CONTEMPORARY POETS

SEVENTH EDITION

Contemporary Writers Series

Contemporary Dramatists
Contemporary Literary Critics
Contemporary Novelists
  (including short story writers)
Contemporary Poets
Contemporary Popular Writers
Contemporary Southern Writers
Contemporary Women Poets
Contemporary World Writers

CONTEMPORARY POETS

SEVENTH EDITION

WITH A PREFACE BY
DIANE WAKOSKI

EDITOR
THOMAS RIGGS

St J

ST. JAMES PRESS

AN IMPRINT OF THE GALE GROUP

DETROIT • NEW YORK • SAN FRANCISCO
LONDON • BOSTON • WOODBRIDGE, CT

Thomas Riggs, *Editor*
Terry Bain, Mariko Fujinaka, *Associate Editors*
Janice Jorgensen, Robert Rauch, *Line Editors*

Margaret Mazurkiewicz, *Project Coordinator*

Michelle Banks, Erin Bealmear, Laura Standley Berger, Joann Cerrito, Jim Craddock,
Steve Cusack, Nicolet V. Elert, Miranda Ferrara, Jamie FitzGerald, Kristin Hart,
Melissa Hill, Laura S. Kryhoski, Carol A. Schwartz, Christine Tomassini, Michael J. Tyrkus
St. James Press Staff

Peter M. Gareffa, *Managing Editor, St. James Press*

Mary Beth Trimper, *Composition and Electronic Prepress*
Evi Seoud, *Assistant Manager, Composition Purchasing and Electronic Prepress*
Dorothy Maki, *Manufacturing Manager*
Rhonda Williams, *Print Buyer*

Kenn Zoran, *Product Design Manager*
Mike Logusz, *Graphic Artist*

ISBN 1-55862-349-3
ISSN 1531-2240

Printed in the United States of America

St. James Press is an imprint of Gale Group
Gale Group and Design is a trademark used herein under license
10 9 8 7 6 5 4 3 2 1
10 9 8 7 6 5 4 3 2 1

CONTENTS

INTRODUCTION

Things fall apart; the centre cannot hold;
Mere anarchy is loosed upon the world . . .

William Butler Yeats wrote these words in his poem "The Second Coming," published in 1921. But as an assessment of our feelings about the state of contemporary poetry, they could as easily have been written in 1990 or in the millennium year of 2000. What now seems clear is that the whole twentieth century has been expansionist and that American poetry can be seen as a paradigm for this infinite annexation of new possibilities, a development that results in a growing sense of extraordinary fragmentation. In retrospect, however, the twentieth century had two golden ages: modernism in the first half of the century, and in the second half the age of the so-called new American poetry. The latter was a constellation formed by the beats, the confessional poets, the New York school, the Black Mountain poets, the black poets, the women poets, and the anti-Vietnam War poets, many from each group overlapping with other groups. Not until the late 1980s did the term "postmodern" begin to creep in and disgruntle us with its varied interpretations.

To no one living through the age of the new American poetry did it seem as if there were a center. Nonetheless, just as we have discovered the patterns of modernism in William Carlos Williams and Wallace Stevens and in T.S. Eliot and Ezra Pound, so we are beginning to see patterns when we regard the confluence of the movements and poetry groups of the 1960s and 1970s. The two halves of the history of poetry in the twentieth century now seem to be sharply distinguished by certain clear and central poetics. What we see on the edge of the new millennium is a kind of tight mainstream for the past few decades. Whether they were women poets, black poets, antiwar poets, confessional poets, beat poets, New York school poets, Black Mountain poets, deep imagist poets, or, later, Native American poets or Asian poets, all shared the idea of the personal poem written in the speaking voice, even the autobiographical or historical voice of the poet. And of course the hallmark of this new American poetry was that it was read out loud. It was an oral poetry, written to be heard or performed. Poetry readings were the news of the second half of the twentieth century.

By the late 1980s this center had come to be called the Whitman tradition, perhaps in recognition that it was an oratorical tradition of poetry we were embracing. But at the same time, just as we had become aware of this oral tradition as a center, the prevalence and power of poetry readings began to diminish. At this point the term "postmodernism" hovered everywhere and began to confound everyone, bound up as it was with contemporary literary discourse and with jargon-bound theory. Some, like David Lehman, wrote brilliantly about it. But no one seemed as interested in what divergent poets shared as what fragmented and distanced them. Adrienne Rich, for example, became a guru for women, at one point not even wanting to allow men into her poetry readings and later taking up one of the primary dogmas of postmodernism, the revision of history, by attempting to show the major roles played by groups other than white males. In response to this another guru, Robert Bly, in an interesting evolution from an imagist poet into a firebrand anti-Vietnam War poet and finally into "Iron John," the icon of the men's movement, continued to fragment the poetry world of the 1980s and 1990s with a New Age self-realization philosophy that moved far beyond poetry or poetics.

The great force of poetry readings in the 1960s and 1970s was produced by a sense of common cause in politics, although practiced not as politics but as ideology. Huge numbers of people read poetry and came to poetry readings because they felt in tune with the ideas emotionally and dramatically presented in the poems and as represented by the lifestyles of the poets. They came to hear and see Gary Snyder represent the back-to-nature world; they flocked to hear Robert Bly, wearing a serape with a tie underneath, declaim his long, ongoing antiwar poem; they surged to hear Nikki Giovanni speak about her black childhood and female desires; they congregated to hear Robert Creeley's syncopated projective verse; and they could not get enough of Allen Ginsberg droning Blake, chanting his own poems, and talking about drugs and sex. The poems were not necessarily political, though many were, but there was a sense of a common cause, a common interest in expressing, asserting, and announcing one's individual and, yes, Whitmanesque "song of myself." The poetry reading was almost as important as the poetry itself.

What was it that changed all of this, gradually throughout the 1980s and then definitively in the 1990s? Perhaps it was political comfort and success in the everyday world. Black poets now seemed to be talking not about common human rights but their own personal ill treatment or lack of privilege. The Vietnam War was over, and pacifism did not seem like something beyond one's personal choice in daily behavior; it was no longer a common cause. In many cases the growing gay and lesbian movements generated an isolationist attitude—"you can't understand us"—and then became so obsessed with the AIDS epidemic that, while one felt sympathetic and even anxious to do something, the groups seemed more like a splintered club of radicals than a common cause people could identify with. In fact, the 1990s showed another swirl of movement coming out of the splintered causes: the obsession with victims. Perhaps it was the Berlin Wall coming down that aroused our international interest in trying once again to understand and respond to the Jewish Holocaust of World War II. Suddenly every disadvantaged person became a victim of Nazi-like persecutors.

By implication the concept of a Whitman tradition emphasized the democratic and individual nature of poets, including the right to change. Thus, by definition the center became a huge, virtually unprioritized array of possibilities, so that by the 1980s there was no clear majority voice at the center of the English-speaking world of poetry. A proliferation of published poets, probably resulting from the many graduate writing programs, splintered any possible audience for poetry, and the lack of a common cause turned people toward individual politics rather than group events. It became equally likely for anyone—from avant-garde writers like John Ashbery, to conservative poets like Henry Taylor and Derek Walcott, to traditional poets like Galway Kinnell and Geoffrey Hill, to poets of color like Yusef Komunyakaa, to AIDS activists like Mark Doty, to nature writers like Mary Oliver, or to old mavericks like Charles Bukowski—to be well reviewed or win major prizes. If there was an establishment, it seemed different every year, lurching from idealizing Allen Ginsberg to lionizing Charles Wright or having a love affair with Rita Dove's poetry. When the American romance with all things Irish began, it became just as matter-of-fact a reality for Seamus Heaney to become Harvard's resident poet and to go on to win a Nobel prize as it was for Gwendolyn Brooks to be awarded more than fifty honorary doctorates or for Robert Pinsky to be seen on national television. Everyone had a cause, but there was no common cause except to give every unheard voice a voice.

With fragmentation a lack of center ensued throughout the commodified 1990s, when even Ginsberg, the supreme beatnik, began to wear three-piece suits. Big-money grants, like the MacArthur, which gave a poet $250,000 for five years, had every poet distracted by dollar signs. If there was a center in the 1990s, it was governed by the professionalization of poetry. The prizes, honors, and money went to poets who were in relatively middle-class university jobs. No more the bohemian world idealized in the 1960s. All of the priorities that might have seemed clear at the big poetry readings of the 1960s and 1970s had broken down.

And the fragmentation became apparent from many sources, including the fact that each year more than three thousand literary magazines were published in England, Canada, and the United States alone. In addition, one was just as likely to find the poetry of new writers like Billy Collins, Sharon Olds, Cathy Song, or Agha Shahid Ah taught in contemporary poetry courses as the work of their older contemporaries.

In the 1980s the most talked about new school of poetry in the United States was the so-called language poetry, which took its name from the journal *L=A=N=G=U=A=G=E,* edited and published for a brief three years, from 1978 to 1981, by Charles Bernstein and Bruce Andrews. Before 1978 there was no such thing as language poetry. There were, of course, many poets writing with postmodernist ideas of structure and form, but they rarely could be labeled, though they might often be referred to as avant-garde. These included, to name only a few, Clark Coolidge, Basil Bunting, Jackson Mac Low, Ron Silliman, Lyn Hejinian, Robert Kelly, Ron Padgett, Michael Davidson, Clayton Eshleman, Susan Howe, and Michael Palmer. Some, like Peter Wild, John Yau, James Tate, or Charles Simic, could be called surrealist poets, though surrealism is a technique more grounded in figure than most of the language poets would embrace. Others, like Robert Creeley, who is primarily identified as a Black Mountain poet, or Michael McClure, identified with the beats, make it clear that this was not a new movement but rather a broader perception of the Pound-Williams axis of poetry in the English language.

Actually, getting language poets to agree on the techniques of writing or even on whether or not they are language poets is problematic. Though the phrase "language poets" has by now been discussed and defined in hundreds of articles and numerous books about contemporary poetry, the biggest disagreement among these writers is not about aesthetics or poetics but about the term itself, which, because it is so convenient, has become common currency. And because language poets attempt to fragment not only the expected linguistic patterns but also personal statements and even the cultural myths that underlie poetic structures, there seems to be only one agreement about what language poetry is. It is abstract, not figurative. For some this means unintelligibility; for others it implies either linguistic or philosophical foundations rather than more personal or literary ones. But for all who either write or read it, language poetry means leaving behind the poetry of anecdote and high metaphor and of personal confession or assertion. It is an interesting extension of the modernist ideal: to move beyond ego is the freedom offered by the technological revolution.

In the 1990s possibly the most interesting manifestation of language poetry was its showing us how to make one of those historic leaps by connecting all, or at least many, of the movements in the poetry scene of the 1960s and 1970s. One can do this through a consideration of one of these groups, the New York school. In his seminal book *The Last Avant-Garde* David Lehman consolidates a strong critical argument for postmodernist inclusiveness—that is, bringing together high and low culture. In doing so, he presents Frank O'Hara, John Ashbery, Kenneth Koch, and James Schuyler as indications of a possible center to twentieth-century poetics.

Not that these poets were this center, but what they represented might be. By extension one sees not just the younger members of the school, like Anne Waldman or Ron Padgett or Lehman himself, as eclectically adding to and thus connecting to this possible center, but one also begins to see the aesthetic connection between poets of many other groups, including Allen Ginsberg, Charles Olson, and Sylvia Plath. Suddenly it seems as if there might be at least an aesthetic center, a new American poetry vortex swirling around in all the disparate groups. It is the democratic need to bring diversities, such as high and low culture, together in the same work.

The other most obvious group of poets to emerge in the 1990s in America is a school made up of people who probably have quite different poetics but who probably would not quarrel about their label. They are the New Formalists. They range from poets like Gjertrud Schnackenberg, who, with her natural and exquisite traditional ear seems like the Richard Wilbur of her generation, to Molly Peacock, who seems to have turned to traditional form precisely because it is unnatural to her and thus a reassuring gesture against chaos, to the erudite Alfred Corn, who like Williams seems to be "searching for a new measure," though within the context of traditional prosody, all the way to a businessman turned poet, Dana Gioia. While the language poets seem to be riding the crest of the feeling that "the centre cannot hold," rejoicing in fragmentation and in the possibility of making a new language construct that will not carry with it bad politics or religion or the economics that pollute the environment, create human inequalities, or make war, the New Formalists want to return to an order that somehow would outlaw the chaos of environmental pollution, human inequalities, and war altogether. Aesthetically they are the opposite, but their political goals are the same. In fact, the center here seems to be politics and not poetics.

Politics, with a lowercase *p*, is probably what overshadowed the world of poetry during the 1990s. Expanding the canon has largely meant reading, teaching, promoting, and publishing the writings of alternative or minority racial, ethnic, and gender groups. We find major anthologies like *The Norton Anthology of Modern Poetry* bragging on their covers about adding more women, Native American, Hispanic, Asian-American, and African-American writers to their rosters. Gertrude Stein has been added probably not because she is the most avant-garde of the modernist writers but because she is a woman. It is ironic that with this greater democracy, something we now see as mandated by the Whitman tradition, poetry has lost any kind of central audience it might have had in the 1960s and 1970s. There are no longer common causes expressed in either the poetry or the poetics.

What one often forgets in respect to the term "New Formalism," however, is that in the 1940s and 1950s, and into the 1960s, there was an assortment of poets who won most of the honors. Perhaps this was the establishment, the fictive center, the beats and others were rebelling or reacting against. They were traditional poets writing formal verse, and they won the majority of the prizes to be had. Notable among them were Robert Penn Warren, Robert Lowell, Anthony Hecht, Richard Wilbur, W.D. Snodgrass, William Meredith, James Merrill, Louis Simpson, Howard Nemerov, John Hollander, John Ciardi, Donald Justice, William Jay Smith, all of the disciples of Theodore Roethke, including James Wright and Carolyn Kizer, and, ironically, Adrienne Rich and Gwendolyn Brooks. Many of them adapted to the various fashions in free verse and continued to occupy the mainstream of American poetry.

The generations who followed these formalists, like my own, learned traditional prosody as young poets and felt the importance of understanding how the new came out of the old and was not simply a reaction against it. This is probably not the case with many of the New Formalists. The force of the New Formalism oddly comes out of the sense of newness, of discovery, it offered to young practitioners like businessman Dana Gioia who obviously had not been educated in its traditions. Thus, the popularity of the movement emanated from the excitement of a nouveau riche, broadcast in a way the poetry of traditionalists like James Merrill or Robert Lowell could not have been. After all, a good education before 1960 decreed that these things were what everyone should know. Gioia, by contrast, has described in "Notes on the New Formalism" pseudo New Formalists in a different way:

> These young poets have grown up in a literary culture so removed from the predominantly oral traditions of metrical verse [sic] that they can no longer hear it accurately. Their training in reading and writing has been overwhelmingly visual not aural, and they have never learned to hear the musical design a poem executes.

Yet Gioia seems to ignore his own lack of awareness of the traditions that made him so excited about his New Formalism. For instance, if one looks at the work of poets who came out of the other big movements of the second half of the twentieth century, one might see an embrace of traditional techniques in poetry and prosody without any sense by many of the practitioners that they were doing something "new." The beat poet Allen Ginsberg routinely required his students at Nairopa to learn the Sapphic stanza and to write in it. Younger New School poets, Anne Waldman and Ron Padgett, along with original New School poets, Kenneth Koch and John Ashbery, have always practiced the regular use and skillful presentation of forms, from the sonnet to the sestina. The Black Mountain poet Robert Creeley, a true descendent of Emily Dickinson, has from the beginning of his career written with her hymn form in mind. The confessional poet Sylvia Plath was a poet of accomplished metrics. And one of the most notable practitioners of the New Formalism, Marilyn Hacker, probably would never have called herself a "New Formalist." In the long tradition of poetry we refer to by way of Ezra Pound, Hacker was simply combining her traditional knowledge with her creative talent "to make it new." Her version of the Petrarchan sonnet should give her pride of place as both an avant-garde poet and a traditionalist. So, like everything else under the sun, the formalism of the New Formalists probably is not very new.

There is, however, one genuinely new movement in American poetry, and it comes perhaps as a result of the fragmentation caused by our political interest in diversity. More and more poets, like Jerome Rothenberg and Gary Snyder, are embracing the idea of ethnopoetics. This might be described as the study of poetry that comes out of the roots of culture and thus is offered as a source, a commonality, a sharing of human experiences. While it focuses on one's tribal, racial, and national or ethnic roots, and perhaps has a bit of a subtext of anthropology driving it, the field of ethnopoetics accepts a commonality of global proportions. It offers an antidote to the fragmentation of the different self-serving political and cultural groups that offer no common ground at all for the many different poetries read, taught, or written. Ethnopoetics is an approach to mend this fragmented condition of the poetry world.

If there are no common heroes and heroines in the world of poetry in 2000, there are also no common enemies (except censorship). The graduate writing programs that once constituted one of the enemies to alternative poets or the avant-garde are now run by writers who represent every possible aesthetic in contemporary poetry. So there are groups and groups and groups of poets. There are regional poets and poetics, just as there are ethnic and racial ones. There are more differences shared by poets than common ground. This makes for a world in which almost anything can happen, and perhaps that is an extremely healthy state of affairs. Oral poetry, the big poetry readings of the 1960s and 1970s, gave poetry a center and helped to create a golden age. But those well-attended readings were generated out of believing that poetry celebrated common causes. Yeats, of course, was worried in "The Second Coming" about what would replace the center in the next millennium:

> And what rough beast, its hour come round at last,
> Slouches towards Bethlehem to be born?

But what if the idea of a center of sameness is the beast itself? More than a hundred years ago Whitman named a different possibility for us in his great poem "Song of Myself":

> and
> I celebrate myself, and sing myself,
> And what I assume you shall assume,
> For every atom belonging to me as good belongs to you.
> Missing me in one place search another,
> I stop somewhere waiting for you.

Whitman's common cause is our differences. Even his common causes have broken down into individual ones, and thus the year 2000 is substantially different from Yeats's 1921. Perhaps we are now in the process of weighing the possibility of a more democratic world of poetry, one that has no heavily weighted center, one genuinely made up of many individual poetics. This would be a world in which no one poet or poetry can, or should want to, speak to or for everyone.

—Diane Wakoski

EDITOR'S NOTE

Contemporary Poets, now in its seventh edition, has been in print since 1970. Although its format has changed over the years, each edition has had the same goal—to provide biographical and bibliographic information, as well as brief critical essays, on some of the world's most important English-language poets.

The seventh edition includes entries on 787 poets who were alive at the beginning of our revision process. The entries are organized into the following sections:

- *Biographical data,* listing, if known, the entrant's nationality, date and place of birth, education, spouse and number of children, career, awards, agent, and address.
- *Bibliography,* listing the title, publisher, and publication date of the entrant's separately published works, including books of verse, novels, collections of short stories or plays, books of nonfiction, and books edited or translated by the entrant. Some entries provide information on media adaptations, manuscript collections, and theatrical activities, as well as a list of critical studies.
- *Personal statement by the entrant (when available),* discussing, for example, early influences, approaches to writing, or views on poetry.
- *Critical essay on the entrant's poetry,* written by an established critic, poet, or editor. The views discussed in the essays are wholly the authors' and should not be seen as those of St. James Press or the editor of this book. Each essay ends with the author's byline.

Contemporary Poets owes its existence to the hard work of many people, some of whom are listed on the staff page. We would like to thank the contributors, not only for writing the essays but also for their patience with the many demands, including deadlines, imposed by St. James Press. We would also like to thank our advisers, who over the years have provided invaluable help in selecting the entrants and contributors and in determining the organization and content of the book.

Finally, special thanks must be given to the poets themselves, who kindly provided biographical and bibliographic information for the entries. Without their poetry and the interest of their readers, this book, of course, would not exist.

—Thomas Riggs
Editor

BOARD OF ADVISERS

CONTRIBUTORS

Dannie Abse
Duane Ackerson
Fleur Adcock
Kathleen Aguero
James Aitchison
Nan Bowman Albinski
Peter Alcock
Michael Andre
Stephen H. Arnold
Jane Augustine

Houston A. Baker, Jr.
Jonathan Barker
Renu Barrett
James Bertram
Jennifer Birkett
Walter Bode
B.J. Bolden
Elmer Borklund
Robert Boyers
Gaynor F. Bradish
Jennifer Brantley
Edward Kamau Brathwaite
Laurence A. Breiner
W.S. Broughton
Lloyd W. Brown
George Bruce
Joseph Bruchac
Hugh Buckingham
Jim Burns
Rose Marie Burwell
George F. Butterick
Don Byrd

Edward Callan
Katie Campbell
Rivers Carew
Hayden Carruth
James Caton
D.D.C. Chambers
Ann Charters
Paul Christensen
Austin Clarke
Anne Cluysenaar
Jeanne Colleran
John Robert Colombo
William Cookson
John R. Cooley
Seamus Cooney
Carlo Coppola
Neil Corcoran
John Cotton
Tony Curtis

Richard Damashek
J.M.Q. Davies
Aidan Day
Cynthia Day
Michel Delville
Terence Diggory
R.H.W. Dillard
Michael Donaghy
Max Dorsinville
David C. Dougherty
David Dowling
Sheila Haney Drain
Louis Dudek
Surjit S. Dulai

Doug Ekelund
Jim Elledge

Edward Foster
Norman Friedman
Robin Fulton

Sally M. Gall
Thomas Gardner
Robert Gaspar
Edward B. Germain
Marty Gervais
James Gibbs
Reid Gilbert
Dana Gioia
Michael Glover
Barry Goldensohn
Lorrie Goldensohn
Lois Gordon
Alvin Greenberg

Ruth Harnett
Thomas Hastings
Burton Hatlen
David M. Heaton
Michael Heller
Geof Hewitt
Douglas Hill
John Hinchey
Susan C. Hines
Philip Hobsbaum
Allen Hoey
Daniel Hoffman
Jan Hokenson
Janis Butler Holm
Ruth Y. Hsu
Theodore R. Hudson
Graham Huggan

Ivor Indyk

Charles L. James
Eldred D. Jones

Susan Kaplan
Rebekah Keaton
Burton Kendle
Bruce King
Devindra Kohli
James Korges
Richard Kostelanetz
Norbert Krapf
B.T. Kugler

Linda Lamont-Stewart
Joan Hutton Landis
Estella Lauter
Geoffrey Lehmann
Harald Leusmann
Stanley W. Lindberg
Carl Lindner
Maurice Lindsay
Rose Lucas
Edward Lucie-Smith
Dennis Lynch

Brian Macaskill
Norman MacCaig
Roy Macnab
Wes Magee
Jacquelyn Marie
Nicole Markotic
Tod Marshall
Roland Mathias
Ashok Mathur
William Matthews
Glyn Maxwell
E.L. Mayo
Thomas McCarthy
Robert McDowell
George McElroy
Martin McGovern
Martin McKinsey
David Meltzer
Bruce Meyer
David Miller
Julie Miller
Tyrus Miller
Ralph J. Mills, Jr.
Christine Miner Minderovic
Robert Miola
R.T. Mole
John Montague
Edwin Morgan

S. Nagarajan
Rudolph L. Nelson
John Newlove
Colin Nicholson

Sean O'Brien
Bernard O'Donoghue
Tanure Ojaide
Michael O'Neill
Lee Oser
Derek Owens
William Oxley

Christine Pagnoulle
Shirley J. Paolini
Joseph Parisi
Derek Parker
Rajeev S. Patke
Jay S. Paul
Ernest Pereira
Marjorie Perloff
Kirsten Holst Petersen
Peter Porter
Sonya B. Posmentier
John Press
Glyn Pursglove

Jed Rasula
David Ray
Liam Rector
John Reibetanz
Julia Reibetanz
John M. Reilly
Alan Riach
Colin Rickards

James K. Robinson
Roger Robinson
Alan Roddick
Judith Rodriguez

Geoff Sadler
Susan Schenk
Andreas Schroeder
Susan M. Schultz
Peter Scupham
Fred Sedgwick
Howard Sergeant
Martin Seymour-Smith
Thomas W. Shapcott
J.N. Sharma
Robert Sheppard
John Shoptaw
Elizabeth Shostak
Alan Shucard
Jon Silkin
Minnie Singh
Sarah Sloane
A.J.M. Smith
Anna Smith
Stan Smith
Kendrick Smithyman
Geoffrey Soar
Jane Somerville
Radcliffe Squires
Aruna Srivastava
Donald Barlow Stauffer
C.K. Stead
Carol Simpson Stern
Anne Stevenson
Anthony G. Stocks

Jennifer Strauss
Rosemary Sullivan
Fraser Sutherland
Martha Sutro
William Sylvester
Julian Symons

John Taggart
Henry Taylor
Myron Taylor
Arthur Terry
Michael Thorn
Saundra Towns
Michael True

Robert Vas Dias
K. Venkatachari

Linda W. Wagner-Martin
Diane Wakoski
William Walsh
Priscilla L Walton
R.J.C. Watt
Eliot Weinberger
Theresa Werner
Nigel Wheale
Patience Wheatley
Margaret Willy
Joseph Wilson
George Woodcock
Derek Wright

Leopoldo Y. Yabes
David Young
Steven Young

CONTEMPORARY POETS

SEVENTH EDITION

LIST OF ENTRANTS

Dannie Abse
Chinua Achebe
Diane Ackerman
Perseus Adams
Robert Adamson
Fleur Adcock
John Agard
Ai
James Aitchison
Meena Alexander
Agha Shahid Ali
A. Alvarez
Moniza Alvi
A.R. Ammons
Michael Anania
Maya Angelou
David Antin
Rae Armantrout
Simon Armitage
John Ash
John Ashbery
Margaret Atwood
Alvin Aubert
Margaret Avison
Kofi Awoonor

Jimmy Santiago Baca
Mary Jo Bang
Gavin Bantock
Amiri Baraka
Douglas Barbour
Elizabeth Bartlett
Edward Baugh
Taner Baybars
Bruce Beaver
Marvin Bell
Michael Benedikt
Louise Bennett
Anne Beresford
Stephen Berg
Carol Bergé
Bill Berkson
Charles Bernstein
Daniel Berrigan
Francis Berry
James Berry
Wendell Berry
James Bertolino
Sujata Bhatt
Frank Bidart
Bill Bissett
David M. Black
Peter Bland
Robin Blaser
Robert Bly

Eavan Boland
Philip Booth
Jenny Bornholdt
Roo Borson
George Bowering
Marilyn Bowering
Edgar Bowers
Alison Brackenbury
John Brandi
Edward Kamau Brathwaite
Kwesi Brew
Elizabeth Brewster
Robert Bringhurst
Lucie Brock-Broido
David Bromige
Gwendolyn Brooks
Olga Broumas
Wayne Brown
Michael Dennis Browne
Alan Brownjohn
George Bruce
Dennis Brutus
Tom Buchan
Michael Bullock
Jim Burns
Stanley Burnshaw
John Burnside
Duncan Bush
Guy Butler
Ron Butlin

Caroline Caddy
Barry Callaghan
Alistair Campbell
Hayden Carruth
Anne Carson
Ciaran Carson
Lorna Cervantes
Fred Chappell
Maxine Chernoff
Syl Cheyney-Coker
Frank Chipasula
Kate Clanchy
John Pepper Clark
Tom Clark
George Elliott Clarke
Gillian Clarke
Harry Clifton
Lucille Clifton
Anne Cluysenaar
Bob Cobbing
Fred Cogswell
Leonard Cohen
Victor Coleman
Wanda Coleman

Don Coles
Billy Collins
John Robert Colombo
Alex Comfort
Stewart Conn
Robert Conquest
David Constantine
Clark Coolidge
Jane Cooper
Wendy Cope
Cid Corman
Alfred Corn
Sam Cornish
Gregory Corso
John Cotton
Jeni Couzyn
Robert Crawford
Robert Creeley
Anthony Cronin
Jeremy Cronin
Kevin Crossley-Holland
Andrew Crozier
Lorna Crozier
Victor Hernández Cruz
Patrick Cullinan
Marcus Cumberlege
Allen Curnow
R.N. Currey
Tony Curtis

Cyril Dabydeen
David Dabydeen
Philip Dacey
Fred D'Aguiar
Beverly Dahlen
Peter Dale
Ruth Dallas
Robert Dana
Keki N. Daruwalla
Kamala Das
Frank Davey
Michael Davidson
Dick Davis
Peter Davison
Bruce Dawe
Madeline DeFrees
Anthony Delius
Ricaredo Demetillo
Jeff Derksen
Eunice de Souza
Christopher Dewdney
Imtiaz Dharker
Pier Giorgio Di Cicco
Peter Didsbury
R.H.W. Dillard

Diane di Prima
Thomas M. Disch
Rosemary Dobson
Stephen Dobyns
Don Domanski
Michael Donaghy
David Dooley
Ed Dorn
Mark Doty
Rita Dove
Charles Doyle
Johanna Drucker
Norman Dubie
Louis Dudek
Carol Ann Duffy
Maureen Duffy
Alan Dugan
Laurie Duggan
Ian Duhig
Helen Dunmore
Douglas Dunn
Stephen Dunn
Paul Durcan
Bob Dylan

Charles Edward Eaton
Richard Eberhart
Michael Echeruo
Lauris Edmond
Murray Edmond
Russell Edson
Alistair Elliot
Kenward Elmslie
James A. Emanuel
John Engels
D.J. Enright
Theodore Enslin
Elaine Equi
Louise Erdrich
Clayton Eshleman
Martin Espada
Mari Evans
Bernardine Evaristo
Peter Everwine
Nissim Ezekiel

Ruth Fainlight
Peter Fallon
U.A. Fanthorpe
Vicki Feaver
Elaine Feinstein
Irving Feldman
James Fenton
Lawrence Ferlinghetti
Edward Field
Donald Finkel
Caroline Finkelstein
Ian Hamilton Finlay
Joan Finnigan

Roy Fisher
Judith Fitzgerald
Roland Flint
Carolyn Forché
Charles Henri Ford
Mark Ford
Gene Fowler
Kathleen Fraser
Anne French
Christopher Fry
John Fuller
Alice Fulton
Robin Fulton

Tess Gallagher
Brendan Galvin
Patrick Galvin
Forrest Gander
Roger Garfitt
Raymond Garlick
George Garrett
David Gascoyne
Greg Gatenby
Gary Geddes
C.H. Gervais
Brewster Ghiselin
Zulfikar Ghose
Reginald Gibbons
Jack Gilbert
Sandra M. Gilbert
Gary Gildner
Valerie Gillies
Dana Gioia
Nikki Giovanni
Peter Gizzi
Duncan Glen
Jon Glover
Louise Glück
Patricia Goedicke
John Gohorry
Albert Goldbarth
Kenneth Goldsmith
Peter Goldsworthy
Lorna Goodison
Alan Gould
Henry Graham
Jorie Graham
Judy Grahn
Robert Gray
Stephen Gray
Jonathan Greene
Lavinia Greenlaw
Linda Gregg
Arthur Gregor
Philip Gross
Barbara Guest
Harry Guest
Thom Gunn
Kristjana Gunnars
Don Gutteridge

Marilyn Hacker
Rachel Hadas
Donald Hall
J.C. Hall
Rodney Hall
Daniel Halpern
Michael Hamburger
Ian Hamilton
Kaiser Haq
Joy Harjo
Michael S. Harper
Michael Harris
Wilson Harris
Jim Harrison
Tony Harrison
J.S. Harry
David Harsent
Kevin Hart
Lee Harwood
Alamgir Hashmi
Robert Hass
Samuel Hazo
Seamus Heaney
John Heath-Stubbs
Anthony Hecht
Lyn Hejinian
Michael Heller
David Helwig
Hamish Henderson
Adrian Henri
Phoebe Hesketh
Dorothy Hewett
William Heyen
Geoffrey Hill
Selima Hill
Brenda Hillman
Daryl Hine
Edward Hirsch
Jack Hirschman
Jane Hirshfield
Tony Hoagland
Philip Hobsbaum
Daniel Hoffman
Michael Hofmann
David Holbrook
John Hollander
Anselm Hollo
Garrett Hongo
Edwin Honig
Jeremy Hooker
Paul Hoover
Chenjerai Hove
Richard Howard
Fanny Howe
Susan Howe
Alejandrino G. Hufana
Glyn Hughes
Coral Hull
Keri Hulme
Michael Hulse

T.R. Hummer
Sam Hunt
Pearse Hutchinson

Mick Imlah
Kevin Ireland

Michael Jackson
Josephine Jacobsen
David Jaffin
Kathleen Jamie
Mark Jarman
Elizabeth Jennings
Rita Joe
Judith Johnson
Linton Kwesi Johnson
Ronald Johnson
Andrew Johnston
George Johnston
Brian Jones
D.G. Jones
Rodney Jones
Erica Jong
June Jordan
Jenny Joseph
Adil Jussawalla
Donald Justice

Sylvia Kantaris
P.J. Kavanagh
Jackie Kay
Judith Kazantzis
Antigone Kefalá
Richard Kell
Anthony Kellman
Robert Kelly
X.J. Kennedy
Brendan Kennelly
Tabish Khair
Mimi Khalvati
Galway Kinnell
John Kinsella
Thomas Kinsella
James Kirkup
Carolyn Kizer
John Knoepfle
Bill Knott
Kenneth Koch
Arun Kolatkar
James Koller
Yusef Komunyakaa
Ted Kooser
Bernard Kops
Richard Kostelanetz
Lotte Kramer
Robert Kroetsch
Shiv K. Kumar
Maxine Kumin
Mazisi Kunene

Stanley Kunitz
Frank Kuppner
Joanne Kyger

Kojo Laing
Patrick Lane
Anthony Lawrence
Irving Layton
Dennis Lee
Don L. Lee
    See Haki R. Madhubuti
Li-Young Lee
David Lehman
Geoffrey Lehmann
Brad Leithauser
Tom Leonard
Douglas LePan
Laurence Lerner
Christopher Levenson
Peter Levi
Philip Levine
Laurence Lieberman
Lyn Lifshin
Maurice Lindsay
Douglas Livingstone
Taban lo Liyong
    See under Taban
Kate Llewellyn
Liz Lochhead
Christopher Logue
Herbert Lomas
Michael Longley
Edward Lowbury
Edward Lucie-Smith
Thomas Lux

Nathaniel Mackey
Alasdair Maclean
Jackson Mac Low
Roy Macnab
Jay Macpherson
Barry MacSweeney
Haki R. Madhubuti
Wes Magee
Sarah Maguire
Jayanta Mahapatra
Derek Mahon
Jennifer Maiden
Clarence Major
David Malouf
Bill Manhire
Chris Mann
Jack Mapanje
E.A. Markham
Daphne Marlatt
Jack Marshall
Roland Mathias
John Matthias
Glyn Maxwell
Gerda Mayer

Seymour Mayne
James J. McAuley
Steve McCaffery
Thomas McCarthy
Michael McClure
Ian McDonald
David McFadden
Roger McGough
Medbh McGuckian
Heather McHugh
Don McKay
Jamie McKendrick
Tom McKeown
Rhyll McMaster
Wesley C. McNair
Florence McNeil
Anthony McNeill
Sandra McPherson
Cilla McQueen
George McWhirter
Matthew Mead
Philip Mead
Paula Meehan
Arvind Krishna Mehrotra
Peter Meinke
David Meltzer
William Meredith
W.S. Merwin
Robert Mezey
James Michie
Christopher Middleton
The Mighty Sparrow
E. Ethelbert Miller
Robert Minhinnick
Judith M. Minty
Sudesh Mishra
Adrian Mitchell
Elma Mitchell
Susan Mitchell
Judith Moffett
John Mole
John Montague
Dom Moraes
Edwin Morgan
Frederick Morgan
Pete Morgan
Robert Morgan
A.F. Moritz
Mervyn Morris
Blake Morrison
Thylias Moss
Andrew Motion
Erin Mouré
Oswald Mtshali
Mudrooroo
Lisel Mueller
Paul Muldoon
Harryette Mullen
Richard Murphy
Les Murray

Rona Murray
Susan Musgrave

Pritish Nandy
Leonard Nathan
John Newlove
Sianne Ngai
Grace Nichols
Eiléan Ní Chuilleanáin
Leslie Norris
Harold Norse
Alice Notley
Naomi Shihab Nye
Robert Nye

Philip Oakes
Joyce Carol Oates
Gregory O'Brien
Sean O'Brien
Bernard O'Donoghue
Dennis O'Driscoll
Desmond O'Grady
John Okai
Gabriel Okara
Sharon Olds
Mary Oliver
Toby Olson
Michael Ondaatje
Frank Ormsby
Gregory Orr
Simon J. Ortiz
Vincent O'Sullivan
Niyi K. Osundare
Richard Outram
Jan Owen
Rochelle Owens
William Oxley

Robert Pack
Ruth Padel
Ron Padgett
Bibhu Padhi
Geoff Page
P.K. Page
Michael Palmer
Greg Pape
R. Parthasarathy
Linda Pastan
Gieve Patel
Alistair Paterson
Don Paterson
Gianna Patriarca
Brian Patten
Raymond R. Patterson
Tom Paulin
Molly Peacock
John Peck
Saleem Peeradina
Bob Perelman

Joyce Peseroff
William Peskett
Lenrie Peters
Robert L. Peters
Paul Petrie
Carl Phillips
Tom Pickard
Marge Piercy
Christopher Pilling
Robert Pinsky
Fiona Pitt-Kethley
Stanley Plumly
Dorothy Porter
Peter Porter
Neil Powell
F.T. Prince
J.H. Prynne
Sheenagh Pugh
Al Purdy
Rodney Pybus

Craig Raine
Kathleen Raine
Carl Rakosi
Julia Randall
Margaret Randall
Tom Raworth
David Ray
Peter Reading
James Reaney
Peter Redgrove
Ishmael Reed
Jeremy Reed
Alastair Reid
Christopher Reid
Donald Revell
Alan Riach
Adrienne Rich
Anne Ridler
Alberto Ríos
Robin Robertson
Paul Roche
Carolyn M. Rodgers
Judith Rodriguez
William Pitt Root
Peter Rose
Joe Rosenblatt
Alan Ross
Jerome Rothenberg
David Rowbotham
Anthony Rudolf
Carol Rumens
Peter Russell
Vern Rutsala
Gig Ryan

Lawrence Sail
Bruce St. John
David St. John
Philip Salom

Mary Jo Salter
Sonia Sanchez
Ed Sanders
Stephen Sandy
Reg Saner
Carole Satyamurti
Leslie Scalapino
William Scammell
Vernon Scannell
Michael Schmidt
Dennis Schmitz
Gjertrud Schnackenberg
John A. Scott
James Scully
Peter Scupham
Fred Sedgwick
Frederick Seidel
Hugh Seidman
Olive Senior
Sipho Sepamla
Mongane Wally Serote
Vikram Seth
Ntozake Shange
Jo Shapcott
Thomas W. Shapcott
David Shapiro
Harvey Shapiro
Brenda Shaughnessy
Richard Shelton
Judith Johnson Sherwin
    See Judith Johnson
Manohar Shetty
Peggy Shumaker
Penelope Shuttle
Leslie Marmon Silko
Ron Silliman
Charles Simic
James Simmons
Louis Simpson
R.A. Simpson
Iain Sinclair
C.H. Sisson
Knute Skinner
Peter Skrzyneckl
David Slavitt
Dave Smith
John Smith
Ken Smith
Vivian Smith
William Jay Smith
Elizabeth Smither
W.D. Snodgrass
Gary Snyder
Gilbert Sorrentino
Gary Soto
Raymond Souster
Wole Soyinka
Barry Spacks
Muriel Spark
Francis Sparshott

Elizabeth Spires
Pauline Stainer
Jon Stallworthy
C.K. Stead
Timothy Steele
Stephen Stepanchev
Alan Stephens
Gerald Stern
Peter Stevens
Anne Stevenson
Ruth Stone
Mark Strand
Jennifer Strauss
Lucien Stryk
Dabney Stuart
Andrew Suknaski, Jr.
C.P. Surendran
Fraser Sutherland
James Sutherland-Smith
Robert Sward
Matthew Sweeney
George Szirtes

Taban lo Liyong
Nathaniel Tarn
James Tate
Andrew Taylor
Henry Taylor
Sharon Thesen
D.M. Thomas
Lorenzo Thomas
R.S. Thomas
Anthony Thwaite
Richard Tillinghast
Charles Tomlinson
John Tranter
David Trinidad
Dimitris Tsaloumas

Lewis Turco
Gael Turnbull
Brian Turner
Hone Tuwhare
Chase Twichell

John Updike

Jean Valentine
Mona Van Duyn
Nance Van Winckel
Robert Vas Dias
Peter Viereck
Ellen Bryant Voigt

Miriam Waddington
David Wagoner
Fred Wah
Jeffrey Wainwright
Diane Wakoski
Derek Walcott
Anne Waldman
Rosmarie Waldrop
Ted Walker
Chris Wallace-Crabbe
Diane Ward
Rosanna Warren
Lewis Warsh
Andrew Waterman
Michael Waters
Robert Watson
Tom Wayman
Alan Wearne
Phyllis Webb
Ian Wedde
Bruce Weigl
Theodore Weiss

Daniel Weissbort
James Welch
Robert Wells
Albert Wendt
David Wevill
Philip Whalen
Kenneth White
Reed Whittemore
John Wieners
Dara Wier
Richard Wilbur
Peter Wild
C.K. Williams
Emmett Williams
Hugo Williams
Jonathan Williams
Miller Williams
Clive Wilmer
Keith Wilson
Hubert Witheford
John Woods
C.D. Wright
Charles Wright
Jay Wright
Judith Wright
Kit Wright

Arthur Yap
J. Michael Yates
John Yau
Al Young
David Young

Benjamin Zephaniah
Paul Zimmer
Fay Zwicky
Jan Zwicky

A

ABSE, Dannie

Nationality: British. **Born:** Cardiff, Glamorgan, 22 September 1923. **Education:** Marlborough Road Elementary School, Cardiff; St. Illtyd's College, Cardiff; University of South Wales and Monmouthshire, Cardiff; King's College, London; Westminster Hospital, London; qualified as physician 1950, M.R.C.S., L.R.C.P. **Military Service:** Royal Air Force, 1951–54: squadron leader. **Family:** Married Joan Mercer in 1951; one son and two daughters. **Career:** Specialist in charge of the chest clinic, Central London Medical Establishment, 1954–82. Senior Fellow in Humanities, Princeton University, New Jersey, 1973–74. Editor, *Poetry and Poverty* magazine, London, 1949–54. President, Poetry Society, 1979–92. **Awards:** Foyle award, 1960; Welsh Arts Council award, 1971, 1987, for play, 1980; Cholmondeley award, 1985. D.Litt.: University of Wales, Cardiff, 1989. Fellow, Royal Society of Literature, 1983. Fellow, Welsh Academy, 1991. **Agent:** Anthony Sheil Associates, 43 Doughty Street, London WC1N 2LF. **Address:** 85 Hodford Road, London N.W.11, England; or, Green Hollows, Craig-yr-Eos Road, Ogmore-by-Sea, Glamorgan, South Wales.

PUBLICATIONS

Poetry

After Every Green Thing. London, Hutchinson, 1948.
Walking under Water. London, Hutchinson, 1952.
Tenants of the House: Poems 1951–1956. London, Hutchinson, 1957; New York, Criterion, 1959.
Poems, Golders Green. London, Hutchinson, 1962.
Dannie Abse: A Selection. London, Studio Vista, 1963.
A Small Desperation. London, Hutchinson, 1968.
Demo. Frensham, Surrey, Sceptre Press, 1969.
Selected Poems. London, Hutchinson, and New York, Oxford University Press, 1970.
Funland: A Poem in Nine Parts. London, Portland University Library, 1971.
Corgi Modern Poets in Focus 4, with others, edited by Jeremy Robson. London, Corgi, 1972.
Funland and Other Poems. London, Hutchinson, and New York, Oxford University Press, 1973.
Lunchtime. London, Poem-of-the-Month Club, 1974.
Penguin Modern Poets 26, with D.J. Enright and Michael Longley. London, Penguin, 1975.
Collected Poems 1948–1976. London, Hutchinson, and Pittsburgh, University of Pittsburgh Press, 1977.
Way Out in the Centre. London, Hutchinson, 1981; as *One-Legged on Ice,* Athens, University of Georgia Press, 1983.
Ask the Bloody Horse. London, Hutchinson, 1986; as *Sky in Narrow Streets,* in *Quarterly Review of Literature Poetry Series* (Princeton, New Jersey), 28, 1987.
White Coat, Purple Coat: Collected Poems 1948–1988. London, Hutchinson, 1989; New York, Persea, 1990.
Remembrance of Crimes Past. London, Hutchinson, 1990; New York, Persea, 1993.

On the Evening Road. London, Hutchinson, 1994.
Selected Poems. London, Penguin, 1994.
Welsh Retrospective. Bridgend, Wales, Seren, and Chester Springs, Pennsylvania, Dufour, 1997.
Arcadia, One Mile. London, Hutchinson, 1998.
Be Seated, Thou: Poems. Riverdale-on-Hudson, New York, Sheep Meadow Press, 1999.

Recordings: *Poets of Wales,* Argo, 1972; *The Poetry of Dannie Abse,* McGraw Hill, n.d.; *Dannie Abse,* Canto, 1984.

Plays

Fire in Heaven (produced London, 1948). London, Hutchinson, 1956; revised version, as *Is the House Shut?* (produced London, 1964); revised version, as *In the Cage,* in *Three Questor Plays,* 1967.
Hands around the Wall (produced London, 1950).
House of Cowards (produced London, 1960). Included in *Three Questor Plays,* 1967; in *Twelve Great Plays,* edited by Leonard F. Dean, New York, Harcourt Brace, 1970.
The Eccentric (produced London, 1961). London, Evans, 1961.
Gone (produced London, 1962). Included in *Three Questor Plays,* 1967; revised version, as *Gone in January* (produced Edinburgh, 1977; London, 1978), in *Madog* (Pontypridd, Glamorgan), 1981.
The Courting of Essie Glass (as *The Joker,* produced London, 1962; revised version, as *The Courting of Essie Glass,* broadcast 1975). Included in *Miscellany One,* 1981.
Three Questor Plays. Lowestoft, Suffolk, Scorpion Press, 1967.
The Dogs of Pavlov (produced London, 1969; New York, 1974). London, Vallentine Mitchell, 1973.
Funland (produced London, 1975).
Pythagoras (produced Birmingham, 1976; London, 1980). London, Hutchinson, 1979.
The View from Row C (includes *House of Cowards, The Dogs of Pavlov,* and *Pythagoras Smith*). Bridgend, Glamorgan, Seren, 1990.

Radio Plays: *Conform or Die,* 1957; *No Telegrams, No Thunder,* 1962; *You Can't Say Hello to Anybody,* 1964; *A Small Explosion,* 1964; *The Courting of Essie Glass,* 1975.

Novels

Ash on a Young Man's Sleeve. London, Hutchinson, 1954; New York, Criterion, 1955.
Some Corner of an English Field. London, Hutchinson, 1956; New York, Criterion, 1957.
O. Jones, O. Jones. London, Hutchinson, 1970.
There Was a Young Man from Cardiff. London, Hutchinson, 1991.

Other

Medicine on Trial. London, Aldus, 1968; New York, Crown, 1969.
A Poet in the Family (autobiography). London, Hutchinson, 1974.
Miscellany One. Bridgend, Glamorgan, Poetry Wales Press, 1981.

A Strong Dose of Myself (essays). London, Hutchinson, 1983.
Under the Influence Of (lecture). Cardiff, University College of Wales, 1984(?).
Journals from the Ant Heap. London, Hutchinson, 1986.
Intermittent Journals. Bridgend, Glamorgan, Seren, 1994.

Editor, with Elizabeth Jennings and Stephen Spender, *New Poems 1956.* London, Joseph, 1956.
Editor, with Howard Sergeant, *Mavericks.* London, Editions Poetry and Poverty, 1957.
Editor, *European Verse.* London, Studio Vista, 1964.
Editor, *Corgi Modern Poets in Focus 1, 3, 5.* London, Corgi, 1971–73.
Editor, *Thirteen Poets.* London, Poetry Book Society, 1973.
Editor, *Poetry Dimension 2–5: The Best of the Poetry Year.* London, Robson, 1974–78; New York, St. Martin's Press, 1976–79; *The Best of the Poetry Year 6–7,* Robson, and Totowa, New Jersey, Rowman and Littlefield, 1979–80.
Editor, *Poetry Supplement, Christmas 1975.* London, Poetry Book Society, 1975.
Editor, *My Medical School.* London, Robson, 1978.
Editor, *Wales in Verse.* London, Secker and Warburg, 1983.
Editor, *Doctors and Patients.* Oxford, Oxford University Press, 1984.
Editor, with Joan Abse, *Voices in the Gallery.* London, Tate Gallery Publications, 1986.
Editor, with Joan Abse, *The Music Lover's Literary Companion.* London, Robson, 1988.
Editor, *The Hutchinson Book of Post-War British Poetry.* London, Hutchinson, 1989.
Editor, with Sandra Anstey, *Listening to Voices from Wales: Short Stories.* Treforest, National Language Unit of Wales, 1992.
Editor, with Anne Stevenson, *The Gregory Anthology, 1991–1993.* London, Sinclair-Stevenson, 1994.
Editor, *Twentieth Century Anglo-Welsh Poetry.* Bridgend, Wales, Seren, 1997.

*

Manuscript Collection: National Library of Wales, Aberystwyth, Dyfed.

Critical Studies: Interviews in *Jewish Quarterly* (London), winter 1962–63, *Flame* (Wivenhoe, Essex), March 1967, *Anglo-Welsh Review* (Tenby), spring 1975, *The Guardian* (London), 31 January 1978, *Good Housekeeping* (London), May 1981, *The Times* (London), 28 February 1983, and *Sunday Times Magazine* (London), 22 May 1983; by Jeremy Robson, in *Corgi Modern Poets in Focus 4,* 1972; "Poet on Poet" by Fleur Adcock, in *Ambit 70* (London), 1977; "The Poetry of Dannie Abse" by Howard Sergeant, in *Books and Bookmen* (London), July 1977; by John Pikoulis and John Tripp, in *Poetry Wales* (Bridgend), October 1977; by David Punter, in *Straight Lines 2* (Norwich), 1979; by Renée Winegarten, in *Jewish Chronicle Literary Supplement* (London), 24 December 1982; *The Poetry of Dannie Abse: Critical Essays and Reminiscences* with contributions by Alan Brownjohn, Vernon Scannell, M.L. Rosenthal, Peter Porter, D.J. Enright, Barbara Hardy, and others, edited by Joseph Cohen, London, Robson, 1983; "Science Poetry: Approaches to Redgrove, Abse, and Ammons" by J.P. Ward, in *Poesis* (Bryn Mawr, Pennsylvania), fall 1984; "Doctor and Magus in the Work of Dannie Abse" by Daniel Hoffman, in *Literature and Medicine* (Albany, New York), 3, 1984;

Dannie Abse by Tony Curtis, Cardiff, University of Wales Press, 1985; by William Oxley, in *The Inner Tapestry* (Salzburg, Austria), 1985; by James A. Davies, in *New Welsh Review* (Lampeter), 6, 1989; by Katherine Soniat, in *Spirit* (South Orange, New Jersey), spring-summer 1989; by J.P. Ward, David Wright, and Richard Poole in *Poetry Wales* (Bridgend), 29(2), 1993; by John Cotton in *The New Reporter* (London), June 1994; by Katie Eramich in *Poetry Wales* (Bridgend), 30(2), 1994.

*   *   *

Dannie Abse is a popular poet without being exactly populist, which is unusual among British poets. Although he has suffered, as have many popular poets since World War I, from critical neglect on account of such popularity, there is an increasing realization that genuine poets can be both popular and serious. In part, Abse's popularity derives from the fact that he is a doctor of medicine and that there is a worldwide interest in anything to do with health. He is also an accessible poet, however, and although he is an avowed believer, like Yeats, in difficulty ("I am committed to the idea of difficulty in writing poetry"), his poems are limpid. As he put it in the introductory note to his 1977 *Collected Poems,* ". . . my ambition has been to write poems which appear translucent but are in fact deceptions." This may be interpreted as the wish to write of complex matters in the simplest and clearest way, as he does.

The reader of his work senses that Abse believes that the best poem, or at least the most appropriate type of poem, is one rooted in the immediate, the visible and day-to-day world. He has written many such poems. Even his "Funland" sequence, for all its surrealism and accent on lunacy, is very much a poem of "the real world." Almost despite his overt intentions, however, the importance of his poems lies not in their concrete descriptive powers or in the moods they evoke but in their ideas, the insights they contain. I do not say that Abse is a highly metaphysical poet, but he is the author of much that can be described as a poetry of ideas. It is a poetry of a quietly enormous range of concern that is informed by fine turns of phrase in flashes, though never using flashy turns of phrase for their own sake.

The persona that Abse projects in his work is an extremely "doubtful" one in the best sense of that term. It is full of doubt and is even self-contradictory, for he is a sincere poet. Abse is self-consciously ambiguous for the sake of truth. This is quite clear from the many-sided poem of alternating currents—by turns negative and positive—called "Poem of Celebration":

> I lean against the air.
> It gives way like unstitched water. I fall in
> but am drowned in air. Now distinctly
> every image reflects the invisible world.
>
> The noise divides from light.
> Bold astronomers who at night
> peep through the window-pane of the colossal skies
> look too far for the farthest star.
> This world confirms my senses.
>
> Swaying and drunk with seeing
> the near magnificence of things,
> I cry out a doxology with surprise
> of a shout, creating maximum silence.

One should note the contradictions and oppositions: "every image reflects the invisible world," "noise divides from light," "a shout, creating maximum silence." Added to this is affirmation that is contradiction piled atop contradiction—"This world confirms my senses"—though he has just demonstrated the insubstantiality of that world. What one has is a poet vitally alive to the mystery of the world and of himself.

This poem, with its urgent questioning of reality, derives from the 1950s. A decade later came "Mysteries," one of Abse's most celebrated poems. The theme is more or less the same, except that the self is increasingly part of his scrutiny as well:

> At night, I do not know who I am
> when I dream, when I am sleeping.
>
> . . . I should know by now that few octaves can be heard,
> that a vision dies from being too long stared at;
>
> . . . that a magnesium flash cannot illumine,
> for one single moment the invisible.
>
> I do not complain. I start with the visible
> and am startled by the visible.

Although Abse starts with "the visible," he is obsessed with "the invisible," an obsession that is fueled by his increasing awareness of his Jewish background. Many of his later poems are influenced by his reading of Judaic literature, which has brought him up against the core of Judaism, which is religious awareness. As a result, Abse's poetry has increasingly sprung from the conflict between his secular beliefs and experience and the deep well of religiosity that lies beneath the surface of Jewish consciousness, the race that Orde Wingate said "invented God."

The pragmatic and empirical side of the secular Abse means, as an interviewer has said, that he "lacks dogmatism" and "confronts experience one step at a time." Other critics have emphasized the sense of his humanity and compassion, which especially show up in his medical poems, though not only there. On birth, Abse is sensitive and beautiful ("The Smile Was" and "The Stethoscope"); on love, tight-lipped but tender and, at times, even tragic ("Portrait of a Marriage" and "The Silence of Tudor Evans") and, once, truly celebratory (in the early poem "Epithalamion"); on death, exact, realistic, and movingly existential ("Pathology of Colours," "Carnal Knowledge," "Millie's Date," "Last Words," and many more). His sense of humanity springs from the anguish of an honest observer of life who, by turns, feels powerlessness and fear in the face of the fact of mortality. There also is a degree of dismay at the way society is organized, but even though Abse comes from a highly political background, his poetry is rarely political as such. Whereas the politician craves ideological solutions, the poet, at least in Abse's case, merely feels compassion and a sense of injustice.

Although I emphasize the more serious aspects of Abse's genius, other critics naturally attend to quite other features of his poetry. He is a gifted anecdotalist, and not a few of his poems are built around this side of his talent. He can take small incidents from life or short tales from Jewish or Greek myth and build them into a quasi narrative in a contemporary setting. He does this, for example, in "A Small Farmhouse near Brno," "Of Rabbi Yose," and "The Victim of Aulis." Even when the setting is not contemporary, the language and tone always are.

This brings one to the great technical virtue of Abse's poems. He is a Welshman by birth, and the craft of his poems springs perhaps as much as anything from that unique awareness of the possibilities of verbal interplay so highly developed in the englyn form of the Welsh language. It surprises me, as I have suggested earlier, that Abse is not considered more of a poet's poet, for he has much to teach his fellow poets. Not least are his ability for the judicious disposition of surprising words and the suggestive phrase. His greatest strength, however, is talent for the discreet organization of sentence into statement and image. Such an effective balance is created that, contrary to Hopkins's advice, we should "admire and (try to) do likewise"—at least, those of us who are his fellow poets. As Peter Porter has put it, "Abse knows just how far to push the insight, how to underlay the fantasy with reality." That he can so effectively achieve this—no matter how varied and wide-ranging his subject matter—is entirely due to his exquisite tact and care in handling words.

Abse's poetry has, as I have suggested, always been known for its humanity and its realism; never exactly despairing, it has been skeptic driven. I have also pointed to its frequent metaphysical undertone, as well as to its Judaic-biblical background. This latter receives masterly treatment in a fine long poem that concludes the volume entitled *Arcadia, One Mile*. The poem, "Events Leading to the Conception of Solomon, the Wise Child," shows a great gift for the extended narrative, which hitherto has not been employed much in his poetry. Likewise, the volume opens with a fine lyric that mixes tenderness with a quietly passionate music of the sort we have not seen since his much-praised "Epithalamion." All of this confirms that the poet's skillful and varied talent remains undimmed even into old age.

—William Oxley

ACHEBE, Chinua

Nationality: Nigerian. **Born:** Albert Chinualumogu in Ogidi, 16 November 1930. **Education:** Government College, Umuahia, 1944–47; University College, Ibadan, 1948–53, B.A. (London) 1953. **Family:** Married Christiana Chinwe Okoli in 1961; two sons and two daughters. **Career:** Talks producer, Lagos, 1954–57, controller, Enugu, 1958–61, and director, Voice of Nigeria, Lagos, 1961–66, Nigerian Broadcasting Corporation; chairman, Citadel Books Ltd., Enugu, 1967. Senior research fellow, 1967–73, professor of English, 1973–81, and since 1984 professor emeritus, University of Nigeria, Nsukka. Visiting professor, 1972–75, and Fulbright Professor, 1987–88, University of Massachusetts, Amherst; visiting professor, University of Connecticut, Storrs, 1975–76; Regents' Lecturer, University of California, Los Angeles, 1984. Editor, 1971–82, *Okike: An African Journal of New Writing,* Nsukka; founding editor, Heinemann African Writers series, 1962–72, and since 1970 director, Heinemann Educational Books (Nigeria) Ltd., and Nwankwo-Ifejika Ltd. (later Nwamife), publishers, Enugu; since 1984 founder and publisher, *Uwa Ndi Igbo: A Bilingual Journal of Igbo Life and Arts.* Member, University of Lagos Council, 1966; chairman, Society of Nigerian Authors, 1966, and Association of Nigerian Authors, 1982–86; member, Anambra State Arts Council, 1977–79; Pro-Chancellor and Chairman of Council, Anambra State University of Technology,

Enugu, 1986–88; director, 1984–90, Okike Arts Center, Nsukka. Since 1981 member of the Executive Committee, Commonwealth Arts Organisation, London; since 1983 member, International Social Prospects Academy, Geneva. Served on diplomatic missions for Biafra during Nigerian Civil War, 1967–69; deputy national president, People's Redemption Party, 1983. **Awards:** Margaret Wrong Memorial prize, 1959; Nigerian National trophy, 1960; Rockefeller fellowship, 1960; Unesco fellowship, 1963; Jock Campbell award (*New Statesman*), 1965; Commonwealth Poetry prize, 1973; Neil Gunn International fellowship, 1974; Lotus award for Afro-Asian writers, 1975; Nigerian National Merit award, 1979; Commonwealth Foundation award, 1984; Champion Award, 1996. Litt.D.: Dartmouth College, Hanover, New Hampshire, 1972; University of Southampton, 1975; University of Ife, 1978; University of Nigeria, 1981; University of Kent, Canterbury, 1982; University of Guelph, Ontario, 1984; Mount Allison University, Sackville, New Brunswick, 1984; Franklin Pierce College, Rindge, New Hampshire, 1985; Ibadan University, 1989; Skidmore College, 1991; City College of New York, 1992; Fichburg State College, 1994; Harvard University, 1996; Binghamton University, 1996; Bates College, 1996. D.Univ.: University of Stirling, 1975; Open University, 1989. LL.D.: University of Prince Edward Island, Charlottetown, 1976; Georgetown University, 1990; Port Harcourt University, 1991. D.H.L.: University of Massachusetts, 1977; Westfield College, 1989; New School for Social Research, 1991; Hobart and William Smith College, 1991; Marymount Manhattan College, 1991; Colgate University, 1993. Honorary Fellow, Modern Language Association (USA), 1975. Member, Order of the Federal Republic of Nigeria, 1979; Honorary Member, American Academy, 1982. Fellow, Royal Society of Literature, 1983. **Address:** Bard College, Annandale-on-Hudson, New York 12504, U.S.A.

PUBLICATIONS

Poetry

Beware, Soul-Brother and Other Poems. Enugu, Nwankwo-Ifejika, 1971; revised edition, Enugu, Nwamife, and London, Heinemann, 1972; revised edition, as *Christmas in Biafra and Other Poems,* New York, Doubleday, 1973.

Novels

Things Fall Apart. London, Heinemann, 1958; New York, McDowell Obolensky, 1959.
No Longer at Ease. London, Heinemann, 1960; New York, Obolensky, 1961.
Arrow of God. London, Heinemann, 1964; New York, Day, 1967.
A Man of the People. London, Heinemann, and New York, Day, 1966.
Anthills of the Savannah. London, Heinemann, 1987; New York, Doubleday, 1988.

Short Stories

The Sacrificial Egg and Other Stories. Onitsha, Etudo, 1962.
Girls at War. London, Heinemann, 1972; New York, Doubleday, 1973.

Other (for children)

Chike and the River. London and New York, Cambridge University Press, 1966.
How the Leopard Got His Claws, with John Iroaganachi. Enugu, Nwamife, 1972; New York, Third Press, 1973.
The Flute. Enugu, Fourth Dimension, 1977.
The Drum. Enugu, Fourth Dimension, 1977.
How Leopard Got His Claws. Nairobi, East African Educational Publishers, 1996.

Other

Morning Yet on Creation Day Essays. London, Heinemann, and New York, Doubleday, 1975.
In Person: Achebe, Awoonor, and Soyinka at the University of Washington. Seattle, University of Washington African Studies Program, 1975.
The Trouble with Nigeria. Enugu, Fourth Dimension, 1983; London, Heinemann, 1984.
Hopes and Impediments: Selected Essays 1965–1987. London, Heinemann, 1988.
The University and the Leadership Factor in Nigerian Politics. Enugu, ABIC, 1988.
Conversations with Chinua Achebe. Jackson, University Press of Mississippi, 1997.
Another Africa, with photographer Robert Lyons. New York, Doubleday, 1999.
Home and Exile. New York, Doubleday, 2000.

Editor, *The Insider: Stories of War and Peace from Nigeria.* Enugu, Nwankwo-Ifejika, and Chatham, New Jersey, Chatham Booksellers, 1971.
Editor, with Dubem Okafor, *Don't Let Him Die: An Anthology of Memorial Poems for Christopher Okigbo.* Enugu, Fourth Dimension, 1978.
Editor, with C.L. Innes, *African Short Stories.* London, Heinemann, 1985.

*

Bibliography: In *Africana Library Journal* (New York), spring 1970; *Chinua Achebe: A Bibliography* by B.M. Okpu, Lagos, Libriservice, 1984; "Chinua Achebe: A Bio-Bibliography" by G. D. Killam, in *Research in African Literature,* 21(4), winter 1990.

Critical Studies: *Chinua Achebe* by Arthur Ravenscroft, London, Longman, 1969, revised edition, 1977; *Chinua Achebe* by David Carroll, New York, Twayne, 1970, revised edition, London, Macmillan, 1980; *Chinua Achebe* by Kate Turkington, London, Arnold, 1977; *Critical Perspectives on Chinua Achebe* edited by Bernth Lindfors and C.L. Innes, London, Heinemann, and Washington, D.C., Three Continents Press, 1978, and *Chinua Achebe* by Innes, Cambridge University Press, 1990; *Postcolonial Literatures: Achebe, Ngugi, Desai, Walcott,* New York, St. Martin's Press, 1995; "Chinua Achebe: Novelist of Cultural Conflict" by Bernth Lindfors, in

America, 175(2), 1996; ''Romanus Okey Muoneke. Art, Rebellion and Redemption: A Reading of the Novels of Chinua Achebe'' by M.M. Goldstein, in *Ariel,* 27(2), 1996; *Chinua Achebe: A Biography* by Ezenwa-Ohaeto, Oxford, James Currey, 1997; *Conversations with Chinua Achebe* edited by Bernth Lindfors, University of Mississippi Press, 1997; ''Close Encounters: Margaret Laurence and Chinua Achebe'' by Clara Thomas, in *Journal of Canadian Studies,* 32(1), 1997; ''Chinua Achebe, a World-Class Writer'' by Essie Baker, in *The Crisis,* 105(3), 1 July 1998; ''Chinua Achebe, History-Teller'' by A. Severac, in *Commonwealth* (Rodez, France), 21(1), 1998; ''Women Writers, Women's Writing—Chinua Achebe Writing Culture: Representations of Gender and Tradition in Things Fall Apart'' by Kwadwo Osei-Nyame, in *Research in African Literature,* 30(2), 1999.

*   *   *

With the publication of his award-winning poetry volume *Christmas in Biafra,* Chinua Achebe showed the kind of mature and sensitive voice that had made his first novel, *Things Fall Apart,* a landmark in African writing fifteen years earlier.

Coming out of the incredible tragedy of the Nigerian civil war, the poems in the collection show remarkable restraint. Their language is simple and careful, yet never lacking in depth. Their imagery, as in the first few lines of ''After a War,'' is exact and intense: ''After a war life catches / desperately at passing / hints of normalcy like / vines entwining a hollow / twig.'' Many of the selections make use of biting irony, as in the title poem, ''Christmas in Biafra,'' in which the seasonal music broadcast over the radio bears messages of ''pure transcendental hate'' and the starving mothers and children stare mutely at a manger where Jesus lies ''plump-looking and rose-cheeked.''

Not all of the poems are about the Biafran conflict, however. Achebe includes personal statements and far-reaching satirical comments on Western foreign policy, as in ''He Loves Me; He Loves Me Not'': ''Harold Wilson he loves / me he gave me / a gun in my time / of need to shoot / my rebellious brother.'' But Achebe's subject matter, as in his other writings, is rooted in the confused landscape of postcolonial Africa, in which political corruption and international deals affect the lives of people who still follow traditional paths. One of his best poems, ''Beware, Soul Brother,'' begins,

> We are the men of soul
> men of song we measure out
> our joys and agonies
> too, our long, long passion week
> in paces of the dance.

This serves as a reminder to the African reader of his connection with the earth and warns against those ''lying in wait leaden-footed, tone deaf / passionate only for the deep entrails / of our soil.'' Yet it is also a poem for all human beings who remember

> where a man's
> foot must return whatever beauties
> it may weave in air, where
> it must return for safety
> and renewal of strength . . .

—Joseph Bruchac

ACKERMAN, Diane

Nationality: American. **Born:** Waukegan, Illinois, 7 October 1948. **Education:** Boston University, 1966–67; Pennsylvania State University, University Park, 1967–70, B.A. in English 1970; Cornell University, Ithaca, New York (Academy of American Poets prize, Corson French prize, Heermans-McCalmon playwriting prize, Corson Bishop prize, Rockefeller fellow), M.F.A. in creative writing 1973, M.A. in English 1976, Ph.D. in English 1978. **Career:** Social worker, New York, 1967; government researcher, University Park, Pennsylvania, 1968; editorial assistant, *Library Journal,* New York, 1970; lecturer, Cornell University, 1971–78; assistant professor, University of Pittsburgh, 1980–83; staff writer, *The New Yorker,* New York, 1988–94. Since 1998 visiting professor at The Society for the Humanities, Cornell University. Writer-in-residence, College of William and Mary, 1982–83, and Ohio University, fall 1983; writer-in-residence, spring 1983, and Director of Writers Program, Washington University, St. Louis, 1984–86; visiting writer, New York University, fall 1986, Columbia University, fall 1986, and Cornell University, spring 1987; master artist-in-residence, Atlantic Center for the Arts, 1988. Contributing editor, *Parade,* and *Travel-Holiday,* both New York. **Awards:** Abbie Copps poetry prize, 1974; National Endowment for the Arts fellowship, 1976, 1986; Creative Artists Public Service fellowship, 1980; *Black Warrior Review* poetry prize, 1981; Pushcart Prize VIII, 1984; Peter I. B. Lavan award, 1985; Lowell Thomas award, Society of American Travel Writers, 1990; Wordsmith award, 1992; New and Noteworthy Book of the Year, *New York Times Book Review,* 1992, for *The Moon by Whale Light,* 1993, for *Jaguar of Sweet Laughter: New and Selected Poems,* 1997, for *A Slender Thread;* ''Literary Lion,'' New York Public Library, 1994; the Explorers Club fellow, 1997; John Burroughs nature award, 1997. Also the recipient of numerous other awards and honors, including Board of Directors, Associated Writing Programs, 1982–85, and Poetry Panel, National Endowment for the Arts, 1991.

PUBLICATIONS

Poetry

The Planets: A Cosmic Pastoral. New York, Morrow, 1976.
Wife of Light. New York, Morrow, 1978.
Lady Faustus. New York, Morrow, 1983.
Jaguar of Sweet Laughter: New and Selected Poems. New York, Random House, and London, Chapman's, 1991.
I Praise My Destroyer. New York, Random House, 1998.

Plays

All Seasons Are Weather, in *Texas Arts Journal* (Dallas), fall 1979.
Reverse Thunder: A Dramatic Poem (produced New Brunswick, New Jersey, 1982). Sections published in *American Poetry Review* (Philadelphia), July-August 1980, and *Denver Quarterly,* winter 1984; published complete, New York, Lumen, 1988.

Other

Twilight of the Tenderfoot: A Western Memoir. New York, Morrow, 1980.
On Extended Wings. New York, Atheneum, 1985.

A Natural History of the Senses. New York, Random House, 1990.

The Moon by Whale Light, and Other Adventures among Bats, Crocodilians, Penguins and Whales. New York, Random House, 1991.

A Natural History of Love. New York, Random House, 1994.

Monk Seal Hideaway. New York, Crown, 1995.

The Rarest of the Rare. New York, Random House, 1995.

Bats: Shadows in the Night, photographs by Merlin D. Tuttle. New York, Crown, 1997.

A Slender Thread. New York, Random House, 1997.

Deep Play. New York, Random House, 1999.

Editor, with Jeanne Mackin, *The Norton Book of Love.* New York, Norton, 1998.

Recordings: *The Naturalists,* Gang of Seven Inc., 1992; *A Natural History of Love,* 1994.

*

Manuscript Collection: Cornell University, Ithaca, New York.

Critical Studies: "By Writing Gracefully about Bats, Birds and Whales, Diane Ackerman Has Become One of Nature's Most Effective Cheerleaders," in *People Weekly,* 36(19), 18 November 1991; "Diane Ackerman: Tight Focus in Small Places" by Barbara Adams, in *Writer's Digest* (Cincinnati, Ohio), 77(9), September 1997.

Diane Ackerman comments:

People sometimes ask me about all of the science in my work, thinking it odd that I should wish to combine science and art and assuming that I must have some inner pledge or outer maxim I follow. But the hardest job for me is trying to keep science out of my writing. We live in a world where amino acids, viruses, airfoils, and such are common ingredients in our daily sense of Nature. Not to write about Nature in its widest sense, because quasars or corpuscles are not "the proper realm of poetry," as a critic once said to me, is not only irresponsible and philistine, it bankrupts the experience of living, it ignores much of life's fascination and variety. I'm a great fan of the Universe, which I take literally: as one. All of it interests me, and it interests me in detail.

Writing is my form of celebration and prayer, but it is also the way in which I inquire about the world. I seem to be driven by an intense, nomadic curiosity; my feeling of ignorance is often overwhelming. As a result, prompted by unconscious obbligatos, I frequently find myself in a state of complete rapture about a field, and rapidly coming down with a book. For as little as six months, perhaps, or as long as three years, I will be obsessed with flying, or whales, love, the senses, or the dark night of the soul, and eagerly learn everything I can. Any facts I might acquire about the workings of Nature fuel my creative work and are secondary to my rage to learn about the human condition, which I don't think we can see whole from any one vantage point. If I hadn't spent a year as a soccer journalist many years ago, to get atmosphere for a novel set in the soccer world, I would never have learned as much as I did about the history of play, and certainly never written the four soccer poems at the end of *Lady Faustus,* which have little to do with soccer, but are really about the rhythm of the mind and what it means to know something.

I try to give myself passionately, totally, to whatever I'm observing, with as much affectionate curiosity as I can muster, as a means to understanding a little better what being human is, and what it was like to have once been alive on the planet, how it felt in one's senses, passions, and contemplations. I think of myself as a nature writer, if what we mean by nature is the full sum of Creation.

Poets tend to be bothered by disturbing questions. Only two questions bother me, but they bother me a lot: 1)How do you start with hydrogen and end up with us? Or, if you like, How did we get from the Big Bang to the whole shebang? and 2)What was it like to have lived? Everything I've written thus far, in poetry or prose, has been an attempt to elaborate or find answers to those two questions. Deep-down, I know they should take from birth to death to answer and include all consciousness. And I suppose some would find that rather overwhelming and fraught with built-in failure. I don't think of it in that way—in terms of goal, success, or self-esteem—but rather as a simple mystery trip. The world revealing itself, human nature revealing itself, is seductive and startling, and that's fascinating enough to send words down my spine.

*   *   *

The work of Diane Ackerman in poetry and prose is a history of her extraordinary enthusiasms. Her memoirs recount her experiences on a cattle ranch (*Twilight of the Tenderfoot*) and in learning to fly (*On Extended Wings*), and, like her later books (*A Natural History of the Senses* and *A Natural History of Love*), they explore in depth and with intensity the full extent of the subject—its history, its detailed ins and outs, its poetry, and ultimately its meaning. She is a prodigious explorer of the world, if by "world" we mean, as she puts it, "the full sum of Creation." Her poetry is distinctive in finding its source in that same enthusiastic energy; she explores the world, inner and outer, with a scientist's poetic eye, recognizing, as the chaos scientist Mitchell Feigenbaum put it, that "art is a theory about the way the world looks to human beings."

Ackerman's book-length poems *The Planets: A Cosmic Pastoral* and *Reverse Thunder: A Dramatic Poem* are the most impressive results of her effort to draw scientific and poetic curiosity (and understanding) together into a unified field of electric language. The first is a long meditation on the planets in our solar system, and the second is a verse play about Juana Inés de la Cruz, a late seventeenth-century Mexican woman who actually lived Ackerman's ideal life as poet, scientist, and genuinely independent and creative thinker.

The Planets: A Cosmic Pastoral is a set of poetic explorations and meditations on the planets, Cape Canaveral, the asteroids, and even the blurry disappointment of the comet Kohoutek. In form and content it ranges widely and well—its science up-to-date and accurate and its poetry a display of dazzling wit. It roused Carl Sagan to say that it demonstrates "how closely compatible planetary exploration and poetry, science and art really are." It bridges the "two cultures" with a vigor and success not witnessed in English and American poetry since the eighteenth century, when Newton's *Opticks* and its implications excited poets and roused their imaginative responses.

At the end of *The Planets,* Ackerman returns to Earth "like a woman who, / waking too early each day, / finds it dark yet / and all the world asleep." This situation also sums up her dilemma as a poet, having pressed poetry into a service far beyond that of most of the poems of her contemporaries and now being faced with the choice of whether to join that sleeping world or to return to planetary exploration. In the poem she concludes, ''But how could my clamorous heart / lie abed, knowing all of Creation / has been up for hours?''

Sister Juana Inés de la Cruz, the heroine of *Reverse Thunder*, faces that same dilemma and answers it in much the same way. She is tragically out of step with her place and time, but she triumphs in the work that she passes down to our time, when she finally can be (or almost can be) fully understood in all her complexity. This fascinating woman, as Ackerman pictures her, draws together in her life as a nun in seventeenth-century Mexico almost all of the conflicting and contradictory strands of life at that time. She is a nun who loves a man passionately, a believing Christian who explores the scientific view of the world, a spiritual and spirited poet who draws her inspiration from both the life of the body and of the mind, and a materialist who comes to understand that matter is so much more than it appears to be:

> If ever there was a good person in this world,
> one just or pure or altruistic or visionary,
> no matter who, or how many, or if only one,
> then purity, or justice or mercy or vision,
> is something of which matter is capable.
> That paradox of the apparent indifference
> of matter to such things as Good and Evil,
> and, yet, at the same time, the reality
> of its complete involvement:
> that's why beauty stuns and touches us.

In her collections of short poems, *Wife of Light* and *Lady Faustus,* and in the fifty-two new poems in *Jaguar of Sweet Laughter: New and Selected Poems,* Ackerman apparently strives to write as Sister Juana would if she were writing today, recognizing no limits to the range of her interests or her voice. Whether she is being earthy, playing a bluesy ''Menstrual Rag'' or singing the true joy of sex with a metaphysical force, or diving under the sea, flying an airplane, brooding over rivers and bridges, confessing the depth of her love, or speculating about the very nature of thought, her wit runs a full range, exhibiting mind, memory, sense, the senses, sensuality, sanity, ingenuity, acumen, real thought, witty banter, and productive persiflage. Her enthusiasm carries her forward but never beyond the bounds of genuine feeling and serious understanding.

As she put it in the title poem of her collection *Lady Faustus:*

> I itch all over. I rage to know
> what beings like me, stymied by death
> and leached by wonder, hug those campfires
>   night allows,
> aching to know the fate of us all,
> wallflowers in a waltz of stars.

—R.H.W. Dillard

ADAMS, Perseus

Nationality: South African and British. **Born:** Peter Robert Charles Adams in Cape Town, 11 March 1933. **Education:** Attended Cambridge, East London, and Sea Town high schools, Cape Town; University of Cape Town, B.A. in psychology and English 1952,

Cert. Ed. 1962. **Career:** Has worked as a journalist, psychologist, clerk, and English teacher in seven countries. **Awards:** South African State Poetry prize, 1963; Festival of Rhodesia prize, 1970; Bridport Arts Festival prize, 1984. **Address:** 7 New End, Hampstead, London N.W.3, England.

PUBLICATIONS

Poetry

The Land at My Door. Cape Town, Human and Rousseau, 1965.
Grass for the Unicorn. Cape Town, Juta, 1975.
Cries & Silences: Selected Poems. Randburg, South Africa, Baobab Books, 1996.

*

Critical Study: In *Momentum: On Recent South African Writing,* edited by M.J. Daymond, J.U. Jacobs, and Margaret Lenta, Pietermaritzburg, South Africa, University of Natal Press, 1984.

Perseus Adams comments:

(1970) Major themes: 1) subjects where the life-death, light-dark juxtaposition is sharply counterpointed; 2) creatures, people or animals, who have been robbed by life; 3) a metaphysical probing to discover our rightful place in the universe.

I employ a free verse with powerful resonant rhythms and complex tones. My style can be harshly decisive or gently lyrical, depending on the subject matter or mood. I have been called my country's ''foremost lyricist,'' but this is not a title I care for.

*   *   *

Perseus Adams is essentially a lyric poet. Even when he has grouped his poems under objective, thematic headings, the personal and subjective element comes through in the rhythms, texture, and structure of his verse. The mood varies from a Hopkinsian delight in nature and the joyful spontaneity of youth to a more introspective frame of mind in which the lessons of experience are mulled over. If this results at times in too explicitly didactic a strain, the poet's seriousness of purpose and lyrical intensity rescue his work from the commonplace or trivial. His first volume, *The Land at My Door,* with its division of poems into ''Morning'' and ''Afternoon,'' reflects the two contrasting moods. It is a grouping reminiscent of Blake's *Songs of Innocence and of Experience* without the conscious parallelism and antithesis. The mood of the ''Morning'' poems is closer to a Wordsworthian sense of awe, as in the closing section of the sonnet ''Dawn on Table Mountain'':

> Nor has there ever been a presence of air to match
> That tumult of impending absence that is
> An African sky, and blue, so blue you feel
> You are gazing at innocence and sacredness blended.
> Now under that dome of an incandescent eye, three play
> Their parts on this altar above the world: Grass,
>   dew and sun
> While joy shivers a watching bush-dove with supernal
>   lightning.

The poems of this first volume are characterized by a somewhat indiscriminate abundance and variety of images, at times giving an impression of contrived ingenuity. The sentiment, too, can be forced and stilted, imposed rather than issuing from the poetic experience; this is true particularly of the closing lines of "Widow" and the self-consciously didactic "A Sky's Blue Innocence." It is worth noting that these failures of tone and technique occur mainly in poems whose subject matter lies outside the writer's range of experience. The clichés and ritual gestures of "The War Veteran," for instance, reveal a sensibility not fully engaged by its subject. Against these one can place poems such as "Crying Baby in a Grocer Shop," in which the apparently commonplace is experienced in a way that invests it with a humane profundity, or "My Grandmother," where the closing stanzas present a beautifully sustained and entirely convincing vision of age advancing toward death and decay.

In *Grass for the Unicorn,* published ten years after *The Land at My Door,* the verbal profusion of the earlier volume has given way to a markedly sparer style and a more austere, controlled expression of feeling. An empathic mode of perception is one of Adams's strengths as a poet, and this is finely realized in "Mountain Protea," which also illustrates his flexible but highly functional command of form:

If—as I'm inclined to believe—
empathy is the art that comes
most naturally to the deeply quiet
                              spiralling out—

this sun pyx has it: high on Devil's Peak
with watch-fire head, all ears pricked
                              it unfolds

to enter into leopard and hawk
accenting their speed, a fleck in their sight
its tense repose, its dovetailing jet
theirs when they hunt . . .

Many of Adams's poems are inspired by his native Cape Town, South Africa, its environs and peoples. He observes keenly but with a sense of humility and awe, as in the fine, and Frost-like, lines of "Bird Shrine," in which the teacher-pupil roles are reversed as the normally backward class truant is transfigured by the "feathered glory" of his pigeons. Satire and protest are foreign to Adams's genius, and when—as in "Indigenous" and "Woltemade"—he resorts to overt social or political comment, he reduces the force and expansiveness of his lyrical gift. Similarly, though his metrical virtuosity is amply illustrated in *Grass for the Unicorn,* his experiments with typography and visual effect are extrinsic to his essentially metaphoric style and have little but novelty to commend them. The precision, force, and clarity encapsulated in a poem such as "Sea Scalpel" point to a salient aspect of Adams's poetry—his craftsmanship—and explain why he selected as a motto for his second volume the remark by the Argentinean poet Arturo Aquino that he preferred poetry to prose because "poetry drops like an eagle and stabs before you know." The other major feature of Adams's poetry is his humanistic vision; he never forgets the Wordsworthian admonition that the poet is a man speaking to men. It is this probing but sympathetic awareness that informs his most successful efforts, as in the poignant "Elegy for the Pure Act."

—Ernest Pereira

ADAMSON, Robert

Nationality: Australian. **Born:** Sydney, New South Wales, 17 May 1943. **Family:** Married 1) Cheryl Adamson in 1973; 2) Juno Gemes in 1988. **Career:** Worked as a pastry cook, fisherman, and journalist in the 1960s; associate editor, 1968–70, editor, 1970–75, and assistant editor, 1975–77, *New Poetry* magazine, Sydney; editor and director, Prism Books, Sydney, 1970–77. Since 1979 founding editor and director, with Dorothy Hewett, Big Smoke Books, Sydney; since 1988 founder, with Michael Wilding, Paper Bark Press. Designer, since 1970, Prism Books and *New Poetry* magazine, and since 1979, Big Smoke Books. **Awards:** Australia Council fellowship, 1976, 1977; Grace Leven prize, 1977. **Address:** 47 Cheero Point Road, Cheero Point, New South Wales 2254, Australia.

PUBLICATIONS

Poetry

Canticles on the Skin. Sydney, Illumination Press, 1970.
The Rumour. Sydney, New Poetry, 1971.
Swamp Riddles. Sydney, Island Press, 1974.
Theatre I-XIX. Sydney, Pluralist Press, 1976.
Cross the Border. Sydney, New Poetry, 1977.
Selected Poems. Sydney, Angus and Robertson, 1977.
Where I Come From. Sydney, Big Smoke, 1979.
The Law at Heart's Desire. Sydney, Prism, 1982.
The Clean Dark. Cheero Point, New South Wales, Paper Bark Press, 1989.
Robert Adamson Selected Poems, 1970–1989. Queensland, University of Queensland Press, 1990.
Zoo. Montmorency, Victoria, Yackandandah Playscripts, 1993.
Waving to Hart Crane. Sydney, Angus and Robertson, 1994.
The Language of Oysters, with photographs by Juno Gemes. Sydney, Craftsman House, 1997.
Black Water: Approaching Zukovsky. Rose Bay, New South Wales, Brandl and Schlesinger, 1999.

Novels

Zimmer's Essay, with Bruce Hanford. Sydney, Wild and Woolley, 1974.
Wards of the State: An Autobiographical Novella. Pymble, New South Wales, Angus and Robertson, 1992.

Other

Editor, with Manfred Jurgensen, *Australian Writing Now.* Indooroopilly, Queensland, Outrider/Penguin, 1988.

*

Manuscript Collection: Australian National Library, Canberra.

Critical Studies: By Dorothy Hewett in *New Poetry 27* (Sydney), no. 1; interview with John Tranter in *Makar 1* (Brisbane), 1979; "Thoughts on Some Recent Poetry," in *Australian Literary Studies* (St. Lucia,

Queensland), 8, 1977, and "Getting Further Away: The Poetry of Robert Adamson," in *Southerly* (Sydney), 38, 1978, both by Dennis Haskell; "'My Name Is Rickeybocky': The Poetry of Robert Adamson and the Spirit of Henry Kendall" by Michael Wilding, in *Southerly* (Sydney), 46(1), March 1986; "Homages and Invocations: The Early Poetry of Robert Adamson," in *Australian Literary Studies* (St. Lucia, Queensland), 14(2), October 1989, and "The Poetry of Robert Adamson," in *Australian Literature Today,* edited by R.K. Dhawan and David Kerr, New Delhi, Indian Society for Commonwealth Studies, 1993, both by Martin Duwell; "Feral Symbolists: Robert Adamson, John Tranter, and the Response to Rimbaud" by David Brooks, in *Australian Literary Studies* (St. Lucia, Queensland), 16(3), May 1994; "Robert Gray and Robert Adamson—A Dialectical Study of Late Australian Romanticism" by Angus Nicholls, in *Antipodes* (Austin, Texas), 11(2), December 1997.

*   *   *

With several major collections, plus two volumes of selected poems, published since 1970, Robert Adamson has claimed for himself a central position among the poets of his generation—a generation that has accomplished a remarkable revitalization of poetic energies in Australia. His work over this period has balanced an overt need to surprise and challenge (or even shock) the reader with an ongoing discovery of the sources of creative nourishment from his personal experience and his background in the Hawkesbury River region. Adamson is not, however, a regional or a confessional poet. His 1979 volume, *Where I Come From,* would seem to be a collection of autobiographical pieces about parents, childhood, and a delinquent adolescence, all related with a sort of deadpan selectivity. It is a carefully contrived game, exploring ways of approaching the self (and themes already uncovered in earlier volumes) that imply a complex relationship not only with the reader but also with the possibility of ever realizing a state beyond "the lie" of the conscious artist. In all of his verse Adamson has sought to transcend the easily ironic stance (or the glibly petulant). His poetry constantly undercuts its own pretensions, but the effect is lacerating, not denigratory. Its surface may range from the artful *simpliste* chronicler of *Where I Come From* to the arty fabulist of "The Grail Poems," but the masks are worn with a wholehearted willingness, a risk taking, that drags us into the exploration and the search. Adamson's work is, in the best sense, self-conscious. It is also consistent in its deeply felt need to seek out, if not to find, some transforming quality from the rawness of observed data and experience.

Adamson's first book, *Canticles on the Skin,* established all of the ongoing concerns he has subsequently followed: poems of prison experience (notably the opening sequence, pointedly titled "The Imitator" and bearing an inscription from Saint Paul that still illuminates his approach to art: "For though I be free from all men, yet have I made myself servant unto all, that I might gain the more"); poems of literary homage; poems of homage to the landscape; and those nervous drug/car/energy poems that were probably his most immediate successes. The book was followed by *The Rumour* in 1971, with its long title centerpiece, pivotal poems of the early 1970s in Australia (the other two being John Tranter's "Red Movie" and Martin Johnston's "The Blood Aquarium"). Though its derivations are clear, "The Rumour" reveals a sense of intense purpose and a drive that carries it into areas almost unexplored in Australian verse. *Swamp Riddles,* though diffuse, includes the first outstanding group of Hawkesbury poems and a much acclaimed set of elegies for his

contemporary Michael Dransfield. *Cross the Border,* ambitious and uneven, attempts a large synthesis but survives through individual achievements. *Where I Come From* is a deliberate turning away from this aesthetic experiment in a self-proclaimed "New Romanticism." It is immediately gripping and seemingly accessible. It is also a progress report.

The Law at Heart's Desire was seen by many to be a retreat into arcane symbolism, much influenced by the work of one of Adamson's early mentors, Robert Duncan. The collection *The Clean Dark,* however, recovers the firm Hawkesbury River concision of *Where I Come From,* thus placing the earlier collection in a new perspective of clarity and certainly reinforcing its centrality as a major statement of Adamson's poetic vision. *The Clean Dark* allows itself more lyric grace and in doing so gives rein to his so-called New Romanticism without overwhelming the reader in misty stances. Adamson's Hawkesbury is a river of sharp, clear lights, not hazy distance.

The Clean Dark won the three major poetry prizes in Australia and reestablished Adamson as a leading poet in a now mature generation. It was succeeded by an autobiographical volume of prose and poetry, titled *Wards of the State* (1992), which also attracted high praise. The collection *Waving to Hart Crane* (1994) continues to utilize the Hawkesbury region as a poetic base for intensely observed metaphysical meditations, while enriching this achievement more overtly with a consciousness of dialogue with the poet's own nominated "peers." The poems include the extraordinary meditation "The Sugar Glider," which, in a ruminative manner perhaps learned from Bruce Beaver, pulls together observations on the work of the poets Michael Palmer and Les Murray with images of rare Australian marsupials and an elegy for lost tribes and species.

The Language of Oysters (1997) offers a consolidation and a synopsis of Adamson's Hawkesbury River poems, being meditations and observations on the river of his childhood and his more recent residence. It includes earlier poems, and in the new context their metaphysical intent is underlined. *Black Water* (1999) maintains Adamson's laconic late tone, but in moving back toward city landscapes the poet reasserts one of his basic beliefs in both the deceit and the power of poetry: "this geodesic discotheque is held together by art alone."

—Thomas W. Shapcott

ADCOCK, Fleur

Nationality: British. **Born:** Papakura, New Zealand, 10 February 1934; immigrated to the United Kingdom in 1963. **Education:** Studied in England, 1939–47; Wellington Girls' College and Victoria University of Wellington, New Zealand, M.A. (honors) in classics, 1956. **Family:** Married Alistair Campbell, *q.v.,* in 1952 (divorced 1958); two sons. **Career:** Temporary assistant lecturer in classics, University of Otago, Dunedin, 1958. Held library posts at University of Otago, 1959–61, and Turnbull Library, Wellington, 1962; assistant librarian, Foreign and Commonwealth Office Library, London, 1963–79. Arts Council creative writing fellow, Charlotte Mason College of Education, Ambleside, Cumbria, 1977–78; Northern Arts fellow, universities of Newcastle upon Tyne and Durham, 1979–81; Eastern Arts fellow, University of East Anglia, Norwich, 1984. **Awards:** Festival of Wellington prize, 1961; New Zealand State

Literary Fund award, 1964; Buckland award, 1967, 1979; Jessie MacKay award, 1968, 1972; Cholmondeley award, 1976; New Zealand Book award, 1984; Arts Council award, 1988. **Address:** 14 Lincoln Road, London N2 9DL, England.

PUBLICATIONS

Poetry

The Eye of the Hurricane. Wellington, Reed, 1964.
Tigers. London, Oxford University Press, 1967.
High Tide in the Garden. London, Oxford University Press, 1971.
The Scenic Route. London, Oxford University Press, 1974.
The Inner Harbour. Oxford, Oxford University Press, 1979.
Below Loughrigg. Newcastle upon Tyne, Bloodaxe, 1979.
Selected Poems. Oxford, Oxford University Press, 1983.
Hotspur: A Ballad for Music. Newcastle upon Tyne, Bloodaxe, 1986.
4-Pack 1: Four from Northern Women, with Maura Dooley, S. J. Litherland, and Jill Maugham. Newcastle upon Tyne, Bloodaxe, 1986.
The Incident Book. Oxford, Oxford University Press, 1986.
Meeting the Comet. Newcastle upon Tyne, Bloodaxe, 1989.
Time-Zones. Oxford, Oxford University Press, 1991.
Looking Back. Oxford, Oxford University Press, 1997.

Other

Editor, with Anthony Thwaite, *New Poetry 4.* London, Hutchinson, 1978.
Editor, *The Oxford Book of Contemporary New Zealand Poetry.* Auckland and Oxford, Oxford University Press, 1982.
Editor, *The Faber Book of Twentieth Century Women's Poetry.* London, Faber, 1987.
Editor and translator, *Hugh Primas and the Archpoet.* Cambridge, Cambridge University Press, 1994.
Editor, with Jacqueline Sims, *The Oxford Book of Creatures.* New York, Oxford University Press, 1996.

Translator, *The Virgin and the Nightingale: Medieval Latin Poems.* Newcastle upon Tyne, Bloodaxe, 1983.
Translator, *Orient Express,* by Grete Tartler. Oxford, Oxford University Press, 1989.
Translator, *Letters from Darkness,* by Daniela Crasnaru. Oxford, Oxford University Press, 1994.

*

Critical Studies: Introduction by Dannie Abse to *Corgi Modern Poets in Focus 5,* 1973; *Fleur Adcock in Context: From Movement to Martians,* by Julian Stannard, Edwin Mellon Press, 1997.

Fleur Adcock comments:

I cannot give a code of my poetic practice or a set of rules by which I have operated; I can only point to certain tendencies and outline an attitude. Poetry is a search for ways of communication. It must be conducted with openness, flexibility, and a constant readiness to listen. The content of my poems derives largely from those parts of my life that are directly experienced: relationships with people or places; images and insights that have presented themselves sharply from whatever source, conscious or subconscious; ideas triggered off by language itself. In recent years I have tended increasingly to use poetry as a method of writing fiction; the narratives of my poems, seldom ever merely autobiographical, often now tell invented stories.

My verse forms are relatively traditional (traditions alter). In general they have moved away from strict classical patterns in the direction of greater freedom, as is usual with most artists learning a trade. It takes courage, however, to leave all props behind, to cast oneself, like Matisse, upon pure space. I still await that confidence. In the meantime I continue to learn and sometimes find it fruitful to return to a rigid metrical form as a discipline and for a different kind of exploration.

I write primarily for the printed page, not for performance, regarding poetry readings as the trailer, not the movie. But because the sound of words is central to the experiencing of a poem, I read my work aloud as it develops and try to remove anything that is clumsy or unacceptable to the ear. As for the eye, the patterns of lines in type do not particularly interest me; words, not their shape on the page, are what matter. If one is fortunate, their destination, like their origin, will be as voices speaking in the mind.

*   *   *

Fleur Adcock is one of the most popular poets in Britain. Though New Zealand born, she spent much of her childhood in wartime England. Her work shows a strong attachment to place, whether it be the English countryside, the beaches of New Zealand, or the dirt tracks of Nepal. Coupled with this is an acute awareness of the barriers between people. Adcock is, by her own admission, a solitary person; with her cool, dispassionate eye and her reluctant nostalgia, she is a true expatriate.

After the war, Adcock's family returned to New Zealand, and it was there that she produced the prizewinning elegy "Flight, with Mountains." The poem is characteristic of her later work in its clear, conversational tone and in its preoccupation with friendship, death, and landscape:

> . . . Another one for the mountains. Another one
> Who, climbing to stain the high snow
> With his shadow, fell, and briefly caught between
> Sudden earth and sun, projected below
> A flicker of darkness . . . .

The poems ends,

> . . . neither
> Rope, nor crumbling ice, nor your unbelieving
> Uncommitted hands could hold you to living.
> Wheels turn; the dissolving air rolls over
> An arc of thunder. Gone is gone forever.

In 1963 Adcock moved back to England. In her first British publication, *Tigers,* she abandoned the romanticism of her earlier works. Influenced by the informality of the 1960s, she experimented with syllabics, discarding conventional meter and rhyme to embrace a more prosy, colloquial style. Although she tends to extrapolate from her own life, Adcock is too reticent to be classed among the confessional poets. Preferring understatement to exaggeration, she tends to suggest rather than plummet. A poem like "Incident" hints at disconcerting truths as the speaker wakes from a nap on the beach to find her lover "waiting for the lapping tide to take me / Watching, and lighting a cigarette." In "Miss Hamilton in London" a spinster goes through her daily rituals, "then went to bed; where for the hours of darkness, / She lay pierced by thirty black spears . . . ." Again the calm, oblique style gives a shocking punch to the poem.

The love poems in this volume are, to say the least, astringent. "Advice to a Discarded Lover" begins by describing a bird's corpse and then goes on to warn the lover that ". . . in you / I see maggots close to the surface. You are eaten up by self-pity, / Crawling with unloveable pathos . . . Do not ask me for charity now: / Go away until your bones are clean." Relationships get equally short shrift in Adcock's next volume, *High Tide in the Garden,* where "Against Coupling" begins,

I write in praise of the solitary act:
of not feeling a trespassing tongue
forced into one's mouth . . .
Pyramus and Thisbe are dead, but
the hole in the wall can still be troublesome.
I advise you, then, to embrace it without encumbrance . . . .

Adcock also draws on the imagery of dreams and mythology. "Afterwards" begins, "We weave haunted circles about each other, / advance and retreat in turn, like witchdoctors / before a fetish . . . ," and the long fantasy "Gas" tackles the theme of the doppelgänger.

In *The Scenic Route,* Adcock explores the Ireland of her ancestors. Death creeps into the volume with "In Memoriam: James K Baxter," but any fear of sentimentality is undercut by the poet's characteristic candor: "I'd write with more conviction about death / if it were clutching at my every breath. / And now we've come to it. The subject's out: / the ineluctable, the all-pervasive . . . / and if so far I've seemed a bit evasive / it's not from cowardice or phoney tact— / it's simply that I can't believe the fact . . . ." In "Kilpeck," the poet and a lover, "dried out and brittle this morning / fragile with continence," examine the grotesques of a Norman church. Although the poem is laced with erotic imagery, the poet affirms her commitment to poetry above all else, presumably including the relationship in question.

Adcock's next volume, *The Inner Harbour,* concentrates on the beginnings and endings of relationships. It also contains some short imagistic pieces, as in the title poem, a sequence of lyrical observations such as:

Under the sand at low tide
are whispers, hisses, long slithers,
bubbles, the suck of ingestion, a soft
snap: mysteries and exclusions . . . .

The volume contains one of Adcock's most poignant poems, "The Soho Hospital for Women," which describes a cancer ward: "Doctor, I am not afraid of a word. / But neither do I wish to embrace that visitor . . . ."

The Incident Book is more outward looking than Adcock's previous collections, with the section "Thatcherland," for example, exploring contemporary Britain. There are ironical reflections on

language and art; "Leaving the Tate" concludes with the line "Art's whatever you choose to frame." Adcock also experiments with voices other than the autobiographical. "On the Land" is written as by a World War I land girl, and in "Drowning" a woman condemned to drown for the murder of her husband ruminates,

Then let the fishes feast on us
and slurp our blood after we're finished:
they'll find no souls to suck from us.
Yours, perhaps, has a safe-conduct:
you're a bishop, and subtle, and Greek.
Well, sir, pray and ponder. But our language has no word
    for dilemma.
Drowning's the strongest word for death.

As this poem suggests, Adcock's work reveals a subtle feminist streak. Over the years her poems have increasingly turned toward the politics of relationships.

In 1987 Adcock edited *The Faber Book of Twentieth Century Women's Poetry.* In her introduction to the anthology she explained that what she values in a poem is "the odd or the unexpected . . . the kind of detail which throws new and startling light . . . often . . . related to another quality I admire: wit." Certainly her work both startles and amuses. Without sacrificing any of its delightful, acerbic humor, with time Adcock's poetry has also become more compassionate.

Time-Zones, Adcock's 1991 collection, is an array of sensitive and intelligent responses to events both small and enormous. In one poem she mourns her father's death and in another witnesses the devastation of the plant by the greenhouse effect. Her flourish is for noticing the link between the domestic and the international, as in "Libya":

When the Americans were bombing Libya
(that time when it looked as if this was it at last,
the match in the petrol-tank which will flare sooner
    or later,
and the whole lot was about to go up)

Gregory turned on the television during dinner
and Elizabeth asked the children to be quiet . . .

Wit, a formal ear, and a strong feminist and global consciousness mark Adcock's significant contribution to the poetry of her country and her language.

—Katie Campbell and Martha Sutro

AGARD, John

Nationality: British (immigrated to England in 1977). **Born:** British Guiana (now Guyana) 1949. **Career:** Has worked as an actor and a performer with a jazz group. **Awards:** Casa de las Américas Poetry prize, Cuba, 1982; Children's Rights Workshop Other award, 1986. **Address:** c/o Hodder & Stoughton, Mill Road, Dunton Green, Sevenoaks, Kent TN13 2YA, England.

PUBLICATIONS

Poetry

Shoot Me with Flowers. Privately printed, 1973.
Man to Pan. Havana, Cuba, Casa de las Américas, 1982.
Limbo Dancer in Dark Glasses. London, Islington Community Press (for Greenhearb), 1983.
Mangoes and Bullets: Selected and New Poems 1972–84. London, Pluto, 1985.
Lovelines for a Goat-Born Lady. London, Serpent's Tail, 1991.

Poetry (for children)

I Din Do Nuttin and Other Poems, illustrated by Susanna Gretz. London, Bodley Head, 1983.
Say It Again, Granny!: Twenty Poems from Caribbean Proverbs, illustrated by Susanna Gretz. London, Bodley Head, 1986.
Lend Me Your Wings, illustrated by Adrienne Kennaway. London, Hodder and Stoughton, 1987.
The Calypso Alphabet, illustrated by Jennifer Bent. New York, Holt, 1989.
Go Noah, Go! London, Hodder and Stoughton, 1990.
Laughter Is an Egg, illustrated by Alan Rowe. London, Viking, 1990.
Life Doesn't Frighten Me at All. New York, Holt, 1990.
The Emperor's Dan-Dan. London, Hodder and Stoughton, 1992.
From the Devil's Pulpit. Newcastle upon Tyne, Bloodaxe Books, 1997.
Get Back Pimple! London, Puffin Books, 1997.

Other

Letters for Lettie and Other Stories (for children), illustrated by Errol Lloyd. London, Bodley Head, 1979.
Dig Away Two-Hole Tim (for children), illustrated by Jennifer Northway. London, Bodley Head, 1981.
Wake Up, Stir About: Songs for Assembly, with others. Cambridge, Massachusetts, Unwin Hyman, 1989.

Editor, with Grace Nichols, *A Caribbean Dozen,* illustrated by Cathie Felstead. Cambridge, Massachusetts, Candlewick Press, 1994.
Editor, with Grace Nichols, *No Hickory, No Dickory, No Dock: A Collection of Nursery Rhymes,* illustrated by Cynthia Jabar. Cambridge, Massachusetts, Candlewick Press, 1994.

*

Critical Study: "A Common Tongue: Interviews with Cecil Abrahams, John Agard, John Harne, and Wole Soyinka" by Siga Asanga, in *Canadian Journal of African Studies,* 24(1), 1990.

*   *   *

Although associated with oral performance and protest poetry, John Agard also writes good love poetry (usually to his wife, the poet Grace Nichols) and books of verse for children. He creates personae unifying his books and has a talent for punning and for finding unexpected metaphors in otherwise dead language. He also has a sense of rhythm and an attractive personal voice. *Shoot Me with Flowers* was self-published in Guyana at the time of flower power and peace and love, the Beatles, Vietnam, and black power. Agard has continued to develop beyond the counterculture and its politics, and his works range from intimate poems to those of *Man to Pan,* a cycle for performance with steel drums.

During 1975 Agard joined All-ah-We, a group of actors and performers in Guyana. This helped him create characters, tell stories, and use Creole, and it improved his ability to work with audiences. He enjoys the surreal invention found in the best calypsos, and his style of performing and use of Creole are calypso-influenced.

Man to Pan, published in Cuba, celebrates the history of the steel band and is largely political. It begins with "Pan Recipe," which claims that the origins of the steel band are found in the response to the centuries-old "rape" of a people as expressed in drums in shantytowns. The poems approximate the various rhythms and tones of pans in a steel band, and there are even visually shaped poems meant to represent rhythms and sounds. Agard wishes to speak for a community, but his politics and his slogans do not always go hand and hand as well as they might with his making of poetry from sounds and rhythms: "and to me octave / is a word dat rhyme with slave." Too much is asserted: "Beethoven to kaiso / shantytownsound turn concerto."

Agard's first volume of poetry for adults published in England was *Limbo Dancer in Dark Glasses,* in which black protest poetry becomes something larger and mythic and more inclusive. The Limbo Dancer moves through various stages from birth to death, with the promise of resurrection. He becomes the dance of life, the survival instinct, sex, even another name for the libido. He combines Frantz Fanon, Marx, and Freud into the black slave's survival dance. The Limbo Dancer, like the Palm Tree King and the Wanted Man, is one of Agard's fanciful personae imagined from street characters, history, the poet, and the revolutionary. "Limbo Dancer's Wombsong" sets the tone of the dancer as an amused and amusing cool cat who speaks English with traits of West Indian dialect: "believe me it was fun / in the primal womb / like great balloon." Born of the "mother of universe," he stretches from Africa to Brazil. He is six million Jews, and he is Stephen Biko, all of the oppressed victims of evil. He is also difficult to interpret. Is he bending over backward in supplication or in aggression? In "Limbo Dancer at Immigration" he is not wanted: "It was always the same / at every border / at every frontier." His dance is a multiple revolution combining Fanon, Che Guevara, Angela Davis, the Kama Sutra, and the joys of natural childbirth. He is part of the masses and is among the children of Soweto and the miners of Gdansk. He is Christ, a black entertainer, someone who will always return.

Mangoes and Bullets consists of new poems under the title "Wanted Man" along with selections from Agard's earlier volumes. It begins with "Dedication": "Remembering Walter Rodney & Maurice Bishop / two of our Caribbean dream-doers." "Immigrant Neighbors" ironically contrasts the horror felt by the white British when "your immigrant neighbours / slaughter a sheep / in view of the street" or a loud all-night party with the viewing of "a video nasty"—"our little ones just love to see / a monster's blood spatter": "Why can't these foreigners / be more like us / why can't they act civilized / and organise a decent fox hunt." Agard amusingly assumes the persona of a wanted man, wanted because of his crimes with Standard English. In "Listen Mr Oxford Don" he says, "I didn't graduate / I immigrate":

I ent have no gun
I ent have no knife

but mugging de Queen's English
is the story of my life
. . .
I ent serving no jail sentence
I slashing suffix in self-defence
I bashing future wit present tense
and if necessary

I making de Queen's English accessory
to my offence.

Lovelines for a Goat-Born Lady is dedicated to Nichols. The term ''goat-born'' refers to the sign under which the ''lady'' was born, and the love poems use many of the usual motifs of such poetry but with a Guyanese difference. She is at times referred to as ''Mudhead woman,'' with a footnote explaining that ''mudhead'' is a Guyanese term of affection for those from the low-lying silted coastland. The poems are charming in their use of West Indian terms and in the many variations Agard finds in writing a love poem: ''Starapple of my eye / my firefly in pitchdense of night.'' In later poems the woman is pregnant: ''Your belly big with child / is geography made new.'' Agard sometimes sounds like a Cavalier poet: ''Lead me to your wanton parts / that I may graze / with holy glee.''

Besides Agard's mischievous poems, *From the Devil's Pulpit* includes delightful drawings of deviltry by Satoshi Kitamura and pages of such quotations and pseudoquotes as ''God is good and The Devil isn't bad either'' (''Irish Proverb'') and ''Spell my name backwards. / Ask yourself: Have you LIVED?'' (''Yours Truly, the Devil''). In ''Book of Temptation'' Agard offers short, witty poems giving the devil's perspective on life. His devil is a social satirist and comedian, and the poems include ''The Seeds of Wimbledon,'' ''The Devil at Carnival,'' ''Glory Glory Be to Chocolate,'' ''Light Up Your Pipes,'' ''Coffee in Heaven,'' ''The Devil's Plenary Address to a Conference,'' and ''I Pity You Your Clocks.'' There also is a section titled ''A Fiend of the Arts'' that includes ''Mona Lisa You Teaser,'' ''Lucifer Relaxes with a Michael Jackson Video,'' and ''Lucifer Addresses Hollywood's Oscar Ceremony.'' At times the poet is a conventional moralist complaining of the horrors of nationalism, ethnic hatred, and civil war in Rwanda, Ireland, and Bosnia. Agard has a philosophy; life consists of balance, opposites, and temptations, and every god needs a devil, every order needs a disorder, and every established hierarchy needs skeptical mockery.

While most of the verses for children in *Get Back, Pimple!* have titles such as ''Exams Blues,'' ''Not-Enough Pocket-Money Blues,'' and ''Blind-Date Blues,'' others, such as ''Angela Davis and Joan of Arc Rap,'' are political.

—Bruce King

AI

Pseudonym: Florence Anthony. **Nationality:** American. **Born:** Albany, Texas, 21 October 1947. **Education:** University of Arizona, Tucson, 1965–69, B.A. 1969; University of California, Irvine, 1969–71, M.F.A. 1971. **Career:** Visiting poet, Wayne State University, 1977–78, George Mason University, 1986, 1987; writer-in-residence, Arizona State University, 1988–89; visiting associate professor, University of Colorado at Boulder, 1996–97. **Awards:** Guggenheim fellowship, 1975; Radcliffe fellowship, 1975; Lamont Poetry Selection, 1978; National Endowment for the Arts fellowship, 1978, 1985; Ingram Merrill fellowship, 1983; St. Botolph Foundation grant, 1986; Before Columbus Foundation American Book Award, 1987, for *Sin*. **Address:** c/o Jill Bialosky, Editor, W.W. Norton, 500 Fifth Avenue, New York, New York 10110–0017, U.S.A.

PUBLICATIONS

Poetry

Cruelty. Boston, Houghton Mifflin, 1973.
Killing Floor. Boston, Houghton Mifflin, 1979.
Sin. Boston, Houghton Mifflin, 1986.
Fate. Boston, Houghton Mifflin, 1991.
Greed. New York, Norton, 1993.

Novel

Black Blood. New York, Norton, 1997.

*

Manuscript Collection: New York Public Library.

Critical Studies: ''The Will to Transcendence in Contemporary American Poet, Ai'' by Rob Wilson, in *Canadian Review of American Studies* (Calgary, Alberta), 17(4), winter 1986; ''A 'Descent toward the Unknown' in the Poetry of Ai'' by Susannah B. Mintz, in *Sage* (Atlanta, Georgia), 9(2), summer 1995; ''Ai's 'Go''' by Michele Leavitt, in *Explicator* (Washington, D.C.), 54(2), winter 1996.

Ai comments:

Ai is the only name by which I wish to be and, indeed, should be known. Since I am the child of a scandalous affair my mother had with a Japanese man she met at a streetcar stop and I was forced to live a lie for so many years, while my mother concealed my natural father's identity from me, I feel that I should not, for all eternity, have to be identified with a man who was only my stepfather.

My writing of dramatic monologues was a happy accident, because I took so much to heart the opinion of my first poetry teacher, Richard Shelton, the fact that the first-person voice was always the stronger voice to use when writing. What began as an experiment in that voice became the only voice in which I wrote for about twenty years. Lately, though, I have been writing poems and short stories using the second person, without, it seems to me, any diminution in the power of my work. Still, I feel that the dramatic monologue was the form in which I was born to write, and I love it as passionately, or perhaps more passionately, than I have ever loved a man.

*   *   *

Ai is a dangerous writer and means to be. Hers is a poetry that aims to be disturbing, and less sophisticated readers may take the violence and sometimes brutal sex that propel her writing at face value. There is considerably more at work, however.

This is poetry about people seeking transformation, a rough sort of salvation, through violent acts. The poems sometimes lift up stones and hurl them at the reader. At other times, especially in her later collections, the poet steps back with her burden so that we can see bits of the national psyche, wriggling and squirming in a new, raw light.

Ai's poems are almost all dramatic monologues. In earlier books like *Cruelty* and *Killing Floor* the voices we hear are often those of the anonymous poor. "Why I Can't Leave You," an early poem from *Cruelty,* Ai's first collection, demonstrates the author's power to suggest erotic entrapment in relationships devoid of tenderness:

I know that we can't give each other any more
or any less than what we have.
There is safety in that, so much
that I can never get past the packing,
the begging you to please, if I can't make you happy,
come close between my thighs
and let me laugh for you from my second mouth.

Killing Floor is in some ways a transitional book, mixing the anonymous voices from the first collection with those of the famous, including Yukio Mishima as he commits hara-kiri and Marilyn Monroe reflecting on her mother's death. In the latter book the acts of violence that fill *Cruelty* and *Killing Floor* become emblems for psychic violence, as in "Guadalajara Cemetery," where the speaker apparently contemplates sex with a widowed man:

It's time to cross the border
and cut your throat with two knives:
you wife, your son . . .
You, me, these withered flowers,
so many hearts tied in a knot,
given and taken away.

In *Fate* and *Greed* speakers often bear the names of real people, many famous to the point of being cultural icons. Ai reinvents each persona, taking real or perceived traits to an even more archetypal extreme. What each says, returning after death, expresses more about the American psyche than about the real figures, and Ai intends it this way. Her speakers include Mary Jo Kopechne, J. Edgar Hoover, Jack Ruby, Jimmy Hoffa, James Dean, Elvis Presley, and Alfred Hitchcock. Characters include both the anointed famous and recipients of Andy Warhol's fifteen minutes of fame, such as the possible rape victim and certain victim of media penetration in "Evidence from a Reporter's Notebook," from *Fate:*

Six straight days, she's front-page news
She makes guest appearances by the dozen
Everybody's cousin wants their piece
of tender meat . . .

By the end of the poem the reporter realizes that she has violated the victim whether an actual rapist has done so or not.

In other poems in the later collections the speakers return to perform other acts of violation, often visited on themselves as much as on real or imagined victims. Sometimes the poems pick up, as does one on Jack Ruby, on scurrilous material published about the notorious, and Ai proceeds to discover the deeper truth lurking even in lies.

In "Oswald Incognito & Astral Travels," from *Greed,* Oswald sees himself vanishing into his own act:

I write my name on the wall
beside the Coke machine. OSWALD
in capital letters.
I erase it with spit and my shirttail,
but it keeps reappearing,
each time the letters get larger,
until the "O" is a hole
I can walk through
and when I finally do, it closes around me
like a mouth around the mouth of a rifle.

In "Miracle in Manila," from *Greed,* a posthumous Ferdinand Marcos reflects on his wife Imelda, who perhaps as much as any contemporary figure has come to personify greed. Here she stages a mock crucifixion, displays phony stigmata on her palms, and then

After a transfusion, a facial,
and a manicure,
she's campaigning again, although it's useless
and I'm back to tap-dancing at her side,
while she proclaims herself
the only candidate
who can rise from the dead.

This is poetry that hardly lays claim to being poetry. It is addressed to ordinary people, not to politicians or academics. Ai faces essential questions and lies about racial and sexual politics with great assurance.

—Duane Ackerson

AITCHISON, James

Nationality: Scottish. **Born:** Stirlingshire, 21 October 1938. **Education:** University of Glasgow, 1956–60, M.A. 1960; University of Strathclyde, Glasgow, 1969–73, Ph.D. 1973. **Family:** Married Norma Nicol in 1960; one son and one daughter. **Career:** Publicity copywriter, Scotsman Publications, Edinburgh; information officer, Strathclyde University, Glasgow, 1979–86; literary journalist, *The Scotsman,* Edinburgh, 1965–75, and *The Herald,* Glasgow, 1981–91; lecturer, Napier University, Edinburgh, 1986–94. **Awards:** Eric Gregory award, 1968; Scottish Arts Council award, 1973. **Address:** 10 Royal Gardens, Stirling FK8 2RJ, England.

PUBLICATIONS

Poetry

Sounds before Sleep. London, Chatto and Windus, 1971.
Spheres. London, Chatto and Windus, 1975.
Second Nature. Aberdeen, Aberdeen University Press, 1990.
Brain Scans. Edinburgh, Scottish Cultural Press, 1998.
Journal of Patrick Napier. N.p., n.d.

Other

The Golden Harvester—The Vision of Edwin Muir. Aberdeen, Aberdeen University Press, 1988.
Guide to Written English. London, Cassell, 1994.
The Cassell Dictionary of English Grammar. London, Cassell, 1996.

Editor, with Alexander Scott, *New Writing Scotland I, II, and III.* Aberdeen, Aberdeen University Press, 1983, 1984, 1985.

*   *   *

Beginning with his first collection, the circumstances James Aitchison depicts in his poems, which generally involve common events and frequently the family, reveal more than they initially promise. Thus, in ''Child in Fairground'' the father puts his child on a horse on a merry-go-round (''roundabout'') that ''sails my child through the wet September evening.'' The child is already out of his control and the impotence of his love hinted at, but nothing untoward happens:

The record ends and slowly the thing
comes round again and all the beasts are still.
He grips the chipped ear and slides down
down from the beast and roundabout to the soft turf.

The wooden horses have become ''beasts'' and the merry-go-round a ''thing,'' suggesting anonymous, threatening powers and a father possessed by anxiety. The poem ends with the line ''And I cannot hear what he says as he takes my hand.'' Despite the final focus on the intensity of the personal experience, however, the low-key writing keeps the merry-go-round and its bored attendant in the foreground throughout:

Sixpence, love-she shuffles them from hand to hand
and does not see the child.

This early poem, from *Sounds before Sleep* (1971), indicates the direction from which Aitchison rarely deviates. The culmination of seeking to be true to the whole experience occurs when the event—place and person—seems to dictate the poem. In ''On Some Islands'' he writes,

When the name is right
it's as if the land had a will of its own
and named itself—
the Bay of Seals, the White Meadow,
Island of the Burned Ground.
. . .
And when you walk in these places
after an absence, after an illness
then each place declares itself to you,
and you to yourself again.

What is required is to be receptive, which depends on the given conditions. Once a person is put at the disposal of the experience, the outer world and the inward world give new perceptions. But the means of perception, words, may degenerate and so must be held up for inspection. In ''Island in the Lake'' the speaker has arrived at the lake with difficulty, and Aitchison writes,

The ruined priory prompted the ruined words:
religion, heritage and history.
It's as if lakes and islands were outlined
in us before we see them; they fill a space
already mapped out for them in our mind.
An island in a lake's a dangerous place—
without looking for them you may find
some other ruined words, life peace or grace.

He discerns illusions and sets aside shibboleths, and although he sets out with an objective he fails to achieve, to the patient, open mind all is gain. Thus, when Aitchison applies his criteria to the portrayal of persons, including himself, the essential experience is in the charity of his interpretations and in the awareness in his people of the marvel of merely being alive.

In ''Off Season'' a visitor discovers an old man in a boarding-house—''You mean you're here the whole year round, she said.'' The poem catches the pitying tone of the visitor and that of the old man disclosing that he can most readily be himself during the off-season, and it concludes,

and nothing could be lovelier than this
December morning with a hint of sun
and sea mist shrinking back into the sea.

It is in a self-portrait, however, ''Picking Sprouts on a Winter Morning,'' that Aitchison puts to the test whether it was a curse or a blessing that he had ''chapped hands'' and that ''sleet or rain / fell while I picked the crop'':

And when I tried to straighten up
I felt the cold and the small hurts
not as a price to pay but part
of a blessing that's familiar
and yet so rare, come from so far
across the mind and from a past
so distant the gift would be lost
were it not for the rain and sleet,
hands raw with frost, wood pigeons' shit
and the wood pigeons in flight
through winter morning's grey half-light.

Yet these poems may be seen as a trial run when set alongside ''Antarctica,'' from the *Journal of Patrick Napier*. Here the impartiality of the documentary style allows the facts of the terrible journey to speak for themselves until the tone modulates to take account of the fantasies of the explorers as they develop under extreme conditions. The movement toward the suggestion of layers of meaning beyond the facts begins subtly with references to the weather:

The snow and ice lie so deep that we walk
not on the earth but on solid weather.
we walk on the weather of many centuries.

Dreams of death and a predatory beast follow, but the narrator survives. The style then returns to a direct simplicity:

And when I awoke and saw the little lamp
And the shadows waltzing on the walls of the tent
I thought myself in God's waiting room.
And I felt the joy of being alive.

The final discovery in all of these poems is that the author exists within a pattern or order of life that, although beyond his comprehension, is not beyond his apprehension. In the simple act of picking sprouts the necessary gesture becomes an ancient ritual. The experience is a by-product of the subject and not within the author's planning. In "Sparrows: A Misreading of Bede" Aitchison writes that

Without parables, without faith
how can we prepare for the merciless places?

In "C.A.D. Imagination as a Primitive System of Computer-Aided Design," the speaker visits a place that though intended to solve problems does not do so for him. The poem begins, appropriately, with cant:

It's mainly files of junk now: junk mail, junk
drafts of abandoned drafts. Sometimes the screen—
this seems to happen more and more—is blank

In the end he escapes from the dry computer air—"I fall in love with words and earth once more." Yet he knows how exposed and vulnerable are his feelings. In "Smooth Edgd Razer"

I sat through *Lears* and *Crucibles*
and tried to deny the rendings of the flesh.

He then plans an escape:

I began to rehearse evasions, practised them
until eluding the smooth edgd razer
became second nature to me,
until my second nature became my first.

I take no risks, cross few thresholds.
I am anonymous, almost invisible.

The cost of the protection is to be less than human. Its attraction is the takeover of first nature by second nature. (The title of the collection, *Second Nature,* helps indicate the significance of the poem.) The distinction of Aitchison's writing, however, is in the creation of characters given unexpected dimension through his compassionate understanding.

Throughout his poetry Aitchison is an explorer, asking questions about the nature of life and generally finding that though chaos threatens to destroy all a controlling order exists. In his collection *Brain Scans,* however, he asks questions about the "territory" in the brain of verbal communication:

But I keep looking, trying to express
in words the nature of the wordlessness
that ripples through forgotten and half-known
channels of the memory's lexicon
where language is inchoate, and the brain

must discover how to write again
WORDS

In "Mr William Sloane," in the sequence "Neurological Rounds," a man is in a hospital after an accident that has almost destroyed his power of speech. With great sensitiveness Aitchison reproduces his partial recovery and discovers a new freshness in the words. He also develops a sequence with other patients. The recognition of our dependence on the physical properties of the brain for verbal communication may be depressing, but this is put in balance by the effect of the will to recover, which brings an unexpected brightness to the poem. It also marks an extension to the art of Aitchison.

—George Bruce

ALEXANDER, Meena

Nationality: American (originally Indian). **Born:** Allahabad, 17 February 1951. **Education:** Unity High School, Khartoum, Sudan, graduated 1964; University of Khartoum, B.A. (honors) 1969; University of Nottingham, Ph.D. in English 1973. **Family:** Married David Lelyveld in 1979; one son and one daughter. **Career:** Tutor in English, University of Khartoum, 1969; lecturer in English, University of Delhi, 1974, and Central Institute of English and Foreign Languages, Hyderabad, 1975–77; CSIR Fellow, Jawaharlal Nehru University, New Delhi, 1975; lecturer, 1977–79, and reader, 1979, University of Hyderabad; visiting fellow, Sorbonne, Paris, 1979; assistant professor of English, Fordham University, Bronx, New York, 1980–87; assistant professor, 1987–89, associate professor, 1989–91, and since 1992 professor, Hunter College and the Graduate Centre, City University of New York. Visiting assistant professor, University of Minnesota, Minneapolis, 1981; lecturer in writing, Columbia University, 1991–99; visiting university grants commission fellow, English Institute, University of Kerala, Trivandrum, 1987; writer-in-residence, Centre for American Culture Studies, Columbia University, New York, 1988; poet-in-residence, American College, Madurai, India, 1994; MacDowell Colony Fellow, 1993. **Awards:** National Endowment for the Humanities travel grant, 1985; New York State Council for the Arts grant, 1988; poetry award, New York State Foundation for the Arts, 1999. **Agent:** Sandra Dijkstra, Sandra Dijkstra Literary Agency, 1155 Camino Del Mar, Suite 515, Del Mar, California 92014. **Address:** English Department, Hunter College, City University of New York, 695 Park Avenue, New York, New York 10021, U.S.A.

PUBLICATIONS

Poetry

The Bird's Bright Ring. Calcutta, Writers Workshop, 1976.
I Root My Name. Calcutta, United Writers, 1977.
Without Place. Calcutta, Writers Workshop, 1978.
Stone Roots. New Delhi, Arnold Heinemann, 1980.
House of a Thousand Doors. Washington, D.C., Three Continents Press, 1988.
The Storm. New York, Red Dust, 1989.

Night-Scene, the Garden. New York, Red Dust, 1989.
River and Bridge. New Delhi, Rupa, 1995.

Play

In the Middle Earth. New Delhi, Enact, 1977.

Novel

Manhattan Music. San Francisco, Mercury House, 1997.

Other

The Poetic Self: Towards a Phenomenology of Romanticism. New Delhi, Arnold Heinemann, 1979; Atlantic Highlands, New Jersey, Humanities Press, 1980.
Women in Romanticism: Mary Wollstonecraft, Dorothy Wordsworth and Mary Shelley. London, Macmillan, 1989.
Nampally Road. San Francisco, Mercury House, 1991.
Fault Lines, New York, Feminist Press, 1993.
The Shock of Arrival: Reflections on Postcolonial Experience. Boston, Southend Press, 1996.

*

Critical Studies: "Exiled by a Woman's Body: Substantial Phenomena in the Poetry of Meena Alexander," in *Journal of South Asian Literature* (East Lansing, Michigan), 21(1), winter/spring 1986, and "The Inward Body: Meena Alexander's Feminist Strategies of Poetry," in *Feminism and Literature,* edited by K. Radha, Trivandrum, University of Kerala, 1987, both by John Oliver Perry; "Poetry, Language and Feminism: The Writings of Meena Alexander" by K. Raveendran, in *Kala Gomati* (Kerala), October 1987; "Meena Alexander's Poetry" by Konnakuzhy Ittira, in *Mathrubhumi* (Kerala), 1989; "Meena Alexander" by Denise Knight, in *Reworlding: Writers of the Indian Diaspora,* Westport, Greenwood Press, 1993; "Towards the Creation of a Vital Aesthetics: A Survey of Contemporary Indian English Poetry and Criticism with Special Reference to Meena Alexander" by Sumitra Mukerji, in *Journal of the School of Languages,* III, 1993; "The Poetry of Multiple Migrations" by Hema Nair, *MS.,* January/February 1994; "The Barbed Wire Is Taken into the Heart" by Ketu Katrak, in *An Interethnic Companion to Asian American Literature,* edited by King-Kok Cheung, Cambridge, Cambridge University Press, 1997; "Portrait of Meena Alexander" by Erika Duncan, in *World Literature Today,* 73(1), winter 1998.

Meena Alexander comments:

Sometimes people one has just met will say, "What sort of poems do you write?" It seems fair enough as a question, but I am always hard put to reply. Poems about childbirth, poems about my grandparent's small town in Kerala, on the southwest coast of India, poems about coming to America, short poems, irregular sonnets, long poems, poems of sexual desire, all of that would be true. But even to say that seems such a bits-and-pieces answer—after all what can one do except move in memory to the dense particularity of each poem? But perhaps I can try now to sketch out a rough map, an internal geography, as it were, formed by the poems.

The volume of poetry *House of a Thousand Doors* I think of as a beginning. The grandmother figure in it is drawn from memory and dream; she stands as a power permitting me to speak in an alien landscape. The sense of newness, of the persistent difficulty of another landscape, another life, becomes in those poems part of a search for a precarious truth. My two long poems *The Storm* and *Night-Scene, the Garden,* both published in 1989, were composed side by side in roughly a year and a half, starting in 1986. Together they form part of a poetic autobiography. The first moves from a vivid childhood memory, my father's father tearing down the ancestral house in Kozencheri to build a modern one. It moves then to the repeated passages away from that first home, taking in airports, dislocations, war. It ends with a "bitten self / cast back into its intimate wreckage." *Night-Scene* I think of as female, dealing with the molten stuff that lies between a mother and a daughter, between a daughter and her maternal home. This poem, which was performed off-off-Broadway in 1988, is set in my mother's ancestral house in Tiruvella in contemporary India. The language takes in the roughness, the crudity of speech. Unlike *The Storm,* which contemplates, frames, this poem swallows chaoses. I think of it, foolishly perhaps, as "unformed," though readers have seen a persistent patterning in it. In my own mind it is related to the poem "Passion," composed in 1986 about the aftermath of childbirth. Now I am working on a series of short poems, 14 to 20 lines in length, which bring together the two landscapes of my life, that of rural Kerala and that of Manhattan, city of subways and dark underground passages.

*　　*　　*

In the 1980 essay "Exiled by a Dead Script," Meena Alexander articulates the dilemma of the Indian poet writing in English. Calling Indian English "a nowhere language," Alexander suggests that the poet "necessarily grasps himself as exiled . . . estranged from the place around him, whose body cannot appropriate its given landscape." In words strikingly similar to those of the Canadian poet Dennis Lee, whose "Cadence, Country, Silence: Writing in Colonial Space" was taken by a generation of Canadian poets to articulate their postcolonial condition of silence, Alexander writes that Indian English poets must "resolutely refuse exile, the language itself must transform. It must contort itself to become mimetic of *muteness— their muteness* which is appropriated as the poet's own." She suggests that her and others' writing in India is marked by two sorts of "terror"—"babble" and "non-sense"—explained by the imperial history of English in India, which "will always remain a colonizing power till those whom it oppresses steal it for themselves, rupture its syntax till it is capable of naming the very structures of oppression."

Thus, Alexander's own poetry is marked by a tension between different traditions of poetry, history, myth, and language. A highly imagistic poetry, her work attempts, at times somewhat romantically (Alexander's academic expertise in English romantic poetry often resonates in her own creative work), to make sense of and create a place in the various worlds the poet finds herself inhabiting:

I learn song is being:

That song might be being as Rilke dreamt
I sing for all who work head bent
close against the great red sun
who labour tooth nail sinew bone
against glass metal paper stone
through sting of sand and lash of snow
they carve this rock to make a sky to breathe in

They forge that land
where Song has second place
and Being thrives alone.

Images, syntax, and structures reminiscent, then, of Coleridge and especially Eliot, of Rilke and Neruda, for the reader trained in a European tradition, are also inflected by Indian rhythms, syntax, structures, and stories. In addition, some of Alexander's best early poetry uncovers the contested space between individual memory, national history, and the poet's attempt to re-create being and identity through writing. In the long poem *The Bird's Bright Ring,* for example, Alexander's typical use of blood, flowers, salt, birds, animals, and other images finds effective and powerful juxtaposition with the consequences of British rule in India:

The writhing subsides
but the dark space
still cuts the air
my sight
          you said

"It was here the shadow fell
the shadow of the British soldiers
here
    here
      they dragged their guns
over the slope to the cleft of the Ridge
1857 a cold bad winter and they broke our backs."
. . . .
"Not only shadows fell that cold hard winter
But bruises like down from hidden veins of porphyry
as the belly of the mother
was torn open
wrought metal
cold cannon
sharp cleft
of bayonet and sword . . ."

Later in the poem, as in other of her verses, contemporary politics also interrupt, often violently. The fourteenth poem in *The Bird's Bright Ring,* for example, consists only of documents: a calendar advertisement, a call for protest, and a newspaper article describing police violence in 1974. Such disjunctures between a poetry rich in imagery and the poet's/speaker's explicit concerns mark the skepticism and hybridization of much postcolonial poetry. In a review of her work Ben Downing has written, "Attracted to both the 'hierarchical unity' of Indian tradition and a modern, Western poetics of rupture, Alexander is faced with the difficult necessity of mediating between them."

This process of poetic mediation and meditation becomes more marked with Alexander's double exile, brought about by her immigration to the United States. Alexander herself suggests that the poems "Hotel Alexandria," "Broadway Poem"—"my first 'American' poem"—and "Waiting for Rain" are attempts to bridge internal cultural displacement and the fragmentation of identity that comes with it. These early "American" poems "permitted an erasure of difference," momentary consolation, even though they simultaneously speak of "the gulf of not-knowing, a pit, a placelessness" that

has doubled and redoubled upon the existing placelessness of being a postcolonial Indian English poet. Although exploring the "discrepant nature of what I found myself to be in America," Alexander has continued to use predominantly Indian images, content, and myth and history.

Alexander's speakers, always female, attempt to articulate these discrepancies by recalling and rewriting specifically female experience. I would argue that, indeed, Alexander is a feminist poet. (Again, her academic work bears out this assertion.) Her populism, her return to the political and historical moment, is often addressed to and for women: "Women of Delhi / You do not see how centuries of dream are flowing from your land / And so I sing knowing poetry to be like bread." The collection *I Root My Name,* containing more intimate poetry, reflects the pain of a woman's experience, as, for instance, in "After the Wedding": "I did not think I would try to die / when yesterday they hennaed my hands / in the patterns of stars and moons / and flowers, for joy."

A longer poem, "A Mirror's Grace" in *Without Place,* rewrites the story of Cleopatra, linking the position of the female speaker/poet to that of Cleopatra who, like the postcolonial poet, finds herself rendered inauthentic in a patriarchal language:

This is a poem about Cleopatra
she did not tell her brilliance
to its mirrors, so broke his wings . . .

A poem by a woman, wiping
her voice dry of fire
and flood, reining it

to speech which is not hers
though its syllables
cut her dusty footsoles.

The poet's remembering through poetry takes the shape of childhood reminiscences in which women—sisters, mothers, and especially grandmothers—figure prominently in the creation of the self. Alexander explains that her "House of a Thousand Doors" is about a poeticized grandmother, citing the poem "Her Garden" to "explain the haunting inexistence of my grandmother": "She died so long / before my birth / that we are one, entirely / as a sky disowned by sun and star: / a bleakness beneath my dreams." For Alexander the recovering or uncovering of personal and cultural history through poetry is archaeological, and the mother or grandmother is a figuration of that unearthing: "Why do I turn to her? . . . Answering my own question backwards. There seems to be no-one else. No-one else, that is, from whom I can draw both the lines of ancestry and poetry. And she both is and is not real." Mother/grandmother/sister also symbolizes for the poet her "mother tongue, which is pure speech." For Alexander this is Malayalam, a language in which she is illiterate and upon whose oral, or childhood, patterns, she overwrites English, "the colonial language which I must melt down to my purposes."

Alexander's work *The Storm* continues in the project of rescuing and re-creating memory. Perhaps more clearly autobiographical than some of her other poetry, this poem is narrated in fragments, echoing in title, in structure, and in the opening metaphoric scene of burial the modernist dream of "shoring fragments against one's ruin," the feminist dream of creating a sense of self and identity through the fragments of a life remembered, and the ongoing poetic project of celebrating and decrying the postcolonial fragmentation of self/culture/nation. It thus aims to create new hybrid and fluid political and personal identities. In this way Alexander manages to provide another temporary appearance of closure and resolution, attempting in her poetry to translate, "in the old sense of transporting, of ferrying across," "the gap, the cleft there between wordless intimacy and functioning script [which] is so co-equal in intensity with the fissures, the sudden cracks in my daily life." *The Storm* thus provides the poetic illusion of mediating between "pure" experience and the act of poetic re-creation:

With the bleached mesh of root
exposed after rainfall
my bitten self cast back
into its intimate wreckage
each jot poised, apart, particular
lovely and rare.
The end of life delved back
into the heart of it all.

—Aruna Srivastava

ALI, Agha Shahid

Nationality: Indian (Kashmiri). **Born:** New Delhi, 4 February 1949. Grew up in Kashmir. **Education:** University of Kashmir, Srinagar, B.A. 1968; University of Delhi, M.A. in English literature 1970; Pennsylvania State University, M.A. in English 1981, Ph.D. 1984; University of Arizona, Tucson, M.F.A. 1985. **Career:** Lecturer in English, University of Delhi, 1970–75; instructor, Pennsylvania State University, 1976–83; graduate assistant, University of Arizona, 1983–85; communications editor, JNC Companies, Tucson, 1985–87; assistant professor of English and creative writing, Hamilton College, Clinton, New York, 1987–93. Visiting professor of creative writing, State University of New York, Binghamton, spring 1989. Associate professor of English, University of Massachusetts, Amherst, 1993—. **Awards:** Breadloaf Writers' Conference scholarship, 1982, 1983; Academy of American Poets prize, 1983: Pennsylvania Council on the Arts fellowship, 1983; Ingram Merrill Foundation fellowship, 1987; New York Foundation for the Arts fellowship, 1993. **Address:** Department of English, Bartlett Hall, University of Massachusetts, Amherst, Massachusetts 01003, U.S.A.

PUBLICATIONS

Poetry

Bone-Sculpture. Calcutta, Writers Workshop, 1972.
In Memory of Begum Akhtar and Other Poems. Calcutta, Writers Workshop, 1979.
The Half-Inch Himalayas. Middletown, Connecticut, Wesleyan University Press, 1987.
A Walk through the Yellow Pages. Tucson, Arizona, Sun/Gemini Press, 1987.
A Nostalgist's Map of America. New York, Norton, 1991.

The Belovéd Witness: Selected Poems. New Delhi, Viking Penguin, 1992.
The Country without a Post Office: Poems. New York, Norton, 1997.

Recordings: *Distinct Traditions, Myths and Voices of the Many Americas,* Poetics Program, SUNY at Buffalo, 1994.

Other

T.S. Eliot As Editor. Ann Arbor, University of Michigan Research Press, 1986.

Translator, *The Rebel's Silhouette: Selected Poems,* by Faiz Ahmed Faiz. Salt Lake City, Peregrine Smith, 1992.

*

Critical Studies: "The Sorrows of a Broken Time" by Emmanuel Nelson, in *Reworlding: Writers of the Indian Diaspora,* Westport, Greenwood Press, 1993; in *Indian Literature,* 145(5), September 1991; by Neile Graham, in *Poet Lore,* 87(1), spring 1992; by Sudeep Sen, in *Poetry Review,* 83(1), spring 1993.

Agha Shahid Ali comments:

My poetry has all along revealed a triple heritage (through certain historical permutations, of course), of which I have only in the past few years become truly conscious: Hindu, Muslim, and Western. This triple heritage has given me and other Indo-English writers a privileged position at this specific postcolonial moment in history, the ability and confidence to breathe something rich and strange into English (for example, I hope readers can detect the music of Urdu in my work), the arrogance, if you will, to reinvent the language and to do so on our own terms.

*   *   *

Agha Shahid Ali is one of the few Indian Muslim poets writing in English and one of the few English-language poets from Kashmir. Long resident in the United States, he has become an American multicultural poet. The books of poems he has published are influenced by his continued uprooting and exile. *Bone-Sculpture* is the work of a promising young poet who has not yet assimilated influences or found a style. Many of Ali's obsessions, however, are already present: memory, death, history, family ancestors, nostalgia for a past he never knew, dreams, Hindu ceremonies, friendships, and self-consciousness about being a poet. Bones are symbolic of a now dead world that will not reply to his interest. In "Dear Editor" he claims, "i am a dealer in words / that mix cultures / and leave me rootless."

In Memory of Begum Akhtar focuses on the old Delhi of the Mughals. There is an elegiac feeling of a rich but lost past. The great singers of the past become symbols for a history Ali cannot live as he attempts to find links and continuity with his origins. "K.L. Saigal" is celebrated as such a link: "Nostalgic for my father's youth, / I make you return / his wasted generation . . . You felt it all." In the title poem the elegy for the great singer Begum Akhtar has the concise, oblique, lyrical qualities and the music and pattern of the oriental ghazel:

feelings are expressed parabolically, statements are left standing on their own, and the poem feels like a song made up of lyric phrases. ''Note Autobiographical-1'' recounts Ali's estrangement from Islam. His parents were modern and secular, read Freud and Marx, and ''ate pork secretly,'' but his grandfather still prayed five times a day. Like many of the Indian Muslims for whom the partition of Pakistan from India was a tragic event, Ali looks backward to a unified culture and nation he has lost and that he tries to maintain in his imagination and verse.

In 1987 Ali published two significant volumes of poetry related to his residence in the United States. The poems show increased verse technique and polish, the use of fantasy, and the ability to work within a wider range of reference. *The Half-Inch Himalayas* is a carefully composed book that, in structure, follows his changes of home from Kashmir to Delhi to the United States. It consists of a prologue and four sections, the first three with eight poems each. Recurring images link the sections. ''Postcard from Kashmir,'' the prologue, introduces the themes of exile, memory, loss of home, and acceptance that one cannot go home again: ''Kashmir shrinks into my mailbox, / my home a neat four by six inches. / / . . . Now I hold / the half-inch Himalayas in my hand. / / This is home. And this the closest / I'll ever be to home.'' Section 1 consists largely of fantasies about the history of his family before he was born or during the days of his childhood. By imagining he hopes to share. The poems move from the Himalayas of ancestral and racial origins and his father's Kashmir down to the plains of India of his mother's side, the plains of the great Urdu culture that preceded partition. The poems in section 2 are concerned primarily with the culture and history of Delhi and the plains. A film of *King Lear* causes the poet to think about the distance between the former splendor of Delhi during the Mughal empire and the poverty of the present: ''Beggars now live here in tombs / of unknown nobles and forgotten saints.''

Section 3 takes place in America and shows an uprooted existence of airplane flights, nights at bars, and changing apartments. Ali's sense of humor is allowed to surface more often, although the metaphor of life in exile as nightmare and death now replaces the earlier symbolic landscape of bones, tombs, and monuments. This is not a land that remembers. In ''Vacating an Apartment,'' for example, the cleaners ''burn my posters / (India and Heaven in flames) . . . make everything new, / clean as Death.'' At five o'clock in the morning on Riverside Drive in New York City he sees a jogger ''bursting . . . suddenly free, / from the air, from himself,'' leaving his heart ''behind him.'' In section 4 there are six dreamlike poems of nostalgia for India written in the United States. The final poem, ''Houses,'' returns to the contrast between imagining home and the actual security of home: ''The man who buried his house in the sand / and digs it up again, each evening / learns to put it together quickly / / and just as quickly to take it apart.'' *The Half-Inch Himalayas* is remarkable for its economy, development, and unity. It is a summing up and distillation of some twenty years of writing poetry.

A Walk through the Yellow Pages is a surreal world of nightmare, fantasy, incongruity, wild humor, and the grotesque. Although the existential anxieties have their source in problems of growing up, leaving home, being a migrant, and dealing with the meeting of cultures, the idiom is American and contemporary. Besides the five ''Bell Telephone Hours'' poems, there is a found poem that slightly reworks an oriental food store's advertisement, two poems called ''Language Games'' (based on Scrabble and charades), a poem based on graffiti (''Poets on Bathroom Walls''), and three poems that

rewrite fairy tales. Each of the ''Bell Telephone Hours'' takes advertising slogans (''Has anyone heard from you lately?'' or ''Call long distance: the next best thing to being there'') to reveal under the social loneliness an existential anxiety: ''He answered, 'God is busy. / He never answers the living. / He has no answers for the dead. / Don't ever call again collect.''' In Ali's version of the fairy tale in ''Hansel's Game'' the mother tells Hansel that ''the womb's no place for a big boy like you'' and pushes him out into the world again on the route ''from the womb to the grave.'' Wiser now, he lives comfortably and keeps the witch in the basement. On special occasions, instead of cake, ''we take portions of her / to serve.'' The icebox in the basement holds the repressed, and fears of the witch are turned into poetry.

While autobiography often starts in a golden age of childhood that is lost in growing up, Ali's obsession with expulsion from the womb, home, and tradition is remarkably intense and results in a poetry symbolic of major cultural and political changes. His poetry about his insecurities has turned into a narrative that itself has become the subject of allegories that elaborate on the story through various metaphors, disguises, and figures. The specificity of his experience and emotions, its acceptance of difference, its feeling of being comfortable yet exiled, of missing something wherever he lives or goes, contributes strongly to the lyrical power of his poetry. The increased technique since his earlier poetry allows him to make use of varied associations, moving rapidly and elliptically, in the style of the ghazel, between layers of feelings, while ordering the poems into complex narratives. There is the music of Urdu in his poetry, a lushness of phrase uncommon to American verse, a variety of theme and subject matter, a trust in his Kashmiri-American voice.

The 104 pages of poetry in *A Nostalgist's Map of America* have a significant organization, with section leading to section, recapitulations of themes and images, and underlying narratives. The prologue, ''Eurydice,'' creates the tone and is followed by four sections. The first section is set in the southwestern United States, and the five poems in it move from the personal to the mythic and anthropological. ''Beyond the Ash Rains'' begins with an announcement of themes: ''When the desert refused my history.'' While section 2 consists of three poems, including ''A Nostalgist's Map of America,'' one of them, ''Evanescence,'' is itself a sequence of eleven poems. The theme of ''Evanescence,'' which unites the section, comes from a poem of Emily Dickinson, quoted as a prologue to section 2. The poems are addressed to a friend in southern California who died of AIDS. Section 3, a sequence of thirteen poems called ''From Another Desert,'' continues the motifs of loss and deserts (here an Islamic desert) and retells an Arabic love story, also common to Persian and Urdu literature, in which Majnoon, the possessed or mad one who has sacrificed everything for love, can be understood as a rebel or revolutionary and the loved one as the revolutionary ideal. In Arabic or Islamic literature love poetry is usually understood to be about love of God, but Ali is in the more modern tradition, in which the significance is understood politically. The eight poems of section 4 return to the desert and such earlier themes and motifs as myth and water while providing a farewell. The concluding poem, ''Snow on the Desert,'' begins with ''Every ray of sunshine is seven minutes old . . . So when I look at the sky I see the past? . . . especially on a clear day'' and moves by various imagistic associations from New York City to Tucson, New Delhi, and Bangladesh.

From the contents of *The Country without a Post Office,* Ali could be taken to be the national poet of a future independent Kashmir. He would probably deny a nationalistic intent, however, and claim to be a humanist concerned with universal justice, which explains his references to Sarajevo, Armenia, and even a Norwegian hostage killed by Kashmiri militants. The poems, each in a different form, offer a loose narrative with repeating images and phrases. The prose poem ''The Blesséd Word: A Prologue'' imagines a time when Kashmir will be free. ''Farewell,'' the opening poem of the first section, is in one-line stanzas. A note reads, ''This poem at one—but only one—level is a plaintive love letter from a Kashmiri Muslim to a Kashmiri Pandit (the indigenous Hindus of Kashmir are called Pandits).'' It might be seen as expressive of a shared culture and history that is asserted throughout the volume: ''In the lake the arms of temples and mosques are locked in each other's reflections.'' There are villanelles and ghazels, even a proper ghazel in which the couplets are linked by the initial *aa* rhyme word, ''Arabic,'' recurring as a rhyme in the second line of each following stanza: ''They ask me to tell them what *Shahid* means- / Listen: It means 'The Belovéd' in Persian, 'witness' in Arabic.'' Desire for and loss of communion with the beloved, God, is understood as part of the longing for home by the exiled and conquered. Ali blends the high lyrical traditions of Islamic poetry with that of Europe, renewing a former link in such Renaissance forms as the canzone.

—Bruce King

ALVAREZ, A(lfred)

Nationality: British. **Born:** London, 5 August 1929. **Education:** Oundle School, Northamptonshire; Corpus Christi College, Oxford (senior research scholar and research scholar of Goldsmiths' Company, 1952–53, 1954–55), B.A. 1952, M.A. 1956; Princeton University, New Jersey (Procter visiting fellow, 1953–54); Harvard University, Cambridge, Massachusetts (Rockefeller fellow, 1955); University of New Mexico, Albuquerque (D.H. Lawrence fellow, 1958). **Family:** 1) Married Ursula Barr in 1956 (marriage dissolved 1961), one son; 2) Married Anne Adams in 1966, one son and one daughter. **Career:** Gauss lecturer, Princeton University, 1957–58; visiting professor, Brandeis University, Waltham, Massachusetts, 1960, and State University of New York, Buffalo, 1966. Advisory poetry editor and poetry critic, *The Observer,* London, 1956–66; editor, *Journal of Education,* London, 1957; drama critic, *New Statesman,* London, 1958–60; advisory editor, Penguin Modern European Poets in Translation, 1965–75; presenter, *Voices* program, Channel 4 television, 1982. **Awards:** Rockefeller fellowship, 1955–56; Vachel Lindsay prize (*Poetry,* Chicago), 1961. **Agent:** Aitken and Stone Ltd., 29 Fernshaw Road, London SW10 OTG, England.

PUBLICATIONS

Poetry

(Poems). Oxford, Fantasy Press, 1952.
The End of It. Privately printed, 1958.
Twelve Poems. London, The Review, 1968.
Lost. London, Turret, 1968.
Penguin Modern Poets 18, with Roy Fuller and Anthony Thwaite. London, Penguin, 1970.

Apparition. St. Lucia, University of Queensland Press, 1971.
The Legacy. London, Poem-of-the-Month Club, 1972.
Autumn to Autumn and Selected Poems 1953–1976. London, Macmillan, 1978.

Play

Screenplay: *The Anarchist,* 1969.

Novels

Hers. London, Weidenfeld and Nicolson, 1974; New York, Random House, 1975.
Hunt. London, Macmillan, and New York, Simon and Schuster, 1978.
Day of Atonement. London, Jonathan Cape, 1991; New York, Random House, 1992.

Other

The Shaping Spirit: Studies in Modern English and American Poets. London, Chatto and Windus, 1958; as *Stewards of Excellence: Studies in Modern English and American Poets,* New York, Scribner, 1958.
The School of Donne. London, Chatto and Windus, and New York, Pantheon, 1961.
Under Pressure: The Artist and Society: Eastern Europe and the U.S.A. London, Penguin, 1965.
Beyond All This Fiddle: Essays 1955–1967. London, Allen Lane, 1968; New York, Random House, 1969.
The Savage God: A Study of Suicide. London, Weidenfeld and Nicolson, 1971; New York, Random House, 1972.
Beckett. London, Fontana, and New York, Viking Press, 1973; revised edition, London, Fontana, 1992.
Life after Marriage: Scenes from Divorce. London, Macmillan, 1982; as *Life after Marriage: Love in an Age of Divorce,* New York, Simon and Schuster, 1982.
The Biggest Game in Town (on gambling). London, Deutsch, and Boston, Houghton Mifflin, 1983.
Offshore: A North Sea Journey. London, Hodder and Stoughton, and Boston, Houghton Mifflin, 1986.
Feeding the Rat: Profile of a Climber. London, Bloomsbury, 1988; Boston, Atlantic Monthly Press, 1989.
Rainforest, with Charles Blackman. Melbourne, Macmillan, 1988.
Night: An Exploration of Night Life, Night Language, Sleep & Dreams. London, Jonathan Cape, and New York, Norton, 1995.
Where Did It All Go Right? An Autobiography. London, Richard Cohen, 1999; New York, Morrow, 2000.

Editor, *The New Poetry: An Anthology.* London, Penguin, 1962; revised edition, 1966.
Editor, *The Faber Book of Modern European Poetry.* London, Faber and Faber, 1992.

*

Critical Studies: Interview with Ian Hamilton, in *New Review* (London), March 1978; interview with Gregory Lestage, in *Poetry*

Review (London), spring 1998; *The Mind Has Mountains: A. Alvarez at 70* edited by Antony Holden and Frank Kermode, Cambridge, Los Poetry Press, 1999.

*   *   *

In volume the published poetry of A. Alvarez is slight indeed, but it is rich in its economy. *Autumn to Autumn and Selected Poems 1953–1976* contained only thirty-seven poems, sixteen published for the first time. Of the new poems eight had been written after 1974, seven of them comprising the section called ''Autumn to Autumn.''

It is a shame that Alvarez, who has done so much to cultivate a climate receptive to the confessional poetry of Lowell, Berryman, and Plath—even though his essay on Plath in *The Savage God* could be criticized for feeding the public's nearly insatiable appetite to feast upon a poet's life to understand her art—and whose writings on Donne and Eliot have done much to clarify their place in the history of contemporary poetry, should be so restrained in his own practice of the art. Perhaps he is too wary of rendering a poetry in the style of the Movement which he so aptly described in his essay ''The New Poetry; or, Beyond the Gentility Principle.'' Does he fear that he cannot heed his own warning and remain ''immune'' to gentility? He complained of the nine poets who formed the so-called Movement that their ''academic-administrative verse, polite, knowledgeable, efficient, polished, and, in its quiet way, even intelligent,'' practiced its own pieties and strove too hard to make the poet appear like the man next door. Although Alvarez has found his own colloquial, modern voice and there is a hard-to-find originality in his novel *Hers,* in his poetry he clings to a compression of style and a formality that seem ultimately to inhibit him. Perhaps the standard he sets at the close of his essay is too high. There he asks that contemporary poetry be like ''Coleridge's Imagination,'' that it ''reconcile a 'more than usual state of emotion' with more than usual order.''

Alvarez's later poems continue the strain and form of the poems in *Lost.* They are poems of ephemera, in which an emotion is briefly isolated, felt, and wafted away, leaving the persona with a sense of perplexity and regret. The poet often depicts mates divided by fears and dreams inhabiting their ''grey untender rooms.'' In ''He Said, She Said,'' from *Autumn to Autumn,* a scent and a presence pass through the bedroom as two autumnal lovers lie together. He names the smell ''hawthorn'' and says that it beckons, ''Come''; she scoffs and says that it said, ''Gone.'' Alvarez closes the poem characteristically, with a note of mild irony:

> A flicker of gold, a smile, a far voice calling
> Confusedly, ''Come,'' ''Gone,'' ''Come.'' The jum-
>   bled scents
> of Spring on the autumn night. ''Our last chance,'' he said
> And she answered, ''You take it without me.''

More than a decade earlier, in another poem of dialogue, ''Autumn Marriage,'' the wife's words were equally matter-of-fact and love-less. Alvarez's range has continued to be narrow.

Autumn to Autumn, containing poetry of two decades, reflects Alvarez's admiration for Donne, Eliot, and Frost and for Plath and Hughes. Several of the poems written in the late 1950s and early 1960s recall Plath's stridency and savage treatment of love's anger. ''Sunstruck'' is such a poem, ''Anger'' another. ''Operation,'' ''Back,''

and ''The Nativity in New Mexico'' recall Plath's ''Tulips'' or ''Cut.'' They shed a harsh, clinical light on a grinning midwife and on thighs sticky with afterbirth. Others use an economy of words to call up ordinary scenes—closing time in a park, a sleeper awakening, the coming of old age. Alvarez's preoccupation with dreams, restlessness, and disintegration mark his modernity, but his verse forms and gift for understatement recall the traditional British poetry of the early twentieth century.

—Carol Simpson Stern

ALVI, Moniza

Nationality: British. **Born:** Lahore, Pakistan, 2 February 1954. **Education:** University of York, 1973–76, B.A. in English (honors) 1976; Whitelands College, London, 1976–77, postgraduate certificate in education 1977; London University Institute of Education, 1982–85, M.A. in education 1985. **Family:** Married Robert Coe in 1995. **Career:** Teacher, Scott Lidgett School, London, 1978–80. Since 1980 teacher, and since 1989, head of English department, Aylwin School, London. **Awards:** The Poetry Business prize (co-winner with Peter Daniels), 1992. **Address:** c/o Oxford University Press, Walton St., Oxford OX2 6DP, England.

PUBLICATIONS

Poetry

Peacock Luggage, with Peter Daniels. London, Smith Doorstop Books, 1992.
The Country at My Shoulder. Oxford, Oxford University Press, 1993.
A Bowl of Warm Air. New York and Oxford, Oxford University Press, 1996.

*

Critical Study: By Linda France, in *Poetry Review,* 84(1), spring 1994.

Moniza Alvi comments:

With *The Country at My Shoulder* I found myself re-creating a past, as if to introduce the possibility of returning in my actual life to my birthplace, Pakistan, which I left when a few months old. Now having made the return visit, I am working on a group of poems centered in my impressions of family and country. The points where East and West converge are crucial. The poems that do not concern my Asian background are equally important to me. I am attracted to the strange seeming and to fantasy and find there some essence of experience. I have written about Pakistan partly because it was, in the first instance, a fantasy. It is difficult to say who has influenced me. Edward Thomas, Jacques Prèvert, and Stevie Smith are amongst those poets who have made a strong impression. When I started writing seriously, I was reading Angela Carter's work and V.G. Ballard's science fiction. I have probably been as much influenced by prose writers as by poets.

*   *   *

Moniza Alvi writes in a beautifully controlled conversational style lit by flashes of fantasy. The titles of some of her poems—"I Was Raised in a Glove Compartment," "I Would Like to Be a Dot in a Painting by Miro," "The Great Pudding"—indicate this. In "A Map of India" she tells us that, when she looks at a map,

> If I stare at the country long enough
> I can prise it off the paper,
> lift it like a flap of skin.

Alvi's idiosyncratic vision can be seen as a way of coming to terms with worlds not only distant geographically but also disparate in cultures and ethos. Her poetry is an exploration toward the reconciliation of these worlds and the discovery of her place in them. Her worlds are also those of inner landscapes, as in the poem "Houdini":

> It is not clear how he entered me
> or why he always has to escape.

More importantly, they are worlds to which the only joint key is the imagination, as in "Afternoon at the Cinema":

> The film—you've seen it before—
> it was a mystery then, and now you've missed
> the sheet with the interpretations on it.

For years Pakistan, where Alvi was born, was an imaginary world to her, for she left it for England when she was only a few months old. It was not until much later that she returned to Pakistan to visit and meet relatives there. Before that time the exploration of the world of her cultural origins had to be via the images in her mind. It is no wonder that she writes,

> There's a country at my shoulder,
> growing larger—soon it will burst,
> rivers will spill out, run down my chest.

These are the first lines of the title poem of her collection *The Country at My Shoulder,* and they set the theme for much of the book.

The poem "Presents from My Aunt in Pakistan" touches on the feeding of the vision of Alvi's imagined world and the sense of contrast and ironies the presents conveyed. While the aunt sent gifts of exotic garments—a *salwar kameez* in peacock blue, embossed slippers, saris, and candy-striped glass bangles, "alien in the sitting room"—these were accompanied by requests for cardigans from Marks and Spencers. These were the clues to the Pakistan that Alvi had to embrace via her imagination and language in "The Country at My Shoulder":

> I water the country with English rain,
> cover it with English words.
> Soon it will burst, or fall like a meteor.

Alvi is aware of the complexity of her intentions, as expressed in these lines from "Hindi Urdu Bol Chaal":

> I introduce myself to two languages,
> but there are so many—of costume,
> of conduct and courtesy.

Her intentions are to discover where her twin cultures converge. It is an exploration that is clearly related to the discovery of her own identity vis-à-vis the two cultures. In "You Are Turning Me into a Novel" she says,

> In the great silent hour
> you are giving me a title
> fashioning me, coaxing me.

It is Alvi's ability to explore and come to terms with her world imaginatively that is the special quality of the poetry. The clarity of her direct and transparently honest approach is what illuminates it.

—John Cotton

AMMONS, A(rchie) R(andolph)

Nationality: American. **Born:** Whiteville, North Carolina, 18 February 1926. **Education:** Wake Forest College, North Carolina, B.S. 1949; University of California, Berkeley, 1950–52. Served in the U.S. Naval Reserve, 1944–46. **Family:** Married Phyllis Plumbo in 1949; one son. **Career:** Principal, Hatteras Elementary School, North Carolina, 1949–50; executive vice president, Friedrich and Dimmock, Inc., Millville, New Jersey, 1952–62; assistant professor, 1964–68, associate professor, 1969–71, and since 1971 professor of English, Cornell University, Ithaca, New York. Visiting professor, Wake Forest University, 1974–75. Poetry editor, *The Nation,* New York, 1963. **Awards:** Bread Loaf Writers Conference scholarship, 1961; Guggenheim fellowship, 1966; American Academy traveling fellowship, 1967, and award, 1977; Levinson prize (*Poetry,* Chicago), 1970; National Book award, 1973, and 1993, for *Garbage;* Bollingen prize, 1974; MacArthur fellowship, 1981; National Book Critics Circle award, 1982; North Carolina award for literature, 1986; Robert Frost medal, Poetry Society of America, 1993; National Institute of Arts and Letters award, 1994; Rebekah Johnson Bobbit National prize for poetry, 1994; Ruth Lilly Poetry prize, 1995. D.Litt.: Wake Forest University, 1972; University of North Carolina, Chapel Hill, 1973. Fellow, American Academy of Arts and Sciences, 1982. **Address:** Department of English, Cornell University, Ithaca, New York 14853, U.S.A.

PUBLICATIONS

Poetry

Ommateum, with Doxology. Philadelphia, Dorrance, 1955.
Expressions of Sea Level. Columbus, Ohio State University Press, 1964.
Corsons Inlet. Ithaca, New York, Cornell University Press, 1965.
Tape for the Turn of the Year. Ithaca, New York, Cornell University Press, 1965.
Northfield Poems. Ithaca, New York, Cornell University Press, 1966.
Selected Poems. Ithaca, New York, Cornell University Press, 1968.
Uplands. New York, Norton, 1970.
Briefings: Poems Small and Easy. New York, Norton, 1971.
Collected Poems 1951–1971. New York, Norton, 1972.
Sphere: The Form of a Motion. New York, Norton, 1974.
Diversifications. New York, Norton, 1975.
The Snow Poems. New York, Norton, 1977.

The Selected Poems 1951–1977. New York, Norton, 1977; revised edition, as *The Selected Poems,* 1986.
Highgate Road. Ithaca, New York, Inkling Press, 1977.
For Doyle Fosco. Winston-Salem, North Carolina, Press for Privacy, 1977.
Poem. Winston-Salem, North Carolina, Press for Privacy, 1977(?).
Six-Piece Suite. Ithaca, New York, Palaemon Press, 1979.
Selected Longer Poems. New York, Norton, 1980.
A Coast of Trees. New York, Norton, 1981.
Worldly Hopes. New York, Norton, 1982.
Lake Effect Country. New York, Norton, 1983.
Easter Morning. Greensboro, North Carolina Humanities Committee, 1986.
Sumerian Vistas. New York, Norton, 1987.
Garbage. New York, Norton, 1993.
Tape for the Turn of the Year. New York, Norton, 1993.
The North Carolina Poems. Rocky Mount, North Carolina Wesleyan College Press, 1994.
Brink Road: Poems. New York, Norton, 1996.
Glare. New York, Norton, 1997.

Other

Set in Motion: Essays, Interviews, and Dialogues. Ann Arbor, University of Michigan Press, 1996.

*

Bibliography: *A.R. Ammons: A Bibliography 1954–1979* by Stuart Wright, Wake Forest, North Carolina, Wake Forest University Press, 1980.

Critical Studies: "A Poem Is a Walk" by the author, in *Epoch* (Ithaca, New York), fall 1968; "A.R. Ammons: When You Consider the Radiance" by Harold Bloom, in *The Ringers in the Tower,* Chicago, University of Chicago Press, 1971; A.R. Ammons issue of *Diacritics* (Ithaca, New York), 1974; *A.R. Ammons* by Alan Holder, Boston, Twayne, 1978; "A Poetry of Restitution" by John Hollander, in *Yale Review* (New Haven, Connecticut), 1981; "A.R. Ammons and *The Snow Poems* Reconsidered" by Michael McFee, in *Chicago Review,* 1981; "The Problem of Freedom and Restriction in the Poetry of A.R. Ammons" by Thomas A. Fink, in *Modern Poetry Studies* (Buffalo, New York), 1982; "A.R. Ammons: Ecological Naturalism and the Romantic Tradition" by Donald H. Reiman, in *Twentieth-Century Literature* (Hempstead, New York), 1985; A.R. Ammons issue of *Pembroke Magazine* (Pembroke, North Carolina), 1986; *A.R. Ammons* edited by Harold Bloom, New York, Chelsea House, 1988; "The Poetry of Ammons" by Nathan A. Scott, Jr., in *The Southern Review* (Baton Rouge, Louisiana), autumn 1988; *A.R. Ammons and the Poetics of Widening Scope* by Steven P. Schneider, Rutherford, New Jersey, and London, Fairleigh Dickinson Press, 1994; *The Spiritual Eye of A.R. Ammons: Mystical Elements in 'Sphere: The Form of a Motion'* (dissertation) by Bertha J. Hanse, University of Arkansas, 1995; "Garbage: A.R. Ammons's Tape for the Turn of the Century" by Lorraine C. DiCicco, in *Papers on Language and Literature* (Edwardsville, Illinois), 32(2), spring 1996; *Set in Motion: Essays, Interviews, and Dialogues* edited by Zofia Burr, Ann Arbor, University of Michigan Press, 1996; "A.R. Ammons's Stevensian Search for a Supreme Fiction in 'Sphere'" by John Adames, in *Twentieth Century Literature* (Hempstead, New

York), 43(1), spring 1997; "Language: The Poet As Master and Servant" by David Young, in *A Field Guide to Contemporary Poetry and Poetics,* edited by Stuart Friebert and others, Oberlin, Ohio, Oberlin College, 1997; "A.R. Ammons and the Whole Earth" by Kevin McGuirk, in *Cultural Critique* (Cary, North Carolina), 37, fall 1997; "Rage for Definition: The Long Poem As 'Sequence'" by Klaus Martens, in *Eichstatter Beitrage,* 20, 1998; "'The World Was the Beginning of the World': Agency and Homology in A.R. Ammons' Garbage" by Leonard M. Scigaj, in *Reading the Earth: New Directions in the Study of Literature and Environment,* edited by Michael P. Branch and others, Moscow, University of Idaho Press, 1998.

*   *   *

A.R. Ammons is an American romantic in the tradition of Emerson and Whitman. He is committed to free and open forms and to the amassing of the exact details experience provides rather than to the extrusion from it of any a priori order. His favorite subject is the relation of a man to nature as perceived by a solitary wanderer along the beaches and rural fields of New Jersey, where Ammons grew up. Because of the cumulative nature of his technique, Ammons's work shows to best advantage in poems of some magnitude. Perhaps the best, and best known, of these is the title poem from *Corsons Inlet,* in which, describing a walk along a tidal stream, the speaker says,

> I was released from forms,
> from the perpendiculars,
> straight lines, blocks, boxes, binds
> of thought
> into the hues, shading, rises, flowing bends and blends of
> sight . . .

Here as elsewhere Ammons accepts only what is possible to a sensibility attuned to the immediacy of experience, for he admits that "scope eludes my grasp, that there is no finality of vision, / that I have perceived nothing completely, / that tomorrow a new walk is a new walk."

Another kind of poem characteristic of Ammons is the brief metaphysical fable, in which there are surprising colloquies between an interlocutor and mountains, winds, or trees, as in "Mansion":

> So it came time
> for me to cede myself
> and I chose
> the wind
> to be delivered to.
> The wind was glad
> and said it needed all
> the body
> it could get
> to show its motions with . . .

The philosophical implications in these poems are explicit in "What This Mode of Motion Said," a meditation upon permanence and change phrased as a cadenza on Emerson's poem "Brahma."

Ammons's *Collected Poems 1951–1971* was chosen for the National Book award in 1973. Not included in this compendious volume is his book-length *Tape for the Turn of the Year,* a free-flowing imaginative journal composed in very short lines and written on a roll of adding machine tape. The combination here of memory, introspection, and observation rendered in ever changing musical phrasing is impressive. Such expansiveness is Ammons's métier. *Sphere: The Form of a Motion* is a long poem in 155 twelve-line stanzas that comprise one unbroken sentence. Taking Whitman and Stevens as his models, Ammons combines the all-inclusive sensibility of the one with the meditative philosophical discourse of the other, as these excerpts may suggest:

> . . . the identifying oneness of populations, peoples: I
> know my own—the thrown peripheries, the stragglers, the
>   cheated,
> maimed, afflicted (I know their eyes, pain's melting
>   amazement)

> the weak, disoriented, the sick, hurt, the castaways, the
> needful needless: I know them: I love them, I am theirs . . .

> the purpose of the motion of a poem is to bring the focused,
> awakened mind to no-motion, to a still contemplation of the
> whole motion, all the motions, of the poem . . .

> . . . by intensifying the alertness

> of the conscious mind even while it permits itself to sink,
> to be lowered down the ladder of structured motions to the
> refreshing energies of the deeper self . . .
> the non-verbal
> energy at that moment released, transformed back through the
> verbal, the sayable poem . . .

Ammons continues to revel in both long wandering poems and shorter lyrics in his volume *Sumerian Vistas.* As he points out in "The Ridge Farm," a meditative poem of fifty-one stanzas, "I like nature poetry / where the brooks are never dammed up . . ." His work is consistent in its experimentation with open forms and in its celebration of living processes and of the identity of man with nature.

Perhaps Ammons's most profound study of culture, human behavior, and the physical world is his 1993 fin de siècle long poem titled *Garbage,* in which he attempts to link science, spirituality, and philosophy as modes through which to evaluate garbage. For Ammons garbage has a force that brings communities together. Refuse expresses something essential about us; it is the originating point of communal consciousness and survival. His desire to know "simple people doing simple things, the normal, everyday routine of life and how these people thought about it" finds him recognizing "a monstrous surrounding of / gathering—the putrid, the castoff, the used, // the mucked up—all arriving for final assessment." Historian, archeologist, culturalist, environmentalist, and—for this book's project—garbologist, Ammons uses the figure of "curvature," which shows that "it all wraps back around," to cast the net wide enough to consider the various angles of garbage, even though the central figure of the book is the garbage dump itself.

Aesthetic involvement in our physical world and the processes of assembly and disassembly are Ammons's perennial concerns. In *Brink Road* he approaches a world largely unpeopled but still in motion and perpetuity: ". . . a snowflake / streaks / out of the hanging gray, / winter's first whitening: white on white let it be, / then, flake / to petal—to hold for a / minute or so." Often compared with Robert Frost and e.e. cummings, Ammons has a voice that sometimes hits a note with a Zen ring to it. In "Saying Saying Away" he revealingly

contends that poems "flow into a place where the distinction / between meaning and being is erased into the meaning of / being."

Winner of the National Book award in both 1973 and 1993 and recipient of the Robert Frost medal of the Poetry Society of America for his life's work, Ammons has had a prolific career that has carried him to his long volume *Glare,* which has the tone of a kind of diary, looping evenly, meditatively, seemingly inconsequentially back to itself. At its best moments it moves with a Wordsworthian grace typical of Ammons's early work:

> if you can
> send no word silently healing, I
> mean if it is not proper or realistic
> to send word, actual lips saying
> these broken sounds, why, may we be
> allowed to suppose that we can work
> this stuff out the best we can and
> having felt out our sins to their
> deepest definitions, may we walk with
> you as along a line of trees, every
> now and then your clarity and warmth
> shattering across our shadowed way.

—Daniel Hoffman and Martha Sutro

ANANIA, Michael

Nationality: American. **Born:** Omaha, Nebraska, 5 August 1939. **Education:** University of Nebraska, Lincoln, 1957–58, and Omaha, B.A. 1961; State University of New York, Buffalo, Ph.D. 1969. **Family:** Married Joanne Oliver in 1960. **Career:** Bibliographer, Lockwood Library, State University of New York, Buffalo, 1963–64; instructor in English, State University of New York, Fredonia, 1964–65, and Northwestern University, Evanston, Illinois, 1965–68. Instructor, 1968–70, and since 1970 assistant professor, then professor of English, University of Illinois, Chicago. Poetry editor, *Audit,* 1963–64, and co-editor, *Audit/Poetry,* 1963–67, Buffalo. Literary editor, Swallow Press, Chicago, 1968–74. **Awards:** Swallow Press New Poetry Series award, 1970. **Address:** Department of English, University of Illinois at Chicago Circle, Chicago, Illinois 60637, U.S.A.

PUBLICATIONS

Poetry

The Color of Dust. Chicago, Swallow Press, 1970.
Set/Sorts. Chicago, Wine Press, 1974.
Riversongs. Urbana, University of Illinois Press, 1978.
Constructions/Variations. Peoria, Illinois, Spoon River Poetry Press, 1985.
The Sky at Ashland. Mt. Kisco, New York, Moyer Bell, 1986.
Selected Poems. Wakefield, Rhode Island, Asphodel Press, 1994.
In Natural Light. Wakefield, Rhode Island, Asphodel Press, 1999.

Recording: *Michael Anania and Mari Evans Reading Their Poems,* Gertrude Clarke Whittall Poetry and Literature Fund, Library of

Congress, 1985; *Illinois Reads: Talks with Illinois Authors: Michael Anania* (videotape), Library Cable Network, 1986.

Novel

The Red Menace. New York, Thunder's Mouth Press, 1984.

Other

In Plain Sight: Obsessions, Morals & Domestic Laughter. Mt. Kisco, New York, Asphodel Press, 1991.

Editor, *New Poetry Anthology 1–2.* Chicago, Swallow Press, 1969–72.
Editor, *Gardening the Skies: The Missouri Writers' Biennial Anthology.* Springfield, Southwest Missouri State University, 1988.

*   *   *

In *The Color of Dust* Michael Anania traces his passage from the timeless to the contemporary, from small-town life by the Missouri River to a state of mind questioning national myths and the consequences of war. By evoking a sense of the land and people and by recognizing the permanence and the regenerative powers of the river, he demonstrates how identity stems from the knitting together of person and place (''We are not confused, / we do not lose our place''). But self-definition may be accomplished only one moment at a time, and periods of doubt inevitably occur (''Am I a songster or a dealer?''). So, too, in his calling the poet attempts to capture and maintain, thereby creating his own dilemma; the writing of a poem means the wresting of something from its organic context. But it is the nature of the creator to utter his vision and, in doing so, to preserve what he perceives. Time and again the poet must confront the realization that all things change; in Robert Creeley's words, ''Everything is water / if you look long enough.''

Anania's attempts to preserve the interrelatedness of experience may be seen metaphorically in ''The Fall'' and dramatically in his war pieces. In the latter he presents the survivors, those men with fragments of mind and those who suffer physical decay. Here Anania successfully weaves a living tapestry as he reveals the tragic operation of causality in human lives. Time goes on, and man improves his weapons; he progresses from shrapnel to napalm. The American hero, a manifestation of national power propagated by the media, wears ''the satin cape / the big red S / meaning, after all, better than.'' Superman's cool efficiency and superior strength symbolize the power of a machine-driven culture.

In *Riversongs* the meaning and metaphor of the river are extended to encompass a sense of the historical past, the passage of time to the present, and the inevitable flow toward death. ''The Riversongs of Arion,'' the ten-poem sequence that gives the book its name, recounts a modern attempt to retrace the Lewis and Clark journey and incorporates excerpts drawn from Lewis's journals. The river of historical time flows into the present and becomes one with the mind of the persona. After all, the first rule of river and mind is motion: ''. . . In time / the river side-winds its banks. / Never the same soil . . .'' Elements of the historical past, of the struggle to settle the frontier, clarify how human experience is continuous and becomes intertwined as it flows into contemporary America, and Lewis's words mingle with references to Billy the Kid, John Wesley Hardin, Wild Bill Hickok, Sacajawea, and Huck Finn. The poem's movement

resembles the outward rippling caused by a stone dropped in water and, simultaneously, a deepening, for every journey is a life quest, individual, uncertain:

> each night I read my Journals
> like a novel, seeking some
> inevitability of plot, a hint
> of form pointing toward an end

The river of memory floats the persona back to the dead fathers of his family (''Reeving'') and forward to present time (''News Notes, 1970'').

Poetry is music that moves like a river, a liquid music flowing and changing. In the play of liquid and light illuminations sparkle like sunlight on wave tips. In *Riversongs* the best of Anania's poems embody the endurance of water wedded to the delicacy of light; things come in waves, they stream past the beholding eye, and they are gone. In the river's continuity and the light playing on its surface, Anania captures and preserves ''those shafts of light / the soul is mirror to.''

—Carl Lindner

ANGELOU, Maya

Nationality: American. **Born:** Marguerita Johnson, St. Louis, Missouri, 4 April 1928. **Education:** Attended schools in Arkansas and California; studied music privately, dance with Martha Graham, Pearl Primus, and Ann Halprin, and drama with Frank Silvera and Gene Frankel. **Family:** Married Tosh Angelos (divorced); 2) married Paul de Feu in 1973 (divorced); one son. **Career:** Actress and singer; associate editor, *Arab Observer,* Cairo, 1961–62; assistant administrator, School of Music and Drama, University of Ghana Institute of African Studies, Legon and Accra, 1963–66; freelance writer for *Ghanaian Times* and Ghanaian Broadcasting Corporation, both Accra, 1963–65; feature editor, *African Review,* Accra, 1964–66; lecturer, University of California, Los Angeles, 1966; writer-in-residence or visiting professor, University of Kansas, Lawrence, 1970, Wake Forest University, Winston-Salem, North Carolina, 1974, Wichita State University, Kansas, 1974, and California State University, Sacramento, 1974. Since 1981 Reynolds Professor, Wake Forest University. Northern coordinator, Southern Christian Leadership Conference, 1959–60. Taught modern dance, Rome Opera House and Hambina Theatre, Tel Aviv. Actress appearing in various television programs. Also composer, television host and interviewer, and writer for Oprah Winfrey television series *Brewster Place.* **Awards:** Yale University fellowship, 1970; Rockefeller grant, 1975; *Ladies Home Journal* award, 1976; Golden Eagle award, 1977; American Academy of Achievement's Golden Plate award, 1990; Essence Woman of the Year, 1992; Horatio Alger award, 1992; Woman in Film award, 1992; Grammy award for best spoken word album, 1994; Spingarn Award NAACP, 1994; Frank G. Wells award, 1995; Southern Christian Leadership Conference of Los Angeles and Martin Luther King, Jr., Legacy Association national award, 1996; W.K. Kellogg Foundation, Expert-in-Residence Program, 1997; Black Caucus of American Library Association, Cultural Keepers award, 1997; Christopher award, 1998; Lifetime Achievement award for literature, 1999. Received Emmy award, National Book award, Pulitzer prize, and

Tony award nominations. Also the recipient of numerous other awards and honors, including the North Carolina Award in Literature, 1987; Langston Hughes award, City College of New York, 1991; Innaugural poet for President Bill Clinton, 1993; poet, Million Man March, Washington, D.C., 1995. Honorary degrees: Smith College, Northampton, Massachusetts, 1975; Mills College, Oakland, California, 1975; and Lawrence University, Appleton, Wisconsin, 1976. **Member:** American Revolution Bicentennial Council, 1975–76; board of trustees, American Film Institute, 1975; advisory board, Women's Prison Association; Harlem Writer's Guild; National Commission on the Observance of International Women's Year; Director's Guild of America; Equity; American Federation Television Radio Artists (AFTRA); Horatio Alger Association of Distinguished Americans; National Society for Prevention of Cruelty to Children, 1992; Ambassador, Unicef International, 1996; Doctors without Borders, 1996; W.E.B. Dubois Foundation, Inc.; National Society of Collegiate Scholars; Lifetime membership, National Association for the Advancement of Colored People (NAACP). **Agent:** Lordly and Dame Inc., 51 Church Street, Boston, Massachusetts 02116–5493, U.S.A.

PUBLICATIONS

Poetry

Just Give Me a Cool Drink of Water 'fore I Diiie. New York, Random House, 1971; London, Virago Press, 1988.
Oh Pray My Wings Are Gonna Fit Me Well. New York, Random House, 1975.
And Still I Rise (also director: produced Oakland, California, 1976). New York, Random House, 1978; London, Virago Press, 1986
Poems. New York, Bantam, 1981.
Shaker, Why Don't You Sing? New York, Random House, 1983.
Now Sheba Sings the Song. New York, Dial Press, and London, Virago Press, 1987.
I Shall Not Be Moved. New York, Bantam Books, 1991
On the Pulse of Morning. New York, Random House, 1993.
Life Doesn't Frighten Me (for children). N.p., Stewart, Tabori, and Chang, 1993.
The Complete Collected Poems of Maya Angelou. New York, Random House, 1994.
Phenomenal Woman: Four Poems Celebrating Women. New York, Random House, 1995.
A Brave and Startling Truth. New York, Random House, 1995.

Recordings: *Miss Calypso,* Liberty, 1957, 1996; *For the Love of Ivy,* Sidney Portier film, 1968; *The Poetry of Maya Angelou,* GWP, 1969; *Women in Business,* University of Wisconsin, 1981; *Georgia, Georgia,* 1972; *All Day Long,* 1974; *And Still I Rise,* 1992; *Been Found,* 1996.

Plays

Cabaret for Freedom (revue), with Godfrey Cambridge (produced New York, 1960).
The Least of These (produced Los Angeles, 1966).
Gettin' up Stayed on My Mind, (produced, 1967).
Ajax, from the play by Sophocles (produced Los Angeles, 1974).

Moon on a Rainbow Shawl, book by Errol John (produced in London, 1988).
King (lyrics only, with Alistair Beaton), book by Lonne Elder III, music by Richard Blackford (produced London, 1990).

Screenplays: *Georgia, Georgia,* 1972; *All Day Long,* 1974.

Television Plays: *Sisters, Sisters,* with John Berry, 1982.

Television Documentaries: *Black, Blues, Black,* 1968; *Assignment America,* 1975; *The Legacy,* 1976; *The Inheritors,* 1976; *Trying to Make It Home* (*Byline* series), 1988; *Maya Angelou's America: A Journey of the Heart* (also host); *Who Cares about Kids, Kindred Spirits, Maya Angelou: Rainbow in the Clouds,* and *To the Contrary* (all Public Broadcasting Service productions).

Other

I Know Why the Caged Bird Sings. New York, Random House, 1970; London, Virago Press, 1984.
Gather Together in My Name. New York, Random House, 1974; London, Virago Press, 1985.
Singin' and Swingin' and Gettin' Merry Like Christmas. New York, Random House, 1976; London, Virago Press, 1985.
The Heart of a Woman. New York, Random House, 1981; London, Virago Press, 1986.
All God's Children Need Traveling Shoes. New York, Random House, 1986; London, Virago Press, 1987.
Mrs. Flowers: A Moment of Friendship (for children). Minneapolis, Redpath Press, 1986.
Wouldn't Take Nothing for My Journey Now. New York, Random House, 1993.
My Painted House, My Friendly Chicken, and Me (for children), N.p., Crown, 1994.
Kofi and His Magic, with photographs by Margaret Courtney-Clark (for children). New York, Clarkson Potter, 1996.

*

Bibliography: "A Maya Angelou Bibliography" by Dee Birch Cameron, in *Bulletin of Bibliography* (Westwood, Massachusetts), 36, 1979.

Manuscript Collection: Wake Forest University, Winston-Salem, North Carolina.

Critical Studies: *Maya Angelou* by Claudia Tate, in *Black Women Writers at Work,* New York, Continuum, 1983; "Transcendence: The Poetry of Maya Angelou" by Pricilla R. Ramsey, in *A Current Bibliography on African Affairs* (Amityville, New York), 17(2), 1984–85; "Maya Angelou: Self and a Song of Freedom in the Southern Tradition" by Carol E. Neubauer, in *Southern Women Writers: The New Generation,* edited by Tonette Bond Inge, Tuscaloosa, University of Alabama Press, 1990; "Singing the Black Mother: Maya Angelou and Autobiographical Continuity" by Mary Jane Lupton, in *Black American Literature Forum,* 24(2), summer 1990; "Breaking Out of the Cage: The Autobiographical Writings of Maya Angelou" by James Robert Saunders, in *Hollins Critic* (Hollins College, Virginia), 28(4), October 1991; *Touch Me, Life, Not Softly: The Poetry of Maya Angelou* (dissertation) by Leila Andrea Walker,

Florida State University, 1994; *The Poetry of Maya Angelou: A Study of the Blues Matrix As Force and Code* (dissertation) by Kathy Mae Essick, Indiana University, 1994; "Racial Protest, Identity, Words, and Form in Maya Angelou's 'I Know Why the Caged Bird Sings'" by Pierre A. Walker, in *College Literature* (West Chester, Pennsylvania), 22(3), October 1995; "Women's Life-Writing and the Minority Voice: Maya Angelou, Maxine Hong Kingston, and Alice Walker" by Suzette A. Henke, in *Traditions, Voices, and Dreams: The American Novel since the 1960s,* edited by Melvin J. Friedman and Ben Siegel, Newark, University of Delaware Press, 1995; "Searching for a Self in Maya Angelou's 'I Know Why the Caged Bird Sings'" by Dana Chamblee-Carpenter, in *Publications of the Mississippi Philological Association* (Cleveland, Mississippi), 1996; *Contemporary American Writers of Desperate Survival: Edward Albee, Maya Angelou, Pat Conroy and Leslie Marmon Silko* (dissertation) by Charlene Knadle, St. John's University, New York, 1998; "Hurston's and Angelou's Visual Art: The Distancing Vision and the Beckoning Gaze" by Marion M. Tangum and Marjorie Smelstor, *Southern Literary Journal* (Chapel Hill, North Carolina), 31(1), fall 1998; *Maya Angelou* by Miles Shapiro, Philadelphia, Chelsea House Publishers, 2000.

Theatrical Activities: Director: **Plays**—*And Still I Rise,* Oakland, California, 1976; *Moon on a Rainbow Shawl* by Errol John, London, 1988; **Film**—*All Day Long,* 1974. Actress: **Plays**—in *Porgy and Bess* by George Gershwin, tour, 1954–55; *Calypso Heatwave,* New York, 1957; *The Blacks* by Jean Genet, New York, 1960; *Cabaret for Freedom,* New York, 1960; *Mother Courage* by Berthold Brecht, Accra, Ghana, 1964; *Medea,* Hollywood, 1966; *Look Away,* New York, 1973; **Film**—*Roots,* 1977; *How to Make an American Quilt,* 1995; *Down in the Delta,* 1998.

*   *   *

In a BBC broadcast—sometime after the 1987 publication of *Now Sheba Sings the Song*—Maya Angelou sang two impromptu, unaccompanied versions of the song "When the Saints Come Marching In." First she sang with a bright, cheerful surface, the "way whites do," and then she sang with a deep contralto, "from the soul," drawing upon the music that flows deep within us all.

William Shakespeare was Angelou's "first white love," but her poems must be heard against a background of black rhythms. She has an uncanny ability to capture the sound of a voice on a page, as in *Just Give Me a Cool Drink of Water 'fore I Diiie.* Vocal, oral, and written aspects blend in her poetry.

It is ironic that her own triumphs have drawn attention from the uniqueness of her poetry. She was named by Martin Luther King, Jr., to be the Northern coordinator for his Southern Christian Leadership Conference and by President Jimmy Carter to be a member of the Commission for the International Women's Year. She has adapted Sophocles' *Ajax* for the stage, television, and film; she appeared in a production of Jean Genet's *The Blacks;* and she had a highly successful career as a dancer. Her books have sold in the millions, but her poetry has received little serious critical attention.

In one sense of the word, however, her poetry is not "serious." Rather it is, as she herself puts it in the title poem of her volume *And Still I Rise,* "sassy." This term, however, has a powerful meaning. "Sassy" implies (we should assume from her own words) that "the impudent child was detested by God, and a shame to its parents and could bring destruction to its house . . ." This use of litotes is congenial with a peculiar sort of "coding," as with kenning. Thus, "God's candle bright" is more of a token for the sun than a metaphor. So, too, the title of her autobiography, *I Know Why the Caged Bird Sings,* is not a sentimental metaphor but a litotes for humiliation. In her poetry understatement is a style for presenting a shared experience in its inconsistency and its energy, and the coding can reinforce the anger implied by the "humor," as in "Sepia Fashion Show":

> Their hair, pomaded, faces jaded
> bones protruding, hip-wise,
> The models strutted, backed and butted,
> Then stuck their mouths out, lip-wise.
>
> They'd nasty manners, held like banners,
> while they looked down their nose-wise,
> I'd see 'em in hell, before they'd sell
> me one thing they're wearing, clothes-wise.
>
> The Black Bourgeois, who all say "yah"
> When yeah is what they're meaning
> Should look around, both up and down
> before they set out preening.
>
> "Indeed" they swear, "that's what I'll wear
> When I go country-clubbing,"
> I'd remind them please, look at those knees
> you got a Miss Ann's scrubbing.

The last line strikes the ear as comic, and we share this sense of it, but then we react as we remember that black women literally had to show their knees to prove how hard they had cleaned. The change—the hearing and then the reaction—is central to Angelou's poetry. We read the understated "nothing happens" in "Letter to an Aspiring Junkie" and then realize that it is a smashing litotes for "violence is everywhere":

> Let me hip you to the streets,
> Jim,
> Ain't nothing happening.
> Maybe some tomorrows gone up in smoke,
> raggedy preachers, telling a joke
> to lonely, son-less old ladies' maids.
>
> Nothing happening,
> Nothing shakin', Jim.
> A slough of young cats riding that
> cold, white horse,
> a grey old monkey on their back, of course
> does rodeo tricks.
>
> No haps, man.
> No haps.
> A worn-out pimp, with a space-age conk,
> setting up some fool for a game of tonk,
> or poker or
> get 'em dead and alive.
>
> The streets?
> Climb into the streets man, like you climb
> into the ass end of a lion.

Then it's fine.
It's a bug-a-loo and a shing-a-ling,
African dreams on a buck-and-a-wing and a prayer.
That's the streets man,
Nothing happening.

The experience is particular; the word "conk" refers to a hairdo—rather like Little Richard's, for example. But the energy comes from the astonishing rhythms and perhaps more accurately from the changes of rhythm.

Angelou has composed poetry from the particulars and the rhythms she knows, and the changes of rhythm themselves become a rhythm, the upsets and restarts in an unsteady state of soul that every life has experienced in some place or other. When we read Angelou's poetry, we share the sense of it. But then we have a reaction from the energy and have to reassess it, so that ultimately, when we hear her poetry, we listen to ourselves.

—William Sylvester

ANTIN, David

Nationality: American. **Born:** Brooklyn, New York, 1 February 1932. **Education:** City College, New York, B.A. 1955; New York University (Lehman Fellow), 1964–66, M.A. in linguistics 1966. **Family:** Married Eleanor Fineman in 1960; one son. **Career:** Freelance editor and translator, 1956–57; chief editor and scientific director, Research Information Service, New York, 1958–60; freelance editor and consultant, Dover Press, New York, 1959–64; curator, Institute of Contemporary Art, Boston, 1967; director of the University Art Gallery and assistant professor, 1968–72, and since 1972 professor of visual arts, University of California, San Diego. Former editor, with Jerome Rothenberg, *Some/Thing,* New York; contributing editor, *Alcheringa,* New York, 1972–80. **Awards:** Longview award, 1960; University of California Creative Arts award, 1972; Guggenheim fellowship, 1976; National Endowment for the Humanities fellowship, 1983; P.E.N. award for poetry, 1984, for *tuning.* **Member:** Editorial board, University of California Press, San Diego, 1972–76, and since 1979, *New Wilderness.* **Address:** P.O. Box 1147, Del Mar, California 92014, U.S.A.

PUBLICATIONS

Poetry

Definitions. New York, Caterpillar Press, 1967.
autobiography. New York, Something Else Press, 1967.
Code of Flag Behavior. Los Angeles, Black Sparrow Press, 1968.
Meditations. Los Angeles, Black Sparrow Press, 1971.
Talking. New York, Kulchur, 1972.
After the War (A Long Novel with Few Words). Santa Barbara, Black Sparrow Press, 1973.
Talking at the Boundaries. New York, New Directions, 1976.
Who's Listening Out There? College Park, Maryland, Sun and Moon Press, 1980.
tuning. New York, New Directions, 1984.
Poèmes Parlés. Paris, Les Cahiers des Brisants, 1984.

Selected Poems 1963–73. Los Angeles, Sun and Moon, 1991.
what it means to be avant-garde. New York, New Directions, 1993.

Recordings: *The Principle of Fit,* 2, Watershed, 1980; *The Archeology of Home,* Astro Artz, 1987.

Other

Translator, *100 Great Problems of Elementary Mathematics: Their History and Solution,* by Heinrich Doerrie. New York, Dover, 1965.
Translator, *The Physics of Modern Electronics,* by W.A. Guenther. New York, Dover, 1967.

*

Critical Studies: "John Cage, Buckminster Fuller, and David Antin" by Barry Alpert, "Some Notes toward a Discussion of the New Oral Poetry" by George Economou, and "A Correspondence between the Editors Robert Kroetsch and William Spanos and David Antin," all in *Boundary* 2 (Binghamton, New York), Spring 1975; interview with Barry Alpert, and articles by Gilbert Sorrentino, Hugh Kenner, Toby Olson, and David Bromige, in *Vort* (Silver Spring, Maryland), Winter 1975; *The Poetics of Indeterminacy* by Marjorie Perloff, Princeton, New Jersey, Princeton University Press, 1982; *So to Speak: Rereading David Antin,* London, Binnacle, 1982, and *In Search of the Primitive,* Baton Rouge, Louisiana State University Press, 1986, both by Sherman Paul; "David Antin and the Oral Poetics Movement," in *Contemporary Literature* (Madison, Wisconsin), Fall 1982, and *The Object of Performance,* Chicago, University of Chicago Press, 1989, both by Henry Sayre; *The Poet's Prose,* Cambridge, University Press, 1983, revised edition, 1991, both by Stephen Fredman; "Professing the Pastoral" by Charles Altieri, in *American Literary History,* 1(4), Winter 1989; *The Jazz Text, Voice and Improvisation in Poetry, Jazz, and Song* by Charles O. Hartman, Princeton, New Jersey, Princeton University Press, 1991; by Marjorie Perloff, in *American Book Review,* 13(5), December 1991–92; "Austin and Antin about 'About'" by Rei Terada, in *SubStance* (Madison, Wisconsin), 24(3), 1995; "Thinking Made in the Mouth: The Cultural Poetics of David Antin and Jerome Rothenberg" by Hank Lazer, in *Picturing Cultural Values in Postmodern America,* edited by William G. Doty, Tuscaloosa, University of Alabama Press, 1995; interview, in *Some Other Fluency: Interviews with Innovative American Authors,* edited by Larry McCaffery, Philadelphia, University of Pennsylvania Press, 1996.

*   *   *

The extraordinary improvisations collected in David Antin's *Talking at the Boundaries, tuning,* and w*hat it means to be avant-garde* and appearing in a spate of periodicals ranging from *Representations* ("The Price") to *Dialog* ("The Messenger") have often been greeted with hostility by readers accustomed to the more traditional lyric modes. Antin's "talk poems" are improvised for particular occasions in particular places, recorded on tape, and only later transcribed on the typewriter. The written texts are described by Antin as "the notations of scores of oral poems with margins consequently unjustified." As scores of actual talks, the texts obviously lack verse form; they do away not only with meter but even with lineation, that last stronghold of free verse. To make matters worse, Antin has expressed a "distrust of ideas of interiority and the whole rhetorical ensemble of notions about 'feelings and emotions.'" Rather, he regards the "art of talking" as essentially the language art, and he is less interested in ethos or pathos than in *dianoia,* which Aristotle defines as "all the thought that is expressed or effected by the words" or, again, as "the ability to say what is possible and appropriate."

Does this mean that an Antin composition is "merely" prose? On the contrary. "Prose," says Antin, "is an image of the authority of 'right thinking,' conveyed primarily through right printing—justified margins, conventional punctuation, and regularized spelling." The distinction between Antin's talking and prose was established in the early 1960s by Northrop Frye in *The Well-Tempered Critic:*

> One can see in ordinary speech . . . a unit of rhythm peculiar to it, a short phrase that contains the central word or idea aimed at, but is largely innocent of syntax. It is much more repetitive than prose, as it is in the process of working out an idea, and the repetitions are largely rhythmical filler.

This "associative rhythm," as Frye calls the rhythm of speech, may be conventionalized in two ways:

> One way is to impose a pattern of recurrence on it; the other is to impose the logical and semantic pattern of the sentence. We have verse when the arrangement of words is dominated by recurrent rhythm and sound, prose when it is dominated by the syntactical relation of subject and predicate.

The interchange between the three basic rhythmic modes provides the combinations that give literature its variety and complexity. When, for example, the associative rhythm is influenced, but not quite organized, by the sentence, we get what Frye calls "free prose," a form that developed much earlier than free verse. Witness the associative monologue found in the personal letter, the diary, in Swift's *Journal to Stella* and in Sterne's *Tristam Shandy.* Beckett's *The Unnamable* is an important modern example.

Antin's talk poems fall into this latter category. Indeed, there is a sense in which Antin is a perfectly traditional writer, his tradition being that not of the romantic or symbolist lyric but of the eighteenth century, particularly the mode of Diderot's *Rameau's Nephew,* which Antin cites as one of his key models. The associative rhythm, Frye remarks, "represents the process of bringing ideas into articulation in contrast to prose or verse, which normally represent a finished product." Just so, Antin's "poetry," even his earlier, more conventionally lineated poems like the elegy "Definitions for Mendy" and "trip through a landscape" (*Selected Poems: 1963–1973*) is a process-oriented art. But this notion of a poem as process must also be qualified. In its written version, which is, of course, the version of the talk poem the reader confronts, one meets a peculiar—and quite postmodern—oscillation between the natural and the artificial, a recognition that writing, no matter how closely it claims to mime speech, is always other. Indeed, the paradox of the talk poem is that it is a formalized text that calls talk itself into question.

In practice the talk poem works in accordance with certain implicit rules. First, just as there are no margins, so there are no complete sentences. The trick is to "keep it moving," in Charles Olson's words, as, for instance, in this passage about cross-country jet travel:

> when i got on the plane i had the feeling   i started
> out early in the day   it was 12 oclock   to be on a
> plane 12 oclock on a plane is in some ways the worst
> possible time to get on a plane because   what happens is
> you start out in the daylight and you wind up in the
> night and there never was any day and its odd you feel
> that youre travelling into the past

The first "when" clause is never completed by a main clause, for the speaker immediately interests himself in what it was like when he got on. The proposition "it was 12 oclock" leads not to the expected account of what happened at twelve o'clock but to a comic sequence about the peculiar feelings attendant upon boarding an eastbound flight at noon. So it goes, with rapid-fire shifts from one image or idea to another. The text is a transcription, not of a character's speech as one might find it, say, in a novel, but of Antin's talk.

But if it is just talk, what makes it art? Here three other rules come in. The first of these is that the talk poem incorporates as many different threads as possible while retaining its improvisatory quality, yet the threads are all relational. The analogy is to a juggling act; as we watch Antin juggle the balls, we gradually realize that they will—or at least should—all be caught. Thus, in "Real Estate" the inquiry into the meaning of the words "real estate" and "currency" seems to get lost as we are given a series of comic narratives about various Antin relatives who did or did not own real estate. These stories are fun in themselves, but, in considering in what sense, if any, a little hotel in the Catskills bought by his eccentric uncle is a "real" estate, Antin leads us right back to the possible meanings of his title.

The second rule is that narrative, but not a "story" in the conventional sense of the term, is an integral part of the talk poem. Pure exposition, rumination, meditation—these undercut the poet's emphasis on the ongoing process of discovery in which one creates the self. Antin's narratives function as parodic examples. They illustrate the points the speaker is making but only because he wants them to, not because they have any sort of objective validity.

Third, the generation of a particular voice is the one fictional element Antin allows himself. If, for example, one were to become ill while visiting San Diego and phoned Antin for advice and help, he would undoubtedly be able to give you practical information as to emergency rooms and so forth. In a talk poem, however, a term like "medical center" is deconstructed. Here is Antin's account of what happened when he and his family first arrived in southern California and found that his then little boy was sick:

> and i said to somebody in a shoestore "what do you do
> if somebody gets sick during lunch?" and they said
> "there's a medical center   right up the hill" and i drove
> to the medical center   and there was a medical center
> in california a medical center is unlike anything youve
> ever seen   unless youre a californian   medical centers
> depend on redwood trees   because theyre made out of
> redwood trees and iceplant   because what they do is level off
> an area   whatever was there they take a bulldozer
> and level it off   if there were eucalyptus trees they knock
> them down they push things out of the way   and then what they
> don't cover with redwood and blacktop they cover with
> iceplant   wherever you go there's iceplant

By this time the reader has all but lost sight of the ostensible purpose of this particular trip, which is to find a hospital, the real focus being a defamiliarized southern California landscape as seen for the first time by an urban poet fresh from the East Coast.

The refusal to claim knowledge either of himself or of his characters has suggested to some readers that Antin is unfeeling, that he refuses to take life "seriously." This is to misunderstand the nature of the talk poems completely. In adopting the stance of a puzzled observer, of the unhabituated eye that sees persons and places as if for the first time, Antin gives us a graphic image of how the mind actually experiences the outside world. He can, moreover, embed such general questions as he wishes to raise—for example, to what extent is the photograph a true reproduction of visual reality? what is the nature of narrative? or what does it mean to be an artist "on the fringe"?—in a set of images or story contexts so that the audience shares his own process of discovery. Antin's "tuning" thus become ours. As he says, "now if you freeze life it's like frozen food," but "when you translate something it changes."

—Marjorie Perloff

ARMANTROUT, (Mary) Rae

Nationality: American. **Born:** Vallejo, California, 13 April 1947. **Education:** California State University, San Diego, 1965–68; University of California, Berkeley, 1969–70, B.A. 1970; California State University, San Francisco, 1972–75, M.A. 1975. **Family:** Married Charles Korkegian in 1971; one son. **Career:** Teaching assistant, California State University, San Francisco, 1972–73; lecturer, California State University, San Diego, 1979–82. Since 1981 lecturer, University of California, San Diego, La Jolla. **Awards:** California Arts Council fellowship, 1989; Fund for Poetry award, 1993, 1999. **Address:** 4774 East Mountain View Drive, San Diego, California 92116, U.S.A.

PUBLICATIONS

Poetry

Extremities. Great Barrington, Massachusetts, The Figures, 1978.
The Invention of Hunger. Berkeley, California, Tuumba, 1979.
Precedence. Providence, Rhode Island, Burning Deck, 1985.
Necromance. Los Angeles, Sun and Moon Press, 1991.
Made to Seem. Los Angeles, Sun and Moon Press, 1995.
Writing the Plots about Sets. Tucson, Arizona, Chax, 1998.
True. Berkeley, California, Atelos, 1998.
The Pretext. Los Angeles, Sun and Moon Press, 1999.

*

Critical Studies: "Armantrout: Extremities" by Susan Howe, in *The L=A=N=G=U=A=G=E Book,* edited by Bruce Andrews and Charles Bernstein, Southern Illinois University Press, 1984; "The Siren Song of the Singular" by Jeffrey Peterson, in *Sagetrieb* (Orono, Maine), 12(3), winter 1993; "See Armantrout for an Alternate View" by Michael Leddy, in *Contemporary Literature,* 35(4), winter 1994; *The Marginalization of Poetry: Language, Writing, and Literary History*

by Bob Perelman, Princeton, New Jersey, Princeton University Press, 1996; "Finding Grace: Modernity and the Ineffable in the Poetry of Rae Armantrout and Fanny Howe" by Ann Vickery, in *Revista Canaria de Estudios Ingleses,* 37, 1998; *A Wild Salience: The Poetry of Rae Armantrout* edited by Tom Beckett and Luigi-Bob Drake, Cleveland, Ohio, Burning Press, 1999.

Rae Armantrout comments:

I began reading poetry seriously in high school. The first poets I responded to were William Carlos Williams and Robinson Jeffers. A little bit later I encountered the work of Robert Creeley, Denise Levertov, and Charles Olson. I studied with Levertov when I was a student at Berkeley. It was there, too, that I met people such as Ron Silliman and Barrett Watten. We formed one nexus of the group later known as language poets.

I am interested in the psychology of perception, especially in the way the mind distinguishes discrete objects. What is a thing? What is a self? I think I deal with this problem mimetically by producing the dubious unity of the poem.

*   *   *

Throughout her career Rae Armantrout has aligned herself with the movement generally known as language poetry, sometimes called, after the title of an important theoretical journal published by this group of writers, L=A=N=G=U=A=G=E poetry. In the years around 1970 a group of poets that included Ron Silliman, Lyn Hejinian, and Charles Bernstein sought to move beyond the search for a unique personal voice that had set the tone of the poetry of the 1960s, both the confessional poetry of Lowell, Plath, and Sexton and the projectivism of Olson and his followers. The leaders of this new avant-garde argued instead that poetry should engage in a critical interrogation of language itself as the mechanism that creates the illusion of an "authentic" subjectivity and thereby trammels us in socially constructed ways of perceiving and acting. The language poets found precedents for their own practices in the syntactic dislocations of William Carlos Williams and Louis Zukofsky and in Gertrude Stein's attempts to probe the limits of referentiality in such works as *Tender Buttons.*

By the mid-1970s language poetry had established itself as a coherent and well-organized movement, with its own journals and publishers, and Armantrout had emerged as a poet within the movement. *In the American Tree,* the 1986 anthology that first brought language poetry to a larger public, includes a substantial selection of her work, and some of her later books were issued by Sun and Moon, a principal publisher of language poetry. In an essay appended to *In The American Tree,* moreover, Armantrout explicitly aligns herself with this movement. She praises Susan Howe for "call[ing] our attention to the effect of linguistic structure on belief," and she salutes Carla Harryman for putting "content at odds with syntactical (or sometimes narrative) structures in order to make these structures stand out, enter our consciousness." "The writers I like," Armantrout declares, "bring the underlying structures of language/thought into consciousness. They spurn the facile. Though they generally don't believe in Truth, they are scrupulously honest about the way word relates to word, sentence to sentence."

Armantrout's own poetry seeks and often achieves many of the qualities that she admires in Howe and Harryman. Armantrout writes lean, almost minimalist poems, and she publishes them in equally lean

31

volumes. While other language poets have experimented with extended prose poems (Silliman, Hejinian, Harryman) or with poetic sequences (Bruce Andrews, both Susan and Fanny Howe), Armantrout has remained faithful to the short poem, usually written in a clipped Creeleyesque line, although her books generally also include occasional forays into the prose poem. Her publisher places her within the tradition of Emily Dickinson, and the comparison is apt. Like Dickinson, Armantrout compresses linguistic structures until they implode. Dickinson saw poetry as a "gift of screws" that wring out the "essential oils," and Armantrout agrees. The work of both poets takes fire from the friction of disparate, even clashing words rubbing up against one another. In part the impulse behind these verbal juxtapositions is simply a spirit of play: Armantrout shares Dickinson's sometimes murderous wit. But both poets want to look at—and thus perhaps to see beyond—the linguistic and social structures that hem us in.

As compared even to the most enigmatic of Dickinson's poems, Armantrout's may seem willfully opaque. Yet if we pay careful attention to her words as they have been placed on the page, without demanding an immediately recognizable human feeling, new possibilities of interconnection begin to come together in our minds. Only by looking in some detail at a specific Armantrout poem can we see how this process takes place. "Family Resemblances" is a relatively simple example:

Old broom,
is it straw-yellow?
stitched with parallel
lightning bolts
like the skirt of a square-dancer

who seems familiar
though she won't notice you,
displaying her do-si-dos
in the flicker
from Lawrence Welk's studio.

The title locates us in a comfortably domestic sphere, and the first phrase of the poem seems to invite a mild nostalgia. Remember when your mother swept the kitchen with a "real" broom made of straw, not a plastic imitation? But the next line reminds us that we live in a realm of commodities. This broom, however old it might be, is perhaps not made of real straw. Rather it is, or it might be, "straw-yellow"—and why, after all, do the manufacturers of plastic brooms almost always make them yellow? The question mark also suggests that we are not sure what color the broom is. We may be seeing not the broom itself but rather a picture of it, perhaps, as the last line of the poem suggests, on a television screen. In any case the fibers of the broom are bound together by two rows of lightning bolt stitches, and the poet notices a similar pattern on the whirling skirt of a square dancer. Hence the title: there is a family resemblance between the broom and the dancer. Both seem familiar. Both speak to our hunger for tradition.

Both broom and dancer, however, are in fact commodities, "ideologically overdetermined" as critical theory might say. The dancer on the screen looks into our eyes and smiles reassuringly but does not really see or know us. The illusion of familiarity, the affirmation of "traditional family values," is a trap. The flicker of the television screen defines our distance from the world of the dancer.

As we recognize the dancer as a commodity, her willingness to display her "do-si-dos" for us becomes obscene, a kind of prostitution. The nominalization of the caller's command to the dancers also enacts a process we may observe throughout the poem. Grammatically, the syntax never quite resolves itself into a sentence, although it seems constantly on the verge of doing so. The failure of the nouns to find a main verb shifts the focus back to the nouns: "broom," "bolts," "skirt," "square-dancer," "do-si-dos," "flicker," "studio." "A noun," Armantrout suggests in another poem, "is a kind of scab." "Family Resemblances" wants not to pull away the scab but to remind us that these nouns are scabs and that there are real wounds under them.

—Burton Hatlen

ARMITAGE, Simon

Nationality: English. **Born:** Huddersfield, West Yorkshire, 26 May 1963. **Education:** Portsmouth Polytechnic, B.A. (honors) 1984; Victoria University of Manchester, certificate of qualification in social work and M.A. 1988. **Career:** Since 1988 probation officer in Manchester. Poetry editor, Chatto and Windus, London. **Awards:** Eric Gregory award, Society of Authors, 1988; Poetry Book Society Choice, 1989; Sunday Times Young Writer of the Year, 1993. **Address:** c/o Faber and Faber, 3 Queen Square, London, England.

PUBLICATIONS

Poetry

The Distance between Stars. N.p., Wide Skirt, 1987.
The Walking Horses. Nottingham, Slow Dancer, 1988.
Human Geography. Huddersfield, Doorstop, 1988.
Zoom. Newcastle upon Tyne, Bloodaxe, 1989.
Around Robinson. Nottingham, Slow Dancer, 1991.
Xanadu. Newcastle upon Tyne, Bloodaxe, 1992.
Kid. London and Boston, Faber, 1992.
Book of Matches. London and Boston, Faber, 1993.
The Anaesthetist: A New Poem. Alton, Prospero Poets, 1994.
Dead Sea Poems. London and Boston, Faber, 1995.
CloudCuckooLand. London and Boston, Faber, 1997.
Killing Time. London, Faber, 1999.

Other

Moon Country: Further Reports from Iceland. London and Boston, Faber, 1996.
All Points North. London, Viking, 1998.

Editor, *Simon Armitage, Sean O'Brien, Tony Harrison.* London and New York, Penguin, 1995.

*

Critical Studies: "On Simon Armitage" by John Whitworth, in *Spectator* (London), 269(8563), 22 August 1992; by Ian Gregson, in

Poetry Review, 83(4), Winter 1994; by John Hartley Williams, in *New Statesman Society* (London), 27 October 1995.

*   *   *

Simon Armitage was nudged into prominence with the publication in 1989 of his first full length volume, *Zoom,* a vibrant collection richly rooted in the northern vernacular and infused with engaging humor. Bringing to mind Philip Larkin's late-career use of vernacular, slang locutions, and telling obscenities, Armitage often turns the commonplace or, especially, the vulgar phrase to epigrammatic effect. In the most successful of such poems he accomplishes a deadpan equivocation, achieved as much from the semantic possibilities of the vulgar phrase itself as from the disjunction between the apparent flippancy of the phrase and the typically serious subject upon which it bears. For instance, "The Peruvian Anchovy Industry," which sympathetically follows the consequences of empty fishing boats, ends with "Hard times for the hake and pilchard, / next on the U.S. shopping list. / Hard times for the Peruvian guano diggers, / no fish: no birds: no shit." The speaker of "Bus Talk," who foresees the bottom of his garden "slumped in the river," complains about official indifference to the subsidence of his house, in particular about the insurance company's refusal to recognize the problem: "No, if that house hasn't dropped a good two inches / this last eighteen months, my cock's a kipper."

Zoom includes occasional lyrics crafted in the line and tone of Robert Creeley, most notably the precisely wrought "Girl." The prevalent affiliation, however, is to an impressive variety of subjects and narrative modes that are often made striking by virtue of something unlikely being put to poetic ends, for instance, the autobiography of a coin ("Ten Pence Story"). Another example, in "Poem by the Boy outside the Fire Station," is the elliptical confession of a young pyromaniac: "Anyway, I'm mad. I know this as a fact / because him in the Post Office said I was / . . . Him at the Post Office knows I'm up to something. / Well, I stink of petrol, and he's seen my matches / and he knows damn well I don't smoke. / But he's frightened to death of saying anything."

Many poems in Armitage's second full collection, *Kid,* inherit the narrative and comic successes of *Zoom,* darkly extending the sometimes black humor of the earlier work's interest in foible. One poem, for instance, captures a distracted student recalling during an examination how one of the girls too good to go out with his kind accidentally abandoned the pillion of her companion's motorcycle ("As he pulled off down the street / she stood there like a wishbone, / high and dry, her legs wide open"), and "Gooseberry Season" tells a macabre tale of how a family gets rid of an out-of-work guest. But *Kid* also begins to address the limits of the earlier volume's more consistently grounded treatment of variety, restlessly searching for a new compound of identities in its reflective and ambitious manipulation of form and theme. Increasingly cautious about words, the issue in "Speaking Terms," these poems often turn to literary issues (using Weldon Kees as a springboard for several "Robinson" poems, a project Armitage furthered on BBC Television) and to occasional metapoetic or political concerns ("The Metaphor Now Standing at Platform 8," "The Guilty," or "Lines Thought to Have Been Written on the Eve of the Execution of a Warrant for His Arrest"). The latter poems suffer from the loss of the energy and directness so close to the heart of most Armitage poems. It seems fair to say that *Kid* is less securely rooted in a sense of place and is more vagrant in its desires.

Armitage's third collection, *Book of Matches,* takes hold of uncertainty, sandwiching a group of poems that identify themselves as descendants of the earlier two volumes between two extended sequences of wry meditation, an opening autobiographical series of mostly childhood reminiscences under the subtitle "Book of Matches" and a closing sequence, "Reading the Banns," patterned around reflections on the poet's wedding ceremonies. Still light in touch, these poems are incrementally enriched by the atmosphere of their evocation and no longer depend on the episodic for the effects they achieve. Paying tribute along the way to a mother ("any distance greater than a single span / requires a second pair of hands") and a father who "thought it bloody queer, / the day I rolled home with a ring of silver in my ear," the opening sequence perspicuously considers aging and its corollaries, fossilization and change: "I'm fossilizing— / every time I rest / I let the gristle knit, weave, mesh":

My dear, my skeleton will set like biscuit overnight,
like glass, like ice, and you can choose
to snap me back to life before first light,
or let me laze until
the shape I take becomes the shape I keep.

Don't leave me be. Don't let me sleep.

Not only the last, most delicate poems of the wedding sequence in *Book of Matches* attest to the fact that this poet has indeed not slept. Beginning with the first of his collections, Armitage has shown a protean vibrancy.

—Brian Macaskill

ASH, John

Nationality: British. **Born:** Manchester, 29 June 1948. **Education:** University of Birmingham, B.A. in English. **Career:** Primary school teacher, 1969–71; research assistant, 1971–75; freelance writer and part-time lecturer, 1975–78; community artist in Manchester, 1978–79; creative writing instructor at primary schools and adult education centers in Manchester, Cheshire, Bedfordshire, and Norwich, England, 1979–85. Full-time writer, 1985—. Visiting writer, University of Iowa Writer's Program, fall 1988. **Awards:** Northwest Arts Association bursary, 1983; Ingram Merrill Foundation grant, 1985; Whiting Foundation award, 1986. **Agent:** Keith Goldsmith, Carcanet Press Ltd., 198 Sixth Avenue, New York, New York 10013. **Address:** c/o Carcanet Press Ltd., 4th Floor, Conavon Court, 12–16 Blackfriars Street, Manchester M3 5BQ, England.

PUBLICATIONS

Poetry

Casino. London, Oasis, 1978.
The Bed and Other Poems. London, Oasis, 1981.
The Goodbyes. Manchester, Carcanet, 1982.
The Branching Stairs. Manchester, Carcanet, 1984.
Disbelief. Manchester, Carcanet, 1987.
The Burnt Pages. Manchester, Carcanet, 1991.
Selected Poems. Manchester, Carcanet, 1996.

Other

The Golden Hoardes: International Tourism and the Pleasure Periphery, with Louis Turner. London, Constable, 1975; New York, St. Martin's Press, 1977.
A Byzantine Journey. New York, Random House, and London, Tauris, 1995.

*

Critical Studies: "Poetry after Penguin" by Michael Hulse, in *Antigonish Review* (Antigonish, Nova Scotia), 60, winter 1985; interview with Andrew McAllister, in *Bete Noire* (Hull, Humberside, England), 8–9, autumn 1989-spring 1990.

*   *   *

With the publication of *The Branching Stairs* in 1984, John Ash firmly established himself as Britain's foremost younger innovative poet, an impressive achievement considering that his first published work had appeared only six years earlier. That first work, a pamphlet titled *Casino,* which Ash called "a kind of homage to Symbolism and the Decadence," uses a somewhat bizarre setting on the Riviera in winter for a series of imaginary portraits based on real figures—Laforgue, Baudelaire, Robert de Montesquieu, and others. The poems are unified by themes of decadence and dissipation.

In his second book, *The Bed and Other Poems,* and in the second part of *The Branching Stairs* Ash's talent frees itself from a restricted theme to lay claim to an original poetic. His poetry calls for more than its share of negative capability on the part of the reader, but the rewards in pure pleasure are munificent. He has a large imagination and uses it to full and varied effect. His is primarily a poetry of ambience and association in which the images, expressed most often in prose speech rhythms, flow thick and fast. The poems' constructs are frequently based on music, film, painting, or architecture. His English-language influences are undoubtedly American and include Wallace Stevens in his use of the exotic and William Carlos Williams in his use of the glancing yet indelible image. The poems' nostalgic tone, the "urban pastoral," and the use of dialogue and such devices as rhetorical questions, image clusters, and the extended, associative meditation can be seen in the work of Frank O'Hara and John Ashbery. Certainly, too, Auden has been a crucial writer for Ash, particularly in elegance, versatility, wit, and the sense of the social anomalies and absurdities of modern life.

Ash is one of Britain's very few "natural" poets. Whatever the work that may have gone into it, each poem appears as an immediate, autonomous, effortless construct that succeeds by constantly developing imagistic materials—"variations with the 'theme' well concealed," in Ash's phrase—to build up a sense of place, persona, style, and event. This is the technique of surrealism, and many poems are surreal, while possessing "a 'sense of reality' that deepens / when realism is abandoned." The method leads to a characteristic unwillingness to ascribe too literal a motive for actions or responses and instead emphasizes appearance, uncertainty, and multiple approaches to the same event. "It has been said," Ash once pointed out in an interview, "that poetry is not for offering solutions but for properly articulating the questions." In "Snow: A Romance," a prose poem in which the persona journeys to the South with a muse-like figure, Ash writes, "He sees resemblances everywhere. It is his trade, his survival technique." Much of the poetry is concerned with a style and way of

life that represents the Midlands English yearning for the warmth and exoticism of the South, that is, the Mediterranean. At the same time Ash, like Auden, expresses a sense of foreboding, an undefined loss, and a threat by the new, the barbarian or those in authority. He is exceedingly conscious of the ruin of civilizations associated with the region. This awareness of decay extends of course to language: "O memoirs, documentaries, mountainous journal! / the text is always and in all places / irretrievably corrupted. Did you think / you could just pick up the language and use it . . . ."

Such an approach to poetry demands a lot from readers. They have to use their own imaginations to fill the gaps, as it were, and sometimes the use of multiple personae, dislocated imagery, and surreal and dream images strains attention and leads to impatience. In this respect, *The Goodbyes* is more demanding than *The Branching Stairs,* for the former seems less assured, more frenetic.

Unlike most contemporary British poets, Ash is cosmopolitan and internationalist in outlook. The culture is primarily European and the methods American-postmodernist. Though he can look backward both to childhood memories and in time to a late nineteenth-century process of dissolution and subsequent rebuilding, the idea of deconstruction is ever present, often expressed in paradoxical images and deliberately archaic words: "As tourists climb, in funiculars, to the apex of the arch, a deck of luxury apartments vanishes far off and silently, in an explosion like a burst of talc." The image is forever "there," in the subconscious, as a city (Beirut?) is deconstructed before our TV tourists' eyes.

Ash's collection *Disbelief* reflects not only his move to America—the structures present are mostly those of New York, where he took up residence—but an increased sureness of hand, an impressive poetic maturity. The work seems freer and simpler in execution, though no less scrupulously assembled. He is more willing to follow up the imaginative implications of moment and place without resorting to exotica and surreal efflorescence. The number of truly successful poems and prose pieces is remarkable—poems such as "A Long Encounter," "October in the Capital," "Rooflines and Riverbells," and "To Illustrate the Day" and the prose pieces "Funeral Preparations in the Provinces" and "Every Story Tells It All." The latter is a beautiful coda—and at the same time an overture—to the work in *Disbelief;* it is a personal essay about how the writer leads his life and about the process of writing and the imagination. Ash's love of the exotic and evocative is located more in the temporal present than in the literary past, as indicated by the list in this essay of the names of East Coast trains—Storm King, Maple Leaf, Sleepy Hollow, or Niagara Rainbow—and by the catalogue poem "The Sky My Husband."

The writing in *Disbelief* is punctuated by the epigrammatic, a quality also of Ash's earlier work but here less calculated to outrage or strive for effect: "We value music because of its ability to *say something and not say it* . . ." ("Every Story Tells It All"), which of course can apply to certain kinds of poetry, namely Ash's. In his poetry,

A word is spoken, an ordinary word,
and it becomes an entire landscape,—
an open and illustrated city.

Ash's approach in his previous books is broadened in the meditative strengths, supple poetics, range, and depth of *The Burnt Pages.* Here the sense of the past and nostalgia for the exotic are transformed via the existential moment into a more philosophical awareness of the place in our lives for the transitory and everyday, as well as the enduring:

> I know I mix the present with the past
> but that's how I like it:
> there is no other way to go on.

While *The Burnt Pages* looks back at the beauty but also the decay and corruption of past civilizations—a kind of Ozymandias point of view in which the predominant idea is of the entropic nature of all things, including human works and relationships—it also looks forward to the immutable and indestructible imagination. The title poem is a brilliant expression of the paradoxical nature of knowledge as it is embodied in art. Bearing in mind the title, one would assume that it is an antipoem of the ''there-are-things-that-are-important-beyond-all-this-fiddle'' variety:

> History reduced to dioramas,
> Technique without utility.

But of course the poem itself is an artifact that may survive its maker and that literary archaeologists will brush off and pore over:

> Now all things must be moving on
> Past the moment of the poem
> Which remains like an empty cast
> For the limbs of a bronze hero—
> An episode in the long history
> Of backward glances.

The Burnt Pages represents a hard-won confidence in the ''purity'' of the individual creative imagination in the face of corruption, decay, and the obliteration of the past.

Ash's by now familiar poetics—his adoption of multiple personae, the seemingly objective accounts of ancient and contemporary real and imaginary civilizations, nostalgia for the past as seen through its great works of art, architecture, and music, and the witty and mordant view of Western suburbanism—are all present in *The Burnt Pages* but are given new power and depth in these marvelously allusive poems. One may still hear echoes of O'Hara, Ashbery, and Auden, but Ash has made his voice his own. His is one of the few successful examples of a North Atlantic poetry—the candid insouciance of the New York school of poets (''Another bunch of fallen gods returning from the 8th Avenue gym,'' begins one of the best poems of the book, ''Twentieth Century'') combined with the preoccupation with the past and ironic view of the European. With his *Selected Poems*, one now has available the best work of a poet at the height of his powers.

—Robert Vas Dias

ASHBERY, John (Lawrence)

Also known as Jonas Berry. **Nationality:** American. **Born:** Rochester, New York, 28 July 1927. **Education:** Deerfield Academy, Massachusetts; graduated 1945; Harvard University, Cambridge, Massachusetts (member of the editorial board, Harvard Advocate), A.B. in English 1949; Columbia University, New York, M.A. in English 1951; New York University, 1957–58. **Career:** Copywriter, Oxford University Press, New York, 1951–54, and McGraw-Hill Book Company, New York, 1954–55; co-editor, *One Fourteen,* New York, 1952–53; art critic, European edition of New York *Herald Tribune,* Paris, 1960–65, and *Art International,* Lugano, Switzerland, 1961–64; editor, *Locus Solus* magazine, Lans-en-Vercors, France, 1960–62; editor, *Art and Literature,* Paris, 1963–66; Paris correspondent, 1964–65, and executive editor, 1965–72, *Art News,* New York; professor of English, 1974–80, and distinguished professor of English, 1980–90, Brooklyn College. Since 1991 professor of English, Bard College, Annandale-on-Hudson, New York. Poetry editor, *Partisan Review,* New Brunswick, New Jersey, 1976–80; art critic, *New York* magazine, 1978–80; art critic, *Newsweek,* New York, 1980–85. **Awards:** Fulbright fellowship, 1955, 1956; Poets foundation grant, 1960, 1964; Ingram Merrill Foundation grant, 1962, 1972; Harriet Monroe memorial prize, 1963, 1974; Guggenheim fellowship, 1967, 1973; National Endowment for the Arts grant, 1968, 1969; American Academy award, 1969; Shelley memorial award, 1973; Frank O'Hara prize, 1974; National Book Critics Circle award, 1976; Pulitzer prize, 1976; National Book award, 1976; Rockefeller grant, for playwriting, 1979–80; English Speaking Union prize, 1979; Bard College Charles Flint Kellogg award, 1983; Academy of American Poets fellowship, 1983; Mayor's award (New York), 1983; Bollingen prize, 1984, 1985; Lenore Marshall-*Nation* award, 1985; Wallace Stevens fellowship, 1985; MacArthur Foundation fellowship, 1985; MLA Common Wealth award in literature, 1986; Creative Arts award, Brandeis University, 1989; Ruth Lilly Poetry prize, *Poetry* magazine, 1992; Robert Frost medal, Poetry Society of America, 1995; Grand prize, Biennales Internationales de Poesie, Belgium, 1996; Gold medal, American Academy and Institute of Arts and Letters, 1997. D. Litt.: Long Island University, Southampton, New York, 1979. **Member:** American Academy, 1980; American Academy of Arts and Sciences, 1983. **Agent:** Georges Borchardt Inc., 136 East 57th Street, New York, New York 10022, U.S.A.

PUBLICATIONS

Poetry

Turandot and Other Poems. New York, Tibor de Nagy, 1953.
Some Trees. New Haven, Connecticut, Yale University Press, and London, Oxford University Press, 1956.
The Poems. New York, Tiber Press, 1960.
The Tennis Court Oath. Middletown, Connecticut, Wesleyan University Press, 1962.
Rivers and Mountains. New York, Holt Rinehart, 1966.
Selected Poems. London, Cape, 1967.
Three Madrigals. New York, Poet's Press, 1968.
Sunrise in Suburbia. New York, Phoenix Book Shop, 1968.
Fragment. Los Angeles, Black Sparrow Press, 1969.
Evening in the Country. San Francisco, Spanish Main Press, 1970.
The Double Dream of Spring. New York, Dutton, 1970.
The New Spirit. New York, Adventures in Poetry, 1970.
Penguin Modern Poets 19, with Lee Harwood and Tom Raworth. London, Penguin, 1971.
Three Poems. New York, Viking Press, 1972; London, Penguin, 1977.

The Vermont Notebook. Los Angeles, Black Sparrow Press, 1975.
The Serious Doll. Privately printed, 1975.
Self-Portrait in a Convex Mirror. New York, Viking Press, 1975.
Houseboat Days. New York, Viking Press, 1977.
As We Know. New York, Viking Press, 1979; Manchester, Carcanet, 1981.
Shadow Train. New York, Viking Press, 1981; Manchester, Carcanet, 1982.
A Wave. New York, Viking Press, and Manchester, Carcanet, 1984.
Selected Poems. New York, Viking, 1985; Manchester, Carcanet, 1986; revised edition, London, Paladin, 1987.
The Ice Storm. New York, Hanuman, 1987.
April Galleons. New York, Viking, 1987; Manchester, Carcanet, 1988.
Three Poems. New York, Ecco Press, 1989.
Flow Chart. New York, Knopf, and Manchester, Carcanet, 1991.
Hotel Lautreamont. New York, Knopf, and Manchester, Carcanet, 1992.
And the Stars Were Shining. New York, Farrar Straus, and Manchester, Carcanet, 1994.
Can You Hear, Bird: Poems. New York, Farrar Straus, 1995.
The Mooring of Starting Out: The First Five Books of Poetry. Hopewell, New Jersey, Ecco Press, 1997.
Wakefulness: Poems. New York, Farrar Straus, 1998.
Girls on the Run: A Poem. New York, Farrar Straus, 1999.

Recording: *The Songs We Know Best,* Watershed, 1989; *Music, Text,* Capstone Records, 1999.

Plays

The Heroes (produced New York, 1952; London, 1982). Included in *Three Plays,* 1978.
The Compromise (produced Cambridge, Massachusetts, 1956). Included in Three Plays, 1978.
The Philosopher (produced London, 1982). Included in *Three Plays,* 1978.
Three Plays (includes *The Heroes, The Compromise, The Philosopher*). Calais, Vermont, Z Press, 1978; Manchester, Carcanet, 1988.

Novel

A Nest of Ninnies, with James Schuyler. New York, Dutton, 1969; Manchester, Carcanet, 1987.

Other

John Ashbery and Kenneth Koch (A Conversation). Tucson, Interview Press, 1966.
R.B. Kitaj: Paintings, Drawings, Pastels, with others. Washington, D.C., Smithsonian Institution, 1981; London, Thames and Hudson, 1983.
Fairfield Porter: Realist Painter in an Age of Abstraction. Boston, New York Graphic Society, 1983.
Rodrigo Moynihan: Paintings and Works on Paper, with Richard Shone. London, Thames and Hudson, 1988.

Reported Sightings: Art Chronicles 1957–1987, edited by David Bergman. New York, Knopf, 1989; Manchester, Carcanet, 1990.
Haibun. Colombes, France, Collectif Generation, 1990.

Editor, *Penguin Modern Poets 24.* London, Penguin, 1973.
Editor, *Muck Arbour,* by Bruce Marcus. Chicago, O'Hara, 1975.
Editor, *The Funny Place,* by Richard F. Snow. Chicago, O'Hara, 1975.
Editor, *The Best American Poetry 1988.* New York, Macmillan, 1988.
Editor, *Pistils,* by Robert Mapplethorpe. London, Cape, and New York, Random House, 1996.

Translator (as Jonas Berry), with Lawrence G. Blochman, *Murder in Montmartre,* by Noël Vexin. New York, Dell, 1960.
Translator, *Melville,* by Jean-Jacques Mayoux. New York, Grove Press, 1960.
Translator (as Jonas Berry), with Lawrence G. Blochman, *The Deadlier Sex,* by Geneviève Manceron. New York, Dell, 1961.
Translator, *Alberto Giacometti,* by Jacques Dupin. Paris, Maeght, 1963(?).
Translator, *Fantomes,* by Marcel Allain and Pierre Souvestre. New York, Morrow, 1986.

*

Bibliography: *John Ashbery: A Comprehensive Bibliography* by David K. Kermani, New York, Garland, 1976.

Critical Studies: *John Ashbery: An Introduction to the Poetry* by David Shapiro, New York, Columbia University Press, 1979; *Beyond Amazement: New Essays on John Ashbery* edited by David Lehman, Ithaca, New York, Cornell University Press, 1980; *The Tribe of John Ashbery and Contemporary Poetry* edited by Susan M. Schultz, Tuscaloosa, Alabama, University of Alabama Press, 1995; *Politics and Form in Postmodern Poetry: O'Hara, Bishop, Ashbery, and Merrill* by Mutlu Konuk Blasing, Cambridge and New York, Cambridge University Press, 1995; *Political Poetics: Revisionist Form in Adrienne Rich, John Ashbery, Charles Wright, and Jorie Graham* (dissertation) by Phyllis Jean Franzek, University of Southern California, Los Angeles, 1995; "Echoes and Moving Fields: Structure and Subjectivity in the Poetry of W.S. Merwin and John Ashbery" by Luke Spencer and Edward Haworth Hoeppner, in *American Literature,* 68(1), 1996; *Dynamics of Being, Space, and Time in the Poetry of Czeslaw Milosz and John Ashbery* by Barbara Malinowska, New York, P. Lang, 1997.

*   *   *

John Ashbery is increasingly taken to be the outstanding American poet of his generation, indeed, perhaps the outstanding poet writing in English today. With the publication of *Flow Chart* in 1991 (and there have been further collections since), Ashbery has been recognized, on the one hand, as a worthy successor to the romantics (see Helen Vendler and Harold Bloom on this connection) and, on the other, as a kind of protolanguage poet. If the more experimental younger poets have preferred the Ashbery of *The Tennis-Court Oath* and *Flow Chart,* while establishment critics opt for the Ashbery of *Self-Portrait in a Convex Mirror,* there is nevertheless a strong consensus on Ashbery's ability to produce memorable representations, however elliptical, enigmatic, and campy their "shifting sands" may be, of what it has meant to be alive in the late twentieth century.

Ashbery's is a style born of the conviction that the world in which we now operate is so strange, so absurd, so heavily sedimented with mediaspeak and characterized by what Umberto Eco calls the "hyperreal," that the poet can hardly present consistent or coherent accounts of subjectivity and individual experience. The romantic lyric of gradual self-revelation, moving toward epiphany and judgment, seems, so Ashbery implies, no longer able to negotiate the slippery slopes of "the familiar interior which has always been there" and that is nevertheless "unknowable." Hence, his version of Wordsworth's *The Prelude* is *Flow Chart,* the title referring to those schematic diagrams used to show the progress of materials through the various stages of a manufacturing process. *Flow Chart* begins with the lines

Still in the published city but not yet
overtaken by a new form of despair . . .

and charts the course whereby the "I" fends off these new forms of despair, sometimes successfully, often not, all the while navigating the shoals of friendship and sexual love, even as he taps "the bloodstream / of our collective memory: here a chicken coop, there a smokestack, / farther on an underground laboratory."

From the first Ashbery's poetry has presented the reader with what he has called, with reference to Gertrude Stein, "an open field of narrative possibilities." Again and again in Ashbery's poems an unspecified "I" (who may just as well be designated as "you") begins an account of something that has happened, only to have his story interrupted by seemingly irrelevant and disparate detail. Or again, as in the fifty-page "Litany," there are two columns of verse (the prayer-and-response form of the genre), and although each column is to be read independently as one moves from page to page, it is often possible to move from left to right (or right to left), creating alternate plots or thought processes, each equally tantalizing and equally possible.

Such indeterminacy has no real precedent in Anglo-American poetry. Wallace Stevens is regularly cited as Ashbery's central precursor, and the early poetry does have the phrasing and accent of the late Stevens, but the two poets have very different sensibilities. A closer model is the Auden of the "Bucolics" and "In Praise of Limestone" ("Rivers and Mountains," for example, echoes Auden's "Mountains"), but Ashbery's landscape is like a comic strip version of Auden's. Indeed, the early modernist closest to Ashbery may well be Eliot, the Eliot of "Prufrock" and *The Waste Land,* those perspectivist poems whose self dissolves into an urban landscape in which pop songs and the classics, pub slang and elevated diction send the reader contradictory and confusing signals. The ominous narrative of "They Dream Only of America," for example, can be read as a postmodern version of Eliot's "Sweeney among the Nightingales." But Eliot's hunger for knowledge is defused in Ashbery's pastiche and parody poems, poems that make no claim to know what a transcendental truth is, much less how the human consciousness can attain the true and the good.

In his introduction to the *Collected Poems* of Frank O'Hara, Ashbery describes the New York climate of the early 1960s, in which O'Hara came of age, as "Picasso and French poetry, de Kooning and Guston, Cage and Feldman . . ." This was also Ashbery's own artistic climate; Cage, for instance, is surely a source for the two-column strategy of "Litany." Having lived in Paris for a decade, Ashbery cast a cold eye on the neosymbolism of his American contemporaries, their mania for what he called "over-interpretation" or "objective correlativitis." In an essay written in French for the special Reverdy issue of *Mercure de France* (1962), he argued that, whereas Eliot and his followers insisted on endowing each word or phrase with symbolic significance, Reverdy's images existed in their own right as "living phenomena," their main characteristic being "transparency."

What we find in Ashbery's enigmatic texts is language on the point of revealing its secret without ever actually doing so. Symbolist poetry, we know, is difficult, but it is not impossible to decode; behind the intricate collage of, say, *The Waste Land,* there is, after all, a coherent core of relational images. In Ashbery's poetry, however, the connections are as likely to be phonemic or graphemic as referential. Thus, we read in the prose text rather perversely called *Three Poems,*

There are some old photographs which show the event. It makes sense to stand there, passing. The people who are there— few, against this side of the air. They made a sign, were making a sign. Turning on yourself as a leaf, you miss the third and last chance. They don't suffer the way people do. True. But it's your last chance, this time, the last chance to escape the ball of contradictions, that is heavier than gravity bringing all down to the level. And nothing to be undone.

The passage begins as a kind of *ekphrasis,* drawing out the meaning of a particular set of photographs. But we are never told what "the event" in question is or where the "there" where it "makes sense to stand" is. By the third sentence the prominence of rhyme ("there"/ "air") all but distracts us from the reality that it is impossible for people to exist "this side of the air." And further, the story now takes on a fairy-tale cast as the poet refers to the "people" making a "sign" and tells the unspecified "you" (himself? a friend?) that he is "miss[ing]" the third and last chance." "They don't suffer the way people do. True" sounds like a popular song, and the rhyme-refrain makes it hard to take the "suffer[ing]" too seriously. In the next sentence we shift back to the language of "last chance[s]," the "ball" to be escaped turning out to be, after the interruption of white space, the cliché "ball of contradictions," even as the familiar words "nothing to be done" become, with the addition of two little phonemes, the parodic "nothing to be undone."

Such rapid-fire tonal, syntactic, and semantic shifts are by no means without "meaning." On the contrary, the passage is concerned with the way we "read" photographs, using them to justify or to explain away particular events, reading into them portentous signs, third and last chances, and so on. Foolish as our constructions of reality are, Ashbery suggests, we continue to indulge in them, to take ourselves too seriously for our own good. As the poet puts it in "October at the Window" (from *April Galleons*),

"My eyes are bigger than my stomach."
And so life goes on happening

As in a frontier novel. One must always
Be quite conscious of the edges of things
And then how they meet will cease
To be an issue, all other things
Being equal, as in fact they are.

The consciousness of the "edges of things," even in the face of "all other things / Being equal," has produced a remarkable body of poetry, in which dream and reality, Walt Disney World T-shirts and Arthur Rackham fairy tales, medieval romance and Elizabethan pageants, Verdi opera and James Dean films coalesce to form Ashbery's distinctive poetic universe. "Pyrography" (the title of one of his finest poems, appearing in the 1977 volume *Houseboat Days*), which is "the process of burning designs on wood and leather with a heated tool," becomes the process of imprinting burning traces of memory and vision on a consciousness so fluid and amorphous that the "heated tool" is likely to slip on its surface. The scene of this particular poem is Cottage Grove (Chicago), the heart of the nation ("This is America calling"), but curiously it is also a fairy-tale world in which "the carriages / Are drawn forward under a sky of fumed oak."

In the second stanza the "we" who are also "they" set out on a journey across the great American continent, first by boxcar through the "gyrating fans of suburbs" and "the darkness of cities," and then the scene suddenly dissolves as the travelers are moving up the Pacific coast to Bolinas, where "the houses doze and seem to wonder why." As the journey continues, one proceeds, not westward or north to Canada, but into an imaginary world. A city has evidently been erected, "built ... Partly over with fake ruins in the image of ourselves: / An arch that terminates in mid-keystone, a crumbling stone pier / For laundresses, an open-air theater, never completed / And only partially designed." Where are we? As with Rimbaud's "Villes" or Ashbery's own "lacustrine cities," these places cannot be specified even as they seem strangely familiar; they emerge as part of a theater decor upon which the curtain may fall any minute. So the poet asks,

How are we to inhabit
This space from which the fourth wall is invariably
    missing,
As in a stage-set or dollhouse, except by staying as we are,
In lost profile, facing the stars ...

This question has haunted Ashbery from the beginning. He has known all along that, as he puts it in the 1956 "Two Scenes," "Everything has a schedule, if you can find out what it is," the difficulty being that one cannot find out. Just so, the question posed in "Pyrography" is rhetorical, for the poet knows that the only way to inhabit a "space from which the fourth wall is invariably missing" is to accept it as the "stage-set or dollhouse" it really is.

In the twenty-five years since "Pyrography" Ashbery's poetry has not so much changed dramatically as it has revealed its scaffolding, has shown us, more limpidly than in the past, how much of the past—poetic, artistic, operatic—goes into the making of the present. A sense of impending death has become increasingly present, although Ashbery treats the theme with his usual indirection, as in "Many Colors" from *Wakefulness,* which begins,

There's a chastening in it,
A hymnlike hemline.
Hyperbole in another disguise.

Dainty foresters walk through it.

And in another poem from this volume the poet thinks ruefully that "once upon a time everybody was here. Then the pellets started to go." Increasingly, the Proustian search for lost time has become Ashbery's subject; the emphasis is now on those moments when "easing through the night we felt scoops / of clay like tired ice cream." Dazzling as were Ashbery's early experiments, the later poetry has a poignancy and depth just short of heartbreak. But the poet always pulls back with a wry smile as he contemplates "the cartoon era of my early life," whose imprint "gasps like a fish on a line." No use, in other words, making a big fuss about it all, for "there is no way to transcribe it." It is this undefined "it," poised on the edge of transcription, that continues to haunt us.

—Marjorie Perloff

ATWOOD, Margaret (Eleanor)

Nationality: Canadian. **Born:** Ottawa, Ontario, 18 November 1939. **Education:** Victoria College, University of Toronto, 1957–61, B.A. 1961; Radcliffe College, Cambridge, Massachusetts, A.M. 1962; Harvard University, Cambridge, Massachusetts 1962–63, 1965–67. **Family:** Divorced; one daughter. **Career:** Lecturer in English, University of British Columbia, Vancouver, 1964–65; instructor in English, Sir George Williams University, Montreal, 1967–68; teacher of creative writing, University of Alberta, Edmonton, 1969–70; assistant professor of English, York University, Toronto, 1971–72. Writer-in-residence, University of Toronto, 1972–73, University of Alabama, Tuscaloosa, 1985, Macquarie University, North Ryde, New South Wales, 1987, and Trinity University, San Antonio, Texas, 1989; Berg Visiting Professor of English, New York University, 1986. Editor and member of the board of directors, House of Anansi Press, Toronto, 1971–73. **Awards:** E.J. Pratt Medal, 1961; President's Medal, University of Western Ontario, 1965; Governor-General's award, 1966, 1986; Centennial Commission prize, 1967; Union League Civic and Arts Foundation prize, 1969, and Bess Hokin prize, 1974 (*Poetry,* Chicago); City of Toronto award, 1976; St. Lawrence award, 1978; Radcliffe Medal, 1980; Molson award, 1981; Guggenheim fellowship, 1981; Welsh Arts Council International Writers prize, 1982; Ida Nudel Humanitarian award, 1986; *Los Angeles Times* Book award, 1986; Arthur C. Clarke Science-Fiction award, for novel, 1987; Commonwealth Writer's prize (regional), 1987, 1994, 1995; Humanist of the Year award, 1987; City of Toronto Book award, 1989; Canadian Bookseller's Association Author of the Year award, 1988; Centennial Medal, Harvard University, 1990; Trillium award, 1992, 1994; Canadian Authors Association Novel of the Year award, 1993; Chevalier dans l'Ordre des Arts et des Lettres, 1994; Norwegian Order of Literary Merit, 1996; the Giller prize, 1996, and Premio Mondello, 1997, for *Alias Grace*; Canadian Booksellers Association author of the year, 1996; National Arts Club medal of honor for literature, 1997. D.Litt.: Trent University, Peterborough, Ontario, 1973; Concordia University, Montreal, 1980; Smith College, Northampton, Massachusetts, 1982; University of Toronto, 1983;

Mount Holyoke College, South Hadley, Massachusetts, 1985; University of Waterloo, Ontario, 1985; University of Guelph, Ontario, 1985; Victoria College, 1987. L.L.D.: Queen's University, Kingston, Ontario, 1974; University of Leeds, Ontario, 1994. Companion, Order of Canada, 1981. Fellow, Royal Society of Canada, 1987. **Member:** American Academy of Arts and Sciences (honorary member), 1988. **Agent:** Phoebe Larmore, 228 Main Street, Venice, California 90291, U.S.A. **Address:** c/o McClelland & Stewart, 481 University Avenue, #900, Toronto, Ontario M5G 2E9, Canada.

PUBLICATIONS

Poetry

Double Persephone. Toronto, Hawkshead Press, 1961.
The Circle Game (single poem). Bloomfield Hills, Michigan, Cranbrook Academy of Art, 1964.
Talismans for Children. Bloomfield Hills, Michigan, Cranbrook Academy of Art, 1965.
Kaleidoscopes: Baroque. Bloomfield Hills, Michigan, Cranbrook Academy of Art, 1965.
Speeches for Doctor Frankenstein. Bloomfield Hills, Michigan, Cranbrook Academy of Art, 1966.
The Circle Game (collection). Toronto, Contact Press, 1966.
Expeditions. Bloomfield Hills, Michigan, Cranbrook Academy of Art, 1966.
The Animals in That County. Toronto, Oxford University Press, 1968; Boston, Little Brown, 1969.
Five Modern Canadian Poets, with others, edited by Eli Mandel. Toronto, Holt Rinehart, 1970.
The Journals of Susanna Moodie. Toronto, Oxford University Press, 1970.
Oratorio for Sasquatch, Man and Two Androids: Poems for Voices. Toronto, Canadian Broadcasting Corporation, 1970.
Procedures for Underground. Toronto, Oxford University Press, and Boston, Little Brown, 1970.
Power Politics. Toronto, Anansi, 1971; New York, Harper, 1973.
You Are Happy. Toronto, Oxford University Press, and New York, Harper, 1974.
Selected Poems. Toronto, Oxford University Press, 1976; New York, Simon and Schuster, 1978.
Marsh, Hawk. Toronto, Dreadnaught, 1977.
Two-Headed Poems. Toronto, Oxford University Press, 1978; New York, Simon and Schuster, 1981.
True Stories. Toronto, Oxford University Press, 1981; New York, Simon and Schuster, and London, Cape, 1982.
Notes Towards a Poem That Can Never Be Written. Toronto, Salamander Press, 1981.
Snake Poems. Toronto, Salamander Press, 1983.
Interlunar. Toronto, Oxford University Press, 1984; London, Cape, 1988.
Selected Poems II: Poems Selected and New, 1976–1986. Toronto, Oxford University Press, 1986; Boston, Houghton Mifflin, 1987.
Morning in the Burned House. Toronto, McClelland and Stewart, and Borton, Houghton Mifflin, 1995.

Recordings: *The Poetry and Voice of Margaret Atwood,* Caedmon, 1977; *Margaret Atwood Reads from A Handmaid's Tale,* Caedmon.

Plays

Radio Play: *The Trumpets of Summer,* 1964.

Television Plays: *The Servant Girl,* 1974; *Snowbird,* 1981; *Heaven on Earth,* with Peter Pearson, 1986.

Novels

The Edible Woman. Toronto, McClelland and Stewart, and London, Deutsch, 1969; Boston, Little Brown, 1970.
Surfacing. Toronto, McClelland and Stewart, 1972; London, Deutsch, and New York, Simon and Schuster, 1973.
Lady Oracle. Toronto, McClelland and Stewart, New York, Simon and Schuster, and London, Deutsch, 1976.
Life before Man. Toronto, McClelland and Stewart, 1979; New York, Simon and Schuster, and London, Cape, 1980.
Bodily Harm. Toronto, McClelland and Stewart, New York, Simon and Schuster, and London, Cape, 1981.
The Handmaids's Tale. Toronto, McClelland and Stewart, Boston, Houghton Mifflin, and London, Cape, 1985.
Cat's Eye. Toronto, McClelland and Stewart, 1988; New York, Doubleday, and London, Bloomsbury, 1989.
The Robber Bride. Toronto, McClelland and Stewart, and New York, Doubleday, 1993.
Alias Grace. Toronto, McClelland and Stewart, London, Bloomsbury, and New York, Doubleday, 1996.

Short Stories

Dancing Girls and Other Stories. Toronto, McClelland and Stewart, and New York, Simon and Schuster, 1977; London, Cape, 1979.
Encounters with the Element Man. Concord, New Hampshire, Ewert, 1982.
Murder in the Dark: Short Fictions and Prose Poems. Toronto, Coach House Press, 1983; London, Cape, 1984.
Bluebeard's Egg and Other Stories. Toronto, McClelland and Stewart, 1983; Boston, Houghton Mifflin, 1985; London, Cape, 1987.
Unearthing Suite. Toronto, Grand Union Press, 1983.
Wilderness Tips. Toronto, McClelland and Stewart, 1991; New York, Doubleday, 1991.
Good Bones. Toronto, Coach House, 1992; New York, Doubleday, 1994.

Other

Survival: A Thematic Guide to Canadian Literature. Toronto, Anansi, 1972.
Days of the Rebels 1815–1840. Toronto, Natural Science of Canada, 1977.
Up in the Tree (for children). Toronto, McClelland and Stewart, 1978.
Anna's Pet (for children), with Joyce Barkhouse. Toronto, Lorimer, 1980.
Second Words: Selected Critical Prose. Toronto, Anansi, 1982; Boston, Beacon Press, 1984.
Margaret Atwood: Conversations, edited by E. Ingersoll. Princeton, New Jersey, Ontario Review Press, 1990.

Editor, *The New Oxford Book of Canadian Verse in English.* Toronto, New York, and Oxford, Oxford University Press, 1982.

Editor, with Robert Weaver, *The Oxford Book of Canadian Short Stories in English.* Toronto, Oxford, and New York, Oxford University Press, 1986.

Editor, *The Canlit Food Book.* Toronto, Totem, 1987.

Editor, with Shannon Ravenel, *The Best American Short Stories 1989.* Boston, Houghton Mifflin, 1989.

*

Bibliography: "Margaret Atwood: An Annotated Bibliography (Prose)" and "(Verse)" by Alan J. Horne, in *The Annotated Bibliography of Canada's Major Authors 1–2* edited by Robert Lecker and Jack David, Downsview, Ontario, ECW Press, 2 vols., 1979–80.

Manuscript Collection: Fisher Library, University of Toronto.

Critical Studies: *Margaret Atwood: A Symposium* edited by Linda Sandler, Victoria, British Columbia, University of Victoria, 1977; *A Violent Duality* by Sherrill Grace, Montreal, Véhicule Press, 1979, and *Margaret Atwood: Language, Text, and System* edited by Grace and Lorraine Weir, Vancouver, University of British Columbia Press, 1983; *The Art of Margaret Atwood: Essays in Criticism* edited by Arnold E. and Cathy N. Davidson, Toronto, Anansi, 1981; *Margaret Atwood* by Jerome H. Rosenberg, Boston, Twayne, 1984; *Margaret Atwood: A Feminist Poetics* by Frank Davey, Vancouver, Talonbooks, 1984; *Margaret Atwood* by Barbara Hill Rigney, London, Macmillan, 1987; *Critical Essays on Margaret Atwood* edited by Judith McCombs, Boston, Hall, 1988; *Margaret Atwood: Vision and Forms* edited by Kathryn van Spanckeren and Jan Garden Castro, Carbondale, Southern Illinois University Press, 1988; "You Are What You Eat: The Politics of Eating in the Novels of Margaret Atwood" by Emma Parker, in *Twentieth Century Literature,* 41(3), 1995; "Trace of a Woman: Narrative Voice and Decentered Power in the Fiction of Toni Morrison, Margaret Atwood, and Louise Erdrich" by Katherine A. Nelson-Born, in *Literature, Interpretation, Theory,* 7(1), 1996; "Margaret Atwood: Writing and Subjectivity" by Alice Palumbo and Colin Nicholson, in *Signs,* 21(3), 1996; "A Rhetoric of Indeterminacy: The Poetry of Margaret Atwood and Robert Bly" by R.A. Kizuk, in *English Studies in Canada,* 23(2), 1997; "Coming-of-Age with Atwood," in *Maclean's,* 111(36), 7 September 1998; "Histones and Historical Fictions—Margaret Atwood and the Edges of History" by Jonathan D. Spence, in *American Historical Review,* 103(5), 1998.

Margaret Atwood comments:

I feel that the task of criticizing my poetry is best left to others (i.e., critics) and would much rather have it take place after I am dead. If at all.

*   *   *

In "This Is a Photograph of Me," the opening poem of Margaret Atwood's *The Circle Game,* the speaker proffers the reader a grainy snapshot. After momentary confusion the photo resolves itself into a recognizable scene:

as you scan
it, you see in the left-hand corner

a thing that is like a branch: part of a tree
(balsam or spruce) emerging
and, to the right, halfway up
what ought to be a gentle
slope, a small frame house.

The picture is banal enough, a familiar evocation of middle-class security, a haven of domesticity nestled in a benevolent nature. Little in the photo, however, is what it initially seems. A sudden parenthesis informs us that the speaker lies drowned, Ophelia-like, in the lake:

I am in the lake, in the center
of the picture, just under the surface.

It is difficult to say where
precisely, or to say
how large or small I am:
the effect of water
on light is a distortion
but if you look long enough
eventually
you will be able to see me.

With a single twist the poem foregrounds our received, perhaps unconscious, habits of reading the world, insisting that a close effort of attention will reveal the idyllic image of home and hearth as a smothering trap for its female victim.

The poem, with its short, free verse lines, its precise, austere diction, and its glancing allusion to myth, is stylistically typical of Atwood's work. But in its insistence on critically examining the images that structure our understanding of the world, it also voices a theme present, in one way or another, in all of her poetry. Like other female poets who came of age in the 1960s, and like other Canadian writers who have long been aware of the political and cultural domination of their country by outside forces, Atwood is extraordinarily sensitive to the ways in which power relations between humanity and nature, between men and women, and between nations shape the modes of representation, the methods of reading and writing, through which we make sense of our lives. Her poetry insists on looking closely enough to identify the marginalized, the hidden, the other, that which has been suppressed or passed over by our inherited maps and legends. Such recognition compels a search for new modes of representation, new ways of writing, that aim to give voice to that which has been silenced. Atwood's poetry thus seeks to move from the old languages of dominance, mastery, and victimization to a new language of tolerance, understanding, and illumination.

This overarching project has played itself out in various registers during the course of Atwood's career. In her early poems, dating from the late 1960s, it often takes the form of a confrontation with the Canadian wilderness, a landscape at once bleak and alien, even hostile, and yet eliciting a strong feeling of identification in the poet. The challenge, broached in many of Atwood's early poems, is to map one's surroundings, find one's place in the world, without denying the otherness and sovereignty of nature, without imposing a false, anthropomorphic pattern on a nonhuman wilderness. It is a difficult project at best, and the characteristically bleak tone of the early poems often proceeds from the failure of Atwood's protagonists to avoid a disastrous ecological imperialism:

He dug the soil in rows,
imposed himself with shovels
He asserted
into the furrows, I
am not random.

The ground
replied with aphorisms:

a tree-sprout
weed, words
he couldn't understand.

The hapless settler described in these lines from "Progressive Insanities of a Pioneer" fails to come to terms with the "ordered absence" that is nature and finds himself overwhelmed by "the green vision, / the unnamed / whale" of the wilderness.

In poems published in the early 1970s Atwood shifted her focus to relations between men and women, relations that, as the title of her book-length cycle *Power Politics* implies, she perceives as equally fraught with the potential for domination and exploitation. The cycle acidly chronicles a stultifying love affair to reveal the pain that lies just behind the traditional tropes of romantic love: "you fit into me / like a hook into an eye / / a fish hook / an open eye." But Atwood is less concerned with documenting male aggression than with delineating the oscillating cycle of victimization practiced by both partners in a relationship dominated by competition, selfishness, and fear and with finding, if possible, some space beyond the old oppressive structures of gender relations in which love might separate itself from power. Such a utopian space seems unimaginable in the world depicted by *Power Politics,* with its couple dissolved, exhausted by each other. But a happier alternative is at least glimpsed in Atwood's next collection, *You Are Happy,* whose final poem rewrites the archetypal image of the sacrificial victim as a vulnerable but trusting lover, unafraid of honest emotional exchange:

On the floor your body curves
like that: the ancient pose, neck slackened, arms
thrown above the head, vital
throat and belly lying
undefended. light slides over you,
this is not an altar, they are not
acting or watching

You are intact, you turn
towards me, your eyes opening, the eyes
intricate and easily bruised, you open

yourself to me gently, what
they tried, we
tried but could never do
before. without blood, the killed
heart. to take
that risk, to offer life and remain

alive, open yourself like this and become whole

You Are Happy can be seen to mark a turning point in Atwood's poetry in other ways as well. Its brilliant cycle "Circe/Mud Poems,"

a feminist recasting of the Circe myth, provides the model for later politically charged reinterpretations of such figures as Orpheus and Eurydice, Giselle, and the Robber Bridegroom. The book's "Songs of the Transformed," a series narrated by creatures half-human and half-animal, inaugurates a slightly less guarded view of the natural world and opens the way for the reverent, almost mystical encounters with nature appearing in *Interlunar* (1984).

Yet if Atwood has managed to attain a guarded confidence, a tentative transcendence in her love and nature poetry, her optimism remains tempered by a keen awareness of the strife and oppression that saturate the modern world. Since *Two-Headed Poems* (1978), Atwood's poetry has increasingly addressed political issues on a national and international level. The title sequence of this volume explores the possibility of a common language that could provide dialogue between English- and French-speaking Canada but concludes, despairingly, that "this is not a debate / but a duet / with two deaf singers." Atwood's involvement with Amnesty International has produced a searing sequence of poems, most notably "Notes towards a Poem That Can Never Be Written," which graphically addresses the continuing practice of torture and political violence. As the title of this poem suggests, these works display a strong continuity with Atwood's earlier efforts in that they question the possibility of accurately representing the reality of torture, especially when one writes in the language of a first world observer who is, if only indirectly, implicated in the violence:

In this country you can say what you like
because no one will listen to you anyway,
it's safe enough, in this country you can try to write
the poem that can never be written,
the poem that invents
nothing and excuses nothing,
because you invent and excuse yourself each day.

As demonstrated in *Power Politics,* Atwood's are among the sharpest eyes of those critiquing late twentieth-century romance. Her contemporary, technically precise, imagistic, and accessible voice suits the terms of middle-aged love and its concerns, which she addresses in her later work. Through the use of goddess myths, history, archeology, dreams, and family stories—the same subjects she has focused on before—she addresses the political consciousness of a sexually liberated generation. One might be reminded of Katherine Hepburn when the speaker in Atwood's "Manet's Olympia" (in her collection *Morning in the Burned House*) states, "She reclines, more or less. / Try that posture, it's hardly languor," or when Helen of Troy conjectures, "There sure a lot of dangerous birds around." The fables and magic that Atwood treasures form the core of her sometimes slightly cynical and lighthearted approaches to crises, which sometimes feel as if they need charms or a spell to break: "You make a cut in yourself, / a little opening / for the pain to get in. / You set loose three drops of your blood." Pervasively nostalgic, the poems of *Morning in the Burned House* are obsessed, sometimes nervously, about the passage of time and how loss configures and reconfigures endlessly within time's flow. The book's title poem resonantly considers the fractured nature of loss and memory:

In the burned house I am eating breakfast. You understand:
     there is no house,
there is no breakfast, yet here I am.

The spoon which was melted scrapes against the bowl
   which was melted also. No
one else is around.

Where have they gone to, brother and sister, mother and
   father? Off along the
shore, perhaps . . .

I can't see my own arms and legs or know if this is a trap
   or a blessing,
finding myself back here, where everything

in this house has long been over, kettle and mirror, spoon
   and bowl, including
my own body,

including the body I had then, including the body I have
   now as I sit at this
morning table, alone and happy,

bare child's feet on the scorched floorboards (I can almost
   see) in my burning
clothes, the thin green shorts

and grubby yellow T-shirt holding my cindery, nonexistent, radiant flesh.
Incandescent.

Even as she acknowledges the limitations of her language, Atwood refuses the option of silence, grimly offering witness to horrors that her words can at best suggest. It is a consistently double consciousness of the limits of language and the necessity of speech that has given all of Atwood's work, no matter what her subject, its complex blend of caution, commitment, irony, and passionate depth. It is her unflinching perception of both the impossibility and necessity of writing that has made Atwood one of our most candid and inspiring poets.

—Anthony G. Stocks and Martha Sutro

AUBERT, Alvin (Bernard)

Nationality: American. **Born:** Lutcher, Louisiana, 12 March 1930. **Education:** Southern University, Baton Rouge, Louisiana, B.A. in English 1959; University of Michigan, Ann Arbor (Woodrow Wilson Fellow), M.A. 1960; University of Illinois, Urbana, 1963–64, 1966–67. **Family:** Married 1) Olga Alexis in 1948 (divorced), one daughter; 2) Bernadine Tenant in 1960; two daughters. **Career:** Instructor, 1960–62, assistant professor, 1962–65, and associate professor of English, 1965–70, Southern University; visiting professor of English, University of Oregon, Eugene, Summer 1970; associate professor, 1970–74, and professor of English, 1974–79, State University of New York, Fredonia; professor of English, 1980–92, and since 1992 professor

emeritus, Wayne State University, Detroit. Member, board of directors, Coordinating Council of Literary Magazines, 1982–86. Advisory editor, *Drama and Theatre,* 1973–75, *Black Box,* 1974–79, *Gumbo,* 1976–78, and *Callaloo,* 1977–83; founder and editor, *Obsidian* magazine, Fredonia, New York, and Detroit, 1975–85; since 1985 senior editorial consultant, *Obsidian II,* Raleigh, North Carolina. **Awards:** Bread Loaf Writers Conference scholarship, 1968; National Endowment for the Arts grant, 1973, 1981; Coordinating Council of Literary Magazines grant, 1979; Annual Callaloo award, 1989. **Address:** 18234 Parkside Avenue, Detroit, Michigan 48221, U.S.A.

PUBLICATIONS

Poetry

Against the Blues. Detroit, Broadside Press, 1972.
Feeling Through. Greenfield Center, New York, Greenfield Review Press, 1975.
South Louisiana: New and Selected Poems. Grosse Pointe Farms, Michigan, Lunchroom Press, 1985.
If Winter Come. Pittsburgh, Carnegie Mellon Press, 1994.
Harlem Wrestler. East Lansing, Michigan, Michigan State University Press, 1995.

Play

Home from Harlem, adaptation of *The Sport of the Gods* by Paul Laurence Dunbar (produced Detroit 1986). Detroit, Obsidian Press, 1986.

*

Bibliography: "Alvin Aubert: A Primary Bibliography," in *Black American Literature Forum* (Terre Haute, Indiana), Fall 1989.

Critical Studies: By J.B., in *Kliatt* (West Newton, Massachusetts), November 1972; by James Shokoff, in Buffalo *Courier-Express,* 8 June 1973; by Herbert W. Martin, in *Three Rivers Poetry Journal* (Pittsburgh), November 1978; by Herbert W. Martin, in *Black American Literature Forum* (Terre Haute, Indiana), Fall 1987; by Tom Dent, in *Black American Literature Forum* (Terre Haute, Indiana), Spring 1988; by Jerry W. Ward, in *Black American Literature Forum* (Terre Haute, Indiana), Fall 1989; by M. Williams, in *African American Review,* 30(3), 1996.

Alvin Aubert comments:
   A poem is a verification of experience in thought and feeling but mostly the latter, for feeling is the means by which essential experience is received and transmitted. If the feeling is right, the intellectual content is also, which is to say that in the poem that works there takes place a mutual verification of thought by feeling, feeling by thought. I am African-American and conscious of my roots in south Louisiana, with its confluence of African, Native American, and European (French and Spanish) cultural influences. My sensitivity is of course African-American, thus leaving no doubt as to the source of the

experiences that verify my poems as well as find verification in them. My thematic concerns are as universal as they are particular. The themes identified by James Shokoff—"death, the shapes of the past, the terror of existence, and the pain of endurance"—are all there and then some. Their particularity is perhaps best identified in Tom Dent's observations about my south Louisiana origin.

*   *   *

The title of Alvin Aubert's first book of poetry, *Against the Blues,* directs us to read his verse against a background of recalled popular sources. For example, "Whispers in a County Church" simulates an exchange of worldly gossip among the pious; "De Profundis" relates the practical plea of a drinker for some sign, less miraculous than a burning bush, to move him to sobriety. These stock comic figures are matched in a pair of poems, opening the book, that invoke Bessie Smith in an allusion to the muse and announce the news of the dispensation of the blues. None of the poems is long. All have the apparent simplicity of direct statement. Except for the references to Smith and, in another poem, Nat Turner, the immediate subjects are personal experiences, just like the blues. The singer-poet presents first-person experiences in ways that will make them typical.

As both singer and poet know, it is not so much the experience itself, though that is surely familiar, as the form in which it is rendered that makes the song and poem typical. Thus, Aubert typifies his poems through the patterns of language. The characters of Zenobia in "Photo Album" or of those in "Uncle Bill" and "Granny Dean" are familiar not only because we may know people like them but because the poet's lines about his characters approximate the habits of speech. Often a use of negatives or identical rhymes echoes the oral games of Black English. Sometimes, as in "Garden Scene," the verse nearly assumes the form of anecdotal exemplum. Of course, it is not to imitate, even to imitate the patterns of spoken language, that Aubert writes. The typicality provided by the linguistic patterns acknowledged by the poet and reader serves as the subject for creative imagination.

Aubert opens *Feeling Through,* his second book of poetry, with "Black Aesthetic," a poem that proposes to reverse Duchamp's *Nude Descending a Staircase* so that it would portray a black man going up, not down. The title poem of the book illustrates Aubert's point, pulling experience up into reflective consciousness and setting it out as the new experience of a poem. With a characteristic syntactic economy, now become almost elliptical, Aubert establishes a situation. He, or his persona, sits on a porch swing, looking through a window at the reflection in a mirror of a carnival photograph. A partial dialogue is overheard but quickly displaced, so that wonder about the old photograph is transformed into a soliloquy on the problem of recapturing the past. The scene and events of "Feeling Through" are the material of a family story. Narrative, however, remains inchoate as the poetic voice plays feelings held in the foreground of mind over the background of anecdote. Thus, the poem is both a gloss on the latent tale of the photograph and the expression of a newly defined experience.

Aubert increasingly attaches subjective significance to his imagery. In poems such as "Economics" from the first volume or "The Opposite of Green" from the second, details explain the mundane appearance of racism, but "Nightmare" and "Levitation," both in the second book, have highly personal references. Still, the tactics of language are consistent throughout Aubert's work. The texts of his poems maintain a continuity with the African-American tradition by simulation and innovation that become a commentary on the richness of his sources and evidence of authentic re-creation.

—John M. Reilly

AVISON, Margaret (Kirkland)

Nationality: Canadian. **Born:** Galt, Ontario, 23 April 1918. **Education:** University of Toronto, B.A. in English 1940, M.A. 1964. **Career:** Worked for North American Life Insurance Company and Gage Press; editor, Canadian Institute of International Affairs, until 1945; staff member, registrar's office and library, 1945–55, and lecturer, for one year, University of Toronto; nursemaid, 1955; worker, Presbyterian Home Missions, Toronto; writer-in-residence, University of Western Ontario, 1972–73; staff member of archives division, Canadian Broadcasting Corporation, 1973–78; staff member, Mustard Seed Mission, Toronto, from 1978. **Awards:** Guggenheim fellowship, 1956; Governor-General's award, 1961, 1990. **Address:** 17 Lascelles Boulevard, Apartment 108, Toronto, Ontario M4V 2B6, Canada.

PUBLICATIONS

Poetry

Winter Sun. Toronto, University of Toronto Press, and London, Routledge, 1960.
The Dumbfounding. New York, Norton, 1966.
Sunblue. Hantsport, Nova Scotia, Lancelot Press, 1978.
Winter Sun/The Dumbfounding: Poems 1940–1966. Toronto, University of Toronto Press, 1982.
No Time. Hantsport, Nova Scotia, Lancelot Press, 1989.
Selected Poems. Toronto and Oxford, Oxford University Press, 1991.
Not Yet but Still. Hantsport, Nova Scotia, Lancelot Press, 1997.

Other

History of Toronto. Toronto, Gage, 1951.
The Research Compendium, with Albert Rose. Toronto, University of Toronto Press, 1964.
A Kind of Perseverance. Hantsport, Nova Scotia, Lancelot Press, 1994.

Translator, with Ilona Duczynska and Karl Polanyi, *The Plough and the Pen: Writings from Hungary 1930–1956.* Toronto, McClelland and Stewart, 1963.
Translator, with Ilona Duczynska, *Acta Sanctorum and Other Tales,* by József Lengyel. London, Owen, 1970.

*

Bibliography: In *The Annotated Bibiliography of Canada's Major Authors,* vol. 6, edited by Jack David and Robert Lecker, Downsview, Ontario, ECW Press, 1985.

Critical Studies: "The Poetry of Margaret Avison" by Martin Wilson, in *Canadian Literature,* Autumn 1959; *Margaret Avison* by E.H. Redekop, Toronto, Copp Clark, 1970; *'Lighting up the Terrain:' The Poetry of Margaret Avison,* Toronto, University of Toronto Press, 1987, *Margaret Avison and Her Works,* Toronto, ECW Press, 1989, "Wholeharted Poetry; Halfhearted Criticism," in *Essays on Canadian Writing* (Toronto), 44, Fall 1991, and in *ECW's Biographical Guide to Canadian Poets,* edited by Robert Lecker, Jack David, and Ellen Quigley, Toronto, ECW, 1993, all by David Kent; *Waiting for the Son: Poetics, Theology, Rhetoric in Margaret Avison's 'Sunblue'* by C.D. Mazoff, Dunvegan, Ontario, Cormorant Books, 1989; "The Avison Collection at the University of Manitoba: Poems 1929–89" by Margaret Calverley, in *Canadian Poetry* (London, Ontario), 28, Spring/Summer 1991; "The Territory of Conscience: The Poetry of Margaret Avison" by R. Sullivan, in *Literary Half-Yearly* (Mysore, India), 32(1), January 1991; "Phoenix from the Ashes: Lorna Crozier and Margaret Avison in Contemporary Mourning" by Deborah Bowen, in *Canadian Poetry,* 40, Spring/Summer 1997.

* * *

It is largely through the work of women poets such as P.K. Page and Phyllis Webb—and even to an extent Margaret Atwood—that a distinctly metaphysical strain has entered into modern Canadian poetry. The writer who perhaps most strikingly manifests this trend is Margaret Avison, and in her case the metaphysical element has been strengthened and shaped by a conversion experience that dominated her second volume, *The Dumbfounding.* This has since added a strong devotional tendency to her poetry and to her life, in which she seeks assiduously to bear witness to her Christianity.

Avison has been writing poetry since the 1950s, and although she did not publish her first collection, *Winter Sun,* until 1960, she had already attracted attention with the poems she had published in periodicals. In fact, her work was the subject of a major critical article (Milton Wilson's "The Poetry of Margaret Avison," in *Canadian Literature* [Vancouver], Autumn 1959) before she had a book in print. Avison has written sparingly and slowly (agonizingly slowly it seems), and by the late 1970s she had published only two further volumes, *The Dumbfounding* and *Sunblue.*

There was never a question of religious faith in itself making Avison a remarkable poet. What Rosemary Sullivan has called "the sophistication and beauty of her linguistic and imagistic gift" were, in fact, most evident at the time when she seemed to be moving away from the religious convictions of her youthful Ontario Methodist background; conversion (or reconversion) seems to have changed her poetry without necessarily enhancing it. The later poems have been more direct, perhaps because the poet ceased to be a searcher in unknown realms. Avison was no longer exploring the dark intricacies of her own mind or the uncertainties of the universe but now moved forward with the assuredness of revealed knowledge.

Many readers prefer the earlier, unconverted Avison. Her poems provide a challenge to those who seek to unravel their introspective intricacy, and they delight with their lambent visuality. Perhaps most of all, the poems project a sense of search and daring, a metaphysical gamble offered, for example, by "The Swimmer's Moment":

> For everyone
> The swimmer's moment at the whirlpool comes,
> But many at that moment will not say,
> "This is the whirlpool, then."

> By their refusal they are saved
> From the black pit, and also from contesting
> The deadly rapids, and emerging in
> The mysterious, and more ample, further waters.
> And so their bland-blank faces turn and turn
> Pale and forever on the rim of suction
> They will not recognize
> Of those who dare the knowledge
> Many are whirled into the ominous centre
> That, gaping vertical, seals up
> For them an eternal boon of privacy,
> So that we turn away from their defeat
> With a despair, not for their deaths, but for
> Ourselves, who cannot penetrate their secret
> Nor even guess at the anonymous breadth
> Where one or two have won:
> (The silver reaches of the estuary).

Those "silver reaches" beyond the whirlpool are the terrain of *The Dumbfounding* and *Sunblue,* and there is a sense, as the poems move through the conversion experience toward the orthodoxy that lies beyond ecstasy, of leveling off into smoother waters. It is there already in "The Dumbfounding," the title poem, in the stripped style as much as in the sense of spiritual certainty:

> Yet you are
> constant and sure,
> the all-lovely, all-men's-way
> to that far country.

> Winning one, you again
> all ways would begin
> life: to make new
> flesh, to empower
> the weak in nature
> to restore
> or stay the sufferer;
> lead through the garden to
> trash, rubble, hill,
> where, the outcast's outcast, you
> sound dark's uttermost, strangely light-brimming, until
> time be full.

Yet one knows that there are dark nights as well as "sunblue" days ahead, for such is the nature of the creative and spiritual life in a poet so naturally metaphysical as Avison.

—George Woodcock

AWOONOR, Kofi

Nationality: Ghanaian. **Born:** Wheta, 13 March 1935. **Education:** University of Ghana, Accra, B.A. 1960; University of London (Longmans Fellow, 1967–68), M.A. 1968; State University of New York, Stony Brook, Ph.D. in comparative literature 1973. **Family:** Six children. **Career:** Research Fellow, Institute of African Studies, Legon, 1960–64; director, Ghana Ministry of Information Film Corporation, 1964–67; poet-in-residence, 1968, assistant professor of

English, 1968–72, associate professor, 1973–74, and chair of Department of Comparative Literature, 1974–75, State University of New York, Stony Brook; visiting professor, University of Texas, Austin, 1972–73. Detained on suspicion of treason, Ghana, 1975–76. Senior lecturer in English, 1975, professor of literature, and dean of the faculty of arts, University of Cape Coast, Ghana, 1977–82. Ghana ambassador to Brazil, 1984–88, and Cuba, 1988–90, and Ghana's ambassador to the United Nations, 1990–94. Since 1997 minister of state, aide to the president, and member of policy management group, Office of the President, Ghana. Formerly editor, *Okyeame,* Accra, co-editor, *Black Orpheus,* Ibadan, and associate editor, *Transition,* 1967–68, *World View,* and *Okike.* **Awards:** Gurrey prize, 1959; Commonwealth poetry award, 1989; Ghana Assocation of Writers distinguished authors award, 1991; ECRAG national award for poetry, 1992, 1994. **Address:** Ambassador, Ghana Mission to the United Nations, 19 East 47th Street, New York, New York 10017, U.S.A.

PUBLICATIONS

Poetry

Rediscovery and Other Poems. Ibadan, Mbari, and Evanston, Illinois, Northwestern University Press, 1964.
Night of My Blood. New York, Doubleday, 1971.
Ride Me, Memory. Greenfield Center, New York, Greenfield Review Press, 1973.
The House by the Sea. Greenfield Center, New York, Greenfield Review Press, 1978.
Until the Morning After: Selected Poems 1963–1985. Greenfield Center, New York, Greenfield Review Press, 1987.
Latin American and Caribbean Notebook. Trenton, New Jersey, Africa World Press, 1992.

Plays

Ancestral Power, and *Lament,* in *Short African Plays,* edited by Cosmo Pieterse. London, Heinemann, 1972.

Novels

This Earth My Brother: An Allegorical Tale of Africa. London, Heinemann, 1970; New York, Doubleday, 1971.
Comes the Voyager at Last: A Tale of Return to Africa. Trenton, New Jersey, Africa World Press, 1992.

Other

In Person: Achebe, Awoonor, and Soyinka at the University of Washington. Seattle, University of Washington African Studies Program, 1975.
The Breast of the Earth: A Survey of the History, Culture, and Literature of Africa South of the Sahara. New York, Doubleday, 1975.
The Ghana Revolution. New York, Oases, 1984.
Ghana: A Political History from Pre-European to Modern Times. Accra, Sedco Publishers, 1990.
Africa: The Marginalised Continent. Accra, Woeli, 1995.

Editor, with Geormbey Adali-Mortty, *Messages: Poems from Ghana.* London, Heinemann, 1970; New York, Humanities Press, 1971.
Editor, *Guardians of the Sacred Word: Ewe Poetry.* New York, Nok, 1974.

Translator, *When Sorrow-Song Descends on You,* by Vinoko Akpalu. Merrick, New York, Cross Cultural, 1981.

*

Bibliography: "Kofi Awoonor: An Annotated Bibliography" by Kwaku Amoabeng and Carol Lasker, in *Africana Journal* (New York), 13, 1982.

Critical Studies: "The Restorative Cycle: Kofi Awoonor's Theory of African Literature" by Rosemary Colmer, in *New Literature Review,* 3, 1977; "Kofi Awoonor: Restraint and Release" by Martin Tucker, in *English in Africa* (Grahamstown, South Africa), 6(1), 1979; "Kofi Awoonor as Poet" by Ayo Mamudu, in *Kiabàrà,* 5(1), 1982; "Myth, History and the Poetry of Kofi Awoonor," in *Toward Defining the African Aesthetic,* edited by Lemuel A. Johnson and others, Washington, D.C., Three Continents, 1982, and "Poetry as Autobiography: Society and Self in Three Modern West African Poets," in *African Literature in Its Social and Political Dimensions,* edited by Eileen Julien, Mildred Mortimer, and Curtis Schade, Washington, D.C., Three Continents, 1986, both by Thomas R. Knipp; "Plights of Contemporary Life in Recent African Fiction" by Jai Shyam, in *Arizona Quarterly* (Tucson, Arizona), 42(3), Autumn 1986; "Rites of Passage in the Poetry of Kofi Awoonor," in *Commonwealth Essays and Studies* (Dijon, France), 8(2), Spring 1986, and "Aspects of Myth in Two Ghanaian Novels," in *Commonwealth Essays and Studies* (Dijon, France), 10(1), Autumn 1987, both by Elaine Saint-Andre Utudjian; "Ritual and Reality in the Novels of Wole Soyinka, Gabriel Okara and Kofi Awoonor" by Derek Wright, in *Kunapipi* (Aarhus, Denmark), 9(1), 1987; "Oral Tradition and the African Novel" by Edward Sackey, in *Modern Fiction Studies* (Baltimore, Maryland), 37(3), Autumn 1991; "Kofi Awoonor as a Prophet of Conscience" by Mary Ebun Modupe Kolawole, in *African Languages and Culture* (Oxford, England), 5(2), 1992; "Landscape as Expression of Alienation: Armab, Awoonor, Soyinka" by Koku Amuzu, in *English in Africa* (South Africa), 20(1), May 1993; "Kofi Awoonor as Critic" by Obi Maduakor, in *Africa Literature Today* (Freetown, Sierra Leone), 19, 1994; "Kofi Awoonor" by Alma Jean Billingslea-Brown, in *Postcolonial African Writers: A Bio-Bibliographical Critical Source Book,* edited by Pushpa Naidu Parekh and Siga Fatima Jagne, Westport, Connecticut, Greenwood, 1998.

Kofi Awoonor comments:

Traditional oral poetry of the Ewes, with its emphasis on lyricism, the chant, repetition of lines, symbolism, and imagery transfused into English through the secondary mediation of Pound, Dylan Thomas, etc.

*   *   *

Kofi Awoonor is Ghana's most famous poet. The pervasive mood of his poetry, keenest in his early work, is lyric lament, expressing the Western-educated African's drifting sense of loss and his anguish of severance from indigenous cultural traditions, cut away by a too hasty, perverting modernization. *Night of My Blood,* which reprints two-thirds of the earlier *Rediscovery,* is permeated by the returning exile's complex aura of nostalgia and fatalism, longing and foreboding, about what he will find. Awoonor's model is the Ewe dirge as performed by the great Anlo dirge singer (or *heno*) Vinoko Akpalu. A recurring motif in Ewe dirge poetry is the myth of the thwarted or desolate return, in which the ancestral pilgrimage leads back to a land of neglected and ruined shrines eaten by termites. Awoonor's much anthologized poem "The Weaver Bird," with its rediscovered shrines defiled by the droppings of foreign religions and false political messiahs, is written in this tradition. In "Dirge" the inarticulacy of the poet's grief over bygone poetic traditions is itself living evidence of their loss.

The persona in the poems of *Night of My Blood* is both liminal and central, and his journey is at once realistic and mythical, leading into himself and his society. The speaking "I" of an Akpalu dirge is simultaneously the grieving individual singer and the whole community plunged into mourning by the death, and though the *heno* lives a socially secluded life, he carries society's collective memory and conscience as part of his *hadzivodoo,* or gift of songs. In his priestlike role he is medium and clairvoyant, vessel and vehicle, of primal energies. Accordingly, Awoonor's imitative elegiac songs are not isolated outbursts of private melancholy but function as expressions of a collective desolation and as a threnody for the spiritual death of an entire culture and the passing of an era. The radial, macrocosmic swell of their nebulous funeral imagery, though attenuating and diffusing its impact, makes for a poetry of remarkable range and resonance, full of daring imaginative syntheses and startling superimpositions.

Onto the dirge archetype of the soul making its moonlit canoe journey across the waters of death are suggestively grafted both the legendary migration of the Ewe people from the Upper Niger to their present home in eastern Ghana (this is the "night" of the poet's "blood" in the title poem) and the modern poet-exile's circular passage of departure and return, rediscovering at last the wisdom of ancestors and of ritual poetic traditions and submerging himself in their sustaining communal ethos. The haunting paradoxical imagery of these delicate lyrics is of flood and the ferryman, drums and bells, cooking fires and sacrificial altars, bitter herbs and incense, and purification and putrefaction, and the constant contextual shifts present the poet-exile in compulsively eschatological terms. The dead man journeys to a new life among the ancestors, the poet to the dead in search of new life for his songs. After the spiritual death of alienation in a foreign culture, the homecoming is a painful initiation, another kind of death that must be endured if a new birth is to be possible. This is sometimes accompanied by the darker perception that the poet's visionary liberation, like the protagonist's in Awoonor's experimental poetic novel *This Earth, My Brother,* is destined to be achieved only by the passage through madness and bodily death, by returning literally to his native earth where his buried birth cord waits to regather him. As the dead man must become an ancestor in order to be put in touch with powers that may be used to benefit the community from a position outside it, the poet, by analogy, must leave his society to acquire the power to revitalize it on his return.

The latter trope—death or exile as mediating agent—and the subsequent retention of what is vital in alien influences are important in this poetry. Awoonor is no cultural purist bent on the retrieval of pristine, precolonial African art forms. On the contrary, he is a great amalgamator and assimilator of experiences and poetic styles, though his syncretism is squarely based within an African cognitive system. *Night of My Blood* contains many distorted and inverted echoes of the Christian liturgy as well as scraps of Hopkins and Eliot. Between the

anvil of Africa and the hammer of the West the poet's pains are transformed "in the forging house of a new life . . . / Into the joy of new songs" ("The Anvil and the Hammer"). Even so, the ominous pun of "forging" suggests that some counterfeiting, falsifying agent may be at work, and in the same poem the refrain "Sew the old days for us, our fathers / That we can wear them under our new garments" images Western and African forms as two separate entities still awaiting combination, giving the impression, as in many of Awoonor's longer and more ambitious poems, of an admixture or juxtaposition rather than a genuine synthesis of influences. Moreover, even the old "garment" of tradition that is worn closest to the poet's skin and heart is the cause of some discomfort.

Though it is a poetry of the speaking (and singing) voice, Awoonor's work is, of course, a print-based approximation to dirge oratory rather than the thing itself (we experience the poet alone on the page, not the singer abroad in the marketplace), and there are many places where the strain of simulation begins to show. Once the poet has denied himself both the natural polytonality of his native Ewe tongue and the external reinforcements of Western metrics (all the poems are written in free verse), the reproduction of the rhythmic counterpoint of the dirge, through the equivalent devices of syntactical parallelism, balanced antithesis, and repetition, is no easy task. Nevertheless, in the best poems of *Night of My Blood* there is a genuine and powerful sense of a voice coming through from another language and culture, progressing from virtual translation through personal adaptations to the creation of entirely new forms. If there is a fault, it is perhaps an excessive and limiting reliance on ready-made ritual formulas, producing poems that are sometimes profound and sometimes trite and empty, and it is perhaps significant that one of the finest poems in the volume is a personal elegy in which the familiar dirge imagery is put to very private use. In "Lament of the Silent Sister," for Christopher Okigbo, Awoonor presents his poetic self as a female persona, artistically immature and unready to be impregnated by Okigbo's uncompromising muse until the moment of the Ibo master's death, when the floods of poetry are released in a state of sexual tumult. The canoe and flood symbolism carried by the poems' rhythmic surge is simultaneously funeral and sexual, telescoping death and procreation, sexual initiation and immolation, ancestral passages and rebirth.

The theme of exile becomes poignantly personal in Awoonor's next volume, *Ride Me, Memory,* which is the fruit of his American experience (1968–1975). Here mellow African memories crowd in alongside American anecdotes and larger political statements. The range of Ewe forms is extended to include the *halo,* the earthy song of abuse, and the praise song, and these are used to paint individual portraits that are, respectively, jocularly caustic and earnestly adulatory (under the first category come meddling first world scholars; under the second black American writers, singers, and jazz musicians). There is in these poems a violent energy together with a tightening of the bonds of political commitment and, along with the greater looseness of form and slighter dependence on hypnotic ritual formulas, a more boldly explicit and less dreamlike imagery. The volume as a whole, however, perhaps because of the preponderance of proper names for people, places, and events, tends toward the diffuseness and breezy thinness of the travelogue.

On his return to Ghana in 1975 Awoonor very quickly found himself in prison on the charge of collusion with a coup plot, and the experiences of his year in Ussher Fort Prison are recounted in *The House by the Sea.* The prison poems at the center of this volume, in their remorseless examination of the nature of political involvement and responsibility, reveal a harsh, distilled intensity, gritty sharpness, and brittle clarity that are new in Awoonor's work. The volume opens out beyond the merely personal to take in political outrage and injustice over the African continent and throughout human history in the world at large, but in the last and most ambitious poem, "The Wayfarer Comes Home," the lyric lusciousness returns (home is simultaneously Eweland, Ghana, and Africa) and the dominant mood is one of affectionate celebration. Awoonor says in the prison poems that the pursuit of political liberty, though it may involve "the possibility of being murdered in a dark cell," is also worth postponing dying for: "On such a day / who would dare think of dying? / So much Freedom means / that we swear we'll postpone dying / until the morning after." These lines provide Awoonor with the title for his volume of collected poems, in which nine new poems offer a mixture of undaunted resilience and stoical resignation in the face of the everyday tragedies of economic ruin, destitution, and early death that continue to devastate modern Africa: "Do not lose heart, / have arms, we have shields . . . / Some rivers there are you cannot swim / some strong rivers there are you cannot ford" ("So the World Changes").

Awoonor's 1992 collection *Latin American and Caribbean Notebook* is the fruit of his diplomatic employment and travels in Brazil, Cuba, and Nicaragua. Awoonor presents himself, self-accusingly, in the historical present as "the braggart loudmouth boastful / uncertain diplomat" who has taken "refuge in an inane occupation," shunted off abroad to serve a country that is being wrecked by fools and criminals back home ("Rio de Janeiro," "Of Home Once More"). In other poems he projects his own sense of displacement upon victims of the black diaspora in other lands and indulges a sentimental adulation of the heroes of the Cuban and Nicaraguan revolutions.

The poems that carry the most conviction in this volume, however, are the nostalgic and delicate love lyrics that wrench subtle reflections upon time and aging from hallucinated childhood memories and the casual affairs of the lonely middle-aged diplomat, condemned to empty beds in alien cities ("Time Revisited," "Distant Home Country," "Lover's Song," "Dream-Again," "Readings and Musings"). The most disappointing efforts are the long, rambling prosy pieces in which obliquely personal reminiscences are randomly interspersed with catalogs of political outrages and scandals (America's impoverished blacks and Britain's homeless in "Betrayers") and with snapshot newspaper headlines (an American-downed Iranian airliner, Arab boys killed by Israeli soldiers in "Of Home and Sea I Already Sang"). Significantly, the most poignantly moving poem in the collection—about the poet's first diplomatic assignment in Cuba and the death of a nineteen-year-old African girl—is one in which the poet confines himself strictly to the experience at hand ("The Girl That Died in Havana"). *Notebook* is Awoonor's most prosily self-indulgent volume. Bearing out the title, many of the poems read like uncoordinated diary jottings, thinly contextualized anecdotes that have not been imaginatively energized into poetry.

—Derek Wright

B

BACA, Jimmy Santiago

Nationality: American. **Born:** Jose Santiago Baca, Santa Fe, New Mexico, 2 January 1952. **Education:** Self-educated; received G.E.D. **Family:** Married; two sons. **Career:** Poet-in-residence, University of California, Berkeley, and Yale University. Writer and farmer. **Awards:** American Book award, Before Columbus Foundation, 1988, for *Martín and Meditations on the South Valley;* Berkeley Regents' fellowship, 1989; Wallace Stevens fellowship, Yale University, 1990; Ludwig Vogelstien award in poetry.

PUBLICATIONS

Poetry

Fired Up with You: Poems of a Niagara Vision, with others. Naco, Arizona, Border Publishing Company, 1977.
Jimmy Santiago Baca. Santa Barbara, California, Rock Bottom, 1978.
Immigrants in Our Own Land. Baton Rouge, Louisiana State University Press, 1979; enlarged edition as *Immigrants in Our Own Land and Earlier Poems,* New York, New Directions, 1990.
Swords of Darkness, edited by Gary Soto. San Jose, California, Mango, 1981.
What's Happening. Willimantic, Connecticut, Curbstone, 1982.
Poems Taken from My Yard. Fulton, Missouri, Timberline, 1986.
Martín and Meditations on the South Valley. New York, New Directions, 1987.
Black Mesa Poems. New York, New Directions, 1989.
In the Way of the Sun. N.p., Grove Press, 1997.
Set This Book on Fire. Mena, Arkansas, Cedar Hill, 1999.

Play

Los Tres Hijos de Julia (produced Los Angeles, 1991).

Other

Working in the Dark. Santa Fe, Red Crane Books, 1991.

*

Critical Studies: "Two Contemporary Chicano Verse Chronicles" by Julian Olivares, in *Americas Review* (Houston, Texas), 16(3–4), Fall/Winter 1988; "Errance et transfert chez Jimmy Santiago Baca" by Yves-Charles Grandjeat, in *Multilinguisme et multiculturalisme en Amerique du Nord: Espace seuils limites,* edited by Jean Beranger and others, Bordeaux, Marillier, 1990; "Carrying the Magic of His People's Heart: An Interview with Jimmy Santiago Baca" by Gabriel Melendez, in *Americas Review* (Houston, Texas), 19(3–4), Winter 1991; "Searching Anaya, Sainz, Fuentes and Baca for a Common, Cultural Center" by Philip J. Davis, in *Confluencia* (Greeley, Colorado), 11(2), Spring 1996.

*   *   *

Jimmy Santiago Baca's *Immigrants in Our Own Land* is a powerful first collection of poetry. A Chicano poet, Baca served a ten-year sentence in an Arizona prison, and his poetry grows out of his experience as a convict. The title poem refers not only to the lot of Chicanos and other minorities but also to convicts as immigrants to a new life in prison:

We are born with dreams in our hearts,
looking for better days ahead.
At the gates we are given new papers,
our old clothes are taken . . .

But in the end, some will just sit around
talking about how good the old world was.
Some of the younger ones will become gangsters . . .

Acknowledging the ruts that prison life can create, Baca chooses not to limit the poems to this experience alone. The poet avoids the specifics of how he got where he is, and he finds value both in remembering previous years of freedom and in looking at his present situation. His poetry is refreshingly free of political rhetoric or self-pity, though Baca does see reforms that could be made in the prison system and lists some of them in "The New Warden":

The government even commissioned some of the convicts
To design patriotic emblems . . .
After the first year, the new warden installed ballot boxes.
A radio and TV shop opened. Some of the convicts' sons
And daughters came into prison to learn from their fathers'
Trades and talking with them about life . . .
Each day six groups of convicts went into the community,
Working for the aged and infirm.
One old convict ended up marrying the governor's mother.

Though some of these poems, like the one just cited, have rhythms close to those of prose, others are very lyrical. Line lengths vary from short to the longer ones of "The New Warden" to even more extended ones that stretch out like Whitman's paragraph-length "lines." Some poems, such as "It Started," blend shorter with longer lines. Here Baca writes of a state-funded poetry workshop in which he gets encouragement from visiting writers to express himself:

I showed you my first poem ever written,
    "They Only Came To See The Zoo"

But you didn't treat me like a wild ape,
Or an elephant. You treated me like Jimmy.
And who was Jimmy?

A mass of moulten fury in this furnace of steel,
and yet, my thoughts became ladles, sifting carefully
through my life . . .

Besides his skill in maneuvering line length, Baca is also adept at switching tone. "So Mexicans Are Taking Jobs from Americans" starts in a playfully satiric vein with "O Yes? Do they come on horses / with rifles, and say, Ese gringo, gimmee your job?'' Several stanzas later, however, the tone becomes more brutal:

> Even on TV, an asthmatic leader
> crawls turtle heavy, leaning on an assistant,
> and from the nest of wrinkles on his face,
> a tongue paddles through flashing waves
> of lightbulbs, of cameramen, rasping
> ''They're taking our jobs away.''

He later achieves a powerful vision of class struggle similar to that in William Carlos Williams's ''The Yachts'':

> Below that cool green sea of money,
> millions and millions of people fight to live,
> search for pearls in the darkest depths
> of their dreams, hold their breath for years
> trying to cross poverty to just having something.

The tone as the poem ends is elegiac, the parting words an epitaph and plea:

> The children are dead already. We are killing them,
> that is what America should be saying;
> on TV, in the streets, in offices, should be saying,
> ''We aren't giving the children a chance to live.''
>
> Mexicans are taking our jobs, they say instead.
> What they really say is, let them die,
> and the children too.

Still, the prevailing feeling is one of hope. Baca brings a compassionate heart to his work, embracing humanity as Whitman did in the nineteenth century and as too few poets have in the twentieth. Here, in ''Joe,'' he describes his ''celly,'' a Vietnam vet:

> Breakage of love bonds between him and his family,
> Sunken cheeks and eyes turning pale
> Like a great bear in hibernation during Spring,
> Streams rot black, berries shrivel, and the sound
> Of gunfire in the distance,
> Tractors plowing under his life
> As he watches from those great pale eyes,
> Tractor blades claw his heart out,
> Remove it slowly like a great mountain, drilling a tunnel
> Right down the middle of it . . .

Like Auden in ''September 1, 1939,'' Baca in his work also says that ''we must love one another or die.'' As he says in ''I Am Offering This Poem,'' his poems are acts of kindness and sharing:

> It's all I have to give,
> and all anyone needs to live,
> and to go on living inside,
> when the world outside
> no longer cares if you live or die;
> remember,
> I love you.

—Duane Ackerson

BANG, Mary Jo

Nationality: American. **Born:** Mary Jo Ward, Waynesville, Missouri, 22 October 1946. **Education:** Northwestern University, Evanston, Illinois, 1969–71, B.A. in sociology (summa cum laude) 1971, M.A. 1975; University of Westminster, London, 1987–89, B.A. in photography 1989; Columbia University, New York, 1993–95, M.F.A. 1998. **Career:** Instructor, Columbia College, Chicago, 1991–93; visiting lecturer, Yale University, New Haven, Connecticut, 1997–98; instructor, The New School, New York, 1998; visiting writer, University of Montana, Missoula, 1999. Since 1999 assistant professor of English, Washington University, St. Louis, Missouri. Co-editor, *Columbia Poetry Review #6,* Columbia College, Chicago, 1992–93; associate editor, 1993–94, and co-editor, 1994–95, *Columbia: A Magazine of Poetry & Prose;* since 1995 poetry co-editor, *Boston Review.* **Awards:** ''Discovery''*The Nation* award, 1995; Bakeless prize, 1996, for *Apology for Want;* New Writers award, Greg Lakes Colleges Association, 1998, for *Apology for Want;* Yaddo fellowship, 1998; Hodder fellowship, Princeton University, 1999–2000; Alice Fay di Castagnola award, Poetry Society of America, 2000.

PUBLICATIONS

Poetry

Apology for Want. Hanover, New Hampshire, University Press of New England/Middlebury College Press, 1997.

*   *   *

Mary Jo Bang's *Apology for Want* addresses desire. The poems remind us that desire is a human condition differentiated from mere animal want or hunger by its insatiability, what Bang calls ''the always ravenous hunger'' (''Persephone Leaving''). Her poems probe desire with a scrupulous gaze and a willful and unabashed attention that avoid self-pity. In this regard the poems break with that strain of twentieth-century confessionalism concerned with the poet's unique personal anguish, often at the expense of intelligibility. Bang's poems suggest a neo-Metaphysical poetics. Harnessing intriguing metaphors, intricate textual allusions, and elaborate wordplay, her poetics hearken back to a more tough-minded and philosophical poetic tradition, one concerned with understanding universal human needs and fears.

Bang's language captivates us with its suggestiveness. We immediately accept the rightness of her metaphors, even though we cannot pin down their aptness precisely, as when she writes, ''once on a backyard swing / I became the sky I meant to be'' (''In St. John's Hospital'') or in her description of a team of surgeons and nurses standing ''like a green sea at the edge of a field of sterility'' (''Open Heart Surgery''). Her polysemous metaphors and short couplets, triplets, and quatrains create a tension. Her poems work to temper desire by framing it within the poetic form and by naming it. Desire is ''the shrouded want to cheek and shoulder / that arms can't reach, throat refuses to ask'' (''In This Business of Touch and Be Touched''). Her figures concretely define objects: ''head lamps crawl'' (''Chicago''), and ''the sea dazes itself'' (''Waking in Antibes''). Reverse personification allows a speaker to define herself in terms of the world, adapting a line of Gerald Manley Hopkins: ''I am the earth, *quartz-fret and sparks of salt*'' (''The Clairvoyant'').

Bang's attention to the possibilities of figurative language and textual allusions suggests a poet concerned with correspondences. Oracular signs and prophetic warnings are part of this order. Whether it is the poem ''Waking in Antibes,'' in which a disfigured baby born in northern India is heralded as the Hindu god Ganesha, or ''The Oracle,'' in which a ''ping'' announces a kitchen fire, such signs and revelations abound in Bang's cosmos and ''can tell you everything you need to know'' if you are attentive enough. Bang does not accept these signs on faith alone but subjects them to reason and tough-minded common sense. She suggests that ''soon we will understand everything—''why our first breath, when our last''—but warns that ''there are few ways / to free the body from desire, all end in anarchy'' (''Apology for Want'').

For Bang being human means being subject to physical and psychological needs, and she cautions balance. Repeatedly we witness the need for physical connection. In ''The Clairvoyant'' the speaker vows, ''I will be pressed against. Known.'' In ''Ashes'' we read, ''in the absence of touch—sight / and sound can compensate only for so long.'' Windows, mirrors, and glass permeate Bang's poems, acting as teasing barriers to the physical contact that might assuage our desire. Bang's barriers, like the poems themselves, set off our wants by framing them. Or worse, they turn on us, reflecting our needy selves. One frustrated speaker complains, the ''mirror tells me nothing, nor how / nor why—won't'' (''In Order Not to Be Eten nor All to Torne'').

Bang's poems suggest that answers are not found in the outer world but are located where ''the outer edge imagined meets real'' (''In This Business of Touch and Be Touched''). ''In St. John's Hospital'' contemplates this place. The speaker waits inside a hospital for a doctor's pronouncement, while

> Outside, red brick divided
> the fabric of late spring. A river limped by
> refusing comfort, a cool *mere*.

By partitioning the landscape, the hospital brick frustrates the speaker's access to the regenerative power of traditional spring images. The river, too, fails to console, as its lethargic limp slows to near stagnation. The stagnant mere reflects back on the speaker, not in ridicule or unfeeling apathy but as a mirror that reflects merely what is.

For Bang life is pain and loss and need. But her poems posit that loss, and the consequent need, defines us. Thus, as in ''In St. John's Hospital,'' an imaginative river provides a mirror that reflects a truer definition of who we are. We are defined merely by our wants, which the speaker only belatedly understands:

> All our lives we carry a condition inside.
> Too late we realize—dry sand
> dust, what might have been a house.

Sand is the material of mirrors. Bang's poem holds out the possibility of a mirror poetics, a space where ''imagined meets real.''

—Rebekah Keaton

BANTOCK, Gavin (Marcus August)

Nationality: British. **Born:** Barnt Green, near Birmingham, Warwickshire, 4 July 1939. **Education:** King's Norton Grammar School; New College, Oxford, M.A. (honors) in English language and literature 1964. **Family:** Married Kyoko Oshima in 1976. **Career:** Head of English department in various private secondary schools in England; professor of English, Reitaku University, Kashiwa-shi, Chiba-ken, Japan, 1969–94. Since 1994 living in the mountains of western Japan, devoting his time to writing and oil painting and directing English dramas with local people. **Awards:** Richard Hillary memorial prize, 1964; Alice Hunt Bartlett prize, 1966; Eric Gregory award, 1969. **Agent:** Peter Jay, 69 King George Street, London SE10 8PX, England.

PUBLICATIONS

Poetry

Christ: A Poem in Twenty-Six Parts. Oxford, Donald Parsons, 1965.
Juggernaut. London, Anvil Press Poetry, 1968.
A New Thing Breathing. London, Anvil Press Poetry, 1969.
Anhaga. London, Anvil Press Poetry, 1970.
Gleeman. Cardiff, Second Aeon, 1972.
Eirenikon. London, Anvil Press Poetry, 1972.
Isles. Feltham, Middlesex, Quarto Press, 1974.
Dragons. London, Anvil Press Poetry, 1979.

Plays

The Last of the Kings: Frederick the Great (produced Edinburgh, 1969).
Blue Tunnel Gateway, A Zen Drama (produced Tokyo, 1982).
Russian Bed Chamber (The Making of Catherine the Great) (produced Tokyo, 1991).

Other

Land of the Setting Sun. Tokyo, Kinseido, 1973.
Disunited Kingdom. Tokyo, Kinseido, 1974.
Twenty Eggs in One Basket. Tokyo, Kinseido, 1975.
Nobler in the Mind. Tokyo, Kinseido, 1976.
Pioneers of English Poetry. Tokyo, Kinseido, 1979.
Dramatic Tales from the Bible. Tokyo, Kinseido, 1981.
Aspects of England. Tokyo, Seibido, 1983.
Towards Humanity. Tokyo, Kinseido, 1985.
English People, English Opinions. Tokyo, Seibido, 1986.
Battling with Words. Tokyo, Kinseido, 1988.
Other People, Other Places. Tokyo, Seibido, 1989.
Towards Wisdom. Tokyo, Kinseido, 1989.
Asking and Answering. Tokyo, Kinseido, 1993.

Translator, with Kyoko Oshima, *Journey of the Wind*, by Tomihiro Hoshino. Tokyo, Rippu Shobo, 1988.
Translator, *Road of the Tinkling Bell,* by Tomihiro Hoshino. Tokyo, Kaiseisha, 1990.

*

Gavin Bantock comments:

Themes and subjects: In *Christ*—Jesus as a man suffering human emotions and human love—a tragic, yet optimistic interpretation of the Gospel Christ.

In middle-length poems, ''Hiroshima,'' ''Juggernaut,'' ''Ichor,'' and ''Person''—examination of the human predicament in a world of intense suffering where there is no God, except violence and destruction, and where life is lived only in the present with no possible planned future. Condemnation of narrow-minded and blindly orthodox people.

Eirenikon is an attack on all those crying for peace and on this rotten Western, capitalistic society—of which the U.S.A. is the chief culprit. Most evils of modern society originate in the U.S.A.

Dragons is a collection of poems, some with Japanese background, emphasizing the unknown behind the known, deepening one's concepts of seemingly ordinary things.

Verse forms, etc.: Usually disciplined free verse based on somewhat elevated speech rhythms; perhaps too much rhetorical usage; trying to eliminate this. (Much early practice in iambic English verse forms.)

Main sources and influences: Anglo-Saxon (I have made numerous translations), the Bible, Ezra Pound, Dylan Thomas, Ted Hughes. *Other strong interests:* Beethoven, Einstein, astronomy, dictators, pipe organs, Japanese archery, gardening, Shakespeare production.

My chief aims are to expose the shortcomings of people who live narrow lives, who are unconscious of the strength of simplicity and of the practical wisdom of the much damned attitude of loving kindness. My attitude to such people is ruthless when they will not listen and sympathetic when they cannot listen. I have great admiration for people with strong wills and powers of endurance; I despise idleness and escapism and irresponsible action in human affairs.

Artistically, I hope to help maintain modern poetry steady in strength and efficiency of words used, in logical forms and order, and in importance of subject. Too much poetry today is formless, trivial, arbitrary, small-minded and does not make use of words or images designed to develop the language; too much of the language of modern poetry is dead and dull.

I believe writing poetry is a skilled craft and must be learned. Too many people write lines of verse without ever making poetry or make ''poetic'' utterances without knowing a thing about versification.

I am trying to make a distinction between the versifying of hippies and layabouts and the making of good poetry by dedicated poets. The public seem to be confused about the values of both.

(1995) Now working on a long autobiographical poem called ''Seamanship,'' utilizing the three elements of the title; plans for novels set in England or Japan; an opera libretto with a Zen theme; and plans for full-length dramas on Alexander the Great and Edward III.

*   *   *

''A bard of the old world living beyond his era''—this quotation from his own poem ''Seer'' might not unfairly be applied to Gavin Bantock himself. The man as revealed in his writings seems totally out of sympathy with the present-day world he inhabits, rejecting our money-dominated society, in which happiness is translated as the accumulation of consumer goods, in favor of a return to older and more austere virtues. His long work *Eirenikon,* in particular, betrays a bitter hatred of all things American, at times becoming a diatribe against the plastic transatlantic pseudoculture that spreads itself like an alien growth over so much of the world. Bantock turns his back on what he regards as a false set of values that have placed arbitrary limits on human growth, seeking his answers in ancient, neglected forms and value systems. Like Kevin Crossley-Holland, he has a keen interest in Old English poetry—*Anhaga* contains many translations from original Saxon writings—and his moral worldview owes much to biblical and Dark Age beliefs. In common with the early English masters, Bantock respects the disciplined ordering of words, regarding poetry as a hard-learned craft whose practice serves further to develop the language and its meaning. There is no room in his scheme of things for those modern poets who rely on a spontaneous outpouring of thoughts and images. Triviality, and its embodiment in the Americanized contemporary lifestyle, is anathema to him and is ruthlessly condemned in a number of his poems.

Basically moralistic in outlook, Bantock frequently writes on a heroic scale—his epic poem *Christ* is an example—where the combination of a preaching tone and the packed solidity of his lines sometimes daunt the reader by their sheer length and weight. Occasionally one feels that the poet is not unduly concerned whether or not his message is understood by the mass of his fellows. He is intent upon mining the potential of his own poetic experience, and humankind tends to come second best. Certainly such works as *Gleeman* and *A New Thing Breathing* present him as a latter-day wandering minstrel, traveling the world from one hall to the next, unsure of his reception but compelled by inner force to sing whatever the response. The central figure of his poems has the same love of wild, uninhabited places as Crossley-Holland shows in his writings, seeking out the bleak terrain of mountains or coasts where high seas break on the edge of the land. Bantock, it appears, communes most easily with the elements, finding hard, uncompromising truths in a wilderness bare of all other life: ''my voice alone shattered the clear air / my breath alone clouded the ringing pinnacles / And no man heard me / so far was I removed from the world of men.''

In place of our current gospel, which despoils the earth in pursuit of money, power, and possessions, Bantock offers the ideals of self-knowledge and loving kindness. These are worthy aims, but one feels that they are presented in a singularly aggressive manner. Bantock's writing has a rugged force and an often bitter edge that sits ill with most Sunday school Christians, having more in common with the Old Testament and the Saxon blood feud. From his Old English models he has refined his language to a strong, honed style that cuts and shapes his poems, the simplicity of utterance serving to emphasize the depths beneath. It is often in his simplest work that Bantock is most effective, as in this account of the poet's craft: ''I have ways of singing worked for every deed / that has in it song somewhere / and every deed has.'' His writing echoes his Saxon forebears in its frequent use of alliteration and its word juggling and wrestling with language. Images persist of the journeying singer, exiled and weeping at the sea's edge, returning to find the hall empty and only the ghost of a song to answer him. Dominating much of his verse is the sea itself, seen as a force for creation and growth, accepted despite its cruelty and destructive power as an integral part of the poet himself, the source of his being. To this, a recurring symbol of his beloved wilderness, Bantock returns continually to renew his own strength and creativity: ''O my music-maker when can I be with you again / and become even from the most sunless places / as a new thing breathing on the shining face of the world.''

—Geoff Sadler

BARAKA, Amiri

Nationality: African-American. **Born:** Everett LeRoi Jones in Newark, New Jersey, 7 October 1934; took name Amiri Baraka in 1968. **Education:** Attended Central Avenue School and Barringer High School, Newark; Rutgers University, Newark, New Jersey, 1951–52; Howard University, Washington, D.C., 1953–54. **Military Service:** U.S. Air Force, 1954–57. **Family:** Married 1) Hettie Roberta Cohen in 1958 (divorced 1965), two daughters; 2) Sylvia Robinson (now Amina Baraka) in 1967, five children; also two stepdaughters and two other daughters. **Career:** Teacher, New School for Social Research, New York, 1961–64, and Summers, 1977–79, State University of New York, Buffalo, Summer 1964, and Columbia University, New York, 1964 and Spring 1980; visiting professor, San Francisco State College, 1966–67, Yale University, New Haven, Connecticut, 1977–78, and George Washington University, Washington, D.C., 1978–79. Assistant professor, 1980–82, associate professor, 1983–84, professor of Africana Studies, 1985–96, and since 1996 professor emeritus, State University of New York, Stony Brook. Founder, *Yugen* magazine and Totem Press, New York, 1958–62; editor, with Diane di Prima, *Floating Bear* magazine, New York, 1961–63; founding director, Black Arts Repertory Theatre, Harlem, New York, 1964–66; founding director, Spirit House, Newark, 1966–70; involved in Newark politics: organized the United Brothers, 1967, and Committee for Unified Newark, 1969–75; chair, Congress of Afrikan People, 1972–76. **Awards:** Whitney fellowship, 1961; Obie award, 1964; Guggenheim fellowship, 1965; Yoruba Academy fellowship, 1965; National Endowment for the Arts grant, 1966, award, 1981; Dakar Festival prize, 1966; Rockefeller grant, 1981, 1989; Before Columbus Foundation award, 1984; American Book award, 1984; Langston Hughes medal, 1989; Ferroni award, Italy, and foreign poet award, 1993; Playwright's award, Black Drama Festival, Winston-Salem, North Carolina, 1997; University of Connecticut Wallace Stevens poetry prize, 1998; One Hundred Black Men, Rutgers University, 1998. D.H.L.: Malcolm X College, Chicago, 1972. **Member:** Black Academy of Arts and Letters. **Address:** Department of Africana Studies, State University of New York, Stony Brook, New York 11794–4340, U.S.A.

PUBLICATIONS (earlier works as LeRoi Jones)

Poetry

April 13. New Haven, Connecticut, Penny Poems, 1959.
Spring and Soforth. New Haven, Connecticut, Penny Poems, 1960.
Preface to a Twenty Volume Suicide Note. New York, Totem-Corinth, 1961.
The Disguise. Privately printed, 1961.
The Dead Lecturer. New York, Grove Press, 1964.
Black Art. Newark, Jihad, 1966.
A Poem for Black Hearts. Detroit, Broadside Press, 1967.
Black Magic: Collected Poetry 1961–1967. Indianapolis, Bobbs Merrill, 1970.
It's Nation Time. Chicago, Third World Press, 1970.
In Our Terribleness: Some Elements and Meaning in Black Style, with Fundi (Billy Abernathy). Indianapolis, Bobbs Merrill, 1970.
Spirit Reach. Newark, Jihad, 1972.
African Revolution. Newark, Jihad, 1973.

Hard Facts. Newark, Peoples War, 1976.
Selected Poetry. New York, Morrow, 1979.
AM/TRAK. New York, Phoenix Book Shop, 1979.
Spring Song. Privately printed, 1979.
Reggae or Not! Bowling Green, New York, Contact Two, 1982.
Thoughts for You! Nashville, Winston Derek, 1984.
The Leroi Jones/Amiri Baraka Reader. New York, Thunder's Mouth Press, 1993.
Transbluesency: The Selected Poems of Amiri Baraka/LeRoi Jones (1961–1995). New York, Marsilio, 1995.
Funk Lore: New Poems, 1984–1995. Los Angeles, Littoral Books, 1996.

Plays

A Good Girl Is Hard to Find (produced Montclair, New Jersey, 1958; New York, 1965).
Dante (produced New York, 1961; as *The 8th Ditch,* produced New York, 1964). Included in *The System of Dante's Hell,* 1965.
The Toilet (produced New York, 1964). With *The Baptism,* New York, Grove Press, 1967.
Dutchman (produced New York, 1964; London, 1967). With *The Slave,* New York, Morrow, 1964; London, Faber, 1965.
The Slave (produced New York, 1964; London, 1972). With *Dutchman,* New York, Morrow, 1964; London, Faber, 1965.
The Baptism (produced New York, 1964; London, 1971). With *The Toilet,* New York, Grove Press, 1967.
Jello (produced New York, 1965). Chicago, Third World Press, 1970.
Experimental Death Unit #1 (also director: produced New York, 1965). Included in *Four Black Revolutionary Plays,* 1969.
A Black Mass (also director: produced Newark, 1966). Included in *Four Black Revolutionary Plays,* 1969.
Arm Yrself or Harm Yrself (produced Newark, 1967). Newark, Jihad, 1967.
Slave Ship: A Historical Pageant (produced Newark, 1967; New York, 1969). Newark, Jihad, 1967.
Madheart (also director: produced San Francisco, 1967). Included in *Four Black Revolutionary Plays,* 1969.
Great Goodness of Life (A Coon Show) (also director: produced Newark, 1967; New York, 1969). Included in *Four Black Revolutionary Plays,* 1969.
Home on the Range (produced Newark and New York, 1968). Published in *Drama Review* (New York), Summer 1968.
Police, published in *Drama Review* (New York), Summer 1968.
The Death of Malcolm X, in *New Plays from the Black Theatre,* edited by Ed Bullins. New York, Bantam, 1969.
Rockgroup, published in *Cricket,* December 1969.
Four Black Revolutionary Plays. Indianapolis, Bobbs Merrill, 1969; London, Calder and Boyars, 1971.
Insurrection (produced New York, 1969).
Junkies Are Full of (SHHH. . .), and *Bloodrites* (produced Newark, 1970). Published in *Black Drama Anthology,* edited by Woodie King and Ron Milner, New York, New American Library, 1971.
BA-RA-KA, in *Spontaneous Combustion: Eight New American Plays,* edited by Rochelle Owens. New York, Winter House, 1972.
Black Power Chant, published in *Drama Review* (New York), December 1972.
Columbia the Gem of the Ocean (produced Washington, D.C., 1973).
A Recent Killing (produced New York, 1973).
The New Ark's a Moverin (produced Newark, 1974).

The Sidnee Poet Heroical (also director: produced New York, 1975). New York, Reed, 1979.

S-1 (also director: produced New York, 1976). Included in *The Motion of History and Other Plays,* 1978.

The Motion of History (also director: produced New York, 1977). Included in *The Motion of History and Other Plays,* 1978.

The Motion of History and Other Plays (includes *S-1* and *Slave Ship*). New York, Morrow, 1978.

What Was the Relationship of the Lone Ranger to the Means of Production? (produced New York, 1979).

At the Dim' crackr Convention (produced New York, 1980).

Boy and Tarzan Appear in a Clearing (produced New York, 1981).

Weimar 2 (produced New York, 1981).

Money: A Jazz Opera, with George Gruntz, music by Gruntz (produced New York, 1982).

Primitive World, music by David Murray (produced New York, 1984).

General Hag's Skeezag. New York, Mentor, 1992.

Screenplays: *Dutchman,* 1967; *Black Spring,* 1967; *A Fable,* 1971; *Supercoon,* 1971.

Novel

The System of Dante's Hell. New York, Grove Press, 1965; London, MacGibbon and Kee, 1966.

Short Stories

Tales. New York, Grove Press, 1967; London, MacGibbon and Kee, 1969.

Other

Cuba Libre. New York, Fair Play for Cuba Committee, 1961.

Blues People: Negro Music in White America. New York, Morrow, 1963; London, MacGibbon and Kee, 1965.

Home: Social Essays. New York, Morrow, 1966; London, MacGibbon and Kee, 1968.

Black Music. New York, Morrow, 1968; London, MacGibbon and Kee, 1969.

Trippin': A Need for Change, with Larry Neal and A.B. Spellman. Newark, Cricket, 1969(?).

A Black Value System. Newark, Jihad, 1970.

Gary and Miami: Before and After. Newark, Jihad, n.d.

Raise Race Rays Raze: Essays since 1965. New York, Random House, 1971.

Strategy and Tactics of a Pan African Nationalist Party. Newark, National Involvement, 1971.

Beginning of National Movement. Newark, Jihad, 1972.

Kawaida Studies: The New Nationalism. Chicago, Third World Press, 1972.

National Liberation and Politics. Newark, Congress and Afrikan People, 1974.

Crisis in Boston!!!! Newark, Vita Wa Watu-People's War Publishing, 1974.

African Free School. Newark, Jihad, 1974.

Toward Ideological Clarity. Newark, Congress of Afrikan People, 1974.

The Creation of the New Ark. Washington, D.C., Howard University Press, 1975.

Selected Plays and Prose. New York, Morrow, 1979.

Daggers and Javelins: Essays 1974–1979. New York, Morrow, 1984.

The Autobiography of LeRoi Jones/Amiri Baraka. New York, Freundlich, 1984.

The Artist and Social Responsibility. N.p., Unity, 1986.

The Music: Reflections on Jazz and Blues, with Amina Baraka. New York, Morrow, 1987.

A Race Divided. New York, Emerge Communications, 1991.

Conversations with Amiri Baraka. Jackson, Mississippi, University Press of Mississippi, 1994.

Eulogies. New York, Marsilio, 1996.

The Autobiography of LeRoi Jones. Chicago, Lawrence Hill, 1997.

Home: Social Essays. Hopewell, New Jersey, Ecco Press, 1998.

Blues People: Negro Music in White America. New York, Morrow, 1999.

The Fiction of Leroi Jones/Amiri Baraka. Chicago, Lawrence Hill, 2000.

Editor, *Four Young Lady Poets.* New York, Totem-Corinth, 1962.

Editor, *The Moderns: New Fiction in America.* New York, Corinth, 1963; London, MacGibbon and Kee, 1965.

Editor, with Larry Neal, *Black Fire: An Anthology of Afro-American Writing.* New York, Morrow, 1968.

Editor, *African Congress: A Documentary of the First Modern Pan-African Congress.* New York, Morrow, 1972.

Editor, with Diane di Prima, *The Floating Bear: A Newsletter, Numbers 1–37.* La Jolla, California, Laurence McGilvery, 1974.

Editor, with Amina Baraka, *Confirmation: An Anthology of African American Women.* New York, Morrow, 1983.

*

Bibliography: *LeRoi Jones (Imamu Amiri Baraka): A Checklist of Works by and about Him* by Letitia Dace, London, Nether Press, 1971; *Ten Modern American Playwrights* by Kimball King, New York, Garland, 1982; *A LeRoi Jones (Amiri Baraka) Bibliography: A Keyed Research Guide to Works by LeRoi Jones and to Writing about Him and His Works* by Theodore R. Hudson, Washington, D.C., The Author, 2001.

Manuscript Collections: Howard University, Washington, D.C.; Beinecke Library, Yale University, New Haven, Connecticut; Lilly Library, Indiana University, Bloomington; University of Connecticut, Storrs; George Arents Research Library, Syracuse University, New York.

Critical Studies: *From LeRoi Jones to Amiri Baraka: The Literary Works* by Theodore Hudson, Durham, North Carolina, Duke University Press, 1973; *Baraka: The Renegade and the Mask* by Kimberly W. Benston, New Haven, Connecticut, Yale University Press, 1976, and *Imamu Amiri Baraka (LeRoi Jones): A Collection of Critical Essays* edited by Benston, Englewood Cliffs, New Jersey, Prentice Hall, 1978; *Amiri Baraka/LeRoi Jones: The Quest for a Populist Modernism* by Werner Sollors, New York, Columbia University Press, 1978; *Amiri Baraka,* Boston, Twayne, 1980, and ''Dreamers and Slaves-The Ethos of Revolution in Walcott and Leroi Jones,'' in *Critical Perspectives on Derek Walcott,* edited by Robert D. Hamner,

Washington, D.C., Three Continents, 1993, both by Lloyd W. Brown; *To Raise, Destroy, and Create: The Poetry, Drama, and Fiction of Imamu Amiri Baraka (LeRoi Jones)* by Henry C. Lacey, Troy, New York, Whitston, 1981; *Theatre and Nationalism: Wole Soyinka and LeRoi Jones* by Alain Ricard, Ife-Ife, Nigeria, University of Ife Press, 1983; *Amiri Baraka: The Kaleidoscopic Torch* edited by James B. Gwynne, New York, Steppingstones Press, 1985; *The Poetry and Poetics of Amiri Baraka: The Jazz Aesthetic* by William J. Harris, Columbia, University of Missouri Press, 1985; *Conscientious Sorcerers: The Black Postmodernist Fiction of Leroi Jones/Amiri Baraka, Ishmael Reed, and Samuel R. Delany* by Robert Elliot Fox, New York, Greenwood Press, 1987; *Amiri Baraka* by Bob Bernotas, New York, Chelsea House, 1991; *Schematic Fusion: An Essay on the Aesthetics of Leroi Jones* (dissertation) by Maurice Angus Lee, Madison, University of Wisconsin, 1993; ''The Black Arts Poets'' by William W. Cook, in *The Columbia History of American Poetry*, edited by Jay Parini and Brett C. Millier, New York, Columbia University Press, 1993; ''Tragedy Elegy Improvisation: Voices of Baraka, II'' by Fred Moten, in *Semiotics 1994*, edited by C.W. Spinks and John Deely, New York, Peter Lang, 1995; by Robert A. Lee, in *American Drama*, edited by Clive Bloom, New York, St. Martin's Press, 1995; *Playing the Audience: Amiri Baraka's Drama and the Performance Text* (dissertation) by Katherine A. Rodowsky, College Park, University of Maryland, 1995; *Three Citizens: Postmodern Identity in the Poetry of Amiri Baraka (Leroi Jones), Adrienne Rich, and James Wright* (dissertation) by Joseph William Heithaus, Indiana University, 1996; *African-American Poets* by Michael R. Strickland, Springfield, New Jersey, Enslow, 1996; *Taking It to the Streets: The Social Protest Theater of Luis Valdez and Amiri Baraka* by Harry J. Elam, Ann Arbor, University of Michigan Press, 1997.

Theatrical Activities: Director: several of his own plays.

Amiri Baraka comments:

(1970) I identify with the black school. My major theme? The evolution of harmony.

(1974) The first step in the United States is revolutionary democracy, then socialism now!

*   *   *

Amiri Baraka's assessment of his own career in the preface to *Black Magic: Collected Poetry 1961–1967* seems from this vantage remarkably accurate. He speaks of his development in these terms:

> You notice [in *The Dead Lecturer* and *Preface to a Twenty Volume Suicide Note*] the preoccupation with death, suicide in the early works. Always my own, caught up in the deathurge of this twisted society . . . .
>
> *Sabotage* [the third, unpublished volume] meant I had come to see the superstructure of filth Americans call their way of life, and wanted to see it fall . . . *Target Study* [the fourth, unpublished volume] is trying really to study, like bomber crews do the soon to be destroyed cities. Less passive now, less uselessly ''literary.''
>
> *Black Art* [the fifth] was the crucial seeing, the decisions, the actual move.

The cover image on *Black Magic* is a blue-eyed, blond-haired, deathly white voodoo doll stuck through the head, throat, heart, groin, and ankles with pins. Baraka's poetry speaks the racial stereotypes assumed by the European tradition but, out of politeness, not spoken of in high art. His crass honesty forces unspoken racism to the surface. Thus, the transactions among the various racial groups are rendered tense and uncomfortable. This is the unpleasant advantage of Baraka's art: the literary quality and the political content fuse.

Since the late 1960s Baraka's tone has been consistently ideological. He has appropriated various vocabularies of Marxism, which is to say the vocabularies of non-black theoreticians, but the ideology has never been consistent. Neither Baraka's art nor his astute social analysis has been more than superficially Marxist. The Marxist jargon, like the use of racial stereotypes, is a provocation, a way of bringing everyone's feelings out into the open. Baraka's poetry is fundamentally musical, not theoretical. Everything but the music is negotiable.

African-American music, which is the emotional and intellectual base of Baraka's poetry, is perhaps the most adequate and complete nongrammatical medium of knowledge to have been created, a medium that does not have its origin in a theoretical Logos. It is a medium not of particles arranged in rule-governed logical hierarchies but of autonomous entities acting freely. Of the music of Ornette Coleman and Cecil Taylor, Baraka writes, ''It considers the *total area* of its existence as a means to evolve, to move, as an intelligently shaped musical concept, from its beginning to its end. This total area is not merely the largely artificial considerations of bar lines and constantly stated chords, but the more musical considerations of rhythm, pitch, timbre, and melody.''

Baraka has been among a small group of poets who, since about 1960, have created a poetry responsible to the total area of its existence. Although the recognition of that area and its most exemplary articulations were the work of black musicians, the totality is not racial. It is distinguished precisely by its dual insistence upon inclusion and autonomy from those limited and limiting systems of music and language that have underwritten the development of European culture. It is in fact large enough, inclusive enough, that the racial issues—the wildly variant emotional systems of distinctive cultures—can arise and state their conflicting contents.

In terms of technique, Baraka's work develops from the projective verse of Charles Olson and Robert Creeley, which itself owed a great deal to the music of Charlie Parker and Miles Davis. It is a language under the control of neither grammar nor subject but of rhythm, breath, and ''the tone-leading of vowels,'' a phrase of Ezra Pound's that was central to the convergence producing the new American poetry. In ''Snake Eyes,'' for example, Baraka's mastery of the mode is clear:

> And what is meat
> to do, that is driven to its end
> by words? The frailest gestures
> grown like skirts around breathing.
>   We take
> unholy risks to prove
> we are what we cannot be. For instance,
>
> I am not even crazy.

The combination of high formality and casualness is a feature of the responsive medium that Baraka and his contemporaries—notable examples being Kenneth Irby, Robert Kelly, and Clayton Eshleman—inherited. Related significantly to music, the verse is still clearly based on speech forms. In the mid-1960s, however, Baraka's forms moved quickly in the direction of free jazz improvisation. In poems such as "Trespass into Spirit," "Form Is Emptiness," and "Vowels 2" formal possibilities that are almost exclusively musical begin to appear:

> The word
>   Raaaaaaaaaaaaaaaaaaaaaaaaaaaaaaaaaaaaaaaaaaaaaaaa
> in all its per
>
> mutations:
>   Raaaa
>   aaaaaaaaaaaaaaaaahhhhhhhhhhhh

The new language was not a moment in an input-output circuit ("A poem is energy transferred from where the poet got it, . . . by way of the poem itself to, all the way over to, the reader," as Charles Olson says) but an emergence from the autonomy of the poet as master of a total area of sound. This marks the most significant development in verse since World War II, an area explored by poets as diverse as Baraka himself, Ntozake Shange, the later Charles Olson, Robert Duncan, Jackson Mac Low, Clark Coolidge, and Charles Stein. In Baraka's later work this complete freedom of sound manages to include the full richness of the black vernacular. In "Jarman Said, 'Our Whole Universe Is Generated by a Rhythm,'" Baraka writes of the total area of artistic action in these terms:

> What is not funky is psychological, metaphysical
> is the religion of squares, pretending no one
> is anywhere.
> Everything gets hot, it is hot now, nothing cold exists
> and cold, is the theoretical line the pretended boundary
> where your eye and hand disappear into desire.

In an important sense the task at hand is to find community with this generative rhythm. The process no doubt involves conflict. Rhythm is a reconciliation of contention and justice. Baraka's testimony in this regard is of immense spiritual and cultural significance.

—Don Byrd

BARBOUR, Douglas

Nationality: Canadian. **Born:** Winnipeg, Manitoba, 21 March 1940. **Education:** Acadia University, Wolfville, Nova Scotia, B.A. in English 1962; Dalhousie University, Halifax, Nova Scotia, M.A. in English 1964; Queen's University, Kingston, Ontario (Canada Council Doctoral grant, 1967–68), Ph.D. in English 1976. **Family:** Married Sharon Nicoll in 1966. **Career:** Teacher of English, Alderwood Collegiate Institute, Toronto, 1968–69; assistant professor, 1969–77, associate professor, 1977–82, and since 1982 professor of English, University of Alberta, Edmonton. Editor, *Quarry,* Kingston, 1965–68; member of the editorial board, *White Pelican,* Edmonton, 1971–76; poetry editor, *Canadian Forum,* Toronto, 1978–80; member of the editorial board, since 1978, NeWest Press, Edmonton, and since 1979, Longspoon Press, Edmonton. Cofounder, with Stephen Scobie,

Re:soundings (sound poetry ensemble). **Address:** 11655 72nd Avenue, Edmonton, Alberta T6G 0B9, Canada.

PUBLICATIONS

Poetry

Land Fall. Montreal, Delta Canada, 1971.
A Poem as Long as the Highway. Kingston, Ontario, Quarry Press, 1971.
White. Fredericton, New Brunswick, Fiddlehead, 1972.
Songbook. Vancouver, Talonbooks, 1973.
He.&.She.&. Ottawa, Golden Dog Press, 1974.
Visions of My Grandfather. Ottawa, Golden Dog Press, 1977.
Shore Lines. Winnipeg, Turnstone Press, 1979.
Vision/Sounding. Toronto, League of Canadian Poets, 1980.
The Pirates of Pen's Chance: Homolinguistic Translations, with Stephen Scobie. Toronto, Coach House Press, 1981.
The Harbingers. Kingston, Ontario, Quarry Press, 1984.
Visible Visions: The Selected Poems of Douglas Barbour, edited by Smaro Kamboureli and Robert Kroetsch. Edmonton, Alberta, NeWest Press, 1984.
Story for a Saskatchewan Night. Red Deer, Alberta, Red Deer College Press, 1989.

Other

Worlds out of Words: The SF Novels of Samuel R. Delany. Frome, Somerset, Bran's Head, 1979.
Canadian Poetry Chronicle: A Comprehensive Review of Canadian Poetry Books. Kingston, Ontario, Quarry Press, 1985.
John Newlove and His Works. Toronto, ECW Press, 1992.
Daphne Marlatt and Her Works. Toronto, ECW Press, 1992.
bpNichol and His Works. Toronto, ECW Press, 1992.
Michael Ondaatje. New York, Twayne Publishers, 1993.

Editor, *The Story So Far Five.* Toronto, Coach House Press, 1978.
Editor, with Stephen Scobie, *The Maple Laugh Forever: An Anthology of Canadian Comic Poetry.* Edmonton, Alberta, Hurtig, 1981.
Editor, with Marni Stanley, *Writing Right: Poetry by Canadian Women.* Edmonton, Alberta, Longspoon Press, 1982.
Editor, *Three Times Five: Short Stories by Harris, Sawai, Stenson.* Edmonton, Alberta, NeWest Press, 1983.
Editor, *Selected and New Poems,* by Richard Sommer. Montreal, Véhicule Press, 1983.
Editor, with Phyllis Gotlieb, *Tesseracts 2: Canadian Science Fiction.* Victoria, British Columbia, Press Porcépic, 1987.
Editor, *Beyond TISH: New Writing Interviews Critical Essays.* Edmonton, NeWest Press, 1992.

*

Critical Studies: "Douglas Barbour: The Land Was Ours before We Were the Land's" by Wayne Tefs, in *Essays on Canadian Writing* (Downsview, Ontario), Summer/Fall 1980; "Shore Lines" by Andrew Brooks, in *Writers News Manitoba* (Winnipeg), December 1982; "'There's More Nothing to Say:' Unspeaking Douglas Barbour's *Story for a Saskatchewan Night*" in *Negation, Critical Theory, and Postmodern Textuality,* edited by D. Fischlin, Netherlands, Kluwer

Academic Publishers, 1994; by B. Leckie, in *English Studies in Canada,* 21(1), 1995.

Douglas Barbour comments:

To entertain possibility in the process of writing the poem—that is my desire. My early poems tended to begin in a clear perception of the outer world—that landscape, that event, that encounter—and I was trying to say something of what I had seen and felt. By the mid-1970s I had, in what I feel are my best works, moved to a more direct encounter with language. If I could listen carefully enough, I would hear something interesting and perhaps be able to transcribe it.

I try to write poems from a poetic stance that proposes that language is alive and not simply a ''tool'' to be ''used'' or ''manipulated'' for some ulterior purpose. I can only discover purpose in the process of writing if I am sufficiently open to what language speaks through me, which is not to say that poems do not mean but that in their wholly grounded being, when I am lucky enough to write a good one, they mean more complexly than ordinary discourse or any conscious ideas I might wish to purvey. It is always more interesting to follow the line of a poem's thought as it leads me on to new discoveries. One of the great arguments of such a poetry discovered and heard in openness is the value of such human openness before the world. This is an ideal, one I try in my writing to live up to.

(1995) In recent years my interest in exploration in language has led me closer to the kind of ''radical artifice'' Marjorie Perloff speaks of in her book of that title. Ways of subverting traditional lyric subjectivity while maintaining some sense of lyric music and rhythm make up one part of my interest in poetic form; another has to do with serial forms. But I still believe in what that great essayist Guy Davenport says: ''Language itself is continually an imaginative act.''

*   *   *

As an undergraduate at Acadia University, Douglas Barbour read and was influenced by William Carlos Williams and the American West Coast poets who published in *Tish.* He began to look for an escape from the language and form of the modernists and a way to replace order and knowledge with exploration and encounter. Lecturing at the Upper Canada Workshop in 1983, he explained that he had used deconstruction to achieve the necessary defamiliarization of language and text. He had discovered new perspectives in intertextual writing, or writing from a pretext, basing a new poem on rearranged elements of an old poem. For instance, the words '';rad os'' might be invented from the title *Paradise Lost* and included, to echo the original, in a new poem.

Barbour's preoccupation with language also led him to explore the possibilities of what was called ''sound poetry.'' He joined forces with Stephen Scobie, a friend and colleague of many years at the University of Alberta, to form Re:sounding, a sound poetry ensemble that has performed in North America and Europe.

The partners then collaborated on what they call homolinguistic translation in *The Pirates of Pen's Chance.* In an afterword they explained that ''these translations take us, as writers, in directions we would never have gone without the stimulus of this process. The poems are unlike any we would ever write in our own voices; they free us from *our* poems. When Tristan Tzara gave his 'recipe' for making a Dada poem by cutting words at random out of a newspaper, he concluded that 'The poem will resemble you.' He was right.''

The poems in *The Pirates of Pen's Chance* illustrate Robert Kroetsch's view that metonymy rather than metaphor is the key to postmodern writing. The poems represent three types of translation: (1) metonymic, in which words of the original text are replaced by words associated with them; (2) acrostic, in which the original text is spelled out either by the first letter of every word or by the first word in every line; and (3) structural, in which all of the words of the new poem are taken from the original text but are chosen by arbitrary methods. The extraordinary thing about these translations is that some are unusually musical, and many are moving. ''Anger Song No. 3,'' based on John Milton's sonnet ''On His Blindness,'' is a structural translation, with one word taken from each line of the original:

Anger Song No. 3

light dark

hide

useless Maker
he denied

Ask God
man's state

thousands rest
wait

In Barbour's selected poems, *Visible Visions,* poems from eight volumes of verse published from 1971 to 1981 appear with new poems. In both the old and new work Barbour displays his two main preoccupations: those of eye/I—perception and internalization; and those of breath/language—sound and meaning. He is deliberately a language poet, using puns and unusual arrangements of punctuation and lines on a page. Language is no longer a tool but a substance in itself. One can generalize to this extent: sharp, immediate images are reflected in sound and repetition.

Barbour is the grandson of a pioneer who became a painter in later life, a man who tried to capture the unique colors and feel of the western Canadian prairie. In the poems taken from *Visions of My Grandfather* the eschewing of capital letters and omission of apostrophes sometimes become confusing: '' & i move deeper into this poem without thinking how ill get to the end.'' The effect is too often prosaic and sometimes breathless. But others of the early poems, particularly those from *Songbook,* restore music to the dryness of postmodernism. Some of the songs are imagistic, like expanded haiku, while other are minimalist, showing the influence of Phyllis Webb, to whom several poems are dedicated. The poems from *White* appear to be an expansion of William Carlos Williams's poem ''Queen Ann's Lace,'' in the spirit of homolingual translation.

One of the grand themes that run through Barbour's selected poems is love—for his wife, for the landscape of the prairie, for the changing seasons. Another is his difficulty in making contact with other people. ''I am awkward among pain,'' he says in ''Song 2'' from *Songbook,* and, later, in ''Song 28,''

They tell me to write
a people poem/a poem
with people in it.
          Not the forest
in which they walk nor the sunset they watch

The poem ends with

> here/hear
> me my friends I love
> you. You
> are always near
> by. In the
> awkward songs where
> you don't appear.

Some of Barbour's later poems are described as "breath ghazals," a type of oriental lyric poetry usually dealing with love and having a distinctive pattern of rhyming, a form first exploited in Canadian poetry by Phyllis Webb. They reproduce the sounds of rain, of lovemaking, of a spring breeze in a beguiling way.

Barbour describes himself aptly in an afterword to *The Pirates of Pen's Chance:*

Douglas Barbour
born, not yet died. tried & not always found wanting. wanting poetry got language; language never languishes, even in translation. translation is what he eventually seeks, but while on this plane, enjoys: language, the listening thereto. to live is to listen: he tries. it is easily borne.

—Patience Wheatley

BARTLETT, Elizabeth

Nationality: British. **Born:** Deal, Kent, 28 April 1924. **Education:** Dover County School for Girls, 1935–39. **Family:** Married Denis Perkins in 1943; one son. **Career:** Clerk, Bells Ltd., 1940–41, Caffyns Ltd., 1941–42, and Barclays Bank, 1942–43, all Lewes, Sussex. Lecturer, Workers Education Association, Burgess Hill, Sussex, 1960–63; receptionist and secretary, West Sussex Health Authority, and home help, West Sussex Country Council, both Burgess Hill, 1966–86. **Awards:** Cheltenham Poetry Competition prize, 1982; Arts Council bursary, 1985; Cholmondeley award, 1996. **Address:** 17 St. John's Avenue, Burgess Hill, West Sussex RH15 8HJ, England.

PUBLICATIONS

Poetry

A Lifetime of Dying. Calstock, Peterloo, 1979.
Strange Territory. Calstock, Peterloo, 1983.
The Czar Is Dead. London, Rivelin Grapheme, 1986.
Instead of a Mass. Liverpool, Headland, 1991.
Look, No Face. Bradford, Redbeck Press, 1991.
Two Women Dancing. Newcastle upon Tyne, Bloodaxe Books, 1995.

Recording: *William Scammell and Elizabeth Bartlett,* Peterloo, 1984.

*

Critical Studies: Interview with Carol Rumens, in *Poetry Review,* 85(1), spring 1995; "Elizabeth Bartlett, Two Women Dancing" by A. Topping, in *Critical Survey* (Oxford), 8(2), 1996.

Elizabeth Bartlett comments:

The poems are linked by one obsession, which is a curiosity about people and their emotions, stimulated originally by a five-year stint of psychoanalysis, with its freedoms and disciplines and its exploration of self. I am drawn to people with maimed personalities because I know I am one myself. I write about what I know, but I also write about imaginary events and people, using whatever the poem needs for its own purpose. I trade in fear and delight, strength and weakness, hate and love, and I'm inclined to agree with Geoffrey Grigson that "the right place for writers of poems, in relation to themselves as poem-writers, is in their poems."

I cannot explain a lifelong passion for this private art, and I have no academic background or qualifications of any kind. The poetry world has been reasonably kind to a rank outsider. I cannot think of anything that has pleased me more than being included in *The Faber Book of Twentieth Century Women's Poetry.*

*   *   *

The strength of Elizabeth Bartlett's poetry lies in its concerns and compassion. It is not poetry of verbal or stylistic innovation. It has a controlled speaking voice whose narratives tend to seize the reader by the lapel after the manner of the Ancient Mariner. This often happens at the outset, as in "Salad Dreams," which begins,

> I am like the lady who dreamed
> she prepared a salad for her guests
> and grated her own skin over it,

or in "Voyeur," which begins,

> Watching from the bed, with a bleeding cunt
> and gin-painted nipples, she saw at last
> what he meant about having had a certain
> nobility in his youth.

The world of Bartlett's poetry is not always a comfortable one, stemming from a world some of us would rather pretend were not there but which in her work in a doctor's office and in social services she has encountered and refused to look away from. It is an intensely and uncompromisingly physical world of blood, bowels, sickness, vomit, menses, and semen, in which people are often deranged. In this world the day of the death of the czar of all Russia is remembered as that when

> Menarche and murder link with fear
> in my mind.

It is a world sometimes on the edge of the precipice of insanity, where the "indefinable odour he carried round with him" was "the smell of loneliness."

What makes the poems acceptable is the compassionate and humane concern that underlies them. The poem "A Plea for Mercy" does not ask God to remake the world or anything so fundamentally unreasonable. All it asks is that some respect be shown and some peace allowed:

From dormitories
to geriatric homes and all the institutions in between,

a fair fantasy, a brief respite, and a dreamless sleep,
before the matrons, doctors, screws and curates muscle in.

It is a plea for a world in which we are allowed the fantasies and illusions that make it bearable and a cri de coeur against the dreaded tendency to institutionalize. As with Willy Loman in Arthur Miller's *Death of a Salesman,* attention should be paid.

It is not, it must be said, a poetry that celebrates the bloody awful but one demanding that compassionate attention be paid. It reveals a world of natural and common human concerns and sensibilities beneath that from which we tend to avert our eyes. Bartlett's poetry is not designed to shock or dismay. Rather, it arouses understanding and recognition and from these compassion. To misquote what is now almost a poetic commonplace, "The poetry is in the compassion."

—John Cotton

BAUGH, Edward

Nationality: Jamaican. **Born:** Edward Alston Cecil Baugh, Port Antonio, 1936. **Education:** University of the West Indies, Mona. **Family:** Married Sheila Baugh. **Career:** Professor of English, University of the West Indies, Mona. Has had several visiting professorships in the United States and Canada. **Address:** University of the West Indies, Mona, Department of English, Kingston 7, Jamaica.

PUBLICATIONS

Poetry

A Tale from the Rainforest. Kingston, Jamaica, Sandberry Press, 1988.

Other

West Indian Poetry, 1900–1970: A Study in Cultural Decolonisation. Kingston, Jamaica, Savacou Publications, 1971.
Derek Walcott: Memory As Vision: Another Life. London, Longman, 1978.

Editor, *Critics on Caribbean Literature.* London, Allen and Unwin, and New York, St. Martin's Press, 1978.
Editor, *Language and Literature in the Commonwealth Caribbean.* Kingston, Jamaica, West Indian Association for Commonwealth Literature and Language Studies, 1979.
Editor, with Mervyn Morris, *Caribbean Theatre.* Kingston, Jamaica, West Indian Association for Commonwealth Literature and Language Studies, 1986.
Editor, *The Caribbean Poem.* Kingston, Jamaica, West Indian Association for Commonwealth Literature and Language Studies, 1989.
Editor, *It Takes a Mighty Fire: Poems,* by H.D. Carberry. Kingston, Jamaica, Ian Randle, 1995.

*   *   *

Edward Baugh is known internationally as an insightful critic of West Indian literature, but he is also a compelling poet. He was one of those included in *Seven Jamaican Poets* (1971), and groups of his poems have appeared since then in *Focus, From Our Yard,* and *The Penguin Book of Caribbean Verse.* Several individual poems are widely admired and anthologized, among them "Truth and Consequence," "The Carpenter's Complaint," and "The Warner Woman."

Baugh's collection *A Tale from the Rainforest* (1988) is especially interested in words that try to efface themselves and in the ironies of human self-exposure. The very first lines pin down the dilemma: "This poem contemplates a time / beyond the consoling agony of words." "Imagine" expresses fond dreams of a time before language, when there was "only gesture that admits no ambiguity." These poems, in complaining against their own medium, imagine worlds beyond or before words, but such is not our world.

Pivoting on the word "gesture," Baugh in some poems turns his attention to drama, that is, to words enmeshed in the world of action and reaction. "Truth and Consequences"—the emphasis is squarely on the "and"—considers a minor player in Shakespeare's *Julius Caesar.* Beset by a mob, the man protests, " . . . I'm Cinna the poet. I never meddled in politics!" But as Baugh comments, the mob knew better, shouting, "Then tear him . . . for his bad verses!" So the poem draws its lesson: "there's no such thing as *only* literature.' / Every line commits you."

Two other poems draw on Shakespeare to reflect upon a declaration by Hamlet: "I am very proud, revengeful, ambitious." Baugh takes this as a revelation of the prince's shocked self-discovery but understands why Claudius and Polonius mistake it for playacting. For "who would believe him? What, the Lord Hamlet? Such a capital chap?" As a group, these Shakespeare poems state the collection's troublesome axioms: every line commits you, but no one believes your revelations.

Baugh never flinches from the recognition that even poets cannot find the words for those they love or those they lose, which is the subject of his most moving work. The poem "Words" unforgettably depicts the moment when a mother and son who share a passion for words (in fact, her legacy to him) are confronted with the unspeakable and find that it takes the form of a word. In "Small Town Story" the poet himself is the "capital chap" unknown to his fellows:

Lectern-glib, tuxedo-smooth
    At after-dinner speech, I find
    No word for mates with whom I roared
The sun to sleep in june-plum days.

Among the fine portrait poems and elegies that dominate the second half of the book, several are concerned with effectually speaking the true word. This is explicit in "For Simon Cole," "The Pulpit Eulogists of Frank Worrell," and especially "Yard-Boy," an homage to a family servant that ends like this: "he polished our shoes. / And I polish these words / from which nothing / accrues to him . . . / and this, I insist, / is a tribute."

Baugh commands many registers of tone. There is plenty of comedy in his work, and there is also the miraculously balanced emotional weight of "Ingrid Bergman's Hat-Brim at the End of Casablanca," a poem even better than its title. Perhaps his greatest tonal resource is his command of spoken Jamaican, arguably the supplest variety of English to be found in the Caribbean. There are no so-called dialect poems here, but even many of the poems that seem to be in Standard English move to discernible Jamaican rhythms. And when the language is entirely Jamaican, Baugh deploys quite distinct voices. Different manners of Jamaican speech serve to express bruised feelings in "The Carpenter's Complaint," bitter, double-edged satire in "Nigger Sweat," and sweet ruminations in "Getting There," a poem about driving perilous roads to visit the tenth muse, a Kingston girl who has moved up into the hills.

Readers may first notice the engagement with Shakespeare, but the collection also makes apparent Baugh's close links with other Caribbean poets. There is certainly an affinity with the magnificent sustained elegy of Ian McDonald's *Mercy Ward*. Baugh shares, too, Dennis Scott's habit of direct talk about what poems are for. "Cold Comfort," an extraordinary poem about reading Philip Larkin in the Caribbean, is certainly part of the ongoing conversation that includes both Mervyn Morris's "Literary Evening: Jamaica" and Scott's "More Poem."

Baugh's poems are funny, intelligent, probing, and full of profound affection. By temperament a private poet, Baugh keeps finding himself in public and still manages to tell the private truth.

—Laurence A. Breiner

BAYBARS, Taner

Nationality: British. **Born:** Nicosia, Cyprus, 18 June 1936. **Education:** Educated privately and at the Turkish Lycée, Nicosia. **Military Service:** Royal Air Force, 1954–55. **Family:** Married Kristin Hughes-Stanton in 1959 (divorced 1977); one daughter. **Career:** Books assistant, 1956–66, book exhibition assistant, 1966–67, periodicals assistant, 1967–72, head of overseas reviews scheme, 1972–81, in design production and publishing department, 1981–82, and book promotion officer, 1983—, British Council, London. **Agent:** MHA Literary Agents, 62 Grafton Way, London W1P 5LD, England. **Address:** 2 rue de l'Eveque, 34360 Saint-Chinian, France.

PUBLICATIONS

Poetry

Mendilin Ucundalier (Corners of a Handkerchief). Nicosia, Cardak Yayinevi, 1953.
To Catch a Falling Man. Lowestoft, Suffolk, Scorpion Press, 1963.
Susila in the Autumn Woods. Rushden, Northamptonshire, Sceptre Press, 1974.
Narcissus in a Dry Pool. London, Sidgwick and Jackson, 1978.
Pregnant Shadows. London, Sidgwick and Jackson, 1981.
Selected Poems. Istanbul, Yapi Kredi, 1997.
Fox and the Cradle Makers. Montpellier, Mossy Well Press, 2000.

Novel

A Trap for the Burglar. London, Owen, 1965.

Other

Plucked in a Far-Off Land: Images in Self Biography. London, Gollancz, 1970.

Editor, with Osman Türkay, *Modern Turkish Poetry.* London, Modern Poetry in Translation, 1971.

Translator, *Selected Poems of Nazim Hikmet.* London, Cape, 1967; New York, Humanities Press, 1968.
Translator, *The Moscow Symphony and Other Poems,* by Nazim Hikmet. London, Rapp and Whiting, 1970; Chicago, Swallow Press, 1971.
Translator, *The Day before Tomorrow,* by Nazim Hikmet. Oxford, Carcanet, 1972.
Translator, *The Snowy Day/Karli bir gün,* by Ezra Jack Keats. London, Bodley Head, 1980.
Translator, *Peter's Chair/Peter'in sandalyasi,* by Ezra Jack Keats. London, Bodley Head, 1980.

*

Critical Studies: "Voice Production" by Frederick Grubb, in *Poetry Review* (London), 1964; "Bigger Than Both of Us" by Bernard Share, in *Irish Times* (Dublin), 12 June 1965; *The Poet Speaks* by Peter Orr, London, Routledge, 1966; "Plucked Untimely" by Raymond Gardner, in *The Guardian* (London), 19 May 1970; "Flame by Flame" by Peter Lewis, in *Times Literary Supplement* (London), 3 October 1978.

Taner Baybars comments:

In my view a poem is the culmination of an intense experience that could not be expressed in any other form. If it could, then it would cease to be a poem, although it might retain the shape of a poem. Also, because of its intense nature a poem is essentially short. There is an obvious difference between poetry and verse, but that difference nowadays is almost always ignored.

* * *

Taner Baybars is a Cypriot whose first book of poems, written in Turkish, was published in Nicosia in 1953. Going to England twelve years later with the expressed intention of studying law (he soon gave up the idea), he decided to stay in London and has adopted English as his literary language with quite remarkable effect. If he experienced any difficulties in writing his poems in a second language, he has enjoyed an advantage over his British contemporaries in that he has remained free of group pressures and influences and has never shown the slightest inclination to follow prevailing fashions in diction or style. His poems, successful or otherwise, have always been quite unlike anyone else's.

The poems in *To Catch a Falling Man* are arranged in chronological order so that it is possible to trace Baybars's development as a poet throughout the volume. The collection begins with the description of a cycle journey through the English countryside, and the early pieces reflect a simplicity and clarity of vision allied to an unusually sophisticated and well-informed outlook. These qualities are reinforced by a creative mind that enables Baybars to evoke the sense in such phrases as "the coquettish wind perambulating in the wheels" or "the waves unkiss the cliff." Though his themes are quotidian— the demolition of an old house, taking barbitone for sleep, the end of a musical concert, spelling out his name, chopping down a tree, or even the sound of a key turning in the lock—he somehow contrives to surround them with a sinister atmosphere, as in ''The Oracle,'' his poem about a computer:

> We are much honoured; we hold conferences and
> discuss what the most fitting question should be;
> when we find it we march and surround the machine;

> the problem is fed in, the drone irregularly
> distends, no answer is laid. We grow old and visit
> every day the clean, compact brain and wait.

In Baybars's later work the simplicity of his earlier style gives way to a search for the unexpected, for what goes on below the surface of human relationships, for the motives beneath the conversation, for the realities underlying appearances. ''Demolishing a House,'' for example, demonstrates Baybars's skill at piling detail upon detail without overwhelming the poem:

> Yet while I ate and poised the fork in the air,
> the noise of a drill shivered the glass facade,
> the fake plants shook, too, a little afraid.
> I had to open my mouth to let the noise out.
> Then I heard the crash of another falling wall.

Narcissus in a Dry Pool begins where *To Catch a Falling Man* concludes stylistically. The individual nature of Baybars's enquiry into the phenomena of existence and his odd and sometimes bizarre approach to his subject lend a sort of piquancy to his poems. For a single volume there is a wide range of styles and types of writing, from the three-line haiku to a series of love poems, ''Explorations,'' to ''The Loneliness of Columbus,'' a dramatic monologue. The description in ''Circumcision Just before Puberty'' leaves nothing to the imagination, but it is nevertheless handled with extraordinary delicacy and understanding. The group of poems ''for Susila Jane,'' his daughter, manifest a new preoccupation, that of observing her gradual introduction to the external world and her development through touch, taste, sight, and smell:

> Seeing your own reflection on a doorknob
> you begin to utter your name, then stop
> in that conflux of brass stained by my hand.
> Who? I hold you against the windowglass.

> You exclaim: Dark! I put you down. You live
> in a galaxy of sounds absorbed by your tongue
> and keeping your name a secret to your tongue
> and grow in full awareness of others.

What seems to impress him most in this exploration of infancy and childhood is the paradox of innocence combined with an almost frightening kind of inner certainty arising from the need for self-fulfillment.

Perhaps most interesting of all are the poems devoted to the relationship between man and woman, the man always being Baybars himself and the woman a particular woman drawn from his private circle. They are, of course, love poems in every sense of the word, yet for Baybars the love relationship is complicated, for his partners are not merely women or lovers. Each, willingly or unwillingly, acquires

a symbolic quality that takes its idiosyncratic scope from an aspect of Baybars's experience—for example, his native country, his childhood, his family, or his adolescence—and that inevitably defines the relationship for him.

—Howard Sergeant

BEAVER, Bruce (Victor)

Nationality: Australian. **Born:** Sydney, New South Wales, 14 February 1928. **Education:** Attended Manly Public School and Sydney Boy's High School. **Family:** Married Kathleen Brenda Bellam, 1963. **Career:** Lived in New Zealand, 1958–62. Has worked as radio program arranger, wages clerk, railway survey assistant, farm laborer, proofreader. Since 1964 freelance writer. **Awards:** *Poetry Magazine* award, Sydney, 1963; Commonwealth literary fellowship, 1967; Captain Cook Bi-Centenary prize, 1970; Grace Leven prize, 1970; Poetry Society of Australia award 1970; Patrick White award, 1982; F.A.W. Christopher Brennan award; A.M. award, 1991. **Address:** 14–16 Malvern Avenue, Manly, New South Wales 2095, Australia.

PUBLICATIONS

Poetry

Under the Bridge. Sydney, Beaujon Press, 1961.
Seawall and Shoreline. Sydney, South Head Press, 1964.
Open at Random. Sydney, South Head Press, 1967.
Letters to Live Poets. Sydney, South Head Press, 1969.
Lauds and Plaints. Poems (1968–1972). Sydney, South Head Press, 1974.
Odes and Days. Sydney, South Head Press, 1975.
Death's Directives. Sydney, New Poetry, 1978.
As It Was. St. Lucia, University of Queensland Press, 1979.
Selected Poems. Sydney, Angus and Robertson, 1979.
Charmed Lives. St. Lucia, University of Queensland Press, 1988.
New and Selected Poems (1960–1990). St. Lucia, University of Queensland Press, 1991.
Anima and Other Poems. St. Lucia, University of Queensland Press, 1994.
Poets and Others. Rose Bay, New South Wales, Australia, Brandl and Schlesinger, 1999.

Novels

The Hot Spring. Sydney, Horvitz, 1965.
You Can't Come Back. Adelaide, Rigby, 1966.

Other

Headlands: Prose Sketches. St. Lucia, University of Queensland Press, 1986.

*

Critical Studies: *New Impulses in Australian Poetry* edited by Thomas W. Shapcott and Rodney Hall, St. Lucia, University of Queensland Press, 1968; ''Gift-Bearing Hands: The Poetry of Bruce

Beaver'' by Craig Powell, in *Quadrant* (Sydney), XII, 5, 1968; ''Bruce Beaver's Poetry'' by Robert D. Fitzgerald in *Meanjin* (Melbourne), September 1969; ''New Australian Poetry'' by James Tulip, in *Southerly* (Sydney), 1970; *Poets on Record 7,* St. Lucia, University of Queensland Press, 1972; ''The 'Livres composés' of Bruce Beaver'' by J. and R.M. Beston, in *WLWE* (Perth), April 1975; ''Images of Ideas, Ideas of Images'' by W.H. New, in *Poetry Australia* (New South Wales), 64, 1977; ''The Poetry of Bruce Beaver'' by Beate Josephi, in *Quadrant* (Sydney), 146, 1979; ''Recent Australian Poetry: The Ordinary and the Extraordinary: Rhyll McMaster, Andrew Taylor, Bruce Beaver, Robert Harris and Jan Owen'' by Alan Gould, in *Quadrant* (Victoria, Australia), 30(10), October 1986; ''To a Live Poet: Bruce Beaver'' by Lawrence Bourke, in *Southerly* (Southerly, Australia), 52(3), 1992; in *Southerly* (Southerly, Australia), 55(1), Autumn 1995.

*   *   *

In his bucolic retrospect *As It Was,* Bruce Beaver writes that ''I had and have no special love of human nature. Pity and disgust are the two emotions it stirs oftenest in me.'' But this characteristically severe self-criticism is belied by his poetry, which reveals a sensibility intuitively and compassionately responsive to ordinary people. He has a ''negative capability,'' one might say, that together with his intense appreciation of the sensory world endorses his claim to be at heart a Keats man. Like Kenneth Slessor a generation earlier, Beaver is a Sydney-sider, but it is as much the pathos of the lives around him as the evanescent moods and spirit of the place that occupies him in his typically low-key, ruminative free verse poems: a man dying unheeded in a crowded office, a flautist banished to a laundry, an aged fisherman and his clan, an eccentric writing ''Eternity'' on Sydney's pavements, a young poet who cries ''My light has gone out!'' as he leaps to his death.

This is not to deny that much of Beaver's poetry is confessional in mode, and at times the act of writing has played a crucially therapeutic role for him. In *As It Was* he vividly recalls his two attempts at suicide and some of his experiences in mental homes, and in an interview with Thomas Shapcott he describes how he wrote *Letters to Live Poets* ''feverishly one poem a day for seven weeks,'' haunted by the fear that he might soon ''turn into a vegetable.'' But Beaver's introspective voyages seem less obsessive than those of some of his American models, such as Robert Lowell or John Berryman, and are more modestly self-deprecating and more genuinely dialogic. In *As It Was* he remarks that ''I was born middle-aged,'' and the vatic persona he projects might be caricatured as a cross between Brennan's romantic Wanderer and T.S. Eliot's Tiresias, a slightly ineffectual, ''melancholy . . . / Tiresias in two minds.'' But Beaver also sees through the ''Shelleyean facade of self-negation,'' and the cumulative effect is of a poet struggling to sustain a balance between self-exploration and participation, between mental and external landscapes, between anguish and thanksgiving.

Letters to Live Poets, with which Beaver achieved recognition as a significant voice in Australian poetry, emanates from the years when opposition to the Vietnam War was escalating, and it is probably his most anguished and politically confrontationist work. It consists of thirty-four free verse epistles addressed in the first place to Frank O'Hara—whose death by being ''crushed on the littered sands'' by a dune buggy epitomized the vulnerability of humanist values—and more broadly to ''the community / world-wide, of live, mortal poets.'' Letter XV is at once a powerful indictment of a ''war

spun out like an incredible / competition between two soap / and cereal kings'' and a poignant expression of vatic impotence: ''how may I, tentatively sane, comment sensibly upon / a wider spread insanity?'' Letter XII exposes the system indirectly through its effects on the poet as society's conscience, on the poet on antidepressants, marginalized like the park methadone drinkers or the imprisoned Ezra Pound, fearful of reverting to the state in which he had ''walked on hands and knees / like Blake's Nebuchadnezzar, scenting the pit.'' Satirical sallies against the banality, complacency, and ugliness of modern consumerism are frequent, occasionally bordering on the grotesque in the manner of A.D. Hope: ''young wives drab, / swelling with hormones,'' old women painted like ''superannuated tigers,'' or executives like ''white worms that seethe in filth.'' Yet considering that Beaver wrote *Letters to Live Poets* in crisis, it is remarkably varied in subject matter, tone, and rhythm. And partly perhaps because he takes seriously Pound's imagist dictum ''No ideas but in things,'' the poetic meditations in which he ''tr[ies] again to learn / how to accept a mutable world'' are all rendered concretely familiar. Like Beaver himself in Letter XIX, where he declares in appropriately measured cadences that ''I welcome the anonymity of middle years, years of the spreading / girth and conversational prolixity,'' on balance these poems are clear-sighted but accepting.

In the interview with Shapcott, Beaver talks of *Lauds and Plaints,* which took him five years to write, as his ''best book'' and one in which he was ''able to include my religious attitudes.'' The book certainly extends his poetic register considerably. Some of the poems (''time to engage / with the radioed day's news / sports results road accidents / election speeches bank robbings / such a busy day to stifle / a yawn at'') retain O'Hara's impromptu casualness or Jack Kerouac's ''words / . . . staccato as jazz notes.'' But more typically the tone is lyrical, and the quotidian is handled with the imaginative daring espoused by Robert Bly. And although Beaver carries his learning lightly, the sophisticated notes of Rainer Maria Rilke and Eliot are often heard. In IV a visit to a cave evokes thoughts of the ''terminal facts'' of womb and tomb and of Blake's ''Urizen trapped in giant / adamantine / obsidian selfhood.'' In VI, inspired by Rilke, Beaver sweeps the ''beautiful / and the hideous horses of creativity'' through several sea changes with Viennese abandon. Sometimes Eliot's influence can be deadening, but more often his cadences have been felicitously assimilated, as in XIX, which begins with ''to stand hushed an hour or two / in that garden is not to redeem / time.'' This poem, which describes how in an Australian ''autumn's summery spring at winter's / wane'' the speaker fancies that he catches ''an oblique glimpse'' of the ''goddess Kore,'' perhaps comes closest to encapsulating the essence of Beaver's religious faith in ''the ordinary miracle of / here and now.'' There is, too, a love of paradox and oxymoron in these poems, of ''shallow mysteries,'' ''a day's eternity,'' or ''empty plenitude.'' And there is a higher incidence of mellifluous phrases than in the earlier volumes, sometimes in the syntactic mode of Berryman or Gerard Manley Hopkins, for example, in glimpses ''of opened to spicy air serene / casements'' or, on a more Australian note, in the ''whipcrack and till-ring of birdsongs.'' At times, however, romanticism and nostalgia are summarily deflated, and a view is merely ''as beautiful as / itself.''

Technically a *prosimetrum* interspersed with family photos, *As It Was* is at once an honest and at times humorous autobiography in the tradition ultimately of William Wordsworth's *The Prelude,* a warm tribute to relatives whose kindness ''helped me continue to live,'' and an evocation of a bygone age of comic books and Dad and Dave and Judy Garland. This is a common impulse in Australian letters, perhaps because the past seems more evanescent than in Europe. The early scenes are set in Manly, but some of the episodes on the uncle's farm seem Wordsworthian even in cadence: "The hawk— for hawk it was—twitched its head to left and right / at the flat concussions of unexpected rifle fire." Others, like the glimpse of a girl spearing eels, are more Keatsian in feel: "I . . . stood there musing / how I so full of Endymion should come upon a true / Diana." More interesting perhaps as a cultural record than as poetry, the volume is full of insights into the Australian mateship syndrome, the sexual imperative, and the alienation of a generation worn down by war, the Depression, and "barely fertile land" and often leading "totally bewildered lives."

Charmed Lives, a later work, is in many respects Beaver's most accomplished. The ardor of *Letters to Live Poets* has mellowed into an acceptance that seems a shade complacent, and there is a new preoccupation with old age and death. But assumed American voices obtrude less frequently, the cultural register is wider, and one is conscious of an often playful exultation in the hard-won mastery of words. The opening "Verse Biography of Raine Maria Rilke," though less effective as a period retrospect than *As It Was,* convincingly portrays the poet as a kindred spirit who "preferred a moderate mania / and a fair degree of poetic constancy / to a normality more nominal than actual." The best poems are in the middle sections titled "Silhouettes" and "Solos," many of them on simple matters like picking apples, flying kites, and singing in the rain. Beaver's insight into people is as keen as ever: "I watch the faces of acquaintances / and see in them a lost child here or there." "A Pair" describes how a promiscuous mother and prudish daughter rally to each other's aid in times of trouble. Many of the poems, as the section titles imply, invite our contemplation of poetry in relation to painting or music, as if to emphasize the humanist end of all of the arts. "Stroll" is a Blakean dream vision in which the poet finds himself in eternity "accepted as a fellow artist" by Edward Elgar and Ralph Vaughan Williams. "A Brave Music" finds the "unsolvable enigma / of life and death, its razor edge of severance / and trumpet summons to the lone review" expressed in a rhapsody by Butterworth. In "Metamorphosis" age has transformed a "slim dark cousin" from a "Modigliani" into a "Rubens." In general, the Keatsian intensity with which the sensory world is evoked confirms the earlier impression that Beaver's art is less often symbolist than sacramental. *Charmed Lives* ends with a series of dramatic monologues in which an androgynous Tiresias appears in different masks, times, and company to suggest the ubiquity of the poetic imagination in its quest for truth. Conceptually, therefore, this last series, though perhaps a little coy in places, is organically related to the earlier sections and brings the volume to an appropriate crescendo.

—J.M.Q. Davies

BELL, Marvin (Hartley)

Nationality: American. **Born:** Brooklyn, New York, 3 August 1937. **Education:** Alfred University, New York, B.A. 1958; Syracuse University, New York, 1958; University of Chicago, M.A. 1961; University of Iowa, Iowa City, M.F.A. 1963. **Military Service:** U.S. Army, 1964–65: Foreign Military Training Officer. **Family:** Married 1) Mary Mammosser in 1958; 2) Dorothy Murphy in 1961; two sons. **Career:** Visiting lecturer, 1965, assistant professor, 1966–69, associate professor, 1969–75, since 1975 professor of English, and since 1986 Flannery O'Connor Professor of Letters, University of Iowa. Visiting professor, Oregon State University, Corvallis, summer 1969, Goddard College, Plainfield, Vermont, summer 1970, University of Hawaii, Honolulu, 1981, and University of Washington, Seattle, winter and spring 1982; Fulbright scholar, in Yugoslavia, 1983, and Australia, 1986; Lila Wallace-Reader's Digest Writing Fellow, University of Redlands, California, 1991–93; visiting fellow, Saint Mary's College, Orinda, California, 1994–95, and Hampden-Sydney College, 1998–99; Woodrow Wilson Visiting Fellow, Nebraska-Wesleyan University, 1996–97. Editor, *Statements* magazine, Rochester, New York and Iowa City, 1959–64; poetry editor, *North American Review,* Mount Vernon, Iowa, 1964–69, and *Iowa Review,* 1969–71. Since 1997 senior poetry editor, *The Pushcart Prize.* Columnist ("Homage to the Runner"), *American Poetry Review,* Philadelphia, 1975–78, 1990–92. **Awards:** Lamont Poetry Selection award, 1969; Bess Hokin prize (*Poetry,* Chicago), 1969; Emily Clark Balch prize (*Virginia Quarterly Review*), 1970; Guggenheim fellowship, 1975; National Endowment for the Arts grant, 1978, 1984; *American Poetry Review* prize, 1982; Award in Literature, American Academy of Arts and Letters, 1994. **Address:** Writers Workshop, University of Iowa, Iowa City, Iowa 52242, U.S.A.

PUBLICATIONS

Poetry

Two Poems. Iowa City, Hundred Pound Press, 1965.
Things We Dreamt We Died For. Iowa City, Stone Wall Press, 1966.
Poems for Nathan and Saul. Mount Vernon, Iowa, Hillside Press, 1966.
A Probable Volume of Dreams. New York, Atheneum, 1969.
The Escape into You: A Sequence. New York, Atheneum, 1971.
Woo Havoc. Somerville, Massachusetts, Barn Dream Press, 1971.
Residue of Song. New York, Atheneum, 1974.
Stars Which See, Stars Which Do Not See. New York, Atheneum, 1977.
These Green-Going-to-Yellow. New York, Atheneum, 1981.
Segues: A Correspondence in Poetry, with William Stafford. Boston, Godine, 1983.
Drawn by Stones, by Earth, by Things That Have Been in the Fire. New York, Atheneum, 1984.
New and Selected Poems. New York, Atheneum, 1987.
Annie-Over, with William Stafford. Rexburg, Idaho, Honeybrook Press, 1988.
Iris of Creation. Port Townsend, Washington, Copper Canyon Press, 1990.
The Book of the Dead Man. Port Townsend, Washington, Copper Canyon Press, 1994.
Ardor: The Book of the Dead Man. Port Townsend, Washington, Copper Canyon Press, 1997.
Poetry for a Midsummer's Night. Seattle, Seventy Fourth Street Productions, 1998.
Wednesday. N.p., Ireland, Salmon Publishing, 1998.

Recording: *The Self and the Mulberry Tree,* Watershed, 1977.

Other

Old Snow Just Melting: Essays and Interviews. Ann Arbor, University of Michigan Press, 1983.
A Marvin Bell Reader: Selected Poetry and Prose. Hanover, New Hampshire, University Press of New England, 1994.

Editor, *Iowa Workshop Poets 1963.* Iowa City, Statements-Midwest Magazine, 1963.

*

Critical Studies: ''The Poetry of Marvin Bell'' by Peter Elfed Lewis, in *Stand* (Newcastle upon Tyne), xiii, 4, 1972; ''Marvin Bell; 'Time's Determinant/Once, I Knew You''' by Arthur Oberg, in *American Poetry Review* (Philadelphia), May-June 1976; ''Not Life So Proud to Be Life: Snodgrass, Rothenberg, Bell, and the Counter-Revolution'' by Larry Levis, in *American Poetry Review* (Philadelphia), January/February 1989; ''Marvin Bell, *New and Selected Poems*'' by Greg Kuzma, in *Prairie Schooner* (Lincoln, Nebraska), summer 1989; ''Exile and Cunning: The Recent Poetry of Marvin Bell'' by Daniel McGuiness, in *Antioch Review* (Yellow Springs, Ohio), summer 1990; ''Containing the Other: Marvin Bell's Recent Poetry'' by Richard Jackson, in *North American Review,* 280(1), Jan/Feb 1995.

*　　*　　*

Marvin Bell's work satisfies a need for every kind of laugh and reminds us that comedy is at least as tough as tragedy. From the outset, however, he has been modulating the balance of amusement and profundity in his poetry. Early on his wit was, by turns, clever and probing, tending at one moment to trivialize his work, at another to deepen it. But over the long haul he has exerted mature control.

His method stresses spontaneity. Verse sections are rarely linked by any kind of discursive rhetoric but often by semiconscious associations arising from imagery and diction. He may organically combine a cliché, an aphoristic biblical phrase, and a straightforward ethical assertion. Trusting his subconscious, Bell does not finally patch his work together with accessible generalizations. He has said that he prefers to go on finding the meaning of a poem after he has finished it. But he has devised structures for his poems that render them both artfully finished and in progress. At worst, and infrequently, a poem is dubiously cryptic, maybe even a willful conundrum, as with ''The Giving In'' (*A Probable Volume of Dreams*). At best a poem unconsciously but overtly relates the visceral experience behind it to the semantic form it has taken, as with ''Life'' (*These Green-Going-to-Yellow*). Bell is also not afraid of social comment, though not as a mentor. In this province he is never as wonderfully nasty as Alan Dugan, but his range of feeling is greater.

The title *A Probable Volume of Dreams* is from ''Treetops,'' in which Bell dreams that his dead father is alive. The collection is largely about the roots of identity. Overarching perhaps is the paradox that we can and cannot perpetuate the dead, bodily and in imagination. The dead especially include the father and the ancestral line, significantly but not parochially Jewish. Nonetheless, as in ''The Delicate Bird Who Is Flying up Our Assess,'' Bell is often the wiseacre.

With *The Escape into You,* Bell came to the love sequence, which regulates the stanza throughout. So much for tradition. Divorce, amorous fatigue, and marital boredom take their place with the faithful heart. The verbal fabric whimsically includes every piece of sexual slang, and belly laughs abound: ''We sold the chairs . . . / then the squeaking sagged- / in-the-center four-poster baby farm . . .'' (''The Auction''). By the end, however, the bawdy merely shares the stage with eroticism and tenderheartedness.

In *Residue of Song* something like midlife encroaches. Thirteen pieces are about the abiding father, proved ''in the distance of a wrist.'' The sequence affectingly moves between the past in Long Island and Russia. Romantic love is other residue. The songs traverse a line from outrageous wisecracking (''Impotence'') though nearly self-aware adolescent yearning (''Set in Hollywood Hills'') to awakening after a great loss (''Dissolution'').

The title poem of *Stars Which See* comments on Seurat's ''La Grande Jatte.'' It catches a poignant relation between our natural yearning and decorum. Animals and trees dominate this elegantly simple collection, freer from prosodic experimentation than earlier volumes. The beautiful ''The Self and the Mulberry'' is approximately Taoist. The final piece, ''Gemwood,'' connects a son's loss of his lab ''rat'' to the parent's projection of losses to come. The authentic sadness and the poet's real attention to children explain why this poem is not merely adroit, as are so many of its ilk.

The gingko's dying leaves supply *These Green-Going-to-Yellow* with its title. The book traces the moribund passage of everything toward autumn. Yet Bell avoids morbidity with frequently uplifting notes of resistance. A doctor's resistance in ''Benny Hooper'' and his own in the exactly bleak landscape of ''At the Airport'' are notable. Trees are meant to dominate, but machines may. The analogies underlying the final two poems, which humanize the willow and the gingko, strain credibility. But the machinery of the grittier ''At the Airport'' and ''The Motor'' is perfectly successful, however grim.

Collected over two years, *Segues* is a poem-by-poem exchange with William Stafford. Its forte is the revelation of one poem's discourse generating another's. But this is also its weakness. It is more difficult than even in an ordinary volume for any piece to stand alone, and the reader may sense an excess of literature over experience as the wellspring of the poems. In addition, Stafford's probes, for good or ill, have elicited much undiluted autobiography in Bell's reactions.

Drawn by Stones is about the habit, after childhood, of not wondering, a death within life: ''I was Taps,'' in a ''youthful half stupor.'' But Bell has been saved, as the last line of the book contends paradoxically: ''it killed me—and almost cost me a life.'' This is why he can wrap up ''To Be'' by saying that ''still a child appears / in the guise of a grownup . . . at story-time.'' The poem sits next to the wonderful ''In Those Days,'' in which Bell discovers the ''mortar in the bloodstream'' that enables one to see that ''Phosphor in the paint on the ceiling / gave constellations their shine . . .''

Humor in the fifteen new poems included in *New and Selected Poems* is of the sort that deflates our facile reductions of experience. In ''Wednesday'' the poet quips that ''through the fervent branches / carried by momentary breezes of local origin, / the palpable Sublime flickered as motes on broad leaves, / while the Higher Good and the Greater Good contended / as sap on the bark of the maples, and even I / was enabled to witness the truly Existential where it loitered / famously in the shadows . . .'' This jesting confirms and revitalizes the experience of the world and of our own minds that lies behind our nominal abstractions of it: ''And of course I went back to work the next morning, / Like you . . . / but now there was a match-head in my thoughts . . . / [and] I saw that the horizon / was an idea of the eye . . .''

This is to say that, while the unalterable quotidian abides, an experience of the natural shapes the capacity of the individual to have a profound reciprocal exchange with the world. This idealist relationship with nature is rooted not in intellect but in the fleeting, revelatory acquaintance with the "dormant regions of the brain, the resonant cavities of not-knowing." In "The Pill" Bell likens these "regions" to the primordial "argument that once raged inside the spiral corridors of a nautilus, at a depth a human being could only imagine . . ." It follows that Bell says in other poems, "The things I did, I did because of trees," and "I am no more stupid now than I ever was."

All of the pieces progress toward a fine (again Taoist) trilogy entitled "In My Nature: 3 Corrective Dialogues." The poet speaks to a tree, the rain, and an island and then receives their artlessly artful and "corrective" replies. Bell is tuned to both the error of anthropomorphic projection upon nature and its necessity. And it fits that the poems comprising the finale address and derive from Tao Yuan-ming and Roethke, both of whom so appreciated this sort of poignancy, wit, and regard for the natural as universal truth, for they remain Bell's gifts to us.

Privacy of vision remains Bell's forte in *Iris of Creation,* even if we struggle at moments to find the emotional core in the poems. Unusual metaphorical connections and surprising word juxtapositions push the writing to the very edge of meaning. The most grounded poems in the collection are those with a defined subject. "The Big Slick," for example, addresses an Alaskan oil spill, and "Big Day at Santa Fe" addresses the downfall of communism. The poet's emotional dilemmas are sharpest and most accessible when he contends with the paradoxical and complex relationship between time, our thoughts of time, and the ways in which the events in our lives respond to time. "A Man May Change," "Victim of Himself," and "Ice" are three poems in which we sense this clarity of sensation.

Bell's collections *The Book of the Dead Man* and *Ardor: The Book of the Dead Man, Vol. 2,* are his most radical and sometimes mystifying contributions to contemporary poetry. In *The Book of the Dead Man* thirty-three sections trace an everyman's observations, ideas, epiphanies, and questions. As a spokesman for the last minute of life, the dead man is "an underground voice trying to soften the blows" who "takes what the world discards." He "will not stay buried, reappearing in disguises that fool no one yet cast doubt." Incantation and repetition mark the style and demonstrate Bell's direct sense for the material of the world. Called a "material mystic" in the introduction of the book, the dead man alternates between nature-driven and market-driven impulses. Through a collapse he undergoes a transformation of self into other: "Whereas formerly the dead man cohered in the usual way, now he thinks dissolution is good for the soul, a form of sacramental undoing viewed through a prism, a kind of philosophic nakedness descending a staircase."

Ardor builds on the momentum of the earlier volume and continues its prophetic, irrepressible litany of the dead man's final moments. In nearly forty two-part poems Bell tours both familiar and unfamiliar hells, from famine in Somalia to war in the former Yugoslavia, trying to find the line that separates the real from the unreal, the shrouded from the illuminated, the living from the dead: "The dead man lives in the flesh, in memory, in absentia, in fact and / fiction, by chance and by nature." The poet and protagonist realize a blurred identity. At one moment Bell suggests that "the dead man is the light that was turned on to study the dark." In *Ardor* Bell, as a dead man, illuminates the shadowy caverns of this world of the living.

—David M. Heaton and Martha Sutro

BENEDIKT, Michael

Nationality: American. **Born:** New York City, 26 May 1935. **Education:** New York University, B.A. in English and journalism 1956; Columbia University, New York, M.A. in comparative literature 1961. **Military Service:** U.S. Army, 1958–59. **Career:** Associate editor, Horizon Press, publishers, New York, 1959–61; New York correspondent, *Art International,* Lugano, 1965–67; associate editor, *Art News* magazine, New York, 1963–72; instructor in language and literature, Bennington College, Vermont, 1968–69; poet-in-residence, Sarah Lawrence College, Bronxville, New York, 1969–73; associate professor of arts and humanities, Hampshire College, Amherst, Massachusetts, 1973–75; Sexton Professor of Poetry, 1975, and visiting professor, 1977–79, Boston University; associate professor, Vassar College, Poughkeepsie, New York, 1976–77. Poetry editor, *Paris Review,* 1974–78. Since 1973 contributing editor, *American Poetry Review,* Philadelphia. **Awards:** Bess Hokin prize (*Poetry,* Chicago), 1968; Guggenheim fellowship, 1969; National Endowment for the Arts prize, 1970, and fellowship, 1979–80; Creative Artists Public Service grant, 1975. **Agent:** Georges Borchardt Inc., 136 East 57th Street, New York 10022. **Address:** 315 West 98th Street, New York, 10025, U.S.A.

PUBLICATIONS

Poetry

Serenade in Six Pieces. Privately printed, 1958.
Changes. Detroit, New Fresco, 1961.
8 Poems. Privately printed, 1966.
The Body. Middletown, Connecticut, Wesleyan University Press, 1968.
Sky. Middletown, Connecticut, Wesleyan University Press, 1970.
Mole Notes (prose poems). Middletown, Connecticut, Wesleyan University Press, 1971.
Night Cries (prose poems). Middletown, Connecticut, Wesleyan University Press, 1976.
The Badminton of Great Barrington; or, Gustav Mahler and the Chattanooga Choo-Choo. Pittsburgh, University of Pittsburgh Press, and London, Feffer and Simons, 1980.

Recording: *Today's Poets 5,* with others, Folkways, 1968.

Plays

The Vaseline Photographer, (playlet; produced New York, 1965).
The Orgy Bureau, in *Chelsea* (New York). 1968.
Box (multi-media event, with others; produced New York, 1970).

Other

Editor, with George E. Wellwarth, *Modern French Theatre: The Avant-Garde, Dada and Surrealism.* New York, Dutton, 1964; as *Modern French Plays: An Anthology from Jarry to Ionesco,* London, Faber, 1965.
Editor, with George E. Wellwarth, *Postwar German Theatre: An Anthology of Plays.* New York, Dutton, 1967; London, Macmillan, 1968.

Editor and translator, *Ring around the World: The Selected Poems of Jean L'Anselme*. London, Rapp and Whiting, 1967; Denver, Swallow, 1968.

Editor, *Theatre Experiment: New American Plays*. New York, Doubleday, 1967.

Editor, with George E. Wellwarth, *Modern Spanish Theatre: An Anthology of Plays*. New York, Dutton, 1968.

Editor, *22 Poems of Robert Desnos*. Santa Cruz, California, Kayak, 1971.

Editor, *The Poetry of Surrealism: An Anthology*. Boston, Little Brown, 1974.

Editor, *The Prose Poem: An International Anthology*. New York, Dell, 1976.

*

Manuscript Collection (1960–68): Humanities Research Center, University of Texas, Austin.

Critical Studies: *Benedikt: A Profile*, Tucson, Grilled Flowers Press, 1978; *The Poetics of the Postmodern American Prose Poem* (dissertation) by Susan Hawkins Miller, n.p., 1981.

Michael Benedikt comments:

(1970) Major theme is probably the relationship of matter and spirit; sometimes the sensual and the "pure." General sources and influences: the French symbolists and surrealists until about 1968; most recently, the English romantic poets. Stylistically, I am interested in the treatment of "difficult" subjects with clarity, since their reality is very clear, at least to me. I am probably as much influenced by contemporary painting, film, and theater as I am by any movement in poetry. I have become interested in the possibilities of the poem in prose as well as verse.

(1995) Newer work is largely in verse and is concerned with the incorporation of more "realistic" materials. Titles of works in progress: *Family Blessings, Family Curses* (narrative poems descriptive of the difficulties of a person undergoing a so-called midlife crisis, including a divorce, and also about the new life and travels that can await him [her]); *Dear Alice/Kate* (one long narrative poem on the subject of two cats who were pets). Also a manuscript of poems on the joys and sorrows of living in an often interestingly technological but always, or almost always, highly materialistic society. The latter MS is intended to be a kind of "survivor's handbook" for myself and others and is tentatively entitled *Of*.

*   *   *

There are many ways to imagine the poet: warbling his native woodnotes wild, legislating unknown to the rest of us, speaking in the language that men do know, giving to airy nothing a local habitation and a name, making things that are palpable and mute. Michael Benedikt typifies the poet as the eternal outsider, the poet against the world. And what a world it is, filled with "traditional poets," "collegiate English instructors," "Women of the Earth" (who use their allure "to snatch at people with"), "Power People" (who shout through loudspeakers, "Get up off your asses and make a revolution!"), guests at garden parties in Scarsdale, "X" (whose lovers are dull, "so that others glimpsing them, and after conversation, would remark, 'Agh! phooey! you wouldn't catch us talking to them at even

the dullest cocktail party ever thrown!' . . ." ["For Love or Money"]). So many cocktail parties; so many references to the Upper West Side of New York; a whole poem devoted to sneering at Troy, New York, which all New York poets know is Nowheresville. I sense in this work a life dedicated to chastising opponents of true culture, true art, true life, whatever that is. In his book *Mole Notes* there is a passage that for me sums up Benedikt's work, expresses the stance he takes toward the world: "Also, at this very moment, there is someone in a Civilian Submarine at the bottom of the Gulf of Mexico whose actions affect us all with their secluded elegance, their secret grandeur, grace, and repose" ("Molar Advent in Retrospect"). In poem after poem Benedikt takes the position of the commander of this submarine, alternatively raving about his enemy the world, lamenting its abysmal ignorance, or pitying its failure to be sensitive, graceful, grand, or elegant. Submarines keep appearing throughout his work, always as outmoded vehicles of transport, whether "civilian" or "pleasure" submarines, the very latest model for the year 1915. These and other images and objects in the work give it a dated air, reminiscent of those surrealist collages that juxtapose steam engines and harpies, corset ads and patent velocipedes.

Benedikt has translated a great deal of surrealist poetry and edited *The Poetry of Surrealism*. It would be surprising if this interest were not reflected in his own poetry. But what does it mean to be writing surrealist poetry in the 1970s, to be guided by an avant-garde aesthetic half a century old? The very objects in many of his poems recall the interiors of early twentieth-century Europe: umbrella stands, mirrors, bowler hats, décolletage. I do not mean to say that Benedikt is a kind of verbal Edward Gorey, camping out among the Edwardians, for many of his poems are set firmly in the present. It is just that he has not always been able to resist using the same things that are familiar to us from that earlier work, and so his poems necessarily partake of the earlier poetry's peculiar historical feel.

Some of Benedikt's poems read like exercises in surrealism. "The European Shoe," for example, consists of fifteen short sections, each having the shoe as its subject: "Tears fall from the eye of the European Shoe as it waves goodbye to us / from the back balcony of the speeding train" (*The Body*). The use of the same incongruous object in a repetitive pattern and the animation of the inanimate (or the other way around) are devices made familiar to us by the surrealists, and to find them in a contemporary poem is to be reminded of the poet's forebears and also to perceive the poem as a crafted thing, a consciously made artifact. Hence my difficulty with this and other poems in *The Body* and in *Sky,* for the surrealists despised the idea of art as craftsmanship. We are confronted here with something that seems very much like the antisurrealist poem. The destruction of what one wishes to celebrate must necessarily accompany the use of surrealism as a style. In "A Beloved Head" Benedikt employs the surrealist device of turning something organic into something mechanical. Here surrealism exists only at the surface of the poem, decorating the straightforward idea that some men manipulate women as if they were machines. André Breton would not have approved.

Mole Notes, an elegantly printed volume of short prose pieces, seems a logical development in Benedikt's work. In *The Body* and *Sky* there is a gradual but noticeable drift toward the long line, a growing sense of paragraphs rather than stanzas or stanzalike forms. But the tone of *Mole Notes* remains consistent with the earlier work, having the sense of a series of collisions, of unexpected juxtapositions. In some of the pieces the comic and the serious work beautifully together ("The Bewitched Lover"):

And whenever you carry me away, it is as if you
were bringing me something! O come to me, true
beloved, so that you can go away in a hurry again!

Here there is a kind of fusion or, better, an alternating current that
expresses exactly the attraction and repulsion cycle of love. But the
common problem of poets who turn to short prose works appears here
as well, the sense that in writing prose the poet can be unbuttoned and
casual and can kick over the traces of form. Many of these mole notes
seem loose to the point of carelessness. ''The Secret of Scotch'' and
''The Pain Alarm'' strike me as being very good stand-up comic
routines, and no doubt they lay them in the aisles at readings, but they
disappoint the reader.

—Steven Young

BENNETT, (Simone) Louise

Also wrote as Louise Bennett-Coverley. **Nationality:** Jamaican.
Born: Kingston, 7 September 1919. **Education:** Studied at primary
and secondary schools in Jamaica; Royal Academy of Dramatic Art,
London (British Council scholarship). **Family:** Married Eric Coverley
in 1954; one daughter and one stepson. **Career:** Worked with the
BBC (West Indies Section) as resident artist, 1945–46 and 1950–53,
and with repertory companies in Coventry, Huddersfield, and
Amersham. Returned to Jamaica, 1955. Drama specialist, Jamaica
Social Welfare Commission, 1955–60; lecturer in drama and Jamai-
can folklore, Extra-Mural Department, University of West Indies,
Kingston, 1959–61. Lecturer and radio and television commentator.
Represented Jamaica at the Royal Commonwealth Arts Festival in
Britain, 1965. **Awards:** Silver Musgrave Medal of the Institute of
Jamaica, 1965; Norman Manley Award for Excellence in the Arts,
1972; Unity award, United Manchester Association, 1972; Gold
Musgrave Medal, 1978; Institute of Jamaica Centenary Medal, 1979.
D.Litt.: University of the West Indies, 1982. M.B.E. (Member, Order
of the British Empire); Order of Jamaica. **Address:** Enfield House,
P.O. Box 11, Gordon Town, St. Andrew, Jamaica.

PUBLICATIONS

Poetry

Dialect Verses. Kingston, Gleaner, 1940.
Jamaican Dialect Verses. Kingston, Gleaner, 1942; enlarged edition,
    Kingston, Pioneer Press, 1951.
Jamaican Humour in Dialect. Kingston, Gleaner, 1943.
Miss Lulu Sez. Kingston, Gleaner, 1948.
Anancy Stories and Dialect Verse, with others. Kingston, Pioneer
    Press, 1950.
*Laugh with Louise: A Potpourri of Jamaican Folklore, Stories,
    Songs, Verses.* Kingston, Bennett City Printery, 1960.
Jamaica Labrish. Kingston, Sangster, 1966.
Anancy and Miss Lou. Kingston, Sangster, 1979.

Selected Poems, edited by Mervyn Morris. Kingston, Sangster, 1982.
Aunty Roachy Seh. Kingston, Sangster, 1993.

Recordings: *Jamaican Folk Songs,* Folkways, 1954; *Jamaican Sing-
    ing Games,* Folkways, 1954; *West Indies Festival of Arts,* Cook,
    1958; *Miss Lou's Views,* Federal, 1967; *Listen to Louise,* Federal,
    1968; *The Honourable Miss Lou,* 1981; *Miss Lou Live,* 1983.

*

Critical Studies: Introduction by Rex Nettlefold, to *Jamaica Labrish,*
1966; ''Noh Lickle Twang: An Introduction to the Poetry of Louise
Bennett'' by Carolyn Cooper, in *World Literature Written in English*
(Arlington, Texas), 17, 1978; '''Long Memoried Women': Caribbean
Women Poets'' by Bruce Woodcock, in *Black Women's Writing,*
edited by Gina Wisker, New York, St. Martin's Press, 1993; ''Riddym
Ravings: Female and National Identity in Jamaican Poetry'' by
Elizabeth A. Wheeler, in *Imagination, Emblems and Expressions:
Essays on Latin American, Caribbean, and Continental Culture and
Identity,* edited by Helen Ryan-Ransom, Bowling Green, Ohio,
Popular, 1993; ''Long Memoried Women: Ooodgeroo Noonuccal
and Jamaican Poet, Louise Bennett'' by Angela Smith, in *Australian
Literary Studies* (St. Lucia, Australia), 16(4), 1994.

Louise Bennett comments:

I have been described as a ''poet of utterance performing
multiple roles as entertainer, as a valid literary figure, and as a
documenter of aspects of Jamaican life, thought, and feeling.'' I
would not disagree with this.

*   *   *

A political commentator, a satirist, and in many ways a social
historian, the Jamaican poet and performing artist Louise Bennett
serves as an articulate voice of her people. No subject is too sacred for
her fancy and biting wit. Her works explore the changing face of
Jamaican politics, the island nation's colonial history, its attainment
of independence, middle-class attitudes, imagination, and a vast array
of other topics. No poet in Jamaica has a better understanding of the
island and its people.

Bennett writes in West Indian English, which is gradually being
recognized by anthropologists and linguistic specialists as a language
with its own grammar, syntax, and rules rather than as a mere dialect.
As the Barbadian poet and novelist George Lamming once put it,
''English is a West Indian language.'' The use of West Indian
English—called ''Creole'' on some islands and ''patois'' on others,
especially on those with a French colonial history)—has enabled
Bennett to get many points across in pithy phrases that would have
taken a whole paragraph to say in standard dictionary terms. Its racy
flavor suits her style. Bennett also employs commonly used words
and phrases that go back to the English of Elizabethan and Cromwel-
lian times.

Bennett's works have rescued from oblivion—often from extinction—a number of Jamaica's folk songs, stories, and sayings, and
her stage productions have put the Jamaican vernacular before large
audiences.

—Colin Rickards

BERESFORD, Anne (Ellen)

Nationality: British. **Born:** Redhill, Surrey, 10 September 1929. **Education:** Studied privately, and attended Central School of Speech Training and Dramatic Art London, 1944–46. **Family:** Married Michael Hamburger, *q.v.,* in 1951 (divorced 1970 and remarried 1974); one son and two daughters. **Career:** Stage actress, 1948–70, and broadcaster, BBC, 1960–70; drama teacher, Wimbledon High School, 1969–73, and Arts Educational School, London, 1973–76; teacher at the Poetry Workshop, Cockpit Theatre, London, 1971–73. Former committee member, Aldeburgh Poetry Festival; member of editorial board, *Agenda* magazine. **Member:** General Council, Poetry Society, 1976–79. **Address:** Marsh Acres, Middleton, Saxmundham, Suffolk IP17 3NH, England.

PUBLICATIONS

Poetry

Walking without Moving. London, Turret, 1967.
The Lair. London, Rapp and Whiting, 1968.
Footsteps on Snow. London, Agenda, 1972.
Modern Fairy Tale. Rushden, Northhamptonshire, Sceptre Press, 1972.
The Courtship. Brighton, Unicorn Bookshop, 1972.
The Curving Shore. London, Agenda, 1975.
Words, with Michael Hamburger. East Bramley, Surrey, Words Press, 1977.
Unholy Giving. Knotting, Bedfordshire, Sceptre Press, 1978.
The Songs of Almut from God's Country. Oxford, Suffolk, Oxford Publications, 1980.
Songs a Thracian Taught Me. London, Boyars, 1980.
The Sele of the Morning. London, Agenda, 1988.
Snapshots from an Album 1884–1895. London, Katabasis, 1992.
Charm with Stones. Germany, Verlag Claudia Gehrke, 1993.
Landscape with Figures. London, Agenda, 1994.
Selected and New Poems. London, Bellew, 1997.
No Place for Cowards. London, Katabasis, 1998.

Plays

Radio Plays: *Struck by Apollo,* with Michael Hamburger, 1965; *The Villa,* 1968.

Television Play: *Duet for Three Voices,* 1983.

Other

Translator, *Alexandros: Selected Poems,* by Vera Lungu, London, Agenda, 1974.

*

Manuscript Collection: Humanities Research Center, University of Texas, Austin.

Critical Studies: ''Anne Beresford'' by Judith Kazantzis, in *Agenda* (London), 34(2), summer 1996; ''Judith Kazantzis and Anne Beresford'' by Michael Tolkien, in *Agenda* (London), 37(1), summer 1999.

Anne Beresford comments:

I don't like to comment on my own work or, for that matter, on other poets—I like to read other poets and hope that they might like to read my work. But I will quote from something David Storey wrote about my poetry: ''The finest of mystic poets, her work is pitched on the very edge of perception: celebratory, frightening, elusive—meditative—and unique.''

*   *   *

Ezra Pound wrote that ''Our life is, in so far as it is worth living, made up in great part of things indefinite, impalpable; and it is precisely because the arts present us these things that we—humanity—cannot get on without the arts.'' Much of the subtlety of Anne Beresford's poetry stems from her attempts to define moments and states of mind of this nature, those aspects of consciousness and daily life that are most impatient of words. Beresford's ''Heimweh'' is short enough to give in its entirety:

> a thrush sings
> every evening
> in the ash tree
>
> it has been singing
> for as long
> as I can remember
> only then
> the tree was probably
> an oak
>
> the song
> aches and aches
> in the green light
> if I knew
> where it was
> I would go
> home

Beresford seldom overstates but is reticent and elliptical. This gives her work an impersonal quality that is rare. At its best her writing expresses an imagination (not fancy) unlike that of any other contemporary poet. This is connected with humor and satire in a strange way. Her irony succeeds because it is not obvious.

A fault present in some poems is a tenuousness of rhythm, where the emotions do not seem strong enough to generate sufficient rhythmic energy. But this is sometimes offset by a clarity and simplicity of imagery that are highly evocative, particularly if the poems are lived with rather than read quickly: ''outside, high on the mountains / is the great plain with wild flowers / wild flowers and air so fresh / one's head goes light'' (''Eurydice''). At times the imagery is menacing: ''You have come to a tower of slate / crumbling into grey sky. / Don't climb, not there . . .'' (''Half-Way''). This is not poetry that strives for immediate effect. Hence, a first reading often misses much of the meaning Beresford's usually very simple words contain.

Beresford never uses dream and myth as an ornament or literary device but rather to express states of mind that are real. Her later work makes use of dramatic monologue and shows a historical conscious-ness that raises her poetry above that of contemporary writers of the short poem, who seem to be incapable of embodying subjects other than the personal and the incidentals of everyday life. ''Nicodemus'' can serve as an example:

> Keeping a sense of proportion
> lip service to what is considered correct
> I have brought what is needed to bury the dead.
> Once again I come to you by night.
> This time to take away all visible proof of my
>   understanding.
> In secret I have applied myself
> to seek out wisdom
> to know what is before my face—
> the inside and the outside are reversed
> that which is
> has become that which is not—
> displaced, troubled
> I live naked in a house that is not my own
> and the five trees of Paradise evade me.

Later books of Beresford, such as *The Sele of the Morning* and *Landscape with Figures,* show a new depth in exploring human relationships, both love and friendship, by using a hard-earned simplicity of language. As the Scottish poet W.S. Milne has written, ''Rarely today does one find such calmness and sanity, such an understanding of life's gifts, in art.''

> Despair stands aside
> prayer is the answer
> in this house
> where a baby is soon to be born
> in the upstairs room.

Landscape with Figures closes with a particularly fine sequence, ''Fragments of a Torn Tapestry,'' and although the poems concern the past, it is their ''nowness,'' to use a word of David Jones, that will make them live. ''London'' is short enough to quote in its entirety:

> In the great city
> is much noise and stench
> of business here
> I can say little
> for in these hard days
> no man is to be trusted.

> Our masters tell us:
> ''Make yourselves friends of Mammon''
> therefore many are betrayed
> Alas! it is true that
> Judas does not sleep

The novelist David Storey has written of Beresford, ''The finest of mystic poets, her work is pitched on the very edge of perception: celebratory, frightening, elusive—meditative—and unique.''

—William Cookson

BERG, Stephen (Walter)

Nationality: American. **Born:** Philadelphia, Pennsylvania, 2 August 1934. **Education:** University of Pennsylvania, Philadelphia; Boston University; University of Iowa, Iowa City, B.A. 1959; University of Indiana, Bloomington. **Family:** Married Millie Lane in 1959; two daughters. **Career:** Formerly instructor in English, Temple University, Philadelphia; also taught at Princeton University, New Jersey, and Haverford College, Pennsylvania. Professor, Philadelphia College of Art. Poetry editor, *Saturday Evening Post,* Philadelphia, 1961–62. Since 1972 founding editor, with Stephen Parker and Rhoda Schwartz, *American Poetry Review,* Philadelphia. **Awards:** Rocke-feller-Centro Mexicano de Escritores grant, 1959–61; National Translation Center grant, 1969; Frank O'Hara prize (*Poetry,* Chicago), 1970; Guggenheim fellowship, 1974; National Endowment for the Arts grant, 1976; Columbia University Translation Center award, 1976. **Address:** 2005 Mt. Vernon Street, Philadelphia, Pennsylvania 19130, U.S.A.

PUBLICATIONS

Poetry

Berg Goodman Mezey. Philadelphia, New Ventures Press, 1957.
Bearing Weapons. West Branch, Iowa, Cummington Press, 1963.
The Queen's Triangle: A Romance. West Branch, Iowa Cummington Press, 1970.
The Daughters. Indianapolis, Bobbs Merrill, 1971.
Nothing in the Word: Versions of Aztec Poetry. New York, Grossman, 1972.
Grief: Poems and Versions of Poems. New York, Grossman, 1975.
With Akmatova at the Black Gates: Variations. Urbana, University of Illinois Press, 1981.
In It. Urbana, University of Illinois Press, 1986.
First Song, Bankei, 1653. Omaha, Nebraska, Cummington Press, 1989.
Crow with No Mouth: Ikkyu, 15th Century Zen Master: Versions. Port Townsend, Washington, Copper Canyon Press, 1989.
Homage to the Afterlife. Omaha, Nebraska, Cummington Press, 1991.
New & Selected Poems. Port Townsend, Washington, and Newcastle upon Tyne, Bloodaxe, 1992.
Oblivion: Poems. Urbana, University of Illinois Press, 1995.
The Steel Cricket: Versions 1958–1997. Port Townsend, Washington, Copper Canyon Press, 1997.
Shaving. Marshfield, Massachusetts, Four Way Books, 1998.
Footnotes to an Unfinished Poem. Washington, D.C., Orchises Press, 2000.

Play

Oedipus the King, with Diskin Clay, adaptation of a play by Sopho-cles (produced New York, 1981). New York and London, Oxford University Press, 1978.

Other

Sea Ice: Versions of Eskimo Songs. Omaha, Nebraska, Cummington Press, 1988.

Editor, with Robert Mezey, *Naked Poetry: Recent American Poetry in Open Forms*. Indianapolis, Bobbs Merrill, 1969.

Editor, with S.J. Marks, *Between People*. Chicago, Scott Foresman, 1972.

Editor with S.J. Marks, *About Women*. New York, Fawcett, 1973.

Editor, with Robert Mezey, *The New Naked Poetry*. Indianapolis, Bobbs Merrill, 1976.

Editor, *In Praise of What Persists*. New York, Harper, 1983.

Editor, *Singular Voices: American Poetry Today*. New York, Avon, 1985.

Translator, with Steven Polgar and S.J. Marks, *Clouded Sky,* by Miklos Radnoti. New York, Harper, 1972.

Translator, *Crow with No Mouth: Ikkyu, 15th-Century Zen Master*. Port Townsend, Washington, Copper Canyon Press, 1989.

*

Critical Studies: "Translation and the Egg" by Deborah Digges, in *Field* (Oberlin, Ohio), 39, Fall 1988; by Frederick Smock, in *American Book Review,* 15(5), December 1993–94; "Stephen Berg: The Passion of Mourning, Part I," in *Denver Quarterly,* 27(3), Winter 1993, and "Stephen Berg: The Passion of Mourning, Part II" in *Denver Quarterly,* 38(2), Fall 1993, both by Laurence Lieberman.

Stephen Berg comments:

All comments on my work—such as the introductions to *Nothing in the Word, Clouded Sky,* and *Grief*—are random and apply to the particular books and poems in question.

*   *   *

Many of the poems in Stephen Berg's 1971 collection, *The Daughters*, break forth with an almost breathless fury of speech, the expression of an agonized, compassionate mind and sensibility confronting the bitter realities of modern existence:

We, the dooms, your future, the bloody fire
between places, dancers on the corpses of who,
we eat what there is. Are you
sitting at a table? Is there food? Us,
the zero washing itself, bones entering the floor,
leaves zigzagging down through silt, through farms
in the lone face of a mirror.

Berg appears to write in the tradition of such poets as Neruda, Vallejo, and Patchen. Like them, he strives for a language and imagery that encompass the irony, fatality, and suffering of a life everywhere overshadowed by mortality, a life unredeemed and unaccounted for either by reason or by any known God. In this endeavor Berg often stretches words and syntax to their extreme limits. Frequently his means of progression—more evident in his longer pieces, which are marked by greater space and freedom—is elliptical and associative rather than logical or merely sequential. Berg's poems sometimes surge and lash out seemingly uncontrollably, yet his works reflect a strong and inventive imagination operating constantly, drawing together disparate details and linking objects and bodies such as love and death, pain and anger. With sudden, vivid, and terrible lightning strokes of vision, he takes his readers to a poetic universe that illuminates their own sense of the world.

Berg's poetry suffers occasional lapses, excesses, and repetitions, but these are minor in comparison with the ambitiousness and force of what he attempts. His later poems show a calmer, more reflective side to his writing. Berg is not only an energetic and highly talented poet but also a translator and editor of considerable accomplishment. As the poet himself once wrote, "I can go anywhere, I can let go forever / and live in the middle of fire, in silence . . ."

—Ralph J. Mills, Jr.

BERGÉ, Carol

Nationality: American. **Born:** Carol Peppis in New York City, 4 October 1928. **Education:** New York University, 1946–52; New School for Social Research, New York, 1952–54. **Family:** Married Jack Bergé in 1955; one son. **Career:** Editorial assistant, Syndicate Publications, Simon and Schuster, *Forbes* magazine, Hart Publishing Company, and Green-Brodie Advertising, New York, 1950–54; assistant to the president, Pendray Public Relations, New York, 1955. Member, COSMEP, 1971–73. Visiting professor at Thomas Jefferson College, Allendale, Michigan, 1975–76; Goddard College, Asilomar, California, 1976; University of California Extension Program, Berkeley, 1976–77; Indiana University, Summer Writers' Conference, Bloomington, 1977; University of Southern Mississippi, Hattiesburg, 1977–78; University of New Mexico, Albuquerque, 1978–79 and 1987; Wright State University, Dayton, Ohio, 1979; and State University of New York, Albany, 1981. Editor, CENTER magazine, 1970–85, *Mississippi Review,* Hattiesburg, 1977–78, and *Paper Branches,* Albuquerque, 1978–79; contributing editor, *Woodstock Poetry Review,* New York, 1977–81, *Shearsman,* 1980–82, Ahsahta Press, Boise, Idaho, 1983, and *Southwest Profile,* 1983. Founder and proprietor, Blue Gate Gallery of Antiques, Santa Fe, New Mexico, 1988–99. Since 1970 editor, CENTER Press and Magazine. **Awards:** MacDowell fellowship (four times); New York State Council on the Arts grant, for editing, 1971–82 (13 grants), for fiction 1974; National Endowment for the Arts grant, 1979. **Address:** 2070 Calle Contento, Santa Fe, New Mexico 87505, U.S.A.

PUBLICATIONS

Poetry

Four Young Lady Poets, with others, edited by LeRoi Jones. New York, Totem-Corinth, 1962.

The Vulnerable Island. Cleveland, Renegade Press, 1964.

Lumina. Cleveland, 7 Flower Press, 1965.

Poems Made of Skin. Toronto, Weed/Flower Press, 1968.

Circles, As in the Eye. Santa Fe, Desert Review Press, 1969.

An American Romance. Los Angeles, Black Sparrow Press, 1969.

The Chambers. Aylesford Priory, Kent, Aylesford Review Press, 1969.

From a Soft Angle: Poems about Women. Indianapolis, Bobbs Merrill, 1972.

The Unexpected. Milwaukee, Membrane Press, 1976.

Rituals and Gargoyles. Bowling Green, Ohio, Newedi Press, 1976.
A Song, A Chant. Albuquerque, Amalgamated Sensitivity Publications, 1978.
Alba Genesis. Woodstock, New York, Aesopus Press, 1979.
Alba Nemesis: The China Poems. Albuquerque, Amalgamated Sensitivity Publications, 1979.

Novels

Acts of Love: An American Novel. Indianapolis, Bobbs Merrill, 1973.
Secrets, Gossip and Slander. Berkeley, California, Reed and Cannon, 1984.

Short Stories

The Unfolding. New York, Theo Press, 1969.
A Couple Called Moebius. Indianapolis, Bobbs Merrill, 1972.
Timepieces. Union City, California, Fault, 1977.
The Doppler Effect. Berkeley, California, Effie's Press, 1979.
Fierce Metronome: The One-Page Novel and Other Short Fiction. Mount Kisco, New York, Window, 1981.

Other

The Vancouver Report: A Report and Discussion of the Poetry Seminar at the University of British Columbia. New York, Peace Eye, 1964.
Zebras, or, Contour Lines. Bowling Green, Ohio, Tribal/Center Press, 1991.

Editor, *The Clock of Moss,* by Judson Crews. Boise, Idaho, Ahsahta Press, 1983.

*

Manuscript Collection: Humanities Research Center, University of Texas, Austin; Jerome Library, Bowling Green State University, Ohio.

Critical Studies: By Hayden Carruth, in *Hudson Review* (New York), 1969; Howard McCord, in *Measure* (Pullman Washington), 1970; by Ishmael Reed, in *Post* (Washington, D.C.), 1973; "A Plethora of Cultural Detail: *Zebras* by Carol Berge" by Barry Silesky, in *American Book Review,* 15(4), October 1993.

Carol Bergé comments:

My poetry, like my fiction, has always dealt in archetypes of human behavior rather than of personal purviews. I am interested in sociological constructs, especially interaction with and response to superimposed forms. I have never been interested in confessional or first-person writings; instead, I have chosen historical perspective. I have not written or published poetry for the past seventeen years. Fiction has absorbed me and attracted my energy, as well as articles about the arts. My major thrusts have been in other fields besides "being a writer" for the past several years. I edit, teach, advise, and do copywriting and other more commercial ventures, often related to my current work as an arts and antiques dealer. This field satisfies my feeling of connection with history, artifacts, and human habits. I am writing a book of fiction (stories) about people in the antiques trade— *ANTICS.* I am continuing as editor of CENTER Press. I am presently editing and compiling *LIGHT YEARS, The N.Y.C. Coffeehouse Poets of the Sixties,* an anthology.

*   *   *

Female intensities of wit, of lust, tenderness, the intelligence of the body, its groping, the ravage and despair, and all in language as varied as the weather—this is Carol Bergé's poetry. Whether in her own voice or in those of dozens of personae, her work, foremost and always female, speaks of the terrible endlessness of sexual need, loving, hating, fighting, forgiving:

> The women breast to breast across empty
> across lava-strewn bitter plains
> facing lidless eyes of the majestic surgeons
> who demand they empty their wombs
> of the quintuplet dolls shaped like "husband"
> Women offering full teats to
> men with infant faces who drink with mouths
> the violet of sleep or of healed circumcision

Bergé's poetry also captures the nuances of observances of self:

> these days
> when you draw back
> as I reach for you
> it is an old wound you rip
> open . . .

Bergé can be and often is talkative. Her verse sometimes seems put together from random images, broken by unlikely shifts of tone and texture with little attempt at lyric unity. But her talk is intelligent, tough, urbane, and original. When she breaks through the talk into genuine poems of her own, they are moving and lucid, and they show a degree of maturity that few contemporary poets can approach.

—Hayden Carruth

BERKSON, Bill

Nationality: American. **Born:** New York City, 30 August 1939.
Education: Brown University, Providence, Rhode Island, 1957–59;
New School for Social Research, New York (Dylan Thomas memorial award 1959), 1959–60; Columbia University, New York, 1959–60;
New York University Institute of Fine Arts, 1960–61. **Family:**
Married 1) Lynn O'Hare in 1975 (divorced 1996), one son and one daughter; 2) Constance Lewallen in 1998. **Career:** Editorial associate, *Portfolio and Art News Annual,* New York, 1960–63; associate producer, *Art-New York* series, WNDT-TV, New York, 1964–65; taught at the New School for Social Research, 1964–69; guest editor, Museum of Modern Art, New York, 1965–69; editor, *Best & Company* magazine, 1969; Teaching Fellow, Ezra Stiles College, Yale University, New Haven, Connecticut, 1969–70; editor, *Big Sky* magazine and Big Sky Books, Bolinas, California, 1971–78; teacher, California Poets in the Schools Program, 1974–84, Naropa Institute, Boulder, Colorado, 1977, New College of California, 1977, 1983,

Southampton College, 1980, and California College of Arts and Crafts, 1983–84. Coordinator of art history, 1988–94, since 1984 professor of art history, and since 1994 director, Letters & Science, San Francisco Art Institute. Since 1988 corresponding editor, *Art in America.* **Awards:** Poets Foundation grant, 1968; Yaddo fellowship, 1968; Coordinating Council of Literary Magazines grants, 1973–77; National Endowment for the Arts grant, 1979; Briarcombe fellowship, 1983; Artspace award in art criticism, 1990. **Address:** 25 Grand View Avenue, San Francisco, California 94114, U.S.A.

PUBLICATIONS

Poetry

Saturday Night: Poems 1960–61. New York, Tibor de Nagy, 1961.
Shining Leaves. New York, Angel Hair, 1969.
Two Serious Poems and One Other, with Larry Fagin. Bolinas, California, Big Sky, 1972.
Recent Visitors. New York, Angel Hair, 1973.
Ants. Berkeley, California, Arif Press, 1974.
Hymns of St. Bridget, with Frank O'Hara. New York, Adventures in Poetry, 1974.
100 Women. Chicago, Simon and Schuchat, 1975.
Enigma Variations. Bolinas, California, Big Sky, 1975.
Blue Is the Hero: Poems 1960–1975. Kensington, California, L Publications, 1976.
Red Devil. Bolinas, California, Smithereens Press, 1982.
Start Over. Bolinas, California, Tombouctou, 1983.
Lush Life. Calais, Vermont, Z Press, 1984.
A Copy of the Catalogue. Vienna, Austria, Labyrinth, 1999.
Young Manhattan, with Anne Waldman. Boulder, Colorado, Erudite Fangs, 1999.
Serenade. Cambridge, Massachusetts, Zoland, 2000.
Fugue State. Cambridge, Massachusetts, Zoland, 2000.

Other

Ronald Bladen: Early and Late. San Francisco, Museum of Modern Art, 1991.
Homage to George Herriman. San Francisco, Campbell-Thiebaud Gallery, 1997.

Editor, *In Memory of My Feelings,* by Frank O'Hara. New York, Museum of Modern Art, 1967.
Editor, with Irving Sandler, *Alex Katz.* New York, Praeger, 1971.
Editor, with Joe LeSueur, *Homage to Frank O'Hara.* Bolinas, California, Big Sky, 1978.
Editor, *What's with Modern Art?* by Frank O'Hara. Mike and Dale's Press, 1998.

*

Manuscript Collection: University of Connecticut, Storrs.

*   *   *

Bill Berkson was a late arrival to the New York ferment that produced such poets as Frank O'Hara, Kenneth Koch, John Ashbery,

and James Schuyler in the 1950s, when abstract expressionism released new energies of awareness for poets as well as painters. Jackson Pollock and Willem de Kooning were giants at the center of this creative apocalypse, and their projections through paint of various states of conscious (and unconscious) experience liberated art from its old logical categories. Suddenly, free and fluid forms of self-expression became the norm of such art, and by the mid-1950s poets applied to syntax and diction the same release and invented a fresh discourse. O'Hara, who as associate curator of the Museum of Modern Art served as a liaison between painting and writing, was the reigning figure of this revolution in poetics.

Berkson came from the next generation, but his credentials were good: born in New York City to upper-class parents, a private school education, a writer for *Art News,* occasional work with the Museum of Modern Art. In addition, Berkson edited a book of O'Hara's poems, *In Memory of My Feelings,* and collaborated with him on a second, *Hymns of St. Bridget.* These are only details of a life, but they add up to a sophisticated apprenticeship for writing a certain style of poetry, one that requires considerable daring and finesse, since much of it is calculated to swing into and well out of ordinary sense. There is about the New York style a punning sense of reality, that objects and events are only tenuously situated in fixity and that the whole texture of one's certainty is as easily disturbed as a creek bed. A delicate, sometimes foolish humor overtakes such lyrics, but behind it is a philosophical impetus—a gnawing frustration with the usual and the vague, a repressed but squirming vitality beneath the mundane and the actual, as in "Leave Canceled":

What we need is a great big vegetable farm!
Every vegetable to stand up and be counted,
and all the farmers to love one another
in their solid, lazy dreams.

Then this would be all knowledge,
all hygiene, and the plants we feel,
and it comes down to Boy and Dad and kind
balloons of sight. The sky's neat sweep.

the irrational, would be this butterfly dish
where lovely woman stacks her arms . . .

Berkson only narrowly skirts sense in his own work, which sets up an interesting tension in reading him. Although the language often seems to be a runaway *logopoeia*—words ordered by sounds alone—with a little scrutiny the thread of a reasoning process is discernible, as in this typical passage:

Are you different from that shelter you
Built for knives? On the side walk, sapphires.
On the fifth floor, fungus was relaxing. I have put on
The crimson face of awareness you gave me.
What is the heart-shaped object that thaws your fingers?
It is a glove and in it a fist.

Sometimes Berkson's experiments break through to a new level of metaphor that ties extraordinary words together ("In the Mean"):

Running water—
it makes you think of all you didn't do

but not regret it, no: *de ma jeunesse.*
You didn't know I was the President
of a great cloud of falling bricks, did you?
Zoom. Bent. The bare stalk of the corn tree plant of
October thirty-one, of November one, November two . . .

In such work, however, the strain for novelty can become an effort, and there is much dogged flippancy in Berkson:

What am I indicting that heads off gardenia?
green green stove-pipe
arm around me stalk wherein pegged a relax bus
globule of often-candelabra in the cake
of soap . . .

And so on. The intention, we might suppose, is to break free of the routines of syntax, lyric formula, the prescribed means by which we translate experience into generalized patterns. The sheer predictability of most poetry tells us that Berkson set out to run off track, to derail his imagination from that groove in which Emily Dickinson tells us the "brain runs evenly—and true" until a splinter sends it reeling forever. It's the outer world the mind borders that Berkson wants to spring toward through derangements of sense and syntax.

Although his later work, as with *Start Over* and *Serenade,* has continued down the same path as before, Berkson, like Ashbery and O'Hara, stands in a prelusive way to the ideas and inventions of the language poets. He is a resource of certain early linguistic ideas, distortions, and strategies by which consciousness found its way out and set off on some sort of trek into the nonformulaic world.

—Paul Christensen

BERNSTEIN, Charles

Nationality: American. **Born:** New York City, 4 April 1950. **Education:** Harvard University, Cambridge, Massachusetts, 1968–72, A.B. in philosophy 1972 (Phi Beta Kappa); Simon Fraser University, Burnaby, British Colombia (King Fellow, 1973–74). **Family:** Married Susan Bee Laufer in 1977; one daughter and one son. **Career:** Writer on medical and health topics. Faculty member and series coordinator, Wolfson Center for National Affairs, New School for Social Research, New York, 1988. Since 1990 David Gray Professor of Poetry and Letters, and director, poetics program, State University of New York, Buffalo. Visiting lecturer, University of Auckland, 1986, and University of California, San Diego, 1987; visiting professor, Queens College, City University of New York, 1988, and City College of the City of New York, 1998; lecturer in creative writing program, Princeton University, New Jersey, 1989 and 1990; Visiting Butler Chair Professor, State University of New York, Buffalo, fall 1989. Editor, with Bruce Andrews, *L=A=N=G=U=A=G=E,* New York, 1978–81, and of poetry anthologies for *Paris Review,* 1982, and *Boundary* 2, 1987. **Awards:** National Endowment for the Arts fellowship, 1980; Guggenheim fellowship, 1985; University of Auckland Foundation fellowship, 1986; New York Foundation for the Arts fellowship, 1990, 1995; Roy Harvey Pearce/Archive for New Poetry Prize of the University of California, San Diego, 1999.

Address: Poetics Program, Department of English, 438 Clemens Hall, State University of New York, Buffalo, New York 14260, U.S.A.

PUBLICATIONS

Poetry

Asylums. New York, Asylum's Press, 1975.
Parsing. New York, Asylum's Press, 1976.
Shade. College Park, Maryland, Sun and Moon Press, 1978.
Poetic Justice. Baltimore, Pod, 1979.
Sense of Responsibility. Berkeley, California, Tuumba Press, 1979.
Legend, with others. New York, Segue, 1980.
Controlling Interests. New York, Roof, 1980.
Disfrutes. Needham, Massachusetts, Poets and Poets Press, 1981.
The Occurrence of Tune, photographs by Susan Bee Laufer. New York, Segue, 1981.
Stigma. Barrytown, New York, Station Hill Press, 1981.
Islets/Irritations. New York, Jordan Davies, 1983; New York, Roof Books, 1992.
Resistance. Windsor, Vermont, Awede Press, 1983.
Amblyopia. Elmwood, Connecticut, Poets and Poets Press, 1985.
Veil. Madison, Wisconsin, Xexoxial, 1987.
The Sophist. Los Angeles, Sun and Moon Press, 1987.
Four Poems. Tucson, Arizona, Chax Press, 1988.
The Nude Formalism. Los Angeles, Sun and Moon Press, 1989.
Senses of Responsibility. Providence, Rhode Island, Paradigm Press, 1989.
The Absent Father in Dumbo. La Laguna, Islas Canarias, Spain, Zasterle Press, 1990.
Rough Trades. Los Angeles, Sun and Moon Press, 1990.
Islets/Irritations. New York, Roof Books, 1992.
Dark City. Los Angeles, Sun & Moon Press, 1994.
The Subject. Buffalo, New York, Meow Press, 1995.
Little Orphan Anagram, with Susan Bee. New York, Granary, 1997.
Reading Red, with Richard Tuttle. Köln, Walther Konig, 1998.
Log Rhythms, with Susan Bee. New York, Granary, 1998.
Republics of Reality: Poems 1975–1995. Los Angeles, Sun and Moon Press, 2000.

Plays

Blind Witness News (opera libretto), music by Ben Yarmolinsky (produced New York, 1990).
The Lenny Paschen Show (opera libretto), music by Ben Yarmolinsky (produced New York 1992).

Other

Content's Dream: Essays 1975–1984. Los Angeles, Sun and Moon Press, 1986.
Artifice of Absorption. Philadelphia, Paper Air, 1987.
A Poetics. Cambridge, Massachusetts, Harvard University Press, 1992.
My Way: Speeches and Poems. Chicago, University of Chicago Press, 1999.

Editor, with Bruce Andrews, *The L=A=N=G=U=A=G=E Book.* Carbondale, Southern Illinois University Press, 1984.

Editor, *The Politics of Poetic Form: Poetry and Public Policy.* New York, Roof, 1990.

Editor, *Close Listening: Poetry and the Performed Word.* New York, Oxford University Press, 1998.

Translator, *The Maternal Drape,* by Claude Royet-Journoud. Windsor, Vermont, Awede Press, 1984.

Translator, *Red, Green, and Black,* by Olivier Cadiot. Windsor, Vermont, Awede Press, 1984.

Translator, with others, *Selected Language Poems=Mei-kuo yu yen pai shih hsuam.* Chengdu, China, Sichuan Literature and Art Publishing House, 1993.

*

Critical Studies: Charles Bernstein issue of *Difficulties* (Kent, Ohio), ii, 1, 1982; "L=A=N=G=U=A=G=E Poetry in the Eighties" by Marjorie Perloff, in *American Poetry Review* (Philadelphia), May-June 1984; "Edit Is Act: Some Measurement for Content's Dream" by Larry Price, in *Line,* 1986; "The Crisis in Poetry," in *Missouri Review* (Columbia), 1986, and "Chalres Bernstein's Dark City: Polis, Policy, and the Policing of Poetry," in *American Poetry Review* (Philadelphia), 24(5), Sept/Oct 1995, both by Hank Lazer; "Pattern as Qualitative Infinity: The Unit as a Book, the Book as a Unit" by Leslie Scalapino, in *Poetics Journal,* 1987; "Private Enigmas and Critical Functions, with Particular Reference to the Writing of Charles Bernstein" by Jerome McGann, in *New Literacy History* (Baltimore), 1990; *Language Poetry: Writing as Rescue* by Linda Reinfeld, Baton Rouge, Louisiana State University Press, 1992; "Reappropriation and Resistance: Charles Bernstein, Language Poetry, and Poetic Tradition" by Christopher Beach, in *ABC of Influence: Ezra Pound and the Remaking of American Poetic Tradition,* Berkeley, University of California Press, 1992; "The Music of Construction: Measure and Polyphony in Ashbery and Bernstein" by John Shoptaw, in *The Tribe of John: Ashbery and Contemporary Poetry,* edited by Susan Schultz, Tuscaloosa, University of Alabama Press, 1995; "(Mis)Characterizing Charlie: Language and the Self in the Poetry and Poetics of Charles Bernstein" by Paul Naylor, in *Sagetrieb* (Orono, Maine), 14(3), winter 1995; *Twenty-five Sentences Containing the Words 'Charles Bernstein', Why Write?* by Paul Auster, Providence, Burning Deck, 1996; "Charles Bernstein: A Dossier" edited by Paul A. Bove, in *Boundary 2* (Pittsburgh), 23(3), fall 1996; "'Rough Trades': Charles Bernstein and the Currency of Poetry" by Kevin McGuirk, in *Canadian Review of American Studies,* 27(3), 1997.

Charles Bernstein comments:

The sense of music in poetry: the music of meaning—emerging, fogging, contrasting, etc. Tune attunement in understanding—the meaning sounds. It's impossible to separate prosody from the structure of the poem. You can talk about strategies of meaning generation, shape, the kinds of sounds accented, the varieties of measurement (of scale, of number, of line length, of syllable order, of word length, of phrase length, of punctuation). But no one has primacy—the music is the orchestrating these into poems, the angles one plays against another, the shading.

My interest in not conceptualizing the field of the poem as a unitary plane: that any prior principle of composition violates the priority I want to give to the inherence of surface, to the total necessity in the durational space of the poem for every moment to count. Writing as a process of pushing whatever way, or making the piece cohere as far as I can: stretching my mind—to where I know it makes sense but not quite why—suspecting relations that I understand, that make the sense of the ready—to hand, i.e., pushing the composition to the very limits of sense, meaning, to that razor's edge where judgment/aesthetic sense is all I can go on (know-how).

*   *   *

Lyn Hejinian published Charles Bernstein's book *Senses of Responsibility,* indeed printed and designed it, on her Tuumba Press in 1979. It is written in a style that could only strike Hejinian as in accord with her own suspended style of discourse, a language intended never quite to touch earth or to assemble in a final pattern of unified meanings. Instead, Bernstein, like Hejinian and vintage John Ashbery, particularly in his double monologue "As You Know," tends to make poetry stand still and accumulate sound, not expository sense. The juxtapositions of sound phrases owe their invention to Gertrude Stein, who stood poetry on its ear in 1914 with the publication of her teasing book *Tender Buttons.*

But there is a doleful, somnolent quality to Bernstein's long lyrics. They seem rooted in American symbolist meditations, the sort T.S. Eliot wrote in the teens, including "The Love Song of J. Alfred Prufrock," "Preludes," and "Portrait of a Lady." The poetry tends to explore the discord of a speaker's mind, the ravaged emotions and confused thinking brought on by an unnamed crisis or impending disaster.

Bernstein explores the sense of disaster obliquely, but at bottom he is working his way toward a consciousness of the Holocaust. As a Jewish poet he is haunted by the past and the terrors of an unfeeling, inattentive society that could allow such horrors to befall an entire race of citizens. In his prose collection *Content's Dream* he carefully dissects the meaning of film as a window through which a passive, protected audience can witness all manner of violence, horror, and sexual degradation without feeling responsible for any of the events. The inconsequentiality of television and movies and the automatism of writing in general make Bernstein's linguistic inventions seem an escape from the conditions in which other holocausts are likely.

Under Bernstein's surface of syntactical disjunction and casual wordplay lies a more urgent script. Following the lead of Stein's earlier prose experiments, in which ordinary experience leaps to life as strange, animistic fields of events, Bernstein reformulates lyric discourse, sending it down logical pathways it has not gone before—to startle, disorient, wake us from moral slumber, and make us heed the precise wording of our social contracts, our information mills, our avalanche of propagandized prose. He means for us to be on the defensive, to be alert, and his poetry is constantly fooling us out of our assumptions so that we pay closer attention:

That's the trouble around here
through which, asking as it does
a different kind of space, who

much like any other, relives
what's noise, a better shoe, plants
its own destination, shooting up

at a vacant—which is forever

unreconstituted—wedding party,
rituals in which, acting out of

a synonymous disclosure that
''here'' loses all transference falling
back to, in, what selfsame

dwelling is otherwise unaccounted for.

Many of Bernstein's speakers are trapped in situations from which there is no escape; they kill time by letting their thoughts range over a tedious catalog of subjects that convey something of the atmosphere of horror waiting to happen. Hannah Arendt made the now famous observation that evil is banal, but reality is merely banal on the surface. Below throb forces and powers that can either mark the way to paradise or purgatory, depending on one's vigilance.

Poetic Justice bears fingerprints on its cover to suggest the booking of a prisoner. It is another of Bernstein's prose sequences on a waiting man, whose resources of language allow him to delicately dissect his every sensation and turn of thought.

Listen. I can feel it. Specifically and intentionally. It does hurt. I like it. Ringing like this. The hum. Words peeling. The one thing. Not so much limited as conditioned. Here. In this.

Spurting. It tastes good. Clogs. Thick with shape. I carry it with me where ever I go. I like it like this. Smears.

In *Parsing* the final fifteen pages are a list of familiar objects, each beginning with ''my.'' The list is preceded by a quote from Swami Sachnananda—''Count the number of things you call mine. This is the distance between you and enlightenment.'' Bernstein's poetry suggests the need to purge oneself of corrupt emotions and habits, dull senses buried under the tawdry wares of a civilization gone to seed. Words are magic, and according to Bernstein they lure one into the remotest intellectual landscapes and cause worlds to turn or be reborn. Bernstein's language poetry, which became a substantial movement in the post-World War II era, argues two issues at once: that the death of language is the death of morality, spirit, and soul; and that the renewal of language is the birth of freedom.

Like Hejinian and Ashbery, Bernstein is a parodist of older styles of writing, The intention is not always satirical but can be affectionate, a subtle form of nostalgia for less complicated worlds, less self-conscious modes of expression. Sometimes, when the tone is light and precise, the effect of merging his voice with those of the past can be haunting:

There is an emptiness that fills
Our lives as we meet
On the boulevards and oases
Of a convenient attachment. Boats
In undertone drift into
Incomplete misapprehension, get
All fired up inside.

In *Rough Trades* Bernstein's parodic skills take on whole passages of lyric in paraphrase, with the result that the sound of much of his phrasing, while saying one thing, or nothing, recalls something else, however unrelated. This happens in ''The Kiwi Bird in the Kiwi Tree,'' where we hear scraps of Omar Khayyám:

. . . The tailor tells
of other tolls, the seam that binds, the trim,
the waste. & having spelled these names, move on
to toys or talcums, skates & scores.

From 1978 to 1981 Bernstein edited *L=A=N=G=U=A=G=E,* the bimonthly journal of poetics and poetry that brought together poets and prose writers attracted to semantic and linguistic experiments. The journal initiated a movement among many interested in turning a reader's concentration to the medium of words instead of the meanings to be abstracted from them. Writers in the journal seem to agree that the language of art has been too well appropriated by others for political and commercial ends and that only by distorting and experimenting with its syntax and grammar can it be renewed for artistic use.

—Paul Christensen

BERRIGAN, Daniel (J.)

Nationality: American. **Born:** Virginia, Minnesota, 9 May 1921. **Education:** Woodstock College, Baltimore, Maryland, 1943–46; Weston (Jesuit) Seminary, Massachusetts: ordained Roman Catholic priest, 1952. **Career:** Teacher of French, English, and Latin, St. Peter's Preparatory School, Jersey City, New Jersey, 1945–49; performed ministerial work in Europe, 1953–54; auxiliary military chaplain, 1954; instructor in French and philosophy, Brooklyn Preparatory School, 1954–57; teacher of New Testament Studies, LeMoyne College, Syracuse, New York, 1957–63; assistant editor, *Jesuit Missions,* New York, 1963–65; director of United Christian Work, Cornell University, Ithaca, New York, 1967–68; jailed for anti-war activities, 1968. From 1972 professor of theology, Woodstock College, New York. Visiting lecturer, University of Manitoba, Winnipeg, 1973; University of Detroit, 1975; University of California, Berkeley, 1976; Yale University, New Haven, Connecticut, 1977; Loyola University, New Orleans, Louisiana, 1988; DePaul University, Chicago, Illinois, 1992, 1994; and Colorado College, Colorado Springs, 1993, 1995. **Awards:** Lamont Poetry Selection award, 1957; Thomas More Association Medal, 1970; Melcher Book award, 1971. **Address:** 220 West 98th Street, Number 7J, New York 10025, U.S.A.

PUBLICATIONS

Poetry

Time without Number. New York, Macmillan, 1957.
Encounters. Cleveland, World, 1960.
The World for Wedding Ring. New York, Macmillan. 1962.
No One Walks Waters. New York, Macmillan, 1966.
False Gods, Real Men: New Poems. New York, Macmillan, 1966.
Love, Love at the End: Parables, Prayers, and Meditations. New York, Macmillan, 1968.
Night Flight to Hanoi: War Diary with 11 Poems. New York, Macmillan, 1968.
Crime Trial. Boston, Impressions Workshop, 1970.
Trial Poems. Boston, Beacon Press, 1970.
Selected and New Poems. New York, Doubleday, 1973.
Prison Poems. Greensboro, North Carolina, Unicorn Press, 1973.

Prison Poems. New York, Viking Press, 1974.

May All Creatures Live. Nevada City, California, Harold Berliner Press, 1984.

Block Island. Greensboro, North Carolina, Unicorn Press, 1985.

Lost & Found. Montclair, New Jersey, Caliban Press, 1989.

Jubilee! 1939–1989: Fifty Years a Jesuit. Greensboro, North Carolina, Unicorn Press, 1990.

Tulips in the Prison Yard. Selected Poems of Daniel Berrigan. Dublin, Ireland, Dedalus Press, 1992.

Homage to Gerard Manley Hopkins. Baltimore, Maryland, Fortcamp Press, 1993.

Minor Prophets Major Themes. Marion, South Dakota, Fortkamp, 1995.

And the Risen Bread: Selected Poems, 1957–1997, edited by John Dear. New York, Fordham University Press, 1998.

Recordings: *America Is Hard to Find,* Cornell University, 1970; *Berrigan Raps,* Caedmon, 1972; *Not Letting Me Not Let Blood: Prison Poems,* National Catholic Reporter, 1976.

Play

The Trial of the Catonsville Nine (produced Los Angeles, 1970; New York and London, 1971). Boston, Beacon Press, 1970.

Other

The Bride: Essays in the Church. New York, Macmillan, 1959.

The Bow in the Clouds: Man's Covenant with God. New York, Coward McCann, and London, Burns Oates, 1961.

They Call Us Dead Men: Reflections on Life and Conscience. New York, Macmillan, 1966.

Consequences: Truth and. . . . New York, Macmillan, and London, Collier Macmillan, 1967.

Go from Here: A Prison Diary (includes verse). San Francisco, Open Space, 1968.

No Bars to Manhood. New York, Doubleday, 1970.

The Dark Night of Resistance. New York, Doubleday, 1971.

The Geography of Faith: Conversations between Daniel Berrigan, When Underground, and Robert Coles. Boston, Beacon Press, 1971.

Absurd Convictions, Modest Hopes: Conversations after Prison with Lee Lockwood. New York, Random House, 1972.

America Is Hard to Find. New York, Doubleday, 1972; London, SPCK, 1973.

Jesus Christ. New York, Doubleday, 1973.

Vietnamese Letter. New York, Hoa Binh Press, 1973.

Lights On in the House of the Dead: A Prison Diary. New York, Doubleday, 1974.

The Raft Is Not the Shore: Conversations toward a Buddhist/Christian Awareness, with Thich Nhat Hanh. Boston, Beacon Press, 1975.

A Book of Parables. New York, Seabury Press, 1977.

Uncommon Prayer: A Book of Psalms. New York, Seabury Press, 1978.

The Words Our Savior Gave Us. Springfield, Illinois, Templegate, 1978.

Beside the Sea of Glass: The Song of the Lamb. New York, Seabury Press, 1978.

The Discipline of the Mountain: Dante's Purgatorio in a Nuclear World. New York, Seabury Press, 1979.

We Die before We Live: Conversations with the Very Ill. New York, Seabury Press, 1980.

Ten Commandments for the Long Haul. New York, Seabury Press, 1981.

Portraits of Those I Love. New York, Crossroad, 1982.

The Nightmare of God. Portland, Sunburst, 1983.

Steadfastness of the Saints: A Journal of Peace and War in Central and North America. Mary Knoll, New York, Orbis, 1985.

The Mission: A Film Journal. New York, Harper, 1986.

To Dwell in Peace (autobiography). New York, Harper, 1987.

The Hole in the Ground: A Parable for Peacemakers. Minneapolis, Minnesota, Honeywell Project, 1987.

Daniel Berrigan: Poetry, Drama, Prose, edited by Michael True. Mary Knoll, New York, Orbis, 1988.

Stations: The Way of the Cross. New York, Harper, 1989.

Sorrow Built a Bridge: Friendship and AIDS. Baltimore, Maryland, Fortkamp Publishing, 1989.

Whereon to Stand: The Acts of the Apostles and Ourselves. Baltimore, Maryland, Fortkamp Publishing, 1991.

Selections from the Writings of Daniel Berrigan. Erie, Pennsylvania, Pax Christi, 1991.

Isaiah: Spirit of Courage, Gift of Tears. Minneapolis, Minnesota, Fortress Press, 1996.

Ezekiel: Vision in the Dust. Maryknoll, New York, Orbis Books, 1997.

Daniel, under the Siege of the Divine. Farmington, Pennsylvania, Plough Publishing, 1998.

Jeremiah: The World, the Wound of God. Minneapolis, Minnesota, Fortress Press, 1999.

The Bride: Images of the Church. Maryknoll, New York, Orbis Books, 2000.

Editor, *For Swords into Plowshares, The Hammer Has to Fall: The Griffiss Plowshares Action.* Piscatoway, New Jersey, Plowshares, 1984.

*

Bibliography: *The Berrigans: A Bibliography of Published Works by Daniel, Philip, and Elizabeth McAlister Berrigan* by Anne Klejment, New York, Garland, 1980.

Critical Studies: *Apologies, Good Friends. . .: An Interim Biography of Daniel Berrigan* by John Deedy, Chicago, Fides Claretian, 1981; *The Writings of Daniel Berrigan* by Ross Labrie, Lanham, Maryland, American University Press, 1989; *Apostle of Peace: Essays in Honor of Daniel Berrigan,* Maryknoll, New York, Orbis Books, 1996; interview by Mark Wagner, *Agni,* 43, 1996.

*   *   *

In spite of his Jesuit training, there is little in Daniel Berrigan's poetry to suggest Gerard Manley Hopkins as a model. Reading the imprimaturs and the *nihil obstats* on the early volumes is surprising to the reader who has come to Berrigan from his later work, where such marks of orthodoxy are so conspicuously absent, perhaps even unavailable. Hopkins was probably too abstractly theological to be a model for Berrigan's taste. Berrigan's early poems have more the feel of seventeenth-century English devotional verse. His references to Simone Weil suggest an indebtedness to her favorite poet among the English writers—George Herbert.

The early volumes brought quick success to Berrigan as a poet:

Style
envelopes a flower like its odor;
bestows on radiant air
the spontaneous word that greets and makes a king.

It is interesting that an early poem addressed to Wallace Stevens accepts the techniques but repudiates the metaphysics that was a part of the Stevens aesthetic:

Awakening
When I grew appalled by love
and promised nothing, but stood, a sick man
first time on feeble knees
peering at walls and weather
like the feeble minded—
the strange outdoors, the house of strangers—
there, there was a beginning.

But even the early poems were dedicated to Dorothy Day, the quiet figure so central to the life of radical Catholicism in America. In their introductions they intone *beata pauperes spiritu* and *beata pacifici,* and Berrigan was to take the words seriously.

Berrigan's opposition to the Vietnam War led him to found Clergy and Laymen Concerned about Vietnam. This ecumenical action so enraged Cardinal Spellman that he exiled Berrigan to South America, a move that proved so unpopular that the cardinal was quickly forced to rescind the action. But the tour through South America—the response to the appalling poverty he saw there—brought Berrigan back to the United States a convinced religious radical. *Consequences: Truth and . . .* is the record of his spiritual and political development during the period.

A post as professor of religion and poetry at Cornell University did not dampen Berrigan's growing involvement with his brother Philip in active opposition to the war. Pouring blood on draft files led to the burning of draft files in Catonsville, Maryland. As he turned increasingly to direct action, Berrigan also turned to prose, his poetry being used to focus his personal reaction to the events he experienced. In *Night Flight to Hanoi* he wrote of holding one child saved from bombing:

Children in the Shelter
Imagine; three of them.
As though survival
were a rat's word.
and a rat's end
waited there at the end
And I must have
in the century's boneyard
heft of flesh and bone in my arms
I picked up the littlest
a boy, his face
breaded with rice (his sister calmly feeding him
as we climbed down)
In my arms fathered
in a moment's grace, the messiah

of all my tears. I bore, reborn
a Hiroshima child from hell.

The play *The Trial of the Catonsville Nine* brought Berrigan worldwide attention, and his prison journals were among the eloquent publications of the last years of the 1960s. *The Dark Night of Resistance,* also published during the period, illustrated the growing influence on Berrigan of Saint John of the Cross, who was read in the 1950s by poets influenced by the religious revival of the time. One has a sense that Berrigan came to understand John in the late 1960s, that he found the saint in his prison experience a model to be lived rather than a style to be imitated.

Berrigan has remained a Roman Catholic and a Jesuit. He has become less active in writing poetry and more active in building a society that can be honestly celebrated in poetry. Despite the serious moral and political issues he forced through his personal involvement, there remains throughout his poetry a sustained joyousness, a marked characteristic of all his work.

—Myron Taylor

BERRY, Francis

Nationality: British. **Born:** Ipoh, Malaya, 23 March 1915. **Education:** Hereford Cathedral School; Dean Close School; University College, Exeter, 1937, 1946; University of London, B.A. 1947; University of Exeter, M.A. 1960. **Military Service:** British Army, 1939–46. **Family:** Married 1) Nancy Melloney Graham in 1947 (died 1967), one son and one daughter; 2) Patricia Thomson in 1970 (marriage dissolved 1975); 3) Eileen Lear in 1979. **Career:** Lecturer, then professor of English, University of Sheffield, 1947–70; professor of English, Royal Holloway College, University of London, Egham, Surrey, 1970–80, now emeritus. Visiting lecturer, Carleton College, Northfield, Minnesota, 1951–52, and University of the West Indies, Jamaica, 1957; British Council Lecturer in India, 1966–67; W.P. Ker Lecturer, University of Glasgow, 1979; visiting fellow, Australian National University, Canberra, 1979; visiting professor, University of Malawi, 1980–81; British Council Lecturer in Japan, 1983; honorary fellow, University of London, 1987. Fellow, Royal Society of Literature, 1968. **Address:** 4 Eastgate Street, Winchester, Hampshire SO23 8EB, England.

PUBLICATIONS

Poetry

Gospel of Fire. London, Mathews and Marrot, 1933.
Snake in the Moon. London, Williams and Norgate, 1936.
The Iron Christ. London, Williams and Norgate, 1938.
Fall of a Tower and Other Poems. London, Fortune Press, 1942.
Murdock and Other Poems. London, Dakers, 1947.
The Galloping Centaur: Poems 1933–1951. London, Methuen, 1952.
Morant Bay and Other Poems. London, Routledge, 1961.
Ghosts of Greenland. London, Routledge, 1967.
From the Red Fort. Bristol, Redcliffe, 1984.
Collected Poems. Bristol, Redcliffe, 1994.

Plays

Radio Plays: *Illnesses and Ghosts at the West Settlement,* 1965; *The Sirens,* 1966; *The Near Singing Dome,* 1971; *Eyre Remembers,* 1982.

Novel

I Tell of Greenland. London, Routledge, 1977.

Other

Herbert Read. London, Longman, 1953; revised edition, 1961.
Poets' Grammar: Person, Time and Mood in Poetry. London, Routledge, 1958; Westport, Connecticut, Greenwood Press, 1974.
Poetry and the Physical Voice. London, Routledge, and New York, Oxford University Press, 1962.
The Shakespeare Inset: Word and Picture. London, Routledge, 1965; New York, Theatre Arts, 1966; revised edition, Carbondale, Southern Illinois University Press, 1971.
John Masefield: The Narrative Poet (lecture). Sheffield, University of Sheffield, 1968.
Thoughts on Poetic Time (lecture). Abingdon-on-Thames, Berkshire, Abbey Press, 1972.

Editor, *Essays and Studies* 22. London, Murray, 1969.

*

Manuscript Collections: Lockwood Memorial Library, State University of New York, Buffalo; Sheffield Public Library; Brotherton Collection, Leeds University Library.

Critical Studies: "Francis Berry," in *Neglected Powers,* London, Routledge, and New York, Barnes and Noble, 1971, and "My Life's Work, with a Discussion of Francis Berry's Poetry," in *Literature and the Art of Creation,* edited by Robert Welch and Suheil Badi Bushrui, Totawa, New Jersey, Barnes and Noble, 1988, both by George Wilson Knight; *Tradition and Experiment in English Poetry* by Philip Hobsbaum, London, Macmillan, and Totowa, New Jersey, Rowman and Littlefield, 1979.

Francis Berry comments:

Have been deeply enchanted by geography—the Mediterranean, the West Indies, Greenland—for the settings it supplies for human actions. Strongest emotion used to be fear in its varieties, especially around sunset or in the night. But even strong noontide sunlight provoked anxiety. Cruelty figures in early poems because I am frightened of cruelty. Have felt responsive to other times as well as other places: so history and myths are also poetic preoccupations. I believe the dead might still care and would not hurt them. It is a gratification to have written any poem that I think is good enough, but the long poem, narrative or dramatic, of lively structure, compact, of varied rhythm, and vivid images, is what I most delight in making: its making sustains the maker day after day during its making and renders tolerable the return of first consciousness each morning.

*   *   *

Francis Berry is a master of the long poem, and his finest work is in that genre. Because of this he has been underrepresented in magazines and anthologies, and his reputation has yet to match the opinion such critics as G. Wilson Knight and Donald Davie have formed of his work.

The Iron Christ tells of a statue made from the guns of the frontier fortresses of Chile and Argentina and the attempt to erect this on the highest point of the Andes as a symbol of peace. The struggle up the mountain is rendered graphically:

> The driver turns his face, his arm to throttle
> Levering steam, but, with a cursing, spin
> The driving-wheels, skidding upon raw rails,
> Circuiting vainly, then grab, heel over rods,
> Pistons pant, valves hiss, wheels grip, groan, grab . . .

Morant Bay deals with an uprising of blacks in Jamaica that was put down ruthlessly by Governor Eyre in 1865. The exotic coloration is instantly compelling:

> . . . On the other side of the ravine
> Rises the opposing flank of another spur,
> Its sandstone swooned from the blurs of that sun,
> Dotted with thorned scrub, roots bedded in stone,
> On which the red spider darts or the lizard waits
> Before his next scurry with a sobbing throat . . .

Equally compelling are the different voices that interweave the narration. One thinks of the diatribe that emanates from the black Deacon Bogle, who denounces the governor and who is echoed by the impassioned responses of his congregation:

> "Der he be
> In dat King's House, an' he eat"—
> *In dat King's House, an' he eat.*
> "He eat fishes an' he eat meat,"
> *He eat fishes an' he eat meat,*
> *War-o, heavy war-o . . .*

Because he uses the voices of his protagonists, Berry is able to enter into their characters and see all sides of the question: Eyre, courageous but bigoted; the instigator of the uprising, Gordon, intelligent and envious; Deacon Bogle, a personification of the superstitious blacks. What is so impressive about this poem upon a vexed subject—race hatred—is that it does not take sides. Instead, it seeks to understand the difficulty of a situation. In many ways *Morant Bay* is a great Catholic poem. It sees the massacre at Morant Bay in terms of original sin, an obeah "whose magic undergoes all manner of transfer / But cannot be cast out."

In *Illnesses and Ghosts at the West Settlement,* Berry's re-creation of voices takes a further step and enters a new terrain. This is the Greenland colonized at the end of the first millennium A.D. by Erik the Red. Plague strikes down the little settlement, smashing the sanctions that govern even this primitive society. The remnant of people staying there becomes demoralized. The whole poem is couched in terms of a recollection by the various ghosts hovering above the colony where they suffered so dreadfully a thousand years before. Gudrid, Erik's daughter-in-law, is the central character. Her voice comes across the centuries in characteristically tentative meters, re-creating a woman's agony in the face of male intransigence:

Illnesses and ghosts.
You founded Greenland, I've seen enough of your Greenland
And I want the sun for a while, husband or no husband.
I want the sun because I am so cold, you know I am so cold,
That I could hear that particular sound again
                                        Oh, I am so old
Before I am hardly girl. Dear Father, Father-in-law,
    help me . . .

It is questionable whether any contemporary poet can offer a greater range of technique and subject matter.

The story does not end with Greenland. ''The Singing Dome,'' which appears in *From the Red Fort,* concerns Shah Jahan, who built the Taj Mahal in memory of his wife. Here is the voice of the dead woman, Mumtaz, interrupting her husband's thoughts, accusing him of wishing her dead in order that he might build his immortal dome:

I died because you wanted me to die.
Or thought you did . . . sometimes. For I could read
That silent thought in the way you looked
At me . . . sometimes. It made me sad—for you
Because I surmised you would be desolate
And helpless . . . I gone. And that you would regret
That thought you had allowed me to discern . . .
Sometimes . . . though you should have not . . .

Note the pondering meter, the quiet dwelling upon the word ''sometimes.'' This is a sparser, more intimate verse than we are used to from Berry. The pain lies nearer the surface. There is a sense of autobiography here not evident, on the whole, in the earlier poems. ''Mbona,'' a narrative concerning a rainmaker, and ''The Banana Plant,'' about a deceased wife who is enshrined in that vegetable, exhibit kindred qualities together with what, for want of a better phrase, might be described as a feeling for nature. Berry has also written successful poems about animals—''The Peacock Senescent,'' ''The Panther,'' and ''Lumping It''—the last an expressionist piece about a boa constrictor.

The process of development with Berry seems to have been a progressive stripping off, so that he has come to confront us with experience at its most personal. One of the most naked of the later poems is called ''Ad Patrem.'' The title is an ironic reference to a text by Milton, who had a father who encouraged him. Berry's history seems to have been quite different. He reverses the direction of Milton's poem, making the father a third-person figure and addressing himself as a second person in a verse as austere as anything he has ever attempted:

He remembers you
Immediate male ancestor
As the declared atheist, son and book hater
The stern and disappointed one
Of whom he was afraid . . .

In 1994 the bulk of this output was gathered together in a truly magnificent *Collected Poems.* The volume was reviewed by David McDuff in *Stand Magazine* (spring 1995), where he termed it ''an extraordinary medley of verse pieces on subjects that range from the Icelandic sagas to the Iron Christ of Chile and Argentina, from the Jamaican riot of Morant Bay to the building of the Taj Mahal.''

In the end it is to the long poems that we turn. Here we have an oeuvre unsurpassed in the later twentieth century. As Robert Nye said of Berry in the *Times* (September 15, 1994), ''He has a rich vein of humanity which makes him interested in verse as a means of storytelling through the use of different voices.'' All we need do is learn from the approach exemplified in Berry's various critical works and attempt to develop an auditory imagination.

—Philip Hobsbaum

BERRY, James

Nationality: British (immigrated to England in 1948). **Born:** Fair Prospect, Jamaica, 1925. **Career:** Overseas telegraphist, Post Office, London, 1951–77. Writer-in-residence, Vauxhall Manor School, London. **Awards:** National Poetry prize, 1981, for ''Fantasy of an African Boy''; C. Day Lewis fellowship; Smarties prize, 1987, for *A Thief in the Village and Other Stories*; Signal Poetry award, for *When I Dance.* **Address:** c/o Hamish Hamilton, 27 Wrights Lane, London W8 5TZ, England.

PUBLICATIONS

Poetry

Fractured Circles. London, New Beacon, 1979.
Lucy's Letters and Loving. London, New Beacon, 1982.
Chain of Days. Oxford, Oxford University Press, 1985.
Hot Earth, Cold Earth. Newcastle upon Tyne, Bloodaxe, 1995.

Poetry (for children)

When I Dance. London, Hamish Hamilton, 1988.
Celebration Song, illustrated by Louise Brierley. London, Hamish Hamilton, and New York, Simon and Schuster, 1994.
Rough Sketch Beginning, illustrated by Robert Florczak. San Diego, Harcourt Brace, 1996.
Playing a Dazzler. London, Hamish Hamilton, 1996; as *Everywhere Faces Everywhere,* New York, Simon and Schuster, 1997.

Short Stories

The Girls and Yanga Marshall. London, Longman, 1987.

Other

A Thief in the Village and Other Stories (for children). London, Hamish Hamilton, 1987; New York, Orchard, 1988.
Anancy-Spiderman (for children). London, Walker Books, 1989; as *Spiderman-Anancy,* New York, Holt, 1989.
The Future-Telling Lady (for children). Northampton, Hamilton, 1991; as *The Future-Telling Lady and Other Stories,* New York, HarperCollins, 1993.
Isn't My Name Magical? (for children). London, BBC Books, 1991.

Ajeemah and His Son (for children). New York, HarperCollins, 1994.
Don't Leave an Elephant to Go and Chase a Bird (for children). New York, Simon and Schuster, 1996.
First Palm Trees (for children). New York, Simon and Schuster, 1997.

Editor, *Bluefoot Traveller: An Anthology of West Indian Poets in Britain*. London, Limestone, 1976; revised edition, 1981.
Editor, *Dance to a Different Drum; Brixton Poetry Festival 1983: Poetry from a Community*. London, Brixton Festival, 1983.
Editor, *News for Babylon: The Chatto Book of West Indian-British Poetry*. London, Chatto and Windus, 1984.
Editor, *Classic Poems to Read Aloud*. New York, Kingfisher, 1995.

*

Critical Studies: ''Learning to Live in London: James Berry'' by Wolfgang Binder, in *Commonwealth Essays and Studies* (Dijon, France), 10(2), spring 1988; ''An Impulse to Write: An Interview with James Berry'' by Brian Merrick, in *Children's Literature in Education* (New York), 27(4), 1996.

*   *   *

A member of the generation that went to England from the West Indies on the SS *Windrush* in 1948, James Berry is one of the pioneers in the development of a black poetry rooted in the British West Indian community and in its speech and experiences. He has edited many of the influential anthologies of West Indian poets in England, including *Bluefoot Traveller*. While some of the nineteen poets included in the 1981 edition were born in England, the anthology continues an older West Indian political and literary culture in which dialect, the peasant, and the village represent authenticity. Berry's own ''Banana Talk'' combines the conventions of political protest with West Indian subject matter and speech. Thus, this is an anthology of cultural assertion by nostalgic or idealizing immigrants concerned with their identity in a foreign land. In his introduction to *News for Babylon: The Chatto Book of West Indian-British Poetry*, Berry declares his purpose as being to make ''another step towards the establishment of Westindian-British writing . . . in its own right.''

Fractured Circles is a selection of poems from two decades, including those from the 1950s about being an immigrant, seeking a room in London, and meeting British whites. Berry is aware of time passing and of making a mark on time. The allegory of the immigrant, combined with a metaphysics of life as being movement in time, suggests a narrative. The first poem begins, ''You can't settle on the ground / like an earth loving rock,'' and it concludes, ''I arrested time: / I moved, unaware of kept movements / to devour me.'' In the next poem the speaker hears Big Ben:

I whisper, man you mek it.
You arrive.
Then sudden like, quite loud, I say,
''Then whey you goin' sleep tenight?''

Berry assumes readers who among themselves speak Jamaican English with its many proverbs. He wants to bring pride to the use of Creole English in poetry.

''Travelling As We Are'' interrupts the interiorized philosophizing. On a London underground train, feeling ''British among Britons,'' the poet encounters two white children and their mother from the American South: ''But this is Europe, Memmy. How come / niggers live here too?'' Although there are no other poems as specific as this one about the history of black-white relations, it is enough to explain the allusions to feelings of anger; there is a past rooted in the slave trade and a slavery that continues to haunt blacks living in the white world. One of Berry's concerns is with memory, and he creates his own memories in contrast to the memories of an older generation. But Berry's memories are often stories about rural Jamaica or longing for an imagined Africa.

In 1981 Berry won the National Poetry prize for ''Fantasy of an African Boy,'' which was followed a year later by his second book of poetry, *Lucy's Letters and Loving*. The amusing poems in the ''Lucy's Letters'' section are in heavily Jamaican English, written by an immigrant to Leela, her friend in rural Jamaica, explaining life in London and concluding with a proverb. The poems contrast the financial advantages of living in England with the natural advantages of what has been lost, such as close friendships and warm weather: ''We get money for holidays / but there's no sun-hot / to enjoy cool breeze.'' The women have jobs and money, are no longer dominated by men, and are influenced by feminists, but they miss dressing up for men. Lucy returns to England after a holiday in the West Indies and worries about losing her past. She is no longer a West Indian but a British West Indian, someone whose identity is being shaped and changed by her life in England. Lucy then decides to save money to buy herself land at home, to which she plans to retire.

The ''Loving'' section of *Lucy's Letters and Loving* consists of love lyrics. Some are set in London, others in a Jamaican village with footnotes explaining the Creole terms. That a poet who has lived for more than thirty years in England should write poems about rural Jamaica in Jamaican English suggests how many of the *Windrush* generation have continued to see themselves as permanent immigrants, never at home in England.

By the time of *Chain of Days* Berry was less likely to become lost in metaphysics. He had become more a poet of statement, but many of the poems are variations on a few basic stylistic mannerisms. For example, ''Two Black Laborers on a London Building Site,'' based on a London underground train crash, has an irony that any minority will recognize:

Who the driver?
Not a black man. Not a black man?
I check that firs'.
Thank Almighty God.
'Bout thirty people dead
An' black man didn' drive?

In *Hot Earth Cold Earth* Berry economically uses dialect, carefully structuring his verse through rhyme, regular stanzas, rhythms based on syllabics and metrics, and even experiments with linked haiku. Some poems have a surreal lyricism that describes the coming and going of the muse. Berry works from an older tradition of protest literature based on class and racial stereotypes: the ballad, folk song, spiritual, and blues. Martin Carter's well-known ''University of Hunger'' is behind the ''I want university'' refrain of ''My Letter to You Mother Africa.'' Berry writes poems about blacks as ''my people'' in which whites are ''robots'' and ''captors'' and the police are "the blue clothes gang." Some poems read like newspaper editorials questioning Africa's role in the diaspora, Africa's lack of interest in its children abroad, and Africa's inability to better itself. The poet sees himself as a mixture of cultures and understands that his Africa is more desire than fact.

There are no clear distinctions between Berry's poems for adults and for children. This is possible because, except for the West Indian dialect, he tends to use older literary forms and phrases, such as Georgian poetic inversions, and older delicacies of manner. Many poems seem like popular song lyrics. In his introduction to *When I Dance* Berry describes his poems as "celebrations" that register "black people's presence in Britain" as a way of helping to create a Caribbean community. Berry affirms the Caribbean origins and speech of black children in England, who in his view should study material from black culture.

—Bruce King

BERRY, Wendell (Erdman)

Nationality: American. **Born:** Henry County, Kentucky, 5 August 1934. **Education:** University of Kentucky, Lexington, A.B. 1956, M.A. 1957; Stanford University, California (Stegner Fellow), 1958–59. **Family:** Married Tanya Amyx in 1957; one daughter and one son. **Career:** Taught at Stanford University, 1959–60, and New York University, 1962–64. Member of the faculty, 1964–70, distinguished professor of English, 1971–72, and professor of English, 1973–77, 1987–93, University of Kentucky. Since 1977 staff member, Rodale Press, Emmaus, Pennsylvania. **Awards:** Guggenheim fellowship, 1951; Rockefeller fellowship, 1965; Bess Hokin prize (*Poetry,* Chicago), 1967; National Endowment for the Arts grant, 1969; first-place winner, Borestone Mountain Poetry Awards, 1969, 1970, 1972; National Institute of Arts and Letters Literary award, 1971; Friends of American Writers award, 1975, for *The Memory of Old Jack;* Jean Stein award, American Academy of Arts & Letters, 1987; Lannan Foundation award for nonfiction, 1989; University of Kentucky Libraries award for intellectual excellence, 1993; Aiken-Taylor award for poetry, *Sewanee Review,* 1994; T.S. Eliot award, Ingersoll Foundation, 1994. Honorary doctorates from Centre College, Transylvania College, Berea College, University of Kentucky, Santa Clara University, and Eureka College. **Address:** Port Royal, Kentucky 40058, U.S.A.

PUBLICATIONS

Poetry

November Twenty-Six, Nineteen Hundred Sixty-Three. New York, Braziller, 1964.
The Broken Ground. New York, Harcourt Brace, 1964; London, Cape, 1966.
Openings. New York, Harcourt Brace, 1968.
Findings. Iowa City, Prairie Press, 1969.
Farming: A Hand Book. New York, Harcourt Brace, 1970.
The Country of Marriage. New York, Harcourt Brace, 1973.
An Eastward Look. Berkeley, California, Sand Dollar, 1974.

To What Listens. Crete, Nebraska, Best Cellar Press, 1975.
Horses. Monterrey, Kentucky, Larkspur Press, 1975.
Sayings and Doings. Lexington, Kentucky, Gnomon, 1975.
The Kentucky River. Monterrey, Kentucky, Larkspur Press, 1976.
There Is Singing around Me. Austin, Texas, Cold Mountain Press, 1976.
Three Memorial Poems. Berkeley, California, Sand Dollar, 1977.
Clearing. New York, Harcourt Brace, 1977.
A Part. Berkeley, California, North Point Press, 1980.
The Wheel. Berkeley, California, North Point Press, 1982.
Collected Poems 1957–1982. Berkeley, California, North Point Press, 1985.
Sabbaths. Berkeley, California, North Point Press, 1987; Ipswich, England, Golgonooza, 1992.
Traveling at Home (includes essay). Berkeley, California, North Point Press, 1989.
A Consent. Monterey, Kentucky, Larkspur Press, 1993.
The Storm. Berkeley, California, Okeanos Press, 1994.
Entries: Poems. New York, Pantheon Books, 1994.
The Farm. Monterey, Kentucky, Larkspur Press, 1995.
Amish Economy. Versailles, Kentucky, Adela Press, 1996.
January, Nineteen Seventy-Five. Monterey, Kentucky, Larkspur Press, 1998.
The Selected Poems of Wendell Berry. Washington, D.C., Counterpoint, 1998.
A Timbered Choir: The Sabbath Poems, 1979–1997. Washington, D.C., Counterpoint, 1998.

Play

The Cool of the Day (produced Louisville, Kentucky, 1984).

Novels

Nathan Coulter. Boston, Houghton Mifflin, 1960; revised edition, Berkeley, California, North Point Press, 1985.
A Place on Earth. New York, Harcourt Brace, 1967; revised edition, Berkeley, California, North Point Press, 1983.
The Memory of Old Jack. New York, Harcourt Brace, 1974.
Remembering. Berkeley, California, North Point Press, 1988.
A World Lost. Washington, D.C., Counterpoint, 1996.

Short Stories

Fidelity: Five Stories. New York, Pantheon Books, 1992.
Watch with Me: And Six Other Stories of the Yet-Remembered Ptolemy Proudfoot (1872–1943) and His Wife, Miss Minnie, née Quinch (1874–1953). New York, Pantheon Books, 1994.

Other

The Rise. N.p., Graves Press, 1968.
The Long-Legged House. New York, Harcourt Brace, 1969.
The Hidden Wound. Boston, Houghton Mifflin, 1970.
The Unforeseen Wilderness: An Essay on Kentucky's Red River Gorge, photographs by Eugene Meatyard. Lexington, University Press of Kentucky, 1971.
A Continuous Harmony: Essays Cultural and Agricultural. New York, Harcourt Brace, 1972.

The Unsettling of America: Culture and Agriculture. San Francisco, Sierra Club, 1977.

Recollected Essays 1965–1980. Berkeley, California, North Point Press, 1981.

The Gift of Good Land: Further Essays Cultural and Agricultural. Berkeley, California, North Point Press, 1981.

Standing by Words: Essays. Berkeley, California, North Point Press, 1983.

The Wild Birds: Six Stories of the Port William Membership. Berkeley, California, North Point Press, 1986.

The Landscape of Harmony: Preserving Wildness and Does Community Have a Value? (lectures). Shenmore, Hereford, Five Seasons, 1987.

Home Economics (essays). Berkeley, California, North Point Press, 1987.

The Work of Local Culture. Iowa City, Iowa Humanities Board, 1988.

The Hidden Wound. San Francisco, North Point Press, 1989.

Harlan Hubbard: Life and Work. Lexington, Kentucky, University Press of Kentucky, 1990.

What Are People For? (essays). Berkeley, California, North Point Press, 1990; London, Rider, 1991.

The Discovery of Kentucky. Frankfort, Kentucky, Gnomon Press, 1991.

Standing on Earth: Selected Essays. Ipswich, England, Golgonooza, 1991.

Sex, Economy, Freedom, & Community: Eight Essays. New York, Pantheon Books, 1993.

Another Turn of the Crank: Essays. Washington, D.C., Counterpoint, 1995.

Two More Stories of the Port William Membership. Frankfort, Kentucky, Gnomon Press, 1997.

Editor, with Wes Jackson and Bruce Coleman, *Meeting the Expectations of the Land: Essays in Sustainable Agriculture and Stewardship.* Berkeley, California, North Point Press, 1984.

*

Critical Studies: *A Secular Pilgrimage: Nature, Place, and Morality in the Poetry of Wendell Berry* (dissertation) by Robert Joseph Collins, Ohio State University, 1978; *Quest for Place: The Poetry of Gary Snyder and Wendell Berry* (master's thesis) by Patrick Dennis Murphy, California State University, Northridge, 1983; *Practicing Resurrection: Wendell Berry's Georgic Poetry, an Ecological Critique of American Culture* (dissertation) by Daniel T. Cornell, Washington State University, 1985; *The Spirituality of Place: Wendell Berry's Poetry and the Ground of Being* (master's thesis) by David C. Wright, Northeast Missouri State University, 1991; by Bruce Bawer, in *New Criterion* (New York), 11(3), November 1992; by Ed Folsom, in *Earthly Words: Essays on Contemporary American Nature and Environmental Writers,* Ann Arbor, University of Michigan Press, 1994; ''Cultivating Wilderness: The Place of Land in the Fiction of Ed Abbey and Wendell Berry'' by Nathanael Dresser, in *Growth and Change,* 26(3), 1995; by John R. Knott, in *Essays in Literature,* 23(1), Spring 1996; interview by Jack Jezreel, in *U.S. Catholic,* 64(6), 1 June 1999.

*   *   *

Except for brief study at Stanford University, a year on a Guggenheim fellowship in Europe, and a few years teaching at New York University, Wendell Berry has stayed close to his own place on earth—in Kentucky, on the Kentucky River not far from where it flows into the Ohio. Berry's poetic world is first the physical and social world of his native region. He is a regionalist, not a provincialist, and a deep sense of place animates all of his works. Berry knows the land firsthand, for he farms it. He understands the cycle of the seasons, planting, tending, harvesting, animal husbandry, country people. Because his ancestors have been in the same region for two centuries, he has an almost unique American feeling for ancestral inheritance. He enunciates the familial bond in ''The Gathering,'' a poem from the 1973 collection *The Country of Marriage*—

> At my age my father
> held me on his arm
> like a hooded bird
> and his father held him so . . .

—and ends with

> My son
> will know me in himself
> when his son sits hooded on
> his arm and I have grown
> to be brother to all
> my fathers, memory
> speaking to knowledge
> finally, in my bones.

Like Edwin Muir, whose poetry and prose he has publicly praised, Berry conveys the story of his life in the context of a fable of a family: faithful watchers guard the traditional day.

Berry's seriousness about small farming is informed and passionate. He is the first real farmer-poet of stature in American history, telling readers clearly and forthrightly how Kentucky land has been overworked and ruined by greedy opportunists. The poet describes the degradation of farmland by agribusiness and the resulting pollution of the soil and air by chemical fertilizers and huge machines.

Berry is a wholly committed environmentalist, a preserver of nature and people. His attack on predators in his Kentucky extends to the whole nation, and his corpus of poetry, novels, essays, and short stories attests to his concern for our vanishing world.

Berry's best poetry appears in *Collected Poems 1957–1982.* Many are long poems, the first being an elegy to his paternal grandfather, Pryor Thomas Berry. The long poem ''History,'' from the 1977 collection *Clearing,* is one of the finest. In it the poet condemns the predators who lead his nation:

> The land bears the scars
> of minds whose history
> was imprinted by no example
> of a forebearing mind, corrected,
> beloved.

A Part consists mainly of short poems. Among the most successful are ''Gary Snyder,'' ''Ripening,'' ''The Way of Pain,'' and ''Horses,'' which ends with the lines

> A dance
> is what this plodding is.
> A song, whatever is said.

The Wheel, a book of poetry published in 1982, closes with Berry's attachment to characteristic themes—the natural world, ancestry, marriage:

> Let the rain come,
> the sun, and then the dark,
> for I will rest
> in an easy bed tonight.

Berry's main subjects are those central to humans—love and death. Perhaps no contemporary American poet is more inclined to, or successful with, the elegy as a poetic form. Berry first attracted national notice with *November Twenty-Six, Nineteen Hundred Sixty-Three,* prompted by the death of President John F. Kennedy. His poems on love are numerous, and although they are mainly deeply serious, some are light and witty, such as "The Mad Farmer's Love Song," in *The Country of Marriage:*

> O when the world's at peace
> and every man is free
> then will I go down unto my love

> O and I may go down
> several times before that.

Berry's style is deceptively simple. Though his language is not actually the language of Kentuckians, it sounds authentic. It would hardly be mistaken, say, for that of a New Englander or a westerner. His prosody is chiefly an open form of "naked," though occasionally, especially in his later work, rhyme and meter figure in.

The characteristic mode of Berry's poetry is instructive, as he goes beyond the nature of things to assert their causes. Over the years his poetry has not changed markedly in theme, style, or intention, but it has grown in sureness, in power, and in passionate directness.

—James K. Robinson

BERTOLINO, James

Nationality: American. **Born:** Hurley, Wisconsin, 4 October 1942. **Education:** University of Wisconsin, Stevens Point, Madison, and Oshkosh, B.S. in English and art 1970; Washington State University, Pullman, 1970–71; Cornell University, Ithaca, New York, 1971–73, M.F.A. 1973. **Family:** Married Lois Behling in 1966 (divorced 1999). **Career:** Teaching assistant, Washington State University, 1970–71; teaching assistant, 1971–73, and lecturer in creative writing, 1973–74, Cornell University; assistant professor, 1974–77, and associate professor of English, 1977–84, University of Cincinnati. Visiting professor, Western Washington University, Bellingham, Winter 1984; instructor in English, Skagit Valley College, Mt. Vernon, Washington, 1984–87; instructor, Shoreline and Edmonds Community Colleges, Seattle, 1988–90; lecturer in creative writing, English department, Western Washington University, 1991–2000; visiting professor, Willamette University, Salem, Oregon, 1998–99. Editor, *Abraxas* magazine and Abraxas Press, Madison, Wisconsin, and Ithaca, New York, 1968–72; editor, *Cincinnati Poetry Review,* 1975–81; poetry editor, *Eureka Review,* New Canaan, Connecticut, 1976–81; co-editor, *Cornfield Review,* 1984. Member of the board of directors, Print Center, 1972–74; member of the editorial board, Ithaca House, New York, 1972–74; member of the board of consultants, Coordinating Council of Literary Magazines, from 1975; member of the literature panel, Ohio Arts Council, 1979–80; member of the board, Washington Center for the Book, Seattle Public Library, 1998–2000. Founder, Elliston Book Award, for small press poetry books, 1976. **Awards:** Hart Crane Memorial Foundation award, 1969; Book-of-the-Month Club award, 1970; YMYWHA Poetry Center Discovery award, 1972; National Endowment for the Arts grant, 1974; James Howard Taft research fellowship, 1976, 1980; Charles Phelps Taft Memorial Fund grant, 1977, 1980; Ohio Arts Council grant, 1979; Betty Colladay award (*Quarterly Review of Literature*), 1986; *Quarterly Review of Literature* book publication award, 1994; Bumbershoot Literary Festival Big Book Competition, Seattle, Washington, 1994; International Merit award in poetry, *Atlanta Review,* 1996. **Address:** P.O. Box 28907, Bellingham, Washington 98228, U.S.A.

PUBLICATIONS

Poetry

Day of Change. Milwaukee, Gunrunner Press, 1968.
Drool. Madison, Wisconsin, Quixote Press, 1968.
Mr. Nobody. Marshall, Minnesota, Ox Head Press, 1969.
Ceremony. Milwaukee, Morgan Press, 1969.
Maize. Madison, Wisconsin, Abraxas Press, 1969.
Stone Marrow. Madison, Wisconsin, Anachoreta Press-Abraxas Press, 1969.
Becoming Human. Oshkosh, Wisconsin, Road Runner Press, 1970.
The Interim Handout. Privately printed, 1972.
Employed. Ithaca, New York, Ithaca House, 1972.
Edging Through. Ithaca, New York, Stone Marrow Press, 1972.
Soft Rock. Tacoma, Washington, Charas Press, 1973.
Making Space for Our Living. Port Townsend, Washington, Copper Canyon Press, 1975.
Terminal Placebos. New York, New Rivers Press, 1975.
The Gestures. Providence, Rhode Island, Bonewhistle Press, 1975.
The Alleged Conception. Southampton, New York, Granite, 1976.
New and Selected Poems. Pittsburgh, Carnegie Mellon University Press, 1978.
Are You Tough Enough for the Eighties? New York, New Rivers Press, 1979.
Precinct Kali, and The Gertrude Spicer Story. St. Paul, New Rivers Press, 1982.
First Credo. Princeton, New Jersey, Quarterly Review of Literature Award Series, 1986.
21 Poems from First Credo. Guemes Island, Washington, Stone Marrow Press, 1990.
Like a Planet. Guemes Island, Washington, Stone Marrow, 1994.
Snail River. Princeton, New Jersey, Quarterly Review of Literature Series, 1995.

Goat-Footed Turtle. Guemes Island, Washington, Stone Marrow Press, 1996.

Other

Editor, *Quixote: Northwest Poets.* Madison, Wisconsin, Quixote Press, 1968.
Editor, *Provisions,* by Anselm Parlatore. Ithaca, New York, Stone Marrow Press, 1971.
Editor, *The Abraxas/5 Anthology.* Ithaca, New York, Abraxas Press, 1972.

*

Manuscript Collections: Murphy Library, University of Wisconsin, La Crosse; Ohio University Library, Athens.

Critical Studies: "Three Good Prospects" by James Naiden, in *Granite* (Hanover, New Hampshire), Autumn 1972; "Observations on a Book of Poetry" by Steven Granger, in *Seizure* (Eugene, Oregon), Fall/Winter 1972; "Employed" by Ripley Schemm, in *Bartleby's Review 2* (Machias, Maine), 1973; "Facing the Eighties with James Bertolino," in *Bluefish* (Southampton, New York), Autumn 1983, and "The Binary Vision of James Bertolino," in *The Duckabush Journal* (Hansville, Washington), 1990, both by Jane Somerville; "James Bertolino: An Overview" by Edward Butscher, in *Poet Lore* (Washington, D.C.), Summer 1984; by Victoria Ballard, in *Crosscurrents* (Lynwood, Washington), Spring 1988.

James Bertolino comments:

I think my poetry has gone through stages that conform to William Blake's three stages of personal evolution: innocence, experience, and radical innocence. I like to feel that my work has entered the third stage.

*   *   *

James Bertolino's work exhibits a variety of directions that are continually developing, expanding, and even doubling back onto themselves. His poetry can be divided into several distinct types, very loosely chronological but also, more importantly, based on subject, theme, and technique.

The subject and viewpoint of Bertolino's earliest work are often distinctly Midwestern and marked by a flatness of language and a matter-of-fact tone. Regardless of the regional focus they display, however, their themes are universal: sexual awakening ("I Had a Packard"), love ("Storms"), maturation ("Changes"), loneliness ("Mom & Sally"), and death ("Salmon Fishing, Boundary Bay"). The poems of this group are solid, quiet, finely honed observations that as often as not owe their success to Bertolino's ability to suggest his meaning effortlessly, or so it seems, and to his remembering to eschew the overt statement.

Bertolino's sociopolitical poetry, the second division of his work, has appeared chiefly, but not exclusively, since the mid-1970s. It does not owe allegiance to any specific political cadre or support any particular group or strata of society over another. Rather, Bertolino's motivation and chief theme is his concern with individuals'—and humankind's—ability to survive the various forces that threaten them. Particularly strong examples of this work include "Killer Chemicals," a found poem; the disturbing, strangely brutal sequence

"Modern Lives"; and "The Nice Guy," the conclusion of which is shocking. A bitterness rivaling that of Weldon Kees's poetry underlies many of the poems of this group, even those in which Bertolino assumes the persona of the malefactor, as in "The Library," which begins chillingly:

I am Harry Truman
& have hurt you more than
you can know.

In his middle period Bertolino's work often takes on a mystical surrealism characteristic of much of his poetry of the 1960s. In such poems he makes a conscious effort to accept—even to embrace wholeheartedly and, at times, blindly—the odd, the quirky, or the bizarre. In "The Eleventh Hour Poem" he perhaps offers a reason for this facet of his work:

Logic
is the formal accident we
will have no part in.

The language of these poems is their most striking characteristic, running the full gamut from a wacky playfulness ("Oh Avis it Hertz!" in "Ontological Pornography"), which is evident even in the serious work of this period, to a high-tech diction ("fear is the black chute, / the nanosecond that never ends" in "St. Irwin, the Martyr"). This work contrasts sharply with, and ultimately satisfies less than, the earlier, more lyrical poems.

Despite their topics and themes Bertolino's later collections remind the reader, to a large degree, of what he produced in the 1960s. There is much in them to admire. Many poems reveal a mature artisan at work, one as conscious of craft as of vision and one capable of combining the two in his most powerful poems. "The Professor," for example, is a double-edged portrait of a man with good intentions who, because of his idealism, is doomed to failure. Similarly, "Home in Ohio" is both succinct and superficially simple, each characteristic camouflaging the complexity of the poem. Unfortunately, however, a number of the poems in his middle period leave much to be desired. While some are strained ("Wine"), pedantic ("Manifest"), or vapid ("American Poetry"), many are simply sophomoric, among them "Fruits and Vegetables."

To some degree Bertolino's full-length volume *Snail River* combines the strongest techniques and characteristics of his previous periods into one collection, revealing the poet at his very best and serving as a capstone to his career. Ranging from the more typical, midsize narrative poems to very short, terse near lyrics, the volume offers precise observations about the experiences of an individual life—sometimes a human being's, often an animal's—that become investigations into the human condition. "Creation Dance," for example, acknowledges a need for order in both nature and society, while simultaneously and ironically recognizing the beauty and, at times, desirability of disorder.

Bertolino also offers the mystical and surreal, the quirky, and the bizarre as metaphor for the human condition, often with shocking results. In "Broken Things," for instance, a young boy's trust in his oddball neighbor is purposefully, inexplicably shattered by that neighbor. "A Boy and His Dog," a coming-of-age poem, not only characterizes the very best of this collection but also of all of Bertolino's poetry. What in a lesser poet's hands might bog down in unrestrained emotion becomes instead a portrait of triumph. At once tense in emotion but never strained, concise yet complete, heart wrenching while never sentimental, this poem, along with others of the collection, deeply affects us by an unexpected, subtly dramatic turn of events, which leaves us clamoring for more.

—Jim Elledge

BHATT, Sujata

Nationality: Indian. **Born:** Ahmedabad, 6 May 1956. **Education:** Goucher College, Baltimore, Maryland, B.A. in philosophy and English 1980; University of Iowa Writers' Workshop, Iowa City, M.F.A. 1986. **Family:** Married Michael Augustin in 1988; one daughter. **Career:** Lansdowne Visiting Writer/Professor, University of Victoria, British Columbia, Spring 1992. Freelance writer and translator. **Awards:** Alice Hunt Bartlett award, 1988; Dillons Commonwealth Poetry prize, 1989; Poetry Society Book Recommendation, 1991, for *Monkey Shadows;* Cholmondeley award, 1991. **Address:** c/o Carcanet Press, 4th Floor, Conavon Court, 12–16 Blackfriars Street, Manchester M3 5BQ, England.

PUBLICATIONS

Poetry

Brunizem. Manchester, Carcanet, and New Delhi, Penguin, 1988.
Monkey Shadows. Manchester, Carcanet, and New Delhi, Penguin, 1991.
Freak Waves (chapbook). Victoria, British Columbia, Reference West, 1992.
The Stinking Rose. Manchester, Carcanet, and New Delhi, Penguin, 1995.
Point No Point: Selected Poems. Manchester, Carcanet, 1997.

*

Critical Studies: "Sujata Bhatt in Conversation with Eleanor Wilner," in *PN Review* (Manchester), 19(4), March-April 1993; in *New Statesman Society* (London), 8(353), 19 May 1995; by Sarag Maguire, in *Poetry Review,* 85(2), Summer 1995.

*   *   *

Sujata Bhatt's is unabashedly a poetry of confession. Born in India, educated in the United States, and living in Germany, Bhatt has found her most compelling subject in the vast disparities of these worlds. Yet she never exploits differences simply to point a neat or ironic juxtaposition, nor is she content with an easy nostalgia. Instead, her best poems wonderingly, and often poignantly, attempt to form an authentically hybrid imaginative whole from experiences that of necessity resist coherence.

Bhatt's poetry insistently returns to a ground note of exile, as when a Bremen flower stall is filtered through the mature speaker's memory of a childhood garden in Poona, India, and simultaneously registered through the eyes of the speaker's half-German newborn daughter ("At the Flower Market"). In the earlier "Go to Ahmedabad," "home" is formulated by an eloquent mnemonic: "for this is the place / I always loved / this is the place / I always hated / for this is the place / I can never be at home in / this is the place / I will always be at home in." In "Devibhen Pathak," one of many poems about Bhatt's ancestors, the poet-speaker meditates (in Germany in the 1980s, we are to assume) on the gold necklace adorned with a swastika, for Hindus a potent religious symbol, that she has inherited from her grandmother: "Oh didn't I love the Hindu Swastika? / And later, one day didn't I start wishing / I could rescue that shape from history?" The interrogative mode permits Bhatt to assume a persona that is simultaneously sincere and wry, and her habitual sensitivity to place is amplified here by the translator's attuned ear for cultural idiom.

An important set of Bhatt's poems anticipates and answers the criticism frequently leveled against Indian poets in English—that genuine poetry cannot be written in a foreign language. The word "brunizem," referring to a prairie soil common to Asia, Europe, and North America, and from which her award-winning first collection takes its name, signals Bhatt's powerfully organic concern with language. Thus, we read in the title poem of the volume,

The other night
I dreamt English
was my middle name.
And I cried, telling my mother
"I don't want English
to be my middle name.
Can't you change it to something else?"
"Go read the dictionary." She said.

Bhatt's method in these poems moves swiftly from the discursive to the imagistic, as in "A Different History":

Which language
has not been the oppressor's tongue?
Which language
truly meant to murder someone?
And how does it happen
that after the torture,
after the soul has been cropped
with a long scythe sweeping out
of the conqueror's face—
the unborn grandchildren
grow to love that strange language.

The long poem "Search for My Tongue" bravely struggles with similar problems:

You ask me what I mean
by saying I have lost my tongue.
I ask you, what would you do
if you had two tongues in your mouth,
and lost the first one, the mother tongue,
and could not really know the other,
the foreign tongue.

In this ambitious experiment in bilingual poetry, English and a remembered Gujarati (the "mother tongue") are pitted against each other in urgently escalating typographic and dialogic conflict. Resolution comes only when the conversational cadences of Bhatt's English freeze into the staccato, extralinguistic rhythms of an accompanying tabla: "I can't (dha) / I can't (dha) / I can't forget I can't forget / (dha dhin dhin dha)'' [with the Gujarati script omitted and typographic exactitude sacrificed].

In her second volume, *Monkey Shadows,* Bhatt finds in the monkey—at once bestial and human, inarticulate and expressive, a dissected object in a laboratory and a living denizen of a childhood garden—a versatile emblem of liminality. Her method is cross-mythologizing, informed by two distinct literary traditions, for in her work Eurydice and Demeter coexist with Hanuman and Ganesh. Other significant poems sketch the emotional localities of a specifi-cally female experience (''Marie Curie to Her Husband,'' ''Clara Westhoff to Rainer Maria Rilke,'' ''Written after Hearing about the Soviet Invasion of Afghanistan,'' ''White Asparagus''). Less suc-cessful, I think, are her later poems after paintings—''Rooms by the Sea,'' ''Sunlight in a Cafeteria,'' ''Portrait of a Double Portrait''— which seem arch and mannered in a self-conscious writing work-shop style.

Bhatt's unrelenting confessional self-examination, with a pas-sionate and fluid free verse line as its unit, announces a new direction in Indian poetry in English, a movement away from the rhythmic control and ironic detachment of a Nissim Ezekiel or an R. Parthasarathy. Finally, no one poem does justice to the complexity of Bhatt's talent, which makes itself known from the accretion of sensory detail sifted through an engaged and vigilant consciousness. She has mastered, and possibly exhausted, her chosen form, the memorializing of intensely lived experience.

—Minnie Singh

BIDART, Frank

Nationality: American. **Born:** 1939. **Education:** Graduated from University of California, Riverside. **Career:** Member of the depart-ment of English, Wellesley College, Massachusetts. Also teaches at Brandeis University, Waltham, Massachusetts. **Awards:** Guggenheim fellowship, 1979; Lila Wallace Reader's Digest Foundation writer's award, 1993; Morton Dauwen Zabel award, 1995; Lannan award, 1998; Rebekka Bobbitt award for poetry, 1998. **Address:** Department of English, Wellesley College, Wellesley, Massachusetts 02181, U.S.A.

PUBLICATIONS

Poetry

Golden State. New York, Braziller, 1973.
Happy Birthday. Cambridge, Massachusetts, Pomegranate Press, 1973.
The Book of the Body. New York, Farrar Straus, 1977.
The Sacrifice. New York, Random House, 1983.
Frank Bidart. New York, Dia Art Foundation, 1988.
In the Western Night: Collected Poems, 1965–1990. New York, Farrar Straus, 1990.
Desire: Collected Poems. New York, Farrar Straus, 1997; Manches-ter, Carcanet, 1998.

*

Critical Studies: ''Two Examples of Poetic Discursiveness'' by Robert Pinsky, in *Chicago Review* (Chicago), 27(1), 1975; ''Wellesley Poets: The Works of Robert Pinsky and Frank Bidart'' by Alan Nadel, in *New England Review and Bread Loaf Quarterly* (Middlebury, Vermont), 4(2), Winter 1981; ''The Sin of the Body: Frank Bidart's Human Bondate'' by Brad Crenshaw, in *Chicago Review* (Chicago), 33(4), Winter 1983; interview by Mark Halliday, in *Ploughshares* (Boston), 9(1), 1983; ''Out Beyond Rhetoric: Four Poets and One Critic'' by David Young, in *Field* (Oberlin, Ohio), 30, Spring 1984; ''Frank Bidart: A Salute'' by Seamus Heaney, in *Agni,* 36, 1992; '''Necessary Thought': Frank Bidart and the Postconfessional,'' in *Contemporary Literature* (Madison, Wisconsin), 34(4), Winter 1993, and *Travel and the Trope of Vulnerability in the Poetry of Elizabeth Bishop, Robert Lowell, Frank Bidart and John Ashbery* (dissertation), University of California, Riverside, 1994, both by Jeffrey Gray; by Stephen Yenser, in *Yale Review* (New Haven, Connecticut), 86(2), 1998; interview by Timothy Liu, in *Lambda Book Report,* 6(9), 1 April 1998.

*   *   *

Frank Bidart's first book of poems, *Golden State,* was published in 1973 as part of the Braziller poetry series, then being edited by the poet Richard Howard. Known for the inroads he himself had made with dramatic monologues, Howard introduced a volume that slipped into the loud circle very quietly but soon created a cultlike audience for its formal and thematic advances. Bidart's verse collection, *The Book of the Body,* appeared in 1977, but it was not until 1983, when *The Sacrifice* was published, that the poet's work began to find the wide readership and attention it deserved from the outset.

For readers who were weaned in America in the post-World War II discourse between free verse and received forms, these three collections came as a revelation and embodied a radical new prosody. *Golden State* contains the dramatic monologue of a rapist named Herbert White; *The Book of the Body* carries forth the voice of the anorexic Ellen West; *The Sacrifice* includes Bidart's most ambitious poem to that point, ''The War of Vaslav Nijinsky.''

Bidart's sense of voice, his sense of ''fastening the voice to the page,'' has always involved both a mimetic action—an ''imitation'' of character and a mirror held up to the psyche of the speaker—and, through the prosody of his poems, actions unto themselves. This is the remarkable achievement of Bidart's contribution to American poetry, and it is at the same time a prosody that has yet to be absorbed in American verse, perhaps because it is inimitable, unassimilable. Bidart's accomplishment stems partly from a learned reinvention of punctuation, capitalization of words, and spacings on the page. It is as if he has made punctuation a character on the page, opened its door and wrung out its possibilities, and in the process wedded punctuation to syntax so that the two are indistinguishable. His skill with the formal properties of language has effected a typography whereby words can actually be heard on the page.

Bidart was for a time a student and compatriot of Robert Lowell and has since taken the ethos of the Lowell generation to an entirely new place, pitch, and mode of composition. His monologues have about them little of the meditative irony that so inspired and plagued an earlier generation of poets. Rather, they are in their earnest melodrama akin to the voice of a Lear, an Augustine staggering through, staging their spiritual autobiographies through their speak-ing voices.

Bidart looks in his poems into the causes of things, the why of what is, and it is the triumph of his art that the forces behind things can be brought forth so seamlessly yet in so obviously constructed and wrought a manner.

In the Western Night: Collected Poems, 1965–1990 includes verse from Bidart's three previous books as well as new work. In its collected context the volume gives readers the opportunity to scrutinize the work of one of the most original poets writing in English.

—Liam Rector

BISSETT, Bill

Nationality: Canadian. **Born:** William Frederick Bissett, Halifax, Nova Scotia, 23 November 1939. **Education:** Dalhousie University, Halifax, 1956–57; University of British Columbia, Vancouver, 1963–65. **Family:** Has one daughter. **Career:** Has worked as a record store clerk, librarian, house painter, ditch digger, gas station attendant, bean picker, disc jockey, construction worker, sign painter, English tutor, fence builder, and hauler. Editor and printer, Blewointmentpress, Vancouver, 1963–83; co-founder, Very Stone Press, Vancouver, 1966–67. Writer-in-residence, University of Western Ontario, London, 1985–86; writer-in-library, Woodstock Library, Ontario. Artist: Individual Shows—Vancouver Art Gallery, 1972, 1984; Western Front Gallery, Vancouver, 1977, 1979; Embassy Cultural House, London, Ontario, 1986; Pizza Rico's, Vancouver, 1986; Neoartism Gallery, Vancouver, 1986; 382A Powell St. Studio, Vancouver, 1986; Selby Hotel, Toronto, 1989. **Awards:** Canada Council grant, 1967, 1968, 1972, 1979, bursary and travel grant, 1971, 1977. **Address:** Box 273, 1755 Robson Street, Vancouver, British Columbia V6G 1C9, Canada.

PUBLICATIONS

Poetry

Th jinx ship nd othr trips: pomes-drawings-collage. Vancouver, Very Stone House, 1966.
we sleep inside each other all (with drawings). Toronto, Ganglia Press, 1966.
Fires in th Tempul (with drawings). Vancouver, Very Stone House, 1967.
where is miss florence riddle. Toronto, Luv Press, 1967.
what poetiks. Vancouver, Blewointmentpress, 1967.
(th) Gossamer Bed Pan. Vancouver, Blewointmentpress, 1967.
Lebanon Voices. Toronto, Weed/Flower Press, 1967.
Of th Land/Divine Service Poems. Toronto, Weed/Flower Press, 1968.
Awake in the Red Desert! Vancouver, Talonbooks, 1968.
Killer Whale. Vancouver, See Hear Productions, 1969.
Sunday Work? Vancouver, Blewointmentpress-Intermedia Press, 1969.
Liberating Skies. Vancouver, Blewointmentpress, 1969.
The Lost Angel Mining Co. Vancouver, Blewointmentpress, 1969.
A Marvellous Experience. Vancouver, Blewointmentpress, 1969(?).
S th Story I to. Vancouver, Blewointmentpress, 1970.

Th Outlaw. Vancouver, Blewointmentpress, 1970.
blew trewz. Vancouver, Blewointmentpress, 1970.
Nobody Owns th Earth. Toronto, Anansi, 1971.
air 6. Vancouver, Air, 1971.
Tuff Shit Love Pomes. Windsor, Ontario, Bandit/Black Moss Press, 1971.
dragonfly. Toronto, Weed/Flower Press, 1971.
what fukin thery. Vancouver, Blewointmentpress, 1971.
drifting into war. Vancouver, Talonbooks, 1971.
Four Parts Sand: Concrete Poems, with others. Ottawa, Oberon Press, 1972.
th Ice bag. Vancouver, Blewointmentpress, 1972.
pomes for yoshi. Vancouver, Blewointmentpress, 1972.
air 10—11—12. Vancouver, Air, 1972.
Polar Bear Hunt. Vancouver, Blewointmentpress, 1972.
Pass th Food, Release th Spirit Book. Vancouver, Talonbooks, 1973.
th first sufi line. Vancouver, Blewointmentpress, 1973.
Vancouver Mainland Ice & Cold Storage. London, Writers Forum, 1973.
whut. Vancouver, Blewointmentpress, 1974.
drawings. Vancouver, Blewointmentpress, 1974.
Medicine my mouths on fire. Ottawa, Oberon Press, 1974.
space travl. Vancouver, Air, 1974.
yu can eat it at th opening. Vancouver, Blewointmentpress, 1974.
Living with the Vishyun. Vancouver, New Star, 1974.
IBM. Vancouver, Blewointmentpress, n.d.
Th fifth sun. Vancouver, Blewointmentpress, 1975.
Image being. Vancouver, Blewointmentpress, 1975.
stardust. Vancouver, Blewointmentpress, 1975.
Venus. Vancouver, Blewointmentpress, 1975.
th wind up tongue. Vancouver, Blewointmentpress, 1976.
Plutonium Missing. Vancouver, Intermedia, 1976.
An Allusyun to Macbeth. Coatsworth, Ontario, Black Moss Press, 1976.
sailor. Vancouver, Talonbooks, 1978.
Five Ways, with Bob Cobbing. Toronto, Writers Forum, 1978.
th first snow. Vancouver, Blewointmentpress, 1979.
soul arrow. Vancouver, Blewointmentpress, 1979.
Sa n th monkey. Vancouver, Blewointmentpress, 1980.
Selected Poems: Beyond Even Faithful Legends. Vancouver, Talonbooks, 1980.
Northern Birds in Colour. Vancouver, Talonbooks, 1981.
Sa n his crystal ball. Vancouver, Blewointmentpress, 1982.
Seagull on Yonge Street. Vancouver, Talonbooks, 1982.
canada gees mate for life. Vancouver, Talonbooks, 1985.
Animal Uproar. Vancouver, Talonbooks, 1987.
what we have. Vancouver, Talonbooks, 1988.
hard 2 beleev. Vancouver, Talonbooks, 1990.
Inkorrect Thots. Vancouver, Talonbooks, 1992.
Th last photo uv th Human Soul. Vancouver, Talonbooks, 1993.
Th Influenza uv Logik. Vancouver, Talonbooks, 1995.
Loving without Being Vulnrabul. Burnaby, British Columbia, Talonbooks, 1997.
Scars on the Seehors. Burnaby, British Columbia, Talonbooks, 1999.
B Leev Abul Char Ak Trs. Burnaby, British Columbia, Talonbooks, 2000.

Recordings: *Awake in the Desert,* See Hear, 1968; *Medicine My Mouths on Fire,* Oberon, 1976; *Northern Birds in Color,* Blewointmentpress, 1982; *Sonic Horses 1,* Underwich, 1984.

Plays

Television Documentaries: *In search of innocence,* 1963; *Strange grey day this,* 1964; *Poets of the 60's,* 1967; *Portrait,* 1984.

Other

Rezoning: Collage and Assemblage, with others. Vancouver, British Columbia, Vancouver Art Gallery, 1989.

Editor, *the Last Blewointment Anthology: 1963–1983.* Toronto, Nightwood, 2 vols., 1985.

*

Critical Studies: ''The Typography of bill bissett'' by bp Nichol, in *we sleep inside each other all,* 1966; *Fires in th Tempul* (exhibition catalogue), Vancouver, Vancouver Art Gallery, 1984; ''Bill Bissett: Controversies and Definitions,'' in *Canadian Poetry* (London, Ontario), 27, fall-winter 1990, and ''Self selected/selected self: bill bissett's Beyond Even Faithful Legends,'' in *Canadian Poetry* (London, Ontario), 34, spring-summer 1994, both by Don Precosky; ''Bill Bissett and His Works'' by Karl Jirgens, in *Canadian Writers and Their Works,* edited by Robert Lecker, Jack David, and Ellen Quigley, Toronto, ECW, 1992.

Bill Bissett comments:

Poet and painter: abt equal time nd involvment, been merging th fields for sum time now, since abt '62 nd previous with concrete poetry, which i early got into with lance farrell, allowing th words to act visually on th page, was aware of such effects before i cud accept th use of say grammatical thot in writing as such appeard too limiting to th singularly amazing development of th person.

    spelling—mainly phonetic

    syntax—mainly expressive or musical rather than grammatic

    visual form—apprehension of th spirit shape of th pome rather than stanzaic nd rectangular

    major theme—search for harmony within th communal self thru sharing (dig Robin Hood), end to war thereby— good luck

    characteristic stylistic device—elipse

    favorite poet—mick jagger

general source—there is only one, nd th variation that spawnd th fingrs of night woven grace issue (romanticism or elevation, i don't feel th I, i.e., ME writes but that i transcribe indications of flow mused spheres sound), from a hoop

        *   *   *

Bill Bissett was a big part of West Coast Canadian counterculture in the 1960s and 1970s. By the late 1980s he had moved to London, Ontario, given up drugs, and cut his hair, but otherwise the same wild spirit reigned.

Bissett claims that he cannot spell or write correctly: ''the way is clear, the free hard path, no correct spelling, no grammar rules.'' Puns

seem to replace meter: ''*hes* closin in all the doors then iul open them yer all stond.'' Drugs, in the period just before crack and AIDS, offered silly, seemingly innocent visions. Stupidity is almost faked and, as in Chaucer, adds to the difficulty of the ''dialect-ic'' of speeding speech:

> did yu blow cock eat cunt make a good
> business deal and still relate were yu are
> yu happy were yu good just once did you today
> have an existential moment in no time were yu
> normal today did yu screw society but found
> sum innocent outlets like no one knew or evry
> one knew did yu buy sum orange pop sticks green
> ones did yu have a treat and were clean were yu
> a dirty outlet for a while managin at th same
> time to find pleasure in nature and read a thot
> conditionin book by a provocative author did . . .

Bissett asks a lot of questions. His monologues are unpunctuated but best when interrogatory. They are written by someone who is outside himself and make rapid connections. Perhaps calling Popsicles ''pop sticks'' is a trifle cutesy; on the other hand, why give free advertisements, even in poems? Bissett draws and paints, writes concrete and political poetry, charming narratives, and sound poetry. But there is sadness, still interrogatory:

> why just when my body nd souls startin to fit
> sum they rip it all up mother i was happy
> in sum of those open spaces why hard times
> again did yu catch me foolin with th images
> now how can i carry any once cross this
> swamp ium sinkin in th deep mud myself

Bissett wears a mask in his poetry; the art in a man's face, the lines, are not fictive. Still, Burroughs and Warhol are distant from Bissett; closer are Patchen or Oppenheimer or, among the ancient modernists, Cummings.

Bissett's 1971 volume *Nobody Owns th Earth* values the earth, love, and country. It may be precisely the down-homeness, the provinciality, of Canada that pushes Bissett beyond sadness into heavy hopelessness:

> there is
> nothing
> to hope
>
> the candul
> yu lit it
> is going
>
> there is
> nothing
> to hope
>
> shut out
> the wind
> flame
>
> there is

nothing
to hope

a sea of
skulls in
th harbor

These lines are from a chant in which Bissett turns from a benign "mother" to give some orders to "flame." His assertive mood is heavy. When he stops asking and hoping, he starts hinting at an apocalypse. Of course, that hinting is itself a hoping, the hope for an end.

—Michael Andre

BLACK, D(avid) M(acleod)

Nationality: British. **Born:** Cape Town, South Africa, 8 November 1941. Moved to Scotland in 1950. **Education:** Edinburgh University, M.A. in philosophy 1966; University of Lancaster, M.A. in Eastern religions 1971. **Career:** Lecturer in liberal studies, Chelsea Art School, London, 1967–70; occupational therapy aide, Friern Psychiatric Hospital, 1973–74. Since 1974 lecturer and supervisor, Westminster Pastoral Foundation, London. Also psychotherapist in private practice. **Awards:** Scottish Arts Council prize, 1968, and publication award, 1969 and 1992; Arts Council of Great Britain bursary, 1968. **Address.** 30 Cholmley Gardens, Aldred Road, London NW6 1 AG, England.

PUBLICATIONS

Poetry

Rocklestrakes. London, Outposts, 1960.
From the Mountains. London, Outposts, 1963.
Theory of Diet. London, Turret, 1966.
With Decorum. Lowestoft, Suffolk, Scorpion Press, 1967.
A Dozen Short Poems. London, Turret, 1968.
Penguin Modern Poets 11, with Peter Redgrove and D.M. Thomas. London, Penguin, 1968.
The Educators. London, Barrie and Rockliff-Cresset Press, 1969.
The Old Hag. Preston, Lancashire, Akros, 1972.
The Happy Crow. Edinburgh, M. Macdonald, 1974.
Gravitations. Edinburgh, M. Macdonald, 1979.
Collected Poems 1964–87. Edinburgh, Polygon, 1991.

*

Manuscript Collection: National Library of Scotland, Edinburgh.

Critical Studies: "The World of D.M. Black" by John Herdman, in *Scottish International 13* (Edinburgh), February 1971; *Contemporary Scottish Poetry* by Robin Fulton, Edinburgh, M. Macdonald, 1974; Andrew Greig, in *Akros 46* (Nottingham), April 1981; *Science and*

Psychodrama: The Poetry of Edwin Morgan and David Black by Robin Hamilton, Frome, Somerset, Bran's Head, 1982; "The Erotic Theme in the Longer Poems of D.M. Black" by W.G. Shepherd, in *The Swansea Review II* (Swansea), Summer 1993.

D.M. Black comments:

My writing career shows signs of dividing into two phases, a first one from about 1960 to 1980, in which I wrote predominantly narrative poems, and a second one, still rather unforeseeable, beginning around 1990. The narrative poems were influenced by many people, including Henri Michaux, Samuel Beckett, and my fellow Scot George MacBeth. Stylistically they followed a trajectory from great formal freedom, not to say disorder, to something much more structured; three long narratives were written in hendecasyllables, a classical meter known to me mainly from Swinburne. I was fascinated for many years by the extraordinary openness created by classical meters, as opposed to the closed quality of the traditional iambic meters of English poetry. The subject matter of these narrative poems also changed in the direction of order and consciousness, starting as rather surrealist and becoming, particularly in *Gravitations,* more large scale and psychologically inquiring.

For personal reasons, I wrote little poetry throughout the 1980s; the *Collected Poems* of 1991 was effectively a summation of the first phase. Since then I have begun writing again. Translations of Goethe, a new departure, have appeared in a number of journals, including *Modern Poetry in Translation* and *Southfields,* and in doing these I have made my peace with the more familiar meters of the last few centuries in Europe. Asked to name admirations at this stage of my career, I would mention first Robert Frost, Richard Wilbur, and another Scot, the technically brilliant Robert Garioch.

*   *   *

The 1960s saw a revived interest in surrealism, and no doubt D.M. Black's earlier poetry reflected this. It was, however, a surrealism of a modified type, laced by side shrieks from George MacBeth's poetry of cruelty, tinged by science fiction and mythmaking, and peppered by the place-names of a hallucinatory Edinburgh. The heady mixture was poured into a flat, deadpan, jerkily enjambed free verse that at moments of stress could take off into lyrical humors and mild, almost pop horror. Long, exotic narratives like "Theory of Diet," "Without Equipment," and "The Rite of Spring," which refuse to come into clear focus, present nightmare explorations of cannibal islands, dwarfs speaking dwarf language, and a prince whose mother is devoured by ants. Among the shorter poems violent and extraordinary fantasies are more successfully related to a ruling idea. In "My Species" it is artificial insemination, in "The Educators" the generation gap, in "The Fury Was on Me" the transforming power of anger, and in "The Eighth Day" the revenge of fruitfulness on asceticism. In some of the most attractive poems fantasy shades off toward reality. For example, "Leith Docks" and "The Red Judge" have evocations of the dramatic northernness and Calvinist tensions of Edinburgh, "With Decorum" celebrates the mysterious sense of renewal in death like a twenty-eight-line *Finnegans Wake,* and "Clarity" turns a track-suited lout into a dancer:

Open the
windows, Jock! My

beauties, my
noble horses—yoked in
pairs, white horses, drawing my great
hearse, galloping and
frolicking over the cropped turf.

In his later work Black has made rather a specialty of the long poem, with a clarifying of style and a leaning toward myth, romance, and fairy tale. In *The Happy Crow*, ''Peter MacCrae Attempts the Active Life'' deals with an incestuous brother-sister relationship, and ''Melusine,'' in a variant of a medieval French legend, tells the story of a count's wife who periodically turns into a fish. In *Gravitations* other long poems start off from the Grimms' fairy tales and the Sumerian Gilgamesh cycle or give the tormented Browningesque confessions of a monk. These are poems of psychological and metaphysical search. Their unusualness can sometimes make them seem to promise more than they actually deliver, but the attempt to revive narrative poetry is to be applauded.

—Edwin Morgan

BLAND, Peter

Nationality: British and New Zealander. **Born:** Scarborough, Yorkshire, 12 May 1934. **Education:** Alleyne's Grammar School, Stone, Staffordshire; Victoria University, Wellington, New Zealand, 1955–59. **Military Service:** Royal Army Education Corps, 1952–54. **Family:** Married Beryl Matilda Connolly in 1956; two daughters and one son. **Career:** Editor, ''Poetry'' program, New Zealand Broadcasting Corporation, 1960–64; co-founder and artistic director, Downstage Theatre Company, Wellington, 1964–68; freelance writer and actor in London. Regular contributor, *London Magazine*, 1964–90. **Awards:** University of New Zealand McMillan-Brown prize, 1958; Melbourne Arts Festival Literary award, 1960; New Zealand Arts Council fellowship, 1968; Cholmondeley award, 1977; Arvon Foundation award, 1980, 1990; GOFTA Best Film Actor award, 1986, for *Came a Hot Friday*. **Address:** 125 Kenilworth Court, Lower Richmond Road, Putney, London SW15, England.

PUBLICATIONS

Poetry

Three Poets, with John Boyd and Victor O'Leary. Wellington, Capricorn Press, 1958.
My Side of the Story; Poems 1960–64. Auckland, Mate, 1964.
Domestic Interiors. Wellington, Wai-Te-Ata Press, 1964.
The Man with the Carpet-Bag. Christchurch, Caxton Press, 1972.
Mr. Maui. London, London Magazine Editions, 1976.
Primitives. Wellington, Wai-Te-Ata Press, 1979.
Stone Tents. London, London Magazine Editions, 1981.
The Crusoe Factor. London, London Magazine Editions, 1985.
Selected Poems. Dunedin, McIndoe, 1987.
Paper Boats. Dunedin, McIndoe, 1990.
Selected Poems. Manchester, Carcanet, 1998.

Plays

Father's Day (produced Wellington, 1967).
George the Mad Ad Man (produced Wellington, 1967; Coventry, 1969).

*

Manuscript Collection: Turnbull Library, Wellington.

Critical Study: ''Poets in Second Grade Heaven: Social Criticism in New Zealand Poetry, 1964–1966'' by Murray Bramwell, in *Poetry of the Pacific Region,* edited by Paul Sharrad, Adelaide, Centre for Research in the New Literature in England, 1984.

Theatrical Activities: Actor: **Plays**—Prahda, Singh in *Conduct Unbecoming* by Barry England, London, 1969; Inspector Ruff in *Don't Just Lie There, Say Something!* London, 1971, and in *A Bit between the Teeth,* London, 1974, both by Michael Pertwee; Sheik Marami in *Shut Your Eyes and Think of England* by Anthony Marriott and John Chapman, London, 1977; Starkey in *Peter Pan* by J.M. Barrie, London, 1982. **Films**—*Came a Hot Friday,* n.d. **Television**—*The Bob Hope Show; The Victoria Wood Show; The Dawson Show; Cribb; The Old Curiosity Shop; Lazarus and Dingwall; Terry and June; Adventurers; The Dave Allen Show; Murder Most Horrid; Heart of the High Country; Savage Play.*

Peter Bland comments:
The main theme of my poetry is one of exile, immigration, or displacement, using invented ''voices'' or surrealist invention to explore the relationship between person and place.

*   *   *

Peter Bland's 1998 *Selected Poems* provides the best access to his forty years of productive writing. It also adds a new dimension to his reputation as a poet of social realism and of displacement. In new work mainly grouped under the heading ''Embarkations,'' his long-standing concern with the tension between roots and nomadism, between belonging and freedom, moves to a deeper enquiry:

. . . but 'belonging' isn't just roots put in,
it's fences falling, fields with no edge,
a looking up that lifts the heart into vagrancy
and leaves it breathless with nomadic bliss.

Belonging and nomadism merge in this later vision. Displacement is now freedom. (Here Bland quotes his friend Louis Johnson in the valedictory poem, with which he won an Arvon award). The later poems reject the obligation to belong to one place, '''digging in' . . . that old Kiwi regressive thing / disguised as growing roots,'' in favor of writing ''poems adrift / like paper boats or messages in bottles, / careless of landfall, happy to be themselves.''
It was for earthbound realism, for suburban social criticism, that Bland first became known. In the 1960s he worked with Johnson in New Zealand to establish a local social realism that ironically or even indignantly contrasted the country's utopian aspirations with the reductive actuality of suburbia. Instead of the conventional romanticism of awe-inspiring landscape, Bland picked out the suburban trivia

of "tin butterflies and plaster gnomes . . . / The cat's paws delicate in new-laid concrete . . ."

Bland and Johnson obliged New Zealand poetry to engage with domestic realities, the pathos of ordinary lives, and the rhythms and diction of the country's elusive vernacular. Bland carried from England an acute ear for dialect and idiolect and a high skill in mimicry. It is no coincidence that by profession he is a successful comic actor. His poetry is distinguished by fine timing, a sometimes complex counterpoint of tones, and an ability to imply but not overstate personal feeling beneath the vigor of the spoken voice.

Bland's ear for the changing accents of everyday life has been further sharpened by his personal shuttlings between England and New Zealand. (He has twice migrated "permanently" to New Zealand but now lives in Sussex.) The robust rhythms and resonant vowels of his native Yorkshire have never left the implied voice of his poetry. They brought a special vigor, sometimes a vehemence, to his early New Zealand work, and they migrated back to England with him to add a contrapuntal duality to such poems as "Mr Maui," the satiric Polynesian impersonation through which he articulated his response to changes in both New Zealand and England in the 1970s:

I'm changing things. My yellow cranes
Dangle office blocks or smash chained suns
On to your rotting wood.

With an increasing tendency to reflect on scenes from memory, Bland has examined his early life in an England extending from the late years of the Depression through World War II to postwar rationing. In "Two Family Snaps," "Northern Funerals 1942," "Lament for a Lost Generation," or the excellent "home front" poem "Recollections of a Ministry of Munition Housing Estate—1944," he movingly reinterprets history from the viewpoint of its forgotten "extras":

We were the make-do-and-menders,

utility-grey men, the last of a line.
You can tell us a mile off even now;
there's a touch of austerity
under the eyes; a hint of carbolic

in our after-shave; a lasting doubt
about the next good time.

Bland's poetic and dramatic skills later focused on migration and displacement, a major twentieth-century subject on whose perplexities he has continued to write with insight and energy. In *The Crusoe Factor* he devolves his own feelings as a returning native into subtly semicomic impersonations of Crusoe, Mrs. Crusoe, and Friday. Several later poems, including "A Last Note from Menton" and "Homage to Van Der Velden," are in the form of letters to his New Zealand friends. He has also projected his own experience into imagined monologues by early New Zealand settlers ("Letters Home—New Zealand 1885," "New Baptized," "Beginnings") and into poems in which migratory movements are intercut with the processes of time and aging ("Let's Meet"). His tone has become more conversational and his rhythms more flexible than in the sometimes overinsistent early work.

Bland's realism has always been subverted by his aphoristic wit and his penchant for the oblique or quirky viewpoint. His imagery hankers habitually after the sea and the possibilities of departure. (He was born in Scarborough, on Yorkshire's east coast). He now often celebrates

what richness arrives when
one's feet aren't 'firmly planted' but
spread out like a well-darned net to catch
whatever the breeze brings in.

Yet he never floats off into introversion, self-delusion, or pretension. The conventions of self-referential language play, so fashionable currently in New Zealand poetry, are satirized in the witty "A Potential Poem for More Than Passing Strangers," in which he remarks, "I miss some sense of a living body / that someone, somewhere, has known and loved."

Bland has continued to develop his mastery of the poetry of the living in virtuoso monologue performances as Gauguin, the New Zealand environmentalist Guthrie-Smith, an amorous middle-aged husband, and an old codger of an aged Dracula. He makes these monologues work dramatically, vocally, visually, and comically. At the same time he does not limit their ability as poems to go beyond, to go again into that extra timeless dimension, "the other silences that go on and on / like the sky through this open window / for ever" ("Bear Dance"), to where "memory trembles with sad occasions, / with crowded wharfs and wayside stations / where the numberless dead wander / lost between trains." Like a great actor, Bland is most moving when he suddenly stops acting.

The late poem "Swimming off Worthing Beach," which is not included in *Selected Poems,* catches the polarities of this confident but still developing poet. It is about floating away from the "beached world" in drifting search for "something to do with space." It keeps a sharp and watchful eye on the changing shoreline clutter of the everyday, while it evokes being adrift, placeless, and timeless, with "gravity taken care of." The swimmer splashes back to the "sharp pebbles," but Bland the poet continues to float poised with an eye on both the pebbles and the void.

—Roger Robinson

BLASER, Robin (Francis)

Nationality: Canadian. **Born:** Denver, Colorado, 18 May 1925; naturalized Canadian citizen, 1972. **Education:** Northwestern University, Evanston, Illinois, 1943, College of Idaho, Caldwell, 1943–44; University of California, Berkeley, B.A. 1952, M.A. 1954, M.L.S. 1955. **Career:** Librarian, Harvard University Library, Cambridge, Massachusetts, 1955–59; assistant curator, California Historical Society, 1960–61; librarian, San Francisco State College Library, 1961–65. Lecturer, 1966–72, professor of English, 1972–86, professor, Centre for the Arts, 1980–84, and since 1986 professor emeritus, Simon Fraser University, Burnaby, British Columbia. Co-founder, *Measure,* Boston, 1957; editor *Pacific Nation,* Vancouver, 1967–69. **Awards:** Poetry Society award, 1965; Canada Council award, 1970, grant, 1989–90. **Address:** 1636 Trafalgar Street, Vancouver, British Columbia V6K 3R7, Canada.

PUBLICATIONS

Poetry

The Moth Poem. San Francisco, Open Space, 1964.
Les Chiméres (versions of Gérard de Nerval). San Francisco, Open Space, 1965.
Cups. San Francisco, Four Seasons, 1968.
The Holy Forest Section. New York, Caterpillar, 1970.
Image-nations 1–12, and The Stadium of the Mirror. London, Ferry Press, 1974.
Image-nations 13–14. Vancouver, Cobblestone Press, 1975.
Suddenly. Vancouver, Cobblestone Press, 1976.
Syntax. Vancouver, Talonbooks, 1983.
The Faerie Queene and The Park. Vancouver, Fissure, 1987.
Pell Mell. Toronto, Coach House Press, 1988.
Muses, Dionysus, Eros. Lawrence, Kansas, Tansy Press, 1990.
The Holy Forest. Toronto, Coach House Press, 1993.

Other

Bach's Belief. Canton, New York, Glover, 1995.

Editor, *The Collected Books of Jack Spicer.* Los Angeles, Black Sparrow Press, 1975.
Editor, *Particular Accidents,* by George Bowering. Vancouver, Talonbooks, 1980.
Editor, with Robert Dunham, *Art and Reality: A Casebook of Concern.* Vancouver, Talonbooks, 1986.
Editor, *Infinite Worlds: The Poetry of Louis Dudek.* Montreal, Véhicule Press, 1988.

*

Bibliography: "A Robin Blaser Checklist" by Miriam Nichols, in *Line,* 3, Spring 1984.

Critical Studies: "Robin Blaser's *Syntax*: Performing the Real" by Miriam Nichols in *Line,* 3, Spring 1984, and "The Poetry of Hell: Jack Spicer, Robin Blaser, Robert Duncan" by Nichols, in *Line,* 12, Fall 1988; "Blaser's Holy Forest" by Brian Fawcett in *Globe & Mail,* Toronto, 29 January 1994; "A Bow to the Numinous" by Phyllis Webb in *Book in Canada,* April 1994; "Rootworks" by Rachel Blau Du Plessis, in *Sulfur* 35, Fall 1994; in *West Coast Line,* 29(2), Fall 1995; interview by Samuel R. Truitt, in *Talisman* (Jersey City, New Jersey), 16, Fall 1996; "In the Shadow of Nerval: Robert Duncan, Robin Blaser, and the Poetics of (Mis)Translation" by Andre Mossin, in *Contemporary Literature* (Madison, Wisconsin), 38(4), Winter 1997.

Robin Blaser comments:

I have two great companions in poetry, Jack Spicer and Robert Duncan. And there is a real debt to Charles Olson.

I have insisted in my work upon a poetry that in its imagery is cosmological. I have tried to include, take in, and bring over in the content of that work images of those worlds to which one is given the possibility of entrance.

I am interested in a particular kind of narrative, what Jack Spicer and I agreed to call in our own work the serial poem—this is a narrative that refuses to adopt an imposed story line and completes itself only in the sequence of poems if, in fact, a reader insists upon a definition of completion that is separate from the poems themselves. The poem tends to act as a sequence of energies that run out when so much of a tale is told. I like to describe this in Ovidian terms as a *carmen perpetuum,* a continuous song, in which the fragmented subject matter is only apparently disconnected. I believe a poet must reveal a mythology that is as elemental as air, earth, fire, and water and that the authors who count take responsibility for a map of those worlds that is addressed to companions of the earth, the world, and the spirit.

*   *   *

Spare and reticent by the common American standards of poetic productivity, Blaser is represented by a body of work scarcely more than two hundred pages long. One might infer that he is a miniaturist, yet on closer inspection we find his lifework proposed as one long poem, "The Holy Forest." Consequently, Blaser's most engaging collection, *Image-nations 1–12,* is regarded by the poet as constituting "intermittent events in the narrative of *The Holy Forest.*" Narrative here is meant to signal something akin to a "composition of the real," a poetics elaborated initially by Blaser with his compatriots Robert Duncan and Jack Spicer in Berkeley, California, in the 1940s. This principle continues to be articulated in terms of companionship in Blaser's sizable book *Pell Mell,* in which is introduced another ongoing series called "Great Companions." These works are narrative in that they compose a story of how the lives and bodies of poetry are "made up," fabricated, enlightened in and by the elusive partnership of language and person. They are, in Duncan's words, "the story told of what cannot be told" and thus have a stake in the invisible, the ineffable, the unknowable.

Blaser's work is situated in the liminal space between himself and others, self and other, his own writing and the work of his comrades, and the written as it is complicitous with the unwritten. A narrative, then, is not so much storytelling as it is the elusive record of wandering and yearning, intimations of a gnosis. "Through the arrangement of words (parataxis)," Blaser writes, "there is a speech along side my speech, which allows a double-speech." In view of this, the relatively diminutive scale of Blaser's publications is deceptive, for his is a "double-speech" that continually evokes the charms and allure of an uncomposed otherness. Behind or beyond each poem is a fugitive other. On one level this implies a spiritual recital, as described by Henry Corbin in his illuminating books on Sufi visionary hermeneutics, but there is a practical, indeed mundane side to this as well. Blaser is the editor of his friend Spicer's *Collected Books,* which must be read not simply as the dutiful arrangement of a deceased poet's lifework but also as a rapturous reinscription within the field of Blaser's own poetics of a double voice. *The Collected Books of Jack Spicer* contains a fifty-page essay, "The Practice of Outside," that is both a thorough presentation of Spicer's poetic practice and an exposition of the nature of Blaser's own aspirations and engagement as a poet. Likewise, Blaser's volume *Syntax* consists almost entirely of the language of others, including graffiti, radio and television voices, and written texts, which he prefaces with the simple but momentous assertion "These poems do not belong to me."

Blaser's sense of belonging is conjugal and heartfelt. Not only does he appear to efface himself in the service of other, but even in the most secure passages of his own poems he returns to his double share, the composer being composed by a language beyond him:

invisible   invisible   invisible   heart
less
      the marvelous   deep   waves   or unbounded
mountain regions
          he effaces himself from
his own language
        the composing is
not so simply himself   agency,
executant   not creator   and
ceremonies
         of a look
      in his bitten heart
     where the heart looks out

The poet's sensitivity to the tenuous grasp of words, reflected in the awesome grip of the hidden and "bitten" heart, is accentuated by the poem's spacing. The words are semantically informative, yet blank spaces are deployed where punctuation might customarily serve. Blaser's meticulous attention to spatial detail reinforces the rhythmic allure of the images. The pages of *Image-nations 1–12* are choreographies, imprints of movement that return the emotions to their transitive order in motion.

The poems in *Pell Mell* return to a left-margin alignment for the most part, reflecting not so much some newfound unity of the poet's own voice but assuaging the reader's encounter with mysteries unassumingly deposited here and there with all the charm of a child's first encounter with a nest of robin's eggs. Consider, for example, "The Sounding Air":

nothing repairs, but that is the
comfort, flowing in what system,
the sounding air of the mind,
refreshment, the caves, the
labyrinthine moment always
the universe, haunted me like
god, but I was inside that
complexity, in the left wrist, and
wondered, such beauty, I said,
where the human form drifts
in the rivers, puzzles or dreams
the solar origins 'see the islands,
rare or fortunate, the work of
chance or necessity' 'the irrational
is mimetic' and the sacred,
after I thought it was beauty, takes
place constantly, ends constantly,
to begin constantly, such violence,
such sacred chance, so 'you' whom
I loved would find the crystal
without difference, would form
and reform the perfection, the
option and come back

Here, as throughout Blaser's work, we are in the secure hands of a most humane poet who accommodates the simple and primary gestures of feeling in a language that takes pains to avoid obscurity yet willingly risks it for the precisions it seeks.

In his early poetic manifesto "The Fire" Blaser proposed that "burning up myself, I would leave fire behind me." That aspiration is misleading in that there are no fireworks, no rhetorical hyperboles, in his work; nor is there any smoky confusion or obfuscation. "The music of the spheres is quite real," he also declared, "but the sound of the earth must meet it." Blaser's is a poetry that demonstrates the humanity of a fire kindled in the heart, absorbing the holy forest of earth in an altogether other harmony.

—Jed Rasula

BLY, Robert (Elwood)

Nationality: American. **Born:** Madison, Minnesota, 23 December 1926. **Education:** St. Olaf College, Northfield, Minnesota, 1946–47; Harvard University, Cambridge, Massachusetts, B.A. (magna cum laude) 1950; University of Iowa, Iowa City, M.A. 1956. **Military Service:** U.S. Naval Reserve, 1944–45. **Family:** Married 1) Carolyn McLean in 1955 (divorced 1979), two daughters and two sons; 2) Ruth Counsell Ray in 1980. **Career:** Since 1958 founding editor, *The Fifties* magazine (later *The Sixties* and *The Seventies*), and the Fifties Press (later The Sixties and The Seventies Press), Madison, Minnesota. From 1966 co-chair, American Writers vs. Vietnam War. **Awards:** Fulbright fellowship, 1956; Amy Lowell traveling fellowship, 1964; Guggenheim fellowship, 1965, 1972; American Academy grant, 1965; Rockefeller fellowship, 1967; National Book award, 1968. **Address:** 308 First Street, Moose Lake, Minnesota 55767, U.S.A.

PUBLICATIONS

Poetry

The Lion's Tail and Eyes: Poems Written out of Laziness and Silence, with James Wright and William Duffy. Madison, Minnesota, Sixties Press, 1962.

Silence in the Snowy Fields. Middletown, Connecticut, Wesleyan University Press, 1962; London, Cape, 1967.

The Light around the Body. New York, Harper, 1967; London, Rapp and Whiting, 1968.

Chrysanthemums. Menomenie, Wisconsin, Ox Head Press, 1967.

Ducks. Menomenie, Wisconsin, Ox Head Press, 1968.

The Morning Glory: Another Thing That Will Never Be My Friend: Twelve Prose Poems. San Francisco, Kayak, 1969; revised edition, 1970; complete version, New York, Harper, 1975.

The Teeth Mother Naked at Last. San Francisco, City Lights, 1970.

Poems for Tennessee, with William Stafford and William Matthews. Martin, Tennessee Poetry Press, 1971.

Water under the Earth. Rushden, Northamptonshire, Sceptre Press, 1972.

Christmas Eve Service at Midnight at St. Michael's. Rushden, Northamptonshire, Sceptre Press, 1972.

Jumping out of Bed. Barre, Massachusetts, Barre, 1973.

Sleepers Joining Hands. New York, Harper, 1973.

The Dead Seal near McClure's Beach. Rushden, Northamptonshire, Sceptre Press, 1973.

The Hockey Poem. Duluth, Minnesota, Knife River Press, 1974.

Point Reyes Poems. San Francisco, Mudra, 1974.

Grass from Two Years, Let's Leave. Denver, Ally Press, 1975.

Old Man Rubbing His Eyes. Greensboro, North Carolina, Unicorn Press, 1975.

The Loon. Marshall, Minnesota, Ox Head Press, 1977.

This Body Is Made of Camphor and Gopherwood: Prose Poems. New York, Harper, 1977.

This Tree Will Be Here for a Thousand Years. New York, Harper, 1979; revised edition, New York, HarperPerennial, 1992.

Visiting Emily Dickinson's Grave and Other Poems. Madison, Wisconsin, Red Ozier Press, 1979.

The Man in the Black Coat Turns. New York, Dial Press, 1981; London, Penguin, 1983.

Finding on Old Ant Mansion. Bedford, Martin Booth, 1981.

The Eight Stages of Translation. Boston, Rowan Tree, 1983.

Four Ramages. Daleville, Indiana, Barnwood Press, 1983.

The Whole Moisty Night. New York, Red Ozier Press, 1983.

Out of the Rolling Ocean and Other Love Poems. St. Paul, Minnesota, Ally Press, 1984.

Mirabai Versions. New York, Red Ozier Press, 1984.

In the Month of May. New York, Red Ozier Press, 1985.

A Love of Minute Particulars. Knotting Bedforshire, Sceptre Press, 1985.

Loving a Woman in Two Worlds. New York, Dial Press, 1985.

Selected Poems. New York, Perennial Library, 1986.

The Moon on a Fencepost. Greensboro, North Carolina, Unicorn Press, 1988.

The Apple Found in the Plowing. Baltimore, Haw River Books, 1989.

What Have I Ever Lost by Dying?: Collected Prose Poems. New York, HarperCollins, 1992.

Gratitude to Old Teachers: Poems. Brockport, New York, BOA Editions, 1993.

Meditations on the Insatiable Soul. New York, HarperPerennial, 1994.

Morning Poems. New York, HarperCollins, 1997.

Holes the Crickets Have Eaten in Blankets. Rochester, New York, BOA Editions, 1997.

Eating the Honey of Words: New and Selected Poems. New York, HarperCollins, 1999.

Recordings: *Today's Poets 5,* with others, Folkways; *For the Stomach: Selected Poems,* Watershed, 1974.

Other

A Broadsheet against the New York Times Book Review. Madison, Minnesota, Sixties Press, 1961.

Talking All Morning: Collected Conversations and Interviews. Ann Arbor, University of Michigan Press, 1979.

A Little Book on the Human Shadow, edited by William Booth. Memphis, Tennessee, Raccoon, 1986.

American Poetry: Wildness and Domesticity. New York, Harper, 1990.

Iron John: A Book about Men. Reading, Massachusetts, Addison Wesley, 1990.

Remembering James Wright. St. Paul, Minnesota, Ally Press, 1991.

The Sibling Society. Reading, Massachusetts, Addison Wesley, 1996.

The Maiden King: The Reunion of Masculine and Feminine, with Marion Woodman. New York, Henry Holt, 1998.

Editor, with David Ray, *A Poetry Reading against the Vietnam War.* Madison, Minnesota, American Writers Against the Vietnam War, 1966.

Editor, *The Sea and the Honeycomb: A Book of Poems.* Madison, Minnesota, Sixties Press, 1966.

Editor, *Forty Poems Touching on Recent American History.* Boston, Beacon Press, 1970.

Editor, *Leaping Poetry: An Idea with Poems and Translations.* Boston, Beacon Press, 1975.

Editor, *Selected Poems,* by David Ignatow. Middletown, Connecticut, Wesleyan University Press, 1975.

Editor, *News of the Universe: Poems of Twofold Consciousness.* San Francisco, Sierra Club, 1980.

Editor, *Ten Love Poems.* St. Paul, Minnesota, Ally Press, 1981.

Editor, *The Winged Life: Selected Poems and Prose of Thoreau.* San Francisco, Sierra Club, 1986.

Co-editor, *The Rag and Bone Shop of the Heart: Poems for Men.* New York, HarperCollins, 1992.

Editor, *The Darkness around Us Is Deep: Selected Poems of William Stafford.* New York, HarperCollins, 1993.

Editor, *The Soul Is Here for Its Own Joy: Sacred Poems of Many Cultures.* Hopewell, New Jersey, Ecco Press, 1995.

Editor, *The Best American Poetry 1999.* New York, Scribner, 1999.

Translator, *The Illustrated Book about Reptiles and Amphibians of the World,* by Hans Hvass. New York, Grosset and Dunlap, 1960.

Translator, with James Wright, *Twenty Poems of Georg Trakl.* Madison, Minnesota, Sixties Press, 1961.

Translator, *The Story of Gösta Berling,* by Selma Lagerlöf. New York, New American Library, 1962.

Translator, with James Wright and John Knoepfle, *Twenty Poems of César Vallejo.* Madison, Minnesota, Sixties Press, 1962.

Translator, *Hunger,* by Knurt Hamsun. New York, Farrar Straus, 1967; London, Duckworth, 1974.

Translator, with Christina Paulston, *I Do Best Alone at Night,* by Gunnar Ekelöf. Washington, D.C., Charioteer Press, 1967.

Translator, with Christina Paulston, *Late Arrival on Earth: Selected Poems of Gunnar Ekelöf.* London, Rapp and Carroll, 1967.

Translator, with James Wright, *Twenty Poems of Pablo Neruda.* Madison, Minnesota, Sixties Press, 1967; London, Rapp and Whiting, 1968.

Translator, with others, *Selected Poems,* by Yvan Goll. San Francisco, Kayak, 1968.

Translator, *Forty Poems of Juan Ramòn Jiménez.* Madison, Minnesota, Sixties Press, 1969.

Translator, *Ten Poems,* by Issa Kobayashi. Privately printed, 1969.

Translator, with James Wright and John Knoepfle, *Neruda and Vallejo: Selected Poems.* Boston, Beacon Press, 1971.

Translator, *Twenty Poems of Tomas Tranströmer.* Madison, Minnesota, Seventies Press, 1971.

Translator, *The Fish in the Sea Is Not Thirsty: Versions of Kabir.* Ithaca, New York, Lillabulero Press, 1971.

Translator, *Night Vision,* by Tomas Tranströmer. Ithaca, New York, Lillabulero Press, 1971; London, London Magazine Editions, 1972.

Translator, *Ten Sonnets to Orpheus,* by Rainer Maria Rilke. San Francisco, Seyhyrus Image, 1972.

Translator, *Lorca and Jiménez: Selected Poems.* Boston, Beacon Press, 1973.

Translator, *Basho.* San Francisco, Mudra, 1974.

Translator, *Friends, You Drank Some Darkness: Three Swedish Poets, Henry Martinson, Gunnar Ekelöf, Tomas Transtömer.* Boston, Beacon Press, 1975.

Translator, *Twenty-Eight Poems,* by Kabir. New York, Siddha Yoga Dham, 1975.

Translator, *Try to Live to See This! Versions of Kabir.* Rushden, Northamptonshire, Sceptre Press, and Denver, Ally Press, 1976.

Translator, *The Kabir Book.* Boston, Beacon Press, 1977.

Translator, *The Voices,* by Rainer Maria Rilke. Denver, Ally Press, and Knotting, Bedfordshire, Sceptre Press, 1977.

Translator, with Lewis Hyde, *Twenty Poems of Vicente Aleixandre.* Madison, Minnesota, Seventies Press, 1977.

Translator, *Twenty Poems of Rolf Jacobson.* Madison, Minnesota, Seventies Press, 1977.

Translator, *Mirabai Versions.* New York, Red Ozier Press, 1980.

Translator, *I Am Too Alone in the World,* by Rainer Maria Rilke. New York, Silver Hands Press, 1980.

Translator, *Canciones,* by Antonio Machado. West Branch, Iowa, Toothpaste Press, 1980.

Translator, *Truth Barriers,* by Tomas Tranströmer. San Francisco, Sierra Club, 1980.

Translator, *Selected Poems,* by Rainer Maria Rilke. New York, Harper, 1981.

Translator, with Coleman Barks, *Night and Sleep,* by Rumi. Cambridge, Massachusetts, Yellow Moon Press, 1981.

Translator, *Letter to Miguel Otero Silva, in Caracas (1948),* by Pablo Neruda. Willimantic, Connecticut, Curbstone Press, 1982.

Translator, with Kirkland, *Selected Poems and Prose,* by Antonio Machado. Buffalo, White Pines Press, 1983.

Translator, *Times Alone: Selected Poems of Antonio Machado.* Middletown, Connecticut, Wesleyan University Press, 1983.

Translator, *Trusting Your Life to Water and Eternity,* by Olav H. Hauge. Minneapolis, Milkweed, 1987.

Translator, *Selected Poems, 1954–1986,* by Tomas Tranströmer, edited by Robert Hass. New York, Ecco Press, 1987.

Translator, *Ten Poems of Francis Ponge.* Riverview, New Brunswick, Owl's Head Press, 1990.

Translator, with Sunil Dutta, *The Lightning Should Have Fallen on Ghalib: Selected Poems of Ghalib.* New York, Ecco Press, 1999.

*

Bibliography: ''Robert Bly Checklist'' by Sandy Dorbin, in *Schist 1* (Willimantic, Connecticut), fall 1973; *Robert Bly: A Primary and Secondary Bibliography* by William Roberson, London, Scarecrow, 1986.

Critical Studies: *Alone with America* by Richard Howard, New York, Atheneum, 1969, London, Thames and Hudson, 1970, revised edition, Atheneum, 1980; *The Inner War: Forms and Themes in Recent American Poetry* by Paul A. Lacey, Philadelphia, Fortress Press, 1972; ''Robert Bly Alive in Darkness'' by Anthony Libby, in *Iowa Review* (Iowa City), summer 1972; ''Robert Bly: Radical Poet'' by Michael True, in *Win* (Rifton, New York), 15 January 1973; *Four Poets and the Emotive Imagination* by Ronald Moran and George Lensing, Baton Rouge, Louisiana State University Press, 1976; *Moving Inward: A Study of Robert Bly's Poetry* by Ingegerd Friberg, Gothenburg, Gothenburg Studies in English, 1977; Charles Molesworth, in *Ohio Review* (Athens), fall 1978; *Of Solitude and Silence: Writings on Robert Bly* edited by Kate Daniels and Richard Jones, Boston, Beacon Press, 1982; *Robert Bly; An Introduction to the Poetry* by Howard Nelson, New York, Columbia University Press, 1984; ''In Search of an American Muse'' by the author, in *New York Times Book Review,* 22 January 1984; *Understanding Robert Bly,* Columbia, University of South Carolina Press, 1989, and *Robert Bly: The Poet and His Critics,* Columbia, South Carolina, Camden House, 1994, both by William V. Davis; *Robert Bly and Randall Jarrell as Translators of Rainer Maria Rilke: A Study of the Translations and Their Impact on Bly's and Jarrell's Own Poetry* by Steven Kaplan, New York, Peter Lang, 1989; *Walking Swiftly: Writings and Images on the Occasion of Robert Bly's 65th Birthday* edited by Thomas R. Smith, St. Paul, Minnesota, Ally Press, 1992; ''Hurt into Poetry: The Political Verses of Seamus Heaney and Robert Bly'' by Jeffery Alan Triggs, in *New Orleans Review,* 19(3–4), fall 1992; ''Robert Bly, Gratitude to Old Teachers'' by Tom Hansen, in *Literary Review,* 39(3), spring 1996; ''A Rhetoric of Indeterminacy: The Poetry of Margaret Atwood and Robert Bly'' by R.A. Kizuk, in *English Studies in Canada,* 23(2), 1997.

*   *   *

Robert Bly emerged from the early 1960s as one of the more stubbornly independent and critical poets of his generation, and wherever forums were open to him, he boldly stated his positions against war and corporate monopoly, broadening federal powers, and crassness in literature. He was a dominating spokesman for antiwar groups during the Vietnam War, staging readings around the United States and compiling (with David Ray) extraordinary poetic protests in the anthology *A Poetry Reading against the Vietnam War.* Throughout his career he has been a cranky but refreshing influence on American thought and culture, as much for the grandeur of his positions as for the force of his artistic individuality.

Although Bly's output has been relatively small in an era of prolific poets, his books follow a deliberate course of deepening conviction and broader conceptions. *Silence in the Snowy Fields,* his first book, is a slender collection of polished, mildly surreal evocations of his life in Minnesota and of the northern landscape, with its harsh winters and huddled townships. Bly's brief poems impute to nature a secret, willful life force, as in this final stanza from ''Snowfall in the Afternoon'':

> The barn is full of corn, and moving toward us now,
> Like a hulk blown toward us in a storm at sea:
> All the sailors on deck have been blind for many years.

Silence in the Snowy Fields has an immediacy of the poet's personal life that reflects the inward shift of poetry during the late 1950s and early 1960s, a direction that Bly then actively retreated from, claiming that poetry deserved a larger frame of experience than the poet's own circumstances and private dilemmas.

The Light around the Body moves into the political and social arena with poems against corporate power and profiteering, presidential politics, and the Vietnam War. These poems are more boldly imaginative and take reckless leaps into a surreal mode of discourse. The poems fuse the banal and the bizarre: ''Accountants hover over the earth like helicopters, / Dropping bits of paper engraved with Hegel's name'' (''A Dream of Suffocation'') or ''Filaments of death grow out. / The sheriff cuts off his back legs / and nails them to a tree'' (''War and Silence'').

To explain his poetics and to give it context, Bly edited an interesting volume of poems entitled *Leaping Poetry,* in which he argued that consciousness has expanded to a new faculty of the brain where memory opens up the mythological experience of human origins. The old nature religions and the archetypes of gods and heroes and the lore of animals, magic, and miracles are there for anyone brave enough to make the descent. In that sense Bly remains true to the original Jungian impulses he started from. At some point late in the 1950s Bly appropriated a nascent movement calling itself "deep image" poetry, after Jung's depth psychology. Bly soon made it his own and drew in other Midwestern poets, among them James Wright, to develop a sense of poetry as coming from interior depths of memory and psychic imagery. In *Sleepers Joining Hands* he suggests that society is returning to a matriarchal order as the foundation of human culture.

Bly later revised his views to argue that men are discovering their own mythological beginnings in certain magical fathers and heroes and are drawing renewed strength in the age of female liberation. *Iron John* and other books counsel men about their traditions and their hidden powers; in a collection of prose entitled *American Poetry: Wilderness and Domesticity* he argues that wilderness has not vanished but only gone underground in a culture of narrow consciousness. In *A Little Book on the Human Shadow* Bly asks, "How much of the darkness from under the earth has risen into poems and stories in [two hundred years]?" The American wilderness was once fully articulated in the Amerindian imagination, but it is, according to Bly, only now finding its way into the minds of white writers.

—Paul Christensen

BOLAND, Eavan

Nationality: Irish. **Born:** Dublin, 24 September 1944. **Education:** Trinity College, Dublin, first-class honors degree 1966. **Family:** Married Kevin Casey in 1969; two daughters. **Career:** Junior lecturer, Trinity College, Dublin, 1967–68; lecturer, School of Irish Studies, Dublin, 1973–88; writer-in-residence, Trinity College, Dublin, 1989, and University College, Dublin, 1991; Hurst Professor, Washington University, St. Louis, Missouri, 1992; Shirley Sutton Thomas Professor, University of Utah, Salt Lake City, 1993; regents lecturer, University of California, Santa Barbara, 1995. Since 1995 professor of English and director of the creative writing program, Stanford University, California. **Awards:** Macaulay fellowship in poetry, 1968; Jacobs award for broadcasting, 1977; Irish American Cultural award, 1983; Ingram Merrill foundation award, 1989; Terrence de Pres award, *Parnassus*, 1993; May Sarton award, New England Poetry Club, 1993; Ireland-American literature award, 1994; Lannan award for poetry, 1994; Irish American literature award, 1994; O'Shaugnessy award for poetry, 1997. D.Litt.: University of Strathclyde, National University of Ireland, and Colby College, all 1997. **Member:** Irish Academy of Letters, 1975. **Address:** c/o English Department, Stanford University, Stanford, California 94305, U.S.A.

PUBLICATIONS

Poetry

23 Poems. Dublin, Gallagher, 1962.
Autumn Essay. Dublin, Gallagher, 1963.
Poetry. Dublin, Gallagher, 1963.

New Territory. Dublin, Alan Figgis, 1967.
The War Horse. London, Gollancz, 1975.
In Her Own Image, illustrations by Constance Short. Dublin, Arlen House, 1980.
Introducing Eavan Boland. Princeton, New Jersey, Ontario Review Press, 1981.
Night Feed. Dublin, Arlen House, and London and Boston, Marion Boyars, 1982.
The Journey. N.p., Deerfield Press, 1983.
The Journey and Other Poems. Manchester, Carcanet, 1987.
Selected Poems. Manchester, Carcanet, 1989.
Outside History: Selected Poems, 1980–90. Manchester, Carcanet, and New York, Norton, 1990.
In a Time of Violence. Manchester, Carcanet, 1994.
An Origin Like Water: Collected Poems 1967–87. New York, Norton, 1996.
The Lost Land: Poems. New York, Norton, and Manchester, Carcanet, 1998.

Other

A Kind of Scar: The Woman Poet in a National Tradition. Dublin, Attic Press, 1989.
Object Lessons: The Life of the Woman and the Poet in Our Time. Manchester, Carcanet, and New York, Norton, 1995.

*

Critical Studies: "A Material Fascination" by Lachlan Mackinnon, in *The Times Literary Supplement* (London), 4403, 21 August 1987; "Toward Her Own Image" by Amy Klauke, in *Northwest Review* (Eugene, Oregon) 25(1), 1987; "'What You Have Seen Is beyond Speech': Female Journeys in the Poetry of Eavan Boland and Eilean Ni Chuilleanain" by Sheila C. Conboy, in *Canadian Journal of Irish Studies* (Saskatoon, Saskatchewan), 16(1), July 1990; "Improvising the Blackbird" by David Walker, in *Field* (Oberlin, Ohio), 44, spring 1991; "Ecriture Feminine and the Authorship of Self in Eavan Boland's 'In Her Own Image'" by Jody Allen-Randolph, in *Colby Quarterly* (Waterville, Maine), 27(1), March 1991; "'We Were Never on the Scene of the Crime': Eavan Boland's Repossession of History" by Patricia L. Hagen, in *Twentieth Century Literature,* 37, winter 1991; "Eavan Boland's Journey with the Muse" by Ellen M. Mahon, in *Learning the Trade: Essays on W.B. Yeats and Contemporary Poetry,* edited by Deborah Fleming, West Cornwall, Connecticut, Locust Hill, 1993; "'Out of Myth into History': The Poetry of Eavan Boland and Eilean Ni Chuilleanain" by Deborah Sarbin, in *Canadian Journal of Irish Studies* (Saskatoon, Saskatchewan), 19(1), July 1993; "Finding a Voice Where She Found a Vision" by Jody Allen-Randolph, in *PN Review* (Manchester), 21(1), September-October 1994; "Anxiety, Influence, Tradition and Subversion in the Poetry of Eavan Boland" by Kerry E. Robertson, in *Colby Quarterly* (Waterville, Maine), 30(4), December 1994; "'An Origin Like Water': The Poetry of Eavan Boland and Modernist Critiques of Irish Literature" by Ann Owens Weekes, in *Bucknell Review* (Cranbury, New Jersey), 38(1), 1994; "Responses to Elizabeth Bishop: Anne Stevenson, Eavan Boland and Jo Shapcott" by David G. Williams, in *English* (Leicester, England), 44(180), fall 1995; "The Diversity of Performance/Performance As Diversity in the Poetry of Laura (Riding) Jackson and Eavan Boland" by Seija H. Paddon, in *English Studies in Canada* (Ottawa), 22(4), December 1996; "First Principles and Last Things: Death and the Poetry of Eavan Boland and Audre Lorde'' by Margaret Mills Harper, in *Representing Ireland: Gender, Class, Nationality,* edited by Susan Shaw Sailer, Gainesville, University Press of Florida, 1997; ''Postcolonialism in the Poetry and Essays of Eavan Boland'' by Rose Atfield, in *Women: A Cultural Review,* 8(2), fall 1997; *Locating in the Actual: The Poetry of Eavan Boland and Adrienne Rich* (dissertation) by Jeannette Elizabeth Riley, University of New Mexico, 1998; ''Eavan Boland: Mazing Her Way'' by David C. Ward, in *Sewanee Review,* 106(2), 1998; ''Dilemmas and Developments: Eavan Boland Re-examined'' by Sarah Maguire, in *Feminist Review,* 62, 1999; Eavan Boland issue of *Colby Quarterly* (Colby, Maine), winter 1999.

*　　*　　*

Eavan Boland is very self-consciously an Irish woman poet. As she said in the 1994 Ronald Duncan lecture, ''I am an Irish poet. A woman poet. In the first category I enter the tradition of the English language at an angle. In the second, I enter my own tradition at an even more steep angle.'' Many of her poetry's strengths, and some of its weaknesses (principally, a tendency to go for flat declarations), derive from the difficult relation to poetic tradition that it articulates. In the midst of, and often propelling, her changes of style is a steady yearning to draw inspiration from a figure addressed in a poem from *Night Feed* (1982) as ''The Muse Mother.'' Here the poet looks at a woman with a child and writes in weighted short lines, a reaction against the careful rhyming of her early work, of her desire ''to be a sibyl / able to sing the past / in pure syllables / . . . / able to speak at last / my mother tongue.''

For all the craving for ''pure syllables,'' the great virtue of Boland's work, like that of Adrienne Rich, is the way it at once contests and negotiates with the impurities of the quotidian. One of her many fine meditations on paintings, ''Self-Portrait on a Summer Evening,'' concludes with ''I am Chardin's woman / edged in reflected light, / hardened by / the need to be ordinary.'' ''Hardened'' implies a strengthening or clarifying that is perilously close to a certain obduracy, and much of Boland's work counts the cost of self-definition. In ''The New Pastoral'' she sees herself, a shade cumbersomely, as a ''displaced person / in a pastoral chaos.'' But the cumbersome is laid aside at the end, where she describes what she sees as ''amnesias / of a rite / I danced once on a frieze.'' Even in this graceful recapturing there is irony, as Boland is compelled to use a traditional pastoral image for her antitraditional sense of a lost self.

Boland's concern with self is, for the most part, unsolipsistic, and her career has been a long struggle to remain true to her own experience and yet to find a way of speaking in more universal terms about ''herstory.'' ''Ode to Suburbia'' is a witty example from her earlier work in which Boland's command of a long sentence spun across a tightly rhymed stanza helps to give the feeling of one experience ''multiplied'':

How long ago did the glass in your windows subtly
Silver into mirrors which again
And again show the same woman
Shriek at a child, which multiply
A dish, a brush, ash . . .

In subsequent poems Boland experiments with a Plath-like voice of controlled ferocity. These poems can, as in ''Woman in Kitchen,'' take on a little too well the blanched hues of the very restrictedness

against which they protest. That said, a poem such as ''Anorexic'' is a superb tour de force, partly because of the conceit it employs of the anorexic speaker seeking to ''slip / back into him again / as if I had never been away.'' More complexly satisfying are Boland's poems of motherhood, found mainly in *Night Feed.* As is the case in Plath's poems about her children, Boland is able to suggest a range of feelings; a credible love is shadowed and intensified by awareness of a range of differences between experience and innocence and between the celebrated moment and the future. ''Night Feed'' lets the silences between its short assertions do most of the poem's work: ''Poplars stilt for dawn / And we begin / The long fall from grace. / I tuck you in.'' Here the final gesture and rhyme hold at bay the saddened onset of a ''fall from grace.''

Boland's best work, however, is written in the longer, fluent line of poems such as ''The Journey.'' The staccato syntax of *Night Feed* yields to a more dreamlike, eddying progression as the poet, possibly influenced by Seamus Heaney's example in *Station Island,* is led in reverie by Sappho into an underworld of ''women and children.'' Boland's characteristic desire to ''''let me at least be their witness'''' is delicately rebuked by Sappho, who replies that ''what you have seen is beyond speech, / beyond song, only not beyond love.'' The moment has a Dantescan ring, yet it also shows how Boland is able to adapt Dante to her own concerns. The poem's movement and atmosphere of dream vision are impressively sustained.

In a Time of Violence (1994) builds on the achievement of *The Journey,* revealing a new appetite for detail and a corresponding ability to weave detail into finely cadenced meditations. This is not to suggest that Boland's poetry has lost its edge, which is quietly apparent in the sequence ''Writing in a Time of Violence.'' But it is to claim for the volume an authority that, in her Duncan lecture, Boland speaks of as hard for her as an Irish woman poet to attain. There is in the collection a hard-won awareness that art can serve not only to express problems but also to provide solutions, however provisional. In ''Time and Violence'' Boland is visited by a (female) voice she ventriloquizes as saying, ''Write us out of the poem. Make us human / in cadences of change and mortal pain / and words we can grow old and die in.'' At this stage in her career Boland is able to span the vast gap between the ruthless imperatives of art and the claims of the ''human'' and to span it in such a way that art begins to seem a qualified source of consolation. Thus, in the final poem, ''The Art of Grief,'' she ends with an implied question that is also a calmly ''unflinching'' statement, the poet wondering ''whether she flinched as the chisel found / that region her tears inferred, / where grief and its emblems are inseparable.''

—Michael O'Neill

BOOTH, Philip

Nationality: American. **Born:** Hanover, New Hampshire, 8 October 1925. **Education:** Dartmouth College, Hanover, A.B. 1948 (Phi Beta Kappa); Columbia University, New York, M.A. 1949. **Military Service:** U.S. Air Force, 1944–45. **Family:** Married Margaret Tillman in 1946; three daughters. **Career:** Instructor, Bowdoin College, Maine, 1949–50; assistant to the director of admissions, 1950–51, and instructor, 1954, Dartmouth College; assistant professor, Wellesley College, Massachusetts, 1954–61; associate professor, 1961–65, and professor of English and poet-in-residence, 1966–86, Syracuse University, New York. Taught at the University of New Hampshire Writers Conference, Durham, 1955; Spencer Memorial Lecturer, Bryn Mawr College, Pennsylvania, 1959; Tufts University Poetry Workshop, Medford, Massachusetts, 1960, 1961. Phi Beta Kappa poet, Columbia University, 1962. **Awards:** Bess Hokin prize (*Poetry,* Chicago), 1955; Lamont Poetry Selection award, 1956; *Saturday Review* prize, 1957; Guggenheim fellowship, 1958, 1965; Emily Clark Balch prize (*Virginia Quarterly Review*), 1964; National Institute of Arts and Letters award, 1967; Rockefeller fellowship, 1968; Theodore Roethke prize (*Poetry Northwest*), 1970; National Endowment for the Arts fellowship, 1980; Academy of American Poets fellowship, 1983; Maurice English award, 1987; Friends of Witherle Memorial Library award, 1985. Litt.D.: Colby College, Waterville, Maine, 1968. **Address:** 95 Main Street, Castine, Maine 04421, U.S.A.

PUBLICATIONS

Poetry

Letter from a Distant Land. New York, Viking Press, 1957.
The Islanders. New York, Viking Press, 1961.
Weathers and Edges. New York, Viking Press, 1966.
Margins: A Sequence of New and Selected Poems. New York, Viking Press, 1970.
Available Light. New York, Viking Press, 1976.
Before Sleep. New York, Viking Press, 1980.
Relations: Selected Poems 1950–1985. New York, Viking Penguin, 1986.
Selves: New Poems. New York, Viking Penguin, 1990.
Pairs. New York, Penguin, 1994.
Lifelines: Selected Poems 1950–1999. New York, Viking, 1999.

Recordings: *Today's Poets 4,* with others, Folkways; *The Cold Coast,* Watershed, 1987.

Other

North by East. Boston, Impressions Workshop, 1966.
Beyond Our Fears. N.p., Georgian Trust, 1968.
Trying to Say It: Outlooks and Insights on How Poems Happen. Ann Arbor, Poets on Poetry, University of Michigan Press, 1996.

Editor, *The Dark Island.* Lunenberg, Vermont, Stinehour Press, 1960.
Editor, *Syracuse Poems,* 1965, 1970, 1973, 1978; and *Syracuse Stories and Poems,* 1983, Syracuse, New York, Syracuse University Department of English, 5 vols., 1965–83.

*

Manuscript Collections: State University of New York, Buffalo; University of Texas, Austin; Special Collections, Dartmouth College, Hanover, New Hampshire.

Critical Studies: *Three Contemporary Poets of New England* by Guy Rotella, Boston, Twayne, 1983; *Forty-Five Contemporary Poems: The Creative Process* edited by Alberta T. Turner, White Plains, New York, Longman Publishing, 1985; interview with Rachel Berghash, *American Poetry Review* (Philadelphia) 18(3), 1989; "Poems after Dreams," in *Dreams Are Wiser Than Men* edited by Richard A. Russo, Berkeley, California, North Atlantic Books, 1987; "Philip Booth, Selves" by Ron Block, in *North Dakota Quarterly* (University of North Dakota), 61(3), summer 1993.

*   *   *

The poetry of Philip Booth, which spans four decades, represents a mighty effort to push through the limits of language into the reality of things. Ever on the edge of reality, clinging to surfaces, he struggles with an intractable world that, though it yields itself to his manipulation, will not allow him to possess it. Frustrated by this condition, Booth hones words to form a bridge across the abyss he feels separates him from true being. For a while, during the period of the 1970s, the process seemed to be wearing him out. But in the 1980s he seemed to find the bridge that achieved the integration he was seeking.

In his early work—*Letter from Distant Land, The Islanders,* and *Weathers and Edges*—Booth forged some of the most disciplined poems of his generation, poems that are eloquent testimonials to the world he knows he must reach but one that seems ever to elude him. Indeed, in an age in which so many others are challenging society and plumbing the depths of the neurotic self, Booth is seeking metaphysical affirmation, an ontological relationship with the world. Hard, disciplined forms, short lines, and cool images carry the weight of his determined search. Booth's poems remind one of the best of the imagists, in their cool detachment in fixing nature in an image, and at the same time of the best of personal poetry in our age. Booth's poems are not an escape from personality but rather a means of establishing it.

Booth found his medium early in *Letter from a Distant Land,* and he then worked it and reworked it in the two succeeding volumes, *The Islanders* and *Weathers and Edges.* The poems in these volumes represent a search for an ineffable reality, a dimly grasped world of being beyond being, a sunlit world of real shapes and truth. But finding the key to that illusive world is like searching for the impossible dream, the dream behind the dream, the dream we call life but that fades to darkness and becomes nothing. The sunlit beaches, the light filtering through the trees, the hard, rocky Maine coast, the muted ancestors whose ghostlike presence can be felt in the earth and in the Booth ancestral home—all merge into a kaleidoscope of images that tumble from the poet's fertile imagination in a lifetime of searching for meaning and existence.

In the volumes *Margins, Available Light,* and *Before Sleep,* the struggle seems to wear the poet out. Progressively hard put to maintain the struggle, Booth retreats to a more and more confined space, literally his ancestral home, where in one room he assesses his struggle and seeks aid and comfort from the generations of his family that have inhabited the house. As the light dims, the desire to sleep after a lifetime of effort becomes an ever growing preoccupation. The entire volume *Before Sleep* carries strong indications of a fatigue so pervasive as to threaten the poet's life. Images of death and decay vie with moments of quickening, of life suddenly revealed, a truth hammered home in silent revelation. Darkness and nothingness creep in like a fog, and the poet finds himself adrift, rudderless, alone, and lost, as in "Fog":

I'm rowing

where measure is lost, I'm barely moving,

in a circle of translucence that moves with me
without compass
                              I can't see out or up into;
I sit facing backwards,
                                        pulling myself slowly
toward the life I'm still trying to get at.

More dangerous still is the condition of the man described in ''Narrative,'' who ''sits all day / on the edge of nothing, / after a while he gets numb and falls in.''

In the five years following the publication of *Before Sleep,* something remarkable must have happened to Booth that gave him a renewed sense of life and that allowed him to make a fresh start in poetry. The first six sections of his *Relations: Selected Poems 1950–1985* include selections from each of his previously published volumes. The seventh section collects new poems demonstrating that he has been able to step back from the abyss, rediscover himself, and find a new joy in living. Although about half of the poems are written in the former mode (for example, ''To Think,'' ''Here, There,'' ''A Man in Maine''), Booth breaks new ground in most of the others. No longer seeing himself as dying, he projects himself as a new man experiencing a new life. The signal for the transformation appears in the poem ''Snapshot,'' in which Booth uses the occasion of looking at a picture of himself at a young age to assess who he is and what he has become. Playfully, he declares that he now knows ''less and better'' and is heavier and less easily pleased, although not tender, harder, more angry, and ''more horny.'' In the remarkable poem ''Public Broadcast'' he describes a cold, wintry afternoon during which he is carrying wood into his house while listening to an opera broadcast over the radio. As he listens to a triumphal march, he fantasizes that he is part of the procession, returning home a conqueror and feeling a sense of victory he ''hasn't felt in fifty years.''

This sense of victory can be felt in the poems ''Dreamboat'' and ''Cycle.'' In ''Dreamboat'' the new feeling is expressed as an escape through music, which allows him to soar ''blowing solo out across the Atlantic.'' ''Cycle'' sounds a challenge of resistance to the forces that for all his life he has projected as working toward his inevitable decay and destruction. He asserts that he finds himself ''miles from where he intended, years from where he has been . . . pumping toward a new country.'' The title of this engaging poem may be read as well as ''full cycle'' or ''recycle'' in relation to the poet's life. In the final poems in the volume—''Saying It,'' ''After the Rebuilding,'' ''Prime,'' ''Creatures,'' and ''Relations''—we are exposed to a profusion of images of rebirth and rebuilding, not only of the poet's life but of his poetry as well. Booth can rest in the satisfaction of having come through a lifetime of struggle to a vision of wholeness, peace, and joy.

—Richard Damashek

BORNHOLDT, Jenny

Nationality: New Zealander. **Born:** Jennifer Mary Bornholdt, Lower Hutt, 1 November 1960. **Education:** Victoria University, Wellington, 1981–84, B.A. in English literature 1984. **Family:** Married Gregory O'Brien in 1994. **Career:** Bookseller, Unity Books, Wellington, 1989–92. Since 1992 copywriter, Haines Recruitment Advertising, Wellington. **Address:** c/o Victoria University Press, P.O. Box 600, Wellington, New Zealand.

PUBLICATIONS

Poetry

This Big Face. Wellington, Victoria University Press, 1988.
Moving House. Wellington, Victoria University Press, 1989.
Waiting Shelter. Wellington, Victoria University Press, 1991.
How We Met. Wellington, Victoria University Press, 1995.
Miss New Zealand: Selected Poems. Wellington, Victoria University Press, 1997.

*

Critical Studies: By Elizabeth Caffin, in *Landfall,* 44(2), June 1990; by Margaret Mahy, in *Landfall,* 46(3), September 1992.

*   *   *

Jenny Bornholdt has begun to accumulate a body of work that is recognizably her own. Her first book, *This Big Face,* shows her experimenting with two kinds of writing: sensitive, intimate lyrics and more outgoing dramatic dialogues, prose poems, and playlets, almost multimedia performance pieces. Both types, however, are informed by sharp observation and precise description of feeling and event.

Here are the first lines from ''Breath'':

Your warm breath
mists up my skin
like glass . . .

The conceit conveys the intimacy of the moment and also delicately hints at a coolness on the part of the speaker. There is a sense of fragility and risk in the third line, which leads on to

quick, finger in the message
write me a note of
your intentions
I have forgotten already
what we are doing here,
why we lie this close
breathing each other's
breath this way

The medium (the misted glass) requires there to be ''the message'' that might help her recover the passion that is ''forgotten already.'' Although this is a slight poem and the tension perhaps dissipates toward the end, it illustrates where Bornholdt's strengths lie.

It is with some assurance that Bornholdt tackles the challenge of the longer sequence in the title poem of *Waiting Shelter* and in ''We will, we do,'' an exploration of family and origins and of the tension between New Zealand, where she was born, and her European heritage. In the shorter lyrics she continues to pursue her own individual vision: ''You approach the world / with open arms and hope / it wants you. Hope to be / asked in to sit amongst the / fine furniture . . . // Here it is. / Here's the world on a good / day, turned slightly / away, but this is no / offence, merely the sun was / in its eyes . . .'' (''The Visit'').

Bornholdt's collection *How We Met* opens with a set of eighteen poems whose titles are those of Estonian folk songs, for example,

"My sister, my little cricket"; "Urging her into the boat"; "My mouth was singing / My heart was worrying." In the last the poem is merely a gloss on the title: "O deceptive mouth / covering up / for the heart like that." In several of these new poems the folk element combines with a surrealism that touched some of the earlier poems. In others she establishes a nicely judged balance of the passionate and the dispassionate, as in "Praising the cook":

> They say the sexual impulse
> is like a fiery horse.
>
> When you break an egg
>   one-handed
> into the frying pan
> it sounds like distant hooves
> crossing a dusty plain.

Bornholdt's published volumes are interesting, if uneven, and it is clear that she enjoys her writing and wants her reader to experience and enjoy the world she creates. Not all of her poems work, but as a collection they show us a young writer with a feel for words, the patterns they make, and the resonances they strike.

—Alan Roddick

BORSON, Roo

Nationality: American and Canadian. **Born:** Ruth Elizabeth Borson, Berkeley, California, 20 January 1952. **Education:** University of California, Santa Barbara, 1970–71; Goddard College, Plainfield, Vermont, 1971–73, B.A. 1973; University of British Columbia, Vancouver, 1975–77, M.F.A. 1977. **Career:** Teacher of writing workshops and writer-in-residence, University of Western Ontario, London, 1987–88, Concordia University, Montreal, 1993–98, and since 1998 University of Toronto. **Awards:** University of British Columbia Macmillan prize, 1977; Canada Council grant, 1982, 1984, 1988, 1991, and 1994; Canadian Broadcasting Corporation Literary award, 1984, 1989, and 1991; National Endowment for the Arts fellowship, 1986. **Address:** c/o Writers' Union of Canada, 54 Ryerson Avenue, Toronto, Ontario M5T 2P3, Canada.

PUBLICATIONS

Poetry

Landfall. Fredericton, New Brunswick, Fiddlehead, 1977.
In the Smoky Light of the Fields. Toronto, Three Trees Press, 1980.
Rain. Moonbeam, Ontario, Penumbra Press, 1980.
A Sad Device. Dunvegan, Ontario, Quadrant, 1981.
Night Walk. Toronto, Missing Link Press, 1981.
The Whole Night, Coming Home. Toronto, McClelland and Stewart, 1984.
The Transparence of November/Snow, with Kim Maltman. Kingston, Ontario, Quarry, Press, 1985.
Intent, or, The Weight of the World. Toronto, McClelland and Stewart, 1989.
Night Walk, Selected Poems. Toronto, Oxford University Press, 1994.
Water Memory. Toronto, McClelland and Stewart, 1996.

Other

Introduction to the Introduction to Wang Wei, with others (Pain Not Bread). London, Ontario, Brick, 2000.

*

Critical Studies: "The Prose Poems of Roo Borson and Robert Priest" by Robert Billings, in *Canadian Fiction Magazine* (Toronto), 56, 1986; "Roo Borson" by Graham Barron, in *Canadian Writers and Their Works,* edited by Robert Lecker, Jack David, and Ellen Quigley, Toronto, Essays on Canadian Writing, 1995.

Roo Borson comments:

(1995) In recent years I've been interested in the interplay of physical sensation and memory; in how the fine distinctions of emotional nuance are encoded or enacted in speech; how rhetoric is made up of rhythm, pitch, tonality, atonality; how consciousness wanders musically.

*   *   *

Roo Borson is one of the young Americans who went north to Canada in the 1970s to take a higher degree. She settled first in Vancouver, where the panorama of islands and snowcapped mountains are as spectacular and beautiful as the scenery of her native California. Later she lived in Toronto. A third-generation poet, she was in her middle twenties when her first book of poems appeared. Other collections followed quickly. At age thirty-two she won first prize in the Canadian Broadcasting Corporation's literary competition with "Folklore," which later appeared as a section of her 1984 collection *The Whole Night, Coming Home.* The book is an evocation of Borson's childhood in Berkeley. The sensual, almost mystical appreciation of the scents and the lush gardens and hillsides and the consciousness of another, working life going on in San Francisco, lit up across the Bay, and in Oakland, the industrial port to the east, invoke a world both beautiful and tough.

Memories of her parents, their love for each other and their children, and the solidarity of her family are luminously symbolized by her mother's beautiful garden, an exotic paradise inhabited by snakes, dogs, spiders, snails, lizards, goldfish, frogs, and, particularly, cats. Occasionally the cumulative effect is powerful. The sweep of memory carries the reader along until, in the last lines of the title poem of the last section, "Folklore," it is summed up:

> And that which now comes alight, the house you
>   grew up in:
> sometimes it is a lantern small enough to carry before in
> one hand.

The Whole Night, Coming Home is also a chronicle of coming-of-age in the California of the reckless 1960s, the world as seen from a speeding car full of flower children. The poems describe the comradeship of the adolescent gang, deeper friendships, and sexual and spiritual awakening, as in the poem "Sixteen":

> She's seen it.
> How the tomcat bites the scruff
> of the female's neck so she can't get away:
> you can hear it hurting her and still she wants it.

The girl doesn't want it though. It's not that
she wants. She wants the part he keeps to himself,
what's back of those eyes.

As Borson matured, her form moved from free verse to prose poems. Density of meaning and concentration of emotion make these later poems as effective, if not more so, than those arranged with varying line lengths and rhythms. There is a consciousness that observes and contemplates, a calm voice presenting the details that are needed for the same flash of understanding.

Borson is an avowed but gentle feminist who has said in an interview in the Montreal literary magazine *Rubicon* that she feels women have been conditioned to find their sense of worth by pleasing others and by acquiring men to look after them; boys, on the other hand, have been conditioned to build and do things. She is against women-only anthologies but feels that women need better access to publication; as it is, women must be unusually accomplished to be recognized and appropriately rewarded. She has admitted that she unconsciously and inadvertently used patriarchal language in her 1981 collection *A Sad Device,* although since then she has been more careful. But she does not, like Erin Mouré and others among her contemporaries, feel the necessity for a new language to express women's concerns; nor does she believe that the language of the patriarchy, in existing before the poem, shapes it and must therefore be reformed.

If there is any criticism of Borson's poetry, it might be that it is too beautiful, too cloying, perfect, and unreal. Perhaps this is why she has turned to the more stringent form of the prose poem, which she handles with such skill, as in this example from *The Whole Night, Coming Home:*

Purple, papery, wisteria wreathed the house, and each
May a white box would arrive, its lid lifting to release not music
but the smell of gardenias, their number compounded by one.
What defines the union this gift symbolized, my father to
my mother, if one who came of it may speak for it? But I can't.
In the end we carry forward only a little of each story.

In the evenings white ginger stood exalted in its leaves, anticipating stars, each point of origin, each needle in a nerve.
Always the freedom, always the need, unresolved.

Whatever came or is yet to come is of this middle realm,
for which the human eye is the inevitable instrument. Awe
and disappointment, unique and to scale. Out of bounds the
unin-habitable regions, both larger and smaller, in which all
of this lies innocently hidden. Just as here among us go
unnoticed those merry-go-rounds whose horses appear or reappear, ghostwise, in the fuschia leaves.

In her collection *Intent, or, The Weight of the World,* Borson continued to explore the beauty and flexibility of the prose poem.

—Patience Wheatley

BOWERING, George (Henry)

Nationality: Canadian. **Born:** Keremeos, British Columbia, 1 December 1936. **Education:** South Okanagan High School, Oliver, British Columbia; Victoria College, British Columbia, 1953–54; University of British Columbia, Vancouver, B.A. 1960, M.A. 1963; University of Western Ontario, London. **Military Service:** Royal Canadian Air Force, 1954–57. **Family:** Married Angela Luoma in 1962: one daughter. **Career:** Has worked for the British Columbia Forest Service and for the Federal Department of Agriculture. Assistant professor, University of Calgary, Alberta, 1963–66; writer-in-residence, 1967–68, and assistant professor of English, 1968–72, Sir George Williams University, Montreal. Since 1972, associate professor, then professor of English, Simon Fraser University, Burnaby, British Columbia. Editor, *Tish,* Vancouver, 1961–63, and *Imago,* 1964–74. Since 1966 editor, Beaver Kosmos Folios. **Awards:** Canada Council grant 1968, 1971, 1977; Governor-General's Award for verse, 1969, for fiction, 1981; Nichol Chapbook award for poetry, 1991, 1992; Canadian Authors' Association award for poetry, 1993. D.Litt.: University of British Columbia, 1994. **Agent:** Denise Bukowski, 125 B Dupont Street, Toronto, Ontario M5R 1V4, Canada. **Address:** 2499 West 37th Avenue, Vancouver, British Columbia V6M 1P4, Canada.

PUBLICATIONS

Poetry

Sticks and Stones. Vancouver, Tishbooks, 1963.
Points on the Grid. Toronto, Contact Press, 1964.
The Man in Yellow Boots. Mexico City, El Corno Emplumado, 1965.
The Silver Wire. Kingston, Ontario, Quarry Press, 1966.
Baseball: A Poem in the Magic Number 9. Toronto, Coach House Press, 1967.
Two Police Poems. Vancouver, Talonbooks, 1969.
Rocky Mountain Foot: A Lyric, A Memoir. Toronto, McClelland and Stewart, 1969.
The Gangs of Kosmos. Toronto, Anansi, 1969.
Sitting in Mexico. Montreal, Imago/Beaver Kosmos, 1969.
George, Vancouver: A Discovery Poem. Toronto, Weed/Flower Press, 1970.
Genève. Toronto, Coach House Press, 1971.
Touch: Selected Poems 1960–1970. Toronto, McClelland and Stewart, 1971.
The Sensible. Toronto, Massasauga, 1972.
Autobiology. Vancouver, New Star, 1972.
Layers 1–13. Toronto, Weed/Flower Press, 1973.
Curious. Toronto, Coach House Press, 1973.
At War with the U.S. Vancouver, Talonbooks, 1974.
In the Flesh. Toronto, McClelland and Stewart, 1974.
Allophanes. Toronto, Coach House Press, 1976.
Poem and Other Baseballs. Coatsworth, Ontario, Black Moss Press, 1976.
The Catch. Toronto, McClelland and Stewart, 1976.
My Lips Are Red. Vancouver, Cobblestone Press, 1976.
The Concrete Island: Montreal Poems 1967–1971. Quebec, Vehicule Press, 1977.
Another Mouth. Toronto, McClelland and Stewart, 1979.
Uncle Louis. Toronto, Coach House Press, 1980.
Particular Accidents: Selected Poems, edited by Robin Blaser. Vancouver, Talonbooks, 1980.
Ear Reach. Vancouver, Alcuin, 1982.
West Window. Toronto, General, 1982.
Smoking Mirror. Edmonton, Longspoon Press, 1982.

Kerrisdale Elegies. Toronto, Coach House Press, 1984; as *Elegie di Kerrisdale,* Rome, Empiria, 1995.

Seventy-One Poems for People. Red Deer, Alberta, Red Deer College Press, 1985.

Delayed Mercy. Toronto, Coach House Press, 1986.

Urban Snow. Vancouver, Talonbooks, 1991.

Do Sink. Vancouver, Pomflit, 1992.

Sweetly. Vancouver, Wuz, 1992.

George Bowering Selected: Poems 1961–1993. Toronto, McClelland and Stewart, 1993.

Blonds on Bikes. Vancouver, Talonbooks, 1997.

A, You're Adorable. Ottawa, Above Ground, 1998.

Plays

A Home for Heroes, in *Prism International* (Vancouver), 1962; in *Ten Canadian Short Plays,* edited by Peter Stevens, New York, Dell, 1975.

Television Play: *What Does Eddi Williams Want?,* 1965.

Novels

Mirror on the Floor. Toronto, McClelland and Stewart, 1967.

A Short Sad Book. Vancouver, Talonbooks, 1977.

Concentric Circles (novella). Coastworth, Ontario, Black Moss Press, 1977.

Burning Water. Toronto, General, and New York, Beaufort, 1980.

En Eaux Troubles. Montreal, Quinze, 1982.

Caprice. Toronto, Viking Penguin, 1987; New York, Viking Penguin, 1988.

Harry's Fragments. Toronto, Coach House, 1990.

Parents from Space. Montreal, Roussau, 1994.

Shoot! Toronto, Key Porter, 1994; New York, St Martin's Press, 1996.

Diamondback Dog. Montreal, Roussan, 1998.

Piccolo Mondo. Toronto, Coach House, 1998.

Short Stories

Flycatcher. Ottawa, Oberon Press, 1974.

Protective Footwear. Toronto, McClelland and Stewart, 1978.

A Place to Die. Ottawa, Oberon Press, 1983.

Spencer and Groulx: from the Forthcoming Novel Caprice. Vancouver, William Hoffer, 1985.

The Rain Barrel. Vancouver, Talonbooks, 1994.

Other

How I Hear "Howl." Montreal, Sir George Williams University, 1968.

Al Purdy. Toronto, Copp Clarke, 1970.

Three Vancouver Writers. Toronto, Coach House Press, 1979.

A Way with Words. Ottawa, Oberon Press, 1982.

The Mask in Place. Winnipeg, Turnstone Press, 1982.

Craft Slices. Ottawa, Oberon Press, 1985.

Errata: I May Be Wrong, But. . . Red Deer, Alberta, Red Deer College Press, 1988.

Imaginary Hand: Some Literary Essays. Edmonton, Alberta, NeWest Press, 1988.

The Moustache: Memories of Greg Curnoe. Toronto, Coach House Press, 1993.

Bowering's B.C. Toronto, Viking, 1996.

Egotists and Autocrats. Toronto, Viking, 1999.

Editor, *Vibrations: Poems of Youth.* Toronto, Gage, 1970.

Editor, *The Story So Far.* Toronto, Coach House Press, 1971.

Editor, *Imago (Twenty) 1964–1974.* Vancouver, Talonbooks, 1974.

Editor, *Great Canadian Sports Stories.* Ottawa, Oberon Press, 1979.

Editor, *Loki Is Buried at Smoky Creek: Selected Poems,* by Fred Wah. Vancouver, Talonbooks, 1980.

Editor, *My Body Was Eaten by Dogs: Selected Poems,* by David McFadden. Toronto, McClelland and Stewart, and Flushing, New York, Cross Country, 1981.

Editor, *The Contemporary Canadian Poem Anthology.* Toronto, Coach House Press, 4 vols., 1983.

Editor, *Sheila Watson and the Double Hook: A Book of Essays, Readings and Reviews.* Ottawa, Golden Dog, 1985.

*

Bibliography: *A Record of Writing: An Annotated and Illustrated Bibliography of George Bowering* by Roy Miki, Vancouver, Talonbooks, 1989.

Manuscript Collections: Douglas Library, Queen's University, Kingston, Ontario; National Library, Ottawa.

Critical Studies: Introduction by the author to *Touch: Selected Poems,* 1971; *A Record of Writing* by Roy Miki, Vancouver, Talonbooks, 1990; *George Bowering: Bright Circles of Colour* by Eva-Marie Kröller, Vancouver, Talonbooks, 1992; *George Bowering and His Works* by John Harris, Toronto, ECW Press, 1992; *A Rhetoric of Reading Contemporary Canadian Narratives: George Bowering, Margaret Atwood, and Robert Kroetsch* (dissertation) by W.F. Garrett-Petts, University of Alberta, Canada, 1993; George's *Fragments: Bowering's Phenomenological Self* (dissertation), Queen's University, 1993, and "The International Politics of Existentialism: From Sartre, to Olson, to Bowering," in *Mosaic* (Canada), 29(1), March 1996, both by Trent Keough; "Postmodern Myth, Post-European History, and the Figure of the Amerindian: Francois Barcelo, George Bowering, and Jacques Poulin" by Marie Vautier, in *Canadian Literature,* 141, summer 1994; "Caprice and No Fixed Address: Playing with Gender and Genre" by Isabel Carrera, in *Kunapipi* (Aarhus, Denmark), 16(1), 1994; "'A Real Historical Fiction': Allegories of Discourse in Canadian Literary Historiography" by Michael Greene, in *Commonwealth Essays and Studies* (Dijon, France), 21(1), autumn 1998.

George Bowering comments:

(1974) I don't think that I will make a "personal statement introducing my work" because I don't write personal poetry. In fact, when personal poetry gets to be confessional poetry, I turn it off & reach for the baseball scores. I'll share with you what I wrote as notes 2 days ago: The snowball appears in hell every morning at seven. Dr Babel contends about the world's form, striking its prepared strings endlessly, a pleasure moving rings outward thru the universe. All sentences are to be served. You've tried it & tried it & it cant be done, you cannot close your ear—i.e., literature must be thought, now. Your knee on class equal poet will like use a simile because he hates ambiguity. The snowball says it: all sentences are imperative.

* * *

George Bowering began to write as an undergraduate in the English Department of the University of British Columbia, where he was an active member of the *Tish* group. The formative influence on this group was the Black Mountain school, especially the "projective verse" and "composition by field" practices identified with Robert Creeley, Charles Olsen, Ed Dorn, and Ronald Duncan.

From the first Bowering had his own voice, which is rather tender and lyrical. At the same time the attitude he takes to his subjects is often that of a rugged West Coaster who crafts his words and lines with the resourcefulness of a lumberjack or carpenter to meet real, everyday needs. Not for him the nuances or reveries associated with the literary writers of the eastern United States and Canada and their preoccupation with the verse of the past.

Storytelling lies at the heart of Bowering's art, and so it is not surprising that his short poems soon began to take on patterns and that the patterns began to predominate. Thus, from *Rocky Mountain Foot* on, his book-length collections have had the feel of books of poems rather than collections of disparate poems. The compulsion to tell the rest of the story or the next story has led him to the longer poem, which is generally a series of linked short lyrical poems.

Because storytelling is more often associated with prose than with poetry in the twentieth century, Bowering has turned to prose and has written successful novels and short stories that are fairly conventional in form.

Consistent with his desire to expand the readership of poetry as well as its range and powers of expression, Bowering has written a great deal of prose about his favorite fellow poets: forewords, prefaces, introductions, dedications, appreciations, explanations, reviews, and so forth. He has been most generous with his praise. As a critic, his range is deeper than it is wide. So moved was he when he learned of the tragic death of his friend the painter Greg Curnoe that within a month he had written an entire book of prose meditations, *The Moustache,* a work full of love, affection, feeling, insight, and appreciation. It is also replete with characteristic Boweringisms ("I remember that Greg Curnoe always knew guys with names like Ernie.")

Bowering will be remembered as a occasional poet, not in the sense of an amateur poet but in the sense of a writer who immortalizes or emblazons the moment as it takes wing. So caught up in the quotidian is Bowering that there is little sense that his poems or his work generally is heading anywhere in particular or has been anywhere in the past. He conveys visceral sensations of the moment, certain emotions, and a few thoughts, but the inner values only lightly touch upon the opposites of memory and imagination. It is as if no one but Bowering had ever written before.

There certainly is a sense of movement in his lines, but there is little or no sense of direction to his work as a whole, despite the arrangement of poems into groups, cycles, and books. This is not a limitation in the short run, but it certainly is a shortcoming when applied to a body of work. Because Bowering does not take himself or the world all that seriously, so easily do things come to him and to it, there is some humor in most of what he writes. It is probably safe to say that he is a major poet who has not written a major poem. (The

sole candidate that comes to mind is the *Kerrisdale Elegies,* a series of poetic meditations that begins with a direct steal from Rilke: "If I complain, who among my friends / would hear?" The question is not answered.) Over the decades the writer has become more adroit and the lines more stylish, but the man behind them has remained much the same bohemian who began writing as an undergraduate at the University of British Columbia in the 1960s.

—John Robert Colombo

BOWERING, Marilyn (Ruthe)

Nationality: Canadian. **Born:** Winnipeg, Manitoba, 13 April 1949. **Education:** University of Victoria, British Columbia, 1966–68, 1969–70, 1971–70, B.A. 1971, M.A. 1973; University of British Columbia, Vancouver, 1968–69; University of New Brunswick, Fredericton, 1975–78. **Family:** Married Michael S. Elcock in 1982; one daughter. **Career:** Radio control room operator, CKDA, Victoria, 1972–73; writer-in-residence, Aegean School of Fine Arts, Paros, Greece, 1973–74; secondary teacher, G.M. Dawson, Masset, British Columbia, 1974–75; instructor in continuing education, University of British Columbia, 1977; lecturer in creative writing, University of Victoria, 1978–80, 1982–86, 1989; editor and writer, Gregson Graham Marketing, Victoria, 1978–80; editor, Noel Collins and Blackwells, Edinburgh, 1980–82; visiting lecturer, 1978–82, lecturer in creative writing, 1982–86, 1989, and visiting associate professor of creative writing, 1993–94, University of Victoria, British Columbia; freelance writer in Seville, Spain, 1990–92; member of the faculty, 1992, and writer-in-electronic-residence, 1993–94, Banff Centre, Banff, Alberta. **Awards:** Canada Council Award, 1972, 1981, 1984, 1986, 1988; National Magazine award, 1978, 1988; Ontario Arts Council award, 1980, 1986. **Address:** c/o Beach Holme Publishing, 226–2040 West 12th Avenue, Vancouver, British Columbia V6J 2G2, Canada.

PUBLICATIONS

Poetry

The Liberation of Newfoundland. Fredericton, New Brunswick, Fiddlehead, 1973.
One Who Became Lost. Fredericton, New Brunswick, Fiddlehead, 1976.
The Killing Room. Victoria, British Columbia, Sono Nis Press, 1977; Victoria, British Columbia, Porcépic, 1991.
Third Child; Zian. Knotting, Bedfordshire, Sceptre Press, 1978.
The Book of Glass. Knotting, Bedfordshire, Sceptre Press, 1978.
Sleeping with Lambs. Victoria, British Columbia, Press Porcépic, 1980.
Giving Back Diamonds. Victoria, British Columbia, Press Porcépic, 1982.
The Sunday before Winter: New and Selected Poetry. Toronto, General, 1984.
Anyone Can See I Love You. Erin, Ontario, Porcupine's Quill, 1987.
Grandfather Was a Soldier. Victoria, British Columbia, Press Porcépic, 1987.
Interior Castle. Victoria, British Columbia, Reference West, 1994.

Autobiography. Victoria, British Columbia, Beach Holme, 1996.
Human Bodies: New and Collected Poems 1987–1999. Vancouver, British Columbia, Porcépic Books, 1999.

Plays

Anyone Can See I Love You (broadcast 1986; produced Victoria, British Columbia, 1988).
Hajimari-No-Hajimari (produced Japan, 1987).

Radio Plays: *Grandfather Was A Soldier,* 1983; *Marilyn Monroe: Anyone Can See I Love You,* 1986; *Laika and Folchakov,* 1987; *A Cold Departure,* 1989.

Novels

The Visitors All Returned. Erin, Ontario, Press Porcépic, 1979.
To All Appearance a Lady. Mississauga, Ontario, Random House, 1989; New York, Viking, and London, Hamish Hamilton, 1990.
Visible Worlds: A Novel. Toronto, HarperCollins, 1997; and New York, HarperCollins, 1998.

Other

Calling All the World; Laika and Folchakov. Victoria, British Columbia, Press Porcépic, 1989.
Love As It Is. Victoria, British Columbia, Beach Holme, 1993.

Editor, with David, *Many Voices: An Anthology of Contemporary Canadian Poetry.* Vancouver, Douglas, 1977.
Editor, *Guide to the Labour Code of British Columbia.* Victoria Government of British Columbia, 1980.

*

Critical Studies: "The Hidden Dreamer's Cry: Natural Force as Point of View" by M. Travis Lane, in *Fiddlehead* (Fredericton, New Brunswick), winter 1977; "Verse into Poetry" by George Woodcock, in *Canadian Literature* (Vancouver, British Columbia), autumn 1983; "The Latitudes of Romance: Representations of Chinese Canada in Bowering's 'To All Appearances a Lady' and Lee's 'Disappearing Moon Cafe'" by Graham Huggan, in *Canadian Literature* (Vancouver, British Columbia), 140, spring 1994.

Marilyn Bowering comments:
My poems, I am told, are full of surprises—the juxtaposition of the metaphysical with the sensuous and the everyday. Not that I am after surprise but that in speculating about the large things I can only use what I know. Serious in intent, certainly, but also with some irony, especially when considering men and women and relatives.
Death remains a favorite topic.
Poetry is always an attempt to make sense and order and is a conjunction of the emotional and physical life with something that "cannot be said." In that sense it attempts to go beyond words yet keeps the pleasure and shock of words as a reward and impetus for the journey. My early work was, as is so often the case, much concerned with the natural world and the past, the links of history and mythology that give the illusion of substance and order to the process of being

alive. Later I became much more interested in exploring consciousnesses other, if that is possible, than my own, in the two verse radio works *Grandfather Was a Soldier* and *Marilyn Monroe: Anyone Can See I Love You,* especially.
I admire poems that suggest story, and this has led me to write more fiction. Most of all I like the dissatisfaction that the best poems encourage, as if there is something just out of reach beyond the edge of perception, and with right risks taken it can be held in the hands.

*   *   *

A prolific writer, Marilyn Bowering remains best known as a poet even though she has also turned her energies to prose. A line in her first book, *The Liberation of Newfoundland,* sums up her poetic predilections: "all things are full of gods." In addition, the aqueous imagery found in this book recurs in much of her later work, as does an obsession with islands, caves, cliffs, dreams, bones, and killing. The early poem "Thera," in *One Who Became Lost,* sets forth this skeletal vision:

> The island hills
> arch grey spines
> from the sea.
> Facing them—
> white jagged ribs of the land,
>
> Bonemakers

Although in other poems she frequently derives her diction from the surrealists, Bowering does not cast their wide net of content. Indeed, her preoccupations appear private, even in their projection into natural forms of sea and land centered on personal agonies. As if to exorcise the latter, she is attracted to fairy tales and often resorts to charms, incantations, spells, and curses as mediums of expression. In her early work, such as *One Who Became Lost,* a certain monotonousness of perception tends to make one poem blur into another, although later books like *Sleeping with Lambs* evidence greater variety and grasp of shape. She adroitly weaves these lines into the title poem of *Giving Back Diamonds:*

> I love you forever
> there's no one like you
> I'd do anything for you
> I want you just as you are
> goodbye forever, goodbye

The repetitive emphasis of this ironic refrain is given extra point by the book's epigraph from Zsa Zsa Gabor: "I never hated a man enough to give diamonds back." Perhaps a title in the "Giving Back Diamonds" section of *The Sunday before Winter* best describes Bowering's attitude to her materials: "Well, it ain't no sin to take off your skin and dance around in your bones."
Anyone Can See I Love You is a cycle of poems as told by Marilyn Monroe about her life. The book has been broadcast and staged—a measure of Bowering's success at re-creating the star's tough but vulnerable voice.
Bowering's later work builds on earlier preoccupations. Inspired by the "fearful wonder" she felt as a child seeing *Sputnik II* in the sky, *Calling All the World* imaginatively and charmingly reconstructs

the epochal journey of Laika, the Soviets' canine cosmonaut and the terrestrial travels of Folchakhov, the dog's trainer. A larger collection, *Love As It Is,* is dominated by a series of dramatic monologues based on the correspondence of George Sand and Frédéric Chopin. Love, she implies, has a dangerous fragility, and the broken pieces of it can cut.

Human Bodies, which samples extensively from previous collections and adds new poems, offers a useful overview of Bowering's strengths and weaknesses. On display are straightforward syntax, flat diction, a certain rhythmic monotony, a monochromatic tone, and a thinness of imagistic reference. If this seems unappealing, Dave Godfrey's introduction rightly calls Bowering's art one of "intelligent indeterminacy" and notes that her poems "almost always put us face to face with people" (or, in the case of Laika, with dogs). Also reaffirmed is the way she smoothly incorporates documentary materials, as when she revisits the battlefields of World War I in *Grandfather Was a Soldier.* Having a structural sensibility, she favors long poems in sections, as in "Letter to Janey":

My mind skitters like metal spoons,
rattling the white plastic.
The words, the prayers, the unknown tongues
are a wind that cores me inside out,
like my grandmother cores an apple.
My insides are scooped out by metal blades.
I'm so light inside my plastic that I scarcely exist at all.

The lines are typical in showing Bowering's reflective mind confronting what to her is the self-evident terror of existence.

—Fraser Sutherland

BOWERS, Edgar

Nationality: American. **Born:** Rome, Georgia, 2 March 1924. **Education:** University of North Carolina, Chapel Hill, B.A. 1947; Stanford University, California, M.A. 1949, Ph.D. 1953. **Military Service:** U.S. Army, 1943–46. **Career:** Instructor, Duke University, Durham, North Carolina, 1952–55; assistant professor, Harpur College, Binghamton, New York, 1955–58; member of the English Department, 1958–91, and since 1991 professor emeritus, University of California, Santa Barbara. **Awards:** Fulbright fellowship, 1950; Swallow Press New Poetry Series award, 1955; Guggenheim fellowship, 1958, 1969; *Sewanee Review* fellowship; Edward F. Jones Foundation fellowship; University of Carolina Institute of Creative Arts fellowship Merrill award, 1974; Brandeis University Creative Arts medal, 1978; Bollingen prize, 1989; Harriet Monroe prize, 1989; American Institute of Arts and Letters award, 1991. **Address:** 1201 Greenwich Street, Apartment 601, San Francisco, California 94109, U.S.A. **Died.**

PUBLICATIONS

Poetry

The Form of Loss. Denver, Shallow, 1956.
Five American Poets, with others, edited by Ted Hughes and Thom Gunn. London, Faber, 1963.

The Astronomers. Denver, Swallow, 1965.
Living Together: New and Selected Poems. Boston, Godine, 1973; Manchester, Carcanet, 1977.
Thirteen Views of Santa Barbara. Woodside, California, Occasional Works, 1987.
Walking the Line. Florence, Kentucky, R.L. Barth, 1988.
Chaco Canyon. Los Angels, Symposium Press, 1988.
For Louis Pasteur. Princeton, New Jersey, Princeton University Press, 1988.
How We Came from Paris to Blois. El Cerrito, California, Jacaranda, 1990.
Collected Poems. New York, Knopf, 1997.

*

Bibliography: *The Published Works of Edgar Bowers, 1948–1988* edited by Jeffrey Akard and Joshua Odell, Florence, Kentucky, R.L. Barth, 1988.

Critical Studies: *Forms Discovery* by Yvor Winters, Denver, Swallow, 1967; *Alone with American* by Richard Howard, New York, Atheneum, 1969, London, Thames and Hudson, 1970, revised edition, Atheneum, 1980; "The Theme of Loss in the Earlier Poems of Catherine Davis and Edgar Bowers," in *Southern Review* 9 (Baton Rouge, Louisiana), and "Contexts for 'Being,' 'Divinity,' and 'Self' in Valéry and Edgar Bowers," in *Southern Review 13,* both by Helen A. Trimpi; "The Early Poems of Edgar Bowers" by Douglas L. Peterson, in *Centennial Review* (East Lansing, Michigan), 42(1), Winter 1998; "The Marriage of Logic and Desire: Some Reflections on Form" by John Foy, in *Parnassus,* 23(1–2), 1998.

*   *   *

The American poet Edgar Bowers has neither sought publicity nor achieved notoriety. He has not written in the modish confessional manner of some of his contemporaries but has simply written some of the great poems of the latter half of the twentieth century. Bowers's work deserves a slow and careful reading, for his poems are worth taking the time to understand.

Bowers's powerful treatment of the themes of deception and honesty, of shadow and lucidity, and of loss and form can be found in his earliest poems, but his depth and range have grown with no diminution of his prosodic mastery. A chief characteristic of his poems, as Yvor Winters pointed out, is that "sensory perception and its significance are simultaneous." This is especially true of "Autumn Shade," a sequence of ten poems that ends the 1965 collection *The Astronomers.* The sequence begins with a sense of destiny that amounts almost to predestination, something that appears in other poems as well:

Now, toward his destined passion there, the strong,
Vivid young man, reluctant, may return
From suffering in his own experience
To lie down in the darkness.

The young man wakes, he works, and he sleeps again, but the first poem ends with a chilling image: "The snake / Does as it must, and sinks into the cold." In another poem the young man lights a fire as the night grows cold:

105

Gently

A dead soprano sings Mozart and Bach.
I drink bourbon, then go to bed, and sleep
In the Promethean heat of summer's essence.

This is pentameter so subtle in modulation that the casual reader may miss a good deal of its technical virtuosity. So much is packed into the subdued, suggestive style that one may overlook the complexity of life and of emotional response to sensations that is being presented. The young man is aware that the things "I have desired / Evade me, and the lucid majesty / That warmed the dull barbarian to life. / So I lie here, left with self-consciousness." Within the sequence the young man's books, his old neighbor who drives through rain and snow, the recollection of Hercules and of his own father, and his view out the window of a Cherokee trail ("I see it, when I look up from the page") all indicate the reality of the external world. The density of reference suggests the presence of the past and the complexity of perception. The young man is trying in this dark night, during these seasons of the soul, to understand his own past and thus his present. His old neighbor's driving in snow prompts him to remember his own driving in war:

Was this our wisdom, simply, in a chance
In danger, to be mastered by a task,
Like groping round a chair, through a door, to bed?

Not many poets in the language could have written these lines. The verbal precision evokes deep resonance of response. Bowers's firm control and stylistic brilliance permit him a potentially dangerous ending for the sequence. It would be trite after this night of darkness and cold to have the sunlight transform the room, and so even shadows become "substantial light." But like all masters, Bowers takes the potentially trite and makes it hugely moving. The man of the sequence survives: "I stay / Almost as I have been, intact, aware, / Alive, though proud and cautious, even afraid." The ending is indicative of one of Bowers's strengths as a man and as a poet—his refusal to be deceived, his almost desperate honesty.

The dramatic monologue "The Prince" is a major examination of what has been termed "German war guilt." In it familial relations serve as the vehicle for a poetic rendering of moral relations:

My son, who was the heir
To every hope and trust, grew out of caring
Into the form of loss as I had done,
And then betrayed me who betrayed him first.

Likewise, in another fine poem, "From J. Haydn to Constanze Mozart (1791)," a verse letter expressing grief becomes a meditation on the rare fusion of mind and body, sense and reason, that Mozart's music embodies: "Aslant at his clavier, with careful ease, / To bring one last enigma to the norm, / Intelligence perfecting the mute keys." These poems, along with "Amor vincit omnia"—the greatest poem on the theme of the magi since Yeats's—"The Mountain Cemetery," and "The Astronomers of Mont Blanc," are part of the enduring body of work that distinguishes Bowers's books. In him we have a poet at once exact and exciting in his use of language. The word always fits the sense, and the sense never exceeds what language is capable of doing: "Whereof we cannot speak, thereof we must be silent."

—James Korges

BRACKENBURY, Alison

Nationality: British. **Born:** Gainsborough, Lincolnshire, 20 May 1953. **Education:** Brigg High School for Girls, Lincolnshire, 1964–71; St. Hugh's College, Oxford, 1972–75, B.A. (honors) in English 1975. **Family:** Married Guy Sheppard in 1975; one daughter. **Career:** Librarian, Gloucestershire College of Arts and Technology, Cheltenham, 1976–83; clerical assistant, Polytechnics Central Admissions System, Cheltenham, 1985–90. Since 1990 electroplater in family business. **Awards:** Eric Gregory award, 1982; Cholmondeley award, 1997. **Address:** c/o Carcanet Press, 4th Floor, Conavon Court, 12–16 Blackfriars Street, Manchester M3 5BQ, England.

PUBLICATIONS

Poetry

Journey to a Cornish Wedding. Walton-on-Thames, Surrey, Outposts, 1977.
Two Poems. London, Many Press, 1979.
Dreams of Power and Other Poems. Manchester, Carcanet, 1981.
Breaking Ground and Other Poems. Manchester, Carcanet, 1984.
Christmas Roses and Other Poems. Manchester, Carcanet, 1988.
Selected Poems. Manchester, Carcanet, 1991.
1829 and Other Poems. Manchester, Carcanet, 1995.
After Beethoven. Manchester, Carcanet, 2000.

Play

Radio Play: *The Country of Afternoon, 1985.*

*

Alison Brackenbury comments:

My poetry is a bad habit of talking to someone who may not be there. It is hard to know what this listener likes. I prefer my very long narrative and very short poems, but expect I will end up represented in anthologies by a single medium-length piece about toads.

I write a good deal about animals—especially unruly horses—gardens, and the past. This sounds comfortable. It is not meant to be. Do you—listener—take your poetry as Ovaltine? Or do you like space: wild grass at the end of the garden; sky, seen suddenly between houses?

I like poetry that is rhythmically supple and pleases by rhyme. I find it very hard to try to write like this. But I think a poem stands a better chance of moving its listener if it stops talking for a moment to sing.

*   *   *

Alison Brackenbury's first collections were dominated by two eponymous long poems (or poem sequences). *Dreams of Power* takes its title from a sequence of eight poems "spoken" by the Elizabethan court lady Arabella Stuart (though perhaps the poems might best be regarded as letters and the sequence seen as a modern continuation of the Ovidian tradition stemming from the *Heroides)*, who is trapped in the suspicions of others. There is much psychological acuteness in the poems, a developing sense of a convincing personality whose sufferings are forcefully presented through sensuously exact imagery. Only occasionally does one feel the obtrusive presence of the researcher's notebook, and for the most part the language achieves a plausible idiom, by no means pastiche Elizabethan, but not anachronistically modern either:

This fugitive and winter love
silvers the lips to frost. I wake, and shine,
The lean trees have no sap to write of us
—nor any rag of leaf, that we may hide . . .

I dare not write. One frozen afternoon—
cold birds—we huddled on the draughty floor.
You kissed my throat in firelight. The logs flowered.
Jasmine, clear yellow for the winter sun
burned on the sills. In darkness, half unsure,
the wind's dogs scratch the thick transparent door.

The title poem of *Breaking Ground* operates more by dialogue than monologue, recounting an imagined visit to John Clare in the asylum. It displays a similar control of iambic pentameter and the same sensitivity to natural detail. Again, the sense of isolation and imprisonment is powerfully evoked. In both sequences, however, there is a certain diffuseness, an occasional loss of focus, which makes the reader long for greater concision. When the sequences turn toward the concentration of lyricism, they are at their most compelling and become more than simply interesting. Nowhere is this more true than in the remarkable lyric "On the Boards," included in *Breaking Ground*, which has the intensity of Clare's own poems of madness without ever being merely imitative:

But He with eyes remote as stars
Reared up to twice my size
With one great blow, He split my head
    and so I sank and died.

[The children] . . . filled the church and stood in rows
to watch the coffin pass
and on the bare and boarded box,
cast every flower there was,

marigolds of sun and flame
light stocks as sweet as women's love
briar roses, frail as wrists of girls,
with every thorn plucked off—

because I faced the sun for them
and cast the dark shapes down
still they will sing me, warm and free,
though I am locked in ground.

The shorter poems of these first two volumes betray an uncertainty of idiom; a few drop into somewhat prosaic anecdote, while others are rather archly poetic. There are, however, some definite successes, especially those poems that enact a kind of memorial invocation, summoning up family ghosts, in "Robert Brackenbury," for example, or renewing mental contact with figures remembered from childhood in "Two Gardeners." The opening lines of this last poem declare that

Too far: I cannot reach them: only gardens.
And stories of the roughness of their lives.

The poet proceeds to retell these stories, and the stories told, the poem can end thus:

Dazzled by dry streets I touch their hands,
Parted by the sunlight, no man's flowers.

Family themes are often at the heart of some of Brackenbury's best poems, such as "My Old," with its almost refrain-like repetition of the poignant phrase "my old are gone," or the attractive poems on her daughter's childhood, such as "Constellations" and "At Night." Equally in evidence is her responsiveness to the natural world, as well as her capacity to find language in which to articulate that response. *Breaking Ground* contains a whole section of poems on horses, and there is much vivid writing in poems such as "Hare" and "Tracking" from Brackenbury's third collection, *Christmas Roses*.

Although this last volume contains no long poem, it is marked by some fine lyrics that have a formal tightness greater than had been consistently present in the earlier collections. There is a genuine and attractive magic to the best of these lyrics, reminiscent of the best of that underrated poet Walter de la Mare or of Edward Thomas. Poems such as "Tower" or "Stopping" have a simplicity not readily found in Brackenbury's earlier work—a simplicity that is the product of considerable sophistication—and they are resonant with unspoken significance. "Owl" is one such poem that belongs in a long tradition of English song and that is not disgraced by comparison with its forebearers:

Love: I heard an owl call:
but none of you were with me,
dearest body or my child,
to hear the owl call.

Deep in the stranger's garden,
where ferns blew, and the wild
blue of tall flowers has gone to dark,
the bird drew near: then called.

The air sinks quietly. Now I shake,
drained, by clean, white walls.
Next day's broad sun will not bring you.
Listen. The owl calls.

Brackenbury's work has been uneven in achievement. Certainly her first two collections contain more than a few poems that one suspects would not appear in a later volume of selected poems. The best of her work, however, testifies to the sharpness of her eye and her intelligence, and she has produced a number of wholly successful poems with a distinctive beauty and power.

—Glyn Pursglove

BRANDI, John

Nationality: American. **Born:** Los Angeles, California, 5 November 1943. **Education:** California State University, Northridge, B.F.A. 1965. **Family:** Two children. **Career:** Member, Peace Corps, South America, 1965–68. Poet-in-the-schools, Arts Division, State of New

Mexico, 1973–90, and State Council of the Arts, Nevada, Montana, and Alaska, 1980–90; poet-in-the-parks, Carlsbad Caverns and Guadalupe Mountains, New Mexico, 1979; writer-in-residence, Just Buffalo/Literary Center, New York, 1989; literature/visual arts residency, Djerassi Foundation, 1990. Poetry, language arts residencies, Navajo Nation, 1986–97. Founder and editor, Tooth of Time Books, Santa Fe, New Mexico. Painter: individual shows—Alla Gallery, Santa Fe, New Mexico, 1984; Thompson Gallery, Albuquerque, 1986; North Columbia Cultural Center, Nevada City, California, 1987; Claudia Chapline Gallery, Stinson Beach, California, 1988; Laurel Seth Gallery, 1991; Woodland-Pattern Book Center, 1995. **Awards:** Portland State Review prize for prose, 1971; P.E.N. writers grant, 1973, 1983; National Endowment for the Arts fellowship, 1980; Witter Bynner translation grant, 1983. **Address:** P.O. Box 2553, Corrales, New Mexico 87048, U.S.A.

PUBLICATIONS

Poetry

Thachapi Fantasy. Privately printed, 1964.

A Nothing Book. Privately printed, 1964.

Poem Afternoon in a Square of Guadalajara. San Francisco, Maya, 1970.

Emptylots: Poems from Venice and LA. Bolinas, California, Nail Press, 1971.

Field Notes from Alaska. Bolinas, California, Nail Press, 1971.

Three Poems for Spring. Bolinas, California, Nail Press, 1973.

August Poems. Bolinas, California, Nail Press, 1973.

San Francisco Lastday Homebound Hangover Highway Blues. Bolinas, California, Nail Press, 1973.

A Partial Exploration of Palo Flechado Canyon. Bolinas, California, Nail Press, 1973.

Smudgepots: For Jack Kerouac. Guadalupita, New Mexico, Nail Press, 1973.

The Phoenix Gas Slam. Bolinas, California, Nail Press, 1974.

Firebook. Virgin River, Utah, Smoky the Bear Press, 1974.

Turning Thirty Poems. Placitas, New Mexico, Duende Press, 1974.

In a December Storm. Bowling Green, Ohio, Tribal Press, 1975.

Looking for Minerals. Cherry Valley, New York, Cherry Valley Editions, 1975.

In a September Rain. Port Townsend, Washington, Copper Canyon Press, 1976.

The Guadalupes: A Closer Look. Carlsbad, New Mexico, Carlsbad Caverns Natural History Association, 1978.

Poems from Four Corners. Fort Kent, Maine, Great Raven, 1978.

Andean Town Circa 1980. Guadalupita, New Mexico, Tooth of Time, 1979.

As It Is These Days. Socorro, New Mexico, Whistling Swan Press, 1979.

Poems for the People of Coyote. Socorro, New Mexico, Distant Longing Press, 1980.

Sky House/Pink Cottonwood. Guadalupita, New Mexico, Tooth of Time, 1980.

At the World's Edge. Tesuque, New Mexico, Painted Stork, 1983.

Zvleika's Book. Santa Barbara, California, Doggerel Press, 1983.

Rite for the Beautification of All Beings. West Branch, Iowa, Toothpaste Press, 1983.

Poems at the Edge of Day. Buffalo, White Pine Press, 1984.

That Crow that Visited Was Flying Backwards. Santa Fe, Tooth of Time, 1984.

That Back Road In: Selected Poems 1972–1983. Berkeley, California, Wingbow Press, 1985.

Circling, with Steve Sanfield. Santa Cruz, California, Exiled-in-America Press, 1988.

Hymn for a Night Feast: Poems 1979–1987. Duluth, Minnesota, Holy Cow Press, 1989.

Shadow Play: Poems 1987–1991. Kenosha, Wisconsin, Light and Dust Books, 1992.

Turning 50 Poems. Pie Town, New Mexico, Age Spot Press, 1993.

Weeding the Cosmos: Selected Haiku. Albuquerque, New Mexico, La Alameda Press, 1994.

Heartbeat Geography: Selected & Uncollected Poems: 1967–1994. Fredonia, New York, White Pine Press, 1995.

No Reason at All. Farmington, New Mexico, Yoohoo Press, 1996.

River Following. Farmington, New Mexico, Yoohoo Press, 1997.

No Other Business Here. Albuquerque, New Mexico, La Alameda Press, 1999.

Short Stories

The Cowboy from Phantom Banks. Point Reyes, California, Floating Island, 1982.

In the Desert We Do Not Count the Days. Duluth, Minnesota, Holy Cow Press, 1990.

A Question of Journey: India, Nepal, Thailand Vignettes. Kenosha, Wisconsin, Light and Dust Books, 1995.

A Question of Journey: Travels in India, Nepal, Thailand & Bali. New Delhi, India, Book-Faith Publishers, 1999.

Reflections in the Lizard's Eye. Santa Fe, New Mexico, Western Edge Press, 2000.

Other

Desde Alla. Santa Barbara, California, Christopher's Press, 1971.

One Week of Mornings at Dry Creek. Santa Barbara, California, Christopher's Press, 1971.

Towards a Happy Solstice: Mine, Yours, Everybody. Santa Barbara, California, Christopher's Press, 1971.

Y Aun Hay Mas: Dreams and Explorations: New and Old Mexico. Santa Barbara, California, Christopher's Press, 1972.

Narrowgauge to Riobamba. Santa Barbara, California, Christopher's Press, 1975.

Memorandum from a Caribbean Isle. Brunswick, Maine, Blackberry, 1977.

Diary from Baja California. Santa Barbara, California, Christopher's Press, 1978.

Diary from a Journey to the Middle of the World. Berkeley, California, Figures, 1980.

Editor, *Chimborazo: Life on the Haciendas of Highland Ecuador.* Rooseveltown, New York, Akwesasne Notes, 1976.

Editor, with Larry Goodell, *The Noose: A Retrospective: Four Decades,* by Judson Crews. Oakland, California, Duende Press, 1980.

Editor, *Dog Day Blues: An Anthology of New Mexico Prison Writing.* Santa Fe, New Mexico, Tooth of Time, 1985.

*

Manuscript Collections: University of California, Davis; Brown University, Providence, Rhode Island; State University of New York, Buffalo.

John Brandi comments:

(1990) *Desde Alla* and *Narrowgauge to Riobamba* are two books akin to two separately painted panels translating the one-same diorama, that of isolated hamlets in the intermountain basins of the remote Andes where I spent a few years living with Quechua Indians.

Whenever I journey, I travel in two separate vehicles. One over the physical landscape, the other within the metaphysical. My writing and painting link the two spheres, migrating back and forth between inner and outer geographies.

My books are geography books, earth primers. Nothing I could have dreamed-up could be more astounding than the reality upon which my poems and paintings are based. They represent purestream, deep-cave, raw-pulse extracts from a realm at once mythic, at once physically accessible. Pen, brush, drops of ink, oil, gouache begin to widen across a blank tablet, dancing in rhythmic steps, disappearing and reappearing in a dream maze, a mirage. Images burn, become a pointed flame, a phoenix whose body joins two wings—one temporal, the other ephemeral; one male, the other female; one spirit, the other flesh; one dark, the other light. The ultimate mystery is to be alive. With each step forward what we walk into disappears. One day we discover something reflected in the mirror which is not our own. Rather, it is a body greater than ours whose image reveals the Body inside the bodies of everyone.

(1995) In 1971, after spending two years in the Andes as a Peace Corps volunteer and another couple of years between Mexico, Alaska, and the California Sierra Nevada as a war resister, I moved to New Mexico. I had grown fond of arid uplifts, particularly those in which humans paid homage—through elaborate systems of ritual drama—to the unseen forces which turn the wheel of life. The Mexican sierras of the Huichol come to mind, as does the altiplano of Bolivia. With its crystal atmosphere, sparse horizon, and elaborate indigenous ceremonies, New Mexico shared a similar identity. It would, over the next twenty years, become a well-suited base, a place where dream and reality converged, where one could live life without a marked division between either.

New Mexico nourished my spirit as a painter, writer, wanderer, and homemaker. Native American traditions of song, dance, and art in acknowledgment to the earth, air, water, and sun that sustain all life reaffirmed my own belief systems. My children—daughter born in Guadalajara, son in a tiny Sangre-de-Cristo adobe house—grew up in the mountains of New Mexico, a rich outback which continues to feed them.

Many poems written during my first decade in the Southwest were collected in *That Back Road In.* I introduced them as "topographic or even typographic projections of the landscape" and viewed the book as a kind of emotional or psychic schematic of territory where "heart, mind, rock and mirage all overlap." I was curious to record everything: what people spoke, how they worked, sang, and played, the look and feel of the land, each place and event that filled me with heightened tranquillity and awe. The poems became a record of exploration: getting to know new territory, finding out who my neighbors were, investigating the hidden canyons of the self. In 1982 a collection of prose called *The Cowboy from Phantom Banks* was issued, later to be expanded and republished as *In the Desert We Do Not Count the Days.* Again, the focus was on the land and the people of the high desert.

From 1979 on, my Southwest travels alternated with journeys into more remote deserts: those of Asia, Rajasthan, Ladakh, the uplands toward Tibet in the Himalayan rain shadow north of Mt. Annapurna. As in the Southwest, these places were filled with sacred sites, venerated waters, and time-tested pilgrimage spots. There were also elaborate ceremonies: tribal, Hindu, Buddhist.

Between 1980 and 1990 I exhibited paintings based on three sojourns to India, Nepal, Burma, and Thailand. Simultaneously, I worked on journal notations which, via letters or in limited-edition xeroxes, were shared with friends. A few poems issued during this period in *Hymn for a Night Feast* and *That Crow That Visited Was Flying Backwards* gave a hint of the Asia experience. But the real work consisted of slowly compiling a book-length prose manuscript.

During this time I discovered the poet Alain Bosquet's words, "essential writing raises wild notions and a challenge." In reading his poems I experienced the same disturbance that overcame me while writing about the world I had traveled in: that it was rapidly shrinking, tilting, clouding; that languages, the power to listen, observe, and speak truthfully had nearly disappeared; that tradition, truths, remembrance, even a realistic concept of mortality, had vanished along with clean water, breathable air, and a once abundant population of beautiful, intelligent, necessary life species.

Such realizations made it clear that we need a psychic or physical transformation and a challenge—unreasoned—to carry us beyond stale boundaries—mental and geographical—imposed by uninspired leaders and enforced by brutal regimes who disguise themselves in suits and ties and work predictable hours in "respectable" offices. One can stay at home and read about the world and realize these disturbances or journey, experience the pathos, feel a small bit of joy in the lives of real people struggling with daily activities in real places and know the tremendous odds presented by a heartbreaking world filled with nuclear arsenals, tree-toppled mountainsides, smuggled arms, slaughtered elephants, horrid atmosphere, and a population that continues to explode. A journey to Indonesia in 1993, focused on the island of Bali, brought me into a culture productively obsessed with art, music, theater, dance, insight, transformation, finding balance within the interplay of good and evil, and maintaining equilibrium within a complex weave of natural and supernatural forces.

"Being is difficult," Bosquet says. "Imagining is fruitful. The poem is tomorrow's truth. It offers the reader a secular prayer through which he can imagine new rapports between man and the universe, man and the void, man and himself." In agreement, I wrote *A Question of Journey* as a means toward the transformation, the metamorphosis that Bosquet implies. Travel, step away from the familiar, touch, be touched. Leave home, let the unpredictability of the road shake your beliefs, find a new way back. Along the way become someone else. Perhaps this new he or she is the you that was there all the time, before you were defined or began to define that person who stares back from the mirror.

*   *   *

John Brandi is an energetically prolific writer-artist whose work restlessly seeks sources of renewal in travel with its disruptions, encounters, labyrinths, mysteries, and delights. His writings embody a naive persona with a shrewder urban self, a curious fusion of *Candide* with Céline. Like many in-flight writers born in postwar American urban sprawl, traces of a self-absorbed relativism and noble savage sentimentality sometimes block the more purely documentary flow of his writing.

Brandi's work exemplifies the impressionistic and telegraphic writing style celebrated by Jack Kerouac. While its surfaces are often attractive, the political and social realities of poverty's enforced lifestyles often get glazed over with a romantic patina. Reflective depth is often absent in Brandi's visceral celebrations of place. His work makes clear that travel is essentially an inward reordering, a pilgrim's quest for a transcendent equilibrium.

That Road Back In: Selected Poems 1972–1983 and *Hymn for a Night Feast: Poems 1979–1987* give an ongoing picture of Brandi's work as a poet, reflecting varied concerns and influences, for example, Gary Snyder, Native American ceremonial song, classical Chinese nature poetry, and Michael McClure's bioenergetic forms, and always reinforced by the quest "to know" writ large à la Ginsberg and Whitman: "Life's a speeding wheel / caught with shadows. Hummingbird here / & gone at my window. / Crosslegged, I listen to cricket & flowers. / And though I inhabit this world / with every sense & sensation, I breathe from / somewhere a deeper light / unlocked from a Perfect Scent. / —all free & a billion times multiplied! / —all sifted finely through the waist / of an hourglass." He sometimes expresses himself in haiku-like discrete exhales of insight: "Trees / for bodies, nests / for heads, we are / mirrors / moving / in the wind."

As Brandi has matured, a sense of time lost and retrospective melancholy has added depth and difficulty to his writings. He is a multifaceted talent whose wide-ranging work—poetry, paintings, illuminated travel journals—is a distinctive history not only of a unique artist but also of a cultural and regional generation of western American poets who emerged during the turbulently utopian 1960s.

—David Meltzer

BRATHWAITE, Edward Kamau

Nationality: Barbadian. **Born:** Lawson Edward Brathwaite, Bridgetown, Barbados, 11 May 1930. **Education:** Harrison College, Barbados; Pembroke College, Cambridge (Barbados Scholar), 1950–54, B.A. (honors) in history 1953, Cert. Ed. 1954; University of Sussex, Falmer, 1965–68, D. Phil. 1968. **Family:** Married Doris Monica Welcome in 1960; one son. **Career:** Education officer, Ministry of Education, Ghana, 1955–62; tutor, University of the West Indies Extra Mural Department, St. Lucia, 1962–63. Lecturer, 1963–76, reader, 1976–82, and since 1982 professor of social and cultural history, University of the West Indies, Kingston. Visiting professor, Southern Illinois University, Carbondale, 1970; University of Nairobi, 1971, Boston University, 1975–76, University of Mysore, India, 1982, Holy Cross College, Worcester, Massachusetts, 1983; and Yale University, New Haven, Connecticut, 1988. Visiting fellow, Harvard University, Cambridge, Massachusetts, 1987. Plebiscite officer in the Trans-Volta Togoland, United Nations, 1956–57. Founding secretary, Caribbean Artists Movement, 1966. Since 1970 editor, *Savacou* magazine, Mona. **Awards:** Arts Council of Great Britain bursary, 1967; Camden Arts Festival prize, London, 1967; Cholmondeley award, 1970; Guggenheim fellowship, 1972; City of Nairobi fellowship, 1972; Bussa award, 1973; Casa de las Américas prize, 1976; Fulbright fellowship, 1982–83, 1987–88; Institute of Jamaica Musgrave medal, 1983. **Address:** Department of History, University of the West Indies, Mona, Kingston 7, Jamaica.

PUBLICATIONS

Poetry

Rights of Passage. London, Oxford University Press, 1967.
Masks. London, Oxford University Press, 1968.
Islands. London, Oxford University Press, 1969.
Penguin Modern Poets 15, with Alan Bold and Edwin Morgan. London, Penguin, 1969.
Panda No. 349. London, Royal Institute for the Blind, 1969.
The Arrivants: A New World Trilogy. London and New York, Oxford University Press, 1973.
Days and Nights. Mona, Jamaica, Caldwell Press, 1975.
Other Exiles. London and New York, Oxford University Press, 1975.
Poetry '75 International. Rotterdam, Rotterdamse Kunststichting, 1975.
Black + Blues. Havana, Casa de las Américas, 1976; revised edition, New York, New Directions, 1995.
Mother Poem. London, Oxford University Press, 1977.
Soweto. Mona, Jamaica, Savacou, 1979.
Word Making Man: A Poem for Nicólas Guillèn, Mona, Jamaica, Savacou, 1979.
Sun Poem. Oxford and New York, Oxford University Press, 1982.
Third World Poems. London, Longman, 1983.
X-Self. London, Oxford University Press, 1987.
Sappho Sakyi's Meditations. Kingston, Jamaica, Savacou Publications, 1989.
Middle Passages. Newcastle upon Tyne, Bloodaxe, 1992.
Trench Town Rock. Providence, Rhode Island, Lost Roads, 1994.

Recordings: *The Poet Speaks 10,* Argo, 1968; *Rights of Passage,* Argo, 1969; *Masks,* Argo, 1972; *Islands,* Argo, 1973; *The Poetry of Edward Kamau Brathwaite,* Casa de las Américas, 1976; *Atumpan,* Watershed, 1989.

Plays

Four Plays for Primary Schools (produced Saltpond, Ghana, 1961–62). London, Longman, 1964.
Odale's Choice (produced Saltpond, Ghana, 1962). London, Evans, 1967.

Other

The People Who Came 1–3 (textbooks). London, Longman, 1968–72.
Folk Culture of the Slaves in Jamaica. London, New Beacon, 1970; revised edition, 1981.
The Development of Creole Society in Jamaica 1770–1820. Oxford, Clarendon Press, 1971.
Caribbean Man in Space and Time. Mona, Jamaica, Savacou, 1974.
Contradictory Omens: Cultural Diversity and Integration in the Caribbean. Mona, Jamaica, Savacou, 1974.
Our Ancestral Heritage: A Bibliography of the Roots of Culture in the English-Speaking Caribbean. Kingston, Carifesta, 1976.
Wars of Respect: Nanny, Sam Sharpe, and the Struggle for People's Liberation. Kingston, API, 1977.
Jamaica Poetry: A Checklist 1686–1978. Kingston, Jamaica Library Service, 1979.
Barbados Poetry: A Checklist, Slavery to the Present. Mona, Jamaica, Savacou, 1979.

Kumina. Mona, Jamaica, Savacou, 1982.
Gods of the Middle Passage. Privately printed, 1982.
National Language Poetry. Privately printed, 1982.
The Colonial Encounter: Language. Mysore, University of Mysore, 1984.
History of the Voice: The Development of a National Language in Anglophone Caribbean Poetry. London, New Beacon, 1984.
Jah Music. Mona, Jamaica, Savacou 1986.
Roots (essays). Havana, Casa de las Americas, 1986.
Barabajan Poems, 1492–1992. Kingston, Jamaica, Savacou, 1994.
DreamStories. Essex, England, and White Plains, New York, Longman, 1994.

Editor, *louanaloa: Recent Writing from St. Lucia.* Castnies, University of the West Indies Department of Extra-Mural Studies, 1963.
Editor, *New Poets from Jamaica.* Mona, Jamaica, Savacou, 1979.
Editor, *Dream Rock.* Kingston, Jamaica Information Service, 1987.

*

Bibliography: *Edward Kamau Brathwaite: His Published Prose and Poetry 1948–1986* by Doris Monica Brathwaite, Mona, Jamaica, Savacou, 1986; *A Descriptive and Chronological Bibliography (1950–1982) of the Work of Edward Kamau Brathwaite* by Doris Monica Brathwaite. London, New Beacon. 1988.

Critical Studies: "The Poetry of Edward Brathwaite" by Jean D'Costa, in *Jamaica Journal* (Kingston), September 1968; *The Chosen Tongue* by Gerald Moore, London, Longman, 1969; "Brathwaite's Song of Dispossession" by K.E. Senanu, in *Universitas* (Accra), March 1969; "The Poetry of Edward Brathwaite" by Damian Grant, in *Critical Quarterly* (London), Summer 1970; "Dimensions of Song" by Anne Walmsley, in *Bim* 51 (Bridgetown, Barbados), July-December 1970; "Three Caribbean Poets" by Maria K. Mootry, in *Pan-Africanist*, ii, 1, 1971; "This Broken Ground" by Mervyn Morris, in *New World Quarterly* (Kingston), v, 3, 1971; "Islands," in *Caribbean Studies* (Rio Piedras, Puerto Rico), January 1971, "Songs of the Skeleton: A Poetry of Fission," in *Trinidad and Tobago Review* (Port of Spain), 1980–81, and *Pathfinder: Black Awakening in "The Arrivants" of Edward Kamau Brathwaite,* Port of Spain, 1981, all by Gordon Rohlehr; "Walcott Versus Brathwaite" by Patricia Ismond, in *Caribbean Quarterly 17* (Kingston), September-December 1971; "A Study of Some Ancestral Elements in Brathwaite's Trilogy" by Samuel Asein, in *African Studies Association of the West Indies Bulletin 4* (Mona, Jamaica), December 1971; "Edward Brathwaite y el neoafricanismo antillano" by G.R. Coulthard, in *Cuadernos Americanos* (Mexico City), September/October 1972; "Odomankoma Kyerema se: A Study of Masks" by Maureen Warner, in *Caribbean Quarterly* (Kingston), June 1973; "E. Brathwaite y su poesia antillana" by Nancy Morejon, in *Bohemia* 22 (Havana), 3 June 1977; "The Cyclical Vision of Edward Kamau Brathwaite" by Lloyd W. Brown, in *West Indian Poetry,* Boston, Twayne, 1978, revised edition, London, Heinemann, 1984; "Edward Brathwaite" by J. Michael Dash, in *West Indian Literature* edited by Bruce King, London, Macmillan, 1979; "Brathwaite and Walcott Issue" of *Caribbean Quarterly 26* (Mona, Jamaica), nos. 1–2, 1980; Robert Bensen, in *Critical Survey of Poetry* edited by Frank N. Magill, Englewood Cliffs, New Jersey, Salem Press. 1983; "'Labyrinth of Past/Present/Future' in Some of Kamau Brathwaite's Recent Poems," in *Crisis and Creativity in the New Literatures in English:*

Cross/Cultures, edited by Geoffrey V. Davis and Hena Maes-Jelinek, Amsterdam, Rodopi, 1990, and "Kamau Brathwaite: A Voice Out of Bounds," in *'Union in Partition': Essays in Honour of Jeanne Delbaere,* edited by Gilbert Debuscher and Marc Maufort, Liege, Belgium, L3, 1997, both by Christine Pagnoulle; *The Recovery of Ancestry in the Poetry of Edward Kamau Brathwaite and Derek Walcott* (dissertation) by June D. Bobb, City University of New York, 1992; Kamau Brathwaite issue of *World Literature Today* (Norman, Oklahoma), 68(4), Autumn 1994; *The Art of Kamau Brathwaite* edited by Stewart Brown, Bridgend, Wales, Seren, 1995; "The Word Becomes Nam: Self and Community in the Poetry of Kamau Brathwaite, and Its Relation to Caribbean Culture and Postmodern Theory" by Elaine Savory, in *Writing the Nation: Self and Country in the Post-Colonial Imagination,* edited by John C. Hawley, Amsterdam, Rodopi, 1996; *The Liberating Imagination: Politics of Vision in the Art of Edward Kamau Brathwaite and Henry Dumas* (dissertation) by Paul Anderson Griffith, Pennsylvania State University, 1995; *Caliban Takes Up His Pen: The Epic Poetry of Kamau Brathwaite, Derek Walcott, and Andrew Salkey* (dissertation) by Michelle Diane Derose, University of Iowa, 1996.

Edward Kamau Brathwaite comments:

What caused the death of the amerindians: the holocaust of slavery: the birth of tom and caliban

in terms of my weltanschauung: my culture-view: it all began with the fall of the roman empire: this imperial achievement had created an equilibrium of material/spirit: metropole/province: law/chaos: which made possible a definition of values with the decline and fall of rome: flux appeared: movements of magic into the metropole: custom replaced statute: gargoyle replaced statue the vikings moved in from the north: the goths, huns, magyars came on from the east; the crescent of islam curved north, african and aztec civilizations began to prophesy disaster christianity (the holy roman empire) attempted to restore/retain the equilibrium but it was impossible: there were too many alternatives: there was mohamet: there were magi: there was the new science of copernicus, the natural philosophers, the medical school at salerno, there was a choice: galilee or galileo: emperor or pope: priest or politician

and then money became the center of this shattered universe: market, bourg, bourse: commerce, ship, merchant, bank: middle class, taxes, nations, mercantilism: travel to new lands: control of new markets: the shift of authority outwards: supported by bullet and bible: but no prayer: but purse: not custom anymore, but curse marco polo overland to china; the portuguese by stepping stone to africa; columbus to san salvador

moctezuma collapsed: chichen itza defeated: geronimo doomed: saskatchewa: mohican: esquimo and ewe whale-worshippers: timbucto, kumasi, ile-ife, benin city, zimbabwe caribs moving towards malaria and syphilis; cherokees moving towards the horse, the weston rifle, the waggon train; ibo and naga to slave ships; zulus towards the locomotive tank; masai towards the jumbo jet, caliban to new york, paris, london town, so that here in the caribbean we have people without (apparent) root: values of whip, of bomb, of bottle: the culture of materialism, not equilibrium

food, flesh, house, harbor: not stone, demon, wilderness, space: extermination of the arawaks

first 10, then 20
first 20, then 200

first 200 then 200,000 africans: slaves, lukumi, tears
200,000: 300,000: 400,000: a million: tears, lukumi
1 million: 2 million: 3 Million: 4 Million: materialism
    buildings hotels, plantation houses
10 million: 20 million: lukumi: lukumi: tears
30 million: 40 million: 50 million: we could go on
    counting: men: money: materialism:
tears: tears: lukumi
the spaniards drained the lake of mexico away: the modern
    city sited in the dust bowl
where are the bison of the prairies: leviathan of the
    pacific indians
where are those 50 million africans: without tongue,
    without mother,without god *can you*
expect us to establish houses here?
to build a nation here? where
will the old men feed their flocks?
where will we make our markets? (Masks, p. 21)

the history of catastrophe requires such a literature to hold a broken
mirror up to broken
nature.

*   *   *

Edward Kamau Brathwaite's solid reputation as a major West Indian poet rests largely on the well-known trilogy *Rights of Passage, Masks,* and *Islands,* reprinted in one volume as *The Arrivants.* But since the publication of the trilogy in 1973, he has produced other important volumes of poetry, including *Other Exiles* and *Mother Poem.*

Other Exiles spans a considerable period of Brathwaite's activity as a poet, more specifically, the twenty-five years before its publication. It is a varied collection reflecting the diversity of interests and techniques that is characteristic of Brathwaite's work as a whole but is often obscured by a prevailing tendency to see him, on the basis of *The Arrivants,* as the monolithic, collective voice of the black diaspora. The collection actually ranges from the exile's intense sense of personal isolation in Europe ("The Day the First Snow Fell") to the satirically detached portrait of the growth of an archetypal young colonial ("Journeys"). In "Conqueror" the personal voice shifts from that of the colonial governor in the Caribbean to the collective consciousness of an emerging Caribbean nationalism, one that has emerged with the West Indian's step from "slave to certain owner."

The collection is also Brathwaite's most uneven work, a reflection perhaps of the degree to which it spans his development from inexperienced writer to mature artist. The precisely drawn portrait of the colonial psyche in "Journeys" is therefore far superior to the self-indulgence and flabbiness of language that mar the word pictures of jazz artists in "Blues." Similarly "Conqueror" demonstrates an acute ear for the discriminating and the effectively appropriate use of language, a quality that is lacking in rather sentimental pieces like "At the Death of a Young Poet's Wife" and "Schooner." On the whole, *Other Exiles* is significant in that, at its best, it reflects those qualities that have become the hallmarks of Brathwaite's mature poetry—the enormous suppleness of language that facilitates a deceptive ease of transition from one viewpoint to the other ("Conqueror"), the complex sense of personality that allows the poet to develop his persona both as a distinctive individual and as the archetype of a

collective experience ("Journeys"), and the imaginative handling of folk language as the expression of a distinctive West Indian culture.

These are the qualities that underlie the success of the trilogy. The ambiguity of Brathwaite's poetic "I" (as both private individual and collective archetype) is perfectly adapted to the poet's exploration of the Caribbean experience in both its private dimension and in its significance to an inclusive West Indian culture. And in turn this ambiguity pinpoints the role of the poet himself, voicing his vision in personal terms that are analogous to and comparable with those of musicians and other artists. At the same time the terms of the personal vision symbolize a group experience in which the creative energies of the culture—like the poetic imagination itself—represent and celebrate the vitality that has persisted in spite of slavery and colonialism.

Rights of Passage, the first section of the trilogy, concentrates on blacks in the Americas, moving from the West Indies to North America and back. In the process the poet discovers affinities between the songs, dances, and language forms through which blacks have responded to a common history, not only in the New World but also in Africa. The exploration of these connections in *Rights of Passage* amounts to a prelude of sorts to the themes of *Masks,* where the poet reverses the historical Middle Passage of slavery by returning from the New World to Africa.

Africa is the source of much that has been explored in *Rights of Passage,* and in *Masks* the poet expands upon the sense of a common source. The continent is simultaneously the historical root and the contemporary essence of a global black presence. The sense of affinities is not only geographical but also temporal. The New World black's return to West Africa is therefore described in terms that recall the forcible departure of the visitor's ancestors into New World slavery, and the sights and sounds of precolonial Africa are at times indistinguishable from those of both contemporary Africa and the modern Caribbean. The past and the present also coexist in *Islands,* where the poet returns to the contemporary West Indies after symbolically retracing the original voyages of enslavement. Here, for the purposes of dramatic contract, the images of slavery and colonialism are juxtaposed with symbols of the new West Indian nationalism.

Finally, the self-conscious use of a variety of language forms (West Indian and American Black English as well as West African) is fundamental to Brathwaite's themes throughout the trilogy. The variety in language enforces the poet's vision of West Indian culture as the diverse product of several sources—Africa, Europe, Asia, and the New World itself. In a similar vein the journey themes dominating the narrative design of the trilogy reinforce a sense of cultural and historical continuities as we move with the poet, through space and time, from one point of the black diaspora to another. And this impression of continuous movement also dramatizes the cultural and psychic progression that gradually culminates in the emergence of a national consciousness that displaces traditional self-hatred and entrenched colonial values.

Mother Poem is actually an intensified and detailed continuation of the themes of *The Arrivants,* for here the progression from a destructive past to a future of creative possibilities is concentrated in Barbados. The mother image that dominates the work, which is a long, continuous poem, is a dual one; it connotes a personal mother, and it reflects the perception of Barbados itself as a mother country, as a cultural source of the poet's perception of self and society. This duality intensifies the vision of growth and change, and the progression is simultaneously cultural in a broad social sense and deeply personal. In turn this sustained duality attests to the persistence of one of Brathwaite's most important assets as poet—his ability to integrate the personal and public voices into a complex poetic language that allows each voice to remain distinctive.

—Lloyd W. Brown

BREW, (O.H.) Kwesi

Nationality: Ghanaian. **Born:** Cape Coast, Ghana, 27 May 1928. **Education:** Attended schools in Cape Coast, Kumasi, Tamale and Accra; University College of the Gold Coast (now the University of Ghana), B.A. 1953. **Career:** Entered the Administrative Service in 1953; government agent at Keta for nearly two years, then assistant secretary in the Public Service Commission. Now in the Ghana Foreign Service: has been ambassador for Ghana to Britain, France, India, Germany, the U.S.S.R., Mexico, and Senegal. **Awards:** British Council prize. Lives in Accra, Ghana. **Address:** c/o Greenfield Review Press, P.O. Box 80, Greenfield Center, New York 12833, U.S.A.

PUBLICATIONS

Poetry

Pergamon Poets 2: Poetry from Africa, with others, edited by Howard Sergeant. Oxford, Pergamon Press, 1968.
The Shadows of Laughter. London, Longman, 1968.
African Panorama. Greenfield Center, New York, Greenfield Review Press, 1981.
Return of No Return and Other Poems. Accra, Ghana, Afram, 1995.
The Clan of the Leopard and Other Poems. Accra, Ghana, Anansesem, 1996.

Play

Screenplay: *The Harvest.*

*

Critical Studies: "Kwesi Brew and His Poetry" by A.W. Kayper-Mensah, in *Legacy,* 3(1), 1976; in *Opon Ifa,* 1(2), 1980.

*   *   *

The Ghanaian poet Kwesi Brew has a much wider range, both of subject and style, than most of his African contemporaries, and over the years he has developed a voice inherently his own. He has written poems about childbirth ("Gamelli's Arm Has Broken into Buds"), childhood memories, youthful indiscretions, and middle-age reflections ("The Middle of the River"), as well as some of the most tender love poems to come out of Africa ("Flower and Fragrance," "The Two Finds," and "The Mesh," to name only a few). Ghanaian folk songs and customs are intricately woven into the tapestry of his poetry, and since Brew has exceptional descriptive gifts, the Ghanaian landscape and idiom come suddenly to life for non-African readers through his works.

Brew has written about such specifically traditional subjects as ancestor worship ("Ancestral Faces") and the passing of the fighting tribes ("Questions of Our Time"), but he has not hesitated to deal with a contemporary event of great significance for his country—the downfall of President Kwame Nkrumah in 1966—in a poem entitled "A Sandal on the Head." In this fascinating poem, which appeared in *Outposts* shortly after the event, Brew maintains a careful distance from his subject by employing an objective correlative appropriate to the situation—the Ghanaian custom of touching the head of a chief with one of his own sandals to declare him "de-stooled." "Ghost Dance," "The Master of the Common Crowd," "The Secrets of the Tribe," "A Plea for Mercy," "The Harvest of Our Life," and other poems draw strongly upon the African way of life and present the conflict between old and new, between tribal instinct and national aspiration, and between the regional and the universal.

—Howard Sergeant

BREWSTER, Elizabeth (Winifred)

Nationality: Canadian. **Born:** Chipman, New Brunswick, 26 August 1922. **Education:** Sussex High School, New Brunswick, graduated 1942; University of New Brunswick, Fredericton, B.A. 1946; Radcliffe College, Cambridge, Massachusetts, A.M. 1947; King's College, London, 1949–50; University of Toronto (Pratt Gold Medal and prize, 1953), B.L.S. 1953; Indiana University, Bloomington, Ph.D. 1962. **Career:** Cataloguer, Carleton University Library, Ottawa, 1953–57, and Indiana University Library, 1957–58; member of the English Department, Victoria University, British Columbia, 1960–61; reference librarian, Mount Allison University Library, Sackville, New Brunswick, 1961–65; cataloguer, New Brunswick Legislative Library, Fredericton, 1965–68, and University of Alberta Library, Edmonton, 1968–70; visiting assistant professor of English, University of Alberta, 1970–71; assistant professor, 1972–75, associate professor, 1975–80, professor of English, 1980–90, and since 1990 professor emeritus, University of Saskatchewan, Saskatoon. **Awards:** Canada Council award, 1971, 1976, 1978, 1985; President's Medal, University of Western Ontario, 1980; Lifetime award, excellence in the arts, Saskatchewan Arts Board, 1995. Litt.D.: University of New Brunswick, 1982. **Address:** Department of English, University of Saskatchewan, Saskatoon, Saskatchewan S7N 0W0, Canada.

PUBLICATIONS

Poetry

East Coast. Toronto, Ryerson Press, 1951.
Lillooet. Toronto, Ryerson Press, 1954.
Roads and Other Poems. Toronto, Ryerson Press, 1957.
Five New Brunswick Poets, with others, edited by Fred Cogswell. Fredericton, New Brunswick, Fiddlehead, 1962.
Passage of Summer: Selected Poems. Toronto, Ryerson Press, 1969.
Sunrise North. Toronto, Clarke Irwin, 1972.
In Search of Eros. Toronto, Clarke Irwin, 1974.
Sometimes I Think of Moving. Ottawa, Oberon Press, 1977.
The Way Home. Ottawa, Oberon Press, 1982.
Digging In. Ottawa, Oberon Press, 1982.
Selected Poems of Elizabeth Brewster, 1944–1984. Ottawa, Oberon Press, 2 vols., 1985.

Entertaining Angels. Ottawa, Oberon Press, 1988.
Spring Again. Ottawa, Oberon Press, 1990.
Wheel of Change. Ottawa, Oberon Press, 1993.
Footnotes to the Book of Job. Ottawa, Oberon Press, 1995.
Garden of Sculpture. Ottawa, Oberon Press, 1998.

Novels

The Sisters. Ottawa, Oberon Press, 1974.
Junction. Windsor, Ontario, Black Moss Press, 1982.

Short Stories

It's Easy to Fall on the Ice. Ottawa, Oberon Press, 1977.
A House Full of Women. Ottawa, Oberon Press, 1983.
Visitations. Ottawa, Oberon Press, 1987.

Other

The Invention of Truth (Stories and Essays). Ottawa, Oberon Press, 1991.
Away from Home (Stories and Essays). Ottawa, Oberon Press, 1995.

*

Critical Studies: "The Poetry of Elizabeth Brewster" by Desmond Pacey, in *Ariel* (Calgary, Alberta), July 1973; "Next Time from a Different Country" by Robert Gibbs, in *Canadian Literature* (Vancouver), autumn 1974; "Speeding towards Strange Destinations: A Conversation with Elizabeth Brewster" by Paul Denham, in *Essays on Canadian Writing* (Downsview, Ontario), summer-fall 1980; "Cadence, Texture and Shapeliness" by J.R. Struthers, in *Journal of Canadian Fiction* (Montreal), 31–32, 1981; "Poems-Elizabeth Brewster," in *Canadian Literature* (Vancouver), 151, 1996.

*   *   *

"I have written poems principally to come to a better understanding of myself, my world, and other people," explains Elizabeth Brewster. Her work dramatizes, again in her own words, "the struggle to lead a human rational life in a world which is increasingly inhuman and irrational."

This credo applies particularly to Brewster's *Passage of Summer: Selected Poems,* which brings together the best work of the writer's earlier collections. Her poems are seen to be sometimes slight, often sentimental, yet ever honest and celebratory, especially of the small things and the little moments and meanings of life. Brewster has been described as a "quiet" poet, and it is true that she prefers the gentle shade to the fierce sun, ironic reflections to strong statements. Often her poems are moving without being at all memorable. Her imagination is more fanciful than imaginative. Yet her work is like a wine that improves with age; its taste mellows in memory.

The critic Morris Wolfe has written, "One has to read a fair bit of Elizabeth Brewster's poetry to realize just how good she is." The opportunity to do so was finally offered with the publication of her *Selected Poems, 1944–1984,* which showcases her finest work. Over the years, it has become apparent, she has found a way to turn fancies and musings into meaningful subjects for poems. At the same time she has mastered the art of the casual aside: "Why do I feel guilty / that I am sometimes bored?" and "Love is never deserved, / is mostly imagination anyway." She has nourished a genius for understatement, and a pleasant wit has taken flower in her garden.

Entertaining Angels offers further evidence of the strength and individuality of Brewster's achievement. This is a likable collection with many strong moments. Indeed, she writes about this fact in the poem "Cloud Formations":

> Some time, I think,
> the perfect arrangement
> of words will come
> (though, even as I write the word,
> I doubt if I would like perfection)
> some time there will be
> the moment of illumination
> (but aren't all moments
> moments of illumination?)

The poem discusses her own background in poetry: the eight-year-old in the attic, writing like Shelley; the ten-year-old copying poems in the scribbler; the twelve-year-old composing "my little poems / as letters to myself . . . written conversations." In the poem "Blue Chair" Brewster finds a homey approach to refer to the wear and tear of the years:

> I like my blue chair, though I can see
> spots which will soon be,
> though they aren't yet,
> shabby.

Throughout the collection there are references to aunts as great storytellers and also to the ghost stories of the Maritimes, the region where Brewster was born and raised, the region she left behind when she moved west to the Prairie Provinces. Perhaps she did not really leave the region behind, for its ghosts flit through a number of her poems written on the prairie. In "The Ungrateful Dead Man," for instance, she describes ghosts as "slipping out of the room / to haunt elsewhere." Ghosts haunt people more than they do places, and the poet herself is among the people they haunt.

It is fair to say that Brewster has succeeded in her resolve to understand herself as well as to write poems that remain in the mind and mellow in the memory.

—John Robert Colombo

BRINGHURST, Robert

Nationality: Canadian. **Born:** Los Angeles, California, 16 October 1946; grew up in the United States, Mexico, and Canada. **Education:** Massachusetts Institute of Technology, Cambridge, 1963–64, 1970–71; University of Utah, Salt Lake City, 1964–65; Defense Language Institute, Monterey, California, 1966–67; Indiana University, Bloomington, 1971–73, B.A. in comparative literature 1973; University of British Columbia, Vancouver, M.F.A. 1975. **Military Service:** U.S.

Army, in California, Israel, and Panama Canal Zone, 1967–69. **Family:** Married Miki Cannon Sheffield in 1974 (divorced 1981); one daughter. **Career:** Journalist in Beirut, Lebanon, 1965–66, and Boston, 1970–71; visiting lecturer in creative writing, 1975–77, and lecturer in English, 1979–80, University of British Columbia; lecturer in typographical history, Simon Fraser University, Burnaby, British Columbia, 1983–84; poet-in-residence, Banff Centre School of Fine Arts, Alberta, 1983, Ojibway and Cree Cultural Centre, Atikokan and Espanola, Ontario, 1985, and Sudbury, Ontario, 1986, and University of Winnipeg, Manitoba, 1986; writer-in-residence and Canada/Scotland Exchange Fellow, University of Edinburgh, 1989–90; Ashley fellow, Trent University, Peterborough, Ontario, 1994; writer-in-residence, University of Western Ontario, 1998–99. Since 1998 conjunct professor, Frost Centre for Native Studies and Canadian Studies, Trent University. General editor, Kanchenjunga Poetry Series, 1973–79; guest editor, *Contemporary Literature in Translation,* Vancouver, 1974, 1976; contributing editor, *Fine Print,* San Francisco, 1985–90. **Awards:** Macmillan prize, 1975; Canada Council arts grant, 1975–76, 1980–81, 1984–85, and 1993–94; Ontario Arts Council grant, 1982; CBC prize, 1985; Guggenheim fellowship, 1987–88; Canada Council Senior Arts grant, 1993–94; Charles Watts award, 1999. **Address:** Box 357, 1917 West Fourth Avenue, Vancouver, British Columbia V6J 1M7, Canada.

PUBLICATIONS

Poetry

The Shipwright's Log. Bloomington, Indiana, Kanchenjunga Press, 1972.
Cadastre. Bloomington, Indiana, Kanchenjunga Press, 1973.
Deuteronomy. Delta, British Columbia, Sono Nis Press, 1974.
Pythagoras. Vancouver, Kanchenjunga Press, 1974.
Eight Objects. Vancouver, Kanchenjunga Press, 1975.
Bergschrund. Delta, British Columbia, Sono Nis Press, 1975.
Jacob Singing. Vancouver, Kanchenjunga Press, 1977.
Death by Water. Vancouver, University of British Columbia Library, 1977.
The Stonecutter's Horses. Vancouver, Standard Editions, 1979.
The Knife in the Measure. Steelhead, British Columbia, Barbarian Press, 1980.
Song of the Summit. Toronto, Dreadnaught Press, 1982.
The Salute by Tasting. Vancouver, Slug Press, 1982.
Tzuhalem's Mountain. Lantzville, British Columbia, Oolichan Press, 1982.
The Beauty of the Weapons: Selected Poems 1972–82. Toronto, McClelland and Stewart, 1982; Port Townsend, Washington, Copper Canyon Press, 1985.
Sahara. Lexington, Kentucky, King Library Press, 1984.
An Augury. Ithaca, New York, Cornell University, 1984.
Rubus Ursinus: A Prayer for the Blackberry Harvest. Mission, British Columbia, Barbarian Press, 1985.
Tending the Fire. Vancouver, Alcuin Society, 1985.
The Blue Roofs of Japan: A Score for Interpenetrating Voices. Mission, British Columbia, Barbarian Press, 1986.
Pieces of Map, Pieces of Music. Toronto, McClelland and Stewart, 1986; Port Townsend, Washington, Copper Canyon Press, 1987.
Conversations with a Toad. Shawinigan, Quebec, Lucie Lambert, 1987.

The Calling: Selected Poems 1970–1995. Toronto, McClelland and Stewart, 1995.
Elements. New York, Kuboaa Press, 1995.

Plays

Jacob Singing (produced Victoria, British Columbia, 1984).
The Blue Roofs of Japan (produced 1986).

Screenplay: *The Spirit of Haida Gwaii,* 1992.

Performance Works:

The Blue Roofs of Japan: A Score for Interpenetrating Voices (produced Missoula, Montana, 1985; radio version produced 1986).
Uddālaka Āruni: A Song for the Weavers (produced Lecce, Apulia, 1990).
New World Suite No. 3 (produced Vancouver, British Columbia, 1990)

Other

The Raven Steals the Light, with Bill Reid. Vancouver, Douglas and McIntyre, and Seattle, University of Washington Press, 1984.
Ocean/Paper/Stone. Vancouver, William Hoffer, 1984.
Shovels, Shoes and the Slow Rotation of Letters: A Feuilleton in Honour of John Dreyfus. Vancouver, Alcuin Society, 1985.
Part of the Land, Part of the Water: A History of the Yukon Indians, with Catherine McClellan and others. Vancouver, Douglas and McIntyre, 1987.
The Black Canoe, photographs by Ulli Steltzer. Vancouver, Douglas and McIntyre, and Seattle, University of Washington Press, 1991.
The Elements of Typographic Style. Vancouver/Port Roberts, Washington, Hartley & Marks, 1992.
Boats Is Saintlier than Captains: Thirteen Ways of Looking at Morality, Language and Design. New York, Edition Rhino, 1997.
Native American Oral Literatures and the Unity of the Humanities: The 1998 Garnett Sedgewick Memorial Lecture. Vancouver, University of British Columbia, 1998.
A Story as Sharp as a Knife: The Classical Haida Mythtellers and Their World. Vancouver and Toronto, Douglas and McIntyre, 1999.
A Short History of the Printed World, with Warren Chappell. Point Roberts, Washington, and Vancouver, Hartley and Marks, 1999.

Editor, with others, *Visions: Contemporary Art in Canada.* Vancouver, Douglas and McIntyre, 1983.

*

Manuscript Collections: National Library, Ottawa; University of British Columbia Library, Vancouver.

Critical Studies: ''The Holes in the Stone'' by William Meads, in *Kayak* (Santa Cruz, California), 44, February 1977; ''Bringhurst's Range: Essential Information'' by Jane Munro, in *CV-II* (Winnipeg), 5(2), winter 1980–81; ''By Persons Unknown'' by Robert Fulford, in

Saturday Night (Toronto), March 1984; ''Recent Canadian Poetry'' by Robin Skelton, in *Poetry* (Chicago), 144(5), 1984; ''Robert Bringhurst'' by Gary Geddes, in his *Fifteen Canadian Poets Times Two,* Toronto, Oxford University Press, 1988; ''Readings of Nothing: Robert Bringhurst's *Hachadura*'' by John Whatley, in *Canadian Literature* (Vancouver), 122/123, 1989; ''Poor Man's Art: On the Poetry of Robert Bringhurst'' by Peter Sanger, in *Antigonish Review* (Antigonish, Nova Scotia), 85/86, 1991; ''The Stonecutter's Horses'' by Francesco M. Casotti, in *La Cultura Italiana e le Letterature Straniere Moderne,* edited by Vita Fortunati, Ravenna, Longo, 1992; *Wisdom of the Mythtellers*, Peterborough, Ontario, Broadview Press, 1994, and ''Polyphonic Myth: A Reply to Robert Bringhurst,'' in *Canadian Literature,* 156, 1998, both by Sean Kane; ''Bringhurst's Presocratics: Lyric and Ecology,''in *Poetry and Knowing,* edited by Tim Lilburn, Kingston, Ontario, Quarry Press, 1995, and ''Being, Polyphony, Lyric: An Open Letter to Robert Bringhurst,'' in *Canadian Literature*, 156, 1998, both by Jan Zwicky.

*   *   *

The poems of Robert Bringhurst seem almost to contradict the statement of method and intentions he makes in a prefatory note to *The Beauty of the Weapons,* a collection that gathers much of his work published by small presses: ''Most of the poems are products more of oral composition than of writing, and have survived into this selection only with repeated performance as a test . . . they exist in the voice, to which the page, though we enshrine it, is in the right order of things a subservient medium.'' Yet in their formal beauty, resembling that of runes and hieroglyphics, Bringhurst's poems almost seem expressly designed for the page and deserving of thick paper and elegant typography. For all his allegiance to air, breath, and music (one of the book's valuable notes says that the poem ''Hachadura'' is intended ''as music, not as cartography. For listening; not, like a map or a roadsign, for reading''), Bringhurst adores indelible materials. Even air becomes substantial (''the chipped air'' and ''black blades of the wind'' in ''Three Deaths''), and he observes ''the stricture/of uncut, utterly / uncluttered light'' (''Poem about Crystal''). Erudite and hard-edged, Bringhurst is a philosophical materialist, and in a note for the section ''The Old in Their Knowing'' praises the pre-Socratics, who ''knew no distinction between physicist, philosopher, biologist and poet.''

For Bringhurst mind becomes visible, as in ''Pherekydes'':

There remains of the mind of Pherekydes
the esker and the glacial milk,
the high spring runoff in the gorge,

and the waterfalls hammered out of cloud
against the mid cliff,
vanishing in the hungry Himalayan air

Although the poet may sometimes be guilty of imagistic overreaching (''quiet as butterflies' bones'' in ''Four Glyphs''), he composes work of carved shapeliness, as in ''A Quadratic Equation'':

Voice: the breath's tooth.
Thought: the brain's bone.
Birdsong: an extension

of the beak of speech:
the antler of the mind.

Using a variety of voices (Francesco Petrarca, an old Coast Salish Indian) and locales (the Old Testament wilderness, El Salvador), Bringhurst consistently meditates on the fundamental, primary, elemental, whether it be the Pentateuch or Aztec mythology or love itself, as in ''Hic Amor, Haec Patria'':

All knowledge is carnal.
Knowledge is meat,
knowledge is muscle.
Old woman, old woman,
what is this hunger
grown hard as a bone?

Bringhurst has always been concerned with the elements of communication, as witnessed by his interest in fine printing and typography. As a poet Bringhurst might be termed, in Gaston Bachelard's system, one whose primary element is earth. His own allegiance remains to the voice. For him, as he says in the foreword to *The Calling,* ''Writing, if it lives, is rooted in speaking, and speaking, if it lives, is rooted in listening for the speech, the calling, of being.'' To that end Bringhurst has increasingly attempted to make ''poems like polyphonic music,'' including in this collection the separately published *The Blue Roofs of Japan* and ''New World Suite No.3,'' for two and three voices, respectively. Though marked by the same strengths as his other poems, these ''layered'' pieces do not make the same impact on the page and tend to project a certain lecturing tone, which on occasion also slightly mars some of his earlier work. In any case, *The Calling* confirms the fact that Bringhurst is a poet of substance.

—Fraser Sutherland

BROCK-BROIDO, Lucie

Nationality: American. **Born:** Pittsburgh, Pennsylvania, 22 May 1956. **Education:** Johns Hopkins University, 1976–79, B.A. The Writing Seminars 1978; M.A. The Writing Seminars 1979; Columbia University, 1979–82, M.F.A. 1982. **Career:** Briggs-Copeland Assistant Professor in Poetry, 1988–93, and director, creative writing program, 1992–93, Harvard University, Cambridge, Massachusetts; associate professor in poetry, Bennington Writing Seminars, 1993–95; visiting professor of poetry, Princeton University, Princeton, New Jersey, 1995. Since 1993 associate professor and director of poetry, Columbia University, New York. **Awards:** Grolier poetry prize, Blacksmith Series, Cambridge, 1983; poetry fellowship, Fine Arts Work Center, Provincetown, 1983; Hoyns fellowship in poetry, University of Virginia, 1984; National Endowment for the Arts poetry fellowship, 1985, 1998; *New Letters* Literary award, 1987; *New England Review* Narrative Poetry award, 1987; Massachusetts Artist fellowship in poetry, 1988, 1996; Harvard-Danforth award for distinction in teaching, 1989, 1990; *American Poetry Review* Jerome Shestack prize for poetry, 1991; Harvard University Phi Beta Kappa Teaching award, 1991; Witter Bynner poetry prize, 1996; John Simon

Guggenheim fellowship in poetry, 1996. **Address:** c/o Dodge Hall, Writing Division, School of the Arts, Columbia University, New York, New York 10027.

PUBLICATIONS

Poetry

A Hunger. New York, Knopf, 1988.
The Master Letters. New York, Knopf, 1995.

*   *   *

A Hunger, Lucie Brock-Broido's first book of poems, was published in 1988 by the major trade house Knopf. One of the more notable debuts of the period, the book had three reprintings between its initial appearance and the autumn of 1994. This is extraordinary given the proliferation of poetry volumes, the generally acknowledged (though much debated) shrinking audience for poetry, and the usual conduct of major trade houses toward poetry (publish a very small number of volumes, then remainder or pulp all but one or two high-octane sellers after twelve months). The commercial performance of Brock-Broido's first book is all the more astonishing when one considers that the poetry clearly evolves from the difficult model of Wallace Stevens. Intense, brooding, and complex, Brock-Broido's poems incessantly probe the terms and terrain of love, depression, friendship, popular culture, and art itself. Such qualities can be seen in these lines from ''Domestic Mysticism'':

When I come home, the dwarves will be long
In their shadows & promiscuous. The alley cats will sneak
Inside, curl about the legs of furniture, close the skins
Inside their eyelids, sleep. Orchids will be intercrossed
    and sturdy.
The sun will go down as I sit, thin armed, small breasted
In my cotton dress, poked with eyelet stitches, a little lace,
In the queer light left when a room snuffs out.

The speaker in this poetry, casting an almost too highly developed eye on detail, brings a merciless honesty to the task of painful witnessing. That the orchids will be ''intercrossed and sturdy'' is an unusual observation, and so is the speaker's attention to the cats' inner eyelids as they sleep. But most accomplished, and perhaps most revealing, is the narrator's description of herself as a small, vulnerable doll both threatened by and part of ''the queer light left when a room snuffs out.'' Although aware of the consequences, the narrator will not avert her glance from the brightness of the sun. Rather, she stares, driven by a belief that the revealing calm resides always at the heart of chaos. She stares, but she does so with full awareness of the inherent danger. Thus, she shares a more than passing sympathy with the intriguing poet Thomas James, who published one volume of verse in 1972 before committing suicide. Brock-Broido acknowledges the bond by quoting one of James's most revealing lines—''I am afraid of what the world will do''—in her poem ''The Beginning of the Beginning.''

Brock-Broido is afraid perhaps, but her vulnerability is not the kind that herds its host into silence and passivity. Her weapon, the tool that separates the chaff from the kernel of truth, is poetry, a language that, though introspective, may lead to accessibility, understanding,

and kinship with a larger audience. If we compare Brock-Broido's poems to those of her contemporary Jorie Graham (whose notes, wordplay, and obfuscation finally make us wonder what if anything such poems have to say), we find in the former a much more productive and meaningful use of the Stevens legacy. Like Sylvia Plath before her, Brock-Broido confronts urgent issues and does so in inventive ways that help her readers confront—and survive—them, too.

—Robert McDowell

BROMIGE, David (Mansfield)

Nationality: Canadian. **Born:** London, England, 22 October 1933. **Education:** University of British Columbia, B.A. (honors) 1962; University of California, Berkeley, M.A. 1964. **Family:** Married 1) Ann Livingston in 1957 (divorced 1961); 2) Joan Peacock in 1961 (divorced 1970), one son; 3) Sherril Jaffe in 1970. **Career:** Worked as a cowman on dairy farms in England, Sweden, and Canada, 1950–53; attendant in mental hospitals in Canada, 1954–55; elementary school teacher in England, 1957–58, and in Vancouver, British Columbia, 1959–62; instructor in English, University of British Columbia, Vancouver, Summer 1964; teaching assistant, 1965–69, extension lecturer, 1969, and instructor in English, 1969–70, University of California, Berkeley; lecturer, California College of Arts and Crafts, Oakland, 1970. Since 1974 assistant professor of English, then associate professor, professor, and professor emeritus, Sonoma State University (California State College), Sonoma. **Awards:** Canadian Broadcasting Corporation Playwriting award, 1961, for ''The Cobalt Poet''; KVOS-TV Playwriting prize, 1962, for ''Save What You Can''; Woodrow Wilson Scholar, 1962–63; Poet Laureate Competition prize, 1964; Canada Council grant, 1965, 1966, and bursary, 1971; James Phelan Scholar in Literature, 1966–67; National Endowment for the Arts prize, 1969. **Address:** 461 High Street, Sebastopol, California 95472, U.S.A.

PUBLICATIONS

Poetry

The Gathering. Buffalo, New York, Sumbooks Press, 1965.
The Ends of the Earth. Los Angeles, Black Sparrow Press, 1968.
Please, Like Me. Los Angeles, Black Sparrow Press, 1968.
The Quivering Roadway. Berkeley, Archangel Press, 1969.
In His Image. N.p., Twybyl Press, 1970.
Threads. Los Angeles, Black Sparrow Press, 1970.
The Fact So of Itself, with others. Los Angeles, Black Sparrow Press, 1970.
They Are Eyes. N.p., Panjandrum Books, 1972.
Birds of the West. Toronto, Coach House Press, 1973.
Ten Years in the Making: Selected Poems, Songs, and Stories, 1961–70. Vancouver, Vancouver Community Press, 1973.
Spells and Blessings. Vancouver, Talonbooks, 1974.
Credences of Winter. Los Angeles, Black Sparrow Press, 1976.
My Poetry. Great Barrington, Massachusetts, The Figures, 1980.
Peace. Berkeley, Tuumba Press, 1981.
Red Hats. Atwater, Ohio, Tonsure Press, 1986.
Desire: Selected Poems, 1963–1987. Santa Rosa, California, Black Sparrow Press, 1988.

Tiny Currents in a World without Scales. London, Ontario, Brick Books, 1991.

A Cast of Tens. Penngrove, California, Avec Books, 1993.

Romantic Traceries. Elmwood, Connecticut, Poets and Poets Press, 1993.

The Harbormaster of Hong Kong. Los Angeles, Sun and Moon Books, 1993.

The Mad Career. Seattle, Grey Spider Press, 1994.

From the First Century (of Vulnerable Bundles). Elmwood, Connecticut, Poets and Poets Press, 1995.

T As in Tether. Tucson, Arizona, Chax Press, 1999.

Short Stories

Three Stories. Los Angeles, Black Sparrow Press, 1973.

Other

Out of My Hands. Los Angeles, Black Sparrow Press, 1974.

Tight Corners and What's around Them. Los Angeles, Black Sparrow Press, 1974.

Men, Women, and Vehicles: Prose Works. Santa Rosa, Black Sparrow Press, 1990.

*

Critical Studies: David Bromige, Ken Irby issue of *Vort* (Silver Spring, Maryland) 1(3), 1973; "The Poet as Language: David Bromige's Tight Corners and What's around Them" by Michael Davidson, in *Credences: A Journal of Twentieth-Century Poetry and Poetics* (Buffalo, New York), 1(2), February 1975.

*   *   *

Born in London, David Bromige worked his way across the Atlantic, first to Canada and then south to the United States. In 1965 he began graduate studies at the University of California at Berkeley, where he received a master's degree. He continued studies there until 1970, but as early as 1965 he had published his first book of poems, *The Gathering.* Three years later his book *Please, Like Me* appeared from one of the principal alternative U.S. presses, Black Sparrow.

Bromige's case is interesting in twentieth-century American letters, which has welcomed other writers from Britain into its higher circles. W.H. Auden, Mina Loy, Christopher Isherwood, the Scottish balladeer Helen Adam, and later Denise Levertov and John Ash have been among them. The lure includes America's experimental energies and its myriad journals devoted to the different edges of the avant-garde. The source of much post-World War II experiment was the figure of Charles Olson, who attracted Levertov and Bromige to venture westward.

Bromige arrived in California during the high noon of postmodern poetry. His models were Olson's open-ended, free-form lyrics and the poetic known variously as Black Mountain poetry or projective verse. Robert Creeley and Robert Duncan were the principal voices of Olson's new poetic, and all three styles are present in Bromige's chatty, quick-changing lyric style. San Francisco was the literary hub of West Coast writing, scene of the San Francisco renaissance and the beat phenomenon. Bromige appropriated the reigning doctrines and applied them with skill from early on.

The anatomy of a Bromige poem goes something like this: a voice fed-up with solitude finds an excuse to relate to someone else, usually a woman, and the result is either a brief sexual encounter or a querulous friendship. It is told to us in language that breaks into interjections, interrupted pathways, commentaries on the self and situation, a joke or two, brief flashes of lyrical music, and a mostly humdrum conversational patter. The poems are not exciting for their finish or intellectual daring; they are not well-made or rigorously composed. Rather, one is given a mind at work, the processes by which a self engages the world to escape from solipsism and fantasy.

A more subtle process is also at work, one that links Bromige to the projective mode. The crabbed syntax, the processual pace of his language, the surface detail, and the steady pace of ideas and perceptions flowing out of mundane subjects are all strategies for breaking down the boundary between the poem and life. This is shown, for example, in "A Call," from *The Ends of the Earth:*

There is built a block in this city
which, when you get to it
very late into the night

first sight tells you every light is out
but can't stop making it
grow bigger, till

a door, you knock on, & nobody comes.
You thought you stood in the street, certainly
your legs were tired & cold, you thought

you lay asleep, up there, the warm
room the knock couldn't reach, your lips
relaxt, yet still

Bromige's early American books are lessons in acquiring the casual, irreverent tonalities of postwar poetry. Duncan's hand is on the poems in which Bromige studies his imagination at work making images and commenting on their accumulating meanings. But the real force at work in shaping Bromige's vision is Creeley. Compared to Bromige, no other poet has quite mastered the intricacy and modesty of Creeley's lyric, as in the brief poem "Some Day Soon, Not Now":

Fierce for one another
that this be for ever
this one time
once more they kiss

only to roll apart
when she alone
drest as for a journey
walks in

to bid goodbye
to nobody at all, bare
bed, a ceiling
& some walls.

English poetry is also about solitude and its furies, resentments, and narcissism, but English poets who find their voice in the United States seem to be looking for the way beyond solitude in some sort of relation to others. The American avant-garde has been formulating such relations from early in the twentieth century, telling us that a world of events includes the human observer and that mind is not isolated from the world but part of its intensity and dynamics. Bromige's lyric is at once self-effacing in its reduction of surface artifice and self-reconstructing in forming its attention to events outside the self. The poetry is a dialogue with objects and landscapes and with others.

The result is a poetry that lessens our sense of self as something interior and subjective and that gives us an awareness made from encounters with the "not-I." The Bromigean self is more like the nerves that are aroused by contact with surroundings; lyric language arises from points of contact from the field, and the poem flows outward to articulate the experience. In another book, *Threads,* the poems achieve richer encounters with the field, and the syntax and diction are all given over to mapping the process of perception as it happens.

—Paul Christensen

BROOKS, Gwendolyn

Nationality: American. **Born:** Topeka, Kansas, 7 June 1917. **Education:** Attended Hyde Park High School, Wendell Phillips High School, and Englewood High School, all Chicago, until 1934; Wilson Junior College, Chicago, graduated 1936. **Family:** Married Henry L. Blakely in 1938; one son and one daughter. **Career:** Publicity director, NAACP Youth Council, Chicago, 1930s. Teacher, Northeastern Illinois State College, Chicago, Columbia College, Chicago, and Elmhurst College, Illinois; Rennebohm Professor of English, University of Wisconsin, Madison; Distinguished Professor of the arts, City College, City University of New York, 1971. Editor, *Black Position* magazine. Consultant in Poetry, Library of Congress, Washington, D.C., 1985–86. **Awards:** Guggenheim fellowship, 1946; American Academy grant, 1946; Pulitzer prize, 1950; Thormod Monsen award, 1964; Ferguson memorial award, 1964; Anisfield-Wolf award, 1968; Black Academy award, 1971; Shelley memorial award, 1976; Frost Medal, 1988; New York Public Library award, 1988; National Endowment for the Arts award, 1989; Society for Literature award, University of Thessaloniki, Athens, Greece, 1990; Aiken-Taylor award, 1992; National Book Foundation medal for lifetime achievement, 1994; National medal of arts, 1995. Has received more than 50 honorary degrees from American universities. Poet Laureate of Illinois, 1968. **Member:** National Institute of Arts and Letters; American Academy of Arts and Letters. **Address:** c/o The Contemporary Forum, 2529A Jerome Street, Chicago, Illinois 60645–1507, U.S.A.

PUBLICATIONS

Poetry

A Street in Bronzeville. New York, Harper, 1945.
Annie Allen. New York, Harper, 1949.
Bronzeville Boys and Girls (for children). New York, Harper, 1956; New York, HarperCollins, 1994.

The Bean Eaters. New York, Harper, 1960.
Selected Poems. New York, Harper, 1963; New York, HarperPerennial, 1994.
We Real Cool. Detroit, Broadside Press, 1966.
The Wall. Detroit, Broadside Press, 1967.
In the Mecca. New York, Harper, 1968.
Riot. Detroit, Broadside Press, 1969.
Family Pictures. Detroit, Broadside Press, 1970.
Black Steel: Joe Frazier and Muhammad Ali. Detroit, Broadside Press, 1971.
Aloneness. Detroit, Broadside Press, 1971.
Aurora. Detroit, Broadside Press, 1972.
Beckonings. Detroit, Broadside Press, 1975.
To Disembark. Chicago, Third World Press, 1981.
Black Love. Chicago, Brooks Press, 1982.
Mayor Harold Washington; and Chicago, the I Will City. Chicago, Brooks Press, 1983.
The Near-Johannesburg Boy and Other Poems. Chicago, David Company, 1986.
Blacks. Chicago, Third World Press, 1987.
Winnie. Chicago, Third World Press, 1988.
Gottschalk and the Grande Tarantelle. Chicago, David Company, 1988.
Children Coming Home. Chicago, David Co., 1991.
Selected Poems. New York, HarperCollins, and London, Hi Marketing, 1999.

Recordings: *The 1987 Consultants' Reunion: Two Evenings of Readings Celebrating the 50th Anniversary of the Consultantship in Poetry,* Gertrude Clarke Whittall Poetry and Literature Fund, 1987; *Poets in Person,* Modern Poetry Association, 1991.

Novel

Maud Martha. New York, Harper, 1953.

Other

A Portion of That Field, with others. Urbana, University of Illinois Press, 1967.
The World of Gwendolyn Brooks (miscellany). New York, Harper, 1971.
Report from Part One: An Autobiography. Detroit, Broadside Press, 1972.
The Tiger Who Wore White Gloves; or, What You Are You Are (for children). Chicago, Third World Press, 1974.
A Capsule Course in Black Poetry Writing, with Don L. Lee, Keorapetse Kgositsile, and Dudley Randall. Detroit, Broadside Press, 1975.
Primer for Blacks. N.p., Black Position Press, 1980.
Young Poets' Primer. Chicago, Brooks Press, 1981.
Very Young Poets. Chicago, Brooks Press, 1983.
Report from Part Two. Chicago, Third World Press, 1996.

Editor, *A Broadside Treasury.* Detroit, Broadside Press, 1971.
Editor, *Jump Bad: A New Chicago Anthology.* Detroit, Broadside Press, 1971.

*

Bibliography: *Langston Hughes and Gwendolyn Brooks: A Reference Guide* by R. Baxter Miller, Boston, Hall, and London, Prior, 1978.

Critical Studies: *Gwendolyn Brooks* by Harry B. Shaw, Boston, Twayne, 1980; *Gwendolyn Brooks; Poetry and the Heroic Voice* by D.H. Melhem, Louisville, University Press of Kentucky, 1987; *A Life Distilled: Gwendolyn Brooks, Her Poetry and Fiction* edited by Maria K. Mootry and Gary Smith, Urbana, University of Illinois Press, 1987; *A Life of Gwendolyn Brooks* by George E. Kent, Louisville, University Press of Kentucky, 1990; *Gwendolyn Brooks,* Mankato, Minnesota, Creative Education, 1993; ''Re-Wrighting Native: Gwendolyn Brooks's Domestic Aesthetic in Maud Martha'' by Malin LaVon Walther, in *Tulsa Studies in Women's Literature* (Tulsa, Oklahoma), 13(1), Spring 1994; *Urban Rage in Bronzeville: Social Commentary in the Poetry of Gwendolyn Brooks, 1945–1960* (dissertation) by Barbara Bolden, University of Illinois, Urbana, 1994; *The Poetics of Enclosure: Emily Dickinson, Marianne Moore, H.D., and Gwendolyn Brooks* (dissertation) by Lesley Wheeler, Princeton University, New Jersey, 1994; *'Not Quite a Lady': Mina Loy, Edna St. Vincent Millay, H.D., Gwendolyn Brooks, and the Poetics of Impersonation* (dissertation) by Susan Nadine Gilmore, Cornell University, Ithaca, New York, 1995; ''Whose Canon? Gwendolyn Brooks: Founder at the Center of the 'Margins''' by Kathryne V. Lindberg, in *Gendered Modernisms: American Women Poets and Their Readers,* edited by Margaret Dickle and Thomas Travisano, Philadelphia, University of Pennsylvania Press, 1996; ''Gwendolyn Brooks at Eighty: A Retrospective'' by Philip Greasley, in *Midamerica* (East Lansing, Michigan), 23, 1996; *On Gwendolyn Brooks: Reliant Contemplation* edited by Stephen Caldwell Wright, Ann Arbor, University of Michigan Press, 1996; ''Native Daughters in the Promised Land: Gender, Race, and the Question of Separate Spheres'' by You-me Park and Gayle Wald, in *American Literature* (Durham, North Carolina), 70(3), September 1998; *The Real Negro: The Question of Authenticity in Twentieth Century African-American Literature* (dissertation) by Shelly Jennifer Eversley, Johns Hopkins University, Baltimore, Maryland, 1998.

*   *   *

In what has since become a well-known episode, Gwendolyn Brooks describes an auspicious turning point in her career, a turning point that came in 1967 when she attended the Second Black Writers' Conference at Fisk University in Nashville. The Pulitzer prizewinning poet was stunned and intrigued by the energy and electricity generated by LeRoi Jones (Amiri Baraka) and Ron Milner, among others, on that predominantly black campus. The excitement was at once surprising, stirring, and contagious, and Brooks admits that from that moment she entered a ''new consciousness.'' She had discovered a new audience: young people full of a fresh spirit and ready, as she characterized them, to take on the challenges. The sturdy ideas that she earlier held were no longer valid in this ''new world,'' and several years later she would untendentiously remark, ''I am trying to weave the coat that I shall wear.''

The older coat that Brooks doffed is made of the material for which she is best known, such vignettes of ghetto people in Chicago as presented in ''The Anniad,'' ''The Sundays of Satin-Legs Smith,'' ''The Bean Eaters,'' or ''We Real Cool.'' They are works of a poet who brings a patrician mind to a plebeian language, a poet always searching for the stirring, unusual coloration of words, the poet in whom Addison Gayle, Jr., has noted what he calls ''a tendency toward obscurity and abstraction'' and ''a child-like fascination for words.'' But like Emily Dickinson, Brooks searched for fresh sounds and imagery produced by word clusters that startle rather than obscure:

> Let it be stairways, and a splintery box
> Where you have thrown me, scraped me with your kiss,
> Have honed me, have released me after this
> Cavern Kindness, smiled away our shocks.

Most of Brooks's poems written before 1967—before the Fisk conference—are her ''front yard songs,'' poems that reflect the self-consciousness of a poet whose audience seeks lessons in a lyric that ostensibly transcends race. They are solid, highly imaginative poems, and if they suggest comparisons with Wallace Stevens, as several critics have noted, they also recall Emily Dickinson's ingenuity with language, including her ironic ambiguities:

> A light and diplomatic bird
> Is lenient in my window tree.
> A quick dilemma of the leaves
> Discloses twist and tact to me.

The poems recall as well the ''grotesques'' who habituate the fictional world of Sherwood Anderson's *Winesburg, Ohio:*

> True, there is silver under
> The veils of the darkness,
> But few care to dig in the night
> For the possible treasure of stars.

But above all there is the unmistakable rhythmic shifting—''My hand is stuffed with mode, design, device. / But I lack access to my proper stone''—and the haunting incongruity—''Believe that even in my deliberateness I was not deliberate.''

The startling Fisk conference may be viewed metaphorically as Brooks's peek at ''the back yard'' (''Where it's rough and untended and hungry weed grows''), the escape, as George Kent says, from the highly ordered and somewhat devitalized life of her ''front yard training.'' The backyard offers a new vitality, a new consciousness. Brooks, around fifty years old at the time of the conference, strikes up a dialogue in free verse with the subjects of her earlier poetry. The distances narrow, and the angles flatten: ''we are each other's / harvest: / we are each other's business: / we are each other's magnitude and bond.''

The angles of vision have changed to suit what Brooks describes as ''my newish voice'': ''[It] will not be an imitation of the contemporary young black voice, which I so admire, but an extending adaptation of today's G.B. voice.'' So there is something of a near elegiac tone in Brooks's ''transcendence'' of her poetic past, but it is elegy without regrets, for she has moved from a place of ''knowledgeable unknowing'' to a place of ''know-now'' preachments:

> I tell you
> I love You
> and I trust You.
> Take my Faith.
> Make of my Faith an engine.
> Make of my Faith
> a Black Star. I am Beckoning.

Still, as Barbara Christian reminds us, there are moments when we need to be admonished to recollect that the "poet has always been a synthesizer and a thermometer, whether she is aware of it or not." By this observation Christian means to suggest that Brooks—attentive poet as she is—intuitively synthesizes her tradition as she goes about taking the measure of the current time.

—Charles L. James

BROUMAS, Olga

Nationality: American. **Born:** Hermoupolis, Greece, 6 May 1949. Immigrated to the United States in 1967. **Education:** University of Pennsylvania, Philadelphia, B.A. 1970; University of Oregon, Eugene, M.F.A. 1973. **Family:** Married Stephen Edward Bangs in 1973 (divorced 1979). **Career:** Instructor in English and women's studies, University of Oregon, 1972–76; visiting associate professor, University of Idaho, Moscow, 1978; poet-in-residence, Goddard College, Plainfield, Vermont, 1979–81, and Women Writers Center, Cazenovia, New York, 1981–82; founder and associate faculty member, Freehand women writers and photographers community, Provincetown, Massachusetts, 1982–87; visiting associate professor, Boston University, 1988–90. Since 1990 Fanny Hurst poet-in-residence, and since 1992 director of creative writing, Brandeis University, Waltham, Massachusetts. Since 1983 licensed bodywork therapist, Provincetown. **Awards:** Yale Younger Poets award, 1977; National Endowment for the Arts grant, 1978; Guggenheim fellowship, 1981–82; Wytter Bynner Translation grant, 1991. **Address:** 162 Mill Pond Drive, Brewster, Massachusetts 02631, U.S.A.

PUBLICATIONS

Poetry

Restlessness (in Greek). Athens, Greece, Alvin Redman Hellas, 1967.
Caritas. Eugene, Oregon, Jackrabbit Press, 1976.
Beginning with O. New Haven, Connecticut, Yale University Press, 1977.
Soie Sauvage. Port Townsend, Washington, Copper Canyon Press, 1980.
Pastoral Jazz. Port Townsend, Washington, Copper Canyon Press, 1983.
Black Holes, Black Stockings, with Jane Miller. Middletown, Connecticut, Wesleyan University Press, 1985.
Perpetua. Port Townsend, Washington, Copper Canyon Press, 1989.
Sappho's Gymnasium, with T. Begley. Port Townsend, Washington, Copper Canyon Press, 1994.
Helen Groves, with T. Begley. Tucson, Arizona, Kore Press, 1994.
Unfolding the Tablecloth of God, with T. Begley. N.p., Red Hydra Press, 1995.
Ithaca, with T. Begley. N.p., Radiolarian Press, 1996.
Rave: Poems, 1975–1999. Port Townsend, Washington, Copper Canyon Press, 1999.

Recording: *If I Yes,* Watershed, 1980.

Other

Translator, *What I Love: Selected Translations of Odysseas Elytis.* Port Townsend, Washington, Copper Canyon Press, 1986.
Translator, *The Little Mariner.* Port Townsend, Washington, Copper Canyon Press, 1988.
Translator, with T. Begley, *Open Papers: Selected Essays,* by Elytis. Port Townsend, Washington, Copper Canyon Press, 1995.
Translator, *Eros, Eros, Eros: Poems, Selected and Last,* by Elytis. Port Townsend, Washington, Copper Canyon Press, 1997.

*

Critical Studies: By Kathleen Norris, in *American Book Review,* 12(4), September 1990; by Lolly Ockerstrom, in *Sojourner* (Cambridge, Massachusetts), 20(6), February 1995; "A New Psychic Geography: Journeying with Olga Broumas and T. Begley" by Deborah L. Repplier, in *Sojourner* (Cambridge, Massachusetts), 20(6), February 1995.

*   *   *

Olga Broumas's collection *Beginning with O* sets sail with "marine / eyes, marine / odors" behind the first letter of her given name. Flicking aside patriarchal constraint along with the patronymic, the book takes on as its subject the naming and shaping body, "a curviform alphabet . . . beginning with O, the O- / mega, horseshoe, the cave of sound." In the omen letter the Greek-born Broumas wills a concentration on beginnings and plots reference points for her voluntary exit from the Greek language and her arrival in English. Her *O* is an open mouth, as the alphabet of the body begins to assemble a language outside the customary configurations of gender, family, and nation.

In her first publications in English Broumas tested a variety of rubrics. The long sequence of poems "Twelve Aspects of God" retrofitted a pantheon of Greek goddesses within feminist and lesbian experience. In homage to Anne Sexton fresh, quirky, and memorable poems replayed fairy tales, reweaving contemporary and mythic events with a keen sense of the painful and radical adjustments of relations to mother, father, sister, and husband that such revision requires. Her Cinderella emerges as a woman

> strung on a windy clothesline a
> mile long. A woman co-opted by promises: the lure
> of a job, the ruse of a choice, a woman forced
> to bear witness, falsely
> against my kind, as each
> other sister was judged inadequate, bitchy, incompetent,
> jealous, too thin, too fat. I know what I know.

Other poems bear dedications to specific women. Everywhere Broumas situates herself within communities of women, the instruments of knowing born of women's pleasure, the earth itself richly female. The following is from "Dactyls":

> Up the long hill, the earth rut steamed in the strange sun.
> We, walking between its labia, loverlike, palm to palm.

Beginning with O invokes Broumas's seaside childhood self. In the birth metaphors that dominate much of her work she emerges from the Greek sea "clean caesarean":

Something immaculate, a chance

crucial junction: time, light, water
had occurred, you could feel your bones
glisten
translucent as spinal fins.

Within the body the bones melt into light burning out time. Again and again the body's transformations are the self's road to understanding, and when the self joins other in erotic conjunction, lovers derive their chief knowledge of the sacred. In *Perpetua* this belief becomes

The text
of sex, word for word and by heart

divined, enacted
in the antechamber of the soul so kindly
also provided me, is my guide and prayer.

Drawn to narrative in the 1980s, Broumas wrote terse, pungent stories in which couples turn into trios and quartets and then, split and scattered, reassemble into other couples, trios, and quartets. Families and conventional marriage then and now are largely seen as sources of misery. The speaker of "Landscape with Driver," from *Soie Sauvage,* has her tubes tied. In "For Every Heart," from *Perpetua,* the speaker says that "I like it when my friend has lovers, their happy moans, / unrestrained, fill the house with the glee of her prowess." Here and elsewhere awareness lights up the salty microrub of parts against and within parts, while Broumas also acknowledges as part of the lyric's subject a glancing penetration of both the metaphysics and the sociology of the erotic. Both early and late the political invades the personal possibility, and all of her books bear witness to the fierce agonies of modern Greek history.

Later poems continue the thematic preoccupations of the early work, even as Broumas varies her formal interests. In sensitive translations of the poems and essays of Odysseas Elytis she indicates the duality of her life in Greece and America, in a culturally stabilizing act reaching across gender and time to an older Greek poet. In *Black Holes, Black Stockings,* written in collaboration with the American poet Jane Miller, she affirms her sense of poetry as emanating from a community of working female artists. Both projects lead to different successes. In the earlier work many beautiful poems are simply autobiographical, but later there is a broader range of portraiture, often with a quietly savage observance of the current historical moment.

Early Broumas poems are occasionally rhythmically awkward and unconvincing, and in their phrasing some poems show their debt too baldly to Adrienne Rich's later declarative style. Broumas's poetry from *Pastoral Jazz* onward experiments more effectively with the timing and pacing of rhythmic units and works with a deliberately varied line length. Developing their own tightly coiled syntax, the later poems unroll their sentences down the page in serene flotillas unimpeded by internal punctuation. Broumas has become increasingly interested in close association with other poets, and the following is a sentence from the prose poetry of Broumas and Miller, its sinuous quick-change virtuosities typical of their work together:

But in the summer she fell back onto the bed where we came over and over to tangle ourselves without mercy, she in my plans for leaving the following autumn, and I in her long legs, white body of summer; and in winter—where having to be clandestine was more difficult—whiter, less floral, except at her lips which were always rose-fair, rose-large, cavernous like the couch she first sat on at the party where we met, in a parlor under the fair shade of her hair.

The aphoristic style of Elytis shows the way to other affinities, other angles of influence, as in this passage from Broumas's translation of *The Little Mariner:* "Few know the emotional superlative is formed of light, not force. That a caress is needed where a knife is laid. That a dormitory with the secret agreement of bodies follows us everywhere referring us to the holy without condescension." The same knowing hand, in a 1994 coauthorship with the classical scholar T. Begley, shapes the brief lyrics that comprise *Sappho's Gymnasium.* This nugget suggests the sharp turns and pleasures of the fusion:

Blueprint I have hearing over knife
prime workshop these forests verbed by breezes

Horizon helicoptera
Lesbian your cups

Hermaphrodite phototaxis

—Lorrie Goldensohn

BROWN, Wayne

Nationality: Trinidadian. **Born:** Trinidad, 18 July 1944. **Education:** University of the West Indies, B.A. (honors) 1968. **Family:** Married Megan Hopkyn-Rees in 1968. **Career:** Staff writer, *Trinidad Guardian,* 1964–65; teacher in Jamaica, 1969; art critic, *Trinidad Guardian,* 1970–71; teacher in Trinidad, 1970–71. Since 1971 writer. **Awards:** Jamaican Independence Festival Poetry prize, 1968; Commonwealth Poetry prize, 1972, for *On the Coast.*

PUBLICATIONS

Poetry

On the Coast. London, Deutsch, 1972.
Voyages. Port of Spain, Trinidad, Inprint Caribbean, 1989.

Other

The Child of the Sea: Stories and Remembrances. Port of Spain, Trinidad, Inprint Caribbean, 1989.

*   *   *

While the Trinidadian poet Wayne Brown was still in his twenties, *On the Coast,* his first collection, appeared with the endorsement of a prestigious publisher and won the Commonwealth prize. The collection is indeed an impressive first book, sophisticated in technique and sensibility. Brown has an islander's discriminating eye for the sea and its weathers, both symbolic and real, and his work is shaped by a distinctively West Indian tradition. Several pieces are dedicated to the leading Jamaican poets of his generation—Anthony McNeill, Mervyn Morris, Dennis Scott—whom he had met during his undergraduate days there, but *On the Coast* as a whole is dedicated to Derek Walcott, and critics have delighted in demonstrating the debt to Walcott in Brown's themes, situations, authorial pose, and even particular phrases. Yet it should probably be said that in this book he writes like Walcott, not like an imitator of Walcott. Brown has the sound of Walcott's voice in his ear, as if Walcott were a local poetic dialect he has mastered. "Crab," for example, exploits Walcott's Technicolor verbs ("a lizard hurls its tongue"), his characteristic similes, and his choppy rhythms ("waves, excitable as spinsters").

These are uniformly adept and cagey poems, and their scope extends beyond the shadow of the master. Walcott's example freed Brown to write a poetry grounded on landscape and meditation at a time when the vision of West Indian poetry was overwhelmingly urban and political. Yet Brown is not unpolitical. In his own depictions of the social landscape of the postcolonial Caribbean, his anger is controlled but not suppressed; in particular the poems on the passing of empire and the discontents of independence fairly crackle with irony. Consider the end of "The Tourists":

> Under that sun
> all is languor, and those who come
> will find nothing unusual, not
> one gesture or motion overdone
>
> But for one parrot fish which turns
> grave somersaults on the stainless steel
> spear that's just usurped its dim
> purpose; which was to swim
> as usual through blue air, in silence, like the sun.

The highly visible trajectory that Brown's first collection seemed to promise was not realized, however, and seventeen years passed before *Voyages* was published, by a small press in Trinidad. The first part of this second volume simply reprints *On the Coast* (dropping three poems and adding two), while the second part offers some two dozen new poems, roughly doubling the small corpus. (It is curious that several uncollected poems that had been published elsewhere are not included.)

As a group the new poems are more withdrawn and confessional, not as public or playful; there are no more of the natural history poems ("Mackerel," "Devilfish," "Vampire") that enliven *On the Coast*. Observed nature has been refined to rudimentary, almost archetypal, landscapes: sea, shore, and breaking wave; earth, moon, and stars. Within these vast spaces there is a sense of narrowed expectations. In such poems as "Rampanalgas," "Facing the Sea," and "Round Trip Back," Brown writes about home, but the emphasis is usually on departures from it and the sea's encroachments upon it. Brown now writes more about love and even about domesticity (so that his affinities with Scott and Morris become clearer), but there is a similar emphasis on estrangement and loss. Here is how "A Letter from Elizabeth" recalls a day at the beach:

> you wading in, all gooseflesh, squeals and wails,
> me, tight-lipped, following; then both of us
> pausing, as if sensing, even then,

> the far advance and rumble of these lines
> I write in desolation for you now.

In Brown's poetry the future has always been a realm of uncanny arrivals and spectral interventions ("The Approach," "The Witness," "Rilke," "Ramon's Dream"). Later poems tend to be retrospective, often nearly remorseful. "Prose" is representative in the way it looks back to a time "when love like life seemed boundless (till time halved it)," a time "of promise not yet unfulfilled." If the backward glance is increasingly one of loss and regret, the poet now looks ahead with something like relish to the final flight from earth ("Voyages," "The Briefing").

Brown's smallish output might lead us to regard him as a minor poet whose reputation must rest on one or two widely reprinted signature pieces. While he has such poems ("Noah" and "Red Hills"), the remarkable fact that more than half of the poems in *Voyages* have been anthologized attests to the consistently high quality of Brown's work.

—Laurence A. Breiner

BROWNE, Michael Dennis

Nationality: American. **Born:** Walton-on-Thames, Surrey, England, 28 May 1940; moved to the United States, 1965; naturalized citizen, 1978. **Education:** St. George's College, Weybridge, Surrey; Hull University 1958–62, B.A. (honors) in French and Swedish 1962; Oxford University, 1962–63, Cert. Ed. 1963; University of Iowa, Iowa City (Fulbright Scholar, 1965), 1965–67, M.A. in English 1967. **Family:** Married Lisa Furlong McLean in 1981; one son and two daughters. **Career:** Visiting lecturer in creative writing, University of Iowa, 1969–71. Visiting assistant professor, 1971–72, assistant professor of English, and since 1989 director of program in creative and professional writing, University of Minnesota, Minneapolis. Writer-in-the-schools, St. Paul Council in Arts and Sciences, Minnesota, 1971–86; visiting professor, Beijing Normal University, Fall 1980; visiting writer, University of South Florida, Tampa, 1987. **Awards:** Hallmark prize 1967; Minnesota State Arts Board fellowship, 1975; National Endowment for the Arts fellowship, 1977, 1978; Bush fellowship, 1981, grant, 1986; Loft-McKnight Writers' award, 1986; Jerome Foundation travel grant, 1988. **Address:** Department of English, University of Minnesota, Lind Hall, 207 Church Street S.E., Minneapolis, Minnesota 55455, U.S.A.

PUBLICATIONS

Poetry

The Wife of Winter. London, Rapp and Whiting, 1970; revised edition, New York, Scribner, 1970.
Fox. Duluth, Minnesota, Knife River Press, 1974.
Sun Exercises. Loretto, Minnesota, Red Studio Press, 1976.
The Sun Fetcher. Pittsburgh, Carnegie Mellon University Press, 1978.
Smoke from the Fires. Pittsburgh, Carnegie Mellon University Press, 1985.
You Won't Remember This: Poems. Pittsburgh, Carnegie Mellon University Press, 1992.

Selected Poems, 1965–1995. Pittsburgh, Carnegie Mellon University Press, 1997.

2 for 5: Two Authors-5 Years. Minneapolis, Minnesota, Frederick R. Weisman Art Museum, 1999.

Recording: *The Poetry of Michael Dennis Browne,* McGraw Hill, n.d.

Plays

How the Stars Were Made (cantata for children), music by David Lord (produced Farnham, Surrey, 1967). London, Chester, 1967.

The Wife of Winter (song cycle), music by David Lord (produced Aldeburgh, Suffolk, 1968). London, Universal, 1968.

The Sea Journey (cantata for children), music by David Lord (produced Farmham, Surrey, 1969). London, Universal, 1969.

Nonsongs, music by David Lord. London, Universal, 1973.

The Snow Queen, adaptation of the tale by Hans Christian Andersen (produced Minneapolis, 1976).

Carol of the Candle, music by Stephen Paulus. N.p., AMSI, 1977.

Carol of the Hill, music by Stephen Paulus. N.p., Hinshaw, 1977.

Mad Book, Shadow Book (song cycle), music by Stephen Paulus (produced Minneapolis, 1977).

Fountain of My Friends (songs for children), music by Stephen Paulus (produced Minneapolis, 1977).

Canticles: Songs and Rituals for Easter and the May, music by Stephen Paulus (produced Minneapolis, 1978).

North Shore (choral work), music by Stephen Paulus (produced St. Paul, Minnesota, 1978).

The Village Singer, music by Stephen Paulus, adaptation of a story by Mary Wilkins Freeman (produced St. Louis, 1979). Valley Forge, Pennsylvania, European-American Music, 1984.

All My Pretty Ones (song cycle), music by Stephen Paulus (produced St. Paul, Minnesota, 1984).

Artsongs (song cycle), music by Stephen Paulus. Valley Forge, Pennsylvania, European-American Music, 1986.

Sitting on the Porch (song cycle), music by Carolyn Jennings (produced Northfield, Minnesota, 1987).

Able-to-Fall (song cycle), music by John Foley (produced Omaha, Nebraska, 1988).

As a River of Light, music by John Foley. Phoenix, Arizona, Epoch Universal, 1989.

Other

Poetry and Hope. St. Joseph, Minnesota, College of Saint Benedict, 1992.

*

Critical Study: By Stephen C. Behrendt, in *Prairie Schooner* (Lincoln, Nebraska), 68(2), Summer 1994.

Michael Dennis Browne comments:

With *You Won't Remember This* I look back over a momentous period of my personal life—my marriage, the birth of my three children, the death of my mother, my fiftieth birthday—and in the life of the world at large, to which my poems are irrevocably committed. Public events that find voice in the poems include the recent repression in China (a country I visited in 1980), the discovery of the bones of Josef Mengele in Brazil, and the slaughter of Jesuit priests in El Salvador, together with happenings close to home such as a civil rights demonstration in Georgia and the issue of censorship.

This manuscript is a crucial document for me in terms of my artistic development. I am coming to a sense of things, of the dimensions and possibilities of experience, for which I am determined to find whole poems, poems that will be able to enter other lives and contribute their reality to them. It is very important to me that my works communicate to others and equally important that the poems reflect the confusions and contradictions of the original experiences. The struggle continues to be to find a focus for sometimes widely disparate elements that propose themselves to the imagination as capable of being (somehow!) combined.

The title poem, "You Won't Remember This," is an extended work in several sections that proceeds from specific childhood memories (my children's, my wife's, my own, intermingled) into speculations on what the dead might remember of earth and what, in the case of certain beloved ones, I would hope they remember. I am also trying to bring into the poem aspects of my own spiritual inquiry, which intensifies with the years.

*   *   *

Michael Dennis Browne is a poet of hard, surprising images. The clarity and suddenness of imagery make real the dreams that fill *The Wife of Winter.* The order of reality is successfully inverted, and the crazy world of the dream is the real, the normal, and not at all nightmarish.

Browne's voice affirms with a kind of joy, although there is a sardonic edge to the war poems and the Michael Morley sequence. He dreams and sings in the face of and despite some nameless, abstract things that underlie the world of the poems:

And you can forget the poems
that have run away from you in horror
like headless birds in the dark
you have not quite killed,

because in this house and place
there are good fresh ghosts,
there are small & near ones here.

The poems are not preoccupied with traditional themes and grand ideas ("The Terrible Christmas") but focus on the naming of things to create his world. He praises a woman because "when the king of ideas advanced through the wood / you fed him an image and he went away." Another woman, the speaker of the excellent title sequence, the "Wife of Winter," finds that waking and the morning are

Dark. A new dark. I am dropped
from the high claw of a dream. Fox

retrieves me, wolf waits.
Who is the owl with wings of snow?
And where is my eagle now?
He is not here, my lady they cry.

Browne leaps past prose with recurring, angry eagles, apples, fox, snow—images that may attain the symbolic in much the same way that Theodore Roethke, one of Browne's strongest influences, created symbols. Browne has learned much from Roethke, which is readily apparent in his rhythms and the songlike quality of many of his poems, even in an occasional image. But Browne's own voice remains clear.

In his work from the late 1970s and beyond, for example in *The Sun Fetcher*, the energy remains clear even while Browne develops other touchstones of his prosody. The narrative, which was submerged or only suggested in *The Wife of Winter*, is strong in such poems as "Fox" and "Uncle Frank." This change in voice diminishes the dream that was at the center of the earlier poems so that now it flickers like a moment's aberration or insight or like an occasional interruption of justifiable paranoia. While some of the images of Browne's poems in the 1970s seem momentary and too topical, the technical experimentation and development of his craft has advanced. A continuation of the Morley character in a sequence, for example, results in a giddy intensification of abrupt, dreamlike humor, which results in high anxiety. There is an ironic sense of celebration in "Paranoia," and the poet is at great pains to reach for vitality—and even, at times, peace—through his work:

> Happier, happier are we not
> both now?
> O painful, painful we people are,
> but once again dancing!

—Joseph Wilson

BROWNJOHN, Alan (Charles)

Nationality: British. **Born:** Catford, London, 28 July 1931. **Education:** Brownhill Road School, London; Brockley County School, London; Merton College, Oxford, 1950–53, B.A. 1953, M.A. 1961. **Family:** Married 1) the writer Shirley Toulson in 1960 (divorced 1969) one son; 2) Sandra Willingham in 1972. **Career:** Teacher, Beckenham and Penge Boys' Grammar School, 1957–65; Wandsworth Borough Councillor, London, 1962–65; Labour Party Parliamentary Candidate, Richmond, Surrey, 1964; senior lecturer in English, Battersea College of Education, later Polytechnic of the South Bank, now South Bank University, London, 1965–79; tutor in Poetry, Polytechnic of North London, 1981–83. Poetry critic, *New Statesman*, London, 1968–76, and *Sunday Times*, London, since 1989. Member, Arts Council Literature Panel, 1967–72; chair of the Greater London Arts Association Literature Panel, 1973–77; deputy chairman, 1979–82, chairman, 1982–88, and deputy president, 1988–91, Poetry Society. **Awards:** Cholmondeley award, 1979; Society of Authors travel scholarship, 1985; Authors' Club (London) award for the best first novel of 1990, for *The Way You Tell Them*. **Address:** 2 Belsize Park, London NW3 4ET, England.

PUBLICATIONS

Poetry

Travellers Alone. Liverpool, Heron Press, 1954.
The Railings. London, Digby Press, 1961.
The Lions' Mouths. London, Macmillan, and Chester Springs, Pennsylvania, Dufour, 1967.
Oswin's Word (libretto for children). London, BBC, 1967.

Sandgrains on a Tray. London, Macmillan, and Chester Springs, Pennsylvania, Dufour, 1969.
Penguin Modern Poets 14, with Michael Hamburger and Charles Tomlinson. London, Penguin, 1969.
Brownjohn's Beasts (for children). London, Macmillan, and New York, Scribner, 1970.
Warrior's Career. London, Macmillan, 1972.
A Song of Good Life. London, Secker and Warburg, 1975.
A Night in the Gazebo. London, Secker and Warburg, 1980.
Collected Poems 1952–1983. London, Secker and Warburg, 1983.
The Old Flea-Pit. London, Hutchinson, 1987.
Collected Poems 1952–1986. London, Hutchinson, 1988.
The Observation Car. London, Hutchinson, 1990.
In the Cruel Arcade. London, Sinclair-Stevenson, 1994.

Play

Radio Play: *Torquato Tasso*, from the play by Goethe, 1982.

Novel

The Way You Tell Them. London, Deutsch, 1990.
The Long Shadows. Stockport, Dewi Lewis Publishing, 1997.

Other

To Clear the River (novel for children; as John Berrington). London, Heinemann, 1964.
The Little Red Bus Book. London, Inter-Action, 1972.
Philip Larkin. London, Longman, 1975.

Editor, *First I Say This: A Selection of Poems for Reading Aloud*. London, Hutchinson, 1969.
Editor, with Seamus Heaney and Jon Stallworthy, *New Poems 1970–1971*. London, Hutchinson, 1971.
Editor, with Maureen Duffy, *New Poetry 3*. London, Arts Council, 1977.
Editor, *New Year Poetry Supplement*. London, Poetry Book Society, 1982.
Editor, with Sandy Brownjohn, *Meet and Write*. London, Hodder and Stoughton, 3 vols., 1985–87.

Translator, *Torquato Tasso*, by Goethe. London, Angel, 1985.
Translator, *Horace*, by Corneille. London, Angel, 1996.

*

Manuscript Collections: Manor House Library (Lewisham Public Library), London; Pennsylvania State University, University Park.

Critical Studies: Review by Peter Porter, in *London Magazine*, October 1969; *The Society of the Poem* by Jonathan Raban, London, Harrap, 1971; Roger Garfitt, in *British Poetry since 1960* edited by Michael Schmidt and Grevel Lindop, Oxford, Carcanet, 1972; Barbara Everett in *London Review of Books*, May 1981; Claud Rawson, in *Poetry Review* (London), April 1984.

Alan Brownjohn comments:

In consulting with Peter Digby Smith, the publisher of my first hardback volume of verse, *The Railings*, I evolved for the dust jacket the simple statement "Poems concerned with love, politics, culture, time."

I think this still defines the themes of my verse, with one or other of these four dominant at different moments. But they all, of course, intersect and interrelate: states of politics or culture affect the values of love; love and time constantly stare at one another, amused, shamefaced, or fatalistic; time watches politics rise to honorable humane achievement or decline into vanity.

I've come to some recent conclusions about the language, tone, and temperament of my poetry which critics might confirm or contradict. Although I am quietly, but very seriously, atheist, socialist, and internationalist, it's the Englishness of what I write that strikes me most as I look back at it—the use of language, the attitudes rehearsed, the codes of honor and styles of reticence employed. I don't feel like making apology for this, because I greatly admire certain English puritan values and feel that English rationalism, democracy, and humanity would be our best postimperial contribution to the world at large, the vehicle for transmission of these values being the English language.

Every poet would like to feel he was writing for, communicating to, the world; and if I ever succeed in doing that, in anything at all, I'd like to feel it was in the above terms and transmitting the above values. But of course we should, and do, receive values from other literatures; and I am aware, more and more as I grow older, of unconscious debts in my own verse to European poetry, e.g., that of France, Germany, and the eastern European countries.

(1995) Entering one's seventh decade is—as for anyone else in any other vocation or trade—a disarming and thought-provoking experience for the poet. I grew up believing that, as with so many of the romantics, poets did not survive as creators—or often as living persons—after forty. Quite naturally, I no longer think that and hope now to diversify and renew whatever talent I have well on into my late years. Fiction, after the modest success of a first novel published at 59, tempts me more these days. But critics have noticed that my verse tends toward the condition of fiction in many of my poems.

(1999) And at the beginning of a new century and millennium I'd see no reason to alter any of the above statements. But I would not want to seem settled, unchanging, or complacent. On the beginning of the year 2000, and at sixty-eight years of age, I would still want to do much, in poetry, fiction, perhaps also in the translation of drama (if I were starting again, I would strive to do more of that). The old values and dilemmas are not altered by a new technology, which gives us, if anything, more diverse problems to face. Confronting such problems is one of the duties—and the pleasures—of persons engaged in the arts. And as "pleasures" is not a word I've used much in writing about my own work, I'd like to conclude this statement by affirming that I've always hoped it would give pleasure.

*   *   *

With the publication of his *Collected Poems 1952–1986,* Alan Brownjohn can now clearly be seen as one of the major talents of contemporary British poetry, a poet of his time and the best of our social poets. Although the subject matter of Brownjohn's poetry ranges widely, taking in such traditional themes as love and childhood, it is the expression of his concern for social issues that marks his work as especially his own. His poem "Knightsbridge Display Window" ends with "sometime we'll get perhaps / A commonwealth of sense, and not with guns," which is in line with his statement that the poem aims "at a kind of cheerful democratic puritanism." It is an

ideal not without a degree of paradox, but that may well be in the nature of most ideals. In his collection *The Railings* Brownjohn's concern can be seen from the beginning as very much a poet's concern:

> Don't look for hunger and disease before
> You blame a country. Stop and listen, now,
> For the unquestioned currency of talk
> Its people handle.

This is the stand that a society is to be judged by the quality of life it engenders. In *The Lions' Mouths* this concern is pursued, and we find that while the view is compassionate it is, nevertheless, allied to an uncompromising critical stance. "Why shouldn't they do as they like?" asks the "fool-libertarian voice" in the poem "A Hairdressers." "No," the poet replies, "I can't wish I were as liberal as that." Here is the puritan speaking, a voice that persists and that we find in the collection *A Song of Good Life,* where in "In Hertfordshire" Brownjohn writes sadly, even harshly, of modern development and new towns:

> It has fangs of reinforced concrete and triple glazing,
> Its eyes are huge stacks of strip-light in Industrial Areas
> Refining precisions to blur life, imprinting so tidy on
> Clicking cards the specific patterns of your death.

Yet the human spirit is more robust than that, as his group of poems in the same collection on the wiles and adventures of the Old Fox would suggest.

In all of Brownjohn's poetry there is the same sharp mind probing and enquiring. The poem "For a Journey" explores the significance of what at first seems an unlikely subject, the naming of country fields—"Topfield," "Third field," and the like—to conclude, "Who knows what could become of you where / No one has understood the place with names?" Brownjohn's need to analyze is reflected in the language he uses. On occasion it can become as complex as the line of thought he pursues, as in "Apology for Blasphemy":

> It is with metaphor
> We can assuage, abolish and
> Create. I will apologise
> With metaphors

The tendency is for such poetry to become abstract in both content and form. Yet in *Sandgrains on a Tray* we find him successfully combating this and developing a clarity and directness that give added strength and purpose to his work, as does his deliberate avoidance of decoration or embellishment. The words are made to work in their own right, consistent again with his cheerful puritanism.

In Brownjohn's collection *Warrior's Career* poems such as "Ode to Centre Point" and "A Politician" see him making his points much more directly, and a new, more personal element emerges in the section of love poems. Meanwhile, the thread of social concern continues in the group of poems in *A Song of Good Life* that present a picture of life in the 1970s through their observation of modern habits and fashions. In *A Night in the Gazebo* the narrative aspect of Brownjohn's poetry comes more to the fore, and via the observations of character and attitude explored in these fictions the oblique questionings and probings of society emerge: "There are too many evils, they race too fast, you lose / Much more than a point if you don't contrive to intercept them."

"Our middle age should have altered a lot of things," Alan Brownjohn writes in his poem "Watermarks." What it has done in his case is to see the production of three more substantial collections of poems: *The Old Flea-Pit, The Observation Car,* and *In the Cruel Arcade.* These new poems contain elements of fantasy and dream:

> And then, one unexpected day, sail back
> With another persona, yes, like someone
> Else altogether, and nothing like myself,
> As an unknown *deus ex machina*

In the end, however, the poems are still firmly rooted in reality. Brownjohn's survival and recovery from a serious illness also has introduced a deeper, more somber note in his work and a greater awareness of time passing. "All the old picture girls are dying," he writes in "On The Death Of Margaret Lockwood," and "Somehow you left us out of your address book" in "Not Known." But the jokey, robustly humorous Brownjohn is still there. Witness the poems "Ballad Form Again" and "A Brighton."

—John Cotton

BRUCE, George

Nationality: British. **Born:** Fraserburgh, Aberdeenshire, Scotland, 10 March 1909. **Education:** Fraserburgh Academy; Aberdeen University, M.A. (honors) in English. **Family:** Married Elizabeth Duncan in 1935 (died 1994); one son and one daughter. **Career:** Teacher of English and history, Dundee High School, 1933–46; general programs producer, Aberdeen, 1946–56, and since 1956 documentary talks producer, BBC, Edinburgh. Fellow in creative writing, Glasgow University, 1971–73; visiting professor, Union Theological Seminary, Richmond, Virginia, 1974; writer-in-residence, Prescott College, Arizona, 1974; visiting professor, College of Wooster, Ohio, 1976–77; and St. Andrews Presbyterian College, Laurinburg, North Carolina, 1985. **Awards:** Scottish Arts Council award, 1968, 1971; Scottish Australian Writing fellowship, 1982. Litt.D.: College of Wooster, 1977. O.B.E. (Officer, Order of the British Empire), 1984. **Address:** 25 Warriston Crescent, Edinburgh EH3 5LB, Scotland.

PUBLICATIONS

Poetry

Sea Talk. Glasgow, Maclellan, 1944.
Selected Poems. Edinburgh, Oliver and Boyd, 1947.
Landscapes and Figures: A Selection of Poems. Preston, Lancashire, Akros, 1967.
The Collected Poems of George Bruce. Edinburgh, Edinburgh University Press, 1970.
The Red Sky Poems. Laurinburg, North Carolina, St. Andrew's Press, 1985.
Perspective: Poems 1970–1986. Aberdeen, Aberdeen University Press, 1987.
Pursuit: Poems 1986–1998. Edinburgh, Scottish Cultural Press, 1999.

Plays

To Scotland, with Rhubarb (produced Edinburgh, 1965).

Radio Play: *Tonight Mrs. Morrison,* music by David Dorward, 1968.

Other

Scottish Sculpture, with T.S. Halliday. Dundee, Findlay, 1946.
Neil M. Gunn. Edinburgh, National Library of Scotland, 1971.
Anne Redpath. Edinburgh, Edinburgh University Press, 1974.
The City of Edinburgh: A Historical Guide. London, Pitkin Pictorials, 1974; revised edition, 1977.
Festival in the North: The Story of the Edinburgh Festival. London, Hale, 1975.
Some Practical Good: The Cockburn Association 1875–1975. Edinburgh, Cockburn Association, 1975.
William Soutar 1898–1943: The Man and the Poet. Edinburgh, National Library of Scotland, 1978.
"To Foster and Enrich": The First Fifty Years of the Saltire Society. Edinburgh, Saltire Society, 1986.

Editor, *The Exiled Heart: Poems 1941–1956,* by Maurice Lindsay. London, Hale, 1957.
Editor, with Edwin Morgan and Maurice Lindsay, *Scottish Poetry One to Six.* Edinburgh, Edinburgh University Press, 1966–72.
Editor, *The Scottish Literary Revival: An Anthology of Twentieth Century Poetry.* London, Collier Macmillan, and New York, Macmillan, 1968.
Editor, with Paul H. Scott, *A Scottish Postbag.* Edinburgh, Chambers, 1986.
Editor, with Frank Rennie, *The Land Out There.* Aberdeen, Aberdeen University Press, 1990.

*

Manuscript Collections: State University of New York, Buffalo; National Library of Scotland, Edinburgh; University of Texas, Austin.

Critical Studies: *The Scottish Tradition in Literature* by Kurt Wittig, Edinburgh, Oliver and Boyd, 1958; *The Scots Literary Tradition* by John Spiers, London, Faber, 1962; "Myth-Maker: The Poetry of George Bruce" by Alexander Scott, in *Akros* (Preston, Lancashire), December 1975; "Sea Talk" by Iain Crichton Smith, in *Towards the Human,* Edinburgh, Macdonald, 1986; "George Bruce at Eighty" by Trevor Royle, in *Scottish Poetry Library Newsletter* (Edinburgh) 13, Summer 1989; "An Impression of Continuity" by Colin Nicholson, in *Poem, Purpose and Place,* Edinburgh, Polygon, 1992; "'Make Marble the Moment': The Poetry of George Bruce" by J.H. Alexander, in *Northern Visions: The Literary Identity of Northern Scotland in the Twentieth Century,* edited by David Hewitt, East Lothian, Tuckwell, 1995.

George Bruce comments:

(1970) I belong, I suppose, to the current Scottish literary revival, though I believe I owe nothing in style to any of my Scottish contemporaries. I have learned the craft of verse especially from Ezra Pound.

From about 1941 to 1953 the main subject matter was life in a sea town and the environment of that life. The approach was definitive rather than descriptive. I was concerned to establish the extraordinary nature of the case, that people continued to believe in life and to make a particular thing of it in circumstances that might have warranted despair, but then should one not despair in any case of human life that is, ipso facto, precariously placed between light and dark?

I came to this subject when the war seemed to confirm by its explicit outrage on human dignity the evidence of Eliot's *The Waste Land*. In these circumstances I found myself—for I did not seek to do so—making a statement in verse about the establishing of life on a minimal basis. I noted the fishermen whose lives were almost continuously threatened by the life-giving and killing element from which they drew their livelihood. To their adaptation to, and acceptance of, their situation they added an apparently unreasonable belief in a personal God. I could not identify myself with their attitudes nor with them. But in looking with particularity at them, the sense of a separate existence came home at a time when the word "object" was almost meaningless to me. I had found an "objective correlative."

I proceeded to apply a craft of verse that I had learned from Ezra Pound, particularly from *Mauberley,* with, as far as I could, clinical exactness. Just as much of my country was mere rock, so my language should be, so the rhythms short and vigorous. When I applied my ear to what I had written, I found the tone and accent an articulation of the words, and sentences related more closely to the manner of speech of the community in which I had been brought up (and to some extent continued about me, for I believe there is a tendency in educated Scottish speech in English to certain general characteristic) than to the implied accent of Pound or to the speech of southern England. A strong emphasis on consonants and a high articulation are characteristic. In my more successful poems of this period I think these elements are present. This was a point of beginning. All my poems were in English.

Then I became increasingly interested in the idea of order. That aspect of nature I knew best, and the irregular characteristic of growth itself threatened order. My poem about St. Andrews, "A Gateway to the Sea," is written as an exposition on the order of a mediaeval town that embodies theological concepts of order in its structure, an order that is threatened by men and by the ravages of the sea. This interest is subordinated in several poems to a rejoicing in the irregularity and variety of creation. It is easy enough to accept that variety as one looks back in history; it is more difficult to accept when the force of life expresses itself in what appears to be brashness and vulgarity. This is the main concern of my poem *Landscapes and Figures.*

(1980) In the 1970s there have been two new developments in my poetry. The one is the use of contemporary events, social and political, as material, on which I have made generally satiric comment. The other is the writing of poetry in Scots, which medium I have also applied to the current social scene. This led Alexander Scott to comment on my having "an uproarious sense of sardonic humor."

(1985) As my poetic interests widened, I came to use a longer line but to incorporate short lines for incantatory or dramatic purposes. Then I included Scots in my poems as the voice of a persona, using the same brief rhythms as I had done in English, the abruptness of the Scots reflecting the utterances of the fishermen under duress. More recently I have written poems in Scots as ironic commentaries on the social scene, but where I have felt most intensely the casual cruelties and injustices of our time, I have made my comment in poems in English, these frequently provoking as counterbalance personal love poems.

(1995) In 1944 my first collection of poems, *Sea Talk,* contained no poems in the vernacular of Scots, which I spoke as a boy, though the poems dealt with the experience of living in the Aberdeenshire coast. I felt then oppressed by the parochial, sentimental character of the verses written in that mode and that I required the clarity of English. Since then my sketches of fishermen in poems in English have accepted their speech. Then I wrote, and continue to write, bilingual poems such as "The Chair," in *Interim,* (University of Nevada, Las Vegas) 10(2), edited by A. Wilber Stevens. Finally, returning to my origins, I write poems in Scots based on the Aberdeenshire vernacular, such as my narrative poem "The Broch," published in *The Five Toons Festival Collection,* edited by George Gunn, Banff & Buchan District Council. This augurs a renewed confidence in the vitality and applicability of Scots to contemporary subjects.

*　　*　　*

The term "regional poet" can either mean a minor writer who celebrates his locality with a certain amount of enthusiasm and charm or a writer who uses the sights and smells and sounds of his native district as imaginative material for containing problems and predicaments that are those of humanity. It is in this second, good, sense that George Bruce is the poet of the northeast of Scotland, with its cold farmlands, its rugged cliffscapes, and its dour and tenacious fishermen.

That tenacity, that necessary, continuing belief in life at its basic food-winning level during the early years of World War II, inspired some of the poems in Bruce's first book, *Sea Talk.* His technique he learned to some extent from T.S. Eliot, though principally from Ezra Pound, especially *Mauberley.* But the tone and timbre of the application of the technique are very much his own, related to those durable qualities among which he had been brought up. "Just as much of my country was mere rock," the poet has explained, "so my language should be, so the rhythms short and vigorous." Comparing the graciousness that allowed Gothic spires to flourish in windswept Balbec and Finistère with the granite knuckle thrust where the Buchan fisherman has his being, Bruce exclaims,

> To defend life thus and so to grace it
> What art! but you, my friend, know nothing of this,
> Merely the fog, more often the east wind
> That scours the sand from the shore,
> Bequeathing it to the sheep pasture,
> Whipping the dust from fields,
> Disclosing the stone ribs of earth—
> The frame that for ever presses back the roots of corn
> In the shallow soil. This wind,
> Driving over your roof,
> Twists the sycamore's branches
> Till its dwarf fingers shoot west,
> Outspread on bare country, lying wide.
> Erect against the element
> House and kirk and your flint face.

Just as the relentless action of wind and waves has shaped his coastline, so past generations have molded his northeast character:

This which I write now
Was written years ago
Before my birth
In the features of my father.

It was stamped
In the rock formations
West of my hometown.
No I write

But perhaps, William Bruce,
Cooper . . .

Against this backcloth of the elements, Bruce sets the hero, determinedly going about his business.

Twenty-three years lie between *Sea Talk* and *Landscapes and Figures*. By the time of the second collection the range and power of the verse have deepened. There is still the hero, "a man of inconsequent build," his "Odyssey the trains between / Two ends of telephone . . ."

There are also clear, objective recollections of the details of childhood, as in the much praised "Tom." In one part of this sequence, "Tom on the Beach," the poet asks himself,

How many years since with sure heart
And prophecy of success
Warmed in it
Did I look with delight on the little fish,

Start with happiness, the warm sun on me?
Now the waters spread horizonwards,
Great skies meet them,
I brood upon uncompleted tasks.

Bruce occasionally uses Scots, though usually only for special colloquial effects in the counterpoint of his verses' rugged music. Henry Moore's sculpture, the impact of distant wars through the television screen, and the experience of an Italian sojourn have given him new thematic material. I doubt if anything can surpass "A Gateway to the Sea," his elegy for the changelessness of change. The "gateway" leads to ruined St. Andrew's Cathedral, where once there was living gossip:

. . . Caesar's politics.
And he who was drunk last night;
Rings, diamants, snuff boxes, warships,
Also the less worthy garments of worthy men!

Here once:

The European sun knew these streets
O Jesu parvule; Christus Victus: Christus Victor.
The bells singing from their towers, the waters
Whispering to the waters, the air tolling
To the air—the faith, the faith, the faith.

But "all that was long ago. The lights / Are out, the town is sunk in sleep . . ." and yet,

Under the touch the guardian stone remains
Holding memory, reproving desire, securing hope

In the stop of water, in the lull of night
Before dawn kindles a new day.

I know of no other so-called regional poet whose treatment of the oldest and most universal theme of all is as powerfully affecting as Bruce's in this poem. The voice is Scottish, but the words are warmed into poetry by a European mind.

At a comparatively advanced age Bruce undertook lecture tours in the United States and in Australia. His European mind responded in verse to these wider experiences, as his collection *Perspective* clearly shows, notably in "Aborigine with Tax Form." "The Desert" is a narrative poem reflecting the bleakness of bigotries and the human wastes they create.

The mother called the children home
in the evening. In the morning the bell
called them to the village school.
Peewits flopped in the air.
Cows rubbed their hairy backs on posts.
In the school the children learned words
so that they could know of the desert far away
that one day would be their desert.

There is also a highly amusing pseudolament for the much heralded demise of the Scots tongue, blown out of its tomb by "a fuff o' win" (wind), leaving the

. . . gran mourners, the Editor o' the Scottish National
Dictionary,
Heid o' the Depairtment o' Scot-Lit.,
President o' the Burns Federation,
President o' the Lallans Society,
President o' the Saltire Society,
a' present in strict alphabetical order . . .

—Maurice Lindsay

BRUTUS, Dennis (Vincent)

Nationality: British (South African exile). **Born:** Salisbury, Rhodesia (now Harare, Zimbabwe), 28 November 1924. **Education:** Paterson High School, South Africa; Fort Hare University, Alice, B.A. in English 1947; Witwatersrand University, Johannesburg, 1963–64. **Family:** Married May Jaggers in 1950; four daughters and four sons. **Career:** High school teacher of English and Afrikaans, Port Elizabeth, 1948–61; journalist in South Africa, 1960–61. Served 18 months in Robben Island Prison, for opposition to apartheid, 1964–65. Left South Africa in 1966. Director, Campaign for Release of South African Political Prisoners, London, 1966–71; staff member, International Defence and Aid Fund, London, 1966–71. Visiting professor, University of Denver, 1970. Moved to the United States in 1971; granted political asylum, 1983. Professor of English, Northwestern University, Evanston, Illinois, 1971–85; Cornell Professor of English literature, Swarthmore College, Pennsylvania, 1985–86. Since 1986 professor and chair, department of black community education, research, and development, University of Pittsburgh, Pennsylvania. Visiting professor, University of Texas, Austin, 1974–75, Amherst College, Massachusetts, 1982–83, Dartmouth College, Hanover, New

Hampshire, 1983, Northeastern University, Boston, 1984. Visiting distinguished humanist, University of Colorado, Center for Studies of Ethnicity in the Americas, Department of English, 1994. Founder-director, Troubadour Press, Del Valle, Texas, 1971. Member of board of directors, Black Arts Celebration, Chicago, 1975. Since 1959 secretary, South African Sports Associations; since 1963 president, South African Non-Racial Olympic Committee; since 1972 chair, International Campaign Against Racism in Sport; since 1975 vice president, Union of Writers of the African Peoples; founding chair, 1975, and since 1979 member of executive committee, African Literature Association; since 1976 member of the editorial board, *Africa Today,* Denver; since 1984 chair, Africa Network. **Awards:** Mbari prize, 1962; Freedom Writers award, 1975; Kenneth Kaunda Humanism award, 1979; Langston Hughes prize, 1988; Paul Robeson award, 1989. D.H.L.: Worcester State College, Massachusetts, 1982; University of Massachusetts, Amherst, 1984. LL.D: Northeastern University, Boston, Massachusetts, 1989. **Address:** 2132 Bluebell Avenue, Boulder, Colorado 80302, U.S.A.

PUBLICATIONS

Poetry

Sirens, Knuckles, Boots. Ibadan, Mbari, 1963; Evanston, Illinois, Northwestern University Press, 1964.
Letters to Martha and Other Poems from a South African Prison. London, Heinemann, 1968.
Poems from Algiers. Austin, University of Texas, 1970.
Thoughts Abroad (as John Bruin). Del Valle, Texas, Troubadour Press, 1970.
A Simple Lust: Selected Poems. London, Heinemann, and New York, Hill and Wang, 1973.
China Poems. Austin, University of Texas, 1975.
Strains, edited by Wayne Kamin and Chip Dameron, Austin, Texas, Troubador Press, 1975; revised edition, 1982.
Stubborn Hope. London, Heinemann, and Washington, D.C., Three Continents Press, 1978; revised edition, Oxford, Heinemann, 1991.
Salutes and Censures. Enugu, Nigeria, Fourth Dimension, and Trenton, New Jersey, Africa World Press, 1984.
Airs and Tributes. Camden, New Jersey, Whirlwind Press, 1989.
Still the Sirens. Santa Fe, New Mexico, Pennywhistle Press, 1993.

Recordings: *The Sounds Begin Again,* Watershed, 1984; *The Writing Life,* Watershed.

Other

Editor, with others, *African Literature, 1988: New Masks.* Washington D.C., Three Continents Press and the African Literature Association, 1990.

*

Manuscript Collections: Northwestern University Library, Evanston, Illinois; Schomberg Collection, New York Public Library.

Critical Studies: *Introduction to African Literature* by Ulli Beier, Evanston, Illinois, Northwestern University Press, 1967; *Who's Who*

in African Literature by Janheinz Jahn, Tübingen, Germany, Erdman, 1972; *African Authors* by Donald Herdeck, Washington, D.C., Black Orpheus Press, 1973; *The Black Mind* by O.R. Dathorne, Minneapolis, University of Minnesota Press, 1974, abridged edition as *African Literature in the 20th Century,* London, Heinemann, 1976; *A Vision of Order* by Ursula Barnett, Amherst, University of Massachusetts Press, 1983; *A People's Voice* by Piniel Shava, London, Zed Press, and Athens, University of Ohio Press, 1989; *Critical Perspectives on Dennis Brutus* edited by Craig W. McLuckie and Patrick J. Colbert, Colorado Springs, Colorado, Three Continents Press, 1995; interview by Lee Nichols, in *ALA Bulletin,* 23(3), Summer 1997; by Craig W. McLuckie, in *Postcolonial African Writers: A Bio-Bibliographical Critical Source Book,* edited by Pushpa Naidu Parekh and Siga Fatima Jagne, Westport, Connecticut, Greenwood, 1998.

Dennis Brutus comments:

(1970) A lyrical poet; protest elements are only incidental, as features of the South African scene obtrude. Favorite poets: John Donne, Browning, Hopkins.

(1985) My concerns have widened to embrace larger social issues, especially nuclear annihilation and the problems of the third world.

*   *   *

Dennis Brutus's life has been marked by both commitment and controversy. As president of the South African Non-Racial Olympic Committee, he was largely responsible for the exclusion of South Africa from international sports competitions. Brutus began his crusade against apartheid while teaching in South Africa; it resulted in his being banned from teaching, writing, and publishing. In 1964, the year after the publication of his first book of poetry, he was arrested, imprisoned for eighteen months, and eventually exiled. Another battle took place in 1983 when he fought deportation from the United States, where he had been teaching for more than a decade. He was finally granted political asylum after a lengthy struggle during which hundreds of Americans, both other writers and those who shared his opposition to racial injustice, rallied to his defense.

Despite his deep political involvement, Brutus's voice as a poet has been marked from his earliest published work by a tone of maturity and restraint. This can be seen most clearly perhaps in the book he wrote following his imprisonment, *Letters to Martha.* The volume's title reflects the fact that he was banned from writing anything of a publishable nature and had to disguise his poems as letters to his sister-in-law. His deft understatement, while presenting the harsh reality of life as a political prisoner, makes the message all the more powerful:

And sometimes one mistook
the weary tramp of feet
as the men came shuffling from the quarry
white-dust-filmed and shambling
for the rain
that came and drummed and marched away.

Although Brutus has experienced personal suffering, which has ranged from the physical suffering of imprisonment on the infamous Robben Island—where he was shot in the back while attempting to escape—to the spiritual suffering caused by the atrocities of apartheid and his own exile, there is never a tone of self-pity in his work. He has even found it possible to write gentle love poems, although the hard truths of history may still intrude. In fact, the powerful last line of an often quoted poem from his first collection, *Sirens, Knuckles, Boots,* might be taken as the philosophy the poet has lived by:

> Patrols uncoil over the asphalt dark
> hissing their menace to our lives,
>
> most cruel, all our land is scarred with terror,
> rendered unlovely and unlovable;
> sundered are we and all our passionate surrender
>
> but somehow tenderness survives.

This is not to say that Brutus is free from anger or even bitterness. Frustration, rage, and great sorrow can be found in his work, but the possibility of redemption, a ''splendid Gethsemane,'' always exists. The world he opposes may be brutal, but his opposition, while strong, is also a celebration of the value of human sensitivity and of individual human lives. His vocabulary is that of a highly educated man, but of one who has not lost touch with the basic reality of ordinary human lives. Thus his tone is both elevated and basic, both passionate and restrained. His literary language is not polite or indirect, however, and he never hesitates to broaden his concerns to include contemporary issues. ''We all live on a Three Mile Island / in a sea / which can transmogrify mankind,'' he says in one poem.

Brutus's poetry from the late 1970s and the 1980s, as seen in the volumes *Stubborn Hope* and *Salutes and Censures,* shows a wider concern for the third world, linking Chile, Nicaragua, and other areas of national struggle with the problems of Africa, specifically South Africa. His poem ''No Matter for History'' takes its title from a statement by Pablo Neruda. Typical of the form of much of Brutus's poetry-free verse marked by cadence and repetition—these lines also embody his views of the inevitability of social democracy and the power of the poet, a power that comes from the people:

> in death
> the generals festered over him
> like blowflies
>
> his voice
> sings on,
> sings men to resistance,
> to hope, to life;
>
> Neruda is dead
> no matter.

Brutus has led many lives, worked continuously for social justice, and visited many lands. His work reflects a diversity of experience and continuity of commitment. His poems of imprisonment are not merely an indictment of the injustice of apartheid but also a statement of the enduring power of the human spirit against adversity. His poems of exile, a long and often painful exile that has taken him to almost every part of the world, are charged with hope. Throughout, he has remained a poet of the highest social commitment, yet one who has seldom sacrificed poetry for polemic.

—Joseph Bruchac

BUCHAN, Tom

Nationality: Scottish. **Born:** Thomas Buchanan Buchan, Glasgow, 19 June 1931. **Education:** Jordanhill College School; Balfron High School; Aberdeen Grammar School; University of Glasgow, 1947–53; M.A. (honors) in English 1953. **Family:** Married Emma Chapman in 1962; two sons and one daughter. **Career:** Teacher, Denny High School, Stirlingshire, 1953–56; lecturer in English, University of Madras, India, 1957–58; warden, Community House, Glasgow, 1958–59; teacher, Irvine Royal Academy, 1963–65; senior lecturer in English and drama, Clydebank Technical College, Glasgow, 1967–70. Co-director, Kalachaitanya Madras, a touring repertory company, in the 1950s and director of the Craigmillar and Dumbarton festivals in the 1970s; editor, *Scottish International,* Edinburgh, 1973–74; member of the Rajneesh Ashram, Poona, in the 1970s. Also printer, Poni Press, Offshore Theatre Company, and Arts Projects, all Edinburgh. **Awards:** Scottish Arts Council award, 1969, 1970. **Agent:** Barbara Hargeaves, Mains of Faillie, Daviot, Invernesshire. **Address:** Scoraig, Dundonnell, Wester Ross IV23 2RE, Scotland.

PUBLICATIONS

Poetry

Ikons. Madras, Tambaram Press, 1958.
Dolphins at Cochin. London, Barrie and Rockliff-Cresset Press, and New York, Hill and Wang, 1969.
Exorcism. Glasgow, Midnight Press, 1972.
Poems 1969–1972. Edinburgh, Poni Press, 1972.
Forwards. Glasgow, Glasgow Print Studio Press, 1978.

Plays

Tell Charlie Thanks for the Truss (produced Edinburgh, 1972).
The Great Northern Welly Boot Show, lyrics by Billy Connolly, music by Tom McGrath (produced Edinburgh and London, 1972).
Knox and Mary (produced Edinburgh, 1972).
Over the Top (produced Edinburgh, 1979).
Bunker (produced Findhorn, Moray, 1980).

Novel

Makes You Feel Great. Edinburgh, Poni Press, 1971.

Other

Editor, with Nora Smith and John Forsyth, *Genie: Short Stories.* Edinburgh, Edinburgh University Press, 1974.

*

Manuscript Collection: Mitchell Library, Glasgow.

*   *   *

Tom Buchan's poetry shows a distinctive and consistent development from his collection *Dolphins at Cochin* to his *Poems 1969–1972.* His distinction, in the first instance, is in his making a true aesthetic response to the machine imagery of the twentieth century. He in no way indulges this response, but it provides the cutting edge to his satire. This is his depiction of "The White Hunter" in *Dolphin at Cochin:*

> The white hunter in his newly laundered outfit
> emerges from the acacias hung about with guns,
> compasses, bandoliers, belts, charms, binoculars,
> Polaroid sun-specs, cameras and a shockproof watch.

The more vividly the equipment displays itself, the greater the doubt cast on the reality of the person encased in it. Buchan's effects are immediate, and their impact is decisive. "The Everlasting Astronauts" begins with

> These dead astronauts cannot decay—
> they bounce on the quilted walls of their tin grave
> and very gently collide with polythene balloons
> full of used mouthwash, excrements and foodscraps.

The hallucinatory effect of the floating bodies is captured, but the emphasis is on doubt as to the values of the achievement of modern man.

The nausea suggested in the last line of the quatrain becomes in Buchan's second collection a more important factor, for this is a book that exhibits passionate indignation, disgust, and contempt at the hypocrisy and callousness of officials in power in modern society. His achievement is in the creation of a nightmare world inhabited by politicians who seem to be caricatures of actual persons. The creations induce belief, and they are seen as we know them projected on the screens of the cinema and television. He presents "Mister Nixon President" in this way:

> announces the U.S. invasion of Cambodia
> (Cambodia) on TV and sincerely his sincere right eye
> fixes the poor old silent US majority
> with Operation Total Myopic Solemnity.

The observation is cruel and comic and with some truth in it. Buchan's "subversive" intention does not limit him to satirizing capitalist politicians, however. In the same poem he hits off Brezhnev:

> meanwhile dateline moss-cow Comrade Leonid
> Nebuchadnezzar Brezhnev in a weird soft hat
> reviews the latest lumpen May Day
> parade with a stiff diminutive wave
> reminiscent of our own dear Queen . . .

The poet undermines the reader's sense of the truth of the observation by injecting into his text such references as CUT and CAM 2, reminding us that for him these are shadows on a screen.

Buchan uses the idea of our seeing the object through a camera lens to a more subtle and profound purpose in his fine poem "The Flaming Man," in which we seem to witness in slow motion the death of a man by burning napalm. Indignation in the poem gives way to compassion, and the result is Buchan at his best. Although he occasionally resorts to political campaigning and to an indulgence in nausea, characteristics that manifest themselves in a strident rhetoric, for the greater part Buchan's rhetoric gives a sinewy strength to his verse.

In *Forwards* Buchan's attention moves beyond politics to the future of man, about which he is optimistic despite the politicians, the institutionalized greed, the corruption of our times, the impotence of those most able to make alterations. He has the conviction that we are on the verge of great changes that will result in a more enlightened consciousness. This is the raw material of Buchan's rhetoric. It calls for a platform delivery, but much of it lacks the image that will carry meaning. When he presents it, it is immediately effective, as in "Sea Crossing":

> I am frightened of that water . . .
> . . .
> And it hides seals, the otter with his stone,
> shark, whales, and the killer whale drifting alongside
> for a moment to inspect the boat
> with his domino mouth pegged out with teeth,
> his playful, mysterious and telepathetic brain-

He comments on "Sea Crossing" that "the image of crossing water for the death-transformation is well known." Where the actual and the symbolic meet, Buchan achieves poetry.

—George Bruce

BULLOCK, Michael (Hale)

Nationality: British. **Born:** London, 19 April 1918. **Education:** Stowe School, Buckinghamshire; Hornsey College of Art, London. **Family:** Married Charlotte Schneller in 1941 (died); one daughter and one son. **Career:** Chairman, Translators Association, London, 1964–67; Commonwealth fellow, 1968, professor of creative writing, 1969–83, and since 1983 professor emeritus, University of British Columbia, Vancouver. McGuffey Visiting Professor of English, Ohio University, Athens, 1968; New Asia Ming Yu visiting scholar, Chinese University of Hong Kong, 1989. Founding editor, *Expression* magazine, London; member of the editorial board, *Canadian Fiction Magazine*, Toronto. Adviser to the New Poetry Society of China, 1994. **Awards:** Schlegel-Tieck translation prize, 1966; Canada Council fellowship, 1968, and translation award, 1979; Social Sciences and Humanities Research Council fellowship, 1981; Okanagan Short Fiction award, 1986. **Address:** 103–3626 West 28th Avenue, Vancouver, British Columbia V6S 1S4, Canada.

PUBLICATIONS

Poetry

Transmutations (as Michael Hale). London, Favil Press, 1938.
Sunday Is a Day of Incest. London and New York, Abelard Schuman, 1961.
World Without Beginning, Amen! London, Favil Press, 1963.
Zwei Stimmen in Meinem Mund (bilingual edition, translated by Hedwig Rohde). Andernach, Germany, Atelier, 1967.
A Savage Darkness. Vancouver, Sono Nis Press, 1969.
Black Wings, White Dead. Fredericton, New Brunswick, Fiddlehead, 1978.
Lines in the Dark Wood. London, Ontario, Third Eye, 1981.
Quadriga for Judy. London, Ontario, Third Eye, 1982.
Prisoner of the Rain: Poems in Prose. London, Ontario, Third Eye, 1983.

Brambled Heart. London, Ontario, Third Eye, 1985.
Dark Water. London, Ontario, Third Eye, 1987.
Poems on Green Paper. London, Ontario, Third Eye, 1988.
Vancouver Moods. London, Ontario, Third Eye, 1989.
The Secret Garden. Victoria, British Columbia, Ekstasis, 1990.
Avatars of the Moon. Victoria, British Columbia, Ekstasis, 1990.
Labyrinths. London, Ontario, Third Eye, 1991.
The Sorcerer with Deadly Nightshade Eyes. Vancouver, Rainbird Press, 1993.
Dark Roses. London, Ontario, Third Eye, 1994.
The Inflowing River. Vancouver, Rainbird Press, 1994.
Moons and Mirrors. Vancouver, Rainbird Press, 1994.
Stone and Shadows. Vancouver, The Poem Factory, 1996.
Erupting in Flowers. Vancouver, Rainbird Press, 1999.
Nocturnes: Poems of Night. Vancouver, Rainbird Press, 2000.

Plays

The Raspberry Picker, adaptation of a play by Fritz Hochwalder (produced London, 1967).
Not to Hong Kong (produced London, 1972). Published in *Dialogue and Dialectic,* Guelph, Ontario, Alive Press, 1973.
The Island Abode of Bliss (produced Vancouver, 1972).
The Coats (produced London, 1975).
Biography: A Game, adaptation of a play by Max Frisch (produced New York, 1979).
Andorra, adaptation of the play by Max Frisch (produced London, 1989).
Sokotra: A Play. Vancouver, Rainbird Press, 1997.

Novels

Randolph Cranstone and the Glass Thimble. London, Boyars, 1977.
Randolph Cranstone and the Veil of Maya. London, Ontario, Third Eye, 1986.
The Story of Noire. London, Ontario, Third Eye, 1987.
Randolph Cranstone Takes the Inward Path. London, Ontario, Third Eye, 1988.
The Walled Garden. Victoria, British Columbia, Ekstasis, 1990.
Voices of the River. Vancouver, Rainbird Press, 1994.

Short Stories

Sixteen Stories as They Happened. Vancouver, Sono Nis Press, 1969.
Green Beginning Black Ending. Vancouver, Sono Nis Press, 1971.
Randolph Cranstone and the Pursuing River. Vancouver, Rainbird Press, 1975.
The Man with Flowers Through His Hands. London, Ontario, Third Eye, 1985.
The Burning Chapel. Victoria, British Columbia, Ekstasis, 1991.
The Invulnerable Ovoid Aura and Other Stories. London, Ontario, Third Eye, 1994.

Other

The Double Ego; Followed by, From Dusk till Dawn. London, Ontario, Melmoth, 1985.
Lifelines. Victoria, British Columbia, Ekstasis, 1990.
Selected Works 1936–1996, edited by Peter Loeffler and Jack Stewart. London, Ontario, Third Eye, 1998.

Translator, with Jerome Ch'ên, *Poems of Solitude.* London and New York, Abelard Schuman, 1961.
Translator, *The Tales of Hoffmann.* London, New English Library, 1962; New York, Ungar, 1963.
Translator, *The Stage and Creative Arts.* Greenwich, Connecticut, New York Graphic Society, 1969.
Translator, *Foreign Bodies,* by Karl Krolow. Athens, Ohio University Press, 1969.
Translator, *Invisible Hands,* by Karl Krolow. London, Cape Goliard Press, and New York, Grossman, 1969.
Translator, with Jagna Boraks, *Astrologer in the Underground,* by Andrzej Busza. Athens, Ohio University Press, 1971.
Translator, *Stories for Late Night Drinkers,* by Michel Tremblay. Vancouver, Intermedia, 1977.
Translator, *The Persian Mirror,* by Thomas Pavel. London, Ontario, Third Eye, 1988.
Translator, *Compulsion,* by Claudette Charbonneau-Tissot. London, Ontario, Third Eye, 1989.
Translator, *Erik Satie Seen Through His Letters,* by Ornella Volta. London, Boyars, 1989.
Translator, *The City in the Egg,* by Michel Tremblay. London, Ontario, Third Eye, 1999.
Other translations include novels and plays by Max Frisch and more than 130 other French and German books.

*

Manuscript Collection: University of British Columbia, Vancouver.

Critical Studies: By John Ditsky, in *Canadian Forum* (Toronto), February 1971; Richard Hopkins, in *British Columbia Library Quarterly* (Victoria), January 1972; "Light on a Dark Wood" by John Reid, in *Canadian Literature* (Vancouver), Autumn 1972; interview with Richard Hopkins, in *British Columbia Library Quarterly* (Victoria), June 1973; *The Incandescent Word: The Poetic Vision of Michael Bullock* by Jack Stewart, London, Ontario, Third Eye, 1990.

Michael Bullock comments:

I consider myself a surrealist, or at least a neosurrealist, in that I base my work upon the free play of the imagination without, however, sacrificing clarity of expression. I seek to use vivid and striking imagery to convey states of mind and emotion and to create an autonomous world freed from the restrictions and limitations of everyday existence. This world and the means I use to give it form remain the same whether I am writing verse, prose, or drama. I believe that my writing in all three genres can with almost equal right be described as poetry. All of it is a vehement rejection of realism. I like to hope that there is some truth in the comment of a reviewer who wrote that my fables "bear witness to one of the most wildly imaginative minds ever to reach the printed page" and in Anaïs Nin's description of my work as "a liberating expansion of what is reality." The two remarks together sum up what I am trying to do.

*   *   *

In the poem "Escape" (*A Savage Darkness*), which might easily stand as his personal manifesto, Michael Bullock explains,

The real surrounds me
with its barbed wire entanglements

Leaping upwards I clutch at a cloud
and stuff it into my head

In a blue haze
figures emerge
and drift
in an endless floating dance

Women with streaming hair
fall downwards
holding burning flowers
Flocks of eyes fly around gazing
and flapping their lids

Stretched out
on the cloud in my mind
I wait for the approach
of the ultimate dream . . .

The poem continues, but the most important catchphrase is "the ultimate dream." For Bullock is a surrealist, almost an orthodox one in fact, and his poetry and his prose insist entirely on the freedom, the total possibility, that is the dream, both as a source and as mode. Bullock's poems are associative, fantastical, alogical; like a free-form dance, they leap and swirl to the arabesques of the imagination. Through his writings Bullock reenacts creation according to his own laws, according to a triumphantly lyrical, nonlineal progression both in time and space:

Out of the air I draw the memory of a bird.
Out of the earth I draw the memory of a tree.
From the memory of the bird
and the memory of the tree
I make the memory of a poem
that weighs lighter than air
and floats away without wind . . .

The result is that Bullock's poetry almost always departs from unexpected places and arrives at unfamiliar destinations. And the means by which it gets there is, needless to say, no less unpredictable.

—Andreas Schroeder

BURNS, Jim

Nationality: British. **Born:** Preston, Lancashire, 19 February 1936. **Education:** Attended local schools and Bolton Institute of Technology, Lancashire, B.A. (honors) 1980. **Military Service:** British Army, 1954–57. **Family:** Married in 1958 (divorced 1973); two sons. **Career:** Worked in mills, offices, and factories, 1952–64. Editor, *Move* magazine, 1964–68, and *Palantir,* 1976–83, both Preston, and jazz editor, *Beat Scene,* since 1992. Since 1964 regular contributor, *Tribune* and *Ambit,* both London; since 1983 part-time tutor in adult education colleges; since 1990 part-time tutor for Manchester University extra-mural department. **Address:** 11 Gatley Green, Gatley, Cheadle, Cheshire SK8 4NF, England.

PUBLICATIONS

Poetry

Some Poems. New York, Crank, 1965.
Some More Poems. Cambridge, R Books, 1966.
My Sad Story and Other Poems. Chatham, Kent, New Voice, 1967.
The Store of Things. Manchester, Phoenix Pamphlet Poets Press, 1969.
A Single Flower. St. Brelade, Jersey, Channel Islands, Andium Press, 1972.
Leben in Preston. Cologne, Palmenpresse, 1973.
Easter in Stockport. Sheffield, Rivelin Press, 1975.
Fred Engels in Woolworths. London, Oasis, 1975.
Playing It Cool. Swansea Galloping Dog Press, 1976.
The Goldfish Speaks from Beyond the Grave. London, Salamander Imprint, 1976.
Catullus in Preston. Cardiff, Cameo Club Alley Press, 1979.
Notes from a Greasy Spoon. Cardiff, University College, 1980.
Internal Memorandum. Bradford, Yorkshire, Rivelin Press, 1982.
The Real World. Cowling, Yorkshire, Purple Heather, 1986.
Out of the Past: Selected Poems 1961–1986. Hungerford, Berkshire, Rivelin Grapheme Press, 1987.
Poems for Tribune. Huddersfield, Yorkshire, Wide Skirt Press, 1988.
The Gift. Bradford, Yorkshire, Redbeck Press, 1989.
Confessions of an Old Believer. Bradford, Yorkshire, Redbeck Press, 1996.
As Good a Reason As Any. Bradford, Yorkshire, Redbeck Press, 1999.

Recording: *Gestures,* Black Sheep, 1984.

Other

Cells: Prose Pieces. Lincoln, Grosseteste Press, 1967.
Saloon Bar: 3 Jim Burns Stories. London, Ferry Press, 1967.
Types: Prose Pieces and Poems. Cardiff, Second Aeon, 1970.
The Five Senses. Oldham, Lancashire, Incline Press, 1999.
Beats, Bohemians, and Intellectuals: Selected Essays. Nottingham, Notts., Trent Editions, 1999.

*

Critical Studies: "The American Influence" by the author, in *New Society* (London), 7 December 1967; "Exit to Preston" by Raymond Gardner, in *The Guardian* (London), 10 August 1972; "A Poet in His Northern Corner" by Bel Mooney, in *Daily Telegraph Magazine* (London), 2 March 1973; "Jim Burns' Poems" by John Freeman, in *Cambridge Quarterly,* 1975; "Mit Poesei Kannst Du Kein Auto Fahren" by Michael Buselmeir, in *Frankfurter Rundschau,* 8 April 1978; "A Northern Master" by Gavin Ewart, in *Ambit* (London), 112, 1988; "How Beat Can You Get?" in *Five Leaves Left* (Leeds), 1988, and "Jim Burns: Poet of 'The Real World,'" in *BOGG* (Arlington, U.S.A. and Filey, England), 1990, both by Andy Darlington; "War, Class War, History and Narrative in the Poetry of Jim Burns" by John Freeman, in *Poetry Wales* (Bridgend), 1996.

Jim Burns comments:

(1970) I suppose my main subject matter tends toward the "domestic," i.e., that which I know best and experience personally.

Brevity and wit are attributes I admire in a poet, and I think (or hope) that some of this comes through in some of my own work.

My main influences have been contemporary American and English poets and some translations from the Chinese and Japanese. I like the directness in these latter. If asked to single out one poet whose work I particularly like and find stimulating I would name Kenneth Rexroth.

I have a deep feeling that the most significant ideas can be expressed in direct and clear language and that the unusual and significant are in the obvious.

The reader may also get an idea of my leanings from the opinions expressed in the articles I have contributed since 1964 to *Tribune* on little magazines and related publications.

(1974) In the past three or four years my poetry has, I think, tended to diversify, both in form and content. I still like brevity and wit but have found that, in order to deal with matters outside the domestic concerns my poems once related to, I've had to become perhaps more discursive. In a sense, as the subject matter widens, so do the forms I use. The lines tend to be longer, the rhythm less precise. Interestingly enough, however, I find that when I do revert to domestic concerns the form tightens again.

(1995) I still continue to write poetry which draws on my personal experience, both past and present. In recent years a number of the poems have referred back to childhood events, army service, and other periods in my earlier life. But at the same time I continue to produce poems which focus on the contemporary scene and on the everyday circumstances of the environment in which I live. Politics and social matters continue to play a part in my poetry, and the title of my new collection, *Confessions of an Old Believer* (forthcoming from Redbeck Press, Bradford, England), may suggest to the reader a basis for my thinking and poetic concerns.

(1999) The comments from 1995 are still relevant, though I would add that the older I get the more I seem to pare poems down to their basics and be as direct as I can with what I want to say.

*   *   *

If one had to find a single word to describe Jim Burns's poems, it would be "anecdotal." Each poem tells a story, and the tone adopted is that of the raconteur, with the impetus relying more on the narrative flow and the ultimate making of a point than on language or rhythm as such. What informs each story is the persona adopted, that of the wryly candid man who, though beguiled by the romantic, is never taken in by it, whether it be romantic love—"Better to make love in bed, turn / your back afterwards. Sleep easy" ("The Way It Is")—or the pretentiousness of romantic politics ("Meanwhile"):

The left wing intellectuals
had fought the Paris Commune, the
General Strike, the Spartacist uprising
and the Spanish Civil War all over
again and would have sung the Red Flag
had they known the words or tune.
Instead, they ordered another round
and the landlord rubbed his hands
and then called time. For everyone.

Indeed, it seems to be Burn's mission to deflate gently the phony and the ostentatious, gently because he too knows the temptations and has sympathy with those who succumb. For this reason the language used avoids the "high flown" to the point of flatness, with Burns's sense of rhythm and the narrative flow carrying the poems on. Nevertheless, the truth must out. "Is a man any less a poet / because he stays at home / with his wife and children," he asks in "A Single Flower." Poetry stands or falls by what is on the page; it is irrelevant if the author washes himself, sleeps with his sister, or has two heads or if he is an archbishop or an arch-Villon:

I once slept out all night
with the homeless, and although
it taught me pity
it did not teach me poetry.

He is right, though there are some who will not forgive him for the statement. But self-depreciatory, honest, and always caring as he is, one cannot help liking the man behind the poems.

The man behind the voice is still there, a voice that can be only his and that dominates the poems in the booklets and in collections such as *The Gift* and *Out of the Past*. The same wry humor is there, cautiously treading the path between deflating the pretentious and the danger of being pretentious itself. For Burns is well aware that satire is a serious business demanding a firm and convinced set of values.

"I am by nature and temperament an urban person," he once said in an interview. He sees the urban landscape and culture as one lived in and shared by real people who deserve celebration. He has no truck with those who wish to run away from it or with those ruralists among young poets who write as if Baudelaire and Eliot had not existed. He pursues what he sees as "an urban mythology for a real world."

—John Cotton

BURNSHAW, Stanley

Nationality: American. **Born:** New York City, 20 June 1906. **Education:** Columbia University, New York, 1924; University of Pittsburgh, B.A. 1925; University of Poitiers, 1927; University of Paris, 1927–28; Cornell University, Ithaca, New York, M.A. 1933. **Family:** Married 1) Irma Robin; 2) Madeline Burnshaw in 1934 (divorced); 3) Lydia Powsner in 1942 (died 1987); one daughter and two stepchildren. **Career:** Advertising copywriter, Blaw-Knox Company, Blawnox, Pennsylvania, 1925–27; advertising manager, The Hecht Company, New York, 1928–32; co-editor and drama critic, *The New Masses,* New York, 1934–36; editor-in-chief, The Cordon Company, publishers, New York, 1937–39; president and editor-in-chief, Dryden Press, New York, 1939–58; vice president, 1958–65, and consultant to the president, 1965–68, Holt, Rinehart and Winston Inc., publishers, New York. Lecturer, New York University, 1958–62; Visiting Regents Lecturer, University of California, Davis, 1980; visiting distinguished professor, University of Miami, 1989. Founding editor (and hand setter), *Poetry Folio* magazine, and Folio Press, Pittsburgh, 1926–29. Contributing editor, *Modern Quarterly,* 1932–33, and *Theatre Workshop* magazine, 1935–38. Director, American Institute of Graphic Arts, 1960–61. **Awards:** American Academy award, 1971. D.H.L.: Hebrew Union College, Cincinnati, 1983. **Address:** 250 West 89th Street, Apt. PH2G, New York, New York 10024, U.S.A.

PUBLICATIONS

Poetry

Poems. Pittsburgh, Folio Press, 1927.
The Great Dark Love. Privately printed, 1932.
The Iron Land: A Narrative. Philadelphia, Centaur Press, 1936.
The Revolt of the Cats in Paradise: A Children's Book for Adults. Gaylordsville, Connecticut, Crow Hill Press, 1945.
Early and Late Testament. New York, Dial Press, 1952.
Caged in an Animal's Mind. New York, Holt Rinehart, 1963.
The Hero of Silence: Scenes from an Imagined Life of Mallarmé. Lugano, Switzerland, Lugano Review, 1965.
In the Terrified Radiance. New York, Braziller, 1972.
Mirages: Travel Notes in the Promised Land: A Public Poem. New York, Doubleday, 1977.

Play

The Bridge (in verse). New York, Dryden Press, 1945.

Novels

The Sunless Sea. London, Davies, 1948; New York, Dial Press, 1949.
The Refusers: An Epic of the Jews. New York, Horizon Press, 1981; part 3 published as *My Friend, My Father,* New York, Oxford University Press, 1986.

Other

A Short History of the Wheel Age. Pittsburgh, Folio Press, 1928.
André Spire and His Poetry: Two Essays and Forty Translations. Philadelphia, Centaur Press, 1933.
The Seamless Web: Language-Thinking, Creature-Knowledge, Art-Experience. New York, Braziller, and London, Allen Lane, 1970.
Robert Frost Himself. New York, Braziller, 1986.
A Stanley Burnshaw Reader. Athens, University of Georgia Press, 1990.

Editor, *Two New Yorkers* (Kruse lithographs and Kreymborg poems). New York, Bruce Humphries, 1938.
Editor, *The Poem Itself: 45 Modern Poets in a New Presentation.* New York, Holt Rinehart, 1960; London, Penguin, 1964; revised edition, New York, Simon and Schuster, 1989.
Editor, *Varieties of Literary Experience: Eighteen Essays in World Literature.* New York, New York University Press, 1962; London, Owen, 1963.
Editor, with T. Carmi and Ezra Spicehandler, *The Modern Hebrew Poem Itself, From the Beginnings to the Present: Sixty-Nine Poems in a New Presentation.* New York, Holt Rinehart, 1965; revised edition, Cambridge, Massachusetts, Harvard University Press, 1989.

*

Manuscript Collection: University of Texas, Austin.

Critical Studies: ''The Great Dark Love'' by André Spire, in *Mercure de France* (Paris), 1 December 1933; ''The Poem Itself'' by Lionel Trilling, in *The Mid-Century* (New York), August 1960; ''On Translating Poetry'' by Herbert Read, in *Poetry* (Chicago), April 1961; ''The Poet Is Always Present'' by Germaine Brée, in *The American Scholar* (Washington, D.C.), summer 1970; ''In the Terrified Radiance,'' in *New York Times Book Review,* 24 September 1972, and ''The Total Act: An Introduction to 'The Seamless Web,' by Stanley Burnshaw,'' in *Carrell* (Coral Gables, Florida), 28, 1990, both by James Dickey; Stanley Burnshaw issue of *Agenda* (London), winter-spring 1983–84; interview with Alan Filreis and Harvey Teres, in *Wallace Stevens Journal* (Potsdam, New York), 13(2), fall 1989; ''Stanley Burnshaw and the Body'' by Robert Zaller, in *Carrell* (Coral Gables, Florida), 28, 1990; ''Stanley Burnshaw: The New Masses Years'' by S.L. Harrison, in *Journal of American Culture* (Bowling Green, Ohio), 17(3), fall 1994.

Stanley Burnshaw comments:

Poetry is the expression of the creator's total organism, or, as I say at the beginning of *The Seamless Web,*

> Poetry begins with the body and ends with the body. Even Mallarmé's symbols of abstract essence lead back to the bones, flesh, and nerves. My approach, then is ''physiological,'' yet it issues from a vantage point different from Vico's when he said that all words originated in the eyes, the arms, and the other organs from which they were grown into analogies. My concern is rather with the type of creature-mind developed by the evolutionary shock which gave birth to what we have named self-consciousness. So far as we know, such biological change failed to arise in any other living creature. So far as we can tell, no other species, dead or alive, produced or produces the language-think of poetry. We are engaged, then, with a unique phenomenon issuing from a unique physiology which seems to function no differently from that of other animals—in a life-sustaining activity based on continuous interchange between organism and environment.

Poetry begins with the body and ends with the body. *The Seamless Web* pursues and confronts the implications of this statement from three different vantage points: (1) language-thinking, (2) creature-knowledge, (3) art-experience. The third (art-experience) offers the clearest introduction to my poetry, especially for the reader who has at hand a copy of my *Caged in an Animal's Mind* and *In the Terrified Radiance;* there are numerous references to the pages in that volume of my poems.

*   *   *

Writing of man's struggle through science and technology to master nature and the culmination of that struggle in the discovery and use of atomic power, Stanley Burnshaw says, ''The war against Nature had been confidently waged and won; and we post-moderns, of 1945-and-after, breathe the spirit of a different epoch, and we have a different terror on our minds: Now that man is victorious, how shall he stay alive?''

This question is a recurring one in his poems, as death, love, and life wage unceasing war, observed by a coal-hard intellect striving relentlessly to illuminate the world, ''this eden,'' through a sense of its kinship with the world of nature. In his long poetry-writing career, Burnshaw has remained contemporary, and in his view of the urgency of confronting man's imminent self-annihilation through the destruction of nature he is in agreement with many poets younger than himself. His collection *In the Terrified Radiance* gives us those parts of his earlier work he wants us to remember, and his oeuvre is made to seem remarkably of a piece. From the beginning he has filled his lyrics with stones, flames, wind, trees, singing, and blood, an imagery suggestive at times of Robinson Jeffers and at others of Theodore Roethke. In all of them, however, Burnshaw is distinctively, if somewhat monotonously and humorlessly, himself.

In Burnshaw's dense, hard-surfaced poems one encounters a harsh, relentless, and totally committed intelligence confronting the mind and senses with the inexorable facts of death and life. The effect is a seamless web (to borrow the title of his book about the physiological origins of the creative act) of images of storm, fire, growth, destruction, and the nourishment of creativity by the forces that destroy. These are not simply poems about the ''good that comes from evil'' or of the cyclical quality of nature; there is something much more elemental in their feeling of primordial unity. Burnshaw, in a paradox of cerebral style and physiological message—what he refers to as creature knowledge—seems a solemn shaman preserving his intellectual detachment while in an ecstasy of sympathy with the tides of being.

Mirages: Travel Notes in the Promised Land is a book-length poem in eight parts chronicling the poet's journey to Israel. He connects biblical events with modern history and modern-day Israel and both to his private life. His response to the turbulence and violence of the ancient and the modern land is to turn again to the body, to life, and to the transcendence of history:

> Since the only certainty is the body out of whose currents
> Clashing and blending,
> Fumes of knowledge may rise—quieting question—
> Leading us out of our nights
> Into untroubled wakefulness.

—Donald Barlow Stauffer

BURNSIDE, John

Nationality: Scottish. **Born:** Dunfermline, Fife, 19 March 1955. **Career:** Software engineer, Enterprise Systems, Thames Ditton, 1988–90; knowledge engineer, Syntelligence, Redhill, Surrey, 1990–94; self-employed, 1994–95; creative writing fellow, University of Dundee, 1995–98; poet in residence, Stirling University, 1999. Since 1999 writer-in-residence, University of St. Andrews, Scotland. **Awards:** Scottish Arts Council Book awards, 1988, 1991, 1995; Geoffrey Faber Memorial prize, 1994, for *Feast Days*.

PUBLICATIONS

Poetry

The Hoop. Manchester, Carcanet, 1988.
Common Knowledge. London, Secker and Warburg, 1991.
Feast Days. London, Secker and Warburg, 1992.
The Myth of the Twin. London, Jonathan Cape, 1994.
Swimming in the Flood. London, Jonathan Cape, 1995.
A Normal Skin. London, Jonathan Cape, 1997.
The Asylum Dance. London, Jonathan Cape, 2000.

Novels

The Dumb House. London, Jonathan Cape, 1997.
The Mercy Boys. London, Jonathan Cape, 1999.

Short Stories

Burning Elvis. London, Jonathan Cape, 2000.

*

Critical Studies: by Ian McMillan, in *Poetry Review,* 84(1), Spring 1994; ''Rencontre avec John Burnside'' by Francoise Abrial, in *Europe,* 75(817), 1997.

John Burnside comments:

I find it difficult to define my work or even to discuss it in the usual terms (e.g., influences). I have mostly written poetry to date, and while I admire many of my contemporaries, I usually look to them for the qualities I lack and would not claim to be ''influenced,'' any more than one is influenced by cinema, or music, or whatever. If pushed, I'd tend to define myself in the negative: that I do not belong to this or that group, that I do not share certain views or interests.

The concerns of my poetry: To begin with I was interested in the question of the real and with the ability of language to express the sense of the sacred, that area of experience that Wittgenstein refers to as the ''mystical'' (the fact of the world's existence). I was also much concerned with the natural world and the cycles of decay and regeneration. In recent work I have been concerned with ideas related to dwelling and to the exploration of just ways of being with others on this earth. What I dream about, and tentatively suggest, is an idea of community, continuity, and acceptance.

*   *   *

With the publication of John Burnside's first book, *The Hoop*, in 1988 it was evident that a new voice, an individual cadence and way of finding words for our perception of the universe, had entered English poetry. These lines are from his poem ''Inside'':

> Sometimes we feel the wind
> against a door; sometimes we speak
> of kinship with the dark, but never step
> beyond the patio, and night is best
> appreciated in this hoop of light
> where dripping is and everybody knows
> magic is somewhere else, where no one goes.

Since *The Hoop* other books have appeared, and with each collection I have a sense that the voltage is increasing. In contrast to the trivia, cleverness, and dull predictability of much current English poetry—emotion without intellect, fancy without imagination—Burnside's poems concern ''the mystery of things'' (to quote Shakespeare's Lear). As in ''Home,'' they express with beauty an interior journey, an attempt to understand our world:

> Like me, you sometimes waken
> early in the dark

thinking you have driven miles
through inward country,

feeling around you still
the streaming trees and startled waterfowl
and summered cattle
swinging through your headlamps.

The poems find words for perceptions "on the borders of language," and, as in "The Forest of Beguilement," they are radiant with mythologies and images from nature:

Nobody travels far, to see
the massed, snow-feathered twig-light
of the wood.

As Ezra Pound wrote, "Some men move in phantasmagoria; the images of their gods, whole countrysides, stretches of hill land and forest, travel with them." These words could have been written about Burnside; he is deeper than being just another pastoral poet. "Nature Poem," which is from his finest book, *The Myth of the Twin*, illustrates this and is short enough to quote entire:

The dark interior. But not the landscape
out beyond the fog

where others go,
and not the greenhouse with its dripping tap

and furred begonias,
but something that resembles both

and neither: a state of mind,
a sense of the mildew and fern

rankness in some corner of the soul
where wounds are healed,

a subtlety that lingers on the skin
through sleep or love, or when the hooded dead

reveal us all as shivers in the wind
gusted on woods and wheatfields after rain.

—William Cookson

BUSH, Duncan

Nationality: Welsh. **Born:** Cardiff, 6 April 1946. **Education:** University of Warwick, 1974–78, First Class Honors in English and European Literature 1978; Wadham College, Oxford, 1978–81. **Family:** Married Annette Jane Weaver in 1981; two sons. **Career:** Since 1984 director of writing program, Gwent College, Wales. **Awards:** Arts Council of Wales Poetry prize, 1984, for *Aquarium,* and 1986 for *Salt;* Arts Council of Wales Book of the Year award, 1995, for *Masks.* **Member:** Welsh Academy, 1982. **Address:** Godre Waun Oleu, Brecon Road, Ynyswen, Penycae, Powys SA9 1YY, Wales.

PUBLICATIONS

Poetry

Aquarium. Bridgend, Poetry Wales Press, 1983.
Salt. Bridgend, Poetry Wales Press, 1985.
Black Faces, Red Mouths. Ynyswen, Bedrock Press, 1986.
Masks. Bridgend, Seren, 1994.
The Hook. Bridgend, Seren, 1997.
Midway. Bridgend, Seren, 1998.

Plays

Cocktails for Three (produced Oxford, 1979).
Ends (produced Cardiff, 1980).
Sailing to America (produced Cardiff, 1982).

Radio Plays: *In the Pine Forest* (adapted from *The Genre of Silence*), 1991; *Are There Still Wolves in Pennsylvania?* (adapted from *Masks*), 1991.

Television Play: *Sailing to America,* 1992.

Novels

The Genre of Silence. Bridgend, Seren, 1988.
Glass Shot. London, Secker and Warburg, 1991.

*

Bibliography: *A Duncan Bush Bibliography* by Alain Sinner, Luxembourg, English Studies, 1994.

Critical Study: "Duncan Bush's Personae" by Richard Poole, in *Poetry Wales* (Bridgend), July 1992.

Theatrical Activities: Director and Actor: **Play**—His own *Cocktails for Three,* Oxford, 1979.

Duncan Bush comments:

Writing is finally like farming. You have a certain area of land of a certain soil type, and all you can hope is to work it all your life. For me this situation means, among other things, not growing potatoes on the same ground two years running. I write not only poetry but fiction and sometimes even drama, and I need to move between these genres. Occasionally they can be combined, as in my first novel, *The Genre of Silence,* which tells the story of a fictional poet in a dangerous time and includes the poems that outlast him. Or in my collection *Masks* there is a sequence of poems that depict a period of crisis in the relationship between a traumatized former soldier and his wife. When writing my second novel, *Glass Shot,* however, I did not write a poem for over a year. This did not worry me, on the principle already mentioned. It is only leaving one of your fields fallow for a season.

In poetry, though, as in prose, it is not how much land you farm. What counts is style, how you write. Yet the only guarantee in style is that the work come in some essential way out of the writer's own changing life or imagination or experience, out of that land you have available to work. Too many young writers start out imitating the style of others, and it is all too easy, so that the world even of published poetry is full of bad to middling, half-guilty pastiches. Good writing also has to be new each time you start and in some ways unpredictable even to its author, which is why so many established writers end up with the other fault, that of imitating themselves.

For me poetry is not merely a matter of running a leg in that old relay race known as influence or tradition. It is a matter of individual authenticity. To be genuinely of his or her day, a poet has to have the courage to be a renegade, a maverick. It is not a matter of postromantic or post-Freudian rebelliousness or anything as simple-minded as that. It is just that a good poet has a more acute critical intelligence and brings it to bear earlier and more radically in the creative process than a bad one. Perhaps this is why some of the poets I admire most are not ordinarily thought of as critics. In them, on the contrary, the critical process has already been subsumed wholesale into the production of a kind of poetry that is not only individually characteristic but decisively modern: Baudelaire and Dickinson, Rimbaud and Cavafy, Hardy and Rilke, Yeats and Owen, William Carlos Williams and Pavese, Plath and Pasolini . . . If these make what appears a set of unlikely combinations, it only enforces the point I am suggesting.

*   *   *

Duncan Bush's poems are memorable for their dramatic touch and for their engagement with issues typical of late twentieth- century post-industrial society. As Richard Poole has pointed out, even in some fairly early poems such as "Pneumoconiosis" Bush adopted the technique of writing through personae, a convenient way of widening his field of enquiry while conveying a sense of immediate experience without raising the suspicion of personal outpourings. The title of his collection *Masks* acknowledges the way he slips into or behind different personalities. Perceptiveness and empathy are equally developed whether his speakers are women or men. It is, for instance, through the farmer's widow and miner's daughter in the short sequence "Farmer's Widow, Tawe Valley" that he manages to express emotions at the destruction of loved places in a way he would probably have shied away from in his own voice. In lines such as

. . . a small black downward dune

of waste high on the valley's side:
the old deciduous woods decayed,
decayed and fallen buried
there, so much prehistory

there is a latent lyricism that contrasts with the detachment with which the death of a falcon is recorded in the next poem, which uses no mediating identified speaker:

it reduces
to a shuttlecock

of pinions
wind aflutter
at the kerbside

of a country road.
And what bears it off is this
long colony of ants.

One notable exception to Bush's dramatic impersonations or apparently unconcerned impersonality occurs in the three-part poem entitled "Coming Back." The piece is suffused with nostalgic sentimentality at his changed relation to his childhood surroundings:

And you
see that tree—long suffering

and safe, like an old horse—
is still tree, and boyhood
boyhood, while you've
changed more than the city.

Yet the emotions it conveys are deflated by the tongue-in-cheek epigraph by Baudelaire that points to changes in the city: "Le vieux Paris n'est plus (la forme d'une ville / Change plus vite, hélàs! que le coeur d'un mortel)."

Bush's impersonations include third-person presentations, as in "The News of Patroclus." Here Achilles, succeeding the Odysseus of his earlier "Ulysses Becalmed," is referred to in the third person, yet the depth of his grief and the danger that now looms upon him are conjured up from inside. The tolling repetition of the two-word sentence "He sat" conveys the numbness that follows the blow, and the opening image of "his silence [hissing] like gas / in the tent" has death lurking around him as it is introduced by "the messenger's apprehensive / useless, lamentory words." While suffering makes him feel invulnerable, he stoops on the way out of his tent to adjust "the loosened sandal at his heel of clay."

Bush's deftness at putting on other people's voices has not led him to full-blown drama. The closest he has come to writing for the stage is the sequence "Are There Still Wolves in Pennsylvania?" This work alternates the voices of a Vietnam War veteran, Wes Ball, and his wife, Linda. Although it was broadcast on BBC Radio 3, it is explicitly called "A poem sequence in ten parts for two voices" rather than a play, and the language used, while having a colloquial touch, is also unmistakably "literary," that is, sustained and economical, pruned and imaginative, in a way "real" speech rarely is. At one point, when Ball has gone alone into the woods on one of his ritual hunting trips, he wonders in the thick of the night whether there are any wolves left in Pennsylvania. The words he uses—"those evil yellow / slant eyes / / in the Disney movies"—combine the unreality of animated cartoons with Asian features that the American subconscious all too easily associates with some archetypal enemy. Toward the end of the same section the hunter remembers one of his awkward attempts at attracting a girl on the day he graduated, but

. . . she was already going
going gone, like all
the women went—water
from a too tense-clenched hand.

The image here is evocative but inaccurate. While the intensive "too tense" adds to the sense of desperation, water flows from a clenched hand whether the clenching is loose or tense. His wife is aggravated by his odd behavior, angered by his willful blindness, and repelled by his persistent need to kill, yet she understands his vulnerability. As he dreams again and again of the fleeing girl he shot dead, he also understands, without the help of "no Dr. Freud or / fucking V.A. shrink," that the horrors he participated in are with him for life and that war has its obdurate ground in male vanity:

```
. . . But
what makes me cry
is: what is it
in us that longs so

to bring down
a running thing,
as if to
just see if we can?
```

Husband and wife are in fact closer to each other than they are aware, and this is part of the poem's underlying irony. The couple have little access to the thoughts and emotions that are fully revealed to readers or listeners.

The Genre of Silence is a kind of writing that baffles classification. It offers a prose frame in the form of biographical information provided by an invented editor for a number of poems allegedly saved from the opus of "Victor Bal," an equally invented poet supposed to have been a Russian dissident. While Bush's novel *Glass Shot,* filled as it is with fantasies that are often close to an appalling reality, can be read as criticism of social absurdities, its best-selling mixture of sex and violence is likely to leave many readers thrilled rather than critically engaged.

The situation is rather different in Bush's many poems confronting contemporary issues directly. Whatever he may say about his not being a political poet, he is clearly aware of the public dimension of human life, even in its most private aspects, and he is committed to exposing the alarming effects on people's lives of widening dissociations. In uncollected poems such as "Café, Rainy Thursday Morning" or, more powerfully still, "August. Sunday. Gravesend" the emptiness and boredom of unemployment combined with very real deprivation lead to a fatal absence of perspective and from there to the lure of destruction for its own sake. "Old Master" elaborates the glossy lie of the painted Dutch winter landscape reproduced on expensive Christmas cards "(for the expensive / / friends)." The accuracy with which ice and snow are depicted suggests "warmth, like the first whisky's," and

```
. . . the rawness of
that wan and waning daylight
only sharpens,

as through a window, looking out,
vicarious and comfortable confirmation
of the Great Indoors . . .
```

But the use of parentheses in the last seven lines undermines the glow of complacency; too many are outside, looking in, sharing in the frustration of the stag faced with the frozen pond.

"Living in Real Time, Summer, 1993" is to me the most remarkable of these vignettes on the way we live. Written in response to the prolonged siege of Sarajevo (like Tony Curtis's poem "From the Hill, the Town"), the poem is less about the war in Bosnia than about the perverse effect of the false sense we have of being permanently and instantly informed. The speaker has stopped in front of the many screens in the window of a television shop in Cardiff's city center to watch "an over of the Trent Bridge test." Slackening interest from the uneven skills of bowler and batsman allows his eyes to slip "to the other channel banked in / other sets." We recognize the familiar view of some snipers' alley in one of those interchangeable

towns turned by civil war into repetitive infernos. The sequence itself—the man running, falling, dying, dead, keened over by "the usual crazed, cradling women"—is a replay ("I realise / I saw these shots two hours ago"). Through some ironic inversion the cricket match is broadcast "in real time," while death in Sarajevo is a repeat. The man will fall and die again and again: "Over and over. And forever / / and forever. No *Amen.*" But the cricket match too, with which the speaker obviously has a far more immediate connection, is ultimately made unreal: "post-modernism [propped up by adequate video techniques] makes all things present, all things post-reality." The last two lines do not apply only to those who watch cricket matches on television but to all of us, willingly turned into resigned spectators. We have opted out of life,

```
trained to the instant replay and the freezeframe:
to the destined fact, knowing there's no way out.
```

Significantly, the speaker here is not felt to be a persona. The "I" is a real "I." The result is that I too, as a reader, feel directly involved, not just in the helplessness but also in the protest implicit in the writing of these lines.

—Christine Pagnoulle

BUTLER, (Frederick) Guy

Nationality: South African. **Born:** Cradock, Cape Province, 21 January 1918. **Education:** Attended local high school; Rhodes University, Grahamstown, M.A. 1939; Brasenose College, Oxford, M.A. 1947. **Military Service:** South African Army in the Middle East, Italy, and the United Kingdom, 1940–45. **Family:** Married Jean Murray Satchwell in 1940; three sons and one daughter. **Career:** Lecturer in English, University of the Witwatersrand, Johannesburg, 1948–50. Professor of English, 1952–86, and since 1987 honorary research fellow, Rhodes University. English editor, *Standpunte,* 1952–54; editor, *New Coin,* 1964–74. Since 1960 advisory editor, *Contrast.* First president, Shakespeare Society of South Africa, 1985. **Awards:** CNA award, 1976; English Academy of Southern Africa Gold Medal, 1989; Lady Usher prize for literature, 1992. D.Litt.: University of Natal, Durban, 1970; University of the Witwatersrand, 1984; University of South Africa, Pretoria, 1989; Rhodes University, Grahamstown, 1994. Honorary Life President, English Academy of South Africa, 1983, Shakespeare Society of South Africa, 1991; Honorary Life Vice-Chairman of National Arts Festival Committee, 1993; Freedom of City of Grahamstown, 1994. **Address:** "High Corner," 122 High Street, Grahamstown 6140, South Africa.

PUBLICATIONS

Poetry

Stranger to Europe; Poems 1939–1949. Cape Town, Balkema, 1952; augmented edition, 1960.
South of the Zambezi: Poems from South Africa. London, Abelard Schuman, 1966.
On First Seeing Florence. Grahamstown, South Africa, New Coin-Rhodes University, 1968.

Selected Poems. Johannesburg, Donker, 1975; revised edition, 1989.
Songs and Ballads. Cape Town, David Philip, 1978.
Pilgrimage to Dias Cross. Cape Town, David Philip, 1987.
Collected Poems. Cape Town, David Philip, 1999.

Plays

The Dam (produced Cape Town, 1953). Cape Town Balkema, 1953.
The Dove Returns (produced Glencoe, Natal 1955). Cape Town, Balkema, and London, Fortune Press, 1956.
Take Root or Die (produced Grahamstown, 1966). Cape Town, Balkema, 1970.
Cape Charade (produced Grahamstown, 1967). Cape Town, Balkema, 1968.
Richard Gush of Salem (produced Grahamstown, 1970). Cape Town, Maskew Miller, 1982.
Demea (produced Grahamstown, 1990). Cape Town, David Philip, 1990.

Novel

A Rackety Colt, or The Adventures of Thomas Stubbs. Cape Town, Tafelberg, 1989.

Short Stories

Tales of the Old Karoo. Johannesburg, Donker, 1989.

Other

An Aspect of Tragedy. Grahamstown, Rhodes University, 1953.
The Republic of the Arts. Johannesburg, Witwatersrand University Press, 1964.
Karoo Morning: An Autobiography 1918–35. Cape Town, David Philip, 1977.
Bursting World: An Autobiography 1936–45. Cape Town, David Philip, 1983.
A Local Habitation: An Autobiography (1945–90). Cape Town, David Philip, 1991.
Guy Butler: Essays and Lectures (1949–1991). Cape Town, David Philip, 1994.
The Prophetic Nun, Lovers of Paint, Sculpture and People. Johannesburg, Random House, 2000.

Editor, *A Book of South African Verse.* London, Oxford University Press, 1959.
Editor, *When Boys Were Men.* Cape Town, Oxford University Press, 1969.
Editor, with Tim Peacock, *Plays from Near and Far: Twelve One-Act Plays.* Cape Town, Maskew Miller, 1973(?).
Editor, *The 1820 Settlers: An Illustrated Commentary.* Cape Town, Human and Rousseau, 1974.
Editor, with Christopher Mann, *A New Book of South African Verse in English.* Cape Town, Oxford University Press, 1979; Oxford, Oxford University Press, 1980.
Editor, with N. Visser, *The Re-Interment on Buffelskop: My Diary, 7–15 June 1921 and 8–29 August 1921* by S.C. Cronwright-Schreiner. Grahamstown, Rhodes University, 1983.

Editor, with David Butler, *Out of the African Ark.* Johannesburg, Donker, 1988.
Editor, with Jeff Opland, *The Magic Tree.* Cape Town, Longman, 1989.

*

Bibliography: In *Olive Schreiner and After: Essays on South African Literature in Honour of Guy Butler* edited by Malvern van Wyk Smith and Don Maclennan, Cape Town, David Philip, 1983; *Guy Butler: A Bibliography* by John Read, Grahamstown, South Africa, National English Literary Museum, 1992.

Manuscript Collection: Thomas Pringle Collection for English in Africa, Rhodes University, Grahamstown; National English Literary Museum, Grahamstown, South Africa.

Critical Studies: *Olive Schreiner and After: Essays on Southern African Literature in Honour of Guy Butler,* edited by Malvern van Wyk Smith and Don Maclennan, Cape Town, David Philip, 1983; "Ghost at a Window Pane: The War Poetry of Guy Butler" by Geoffrey Hutchings, in *English in Africa* (Grahamstown, South Africa), 15(2), October 1988; "Soliciting the Other: Interpenetration of the Psychological and the Political in Some Poems by Guy Butler" by Dirk Klopper, in *English in Africa* (Grahamstown, South Africa), 21(1–2), July 1994; "The Drama of Country and City: Tribalization, Urbanization and Theatre under Apartheid" by Loren Kruger, in *Journal of Southern African Studies,* 23(4), 1997.

Guy Butler comments:

(1990) Much of my poetry, but by no means all, is generated by the European-African encounter as experienced by someone of European descent who feels himself to belong to Africa. I am, I think, a product of the old, almost forgotten Eastern Cape frontier tradition, with its strong liberal and missionary admixture. The nature of the frontier has changed and spread, until all articulate men, but particularly artists, are frontiersmen and/or interpreters. English, as the chosen language of literature of millions of blacks, has a great and exciting future in Africa, and I have made it my life's business to encourage its creative use in this corner of the world.

(1995) From its inception I have been involved in the design and use of the 1820 Settlers National Monument in Grahamstown as a cultural and educational center. I organized the first festivals (1970–74). The Arts Festival is now regarded by many as the premier event in the South African cultural calendar.

*   *   *

Guy Butler's work is a sustained endeavor to distinguish and reconcile the two strains of Europe and Africa, chiefly, but not merely, in the southern part of the continent; to record and interpret the local scene; to find appropriate media in vocabulary, imagery, and forms through which to discover and express something of the African essence and primitive consciousness; to establish an African mythology and archetypes (Livingstone, Camoens, the last trekker); and to acclimatize as far as possible "the Grecian and Mediaeval dream." Orpheus has an "African incarnation" ("Myths"), and Apollo must come to "cross the tangled scrub, the uncouth ways" ("Home Thoughts") and join the Dionysian dance.

Africa almost becomes an image for a state of mind in which the poet's imagination tries to find dwelling and the human being strives to come to terms with himself, a testing ground for his beliefs and values. The inescapable preoccupation of the modern artist to find his place in his world is for the English poet in Africa, sensitive to European history, art, and thought, perhaps more dramatically evident than for his British counterpart. The struggle to articulate, clarify, harmonize, and balance contending forces and to be true to experience informs Butler's poetry with tension and some anguish and lifts it above trivialities. Circumstances tempt the South African writer to exploit rather than explore his material, to be self-conscious or self-pitying, to address too limited a home audience, or to slide into fashionable political or literary cant. Butler rarely succumbs.

T.S. Eliot observes of the genuine poet that "his strict duty is to his *language,* first to preserve, and second to extend and improve." Butler's responsible and experimental use of language is grounded in such an awareness of literary tradition. This leads him to genres other than the ubiquitous meditative lyric, to the ballad, song, sonnet, elegy, narrative, and metaphysical debate, in a variety of measures. He is particularly at home in the long poem, where he shows a not inconsiderable architectonic skill. Besides verse drama there is the seemingly casual free verse anecdote ("Sweet-Water") and the formal symphonic poem in fairly elaborate stanzas ("Bronze Heads"). With an understanding of neoclassic decorum, he uses a range of styles in prismatic or transparent language and in a speaking voice or singing roles. Sometimes regarded as an old-fashioned versifier playing safe, he is in fact often taking risks with rhyme, intricate verse and image patterns, colloquialisms, clichés, plain statements, or rhetorically splendid utterances. The long poem "On First Seeing Florence" is a complex structure of varied styles, rhythms, and images that eloquently presents a moment of vision.

Because of his readiness to undertake the hazardous and difficult, because of his range, breadth, and technical skill, and because he has something to say, Butler may be the most significant poet writing in South Africa. Others may reach greater heights in individual poems, but few can present a body of work that has such wholeness, complexity, variety, and approachability. Nor is his appeal merely local, though certain poems may have a particular poignancy for his countrymen. A lyric like "Stranger to Europe" or a meditation like "Myths" is read wherever poetry is recognized.

—Ruth Harnett

BUTLIN, Ron

Nationality: Scottish. **Born:** Edinburgh, 17 November 1949. **Education:** Dumfries Academy, 1960–66; University of Edinburgh, 1970–77, M.A. 1975, Dip.Ed. 1977. **Career:** Has worked as a footman, model, computer operator, security guard, laborer, and city messenger. Writer-in-residence, University of Edinburgh, 1982, 1985, and for Midlothian Region, 1989–90; Scottish/Canadian Exchange Writing fellow, University of New Brunswick, Fredericton, 1984–85, University of Stirling, 1993, and University of St. Andrews, 1998–99; Craigmillar Literacy Trust Instep Project, 1997–98. **Awards:** Scottish Arts Council bursary, 1977, 1987, and Book award, 1982, 1984, 1985, 1994, 1999. **Agent:** Mic Cheetham, 11–12 Dover Street, London W1X 3PH, England. **Address:** 7 West Newington Place, Edinburgh EH9 1QT, Scotland.

PUBLICATIONS

Poetry

Stretto. Edinburgh, Outlet Design Service, 1976.
Creatures Tamed by Cruelty. Edinburgh, University of Edinburgh Student Board, 1979.
Ragtime in Unfamiliar Bars. London, Secker and Warburg, 1985.
Histories of Desire. Newcastle upon Tyne, Bloodaxe, 1995.

Play

Blending In, adaptation of a play by Vinaver (produced Edinburgh, 1989).

Radio Play: *Blending In,* 1990.

Novels

The Sound of My Voice. Edinburgh, Canongate, 1987.
Night Visits. N.p., Scottish Cultural Press, 1997.

Short Stories

The Tilting Room. Edinburgh, Canongate, 1983.

Other

Editor, *Mauritian Voices.* N.p., Flambard Press, 1996.
Editor, *When We Jump We Jump High!* N.p., Craigmiller Literacy Trust, 1998.

Translator, with Kate Chevalier, *The Exquisite Instrument: Imitations from the Chinese.* Edinburgh, Salamander Press, 1982.

*

Critical Studies: "Metaphors for the Fall and Afterwards" by Colin Nicholson, in *The Weekend Scotsman* (Edinburgh), 15 June 1985; "Loneliness and Resurrection" by Andrew Sparrow, in *The Student* (Edinburgh), 17 April 1986; "Ron Butlin's Writing" by Nicholson, in *Cencrastus* (Edinburgh), 24, autumn 1986; "Lost Classic" by Irvine Welsh, in *New York Village Voice Literary Supplement* (New York City), spring 1997; "Ron Around" by Nicholab Royle, in *Time Out* (London), 2 September 1998.

Ron Butlin comments:

My work is my way of trying to get to grips with what is going on around me and inside me. It is my attempt to see and—hopefully—to feel, clearly. The demands that the craft of poetry makes upon me, that intimacy with the sound and weight of words, sharpen my sensitivity, I hope—and my eyesight! There are no "messages" in my work—if there is any message, it is all around us all the time, and, for me, trying to write poetry is my way of trying to read what is already written here.

*   *   *

An autobiographical myth informs Ron Butlin's poetry, and a convenient entry to his work is through the group of poems that closes his volume *Ragtime in Unfamiliar Bars.* Three of these poems, "The Colour of My Mother's Eyes," "Poem for My Father," and "My Grandfather Dreams Twice of Flanders," are incorporated from Butlin's first collection, *Creatures Tamed by Cruelty,* and together with three other poems written at different times over several years— "Inheritance," "Claiming My Inheritance," and "My Inheritance"— they allow us access to recurrent themes. In "Inheritance" an older self consoles his younger counterpart about the sense of loss caused by the crushing of birds' eggs in childhood. The poem ends with

> This is your inheritance:
> your fist clenched on yolk and broken shell,
> on fragments of an unfamiliar tense

and shows the child's entry into compromised and compromising time. To extend this theme, when "Claiming my Inheritance" ends, the sense of unease, "as if the present tense were happening too soon," is sharpened:

> The older I become the more
> I am aware of exile, of longing for—
> I clench my fist on nothing and hold on.

Not until *Ragtime*'s final poem, "My Inheritance," does "every tense / become a plaything we can share." And while the speaker is still left at one point to "cling . . . to my despair," developments within the structure of the poem directly affect the nature of this despair. The tenth anniversary of his father's death leads him to recall the absence of Odysseus, leaving his son Telemachus idle and his wife Penelope weaving and unweaving her tapestry for the same length of time. A mythic frame of reference enables Butlin to situate, distance, and so explore more fully his sense of origination, identity, and relationship. Within these extended parameters, a life becomes available for interpretation in different ways.

His collections show Butlin precariously but insistently coming to terms with his poetic self's corruption. In this perspective his writing has been sweated out of a personal experience that generates a painful iconography of loss and turmoil. A metaphoric fall from grace achieves biographical endorsement in a move from the country to the city. Although Butlin was born in Edinburgh, before his first birthday he was living in the village of Hightae on the coastal fringe of the southern uplands of Scotland. He grew up there until he left home at the age of sixteen and headed for London, a classic journey of separation, exile, and alienation for which the metaphor of the fall seems appropriate.

If that is the case, then in one aspect the poetry forges a paradigm of regeneration, since it is characterized as much by its altruistic expression of a world of sensuous pleasure—Butlin is also a love poet of grace and felicity—as it is by the private stress of his emotions. His first collection takes its title from a poem called "I Shall Show You Glittering Stones," which demonstrates an ability to generate public resonance from personal intensities:

> I shall tell you that the sky
> is the underbelly of a crouched animal,
> I shall tell you that it tunnelled once
> upon a time into the daylight,

and that it stayed there
> tense and afraid:
> —then we will become whatever our embrace
> can liken to ourselves

> and to that creature as it turns upon us.

Animal warmth and feral wariness form an uneasy dialectic, prefiguring the struggle of experience into expression that threatens the making even in the process of being made.

A determining continuity of image in the writing is a father figure of usually destabilizing, often threatening dimensions. "Time and again his dead hand reaches for mine," according to "Poem for My Father," and in "Two Landscapes: Father and Son," we read,

> My father becomes a forest without birdsong
> where sometimes the wind keens in the high branches:
> but down here where I am
> it is sunless and silent
> until he dies.

The figure haunts a life of writing, jeopardizing a secure sense of self, and in the reconstruction of that self through verbal artifact, a use of poetic inscription in a process of self-definition, history and personality interact. In this text, as the written reconstruction proceeds, and against the ruin that threatens his stable voice, he shores fragments from wherever they may be found. In its precise image of evanescence, sunlight playing to its own reflection through a phantasm of mist, the second part of "Two Landscapes" conjures the chimera of solution-dissolution-resolution that is a repeated concern in these poems: an insubstantiality endlessly caught and released in the moment of imagistic configuration.

Then, at a time that formed a watershed in his work, Butlin returned to the native strains of a Scots voice and inaugurated a different reintegration, a more radical relocation. In "The Wonnerful Warld O John Milton," Butlin's strategy is to mock with a jester's irreverence and to goad with the provocations of an Elizabethan fool. Autobiographical pressures and literary-historical precedent coincide, with Milton becoming the father to be circumscribed, the voice to be dumbfounded, as a Scots volubility mouths its dissent and utters its now mischievous, now philosophical opposition. The poem "Ootlins," in its sympathetic identification with the outcasts of Eden, already prepares us for a radically alternative moral promise, and in these tensions a distinctive voice makes itself felt:

> I canna conceive Milton's view o things withoot distress,
> fer ony man become a prince o his ain darkness
> wad blindly mak Paradise just fer hissel
> an mak each warld Milton's Hell.

Further evidence of Butlin's tactical deployment of writing as the self's conspectus comes in his collection of poems from the Chinese, *The Exquisite Instrument,* where he is able to examine an emotional world of loss and separation that is his existentially at the same time as it is subordinated within and distanced through the frame of an adopted empire of feeling. Freed from the encumbrance of immediacy, a greater clarity of utterance situates painful or desolate images within the medium of sympathetic sensibilities: "for these silent harmonies replace the clamour / and din of men's unhappiness.'' As the title poem implies, language suitably orchestrated promises self-transcendence:

> —But when this exquisite instrument is tuned,
> then I shall play howsoever I please
> upon its fifty strings.

—Colin Nicholson

C

CADDY, Caroline

Nationality: Australian. **Born:** Caroline Mavis Rumple, Perth, Western Australia, 20 January 1944. **Education:** Received high school diploma of dental nursing. **Family:** Married Daniel C. Caddy in 1965 (died 1972); one son and one daughter. **Career:** Dental nurse, Perth, 1960–65. Since 1965 self-employed in farming, teaching writing workshops, and working at clerical jobs. **Awards:** Western Australian Literary Week award, 1991, for *Beach Plastic;* National Book Council Banjo Patterson award, and Phillips Fox Turnbull award, 1992, for *Conquistadors.* **Address:** 709/34 Wentworth Street, Glebe, New South Wales 2037, Australia.

PUBLICATIONS

Poetry

Singing at Night. Perth, Fremantle Arts Centre Press, 1981.
Letters from the North. Perth, Fremantle Arts Centre Press, 1984.
Beach Plastic. Perth, Fremantle Arts Centre Press, 1990.
Conquistadors. Perth, Penguin Australia, 1991.
Bushnights: Poems & Photos. Beaumaris, Victoria, Lichtbild, 1994.
Antarctica: Poems. South Fremantle, Western Australia, Fremantle Arts Centre Press, 1996.
Working Temple: Poems. South Fremantle, Western Australia, Fremantle Arts Centre Press, 1997.
Editing the Moon. Fremantle, Western Australia, Fremantle Arts Centre Press, 1999.

*

Caroline Caddy comments:

My need to be able to read my work aloud to my own satisfaction was a big impetus to my development as a poet. Although I knew I had achieved the poem on the page, I felt it was not complete unless I could read to an audience and have my voice come off the page, the script to translate truly into sound. It was not till I had begun to work in the form and pacing of my later books, *Beach Plastic* being transitional, that I felt able to ''voice'' my poetry.

Some of my later poems, especially in *Conquistadors,* have been seen by critics as obscure or difficult. I believe that the imagery used should not be private to the poet and aim in my work for the universal or the universal embedded in the idiosyncratic. No, no, I hear you say, not the dreaded word ''symbol.'' Sometimes I feel I am trying to steer my poetry around the dreaded word and come up with a silhouette of sight, smell, and touch like those popular 3-D pictures that you have to go into a brown study to see.

My latest books, drawn from time spent in Antarctica and China, are more easily accessed, with many of the poems close to what I would call lyric essays.

*   *   *

The Western Australian poet Caroline Caddy has had a slow rise to national visibility. This is perhaps partly owing to a childhood spent in the United States and to country jobs and a country address in Australia since then.

Singing at Night announces Caddy's interest in different traditions (Japanese, Chinese, Tarzan after the jungle) and her tendency to look for a structure, a larger grouping (the title sequence of eight poems). Although ''The Lions of Ghir'' is perhaps the best early poem, the short poem ''Rain,'' with its flexible phrasing and scattered layout between the two margins of the column of print, points the way to her later work.

Caddy finds voices in *Letters from the North.* The title sequence, about the rough life of mining workers and the isolation of their families in corporation towns of the northwestern Australian desert, consists of the abrupt, sometimes banal remarks—verbal jottings—of a colloquial voice. Another sequence, ''A Member of the Tribe,'' sketches seven deprived lives as monologue ''testaments'' in the mode of Edgar Lee Masters's *Spoon River Anthology.* The distance between the dialect of the North Americans of Masters's work and the Australian voices of Caddy's sequence is an impressive measure of her skill.

Beach Plastic, like all of Caddy's books spanning a wide range of interests, is nonetheless keyed to her knowledge of bushland and of the coast of southwestern Australia. In this book she definitively claims the constraints and liberties of the columnar poem: both margins are justified, and both long and short lines are placed within the column, with some free at either end and others stayed at the margin. In her early work Caddy insisted on the exact placing of the lines and letters to conform with her typescript, to the point of demanding a typewriter font, for its equal letter spaces, in her fourth book.

Not just the form she has developed but also a restless ingenuity with language guarantee the energy of Caddy's voice, as in ''Fire 3'':

Down one side of the house
piston backs hoe a wall of flame
while I
filling buckets and can't helping it
make aghast in my own head
lines of poetry
Now I've had it!
Three trees fall at my presumption.
Away from the house! Who's got who licked.
Negative negative We have lift-off
and the whole hill erupts
phlogists our backs our necks—
shoulders imp with ash-sting
and the sun
IS GONE . . .
Oh Wiz Oh Witcher hear me cry
with everybody
bring back the light!
no! no! not this that . . .
–the Heavenly Disc–(whispered).

Doctrine, desire, and the powers in one's life occupy Caddy in several of the poems of *Conquistadors,* winner of the Phillips Fox Turnbull national award for poetry. Her travels to Antarctica and China are reflected in three later collections, *Antarctica* (1996), *Working Temple* (1997), and *Editing the Moon* (1999).

Despite the verbal and vocal virtuosity of Caddy's work and despite her effectiveness as a reader, she is rarely scheduled to perform. Her writing, too, may seem arcane if the reader opens it with the idea of merely being entertained. She is a poet with ambitious projects whose time is perhaps yet to come. Quite apart from the riches of what Caddy observes and has to say, her stubborn labor to control her own responsive form will not go out of fashion and has remained a defining point in her work.

—Judith Rodriguez

CALLAGHAN, Barry

Nationality: Canadian. **Born:** Toronto, Ontario, 5 July 1937. **Education:** St. Michael's College School, Toronto; Assumption University, Windsor, Ontario, 1957–58; University of Toronto, B.A. 1961, M.A. 1963. **Family:** Married Nina Ann Rabchuck in 1965 (separated 1969); one son. **Career:** Teaching fellow, University of Toronto, 1960–64. Since 1965 professor, York University, Toronto. Literary critic, "Umbrella" program, 1964–66, co-host, "The Public Eye," 1966–68, senior producer of current affairs, 1967–71, and war correspondent in Lebanon and Jordan, 1969–71, all Canadian Broadcasting Corporation Television; war correspondent in Rhodesia and South Africa, 1976, Villon Films. Co-owner, Villon Films, 1972–76. Critic of contemporary affairs, CTV network, 1976–82; host of dramatized novels series, OECA-TV, 1977. Literary editor, Toronto *Telegram,* 1966–71; since 1972 founder and publisher, *Exile* magazine, and since 1976 publisher, Exile Editions, both Toronto. Contributing editor, 1978–90, *Toronto Life Magazine.* Artist. Individual shows: Isaacs Gallery, Toronto, 1978; Carleton University Gallery, Ottawa, 1998. **Awards:** Prix Italia, 1977; National Magazine award, 1977, 1978, 1979, 1980, 1983, 1984, 1985, 1988; National Magazine Award President's Medal, for excellence in journalism, 1982, 1985, 1988; CBC fiction award, 1985; Canadian Periodical Publishers award, for fiction, 1986; Ontario Arts Council award, 1987; White award, for journalism, 1988; Toronto Arts Foundation award, 1993; inaugural W.O. Mitchell award, 1998. LL. D.: State University of New York at Buffalo, 1999. **Address:** 20 Dale Avenue, Toronto, Ontario M4W 1K4, Canada.

PUBLICATIONS

Poetry

The Hogg Poems and Drawings. Don Mills, Ontario, General, 1978.
As Close As We Came. Toronto, Exile, 1982.
Stone Blind Love. Toronto, Exile, 1988.
Hogg: The Poems and Drawings. Toronto, McArthur and Company, 1998.

Novels

The Way the Angel Spreads Her Wings. Toronto, Lester and Orpen Dennys, 1989; Toronto, Little, Brown, 1995.
When Things Get Worst. Toronto, Little Brown, 1993.

Short Stories

The Black Queen Stories. Toronto, Lester and Orpen Dennys, and Princeton, New Jersey, Ontario Review Press, 1982.
A Kiss Is Still a Kiss. Toronto, McArthur and Company, 1997.

Other

Barrelhouse Kings. Toronto, McArthur and Company, 1998.

Editor, *Sights and Sounds: The Poetry of W.W.E. Ross.* Toronto, Longuans, 1966.
Editor, *The Selected Poems of Frank Prewett.* Toronto, Exile, 1982.
Editor, *Lords of Winter and of Love: A Book of Canadian Love Poems in English and French.* Toronto, Exile, 1983.
Editor, *Canadian Travellers in Italy.* Toronto, Exile, 1989.
Editor, *Exile: The First Fifteen Years,* three volumes. Toronto, Exile, 1992.
Editor, with David Lampe, *An Occasion of Sin: Stories by John Montague.* Buffalo, New York, White Pine Press, 1992.
Editor, with Margaret Atwood, *The Selected Poems of Gwendolyn MacEwen,* two volumes. Toronto, Exile, 1995.
Editor, *This Ain't No Healing Town: Toronto Stories.* Toronto, Exile, 1995.
Editor, *The Annesley Drawings.* Toronto, Exile, 1999.

Translator, *Atlante* by Robert Marteau. Toronto, Exile, 1979.
Translator, *Treatise on White and Tincture* by Robert Marteau. Toronto, Exile, 1979.
Translator, *Interlude* by Robert Marteau. Toronto, Exile, 1982.
Translator, *Singing at the Whirlpool and Other Poems* by Miodrag Pavlovic. Toronto, Exile, 1983.
Translator, *A Voice Locked in Stone* by Miodrag Pavlovic. Toronto, Exile, 1985.
Translator, *Fragile Moments* by Jacques Brault. Toronto, Exile, 1986.
Translator, *Flowers of Ice: Selected Poems* by Imants Ziedonis. Toronto, Exile, 1987; New York, Sheep Meadow Press, 1990.
Translator, with Ray Ellenwood, *Wells of Light: Selected Poems by Fernand Ouellette.* Toronto, Exile, 1989.
Translator, *Eidolon,* by Robert Marteau. Toronto, Exile, 1992.

*   *   *

Barry Callaghan has a diverse literary talent as poet, prose writer, and editor of *Exile,* one of the most inventive literary magazines of the age, perhaps the only one to rival the pioneer efforts of the 1920s. Behind such activity there lies a central thrust of energy. Callaghan is a big man who likes many things—traveling, gambling, listening to the blues, pushing the work of writers and artists he admires. He is like a Canadian Diaghilev.

Callaghan's own work gleams like the sun dancing on his native ice but also like an exotic reaction to seasonal claustrophobia. Like the character in *The Waste Land,* he "reads much of the night and goes south in the winter." But this is the surface texture. Beneath is a major theme, an odyssey in search of love and meaning that leads to strange places, as in his work in which a leper colony in Africa is illuminated with the self-denying light of sacrifice.

In *The Hogg Poems* the protagonist leaves "this land of eelgrass / and icedrifts and snow" to go to the many-layered city of Jerusalem, where he falls in love. The baroque rhetoric of "their days of"

undress and incantation
when love swung through the air
like a great bell and he sought
the shape of singularity

made the Hogg poems an astonishing debut. Except for a few poems by Margaret Atwood on love and survival, I cannot easily find anything like it in Canadian literature. One turns for comparison to sequences like *Crow,* by the English poet Ted Hughes, or the American poet Galway Kinnell's *The Book of Nightmares.*

Hurt by silence into a series of strange Bosch-like drawings, Hogg returns to his old stomping ground, Toronto's underworld. The basis of Callaghan's aesthetic is jazz, but his riffs are colored by a knowledge of literature, both biblical and modern. The blend of the blues and the Browningesque make "Judas Priest" and "John the Conqueroo" tours de force in two traditions. Other poems reach toward ritual, amulets, incantations, and hymns from the book of Hogg. *As Close As We Came* brings us into the frozen heart of eastern Europe. (People tend to forget that Russia and Canada are the two coldest and largest countries in the world.) Ice also begins this book, thawed a little by the presence of a Russian muse. Again, the poems are shaped like canticles of praise or invocations against evil, hesitating between the stolen embrace and the official silence:

We rose tight-lipped
as police in grey mutton hats thumbed
our papers.

Around this time Callaghan began to translate the dense lyrics of the French alchemist-poet Robert Marteu from the Charente. Thus, his third volume, *Stone Blind Love,* is another poem cycle on the search for love, but through the unlikely substance of stone pictured in a surrealism as strange as Chagall:

Stones, like horses, hunger for women
and sprout wings
They stamp their moon-faced hoofs.

—John Montague

CAMPBELL, Alistair (Te Ariki)

Nationality: New Zealander. **Born:** Rarotonga, Cook Islands, 25 June 1925; immigrated to New Zealand in 1933. **Education:** Anderson's Bay School, 1933–39; Otago Boys' High School, Dunedin, 1940–43; University of Otago, 1944; Victoria University, Wellington, 1945–47, 1951–52, B.A. in Latin and English; Wellington Teachers College, diploma in teaching. **Family:** Married 1) Fleur Adcock, *q.v.,* in 1952 (divorced 1957), two sons; 2) Meg Andersen in 1958, one son and two daughters. **Career:** Staff member, Health Department Records Office, Wellington, 1944; gardener, Mowai Red Cross Hospital, Wellington, 1948–49; teacher, Newtown Primary School, 1954; editor, Department of Education School Publications Branch, Wellington, 1955–72; senior editor, New Zealand Council for Educational Research, Wellington, 1972–87. Poetry consultant, writer's workshop, University of South Pacific, Suva, 1974, and Lautoka, Fiji, 1980; president, P.E.N. New Zealand Centre, 1976–79; guest writer, Adelaide International Festival of the Arts, 1978. **Awards:** La Spezia Film Festival Gold Medal, 1974; New Zealand Book award, 1982; President of Honour, P.E.N. New Zealand Centre, 1989; Arts Council Scholarship in Letters, 1990; Writer's Fellow, Victoria University, 1992; Pacific Islands Artist award, 1998. D.Litt.: Victoria University of Wellington, 1999. **Address:** 4B Rawhiti Road, Pukerua Bay, Wellington, New Zealand.

PUBLICATIONS

Poetry

Mine Eyes Dazzle: Poems 1947–49. Christchurch, Pegasus Press, 1950; revised edition, 1951, 1956.
Wild Honey. London, Oxford University Press, 1964.
Blue Rain. Wellington, Wai-te-ata Press, 1967.
Drinking Horn. Paremata, Bottle Press, 1970.
Walk the Black Path. Paremata, Bottle Press, 1971.
Kapiti: Selected Poems 1947–71. Christchurch, Pegasus Press, 1972.
Dreams, Yellow Lions. Waiura, Alister Taylor, 1975.
The Dark Lord of Savaiki. Pukerua Bay, Te Kotare Press, 1980.
Collected Poems 1947–1981. Martinborough, Alister Taylor, 1981.
Soul Traps: A Lyric Sequence. Pukerua Bay, Te Kotare Press, 1985.
Stone Rain: The Polynesian Strain. Christchurch, Hazard Press, 1992.
Death and the Tagua. Wellington, Wai-te-ata Press, 1995.
Pocket Collected Poems. Christchurch, Hazard Press, 1996.
Gallipoli and Other Poems. Wellington, Wai-te-ata Press, 1999.

Recording: *The Return and Elegy,* Kiwi.

Plays

Sanctuary of Spirits (broadcast, 1963). Wellington, Victoria University-Wai-te-ata Press, 1963.
The Suicide (broadcast, 1965). Published in *Landfall 112* (Christchurch), 1974.
When the Bough Breaks (produced Wellington, 1970). Published in *Contemporary New Zealand Plays,* edited by Howard McNaughton, Wellington, Oxford University Press, 1974.

Radio Plays: *Sanctuary of Spirits,* 1963; *The Homecoming,* 1964; *The Proprietor,* 1964; *The Suicide,* 1965; *Death of the Colonel,* 1966; *The Wairau Incident,* 1967.

Television Documentaries: *Island of Spirits,* 1973; *Like You I'm Trapped,* 1975.

Novels

The Frigate Bird. Auckland, Heinemann Reed, and London, Methuen, 1989.
Sidewinder. Auckland, Reed Books, 1991.
Tia. Auckland, Reed Books, 1993.
Fantasy with Witches. Christchurch, Hazard Press, 1998.

Other

The Fruit Farm (for children). Wellington, School Publications Branch, 1953.
The Happy Summer (for children). Christchurch, Whitecomb and Tombs, 1961.
New Zealand: A Book for Children. Wellington, School Publications Branch, 1967.
Maori Legends. Wellington, Seven Seas, 1969.
Island to Island (memoirs). Christchurch, Whitcoulls, 1984.

*

Manuscript Collections: University of Canterbury, Christchurch; Alexander Turnbull Library, National Library, Wellington; Archives, Library, Victoria University of Wellington.

Critical Studies: By James Bertram, in *Comment* (Wellington), January-February 1965; ''Alistair Campbell's *Mine Eyes Dazzle:* An Anatomy of Success'' by David Gunby, in *Landfall* (Christchurch), March 1969; ''Alistair Campbell's *Sanctuary of Spirits:* The Historical and Cultural Context'' by F.M. McKay, in *Landfall* (Christchurch), June 1978; *Introducing Alistair Campbell* by Peter Smart, Auckland, Longman Paul, 1982; ''The Polynesian Voice'' by K.O. Arvidson, in *The Reviews Journal* (Flinders University of South Australia), 1993; ''Linguistics, Philology, Chickens and Eggs'' by Richard Hogg, in *English Historical Linguistics 1992,* edited by Francisco Fermandez, Miguel Fuster, and Juan Jose Calvo, Amsterdam, Benjamins, 1994.

Alistair Campbell comments:

When I began writing verse, like many other poets I came under the influence of W.B. Yeats and, later, Ezra Pound. Then I learned from certain Spanish, like Lorca, and Latin American poets, like Neruda, to write directly about my feelings. From American poets like James Wright, whose verse I considered attractive and fresh, I learned to loosen my lines and write simple, evocative lyrics drawing on the richness of the natural world.

Later I went to Maori history and my own family genealogy and traditions for Polynesian myths and legends that provided me with imagery for my personally charged dramatic lyrics, which are among my best work. In my family poems I explore the more painful aspects of my childhood and later family life. These are simple, straightforward poems written in gently paced blank verse. They are inward looking, owing little to outside influences.

More recently I have written contrasting lyric sequences, the first, ''Gallipoli,'' on the disastrous campaign of 1915, in which I explore themes of violence, courage, comradeship, and folly in a classical setting, with overtones of the Trojan War. In the second sequence, ''Cages for the Wind,'' the violence of war gives way to peace and quiet. I write about love for my wife, for our wind-swept landscape and the creatures we share it with. These are poems of old age, observed with humor, affection, and tolerance but with an underlying awareness of the darker side of things.

*   *   *

Since his seventieth birthday in 1995, three major books have revived and redefined Alistair Te Ariki Campbell as a poet. The valedictory *Death and the Tagua* (1995), filled with retrospection and images of departure, is an address to the poet's lost family that weaves personative, narrative, and Polynesian elements into a resonant lyricism new even for this subtle master of word music. The *Pocket Collected Poems* (1996) gives summative shape to a body of work that has always been profoundly personal, and often deeply painful, while also highlighting the sustained Polynesian strain that is now made evident even in the early poems. His extraordinary continuing development is then shown in *Gallipoli and Other Poems* (1999). Here two sequences, one of war and the other of love, confirm a wholly contemporary mastery of flexible lyricism, wit, and conversational comedy as well as a courage that is now rare in New Zealand poetry to tackle big themes: history, tragedy, age, passion, loss.

Campbell (he first elected to use his full name in 1992) was born on Rarotonga, one of the Cook Islands, of a Scottish father, an accountant turned Pacific trader after the trauma of Gallipoli and the Somme, and the daughter of a Rarotonga elder. Both parents died before he was eight, and Campbell was educated in New Zealand, growing up as an orphan and exile and learning a new language and culture. The rich magic of English verse became his talisman, and his own poems were to seek compulsively for ideal and timeless love, to reconcile the inevitability of loss with ''impossible yearnings'' across seas that ''stretch / quivering with dreams / towards ever-receding / landfalls.''

From the outset, Campbell was an elegiac poet of extraordinary force. Loss sounds through early poems such as ''Lament,'' ''Fragment,'' and the well-known ''Elegy'' sequence of 1948–49 and on through ''Personal Sonnets'' and ''Elegy for Anzac Day'' to ''Death and the *Tagua.*'' Even the most ecstatic or erotic outbursts (and Campbell does both well) take added intensity from the threat or fear of loss. Vitality in counterpoint with mortality gives power to poems from the early ''August'' to the late ''Wairaka Rock.'' ''Blue Rain'' is perhaps its finest rendering, with its lovers ''merry as thieves'' who have nothing to fear but collapse and ruin. Even the rich coloring of ''Love Song for Meg'' is tinged for a moment by the ''dull silver / of decaying trees.'' Through ecstasy there is always the glimpse of grief.

Campbell has often been called an ''animistic'' poet, and key poems like ''The Return'' indeed have an almost instinctual appeal, a *duende* drawn from a rare mythopoeic power. Although he is deeply read, Campbell uses nothing ready-made. A mythology's gods may become the poet's demons, and the Greek, Polynesian, and other myths are reforged in the smithy of his own often tortured soul. Thus animism and celebrations of love and landscape are intercut with mortality and loss. Even in ''The Return'' the hulks are spent, Dionysus drowned, the fires gone out, and the mist moving over the land.

Poems of Campbell's midcareer, grouped in the *Collected Poems* as ''Personal Sonnets,'' make some autobiographical matters explicit. Full of unresolved questions and images of wrenching loss, they date from a period of psychiatric treatment and belong with the agonized conflicts and self-castigation of the poet's radio plays. The same tortured psyche, crying for exorcism or extinction, then produced the landmark ''Sanctuary of Spirits'' and other conjurings of the destructive spirit of the Maori warlord Te Rauparaha. Poems from the later 1960s through the 1980s brought a change from psychic rage to a more poignant or sorrowful mood, while also showing a more versatile talent than before. Their tone varies from rapturous to wry, from satiric to sexy, and the craft encompasses poignant wordplay in ''Reflections on the Verb 'To Be,''' evocative minimalism in ''Dream, Yellow Lions,'' and the impeccably modulated long line of ''That Thing.'' While Campbell is always lyric, his poems are also dynamic and dramatic. They are not just songs; they move. Ecstasy verges into loss, the door closes, the bittern booms, the earth tilts, the child who might have been lost comes "Home from Hospital."

A pilgrimage to Tongareva (Penrhyn) in 1979 released Campbell's Polynesian self openly into his work, which now includes autobiography and Polynesian novels as well as poems that have drawn on Tongarevan myths and ancestral chants. (They also draw on Latin American and Spanish poetry, for Campbell is never facile.) His later poems inscribe the South Pacific in image after image of a wholly distinctive vividness: "The trade winds / are your fingers / on my eyelids," or "atolls in their green birth / pricking the white horizon." Because such images are known from within, they can have wit: "Who but a goofy goddess / could scatter pebbles / all over the Pacific / and call them land?" They also have cruelty and darkness, as in the "Dark Lord of Savaiki" sequence, in which nine painful poems must be endured before the final cathartic image: "Father and mother / walking hand in hand / across the swirling waters / of Taruia Passage, / where the leaping dolphins / celebrate the dawn." We recognize now how often, even in the early poems, Campbell has been making the effort to record such fundamental Polynesian images as the sound of the Pacific shore, the encounter of ocean with land, "the surf-loud beach."

From his first collection, *Mine Eyes Dazzle* (1950), Campbell's charismatic voice has won an unusually broad range of admirers. Although he is still excluded from some academic orthodoxies, he gets substantial treatment in the *Oxford Companion to New Zealand Literature* (1998). He is that rare kind of writer who may seem superficially conventional while responding to a deeper originality and more finely attuned sense of the time. (One thinks, for example, of Hardy.) The lyric, resonant, and now identifiably Polynesian strain in Campbell's voice, from "Lament" and "The Return" to "Tongareva" and "Gift of Dreams," may prove more central than the fashions of cerebral and ludic sparseness and at the least provide a wholly distinctive pleasure to the ear and inward eye.

—Roger Robinson

CARRUTH, Hayden

Nationality: American. **Born:** Waterbury, Connecticut, 3 August 1921. **Education:** University of North Carolina, Chapel Hill, B.A. 1943; University of Chicago, M.A. 1947. **Military Service:** U.S. Army Air Corps during World War II. **Family:** Married 1) Sara Anderson in 1943, one daughter; 2) Eleanore Ray in 1952; 3) Rose Marie Dorn in 1961, one son; 4) Joe-Anne McLaughlin in 1989. **Career:** Editor, *Poetry,* Chicago, 1949–50; associate editor, University of Chicago Press, 1950–51, and Intercultural Publications Inc., New York, 1952–53. Visiting professor, Johnson State College, Vermont, 1972–74, University of Vermont, Burlington, 1975–78, and St. Michael's College, Winooski, Vermont, 1978–79; professor of English, Syracuse University, New York, 1979–84 and 1986–91, and Bucknell University, 1985–86. Poetry editor, *Harper's,* New York, 1977–82. Member of the editorial board, *Hudson Review,* New York, 1971—. **Awards:** Vachel Lindsay prize, 1954, Bess Hopkin prize, 1956, Levinson prize, 1958, Eunice Tietjens memorial prize, and Morton Dauwen Zabel prize, 1968 (*Poetry,* Chicago); Harriet

Monroe award, 1960; Bollingen fellowship, 1962; Carl Sandburg prize, 1963; Emily Clark Balch prize (*Virginia Quarterly Review*), 1964; Guggenheim fellowship, 1965, 1979; National Endowment for the Arts grant, 1967, 1968, 1974, 1984, fellowship, 1988; Shelley memorial award, 1978; Lenore Marshall prize, 1979; Whiting Foundation award, 1986; Ruth Lily prize, 1990; National Book Critics' Circle award for poetry, 1993; Poetry Center prize, Passaic County Community College, 1995; Lannan Foundation award, 1995; National Book award for poetry, 1996. **Address:** RD 1, Box 128, Munnsville, New York 13409, U.S.A.

PUBLICATIONS

Poetry

The Crow and the Heart, 1946–1959. New York, Macmillan, 1959.
In Memoriam: G.V.C. Privately printed, 1960.
Journey to a Known Place. New York, New Directions, 1961.
The Norfolk Poems, 1 June to 1 September 1961. Iowa City, Prairie Press, 1962.
North Winter. Iowa City, Prairie Press, 1964.
Nothing for Tigers: Poems 1959–64. New York, Macmillan, 1965.
Contra Mortem. Johnson, Vermont, Crow's Mark Press, 1967.
For You. New York, New Directions, 1970; London, Chatto and Windus, 1972.
The Clay Hill Anthology. Iowa City, Prairie Press, 1970.
From Snow and Rock, From Chaos: Poems 1965–1972. New York, New Directions, and London, Chatto and Windus, 1973.
Dark World. Santa Cruz, California, Kayak, 1974.
The Bloomingdale Papers. Athens, University of Georgia Press, 1974.
Loneliness: An Outburst of Hexasyllables. West Burke, Vermont, Janus Press, 1976.
Aura. West Burke, Vermont, Janus Press, 1977.
Brothers, I Loved You All. New York, Sheep Meadow Press, 1978.
Almanach du Printemps Vivarois. New York, Nadja, 1979.
The Sleeping Beauty. New York, Harper, 1982; revised edition, Port Townsend, Washington, Copper Canyon, 1990.
The Mythology of Dark and Light. Syracuse, New York, Tamarack, 1982.
If You Call This Cry a Song. Woodstock, Vermont, Countryman Press, 1983.
Asphalt Georgics. New York, New Directions, 1985.
Mother. Syracuse, New York, Tamarack Press, 1985.
The Oldest Killed Lake in North America: Poems 1979–1981. Grenada, Mississippi, Salt-Works Press, 1985.
Lighter than Aircraft. Lewisburg, Pennsylvania, Bucknell University, 1985.
The Selected Poetry of Hayden Carruth. New York, Macmillan, and London, Macmillan, 1985.
Tell Me Again How the White Heron Rises and Flies across the Nacreous River at Twilight toward the Distant Islands. New York, New Directions, 1989.
Sonnets. Lewisburg, Pennsylvania, Press of Appletree Alley, 1989.
Collected Shorter Poems. Port Townsend, Washington, Copper Canyon, 1992.
Collected Longer Poems. Port Townsend, Washington, Copper Canyon, 1994.

A Summer with Tu Fu. N.p., Brooding Heron Press, 1996.
Scrambled Eggs & Whiskey, Poems 1991–1995. Port Townsend,
   Washington, Copper Canyon, 1996.

Recording: *Eternity Blues,* Watershed, 1987.

Novel

Appendix A. New York, Macmillan, 1963.

Other

After "The Stranger": Imaginary Dialogues with Camus. New York,
   Macmillan, 1965.
Working Papers: Selected Essays and Reviews, edited by Judith
   Weissman. Athens, University of Georgia Press, 1982.
*Effluences from the Sacred Caves: More Selected Essays and Re-
   views.* Ann Arbor, University of Michigan Press, 1983.
Sitting In: Selected Writings of Jazz, Blues, and Related Topics. Iowa
   City, University of Iowa Press, 1986; revised edition, 1994.
Suicides and Jazzers. Ann Arbor, University of Michigan Press,
   1992.
Selected Essays & Reviews. Port Townsend, Washington, Copper
   Canyon, 1996.
Reluctantly, Autobiographical Essays. Port Townsend, Washington,
   Copper Canyon, 1998.
Beside the Shadblow Tree: A Memoir of James Laughlin. Port
   Townsend, Washington, Copper Canyon, 1999.

Editor, with James Laughlin, *A New Directions Reader.* New York,
   New Directions, 1964.
Editor, *The Voice That Is Great within Us: American Poetry of the
   Twentieth Century.* New York, Bantam, 1970.
Editor, *The Bird/Poem Book: Poems on the Wild Birds of North
   America.* New York, McCall, 1970.

*

Manuscript Collection: Guy W. Bailey Library, University of
Vermont, Burlington.

Critical Studies: "The Real and Only Sanity" by Geoffrey Gardner,
in *American Poetry Review* (Philadelphia), January-February 1981;
"The Odyssey of Hayden Carruth" by R.W. Flint, in *Parnassus*
(New York), summer 1984; Hayden Carruth issue of *Seneca Review*
(Geneva, New York), 19(1), spring 1990; *Existentialism and New
England: The Poetry and Criticism of Hayden Carruth* (dissertation)
by Anthony Jerome Robbins, Louisiana State University, 1991;
interview with Anthony Robbins, in *American Poetry Review* (Philadelphia), 22(5), September-October 1993; "Carruth against the Grain"
by Marshall Rand, in *Minnesota Review* (Greenville, North Carolina),
43–44, fall 1994-spring 1995; "Beautiful Dreamers: Helen in Egypt
and the Sleeping Beauty" by Charlotte Mandel, in *Clockwatch
Review* (Bloomington, Illinois), 9(1–2), 1994–95; "Propositions in
the Margins of Hayden Carruth's 'Collected Shorter Poems'" by
Mark Rudman, in *American Poetry Review* (Philadelphia), 24(2),
March-April 1995; "Hayden Carruth: The Gift of Self" by Roy
Scheele, in *Poets & Writers,* 24(3), 1 May 1996; "A Love Supreme:

Jazz and the Poetry of Hayden Carruth" by M. Miller, in *Midwest
Quarterly,* 39(3), 1998.

*   *   *

At the center of Hayden Carruth's first book, *The Crow and the
Heart,* is the important long poem "The Asylum," which establishes
one of the central themes and concerns of his poetry: the interplay
between so-called madness and sanity. Like most of his early work,
"The Asylum" is tightly controlled verse dominated by iambic lines
and consistent rhyme schemes. He describes a long winter spent in a
mental institution, where he struggles through nightmare and chaos:
"how hard the search here for the self at last!" He comes to the
painful conclusion that, if nothing else is possible, what is important
is to *"Save thou thyself."* The poem slowly enlarges to encompass
America in its own illness. "This land once was asylum when we
came . . . ," but madness and decay now grow throughout the country.
Leaving the asylum, he rebuilds his life "on a windy knoll" and is
held in check by labor and the land. He discovers that in this "house
of pain" called life we each have "our particular hells" to endure. On
this foundation of pain and understanding he rebuilds: "we lie all
nailed and living, love's long gain." The poem is central to the
reader's engagement with Carruth's later work, for it establishes his
crucial and complex interplay between chaos and order, between the
nightmare of the asylum and the relative control that comes from farm
labor and the cycle of the seasons.

In *From Snow and Rock, From Chaos* we learn a landscape of
Vermont place-names and farm laborers and meet more than one
"tough minded Yankee." His poems here are like fragments wrested,
torn from tree, rock, and earth and forced into verse, like a leaf torn in
two, "one leaf / torn to give you half / showing . . . love's complexity
in an act . . . ." In many of these poems we witness pain being
endured through suffering and waiting until a release brings wider
vision and moments of intense love.

Brothers, I Loved You All contains some of Carruth's finest
work. He captures here, as in many earlier poems, sharply etched
images of momentary events. Some of these, notably the long poem
"Vermont" and several that follow it, are Frostian in theme. The
volume ends with "Paragraphs," a twenty-eight-part poem in
improvisational style that honors Carruth's favorite musicians. But
his subject is best expressed by the line "RAVAGE, DEVASTATE,
SACK." It is with shock and rage that he sees even the pastoral hills
of Vermont ravaged and devastated by the greedy and shortsighted.
He reproaches his neighbors by name for selling their farms to make
way for stores and trailer parks and "for a hot pocketful of dollars."
Through them he accuses all America: "your *best* is what you gave
them / o my friends— / your lives, your farms." With this poem a
much more direct and forceful public voice emerges, crying forcefully against the environmental destructiveness of American culture.
Thus, we see Carruth not only as a survivor of chaos but also as a
revolutionary poet who sees "all dark ahead and behind, his fate / a
need without hope: *the will to resist."*

Carruth's move to Syracuse, New York, in 1979 resulted in a
shift of idiom and locale first apparent in *Asphalt Georgics* (1985), a
group of poems written in syllabic ballad stanzas employing frequently hyphenated enjambments, and later in the Whitmanesque-
lined and loopingly discursive poems from *Tell Me Again How the
White Heron Rises and Flies across the Nacreous River at Twilight
toward the Distant Islands* (1989). The first of these volumes laments
the passing of the agrarian lifestyle that provided the basis for

traditional georgics while celebrating the persistence of human life amid the suburban sprawl that threatens this spirit. The poems are lengthy and build through strategies of apparent tangent and indirection. ''Names,'' the first poem of what might be read as a loose sequence, introduces the form and a sense of the intermingling of lives and histories as one speaker flows into another, the shift signaled by the changing names of what seems to be a single speaker over the poem's sixteen pages. The strict form allows Carruth considerable flexibility in presenting conversational speech. In the second collection such strategies evolve into structures that accumulate like jazz riffs and motifs, the poems seeming to diverge wildly from the ''point'' only to swoop around at the end to enlarge the idea. Many of the poems consider the poetic process from the vantage point of an aging poet who wonders what his life has meant for himself as well as for aging or dead friends, James Wright, Raymond Carver, John Cheever, and Galway Kinnell among them.

In 1994 Carruth gathered all of his longer poems composed between 1957 and 1983 in *Collected Longer Poems.* Three are written in Carruth's trademark ''para-graphs,'' rhymed, variably metered fifteen-line stanzas. These include *The Sleeping Beauty,* the heart of Carruth's oeuvre. Others are written in sprawling Whitmanesque lines, tercets, free verse lyrics, and loosened blank verse, the chosen form answering the demands of the subject matter. Carruth's use of the paragraph evolves from the period academic treatment of ''The Asylum'' to incorporate elements reminiscent of the other school of American poetry, particularly the work of such post-Poundians as Denise Levertov and Robert Creeley. Finally, in *The Sleeping Beauty* he achieves even greater flexibility of line, including caesura and enjambment, emphasis and phrasing, in both their poetic and musical senses. His fundamental concern with the tough issues remains steadfast, however. Yet they are issues in plural, a life's work to ponder and puzzle, to grapple with again and again: madness, the riddle of being, the paradoxically ennobling and damaging romantic myth. Certainly for Carruth ''the poem keeps moving,'' fluid, flexible, bearing witness.

The fruits of Carruth's forty-five years of labor as a critic and literary journalist have been gathered in *Selected Essays & Reviews* (1996). Carruth's essays, taken either individually or as a whole, betray the pervasive influence of a variety of thinkers, including Nikolay Berdyayev, Max Stirner, Arthur Schopenhauer, and Albert Camus. Existence precedes essence; life comes before form, and the poet has multiple considerations, as Carruth writes in his remarkable ''A Meaning of Robert Lowell,'' ''prior to poetry.'' Precise definition is crucial for Carruth, and he is both ruthless and exhaustive in rendering meaning clear. He demonstrates a near encyclopedic memory for literature and philosophy (notably Western), but the essays never seem cerebral set pieces; his knowledge operates as an instrument for ethical discrimination. In this regard he is a disciple, as well, of William James, not in the sloppy application of relativism but in the clear regard of context and applicability. Special note should be made of ''The Nature of Art,'' which provides a representative taste of Carruth's pragmatism. Of the relationship between nature and art, he notes,

> no relationship pertains between nature and art at all. . . .
> Relationships can exist only among things in nature, and art is
> one of them. Nature is everything, ok? It is all material reality,
> and material reality includes absolutely everything, all there is,
> not merely stones and oceans, butterflies and flowers, but
> ideas, poems, dreams, spiritual intimations. I neither know nor

need a supernatural, an other-than-natural. The supernatural is by definition inconceivable, and the inconceivable is of no use to poetry—shy; or to anything.

This insight leads to awareness of the ultimate devastation—death. And such awareness leads to ''lucidity'' and ''authenticity,'' terms borrowed from Camus and Sartre, respectively: ''the two ideal virtues toward which conscious humanity, personally and collectively, must strain, coming even before honesty and ordinary decency, immensely important though these are.'' Such is the spirit that animates all of the pieces gathered in this overdue compilation as completely as his collected poems.

Scrambled Eggs & Whiskey, which won the National Book award, extends Carruth's already considerable accomplishment and reveals a heretofore underdeveloped aspect—the depth and breadth of his sense of humor. While many of his Vermont poems display characteristic Yankee wryness and dryness, Carruth's humorous repertoire includes the epigrammatic, as in ''The Last Poem in the World'':

> Would I write it if I could?
> Bet your glitzy ass I would.

Sly humor also runs through the moving sequence ''A Summer with Tu Fu,'' in which Carruth conducts a dialogue across the centuries and an ocean with the Chinese poet, a chat between friends over chilled white wine as they look out over their respective vistas:

> A swallow here
> zooms across the pond, becoming
> a winter jay on the farther shore.
> Snow whirls in the pass, torrential
> rain drenches the cabbage fields,
> the palace grounds are enshrouded
> with mist. Old age and final illness
> come with the swiftness of the Yangtze
> flooding in springtime, or like
> the quick unreeling cinematograph.

Note the compression of time and space, the seamless movement through seasons and eras, and the adept cross-cultural figures for rapid, ineluctable change. Even the doubling of the final figure reinforces the distance between the two cultures, the displacement of a natural metaphor by a mechanical one. In addition, the specific technological reference is not just mechanical but a mechanism for producing artificial imagery that itself displaces immediate experience. More than mere difference, more than impoverishment, is implied.

Many of the poems are clearly autobiographical, yet rarely does the book seem self-indulgent and never merely ''confessional.'' These poems from late in the author's life show vigor, rigor, experimental suppleness, and rare candor. Always original and thoughtful, Carruth realizes himself in this book even more fully than before, like Yeats's ''wild old wicked man'' coming into his element without apology and with the confidence that only the enthusiasm of the constant beginner can engender and that only lifelong devotion to the art and craft can support.

In *Reluctantly* Carruth provides fragments of autobiography, including an excruciating study of his own nearly successful suicide, titled simply ''Suicide.'' Not since Camus's ''The Myth of Sisyphus'' has an author examined this issue as directly and bluntly. Carruth neither sentimentalizes his act nor shies away from painful detail but achieves a masterful balance. Finally, he believes that he "discovered in suicide a way to unify [his] sense of self, the sense which had formerly been so refracted and broken up":

> Suicide is not only what I did but what I was capable of doing. Elemental though it may be, it still gives shape, integrity, and certain fullness to the figure of myself—minuscule, of course—that I see out there in history. It isn't much, but it's more than I had before. And this is a real and significant feeling in me, no matter how other people may recoil from it, as I myself would have recoiled if it had been presented to me in my ante-suicidal ignorance.

The other fragmentary pieces, though less pervasively intense, provide an insight into the life and mind of one of the great poets of our age.

Carruth's *Beside the Shadblow Tree* is a memoir of his complex friendship with James Laughlin. The value of the book is not its factual accuracy, for Carruth uses his first footnote to advise readers, "I'm writing this entirely from memory. No research. Conditions are not the best." Toward the end of the book, after recalling dates and persons earlier forgotten and uncovering evidence to suggest that chronology was other than he recalled, Carruth wonders about his method:

> Should I go back to the beginning and rewrite this memoir to make it more accurate? That is what Jas [Carruth's name for Laughlin] would have suggested. He was a stickler not only for accuracy but for tidiness. But this is my work, not his. I could and did mimic his style in language, though not in other things, when I needed to, but my own poetry and prose were always naturally different from his, to say the least. This is a matter of esthetic, not moral, judgment. To my mind the value of the kind of writing I'm doing here, if it has any, is in its spontaneity, its closeness to the actual mental flow, which is a virtue that Jas did not appraise highly. I will leave this thing the way it is.

This passage, as the work as a whole, reveals more about Carruth than about Laughlin, though certainly the careful distinction—also characteristic of Carruth—made between the author's working method and that of his subject provides a miniature of Laughlin as well as Carruth—or at least Laughlin as Carruth recalls him. Their friendship spanned the better part of both their adult lives and spanned social differences as well: Laughlin the moneyed sophisticate and Carruth the poor and stymied rustic. If these caricatures fail to apprehend either of the parties fully, they structure much of Carruth's treatment of the friendship. For readers interested in twentieth-century poetry of the past half century, this small memoir will prove indispensable.

—John R. Cooley and Allen Hoey

CARSON, Anne

Nationality: Canadian. **Born:** 1950. **Education:** University of Toronto, Ph.D. 1981. **Career:** Has taught at Princeton University, Emory University, and University of California, Berkeley. Professor of classics, McGill University, Montreal. **Awards:** Rockefeller Foundation fellowship; Guggenheim Foundation fellowship; Djerassi Foundation fellowship; Pushcart prize, 1997.

PUBLICATIONS

Poetry

Short Talks. London, Ontario, Brick Books, 1992.
Plainwater: Essays and Poetry. New York, Knopf, 1995.
Glass, Irony and God: Essays and Poetry. New York, New Directions, 1995.
Wild Workshop, with Kay Adshead and Bridget Meeds. London, Faber, 1997.
Glass and God. London, Cape Poetry, 1998.
Autobiography of Red: A Novel in Verse. New York, Knopf, 1998.
Men in the Off Hours. New York, Knopf, 2000.

Other

Eros the Bittersweet: An Essay. Princeton, New Jersey, Princeton University Press, 1986.
Economy of the Unlost: Reading Simonides of Keos with Paul Celan. Princeton, New Jersey, Princeton University Press, 1999.

*

Critical Studies: By Guy Davenport, in *Grand Street* (Denville, New Jersey), 6(3), spring 1987; "Fickle Contracts: The Poetry of Anne Carson" by Adam Phillips, in *Raritan* (New Brunswick, New Jersey), 16(2), fall 1996; "An Introduction to Anne Carson" by Jorie Graham, and interview with John D'Agata, both in *Brick,* 57, fall 1997.

*   *   *

"The Canadian writer Anne Carson is among the most interesting of contemporary English-language poets." So wrote Oliver Reynolds in the *Times Literary Supplement.* The front cover of Carson's book *Autobiography of Red* offers an encomium from Michael Ondaatje: "Anne Carson is, for me, the most exciting poet writing in English today."

Carson's books of prose and poetry are issued by major publishing houses in New York and London; she and her work are profiled and praised in leading newspapers and literary magazines; and she has held a series of academic fellowships and received a number of major literary awards. Yet Carson has received little appreciation in her native Canada. As Richard Teleky wrote in the second edition of *The Oxford Companion to Canadian Literature* (1997), "That a writer of Carson's importance should be almost unknown in her own country attests to the eccentricities of contemporary Canadian literary culture."

The lapse is odd and inexplicable (like much of the poet's work). Carson was born in Toronto, holds three degrees from the University of Toronto, and since 1988 has been a professor of classics at McGill University in Montreal. She has no Canadian publisher, and it was not until the appearance of *Autobiography of Red* that the country's reviewers and critics took notice of her unique achievement.

"Anne Carson is the real thing," Rachel Barney wrote in the *National Post,* "but just what thing it is hard to say." Perhaps the best way to discuss the "real thing" is to describe the idiosyncratic books she has published to date. Certainly reviewers and critics delight in doing so.

Eros the Bittersweet: An Essay (1986) is a critical study of Sappho that examines sexual desire, poetry, and the Greek alphabet. *Short Talks* (1992) is a chapbook collection of prose poems (with a discussion of prepositions as among the world's "major things") later included with essays in *Plainwater: Essays and Poetry* (1995). Prose and poetry are also integrated in *Glass, Irony and God: Essays and Poetry* (1995). She contributed "The Glass Essay" to the anthology *Wild Workshop* (1997), which also features other long poems by Kay Adshead and Bridget Meeds. *Autobiography of Red: A Novel in Verse* (1998) is not a novel but rather a free verse narrative about a winged red monster named Geryon as described by the Greek poet Stesichoros (who introduced the antiheroic mode to literature), reimagined and set in the main in the 1950s. *Economy of the Unlost: Reading Simonides of Keos with Paul Celan* (1999), a book of literary criticism, compares and contrasts the ancient Greek poet Simonides and the modern Romanian poet Paul Celan, who lived in Paris and wrote in German. *Men in the Off Hours* (2000) is a relatively straightforward collection of poems. The poems, however, are not straightforward, but clipped and curious. Indeed, they are replete with contemporary and classical references to Lazarus, Catherine Deneuve, Thucydides, and Virginia Woolf, among others.

Reading Carson's writing, whether prose or poetry (or more likely a combination of the two), brings to mind the experience of reading the poetry of John Ashbery. Ashbery's writing has no subject matter per se (it makes no statements ad hoc), but it offers the reader the expression of one poet's remarkably refined sensibility and seemingly unlimited range of reference. Carson too writes out of her sensibility, but the writing has been made pungent, rather than seasoned, with learning. Her temperament, like Ashbery's, is decidedly postmodern in the sense that there is no continuity except what is provisionally imposed by the sensibility. Ashbery's style has been described as "language-based"; Carson's is based on commentaries and fragments of information from the past and the present. Ashbery delights in shifts in levels of language and popular references, whereas Carson enjoys displays of erudition. If Ashbery sounds smug, Carson sounds cocky.

An instance of her tone is her amusing statement about the Greek poet Stesichoros: "He came after Homer and before Gertrude Stein, a difficult interval for a poet." The sentence is meaningless, but it is not senseless; it makes one giggle along with the poet. An instance of her showy use of scholarly practice is writing appendixes A, B, and C to a narrative poem and then perversely placing them before rather than after the narrative itself.

Carson shares with Ashbery the technique of the free association of words and phrases to segue the reader from meaning to meaning in the general direction of whatever overall meaning may be present. In the introduction to "Short Talks," included in *Plainwater,* she writes,

> Early one morning words were missing. Before that, words were not. Facts were, faces were. In a good story, Aristotle tells us, everything that happens is pushed by something else . . . You can never know enough, never work enough, never use the infinitives and participles oddly enough, never impede the movement harshly enough, never leave the mind quickly enough.

The passage makes incremental sense, but whether the sense of it adds up to more than a sensitivity to suggestive phrases is anyone's guess.

Many of her effects are subtle indeed. Here is a couplet from "One-Man Town" from the same collection:

> It's Magritte weather today said Max.
> Ernst knocking his head on a boulder.

What is surprising about those lines is the period that unexpectedly appears following the painter's given name, Max. Who is Max? Oh, Max Ernst the artist. Is his full name Maxwell? The reader is sidetracked, buffaloed.

The poet is quick on the uptake. Here are sentences from the introduction to "The Anthropology of Water" from *Plainwater:*

> Water is something you cannot hold. Like men. I have tried.

Anne Carson is certain to have an influence on how academic poets write, read, and teach poetry in the future throughout the English-speaking world (and even in Canada). It is hard to imagine that there exists a wide public for her writing, yet her erudition, imagination, spirited nature, and cultural sensitivities guarantee her an elite reading public. One wonders what literary delight she will dream up next.

—John Robert Colombo

CARSON, Ciaran

Nationality: Irish. **Born:** Belfast, Ireland, 9 October 1948. **Education:** Queens University, Belfast, B.A. **Family:** Married Deirdre Shannon in 1982; two sons and one daughter. **Career:** Since 1975 traditional arts officer, Arts Council of Northern Ireland. **Awards:** Eric Gregory award; Alice Hunt Bartlett award; *Irish Time*/Aer Lingus award. **Address:** Arts Council of Northern Ireland, 181 A Stranmills Road, Belfast BT9 5DU, Northern Ireland.

PUBLICATIONS

Poetry

The New Estate. Winston-Salem, North Carolina, Wake Forest University Press, 1976.
The Irish for No. Dublin, Gallery Press, 1987.
The New Estate, and Other Poems. Oldcastle, Meath, Gallery Press, 1988.
Belfast Confetti. Madison, Wisconsin, Silver Buckle Press, 1993.
First Language: Poems. Winston-Salem, North Carolina, Wake Forest University Press, 1994.
Letters from the Alphabet. Oldcastle, Meath, Gallery Press, 1995.
Opera Et Cetera. Oldcastle, Meath, Gallery Press, and Winston-Salem, North Carolina, Wake Forest University Press, 1996.
The Twelfth of Never. Winston-Salem, North Carolina, Wake Forest University Press, and Oldcastle, Meath, Gallery Press, 1998.
Fishing for Amber. London, Granta, 1999.
The Ballad of HMS Belfast: A Compendium of Belfast Poems. Oldcastle, Meath, Gallery Press, 1999.

Other

Irish Traditional Music. Belfast, Appletree Press, 1986.
Last Night's Fun: A Book about Irish Traditional Music. London,
 Jonathan Cape, 1996; as *Last Night's Fun: In and Out of Time with
 Irish Music,* New York, North Point Press, 1997.
The Star Factory. London, Granta, 1997; New York, Arcade, 1998.
*The Alexandrine Plan: Versions of Sonnets by Baudelaire, Mallarmé,
 and Rimbaud.* Winston-Salem, North Carolina, Wake Forest
 University Press, and Loughcrew, Ireland, Gallery Press, 1998.

*

Critical Studies: "Threaders of Double-Stranded Words: News
from the North of Ireland" by John Drexel, in *New England Review
and Bread Loaf Quarterly* (Middlebury, Vermont), 12(2), winter
1989; "One Step Forward, Two Steps Back: Ciaran Carson's 'The
Irish for No'" by Neil Corcoran, in *The Chosen Ground: Essays on
the Contemporary Poetry of Northern Ireland,* edited by Neil Corcoran,
Bridgend, Seren, 1992; "The Dismembering Muse: Seamus Heaney,
Ciaran Carson, and Kenneth Burke's 'Four Master Tropes'" by Rand
Brandes, in *Bucknell Review* (Cranbury, New Jersey), 38(1), 1994;
"Ciaran Carson's Parturient Partition: The 'Crack' in MacNeice's
'More Than Glass'" by Guinn Batten, in *Southern Review* (Baton
Rouge, Louisiana), 31(3), summer 1995; "'Everything Provisional':
Fictive Possibility and the Poetry of Paul Muldoon and Ciaran
Carson" by Jonathan Allison, in *Etudes Irlandaises* (Sainghinen en
Melantois, France), 20(2), autumn 1995; "Earth Writing: Seamus
Heaney and Ciaran Carson" by John Kerrigan, in *Essays in Criticism,*
48(2), 1998; "The Evolving Art of Ciaran Carson" by Ben Howard,
in *Shenandoah,* 48(1), spring 1998.

*   *   *

Ciaran Carson's first book, *The New Estate,* was quiet in tone,
with evocations of "The Insular Celts" and the monastic life of Saint
Ciaran, his namesake. But present-day Belfast intruded with "The
Bomb Disposal," a backdrop where "the city is a map of the city /
Its forbidden areas changing daily." In time this would become Carson's
main theme. In *The Irish for No* and *Belfast Confetti,* he is the
laureate of a city

where nothing is permanent.
When someone asks me where I live, I remember where I
 used to live.
Someone asks me for directions, and I think again. I turn into
A side-street to try to throw off my shadow, and history is
 changed.

After more than a decade of brooding Carson had found ways to
deal with a nearly impossible subject, the urban violence of the late
twentieth century, Belfast as Beirut. One way is the long, meandering
line of the storyteller. Carson is a traditional musician who has
learned how to introduce the wandering note that, as in the slow air,
seems lost before it surfaces again. Thus a rural art is transposed to the
grim world of Belfast pub life, with its details of blasts and deaths.

Carson also expands or shrinks the sonnet form to suit the harsh
material. In his later work, *First Language* and *Letters from the
Alphabet,* he proceeds from the breaking down of buildings to the
breaking down of language. Ovid and Rimbaud are drafted into this

deft enterprise, the most extensive and elaborate linguistic display
since Austin Clarke. Now he has moved from Saint Ciaran to the
Ulster of Edward Carson, a second namesake:

Eyes. The seraphic frown. The borders and the chains contained
 therein. The fraternal
Gaze of the Exclusive Brethren: orange and bruised purple,
 cataleptic.

I once said that no one could make sense out of present-day
Belfast. Carson has made me eat at least some of my words.

—John Montague

CERVANTES, Lorna Dee

Nationality: American. **Born:** San Francisco, 6 August 1954. **Education:** San Jose State University, California, B.A. 1984; University
of California, Santa Cruz, 1985–88. **Career:** Instructor of creative
writing, University of Colorado, Boulder. Founder, Mango Publications, and editor, *Mango* literary review; founder and editor, *Red Dirt*
magazine. Has been active in the American Indian and Chicano
movements since the 1970s. **Awards:** National Endowment for the
Arts grant, 1978, 1989; American Book award, 1982, for *Emplumada;*
Hudson D. Walker fellowship, Fine Arts Work Center, Provincetown; Pushcart prize. **Address:** Department of English, University of
Colorado, Box 226, Boulder, Colorado 80309–0226, U.S.A.

PUBLICATIONS

Poetry

Emplumada. Pittsburgh, Pennsylvania, University of Pittsburgh Press,
 1981.
From the Cables of Genocide: Poems of Love and Hunger. Houston,
 Arte Publico Press, 1991.

Recording: *An Evening of Chicano Poetry,* Archive of Recorded
 Poetry and Literature, 1986.

*

Critical Studies: "Soothing Restless Serpents: The Dreaded Creation and Other Inspirations in Chicana Poetry" by Tey Diana Rebolledo,
in *Third Woman* (Berkeley, California), 2(1), 1984; "Notes toward a
New Multicultural Criticism: Three Works by Women of Color" by
John F. Crawford, in *A Gift of Tongues: Critical Challenges in
Contemporary American Poetry,* edited by Marie Harris and Kathleen Aguero, Athens, University of Georgia Press, 1987; "Chicana
Literature from a Chicana Feminist Perspective" by Yvonne Yarbro-Bejarano, in *Chicana Creativity and Criticism: Charting New Frontiers in American Literature,* edited by Maria Herrera-Sobek and
Helena Maria Viramontes, Houston, Arte Publico, 1988; "Lorna Dee
Cervantes's Dialogic Imagination," in *Annales du Centre de
Recherches sur l'Amerique Anglophone* (Cedex, France), 18, 1993,

and ''Bilingualism and Dialogism: Another Reading of Lorna Dee Cervantes's Poetry,'' in *An Other Tongue: Nation and Ethnicity in the Linguistic Borderlands,* edited by Alfred Arteaga, Durham, North Carolina, Duke University Press, 1994, both by Ada Savin; ''Divided Loyalties: Literal and Literary in the Poetry of Lorna Dee Cervantes, Cathy Song and Rita Dove'' by Patricia Wallace, in *MELUS* (Amherst, Massachusetts), 18(3), fall 1993; '''An Utterance More Pure Than Word': Gender and the Corrido Tradition in Two Contemporary Chicano Poems'' by Teresa McKenna, in *Feminist Measures: Soundings in Poetry and Theory,* edited by Lynn Keller and Cristanne Miller, Ann Arbor, University of Michigan Press, 1994.

*   *   *

In the 1970s Lorna Dee Cervantes became part of the new Chicano movement, which at the time was largely male. Interested in the conundrums of race and race relations—in part because her heritage was both Native American and Mexican—Cervantes became a publisher. In the mid-1970s she founded Mango Publications, a small press designed to publish the work of Chicano and Chicana writers. One outlet for this work was the little magazine *Mango.* Receiving grants from the National Endowment for the Arts, she maintained her publications projects while she polished the craft of writing poetry. By the time *Emplumada,* her first collection, appeared in 1981, she was widely published in little and Chicano magazines. When her collection won the 1982 American Book award, she was guaranteed prominence in the increasingly multicultural U.S. arts scene.

After Cervantes graduated from San Jose State University in 1984, she studied for four years as a graduate student in the history of consciousness program at the University of California at Santa Cruz. Itself a unique contribution to the interdisciplinary movement, this graduate program allowed students to combine specializations in the study of history, culture, literature, art, and politics. It led Cervantes into a number of avenues for her work, including the editing of *Red Dirt,* a magazine of multicultural literature, and teaching creative writing at the University of Colorado at Boulder.

Often anthologized, the poems of Cervantes make an explicit statement about race and sexuality. In *Emplumada* she uses untranslated Spanish words and phrases within the English, giving readers the message that no single language can express all of the feelings and knowledge of living in the United States. The title of the book, translated as a combination of ''feathered'' and ''pen flourish,'' strikes many readers as both exotic and metaphorically persuasive. The poet's claim to be creating a new language is a message as old as print. Long before the political and educational struggles over bilingualism, Cervantes's poems gave body to the ideas of the movement. Linguists call her practice ''code-switching''; writers and readers appreciate her deft use of a blend of languages, each operative within the Americas.

Cervantes's second collection, *From the Cables of Genocide: Poems of Love and Hunger,* was published in 1991. Many of the themes from her first book reappear, but the new density of the metaphoric texture shows that Cervantes is no longer interested in creating too direct, or too simple, a commentary. Whereas several of the *Emplumada* poems—''Beneath the Shadow of the Freeway'' and ''Poem for the Young White Man Who Asked Me How I, an Intelligent, Well-Read Person Could Believe in the War between Races''—set the tone for the keen expression of the Chicano movement, her later poetry focuses more intently on male-female relationships. Sexuality and its various powers seem to have usurped the

battlefield of racial conflict. In ''Beneath the Shadow of the Freeway'' Cervantes had prefigured her later themes. Here the ''soft'' woman laments the loss of her lover, even as her magnificently eloquent mother tells her to live for herself. The poem pictures the matriarchs of the family, stanza by stanza, voicing their wisdom to the young protagonist. It is the grandmother who ''trusts only what she builds / with her own hands.'' But she also has lived too many years with a man who has been waiting to kill her. Untold, but insistently paralleled, the concluding chapter of the protagonist's life haunts the reader. Playing against the stereotype of women's need to learn from their female ancestors in order to find wisdom, Cervantes creates a tapestry of affirmation and denial that shows the complex negotiations necessary for women within a culture on the other side of American prosperity. Economics is the unwritten player in many of Cervantes's poems.

In *From the Cables of Genocide* ''Macho'' gives a sharp, humorous twist to the male subject, ostensibly ''a man of gristle and flint'' whose ''lure'' is ''potent.'' Intellectualism cannot subvert the physical realities of a human life, and in her later poem ''Bananas'' Cervantes brings together both pervasive themes. This five-part poem moves from Estonia, where a man takes his children to the Dollar Market to look at bananas (so dear he could never buy one for them to taste) to Boulder (with her Dia de los Muertos celebration) to Kwajalein (a Pacific atoll) to Colombia, where the carnage of the 1928 United Fruit Company strike (and the ''bananas, black on the stumps, char into odor'') centers the poet's memory: ''The murdered Mestizos have long been cleared / and begin their new duties as fertilizer for the plantations. / Feathers fall over the newly spaded soil: turquoise, / scarlet, azure, quetzal, and yellow litters / the graves like gold claws of bananas.'' The metaphor of Cervantes's *Emplumada* returns to force the reader to see beneath the brilliance of the exotic culture into its harsh mounds of death.

—Linda Wagner-Martin

CHAPPELL, Fred

Nationality: American. **Born:** Canton, North Carolina, 28 May 1936. **Education:** Duke University, Durham, North Carolina, 1954–61, 1961–64, B.A. 1961, M.A. 1964. **Family:** Married Susan Nicholls in 1959; one son. **Career:** Professor of English, University of North Carolina, Greensboro. **Awards:** Rockefeller grant, 1967–68; National Institute of Arts and Letters, 1968; Roanoke-Chowan poetry award, 1972, 1975, 1979, 1980, 1985; Prix de Meilleur des Livres Estrangers (Academie Francaise), 1972; Sir Walter Raleigh prize, 1972; Oscar A. Young Memorial award, 1980; North Carolina award in literature, 1980; Zoe Kincaid Brockman award, 1981; Bollingen prize, 1985; Endowed Chair: The Burlington Industries Professorship, 1988; O. Max Gardner award, the Universities of North Carolina, 1987; Ragan-Rubin award, North Carolina English Teachers Association, 1989; Thomas H. Carter award, *Shenandoah,* 1991; World Fantasy award for best short story, 1992, 1994; T.S. Eliot prize, Ingersoll Foundation, 1993; Aiken Taylor award in poetry, 1996; North Carolina poet laureate, 1998. **Member:** Fellowship of Southern Writers. **Agent:** Rhoda Weyr, 151 Bergen Street, Brooklyn, New York 11217, U.S.A. **Address:** 305 Kensington Road, Greensboro, North Carolina 27403, U.S.A.

PUBLICATIONS

Poetry

The World between the Eyes. Baton Rouge, Louisiana State University Press, 1971.
River. Baton Rouge, Louisiana State University Press, 1975.
The Man Twice Married to Fire. Greensboro, North Carolina, Unicorn Press, 1977.
Bloodfire. Baton Rouge, Louisiana State University Press, 1978.
Awakening to Music. Davidson, North Carolina, Briarpatch Press, 1979.
Wind Mountain. Baton Rouge, Louisiana State University Press, 1979.
Earthsleep. Baton Rouge, Louisiana State University Press, n.d.
Driftlake: A Lieder Cycle. Emory, Virginia, Iron Mountain Press, 1981.
Midquest. Baton Rouge, Louisiana State University Press, 1981.
Castle Tzingal. Baton Rouge, Louisiana State University Press, 1988.
First and Last Words. Baton Rouge, Louisiana State University Press, 1988.
C: 100 Poems. Baton Rouge, Louisiana State University Press, 1993.
Spring Garden: New and Selected Poems. Baton Rouge, Louisiana State University, 1995.

Novels

It Is Time, Lord. New York, Atheneum, 1963.
The Inkling. New York, Harcourt Brace, 1965.
Dagon. New York, Harcourt Brace, 1968.
The Gaudy Place. New York, Harcourt Brace, 1972.
I Am One of You Forever. Baton Rouge, Louisiana State University Press, 1985.
Brighten the Corner Where You Are. New York, St. Martin's Press, 1989.
Farewell, I'm Bound to Leave You. New York, Picador, 1996.
Look Back All the Green Valley. New York, Picador, 1999.

Short Stories

Moments of Light. Los Angeles, New South, 1980.
More Shapes than One. New York, St. Martin's Press, 1991.

Other

The Fred Chappell Reader. New York, St. Martin's Press, 1987.
Plow Naked: Selected Writings on Poetry. Ann Arbor, University of Michigan Press, 1993.
A Way of Happening: Observations of Contemporary Poetry. New York, Picador, 1998.

*

Manuscript Collection: Duke University, Durham, North Carolina.

Critical Studies: "Letters from a Distant Lover: The Novels of Fred Chappell" by R.H.W. Dillard, in *Hollins Critic* (Hollins College, Virginia), 10(2), 1973; "A Writer's Harmonious World" by Kelly Cherry, in *Parnassus* (New York), 9(2), fall-winter 1981; "Quest and Midquest: Fred Chappell and the First-Person Personal Epic" by Alan Nadel, in *New England Review and Bread Loaf Quarterly* (Middlebury, Vermont), 6(2), winter 1983; "Images of Impure Water in Chappell's River" by Donald Secreast, in *Mississippi Quarterly* (Mississippi State), 37(1), winter 1983–84; "A Few Things about Fred Chappell" by George Garrett, in *Mississippi Quarterly* (Mississippi State), 37(1), winter 1983–84; "Walking the Intellectual Hills" by Paul Rice, in *Chattahoochee Review,* 11(1), fall 1990; "Tributes to Fred Chappell" by Sam Ragan and others, in *Pembroke Magazine* (Pembroke, North Carolina), 23, 1991; "Spiritual Matter in Fred Chappell's Poetry: A Prologue" by Dabney Stuart, in *Southern Review* (Baton Rouge, Louisiana), 27(1), winter 1991; "Fred Chappell's I Am One of You Forever: The Oneiros of Childhood Transformed" by Amy Tipton Gray, in *The Poetics of Appalachian Space,* edited by Parks Lanier, Jr., Knoxville, University of Tennessee Press, 1991; "Friend of Reason: Surveying the Fred Chappell Papers at Duke University" by Alex Albright, in *North Carolina Literary Review,* 1(1), summer 1992; "Fred Chappell's Castle Tzingal: Modern Revival of Elizabethan Revenge Tragedy" by Edward C. Lynskey, in *Pembroke Magazine* (Pembroke, North Carolina), 25, 1993; "Fred Chappell's Urn of Memory: I Am One of You Forever" by Hilbert Campbell, in *Southern Literary Journal* (Chapel Hill, North Carolina), 25(2), spring 1993; "Fred Chappell" by Tersh Palmer, in *Appalachian Journal* (Boone, North Carolina), 19(4), summer 1992; "Chappell's Continuities: First and Last Words" by Peter Makuck, in *Virginia Quarterly Review* (Charlottesville, Virginia), 68(2), spring 1992; *The Appalachian Literary Tradition and the Works of Fred Chappell: Three Essays* (dissertation) by Susan O'Dell Underwood, Florida State University, 1995; "Fred Chappell: From the Mountains to the Mainstream" by Jennifer Howard, in *Publishers Weekly,* 243(40), September 1996; *Folklore and Literature: The Poetry and Fiction of Fred Chappell* (dissertation) by Carmine David Palumbo, University of Southwestern Louisiana, 1997; *Dream Garden: The Poetic Vision of Fred Chappell* edited by Patric Bizzaro, Baton Rouge, Louisiana State University Press, 1997; "Fred Chappell: Midquestions" by Randolph Paul Runyon, in *Southern Writers at Century's End,* edited by Jeffrey Folks and James Perkins, Lexington, University Press of Kentucky, 1997.

Fred Chappell comments:

As my purposes in poetry are simple—to entertain and to instruct—so do I try to keep my aesthetic philosophy simple. I believe that every poem or group of poems generates its own aesthetic standards and it is by these that work is to be judged. The hard task is to discover these standards and then to find means of composition that can make them clear and dramatic.

For these reasons I trust in poetry that is thoroughly modeled, highly finished—but which strives for a spirit of spontaneity. Both formal verse and free verse can achieve these largest ends, though not, of course, by means of the same effects.

Fashions in poetry, whether passé or prevailing, hold but amusement for me, or at least an academic interest. I have only a naturalist's curiosity about different schools of poetry and lives of poets. The work itself is important: the line, the phrase, the word.

* * *

Fred Chappell's central poetic achievement is *Midquest,* the long poem that first appeared from 1975 to 1980 as four separate volumes—*River, Bloodfire, Wind Mountain,* and *Earthsleep*—each the size of a normal collection of poems. At the midpoint of his life, as Dante put it, the speaker looks at his past and present, considering especially his love for his wife Susan, the various personae he has tried on as he has become his own man, and the significance of place, family, friendship, music, and literature. The poem is autobiographical fiction, and so it is fair for the author to say that "Fred" is no more or less Fred Chappell than any of his other fictional characters (Chappell is also an excellent novelist).

Each section of *Midquest* contains eleven poems, and in its own way each volume recounts the same twenty-four hours in the author's life on the day of his thirty-fifth birthday. The most apparent tension in the poem is perhaps that between the speaker's rural Appalachian childhood and his urban, academic adulthood. It is not that the two worlds cannot connect but that they connect on so many levels, distant as they sometimes seem. The speaker's grandmother is a source of lore and inspiration, as is "a garrulous old gentleman" named Virgil Campbell, who in each of the volumes gets a section in which he presents some boisterous recollections. Over against these recollections of rural adventure and misadventure are poems exploring the origins and the persistence of the speaker's literary urges and ambitions. These are made with great delicacy and freedom from self-indulgence. *Midquest* is a poem celebrating the world most of us live in and the play of mind and language over it.

Midquest was preceded by *The World between the Eyes,* which appeared after Chappell had already published three novels. He has continued to publish both fiction and poetry, and increasingly the two genres seem to converse, as later novels recapitulate some of the scenes in *Midquest.* He has allowed himself some room for unusual experiments in later collections, however, beginning with *Castle Tzingal,* a sequence of soliloquies set in an impossibly remote and mythical principality fraught with alchemy, royal treachery, and lost love. Without the slightest insistence, the work edges toward being a parable for our threat-haunted time.

Source contains scenes more explicit in their author's consciousness of the trouble our technology portends, but it also moves deeply toward acceptance of death, especially in "Forever Mountain," a poignant farewell to the poet's father. This book is Chappell's seventh, but it is only his second to collect a group of poems written one at a time, in the manner of most collections of poetry. Furthermore, his eighth, *First and Last Words,* undertakes another experiment in making a sequence of related poems that are presented as forewords or afterwords to various works of literature. Some of the works, like Hardy's *The Dynasts,* do not come to mind in profuse detail, but Chappell treads with confidence that thin and unsteady line between making us think that we might go back to the originals one day and frustrating us because we need more familiarity with the works he writes about. *First and Last Words* comes as close to complete independence as any book of poems can, but it is unusually direct in its acknowledgment that poems are made, in part, from other poems.

Chappell's collection *C* gets its title from the Roman numeral for one hundred. The book contains one hundred short poems, mostly epigrams and translations of epigrams, that are remarkably supple and various in tone and form. In such an enterprise a certain unevenness might be more apparent than in a good collection of thirty poems, but there is an abundance of wit in this collection, as in all of Chappell's deeply humane and brilliantly crafted poetry.

—Henry Taylor

CHERNOFF, Maxine

Nationality: American. **Born:** Maxine Hahn, Chicago, Illinois, 24 February 1952. **Education:** University of Illinois, Chicago, 1968–74, B.A. 1972; M.A. 1974. **Family:** Married 1) Arnold Chernoff in 1971 (divorced 1972); 2) Paul Hoover in 1974; one daughter and two sons. **Career:** Lecturer, University of Illinois, Chicago, 1977–80; instructor, Columbia College, Chicago, 1977–85; assistant professor, 1980–87, and associate professor, 1987–94, Chicago City Colleges; adjunct associate professor, Art Institute of Chicago, 1990–94; associate professor of creative writing, 1994–97, and since 1997 professor and chair of creative writing, San Francisco State University. **Awards:** Carl Sandburg award, 1985, for *New Faces of 1952;* Friends of American Writers award, 1987; PEN Syndicated Fiction award, 1988; *Southern Review*/Louisiana State University Short Story award, 1988; *Sun-Times* Friends of Literature award, 1993; faculty affirmative action grant, San Francisco State University, 1995; and five Illinois Arts Council fellowships. Since 1989 honorary fellow, Simon's Rock of Bard College, Annandale-on-Hudson, New York. **Address:** 369 Molino Avenue, Mill Valley, California 94941, U.S.A.

PUBLICATIONS

Poetry

A Vegetable Emergency. Venice, California, Beyond Baroque Foundation, 1976.
Utopia TV Store. Chicago, Yellow Press, 1979.
New Faces of 1952. Ithaca, New York, Ithaca House, 1985.
Japan. Bolinas, California, Avenue B Press, 1988.
Leap Year Day: New and Selected Poems. Chicago, ACM, 1990.
Next Song: A Chapbook. Saratoga, California, Instress, 1998.

Novels

Plain Grief. New York, Simon and Schuster, 1991.
American Heaven. Minneapolis, Minnesota, Coffee House Press, 1996.
A Boy in Winter. New York, Crown, 1999.

Short Stories

Bop. Minneapolis, Minnesota, Coffee House Press, 1986.
Signs of Devotion. New York, Simon and Schuster, 1993.

Other

In the News, with Ethel Tiersky. Chicago, National Textbook Company, 1991.
Attractions, with Ethel Tiersky. Chicago, Contemporary Books, 1993.

*

Critical Studies: "Fiction As Language Game: The Hermeneutic Fables of Lydia Davis and Maxine Chernoff" by Marjorie Perloff, in *Breaking the Sequence: Experimental Women Fiction Writers.* Princeton, New Jersey, Princeton University Press, 1989; *Writing Illinois* by James Hurt, Urbana, University of Illinois Press, 1992; *Interviews* *with American Women Writers* by Aruna Sitesh, New Delhi, East-West Press, 1994.

Maxine Chernoff comments:

I began as a writer with the prose poem, a form that spans two genres. I was drawn to the prose poem as a means to explore the metaphysical in the manner of the great French and Latin American practitioners of the form. I spent ten years exploring its strengths and limitations. It was an excellent mode to express my then attitudes about human experience and societal chaos: the Vietnam War and the Watergate era exerted huge pressures on me to account for ''truth.'' The turns of mind of the short, terse, self-limiting form were appropriate to my probing social consciousness, as were its natural ironies, evasions, and allusions.

As I matured as a writer, I sought to inform my writing with a means to examine human behavior, particularly on the miniature level of communication, how language bends and sometimes breaks as it is called upon to articulate and analyze relationships. My movement from the prose poem to the short story attempted to account for this realm of social interaction, the adequacy and the inadequacy of language spoken to create a moment and internalized to reflect upon that moment. It signaled a turning inward for me, away from public ceremonies toward private rituals. It represented more careful listening on my part to the way people ''whisper'' about their lives.

After nearly a decade of story writing, I decided that I needed the space a novel would provide to let experience through language take the twists and turns that might honor its fullness. All three of my novels are about stalemate—the difficulties of communicating and the loss we experience if we stop trying.

The more I write prose, the more poetry's ''proper'' aims separate for me. My poems now, taut and tense with the difficult of choosing the words we need and the stumbling that results, feel like songs that come to me in a language I don't fully understand. I let my instincts here serve the mystery of their articulation.

The older and more practiced I become, the more awe I feel for the act of creation, its perils, its incompleteness, its contingency, its defeatedness, its attempt to light up a small corner through empathy.

*   *   *

Maxine Chernoff's poems skate and glide from aperçu to insight to witticism and on to surreal conclusion. They are usually leavened by ingratiating perkiness. She starts spinning words that, in her best poems, turn into stories and finally myths. But her work is uneven and has evolved choppily. She has been influenced by the New York school of O'Hara via Berrigan, as well as by the Coolidge-like language school, but she seems truly inspired only by the prose of Russell Edson.

It is useful to begin with Chernoff's weakest work, *Japan,* published in 1988. Its final poem is ''Zones'':

Sun
    shut Wednesday
swank of
    missing
ball-point
    dodger
radiant mud
    moving
poor

    a quiet
lapse
    austerely
yours
    endured colossal
sleep
    to reckon
bliss by
    curtained
hearty
    thinness
child's word
    wavers
thinking world
    to open
languor's
    naked
door

Within the book are twenty-six aleatory language-oriented poems arranged alphabetically by title, one per letter. They run a weary gamut, utterly unlike. Consider, for example, her witty ''Abridged Bestiary'':

The aardvark and the zebra were the only animals that the concise Noah allowed to join him. ''Bears to yaks be damned,'' he shouted . . .

The work recalls David Rosenberg's much earlier *39 Excellent Articles of Japan,* which simply consists of found poems from a Japanese catalog written in pidgin English. While his work is wacky and camp, Chernoff's *Japan* seems to be an aesthete's abecedarium. If the poems of *Japan* have themes, they are generated, as Chomsky would say, by the tendency language has to mean. Abandon all hope ye who interpret here.

In contrast, Chernoff's poem ''For My Father'' is forceful and strong, beginning, ''He was my face on a necessary white.'' Chernoff's local allusions to Chicago, her home for many years, also glow, as in ''April Fool,'' for a certain dean at the University of Chicago:

The Early Warning System buzzed
the TV screen while I made
coffee: Oh good, the end of
the world. Then I told my mother
we'd have lunch at two.
Happy April Fools',
Professor Wayne C. Booth
who claims our use of irony
shows our fear of God
the Father not liking
his smirking children.

Chernoff can also write excellent prose. Her shortest prose she calls prose poetry, the kind of work of which Edson is the preeminent contemporary master. Her best pieces, such as ''The Last Auroch,'' twist a tall tale into a myth. In ''The Apology Store,'' for example, she tries to buy an all-purpose apology, but the store will not accept her currency and then claims to be sold out until spring or until a strike is over or until whenever. She finally asks the store to phone when they can help. ''I'm sorry,'' the clerk says, ''we don't have a phone.''

Chernoff's first book of short stories, *Bop,* was published in 1986. Although she has since been making a mark with her fiction, there is always something buoyant and exceptional in her best poetry, such as "Leap Year Day," the title poem from her 1991 book of new and selected poems:

The paleolithic heart might burst
with news of slowness, news of feathers.
All the softness listed in the register
you keep: day of finite crashing.
Who's to say the deafness that you wore
was needed by the Greeks? Depression
sounded like a whole note sewn with
lilac thread. I wanted to assure you
that the small biology of kissing
would not last until the pebble dried
and a flag wobbled and a list faded and a map
was drawn and a green planet drifted
under your lens. The elbowed dawn lifted,
and you said nothing of the storm that flashed
off-shore, as if to mean, forgotten winter
without signs. You will not fade.
I believe your wholeness as it rests its future
on our lengthening half-lit letters.

—Michael Andre

CHEYNEY-COKER, Syl

Nationality: Sierra Leonean. **Born:** Freetown, 28 June 1945. **Education:** University of Oregon, Eugene, 1967–70; University of California, 1970; University of Wisconsin, Madison, 1971–72. **Career:** Worked as a drummer; factory and dock worker; journalist, Eugene *Register Guard,* Oregon, 1968–69; teaching assistant, University of Wisconsin, 1971; head of cultural affairs, Radio Sierra Leone, 1972–73; freelance writer, 1973–75; visiting professor of English, University of the Philippines, Quezon City, 1975–77. Lecturer, 1977–79, and since 1979 senior lecturer, University of Maiduguri, Nigeria. **Awards:** Food Foundation grant, 1970. **Address:** Department of English, University of Maiduguri, P.M.B. 1069, Maiduguri, Nigeria.

PUBLICATIONS

Poetry

Concerto for an Exile. New York, Africana, 1972; London, Heinemann, 1973.
The Graveyard Also Has Teeth. London, New Beacon, 1974.
The Blood in the Desert's Eyes: Poems. Portsmouth, New Hampshire, Heinemann, 1990.

Novel

The Last Harmattan of Alusine Dunbar. Oxford and Portsmouth, New Hampshire, Heinemann, 1990.

*

Critical Study: "Syl Cheyney-Coker, Concerto for an Exile" by M.J. Salt, in *African Literature Today* (Freetown, Sierra Leone), 7, 1975.

Syl Cheyney-Coker comments:

(1974) I hold the terrible distinction of being the only poet from my country who has published a sizable volume of poems. I say "terrible" not in the pejorative sense but from a feeling of painful awareness that before my appearance my country was a ghetto of silence.

A popular awareness of self and the creation of different modes of expression of our social and cultural needs seem to me to be the immediate task of the Sierra Leonean writer. We are a strange people; our history, language, and culture are not to be confused with those of other English-speaking Africans.

The admixture of English philanthropy and African exotica that has produced and shaped the Sierra Leonean creole is for me the makeup of any genuine Sierra Leonean literature.

My Afro-Saxon heritage has meant a lot for me as I summarize my passion, and I hope it will convey something of the strangeness of my people to the reader.

*   *   *

The question of ancestry is a central concern in the writing of many third world poets. In the poems of Syl Cheyney-Coker, especially those collected in his 1972 book *Concerto for an Exile,* this concern becomes a fixation. He writes of his

. . . Creole ancestry
which gave me my negralised head
all my polluted streams

providing the impulse for poems that, in the extravagance and precise violence of their imagery, match some of the best writing of Vallejo and U'Tamsi, two poets whom Cheyney-Coker acknowledges as influences.

There are also definite echoes of the negritude school and the poems of David Diop. The "Africa, My Africa" of Diop's poems has, however, been narrowed down to a specific nation, Sierra Leone, the land of freed slaves where a patois language and a Western-influenced capital, Freetown, are ironic heritages of the colonial era:

In my country the Creoles drink only
Black and White with long sorrows
hanging from their colonial faces . . .

Cheyney-Coker's poems are cries of bitter agony and bright illumination at one and the same time. They present the picture of a nation and a poet tortured by a culture and a religion imposed upon them, but a nation and a poet who may find salvation through defiance. This can be seen, for example, in "Agony of the Dark Child" or in "Misery of the Convert":

I was a king before they nailed you on the cross
converted I read ten lies in your silly commandments
to honour you my Christ
when you have deprived me of my race . . .

"Painful" is a word that can readily be applied to much of Cheyney-Coker's writing, just as another word—"truthful"—can also be applied to the same poems. Through a wrenching examination of personal and national histories, he attempts to create a new vision, a more honest world. In his poem "Guinea," written on the unsuccessful invasion of that nation by Portuguese mercenaries, he defines his role:

I am not the renegade
who has forsaken your shores
I am not the vampire
gnawing at your heart
to feed capitalist banks
I am your poet
writing No to the world.

—Joseph Bruchac

CHIPASULA, Frank (Mkalawile)

Nationality: Malawian. **Born:** Luanshya, Zambia, 16 October 1949. **Education:** University of Malawi, 1970–73; University of Zambia, B.A. 1976; Brown University, M.A. in creative writing 1980; Yale University, M.A. in Afro-American Literature 1982. **Family:** Married Stella Patricia Banda in 1976; one son. **Career:** Freelance broadcaster, Malawi Broadcasting Corporation, Blantyre, 1971–73; English editor, National Educational Company of Zambia, 1976–78. Since 1964 writer. First organizer of Writers' Group, Chancellor College, University of Malawi, 1970–73. **Awards:** Fulbright travel grant, 1978–80; Noma award honorable mention, African Book Publishing Record, 1985, for *O Earth, Wait for Me.* **Address:** Department of English, Brown University, Box 1852, Providence, Rhode Island 02912, U.S.A.

PUBLICATIONS

Poetry

Visions and Reflections. Lusaka, National Educational Company of Zambia, 1972.
O Earth, Wait for Me. Athens, Ohio University Press, 1984.
Nightwatcher, Nightsong. Peterborough, Paul Green, 1986.
Whispers in the Wings: Poems. London and Portsmouth, New Hampshire, Heinemann, 1991.

Other

Editor, *A Decade of Poetry.* Lusaka, National Educational Company of Zambia, 1980.
Editor, *When My Brothers Come Home: Poems from Central and Southern Africa.* Middletown, Connecticut, Wesleyan University Press, 1985.
Editor, *A Decade in Poetry.* Lusaka, Kenneth Kaunda Foundation, 1991.
Editor, with Stella Chipasula, *Heinemann Book of African Women's Poetry.* Oxford, Heinemann, 1995.

*

Critical Studies: "Singing in the Dark Rain" by James Gibbs, in *Index on Censorship* (London, England), 17(2), February 1988; "Poetry and Liberation in Central and Southern Africa" by Anthony Nazmobe, in *Literature, Language and the Nation,* edited by Emmanuel Ngara and Andrew Morrison, Harare, Atoll and Baobab Books, 1989.

*   *   *

The Malawian Frank Chipasula is a major voice in the new generation of African poets. After his early education at Chancellor College at the University of Malawi and at the University of Zambia, where he was awarded a B.A. degree, he received an M.A. in creative writing from Brown University. While he was at Chancellor College, he was a founding member of the Writers' Group, which included the well-known Malawian poets Jack Mapanje, Lupenga Mphande, and Steve Chimombo. Chipasula's volumes of poetry include *Visions and Reflections* (1972) and *Whispers in the Wings* (1991). His poems also appear in, among other books, *When My Brothers Come Home: Poems from Central and Southern Africa* (1985), which he edited, and the *Heinemann Book of African Poetry in English* (1990).

Highly conscious of the artist's role in society, Chipasula assumes the responsibility of truth, which he bluntly portrays in "Manifesto on Ars Poetica":

I will not clean the poem to impress the tyrant;
I will not bend my verses into the bow of a praise song.
I will put the symbols of murder hidden in high offices
In the centre of my crude lines of accusations.
I will undress our land and expose her wounds.

Whether he writes in Malawi or elsewhere, Chipasula's poetry is centered on his home country, the small southeastern African nation that was ruled for more than three decades by the autocratic Hastings Kamuzu Banda, who unleashed a reign of terror upon his people. In his poetry, most of which has been written in exile, Chipasula affirms his love of his homeland, as in "A Love Poem for My Country," and exposes the cruelty of Banda. He laments a beautiful land that has become "stale" and "ravaged" and whose "flowers" are mangled. He uses copious images of violence and torture, including "burning calyx of sorrow," "bullet-riddled stalks," "chipped genitals," and "merciless knife." He accuses the sadistic and neurotic Banda of putting stones in prison for failing to sing his praises, and he accuses the colonizers of complicity in setting precedents for Banda, who learned from their violent repression of Africans, as shown by the Portuguese atrocities in "Wiriyamu" and "Nhazonia." In *Whispers in the Wings* he draws parallels between what has happened in Malawi and in countries such as Ethiopia, Mozambique, South Africa, Sudan, and Uganda. In "Shrapnel" and other poems he portrays violence as a worldwide phenomenon that needs to be eradicated wherever it rears its head.

Chipasula's poems about his American experiences mainly reflect on his situation as an exile. He compares what is happening in his homeland with the historical antecedents of slavery, past atrocities in the West Indies committed by Europeans, and the humiliation of black peoples like the Congolese Pygmy in the Bronx Zoo and the Hottentot Venus, whose experiences he shares.

While graphically presenting evil, the poet is hopeful of positive change at home and elsewhere. He intends to "resurrect the gaunt sun from its sickbed / And scatter this darkness with one flaming sword of light.'' He is confident of happier times; hence, ''I know a day will come and wash away my pain / And I will emerge from the night breaking into song / Like the sun, blowing out these evil stars.'' The poet confronts evil wherever he sees it and expects through struggle that things will change for the better.

Chipasula uses highly descriptive language to convey the evil perpetrated in Malawi and elsewhere. Many of his images are symbolic, and the irony and paradox of his language helps to undermine the perpetrators of evil. In some of his early poems he experiments with traditional African poetic styles. Because he is constantly accusing dictators and cataloguing their atrocities, his voice is often maudlin and rarely varied. As has been noted, his ''bluntness shocks the reader into a realization of the ugly reality of his brutalized homeland. He is the memory of his society and is faithful to the experience of the Banda era of Malawi's history.'' Without doubt Chipasula's poetry carries perhaps the strongest exilic voice in contemporary verse, and despite the nightmarish experiences he portrays, the hope he envisions has been vindicated in the improved state of present-day Malawi.

—Tanure Ojaide

CLANCHY, Kate

Nationality: British. **Born:** Katharine Sarah Clancy, Glasgow, 6 November 1965. **Family:** Married Matthew Reynolds in 1999. **Career:** Teacher of English and drama, Copthall Comprehensive School, Barnet, 1988–90; teacher at various schools in the Lothian region, 1990–91; teacher of English, 1992–94, teacher of English and writer-in-residence, 1994–98, Havering Sixth Form College, Essex; teacher-trainer for network training, the Poetry Library, Oxford University Department of Education, 1998–99. Since 1999 lecturer, Keble College, Oxford. **Awards:** Eric Gregory award, Society of Authors, 1994; New London Writers award, 1996; Scottish Autumn Book award, London Arts Board, 1996; Forward prize, Scottish Arts Council, 1996; Scottish First Book of the Year award, Saltire Society, 1996; Somerset Maugham award, Society of Authors, 1997; Scottish Spring Book award, Scottish Arts Council, 2000.

PUBLICATIONS

Poetry

Slattern. London, Chatto and Windus, 1996.
Samarkand. London, Picador, 1999.

*   *   *

Either in life or in letters, the usual methods of definition do not apply to Kate Clanchy. Her first book, *Slattern,* joined a metaphysical sense of language to a quite startling apprehension of matters either passed over or not hitherto thought worth writing about. Hers is an exquisitely feminine consciousness, and it reminds us that whole areas of experience have been brought to awareness by poets arriving in the wake of Adrienne Rich and Sylvia Plath, bold enough to write

about that which needs to be written about, no matter how slight, no matter how wounding.

''Poem for a Man with No Sense of Smell'' definitely breaks new ground, smell not being a prime constituent of poetry. The speaker defines each area of her body much as Marvell grazed the face and bosom of his coy mistress, but she does so in terms of olfactory sensations: the ''bass note'' of the armpits, the ''wet flush'' of her fear, the delicate hairs on the nape of her neck that ''hold a scent frail and precise as a fleet / of tiny origami ships, just setting out to sea.''

This image is a kind of norm that emerges at intervals through an output notable for its variegation. With elegant poise ''For a Wedding'' runs through the difficulties and pleasures that may be conjectured of the married state and ends with a vision at once of relaxation and of precariousness:

I wish you years that shape, that form,
and a pond in a Sunday, urban garden;
where you'll see your joined reflection tremble,

stand and watch the waterboatmen
skate with ease across the surface tension.

A similar image, of tiny waterborne creatures, sounds a note of warning in ''Patagonia'': ''the last clinging barnacles, / growing worried in the hush, had / paddled off in tiny coracles . . .'' The breakup of a love affair affords a theme available to both sexes, but in the poetry of a writer such as Clanchy the situation is approached sideways. The poem is definite in feeling but, on first reading, elusive in narrative structure.

Here Patagonia is a name, not a land. It stands for a belief that two people can be idyllically happy in their own world. But what is this world? It is full of contradictions, a peninsula wide enough for a couple of ''ladderback chairs,'' presumably the furniture, such as it is, that the couple have in their room. The poem, couched in a masterly free verse, is not speech in the usual sense but rather a meditation in the mind of the protagonist, and it seems that her partner is paying her little attention. There is a remarkable transition from the fauna— ''restless birds''—to the lover's hands. One implication may be that he is about to administer the coup de grâce. The woman anticipates this, crying,

When I spoke of Patagonia, I meant

skies all empty aching blue. I meant
years, I meant all of them with you.

The effect is to intensify the troubled hope of the earlier lines into something very like despair. There is a triple ''I meant'': ''I meant skies''; ''I meant years''; ''I meant all of them.'' It is too late, however, for her to say what she meant. Whatever she meant, none of it is going to happen now. It is the intensification of hopelessness achieved by these doubts and these repetitions that renders the lines a key to the whole, highly original poem.

The critic Gerald Woodward has written, ''Clanchy's real gifts . . . are an ear perfectly tuned to the rhythms and sonorities of the poetic line, an eye that is able to catch fresh glimpses of the world, and a facility with metaphor that casts up delightful conceits.'' Perhaps her second book, *Samarkand,* which Woodward was reviewing, does not quite live up to the promise of the first. The amount of whimsy in relation to thought has increased. In "The Acolyte," for example, Clanchy pictures herself humorously as a humble woman at the foot of a phallic pillar, on top of which is her lover "surveying a perfect circumference of sunset." In the promisingly named "War Poetry" a class of boys, who under other circumstances would enlist to fight for their country, sit abashed as they watch through the safety of glass a menacing swarm of wasps that have been disturbed. Somehow the later poems live a little too comfortably within the protection of their author's irreproachable style and flawless technique. It seems that the questioning and disturbance that gives such power to the first book has somewhat abated.

Nonetheless, Clanchy has shown extraordinary talent. Based on what she has achieved, she stands out among the significant poets of the past thirty years or so.

—Philip Hobsbaum

CLARK, John Pepper

Also writes as J.P. Clark Bekederemo. **Nationality:** Nigerian. **Born:** Kiagbodo, 6 April 1935. **Education:** Warri Government College, Ughelli, 1948–54; University of Ibadan, 1955–60, B.A. (honors) in English 1960, and graduate study (Institute of African Studies fellowship), 1963–64; Princeton University, New Jersey (Parvin fellowship). **Family:** Married Ebun Odutola Clark; three daughters and one son. **Career:** Information officer, Government of Nigeria, 1960–61; head of features and editorial writer, Lagos *Daily Express,* 1961–62; research fellow, 1964–66, and professor of African literature, 1966–85, University of Lagos. Founding editor, *Horn* magazine, Ibadan; co-editor, *Black Orpheus,* Lagos, from 1968. Founding member, Society of Nigerian Authors. **Agent:** Andrew Best, Curtis Brown, 162–68 Regent Street, London W1R 5TB, England.

PUBLICATIONS

Poetry

Poems. Ibadan, Mbari, 1962.
A Reed in the Tide: A Selection of Poems. London, Longman, 1965; New York, Humanities Press, 1970.
Casualties: Poems 1966–68. London, Longman, and New York, Africana, 1970.
Urhobo Poetry. Ibadan, Ibadan University Press, 1980.
A Decade of Tongues: Selected Poems 1958–1968. London, Longman, 1981.
State of the Union (as J.P. Clark Bekederemo). London, Longman, 1985.
A Lot from Paradise (as J.P. Clark). Ikeja, Malthouse Press, 1999.

Plays

Song of a Goat (produced Ibadan, 1961; London, 1965). Ibadan, Mbari, 1961; in *Three Plays,* 1964; in *Plays from Black Africa,* edited by Frederic M. Litto, New York, Hill and Wang, 1968.
Three Plays. London, Oxford University Press, 1964.
The Masquerade (produced London, 1965). Included in *Three Plays,* 1964.

The Raft (broadcast 1966; produced New York 1978). Included in *Three Plays,* 1964.
Ozidi. Ibadan, London, and New York, Oxford University Press, 1966.
The Bikoroa Plays (as J.P. Clark Bekederemo) (includes *The Boat, The Return Home, Full Circle*) (produced Lagos, 1981). Oxford, Oxford University Press, 1985.

Radio Play: *The Raft,* 1966.

Screenplay: *The Ozidi of Atazi.*

Other

America Their America. London, Deutsch-Heinemann, 1964; New York, Africana, 1969.
The Example of Shakespeare: Critical Essays on African Literature. London, Longman, and Evanston, Illinois, Northwestern University Press, 1970.
The Hero as a Villain. Lagos, University of Lagos Press, 1978.

Editor and Translator, *The Ozidi Saga,* by Okabou Ojobolo. Ibadan, University of Ibadan Press, 1977.

*

Critical Studies: *Three Nigerian Poets: A Critical Study of the Poetry of Soyinka, Clark, and Okigbo* by Nyong J. Udoeyop, Ibadan, Ibadan University Press, 1973; *A Critical View on John Pepper Clark's Selected Poems* by Kirsten Holst Petersen, London, Collings, 1981; *John Pepper Clark* by Robert M. Wren, Lagos, Nigeria, Lagos University Press, 1984; "The Lagos Scene," in *West Africa* (London), 3574, 16 December 1985; "The 'Sharp and Sided Hail': Hopkins and His Nigerian Imitators and Detractors" by Emeka Okeke-Ezigbo, in *Hopkins among the Poets: Studies in Modern Responses to Gerard Manley Hopkins,* edited by Richard F. Giles, Hamilton, Ontario, International Hopkins Assocation, 1985; "Poetry as Autobiography: Society and Self in Three Modern West African Poets" by Thomas R. Knipp, in *African Literature in Its Social and Political Dimensions,* edited by Eileen Julien and others, Washington, D.C., Three Continents, 1986; *An Investigation of John Pepper Clark's Drama as an Organic Interaction of Traditional African Drama with Western Theatre* (dissertation) by Thomas Vwetpak Anpe, n.p., 1986; "African Religious Beliefs in Literary Imagination: Ogbanje and Abiku in Chinua Achebe, J.P. Clark, and Wole Soyinka" by Chidi T. Maduka, in *Journal of Commonwealth Literature* (East Sussex, England), 22(1), 1987; "J.P. Clark as a Poet," in *Literary Criterion* (Bangalore, India), 23(1–2), 1988, and *The Poetry of J.P. Clark Bekederemo,* Lagos, Longman, 1989, both by Isaac Eliminian; "The Poet and His Art: The Evolution of J.P. Clark's Poetic Voice" by Aderemi Bamikunle, in *World Literature Today* (Norman, Oklahoma), 67(2), spring 1993; "J.P. Clark's Romantic 'Autotravography'" by Tony E. Afejuku, in *Literature Interpretation Theory* (New York), 4(2), 1993; "J.P. Clark-Bekederemo and the Ijo Literary Tradition" by Dan S. Izevbaye, in *Research in African Literatures* (Bloomington, Indiana), 25(1), spring 1994; "J.P. Clark's Dramatic Art: The Experimental Stage of His Dramatic Writing" by Daniel Nwedo Uwandu, in *Literary Half-Yearly* (India), 36(2), July 1995; *The Tragedy of Uncertain Continuity: John Bekederemo and Wole Soyinka* (dissertation) by Camille Aljean Willingham, Brown University, 1998; by Emevwo Biakolo, in *Postcolonial African Writers: A Bio-Bibliographical Critical Source Book,* edited by Pushpa Naidu Parekh and others, Westport, Connecticut, Greenwood, 1998.

*   *   *

John Pepper Clark is a dramatist as well as a poet, but whereas his drama production is held together by a certain unity of theme and style, his poetry is not. *A Reed in the Tide* is a collection of occasional poems, each one seemingly inspired by an actual occurrence in the poet's life such as watching Fulani cattle, seeing a girl bathing in a stream, or flying across the United States. The incidents take on a symbolic and sometimes a moral value that is worked out in the poems partly through description and partly through explicit commentary. In "Agbor Dancer," for example, Clark describes seeing a girl dance the traditional Agbor dance—"See her caught in the throb of a drum . . . entangled in the magic maze of music . . ."—and this leads him to a feeling of loss. He can no longer do the dance and is alienated from tribal life, but he wishes for reintegration: "Could I, early sequester'd from my tribe, / Free a lead-tether'd scribe / I should answer her communal call . . ."

The idea of cultural integration that runs through some of Clark's verse is supported by poems that deal with traditional African themes or that evoke Clark's native Nigerian town and landscape. The last section of *A Reed in the Tide* contains the most successful poems of the collection. The Ezra Pound-inspired poem about Ibadan and the sensitive depiction of the wet tropical Niger delta in "Night Rain," both excellent visual descriptions, are free of philosophical tags. The poems dealing with modern American life provide a logical contrast to the loving concern with traditional life. Clark dwells on the alienating effects of technology in "Service," about the slot machine, and in "Cave Call," on the underground train.

Clark's collection *Casualties: Poems 1966–68* deals with the Biafran war. The poet took part in the war, intervening on behalf of a friend, and was personally acquainted with several of the most important leaders in the conflict. An intimate knowledge of the details of the clash is necessary for an understanding of the poetry, which is mainly narrative and argumentative. Clark has felt obliged to provide footnotes to most of the poems to explain the details, for instance, that the crocodile in "The Reign of the Crocodile" is Major General Ironsi, who carried a stuffed crocodile as a swagger stick. The collection suffers badly from its concern with the actual details of the war, and one can only agree with Clark when he writes in the preface to the book's notes that "I sometimes wish I had written in prose this personal account . . ." Some of the poems, however, are transfused with a sadness that transcends the details and brings across not just the misery of war but also the particular misery of civil war, in which friendships and family ties are tested and broken.

Clark's pessimism is at its most acute in the 1985 collection *State of the Union.* In the book's first section, "State of the Union," which focuses on Nigerian sociopolitical and economic problems, the tone of the poems is clear: "Services taken / For granted elsewhere either break down / Or do not get started at all / When introduced here." The problem, Clark maintains, lies with the citizens of the country ("something there must / Be in ourselves"), who cannot commit themselves to a social paradigm. But his purpose is not just to point a finger in familiar ways, and in "The Sovereign," the last poem of the first section, he makes his most complex claim. Nigeria has never been a sovereign nation, "never a union," nothing but "an

amalgamation" of "four hundred and twenty three" states, "all spread / Between desert and sea," and it never will be a complete whole: "Hammer upon / Anvil may strike like thunder . . . but all is alchemy / Trying to sell as gold in broad daylight / This counterfeit coin called a sovereign." Clearly, as both Nigerian history and Clark's career have proceeded, his poetry has grown, its approach shifting according to political and historical circumstances and according to the unusual stance of this vital poet.

—Kirsten Holst Petersen and Martha Sutro

CLARK, Tom

Nationality: American. **Born:** Thomas Willard Clark, Chicago, Illinois, 1 March 1941. **Education:** University of Michigan, Ann Arbor (Hopwood prize, 1963), B.A. 1963; Cambridge University (Fulbright fellow, 1963–65), 1963–65; University of Essex, Wivenhoe, 1965–67. **Family:** Married Angelica Heinegg in 1968; one daughter. **Career:** Poetry editor, *Paris Review,* 1963–73; instructor in American poetry, University of Essex, 1966–67; senior writer, *Boulder Monthly,* Colorado. Since 1987 instructor in poetics, New College of California. **Awards:** Bess Hokin prize, 1966, and George Dillon memorial prize, 1968 (*Poetry,* Chicago); Poets Foundation award, 1967; Rockefeller fellowship, 1968; Guggenheim fellowship, 1970; National Endowment for the Arts grant, 1985. **Address:** c/o Black Sparrow Press, 24 Tenth Street, Santa Rosa, California 95401, U.S.A.

PUBLICATIONS

Poetry

Airplanes. Brightlingsea, Essex, Once Press, 1966.
The Sand Burg. London, Ferry Press, 1966.
Bun, with Ron Padgett. New York, Angel Hair, 1968.
Chicago, with Lewis Warsh. New York, Angel Hair, 1969.
Stones. New York, Harper, 1969.
Air. New York, Harper, 1970.
Green. Los Angeles, Black Sparrow Press, 1971.
The No Book. Wivenhoe Park, Essex, Ant's Forefoot, 1971.
Back in Boston Again, with Ted Berrigan and Ron Padgett. Philadelphia, Telegraph, 1972.
John's Heart. London, Cape Goliard Press, and New York, Grossman, 1972.
Smack. Los Angeles, Black Sparrow Press, 1972.
Blue. Los Angeles, Black Sparrow Press, 1974.
Suite. Los Angeles, Black Sparrow Press, 1974.
At Malibu. New York, Kulchur, 1975.
Baseball. Berkeley, California, Figures, 1976.
Fan Poems. Plainfield, Vermont, North Atlantic, 1976.
An Arthur Flegenheimer Sachet. Privately printed, 1977.
35. Berkeley, California, Poltroon Press, 1977.
How I Broke In/Six Modern Masters. Bolinas, California, Tombouctou, 1978.
When Things Get Tough on Easy Street: Selected Poems 1963–1978 Santa Barbara, California, Black Sparrow Press, 1978.
Heartbreak Hotel. West Branch, Iowa, Toothpaste Press, 1981.
Journey to the Ulterior. Santa Barbara, California, Am Here/Immediate, 1981.

Nine Songs. Isla Vista, California, Turkey Press, 1981.

The Rodent Who Came to Dinner. Santa Barbara, California, Am Here/Immediate, 1981.

A Short Guide to the High Plains. Santa Barbara, California, Cadmus, 1981.

Under the Fortune Palms. Isla Vista, California, Turkey Press, 1982.

Dark As Day. Bolinas, California, Smithereens Press, 1983.

After Dante. Santa Barbara, California, Handmade, 1984.

How It Goes. Santa Barbara, California, Handmade, 1984.

Paradise Resisted: Selected Poems 1978–1984. Santa Barbara, California, Black Sparrow Press, 1984.

Property. Los Angeles, Illuminati, 1984.

Technology. Santa Barbara, California, Handmade, 1984.

The Border. Minneapolis, Coffee House Press, 1985.

Disordered Ideas. Santa Rosa, California, Black Sparrow Press, 1987.

Easter Sunday. Minneapolis, Coffee House Press, 1987.

Fractured Karma. Santa Rosa, California, Black Sparrow Press, 1990.

Sleepwalker's Fate. Santa Rosa, California, Black Sparrow Press, 1992.

Junkets on a Sad Planet: Scenes from the Life of John Keats. Santa Rosa, California, Black Sparrow Press, 1994.

Like Real People. Santa Rosa, California, Black Sparrow Press, 1995.

Empire of Skin. Santa Rosa, California, Black Sparrow Press, 1997.

White Thought. West Stockbridge, Massachusetts, Hard Press/The Figures, 1997.

Play

The Emperor of the Animals. London, Goliard Press, 1967.

Novels

The Master. Markesan, Wisconsin, Pentagram, 1979.

Who Is Sylvia? Eugene, Oregon, Blue Wind Press, 1979.

The Spell: A Romance. Santa Rosa, California, Black Sparrow Press, 2000.

Short Stories

The Last Gas Station and Other Stories. Santa Barbara, California, Black Sparrow Press, 1980.

Other

Neil Young. Toronto, Coach House Press, 1971.

Champagne and Baloney: The Rise and Fall of Finley's A's. New York, Harper, 1976.

No Big Deal, with Mark Fidrych. Philadelphia, Lippincott, 1977.

A Conversation with Hitler. Santa Barbara, California, Black Sparrow Press, 1978.

The World of Damon Runyon. New York, Harper, 1978.

The Mutabilitie of the Englishe Lyrick (parodies). Berkeley, California, E Typographeo Poltroniano, 1978.

One Last Round for the Shuffler: A Blacklisted Ball Player's Story. St. Paul, Minnesota, Truck, 1979.

The Great Naropa Poetry Wars. Santa Barbara, California, Cadmus, 1980.

Jack Kerouac. New York, Harcourt Brace, 1984.

Late Returns: A Memoir of Ted Berrigan. Bolinas, California, Tombouchtou, 1985.

Kerouac's Last Word: Jack Kerouac in Escapade. Sudbury, Massachusetts, Water Row Press, 1986.

The Exile of Céline. New York, Random House, 1986.

Charles Olson: The Allegory of a Poet's Life. New York, Norton, 1991.

Robert Creeley and the Genius of the American Common Place. New York, New Directions, 1993.

Things Happen for a Reason: The True Story of an Itinerant Life in Baseball, with Terry Leach. Berkeley, California, Frog Ltd., 2000.

*

Manuscript Collection: University of Connecticut, Storrs; University of Kansas, Lawrence; University of Michigan, Ann Arbor.

Critical Studies: "Tom Clark: Inertia and the Highway Patrol" by Pat Nolan, in *Sun & Moon* (College Park, Maryland), 5, 1979; interview with Tom Clark by Lynn Gray, in *FM Five* (San Francisco), 3(3), winter 1986; "Tom Clark: A Checklist" by Timothy Murray, in *Credences* (Buffalo, New York), 1(1), n.d.

* * *

Tom Clark's poetry published in the 1960s can give the impression of the man who got on his horse and rode off in all directions at once. The look of the poems is frequently reassuring, the lines of more or less equivalent length grouped into equivalent units on the page, promising a rational structure. But within these units chaos sometimes reigns. The thin or nonexistent punctuation often creates syntactical confusion. There is also a certain fondness for quirky modifiers, as though the poet were a computer choosing at random from a bank of nouns and a bank of adjectives and combining the results. To place a "secretive tambourine" and a "sober dog" back-to-back in the poem "Comanche," from *Stones,* suggests an interest more in the way words can collide than in their potentiality for pleasing combinations or for meaning. This fondness for playing with words surfaces in some poems in the form of jingly sound effects. In addition, Clark seems fond of the chain poem, in which the repetition of a single word or phrase in each section ties the whole together, as in his brash parody of Wallace Stevens's famous blackbird poem, "Eleven Ways of Looking at a Shit Bird" (*Stones*).

The poems published during the 1970s move away from these scattergun effects. This work seems clearer and cleaner, although it has the same drive and energy, the general feeling being that Clark is perpetually en route. In addition, the range of subjects is wider, with the introspection of the earlier work giving way to a concern with things and people in the world. One of my favorites is "To Kissinger" (*When Things Get Tough on Easy Street*), a wacky series of insults that make a forceful political point with humor. In the same collection are a number of poems about running, some short, throwaway pieces, others, such as "Morning Leaves Me Speechless," expressing beautifully the euphoria that can appear on the other side of physical exertion.

In a number of books published during this time Clark seems overly fond of the tiny poem. *Green* and *Blue* contain a number of poems that consist of one sentence or even less; *Smack* is made up entirely of single sentences arranged vertically on the page. These efforts at minimal art via the word are not always successful; they give the impression of notebook jottings, casual ideas that might grow into poems. There is a throwaway streak in Clark's work, a willingness to let things go, to gallop on to the next poem, to get on down the road. While this tendency may undermine the shorter poems, in the longer ones, where there is room for discursive, casual, or colloquial effects, it can produce exciting poetry. A good example of this is ''Chicago'' (*When Things Get Tough on Easy Street*), an extended recollection of the poet's youthful experiences as an usher at various stadiums, ballparks, and convention halls in the Chicago area that ends by evoking an entire era—that strange period of American history known as ''the fifties.'' There is an interesting and unexpected idea implied in the poem, that poets and ushers have something in common. Both are employed spectators, in it for more than entertainment.

Clark is a world-class spectator, his work a grand record of his passionate looking on. In many of his sports poems, especially those dealing with baseball, he tries to invest the game with a meaning far beyond its position in American society as entertainment. Clark is a fan; he does not write about baseball but celebrates it. The poems belong to the tradition of the encomium, and the names of the players ring through them like a Homeric roll call: Orestes Minoso, Catfish Hunter, Vida Blue, Bert Campaneris, Bill Lee. The poem on Lee is perhaps the best of these, a long, warm appreciation of the player's eccentric intelligence.

Clark ultimately seems to have been released from his focus on baseball as a subject, perhaps because he has been able to celebrate the sport in prose in a number of books and articles, although his fondness for the encomium persists in some of his poems about artists in other fields—two on Reverdy and one each on Ungaretti, Vuillard, Kafka, and Lenny Bruce. But his midcareer work is not all hero worship. For example, in ''How I Broke In,'' the poem sequence that concludes *When Things Get Tough on Easy Street,* Clark shuffles and reshuffles a number of images, allusions, and individual lines, upping the ante in each section and increasing the pressure until one begins to wonder how he can sustain it and keep going. To read this sequence is to confront something powerful, even dangerous, something barely held in control.

Clark's combination of a West Coast, postbeat identity with a slightly harder, more scholarly edge has been characteristic of much of his career. In *Junkets on a Sad Planet: Scenes from the Life of John Keats,* Clark turns directly toward poetic tradition and by doing so takes spectatorship to a new level. In this collection of 127 poems and prose pieces, Clark attempts both to mimic Keats as well as to redraw him into something of a Clarkian modernist-romantic. Thus, heightened swoons such as ''She comes, she comes again, sighing like a ringdove / in the pallid moonshine, or tongueless Philomel / who cannot utter her ravisher's name / because he has stolen away her articulation'' are conflated with raw, aggressive lines such as ''His endless suspicions and moods, as though everything / He had were about to be taken from him. And it was.'' It is interesting that in the prose sections Clark offers astute conjectures about Keats's life. Clark is impressive in his mastery of a range of poetic voices. The last section, ''Coda: Echo and Variation,'' an extended, twelve-part deathbed song, is a Keatsian retrospection of a brief, tragic life and the most passionate and sad part of the collection.

Clark both resists and subscribes to the formal aspects of poetry. In *Like Real People,* a largely autobiographical collection of poems, the first section, ''Happy Talk,'' consists of fourteen-line poems that clearly nod to the sonnet form, but not beyond their line count and rough line length. They read almost like an early Pollack painting, as surfaces crowded with small spots of various color. Although they are somewhat disjointed in their thinking, as a section they create atmospheric human yearning or nostalgia for childhood. The childhood poems, in a section called ''Torn from an Old Album,'' are largely written in concrete, precise imagery. It is often the poems in ''Reflections,'' written in longer, more prosaic lines, that are the most convincing pieces of the collection. Mixing prose into his books with characteristic flourish, Clark closes out this collection with the prose section ''Confessions,'' in which he recalls his midcentury childhood and adolescence, his schooling in England, and his political and poetic life in the company of Ted Berringan and others.

—Steven Young and Martha Sutro

CLARKE, George Elliott

Pseudonyms: Nahum Shaka; Nattt Moziah Shaka. **Nationality:** Canadian. **Born:** George Elliott Johnson, Windsor, Nova Scotia, 12 February 1960. **Education:** University of Waterloo, Ontario, 1979–84, B.A. (honors) 1984; Dalhousie University, Halifax, Nova Scotia, 1986–89, M.A. 1989; Queen's University, Kingston, Ontario, 1990–93, Ph.D. 1993. **Family:** Married Geeta Paray-Clarke in 1998. **Career:** Legislative researcher, Provincial Parliament, Toronto, 1982–83; library assistant, Halifax Memorial Library, Nova Scotia, 1983; newspaper editor, University of Waterloo, Ontario, 1984–85; social worker, Black United Front, Dartmouth, Nova Scotia, 1985–87; parliamentary aide, House of Commons, Ottawa, Ontario, 1987–91; freelance writer, Kingston and Ottawa, Ontario, 1991–94; assistant professor of English, Duke University, Durham, North Carolina, 1994–99. Assistant professor of English, University of Toronto, Ontario, 1999—. **Awards:** First prize in poetry, Writers' Federation of Nova Scotia, 1981; second prize, Bliss Carman award, 1983; Archibald Lampman award, 1991, for *Whylah Falls;* Portia White prize, 1998; Rockefeller Foundation Bellagio Center fellow, 1998. LL.D: Dalhousie University, 1999. D.Litt.: University of New Brunswick, 2000. **Agent:** The Bukowski Agency, Toronto, Ontario. **Address:** 7 King's College Circle, Department of English, University of Toronto, Toronto, Ontario M5S 3K1, Canada.

PUBLICATIONS

Poetry

Saltwater Spirituals and Deeper Blues. Halifax, Nova Scotia, Pottersfield Press, 1983.
Whylah Falls. Vancouver, Polestar Books, 1990.
Lush Dreams, Blue Exile. Halifax, Nova Scotia, Pottersfield Press, 1994.

Plays

Whylah Falls: The Play. Toronto, Playwrights Canada Press, 1999.
Beatrice Chancy. Vancouver, Polestar Books, 1999.

Screenplays: *One Heart Broken into Song,* 1999; *Beatrice Chancy: The Opera,* 2000.

Other

Editor, *Fire on the Water: An Anthology of Black Nova Scotian Writing.* Halifax, Nova Scotia, Pottersfield Press, 2 vols., 1991–92.
Editor, *Borderlines.* Toronto, Copp-Clark, 1995.
Editor, *Eyeing the North Star.* Toronto, McClelland and Stewart, 1997.

*

Critical Studies: "An Unimpoverished Style" by M. Travis Lane, in *Canadian Poetry* (London, Ontario), 1985; "Whylah Falls" by Arnold Davidson, in *Wissenschaftlicher Verlag Trier* (Stuttgart, Germany), 1997; "A Rose Grows in Whylah Falls" by Dorothy Wells, in *Canadian Literature* (Vancouver), 1997; "Even the Stars Are Temporal" by Wayde Compton, in *West Coast Line* (Vancouver), 1997; "Some Aspects of Blues Use" by H. Nigel Thomas, in *CLA Journal,* 1999; "G.E. Clarke's Redemptive Vision" by Maureen Moynagh, in *Playwrights Canada* (Toronto), 2000.

George Elliott Clarke comments:

I come to poetry as a dreaming singer. I have spirituals in my blood, blues in my heart. I keep striving to get trumpets, pianos, guitars, and drums into my poetry. I can only think of it as song. My poetics is revelation.

I embrace all the poetic forms—from *vers blanc* to *vers libre,* from haiku to rap, from epic to proverb. For me poetry is whatever a poet chooses to do.

My first influence was my mother's voice and then the King James Version of the Bible, which I have read thrice. Now I read everything: the British—Shakespeare, Shelley, Clare, Yeats, Walcott; the Canadian; and the African American—Toomer, Hayden, Baraka, and the "Ugly American"—Pound.

In the end I am interested in singing the Bible and dreams of Africadia, a portion of Nova Scotia settled by African Americans more than two centuries ago. But I also just like to sing.

*   *   *

George Elliott Clarke comes from and writes about the long-established black community of Nova Scotia, some of whose members are descended from Loyalists who fled north during and after the American Revolution and the War of 1812. This genealogy of the "Africadians" (to use a word Clarke has coined) is important because, together with a strong lyrical and rhetorical impulse, the poet clearly sees himself as a witness for, and chronicler of, his people. To that end he often intersperses local archival photos among his poems. Yet Clarke is never insular. Not only does he take account of the Scots and the indigenous Micmacs, but he also draws on the wider African-American heritage of glorious gospel and blues. He reaches out to American expatriates in Paris and touches on the Africadians who migrated to West Africa in 1792 to found what became the nation of Sierra Leone.

Clarke's first collection, *Saltwater Spirituals and Deeper Blues,* commemorates the cohesive and energizing role of black churches in an alien land and laments the destruction of Africville, an economically stricken but culturally vibrant community in the Halifax area. In "Campbell Road Church" a railway porter remembers the

shabby shacktown of
shattered glass and promises,
rats rustling like a girl's loose dress.
he rages to recall
the gutting death of his genealogy,
to protest his home's slaughter
by butcher bulldozers
and city planners molesting statistics.

The lament becomes a personal one in "Crying the Beloved Country" when he considers what amounts to his own expatriation from his province's "sea-bound beauty / shale arms and red clay lips / sipping fundy streams":

why can i not depart from you
like any proud, prodigal son,
ignoring your eyes'
black baptist churches?
what keeps me from easy going?
Mother, is it your death
i fear
or my life?

In any case Clarke aims to achieve the vigor and syncretism of what in "East Coasting" he calls "bagpipe jazz hymns."

Whylah Falls, a verse novel later adapted as a stage play, assembles a busy and complex cast of characters in a fictional village founded by black Loyalists, a place that Clarke terms a kind of northern Mississippi, "with blood spattered, not on magnolias, but on pines, lilacs and wild roses." Here his documentary tendencies take a different turn: "These poems are facts presented as fiction. There was no other way to tell the truth save to disguise it as a story." The interwoven tales of violence, persecution, and love are told in voices that alternate between romance and realism. One of them, Cora's, leans toward realism. In "Cora's Testament" we read,

Uncle was sniffin' me, and I'd be damned
If I 'lowed him to stir my sugar bowl,
And I shushed a cryin' doll; so when a skirt-
Crazed Saul, who trudged nine miles and back to spade
Gypsum, came courtin' me, I swept his house,
Slept in his bed.

In *Lush Dreams, Blue Exile* Clarke organizes his poems in sections, giving them place-names that, he tells us, "refer to states of mind, not actual geographies." For example, the section "Axum-Saba" derives from "ancient African-Arabian kingdoms ruled by Queen Saba (*Sheba*), the beautiful Panther-in-the-Blossom" and consists of love poems. This wide-ranging collection includes the stronger poems from *Saltwater Spirituals and Deeper Blues* and in the aptly named "Gehenna" section encompasses public, indeed historical, events like the assassinations of García Lorca, Martin Luther King, Jr., the Kennedy brothers, and Indira Gandhi. In "April 3–4, 1968" Clarke shows King preaching in church and then, the next day,

After the rain, he steps into the cool
Dusk, into the cool, wet, Tennessee dusk.
Andy dreams he hears an engine crackle.
Ralph jumps instinctively, then turns, then turns,

And sees King, his arms outstretched, blood blazing
From the hole the bullet's punched through his neck.

Yet no matter how somber his subject matter may be, Clarke always strikes the celebratory note. On April 3 he has King tell his rapt audience, "I've been to the mountaintop," and he makes another preacher, Richard Preston in *Saltwater Spirituals and Deeper Blues,* exhort his flock to "go sound the jubilee."

—Fraser Sutherland

CLARKE, Gillian

Nationality: Welsh. **Born:** Gillian Williams, Cardiff, Glamorgan, 8 June 1937. **Education:** St. Clare's Convent, Porthcawl, Glamorgan; University College, Cardiff, B.A.(honors) in English 1958. **Career:** News researcher, BBC, London, 1958–60, and since 1960 occasional broadcaster. Since 1985 freelance writer. Lecturer in art history, Gwent College of Art and Design, Newport, 1975–84; writing fellow, St. David's University College, Lampeter, Dyfed, 1984–85. Editor, *Anglo-Welsh Review,* 1976–84. Chair, since 1988, Welsh Academy, and since 1989, Taliesin Trust. President, Writer's Centre, Ty Newydd. **Address:** Carcanet Press, 4th Floor, Conavon Court, 12–16 Blackfriars Street, Manchester M3 5BQ, England.

PUBLICATIONS

Poetry

Snow on the Mountain. Swansea, Christopher Davies, 1971.
The Sundial. Llandysul, Dyfed, Gomer, 1978.
Letter from a Far Country. Manchester, Carcanet, 1982.
Fires on Llyn. Leamington Spa, Warwickshire, Other Branch Readings, 1984.
Selected Poems. Manchester, Carcanet, 1985.
Letting in the Rumour. Manchester, Carcanet, 1989.
The King of Britain's Daughter. Manchester, Carcanet Press, 1993.
Collected Poems. Manchester, Carcanet, 1997.
Banc Sîon Cwilt: A Local Habitation and a Name. Newtown, Powys, Gwasg Gregynog, 1998.
Five Fields. Manchester, Carcanet, 1998.
The Animal Wall: And Other Poems. Llandysul, Pont Books, 1999.

Plays

The King of Britain's Daughter (libretto for cantata), 1993.

Radio Poems: *Talking in the Dark,* 1975; *Letter from a Far Country,* 1979.

Other

Editor, *The Poetry Book Society Anthology 1987–1988.* London, Hutchinson, 1987.
Compiler, *The Whispering Room: Haunted Poems.* New York, Kingfisher, 1996.

*

Critical Studies: "Grafting the Sour to Sweetness: Anglo-Welsh Poetry in the Last Twenty-Five Years" by Tony Curtis, in his *Wales: The Imagined Nation—Studies in Cultural and National Identity,* Bridgend, Mid Glamorgan, Poetry Wales, 1986; "Two Welsh Poets: Gillian Clarke and Tony Curtis" by Michael Hulse, in *Quadrant* (Victoria, Australia), 32(1–2), January-February 1988; "Incoming Tales: The Poetry of Gillian Clarke" by Linden Peach, in *New Welsh Review* (Cardiff, Wales), 1(1), summer 1988; by Roger Garfitt, in *Poetry Review,* 84(2), summer 1994; "The Poetry of Gillian Clarke" by K.E. Smith, in *Poetry in the British Isles: Non-Metropolitan Perspectives,* edited by Hans-Werner Ludwig and Lothar Fietz, Cardiff, University of Wales Press, 1995; "Women Poets and 'Women's Poetry': Fleur Adcock, Gillian Clarke and Carol Rumens" by Lyn Pykett, in *British Poetry from the 1950s to the 1990s: Politics and Art,* edited by Gary Day and Brian Docherty, London, Macmillan, and New York, St Martin's Press, 1997.

*   *   *

Gillian Clarke writes of her native Wales, of the elements that form and shape it: "It is not easy. / There are no brochure blues or boiled sweet / Reds. All is ochre and earth and cloud-green / Nettles tasting sour and the smells of moist earth and sheep's wool . . ." ("Blaen Cwrt"). Rain, unyielding stone, the "uncountable miles of mountains," and the "big, unpredictable sky" underlie her work. Beneath her apparently artless syntax is a complex system of assonance; repeated vowels and consonants keep the poems both tight and resonant. Many of Clarke's syntactical experiments are based on the metrical devices of traditional Welsh poetry.

Clarke's collection *The Sundial* deals with death, abandonment, and time passing, and there is a constant sense of people pushing back the wilderness, keeping primordial forces at bay. But these huge themes are carefully concealed in domestic disguises. For example, in the title poem a young son's sundial gives rise to the final stanza:

All day we felt and watched the sun
Caged in its white diurnal heat,
Pointing at us with its black stick.

Though rural life looms large, this is the province of primitive archetypes rather than country idylls. In "Storm Awst"

. . . This then is the big weather
They said was coming. All the signs
Were bad, the gulls coming in white,
Lapwings gathering, the sheep too
Calling all night. The gypsies
Were making their fires in the woods
Down there in the east . . . always
A warning . . .

There is no comfort in this world, and even in the secure setting of "Baby-Sitting" the speaker fears the waking of her charge:

. . . To her I will represent absolute
Abandonment. For her it will be worse
Than for the lover cold in lonely
Sheets; worse than for the woman who waits
A moment to collect her dignity
Beside the bleached bone in the terminal ward.

167

As she rises sobbing from the monstrous land
Stretching for milk-familiar comforting,
She will find me and between us two
It will not come. It will not come.

Clarke's second major collection, *Letter from a Far Country,* exhibits the same preoccupations though the tone is less intense, more refined. Here the rhythms of rural life prevail in poems like "Scything," "Buzzard," and "Friesian Bull." Death is always close, but there is an acceptance of it, as in "The Ram," which begins, "He died privately. / His disintegration is quiet. / Grass grows among the stems of his ribs . . ."

The title poem of the collection is a wonderful rambling meditation written originally for radio. Centered around a real parish in Wales, it explores "the far country" of the past and the imagined lives of its women inhabitants. Clarke reveals a remarkable eye for detail: ". . . sea-caves, cellars; the back stairs / behind the chenille curtain; the landing when the lights are out; / nightmares in hot feather beds . . ." or "A stony track turns between ancient hedges, narrowing, / like a lane in a child's book. / Its perspective makes the heart restless / . . . The minstrel boy to the war has gone. / But the girl stays. To mind things. / She must keep. And wait. And pass time. / There's always been time on our hands . . ." In such discreet phrases Clarke voices women's discontent: "The gulls grieve at our contentment. / It is a masculine question. / 'Where' they call 'are your great works?' / They slip their fetters and fly up / to laugh at land-locked women. / Their cries are cruel as greedy babies . . ."

In its solemn, reticent way this poem celebrates the lives of women: "It has always been a matter / of lists. We have been counting, / folding, measuring, making, / tenderly laundering cloth / ever since we have been women." The poem concludes with an easy rhythmical verse that, for all its lightness of touch, expresses a profound confusion about the choices facing contemporary women: "If we launch the boat and sail away . . . Who'll catch the nightmares and ride them away . . . Will the men grow tender and the children strong? . . . Who will do the loving while we're away?"

The new poetry in Clarke's 1985 *Selected Poems* is more lyrical than her previous work. There is a maturity about these poems. For example, in "October" the poet proclaims, ". . . I must write like the wind, year after year / passing my death day, winning ground." And "Climbing Cader Idris" begins, "You know the mountain with your body, / I with my mind, I suppose. / Each, in our own way, describes / the steepening angle of rock . . ." Here nature is no longer the vengeful adversary, but rather more an accomplice. Poems like "Epithalamium" reveal unbridled, joyful celebration, and even the stark, sad "The Hare," written in memory of the poet Frances Horovitz, ends on a note of calm acceptance:

. . . When they hand me insults or little hurts
and I'm on fire with my arguments

at your great distance you can calm me still.
Your dream, my sleeplessness, the cattle
asleep under a full moon,

and out there
the dumb and stiffening body of the hare.

—Katie Campbell

168

CLIFTON, Harry

Nationality: Irish. **Born:** Dublin, 15 August 1952. **Education:** University College, Dublin, 1974–76, B.A. in English literature and philosophy 1974, M.A. in philosophy 1975, H.Dip. in education 1976. **Career:** Teacher of English and English literature, Government Teacher's College, Keffi, Nigeria, 1976–78; teacher of English and French, Blackrock College, Dublin, 1979–80; working in Irish Civil Service, 1980–88, including period of secondment working in Thailand with refugee aid programs, 1980–82; teacher of English and English literature, The New School, Assisi, Italy, 1989–91; teacher of English and media studies, St. Charles Sixth Form College, London, 1992–93; lecturer on Irish literature, University of Bremen, Germany, spring 1994; writer-in-residence, University of Bordeaux, France, spring 1996. **Awards:** Patrick Kavanagh award, 1981; Arts Council bursary in literature, 1982. Irish fellow, Iowa International Writer's program, 1985; fellowship at Foundation Binz 39, Scuol, Switzerland, 1991; fellowship at Atelierhaus Worpswede, Germany, 1993–94. **Address:** 6 rue du Pierre Brossolette, 92320 Châtillon, Paris, France.

PUBLICATIONS

Poetry

Null Beauty. Belfast, Honest Ulsterman, 1975.
The Walls of Carthage. Dublin, Gallery Press, 1977.
Office of the Salt Merchant. Dublin, Gallery Press, 1979.
Comparative Lives. Dublin, Gallery Press, 1982.
The Liberal Cage. Dublin, Gallery Press, 1988.
At the Grave of Silone. Belfast, Honest Ulsterman, 1993.
The Desert Route: Selected Poems 1973–88. Dublin and Newcastle upon Tyne, Gallery Press/Bloodaxe, 1993.
Night Train through the Brenner. Loughcrew, County Meath, Gallery Press, 1994.

Other

On the Spine of Italy: A Year in the Abbruzzi. London, Macmillan, 1999.

*

Critical Study: "The Permanent City: The Younger Irish Poets" by Gerald Dawe, in *The Irish Writer and the City,* edited by Maurice Harmon, Gerrards Cross, Buckinghamshire, and Totowa, New Jersey, Smythe, 1984.

Harry Clifton comments:

The poems in *The Desert Route* were written over a period of fifteen years and are drawn from my four collections published in Ireland over that time. I say collections rather than books, for in a very real sense this is the first book I have published, if by the term "book" is meant something other than the mechanical entity made up of sixty-four printed pages. I like to think that, between us, my editor Peter Fallon and I have been able to abstract the real structure that underlay those earlier texts and to arrive at something whole and integral, an unforced unity of experience.

As it happens, I have traveled a good deal and lived in places not normally included within the psychic space of an Irish poet. Africa, where my postuniversity wanderings led me in the late seventies as a fledgling teacher—a raw, vivifying reality after the cerebral hush of graduate studies, an awakening to sex and death, and the violence and innocence of political change. Later in the Far East, where I worked in the administration of aid programs for the hundreds of thousands of Cambodian refugees camped inside the Thai border and wrote dark, disaffected poems on the side of sexual and political compromise. The flip side, as I see it now, of a misplaced idealism akin to that of the thirties poets seeking to unite the active with the contemplative. Thailand in the early eighties was my Spain—it exposed a falseness in me through which flowed the seven devils of the id. I hope the African, and more particularly the Asian, poems included here convey some sense of a Western consciousness enlarged and threatened by these new psychic spaces.

In between, of course, there has always been Ireland—the "distaff side" to the wanderings. A home to come back to, albeit temporarily, and consolidate before sallying forth again. I am struck by how often over the years I have written of returning to Ireland as an ever diminishing reality which never quite reaches the vanishing point, and probably never will. Which is why, I suppose, my ideal "Irish" poet would probably be someone like Louis MacNeice, for whom Ireland is a province of his imagination, as are Sri Lanka, Norway, Iceland, Italy, or wherever he happens to be, but whose primary allegiance is to the English language itself.

Years ago a priest who is now one of the highest religious authorities in Ireland confided in me that he had never once, in forty years of living, had an experience of the Absolute. He described himself, quoting Saint Augustine, as one condemned to shuttle endlessly back and forth across the desert between Carthage and Alexandria to compare their walls—the desert, of course, being the desert of relative values. Out of that image I wrote "The Walls of Carthage," one of the earliest poems in this selection and one which in a sense defines all the journeyings of *The Desert Route*—for the polarities called Alexandria and Carthage might just as easily be North and South, id and consciousness, the West and elsewhere. And the desert between them, physical and fleshed out though I hope it is in these poems, no more than a state of mind.

*   *   *

"Coincident worlds / Are meshing into gear / At intersections only a god might see / Or a stationmaster," writes Harry Clifton in "Experience," the opening poem of his collection *The Liberal Cage*. But Clifton's poems reveal that these "coincident worlds" are visible to one more person—the poet, for whom surveying the often imperceptible or seamless overlap between disparate worlds and different measures of experience is a persistent preoccupation. Clifton has traveled extensively beyond his native Ireland, particularly to places—Africa, Asia, America—whose geography, psychic and actual, is vast and uncertain. Usually the journey is unsettling, whether "somewhere in Africa," where the "barking of primates, desolate after rain, came floating from graveyards of lorries" ("Vladimir and Estragon"), or in the "loveless, extraterrestrial space" of Middle America ("Euclid Avenue").

The varied but often jagged landscapes Clifton describes make him a writer with a particular affinity for the poetry of place, a genre, as Seamus Heaney has described it, that is known in Irish poetry as *dinnseanchas*. This fascination with the actual, psychic, and mythical dimensions of locale allows Clifton to use place in his poetry to negotiate the extremes of experience deftly and quietly amid the problematic terrain of the human heart in joy and despair, in and out of love, anywhere. Thus in Clifton's poems speakers characteristically attempt both to come to terms with the self as well as to understand what is external and opaque.

Not surprisingly, Clifton, the great-grandson of a Fenian exile, renders a sense of isolation just as discerningly as he does a sense of place. The isolation is both ethical and philosophical. The ethical sense is apparent throughout his work, and it is one particularly sensitive to the wreckage left by colonial and imperial presences. In the elegantly crafted "Monsoon Girl," for example, the anesthetizing hedonism of a night with a pleasure girl is jarred by lights, dope squads, the "poor starting early," and a pervasive sense of a miscarriage of justice. In the equally admirable "Walls of Carthage" the speaker is no hedonist, but he remains an isolate, this time a priest in his late forties who is "still / In the desert, still / Relativity's fool." Posting Alexandria and Carthage as the philosophical points between which he must shuttle with his "speech of failure" and "groundless visions," the priest concludes that

> We, in inferior reason
> Travel until we fall,
> To compare in a desert season,
> The beauty of their walls.

Formal, technically subtle, with a craftsman's facility for understated rhyme, most frequently cast in quatrains, Clifton's poetry derives its power from a philosophical complexity, a stoic's sensibility, an observable maturation of voice and attitude, and a bearing that is both passionate and compassionate. Like his better-known countrymen, Clifton left Ireland to write of foreign places, of journey, and of exile, while nonetheless invoking his native land as a place he can never wholly leave emotionally. "The Distaff Side" might be taken as an allegorical representation of his Irish and exiled selves. In the poem the red-haired "runaway daughter" has insisted that the couple return to Ireland, where "nobody knows him" and his rages

> Are all domestic, tantrums at bad little girls
> Upsetting the basket of eels he gathered for ages
> And starting their passionate journeys back to the world.

The analogues to Joyce and to Joyce's own journeyman, Leopold Bloom, are repeated in "Eccles Street, Bloomsday 1982," where, as in the poem "Ireland," breakthrough and release remain largely elusive. Nonetheless, the speaker's own "arc of odyssey" and "invisible yearning" are the prefigured but wholly possible steps taken when his love and he unsentimentally "weigh anchor at last, and go away."

Clifton's poems of exile and return are insufficiently known in some of the places—the United States preeminently—he describes so acutely. They are extraordinary works, small masterpieces of concrete description and philosophical rumination, and are deserving of a wider readership. Most fortuitously perhaps, the poet, though no longer an "Upstairs Child," still has "all the time in the world / To compose myself, and quite self-consciously."

—Sheila Haney Drain and Jeanne Colleran

CLIFTON, (Thelma) Lucille

Nationality: American. **Born:** Thelma Lucille Sayles, Depew, New York, 27 June 1936. **Education:** Howard University, Washington, D.C. 1953–55; Fredonia State Teachers College, New York, 1955. **Family:** Married Fred J. Clifton in 1958 (died 1984); four daughters and two sons. **Career:** Claims clerk, New York State Division of Employment, Buffalo, 1958–60; literature assistant, U.S. Office of Education, Washington, D.C., 1969–71; professor of literature and creative writing, University of California, Santa Cruz, 1985–89. Since 1989 distinguished professor of humanities, St. Mary's College of Maryland, and professor of writing, Columbia University, 1994–96. Visiting writer, Columbia University School of the Arts; poet-in-residence, Coppin State College, Baltimore, 1972–76; visiting writer, George Washington University, Washington, D.C. 1982–83; Distinguished visiting professor, St. Mary's College, Maryland, 1989–91. Poet Laureate for the State of Maryland, 1976–85. **Awards:** YM-YWHA Poetry Center Discovery award, 1969; National Endowment for the Arts grant, 1970, 1972; Juniper prize, 1980; American Library Association Coretta Scott King award, 1984; Lannan literary award for poetry, 1996, for *The Terrible Stories*. Honorary degrees from University of Maryland and Towson State University. **Agent:** Marilyn Marlow, Curtis Brown, 10 Astor Place, New York, New York 10003, U.S.A. **Address:** St. Mary's College of Maryland, St. Mary's City, Maryland 20686, U.S.A.

Publications

Poetry

Good Times. New York, Random House, 1969.
Good News about the Earth. New York, Random House, 1972.
An Ordinary Woman. New York, Random House, 1974.
Two-Headed Woman. Amherst, University of Massachusetts Press, 1980.
Good Woman: Poems and a Memoir, 1969–1980. Brockport, New York, BOA, 1987.
Next. Brockport, New York, BOA, 1987.
Ten Oxherding Pictures. Santa Cruz, California, Moving Parts Press, 1989.
Quilting: Poems, 1987–1990. Brockport, New York, BOA, 1991.
The Book of Light. Port Townsend, Washington, Copper Canyon Press, 1993.
The Terrible Stories. Brockport, New York, BOA, 1996.

Recordings: *The Place for Keeping* (audiocassette), Watershed, 1977; *Lucille Clifton* (video), reading and interview with Lewis MacAdams, The Lannan Foundation in association with Metro Pictures and EZTV, 1989; *Where the Soul Lives* (video), from *The Power of the Word* with Bill Moyers, Public Affairs TV and David Grubin, 1989; *Everett Anderson's Goodbye,* American Printing House for the Blind, 1996.

Other (for children)

The Black BC's. New York, Dutton, 1970.
Some of the Days of Everett Anderson. New York, Holt Rinehart, 1970.

Everett Anderson's Christmas Coming [Year, Friend, 1–2-3, Nine Month Long, Goodbye]. New York, Holt Rinehart, 6 vols., 1971–83.
Good, Says Jerome. New York, Dutton, 1973.
All Us Come Cross the Water. New York, Holt Rinehart, 1973.
Don't You Remember. New York, Dutton, 1973.
The Boy Who Didn't Believe in Spring. New York, Dutton, 1973.
The Times They Used to Be. New York, Holt Rinehart, 1974.
My Brother Fine with Me. New York, Holt Rinehart, 1975.
Three Wishes. New York, Viking Press, 1976.
Amifika. New York, Dutton, 1977.
The Lucky Stone. New York, Delacorte Press, 1979.
My Friend Jacob. New York, Dutton, 1980.
Sonora Beautiful. New York, Dutton, 1981.
Dear Creator: A Week of Poems for Young People and Their Teachers. New York, Doubleday Book for Young Readers, 1997.

Other

Generations. New York, Random House, 1976.

*

Critical Studies: "The Theme of Celebration in Lucille Clifton's Poetry" by Joyce Johnson, in *Pacific Coast Philology* (Malibu, California), 18(1–2), November 1983; "Tell the Good News: A View of the Works of Lucille Clifton" by Audrey T. McCluskey, and "Lucille Clifton: Warm Water, Greased Legs, and Dangerous Poetry" by Haki Madhubuti, both in *Black Women Writers (1950–1980): A Critical Evaluation*, edited by Mari Evans, Garden City, New York, Anchor-Doubleday, 1984; "Lucille Clifton: A Changing Voice for Changing Times" by Andrea Benton Rushing, in *Coming to Light: American Women Poets in the Twentieth Century,* edited by Diane Wood Middlebrook and Marilyn Yalom, Ann Arbor, University of Michigan Press, 1985; *Four Contemporary Black Women Poets: Lucille Clifton, June Jordan, Audre Lorde, & Sherley Anne Williams* (dissertation) by Doris Davenport, n.p., 1987; "Blackness Blessed: The Writings of Lucille Clifton" by Hank Lazer, in *Southern Review* (Baton Rouge, Louisiana), 25(3), summer 1989; "The Chronicling of an African-American Life and Consciousness: Lucille Clifton's Everett Anderson Series," in *Children's Literature Association Quarterly* (Battle Creek, Michigan), 14(3), winter 1989, and "Perspectives on Unity and the African Diaspora: Examples from the Children's Literature of Lucille Clifton and Rosa Guy," in *Work and Play in Children's Literature: Selected Papers from the 1990 International Conference on the Children's Literature Association,* edited by Susan R. Gannon and Ruth Anne Thompson, Pleasantville, New York, Pace University, 1990, both by Dianne Johnson; *The Poetics of Maternal Affiliation in Sylvia Plath, Anne Sexton, Adrienne Rich, Lucille Clifton and Judy Grahn* (dissertation) by Andrea Susan Musher, n.p., 1990; "Kin and Kin: The Poetry of Lucille Clifton" by Alicia Ostriker, in *American Poetry Review* (Philadelphia), 22(6), November-December 1993; "Healing Our Wounds: The Direction of Difference in the Poetry of Lucille Clifton and Judith Johnson" by Jean Anaport-Easton, in *Mid-American Review* (Bowling Green, Ohio), 14(2), 1994; "Poets against Marginalization" by Thomas Fink, in *Minnesota Review* (Greenville, North Carolina), 43–44, fall 1994-spring 1995; "The Poetics of Matrilineage: Mothers and Daughters in the Poetry of African American Women, 1965–1985" by Fabian

Clements Worsham, in *Women of Color: Mother-Daughter Relationships in 20th-Century Literature,* edited by Elizabeth Brown-Guillory, Austin, University of Texas Press, 1996; "Channeling the Ancestral Muse: Lucille Clifton and Dolores Kendrick," in *Female Subjects in Black and White: Race, Psychoanalysis, Feminism,* edited by Elizabeth Abel and others, Berkeley, University of California Press, 1997, and "In Her Own Images: Lucille Clifton and the Bible," in *Dwelling in Possibility: Women Poets and Critics on Poetry,* edited by Yopie Prins and Maeera Shreiber, Ithaca, New York, Cornell University Press, 1997, both by Akasha Gloria Hull; "Sharing the Living Light: Rhetorical, Poetic, and Social Identity in Lucille Clifton" by Mark Bernard White, in *College Language Association Journal* (Atlanta, Georgia), 40(3), March 1997; *The Representation of the Female Subject by Three American Women Artists: Painter Alice Neel, Poet Lucille Clifton, and Filmmaker Claudia Weill, 1970–1980* (dissertation) by Denise Bauer, New York University, 1998; interview with Charles H. Rowell, in *Callaloo,* 22(1), winter 1999.

Lucille Clifton comments:
I am a black woman poet, and I sound like one.

* * *

Lucille Clifton creates a poetry of ideas in which the ordinary is revealed to be extraordinary, in which the indigenously commonplace yields universal truth. Two realities influence the mode and substance of her poetry: she is African-American, and she is a woman. "I write," she asserts, "what I know."

Early in her career, in "after Kent State," Clifton wrote, "white ways are / the ways of death / come into the / Black / and live." In a later volume, in a poem titled "To Ms. Ann" (a historically ubiquitous title and name applied derisively to white "ladies"), she wrote, "you have never called me sister / and it has only been forever and / i will have to forget your face." Thus, she turned from whiteness to affirm and celebrate blackness.

The optimism that pervades Clifton's poetry is rooted in her ethnic heritage and milieu. She teaches that black life is, indeed, fraught with danger and adversity: "i went into my mother as / some souls go into a church / . . . listen, eavesdroppers, there is no such thing / as a bed without affliction; / the bodies all may open wide but / you enter at your own risk." Still, one must take the risks: "I'm trying for the lone one mama, / running like hell and if i fall / i fall / i fall." The result is that

> i survive
> survive
> survive.

One must see the beauties and lessons in the lives of forerunners, and, Clifton teaches, one must see the beauties and possibilities in one's own life. In "Last Note to My Girls" she says, "i command you to be / good runners / to go with grace."

In the autobiographical prose work *Generations* Clifton asserts, "Things don't fall apart. Things hold. Lines connect in thin ways that last and last and lines become generations made out of pictures and words just kept." This heritage-inspired, almost mystical, faith and motivation are common in her poetry, as in the lines "someone calling itself Light / has opened my inside, / i am flooded with brilliance / mother, / someone of it is answering to / your name."

Clifton's sense of extended black family is especially strong in poems written from a female writer's or persona's point of view. Her feminism manifests itself neither in a strident voice of protest nor in concepts of fragile daintiness, shielded vision, protective seclusion, or cloying sentimentality. Hers is a dignified, active, poised, self-assured, insightful, and sensitive womanness. Poems such as "the lost baby poem," about an abortion, and "Conversation with My Grandson, Waiting to Be Conceived" obviously were written by such a woman. She sees her woman's strength, resolve, and independence in generations to come:

> sing the names of the women sing
> the power full names of the women sing
> White Buffalo Woman who brought the pipe
> Black Buffalo Woman and Black Shawl
> sing the names of the women sing
> the power of name in the women sing
> the name i have saved for my daughter sing . . .
> the name of my daughter sing she is
> They Are Afraid of Her.

The settings and situations that inform Clifton's poetry are those in which "little" people endure and function admirably, even heroically. The heroes who inspire or populate her poetry are public African-Americans such as Angela Davis, Little Richard, and, more important, unexpected and unsung people such as "Miss Rosie," a "wet brown bag of a woman."

That religion is a source of Clifton's optimism is evident in her poems. A number of them are built upon metaphorical constructs derived from the Bible. In one poem, immediately after confessing that "i am not equal to the faith required," the speaker reports that, although "i try to run from such surprising presence; / the angels stream before me / like a torch." Clifton's God, it might be said, can be perceived by black people. In one poem the biblical Mary speaks with syntax and grammar identified with African-Americans, and in "Palm Sunday" the people lay "turnips / for the mule to walk / on waving beets / and collards in the air." In keeping with African-American religious traditions, it is a beatific faith.

Consistent with the prevailing theme of survival in her work, Clifton's essay "A Letter to Fred" reflects poignant memories of the life she shared with her deceased husband and responds to the persistent question, posed by family and friends, of whether or not she will remarry:

> Why shouldn't I? Why do they think that I wouldn't? Or shouldn't? After more than 30 years I know how to mate almost better than anything. Why would anyone learn something well, then promptly decide not to do it?

Poetically, Clifton shows resolution and insight as she clarifies death as new life. The male speaker in "the death of fred clifton" states that

> i seemed to be drawn
> to the center of myself
> leaving the edges of me
> in the hands of my wife
> and i saw with the most amazing
> clarity

so that i had not eyes but
sight,
and, rising and turning
through my skin,
there was all around not the
shapes of things
but oh, at last, the things
themselves.

The themes of womanness, history, and religion create a symmetry of survival in Clifton's *Quilting: Poems, 1987–1990,* where the shared and intertwined histories of women are replicated in sections named for traditional quilt designs: "log cabin," "catalpa flower," "eight-point star," and "tree of life." The opening poem, "quilting," is suggestive of that history:

in the unknown world
the woman threading together her need
and her needle
nods toward the smiling girl
remember
this will keep us warm.

In "at the cemetery, / walnut grove plantation, south carolina, 1989," Clifton celebrates the histories of unnamed slave women: "some of these dark / were slaves / some of these slaves / were women . . . / tell me your names." She acknowledges the dichotomies of women's unique gifts in poems such as "poem in praise of menstruation," "poem to my uterus," and "to my last period." The poet's wry humor is evident in "wishes for sons," in which the speaker announces that "i wish them hot flashes / and clots like you / wouldn't believe."

In several poems Clifton's religious optimism is tinged with ambivalence. In "wild blessings" she weaves her lyrical voice with biblical imagery to create an analogy of the dubious virtues of knowledge. The speaker is clearly discomfited with the gift of insight: "i am grateful for many blessings / but the gift of understanding, / the wild one, maybe not." In the section "tree of life" the speaker frets over the loss of innocence created by Lucifer's fall from grace and the resulting "perpetual evening" of carnal knowledge that has had an impact on the world:

i the only lucifer
light-bringer
created out of fire
illuminate i could
and so
illuminate i did.

Ultimately Clifton's rock-like faith is clear. In "still there is mercy, there is grace" the speaker states, "how otherwise / could i . . . curl one day safe and still / beside You / at Your feet, perhaps, / but amen, Yours." The final section of the work, "Prayer," injects a note of quiet religious faith as the speaker suggests, "and may you in your innocence / sail through this to that."

In her work *The Book of Light* Clifton creates an extended metaphor of survival by suggesting that the light is the path to personal survival: "woman, i am lucille, which stands for light." In

short signature poems she acknowledges heroes and antiheroes, but in the poem "final note to clark" there is a clear disclaimer of superheroes: "why did i think you could fix it?" Finally, in "she lived" the speaker accepts personal responsibility: "she walked away / from the hole in the ground / deciding to live. and she lived."

Clifton's poems are short, graceful, incisive. They continue to open as the reader contemplates or reexperiences them. Their understated yet insistent, and occasionally wryly humorous, endings often surprise. The best generic term to characterize their form and technique is free verse. Her lines are sinewy, lithe, rather matter-of-fact, and her diction is clear, precise, often in the idioms of black Americans.

In *The Terrible Stories* Clifton creates a mosaic of chilling places and events that stain the American landscape. The book is comprised of five parts, but it is in part 4, "In the Meantime," that the poet/narrator compresses the torment and frustration of a lifetime into a single unpunctuated question and seeks solace from her "dead once husband": why / cancer and terrible loneliness / and the wars against our people." Throughout the book Clifton builds on this theme and tackles the fear, pain, and loneliness of cancer; America's shameful history of enslavement and its dire aftermath; family lives; and, finally, in "From the Book of David," biblical history.

In the first part, "A Dream of Foxes," Clifton establishes the human terrain of unabated hunger and unresolved loneliness that threaten the contentment of both the speaker and her "sister fox." The speaker queries, "who / can blame her for hunkering / into the doorwells at night" with "her little bared teeth?" Yet the fox recognizes and understands the human hunger and "barks her compassion." In one of the most potent sections of the book, part 2, "From the Cadaver," the poet/narrator deftly examines the emotional and physical scars that result from cancer and a mastectomy. Breast cancer survivors surround the speaker in the poem as "amazons": "my sisters swooped in a circle dance / audre was with them and I / had already written this poem." The speaker also examines the terrible stories in a woman's responses to a lumpectomy, radiation, and loss. In "scar" the speaker articulates the finality of breast cancer surgery: "woman I ride / who cannot throw me / and I will not fall off."

In the third section, "Memphis," Clifton takes the reader on an emotional historical journey that includes black enslavement in America, the antebellum culture, and the continued pattern of contemporary human horrors. In "auction street" the speaker recalls the collective voices of those who feel slavery "throbbing up through our shoes," moved by the many African slaves "led in a [slave] coffle / to the [auction] block," in contrast to Moses, "who heard from the mountaintop: / take off your shoes / the ground you walk is holy." And in poems like "slaveships," "memphis," and "the son of medgar," the poet, still haunted by history, begins with African slaves who were "loaded like spoons" and later ruminates over the deaths of three civil rights workers in Mississippi—Michael Schwerner, James Chaney, and Andrew Goodman—and of the death of Medgar Evers, who was gunned down in front of his Mississippi home.

The work is powerful in its understated passion and persistently questioning tone. Clifton crosses poetic and historical boundaries as she unearths the calamities that have befallen humanity. And although the poet offers no startling conclusions, she has given life and voice to the terrible stories of human life that may confront and alarm us all.

—Theodore R. Hudson and B.J. Bolden

CLUYSENAAR, Anne (Alice Andrée)

Nationality: Irish. **Born:** Brussels, Belgium, 15 March 1936. **Education:** Trinity College, Dublin (Vice-Chancellor's prize, 1956), B.A. (honors) in English and French 1957; University of Edinburgh, diploma in general linguistics 1963. **Family:** Married Walter Freeman Jackson in 1976; three stepchildren. **Career:** Reader to the writer Percy Lubbock for one year; assistant lecturer, Manchester University, 1957–58, and King's College, Aberdeen University, 1963–65; lecturer in general linguistics, Lancaster University, 1965–71; senior lecturer in language and literature, Huddersfield Polytechnic, Yorkshire, 1972–73; lecturer in linguistics, Birmingham University, 1973–76; senior lecturer, then principal lecturer in English Studies, Sheffield City Polytechnic, 1976–87. Chair, Verbal Arts Association, 1983–86; active in National Poetry Society Poets-in-Schools workshops. Formerly general editor, *Sheaf,* and regular poetry reviewer, *Stand,* Newcastle upon Tyne. Tutor in creative writing, University of Wales, Cardiff, and freelance song writer and librettist. **Address:** Little Wentwood Farm, Llantrisant, Usk, Gwent NP5 1ND, Wales.

PUBLICATIONS

Poetry

A Fan of Shadows. Manchester, David Findley Press, 1967.
Nodes. Dublin, Dolmen Press, 1969.
Double Helix, with Sybil Hewat. Manchester, Carcanet, 1982.
Time-Slips: New and Selected Poems. Manchester, Carcanet, 1997.

Other

Introduction to Literary Stylistics: A Discussion of Dominant Structures in Verse and Prose. London, Batsford, 1976; as *Aspects of Literary Stylistics,* New York, St. Martin's Press, 1976.
Verbal Arts: The Missing Subject. London, Methuen, 1985.

Editor, *Selected Poems,* by Burns Singer. Manchester, Carcanet, 1977.
Editor, *Of Sawn Grain: Poems 1993–1996.* Abergavenny, Collective Press, 1997.

*

Critical Study: "'So Truth Be in the Field': Milton's Use of Language" by Colin MacCabe, in *Teaching the Text,* edited by Susanne Kappeler and Norman Bryson, London, Routledge, 1983.

Anne Cluysenaar comments:

(1985) I consider *Double Helix* the best I have done so far. In a review of *Double Helix* in *Writing Women* Linda Anderson caught exactly what I had hoped would be the effect of the book. In particular, she sees my mother's memoirs, together with other family documents, letters, and photographs, as providing "an eloquent record of family history reaching back over three generations." My poems seek to interpret this in terms of "the boundaries of self and others." They are "meditations ... on precisely those gaps and silences where lives meet and separate, where writing begins and ends." In writing the book, I was attempting to set down only what

appeared to me to be literally true and to find poetry in such reality. Without, of course, believing that this is the only way in which poetry can be written, I felt the need to assure myself that poetry is not so much a sophisticated fiction as a simple, everyday experience shared by everyone if not always recognized for what it is. I hoped *Double Helix* would be receivable as this reviewer received it: "What the reader experiences is the repeated sense of overlapping subjectivities—not just what can be created and told of another life but also where that understanding ends. The gaps, absences, differences between the various texts create space for the reader and necessitate a kind of collaborative reading experience, the meeting of our own subjectivity with that evidenced by the text," so that the reader's realities come to enrich those whose traces survive on the written page.

(1995) Certain dimensions of family history that I explored in *Double Helix* were to lead me into human prehistory and geology. Again, I was concerned with crossing the boundaries of self and others but in wider terms. By this time I was living in the border country of Wales, where landscape and ways of living inevitably take on political and linguistic implications and are especially moving to someone like myself who in the last World War lost both her original language and her original country. The resulting sequence, "Time-Slips," is the title sequence of my forthcoming new and selected poems (Carcanets, Manchester, England), which will also contain a sequence of poems exploring personal experience in the context of a reading of the seventeenth-century poet Henry Vaughan, who lived nearby and suffered during the British Civil War. In particular, "Vaughan Variations" attempts to relate the pressures of personal and social coincidence to those "quick vibrations" (Henry's phrase) that may seem to connect us less haphazardly to our natural surroundings.

*   *   *

Anne Cluysenaar's earlier poetry belongs to the school of Valéry and Beckett. Her poems evoke formally what it is to be human—the perceiving center, constantly changing, of a universe itself in a constant state of flux. *A Fan of Shadows* is a collection of models of the human condition, explained in appended notes as figures of "continuous creation" or "radiations from an occasionally moving centre." In "Figures" the image of Derwentwater is "love's point of balance" between opposites—stillness and movement, presence and absence, love and solitude, liquid and solid:

The variant self awakes
To hills, fields, open water
Newly aware of their stillness.

Between a kiss and the stillness
Of lonely thought, water
Off balance on a stony shore.

In "Sea" the stillness of midocean is complemented by the moving tides; in "Petrarch" the "still pool" is speechless and knows itself only in its overflow, "river-song." The sameness of experiences is underlined by the accumulation of archetypes of desire—Orpheus, Laura, Balder—and by a repetition of words, phrases, and whole verses that in several poems dictate the entire structure. The love lyric "Sea" falls into two near mirror halves; "Epithalamium" opens as ''the rings of the sun rise'' to close on an echo: ''The rings of the winter sunrise.'' The details of the differences are what make the present moment, which Cluysenaar seeks to flesh out, charting, in the words of ''La Belle Otero,'' what she calls ''the strangely similar gaze in two chance moments.''

The changes in the quality of Cluysenaar's perceptions of the present are what distinguish her development and progress as a poet. In her earlier work she does not always successfully cross the divide between eternal verity and dead cliché. Her landscapes remain abstract, shot through by mind rather than sensuous matter. In its separate moment a poem like ''Figures'' can pinpoint an interesting and self-defining interpretation of thinker and perceived world:

> A slim wave's shadow
> Sinks into the hammered gold
> Of dry stone creased with water.
>
> Fish become concentrations
> Of light, on which waves wind
> Tongue-rolls of clear water.

But the vein it works is limited, and the strain of avoiding the twin evils of banality and preciosity constantly shows through. In later works there is more warmth, and a personal voice finally makes itself heard. ''Maker'' recognizes the poet's problem—the distance between the vivid color of the real world and the abstractly arid version on the dead paper before him. ''The May Fox'' solves the problem through a surprise confrontation with death (the narrow escape of a fox caught in the car's headlights) that turns into love, a moment of shared human and animal warmth that dramatically reenacts the exchange of meaning between man, nature, and the ideas and objects of man's creation.

Double Helix is a blend of letters, photographs, family documents, and poems that raise all human experience to the level of lyric. The voice of ''the unnecessary poet'' (''In Time-Lapse'') blends with others, past and present, in a celebration of human community where ''I'' is no more or less than the individual inflection of the ''universal experiences,'' the ''natural signs,'' of all daily life. To be human is to re-create from the abstract flow the sensuous detail of reality, ''the stream / whose tiny, illegal trout / come to fingers patient with memories'' (''Resting the Ladder''). In ''The Line on the Map'' the line ''has become hills, trees / A place not a direction.'' This place is not circumscribed, and its expanding ripples reach out to include whole literary traditions (Milosz, Housman), cross the frontiers of class, nation, and politics, and abolish all limits, even those of death. Where private possession is abolished by community, as in ''Resting the Ladder,'' there is no loss:

> Watching, this first year, the swallow
> change to a silent icicle
> over the stable door,
> and knowing this will be the view
> of my old age, I warn myself
> we shall never own this place outright.

Cluysenaar's poetry reserves its anger for the merchants of loss and destruction, the authors of the concentration camps, the atom bomb, unemployment, repression. Against these her closing pages

rise to a dignified rage that twists syntax but not sense, linking indissolubly poetic, personal, and political value, as in ''7 September—Ready to Leave'':

> What duty can we meantime fulfil
> other than that which has always been ours?
> To grow with such persistent angry will
> that what is to be killed is worth dying for?

Whereas *Double Helix* draws on the strength of past lives, Cluysenaar's later poems, which are experiments in sonnet form, look to the future. The child of ''Double'' reveals the real terrors concealed by the familiar language and rituals of everyday life. ''In the Midst,'' with its schemes of mirrorlike patterns constraining writhing, broken rhythms, points to the destructive nature of abstract and abstracted adult language, ''the lip nice / on shattering syllables,'' for which the sole remedy is the baby's primitive scream: ''It cries, and their mimed fear / Is as nothing to the real, modern horror. / It cries, we laugh. We catch our breath.''

—Jennifer Birkett

COBBING, Bob

Nationality: British. **Born**: Enfield, Middlesex, 30 July 1920. **Education:** Enfield Grammar School; Bognor Training College, teaching certificate 1949. **Family:** Married Jennifer Pike in 1963; three sons and two daughters from previous marriages. **Career:** Civil servant, 1937–41; farmer, 1942–43; teacher in Swindon, Wiltshire, 1944–47, and London, 1949–64; manager, Better Books Poetry Bookshop, London, 1964–67. Since 1967 freelance writer and performer. Since 1954 co-editor, *And;* since 1963 publisher, Writers Forum, London. Performer with abAna group and Australian Dancers, both now inactive, and with Konkrete Canticle Birdyak, and Domestic Ambient Buoys. Founding member and vice president, Association of Little Presses. **Awards:** C. Day Lewis fellowship, Goldsmiths' College, 1973. **Address:** 89A Petherton Road, London N5 2QT, England.

PUBLICATIONS

Poetry

Massacre of the Innocents, with John Rowan. London, Writers Forum, 1963.
Sound Poems: An ABC in Sound. London, Writers Forum, 1965.
Eyearun. London, Writers Forum, 1966.
Chamber Music. Stuttgart, Hansjörg Mayer, 1967.
Kurrirrurriri. London, Writers Forum, 1967.
SO: Six Sound Poems. London, Writers Forum, 1968.
Octo: Visual Poems. London, Writers Forum, 1969.
Whisper Piece. London, Writers Forum, 1969.
Why Shiva Has Ten Arms. London, Writers Forum, 1969.
Whississippi. London, Writers Forum, 1969.
Etcetera: A New Collection of Found and Sound Poems. Cardiff, Vertigo, 1970.
Kwatz. Gillingham, Kent, Arc, 1970.
Sonic Icons. London, Writers Forum, 1970.

Triptych One: Are Your Children Safely in the Sea [Two: Undum Eidola; Three; Four: Three Tables; Five: Feathered; Six: Variations on a Theme; Seven: A Sense of (Japanese) Dress; Eight: Clippings and Trimmings; Nine: Vestimentiferan; Ten: For Eric]. London, Writers Forum, 10 vols., 1970–95.

Kris Kringles Kesmes Korals. Cardiff and London, Vertigo-Writers Forum, 1970.

Three Poems for Voice and Movement. London, Writers Forum, 1971.

Konkrete Canticle. London, Covent Garden Press, 1971.

Beethoven Today. London, Covent Garden Press, 1971.

Spearhead. London, Writers Forum, 1971.

Five Visual Poems. London, Writers Forum, 1971.

The Judith Poem. London, Writers Forum, 1971.

Poster No.2. Brighton, Judith Walker Poster, 1971.

Songsignals. Cardiff, Second Aeon, 1972.

Tomatomato. Kettering, Northamptonshire, All-In, 1972.

15 Shakespeare-Kaku. London, Writers Forum, 1972.

Trigram. London, Writers Forum, 1972.

Ecolony. London, Writers Forum, 1973.

Circa 73–74. London, Writers Forum, 1973.

Alphapitasuite. London, Writers Forum, 1973.

In Any Language. London, Writers Forum, 1973.

The Five Vowels. London, Writers Forum, 1974.

Picture Sheet One. London, Good Elf, 1974.

A Winter Poem. (nos. 1–23). London, Writers Forum, 23 vols., 1975–99.

Five Performance Pieces. London, Writers Forum, 1975.

Yedo Keta Waro. London, Writer Forum, 1975.

Hydrangea. London, Writers Forum, 1975.

Kyoto to Tokyo. London, Good Elf, 1975.

A Round Dance. Stockholm, Writers Forum, 1976.

Poems for the North West Territories. London, Writers Forum, 1976.

Bill Jubobe: Selected Texts 1942–1975. Toronto, Coach House Press, 1976.

Jade-Sound Poems. London, Writers Forum, 1976.

Furst Fruts Uv 1977, with Lawrence Upton. London, Good Elf— Writers Forum, 1977.

Title: Of the Work. London, Writers Forum, 1977.

Number Structures. Stockholm, Writers Forum, 1977.

Tu To Ratu: Earth Best. London, Writers Forum, 1977.

Cygnet Ring: collected poems 1. London, Tapocketa Press, 1977.

And Avocado. London, Writers Forum, 1977.

Bob Cob's Rag Bag. London, Writers Forum, 1977.

Anan An'Nan. London, Writers Forum, 1977.

Scorch Scores. London, Writers Forum, 1977.

Citycisms. London, Writers Forum, 1977.

Windwound. London, Writers Forum, 1977.

Voice Prints. London, Writers Forum, 1977.

Janus. London, Writers Forum, 1977.

Fingrams. London, Writers Forum, 1977.

Fracted. London, Writers Forum, 1977.

Cuba. London, Writers Forum, 1977.

Towards the City, with Jeremy Adler. London, Writers Forum, 1977.

Five Ways, with Bill Bissett. Toronto, Writers Forum, 1978.

Niagara. London, Writers Forum, 1978.

A Movie Book. London, Writers Forum, 1978.

Two Leaf Book. London, Writers Forum, 1978.

Found: Sound. London, Tapocketa Press, 1978.

Principles of Movement. London, Writers Forum, 1978.

Meet Bournemouth. London, Writers Forum, 1978

Fugitive Poems No. X. London, Writers Forum, 1978.

Game and Set. London, Writers Forum, 1978.

Ginetics. London, Writers Forum, 1978.

A B C/Wan Do Tree: collected poems 2. London, El Uel Uel U, 1978.

Sensations of the Retina. Toronto, Gronk, 1978.

A Peal in Air: collected poems 3. Toronto, Anonbeyondgr Onkontaktewild Presses, 1978.

Grin. London, Writers Forum, 1979.

A Short History of London, with Jeremy Adler. London, Writers Forum, 1979.

The Kollekted Kris Kringle (collected poems 4). London, Anarcho Press, 1979.

Pattern of Performance. London, Writers Forum, 1979.

Notes from the Correspondence, with Jeremy Adler. London, Writers Forum, 1980.

Voicings. London, Writers Forum, 1980.

The Sacred Mushroom. London, Writers Forum, 1980.

Statue of Liberty Suite. Leamington Spa, Other Branch Readings, 1980.

(Soma) Light Song. London, Writers Forum, 1981.

Serial Ten (Portraits). London, Writers Forum, 1981.

Four Letter Poems. London, Writers Forum, 2 vols., 1981.

Fencott and Cobbing in Miami [Baltimore, New York, Buffalo, Toronto, at Bay, San Diego, Clyde Dunkob in Vancouver]. Miami, Baltimore, New York, Buffalo, Toronto, San Francisco, San Diego, and Vancouver, El Uel Uel U-Writers Forum, 8 vols., 1982.

In Line. London, Writers Forum, 1982.

Sound of Jade. London, Writers Forum, 1982.

Baker's Dozen. London, Writers Forum, 1982.

Processual One [Two, 3, four, Quintet, Spin-Off, Novation: The Seventh Assignment, Double Octave, Spin-Off Two, Nonny-Nonny Swart Process U.A.L. (paper) 10, Summation, Supplement, (Almost) Random Snippets from Works in Progress, A Processual Notation]. London, Writers Forum, 15 vols., 1982–85.

Lightsong Two. London, Writers Forum, 1983.

Bob Cobbing's Girlie Poems: collected poems 5. London, Good Elf, 1983.

Prosexual. Milan, Writers Forum, 1984.

Homage to Theocritus, with Jeremy Adler. London, Writers Forum, 1985.

Sockless in Sandals: collected poems 6. Cardiff, Second Aeon, 1985.

Vowels and Consequences: collected poems 7. Newcastle upon Tyne, Galloping Dog Press, 1985.

Metamorphosis for bpNichol. London, Writers Forum, 1986.

Poetry into Music. London, Writers Forum, 1986.

Point of Departure. London, Writers Forum, 1986.

Variations on a Theme. London, Writers Forum, 1986.

Portrayed. London, Dirty, 1986.

Lame, Limping, Mangled, Marred and Mutilated: collected poems 9. London, David Barton, 1986.

Astound and Risible: collected Poems 8. Oakland, California, Ink Blot, 1987.

Processual: collected poems 10. London, New River Project, 1987.

Entitled: Entitled: collected poems 11. London, Micro-Brigade, 1987.

Wan, Do, Tree, Grin. London, Writers Forum, 1987.

Twelve. London, Writers Forum, 1987.

Six Computer Score. London, Writers Forum, 1987.

Both Both, with Bruce Andrews. London, Writers Forum, 1987.
Computer Poems. London, Writers Forum, 1988.
Stracci 1 [2,3]. London, Writers Forum, 3 vols., 1988.
Dress Sense. London, Writers Forum, 1989.
Raddle. London, Writers Forum, 1989.
Self-Portrait with Glasses. London, Writers Forum, 1989.
A Choice of Whiskies (as Connie Sirr). London, Writers Forum, 1989.
Improvisation Is a Dirty Word: collected poems 12. Heptonstall, Yorkshire, Magenta, 1990.
Bob Jubile. London, New River Project, 1990.
Codes and Diodes, with Robert Sheppard. London, Writers Forum, 1991.
Life, The Universe and Everything. London, Interim Books, 1992.
Fuerteventura. London, Writers Forum, 1992.
Ulli's Sett. London, Micro Brigade, 1993.
Open Folios. London, Writers Forum, 1993.
Voice Prints: collected poems 13. Seaham, Amra Imprint, 1993.
Score. London, Writers Forum, 1994
Electrografien. Berlin, Hybriden Verlag, 1994.
Domestic Ambient Noise, with Lawrence Upton. London, Writers Forum, 257 vols., 1994–99.
Pitchblend. London, Writers Forum, 1995.
Poems by R W C for R W C: collected poems 14. Sutton, R W C, 1996.
Gibbering His Wares: collected poems 15. Glasgow, Object Permanence, 1996.
Ow, Ow 2, Ow 3. London, Writers Forum, 3 vols., 1996–97.
Glossolalie un hallali. London, Writers Forum, 1997.
In Just Intonation. London, Writers Forum, 1997.
Undum Eidola. London, Writers Forum, 1997.
Fuming, with Lawrence Upton. London, Writers Forum, 1997.
Sound of Colour, Colour of Sound. London, Writers Forum, 1997.
Vispo for Eric. London, Writers Forum, 1997.
Cylinder Head, with Jennifer Pike. London, Writers Forum, 1997.
15 Shakespeare-Kaku (augmented edition). London, Writers Forum, 1998.
Kikaku Revisited. London, Writers Forum, 1998.
Are Your Children Safe in the Sea? London, Writers Forum, 1998.
Circuit. London, Writers Forum, 1998.
Morris Dance. London, Writers Forum, 1998.
System and Random. London, Writers Forum, 1999.
Ein Noise Project, with Serge Segay. London, Writers Forum, 1999.
Voices. London, Writers Forum, 1999.
Kob Bok Selected Texts 1948–1999. Buckfastleigh, Etruscan Books, 1999.
Shrieks and Hisses: collected poems 16. Buckfastleigh, Etruscan Books, 1999.

Recordings: *An ABC in Sound,* with Ernst Jandl, Writers Forum, 1965; *Chamber Music,* Swedish Radio-Fylkingen, 1968; *Whississippi,* Swedish Radio-Fylkingen, 1969; *Marvo Moves Natter and Spontaneous Appealinair Contemprate Apollinaire,* Ou, 1969; *Variations on a Theme of Tan,* Stedelijk Museum, Amsterdam, 1970; *As Easy,* Swedish Radio-Fylkingen, 1971; *Ga(il s)o(ng), Suesequence, Poem for Voice and Mandoline and Poem for Gillian, Hymn to the Sacred Mushroom,* Arts Council, 1971; *Khrajrej,* Opus Magazine, 1973; *E colony,* Typewriter Magazine, 1973; *Hymn to the Sacred Mushroom,* CBS/Sugar, 1975; *Portrait of Robin Crozier,* Fylkingen, 1977; *15 Shakepeare-kaku,* with Laurence Casserley, Cramps, 1978; *Vive Rabelais,*

with Henri Chopin, Pipe, 1980; on cassette: *Bob Cobbing and abAna,* Polytechnic of Central London, 1975; *Slowly Slowly The Tongue Unrolls,* Balsam Flex, 1979; *Trigram,* Balsom Flex, 1979; *An ABC in Sound,* Balsam Flex, 1980; *Cobbing at Orpington, and at King's College,* Herne Tapes, 1981; *abAna,* Writers Forum, 1982; *Scrambles,* with Clive Fencott, Writers Forum, 1982; *Various Throats,* with Steve Smith and Keith Musgrove, Underwhich 1982; *Oral Complex at the October Gallery [at L.M.C.],* Writers Forum, 1982–83; *Aberration,* Klinker Zoundz, 1988; *Green Computer,* Klinker Zoundz, 1988; *E Colony; from A Processual Double Octave,* Klinker Zoundz, 1988.

Other

Three Manifestos. London, Writers Forum, 1970.
Concrete Sound Poetry. London, Writers Forum, 1974.
Some Myths of Concrete Poetry, with Peter Mayer. London, Writers Forum, 1976.
Some Statements on Concrete Sound Poetry. London, Writers Forum, 1978.
Concerning Concrete Poetry (omnibus), with Peter Mayer. London, Writers Forum, 1978.
Changing Forms in English Visual Poetry. London, Writers Forum, 1988.
Serious Dissertations on Something or Other. London, Anarcho Press, 1989.

Editor, *Pamphlet One.* London, Writers Forum, 1968.
Editor, *A Typographical Problem.* London, Writers Forum, 1969.
Editor, *Free Form Poetry I and II.* London, Writers Forum, 2 vols., 1970–71.
Editor, *Samples of Concrete Poetry.* London, Writers Forum, 1970.
Editor, *British Modernism: Fact or Fiction?* London, Writers Forum, 1971.
Editor, with Peter Mayer, *International Concrete Poetry.* London, Writers Forum, 1971.
Editor, *Gloup and Woup: A Folio of Concrete Poetry.* Todmorden, Lancashire, Arc, 1974.
Editor, *Prospects.* London, Writers Forum, 1986.
Editor, *Songs: All Over the Place.* London, Writers Forum, 1986.
Editor, *Seevic's Feat.* London, Writers Forum, 1989.
Editor, with Bill Griffiths, *VerbiVisiVoco—A Performance of Poetry.* London, Writers Forum, 1992.
Editor, with Bill Griffiths, *Motley for Mottram.* London, Writers Forum, 1994.
Editor, *In Memoriam Dsh.* London, Writers Forum, 1995.
Editor, *Gifts for Three Sheppards.* London, Writers Forum, 1996.
Editor, with Lawrence Upton, *Word Score Utterance Choreography.* London, Writers Forum, 1998.

*

Manuscript Collections: State University of New York, Buffalo; Ruth Marvin Sackner Archive of Concrete and Visual Poetry, Miami.

Critical Studies: By Dom Sylvester Houédard, in ''Bob Cobbing Issue'' of *Extra Verse 17* (London), 1966; by Eric Mottram, in *Second Aeon 16–17* (Cardiff), 1973; *Bob Cobbing and ''Writers Forum''* edited by Peter Mayer, Sunderland, Ceolfrith Press, 1974.

Bob Cobbing comments:

(1975) My earlier poems "might seem to be conventionally linear; but their urge is towards stabilized diagram, itemised pieces of information in a spatial lay-out which is, in fact, the syntax" (Eric Mottram). In later poems the dance of letters, half-letters, syllables, and words on the page is score for "a ballet of the speech organs" (Victor Shklovsky). In still later poems the scores are for instrumental as well as vocal poetry, for a ballet of the whole body and not just the voice.

I have been described as "a lettriste, thirty years out of date" (François Dufrêne), and it is true that I value *lettriste* principles, but not solely. My work derives equally from Joyce, Stein, and the Kerouac of "Old Angel Midnight"; from François Dufrêne's post-*lettriste cri-rythmes* and the vocal microparticles of Henri Chopin. This leads Dom Sylvester Houédard to note the range of my personal scale (a) from eye to ear, (b) from most to least abstract.

At present I am working on single-voice poems; multivoiced poems; poems based on words; poems not using words or even letters; poems for electronic treatment on tape; poems for "voice as instrument and instruments as speaking voices" (*Time Out* magazine, concerning the group abAna with which I performed); poems as scores for dance or drama, invitations to act out an event in space, sound and choreography.

"History points to an origin that poetry and music share in the dance that seems to be a part of the make-up of homo sapiens and needs no more justification or conscious control than breathing" (Basil Bunting). This attitude is always worth exploring and means both a going back and a going forward.

*   *   *

Bob Cobbing is a senior and major exponent of the international concrete poetry movement in Great Britain. What is immediately impressive about his large body of work, in comparison with that of other poets in the field, is its range, and the published texts, which are freestanding visual poems, are also scores for vocal performance as sound poems. One of Cobbing's titles, *Sonic Icons,* stresses the interdependence of the two sides of his work through its appropriate anagram. His division of labor between self-publishing and performance ensures the unity of a creative project of great importance, yet his quest for new materials, techniques, and processes remains undiminished in energy and innovation.

Coming from a family of sign writers may have enabled Cobbing to disregard divisions between design and inscription, but he was a visual artist before he was a poet. His earliest duplicator print of 1942 presages his later work and his interest in the mechanics and accidents of printing. But it was not until 1965, with the alliterative sequence *An ABC in Sound,* that Cobbing came to maturity. Perhaps the best-known poem from this work is "Tan Tandinanan," a complex series of mantric variations for chanting that begins with

tan tandinanan tandinane
tanan tandina tandinane
tanare tandita tandinane
tantarata tandina tandita . . .

At about this time Cobbing began to make visualizations of earlier, often conventional poems, utilizing the ink duplicator as a medium. Thus, the mimetic crawling superimposition of "WORM" (1964) is based on a 1954 linear original. He used letters as elements in a visual design, but although he used his artistic skills, his materials remained anchored to language. Accepting these "signs" as if they were hieroglyphs of a forgotten language, one could freely interpret them as sound. As the texts became less lexical and more like black-and-white abstracts, suggestive landscapes of sound, so the emphasis moved away from phonetics toward the use of "vocal micro-particles," anything from a whisper to a bellow. The lip prints used for "U" from *The Five Vowels* might be considered as the most direct and primitive of linguistic signs. The semantic element, slenderly present in "WORM," for example, rarely surfaces in later work, where interpretation is no longer a matter of literary hermeneutics but of performance. Rather than a series of works, Cobbing's poetry is a continuing activity.

Cobbing performs in various ensembles, sometimes with improvising musicians but often with other sound poets. As with any form of improvised art, rapport between performers is essential to the fluency and unity of the work. A group can develop techniques and procedures, and possibly even conventions of translating marks on the page into sound, but the surprises of spontaneous improvisation are still the joys of such work. However much the sound poetry approaches contemporary music, the emphasis is always more linguistic than musical, even in works where the voice is modified by electronics or accompanied by musical instruments. In one of the "Three Variations on a Theme of *Tan*" paralinguistic, but nonmusical, sounds such as grunting, panting, and coughing take over the rhythm of the poem. Whenever professional singers perform the piece, they tend to regulate the pitch, harmony, articulation, and timbre according to musical criteria, whereas Cobbing is most interested in the full potentialities of the human voice.

This exploratory work, extending toward other art forms, can be usefully considered as one of the enduring (and most pleasurable) forms of multimedia and performance art from the 1960s and 1970s. Yet Cobbing has frequently asserted that his work belongs to a centuries-long tradition of phonological and graphological invention within the mainstream of literature. His work can therefore be seen as the result of experiments in foregrounding one or more of the conventional units of poetic structure (such as rhyme and alliteration or line and layout), allied to a concentration upon the materiality of language as sound or sign. While he makes sophisticated use of the technologies of printing and electronics, Cobbing believes his work to be essentially primitive, a direct mode of communication at times verging on the prelinguistic. He insists that poetry belongs not just to the vocal chords but to the whole body, and, in works such as *Three Poems for Voice and Movement,* he has scored for dancing as well.

In his work of the late 1970s and early 1980s Cobbing began to use nonlinguistic marks, both natural forms and man-made objects, as though they were significant linguistic signs. In performance these inky maps became scores for the various groups he formed. In a series of pamphlets and sheets entitled "Processual," made between 1982 and 1985 and issued in 1987 as a boxed set called *Processual: collected poems 10,* Cobbing used his new photocopier as both a poetic tool and as the latest mode of production for Writers Forum, his veteran little press. "Processual" refers directly to the processing of materials by photocopying, which was a major development in his work. This led to a transformational, almost impersonal, series of texts. The systematic magnification and reduction of images suggest both microscopic and cosmic forms, but in fact they are often produced by a mundane object such as a wine glass on the copy board.

While Cobbing has continued to produce many smaller items and has developed his techniques by moving text during the photo-copying process, since the mid-1990s his work with Lawrence Upton has resulted in an astounding collaboration on both texts and performances that threatens to dwarf "Processual." Called *Domestic Ambient Noise,* the completed project is projected to consist of three hundred booklets, each processing a single theme drawn from the other poet's work to produce six-page variations, which in turn may be selected as themes. The risky dialogue between the two writers ensures the injection of unpoetic materials, even by Cobbing's standards: packaging, clip art, Marmite smears as well as calligraphy, found texts, and even composed texts. Cobbing and his latest photo-copier can process any materials he is challenged with (Upton often produces computer-generated images and text) and transform them into surprising and even beautiful texts.

By the year 2000 Writers Forum had produced about a thousand booklets and pamphlets. The anthology *VerbiVisiVoco* gives some idea of the scope of the press and of the associated workshop that Cobbing has run in London since 1954.

—Robert Sheppard

COGSWELL, Fred(erick William)

Nationality: Canadian. **Born:** East Centreville, New Brunswick, 8 November 1917. **Education:** Provincial Normal School, 1937; Carleton Vocational School, graduated 1939; University of New Brunswick, Fredericton (Bliss Carman medal, 1946, 1947, Douglas Gold medal, 1949), B.A. (honors) 1949, M.A. 1950; University of Edinburgh (I.O.D.E. Overseas fellowship, 1950–52), Ph.D. 1952. **Military Service:** Canadian Army, 1940–45: sergeant. **Family:** Married 1) Margaret Hynes in 1944 (died 1985), two daughters (one deceased); 2) Gail Fox in 1985 (divorced 1997); 3) Adele Bartleton in 1997. **Career:** Assistant professor, 1952–57, associate professor, 1957–61, professor of English, 1961–83, and since 1983 professor emeritus, University of New Brunswick. Editor, *Fiddlehead* magazine, 1952–66, Fiddlehead Poetry Books, 1960–82, and *Humanities Association Bulletin,* 1967–72, all in Fredericton. President, Association of Canadian and Quebec Literatures and Atlantic Publishers Association, both 1978–80. **Awards:** Nuffield fellowship, 1959; Canada Council fellowship, 1966; Canadian-Scottish writing fellowship, University of Edinburgh, 1983–84; Aiden Nowlan Award for Literary Excellence, New Brunswick Legislature, 1995. LL.D.: St. Francis University, Antigonish, Nova Scotia, 1982; Mount Allison University, Sackville, New Brunswick, 1988. D.C.L.: King's College, Halifax, Nova Scotia, 1985; Confederation Medal, 1967–92. **Member:** Order of Canada, 1981. **Address:** 31 Island View Drive, Douglas, New Brunswick E3A 7R7, Canada.

PUBLICATIONS

Poetry

The Stunted Strong. Fredericton, New Brunswick, Fiddlehead, 1954.
The Haloed Tree. Toronto, Ryerson Press, 1956.
Descent from Eden. Toronto, Ryerson Press, 1959.

Lost Dimension. London, Outposts, 1960.
Five New Brunswick Poets, with others, edited by Cogswell. Fredericton, New Brunswick, Fiddlehead, 1962.
Star-People. Fredericton, New Brunswick, Fiddlehead, 1968.
Immortal Plowman. Fredericton, New Brunswick, Fiddlehead, 1969.
In Praise of Chastity. Fredericton, New Brunswick, Chapbooks, 1970.
The Chains of Liliput. Fredericton, New Brunswick, Fiddlehead, 1971.
The House without a Door. Fredericton, New Brunswick, Fiddlehead, 1973.
Light Bird of Life: Selected Poems. Fredericton, New Brunswick, Fiddlehead, 1974.
Against Perspective. Fredericton, New Brunswick, Fiddlehead, 1977.
A Long Apprenticeship: Collected Poems. Fredericton, New Brunswick, Fiddlehead, 1980.
Our Stubborn Strength. Toronto, League of Canadian Poets, 1980.
Selected Poems. Montreal, Guernica, 1983.
Pearls. Charlottetown, Prince Edward Island, Ragweed Press, 1983.
Meditations: 50 Sestinas. Charlottetown, Prince Edward Island, Ragweed Press, 1986.
An Edge to Life. Saint John, New Brunswick, Purple Wednesday Society, 1987.
The Best Notes Merge. Ottawa, Borealis Press, 1988.
The Black and White Tapestry. Ottawa, Borealis Press, 1989.
Watching an Eagle. Ottawa, Borealis Press, 1991.
When the Right Light Shines. Ottawa, Borealis Press, 1992.
In Praise of Old Music. Ottawa, Borealis Press, 1992.
In My Own Growing. Ottawa, Borealis Press, 1993.
As I See It. Ottawa, Borealis Press, 1994.
The Trouble with Light. Ottawa, Borealis Press, 1996.
Folds. Ottawa, Borealis Press, 1996.
A Double Question. Ottawa, Borealis Press, 1999.
With Vision Added. Ottawa, Borealis Press, 2000.

Recording: *Fred Cogswell: A Poetry Reading,* League of Canadian Poets, 1980.

Other

Sir Charles G.D. Roberts and His Works. Toronto, ECW Press, 1983.
The Bicentennial Lectures on New Brunswick Literature, with Malcolm Ross and Marguerite Maillet. Sackville, New Brunswick, Mount Allison University, 1985.
Charles Mair and His Work. Toronto, ECW Press, 1988.

Editor, *A Canadian Anthology.* Fredericton, New Brunswick, Fiddlehead, 1960.
Editor, *Five New Brunswick Poets.* Fredericton, New Brunswick, Fiddlehead, 1962.
Editor, with Robert Tweedie and S.W. MacNutt, and contributor, *The Arts in New Brunswick.* Fredericton, University of New Brunswick, 1966.
Editor, with Thelma Reid Lower, *The Echanted Land: Canadian Poetry for Young Readers.* Toronto, Gage, 1967.
Editor and translator, *One Hundred [and A Second Hundred] Poems of Modern Quebec.* Fredericton, New Brunswick, Fiddlehead, 1970–71.

Editor, *The Home Place,* by Marion McLellan. Charlottetown, Prince Edward Island, 1973.

Editor and translator, *The Poetry of Modern Quebec.* Montreal, Harvest, 1975.

Editor, with Kay Smith and Constance Soulikias, *Mysterious Special Sauce.* Ottawa, Canadian Council of Teachers of English, 1982.

Editor and translator, *The Complete Poems of Emile Nelligan.* Montreal, Harvest, 1983.

Editor, *The Atlantic Anthology: Poems and Prose, Past and Present.* Charlottetown, Prince Edward Island, Ragweed Press, 3 vols., 1984–85.

Editor and translator, with Jo-Anne Elder, *Unfinished Dreams: Contemporary Poetry of Acadie.* Fredericton, New Brunswick, Goose Lane Editions, and Moncton, Editions d'Acadie, both 1990.

Translator, *The Testament of Cresseid,* by Robert Henryson. Toronto, Ryerson Press, 1957.

Translator, *Confrontation,* by G. Lapointe. Fredericton, New Brunswick, Fiddlehead, 1973.

Translator, with Jo-Anne Elder, *Climates,* by Herménégilde Chiasson. Fredericton, New Brunswick, Goose Lane Editions, 1999.

*

Manuscript Collection: University of New Brunswick, Fredericton.

Critical Studies: *Four Maritime Poets: A Survey of the Works of Alden Nowlan, Fred Cogswell, Raymond Fraser and Al Pittman As They Reflect the Spirit and Culture of the Maritime People* (thesis) by Margie Williamson, Halifax, Nova Scotia, Dalhousie University, 1972.

Fred Cogswell comments:

My poetry is a response, as a rule, to direct personal experience. It finds its own form instinctively out of the various forms which I have encountered, either traditional or modern. It is marked by directness, economy, sincerity, and the avoidance of long words.

*   *   *

Fred Cogswell belongs to a generation of Canadian poets whose lives revolved around the academy and the professions. Their center was Montreal, where Louis Dudek, Frank Scott, P.K. Page, A.M. Klein, and John Sutherland were leaders. The poets' backgrounds were middle-class and their tastes intellectual.

A Long Apprenticeship: Collected Poems makes an allegory of the struggle of a skeptical intelligence against ingrained religion, of a loss of innocence and paradise partially regained. The rich variety of forms suits Cogswell's epigrammatic, ironic style. He ranges from the villanelle through imagism to sestinas. Early poems are controlled lyrics with careful rhyme schemes. A favorite form is the sonnet, usually with an octet for the initial deliberation and a sestet for the turn of thought or change of key or mood. Sometimes a couplet puts a sting in the tail.

The themes range from sacred and profane love to the expression of love for the natural world and particularly the New Brunswick countryside. Cogswell shares with the American poet Edwin Arlington Robinson the ability to write about country folk of northeastern North America with clear-sighted compassion, as in the sonnet "Valley Folk":

O narrow is the house where we are born,
And narrow are the fields in which we labour,
Fenced in by rails and woods that low hills neighbour
Lest they should spill their crops of hay and corn.
O narrow are the hates with which we thorn
Each other's flesh by gossip of the Grundies,
And narrow are our roads to church on Sundays,
And narrow too, the vows of love we've sworn.

But through our fields the Saint John River flows
And mocks the patterned fields that we enclose;
There sometimes pausing in the dusty heat
We stretch cramped backs and lean upon our hoes
To watch a sea-gull glide with lazy beat
To wider regions where the river goes.

Another of Cogswell's favorite forms, as demanding in its elusive and allusive way as the sonnet, is the haiku:

coin-silver on a
dark rich tablecloth, who will
pick you up, full moon?

To read *A Long Apprenticeship* is to be admitted to the friendship of a thoughtful, modest, passionate, scholarly man. Graceful, epigrammatic, rhymed lyrics mature as the years go by into freer, unrhymed, but always controlled stanzas—a testament to the examined life. Themes of love remembered, time passing inexorably, the close approach of death are turned and twisted in the bright light of the poet's mind to give off flashes of truth. In the natural world Cogswell is a butterfly catcher who entraps images. He is also a classicist, steeped in the mythology of Greece, Rome, the Middle East, and Christianity.

Meditations: 50 Sestinas amply illustrates Cogswell's fascination with, and mastery of, form. Here, in the spirit of Wordsworth's "Scorn not the Sonnet . . ." is part of the opening poem, "The Sestina":

You ask me why I write Sestinas now.
The form is out of fashion and it makes
Another barrier to the flow of thought.
Why not write free verse? Surely images
And the natural rhythms of our speech
Are enough to suit the needs of poesy.

I answer that the house of poesy
has many rooms. The one most crowded now
Is that you name. So thronged it is with speech
You can hardly tell the sound one poet makes
among the general din, and images
Are not the only means to capture thought.

Cogswell's verse is always musical, perhaps too musical for postmodern taste. Occasionally there are lapses, which probably illustrate nothing more than the change in poetic diction since the 1930s and 1940s.

Well along in his eighth decade, Cogswell has edited and translated a new collection of Acadian French poetry. He has, as well, produced yearly a new book of poetry in which postmodern prose poems form an intriguing part of the repertoire.

—Patience Wheatley

COHEN, Leonard (Norman)

Nationality: Canadian. **Born:** Montreal, Quebec, 21 September 1934. **Education:** McGill University, Montreal, B.A. 1955; Columbia University, New York. **Family:** Has lived with Suzanee Elrod, one son and one daughter; has lived with Rebecca De Mornay. **Career:** Composer and singer: has given concerts in Canada, the United States, and Europe. **Awards:** McGill University literary award, 1956; Canada Council award, 1960; Quebec literary award, 1964; Governor-General's award, 1969 (refused), 1993; Canadian Authors Association award, 1985. Order of Canada, 1992. D.L.: Dalhousie University, Halifax, Nova Scotia, 1971. Lives in Montreal and Greece. **Address:** c/o Stranger Management Inc., 419 North Larchmont Boulevard, Suite 88, Los Angeles, California 90004–3013, U.S.A.

PUBLICATIONS

Poetry

Let Us Compare Mythologies. Montreal, Contact Press, 1956.
The Spice-Box of Earth. Toronto, McClelland and Steward, 1961; New York, Viking Press, 1965; London, Cape, 1971.
Flowers for Hitler. Toronto, McClelland and Steward, 1964; London, Cape, 1973.
Parasites of Heaven. Toronto, McClelland and Stewart, 1966.
Selected Poems 1956–1968. New York, Viking Press, 1968; London, Cape, 1969.
Leonard Cohen's Song Book. New York, Collier, 1969.
Five Modern Canadian Poets, with others, edited by Eli Mandel. Toronto, Holt Rinehart, 1970.
The Energy of Slaves. Toronto, McClelland and Stewart, and London, Cape, 1972; New York, Viking Press, 1973.
Two Views. Toronto, Madison Gallery, 1980.
Book of Mercy. Toronto, McClelland and Steward, London, Cape, and New York, Villard, 1984.
Stranger Music: Selected Poems and Songs. New York, Pantheon, 1993.
Dance Me to the End of Love. New York, Welcome Book, 1995.

Recordings: *The Songs of Leonard Cohen,* Columbia, 1968; *Songs from a Room,* Columbia, 1969; *Songs of Love and Hate,* Columbia, 1971; *Live Songs,* Columbia, 1973; *New Skin for the Old Ceremony,* Columbia, 1974; *The Best of Leonard Cohen,* Columbia, 1975; *Death of a Lady's Man,* Warner Brothers, 1977; *Recent Songs,* CBS, 1979; *Various Positions,* CBS, 1985; *I'm Your Man,* CBS, 1987; *Leonard Cohen Takes Manhattan,* Sony Music, 1992; *Tower of Song,* Sony Music, 1995.

Plays

The New Step (produced Ottawa and London, 1972). Included in *Flowers for Hitler,* 1964; in *Selected Poems,* 1968.
Sisters of Mercy: A Journey into the Words and Music of Leonard Cohen (produced Niagara-on-the-Lake, Ontario, and New York, 1973).
A Man Was Killed, with Irving Layton, in *Canadian Theatre Review* (Downsview, Ontario), spring 1977.

Novels

The Favorite Game. New York, Viking Press, and London, Secker and Warburg, 1963.
Beautiful Losers. Toronto, McClelland and Steward, and New York, Viking Press, 1966; London, Cape, 1970.

Other

Death of Ladies' Man (novel-journal). Toronto, McClelland and Stewart, 1978; London, Deutsch, and New York, Viking Press, 1979.
Fingerpicking Leonard Cohen. New York, Amsco Publications, 1989.
Leonard Cohen Anthology. New York, Amsco Publications, 1991.
You Do Not Have to Love Me. Outremont, Quebec, J. Trépanier, 1996.
The Concise Leonard Cohen. London, Wise Publications, 1997.

*

Bibliography: By Bruce Whiteman, in *The Annotated Bibliography of Canada's Major Authors 2* edited by Robert Lecker and Jack David, Downsview, Ontario, ECW Press, 1980.

Manuscript Collection: University of Toronto.

Critical Studies: *Leonard Cohen* by Michael Ondaatje, Toronto, McClelland and Stewart, 1970; *The Immoral Moralists: Hugh MacLennan and Leonard Cohen* by Patricia Morley, Toronto, Clarke Irwin, 1972; *Leonard Cohen: The Artist and His Critics* edited by Michael Gnarowski, Toronto, McGraw Hill Ryerson, 1976; *Leonard Cohen* by Stephen Scobie, Vancouver, Douglas and McIntyre, 1978; *Leonard Cohen: Prophet of the Heart* by L.S. Dorman and C.L. Rawlins, London, Omnibus Press, 1990; "Canadian Cryptic: The Sacred, the Profane, and the Translatable" by Sylvia Soderlind, in *ARIEL* (Calgary, Alberta), 22(3), July 1991; "Leonard Cohen, Phyllis Webb, and the End(s) of Modernism," in *Canadian Canons: Essays in Literary Value,* edited by Robert Lecker, Toronto, University of Toronto Press, 1991, and "The Counterfeiter Begs Forgiveness: Leonard Cohen and Leonard Cohen," in *Canadian Poetry* (London, Ontario), 33, Fall-Winter 1993, both by Stephen Scobie; "Leonard Cohen and His Works" by Linda Hutcheon, in *Canadian Writers and Their Works,* edited by Robert Lecker and others, Toronto, ECW, 1992; *Discoveries of the Other: Alterity in the Work of Leonard Cohen, Hubert Aquin, Michael Ondaatje, and Nicole Brossard* (dissertation) by Winfried Siemerling, University of Toronto, 1993; "The Proceedings of the Leonard Cohen Conference,

Red Deer College, October 22–24, 1993," in *Canadian Poetry* (London, Ontario), 33, fall-winter 1993; *Take This Waltz: A Celebration of Leonard Cohen* edited by Michael Fournier and Ken Norris, Ste. Anne de Bellevue, Quebec, Muses, 1994; *Leonard Cohen: A Life in Art* by Ira Nadel, Toronto, ECW, 1994; "Neurotic Affiliations: Klein, Layton, Cohen, and the Properties of Influence" by Michael Abraham, in *Canadian Poetry* (London, Ontario), 38, spring-summer 1996; "Irving Layton, Leonard Cohen, and Other Recurring Nightmares" by David Layton, in *Saturday Night,* 111(2), March 1996; "Leonard Cohen's Traffic in Alterity in Beautiful Losers" by Andrew Lesk, in *Studies in Canadian Literature,* 22(2), 1997.

*   *   *

The figures of Leonard Cohen's poems rise like figures in Chagall, transformed from the ordinary, surprised into a world of visionary experience. Out of the junk of the everyday—"the garbage and the flowers"—the magical world of the imaginative is created. There is a strong sense that his poetry is a prodigious search of experience for the exit from the ordinary, but it is not always violently so. Some of the earlier works—"Go by Brooks," for instance—have a simple lyricism that is also intense. Occasionally it slopes off into a characteristic wry humor. More often its apparent Emily Dickinson-like simplicities conceal a toughness and a danger for which only the ballad form is adequate. And it is in the ballad that Cohen's greatest strength lies. The concentration of the imagery and the force of the rhyme give a telling intensity to the surrealist experiences of his imagination, an intensity that becomes at times almost gnomic:

History is a needle
for putting men asleep
anointed with the poison
of all they want to keep.

Certain themes preoccupy Cohen as certain images haunt his imagination. His search is for the sensual heaven of "The Sisters of Mercy," not the skeletal world of the ideal, the astringent dead world of "I Have Not Lingered in European Monasteries." Indeed, his religion is the rejection of the suffering ascetic—"I disdain God's suffering. / Men command sufficient pain"—for a world in which liturgical celebrations are the extreme of the physical, a "constant love / and passion without flesh." But even in the physical world his fear of entrapment by the deadly females of such poems as "The Unicorn Tapestries" or "I Long to Hold Some Lady" is strong. In his poetic fabric they become the creatures of the liturgy of death. "The Story of Isaac" lurks behind the sacrificial metaphors to which he recurs. What is most telling in this balladic preoccupation with the undefined horror is Cohen's recognition of it not as external to himself but as part of his own psyche. Dachau is everyday Montreal, and the amatory is also the murderous—"tasting blood on your tongue / does not shock me." So the poetry is exculpatory, especially in the 1964 book *Flowers for Hitler,* and the desire to escape from the "ape with angel glands" the more intense.

In Cohen's later poetry there is a sense of imminence. The partisan's retreat is more embattled even than "the small oasis where we lie" of his earlier love poems. His concern with freedom, his feeling of the "incomparable sense of loss" to which he refers in "Queen Victoria and Me," is more than nostalgia for a lost land of freedom and the spirit. It is a matter of skirmishes in the hills "on the side of the ghost and the king," a matter of escaping from the horrific city whose terrors are also the terrors of "the armies marching still" toward the war that must surely come.

A mode like Ferlinghetti's saves such poems as "The Killers That Run Other Countries" from sentimentalism. And Cohen's "Song for My Assassin," another ballad, has the same wryness as his love songs, a wryness that recognizes that the pretty fictions, even his women, are in large measure self-amusements. Occasionally he slips from his customary Horatian tone to a heavy-handed Juvenalian, and when feeling is too close to be contained, the poem can be very flat indeed. But even in the ostensible absence of the muse Cohen can write a fine poem, of which "The Poems Don't Love Us Anymore" (in *The Energy of Slaves*) is a good example.

Cohen's voice is most sympathetic and most telling in his celebrations of the poet's capacity not only to hold out against the faceless butchers but also to make acclaim of "orange peels, / cans, discarded guts." The surrealism that is so much a part of the Canadian sensibility provides him with a new way of seeing the ordinary transformed: "One of the lizards / was blowing bubbles / as it did pushups on the carpet." The conclusion to this poem is that "I believe the mystics are right / when they say we are all One." Cohen's voice celebrates the beauty, entirely human, that prevails over "the clubfoot crowds." Its affirmation is that not only all poets but also "all men will be sailors."

—D.D.C. Chambers

COLEMAN, Victor (Art)

Pseudonyms: Vic d'Or; Lee Enfield. **Nationality:** Canadian. **Born:** Lvov, Poland, 11 September 1944. **Education:** State University of New York, Buffalo, 1963–65; University of California, Berkeley Poetry Conference, summer 1965. **Family:** Married 1) Elizabeth Toon in 1963 (divorced 1967), two daughters and one son; 2) Sarah Miller in 1968 (divorced 1972), one daughter; 3) Jan-Marie Cooke in 1970; one daughter. **Career:** Copy clerk, *Toronto Star,* Toronto, 1962–64; assistant production manager, Oxford University Press, Toronto, 1965–66; senior editor/production manager, The Coach House Press, Toronto, 1967–74; artistic director, A Space, Toronto, 1975–78; programmer/administrator, National Film Theatre, Kingston, Ontario, 1980–82; programmer/publicist, The Music Gallery, Toronto, 1983–86; producer, Coach House Talking Books, Toronto, 1989–90. Since 1992 executive director, Toronto Small Press Group, Toronto. **Awards:** Canada Council Arts award, 1974, 1977; Ontario Arts Council Writer's Project grant, 1990, and Works in Progress grant, 1991.

PUBLICATIONS

Poetry

From Erik Satie's Notes to the Music: "Nine Poems." Toronto, Island Press, 1965.
one/ eye/ love. Toronto, Coach House Press, 1967.

Light Verse. Toronto, Coach House Press, 1969.

Back East. Montreal, Quebec, Bowering, 1970.

Old Friends' Ghosts: Poems 1963–68. Toronto, Weed/Flower Press, 1970.

Some Plays: On Words. Buffalo, New York, Intrepid Press, 1971.

Strange Love. Toronto, Coach House Press, 1972.

Parking Lots. Vancouver, Talonbooks, 1972.

America: A Government Publication. Toronto, Coach House Press, 1972.

Stranger. Toronto, Coach House Press, 1974.

Speech Sucks. Vancouver, Talonbooks, 1974.

Terrific at Both Ends. Toronto, Coach House Press, 1978.

Captions for the Deaf. Toronto, Rumour, 1979.

From the Dark Wood: Poems 1977–83. Toronto, Underwhich Editions, 1985.

Corrections: Rewriting Six of My First Nine Books. Toronto, Coach House Press, 1985.

Honeymoon Suite, with David Bolduc. Toronto, Underwhich Editions, 1990.

Waiting for Alice. Toronto, Eternal Network, 1993.

Lapsed W.A.S.P.: Poems 1978–89. Toronto, ECW Press, 1994.

Letter Drop: An Alphabet of Lipograms. Toronto, Coach House Press, 1999.

The Exchange: Poems, 1984–95. Toronto, Eternal Network, 1999.

Recording: *Nothing Heavy or Fragile,* Coach House/Music Gallery Talking Books, 1990.

Plays

The Party (produced 1981).

Screenplay: *125 Rooms of Comfort,* 1974.

Radio Play: *Audiothon,* 1975.

*

Manuscript Collections: The National Library of Canada, Ottawa, Ontario; Simon Fraser University Library, Special Collections, Burnaby, British Columbia.

* * *

Perhaps the truest lines ever written about Victor Coleman and his work come from the American poet Allen Ginsberg:

Head music for study
Tun'd after Zukofsky
Syllables broken to the eye
Ear rythm [sic] choppy mind very high
Acerb repugnant honesty.

These lines, titled "Coleman's America," are reproduced in his collection *America: A Government Publication* (1972). It is worthwhile pondering each of the insights in turn, for, despite their age, they are as apt today as when they were originally penned.

"Head music." Coleman enjoys playing games, rather in the manner of the French composer Erik Satie. In *Terrific at Both Ends* (1978) there is a poem called "Flood: Hologram," which includes these lines:

I separate
my thoughts
with stars

What the poet has in mind are not the stars in the heavens but the asterisks on the page that separate the *pensées.*

"For study." Much thought is given to the appearance of the words and lines on the page. In fact, positions are calculated in advance. The books themselves seem to be archives of attitudes. *Speech Sucks* (1974), for instance, includes the line "This book exported to Mars." Why Mars? No reason is given. Either the poet is engaging in foolishness, or he has the expectation that his work will endure and be studied when there are flights to the red planet.

"Tun'd after Zukofsky." Ginsberg's reference is to the American objectivist poet Louis Zukofsky, who fine-tuned the sounds of his own work, even rewriting phonetically Shakespeare's sonnets. Coleman is definitely writing in the wake of Zukofsky's literalism.

"Syllables broken to the eye." Ginsberg sees the words rather than hearing the poems. In the poem "Flood: Hologram" Coleman writes about survival: "Victor, victim / of vacuity." Everything here is reduced to alliteration. Elsewhere the poet chops at the words, extracting their syllables of sense.

"Ear rythm [sic] choppy mind very high." Ginsberg, like Whitman before him, enjoys misspelling the word "rhythm." Nonetheless, there is something "choppy," or intermittent, about Coleman's way of writing. At the same time the poet is quite aware, though certainly not "high-minded," about this. He is very observant, as in "From the Realms of the Unseen Father" in *Terrific at Both Ends,* "to convince us that the form is legitimate / a uniform is worn," "we all call it home no matter what / the numbers on the houses," and "one sixteenth of a second on the celluloid / a burp in time made permanent by chemicals."

"Acerb repugnant honesty." Ginsberg's words are well chosen. Acerbity is hard to take in quantity, and repugnance may be based on what is said, on how it is said, or on both. Yet it may be worth enduring both acerbity and repugnance if they are coupled with honesty.

Coleman's debt to Zukofsky is apparent in "After Reading Spring & All, All in All, & All," included in *Old Friends' Ghosts: Poems 1963–68* (1970):

Zuk
of
sky's
lyre's
no
liar

no
Lear
no
lair

I
sing

one
air

Coleman goes beyond the objectivist stance in the imprecation or exorcism called "Disengagement Ritual," which in the summer of 1976 was performed at the Parachute Centre for Cultural Affairs in Calgary. The work consists of lines like "I want to forget your face, your hands." There are seventy-three such lines, culminating in a gridlock contradiction: "I can't / Forget . . . I won't / Forget." It leaves the reader or listener about where he or she began in the first place.

—John Robert Colombo

COLEMAN, Wanda

Nationality: American. **Born:** Los Angeles, 13 November 1946. **Education:** Attended Valley Junior College, Van Nuys, California, and California State University, Los Angeles. **Family:** Married Austin Straus in 1981. **Career:** Writing team member, *Days of Our Lives* daytime drama series, Los Angeles, 1975–76; instructor, fiction writing workshop, UCLA Extension Program, Los Angeles, fall 1989; instructor, Otis-Parsons, Los Angeles, winter 1991; Fletcher Jones Endowed Chair in Literature & Writing, Loyola Marymount University, Los Angeles, 1994–96; lecturer, department of black studies, California State University, Long Beach, spring 1997. Editorial coordinator, Studio Watts Arts Newsletter, 1968–70; poetry editorial consultant, *Black Issues Magazine,* New York/Washington, D.C., 1998–99. Editorial advisory board member, *African American Review,* Indiana, 1995—. **Awards:** Studio Watts grant, 1968–69; Emmy award for best writing in daytime drama, *Days of Our Lives,* 1976; National Endowment for the Arts fellow, 1981–82; Guggenheim fellow, poetry, 1984; Vesta award in writing, 1988; Poet of the Year, Pasadena City College, 1989; California Arts Council fellowship grant, 1989; Harriette Simpson Arnow prize, *American Voice,* 1990; Writer's Residency, Djerassi Foundation, 1990–91; Founders Literary Achievement award, International Black Writers & Artists, 1994; Lenore Marshall National Poetry prize, 1999, for *Bathwater Wine.* **Address:** P.O. Box 11223, Marina del Rey, California 90295–7223, U.S.A.

PUBLICATIONS

Poetry

Art in the Court of the Blue Fag. Santa Rosa, California, Black Sparrow Press, 1977.
Mad Dog Black Lady. Santa Rosa, California, Black Sparrow Press, 1979.
Imagoes. Santa Rosa, California, Black Sparrow Press, 1983.
24 Hours in the Life of Los Angeles, with Jeff Spurrier. New York, Alfred Van Der Marck Editions, 1984.
Heavy Daughter Blues: Poems & Stories, 1968–86. Santa Rosa, California, Black Sparrow Press, 1987.
The Dicksboro Hotel & Other Travels: Poems. Tarzana, California, Ambrosia Press, 1989.

African Sleeping Sickness: Stories & Poems. Santa Rosa, California, Black Sparrow Press, 1990.
Hand Dance. Santa Rosa, California, Black Sparrow Press, 1993.
American Sonnets. Kenosha, Wisconsin, Woodland Pattern/Light and Dust Press, 1994.
Bathwater Wine. Santa Rosa, California, Black Sparrow Press, 1998.

Recordings: *Voices of the Angels,* Freeway Records, 1981; *English as/a Second Language,* Freeway/Enigma, 1982; *Neighborhood Rhythms,* Freeway/Rhino Records, 1984; *Twin Sisters,* Freeway/Rhino Records, 1985; *Black Angeles,* New Alliance, 1988; *High Priestess of Word,* BarKubCo/New Alliance, 1989; *Hollyword,* BarKubCo/Rhino Records, 1990; *Black & Blue News,* BarKubCo/Idiot Savant/Widowspeak Records, 1991; *Black & Tan,* BarKubCo/New Alliance, 1991; *Jazzspeak,* BarKubCo/New Alliance, 1991; *Berserk on Hollywood Boulevard,* New Alliance/BarKubCo/Idiot Savant Records, 1991; *Our Souls Have Grown Deep Like the Rivers: Black Poets Read Their Work,* Rino World Beat/Rhino Records, 2000.

Novel

Mambo Hips & Make Believe. Santa Rosa, California, Black Sparrow Press, 1999.

Short Stories

A War of Eyes & Other Stories. Santa Rosa, California, Black Sparrow Press, 1988.

Other

Native in a Strange Land: Trials & Tremors. Santa Rosa, California, Black Sparrow Press, 1996.

*

Critical Studies: "Doing Battle with the Wolf: A Critical Introduction to Wanda Coleman's Poetry" by Tony Magistrale, in *Black American Literature Forum,* 23(3), fall 1989; "The Anger of an Artist without Sanction: Wanda Coleman" by Kirk Silsbee, in *L.A. Style* (Los Angeles), March 1991; "So They Can See Me: Talking to Wanda Coleman" by Hillary Fielding, in *Poetry Flash* (Berkeley, California), January-February 1994; "Wanda Coleman: Featured Poet" by Rebecca Bush, in *Slack* (Boulder, Colorado), 1994; "Wanda Coleman: Native in a Strange Land" by Carol Schwalberg, in *Poets & Writers,* 26(5), September/October 1998; "Trash, Art, and Performance Poetry: Wanda Coleman" by Eric Murphy Selinger, in *Parnassus* (New York), 1998; "Revisit Western Criticism through Wanda Coleman" by Krista Comer, in *Western American Literature* (Logan, Utah), 33(4), winter 1999; interview with Rachel Levine, in *ACM/Another Chicago Magazine* (Chicago), 35, 1999; by S.K. Stanley, in *African American Review,* 33(2), 1999.

Wanda Coleman comments:
My influences are many and varied, and I use them depending on my intent at the moment of writing. My primary influences are those

of writers encountered during my school years and those I discovered on my own as I matured. These writers cross the literary spectrum from Shakespeare to Camus, from Sartre to Melville. The French existentialists have probably had the greatest impact on me overall. Too, since I am black and multiply gifted, there are other influences equally powerful: those of music, dance, and visual art, particularly graphic design.

Although my parents were working-class poor, they struggled to provide me and my siblings with a culturally rich environment and succeeded. I use some of my musical training in performance, not to mention years spent in speech and debate. My musical training was classical, voice and the violin and piano (some dabbling on the cello, viola, and guitar). My dance background includes ballet and experimental dance theater (Beck and Molina, Anna Halprin). My father taught me his skills as a graphic artist, advertising man, and painter. As the writing has become dominant in my life, I have learned to channel all of my other loves into it in a jazzlike style. I like to think of myself as a fusionist in a broader usage of the term. My mother was a singer and played the piano, so she gave me my earliest piano lessons. I was an avid reader and was encouraged to read by both parents and was taken to concert halls, museums, and galleries all through my childhood. Coming of age in Los Angeles has been very difficult, and life as a poet here has proved more a trial than a pleasure. Yet I have survived to become the most prolific African-American poet in the history of Western verse.

Unlike the introvert who is my true nature, my poetry is urban and concerned with the material world as I rage against it and through it. Often my poems are also the stories of those I encounter along the way. Often my poems address those aspects of black consciousness still largely ignored, even by my African-American peers, that is, those of slave origin. I have lived long enough to become an influence myself and have inspired younger voices in this region. Others often use the word "uncompromising" to describe my work. I find that quite pleasing. Oh, while my musical bent was classical and gospel, I love modern jazz, rock and roll, folk music of the southern U.S., fado, and virtually anything else of quality. I have been a primary participant in the Los Angeles poetry renaissance that has largely gone undocumented for thirty years. This happenstance infuriates me, and that anger, among others, has gone into my work, not as therapy but as transformation into art.

*   *   *

Wanda Coleman's published works, including her collections of poetry, represent a quarter of a century of writing in Los Angeles. On the West Coast she is known as a "powerhouse poet," acclaimed more for the strident voice of her spoken word performances than for her published works, and she has made a number of recordings. In her poetry, as well as in her short stories and essays, Coleman persistently creates a desolate landscape of a torn humanity ravaged by racial injustice, economic oppression, failed relationships, and physical, psychological, and sexual abuse. There is no prospect of repair, healing, or reconciliation. Although she is most often cited for the anger and rage in her poetry, her canon reveals her to be a regional poet sensitive to the racial inequalities and economic disparities of black Americans. Her writings convey her keen ear for the urban vernacular and show her penchant for a clear, direct, and raw poetic style, yet her work has received little critical attention.

Coleman has said that *Imagoes,* published in 1983, "was my watershed book in which I acknowledged my full womanhood and attempted to place childhood in perspective." In the work she assumes an autobiographical stance that details her growth from girlhood to womanhood as she witnesses the disrespect accorded black men in America. In "Daddyboy" a father halts his children's use of their childhood term of endearment for him, snapping, "don't call me that no more!" In an attempt to explain the racial encoding behind the term, the mother states, "your father's black. white people disrespect black men by calling them boy / call him anything but."

As she reports on America's excluded underclass of the black urban poor, Coleman's poetic voice becomes editorial and repetitious in content, language, and structure. She avoids much of the compression common to poetry and opts for a prosaic rather than a lyrical form. Coleman's speakers, with whom she readily identifies, emit raw, blunt, streetwise, matter-of-fact details of the grim and painful episodes in the perilous subsistence of the black residents of Los Angeles. In "Under Arrest" a policeman itches to shoot a woman he has stopped: "freeze. freeze! that's right! freeze before I take / your head off. freeze! come on and raise. raise those / arms. get 'em up. let me see you raise those arms. high / or I'll take your head off. higher. higher! or / I'll spill your blood all over the sidewalk." *Imagoes* is stark in its statements on the dismal frustrations and the futility of black life in America, and Coleman's flat linguistic thrust depicts a world of infinite anguish. "The Big Empty—for Kalin" ends with "tear me from this cross / end my pain / wash it away in blood / take this towel / my life / throw it in."

Heavy Daughter Blues: Poems & Stories, 1968–1986 (1987) counters the theme in *Imagoes* of giving up with an air of stoicism, evident, for example, in the opening poem, "Some Rock Lady." Here the woman takes "stone injections" to steel herself "against the world" and emerges "solid as gibraltar." In "El Hajj Malik El-Shabazz," a poetic tribute to Malcolm X, strength and artistic responsibility are apparent. The speaker asserts that Malcolm X lives on despite his assassination: "blood spilled out of you that day / blood running out and spilling / into us / where you live / where the black phoenix rises in our hearts / forever."

Heavy Daughter Blues is also ripe with the subject of betrayal in relationships, as well as women's overt sexuality, something that flavors much of Coleman's work. In "The Gossip" the speaker eagerly reveals the progress of a woman's ex in his new relationship: "she calls me up and tells me / she saw him just the day before and asks / how things are between us / all giggles . . . / she left her message / clawed into my heart with that long lush crimson / tongue of hers / which is why I never call back / she gets off in my ear." And in "Death 211" a woman who sees her lover with another woman longs to kill him: "I am still seeing them together / am blinded by her thighs across his / and the desire to kill." There is gender reversal in "Jerry 1969," in which a woman bids goodbye to her lover, pledging her love and promising to join him soon. But upon his departure the woman acts out her betrayal, stating, "and I was relieved that my act was over and made / my way to the nearest pawn shop / to hock my flawed solitaire." "Barry's Goodbye" is one of many Coleman poems that gives explicit testimony to women's sexuality, and in this respect it is similar to earlier poems like "Mama's Man" and "Kate."

Beginning in 1989 and continuing into the 1990s Coleman published a number of collections, including *The Dicksboro Hotel & Other Travels: Poems* (1989), *African Sleeping Sickness: Stories & Poems* (1990), *Hand Dance* (1993), and *American Sonnets,* a chapbook of 24 poems (1994). These volumes feature often anthologized poems like "Emmett Till" (1990), "American Sonnet 10" (1993), and "Today I Am a Homicide in the North of the City" (1990). Yet it was not until Coleman published *Bathwater Wine* in 1998 that she won national acclaim for her work. This volume earned Coleman the 1999 Lenore Marshall National Poetry prize from the Academy of American Poets.

A five-part bildungsroman, *Bathwater Wine* features a young black girl's uneasy transition to womanhood amid urban strife and luckless relationships. The first and second parts, "Dreamwalk" and "Disclosures," define the growing pains of a young girl's elementary and junior high school years, profile her father's futile struggles to halt the grinding poverty of their lives, and document her introduction to racial prejudice. In "Chapter 2 of the Story" a ten-year-old black girl is plagued by a white librarian whose "gray eyes policed me thru the stacks like dobermans" until the librarian finally "decided / she'd misjudged her little colored girl." The third section is titled "More American Sonnets (26–86)," and the fourth part "God Bless the Fire." In the fifth section, "Thirteen Ways of Looking at a Bluesbird," the girl responds to the riveting blues of adulthood. The poems in this section reflect the irony, anger, and outrage that epitomize Coleman's poetry. The opening poem, "Late Broadcast News," features the lines "six black men were killed and more than a hundred blacks were arrested when rioting started following the death of a 16-year-old mentally retarded black detainee in the country prison . . . the dead were all shot in the back."

In *Bathwater Wine,* as in many Coleman volumes, much of the urban action is centered in and around cars, the single visible possession of the economically deprived characters. In poems like "I Remember Romance in the Chevy Graveyard" a teenage girl recalls how "the spurs on his black leather boots jangled as / one scratched the door handle and the other / kept hitting the brake pedal." In "The Broken Car Window" a young couple tries to recapture teenage romance at a drive-in movie, and in "Closing Time" a work-weary waitress locking up the restaurant mulls, "at Trinity & Santa Barbara / the last clunker on the black top is mine." These poems recall earlier Coleman poems with cars as riveting images, as, for example, when the speaker in "I Live for My Car" states, "can't let go of it. to live is to drive." The poem "Parked" opens, "loud. Funk blast thru walls / I feel it clear across the street / in the car."

Coleman has not received the critical attention that is essential for a full explication of her work, perhaps because she crafts her poetry as recordings and photographs of America's voiceless and invisible impoverished underclass of blacks, the poor, women, and children. Coleman's stance is tough, but her work reflects a poet committed to honing a craft that gives voice and visibility to a little known community of Americans.

—B.J. Bolden

COLES, Don

Nationality: Canadian. **Born:** Woodstock Ontario, 12 April 1928. **Education:** University of Toronto, B.A. 1949, M.A. 1952; University of Cambridge, M.A. 1954. **Family:** Married Heidi Goelnitz in 1959; one daughter and one son. **Career:** Worked as a translator in Scandinavia, Italy, and Germany, 1954–65; instructor, 1965–66, lecturer, 1966–68, assistant professor, 1968–71, associate professor, 1971–81, since 1979 director of program in creative writing, and since 1981 professor of humanities and creative writing, York University, Toronto. Since 1985 poetry editor, Banff Centre for the Fine Arts, Alberta. **Awards:** Canada Council grants; CBC Literary award, 1980; National Magazine award, 1986; Governor General's prize, 1993, for *Forests of the Medieval World;* John Glassco prize, 1996, for translation of *For the Living and the Dead* by Tomas Tranströmer. **Address:** 122 Glenview Avenue, Toronto, Ontario M4R 1P8, Canada.

PUBLICATIONS

Poetry

Sometimes All Over. Toronto, Macmillan, 1975.
Anniversaries. Toronto, Macmillan, 1979.
The Prinzhorn Collection. Toronto, Macmillan, 1982.
Landslides: Selected Poems 1975–1985. Toronto, McClelland and Stewart, 1986.
K. in Love. Montreal, Signal, 1987.
Little Bird. Montreal, Véhicule Press, 1991.
Forests of the Medieval World. Erin, Ontario, Porcupine's Quill, 1993.
Someone Has Stayed in Stockholm, New and Selected Poems. Todmorden, England, ARC-Publications, 1994.

Other

Editor, *The Moment Is All: Selected Poems 1944–1983* by Ralph Gustafson. Toronto, McClelland and Stewart, 1983.

*

Critical Studies: "Attending the Masses" by Paul Stuewe, in *Queen's Quarterly* (Kingston, Ontario), winter 1983; "'All in War with Time': The Poetry of Don Coles" by Susan Glickman, in *Essays on Canadian Writing* (Toronto), 35, winter 1987.

*   *   *

In a poem from *Landslides* called "What Will Happen to Us Both?" Don Coles voices the central concern of his poetry: "Time leans close." Throughout his career his poems have turned and returned to deal with this invisible element in which we live and which buffets and shapes our bodies and our hopes.

The theme is not a new one, and its presence in Coles's poetry is one of the ways his work reveals its comprehension and assimilation of the main traditions of classical and modern literature; his is a Canadian poetry informed by the heart and mind of Europe. Thus, his handling of time reminds us of Horace's efforts to build poetic structures that can afford monumental shelter against time's storms, of Shakespeare's lines of defense against the "bloody Tyrant," or of the "pretty rooms" that Donne builds deep inside his sonnets. Yet Coles's treatment of the theme is utterly new, and it contributes much to the distinct resonance of his voice among modern Canadian poets.

The poems often begin by plunging us into the currents of time. "My God how we all swiftly, swiftly / unwrap our lives" begins the first poem in his first collection, *Sometimes All Over,* and it proceeds to compare our rampage through time with the blitzkrieg of small children through the wrappings of their birthday presents. But "compare" is too tame a word to convey the poem's workings. Rather, it involves us in the unravelings of time: only three sentences unwind over nineteen lines; none but the last line is end-stopped; and all but three of the other lines hurtle forward without even a comma or a dash. The result is that the poem picks us up and carries us along, making us realize viscerally the point it insinuates rather than states: even as we think we are moving forward in control of our birthdays and our presents, it is time that rolls us along and controls our every turn. Yet we are not helpless. The sheer imaginative energy of the poem's unfurling metaphor and the momentum of its syntax testify—as surely as Horace's or Shakespeare's monuments—to a creative power that takes on the assaults of time and will not surrender easily, achieving a temporary victory in the controlling shape of the poem itself.

Such shapes have allowed Coles to move beyond the territory of personal history, in which many of the encounters with time took place in his first volume in such poems as "Photograph" or "My Grandfather, My Grandmother." His second collection, *Anniversaries,* unreels its comprehending skeins of language through the times of a "dim old dawdler, / Main Street gazer" ("Codger"), a widow and a "Gentleman, 50'ish" ("Lonelyhearts"), and the artists and heroes of medieval France ("Guide Book"). It unfolds the life dormant in "a yellowed and torn half-page of an unidentifiable newspaper" in "Mrs. Colliston," and it searches out the life behind a stone monument in another poem whose very title embodies its process of rescuing experience from time: "On a Bust of an Army Corporal Killed on His Twenty-first Birthday Driving a Munitions Wagon in the Boer War."

Both *Anniversaries* and *The Prinzhorn Collection* also show Coles traveling through the histories, real and imagined, of such writers as Tolstoy, Rilke, Mann, Ibsen, and James. Most successful is the long poem that gives *The Prinzhorn Collection* its title, a searing look into the drawings, letters, and journals of the inmates of a nineteenth-century madhouse. The poem's short but unstoppable lines trace a narrowing orbit, from the obscene drawings of the madwomen through the men's "complaints, / Threats, fawnings, explanations, / Prayers. Rational and irrational / Proposals." They move across "the borders of despair" to center on the anguished cries of a single inmate, Joseph Grebing. Coles's lines compress the twelve years of Grebing's unanswered petitions for his family's love into a core of agony at the heart of the poem, all the more effective because it avoids a direct and potentially bathetic approach in favor of a terrifying sweep around the margins of chaos: "A thin, / Leaf-coloured tendril winds from / One beflowered upper-case letter / To the next, and contains, like / An icon'd saint's girdle, messages—/ To speak plainly, just one message, / Of unmistakable awfulness." Coles makes the inmate's grief speak so movingly across a hundred years that it comes as a shock, a last, wrenching turn of the screw, when he reminds us that "nothing of it / Was ever mailed, or we should not / Now have it." But this temporary triumph of oblivion is offset by the knowledge that we do have it, thanks to Coles's art; his poem has rescued Grebing's voice from the dead silence of time.

The poems of *K. in Love* mark a radical departure from Coles's earlier work in both design and implications. Short (most no more than eight or ten lines), untitled, confessional, they are love notes ostensibly written by Franz Kafka. The poems offer a seizing of instants, and they embody a new awareness of the power of individual words to leap off the page, alive, and to influence reality rather than merely record it. Thus, in "It's so lonely here," "Every word on the page / Bursts into tears," or "When you refer in today's letter / To 'our love', completely new / Images of home / Drift near." Coles has discovered in these poems perhaps the most effective weapon against time: the creative potential of the word to escape the frozen, photographic contours of history and to make a fresh time of its own. The discovery anticipates the last line of *Forests of the Medieval World* ("an hour's immortal even if a life isn't"), and it carves out the primary line followed in that volume and in its immediate predecessor, *Little Bird.* The latter book takes the sharp moments of *K. in Love* and joins them—without blunting them—into the sequence "Last Letter to My Father." Through heavily enjambed quatrains that are irregular in rhythm and rhyme, Coles pursues a dialogue between his own imaginative language and his father's polite middle-class silence, and in the process he manages both to demonstrate the grounds of his love for his father and to justify a life devoted to poetry. The quatrains achieve a superb tonal balance, keeping us distant from sentimentality through their wit ("heart I" rhymes with "Sparta," and "Word" with "blurred") as they effect "*a kind of / binding of / silence / & language*" that enmeshes love.

Such a balance also carries us through the more diverse loves (friendly, paternal, passionate, filial) of Coles's most chronologically and geographically inclusive volume, *Forests of the Medieval World.* Winner of the Governor General's award, this collection staves off time by comprehending much of its offerings, the sights and sounds of a lifetime given the ringing solidity of bronze through the pressure of Coles's art. His language can rise without apparent effort from the commonplace ("Way to look, Gary, way to look") to the metaphorical ("your tongue / harried my mouth's bays and inlets"), or it can hover magically to include both at once, as when the baseball coach of "Night Game" sits "staring into the evening diamond." As we move from Edvard Munch's Norway to G.A. Henty's India, from the Wren Library at Cambridge to the Triple Star Cleaners of small-town Ontario, time rolls more powerfully than ever through the aged or aging figures of *Forests of the Medieval World,* but in this most accomplished and resonant of Coles's works "their brief voices / Are vibrant and near."

—John Reibetanz

COLLINS, Billy

Nationality: American. **Born:** New York City, 22 March 1941. **Education:** Holy Cross College, Worcester, Massachusetts, 1959–63, B.S. in English 1963; University of California, Riverside, 1963–67, Ph.D. 1971. **Family:** Married Diane Collins in 1979. **Career:** Since 1969 professor, Lehman College, City University of New York, Bronx, and visiting writer, Sarah Lawrence College, Bronxville, New York, 1997—. Vice president, Poetry Society of America, 1999—. **Awards:** New York Foundation for the Arts poetry fellow, 1986; National Endowment for the Arts creative writing fellow, 1988; Bess Hokin prize, *Poetry,* 1991; Guggenheim Foundation fellow, 1993; Oscar Blumenthal prize, *Poetry,* 1993; Literary Lion award, New York Public Library, 1993; Levinson prize, *Poetry,* 1995; J. Howard and Barbara M. J. Wood prize, *Poetry,* 1999; Paterson Poetry prize, 1999, for *Picnic, Lightning.* **Agent:** Chris Calhoun, Sterling Lord, 65 Bleeker Street, New York, New York 10012.

PUBLICATIONS

Poetry

Pokerface. Los Angeles, Kenmore Press, 1977.
The Video Poems. Los Angeles, Applezaba Press, 1981.
The Apple That Astonished Paris. Fayetteville, University of Arkansas Press, 1988.
Questions about Angels. New York, Morrow, 1991; revised edition, Pittsburgh, Pennsylvania, University of Pittsburgh Press, 1998.
The Art of Drowning. Pittsburgh, Pennsylvania, University of Pittsburgh Press, 1995.
Picnic, Lightning. Pittsburgh, Pennsylvania, University of Pittsburgh Press, 1997.
Taking Off Emily Dickinson's Clothes: Selected Poems. London, Picador, 2000.
Sailing Alone around the Room: New and Selected Poems. New York, Random House, 2000.

Recording: *The Best Cigarette,* E. Antonow, 1993, Cielo, 1997.

*   *   *

Billy Collins's poetry has received a great deal of critical acclaim and several prestigious awards. From his first mature work in *The Apple That Astonished Paris* to his later *Sailing Alone around the Room: New and Selected Poems,* he has adopted a voice that is both philosophical and comic, intellectually stimulating yet accessible. In fact, Collins's attraction to performance poetry (his CD audio book *The Best Cigarette* sold well) and his reasonably large popular appeal might seem antithetical to the critical acclaim he has received. To put it another way, the accessibility of Collins's work and the emphasis by the poet and his publishers on his stature as a mainstream poet are quite unexpected in the work of one who is also so celebrated by academic critics.

Whatever the case may be, Collins's work is connected to the recent literary past and should be considered within the same context as the meditative lyrical practices of poets ranging from Wordsworth to Auden to the contemporaries Stephen Dunn and Linda Pastan. Frequently beginning with a subjective encounter with the external world, Collins's poems then embark upon ruminations that may allude to literary figures (Dickinson, Wordsworth, Yeats, and others) or to philosophy and religion. Collins has found a great deal of success with this mode, and perhaps the only criticism that should be levied against his work is that it seems from *Questions about Angels* to *Picnic, Lightning* that there has been little exploration in form or in terms of themes and subjects. Considering a few of the titles in *Questions about Angels* illustrates Collins's meditative lyrical practice. ''Reading Myself to Sleep,'' ''The Norton Anthology of Literature,'' ''Going Out for Cigarettes,'' and ''Weighing the Dog'' are all poems that begin with a mundane experience and then move outward to a consideration of something meditatively engaging or philosophically puzzling.

Another aspect of Collins's work that separates him from a great many contemporary poets is the fact that he is also unabashed about using satire and humor, and his meditative lyrics utilize a range of tones, from the absurd to the highly serious. Consider, for instance, these lines from ''Marginalia'' in *Picnic, Lightning.* The speaker asks all those who ''have managed to graduate from college / without ever having written 'Man vs. Nature''' in a margin to step forward, comically undercutting the pedantic aspects of teaching literature. In another poem, however, Collins writes:

> And the soul is up on the roof
> in her nightdress, straddling the ridge,
> singing a song about the wildness of the sea
> until the first rip of pink appears in the sky.
> Then, they all will return to the sleeping body
> the way a flock of birds settles back into a tree.

This poem has a tone that is much closer to the lyrical mode of a poet like Wallace Stevens, and, coupled with the comic riffs Collins uses elsewhere, it is illustrative of his tonal range. The voice in these poems is always intimate, however, in a way that Stevens's work would never attempt to be. Perhaps this intimacy, as well as the frequent use of humor, is connected to Collins's emphasis on the performance dimensions of poetry and on his use of CDs and public readings to promote his work.

Collins makes frequent references to jazz and to musicians. This is another aspect of his interest in the performance possibilities of poetry and in the guise of improvisation his poems seem to aspire toward. The effects can be engaging if not always completely compelling as powerful poetry. Consider these lines from ''I Chop Some Parsley While Listening to Art Blakey's Version of 'Three Blind Mice''':

> And I start wondering how they came to be blind.
> If it was congenital, they could be brothers and sister,
> and I think of the poor mother
> brooding over her sightless young triplets.
>
> Or was it a common accident, all three caught
> in a searing explosion, a firework perhaps?
> If not,
> If each came to his or her blindness separately,
>
> how did they ever manage to find one another?
> Would it not be difficult for a blind mouse
> to locate even one fellow mouse with vision
> let alone two other blind ones?

There is doubt that this is clever, and it is popular. But many poets have attracted reasonably wide readership only to suffer anonymity in fifty years—or less. Whether Collins's work will avoid such a fate is still a question, one perhaps connected to whether or not he is willing to depart from his previously praised modes and develop his abilities in different directions.

—Tod Marshall

COLOMBO, John Robert

Nationality: Canadian. **Born:** Kitchener, Ontario, 24 March 1936. **Education:** Waterloo College, Ontario, 1956–57; University College, University of Toronto, 1958–60, B.A. (honors) 1959. **Family:** Married Ruth Brown in 1959; one daughter and two sons. **Career:** Editorial assistant, University of Toronto Press, 1957–60; assistant editor, Ryerson Press, 1960–63; senior advisory editor, McClelland

and Stewart, Toronto, 1964–70. Former editor, *The Montrealer, Exchange,* and *Tamarack Review,* Toronto; occasional instructor, York University, Toronto, 1963–66; writer-in-residence, Mohawk College, Hamilton, Ontario, 1978; host, *Colombo's Quotes* television series, 1978. Occasional columnist, Toronto *Star,* Toronto *Voice, Danforth Report.* **Awards:** Canada Council grant, 1967, 1971; Centennial medal, 1967; Harbourfront Literary award, 1987. D.Litt.: York University, 1998. **Member:** Ontario Arts Council Advisory Panel, 1966–67; Canada Council Arts Advisory Panel, 1968–70. **Address:** 42 Dell Park Avenue, Toronto, Ontario M6B 2T6, Canada.

PUBLICATIONS

Poetry

Fragments. Privately printed, 1957.
Variations. Kitchener, Ontario, Hawkshead Press, 1958.
This Citadel in Time. Kitchener, Ontario, Hawkshead Press, 1958.
This Studied Self. Kitchener, Ontario, Hawkshead Press, 1958.
In the Streets (as Ruta Ginsberg). Toronto, Hawkshead Press, 1959.
Poems and Other Poems. Toronto, Hawkshead Press, 1959.
Two Poems. Toronto, Hawkshead Press, 1959.
This Is the Work Entitled Canada. Toronto, Purple Partridge Press, 1959.
Fire Escape. Toronto, Hawkshead Press, 1959.
The Impression of Beauty. Toronto, Hawkshead Press, 1959.
Poems to Be Sold for Bread. Toronto, Hawkshead Press, 1959.
Lines for the Last Day. Toronto, Hawkshead Press, 1960.
The Mackenzie Poems. Toronto, Swan, 1965.
The Great Wall of China: An Entertainment. Montreal, Delta Canada, 1966.
Abracadabra. Toronto, McClelland and Stewart, 1967.
Miraculous Montages. Toronto, Heine, 1967.
John Toronto: New Poems by Dr. Strachan, Found by John Robert Colombo. Ottawa, Oberon Press, 1969.
Neo Poems. Vancouver, Sono Nis Press, 1970.
The Great San Francisco Earthquake and Fire. Fredericton, New Brunswick, Fiddlehead, 1971.
Praise Poems and Leonardo's Lists. Toronto, Weed/Flower Press, 1972.
Translations from the English. Toronto, Peter Martin, 1974.
The Sad Truths. Toronto, Peter Martin, 1974.
The Great Collage. Oakville, Ontario, Oasis Press, 1974.
Proverbial Play. Toronto, Missing Link Press, 1975.
Mostly Monsters. Toronto, Hounslow Press, 1977.
Variable Cloudiness. Toronto, Hounslow Press, 1977.
Private Parts. Toronto, Hounslow Press, 1978.
The Great Cities of Antiquity. Toronto, Hounslow Press, 1979.
Recent Poems. Toronto, League of Canadian Poets, 1980.
Selected Poems. Windsor, Ontario, Black Moss Press, 1982.
Selected Translations. Windsor, Ontario, Black Moss Press, 1982.
Off Earth. Toronto, Hounslow Press, 1987.
Luna Park/ One Thousand Poems. Toronto, Hounslow Press, 1994.
Space Poems. Toronto, Colombo and Company, 1995.
Contrails. Toronto, Colombo and Company, 1996.
Earlier Lives. Toronto, Colombo and Company, 1996.
Ether/Rewords. Toronto, Colombo and Company, 1997.
What Is What. Toronto, Colombo and Company, 1998.
Interspaces. Toronto, Colombo and Company, 1999.

Half a World Away: Poems and Effects. Toronto, Colombo and Company, 2000.
Impromptus: One Thousand Poems. Toronto, Colombo and Company, 2000.

Other

CDN SF & F:A Bibliography of Canadian Science Fiction and Fantasy. Toronto, Hounslow Press, 1979.
Blackwood's Books: A Bibliography Devoted to Algernon Blackwood. Toronto, Hounslow Press, 1981.
Canadian Literary Landmarks. Toronto, Hounslow Press, 1984.
Great Moments in Canadian History. Toronto, Hounslow Press, 1984.
Toronto's Fantastic Street Names. Toronto, BAKKA, 1982.
1001 Questions About Canada. Toronto, Doubleday, 1986.
Mysterious Canada: Strange Sights, Extraordinary Events and Peculiar Places. Toronto, Doubleday, 1988.
999 Questions About Canada. Toronto, Doubleday, 1989.
Semi-Certainties: Some Aphorisms of John Robert Colombo. Toronto, Colombo and Company, 1998.
Lambert's Day. Toronto, Colombo and Company, 1999.
Mysteries of Ontario. Toronto, Hounslow, 1999.
Self-Schrift. Toronto, Colombo and Company, 1999.
Open Secrets: Aphorisms of John Robert Colombo. Toronto, Colombo and Company, 2000.

Editor, *Rubato: New Poems by Young Canadian Poets.* Toronto, Purple Partridge Press, 1958.
Editor, *The Varsity Chapbook.* Toronto, Ryerson Press, 1959.
Editor, with Jacques Godbout, *Poésie 64/Poetry 654.* Toronto and Montreal, Ryerson Press-Editions du Jour, 1963.
Editor, with Raymond Souster, *Shapes and Sounds: Poems of W.W.E. Ross.* Toronto, Longman, 1968.
Editor, *How Do I Love Thee: Sixty Poems of Canada (and Quebec)* . . . Edmonton, Hurtig, 1970.
Editor, *New Direction in Canadian Poetry.* Toronto, Holt Rinehart, 1970.
Editor, *Rhymes and Reasons: Nine Canadian Poets Discuss Their Work.* Toronto, Holt Rinehart, 1971.
Editor, *An Alphabet of Annotations.* Montreal, Gheerbrant, 1972.
Editor, *Colombo's Canadian Quotations.* Edmonton, Hurtig, 1974; as *Colombo's Concise Canadian Quotations,* 1976.
Editor, *Colombo's Little Book of Canadian Proverbs, Graffiti, Limericks, and Other Vital Matters.* Edmonton, Hurtig, 1975.
Editor, *Colombo's Canadian References.* Toronto, Oxford University Press, 1976; London and New York, Oxford University Press, 1977.
Editor and translator, with Nikola Roussanoff, *The Balkan Range: A Bulgarian Reader.* Toronto, Hounslow Press, 1976.
Editor and translator, *East and West: Selected Poems,* by George Faludy. Toronto, Hounslow Press, 1978.
Editor, *The Poets of Canada.* Edmonton, Hurtig, 1978.
Editor, *Colombo's Book of Canada.* Edmonton, Hurtig, 1978.
Editor, *Colombo's Names and Nicknames.* Toronto, NC Press, 1978.
Editor, *Colombo's Book of Marvels.* Toronto, NC Press, 1979.
Editor, *Other Canadas: An Anthology of Science Fiction and Fantasy.* Toronto, McGraw Hill Ryerson, 1979.
Editor, *Dark Times,* by Waclaw Iwaniuk, translated by Jagna Boraks. Toronto, Hounslow Press, 1979.

Editor, *Colombo's Hollywood.* Toronto, Collins, 1979; as *Wit and Wisdom of the Moviemakers,* London, Hamlyn, 1979; as *Popcorn in Paradise,* New York, Holt Rinehart, 1980.

Editor, *The Canada Colouring Book.* Toronto, Hounslow Press, 1980.

Editor, 222 *Canadian Jokes.* Cobalt, Ontario, Highway Book Shop, 1981.

Editor, *Far from You: Poems,* by Pavel Javor, translated by Rom Banerjee. Toronto, Hounslow Press, 1981.

Editor, *Friendly Aliens.* Toronto, Hounslow Press, 1981.

Editor, *Poems of the Inuit.* Ottawa, Oberon Press, 1981.

Editor, with Michael Richardson, *Not to Be Taken at Night: Classic Canadian Tales of Mystery and the Supernatural.* Toronto, Lester and Orpen Dennys, 1981.

Editor, *Years of Light: A Celebration of Leslie A. Croutch.* Toronto, Hounslow Press, 1982.

Editor, *Colombo's Last Words.* Cobalt, Ontario, Highway Book Shop, 1982.

Editor, *Colombo's Laws.* Cobalt, Ontario, Highway Book Shop, 1982.

Editor, *Windigo: An Anthology of Fact and Fantastic Fiction.* Saskatoon, Saskatchewan, Western Producer, 1982, and Lincoln, University of Nebraska Press, 1983.

Editor, *Colombo's Canadiana Quiz Book.* Saskatoon, Saskatchewan, Western Producer, 1983.

Editor, *Colombo's 101 Canadian Places.* Toronto, Hounslow Press, 1983.

Editor, *René Lévesque Buys Canada Savings Bonds and Other Great Canadian Graffiti.* Edmonton, Hurtig, 1983.

Editor, *Songs of the Indians.* Ottawa, Obereon Press, 2 vols., 1983.

Editor and translator, with George Faludy, *Learn This Poem of Mine by Heart,* by Faludy. Toronto, Hounslow Press, 1983.

Editor, *The Toronto Puzzle Book.* Toronto, McClelland and Stewart, 1984.

Editor, with Michael Richardson, *We Stand on Guard: Poems and Songs of Canadians in Battle.* Toronto, Doubleday, 1985.

Editor, *Colombo's New Canadian Quotations.* Edmonton, Alberta, Hurtig, 1987.

Editor, *Extraordinary Experiences.* Toronto, Hounslow Press, 1989.

Editor, *Songs of The Great Land.* Ottawa, Oberon Press, 1989.

Editor, *Mysterious Encounters.* Toronto, Hounslow Press, 1990.

Editor, *Voices of Ram.* Ottawa, Oberon Press, 1990.

Editor, with Cyril Greenland, *Walt Whitman's Canada.* Toronto, Hounslow Press, 1992.

Editor, *Close Encounters of the Canadian Kind.* Toronto, Colombo and Company, 1994.

Editor, *Voices of Rama.* Toronto, Colombo and Company, 1994.

Editor, *Ghosts Galore!* Toronto, Colombo and Company, 1994.

Editor, *Strange Stories.* Toronto, Colombo and Company, 1994.

Editor, *Ogdenisms.* Toronto, Hounslow Press, 1994.

Editor, *Ghost Stories of Ontario.* Toronto, Hounslow Press, 1995.

Editor, *Erotica Canadiana.* Toronto, Colombo and Company, 1995.

Editor, *Metro's Goldwyn Mayor.* Toronto, Colombo and Company, 1995.

Editor, *Haunted Toronto.* Toronto, Hounslow Press, 1996.

Editor, 666 *Canadian Jokes.* Toronto, Colombo and Company, 1996.

Editor, *The Stephen Leacock Quote Book.* Toronto, Colombo and Company, 1996.

Editor, *Slightly Higher in Canada.* Toronto, Colombo and Company, 1996.

Editor, *Iron Curtains.* Toronto, Colombo and Company, 1996.

Editor, with Cyril Greenland, *The New Consciousness.* Toronto, Colombo and Company, 1997.

Editor, *Marvellous Stories.* Toronto, Colombo and Company, 1998.

Editor, *Closer Than You Think.* Toronto, Colombo and Company, 1998.

Editor, *All about Us.* Toronto, Colombo and Company, 1998.

Editor, *More Iron Curtains.* Toronto, Colombo and Company, 1998.

Editor, *Conjuring Up the Owens.* Toronto, Colombo and Company, 1999.

Editor, *The Occult Webb.* Toronto, Colombo and Company, 1999.

Editor, *Three Mysteries of Nova Scotia.* Toronto, Colombo and Company, 1999.

Editor, *Singular Stories.* Toronto, Colombo and Company, 1999.

Editor, *The UFO Quote Book.* Toronto, Colombo and Company, 1999.

Editor, *Weird Stories.* Toronto, Colombo and Company, 1999.

Editor, *Ghosts in Our Past.* Toronto, Colombo and Company, 2000.

Editor, *Small Wonders.* Toronto, Colombo and Company, 2000.

Editor, *Canadian Capers.* Toronto, Colombo and Company, 2000.

Translator, with Robert Zend, *From Zero to One,* by Zend. Vancouver, Sono Nis Press, 1973.

Translator, with Nikola Roussanloff, *Under the Eaves of a Forgotten Village: Sixty Poems from Contemporary Bulgaria.* Toronto, Hounslow Press, 1975.

Translator, with Nikola Roussanoff, *The Left-Handed One,* by Lyubomir Levchev. Toronto, Hounslow Press, 1977.

Translator, with Nikola Roussanoff, *Remember Me Well,* by Andrei Germanov. Toronto, Hounslow Press, 1978.

Translator, with Nikola Roussanoff, *Depths,* by Dora Gabe. Toronto, Hounslow Press, 1978.

Translator, with Waclaw Iwaniuk, *Such Times: Selected Poems,* by Ewa Lipska. Toronto, Hounslow Press, 1981.

Translator, with Robert Zend, *Beyond Labels,* by Zend. Toronto, Hounslow Press, 1982.

Translator, with Petronela Negosanu, *Symmetries,* by Marin Sorescu. Toronto, Hounslow Press, 1982.

*

Manuscript Collection: Mills Memorial Library, McMaster University, Hamilton, Ontario.

Critical Studies: By Northrop Frye, in *University of Toronto Review,* July 1959; by Al Purdy, in *Toronto Globe and Mail,* 4 June 1966; by George Woodcock, in *Canadian Literature* (Vancouver), summer 1966; by Louis Dudek, in *Montreal Gazette,* 22 October 1966; by Miriam Waddington, in *Toronto Globe and Mail,* 18 March 1967; by Hugh MacCallum, in *University of Toronto Review,* July 1967 and July 1968; "John Robert Colombo: Documentary Poet as Visionary" by Jean Mallinson, in *Essays on Canadian Writing* (Downsview, Ontario), 5, 1976; "Redeeming Prose: Colombo's Found Poetry" by Manina Jones, in *Canadian Poetry* (London, Ontario), 25, fall-winter 1989; "Redeeming Riel" by Loise Drew, in *Canadian Poetry* (London, Ontario), 31, fall-winter 1992; "A Publishing Giant . . ." by Robert Fulford, in *The Globe and Mail* (Toronto), 17 April 1999; *The Dictionary of the Avant-Gardes* by Richard Kostelanetz, New York, Schirmer Books, 2nd edition, 2000.

John Robert Colombo comments:

I have written, translated, and compiled more than 140 books, and I have edited more than 125 for Canadian publishing houses. I discuss all of this in my memoir *Self-Schrift* (1999). I am nationally known as the "Master Gatherer" for my compilations of Canadiana. Lately I have been called (by Robert Girard of Arcturus Books) "Canada's Mr. Mystery" for my books about paranormal Canadiana. As well, I have done a fair amount of column writing and broadcasting. Finally, I have written and translated and compiled a great deal of poetry. I have chosen not to live the life of the poet. An old adage goes, "You have to choose between living like an artist or being an artist." I opted for the latter way of life. To me the artist is the artisan of awareness and the transmitter rather than the originator of wonders. All of these activities are to me complementary concerns, for they arise out of my desire and need to raise the awareness of Canadians and others of the continuity and complexity of the various words that we inhabit. The words are largely comprehended through words, all of which take form and wondrously appear on one of my computer screens!

*   *   *

Although John Robert Colombo's activities as an accomplished editor and prolific anthologist have obscured his work as a poet, the latter is of a piece with the former. Not only are the same eclectic interests at play—quotations, proverbs, translations, science fiction, fantasy, the paranormal—but the same procedures of selection and combination are apparent. Colombo plainly does not regard his use of found or documentary materials as any less creative than the more or less spontaneous generation of original poems, even his own. We find Colombo's muse less hovering over his shoulder than wherever he casts his eye.

Colombo attempts to produce what Viktor Shklovsky called "defamiliarization"—the making strange of the familiar. The found poem, reproducing the words of others while framing them in a different context, lends itself to this strategy, and Colombo was one of the first Canadian practitioners of the form. *The Mackenzie Poems* and *John Toronto* recast the words of two early nineteenth-century political rivals, William Lyon Mackenzie and Bishop John Strachan. In many other collections, including the significantly titled *Translations from the English,* Colombo raids heterogeneous sources for his rearrangements, usually for comic or ironic effect. *The Great San Francisco Earthquake and Fire* manipulates James Russel Wilson's prose account of the disaster:

> Weddings in great number
> resulted from the disaster.
> Women, driven out of their homes
> and left destitute,
> appealed to the men to whom
> they were engaged,
> and immediately marriages were effected.
> "I don't live anywhere,"
> was the answer given in many cases
> when the applicant for a licence
> was asked where his residence is.
> "I used to live in San Francisco."

Similarly, a sequence of messages on cards in the Monopoly board game, for example, culminates in the following:

YOU HAVE WON SECOND PRIZE
IN A BEAUTY CONTEST
COLLECT $11.00

The list poem, often of clichés, proverbs, and catchphrases, is another favorite device, especially in *Abracadabra, Neo Poems,* and *Leonardo's Lists.* Colombo is unafraid of such material, and as he says in *The Great Wall of China,* "All the truisms / are true . . ." The risk he takes is that sometimes the banal original simply cannot be redeemed. Then, too, his methods sometimes seem too mechanical or schematic, as in "After Stesichorus" in *The Sad Truths,* in which historical facts (e.g., the fall of Troy and Columbus's voyage) are stated, then intermingled ("Feudalism rose and the Renaissance fell").

Although *Selected Poems* conveniently presents the wide range of his work, *Abracadabra* may be the best single collection, including, as it does, the wonderfully witty "Recipe for a Canadian Novel," which ends,

> Slice or leave whole.
> Serves twenty million all told—
> when cold.

Colombo typically states a theme and then gives variations or else resolves game-playing or puzzle-making rules he has stated or implied at the outset. Anagrams, concrete poems, and verse forms like the haiku or its parodic version, the senryu, all are in Colombo's grab bag of what he calls in *Off Earth* "poems and effects."

The effects are lavishly displayed in a large-format, limited-edition selection that includes *Luna Park* and the arrestingly titled *One Thousand Poems.* The latter, true enough, consists of one thousand (alphabetized) poems, but each is no longer than four words or so, and many are just one. Here are a few:

> ADULTery
> affluenza
> Bang Cock, Thigh Land
> ex ile
> Jacques Lacan't
> liarwyer
> Mao Tse Ching
> SalMAN RushDIE
> United States of AmerCIA

If the puns and wordplay are sometimes juvenile or otherwise ill judged, the performance remains remarkable.

Colombo's philosophical bent and love of paradox hold abundant sway in *What Is What* and *Half a World Away.* His date-lined "poems and effects," each book written over one calendar year and ordered, respectively, by the seasons and by zodiacal signs, record the interplay of words and worlds. Terms "effects" as "poetic undertakings," Colombo gives poems no precedence over them. In both cases he typically uses parallelism and "hypallage," which in "Muses" he helpfully defines as "the interchange of two elements / In a proposition or statement." Sometimes these rhetorical devices are combined, as in the two-line poem (or is it an effect?) "Intimacy":

> Her here
> His her

Social comment, elegies, quotations, and travel notes mingle in these poetic daybooks, as do aphorisms and banality. Colombo is, in fact, a connoisseur of the banal, noting in "Proem" that "some things are so predictable that their occurrence is always slightly surprising." With its tone of cheerful pessimism, which is suitably paradoxical, Colombo's work essentially concerns transformation, a two-way metamorphosis of "the real world of consensual reality and the equally real world of imaginal reality," as he puts it in the preface to *Half a World Away.* The poet is a coolheaded observer of both.

Most of Colombo's poems are in a sense translations, but he also does straightforward renditions from other languages. *Collected Translations* renders sixty-five poems from eleven languages, including Bulgarian, Romanian, and Inuktitut. Some are "co-translations" with native speakers, and all are arranged "as if they would be in a book of original poems by a single author." If Colombo's entire oeuvre has a metaphysical subtext, it may be that the universe itself is the work of a single author—a highly quotable one.

—Fraser Sutherland

COMFORT, Alex(ander)

Nationality: British. **Born:** London, 10 February 1920. **Education:** Highgate School, London, 1932–36; Trinity College, Cambridge (Styring scholar; Senior scholar), 1938–40, M.B., B.Ch. 1944, M.A. 1945; London Hospital (Scholar), M.R.C.S. and L.R.C.P. 1944, D.C.H. 1945, Ph.D. in biochemistry 1949, D.Sc. in gerontology 1963. **Family:** Married 1) Ruth Muriel Harris in 1943 (marriage dissolved 1973), one son; 2) Jane Tristram Henderson in 1973 (died 1991). **Career:** House physician, London Hospital, 1944; resident medical officer, Royal Waterloo Hospital, London, 1944–45; lecturer in physiology, 1945–51; honorary research associate, department of zoology, 1951–73, and director of research on the biology of aging, 1966–73, University College, London; lecturer in psychiatry, Stanford University, California, 1974–83; senior fellow, Institute for Higher Studies, Santa Barbara, California, from 1975; professor of pathology, University of California School of Medicine, Irvine, 1976–78; consultant psychiatrist, Brentwood Hospital, Los Angeles, 1978–81; adjunct professor, Neuropsychiatric Institute, University of California, Los Angeles, from 1980; consultant, Ventura County Hospital (Medical Education), California, from 1981. Editor, with Peter Wells, Poetry Folios, Barnet, Hertfordshire, 1942–46. President, British Society for Research on Ageing, 1967. **Awards:** Nuffield research fellowship, 1952; Ciba Foundation prize, 1958; Borestone Mountain poetry award, 1962; Karger memorial prize in gerontology, 1969. **Address:** Chacombe House, Chacombe Near Banbury, Oxon OX17 2SL, England. **Died:** 29 March 2000.

PUBLICATIONS

Poetry

France and Other Poems. London, Favil Press, 1941.
Three New Poets, with Roy McFadden and Ian Serraillier. Billericay, Essex, Grey Walls Press, 1942.
A Wreath for the Living. London, Routledge, 1942.
Elegies. London. Routledge, 1944.

The Song of Lazarus. Barnet, Hertfordshire, Poetry Folios, and New York, Viking Press, 1945.
The Signal to Engage. London, Routledge, 1947.
And All but He Departed. London, Routledge, 1951.
Haste to the Wedding. London, Eyre and Spottiswoode, 1962; Chester Springs, Pennsylvania, Dufour, 1964.
Poems for Jane. London, Mitchell Beazley, and New York, Crown, 1979.
Mikrokosmos. London, Sinclair-Stevenson, 1994.

Plays

Into Egypt: A Miracle Play. Billericay, Essex, Grey Walls Press, 1942.
Cities of the Plain: A Democratic Melodrama. London, Grey Walls Press, 1943.

Television Play: *The Great Agrippa,* 1968.

Novels

The Silver River, Being the Diary of a Schoolboy in the South Atlantic, 1936. London, Chapman and Hall, 1938.
No Such Liberty. London, Chapman and Hall, 1941.
The Almond Tree: A Legend. London, Chapman and Hall, 1942.
The Power House. London, Routledge, 1944; New York, Viking Press, 1945.
On This Side Nothing. London, Routledge, and New York, Viking Press, 1949.
A Giant's Strength. London, Routledge, 1952.
Come Out to Play. London, Eyre and Spottiswoode, 1961; New York, Crown, 1975.
Tetrarch. Boulder, Colorado, Shambhala, 1980; London, Wildwood House, 1981.
Imperial Patient: The Memoirs of Nero's Doctor. London, Duckworth, 1987.
The Philosophers. London, Duckworth, 1989.

Short Stories

Letters from an Outpost. London, Routledge, 1947.

Other

Peace and Disobedience. London, Peace News, 1946.
Art and Social Responsibility: Lectures on the Ideology of Romanticism. London, Falcon Press, 1946.
The Novel and Our Time. Letchworth, Hertfordshire, Phoenix House, and Denver, Swallow, 1948.
Barbarism and Sexual Freedom: Six Lectures on the Sociology of Sex from the Standpoint of Anarchism. London, Freedom Press, 1948.
First-Year Physiological Techniques. London, Staples Press, 1948.
The Pattern of the Future. London, Routledge, and New York, Macmillan, 1949.
The Right Thing to Do, Together with the Wrong Thing to Do. London, Peace News, 1949.

Authority and Delinquency in the Modern State: A Criminological Approach to the Problem of Power. London, Routledge, 1950; revised edition, as *Authority and Delinquency,* London, Sphere, 1970.

Sexual Behavior in Society. London, Duckworth, and New York, Viking Press, 1950; revised edition, as *Sex in Society,* Duckworth, 1963; New York, Citadel Press, 1966.

Deliquency (lecture). London, Freedom Press, 1951.

Social Responsibility in Science and Art. London, Peace News, 1952.

The Biology of Senescence. London, Routledge, and New York, Rinehart, 1956; revised edition, as *Ageing: The Biology of Senescence,* 1964; revised edition, as *The Biology of Senescense,* Edinburgh, Churchill Livingston, and New York, Elsevier, 1979.

Darwin and the Naked Lady: Discursive Essays on Biology and Art. London, Routledge, 1961; New York, Braziller, 1962.

The Process of Ageing. New York, New American Library, 1964; London, Weidenfeld and Nicolson, 1965.

The Nature of Human Nature. New York, Harper, 1965; as *Nature and Human Nature,* London, Weidenfeld and Nicolson, 1966.

The Anxiety Makers: Some Curious Preoccupations of the Medical Profession. London, Nelson, 1967.

What Rough Beast? and What Is a Doctor? (lectures). Vancouver, Pendejo Press, 1971.

The Joy of Sex: A Gourmet's Guide to Love Making. New York, Crown, 1972; London, quartet, 1973; revised edition, New York, Pocket Books, 1987.

More Joy: A Sequel to "The Joy of Sex." London, Mitchell Beazley, 1973; New York, Crown, 1974; revised edition, 1987.

A Good Age. New York, Crown, 1976; London, Mitchell Beazley, 1977.

The Facts of Love: Living, Loving, and Growing Up (for children), with Jane Comfort. New York, Crown, 1979; London, Mitchell Beazley, 1980.

I and That: Notes on the Biology of Religion. London, Mitchell Beazley, and New York, Crown 1979.

What Is a Doctor? Essays on Medicine and Human Natural History. Philadelphia, Stickley, 1980.

Practice of Geriatric Psychiatry. New York, Elsevier, 1980.

What about Alcohol? (textbook), with Jane Comfort. Burlington, North Carolina, Carolina Biological Supply Company, 1983.

Reality and Empathy; Physics, Mind, and Science in the 21st Century. Albany, State University of New York Press, 1984.

Say Yes to Old Age: Developing a Positive Attitude toward Aging. New York, Crown, 1990.

Science, Religion and Scientism. N.p., South Place Ethical Society, 1990.

The New Joy of Sex. New York, Crown, 1991.

Against Power and Death: The Anarchist Articles and Pamphlets of Alex Comfort. London, Freedom Press, 1994.

Sexual Positions. London, Mitchell Beazley, and New York, Crown, 1997.

Kisses and Caresses. London, Mitchell Beazley, 1997.

Sexual Fantasies. London, Mitchell Beazley, 1997.

Sexual Foreplay. London, Mitchell Beazley, and New York, Crown, 1997.

Editor, with Robert Greacen, *Lyra: An Anthology of New Lyric.* Billericay, Essex, Grey Walls Press, 1942.

Editor, with John Bayliss, *New Road 1943 and 1944: New Directions in European Art and Letters.* London, Grey Walls Press, 2 vols., 1943–44.

Editor, *History of Erotic Art 1.* London, Weidenfeld and Nicolson, and New York, Putnam, 1969.

Editor, *Sexual Consequences of Disability.* Philadelphia, Stickley, 1978.

Translator, with Allan Ross Macdougall, *The Triumph of Death,* by C.F. Ramuz. London, Routledge, 1946.

Translator, *The Koka Shastra.* London, Allen and Unwin, 1964; New York, Stein and Day, 1965.

Translator, *The Illustrated Koka Shastra: Medieval Indian Writings on Love Based on the Kama Sutra.* New York, Simon and Schuster, 1997.

*

Bibliography: "Alexander Comfort: A Bibliography in Progress" by D. Callaghan, in *West Coast Review* (Burnaby, British Columbia), 1969.

Critical Studies: *The Freedom of Poetry* by Derek Stanford, London, Falcon Press, 1947; "The Scientific Humanism of Alex Comfort" by Wayne Burns, in *The Humanist 11* (London), November-December 1951; "The Anarchism of Alex Comfort" by John Ellerby, "Sex, Kicks and Comfort" by Charles Radcliffe, and "Alex Comfort's Art and Scope" by Harold Drasdo, all in *Anarchy 33* (London), November 1963; *Alex Comfort* by Arthur E. Salmon, Boston, Twayne, 1978.

* * *

Alex Comfort's best-known poems are concerned with sexual love, with a sometimes tender, sometimes bawdy exploration of the sexual impulse in men and women. If other poets have occasionally explored this subject, Comfort is, apart from his contemporary Gavin Ewart, the only poet who is known almost exclusively for it. This is partly because of his extrapoetic writing, often about sexual psychology and physiology, and partly through the continual anthologizing of his fine poem "For Ruth" ("There is a white mare that my love keeps / unridden in a hillside meadow . . .'').

Comfort's earlier poems, owing much to T.S. Eliot, often consisted of meditations on death, not only on violent death in war, as in the 1944 *Elegies,* but also on death as seen lurking in natural landscapes: "The condemned cell of the woods lies round our doors, / the trees are bars, and barbs the bramble carries . . ." Comfort's subsequent war poems, in *The Signal to Engage,* were as bitter as those of Siegfried Sassoon a generation earlier. But it was later, in the 1960s, that Comfort found the theme and the style, sometimes extrovert, sometimes interior, that enabled him to write the poems in which he is seen at his most amusing, accomplished, and wise. His range within this theme is considerable and ranges from the lyrical to the epigrammatic ("Babies' and lovers' toes express / ecstasies of wantonness. / That's a language which we lose / with the trick of wearing shoes").

Comfort's technical range is not great, but he commands a technique that enables him to make his points in a sinewy and terse language that is only occasionally marred by sentimentality. His anecdotes—often telling a short story that might have appealed to Guy de Maupassant—are succinct, and if he turns his hand to a purposely made piece, as in *Haste to the Wedding,* the note is never false.

Comfort's attitude toward love, increasingly shared by his younger readers, is celebrated in poetry like none that has been written since the Restoration. It is direct and uncompromising, with a note of wholehearted enjoyment. He is tired of "the best pentameters," of "eloquence overdone": "That first act of our own / is still the best act left. Let's go to bed." Of course this means that there are limitations, and Comfort has perhaps never wholly recaptured the tenderness of "For Ruth." But while many other poets have written single poems of considerable beauty, not so many have written, for instance, a complaining elegy on bed manufacturers: "Surely the trade has one Stradivarius? / If not, I know why in Neolithic days / the Goddess was steatopygic. / For the meantime let us unroll the rug."

Comfort's later love poems succeed perhaps because they lack the painful intensity of longing that pierces the verse of poets both less happy as lovers and more intent on their poetry. Comfort's verse celebrates, not mourns or yearns. His words "serve to fill the space / between meeting and meeting— / this is the eloquent thing / that they are celebrating / and nothing that we write / myself or any other / matches the fine content / of what we do together."

—Derek Parker

CONN, Stewart

Nationality: British. **Born:** Glasgow, Scotland, 5 November 1936. **Education:** Attended Kilmarnock Academy and Glasgow University. **Military Service:** Royal Air Force. **Family:** Married Judith Clarke in 1963; two sons. **Career:** Radio drama producer, Glasgow, then head of Drama (Radio), BBC, Edinburgh, 1962–92. Literary adviser, Edinburgh Royal Lyceum Theatre, 1973–75. Has served on literature and drama panels of the Scottish Arts Council. **Awards:** Eric Gregory award, 1963; Scottish Arts Council poetry prize and publication award, 1968; Poetry Book Society choice awards, 1972, 1978, 1992; Edinburgh Festival Fringe award, for drama, 1981, 1988. Fellow, Royal Scottish Academy of Music & Drama, 1990. **Agent:** Lemon Unna and Durbridge Ltd., 24–32 Pottery Lane, London W11 4LZ, England.

PUBLICATIONS

Poetry

Thunder in the Air. Preston, Lancashire, Akros, 1976.
The Chinese Tower. Edinburgh, M. Macdonald, 1967.
Stoats in the Sunlight. London, Hutchinson, 1968; as *Ambush and Others Poems,* New York, Macmillan, 1970.
Corgi Modern Poets in Focus 3, with others, edited by Dannie Abse. London, Corgi, 1971.
An Ear to the Ground. London, Hutchinson, 1972.
Under the Ice. London, Hutchinson, 1978.
In the Kibble Palace: New and Selected Poems. Newcastle upon Tyne, Bloodaxe, 1987.

The Luncheon of the Boating Party. Newcastle upon Tyne, Bloodaxe, 1991.
At the Aviary. Newcastle upon Tyne, Bloodaxe, 1995.
In the Blood. Newcastle upon Tyne, Bloodaxe, 1995.
Stolen Light: Selected Poems. Newcastle upon Tyne, Bloodaxe, 1999.

Plays

Break-Down (produced Glasgow, 1961).
Birds in a Wilderness (produced Edinburgh, 1964).
I Didn't Always Live Here (produced Glasgow, 1967). Included in *The Aquarium, The Man in the Green Muffler, I Didn't Always Live Here,* 1976.
The King (produced Edinburgh, 1967; London, 1972). Published in *New English Dramatists 14,* London, Penguin, 1970.
Broche (produced Exeter, 1968).
Fancy Seeing You, Then (produced London, 1974). Published in *Playbill Two,* edited by Alan Durband, London, Hutchinson, 1969.
Victims (includes *The Sword, In Transit,* and *The Man in the Green Muffler*) (produced Edinburgh, 1970). *In Transit,* published New York, Breakthrough Press, 1972; *The Man in the Green Muffler,* included in *The Aquarium, The Man in the Green Muffler, I Didn't Always Live Here,* 1976.
The Burning (produced Edinburgh, 1971). London, Calder and Boyars, 1973.
A Slight Touch of the Sun (produced Edinburgh, 1972).
The Aquarium (produced Edinburgh, 1973). Included in *The Aquarium, The Man in the Green Muffler, I Didn't Always Live Here,* 1976.
Count Your Blessings (produced Pitlochry, Pertshire, 1975).
Thistlewood (produced Edinburgh, 1975). Todmorden, Lancashire, Woodhouse, 1979.
The Aquarium, The Man in the Green Muffler, I Didn't Always Live Here. London, Calder, 1976.
Play Donkey (produced Edinburgh, 1977). Todmorden, Lancashire, Woodhouse, 1980.
Billy Budd, with Stephen Macdonald, adaptation of the novel by Melville (produced Edinburgh, 1978).
Hecuba (produced Edinburgh, 1979; revised version produced Glasgow, 1989).
Herman (produced Edinburgh, 1981; London, 1986).
By the Pool (produced Edinburgh, 1988; London, 1989).
Hugh Miller (produced Edinburgh, 1988).
The Dominion of Fancy (produced Pitlochry, Pershire, 1992).
Mission Boy (produced Grahamstown, South Africa, 1996; Edinburgh, 1998).
Clay Bull (produced Edinburgh, 1998).

Radio Plays: *Any Following Spring,* 1962; *Cadenza for Real,* 1963; *Song of the Clyde,* 1964; *The Canary Cage,* 1967; *Too Late the Phalarope,* from the novel by Alan Paton, 1984; *Beside the Ocean of Time,* from the novel by George Mackay Brown, 1997; *Greenvoe,* from the novel by George Mackay Brown, 1998.

Radio Broadcast: *The Living Poet,* 1989.

Television Plays: *Wally Dugs Go in Pairs,* 1973; *The Kite,* 1979; *Blood Hunt,* 1986.

Other

Twelve More Modern Scottish Poets, edited by Charles King and Iain Crichton Smith. London, Hodder & Stoughton, 1986.

Editor, *New Poems 1973–74.* London, Hutchinson, 1974.
Editor, with Ian McDonough, *The Ice Horses.* Edinburgh, Scottish Cultural Press, 1996.

*

Manuscript Collection: Scottish National Library, Edinburgh.

Critical Studies: Interviews with James Aitchison in *Scottish Theatre* (Edinburgh), March 1969, Allen Wright in *The Scotsman* (Edinburgh), 30 October 1971, and Joyce McMillan in *Scottish Theatre News* (Glasgow), August 1981; "Bound by Necessity" by George Bruce, in *Akros,* 1979; "Towards the Human," in *Towards the Human* by Iain Crichton Smith, Edinburgh, MacDonald, 1986.

Theatrical Activities: Director: **Radio**—many plays, including *The Dirt under the Carpet* by Rona Munro, 1987; *Not about Heroes* and *In the Summer of 1918* by Stephen MacDonald; *Potestad* by Eduardo Pavlovsky; *Andromache* by Douglas Dunn, 1989; *Good* by C.P. Taylor, 1989; *Carver* by John Purser, 1991; *Yosemite* by James Rankin, 1993.

*   *   *

At the age of twenty-six Stewart Conn wrote "Todd," a characterization of an uncle who had a passionate love for horses. In its effect of concentrated intensity it is a remarkable poem. It begins,

My father's white uncle became
  Arthritic and testamental in
Lyrical stages . . .

The "white uncle," at once legendary in its suggestion, almost immediately becomes suffering actuality in "arthritic" before turning Old Testament prophet in "testamental," but this prophet's fires burn in his passion for horses. Yet the horses themselves are "a primal extension of rock and soil," though equally they have "cracked hooves" and are fed on "bowls of porridge." The world of the stable is activated in sounds—"thundered nail"—and in smells—"his own horsey breath"—the uncle's breath, as horse and he are one. The words are charged with meaning as they flow to and fro between the actual and the mythical. The people from Conn's childhood, purposeful and vigorous, become vividly alive in the poems:

From the byre, smack on time
Old Martha comes clattering out,
  With buttered bannocks and milk in a pail.

About the same time as Conn was writing poems bred from his community, he wrote laconic dramatic poems dealing with barbarities and evoking in the reader repulsion and nausea. I frequently find these historical or quasi-historical episodes contrived, but they were a genuine endeavor to accept alienation into Conn's oeuvre, a necessary move if his poetry was to respond to contemporary conditions. In any case his domestic themes increasingly committed Conn to deal with suffering. The poem "Crippled Aunt" ends with the poet observing the aunt, who is paralyzed from the waist down, in church:

Watching them wheel you down the aisle, I am humble.
  I, who would curse the fate
    That has twisted you into what
You are, shudder to hear you say life's ample
For your needs, Christian by such example.

But this situation still belongs to Conn's past. His finer achievement, as in his collection *Under the Ice,* for the most part uses domestic situations of the present as a means of contemplating contemporary distresses and perplexities. When the horror story is told now, as in "Reawakening," it is no longer an attempt to create a cruel past; it is related to the frightening unguided missile in which we travel through space and time. The only answer that proposes itself to the poet is to be found in love between two people, but no sooner is the idea proposed, as in "Arrivals," than it is questioned:

The plane meets
its reflection on the wet
runway, then crosses
to where I wait
behind plate glass.

I watch
with a mixture
of longing and despair
as you re-enter
the real world.

The poet's beloved returns to him, who is at a remove behind glass. She returns to the "real world," but we are left wondering where that is. Conn can now put a fine edge on daily experiences, guiding the reader to recognize the strangeness of existence but not allowing a refuge in simple statements. The ambiguities and perplexities remain but are refined into poetry.

In the books that follow a widening of subjects yields a more relaxed view of communal activities. In the title poem of *The Luncheon of the Boating Party,* Conn as dramatist-poet enters with gentle humor into the personas of Renoir's painting. Here is an extension of his enjoyment of character drawn from the personal experience of a rural Scottish community, which still plays a significant part in this book and in *In the Blood.* Conn's peculiar achievement, however, is in recording violations of humanity. When a community is violated, as was Lockerbie by the exploding bomb in the plane, he notes the event in restrained, accurate observation. In the poem "Breach of Privacy" he is in anguish at another violation, that by the media. Conn asks, "How at such a time dare a lens intrude?"

Conn applies his disciplined, economic verse in *At the Aviary* to his encounter with the cruelty and hatred he experienced in his first visit to South Africa in 1984, setting such exigencies in the context of the beauty of the country and of animal creation. Even so, the situation with the greatest tragic force is that which occurs against the background of ordinary days at home. In "Losing Touch," from *In the Blood,* he notes of an aging woman,

   . . . the loss of dignity
entailed; her window the wall of an aquarium

hemming her in. With no warning,
a pang of pain spans the space between.

Conn is to be respected for allowing himself to remain vulnerable and so now to accept the full impact of such situations as seen in the context of human failures:

Nowhere
Man cannot render unfit for habitation.

In praising an artist in "Choosing a Drawing" he describes his own achievement:

I marvel
how in pen and ink or granite, he can impose
such order; through controlled frenzy, convey
the tenderness and terror of his inner eye.

Conn has equipped himself to deal with the widest possible range of subjects. This can be seen, for example, in his response to the social and political situation in South Africa and to the flora and fauna of that country. But his diversity never leads to diffusion, for a concerned and humane mind is always present. In the midst of the hype and sound bites of the present time, perhaps the greatest benefaction the poet can give us are works that demand consideration in their reading.

—George Bruce

CONQUEST, (George) Robert (Acworth)

Pseudonyms: Ted Parker, Victor Gray. **Nationality:** American. **Born:** Great Malvern, Worcester, 15 July 1917. **Education:** Winchester College; Magdalen College, Oxford, B.A. 1939; University of Grenoble, 1935–36. **Military Service:** Served in the Oxfordshire and Buckinghamshire Light Infantry, 1939–46. **Family:** Married 1) Joan Watkins in 1942 (divorced 1948), two sons; 2) Tatiana Mihailova in 1948 (divorced 1962); 3) Caroleen Macfarlane in 1964 (divorced 1977); 4) Elizabeth Neece in 1979. **Career:** Member of the U.K. Diplomatic Service, 1946–56; fellow, London School of Economics, 1956–58; visiting poet, University of Buffalo, 1959–60; literary editor, *The Spectator,* London, 1962–63; senior fellow, Columbia University, New York, 1964–65; fellow, Woodrow Wilson Center, Washington, D.C., 1976–77; visiting scholar, Heritage Foundation, Washington, D.C., 1980–81. Senior research fellow, 1977–79, and since 1981 scholar-curator of the Russian and CIS collection, Hoover Institution, Stanford, California. Since 1981 research associate, Ukrainian Research Institute, Harvard University, Cambridge, Massachusetts; since 1983 adjunct fellow, Center for Strategic and International Studies, Washington, D.C. Editor, *Soviet Analyst,* London, 1971–73. **Awards:** P.E.N. prize, 1945; Festival of Britain prize, 1951; Mencken award, 1987; Shevcenko award, 1991; Jefferson Lecturer in the Humanities, 1993; Alexis de Tocqueville award, 1994; American Academy of Arts and Letters award for light verse, 1997; Richard M. Weaver prize, 1999. M.A. 1972, and D. Litt. 1975: Oxford University. Fellow, Royal Society of Literature, 1972, and British Academy, 1994. O.B.E. (Officer, Order of the British Empire), 1955. C.M.G.

(Companion, Order of St. Michael and St. George), 1996. **Address:** Hoover Institution, Stanford, California 94305–2323, U.S.A.

PUBLICATIONS

Poetry

Poems. London, Macmillan, and New York, St. Martin's Press, 1955.
Between Mars and Venus. London, Hutchinson, and New York, St. Martin's Press, 1962.
Arias from a Love Opera. London, Macmillan, and New York, Macmillan, 1969.
Casualty Ward. London, Poem-of-the-Month Club, 1974.
Coming Across. Menlo Park, California, Buckabest, 1978.
Forays. London, Chatto and Windus, 1979.
New and Collected Poems. Irvine, California, C. Schlacks, 1986; London, Century Hutchinson, 1988.
Demons Don't. London, London Magazine Editions, 1999.

Novels

A World of Difference. London, Ward Lock, 1955; New York, Ballantine, 1964.
The Egyptologists, with Kingsley Amis. London, Cape, 1965; New York, Random House, 1966.

Other

The Soviet Deportation of Nationalities. London, Macmillan, and New York, St. Martin's Press, 1960; revised edition, as *The Nation Killers: The Soviet Deportation of Nationalities,* London, Macmillan, and New York, St. Martin's Press, 1970.
Common Sense about Russia. London, Gollancz, and New York, Macmillan, 1960.
Courage of Genius: The Pasternak Affair. London, Collins-Harvill Press, 1961, Philadelphia, Lippincott, 1962.
Power and Policy in the U.S.S.R. London, Macmillan, and New York, St. Martin's Press, 1961.
Russia after Khrushchev. London, Pall Mall Press, and New York, Praeger, 1965.
The Great Terror: Stalin's Purge of the Thirties. London, Macmillan, and New York, Macmillan, 1968; revised edition, 1973.
Where Marx Went Wrong. London, Stacey, 1970.
Lenin. London, Fontana, and New York, Viking Press, 1972.
Kolyma: The Arctic Death Camps. London, Macmillan, and New York, Viking Press, 1978.
Present Danger: Towards a Foreign Policy. Oxford, Blackwell, and Stanford, California, Hoover Institution, 1979.
The Abomination of Moab. London, Temple Smith, 1979.
We and They: Civic and Despotic Cultures. London, Temple Smith, 1980.
What to Do When the Russians Come: A Survivor's Guide, with Jon Manchip White. New York, Stein and Day, 1984.
Inside Stalin's Secret Police: NKVD Politics 1936–1939. Stanford, California, Hoover Institution Press, and London, Macmillan, 1985.
The Harvest of Sorrow: Soviet Collectivization and the Terror-Famine. New York, Oxford University Press, and London, Century Hutchinson, 1986.

Stalin and the Kirov Murder. New York, Oxford University Press, and London, Century Hutchinson, 1989.

Tyrants and Typewriters. London, Century Hutchinson, and San Diego, Lexington, 1989.

The Great Terror Reassessed. New York, Oxford University Press, and London, Century Hutchinson, 1990.

Stalin, Breaker of Nations. New York, Viking, and London, Werdenfeld, 1991.

Reflections on a Ravaged Century. New York, Norton, and London, John Murray, 1999.

Editor, *New Lines 1–2.* London, Macmillan, 2 vols., 1956–63.

Editor, *Back to Life: Poems from Behind the Iron Curtain* (anthology). London, Hutchinson, and New York, St. Martin's Press, 1958.

Editor, with Kingsley Amis, *Spectrum [1–5]: A Science Fiction Anthology.* London, Gollancz, 5 vols., 1961–65; New York, Harcourt Brace, 5 vols., 1962–67.

Editor, *Soviet Studies Series.* London, Bodley Head 8 vols., 1967–68; New York, Praeger, 8 vols., 1968–69.

Editor, *A Childhood in Prison* by Pyotr Yakir. London, Macmillan, 1972; New York, Coward McCann, 1973.

Editor, *The Robert Sheckley Omnibus.* London, Gollancz, 1973.

Editor, *The Russian Tradition,* by Tibor Szamuely. London, Secker and Warburg, 1974; New York, McGraw Hill, 1975.

Editor, *The Last Empire: Nationality and the Soviet Future.* Stanford, California, Hoover Institution Press, 1986.

Translator, *Prussian Nights,* by Alexander Solzhenitsyn. London, Collins-Harvill Press, and New York, Farrar Straus, 1977.

*

Critical Studies: In *Times Literary Supplement* (London), 30 May 1955; by D.J. Enright, in *The Month* (London), May 1956; John Holloway, in *Hudson Review* (New York), xiv, 4, 1961; Thom Gunn, in *The Spectator* (London), 4 May 1962; ''The Movement against Itself: British Poetry of the 1950s'' by Florence Elon, in *Southern Review* (Baton Rouge, Louisiana), 19(1), winter 1983; ''Robert Conquest and Science'' by Jerry Bradley, in *Readerly/Writerly Texts* (Portales, New Mexico), 4(1), 1996.

Robert Conquest comments:

I suppose my main theme is the poet's relationship to the phenomenal universe, in particular to landscape, women, art, and war. Forms usually, though not always, traditional. Sometimes straight lyric, more often with development of a train of thought, an attempt to master, or transmit, a presented reality in intellectual and emotive terms simultaneously. The vocabulary often runs to words—not specialist ones—drawn from the technical, scientific, and philosophical spheres and mediatized into the ordinary language.

Since all this is in principle a complex and difficult process, a strong effort goes into keeping it as comprehensible as possible, avoidance of forced obscurities and provision of a rigorous guidance of sound and structure.

(1995) The above now sounds rather dry and scholastic. ''Rigor'' is too strong, though form (usually) valuable. Lyrical, sensuous rhetoric, now rare, needed. Fashions in free, wry, minor-key-personal make for criticasters' or academics' private-plot versicles.

Have also published much light verse under various pseudonyms, mainly Ted Parker and Victor Gray.

*   *   *

Robert Conquest's reputation as a historian of the Soviet Union has overshadowed his poetic achievement, even though his *New and Collected Poems* assembled the contents of five volumes that had appeared between 1955 and 1979, together with poems from a variety of printed sources and a number of new poems. He also edited *New Lines,* arguably the most influential anthology of contemporary poetry that has appeared since the end of World War II. His introduction to the anthology was not primarily a manifesto or an attempt to promote a new school; it was instead a reasoned and persuasive criticism of certain poetic theories and practices that Conquest held to be deleterious and an assertion that good sense, lucidity, rational control of language, and the traditional use of rhyme, meter, and formal patterns may be valuable servants of the poetic imagination.

At its best Conquest's own verse exemplifies his precepts. It would be wrong to think of him as antiromantic or as an apologist for a neo-Augustan revival. Indeed his range of sympathies is wide, embracing such diverse figures as Catullus, Ovid, nineteenth-century English romantic poets, Chateaubriand, Stendhal, Lamartine, Turgenev, and Hart Crane, along with painters ranging from Salvator Rosa to Paul Klee. But he draws the line at Ezra Pound.

Conquest was attached to the Soviet Army Group in 1944–45, watched the takeover of Bulgaria by the Communists, and returned there after the war as a member of the British embassy. In *Poems* and in his second collection, *Between Mars and Venus,* he draws on some of his Balkan experiences, evoking not so much political events as the countryside, the historical associations of places, and the prevalence of bedbugs. Many of the themes in his first two volumes—guided missiles, international politics, travel, music, painting, major writers, love between men and women—reflect his public concerns and his sensuous temperament.

Arias from a Love Opera and *Forays* represent an advance on their predecessors, commanding a widening range of subject matter and a greater emotional richness. In ''Seal Rock: San Francisco'' Conquest discerns analogies between the gyrations of the seals and the workings of the shaping spirit of imagination. Two of the finest poems in *Arias from a Love Opera* are a tribute to Coleridge and a plangently romantic meditation, ''Chateaubriand's Grave'':

Silly or not, conventions cannot hide
The sea's huge swirl of glitter and of gloom,
Nor pour oblivion on the baffled pride
That thrusts the memoirs from beyond the tomb.

Forays resumes and develops some of the themes from Conquest's earlier collections and explores new themes. ''To Be a Pilgrim'' has nothing to do with Bunyan but brings together a number of Conquest's favorite preoccupations—scenery, attractive young women, and great men from the past, especially poets. The narrator spends two nights with his girlfriend on the Isle of Wight, whose associations with Tennyson, Swinburne, and Garibaldi enrich his pleasure in the girl's company. The tone throughout is lighthearted and ironic:

And then why don't we drive across
To seek through scent of salt and rose

The chime-hid church where Swinburne was
—Baptised? buried? One of those.

Even more nostalgic is ''Then and There''—a youthful memory
of a prostitute whose beat was opposite St. Anne's Church, Soho:

Most tarts were awful. Still, there were
A nereid up on Soho Square,
An empress by the Caves de France . . .
But she who really took the glance
Moved in the semblance of a bride
Along the sunlit stretch outside
That restaurant opposite St Anne's
(As if that's where they'd called her banns).

The poet never so much as spoke to her, but despite, or because of, this her image haunts him still.

Conquest's virtuosity as a writer of light verse and of pastiche is demonstrated in nine limericks printed under the pseudonym Victor Gray in Kingsley Amis's *The New Oxford Book of Light Verse* and in the four poems attributed to Ted Pauker that end Conquest's *New and Collected Poems*. ''A Grouchy Good Night to the Academic Year,'' a marvelous pastiche of W.M. Praed, is a witty, high-spirited attack on progressive theories of higher education. ''Garland for a Propagandist (Air: The Vicar of Bray)'' is equally adroit and far more savage, because it conveys, like so many of Conquest's prose works, his cold detestation of the cruelty that pervaded Communist rule in the Soviet Union:

When Yezhov got it in the neck
(In highly literal fashion)
Beria came at Stalin's beck
To lay a lesser lash on;
I swore our labour camps were few,
And places folk grew fat in;
I guessed that Trotsky died of flu
And colic raged at Katyn.

Conquest's poetry is marked by intellectual clarity, technical skill, the assertion of traditional values, and a strongly romantic sensibility, all of which lend firmness and coherence to his most accomplished work. His poetry, which yields a keen, civilized pleasure, bears witness to the values and traditions in which he believes.

—John Press

CONSTANTINE, David (John)

Nationality: British. **Born:** Salford, Lancashire, 4 March 1944. **Education:** Manchester Grammar School, 1955–62; Wadham College, Oxford, 1962–66, B.A. (honors) in modern languages 1966, Ph.D. 1971. **Family:** Married Helen Best in 1966; one daughter and one son. **Career:** Lecturer, then senior lecturer in German, University of Durham, 1969–81. Since 1981 fellow in German, Queen's College, Oxford. Literary editor, *Oxford Magazine*. **Awards:** Alice Hunt Bartlett prize, 1984; Sir Steven Runciman prize, for nonfiction, 1984; Southern Arts Literature prize, 1987. **Address:** 1 Hill Top Road, Oxford OX4 1PB, England.

PUBLICATIONS

Poetry

A Brightness to Cast Shadows. Newcastle upon Tyne, Bloodaxe, 1980.
Watching for Dolphins. Newcastle upon Tyne, Bloodaxe, 1983.
Talitha Cumi, with Rodney Pybus. Newcastle upon Tyne, Bloodaxe, 1983.
Mappa Mundi. Hereford, Five Seasons Press, 1984.
Madder. Newcastle upon Tyne, Bloodaxe, 1987.
Selected Poems. Newcastle upon Tyne, Bloodaxe, 1991.
Caspar Hauser. Newcastle upon Tyne, Bloodaxe, 1994.
The Pelt of Wasps. Newcastle upon Tyne, Bloodaxe, 1998.

Novel

Davies. Newcastle upon Tyne, Bloodaxe, 1985.

Short Stories

Back at the Spike. Keele, Ryburn Publishing, 1994.

Other

The Significance of Locality in the Poetry of Friedrich Hölderlin. London, Modern Humanities Research Association, 1976.
Early Greek Travellers and the Hellenic Ideal. Cambridge, Cambridge University Press, 1984.
Hölderlin. Oxford and New York, Oxford University Press, 1988.
Friedrich Hölderlin. Munich, Beck, 1992.

Editor, *German Short Stories 2.* London, Penguin, 1976.
Translator, *Selected Poems of Hölderlin.* Newcastle upon Tyne, Bloodaxe, 1990.
Translator, with Helen Constantine, *Henri Michaux: Déplacements Dégagements.* Newcastle upon Tyne, Bloodaxe, 1990.
Translator, with Mark Treharne, *Pensées sous les Nuages,* by Philippe Jaccottet, Newcastle upon Tyne, Bloodaxe Books, 1994.
Translator, *Die Wahlverwandtschaften.* Oxford and New York, Oxford University Press, 1994.
Translator, *Selected Writings of Heinrich von Kleist.* London, Dent, 1997.

*

Critical Study: ''Arcadia Revisited: An Interview with David Constantine'' by Bruce Meyer, in *Waves* (Richmond Hill, Ontario), 14(4), spring 1986.

David Constantine comments:

I have written poems as a way of dealing with the world I live in. I like to be tangible and close, having perhaps a particular place or a particular person in mind, but the expression I arrive at may often be oblique (I like the myths, their characters and structures). I try to give my poems a definite shape; formlessness makes me uneasy. I think of writing as a way of combating the sort of ideology we have lived under in Britain for too many years. I think that poetry is intrinsically, in its rhythms, a gesture in favor of generous and passionate life.

*   *   *

After the publication of his first full-length volume in 1980 when he was thirty-six, David Constantine's reputation developed rapidly, to a point where by the end of the 1980s he was regarded as one of England's most important poets. This is despite the fact that he is the most un-English of poets in several respects. The principal influences on him are classical poetry and modern German and French writers, with the result that he is entirely free of the elegant, self-constraining ironies characteristic of contemporary English poetry. In Alvarez's terms, he is farther from "the gentility principle" than almost anyone writing seriously in English. This is not accidental; both major tendencies of his writing—toward the overtly sensual and toward social observation—are determinedly opposed to genteel restraints.

This program was already in evidence in *A Brightness to Cast Shadows,* the blurb of which called the poetry "direct and uncomplicated." The main impression here is of a writer who is *l'homme moyen sensuel,* often, indeed, more than *moyen.* But the sensuality has to be seen in the context of the overall meaning of the poetry. It is as much tactile as sexual (as in "Streams"), and it is only one insistent aspect of human fulfillment as a whole, no more or less significant than the intellectual, though it is more prominent at this stage. Several technical features of the poetry recall German poets such as Heine and Hölderlin (the latter translated by Constantine to great critical acclaim), taking a poem's opening words as the title, for example, or starting in medias res—both techniques evidenced in "But Most You Are Like." And it is not only nineteenth-century German poetry that is evoked. It is hardly an overstatement, for example, to call Constantine a courtly love poet in the way the word "mercy" is used with a subtle ambivalence between the amorous and the religious. Other characteristics of the earlier poems, sustained in his later work, are an objectivity achieved by a varying persona and a marked social concern in a series of poems about down-and-outs. The volume is dominated by a single poem (in a way that his later volumes have not been), an impressive sequence about the death of his grandfather in World War I, "In Memoriam 8571 Private J.W. Gleave." All of Constantine's strengths are in evidence here— precision, formality, and unsentimental compassion. It tends perhaps to overbalance the book; only the long Aphrodite poem, "Among Those Fortunate Dwellers," does not seem dwarfed by the sequence.

Admired as this first volume was, Constantine's second, *Watching for Dolphins,* was immediately recognized as a more impressive achievement, and it won the 1984 Alice Hunt Bartlett prize. The individual poems are both larger and more complex, and the volume cannot be called "direct and uncomplicated." There is a higher proportion of mythological poems, providing a weightier start to the volume, and it ends with a series of fine translations, including some brilliant versions of Sappho. Most impressively, the volume gains authority by its greater stylistic uniformity. The opening in medias res has great sureness and expertise and is often evocative, perhaps coincidentally, of Meredith's *Modern Love:* "But then her name, coming to her averted" ("Bluebells"). Significant of the increased

ambition is the way a haunting poem from the first book, "The Drowned," finds its place among a group of even stronger poems in a series here called "Islands." Both as a whole and in its individual poems, of which the title poem has achieved celebrity, *Watching for Dolphins* shows greater power and confidence. The use of Christian-derived and classical mythology in collaboration in the sensual personal poems creates a consistent humanist philosophy, expressed across a wide eclectic range.

Constantine's book *Madder* builds on these strengths to achieve an even more persuasive wholeness. The socially conscious element, which also is powerfully evident in Constantine's novel, *Davies,* is integrated into the humanist philosophy, with economic privation held to be deplorable because it denies its victims the capacity to achieve full humanity. Tactile sensuality or imaginative exultation in nature cannot be achieved where the violence and injustice coldly faced in poems like "Eldon Hole" and "Pictures" prevail. Constantine's established themes and subjects are found here: shells, mercy, streams, solitude, sexual closeness. "Sols," a long, imaginative elegy on the death of the poet's three-week-old cousin, born a year before him, is possibly his finest single poem. The virtue of the volume is that the technical skills and devices that earlier had excited admiration, sometimes at the expense of calling attention to themselves, have now settled into a light but telling artlessness, as at the ambiguous end of "Donn' Elvira" from the "Don Giovanni" sonnets:

> I am the widow of a man at whom
> I never smiled as though I were his whore.

It is a poetry in which the public and private sides of life are in equilibrium and that presents the world, seen in its fullness, as always worth living in.

This drive toward humane seriousness Constantine sees as a restoration of English poetry to its true traditions in an age that desperately needs it. He would claim, after all, to be an archetypally English poet of an ageless school.

—Bernard O'Donoghue

COOLIDGE, Clark

Nationality: American. **Born:** Providence, Rhode Island, 26 February 1939. **Education:** Brown University, Providence, 1956–58. **Family:** Married Susan Hopkins in 1967; one daughter. **Career:** Editor, *Joglars* magazine, Providence, 1964–66; producer of weekly radio program of new poetry, KPFA-FM, Berkeley, California, 1969–70. **Awards:** National Endowment for the Arts grant, 1966; New York Poets Foundation award, 1968. **Address:** c/o The Figures, 5 Castle Hill, Great Barrington, Massachusetts 01230, U.S.A.

PUBLICATIONS

Poetry

Flag Flutter and U.S. Electric. New York, Lines, 1966.
(Poems). New York, Lines, 1967.
Ing. New York, Angel Hair, 1969.

Space. New York, Harper, 1970.

The So. New York, Boke, 1971.

Moroccan Variations. Bolinas, California, Big Sky, 1971.

Suite V. New York, Boke, 1973.

The Maintains. San Francisco, This Press, 1974.

Polaroid. New York, Boke, 1975.

Quartz Hearts. San Francisco, This Press, 1978.

Own Face. Lenox, Massachusetts, Angel Hair, 1978.

Smithsonian Depositions, and Subject to a Film. New York, Vehicle, 1980.

American Ones. Bolinas, California, Tombouctou, 1981.

A Geology. Needham. Massachusetts, Potes and Poets Press, 1981.

Research. Berkeley, California, Tuumba Press, 1982.

Mine: The One That Enters the Stories. Berkeley, California, Figures, 1982.

Solution Passage: Poems, 1978–1981. Los Angeles, Sun and Moon Press, 1986.

The Crystal Text. Great Barrington, Massachusetts, Figures, 1986.

Mesh. Detroit, Michigan, In Camera, 1988.

At Egypt. Great Barrington, Massachusetts, The Figures, 1988.

Sound as Thought: Poems 1982–1984. Los Angeles, Sun and Moon Press, 1990.

The Book of During. Great Barrington, Massachusetts, 1991.

Odes of Roba. Great Barrington, Massachusetts, 1991.

Baffling Means. Stockbridge, Massachusetts, O-blek Editions, 1991.

On the Slates. New York, Flockophobic Press, 1992.

Lowell Connector: Lines & Shots from Kerouac's Town. West Stockbridge, Massachusetts, Hard Press, 1993.

Own Face. Los Angeles, Sun and Moon Press, 1993.

Registers: (People in All). Bolinas, California, Avenue B, 1994.

The ROVA Improvisations. Los Angeles, Sun and Moon Press, 1994.

Keys to the Caverns. Canary Islands, Zasterle Press, 1995.

Book of Stirs. Los Angeles, Seeing Eye Books, 1998.

Play

To Obtain the Value of the Cake Measure from Zero, with Tom Veitch. San Francisco, Paints Press, 1970.

Other

Now It's Jazz: Writings on Kerouac & the Sounds. Albuquerque, New Mexico, Living Batch Press, 1999.

Editor, *Heart of the Breath: Poems, 1979–1992,* by Jim Brodey. West Stockbridge, Massachusetts, Hard Press, 1996.

*

Bibliography: "Clark Coolidge: A Selected Bibliography" by Edward Foster, in *Talisman,* 3, fall 1989.

Critical Studies: Clark Coolidge issue of *Big Sky 3* (Bolinas, California), 1972; interview in *This 4* (San Francisco), spring 1973; *The End of Intelligent Writing* by Richard Kostelanetz, New York, Sheed and Ward, 1974; "A Symposium on Clark Coolidge," in *Stations 5* (Milwaukee, Wisconsin), winter 1978; "Notes on Coolidge, Objectives, Zukofsky, Romanticism, and &" by Robert Grenier, in *In the American Tree,* edited by Ron Silliman, Orono, Maine, National Poetry Foundation, 1986; "Clark Coolidge" by Lee Bartlett, in his *Talking Poetry: Conversations in the Workshop with Contemporary Poets,* Albuquerque, University of New Mexico Press, 1987; Clark Coolidge issue of *Talisman,* 3, fall 1989; "'All the Movement Still My Own': Clark Coolidge's Mesh" by Bruce Campbell, and "Word for Sign: Poetic Language in Coolidge's 'The Crystal Text'" by Krzysztof Ziarek, both in *Sagetrieb* (Orono, Maine), 10(1–2), spring-fall 1991; by William Corbett, in *Arts,* 65(10), summer 1991; "Clark Coolidge and a Jazz Aesthetic" by Aldon L. Nielsen, in *Pacific Coast Philology* (Malibu, California), 28(1), September 1993; "Teaching American Poetry in Context: Emerson and the Non-American Reader" by Edwrad Halsey Foster, in *American Literature for Non-American Readers: Cross-Cultural Perspectives on American Literature,* edited by Meta Grosman, Frankfurt, Peter Lang, 1995.

Clark Coolidge comments:

The context of my works is the tonality of language (seen, heard, spoken, thought) itself, a tonality that centers itself in the constant flowage from meaning to meaning and that sideslippage between meanings. All the books we shall perhaps never read again form a constant background of reference points. We are free now to delight in the surface of language, a surface as deep as the distance between, for instance, a noun (in the mind or in a dictionary) and its object somewhere in the universe.

*   *   *

None of the experimental poets in America has been as various, intelligent, and prolific as Clark Coolidge, who also edited one of the few genuinely avant-garde literary magazines of the 1960s, *Joglars.* His opening book, *Flag Flutter and U.S. Electric,* collected his early forays into post-Ashberyan acoherence, in which the poet tries to realize a semblance of literary coherence without resorting to such traditional organizing devices as meter, metaphor, exposition, symbolism, consistent allusion, declarative statements, or autobiographical reference. (The key Ashbery work in this vein is his 1960 poem "Europe," collected in *The Tennis Court Oath.*) In a theoretical statement contributed to Paul Carroll's anthology *The Young American Poets* (1968), Coolidge wrote that "words have a universe of qualities other than those of descriptive relation: Hardness, Density, Sound-Shape, Vector-Force, & Degrees of Transparency/Opacity," and his earlier poems reveal rather exceptional linguistic sensitivities, especially regarding the selection and placement of words. The intelligence informing his creative processes is radically poetic, precisely because it is not prosaic.

In subsequent work Coolidge pursued not just varieties of acoherence but also reductionism, joining Kenneth Gangemi and Robert Lax among America's superior minimal poets. In the back sections of Coolidge's retrospective *Space* are several especially severe examples, such as the untitled poem beginning "by a I," which contains individually isolated words, none more than two letters long, that are scattered across the space of a single page (Coolidge's primary compositional unit). These words are nonetheless related to one another, not only in terms of diction and corresponding length (both visually and verbally) but also by spatial proximity, and if the individual words were arranged in another way, both the poem and the reading experience would be different. It should also be noted that Coolidge's work extends radically the

Olsonian traditions both of "composition by field," as opposed to lines, and of emphasizing syllable rather than rhyme and meter.

Like all genuinely experimental artists, Coolidge accepted the challenge of an inevitable next step, extending his delicate reductionist technique into two of the most remarkable long poems of the 1960s: "AD," originally published in *Ing* and then reprinted in *Space,* and *Suite V,* which appeared as a booklet in 1973, although it was initially composed several years before. "AD" begins in the familiar Coolidgean way, with stanzas of superficially unrelated lines, but the poetic material is progressively reduced over twenty pages (thereby reca-pitulating Coolidge's own poetic development in a kind of formalist autobiography) until the poem's final pages contain only vertically ordered fragments of words. *Suite V* is yet more outrageously spartan, containing nothing more than pairs of three-letter words in their plural forms, with one four-letter word at the top and the other at the bottom of otherwise blank pages.

Whereas Coolidge once seemed the avatar of what came to be called language poetry, his presence has by now receded. His work does not receive as much critical attention as does that of Charles Bernstein or even Ron Silliman, to cite two younger writers who learned from Coolidge's innovations without significantly surpassing them. Nonetheless, Coolidge has continued to publish prolifically, all of his later books appearing from smaller presses (one measure of his integrity). In my judgment none of the later work is quite as avant-garde or as consequential as his opening moves. One of the thicker collections, *Solution Passage: Poems, 1978–1981* (1986), contains what seem to be riffs upon Noam Chomsky's "colorless green ideas sleep furiously," which is to say, phrases that are syntactically acceptable without making semantic sense.

—Richard Kostelanetz

COOPER, Jane (Marvel)

Nationality: American. **Born:** Atlantic City, New Jersey, 9 October 1924. **Education:** Vassar College, Poughkeepsie, New York, 1942–44; University of Wisconsin, Madison, B.A. 1946 (Phi Beta Kappa); University of Iowa, Iowa City, M.A. 1954. **Career:** Professor of literature and writing, poet-in-residence, Department of English, Sarah Lawrence College, Bronxville, New York, 1950–87. **Awards:** Guggenheim fellowship, 1960; Lamont Poetry Selection award, 1968; Ingram Merrill Foundation grant, 1971; Creative Artists Public Service grant 1974; Shelley memorial award, 1978; National Endowment for the Arts grant, 1982; Maurice English award, 1985; Bunting fellowship (Radcliffe College), 1988–89; American Academy of Arts and Letters award in literature, 1995; New York State poet, 1995–97. **Address:** 545 West 111th Street, Apt. 8K, New York, New York 10025, U.S.A.

PUBLICATIONS

Poetry

The Weather of Six Mornings. New York, Macmillan, 1969.
Maps and Windows. New York, Macmillan, 1974.
Threads: Rosa Luxemburg from Prison. New York, Flamingo Press, 1979.

Scaffolding: New and Selected Poems. London, Anvil Press Poetry, 1984; as *Scaffolding: Selected Poems.* Gardiner, Maine, Tilbury House, 1993.
Green Notebook, Winter Road. Gardiner, Maine, Tilbury House, 1994.
The Flashboat: Poems Collected and Reclaimed. New York, Norton, 1999.

Other

Editor, with others, *Extended Outlooks: The "Iowa Review" Collection of Contemporary Women Writers.* New York, Macmillan, 1982.
Editor, with others, *The Sanity of Earth and Grass: Complete Poems of Robert Winner.* Gardiner, Maine, Tilbury House, 1994.

*

Manuscript Collection: Berg Collection, New York Public Library.

Critical Studies: "An Ecstasy of Space" by Rachel Hadas, in *Parnassus: Poetry in Review* (New York), 15 (1), 1989; "The Practiced Hand" by Jan Clausen, in *Women's Review of Books,* 7, 1995; interview with Eric Gudas, in *The Iowa Review* (Iowa City), 25(1), winter 1995.

Jane Cooper comments:

(1995) *Green Notebook, Winter Road* deals with friendship, aging, the lives of girls and women, the humor and "complex shame" of a white Southern heritage, illness, and the enduring mysteries of art. It is a book that is meant to be very fluid, as the private and public worlds intersect, the present is opened out by glimpses of the past (and not just the personal past but the inherited or hearsay past as well), and song exists side by side with speech (long lines, prose lines). The book has an epigraph from Emily Dickinson's *Letters,* "My friends are my 'estate,'" but I suppose the real quest is to find out who the self is—to delve deep into the wisdom of the body, intuition, and dreams and at the same time to record accurately, with loving if sometimes skeptical attention, details of social life, history, family, race, class. Someone complained that there is too much death in the poems. Not at all. I am 70, and I celebrate "ongoingness."

(2000) Now, in the year 2000, what is there to add? *The Flashboat: Poems Collected and Reclaimed* continues the same adventure, asking the same questions in a somewhat larger context. Or, as one poem has it, "I'm trying to write a poem that will alert me to my real life."

*   *   *

Jane Cooper's *Maps and Windows* of 1974 pulled a group of twelve poems from the decades-old oblivion of an unpublished manuscript, just as in 1984 *Scaffolding* reached back to acknowledge yet other early work, reclaiming a group of five poems written between 1954 and 1969. The rescued poems became part of Cooper's drive to make her own chronologies match a constantly changing but governing preoccupation with historical patterning. Never quite syn-chronous, the author's life and her awareness of its shaping forces moved in charged interchange, and within each successive book an older self of the writer confronted the current self, soberly and self-consciously rearranging its canon to reflect different urgencies, newly promising directions. In 1994, against time's mounting losses, *Green Notebook, Winter Road* continues and triumphantly intensifies this prodding and testing of Cooper's relations to persons, places, and traditions as the poet reorders the psyche's props for survival, altering the earlier confrontation of self against self to reflect instead a greater concern for the fit of the writing self within a tradition of women artists. Packed densely with reference to works and lives, Cooper's short, clustered jewel-like lyrics dedicated to Georgia O'Keeffe (''The Winter Road'') and Willa Cather (''Vocation: A Life'') speak about the inevitable sexual and psychosocial crises and conflicts that existed so painfully for these women who were primary makers.

The earlier *Scaffolding* put Cooper's need to contextualize in place. Within a sequence entitled ''Dispossessions'' Cooper quotes from Rilke's *Malte Laurids Brigge:* ''it is not enough / to have memories, they / must turn to blood inside you.'' While people die, houses remain husks, and things speak mutely only as things, poetry remains the constant. Yet the troubled search for vocation, for its lifeblood, becomes the fluid scaffolding of Cooper's poetry.

Scaffolding includes an essay, rather formidably entitled ''Nothing Has Been Used in the Manufacture of This Poetry That Could Have Been Used in the Manufacture of Bread,'' in which the Cooper of 1974 traces the growth of her poetry away from its initial focus on war and heroic themes to what she calls ''the poetry of development.'' The impulse of both the essay and the collecting process is recursive and meditative. The whole of *Scaffolding* insists stubbornly but without vanity on tracing the particular figure of a career shaped by the facts of gender, culture, and history, refusing to fracture the tender sinuosities of the life it records.

As Cooper draws the connecting links in both prose and poetry, her early work and its intentions bear witness for a generation of American women growing up directly in the aftermath of World War II. It was a generation of women writers for whom, she comments, ''The men's lives seemed more central than ours, almost more truthful. They had been shot down, or squirmed up the beaches. We had waited for their letters.'' Sojourning as a student of twenty-two in Oxford in the summer of 1947, Cooper marked the years as the opening of a struggle to sustain herself as a poet, a struggle sharply linked to the cultural circumscription of women's lives: '''Didn't anyone ever tell you it was all right to write?' asked the psychiatrist who came along much later. 'Yes, but not to be a writer,''' she says. In ''The Knowledge That Comes through Experience'' she asks sardonically,

When shall I rest, when shall I find myself
The way I'll be, iced in a shop window?

Failing to find herself reflected as the edible woman desired by her time, she concludes,

Meanwhile I use myself. I am useful
Rather foolishly, like a fish who yearns
Dimly toward daylight. There is much to learn
And curiosity empties our rewards.
It seems to me I may be capable,
Once I'm a skeleton, of love and wars.

The poet remained a woman who, strip as she might, could never divest herself of a problematic feminine creativity bound to collide with cultural convention. ''Obligations'' blends sensuousness and watchful sobriety as it tracks ''the dark home of our polarities / And our defense, which we cannot evade.''

While a number of early poems dealing with gender relations have their own quietly wicked bite, others have the glassy good manners of the 1950s. All of the poems are solid affairs, with skillful construction and impeccable diction, and if they are occasionally too elliptical and understated, the personal and domestic themes are always perceptively treated.

After the more tentative 1950s an appealing rawness and fresh innocence dominate Cooper's middle and later work. In both prose and poetry there is a plain, stripped, almost severe speech whose truthfulness is always enhanced by delicacy of feeling. The poems press meaning through pauses and silences, through the white spaces of short lines and brief stanzas. Cooper's poems continue to represent the conflicts between our needs as separate people and the claims that we necessarily allow others to make on us as friends, lovers, family members, and citizens. There are scalding poems about childlessness. Several of the best, like ''My Young Mother'' and ''Hunger Moon,'' practice a curious detachment in which a disembodied poet-speaker moves back before her own birth or observes a stage set with past selves. This characteristic gesture, used with an eerie flash, concludes the 1985 poem ''Estrangement'': ''You watch your own back growing smaller up the beach.''

Scaffolding closes with ''Threads: Rosa Luxemburg from Prison,'' a dramatic monologue written as a sequence. ''Threads'' stretches the poet's early absorption with war, recovering the heroic for a perspective now both emphatically female and pacifist. It is Luxemburg's voice speaking persuasively from beginning to end, but it is Cooper's achievement that from within poems both restrained and passionate continuities of style and vision weld the sequence to the rest of her own writing life.

By 1994 Cooper's meditations on the trajectory of female lives touched on colleagues and writing friends, most notably Muriel Rukeyser. The spine of *Green Notebook, Winter Road* is elegy. The same empathy, insight, and imaginative historical intelligence that were joined with lyricism in ''Threads'' now freely and authoritatively move back and forth between prose and poetry, and a new comic deftness leavens the pieces about Cooper's Jacksonville family. The poet's probes into the ongoing trauma of her troubled health also expand the emotional compass of her work, and both the internal and external perspectives increasingly enlarge and brighten to produce a poetry more compelling and interesting with each subsequent book.

—Lorrie Goldensohn

COPE, Wendy

Nationality: British. **Born:** Erith, Kent, 21 July 1945. **Education:** Farringtons School, Chislehurst, Kent, 1957–62; St. Hilda's College Oxford, B.A. in history 1966, M.A. 1970; Westminster College of Education, Oxford, Dip Ed. 1967. **Career:** Teacher, Portway Junior School, London, 1967–69, Keyworth Junior School, London 1969–73, Cobourg Primary School, 1973–81, and Brindishe Primary School, 1984–86; arts editor, *ILEA Contact* teachers' newspaper, 1982–84.

Since 1986 freelance writer. **Awards:** Cholmondeley award, 1987; Michael Braude award for light verse, American Academy of Arts and Letters, 1995. Fellow, Royal Society of Literature, 1993. D.Litt.: University of Southampton, 1999. **Agent:** Pat Kavanagh, Peters Fraser and Dunlop, Drury House, 34–43 Russell Street, London WC2B 5HA, England.

PUBLICATIONS

Poetry

Across the City. Berkhamsted, Hertfordshire, Priapus, 1980.
Hope and the 42. Leamington Spa, Warwickshire, Other Branch Readings, 1984.
Making Cocoa for Kingsley Amis. London and Boston, Faber, 1986.
Poem from a Colour Chart of Housepaints. Berkhamsted, Hertfordshire, Priapus, 1986.
Men and Their Boring Arguments. Winchester, Hampshire, Wykeham Press, 1988.
Does She Like Word-Games? London, Anvil Press Poetry, 1988.
Twiddling Your Thumbs (for children). London, Faber, 1988.
The River Girl. London and Boston, Faber, 1990.
Serious Concerns. London and Boston, Faber, 1992.

Other

Editor, *Is That the New Moon?: Poems by Women Poets.* London Collins, 1989.
Editor, *The Orchard Book of Funny Poems.* London, Orchard, 1993.
Editor, *The Funny Side: 101 Humorous Poems.* London, Faber, 1998.
Editor, *The Faber Book of Bedtime Stories.* London, Faber, 2000.

*

Critical Studies: ''Dana Gioia on Wendy Cope'' by Dana Gioia, in *Poetry Review,* 82(4), winter 1993; ''Wendy Cope's Use of Parody in Making Cocoa for Kingsley Amis'' by Marta Perez Novales, in *Miscelanea* (Saragossa, Spain), 15, 1994; ''Poetic Assessment'' by Gerry Cambridge, in *Acumen* (Brixham, England), 26, September 1996.

Wendy Cope comments:

(1990) I began writing poems in the early 1970s when I was twenty-seven. My earliest poems were short, lyrical, and intense. Many of them were in free verse; some were haiku. None of them rhymed. There were no jokes in them. After about six years I began to allow my sense of humor into my poems. I invented an unpleasant South London poet called Jason Strugnell who wrote Shakespearean sonnets about the trials and tribulations of a middle-aged man of letters. He was also influenced by some of his contemporaries, and a series of parodies of living poets was published under his name.

At around the same time I became interested in using rhyme and traditional rhyming forms. At first the subject matter of these poems was mostly literary. Then I began to use rhyming forms to write more personal poems, many of them about love affairs.

(1995) My second full-length collection, *Serious Concerns,* is a bleaker book than my first, *Making Cocoa for Kingsley Amis.*

Although it includes quite a few humorous poems, those who perceive it as a volume of comic verse are overlooking a fair proportion of the contents.

*   *   *

Wendy Cope's *Making Cocoa for Kingsley Amis* was greeted with acclaim, and, skillfully marketed, it became a best-seller. ''The most accomplished parodist since Beerbohm,'' wrote an enthusiastic blurb writer. This is not without truth, for Cope is a brilliant parodist. There are, for example, the splendidly Shakespearean sonnets:

Not only marble, but the plastic toys
From cornflake packets will outlive this rhyme . . .

With ''Budgie His Voice'' (Hughes), the ''Wasteland Limericks'' (Eliot), and ''The Strugnell Rubaiyat,'' *Making Cocoa for Kingsley Amis* is replete with parodies.

I would maintain, however, that Cope is more than a parodist. She is an original, needle-sharp satirist. Jason Strugnell, the ''author'' of so many of the parodies and an honorable member of a long line of fictional poets, together with Enoch Soames and Sebastian Arrurruz, is a brilliant invention. He epitomizes a particular type of suburbanite with certain attitudes toward poetry and art. He is a cousin of Ann Whickham's ''Croydon Man'' and is Matthew Arnold's philistine writ large. He is delightfully funny as he reveals a whole vista of the British spiritual malaise. We can sense which way he would vote, the newspaper he reads, his attitude to life in general, all linked to the enterprise culture as expressed in

I need a woman, honest and sincere,
Who'll come across on half a pint of beer.

Cope's Strugnell is a razorlike dissection of certain British attitudes, and through him she sends up beautifully the convention of British anti-intellectualism. It is good to see such subversive stuff attracting such acclaim.

After *Making Cocoa for Kingsley Amis* Cope published two booklets of verse, besides one for children, *Twiddling Your Thumbs.* One booklet, *Does She Like Word-Games?,* was nicely produced by Anvil Press; the other, *Men and Their Boring Arguments,* was rather badly designed and printed by Wykenham Press. (Cope's work deserves better.) Both contain acidly sharp and neatly crafted verses. Those concerned with the attitudes of men are specially keen edged and perceptive—

Bloody men are like bloody buses—
You wait for about a year
And as one approaches your stop
Two or three others appear

or

If you want to be one who's irresistibly appealing,
Don't change the subject when she tells you how she's feeling.

Good as they are of their kind, however, there is a worrying aspect. Is Cope in danger of being typecast by publishers' marketing departments as a witty squib writer, as a sort of comedienne, an intellectual Pam Ayres? I hope not, for long before the publication of *Making Cocoa for Kingsley Amis* Cope published a small Priapus Press booklet, *Across the City,* in which she explored her own feelings and concerns. They were the tentative poems of a new writer feeling her way, but they expressed a truth of feeling that I hope does not get lost or neglected. For instance, consider these lines from "From Your High Window":

> Alone in your room
> I have abandoned
> this day's plans, attempts
> to regulate the
> tide, it carries me.
>
> And you are warm stones
> on a shore, my palms
> remember every
> curve of bone, I taste
> traces of sea spray.

Not that there are no hints of such feelings in *Making Cocoa for Kingsley Amis.* "Tich Miller," for example, in spite of its jaunty-jokey style and seemingly offhand ending, is a poem deep with concern and feeling. Further, the title of Cope's second major collection, *Serious Concerns,* suggests a shift in emphasis. This book contains a fair proportion of squibs and jokes even while it rebuts the criticism that she "writes to amuse":

> Write to amuse? What an appalling suggestion!
> I write to make people anxious and miserable and to
>   worsen their indigestion.

In the fourth section of *Serious Concerns* there are several deeply felt, if sometimes not quite achieved, love poems and poems of even more profound feelings, as seen in "Leaving":

> Next summer? The summer after?
> With luck we've a few more years
> Of sunshine and drinking and laughter
> And airports and goodbyes and tears.

Since then Craig Raine's new literary journal, *Arete,* has published a group of Cope's poems in which her "serious concerns" are extended. In these poems there are some finely expressed close observations—

> At first I'm startled by the sound of bicycles
> Above my head. And then I see then, two swans
> Flying in to their runway behind the reeds.

—that provoke reflections about the Christmas just passed and the emotions that were stirred:

> If only this could be Christmas now—
> These shining meadows,
> The hum of huge wings in the sky.

Cope rightly reminds me that her beautifully constructed and incisively witty poems, for which she is probably best known, are not without their serious concerns. Nevertheless, it is good to see this other facet of her poetry develop.

—John Cotton

CORMAN, Cid

Nationality: American. **Born:** Sidney Corman, Boston, Massachusetts, 29 June 1924. **Education:** Boston Latin School; Tufts College, Medford, Massachusetts, A.B. 1945 (Phi Beta Kappa); University of Michigan, Ann Arbor (Hopwood award, 1947), 1946–47; University of North Carolina, Chapel Hill, 1947; Sorbonne, Paris (Fulbright Fellow), 1954–55. **Family:** Married Shizumi Konishi in 1965. **Career:** Poetry broadcaster, WMEX, Boston, 1949–51; teacher in Italy, 1956–67, and at Kyoto Joshidai, Japan, 1958–60, Ryukoku University, Kyoto, 1962–64, and Doshisha University, Kyoto, 1965–66. Since 1951 editor, *Origin* magazine and Origin Press, Ashland, Massachusetts, and Kyoto. Owner, Cid Corman's Dessert Shop, Kyoto, 1974–79, and Sister City Tea Shop, Boston, since 1981. **Awards:** Chapelbrook Foundation grant, 1967–69; Co-ordinating Council of Little Magazines grant, 1970, 1978; National Endowment for the Arts grant, 1974; Lenore Marshall memorial prize, 1975. **Address:** c/o Coffee House Press, Box 10870, Minneapolis, Minnesota 55440, U.S.A.

PUBLICATIONS

Poetry

subluna (juvenilia). Privately printed, 1945.
Night Claims (song), music by Hugo Calderón. New York, Shirmer, 1950.
A Thanksgiving Eclogue from Theocritus. New York, Sparrow Press, 1954.
Ferrini and Others, with others. Berlin, Gerhardt, 1955.
The Precisions. New York, Sparrow Press, 1955.
The Responses. Ashland, Massachusetts, Origin Press, 1956.
Stances and Distances. Ashland, Massachusetts, Origin Press, 1957.
The Marches. Ashland, Massachusetts, Origin Press, 1957.
Clocked Stone. Ashland, Massachusetts, Origin Press, 1959.
A Table in Provence. Kyoto, Origin Press, 1959.
The Descent from Daimonji. Kyoto, Origin Press, 1959.
For Sure. Kyoto, Origin Press, 1960.
Sun Rock Man. Kyoto, Origin Press, 1962; New York, New Directions, 1970.
For Instance. Kyoto, Origin Press, 1962.
In No Time. Privately printed, 1963.
In Good Time. Kyoto, Origin Press, 1964.
For Good. Kyoto, Origin Press, 1964.
All in All. Kyoto, Origin Press, 1964.
Nonce. New Rochelle, New York, Elizabeth Press, 1965.
For You. Kyoto, Origin Press, 1966.
Stead. New Rochelle, New York, Elizabeth Press, 1966.
For Granted. New Rochelle, New York, Elizabeth Press, 1967.
Words for Each Other. London, Rapp and Carroll, 1967.

& *without End.* New Rochelle, New York, Elizabeth Press, and London Villiers, 1968.

No Less. New Rochelle, New York, Elizabeth Press, 1968.

Hearth. Kyoto, Origin Press, 1968.

The World as University. Kyoto, Origin Press, 1968.

No More. New Rochelle, New York, Elizabeth Press, 1969.

Plight. New Rochelle, New York, Elizabeth Press, 1969.

Nigh. New Rochelle, New York, Elizabeth Press, 1970.

Livingdying. New York, New Directions, 1970.

Of the Breath of. Berkeley, California, Maya, 1970.

For Keeps. Kyoto, Origin Press, 1970.

For Now. Kyoto, Origin Press, 1971.

Cicadas. Amherst, New York, Slow Loris Press, 1971.

Out and Out. New Rochelle, New York, Elizabeth Press, 1972.

Be Quest. New Rochelle, New York, Elizabeth Press, 1972.

A Language without Words. Saffron Walden, Essex, Byways, 1973.

So Far. New Rochelle, New York, Elizabeth Press, 1973.

Poems: Thanks to Zuckerkandl. Rushden, Northamptonshire, Sceptre Press, 1973.

Breathings. Tokyo, Mushinsha, 1973.

Three Poems. Rushden, Northamptonshire, Sceptre Press, 1973.

Yet. New Rochelle, New York, Elizabeth Press, 1974.

RSVP. Knotting, Bedfordshire, Sceptre Press, 1974.

O/I. New Rochelle, New York, Elizabeth Press, 1974.

For Dear Life. Los Angeles, Black Sparrow Press, 1975.

Once and for All: Poems for William Bronk. New Rochelle, New York, Elizabeth Press, 1975.

Not Now. N.p., Moschatel Press, 1975.

Unless. Kyoto, Origin Press, 1975.

'S. New Rochelle, New York, Elizabeth Press, 1976.

For the Asking. Santa Barbara, California, Black Sparrow Press, 1976.

Any How. Nagoya, Kisetsusha, 1976.

Leda and the Swan. Paris, Hocguard, 1976.

Be Longings. Boston, Origin Press, 1977.

Antics. Boston, Origin Press, 1977.

Gratis. Boston, Origin Press, 1977.

Auspices. Milwaukee, Pentagram Press, 1978.

Of Course. Boston, Origin Press, 1978.

So. Boston, Origin Press, 1978.

At Their Word. Santa Barbara, California, Black Sparrow Press, 1978.

In the Event. Bangor, Maine, Theodore Press, 1979.

Tabernacle. Boston, Origin Press, 1980.

Manna. West Branch, Iowa, Toothpaste Press, 1981.

At Least (2). Iowa City, Corycian Press, 1981.

Identities. Vineyard, Massachusetts, Salt-Works Press, 1981.

Tu. West Branch, Iowa, Toothpaste Press, 1983.

Aegis: Selected Poems 1970–1980. Barrytown, New York, Station Hill Press, 1984.

In Particular: Poems, New and Selected. Dunvegan, Ontario, Cormorant, 1986.

Root Song. Elmwood, Connecticut, Potes and Poets Press, 1986.

And the Word. Minneapolis, Coffee House Press, 1987.

Tel 2 let. Charleston, Illinois, Tel-let, 1988.

Yea. Los Angeles, Lapis, 1989.

Of. Venice, California, Lapis, 1990.

All Yours. New York, The Cooper Union for the Advancement of Science & Art, 1991.

Nothing to Nothing. Charleston, Illinois, Tel-let, 1991.

The Revolt of the Poet. Jamaica, Vermont, Bull Thistle Pres, 1995.

How Now: Poems. Boulder, Colorad, Cityful Press, 1995.

Marginalia. Plymouth, Shearsman Books, 1996.

No Shit. Abiko, Chiba, Japan, Abiko Literary Press, 1996.

Pith Water. Charleston, Illinois, Tel-let, 1997.

God or Buddha. Green River, Vermont, Longhouse, 1998.

You Don't Say. Pittsburgh, Pennsylvania, Lilliput Review, 1998.

Going Going. Berkeley, California, Tangram, 1999.

Tributary: Poems. New York, Edgewise Press, 1999.

Nothing Doing. New York, New Directions, 1999.

Nothing at All. Brooklyn, New York, MEB/PNY, 1999.

Other

At: Bottom. Bloomington, Indiana, Caterpillar, 1966.

William Bronk: An Essay. Carrboro, North Carolina, Truck Press, 1976.

The Act of Poetry and Two Other Essays. Santa Barbara, California, Black Sparrow Press, 1976.

Word for Word: [At Their Word:] Essays on the Art of Language. Santa Barbara, California, Black Sparrow Press, 2 vols., 1977–78.

Projectile, Percussive, Prospective: The Making of a Voice. Portree, Isle of Skye, Aquila, 1982.

Where Were We Now: Essays & Postscriptum. Seattle, Broken Moon Press, 1991.

The Practice of Poetry: Reconsiderations of Louis Zukofsky's A Test of Poetry. Vermont, Longhouse-Origin, 1998.

Editor, *The Gist of "Origin": An Anthology.* New York, Grossman, 1975.

Editor, *The Granite Pail: The Selected Poems of Lorine Niedecker.* Berkeley, California, North Point Press, 1985.

Translator, *Cool Melon,* by Bashō. Ashland, Massachusetts, Origin Press, 1959.

Translator, *Cool Gong.* Ashland, Massachusetts, Origin Press, 1959.

Translator, with Susumu Kamaike, *Selected Frogs,* by Shimpei Kusano. Kyoto, Origin Press, 1963.

Translator, *Back Roads to Far Towns,* by Bashō. Tokyo, Mushinsha, 1967; New York, Grossman, 1971.

Translator, with Susumu Kamaike, *Frogs and Others: Poems,* by Shimpei Kusano. Tokyo, Mushinsha, 1968; New York, Grossman, 1969.

Translator, *Things,* by Francis Ponge. Tokyo, Mushinsha, and New York, Grossman, 1971.

Translator, *Leaves of Hypnos,* by René Char. Tokyo, Mushinsha, and New York, Grossman, 1973.

Translator, *Breathings,* by Philippe Jaccottet. New York, Grossman, 1974.

Translator, with William Alexander and Richard Burns, *Roberto Sanesi: A Selection.* Pensnett, Staffordshire, Grosseteste, 1975.

Translator, *Peerless Mirror: Twenty Tanka from the Manyoshu.* Cambridge, Massachusetts, Firefly Press, 1981.

Translator, with Susumu Kamaike, *Asking Myself/Answering Myself,* by Shimpei Kusano. New York, New Directions, 1984.

Translator, *One Man's Moon* (version of haiku). Frankfort, Kentucky, Gnomon Press, 1984.

Translator, with Takashi Kojiba and Will Petersen, *Hell Screen Cogwheels, and a Fool's Life,* by Ryunosuke Akutagawa. Hygiene, California, Eridanos Press, 1988.

Translator, *Born of a Dream: 50 Haiku*. Frankfort, Kentucky, Gnomon Press, 1988.

Translator, *Little Enough: 49 Haiku*. Frankfort, Kentucky, Gnomon Press, 1991.

Translator, *Walking into the Wind*, by Santoka. N.p., Cadmus Editions, 1994.

Translator, with others, *Back Roads to Far Towns: Basho's Oku no hosomichi*. Hopewell, New Jersey, Ecco Press, 1996.

*

Manuscript Collections: University of Texas, Austin; Kent State University, Ohio; Indiana University, Bloomington; New York University; State University of New York, Buffalo.

Critical Studies: ''Cid Corman Issue'' of *Madrona* (Seattle), December 1975; ''A Selection from the Correspondence: Charles Olson and Cid Corman, 1950'' edited by George Evans, in *Origin* (Orono, Maine), 1, fall 1983; *'Between Your House and Mine': The Letters of Loraine Niedecker to Cid Corman, 1960–1970* (dissertation) by Lisa Pater Faranda, n.p., 1984; ''Getting the Secret Out of Cid Corman'' by Gregory Dunne, in *Kyoto Journal*, 31, 1996.

Cid Corman comments:

My work has developed from the pioneer poetry of Pound-Williams-Stevens, but much also from contact with French poetry. No forms, but a strict sense of the sounded meaning of words, pauses, verses, etc., and the felt thought that poetry is. Brevity, immediacy, clarity. A poetry that makes the role of the critic pointless, needless. The ideal, always, to join that most human society of poets whose work is published under the title of ANON.

Poetry calls for anonymity. It appeals, in short, to the each in all and the all in each. Its particularity must become yours. Autobiography is implicit in anyone's work and may be taken for granted, but what has been realized and so set out as to be shared loses itself in the self that is found extended without end in song.

As the author has elsewhere put it: ''If I have nothing to offer you in the face of death—in its stead—the ache behind every ache, the instant man knows, I have no claim as poet. My song must sing into you a little moment, stay in you what presence can muster—of sense more than meaning, of love more than sense, of giving the life given one with the same fullness that brought each forth, each to each from each, nothing left but the life that is going on.''

*   *   *

Cid Corman's poems are tight, reticent, and resonant. He demonstrates how evocative the minimal registration of specifics can be, and he has combined with this his own lifelong concern for the sound of poetry, syllable by syllable. (Louis Zukofsky is for him, as for Robert Creeley, a measure of such possibilities.) The result, both in the longer more discursive poems of *Sun Rock Man* or *& without End* and in the short haiku-like poems of such books as *Nonce*, *Stead*, and *Nigh*, is a poetry of considerable grace and strength.

Corman's early poems seem to cry out for the compression of his later style. ''First Farm North'' from *The Precisions* begins with the line ''I stood above at the bathroom window'' and goes on, in leisurely anecdotal style, to evoke a mood by careful accumulation of detail, ending with

The mirror was thawed into the scene
and the brightness of the morning
pressed a cool handful of water
into my eyes and my pulse raced song.

While retaining a sense of measure in these lines, Corman is already free of iambic regularity, but the poem, though charming, is diffuse. Other poems feature a 1950s elegance (''Leaves discuss the wind'') consorting somewhat uneasily with touches of what has come to seem Corman's characteristic sensibility (''It takes all my time, and my father's, / to let life go'').

Between such early work and the development seen in the 1962 *Sun Rock Man*, there intervenes a Japanese influence and the translations from Bashō and others published in *Cool Gong* and *Cool Melon*. A gain in expressive means—shorter lines, barer statement, more fluid syntax—is seen throughout *Sun Rock Man*. In ''The Gift'' Corman writes,

First night in a
strange town to
be going home

passing a
strange girl saying
goodnight to me

how night is
when she says so
suddenly good

The line breaks are like Creeley's; the syntax, with its dangling participles and the canny deployment that gets the clinching phrase at the end, owes something to William Carlos Williams (''As the cat / climbed over . . .'' in ''Poem''); and the syllabic grid (4=3-4, 3=4-4, 3=4-4) suggests the style of Marianne Moore. But in its feelings the poem is wholly Corman's. And the entire book, its sum exceeding its parts as a tribute to a place and people—the Italian town where the poet spent a year teaching English—marks the emergence of Corman's mature voice.

In *For Instance*, also published in 1962, the reader finds more specific oriental influences in content, tone, and technique. ''Number 7'' reads,

gong gone
odor of cherry tolling
eventide

The juxtaposed verbless phrases evoke a mood of contemplative harmony with natural surroundings, a mood often associated with Japanese poetry. Though a haiku translation, Corman's poem is nevertheless Western in its reliance on metaphor, assonance, and connotative language.

Corman's later work has continued along the lines of *Sun Rock Man* and *For Instance*. It cannot be denied that his emotional range is narrow and that his tone can verge on too easy a plangency, too self-indulgent an acquiescence in the drift toward dissolution. For instance, ''The Mystery,'' a poem about swallows from the 1964 collection *In Good Time*, ends with ''How each / pursued / / each, / pursued / by a green sky / as the sun settles, / / desperate / to let themselves / go, O / against night.'' It has been suggested that the melodramatic ''desperate'' and the moaning ''o'' sounds produce too

205

facile a pathos and distract attention from the things seen to the emoting observer. Contrast the restraint of a successful poem on roughly the same thing:

> Someone will
> sweep the fallen
> petals away
>
> away. I know,
> I know. Weight of
> red shadows.

Here the talking voice is never swamped, and the tone plays against and makes more convincing the feelings that weigh on the speaker. Even more fully impersonal is the following, taken from *Nonce:*

> The leaf that moved with the wind
>   moves
> with the stream.

The energy is released by so simple a means as a change in tense. And the emotional effect is complex—transience is recognized, as is cyclical renewal—and all is made to inhere in the thing seen. When he writes like this, and he does it often enough for every book to be rewarding, Corman's is a voice that earns our careful attention.

There is no mistake that Corman's verse continues to be associated with Japanese poetry. In his 1987 collection *And the Word* he retains metrical integrity and, in his best moments, operates without ulterior motives:

> *Like* a child again
> holding a round stone
> in my hand until
>
> the warmth of my hand
> warms the stone and I
> feel comprehended.

Simplicity, stasis and acute metaphorical renderings are the guiding principles of Corman's extraordinary writing.

—Seamus Cooney and Martha Sutro

CORN, Alfred

Nationality: American. **Born:** Bainbridge, Georgia, 14 August 1943. **Education:** Emory University, Atlanta, 1961–65, B.A. in French 1965; Columbia University, New York (Woodrow Wilson Fellow; Faculty Fellow), 1965–67, M.A. 1967; Fulbright Fellow, Paris, 1967–68. **Family:** Married Ann Jones in 1967 (divorced 1971). **Career:** Preceptor, Columbia University, 1968–70; associate editor, *University Review,* New York, 1970; staff writer, DaCapo Press, New York, 1971–72; assistant professor, 1978, and visiting lecturer, 1980–81, Connecticut College, New London; visiting lecturer, Yale University, New Haven, Connecticut, 1977, 1978, 1979, Columbia University, 1983, 1985, 1986, 1987, and City University of New York, 1983, 1985; Elliston Professor of poetry, University of Cincinnati, Ohio, 1989; visiting professor, University of California, Los

Angeles, and Ohio State University, 1990; resident, Thurber House, Columbus, Ohio, 1990; Bell Professor, University of Tulsa, 1992; Hurst Resident in Poetry, Washington University, 1994; instructor, graduate writing division, Columbia University, 1991–95. **Awards:** Ingram Merrill Foundation fellowship, 1974; George Dillon prize, 1975, Oscar Blumenthal prize, 1977, National Endowment for the Arts fellowship, 1980, 1991; Levinson prize, 1982 (*Poetry,* Chicago); Davidson prize, 1982; American Academy award, 1983; Academy of American Poets fellowship, 1987. **Address:** 720 Fort Washington Avenue, New York, New York 10040–3708, U.S.A.

PUBLICATIONS

Poetry

All Roads at Once. New York, Viking Press, 1976.
A Call in the Midst of the Crowd. New York, Viking Press, 1978.
The Various Light. New York, Viking Press, 1980.
Notes from a Child of Paradise. New York, Viking Press, 1984.
An Xmas Murder. New York, Sea Cliff Press, 1987.
The West Door. New York, Viking, 1988.
Autobiographies. New York, Viking, 1992.
Present. Washington, D.C., Counterpoint, 1997.
Stake: Selected Poems, 1972–1992. Washington, D.C., Counterpoint, and Plymouth, Plymbridge, 1999.

Novel

Part of His Story. Minneapolis, Mid-List Press, 1997.

Other

The Metamorphoses of Metaphor: Essays in Poetry and Fiction. New York, Viking 1987.
The Poem's Heartbeat: A Manual of Prosody. Brownsville, Oregon, Story Line Press, 1997.

Editor, *Incarnation: Contemporary Writers on the New Testament.* New York, Viking, 1990.
Editor, *Walking Liberty,* by James Haug. Boston, Northeastern University Press, 1999.

*

Critical Studies: "Alfred Corn's Speaking Gift" by George Kearns, in *Canto* (Andover, Massachusetts), fall 1978; "In the Place of Time" by G.E. Murray, in *Parnassus* (New York), spring-summer 1983; "The Traveler: On the Poetry of Alfred Corn" by Richard Abowitz, in *The Kenyon Review,* fall 1993; by Robyn Selman, in *Boston Review* (Cambridge, Massachusetts), 20(2), April 1995.

Alfred Corn comments:

(1990) Observers have noted that books of mine have an upward or downward direction. If *Notes from a Child of Paradise* was in the mode of ascent, then *The West Door* is in the mode of descent, many of the poems concerned with incarnational themes. To go out of the west door of the sanctuary is an entry into a world of physicality, of suffering and death. The book is dedicated to David Kalstone, critic and teacher, who died of AIDS in 1986. The collection's longest poem is "An Xmas Murder," a narrative and dramatic poem set in Vermont, recounting a crime and its aftermath in the life of one of the characters. There are two extended sequences in the book, "Tongues on Trees," a pastoral exploration of nature and language, and "After Ireland," a series of Irish subjects. "New Year," the volume's concluding lyric, is in the tradition of sunset poems such as Baudelaire's "Recueillement."

(1995) *Autobiographies* is in two parts, an opening section of metered lyrics and medium-length poems, including "My Neighbor, the Distinguished Count," a characterized monologue in the voice of a young woman initiated into vampirism by Dracula; and "Contemporary Culture and the Letter K," a comic survey of recent history ending with a serious reflection concerning the AIDS epidemic. "La Madeleine" is a poetic sequence around the theme of Mary Magdalene and Proust's "petite madeleine," in which loss is balanced by the redemptive powers of memory and faith. "The Jaunt" is a twilight meditation on a boat trip not taken, to be understood as an allegory for the surprising directions imposed by the poet's private sense of calling.

The volume concludes with "1992," a long autobiographical sequence in twenty sections with dates for their titles, the earliest 1949, the latest 1992. Each section juxtaposes an incident from the narrator's life with an incident from the life of a series of fictional characters in different parts of America. In fact, every state of the Union is mentioned during the course of the poem. The sequence provides something like a portrait of the United States in the latter half of the twentieth century, concluding with the quincentennial year of the Columbian voyage.

*   *   *

"Getting Past the Past" is both a title and a leitmotiv in Alfred Corn's impressive first book, *All Roads at Once*. Both in style and subject matter, past is present—or, as he puts it, "the past is a project / To be continued"—viewed and revised by a keenly individual sensibility: "We invent / The world and a wide cup to catch it in." Whether remembering childhood reading of and identification with fairy tales or traveling in Italy, France, and the Caribbean, the poet is caught by an evanescent past beyond recapture, if not recall, by the gift of imagination: "Yet somehow it's lost. / The instinct to save, to fix in words, / Drains color, excitement dying to be / Art for others, from which you withdraw, / Victim of an imagination." This explains the artist's awareness of his vocation and his ambivalence about it, joy and inevitable disappointment, and meanwhile the hope in this "double life, to be read and dreamed / Until the secret order appears."

Creating "poems across the trenches / of time" is one way to impose an order on "the curve of history" while waiting for the indefinite future. Already Corn demonstrates master craftsmanship in the traditional poetic forms. If in his sophistication he sometimes sounds too world-weary, even languid, the sharpness of his observations and aperçus, his wit and wordplay (often twisting clichés and turning puns into newer and neater truisms) prevent these poems from being merely facile, though not always from being mannered. Corn's verbal ability and technical virtuosity are reminiscent of James Merrill, as his gift for evoking associative meaning through catalog and astute juxtaposition owe more than a little to John Ashbery. The weights of tradition, however, like those of his own past, are not so much burdens as influences transformed into a distinctive identity. Thus, Hart Crane's *The Bridge* helps Corn make his own philosophical and spiritual connections, while "Passages from a Voyage," the

brilliantly sustained long poem that concludes the volume, uses Darwin's account of his journey as a basis for personal poetic explorations of the duality of man's life, the ambiguity of consciousness and the body's "ignorant optimism," and mutability and its terrors, the whole becoming an "experience arranged in a splendid contraption."

With *A Call in the Midst of the Crowd* Corn continues to develop his themes of love and loss, but here self-assuredness replaces the self-consciousness of his earlier work. Again we find the subtle allusions to illustrious predecessors, the bright phrases and descriptive catalogs, but now the abstract and concrete combine in lyrics capable of capturing the most elusive mood or the immensity and diversity of a great city. Once again, travel is a subject, the dislocation provoking unease as "thoughts come stunned / And out of order." But the very disarray proves a creative stimulus. Though the "world of object perpetually / Closes in," Corn has many a "rare moment when seeing comes of age," particularly in the long title poem on New York City that makes up most of the book. The four-part poem is itself half made up of astutely selected and cleverly arranged quotations from Crane, Henry James, Poe, Melville, Whitman, Tocqueville, and Wallace Stevens, whose comments play counterpoint to Corn's own observations about the city, its effect on the individual adventurer (or exile) there, and the course of a broken but then mended romance. As the poem progresses, often ironically, through the seasons of love, it reveals the infinite possibilities for achievement and failure, the chaos, distractions, and sheer abundance that make the excitement and danger of the city. As long urban history merges with the individual present with oblique significance, we are told, "Our births choose us; then our lives; then our deaths." For all that, however, the city grants freedom to the poet, for here he is "free once more to stroll where I'm drawn, hero / Of my own story." The promise Corn finds in the city is the same the book holds for its author: "The speaking gift that falls to one who hears / A word shine through the white noise of the world."

In *Present,* his 1997 collection, Corn turns from addressing travel at home and abroad to focus on time. A study and appreciation of the present moment becomes the way to live more wholly in the future. The notion of "present" is also scrutinized as "gift," the gift of God's love, the gift of the artist's expression, and the gifts of self and love. In "Stepson Elegy" a woman Corn remembers from his childhood in Georgia makes an offering of "the double handicap of work / And housework in our poorly sited little house." In the prose passage of "A Goya Reproduction" Corn addresses Don Manuel Osorio Manrique de Zuniga, a figure in the painting depicted on the book's cover. Spiritual intuitions are rendered concrete in the poem via the evocations of doom and innocence. Art is also rendered spiritually sacred in "Musical Sacrifice," a sequence that compares Kafka and Bach by tracing their lives. The poem ambitiously plays on meditations on music, German history, and details from the lives of the composer and the novelist. Corn describes the tonal qualities of Bach's concertos as "hard-pressed determination, the soul testing its powers of understanding when confronted with Creation from the first night until this, the Dorian mode's rugged heft mustered to convey a sense of ineluctable will accomplishing its ends in a world of mute suffering." As if in sympathy with Bach and Kafka, Corn seems to be expressing his tenant of the artist's responsibility: artists must refuse the complacencies of a hidden life and take a stand for their own personal expression.

For Corn writing and autobiography are inseparably linked. *Stake: Selected Poems, 1972–1992* is an examination of a long-term fascination with both the symbiotic and the antagonistic relationship between these two forces. One section of "Notes from a Child of Paradise," a book-length poem, examines how a trip to the Grand Canyon renders the poet so disconnected from himself that he is forced to speak in the third-person plural, "staggered, trying then also / To find words that would fall in love with what they saw." The long poem "1992" uses personal anecdotes of cross-country trips mixed with small frames of imagined lives of everyday people to express the transitory and inherently meaningful: "Trees rushing by, / a sinking sun caught in them. Wordlessness, / more than anything else, was how we communicated." The poet's voice, both brave and historical, renders contemporary life at its most intelligent and complex.

—Joseph Parisi and Martha Sutro

CORNISH, Sam(uel James)

Nationality: American. **Born:** Baltimore, Maryland, 22 December 1935. **Education:** Attended Booker T. Washington High School and Douglass High School, both Baltimore; Goddard College, Plainfield, Vermont; Northwestern University, Evanston, Illinois. **Military Service:** U.S. Army Medical Corps, 1958–60. **Family:** Married Jean Faxon in 1967. **Career:** Writing specialist, Enoch Pratt Library, Baltimore, 1965–66 and 1968–69; bookseller, 1966–67; editorial consultant, CARE, U.S. Office of Education, Washington, D.C., 1967–68; from 1969 teacher of creative writing, Highland Park Free School, Roxbury, Massachusetts; staff adviser and consultant on children's writing, Education Development Center, Newton, Massachusetts, 1973–78. Instructor in Afro-American Studies, Emerson College, Boston. Former editor of the Enoch Pratt Library publication *Chicory,* and *Mimeo* magazine. Former consultant in elementary-school teaching, Central Atlantic Regional Educational Laboratories Humanities Program. **Awards:** National Endowment for the Arts grant, 1967, 1969. **Address:** Department of English, Emerson College, 100 Beacon Street, Boston, Massachusetts 02116, U.S.A.

PUBLICATIONS

Poetry

In This Corner: Sam Cornish and Verses. Baltimore, Fleming McAllister, 1961.
People Beneath the Window. Baltimore, Sacco, 1962.
Generations (single poem). Baltimore, Beanbag Press, 1964.
Angles. Baltimore, Beanbag Press, 1965.
Winters. Cambridge, Massachusetts, San Souci Press, 1968.
Short Beers. Cambridge, Massachusetts, Beanbag Press, 1969(?).
Generations (collection). Boston, Beacon Press, 1971.
Streets. Chicago, Third World Press, 1973.
Sometimes: Ten Poems. Cambridge, Massachusetts, Pym Randall Press, 1973.
Sam's World. Washington, D.C., Decatur House, 1978.
Songs of Jubilee: New and Selected Poems 1969–1983. Greensboro, North Carolina, Unicorn Press, 1986.
Folks like Me. Cambridge, Massachusetts, Zoland Books, 1993.
Cross a Parted Sea: Poems. Cambridge, Massachusetts, Zoland Books, 1996.

Other

Your Hand in Mine. New York, Harcourt Brace, 1970.
Grandmother's Pictures (for children). Lenox, Massachusetts, Bookstore Press, 1974.
My Daddy's People Were Very Black. Newton, Massachusetts, Educational Development Center, 1976.
Walking the Street with Mississippi John Hurt (for children). Scarsdale, New York, Bradbury Press, 1978.
1935: A Memoir. Boston, Massachusetts, Ploughshares Books, 1990.

Editor, with Lucian W. Dixon, *Chicory: Young Voices from the Black Ghetto.* New York, Association Press, 1969.
Editor, with Hugh Fox, *The Living Underground: An Anthology of Contemporary American Poetry.* East Lansing, Michigan, Ghost Dance Press, 1969.

*

Critical Studies: Introduction by Ron Shreiber to *Winters,* 1968; "Kinship and History in Sam Cornish's *Generations*" by C.K. Doreski, in *Contemporary Literature* (Madison, Wisconsin), 33(4), winter 1992; "Make a Drumbeat" by William Doreski, in *Pembroke* (Pembroke, North Carolina), 30, 1998.

Sam Cornish comments:

Most of my major themes are of urban life, the Negro predicament here in the cities, and my own family. I try to use a minimum of words to express the intended thought or feeling, with the effect of being starkly frank at times. Main verse form is unrhymed, free. Main influences—Lowell, T.S. Eliot, LeRoi Jones.

*   *   *

Sam Cornish feels that T.S. Eliot, Robert Lowell, and LeRoi Jones have influenced him, and this influence is evident in his thematic affinity with Jones and the subtle irony of his poetry, a quality so significant in Eliot and Lowell. The three dominant themes in Cornish's works are urban life, the situation of people of color, and his own family. In form his poetry is strikingly concise—even terse—and his verse unrhymed. The short poem "Sam's World" is a representative sample of the poet's sharp consciousness of black people's plight and, simultaneously, his perception of the identity and dignity possible even in that plight:

sam's mother has
grey combed hair

she will never touch
it with a hot iron
she leaves it
the way the lord
intended

she wears it proudly
a black and grey
round head of hair

In comments on his well-known "Generations 1" Cornish says that he "walked to the east side of Baltimore trying to find and remember the boys that grew up with me and were still living on the streets: laughing, talking and thinking about the streets, the playgrounds that had turned into parking lots, or weeded places after the riots. The poem grew out of those meetings and remembering what it was like to grow up alone, how I felt about women, the church, what I wanted to do with my life.'' Remembered, relived, and reflected-upon events provide a major basis for his poetry. The unrecognizable and beautiful transformations of these events into poetry is obvious in ''Generations 1.'' Specific details about the familiar figures of everyday life become highly generalized and evocative in such lines as these:

> he would come into her cold apartment
> wondering if he had the special knowledge
> that women wanted from men
> endured the pain she moaned
> the odor between her breasts
>
> and wanted god to remember
> he was young
> and in much trouble
>
> with himself

Cornish's poetry shows an intense awareness of what it means to be human and, especially, to be black in contemporary America. It fuses in a complex way a tender awareness of intimate man-woman relations, close family ties, and a sympathy and understanding for fellow blacks. As an African-American poet, Cornish suffers the anguish of his people and writes about it in a way that combines the immediacy of one sharing the experience and the control of the detached observer. It is this tone of wistfulness and this control that make his poetry deeply moving without being shriekingly militant.

—J.N. Sharma

CORSO, (Nunzio) Gregory

Nationality: American. **Born:** New York City, 26 March 1930. **Family:** Married 1) Sally November in 1963 (divorced), one daughter; 2) Belle Carpenter in 1968, one daughter and one son; 3) Jocelyn Stern, one son. **Career:** Manual laborer, 1950–51; reporter, *Los Angeles Examiner,* 1951–52; merchant seaman, 1952–53. Member of the department of English, State University of New York, Buffalo, 1965–70. **Awards:** Longview Foundation award; Poetry Foundation award. **Address:** c/o New Directions, 80 8ᵗʰ Avenue, New York, New York 10011–5126, U.S.A.

PUBLICATIONS

Poetry

The Vestal Lady on Brattle and Other Poems. Cambridge, Massachusetts, Richard Brukenfeld, 1955.
Gasoline. San Francisco, City Lights, 1958.
Bomb. San Francisco, City Lights, 1958.

A Pulp Magazine for the Dead Generation with Henk Marsman. Paris, Dead Language, 1959.
The Happy Birthday of Death. New York, New Directions, 1960.
Minutes to Go, with others. Paris, Two Cities, 1960.
Selected Poems. London, Eyre and Spottiswoode, 1962.
Long Live Man. New York, New Directions, 1962.
Penguin Modern Poets 5, with Lawrence Ferlinghetti and Allen Ginsberg. London, Penguin, 1963.
The Mutation of the Spirit: A Shuffle Poem. New York, Death Press, 1964.
There Is Yet Time to Run through Life and Expiate All That's Been Sadly Done. New York, New Directions, 1965.
The Geometric Poem: A Long Experimental Poem, Composite of Many Lines and Angles Selective. Privately printed, 1966.
10 Times a Poem. New York, Poets Press, 1967.
Elegiac Feelings American. New York, New Directions, 1970.
Egyptian Cross. New York, Phoenix Book Shop, 1971.
Ankh. New York, Phoenix Book Shop, 1971.
(Poems). New York, Phoenix Book Shop, 1971.
The Night Last Night Was at Its Nightest. New York, Phoenix Book Shop, 1972.
Earth Egg. New York, Unmuzzled Ox, 1974.
Herald of the Autochthonic Spirit. New York, New Directions, 1981.
Writings from Unmuzzled Ox Magazine. New York, Unmuzzled Ox, 1981.
Four Poems. New York, Paradox Bookshop, 1981.
Wings, Wands, Windows. Englewood, Colorado, Howling Dog Press, 1982.
Hitting the Big 5–0. New York, Catchword, 1983.
Mindfield: New and Selected Poems. New York, Thunder's Mouth, 1989.
Gasoline & The Vestal Lady on Brattle. San Francisco, City Lights Books, 1992.

Plays

In This Hung-Up Age (produced Cambridge, Massachusetts, 1955). Published in *New Directions 18,* edited by James Laughlin, New York, New Directions, 1964.
Standing on a Streetcorner, in *Evergreen Review 6* (New York), March-April 1962.
That Little Black Door on the Left, in *Pardon Me Sir, But Is My Eye Hurting Your Elbow?,* edited by Bob Booker and George Foster. New York, Geis, 1968.
Way Out: A Poem in Discord. Kathmandu, Nepal, Bardo Matrix, 1974.

Novel

The American Express. Paris, Olympia Press, 1961.

Other

The Minicab War (parodies), with Anselm Hollo and Tom Raworth. London, Matrix Press, 1961.
Some of My Beginnings and What I Feel Right Now. Portree, Isle of Skye, Aquila, 1982.
Poems, Interview, Photographs. Louisville, Kentucky, White Fields Press, 1994.

Editor, with Walter Höllerer, *Junge Amerikanische Lyrik.* Munich, Hanser, 1961.

*

Bibliography: *A Bibliography of the Works of Gregory Corso 1954–1965* by Robert A. Wilson, New York, Phoenix Book Shop, 1966.

Manuscript Collections: Columbia University, New York; University of Texas, Austin; State University of New York, Buffalo; University of Kansas, Lawrence.

Critical Studies: *Riverside Interviews 3* edited by Gavin Selerie, London, Binnacle Press, 1982; *Exiled Angel: A Study of the Work of Gregory Corso* by Gregory Stephenson, London, Hearing Eye, 1989; ''Ethnos and the Beat Poets'' by Steve Harney, in *Journal of American Studies* (Cambridge, England), 25(3), December 1991; ''Unleashing Language: The Post-Structuralist Poetics of Gregory Corso and The Beats'' by Robert C. Timm, in *Kerouac Connection,* 27, winter 1995; ''Una Testa Dura-On Being Gregory Corso and Being Italian'' by Vincent Zangrillo, in *Voices in Italian Americana* (Chicago), 7(1), 1996; ''On Gregory Corso'' by Iain Sinclair, in *London Review of Books,* 18(11), 1996; *'A Clown in the Grave': Complexities and Tensions in the Works of Gregory Corso* by Michael Skau, Carbondale, Illinois, Southern Illinois University Press, 1999.

Gregory Corso comments:

[I am a] mental explorer, un-Faustian.

[My verse is] hopeful—naive—strange—sweet—soon smart— why not.

*   *   *

Gregory Corso was one of the beat generation's most ardent apologists. But with the others—Ginsberg, Ferlinghetti, Kerouac, Snyder—he shared that antisocial, apocalyptic, love-centered, freedom-loving mystique that has become so familiar to us. With Ginsberg and Kerouac, Corso was part of a kind of beat triumvirate, each encouraging and supporting the other and his work. If Kerouac was the father figure and Ginsberg the rabbi figure, Corso was the child figure and the clown.

Born into a poor immigrant family in Manhattan, Corso grew up as an underprivileged kid and became a juvenile delinquent. Before he was twenty years old, he had spent three years in prison for attempted robbery. Corso read widely and voraciously in prison. After his release he eventually found his way to the Harvard Library, where he continued his self-education and was taken up by local students and writers, who subsidized and saw through the press his first book of poems, *The Vestal Lady on Brattle.* It was at this point that Ginsberg and Kerouac ''discovered'' him.

Corso's poems are a mixture of powerful statement and bombast. He can be funny, maudlin, original, hackneyed, outrageous, and sentimental, sometimes all in one poem. His stance is that of the sophisticated child looking about him at a world gone mad and wondering why he is a part of it. But madness is also a virtue, since it is a response to and release from the sanity and conformity of the suburban 1950s against which the beats were reacting. As Corso put it, ''Man is great and mad, he was born mad and wonder of wonders the sanity of evolution knoweth not what to do.''

Corso thinks of himself rather self-consciously as a poet, which leads him into excesses of language, archaisms, ''poetic'' phrasing, and unusual words. As one might expect of an autodidact, he wears his learning somewhat heavily, scattering literary and mythological allusions through his work. He likes to use words like ''swipple,'' ''precocial,'' ''spatchcock,'' and the like. He can use a word like ''writ'' without apparent irony, and he seems to want such lines as ''Life has meaning and I do not know the meaning'' to be taken at face value. We can see the strong influence of Kerouac at work here in the belief of letting it all hang out and writing without revision. This hit-or-miss technique of composition sometimes results in powerfully expressed feelings and ideas, but it often falls wide of the mark. Corso is not afraid to take chances, and there is something both endearing and annoying about his mixture of prosy language and verbal excess. Here is a typical piece of fustian taken at random:

O walking crucifixes hooded and bowed
treking catacombic apothecaries
Grains drams and ounces of aphasia
Etherized Popes their desperado nods
raise welts of confessional memories on my lips

Corso's subjects include large ones such as the plight of humanity and American society, Zen Buddhism, Egyptian religion, and art and smaller ones such as travel in Europe and Africa, his childhood, and the literary life. His most frequently anthologized poem, the funny-sad meditation called ''Marriage,'' is his best. The famous ''Bomb'' poem, printed in the shape of a mushroom cloud, shows a richness of invention, which is one of his hallmarks, and an obsession with death, which is another. The title of one of his collections is *The Happy Birthday of Death,* a title ostensibly chosen from a long list of possibilities such as ''Fried Shoes,'' ''Gargoyle Liver,'' ''The Rumpled Backyard,'' and ''Radiator Soup.''

Other good poems include ''Giant Turtle,'' which describes a turtle laying eggs, ''Hair,'' another repetitious but inventive verse, and ''Seed Journey.'' Two long efforts in *Elegiac Feelings American* should be noted. The title poem, inscribed ''for the dear memory of John Kerouac,'' is an attack on America and its destruction of Kerouac that is rather incoherent in its excesses and logical inconsistencies. ''The Geometric Poem'' is a facsimile reproduction of a long handwritten manuscript complete with cartoonlike illustrations and hieroglyphics drawn by the poet, an elaborate and not wholly successful evocation of Egyptian culture and religion.

Corso's best poems combine his original and zany humor with an innocent tenderness. He is also capable, however, of rage against AIDS, pity for the homeless, and a lingering distrust, typical of the beat generation, of such middle-class phenomena as cops, the suburbs, and literary agents. Many of these conflicting ideas and moods occur in the ambitious kaleidoscopic poem ''Field Report,'' collected in the 1989 *Mindfield.* This is a report from the front lines of ''poesia,'' a mythical but very real territory where Corso appears to feel simultaneously beleaguered, entrenched, and at home.

It is difficult not to like Corso as a person seen through his poems. He is the perennial bad boy, jack-off (a recurrent but minor theme), hipster, clown, rebel, *poète maudit,* and misty-eyed romantic. Yet some of these images seem rather dated and quaint. By the 1990s Corso had become an aging, but engaging, clown, a child-man in an aging body who looks in the mirror and cannot believe what he sees. Strenuously resisting death and aging, he humorously and half-seriously denies them both. As the father of two children and the husband of a woman much younger than himself, he has contemplated the grotesquerie of himself in the year 2000 at age seventy, his wife in her forties, his son in his twenties.

—Donald Barlow Stauffer

COTTON, John

Nationality: British. **Born:** London, 7 March 1925. **Education:** University of London, B.A. (honors) 1956. **Military Service:** Royal Naval Commando in the Far East, 1942–46. **Family:** Married Peggy Midson in 1948; two sons. **Career:** Teacher with the Middlesex Education Authority, 1947–58; head of the English Department, Southall Grammar Technical School, Middlesex, 1957–63; headmaster, Highfield Comprehensive School, Hemel Hempstead, Hertfordshire, 1963–85. Founder, with Ted Walker, and editor, 1962–72, *Priapus* magazine; editor, *The Private Library,* 1969–79. Since 1975 publisher, Priapus Press. Chair, 1972–74, 1977, and treasurer, 1986–89, The Poetry Society, London. **Awards:** Arts Council award, 1971. Appointed Deputy Lieutenant of the County of Hertfordshire, 1989. **Address:** 37 Lombardy Drive, Berkhamsted, Hertfordshire HP4 2LQ, England.

PUBLICATIONS

Poetry

Fourteen Poems. Berkhamsted, Hertfordshire, Priapus, 1967.
Outside the Gates of Eden and Other Poems. Bushey Heath, Hertfordshire, Taurus Press, 1969.
Ampurias. Berkhamsted, Hertfordshire, Priapus, 1969.
Old Movies and Other Poems. London, Chatto and Windus-Hogarth Press, 1971.
Columbus on St. Cominica. Rushden, Northamptonshire, Sceptre Press, 1972.
Preludes: San Martin. Northamptonshire, Sceptre Press, 1973.
Roman Wall. Richmond, Surrey, Keepsake Press, 1973.
Photographs. Oxford, Sycamore Press, 1973.
Kilroy Was Here: Poems 1970–74. London, Chatto and Windus-Hogarth Press, 1975.
Places. Berkhamsted, Hertfordshire, Priapus, 1976.
Fragments 11, 12, and 13. Knotting, Bedfordshire, Sceptre Press, 1976.
Powers. Berkhamsted, Hertfordshire, Priapus, 1977.
A Berkhamsted Three, with Fred Sedgwick and Freda Downie. Berkhamsted, Hertfordshire, Priapus, 1978.
Piers. Leicester, New Broom Press, 1979.
A Letter for a Wedding. Berkhamsted, Hertfordshire, Priapus, 1980.
Somme Man. Berkhamsted, Hertfordshire, Priapus, 1980.
Wishful Thinking. Leicester, New Broom Press, 1980.
Poems for a Course, with Wes Magee. Berkhamsted, Hertfordshire, Priapus, 1980.
The Totleigh Riddles. Berkhamsted, Hertfordshire, Priapus, 1981.
Catullus at Sirmio. Berkhamsted, Hertfordshire, Priapus, 1982.
Day Book Continued. Leicester, New Broom Press, 1982.

The Highfield Write-a-Poem, with Bevis Cotton. Berkhamsted, Hertfordshire, Priapus, 1982.
Day Book. Berkhamsted, Hertfordshire, Priapus, 1983.
The Storyville Portraits. West Kirby, Merseyside, Headland, 1984.
Dust. Hitchin, Hertfordshire, Starwheel Press, 1986.
Oh Those Happy Feet. Hatch End, Middlesex, Poet and Printer Press, 1986.
The Poetry File. London, Macmillan, 1988.
Here's Looking at You Kid: New and Selected Poems. West Kirby, Merseyside, Headland, 1990.
That's It. Ipswich, The James Daniel Daniel John Press, 1994.

Poetry (for children)

The Crystal Zoo, with U.A. Fanthorpe and L.J. Anderson. Oxford, Oxford University Press, 1985.
The Biggest Riddle in the World, with Fred Sedgwick. London, Mary Glasgow, 1990; with *Hey!,* as *Two by Two,* 1990.
Hey! with Fred Sedgwick. London, Mary Glasgow, 1990; with *Biggest Riddle in the World,* as *Two by Two,* 1990.
First Things. Walton-on-Thames, Nelson, 1993.
Oscar the Dog and Friends. Harlow, Essex, Longmans, 1994.
Christmas Riddles: For Young Friends. Berkhamsted, Priapus Press, 1997.
The Sukey Poems: For Young Friends: Christmas 1998. Berkhamsted, Priapus Press, 1998.

Other

British Poetry since 1965. London, National Book League, 1973.

Editor, *I Am the Song* (poetry for young people). Walton-on-Thames, Nelson, 1996.

*

Critical Studies: In *Poetry Book Society Bulletin 69* and *84* (London), 1971, 1975; by Anne Cluysenaar, in *Stand* (Newcastle upon Tyne), xiv, 1, 1972; by Fred Sedgwick, in *Hertfordshire Countryside* (Hitchin), December 1979; interview with Moira Andrew, in *School's Poetry Review,* 1984.

John Cotton comments:

Overstatement is the obvious and inherent danger in writing a piece of this kind. I expect I may not avoid it! Basically I write as a way of exploring what I experience and what I think and feel about that experience. I explore my emotions and attitudes and, of course, the language in which I express them. If I succeed in this, it is for others to judge. But personally I find the process itself of immense value.

Yet if it sounds pretentious to go on to say that my pursuit of the art constitutes an exploration of that area, that borderline, between our wish to make things last forever and our consciousness that they never can. That in this it is a way of comprehending and reconciling ourselves to the universal mutability of things, ideas, and concepts.

That the serious side of our work, and frequently the comic side, is an extension of our quarrel with God. Then I can only plead that is the nearest I can get to an explanation of what I attempt to do.

Having gone thus far, I may as well compound things by saying that with Aristotle I look upon one of the purposes of our fictions as a means of bringing or finding some sort of order to the plethora of disparate experiences to which we are all subjected.

In mitigation, I would quickly add that while I take the art seriously I do not take myself so.

* * *

John Cotton's work strikes one as utterly English. The poems seem rooted in the attributes of decency and compassion, and there is evidence of a square-shouldered stance in the face of the inevitable enemy. English, yes, even though Cotton ranges far for his subject matter—outer space (in ''Report Back''), New Orleans (in *The Storyville Portraits*), or Spain (in *Kilroy Was Here*). Despite this wanderlust, Cotton remains the careful, considerate, and deliberate poet with feet firmly planted on the English landscape.

He prefers a ''natural'' line length, which can look untidy and unformed but which reads well. A resonant tone echoes through the poems whatever their lengths. He is adept with the brief landscape sketch (''Moorland Signals'') and the extended sequence, as, for instance, in *Day Book,* thirty-two ''fragments.'' While reluctant to let himself go on the page, there is, nevertheless, occasion for humor, for the belly laugh, for the sensual, as in ''Old Movies'':

And their apartments,
vast as temples,
full of unused furniture,
the sideboards bending with booze,
and all those acres of bed!
She, in attendance, wearing
diaphanous, but never quite
diaphanous enough, nightwear.

At times Cotton can be clumsily poetic (''Did the grey climacteric beast have to choose''), but instances of such overwriting are rare. More common is a clear diction, a feeling that each poem knows exactly where it is going. His later work has darkened, and human situations are presented without camouflage, as in the moving ''The Night Ward.'' Here Cotton spells out without stridency or blather the dread experienced by those being stalked by death. The observations are sharp, the compassion palpable:

The drip measures it
As it feeds down into the arm,
Spelling out its fractions
By the bobbing of a small plastic ball.
Listen. You might just hear it.
God help the heart that is as quiet.
We wait for dawn from the trenches of our beds.

Cotton not only moves but also entertains the reader. He is not one to stick with gloom, and past experiences in the cinema and poems such as ''The Westerners'' are packed with incident and good lines. Like the washing on the line in ''Moorland Signals,'' Cotton's poems are ''a bright bunting / of challenge to the grey power . . .''

—Wes Magee

212

COUZYN, Jeni

Nationality: Canadian. **Born:** South Africa, 26 July 1942; became Canadian citizen, 1975. **Education:** University of Natal, B.A. 1962, B.A. (honors) 1963. **Career:** Drama teacher, Rhodesia, 1964; producer, African Music and Drama Association, Johannesburg, 1965; teacher, Special School, London, 1966; poetry organizer and gallery attendant, Camden Arts Centre, London, 1967. Since 1968 freelance poet, lecturer, broadcaster, and psychotherapist. Writer-in-residence, University of Victoria, British Columbia, 1976. **Awards:** Arts Council grant, 1971, 1974; Canada Council grant, 1977, 1984. **Address:** c/o Bloodaxe Books, P.O. Box 1SN, Newcastle upon Tyne NE99 1SN, England.

PUBLICATIONS

Poetry

Flying. London, Workshop Press, 1970.
Monkeys' Wedding. London, Cape, 1972; revised edition, Vancouver, Douglas and McIntyre, and London, Heinemann, 1978.
Christmas in Africa. London, Heinemann, 1975.
House of Changes. London, Heinemann, 1978.
The Happiness Bird. Victoria, British Columbia, Sono Nis Press, 1978.
A Time to Be Born. London, Heinemann, 1981.
Life by Drowning: Selected Poems. Toronto, Anansi, 1983; revised edition, Newcastle upon Tyne, Bloodaxe Books, 1985.
In the Skin House. Newcastle upon Tyne, Bloodaxe, 1993.

Other

Ton-Cat-Lion (for children). London, Gollancz, 1987.
Bad Day (for children). London, Gollancz, 1988.

Editor, *Twelve to Twelve: Poems Commissioned for Poetry D-Day, Camden Arts Festival 1970.* London, Poets' Trust, 1970.
Editor, *The Bloodaxe Book of Contemporary Women Poets.* Newcastle upon Tyne, Bloodaxe, 1985.
Editor, *Singing Down the Bones: A Poetry Collection.* London, Women's Press, 1989.

*

Critical Studies: Interview with Leon de Kock, in *Donga,* 7, 1977; ''Poet in Africa: Jeni Couzin'' by E. Pereira, in *Unisa English Studies* (Pretoria, South Africa), 16(1), 1978; by Kevan Johnson, in *Poetry Review,* 83(4), winter 1994; ''A Woman's Poet Journey into Life: On Jeni Couzyn's Poems'' by Eunwon Han, in *Journal of English Language and Literature* (Seoul, Korea), 41(4), winter 1995.

Jeni Couzyn comments:

I am interested in using symbol rather than image and tend to write with as much clarity as I can. I am at times monosyllabic and look for the shortest and simplest words I can find. I believe poetry should be ''true'' at the deepest possible level and dislike the kind of poetry that appears to be complex on the surface, crammed with learned references and tricky images but that finally has little to say.

I write in free verse, using rhythm and stress to underline meaning and to counterpoint the sense whenever I can. Similarly, I use rhyme for surprise and emphasis rather than in any metrical pattern. I am particularly fond of imperfect rhymes, especially where the rhyming syllable falls on the unstressed part of the word.

I believe that poetry should be spoken and read on the page only as a kind of specialized reference, as music is written to be played and listened to. Reviewers at this time in the history of poetry use the words "poetry circuit" as a dirty word, as though it were some kind of big roundabout that only the common and the simple people climbed aboard. The simply expressed but profound truth of a poem like Robert Frost's "Nothing Gold Can Stay" is what I most admire in poetry and most seek for. The criteria I use to judge my own work are, Is it interesting? Is it relevant to other people's lives? Is it music? Is it true in the deepest sense, in a lasting way? To the extent that these criteria are approached, I am pleased or displeased with a poem.

In sound I have been most influenced by Dylan Thomas, not so much in his technique as in his courage in defying the dry tradition of poetry he was born into.

That I am a poet in an age where the "unintellectual" (i.e., almost everybody) think of poetry as something they did not like when they were at school, and the intellectual think it something the masses should be excluded from, is sad for me. This age has too much reverence for poetry and too little respect, for by the same token it is very difficult indeed to earn a living from poetry. Nor are poets considered valid members of the community. You will never see a panel set up to discuss drug usage, for example, or terrorism in Ireland, with a poet among the psychiatrists, students, businessmen, clergy, and housewives being asked to give their view.

For me being a poet is a job rather than an activity. I feel I have a function in society neither more nor less meaningful than any other simple job. I feel it is part of my work to make poetry more accessible to people who have had their rights withdrawn from them. Standing in the way of this are the poetry watchdogs who bark in the Sunday reviews, trying to preserve their sterile territory. Also it is necessary to overcome the apathy and ignorance of a whole society with a totally untrained ear and a profoundly sluggish imagination.

*   *   *

The first book published by Jeni Couzyn was called *Flying.* Few of the poems contained in it had at the time reached the usual magazines and anthologies. Couzyn, however, was already known for her appearances on the recital circuits, where she had been a handsome presence. *Flying* consisted of reflections on the author's South African background, descriptions of the gray suburbia she found in London, dramatizations of love relationships, and revelations of mental stress.

The poems on this last subject were at their best when the author expressed her internal conflicts through a flow of exotic imagery. For example, "The Farm" deals with what seems to be depressive illness, but it does so in terms almost of a child's holiday:

> On the farm there are two
> cows.
> And a lot of
> trees. They change their leaves
> whenever they like. When they change their leaves you
> know
> That it is autumn. The two cows have a calf and then you

> know
> that it is spring.
> You can take your cat with you to the farm or whatever
> you like. You can take your
> bicycle
> or your
> typewriter
> or all your books
> you can take whatever you like with you to the farm . . .

The patient monosyllables ratify a childlike acceptance of what becomes more abnormal the further the poem proceeds. It is not a child speaking, however, and the resulting conflict between the innocent and the sinister sets up an uneasy tension in the reader. This transmutes the mind's cliffs of fall into a parable.

Couzyn's second book, *Monkeys' Wedding,* suffers a little from overexplicitness. Despite this, the collection includes some powerful work, most notably "The Babies," a painful poem about contraception and abortion: "On the table the baby lay / pulped like a watermelon, a few / soft bits of skull protruding from the mush . . ." Perhaps the skin of fiction is stretched too thinly over the agony, for we are more conscious of outcry than of experience. If it is not to seem shrill, emotion of this sort demands something more substantial by way of narrative.

Some such narrative is sought in Couzyn's next book, *Christmas in Africa.* Here she makes considerable use of science fiction, notably the work of Brian Aldiss. In "Marapper the Priest" she writes, "I am your priest and your prophet. / May the long journey end / may the ship come home . . ." Surely, however, this would be obscure to a reader who did not know Aldiss's *Non-Stop.* Further, the reader who does know this superb novel may wonder why he or she has need of Couzyn's poem. More striking are what seem to be reminiscences of Couzyn's childhood in South Africa. "In the House of the Father" tells us, "The snakes were the price. In their hundreds they inhabited / our world at Christmas. They were the hazard / in the garden. And they were everywhere . . ." Sharp as such details seem, they may not be felt to have the pressure of implication found in the imagery of *Flying.* Nor do they seem to attain a sufficiently decisive form, and some readers may find the verse discursive.

In Couzyn's fourth book, *House of Changes,* there is a paucity of sharp detail. Imagery has given way to incantation: "Leprechaun take back thy curse / Leprechaun take back thy curse . . ." This seems to be wrenched from a context, but no adequate background is given. Although there are more science fiction poems, they are even more dependent upon Philip K. Dick than the earlier ones were upon Aldiss. Sometimes, however, the poet succeeds in relating the areas of poetry and science fiction: "Insatiable one. I'm exhausted with eating / I'm a bag of bones, I am all stomach. Bloated / I lie here unable to move in my sea of flesh." This, from a poem titled "I and Wolverine," appears to be a dialogue between an exhausted woman and the unappeasable sexuality that devours her.

In *Life by Drowning: Selected Poems,* Couzyn appears to favor her more mystical poems at the expense of some earthy and domestic ones, most of which have been dropped. The effect is to render her work more abstract and less humorous than it seems to be if the books are read in progression. This adverse effect is exaggerated by the fact that the poems are arranged thematically rather than chronologically. The situation is not helped by the preface to a later book, *In the Skinhouse,* which describes Couzyn as "surrendering the mystery of the soul'' and compares her work with the revelation accorded to Mary Magdalene. This may be held to describe the pieces in this particular collection: "Each mandala of lives / has a single life / at its centre." Such writing has not been conducive to the poet's reputation as a whole.

Africa, however, has been a redeeming feature throughout Couzyn's uneven career. The late book *Homecoming* is in some ways the best collection since *Flying*. The book is an account of a personal journey through contemporary South Africa. It begins by responding to the paintings of Cecil Skotnes and goes on to draw upon the work of Pippa Skotnes and Lucy Lloyd with respect to the San, a people now almost extinct. Here there is not that dependence found in Couzyn's earlier adaptations of science fiction, for these poems are self-substantive, with a specific grasp of imagery. "The Meaning of a Name," for instance, mourns the destruction of District Six in Cape Town with a power and certainty seldom equaled in poems of our time. This is what the English language tends to lack, a truly political—not a partisan political—poetry:

I photograph Violet Pogo in her half-finished house
squeezed among shanties spread across the flats
to the horizon like broken shells.

It's big, prompts Violet,
Well built. Rusty walls riddled with holes
nailed to flimsy beams . . .

This is mourning but also celebration. South Africa has replaced the science fiction analogues and the incantations that were a substitute for narrative in Couzyn's earlier poetry. *Homecoming* ends with an extended tribute to Nelson Mandela, not at all mystical and wholly appropriate to its eminent subject. This is work by a remarkable poet that exhales a fresh sense of discovery in exploring the world outside.

—Philip Hobsbaum

CRAWFORD, Robert

Nationality: Scottish. **Born:** Bellshill, Lanarkshire, 23 February 1959. **Education:** West Coats Primary School, Cambuslang, Glasgow, 1964–69; Hutchesons' Grammar School, Glasgow, 1969–77; University of Glasgow, 1977–81, M.A. (honors) 1981; University of Oxford, 1981–84, D.Phil. 1985. **Family:** Married Alice Wales in 1988; one son and one daughter. **Career:** Elizabeth Wordsworth Junior Research Fellow, St. Hugh's College, Oxford, 1984–87; British Academy postdoctoral fellow, University of Glasgow, 1987–89. Lecturer, 1989–95, and since 1995 professor of modern Scottish literature, University of St. Andrews, St. Andrews, Fife. **Awards:** Eric Gregory award, 1988; Poetry Book Society Recommendation, 1990, for *A Scottish Assembly,* 1992, for *Talkies,* 1996, for *Masculinity;* New Generation Poet, UK Arts Council, 1992; Scottish Arts Council Book award, 1994, for *Identifying Poets,* 1999, for *Spirit Machines.* Fellow, Royal Society of Edinburgh, 1999, and the English Association, 1999. **Agent:** David Godwin, 55 Monmouth Street, London WC2H 9DG, England. **Address:** School of English, University of St. Andrews, St. Andrews, Fife, KY16 9AL, Scotland.

PUBLICATIONS

Poetry

A Scottish Assembly. London, Chatto and Windus, 1990.
Sharawaggi: Poems in Scots, with W.N. Herbert. Edinburgh, Polygon, 1990.
Talkies. London, Chatto and Windus, 1992.
Masculinity. London, Cape, 1996.
Spirit Machines. London, Cape, 1999.

Other

The Savage and the City in the Work of T.S. Eliot. Oxford, Oxford University Press, 1987.
Devolving English Literature. Oxford, Oxford University Press, 1992.
Identifying Poets: Self and Territory in Twentieth-Century Poetry. Edinburgh, Edinburgh University Press, 1993.
Literature in Twentieth-Century Scotland: A Select Bibliography. London, British Council, 1995.

Editor, *Other Tongues: Young Scottish Poets in English, Scots and Gaelic.* St. Andrews, University of St. Andrews Press, 1990.
Editor, *About Edwin Morgan.* Edinburgh, Edinburgh University Press, 1990.
Editor, *The Arts of Alasdair Gray.* Edinburgh, Edinburgh University Press, 1991.
Editor, *Reading Douglas Dunn.* Edinburgh, Edinburgh University Press, 1992.
Editor, *Liz Lochhead's Voices.* Edinburgh, Edinburgh University Press, 1993.
Editor, *Talking Verse.* St. Andrews, University of St. Andrews, 1995.
Editor, *Robert Burns and Cultural Authority.* Edinburgh, Edinburgh University Press, and Iowa City, University of Iowa Press, 1997.
Editor, *Launch-site for English Studies.* St. Andrews, Verse, 1997.
Editor, *The Scottish Invention of English Literature.* Cambridge, Cambridge University Press, 1998.
Editor, *The Penguin Book of Poetry from Britain and Ireland since 1945.* Hammondsworth, Penguin, 1998.
Editor, *The New Penguin Book of Scottish Verse.* Hammondsworth, Penguin, 2000.
Editor, *Scottish Religious Poems.* Edinburgh, St. Andrews Press, 2000.

*

Manuscript Collection: St. Andrews University Library, St. Andrews, Fife.

Critical Studies: By Anthony Woodward, in *Review of English Studies,* February 1990; review of 'Devolving English Literature' by Michael Baron, in *English,* 42(172), spring 1993, and by Fiona Stafford, in *Review of English Studies,* 46(181), February 1995; in *Poetry Review,* 84(1), spring 1994.

*   *   *

Sometimes obliquely, often with energizing directness, Robert Crawford's poetry addresses Scotland, its past, present, and future. In the title poem of *A Scottish Assembly* the poet describes not being able to say "why I came back here to choose my union / On the side of the ayes, remaining a part / / Of this diverse assembly—Benbecula, Glasgow, Bow of Fife— / Voting with my feet, and this hand." The phrase "this hand" is an emphatic but controlled gesture and shows Crawford to be a poet with a sense of a mission—to affirm the worth and potential of Scotland's "democratic intellect" ("Scotland"). The deft allusion to "this warm scribe my hand" in Keats's *The Fall of Hyperion* reveals Crawford's ability to make the English literary tradition serve his own ends. But the words "to choose my union / On the side of the ayes" are not without a hint of the *voulu*, despite the poem's disinclination to provide "rhyme or reason." There are moments when Crawford's identification between Scotland and some techno-poststructuralist utopia seem willed.

The main virtues of Crawford's work are its passages of surreal or satiric inventiveness (though these can pall), its heterogeneous mix of dictions, its fascination with what language reveals or betrays about a culture, and its valuable note of democratic celebration. A good example of the last quality is "Rain." In this poem the pressure to affirm a collective sense of identity challenges the mood of "solitude, and me / Remembering again that I shall die" in Edward Thomas's famous poem of the same title. The weaknesses of Crawford's work are its rhythmic prosiness (which is not deny momentum and rhetorical drive to his poems), its lack of formal variety, and its unsure touch when it enters the subjective realm. Crawford is a poet of gusto rather than nuance; his sentence shapes are declarative rather than exploratory. He always animates his subject, but he moves his reader less frequently. The end of "A Saying," one of the better personal poems in *A Scottish Assembly*, displays Crawford's interest in the local, in a person's culturally shaped "voiceprint." In its coy allusion to a well-known pop song, however, it ducks the emotional challenge it sets itself: "Through the machine I hear your Glasgow accent, / Your voiceprint. I just called, to say." In fact, Crawford is, glimmeringly more affecting in his contributions to *Sharawaggi: Poems in Scots,* a 1990 volume he wrote with W.N. Herbert. Little of his work in English has the force, in context, of these lines from the close of "Allerish": "Menkit, menkit, menkit, menkit, menkit! / / An noo thi twa o us, schedded" ("Joined, joined, joined, joined, joined! / / And now the two of us, parted" in Crawford's translation). He is capable, however, of a quiet dignity in his more public work, in "Nec Tamen Consumebatur" shifting laterally and, in the end, powerfully between respect for nationalist pride and political compassion for "small peoples." The poem concludes with lines that use well the pauses and weightings allowed by Crawford's favored two-line stanza:

When you spoke about poems in Vietnamese
I heard behind the pride in your voice

Like a ceilidh in an unexpected place
The burning violins of small peoples.

Talkies, Crawford's second full collection in English, goes full pelt in pursuit of the "new voice" that, in "Radio Scottish Democracy," "starts to come unjammed / / Against a rout of white-noise, Floddens, / Cullodens, nostalgias that rhyme." The suspicion of hackneyed "nostalgias" does much to make Crawford's own poetic nationalism worthwhile. The volume mixes generalization with illustrative detail and at its best moves easily between the two. "WS," like other poems by Crawford, concerns itself with the writer's duty to attend to "famous non-celebrities, characters not in Smollett, /

Sources never to be revealed / / Without whom you could neither speak nor listen." Here the playful phrasing just about keeps at bay the danger of self-importance. Crawford's is a significant poetic task whose difficulties are suggested by the end of "Next Move," where he is "aware each step I took down the street / How much the next move would cost me."

The next move after *Talkies* was in the direction of a more personal poetry. In *Masculinity,* organized in the form of four loosely thematic sections, Crawford concentrates on domestic themes from a perspective shaped by gender politics as well as by an abiding concern with Scottish culture. As he takes snapshots of marriage and fatherhood, Crawford finds himself, with an often subtly managed balance, suggesting that he has experienced life as a series of stereotypes even when he wishes to show himself undoing stereotypes. The beginning of "Gym"—"Here they are again: men who are ill-at-ease / In rooms without wallbars or white lines painted on the floor"—plays with the fact that here, indeed, they are again crude representations of men. The poem finally works its way to a point where it can reinvest the hackneyed phrase "like a man" with meaning. Elsewhere the volume manages changes of tone and attitude with sensitivity and skill. "Winter" describes attending an adoption meeting in a way that shows off Crawford's new ability to blend statement with understatement. Here, as elsewhere, there is much to admire in his use of line breaks, rephrasings ("I couldn't really tell / Just what I wanted. I wanted too much") and deadpan detail (the couples wanting to adopt babies sit "in a semi-circle on bright scatter-cushions").

For all its many virtues *Masculinity* represents a certain curtailing, on Crawford's part, of ambition, both thematically and linguistically. There is no shortage of ambition in *Spirit Machines,* perhaps his finest achievement to date. The volume combines the personal and cultural emphases apparent in his previous collection with a going-for-broke verbal excitement in the long poem "Impossibility," a fantasia on the life of Margaret Oliphant. Almost too programmatically, "The Result" refers at once to relief at good personal and political news. But it is telling that the poem is faced by "The Balance," a wry piece that speaks of how bank tellers would work on "if one thing in the balance for the day / Did not work out exactly," and the collection is vividly aware of things not working out. Thus, in "Bereavement" Crawford elegizes with stoical acceptance: "I walk the same roads far ahead of you, / So slowly, but you never catch me up." If, like his speaker in "Impossibility," Crawford might say, "I am a pearl and Scotland is a pearl," he never loses sight of the necessary grit that pearls require.

—Michael O'Neill

CREELEY, Robert (White)

Nationality: American. **Born:** Arlington, Massachusetts, 21 May 1926. **Education:** Holderness School, Plymouth, New Hampshire; Harvard University, Cambridge, Massachusetts, 1943–44, 1945–46; Black Mountain College, North Carolina, B.A. 1954; University of New Mexico, Albuquerque, M.A. 1960. **Military Service:** American Field Service in India and Burma, 1944–45. **Family:** Married 1) Ann MacKinnon in 1946 (divorced 1955), two sons and one daughter, 2) Bobbie Louise Hall in 1957 (divorced 1976), three daughters; 3) Penelope Highton in 1977, one son and one daughter. **Career:** Farmer near Littleton, New Hampshire, 1948–51; lived in France, 1951–52, and Mallorca, 1952–53; instructor, Black Mountain College, spring 1954 and fall 1955; teacher in a boys school, Albuquerque, 1956–59, and on a finca in Guatemala, 1959–61; visiting lecturer, 1961–62, and visiting professor, 1963–66, 1968–69, 1978–80, University of New Mexico; lecturer, University of British Columbia, Vancouver, 1962–63; visiting professor, 1966–67, professor 1967–78, Gray Professor of Poetry and Letters, 1978–89, and since 1989 Samuel P. Capen Professor of poetry and humanities, State University of New York, Buffalo. Visiting Professor, San Francisco State College, 1970–71, and State University, of New York, Binghamton, 1985, 1986. Operated the Divers Press, Palma de Mallorca, 1953–55; editor, *Black Mountain Review,* North Carolina, 1954–57, and associated with *Wake, Golden Goose, Origin, Fragmente, Vou, Contact, CIV/n,* and *Merlin* magazines in early 1950s, and other magazines subsequently; advisory editor, since 1983, *American Book Review* and *Sagetrieb,* and since 1984, *New York Quarterly;* since 1984 contributing editor, *Formations.* **Awards:** D.H. Lawrence fellowship, 1960; Guggenheim fellowship, 1964, 1971; Rockefeller grant, 1965; Shelley memorial award, 1981; National Endowment for the Arts grant, 1982; DAAD fellowship, 1983, 1987; Leone d'Oro Premio Speziale (Venice), 1984; Frost Medal, 1987. New York State poet, 1989–91; Distinguished Professor award, State University of New York, Buffalo, 1989; Horst Bienek Preis fur Lyrick, Munich, 1993; the America award for poetry, 1995; Lila Wallace Reader's Digest Writers' award, 1996; Bollingen prize, 1999; Chancellor's medal, SUNY, Buffalo, 1999. **Member:** American Academy, 1987. **Address:** 313 Clemens, State University of New York, Buffalo, New York 14260, U.S.A.

PUBLICATIONS

Poetry

Le Fou. Columbus, Ohio, Golden Goose Press, 1952.
The Kind of Act of. Palma, Mallorca, Divers Press, 1953.
The Immoral Proposition. Karlisruhe-Surlach, Germany, Jonathan Williams, 1953.
A Snarling Garland of Xmas Verses. Palma, Mallorca, Divers Press, 1954.
All That Is Lovely in Men. Asheville, North Carolina, Jonathan Williams, 1955.
Ferrini and Others, with others. Berlin, Gerhardt, 1955.
If You. San Francisco, Porpoise Bookshop, 1956; London, Lion and Unicorn Press, 1968.
The Whip. Worcester, Migrant Press, and Highlands, North Carolina, Jonathan Williams, 1957.
A Form of Woman. New York, Jargon-Corinth, 1959.
For Love: Poems 1950–1960. New York, Scribner, 1962.
Distance. Lawrence, Kansas, Terrence Williams, 1964.
Two Poems. San Francisco, Oyez, 1964.
Hi There! Urbana, Illinois, Finial Press, 1965.
Words (single poem). Rochester, Minnesota, Perishable Press, 1965.
About Women. Los Angeles, Gemini, 1966.
Poems 1950–1965. London, Calder and Boyars, 1966.
For Joel. Madison, Wisconsin, Perishable Press, 1966.
A Sight. London, Cape Goliard Press, 1967
Words (collection). New York, Scribner, 1967.
Robert Creeley Reads (with recording). London, Turret-Calder and Boyars, 1967.
The Finger. Los Angeles, Black Sparrow Press, 1968.

5 Numbers. New York, Poets Press, 1968.
The Charm: Early and Uncollected Poems. Mount Horeb, Wisconsin, Perishable Press, 1968; London, Calder and Boyars, 1971.
The Boy. Buffalo, Gallery Upstairs Press, 1968.
Numbers. Stuttgart and Dusseldorf, Domberger-Galerie Schmela, 1968.
Divisions and Other Early Poems. Mount Horeb, Wisconsin, Perishable Press, 1968.
Pieces. Los Angeles, Black Sparrow Press, 1968.
Hero. New York, Indianakatz, 1969.
A Wall. New York and Stuttgart, Bouwerie-Domberger, 1969.
Mazatlan: Sea. San Francisco, Poets Press, 1969.
Mary's Fancy. New York, Bouwerie, 1970.
In London. Bolinas, California, Angel Hair, 1970.
The Finger: Poems 1966–1969. London, Calder and Boyars, 1970.
For Betsy and Tom. Detroit, Alternative Press, 1970.
For Benny and Sabina. New York, Samuel Charters, 1970.
As Now It Would Be Snow. Los Angeles, Black Sparrow Press, 1970.
America. Miami, Press of the Black Flag, 1970.
Christmas: May 10, 1970. Buffalo, Lockwood Memorial Library, 1970.
St. Martin's. Los Angeles, Black Sparrow Press, 1971.
Sea. San Francisco, Cranium Press, 1971.
1.2.3.4.5.6.7.8.9.0. Berkeley, California, and San Francisco, Shambala-Mudra, 1971.
For the Graduation. San Francisco, Cranium Press, 1971.
Change. San Francisco, Hermes Free Press. 1972.
One Day after Another. Detroit, Alternative Press, 1972.
A Day Book (includes prose). New York, Scribner, 1972.
For My Mother. Rushden, Northamptonshire, Sceptre Press, 1973.
Kitchen. Chicago, Wine Press, 1973.
His Idea. Toronto, Coach House Press, 1973.
Sitting Here. Storrs, University of Connecticut Library, 1974.
Thirty Things. Los Angeles, Black Sparrow Press, 1974.
Backwards. Knotting, Bedfordshire, Sceptre Press, 1975.
Away. Santa Barbara, California, Black Sparrow Press, and Solihull, Warwickshire, Aquila, 1976.
Selected Poems. New York, Scribner, 1976.
Myself. Knotting, Bedfordshire, Sceptre Press, 1977.
Thanks. Deerfield, Massachusetts, Deerfield Press, 1977.
The Children. St. Paul, Truk Press, 1978.
Hello: A Journal, February 23—May 3, 1976. New York, New Directions, and London, Boyars, 1978.
Later (single poem). West Branch, Iowa, Toothpaste Press, 1978.
Desultory Days. Knotting, Bedfordshire, Sceptre Press, 1978.
Later: New Poems. New York, New Directions, 1979; London, Boyars, 1980.
Corn Close. Knotting, Bedfordshire, Sceptre Press, 1980.
Mother's Voice. Santa Barbara, California, Am Here-Immediate, 1981.
The Collected Poems of Robert Creeley 1945–1975. Berkeley, University of California Press, 1982; London, Boyars, 1983.
Echoes. West Branch, Iowa, Toothpaste Press, 1982.
A Calendar. West Branch, Iowa, Toothpaste Press, 1983.
Mirrors. New York, New Directions, 1983; London, Boyars, 1984.
Memories. Durham, Pig Press, 1984.
Four Poems. Santa Barbara, California, Handmade, 1984.
Memory Gardens. New York, New Directions, 1986; London, Boyars, 1987.
7 & 6. Albuquerque, New Mexico, Hoshour Gallery, 1988.

Gedichte (German & English). Salzburg, Residenz, 1988.
The Company. Providence, Rhode Island, Burning Rock, 1988.
Windows. New York, New Directions, 1990; London, Boyars, 1991.
Places. Buffalo, New York, Shuffalof Press, 1990.
Have a Heart. Boise, Idaho, Limberlost Press, 1990.
Gnomic Verses. La Laguna, Tenerife, Islas Canarias, Zasterle Press, 1991.
Selected Poems 1945–1990. Berkeley, University of California Press, and London, Boyars, 1991.
Life & Death. New York, Gagosian Gallery, 1993.
Loops: Ten Poems. Kripplebush, New York, Nadja, 1995.
Echoes. New York, New Directions, 1994; London, M. Boyars, 1995.
Four Days in Vermont. Durham, England, Pig Press, 1995.
Robert Creeley. Brattleboro, Vermont, Longhouse, 1995.
The Dogs of Auckland. Buffalo, New York, Meow Press, 1996.
So There: Poems 1976–1983. New York, New Directions, 1998.
Personal: Poems. Berkeley, California, Peter Koch, 1998.
Life & Death. New York, New Directions, 1998.
Edges. New York, Blum, 1999.
En Famille: A Poem. New York, Granary, 1999.

Recordings: *Today's Poets 3,* with others, Folkways; *Robert Creeley Reads,* Turret-Calder and Boyars, 1967.

Play

Listen (produced London, 1972). Los Angeles, Black Sparrow Press, 1972.

Novel

The Island. New York, Scribner, 1963; London, Calder, 1964.

Short Stories

The Gold Diggers. Palma, Mallorca, Divers Press, 1954.
Mister Blue. Frankfurt, Insel, 1964.
The Gold Diggers and Other Stories. London, Calder, and New York, Scribner, 1965.

Other

An American Sense (essay). London, Sigma, 1965(?).
Contexts of Poetry. Buffalo, Audit, 1968.
A Quick Graph: Collected Notes and Essays. San Francisco, Four Seasons, 1970.
A Day Book. Berlin, Graphics, 1970.
Notebook. New York, Bouwerie, 1972.
A Sense of Measure (essays). London, Calder and Boyars, 1973.
The Creative. Los Angeles, Black Sparrow Press, 1973.
Contexts of Poetry: Interviews 1961–1971, edited by Donald Allen. Bolinas, California, Four Seasons, 1973.
Inside Out: Notes on the Autobiographical Mode. Los Angeles, Black Sparrow Press, 1973.
Presences: A Text for Marisol. New York, Scribner, 1976.
Mabel: A Story, and Other Prose. London, Boyars, 1976.
Was That a Real Poem or Did You Just Make It Up Yourself. Santa Barbara, California, Black Sparrow Press, 1976.
Was That a Real Poem and Other Essays, edited by Donald Allen. Bolinas, California, Four Seasons, 1979.

Charles Olson and Robert Creeley: The Complete Correspondence, edited by George F. Butterick. Santa Barbara, California, Black Sparrow Press, 8 vols., 1980–87.
The Collected Prose of Robert Creeley. New York and London, Boyars, 1984.
The Collected Essays of Robert Creeley. Berkeley, University of California Press, 1989.
Autobiography. Madras, New York, Hanuman Books, 1990.
Tales out of School: Selected Interviews. Ann Arbor, University of Michigan Press, 1993.
Day Book of a Virtual Poet. New York, Spuyten Duyvil, 1998.
In Company: Robert Creeley's Collaborations. Greensboro, North Carolina, University of North Carolina Press, 1999.

Editor, *Mayan Letters,* by Charles Olson. Palma, Mallorca, Divers Press, 1953; London, Cape, and New York, Grossman, 1968.
Editor, with Donald Allen, *New American Story.* New York, Grove Press, 1965.
Editor, *Selected Writings,* by Charles Olson. New York, New Directions, 1966.
Editor, with Donald Allen, *The New Writing in the U.S.A.* London, Penguin, 1967.
Editor, *Whitman.* London, Penguin, 1973.
Editor, *Going On: Selected Poems 1958–1980,* by Joanne Kyger. New York, Dutton, 1983.
Editor, *The Essential Burns.* New York, Ecco Press, 1989.
Editor, *Selected Poems* by Charles Olson. Berkeley, University of California Press, 1993.

*

Bibliography: *Robert Creeley: An Inventory 1945–1970* by Mary Novik, Montreal, McGill-Queen's University Press, 1973.

Manuscript Collection: Washington University, St. Louis.

Critical Studies: *Measures: Robert Creeley's Poetry* by Ann Mandel, Toronto, Coach House Press, 1974; "Robert Creeley Issue" of *Boundary 2* (Binghamton, New York), spring-fall 1978; *Robert Creeley's Poetry: A Critical Introduction* by Cynthia Edelberg, Albuquerque, University of New Mexico Press, 1978; *Robert Creeley* by Arthur L. Ford, Boston, Twayne, 1978; *The Lost America of Love: Rereading Robert Creeley, Edward Dorn, and Robert Duncan* by Sherman Paul, Baton Rouge, Louisiana State University Press, 1981; *Poet's Prose: The Crisis in American Verse* by Stephen Fredman, Cambridge, Cambridge University Press, 1983; *Robert Creeley: The Poet's Workshops* edited by Carroll F. Terrell, Orono, Maine, National Poetry Foundation, 1984; *Robert Creeley's Life and Work: A Sense of Increment,* edited by John Wilson, Ann Arbor, University of Michigan Press, 1987; *The Lyric and Modern Poetry: Olson, Creeley, Bunting* by Brian Conniff, New York, P. Lang, 1988; *Robert Creeley, Edward Dorn, and Robert Duncan: A Reference Guide* by Willard Fox III, Boston, G.K. Hall, 1989; *Poet's Prose: The Crisis in American Verse* by Stephen Fredman, Cambridge, England, Cambridge University Press, 1990; *Robert Creeley and the Genius of the American Common Place: Together with the Poet's Own Autobiography* by Tom Clark, New York, New Directions, 1993; *Understanding the Black Mountain Poets* by Edward Halsey Foster, Columbia,

University of South Carolina Press, 1994; ''Awake to Particulars: The Prose of Robert Creeley'' by D. Barone, in *Review of Contemporary Fiction,* 15(3), 1995; by Alistair Wisker, in *American Poetry: The Modernist Ideal,* edited by Clive Bloom and Brian Docherty, New York, St Martin's Press, 1995; Robert Creeley issue of *Review of Contemporary Fiction* (Normal, Illinois), 15(3), fall 1995; ''Love and Frangibility: An Appreciation of Robert Creeley'' by Heather McHugh, in *American Poetry Review* (Philadelphia), 26(3), 1997; ''Robert Creeley and Robert Duncan: A World of Contradiction'' by Alice Entwistle, in *Journal of American Studies,* 32(2), 1998; interview in *Salt Hill Journal* (Syracuse, New York), 5, 1998.

Robert Creeley comments:

I write to realize the world as one has come to live in it, thus to give testament. I write to move in words, a human delight. I write when no other act is possible.

* * *

In a note from 1960 Robert Creeley writes, ''I believe in a poetry determined by the language of which it is made . . . I look to words, and nothing else, for my own redemption . . . I mean then *words,* as opposed to content.'' Creeley speaks of words as the abstract expressionist painters spoke of paint. The poems are, as it were, events, physiological events, movements. This can be seen, for example, in ''Water Music'':

The words are a beautiful music.
The words bounce like in water.
Water music,
loud in the clearing

off the boats,
birds, leaves.

They look for a place
to sit and eat—

no meaning,
no point.

This, like Creeley's other poems, does not belong to the same art as, for example, the poems of A.R. Ammons. As it turns out, the terms ''underground'' and ''academic,'' as they were applied to American poetry in the 1950s, marked a profound and enduring division. But Creeley and many of the other so-called underground poets have turned out to make their livings in the universities. The distinction, which has still not been adequately named, is between two kinds of attention. The academic poets, to paraphrase Gertrude Stein, write writing as it is prepared, whereas Creeley writes writing as it is written. Or, in terms suggested by Creeley's contemporary and friend Robert Duncan, academic writing is conventional, while Creeley's writing is formal. Thus, Creeley's art is improvisatory, responsive not to a tradition of poetry but to an immediate engagement with language in the crisis of living. Although the quatrains that are common in Creeley's earlier work superficially resemble a preferred stanzaic convention of the academics, his use of them is utterly different. Creeley gives the convention the same respect (and disrespect) that

jazz musicians such as Charlie Parker and Bud Powell gave the show tunes on which they based their improvisations:

Comes the time when it's later
and onto your table the headwaiter
puts the bill, and very soon after
rings out the sound of lively laughter—

Creeley's is an art not of preparation but of discovery. In this playful, ironic poem, ''The Wicker Basket,'' the implicit closure of the tight rhymes is not a requirement of the convention Creeley has chosen to obey but rather a function of the subject matter. In a statement quoted by Charles Olson in the influential essay ''Projective Verse,'' ''Form is never more than an extension of content.'' This practical poetic advice inverts the conventional wisdom not only of the literary tradition but also of the entire Western philosophical tradition. Obviously related to the existentialist dictum that existence is prior to essence, Creeley's formulation has the advantage of posing the work not in relation to will but in relation to process. In another poem, ''Kore,'' addressed to the feminine archetype, he writes,

It was a lady
    accompanied
by goat men
    leading her.

Her hair held earth.
    Her eyes were dark.
A double flute
    made her move.

''O love,
    where are you
leading
    me now?''

The beautifully articulated, discrete poems from the volumes *For Love* and *Words* (1967), including ''Kore,'' give way in the 1968 *Pieces* to a poetry of pure process. The opening passage is at once the proposition of the work and a demonstration of it:

As real as thinking
wonders created
by the possibility—

forms. A period
at the end of a sentence
which
began it was
into a present,
a presence

saying
something
as it goes.

In *Pieces* Creeley arrives at a certain mastery in which poetry is not assertion but choice. All of the possibilities are available to be used:

Here we are.
There are five
ways to say this.

The poem is no longer the occasion of a masterpiece in which incoherence must be overwhelmed by force. All of the possibilities are available, and thus no ad hoc metaphors or symbolic vaguenesses need be employed. Meaning exists through itself, not by reference to some deferred thing:

—it
it—

For the reader who seeks flash and dazzle in poetry, of course, this will not satisfy, but for those who want poetry to tune itself constantly to the in-itselfness of things, this little measure, marking the rhythm of all to which the impersonal pronoun refers, is an exhilarating salute to the medium poetry modulates.

Creeley is the Mallarmé of the new poetry. He represents this particular poetic possibility at its least compromising. The other Black Mountain poets, notably Charles Olson, Robert Duncan, Denise Levertov, and Edward Dorn, while firmly grounded in the immediacy of the poem itself, are speculative, each in his or her own way addressing the world as a larger construct. When Creeley's poetry is dull, as it sometimes is, it is the dullness of the real, and when it is exciting, as it often is, it is the excitement of the real. In the preface to *Words* (1967) Creeley writes, "Things continue, but my sense is that I have, at best, simply taken place with that fact."

Creeley's influence on the generation of poets who came into their maturity in the 1970s was immense, especially the poets of the language school, including Robert Grenier, Michael Palmer, and Charles Bernstein. They were attracted to the fact that Creeley's work, especially in *Pieces* and after, is nonrepresentational, not fundamentally exemplary of speech or ideal emotion. One might say that Creeley's most characteristic late work is a series of very short pieces—one-liners—engraved on a series of sculptural pieces. They address their readers with questions, conundrums, and assertions from some completely nonpersonal vantage, as if they occur somehow in the air.

—Don Byrd

CRONIN, Anthony

Nationality: Irish. **Born:** Enniscorthy, County Wexford, 28 December 1926. **Education:** Blackrock College, Dublin, 1939–45; University College, Dublin, 1945–48, B.A. **Family:** Married Thérèse Campbell in 1955; two daughters. **Career:** Associate editor, *The Bell,* Dublin, 1952–54; literary editor, *Time and Tide,* London, 1956–58; visiting lecturer, University of Montana, Missoula, 1966–68; poet-in-residence, Drake University, Des Moines, Iowa, 1968–70. Cultural and artistic adviser to the Irish Prime Minister, 1980–83; member, Aosdána. Since 1987 columnist, *Irish Times,* Dublin, 1973–86. **Awards:** Marten Toonder award, 1983. **Agent:** Reg Davis-Poynter, 118 St. Pancras, Chichester, West Sussex PO19 4LH, England. **Address:** Office, 18 Curzon Street, Dublin 8, Ireland.

PUBLICATIONS

Poetry

Poems. London, Cresset Press, 1957.
Collected Poems, 1950–1973. Dublin, New Writers' Press, 1973.
Reductionist Poem. Dublin, Raven Arts Press, 1980.
R.M.S. Titanic. Dublin, Raven Arts Press, 1981.
41 Sonnet-Poems 82. Dublin, Raven Arts Press, 1982.
New and Selected Poems. Dublin, Raven Arts Press, and Manchester, Carcanet, 1982.
Letter to an Englishman. Dublin, Raven Arts Press, 1985.
The End of the Modern World. Dublin, Raven Arts Press, 1989.
Relationships. Dublin, New Island Books, 1994.
The Minotaur: And Other Poems. Dublin, New Island Books, 1999.

Plays

The Shame of It (produced Dublin, 1973). Published in *Dublin Magazine,* 1971

Screenplay: *The Chief,* 1976.

Novels

The Life of Riley. London, Secker and Warburg, and New York, Knopf, 1964.
Identity Papers. Dublin, Irish Writers' Cooperative, 1979.

Other

A Question of Modernity (essays). London, Secker and Warburg, 1966.
Dead As Doornails: A Chronicle of Life. Dublin, Dolmen Press, and London, Calder and Boyars, 1976.
Heritage Now: Irish Literature in the English Language. Dingle, County Kerry, Brandon, 1982; New York, St. Martin's Press, 1983.
An Irish Eye (essays). Dingle, County Kerry, Brandon, 1985.
Ireland: A Week in the Life of a Nation, edited by Red Saunders and Syd Shelton. London, Century Hutchinson, 1986.
Art for the People? Dublin, Raven Arts Press, 1988.
No Laughing Matter: The Life and Times of Flann O'Brien. London, Grafton, 1989.
Samuel Beckett: The Last Modernist. London, HarperCollins, 1996; New York, HarperCollins, 1997.

Editor, *The Courtship of Phelim O'Toole* by William Carleton. London, New English Library, 1962.

*

Manuscript Collection: University of Texas, Austin.

Critical Studies: "The Disinherited Muse" by Michael Kane, in *The Dublin Magazine* (Dublin), July 1970; "A Vision of Reality" by Paul Durcan, in *Structure* (Dublin), 2(2), 1973; "Anthony Cronin: Artistic Essences" by Anthony Burgess, in *In Dublin* (Dublin), 17 December 1982; by R. Tillinghast, in *New Criterion* (New York), 17(1), 1998.

Anthony Cronin comments:

Fortunately for us all, there is a lot of free-floating poetry in the world. The poet's object is to trap some of this floating poetry, to bottle it you could say. But such poetry is not always immediately recognizable in its raw state. One person's floating poetry may be another person's poisonous fog. Only after it has been successfully bottled will others recognize it as poetry: Baudelaire's urban imagery, Yeats's phases of the moon, Eliot's ignobilities, Auden's pumping engines.

Most of the floating poetry of the world has never been bottled by anybody, but those who write poetry are generally so responsive to the potency of their predecessors' bottled products that they incline to overlook their own most immediately to-hand raw material. They go on searching for and bottling that which others have already made unmistakably their own rather than that which is under their noses.

One of the best things about being at it for some time is that you begin to recognize more quickly where your own poetry is not to be found, however much you think it should be, and where it is, however unpromising, unworthy, and unpoetic the raw stuff may seem to others. The bottling process involves bringing this free-floating poetry into combination with the inherent poetry of words so that it undergoes a chemical change that will enable others ultimately to recognize it for what it is. But one has to do this in such a way that it does not leak, or explode, or lose its efficacy. And that of course is the difficulty.

*　　*　　*

Anthony Cronin's poetic career has been molded by an ambition to combine the political and philosophical in his work. He is a philosopher by nature, and his effort to understand both his own country and the modern world is chronicled in his poetry. He has resisted Irish categories, distrusting the peasant mold and the society created by ''peasant proprietors,'' both commercial and academic. Therefore, he has made poetry on a grand scale and shunned the local and the precious. ''You could put anything into poems—one's attitudes about society, one's feelings about religion, even about art and literature, why not?'' he said to Fintan O'Toole in an interview. The great pleasure of his work then is in its broad sweep:

> For the heart cannot rest among the ill-considered
>   spaces of the suburbs
> Where the Spring wind twitches the bushes
> And the fearful but ambitious families live, each
>   behind its fence,
> Nor among the high-rise towers which have size
>   without permanence
> And are homes without reassurance.

A constant search for some believable artistic and political pattern has produced Cronin's best works, *R.M.S. Titanic* and *The End of the Modern World.* In a preface to the former work Paul Durcan wrote that ''R.M.S. Titanic stands in relation to 20th-Century Western Society as does *The Deserted Village* to 18th-Century Western Society; in proportion and scale, in tenor and scope . . .'' Cronin himself has said that the immediate inspiration for the poem was the film *A Night to Remember,* with Kenneth More as Third Officer Lightoller. Within the narrative of the *Titanic*'s sinking Cronin has woven oral antipapist slogans, traditional songs, and general social history: ''Sick in the bilboes of the world the poor /

Cling to each other . . .'' The *Titanic*'s sinking confirms the poet's unease about Western society as a class-ridden vessel is wrecked at the very nadir of modern arrogance: ''The lights were suddenly darkened, / Bringing the consciousness of error.''

Cronin's later work continues the exploration of anxiety and political decline. In his *Irish Times* essays and in books like the novel *Identity Papers* and *A Question of Modernity,* a collection of essays, he ventilates his philosophical positions. He speaks out against tyranny of every kind with an almost undergraduate fearlessness. Contrary to what his enemies have said, Cronin is his own man. Like many socialists, he has attached himself to popular-front personalities as a method of immediately influencing Irish society. There are few cultural commentators in Ireland with Cronin's combination of Joycean learning and Malraux-like pragmatism, and there are no literary critics capable of understanding the creativeness of his involvement in cultural politics. It is strange that those who are brought up on the poems of Yeats, the poet who was duty bound to his country and ''the management of men,'' cannot make the imaginative leap required to understand Cronin's work in government. Of course, like all things in Ireland, there is a great deal of personal envy involved when peers judge Cronin's work.

In his book-length sonnet sequence *The End of the Modern World* Cronin gathers up all of the material of thirty years of thought, combines all of his reading in European philosophy and history, and tats the lot into an autobiographical sonnet web. He focuses upon personal aspects of world events, upon artists as witnesses: Baudelaire, de Sade, Rilke, Gauguin, Yeats, Elvis Presley. Poetry, or rather the comprehending artist as witness, is the hero of the sequence. The poet's personal life breaks through as an antidote to grand gestures:

> I joined the NUJ. I wrote long pieces
> About the need of state support for artists,
> Tried to define an order in which art
> Might find itself the breath of common being.

In keeping with Cronin's fearlessness, the sequence is an ambitious one. It closes with a series of sonnets that are wholly concerned with art, with Gauguin and Van Gogh. The last poem presents us with an image of Manhattan as ''meaningless, astonishing and simple.'' As always, the cast of Cronin's mind is philosophical. His prosody is often awkward, and there is a sameness in his verbal technique, but his poems soar with the helium of ideas. It is through complex speculation that he has escaped the literary meanness of Ireland.

—Thomas McCarthy

CRONIN, Jeremy

Nationality: South African. **Born:** 1949. **Education:** University of Cape Town; the Sorbonne, Paris, M.A. in philosophy. **Career:** Lecturer in philosophy and politics department, University of Cape Town, until his 1976 arrest and imprisonment for having carried out African National Congress underground work; released from prison in 1983 and spent three years in exile in London and Lusaka before returning to South Africa in 1990. Member of the executive, South African Communist Party. **Awards:** Ingrid Jonker prize, 1984, for *Inside.*

PUBLICATIONS

Poetry

Inside. Johannesburg, Ravan Press, 1984; London, Cape, 1987.
Even the Dead: Poems, Parables, and a Jeremiad. Bellville, South Africa, Mayibuye Books, 1997.
Inside & Out: Poems from Inside and Even the Dead. Cape Town, David Philip, and London, Global, 1999.

Other

Ideologies of Politics. Cape Town, Oxford University Press, 1975.

*

Critical Studies: "Inside" by Stephen Gray, in *Index on Censorship* (London), 13(3), June 1984; "South African Prison Literature" by Sheila Roberts, in *Ariel* (Calgary, Alberta), 16(2), April 1985; "Written Poetry for Performance" by Peter Horn, in *Emerging Literatures,* edited by Reingard Nethersole, Bern, Switzerland, Peter Lang, 1990; "Confession and Solidarity in the Prison Writing of Breyten Breytenbach and Jeremy Cronin" by David Schalkwyk, in *Research in African Literatures* (Bloomington), 25(1), spring 1994; by B. Harlow, in *Race & Class,* 40(1), 1998; "Inside Out: Jeremy Cronin's Lyrical Politics" by Brian Macaskill, in *Writing South Africa: Literature, Apartheid, and Democracy, 1970–1995,* edited by Derek Attridge and Rosemary Jolly, Cambridge, England, Cambridge University Press, 1998.

*   *   *

Jeremy Cronin's poems address the relation between the public and the private, keenly rearticulating a tension common to contemporary South African literature: the disparity, perhaps only an ostensible disparity, of demands for revolutionary struggle on the one hand and aspirations for a more private aesthetic on the other. Charged in 1976 under the Terrorism Act for his participation in the then banned African National Congress, Cronin was sentenced to seven years' imprisonment, part of which he served with death row inmates at a maximum security prison. In an interview with Stephen Gray after his release in 1983 Cronin expressed how incarceration freed him from fears that a lyricism "concentrated largely on subjective feelings and emotions" is self-indulgent in the context of oppression: "one of the advantages of being in prison, at least for me, was that I suddenly felt that it wasn't such an indulgence to be able to write about my own personal feelings; what I was experiencing in prison was to a large extent the effect of the apartheid system, of which I too was a minor victim" (*Index on Censorship*).

Inside, Cronin's volume of poems illegally recorded in prison and either smuggled out or memorized for later reworking, bears testimony in its strongest constituents to a surprising symbiosis of autobiography, lyricism, narrative, oral performance, and political commitment. The sense of surprise the volume evokes begins with some of the thematic turns of the title of the collection. "Inside," of course, refers in one sense to the documentation of solidarity with political prisoners inside a contaminated penal system: "Every time they cage a bird / the sky shrinks. A little" ("For Comrades in

Solitary Confinement"). But "inside" also refers to the autobiographical interiority of love poems written for the wife who died while Cronin was imprisoned, an interiority that fuels the lyricism of such poems as "A Prayer in Search of Beads," in which the function of a rosary's mnemonic beads—to recall words of spiritual praise—is substantiated by inversion, since words now seek to invoke a carnal palpability:

> *Un zip . . . Un zip* I intone
> fumbling with its sounds
> as if I hoped to touch
> in that word, bump, bump,
> the tingling, the warm
> rosary down your spine.

While the conjunction of these two senses of "inside" is not in itself exceptional, the linkages Cronin effects ring delicately true. For instance, consider "when to say plainly: / 'I love you' / is also / a small act / of solidarity with all the others" ("Itchy with its . . ."); "That's better, she says, but / Why all this delicate nature stuff? It wasn't / A flower that taught you how to drive" ("A Love Poem"); or "Your death, my wife, / one crime they managed / not to perpetrate / on the day that you died" ("I Saw Your Mother"). What remains exceptional in the coupling of the personal and institutionalized senses of "inside" operative in *Inside* is that the titular metaphor of the collection turns out to refer neither to private lyricism nor to public politics in any disjunctive sense. More than merging the private with the political, *Inside* turns inside outward, to a physical or sometimes metaphysical "outside" that the landscape and nature poems especially show to be contiguous with the inside. This can be seen, for example, in "Chapman's Peak," a love poem to the mountains that mark what was once known as the Cape of Good Hope, rendered in the poem as a figure of freedom, or in "Chameleon," the "confuser of nature's / metaphysical divides" that the poem addresses, having seen "you / finally old with age / tiptoe to the end / turn a deep brown and wear / your own death / like another disguise."

Despite the dangers of sentimentalism and ideological dissimulation that might be expected to attend a project like Cronin's, dangers that do threaten some of the poems, the turning inside out, or metamorphoses, from isolation and despair to community and hope typically produce a remarkable record of resilience and beauty. Refusing to be limited by constrictions of the present, these poems look with respect to the past and with hope to the future, making their linguistic insides serve materialist hopes for a world outside. In metapoetic fashion several of the poems explicitly conjure attempts "to prise carefully / sound / from sound / to honour by speaking / (and sometimes to discard) / . . . shells of meaning / left in our mouths / by thousands of years of / human occupation" ("Cave-Site"). Others offer themselves as a litany to and for the tongue ("tchareep tchareep tchareep / Protrusible Shadow / Tree of Tastebuds / kree-kree-kree-kree / sssszzzz / from this jungle of unmapped sounds / you arise / Elastic Denizen" ["Litany"]) or link a mountain spring to speech ("dropping dental, lateral / Clicking in its palate") and then to the flow of history, agriculture, and industrial labor, all to identify a river in "The River That Flows through Our Land."

The river that flows through the land Cronin shares with his fellow South Africans is, as the poem insists, "a river that carries many tongues in its mouth." Although Cronin's tongue has been schooled partly by international voices—by poets like Seamus Heaney and César Vallejo and by the semiologists and theorists of Marxism who inform his critical essays on culture—its dexterity has more profoundly been coached by the many tongues of South Africa, not only by those of Mongane Serote, Mafika Gwala, and other performance poets and by the metaphysical poems of Douglas Livingston, say, but also by the rhythms of countless everyday voices inside and outside prison. To these voices, many and diverse, Cronin's poems remain true as they humbly struggle ''to learn how to speak / With the voices of this land.''

—Brian Macaskill

CROSSLEY-HOLLAND, Kevin (John William)

Nationality: British. **Born:** Mursley, Buckinghamshire, 7 February 1941. **Education:** Bryanston School; St. Edmund Hall, Oxford, M.A. (honors) in English language and literature 1962. **Family:** Married Linda Marie Waslien; two sons and two daughters by previous marriages. **Career:** Editor, Macmillan publishers, London, 1962–71; Gregory Fellow, University of Leeds, 1969–71; talks producer, BBC, London, 1972; editorial director, Victor Gollancz publishers, London, 1972–77; English lecturer, University of Regensburg, 1978–80. General editor, Mirror of Britain series, André Deutsch publishers, London, from 1975; editorial consultant, Boydell and Brewer publishers, Woodbridge, Suffolk, 1983–89. Lecturer in English, Tufts in London program, 1967–78; Arts Council Fellow in English, Winchester School of Art, 1983, 1984; Visiting Fulbright Professor of English, St. Olaf College, Northfield, Minnesota, 1987–88, 1989–90. Chair Literature Panel, Eastern Arts Association, 1986–89; trustee and chair, Friends of Wingfield College, 1989; Endowed Chair in Humanities and Fine Arts, University of St. Thomas, St. Paul, Minnesota, 1990–95. Since 1998 co-founder and chair, Poetry-next-the-Sea. **Awards:** Arts Council award, 1968, 1977, 1978; Library Association Carnegie Medal, 1986; Nottinghamshire book award, 1999; fellow, Royal Society of Literature. **Agent:** Rogers Coleridge and White, 20 Powis Mews, London W11 1JN. **Address:** Clare Cottage, Burnham Market, Norfolk PE31 8HE, England.

PUBLICATIONS

Poetry

On Approval. London, Outposts, 1961.
My Son. London, Turret, 1966.
Alderney: The Nunnery. London, Turret, 1968.
Confessional. Frensham, Surrey, Sceptre Press, 1969.
Norfolk Poems. London, Academy, 1970.
A Dream of a Meeting. Frenshman, Surrey, Sceptre Press, 1970.
More Than I Am. London, Steam Press, 1971.
The Wake. Richmond, Surrey, Keepsake Press, 1972.
The Rain-Giver and Other Poems. London, Deutsch, 1972.
Petal and Stone. Knotting, Bedfordshire, Sceptre Press, 1975.
The Dream-House and Other Poems. London, Deutsch, 1976.
Between My Father and My Son. Minneapolis, Black Willow Press, 1982.

Time's Oriel and Other Poems. London, Hutchinson, 1983.
Above the Springline. London, Francis Kyle Gallery, 1986.
Waterslain and Other Poems. London, Hutchinson, 1986.
The Painting-Room and Other Poems. London, Century Hutchinson, 1988.
East Anglian Poems. Colchester, Jardine, 1988.
Oenone in January. Llandogo, Old Stile Press, 1988.
New and Selected Poems 1965–1990. London, Hutchinson, 1991.
Eleanor's Advent. Llandogo, Old Stile Press, 1992.
The Language of Yes. London, Enitharmon, and Chester Springs, Pennsylvania, Dufour, 1996.
Poems from East Anglia. London, Enitharmon, 1997.

Plays

The Green Children (libretto), music by Nicola LeFanu (produced London, 1990).
The Wildman (libretto), music by Nicola LeFanu (produced London, 1995).
The Wuffings, with Ivan Cutting (produced London, 1997). London, Runetree Press, 1999.

Other (for children)

Havelok the Dane. London, Macmillan, 1964; New York, Dutton, 1965.
King Horn. London, Macmillan, 1965; New York, Dutton, 1966.
The Green Children. London, Macmillan, 1966; New York, Seabury Press, 1968.
The Callow Pit Coffer. London, Macmillan, 1968; New York, Seabury Press, 1969.
Wordhoard: Anglo-Saxon Stories, with Jill Paton Walsh. London, Macmillan, and New York, Farrar Straus, 1969.
The Pedlar of Swaffham. London, Macmillan, 1971; New York, Seabury Press, 1972.
The Sea-Stranger. London, Heinemann, 1973; New York, Seabury Press, 1974.
The Fire-Brother. London, Heinemann, and New York, Seabury Press, 1975.
Green Blades Rising: The Anglo-Saxons. London, Deutsch, 1975; New York, Seabury Press, 1976.
The Earth-Father. London, Heinemann, 1976.
The Wildman. London, Deutsch, 1976.
The Dead Moon and Other Tales from East Anglia and the Fen Country. London, Deutsch, 1982.
Beowulf. Oxford, Oxford University Press, 1982.
Tales from the Mabinogion, with Gwyn Thomas. London, Gollancz, 1984.
Axe-Age, Wolf-Age: A Selection from the Norse Myths. London Deutsch, 1985.
Storm. London, Heinemann, 1985.
British Folk Tales: New Versions. London and New York, Orchard, 1987; selections as *Boo!, Dathera Dad, Piper and Pooka,* and *Small-Tooth Dog,* London, Orchard, 4 vols., 1988.
The Quest for Olwen, with Gwyn Thomas. Cambridge, Lutterworth Press, 1988.
Wulf. London, Faber, 1988.
Under the Sun and Over the Moon. London, Orchard, and New York, Putnam, 1989.

Sleeping Nanna. London, Orchard, 1989; New York, Ideal, 1990.

Sea Tongue. London, BBC Publications, 1991.

Tales from Europe. London, BBC Publications, 1992.

Long Tom and the Dead Hand. London, Deutsch, 1992.

The Labours of Herakles. London, Orion, 1993.

The Green Children. London, Oxford University Press, 1994.

The Old Stories: Tales from East Anglia and the Fen County. Cambridge, Colt Books, 1997.

Short! A Book of Very Short Stories. London, Oxford University Press, 1998.

The King Who Was and Will Be. London, Orion, and as *King Arthur and His Court,* New York, Dutton, 1999.

Other

Pieces of Land: Journeys to Eight Islands. London, Gollancz, 1972.

The Norse Myths: A Retelling. London, Deutsch, and New York, Pantheon, 1980.

The Stones Remain: Megalithic Sites of Britain, photographs by Andrew Rafferty. London, Rider, 1989.

Editor, *Running to Paradise: An Introductory Selection of the Poems of W.B. Yeats.* London, Macmillan, 1967; New York, Macmillan, 1968.

Editor, *Winter's Tales for Children 3.* London, Macmillan, 1967.

Editor, *Winter's Tales 14.* London, Macmillan, 1968.

Editor, with Patricia Beer, *New Poetry 2.* London, Arts Council, 1976.

Editor, *The Faber Book of Northern Legends [Northern Folktales]* (for children). London, Faber, 2 vols., 1977–80.

Editor, *The Riddle Book* (for children). London, Macmillan, 1982.

Editor, *Folk-Tales of the British Isles.* London, Folio Society, 1985; New York, Pantheon, 1988.

Editor, *The Oxford Book of Travel Verse.* Oxford and New York, Oxford University Press, 1986.

Editor, *Northern Lights: Legends, Sagas and Folk-Tales.* London, Faber, 1987.

Editor, *Medieval Lovers: A Book of Days.* London, Century Hutchinson, and New York, Weidenfeld and Nicolson, 1988.

Editor, *Medieval Gardens: A Book of Days.* London, Garamond, and New York, Rizzoli, 1990.

Editor, *Peter Grimes: The Poor of the Borough.* London, Folio Society, 1990.

Editor, *The Young Oxford Book of Folk-Tales.* London, Oxford University Press, 1998.

Editor, with Lawrence Sail, *The New Exeter Book of Riddles.* London, Enitharmon, 1999.

Translator, *The Battle of Maldon and Other Old English Poems,* edited by Bruce Mitchell. London, Macmillan, and New York, St. Martin's Press, 1965.

Translator, *Beowulf.* London, Macmillan, and New York, Farrar Straus, 1968.

Translator, *Storm and Other Old English Riddles* (for children). London, Macmillan, and New York, Farrar Straus, 1970.

Translator, *The Exeter Riddle Book.* London, Folio Society, 1978; as *The Exeter Book of Riddles,* London, Penguin, 1979.

Translator, *The Anglo-Saxon World.* Woodbridge, Suffolk, Boydell Press, 1982; New York, Barnes and Noble, 1983.

Translator, with Susanne Lugert, *The Fox and The Cat: Animal Tales from Grimm.* London, Andersen Press, 1985; New York, Lothrop, 1986.

Translator, *The Wanderer.* Colchester, Jardine, 1986.

Translator, *The Seafarer.* Llandogo, Old Stile Press, 1987.

Translator, *The Old English Elegies.* London, Folio Society, 1988.

*

Manuscript Collections: Brotherton Collection, University of Leeds; Lillian H. Smith and Osborne Collections, Toronto Public Library.

Critical Study: "Word-Formation and Poetic Language: Non-Lexicalized Nominal Compounds in the Poetry of Kevin Crossley-Holland" by Jean Boase-Beier, in *Functionalism in Linguistics,* edited by Rene Dirven and Vilem Fried, Amsterdam, Benjamins, 1987.

Kevin Crossley-Holland comments:

(1974) If the society reflected in Old English poetry now seems alien, many of its moods are wholly familiar, essentially English: an out-and-out heroism, a dogged refusal to surrender, a love of the sea, an enjoyment of melancholy, nostalgia. In translating it, my staple diet has been a nonsyllabic four-stress line controlled by light alliteration. There are plenty of cases, though, where I have not conformed to this pattern; my concern has been to echo rather than slavishly to imitate the originals. My diction inclines to the formal, though it certainly is less formal than that of the Anglo-Saxon poets; it seemed to me important at this time to achieve truly accessible versions of these poems that eschewed the use of archaisms, inverted word orders, and all "poetic" language. I have not gone out of my way to avoid words that spring from Latin roots, but the emphasis has fallen naturally on words derived from Old English. My translations are, I believe, faithful by and large to the letter of the originals, but it is the mood I have been after. And if I have not caught anything of it, then I have not succeeded in my purpose.

*   *   *

In Kevin Crossley-Holland one encounters a poet whose vision covers a wide sweep of history, one to whom remote past and immediate present reveal themselves as a continuous, related process. He is an accomplished translator of Old English literature, and his work demonstrates a definite kinship with the Anglo-Saxon poets and an admiration for the traditional virtues embodied in their writings. The qualities of rugged individualism, stoical endurance, loyalty, and truthfulness appear constantly in his poems, celebrated in a hard, laconic style pruned of all superfluities. Crossley-Holland has a storyteller's gifts, and such works as "Dead Moon," a retelling of East Anglian folktales, or his superb version of *Beowulf* for younger readers are proof of his ability. As a poet, he uses language that is at once spare and richly descriptive, with an inspired use of alliteration that is rendered effective in contemporary as well as historical contexts. In common with earlier writers, he is aware of the unyielding strength of the earth and of those bleak landscapes where man must either adapt or struggle to survive. Poems like "Hills" and "Fortification" emphasize the harshness of nature, its intractability to man, and his efforts to change it: "No little people come out of that hill. / It is gaunt grey whale. / Taking light, killing it, offering nothing.'' Yet for all their grimness, Crossley-Holland sees these forbidding regions as places of magic and is irresistibly drawn to them, regarding them as in some way essential to his own fulfillment and growth: ''Yet here I come. Here alone I cannot sham. / The place insists that I know who I am.''

This image of wasteland as heartland is further reinforced in Crossley-Holland's collections *The Painting-Room and Other Poems, Waterslain and Other Poems,* and *East Anglian Poems.* The last two works in particular reaffirm the poet's spiritual identification with the bare, marshy Norfolk coast, where land and sea merge uneasily together at the mercy of fierce winds and tides. Crossley-Holland's vision of his adopted homeland is tough and unsentimental, but this does not prevent him from finding beauty there: ''The blue hour ends, this world / floats on a great stillness. / / I can only guess where marsh / finishes and sky begins, / / each grows out of the other.'' Yet even here danger lurks, the tide encroaching slowly to drown the last outposts of land, as when in ''Shadows'' the poet watches the sun set over the marsh: ''O most loved when almost lost, / This most uncommon common place, / / Still at dark mysterious, / My sea-threatened wilderness.'' Making frequent use of half rhymes and tersely worded couplets, Crossley-Holland celebrates the elemental, untamed wasteland as something set apart from human life, a force that defies and outlasts man but at the same time continues to exercise a compelling hold upon him. Again and again he is drawn back to ''this flux, this anchorage,'' which fuels his own growth as a writer: ''Here you watch, you write, you tell the tides. / / You walk clean into the possible.''

Practical and physical in his approach, an amateur archaeologist collecting history's evidence, Crossley-Holland has an outward toughness countered by his sensitivity when dealing with human relationships, the tenderness toward loved ones shown in such poems as ''Rapids'' or ''A Wreath.'' He loves riddles, and humor surfaces occasionally in his work, as seen, for example, by his wry appraisal of three pretty archaeology students in ''A Small Ritual.'' Able to portray the acts of heroes when required, he is also wary of hymning their glories. ''At Mycenae,'' with its evocation of shepherds and flocks untroubled by the strife of gods or kings, reaffirms his commitment to more common lives. His writing concentrates on the universal themes of love and death, loneliness and exile, whether that of the Saxon ''Wanderer,'' or the aging survivor of the British Raj in ''Postcards from Kodai.'' Crossley-Holland's poems sometimes appear to compose themselves from a mass of fragments, the sharply observed images coalescing to form a distinctive whole. With equal assurance he presents visions of bare hillsides and remote marshlands, the reflections of a monk in pursuit of salvation, the terror of an old woman faced with death. In ''Neenie'' the random, disconnected utterances of his dying grandmother are made to take on the nature of a revelation: ''I listen and think you are telling something / Greater than its parts, a breath and sum / of life itself, the ego dispossessed.''

In Crossley-Holland's collections *The Language of Yes* and *Poems from East Anglia* love of family and community are further confirmed in such poems as ''Still Life'' and ''Eleanor with Field Flowers,'' while elsewhere the poet ranges wider with tributes to the long-vanished Anasazi women of the American Southwest or, in ''Alfred in the Alps,'' with visions of a Saxon king at a moment of crisis. Crossley-Holland calls up personal images and memories from references on a Victorian tithe map, hears music in unofficial venues during the Aldeburgh Festival, and visualizes an overgrown field as a Viking war host. His poetry reflects his abiding distrust of words for their own sake, the hollow promises of politicians denounced in the title poem of *The Language of Yes.* Instead he strives to reach and release the core of meaning that lies beneath sound or speech, striking resonances from harsh Old English materials, the ''earth-words'' evoked in ''Translation Workshop: Grit and Blood,'' where he essays a translation of ''The Battle of Maldon.'' Never losing his wry humor, he pokes fun at himself in ''The Fox and the Poet,'' where he and his literary fellows are seen as a kind of vampire: ''They are shape-changers. They dream and devour. / They translate you and take away your power.'' All the same, Crossley-Holland's is an intent, serious quest whose purpose is effectively stated in ''One End of Singing'' as a search for ''not what words signify, but what they are, / each itself, each singular.''

Poems from East Anglia brings together items from seven collections with some previously unpublished poems and celebrates the spiritual landscape that pervades so much of its author's writing. Central to it are the twenty-five poems from *Waterslain,* snapshot portraits of locations, characters, tales, and memories through which the atmosphere of the vast, bleak stretch of marsh and sky echoes with hypnotic power. Again Crossley-Holland creates affectionate family pictures and ponders the nature of his work, deciding that unease and discomfort are essential to his muse. ''To the Edge,'' a new poem that ends the collection, reminds the reader that the poet's quest continues: ''To an innocent page, damp and salty, and this fitful / pen / / To the edge that's always uncomfortable.''

—Geoff Sadler

CROZIER, Andrew

Nationality: British. **Born:** 1943. **Education:** Cambridge University, M.A.; University of Essex, Wivenhoe, Ph.D. **Career:** Reader in English, University of Sussex, Brighton. **Address:** Arts Building, University of Sussex, Brighton, Sussex BN1 9QN, England.

PUBLICATIONS

Poetry

Loved Litter of Time Spent. Buffalo, Sumbooks, 1967.
Train Rides: Poems from '63 and '64. Pampisford, Cambridgeshire, R., 1968.
Walking on Grass. London, Ferry Press, 1969.
In One Side and Out the Other, with John James and Tom Phillips. London, Ferry Press, 1970.
Neglected Information. Sidcup, Kent, Blacksuede Boot Press, 1973.
The Veil Poem. Providence, Rhode Island, Burning Deck, 1974.
Printed Circuit. Cambridge, Street, 1974.
Seven Contemporary Sun Dials, with Ian Potts. Brighton, Ian Potts, 1975.
Pleats. Bishops Stortford, Hertfordshire, Great Works, 1975.
Duets. Guildford, Surrey, Circle Press, 1976.
Residing. Belper, Derbyshire, Aggie Weston's, 1976.
High Zero. Cambridge, Street, 1978.
Were There. London, Many Press, 1978.

Utamaro Variations. London, Tetrad, 1982.
All Where Each Is. Edinburgh, Agneau 2, 1985.
Ghosts in the Corridor, with Donald Davie and C.H. Sisson. London, Paladin, 1992.

Other

Editor, with Tim Longville, *A Various Art.* Manchester, Carcanet, 1987.
Editor, *Poems 1923–1941*, by Carl Rakosi. Los Angeles, Sun and Moon Press, 1995.
Editor, *Poems and Adolphe 1920,* by John Rodker. Manchester, Carcanet, 1996.

*   *   *

When Alan Halsey of the Poetry Bookshop in Haye-on-Wye handed us the 310-page collection of Andrew Crozier's poetry, we were immediately impressed by the effectively condensed, extraordinarily pertinent title—*All Where Each Is.* This notion (*Begriff*) moves through his oeuvre. The collection literally begins with ''each'' and ends with ''all.'' The first poem starts with the isolated individual:

Man's energies have such bounds
he turns in

The last word in the book, however, is ''together''—''go separately together.'' The sense of ''each'' and ''all'' is central to a poet and an editor.

As an editor and as a collaborator, Crozier has provided occasions for poetry by others, and generosity informs his own poetry. In many collections over the years his poems move from the I outward to bestow a sense of sharing.

What do I know? I know that I perceive, and the process of perception moves from the I to the outer world. The process is complex, as the poem ''Marriage'' demonstrates with a beautifully strange, ironic sheen. More directly, perhaps, there is

More to be learnt
looking from the window of a train
riding through north London into the fields
than from prolonged scrutiny of the
others in the buffet car.

Velocity is a derivative of space with respect to time, or the motion of space itself involves time: ''The Shores of Romney Marsh / have probably been here since the sea / withdrew . . .'' The perception of motion involves the perception of space, space involves the past, and perceiving the past brings us back to the present or, in the words of Charles Olson, ''The chain of memory is resurrection.'' From the past, the present shore, the slope was

. . . sheltering me as I walked
along its contour to enter Rye
across the sluice
from the other side.

How can I tell what I know? What I know belongs to how I know, and how involves the act of telling, which changes through time:

Yes that's true very good
more beautiful
and no less true
than ever before.

Say it again
You cannot say it again

The I implies everybody. Listening and seeing re-create the outer world, as in ''Grand Hotel'':

The three old men are silent
listening to the sound of laughter
happy voices rise from lighted windows
the murmured song of the sea
blends with the gramophone.

Many of Crozier's collections are beautifully printed, and this is particularly true of *Utamaro Variations,* printed in 18-point Baskerville on Somerset Cream paper, with a strict orthogonality of lines in Ian Tyson's art creating an interesting dialogue of inner spaces and outer space. The poems move in an unexpected terza rima, recalling the poet of light and of moving light:

The colours break out and float
In the appearance of a world
Reflecting the shadows of a boat

As though an inner life unfurled
Like waves and eddying water
In a photograph its edges curled

With age . . .

The ''inner life'' has to move out, has to be ''unfurled.'' Perception moves, and awareness of motion is perception, the motion of ''curled'' from age:

The End of a Row of Conjectural Units

Formerly the pure element of itself, it might last forever and seem as indistinct as the glare of the sun on a white wall before the thought of shadows has fallen across it; as if the flood of natural light surfacing the bricks, the cement, and paintwork had absorbed them all in unimpeded descent and could keep on going: absolute space.

In 1967 Stephen Rodefer, a poet whose ''inner life unfurled'' has continued to give birth to poems, noticed what Crozier essentially shares with the reader:

What you see is not what you know. And what you know you may not, you probably do not, understand. But you do know it. You have it. You carry it with you. It is what is yours most dearly.

—William Sylvester

CROZIER, Lorna

Also writes as Lorna Uher. **Nationality:** Canadian. **Born:** Swift Current, Saskatchewan, 24 May 1948. **Education:** University of Saskatchewan, Saskatoon, B.A. 1969; University of Alberta, Edmonton, M.A. 1980. **Family:** Lives with the poet Patrick Lane, *q.v.* **Career:** High school English teacher, Glaslyn, Saskatchewan, 1970–72, and Swift Current, 1972–77; creative writing teacher, Saskatchewan Summer School of the Arts, Fort San, 1977–81; writer-in-residence, Cypress Hills Community College, Swift Current, 1980–81, Regina Public Library, Saskatchewan, 1984–85, and University of Toronto, 1989–90; director of communications, Saskatchewan Department of Parks, Culture, and Recreation, Regina, 1981–83; broadcaster and writer, Canadian Broadcasting Corporation Radio, 1986; guest instructor, Banff School of Fine Arts, Alberta, 1986, 1987; special lecturer, University of Saskatchewan, 1986–91. Associate professor, 1991–97, and since 1997 professor, University of Victoria, Canada. Vice president, Saskatchewan Writers' Guild, 1977–79; committee president, Saskatchewan Artists' Colony, 1982–84. **Awards:** CBC prize, 1987; Governor General's award for poetry, 1992; Canadian Author's award for poetry, 1992; The League of Canadian Poets' Pat Lowther award, 1992; National Magazine Gold Medal award for poetry, 1996; Mothertongue Chapbook winner, 1996, for *The Transparency of Grief.* **Address:** c/o McClelland and Stewart Inc., 481 University Avenue, Suite 900, Toronto, Ontario M5G 2E9, Canada.

PUBLICATIONS

Poetry

Inside Is the Sky (as Lorna Uher). Saskatoon, Saskatchewan, Thistledown Press, 1976.

Crow's Black Joy (as Lorna Uher). Edmonton, Alberta, NeWest Press, 1978.

No Longer Two People (as Lorna Uher), with Patrick Lane. Winnipeg, Manitoba, Turnstone Press, 1979.

Animals of Fall (as Lorna Uher). Vancouver, Very Stone House, 1979.

Humans and Other Beasts (as Lorna Uher). Winnipeg, Manitoba, Turnstone Press, 1980.

The Weather. Moose Jaw, Saskatchewan, Coteau, 1983.

The Garden Going On without Us. Toronto, McClelland and Stewart, 1985.

Angels of Flesh, Angels of Silence. Toronto, McClelland and Stewart, 1988.

Inventing the Hawk. Toronto, McClelland and Stewart, 1992.

Everything Arrives at the Light. Toronto, McClelland and Stewart, 1995.

The Transparency of Grief. Salt Spring Island, British Columbia, Other Tongue Press, 1996.

A Saving Grace: The Collected Poems of Mrs. Bentley. Toronto, McClelland and Stewart, 1996.

What the Living Won't Let Go. Toronto, McClelland and Stewart, 1999.

Play

If We Call This the Girlie Show, Will You Find It Offensive, with Rex Deverel, Denise Ball, and David Miller (produced Regina, 1984).

Other

Editor, with Gary Hyland, *A Sudden Radiance: Saskatchewan Poetry.* Regina, Saskatchewan, Coteau, 1987.

Editor, with Patrick Lane, *Breathing Fire: The New Generation of Canadian Poets,* Pender Harbour, British Columbia, Harbour Publishers, 1995.

Editor, with Patrick Lane, *The Selected Poems of Alden Nowlan.* Toronto, Anansi, 1995.

*

Critical Studies: Interview by Doris Hillis, in *Prairie Fire,* 6(3), summer 1985; by Nathalie Cooke, in *Canadian Writers and Their Works,* edited by Robert Lecker and others, Toronto, ECW, 1995; ''Phoenix from the Ashes: Lorna Crozier and Margaret Avison'' by Deborah Bowen, in *Canadian Poetry,* 40, spring-summer 1997.

*   *   *

Since her emergence from the so-called Moose Jaw movement in the mid-1970s, Lorna Crozier has earned a significant place in Canadian poetry, not only for the penetrating wit of her poetry and impressive command of satirical skills but also for the depth of perception and feeling she infuses into her work. In later books such as *The Weather, The Garden Going On without Us,* and *Angels of Flesh, Angels of Silence,* Crozier has become a spokesperson for the feminist heterosexual woman, a keen observer not only of the consequences of relationships but also of their dynamics and an apologist for desire, love, and caring.

Crozier is not the typical prairie poet. Her terrain, aside from the use of her native Saskatchewan landscape as a backdrop for poems such as ''The Photograph I Keep of Them'' in *The Garden Going On without Us,* is the realm of metaphysics and the metaphysical complexities of time, place, history, thought, and emotions:

> Behind them the prairies
> tells its spare story of drought.
>
> They tell no stories.
> Not how they feel
> about one another
> or the strange landscape
> that makes them small.
>
> I can write down only this
> for sure:
> they have left the farm
> they are going somewhere.

Poems such as ''The Women Who Survive'' and ''My Aunt's Ghost'' are written in the voice of a small-town Saskatchewan woman, an effort on Crozier's part that reflects a growing movement in Canadian poetry away from a purely physical depiction of external landscape to a more intimate, psychological, and internalized recreation of the voices that inhabit both the inner and outer worlds. As she once noted in an interview, her poems arise out of an ''emotional response to what is going on in the world . . . filtered through my way of seeing things.''

Crozier examines her subjects with the intricacy of a ''freeze-frame philosopher'' who has forsaken pure reason for the culs-de-sac of possibility, political points, and verity of truth through feeling, as in ''A Poem about Nothing'' in *The Garden Going On without Us:*

When the Cree chiefs
signed the treaties on the plains
they wrote X
beside their names.

In English, X equals zero.

While still political in its tone and preoccupation—whether in the sense of sexual politics or, as in the case of ''A Poem about Nothing,'' in the traditional sense—Crozier's work has become more playful. In her later writing she has shown a marked movement away from the dark overtones of her earlier books, when she shared many of the solemn concerns and motivations found in Margaret Atwood's verse. In retrospect the change seems to have taken place with publication of her pivotal *No Longer Two People,* a volume of dialogues between a male and a female poetic anima that she coauthored with Patrick Lane. The book, the result of a reconciliation after a disagreement, took its title from a quote by Picasso: ''They are no longer two people, you see, but forms and colours; forms and colours that have taken on, meanwhile, the idea of two people and preserve the vibration of life.'' *No Longer Two People,* which was unjustly maligned by critics when it appeared, has taken on an important role in Crozier's canon for two reasons. First, it shifted the focus of her work onto the details of the male-female relationship and allowed her to redefine her own femininity and her partner's masculinity within that context, and, second, it brought to her work an idea of ''metamorphosis,'' which has become a key element in her later collections.

''The Penis Poems'' in *Angels of Flesh, Angels of Silence,* for example, or ''The Sex Lives of Vegetables'' in *The Garden Going On without Us* are sequences of poems that approach human sexuality with a partially satirical, partially magical sense of wit and metamorphosis. In ''The Penis Poems'' the male phallus is subjected to a range of speculative possibilities, some historical, some sensual, some mythical, and all humorous. To accomplish this, Crozier has taken up the poetic sequence as her forte, and, as in ''The Foetus Dreams'' in *The Garden Going On without Us,* she explores her subjects by ''taking more than one look at something.'' In this sense Crozier is a refreshingly cinematic poet who offers different angles and variations on the same subject, the same theme, without cumbersome repetition. For her, poetry is not a linear experience but a range of experiences, just as her perception of the prairie, the landscape of her psychological orientation, is not linear or even infinitely horizontal but rather multidimensional, metaphysical, and playfully pliable.

Mythology, both as a literary source and as a model for metamorphosis, has become increasingly important to her work as it represents the impossible within the realm of the possible. Whether she is writing about Icarus or penises, classical mythology or personal biography, the sheer delight that comes from a playful transformation is one of the rewards of Crozier's work. The need to transform, in essence the need to mythologize, to identify and re-create wonder, is at the core of her work, so that her poems ultimately are retellings of known stories, accepted facts, and plotable landscapes. In ''Icarus in the Sea'' from *Angels of Flesh, Angels of Silence,* she concludes,

He is what moves under
green shadows in prairie sloughs,
what nests in blue
reflections in mountain lakes . . .

Icarus of sky and water,
you who know the paths of birds
and spawning fish,
we will think of you
as the one we cannot catch,
the one that keeps us
dreaming, the broken
line, the
Ah!

The same sense of wonder, of making old things new, is extended in Crozier's work to the realm of the domestic, where small everyday objects and tasks are scrutinized with a warmth and sensitivity that lift them above the level of the merely mundane. In the found poem ''Dreaming Domestic,'' in *Angels of Flesh, Angels of Silence,* commonplace dreams are elevated by the sense of possibilities they foretell for the women who dream them:

A young woman dreaming of eating pickles
foretells an unambitious career.
If she dreams of basting meats
she will determine her expectations
by folly and selfishness.

Crozier's images are those of the concrete rather than the abstract world, the temporal rather than the extemporal. When she allows herself excursions into the biography of others, as in such Russian-influenced poems as ''Pavlova'' and ''Nijinsky'' in *The Garden Going On without Us,* it is to explore the details of the everyday lives of her subjects, which in turn humanizes them. It is this sense of humanizing the subject, of making the real more real by making it magical and believable, that gives Crozier's work its life.

—Bruce Meyer

CRUZ, Victor Hernández

Nationality: Puerto Rican. **Born:** Aguas Buenas, 6 February 1949. Immigrated to the United States in 1954. **Education:** Benjamin Franklin High School, New York. **Family:** Divorced; one son and one daughter. **Career:** Editor, *Umbra* magazine, 1967–69; co-founder, East Harlem Gut Theatre, New York, 1968; guest lecturer, University of California, Berkeley, 1970; member of ethnic studies Department, San Francisco State College, 1971–72. Visiting professor, literature department, University of California, San Diego, winter 1993, University of Michigan, Ann Arbor, program in Caribbean culture and literature, winter 1994. Also worked for the San Francisco Art

227

Commission, 1976, and Mission Neighborhood Center, San Francisco, 1981. Founder, with Ishmael Reed, Before Columbus Foundation. **Awards:** Creative Arts Public Service award, 1974; National Endowment for the Arts fellowship, 1980; New York Poetry Foundation award, 1989; Guggenheim award (Latin America and the Caribbean), 1991. **Address:** P.O. Box 1047, Aguas Buenas, Puerto Rico 00703.

PUBLICATIONS

Poetry

Papo Got His Gun. New York, Calle Once, 1966.
Doing Poetry. Berkeley, California, Other Ways, 1968.
Snaps. New York, Random House, 1969.
Mainland. New York, Random House, 1973.
Tropicalization. Berkeley, California, Reed Cannon and Johnson, 1976.
By Lingual Wholes. San Francisco, Momo's Press, 1982.
Rhythm, Content and Flavor: New and Selected Poems. Houston, Arte Publico Press, 1988.
Red Beans. Minneapolis, Minnesota, Coffee House Press, 1991.
Panoramas. Minneapolis, Minnesota, Coffee House Press, 1997.

Other

Editor, with Herbert Kohl, *Stuff: A Collection of Poems, Visions and Imaginative Happenings from Young Writers in Schools—Opened and Closed.* Cleveland, World, 1970.

*

Critical Studies: "Latin Popular Music in the Poetry of Victor Hernández Cruz" by Frances Aparicio, in *MELUS,* 16(1), spring 1990; by Anne C. Bromley, in *American Book Review,* 13(6), February 1992.

Victor Hernández Cruz comments:

I was born via midwife in a small wooden house some two hundred miles from the equatorial line of the planet on the island of Puerto Rico in a small town of agricultural habits, Aguas Buenas. My grandfather Julio, "El Bohemio," was a tobacconist; that is, he rolled cigars. Tobacconists are notorious spinners of tales, and they have a tradition of reading literature out loud while they work. This was my introduction to expression through readers of Cervantes and the Bible in the *chin-chal* (tobacco workshop) and the practitioners of oral poetry—declaimers and the singers of the bolero. When the agricultural system of the island broke down due to bad management, it left a great portion of the interior campesino population displaced. These were my folks, and we became a part of some kind of massive forced migration. We left the mountains with our songs, spiritism, humor, and our Caribbean spaced-out heads and headed toward cities like New York and Chicago. At the age of five I was staring out a window on the Lower East Side of Manhattan, locked in the house until my mother made certain that it was okay to go out while white coconut meat fell frozen from the sky. At the age of fifteen I began to write, feeling a very deep impulse to do so. I really had to balance a lot of worlds together, for I was feeling and looking at the culture of my parents and the new and modern culture of New York, its architecture,

its art, and its fervent intellectual thought. I have been comparing things silently inside myself ever since. I feel like an eternal immigrant, leaving a past and going toward a future. I practice folkloric experimentation and hope that I can rescue the old stories to tell them in the houses of the future.

(1995) Coming from a Caribbean culture, I am at the center of cultural and racial syntheses. This includes psychology, religion, spirituality, music, languages, dances, gestures. It is a great place from which to write and make music because so much of world culture has come through here to be molded and changed. We are truly one of the greatest cosmopolitan centers of the planet. Before leaving to the United States and thus to English, the Spanish of my upbringing was full of Taino words, Arabic and African words. Speaking or writing, it was like making the story of my mestizo body vibrate in the sounds. The language was full of the conquest, slavery, the hacienda, and other forms of *encomiendas,* a Spanish word for "migration." In New York City I came into contact with different forms of English—Yiddish-influenced English, African-American English, all sorts of working-class speech from the great community of immigrants on the Lower East Side of Manhattan. Language for me is always migration and translation. History for me is many epochs and social attitudes, one within the other. Out of all these elements I have forged a poetry that contains both tradition and experiment, a marriage between oral and literate forms, the popular and the cultivated. Writing is a strong individual freedom. The poet deciphers his psychological, emotional, and historical position for himself and others (for language is always a social bridge) within the rhythms of his culture, the culture that he was born into and the culture that he continuously acquires. Writing is making oneself up from what one has toward what one dreams.

* * *

Victor Hernández Cruz, a Puerto Rican émigré and bilingual poet of cultural collisions and fusions, emerged as a vital and distinctive poetic voice during the early 1970s. His is a major voice in the so-called Newyorican school of émigré poets. Key to his work is his use of English in relation to his native Spanish. His early books—*Snaps* and *Mainland*—reflect the immigrant experience with verve, desire, and irony, moving back and forth from Puerto Rico to New York to California: "I am quiet / Still / Like the owls who sit atop / telephone poles."

Cruz's poems move easily in and out of barrio pop song infusions with post-Lorca *odas delire,* an insistence on place and displacement, the graftings of multicultural urban voices and images, and the poet as alien eyes and ears observing and rewriting the world he wanders through. Cruz plays with syntactical and grammatical conventions in both English and Spanish, weaving fascinating bifurcated chaos that he transcends, offering a diffracted synthesis allowing for more complex pleasures.

By Lingual Wholes is a comprehensive collection of Cruz's work and the place where his language play is most contagious and extensive. American and Spanish vernaculars bruise and caress often traditional rhythms and sentiments. The poet sees through the torn world to green paradises of perfection: "The greater cities are / surrounded by woods / Jungles secretly / of America // Behind lights / the green / Green eyes of Tree gods / Rhythm we would call it Puerto Rico / But it doesn't begin to be as real."

—David Meltzer

CULLINAN, Patrick

Nationality: South African. **Born:** Pretoria, 21 May 1932. **Education:** Charterhouse, Surrey; Magdalen College, Oxford, 1950–53, B.A. and M.A. in Italian and Russian 1953. **Career:** Farmer and sawmiller, eastern Transvaal, 1953–79. Since 1963 freelance writer. Co-founder of Bateleur Press; editor, *The Bloody Horse*, 1980–81; lecturer, English department, University of the Western Cape, 1982–92. **Awards:** Olive Schreiner award, 1980; Pringle prize, 1983, 1984, 1990; Sanlam Literary award, 1989. **Address:** Silver Spring, Hout Bay Road, Constantia 7800, South Africa.

PUBLICATIONS

Poetry

The Horizon Forty Miles Away. Johannesburg, Polygraph, 1973.
Today Is Not Different. N.p., 1978.
The White Hall in the Orchard. Cape Town, David Philip, 1984.
Selected Poems 1961–1991. Johannesburg, Artists' Press, 1992.
Selected Poems, 1961–1994. Plumstead, South Africa, Snailpress, 1994.
Transformations. Plumstead, South Africa, Carapace Pets, 1999.

Short Stories

Surprisingly Short Stories. London, Minerva, 1998.

Other

Robert Jacob Gordon 1743–1795: The Man and His Travels at the Cape. Cape Town, Winchester-Struik, 1992.

*

Critical Study: "The Maker and the Job," in *Momentum: On Recent South African Writing,* edited by M.J. Daymond and others, Pietermaritzburg, South Africa, University of Natal Press, 1984.

*   *   *

Patrick Cullinan is unique among South African poets in that his work, though reflecting the country of his birth and the place where he lives, reveals a sophistication and modernism that give it a dimension far beyond the local. This comes from his profound knowledge of the cultures and literatures of Europe and his fluency in Italian, French, and Russian, with consequent influences of Dante, Montale, Rimbaud, and Mandelstam among others. He has also resisted the pressure of fashion, in his view the enemy of art, that would make poetry the servant of politics. His work may therefore survive in the postapartheid South Africa, when much of what his contemporaries have written comes to be filed as sociopolitical history.

Some of this can be explained by Cullinan's origins and unusual upbringing, the irony of which has not been lost on him and which he refers to with wit in such poems as "Sir Tom" and "The Billiardroom." His grandfather Sir Thomas Cullinan, whose name is associated with the famous diamond that is part of the British crown jewels, created a colonial family dynasty with a great fortune from mining and industry. It was an unlikely environment in which to nurture a poet, and Cullinan's father was to show little more than contempt for his son's inclinations. Soon after World War II the son was sent to school at Charterhouse, in England, surprisingly since by that time South Africa's English-speaking elite had ceased to send their children "home" to be educated. Then came Oxford. Cullinan was twenty-one by the time he returned to South Africa. But with his European languages and the works of Europe's literary giants in his baggage he had treasure greater than family diamonds that he would call on in his work over the following years.

Was Cullinan now an exile from Europe or an African? One night in a cottage in the eastern Transvaal, confronted no doubt by the physical power of Africa, he had his answer. "I was an African and always would be," he recalled, "but that I have an enormous amount of Europe in my make-up is something that I would never want to deny." His African identity reveals itself in his poetry not so much as an evocation of the physical Africa, its landscapes, sights, and sounds, as in its history, particularly that of its early explorers and travelers. He has written a fine poem about the eighteenth-century French naturalist and explorer François Le Vaillant. (The Frenchman applied a certain poetic imagination, license even, in describing what he said he saw, which no doubt appealed to his great nephew Charles Baudelaire, who went to the Cape of Good Hope in 1847 and took a look himself.) Robert Jacob Gordon, another explorer of the same period, has long fascinated Cullinan, who spent fourteen years producing an impressive biography on him.

Cullinan, however, is above all a metaphysical poet, as his later poetry clearly shows. His preoccupation is with what one critic called a "modern sense of disquiet," an echo again of Montale and a search for answers to those eternal questions that like-minded poets ask themselves wherever they may be. From this Cullinan reflects upon the nature of poetry, how and why it is written; he writes poems about poems. What also emerges is Cullinan's skill in crafting verse, the infinite pains he takes to pare down his lines to the bare bones of sense and sound, as in some of his haunting love poems.

—Roy Macnab

CUMBERLEGE, Marcus (Crossley)

Nationality: British. **Born:** Antibes, France, 23 December 1938. **Education:** Sherborne School, Dorset; St. John's College, Oxford, B.A. 1961. **Family:** Married 1) Ava Nicole Paranjoti in 1965 (divorced 1972), one daughter; 2) Maria Lefever in 1973. **Career:** Teacher, British Council, Lima, Peru, 1957–58, 1962–63; advertising executive, Ogilvy and Mather, London, 1964–67; advertising assistant, British Travel Authority, London, 1967–68; English teacher, Lycée International, St. Germain-en-Laye, 1968–70. Since 1978 visiting lecturer in poetry and oriental studies, International University of Lugano, Hilversum, and University of Limburg. Since 1976 translator of Flemish tourist literature, West Flanders. Editor, with Scott Rollins, *Dremples,* Amsterdam, 1977. **Awards:** Eric Gregory Award, 1967. **Address:** Eekhoutstraat 42, 8000 Bruges, Belgium.

PUBLICATIONS

Poetry

Oases. London, Anvil Press Poetry, 1968.
Poems for Quena and Tabla. Oxford, Carcanet, 1970.
Running towards a New Life. London, Anvil Press Poetry, 1973.
Firelines. London, Anvil Press Poetry, 1977.
The Poetry Millionaire. Swanage, Dorset, Dollar of Soul Press, 1977.
La Nuit Noire. Bruges, Manufaktuur, 1977.
XX Vriendelijke Vragen. Bruges, Ganzespel, 1977.
Bruges/Brugge, with Owen Davis. Bruges, Orion, 1978.
Northern Lights. Bruges, Manufaktuur, 1981.
Life Is a Flower. Bruges, Drukkerij Setola, 1981.
Vlaamse Fabels. Bruges, Manufaktuur, 1982.
Sweet Poor Hobo. Bruges, Manufaktuur & Babel, 1984.
Things I Cannot Change. Bruges, Limited Editions, 1993.
The Best Is Yet to Be? Bruges, Manufaktuur, 1997.
The Moon, the Blackbird and the Falling Leaf. Bruges, Paper Tiger Press, 1999.
Once I Had a Secret Love. Bruges, Paper Tiger Press, 2000.

*

Critical Study: ''Fur die Schule ungeeignet? 'Horse' von Marcus Cumberlege'' by Inge Leimberg, in *Literatur in Wissenschaft und Unterricht* (Wurzburg, Germany), 20(1), 1987.

Marcus Cumberlege comments:

(1980) Major influences: César Vallejo, the French symbolists, Lorca, Blake, Rilke, Eliot, Yeats. Later influences: Gautier, Pessoa, Van Ostaijen and Flemish expressionism; Basho, Wang Wei, Rumi; Mellie Uyldert and Henri van Praag.

Earlier themes: (1) survival of ''human beings'' in urban society, compassion for the former while satirizing shortcomings of the latter; (2) automatic poetry attempting to situate the poet geographically and define his role as interpreter of mysteries; (3) original poetry in Spanish, French, and Dutch; translation from contemporary Latin American poets. Recent themes: Connemara and West Flanders: haiku; he remains an experimentalist in practice, and his poetry is concerned with changing the quality of life at an environmental level, partly through direct cooperation with musicians and graphic artists. He is conscious of poetry's educational function, and although he treats writing as an act of personal spiritual discipline, he regards his books as an extended physical manifestation of his own personality, seeking through publication to serve, delight, and ultimately enlighten others.

(1985) More recently I began to make free use of Dutch, French, Spanish, and Irish in my original work, with a return to automatic writing.

(1995) Back to haiku and rhyming twelve-line lyrics. One hundred of these published in 1993 in *Things I Cannot Change,* poems (sometimes humorous) based on my recovery from alcoholism and manic depression. I now get great enjoyment and release from my own writing, which has something of a therapeutic quality about it. The use of language is simplified and spontaneous. There is no more striving for perfection.

(2000) Writing my silly little poems, at age sixty, has become second nature to me. This often nocturnal activity is now as inescapable as thought itself and as necessary as breathing. The lyrics in *Firelines* (1977) sometimes took six weeks to compose. Those in *Once I Had a Secret Love* (2000) are often completed in fifteen minutes. Still, the message, or cry, always seems to be urgent and vital.

*   *   *

Marcus Cumberlege had been writing poems for about ten years before the publication of his first major collection, *Running towards a New Life,* in 1973, though his smaller collections, *Oases* and *Poems for Quena and Tabla,* had introduced his work to the public. During this period it seemed that he was working toward the development of an individual voice, experimenting with various styles, ideas, and forms and with the use of language to obtain different effects. The result was that *Running towards a New Life,* covering the whole of the period, gives the impression that his work was a great deal more uneven than it had become by the time of publication.

Sometimes the influences are a little too obvious in the earlier poems—one can identify the Auden style and the Brian Patten manner, for instance—but there is a calm assurance about the later poems in the book, which has a roughly chronological sequence. Nevertheless, whatever the style or tone, Cumberlege has always written civilized verse, work that is witty, sophisticated, and rooted in European poetry, demonstrating a wide reading of classical and modern poetry. The polished couplets of ''Mural for the Country Residence of a Latin American President,'' with its deliberate connection with Eliot's ''Prufrock'' at the beginning, is still one of the best things he has done. His knowledge of technique is remarkable, but his most striking characteristic is a capacity for finding the startlingly apt image or metaphor; when he manages to combine these qualities with a driving theme, he can be superb. In ''There Are Days'' he shows his real potential.

Having worked his way systematically through the relatively long process of experimentation, Cumberlege appears to be reaping the benefit, if one can judge from his second major collection, *Firelines.* The volume is divided into five sections—''The SunDial,'' ''The Ram,'' ''Harmonia's Necklace,'' ''The Murmuring Branches,'' and ''Errisberg''—each with its dedication, epigraph, and poetic style. He exerts a firmer control over material, manipulates language in a more effective manner, and gives more attention to precision of statement, while demonstrating his versatility in a range of styles. The first section is more structured than the rest and more traditionally lyrical—

No South or North. I turn.
Sun breathes, warm as a dog
Chasing sheep into rock. The moon
Thrusts its slane into the bog

—but one might hazard a guess that these poems are from an earlier phase. ''Oasis'' and ''Lord Dunsany'' are, in fact, included in *Oases,* published nine years earlier. One can certainly imagine that Cumberlege would not now be content with the following stanza from ''Hesperides'':

Sun dips a brush in darkness.
The paintbox in the west
Closing, one drop of scarlet
Splashes the robin's breast.

Still, there are some attractive pieces in which the rhyming or half-rhyming pattern lends deceptive simplicity ("Eclipse"):

The river clambers to its source,
Apples awaken as they fall.
Ghosts of the famine stalked our house
And whispered through a moonlit wall.

"The Ram" section, which links astrological symbols and tarot concepts with "fierced-eyed Mrs. Mop," "the Connaught moon," the "Moorish dreams of Potocki," "the Western Buddha," "The House of Opposites," and Saint John, has striking phraseology here and there, but with its slightly surrealistic use of imagery it is likely to be inaccessible to many readers. The most outstanding poems—"The Connemara Cradle," "A Hot Chestnut," "Questions for Goldilocks," "The Perfect Man," and "Coole Park and Ballylee, Winter"—are all collected in the "Harmonia's Necklace" section.

Cumberlege lived part of his childhood in Ireland and later spent some time on the west coast of Ireland. It is not surprising that this experience seems to have made a strong impact upon his poetry. "The Murmuring Branches" section contains his fine translations from the Spanish of Lorca (including "The Faithless Wife") and Carlos Bousoño, the Flemish of Herman Leys, and the French of Jacques Prévert.

—Howard Sergeant

CURNOW, Allen

Nationality: New Zealander. **Born:** Timuru, 17 June 1911. **Education:** Christchurch Boys' High School, 1924–28; University of Canterbury, Christchurch, 1929–30; University of Auckland, 1931–33, B.A. 1938; St. John's College (Anglican theological), Auckland, 1931–33. **Family:** Married 1) Elizabeth J. LeCren in 1936 (divorced 1965), three children; 2) Jenifer Mary Tole in 1965. **Career:** Cadet journalist, Christchurch *Sun*, 1929–30; reporter and sub-editor, 1935–48, and dramatic critic, 1945–47, *The Press,* Christchurch; reporter and sub-editor, News Chronicle, London, 1949. Lecturer in English, 1951–66, and associate professor of English, 1967–76, University of Auckland. **Awards:** New Zealand Literary Fund travel award, 1949; British Council grant, 1949; Carnegie grant, 1950; New Zealand Book award, 1958, 1963, 1975, 1980, 1983, 1987; Fulbright grant, 1961; Library of Congress Whittall Fund award, 1966, 1974; Katherine Mansfield memorial fellowship, 1983; Commonwealth Poetry Prize, 1989; Queen's Gold Medal, 1989. Litt.D.: University of Auckland, 1966; University of Canterbury, 1975. C.B.E. (Commander, Order of the British Empire), 1986; O.N.Z. (Order of New Zealand), 1990. **Agent:** Curtis Brown (Australia) Pty. Ltd., P.O. Box 19 Paddington, New South Wales 2021, Australia. **Address:** 62 Tohunga Crescent, Parnell, Auckland 1, New Zealand.

PUBLICATIONS

Poetry

Valley of Decision. Auckland, University College Press, 1933.
Three Poems. Christchurch, Caxton Press, 1935.
Another Argo, with Denis Glover and A.R.D. Fairburn. Christchurch, Caxton Press, 1935.
Enemies: Poems 1934–36. Christchurch, Caxton Press, 1937.
Not in Narrow Seas. Christchurch, Caxton Press, 1939.
A Present for Hitler and Other Verses (as Whim-Wham). Christchurch, Caxton Press, 1940.
Recent Poems, with others. Christchurch, Caxton Press, 1941.
Island and Time. Chirstchurch, Caxton Press, 1941.
Verses, 1941–42 (as Whim-Wham). Christchurch, Caxton Press, 1942.
Verses 1943 (as Whim-Wham). Wellington, Progressive, 1943(?).
Sailing or Drowning. Wellington, Progressive, 1943.
Jack Without Magic. Christchurch, Caxton Press, 1946.
At Dead Low Water, and Sonnets. Christchurch, Caxton Press, 1949.
Poems 1949–57. Wellington, Mermaid Press, 1957.
The Hucksters and the University. Auckland, Pilgrim Press, 1957.
Mr. Huckster of 1958. Auckland, Pilgrim Press, 1958.
The Best of Whim-Wham. Hamilton, Paul's Book Arcade, 1959.
A Small Room with Large Windows: Selected Poems. Oxford, Oxford University Press, 1962.
Trees, Effigies, Moving Objects: A Sequence of Poems. Wellington, Catspaw Press, 1972.
An Abominable Temper and Other Poems. Wellington, Catspaw Press, 1973.
Collected Poems 1933–73. Wellington, Reed, 1974.
An Incorrigible Music: A Sequence of Poems. Auckland, Auckland University Press-Oxford University Press, 1979; Oxford, Oxford University Press, 1980.
You Will Know When You Get There: Poems 1979–81. Auckland, Auckland University Press-Oxford University Press, 1982.
Selected Poems. Auckland, Penguin, 1982.
The Loop in the Lone Kauri Road: Poems 1983–1985. Auckland, Auckland University Press, and Oxford, Oxford University Press, 1986.
Continuum: New and Later Poems 1972–1988. Auckland, Auckland University Press, 1988.
Selected Poems. London, Viking, 1990.

Plays

The Axe: A Verse Tragedy (produced Christchurch, 1948). Christchurch, Caxton Press, 1949.
Moon Section (produced Auckland, 1959).
The Overseas Expert (broadcast, 1961). Included in *Four Plays,* 1972.
Doctor Pom (produced Auckland, 1964).
The Duke's Miracle (broadcast, 1967). Included in *Four Plays,* 1972.
Resident of Nowhere (broadcast, 1969). Included in *Four Plays,* 1972.
Four Plays (includes *The Axe, The Overseas Expert, The Duke's Miracle,* and *Resident of Nowhere).* Wellington, Reed, 1972.

Radio Plays: *The Overseas Expert,* 1961; *The Duke's Miracle,* 1967; *Resident of Nowhere,* 1969.

Other

New Zealand Through the Arts, with Sir Tosswill Woollaston and Witi Ihimaera. Wellington, Friends of the Turnbull Library, 1982.
Look Back Harder: Critical Writings 1935–1984, edited by Peter Simpson. Auckland, Auckland University Press, 1987.

Editor, *A Book of New Zealand Verse 1923–45.* Christchurch, Caxton Press, 1945; revised edition, 1951.
Editor, *The Penguin Book of New Zealand Verse.* London, Penguin, 1960.

*

Manuscript Collection: Turnbull Library, Wellington.

Critical Studies: "Allen Curnow's Poetry (Notes towards a Criticism)" by C.K. Stead, in Landfall (Christchurch), March 1963; "Conversation with Allen Curnow" by MacDonald P. Jackson, in *Islands* (Auckland), winter 1973; "Allen Curnow: Forty Years of Poems" by Terry Sturm, in *Islands* (Auckland), autumn 1975; *Allen Curnow* by Alan Roddick, Wellington, Oxford University Press, 1980, Oxford, Oxford University Press, 1981; "Allen Curnow: Further Out" by Chris Wallace-Crabbe, in *Scripsi* (Melbourne), spring 1983; "That Second Body: An Australian View of Allen Curnow's Progress" by Chris Wallace-Crabbe, in *A Review of English Literature* 16(4), 1985; "'Errors and Omissions Excepted:' Allen Curnow's Philosophical Skepticism" by Trevor James, in *Journal of Commonwealth Literature* (London), 22(1), 1987; "Second Wind: Allen Curnow's *Continuum*" by C.K. Stead, in *London Review of Books,* 16 February 1989; "Allen Curnow: *Continuum, New and Later Poems 1972–1988*" by Thomas Crawford, in *British Review of New Zealand Studies,* 2 1990; "Some Remarks on Allen Curnow" in *Allen Curnow at Eighty: A Celebration,* edited by Michael Hulse, in *Verse,* 8(2), 1991, "An Appreciation of Allen Curnow" in *The Spectator* (London), 269(8557), 11 July 1992, and "Allen Curnow, Memory and Avro 504K" in *Review Journal of the Centre for Research into the New Literature in English* (Adelaide) 1, 1993, all by Michael Hulse; "Where Tomorrow Was, Encloses Me Now: Allen Curnow's Recent Poetry of Recollection" by Michael Faherty, in *Verse* 8(2), 1991; "Postmodernism and Allen Curnow" by Donald Davie, in *PN Review* (Manchester), 1991; "Writing an Island's Story: The 1930s Poetry of Allen Curnow" by Stuart Murray, in *Journal of Commonwealth Literature* (London), 30(2), 1995.

Allen Curnow comments:

I don't know of any school I would care to belong to. New Zealand is difficult enough for me.

I don't know anything about themes, subjects, etc., only that occasions for poems or plays crop up as one feels a need (intermittently) to touch something, to check on its existence or one's own.

I don't know about influences either but sometimes think of Yeats's dictum "All that is personal soon rots; it must be packed in ice or salt. Ancient salt is best packing." This is bound to be misinterpreted. I would like to be a poet writing verse so radically old that it looks radically new. I would have to be a much better poet than I am.

Half a century ago I wrote a good few poems "about" New Zealand, as much to find out what I was as what it was. Worry about one's country is one of the major human worries; of course, one can think of universality and worry about that instead, but it's an arid

ground for poetry. One learns to live with the oddity of one's country, like Byron's lame foot or Wallace Stevens's insurance company, and these universal poems record the learning process. Poetry won't bear too much accidental stuff, but must have some. Warning: do not exceed the stated dose.

*   *   *

Allen Curnow is a central figure in modern New Zealand poetry. His *A Book of New Zealand Verse 1923–1945,* a selection of poems supported by an impressive introduction, made apparent for the first time that New Zealand's modern poets had produced the beginnings of a distinct tradition. Curnow's point was that the period of colonial literature was over, demonstrated by the fact that the poets were no longer romanticizing their environment with an eye to, or with the eyes of, English readers but were coming to terms with it as it was. Curnow's argument was further supported by an enlargement of his anthology in 1951 and was extended in his 1960 *Penguin Book of New Zealand Verse.*

Curnow's critical writing went hand in hand with the writing of his poetry, contributing to the development of his subject matter, which had always, however personal its origins, reached toward public statement. In the 1930s, while still finding his voice, he wrote political and social satire. But his characteristic middle style, as he found it in the 1940s, was one of ironic perplexity, brooding over one or another distinctly New Zealand scene or historical event, making its detail sharply present to the senses, yet working at it verbally until its particulars rendered up a broader significance. A sonnet in memory of a cousin killed in North Africa begins with these lines: "Weeping for bones in Africa, I turn / Our youth over like a dead bird in my hand." By the end the dead soldier has assumed not heroic but national proportions:

> But O if your blood's tongued it must recite

> South Island feats, those tall, snow-country tales
> Among incredulous Tunisian hills.

A recording of a Beethoven quartet becomes "Your 'innermost Beethoven' in the uttermost isles." The skeleton of the extinct moa "on iron crutches" in a museum suggests a vision of the New Zealand poet: "Not I, some child, born in a marvellous year / Will learn the trick of standing upright here." Even in his more difficult poems Curnow's gift for dazzling phrase arrests and holds attention. His lines have the ring of major statement: "Small gods in shawls of bark, blind, numb and deaf, / But buoyant, eastward, in the blaze of surf."

In poems written mostly in the mid-1950s very different occasions or "subjects" seem to have led Curnow consistently to the same preoccupation, weighing objective against subjective, real against ideal. In the real—the present time and place—and in that alone our salvation, or more simply our satisfaction, lies. It is the pursuit of the ideal that damns us. The self is discovered and defined only as it confronts what exists out there:

> A kingfisher's naked arc alight
> Upon a dead stick in the mud
> A scarlet geranium wild on a wet bank
> A man stepping it out in the distance
> With a dog and a bag.

In the 1950s Curnow's anthologies brought him into conflict with a younger generation of poets. Then (the two facts are not necessarily connected) for 15 years, beginning in 1957, he published almost no new poems. In 1972, the year of James K. Baxter's death, there appeared Curnow's sequence *Trees, Effigies, Moving Objects: A Sequence of Poems,* which put him back into the center of new developments in New Zealand poetry. This was followed by a less striking collection, *An Abominable Temper and Other Poems,* in 1973 and by the extraordinary and powerful sequence *An Incorrigible Music: A Sequence of Poems* in 1979. In the latter book Curnow juxtaposes images of coastal New Zealand with modern urban Italy and a Borgia murder with that of the Italian statesman Aldo Moro exactly 500 years later. The mind and the poetic skills are cast wide to bring together these various realities, each of them a means of confronting death in a new way. Curnow has never written better.

Yet it is possibly the less spectacular (in terms of subject matter) but more homegrown poems of Curnow's 1982 collection, *You Will Know When You Get There: Poems 1979–81,* that will be seen to have quarried most deeply the vein of experience and reflection central to his writing. Self and place, self in place, and place in self, the sense of a soul lost at the altar and found in action, being in love, pissing by moonlight, or walking among trees down to a wild coast—these are the mysteries he comes back to when he is writing at his best. His habit has been to waste no energy on peripheral things, to write slowly and carefully, and to publish only when something finished has been achieved. *The Loop in the Lone Kauri Road* and the half-dozen poems in *Continuum* show Curnow writing only three or four poems a year but still at the top of his form.

—C.K. Stead

CURREY, R(alph) N(ixon)

Nationality: British. **Born:** Mafeking, South Africa, 14 December 1907. **Education:** Studied at government schools in South Africa, and at Kingswood School, Bath; Wadham College, Oxford, 1927–30, B.A. (honors) in modern history 1930, M.A. 1938. **Military Service:** British Army, 1941–46; commissioned with the Royal Artillery; wrote and edited Army Bureau of Current Affairs publications; Staff Major, 1945. **Family:** Married Helen Estella Martin in 1932; two sons. **Career:** Senior English master, 1946–72, and senior master for arts subjects, 1964–72, Royal Grammar School, Colchester, Essex. President of the Suffolk Poetry Society, Ipswich, 1967–79. **Awards:** Viceroy's prize, 1945; South African poetry prize, 1959. Fellow, Royal Society of Literature, 1970; fellow, English Centre of P.E.N.. **Address:** 3 Beverley Road, Colchester, Essex CO3 3NG, England.

PUBLICATIONS

Poetry

Tiresias and Other Poems. London, Oxford University Press 1940.
This Other Planet. London, Routledge, 1945.
Indian Landscape: A Book of Descriptive Poems. London, Routledge, 1947.
The Africa We Knew. Cape Town, David Philip, 1973.
Collected Poems and Translations. Oxford, James Currey, forthcoming.

Plays

Radio Plays: *Between Two Worlds,* 1948; *Early Morning in Vaaldorp,* 1961.

Other

Poets of the 1939–1945 War. London, Longman, 1960; revised edition, 1967.
Vinnicombe's Trek: Son of Natal, Stepson of Transvaal 1854–1932. London, James Currey, 1989; Pietermaritzburg, University of Natal Press, 1989.

Editor, with R.V. Gibson, *Poems from India by Members of the Forces.* Bombay, Oxford University Press, 1945; London Oxford University Press, 1946.
Editor, *Letters and Other Writings of a Natal Sheriff: Thomas Phipson 1815–1876.* Cape Town and London, Oxford University Press, 1968.

Translator, *Formal Springs: French Renaissance Poems.* London, Oxford University Press, 1950; New York, Books for Libraries, 1969.

*

Critical Studies: *A Critical Survey of South African Poetry in English* by G.M. Miller and Howard Sergeant, Cape Town, Balkema, 1957; by W.G. Saunders, in *South African Poetry: A Critical Anthology* edited by D.R. Beeton and W.D. Maxwell-Mahon, Pretoria, University of South Africa Press, 1966; by Jack Cope, in *Companion to South African English Literature,* edited by D. Adey, Johannesburg, Ad Danker, 1986; *War Like a Wasp* edited by A. Sinclair, Middlesex, Hamish Hamilton, 1989; *The War Decade* edited by A. Sinclair, Middlesex, Hamish Hamilton, 1989; by Iain R. Smith, in *African Affairs,* 89(355), April 1990.

R.N. Currey comments:

It takes a lifetime to discover what kind of poet one is. I appear to be an occasional poet, having written much more at some periods of my life than at others.

In the war I found myself placed, quite unprepared by any previous technical training, in a highly-technical branch of warfare, in which destruction was carried out impersonally at a distance. I received from this experience an intense impression of what I take to be the likely warfare of the future, in which it will require a strong effort of imagination on the part of the killer to realize what he is doing. I wrote of this in *This Other Planet* and in *Between Two Worlds* and am intrigued to find out that some of the poems in which I tried to express my response to this are now being anthologized more often than the conventional war poems that found more favor at the time.

When I was posted to India, I found there, still going on, the Middle Ages I had read about when studying history at Oxford. Indians still went on pilgrimage, as people did in the England of Chaucer's time, and my antiaircraft gunners, who had the same names as the gods in the Indian temples, belonged to the same preindustrial world. The excitement of this theme is still with me, and I hope to write about it again. Translating French poems of the Renaissance and

Middle Ages has also given me an entry into those preindustrial times, and I am glad to find that these poems, too, have the vitality that gets them reprinted many years after first being published.

I have written other topographical poems about places of special importance to me. South Africa, where I spent my boyhood and where I have a long family connection, has underlined contrasts and aroused tensions of the sort that produced poetry. *The Africa We Knew* is a book of South African poems, most of which have been printed and broadcast both in England and in South Africa. I have also edited the letters of a great-grandfather, Thomas Phipson, who landed in Natal in the first year of British settlement, 1849, and have done a biographical study of a grandfather, Thomas Vinnicombe, who kept a remarkable record, most of it in verse, of the crucial years leading to the Anglo-Boer War of 1899–1902. In a life spent on horseback and with wagons he used verse for its original purpose of record.

I find that I have to go to a new country to discover the one in which I live, to move for a while into a different period in order to come to terms with the present. Both North Africa and the western United States have given me new viewpoints from which to see the imperial world in which I grew up.

I have published poems, at different times in my life, in different countries, mainly in England but also in the United States, India, South Africa, and Ireland. For many years I have done my writing and broadcasting alongside teaching English and running an English department at a grammar school.

During our long married life, my wife and I closely shared many writing interests, and I was able to take part with her in the editing and production of her father's children's classic—the *Uncle* series by J.P. Martin (London, Jonathan Cape, 1964–73).

Although I have never been one of a group of writers, I have had enough generous encouragement from David Cecil, Edward Thompson, John Arlott, T.S. Eliot, Dylan Thomas, Ronald Blythe, as well as Roy Campbell, Roy McNab, Guy Butler, Jack Cope, and other South African writers.

*   *   *

T.S. Eliot said of R.N. Currey that he was the best war poet, in the precise sense of the term, that World War II produced. This was high praise since between 1939 and 1945 some very distinguished verse appeared in the little reviews and the numerous anthologies of the period. But the war poems collected in Currey's volume *This Other Planet*, reconsidered some fifty years later, seem still to hold the essence of their period in what was felt and thought by those who were the dramatis personae of "this damned unnatural sort of war," where so much was remote and impersonal. Like the enemy pilot,

To us he is no more than a machine
Shown on an instrument; what can he mean
In human terms?—a man, somebody's son,
Proud of his skill; compact of flesh and bone,
Fragile as Icarus—and our desire
To see that damned machine come down on fire.

It was as a war poet that Currey really established his reputation, and it is significant that he was chosen by the British Council to write its publication *Poets of the 1939–1945 War*. Nevertheless, it is largely as a South African poet that he developed. He finds his themes in and feeds his imagination on the physical Africa that he knew as a boy and on the history of men and things in that complicated but fascinating Euro-African world with its odd duality: "Eating our Christmas pudding beneath the grace / Of feminine willows on the vivid grass," or "My father, all that tawny homeward run, / Remembering snow as I remember sun."

Although Currey has lived most of his adult life in Britain, he has gone home from time to time, and his long work *Early Morning in Vaaldorp*, successfully broadcast by the BBC, is in a sense a tribute to his South African oeuvres, "which could not have been written if I had not come from a long South African tradition and spent most of my impressionable years there." North Africa, particularly Morocco, has been responsible for other impressive poems by Currey, who claims to be able to see the Southern Cross from both ends of the continent, a kind of unifying light in his work. India, too, where he spent much of the war years, makes a further link in this chain of poetic topography.

Some of Currey's most memorable poems, of love particularly, have a lyric poignancy that are devoid of any particular context of time or place and that achieve a universality of appeal. Such is his beautifully constructed "Song," revealing how truth emerges only from the tug-of-war of contrasts:

There is no joy in water apart from the sun,
There is no beauty not emphasized by death,
No meaning in home if exile were unknown;
A man who lives in a thermostat lives beneath
A bell of glass alone with the smell of death.

In poems such as these Currey reveals himself as a poet of considerable artistry, taking infinite pains with his verse-making to derive the maximum impact from word or image. He is an observer of life or landscape with very particular vision.

—Roy Macnab

CURTIS, Tony

Nationality: British. **Born:** Carmarthen, 26 December 1946. **Education:** Queen Elizabeth Grammar School, Carmarthen, 1957–60; Greenhill School, Tenby, 1960–65; University College of Swansea, 1965–69, B.A. (honors) in English 1968, Post-Graduate Certificate in Education 1969; Goddard College, Plainfield, Vermont, 1979–80, M.F.A. in creative writing 1980. **Family:** Married Margaret Blundell in 1970; one son and one daughter. **Career:** Assistant master, Wilmslow Grammar School for Boys, Cheshire, 1969–71; second in charge of the English Department, Maltby School, West Riding, 1971–74; lecturer in English, South Glamorgan College of Education, Barry, 1974–79. Since 1979 senior lecturer in English, Polytechnic of Wales, Pontypridd. Scheme leader, M.A. in writing, 1993, and professor of poetry, 1994, University of Glamorgan. Founder, Edge Press, 1977–80; editor, *Madog Arts Magazine*, 1977–81; chair, Welsh Academy, 1984–88; director, Cardiff Literature Festival, 1986. **Awards:** Eric Gregory award, 1972; Welsh Arts Council Young Poets prize, 1974; National Poetry Competition prize, 1984; Greenwich Festival prize, 1990; Dylan Thomas award, 1993. **Address:** "Pentwyn," 55 Colcot Road, Barry, South Glamorgan CF6 8BQ, Wales.

PUBLICATIONS

Poetry

Peveril Castle. Frensham, Surrey Sceptre Press, 1971.

Walk Down a Welsh Wind. Manchester, Phoenix Pamphlet Poets Press, 1972.

Home Movies: A Poem Sequence from the U.S.A. 1972. Winchester, Hampshire, Platform/Green Horse, 1973.

Album. Llandybie, Carmarthen, Christopher Davies, 1974.

Three Young Anglo-Welsh Poets, with Duncan Bush and Nigel Jenkins. Cardiff, Welsh Arts Council, 1974.

The Deerslayers. Neath, Glamorgan, Cwm Nedd Press, 1978.

Carnival. Port Talbot, Glamorgan, Alun, 1978.

Preparations: Poems 1974–1979. Llandysul, Dyfed, Gomer, 1980.

Letting Go. Bridgend, Glamorgan, Poetry Wales Press, 1983.

Selected Poems, 1970–1985. Bridgend, Glamorgan, Poetry Wales Press, 1986.

Poems Selected and New. Santa Cruz, California, Story Line Press, 1986.

The Last Candles. Bridgend, Glamorgan, Seren, 1989.

Taken For Pearls. Bridgend, Glamorgan, Seren, 1993.

War Voices. Bridgend, Glamorgan, Seren, 1995.

The Arches. Bridgend, Glamorgan, Seren, 1998.

Play

Radio Play: *Islands,* 1975.

Other

Out of the Dark Wood: Prose-Poems, Stories. Barry, Glamorgan, Edge Press, 1977.

Dannie Abse. Cardiff, University of Wales Press, 1985.

How to Study Modern Poetry. London, Macmillan, 1990.

Welsh Painters Talking. Bridgend, Glamorgan, Seren, and Chester Springs, Pennsylvania, Dufour Editions, 1997.

Editor, *Pembrokeshire Poems.* Fishguard, Pembrokeshire Handbooks, 1975.

Editor, *The Art of Seamus Heaney.* Bridgend, Glamorgan, Poetry Wales Press, 1982; second edition, Poetry Wales Press, and Chester Springs, Pennsylvania, Dufour, 1985; third edition, Bridgend, Glamorgan, Seren, 1994.

Editor, with Cliff James, *Writing in Wales: A Welsh Academy Resource Pack.* Cardiff, Welsh Academy, 1985.

Editor, *Wales: The Imagined Nation: Essays in Cultural and National Identity.* Bridgend, Glamorgan, Poetry Wales Press, 1986.

Editor, *The Poetry of Pembrokeshire [Snowdonia].* Bridgened, Glamorgan, Seren, 2 vols., 1989.

Editor, with Sian James, *Love from Wales: An Anthology.* Bridgend, Glamorgan, Seren, 1991.

Editor, *How Poets Work.* Bridgend, Glamorgan, Seren, 1996.

Editor, with Christine Pagnoulle, *Sans Dragon et Moutons.* Namur, Belgium, Sources, 1994.

Editor, *Coal: An Anthology of Mining.* Bridgend, Glamorgan, Seren, 1997.

*

Critical Studies: "Tony Curtis: Frontiersman of Anglo-Welsh Poets" by Mercer Simpson, in Poetry Wales (Bridgend Glamorgan), 20(3), 1985; "Imagination's Roosting Place: *Selected Poems, 1970–1985*" by Anthony Conran, in Planet (Aberystwyth), 67, 1987; "Interview: Tony Curtis" by Robert Minhinnick, in *New Welsh Review* (Lampeter), 2(4), Spring 1990; "Tony Curtis: An Appreciation" by Anne Stevenson, in *New Welsh Review* (Lampeter), 2(4), Spring 1990; "History Books: The Poetry of Tony Curtis" by Tony Brown, in *New Welsh Review* (Lampeter), 2(4), Spring 1990; "Tony Curtis: A Bio-Critical Essay" by Sam Adams, in *Cimarron Review,* 126–127, Winter/Spring 1999.

Tony Curtis comments:

I write because it is easier than not writing. It makes sense. Poetry is the most effective way I know of recording, in a considered way, my ideas and experiences and of introducing myself to myself. I am not talking about confessional poetry. I have written directly about myself on few occasions in the last ten years, and since a number of poems dealing with my father's death. Through the 1980s, and now at the beginning of a new decade, I am working at the craft of a poetry that performs as interesting a role as fiction. I am speaking in new voices, other people's voices, and am attempting to create and re-create stories. At the same time I am enjoying more and more the challenges and rewards of formal verse forms and the use of rhyme.

Why don't I write these ideas and experiences, albeit vicarious experiences, directly as short stories? Well, I have done that too and may well turn to the short story again. It does, however, seem to be more compelling, more natural, for me to explore people and their situations through poetry at the moment. More natural? How can poetry, that most wrought of the written arts, foregrounding as it does language in all its flashy, far-fetched manifestations, how can poetry be natural? Well, perhaps it is simply that it has become for me the obvious place to go with my thoughts, my ideas, and the stories I have taken from others.

I realize that this fictive approach may well disturb and disappoint some readers. As we reach the end of the twentieth century, I am aware that whatever audience there might still be for poetry retains expectations rooted in the nineteenth century. The legacy of the romantics is still alive. Poets are sensitive beings, meditating or raging at the center of a cruel or indifferent universe. Souls are to be bared, secrets recognized and shared. Frequent performers of their poetry, a practice that is currently the only sure way to make money as a poet, develop catchphrases, witty off-the-cuff asides sprinkled like yeast to work the considered weight of their words. It is now my practice to say that I wish an audience to leave my reading knowing little more about me than when they entered. If I am really trying to impress, I throw out a reference to Keats and "negative capability." "My life is boringly regular, but the world around is not," I say. I cite Browning's wonderful dramatic monologues, pass on my enthusiasm for the contemporary American Norman Dubie. Like all acts, it is rehearsed and brittle, but until the next death, the next X ray, the fresh pain, it will do.

*   *   *

After early collections in which his diction occasionally carried overtones of Dylan Thomas, Tony Curtis has moved toward the variety of topics and the modulation of voices and versatility in form evidenced in his collections *The Last Candles* and *Taken for Pearls.* Most of his poems are short narratives building toward a dramatic climax and exploring common emotions, however exceptional some of the situations he starts from may be. His inspiration is triggered with equal felicity by small domestic occurrences such as the sudden awareness that a daughter is growing into a woman ("Games with My Daughter" in *The Last Candles*) or the discovery of a fledgling's corpse in a watering can ("At the Border" in *Taken for Pearls*), by photographs or paintings (Winslow Homer, Andrew Wyeth, Hans Theo Richter, and Edvard Munch being frequent sources), and by reports (news items, books, or stories he was told) of often dramatic historical events, frequently associated with one of the two world wars.

Even in a poem that seems blissfully free of violence, like "The Portrait of the Painter Hans Theo Richter and His Wife Gisela in Dresden 1933," which is supposed to celebrate "the perfect moment of love" (although on looking at the painting reproduced on the cover of the collection I find a typical imbalance between the wife's pliant concern and the man's absentminded concentration), war is recalled in several ways: place and time, ominous anticipation of the wife's death by fire, and the last lines recording "the sounds of the day"— "a neighbour's wireless playing marches, then a speech." Conversely, the polished innocuousness of the guided tour offered around Terezín (Theresienstadt) in slightly awkward English is undermined by what is heard beyond the speaker's words:

Look at the children's pictures. You see—
houses with fences. The chimneys smoke
—there are families inside.

Or again, in the same poem,

Where a child's mind flies, yes?
This one has played the gallows game.
Or it could be a door.

In his later work more than in his earlier collections other wars are called up too, closer to us in time though some may be more distant in space: guerrilla warfare in Southeast Asia, internecine fighting in Yugoslavia, perhaps also the Persian Gulf War indirectly in the choice to translate poems from a colloquial Iraqi dialect.

Using a neat chiasmus (things are never quite as neat as they seem when one dives into the works), Curtis's poems, one could say, bring out the common core of human emotion even in extreme situations. Conversely, they show up the uniqueness of each pattern of experience even in the most everyday circumstances.

Many of Curtis's protagonists, whether referred to in the third person or speaking in their own voices, are people he does not know personally, people whom he has read or heard about and yet whose experiences he re-creates from the inside. Some are about people he is personally involved with. Remarkably, whether or not personal elements are involved, there is no hiatus in the quality and intensity of the emotion called up by the lines. Readers, though presumably not the writer, may feel moved in similar ways, say, by the story of the nurse with a dying baby girl ("Incident on a Hospital Train from Calcutta, 1944") and by the fresh recollection of a friend's unexpected death ("Playing for Vince"). In grim keeping with the pervasive concern with loss and separation, the figure of Curtis's dead father appears in his poems, mainly in the collection called *Preparations: Poems 1974–1979,* in which the recurring reference to the scattering of his father's ashes from the Pembrokeshire cliff top is first

introduced. Grief is unobtrusively expressed through recollections of the life his father had lived, his mastery of the art of bell ringing or the weather vane he so skillfully contrived. Curtis's grandmother is also present in a number of poems written after her death, notably in "My Grandmother's Cactus" (*Letting Go),* where his grief for her absence makes him welcome the injuries inflicted by the plant's spikes. In "Under the Yew" (*Taken for Pearls*), a poem that records the relaxed conversation he has with her in the churchyard where she is buried, he acknowledges the importance of belonging:

the string is tied back here, as they say—
apron strings . . . heart strings, a way through the maze.

Thanks to and out of this sense of belonging he can confidently venture into the lives of others without ever seeming to intrude.

Considering that most of Curtis's poems, hardly any of them over fifty lines, are rounded stories, complete with circumstances and the last-minute inclusion of yet another strand, a particular gift for compression undoubtedly counts among his achievements. But this is one he shares with many contemporary poets writing in English. His appeal to common experience and his use of a direct, sometimes colloquial language that he does not refine or rarefy into a sophisticated idiom are features that may be reminiscent of Philip Larkin, but without Larkin's bitter sarcasm or slip into deliberate coarseness. His attitude to conventional forms is different too. While Larkin shapes the surface of his texts on strict prosodic and rhyming patterns, simultaneously erasing them in his use of syntax, Curtis rarely forces his lines into outward regularity; he allows sounds and rhythms to inform them from inside. The notable exception to the apparent freewheeling nature of his verse is his use of villanelles, a form in which the repetition of lines, associated with variations on a cluster of images, makes for an indirect approach to the emotion at the core of the poem.

Curtis's poems are most satisfactory when they are understated. Attitudes and emotions, sometimes even facts, are suggested through one or two apt images or comparisons rather than being developed. Readers are expected to supplement and complement what is given. Does the Thai girl's body adrift on the hotel bed call up the spread corpse of the European male who bought her for a couple of weeks and who was last seen hanging onto his pole in a frenzy of terror on a raft surrounded by desperately determined guerrillas ("Summer in Bangkok" in *Taken for Pearls*)? In "Home Front" (*The Last Candles*) the irony of the mother's readiness to gas herself and her children in order to escape the Nazis is not stated. In "Soup," an early prizewinning poem telling of a Jewish boy in a concentration camp, readers are left to decide whether the storyteller is genuinely reluctant to tell his story. How much should be made of the apple in the Sarajevo poem ("From the hills, the town" in *Taken for Pearls*), which the watching officer first divides into two with a twist of his hands, then fits back together before biting impartially from both halves?

While there is never any doubt about where his sympathies lie, Curtis eludes stark simplifications. Not all victims of persecution, for example, are heroes. Even self-satisfied chauvinistic males or sports figures such as the racing driver Richard Beattie-Seaman, who compromised himself with Nazi leaders when he won the Nürburgring race in 1938, can be embraced in our compassion because of their fear or suffering. His poems recurringly appeal to a compassion that is never cloyingly self-righteous. Many explore a sense of bereavement, dispossession, or loss, as in the poem called "Public Sale" on the plight of the husband who has lost his wife. The italicized lines

When a man's left alone, seems like
his fields pull further towards the sky-line,
the earth fights harder against the plough

are quietly contrasted with the terrible ease with which those preying on "another man's loss" seem to turn over the land:

One by one their laden trucks leave,
churning the dirt road into furrows
that a man could plant so easily.

Even Curtis's apparently detached interest in traditional funeral rites as they can still be observed in villages in South Wales ("Preparations") includes a personal involvement in the strategies developed to counter grief. The final comparison of the women in the house counting "over and over" the places for the guests at the funeral meal makes it clear that there is something sacramental in the material gestures of preparing sandwiches and laying the table, some way of conjuring death.

Within twenty-four lines a poem such as "The Night-Trees" offers a neat instance of the power of indirection to convey emotions.

Parents who presumably belong to an Asian community are about to kill their second baby girl at birth, something that calls for only indignation. The situation is not condoned, but it is understood from inside. The resigned unhappiness of both the father and mother can be felt in their separate vigils, the mother further softening her grief in the fairy-tale fantasy of girls whispering "one to the other" while one is dead and buried and the other still to be born and disposed of.

Notwithstanding the apparent straightforwardness in most of his story poems, allusive indirectness is thus a key notion in approaching Curtis's work. He is obviously critical of a social system flaunting material success and efficiency in business as supreme values, made clear in texts such as "Summer in Greece" and "The Immortality of Birds." But his poems are never political slogans. Whereas slogans consolidate what should be removed or altered, simply telling a story may lead to awareness and so, perhaps, to change. Similarly, Curtis repeatedly suggests symbols, but he stays clear of a reassuring neatness that would preclude the messiness and confusion of the real world, Yeats's mire and blood.

—Christine Pagnoulle

D

DABYDEEN, Cyril

Nationality: Canadian. **Born:** Canje, Berbice, Guyana, 15 October 1945. **Education:** St. Patrick's Anglican School, Berbice, Guyana, 1951–58; Lakehead University, 1970–73, B.A. in English (honors), 1973; Queen's University, Ontario, 1973–75, M.A. in English 1974, Master of Public Administration 1975. **Family:** Married Claire McCaughey in 1989; one daughter. **Career:** School teacher, Berbice, Guyana, 1961–70; lecturer in English/communications, Algonquin College, Ottawa, 1976–81; race relations specialist with municipal and federal governments of Canada, 1984–99. Since 1987 lecturer in English and creative writing, University of Ottawa. **Awards:** Sandbach Parker Gold medal for poetry in Guyana, 1964; A.J. Seymour Lyric Poetry prize, Guyana, 1967; Queen's University fellowship, 1973–74; Poet Laureate of Ottawa, 1984–87; Certificate of Merit for contribution to the arts, Government of Canada, 1989; Canada Council and Ontario Arts Council award for writing. **Address:** 106 Blackburn, Ottawa, Canada KIN 8A7.

PUBLICATIONS

Poetry

Goatsong. Toronto, Mosaic Press, 1977.
Distances. Vancouver, Fiddlehead Press, 1977.
This Planet Earth. Ottawa, Borealis Press, 1980.
Heart's Frame. Cornwall, Vesta Publications, 1982.
Islands Lovelier than a Vision. Leeds, Yorkshire, Peepal Tree Press, 1988.
Elephants Make Good Stepladders. London, Ontario, Third Eye Publications, 1986.
Coastland: New and Selected Poems. Toronto, Mosaic Press, 1989.
Stoning the Wind. Toronto, Tsar Publications, 1994.
Born in Amazonia. Toronto, Mosaic Press, 1995.
Discussing Columbus. Leeds, Yorkshire, Peepal Tree Press, 1997.

Novels

Dark Swirl. Leeds, Yorkshire, Peepal Tree Press, 1989.
The Wizard Swami. Leeds, Yorkshire, Peepal Tree Press, 1989.
Sometimes Hard. London, Longman, 1994.

Short Stories

Still Close to the Island. Ottawa, Commoners Press, 1980.
To Monkey Jungle. London, Ontario, Third Eye Publications, 1988.
Jogging in Havana. Toronto, Mosaic Press, 1992.
Black Jesus and Other Stories. Toronto, Tsar, 1996.
Berbice Crossing. Leeds, Yorkshire, Peepal Tree Press, 1997.

Other

Editor, *A Shapely Fire: Changing the Literary Landscape.* Toronto, Mosaic Press, 1987.
Editor, *Another Way to Dance: Asian Canadian Poetry.* Toronto, Williams-Wallace, 1991.
Editor, *Another Way to Dance: Contemporary Asian Poetry in Canada and the U.S.* Toronto, Tsar, 1997.

*

Critical Studies: "The Poetry of Michael Ondaatje and Cyril Dabydeen: Two Responses to Otherness" by Arun Mukherjee, in *Journal of Commonwealth Literature* (London) 26(1), 1986; "The Fictions of Cyril Dabydeen," in *SPAN: Journal of South Pacific Association for Commonwealth Literature and Language Studies* 36, 1993, and "Cyril Dabydeen: from National to Multicultural Voice," in *Commonwealth Essays and Studies* (Dijon, France), 19(1), 1996, both by Alan McLeod, and "Cyril Dabydeen: Remembrance of Things Indian," in *The Literature of the Indian Diaspora,* edited by McLeod, New Delhi Publishers, 1999; "Cyril Dabydeen: Here and There" by Frank Birbalsingh, in his *Frontiers of Caribbean Literatures in English,* New York, St. Martin's Press, 1996.

Cyril Dabydeen comments:

I began writing in a colony in South America—one considered part of the English-speaking Caribbean geographical, social, and historical milieu. Thus, from early on all the major British (and American) poets became my accustomed reading material: Louis MacNeice, W.H. Auden, Stephen Spender, Eliot, Whitman, Lowell, etc. Many of these authors' works I would come across in the British Council Library reading room in New Amsterdam, Guyana. At the same time, in the midst of political and social turmoil in the Caribbean and the third world as a whole, I became strongly imbued with the sense of nationalism and self-identification and self-assertion manifested in the arts; thus, the powerful voices of Caribbean and other third world poets and thinkers became my regular reading: Martin Carter, A.J. Seymour, Derek Walcott (of the poets), and essayists and novelists such as Sam Selvon, George Lamming, C.L.R. James, Frantz Fannon, etc. (See my article "Where Doth the Berbice Run," *World Literature Today,* summer 1994.) In Canada my writing has become more direct, perhaps less metaphorically wrought. I also read a great deal of the contemporary confessional poets, such as Sexton, Ted Hughes, Lowell, Roethke, Sylvia Plath (I wrote an M.A. thesis on her), and became immersed in most of the major and minor talented Canadian poets as I interact with them and share "the stage" with them as a reader of my own poetry. This includes poets such as Michael Ondaatje, bpNichol, Seymour Mayne, Dorothy Livesay, Miriam Waddington, Rienzi Crusz, and Joy Kogawa.

I am now concerned as a poet with evoking hinterland landscapes and memory and in giving voice to experience that is still muted, silent, which hopefully would become part of the currency of wider experience and therefore universal. I also draw from my (so-called) three identities—my Indian heritage, my South American-Caribbean roots, and my Canadian (Great White North) influences—all of which fuse and become embroidered or symbiotic in verse and fiction. Movements of peoples and all of our common ancestry take shape and form in my quest to depict inner selves and manifold experiences of place and the human spirit. (See my article "Places We Come From: Voice of Caribbean-Canadian Writers and Multicultural Contexts," *World Literature Today,* spring 1999.)

*   *   *

Two cultures enrich the poetry of Cyril Dabydeen. There is the culture of his homeland (he was born in British Guiana, now Guyana, in 1945), and there is the culture of his adopted land (he settled in Canada in 1970). Movements, rhythms, sensations, emotions, and images from the Caribbean, from South America, and from Canada enliven his poems. Such emotions as loneliness, homelessness, displacement, and anxiety may be said to lurk between the lines. That Dabydeen has had acceptance in his newfound land is borne out by the honor he received when he was appointed the first poet laureate of Ottawa (1984–87). As Jeremy Poynting wrote in the preface to Dabydeen's impressive collection *Coastland: New and Selected Poems* (1989), "He is truly a poet of the New World."

Coastland bristles with energy and bursts with light. It is a generous book that brings together the more than eighty poems the poet wished to preserve from the years from 1973 to 1987. Yet, after reading the collection, one is left with the paramount impression not of reading a book of separate poems so much as of sampling a single long poem that has been broken up and offered in short bites or takes—a kind of odyssey or record of Dabydeen's impressions and images.

Despite the shapeliness of many of the poems, the work as a whole feels somewhat ungainly, rushed, improvised. Ungainliness is not necessarily bad. After all, Walt Whitman pioneered the ungainly, sprawling, occasional, personal style. While Dabydeen may lack the range and resources of a Whitman—he is not alone in this—he does not bring to the manner anything that is stylistically new or interesting except his own enthusiasm and personality.

For this reason *Coastland,* as representative of all of Dabydeen's writing, is a collection of occasional poetry that is more interesting for the author's impressions than it is for his ideas. Yet on this level it is an engrossing work. No Canadian poet gives better expression to what Dabydeen calls "all our fateful diversities." Coming from the South, living in the North, he continues to cast about for some place under the sun that will correlate all of these diversities. He writes about this in "Passion Play":

> Heart, take me there where I know myself—
> Take me to the wide rivers once again.
> Brown, the waters, the raft plying,
> The shadow of the hand, mighty oars; take me
> Where I am also the flower bursting out
> From a ribbed cage—
> The boa-constrictor coils and uncoils.

Places "where I know myself" are plentiful. There are evocations of Guyana, Jamaica, Barbados, Trinidad, Soweto, Havana, Florida, and places closer to home—Newfoundland, Halifax, the Fraser River, Lake Nipigon, and Atikokan, among others. Locales are evoked in phrases. In one poem the poet happily comments that "green is green / in a forest / nondescript / as coconuts." Coconuts may be nondescript in tropical forests, but in Canada they are to be

remarked on. He may be a too well seasoned traveler, for he writes as follows in "Foreign Legions":

> This is a surfeit, believe me—
> I am circumscribed in the desire to traverse
> whole landmarks . . .

Dabydeen has emerged as a fine writer of travel poems and of poems of local color who catches a salient characteristic of a place through a characteristic response to its appearance or its culture. Curiously, for all the traveling, there are hardly any references in the collection to Ottawa, Dabydeen's adopted city, which is too bad.

—John Robert Colombo

DABYDEEN, David

Nationality: Guyanese and British. **Born:** British Guiana, 9 December 1956. Immigrated to the United Kingdom in 1969. **Education:** Cambridge University, B.A. (honors) in English literature, 1978; London University, Ph.D. in English literature 1982; Wolfson College, Oxford, 1983–87. **Career:** Community education officer, Wolverhampton, 1982–84. Since 1984 lecturer in Caribbean studies, Warwick University, Coventry. President, Association for the Teaching of Caribbean, African, and Asian Literature, 1985–87. **Awards:** Cambridge University Quiller-Couch prize, 1978; Yale University Center for British Art resident fellowship, 1982; Commonwealth Poetry prize, 1984. **Agent:** Curtis Brown Ltd., Haymarket House, 28/29 Haymarket, London SW1Y 4SP. **Address:** Centre for Caribbean Studies, University of Warwick, Coventry CV4 7AL, England.

PUBLICATIONS

Poetry

Slave Song. Mundelstrup, Denmark and Kingston, Surrey, Dangaroo Press, 1984.
Coolie Odyssey. Mundelstrup, Denmark and Kingston, Surrey, Dangaroo Press, 1988.
Turner: New & Selected Poems. London, Cape, 1994.

Novels

The Intended. London, Secker and Warburg, 1990.
Disappearance. London, Secker and Warburg, 1993.
The Counting House. London, Cape, 1996.
A Harlot's Progress. London, Cape, 1999.

Other

Hogarth's Blacks: Images of Blacks in Eighteenth-Century English Art. Mundelstrup, Denmark and Kingston, Surrey, Dangaroo Press, 1985; Athens, University of Georgia Press, 1987.
Hogarth, Walpole and Commercial Britain. London, Hansib, 1988.
Black Writers in Britain, with Paul Edwards. Edinburgh, Edinburgh University Press, 1991.

Editor, *The Black Presence in English Literature.* Wolverhampton, Wolverhampton Council for Community Relations, 1983; revised edition, Manchester, Manchester University Press, 1985.

Editor, with Brinsley Samaroo, *India in the Carribean.* London, Hansib, 1987.

Editor, *A Handbook for Teaching Carribean Literature.* London, Heinemann, 1988.

Editor, *Rented Rooms.* Mundelstrup, Denmark and Kingston, Surrey, Dangaroo Press, 1988.

Editor, with Nana Wilson-Tagoe. *A Reader's Guide to West Indian and Black British Literature.* London, Hansib, 1988.

*

Critical Studies: "The Other Triangle" by Fred D'Aguiar, in *Poetry Review* (London), 78(2), 1988; "Between Creole and Cambridge English: The Poetry of David Dabydeen" by Benita Parry, in *Kunapipi* (Aarhus, Denmark), 10(3), 1988–89; "David Dabydeen: Coolie Odyssey" by Frank Birbalsingh, in his *Frontiers of Caribbean Literatures in English,* New York, St. Martin's Press, 1996; *The Art of David Dabydeen* edited by Kevin Grant, n.p., Peepal Tree Press, 1997; "Gender and Hybridity in Contemporary Caribbean Poetry" by Jana Gohrisch, in *Anglistentag 1997 Giessen,* edited by Raimund Bormeier, Herbert Grabes, and Andreas H. Jucker, Trier, Germany, Wissenschaftlicher Verlag Trier, 1998.

David Dabydeen comments:

I write in English and in a creolized English on two subjects: the colonial experience, specifically the erotic and pornographic dimensions of empire; and the experience of migration, exploring the transformations of language, identity, and sexuality that result from such migration. As with many writers from the Caribbean, my work has been influenced by two literary texts—*The Tempest* and *Heart of Darkness.*

My ancestors came from India to the Caribbean from 1838 onwards to work in the British sugar plantations there. In the twentieth century most of us left for England and North America. I would like to move back to India to complete the triangle in real life, not just in poetry.

*   *   *

In the introduction to his first book, *Slave Song,* David Dabydeen expresses surprise at the lack of poetry written in Creole. He duly wrenches it from the ground by the roots to enact a simple, violent, and often spellbinding drama of oppression, agony, lust, and sweat among the sad and brutalized cane cutters of Guyana. Dabydeen uses limited diction and a simple oral rhythm to such compelling effect that one can only share his surprise.

Slave Song has the claustrophobic darkness of a Jacobean blood tragedy. It employs a handful of raw, day-to-day sensory experiences—the cloying sweetness of cane, the crackle of the cutters' bare feet killing frogs, the workers accidentally gashing themselves with their own cutlasses, and murderous, surging lust for the white mistress ("Bu when night come how me dream . . . / Dat yu womb lie like starapple buss open in de mud / An how me hold yu dung, wine up ya waiss / Draw blood from yu patacake, daub am all over yu face / Till yu dutty like me an yu halla"). These experiences are all Dabydeen needs to give his songs the resonating pity and humanity they demand in order to ring true.

What moves under the hot sun oozes, rots, drips, and spurts. This description of a girl found dead in a swamp, merging sex and blood in the shape of lush fruit, typifies the voices, concerns, and techniques of *Slave Song:*

Yesterday she womb bin live an stirrin wid clean bright blood
Like starapple inside, full flesh when yu squash it open
An all de ripe juice run dung ya finga, dung yu arm an troat.
Now she hollow, now she float.

Dabydeen can infuse single images with such color and vitality that they take on the Marvellian power to change a poem's course, whether universalizing to the racial, dimming to the tenderly personal, or swerving to the explicitly sexual. The hot sun turns into an overseer, the mistress's silk frock into a waterfall, and her unattainable sex into the "baigan-chokey," the too-ripe aubergine.

Within these glaring confines Dabydeen displays impressive range. He can take us quickly into the shade: "Leh we go sit dung riverside, dip, dodo, die— / Shape deep in cool deh." The language is clear enough in its alliteration and assonance to wave-off English annotation.

In the following two stanzas we hear the familiar voice of the worker after his work, though, as with all of Dabydeen's characters, it is a voice of extreme pain and extreme relief, followed by the equally universal sound of the melancholy drinker hours later. The stanza break itself does the work of three hours lost with the bottle:

Tank Gaad six a'clack!
Me go home
And me go bade
An me go comb
An me go rock
In hammock
Cassava, pepperpot,
Drink some rum an coconut!

. . . When me soul saaf and me eye wet
An de breeze blow an me eye shet
An de bakle na ga mo rum
Den leh yuh come
An tek me wey, wheh
Chain na deh, wheh
Cane na deh . . .

Out of these two voices, blending effortlessly and pitifully into one man, we feel the dirt and pain of his job, the pathetic joy of the exhausted in simplest pleasures (this is the work of the exclamation mark after "coconut"), the pathos of the habitual rum drinker, and what lies beneath every word spoken in this book, the dull misery of enslavement.

In Dabydeen's work, as with Derek Walcott's, the tongue chosen is itself a character in the drama, the tension between native patois and colonial English loading every word with personal, racial, or political significance. *Coolie Odyssey,* the second of his books, charts the last stage of the immigrant's journey to England and duly enrobes itself in that language. Everything of importance in the first work is expertly carried over: the joy of song, some of the starkest images (the raw lust of the cane cutters becomes, for example, in the context of England and its literature the eyes of Caliban on Miranda—"And the sun resumed its cruelty / And the sun shook with imperial glee / At the fantasy''), and the transfiguring capacity of simple objects. Dabydeen's work in English loses none of this quality, so that, while it describes the troubled racial feeling, the use of English and the absence of Creole themselves perform it:

> [We] confess the lust of beasts
> In rare conceits
> To congregations of the educated
> Sipping wine, attentive between courses—
> See the applause fluttering from their hands
> Like so many messy table napkins.

When Dabydeen employs a cross between the tongues (roughly speaking, English diction with Creole grammar), the effect is even stronger. What we hear sounds exactly like what it is, the divided voice of the displaced immigrant knowing two cultures and at home in neither. Nowhere is this better evinced than in his description of the legendary batsman Kanhai, where, in the poem as a whole, cane cutting, cricket, the colonial past and hoped-for future, and the indignation, pride, and fury of the race draw every line as taut as can be:

> . . . round night radio we huddle to catch news
> Of Kanhai batting lonely in some far country
> Call Warwick-Shire, and every ball blast
> Is cuff he cuffing back for we,
> Driving sorrow to the boundary
> Every block-stroke is paling in a fence
> He putting down to guard we,
> And when century come up, is like dawn!

The work of Dabydeen, native Guyanese and now a teacher in England (''where it snows but we still born brown''), powerfully voices the enslavement, odyssey, and modern dilemmas of his people. The voice is as articulate in the mouth of the slave boy or cane cutter as in that of the naive immigrant or educated poet.

—Glyn Maxwell

DACEY, Philip

Nationality: American. **Born:** St. Louis, Missouri, 9 May 1939. **Education:** St. Louis University, B.A. 1961; Stanford University, California, M.A 1967; University of Iowa, Iowa City, M.F.A. 1970. **Family:** Married Florence Chard in 1963 (divorced 1986); two sons and one daughter. **Career:** U.S. Peace Corps volunteer in Eastern Nigeria, 1963–65; instructor in English, University of Missouri, St. Louis, 1967–68. Since 1970 member of the department of English, Southwest State University, Marshall, Minnesota. Distinguished writer-in-residence, Wichita State University, Kansas, 1985; distinguished visiting writer, University of Idaho, 1999. Editor, *Crazy House,* 1971–76. **Awards:** Woodrow Wilson fellowship, 1961; New York YM-YWHA Discovery award, 1974; National Endowment for the Arts fellowship, 1975, 1980; Minnesota State Arts Board fellowship, 1975, 1983; Bush Foundation fellowship, 1977; Loft-McKnight fellowship, 1984; Fulbright lectureship, 1988. **Address:** 2250 Co. Rd. 25, Lynd, Minnesota 56157, U.S.A.

PUBLICATIONS

Poetry

The Beast with Two Backs. Milwaukee, Gunrunner Press, 1969.
Fist, Sweet Giraffe, The Lion, Snake, and Owl. Poquoson, Virginia, Back Door Press, 1970.
Four Nudes. Milwaukee, Morgan Press, 1971.
How I Escaped from the Labyrinth and Other Poems. Pittsburgh, Carnegie Mellon University Press, 1977.
The Boy under the Bed. Baltimore, Johns Hopkins University Press, 1979.
The Condom Poems. Marshall, Minnesota, Ox Head Press, 1979.
Gerard Manley Hopkins Meets Walt Whitman in Heaven and Other Poems. Great Barrington, Massachusetts, Penmaen Press, 1982.
Fives. Peoria, Illinois, Spoon River Poetry Press, 1984.
The Man with Red Suspenders. Minneapolis, Milkweed, 1986.
The Condom Poems II. Peoria, Illinois, Spoon River Poetry Press. 1989.
Night Shift at the Crucifix Factory. Iowa City, University of Iowa Press, 1991.
Notes of an Ancient Chinese Poet. Bemidji, Minnesota, Loonfeather Press, 1995.
What's Empty Weighs the Most: 24 Sonnets. Elgin, Illinois, Black Dirt Press, 1997.
The Deathbed Playboy. Spokane, Eastern Washington University Press, 1999.
The Paramour of the Moving Air. Princeton, *Quarterly Review of Literature, 1999.*

Other

Editor, with Gerald M. Knoll, *I Love You All Day: It Is That Simple.* St. Meinrad, Indiana, Abbey Press, 1970.
Editor, with David Jaus, *Strong Measures: Contemporary American Poetry in Traditional Forms.* New York, Harper, 1986.

*

Manuscript Collection: Harry Ranson Humanities Research Center, University of Texas, Austin.

Critical Studies: By Dabney Stuart, in *Shenandoah* (Lexington, Virginia), winter 1971; David Jauss, in *Great River Review* (Minneapolis), fall 1977; Vernon Young, in *Hudson Review* (New York), December 1977; Leonard Nathan, in *Parnassus* (New York), fall/winter 1978; Joseph B. Wagner, in *Tar River Poetry* (Greenville, North Carolina), spring 1979; interview, in *Voices* (Marshall, Minnesota), April-May 1979; Philip Jason, in *Poet Lore* (Boston), fall 1979 and winter 1981–82; Bob Fauteux, in *Minnesota Daily* (Minneapolis), 16 June 1981; Barton Sutter, in Minneapolis *Tribune,* 8 May 1983; Orval Lund, in *Great River Review* (Minneapolis), fall 1986; James Bertolino, in *Bellingham Review* (Bellingham, Washington), spring 1987; Frank Allen, in *American Book Review,* August 1992; *Literary Review,* winter 1995.

Philip Dacey comments:
    As a young boy I dreamed of being a novelist—in vain, as a few sorry half-attempts later indicated. In my mid-twenties, largely at sea as to my career and goals, I was amazed to find myself writing poems

(poetry never was a favorite literary genre of mine), then more poems and in time growing into a practicing professional poet. Poetry came unbidden into my life and gave it shape, meaning, direction. I am deeply grateful to it. I have since then, about twenty-five years ago, tried to serve the art well and develop as best I could whatever gift for it I have. I hope to have another twenty-five years to further my commitment and partially repay poetry for all it has given me.

*   *   *

Philip Dacey's collections provide a compendium of poetic delights: wit, wisdom, and the full spectrum of feeling. He is equally at home in the natural world and in the realm of meditation. His language may consist of spare, flat diction or involve rich, flowing imagery, but it is always right, always evocative of a sensibility and a moment.

How I Escaped from the Labyrinth and Other Poems is too accomplished to be labeled a first volume. Dacey's poems have a way of lingering. They haunt with their gentleness, lift with their lightness. How much he packs into his one-line poem "Thumb" ("The odd, friendless boy raised by four aunts"). How imaginatively he fashions, then exploits, the metaphor of pornography in "Porno Love" to explore the elements of artistic and personal risk: "I've been exposing my genitals / in poems for a long time now, / at least when they're good." It is by risking that the artist (the lover) declares, "I trust you." Thus, we see "how certain private parts / made vulnerable / give greatest pleasure / in a consummation / of good will." In "Learning to Swim in Mid-Life" the speaker is able at last to give himself to water (to woman, to others, ultimately to himself): "So I enter you / and you keep me up, / longer than I have / ever expected." The swimmer now feels that "for once it would be easy / to carry myself. / With no strain, / I could give myself / to others. / I would say, Here, / take me. It would be that simple." By themselves his hands "are taking / what they need / to pull me forward." At last "I am wet / with your wetness."

The Boy under the Bed considers a group of themes that are personal and universal: the tension between self-preservation and one's need for others; the struggle to maintain love against the onslaught of time; the revelation of freedom deriving from one's ability to have faith. "The Door Prohibited" dramatizes life as a series of doors and rooms. If one is tempted to open doors, there is also the need to keep at least one door closed. "The Orgy" masterfully conveys sexual innuendo in simple diction as it underscores the not-so-simple questions of whether and when to risk a new experience: "What would we do / without the line / that runs between / your piece and mine?" With regret the speaker declines the invitation ("Better stay home / in certain nooks"), but his sense of lost opportunity is offset by the arrival of another invitation. Life is rich in possibilities.

"Watching a Movie in a Foreign Language without Subtitles" captures the speaker's sense of displacement, alienation, and failed communication. The poem opens with the lines "For years now, you have starred / In your own foreign movie." A family man, the "I" sadly realizes that he now comprehends strangers better than his own wife and children. In "The Last Straw" the speaker's marriage has collapsed: "One minute the camel was standing there, / then it was not. I said it was her / straw that did it, she said it was mine. / The fact is, if any one / of all those previous straws had been withheld, / the camel would not now be dead. / So who can assign responsibility?" Dacey breathes life into a cliché through a combination of bold, exact metaphor and colloquial, connotative language.

Not only does Dacey craft poems that breathe free of artifice, but he also buoys the spirit as he dramatizes how faith and self-trust are ultimately the same. In "Levitation" the speaker is in love with the magician's assistant and her "faith in air." After she tells him, "You have nothing to rely on," she instructs him to "go higher / higher." Dacey does just that. In "The Runner" he becomes thinner, refines himself; his bones surface, "coming forward to meet / the eye. Or slowly developing like / a picture in a darkroom or the features / of a darkened room to a would-be sleeper. / The flesh was all a lie. The bones were true / and now were rising as he ran." Death and the speaker run together as partners, "the two of them. The one he'd come to meet / beside him. That shadow, scything the flowers / and leaving them intact." As he hears the surprising off-rhyme of "health and death," the shadow finally becomes "a lover. And he / had come to rendezvous." Poems like "Proofreading" and "The Way It Happens" develop and reinforce this willingness to trust, this giving over that makes possible the acts of transcendence and transformation.

Gerard Manley Hopkins Meets Walt Whitman in Heaven and Other Poems consists of a sequence based on the historical and imagined life of the British poet. Dacey is marvelous in re-creating moments and circumstances related to Hopkins's life. Employing Hopkins's own vocabulary and sprung rhythm, he succeeds not only in making accessible but also in resurrecting Hopkins's sensibility for the reader. The title poem, a combination painting and stage play, depicts heaven as a swimming hole where the two poets meet, grapple, and join at last to strike an appropriately Whitmanesque pose.

In *Fives* and *The Man with Red Suspenders* Dacey continues his exploration of identity, process, and relationship. Highly structured (five sections of five poems, each poem in five cinquains), *Fives* focuses on growth and completion. Dedicated to the daughter "who made us five," the book's opening poem has the speaker-poet musing on the various names assigned him, how name and self become each other. "Not Correcting His Name Misspelled on the Mailing Label" concludes with his longing to be called "Cyaed": "a Welsh verse form / impossible to pronounce, / a near forgotten / arrangement of sounds / some few mouths can enjoy." The name, like the self, is capable of transformations; out of what is given, a man creates his being. In Dacey's poems transformation and faith make each other possible, as in "The Pianist," where "one thing led to another / not thing. The music couldn't be seen, / even when found. He had to believe in it / like any ghost / to give himself a past, / that is, a future." His sense of life's connectedness and flow appears in "Arriving Late for a Movie": "If you miss the beginning, / you miss the end. / The end is in the beginning." Dacey reminds us that life and love will not be divided or compartmentalized. In "Mobius" he presents "our love / with no inside or outside / or no clear / line dividing so." Always the self continues its journey, evolving, ascending, as in "The Body," which ". . . always / rights itself." Kept on track by "the gyroscope / of the spirit / . . . / Even in death / the body flourishes, / . . . / the limbs flailing / . . . / but actually / the body's flying." Thus, going down is arising, and the dance of death is paradoxically the dance of freedom. Dacey's poems are rich in paradox and surprise. *Fives* concludes with the self's need to yield in order to transform itself into something more. One must be willing to get "down on all fours" with one's "forehead / touching the earth." As described in "The Position," by being "open / to attack / or love," one may discover "a larger number— / or one / just like him— / into which he can go / and leave nothing over." Transcendence comes with giving over to another as large as, or larger than, oneself.

Perhaps Dacey's penchant for paradox, coupled with his highly distinct voice and vision, reveals him to be a twentieth-century transcendentalist, a secular priest finding his own way. In *The Man with Red Suspenders* Dacey again brings together Hopkins and Whitman, two men of faith but two men of widely differing sensibilities. These men are Dacey's mentors and, in a way, the poles of his poetic being. Between them they generate the current of imagery that flows from Dacey. Seeming opposites are necessary to complete the circuit, to achieve wholeness.

Being open to the other, without or within, is risky business. In "The Hitchhiker" the driver is warned, "I am dangerous. / I could change your life." To travel and to grow requires keeping open, as in "Whitman's Answering Service," which ends with "remember, the only phone company / is yourself." If one tries to overcontrol one's life, to lock every drawer, as in "The Office Manager Locking Up," then "the silence says / murder / and order / as if they were one word." Hence, the manager locks himself up. But for the poet—and for Hopkins and Whitman—life is a gift. "Placating the Gods" concludes, "Spend the day / finding yourself. / Say thank you." In "The Rules" it is ". . . be glad / You got what you got." Loving this life means having faith, whose signs are everywhere, as in "Pac-Man," which tells us that "when you die, / . . . / transformation is taking place, / which means eyes set free / to float, and see." Like our own hopes for ascension and transfiguration, the creatures in "The Fish in the Attic" mysteriously swim and fly overhead, "making an untranslatable / pattern amidst / what you have discarded / or do not know you need yet." Like us they wait just below the ice-covered roof "for a fisherman to cut the hole / they can escape through." Even, perhaps especially, the moment of impending death brings a flood of self-awareness and transcendence, as in "The Safe," which hurtles downward toward the speaker, who sees "the great / black open womb bearing down, passionate / to a fault." He sees, mirrored, his own creative interior, "wombish" too, "rising to meet in an open rush, / its perfect mate." Beholding his inner wealth, his glory, he feels that it is "a privilege to die like that, / the victim of treasure, inside and out." The self's treasure, Dacey assures us, is virtually inexhaustible. Because Dacey's poems reveal the godhead within, they achieve transcendence and are themselves acts of faith.

With his book *Night Shift at the Crucifix Factory*, Dacey secures his place as a major voice in contemporary poetry. This award-winning volume continues Dacey's quixotic journey in the realms of matter and imagination. While the poet repeatedly pokes fun at the Roman Catholic tradition that no longer binds him, he remains a serious searcher for faith. Dacey arranges his material in three sections, a personal trinity that presents the hero-poet's own life path and quest.

In the first section, "On Donk's Row," Dacey acknowledges and explores contributions and connections involving various family members, starting with his grandfather who, the speaker ". . . love[s] to say / . . . mined for coal / in southern Illinois, / I with my ink-stained / fingers that dig / and dig in air / for air." Mother and father are here, too, along with Whitman. In the imagined narrative "Thomas Eakins: The Secret Whitman Sitting," the artist reflects on the sleeping poet-subject: ". . . I had seen that posture before. / That slump. Almost as if I had created it. / And then I remembered: I had. It was my Christ's. / Twice crucified. // The critics bled him, too, / for being first a man, no god, unless / all men and women were equally gods."

In the second section, "Positively No," the poet moves forward to test and claim his identity. Learning to listen even more attentively,

he imagines the colloquy between "the ear and mouth, old cousins / from an old country where words go in and out / like lovers, and two are one, and one— / one listens in order to speak." If loss is inevitable, gratitude for what has been is a positive and appropriate response: "The voices come bearing their own deaths / as gifts, and the hand of the ear / says thank you, by opening like a grave."

"In Yugoslavia: Two Islands and a Hill" is the centerpiece of this section, a trilogy in which the second poem, "Pilgrimage to Medugorje," speaks to the quest for faith most directly. The poet visits a remote village where local children claim to have seen the Virgin Mary and observes of the crowd, ". . . It was Times Square / with a halo, milling pilgrims everywhere, / and Mass a sellout, S.R.O." The speaker narrates with wry irony:

I didn't stay but went instead to find
the place where six teenagers lost their minds
and hearts to God. I saw two arrowed signs:
"This Way to the Hill of Apparitions,"
"This Way to the Toilets." And I, I took
the way less traveled by, no doubt, to hike
the hill where Holy Mary came, they say.

The speaker climbs and looks but does not have a religious vision: ". . . Out of a fine mist, / nothing appeared to me, who craved a sign, / except a begging dog, all skin and bone, / whose head I scratched." Thus, ". . . I climbed back down, / my faith unrenewed. I hadn't seen one / miracle, unless everything was it." This, of course, is the point, but it would not be Dacey without something also tangible, and so the poem concludes, ". . . And, oh / yes, while at Medugorje, looking for truth, / I had some great fried chicken at a booth." The poet says no to the traditional—the institutional—answers, finding his own instead. There is gratitude and reverence for being, his own as well as all that exists about him.

There also is a fierce determination to protect and nurture the hard-won and unique self. Like poems, the self is its own reason for being and deserving of valuation. The speaker-poet in "Translated from the" lives in an oppressive culture and says defyingly,

. . . I love my poems because
they are not published.
To live like outlaws
is their success.
They are my secret life,
illegal, punishable
not publishable, a threat
to whom they may concern.

Any institution—sacred or secular—no matter how benevolent, poses a threat to the individual life, which by definition is creative and itself a work of art.

Creating is the supreme act of celebration. The poet is both attendant priest and deity, bringing artifacts into being and thereby engaging in the ongoing process of creating the self. It is divine work by which the artist elevates himself—and perhaps his audience. Hell, on the other hand, is doing the same task over and over for money, crucifying the self to keep the body alive. In "The Feet Man," the poem from which the collection's title is derived, the speaker's job is to nail "Jesus' feet to the cross on the / assembly line," which translates into striking those nails "... more than two thousand times / a day."

The real task, for the individual and the artist, is to become oneself, difficult and painful as the process must be: "The point is / you can't fool God. / The point is / you can't fool yourself" ("The Sacrifice"). One lets go of the old ways, the old relationships, only to find them articulated and manifested in new forms and experiences. The stripper in a bar, moving to Pachelbel's canon "... performed it, too, / each move as practiced as a halfback's fake / or priest's elevation of the Host at Mass." The speaker "... felt I could have been in church, albeit / a church like none my mother took me to," and, oh, that stripper, "... once she touched her breasts and crotch with what / seemed to me, in my enthusiasm, / liturgical significance. Ah, men!" ("Strip Pachelbel"). Becoming oneself requires the freedom to say no, as in "Not Answering the Telephone." One declines the world's invitations and distractions in order to continue a particular activity, affirming thereby the self's high priority.

When the price of individuation seems unbearably high, in the sundering of the dearest ties, as in the loss of joint custody of children in a divorce judgment, a person is not entirely alone if he can remain open and trusting. In "Vigil Strange" the speaker, crushed and stunned as is any casualty of the marital wars, gropes for comfort in *Leaves of Grass* and finds it in the words of Whitman, the most compassionate of nurses:

and the dream has long persisted of a ghost
brooding over me that night, the low cloud
of his beard like weather, universal breath,
all my air a great mothering body of words.

The last section—"The Stories They Told"—finds the poet returning from his dangerous but life-creating journey to tell of his discoveries. In "Lies" the poet explores the relationship between art and truth; addressing his neighbor Arthur, who only likes "movies that really happened," the poet begins, "I know how it is, Art." The truth that what art tells is truer than truth, made up as it is of the things of the world, selected, heightened, rearranged, imagined, all to take us deeper into that mine where nuggets abound. "Jill, Afterward" tells how the girl's boyfriend had nothing in his pail, despite his story to the contrary. But since she went up the hill with him to see "... whether / He had anything in his pants," she learned to her chagrin that "... damn, too, if his pants weren't full." She adds that "I've got these kids to prove that story." Imagination is potent and fertile in ways that never fail to surprise.

The final poem is "Endpapers," which reminds us that at the end of every tale, lived or written, is the blank page: "At the end of every storybook, it snows. / The white endpaper has the final word." Rather than this being the blank face of dismay, emptiness, or ambiguity, however, it becomes a joke for the poet-speaker and his real-life daughter. Truth and art always and forever dance.

Two more books of poems, The *Paramour of the Moving Air* and *The Deathbed Playboy,* were published in 1999. Running like a rich river through *Paramour* is Dacey's love affair with language. For the poet language is living and palpable, always moving, the flow of music the self makes in response to the symphony of the world. Looking back to his origins in the first poem ("Inheriting the Gift of Blarney"), he has come to learn that "I grew up inside the word, / though I did not know it then. / My place was green with vowels, / and waves against the cliffs of Moher / were consonants." The sheer act of writing words on paper is a rapture, as the poet muses in "The Lost Art" (of penmanship): "It must have been like love / the hand moving with just the right / pressure and angle, / following the contours / of a name, a long body of names."

The second section, "A Little Night Music," continues the focus on language, sometimes through analogy, sometimes offhand and indirectly, but it is always present. Consider "Amherst with Fries" in which, after giving his order and hearing the bored cashier in a Massachusetts Burger King wonder ("at least a little") at "how 'Whopper' and 'water' sound alike,'" the speaker reminds us

... that language is always
and in any state the special of the day,
and that although few people full-rhyme
all people off-rhyme, that any is more at home
with any other, or should be, then either is
with Styrofoam cups or a plastic tray.

At any moment the miracle of language can leap into view, as evidenced here by the minimum wage cashier with her "surprising— even to her, I bet— / regard for what daily commercial use / has reduced to near invisibility: our life- / giving diet of vowel and consonant cluster." And so, like this young woman mostly going through the motions of a mindless job, any of us is capable of

playing the role of an intelligent ear,
a kind of subversive rational weapon,
a uniformed and smiling stealth poet,
listening with great discrimination
as a line forms all day in front of her.

Dacey is indeed wedded to language. Poetry for him is much more than a medium; it is the water of life, the air we breathe, and the most significant other, the muse as the beloved.

Published almost simultaneously with *Paramour, The Deathbed Playboy* opens with "Recorded Message," a poem that sets the tone and subject matter for much of what follows—a wryly serious look at contemporary American culture and what it means to be an individual living in it. Taking up a familiar experience, "Recorded Message" provocatively dramatizes how communication has become trivialized and depersonalized, how language has become commercialized in a techno-business culture. And then the poems immediately following display language's emotive power as Dacey reflects upon experiences involving family members and does so lovingly and with a clarity and control that evoke deep and resonant feelings from the reader: Dacey's brother at the dying sister's bedside during her last months; his ninety-year-old father remembering how, newly divorced and living in a tiny rented room, he would rub noses with the young poet-to-be during Friday night stayovers ("Eskimo Joe"). It is dangerous material that could easily bog down in the slough of sentimentality, but for Dacey, with his discipline and surety of language, it does not. As the bonds of familial love connect the poet with his kin, the reader feels drawn into the family circle, welcomed into another branch of his family he did not know was there.

At the same time Dacey weaves in the elements of late twentieth-century America—*Candid Camera,* Baryshnikov, the *Trident II* submarine, George Bush and Saddam Hussein—as he muses how "maybe like any modern / I love fragments" ("Reading While

Driving''). In the next poem (''For the God Poseidon'') Dacey identifies modern man's condition and location as a species ''between beliefs / between the knellings of a bell.'' Dacey's most powerful indictment comes in ''The New American Stations of the Cross.'' Although the poem deserves to be quoted entire, a few excerpts suggest the its concerns: ''Jesus' side is pierced / by the dull rhetoric / of presidential candidates, / who drink his blood.'' ''Japan offers to carry / Jesus' cross / at a very attractive interest rate.'' ''Jesus, who carries no cash / in his small loin cloth, / is stripped of his credit cards / which have no limits.'' ''Jesus is nailed to a cross / of wood from an old-growth forest.'' ''Jesus is taken down / from the cross / because 64% of the people / surveyed in a Gallup poll / approve of such action / while only 32% disapprove / and 4% don't know what they think.'' ''Jesus is laid / in a tome / converted from / a defunct / Savings and Loan / vault.'' ''The Supreme Court rules / God is guilty / of reverse discrimination / in letting only a Jew / rise from the dead.''

With some half-dozen chapbooks (two of them—*Fives* and *What's Empty Weighs the Most: 24 Sonnets*—quite substantial) in addition to his full-length collections in print, Dacey has amassed an impressive body of work. The poet has Whitman's compassion and involvement with human concerns, Dickinson's eccentricity and boldness, and Frost's ear for spoken language that reveals the inner life. Most of all, however, Dacey's poetry is always his own. Laced and leavened with an unsparing wit, along with a spirit of openness and curiosity at what life has to offer and always the willingness to explore, this is poetry of the highest order.

—Carl Lindner

D'AGUIAR, Fred

Nationality: British. **Born:** London, 2 February 1960. Brought up in Guyana. **Education:** University of Kent, Canterbury, B.A. in English; Cambridge University (Judith E. Wilson fellow), 1989–90. **Career:** Trained and worked as a psychiatric nurse. Writer-in-residence, London Borough of Lewisham, 1986–87, and Birmingham Polytechnic, 1988–89; visiting writer, Amherst College, 1992–94; assistant professor of English, Bates College, 1994–95, and since 1995 University of Miami, Florida. Editor, *Artrage* magazine, London. **Awards:** Minority Rights Group award, 1983; University of Kent T.S. Eliot prize, 1984; G.L.C. literature award, 1985; Guyana Poetry prize, 1987; David Higham First Novel award, Book Trust, London, 1995, and Whitbread award, Booksellers Association of Great Britain and Ireland, 1995, both for *The Longest Memory*. **Address:** c/o Chatto and Windus Ltd., 20 Vauxhall Bridge Road, London SW1V 2SA, England.

PUBLICATIONS

Poetry

Mama Dot. London, Chatto and Windus, 1985.
Airy Hall. London, Chatto and Windus, 1989.
British Subjects. London, Chatto and Windus, 1992.
Bill of Rights. London, Chatto and Windus, 1998.

Plays

High Life (produced London, 1987).
A Jamaican Airman Foresees His Death. London, Methuen, 1995.

Novels

The Longest Memory: A Novel. London, Chatto and Windus, and New York, Pantheon, 1994.
Dear Future. London, Chatto and Windus, and New York, Pantheon, 1996.
Feeding the Ghosts. London, Chatto and Windus, 1997; Hopewell, New Jersey, Ecco Press, 1999.

Other

Editor, with Gillian Allnutt, Ken Edwards, and Eric Mottram, *The New British Poetry 1968–1988.* London, Paladin, 1988.
Editor, *The West Indies and the Spanish Main,* by Anthony Trollope. New York, Carroll and Graf, 1999.

*

Critical Studies: Interview with Frank Birbalsingh, in *Ariel* (Calgary, Alberta, Canada), 24(1), January 1993; by Michael Horovitz, in *Poetry Review,* 83(4), winter 1994; by M. Simpson, in *Critical Survey* (Oxford, England), 6(3), 1994; by Paula Burnett, in *New Statesman Society* (London), 22 March 1996; by Sean O'Brien, in *London Review of Books,* 18(11), 1996; '''Tricksters of Heaven': Visions of Holocaust in Fred D'Aguiar's 'Bill of Rights' and Wilson Harris's 'Jonestown''' by Hena Maes-Jelinek, in *'Union in Partition': Essays in Honour of Jeanne Delbaere,* edited by Gilbert Debusscher and Marc Maufort, Liege, Belgium, L3, 1997; ''Remembering Slavery: History As Roots in the Fiction of Caryl Phillips and Fred D'Aguiar'' by Benedicte Ledent, in *The Contact and the Culmination,* edited by Marc Delrez and Benedicte Ledent, Liege, Belgium, L3, 1997; by H. Hathaway, in *African American Review,* 32(3), 1998; ''Anonymity, Naming and Memory in Fred D'Aguiar's 'Feeding the Ghosts': Islands of Fiction in a Sea of History'' by Carole Froude-Durix, in *Commonwealth Essays and Studies* (Dijon, France), 21(1), autumn 1998.

*   *   *

Fred D'Aguiar was born in London of Guyanese parents. His early years were spent in Guyana, but his secondary education was in London. He is a leading name among the now established generation of black poets who have contributed a wide variety of new energies and rhythms to British poetry during the 1980s and 1990s. D'Aguiar's poetry represents a cross-cultural synthesis of two traditions: one predominantly oral and belonging to the Caribbean, and the other the mainstream written literary tradition. The Caribbean has fostered major writing in both traditions, but its impressive performance-based oral tradition was not widely known in Britain until the 1980s, when it proved something of a revelation to many, especially younger, contemporary poetry readers.

The two traditions can be seen in D'Aguiar's first book, *Mama Dot.* Through the persona of Mama Dot, D'Aguiar creates a living metaphor for the Caribbean region, part possibly an actual person, part archetypal mother figure, but most importantly a spirit of place, as in the title poem "Mama Dot":

Born on a Sunday
in the kingdom of Ashante

Sold on Monday
into slavery

Ran away on Tuesday
cause she born free

Lost a foot on Wednesday
when they catch she

Worked all Thursday
till her head grey

Dropped on Friday
where they catch she

Freed on Saturday
in a new century

In "The Day Mama Dot Takes Ill," another poem in the sequence, "The continent has its first natural disaster: / Chickens fall dead on their backs, / But keep on laying rotten eggs . . ." When Mama Dot returns to health, the natural world celebrates: "She throws open her window / To a chorus and rumpus of animals and birds, / And the people carnival for a week."

The volume *Mama Dot* is divided into three sections, of which the title sequence is the first. The poem "Roots Broadcast," from which the second sequence takes its title, is written in the Caribbean and Guyanese oral vernacular idiom that was named by Edward Kamau Brathwaite "nation-language" (the book has a one-page glossary of these words):

No sun nah come up
dese days yet sun muss deh
some weh shinin pan somebady
else back wen all we gat
is hevy cloud redy fe bruk
pan we head an memry
of how sun wuk cawn dead
fo dis ya roots broadcast
pickin up pickin up

The third section of the book is taken up with "Guyanese Days," a long autobiographical poem on D'Aguiar's recollections of his early days in Guyana. It is written in Standard English, in itself a comment on his own mixed cultural and ethnic heritage. The poem is a tour de force and something of a virtuoso performance in language, equally eloquent and direct and providing impressive evidence of D'Aguiar's talent.

D'Aguiar's second book, *Airy Hall*, is also carefully divided into three sections. Although just as fastidiously written as *Mama Dot*, the

volume has an altogether stronger feeling of magic realism. The first part is taken up by the "Airy Hall" sequence, which, like "Guyanese Days," seems based on the poet's early memories of Guyana, although the poems are altogether more mysterious and imaginative in their evocations. The sequence reflects different aspects of the place, with titles such as "Airy Hall's Dynasty," "Airy Hall's Dark Age," and "Airy Hall Isotope," where the Western world and the third world meet:

Consider our man in a hovel
With no windows, a shack our missiles
Sail through; cracks that do not interrupt
The flow of moonlight or sunlight,
Seen here washing or baking his floor

The second section of *Airy Hall* includes the poem "El Dorado Update," a title referring to the abundant unmined gold in the interior of the Guyanese rainforest. The poem comments on the financial and other problems of third world nations, and stylistically it is a new departure, mixing lines from children's rhymes with phantasmagoric imagery to create a dream atmosphere in which fantasy and reality coexist:

Riddle me, riddle me, riddle.
One people, one nation, one destiny?
    Let's take a walk
    not to stay, just to see

You pass a man at Customs,
returning from an island;
he wears several tin chains,
tin rings on every finger,
and tin bracelets that jingle
as his arms swing.

Customs ensure
what he declares
tallies with their list made
when he departed
with identical amounts
of gold.

The third part of *Airy Hall* consists of the long poem "The Kitchen Bitch," which, more than any other part of the book, puzzled reviewers on its publication. The poem is complex, interweaving images of Guyana and the Caribbean with more phantasmagoric imagery and with dislocations of the narrative. A note to the poem explains that "kitchen bitch" is the name for a tin kerosene lamp used by Jamaican peasants. The poem tells the story of an expedition high up in the rainforest of the Guyanese interior, apparently following in the tracks of the half real, half legendary figure of Albert Collier. It is best read the way one reads, say, a Wilson Harris novel or a Jorge Luis Borges story, trusting to its own logic rather than to any linear narrative. *Airy Hall* is an ambitious and adventurous book that deserves to be better known, for it shows D'Aguiar broadening his range to look into the mysterious and enigmatic Amerindian past of Guyana.

D'Aguiar's *British Subjects* takes a long look at his birthplace of Britain, which he loves and yet where he most keenly experiences what he has called the black British poet's "sense of being 'other.'" The book does not have the brilliance of imagery of his earlier work and chooses to focus instead on the everyday feel of the "grey light and close skies" of urban Britain. In "Home" he explores his love for the red telephone boxes, "chokey streets, roundabouts and streetlamps / with tyres chucked round them" that he misses when he is away. His happiness as his plane touches down at Heathrow is short-lived when he arrives at customs "to the usual inquisition":

> my passport photo's too open-faced,
> haircut wrong (an afro) for the decade;
> the stamp, British Citizen not bold enough
> for my liking and too much for theirs.

"At the Grave of the Unknown African" is a moving and accomplished poem in couplets that is set in Bristol at the grave of a slave dead for 250 years. In the first part the poet meditates on the past "souls for sale in Bristol's port" and juxtaposes this with images of urban riots and skinheads in modern Bristol. In the second part an unnamed African slave answers the poet and urges him to

> Say what happened to me and countless like me, all anon.
> Say it urgently. Mean times may bring back the water cannon.

> I died young, but to age as a slave would have been worse.

The tone of the poem is assured, and the quiet dignity of the slave is allowed to speak out plainly.

British Subjects also includes several sequences: "Sonnets from Whitley Bay," a series of well-wrought love poems; "Frail Deposits," a series of four poems for Wilson Harris; "The Body in Question," addressed to various parts of the body; and "Notting Hill," an evocation of the annual celebratory Caribbean carnival in the Notting Hill area of London.

In the 1990s D'Aguiar published three distinguished novels— *The Longest Memory* (1994), *Dear Future* (1996), and *Feeding the Ghosts* (1997)—that met with critical acclaim in Britain. The distinction of his prose writing might have led to the confidence of address that is found in D'Aguiar's book of poetry *Bill of Rights,* published in 1998 and his most ambitious work to date. The book consists of an interlinked sequence of poems that make up a single dramatic narrative of an event in contemporary Guyanese history, the mass suicide in Jonestown of the followers of Jim Jones, the charismatic leader of a doomed religious sect. Place-names and scenes shift between a remembered London and present-day Guyana, creating the feeling of a disjointed life. The book is told from the point of view of a member of the cult whose personal history is intermixed with that of the group and whose voice we follow through illness and the birth of a child with his partner. We are given glimpses of the warped sexual morality of Jones and see the chilling mass suicide of the group, ". . . an excursion to God's theme park," which, miraculously, the speaker survives.

The book reminds us how many dramatic voices we find in the poems of D'Aguiar (he also has written plays), and the dramatic voices in *Bill of Rights* lead the reader through the experience in a exhilarating progression. Yet craft is present throughout, and contrasting sections use both the oral and the literary traditions. The poem is full of echoes of other poets, including W.H. Auden, W.B. Yeats,

Derek Mahon, Tom Paulin, Benjamin Zephaniah, Linton Kwesi Johnson, and Bob Dylan.

D'Aguiar's achievement is substantial, and he has shown himself to be an ambitious, original, and subtly experimental writer in the mainstream of contemporary poetry in Britain.

—Jonathan Barker

DAHLEN, Beverly

Nationality: American. **Address:** 15 Mirabel Avenue, San Francisco, California 94110.

PUBLICATIONS

Poetry

Out of the Third. San Francisco, Momo's Press, 1974.
A Letter at Easter: To George Stanley. Emeryville, California, Effie's Press, 1976.
The Egyptian Poems. Berkeley, California, Hipparchia Press, 1983.
A Reading (1–7). San Francisco, Momo's Press, 1985.
A Reading (11–17). Elmwood, Connecticut, Poets and Poets Press, 1989.
A Reading (8–10). Tucson, Arizona, Chax Press, 1992.

*

Critical Studies: "For the Body Which Deepens in Silence: The Early Works of Beverly Dahlen" by Mark Linenthal, in *Ironwood* (Tucson, Arizona), 14(1), Spring 1986; *Skirting the Subject: Pursuing Language in the Works of Adrienne Rich, Susan Griffin, Beverly Dahlen* (dissertation) by Alan Shima, Uppsala, Sweden, Uppsala University, 1993.

*   *   *

Though often included in that large and varied body referred to as language poetry, the poetry of Beverly Dahlen has consistently distinguished itself by its technical resourcefulness, its vigorous intimacy, and the coherence and development of its ambitious project. Dahlen's talents as a poet are considerable, and the menace and lyricism of these lines from *A Reading (1–7)* are exemplary: "in the myth of the unicorn the lady collaborates. she, lovely, is working for / the enemy, a spy, a trap, a snare. a man's lady. / she comes on the scene. of / course the unicorn is innocent, the child's body, slain. for her sake." The very seduction of such lyricism, however, and indeed the capacity of language itself to impose a meaning upon an experience, to reduce the subject to a voice, and to persuade form from the formless evoke an apprehension in Dahlen through which all her work is refracted ("this is talk. talk is cheap"). Concurrent with this apprehension of language, however, is the recognition that the power of speech to create meaning has been an exclusively male possession. Throughout Dahlen's work we find women choked, gagged, bruised about the throat, with mouths bloody or dry and empty of words. "Gesture," the first poem in her first book, *Out of the Third,* presents us with a mannerism the speaker has acquired from her mother:

I am trying to remember
what she
was afraid to say
all those

years, fingers folded
against her mouth,
head turned away.

Out of the Third is a book concerned with origins. There is the migration of the poet's family to the West Coast, which left behind "The Great Plains a burial mound. / The ditched bodies of women / and Indians." There is also a migration in language, a searching and a leaving behind. Dahlen asserts, almost haltingly,

I am trying
to learn
to speak
the American language

Though she acknowledges that "this is my mother tongue / this is my mother's tongue," the poet cannot accept it the way it has been prepared: ". . . roasted / sliced fan-shaped / she calls it flank steak." It is a pathetic figure, a tongue that misrepresents itself, and Dahlen concludes, "I know it's heart / I won't eat it." "The Occupation," a powerful poem that tells of the death of the poet's grandmother, also confronts this numbing speech: "My father at home naming all the vegetables / growing in his garden," and "No one says the word *dying.*" Language is itself an occupying force, keeping "everything in order. / Eating and dying":

How they talk. She passed away.
Gone in the rainy air.

To engage this language, both as everyday speech and as a poetic tradition, to counter the language that trivializes experience and attempts to silence women, is perceived as a political imperative: "I will make a voice. / It will be alone. You will hear it all night long falling away / towards the west. It will carry you." The making of this voice, however, the identification of its source and the choice of its texture, provides the problem that energizes much of Dahlen's work, and indeed this very question has become a touchstone for critics concerned to differentiate among language poets as a group. For Dahlen language is a thing that endlessly recedes. *A Reading (1–7)* commences with the words "before that and before that. everything in a line." Yet she does not conclude from this that language is the limit of consciousness. With Julia Kristeva, Dahlen understands language to signify an absence. The following is from *Out of the Third:*

Beginning at the skin
I work my way inward along the branches
looking for the one that leads to the ground.
I have been out here a long time now.

Dahlen's poetry, then, is most compelling as an intensely personal search for this "ground." In *A Letter at Easter: To George Stanley,* Dahlen finds the terms for such a search in an intimate correspondence that is liberating in the imaginative scope it affords but frustrating in its exclusion from the "real world": "This old

mothering split. The crack of doom in which / we speak to each other." In *The Egyptian Poems* this split becomes wider but to luminous effect. Here the poetry is compact, calm with a sense of its own power, the rhythm of its stanzas giving a sense of incantation. The gods have been invoked, and through poetry their attributes may be incorporated:

Eat the heart, the leg, the thigh,
all the parts. Take into the darkness of your mouth
this eye. It will be enough light.

It seems that the ground has been achieved, or at least the means to speak it and to see it, with the eye in the mouth now the same thing, have been. In her three later books, each entitled *A Reading,* Dahlen explores experience with a language that generates possibilities, that invites rather than establishes meaning. As Rachel Blau DuPlessis has noted in her excellent essay on Dahlen, the poetry of *A Reading* works metonymically to frustrate closure and encourage multiple readings. It resists participation in the reflex repressions that normally accompany all acts of language: "that's where the wind comes, for wind read calm, and the darkness, and for / darkness read light. that's where she is one or another so must be both. / the murdered or murderer."

The three volumes of *A Reading* are impressive, perhaps essential, works of postmodern poetry. Written in a form that combines the journal with the long poem, released from the constraints of stanza and line, given instead to a constantly rearranging lyricism, and cast with a truly multivocal feminist subject, this poetry is Dahlen's invitation to the reader to join her in learning to speak the American language.

—James Caton

DALE, Peter (John)

Nationality: British. **Born:** Addlestone, Surrey, 21 August 1938. **Education:** Strode's School, Egham, Surrey; St. Peter's College, Oxford, 1960–63, B.A. (honors) in English 1963. **Family:** Married Pauline Strouvelle in 1963; one son and one daughter. **Career:** Hospital porter and orderly, 1958–60; assistant teacher of English, Knaphill County Secondary School, Woking, Surrey, 1963, and Howden Comprehensive Secondary School, East Yorkshire, 1964–65; English master, 1965–71, and head of English, 1971–72, Glastonbury High School, Sutton, Surrey. Head of English, Hinchley Wood School, Esher, Surrey, 1972–93. Since 1993 full-time writer. Associate editor, 1971–82, and co-editor, 1982–96, *Agenda* magazine, London. Since 1997, with Ian Hamilton, Philip Hoy, on editorial board of *Between the Lines,* and since 1998, editor of poetry column in *Oxford Today.* **Awards:** Arts Council bursary, 1969. **Address:** 10 Selwood Road, Sutton, Surrey, England.

PUBLICATIONS

Poetry

Nerve. Privately printed, 1959.
Walk from the House. Oxford, Fantasy Press, 1962.
The Storms. London, Macmillan, and Chester Springs, Pennsylvania, Dufour, 1968.

Mortal Fire. London, Macmillan, and Chester Springs, Pennsylvania, Dufour, 1970; revised edition, London, Agenda, and Athens, Ohio University Press, 1976.

Cross Channel. Sutton, Surrey, Hippopotamus Press, 1977.

One Another: A Sonnet Sequence. London, Agenda, 1978.

Too Much of Water: Poems 1976–82. London, Agenda, 1983.

A Set of Darts, with W.S. Milne and Robert Richardson. Grimsby, England, Big Little Poems Books, 1990.

Earth Light. Frome, England, Hippopotamus Press, 1991.

Edge to Edge: Selected Poems. London, Anvil Press Poetry, 1996.

Da Capo: A Sequence of Poems. London, Agenda/Poets and Painters Press, 1997.

Plays

The Cell, in *Agenda* (London), 13(2), 1975.

Sephe, in *Agenda* (London), 18(1), 1981.

The Dark Voyage, in *Agenda* (London), 29(1–2), 1991.

Other

An Introduction to Rhyme. London, Bellew Publishing, 1998.

Translator, *The Legacy and Other Poems of François Villon*. London, Agenda, 1971; revised edition, as *The Legacy, The Testament, and Other Poems,* London, Macmillan, and New York, St. Martin's Press, 1973.

Translator, with Kokilam Subbiah, *The Seasons of Cankam: Love Poems Translated from the Tamil*. London, Agenda, 1975.

Translator, *Selected Poems of Villon*. London, Penguin, 1978.

Translator, *Narrow Straits: Poems from the French*. Sutton, Surrey, Hippopotamus Press, 1985.

Translator, *Poems,* by Jules Laforgue. London, Anvil Press Poetry, 1986.

Translator, *Selected Poems of François Villon*. London, Penguin, 1988; New York, Viking, 1989; revised edition, 1994.

Translator, *Dante: The Divine Comedy*. London, Anvil Press Poetry, 1996; revised edition, 1998.

Translator, *Poems of Jules Laforgue*. London, Anvil Press Poetry, 2000.

Translator, *Poems of François Villon*. London, Anvil Press Poetry, 2000.

* * * * *

Critical Studies: *"Notes on the Poetry of Peter Dale,"* in *Agenda* (London), viii, 3–4, 1970, and "The Poetry of Peter Dale," in *PNR,* 119, 1998, both by William Cookson; "The Poetry of Peter Dale" by Terry Eagleton, in *Agenda* (London), xiii, 3, 1975; "Father's Story" by Donald Davie, in *The Listener* (London), October 1976; "The Poetry of Ordinariness," in *Agenda* (London), xiv, 4-xv, I, 1977, and "Fathers and Sons: Peter Dale's *Mortal Fire,*" in *Southern Review* (Baton Rouge, Louisiana), Winter 1979, both by William Bedford; "Reciprocals: Peter Dale and Timothy Steele" by Wyatt Prunty, in *Southern Review* (Baton Rouge, Louisiana), July 1981; Peter Dale issue of *Agenda* (London), 26(2), Summer 1988; Peter Dale issue of *Outposts* (Frome, England), 156, Spring 1988; "Solipsism Transcended" by W.G. Shepherd, in *Agenda* (London), xxxi(1), 1995.

Peter Dale comments:

Within the constraints of such a volume as this, not much of significance or assistance may be said about one's verse. It's the job of poems, not poets, to speak for themselves—and the chief problem with that idea in our modern cultures is the difficulty a poem has in getting any distribution, let alone a decent hearing. This isn't helped by the thought that a true poem is a needle in a haystack. Searching for it is no use; it has to find you—and many a thing pricks which is no poem. (The Internet itself, in terms of distribution, is a madly made haystack). Young, you'd set out with a commitment to firm ideas of what you wanted to write; older, in retrospect, in your selected poems, you end up shocked, though often agreeably, at where the vagaries of the imagination have taken you in disregard of the intention. Conscious intention, contemporary acclaim, or dismissal have little to do with poems. A poet's commitment is to giving life, an ineradicable emotion, to a few words that will carry over the years and speak directly to a reader or hearer in the inner voice of mind and imagination. It's almost impossible. Even great poets do it rarely. The commitment remains but, as Larkin remarked, you write not what you like but what you can. And given the cultural situation, you hope—adapting Eliot—"My words echo / Thus in your mind." Though you read on: "But to what purpose / Disturbing the dust on a bowl of rose-leaves . . ." It's no consolation to substitute "computer screen" for "bowl."

*   *   *

In "'Where All the Ladders Start,'" an essay on Yeats, Peter Dale writes, "For me, the important Yeats is the questioning, observing one who analyses moments—and what poet was given better moments?—rather than the systemising, abstracting one." He offers "After Long Silence" as his initial example of Yeats at his best. The lyric analysis of "moments" is Dale's own great strength as a poet, and it is significant that "After Long Silence" contains much that one finds in Dale's work too: powerful emotion expressed indirectly, an awareness of the mutability of things, the recognition of the past in the present, an attraction to occasions of oblique or transitional light, repetition of word and phrase within a stanza marked by subtle rhymes. Such qualities are evident even in so short a poem as "Crocuses":

Delicate, firm as porcelain, with that dram
Of stillness till they lapse back from the rim.

Love, love, yes, something once, never enough,
nor you, nor I—today they touch a nerve.

The exact hesitancy of the rhythm enacts in microcosm what Dale has elsewhere, in the foreword to *One Another,* called "the morphology of an emotion." The internal rhyme ("stillness"/"till"), the repetition ("love, love"/"nor you, nor I"), the gracefulness of the rhyming—of which Dale has been theorist as well as skilled practitioner—all have a heightened naturalness of idiom that is the product of a sure technique. Dale's earlier work includes both poems in traditional forms (e.g., "The Storms") and some minimalist free verse. The later work brings together the virtues of both. The encounter with minimalism certainly helped to develop an alertness to the eloquence of the natural image, as in "Dusk":

Moon a sliver of apple
blue on a knife-blade.

Light enough for a known face
I touch shadow round your eyes.

The recurrent themes that mark Dale's mature work are, in a sense, nothing other than the high commonplaces of the poetic tradition—love and death. A repeated image—reflections in a window—provides a clue to what is most individual in Dale's treatment of these themes. The sequence "Mirrors, Windows" in *Earth Light* (first published in *Agenda* in 1988) is made up of ten sonnets. These impressive poems take as their starting point a situation in which "a middle-aged man observes his dead father's features in the window pane." Reflection, in more than one sense, is the central concern. The window reflects, but it also can be seen through; it combines opacity and transparency; we see in it both what is within and what is outside. Images are thus superimposed, and poetically the window becomes a means to articulate the simultaneous or alternating presences of past, present, and future. In *One Another* a central concern is with "the years in the window pane" (from "Dusk"—not the poem quoted above), with attempts to grasp the "see-through stuff of memory" ("Memorial"), and the sequence ends with "Window," a poem that begins with the characteristic ambiguity of "your eyes, child, in the window."

Dale's finest work is that in which memory attempts to recall to language the moment of experience, to put wordless epiphany into words. The moments of epiphany are those in which a kind of "double exposure" makes available to the seeing mind the past or the future in the present, in memory or imagination, so that the moment itself becomes timeless, an awareness of mutability coexisting with an apprehension of something outside time. The longer reflective poems examine such questions, although not in a coldly intellectual fashion, establishing an emotional metaphysics of seeing and remembering, recording the activity of the "merciless eye, that nothing can assuage" ("Recapitulation") of the subjectivity of meaning:

There is no voice in the stream's whispered hearsay.
    There is no beauty here. It's all my eye.

"Summer Shadows," which closes *Too Much of Water: Poems 1976–82,* is a major poem in which particularity of observation is perfectly married to a searching mind. The language, for all its seeming clarity, is richly teasing in its implications.

Dale is a love poet of the greatest tenderness, whether in the magnificent sonnets of *One Another: A Sonnet Sequence* or in lyrics that continue the great English tradition, as in "Occasions":

I wasn't there to look
    the time you saw the lightning sear
the crooked oak.
    I had your fear for it.

I wasn't there the day
    you found a wind-cast blossom shadow
spread from the may.

Your joy I had for that.

—You let the bird go free.
    I couldn't see the blood that welled
but it seemed to me
    a bulb you held had burst . . .

When the love that I swear
    is a dry husk on the wind's breath,
I shan't be there.
    You'll have my death for it.

It is in the precision of his language, its economy and its shapeliness, that Dale creates his poetic idiolect. The emotional and psychological states with which it deals are often at the edge of the poet's knowledge. There is, consequently, obliqueness in the achieved precision, a sense of discoveries, and recoveries, being made.

Though *Mortal Fire* contains much of value, it is on *One Another*, *Too Much of Water*, and *Earth Light*, particularly in the sequences "Like a Vow" and "Mirrors, Windows," that a claim for Dale's importance as a poet should be based. An equally forceful claim might be made on the strength of his work as a translator. Donald Davie has praised Dale's versions of Villon as the work of an "exceptionally thoughtful and enterprising translator." Dale's remarkable translations of Jules Laforgue certainly demonstrate both thought and enterprise of a high order. So do many of his other translations from the French, notably of Tristan Corbière, and he has published his translation of Dante. Dale is a self-effacing translator; his own personality does not intrude between the reader and the translated text. Elsewhere we often feel, say, that we are reading Marianne Moore as much as La Fontaine, Craig Raine rather than Racine. Dale has no truck with Poundian doctrines of imitation; his is a courageous attempt to find English equivalents for the form, content, and spirit of the original. To have successfully translated such writers as often as Dale has done is an astonishing achievement, and there is courage in his insistence on printing his translations with their originals on the facing page. This kind of courage might have been no more than foolhardiness, but such is Dale's critical intelligence and his technical skill and inventiveness that the results are among the major achievements of modern verse translation. They are the work of a conscientious, and poetically gifted, craftsman.

Dale's work both as original poet and as translator puts him in the first rank of contemporary English poets.

—Glyn Pursglove

DALLAS, Ruth

Pseudonym for Ruth Mumford. **Nationality:** New Zealander. **Born:** Invercargill, 29 September 1919. **Education:** Southland Technical College, Invercargill. **Awards:** New Zealand Literary Fund achievement award, 1963; University of Otago Robert Burns fellowship, 1968; New Zealand Book award, 1977; Buckland award, 1977; Achievement award for literature, Royal New Zealand Foundation for the Blind, 1999. Litt.D.: University of Otago, Dunedin, 1978. C.B.E. (Commander, Order of the British Empire), 1989. **Address:** 392 Bay View Road, St. Clair, Dunedin, New Zealand.

PUBLICATIONS

Poetry

Country Road and Other Poems 1947–1952. Christchurch, Caxton Press, 1953.
The Turning Wheel. Christchurch, Caxton Press, 1961.
Experiment in Form. Dunedin, University of Otago Bibliography Room, 1964.
Day Book: Poems of a Year. Christchurch, Caxton Press, 1966.
Shadow Show. Christchurch, Caxton Press, 1968.
Song for a Guitar and Other Songs, edited by Charles Brasch. Dunedin, University of Otago Press, 1976.
Walking on the Snow. Christchurch, Caxton Press, 1976.
Steps of the Sun. Christchurch, Caxton Press, 1979.
Collected Poems. Dunedin, University of Otago Press, 1987.

Short Stories

The Black Horse and Other Stories. Dunedin, University of Otago Press, 2000.

Other

Curved Horizon (autobiography). Dunedin, University of Otago Press, 1991.

Other (for children)

Sawmilling Yesterday. Wellington, Department of Education, 1958.
The Children in the Bush. London, Methuen, 1969.
Ragamuffin Scarecrow. Dunedin, Otago University Bibliography Room, 1969.
A Dog Called Wig. London, Methuen, 1970.
The Wild Boy in the Bush. London, Methuen, 1971.
The Big Flood in the Bush. London, Methuen, 1972; New York, Scholastic, 1974.
The House on the Cliffs. London, Methuen, 1975.
Shining Rivers. London, Methuen, 1979.
Holiday Time in the Bush. London, Methuen. 1983.

*

Manuscript Collection: Hocken Library, University of Otago, Dunedin, New Zealand.

Critical Studies: By James Bertram, in *Landfall 29* and *62* (Christchurch), March 1954, and June 1962; introduction by Charles Brasch to *Song for a Guitar,* 1976; ''The Rhythm of Change: Comments on the Work of Ruth Dallas'' by John Gibb, in *Pilgrims 3* (Dunedin), nos. 1–2, 1978; Basil Dowling, in *Landfall* (Christchurch), December 1980.

Ruth Dallas comments:

I am sometimes rather frowningly called a ''nature poet,'' but I have never lived in a large city and been separated from the life of the earth and the coming up and going down of the sun in unpolluted skies; so I take my imagery where I find it. I have tried to keep in the forefront of my mind my position in space and time; I want never to forget that I am on a remote small planet in space and never to forget that I am on it at present and must soon leave. And who is to say that I am to write twentieth-century poetry, or any other kind of poetry? It is chance that I was born in the twentieth century and not the tenth, and chance that I was born in New Zealand and not Scandinavia or China. I care nothing for fashion in poetry and think a poem should be as free as one of the far-ranging seabirds I have watched by the hour flying in storm and calm about the coasts of New Zealand. A bird is not always flying; when it is still, it is very still, but you know what it can do.

Perhaps for this reason I have been attracted to the ancient meditative poems of the Chinese and Japanese, who used words with as much thought as they used the brush strokes from which their poems are hardly separable. I, too, like to use words sparingly and to make them carry as many overtones as possible, but all should seem spontaneous.

A poem is a human utterance, like dance and song, or an involuntary cry. What would please me most would be to find that my poems appeared effortless, however hard I work on them. But if I fail, it is difficult to believe that it matters. Poetry runs in our veins and over the centuries will flower now here, now there. If it does not come from my pen, it will come from another's. *Steps of the Sun* shows less Chinese influence and more exploration of the possibilities of the imagination.

*　　*　　*

Ruth Dallas first became known as a regional poet, a meditative recorder of rural life and incident in Southland, the lonely province at the bottom of New Zealand that looks inland to small farms, mountain lakes, and brooding beech forests and south to Antarctica. This is hard country (central Otago concentrates wilderness, orchards, and climatic extremes), and a girl growing up in intellectual isolation, threatened with blindness and with an ailing mother to care for, had to develop her own inner discipline and self-reliance. The result was a lyrical poetry of plain statement and diction, responsive to the play of natural and historical forces on human lives. *Country Road* has several poems (''Milking before Dawn,'' ''Grandmother and Child,'' ''The World's Centre'') that soon became stock New Zealand anthology pieces, and Dallas was conveniently typed as a nature poet with a limited range.

Eight years later, however, *The Turning Wheel* revealed a more restless and capacious mind. The title sequence is still concerned with seasonal growth and change, but ''Letter to a Chinese Poet'' (Po Chü-i) is a much more ambitious sequence, in which local and personal material is assimilated into a cultural and metaphysical synthesis of real power and intensity. An autobiographical essay, ''Beginnings'' (*Landfall,* December 1965), describes the independent reading that led to a new interest in Buddhist influences on Indian, Chinese, and Japanese literature: ''Through my lack of formal, dogmatic education, there were no walls to break down, and I was able to pass as freely into one culture as into another.'' Dallas's first writing in Invercargill had been encouraged by the critic and editor M.H. Holcroft, and when she moved to Dunedin, she began a long association with the poet Charles Brasch in the editing of *Landfall,* which is clearly traceable in the development of her thought. It would be misleading to describe her as a philosophical poet; she is no system maker, and her best work remains concentrated in short lyrical forms. But like Ruth Pitter perhaps, Dallas has produced a considerable body of lyrical work, often experimental in shape and texture and apparently purely decorative or musical, that carries a gravity of thought and perception quite disproportionate to its limited compass.

During the 1970s Dallas had some international success with her stories for children, and she came to be considered a creative prose writer as well as a poet. Yet her verse volume *Walking in the Snow* won the New Zealand Book award for poetry in 1977, and there is evidence, particularly with the publication of her *Collected Poems* in 1987, of a steadily widening appreciation of her distinctive lyrical achievement. She is one of the most independent and unfashionable of New Zealand writers, but her purity of diction and clear singing note seem likely to preserve her work when more aggressively modern verse is forgotten. She has no doubts about what she is striving for—the unassuming mastery of a Japanese jar glimpsed in a pottery kiln: "The jar was uneven, casual, easy, nonchalant; it seemed almost accidental, but was not. That's how I should like my finished work to appear."

—James Bertram

DANA, Robert (Patrick)

Nationality: American. **Born:** Allston, Massachusetts, 2 June 1929. **Education:** Drake University, Des Moines, Iowa, B.A. 1951; University of Iowa, Iowa City, M.A. 1954. **Military Service:** Radioman in U.S. Navy, 1946–48. **Family:** Married 1) Mary Kowalke in 1951, two daughters and one son; 2) Peg Sellen. **Career:** Instructor, 1954–58, assistant professor, 1958–62, associate professor, 1962–68, and professor of English, 1968–94, Cornell College, Mount Vernon, Iowa; editor, Hillside Press, 1957–67, and *The North American Review,* 1964–68, both Mount Vernon; contributing editor, *American Poetry Review,* 1973–88, *New Letters,* 1980–83, and since 1991 *The North American Review.* **Awards:** Danforth grant, 1959; Rinehart Foundation fellowship, 1960; Ford-ACM grant, 1966; Rainer Maria Rilke prize, 1984; National Endowment for the Arts fellowship, 1985, 1993; Delmore Schwartz memorial award, 1989; Carl Sandburg medal, 1994; Pushcart Prize XXI, 1996. **Address:** 1466 Westview Drive, Coralville, Iowa 52241, U.S.A.

PUBLICATIONS

Poetry

My Glass Brother and Other Poems. Iowa City, Constance Press, 1957.
The Dark Flags of Waking. Iowa City, Qara Press, 1964.
Journeys from the Skin: A Poem in Two Parts. Iowa City, Hundred Pound Press, 1966.
Some Versions of Silence. New York, Norton, 1967.
The Power of the Visible. Chicago, Swallow Press, 1971.
The Watergate Elegy. Chicago, Wine Press, 1973.
Tryptych. Chicago, Wine Press, 1974.
Winter Poems, with Debora Greger and George O'Connell. Lisbon, Iowa, Penumbra, 1977.
In a Fugitive Season. Iowa City, Windhover Press, 1979.
On a View of Paradise Ridge from a Rented House. Kendrick, Idaho, Two Magpies Press, 1980.

Keats in Detroit to Byron in California. Privately printed, 1982.
What the Stones Know. Iowa City, Seamark Press, 1984.
Blood Harvest. Iowa City, Windhover Press, 1987.
Starting Out for the Difficult World. New York, Harper, 1987.
What I Think I Know: New & Selected Poems. Chicago, Another Chicago Press, 1991.
Yes, Everything: New Poems. Chicago, Another Chicago Press, 1994.
Hello, Stranger. Tallahassee, Florida, Anhinga Press, 1996.
Summer. Tallahassee, Florida, Anhinga Press, 2000.

Other

Editor, *Against the Grain: Interviews with Maverick American Publishers.* Iowa City, University of Iowa Press, 1986.
Editor, *A Community of Writers: Paul Engle and the Iowa Writers' Workshop.* Iowa City, University of Iowa Press, 1999.

*

Bibliography: *Voyages to the Inland Sea 3* edited by John Judson, La Crosse, University of Wisconsin Press, 1973.

Critical Studies: "A World that Comes Apart like a Surprise" by Anselm Hollo, in *New Letters* (Kansas City, Missouri), summer 1973; "From Deep Space: The Poetry of Robert Dana" by Edward Brunner, in *The Iowa Review,* 22(3), fall 1992.

Robert Dana comments:

I see myself as a poet—I don't believe in poets as prophets, or priests, or even as people of superior intelligence and feeling. Though I'm sure I once did and once in a while still do. Ultimately, I think, I believe what Auden and Cunningham have believed before me—that the poet's only magic is with words. He begins life with a natural gift for handling them and hearing them. He loves them for their sounds, their taste, their soft or their steel feel. And for their enduring strangeness. Each word has, for him, its own perfect story.

Much later, when the poet begins to develop a style, he comes to recognize that style is not just a way of saying things but a way of seeing things. And seeing them with the whole being at once. Poetry is felt thought, Eliot once said. And so it is. But being both at once, it is neither. A poem is an experience of a total kind in which the transitory in our existence passes into permanence.

*   *   *

In *ABC of Reading* Ezra Pound lists six categories of poets, ending with "starters of crazes." Robert Dana has never started a craze. He is not an inventor either, a poet who creates a brand new process, but he has learned from such poets, assembling and assimilating techniques and poetic strategies so well that he earns a place in Pound's second category—master craftsman.

Dana's first book describes our perishing world as it becomes part of his inner life, an ironic charting of his country's taste for concrete images "Unlikely as Chicago." He skewers Americans' view of nature:

Pigs blister the hillside . . .
Morning may strike us anywhere.

Dana looks for balance in another direction, toward the Tang poets he translates or to

> The grace of simple food . . .
> . . . the table wooden as the loneliness of plain fact

> And bread of the moon
> the heart's small loaf.

The tension between the two worlds is sometimes manifest in Dana's silences, and it may occur in the "zag zag zag of sodium lamps / blue across the causeways." In his second book the tension turns toward dreams, becoming metamorphic:

> And I am driving into my own sleep
> of white chickens
> past barnyard harvest of junked cars
> the wind slumps through the empty eyes of cows.

Landscapes begin to flash surrealistically: Los Angeles sloshes into the ocean after nine days of rain, Kennedy is assassinated again, "razors could not cut the rain from the glass." Without reveling in vatic zeal or surreal petulance, however, the poet "whistles under the true sky of his troubles / walking slowly / inside himself," realizing that, regardless of the emotions that flood him, he gains only a measured wisdom:

> I see that I am what I always was
> that ordinary man on his front steps
> bewildered under the bright mess of the heavens
> by the fierce indecipherable language of its stars.

In the books that have followed, Dana has steadily sharpened and broadened this perspective. The voice that now comes from his page is assured in its puzzlement, not distracted even by artifice. "These Days," from *What I Think I Know,* describes two people fishing on a beach and records their banal conversation until Dana announces candidly, "You're reading a translation. / The beach is empty." He continues with

> I'm swirling
> my wind-chilled whiskey
> in its glass, and watching the sun

> collapse in heaven-fire,
> or wild glory, or whatever
> passes for that these days.

It is bitter, passionate realism, not drunk on nature, self-pity, romanticism, salvation schemes, whiskey, or a dream of poetry.

The poem "Gebra's Story" shows how far Dana has come. Gebra, his guide on an expedition, tells him about Kilimanjaro—"Not the House of God, / just another great stone / in a land of stones"—and about a climb into whiteout conditions:

> . . . we lost our way
> and couldn't see.
> My tears froze in my eyes.

Gebra has told his icy story in the "suffocating shade" of a desert below the "sacred / mountain of the Masai, / soaring in the filthy heat." Dana sits "amid flies," listening, and when it is over, he says simply, "I believe his story . . . and you can believe mine." Dana then tells about the prior night on the desert:

> last night, I shat where
> lion shit and jackal.

Again we listen, for the poem is about listening and telling. It is about being in "God's house," lost in the snow or exhausted by dysentery, about

> squatting there without
> benefit of gun
> or prayer,

> under lightning, with sudden, torrential rain

> sluicing my scarred arms in long bright shivers.

We believe his story.

—Edward B. Germain

DARUWALLA, Keki N(asserwanji)

Nationality: Indian. **Born:** Lahore, Pakistan, 24 January 1937. **Education:** Government College, Ludhiana; University of the Punjab, Lahore, M.A. in English. **Family:** Married; one child. **Career:** Since 1958 member of the Indian Police Service, and since 1962 superintendent of police. **Address:** c/o Oxford University Press, Post Box 43, YMCA Library Building, 1st Floor, Jai Singh Road, New Delhi 110 001, India.

PUBLICATIONS

Poetry

Under Orion. Calcutta, Writers Workshop, 1970; revised edition, New Delhi, Indus, 1991.
Apparition in April. Calcutta, Writers Workshop, 1971.
Crossing the Rivers. New Delhi, Oxford University Press, 1976.
Winter Poems. New Delhi, Allied, 1980.
The Keeper of the Dead. New Delhi, Oxford University Press, 1982.
Landscapes. New Delhi, Oxford University Press, 1987.
A Summer of Tigers: Poems. New Delhi, Indus, 1995.

Short Stories

Sword and Abyss. Sahibabad, Vikas, 1979.
The Minister for Permanent Unrest & Other Stories. Delhi, Ravi Dayal Publishers, 1996.

Other

Editor, *Two Decades of Indian Poetry 1960–1980.* Sahibabad, Vikas, 1980.

*

Critical Studies: *Critical Spectrum: The Poetry of Keki N. Daruwalla* edited by F.A. Inamdar, New Delhi, Mittal Publications, 1991; *Keki N. Daruwalla: Assessment As a Poet* by R.A. Singh, Bareilly, Prakash Book Depot, 1992.

Keki N. Daruwalla comments:

(1970) There is very little that is urbane or sophisticated about my poetry. I avoid a well-groomed appearance and strive for a sort of earthy poetry, "immersed in site." A long, irregular line helps me in my descriptive passages. I tend to make my verse as condensed and harsh as possible. Exile, rootlessness, and death—as a ritual that presides over our buried lives—are themes that come naturally to me. Significant incidents I turn into what I call "incident-poems." However, I try and involve myself with attitudes to things rather than the incident itself, e.g., an earthquake, drought ("Food and Words"), ritual murder ("Caryak"), death of a child ("Fire-Hymn"). My ambition is to write a series of intensely personal poems, all interconnected and nailed round the scaffolding of a personal myth.

*   *   *

Although the Indian writer Keki N. Daruwalla has published short stories and dabbles in literary journalism, he is primarily a poet. Since *Under Orion,* his first volume of poems, he has shown consistency in rigor of style and an admirable skill in combining traditional prosody with free verse, narrative flow with the introspective, and the lyrical with the satirical. Possessing an urban sensibility, Daruwalla is a poet of "the octopus city," and even his perceptions of nature are conveyed through urban analogies: "the streets of dawn," "the street of virginity," "the spear-grass street."

Given his literary background, the echoes of Blake and Yeats ("gongs sound like hammered gold"), Auden ("let me hold tight to the angst, the fear / it's all I have my dear"), and Hopkins and Ted Hughes ("I saw the wild hawk-king this morning / riding an ascending wind / as he drilled the sky") are perhaps inevitable, though the use of literary references like the one to Dante in "Boat-Ride," for example, do not always seem to work. Words like "ere" and "whence," which slip in occasionally, introduce an element of archaism that jars with the otherwise exemplary terse modernism.

Despite these conscious or unconscious stylistic echoes, Daruwalla's poetry is distinguished by sharp, articulate imagery, an eye probing for meaning behind the details of everyday life, and a concern with social, political, and religious values, in particular "the spider-thread of ritual." His is a distinctly contemporary voice in Indian poetry, free from self-indulgence and from a temptation to mythologize the sordid and disturbing present through romantic images of the past. On the other hand, there is throughout his poetry an element of skepticism, often salutary but sometimes rendered hollow by a failure to see that his kind of probing can be self-limiting. It is possible that his experiences in the police services have contributed to this in some way. He is unshakably committed to his everyday environment and struck by the ubiquitousness of violence, even in

sexual experience, as illustrated in "Fish in Speared by Night." His "bitter, scornful, satiric tone," as Nissim Ezekiel describes it, determines the scope of his irony and is both his strength and his weakness.

Another feature that runs through different collections of Daruwalla's poems is his acceptance of the physical reality of his environment and his belief that "destiny, stars, fate / we don't measure up to such words." For example, these lines from *Under Orion*—"if fate were to squeeze me hard / all that would remain of me / would be a bit of turd"—are echoed in his futuristic vision of the death of the river in the 1976 *Crossing the Rivers,* where three spacemen from another planet "dig through your silt-flanks / and come upon a half-burnt skull / as the Magi came upon the Christ."

Crossing the Rivers is astonishingly authentic, both in its portrayal of the sordidness of Varanasi, the sacred city of the Hindus, and in its controlled anger at its decadence, of which people seem to be unmindful. His ironic invocation of the river Ganges, through razor-sharp language and a wry humor, contrasts with that of Jawaharlal Nehru, a self-confessed agnostic equally distrustful of the empty husk of ritual, in his *Will.* For the latter the river is still a valued poetic layer of his racial memory, even though its religious function is suspect, but for Daruwalla "the river will not yield her secrets: / the flowers of her body withhold their perfume."

Daruwalla's definition of a poet would seem to involve the role of a social commentator. That he can transmute social comment into poetry as social gesture gives to his poetry a double-edged quality and reflects a view of life that requires a toughness of the spirit for survival. This, however, is implicit. His poems often end with a question, and even when it is not ostensibly so, the ending reads more like an opening out to a question than a flat statement, as for example in "Mother."

The enigma of survival is Daruwalla's central concern. Such is the poet's aversion to abstraction that his words become sensory images in the process of their poetic articulation. The refusal, however, to look inward, which is evident in the poems about the Ganges in *Crossing the Rivers,* is less apparent in poems such as "The Parsi Hell," "Mehrab," and "The Keeper of the Dead" and in the poems in the section entitled "In the Shadow of the Imambara," which draw directly from Daruwalla's Zoroastrian background even though they, too, are colored by his satiric skepticism.

Daruwalla achieves an inwardness of feeling and a suppleness of language and form whenever he deals with a human situation, a specific personage, or a place or landscape and attempts to relate this to the world of his dreams and memory.

—Devindra Kohli

DAS, Kamala

Nationality: Indian. **Born:** Kamala Nair in Malabar, South India, 31 March 1934; took name Suraiya in 1999. **Education:** Studied privately. **Family:** Married K. Madhava Das in 1949; three sons. **Career:** Poetry editor, *Illustrated Weekly of India,* Bombay, 1971–72, 1978–79; former editor, *Pamparam,* Trivandrum, Kerala; former director, Book Point, Bombay; former president, Jyotsha Art and Education Academy, Bombay; former member Governing Council, Indian National Trust for Cultural Heritage, New Delhi, and State Planning Board Committee on Art, Literature, and Mass Communications. Independent Candidate for Parliament, 1984. Chair, Forestry

Board, Kerala. **Awards:** P.E.N. prize, 1964; Kerala Sahitya Academy award, for fiction, 1969; Chaiman Lal award, for journalism, 1971; Asian World prize for literature, 1985; Indira Priyadarsini Vrikshamitra award, 1988. Hon.Doc.: World Academy of Arts and Culture, Taiwan, 1984. **Address:** Royal Stadium Mansion, Gandhi Nagar, Cochin 20, India.

PUBLICATIONS

Poetry

Summer in Calcutta: Fifty Poems. Delhi, Everest Press, 1965.
The Descendants. Calcutta, Writers Workshop, 1967.
The Old Playhouse and Other Poems. Madras, Longman, 1973.
Tonight This Savage Rite: The Love Poetry of Kamala Das and Pritish Nandy. New Delhi, Arnold-Heinemann, 1979.
Collected Poems. Privately printed, 1984.
The Best of Kamala Das. Kozhikode, Bodhi Publishing House, 1991.
Only the Soul Knows How to Sing. Kottayam, D.C. Books, n.d.

Novels

Alphabet of Lust. New Delhi, Orient, 1977.
Madhavikkuttiyute munnu Novalukal (three novels; for children). Trivandrum, Navadhara, 1977.
Manomi. Trichur, Current Books, 1987.
Chandana Marangal (The Sandalwood Tree). Kottayam, D.C. Books, 1988.
Katalmayuram: Munnu Ceru Novalukal. Kottayam, Current Books, 1991.

Short Stories

Pathu Kathakal (Ten Stories), *Tharisunilam* (Fallow Fields), *Narachirukal Parakkumbol* (When the Bats Fly), *Ente Snehita Aruna* (My Friend Aruna), *Chuvanna Pavada* (The Red Skirt), *Thanuppu* (Cold), *Rajavinte Premabajanam* (The King's Beloved), *Premathinte Vilapa Kavyam* (Requiem for a Love), *Mathilukal* (Walls). Trichur, Kerala, Current Books, 1953–72.
A Doll for the Child Prostitute. New Delhi, India Paperbacks, 1977.
Ente Kathakal. Calcutta, Mathrubhumi, 2 vols., 1985.
Palayanam: Kathakal. Trichur, Current Books, 1990.
Padmavati, the Harlot and Other Stories. New Delhi and New York, Sterling Books, 1992.

Other

Driksakshi Panna (Eyewitness) (for children). Madras, Longman, 1973.
My Story. New Delhi, Sterling, 1976; London, Quartet 1978.
Bhayam Ente Nisavastram (Fear Is My Nightgown). Calcutta, Mathrubhumi, 1986.
Balyakala Smaranakal (Childhood Reminiscences). Kottayam, D.C. Books, 1987.
Varshangalku Mumbu (Years Ago). Trichrur, Kerala, Current Books. 1989.
Nirmatalam Puttakalam. Kattayam, D.C. Books, 1993.

*

Critical Studies: *Kamala Das* by Devindra Kohli, New Delhi, Arnold-Heinemann, 1975; *Expressive Form in the Poetry of Kamala Das* by Anisur Rahman, New Delhi, Abhinav, 1981; *Kamala Das and Her Poetry* by A.N. Dwivedi, New Delhi, Doaba, 1983; *Kamala Das,* Bedford Park, South Australia, Flinders University, 1987; *Untying and Retying the Text: An Analysis of Kamala Das's* My Story, New Delhi, Bahri Publications, 1990, and *Feminist Revolution and Kamala Das's* My Story, Patiala, Century Twentyone Publications, 1992, both by Kaura Ikabala; *Contemporary Indian Poetry in English: With Special Reference to the Poetry of Nissim Ezekiel, Kamala Das, A.K. Ramanujan, and R. Parthasarathy,* by P.K.J. Kurup, New Delhi, Atlantic Publishers & Distributors, 1991; *The Poetry of Kamala Das,* by K.R. Ramachandran Nair, New Delhi, Reliance Publishing House, 1993; *The Endless Female Hungers: A Study of Kamala Das,* by Vrinda Nabar, New Delhi, Sterling Publishers, 1994; "Self Revealed and Self Mythified: The Autobiographies of Maya Angelou and Kamala Das" by D. Maya, in *Literary Criterion* (India), 32(3), 1996.

Kamala Das comments:

(1970) I began to write poetry with the ignoble aim of wooing a man. There is therefore a lot of love in my poems. I feel forced to be honest in my poetry. I have read very little poetry. I do not think that I have been influenced by any poet. I have liked to read Kalidasa. When I compose poetry, whispering the words to myself, my ear helps to discipline the verse. Afterwards, I count the syllables. I like poetry to be tidy and disciplined.

(1974) My grand-uncle is Nalapat Narayana Menon, the well-known poet-philosopher of Malabar. My mother is the well-known poetess Nalapat Balamani Amma. I belong to the matriarchal community of Nayars. Our ancestral house (Nalapat House) is more than four hundred years old and contains valuable palm leaf manuscripts like the *Varahasamhita, Susrutha Samhita,* and books of mantras.

As I have no degree to add to my name, my readers considered me in the beginning like a cripple. My writing was like the paintings done by "foot-and-mouth" painters or like the baskets made by the blind. I received some admiration, but the critics, well-known academicians, tore my writing to shreds. This only made my readers love me more. All I have wanted to do is to be real and honest to my readers.

(1999) I embraced the religion of Islam in December 1999. I shall visit other lands to propagate Islam. I relinquished the freedom granted by lenient Hinduism to serve my master Allah. I am happy at last.

*   *   *

Kamala Das is bilingual, and she writes poetry in English and fiction and autobiography in Malayalam and English. Her first book of poems, *Summer in Calcutta,* with its spontaneous speech rhythms and individual tone of voice, established her as a distinctly contemporary and refreshingly original poet. As an expression of a married Indian woman's search for "an identity that was loveable," her poetry has opened up new possibilities for other Indian women writers.

At the age of fifteen Das was forced into a traumatic arranged marriage, one devoid of love and companionship. This experience brought the rebel in her to the surface. In "The Blood-Stained Moonlight," a chapter of her autobiographical *My Story,* she reveals the powerful link between her marriage and her need to write poetry. Thus, "confessing / By peeling off my layers" or by "letting my mind striptease,'' she wrote with an uncompromising honesty poems that "flaunt a grand, flamboyant lust.'' To see this aspect of her poetry as mere sensational self-dramatization is to overlook its underlying sensitivity; she suggests this herself when she declares, "I'm too emotional to be pornographic.'' Her frequently quoted poem "An Introduction" is doubtless confessional to a degree, but it is also an assertion of a writer's freedom. It transforms an Indo-English woman writer's alienation from "critics, friends, visiting cousins''—who, as spokesmen of the patriarchal culture, tell her not to write in English and advise her to conform—into a larger and more universal alienation—sexual, social, and artistic—that is perhaps at the heart of any attempt at self-exploration and self-integration:

> . . . I met a man, loved him. Call
> Him not by any name, he is every man
> Who wants a woman, just as I am every
> Woman who seeks love. In him . . . the hungry haste
> Of rivers, in me . . . the ocean's tireless
> Waiting. Who are you, I ask each and everyone,
> The answer is, it is I. Anywhere and
> Everywhere, I see the one who calls himself
> I; in this world, he is tightly packed like the
> Sword in its sheath.

Das has often been criticized, ironically by her own countrywomen, for not conforming to the norms of traditional grammar and for not being conscious of technique. Indeed, she lacks an academic background, and she rarely revises her poems. One looks in vain for literary echoes in her work. On the positive side, however, her style derives its authenticity precisely from its linguistic "distortions'' and "queernesses'' and from her innate rhythms, which are part of the process of the Indianization of English that Raja Rao prophesied in his preface to *Kanthapura* (1938) as being both desirable and inevitable.

Das's favorite theme has always been the shadowy borderline between fulfillment and lack of fulfillment in love, between the point where lust ends and spiritual love begins, as experienced by a married Indian woman. Poems such as "In Love,'' "Summer in Calcutta,'' "The Freaks,'' "The Fear of the Year,'' "A Relationship,'' "An Apology to Goutama,'' "Winter,'' "Spoiling the Name,'' "With Its Quiet Tongue,'' "The Sea Shore''—all from *Summer in Calcutta*—demonstrate this amply. In these poems Das synthesizes the changing reality of her private passion and the apparently unchanging reality of the Indian sun and landscape.

Das's concern with disease, illness, aging, fragmentation, and death—dominant themes in her second volume, *The Descendants*—recurs in many of her later poems, including "Life's Obscure Parallel,'' "Death Is So Mediocre,'' "The Sensuous Woman, III,'' "Woman without Her Shadow,'' "Words Are Birds,'' and "I Shall Not Forget.'' In the latter, memories of happiness and the sense of imminent death are interwoven to produce a more focused and mellow acceptance of life as it is.

In the 1973 volume *The Old Playhouse and Other Poems*, however, Das deals with the way in which a broken marriage makes a woman conscious of the need to create a space of her own. In "The Stone Age,'' for example, the husband, an "old fat spider weaving webs of bewilderment'' around the female persona, turns her into "a bird of stone, a granite dove.'' He becomes an unwelcome intruder into the privacy of her mind: "With loud talk you bruise my premorning sleep, / You stick a finger into my dreaming eye.'' Other men who haunt her mind "sink / like white suns in the swell of my

Dravidian blood.'' She drives along the sea and climbs "the forty steps to knock at another's door.'' At this point, the act of defiance having taken place and the dull cocoon of domesticity assaulted, the poem becomes alive with energetic questioning, and the theme of winning and losing asserts itself.

Under Das's deceptively simple surfaces lies a complexity that is imperfectly controlled, and she defies categorizations that are not heavily qualified. While she empathizes with the rebel, she can also celebrate her rootedness in her tradition. Outspoken about her womanhood, she does not, however, typecast genders. When she speaks of love outside marriage, she is not recommending adultery but merely searching for a relationship that gives both love and security and preserves her individuality. Her focus is not on the sexual act. In "I Shall Some Day'' she visualizes taking refuge in the cocoon the husband builds around her with morning tea, "in your nest of familiar scorn,'' after her world has become "just a skeletal thing.'' Some of Das's better poems deal with the memories of her childhood, of her grandmother's house and of "the warmth that she [her great-grandmother] took away,'' in contrast to "the great brown thieving hands [that] groped beneath my / Clothes, their fire was that of an arsonist's, / Warmth was not their aim . . .''

Das is capable of intense detachment and can empathize with the larger world of ordinary people, the victims in one way or another of the same system. Her rebellion is evident in such early poems as "The Child in the Factory,'' "The Flag,'' "Someone Else's Song,'' "The Sunshine Cat,'' "Forest Fire,'' "A Hot Noon at Malabar,'' and "Visitors to the City.'' The social awareness of some of her later poems, including "The House Builders,'' "The Lunatic Asylum,'' and poems provoked by the politically charged ethnic situation in Sri Lanka, all from *Collected Poems,* is evidence of the same quality of detachment.

—Devindra Kohli

DAVEY, Frank(land Wilmot)

Nationality: Canadian. **Born:** Vancouver, British Columbia, 19 April 1940. **Education:** University of British Columbia, Vancouver, 1957–63, B.A. (honors) 1961, M.A. 1963; University of Southern California, Los Angeles (Canada Council fellow), 1965–68, Ph.D. 1968. **Family:** 1) Helen Simmons in 1962 (divorced 1969); 2) Linda McCartney in 1969, one son and one daughter. **Career:** Teaching assistant, University of British Columbia, 1961–63; lecturer, 1963–66, and assistant professor, 1967–69, Royal Roads Military College, Victoria, British Columbia; writer-in-residence, Sir George Williams University, Montreal, 1969–70; assistant professor, 1970–72, associate professor, 1972–79, coordinator of the creative writing program, 1976–79, professor of English, 1980–90, and chair of the department of English, 1985–90, York University, Toronto. Since 1990 Carl F. Klinck Professor of Canadian Literature, University of Western Ontario, London. Visiting professor, Shastri Indo-Canadian Institute, Karnatak University, India, 1982. Founding editor, *Tish* magazine, Vancouver, 1961–63. Since 1965 founding editor, *Open Letter,* Toronto; general editor, Quebec Translations series, 1973–90, and since 1975 member of the editorial board, Coach House Press, Toronto; since 1977 general editor, New Canadian Criticism series, Talonbooks, Vancouver; director, *Swift Current* literary database and magazine project, 1984–90. President, the Association of Canadian College and University Teachers of English, 1994–96. **Awards:** Macmillan prize, 1962; Department of National Defence arts research grant, 1965, 1966, 1968; Humanities Research Council of Canada grant, 1974, 1981; Canada Council travel grant, 1966, 1971, 1973, and fellowship, 1966, 1974; Canadian Federation for the Humanities grant, 1979 and 1992; Social Sciences and Humanities Research Council fellowship, 1981. **Address:** University of Western Ontario, Department of English, London, Ontario N6A 3K7, Canada.

PUBLICATIONS

Poetry

D-Day and After. Vancouver, Tishbooks, 1962.
City of the Gulls and Sea. Privately printed, 1964.
Bridge Force. Toronto, Contact Press, 1965.
The Scarred Hull. Calgary, Imago, 1966.
Four Myths for Sam Perry. Vancouver, Talonbooks, 1970.
Weeds. Toronto, Coach House Press, 1970.
Griffon. Toronto, Massasauga, 1972.
King of Swords. Vancouver, Talonbooks, 1972.
L'An Trentiesme: Selected Poems 1961–1970. Vancouver, Community Press, 1972.
Arcana. Toronto, Coach House Press, 1973.
The Clallam; or, Old Glory in Juan de Fuca. Vancouver, Talonbooks, 1973.
War Poems. Toronto, Coach House Press, 1979.
The Arches: Selected Poems, edited by B.P. Nichol. Vancouver, Talonbooks, 1980.
Capitalistic Affection! Toronto, Coach House Press, 1982.
Edward and Patricia. Toronto, Coach House Press, 1984.
The Louis Riel Organ and Piano Company. Winnipeg, Manitoba, Turnstone Press, 1985.
The Abbotsford Guide to India. Victoria, British Columbia, Press Porcépic, 1986.
Postcard Translations. Toronto, Underwhich, 1988.
Popular Narratives. Vancouver, Talonbooks, 1991.

Other

Five Readings of Olson's "Maximus." Montreal, Beaver Kosmos, 1970.
Earle Birney. Toronto, Copp Clark, 1971.
From There to Here: A Guide to English-Canadian Literature since 1960. Erin, Ontario, Press Porcépic, 1974.
Louis Dudek and Raymond Souster. Vancouver, Douglas and McIntyre, 1980; Seattle, University of Washington Press, 1981.
Surviving the Paraphrase: Essays on Canadian Literature. Winnipeg, Turstone Press, 1983.
Margaret Atwood: A Feminist Poetics. Vancouver, Talonbooks, 1984.
Reading Canadian Reading. Winnipeg, Manitoba, Turnstone Press, 1988.
Post-National Arguments: The Politics of the Anglophone-Canadian Novel Since 1967. Toronto, University of Toronto Press, 1993.
Reading "KIM" Right. Vancouver, Talonbooks, 1993.
Literary Power: Essays on Anglophone-Canadian Literary Conflict. Edmonton, NeWest Press, 1994.

Karla's Web: A Cultural Examination of the Mahaffy-French Murders. Toronto, Viking/Penguin, 1994; revised edition, 1995.
Cultural Mischief: A Practical Guide to Multiculturalism. Burnaby, British Columbia, Talonbooks, 1996.

Editor, *Tish 1–19.* Vancouver, Talonbooks, 1975.
Editor, *Mrs. Dukes' Million,* by Wyndham Lewis. Toronto, Coach House Press, 1977.
Editor, *The Browser's Opal L. Nations.* Toronto, Coach House Press, 1981.
Editor, *Given Names: New and Selected Poems 1972–1985,* by Judith Fitzgerald. Coatsworth, Ontario, Black Moss Press, 1985.
Editor, with Fred Wah, *The Swiftcurrent Anthology.* Toronto, Coach House Press, 1986.
Editor, *Deeds/Nations,* by Greg Curnoe. London, ON, London Chapter of the Ontario Archeological Society, 1994.

*

Manuscript Collection: Simon Fraser University, Burnaby, British Columbia.

Critical Studies: Interviews with Elizabeth Komisar in *White Pelican* (Edmonton, Alberta), 1975, George Bowering in *Open Letter* (Toronto), 4(3), Spring 1979, Gale Scott, in *Spirale* (Montreal), 1981, and Fred Gaysek, in *Artviews* (Toronto), 1988; ''Frank Davey: Finding Your Voice to Say What Must Be Said'' by Douglas Barbour, in *Brave New Wave* edited by Jack David, Windsor, Ontario, Black Moss Press, 1978; ''*Frank Davey, Critic As Autobiographer*'' by E.D. Blodgett, and ''War Poetry: Fears of Referentiality'' by Lynette Hunter, both in *Beyond Tish,* edited by Douglas Barbour, Edmonton, NeWest Press, 1991; ''Nobody Gets Hurt Bullfighting Canadian Style: Rereading Frank Davey's 'Surviving the Paraphrase''' by Robert Lecker, in *Studies in Canadian Literature* 18(3), 1993; ''Post-National Arguments: The Politics of the Anglophone-Canadian Novel since 1967'' by C. Hunter, in *Ariel,* 25(3), 1994; ''Mastering the Mother Tongue: Reading Frank Davey Reading Daphne Marlatt's How Hug a Stone'' by Julie Beddoes, in *Canadian Literature,* 155, Winter 1997; ''The Presumption of Culture and Ideas of North: A Reply to Frank Davey'' by T. Henighan, in *English Studies in Canada,* 24(4), 1998.

Frank Davey comments:

Since 1964 my poetry has been written mostly in sequences of from ten to one hundred pages. I have been especially interested in the politics of the abrupt shifts of tone and diction that are possible between the sections of a serial poem and in the writing of European (*King of Swords, Weeds*) or United States (*The Clallam, Capitalistic Affection!*) mythology from a Canadian perspective. Recently I have been connected with the collapse of poetry as a socially instrumental discourse and have been experimenting with poems disguised as prose (*The Abbotsford Guide to India*). Most of my writing, verse or criticism, has been concerned with the decentralization of literary mythologies and the enabling and creation of alternative texts.

*   *   *

Frank Davey has managed to emerge with three careers: he is a poet who writes with some degree of originality and interest; he is a postmodernist critic in Canadian letters; and he is a social and cultural commentator with a sharp eye for the imagery of everyday life. The three careers could be couched in three different tenses—the past to refer to the poet, the present to refer to the critic, and the future to refer to the commentator—though that would lead one to the conclusion that the activities have been successive. Instead, they overlap.

As a poet Davey is best known for his espousal of the values of the Black Mountain school in Canada, introduced through the monthly mimeographed newsletter *Tish*, continued from 1965 through the triannual *Open Letter*, and embodied in his teaching and in articles, reviews, and the pages of *From There to Here: A Guide to English-Canadian Literature since 1960*, a once useful though quite opinionated handbook. His poetry, judged by *L'An Trentiesme: Selected Poems 1961–1970* and *Arcana*, is not at all doctrinaire, contrary to what George Bowering is quoted as saying in *From There to Here*, but rather light and lyrical. As Davey himself says in ''out &/on,'' a poem from the ''Bridge Force'' part of the selected poems, ''description / is a bird who comes down / all too easy.'' *Arcana* includes occasional poems plus chic meditations on the tarot cards. On the basis of these works it could be maintained that Davey is essentially an occasional poet. Yet he has written semidocumentary, semilyrical poems on a number of marine disasters, culminating in *The Clallam; or, Old Glory in Juan de Fuca*, a long poem that successfully re-creates the sinking of the ship of that name. Perhaps his credo is best summed up in ''The Mirror XIV'' from *Arcana*:

> I write these words
> that someone, will remember me,
> or at least finding me here
> poisd, burnd, loved, unloved, will see words
> moving.

With later books the reader senses that Davey, having decided to direct the Muse a bit in her deliberations, has engaged more than his sensibility. *The Louis Riel Organ and Piano Company* is a long, rambunctious poem full of humor and fine effect:

> What T.S. Eliot forgot
> was that Homer was just
> a small-town boy. James Joyce
> didn't forget.

Capitalistic Affection!—note the exclamation mark—is a loving and nostalgic look at comic book and other characters of contemporary mythology as figures of fun but also as guides and guardians of morality: ''What Chester Gould told me / was that all criminals have ugly faces.'' In that context the collection's Canadian literature sequence simply seems out of place.

The liveliest of all of Davey's books is *Edward and Patricia*, a riotously funny sequence of poems about early married life. For its pinpointing of the niceties and naughtiness that characterize the days and nights of the contemporary urban couple, Davey deserves a prize from John Updike.

Davey must have cheered the day the term ''postmodernism'' surfaced, because with it came a theory, or set of considerations, that would enable him to organize longtime concerns. These include continuity and discontinuity in life and art, personality and impersonality in literary works, the interactivity of the whole and the part, and self-reference.

In 1990 Davey was appointed to the Carl F. Klinck chair as professor of Canadian literature at the University of Western Ontario

in London. During this period he wrote a literary-social-critical study of Prime Minister Kim Campbell, comparing her to the heroine of *Anne of Green Gables*, and a widely discussed consideration of the effects of censorship, based on the notion of prior restraint, in contemporary society.

—John Robert Colombo

DAVIDSON, Michael

Nationality: American. **Born:** Oakland, California, 18 December 1944. **Education:** San Francisco State University, 1963–67, B.A. 1967; State University of New York, Buffalo, 1967–71, Ph.D. 1971; post-doctoral fellow, University of California, Berkeley, 1974–75. **Family:** Married 1) Carol Wikarska in 1970 (divorced 1974); 2) Lori Chamberlain in 1988; two children. **Career:** Visiting lecturer, San Diego State University, 1973–76. Curator, Archive for New Poetry, 1975–85, and since 1977 professor of literature, University of California, San Diego. Advisory editor, *Fiction International*, Canton, New York; advisory editor, *Sagetrieb, River City*; editor, *The Archive Newsletter* and *Documents for New Poetry*, both in La Jolla, California. **Award:** National Endowment for the Arts grant, 1976. **Address:** Department of Literature, University of California at San Diego, La Jolla, California 92093, U.S.A.

PUBLICATIONS

Poetry

Exchanges. Los Angeles, Prose and Verses Press, 1972.
Two Views of Pears. Berkeley, California, Sand Dollar, 1973.
The Mutabilities, and The Foul Papers. Berkeley, California, Sand Dollar, 1976.
Summer Letters. Santa Barbara, California, Black Sparrow Press, 1976.
Grillwork. Montreal, M.B.M. Monographs, 1980.
Discovering Motion. Berkeley, California, Little Dinosaur Press, 1980.
The Prose of Fact. Berkeley, California, Figures, 1981.
The Landing of Rochambeau. Providence, Rhode Island, Burning Deck, 1985.
Analogy of the Ion. Great Barrington, Massachusetts, Figures, 1988.
Post Hoc. San Francisco, Avenue B, 1990.
Leningrad. San Francisco, Mercury House, 1991.
The Arcades. Oakland, California, O Books, 1998.

Other

The San Francisco Renaissance: Poetics and Community at Mid-Century. Cambridge University Press, 1989.
Ghostlier Demarcations: Modern Poetry and the Material Word. Berkeley, University of California Press, 1997.

*

Critical Studies: *The Dance of the Intellect: Studies in the Poetry of the Pound Tradition* by Marjorie Perloff, New York, Cambridge

University Press, 1985; *Poet's Prose* by Steve Fredman, New York, Cambridge University Press, 1993; *Palmer/Davidson: Poets and Critics Respond to the Poetry of Michael Palmer and Michael Davidson,* edited by P. Michael Campbell, Berkeley, Occident Press, 1992.

Michael Davidson comments:

My first encounters with poetry occurred, as they did for most of my generation, via Brooks and Warren's *Understanding Poetry.* As I remember, "classic" poems were presented, followed by four or five seminal questions that, once answered by the bright literature student, would solve the curious riddle hidden, intentionally, no doubt, in the poem. Such an approach to poetry was pretty intimidating for a young writer. After all, the poet presumably had thought these strategies out before sitting down to write, and my early practice simply involved writing "toward" some vaguely formed idea. The Brooks and Warren method of literary analysis was accompanied in creative writing workshops by stern lectures on what was then called the "craft" of poetry, that is, the poet's ability to exert his will to power over form. The supreme poet, then, was one who could channel the multifarious happenings of daily life into a series of discrete, oblique figures, usually involving some part of the poet's inner organs or perhaps his ancestral origins. This rather inhospitable atmosphere was an important formulating experience for my own work, but under the salutary influence of the poetry renaissance of the late 1950s and early 1960s in San Francisco I resumed the practice of writing toward some vaguely formed idea.

I would like to think of my work as an interrogation or exploration of its own processes, not for the sake of formalist exercise but in order to test the thresholds of meaning. In this sense poetry is a profoundly human activity since it refuses to take the world for granted while believing utterly in its multifaceted character. The most difficult task for the poet, as Jack Spicer pointed out, is avoiding what you want to say since this invariably results in a trivializing of that initial charge that drove you to write in the first place. And oddly enough, the result is something extremely personal, if only because the writing embodies the wandering, desultory quality of one's thoughts. At times this "tracing" involves areas of interruption and semantic breakdown since it is often where language fails to provide necessary information, or where it provides the unwanted figure, slip of tongue, or typo, that it most reveals. How, then, to capture that quality? At the simplest level, by being open to the qualities and textures and confusions of one's own language as it struggles with difficult material and alternately by avoiding the lure of an imperializing rhetoric that yearns to "temper" that experience by subordinating its semantic plurality. This may not be a practical solution, but it is at least the atmosphere in which the various solutions offered in my writing have been nurtured.

(1995) The emphasis above is on writing as an "interrogation or exploration of its own processes," and while I still stand by those remarks, I would qualify them by adding that there are no processes that are writing's own. Language is social, even in those moments when it is being used to provide sanctuary from the social. Linguistic interrogation and exploration must also attend to the social idiolects in which writing appears—the voices, dialects, and rhetorics of people in groups. Testing the thresholds of meaning cannot be done in a vacuum. Meaning is a collaborative activity among individuals, not something congealed in a text. Any challenge to sedimented usage is simultaneously an attack on the institutions for which it has become normalized. This does not mean that individual expression is dead,

only that it achieves its authority by acknowledging its contingent, dialogic, and tenuous nature.

*   *   *

"To 'do' one's art," Michael Davidson writes, "means to solve problems in a language which the art establishes as it is being created. Its grammar and lexicon emerge less as a result of a commitment to prior forms and more as a response to immediate necessity." The locus of interest in Davidson's *The Mutabilities, and The Foul Papers* is precisely in watching the response to immediate necessity unfold. The poems are, as it were, live performances.

The epigraph to the volume is from Laurence Sterne's *Tristram Shandy,* and the pervading tone is Shandean. Davidson's poetry turns on a sense of language as a persistent but unreliable medium. Above all, "I"—the sign that traditionally holds a privileged place in language as the center of control—is very slippery and unstable. It would not be an oversimplification to say that Davidson's work is an investigation of language in which the "I" becomes as much a matter of conjecture as everything else:

> Marking this way
> as a direction one comes to know
> one is known,
> hence you are still you
> and I
> am not so sure.

Lacking a dependable ordering ego, the poems are variations on unstated—and unstatable-themes, or, as in "Often he felt uncomfortable," on a theme that is itself mutable. The idiomatic phrase "to come out" is loaded with ambiguities, and in this poem Davidson uses it in a half-dozen or more different senses. The central matter of conjecture, however, is how words come out. Of all things their coming out is most mysterious: "and the vipers and bats and lizards come out of nowhere / which is a word out of which other words come out." The origins of language are completely concealed by the fact that whatever they might be can only be stated in language:

> in the beginning was the word and when it was out
> there was a space projected like a little star
> out of which all the light we have ever seen came pouring
> one word at a time.

There is nothing occult, nothing hidden, in Davidson's poetry. It is, like the poetry of Michael Palmer, a poetry of surfaces.

"The Foul Papers" *(The Mutabilities)* are prose poems, but their strategies are fundamentally like those found in Davidson's other work. In the title piece of the section, for example, there are seven paragraphs about some unnamed "he" who is, however, "close to," if not identical with, the "I" who gives the account. Although the paragraphs are very loosely organized, they do have centers of concerns. The first is about his loss of virginity, the second a concert by the Coasters, the third his "47 Plymouth with blue Satin seat covers," the fourth the cat odors in his house, the fifth a list of things he has to do on some relatively uneventful day, the sixth a love affair (perhaps with the woman with whom he speaks in the second), and the last a conversation with another woman. Although it is possible to trace several lines of connection through the piece, one of the primary conjectural centers has to do with smell. The piece concludes with "so their conversation draws on into empty night, the prospect emptying itself into their conversation until only smells remain and which, in time, take on the unexpected pressure of beauty." It is just that "unexpected pressure of beauty," issuing from what seems rather unpromising material, that is the dominant effect of Davidson's work.

The so-called language movement with which Davidson's work is identified has run the course of its initial impulse. Unlike some of the other language poets, such as Bruce Andrews, who have been drawn more to performance, Davidson's work seems increasingly to demonstrate philosophical and critical points. *Analogy of the Ion,* for example, could almost be used as a text in a graduate seminar in literary theory, for in its ironic mode it touches on many of the major points.

—Don Byrd

DAVIS, Dick

Nationality: British. **Born:** Portsmouth, Hampshire, 18 April 1945. **Education:** King's College, Cambridge, 1963–66, B.A. in English 1966, M.A. 1970; University of Manchester, Ph.D. in Persian 1988. **Family:** Married Afkham Darbandi in 1974; two daughters. **Career:** Teacher in Greece, 1967–68, Italy, 1968–69, Margaret McMillan College, Bradford, Yorkshire, 1969–70, Tehran University, 1970–71, and College of Literature and Foreign Languages, Tehran, 1971–78; Northern Arts Literary Fellow, Universities of Durham and Newcastle, 1985–87; poet-in-residence, 1985, and visiting associate professor, 1987–88, University of California, Santa Barbara; assistant professor of Persian, 1988–1992, associate professor of Persian, 1993–98, and since 1998 professor of Persian, Ohio State University, Columbus. Reviewer, *PN Review,* Manchester, 1975–86, and *The Listener,* 1980–87, and *Times Literary Supplement,* both London. **Awards:** Arts Council grant, 1979; Royal Society of Literature Heinemann award, 1981; British Institute of Persian Studies grant, 1982–83; Ingram Merrill award, 1993; Guggenheim award, 1999. **Address:** NELC, 203 B+2, 1735 Neil Avenue, Ohio State University, 190 North Oval Mall, Columbus, Ohio 43210, U.S.A.

Publications

Poetry

Shade Mariners, with Clive Wilmer and Robert Wells. Cambridge, Gregory Spiro, 1970.
In the Distance. London, Anvil Press Poetry, 1975.
Seeing the World. London, Anvil Press Poetry, 1980.
The Covenant. London, Anvil Press Poetry, 1984.
Visitations. Colchester, Ampersand Press, 1983; as *Four Visitations,* West Chester, Pennsylvania, Aralia Press, 1985.
What the Mind Wants. Florence, Kentucky, Barth, R.L. 1984.
Lares. N.p., Sea Cliff Press/Cummington Press, 1986.
Devices and Desires: New and Selected Poems 1967–1987. London, Anvil Press Poetry, 1989.
A Kind of Love: New & Selected Poems. Fayetteville, University of Arkansas Press, 1991.
Touchwood. London, Anvil Press Poetry, 1996.

Other

Wisdom and Wilderness: The Achievement of Yvor Winters. Athens, University of Georgia Press, 1983.
Epic & Sedition: The Case of Ferdowsi's Shahnameh. Fayetteville, University of Arkansas Press, 1992.

Editor, *The Selected Writings of Thomas Traherne.* Manchester, Carcanet, 1980.
Editor, with David Williams, *New Writing from the North.* Ashington, Northumberland, MidNAG, 1988.
Editor, *The Ruba'iyát of Omar Khayyám,* translated by Edward FitzGerald. London, Penguin, 1989.

Translator, with Afkham Darbandi, *The Conference of the Birds,* by Attar. London, Penguin, 1984.
Translator, *The Little Virtues,* by Natalia Ginzburg. Manchester, Carcanet, 1985; New York, Seaver, 1986.
Translator, *The City and the House,* by Natalia Ginzburg. Manchester, Carcanet, 1986; New York, Seaver, 1987.
Translator, *The Legend of Seyavash,* by Ferdowsi. New York, Penguin Classics, 1992.
Translator, *Borrowed Ware: Medieval Persian Epigrams.* London, Anvil Press Poetry, 1996; Washington, D.C., Mage, 1997.
Translator, *My Uncle Napoleon,* by Iraj Pezeshkzad. Washington, D.C., Mage, 1997.
Translator, *The Lion and the Throne: Stories from the Shahnameh of Ferdowsi.* Washington, D.C., Mage, 1998.

*

Critical Studies: "Immersions" by Thom Gunn, in *British Poetry since 1970: A Critical Survey,* edited by Peter Jones and Michael Schmidt, New York, Persea, 1980; "Dick Davis, *A Kind of Love: Selected and New Poems*" by David Middleton, in *Classical Outlook,* 70(3), spring 1993.

Dick Davis comments:

My themes are love, travel, and the meeting of cultures; my technique is formal to the point of pedantry. I admire wit and sentiment in poetry; I dislike obfuscation, density of texture at the expense of clarity, whatever cannot be paraphrased. I aim to write good verse.

*   *   *

With the publication of a volume of selected poems in 1989, it is possible to give more than a merely provisional account of the poetry of Dick Davis, whose first full-length collection, *In the Distance,* was published only in 1975. Nonetheless, certain distinctive features were apparent in the first volume and in his next, *Seeing the World.* In poems like "The Diver" or "A Mycenean Broach" one can see his early work as definitely inheriting the mantle of the so-called tight-lipped school of the late 1960s, plus that movement's inevitable tendency toward a minimalist art, exemplified in such pieces of Davis's as "Service," "Desire," or the positively paltry "An Affair . . ." A number of the poems of *In the Distance* are marred by a vagueness derived from either too much abstraction or an overanxiety for precision that leads to a gnomic and static utterance. Sometimes, too, there is a carelessness of syntax, as in ''The Shore''—''he rolls / Aside to watch the deep / Thought may not sound''—or in ''Old Man Seated before a Landscape''—''each separate / Discrete particular, an animate / Uncertain will claiming attention: no.'' In or out of context these lines verge on syntactical nonsense.

On the other hand, several of the poems in Davis's initial volume are fully achieved pieces. Particularly accomplished is the mythologically dreamlike ''Diana and Actaeon,'' ''Odysseus in Ithaca,'' and ''A Memory,'' the last showing a lyrical propensity. In ''Love in Another Language'' the lines ''The meaning crammed / Through unfamiliar channels, in new tones, / With a choked force'' are an excellent summary of both Davis's problem with craft and that of modern poets in general.

Persisting, however, with his intolerable wrestle with words and form, Davis advances considerably with his second volume. There is more inevitability and less academic forcing about the poems. His gift for discovering the fine line, the meaningful and memorable utterance, is further developed; only now he is able, in poem after poem, to find a perfectly supportive context for his insights. ''Marriage as a Problem of Universals'' is quite brilliant. It is a poem on large abstractions that works on the practical level, the form being turned and turned in masterly fashion. In ''Desert Stop at Noon'' thought and compassionate feeling are communicated readily to the reader, and ''Baucis and Philemon'' and ''Semele'' further reinforce the sense of a sensitive and maturing talent, one informed by a serious authority.

If one may be permitted to generalize, there are several identifiable thematic strands in Davis's work, several distinct personae, as it were. There is the academic persona of ''Art Historian'' or of ''The Epic Scholar,'' one ''desolate with love'' of his subject and with the past, one who would willingly ''rest here and fantasize the willing past.'' Then, too, there is something of the philosopher in Davis. Indeed, there has to be to enable him to write ''Marriage as a Problem of Universals,'' though the success of this particular poem also requires the poet to be celebrant, to be a man in love with not just the nuptial state (as a moralist or a philosopher might be) but with a real live woman too. In addition, the man who early perceived the limits of irony (''Irony does not save'') is clearly on the way to some sort of religious awareness, and I think that there are pointers toward that end in many of the poems. I conclude this not just because of the occasional religious poem, such as ''The Virgin Mary'' or ''St. Christopher,'' but also because of the more subtle evidence of a growing wisdom in the poet, the wisdom that always uncovers the divine in things. A yet further persona of Davis is concerned with classical myth, and even poems that make no reference to the Greco-Roman world—for example, ''Scavenging after a Battle'' or ''Touring a Past''—strongly suggest a poet who has wandered, like Keats, much in the golden realms of Homer.

Consequently, in Davis we encounter a varied talent and one that, combining ''imaginative ambitiousness with technical honesty'' (to borrow the words of the *Times Literary Supplement* about his first volume), should suggest a sound poetic future. Provided that Davis can find things to say, it would seem that his future should be assured, for clearly his is a soundly based and intelligent talent. To borrow Michael Robert's famous pointer of genuine poetry, there is a certain ''elegance'' about Davis's writing.

Devices and Desires: New and Selected Poems 1967–1987 brings together all of Davis's best poems, some of which have been discussed above, and it is quite easy to appreciate the eulogies that have been lavished on his work by the likes of Thom Gunn (''Davis is one of the best poets around''), Michael Schmidt (''he belongs to an English and a European tradition of writing in which 'purity' of diction, of thought and theme, are virtues of the highest order''), and Glyn Pursglove (''Davis . . . is undoubtedly one of the most accomplished and most rewarding . . . of the younger English poets''). Indeed, Davis is one of the most deft and delicate technicians now writing in traditional forms. But what we can see—and began to suspect with *The Covenant*—is that Davis is increasingly in what I may term ''inspirational difficulty.'' As he puts it in one of the new poems appended to the selected poems, entitled significantly ''To the Muse,'' ''I can't complain / If you disdain / To visit me— / Too often I / Tried to deny / Your quiddity.'' There is a distinct possibility that Davis's work as a lecturer and translator of Persian language and literature may have begun to dry up his fount of poetry and, to some extent at least, be turning his considerable linguistic skills away from poetry. Indeed, the appearance in 1992 of his lengthy translation of *The Legend of Seyavash* by Ferdowsi, which is part of the great epic poem of Iran, *The Book of Kings*—a considerable and accomplished undertaking—along with subsequent translations, would seem to indicate such a move.

—William Oxley

DAVISON, Peter (Hubert)

Nationality: American. **Born:** New York City, 27 June 1928. **Education:** Fountain Valley School, Colorado Springs; Harvard University, Cambridge, Massachusetts, A.B. (magna cum laude) 1949 (Phi Beta Kappa); St. John's College, Cambridge (Fulbright Scholar), 1949–50. **Military Service:** U.S. Army, 1951–53. **Family:** Married 1) Jane Truslow in 1959 (died 1981), one son and one daughter; 2) Joan E. Goody in 1984. **Career:** Page in the U.S. Senate, 1944; editorial assistant, 1950–51, and assistant editor, 1953–55, Harcourt Brace publishers, New York; assistant to the director, Harvard University Press, 1955–56; associate editor, 1956–59, executive editor, 1959–64, director, 1964–79, and senior editor, 1979–85, Atlantic Monthly Press, Boston; consulting editor, Houghton Mifflin publishers, Boston, 1985–98. Member of advisory board, National Translation Center, 1965–68. Since 1972 poetry editor, *Atlantic Monthly,* Boston. **Awards:** Yale Series of Younger Poets award, 1963; American Academy of Arts and Letters award, 1972; Academy of American Poets award, 1981, 1985; New England Booksellers award, 1995. **Address:** 70 River Street, Boston, Massachusetts 02108, U.S.A.

PUBLICATIONS

Poetry

The Breaking of the Day and Other Poems. New Haven, Connecticut, Yale University Press, 1964.
The City and the Island. New York, Atheneum, 1966.
Pretending to Be Asleep. New York, Atheneum, 1970.
Dark Houses. Cambridge, Massachusetts, Halty Ferguson, 1971.
Walking the Boundaries: Poems 1957–1974. New York, Atheneum, and London, Secker and Warburg, 1974.
A Voice in the Mountain. New York, Atheneum, 1977.

Barn Fever and Other Poems. New York, Atheneum, 1981; London, Secker and Warburg, 1982.
Praying Wrong: New and Selected Poems 1957–1984. New York, Atheneum, 1984; London, Secker and Warburg, 1985.
The Great Ledge. New York, Knopf, 1989.
The Poems of Peter Davison, 1957–1995. New York, Knopf, 1995.
Breathing Room: New Poems. New York, Knopf, 2000.

Recording: *Paradise as a Garden,* Watershed.

Other

Half Remembered: A Personal History. New York, Harper, 1973; London, Heinemann, 1974; revised edition, Brownsville, Oregon, Story Line Press, 1991.
One of the Dangerous Trades: Essays on the Work and Workings of Poetry. Ann Arbor, University of Michigan Press, 1991.
The Fading Smile: Poets in Boston, 1955–1960. New York, Knopf, 1994.

Editor, *Hello Darkness: The Collected Poems of L.E. Sissman,* Boston, Little Brown, and London, Secker and Warburg, 1978.
Editor, *The World of Farley Mowat: A Selection from His Works.* Toronto, McClelland and Stewart, and Boston, Little Brown, 1980.

*

Manuscript Collection: Beinecke Library, Yale University, New Haven, Connecticut.

Critical Studies: Foreword by Dudley Fitts to *The Breaking of the Day and Other Poems,* 1964; *Three Contemporary Poets of New England* by Guy Rotella, Boston, Twayne, 1983; "Studying Interior Architecture by Keyhole: Four Poets" by Reg Saner, in *Denver Quarterly,* 20(1), summer 1985.

Peter Davison comments:

Between 1950 and 1998 I worked as an editor, reading other people's manuscripts, encouraging other people's muses, discouraging those—both prose and poetry—that seemed to be unsuited to a partnership between us, helping bring texts into publishable condition, attempting to make the delicate compromise between publishing books of some degree of excellence and books sufficiently profitable to keep me employed and to keep their authors published. Editing came to me before poetry did, by a few years, yet I was raised in an atmosphere that positively reeked of poetry, a fragrance as strong as that of my father's cigars. I have never been able, despite years of interior struggle, fully to separate the processes of editing and poetry, though the conduct of each craft differs profoundly from the other and emerges from entirely different regions of the soul. Yet such are the perils of appearances, I have by and large been seen as a poet by editors and as an editor by poets . . .

To the extent that we give ourselves to poetry, we give up the safety of trades, we deny ourselves economic value in order to claim a value of another, and, we believe, higher, kind. That may be the most dangerous claim of all, for to give yourself to poetry you have to bet your life on it, as Frost used to say. He, in turn, in his most profound poem, "Directive," referred us to St. Mark, who quotes Jesus as saying, again and again, "He that hath ears to hear, let him hear," and then, "Whosoever will save his life shall lose it . . ."

Not a dangerous trade? The hell you say.

*   *   *

Most of Peter Davison's poetry has an even, gemlike quality that typifies intelligent academic verse. Davison's work, generously laden with mythical allusions, is often rhymed and carefully metered. At its best the poetry illuminates a moment or an observation from the poet's life without straining toward an undeserved depth. In "Lunch at the Coq D'Or," for example, Davison portrays a fancy restaurant where "each noon at table tycoons crow / And flap their wings around each other's shoulders." He is waiting for an associate, Purdy, who eventually "is seated with his alibis":

I know my man. Purdy's a hard-nosed man.
Another round for us. It's good to work
With such a man. "Purdy," I hear myself,
"It's good to work with you." I raise
My arm, feathery in the dimlight, and extend
Until the end of it brushes his padded shoulder.
"Purdy, how are you? How you doodle do?"

Here Davison has included himself among the blamed by repeating the feather-wing imagery of the tycoons and then his own arm of luncheon goodwill. The humor of his concluding line emphasizes the nonsense encountered in daily business intercourse.

Too often Davison lacks this detachment and becomes merely a clever man with a pen, rhyming when he should be working his guts in ink. His position is sometimes ambiguous. Surely "Conviction Means Loss of License" deals with a serious subject, but Davison seems only to consider the fatal car crash of three brothers an opportunity to exercise his wit. Worse, he preaches in the sardonic manner of a radar cop:

For they were faithful to the plan
That nature must make way for man
And fed their faith in this great cause
By putting speed above the laws
Designed to neither help nor hurt.

Inertia rendered them inert.

In other poems Davison seems too pat, for example, in "Intacta," where he tells the familiar story of a seemingly virginal but actually permissive girl, and in "Winter Fear," which ends with the lines "The weather tells of famine and defeat, / Of lying leaves and how we were betrayed / By spring. But winter never yet has won." How, after all, does he know that the girl of "Intacta" is loose? Although it is true that winter "never yet has won," neither has any season (or condition of mind, the poem suggests to me) triumphed over winter. In short, Davison refuses to confess his own possible guilt or confusion.

These comments are perhaps unfairly negative, for there is much to admire in the body of Davison's work. "The Breaking of the Day," the title poem of his first collection, is a perfect refutation of the criticisms I levy against the least successful of his poems. Here the poet takes the risk of baring himself to the reader, acknowledging his doubts: ''I shall never know myself / Enough to know what things I half believe / And, half believing, only half deny.'' In a poem such as this the fusion of craft and insight is fully realized, and Davison proves himself the poet of skill his reputation holds him to be.

Dark Houses is a seven-part retrospective in verse on the life of his father, the poet Edward Davison, whose presence is fully documented in the son's *Half Remembered: A Personal History,* an autobiography. *Dark Houses* is a very good poem, crafted with a precision less and less evident among contemporary poets:

> And now his thirsty body
> Is part of the land at last, land of his children,
> Where the grey ungiving stone can always stand
> For fathers, thrusting up above the fields
> Not ever his own, though dearer than the land
> That gave him birth but never knew his name.

—Geof Hewitt

DAWE, (Donald) Bruce

Nationality: Australian. **Born**: Geelong, Victoria, 15 February 1930. **Education:** Northcote High School; Melbourne University; Queensland University, Brisbane, B.A. 1969, M.A. 1975, Ph.D. 1980; University of New England, Armidale, New South Wales, Litt.B. 1973. **Military Service:** Royal Australian Air Force, 1959–68. **Family:** Married Gloria Desley in 1964; two sons and two daughters. **Career:** Worked as a laborer, gardener, and postman. Senior lecturer, then associate professor, in literature, University College of Southern Queensland (formerly Darling Downs Institute of Advanced Education), Darling Heights, Toowoomba, 1980–93. **Awards:** Myer prize, 1966, 1969; Ampol Arts award, 1967; Mary Gilmore medal, 1971; Grace Leven prize, 1978; Patrick White Literary award, 1980; Christopher Brennan award, 1984. A.O. (Order of Australia), 1992. D.Litt.: University of Southern Queensland, 1995; University of New South Wales, 1997. **Address:** 30 Cumming Street, Toowoomba, Queensland 4350, Australia.

PUBLICATIONS

Poetry

No Fixed Address. Melbourne, Cheshire, 1962.
A Need of Similar Name. Melbourne, Cheshire, 1965.
An Eye for a Tooth. Melbourne, Cheshire, 1968.
Beyond the Subdivision. Melbourne, Cheshire, 1969.
Heat-Wave. Melbourne, Sweeney Reed, 1970.
Condolences of the Season. Melbourne, Cheshire, 1971.
Just a Dugong at Twilight: Mainly Light Verse. Melbourne, Cheshire, 1975.
Sometimes Gladness: Collected Poems 1954–1978. Melbourne, Longman Cheshire, 1978; revised edition, 1983, 1988; as *Sometimes Gladness: Collected Poems 1954–1992.* Longman Cheshire, 1993.
Selected Poems. London, Longman, 1984.

Towards Sunrise: Poems 1979–1986. Melbourne, Longman Cheshire, 1986.
This Side of Silence: Poems 1987–1990. Melbourne, Longman Cheshire, 1990.
Mortal Instruments: Poems 1990–1994. Melbourne, Longman Cheshire, 1995.
A Poet's People. South Melbourne, Addison Wesley Longman, 1998.

Short Stories

Over Here, Harv! and Other Stories. Melbourne, Penguin, 1983.

Other

Five Modern Comic Writers. Toowoomba, Queensland, Darling Downs Institute of Advanced Studies, 1981.

Editor, *Dimensions.* Sydney, McGraw Hill, 1974.
Editor, *Speaking in Parables.* Melbourne, Longman Cheshire, 1987.

*

Manuscript Collection: Fryer Library, University of Queensland, St. Lucia.

Critical Studies: *The Man down the Street,* edited by Ian V. Hansen, Melbourne, V.A.T.E., 1972; *Times and Seasons: An Introduction to Bruce Dawe* by Basil Shaw, Melbourne, Cheshire, 1974; *Adjacent Worlds: A Literary Life of Bruce Dawe* by Ken Goodwin, Melbourne, Longman Cheshire, 1988; *Bruce Dawe: Essays and Opinions,* edited by K.L. Goodwin, Melbourne, Longman Cheshire, 1990; *Bruce Dawe* by Peter Kuch, Oxford, Oxford University Press, 1995.

Bruce Dawe comments:

The themes I deal with are the common ones of modern civilization—loneliness, old age, death, dictatorship, love. I like the dramatic monologue form and use it in free, blank, and rhymed verse forms, attempting at the same time to capture something of the evanescence of contemporary idiom, which is far richer and more allusive than the stereotyped stone-the-crows popular concept of Australian speech would have people believe.

*   *   *

Bruce Dawe was certainly the most central and pivotal poet in Australia during the decade of the 1960s. His work first appeared in Melbourne in the late 1950s, and it broke through to a wide audience with *No Fixed Address,* his first collection. *No Fixed Address* displayed a freshness and gaiety quite unusual in Australian literature at the time and, more importantly, demonstrated a highly developed sense of local speech cadence and inflection. Dawe has always been concerned with the celebration of the maligned denizens of the great sprawl of outer suburbs that surround our cities. He views them with affection, sympathy, and wit and with an ear attuned to natural speech rhythms that is more precise and more immediately convincing than that of any other poet. This perceptiveness is coupled with a brilliant feeling for language and, particularly, for image.

Dawe broke through to a whole new generation of Australian readers, and his popularity has been gained without any loss of integrity or style. Indeed, because of the genuineness of his essential attitudes, such popularity is a natural aspect of his poetic justification. In later volumes Dawe became concerned with developing his initial vision and perceptions. He has been one of the few Australian poets to find a convincing method of dealing with contemporary political events and issues without loss of poetic validity. This is an area in which Australian poetry has always been backward and undeveloped. In 1971 a selected volume, *Condolences of the Season,* offered readers a summary of Dawe's work. His later poems tend to employ a more elegiac cadence, but though the subject matter is often eclectic and wide flung, it still seems that his contribution is primarily related to the admission into the corpus of Australian poetry of an area of suburban reality and liveliness that had only been approached in the most awkward and uncomfortable way by his predecessors.

Sometimes Gladness: Collected Poems 1954–1978, which has been revised more than once, is perhaps the most successful book of verse by a contemporary Australian poet. It continues as the quintessential Dawe compendium. Later collections remain more as postscripts to the earlier work. There are adroit political poems written on major and minor crises and often with effective, but repetitive, reliance on Old Testament rhetoric. There are poems on social issues, particularly abortion, written in conventional quatrains. The best poems, though, still capture the laconic sage of the backyard larrikin turned head of the family, with an occasional day off. *Mortal Instruments* and *A Poet's People* confirm that in his later work Dawe has as sharp an eye as ever on the quiddities of people and of politics, though the tone and the cadence have become as familiar as a ribald old grandfather.

—Thomas W. Shapcott

DeFREES, Madeline

Pseudonyms: Sister Mary Gilbert. **Nationality:** American. **Born:** Mary Madeline DeFrees, Ontario, Oregon, 18 November 1919. **Education:** Marylhurst Normal, Oregon, 1936–43; Marylhurst College, Marylhurst, 1943–48, B.A. 1948; University of Oregon, Eugene, 1949–50, M.A. 1951. **Career:** Member, Sisters of the Holy Names of Jesus and Mary, 1937–73. Elementary school teacher, Bend, Oregon, 1938–39, St. Monica's School, Coos Bay, Oregon, 1939–40, St. Francis School, Portland, Oregon, 1940–42; high school teacher, St. Mary's Academy, Medford, Oregon, 1942–44, 1946–49; St. Mary's, The Dalles, Oregon, 1944–46; instructor, 1950–55, assistant professor, 1955–63, and associate professor, 1963–67, Holy Names College, Spokane, Washington. Visiting associate professor, Seattle University, Washington, 1965–66; visiting associate professor, 1967–69, associate professor, 1969–72, and professor, 1972–79, University of Montana, Missoula; professor of English, 1979–85, and director of creative writing program, 1980–83, University of Massachusetts, Amherst. Since 1985 self-employed writer. Poet-in-residence, Bucknell University, spring 1988; distinguished visiting writer, Eastern Washington University, spring 1988; distinguished visiting writer, Wichita State University, April 1993. Contributor to *The San Diego Weekly Reader,* 1994–96. Taught creative writing classes two quarters at The Richard Hugo House, Seattle, 1998–99. **Awards:** T. Neil Taylor award for journalism research, University of Oregon, 1950; Indiana University Writer's Conference Poetry prize, 1961; co-winner, Abbie M. Copps Poetry prize, Olivet College, Michigan,

1973; Hohenberg Foundation for best poem, 1979; National Endowment for the Arts fellowship, 1981–82; Guggenheim fellowship, 1980–81; co-winner, Consuelo Ford award, Poetry Society of America, 1982; Carolyn Kizer award, *Calapooya Collage,* 1994; Ann Stanford Poetry Prize, 1998. D.Litt: Gonzaga University, Spokane, Washington, 1959. **Address:** 7548 11th Avenue Northwest, Seattle, Washington 98117, U.S.A.

PUBLICATIONS

Poetry

From the Darkroom. New York, Bobbs Merrill, 1964.
When Sky Lets Go. New York, George Braziller, 1978.
Imaginary Ancestors. Missoula, Montana, CutBank/SmokeRoot Press, 1978.
Magpie on the Gallows. Port Townsend, Washington, Copper Canyon Press, 1982.
The Light Station on Tillamook Rock. Corvallis, Oregon, Arrowood Books, 1990.
Possible Sibyls. Amherst, Massachusetts, Lynx House Publishers, 1991.
Double Dutch. West Sacramento, Red Wing Press, 1999.

Recordings: *Black Box 11,* Watershed, 1976; *Existing Light,* Watershed, 1980.

*

Manuscript Collection: University of Massachusetts, Amherst; University of Oregon, Eugene; Lockwood Memorial Library, Buffalo, New York.

Critical Studies: "Domesticating Two Landscapes: The Poetry of Madeline DeFrees" by M.L. Lewandowska and Susan Baker, in *Woman Poet: The West, Volume One,* Reno, Nevada, Women-in-Literature, 1980; in *Poet Lore* by Sheila Bender, winter 1993.

Madeline DeFrees comments:

My strongest early influences were Gerard Manley Hopkins and Emily Dickinson, both excellent poets but bad models, especially for beginners. By the time I discovered Hopkins I had already taught myself the rudiments of versification, putting to use the scansion I had learned in high school English and Latin classes. I read the Untermeyer anthologies, and when I found a poem I admired, modeled one on the same rhythmic and grammatical structure. I sought out books on prosody and practiced the various forms in a poetry notebook.

After I entered the convent, I wrote reams of light verse for the "simplicities" we planned to entertain the professed sisters. During Canonical Year (1937–38), when our reading of secular literature was very severely restricted, I concentrated on Hopkins, meditating on lines from the "terrible sonnets" and writing bad imitations. Of this apprenticeship two traces survive: a penchant for juxtaposed stresses and a fondness for hard *c* and *k* sounds. When I emerged from the Hopkins spell, I began submitting poems to *Spirit,* a Catholic poetry magazine and eventually scored an acceptance in 1949. From then on I contributed regularly to that magazine and to the *New York Times* until 1959, when I took a poetry workshop from Karl Shapiro at

Portland State University. Shapiro helped me to break out of form, urged me to publish in the quarterlies, and promised to take poems for *Prairie Schooner.*

My poems, as well as my short stories, are largely generated by a love of language. I am keenly interested in words: their derivations, connotations, changing histories, affinities with words of other languages. I like to hide small bonuses in lines of a poem, as when I write, "There's a welt on my shoulder . . . ," having in mind the German word for "world." Or "small fins / winnowing the ear," in which fins are part of a watery world but also "ends," as in the French. Finally, I see the poem as the most important verbal structure able to hold contradictories in balance and, therefore, the truest of all linguistic forms.

*   *   *

Madeline DeFrees's poetry is witty, erudite, and filled with careful observation and keen perceptions about the two worlds she has lived in—the religious and the secular. Her poems are not just intellectual exercises; they are also passionate. Like the English Metaphysical poets, she manages to fuse the worlds of flesh and spirit.

For thirty years the poet was a member of the Sisters of the Holy Names of Jesus and Mary. Her first poetry collection, *From the Darkroom,* was published under the name Sister Mary Gilbert. Now retired from both the convent and teaching, she publishes as Madeline DeFrees.

The poems in *When Sky Lets Go* and *Possible Sibyls* often reflect on DeFrees's religious calling, as in "The Ventriloquist's Dummy" in the latter collection:

> I was tired of being
> a mouthpiece, the body stuffed sawdust. The head
> hard rubber: it would
> stretch . . .
>
> *This dummy,* the legend swore, *could*
> save a life. Could you?
>
> In the undeclared war
> I could save my own, the heart
> gone out of it, breath so faint the mirror
> refused to cloud. I tried CPR,
> turned up the volume, put away the shroud, spoke
> at last in my native tongue.

Such excerpts may catch the intensity and bold imagery of DeFrees's poetry, but they fail to capture the way in which, like John Donne, she is able to link disparate things. In "The Ventriloquist's Dummy," for example, the lines "Soul flung a diffident / thread away from earth, anchored on God, on Heaven" manage to suggest both a spider producing its web and the strings a puppet dangles from, the paradoxical sense of at once controlling one's fate and being controlled externally. Other lines play off other contradictions: "All those years perfecting my circus act / were sawing a woman in half." In the above lines she also associates the ventriloquist's dummy with another, potentially lifesaving CPR dummy.

DeFrees's talent extends beyond the short lyric to longer poems. One of these, in *Possible Sibyls,* is the five-part "The Garden of Botanical Delights." In one section she blends botany, dream psychology, and devotional diction:

> Here is my act of faith in the secret life of
> plants, the still more secret
> lives we harbor in our sleep when images
> float upward into light
> and everything that grows
> begins to speak: *tension along the midriff,*
>
> *consternation among the broccoli, the several*
> *heads rising from a single*
> *stalk, the many voices of bok choy.*

DeFrees has written even longer poems, including the book-length *The Light Station on Tillamook Rock,* which draws on a year of living on the Oregon coast near a former lighthouse. The poem displays considerable research into marine life and the nautical history of the coastal area. In the seventh part, "Scene Out of Sequence: What the Coastwise Know," she juxtaposes the romance of the sea with what it can do to its victims:

> Don't invent a necklace
> of anemones, starfish worn like a badge
> or barrette. Widows and cosmeticians have been
> known to faint, regarding three days'
> changes. Water-logged, we say, speaking of
> boats and floating timber, not unlike
> the swollen bulbs of kelp: shape of an amber
> beet tossed up by the tide.

In many of DeFrees's poems language is rich and imagery layered, and these works become more rewarding with each return visit. The tone is sometimes tormented and angry, understandable emotions in someone who comes to question her sacrifice in choosing a particular path for thirty years. But she can also distance herself and be playful about such matters. "With A Bottle of Blue Nun to All My Friends," in *When Sky Lets Go,* delights in ludicrous situations, a sort of religious burlesque:

> The parachute
> surrounds her like a wimple.
> That's what happens when Blue Nuns
> bail out.
> It's that simple.

Elsewhere her voice turns more satirical, as when she describes in "Monasticism in the Western World," in *Possible Sibyls,* how

> To support the contemplative life, the Order of
> St. Clare in Corpus Christi, Texas,
> mixes pleasure & business, breeds miniature
> horses.

The poem concludes,

> Whether you want
> a pet or mascot, why not join the parade
> to the monastery? You can depend on these
>
> faithful companions, so easy to control, so

willing, pulling the sulkies past
the grandstand. Anyone at all can handle them.

In *Possible Sibyls* DeFrees also addresses her decision to leave
the order, telling in "Denby Romany" of a woman torn between
religious and secular passion:

The stained glass shed its burden—gold, rose-
red, garnet. Like Renoir

she found richer colors in refusal of the perfect
light.

In the last poem of the collection, "The Auger Kaleidoscope,"
DeFrees pictures her own personal resurrection:

I am
the daughter come back from the tomb to a dream
of light on the mountain, each rolled-away
stone semi-precious, hand-crafted, hand-cast,
fit for sending a traveler on his way.

—Duane Ackerson

DELIUS, Anthony (Ronald St. Martin)

Nationality: South African. **Born:** Simonstown, 11 June 1916.
Education: St. Aidan's College, Grahamstown; Rhodes University,
Grahamstown, B.A. 1938. **Military Service:** South African Intelli-
gence Corps, 1940–45: captain. **Family:** Married Christina Truter in
1941; one daughter and one son. **Career:** Co-founder, 1947, and
editor and political correspondent, Port Elizabeth *Saturday Post* (later
Evening Post); parliamentary correspondent, *Cape Times,* Cape Town,
1951–54 and 1958–67. Banned from the South Africa House of
Assembly for his *Cape Times* political commentary. Writer, BBC
Africa Service, London, 1968–77. Since 1977 freelance writer.
Former co-editor, *Standpunte,* Cape Town. Since 1962 member of the
editorial board, *Contrast* magazine, Cape Town. **Awards:** South
African poetry prize, 1960; CNA Literary Award, 1977. **Address:** 30
Graemesdyke Avenue, London SW14 7BJ, England.

PUBLICATIONS

Poetry

An Unknown Border. Cape Town, Balkema, 1954.
The Last Division. Cape Town, Human and Rousseau, 1959.
A Corner of the World: Thirty-Four Poems. Cape Town, Human and
    Rousseau, 1962.
Black South-Easter. Grahamstown, New Coin, 1966.

Play

The Fall: A Play about Rhodes. Cape Town, Human and Rousseau,
    1957.

Novels

The Day Natal Took Off: A Satire. Cape Town, Human and Rousseau,
    and London, Pall Mall Press, 1963.
Border. Cape Town, David Philip, 1976.

Other

The Young Traveller in South Africa. London, Phoenix House, 1947;
    revised edition, 1959.
The Long Way Round (travel in Africa). Cape Town, Timmins, 1956.
Upsurge in Africa. Toronto, Canadian Institute of International
    Affairs, 1960.

*

Manuscript Collection: Rhodes University, Grahamstown.

Critical Studies: Interview with Mike Popham, in *Contrast* (Cape
Town, South Africa), 11(2), 1977; "To Be a Man Is Very Hard:
Anthony Delius's Border" by S.G.M. Ridge, in *Standpunte*
(Stellenbosch, South Africa), 134, 1978.

*   *   *

Anthony Delius has described himself as one of the most
indoctrinated of South Africans, a misleading description since it
would imply an acceptance of certain sociopolitical attitudes that are
the opposite of what he believes. What one can properly say,
however, is that of the poets of his country writing in English he is
probably the most consciously South African. Despite the title of his
1962 collection, *A Corner of the World,* it is the African continent as a
whole, many of his poems reflecting his travels, and not just his own
country with which he identifies. From his early poems, including the
long, impressive "Time in Africa," written during World War II,
Delius has shown himself fascinated by what living in Africa has
accumulated over the centuries, seeing history as a continuous
process working on his own contemporary experience and on into the
future like a prophecy.

In "Black South-Easter," probably the best long poem produced by a South African in a generation, Delius, twenty years after
"Time in Africa," succeeded in using history as a poet should, taking
imagination as the catalyst to produce a recipe for the making of myth.
The poet, struggling through the windy Cape night, is confronted by
historical ghosts, by symbolical figures of contemporary values, the
millionaire and the actress, and by his own many-sidedness, his own
"Indian file of selves," while his mind and memory are swept
dramatically on a course of their own through a wider and deeper
disorder of time and circumstance. For instance, he sees the fifteenth-
century navigator Dias in this way:

His niche was the stern
Of a torpedoed tanker, cliff-hung
Like an opera box.

Here is a tremendously ambitious poem; that it succeeds is a measure
of the poet's power to use language to control a variety of influences
working on the imagination at the same time. If Delius has proved his

staying power in attempting the long distances (since *The Lusiads* the Cape presents a surviving challenge to South African poets to go for the big theme), yet his enduring reputation may well lie among some of his short poems, such as the exquisite "The Gamblers," about Cape Coloured fishermen, a popular anthology piece since it first appeared in the *New Yorker:*

> Day flips a golden coin—but they mock it.
> With calloused, careless hands they reach
> Deep down into the sea's capacious pocket
> And pile their silver counters
> on the beach.

"Deaf and Dumb School" is another poem beautifully conceived to express the poet's compassion: "Silence like a shadow shows the room / Of minds that make their signs and mouth their cries."

Delius's poetry shows another kind of compassion, perhaps of the best kind, that which comes after clear vision has stripped away from situations and people the humbug, false myth, and sloth that have accumulated about them. In this process satire acts like a paint stripper, and Delius, as satirist, has long been active in the South African context. Though echoes of Roy Campbell sometimes interrupt originality, there are parts of *The Last Division* whose humor will preserve it long after the lampooned figures of politics have been forgotten.

—Roy Macnab

DEMETILLO, Ricaredo

Nationality: Filipino. **Born:** Dumangas, Iloilo, 2 June 1920. **Education:** Silliman University, Dumaguete City, A.B. in English 1947; University of Iowa, Iowa City, M.F.A. in English and creative writing 1952. **Family:** Married Angelita Delariarte in 1944; four children. **Career:** Assistant professor, 1959–70, chairman of the Department of Humanities, 1961–62, associate professor, 1970–75, professor of humanities, 1975–85, and since 1986 professor emeritus, University of the Philippines, Diliman, Quezon City. **Awards:** Rockefeller fellowship, 1952; University of the Philippines Golden Jubilee award; Philippines Republic Cultural Heritage award, 1968; Palanca award, for play, 1975; South-East Asia Writer's award, 1985; Writer's Union of the Philippines award, 1991. **Address:** 38 Bulacan Street, West Avenue, Quezon City, Philippines.

PUBLICATIONS

Poetry

No Certain Weather. Quezon City, Guinhalinan Press, 1956.
La Via: A Spiritual Journey. Quezon City, Diliman Review, 1958.
Daedalus and Other Poems. Quezon City, Guinhalinan Press, 1961.
Barter in Panay. Quezon City, University of the Philippines Office of Research Coordination, 1961.
Masks and Signature. Quezon City, University of the Philippines Press, 1968.
The Scare-Crow Christ. Quezon City, Diliman Review, 1973.

The City and the Thread of Light and Other Poems. Quezon City, Diliman Review, 1974.
Lazarus, Troubadour. Quezon City, New Day, 1974.
Sun, Silhouettes, and Shadow, photographs by B. David Williams, Jr. Quezon City, New Day, 1975.
First and Last Fruits. Quezon City, New Day, 1989.

Play

The Heart of Emptiness Is Black (produced Quezon City, 1973). Quezon City, University of the Philippines Press, 1975.

Novel

The Genesis of a Troubled Vision. Quezon City, University of the Philippines Press, 1976.

Other

The Authentic Voice of Poetry. Quezon City, University of the Philippines Office of Research Coordination, 1962.
My Sumakwelan Works in the Context of Philippine Culture. Quezon City, University of the Philippines Press, 1976.
Major and Minor Keys. Quezon City, New Day, 1985.

*

Critical Studies: "The Wounded Diamond," in *Bookmark* (Manila), 1964, and article in *Solidarity Magazine* (Manila), 1968, both by Leonard Casper; *A Native Clearing* edited by Germino H. Abad, Quezon City, University of the Philippines Press, 1993.

Ricaredo Demetillo comments:

(1970) My poetry has been much influenced by the New Criticism in America, but I do not belong to any school.

My poetry has been concerned with the following major themes: the rebellion of the young against the conventional values of an overly repressive society; the modern journey of the individual from lostness to wholeness and fullest creativity; the rise and fall of civilization, using the myth of Daedalus in ancient Crete to objectify and evoke the human condition; and the important position of the artists as the bearers and the creators of volumes necessary to the renewal of society. To project all these themes, I have used the lyric, the elegiac, the poetic essay, the epic, etc., with relatively good success. Always I have been concerned with the human condition and also celebrated the hierarchy of light. Strongest influences: Homer, Dante, Baudelaire, Dylan Thomas, W.B. Yeats, and Auden, not to mention myths of all sorts, including the Filipino ones.

(1974) My recent book *The Scare-Crow Christ* was written mostly during the troubled period of student activism in Manila and contains poems objectifying the poverty and the spiritual confusion of the time. One poem speaks of the indifference of the average man to the welfare of the "diminished, unfulfilled" man and asks, "Are you not Judas to his scare-crow Christ?" Still another one pays "tall tribute to the hardihood of man" that is able to survive the horrors of war in Vietnam and elsewhere.

But these new poems are evocations, not propagandistic statements.

My verse drama *The Heart of Emptiness Is Black,* really a sort of sequel to *Barter in Panay,* deals centrally with the conflict between tribalism and emergent individualism, which may have relevance to the present situation of the Philippines under martial law. I chose the drama as a form so that I can be heard by the public, for poetry locally is mostly unheard and unread, if not dead.

The City and Other Poems objectifies or evokes the lostness of man in the modern city and the poet's search for any available meaning in the human condition today.

*   *   *

Ricaredo Demetillo's poetry, fiction, and criticism belong to a tradition that is both East and West, and his work is being recognized, though a bit slowly, as a distinct part of the world cultural heritage, a blending of oriental and occidental values. His writings offer a rich mine for the student and the science of culture.

Demetillo deals with a variety of themes: the revolt of youth against oppressive society, the rise and fall of civilizations, the spiritual bankruptcy of language that presages political violence and economic distress, the poet's Dantean/Faustian journey through the morass of living to the higher life. An important work, the poet himself says, "evokes and proclaims the life-forwarding sacrifices of the artists, the 'unstable men,' who are the harbinger of the truths—and values—that invigorate and renew society during critical epochs." Another critic has observed that his early *La Via: A Spiritual Journey* is the most sustained argument in verse in any language by a Filipino.

What many consider Demetillo's most ambitious work is the literary epic sequence he adapted from the ethnolinguistic legend popularly know as *Maragtas.* He has rewritten the story in three parts, each complete in itself. *Barter in Panay,* the first of the three, concerns the pseudohistorical settlement of the island of Panay, in central Philippines, by several boatloads of people from Borneo, not through armed conquest but peacefully through friendly barter (gold for land) with an earlier group of settlers. The story is transformed into a serious literary epic with the intention to project not crudely tribal values but rather national, even international, ideals about justice, liberty, racial harmony, democratic government, and the interrelationships of people whose leaders act only with the consent of the governed. The principles of freedom and democracy expressed in the traditional story of *Barter in Panay* remain applicable today.

In the second part of the sequence, *The Heart of Emptiness Is Black,* Demetillo dramatizes the tragic conflict between the lovers Kapinanga and Guronggurong, on the one hand, and the oppressive authority of the leader of the expedition, Datu Sumakwel, and the priest Bangutbanwa, on the other. Kapinanga's adultery with Guronggurong leads to his death and her exile, as decreed by her husband, Sumakwel. In the third part both Kapinanga and Sumakwel have been chastened by their experiences, which leads to reconciliation. What started out as a bucolic narrative and continued as high tragedy winds up as romantic melodrama.

One may discern in the lifework of Demetillo an eloquent argument for the integrity of the artist as both individual human being and as social person. José Garcia Villa, the other major Philippine poet of the twentieth century, may be patronizing toward Demetillo's social commitments, but Demetillo, while recognizing the superior quality of Villa's personal lyricism, is proud of his stand. Although both Villa and Demetillo accept the centrality of the formal, or aesthetic, values in a work of art, Villa stops there. Demetillo, however, goes further, looking for additional values that may enhance the beauty and significance of human life. As a poet Demetillo has attained a stature that in Philippine literature is hard to erode and difficult to surpass.

—Leopoldo Y. Yabes

DERKSEN, Jeff

Nationality: Canadian. **Born:** Murrayville, British Columbia, 1958. **Education:** David Thompson University Centre, Nelson, British Columbia, 1980–84, B.A. 1984; University of Calgary, Calgary, Alberta, 1993–95, M.A. 1995. **Career:** Founding board member, Artspeak Gallery, Vancouver, British Columbia, 1986–95; board member, The New Gallery, Calgary, Alberta, 1994–95; editor, *Writing* magazine, Vancouver, British Columbia, 1989–93. Since 1984 founding board member, Kootenay School of Writing, Vancouver, British Columbia. **Awards:** Dorothy Livesay Poetry award, 1991; British Columbia Book prize, 1991, for *Down Time;* Alberta Writers' Guild Poetry prize, 1994, for *Dwell.* **Address:** P.O. Box 61102, Kensington Postal Outlet, Calgary, Alberta T2N 456, Canada.

PUBLICATIONS

Poetry

Memory Is the Only Thing Holding Me Back. Nelson, British Columbia, DTUC Press, 1984.
Until (chapbook). Vancouver, Tsunami Editions, 1987.
Down Time. Vancouver, Talonbooks, 1990.
Selfish (chapbook). Vancouver, Pomeflit, 1993.
Dwell. Vancouver, Talonbooks, 1994.

*

Jeff Derksen comments:

Often I am asked why, if I intend the reader to be the primary agent of meaning in my texts, do I make the poetry so "hard." My reply is that my poetry is no harder to understand than a boat ride, say, a canal tour of historical Amsterdam.

*   *   *

There is a restless subjectivity in Jeff Derksen's poetry that refuses the central figure of a stable self. Using a variety of social voices, he blends newscasts, financial and economic statistics, overheard conversations, intertextual references to other poets and their poetry, and information on pop culture. His work investigates excess rather than closure. Disjunctively presented, the voices shift so that it is impossible to identify any single speaker as the ultimate authority, any one voice as representative of a unified whole. Instead, the persistence of the multiple voices motivates the reader to understand and accept a writing that formally challenges notions of the lyric tradition.

In addition to his poetry, Derksen is known as one of the organizers of Vancouver's Kootenay School of Writing, a collective based on and engaged in supporting and perpetuating language-based writing, and for editing the literary magazine *Writing*. He has also written essays on contemporary poets and thinkers.

In *Down Time* and *Dwell* Derksen combines the long poetry form with formally unrelated texts. These diverse pieces come together within each book by playing off and against one another as singular, isolated poems, so that the effect of reading is cumulative, from the micro to the macro. In "Blind Trust," a piece that embodies the internal dialogue between the materiality of the words by dividing two discrete prose sections with a huge gap of white space, Derksen presents the dialogic possibilities of language itself. "They will recognize others as outsiders," he says at the top of the page: "Coddled, malignant." Then, at the bottom of the page he says, "A chemical engineer and a bank president may sound very much alike. Adjutant, addled." Thus his poetry becomes not only social commentary on a capitalist and homogenizing humanity but also metacommentary on its own processual methodology.

Derksen often plays with the formal construct of justified left margins and ragged-right line breaks. The pieces shift from sentences in paragraphs to numbered stanzas to minimal words composed on the abundance of space on the page. For example, in "Neighbourhood" the justified-left/ragged-right pattern of lyric poetry is turned on its ear. Each word of the poem outside the square brackets, which operate as external social commentary, carries equal weight, and there is not much emphasis or pivot on the line break:

> general lap pad data
> tackles seam manager [a
> qualified control] oligarchy chyme
> me menial detail

Moreover, each word is generated by the last few letters in the previous word, so that the act of reading relies on a word's relationship to surrounding words rather than on meaning or narrative connections.

In contrast, Derksen's other pieces in *Dwell* range from short lyrics to travelogues to celebratory sentence performances. In "If History Is the Memory of Time What Would Our Monument Be" Derksen develops an assortment of disjunctive declarations, ranging from observation on the business world to cancer treatment to gender construction:

> That pulp and paper are "in my blood" is the
> patriarchal view.

> What happens to the poetics of place when your
> only "place" is your body and it's not moving.

> Still, I'd rather be a statistic than a metaphor.

Derksen's poetry is grounded in his use of irony, which builds on an accumulation of events and information, images, and interruptive narratives that provide the context through which it is to be read. In addition, the heteroglossia that can be found in his poems oppose the tradition of the individual perceiving consciousness and emphasize instead the blurred boundary between world and text.

—Nicole Markotic

de SOUZA, Eunice

Nationality: Indian. **Born:** Poona, 1 August 1940. **Education:** University of Bombay, B.A. (honors) 1960, Ph.D. 1988; Marquette University, Milwaukee, Wisconsin, M.A. 1963. **Career:** Since 1969 lecturer in English, and since 1990 head of the Department of English, St. Xavier's College, Bombay. Arts columnist, *Economic Times*, Bombay, 1973–84; literary editor, Indian Post, Bombay, 1987. **Address:** St. Xavier's College, Bombay 400 001, India.

PUBLICATIONS

Poetry

Fix. Bombay, Newground, 1979.
Women in Dutch Painting. Bombay, Praxis, 1988.
Ways of Belonging: Selected Poems. Edinburgh, Polygon, 1990.
Selected and New Poems. Bombay, St. Xavier's College, 1994.

Other (for children)

All about Birbal. Bombay, India Book House, 1969.
Himalayan Tales. Bombay, India Book House, 1973.
More about Birbal. Bombay, India Book House, n.d.
Tales of Birbal. Bombay, India Book House, n.d.

Other

Talking Poems: Conversations with Poets. New Delhi, Oxford University Press, 1999.

Editor, with Adil Jussawalla, *Statements: An Anthology of Indian Prose in English.* Bombay, Orient Longman, 1976.
Editor, *Nine Indian Women Poets: An Anthology.* Delhi, Oxford University Press, 1997.

*

Critical Studies: "Three Poets Come of Age" by Kersey Katrak, in *Sunday Observer* (Bombay), 12 December 1982; in *Modern Indian Poetry in English* by Bruce King, Oxford, Oxford University Press, 1987; by Elizabeth Reuben, in *Indian* P.E.N., April-June 1989; "'One Long Cry in the Dark'?: The Poetry of Eunice de Souza" by Veronica Brady, in *Literature & Theology* (Oxford, England), 5(1), March 1991.

Eunice de Souza comments:

The first poems I wrote were about what it was like to grow up in Poona, in a conservative Goan Roman Catholic milieu. Most of these poems are in the form of dramatic monologues. I generally like to use the speaking voice when I write, and many poems are in the form of conversations about relationships, about critics who tell me how to write, and so forth. I like poems to be spare and economical. There are a number of poets whose work I feel close to, particularly the medieval saint poets in India and Emily Dickinson.

*   *   *

In her first collection, *Fix*, Eunice de Souza established herself as a writer of short poems in which a surface structure of controlled irony masks an often painful and violent subject matter. The title is instructive, suggesting both a problem and the repair work that is needed. As a satirist of Roman Catholic, middle-class hypocrisy in the Goa of her birth and upbringing, de Souza favors a conversational idiom, urbane and seemingly matter-of-fact and with very English cadences, that at first conceals and then reveals an often extreme distress. Beneath a fluent and knowing utterance there stir feelings of anger, confusion, and desolation. The opening poem, ''Catholic Mother,'' focuses initially upon the father of a large Catholic family but then turns from apparent celebration of the male to the mother whose silence speaks volumes:

Pillar of the Church
says the parish priest
Lovely Catholic Family
says Mother Superior

the pillar's wife
says nothing.

Such understatement is typical as de Souza, taught by Irish nuns in a convent school in Poona in Maharashtra state, brings an astringent wit to bear upon tensions and stresses that are in part a legacy of Portuguese colonialism. ''Marriages Are Made'' explores the peculiar mingling of Indian and Christian practices as the life of a young woman is arranged for her in ways that reduce her to the status of an animal being examined for possible faults in pedigree, while ''Feeding the Poor at Christmas'' exposes the self-serving and unfeeling elements in supposedly Christian charity. In similarly dry, laconic tones ''Sweet Sixteen'' presents the fear and ignorance of sexuality promoted by a Catholic upbringing as it affects young girls:

At sixteen, Phoebe asked me:
Can it happen when you're in a dance hall
I mean, you know what,
getting *preggers* and all that, when
you're dancing?
I, sixteen, assured her
you could.

In different ways de Souza examines problems and uncertainties associated with color and with ethnic divergences. The aging Anglo-Indian of ''Miss Louise'' lives in a world of fantasy, where she retains the sexually desirable attractiveness she had dreamed of all her life. The light-skinned woman in ''Mrs. Hermione Gonsalvez'' reveals other aspects of nostalgia and of male oppression:

In the good old days
I had looks *and* colour
now I've only got colour
just look at my parents
how they married me to a dark man
on my own I wouldn't even have
looked at him.

As she dramatizes these voices, de Souza's ear for the trick of speech in Anglicized middle-class Indians lends conviction to her portrayals. ''Conversation Piece,'' which generated considerable hostility in the Indian press from Hindus angry at what they took to be an insult to their religion, quietly registers cross-cultural divisions and misunderstandings when a Portuguese-bred aunt picks up a clay lingam, a phallic representation of Siva, and asks,

Is this an ashtray?
No, said the salesman,
This is our God.

It is clear that de Souza's brief inscriptions, often seemingly casual in their mode of delivery, are taut with repressed levels of deep anxiety. Her father died when she was a young child, and difficulties related to this can surface in a traumatizing imagery of cutting, slashing, and sometimes self-laceration. ''Forgive me, Mother'' is one such poem, tracing complications in the developing and sustaining of a relationship: ''I was never young. / Now I'm old, alone. / In dreams / I hack you.'' The poem ''Autobiographical,'' which affects a cavalier, distancing stance at the beginning—''Right now, here it comes. / I killed my father when I was three''—goes on to chart deeper senses of failure and self-recrimination, including suicidal urges, and ''One Man's Poetry'' encodes an imagery of disintegration—''My limbs begin to scatter / my face dissolve.''

De Souza's second volume, *Women in Dutch Painting*, much of it written during a six-month visit to England in 1983–84, presents a somewhat more relaxed countenance to the world as she broadens her horizons and produces poems of more measured self-interrogation. ''The Hills Heal'' draws strength from a natural environment and acknowledges therapeutic value in the writing of a poetry that can contain destructive impulses by giving them form:

Yet the world will maul again, I know,
and I'll go gladly for the usual price,

Emerge to flay myself in poems,
The sluiced vein just a formal close.

In a similar gesture, which nonetheless retains discomfiting elements, ''She and I'' returns to a maternal relationship where, after a lifetime's silence between them on the subject of the father's/husband's death, the mother begins to speak about him. The release seems to portend her own death, thereby creating a further complication between mother and daughter, as the poem acknowledges: ''I am afraid / for her, for myself, / but can say nothing.''

If *Women in Dutch Painting* is generally more composed in its attitudes, it is still a record of troubled feelings. Although ''Another Way to Die'' ends on a restorative note, its imagery of dissolution picks up a thread of concern from *Fix*, and while ''The Road'' can contemplate a Catholic childhood with greater equanimity, it also recognizes continuing uncertainties. ''Songs of Innocence'' traverses the enclosing securities of a catechized childhood only to register the gap of difference between then and now. Its fourth section tells of a return to Goa, ''searching for roots'' but finding instead a crumbling place of origination that no longer sustains a sense of self. But in the fourth poem of the sequence ''Return,'' de Souza discovers different ways of relating to a domestic community. Referring to a newspaper account of an attempt by Bombay prostitutes to break with their past and improve their life prospects, the poem wryly concludes, ''I know something / of how you feel.'' It seems, too, in the poem ''Notations'' that de Souza can find in ballads a way of locating her own very different writing in a tradition that may offer sustenance. At least she discerns in ballad writing qualities to which her own poetry can respond: ''No cut to abstractions. / It happened: that is all they say. / It happened.''

—Colin Nicholson

DEWDNEY, Christopher

Nationality: Canadian. **Born:** London, Ontario, 9 May 1951. **Education:** Attended South and Westminster Collegiate Institutes, London, Ontario; H.B. Beal Art Annex, London, Ontario. **Family:** Married 1) Suzanne Dennison in 1971 (dissolved 1975), one daughter; 2) Lise Downe in 1977, one son. **Career:** Associate fellow, Winters College, York University, Toronto, 1984; Éminence Verte, Society for the Preservation of Wild Culture, Toronto, 1987; poetry editor, Coach House Publishing, Toronto, 1988. President, Forest City Gallery Artists Association, 1978, 1979. **Awards:** Design Canada award, 1974; Canada Council grant, 1974, 1976, 1981, 1985; CBC prize, 1986. **Address:** c/o McClelland and Stewart Inc., 481 University Avenue Suite 900, Toronto, Ontario M5G 2E9, Canada.

PUBLICATIONS

Poetry

Golders Green. Toronto, Coach House Press, 1972.
A Paleozoic Geology of London, Ontario. Toronto, Coach House Press, 1973.
Fovea Centralis. Toronto, Coach House Press, 1975.
Spring Trances in the Control Emerald Night. Berkeley, California, Figures, 1978.
Alter Sublime. Toronto, Coach House Press, 1980.
The Cenozoic Asylum with Spring Trances in the Control Emerald Night. Berkeley, California, Figures, 1982; *The Cenozoic Asylum* published separately, Liverpool, Délires, 1983.
Predators of the Adoration: Selected Poems 1972–1982. Toronto, McClelland and Stewart, 1983.
Permugenesis. Toronto, Nightwood, 1987.
The Radiant Inventory. Toronto, McClelland and Stewart, 1988.
Demon Pond: Poems. Toronto, McClelland and Stewart, 1994.
Signal Fires. Toronto, McClelland and Stewart, 2000.

Recording: *Video Marquee.* Toronto, Coach House/Music Gallery Talking Books, 1990.

Play

Hand in Glove with an Old Hat (produced Toronto, 1982).

Other

The Immaculate Perception. Toronto, Anansi, 1986.
Recent Artifacts from the Institute of Applied Fiction. Montreal, McGill University Libraries, 1990.
Concordant Proviso Ascendant: A Natural History of Southwestern Ontario, Book III. Great Barrington, Massachusetts, The Figures, 1991.

The Secular Grail. Toronto, Somerville House, 1993.
Last Flesh: Life in the Transhuman Era. Toronto, HarperCollins, 1998.

Editor, *The Skin of Culture: Investigating the New Electronic Reality,* by Derrick De Kerckhove, Toronto, Somerville House, 1995.

*

Manuscript Collection: McLennan Library, McGill University, Montreal.

Critical Studies: ''Strata and Strategy: Pataphysics in the Poetry of Christopher Dewdney'' by Steve McCaffery, in *North of Intention: Critical Writings 1973–1986,* Toronto, Nightwood, 1986; ''Manifold Destiny: Metaphysics in the Poetry of Christopher Dewdney'' by Alistair Highet, in *Essays on Canadian Writing* (Toronto), 34, Spring 1987; ''Give Yourself Up: Christopher Dewdney's Poetry'' by Robert Lecker, and ''As If Paradise Renewed a Tangible and Immaculate Perception: Dewdney's Textbook'' by Bruce Whiteman, both in *Sagetrieb* (Orono, Maine), 7(1), Spring 1988; ''Radiant Inventories: A Natural History of the Natural Histories,'' in *Canadian Poetry* (London, Ontario), 32, Spring/Summer 1993, and ''The Word Entrances: Virtual Realities in Dewdney's Log Entries,'' in *Studies in Canadian Literature* (Fredericton, New Brunswick), 18(2), 1993, both by Christian Bok.

Christopher Dewdney comments:

It is a warm, gray afternoon in August. You are in the country, in a deserted quarry of light gray Devonian limestone in southern Ontario. A powdery luminescence oscillates between the rock and sky. You feel sure that you could recognize these clouds, with their limestone texture, out of random cloud photographs from all over the world.

You then lean over and pick up a flat piece of layered stone. It is a rough triangle about one foot across. Prying at the stone, you find the layers come apart easily in large flat pieces. Pale gray moths are pressed between the layers of stone. Freed, they flutter up like pieces of ash caught in a dust devil. You are splashed by the other children but move not.

*   *   *

Critics of Christopher Dewdney's poetry have most often felt compelled to preface their readings with acknowledgment of the work's inherent difficulty. Indeed, Dewdney's books of poetry and prose poems can be daunting in their overt cerebration, their use of scientific nomenclature, and their immersion in such seemingly arcane worlds as paleontology, brain anatomy, and information theory. Equally common among Dewdney's commentators, however, is the enthusiasm with which they have responded to his body of work, both for the vitality and richness of its poetry and for the elaborately suggestive cosmology the poet has envisioned.

Dewdney's concerns and ability are fully evident in early poems such as ''The Memory Table'' and ''Transubstantiation'' (from *A Paleozoic Geology of London, Ontario*). In the latter the poet deftly achieves a characteristic resonance of imagery:

Devoid of perception the
blind form of the fossil

exists post-factum.
Its movement planetary, tectonic.
The flesh of these words
disintegrates.

Here explorations of the physical world at once ascribe to that world an existential autonomy—a "blind form"—and reveal a correlative function of the poetic process, an autonomy of its own but also a fossilization in the movement from perception to form.

This correlation of the poetic to the prehistoric is a postulate throughout Dewdney's work, and the metaphoric substratum from which the two assert their influence is designated as the "memory table," whose "shafts / by which we remember / are called / 'wishing wells' by some." For Dewdney, then, "what is beneath . . . / is only hinted at" ("Glass"), and one of the functions of poetry is to embody "a primaeval history uncorrupted by humans," to insist upon its own incarnation as a living memory of that "blind form," radical and liberating in the face of perceptual and linguistic convention. This is the sense of "Anecessity" (from *Alter Sublime*), in which the poet asserts, "There is no oral tradition. / There is amoral tradition." Wordplay is not entirely déclassé here; rather it is embraced by a poetry concerned to expose the commingling "haloes" that irradiate the taxonomic "kernels" of words to reveal the fleshy texture of language. In "Anecessity" Dewdney displays his poetic mastery at conjuring this texture of language with adroit turns of thought, crisp imagery, and a delicate sense of line:

Instinct. A sense
of concentric liqueurs
mutually arriving at their
respective levels.
That's a moral. A thorn
breaking off just under the skin.

In the world of "amoral tradition" and in the service of a subversive logic of "anecessity," the poem is a necessity, a memory lodged by the poet beneath the skin—"Barbs relying on / your movement / to work their way in." For Dewdney this process is sacral, and the movement of these poetic barbs is comparable to the tectonic movement of fossils.

The tension between a blind primeval order and a linguistically codified human consciousness, a tension that consistently manifests itself with startling variety and complexity, informs the whole of Dewdney's work. It is its motor, the purpose of a poetry that eschews and undermines the very languages of purpose. In this sense, then, Dewdney's poetry sets itself a task that is at once destructive and self-destructive. "The poet hosts a parasite," we are told in "Parasite Maintenance" (from *Alter Sublime*), a fascinating and fun treatise that is at once a scientific discourse and a metaphysical conceit. Here Dewdney envisions an autonomous "living language" that exists symbiotically with human consciousness and imposes upon that consciousness a "governor," a barrier to "certain higher forms of perceptual reasoning." The parasite, then, is the condition peculiar to the poet, the means by which the governor may be engaged in battle. The spoils of this contest "are those bits of information from beyond the limits of science and madness." In this light Dewdney's conception of the role of poetry might be seen to have its direct predecessors in the romanticist and surrealist movements. But the relationships Dewdney has articulated between nature and poetry, between the physical and the linguistic, bear decidedly original characteristics.

If the tensions that engender Dewdney's poetry appear conspicuously intellectualized in description, the substance of his poetry is consistently visceral and luminous. Given the sheer power of Dewdney's imagination, the reader has almost always a sense of confronting the uncanny. In "The Drawing Out of Colour" (from *Fovea Centralis*), for instance, "the voice of cicada" in "the silent radar forest" becomes ". . . the long sustained note / of an indeterminate philosophy / in a court where the evidence / neither confirms nor denies its testimony." And while the confessional voice is refreshingly alien to Dewdney, one nonetheless has the sense that throughout his poetry there is a great deal at stake, a reverence, often with an indeterminate syntax to give voice to the "indeterminate philosophy." Witness these lines from "United" (in *Alter Sublime*):

I am surrounded by unendurable beauty
endless a succession of this truth.
Manifold destiny. May the cradle of the ocean
spawn our likeness in years to come.

Though limited in its appeal by the particular rigors of its cosmology, Dewdney's poetry evinces a rare combination of postmodern intellectual concerns with a spectacular imagistic and verbal freshness. He is rightly considered one of Canada's most important avant-garde writers.

—James Caton

DHARKER, Imtiaz

Nationality: Indian. **Born:** Pakistan, 31 January 1954. **Family:** Married; one daughter. **Career:** Poet, visual artist, and filmmaker; has had six solo exhibitions of drawings. **Address:** B-2, Purshottam Bhavan, Little Gibbs Road, Malabar Hill, Bombay 400 006, India.

PUBLICATIONS

Poetry

Purdah: And Other Poems. New Delhi and Oxford, Oxford University Press, 1988.
Postcards from God. New Delhi and New York, Viking, 1994; Newcastle upon Tyne, Bloodaxe, 1997.

*

Critical Studies: "Discreet Rebellion: The Poetry of Imtiaz Dharker" by A.K. Tiwari, and "Unveiling Womanhood: Dharker's 'Purdah'" by Rashmi Chaturvedi, both in *Women's Writing: Text and Context,* edited by Jasbir Jain, Jaipur, India, Rawat, 1996.

*   *   *

Imtiaz Dharker's maturation as a poet is an impressive phenomenon in contemporary Indian writing in English. She has moved from the frankly polemical diatribes that made up her first collection, *Purdah: And Other Poems,* to a highly condensed, prophetic utterance able to combine directness with obliquity. Her indignation at oppressive social structures has by no means lost its force, but the outrage has found a new fluency and a medium that can fully bear its weight.

Even Dharker's early writing sometimes shows an adroit handling of form. Thus, in ''Grace'' the doorkeeper of a mosque decries the defiling presence of a menstruating woman:

He rolls his reason on his tongue
and spits it out.
You know again the drought
the blazing eye of faith
can bring about.

Another example is seen in these lines from ''Purdah I'':

She half-remembers things
from someone else's life,
perhaps from yours, or mine—
carefully carrying what we do not own:
between the thighs, a sense of sin.

The controlled intimacy of tone, which is achieved by casual and partial rhymes, a line adapted to speech, and a sly manipulation of the reader's complicity, persists in Dharker's second, breakthrough collection, *Postcards from God.* The eponymous series of twenty-eight poems that make up the first part of the book is organized by what might have been little more than a witty conceit: a carefully lowercase god addresses his/her human constituents as a fellow traveler. It is remarkable that Dharker pulls off this risky device, for it is no mean feat to play god in a manner neither Olympian nor coy. Some of the poems are illustrated by Dharker's own Kathe Kollwitz-like drawings, mostly of the human face in agony. But their power comes from the vivid colloquialism of Dharker's images. In ''Question I'' god has ''the biggest remote control / of all.'' In ''Taking the Count'' god is a *dhobi,* a washerman ''bow-legged from carrying a bundle / that has always been too big for me'':

Every day, I take the count,
I separate the dusters from the sheets,
I beat and rinse and squeeze and pound

till each one is ready to be thrown free,
laid across the ground
under the white-hot critical eye.

Rows of souls washed clean,
all accounted for,
spread out to dry.

Dharker's vision is mystical, but at its most sharply realized her poetry approaches the jeremiad, its political criticism raised by moral fervor to an intense rhetorical pitch. ''6 December 1992,'' which allusively commemorates the outbreak of communal violence in Bombay, visualizes ''the whole world / changed to glass'':

Glass leaders laugh
and the whole world can see

right through their faces
into their black tongues.

And through the crystal night
the bodies begin to burn.

Dharker's poetic grasp is occasionally less sure, however, as in ''Adam from New Zealand,'' where the speaker refuses to collaborate in a visiting journalist's quest for information about the Bombay poor:

How can I serve up Zarina
or her brother Adam
to their random cameras?
They will smile shyly.
The aperture will open
to swallow up their souls.

The self-righteous ''I'' is problematical, permitting the poetry of protest to slip into an anecdotal sensationalism.

Dharker's writing always recognizes the centrality of the image. A filmmaker as well as a visual artist and poet, she is painfully aware of the proliferation of the image through the mass media, particularly in Bombay, the established center of the Indian film industry. As god remarks in ''Aperture,'' one of his postcards,

I placed eyes everywhere.
Men added more.
The pupil, dilated,
the open aperture, the watching lens.

The wound in the forehead,
flashing fire.

These are the organs
of a predatory power.

''Question II'' gnomically asks, ''Did I create you / in my image / / or did you create me / in yours?'' Against the manifold images propagated by neofundamentalist religion and corrupt politics, in ''Living Space'' Dharker shores up the timely and uncompromising integrity of her art:

Into this rough frame,
someone has squeezed
a living space

and even dared to place
these eggs in a wire basket,
fragile curves of white
hung out over the dark edge
of a slanted universe, gathering the light
into themselves,
as if they were
the bright, thin walls of faith.

—Minnie Singh

Di CICCO, Pier Giorgio

Nationality: Canadian. **Born:** Arezzo, Italy, 5 July 1949. Immigrated to Canada in 1952. **Education:** University of Toronto, B.A. 1972, B.Ed. 1973; St. Paul's University, Bachelor of Sacred Theology, 1990; University of Toronto, Master of Divinity, 1990. **Career:** Bartender, Toronto, 1972–75; founder and poetry editor, *Poetry Toronto Newsletter,* 1976–77; associate editor, *Books in Canada,* Toronto, 1976–79; co-editor, 1976–79, and poetry editor, 1980–82, *Waves,* Richmond Hill, Ontario. Since 1993 ordained Roman Catholic priest and associate pastor of St. Anne's Church, Brampton, Ontario. Contributing editor, *Argomenti Canadesi,* Rome, and *Italia-America,* San Francisco. Former editor, *Descant,* Toronto, and *Poetry View.* Sessional poetry instructor, Three Schools of Art, Toronto, 1977–78; part-time instructor, Humber College, Toronto, 1981–82, 1984; sessional instructor in creative writing, Columbus Centre, Toronto, 1985. Has also worked as a chemist, detective, and teacher. Brother in the Order of St. Augustine. **Awards:** Canada Council award, 1974, 1976, 1980; Carleton University Italo-Canadian Literature award, 1979. **Address:** P.O. Box 839, Station P, Toronto, Ontario M5S 2Z1, Canada.

PUBLICATIONS

Poetry

We Are the Light Turning. Scarborough, Ontario, Missing Link Press, 1975; revised edition, Birmingham, Alabama, Thunder City Press, 1976.
The Sad Facts. Vancouver, Fiddlehead, 1977.
The Circular Dark. Ottawa, Borealis Press, 1977.
Dancing in the House of Cards. Toronto, Three Trees Press, 1977.
A Burning Patience. Ottawa, Borealis Press, 1978.
Dolce-Amaro. Tuscaloosa, Alabama, Papavero Press, 1979.
The Tough Romance. Toronto, McClelland and Stewart, 1979.
A Straw Hat for Everything. Birmingham, Alabama, Angelstone Press, 1981.
Flying Deeper into the Century. Toronto, McClelland and Stewart, 1982.
Dark to Light: Reasons for Humanness: Poems 1976–1979. Vancouver, Intermedia Press, 1983.
Women We Never See Again. Ottawa, Borealis Press, 1984.
Twenty Poems. Guadalajara, Mexico, University of Guadalajara Press, 1985.
Post-Sixties Nocturne. Vancouver, Fiddlehead, 1985.
Virgin Science: Hunting Holistic Paradigms. Toronto, McClelland and Stewart, 1986.
The City of Unhurried Dreams: Poems, 1977–1983. Montreal, Guernica, 1993.

Other

Editor, *Roman Candles: An Anthology of 17 Italo-Canadian Poets.* Toronto, Hounslow Press, 1978.

*   *   *

The course of Pier Giorgio Di Cicco's career may be imaged as a series of concentric circles. At their center is the smallest circle, representing his earliest work. Later collections fan out, each inscribing a wider arc and covering greater breadth, but each radiating from the same remarkably consistent core of values and artistry.

The earliest poems are mostly love poems, possessed of an imaginative vitality that resembles more the fiction of a García Márquez or a Borges than anything previously found in Canadian poetry. They are often surreal in effect, with exuberant emotion that pushes the contours of their imagery into constantly rippling, metamorphosing shapes, bursting and reshaping themselves with dazzling resourcefulness. This can be seen, for example, in ''The Dream of His Head,'' from *Dancing in the House of Cards:* ''The boat between them, and / the rivers of their bodies flowed into endless night. The light / moon sat on the sill, shaking its hands, telling them / to go back. / They blinked, and in that moment, the rivers turned into / alcoves, where trees were growing like children.''

Di Cicco's early poems invite us into a world warmed and softened by the powers of an imagination as intense as the sunlight of his native Italy. Reality becomes transfigured by a kind of seeing that Di Cicco, in ''The Reality Pill,'' insists is not magic: ''I do not believe in magic. / I believe the doorsteps / of the city ascend the heaven, where angels / polish them into dust.'' It is this confidence in the transforming energy of imaginative vision that sustains Di Cicco's extraordinarily prolific output and that enables his poetry to comprehend an increasingly large portion of the world around it. As he writes in ''Son of Man,'' from *A Burning Patience,* ''My imagination is a stone's throw from desire; I hear it / in my sleep, winding its engines, for the barrelling / through the dark corner of things.''

Many of Di Cicco's poems from the late 1970s barrel through the dark corners of his own background, focusing on the immigrant experience of his and other families. ''America,'' in *The Tough Romance,* personifies his newfound continent as ''a good whore—nothing to fall in love with,'' but it sympathizes with her sentimental attachments as ''she took / me around like a sweetheart showing off her home town'' and winds up respectful of her power to win a permanent place in the hearts of her lovers. Other poems in the volume emphasize the painful isolation of the new immigrant, and they do so in little narratives made bearable only by the affirmations that the imagination wrings from them. ''The Man Called Beppino,'' for instance, paints a poignant image of an impoverished, dying father (''It is this man who sits under his mimosa / by the highway, fifty pounds underweight, with no / hospital''), but it will not leave this picture without insisting that we finally focus on it, as Beppino himself has done, with imaginative vision: ''look / there are great white roses in his eyes.''

The poems of *Flying Deeper into the Century* witness the first of two more radical extensions of Di Cicco's purview. They fly deeper into the day-to-day life around the poet, frequently drawing their words and images from newspapers and television and turning a satiric scrutiny on the tendency in the 1970s and 1980s to ignore social and moral issues. Di Cicco's outrage at the pervasive materialism and a lack of moral commitment (both, after all, are threats to the creative spirit of his earlier poetry) often expresses itself in Whitmanesque catalogues. In ''Armageddon,'' for instance, he laments—under the shadow of the imminent mushroom cloud—the pointlessness of ''more music, more money, more libraries, huge indestructible libraries / where they will freeze blades of grass for Martians.'' Or turning to social mores, ''Relationships'' casts a cold eye on how ''convenience'' has blurred important distinctions by veiling them under a buzzword: ''the / strong relationship, the superficial relationship, / the relationship between two people, an honest / relationship, the mature relationship, the dead / relationship.'' Sometimes this technique can be very powerful, but occasionally it blunts the cutting edge of the poems by embodying the imprecision it seeks to oppose, as at the end of ''Failsafe: The Movie'': ''Almost as if we don't have / to go through it again. Almost as if films / could tell us something. Almost as if art / weren't the worst kind of lie.'' Language and cadence are certainly colloquial, but memorable poems usually avoid speaking like this.

Di Cicco's poetic footing is usually surer when he turns to the experience of love that, like his recurrent references to roses, forms the solid, affirmative core of every one of his collections. With its movingly plain diction and its sudden expanded vistas, the conclusion of ''The Express Sunlight,'' from *Women We Never See Again,* typifies such strengths: ''the irreparable itch begins. I want to sing. You haven't ears / enough, I haven't voice enough, but between us the earth gapes, / and that slender-footed desire comes up. It is an angel, and it goes / by the name of any day of the week.''

The second and more significant extension of Di Cicco's poetic vision occurs in the poems of *Virgin Science: Hunting Holistic Paradigms,* in which his art reaches out to the theories of postclassical physics. The spirit of joy that infuses the volume stems from Di Cicco's recognition that ''physics has become meta-poetry'' (''Towards a Transforms Glossary''). A Blakean type of poetic vision, in which matter is animated and the perceiver of it helps define it in the process of perception, had always been accepted on faith as the center of Di Cicco's poetic credo. He now finds that the world his poems have been reaching toward is in fact the reality of modern, post-Cartesian science. Matter only ''appears solid because electrons / rotate at 600 miles per second'' (''Searching the Light Cone''), and as the prose poem at the beginning of ''A Holographic Theory of Consciousness'' puts it, ''Material objects are the result of two or more intersecting waves married into three-dimensional forms by the act of consciousness.'' It is a marriage that his entire oeuvre has brought to consummation.

—John Reibetanz

DIDSBURY, Peter

Nationality: British. **Born:** Fleetwood, 10 April 1946. **Education:** Balliol College, Oxford, 1964–68. **Family:** Married 1) Susan Raleigh (divorced); 2) Patricia Ann Cooley in 1982, two daughters and one son. **Career:** High school teacher, Hull, 1973–81. Since 1982 archaeologist, Hull Museums, Hull. **Address:** 16 Ventnor Street, Hull, North Humberside HU5 2LP, England.

PUBLICATIONS

Poetry

The Butchers of Hull. Newcastle upon Tyne, Bloodaxe, 1982.
The Classical Farm. Newcastle upon Tyne, Bloodaxe, and Chester Springs, Pennsylvania, Dufour Editions, 1987.
That Old Time Religion. Newcastle upon Tyne, Bloodaxe, 1994.

*

Critical Studies: ''Epigraphs for Epigones; John Ashbery's Influence in England'' by Ian Gregson, in *Bete Noire* (Hull, Humberside), 4, winter 1987; Peter Didsbury issue of *Bete Noire* (Hull, Humberside), 6, winter 1988; by Ian McMillan, in *Poetry Review,* 84(2), summer 1994.

*   *   *

Peter Didsbury is closely associated with Hull, where he moved at the age of six and where his occupations as a teacher and an archaeologist have thoroughly immersed him in the urban and domestic life of that city. It is the images of Hull's rain-drenched farms, ditches, drains, and dykes that are so powerfully depicted in his writing. The city has come a long way in its public and literary consciousness since the early 1950s. Hull poets have been labeled ''provincial'' with respect to London and Oxbridge, which are centers of conservatism in poetry. Nonetheless, the leading consortium of Hull poets—Peter Didsbury, Tony Flynn, Douglas Houston, and Sean O'Brien—are drawn to more radical European and American styles even while they remain loyal to working-class values and hostile to the presumptions of the metropolis.

Of the influences on his writing Didsbury has said, ''I started writing poetry at school. Just before going to the university. An exceptionally gifted English teacher set us to imitate Gerard Manley Hopkins as a literary exercise. Like many poets, I was largely concerned with epiphanies at first and then with the self-justifying products of the autonomous imagination. It's the dangers of the latter that have begun to be borne in upon me more recently . . . .''

Didsbury is considered to be a postmodernist poet, one influenced by the American John Ashbery. His technique of rendering the complexity of experience with the mind's bafflement in the face of it, and with its difficulty in finding significant connections between one experience and another, is an element used by Ashbery. This is applied to phenomena when objects clear for a moment and then blur, resulting in a puzzling homogeneity in which adjacent outlines turn illegible. Didsbury also has learned some technical elements from Ashbery: rhythmical flexibility and colloquial nonchalance, an outlook on subject matter, a belief in a self-conscious inclusiveness, and an apparent openness to experience as the poem is being written that can allow for improvisation.

In ''The Flowers of Finland,'' from *The Butchers of Hull,* Didsbury uses Ashbery's method when he evokes the moment of composition in which ideas are proposed and then modified or even erased:

Taken. Under-taken. Taken.
Words from a dream . . .
Stop. All wrong.
Words from a reverie.
Work on in Shapeland

Anywhere will do to start
It always has.
Language is the propensity.
We have the template,
then anything you care to mention.

Other ideas whose status is in doubt are introduced, and there are bits of narrative or metaphors for what proceeds or follows them:

After my head hit the windscreen
I thought of Auden's words
that without a cement of blood they would not safely stand.

Didsbury is a creative and original poet in his handling of language. He uses language as a medium of delight but is very much a maker of poems and of crafted objects. He uses devices that can be labeled as "historical-surrealist" and as "anecdotal-pastoral." In "The Specialist Heart" he exploits a cultivated disparity between flatness of tone and a soaring, playful imagination:

My inside pocket is my specialist heart.
I feed it with papers.
We have filled our jackets with regularity
my fathers and I,
we make wardrobes into libraries . . .
Our pockets swell to the old afflatus
of a war against women:
hushed tones, and angry glances.
Once a year, on Mischief Night
we frighten ourselves on the old stories
of female victories: jackets gone to jumble
and vanished patrimonies.

Didbury's prose poem "A White Wine for Max Ernst" is a surrealist and allegorical work in which he bares his imagination in the same way as the objects he writes about are laid bare in a tactile environment, although the two are dissociated from each other: "A clockwork train on the green tiled floor of a swimming pool. A loco / pulling just three carriages chugs busily around in chlorinated wine. The / bath is square and uniformly six feet deep. There are not tracks. The large / key . . . It is large / enough with its butterfly wings for a child's small fingers . . . From here I can only taste it."

In *The Classical Farm* Didsbury continues a further aspect of Ashbery's method. "The Smart Chair" questions the way in which poems connect distinct experiences. Its improvisational quality emerges from this because the experiences appear to enter randomly, so that the poem links a remark by an eleven-year-old girl and a visit to a small island. The prosaic experience is juxtaposed with the conventional poetic experience:

My chair looked smart because it had a tie hanging over
    the back.
She's eleven years old, and although she knows that I
    don't wear ties
she didn't know I'd been to a funeral, wearing that tie
which now improves my furniture.

The second experience is made more "poetic" by having a fantasy attached to it:

. . . a white farmhouse stood in the middle of the bay
on a rock that was little larger than itself. *Not* a farmhouse,
unless they farmed seaweeds, rats, and the voices of
    drowned sailors—
there wasn't enough room—

In *That Old Time Religion* Didsbury writes with the same sense of adventure and imagination as in his other two collections. His inventiveness is surrealist and powerful. In this work there is a glimpse of an alternative history in which Catholic Europe and the East are strangely mixed, in which matters of faith and damnation are still alive yet meaningless. A vision of pastoral England is also apparent in his invention of pure play in which there are disparate celebrations of estuaries, farms, estates, and city streets.

Didsbury sums up his poetical beliefs in statements such as these:

I have a strong belief in the poem as a "made thing," a coherent, independent object that it is necessary to release from the "stone" of the world . . . Linguistics and history (in its broadest sense) are the vehicles in which my poems travel.

For me, the writing of poetry is essentially a spiritual undertaking, and I have slowly come to realize that I have a "religious" nature that can find no other formal expression.

—Renu Barrett

DILLARD, R(ichard) H(enry) W(ilde)

Nationality: American. **Born:** Roanoke, Virginia, 11 October 1937. **Education:** Roanoke College, Salem, Virginia, 1955–58, B.A. 1958 (Phi Beta Kappa); University of Virginia, Charlottesville (Woodrow Wilson Fellow, 1958–59; DuPont Fellow, 1959–61), M.A. 1959, Ph.D. 1965. **Family:** Married 1) Annie Doak in 1965 (divorced 1975); 2) Cathy Hankla in 1979. **Career:** Instructor in English, Roanoke College, summer 1961, and University of Virginia, 1961–64. Assistant professor, 1964–68, associate professor, 1968–74, since 1971 chair of the graduate program in contemporary literature and creative writing, and since 1974 professor of English, Hollins College, Virginia. Since 1973 vice-president, *Film Journal,* New York. Contributing editor, *Hollins Critic,* Hollins College, Virginia, 1966–77. Since 1992 editor-in-chief, *Children's Literature.* Member of literary board, Virginia Center of the Creative Arts; member of editorial advisory board, *New Virginia Review.* Member of Roanoke County Democratic Committee and delegate to state political conventions. **Awards:** Academy of American Poets prize, 1961; Ford grant, 1972; O.B. Hardison, Jr. Poetry award of the Folger Shakespeare Library, 1994. **Agent:** Blanche C. Gregory, 2 Tudor City Place, New York, New York 10017. **Address:** Box 9671, Hollins College, Virginia 24020, U.S.A.

PUBLICATIONS

Poetry

The Day I Stopped Dreaming about Barbara Steele and Other Poems. Chapel Hill, University of North Carolina Press, 1966.
News of the Nile. Chapel Hill, University of North Carolina Press, 1971.
After Borges. Baton Rouge, Louisiana State University Press, 1972.
The Greeting: New and Selected Poems. Salt Lake City, University of Utah Press, 1981.
Just Here, Just Now. Baton Rouge, Louisiana State University Press, 1994.
A New Pleiade: Selected Poems. N.p., 1998.

Play

Screenplay: *Frankenstein Meets the Space Monster,* with George Garrett and John Rodenbeck, 1966.

Novels

The Book of Changes. New York, Doubleday, 1974.
The First Man on the Sun. Baton Rouge, Louisiana State University Press, 1983.

Short Stories

Omniphobia. Baton Rouge, Louisiana State University Press, 1995.

Other

Horror Films. New York, Monarch Press, 1976.
Understanding George Garrett. Columbia, University of South Carolina Press, 1988.

Editor, with Louis D. Rubin, Jr., *The Experience of America: A Book of Readings.* New York, Macmillan, and London, Collier Macmillan, 1969.
Editor, with George Garrett and John Rees Moore, *The Sounder Few: Essays from ''The Hollins Critic.''* Athens, University of Georgia Press, 1971.

*

Critical Studies: ''Watersmeet: Thinking about Southern Poets'' by Kelly Cherry, in *Book Forum* (New York), 3, 1977; ''Ladies in Boston Have Their Hats: Notes on WASP Humor'' by George Garrett, in *Comic Relief: Humor in Contemporary American Literature,* edited by Sarah Blacher Cohen, Urbana, University of Illinois Press, 1978; in *The Writer's Mind: Interviews with American Authors* edited by Irv Broughton, Fayetteville, University of Arkansas Press, 1990.

R.H.W. Dillard comments:

Although I have thought a good deal about what I am doing in my poems, I do not know that I really am able to express the results of that thinking very clearly, except (I hope) in the poems themselves. Allow me, then, to offer in place of an introductory statement about my poetry excerpts from three poems that might do the job.

The first, from the poem ''News of the Nile,'' is just a description of the source of my poems' experience in the broadest sense: ''All these things I have read and remembered, / Witnessed, imagined, thought and written down . . .''

The second, from the poem ''Construction,'' may be a bit more helpful, for it is as close as I have come to an explicit esthetic statement, and it also makes explicit my central concern with the vital involvement of seeing and saying, of action and belief:

To say as you see. To see as by stop-action,
Clouds coil overhead, the passage of days,

Trees bend by the side of the road
Like tires on a curve, plants uncurl,

How the world dissolves in the water of the eye:
The illusion speed produces. The reality of speed.

A result: to see as you say,
As gravity may bend a ray of light.

To say the earth's center is of fire:
Life leaps from the soil like sun flares.

To see the world made true,
An art of rocks and stones and trees,

Real materials in real space,
L'esthétique de la vitesse.

The third, from the long poem *January: A Screenplay,* is a prayer that states briefly the faith and the humility that I hope is at the heart of everything I do:

For my sorrow in this depth of joy,
Gift beyond reward, I'm sorry.
For the joy I feel in this broken world,
This sorrow, this woe, I thank you,
I thank you.

*   *   *

Taking work from his first three books, R.H.W. Dillard's *The Greeting: New and Selected Poems* (1981) established him as an unusual and important contemporary poet. The earliest of the three volumes, *The Day I Stopped Dreaming about Barbara Steele and Other Poems* (1966), is a highly sophisticated and humorous collection. Also his most traditionally formal, it is impressive in its sardonic rendering of a wide range of experiences. Sometimes, however, in labored attempts to charge the ephemeral with beauty and significance, Dillard comes across as an overly witty aesthete, thus compromising some of the emotional qualities of the poems.

News of the Nile (1971) develops Dillard's voice in a different, interesting direction. The witty, stylized, intellectual voice of the first volume becomes more autobiographical and personal, even troubled. Influenced by his study of horror movies, Dillard examines the perverse side of human nature—blood lust, cannibalism, the macabre. Such poems as ''Night of the Living Dead,'' ''Event: A Gathering; Vastation,'' and ''Act of Detection'' revel in the horrific. Not all of the poems in the volume deal with such subjects, and some give poignant accounts of a more personal nature.

Dillard's third book, *After Borges* (1972), represents a mature achievement, arising out of a profound experience with the Argentine writer's work. Returning to the wit that fueled his first volume, such poems as ''Round Ruby,'' ''What Can You Say to Shoes,'' ''Sweet Strawberries,'' and ''Wings'' express joy and pathos at life's absurdities and trivialities as well as at its beauties. The series of poems that purport to be ''after the Spanish of Jorge Luis Borges''—''Limits,'' ''The Other Tiger,'' ''Argumentum Ornithologicum,'' and ''Epilogue''—are more introspective, serious, and complex. ''Epilogue,'' for instance, gives an introspective account of the poet setting ''out to shape a world''; the poem ends in self-confrontation at a ''face, wearing / And worn, warm as worn stone. / A face you know: your own.'' It is not surprising that Dillard is attracted to the intellectual labyrinths of Borges, but what makes the book interesting is how

Dillard's poems appropriate Borges's musings and reshape them into a felt, personal response to the work of the Argentine writer.

In *The Greeting: New and Selected Poems* Dillard shows the versatility of his published work as well as the direction of his later poems. Indeed, the collection brings together much of the best work from his earlier books. One of its most interesting achievements is a sixty-page screenplay in verse. Called *January,* it tells a story of two lovers who are forced to carry on a long-distance relationship across the Atlantic. Adopting a style reminiscent of Yeats's dreamy dramas of the romantic Irish past and of Robbe Grillet's film *Last Year at Marienbad,* Dillard depicts a hazy, rose-colored world of vague emotions, shifting settings, and constant longing. Although the conclusion, which emphasizes the message ''The only knowledge is love,'' is somewhat banal and some of the language is flat, the parameters of the project are ambitious. The screenplay illustrates not only Dillard's devotion to film but also his interest in expanding the genre confines of poetry. It is worth noting that he attempts such expansion again in his novel *The First Man on the Sun* (1983) by including a long section of poetry by one of the characters.

In *Just Here, Just Now* (1994) Dillard combines several of the qualities of his earlier books. Returning to the techniques of his second volume, in which he used a great many references to horror films, and of his third, in which he appropriated Borges, *Just Here, Just Now* relies heavily upon allusions to film, culture, and art for its success. Although there are places where Dillard's strong personal voice shines through, the reliance on allusion can seem overly cerebral:

> And my case, in fact, will seem
> Quite insecure if I depend
> Only on the *Tractacus*
> Or make Whitehead and Russell
> My solid ground, my fact . . .

In addition to these, there are allusions to Hart Crane, Poe, Rousseau, Frankenstein, Lawrence Becker, and George Garrett—all in the first seventeen pages. Even so, Dillard at his best can be found in this rather brief book, especially in the epistolary poems ''Autumn Letter to London,'' ''Winter Letter to Bluefield,'' and ''Spring Letter to Paradise,'' which successfully combine his erudition with a strong, emotional voice.

—Richard Damashek and Tod Marshall

di PRIMA, Diane

Nationality: American. **Born:** New York City, 6 August 1934. Attended Swarthmore College, Pennsylvania, 1951–53. **Family:** Married 1) Alan S. Marlowe in 1962 (divorced 1969) 2) Grant Fisher in 1972 (divorced 1975); has four daughters and one son. **Career:** Contributing editor, *Kulchur* magazine, New York, 1960–61; co-editor, with LeRoi Jones, 1961–63, and editor, 1963–69, *Floating Bear* magazine, New York; also associated with *Yugen, Signal, Guerilla,* San Francisco *Sunday Paper,* and *Rallying Point.* Publisher, Poets Press, 1964–69, and Eidolon Editions, San Francisco, since 1974. Affiliated with Wingbow Press, Berkeley, California. Founder, with Alan Marlowe and others, New York Poets Theater, 1961–65. Teacher in the Poetry-in-the-Schools program, 1971–75; visiting faculty member, Naropa Institute, Boulder, Colorado; artist-in-residence, Napa State Hospital, 1976–77. Member of the Core Faculty, New College of California, San Francisco, 1980–87. Since 1981 working privately as a psychic and healer. Founded in 1983, with Janet Carter, Carl Grundberg, and Sheppard Powell, and worked as writer and teacher, 1983–91, San Francisco Institute of Magical and Healing Arts. Senior lecturer, California College of Arts and Crafts, Oakland, 1990–92; visiting faculty, San Francisco Art Institute, 1992; adjunct faculty, California Institute of Integral Studies, 1994. Columnist, *Mama Bear's News and Notes,* 1987–93, and *Harbin Quarterly,* 1992–93. Artist: Individual shows—Museum of Modern Art, San Francisco, 1974; Point Reyes Dance Palace, 1977; San Francisco Dharmadhatu, 1985; Naropa Institute, 1989. **Awards:** National Endowment for the Arts grant, 1966, 1973; Coordinating Council of Little Magazines grant, 1967, 1970; Lapis Foundation, 1978, 1979; Institute for Aesthetic Development, 1986; Lifetime Service award, National Poetry Association, 1993. **Address:** c/o Wingbow Press, 2940 West 7th Street, Berkeley, California 94710, U.S.A.

PUBLICATIONS

Poetry

This Kind of Bird Flies Backward. New York, Totem Press, 1958.
The Monster. New Haven, Connecticut, Penny Poems, 1961.
The New Handbook of Heaven. San Francisco, Auerhahn Press, 1963.
Unless You Clock In. Palo Alto, California, Patchen Cards, 1963.
Combination Theatre Poem and Birthday Poem for Ten People. New York, Brownstone Press, 1965.
Haiku. Topanga, California, Love Press, 1967.
Earthsong: Poems 1957–59, edited by Alan S. Marlowe. New York, Poets Press, 1968.
Hotel Albert. New York, Poets Press, 1968.
New Mexico Poem, June-July 1967. New York, Roodenko, 1968.
The Star, The Child, The Light. Privately printed, 1968.
L.A. Odyssey. New York, Poets Press, 1969.
New As. . . . Privately printed, 1969.
The Book of Hours. San Francisco, Brownstone Press, 1970.
Kerhonkson Journal 1966. Berkeley, California, Oyez, 1971.
Prayer to the Mothers. Privately printed, 1971.
So Fine. Santa Barbara, California, Yes Press, 1971.
XV Dedications. Santa Barbara, California, Unicorn Press, 1971.
Revolutionary Letters. San Francisco, City Lights, 1971.
The Calculus of Letters. Privately printed, 1972.
Loba, Part 1. Santa Barbara, California, Capra Press, 1973.
Freddie Poems. Point Reyes, California, Eidolon, 1974.
North Country Medicine. Privately printed, 1974.
Brass Furnace Going Out: Song, After an Abortion. Syracuse, New York, Pulpartforms-Intrepid Press, 1975.
Selected Poems 1956–1975. Plainfield, Vermont, North Atlantic, 1975; revised edition, 1977.
Loba as Eve. New York, Phoenix Book Shop, 1975.
Loba, Part 2. Point Reyes, California, Eidolon, 1976.
Loba, Parts 1–8. Berkeley, California, Wingbow Press, 1978.
Wyoming Series. San Francisco, Eidolon Editions, 1988.
The Mysteries of Vision. Santa Barbara, California, Am Here Books, 1988.
Pieces of a Song: Selected Poems. San Francisco, City Lights, 1990.
Seminary Poems. Point Reyes, California, Floating Island, 1991.

The Mask Is the Path of the Star. Louisville, Kentucky, Thinker Review International, 1993.
22 Death Poems. Ellsworth, Maine, Backwoods Broadsides, 1996.
Loba. New York, Penguin, 1998.

Plays

Paideuma (produced New York, 1960).
The Discontentment of the Russian Prince (produced New York, 1961).
Murder Cake (produced New York, 1963).
Like (produced New York, 1964).
Poets Vaudeville, music by John Herbert McDowell (produced New York, 1964). New York, Feed Folly Press, 1964.
Monuments (produced New York, 1968).
The Discovery of America (produced New York, 1972).
Whale Honey (produced San Francisco, 1975; New York, 1976).
ZipCode: Collected Plays. Minneapolis, Minnesota, Coffee House Press, 1994.

Novels

The Calculus of Variation. New York, Poets Press, 1966.
Spring and Autumn Annals. San Francisco, Frontier Press, 1966.
Memoirs of a Beatnik. New York, Olympia Press, 1969.

Short Stories

Dinners and Nightmares. New York, Corinth, 1961; revised edition, 1974.

Other

Notes on the Summer Solstice. Privately printed, 1969.

Editor, *Various Fables from Various Places.* New York, Putnam, 1960.
Editor, *War Poems.* New York, Poets Press, 1968.
Editor, with LeRoi Jones, *The Floating Bear: A Newsletter, Numbers 1–37.* La Jolla, California, Laurence McGilvery, 1973.

Translator, with others, *The Man Condemned to Death,* by Jean Genet. New York, Poets Press, 1963.
Translator, *Seven Love Poems from the Middle Latin.* New York, Poets Press, 1965.

*

Manuscript Collection: Southern Illinois University, Carbondale.

Critical Studies: Interview with Anne Waldman, in *The Beat Road,* edited by Arthur Winfield Knight and Kit Knight, California, Pennsylvania, Unspeakable Visions of the Individual, 1984; ''Diane di Prima: Extending La famiglia'' by Blossom S. Kirschenbaum, in *MELUS* (Amherst, Massachusetts), 14(3–4) Fall/Winter 1987; by Carl Solomon, in *American Book Review,* 13(2), June 1991; by Charles Marowitz, in *American Book Review,* 15(2), June 1993.

*   *   *

Diane di Prima is, sadly, the only major female poet to emerge out of the beat generation's upheaval in American poetry. Her work lucidly reflects as well as transcends beat assumptions, however, as radical spirits permeate her writing, including emancipatory romanticism, anarchism, feminism, and chthonic esotericism. A resilient web of assertive traditions and practices informs her work, revealing a powerful and uncompromising history of herself as woman, artist, citizen, and sage. Early beat collections like *This Kind of Bird Flies Backward* retain their clarity and unity of purpose. The magical poems in *The New Handbook of Heaven* do not cancel out the polemics of *Revolutionary Letters,* and the exacting lyric particulars of *Kerhonkson Journal 1966* complement the transgressive charm of *Memoirs of a Beatnik.*

Loba is a major serial poem that synthesizes much of di Prima's earlier work and enters more deeply into ritual realms and the hermetic. Through meta-actual female myths and symbols expressed and embodied in Loba, Lilith, Eve, Iseult, and Persephone, the poet restores disallowed literary and mythic examples of female power and history into a grand narrative. The dialectic of wildness and civilization as feminine spheres of action and re-creation is compellingly sustained.

Di Prima's work has participated in and contributed to many critical schisms in American culture—the 1950s beat movement, the 1960s countercultural carnivals of self and collective politics, the redefining of feminine consciousness during the 1970s, and the teaching of esoteric praxis and healing arts in the 1980s. The poet has begun work on her autobiography, to be titled *Recollections of My Life as a Woman,* which should provide a broader experiential knowledge of these epochs, just as her poetic work has offered a richly emblematic unfolding of significant visible and invisible histories.

— David Meltzer

DISCH, Thomas M(ichael)

Nationality: American. **Born:** Des Moines, Iowa, 2 February 1940. **Education:** St. Paul's Convent School, Fairmont, Minnesota; Central High School, St. Paul, Minnesota; Cooper Union, New York, and New York University, 1959–62. **Career:** Part-time checkroom attendant, Majestic Theatre, New York, 1957–62; copywriter, Doyle Dane Bernbach Inc., New York, 1963–64. Since 1964 freelance writer and lecturer. Theatre critic, *The Nation,* 1987–91, and since 1993, *New York Daily News.* Since 1996 artist-in-residence, College of William and Mary. **Awards:** O. Henry prize, 1975, 1979; John W. Campbell Memorial award, 1980; *Locus* award, 1981; British Science-Fiction award, for short stories, 1981. **Agent:** Karpfinger Agency, 500 Fifth Avenue, Suite 2800, New York, New York 10110, U.S.A.

PUBLICATIONS

Poetry

Highway Sandwiches, with Marilyn Hacker and Charles Platt. Privately printed, 1970.
The Right Way to Figure Plumbing. New York, Basilisk Press, 1972.
ABCDEFG HIJKLM NOPQRST UVWXYZ. London, Anvil Press Poetry, 1981.

Burn This. London, Hutchinson, 1982.

Orders of the Retina. West Branch, Iowa, Toothpaste Press, 1982.

Here I Am, There You Are, Where Were We. London, Hutchinson, 1984.

Yes, Let's: New and Selected Poems. Baltimore, Maryland, Johns Hopkins University Press, 1989.

Dark Verses & Light. Baltimore, Johns Hopkins University Press, 1991.

Haikus of an AmPart. Minneapolis, Coffee House Press, 1991.

The Hawk & the Metaphor. Chester, Pennsylvania, Aralia Press, 1993.

The Dark Old House. Edgewood, Kentucky, Barth, 1996.

A Child's Garden of Grammar (as Tom Disch). Hanover, New Hampshire, University Press of New England, 1997.

Novels

The Genocides. New York, Berkley, 1965; London, Whiting and Wheaton, 1967.

Mankind under the Leash. New York, Ace, 1966; as *The Puppies of Terra,* London, Panther, 1978

The House That Fear Built (as Cassandra Knye), with John Sladek. New York, Paperback Library, 1966.

Echo round His Bones. New York, Berkley, 1967; London, Hart Davis, 1969.

Camp Concentration. London, Hart Davis, 1968; New York, Doubleday, 1969.

Black Alice (as Thom Demijohn), with John Sladek. New York, Doubleday, 1968; London, W. H. Allen, 1969.

The Prisoner. New York, Ace, 1969; London, Dobson, 1979.

334. London, MacGibbon and Kee, 1972; New York, Avon, 1974.

Clara Reeve (as Leonie Hargrave). New York, Knopf, and London, Hutchinson, 1975.

On Wings of Song. New York, St. Martin's Press, and London, Gollancz, 1979.

Triplicity (omnibus). New York, Doubleday, 1980.

Neighboring Lives, with Charles Naylor. New York, Scribner, and London, Hutchinson, 1981.

The Businessman: A Tale of Terror. New York, Harper, and London, Cape, 1984.

Amnesia. N.p., Electronic Arts, 1985.

The Priest: A Gothic Romance. London, Millenium, 1994.

The Sub: A Study in Witchcraft. New York, Knopf, 1999.

Short Stories

One Hundred and Two H-Bombs. London, Compact, 1966; New York, Berkley, 1971; enlarged edition, as *White Fang Goes Dingo and Other Funny S. F. Stories,* London, Arrow, 1971.

Under Compulsion. London, Hart Davis, 1968; as *Fun with Your New Head,* New York, Doubleday, 1971.

Getting into Death. London, Hart Davis MacGibbon, 1973; New York, Knopf, 1976.

The Early Science Fiction Stories of Thomas M. Disch. Boston, Gregg Press, 1977.

Fundamental Disch. New York, Bantam, 1980; London, Gollancz, 1981.

The Man Who Had No Idea. London, Gollancz, 1982.

Ringtime: A Story. West Branch, Iowa, Toothpaste Press, 1983.

Torturing Mr. Amberwell. New Castle, Virginia, Cheap Street, 1985.

The Silver Pillow: A Tale of Witchcraft. Willimantic, Connecticut, Ziesing, 1987.

The M.D.: A Horror Story. New York, Grafton, 1991.

Other

The Brave Little Toaster (for children). New York, Doubleday, and London, Grafton, 1986.

The Tale of Dan De Lion: A Fable (for children). Minneapolis, Coffee House Press, 1986.

The Brave Little Toaster Goes to Mars (for children). New York, Doubleday, 1988.

The Dreams Our Stuff Is Made of: How Science Fiction Conquered the World. London and New York, Free Press, 1998.

Editor, *The Ruins of Earth: An Anthology of the Immediate Future.* New York, Putnam, 1971; London, Hutchinson, 1973.

Editor, *Bad Moon Rising.* New York, Harper, 1973; London, Hutchinson, 1974.

Editor, *The New Improved Sun: An Anthology of Utopian Science Fiction.* New York, Harper, 1975; London, Hutchinson, 1976.

Editor, with Charles Naylor, *New Constellations.* New York, Harper, 1976.

Editor, with Charles Naylor, *Strangeness.* New York, Scribner, 1977.

Editor, *The Castle of Indolence: On Poetry, Poets, and Poetasters.* New York, Picador, 1995.

*

Bibliography: *Thomas M. Disch: A Preliminary Bibliography* by David Nee, Berkeley, California, Other Change of Hobbit, 1982; *Tom Disch Checklist* by Chris Drumm, San Bernadino, California, Borgo Press, 1989.

Critical Studies: ''Naturalism, Aestheticism and Beyond: Tradition and Innovation in the Work of Thomas M. Disch'' by Thomas L. Wymer, in *Voices for the Future, III,* edited by Thomas D. Clareson and Wymer, Bowling Green, Ohio, Popular, 1984; ''Dystopia or Dischtopia: The Science-Fiction Paradigms of Thomas M. Disch'' by Peter Swirski, in *Science-Fiction Studies* (Greencastle, Indiana), 18(2), July 1991.

*   *   *

It is a swan dive from the warm sincerity of most American poetry into the cool astringency of Thomas M. Disch's formal negotiations. Disch has produced some of the most wildly imaginative science fiction ever written, an interactive novel on computer disk, children's books about the Brave Little Toaster, and a novelization of the *Prisoner* television series. The same baroque invention, erudition, and camp black humor are coupled with virtuoso technique in such poems as ''At the Grave of Amy Clampitt,'' the sestina ''Prayer to Pleasure,'' and a villanelle on the death of the universe from heat.

A certain percentage of Disch's poetry admittedly falls into the category of light verse. His work frequently leaves itself open to the charge of empty ingenuity, and he has been criticized as being glib. It is, however, a quality that Randall Jarrell identified as ''The Higher Glibness,'' for although Disch is almost always funny, he is never just clever; there usually is a serious philosophical issue driving the wit. Consider this gem of advice from "How to Behave When Dead," couched in the language of an etiquette manual: "Remember: / sincerity and naturalness / count for more than wit / His jokes may strike you as / abstruse. / Only laugh if He does." Only when "He" is parenthetically described as "a bronze skull gorging on a snake" do we realize that we are not in heaven.

For some time Disch's talent as a poet went largely unacknowledged in the United States. His second collection was published in Britain by the perspicacious Anvil Press because American publishers, for whom sincerity and naturalness may often count for more than wit, were not interested. Perhaps this is because mainstream American readers often have difficulty distinguishing nuances of irony and are apt to be confused and disturbed by moral ambiguity. Poets like Disch, who habitually shift register from the frivolous to the serious and produce titles like "Light Verses for the Vietnam War Dead" and "The Rapist's Villanelle" belong to a minority strand in American poetry.

The strongest current in mainstream American verse demands a program of romantic sincerity couched in open forms, and mainstream critics are suspicious of poets who flaunt technique. The most successful resistance to the status quo has come from those poets directly influenced by Auden—James Merrill, John Hollander, Anthony Hecht, and Richard Howard. Like them Disch is drawn to traditional forms. But in terms of tone and composition he is clearly an heir of the New York school of poets, which included John Ashbery, Barbara Guest, James Schuyler, Kenneth Koch, and principally Frank O'Hara. In fact, one way of characterizing Disch's work would be to say that he uses the technique of the Byron of *Don Juan* as channeled through the voice of O'Hara.

Although he appears to take the challenge of form lightly, Disch is a formalist par excellence. He delights in the restrictions of rhyme, meter, and numerous less conventional rules. In his second collection, *ABCDEFG HIJKLM NOPQRST UVWXYZ,* for example, all of the poems appear in strict alphabetical order, beginning with "Abcedary" ("A is an apple, as everyone knows. / But B is a . . . What do you suppose? / A Bible? A Barber? A Banquet? A Bank? / No B is this Boat, the night that it sank . . ."). The collection ends with a kind of mirror image catalog of alphabetical invention, "Zewhyexary" ("Z is the Zenith from which we decline / While Y is the Yelp as you're twisting your spine."). Both poems are loosely narrative series of associations in rhyming couplets, and both are shamelessly concerned with their own composition, which is exactly the point. This reliance on lists and verbal formulas is a recurrent feature in Disch's work, as in "Slides," which takes the form of comments on individual holiday snapshots: "Marilyn and me / / Charles and Marilyn / / me and Charles / with the sign at the exit behind us. / / And this is the last one. / They say it's a mile deep."

Disch is also a fatally accurate parodist. "High Purpose in Poetry: A Primer," for example, is dedicated to A.R. Ammons in the sense that *Don Juan* was dedicated to Robert Southey. Disch lampoons Ammons's easy cosmic affirmations: "Only one thing is needed: to speak of matters elemental. / . . . of anything as basic / As water, fire, earth, or air: to lift it up and say of it, / There! Behold!" Disch is enormously skilled in the art of graceful deflation. In "Skydiver" the grand romanticism of the parachutist's leap is undermined by the poet's description, "and though / That may sound snide or flip, it's just my way / Of talking: I honestly feel amazement, only that." Characteristically, this very assurance puts us at once on our guard, so that we are prepared for the final lines of the poem when

Disch praises skydiving as the ultimate expression "of faith in things unseen: the wind, / The mind, the patient skill of seamstresses / Running immense lengths of nylon / Through their clamoring machines."

—Michael Donaghy

DOBSON, Rosemary (de Brissac)

Nationality: Australian. **Born:** Sydney, New South Wales, 18 June 1920. **Education:** Frensham, Mittagong, New South Wales; Sydney University. **Family:** Married A.T. Bolton in 1951; one daughter and two sons. **Awards:** *Sydney Morning Herald* prize, 1946; Myer award, 1966; Robert Frost award, 1979; Australia Council fellowship, 1980; Patrick White award, 1984; Grace Leven award, 1984; Victorian Premier's literary award, 1984. Officer, Order of Australia, 1987. **Agent:** Curtis Brown (Australia) Pty. Ltd., P.O. Box 19, Paddington, New South Wales 2021. **Address:** 61 Stonehaven Crescent, Deakin, Canberra, ACT 2600, Australia.

PUBLICATIONS

Poetry

Poems. Mittagong, New South Wales, Frensham Press, 1937.
In a Convex Mirror. Sydney, Dymock's Book Arcade, 1944.
The Ship of Ice and Other Poems. Sydney, Angus and Robertson, 1948.
Child with a Cockatoo and Other Poems. Sydney, Angus and Robertson, 1955.
(Poems), selected and introduced by the author. Sydney, Angus and Robertson, 1963.
Cock Crow. Sydney, Angus and Robertson, 1965.
Rosemary Dobson Reads from Her Own Work (with recording). St. Lucia, University of Queensland Press, 1970.
Selected Poems. Sydney, Angus and Robertson, 1973; revised edition, 1980.
Greek Coins: A Sequence of Poems. Canberra, Brindabella Press, 1977.
Over the Frontier. Sydney, Angus and Robertson, 1978.
The Continuance of Poetry. Canberra, Brindabella Press, 1981.
Journeys, with others, edited by Fay Zwicky. Melbourne, Sisters, 1982.
The Three Fates and Other Poems. Sydney, Hale and Iremonger, 1984.
Collected Poems. Sydney, Angus and Robertson, 1991.
Untold Lives. Canberra, Brindabella Press, 1992.

Other

Focus on Ray Crooke. St. Lucia, University of Queensland Press, 1971.
A World of Difference: Australian Poetry and Painting in the 1940's (lecture). Sydney, Wentworth Press, 1973.
Summer Press (for children). St. Lucia, University of Queensland Press, 1987.

Editor, *Australian Poetry 1949–1950.* Sydney, Angus and Robertson, 1950.

Editor, *Songs for All Seasons: 100 Poems for Young People.* Sydney, Angus and Robertson, 1967.

Editor, *Australian Voices: Poetry and Prose of the 1970's.* Canberra, Australian National University Press, 1975.

Editor, *The Grammar of the Real: Selected Prose, 1959–1974,* by James P. McAuley. Melbourne, Oxford University Press, 1975.

Editor, *Sisters Poets 1.* Carlton, Victoria, Sisters, 1979.

Translator, with David Campbell, *Moscow Trefoil.* Canberra, Australian National University Press, 1975.

Translator, with David Campbell, *Seven Russian Poets.* St. Lucia, University of Queensland Press, 1979.

*

Manuscript Collections: National Library of Australia, Canberra; Fryer Memorial Library, University of Queensland, Brisbane.

Critical Studies: "The Poetry of Rosemary Dobson" by James McAuley, in *The Grammar of the Real,* London, Oxford University Press, 1975; "A Frame of Reference: Rosemary Dobson's Grace Notes for Humanity" by Adrian Mitchell, in *Australian Literary Studies* (St. Lucia, Queensland), May 1981; "Reclusive Grace: The Poetry of Rosemary Dobson" by Fay Zwicky, in *The Lyre in the Pawnshop: Essays on Literature and Survival 1974–1984,* Nedlands, University of Western Australia Press, 1986; "Rosemary Dobson's Modernist Elegies: A Reading of *The Three Fates*" by James Tulip, in *Southerly* (Sydney), 1985; "Speaking the Silence: Contemporary Poems on Paintings," in *Word & Image* (Basingstoke, England), 5(2), April-June 1989, "Vision, Language, and the Land in Rosemary Dobson's Poetry," in *Antipodes* (Brooklyn, New York), 10(2), December 1996, and "'Put Past to Present Purpose': Time and Temporality in the Poetry of Rosemary Dobson," in *Commonwealth Essays and Studies* (Dijon, France), 21(1), autumn 1998, all by Werner Senn; "Austerity and Light. A Tribute to Rosemary Dobson" by Barbara Giles, in *Southerly* (Sydney), 52(3), 1992; "'The Folds of Unseen Linen': The Fabric of Rosemary Dobson's Poetry" by Marie-Louise Ayres, in *Australian Literary Studies* (St. Lucia, Queensland), 17(1), May 1995; "'Looking into the Landscape': The Elegiac Art of Rosemary Dobson" by David McCooey, in *Westerly* (Westerly, Australia), 40(2), winter 1995.

Rosemary Dobson comments:

At various times I have been asked for statements about the writing of poetry. The following are extracts from these.

I have always regarded the writing of poetry as a vocation, believing that in writing poetry one enters a world of privilege. This is perhaps not a widely accepted attitude but I stand by it.

Poetry is an act of communication between writer and reader to which both contribute.

Of all those who value freedom of expression poets are the best equipped to assert and defend it.

I early determined to write with clarity, and an edge of wit, or as close as I could come to it. That wish for clarity has developed into an appreciation of, and an aim towards, the austere—perhaps desirable in many other areas besides literature in our time.

* * *

Rosemary Dobson wrote, designed, and printed her first collection of poems in 1937, while she was still in school. Although the poems are juvenilia, a sense of purpose and a quiet elegance are already apparent, and the book is a beautifully designed small volume. *In a Convex Mirror* is to a large extent made up of poems originally published in the *Sydney Bulletin;* they attracted considerable interest by their vivacity and concern with an immediately experienced world without loss of lyric poise. The title poem, which takes as its starting point a famous Vermeer interior, is significant also for its preoccupation with time, a subject that became of overriding concern for a number of poets in this period of dramatic upheaval.

For Dobson time was most fully explored in the long title poem of her next collection, *The Ship of Ice and Other Poems,* which begins with the line "Time is a thief at the end of a road, is a river" and which maintains a fine balance between wit and tension. The book also contains the vivacious sequence "The Devil and the Angel," which broke new ground in Australian writing of the period with its joyful irony and alert conversational tone. But it was in her next volume, *Child with a Cockatoo and Other Poems,* that Dobson fully explored what has become her most admired achievement, the "Poems from Paintings." Art has always played an important part in her concerns, and its particular capacity to exist, as it were, outside time provides the essential frisson behind these witty and perceptive poems. The underlying sensibility remains elegant and alert, though perhaps the poems in monologue form most sharply retain that particular freshness that made their first appearance so notable.

It was to be ten years before Dobson's next publication, *Cock Crow.* There is a considerable deepening of feeling in the opening poems "Child of Our Time" and "Out of Winter," works of personal apprehension reminiscent perhaps of the work of Judith Wright. Dobson has always been careful about intruding the naked personality into her poems, and the first section of *Cock Crow* represents, through its attempts at overcoming a natural reticence, a moving testament to the poet's inner agony. The second section of the book is more playful, especially in the poems that translate figures from classical mythology into thoroughly Australian settings.

Another long period of silence intervened before the publication of *Selected Poems.* This volume contained twenty-six new poems, some written in England and some in Greece and Crete. Their firm lyrical tone and occasional moments of witty observation place them securely in the characteristic Dobson style. *Over the Frontier* was published in 1978. Its most engaging quality is still that carefully modified informality, as in "Callers at the House" or "Oracles for a Childhood Journey," as well as the more overtly lyrical "Canberra Morning" or poems that explore classical, literary, and even scientific themes. Her translation, with David Campbell, of contemporary Russian poets, *Moscow Trefoil,* has added a subtle flavor and tension to the best of her own work. This is most notable in the title poem of the collection, though the centerpiece is the sequence "Poems from Pausanias." Attracted by the immediate vividness of Pausanias's *Guide to Greece,* she has used her own response to renegotiate its immediacy. Thus the theme of time, always essential to her vision, becomes a subtly recurring third theme explored here, and the reader becomes part of an ongoing chain of recognition and discovery.

The Three Fates and Other Poems, which received a Victorian Premier's literary award in 1984, is widely regarded as Dobson's most important volume since *Cock Crow* in 1965. In it she shows a subtle attunement to contemporary practices without in any way impairing her long-defined sense of precision and tautness. It is a book in which an implicit elegiac tone is balanced with a mature and warm, often playful, sensibility. *The Three Fates and Other Poems,* though it deals with subjects and responses firmly within her established framework of reference, shows the poet once more as one of the leaders of her generation in Australian literature.

—Thomas W. Shapcott

DOBYNS, Stephen

Nationality: American. **Born:** Orange, New Jersey, 19 February 1941. **Education:** Shimer College, Mount Carroll, Illinois 1959–60; Wayne State University, Detroit,1961–64, B.A. 1964; University of Iowa, Iowa City, 1964–65, 1966–67, M.F.A. 1967. **Family:** Married; two children. **Career:** Instructor in English, State University of New York College, Brockport, 1968–69; reporter, *Detroit News,* 1969–71; visiting writer, University of New Hampshire, Durham, 1973–75, University of Iowa, 1977–78, Boston University, 1978–79, 1980–81, and Syracuse University, 1986; faculty member, department of creative writing, Goddard College, Plainfield, Vermont, 1978–80; creative writing staff, Warren Wilson College, Swannanoa, North Carolina, 1981–97; professor of English, 1987–95, and director of M.F.A. program in creative writing, 1989–94, Syracuse University, New York. Since 1995 guest writer, *San Diego Weekly Reader,* California. **Awards:** Lamont Poetry Selection award, 1971; MacDowell Colony fellowship, 1972, 1976; Yaddo fellowship, 1972, 1973, 1977, 1981, 1982; National Endowment for the Arts grant, 1974, 1981; Guggenheim fellowship, 1983; National Poetry Series prize, 1984; Levinson prize, 1999, for *Pallbearers Envying the One Who Rides.* **Address:** 136 Barnard Avenue, Watertown, Massachusetts 02172, U.S.A.

PUBLICATIONS

Poetry

Concurring Beasts. New York, Atheneum, 1972.
Griffon. New York, Atheneum, 1976.
Heat Death. New York, Atheneum, 1980.
The Balthus Poems. New York, Atheneum, 1982.
Black Dog, Red Dog. New York, Holt Rinehart, 1984.
Cemetery Nights. New York, Viking, 1987; London, Bloodaxe, 1991.
Body Traffic. New York, Penguin, 1991.
Velocities: New and Selected Poems, 1966–1992. New York, Viking, 1994; London, Bloodaxe, 1995.
Common Carnage. New York, Viking, 1996; London, Bloodaxe, 1997.
Pallbearers Envying the One Who Rides. New York, Penguin, and London, Bloodaxe, 1999.

Novels

A Man of Little Evils. New York, Atheneum, 1973; London, Davies, 1974.
Saratoga Longshot. New York, Atheneum, 1976; London, Hale, 1978.

Saratoga Swimmer. New York, Atheneum, 1981; London, Allison and Busby, 1986.
Dancer with One Leg. New York, Dutton, 1983.
Saratoga Headhunter. New York, Viking, 1985; London, Allison and Busby, 1986.
Cold Dog Soup. New York, Viking, 1985.
Saratoga Snapper. New York, Viking, 1986; London, Century Hutchinson, 1988.
A Boat Off the Coast. New York, Viking, 1987.
The Two Deaths of Señora Puccini. New York and London, Viking, 1988.
Saratoga Bestiary. New York, Viking, 1988; London, Mysterious Press, 1989.
The House of Alexandrine. Detroit, Wayne State University Press, 1989.
Saratoga Hexameter. New York, Viking, 1990.
After Shocks/Near Escapes. New York, Viking, 1991.
Saratoga Haunting. New York, Viking, 1993.
The Wrestler's Cruel Study. New York, Norton, 1993.
Saratoga Backtalk. New York, Norton, 1994.
Saratoga Fleshpot. New York, Norton, 1995.
Saratoga Trifecta. New York, Penguin, 1995.
The Church of Dead Girls. New York, Henry Holt, and London, Viking, 1997.
Saratoga Strongbox. New York, Viking, 1998.
Boy in the Water. New York, Henry Holt, and London, Viking, 1999.

Other

Reading Raymond Carver, with Randolph Paul Runyon, New York, Syracuse University Press, 1992.
Best Words, Best Order: Essays on Poetry. New York, St. Martin's Press, 1996.

*

Critical Studies: "Can We Talk? The Welcome Poetries of Dunn and Dobyns" by Dave Smith, in *New England Review,* 17(2), Spring 1995; *Uncertainty & Plentitude: Five Contemporary Poets* by Peter Stitt, Iowa City, University of Iowa Press, 1997; "Story Tellers" by Louise Gluck, in *American Poetry Review* (Philadelphia), 26(4), 1997; "Poetic Positionings: Stephen Dobyns and Lyn Hejinian in Cultural Context" by Christopher Beach, in *Contemporary Literature* (Madison, Wisconsin), 38(1), Spring 1997.

*   *   *

Stephen Dobyns's preoccupations as a poet are suggested by two quotations that appear at the front of his award-winning first collection, *Concurring Beasts* (1972). The first quotation, from Walter Pater, refers to "the individual in his isolation, each mind keeping as a solitary prisoner its own dream of the world." The second quotation is from Gérard de Nerval, in which the poet says that he asked God for "the power to create my own universe, to govern my dreams, instead of enduring them." Such sentiments characterize the aesthetic of many artists, but few poets use them to such valuable purpose as does Dobyns.

Although Dobyns's competence as a poet is evident in the early poems, they hardly prepare one for the extraordinary vigor, assuredness, and penetrating wit of the later work, which is well and handsomely represented in *Velocities: New and Selected Poems, 1966–1992* (1994). By the end of the 1990s he was the author of ten books of poetry and of twenty-one novels, and he has come to hold a special claim on the reader's attention as one of America's most accomplished poets.

The private agonies of the typical Dobyns character are rendered naturalistically and with merciless honesty. The philosophical position that informs many of his poems rests somewhere between the "inhumanism" of Thomas Hardy or Robinson Jeffers and the wacky surrealism of David Ignatow or Russell Edson. In Dobyns's "The Nihilist," for example, God appears as "that vacancy between the stars." To those who regard God's dwelling place as "an empty room," the speaker responds, "wrong, wrong again. Listen carefully, hear the laughter."

An early poem reminiscent of the surrealists, on the other hand, is "Seeing Off a Friend," in which the narrator talks with a man who has just jumped to his death from the twentieth floor of a building. When the speaker asks the man in midflight, at the tenth floor and again at the fifth, what he has learned in his travels,

> He smiles again, basically cheerful
> but shakes his head. These answers
> are slow in approaching, he says,
> perhaps it is too soon to tell.

In a random universe, a place where "it's so difficult / to find something to hold on to," our consolations are fleeting. They are "fragments," as Dobyns calls them in a beautiful, if uncharacteristic, lyric to a friend on the death of his daughter. Throughout *Body Traffic* he provides brilliant reflections on the psychic wounds and pleasures of the human body (noses, fingernails, bellies, tongues), along with a series of poems on Paul Cézanne, the master painter of the human form. The former are written in Dobyns's characteristic free verse of ten to fifteen syllables; the latter are sonnets in varied and occasionally intricate rhyme.

In Dobyns's world sex is a major consolation, its joys acknowledged and even extolled in various poems. In "Cemetery Nights VI," for example, after telling about a dead man who imagines his widow in bed with a new lover, the narrator compares a breeze at the lovers' window to a "vast legion of the dead . . . with their unbearable jumble of envy and regret," who watch "the man as he drops his head, presses his mouth to the erect nipple."

Such pleasures, however, are temporary. "The Body's Curse," for example, speaks of "sexual hunger" among men

> thirsting for ladies as a bowling ball thirsts for pins
> then casting them aside, the beauty forgotten
> while still clasped in a post-orgasmic embrace.

"Tenderly" describes a hapless, even desperate man in a restaurant who

> leaps onto his tabletop,
> whips out his prick and begins sawing at it

> with a butter knife. I can't stand it
> anymore! he shouts.

The thirty patrons in the café, with burdens of their own to shoulder, are now "linked / as a family is linked—through a single portrait." Compassionate, they hope that he might enjoy better times, perhaps

> on a topless foreign beach with a beauty
> clasped in his loving arms breathing heavily, Oh,
> darling, touch me there, tenderly, one more time!

"The Body's Joy" also is about people caught in "the tyranny of desire," wishing "for some relief from the self." Although lovers "cannot make our Sun / Stand still" or even "make him run," in Andrew Marvell's words, their bodies do offer momentary hopes and pleasures that defeat "the steady gallop of time," making it "dance like a ball / balancing on a spume of water in sunlight." One of the best poems, "Desire," after mentioning a man who at ninety swears that his sexual longing remains undiminished, recommends that men remain "bad and unrepentant," celebrating

> each difference, not to be cruel or gluttonous
> or over-bearing, but full of hope and self-forgiving.

The dominant attitude in a Dobyns poem is, nonetheless, the tension evident in the final lines of "Pastel Dresses," as the narrator remembers his excitement at age fourteen over a first dance party:

> How can we not love
> this world for what it gives us? How
> can we not hate it for what it takes away?

Dobyns is so good at what he does that one hesitates to suggest limitations. An admiring reader, however, looks forward to a somewhat broader perspective than the one he has mastered—not high seriousness necessarily but poems about injustices created or sustained by human beings, however hapless, even blameless they may be.

—Michael True

DOMANSKI, Don Rusu

Nationality: Canadian. **Born:** Sydney, Nova Scotia, 29 April 1950. **Family:** Married Mary M. Meidell in 1969. **Awards:** Canadian Literary award, 1999.

PUBLICATIONS

Poetry

The Cape Breton Book of the Dead. Toronto, House of Anansi Press, 1975.
Heaven. Toronto, House of Anansi Press, 1978.
War in an Empty House. Toronto, House of Anansi Press, 1982.
Hammerstroke. Toronto, House of Anansi Press, 1986.
Wolf-Ladder. Toronto, Coach House Press, 1991.
Stations of the Left Hand. Toronto, Coach House Press, 1994.
Parish of the Physic Moon. Toronto, McClelland and Stewart, 1998.

*   *   *

Uniquely among Canadian poets, Don Domanski puts surrealism at the service of meditation. His poems typically dwell in the midst of dream, sleep, night, and shadow, and they are marked by spare punctuation, smooth cadences, and quietly aphoristic endings. The effect is that of some mystical vade mecum or atlas of the spirit.

The devices and imagistic apparatus remain traditional. Domanski is especially fond, for example, of insects and spiders. In "A Spider Standing Nude before a Mirror," from *Hammerstroke,* the feminine subject

. . . was made in the shape of Rome
that city of spiders and the gods of spiders
and the spidery light of dead things
drifting down to paradise

Indebted to surrealism as it is, Domanski's work does not display the wild scribblings of the unconscious, even though at times he is guilty of overreaching, as in "Necropolis" from his first collection, *The Cape Breton Book of the Dead:* "the rat's stomach is opened to the stars / a nebula placed in its bowel." Usually, however, his poems are descriptively apposite, and they are sometimes anchored to actual places. In "A Town of Weights," from *Hammerstroke,* he writes of Wolfville, Nova Scotia:

last night the souls of the dead
were thrown back into their bodies
and allowed to fly one more time
around the town
their eyes rouged with roses
their feet painted with ale

Moreover, Domanski's version of surrealism is inflected with implied moral values. In "The Farm at Four A.M."

in the barn there are
two hogs hanging
from black ropes in the air

they are the old weights
the old judgments against us

Likewise, in "Flies," from *The Cape Breton Book of the Dead,* he observes that

they arrive with a talent like men
for living
for carrying their purpose to its extreme

Domanski's style and preoccupations have altered little since his first book. In it are found the flashes of wit that recur in subsequent collections. In "Old Women" he notes that

only the wedding ring or the coffin
bring them together like this
to share a darkening room

Only these two objects

flush them out of the tall grass
where they hide (drowned sparrows)
from the rock and the tom cat

Domanski often concerns himself with dystopias, utopias, deities, and visible and invisible cities. In "Bat Song," from *Heaven,* he says that "among the emplacement of stars / heaven dreams its amorous skin." Always present are the timeless processes of transformation, often seen through the vehicle of dreams. In "Dreamtime," from *War in an Empty House,* he says that

in sleep there are many diners
where Cathars drink the coffee your mother
made for you twenty years before

In "Close of Day," from *Hammerstroke,* he describes how a woman

. . . turns a square knob
on the radio
and instantly the apples
darken in their bowl

Domanski's poems are never explicitly autobiographical, and *Parish of the Physic Moon,* his 1998 collection, exhibits not his personal, individual self as a universal Self that encompasses everyone. When the poet uses the first person, it is the mystical "I," at once everyone and no one. A consequence is that his poems often have great beauty but a certain interchangeability, even monotony, although this is relieved at moments by marvelously right images, as in "Writing," the book's opening poem:

in vacant office towers across town
elevators are stables where horses and hay
are lowered slowly to the Underworld

cables surrounded by a pause in this poem
allow for their descent.

Domanski puts strong emotions—grief, anger, joy—in his work, but they are woven into a cosmological tapestry of life, death, and eternity. The following lines are from "Sleep's Ova":

I was born because millions of years ago communities
grew out of ponds   because ponds need a way to
    say goodbye
because I'm always saying goodbye   and so are you

In "Child of the Earth," the book's last poem, Domanski sums up his vision of the self, first noting that

so many selves make up the nightly routine   so many
fall with the snow upon,   drown in the wintry sea

but concluding that the wind will

blow your particles into empty space   O empty space
this is the self   all worlds   the single place.

—Fraser Sutherland

DONAGHY, Michael (John)

Nationality: American. **Born:** Bronx, New York, 24 May 1954. **Education:** Fordham University, New York, 1972–76, B.A. 1976; University of Chicago, 1977–79, M.A. 1979. **Career:** Doorman, New York, 1972–77; musician, Chicago, 1978–85 and since 1986, London. Since 1988 teacher, Birkbeck College, University of London. **Awards:** Whitbread award for poetry, 1989; Geoffrey Faber award, 1990; Ingram Merrill Foundation grant, 1995. **Address:** 88 Umfreville Road, London N4 1SA, England.

PUBLICATIONS

Poetry

Slivers (chapbook). Chicago, Thompson Hill Press, 1985.
O'Ryan's Belt (chapbook). Madison, Wisconsin, Silver Buckle Press, 1991.
Machines (pamphlet). Guildford, England, Circle Press, 1987.
Shibboleth. Oxford, Oxford University Press, 1988.
Errata. Oxford, Oxford University Press, 1993.

Other

Editor, *Michael Donaghy, Andrew Motion, Hugo Williams.* London and New York, Penguin, 1997.

*

Critical Studies: "Other Irish Writing" by Cathal Dallat, in *Verse* (St. Andrews, Scotland), 9(3), winter 1992; by Michael Hulse, in *Poetry Review,* 83(2), summer 1993.

Michael Donaghy comments:

I want to say that my poems speak for themselves. I expect we all do. They have their own lives to lead. For those of you who do not know my poems, there is a lot of memory in them. Memory and history and music and sex and drinking. I hope you find them memorable—or at least memorizable.

A hostile reviewer dismissed them like this: "His poems are not confessional, but it helps to think of a Confessional—a little box with a screen separating two parties. Think of that screen as the page. A voice seems to come from behind the screen, but if you read the poems aloud the only voice you hear is your own" (Florence Olsen, *Haymarket).* I can live with that.

My principal influences are not twentieth-century. But there is no escaping that lunatic Yeats (*The Tower*). Paul Muldoon redirected me to Frost, his ear, his palimpsest ironies (*Complete Poems,* 1949). For my third choice I considered prose (Borges) or the collected Bishop or MacNeice, but Derek Mahon's *The Snow Party* brought me back to poetry when I thought I had almost given up.

*   *   *

In the blurb on the back cover of Michael Donaghy's prizewinning first collection, *Shibboleth* (1988), we read that "his work has a wit and grace reminiscent of the metaphysical poets." Like most statements in blurbs, this mistakes a wish for reality. Donaghy does imitate the gestures of Metaphysical poetry, but his conceits do not match in intensity or depth of feeling those in Donne and company. Heterogeneous things violently yoked together give way in "Machines," the first poem in *Shibboleth,* to something more self-preening: "Dearest, note how these two are alike: / This harpsichord pavane by Purcell / And the racer's twelve-speed bike." But the poem is saved from self-approval by its awareness of risk, and it attains an odd kind of "balance," to use its own word, by failing to be as slickly clever as, in one sense, it needs to be.

Indeed, Donaghy is a poet who often succeeds by failing. The bard who survived Odysseus's shoot-out speaks the finely antiheroic "Remembering Steps to Dances Learned Last Night." The poem begins with a spirited pastiche in the Homeric manner, but at the climax a more downbeat, colloquial tone makes itself heard: "I know you came to hear me sing about the night the king came home, / . . . / I can't." Donaghy's most authentic notes can emerge from moments that seem inauthentic and certainly are scarcely distinguishable from his interest in playing games, fooling around, showing off. Among the fascinations of "'Smith'" is its sideways glance at Donaghy's predicament as a poet: "Why does it seem to take a forger's nerve / To make my signature come naturally?" These jokey yet jittery pentameters are followed by the question "Naturally?"—revealing Donaghy's sense that the truest poetry may be the most feigning.

Such a stance can lead to a tedious, would-be poker-faced stress on fictiveness, as in "Analysand," which opens in writing workshop style: "I've had an important dream. But that can wait." More powerfully, the close of "'Smith'" at once sustains the view of the poet as forger and tries to recapture "a moment so pure." Those who live by irony have a tendency to die by it too, and the poem's ending is typical of some of the most compelling yet ambivalent passages in Donaghy's work; it shows the poet's palpable unease with an ironic manner he cannot quite disown. The collection's most impressive poem, "Letter," includes but triumphs over the poet's anxieties about writing, speech, and authenticity, anxieties parceled out in the poem between the poet and his elegized father: "No relics here of how you felt; / Maybe writing frightened you, the way it fixed a whim." The poem combines different line lengths skillfully, its avoidance of polished metrics and rhymes freeing Donaghy from posturing. In this piece the search for precision is helpful rather than merely precious. Thus the ending, as in Coleridge's "Frost at Midnight," suggests a distinction between "silence" and "quiet" and then, touchingly, makes the words synonyms: "Your breath / Making the blizzard silent, / The silence quiet, at last, / The quiet ours."

Failure and error lie close to the thematic heart of *Errata,* Donaghy's second collection. In "The Commission" the speaker, a Renaissance artist, says of the pope that "all of my efforts to stay in his favour / were wasted." In "Cruising Byzantium" "firemen say the saved are sometimes wrong," and "City of God" begins, "When he failed the seminary he came back home." In "The Chamber of Errors" the speaker says, "I spend my life repairing details." In the three sections of "True" Donaghy offers a wry emblem of the way disaster is made the stuff of art's entertainment. The word "true" can, as the poem's epigraph points out, mean "to adjust so as to make true," and Donaghy writes with acute sympathy in this volume about the human endeavor to "make true" what needs adjusting. The result is to alert us to the crooked nature of desire and achievement, as in "A Reprieve," in which the police chief, Francis O'Neil, cuts a deal with a suspect so that he can augment his collection of Irish folk music. The poem ends with an ampler lilt and mood of forgiveness than is customary in Donaghy's work:

But there's music here in this lamplit cell,
and O'Neil scratching in his manuscript like a monk
at his illuminations, and Nolan's sweet tone breaking
as he tries to phrase a jig the same way twice:
'The Limerick Rake' or 'Tell her I am' or 'My Darling
    Asleep'.

For all the earlier collection's sporadic brilliance, *Errata* generally shows a maturity lacking in *Shibboleth*.

—Michael O'Neill

DOOLEY, David (Allen)

Nationality: American. **Born:** Knoxville, Tennessee, 3 November
1947. **Education:** University of Tennessee, 1964–67, and in the late
1970s, M.A. in English; Johns Hopkins University, 1967–68, B.A.
1968. **Career:** Since 1982 paralegal, Matthews and Branscomb, San
Antonio. **Awards:** Nicholas Roerich prize, 1988, for *The Volcano
Inside*.

PUBLICATIONS

Poetry

The Volcano Inside. Brownsville, Oregon, Story Line Press, 1988.
The Revenge by Love. Brownsville, Oregon, Story Line Press, 1995.

*   *   *

David Dooley's extraordinary debut volume, *The Volcano Inside,* won the inaugural Nicholas Roerich Poetry prize. Published in
1988, it inspired the critic Helen Vendler to declare on National
Public Radio that its author was one of the most exciting new poets
she had come across in years. Poet-critic Allen Hoey claimed that the
poems "... cut out a territory for themselves foreign to most people
writing poems today—to say that they are the product of an individual
voice would not reduce [Dooley's] accomplishment to a platitude but
would belie the multiplicity of voices he has mastered in the volume." This last comment is particularly accurate, for to quote any one
segment from *The Volcano Inside* is to risk overlooking the poet's
exuberant versatility:

So I'd give her the kind of fucking she was meant for
and afterwards sometimes I'd go to the typewriter buck naked
and start writing till she bitched about the noise
though more than once she fell asleep and honked like a flight
    of geese
but she'd bitch so I'd open a notebook and while she slept,
on summer nights the windows open and she lay there naked
    asleep
the covers tangled down at her knees till I wouldn't know
if I were writing with my pen or my cock, I'd use
whatever tool I needed. There were no answers
because there were never any questions. If you write,
You need books and paper and food and cunt and drink

and that's it. By daybreak there'd be pages of Olga in the
    typewriter,
pages of Olga in the notebook, and squirming in the bed
she'd be rubbing the yellow muck out of her big cow eyes.

These lines from "How I Wrote It" are part of an older writer's
earthy monologue. Part confession, part harangue, the comments are
directed at a younger person, presumably an aspiring writer. The
speaker's point of view is refreshingly uncomplicated yet avoids the
shallow simplicity from which so much current opinion bubbles to the
surface. His vision is also essentially compassionate, a key point that
may be overlooked as a result of his consistent vulgarity. But careful
reading reveals the compassion in his genuine affection for his
inspiration-whore-companion and in his love of writing and the things
of the common world: "I knew how to live with the grime, you see. /
The grime on a tenement is as beautiful as the sunrise."

This writer, and the poet who created him, descends from
George Crabbe and Robert Browning and, later, from the American
tradition of Frost and Jeffers. Literary schools and theories hold little
interest for them, but real life, lived by real people, contains the stuff
of poetry. Donald Hall recognized this in the *Harvard Book Review*
when he declared, "David Dooley's poetry is not like anybody else's:
It is energetic, often long-lined and propulsive, with a headlong
compelling rhythm ... Dooley uses justly-observed speech to fix
character." In long lines that drive through subjects with the haunting
echo of classic blank verse or in clipped, short-lined stanzas, Dooley
gives eloquent voice to lovers, parents, and loners and to mind
readers, movie makers, joggers, country and western singers, and so
many overlooked "others" who make up our world, the people we
see when we look in the mirror.

Dooley's second volume, *The Revenge By Love* (1995), features
a compelling eleven-poem sequence about the great American painter
Georgia O'Keeffe and her mentor, lover, and eventual husband, the
photographer Alfred Stieglitz. In other poems an emotionally devastated Saint-Saëns spends a winter in Egypt, a wealthy gay man
chooses a life of hedonism over a political career, a woman's attitudes
toward love and marriage are revealed in her relationship with food,
and a young writer begins to understand the implications of sleeping
with his best friend's girl. This narrative, dramatic verse, exploring
the depths of human relationships, is unusually accessible. It satisfies
even more with repeated reading:

Far out in the dark are hills which turn angry red
when a cloud passes. Oh, but in other lights
they are pink as flesh. What will tomorrow's first colors be?
Coral? Peach? Pale yellow? Opalescent blue?
And then the sun will rise.

—Robert McDowell

DORN, Ed(ward Merton)

Nationality: American. **Born:** Villa Grove, Illinois, 2 April 1929.
Education: University of Illinois, Urbana, 1949–50; Black Mountain
College, North Carolina, 1950–51, 1954–55. **Family:** Married 1)
Helene Dorn; 2) Jennifer Dunbar in 1969. **Career:** Reference librar-
ian, New Mexico State Library, Santa Fe, 1959; taught at Idaho State

University, Pocatello, 1961–65; visiting professor of American Literature (Fulbright Lecturer, 1965–66, 1966–67), University of Essex, Wivenhoe, England, 1965–68, 1974–75; visiting poet, University of Kansas, Lawrence, 1968–69; taught at Northeastern Illinois University, Chicago, 1970–71, and Kent State University, Ohio, 1973–74; Regents Lecturer, University of California, Riverside, 1973–74; writer-in-residence, University of California at San Diego, La Jolla, 1976, and since 1977, University of Colorado, Boulder. Editor, *Wild Dog* magazine, Salt Lake City, 1964–65; editor, *Rolling Stock* newspaper; since 1983 editor *Rolling Rock* magazine. **Awards:** National Endowment for the Arts grant, 1966, 1968; D.H. Lawrence fellowship, 1969. **Address:** Department of English, Campus Box 226, University of Colorado, Boulder, Colorado 80309, U.S.A. **Died:** 10 December 1999.

PUBLICATIONS

Poetry

Paterson Society. Privately printed, 1960.
The Newly Fallen. New York, Totem Press, 1961.
From Gloucester Out. London, Matrix Press, 1964.
Hands Up! New York, Totem-Corinth, 1964.
Idaho Out. London, Fulcrum Press, 1965.
Geography. London, Fulcrum Press, 1965; revised edition, 1968.
The North Atlantic Turbine. London, Fulcrum Press, 1967.
Song. Newcastle upon Tyne, Northern Arts, 1968.
Gunslinger, Book I. Los Angeles, Black Sparrow Press, 1968.
The Midwest Is That Space Between the Buffalo Statler and the Lawrence Eldridge. Lawrence, Kansas, Terrence Williams, 1968.
Gunslinger, Book II. Los Angeles, Black Sparrow Press, 1969.
Gunslinger 1 and 2. London, Fulcrum Press, 1969.
Twenty-Four Love Songs. San Francisco, Frontier Press, 1969.
The Cosmology of Finding Your Spot. Lawrence, Kansas, Cottonwood, 1969.
Ed Dorn Sportcasts Colonialism. Privately printed, 1969 (?).
Songs: Set Two, A Short Count. West Newbury, Massachusetts, Frontier Press, 1970.
Spectrum Breakdown: A Microbook. LeRoy, New York, Athanor, 1971.
A Poem Called Alexander Hamilton. Lawrence, Kansas, Tansy-Peg Leg Press, 1971.
The Cycle. West Newbury, Massachusetts, Frontier Press, 1971.
The Kultchural Exchange. Seattle, Wiater, 1971.
Old New Yorkers Really Get My Head. Lawrence, Kansas, Cottonwood, 1972.
The Hamadryas Baboon at the Lincoln Park Zoo. Chicago, Wine Press, 1972.
Gunslinger, Book III: The Winterbook Prologue to the Great Book IIII Kornerstone. West Newbury, Massachusetts, Frontier Press, 1972.
Recollections of Gran Apacheria. San Francisco, Turtle Island, 1974.
Gunslinger, Books I, II, III, IV. Berkeley, California, Wingbow Press, 1975; revised edition, as *Gunslinger,* Durham, North Carolina, Duke University Press, 1989.
The Collected Poems 1956–1974. Bolinas, California, Four Seasons, 1975.
Manchester Square, with Jennifer Dunbar. London, Permanent Press, 1975.

Slinger. Berkeley, California, Wingbow Press, 1975.
Hello La Jolla. Berkeley, California, Wingbow Press, 1978.
Selected Poems, edited by Donald Allen. Bolinas, California, Grey Fox Press, 1978.
Yellow Lola: Formerly Tilted Japanese Neon (Hello, La Jolla, Book II). Santa Barbara, California, Cadmus, 1981.
Captain Jack's Chaps, or, Houston, MLA. Madison, Wisconsin, Black Mesa Press, 1983.
Abhorrences. Berkeley, California, Handmade, 1984; revised edition, Santa Rosa, California, Black Sparrow Press, 1990.
From Abhorrences: A Chronicle of the 80ies. Boise, Idaho, Limberlost Press, 1989.
The Denver Landing. Buffalo, New York, Uprising Press, 1993.
High West Rendezvous. Hereford, West House Books, 1996.

Recording: *Edward Dorn Reads from "The North Atlantic Turbine,"* Livingdiscs, 1967.

Short Stories

Some Business Recently Transacted in the White World. West Newbury, Massachusetts, Frontier Press, 1971.

Other

What I See in the Maximus Poems. Ventura, California, and Worcester, Migrant Press, 1960.
Prose 1, with Michael Rumaker and Warren Tallman. San Francisco, Four Seasons, 1964.
The Rites of Passage: A Brief History. Buffalo, New York, Frontier Press, 1965; revised edition, as *By the Sound,* Mount Vernon, Washington, Frontier Press, 1972; revised edition, Santa Rosa, California, Black Sparrow Press, 1991.
The Shoshoneans: The People of the Basin-Plateau. New York, Morrow, 1967.
Bean News. San Francisco, Free Press, 1972.
The Poet, The People, The Spirit, edited by Bob Rose. Vancouver, Talonbooks, 1976.
Roadtesting the Language: An Interview, with Stephen Fredman. San Diego, University of California Archive for New Poetry, 1978.
Views, Interviews, edited by Donald Allen. Bolinas, California, Four Seasons, 2 vols., 1980.
Way West: Stories, Essays & Verse Accounts. Santa Rosa, California, Black Sparrow Press, 1993.

Translator, with Gordon Brotherston, *Our Word: Guerrilla Poems from Latin America.* London, Cape Goliard Press, and New York, Grossman, 1968.
Translator, with Gordon Brotherston, *Tree Between Two Walls,* by José Emilio Pacheco. Los Angeles, Black Sparrow Press, 1969.
Translator, with Gordon Brotherston, *Selected Poems,* by César Vallejo. London, Penguin, 1976.
Translator, *Image of the New World: The American Continent Portrayed in Native Texts,* edited by Gordon Brotherston. London, Thames and Hudson, 1979.
Translator, with Gordon Brotherston, *The Sun Unwound: Original Texts from Occupied America.* Berkeley, California, North Atlantic Books, 1999.

*

Bibliography: *A Bibliography of Ed Dorn* by David Streeter, New York, Phoenix Book Shop, 1973.

Manuscript Collection: Northwestern University, Evanston, Illinois.

Critical Studies: "An Interview with Ed Dorn," in *Contemporary Literature* (Madison, Wisconsin), 15, 3; *The Lost America of Love: Rereading Robert Creeley, Edward Dorn, and Robert Duncan* by Sherman Paul, Baton Rouge, Louisiana State University Press, 1981; *Internal Resistances: The Poetry of Ed Dorn* by Donald Wesling, Berkeley, University of California Press, 1985; *Edward Dorn* by William McPheron, Boise, Idaho, Boise State University, 1988; *Robert Creeley, Edward Dorn, and Robert Duncan: A Reference Guide,* by Willard Fox III, Boston, Massachusetts, G.K. Hall, 1989; "The Relation between Open Form and Collective Voice: The Social Origin of Processual Form in John Ashbery's Three Poems and Ed Dorn's Gunslinger" by Anne Dewey, in *Sagetrieb* (Orono, Maine), 11(1–2), spring-fall 1992.

*   *   *

Ed Dorn's work has been widely praised in both England and the United States. Russell Banks, writing in *Lillabulero,* has compared him to Olson, Williams, and Pound. A. Alvarez has suggested that Dorn has produced "a handful of beautifully pure and unaffected love-songs, and an intriguing long poem about a drive, 'Idaho Out,' in which cultural worry loses out to a kind of anarchic, footloose vitality and a feeling for the vast, frozen emptiness of the American West." Dorn's work reminds Alvarez of Hemingway, and it is true that Dorn is concerned with capturing idiomatic speech accurately. But he also indulges a kind of jam-pack jumbling of observations that is more the poetic counterpart of exuberant and excited writers like Thomas Wolfe. Dorn's recall of childhood, his feeling for places and writers, his political convictions, his tourism—all find their way, in cascades of energy, into his loose, straying verse.

Dorn's reactions to England, where he lived for some time, are particularly sensitive:

> As we go
> through Sussex, hills are round
> bellies are the downs
> pregnantly lovely
> the rounds of them, no towns
> the train passes
> shaking along the groove
> of the countryside.

He purports "to love / that, and retain an ear for / the atrocities of my own hemisphere," criticizing, with simplistic pessimism, almost everything about the United States:

> The thorn however
> remains, in the desert
> of american life, the thorn
> in the throat of our national hypocrisy.

And yet Dorn is also sentimental at will about his native land: "And yes Fort Benton is lovely / and quiet, I would gladly give it as a gift / to a friend / . . ." At his best, he is a sentimentalist for the America he denounces:

> Bitterly cold were the nights.
> The journeymen slept in the lots of filling stations
> and there were the interrupting lights
> of semis all night long as those beasts
> crept past or drew up to rest their motors
> or roared on.

Dorn's *Gunslinger* seems to be built on these strong native feelings. It is an effort at building a comic epic on the western, in which Dorn finds the archetypal characters and enthusiasms that reveal America:

> And why do you have a female horse
> Gunslinger? I asked. Don't move
> he replied
> the sun rests deliberately
> on the rim of the sierra.

This work also moves away from the ego as center, a practice that was somewhat problematic in earlier long poems in which Dorn spoke as a seer. One does not, however, want to lose other qualities of his earlier work—his exuberance, puritanical anger, and authority about his enthusiasms.

—David Ray

DOTY, Mark (A.)

Nationality: American. **Born:** Maryville, Tennessee, 10 August 1953. **Education:** University of Arizona, Tucson, 1970–71; Drake University, Des Moines, Iowa, 1976–78, B.A. 1978; Goddard College, Plainfield, Vermont, 1978–80, M.F.A. 1980. **Family:** Married 1) Ruth Doty in 1971 (divorced 1980); 2) lived with Wally Roberts 1982–94 (died 1994); 3) has lived with Paul Lisicky since 1995. **Career:** Faculty member, Goddard College, Plainfield, Vermont, 1985–90; faculty, M.F.A. Writing Program, Vermont College, 1981–94; guest faculty, Sarah Lawrence College, 1990–94; professor, creative writing program, University of Utah, 1996–98; since 1998 professor, creative writing program, University of Houston, Texas. Fannie Hurst Visiting Professor, Brandeis University, fall 1994; visiting faculty, graduate writing program, Columbia University, New York, and Sarah Lawrence College, spring 1996; visiting faculty, Writers Workshop, University of Iowa, fall 1995, fall 1996. **Awards:** Massachusetts Artists Foundation fellowship, 1985; Vermont Council on the Arts fellowship, 1986; Theodore Roethke prize, Poetry Northwest, 1986; Pushcart prize, 1987, 1989; James Wright prize, *Mid-American Review,* 1991; National Poetry Series publication, 1993, *Los Angeles Times* Book Award for poetry, 1993, National Book Critics' Circle Award for best book of poetry, 1994, and T.S. Eliot Prize for best book of poetry published in the U.K., 1995, all for *My Alexandria;* Ingram Merrill Foundation award, 1994; John Simon Guggenheim Memorial Foundation Fellowship, 1994–95; Giles Whitney Foundation Award for Particularly Promising Writers, 1995; Rockefeller Foundation fellowship, 1995; Whiting Writers award, 1995; National Endowment for the Arts fellow, 1995–96; Lambda Literary Award for Gay Men's Poetry, 1996, and *Boston Review* Poetry prize, 1996, both for *Atlantis;* Witter Bynner Poetry prize, 1997; PEN/Martha Albrand Award for first book of nonfiction, 1997, for *Heaven's*

Coast; Cohen award for poetry, *Ploughshares,* 1998; Notable Book of the Year, American Library Association, 1998, and Books to Remember award, New York Public Library, 1999, both for *Sweet Machine;* Nonfiction Honor Book, Gay, Lesbian, Bisexual and Transgendered Book awards, American Library Association, 2000, for *Firebird;* Lila Wallace-Readers Digest Foundation fellowship, 2000–03. **Agent:** William Clegg, The Robbins Office, 405 Park Avenue, New York, New York 10022. **Address:** 19 Pearl Street, Provincetown, Massachusetts 02657, U.S.A.

PUBLICATIONS

Poetry

Turtle, Swan: Poems. Boston, Godine, 1987.
Bethlehem in Broad Daylight. Boston, Godine, 1991.
My Alexandria. Urbana, University of Illinois Press, 1993; London, Cape Poetry, 1995.
Atlantis. New York, HarperCollins, 1995; London, Jonathan Cape, 1996.
Favrile. New York, Dim Gray Bar Press, 1997.
Sweet Machine. New York, HarperCollins, and London, Cape Poetry, 1998.
An Island Sheaf. New York, Dim Gray Bar Press, 1998.
Turtle, Swan, and Bethlehem in Broad Daylight: Two Volumes of Poetry. Urbana, Illinois, University of Illinois Press, 2000.

Recordings: *Mark Doty,* Anne Newman Sutton Weeks poetry series, 1997; *Mark Doty,* Lannan Foundation, 1999.

Other

Tell Me Who I Am: James Agee's Search for Selfhood (as Mark A. Doty). Baton Rouge, Louisiana, Louisiana State University Press, 1981.
Heaven's Coast: A Memoir. New York, HarperCollins, and London, Jonathan Cape, 1996.
White Kimono. Tuscaloosa, Alabama, Enstar Press, 1997.
Firebird: A Memoir. New York, HarperCollins, and London, Jonathan Cape, 1999.

*

Critical Studies: "The Poetry of August Kleinzahler and Mark Doty" by Helen Vendler, in *The New Yorker* (New York), 8 April 1996; "Creatures of the Rainbow: Wallace Stevens, Mark Doty, and the Poetics of Androgyny" by David R. Jarraway, in *Mosaic: A Journal for the Interdisciplinary Study of Literature* (Canada), 30(3), September 1997; "Mercurial and Rhapsodic: Manifestations of the Gay Male Body in the Poetry of Mark Doty and Wayne Koestenbaum" by William Joseph Reichard, in *The Humanities and Social Sciences* (Ann Arbor, Michigan), 58(4), October 1997.

*　　*　　*

Although the poet and memoirist Mark Doty includes gay themes and issues in his poetry, he has not been typecast as an exclusively gay poet. His poems, often lyrical and detailed, transcend the gay experience. He does sometimes write to other gay men because their experience, explains Doty, "often overlaps with mine." And he sometimes feels compelled to write about the gay experience because he believes that, for the most part, it is "stereotyped, misrepresented, falsely homogenized, or erased."

The volume *Turtle, Swan* (1987) contains poems about Doty's early life and shares his coming-of-age and young adulthood. In "A Replica of the Parthenon" he uses his memory of a book on archaeology to discuss the inevitability of death:

> . . . we know that we will lie down in our own bodies and
> someone will fold our hands . . .

"Rocket" and "In the Form of Snow" are based on experiences in jobs he had as a young man. "Hair" is a breathtaking account of a scene from a film shot at a concentration camp days after its liberation. Essentially the poem describes the shock of someone discovering his or her own mortality:

> . . . Though her gesture is effortless
> it seems also for the first time,
> as if she has just remembered
> that she has long hair, . . .
>
> At a time the arms and hands
> and face remember, the scalp
> remembers that her hair
> is a part of her, her own.

Following *Turtle, Swan,* Doty began to speak more directly on the gay experience. The books *Bethlehem in Broad Daylight* (1991), *My Alexandria* (1993), and *Atlantis* (1995) demonstrate his maturation as a man and as a poet. During this time Doty met his lover and partner Wally Roberts, who in 1994 died from AIDS. As Doty explained to *Salon,* "Before Wally's diagnosis, lots of my work had been about memory and trying to gain some perspective on the past. Suddenly that was much less important and I felt pushed to pay attention to now, what I could celebrate or discern in the now . . . There's no time to fool around." While some of the poems written during this period are unquestionably melancholic, Doty manages to speak of death without poisonous anger or grief so that readers are left with the essential beauty of love. "The Embrace" ends in this way:

> Bless you. You came back so I could see you
> once more, plainly, so I could rest against you
> without thinking this happiness lessened anything,
> without thinking you were alive again.

When Doty has been asked how he writes poetry, he explains that first he is presented with a metaphor, even though he does not always know what the image represents. He then begins to describe the image and decipher its meaning. In an interview in *Lavender Magazine* he pointed out, "My metaphors know more than I do. I begin with a description, and things float up from there."

For a time after the death of his partner Doty was unable to read or write poetry. Since then, however, he has published additional volumes of poetry, including *Sweet Machine,* and two volumes of memoirs. Doty is clearly striving to write about what preoccupies him at the present and to describe the common conditions of American life in our particular moment.

—Christine Miner Minderovic

DOVE, Rita (Frances)

Nationality: American. **Born:** Akron, Ohio, 28 August 1952. **Education:** Miami University, Oxford, Ohio, B.A. (summa cum laude) 1973 (Phi Beta Kappa); University of Tübingen, West Germany (Fulbright/Hays fellow), 1974–75; University of Iowa, Iowa City, M.F.A. 1977. **Family:** Married Fred Viebahn in 1979; one daughter. **Career:** Research assistant, 1975, and teaching assistant, 1976-77, University of Iowa; assistant professor of creative writing, 1981–84, associate professor, 1984–87, professor of English, Arizona State University, Tempe, 1987–89. Since 1989 professor of English, and since 1993 Commonwealth Professor of English, University of Virginia, Charlottesville. Writer-in-residence, Tuskegee Institute, Alabama, 1982; Rockefeller Foundation residency, Bellagio, Italy, 1988. Member of the editorial board, *National Forum,* 1984–89; advisory editor, 1987–92, and associate editor, 1989–98, *Callaloo;* advisory editor, *Gettysburg Review,* 1987–92; editor since 1988, *TriQuarterly,* since 1990 *Ploughshares,* and since 1994 *The Georgia Review.* Since 1987 commissioner, Schomburg Center for the Preservation of Black Culture, New York Public Library. Member of the Board of Directors, Associated Writing Programs, 1985–88 (president 1986–87); member of the advisory board, North Carolina Writers' Network, 1991–99; since 1994 member, Council of Scholars, Library of Congress. Final judge, Walt Whitman award, 1990; juror, Ruth Lilly prize, National Book award (poetry), and Pulitzer prize in poetry, 1991, Newman's Own/First Amendment award, PEN American Center, 1994, and since 1992 Anisfield-Wolf Book awards. U.S. Poet Laureate/Consultant in Poetry, Library of Congress, 1993–95. **Awards:** Fulbright fellowship, 1974–75; National Endowment for the Arts grant, 1978, fellowship, 1982; Ohio Arts Council grant, 1979; Guggenheim fellowship, 1983; Lavan Younger Poets award, 1986; Pulitzer prize for *Thomas and Beulah,* 1987; Mellon fellowship, 1988–89. National Endowment for the Arts Creative Writing fellowship, 1989; Ohioana award for *Grace Notes,* 1990, for *Selected Poems,* 1994; "Literary Lion," New York Public Library, 1991, Phi Beta Kappa poet, Harvard University, 1993; Virginia College Stores Association Book award for *Through the Ivory Gate,* 1993; Women of the Year award, *Glamour* magazine, 1993; NAACP Great American Artist award, 1993; Renaissance Forum award for leadership in the literary arts, Folger Shakespeare Library, 1994; Golden Plate award, American Academy of Achievement, 1994; Carl Sandburg award, International Platform Association, 1994; Fund for New American Plays grant, Kennedy Center, 1995; Charles Frankel prize, 1996; National Medal in the Humanities, 1996; Heinz award in the arts and humanities, 1996; Levinson prize, *Poetry,* 1998. U.S. Poet Laureate/Consultant in Poetry, Library of Congress, 1993–95. H.D.L.: Miami University, 1988; Knox College, 1989; Tuskegee University, Alabama, 1994; University of Miami, Florida, 1994; Washington University, St. Louis, Missouri, 1994; Case Western Reserve University, Cleveland, Ohio, 1994; University of Akron, Ohio, 1994. **Address:** Department of English, Bryan Hall, University of Virginia, Charlottesville, Virginia 22903, U.S.A.

PUBLICATIONS

Poetry

Ten Poems. Lisbon, Iowa, Penumbra Press, 1977.
The Only Dark Spot in the Sky. Tempe, Arizona, Inland Porch, 1980.
The Yellow House on the Corner. Pittsburgh, Pennsylvania, Carnegie-Mellon University Press, 1980.
Mandolin. Athens, Ohio Review, 1982.
Museum. Pittsburgh, Pennsylvania, Carnegie-Mellon University Press, and London, Feffer and Simons, 1983.
Thomas and Beulah. Pittsburgh, Pennsylvania, Carnegie-Mellon University Press, 1986.
The Other Side of the House. Tempe, Arizona, Pyracantha Press, 1988.
Grace Notes. New York, Norton, 1989.
Selected Poems. New York, Pantheon, 1993.
Lady Freedom among Us. West Burke, Vermont, Janus Press, 1994.
Mother Love. New York, Norton, 1995.
Evening Primrose. Minneapolis, Minnesota, Tunheim-Santrizos, 1998.
On the Bus with Rosa Parks. New York, Norton, 1999.

Plays

The Siberian Village. In *Callaloo* (Charlottesville, Virginia), 14(2), 1991.
The Darker Face of the Earth (produced Ashland, Oregon, 1996; London, 1999). Ashland, Oregon, Story Line Press, 1994; revised edition, Ashland, Oregon, Story Line Press, 1996; revised edition, London, Oberon Press, 1999.

Musicals: *The House Slave,* music by Alvin Singleton (produced Spelman College, Atlanta, Georgia, 1990); *Under the Resurrection Palm*, with Linda Pastan, music by David Liptak (1993); *Singin' Sepia,* music by Tania Leon (produced New York, 1996); *Umoja,* music by Alvin Singleton (produced Atlanta, Georgia, 1996); *Grace Notes,* music by Bruce Adolphe (produced New York, 1997); *The Pleasure's in Walking Through,* music by Walter Ross (produced Charlottesville, Virginia, 1998); *Seven for Luck,* music by John Williams (produced Tanglewood, Massachusetts, 1998).

Short Stories

Fifth Sunday. Lexington, University of Kentucky, 1985.

Novel

Through the Ivory Gate. New York, Pantheon Books, 1992.

*

Critical Studies: "A Conversation with Rita Dove" by Stan Rubin and Earl Ingersoll, in *Black American Literature Forum* (Terre Haute, Indiana), 20(6), fall 1986; "The Assembling Vision of Rita Dove," in *Callaloo* (Charlottesville, Virginia), 9(1), 1986, and "The Assembling Vision of Rita Dove," in *Conversant Essays: Contemporary Poets on Poetry,* edited by James McCorkle, Detroit, Michigan, Wayne State University Press, 1990, both by Robert McDougall; "The Poems of Rita Dove" by Arnold Rampersand, in *Callaloo*

(Charlottesville, Virginia), 9(1), 1986; "Rita Dove: Crossing Boundaries" by Ekaterini Georgoudaki, in *Callaloo* (Baltimore, Maryland), 14(2), spring 1991; "Folk Idiom in the Literary Expression of Two African American Authors: Rita Dove and Yusef Komunyakaa" by Kirkland C. Jones, in *Language and Literature in the African American Imagination,* edited by Carol Aisha Blackshire-Belay, Westport, Connecticut, Greenwood, 1992; *Coming to Consciousness: Lyric Poetry As Social Discourse in the Work of Charles Simic, Seamus Heaney, Tom Paulin, Tony Harrison, and Rita Dove* (dissertation) by Jonathan Hufstader, Cambridge, Massachusetts, Harvard University, 1993; "Divided Loyalties: Literal and Literary in the Poetry of Lorna Dee Cervantes, Cathy Song and Rita Dove" by Patricia Wallace, in *MELUS* (Amherst, Massachusetts), 18(3), fall 1993; *Creative Composing: The Verbal Art of Rita Dove, the Visual Art of Stephen Davis and the Filmic Art of Stanley Brakhage* (dissertation) by Susan Shibe Davis, Arizona State University, 1994; "The African American Kunstlerroman" by Madelyn Jablon, in *Diversity,* 2, 1994; "Rita Dove: Identity Markers" by Helen Vendler, in *Callaloo* (Baltimore, Maryland), 17(2), summer 1994; "No Vers Is Libre" by Scott Ward, in *Shenandoah* (Lexington, Virginia), 45(3), fall 1995; "Portraits of a Diasporan People: The Poetry of Shirley Campbell and Rita Dove" by Janet Jones Hampton, in *Afro-Hispanic Review* (Columbia, Missouri), 14(1), spring 1995; "Rita Dove: Taking the Heat" by Brenda Shaughnessy, in *Publishers Weekly,* 246(15), 12 April 1999; "Sitting the Poet: Rita Dove's Refiguring of Traditions" by Susan R. Van Dyne, in *Women Poets of the Americas: Toward a Pan-American Gathering,* edited by Jacqueline Vaught Brogan, Notre Dame, Indiana, University of Notre Dame Press, 1999; "Rita Dove's Shakespeares" by Peter Erickson, in *Transforming Shakespeare: Contemporary Women's Re-Visions in Literature and Performance,* edited by Marianne Novy, New York, St Martin's Press, 1999.

*　　*　　*

Rita Dove's poetry is concerned with history. Skimming the titles of her poems reveals such figures as Catherine of Alexandria, Nestor, Boccaccio, Shakespeare, and Schumann, as well as Dove's grandparents, Thomas and Beulah. Yet historical fact—and, at times, mythological model—plays a smaller role in Dove's poetry than does lyrical truth. She seeks the untold moments of life that, once discovered, reveal and illuminate more than a historical narrative could. In "Robert Schumann, Or: Musical Genius Begins with Affliction," the moment is a tormented encounter with a prostitute during which the music in the composer's head becomes an alarm and "pulls higher and higher, and still / each phrase returns to *A* / no chord is safe from *A*." In "Boccaccio: The Plague Years" the moment that reveals Boccaccio's passion for Fiammetta originates in the collection of corpses:

> . . . He closed his eyes
> to hear the slap
> of flesh onto flesh, a
> liquid crack like a grape
> as it breaks on the tongue.

Because of its grisly contrast, this image embodies the need to live fully in the senses, to love most passionately when surrounded by death.

Dove's poetry also explores the history of the African-American experience. The poems in the third section of *The Yellow House on the Corner* are written from the point of view of American slaves. The Pulitzer prizewinning *Thomas and Beulah* recounts the story of Dove's grandparents from courtship to death. Just as "these poems tell two sides of a story," the selection from the Dove family history tells a second story of the American experience: Thomas "heading North, straw hat / cocked on the back of his head" ("Jiving"), and Beulah waiting in Akron, Ohio, "Papa's girl, / black though she was" ("Taking in Wash"). Their lives become a part of our collective history. In *Grace Notes* Dove discovers a metaphor for the African-American experience in the buckeye, "its fruit / so useless, so ugly":

> We piled them up
> for ammunition.
> We lay down
>
> with them
> among the bruised leaves
> so that we could
>
> rise, shining.

In "Crab-boil" the speaker remembers being on a whites-only beach, but she refuses to be like the crabs scratching uselessly in the bucket:

> I decide to believe this: I'm hungry.
> Dismantled, they're merely exotic,
> a blushing meat . . . If
> we're kicked out now, I'm ready.

The discovery of the buckeye or the crabs is more than the means of articulating the speaker's experience; it becomes the experience itself. The poems reenact discovery.

Just as Dove's poetry explores history through the individual, it also explores time through the moment. Within the moment lies possibility. In "The Fish in the Stone," for example, the fossil is no longer trapped in stone but is permitted for a moment to come alive:

> In the ocean the silence
> moves and moves
>
> and so much is unnecessary!
> Patient, he drifts
> until the moment comes
> to cast his
> skeletal blossom.

For the fish, analysis discovers "the small predictable truths"; the real mystery of life is found only by living. In "Canary" Dove writes, "If you can't be free, be a mystery," because mystery, an essential quality of human life, is liberating. Dove's poems enter the mysterious by opening themselves to the moment of discovery. The discovery usually is not rational but rather emotional or physical. In "Pastoral" the speaker describes breast-feeding, her daughter "like an otter, but warm, / . . . eyes / unfocused and large: milk-drunk." She discovers

> what a young man must feel
> with his first love asleep on his breast:
> desire, and the freedom to imagine it.

What allows the poetry "desire, and the freedom to imagine it" is Dove's ability to sublimate her own will to the will of the poem, to surrender historical fact to greater truth. In doing so, Dove gives up the security of what she knows through logic to the greater assurance of what she discovers through prosody and the integrity of the line. The poem "Silos," for example, is not satisfied with silos in their prosaic function as warehouses for grain; they become "martial swans in spring paraded against the city sky's / shabby blue." In the end they become "the ribs of the modern world." In "Ars Poetica" Dove writes,

What I want is this poem to be small,
a ghost town
on the larger map of wills.
Then you can pencil me in as a hawk:
a traveling x-marks-the-spot.

As the hawk's eyes detect movement even in a ghost town, so Dove's poems, though sharply focused in the subjective moment, see our history far and wide. In *On the Bus with Rosa Parks* the former U.S. Poet Laureate (1993–95) scrutinizes the way individual lives figure in the tide of history. The blessing of freedom is considered in "Maple Valley Branch Library, 1967" as the poem implores, "tell me what you've read that keeps / that half smile afloat / above the collar of your impeccable blouse."

Drawing links between a mythical past and a tough and unforgiving present is a timeless concern for Dove. Perhaps all major poets who address the concern of equations—between two people, between human and earth, between past and present—find themselves expressing their thoughts in the form of the sonnet. In the introduction to *Mother Love,* Dove cites Rilke's *Sonnets to Orpheus* as her model. A daughter as well as the mother of a daughter, Dove draws on the timeless tragedy of Demeter and Persephone to demonstrate the range of dynamics between mothers and daughters. She notes that the tightly constrained sonnet form helps her narrators address their dilemmas because mothers and daughters are "struggling to sing in their chains." In a contemporary and ironic way the sonnets depict hell as faux-cultured Parisian society or as an Italian grotto. The narrator confronts a "gatekeeper" by imploring, "hasn't he seen an American Black / before? We find a common language: German." Dramatic and inventive, the poems also resound from small town America and the expanses of Mexico. As in all of her work, Dove sees the power of ancient sorrows and old truths in the pulse of our contemporary and in the momentary.

—Julie Miller and Martha Sutro

DOYLE, Charles (Desmond)

Verse published after 1970 as Mike Doyle. Nationality: British and Canadian. **Born:** Birmingham, Warwickshire, 18 October 1928. **Education:** Wellington Teachers College, New Zealand, Dip. Teach. 1955; Victoria University College, University of New Zealand (Macmillan Brown prize, 1956), B.A. 1956, M.A. 1958; University of Auckland, Ph.D. 1968. **Military Service:** Royal Navy. **Family:** Married 1) Helen Merlyn Lopdell in 1952 (died); 2) Doran Ross Smithells in 1959 (divorced); three sons and one daughter; 3) Rita Jean Brown in 1992. **Career:** Lecturer, 1961–66, and senior lecturer

in English and American literature, 1966–68, University of Auckland; visiting fellow, Yale University, New Haven, Connecticut (American Council of Learned Societies fellowship), 1967–68. Associate professor, 1968–76, professor of English, 1976–93, and since 1993 professor emeritus, University of Victoria, British Columbia. Editor, *Tuatara* magazine. **Awards:** Jessie Mackay memorial prize, 1955; Unesco Creative Artists fellowship, 1958; Canada Council grant, 1971, 1972, fellowship, 1975, 1982, 1986. **Address:** 641 Oliver Street, Victoria, British Columbia V8S 4W2, Canada.

PUBLICATIONS

Poetry

A Splinter of Glass Poems 1951–55. Christchurch, Pegasus Press, 1956.
The Night Shift: Poems on Aspects of Love, with others. Wellington, Capricorn Press, 1957.
Distances: Poems 1956–61. Auckland, Paul's Book Arcade, 1963.
Messages for Herod. Auckland, Collins, 1965.
A Sense of Place. Wellington, Wai-te-ata Press, 1965.
Earth Meditations: 2. Auckland, Aldritt, 1968.
Noah, with Quorum, by Robert Sward. Vancouver, Soft Press, 1970.
Earth Meditations. Toronto, Coach House Press, 1971.
Abandoned Sofa. Victoria, British Columbia, Soft Press, 1971.
Earthshot. Exeter, Exeter Books, 1972.
Preparing for the Ark. Toronto, Weed/Flower Press, 1973.
Planes. Toronto, Seripress, 1975.
Stonedancer. Auckland, Auckland University Press/Oxford University Press, 1976.
A Month Away from Home. Victoria, British Columbia, Tuatara, 1980.
A Steady Hand. Erin, Ontario, Porcupine's Quill, 1982.
The Urge to Raise Hats. Victoria, British Columbia, Tuatara, 1989.
Separate Fidelities. Victoria, British Columbia, Hawthorne Society, 1991.
Intimate Absences, Selected Poems 1954–1992. Victoria, British Columbia, Beach Holme Publishing, 1993.
Trout Spawning at Lardeau River: Poems. Victoria, British Columbia, Ekstasis Editions, 1997.

Other

Small Prophets and Quick Returns: Reflections on New Zealand Poetry. Auckland, New Zealand Publishing Society, 1966.
R.A.K. Mason. New York, Twayne, 1970.
James K. Baxter. Boston, Twayne, 1976.
William Carlos Williams and the American Poem. London, Macmillan, and New York, St. Martin's Press, 1982.
Richard Aldington: A Biography. Carbondale, Southern Illinois University Press, and London, Macmillan, 1989.

Editor, *Recent Poetry in New Zealand.* Auckland, Collins, 1965.
Editor, *William Carlos Williams: The Critical Heritage.* London, Routledge, 1980.
Editor, with Warren Magnusson and others, *The New Reality: The Politics of Restraint in British Columbia.* Vancouver, New Star, 1984.

Editor, *Wallace Stevens: The Critical Heritage.* London, Routledge, 1985.

Editor, with Warren Magnusson and others, *After Bennett: A New Politics for British Columbia.* Vancouver, New Star, 1986.

Editor, *Richard Aldington: Reappraisals.* Victoria, British Columbia, University of Victoria, ELS Monographs, 1990.

*

Manuscript Collection: Hocken Library, Otago University, Dunedin, New Zealand.

Critical Studies: *Aspects of New Zealand Poetry* by James K. Baxter, Christchurch, Caxton Press, 1967; "Earth Meditations One to Five" in *Quarry* (Kingston, Ontario), summer 1972; "Le Longue Voyage de Mike Doyle" by John Greene, in *Ellipse* (Quebec), 1977; "Quiet Islands," in *Anthos* (Ottawa), winter 1978; "Poetic Journeys," in *Canadian Literature 79* (Vancouver), 1979; "Mike Doyle and the Poet's Progress" by David Dowling, in *West Coast Review* (Vancouver), winter 1981; "Reality's Outer Limit" by Charles Jillard, in *Reference West* (Victoria, British Columbia), 1989.

Charles Doyle comments:

My central interest is still in the life of poetry. Contemporary poetry is perplexingly full of riches on the one hand and poetasters on the other, loaded with hype and competition. Having been within viewing distance of the high ground and having lived through avant-garde ambitions into a late quietism, I am indeed fortunate in retaining a live and committed sense of poetry and the poem. It rejoices me that there is so much poetry and the life of poetry to continue to be excited by.

*   *   *

Because of his residence in Britain, New Zealand, the United States, and Canada and his occupation as academic, critic, and editor, Charles Doyle's poetic career might well be described in the words of the acknowledged master W.C. Williams as the attempt to "find a local speech." A sense of geographical displacement in the 1950s was exchanged for a sense of intellectual displacement in the 1960s, while in the 1970s the search for poetic form dominated. His best poetry results when a balance between inventive form, philosophical reflection, and deeply felt personal experience is achieved.

Doyle's earlier lyrics contrast Europe ("our derelict hearts abandoned in distant places") with New Zealand as he wonders why "in a green country / where the cricket sings / there is such heartache / at the heart of things." When he does attempt to verbalize the here and now, the real says, "I am a thing, and that / Defeats you utterly." *In Messages for Herod* Doyle is vividly capable of evoking the present in dramatic lyrics, as in the poem in which the clear smile of a hitchhiker is glimpsed from a car window. But the title poem shows the poet's dread of the personal as the parochial; Herod slaughters the children because one of them denies that Auckland is the center of the universe.

Doyle seeks a solution in a Yeatsian Byzantium—"To make is to discover." *Earth Meditations* is a sustained intellectual mosaic, like *The Waste Land* welding together disparate fragments of form—concrete, imagist, lyric—and aesthetic idea—Magritte ("woid voice us imidge"), Joyce, Spinoza, Butler—in a search for meaning. For all

its linguistic inventiveness the sequence affirms the real in theory ("Could you have made / that same daub / without the dame?" the poet asks Magritte) and in practice through autobiography (life in New Zealand as sitting on "a cairn / of sheep currants").

More arid experimentation is found in *Earthshot* and in *Noah, with Quorum,* another long sequence that betrays Doyle's occasionally mawkish naïveté ("all that water?" or "Perhaps paradise / is always / what is lost?"). Yet even here there are superb moments in which emotion is crisply captured, as when the speaker laments separation from his love and "arms in my head / grow long three thousand miles" or in *Noah, with Quorum* in the lines "Even the windowpanes / wept."

All of these volumes may be seen as a long apprenticeship for the flowering of *Stonedancer.* Written in a remarkable variety of forms, these poems are wedded to occasional as well as more profound mediations with the sculptural simplicity, grace, and rightness of the Gaudier-Brzeska work of the title. A comparison of the title poem of Doyle's first volume—

I have shed an abstruse skin, and my bone's necrosis
Leaves Love's uncomplicated land to rediscover
Simple as still water or a moving tree

—with the last poem of *Stonedancer,* "The Journey of Meng Chiao"—

I must leave you here by the pinewoods under the sky.
I must go now. What do I hope to find when I arrive?
If I am lucky, the pinewoods under the sky

—shows his advance in philosophy and technique. An oriental simplicity of form and acceptance of emotion pervade the volume, as in "Shen Kua's Specifications for Travel" or the bliss of fulfilled love: "And on the hill slope, look / at the beautiful skiers. / See them go, see them go / over the frozen snow."

Much of the volume achieves Doyle's new ideal of the "poem as breathing" ("I dig those small / thin poems," he says) but also as "Dionysiac ravings." Fortunately Doyle escapes mystic platitudes by retaining the vigorous engagement with the world that has always marked his poetry. For example, there is a superb poem about the torture of an innocent African that ends with the lines "It was nobody's fault / that, as far as life is concerned, by the end of it / he knew everything else there was to know."

This volume suggests that Doyle "may have saved / the fullest wine until / gross appetite's discarded / its first, careless edge." Like a unique bouquet, his speech is local to each poem. Such versatility in thought, feeling, and technique is rare among modern poets. For all his academic fluency Doyle can always be relied upon to give us in each poem Williams's ideal—"a new world that is always 'real.'"

The volume *A Steady Hand* belies its title in a restless variety of forms and themes. Doyle is best when looking at the "simple history" of the natural world, evoking it through the aesthetic theory of a Klee ("*I am possessed by colour*") or polishing set pieces like "The Journey of Meng Chiao" or the powerful political protest of "The Inquisitor." But along with this mastery of form and tone go many uninspired lyrics, including a long separation sequence, suggesting a restless talent that is uncommitted, unfulfilled.

—David Dowling

DRUCKER, Johanna (Ruth)

Nationality: American. **Born:** Philadelphia, 30 May 1952. **Education:** University of Rochester, New York, 1969–70; California College of Arts and Crafts, Oakland, 1970–73, B.F.A. 1973; University of California, Berkeley, 1980–86, M.A. 1982, Ph.D. 1986. **Family:** Married Brad Freeman in 1991. **Career:** Lecturer, San Francisco State University, California, 1984, and University of California, Berkeley, 1985–86; assistant professor, University of Texas, Richardson, 1986–88; Mellon fellow, Harvard University, Cambridge, Massachusetts, 1988–89; assistant professor, Columbia University, New York, 1989–94; associate professor of art history, Yale University, New Haven, Connecticut, 1994–98; professor of art history, Purchase College, State University of New York, 1998–99. Since 1999 Robertson Professor of Media Studies, University of Virginia, Charlottesville. **Awards:** Regents fellowship, 1980–81, 1981–82, 1983–84; Fulbright fellowship, 1984–85; Getty fellowship, 1992–93. **Agent:** Steve Clay, Granary Books, 307 Seventh Avenue, Suite 1401, New York, New York 10001, U.S.A.

PUBLICATIONS

Plays

First Person Singular (produced San Francisco, 1975).
Any Other (produced Berkeley, California, 1977).
Queenie and the Prince (produced San Francisco, 1981).
Family Life (produced San Francisco, 1983).
Through the Dark End of Daylight (produced Berkeley, California, 1984).

Novels

History of the/My Wor(l)d. New York, Druckwerk, 1989.
Simulant Portrait. Riverdale, Maryland, Pyramid Atlantic, 1990.
Otherspace: Martian Typography, with Brad Freeman. Atlanta, Nexus Press, 1992.
Narratology. New York, Druckwerk, 1994.
Dark Decade. St. Paul, Detour Press, 1995.
Nova Reperta, with Brad Freeman. New Haven, Connecticut, JAB Books, 1999.

Other

The Visible Word. Chicago, University of Chicago Press, 1994.
Theorizing Modernism. New York, Columbia University Press, 1994.
The Alphabetic Labyrinth. London, Thames and Hudson, 1995.
The Century of Artists' Books. New York, Granary, 1995.
Figuring the Word. New York, Granary, 1998.

*

Critical Studies: "Johanna Drucker's Herstory" by Marjorie Perloff, in *Harvard Library Bulletin* (Cambridge), 1992; "Through Light and the Alphabet: An Interview with Johanna Drucker" by Matthew G. Kirschenbaum, in *Postmodern Culture* (Charlottesville, Virginia), 7(3), May 1997.

Theatrical Activities: Director: **Plays**—*Queenie and the Prince,* San Francisco, 1981; *Through the Dark End of Daylight,* Berkeley, California, 1984. Actor: **Plays**—role in *First Person Singular,* San Francisco, 1975; role in *Any Other,* Berkeley, California, 1977.

Johanna Drucker comments:

As a creative writer I have two main concerns: the structure of narrative and the relation between format and meaning. In a number of my works these two issues have been integrated, while in others one or the other dominates.

My interest in layout and format (the structural features of the text on the page) grew out of my direct involvement with letterpress printing. My direct involvement in hand setting type allowed me to experiment with the presentation of the text in ways which are not possible within a conventional publication. I began printing in 1972 with the publication of *Dark,* which contained stone lithographs and hand-set type. In the 1976 publication *Twenty-Six '76,* a book about a trip to Los Angeles, I used typographic formats to explore ways to differentiate linguistic themes within a narrative account. Individual fonts and sizes were used to distinguish quoted language, descriptive passages, overheard conversation, and interior reflections. The pages of this work looked more like a skeleton than a book text—as if all the extraneous flesh of experience had been eroded and only the structure of the experience remained. Since that time I have produced more than twenty works whose formats and language are interrelated. My work has some connection to that of other contemporary poets engaged with the visual representation of language, such as Steve McCaffery or Susan Howe, and other writers engaged with the structure of the book or with the materiality of language in verbal or visual form, but few are producers of books. My interest in the history of printing, the alphabet, and critical concerns about the visual representation of language grew directly out of my activities as a printer and writer. In the last fifteen years the two domains—that of scholarly and critical research and that of creative publication—have worked to feed and stimulate each other.

An interest in narrative form and prose structure has always been at the basis of my writing practice. My engagement with theoretical concerns in the context of the Bay Area language poetry scene in the 1970s transformed my belief in conventional fiction and prose, infusing my work with self-consciousness about form and structure as well as language. In the 1980s I came under the influence of feminist critical theory and began to see my own experiments with received form, particularly my interest in subverting the linearity of conventional prose through complex formats, within the framework of feminist writing. Both in terms of structure and in terms of subject matter, my work from *Against Fiction* (1984) to *History of the/My Wor(l)d, Simulant Portrait,* and *Narratology* displays overt feminist concerns. Specifically, these include an interest in the construction of a feminist subjectivity.

*   *   *

Johanna Drucker is a prominent experimental artist whose work can be classified under a variety of genres. A particular book might be considered a novel, a play, poetry, or simply "book" art. Although none of her books is listed above as verse, she shares with modern poets a number of concerns, including the relation between format and meaning. What her books look like and what they say interact in many possible ways so that the reader's subjectivity becomes a part of the work itself.

Drucker's name in German means "printer," and at times she calls her printing Druckwerk. Her books have an immediate visual effect, sometimes with a counterpoint of colors. In some magenta and black seem to predominate, in others yellows and blues. One "book," for example, is a blue box containing separate sheets of ivory paper. Drucker uses a variety of visual techniques—type fonts, clip-art decorations, pictures, and patterns—all of which are potentially disruptive from a more traditional point of view.

What Drucker prints can be interpreted in various ways, and in a sense one cannot read or even quote from her books. For example, when Drucker writes "S crap 's ample," should one read it as "Scrap is ample," "crap sample," or "Is crap a sample" or in some other way? Whatever the words mean, they trigger the reader's tendency to supply sounds, to fill the gaps left by an apostrophe. The reader thus becomes part of the creative process, a participant in the creation of meaning, or, to use the language of computers, the process becomes "interactive."

The printing and layout can be so spatially disruptive that, depending on the reader's physical distance from the page, the words seem to fall into several sequences. The title of one of Drucker's books is *History of the/my Wor(l)d* (1989). The slash in the title, used to suggest the possibilities of multiple responses, implies either/or or both. The letters of the title are printed in different type sizes on the cover. Viewed from a middle distance, the title appears to be simply a large *W*. The closer one gets to the book, the more the other letters come into focus, but the dominant *W*, positioned, or displaced, to the left, tends to pull the eye to read *Word* first, encouraging another response, *Word History*.

Drucker's presentations—in which she reads, talks, and displays her work on a screen—draw enthusiastic audiences, and her work arouses keen enthusiasm among experimental practitioners. An emerging talent among these poets is William Howe, whose book *tripflea* employs a black clip-art flea printed on pages of gray paper scented with the insecticide Raid. The paper can be shuffled to form different sequences. Another poet, Lewis MacAdams, has baked cookies in the shapes of letters, arranged the letters into a poem, read the poem, and thrown the cookies to the audience so that they could eat the poem.

Some might say such experiments have been done before, for example, in Ezra Pound's "Blast," by the surrealists, and even quasi-commercially in "The Tiger's Eye." One can respond, however, that these earlier works were essentially aimed at supporting a text, while Drucker's far wider use of technology shifts the attention so that neither the text nor the technology has primacy. This is not unlike Charles Rosen's finding an "inaudible" melody between the mathematical patterns of music and the sound a listener actually hears.

—William Sylvester

DUBIE, Norman (Evans, Jr.)

Nationality: American. **Born:** Barre, Vermont, 10 April 1945. **Education:** Goddard College, Plainfield, Vermont, 1964–69, B.A. 1969; University of Iowa, Iowa City, 1969–71, M.F.A. 1971. **Family:** Married 1) Francesca Stafford in 1969 (divorced 1973), one daughter; 2) Pamela Stewart in 1974 (divorced 1979); 3) Jeannine Savard in 1981. **Career:** Teaching assistant, 1969–71, and lecturer in creative writing, 1971–74, University of Iowa; assistant professor, Ohio University, Athens, 1974–75. Writer-in-residence, 1975–76, director of the Graduate Writing Program, 1976–77, associate professor, 1978–82, professor, 1982–91, and since 1991 Regents Professor of English, Arizona State University, Tempe. Poetry editor, *Iowa Review,* 1971–72, and *Now,* 1973–74. Poetry director, Prison Writers and Artists Workshop, Iowa City, 1973–74. **Awards:** Bess Hokin prize (*Poetry,* Chicago), 1976; Guggenheim grant, 1977; National Endowment for the Arts grant, 1986; Ingram Merrill Foundation grant, 1987. **Address:** Department of English, Arizona State University, Tempe, Arizona 85281, U.S.A.

PUBLICATIONS

Poetry

The Horsehair Sofa. Plainfield, Vermont, Goddard Journal, 1969.
Alehouse Sonnets. Pittsburgh, University of Pittsburgh Press, 1971.
Indian Summer. Iowa City, Elizabeth Press, 1974.
The Prayers of the North American Martyrs. New York, Penumbra Press, 1975.
Popham of the New Song and Other Poems. Port Townsend, Washington, Graywolf Press, 1975.
In the Dead of the Night. Pittsburgh, University of Pittsburgh Press, 1975.
The Illustrations. New York, Braziller, 1977.
A Thousand Little Things and Other Poems. Omaha, Cummington Press, 1977.
Odalisque in White. Seattle, Porch, 1979.
The City of the Olesha Fruit. New York, Doubleday, 1979.
The Everlastings. New York, Doubleday, 1980.
The Window in the Field. Copenhagen, Razorback Press, 1981.
Selected and New Poems. New York, Norton, 1983.
The Springhouse. New York, Norton, 1986.
Groom Falconer. New York, Norton, 1989.
Radio Sky. New York, Norton, 1991.
The Clouds of Magellan (Aphorisms). Santa Fe, New Mexico, Recursos Press, 1992.
The Funeral. Calais, Vermont, Z Press, 1998.

*

Manuscript Collection: University of Iowa Special Collections, Iowa City.

Critical Studies: Interview in *American Poetry Review* (Philadelphia), July-August 1978, and November-December 1989; "A Generous Salvation: The Poetry of Norman Dubie" by David St. John, in *Conversant Essays: Contemporary Poets on Poetry,* Detroit, Wayne State University Press, 1990; "My Dubious Calculus" by William Slattery, in *The Antioch Review* (Yellow Springs, Ohio), 52, winter 1994; "Dubie's 'Amen'" by Michele Leavitt, in *Explicator* (Washington, D.C.), 56(1), fall 1997.

*   *   *

The American poet Norman Dubie has been justifiably praised by his contemporaries and has attracted awards and endowments from the literary establishment. I regard him as possibly the most accomplished practitioner of narrative poetry currently working in the English language, yet he remains unpublished and unrecognized in

Britain. The Atlantic pond, it seems, is wider and deeper than it should be.

What so many readers outside the United States have missed is a body of work that is lyrical and documentary, learned and eclectic, determinedly researched, and yet revelatory and epiphanic in a way associated more with the modern short story. In "Elegy to the Sioux" and "The Scrivener's Roses" Dubie has written poems that rank with the best of Lowell and Ginsberg in their power to evoke uniquely American experiences and in their grasp of critical episodes from American history. That having been said, unlike Ginsberg, Lowell, and the confessional poets, Dubie himself remains healthily absent from the poetry. His work is refreshingly distanced from the confines of postwar American confessional poetry; he is more specific than Bly and more accessible than Ashbery. Here there is no *Life Studies,* no *Howl,* no *Dream Songs.* Instead, the consequence of a narrative strategy is to bring characters and events to the foreground and to confirm the "negative capability" of the poet.

"The Scrivener's Roses" has qualities that both perplex and astound. It is a long poem of some 153 lines that weaves apparently unconnected characters and events from the American Civil War into a rich narrative of details and essences. The poem opens with an amputation by a surgeon. The young boy on whom he operates has a sister who works in a paper mill in New England, where

They often said that April snow was a poor man's manure.

Letters written on that paper may, given the war, end up undelivered and discarded in the dead letter office in Washington, D.C., which Herman Melville visits and writes a story about. At this time Sherman's Union troops are pushing further into Confederate Georgia, ravaging people and places as they go:

. . . At dusk, searching for women, they
Arrive at the churchyard—with bayonets they open the fresh mounds
Where the sisters were hurriedly buried.
. . . The dancing soldiers are laughing

With the rigid partners in moonlight—you can hear dry bones
Breaking! Some of the women are shaven, one has long red hair.
Their white breasts bouncing in the chill night air . . .

Dubie is undoubtedly drawn to the bizarre and the macabre, but "The Scrivener's Roses" is also representative of his ability to resolve the darker aspects of human behavior and the human soul. He does this not explicitly but in the very act of making manifest the underlying connections between historical events and personal perceptions. As E.M. Forster insisted, "Only connect." One is left at the end of the poem with a profound sense of unease and confirmation.

In "Elizabeth's War with the Christmas Bear," "The Huts at Esquimaux," "La Pampa," and many other poems, Dubie draws the reader into the lives of people in strange places at significant moments. He skillfully gives voice to others through his dramatic monologues, for example, "The Pennacesse Leper Colony for Women, Cape Cod: 1922," "The Czar's Last Christmas Letter: A Barn in the Urals," and "Aubade of the Singer and Sabateur, Marie Triste." Such writing does much to redress the imbalance set up by the preeminence of the confessional mode in contemporary American poetry.

Another central strand in Dubie's work is his reconsideration of the lives of other artists and writers—Chekhov, Proust, Ingmar Bergman, Rodin, the photographers Weston and Brassai, and many more. There are some readers who may regard this as parasitic or irritatingly arch. To me, however, the compelling reenactment of pain and passion in such poems as "Sun and Moon Flowers: Paul Klee, 1879–1940," "After Three Photographs of Brassai," and "The Duchess' Red Shoes" seems to justify the exercise. In any case, his later poems engage more directly with contemporary events, especially the political traumas of South and Central America. There also are poems in which his wife and family appear, though Dubie rarely satisfies the expectations of readers looking for the personal lyric in the tradition that runs from the romantics to Seamus Heaney and Galway Kinnell.

The only misgiving I have concerns Dubie's use of the line and the paragraph break, both of which appear at times quite arbitrary. This, however, may be another example of the problems one encounters when discourses and signifiers have to travel across oceans.

Dubie has constructed a body of work that offers different challenges and distinct rewards. His *Selected and New Poems,* published when he was in his mid-30s, clearly established him as an original American voice, and his subsequent collections have confirmed him as a poet deserving of an international audience.

—Tony Curtis

DUDEK, Louis

Nationality: Canadian. **Born:** Montreal, Quebec, 6 February 1918. **Education:** Montreal High School; McGill University, Montreal, B.A. 1939; Columbia University, New York, M.A. in history 1946, Ph.D. in English and comparative literature 1955. **Family:** Married 1) Stephanie Zuperko in 1943 (divorced 1965); 2) Aileen Collins in 1970; one son. **Career:** Instructor in English, City College of New York, 1946–51. Lecturer, 1951–53, associate professor, 1953–69, Greenshields Professor of English, 1969–84, and since 1984 professor emeritus, McGill University. Associated with *First Statement* magazine, Montreal, 1943; editor, McGill Poetry Series, 1956–66, and *Delta,* Montreal, 1957–66; former publisher, Contact Press, Toronto, and Delta Canada Press, Montreal. Currently publisher, DC Books, Montreal. Former director-at-large, Canadian Council of Teachers of English; former member of Humanities Research Council of Canada. **Awards:** Quebec Literary award, 1968. D.L.: York University, Toronto, 1983; Hon. Dip.: Dawson College, Montreal, 1984. D.H.L.: St. Francis Xavier University, Antigonish, Nova Scotia, 1995. Officer, Order of Canada, 1984. **Address:** 5 Ingleside Avenue, Montreal, Quebec H3Z 1N4, Canada.

PUBLICATIONS

Poetry

Unit of Five, with others, edited by Ronald Hambleton. Toronto, Ryerson Press, 1944.
East of the City. Toronto, Ryerson Press, 1946.
The Searching Image. Toronto, Ryerson Press, 1952.
Cerberus, with Irving Layton and Raymond Souster. Toronto, Contact Press, 1952.

Twenty-Four Poems. Toronto, Contact Press, 1952.
Europe. Toronto, Laocoon Press, 1954.
The Transparent Sea. Toronto, Contact Press, 1956.
En México. Toronto, Contact Press, 1958.
Laughing Stalks. Toronto, Contact Press, 1958.
Atlantis. Montreal, Delta Canada, 1967.
Collected Poetry. Montreal, Delta Canada, 1971.
Epigrams. Montreal, DC Books, 1975.
Selected Poems. Ottawa, Golden Dog Press, 1975.
Cross-Section: Poems 1940–1980. Toronto, Coach House Press, 1980.
Poems from Atlantis. Ottawa, Golden Dog Press, 1980.
Continuation 1. Montreal, Véhicule Press, 1981.
Zembla's Rocks. Montreal, Véhicule Press, 1986.
Infinite Worlds, edited by Robin Blaser. Montreal, Véhicule Press, 1988.
Continuation II. Montreal, Véhicule Press, 1990.
Small Perfect Things. Montreal, DC Books, 1991.
A Last Stand: Poems. Montreal, Véhicule Press, 1995.
The Caged Tiger. Montreal, Empyreal Press, 1997.
The Poetry of Louis Dudek: Definitive Edition, Kemptville, Ontario, Golden Dog Press, 1998.

Recording: *The Green Beyond,* CBC, 1973.

Other

Literature and the Press: A History of Printing, Printed Media, and Their Relation to Literature. Toronto, Ryerson Press-Contact Press, 1960.
The First Person in Literature. Toronto, CBC Publications, 1967.
Selected Essays and Criticism. Ottawa, Tecumseh Press, 1978.
Technology and Culture. Ottawa, Golden Dog Press, 1979.
Ideas for Poetry. Montreal, Véhicule Press, 1983.
In Defence of Art: Critical Essays and Reviews, edited by Aileen Collins. Kingston, Ontario, Quarry Press, 1988.
Paradise: Essays on Myth, Art, & Reality. Montreal, Véhicule Press, 1992.
Notebooks, 1960–1994. Ottawa, Ontario, Golden Dog Press, 1994.
The Birth of Reason. Montreal, DC Books, 1994.
1941 Diary. Montreal, Empyreal, 1996.
Reality Games. Montreal, Empyreal, 1998.

Editor, with Irving Layton, *Canadian Poems 1850–1952.* Toronto, Contact Press, 1952; revised edition, 1953.
Editor, *Selected Poems,* by Raymond Souster. Toronto, Contact Press, 1956.
Editor, *Montréal, Paris d'Amérique/Paris of America,* photographs by Michel Régnier. Montreal, Editions du Jour, 1961.
Editor, *Poetry of Our Time: An Introduction to Twentieth-Century Poetry, Including Modern Canadian Poetry.* Toronto, Macmillan, 1965.
Editor, with Michael Gnarowski, *The Making of Modern Poetry in Canada: Essential Articles on Contemporary Canadian Poetry in English.* Toronto, Ryerson Press, 1967.
Editor, *All Kinds of Everything: Worlds of Poetry.* Toronto, Clarke Irwin, 1973.
Editor, *Dk—Some Letters of Ezra Pound.* Montreal, DC Books, 1974.

*

Bibliography: *Louis Dudek: A Check-list* by Karol W.J. Wenek, Ottawa, Golden Dog Press, 1975.

Critical Studies: "A Critic of Life: Louis Dudek As Man of Letters" by Wynne Francis, in *Canadian Literature* (Vancouver), autumn 1964; "Louis Dudek Issue" of *Yes 14* (Montreal), September 1965; *The Oxford Anthology of Canadian Literature* edited by Robert Weaver and William Toye, Toronto, Oxford University Press, 1973; *Louis Dudek and Raymond Souster* by Frank Davey, Vancouver, Douglas and McIntyre, 1980, Seattle, University of Washington Press, 1981; "Louis Dudek: Texts and Essays" edited by B.P. Nichol and Frank Davey, in *Open Letter* (Toronto), summer 1981; by Terry Goldie, in *Canadian Writers and Their Works,* edited by Robert Lecker and others, Toronto, ECW Press, 1985; "Infinite Worlds: The Poetry of Louis Dudek" by Robin Blaser, in *Sagetrieb* (Orono, Maine), 7(1), spring 1988; *The Place of American Poets in the Development of Irving Layton, Louis Dudek and Raymond Souster* (dissertation) by Sabrina Lee Reed, n.p. 1989; "Dudek on Frye or, Not a Poet's Poetics" by Nicola Vulpe, in *Canadian Literature* (Vancouver, British Columbia), 136, spring 1993.

*   *   *

When Robin Blaser introduced the quasi-definitive selection of Louis Dudek's poems, *Infinite Worlds,* he claimed that "Dudek is Canada's most important—that is to say consequential—modern voice." This is not the place for the ranking of poets, but the really significant part of Blaser's statement can be taken as true. Throughout a long career Dudek has been perhaps Canada's most consistent defender and practitioner of the classic modern mode.

There are two ways in which Dudek's modernism has been manifest, first in his devotion to imagism, which dominated the earlier part of his poetic career, and then in his insistence that in poetry perception (the discovery of the right image) must be disciplined and shaped by thought. More than most Canadian poets, Dudek has been a deliberately intellectual artificer, consciously concerned with the propagation of an essentially elitist literary attitude.

Here one comes to the main and most abiding influence on Dudek as a poet, that of Ezra Pound. Dudek began writing verse at the end of the 1930s, though his first volume, *East of the City,* did not appear until 1946. In 1943 he joined John Sutherland and Irving Layton in editing the poetry magazine *First Statement,* which Sutherland had founded in 1942, and he helped launch a movement that would liberate Canadian poetry from the British past, giving it at least a North American if not a very specifically Canadian character.

At this time Dudek already regarded himself as an imagist, and for a long time he argued that imagism was "the central antidote to the ills of Canadian poetry: the insistence on the clarity of imagery, contemporary imagery." One of his earliest books was actually called *The Searching Image,* and it presents some almost naively direct examples of imagist practice, for example, "A Small Rain," which I quote whole:

Evening. With the thin rain falling,
a sky like moonstone.
And here, a slender tree, at street-edge
   one branch pointing left
      skyward,
      Another, thin, slanting to the right.

And in the pale-light-filled street
     the first lamps, far
    pearly, light blue
      light green, red
   of all colours
      of all dimensions.

The resemblance to the early Pound is evident, and there is no doubt that Dudek has combined the role of disciple and original creator in an unusual way. As the Canadian critic Milton Wilson once remarked, Pound had been "both the hero and the villain of his story." In the late 1940s, when Dudek studied and taught in New York for a while, he began a correspondence with Pound that he eventually published. Not only did he follow Pound into imagism, but Dudek also labored diligently to acquire the kind of omnivorous erudition Pound displayed in his *Cantos*. Eventually the later Dudek came to resemble the later Pound, for it was the influence of *The Cantos* that led Dudek in the direction that most clearly marked his originality among Canadian poets, the creation of the long meditative poem as distinct from the long narrative poem, which already had a considerable Canadian history.

At their best Dudek's long poems of the 1950s and 1960s—*Europe, En México,* and *Atlantis*—move out from the shadow of *The Cantos* to become fine examples of philosophic verse filtered through a highly individual sensibility. Such poems, though they are formally modeled on journeys, have been criticized for their lack of narrative development, but this is the application of a prose criterion to a kind of writing that is, in fact, following an essentially poetic pattern, substituting for the quasi-chronological development of an argument the juxtaposition of situations, incidents, epiphanies, and revelations that are united tonally by the reflective manner. In them one finds examples of the poetry of philosophic statement such as few other Canadians have bettered. This Heraclitean reflection from *Atlantis* is an example:

I seem to peer through time, as through a tottering mansion,
to glimpse the shapes beyond, the spectral bone-men
     who lived, and died, and believed.

And see the new religion fearfully replacing the old,
      burning temples,
knowing, past cure, how sure their reasons were
     against the old idols,
who are now burned themselves, with the sure fire of reason.

Nothing stands, we say, we moderns.
All's flux, an art of mathematics—of fiery matter,
while the old gods gutter and die in the flames.

With the writing of these long works Dudek's production of short lyric poems declined, and for more than twenty years, between 1958 (*Laughing Stalks*) and 1980 (*Cross-Section: Poems 1940–1980*), he published no collections of shorter poems. But it would be a mistake to assume that in giving an example to younger Canadian poets of the writing of long poems, which many of them have since followed, he entirely abandoned the lyric mode. One can find passages in the major poems, like the following from *En México,* that show his continued devotion to simple imagism and that in this way declare the unity of his work:

All the green blanketing the hills,
the braided streams,
and the brown sands bleaching;
horses with heads akimbo,
small lambs that leap,
children with huge eyes,
and lovers shy in their look;
   praise these to the bewildering heavens,
knowing no other tongue but praise.

—George Woodcock

DUFFY, Carol Ann

Nationality: British. **Born:** Glasgow, 23 December 1955. **Education:** St. Joseph's Convent, Stafford, Staffordshire; Stafford Girls' High School; University of Liverpool, 1974–77, B.A. (honors) in philosophy. **Career:** Since 1983 poetry editor, *Ambit* magazine, London. Visiting fellow, North Riding College, Scarborough, 1985; writer-in-residence, Southern Arts, Thamesdown, 1987–88. **Awards:** C. Day Lewis fellowship, 1982–84; National Poetry Competition award, 1983; Gregory award, 1984; Scottish Arts Council award, 1986; Somerset Maugham award, 1988; Dylan Thomas award, 1989. **Agent:** Tessa Sayle Ltd., 11 Jubilee Place, London SW3 3TE. **Address:** 4 Camp View, London SW19 4UL, England.

PUBLICATIONS

Poetry

Fleshweathercock and Other Poems. Walton-on-Thames, Surrey, Outposts, 1973.
Fifth Last Song. Wirral, Merseyside, Headland, 1982.
Standing Female Nude. London, Anvil Press Poetry, 1985.
Thrown Voices. London, Turret, 1986.
Selling Manhattan. London, Anvil Press Poetry, 1987.
The Other Country. London, Anvil Press Poetry, 1990.
William and the Ex-Prime Minister. London, Anvil Press Poetry, 1992.
Mean Time. London, Anvil Press Poetry, 1993.
Selected Poems. London, Penguin, 1994.
Meeting Midnight: Three Young Poems. Holybourne, Alton, Hampshire, Clarion Publishing, 1995; as *Meeting Midnight,* London, Faber, 1999.
The Pamphlet. London, Anvil Press Poetry, 1998.
The World's Wife: Poems. London, Picador, 1999; New York, Faber, 2000.

Plays

Take My Husband (produced Liverpool, 1982).
Cavern of Dreams (produced Liverpool, 1984).
Little Women, Big Boys (produced London, 1986).

Radio Play: *Loss,* 1986.

Other

Editor, *Home and Away.* Thamesdown, Southern Arts, 1988.
Editor, *I Wouldn't Thank You for a Valentine: Poems for Young Feminists.* London, Viking, 1992; New York, Holt, 1993.
Editor, *Grimm Tales.* London, Faber, 1996.
Editor, *Stopping for Death: Poems of Death and Loss.* New York, Holt, 1996.
Editor, with others, *Five Finger-Piglets: Poems* (for children). London, Macmillan, 1999.
Editor, *Rumpelstiltskin and Other Grimm Tales.* London, Faber, 1999.
Editor, *Time's Tidings: Greeting the Twenty-First Century.* London, Anvil Press Poetry, 1999.

*

Critical Studies: "The Poetry of Carol Ann Duffy" by Jane E. Thomas, in *Bête Noire* (Hull) 6, 1989; *Taking Their Word: Twentieth-Century Women Reinvent the Victorian* (dissertation) by Danette DiMarco, Duquesne University, 1995.

*   *   *

Speaking of the poet's "eye" and "ear" are familiar commonplaces of contemporary criticism. These terms readily suggest the sister arts of poetry and painting and the obvious relationship of poetry to the formal measures of music. But as poets and critics we all too often neglect the equally important analogy of poetry and drama. One of Britain's most popular and highly regarded poets, Carol Ann Duffy, launched her career with two plays staged at the Liverpool Playhouse, and her best verse evinces the most valuable skills of the playwright—dramatic timing and characterization.

Duffy has covered an impressive range of styles throughout her collections, from love lyrics (the critic Robert Nye remarked that she writes love poems "as if she were the first to do so") to razor-sharp political satire. But the hallmark of her work remains the dramatic monologue. Most poets who attempt this genre fail because they cannot resist imposing clever metaphors and well-wrought similes—in effect their own voices—on the character's diction. The trick of the successful dramatic monologue, however, consists of elevating speech to poetry without leaving the closed set of the character's vocabulary. Duffy handles this easily, coaxing pathos and a rarefied music from the sentence fragments of maniacs or, as in "Words of Absolution," the neologisms of the senile: "Blessed art thou among women even if / we put you in a home. Only the silent motion / of lips and the fingering of decades. / How do we show that we love God? / Never a slack shilling but good broth / always on the table. Which are the fasting days? / Mary Wallace, what are the days of abstinence?"

Duffy's first collection, *Standing Female Nude,* is heavily weighted with such points of view. There are war photographers, immigrant schoolchildren, and Franz Schubert, and there is even a poem from the point of view of a pair of dolphins confined in an aquarium. But the most intriguing and formally engaging of these poems are spoken by morally ambiguous personalities. (It is safe to say that the most successful dramatic monologues from Browning on deal with speakers who are in some way reprehensible.) The fact that a poem is a monologue helps to determine our sympathy for the speaker—since we must adopt his viewpoint as our entry into the poem—and Duffy exploits the effect created by this tension between sympathy and moral judgment in poems spoken by murderers and crypto-Nazis.

In a poem like "Education for Leisure," for example, we can trace the character's progressive degeneration from alienation ("Once a fortnight, I walk the two miles into town / for signing on. They don't appreciate my autograph") to dangerous psychosis ("The pavements glitter suddenly. I touch your arm"), but there is something unmistakably attractive in his grim humor. We are drawn to the character even as we are repelled: "Today I am going to kill something. Anything . . . / I squash a fly against the window with my thumb. / We did that at school. Shakespeare. It was in / Another language and now the fly is in another language. / I breathe out talent on the glass to write my name." This last image recurs in a number of poems, for example, in "Psychopath," where the fairground speaker says, "My breath wipes me from the looking glass." It is almost an emblem of dramatic irony; we know more than the character because he is kept from self-knowledge by his own words.

Duffy frequently collects a chorus of voices in a single poem to produce a kind of dramatic collage. For example, in "Dies Natalis," from *Selling Manhattan,* she adopts a series of markedly different dictions as one personality undergoes a succession of reincarnations as an Egyptian queen's cat, an albatross, a man, and a baby. She returns to this form throughout her collections, with "Comprehensive," "A Clear Note," and "Model Village" being further examples.

The menacing ventriloquist's prop of "The Dummy" in *Selling Manhattan* recalls the film *Dead of Night,* and its presence in the collection redirects our attention to Duffy's whole voice-throwing enterprise. It is a brilliantly conceived poem in which a persona has finally turned on the poet herself:

> Balancing me with your hand up my back, listening
> to the voice you gave me croaking for truth, you keep
> me at it. Your lips don't move, but your eyes look
> desperate as hell. Ask me something difficult.

Duffy's collection *The Other Country* contains fewer dramatic monologues, but "The Way My Mother Speaks" offers another insight into her uncanny facility with the genre: "I say her phrases to myself in my head / or under the shallows of my breath, / restful shapes moving." No other poet writing in Britain listens so carefully.

—Michael Donaghy

DUFFY, Maureen (Patricia)

Also wrote as D.M. Cayer. Nationality: British. **Born:** Worthing, Sussex, 21 October 1933. **Education:** Trowbridge High School for Girls, Wiltshire; Sarah Bonnell High School for Girls; King's College, London, 1953–56, B.A. (honors) in English 1956. **Career:** Schoolteacher for five years. Co-founder, Writers Action Group, 1972; joint chair, 1977–78, and president, 1985–89, Writers Guild of Great Britain; chair, Greater London Arts Literature Panel, 1979–81; vice-chair, 1981–86, and since 1989 chair, British Copyright Council; since 1982 chair, Authors Lending and Copyright Society; vice president, Beauty Without Cruelty; fiction editor, *Critical Quarterly,* Manchester, 1987. **Awards:** City of London Festival Playwright's prize, 1962; Arts Council bursary, 1963, 1966, 1975; Society of Authors traveling scholarship, 1976. Fellow, Royal Society of Literature, 1985. **Agent:** Jonathan Clowes Ltd., Ironbridge House, Bridge Approach, London NW1 8BD. **Address:** 18 Fabian Road, London SW6 7TZ, England.

PUBLICATIONS

Poetry

Lyrics for the Dog Hour. London, Hutchinson, 1968.
The Venus Touch. London, Weidenfeld and Nicolson, 1971.
Actaeon. Rushden, Northamptonshire, Sceptre Press, 1973.
Evesong. London, Sappho, 1975.
Memorials of the Quick and the Dead. London, Hamish Hamilton, 1979.
Collected Poems. London, Hamish Hamilton, 1985.

Plays

The Lay-Off (produced London, 1962).
The Silk Room (produced Watford, Hertfordshire, 1966).
Rites (produced London, 1969). Published in *New Short Plays 2,* London, Methuen, 1969.
Solo, Olde Tyme (produced Cambridge, 1970).
A Nightingale in Bloomsbury Square (produced London, 1973). Published in *Factions,* edited by Giles Gordon and Alex Hamilton, London, Joseph, 1974.

Radio Play: *Only Goodnight,* 1981.

Television Play: *Josie,* 1961.

Novels

That's How It Was. London, Hutchinson, 1962; New York, Dial Press, 1984.
The Single Eye. London, Hutchinson, 1964.
The Microcosm. London, Hutchinson, and New York, Simon and Schuster, 1966.
The Paradox Players. London, Hutchinson, 1967; New York, Simon and Schuster, 1968.
Wounds. London, Hutchinson, and New York, Knopf, 1969.
Love Child. London, Weidenfeld and Nicolson, and New York, Knopf, 1971.
I Want to Go to Moscow: A Lay. London, Hodder and Stoughton, 1973; as *All Heaven in a Rage,* New York, Knopf, 1973.
Capital. London, Cape, 1975; New York, Braziller, 1976.
Housespy. London, Hamish Hamilton, 1978.
Gor Saga. London, Eyre Methuen, 1981; New York, Viking Press, 1982.
Scarborough Fear (as D.M. Cayer). London, Macdonald, 1982.
Londoners: An Elegy. London, Methuen, 1983.
Change. London, Methuen, 1987.
Illuminations. London, Flamingo, 1992.
Occam's Razor. London, Sinclair-Stevenson, 1993.
Restitution. London, Fourth Estate, 1998.

Other

The Erotic World of Faery. London, Hodder and Stoughton, 1972.
The Passionate Shepherdess: Aphra Behn 1640–1689. London, Cape, 1977; New York, Avon, 1979.
Inherit the Earth: A Social History. London, Hamish Hamilton, 1980.
Men and Beasts: An Animal Rights Handbook. London, Paladin, 1984.
A Thousand Capricious Chances: A History of the Methuen List 1889–1989. London, Methuen, 1989.
Henry Purcell. London, Fourth Estate, 1994.

Editor, with Alan Brownjohn, *New Poetry 3.* London, Arts Council, 1977.
Editor, *Oroonoko and Other Stories,* by Aphra Behn. London, Methuen, 1986.
Editor, *Love Letters Between a Nobleman and His Sister,* by Aphra Behn. London, Virago Press, 1987.
Editor, *Five Plays/Aphra Behn: Selected and Introduced by Maureen Duffy.* London, Methuen Drama, 1990.

Translator, *A Blush of Shame,* by Domenico Rea. London, Barrie and Rockliff, 1968.

*

Manuscript Collection: King's College, University of London.

Critical Studies: By Dulan Barber, in *Transatlantic Review 45* (London), spring 1973; *Guide to Modern World Literature* by Martin Seymour-Smith, London, Wolfe, 1973, as *Funk and Wagnalls Guide to Modern World Literature,* New York, Funk and Wagnalls, 1973; *A Female Vision of the City: London in the Novels of Five British Women,* Knoxville, University of Tennessee Press, 1989, and "Virginia Woolf As Modernist Foremother in Maureen Duffy's Play 'A Nightingale in Bloomsbury Square,'" in *Unmanning Modernism: Gendered Re-Readings,* edited by Elizabeth Jane Harrison and Shirley Peterson, Knoxville, University of Tennessee Press, 1997, both by Christine W. Sizemore; "'Keepers of History': The Novels of Maureen Duffy" by Lyndie Brimstone, in *Lesbian and Gay Writing: An Anthology of Critical Essays,* edited by Mark Lilly, Philadelphia, Temple University Press, 1990; "Mary and the Monster: Mary Shelley's Frankenstein and Maureen Duffy's Gor Saga" by Jenny Newman, in *Where No Man Has Gone Before: Women and Science Fiction,* edited by Lucie Armitt, London, Routledge, 1991; "Fiction As Historical Critique: The Retrospective World War II Novels of Beryl Bainbridge and Maureen Duffy" by Phyllis Lassner, in *Phoebe,* 3(2), fall 1991; "Three Recent Versions of the Bacchae" by Elizabeth Hale Winkler, in *Madness in Drama,* edited by James Redmond, Cambridge, Cambridge University Press, 1993; "Maureen Duffy: A Polyphonic Sub-Version of Realism" by Christoph Bode, in *Anglistik* (Bochum, Germany), 60, 1997.

*   *   *

Best known for her novels and her championing of social causes, Maureen Duffy has also written poems that echo her humane and libertarian views. Whether speaking out forcefully on women's rights, animal rights, or the horrors of famine, homelessness, and poverty, the voice is recognizable from the earliest of her published work to the mature expression of her later collections. Above all, her writings celebrate the liberating power of physical love, in particular the love between women. Such themes are hinted at in her early poems, where tributes to political and literary giants are mingled with keener insights into the nature of various types of women and the growth of sexual awareness. Duffy's first efforts include the sobering study "My Sisters the Whores" that is counterbalanced by her vision of the drab, imprisoned existence of young housewives in "A Woman's World": "Their lives, a mesh / / Of tiny incident, entrap and bind / Them." Elsewhere, in her "Women" sequence of poems, Duffy explores the burgeoning sexuality of girls dancing together and the repressed longings of love-starved spinster schoolteachers, where "Love is an outcast, beauty hides away / Behind a gymslip or a manly tie." The same early writings include other significant thematic devices, the poet using fairy-tale conventions and Greek legends to express personal and contemporary concerns. "Rapunzel" and "Ulysses" are notable examples of a method that Duffy uses more subtly in later collections to describe the overwhelming joys and pangs of love.

Love in its physical and spiritual forms is central to Duffy's writing and provides her with the core of her finest work. Its passion imbues the bulk of her poetry, with collections like *Lyrics for the Dog Hour, The Venus Touch,* and *Evesong* almost totally given over to an expression of its strength, its violence, and its ultimate fulfillment. Duffy presents herself as being caught helplessly in the grip of an awesome cataclysmic act, compared directly at times to a nuclear attack or to some kind of trench warfare: "And we renew our love / Under the whine of the guns." Liberated by forbidden pleasure to a paradisal state beyond the reach of others, she remains fearfully aware of her own vulnerability in the face of loss and separation, the pain rendered more bitter after the joys that have been shared: "I hoard now against our winter, / Pack in the black hole of my heart / And stamp down hard, / Words, looks to nourish / When I stir in the long sleep / Troubled by dreams / And all is bitter outside."

Classical allusions to legends and to musical and artistic masterpieces abound. Duffy and her beloved are hymned as Orpheus and Eurydice, Minotaur and labyrinth, while through their acts of passion the love goddess Venus, the liberated female of the Olympian age who serves as their spiritual ancestress, is continually invoked. Yet however ecstatic the transports, the poet retains a sense of proportion throughout, finding time to explore the old myths with a less than flattering eye, especially in her cynical commentary on the *Iliad* in "Helen and the Historians": "The whole affair was just a trick of trade / Paris not prince of course / but merchant chief. / Achilles, Patroclus two / banking firms; his rage / takeover bid; his death a crash." In other poems Duffy gives vent to self-mockery, deriding her mannish walk and big backside, claiming that "I have been / a bull in a porcelain shop trampling china roses." Imagining herself as a "beast" to the beloved's "beauty," she prepares once more for the bruising but desired encounter: "Waiting on love I flex / thews, thighs like a dancer / or boxer knowing / I will get as good as I give.

Other concerns intrude in *Memorials of the Quick and the Dead,* where Duffy looks outward to the world and its wrongs. In a series of hard, clear-cut verses she traces her origins in an Irish graveyard and attacks her own government for its neglect of writers and homeless children. The rule of the Greek colonels is condemned in "Antigone," while in "Lemonchic" the author mourns the death in space of the dog Laika. Duffy comments on the environmental problems of drought and Dutch elm disease and admits a sad kinship with Nigerian rebels whose execution she witnesses on her television screen: "Three thousand miles away / by satellite I mourn / the rest of their lives unborn / those islands of flesh and bone / mine / whatever they had done." Tributes to Benjamin Britten and Gracie Fields are offset by "Bestialry," with its fierce impassioned outcry against the cruelty of humans to other creatures, the author detailing the atrocities inflicted on rabbits and battery hens. Yet in the end it is to love and its healing power that Duffy returns, affirming in the latter part of *Memorials of the Quick and the Dead* and subsequently in "The Garland" section of *Collected Poems* her allegiance to the goddess: "But you brought me up in your worship / though I'm old and ridiculous too / to be panting after your favours / what else am I to do." The range of her poetry—from neat, poised classical verse to a loose, conversational style—the variety of subjects covered, and the pure, intense clarity of her vision lift her work above the ordinary, giving to it the quality of a personal testament.

—Geoff Sadler

DUGAN, Alan

Nationality: American. **Born:** Brooklyn, New York, 12 February 1923. **Education:** Queens College, New York; Olivet College, Michigan; Mexico City College, B.A. 1951. **Military Service:** U.S. Army Air Force during World War II. **Family:** Married to Judith Shahn. **Career:** Worked in advertising, publishing, and for a medical supply company; taught at Sarah Lawrence College, Bronxville, New York, 1967–71. Since 1971 staff member for poetry, Fine Arts Work Center, Provincetown, Massachusetts. **Awards:** Yale Series of Younger Poets award, 1961; Pulitzer Prize, 1962; National Book award, 1962; American Academy in Rome fellowship, 1962; Guggenheim fellowship, 1963, 1972; Rockefeller fellowship, 1966; Levinson prize (*Poetry,* Chicago), 1967; Shelley memorial award, 1982; Melville Cane award, 1984; American Academy award, 1985. **Address:** c/o Ecco Press, 26 West 17th Street, New York, New York 10011, U.S.A.

PUBLICATIONS

Poetry

General Prothalamion in Populous Times. Privately printed, 1961.
Poems. New Haven, Connecticut, Yale University Press, 1961.
Poems 2. New Haven, Connecticut, Yale University Press, 1963.
Poems 3. New Haven, Connecticut, Yale University Press, 1967.
Collected Poems. New Haven, Connecticut, Yale University Press, 1969; London, Faber, 1970.
Poems 4. Boston, Little Brown, 1974.
Sequence. Cambridge, Massachusetts, Dolphin, 1976.
New and Collected Poems 1961–1983. New York, Ecco Press, 1983.
Poems 6. New York, Ecco Press, 1989.

*

Critical Studies: Interview with Michael Ryan, in *Iowa Review* (Iowa City, Iowa), 4(3), 1973; "Alan Dugan: The Poetry of Surviv- al" by Robert Boyers, in his *Contemporary Poetry in America: Essays and Interviews*, New York, Schocken, 1974; "Christian Symbology in Alan Dugan's 'Morning Song,'" by Wayne McGinnis, in *Nassau Review* (Garden City, New York), 3(3), 1977; by David Wojahn, in *Western Humanities Review* (Salt Lake City, Utah), 38(3), autumn 1984; "'Pieces of Harmony': The Quiet Politics of Alan Dugan's Poetry" by John Gery, in *Politics and the Muse: Studies in the Politics of Recent American Literature,* edited by Adam J. Sorkin, Bowling Green, Popular, 1989.

*   *   *

Alan Dugan is a fine poet who has created a significant body of work while cultivating a confining style and exercising his caustic intelligence on a relatively narrow range of subjects. Though few critics get terribly excited about his work, most concede that it successfully inhabits the middle ground of experience that our best contemporary poets seem too loathe to admit. In Dugan, at least, if one is able to hope at all, one hopes to endure rather than to triumph. If one feels trapped, one will strive not for ultimate freedom and total independence but for the sensation of freedom—temporary, imper- fect, illusory. Dugan's spirit is best expressed in the conditional, which is to say that nothing he feels or thinks is very far removed from regret for what might have been. It has been generally accepted that Dugan is something of a moralist, if we understand a moralist to be someone who experiences convulsive fits of nausea whenever he remembers what he is and to what he has given his approval, if only by means of undisturbed acquiescence.

Dugan's is an intensely private, almost a claustrophobic, vision. His poems usually communicate small perceptions appropriate to the lives of small people, so that we listen not because of any glittering eye but because we feel we should. The voice that apprehends us is as earnest as any we might hope to encounter, and the combination of brittle surfaces and an underlying warmth is relentlessly imposing.

Dugan's poems have variety, but they might all be drawn together as a single long poem. The same alert but static sensibility is operant in all of them, and the speaker rarely indulges the sort of emotional extremism that might distinguish his more inspired from his more characteristically quotidian utterances. Particulars in the work are easily reducible to an elementary abstraction in which polarities are anxiously opposed until, under the wry focus of Dugan's imagination, they somehow coalesce. Alternatives become merely matters of perspective, and the wise man gradually learns that, as between one choice and another, we had best avoid choices altogether.

The predictable, low-keyed humor does little to mitigate the stinging venom of self-contempt that courses through so much of Dugan's work. His is a bitter eloquence. If the cadence is austere, it is rarely impoverished, and the muscular flow of his terse diction is rarely purchased at the expense of complexity. Dugan invites us to witness with him, without any redemptive qualification, the sordid spectacle of our common humiliation. It is a strangely unimpassioned witnessing, but the amusement of ironic detachment has much to recommend it. What Dugan fears most is the neutrality that predicts the death of the spirit, but more and more it appears to him that this is, indeed, his most authentic reality.

—Robert Boyers

DUGGAN, Laurie

Nationality: Australian. **Born:** Laurence James Duggan, Melbourne, 30 May 1949. **Education:** Monash University, Melbourne, B.A. 1976; Sydney University, 1973–74; Melbourne University since 1991 (Ph.D. in progress). **Career:** Lecturer in media studies, Swinburne College, 1976, and the Canberra College of Advanced Education, 1983; freelance scriptwriter, 1978–83; art critic, *The Times on Sun- day,* Melbourne, 1986–87; poetry teacher, Victoria University of Technology, Melbourne, 1994. **Awards:** Anne Elder award for a first book of poems, 1978; ANZ New Writing award, 1988; Wesley Michel Wright award, 1988.

PUBLICATIONS

Poetry

East: Poems 1970–1974. Melbourne, Rigmarole, 1976.
Under the Weather. Sydney, Wild and Woolley, 1978.
Adventures in Paradise. Adelaide, Experimental Art Foundation, 1982.
The Great Divide: Poems 1973–83. Sydney, Hale and Iremonger, 1985.
The Ash Range. Sydney, Picador, 1987.
All Blues. London, Northern Lights, 1989.
The Epigrams of Martial. Melbourne, Scripsi, 1989.
Blue Notes. Sydney, Picador, 1990.
Memorials. Adelaide, Little Esther, 1995.
Selected Poems. St. Lucia, University of Queensland Press, 1996.
New and Selected Poems, 1971–1993. St. Lucia, University of Queensland Press, 1996.

*

Critical Studies: *Topopoesis: Laurie Duggan's "The Ash Range"* by Philip Mead, Melbourne, Scripsi, 1988; "A Place in History: The Ash Range, Landscape and Identity" by Lawrence Bourke, in *West- erly* (Nedlands, Australia), 38(1), autumn 1993.

*   *   *

Laurie Duggan is one of a group of poets associated with Monash University in Melbourne, which in the 1960s was a center of student unrest and challenge. Other poets connected with this group are Alan Wearne and John A. Scott, both of whom have established strong claims to attention in extended book-length verse sequences.

Duggan is best known for his book-length collage of poetry and documentation, *The Ash Range* (1987), which won the Victoria Premier's award. It is a personal and historical exploration of Gippsland, home of his forebears. The book has a clear ancestry in precedents set by William Carlos Williams and Charles Olson in America, and Duggan contributes significantly to the adaptation of such precursors to an Australian context and tone. The tenor of quizzicality and fascination with the ruthlessness of settlement that displaced Aboriginal cultures brings the work into the Australian preoccupation with invasion and the largely unacknowledged guilt that falsified earlier records. Since the bicentenary of white settlement (invasion) in 1988, this has become one of the overriding subjects in Australian writing.

From the perspective of *The Ash Range* it is possible to reexamine Duggan's earlier volumes—*East: Poems 1970–1974* (1976), *Under the Weather* (1978), *Adventures in Paradise* (1982), and *The Great Divide* (1985). The early work is characterized by a playful and fanciful enjoyment of language and a determined refusal to be trapped in the serious. These qualities are characteristic of much writing of the so-called Generation of '68, but from the outset Duggan reveals real technical skill and finesse. His parodies of contemporary Australian poets are rare for their accurate pitch of voice, and they also reveal a poet with an intelligence lively enough to engage in such badinage with cultural predecessors. Throughout these volumes there is an anticipation of the techniques of organization that reach their summit in *The Great Divide:* juxtaposition; notation of minutiae of observation; a fine ear for the niceties of laconic Australian speech inflection, whether of city or country; and the skilled placement of words, lines, and phrases so as to have minimum text achieve maximum effect.

In 1989 Duggan published a highly acclaimed series of modern versions of Martial's epigrams that revealed him to be a challenger to the esteemed older Australian poet Peter Porter in this area. *Blue Notes* (1990) includes more versions from the Italian futurists and a return to Gippsland territoriality.

—Thomas W. Shapcott

DUHIG, Ian

Nationality: British. **Born:** 9 February 1954. **Education:** Leeds University, Yorkshire, 1974–77, B.A. 1977. **Family:** Married Jane Vincent; one son. **Career:** Hostel worker, Roma Drugs Project, London, 1977–79; hostel manager, Extern, Belfast, Northern Ireland, 1979–81, and Derwent House, Leeds, Yorkshire, 1981–84; director, Leeds Housing Concern, Leeds, Yorkshire, 1984–87; co-ordinator, Pgasfholme Project, York, Yorkshire, 1987–91. Since 1991 freelance writer. **Awards:** Winner, National Poetry Competition, 1987, for *Nineteen Hundred & Nineteen;* Writer's award, Arts Council of Great Britain, 1996, for *Nominies;* shortlisted for Whitbread and Forward awards, 1992; T.S. Eliot prize, 1996. **Address:** 16 Pasture Terrace, Leeds LS7 4QR, Yorkshire, England.

PUBLICATIONS

Poetry

The Bradford Count. Newcastle upon Tyne, Bloodaxe, 1991.
The Mersey Goldfish. Newcastle upon Tyne, Bloodaxe, 1995.
Nominies. Newcastle upon Tyne, Bloodaxe, 1998.

Other

Editor, *The Nightwatchgirl of the Moon.* Ilkley, Yorkshire, ILF Press, 1998.
Editor, *One.* Ilkley, Yorkshire, ILF Press, 1998.

*

Critical Studies: In *Public and Private in Contemporary British Poetry,* by Peter Porter, London, Vintage, 1995; in *Poetry Today,* by Anthony Thwaite, London, Longman, 1996.

Ian Duhig comments:

I write out of the experience of the Irish diaspora and so appear in anthologies in two countries (*Modern Irish Poetry,* ed. Patrick Crotty, Blackstaff, Northern Ireland, 1995, and also *The Penguin Book of Poetry since 1945,* ed. Crawford and Armitage). I attempt to link this with my work among homeless people, especially in my most recent book (*Nominies,* 1998). This gives me an excuse to roam the world and use all registers, including, I hope, humor.

*   *   *

Born in England of Irish ancestry, Ian Duhig brings to his work a keen sense of postcolonial irony. Steeped in history, his poems reveal the arrogance and deceit within the power dynamics of institutionalized religion, politics, and language. At times Duhig's historical references are overly obscure and poorly contextualized. Often, however, the poet achieves a provocative juxtaposition of Old World and postmodern views. His speakers are likely to be victims or outsiders: an exiled transsexual anarchist in revolutionary Mexico, Irish patriots caught in a maze of betrayals, or a Japanese mother starving during a wartime blockade. In ''From the Plague Journal,'' from *The Bradford Count,* the mother states simply,

I sold my son's thousand-stitch belt
for peaches and eggs which I mashed and strained,
mashed and strained. Still my children died . . .

More typically, however, Duhig grafts the detached and mocking point of view of the late twentieth century onto his historical figures. In ''The Irish Slave,'' for example, also in *The Bradford Count,* a priest kidnapped from Ireland and living in a sultan's palace compares his present life with the austerity that would have been his lot in Ireland and concludes, ''Castration has been a good career move.'' Similarly, ironic references pervade the speech of the disgraced court attendant who, in ''Note,'' from *The Mersey Goldfish,* relates that he was given

. . . an offer I couldn't refuse,
the chance of a new position. It was missionary
. . .
not as hard as the conversion of the Jews;
remote, but the word was leprosy was dropping off.

Duhig's irreverent tone is effective here in uncovering the hidden ugliness he sees in colonialist attitudes.

Conflicts over language also figure prominently in Duhig's poems. Several deal directly with the English suppression of Irish words or the inevitable mutability of common expressions. In ''Nothing Pie,'' from *Nominies,* the poet observes how his native Yorkshire speech differs from his Irish father's and from his own son's, while ''Talking God,'' from the same collection, relates a conversation between the deity and a Navajo ''code talker'' from World War II. When the Navajo asks, ''—What of the Dogfaces who ordered our ancestors into a land where nothing grew but shadows, to share insects and weave bird-traps from each other's hair, to lose the robe of dawn, the robe of blue sky, the robe of yellow evening light and the robe of darkness?'' God answers with ''—*Shit happens*.'' In this case Duhig's use of a *Forrest Gump*-like banality is at odds with the gravity and urgency of the subject.

Throughout his work Duhig displays an interest in vernacular forms, particularly the ballad and the song. Indeed, several pieces in *Nominies,* which itself is the Yorkshire term for children's chants, were originally conceived as part of a musical presentation. While not structurally complex, these poems use the seeming innocence of singsong rhythm and rhyme to accentuate the presence of evil in daily life. This can be seen, for example, in the title poem:

I've heard of the children poisoned,
I've heard of the children shot—
I've even heard some call this love
but I think not.

Hints of ancient alliterative verse patterns can also be found in Duhig's work, as in ''Brut,'' his version of the story of Helen of Troy in *The Mersey Goldfish-*

For horned Menelaus
the Greeks took Old Troy,
salted its vineyards,
slaughtered its folk,
poor innocent bastards

—or, less obviously, in ''Reforma Agraria,'' in *The Bradford Count,* in which

the light oil of the gun
like watchmaker's oil,
. . .
ran from the Lugers,
ran from Berettas,
down into the eyes
of wounded land-leaguers . . .

Though in these pieces Duhig uses a line break rather than a caesura to separate pairs of initial stresses and does not employ strict alliteration, the rhythmic toll of Old Saxon and Old Celtic verse remains.

Duhig's work can sometimes be cryptic, but it is often playful, and it is distinguished throughout by an acerbic wit. His explorations of power and conflict reveal a passion for language and truth.

—Elizabeth Shostak

DUNMORE, Helen

Nationality: British. **Born:** Yorkshire, 1952. **Education:** York University, B.A. in English 1973. **Family:** Married; one son, one daughter, and one stepson. **Career:** Has worked as a nursery teacher. Since 1979 full-time author. **Awards:** Poetry Book Society Choice; Poetry Book Society Recommendation, 1991, for *Short Days, Long Nights;* Alice Hunt Bartlett award; Orange prize for fiction, 1996. **Address:**

c/o Bloodaxe Books, P.O. 1SN, Newcastle upon Tyne NE99 1SN, England.

PUBLICATIONS

Poetry

The Apple Fall. Newcastle upon Tyne, Bloodaxe, 1983.
The Sea Skater. Newcastle upon Tyne, Bloodaxe, 1986.
The Raw Garden. Newcastle upon Tyne, Bloodaxe, 1988.
Short Days, Long Nights: New & Selected Poems. Newcastle upon Tyne, Bloodaxe, 1991.
Secrets (for children). London, Bodley Head, 1994.
Recovering A Body. Newcastle upon Tyne, Bloodaxe, 1994.
Bestiary. Newcastle upon Tyne, Bloodaxe, 1997.

Novels

Zennor in Darkness. Harmondsworth, England, Penguin, 1993.
Burning Bright. Harmondsworth, England, Penguin, 1994.
A Spell of Winter. Harmondsworth, England, 1995.
Talking to the Dead. Harmondsworth, England, Penguin, 1996.
Love of Fat Men. Harmondsworth, England, Penguin, 1997.
Your Blue-eyed Boy. Harmondsworth, England, Penguin, 1998.
With Your Crooked Heart. Harmondsworth, England, Penguin, 1999.

Other

Going to Egypt (for children). London, Random House, 1994.
In the Money (for children). London, Random House, 1995.
Amina's Blanket (for children). N.p., Reed Books, 1996.
Go Fox (for children). N.p., Transworld, 1996.
Fatal Error (for children). N.p., Transworld, 1996.
Allie's Apples (for children). N.p., Reed Books, 1997.
Great-Grandma's Dancing Dress (for children). Cambridge University Press, 1998.
Clyde's Leopard (for children). Cambridge University Press, 1998.
Brother Brother, Sister Sister (for children). N.p., Scholastic, 1999.
Allie's Rabbit (for children). N.p., Egmont Books, 1999.

*   *   *

Since her first collection of poems, *The Apple Fall,* appeared in 1983, Helen Dunmore has proved herself a prolific and versatile writer, publishing novels and children's verse as well as further volumes of poetry. *The Apple Fall* introduced a poet who, at thirty-one, was already clearly in possession of her own intense, humane, and individual voice. Dunmore's sensitivities respond acutely to a broad spectrum of concerns that runs from the political to the domestic, from the abstract to the anecdotal. Themes as diverse as recollections of Proust, Berlin in the last days of the wall, the development of a baby within her own body, or a man waiting for a heart operation all engage her creativity. More than most, perhaps, Dunmore's is a world in which sensation plays a central role:

It's not that I'm afraid,
but that I'm still gathering
the echoes of my five senses—

how far they've come with me, how far
they want to go on.

Dunmore frequently writes from a perspective that reverses the stereotypical viewpoint. A poem about a child escaping from bed to interrupt the adults watching television presents the writing of poetry as a mundane activity when contrasted with the child's exploration of its dreamworld:

. . . the nightly row of the typewriter
and piles of discontented paper by the table.
I make poetry common as floor washing

but still you wade in, thigh-deep in dreams
at nine-thirty, while we are doped
on one sofa, numb to excellent acting.

In *The Raw Garden* (1988) Dunmore aimed at producing an elaborately structured, thematically linked work. The poems discuss perceived ideas of the natural and unnatural in the context of landscape and, in her own words, are "intended to speak to, through, and even over each other." Wide, occasionally surreal leaps of the imagination come to Dunmore with sometimes disconcerting ease. There can be an almost cinematic abruptness to her changes of focus, though the technique often produces images of startling power. In "Permafrost" a close-up of "frozen things / snowdrops and Christmas roses" pulls back to "nuclear snowsuits bouncing on dust" and then

. . . moon-men lost on the moon
watching the earth's green flush

tremble and perish.

Recovering a Body (1994) is built around another community of concerns, this time those related directly to the body: "Sexuality, aging, death, reproduction." The title poem fantasizes about a woman waking in the morning to find her body gone and then recounts the various stratagems she employs to retrieve it. This poem and many of its companion pieces are a striking demonstration of Dunmore's sensitivity to nuance and her insight into these vital areas of human feeling. The shorter poems in particular convey intense emotion in language that eschews rhetoric in favor of economy and precision:

meet me where the fire
lights the bayou

watch my sweat shine
as I play for you.

It is for you I play
my voice leaping the flames,

if you don't come
I am nothing.

Dunmore is generally at her best when working on a relatively miniature scale. The creative territory she occupies is one of markedly fluid boundaries, and it may be because of this that her longer poems, with their sometimes unwieldy structures, can seem too improvisatory and discursive for their own good.

—Rivers Carew

DUNN, Douglas (Eaglesham)

Nationality: British. **Born:** Inchinnan, Renfrewshire, 23 October 1942. **Education:** Renfrew High School; Camphill School, Paisley; Scottish School of Librarianship; University of Hull, 1966–69, B.A. in English 1969. **Family:** Married 1) Lesley Balfour Wallace in 1964 (died 1981); 2) Lesley Jane Bathgate in 1985; one son and one daughter. **Career:** Library assistant, Renfrew County Library, Paisley, 1959–62, and Andersonian Library, Glasgow, 1962–64; assistant librarian, Akron Public Library, Ohio, 1964–66; librarian, Chemistry Department Library, University of Glasgow, 1966; assistant librarian, Brynmor Jones Library, 1969–71, and fellow in creative writing, 1974–75, University of Hull; fellow in creative writing, 1981–82, and honorary visiting professor, University of Dundee, 1987–89; writer-in-residence, University of New England, Armidale, New South Wales, and Scottish Arts Council-Australia Council Exchange fellow, 1984. Since 1991 professor of English, University of St. Andrews, and since 1993 director, St. Andrews Scottish Studies Institute. Poetry reviewer, *Encounter* magazine, London, 1971–78. **Awards:** Eric Gregory award, 1966; Scottish Arts Council award, 1970, 1984; Somerset Maugham award, 1972; Faber memorial prize, 1976; Hawthornden prize, 1982; Whitbread award, 1985, and Book of the Year award, 1986; Cholmondeley award, 1989. D.Litt.: University of Hull, 1996. LL D: University of Dundee, 1987. Fellow, Royal Society of Literature, 1981. **Agent:** Peters Fraser and Dunlop Group Ltd., Drury House, 34–43 Russell Street, London WC2B 5HA, England. **Address:** School of English, University of St. Andrews, St. Andrews, Fife KY16 9AL, Scotland.

PUBLICATIONS

Poetry

Terry Street. London, Faber, 1969; New York, Chilmark Press, 1973.
Corgi Modern Poets in Focus 1, with others, edited by Dannie Abse. London, Corgi, 1971.
Backwaters. London, The Review, 1971.
Night. London, Poem-of-the-Month Club, 1971.
The Happier Life. London, Faber, and New York, Chilmark Press, 1972.
Love or Nothing. London, Faber, 1974.
Barbarians. London, Faber, 1979.
St. Kilda's Parliament. London, Faber, 1981.
Europa's Lover. Newcastle upon Tyne, Bloodaxe, 1982.
Elegies. London, Faber, 1985.
Selected Poems 1964–1983. London, Faber, 1986.
Northlight. London, Faber, 1988.
New and Selected Poems 1966–1988. New York, Ecco Press, 1989.
Dante's Drum-Kit. London, Faber, 1993.
The Donkey's Ears. London, Faber, 2000.
The Year's Afternoon. London, Faber, 2000.

Recording: *Douglas Dunn and Philip Larkin,* Faber, 1984.

Plays

Screenplays (verse commentaries): *Early Every Morning,* 1975; *Running,* 1977; *Anon's People,* 1984; *Dressed to Kill,* 1992.

Radio Plays: *Scotsmen by Moonlight,* 1977; *Wedderburn's Slave,* 1980; *The Telescope Garden,* 1986; *Andromache,* adaptation of the play by Racine, 1989.

Television Plays: *Ploughman's Share,* 1979; *Anon's People,* 1984; *Dressed to Kill,* 1992.

Short Stories

Secret Villages. London, Faber, and New York, Dodd Mead, 1985.
Boyfriends and Girlfriends. London and Boston, Faber, 1995.

Other

Under the Influence: Douglas Dunn on Philip Larkin. Edinburgh, Edinburgh University Library, 1987.
Poll Tax, the Fiscal Fake: Why We Should Fight the Community Charge. London, Chatto and Windus, 1990.

Editor, *New Poems 1972–73.* London, Hutchinson, 1973.
Editor, "British Poetry Issue" of *Antaeus 12* (New York), 1973.
Editor, *A Choice of Byron's Verse.* London, Faber, 1974.
Editor, *Two Decades of Irish Writing.* Manchester, Carcanet, and Philadelphia, Dufour, 1975.
Editor, *What Is to Be Given: Selected Poems of Delmore Schwartz.* Manchester, Carcanet, 1976.
Editor, *The Poetry of Scotland.* London, Batsford, 1979.
Editor, *Poetry Supplement 1979.* London, Poetry Book Society, 1979.
Editor, *A Rumoured City: New Poets from Hull.* Newcastle upon Tyne, Bloodaxe, 1982.
Editor, *To Build a Bridge: A Celebration of Verse in Humberside.* Lincoln, Lincolnshire and Humberside Arts, 1982.
Editor, *Scotland, An Anthology.* New York, HarperCollins, 1991.
Editor, *Faber Book of Twentieth Century Scottish Poetry.* London, Faber, 1992.
Editor, *Oxford Book of Scottish Short Stories.* Oxford and New York, Oxford University Press, 1995.
Editor, *20th Century Scottish Poems.* London, Faber, 2000.

Translator, *Andromache,* by Racine. London, Faber, 1990.

*

Manuscript Collection: Brynmor Jones Library, University of Hull.

Critical Studies: *Reading Douglas Dunn* edited by R. Crawford and D. Kinlock, Edinburgh, Edinburgh University Press, 1992; *The Uses of the Commonplace in Contemporary British Poetry: Larkin, Dunn and Raine* by Jerzy Jarniewicz, Lodz, Poland, Wydawnictwo Uniwersyteto Lodzkiego, 1994; "The Englishman's Scottishman, or Radical Scotsman?: Reading Douglas Dunn in the Light of Recent Reappraisal of Philip Larkin" by Rebecca Smalley, in *Scottish Literary Journal* (Aberdeen, Scotland), 22(1), May 1995; "Secrets: On Translating Douglas Dunn's Elegies into German" by Evelyn Schlag, in *Forum for Modern Language Studies* (Scotland), 33(1), January 1997.

*   *   *

Douglas Dunn's first book, *Terry Street,* became famous almost before publication for its deft evocation of life in a working-class suburb of Hull. Bikes, dog shit, perms, cheap perfumes, "old men's long underwear /(Dripping) from sagging clotheslines"—these dour, unrhymed poems, full of lists, filled corners of pages in the *Times Literary Supplement,* the *New Statesman,* and *London Magazine* in the late 1960s. They seemed to inhabit part of Larkin's terrain.

Right from the start, however, Dunn had a way of lifting the end of a poem with an utterly surprising symbol that made the epithet "realist" inappropriate. The second part of the book confirmed that he would not be trapped in a post-Movement stance. Notice, for example, the daring rightness of the first two lines of "Love Poem" and the telling glance at time in the last line:

I live in you, you live in me;
We are two gardens haunted by each other.
Sometimes I cannot find you there,
There is only the swing creaking, that you have just left,
Or your favourite book beside the sundial.

The first line echoes with disturbing effect the petition for humble access in *The Book of Common Prayer:* "that we may evermore dwell in him, and he in us." The whole piece sets up a world of implication and nuance that goes way beyond the minimalist writing of the post-Movement poets of the time.

After some uncertainty with two transitional books, *Barbarians* confirmed that Dunn is one of the very best poets we have. An elegant, technically highly achieved verse is concerned with obscure people, like the inhabitants of Terry Street, who have dragged themselves out of their "holes in the ground somewhere" to wave their "quaint and terrible grudges" at their masters. A quasi-Marxist presence haunts many of the poems—"Gardeners," for example, with its angry ending, "The Student," and "An Artist Waiting in a Country House." "Transcendance" has this presence but echoes *Terry Street* in more than one way:

Fish-smelling bedroom of the gutted heart;
A port town built for departures, dockside bars—
Flat town, that's warm and sleazy, here's your art:
A climb on excrement to reach the stars.

St. Kilda's Parliament also looks at the problems of the obscure—"That absinthe drinker and his sober wife"—but more often than before through the eyes of art. Dunn's vision of the ordinary man has matured, and the rhythms have tightened, taking our attention from the first lines of the opening poem ("On either side of a rock-paved lane, / Two files of men are standing barefoot, / Bearded, waistcoated . . .") to the last poem, a partly self-mocking, sensuous meditation on Ratatouille, love, and the terrible danger implicit for us all in modern politics.

The candor of the poems in Dunn's *Elegies*—their unremitting look at the emotions following the death of a wife—makes them hard to read without tears. But it is art's job not to flinch, and Dunn's art never does. Neither should the reader:

They called me in. What moment worse
Than that young doctor trying to explain?
"It's large and growing." "What is?" "Malignancy."
"Why *there?* She's an artist!"

This is a poetry of, as Dunn says of his late wife, "honesty at all costs." It is also art's duty to transform, however, and Dunn ends the book by celebrating his wife and their love: "I call her name, / And it is very strange and wonderful."

The poem "Larksong" is an example of Dunn's Hardy- and Porter-haunted beauty of manner:

A laverock in its house of air is singing
May morning, May morning, and its trills drift
High on the flatland's abstract hill
In the down-below of England.
I am the aerial photograph it takes of me
On a sonar landscape
And it notates my sorrow
In Holderness, where summer frost
Melts from the green like her departing ghost.

Dunn, like Hardy before him, has always been interested in images of clothes. "All that time," he writes in *Terry Street,* "I had been in love with a coat," and later he observes himself infatuated with Billie Holiday and impersonating a sophisticate "in my white tuxedo." In *Elegies,* however, his poems talk of "empty, perfumed wardrobes" where ". . . once hung the silks and prints of 'If/Only', and the clothes she gave to her friends." *Elegies* is a commanding, wonderful book.

Northlight has a different richness, a resemblance to a genre painter's interest in rooms and their contents. *Dante's Drum-Kit* presents problems to those easily irritated by the overuse of Scottish dialect and a delight in the display of playful language gifts for their own sake. But its middle section contains moving poems expressing something that has always been implicitly present in Dunn's work—a profound, eloquent compassion for the underdogs in the fact of the cruelty of late twentieth-century British politics:

Not down-and-outs
Though some come close,
Nor layabouts
Trading pathos
For tea and bread
But simply poor
In this lowered epoch . . .

We are back in Terry Street, but Dunn is angrier now, the author of an attack on callous government fiscal policies. The sparer his language and forms, the clearer that anger comes across.

—Fred Sedgwick

DUNN, Stephen

Nationality: American. **Born:** New York City, 24 June 1939. **Education:** Hofstra University, Hempstead, New York, 1958–62, B.A. in history 1962; New School for Social Research, New York, 1964–66;

Syracuse University, New York, 1968–70, M.A. in creative writing 1970. **Military Service:** U.S. Army, 1962. **Family:** Married Lois Kelly in 1964; two daughters. **Career:** Professional basketball player for the Williamsport Billies, Pennsylvania, 1962–63; copywriter, National Biscuit Company, New York, 1963–66; assistant editor, Ziff-Davis publishers, New York, 1967–68; assistant professor of creative writing, Southwest Minnesota State College, Marshall, 1970–73. Associate professor, then professor, 1974–90, and since 1990 Trustee Fellow in the Arts, Stockton State College, New Jersey. Visiting poet, Syracuse University, 1973–74, and University of Washington, Seattle, winter 1980; adjunct professor of poetry, Columbia University, 1983–87. **Awards:** Academy of American Poets prize, 1970; National Endowment for the Arts fellowship, 1973, 1982, 1989; Bread Loaf Writers Conference Robert Frost fellowship, 1975; Theodore Roethke prize (*Poetry Northwest*), 1977; New Jersey Arts Council fellowship, 1979, 1983; Helen Bullis prize, 1982; Guggenheim fellowship, 1984; Levinson prize (*Poetry*), 1988; Oscar Blumenthal prize (*Poetry*), 1991; James Wright prize (*Mid-American Review*), 1993; American Academy of Arts & Letters award, 1994. **Agent:** Philip G. Spitzer Literary Agency, 111–25 76ᵗʰ Avenue, Forest Hills, New York 11375. **Address:** 445 Chestnut Neck Road, Port Republic, New Jersey 08241, U.S.A.

PUBLICATIONS

Poetry

Five Impersonations. Marshall, Minnesota, Ox Head Press, 1971.
Looking for Holes in the Ceiling. Amherst, University of Massachusetts Press, 1974.
Full of Lust and Good Usage. Pittsburgh, Carnegie Mellon University Press, 1976.
A Circus of Needs. Pittsburgh, Carnegie Mellon University Press, 1978.
Work and Love. Pittsburgh, Carnegie Mellon University Press, 1981.
Not Dancing. Pittsburgh, Carnegie Mellon University Press, and London, Feffer and Simons, 1984.
Local Time. New York, Quill, 1986.
Between Angels. New York, Norton, 1989.
Landscape at the End of the Century. New York, Norton, 1991.
New & Selected Poems: 1974–1994. New York, Norton, 1994.
Loosestrife: Poems. New York, Norton, 1996.
Winter at the Caspian Sea: Poems. Aiken, South Carolina, Palanquin, 1999.

Other

Walking Light: Essays & Memoirs. New York, Norton, 1993.
Riffs & Reciprocities: Prose Pairs. New York, Norton, 1998.

Editor, *A Cat of Wind, An Alibi of Gifts* (anthology of children's poetry). Trenton, New Jersey State Council on the Arts, 1977.
Editor, *Silence Has a Rough, Crazy Weather* (poems by deaf children). Trenton, New Jersey State Council on the Arts, 1979.

*

Critical Studies: "Four from Prospero" by David Wojahn, in *Georgia Review* (Athens, Georgia), 43(3), fall 1989; "Finding,

Discovering, Pursuing: Poets on Poetry'' by Sanford Pinsker, in *Gettysburg Review* (Gettysburg, Pennsylvania), 7(1), winter 1994; ''Precarious Balances: A Conversation with Stephen Dunn'' by David Elliott, in *Mid-American Review* (Bowling Green, Ohio), 15(1–2), 1995.

Stephen Dunn comments:

I write what I discover to be true or effective or moving in the act of writing. Then I rewrite for coherence and, ideally, beauty. Certain obsessions emerge. I have a vague idea what they are, but I do not wish to know them too consciously. I want the poem to emerge from my own imperatives and reach out to the reader, naturally, clearly, as if I had cut through all the sanctioned lies and was simply speaking.

*   *   *

The voice of Stephen Dunn's poems is sure, lyric, and comic, in language that is both intelligent and deceptively simple. Much of the joy of his poems arises from their insistence on the ''thisness'' of the body and a refusal to ignore its pleasures in the midst of awkwardness, even pain.

The characteristic speaker in a Dunn poem wants, like most of us, to wear his body naturally and pleasantly, though someone or something keeps reminding him that it is seldom possible to do so. In ''Modern Dance Class,'' for example, ''the instructor looks at me / the way gas station attendants / looks at tires whose treads are gone.'' The determined dancer, knowing that ''grace / is what occurs after technique / has been loved a long while / and then forgotten,'' tries hard to pull himself together. A reader's delight in such poems is a direct result of the poet's accurate rendering of his (and our) failure to accomplish that recovery.

Dunn has described the typical speaker in his poems as ''the normal man, gone public,'' the person whose ''private little efforts / to fulfill himself / are / not unlike yours, or anyone's.'' There is something approaching perfection in his ''inventive mixture of wit and pathos,'' as one reviewer has said. Happiness, after all, is perpetually there and not there,

> A state you must dare not enter
>   with hopes of staying . . .
>
> with its perfect bridge above
>   the crocodiles,
> and its doors forever open.

In ''Truck Stop: Minnesota,'' an early poem, the speaker struggles to feel at home in an inhospitable world. ''The waitress looks at my face as if it were a small tip,'' he says, trying to win a friendly response from a woman treated familiarly by other customers—truckers—who call her ''sweetheart . . . Honey. Doll.'' The poem ends with a familiar complaint, in a line that Dunn chose as the title for his second collection, ''I'm full of lust and good usage, lost here.''

Ordinary pleasures lead Dunn to ask unexpected questions, as in ''A Private Man Confronts His Vulgarities at Dawn.'' He walks the beach,

>   my cock
> rubbing against my pants
> in this public sun, these various doors

swinging in my chest . . .
I want to know how
to cherish all this,

and just how many debts
a body is allowed.

In Dunn's best poems the speaker's lust for life keeps him ill at ease among people with little or no appreciation for the small anxieties and delights of daily living. He remains wary, attentive both to an occasionally unfriendly world and to troublesome intrusions, like death. Throughout, the poems of love and recollection, such as ''Those of Us Who Think Who Know'' and ''Tenderness,'' are as beautiful in their rightness as the comic ones.

In collections that appear with a regularity Dunn has extended himself to new subjects, the subtle and not so subtle conflicts between men and women in *Local Time* and the lingering sense of spirituality in a secular world in *Between Angels*. ''Other angels have urged us / to change our lives,'' he writes in a characteristically offhand manner,

> but you seem to know
> we drift, stumbling
> toward even the smallest
>
> improvement.

Dunn asks and expects little of human nature. Nor does he take for granted the minor pleasures that ordinary people, ordinary lives are allowed.

For his lyricism to work, however, Dunn, like Robert Herrick, has to ignore significant corners of the world. Conflict and consummate evil remain at some distance. On occasion a hint of complacency undermines Dunn's claim on our attention. In the latter poems, for example, when he tries to extend himself to something beyond private experience, he occasionally loses his way. In ''When the Revolution Came,'' about the transformation in eastern Europe in 1989, he can only ask, ''Were we thinking of ourselves . . . And did we feel a little smug?''

Dunn's forte is a kind of comedy of manners in which fundamental or visible economic or political evils seldom intrude. ''Altruism,'' he writes in ''Mon Semblable,'' ''is for those / who can't endure their desires.'' Is it for no one else?

—Michael True

DURCAN, Paul

Nationality: Irish. **Born:** Dublin, 16 October 1944. **Education:** Gonzaga College, Dublin; University College, Cork, 1971–74, B.A. (honors) in archaeology and medieval history. **Family:** Married Nessa O'Neill in 1969 (separated 1983); two daughters. **Career:** Poet-in-residence, The Frost Place, Franconia, New Hampshire, 1985; writer-in-residence, Trinity College, Dublin, 1990. Founder, with Martin Green, *Two Rivers* literary magazine, 1969; member, Aosdána. **Awards:** Patrick Kavanagh award, 1975; Irish Arts Council bursary, 1976, 1980; Irish-American Cultural Institute award, 1989; Whitbread award for poetry, 1990. **Address:** 14 Cambridge Avenue, Ringsend, Dublin 4, Ireland.

PUBLICATIONS

Poetry

Endsville, with Brian Lynch. Dublin, New Writers Press, 1967.
O Westport in the Light of Asia Minor. Dublin, Anna Rivia, 1975; revised edition, London, Harvill, 1995.
Teresa's Bar. Dublin, Gallery Press, 1976; revised edition, 1986.
Sam's Cross. Dublin, Profile Poetry, 1978.
Jesus, Break His Fall. Dublin, Raven Arts Press, 1980.
Ark of the North. Dublin, Raven Arts Press, 1982.
The Selected Paul Durcan, edited by Edna Longley. Belfast, Blackstaff Press, 1982.
Jumping the Train Tracks with Angela. Dublin, Raven Arts Press, 1983.
The Berlin Wall Café. Belfast, Blackstaff Press, 1985; London, Harvill Press, 1995.
Going Home to Russia. Belfast, Blackstaff Press, 1987.
Jesus and Angela. Belfast, Blackstaff Press, 1988.
In the Land of Punt. Dublin, Clashganna Mills Press, 1988.
Daddy, Daddy. Belfast, Blackstaff Press, 1990.
Crazy about Women. Dublin, National Gallery of Ireland, 1991.
A Snail in My Prime. London, Harvill Collins, 1993; New York, Viking Penguin, 1995.
Give Me Your Hand. London, MacMillan, 1994.
Christmas Day, with *A Goose in the Frost.* London, Harvill, 1996.
Greetings to Our Friends in Brazil: One Hundred Poems. London, Harvill, 1999.

Other

At the Edge of the Edge of Mark Joyce. Dublin, Green On Red Gallery, 1998.

*

Critical Studies: "The Permanent City: The Younger Irish Poets" by Gerald Dawe, in *The Irish Writer and the City,* edited by Maurice Harmon, Buckinghamshire, Smythe, and Totowa, New Jersey, Barnes and Noble, 1984; "Masks and Voices: Dramatic Personas in the Poetry of Paul Durcan" by Kathleen McCracken Gahern, in *Canadian Journal of Irish Studies* (Saskatoon, Canada), 13(1), June 1987; "Poetic Forms and Social Malformations" by Edna Longley, in *Tradition and Influence in Anglo-Irish Poetry,* edited by Terence Brown and Nicholas Grene, Totowa, New Jersey, Barnes and Noble, 1989; *The Kilfenora Teaboy: A Study of Paul Durcan* edited by Colm Toibin, Dublin, New Island, 1996; "Ekphrasis and Textual Consciousness" by Elizabeth Bergmann Loizeaux, in *Word & Image* (Philadelphia, Pennsylvania), 15(1), January-March 1999.

*   *   *

Paul Durcan has emerged as the most dynamic, distinctive, and urgent voice in contemporary Irish poetry. His voice has become so rooted in southern Irish experience that one forgets his years of exile and obscurity. His earlier poetic years were spent wandering London looking for work, eventually editing the literary magazine *Two Rivers.* His years in Cork, fathering two children and studying at the university, were spent in the same hermetic privacy. Yet he was writing all the time. In 1985, eighteen years after publishing his first

book, he published *The Berlin Wall Café.* He had finally reached a wide and appreciative audience. The core of the collection was a group of poems celebrating a marriage that had just ended. Poems like "The Jewish Bride," "Raymond of the Rooftops," and "The Pieta's Over" had a profound effect on those who read them:

> it is Easter all over our lives:
> The revelation of our broken marriage, and its resurrection;
> The breaking open of the tomb, and the setting free . . .

Durcan laid bare the punctured flesh of relationships. The poems were full of the energy of human conflict, an energy of integrity because of the poet's self-loathing and defense of the beloved: This exposure of the purely personal—personal suffering without the camouflage of myth or evasiveness of metaphor—was new in Irish poetry. There was neither Leda nor the Swan, Diarmuid nor Grainne, but the named human principals involved. A number of critics reacted angrily to this kind of poetry. Yet Durcan had spent twenty years perfecting his narrative gift, and the charged narratives of *The Berlin Wall Café* came at the end of a long line of determined narrative clusters in five previous books. In a series of intense monologues over many years he had sharpened his own sensibility and trained himself as a pensive witness: "Now he will grope back into the abode and crouch down; / Another dry holocaust in the urban complex over" or "And I think of all the nationalities of Israel / And of how each always clings to his native hat, / His priceless and moveable roof . . ."

The cadence of Durcan's later poems, his ability to create monologues that seem like the product of eavesdropping, is present in smaller moments in the earlier poems. Much has been made of Durcan's surrealism as well as his capacity for outrageous description and hyperbole. Yet he himself has said that surrealism is too restrictive a category: "Surrealism was a technique for a short period of history; I don't think I'm using technique at all. I prefer to think of it as metamorphosis." His poems often begin in a bland narrative manner, as in a provincial newspaper report, and then undergo metamorphosis:

> When you analyse it, like Dr. Ronan W,
> You can see that she and me—
> That we're quite a pair of trapeze artists, the pair of us,
> Pipistrelles on bars—the city falling down all around us.

It is in the ordinary places—pubs, railway stations, courtrooms, and kitchens—that a point of departure is reached. Durcan often uses the banal Hemingway tone of cables to dampen our expectations and create room for conflict. Like the Cork poet Patrick Galvin, who employed brilliant theater tricks in a previous generation, Durcan sometimes uses outrageous titles like "Archbishop of Kerry to Have an Abortion" or "Wife Who Smashed Television Gets Jail" to create a mood and grab attention. In his poetry he has absorbed all of the pathos and drama of Nell McCafferty's famous *Irish Times* column "In the Eyes of the Law," which was so influential in the 1970s:

> A forty-two-year-old parish priest—Fr. Francey Mulholland—
> Was charged yesterday in the Circuit Criminal Court
> With not wearing a condom, and with intent
> To cause an unwanted pregnancy.

But what Durcan has created is a unique body of work, entirely personal and forged out of an area where traditionalists would never dare to tamper. He has allowed the culture of the Irish south to intrude upon his life, and, even when dealing with the most painful personal crisis, he has created ripples that wash against Irish society in general.

—Thomas McCarthy

DYLAN, Bob

Nationality: American. **Born:** Robert Allen Zimmerman in Duluth, Minnesota, 24 May 1941. **Education:** University of Minnesota, Minneapolis, 1959–60. **Family:** Married Sara Lowndes in 1965 (divorced 1977), three sons and two daughters. **Career:** Composer and performer. **Awards:** Emergency Civil Liberties Committee Tom Paine award, 1963; Grammy award, 1980, 1993; American Society of Composers, Authors, and Publishers Founder's award, 1986; Légion de l'Ordre des Arts et Lettres (France), 1990; Lifetime Achievement award, National Academy of Recording Arts and Sciences, 1991; Arts award, Dorothy and Lillian Gish Prize Trust, 1997; Lifetime Achievement award, John F. Kennedy Center honors, 1997; 3 Grammy awards, National Academy of Recording Arts and Sciences, for Album of the Year, Best Male Rock Performance, and Best Contemporary Folk Album, 1998, for *Time out of Mind*. Named to the Rock 'n' Roll Hall of Fame, Cleveland, Ohio, 1988. D. Mus.: Princeton University, New Jersey, 1970. **Address:** c/o Jeff Rosen, P.O. Box 870, Cooper Station, New York, New York 10276, U.S.A.

PUBLICATIONS

Poetry

Tarantula. New York, Macmillan, 1966.
Approximately Complete Works. Amsterdam, De Bezige Bij-Thomas Rap, 1970.
Poem to Joanie. London, Aloes Press, 1972.
Words. London, Cape, 1973.
Writings and Drawings. New York, Knopf, and London, Cape, 1973.
The Songs of Bob Dylan 1966–1975. New York, Knopf, 1976.
XI Outlined Epitaphs, and Off the Top of My Head. London, Aloes Seola, 1981 (?).
Lyrics 1962–1985. New York, Knopf, 1985; London, Cape, 1986.

Scores: *Oh Mercy,* New York, Amsco, 1989; *Fingerpicking Dylan,* London and New York, Amsco, 1990; *Bob Dylan Anthology,* New York, Amsco, 1990; *Bob Dylan Rock Score,* London and New York, Wise, 1990; *Under the Red Sky,* New York, Amsco, 1990; *Classic Dylan,* New York, Amsco, 1991; *The Harp Styles of Bob Dylan,* London and New York, Amsco, 1992; *Bob Dylan,* New York, Amsco, 1993; *The Very Best,* New York, Amsco, 1993; *The Songs of Bob Dylan: From 1966 through 1975,* New York, Knopf/ Cherry Lane, 1994; *Bob Dylan's Greatest Hits,* New York, Amsco, 1994; *World Gone Wrong,* New York, Amsco, 1994; *Greatest Hits, Songtab Edition, Volume 2,* New York, Amsco, 1999.

Recordings: *Bob Dylan,* Columbia, 1962; *The Freewheelin' Bob Dylan,* Columbia, 1963; *The Times They Are A-Changin',* Columbia, 1964; *Another Side of Bob Dylan,* Columbia, 1964; *Bringing It All Back Home,* Columbia, 1965; *Highway 61 Revisited,* Columbia, 1965; *Blonde on Blonde,* Columbia, 1966; *Bob Dylan's Greatest Hits,* Columbia, 1967; *John Wesley Harding,* Columbia, 1968; *Nashville Skyline,* Columbia, 1969; *Self Portrait,* Columbia, 1970; *New Morning, Columbia,* 1970; *Bob Dylan's Greatest Hits, vol. 2,* Columbia, 1971; *Dylan,* Columbia, 1973; incidental music for the film *Pat Garrett and Billy the Kid,* 1973; *Planet Waves,* Asylum, 1974; *Before the Flood,* Asylum, 1974; *Blood on the Tracks,* Columbia, 1975; *The Basement Tapes,* CBS, 1975; *Desire,* Columbia, 1976; *Hard Rain,* CBS, 1976; *Masterpieces,* CBS/ Sony, 1978; *Street Legal,* CBS, 1978; *Bob Dylan at Budokan,* Columbia, 1979; *Slow Train Coming,* Columbia, 1979; *Saved,* Columbia, 1980; *Shot of Love,* Columbia, 1981; *Infidels,* Columbia, 1983; *Real Live,* Columbia, 1984; *Empire Burlesque,* Columbia, 1985; *Biograph,* Columbia, 1985; *Knocked Out Loaded,* Columbia, 1986; *Dylan & The Dead,* Columbia, 1987; *Hearts of Fire,* Columbia, 1987; *Down in the Groove,* Columbia, 1988; *Emotionally Yours,* EMI, 1988; *Oh Mercy,* Columbia, 1989; *The Songs of Bob Dylan,* Start, 1989; *All the Way Down to Italy,* Templar, 1991; *The Bootleg Series, vols. 1–3,* Columbia, 1991; *Good As I Been to You,* Columbia, 1992; *Hammersmith Highlights,* One Over the Gate, 1993; *Oh Mercy,* Columbia, 1989; *Bob Dylan and Johnny Cash,* Yellow Dog, 1994; *Bob Dylan's Greatest Hits, vol. 3,* Columbia, 1994; *MTV Unplugged,* Columbia, 1995; *Time out of Mind,* Columbia, 1997; *Bob Dylan's Greatest Hits, vol. 2,* Columbia, 1999.

Other

Bob Dylan in His Own Words, compiled by Miles, edited by Pearce Marchbank. London, Omnibus Press, and New York, Quick Fox, 1978.
Save!: The Gospel Speeches of Bob Dylan. Madras and New York, Hanuman Books, 1990.
Drawn Blank. New York, Random House, 1994.

*

Bibliography: *Bob Dylan, American Poet and Singer: An Annotated Bibliography and Study Guide of Sources and Background Materials, 1961–1991,* Greenburg, Pennsylvania, Eadmer Press, 1991; *Bob Dylan: A Bio-Bibliography* by William McKeen, Westport, Connecticut, Greenwood Press, 1993; *Bob Dylan: A Descriptive, Critical Discography and Filmography, 1961–1993* by John Nogowski, Jefferson, North Carolina, McFarland, 1995.

Critical Studies: *Bob Dylan: A Retrospective* edited by Craig McGregor, New York, Morrow, 1972, revised edition, London, Angus and Robertson, 1980; *Bob Dylan* by Anthony Scaduto, New York, New American Library, 1973; *Rolling Thunder Logbook* by Sam Shepard, New York, Viking Press, 1977, London, Penguin, 1978; *Bob Dylan: An Illustrated History* by Robert Alexander, London, Elm Tree, 1978; *Bob Dylan: His Unreleased Works* by Paul Cable, London, Scorpion-Dark Star, 1978, New York, Associated Music, 1980; *The Art of Bob Dylan, Song and Dance Man* by Michael Gray, London, Hamlyn, and New York, St. Martin's Press, 1981; *Twenty Years of Recording: The Bob Dylan Reference Book* by Michael Korgsgaard, Copenhagen, Scandinavian Institute for Rock Research, 1981; *Bob Dylan: From a Hard Rain to a Slow Train* by Tim Dowley, Tunbridge Wells, Kent, Midas, 1982; *Voice without Restraint: A Study of Bob Dylan's Lyrics and Their Background* by John Herdman, Edinburgh, Harris, and New York, Delilah, 1982; *Performed Literature: Words and Music by Bob Dylan* by Betsy

Bowden, Bloomington, Indiana University Press, 1982; *Blood on the Tracks: The Story of Bob Dylan* by Chris Rowley, New York, Proteus, 1983; *A Darker Shade of Pale: A Backdrop to Bob Dylan* by Wilfrid Mellers, London, Faber, 1984, New York, Oxford University Press, 1985; *Dylan* by Jonathan Cott, New York, Doubleday, and London, Vermilion, 1984; *Bob Dylan: Escaping on the Run* by Aidan Day, Bury, Wanted Man, 1984, and *Jokerman: Reading the Lyrics of Bob Dylan* by Day, Oxford and New York, Blackwell, 1988; *The Bible in the Lyrics of Bob Dylan* by Bert Cartwright, Bury, Wanted Man, 1985; *No Direction Home: The Life and Music of Bob Dylan* by Robert Shelton, London, New English Library, 1986; *Jokermen and Thieves: Bob Dylan and the Ballad Tradition* by Nick De Somogyi, Bury, Wanted Man, 1986; *Dylan: A Biography* by Bob Spitz, New York, McGraw Hill, 1988; *Dylan: Stolen Moments*, Romford, Wanted Man, 1988, and *Dylan: Behind the Shades*, London, Penguin, 1992, both by Clinton Heylin; *Performing Artist: The Music of Bob Dylan 1960–1973* (vol. 1) by Paul Williams, Lancaster, Pennsylvania, Underwood Miller, 1990; The *Dylan Companion* edited by Elizabeth Thomson and David Gutman, London, Macmillan, 1990; *Bob Dylan: Performing Artist* by Paul Williams, London, Omnibus, 1990; *Oh No! Not Another Bob Dylan Book* by Patrick Humphries, Brentwood, Square One, 1991; *Bob Dylan: A Portrait of the Artist's Early Years* by Daniel Kramer, N.p., Plexus, 1991; *Bob Dylan: Performing Artist: The Middle Years, 1974–1986,* Novato, California, Underwood-Miller, 1992; *Hard Rain: A Dylan Commentary* by Tim Riley, New York, Vintage Books, 1992; *Wanted Man: In Search of Bob Dylan* by John Bauldie, London, Penguin, 1992; *The Bob Dylan Concordance* by Steve Michel, Grand Junction, Colorado, Rolling Tomes, 1992; *Bob Dylan* by Jay Allen Sanford, San Diego, California, Revolutionary Comics, 1992; *Dylan: A Man Called Alias* by Richard Williams, London, Bloomsbury, 1992; *Jewels & Binoculars* by Phil Bowen, Exeter, Stride/Westwords, 1993; *The Cracked Bells: A Guide to Tarantula* by Robin Witting, Scunthorpe, Exploding Rooster Books, 1993; *Bob Dylan* by Susan Richardson, New York, Chelsea House, 1995; ''Methane Emissions'' by David Partenheimer, in *McNeese Review* (Lake Charles, Louisiana), 34, 1995–96; '''Read Books, Repeat Quotations': A Note on Possible Conradian Influences on Bob Dylan's 'Black Diamond Bay''' by Allan H. Simmons, in *The Conradian* (London), 20(1–2), spring-autumn 1995; ''Synergies and Reciprocities: The Dynamics of Musical and Professional Interaction between the Beatles and Bob Dylan'' by Ian Inglis, in *Popular Music and Society,* 20(4), winter 1996; ''(Pass through) The Mirror Moment and Don't Look Back: Music and Gender in a Rockumentary'' by Susan Knobloch, in *Feminism and Documentary,* edited by Diane Waldman and Janet Walker, Minneapolis, University of Minnesota Press, 1999.

Theatrical Activities: Actor: **Films**—*Don't Look Back,* 1965; *Eat the Document,* 1966; *Pat Garrett and Billy the Kid,* 1973; *Renaldo and Clara,* 1978; *Hearts of Fire,* 1987.

*   *   *

Bob Dylan's lyrics show the influence of a remarkably eclectic range of styles, from the blues, folk songs, and the American popular song to the Bible and symbolist and modernist poetry. His integration of these influences is unparalleled. Dylan has never sacrificed the musical side of his inspiration; his is a song-poetry and is written not to an accentual syllabic but to a strongly accentual meter, supported by a sophisticated sense of rhyme. At the same time he has repeatedly demonstrated that songs may bear the same load of meaning as conventional poetry. His career has been marked by the relentless adoption and abandonment of different lyrical and musical stances, so that looking back over his career one sees a bewildering series of lyric identities. As far as it is possible to distinguish them, his main themes—often overlapping in the same song—are social and political commentary, love, religion, and the nature of personal identity.

First there was the Dylan whose political lyrics helped galvanize the New Left in the early 1960s. This was the Dylan who extended the ironic wit and gravity of the talking blues form in ''Talkin' World War III Blues'' (*The Freewheelin' Bob Dylan*) or who wrote a finely constructed piece on the murder of a Baltimore waitress in ''The Lonesome Death of Hattie Carroll'' (*The Times They Are A-Changin'*). In songs on his second album of 1964 (*Another Side of Bob Dylan*) he began to show a distinct unease with direct social and political statement, and the 1965 album *Bringing It All Back Home*—which includes ''Mr. Tambourine Man,'' an excellent piece on the nature of poetic inspiration—marks Dylan's decisive movement into a lyric mode characterized by indirection and obscurity. This was a mode also dominating, in different forms, *Highway 61 Revisited,* which includes ''Desolation Row,'' a highly allusive reading of personal and cultural identity; *Blonde on Blonde,* which has ''Visions of Johanna,'' one of Dylan's most surrealistic lyrics, dealing with the question of subjectivity; and *John Wesley Harding,* which reveals Dylan concentrating on vividly drawn and peculiarly compact narratives.

After these four, frequently lyrically recondite albums Dylan reemphasized, as he was to do at periodic intervals, his place within the tradition of American popular music by recording a set of almost sublimely banal country songs (*Nashville Skyline*) and a group of cover versions of other people's songs on an album ironically titled *Self Portrait.* He then just kept on changing. By 1975 he had released *Blood on the Tracks,* which investigates love and personal identity in a series of complex and elusive narratives distinguished as much by what they leave out as by what they contain. Two more albums, *Desire* and *Street Legal,* show him experimenting further with modernist effects, particularly in ''Isis'' on *Desire* and ''Changing of the Guards'' on *Street Legal.* By the end of the 1970s, however, Dylan was to adopt yet another verbal register when he began recording three explicitly Christian albums(from *Slow Train Coming* to *Shot of Love*), all of which are charged by insecurity as much as by a security of vision.

Along with shifting personae, themes, and tones there are, of course, reinterpreted consistencies in Dylan's lyric concerns. There is the reiterated acuity and severity of his writing about love and relationships, for instance, from the sharply straightforward ''Positively 4th Street'' to the sharp but more arcane manner of the dramatic monologue ''Idiot Wind'' from *Blood on the Tracks.* Another of Dylan's recurrent themes is his uneasy preoccupation with apocalypse. Even his work of the early 1960s distanced itself from the naively optimistic millenarianism of the times. In ''A Hard Rain's A-Gonna Fall'' (*The Freewheelin' Bob Dylan*), for example, he drew simultaneously on both the ballad tradition and the Bible to compose a picture of a world on the verge of Armageddon. But the song merely warns of the ''hard rain'' that will fall like the pestilences in Revelation. Unlike Revelation, however, there is no machinery of renovation to offset the doom. A comparable kind of darkness underlies many of Dylan's more complicated songs of the mid-1960s. In ''Desolation Row'' the state of Western culture is envisaged in terms of the voyage of the *Titanic:* ''Praise be to Nero's Neptune / The

Titanic sails at dawn.'' Here the Neptune belonging to the drowned passengers of the *Titanic* also belongs to Nero, who presided over Rome while it burned. The end of an overproud culture is to come to an apocalyptic conflux of water and fire.

The dominant tendency of Dylan's use of apocalyptic imagery in the 1960s—to express apocalyptic despair—shadows his use of similar imagery in his later songs. The religious lyrics identify the possibility of an ultimate hope, but the Christian lyrics never hold such perspectives simply or easily. The closing lines of ''Jokerman,'' from *Infidels,* again recall Revelation (''a woman . . . upon a scarlet colored beast'') as they picture the birth of an Antichrist. But in the final verse ultimate outcomes are left radically uncertain as the figure of the Jokerman, the questionable spirit of human nature, responds with an ambiguous lack of response:

> It's a shadowy world, skies are slippery gray,
> A woman just gave birth to a prince today and dressed him in
>   scarlet.
> He'll put the priest in his pocket, put the blade to the heat,
> Take the motherless children off the street
> And place them at the feet of a harlot.

> Oh, Jokerman, you know what he wants,
> Oh, Jokerman, you don't show any response.

Apocalyptic tonalities reappear on Dylan's 1989 album *Oh Mercy* in a song of reflection on past life and present circumstance: ''It's the last temptation, the last account, / The last time you might hear the Sermon on the Mount, / The last radio is playing . . .'' It is a sense of urgency like this that fires Dylan's best lyrics, whatever their subject.

One of the greatest of Dylan's albums, the 1997 *Time out of Mind* explores the experience of aging, the experience of no longer being young and of yet still being driven by the harrowing energies of love. The urgency of the album is founded in a very personal sense of death bearing down (''It's not dark yet, but it's getting there''). But despair is not given free rein. The last song of the collection, ''Highlands,'' alludes to and massively elaborates and complicates Robert Burns's ''My Heart's in the Highlands.'' Whereas Burns looks back nostalgically to a lost ideal, Dylan's future-oriented lyric uses the image of the Highlands to suggest a condition yet to be achieved: ''There's a way to get there, and I'll figure it out somehow / But I'm already there in my mind / And that's good enough for now.''

—Aidan Day

E

EATON, Charles Edward

Nationality: American. **Born:** Winston-Salem, North Carolina, 25 June 1916. **Education:** Duke University, Durham, North Carolina, 1932–33; University of North Carolina, Chapel Hill, 1933–36, B.A. 1936 (Phi Beta Kappa); Princeton University, New Jersey, 1936–37; Harvard University Cambridge, Massachusetts, 1938–40, M.A. in English 1940. **Family:** Married Isabel Patterson in 1950. **Career:** Instructor, Ruiz Gandia School, Poncé, Puerto Rico, 1937–38; instructor in creative writing, University of Missouri, Columbia, 1940–42; vice consul, American Embassy, Rio de Janeiro, Brazil, 1942–46; professor of creative writing, University of North Carolina, 1946–52. Art critic and organizer of art shows. **Awards:** Bread Loaf Writers Conference, Robert Frost fellowship, 1941; Boulder, Colorado, Writers Conference fellowship, 1942; Ridgely Torrence memorial award, 1951; Gertrude Boatwright Harris award, 1955; *Arizona Quarterly* award, 1956, 1975, 1977, 1979, 1982; Roanoke-Chowan award, 1970, 1987, 1991; Oscar Arnold Young award, 1971; New England Poetry Club Golden Rose, 1972; O. Henry award, for fiction, 1972; Alice Fay di Castagnola award, 1974; Arvon Foundation award, 1980; *Hollins Critic* award, 1984; Brockman award, 1984, 1986; *Kansas Quarterly* award, 1987; North Carolina literature award, 1988; Fortner award, 1993. D.Litt.: St. Andrews College, 1998. **Membership:** American Academy of Poets. **Address:** 808 Greenwood Road, Chapel Hill, North Carolina 27514, U.S.A.

PUBLICATIONS

Poetry

The Bright Plain. Chapel Hill, University of North Carolina Press, 1942.
The Shadow of the Swimmer. New York, Fine Editions Press, 1951.
The Greenhouse in the Garden. New York, Twayne, 1956.
Countermoves. New York and London, Abelard Schuman, 1963.
On the Edge of the Knife. New York and London, Abelard Schuman, 1970.
The Man in the Green Chair. South Brunswick, New Jersey, A.S. Barnes, and London, Yoseloff, 1977.
Colophon of the Rover. South Brunswick, New Jersey, and New York, A.S. Barnes, and London, Thomas Yoseloff, Ltd., 1980.
The Thing King. New York, Cornwall, 1983.
The Work of the Wrench. New York, Cornwall, 1985.
New and Selected Poems 1942–1987. New York, Cornwall, 1987.
A Guest on Mild Evenings. New York, Cornwall, 1991.
The Country of the Blue. New York, Cornwall, 1994.
The Fox and I. New York, Cornwall, 1996.
The Scout in Summer. New York, Cornwall, 1999.
The Jogger by the Sea. New York, Cornwall, 2000.

Play

Sea Psalm (produced Chapel Hill, North Carolina, 1933). Published in *North Carolina Drama,* Richmond, Virginia, Garrett and Massie, 1956.

Novel

A Lady of Pleasure. New York, Cornwall, 1993.

Short Stories

Write Me from Rio. Winston-Salem, North Carolina, John F. Blair, 1959.
The Girl from Ipanema. Lunenburg, Vermont, North Country, 1972.
The Case of the Missing Photographs. South Brunswick, New Jersey, A.S. Barnes, 1978.
New and Selected Stories, 1959–1989. New York, Cornwall, 1989.

Other

Charles and Isabel Eaton Collection of America Paintings. Chapel Hill, University of North Carolina, 1970.
Karl Knaths. Washington, Connecticut, Shiver Mountain Press, 1971.
Karl Knaths: Five Decades of Painting. Washington, D.C., International Exhibitions Foundation, 1973.
Robert Broderson: Paintings and Graphics. Washington, Connecticut, Shiver Mountain Press, 1975.

*

Manuscript Collections: (verse) Southern Historical Collection, University of North Carolina, Chapel Hill; (prose) Mugar Memorial Library, Boston University.

Critical Studies: By Louis Untermeyer, in *Yale Review* (New Haven, Connecticut), winter 1944; by Robert Hillyer, in *New York Times Book Review,* 22 July 1951; ''The Poetry of Charles Edward Eaton'' by W.W. Davidson, in *Georgia Review* (Athens), spring 1953; by Gerard P. Meyer, in *Saturday Review* (New York), 31 March 1956; in *Booklist* (Chicago), 1 May 1956; by May Swenson, in *Poetry* (Chicago), March 1957; ''The Greenhouse in the Garden'' by William Carlos Williams, in *Arizona Quarterly* (Tucson), spring 1957; Wallace Fowlie, in *New York Times Book Review,* 12 May 1963; by John Engels in *Poetry* (Chicago), September 1963; by F.C. Flint, in *Virginia Quarterly Review* (Charlottesville), autumn 1963; ''Betwixt Tradition and Innovation'' by Robert D. Spector, in *Saturday Review* (New York), 26 December 1970; ''The Crisis of Regular Forms'' by John T. Irwin, in *Sewanee Review* (Tennessee), winter 1973; ''The Shining Figure: Poetry and Prose of Charles Edward Eaton'' by Dave Smith, in *Meanjin* (Melbourne), summer 1974; Robert Miola, in *Commonweal* (New York), 18 August 1978; by M.L. Hester, in *Southern Humanities Review* (Auburn, Alabama), fall 1979 and fall 1981; by John Hollander, in *Yale Review* (New Haven, Connecticut), autumn 1983; by Walter Shear, in *Midwest Quarterly* (Pittsburg, Kansas), summer 1989; by Harold Witt, in *The Chariton Review* (Kirksville, Missouri), spring 1990 and fall 1992; by Cynthia Wong, in *The Cream City Review* (Milwaukee, Wisconsin), summer 1990; in *The Arts Journal* (Asheville, North Carolina), June 1990, in *Paintbrush* (Kirksville, Missouri), spring 1992, and '''The Machete Working in the Fields of Grace': An Essay on Three Recent Books by Charles Edward Eaton,'' in *Pembroke Magazine* (North Carolina),

30, 1998, all by Judy Hogan; by Glenn B. Blalock, in *Poets, Dramatists, Essayists and Novelists of the South,* edited by Robert Bain and Joseph Flora, Westport, Connecticut, Greenwood, 1994; by Walter Shear, in *Midwest Quarterly* (Pittsburg, Kansas), August 1997.

Charles Edward Eaton comments:

Though I am resistant in general to definitions of poetry and poets as too limiting, if pressed I might admit to being a modern formalist, but I should insist on the importance of the qualifying adjective. I compose in a number of verse forms and write lyrical as well as dramatic poetry, but I do not lean on any poet of the past or present for technical inspiration. I believe that each poet must develop his own organic sense of form and adapt even the most conventional meter to his personal rhythm. For example, a number of my poems are written in triptychs, their long lines rhyming every other line, modulated in an entirely individual way. William Carlos Williams, in a study of my work, called this three-line stanza an Americanization of terza rima. Perhaps he felt it was very American in its love of freedom and yet somewhat European in its formal allegiance. There is no doubt that I like poetry that is both vigorous and controlled.

In this respect I think the best short statement about my work has been made by Robert D. Spector in *Saturday Review:* ''Charles Edward Eaton may not belong at all in the category of unconventional poets, and yet, it seems to me, his use of conventions becomes a very personal thing that removes him from tradition . . . If Eaton's poetry, with its use of rhymed stanzas, appears superficially to belong to a formal tradition, his long, free lines and sometimes brutal imagery and diction, pushing his feelings to their limit, suggest otherwise. *On the Edge of the Knife* combines conventional and unconventional in such a way that it is finally the poet's own work. Perhaps, after all, that is the way of poetry. Whether bound to tradition or not, its value rests on the peculiar virtues of the poet.''

I am in emphatic accord with any statement about my work which indicates that I believe in working powerfully and freely on one's own terms within the entire range of poetry. I am in no sense a reductionist, but have confidence in the fundamental richness of poetry and the surprise lurking in its possibilities. Form should be an energetic expression of the poet's own psychology, not an artificial imposition, and the poem should convey some sense of the struggle which went into the formal achievement: ''I have a powerful nature in pursuit of pleasure. / Peace, good will, and I do not share / My time's contempt for passion balanced by strict measure.'' An extension of what is involved in this position is given at the conclusion of ''The Turkey'': ''So the bird I know is like a gaudy catafalque. / If you should carry a secret hump upon your back, / You, too, would have a burdened and uncertain walk. / This is what it is to spread an image in the sun— / This is how we teach thick, precarious balance as if the land moved like a ship / And one set sail heavily, slowly, encumbered with imagination.''

As to my subject matter, it is greatly influenced by where I am living and what I am doing at any given time. In this sense it is always around me, and it moves forward with me as I go along. Almost every poem, hidden though it may be to the reader, has its donnée from some aspect of experience. Landscape wherever I have lived (North Carolina, Puerto Rico, Brazil, Connecticut, etc.) comes strongly into my work, but I do not consider myself a nature poet. Animals and flowers are continuous with and contiguous to my interest in human beings and are a constant motif in my work, but I am not interested in fauna or flora per se and am in no sense a botanical or zoological poet. All of my subjects are finally a way of talking about people in the expanding enclave of interest and experience I have chosen to explore. I have been amused by one magazine editor's recognition of my predilection for ''all things, great and small'' in welcoming a new submission as another poem from ''the Garden of Eaton.''

Painting has been another seminal influence, and I have long enjoyed what John Singleton Copley called ''the luxury of seeing.'' This interest is the specific motivation in such poems as ''The Gallery,'' ''The Museum,'' ''Homage to the Infanta,'' and ''Nocturne for Douanier Rousseau,'' among others, but it is a constantly underlying, energizing source. ''Five Études for the Artist'' *(Art International,* November 1972) is an extended statement of this pictorial dedication which has been noted by numerous artists, including the New England painter Karl Knaths, who has commented at length on the ''vital imaginative reality'' of the visual qualities of the poems.

The intellectual content of my poetry and its final outlook and credo have been greatly strengthened by the study of philosophy. Writing in the *New York Times* about *Countermoves,* Wallace Fowlie recognized this influence when he said, ''Charles Eaton demonstrates an admirable technical control over the effects he wishes to make, and a clear awareness of at least one major function of poetry. This would be the art of questioning everything, and of questioning in particular the power of poetry.''

Fowlie's acknowledgment of the power of sentiment as balancing the intellectual in the poetry is reflected in a line from my long poem ''Robert E. Lee: An Ode'': ''I believe in the world seen through a temperament.'' I am certain that it is always the task of the writer to give us his personal vision of reality. This means an uncommon dedication, a determination to keep the fine arts fine, a perpetual sense of renewal and reaffirmation. One must constantly ask oneself in times of discouragement, Who will do my particular kind of writing if I don't? Who will take care of my dreams when I am gone? In our dispersive time it is not easy to keep a sense of personality and purpose, and, as a consequence, attention to the disciplines of character is equally important with ability. Probably more writers fail through lack of character than of ability. Morale is one of the essential fibers of a meaningful life. Cézanne reminded himself every morning to be *''Sur le motif!''* So must the poet.

*   *   *

The poetry of Charles Edward Eaton ranges from the quiet, reflective, and calmly precise to the colorful, daring, gripping, and raw. The best of his work provides the reader with a delightful though sometimes disturbing experience: he advances confidently, secure in the carefully controlled rhythms, the superbly disciplined energies of syntax, until of a sudden he loses his balance. Upon recovering it the reader discovers that he has been walking on a tightrope, stretched precariously between the world as he usually sees it and the world as it really is.

Eaton is a poet who allows his mind and heart to play upon experience. He sings of ordinary things: the amber light of the sun, the fading fragrance of purple lilacs, the red fire of October, the bodies of swimmers, golden and hard muscled, a day in spring ''. . . like a bell / Rung suddenly in many tones of green, / Sprung full and clear-toned well / Into the rounded air . . .'' He sings also of extraordinary things: a giggler, voyeur, centaur, eunuch, cowboy, woman with a scar, dagger thrower's assistant, and Madame Midget, ''Her tiny heart, loaded with feeling close as a plum is to its stone.'' Repeatedly, through skillful use of conventional form and variations, the poet demonstrates how tenuous and fluctuating is the distinction between the two. For Eaton all experience, the ordinary as well as the extraordinary, the painful as well as the pleasant, is matter for poetry to assimilate and rearrange. "From bee-sting, spider-bite, thorn-prick, hammer-bruise," no less than from "lip-brush" and "hand-grasp," the flesh learns and "grows wise."

On the Edge of the Knife and *The Man in the Green Chair* explore with increasing boldness and vigor the abnormality of the normal. They reveal the bestial power of Eros and descend into the primitive darkness deep within each of us. The verse, like the song of the tree frog, is often "raw with harsh and heartfelt music," a music that reverberates through the intelligent verse paragraphs, the chiseled quatrains, the unorthodox, long-lined triptychs. Such rawness never chafes or offends. Eaton's mastery of form, achieved by years of experience and adapted to the distinctive sound of the poet's individual voice, finally teaches the heart the lesson it learns in "Della Robbia in August," not only to grieve but also to rise "in a brilliant form of care."

—Robert Miola

EBERHART, Richard (Ghormley)

Nationality: American. **Born:** Austin, Minnesota, 5 April 1904. **Education:** University of Minnesota, Minneapolis, 1922–23; Dartmouth College, Hanover, New Hampshire, B.A. 1926; St. John's College, Cambridge, B.A. 1929, M.A. 1933; Harvard University, Cambridge, Massachusetts, 1932–33. **Military Service:** U.S. Naval Reserve, 1942–46: Lieutenant Commander. **Family:** Married Helen Butcher in 1941; one son and one daughter. **Career:** Basement floorwalker, Marshall Field and Company, Chicago, 1926–27; slaughterhouse worker, New York, 1929. Tutor to the two daughters of the Proctors (of Proctor and Gamble), 1929–30, the son of King Prajadhipok of Siam, 1930–31, and the son of Prime Minister Kridakava. English teacher, St. Mark's School, Southboro, Massachusetts, 1933–41, and Cambridge School, Kendal Green, Massachusetts, 1941–42. Assistant manager to vice president, Butcher Polish Company, Boston, 1946–52: now honorary vice president and member of the board of directors. Visiting professor, University of Washington, Seattle, 1952–53, 1967, 1972; professor of English, University of Connecticut, Storrs, 1953–54; visiting professor, Wheaton College, Norton, Massachusetts, 1954–55; resident fellow in creative writing and Gauss Lecturer, Princeton University, New Jersey, 1955–56. Professor of English and poet-in-residence, 1956–68, Class of 1925 Professor, 1968–70, and professor emeritus, 1970–80, and since 1986 poet-in-residence, Dartmouth College. Elliston Lecturer, University of Cincinnati, 1961; visiting professor, Columbia University, New York, 1975, University of California, Davis, 1975, and University of Florida, Gainesville, winter term, 1974–82; Wallace Stevens Fellow, Timothy Dwight College, Yale University, New Haven, Connecticut, 1976; honorary fellow, St. John's College, Cambridge, 1986. Founder, 1950, and first president, Poets' Theater, Cambridge, Massachusetts; member, 1955, and since 1964 director, Yaddo Corporation. Consultant in poetry, 1959–61, and honorary consultant in American letters, 1963–69, Library of Congress, Washington, D.C. **Awards:** Guarantor's prize, 1946, and Harriet Monroe memorial prize, 1950 (*Poetry*, Chicago); New England Poetry Club Golden Rose, 1950; Shelley

memorial award, 1952; Harriet Monroe memorial award, 1955; American Academy grant, 1955; Bollingen prize, 1962; Pulitzer prize, 1966; Academy of American Poets fellowship, 1969; National Book award, 1977; President's Medallion, University of Florida, 1977; World Academy of Arts and Letters diploma award, 1981; Sarah Josepha Hale award, 1982; Robert Frost Medal, 1986. D. Litt: Dartmouth College, 1954; Skidmore College, Saratoga, New York, 1966; College of Wooster, Ohio, 1969; Colgate University, Hamilton, New York, 1974; D.H.L.: Franklin Pierce College, Rindge, New Hampshire, 1978; St. Lawrence University, Canton, New York, 1985; Plymouth State College, New Hampshire, 1987. Poet Laureate of New Hampshire, 1979. Since 1972 honorary president, Poetry Society of America. **Member:** American Academy, 1960, and American Academy of Arts and Sciences, 1967. **Address:** 80 Lyme Road, #161, Hanover, New Hampshire 03755, U.S.A.

PUBLICATIONS

Poetry

A Bravery of Earth. London, Cape, 1930; New York, Cape and Smith, 1931.

Reading the Spirit. London, Chatto and Windus, 1936; New York, Oxford University Press, 1937.

Song and Idea. London, Chatto and Windus, 1940; New York, Oxford University Press, 1942.

A World-View. Medford, Massachusetts, Tufts College Press, 1941.

Poems, New and Selected. New York, New Directions, 1944.

Rumination. Hanover, New Hampshire, Wayzgoose Press, 1947.

Burr Oaks. New York, Oxford University Press, and London, Chatto and Windus, 1947.

Brotherhood of Men. Pawlet, Vermont, Banyan Press, 1949.

An Herb Basket. Cummington, Massachusetts, Cummington Press, 1950.

Selected Poems. New York, Oxford University Press, and London, Chatto and Windus, 1951.

Undercliff: Poems 1946–1953. London, Chatto and Windus, 1953; New York, Oxford University Press, 1954.

Great Praises. New York, Oxford University Press, and London, Chatto and Windus, 1957.

The Oak. Hanover, New Hampshire, Pine Tree Press, 1957.

Collected Poems 1930–60, Including 51 New Poems. New York, Oxford University Press, and London, Chatto and Windus, 1960.

The Quarry: New Poems. New York, Oxford University Press, and London, Chatto and Windus, 1964.

The Vastness and Indifference of the World. Milford, New Hampshire, Ferguson Press, 1965.

Fishing for Snakes. Privately printed, 1965.

Selected Poems 1930–1965. New York, New Directions, 1965.

Thirty One Sonnets. New York, Eakins Press, 1967.

Shifts of Being. New York, Oxford University Press, and London, Chatto and Windus, 1968.

The Achievement of Richard Eberhart: A Comprehensive Selection of His Poems, edited by Bernard F. Engle. Chicago, Scott Foresman, 1968.

Three Poems. Cambridge, Massachusetts, Pym Randall Press, 1968.

Fields of Grace. New York, Oxford University Press, and London, Chatto and Windus, 1972.

Two Poems. West Chester, Pennsylvania, Aralia Press, 1975.

Collected Poems 1930–1976, Including 43 New Poems. New York, Oxford University Press, and London, Chatto and Windus, 1976.
Poems to Poets. Lincoln, Massachusetts, Penmaen Press, 1976.
Hour, Gnats. Davis, California, Putah Creek Press, 1977.
Survivors. Brockport, New York, Boa, 1979.
Ways of Light: Poems 1972–1980. New York, Oxford University Press, and London, Chatto and Windus, 1980.
New Hampshire: Nine Poems. Roslindale, Massachusetts, Pym Randall Press, 1980.
Four Poems. Winston-Salem, North Carolina, Palaemon Press, 1980.
Florida Poems. Gulfport, Florida, Konglomerati Press, 1981.
The Long Reach: New and Uncollected Poems 1948–1984. New York, New Directions, 1984.
Snowy Owl. Winston-Salem, North Carolina, Palaemon Press, 1984.
Throwing Yourself Away. Roslyn, New York, Stone House Press, 1984.
Spite Fence. Charleston, West Virginia, Mountain State Press, 1984.
Collected Poems 1930–1986. New York and Oxford, Oxford University Press, 1988.
Maine Poems. New York, Oxford University Press, 1989.
New and Selected Poems 1930–1990. New York, Blue Moon Press, 1990.

Recording: *Richard Eberhart Reading His Own Poems,* Caedmon, 1966.

Plays

The Apparition (produced Cambridge, Massachusetts, 1951). Included in *Collected* Verse Plays, 1962.
The Visionary Farms (produced Cambridge, Massachusetts, 1952). Included in *Collected Verse Plays,* 1962.
Triptych (produced Chicago, 1955). Included in *Collected Verse Plays,* 1962.
The Mad Musician, and Devils and Angels (produced Cambridge, Massachusetts, 1962). Included in *Collected Verse Plays,* 1962.
Collected Verse Plays (includes *Triptych, The Visionary Farms, The Apparition, The Mad Musician, Devils and Angels, Preamble I and II*). Chapel Hill, University of North Carolina Press, 1962.
The Bride from Mantua, adaptation of a play by Lope de Vega (produced Hanover, New Hampshire, 1964).
Chocurua. New York, Nadja Press, 1981.

Other

Poetry As a Creative Principle (lecture). Norton, Massachusetts, Wheaton College, 1952.
Of Poetry and Poets. Urbana, University of Illinois Press, 1979.

Editor, with others, *Free Gunner's Handbook,* revised edition. Norfolk, Virginia, Naval Air Station, 1944.
Editor, with Selden Rodman, War *and the Poet. An Anthology of Poetry Expressing Man's Attitude to War from Ancient Times to the Present.* New York, Devin Adair, 1945.
Editor, . . . *Dartmouth Poems.* Hanover, New Hampshire, Dartmouth Publications-Butcher Fund, 12 vols., 1958–59, 1962–71.
Editor, *To Eberhart from Ginsberg: A Letter About "Howl" 1956.* Lincoln. Massachusetts. Penmaen Press. 1976.

*

Bibliography: *Richard Eberhart: A Descriptive Bibliography, 1921–1987* by Stuart Wright, assisted by Charles and Stephanie Lovett, Westport, Connecticut, Meckler, 1989.

Manuscript Collection: Dartmouth College Library, Hanover, New Hampshire.

Critical Studies: "Richard Eberhart" by Ralph J. Mills, Jr., in *Contemporary American Poetry,* New York, Random House, 1960, and *Richard Eberhart* by Mills, Minneapolis, University of Minnesota Press, 1966; introduction to *The Achievement of Richard Eberhart,* 1968, and *Richard Eberhart,* New York, Twayne, 1972, both by Bernard F. Engle; "The Cultivation of Paradox: The War Poetry of Richard Eberhart" by Richard J. Fein, in *Forum* (Muncie, Indiana), spring 1969; *Richard Eberhart: The Progress of an American Poet* by Joel Roache, New York, Oxford University Press, 1971; *Richard Eberhart* (film), directed by Samuel Mandelbaum, New York, Tri-Pix, 1972; *Richard Eberhart* (film), directed by Irving Broughton, Seattle, University of Washington, 1974; *Richard Eberhart: A Celebration,* edited by Sydney Lea and others, n.p., Kenyon Hill, 1980; "A Tribute to Richard Eberhart" by Cleanth Brooks, in *South Atlantic Review* (Atlanta, Georgia), 50(4), November 1985; "Light in Richard Eberhart's Verse" by Donald Gutierrez, in *Ball State University Forum* (Muncie, Indiana), 27(1), winter 1986; "Richard Eberhart Symposium Issue" edited by Sue Brannan Walker and Jane Mayhall, in *Negative Capability,* 6(2–3), spring-summer 1986.

Richard Eberhart comments:

My poetry celebrates life, which does not last long, and mankind, which is temporal as well, through understanding and perception of my times, insofar as I am able to create poems that may communicate values and meanings I can know.

*   *   *

Throughout the years Richard Eberhart has pursued a romantic poetry in the tradition of Blake, Wordsworth, and Whitman. He has been concerned with understanding and transcending concrete experience, and his predominant themes have centered around the brutal reality of death. Eberhart's goal has remained constant: to achieve a connection with the unifying force that runs through all things. He has accomplished this most frequently in the act of writing his verse, and his poetry has become the vehicle for intimations of immortality.

Eberhart is an "inspirational" poet. As he puts it, "The poet breathes in maybe God," and poetry is "dynamic, Protean." The result, however, as even his most ardent admirers admit, is an unevenness in quality. One finds stirring and exquisite lines alongside phrases marred by sentimentality, pedantic diction, and banal abstraction. "The poet's mind is a filament informed with the irrational vitality of energy, as it was discovered in our time in quantum mechanics," he continues, and "the quanta may shoot off any way." Needless to say, one looks to the poems of steady inspiration, where "the poet writes with a whole clarity," able to "aggravate" perception into life.

Eberhart's best work results from his ability to transform keenly felt perceptions through the very language of the senses into moral, metaphysical, and sometimes even religious experience. His most moving poems retain the urgency and exaltation of the felt moment as they simultaneously transform that moment into something abstract and often mystical. As Eberhart explains, the successful poet "makes the world anew; something grows out of the old, which he locks in words'' (''Big Rock'').

The early and well-known ''This Fevers Me'' expresses Eberhart's unbounded wonder at nature and the fierce exhilaration that ''lyric'' and ''lovely'' nature arouses in him. God ''incarnate'' resides in the external world, and, as such, ''This fevers me, this sun on green. / On grass glowing, this young spring. / The secret hallowing is come, / Regenerate sudden incarnation, / Mystery made visible / In growth.'' Such an intimate connection to physical nature involves the poet in the cycles of growth and decay, and he must therefore search for a transcendent significance. Thus, although all of nature ultimately wastes and decays, like the lamb that lies ''putrid'' on ''the slant hill'' (''For a Lamb''), the poet knows that there is a fundamental continuity for all natural things. The lamb, he believes, is ''in the wind somewhere, / . . . There's a lamb in the daisies.''

''The Groundhog,'' his most frequently anthologized poem, goes even further in expressing Eberhart's wild and exhilarated transcendence in the face of physical decay. The poet has returned regularly to the site of a dead groundhog in order to observe its disintegration and absorption into natural processes. As a result, as its bones lie ''bleaching in the sunlight,'' they seem to be as ''beautiful as architecture.'' Witnessing the groundhog's metamorphosis during his own aging process has transformed the poet as well—from a sense of ''naked frailty'' to one of ''strange love'' and even ''fever''—to a ''passion of the blood.'' His confrontation with and then articulation of death—his poetry—have given him the ''immense energy'' of ''the sun.'' He also sees himself in the company of historical figures who have similarly transcended the ravages of time through imagination and concludes with the shared ecstasy of ''Alexander in his tent; / . . . Montaigne and his tower, / . . . Saint Theresa in her wild lament.''

Another of Eberhart's familiar themes is represented in ''If I Could Only Live at the Pitch That Is Near Madness.'' He writes of the intensity of childhood, of the time of ''incomparable light,'' when ''everything'' was ''violent, vivid, and of infinite possibility.'' Nevertheless, although childhood was a time of visionary possibility, the grown man accepts and indeed delights in the obligations of adulthood. Thrust ''into [the] realm of complexity,'' he even embraces the responsibilities of maturity. For Eberhart there is a compensatory joy in ''the moral answer,'' in understanding and performing the responsibilities of adulthood.

Age brings with it, for example, the awareness of human cruelty, and many of Eberhart's poems treat the varieties of human suffering that grow out of social, political, and family strife. One is obliged, he states in his famous ''Am I My Neighbor's Keeper?,'' to care for his fellow humans. In his ''The Fury of Aerial Bombardment'' he asks what sort of God would permit the barbarism of war: ''You would feel that after so many centuries / God would give man to relent.''

Many of Eberhart's poems lament the weariness and loneliness of old age and the poet's despair when he senses an indifferent universe. ''A name may be glorious but death is death,'' he writes in ''I Walked over the Grave of Henry James,'' incapable of intuiting for James the transcendence of his lamb or groundhog. Similarly, when intellect rules spirit, it ''kills all delight / [and] brings the solemn inward pain / Of truth into the heart again'' (''In a Hard Intellectual Light''). In ''The Goal of Intellectual Man'' he explains that love is ''difficult, dangerous, pure, [and] clear,'' but love alone is the ''truth of the positive hour / Composing all of human power.''

Virtually overlooked in the Eberhart oeuvre are the verse plays, which were published in collected form in 1962. Eberhart admits that in writing these ''the motives are the same as those for lyric poetry, . . . a basic split in the soul and a need to create, to compensate, to make a whole world.'' He also adds the revealing comment that ''verse drama with me has been a thrust of the whole man,'' his effort toward ''more control of emotion.'' *Triptych* has virtually no action and consists entirely of poetry. It is a modern morality play with a woman in dialogue with both an airy sprite and a man of sense:

Percy: Reason and treason are the same thing to me . . .
John: You merely rave against what you love.
Percy: If I rave against what I love,
    You fail me in reciprocal
       Love of what you hate.
Priscilla: What sport is this?

Choosing a Monument is another three-way dialogue, this time between a sister and her two brothers. In *Preamble I* a poet and a writer exchange ideas about the problems facing the modern generation. In *Preamble II* two authors further discuss the problems of the age. Eberhart's other plays include *The Apparition, The Visionary Farms* (his first effort to include a plot), *Devils and Angels,* and *The Mad Musician.* Eberhart's endeavors in verse drama lasted primarily from the mid-1930s through the mid-1950s.

Some of Eberhart's best poems in later volumes like *Ways of Light* address ''love and the challenge of time.'' Eberhart listens to the owl cry (''Who'') and returns to the ''rowboat'' image of his youth to contemplate the concrete and visionary worlds, the seals and ''loon's cry far beyond the human.'' *The Long Reach* stresses the fragility of life, not just the immutability of death. Once again, in his typically nonironic, direct, and occasionally naive terms, Eberhart accepts the conditions of love and responsibility that are imposed by life. He also reflects on what he has come to define as the oblivion of death.

Maine Poems, a collection of verse published throughout his career, reminds us of Eberhart's uncertainty concerning the future. In ''Old Tree by the Penobscot,'' as the poet identifies once again with a natural object, he observes how a strong, beautiful, and well-rooted tree has endured a kind of ''stalwart declination.'' Will he, the poet asks, like the tree, change in form and grow to be unrecognizable? Will he become ''a myth of time''? In the end one can only ''raise his hands to God'' (''Death in the Mines''), although Eberhart seems relatively confident that both nature and poetry assure immortality: ''A wind will spring up, a spirit arise / And ride on the air lightly, supremely clear, / In other centuries, and in other civilizations.'' One of the most moving and direct poems here, ''Looking at the Waters,'' concludes with ''Can you say anything new about looking at the waters? / . . . I wish I could figure out the nature of the world, / Why one boat heads one way, why one heads another, / What is the current that shapes our direction.'' As though writing an answer to all of his earlier queries, the poem ends with the lines ''No moment is so good as a sure moment / When words take on a supernatural mystery, / And wherever the sea and we are going, / Ultimately the best is not knowing.''

—Lois Gordon

ECHERUO, Michael (Joseph Chukwudalu)

Nationality: Nigerian. **Born:** Umunumo, Mbano Division, 14 March 1937. **Education:** Stella Maris College, Port Harcourt, 1950–54; University College, Ibadan, 1955–60, B.A. (honors) 1960; Cornell University, Ithaca, New York (Phi Beta Kappa), 1962–65, M.A. 1963, Ph.D. 1965. **Family:** Married Rose N. Ikwueke in 1968; five children. **Career:** Lecturer, Nigerian College of Arts and Technology, Enugu, 1960–61. Lecturer, 1961–70, senior lecturer, 1970–73, and professor, 1973–74, University of Nigeria, Nsukka; professor of English, 1974–80, and dean of the Postgraduate School, 1978–80, University of Ibadan. Vice-chancellor, Imo State University, Owerri, 1981–89. Visiting professor, Indiana University, Bloomington, 1989–90. Since 1990 William Safire Professor of Modern Letters, Syracuse University, New York. Since 1977 founding president, Nigerian Association for African and Comparative Literature. **Awards:** All-Africa Poetry Competition prize, 1963. D.Litt.: University of Nebraska, 1992. **Address:** Syracuse University, Department of English, 410 Hall of Languages, Syracuse, New York 13244, U.S.A.

PUBLICATIONS

Poetry

Mortality. London, Longman, 1968.
Distanced: New Poems. Enugu, I.K., 1975.

Other

Joyce Cary and the Novel of Africa. London, Longman, and New York, Africana, 1973.
Victorian Lagos: Aspects of Nineteenth-Century Lagos Life. London, Macmillan, 1977; New York, Holmes and Meier, 1978.
Poets, Prophets, and Professors. Ibadan, Ibadan University Press, 1977.
The Conditioned Imagination from Shakespeare to Conrad: Studies in the Exo-Cultural Stereotype. London, Macmillan, and New York, Holmes and Meier, 1978.
Joyce Cary and the Dimensions of Order. London, Macmillan, and New York, Barnes and Noble, 1979.

Editor, *Igbo Traditional Life, Literature, and Culture.* Austin Texas, Conch, 1972.
Editor, *The Tempest,* by Shakespeare. London, Longman, 1980.
Editor, *Igo-English Dictionary: A Comprehensive Dictionary of the Igbo Language.* New Haven, Connecticut, Yale University Press, 1998.

*

Critical Studies: Interview with Bernth Lindfors, in *Greenfield Review* (Greenfield Center, New York), 3(4), 1974; "The Dignity of Intellectual Labor: A Fiftieth Birthday Tribute" by Isidore Okpewho, in *The Gong and the Flute: African Literary Development and Celebration,* edited by Kalu Ogbaa, Westport, Connecticut, Greenwood, 1994.

*   *   *

From the crossroads experience of an African heritage and a "European" education, the Nigerian writer Michael Echeruo, like his late countryman Christopher Okigbo, has forged poetry that is wide-ranging, deceptively simple, and highly individual. Although the poems in his first volume, *Mortality,* often come out of his experiences as a master's and doctoral student in the United States, they are still like trees with their roots deep in African soil, no matter how high their branches reach into a foreign sky. The return to Africa, whether physically or metaphorically, is implicit, as in the first poem in the book, "Debut":

> Have we not looked the whole world out,
>   searched the whole hearth out
>   till we saw the palm-nuts again
> by which we were to live?

It is, therefore, no accident that an entire section of his book is titled "Defections" and that he says in the poem "Harvest Time," "Village maidens / are the bearers of my harvest . . ."

Wit and irony also figure strongly in Echeruo's poetry, along with a sense of what it is to be an African poet in a foreign land:

> . . . like an unfeathered bird
> in their spring—
> white and spruce and clean—
> . . . like an unclassified gift
> to their museums
> where they spin out fine tall tales
> all day long
> amid the blistering flurries
> of their bleak December days.

Although Nigeria figures strongly in his verse, Echeruo also ranges capably throughout Western literature, bringing in such diverse sources as the Bible, D.H. Lawrence, Joyce, and St. John of the Cross. His poem "The Signature," which revolves around the figure of O'Brien (who seems to be an Irish priest like the Flannagan of Chris Okigbo's "Limits"), draws a picture of African ceremonies in conjunction with Catholic rites and reaches the conclusion that "the priests and elders of my past / would love to see O'Brien's paradise."

Whether ironic or celebratory, whether a poem of love or a poem of satire, there is a current of lyricism that runs through all of Echeruo's verse, a lyricism that can be felt in the lines from his poem "Wedding." These lines speak of birth and stress again the poet's ties to the soil:

> Tap roots beneath the giant
> speak like the gods
> and life comes
> like a spasm of light . . .

—Joseph Bruchac

EDMOND, Lauris (Dorothy)

Nationality: New Zealander. **Born:** Lauris Dorothy Scott on 2 April 1924. **Education:** Napier Girls High School, 1937–41; University of Waikato, Hamilton, B.A. 1968; Victoria University, Wellington,

M.A. (honors) 1972. **Family:** Married Trevor Edmond in 1945; four daughters and one son. **Career:** Teacher, Huntly College, 1968–69, and Heretaunga College, Wellington, 1970–72; editor, Post-Primary Teachers Association, Wellington, 1973–80. Since 1980 off-campus tutor and lecturer, Massey University, Palmerston North. Writer-in-residence, Deakin University, Melbourne, 1985. Founded periodical, *New Zealand Books,* 1990. **Awards:** New Zealand P.E.N. award, 1975; Katherine Mansfield-Menton fellowship, 1981; Commonwealth poetry prize, 1985; Lilian Ida Smith award, 1987; A.W. Reed Lifetime Achievement award, 1999. D.Litt.: Massey University, 1988. O.B.E. (Officer, Order of the British Empire), 1986. **Address:** 22 Grass Street, Oriental Bay, Wellington, New Zealand. **Died:** 28 January 2000.

PUBLICATIONS

Poetry

In Middle Air. Christchurch, Pegasus Press, 1975.
The Pear Tree and Other Poems. Christchurch, Pegasus Press, 1977.
Salt from the North. Wellington, Oxford University Press, 1980.
Seven. Wellington, Wayzgoose Press, 1980.
Wellington Letter. Wellington, Mallinson Rendel, 1980.
Catching It. Auckland, Oxford University Press, 1983.
Selected Poems. Auckland, Oxford University Press, 1984.
Seasons and Creatures. Auckland, Oxford University Press, and Newcastle upon Tyne, Bloodaxe, 1986.
Summer near the Arctic Circle. Auckland, Oxford University Press 1988.
New and Selected Poems. Auckland, Oxford University Press, and Newcastle upon Tyne, Bloodaxe, 1991.
Scenes from a Small City. N.p., Daphne Brasell Associates, 1994.
Selected Poems 1975–1994. N.p., Bridget Williams Books, 1994.
A Matter of Timing. Auckland University Press, 1996.
In Position. Newcastle upon Tyne, Bloodaxe, 1996.
50 Poems. N.p., Bridget Williams Books, 1999.

Plays

Between Night and Morning (produced Wellington, 1980).

Radio Plays: *The Mountain* (cycle of 4 plays), 1980–81.

Novel

High Country Weather. Sydney, Allen and Unwin, and Wellington, Port Nicholson Press, 1984.

Other

Autobiographical Series:

Hot October: An Autobiographical Story. Sydney, Allen and Unwin, 1989.
Bonfires in the Rain. N.p., Bridget Williams Books, 1991.
The Quick World. N.p., Bridget Williams Books, 1992.
An Autobiography. N.p., Bridget Williams Books, 1994.

Editor, *Dancing to My Tune: Verse and Prose,* by Denis Glover. Wellington, Catspaw Press, 1974.
Editor, *Young Writing.* Wellington, P.E.N. New Zealand Centre, 1979.
Editor, *A Remedial Persiflage,* by Chris Ward. Wellington, Post Primary Teachers Association, 1980.
Editor, *The Letters of A.R.D. Fairburn.* Wellington, Oxford University Press, 1981.
Editor, with Carolyn Milward, *Women in Wartime: New Zealand Women Tell Their Story.* Wellington, Government Printing Office, 1986.
Editor, with Bill Sewell and Harry Ricketts, *Under Review: A Selection from 'New Zealand Books' 1991–1996.* N.p., Daphne Brasell Associates, 1997.

*

Manuscript Collection: Alexander Turnbull Library, Wellington.

Critical Studies: In *New Zealand Listener* (Wellington), 11 June 1983; *Landfall* (Christchurch), September 1983; ''A Fine Flowering'' by Barbara Giles, in *Overland* (Melbourne), 103, July 1986; ''Top of the Poets'' by Gillian Mawrey, in *Commonwealth*, 28(4), March 1986; ''Privileged Happyland?'' by Bernard O'Donoghue, in *Poetry Review* (London), 78(1), spring 1988.

Lauris Edmond comments:

(1984) I came to poetry publishing late—though I had always written some, even during the busiest years when I lived in country towns and brought up my six children. In 1974 I first sent poems to an editor (of *Islands,* a New Zealand literary journal); they were accepted, and I began seriously to work on half-finished drafts and notes. By 1975 I had a manuscript ready for publication, and I have published five further volumes since then, with a *Selected Poems* this year.

The chief effect of this pattern of living my life first, as it were, and becoming a committed writer second is that all my work is filled with a sense of relationship. This is sometimes with people but also with events, experiences, the natural world; I don't think I write anything without this sense of being a part of a larger experience, and in relationship with it, being expressed in some way.

This quality is reflected in the process of writing by my awareness that the creation of a poem is as much a matter of listening as speaking; the experience which lies at the center of the poem has from the moment of inception its own life, to which I as poet respond. Since I have an abiding sense of the living quality in the natural environment, and the psychological environment in which I live, it seems natural to me to find this relationship again and again, even in the smallest details of existence, each of which has its own uniqueness.

I wrote my first novel because I was awarded the writer's fellowship which sends a New Zealand writer to the south of France for a year, to live in Menton. I do not believe that poetry can be written according to any kind of organized program, so I wrote a novel, and having done so, I intend to write others. I found an immediate parallel between the vitality of the ''world of the poem'' and that of the fictional world of my novel, though many of the details of the writing process were different.

Beginning late has some obvious advantages, though I didn't do it by conscious choice. The main one is that the maturity that one hopes has been learned in thirty years of adult life forms the basic outlook or point of view in everything I write. Some kinds of apprenticeship, it seems, do not have to be passed through. There is also a considerable sense of urgency, which I think may give pace and energy to my writing. The volume of *Selected Poems* shows rather less variation between early and later poems than a poet who began writing in youth would display. And I could never regret my children!

(1995) During the last six years I have been working on a three-volume autobiography, recently reissued as a single volume. I have found the process extraordinarily revealing as a way of understanding why my writing began so late. It has aroused a major response and has been seen as a central story of women of my generation. Now that the work is finished my concern has been to discover if—and in what ways—this has affected my poetry writing. Certainly the internal reverberations have taken a long time to settle, and only in the last few months have I been able to go back—or move on—to a new departure in poetry. I find that writing poems is still my first choice of occupation, rather than the fiction I thought I would return to. I am working at present on a long sequence of poems that document in various ways the moral, intellectual, and spiritual journeys of my later life.

*   *   *

Lauris Edmond's outpouring of poetry, including a volume of selected poems that won the 1985 Commonwealth poetry prize, comes comparatively late in a life devoted initially to a large family in a small New Zealand town. While recognizing in her *Landfall* interview that she has "the powerful enthusiasm of the late starter," Edmond is pleased to have been able to experience a "personal life" and then a career.

Her first volume, *In Middle Air,* sounds recurrent themes: the brutality of rural living (of a sensitive boy it is sneered, "He'll roughen up"), the cold alienness of the physical environment, the ravages of time, and the necessity for love ("We starve alone") and for putting observation into words. There is, however, a strain of high romantic lyricism that is at odds with the more supple, intimate dramatic sense that was slowly to emerge as the poet's distinctive voice, along with an uncertainty of line. In *The Pear Tree* the line fits more naturally a more forthright voice, often addressing friends (male or female) as "you" and arguing for philosophical positions such as the importance of the here and now. A series of portraits of older women forms a minor theme in Edmond's writing, as in "At Mary's House," which typically draws analogies between body, spirit, and the natural landscape ("nobody / has weeded here for a long time").

In *Wellington Letter* the poet criticizes her people—"we cultivate mind's middle distances." Instead, Edmond tries to move up close to experience or to stand back and make a crisp generalization, for instance, that the great poets had "unshakeable courage." The dangers of bald poetic philosophizing are obvious, and Edmond has since wisely moved toward the quotidian—"it was not anything achieved; / the art was just to let it happen." Thus the first half of *Salt from the North* shows a surer focus and sense of line and an unforced completeness in each poem. Unfortunately, in the second half of that volume and in *Catching It* the moralizing creeps in, effective only

when it proceeds from a vivid personal setting, as, for example, in "Latter Day Lysistrata," an antiwar poem in which the poet in her garden protests male folly:

> Let us show them the vulnerable
> earth, the transparent light that slips
> through slender birches falling over
> small birds that sense in the minuscule
> threads of their veins . . .

Many of Edmond's poems are about trees, their rootedness and memories. The 1981 Mansfield fellowship in Menton gave her roots and a perspective from elsewhere to revitalize her poetry. In *Catching It* the lines are often shorter and surer, the moment or performance brought off more often. Whether she is gazing back home ("I am the child of exiles who dreamt / of the lost garden") or at Frenchmen sitting in a town square, she "catches it." Her dominant sense of transience and death finds strong dramatic form in the poem "At Delphi," in which she imagines the sacrifice of an older woman.

Although Edmond's work in poetry slowed while she wrote her multivolume autobiography, she has consolidated her reputation as one of New Zealand's foremost poets with several further volumes, including *Seasons and Creatures* and *Summer near the Arctic Circle.* While *Seasons* continues to use as subject matter the things of daily life—flowers, cats, cows, family, neighbors—*Summer,* as its title suggests, often goes further afield, indicating a widening scope and audience. In "Commonwealth Poetry Tour" Edmond acknowledges this movement outward: "So it grew, tiny convincing universe / feeling its frailty, marvelling at its passion . . ."

Less varied in tone and subject matter than her countrywoman Fleur Adcock, less philosophically inclined than Judith Wright, Edmond also sometimes lacks the metrical variety of each of these poets, but this is the distinguished company in which she now belongs. She has built up a commanding body of work, and her voice has always been crisp, clear, and articulate. If her writing seems addressed primarily to her own pleasure, as is evidenced by "Cows"—

> They do not suppose this matters,
> nor that anything else does—indeed,
> they do not suppose. Their time is entirely
> taken up with the delicious excruciating
> digestion of existence
> and if they please me on the by-pass road
> in the ripening sun this morning
> that is wholly my affair.

—then we are privileged to be party to it.

—David Dowling and Theresa Werner

EDMOND, Murray (Donald)

Nationality: New Zealander. **Born:** 1949. **Career:** Writer, actor, and director, Town and Country Players, Wellington. Since 1991 lecturer in drama, University of Auckland. Editor, *Freed,* 1970–71. **Address:**

English Department, University of Auckland, Private Bag 92019, Auckland, New Zealand.

PUBLICATIONS

Poetry

Entering the Eye. Dunedin, Caveman Press, 1973.
Patchwork. Days Bay, Hawk Press, 1978.
End Wall. Auckland, Oxford University Press, 1981.
Selected Poems. Auckland, Oxford University Press, 1984.
Letters and Paragraphs. Christchurch, Caxton Press, 1987.
From the Word Go: Poems. Auckland, Auckland University Press, 1992.
The Switch: A Long Poem. Auckland, Auckland University Press, 1994.

Other

Editor, with Mary Paul, *The New Poets of the 80's: Initiatives in New Zealand Poetry.* Wellington, Allen and Unwin, 1987.

*

Critical Study: By Chris Price, in *Landfall,* 46(4), December 1992.

* * *

Murray Edmond's poetry began its rise to prominence in New Zealand in the early 1970s, after a decade in which the choices open to New Zealand poets had been defined by Allen Curnow's traditionalist *The Penguin Book of New Zealand Verse* and Donald Allen's innovative anthology *The New American Poetry,* both of which appeared in 1960. In his association with and editorship of the little magazine *The Word Is Freed* (known locally as *Freed*), Edmond helped keep open the doors to the American influence that conspicuously revitalized the New Zealand poetry scene at the end of the 1960s. Whereas Curnow had stressed the poem as a well-made object, Edmond and a number of his contemporaries sought in their verse to remain open to the shifting identities of their situation.

In his early poetry Edmond accepted the technical opportunities made available by Williams, O'Hara, Duncan, Creeley, and Olson—the variable foot, the unpredictable length of the line, rhythms that are deliberately uncertain, and the use of the ampersand and of the oblique. The strength his poetry shares with Curnow's is an attention to the local and specific, but whereas Curnow's sense of the local and specific is derived from a Yeatsian understanding of national destiny (instead of Ireland's reality, there is New Zealand's), Edmond eschews such grandiose notions. He has developed an interest in oriental culture, yet his poetry often deals with situations that are domestic and familiar.

Edmond's language itself is domestic, familiar, lightly empowered, and used with a care born of nervous caution. He attempts to maintain a familiar regard without becoming merely blasé and contemptuous. "Night-Shift 1" is a good example:

I get up at 4.00 p.m.
& buy a cheese

3 tomatoes, an orange, & a tin of fruit juice
as usual:
also a paper.
I return to the kitchen
& put 2 tomatoes in the fridge for midnight,
cut off a piece of cheese
& put the rest in the fridge,
also for midnight . . .

Here the varied lengths of the lines register an erratic attention, while the tone is kept balanced and stable by its forward movement through the list of small accomplished deeds.

Edmond's poetry also departs from more traditional New Zealand verse by frequently referring to an urban or suburban environment:

2 men in blue jeans
& strawhats
shovelling hay
into a great trench
transversing the new
lay of the motorway

Images drawn from the farmyard and paddock shift into a world of cars, engines, and asphalt. This is "transversing" indeed.

What makes Edmond's verse more remarkable still is the degree to which he has worked to achieve a dissolution of the egocentric self, even in ostensibly personal poetry. His sense of the familial has counterpointed his sense of the international, and he understands how both structures are as fragile as they are powerful. "My Return to Czechoslovakia" begins,

Twice in my life I have felt utterly
foreign, staying in a place.
The first was in Prague.

The second, it turns out, was in Christchurch, where, having "thought of all the people who went into my making," he "looked right through the window of the moon / —right through into Czechoslovakia." The two moments, which pinpoint an isolated personal identity, are thereby brought together by different sets of geographical, political, and national identities and histories and through the mixed blessings of his Scottish forebears.

The precarious balance thus set up may be provisional, but it appears to give pleasure. "In inflationary times," the poet says, "it would be good to live in a shack," for a shack "hardly exists. / You are out the exit / before you are in the entrance . . . Let us be done with concrete and steel . . ." Even in a slightly less impermanent dwelling, as in "House," the tentative nature of the structure of reality is described in long lines, the strength of which is concurrent with their tenuousness:

Here I live on a cliff in a tiny house at the end of the
island . . .
and you are there asleep in the bed curled to the end wall of the
house . . .
your dreaming holding up the whole fabric of paint and wood and
tin . . .
Tonight I embrace you and trust the roof will hold up till
morning.

This has the tone of a prayer, and Edmond's statement that the "end wall" is "a structure which allows the rest of the world to begin" balances an acknowledged grandness against a convincing humility. The simplicity of his language leads away from the magniloquent assertions flung off the superstructures of selfhood and toward a more cautious appreciation of experience that is tempered by the pressures of hard work, profit and loss, lack of pretension, piety, and, in his own words, "investment, worry ... ownership, exploitation, and the nervous longing for family ..." Edmond has carried these concerns through to the "family" poems and the playfully philosophical and linguistically self-conscious poems in *Letters and Paragraphs*.

Throughout the 1970s and 1980s Edmond's academic career as a university teacher and his career as a dramatist and actor (taking theatrical productions on tour in New Zealand, out of the conventional theatrical venues) went hand in hand with his poetic accomplishment. He has also edited (with Mary Paul) a timely anthology of contemporary New Zealand verse, *The New Poets of the 80's: Initiatives in New Zealand Poetry*, whose project was to be "anti-absolute, anti-hierarchical" and to stress "the energy, the commitment, the intensity, and, above all, the variety of the emerging scene." Edmond's own response to what he describes as "the breakdown of consensus, the loss of literary homogeneity and traditional control of literary genealogy" in New Zealand poetry has been, like that of most of the poets represented in the anthology, one of welcoming enthusiasm.

—Alan Riach

EDSON, Russell

Nationality: American. **Born:** 9 April 1935. **Education:** Art Students League, New York; New School for Social Research, New York; Columbia University, New York; Black Mountain College, North Carolina. **Family:** Married Frances Edson. **Awards:** Guggenheim fellowship, 1974; National Endowment for the Arts grant, 1976, fellowship, 1982; Whiting Foundation award, 1989. **Agent:** Georges Borchardt Inc., 136 East 57th Street, New York, New York 10022. **Address:** 149 Weed Avenue, Stamford, Connecticut 06902, U.S.A.

PUBLICATIONS

Poetry

Appearances: Fables and Drawings. Stamford, Connecticut, Thing Press, 1961.
A Stone Is Nobody's: Fables and Drawings. Stamford, Connecticut, Thing Press, 1961.
The Boundry (sic). Stamford, Connecticut, Thing Press, 1964.
The Very Thing That Happens: Fables and Drawings. New York, New Directions, 1964.
The Brain Kitchen: Writings and Woodcuts. Stamford, Connecticut, Thing Press, 1965.
What a Man Can See. Highlands, North Carolina, Jargon, 1969.
The Childhood of an Equestrian. New York, Harper, 1973.
The Clam Theatre. Middletown, Connecticut, Wesleyan University Press, 1973.
A Roof with Some Clouds behind It. Hartford, Connecticut, Bartholomew's Cobble, 1975.

The Intuitive Journey and Other Works. New York, Harper, 1976.
The Reason Why the Closet-Man Is Never Sad. Middletown, Connecticut, Wesleyan University Press, 1977.
Edson's Mentality. Chicago, Oink Press, 1977.
The Traffic. Madison, Wisconsin, Red Ozier Press, 1978.
The Wounded Breakfast: Ten Poems. Madison, Wisconsin, Red Ozier Press, 1978.
With Sincerest Regrets. Providence, Rhode Island, Burning Deck, 1981.
Wuck Wuck Wuck! New York, Red Ozier Press, 1984.
The Wounded Breakfast. Middletown, Connecticut, Wesleyan University Press, 1985.
Tick Tock. Minneapolis, Minnesota, Coffee House Press, 1992.
The Tunnel: Selected Poems. Oberlin, Ohio, Oberlin College Press, 1994.

Plays

The Falling Sickness: A Book of Plays. New York, New Directions, 1975.

Novels

Gulping's Recital. Rhinebeck, New York, Guignol, 1984.
The Song of Percival Peacock. Minneapolis, Minnesota, Coffee House Press, 1992.

*

Critical Studies: *A Prose Poem Anthology* edited by Duane Ackerson, Pocatello, Idaho, Dragonfly Press, 1970; "Prose Poems" by William Matthews, in *New American and Canadian Poetry 15* (Trumansburg, New York), 1971; "I Am Sure Happiness Is Not Too Far Away" by Thomas Meyer, in *Parnassus* (New York), 2(1), 1974; "On Russell Edson's Genius" by Donald Hall, in *American Poetry Review 6* (Philadelphia), 5, 1977; "Portrait of the Writer As a Fat Man: Some Subjective Ideas or Notions on the Care and Feeding of Prose Poems" by the author, in *Claims for Poetry*, edited by Donald Hall, Ann Arbor, University of Michigan Press, 1982; "The Essential Russell Edson: A Surrealist Reading" by Larry Smith, in *Stardancer 7* (New York), 1983; "Russell Edson's Humor: Absurdity in a Surreal World" by Donald E. Hardy, in *Studies in American Humor* (San Marcos, Texas), 6, 1988; "Structural Politics: The Prose Poetry of Russell Edson" by Lee Upton, in *South Atlantic Review* (Atlanta, Georgia), 58(4), November 1993.

Russell Edson comments:

I write short prose pieces that are neither fiction nor reportage. Perhaps the currently popular term in America (although we certainly did not originate it), "prose poem," is vague enough to describe the blurred borders of my gross generality. But as soon as I say this, I want to shout that I refuse to write prose poems, that I want to write the work that is always in search of itself, in a form that is always building itself from the inside out.

In that I am more at home in my work than in describing it, I offer an example below, "A Chair":

A chair has waited such a long time to be with its person. Through shadow and fly buzz and the floating dust it has waited such a long time to be with its person. What it remembers of the forest it forgets, and dreams of a room where it waits—Of the cup and the ceiling—Of the animate one.

*   *   *

Russell Edson is a central exponent of the American prose poem, a form to which he has devoted himself for some forty years. He has never been quite at ease with the term, however, preferring to describe his inventions as short prose or to speak of an undefined form discovered in the act of writing. His distinctive paragraphs appear in both poetry anthologies and in collections of short-short fiction.

Edson's work has changed little since he began to publish in the early 1960s. Derived from surrealism and the absurd, his verse paragraphs are capricious, provocative, irreverent, and hilarious. Because they are often peopled by animals, they are sometimes called fables, but they might better be called antifables, for they release energies opposite to the comforting morality of the traditional fable. They can be called moral lessons only in the obverse, since they define an amoral world, a theater of cruelty that is comically perverse, threatening, and incoherent.

There are exceptions, and one can discover conventional sentiments in the Edson oeuvre. For instance, a man looking for love is told that he will never find it ''because it was anywhere you went, but you kept going because you will love nothing.'' One can even find an occasional soft image that suggests the influence of oriental poetry: ''In the end only dough, a soft white boulder . . . / Faint dawn, the cry of birds . . .'' But the haiku-like suspension of the ending is corrected by its outlandish context. The poem is about a woman who gets so caught up in kneading that her hands become part of the dough and are ''worn to white wrist stumps.'' Finally she disappears.

The impetus in Edson is narrative and dramatic, not descriptive. Description, after all, requires stasis, but in Edson things rarely hold still long enough to be pictured. Landscape is insignificant, a ''large place out the window.'' Characters dominate and include people, animals, and objects: a man who keeps his father in a sack, a bird that decides to become a Greek statue, a toilet that demands to be loved. Leveling is a key strategy. For example, one Edson character explains that he ''no longer tells up from down''; they are ''mirror images of equal value.'' Everything is alive with feeling and significance, but nothing is valorized.

Individual pieces range in tone and subject matter from gentle caprice to sheer foolishness to rude violence. But the emblem of Edson's oeuvre as a whole is an iconoclastic, cynical-whimsical stance, the manifestation of a fictive realm that is not merely askew but also unstable at its core.

Donald Hall has called the Edson cosmos ''pure surrealism,'' not the surreal twist of plot or description used to surprise but ''a whole irrational universe.'' This inside-out cosmos goes beyond confusion to celebrate coincidence and make the alogical seem everyday. Primal and infantile, it writhes with loony metamorphosis, good-natured cannibalism, lighthearted bestiality, and comic violence. Edson's world includes a rat who ''wanted to put its tail in an old woman's vagina'' to keep it from getting stepped on, identical twins who have to take turns being alive, a woman who beats an ox to death with her apron strings, a man who has a mouse for a daughter and, while teaching her to dance, steps on her and then presses her like

a flower into a book. Nonsensical as they are, the stories are not meaningless. They hold meanings we recognize but rarely acknowledge; they are subtext made surface.

Edson's most persistent target is the myth of the happy family, which he defines as a falsehood:

A husband and wife discover that their children are fakes.
Mildred is not a real daughter.
Nor is Frederick a real son.
But then the husband discovers that his wife is not a real wife, even as she discovers that he is not a real husband.
So it's all right if a fake husband and a fake wife have fakes for children.
Even their neighbors are fakes . . .

In particular, Edson likes to debunk the beatification of motherhood:

There was also a huge face on mother's back which was her real face. The other little face was a phoney little face that pretends kindness on the front of her head. The huge face looks at one as mother pretends to be washing dishes at the sink, it is the big ugly man that looks out of her back, her apron tied in the back to effect a bow tie effect for the big ugly man.

Most of Edson's mothers are absurdist recapitulations of tired Freudian dogma, and the destructive mythic mother appears again and again. In one selection a young man becomes infatuated with a piece of toast, which his mother eats: ''In a moment's time mother had eaten the only thing that I had ever come near to loving.'' He grabs another piece as a substitute: ''Mother seeing my happiness and admiring my grownupness slapped me with affection across the mouth.''

Eating—devouring—is central in Edson's writing. Everything feeds on everything else. A cookie eats a man ''with a glass of milk and a kind word from the man's mother.'' An old woman cooks her dog for his own dinner and then realizes that he cannot eat himself. A physician, called to heal a poor duck that got cooked by mistake, eats his patient part by part, suggesting prosthetic replacements for each eaten leg and wing; when he has eaten all of it, he suggests that a rubber duck could take its place. Edson defines his province as ''a land'' that is ''eating itself'' and ''forming itself.'' At the center of this universe God is eating a jelly sandwich.

Edson's plot is the familiar twentieth-century story of alienation and outrage. Yet Edson is an original among the many iconoclasts who unmask our nice ideas. He has taken forms typical of absurd drama and surreal film or fiction and embedded them in the prose poem. His zany realm is closer to Chaplin, Pynchon, or Vonnegut than to the territory of most poets. His odd, flat, jerky, childish syntax; his distinct manner, which combines a chuckle, a scream, and a shrug; the pure otherness of his world—these combine to provide a remedy to sweet, harmless verses.

—Jane Somerville

ELLIOT, Alistair

Nationality: British. **Born:** Liverpool, Lancashire, 13 October 1932. **Education:** Attended schools in Wigan, Hoylake, and the United States, 1941–45; Fettes College, Edinburgh, 1946–50; Christ Church, Oxford, B.A. 1955, M.A. 1958. **Family:** Married Barbara Demaine in 1956; two sons. **Career:** Actor and stage manager, English Children's Theatre, London, 1957–59; assistant librarian, Kensington, London, 1959–61; cataloguer, Keele University Library, 1961–65; accessions librarian, Pahlavi University Library, Shiraz, Iran, 1965–67; special collections librarian, Newcastle upon Tyne University Library, 1967–82. Since 1983 freelance writer. **Awards:** Arts Council grant, 1979; Prudence Farmer award (*New Statesman*), 1983, 1991; Ingram Merrill Foundation fellowship, 1983; Djerassi Foundation fellowship, 1984. **Agent:** Nicki Stoddart, Peters Fraser and Dunlop, Drury House, 34–43 Russell Street, London WC2B 5HA, England. **Address:** 27 Hawthorn Road, Newcastle upon Tyne NE3 4DE, England.

PUBLICATIONS

Poetry

Air in the Wrong Place. Newcastle upon Tyne, Eagle Press, 1968.
Contentions. Sunderland, Ceolfrith Press, 1977.
Kisses. Sunderland, Ceolfrith Press, 1978.
Talking to Bede. Ashington, Mid-Northumberland Arts Group, 1982.
Talking Back. London, Secker and Warburg, 1982.
On the Appian Way. London, Secker and Warburg, 1984.
My Country: Collected Poems. Manchester, Carcanet, 1989.
Turning the Stones. Manchester, Carcanet, 1993.
Facing Things. Manchester, Carcanet, 1997.

Play

Medea, translation of the play by Euripides (produced London, 1992; New York, 1994). London, Oberon Books, 1993.

Other

Editor, *Poems by James I and Others.* Newcastle upon Tyne, Eagle Press, 1970.
Editor, *Lines on the Jordan.* Newcastle upon Tyne, Eagle Press, 1971.
Editor, The *Georgics with John Dryden's Translation,* by Virgil. Ashington, Mid-Northumberland Arts Group, 1981.
Editor and translator, *French Love Poems* (bilingual). Newcastle upon Tyne, Bloodaxe, 1991.
Editor and translator, *Italian Landscape Poems* (bilingual). Newcastle upon Tyne, Bloodaxe, 1993.

Translator, *Alcestis,* by Euripides. San Francisco, Chandler, 1965.
Translator, *Peace,* by Aristophanes, in *Greek Comedy.* New York, Dell, 1965.
Translator, *Femmes/Hombres, Women/Men,* by Paul Verlaine. London, Anvil Press Poetry, 1979; New York, Sheep Meadow Press, 1984.
Translator, *The Lazarus Poems,* by Heinrich Heine. Ashington, Mid-Northumberland Arts Group, 1979.

Translator, *Medea,* by Euripides. London, Oberon Books, 1993.
Translator, *La Jeune Parque,* by Paul Valéry. Newcastle upon Tyne, Bloodaxe, 1997.

*

Manuscript Collection: Literary and Philosophical Society, Newcastle upon Tyne.

Critical Studies: By Alan Hollinghurst, in *Times Literary Supplement* (London), 30 September 1983; by Peter Jones, in *The Times* (London), 18 July 1984; by Peter Porter, in *The Observer* (London), 29 July 1984.

Alistair Elliot comments:

My poems are usually in traditional forms, and either with full or half-rhymes, because I think I perform better on a frame than when just jumping about.

Their contents are fairly varied: for example, a modern party explained to a long dead poet; walking instead of driving to work; meeting someone who has the exact voice of someone I once loved; a blanket spun and woven by my grandmother; clipping toenails as an activity common to all human cultures and times; and most recently a journey from Rome to Brindisi, a book-length poem.

I don't think there are limits on what one can write "about"—lately I have begun to feel that perhaps when I die I can take with me anything I have mentioned in a poem, so I think about furnishing my afterlife. On the other hand, the insurable contents of a poem are not, it seems, entirely in the poet's control. I used to see it as a matter of pulling a poem from its hiding place by the tail, knowing it can shed the tail and get away. Now it seems more as if I am trying to mind read the Muse, who has seen the unwritten poem somewhere in a book of the future.

I try hard to make my work clear and comprehensible; at least the gist of a poem should come across when read aloud to an audience. But I think that should make the audience feel eager to meet the poem itself, that is, the poem on the page, the real whole poem as opposed to one of its sonic shadows. I don't see this audience, these creatures feeding round the pool of general knowledge, in very definite terms—I just expect they will be like me, members of a species that on the whole delights in language, in stories about itself, in nifty problems, in imagined and described things. Some poets try to use verse to change or fortify their readers' point of view. I don't seem to be interested in that, in general, but I have written the odd argumentative poem.

(1995) Translation takes much longer than original writing, perhaps four times as long. I am quite surprised it is possible, since I have never been able to write a poem suggested by another person, and a translation is precisely that, writing something to detailed specifications. I like to think I take at least as much trouble over a translation text as a critic or a textual editor does; though I may have to cut through a Gordian uncertainty with alexandrine gusto and perhaps even give myself the license a cook inevitably takes with a recipe, I normally attempt to read everything my author wrote, or as much as I can in the time I am working on him, so that I feel confident I know what the main drift is as well as what each sentence means. For example, I read all of Euripides for *Medea* and Verlaine's prose books as well as his verse. I have a habit of reading foreign verse in bed first thing in the morning—it sets me up for the day—and I sometimes have to sit down afterwards and translate something difficult in order to force an understanding. To me, then, translation is a form of critical reading, among other things.

*   *   *

In his first full-length book, *Contentions,* Alistair Elliot hardly prepared his readers for the extraordinary accomplishment of his second, *Talking Back.* Elliot's talent needed time to come into its own. At first sight the poems in *Talking Back* might perhaps appear bookish or overly scholarly (titles such as ''Talking to Horace'' or ''The Aegean: Summer 493 B.C.'' hardly help dispel this impression), but once read with care and a feeling intelligence, they begin to reveal their depths as well. As Dick Davis has pointed out, ''Elliot writes as if we still (just) share a common culture and care about what happens to it.'' Elliot certainly sees nothing wrong in writing poetry that appeals to the intellect and even presupposes from the reader a degree of knowledge within a living literary tradition. Of the twenty-four pages in the pamphlet publication of *Talking to Bede,* three consist of a chronology of useful dates from A.D. 547 to 1370, and six are notes on the poem. What is surprising, given these facts, is the poem's essential liveliness of idiom and tone, for it seems actually to be talking with Bede and the reader:

You think historians must be keen to see
What followed their escape from history?
You think we can't find out? I'd rather hear
The earth described. Remind us of the Wear,
The creatures, plants and light where I began
To look around the domicile of man,
The home I only saw till I was seven.

Thus Elliot gives Bede a local habitation in his poem. This is the very best use of scholarship in poetry. Learning is never on display to impress but rather is always born of an enthusiasm for bringing history to life in the present. This side to Elliot is counterbalanced by his ability—already independently achieved by his contemporary Tony Harrison—to write plainly and also movingly about matters of his own family history. The poem ''John Elliot'' maintains a correlation between events in history contemporaneous with events in the personal history, from birth to death, of his grandfather, linking the private life with public events. It ends with a stark image:

Still never losing your temper,
you grew old in the long beard,
and died, before my parents met.
Years later, my father recognised your arm-bone
held out in the grave
at his mother's funeral:
I'd have seen you—if I'd gone.

The care that has gone into making this poem and its truthfulness to a family memory allow the image to have a sensitive delicacy of emotion. As the wife rejoins her husband in a grave, the dead are allowed dignity without a trace of sentimentality. Those who say that Elliot's imagination is most forcefully fueled by Virgil, Horace, Livy, and other classical writers should bear in mind poems such as this or the equally moving ''Bless the Bed That I Lie On,'' written for his grandmother Marion Elliot. The poem, which is collected in *My*

Country: Collected Poems, uses the image of a blanket made by his grandmother to record another instance of the loving kindness that binds together husband and wife in life and death. Elliot's virtuosity with language controls and shapes powerful personal emotion in such poems:

The history of this blanket's partly known:
You made it—starting not from yarn but wool
Sheared perhaps from a known sheep in Glencoul,
And lichen, from the ultrabasic stone.

On the Appian Way, originally a book-length poem, traces Elliot's journey in Italy along the route taken from Rome by the poet Horace in 37 B.C. The poem combines Elliot's usual liveliness of narration with an effortless and urbane artistry. It celebrates everyday things such as, for instance, breakfast in a bar, while also including enough allusions to Horace's poem on the same journey to fill twelve pages of notes on a work the author claims ''is as unobscure and impersonal as I could make it.'' The poem, divided into fifteen sections, each marking one day and the places seen, is in heroic couplets; the tone, perhaps reminiscent of Arthur Hugh Clough's masterpiece ''Amours de Voyage,'' allows Elliot to be both formal and relaxed:

These are the hardest hours to justify,
Not envied by the dead—the hours I pass
Gaping at their possessions behind glass,
Windowshopping like Tantalus, an ape
That, hands in pockets, comprehends pure shape
Vacuously.

My Country includes, in addition to the works discussed here, ''The American Poems,'' a substantial group from a journey in the United States in 1983–84, taking in places as diverse as Arizona, California, Florida, and New York. The forms and subjects are as various as the places seen, and—as in *On the Appian Way*—the poems, alternately ironic and entertaining, incorporate the detail of daily life for the traveler, as in ''Reasons for Happiness in San Francisco'':

There are pleasures in maintenance:
Buying stationery (on Haight);
Leaving my Harris wool
Sportsjacket to be cleaned, by a Chinese,
Of its American dust

There also is good work in the other new poems in the collection. These include the already mentioned ''Bless the Bed That I Lie On'' and other firmly controlled, yet deeply moving poems on his grandparents and family.

Elliot's book *Turning the Stones* contains further evidence of the development of his talent along a range of themes. The book contains fine poems touching on classical themes, including ''Homer,'' ''Cornelia,'' and ''My Brown Boots,'' the last a long and quirkily entertaining poem on the loss of a pair of old ''coffee-boots'' in an excursion around Arcadia. It also includes poems on visits to the United States and two poems on horses. One of these, ''At Appleby Horse Fair,'' is an outstanding example of Elliot's ability to write clearly about an activity—here the long-surviving outdoor horse market at Appleby-in-Westmoreland in northern England—and to provide the reader with a real insight into the meaning it offers for our lives. The poem explains the close relationship between the young men and the horses they are there to sell. ''Selling your friends is a hard job; / it helps to do it with style,'' the poem concludes.

Some of the best poems in *Turning the Stones* look back in time to make connections with members of the poet's Scottish family or with Elliot's own early days. An example is ''Remains of Mining in the Upper Peninsula, Michigan,'' in which he detects among an old log cabin the domestic scent of his grandmother's farmhouse. In these thoughtful and understated poems the reader is allowed an insight into what Elliot calls ''the bounty of the past'' and the vitality of past lives as remade in the present.

Elliot's poems, those of his first book aside, are throughout—and often simultaneously—literate entertainment, a moving documentation of life, and high art. His reputation has grown steadily over the years and has spread among those who care for poetry.

—Jonathan Barker

ELMSLIE, Kenward (Gray)

Nationality: American. **Born:** New York City, 27 April 1929. **Education:** Harvard University, Cambridge, Massachusetts, B.A. 1950. **Career:** Worked with the Karamu Inter-Racial Theatre, Cleveland. Art critic, *Art News*, New York, 1966–67. Since 1972 publisher and editor, Z Press, and editor, *Z Magazine*, 1973–77, Calais, Vermont. **Awards:** Ford grant, 1964; National Endowment for the Arts grant, 1966, 1978; 1980; Frank O'Hara award, 1971; Cynthia Weir Librettist award, 1998. **Address:** Poets Corner, Calais, Vermont 05648, U.S.A.

PUBLICATIONS

Poetry

Pavilions. New York, Tibor de Nagy, 1961.
Power Plant Poems. New York, ''C'' Press, 1967.
The Champ. Los Angeles, Black Sparrow Press, 1968; Pittsfield, Massachusetts, The Figures, 1994.
Album, New York, Kulchur, 1969.
Circus Nerves. Los Angeles, Black Sparrow Press, 1971.
Motor Disturbance. New York, Columbia University Press, 1971.
Girl Machine. New York, Angel Hair, 1971.
Penguin Modern Poets 24, with Kenneth Koch and James Schuyler. London, Penguin, 1973.
Tropicalism. Calais, Vermont, Z Press, 1975.
Topiary Trek. N.p., Topia Press, 1977.
Communications Equipment. Providence, Rhode Island, Burning Deck, 1979.
Moving Right Along. Calais, Vermont, Z Press, 1980.
Sung Sex. New York, Kulchur, 1989.
Champ Dust. Boulder, Colorado, The New Censorship, 1994.
The Champ, with Joe Brainard. Lenox, Massachusetts, The Figures, 1994.
Bare Bones. Flint, Michigan, Bamberger, 1995.

Routine Disruptions, Selected Poems & Lyrics. Minneapolis, Minnesota, Coffee House Press, 1999.
Cyberspace, with Trevor Winkfield. New York, Granary, 2000.
Nite Soil. New York, Granary, 2000.

Recordings: *Lizzie Borden,* Desto, 1967; *The Sweet Bye and Bye,* Desto, 1970; *The Grass Harp,* Painted Smiles, 1972; *Rare Meat,* Watershed, 1979; *Highlights from ''Miss Julie,''* Painted Smiles, 1980; *Kenward Elmslie Visited,* Painted Smiles, 1982; *Palais Bimbo Lounge Show,* Painted Smiles, 1985; *Lola,* Painted Smiles, 1985; *Three Sisters,* Painted Smiles, 1986; *26 Bars,* Z Press, 1987; *Miss Julie,* Newport Classic, 1998; *Postcards on Parade,* Harbinger Records, 1999.

Plays

The Sweet Bye and Bye, music by Jack Beeson (produced New York, 1956). New York, Boosey and Hawkes, 1966.
Unpacking the Black Trunk with James Schuyler (produced New York, 1965).
Lizzie Borden, music by Jack Beeson (produced New York, 1965, revived 1999 and televised *Live from Lincoln Center,* PBS). New York, Boosey and Hawkes, 1966.
Miss Julie, music by Ned Rorem (produced New York, 1965, revised version, San Francisco, 1999). New York, Boosey and Hawkes, 1965.
The Grass Harp, music by Claibe Richardson, adaptation of the novel by Truman Capote (produced New York, 1971). New York, French, 1971.
City Junket (produced New York, 1974). New York, Boke, 1972.
The Seagull, music by Thomas Pasatieri, adaptation of the play by Chekhov (produced Houston, 1974). Melville, New York, Belwin Mills, 1974.
Washington Square, music by Thomas Pasatieri, adaptation of the novel by Henry James (produced Detroit, 1976). Melville, New York, Belwin Mills, 1976.
Lola, music by Claibe Richardson (produced New York, 1982).
Three Sisters, music by Thomas Pasatieri (produced Columbus, Ohio, 1986). Calais, Vermont, Z Press, 1986.
Postcards on Parade, music by Steven Taylor (produced New York, 2000). Flint, Michigan, Bamberger Books, 1993.

Novel

The Orchid Stories. New York, Doubleday, 1973.

Other

The Baby Book. New York, Boke, 1965.
The 1967 Gamebook Calendar. New York, Boke, 1967.
Shiny Ride. New York, Boke, 1972.
The Alphabet Work. Washington, D.C., Titanic Press, 1978.
Bimbo Dirt. Calais, Vermont, Z Press, 1981.
Palais Bimbo Snapshots. Grindstone City, Michigan, Alternative Press, 1982.
Stage-Duo, with Anne Waldman. Cherry Valley, New York, Rocky Ledge, 1983.
26 Bars. Calais, Vermont, Z Press, 1987.
Pay Dirt, with Joe Brainard. Flint, Michigan, Bamberger Books, 1992.

Editor, *Miltie Is a Hackie: A Libretto,* by Edwin Denby. Calais,
   Vermont, Z Press, 1973.
Editor, *Mobile Homes,* by Rudy Burckhardt. Calais, Vermont, Z
   Press, 1979.
Editor. *Tulsa Kid.* Calais. Vermont, Z Press, 1980.

*

Bibliography: *Kenward Elmslie, A Bibliographical Profile* by William C. Bamberger, Flint, Michigan, Bamberger Books, 1993.

Critical Studies: "Poetry and Public Experience" by Stephen Donadio, in *Commentary* (New York), February 1973; "Figure in the Carport" by John Ashbery, in *Parnassus* (New York), Summer 1976; "A Tribute to Kenward Elmslie" by Michael Silverblatt, in *Blarney* (Los Angeles), Spring 1984; "Poets Corner" by Brad Gooch, in *House and Garden* (New York), November 1986; "Millennium Plainsongs" by Bill Berkson, in *New York Native,* 14 April 1986; by Robert Peters, in *Review of Contemporary Fiction,* Summer 1994; "One Sings, the Other Doesn't" by Christopher Luna, in *Colorado Daily,* 106(185), 19 November 1998; by Gary Sullivan, in *Rain Taxi,* 3(4), Winter 1998–99; by Alice Notley, in *Poetry Project Newsletter,* 173, March 1999; "Poetry, Libretto & Song" by Scott Hreha, in *Minnesota Daily,* 11 April 1999.

Kenward Elmslie comments:

   Since about 1961 I have considered myself primarily a poet; before that I thought of myself, and was, primarily a writer of lyrics for theater songs. I have continued to write for the theater, have ventured into fiction, but I feel most centered as a writer when working on a poem. I enjoy collaborating with composers and visual artists, and, increasingly, I have begun singing poem-songs, set to music I have made up. I am sometimes listed as a member of the New York school of poets, an outgrowth of friendship with the founders—Kenneth Koch, John Ashbery, the late James Schuyler, and Frank O'Hara—but it makes me uneasy to think of my work thus conjoined, partly because of the range of influences that have been of use: Wallace Stevens, John Latouche, Bert Brecht, Ron Padgett, Jane Bowles, John Ashbery, Frank O'Hara, Kenneth Koch, Evelyn Waugh, Lorenz Hart, Ira Gershwin, Alex Katz, Red Grooms, Joe Brainard, Ken Tisa, Donna Dennis, and the films of Jacques Tati.

*   *   *

   Poet, librettist, and novelist, Kenward Elmslie has affinities with the New York school, with O'Hara and Ashbery or perhaps Ted Berrigan and Joe Brainard. His poems and prose poems (the opera libretti are rather different) are characterized by the juxtaposition of precise, and yet bizarre, sensory observations, as in "Tropicalism":

   Ate orange.
   Legs stained . . . stains turn into fur patches . . .
   fur patches turn into puma hide . . . palaver re
   escape route . . . boy's lips . . . chicken feather along
   outer perimeter of lower redder one, with
   up-and-down wrinkles fly is negotiating . . .
   too much pursing . . . spooky profiles peer
   sideways on high-rise balconies . . .

Elmslie is a poet of transformation and metamorphosis, and things flow into things with an almost delirious momentum. Experience has no order that might allow the observer to stand at a discreet distance from the observed, as shown in "Olden Scrapple Sonnet":

   Wept at the way they gave of theirselves,
   the flasher's midriff entangled in cobwebs,
   the way Thebes, roped off, mazurka-polka'd,
   sex nuances forgotten for glitz of vernal equinox.
   Then by bad roads out of the sad mountains,
   lit-up arrows arching into stage-shows,
   Bijou: self-acting clogs in orphanage orangerie,
   Palace: abandoned. Lugged myself to primal hut.

   Elmslie writes of the "maelstrom of remembered sights and sounds" ("Long Haul"), and at times there emerges from the seeming modernity of his linguistic usage an atmosphere of whimsy and nostalgia that can verge on the sentimentally lyrical. Poetic structure is a problem; at times syntax is abandoned, while some poems retain a more or less orthodox syntactical organization. One interesting development has been the use in poems such as "Regret Space Not Include" and "One Hundred I Remembers" of a formal device whereby each "verse" begins with the same verbal formula, rather in the manner, say, of Christopher Smart's *Jubilate Agno.* It is here perhaps that many readers find Elmslie most accessible. His confrontation with life's particularities is described in "Black Froth":

   Disjointed a necessary mode of life ill-prepared for.
   Eager for the seamlessness underneath.

The search for the "seamlessness" produces challenging verbal constructions that occasionally exclude the reader. At his best, however, Elmslie's energy and invention combine to create records of a very individual sensibility.

—Glyn Pursglove

EMANUEL, James A(ndrew, Sr.)

Nationality: American. **Born:** Alliance, Nebraska, 15 June 1921. **Education:** Alliance High School, 1935–39; Howard University, Washington, D.C., 1946–50, B.A. (summa cum laude) 1950; Northwestern University, Evanston, Illinois, 1950–53, M.A. 1953; Columbia University, New York, 1953–62, Ph.D. 1962. **Military Service:** 93rd Infantry Division, U.S. Army, 1944–46: Sergeant; Army Commendation Ribbon. **Family:** Married Mattie Johnson in 1950 (divorced 1974); one son (deceased 1983). **Career:** Canteen steward, Civilian Conservation Corps, Wellington, Kansas, 1939–40; elevator operator, Des Moines, Iowa, 1940–41; weighmaster, Rock Island, Illinois, 1941–42; confidential secretary, Office of the Inspector General, U.S. War Department, Washington, D.C. 1942–44; civilian chief, Pre-Induction Section, Army and Air Force Induction Station, Chicago, 1950–53; instructor, Harlem YWCA Business School, New York, 1954–56; instructor, 1957–62, assistant professor, 1962–70, associate professor, 1970–72, and professor of English, 1973–84, City College of New York; Fulbright Professor of American Literature, University of Grenoble, 1968–69, and University of Warsaw, 1975–76; visiting professor of American Literature, University of

Toulouse, 1971–73, 1979–81. General Editor, Broadside Critics Series, Detroit, 1969–75. **Awards:** John Hay Whitney fellowship, 1952, 1953; Saxton memorial fellowship, 1964; *Black American Literature Forum* Special Distinction award (for poetry), 1978. **Address:** B.P. 339, 75266 Paris Cedex 06, France.

PUBLICATIONS

Poetry

The Treehouse and Other Poems. Detroit, Broadside Press, 1968.
At Bay. Detroit, Broadside Press, 1969.
Panther Man. Detroit, Broadside Press, 1970.
Black Man Abroad: The Toulouse Poems. Detroit, Lotus Press, 1978.
A Chisel in the Dark: Poems, Selected and New. Detroit, Lotus Press, 1980.
A Poet's Mind. New York, Regents, 1983.
The Broken Bowl: New and Uncollected Poems. Detroit, Lotus Press, 1983.
Deadly James and Other Poems. Detroit, Lotus Press, 1987.
The Quagmire Effect. Paris, American College, 1988.
Whole Grain: Collected Poems, 1958–1989. Detroit, Lotus Press, 1991.
De la rage au coeur, bilingual with French translations by Jean Migrenne. Thaon, France, Amiot Lenganey, 1992.
Blues in Black and White, with Godelieve Simons. Brussels, Belgium, privately printed, 1992.
Reaching for Mumia: 16 Haiku. Paris, L'insomniaque éditeur, 1995.
JAZZ from the Haiku King. Detroit, Broadside Press, 1999.

Recordings: *The Treehouse and Other Poems,* Broadside Voices, 1968; *Panther Man,* Broadside Voices, 1970.

Other

Langston Hughes. New York, Twayne, 1967.
How I Write 2, with MacKinlay Kantor and Lawrence Osgood. New York, Harcourt Brace, 1972.

Editor, with Theodore L. Gross, *Dark Symphony: Negro Literature in America.* New York, Free Press, 1968.

*

Manuscript Collection: Jay B. Hubbell Center, Perkins Library, Duke University, Durham, North Carolina; Manuscript Division, The Library of Congress, Washington, D.C.

Critical Studies: In *Road Apple Review* (Oshkosh, Wisconsin), Winter 1971–72; "James A. Emanuel: The Perilous Stairs," in *Caliban* (Toulouse, France), 12, 1976, and "Black Man Abroad: James A. Emanuel," in *Black American Literature Forum* (Terre Haute, Indiana), Fall 1979, both by Marvin Holdt; *Black American Poetry: A Critical Commentary* by Ann Semel and Kathleen Mullen, New York, Monarch Press, 1977; *La Rive Noire: De Harlem à la Seine* by Michel Fabre, Paris, Lieu Commun, 1985; "A Poet's Self: Restructuring the Fragments" by Anthony Suter, in *Caliban* (Toulouse, France), 23, 1986; "James Emanuel: A Poet in Exile" by Michael Fabre, in his *From Harlem to Paris: Black American Writers in France, 1840–1980,* Urbana and Chicago, University of Illinois Press, 1991; "Sanctuary" by Toni Y. Joseph, in *One Voice,* Dallas, The Dallas-Fort Worth Association of Black Communicators, 1994.

James A. Emanuel comments:

(1974) Some of the personal history and many of the ideas reflected in my poetry can be found in my contribution to the book *How I Write* 2. By now writing poetry is my principal method of finding and expressing what life means. From the time that I began to write poetry steadily, in the late 1950s, the exacting labor and the large mysteries of that activity—usually carried on late at night—have centered upon vital, everyday matters. The categories into which my poems can be divided describe areas of experience and thought with which ordinary men are well acquainted, and I have wanted my poetry to be fundamentally clear to the largest possible audience. Recurrent subjects are youth (centrally my son, James) and miscellaneous black experience; other subjects include writers, anti-Semitism, blues, war, etc. The lyrics continue philosophical, descriptive, and personal themes. The tone is usually serious, sometimes satirical, once in a while humorous; the form varies from strict sonnets to free verse that attempts to catch nuances of black American speech patterns that might be heard on a Harlem street. My poetry runs roughly parallel to my life: a movement from the reflective traditional to the compressed tensions of the 1970s, with inevitably special emphasis on racism but also with constantly interspersed lyrics that have little to do with our perilous decades. Thus I hope that my poetry, in its unplanned evolution and variety, attests the crucial, dual role of the black poet: to struggle as embroiled man but to reflect as clear mind; to denude and expose as destroyer yet to clothe and grace as creator; to live as black and therefore made for the wide world yet American and therefore made for the narrow cauldron that our nation has become.

My latest work, especially "The Toulouse Poems" and generally those written in and after 1972, might well suggest that three loves develop in my work: parental, racial, and romantic. These common passions are the staple of my poetry. Trying to fathom them and to transform them into art, I am content to be judged by that mass of readers who feel as strongly as they think and who are drawn to what I want increasingly to keep in my poetry: the bite and song of reality.

(1980) Reviewing my poems written recently in London and Paris, I find experiments with antirealism coming into my work, perhaps as an intensification of my grappling with such subjects as tyranny, art, and time.

(1995) Having published my first college poem almost fifty years ago, I have a long backward glance covering facts that would crowd this entry: my poems in over 120 anthologies; M.A. theses on them; thirty-odd years of public readings of them; translations of them; art exhibits abroad with American and foreign artists' work based on them; radio discussions of them on France Culture's *Panorama* program; my public launching of my new creations, "jazz haiku" and "blues haiku," in 1993; my life and works treated in fifty reference books; my fourteen awards from international biographical centers in the past four years; and my university-archived autobiographies, *From the Bad Lands to the Capital* (1943–44) and *Snowflakes and Steel: My Life as a Poet, 1971–1980* (1981).

Yet, as C. Day Lewis suggested in his preface to the first edition of *Contemporary Poets,* perhaps 10 percent, perhaps only 1 percent, of us in this book will survive as "names" in poetry. Our lifetime facts, like mine above, will disappear if not steadily absorbed into remembered, reread poems. Since this absorption occurs outside the powers of us who are neither leaders nor wheelhorses in the fields where literary reputations are raised, we have placed our hopes on durable themes and proven craftsmanship.

The 215 poems in my collection *Whole Grain* (1991) reveal at least twenty-one large thematic categories, none foretelling my innovative jazz and blues forms. My innumerable poem drafts record my craving for the exact word, the breathing image, the pared-down line, the harnessed rhythm. These hard demands are matched in sincerity by my hope that critics worth their salt will follow the lead of Marvin Holdt, Anthony Suter, and Michel Fabre in France, the efforts of Douglas Watson and James de Jongh in the U.S.A., by searching the substance and methods of my best poems, which I have labeled in my files as "the top ten percent." Going that far, may they go farther.

(2000) As this third millennium begins, my hindsight should have the merit of age, and my foresight risks little. After over forty years of publishing, I believe that my best contributions to prose are *Langston Hughes* (1967) and my later essays on that author; *Dark Symphony: Negro Literature in America* (1968), done with Theodore Gross; and "A Force in the Field," in *Contemporary Authors Autobiography Series,* vol. 18 (1994). I think, then, that my critical faculties, my comprehension of the accomplishments of my brother-writers, and my grasp of the meaning of my own life have been well-recorded.

Nothing remains as a hard literary task except the extended expression of my force as a poet, largely with the expected creative collaboration (in art-plus-poetry books) of Godelieve Simons of Brussels, the authority on women engravers in her country.

*   *   *

James A. Emanuel's sympathies are clear even without his statement in *Panther Man* that young people are "the only people whom I tend to respect as a group." Poems like "A Clown at Ten," "The Young Ones, Flip Side," "Fourteen," "Sixteen, Yeah," and "Fisherman" celebrate with an understanding smile the passion and energy of youth while they steer clear of Housmanian idolatry and pathos. Young adulthood is pain, punching, and confusion for the poet, the hopeful stage through which the world passes to confrontation. Behind it stretches the prelapsarian vista of childhood. The poet captures the antics of the bathtub sailor in "The Voyage of Jimmy Poo," a time of sterling memory in "I Wish I Had a Red Balloon," and the joy of answering children's questions in "For the 4th Grade, Prospect School: How I Became a Poet."

Manhood brings a different order: understanding, rebellion, militancy, anguish, and death. "Emmett Till," "Where Will Their Names Go Down," and "For Malcolm, U.S.A." pay tribute to the victims, while "Panther Man," "Animal Tricks," "Crossover: for RFK," and "Black Man, 13th Floor" speak in strident—sometimes black and idiomatic—tones of the growth of a generation of men who are rising to take control.

Surrounding and undergirding all stages, however, is the essential romantic humanism of the poet. "Nightmare" and "Christ, One Morning" let us know that all is in the hands of man; there is no God who can be trusted. Ceaselessly, Emanuel reaffirms the power of the imaginative intellect to scale the heights of its own tree house and to dream ("A Negro Author" and "The Treehouse") or to bring the

authoritarian assumptions of the world down with a wince ("Black Poet on the Firing Range"). The poems from Toulouse show a sweep and maturity that combine this essential vision with a firm formal mastery.

—Houston A. Baker, Jr.

ENGELS, John (David)

Nationality: American. **Born:** South Bend, Indiana, 19 January 1931. **Education:** University of Notre Dame, Indiana, A.B. 1952; University College, Dublin, 1955; University of Iowa, Iowa City, M.F.A. 1957. **Military Service:** U.S. Navy, 1952–55: Lieutenant. **Family:** Married Gail Jochimsen in 1957; two daughters and four sons (one deceased). **Career:** Instructor in English, Norbert College, West De Pere, Wisconsin, 1957–62. Assistant professor, 1962–70, and since 1970 professor of English, St. Michael's College, Winooski Park, Vermont. Visiting lecturer, University of Vermont, Burlington, 1974, 1975, 1976; Slaughter Lecturer, Sweet Briar College, Virginia, 1976; writer-in-residence, Randolph Macon Woman's College, Virginia, 1992. Secretary, 1971–72, and trustee, 1971–75, Vermont Council on the Arts. **Awards:** Bread Loaf Writers Conference scholarship, 1960, and Robert Frost fellowship, 1976; Guggenheim fellowship, 1979. **Address:** Department of English, St. Michael's College, Winooski Park, Vermont 05404, U.S.A.

PUBLICATIONS

Poetry

The Homer Mitchell Place. Pittsburgh, University of Pittsburgh Press, 1968.
Signals from the Safety Coffin. Pittsburgh, University of Pittsburgh Press, 1975.
Vivaldi in Early Fall. Burlington, Vermont, Bittersweet Press, 1977.
Blood Mountain. Pittsburgh, University of Pittsburgh Press, 1977.
Vivaldi in Early Fall (collection). Athens, University of Georgia Press, 1981.
The Seasons in Vermont. Syracuse, Tamarack, 1982.
Weather-Fear: New and Selected Poems 1958–1982. Athens, University of Georgia Press, 1983.
Cardinals in the Ice Age. St. Paul, Minnesota, Graywolf Press, 1987.
Walking to Cootehill: New and Selected Poems, 1958–1992. Hanover, New Hampshire, University Press of New England, 1993.
Big Water. New York, Lyons & Burford, 1995.
Sinking Creek: Poems. New York, Lyons Press, 1998.

Other

Writing Techniques, with Norbert Engels. New York, McKay, 1962.
Experience and Imagination, with Norbert Engels. New York, McKay, 1965.

Editor, *The Merrill Guide to William Carlos Williams.* Columbus. Ohio. Merrill, 1969.

Editor, *The Merrill Checklist of William Carlos Williams*. Columbus, Ohio, Merrill, 1969.

Editor, *The Merrill Studies in Paterson*. Columbus, Ohio, Merrill, 1971.

*   *   *

Through eight full volumes—the fifth and seventh selections spanning, respectively, twenty-five and thirty-five years of work— John Engels's poems reveal themselves to be parts of one long, complex, and intense meditation on the struggle of mind with matter, earth with air, death with love. The poems, varied in subject and manner, never arrive at easy answers but rather pause at the soul's leap into air or recoil at the earth's deadly bull's-eye or end in a terrible balance between brute fact and injured thought.

The poems in the first five books all center in the consciousness of a man living for many years in a single house in Vermont, aware always of the stagnant water seeping into his cellar and up into his living air, wary and worried by winter's deadly encroachments, wounded beyond solace by the death of his baby son, and yet still able to count over the names of his living family, wife and children, still able to make the act of love, which consists of his continuing attempts to name the world, to give it words by which to live. The scope of his poetry is, then, small—this house, these people, these doubts and concerns. But its range and depth are enormous as Engels worries these simple subjects into a poetry as disciplined and intense and deeply meaningful as that of any modern poet.

Engels is never content with the results of his words' wrestle with matter. From his first book, *The Homer Mitchell Place*, to *Big Water* he has returned to the same subjects, themes, and images, reshaping them, restating them, reassessing them, always pressing them deeper toward a continually elusive meaning. In *Weather-Fear* he reworked and relined poems, compressing them on the page, holding back the flow of their rich rhythms, aware always that they still do not say enough of what they must say if they are to push away from the earth's grave downpulling into the soul's freed flight. This dissatisfaction, which is at the heart of his poetry's dynamic tension, emerges explicitly in the long and central poem "Interlachen," with which he ends *Weather-Fear*:

I tend to speak, though lacking
clarity, not knowing
the names, not having in need
the language, given to interminable
revision of the text. And this is where
the true anger locates itself,
that I have no ability or hope
that I may speak to the ordinary with much
in the way of truth or generosity.
And it must seem I make these rituals
as if they were sole judge of the truth,
not merely sanctimonies of procedure, noble
appearances of moral care
by reason of which the names refuse themselves,
and it all ends
in such unsatisfactory obliquities as this.

Despite and perhaps because of his sense of inadequacy in the face of the overwhelming task, Engels's speaking "to the ordinary" has, as he described Mozart's music, "seized in the real and made to

flash forth / the mute transparencies / of matter." In *Cardinals in the Ice Age* he extends his personal voice and local concerns into other voices and into eastern Europe, to Subotica and Slovenj Gradec, Bohinj and Skopje, a ranging out that he continues in *Walking to Cootehill*. But in alien places with difficult names he finds himself struggling with the same problems, shaping them into words and into vital form. Still only "a whisker from / annihilation," he finds himself in a living museum of horrors and wonders, having no choice but to trust the loud stranger at the taxi's wheel because in this strange world he is "unable / with clarity to see enough ahead / to mark our proper turnings / and prepare for them."

Engels is a major voice in American poetry, one not given proper credit at a time when simple anecdote or surreal political statement is accorded lavish critical attention. Yet his sure growth from the controlled metrical force of his early poems through the mythic breakthrough of the poems in *Blood Mountain* to the sustained musical visions of the later poems in *Vivaldi in Early Fall,* the grand reassessments of *Weather-Fear,* the new locales and voices in *Cardinals in the Ice* Age, and the careful unifying of his work (poems old and new taking proper places in the design) in *Walking to Cootehill* and *Big Water* (a gathering of old and new poems about fishing) is that of a serious craftsman and a genuinely visionary artist. Like the other artists of whom he has written—Mozart and Vivaldi, Mahler and van Gogh—he has produced a body of work in which change and sustained vision are in total harmony, in which we dare name our darkness, know the shock of our fall that made the whole earth shake, and feel the bruise that congeals at the very root of our being.

What Engels finally gives us is our most basic fear made tangible, grounded in a language of weight and substantial gravity, and from that ground he forces us aloft, lifts our gaze from the sealed grave and gaping cellar hole to a vision earned in all that painful darkness, a moment, as he puts it in "The Disconnections,"

in the dazzling, translucid sea-light, union of particles
beyond all series, never so light as then, the earth
closed on itself and centered, gravid
with bodies, trembling to give birth.

—R.H.W. Dillard

ENRIGHT, D(ennis) J(oseph)

Nationality: British. **Born:** Leamington, Warwickshire, 11 March 1920. **Education:** Leamington College; Downing College, Cambridge, B.A. (honors) in English 1944, M.A. 1946; University of Alexandria, Egypt, D.Litt. 1949. **Family:** Married Madeleine Harders in 1949; one daughter. **Career:** Lecturer in English, University of Alexandria, 1947–50; organizing tutor, Extra-Mural Department, Birmingham University, 1950–53; visiting professor, Konan University, Kobe, Japan, 1953–56; Gastdozent, Free University, West Berlin, 1956–57; British Council Professor of English, Chulalongkorn University, Bangkok, 1957–59; professor of English, University of Singapore, 1960–70; temporary lecturer in English, University of Leeds, Yorkshire, 1970–71; honorary professor of English, University of Warwick, Coventry, 1975–80. Since 1982 freelance writer. Coeditor, Encounter magazine, London, 1970–72; editorial adviser, 1971–73 and member of the board of directors, 1973–82, Chatto and Windus publishers, London. **Awards:** Cholmondeley Award, 1974;

Society of Authors traveling scholarship, 1981; Queen's Gold Medal for Poetry, 1981; companion of literature, 1999. H.D.L.: University of Warwick, 1982; H.D. Univ.: University of Surrey, Guildford, 1985. Fellow, Royal Society of Literature, 1961. OBE (Officer, Order of the British Empire), 1991. **Agent:** Watson Little Ltd., Capo di Monte, Windmill Hill, London NW3 6RJ. **Address:** 35-A Viewfield Road, London SW18 5JD, England.

PUBLICATIONS

Poetry

Season Ticket. Alexandria, Editions du Scarabée, 1948.
The Laughing Hyena and Other Poems. London, Routledge, 1953.
The Year of the Monkey. Kobe, privately printed, 1956.
Bread Rather Than Blossoms. London, Secker and Warburg, 1956.
Some Men Are Brothers. London, Chatto and Windus, 1960.
Addictions. London, Chatto and Windus, 1962.
The Old Adam. London, Chatto and Windus, 1965.
Unlawful Assembly. London, Chatto and Windus, and Middletown, Connecticut, Wesleyan University Press, 1968.
Selected Poems. London, Chatto and Windus, 1969.
The Typewriter Revolution and Other Poems. New York, Library Press, 1971.
In the Basilica of the Annunciation. London, Poem-of-the-Month Club, 1971.
Daughters of Earth. London, Chatto and Windus, 1972.
Foreign Devils. London, Covent Garden Press, 1972.
The Terrible Shears: Scenes from a Twenties Childhood. London, Chatto and Windus, 1973; Middletown, Connecticut, Wesleyan University Press, 1974.
Rhyme Times Rhyme (for children). London, Chatto and Windus. 1974.
Sad Ires and Others. London, Chatto and Windus, 1975.
Penguin Modern Poets 26, with Dannie Abse and Michael Longley. London, Penguin, 1975.
Paradise Illustrated. London, Chatto and Windus, 1978.
A Faust Book. London, Oxford University Press, 1979.
Walking in the Harz Mountains, Faust Senses the Presence of God. Richmond, Surrey, Keepsake Press, 1979.
Collected Poems. Oxford and New York, Oxford University Press, 1981.
Instant Chronicles. Oxford and New York, Oxford University Press, 1985.
Collected Poems 1987. Oxford and New York, Oxford University Press, 1987.
Selected Poems 1990. Oxford and New York, Oxford University Press. 1990.
Under the Circumstances. Oxford and New York, Oxford University Press, 1991.
Old Men and Comets. Oxford and New York, Oxford University Press, 1993.
Collected Poems 1948–1998. Oxford and New York, Oxford University Press, 1998.

Novels

Academic Year. London, Secker and Warburg, 1955.
Heaven Knows Where. London, Secker and Warburg, 1957.

Insufficient Poppy. London, Chatto and Windus, 1960.
Figures of Speech. London, Heinemann, 1965.

Other

A Commentary on Goethe's "Faust." New York, New Directions, 1949.
The World of Dew. Aspects of Living Japan. London, Secker and Warburg, 1955; Chester Springs, Pennsylvania. Dufour, 1959.
Literature for Man's Sake: Critical Essays. Tokyo, Kenkyusha, 1955.
The Apothecary's Shop. London, Secker and Warburg, 1957; Chester Springs, Pennsylvania, Dufour, 1959.
Robert Graves and the Decline of Modernism (address). Singapore, Craftsman Press, 1960.
Conspirators and Poets. London, Chatto and Windus, and Chester Springs, Pennsylvania, Dufour, 1966.
Memoirs of a Mendicant Professor. London, Chatto and Windus, 1969.
Shakespeare and the Students. London, Chatto and Windus, 1970; New York, Schocken, 1971
Man Is an Onion: Essays and Reviews. London, Chatto and Windus, 1972; LaSalle, Illinois, Library Press, 1973.
A Kidnapped Child of Heaven: The Poetry of Arthur Hugh Clough (lecture). Nottingham, University of Nottingham, 1972.
The Joke Shop (for children). London, Chatto and Windus, and New York, McKay, 1976.
Wild Ghost Chase (for children). London, Chatto and Windus, 1978.
Beyond Land's End (for children). London, Chatto and Windus, 1979.
A Mania for Sentences. London, Chatto and Windus, 1983; Boston, Godine, 1985.
The Alluring Problem: An Essay on Irony. Oxford and New York, Oxford University Press, 1986.
Fields of Vision: Essays on Literature, Language, and Television. Oxford and New York, Oxford University Press, 1988.
Interplay: A Kind of Commonplace Book. Oxford and New York, Oxford University Press, 1995.
Play Resumed: A Journal. Oxford and New York, Oxford University Press, 1999.

Editor, *Poets of the 1950's: An Anthology of New English Verse.* Tokyo, Kenkyusha, 1955.
Editor, with Takamichi Ninomiya, *The Poetry of Living Japan.* London, Murray, and New York, Grove Press, 1957.
Editor, with Ernst de Chickera, *English Critical Texts: 16th Century to 20th Century.* London and New York, Oxford University Press, 1962.
Editor, *A Choice of Milton's Verse.* London, Faber, 1975.
Editor, *Rasselas,* by Samuel Johnson. London, Penguin, 1976.
Editor, *The Oxford Book of Contemporary Verse 1945–1980.* Oxford, Oxford University Press, 1980.
Editor, *The Oxford Book of Death.* Oxford and New York, Oxford University Press, 1983.
Editor, *Fair of Speech: The Uses of Euphemism.* Oxford and New York, Oxford University Press, 1985.
Editor, *The Faber Book of Fevers and Frets.* London, Faber, 1989.
Editor, with David Rawlinson, *The Oxford Book of Friendship.* Oxford and New York, Oxford University Press, 1991.
Editor, *The Oxford Book of the Supernatural.* Oxford and New York, Oxford University Press, 1994.

Translator, with Madeleine Enright, *Nature Alive,* by Colette Portal. London, Chatto and Windus, 1980.

Translator/Reviser, with Madeleine Enright, *In Search of Lost Time,* by Marcel Proust. London, Chatto and Windus, and New York, Random House, 1992.

*

Critical Studies: *D.J. Enright: Poet of Humanism* by William Walsh, London, Cambridge University Press, 1974; "No Easy Answer: The Poetry of D.J. Enright" by Shirley Chew, in *New Lugano Review* (Lugano, Switzerland), vol. 3, no. 1–2, 1977; Anthony John Harding, in *Poets of Great Britain and Ireland 1945–1960,* edited by Vincent B. Sherry, Jr., Detroit, Gale, 1984; *Life by Other Means: Essays on D.J. Enright* edited by Jacqueline Simms, Oxford, Oxford University Press, 1990.

*   *   *

The chief stimulus for the highly individual talent of D.J. Enright has been the landscape and people of the countries, mainly in the Far East, where he has spent most of his working life. Some characteristic attitudes already apparent in early poems about his native Black Country—in, for example, his pointing to the incongruity between the idyllic name and dreary reality of Swan Village—have persisted in later work like the disenchanted cameos of commuter London in *Sad Ires* or of the contemporary English scene satirized in *Paradise Illustrated.*

But it is through Enright's pictures of life abroad that his sense of ironic contrast is most memorably communicated, as in "The Beach at Abousir" between vacationers and those "pointed shapes, like trees in winter— / Aged men and ancient children" patiently waiting their chance to pilfer from the prosperous. In Japan the cherry "comes to its immaculate birth" amid poverty, hunger, and disease. A beautiful peasant girl is found to be a perfect subject by filmmakers "except for the dropsy / Which comes from unpolished rice" (the grim wordplay of the title, "A Polished Performance," is typical). Ragged subway sleepers, tensely "hectic rice-winners" commuting on the subway, and the ragman who "picks his comfort" in the gentle beauty of the Kyoto autumn make their silent but uncompromising comment on a society of extremes. In "A Pleasant Walk," contrasting the rows of banks lining "a noble promenade . . . paved in gold from every nation" with "the brutal village sunk in slush," Enright bitterly observes that "high commerce civilizes, there's no doubt of that." The banker of "Happy New Year," bemoaning the falling yen as he shows off his opulent house and art treasures, is relentlessly juxtaposed with the empty-pocketed "masters of their fourpenny kites / That soar in the open market of the sky"; the "moderate ambitions" of princes and generals for an air-conditioned palace, a smarter general headquarters, are shown against the refugees of "Brush-Fire" in flight from their burning shacks, pushing bicycles piled with small bundles. The controlled anger of "The Monuments of Hiroshima" is matched by the deadly fairy-tale idiom employed to recount a bombing error in "The Pied Piper of Akashi."

To Enright's acute, compassionate eye the great enemy is indifference to suffering, whether in the anonymous multitude or in the individual tragedy like that of the thirteen-year-old suicide who found rat poison cheaper than aspirin. In his dry, amused relish of the ludicrous he can often be very funny, but it is a humor, as in the caustic comment of "Public Address System" on the grotesqueries of excessive official politeness, from which the biting edge is seldom absent. "Simply, he was human, did no harm, and suffered for it" is his epitaph for the poor and oppressed; his sense of the common sadness of the human condition is most poignantly crystallized in the diffident, fragile nocturnal melody, at once elegiac and celebrating survival, of "The Noodle-Vendor's Flute."

The shock of large-scale misery and squalor to a caring Western sensibility is frequently registered through the accent of deliberate, almost casual understatement that allows the recorded fact to speak for itself, and this powerful restraint serves to intensify by contrast the impassioned force of the writer's pity and indignation. In common with his fellows of the so-called Movement, Enright has resolutely refused to sentimentalize the apparently picturesque, rejecting "epochs of parakeets, of peacocks, and paradisaic birds" for unembellished "images that merely were." This is reflected in his astringent advice in "Changing the Subject" and the wry self-mockery of an acknowledged poetic temptation in "Displaced Person Looks at a Cage-Bird," while both "Nature Poetry" and the enchanting "Blue Umbrellas" survey our distortions of reality by "the dishonesty of names."

Slyly quizzical, irreverent, socially inconvenient in his impatience of humbug, Enright directs the same remorseless wit toward his own shortcomings, as in "The Fairies," "The Ageing Poet," and "A Commuter's Tale," the barbs part of his scrutiny of the human sham, from minister of state to theorizing anarchist or romanticizing poet. A skeptical inner voice prompts him to question whether his own persistent choice of exotic backgrounds might not represent an escapist "rest from meaning." The answer is provided by his characteristic affirmation that "nothing is exotic, if you understand, / If you stick your neck out for an hour or two." The special tone of this civilized, ironic, unostentatious voice is invoked in "Elegy in a Country Suburb":

> Wholly truthful, intimate
> And utterly unsparing,
> A man communing with himself.

—Margaret Willy

ENSLIN, Theodore (Vernon)

Nationality: American. **Born:** Chester, Pennsylvania, 25 March 1925. **Education:** Attended public and private schools; studied composition with Nadia Boulanger, 1943–44. **Family:** Married 1) Mildred Marie Stout in 1945 (divorced 1961), one daughter and one son; 2) Alison Jane Jose in 1969, one son. **Career:** Columnist ("Six Miles Square"), The Cape Codder, Orleans, Massachusetts, 1949–56. **Awards:** Nieman award, for journalism, 1955; National Endowment for the Arts grant, 1976. **Address:** R.F.D. Box 289, Kansas Road, Milbridge, Maine 04658, U.S.A.

PUBLICATIONS

Poetry

The Work Proposed. Ashland, Massachusetts, Origin Press, 1958.

New Sharon's Prospect. Kyoto, Japan, Origin Press, 1962.

The Place Where I Am Standing. New Rochelle, New York, Elizabeth Press, 1964.

This Do (and The Talents). Mexico City, El Corno Emplumado, 1966.

New Sharon's Prospect and Journals. San Francisco, Coyote's Journal, 1966.

To Come to Have Become. New Rochelle, New York, Elizabeth Press, 1966.

The Four Temperaments. Privately printed, 1966.

The Dependencies. New York, Caterpillar, 1966.

Characters in Certain Places. Portland, Oregon, Prensa da Lagar-Wine Press, 1967.

The Diabelli Variations and Other Poems. Annandale-on-Hudson, New York, Matter, 1967.

2/30–6/31: Poems 1967. Cabot, Vermont, Stoveside Press, 1967.

Agreement and Back: Sequences. New Rochelle, New York, Elizabeth Press, 1969.

The Poems. New Rochelle, New York, Elizabeth Press, 1970.

Forms. New Rochelle, New York, Elizabeth Press, 5 vols., 1970–74.

Views 1–7. Berkeley, California, Maya, 1970.

The Country of Our Consciousness. Berkeley, California, Sand Dollar, 1971.

Etudes. New Rochelle, New York, Elizabeth Press, 1972.

Views. New Rochelle, New York, Elizabeth Press, 1973.

Sitio. Hanover, New Hampshire, Granite, 1973.

In the Keepers House. Dennis, Massachusetts, Salt Works Press, 1973.

With Light Reflected. Fremont, Michigan, Sumac Press, 1973.

The Swamp Fox. Dennis, Massachusetts, Salt Works Press, 1973.

The Mornings. Berkeley, California, Shaman/Drum, 1974.

Fever Poems. Brunswick, Maine, Blackberry, 1974.

The Last Days of October. Dennis, Massachusetts, Salt Works Press, 1974.

The Median Flow: Poems 1943–73. Los Angeles, Black Sparrow Press, 1974.

Synthesis 1–24. Plainfield, Vermont, North Atlantic, 1975.

Ländler. New Rochelle, New York, Elizabeth Press, 1975.

Some Pastorals. Dennis, Massachusetts, Salt Works Press, 1975.

Papers. New Rochelle, New York, Elizabeth Press, 1976.

Carmina. Dennis, Massachusetts, Salt Works Press, 1976.

The Further Regions. Milwaukee, Pentagram Press, 1977.

Ascensions. Santa Barbara, California, Black Sparrow Press, 1977.

Circles. Lewiston, Maine, Great Raven Press, 1977.

Concentrations. Dennis, Massachusetts, Salt Works Press, 1977.

Ranger CXXII and CXXVIII. Rhinebeck, New York, Station Hill Press, 1977.

Tailings. Milwaukee, Pentagram Press, 1978.

16 Blossoms in February. Brunswick, Maine, Blackberry, 1979.

Ranger, Ranger 2. Richmond, California, North Atlantic, 2 vols., 1979–80.

May Fault. Lewiston, Maine, Great Raven Press, 1979.

Opus 31, No. 3. Milwaukee, Membrane Press, 1979.

A Root in March. Orono, University of Maine Press, 1979.

The Flare of Beginning Is in November. New York, Jordan Davies, 1980.

The Fifth Direction. Milwaukee, Pentagram Press, 1980.

Star Anise. Milwaukee, Pentagram Press, 1980.

Two Geese. Milwaukee, Pentagram Press, 1980.

In Duo Concertante. Milwaukee, Pentagram Press, 1981.

Markings. Milwaukee, Membrane Press, 1981.

Opus O. Milwaukee, Membrane Press, 1981.

Processionals. Dennis, Massachusetts, Salt Works Press, 1981.

Knee Deep in the Atlantic, with others. Milwaukee, Pentagram Press, 1981.

September's Bonfire. Elmwood, Connecticut, Potes and Poets Press, 1981.

Axes 52. Willimantic, Connecticut, Ziesing Brothers, 1981.

To Come Home (To). Lewiston, Maine, Great Raven Press, 1982.

Meditations on Varied Grounds. Hartford, Connecticut, Potes and Poets Press, 1982.

Passacaglia. Bayonne, New Jersey, Beehive Press, 1982.

"F.P." Willimantic, Connecticut, Ziesing Brothers, 1982.

A Man in Stir. Milwaukee, Pentagram Press, 1983.

Grey Days. N.p., Last Straw Press, 1984.

Songs Without Notes. Grenada, Mississippi, Salt-Works Press, 1984.

Music for Several Occasions. Milwaukee, Membrane Press, 1985.

The Weather Within. Madison, Wisconsin, Landlocked Press, 1985.

Meeting at Jal, with Keith Wilson. N.p., Southwestern American Literature Association, 1985.

For Mr. Walters, Master Mechanic. Warrenville, Connecticut, Shirt Pocket Press, 1985.

I Am You Are. Brattleboro, Vermont, Green River, 1985.

The Path Between. South Harpswell, Maine, Blackberry, 1986.

The Waking of the Eye. Weymouth, Stingy Artist/Last Straw Press, 1986.

Case Book. Elmwood, Connecticut, Potes and Poets Press, 1987.

From near the Great Pine. Peoria, Illinois, Spoon River Press, 1988.

Love & Science. Kenosha, Wisconsin, Light and Dust Books, 1990.

Gamma Ut. Charleston, Illinois, Tel Let, 1992.

A Sonare. Green River, Vermont, Longhouse, 1994.

Communitas. Hobbs, New Mexico, Writers on the Plains, 1996.

Skeins. Brattleboro, Vermont, Longhouse-Origin, 1998.

Re-Sounding: Selected Later Poems. Jersey City, New Jersey, Talisman House, 1999.

Sequentiae. London, Stop Press, 1999.

Then and Now: Selected Poems, 1943–1993. Hanover, New Hampshire, University Press of New England, 1999.

Play

Barometric Pressure 29.83 and Steady (produced New York, 1965).

Short Stories

2 + 12. Dennis, Massachusetts, Salt Works Press, 1979.

Other

Mahler. Los Angeles, Black Sparrow Press, 1975.

The July Book. Berkeley, California, Sand Dollar, 1976.

Editor, *The Selected Poems of Howard McCord 1961–1971.* Trumansburg, New York, Crossing Press, 1975.

Translator, *Fragments/Epigrammata,* by Pindar and Calimachus. Dennis, Massachusetts, Salt Works Press, 1982.

*

Manuscript Collection: Fales Collection, New York University Libraries.

Critical Studies: "The Frozen State" by the author, in *Elizabeth* (New Rochelle, New York), 1965; Theodore Enslin issue of *Truck 20* (St. Paul), 1978; Theodore Enslin issue of *Talisman* (Hoboken, New Jersey), 12, 1994; "Toward a Common Ground: Versions of Place in the Poetry of Charles Olson, Edward Dorn, and Theodore Enslin" by Burton Hatlen, in *Sagetrieb* (Orono, Maine), 15(3), winter 1996.

Theodore Enslin comments:

I suppose I would classify as a nonacademic and have been allied with those who broke with the New Criticism in the early 1950s.

Perhaps, as Cid Corman once said, I write more "you" poems than anyone else now alive. My themes are what I find around me, and since I live in the country, this has sometimes led to thinking that I am in some way a nature poet. I heartily disavow this. My poems are intensely introspective, from which I attempt to produce the impersonality/personality that I feel necessary to any valid work of art. My formal structure is based on sound, and I feel that my musical training has shaped this more than anything else. The line breaks/stresses are indicated as a type of notation, something that concerns me since I believe we have no adequate notation for poetry and I conceive of any poem as requiring a performance. It should be read aloud. In ways, some important to me and some to the work itself, I would say that Rilke, W.C. Williams, Thoreau, and latterly Louis Zukofsky were influences. The rest must be said in the poems themselves.

(1995) I am increasingly dismayed at the neglect of poetry—the text itself—in favor of criticism, often ill informed. May I make a plea? Return to the work itself. It may bring pleasant surprises.

*   *   *

Theodore Enslin's work became known in the pages of *Origin,* the seminal magazine edited by Cid Corman, who also published Enslin's first book. It is not surprising, then, to find a continuity between the work of the two men. Both write spare, quiet post-Williams poems grounded in a shared respect for the otherness and autonomy of natural things and a distrust of the romantic ego. A basic premise is that the sufficiently careful naming of phenomena can by itself energize attention. But Enslin is more diffuse than Corman. Many of his poems read quickly seem merely flat, no more than prose jottings. Reread, however, with due attention to the lineation and sound, the best of them take on a pondered weight and become meditations rather than mere statements. His method of condensing daily experience and observation into poems can be seen in the charming *New Sharon's Prospect,* which gives both the prose anecdotes and sketches and the poems that crystallize out of them.

Enslin's work is filled with the places, people, and things of rural New England, where he lives. If at times it reminds you of a Frost landscape, it is free of Frost's often intrusive personality. Others of his poems are more abstract notations of emotion or of the problematic relations of observer and external reality. The following is from *The Place Where I Am Standing:*

I turned once to the window
and once
to you
        not here.
I would have shown you
a world I see there,
but it would not have been your world.
It is better this way
In absence, you come to the window,
look out on just those things
I have shown you.

The five volumes of *Forms,* a long open-structure poem, are the product of "sixteen years of experiment and discovery" that Enslin describes as "my apperception of art, of history, of experience, whatever any of it may have been worth, and no matter how limited." First acquaintance suggests that this is less rewarding than the short poems, but the interest of the latter is grounds enough for thinking that the long work will deserve frequentation.

—Seamus Cooney

EQUI, Elaine

Nationality: American. **Born:** Chicago. **Education:** Columbia College, Chicago, M.A. in writing. **Family:** Married Jerome Sala. **Career:** Teacher, New School and the Writers Voice, New York.

PUBLICATIONS

Poetry

Federal Woman. Chicago, Danaides Press, 1978.
Shrewcrazy: Poems. Los Angeles, Little Caesar Press, 1981.
The Corners of the Mouth. Culver City, California, Iridescence, 1986.
Accessories. Great Barrington, Massachusetts, The Figures, 1988.
Surface Tension: Poems. Minneapolis, Coffee House Press, 1989.
Decoy: Poems. Minneapolis, Coffee House Press, 1994.
Voice-Over: Poems. Minneapolis, Coffee House Press, 1998.
Friendship with Things. Great Barrington, Massachusetts, The Figures, 1998.

*

Critical Study: "Rooted: Staying Home with Elaine Equi and Susan Gervitz" by the author and Gervitz, in *Village Voice Literary Supplement* (New York), 124, April 1994.

*   *   *

Here is a poem from Elaine Equi's volume *Surface Tension* (1989) entitled "Last Night of the Year":

Listen with your eyes
With all the senses

Take things home
to the present tense

Black coffee
Green grapes
        Paper
White narcissus

Lines that intersect
create their own drama
and the distance
between is actually
a form of participation

You didn't know that
not really
        until now
or you wouldn't
have insisted
on adding so much

Equi is a poet who listens "with all the senses," her eyes especially, and "take(s) things home" into the present. Her images "create their own drama," and "the distance between" them is the reader's participation in the poem. Indeed, readers get into trouble if they do not realize this and try to move within the poems without adding anything. When Equi, especially in her earlier works, writes lines like "generic / as a puff / of flag / / or the bullet-headed / beam / of an apple," it is difficult to make the brain bend around such images, to make even the vaguest sort of linear sense out of them. As she says in the poem "Summary," "it's the words / that are important / but there aren't any." Of course there are words, but in some poems the words are beside the point. The point lies somewhere in between the words.

Although she grew up in Chicago, Equi identifies herself as a New York poet, and she is a tremendous fan of Frank O'Hara. She owes much to his work, and hers contains the same positive bounce, extroversion, conversational banter, and verbal ease. She is at her best in her later poems, which seem to enjoy greater cohesion, as in the delightful "Lesbian Corn":

In summer
I strip away
Your pale kimono.
your tousled hair too,
comes off in my hands
leaving you
completely naked.
All ears and
tiny yellow teeth.

And as her work has progressed, cohesiveness has become the norm, or perhaps it has simply become easier to recognize. Nevertheless, the more random poems are always fun, even if they seem to lie just beyond any possibility of intellectual grasp. The poems leap from a nervy kind of sophistication to a fresh, street-smart, pop-conscious hopefulness.

From the volume *Decoy* (1994) comes the poem "This Is Not a Poem":

the poem exists
always and only
in the mind
of the reader

and these words
can never be more than
arrows, breadcrumbs

a map of abbreviations
however crude or elaborate

the poem comes into being
as the writer reads
and the reader anticipates

one can fill every inch
with writing and still
be no closer to the poem

as it lies there
a liar with a beautiful voice
that is often mistaken for silence

This poem, more contemplative than most of Equi's writings, reminds the reader of the importance of seeing the poem as "a map of abbreviations" that calls upon the reader to spell out the words in their entirety.

Yet Equi has matured into gracefulness without sacrificing buoyancy. It is as if she has taken to heart her own observation from the title poem in the volume *Voice-Over* (1998): "In poetry too / we like our lyricism / minus the garlic / on the poet's breath."

—Judy Clarence

ERDRICH, (Karen) Louise

Nationality: American (Native American: Turtle Mountain Band of Ojibwa). **Born:** Little Falls, Minnesota, 7 June 1954. **Education:** Dartmouth College, Hanover, New Hampshire, B.A. 1976; Johns Hopkins University, Baltimore, Maryland, M.A. 1977. **Family:** Married Michael Dorris in 1981 (died 1997); two sons and four daughters. **Career:** Visiting poetry teacher, North Dakota State Arts Council, 1977–78; creative writing teacher, Johns Hopkins University, 1978–79; communications director and editor of *Circle,* Boston Indian Council, Massachusetts, 1979–80; text book writer, Charles-Merrill Company, 1980; visiting fellow, Dartmouth College, 1981. Also has worked as a beet weeder in Wahpeton, North Dakota; waitress in Wahpeton, Boston, and Syracuse, New York; psychiatric aide in a Vermont hospital, poetry teacher in prisons; lifeguard; and construction flag signaler. **Awards:** MacDowell fellowship, 1980; Yaddo fellowship, 1981; Nelson Algren award, 1982; National Book Critics Circle award, 1984; Virginia Scully prize, 1984; Sue Kaufman award, 1984; *Los Angeles Times* Book award, 1985; Guggenheim fellowship, 1985. **Member:** American Academy of Arts and Letters; American Academy of Arts and Sciences. **Address:** c/o HarperCollins, 10 East 53rd Street, New York, 10022, U.S.A.

PUBLICATIONS

Poetry

Jacklight. New York, Holt, 1984.
Baptism of Desire. New York, HarperCollins, 1989.

Recordings: *Louise Erdrich and Michael Dorris with Paul Bailey* (videotape), Roland Collection of Films on Art, 1980; *Conversations with Louise Erdrich and Michael Dorris,* Jackson, University Press of Mississippi, 1994.

Novels

Love Medicine. New York, Holt, 1984; London, Deutsch, 1985.
The Beet Queen. New York, Holt, 1986; London, Hamish Hamilton, 1987.
Tracks. New York, Holt, and London, Hamish Hamilton, 1988.
Crown of Columbus, with Michael Dorris. New York and London, HarperCollins, 1991.
The Bingo Palace. London, Flamingo, 1994.
Tales of Burning Love. New York, HarperCollins, 1997.
The Antelope Wife. New York, HarperCollins, 1998.

Other

Route 2, with Michael Dorris. Northridge, California, Lord John Press, 1990.
The Bluejay's Dance: A Birth Year. New York, HarperCollins, 1995.
Grandmother's Pigeon (for children). New York, Hyperion, 1996.
The Birchbark House (for children). New York, Hyperion, 1999.

Editor, with David Solheim, *Plainsong: Writings from North Dakota's Poets-in-the-Schools Program, 1975–1977.* Fargo, North Dakota, North Dakota Council on the Arts, 1978.

*

Critical Studies: ''Transactions in a Native Land: Mixed-Blood Identity and Indian Legacy in Louise Erdrich's Writing'' by Daniela Daniele, in *RSA Journal,* 3, 1992; ''Working (In) the In-Between: Poetry, Criticism, Interrogation, and Interruption'' by Jeannie Ludlow, in *Studies in American Indian Literatures* (Virginia), 6(1), Spring 1994; ''The Construction of Gender and Ethnicity in the Poetry of Leslie Silko and Louise Erdrich'' by Susan Perez Castillo, in *ICLA '91 Tokyo: The Force of Vision, II: Visions in History; Visions of the Other,* edited by Earl Miner and others, Tokyo, International Comparative Literature Association, 1995; ''Sacramental Language: Ritual in the Poetry of Louise Erdrich'' by P. Jane Hafen, in *Great Plains Quarterly* (Lincoln, Nebraska), 16(3), Summer 1996.

* * *

Louise Erdrich's standing as a poet rests with the two volumes of poetry that she published in the 1980s, *Jacklight* (1984) and *Baptism*

of Desire (1989). Even if she were to continue to concentrate on writing prose fiction, as she has done since then, and never publish another collection of her poems, her reputation as a poet would be solid. She has already established herself with the truthful intensity of her poetic expression, her fearlessness in the use of myth to express the realities of the human heart, and the imaginative exactness of her language.

Of Ojibwa (Chippewa) and German heritage (she is a member of the Turtle Mountain band of Ojibwa), Erdrich was raised in Wahpeton, North Dakota, and she uses all of these elements of ancestry and place in her poetry. The *Jacklight* poems tend to fall into five overlapping thematic categories: poems of Indian heritage in conflict with the dominant white culture; poems of sisterhood and family; love poems; poems peopled with the shadows of figures from her past; and mythic poems that draw upon Native American myths and the habit of mythmaking.

Among the poems of tension between the Indian and white worlds are some of Erdrich's best and most frequently anthologized poems, including ''Indian Boarding School: The Runaways,'' which recounts the habitual running away of children from an Indian boarding school to the Indian place of their dreams ''just under Turtle Mountains.'' They know that the sheriff will be ''waiting at midrun / to take us back,'' but ''home's the place we head for in our sleep.'' Like the tracks on the land of the railroad they ride, ''the worn-down welts / of ancient punishments lead back and forth.'' ''Dear John Wayne'' presents the reaction of young Indians to a John Wayne western at a drive-in movie. When it is over, they continue to hear his voice speaking its real message: *''Come on, boys, we got them / where we want them, drunk, running. / They'll give us what we want, what we need.''*

''A Love Medicine'' represents Erdrich's sisterhood-family poems. When ''this dragonfly, my sister'' feels the boot of her man planting ''its grin / among the arches of her face,'' the speaker responds with her whole feminine being: *''Sister, there is nothing / I would not do.''*

Erdrich's love poems tend to have a poignantly sad note that is echoed in ''Train'': ''Here is the light I was born with, love. / Here is the bleak radiance that levels the world.'' Mary Kröger is the most powerful figure in the character poems of ''The Butcher's Wife'' section of *Jacklight.* Futilely pursued by Rudy J.V. Jacklitch, the sheriff who crashed his truck and died cursing her, Mary hears her name destroyed by the townspeople until she ''feared to have it whispered in their mouths!''

Among the best poems in the fine ''Myths'' section of *Jacklight* is ''Whooping Cranes,'' a haunting poem about a foundling boy, ''strange and secret among the others, / killing crows with his bare hands / and kissing his own face in the mirror,'' who ends up flying into the mystical formation of whooping cranes that ''sailed over / trumpeting the boy's name.'' Noteworthy, too, is the Potchikoo mythical prose poem cycle about a man born as a ''potato boy'' after ''a very pretty Chippewa girl'' is raped by the sun in a potato field. Archetypally, Potchikoo dies when his three lovely daughters visit him in his old age, sit on his lap, and block the sun from him: ''He hardly knew it when all three daughters laid their heads dreamily against his chest. They were cold, and so heavy that his ribs snapped apart like little dry twigs.''

Baptism of Desire projects very much the same range and depth as the earlier volume. Indeed, some of the same characters—Rudy

J.V. Jacklitch, Mary Kröger, the mythic Potchikoo—do encore appearances, for which readers of *Jacklight* must be grateful. The main change is that *Baptism* is, paradoxically, even more spiritual in its earthiness. In "The Sacraments," for example, a richly portrayed rain dance merges with the Christian sacraments. In "Mary Magdalene," after she washes "your ankles / with my tears," Mary sardonically resolves to "drive boys / to smash empty bottles on their brows. / I will pull them right off of their skins." She concludes with an observation that is at once earthy and spiritually rebellious: "It is the old way that girls / get even with their fathers— / by wrecking their bodies on other men."

The poet and critic Simon Ortiz has summed up the strength of Erdrich's poetry succinctly: ". . . by knowing a bit of truthful fear we may know courage, love, faith, life. That is the way I experience Erdrich's poems of revelation. She is a remarkable, remarkable writer."

—Alan Shucard

ESHLEMAN, Clayton

Nationality: American. **Born:** Indianapolis, Indiana, 1 June 1935. **Education:** Indiana University, Bloomington, 1953–61, B.A. in philosophy 1958, M.A. in creative writing 1961. **Family:** Married 1) Barbara Novak in 1961 (divorced 1967), one son; 2) Caryl Reiter in 1969. **Career:** Instructor, University of Maryland Eastern Overseas Division, Taiwan, Korea, and Japan, 1961–62; instructor in English, Matsushita Electric Corporation, Osaka, Japan, 1962–64; lived in Peru, 1965; instructor, New York University American Language Institute, 1966–68; member of the School of Critical Studies, California Institute of the Arts, Valencia, 1970–72; taught at University of California, Los Angeles, 1975–77; taught in a black ghetto high school in Los Angeles (California Arts Council grant), 1977–78; visiting lecturer in creative writing, University of California, San Diego, Riverside, Los Angeles, and Santa Barbara, 1979–86; Dreyfuss poet-in-residence, and lecturer, California Institute of Technology, Pasadena, 1979–84. Since 1986 professor of English, Eastern Michigan University, Ypsilanti. Editor, *Folio,* Bloomington, Indiana, 1959–60; publisher, Caterpillar Books, 1966–68, and editor, *Caterpillar* magazine, New York, 1967–70, and Sherman Oaks, California, 1970–73; reviewer, *Los Angeles Times Book Review,* 1979–86. Since 1981 founder and editor, *Sulfur* magazine, Pasadena, then Ypsilanti, Michigan. **Awards:** National Translation Center award, 1967, 1968; Union League Civic and Arts Foundation prize (*Poetry,* Chicago), 1968; National Endowment for the Arts grant, 1969, fellowship, 1979, 1981; Coordinating Council of Literary Magazines grant, 1969, 1970, 1971, 1975; P.E.N. award, for translation, 1977; Guggenheim fellowship,1978; National Book award, for translation, 1979; National Endowment for the Humanities grant, 1980, fellowship, 1981; Soros Foundation travel grant, 1986; Cooper fellow, Swarthmore College, 1987; National Endowment for the Arts translation fellowship, 1988; Michigan Arts Council grant, 1988; Distinguished Faculty Research/Creativity award, 1989, and Faculty Research fellowship, 1990, Eastern Michigan University; Michigan Artists award, the

Arts Foundation of Michigan, 1992; Academic Specialist grant, U.S.I.A., Mexican Translation Project, 1992. **Address:** 210 Washtenaw Avenue, Ypsilanti, Michigan 48197, U.S.A.

PUBLICATIONS

Poetry

Mexico and North. Privately printed, 1962.
The Chavin Illumination. Lima, Peru, and La Rama, Florida, 1965.
Lachrymae Mateo: 3 Poems for Christmas 1966. New York, Caterpillar, 1966.
Walks. New York, Caterpillar, 1967.
The Crocus Bud. Reno, Nevada, Camels Coming, 1967.
Brother Stones. New York, Caterpillar, 1968.
Cantaloups and Splendour. Los Angeles, Black Sparrow Press, 1968.
T'ai. Cambridge, Massachusetts, Sans Souci Press, 1969.
The House of Okumura. Toronto, Weed/Flower Press, 1969.
Indiana. Los Angeles, Black Sparrow Press, 1969.
The House of Ibuki: A Poem, New York City, 14 March-30 Sept. 1967. Fremont, Michigan, Sumac Press, 1969.
Yellow River Record. London, Big Venus, 1969.
A Pitchblende. San Francisco, Maya, 1969.
The Wand. Santa Barbara, California, Capricorn Press, 1971.
Bearings. Santa Barbara, California, Capricorn Press, 1971.
Altars. Los Angeles, Black Sparrow Press, 1971.
The Sanjo Bridge. Los Angeles, Black Sparrow Press, 1972.
Coils. Los Angeles, Black Sparrow Press, 1973.
Human Wedding. Los Angeles, Black Sparrow Press, 1973.
The Last Judgment: For Caryl Her Thirty-First Birthday, The End of Her Pain. Los Angeles, Plantin Press, 1973.
Aux Morts. Los Angeles, Black Sparrow Press, 1974.
Realignment. Providence, Rhode Island, Treacle Press, 1974.
Portrait of Francis Bacon. Sheffield, Rivelin Press, 1975.
The Cull Wall: Poems and Essays. Los Angeles, Black Sparrow Press, 1975.
Cogollo. Newton, Massachusetts, Roxbury, 1976.
The Woman Who Saw Through Paradise. Lawrence, Kansas, Tansy Press, 1976.
Grotesca. London, New London Pride, 1977.
On Mules Sent from Chavin: A Journal and Poems 1965–66. Swansea, Galloping Dog Press, 1977.
Core Meander. Santa Barbara, California, Black Sparrow Press, 1977.
The Name Encanyoned River. New Paltz, New York, Treacle Press, 1977.
The Gospel of Celine Arnauld. Willits, California, Tuumba Press, 1978.
What She Means. Santa Barbara, California, Black Sparrow Press, 1978.
A Note on Apprenticeship. Chicago, Two Hands Press, 1979.
The Lich Gate. Barrytown, New York, Station Hill Press, 1980.
Nights We Put the Rock Together. Santa Barbara, California, Cadmus, 1980.
Our Lady of the Three-Pronged Devil. New York, Red Ozier Press, 1981.
Hades in Manganese. Santa Barbara, California, Black Sparrow Press, 1981.
Foetus Graffiti. East Haven, Connecticut, Pharos Press, 1981.

Fracture. Santa Barbara, California, Black Sparrow Press, 1983.

Visions of the Fathers of Lascaux. Los Angeles, Panjandrum, 1983.

The Name Encanyoned River: Selected Poems 1960–1985. Santa Barbara, California, Black Sparrow Press, 1986.

Hotel Cro-Magnon. Santa Rosa, California, Black Sparrow Press, 1989.

Under World Arrest. Santa Rosa, California, Black Sparrow Press, 1994.

Nora's Roar. Boulder, Colorado, Rodent Press, 1996.

From Scratch. Santa Rosa, California, Black Sparrow Press, 1998.

Other

Antiphonal Swing: Selected Prose 1962–1987. Kingston, New York, McPherson, 1989.

Novices: A Study of Poetic Apprenticeship. Los Angeles, Mercer and Aitchison. 1989.

Editor, *A Caterpillar Anthology: A Selection of Poetry and Prose from Caterpillar Magazine.* New York, Doubleday, 1971.

Editor, *The Parallel Voyages,* by Paul Blackburn. Tucson, Arizona, Sun/Gemini Press, 1987.

Editor and Translator, *Conductors of the Pit: Major Works by Rimbaud, Vallejo, Césaire, Artaud, and Holan.* New York, Paragon House, 1988.

Translator, *Residence on Earth,* by Pablo Neruda. San Francisco, Amber House, 1962.

Translator, with Denis Kelly, *State of the Union,* by Aimé Césaire. Bloomington, Indiana, Caterpillar, 1966.

Translator, *Seven Poems,* by Cesar Valléjo. Reno, Nevada, Quark, 1967.

Translator, *Poémas Humanos/Human Poems,* by Cesar Vallejo. New York, Grove Press, 1968; London, Cape, 1969.

Translator, with José Rubia Barcia, *Spain, Take This Cup from Me,* by César Vallejo. New York, Grove Press, 1974.

Translator, *Letter to André Breton,* by Antonin Artaud. Los Angeles, Black Sparrow Press, 1974.

Translator, with Norman Glass, *To Have Done with the Judgement of God,* by Antonin Artaud. Los Angeles, Black Sparrow Press, 1975.

Translator, with Norman Glass, *Artaud the Momo,* by Antonin Artaud. Santa Barbara, California, Black Sparrow Press, 1976.

Translator, with José Rubia Barcia, *Battles in Spain,* by César Vallejo. Santa Barbara, California, Black Sparrow Press, 1978.

Translator, with José Rubia Barcia, *The Complete Posthumous Poetry,* by César Vallejo. Berkeley, University of California Press, 1978.

Translator, with Annette Smith, *Notebook of a Return to the Native Land,* by Aimé Césaire. New York, Montemora, 1979.

Translator, with Norman Glass, *Four Texts,* by Antonin Artaud. Los Angeles, Panjandrum, 1982.

Translator, with Annette Smith, *The Collected Poetry,* by Aimé Césaire. Berkeley, University of California Press, 1983.

Translator, *Given Giving: Selected Poems of Michel Deguy.* Berkeley, University of California Press, 1984.

Translator, with A. James Arnold, *Chanson,* by Antonin Artaud. New York, Red Ozier Press, 1985.

Translator, with Annette Smith, *Lost Body,* by Aimé Césaire. New York, Braziller, 1986.

Translator, *Sea-Urchin Harakiri,* by Bernard Bador. Los Angeles, Panjandrum, 1986.

Translator, with Annette Smith, *Lyric and Dramatic Poetry 1946–1982,* by Aimé Césaire. Charlottesville, University Press of Virginia, 1990.

Translator, *Trilce,* by César Vallejo, New York, Marsilio, 1992.

Translator, *Watchfiends & Rack Screams,* by Antonin Artaud. Boston, Exact Change, 1995.

*

Manuscript Collections: Lilly Library, Indiana University, Bloomington; Fales Collection, New York University; University of California, San Diego.

Critical Studies: ''Altars and a Caterpillar Anthology'' by Hayden Carruth, in *New York Times Book Review,* 13 February 1972; Clayton Eshleman issue of *Oasis 19* (London), 1977; ''Hades in Manganese'' by Donald Wesling, in *American Book Review* (New York), May/June 1982; ''Inscribing the Fall'' by A. James Arnold, in *Virginia Quarterly Review* (Charlottesville), winter 1983; ''The Visionary Poetry of Clayton Eshleman'' by Diane Wakoski, in *American Poetry 3* (Albuquerque),1984; ''Black Themes in Surreal Guise'' by Serge Gavronsky, in *New York Times Sunday Book Review,* 19 February 1984; ''Back to the Mind Cradles,'' in *Bluefish* (Southampton, New York), 2, 1984; and *Minding the Underworld: Eshleman and Late Post-Modernism,* Santa Rosa, California, Black Sparrow Press, 1991, both by Paul Christensen; ''Through a Glass Darkly'' by Christopher Maurer, in *The New Republic* (Washington, D.C.), 22 July 1993; ''Impenetrable'' by Jason Wilson, in *Times Literary Supplement* (London), 23 July 1993; ''Spinal Traffic'' by Kenneth Warren, in *American Book Review* (New York), June 1996; ''On-Site Inspection'' by John Olson, in *American Book Review* (New York), December/January 1996–97.

Clayton Eshleman comments:

As species disappear, the Paleolithic grows on us; as living animals disappear, the first outlines become more dear, not as reflections of a day world but as the primal contours of psyche, the shaping of the underworld at the point Hades was an animal. The new wilderness is thus the spectral realm created by the going out of animal life and the coming in of these primary outlines. Our tragedy is to search further and further back for a common nonracial trunk in which the animal is not separated out of the human while we destroy the turf on which we actually stand.

My poetics are based on a belief that there is an archetypal poem and that its most ancient design is probably the labyrinth. One suddenly cuts in, leaving the green world for the apparent stasis and darkness of the cave. The first words of a poem, from this viewpoint, propose and nose forward toward a confrontation with what the writer is only partially aware of, or may not be prepared to address until it emerges, flushed forth by meanders and dead ends. Poetry twists toward the unknown and seeks to realize something beyond the poet's initial awareness. What it seeks to know might be described as the unlimited interiority of its initial impetus.

*   *   *

For any reader interested in a poet's processes of self-discovery, Clayton Eshleman must be a primary figure. Since 1962, when he published his first chapbook of poems, Eshleman has been searching—in private ways through Reichian therapy, Scientology, and Jungian theory; in literary ways through translating the works of César Vallejo and Aimé Césaire; in critical ways through editing his magazines *Caterpillar* and *Sulfur;* and in historical ways through his researches into Paleolithic caves in France—for a means to throw off the swaddled, bourgeois Midwestern American identity he was born with and to emerge as a completely self-created new man.

What an odyssey Eshleman has made, from Indiana through Mexico and Peru, then Japan, New York, and Los Angeles, and finally back to the Midwest. Eshleman himself calls his journey a "meander" rather than an odyssey, one that follows the contours of the earth rather than a man-made course, but his journey has been one of self-creation as much as self-discovery. Eliot Weinberger, in his excellent and useful introduction to *The Name Encanyoned River,* Eshleman's selected poems, describes his poetry and life as "a river that springs up in the arid wilderness of Indiana and flows toward a Utopic vision of personal and global wholeness; a river that is nearly all rapids and is flanked by canyon walls. Along the way one writes, paints, leaves one's mark on the walls: both an act of testimony for the community (this is where we are) and an imaginative leap to the other side." Because Eshleman's meander is complex, his poems have acquired a reputation for being difficult and even obscure. Their densely textured surfaces might lead one to place his work in the tradition of Ezra Pound's *Cantos,* though Eshleman's vision always leads back to self, not to history, as does Pound's.

In speaking of Eshleman's literary origins and practices, Hayden Carruth has written, with great accuracy,

> His verbal practice, based on the isolated phrase, with many elisions and enjambments, a free cadence, strange juxtapositions, and extremes of diction, places him pretty squarely in our native Black Mountain tradition. Unlike some other Black Mountain poets, however, such as Robert Duncan, Denise Levertov or Robert Kelly, Eshleman aims for conceptual discrimination. Sometimes this leads to mere fussiness, sometimes to genuine analytical elegance. But always his tone is tough, involuted and dense with separate movements of feeling characteristically sustained over rather long passages.

One problem with locating Eshleman in the Black Mountain tradition, however, is that all Black Mountain theory leads to linguistics. When Olson bids us to go back to pre-Socratic times and relearn the possibilities of poetry, he really means to relearn the possibilities of poetic speech. But Eshleman is exploring Paleolithic drawings and cave paintings psychologically, not linguistically. His goal, as Weinberger says, is a Utopian personal and global vision. For Eshleman the personal (the psychological) is political. When the reader understands this, Eshleman's obsession with the sexual can be recognized by any feminist theorist and his convoluted language of ecstatic lyricism revealed as grappling constantly with the buried female, as in this excerpt from "Scorpion Hopscotch":

Unexpectedly this morning I grasped
my orgasm and held it for a moment in my hands,
outwardly a crystal ball—yet as I looked
I penetrated my own reflection and glimpsed
its marvelous inner workings, death
was happy, a gold fluid that streamed
through the crystal complexity of what I saw.

For Eshleman true maleness comes through the purity and intensity with which it longs for the female, as in "Scarlet Experiment":

The apple dangling from the lovely fingers of a branch is red
all the way through, its seeds
tiny beings carousing in Eve's rich heart.
The earth, as well as woman, menstruates—
the evidence is flowers, especially roses.
Against green or brown, they take on a rusty,
delicious tenor, scarlet experiments
in league with liquid blackness, or that imperfect
circle of pebbles a male octopus arranges on the ocean floor,
to invite one in heat inside such a circle
to mate motionless changing colors for hours.

Eshleman's work uses the double paradigm of rooting into the self for discovery of the primal male-female entity and of burrowing down into the earth. The latter is seen particularly as he explores Paleolithic caves containing the earliest visual art made by mankind so as to locate a vision of humanity that will not be war-death-patriarchal-nuclear/holocaust-bound. The theme of the coiled serpent, of the intestines, and of the phallus strangling the world is one that recurs often in Eshleman's work, as he sees clearly the troubles of a masculine, male-dominated civilization taking the hunter's and killer's power to rule the world.

From the very beginning of his meander into poetry, Eshleman has believed that it is important to be part of a global community. Not only does he read and translate poetry from several other languages, but he also has traveled extensively, participating generously in international conferences and events and offering hospitality to foreign poets both personally and for their work in *Sulfur* magazine. He has returned religiously, as a pilgrim, to the Dordogne, usually staying at the Cro-Magnon Hotel, the title of a collection of poetry from which these lines of "Keriescan, 1985" come:

the opened   loaded
        field

Neanderthal muscle, a return of
the repressed struggle against opacity

From there he explores the caves, looking for inspiration and new vision for his personal and global Utopia.

—Diane Wakoski

ESPADA, Martin

Nationality: American. **Born:** Brooklyn, New York, 1957. **Career:** Has worked as an attorney. Instructor in English, University of Massachusetts, Amherst. **Awards:** PEN/Revson award, 1989, for *Rebellion Is the Circle of a Lover's Hands*; National Endowment for the Arts fellowship; Massachusetts Artists fellowship; Paterson Poetry prize; American Book award, Before Columbus Foundation, for *Imagine the Angels of Bread*. **Address:** Department of English, Bartlett Hall, University of Massachusetts, Amherst, Massachusetts 01003, U.S.A.

PUBLICATIONS

Poetry

The Immigrant Iceboy's Bolero, with photographs by father, Frank
Espada. Madison, Wisconsin, Ghost Pony Press, 1982.
Trumpets from the Islands of Their Eviction. Tempe, Arizona, Bilin-
gual Press, 1987.
Rebellion Is the Circle of a Lover's Hands. Willimantic, Connecticut,
Curbstone Press, 1990.
City of Coughing and Dead Radiators: Poems. New York, Norton,
1993.
Imagine the Angels of Bread: Poems. New York, Norton, 1996.
A Mayan Astronomer in Hell's Kitchen: Poems. New York, Norton,
2000.

Other

Zapata's Disciple: Essays. Cambridge, Massachusetts, South End
Press, 1998.

Editor, *Poetry Like Bread: Poets of the Political Imagination from
Curbstone Press.* Willimantic, Connecticut, Curbstone Press, 1994.
Editor, *El Coro: A Chorus of Latino and Latina Poetry.* Amherst,
University of Massachusetts Press, 1997.

*

Critical Studies: "With Martin Espada" by Mireya Perez-Erdelyi,
in *Americas Review* (Houston), 15(2), summer 1987; "'Lengua,
Cultura, Sangre': Song of the New Homeland" by Marguerite Maria
Rivas, in *Americas Review* (Seattle), 21(3–4), fall-winter 1993; in
Literary Cavalcade, 47(2), October 1994; by Matthew Rothschild, in
Progressive, 58(5), May 1994; by Roger Gilbert, in *Partisan Review*
(New York), LXI(1), winter 1994; by Frank Allen, in *Poet Lore,*
90(1), spring 1995; interview with Elizabeth Gunderson, in *Poets &
Writers,* 23(2), March 1995.

*   *   *

Before becoming a tenants' rights lawyer and then a professor of
English, Martin Espada held many jobs, including gas station attendant, printing bindery worker, bartender, telephone solicitor, mental
patient advocate, transient hotel desk clerk, and bouncer. The class
dynamics of this generally disrespected and poorly paid work figure
prominently in Espada's poems, many of which reveal the daily
oppression of the powerless at the hands of bosses, corporate interests, landlords, colonizers, and the police. By bearing witness to such
injustice, Espada insists on the essential dignity of lives that poverty
degrades.

Espada, a native of Brooklyn, New York, whose father came
from Puerto Rico, belongs to the Neorican, or Nuyorican, tradition.
Neorican writers are of Puerto Rican descent and concern themselves
with Puerto Rican themes, but they write in English or sometimes
switch between English and Spanish within a piece. Puerto Rico
itself, "the Island," remains a central focus in this tradition. Espada
locates numerous poems there, and in other works he uses the island
as a symbol of the exile's lost fatherland and of the hope of return.
"The Spanish of Our Out-Loud Dreams," in *Trumpets from the*

Islands of Their Eviction, evokes both this redemptive image and the
pain of the "eviction" from home. In the poem the speaker addresses
a woman who takes her dying father from a hospital in the Bronx back
to an island of refuge and comfort. The island offers what is natural
(palm trees and the mother tongue) as opposed to the harsh sterility of
exile (failed radiation treatments in the Bronx). It suggests the hope of
reunion after a lifetime "wander[ing] with stuffed bags, / not staying
long enough / to learn the language." Similarly, "We Live by What
We See at Night" evokes the pain and longing of exile. The poet,
addressing his father, imagines the old man's dreams of home:

> When the mountains of Puerto Rico
> Flickered in your sleep
> With a moist green light,
> When you saw green bamboo hillsides
> Before waking up to East Harlem rooftops
> Or Texas barracks,
> . . .
> the craving for that island birthplace
> burrowed, deep
> as thirty years' exile,
> constant as your pulse.

The clipped syllables of "Texas barracks," following the mellow
description of the island's beauty, are as sharp as gunshots. Echoing
the language of the first stanza, the poet reveals how, through his
father's dreams, the boy recognizes a home he has never seen.

Though Espada writes within the Neorican tradition, he does not
focus exclusively on the experience of Puerto Rican exiles. He writes
about Mexican migrant workers, Nicaraguan and El Salvadoran
peasants terrorized by government death squads, unskilled laborers
hoping to find jobs, and mental patients. Often Espada chooses
overtly political themes. He skewers social hypocrisy in "For the Jim
Crow Mexican Restaurant in Cambridge, Massachusetts Where My
Cousin Esteban Was Forbidden to Wait Tables Because He Wears
Dreadlocks," from *A Mayan Astronomer in Hell's Kitchen.* "I am
aware of your T-shift solidarity / with the refugees of the Americas,"
the poet sneers, and the poem swells to a litany of curses that smartly
put tortilla white exploiters of Mexican culture in their place: ". . .
and may the Aztec gods pinned like butterflies / to the menu wait for
you in the parking lot / at midnight, demanding that you spell their
names." Less satisfying is "The Eleventh Reason," which considers
the controversial case of Julius and Ethel Rosenberg. The poem
expresses predictable outrage but adds nothing essentially new to
the story.

Similarly condemning are Espada's poems about death row
inmate Mumia Abu-Jamal, a onetime Black Panther convicted—
erroneously, he maintains—of murdering a police officer. "Another
Nameless Prostitute Says the Man Is Innocent," commissioned by
National Public Radio but never aired, intones, "The board-blinded
windows knew what happened; / the pavement sleepers of Philadelphia . . . / . . . knew what happened," creating through these and
similar repetitions of phrases a solemnity of tone that suggests the
coverup of a grave injustice. Mumia is heroized (he has "thinking
dreadlocks" and is described sharing meals and calling out his
friends' names), whereas the police are demonized (they speak in
"fanged whispers"). Certain that Mumia has been made a martyr,
Espada assures the prisoner that after death he will be welcomed by
the spirit of Walt Whitman, at whose tomb ". . . the granite door is
open / and fugitive slaves may rest."

Hard-hitting as his openly political poems are, Espada can be tender and funny as well. One humorous poem explains that he would not have accidentally hit his love in the eye with a poison ivy-wrapped crayfish if he had not grown up in an area so polluted that he does not know the first thing about nature (''I Apologize . . .'' from *Mayan Astronomer*). And in ''Rednecks,'' a moving piece made all the more lovely for its reversal of usual stereotypes, a group of teenagers jeering at rednecks are humbled when they see a simple farmer lovingly kiss the deformed face of a woman scarred by fire. Adrienne Rich and David Lehman selected it as among the best American poems of 1996.

—Elizabeth Shostak

EVANS, Mari

Nationality: American. **Born:** Toledo, Ohio, 16 July 1923. **Education:** University of Toledo. **Family:** Divorced; two sons. **Career:** Writer-in-residence and instructor in black literature, Indiana University-Purdue University, Indianapolis, 1969–70; assistant professor of black literature and writer-in-residence, Indiana University, Bloomington, 1970–78, and Purdue University, West Lafayette, Indiana, 1978–80; writer-in-residence and visiting assistant professor, Northwestern University, Evanston, Illinois, 1972–73; visiting professor, Washington University, St. Louis, 1980, Cornell University, Ithaca, New York, 1981–84, University of Miami, Coral Gables, 1989, and writer-in-residence, Spelman College, Atlanta, 1989–90. Associate professor, 1985–86, State University of New York, Albany. Producer, writer, and director, The Black Experience television program, Indianapolis, 1968–73. Consultant in ethnic studies, Bobbs Merrill publishing company, Indianapolis 1970–73 and 1978–83. **Awards:** John Hay Whitney fellowship, 1965; Woodrow Wilson Foundation grant, 1968; Black Academy of Arts and Letters award, 1971; MacDowell fellowship, 1975; Builders award (Third World Press), 1977; Indiana Committee for Humanities grant, 1977; Kuumba Theatre Workshop Black Liberation award, 1978; Copeland fellowship, 1980; National Endowment for the Arts award, 1981; Black Arts Celebration award, 1981; Yaddo fellowship, 1984. L.H.D.: Marion College, Indianapolis, 1975. **Address:** P.O. Box 483, Indianapolis, Indiana 46206, U.S.A.

PUBLICATIONS

Poetry

Where Is All the Music? London, Paul Breman, 1968.
I Am a Black Woman. New York, Morrow, 1970.
Whisper. Los Angeles, Center for Afro-American Studies, 1979.
Nightstar. Los Angeles, Center for Afro-American Studies, 1981.
A Dark and Splendid Mass. New York, Harlem River Press, 1992.

Plays

River of My Song adaptation of the novel *Their Eyes Were Watching God* by Zora Neale Hurston (also director: produced Indianapolis, 1977). *Eyes* (produced New York, 1979).

Other

Rap Stories (for children). New York, Third World Press, 1973.
J.D. (for children). New York, Doubleday, 1973.
I Look at Me. Chicago, Third World Press, 1974.
Singing Black (for children). Indianapolis, Reed, 1976.
Jim Flying High (for children). New York, Doubleday, 1979.
Dear Corinne, Tell Somebody! Love, Annie: A Book about Secrets (for children). East Orange, New Jersey, Just Us Books, 1999.

Editor, *Black Women Writers 1950–1980: A Critical Evaluation.* New York, Doubleday, 1984; as *Black Women Writers 1950–1980: Arguments and Interviews,* London, Pluto, 1985.

*

Critical Study: ''Mari Evans: Consciousness and Craft'' by Robert P. Sedlack, in *College Language Association Journal* (Atlanta, Georgia), 15, 1972.

*   *   *

Mari Evans has revealed that when she was ''about ten'' she discovered Langston Hughes's first book of poems, *The Weary Blues,* and that she was bright eyed with astonishment because Hughes was ''writing about me!'' She went on to explain that he introduced her ''to a Black literary tradition that began with the inception of writing in the area of Meroë on the African continent many millennia ago.'' This rhapsodic recollection speaks generously to the nature of Evans's lifetime of inspiration and professional commitment.

No less a personage than Margaret Walker has recognized Evans's pivotal place between the poets of the 1930s and 1940s and those of the 1960s and 1970s. In an interview with Nikki Giovanni, Walker recalled Evans's striking 1972 phrase ''Our Black Family Nation,'' an allusion to black spiritual unity and the expression of her concern that ''black life be experienced throughout the diaspora on the highest, most rewarding, most productive levels.'' This is not inflated rhetoric, for Evans's literary maturity emerges full-fledged from the embers of the 1960s civil rights era, the unique condition when moment, voice, and audience converged. But it was an evolving emergence, and Evans's earlier expression of sociopolitical awareness is evident, for instance, in Arna Bontemps's 1963 anthology *American Negro Poetry:*

> Hope I lives till I get
> home
> I'm tired of eatin'
> What they eats in Rome . . .

Such deceptively simple and properly idiomatic expressions represent the hallmark of the blues mode made popular in poetry by Hughes, combining humor with revelation. The lines are from ''When in Rome,'' a poem reprinted in Evans's 1970 collection *I Am a Black Woman.* The full corpus of Evans's poems, however, is many voiced, ranging from the personal to the public, from the colloquial to the formal, from the private to the political, all carefully manipulated perceptions and rhetoric:

> Your eye warm to mine shared
> presentpast and ancient source

Black unison
our heartbeats

or

El Hajj Malik Shabazz / who went through the changes
and became a Truth / and a positive action / and more than
a voice in the wind

Yet, as David Dorsey has so aptly pointed out, it is often
necessary "to emphasize that [Evans's] thematic unity depends on an
ever expanding concept of love which comes to embrace the whole
community." It is in light of this love for community that the title
poem of *I Am a Black Woman* proves to be Evans's most representative verse:

I
am a black woman
tall as a cypress . . .
Look
    on me and be
renewed.

This is mother and spirit, protector and enabler. Evans is a poet in the
African tradition who, like the priestess, uses language to transform
symbol into reality. There is probably no American poet who takes on
her charge with greater responsibility.

—Charles L. James

EVARISTO, Bernardine

Nationality: British. **Born:** London, 1959. **Career:** Poet-in-residence, Museum of London, 1999. **Awards:** Emma Best book award,
for *Lara*; Arts Council Writers award, 2000.

PUBLICATIONS

Play

Moving Through (produced London, 1982).

Novel

Lara. Turnbridge Wells, Kent, Angela Royal, 1997.

*   *   *

Bernardine Evaristo combines a highly textual sense of form
with oral performance poetry. She can mix autobiography with fiction
and appear objective and noncommitted while observing through
black feminist eyes. Her volume *Island of Abraham* often recalls what
otherwise might be ignored as not belonging to the way in which
history is recorded by whites and Europeans. Even when this non-
European past is brought to attention by, say, an archaeologist, it

becomes a tourist's view of strange ruins without recapturing the
actual nature of what it was like. "Epitaph," with its awareness of
loss, is like Keats's "Ode on a Grecian Urn":

Ethiopian, Aztec, Ashanti,
Mongol, Ottoman, Shang,
Inca, Moor, Mayan.
Your years did not stand still
like upright Corinthian pillars
but were flowing rivers
carrying the memories of your deeds.

A poem of black third world protest becomes an elegy on the decay
and death of civilizations, which end in ruins: "Nothing lasts forever. / Europe's empires dissolved to dust, / . . . for all great civilisations
live and die." The tone, voice, and movement of the poem, the feeling
of balance, and even the piling up of rich sounding nouns and the use
of time as a river seem influenced by Derek Walcott, especially the
Walcott of "A Far Cry from Africa" and "Ruins of a Great House."

Other poems have Walcott's measured, elegiac way of treating
topics through distance and respect. One of Evaristo's recurring
themes is her mixed ancestry and how little she knows of her Nigerian
father. In "Father, My Father" she says, "Daddy, I cannot read your
eyes. / Those brown orbs of Yoruba history." In many of the poems
the poet is an outsider in other lands, a traveler familiar with fear and
with overcoming it. It is this knowledge that allows the speaker to feel
superior to her "male, white and young" Spanish-speaking acquaintance in "Spanish Blues," which concludes with her entering a café
in Grenada full of paintings of symbols of masculinity, where "I
order a whisky, marvel at the measure, / swallow the fire easily, this
time." In the poem "Island of Abraham" she flies to Sainte Marie
Island, off mainland Madagascar. This is one of several poems in
which the speaker desires to be one with the natives, only to be
regarded as another rich foreign tourist, a colored white. She imagines
herself as a small girl in 1666 watching the arrival of pirates, the first
white men: "the island would never be the same again, / its virginal
membrane broken." The results of history are "recalled now in the
green-eyed, / dark skinned boy."

This is in part Evaristo's situation. She is a product of Europe's
encounter with other people, and although she attempts to identify
with the others, she is herself a tourist from England enjoying herself
on this island off the coast of Madagascar. There is a desire for
rootedness, community, belonging, and continuity. This is associated
with family, females, and being black and is contrasted with strangers, male culture, and whites. "Antique Gold and Burning Rose"
speaks once more of "memory" and speaks of visions of African
women in the Sudan and Egypt: "I recall Cleopatra, Seacole, /
Tubman, Bricktop and Baker." In the next poem, "Simple Scribe,"
Evaristo imagines herself and her poetry as being like a scribal writer
in the past, "trying to learn so that I can pass on / trying to listen so
that I can hear / trying to move so that I can enter."

Lara, a novel in verse, is part of an attempt to rediscover and
invent a usable past. On her mother's side Omilara is the product of a
poor Irish Catholic family that moved to England in the nineteenth
century and that tried to raise itself out of illegitimacy to the security
of the middle class. This was what was intended for Ellen, Lara's
mother, until she met and married an African, one of the black
immigrants who arrived in England after World War II in search of a
higher education and with a desire to be at the center of the British
Empire. Taiwo, a Nigerian, is from a Lagos Yoruba family earlier

taken as slaves to Brazil, from whence some had returned to Africa after emancipation to form a small, elite enclave during the later nineteenth and early twentieth centuries. As these two stories might suggest, although the history of slavery and white domination are the main focus of black-white race relations, the actual history is more complex. The story of the Irish and the working class often has its parallels in black history, while the continuing movement of people of African descent back and forth across the Atlantic and to England has taken place over several centuries and has resulted in a complex black history of class and cultural differences.

The first half of *Lara* is concerned with the history of the girl's white family and with her life in England. It is a story about Irish Catholics in what to them is a harsh world with few comforts except family and church. This must be one of the last portraits of a way of life that is now passing. It feels solidly present in the poems, as do the attraction of Ellen toward Taiwo, the mixture in Ellen's mother of racial prejudice and the fear of losing class status if her daughter marries a black man, life in England immediately after World War II, Lara's youth in a large household in a working-class suburb, and her experience of the cultural and political fashions that followed the swinging 1960s.

Ellen experiences discrimination for marrying a black man and is rejected by her mother until the children are born, when there is a semireconciliation. Lara's own childhood is both typical and troubled by racial hurts, but more often she is bothered by being different, so that naive questions of where she is from can wound her. She wants to be like everyone else until, sexually awakened, she also becomes conscious of color and has an affair with a black Etonian. She then plunges into black England, trying to find a supportive identity, and toward the end of the book travels to Nigeria and Brazil and then back to Nigeria before returning to England. This symbolically recapitulates the journey of her black ancestors and is emotionally cleansing, allowing her to face London reborn, knowing who she is, a product of several cultures, each with its own complex history.

—Bruce King

EVERWINE, Peter (Paul)

Nationality: American. **Born:** Detroit, Michigan, 14 February 1930. **Education:** Northwestern University, Evanston, Illinois, B.S. 1952; Stanford University, California, 1958–59; University of Iowa, Iowa City, Ph.D. 1959. **Military Service:** U.S. Army, 1952–54. **Family:** Divorced; two children. **Career:** Instructor in English, University of Iowa, 1959–62. Since 1962 professor of English, California State University, Fresno. **Awards:** Lamont Poetry Selection award, 1972; Guggenheim fellowship, 1976. **Address:** Department of English, California State University, Fresno, California 93710, U.S.A.

PUBLICATIONS

Poetry

The Broken Frieze. Mt. Vernon, Iowa, Hillside Press, 1958.
In the House of Light: Thirty Aztec Poems. Iowa City, Stone Wall Press, 1970.
Collecting the Animals. New York, Atheneum, 1973.
Keeping the Night. New York, Atheneum, 1977.

Other

Editor and Translator, with Shulamit Yasny-Starkman, *The Static Element: Selected Poems of Natan Zach.* New York, Atheneum, 1982.

* * *

The quantity of Peter Everwine's poetry is slight, but the quality is gemlike. Some of the poems in *Keeping the Night* were anthologized earlier in *The New Naked Poetry.* "Nude" would have been a more fitting adjective to describe his art. His poetry is neither raw nor bare. It is subtler—precise but unadorned, palpable, and dumb. It achieves its effect slowly. It wants to be read over and over. It unfolds in silence and in empty spaces. "Night," from *Keeping the Night,* which is quite like haiku, is typical of Everwine's manner:

In the lamplight falling
on the white tablecloth
my plate
my shining loaf of quietness.

I sit down.
Through the open door
all the absent I love enter
and we eat.

At its best Everwine's poetry is deceptively simple. Largely monosyllabic, invariably brief, his poems mold speech to express unspoken, deeply felt truths found in moments selected from ordinary life, either his own or that of his kin.

The earlier volume *In the House of Light* is made up of Everwine's translations of Spanish transcriptions of poems of the Nahuatl-speaking peoples of Mexico. Everwine observed that one of the words used for a poet in Nahuatl is *tlamatine* (one who knows something), and in his verse translations he offers "an attempt to locate that ancient presence in my own speech" *(Collecting the Animals).* He succeeds brilliantly.

The seeming simplicity of Everwine's work establishes an aura of trust and candor rarely found in contemporary poetry. His poetry is unmarred by self-consciousness. There is no stridency, no verbal fireworks, no exhibitionism. Nor is there any hint of sentimentality in the many memories he evokes. In "Drinking Cold Water," from *Collecting the Animals,* the re-creation of his tough-spirited grandmother who "lay down in the shale hills of Pennsylvania" years before is completely authentic:

all I can think of is your house—
the pump at the sink
spilling a trough of clear
cold water from the well—
and you, old love,
sleeping in your dark dress
like a hard, white root.

His Italian grandfather, who immigrated to the United States and spat in the wind, quit his job, and returned to Italy every time his bosses maddened him, is depicted with equal vividness in "Paolo Castelnuova," from *Keeping the Night.* The poem ends with the grandson, the persona, penning the will the old man did not leave:

I, Paolo, give my stone to the priests.
Tell them to make it bread.

Water I give to those loving how money sweats.

Fire I leave to my children

As for air,
give it to the buzzard who is the first
and last of kings.

The other portraits in *Keeping the Night* and *Collecting the Animals*—
of Dorothy, "her ass rubbed raw through half the fields in Armstrong
County," of his immigrant mother who was never really American
until grass closed over her gravestone, of his sons—are equally
precise and real.

Whether Everwine searches for a language to hold the night's
secrets, childhood recollections, or the paradoxical condition of a man
who eats dinner while talking with his guests of the dead past and
never looking at "the axe lying in the courtyard, a crust of blood and
feathers on its edge" ("The Dinner" from *Keeping the Night*), he
catches exactly the experience he knows. He has learned his experience and his craft "hand over hand," as he says in another poem in a
slightly different context.

—Carol Simpson Stern

EZEKIEL, Nissim

Nationality: Indian. **Born:** Bombay, 16 December 1924. **Education:**
University of Bombay (Lagu prize, 1947), 1941–47, M.A. 1947.
Family: Married Daisy Jacob in 1952; two daughters and one son.
Career: Lecturer, Khalsa College, Bombay, 1947–48; professor of
English and vice-principal, Mithibai College, Bombay, 1961–72;
reader, 1972–81, and professor of American literature, 1981–85,
University of Bombay. Visiting professor, University of Leeds, 1964,
and University of Chicago, 1967; writer-in-residence, National Uni-
versity of Singapore, 1988–89. Editor, *Quest* magazine, 1955–57;
associate editor, *Imprint* magazine, 1961–67; art critic, *The Times of
India,* Bombay, 1964–67. Since 1985 editor, Indian P.E.N. Lived in
London, 1948–52. **Awards:** Farfield Foundation travel grant, 1957;
National Academy award, 1983; Padma Shree, 1988. **Address:** 18
Kala Niketan, 6th Floor, 47-C, Bhulabhai Desai Road, Bombay
400026, India.

PUBLICATIONS

Poetry

A Time to Change and Other Poems. London, Fortune Press, 1952.
Sixty Poems. Bombay, Strand Bookshop, 1953.
The Third. Bombay, Strand Bookshop, 1959.
The Unfinished Man: Poems Written in 1959. Calcutta, Writers
Workshop, 1960.
The Exact Name: Poems 1960–1964. Calcutta, Writers Workshop,
1965.

Pergamon Poets 9, with others, edited by Howard Sergeant. Oxford,
Pergamon Press, 1970.
Hymns in Darkness. New Delhi and London, Oxford University
Press, 1976.
Latter-Day Psalms. New Delhi, Oxford University Press, 1982.
Collected Poems 1952–1988. New Delhi and Oxford, Oxford Univer-
sity Press, 1989.

Plays

Three Plays (includes *Nalini, Marriage Poem, The Sleep-walkers*)
(produced Bombay, 1969). Calcutta, Writers Workshop, 1969.
Don't Call It Suicide: A Tragedy. Madras, Macmillan India, 1993.

Other

The Actor: A Sad and Funny Story for Children of Most Ages.
Bombay, India Book House, 1974.
Our Cultural Dilemmas: Tagore Memorial Lectures 1981–82.
Ahmedabad, Gujarat University, n.d.
Selected Prose. Delhi and Oxford, Oxford University Press, 1992.

Editor, *Cultural Profiles.* Bombay, International Cultural Centre, 1961.
Editor, *A New Look at Communism.* Bombay, Indian Committee for
Cultural Freedom, 1963.
Editor, *Indian Writers in Conference.* Mysore, P.E.N. All India
Writers Conference, 1964.
Editor, *Writing in India.* Lucknow, P.E.N. All India Writers Confer-
ence, 1965.
Editor, *An Emerson Reader.* Bombay, Popular Prakashan, 1965.
Editor, *A Martin Luther King Reader.* Bombay, Popular Prakashan,
1969.
Editor, *All My Sons,* by Arthur Miller. Madras, Oxford University
Press, 1972.
Editor, with Ursula Bickelmann, *Artists Today/East-West Visual Arts
Encounter.* Bombay, Marg Publications, 1987.
Editor, with Meenakshi Mukherjee, *Another India: An Anthology of
Contemporary Indian Fiction and Poetry.* Delhi, Penguin, 1990.

*

Critical Studies: *The Poetry of Nissim Ezekiel* by Meena Belliapa
and Rajeev Taranath, Calcutta, Writers Workshop, 1966, and article
by Taranath, in *Quest 74* (Bombay), January-February, 1972; *Nissim
Ezekiel: A Study* by Chetan Karnani, New Delhi, Arnold-Heinemann,
1974; Nissim Ezekiel issue of *Journal of South Asian Literature*
(Rochester, Michigan), September-December 1974; *The Poetry of
Encounter: Three Indo-Anglian Poets* by Emmanuel Narendra Lall,
New Delhi, Sterling, 1983; *Perspectives on Nissim Ezekiel: Essays in
Honour of Rosemary C. Wilkinson* edited by Suresh Chandra Dwivedi,
Delhi, K.M. Agencies, 1989; *Three Indian Poets: Nissim Ezekiel,
A.K. Ramanujan, Dom Moraes* by Bruce King, Madras, Oxford
University Press, 1991; *Nissim Ezekiel, Poet of Human Balance* by
Harish Raizada, Ghaziabad, India, Vimal Prakashan, 1992; *Essays on
Nissim Ezekiel* edited by Ted Shrama, Meerut, Shalabha Prakashan,
1994; "Nissim Ezekiel: Quest for Linguistic Identity" by R.S.
Pathak, in *Creative Forum* (New Delhi), 5(1–4), 1995; "Irony in the
Poetry of Nissim Ezekiel" by Niranjan Mohanty, in *World Literature
Today* (Norman, Oklahoma), 69(1), winter 1995.

Nissim Ezekiel comments:

(1974) I do not identify myself with any particular school of poetry. Labeled ''Indo-Anglian'' or ''Indo-English,'' i.e., an Indian poet writing in English, I accept the label. I am satisfied at present to be included among the poets of the Commonwealth but hope to be better known in the U.K. and U.S.A. as an Indian poet. I consider myself a modernist but not avant-garde.

I have written in the traditional verse forms as well as in free verse. Major influences: Pound, Eliot, Auden, MacNeice, Spender, Yeats, and modern English and American poetry in general. My latest poetry, 1966–73, is beyond all influences. Some of my recent poems are in Indian English. I have written found poems on scientific subjects and several on newspaper reports and personal letters. Major themes: love, personal integration, the Indian contemporary scene, modern urban life, spiritual values. I aim at clarity above all, claim never to have written an obscure poem. I like to make controlled, meaningful statements, avoiding extremes of thought and expression.

(1995) I believe that it is possible to have a full and final view of the nature of poetry. The search for the essential in poetry has its positive value, as it rejects diffuseness and abstraction in favor of the concentrated and the concrete. But it tends to overemphasize image, form, and music in poetry, treating its substantial content as of secondary value. The human ethos is sacrificed to mere method. A reasonable view of poetry on the other hand would not insist on purity but on integrity. It would allow for the functional role of different elements in poetry, including the role of ideas.

*   *   *

The jacket of his *Collected Poems 1952–1988* describes Nissim Ezekiel as India's best-known English-language poet. The claim is probably justified. Certainly justified is the claim that he helped initiate the postromantic phase of modern Indian poetry in English. Although there are signs of a reaction against his mode of poetry and even a reevaluation of his role in the history of English-language poetry in India, his place is secure.

Ezekiel's poems are Indian in their use of urban landscape, their imagery, and their themes. The themes are related mostly to urban life in India, particularly Bombay, where Ezekiel lives. He deals with these themes in a spirit of ironical detachment, skepticism, amusement, and mockery, sometimes self-mockery. Often there is a deflating comment that is made part of the narrating voice and tone. His critical intelligence is especially aroused by all forms of hypocrisy, hard-heartedness, bogus spirituality, middle-class smugness, social and political dogma, religious bigotry, and received wisdom that has not been freshly examined. His commitments are to the value of the human individual, to living in India, with all of its pains, pleasures, and discomforts, and to the importance of poetic speech. His style is distinguished by precision, economy, and clarity. The tone is usually that of easy, informal conversation, but with none of the carelessness of conversation.

Ezekiel has succeeded in creating and developing a distinct personality in his work. His love poems render the many moods of love with honesty, frankness, and a conspicuous lack of romanticism. (One misses, however, a note of tenderness and gratitude.) His religious poems are skeptical and questioning; they do not scoff at belief or reject it but rather seek valid and reliable bases for belief. Ezekiel's social verse shows a keen eye for all forms of highfalutin humbug, hypocrisy, and corruption, and the poems are informed with compassion and a keen awareness of suffering and exploitation. No remedial action is proposed, however, for Ezekiel is not that kind of writer. He has written some amusing and effective dramatic monologues on certain Indian character types by exploiting poetically common Indian misuses of English idiom. Ezekiel has written both regular and free verse.

No notice of Ezekiel is complete without gratefully acknowledging the help and encouragement he has given new writers, both informally and as an editor of verse magazines.

—S. Nagarajan

F

FAINLIGHT, Ruth

Nationality: American. **Born:** New York City, 2 May 1931. **Education:** Attended schools in America and England; studied at Birmingham and Brighton colleges of art. **Family:** Married Alan Sillitoe, *q.v.,* in 1959; one son and one adopted daughter. **Career:** Poet-in-residence, Vanderbilt University, Nashville, Tennessee, 1985, 1990. **Award:** Cholmondeley award, 1994. **Address:** 14 Ladbroke Terrace, London W11 3PG, England.

PUBLICATIONS

Poetry

A Forecast, A Fable. London, Outposts, 1958.
Cages. London, Macmillan, 1966; Chester Springs, Pennsylvania, Dufour, 1967.
18 Poems from 1966. London, Turret, 1967.
To See the Matter Clearly and Other Poems. London, Macmillan, 1968; Chester Springs, Pennsylvania, Dufour, 1969.
Poems, with Alan Sillitoe and Ted Hughes. London, Rainbow Press, 1971.
The Region's Violence. London, Hutchinson, 1973.
21 Poems. London, Turret, 1973.
Another Full Moon. London, Hutchinson, 1976.
Two Fire Poems. Knotting, Bedfordshire, Sceptre Press, 1977.
The Function of Tears. Knotting, Bedfordshire, Sceptre Press, 1979.
Sibyls and Others. London, Hutchinson, 1980.
Two Wind Poems. Knotting, Bedfordshire, Martin Booth, 1980.
Climates. Newcastle upon Tyne, Bloodaxe, 1983.
Fifteen to Infinity. London, Hutchinson, 1983.
Selected Poems. London, Century Hutchinson, 1987.
Three Poems. Child Okeford, Dorset, Words Press, 1988.
The Knot. London, Century Hutchinson, 1990.
Sibyls, with woodcuts by Leonard Baskin. Searsmont, Maine, Gehenna Press, 1991.
This Time of Year. London, Sinclair-Stevenson, 1994.
Selected Poems. London, Sinclair-Stevenson, 1995.
Pomegranate, with mezzotints by Judith Rothchild. Ceret, France, Editions de l'Eau, 1997.
Sugar-Paper Blue. Newcastle upon Tyne, Bloodaxe, 1997; Chester Springs, Pennsylvania, Dufour, 1998.
Leaves/Feuilles, with French versions of poems by M. Duclos and mezzotints by Judith Rothchild. Octon, France, Editions Verdigris, 1998.

Plays

All Citizens Are Soldiers, with Alan Sillitoe, adaptation of a play by Lope de Vega (produced London, 1967). London, Macmillan, and Chester Springs. Pennsylvania, Dufour, 1969.
The Dancer Hotoke (opera libretto), music by Erika Fox (produced London, 1991). Included in *Selected Poems,* London, Sinclair-Stevenson, 1995.
The European Story (opera libretto), music by G. Alvarez (produced London, 1993). Included in *Selected Poems,* London, Sinclair-Stevenson, 1995.

Short Stories

Penguin Modern Stories 9, with others. London, Penguin, 1971.
Daylife and Nightlife. London, Deutsch, 1971.
Dr. Clock's Last Case. London, Virago Press, 1994.

Other

Editor, *Selected Poems,* by Harry Fainlight. London, Turret, 1987.
Editor, *Journeys,* by Harry Fainlight. London, Turret, 1992.

Translator, *Navigacions,* by Sophia de Mello Breyner Andresen. Lisbon, Casa da Moeda, 1983.
Translator, *Marine Rose,* by Sophia de Mello Breyner. Redding Ridge, Connecticut, Black Swan, 1989.

*

Critical Studies: By Michèle Duclos, in *La Traductiere 10* (Bordeaux, France), June 1992; by Barbara Hardy, in *New European Review* (London), 8/9, 1992; by Janet Barron, in *New Statesman Society,* 7(308), 24 June 1994.

Ruth Fainlight comments:

I try to keep the words of a poem close to the feelings and sensations that inspired it in the hope that it will inspire the same feelings, recognitions, and memories in its reader. In this way he or she becomes involved in its reality, even a participant in its creation, because reading is an active relationship between reader and writer. But writing is a relationship between writer and language. A poem develops organically from the first inspiring phrase. That phrase, or cluster of words, includes every essential element, and my work is to allow all its potential of sound and meaning to realize themselves. And like every other living organism, its development is a unique combination of unassailable laws and the entirely unexpected.

(1995) Though I appreciate the arguments of those who believe that a poem should be left in its first published state, I feel that the relationship between poet and poem, like a living marriage, is continually changing and so have taken the opportunity to revise some of the work. As in any relationship, it is very hard to know if one's actions will have good or bad results.

(2000) My mother tongue is English, my ancestry Eastern European; I grew up in the United States. With such a background, I am a good example of what is often referred to as a "rootless cosmopolitan." Although, or perhaps because, that label is often used pejoratively, I accept it with pleasure. It is easy for me to feel connections with people from any part of the world. My writing is the expression of all the factors that combine to make me what I am. As a poet my prime allegiance is to the language in which I write. The literature of the English language is what has nourished, delighted, and instructed me. I prefer not to have any qualifying word attached to "poet" in reference to myself, unless it is to create a new category: not English, American, Jewish, female, feminist, or anything else but an English-language poet.

* * *

The poetry of Ruth Fainlight reflects a systematic mining of personal experience. Central to her work are the interwoven themes of the poet's role in "normal" life and that of a woman in a world whose standards are still defined by men. Both of these concerns are explored directly, the woman-poet giving evidence of their effect upon her. As a writer, Fainlight is conscious of herself as being in possession of a gift that to some extent distances her from the ordinary world. It is a mixed blessing, for the compulsive urge for expression devours her own existence as its raw material. The force of this need within her and the paralyzing frustration in those arid periods when she is unable to write are keenly observed in a number of poems, not least in the hospital convalescence of "Late Afternoon." Warring with the poetic urge is the harder, more practical side of Fainlight's nature, what she refers to as "My Stone-Age Self," its earth-bound cynicism denying all spiritual values, insisting that "nothing / but the body's pleasure, / use, and comfort, matters." Such works as "Passenger" indicate that on more than one occasion the poet has found herself wondering if creativity is worth the trouble, if it would not in fact be better if she were a nonpoetic person, unravaged by the debilitating forces that cannibalize the self.

The roles of woman and poet interlock once more in Fainlight's relationship with her mother, which is presented in several of her poems. The relationship is seen as ambivalent, varying somewhere between love and resentment, and in some ways it is equated with her attitude toward poetry itself; it is significant that Fainlight regards the muse as a mother figure whose status she is not always willing to acknowledge. Similarly, in the case of love, while responding to the compulsive urge, she is aware of the threat it poses, the gradual absorption of the self into family life. "Here" presents domesticity as at once a prison and a dangerous lure, the attractions of which compel her to accept it against her better judgment. The male-female confrontation, its conflict and resolution, is tracked by Fainlight back into the looming shadow of myth and fairy tale, imaged in Adam's Fall or in "Beauty and the Beast." At once a wife and mother and an individual, she balances the warring opposites with a clear, unjaundiced vision, setting them down in measured polarities in her verse.

More than second-class citizenship or lack of inspiration, death is the final restriction, the limit placed on all created things. Robbed of her loved brother, a fellow poet who died young, Fainlight is aware of death as a constantly lurking threat, reminders of its presence appearing when least expected in a chance sighting of the moon in the night sky, for example, or in the coming of another spring. In her account of her brother's funeral, the sudden breaking of a storm matches her grief, his death the crucial event that convinces her of the fearful end to everything: "I shall not meet my dead again / as I remember them / alive, except in dreams or poems. / Your death was the final proof / I needed to accept that knowledge."

This Time of Year reexamines the familiar themes with a growing depth and intensity of expression. In the sequence of poems "Twelve Sibyls" Fainlight evokes a range of archetypal female figures who are gifted with the power of utterance and self-creation yet who are still denied, frozen, and curbed by the controlling strength of the male "god." "This Time of Year" blends the fallen leaves of autumn with recollections of her dead parents, the images subtly and indissolubly woven together in a few words, while "Tosca" depicts the memory of other relatives and their everyday talismans. Fainlight subjects herself to ironic self-analysis in "The Author" and "Reflection," humorously visualizing her mirror image in the latter poem as "all contrary." Her ambiguous view of domesticity surfaces once more in "Romance," where she warns of the enslaving properties of

fairy tales; the contrasting vision is shown in "Art," where her musings on the preparation of food recall the earlier "Box and Sampler," with its message of shared ritual as a liberating influence.

Fainlight compares her relationship to her poetry with that of a living marriage, subject to constant change, and this is clearly shown in the enlarged *Selected Poems* of 1995, where several of her earlier works appear in revised form. The collection also confirms the breadth of her talent, including translations of French and Portuguese poetry and texts of libretti written for the Royal Opera's *The Garden Venture*. It comes over as an impressive blend of her best work, drawn from most of her past collections.

Her versatility is further shown in *Sugar-Paper Blue*, Fainlight the short story writer adding a handful of prose pieces to this volume of poems. Her subtle use of symbols is seen in "Pomegranate," where the act of eating the fruit is linked to Greek mythology and to the Spanish sisters she visits again after a separation of twenty years and finds to be "strange, yet closer" than before. Inevitably, it is the inexorable advance of old age that dominates Fainlight's later writing. She reflects sadly on her vanished youth in "Friends' Photos" and "Young Men," contemplates short-term memory loss in "Whatever It Was," and in "Whatever" ponders on her increasing demands on life ("This urgent impatience comes with getting older. / I'm sure I once was able to hold out longer, / pace my pleasures and accept postponement. / These days though, I crave them instant, constant.") The aches and pains that flesh is heir to, whether unwelcome encounters with the dentist in "Bruises" and her prose piece "The Tooth Fairy" or an injured toe that refuses to heal in "Jade," are recalled with sad resignation, while in "The Gates" Fainlight is forced to admit the oncoming threat of death: "Still to come is the work / of leaving life."

The title poem once more displays Fainlight's skill in weaving complex associations from the simplest of materials. From her statement "But I thought everyone knew / what was meant by sugar-paper blue" the movement of the poem shifts quickly to her immigrant aunt and mother filling sugar bags in a chilly New York grocery store and on to the blue-painted walls of a house in Leningrad in 1965 where Fainlight—a guest—is suddenly made aware that the poetess Anna Akhmatova lives there and is walking around in the room above. Turning to poetry as a means of liberation and healing, Fainlight finds herself wishing that she could compact all of the world's misery—her relatives' drudgery, Akhmatova's imprisonment, the gulags, and the murder of dissidents—into a stone wrapped in blue sugar paper and throw it away. She knows that it cannot be, in the same way she is prevented from seeing Akhmatova, but the image and the feeling behind it retain their power over the reader and poet alike. The most impressively sustained poem of an excellent collection, "Sugar-Paper Blue" is clear proof of the poet's continuing attempt to set down her markers in the face of oblivion.

—Geoff Sadler

FALLON, Peter

Nationality: Irish. **Born:** Osnabrück, West Germany, 26 February 1951. **Education:** St. Gerard's School, Glenstal Abbey; Trinity College, Dublin, B.A. (honors) 1975. **Career:** Since 1970 editor and publisher, Gallery Press, Dublin. Since 1980 fiction editor, O'Brien Press, Dublin, and since 2000 Heimbold Professor of Irish Studies,

Villanova University, Pennsylvania. Poet-in-residence, Deerfield Academy, Massachusetts, 1976–77, 1996–97. Co-editor, *Ocarina*. **Awards:** Irish Arts Council bursary, 1981; Meath Personality of the Year for Culture, 1987; O'Shaughnessy poetry award, Irish American Cultural Institute, 1993. **Address:** Gallery Press, Loughcrew, Oldcastle, County Meath, Ireland.

PUBLICATIONS

Poetry

Among the Walls. Dublin, Tara Telephone, 1971.
Co-incidence of Flesh. Dublin, Gallery Press, 1972.
The First Affair. Dublin, Gallery Press, 1974.
Finding the Dead. Deerfield, Massachusetts, Deerfield Press, 1978.
The Speaking Stones. Dublin, Gallery Press, 1978.
Winter Work. Dublin, Gallery Press, 1983.
The News and Weather. Dublin, Gallery Press, 1987.
Eye to Eye. Loughcrew, Oldcastle, Gallery Press, 1992.
News of the World: Selected Poems. Winston-Salem, North Carolina, Wake Forest University Press, 1993.

Other

Essentials of Writing: A Programmed Text in English Grammar and Syntax. Malvern, E-W Commercial Publications, 1992.

Editor, *New and Selected Poems* by Brendan Kennelly. Dublin, Gallery Press, 1976.
Editor, *A Farewell to English* by Michael Hartnett. Dublin, Gallery Press, 1978.
Editor, *The Headgear of the Tribe: Selected Poems* by Desmond O'Grady. Dublin, Gallery Press, 1979.
Editor, *The First Ten Years: Dublin Arts Festival Poetry.* Dublin, Dublin Arts Festival, 1979.
Editor, with Seán Golden, *Soft Day: A Miscellany of Contemporary Irish Writing.* Dublin, Wolfhound Press, and Notre Dame, Indiana, University of Notre Dame Press, 1980.
Editor, *The Writers: A Sense of Ireland: New Work by 44 Irish Writers.* Dublin, O'Brien Press, and New York, Braziller, 1980.
Editor, *After the Wake: 21 Prose Works* by Brendan Behan. Dublin, O'Brien Press, 1981.
Editor, *The Second Voyage* by Eiléan Ní Chuilleanáin. Dublin, Gallery Press, and Newcastle upon Tyne, Bloodaxe, 1986.
Editor, with Derek Mahon, *The Penguin Book of Contemporary Irish Poetry.* London, Penguin, 1990.

*

Critical Studies: "A Miscellany of Contemporary Irish Writing by Peter Fallon and Sean Golden" by Knute Skinner, in *Concerning Poetry* (Bellingham, Washington), 14(2), fall 1981; "Peter Fallon: Contemporary Irish Poet, Editor, and Publisher" by Jerry B. Lincecum, in *Notes on Modern Irish Literature* (Butler, Pennsylvania), 3, 1991; "Chosen Home: The Poetry of Peter Fallon" by Eamon Grennan, in *Eire-Ireland* (St. Paul, Minnesota), 29(2), summer 1994.

*   *   *

Peter Fallon has taken to heart more than any other Irish writer Patrick Kavanagh's rather Polonian observations about the virtues of the parochial: writers who take their material from their own parish are true to their experience, and they offer the world a knowledge in detail to which it otherwise could not have access. Fallon has always rooted his poetry in the events, personalities, and language of his home terrain in County Meath, and his 1978 collection, *The Speaking Stones,* defeats all charges of the dangers of provincialism. Fallon's 1987 volume, *The News and Weather,* is a triumphant justification of his concentration on what he has called, in an Irish idiom, his "care"—the things that it falls to him to look after.

Fallon's career suggests a paradox. His early work tries too hard to draw the universal moral from the stories in his world and consequently seems too narrow an expression of the poet's view; his later work is much simpler and never forces the moral, leaving an air of universality to be inferred. The poems in *The Speaking Stones* are both too long and too elaborate; there is simply too much fact in them for direct impact. For example, too many details of the arcane arts of water divining are itemized in "Finding the Dead," dissipating the impact of its strongest lines:

> In time the unfound dead
> will gather in the maps.

Winter Work, published in 1983, displays far more compression and a new imaginativeness, as in the hideous surrealism of "Water-Dogs," about the traditional Irish country practice of drowning unwanted dogs. When the sheepdogs who attack sheep are caught,

> they're put to water, rounding fishes,
> long sleep and dreams of cold-blooded killings.

There is a metaphorical resonance here, a sense of something beyond the letter of the narrative that Fallon's earlier work does not often suggest. *Winter Work* also takes up the charge of provincial narrowness and argues with it as expressly as a poet dares in the poem "The Lost Field," which can be read as a gloss on Kavanagh's case for parochialism:

> Think of all that lasts. Think of land . . .

> Imagine the world
> the place your own windfalls could fall.

> I'm out to find that field, to make it mine.

Fallon is serving notice here of his determination to proceed in the same vein. Yet the style of *The News and Weather* marks an enormous advance. It is a shorter book, made up of short poems, but its impact is much more forceful. The same strange stories are told but with a new force that comes from understatement. Both the expansiveness of *The Speaking Stones* and the tendency of *Winter Work* to draw on Gaelic poetry, not always usefully, have been dropped. Fallon is suddenly his own man, with confidence in himself. The pared-back brevity serves his purposes, and the formal structures (sonnets, quatrains), which in earlier work occasionally seem forced and an end in themselves, are now a perfect container for his humorous wisdom poems. Even a punch line poem like "The Late Country," which Fallon, who is a celebrated reader of poetry, performs to great humorous effect, uses local idiom with classical epigrammatic terseness:

> He is drinking to forget.
> He has yet to learn that bad beats worse.

But the intimations of universality in the local are everywhere here. In "Caesarean," about the deaths of twin lambs, he writes,

> We knelt close to hear a heart,
> heard our own and thought it one of theirs.

Local references add to the storehouse of language, but they do not diminish their subjects. It may not be too sophistical to suggest that the charge of provincialism against Fallon is itself evidence of a fear of narrowness. Such fear has often led to a desperate wish for cosmopolitanism in Irish writing, but such a cultivated style would be unconvincing.

Fallon has the virtue of writing about what he knows best. When his subjects are allowed to carry the weight, as in the two haunting poems about the Irish disaster of unwanted pregnancy, Fallon has more to teach than writers of more declared ambition.

—Bernard O'Donoghue

FANTHORPE, U(rsula) A(skham)

Nationality: British. **Born:** Lee Green, London, 29 July 1929. **Education:** St. Anne's College, Oxford, 1949–53, B.A. 1953, M.A. 1958; University of London Institute of Education, 1953–54, Dip.Ed. 1954; University College, Swansea, diploma in school counseling 1971. **Career:** Assistant English teacher, 1954–62, and Head of English, 1962–70, Cheltenham Ladies' College, Gloucestershire; clerk in various businesses in Bristol, 1972–74; hospital clerk and receptionist, Bristol, 1974–83. Arts Council creative writing fellow, St. Martin's College, Lancaster, 1983–85. **Awards:** Society of Authors traveling scholarship, 1984; Hawthornden fellowships, 1987, 1997; Arts Council Writers award, 1994; Cholmondeley award, 1995. D.Litt.: University of the West of English Bristol, 1995. Fellow, Royal Society of Literature, 1987. **Address:** Culverhay House, Wotton under Edge, Gloucestershire GL12 7LS, England.

PUBLICATIONS

Poetry

Side Effects. Liskeard, Cornwall, Harry Chambers/Peterloo Poets, 1978.
Four Dogs. Liskeard, Cornwall, Treovis Press, 1980.
Standing To. Liskeard, Cornwall, Harry Chambers/Peterloo Poets, 1982.
Voices Off. Liskeard, Cornwall, Harry Chambers/Peterloo Poets, 1984.
The Crystal Zoo (for children), with John Cotton and L.J. Anderson. Oxford, Oxford University Press, 1985.
Selected Poems. Calstock, Cornwall, Peterloo Poets, 1986.
A Watching Brief. Calstock, Cornwall, Peterloo Poets, 1987.
Neck Verse. Calstock, Cornwall, Peterloo Poets, 1992.

Safe As Houses. Calstock, Cornwall, Peterloo Poets, 1995.
Consequences. Calstock, Cornwall, Peterloo Poets, 2000.

Recordings: *Double Act,* with R.V. Bailey, Penguin, 1997.

*

Critical Studies: *Taking Stock: A First Study of U.A. Fanthorpe* by Eddie Wainwright, Calstock, Cornwall, Peterloo Poets, 1994; "Hearing the Other: Voices in U.A. Fanthorpe's Poetry" by Paul Delaney, in *Christianity and Literature* (Carrollton, Georgia), 46(3–4), spring-summer 1997.

*   *   *

U.A. Fanthorpe had an Oxford education and went on to teach at a prestigious school. She gave this up to become, after various temporary jobs, a clerical worker at a hospital. Such a biography may sound like that of an English eccentric. There is nothing, however, eccentric about Fanthorpe's verse. She gives more than a passing nod to Betjeman and is aware of the comedic aspects of Auden, but such affinities are a matter of rivalry rather than imitation. Her most obvious literary relationship seems to be with a phase of poetry, colloquial and acidulous, that began in Britain soon after World War II. By that time Fanthorpe was already a young adult, but she had many years to go before she published a book of her own. Further, behind many of the more palpable analogues are the poets preserved for Fanthorpe's generation in the attractively bound Oxford Editions of Standard Authors.

In several respects, however, Fanthorpe's verse is not related to the classics. This is a result of her subject matter, which, socially speaking, is rather down-market. Wordsworth had some odd encounters, and so did Coleridge, but they never met Julie the encephalitic or Alison with the damaged brain. Tennyson wrote of sickbeds, but not in the vein of Fanthorpe: "The smashed voice roars inside the ruined throat / Behind the mangled face . . ." Yet the standard authors are not entirely forgotten. That poem, ironically entitled "Linguist," modulates into a style Tennyson would have recognized: "A silent clock that speaks / The solemn language of the sun . . ." All of this goes to show how genuinely inclusive is the English tradition in which Fanthorpe works.

Fanthorpe's world, though fraught with wit, is not a cosy one. Functionaries in her poems deal with sickness and death at close quarters. The hospital secretary requires a sense of order in typing out her fatal lists, and the clerk needs a strong back to tote her files. Moreover, all of this takes place in a busily social atmosphere. Almost the best of these poems is "Lament for the Patients." Here a startling use is made of interpolated statement:

> To me came the news of their dying:
> From the police (*Was this individual*
> *A patient of yours?*); from ambulance
> Control (*Our team report this patient*
> *You sent us to fetch is deceased already*);
> From tight-lipped telephoning widowers
> (*My wife died in her sleep last night*);
> From carboned discharge letters (*I note*
> *That you have preserved the brain. We would certainly*
> *Be very interested in this specimen*);
> From curt press cuttings (*Man found dead.*

Foul play not suspected). I annotated their notes
With their final symptom: *Died*.
Therefore I remember them.

An ironic effect is gained through the way in which natural language is displaced by official language, causing some odd ambiguities. The word "individual," necessarily used by the police, fortuitously drains the patient of individuality. The "deceased" is no longer a person but has, precipitately, become a corpse. Further, all of this is contrasted with the central persona, the speaker of the poem, who has to cope with these incoming calls and who does so succinctly and with a degree of alliterative skill: "I annotated their notes . . ." That, in its turn, may remind the reader of the breakthrough in the early 1950s when James Kirkup inaugurated a new mode in poetry with "A Correct Compassion" and when D.J. Enright sent back his wry dispatches from Egypt and Japan.

Much of what Fanthorpe writes about may seem as drab and basic as the topics chosen by Kirkup and Enright. Characteristically, however, each subject is irradiated by an enlivening gleam. What Fanthorpe says of the winter adventurers in her poem "Hang-Gliders in January" is also true of her own verse: "Like all miracles, it has a rational / Explanation . . ." Here, as elsewhere in her work, it is the naturalistic detail that seems to carry the vital charge: "We saw the aground flyers, their casques and belts / And defenceless legs . . ." This gives an ironic turn to the immediately preceding statement: "It was all quite simple, really." The poem tempts the reader beyond its literal meaning. Fanthorpe's skill makes her appear, among the hopeless flops of some latter-day versifiers, "like a bird at home in the sky."

Fanthorpe's later verse does not so much develop the earlier technique as merely add to it. There is no diminution of skill, but there is a tendency to retreat from the immediate and particular world to topics that are literary and historical. This sometimes results in poems that are both moving and ambitious, as in the poem "Tyndale in Darkness." At the same time the immediacy of the first two books seems to have dispersed itself into allusion and reminiscence.

In an interview with Eddie Wainwright, who in *Taking Stock* has written a fine preliminary study of her poetry, Fanthorpe says, "What's important to me is *people* . . ." Perhaps it is the people in her hospital wards who gave rise to her best pieces rather than Edward the Confessor, Titania, John Clare, or W.B. Yeats, figures of a type that increasingly tend to throng her verse. If this is to say that *Side Effects* and *Standing To* are her best collections, it is also to say that poems such as "Jobdescription," "Linguist," "After Visiting Hours," and "Lament for the Patients" are masterpieces of irony, observation, and, most of all, compassion.

—Philip Hobsbaum

FEAVER, Vicki

Nationality: British. **Born:** Vicki Turton, Nottingham, 14 November 1943. **Education:** University of Durham, B.A. (honors) 1962, and University of London, M.A. 1982. **Family:** Married William Andrew Feaver in 1960 (divorced); three daughters, one son. **Career:** Creative writing instructor, Chichester Institute of Higher Education; British television writer of subtitles for the deaf. **Awards:** Arvon Competition prize winner, 1992; Forward prize, 1993; Heinemann prize, 1994, for *The Handless Maiden;* Cholmondeley award.

PUBLICATIONS

Poetry

Close Relatives. London, Secker and Warburg, 1981.
The Handless Maiden. London, Cape Poetry, 1994.

*

Critical Studies: By Philip Gross, in *Poetry Review,* 84(2), summer 1994; in *Poetry Review,* 85(1), spring 1995; by the author, in *How Poets Work,* edited by Tony Curtis, Bridgend, Seren, 1996.

*   *   *

I first encountered Vicki Feaver's poetry in the Tate Gallery Anthologies, in which poems are paired with paintings. Feaver's "Oi Yoi Oi" was paired with Roger Hilton's painting of the same name. The immediate impression of Feaver's poem, like that of the painting, is of one of energy and movement:

The lady has no shame.
Wearing not a stitch
she is lolloping across
an abstract beach
towards a notional sea.

The poem catches the spirit of the painting beautifully.

The same can be said of another Feaver poem, this one about a deeply contrasting painting, Lucian Freud's near still life *Naked Girl with an Egg.* Energy also intrudes here, but this time it is in the portrayal of the act of painting itself:

his brush
slithering over lustrous flesh,
the coarse dark hair between her legs,
like a tongue seeking salt.

It is a poem in which energy and sensuality are splendidly interrelated.

Indeed, energy and the physical enjoyment of life are the hallmarks of many of Feaver's poems. Domestic subjects, as in "Ironing," throb with images of movement and physical involvement:

I used to iron everything
my iron flying over sheets and towels
Like a sledge chased by wolves over snow.

Feaver's poetry revels in a joyous embrace of life itself and celebrates with the reader a fundamentally real world of sensual pleasures, as in "Ruben's Bottom"—"in my rawness, named Flesh."

Another thread running through Feaver's poetry is that of the stuff of legend and folklore. There are biblical heroines such as Judith and Esther and other stories deep in the Western tradition, such as those of Circe and of the handless maiden. Feaver's poems bring to such subjects the immediacy of feeling and emotion:

And I cried for my hands that sprouted
in the red-orange mud—the hands
that write this, grasping
her curled fists.

In addition, Feaver creates and celebrates her own domestic folklore out of the home truths and mythology of everyday life—of wasps, ironing, menstruation, wood pigeons, and a grandmother dying. It is an acceptance of a world of wonder in the ordinary fabric of life, informed by a cheerful energy of purpose and illuminated by the forces of imagination and verbal energy that make it the stuff of poetry.

—John Cotton

FEINSTEIN, Elaine

Nationality: British. **Born:** Bootle, Lancashire, 24 October 1930. **Education:** Wyggeston Grammar School, Leicester; Newnham College, Cambridge, B.A. in English 1952, M.A. 1955. **Family:** Married Arnold Feinstein in 1956; three sons. **Career:** Editorial staff member, Cambridge University Press, 1960–62; lecturer in English, Bishop's Stortford Training College, Hertfordshire, 1963–66; assistant lecturer in literature, University of Essex, Wivenhoe, 1967–70. Writer in residence for the British Council in Singapore, 1993. **Awards:** Arts Council grant, 1970, 1979, 1981; Daisy Miller prize, 1971, for fiction; Kelus prize, 1978; Cholmondeley award, 1990. D.Litt: University of Leicester, 1990. Fellow, Royal Society of Literature, 1980. **Agent:** Gill Coleridge, Rodgers, Coleridge & White, 20 Powis Mews, London W11, England; (plays and film) Lemon Unna and Durbridge, 24–32 Pottery Lane, London W11 4LZ, England.

PUBLICATIONS

Poetry

In a Green Eye. London, Goliard Press, 1966.
The Magic Apple Tree. London, Hutchinson, 1971.
At the Edge. Rushden, Northamptonshire, Sceptre Press, 1972.
The Celebrants and Other Poems. London, Hutchinson, 1973.
Some Unease and Angels: Selected Poems. London, Hutchinson, and University Center, Michigan, Green River Press, 1977.
The Feast of Euridice. London, Faber, 1980.
Badlands. London, Hutchinson, 1986.
City Music. London, Hutchinson, 1990.
Selected Poems. Manchester, Carcanet, 1994.
Daylight. Manchester, Carcanet, 1997.
Gold. Manchester, Carcanet, 2000.

Plays

Lear's Daughters (produced London, 1987).

Radio Plays: *Echoes,* 1980; *A Late Spring,* 1982; *A Captive Lion,* 1984; *Marina Tsvetayeva: A Life,* 1985; *A Day Off,* from the novel by Storm Jameson, 1986; *If I Ever Get on My Feet Again,* 1987;

The Man in Her Life, 1990; *Foreign Girls,* 1993; *Winter Meeting,* 1994.

Television Plays: *Breath,* 1975; *Lunch,* 1982; *Country Diary of an Edwardian Lady* series, from work by Edith Holden, 1984; *A Brave Face,* 1985; *The Chase,* 1988; *A Passionate Woman* series, 1989.

Novels

The Circle. London, Hutchinson, 1970.
The Amberstone Exit. London, Hutchinson, 1972.
The Glass Alembic. London, Hutchinson, 1973; as *The Crystal Garden,* New York, Dutton, 1974.
Children of the Rose. London, Hutchinson, 1975.
The Ecstasy of Dr. Miriam Garner. London, Hutchinson, 1976.
The Shadow Master. London, Hutchinson, 1978; New York, Simon and Schuster, 1979.
The Survivors. London, Hutchinson, 1982.
The Border. London, Hutchinson, 1984.
Mother's Girl. London, Century Hutchinson, 1988.
All You Need. London, Century Hutchinson, 1989.
Loving Brecht. London, Hutchinson, 1992.
Dreamers. London, Hutchinson, 1994.
Lady Chatterley's Confession. London, Macmillan, 1995.

Short Stories

Matters of Chance. London, Covent Garden Press, 1972.
The Silent Areas. London, Hutchinson, 1980.

Other

Bessie Smith. London, Penguin, 1985.
A Captive Lion: The Life of Marina Tsvetayeva. London, Century Hutchinson, and New York, Dutton, 1987.
Marina Tsvetayeva. London, Penguin, 1989.
Lawrence's Women. New York and London, Harper Collins, 1993.
Pushkin. London, Weidenfeld and Nicolson, 1998; as *Pushkin: A Biography,* New York, Ecco Press, 1999.

Editor, *Selected Poems of John Clare.* London, University Tutorial Press, 1968.
Editor, with Fay Weldon, *New Stories 4.* London, Hutchinson, 1979.
Editor, *PEN New Poetry.* London, Quartet, 1988.
Editor, *After Pushkin: Versions of the Poems of Alexander Sergeevish Pushkin by Contemporary Poets.* Manchester, Carcanet, 1999.

Translator, *The Selected Poems of Marina Tsvetayeva.* London, Oxford University Press, 1971; revised edition, Oxford and New York, Oxford University Press, 1981; revised edition, Oxford and New York, Oxford University Press, 1993.
Translator, *Three Russian Poets: Margarita Aliger, Yunna Moritz, Bella Akhmadulina.* Manchester, Carcanet, 1979.
Translator, with Antonia W. Bouis, *First Draft: Poems,* by Nika Turbina. London, Boyars, 1988.
Translator, *Marina Tsvetaeva: Selected Poems.* Manchester, Carcanet, 1999.

*

Manuscript Collection: Cambridge University.

Critical Studies: "Modes of Realism: Roy Fisher and Elaine Feinstein" by Deborah Mitchell, in *British Poetry since 1970* edited by Michael Schmidt and Peter Jones, Manchester, Carcanet, and New York, Persea, 1980; Peter Conradi, in *British Novelists since 1960* edited by Jay L. Halio, Detroit, Gale, 1983.

Elaine Feinstein comments:

When I began writing in the early 1960s, I felt the influence of the Americans—Stevens and perhaps even Emily Dickinson as much as W.C. Williams—and I suppose the turning point in finding a voice of my own arose, paradoxically, from working on the translations of Marina Tsvetayeva and other modern Russian poets. And perhaps also from writing prose, which began at first as an extension of the poetic impulse but, after several novels, works as a channel for the exploration of my humanist concerns and leaves me freer now to take greater risks with language when I choose to write lyric poetry. Perhaps both experiences have encouraged me to write longer poems, such as the title poem of *The Celebrants* and more recently "New Poems for Dido and Aeneas," and to find longer lines and new rhythms as well as richer subject matter.

(1995) I find my poems get bonier and more bare as I get older and usually spring from some experience in my own life, as if the impulse to make poems now has to connect with a need to puzzle out personal thoughts and feelings. And I want the verse to be clear and quiet, even though lyric poetry rises most powerfully from intense emotion, and it is the lyric I love. I have no ambition to write a long poem. If I am going to tell stories, I would rather write novels.

The poets I most read are still, above all, lyric poets. Herbert's simplicity, Pound's marvelous ear for syllables, Lawrence's sharpness of response, and Charles Reznikoff's humanity remain my models. My onetime Black Mountain mentors had some of these virtues too, but neither their passion for geography and local history nor their insistence on uncorrected spontaneity was ever truly mine. And they were often obscure even on a close reading.

These days I work most of all for directness and lucidity. I do not want the music of the lyric to drown what has to be said. There is always a tug between speech and music in poetry. What I am looking for is a music that has the natural force of spoken feeling, the Wordsworthian "language really used by men," though I confess I enjoyed the street language of slang rather more in the days when it was not so smart to make use of it.

It was from Tsvetayeva I first learned to use personae, finding mythical figures particularly useful as vehicles for the passions. Like characters in fiction, personae allow poets to go outside autobiography without forfeiting their own patterns of feeling. It is rather like writing drama. I do not know whether I will do more.

Tsvetayeva thought a poet had to let "the hand race, (and when it doesn't race to stop)," and I may well write fewer poems of any kind. It is hard to predict. I shall probably not do many more translations. The pressure is elsewhere, in the work of understanding, assessing, and confronting the passage of time.

I am not conscious at the moment of being part of any particular grouping, nor have I been since the English Intelligencer poets who followed Jeremy Prynne came and sat on my Trumpington floor in the sixties, and even then I am not sure how much I shared with them. Over the last twenty years or so my closest literary friendships have been with novelists. But I am very much aware of the good women poets who are writing now. When I began writing, there were so few

of us, and now some of the best young poets are women. And I have not written many overtly political poems. I continue to feel a poet should serve poetry rather than putting his art at the service of any politics.

*   *   *

"Anniversary," which opens the collection *The Magic Apple Tree,* expresses the act of faith in humanity on which all Elaine Feinstein's poetry is posited:

> Listen, I shall have to whisper it
> into your heart directly: we are all
> supernatural/every day
> we rise new creatures/cannot be predicted.

Confronting the banal, flat surfaces of modern existence, symbolized by the mud, mists, and rain of the East Anglian fens, "our brackish waters" ("The Magic Apple Tree"), she acknowledges the limitations set for humans by "the tyranny of landscape" ("Moon") and by our rooting in a particular and all-pervasive present—"How do you change the weather in the blood?" ("I Have Seen Worse Days Turn"). The techniques of poetry are the "alembic," the alchemist's vessel that effects a transformation that is not the transcendence but a sharpening of the real, the celebration of "what in the landscape of cities / has to be prized" ("Some Thoughts on Where"). Feinstein shares with the reader the liberating power of new perceptions: "We have broken some magic barrier" to become "open to the surprises of the season" ("Renaissance February 7"). She delights in the surprises of imagery, color, syntax, tone, and rhythms that set "your own East Anglian children / . . . dancing. To an alien drum" ("Moon"). "Our Vegetable Love Shall Grow" develops the surrealist quality of Marvell's image in the mock horror of a vampire crocus, grotesquely yoking the energies of nature and the city to drain away the lesser vitality of the human. Black humor is the vehicle for modern man and woman to reassert dominance of a reality that threatens to overwhelm. The invocation of Buster Keaton ("Out") is no accident, nor is the marvelous punning cynicism of "West," whose hesitating and stabbing rhythms embrace exactly the bitterly revealing twists of Mae West's comedy.

Feinstein moves incessantly between creative turmoil and a sense of peace, carrying the poet's burden of personal responsibility for the remaking of harmony and unity out of a torn, disjointed world. The broken utterances of "Marriage" catch the pain of human separateness on an intensely personal note:

> tender whenever we touch   what
> else we share   this flesh   we
> bring together   it hurts to
> think of dying as we lie close

In the realm of private loves Feinstein can convey the kind of rare emotion she finds in Marina Tsvetayeva, whom she praises in the introduction to her translations for the "wholeness of her self-exposure." Feinstein also goes beyond the purely personal, however. *At the Edge* evokes a new understanding reached through the "lyric daze'' of carnal passion but makes it clear that the knowledge gained at these frontiers can be kept only through the interpretative but distancing medium of poetic language: ''We were washed in salt on the same pillow together / and we watched the walls change level gently as water . . .''

The title poem of *The Celebrants* recounts the perpetual struggle for meaning through love, science, art, and religion, seeking to evade the limits of death and corruption bounding the world of the body, waiting for the gratuitous moment of poetic surprise ''to free us from the / black drama / of the magician.'' The other poems in the volume have a darker tone than earlier work, a deeper and richer seriousness, and a more biting and bitter humor. *Some Unease and Angels,* essentially a well-chosen retrospect with some new poems, confirms Feinstein's determination to create through language a new balance of man, woman, and their world with nature and its warring elements, as in ''Watersmeet'':

> everywhere plant flesh
> and rich ores had eaten into each other, so that
> peat, rain, green leaves and August fused
> even the two of us together; we took
> a new balance from the two defenceless
> kingdoms bonded in hidden warfare underfoot.

In Feinstein's later work, including *The Feast of Euridice* and the ''Nine Songs for Dido and Aeneas,'' the perspective of myth and legend throws the balance back into question. Virgil's epic celebration of empire is brilliantly turned into a denunciation of the devouring lust for power and possession that drives the imperialist hero. Dido's ancient, orderly kingdom, freely offering its nurturing affections to exorcise Aeneas's ghosts, is laid waste by his ambitions. But at the end it is Dido who wins immortality, not by any witch's magic but by natural powers of endurance and love.

Badlands collects together, across time and space, landscapes of exile, suffering, and loss. Present-day California is given over to ''entrepreneurs and bandits''; in England ''the old gods are leaving''; in Carthage and Ithaca, or deep in the volcanic passage to Hades, Dido, Penelope, and Eurydice yearn toward hopelessly lost loves; in dream and in reality childhood homes or empty lodging house rooms enshrine the absence of dead parents or of poet friends. Again the volume pays tribute to the necessary pain of poetry. Mute matter must be forced to speak; to release the dead soul in ''England,'' the poet must ''crack the / tarmac of the language.'' The poet, too, must constantly ''fight for breath'' (''Park Parade, Cambridge''). Turn and turn about, Feinstein's poetry demonstrates its double face: the cool Apollonian ''weaving and waiting,'' practiced by the waking Penelope, and the frenzied onslaught on language in Penelope's dream, presided over by Dionysus or by ''Hermes, the twister, the pivoter'' (''Three Songs for Ithaca''). The god-magician enters Penelope's sleep with language that embodies the cruel mystery of poetic creation ''to remind me of strangers, returning, who speak in the language / of timberwolves, feeding on human flesh, sorcerer's prey.'' The loose, twisting syntax and the savage, melodramatic vocabulary generate a radical disturbance that evokes the sacred terror of the poetic experience: ''I blench at his voice.''

—Jennifer Birkett

FELDMAN, Irving (Mordecai)

Nationality: American. **Born:** Brooklyn, New York, 22 September 1928. **Education:** City College of New York, B.S. 1950; Columbia University, New York, M.A. 1953. **Family:** Married Carmen Alvarez del Olmo in 1955; one son. **Career:** Taught at the University of Puerto Rico, Rio Piedras, 1954–56; University of Lyons, France, 1957–58; and Kenyon College, Gambier, Ohio, 1958–64. Since 1964 distinguished professor of English, State University of New York, Buffalo. **Awards:** Jewish Book Council of America Kovner award, 1962; Ingram Merrill Foundation grant, 1963; American Academy grant, 1973; Guggenheim fellowship, 1973; Creative Artists Public Service grant, 1980; Emily Clark Balch poetry prize, 1983; Academy of American Poets fellowship, 1986; National Endowment for the Arts grant, 1987; MacArthur fellow, 1992. **Address:** Department of English, State University of New York, Buffalo, New York 14260, U.S.A.

PUBLICATIONS

Poetry

Work and Days and Other Poems. Boston, Little Brown, and London, Deutsch, 1961.
The Pripet Marshes and Other Poems. New York, Viking Press, 1965.
Magic Papers and Other Poems. New York, Harper, 1970.
Lost Originals. New York, Holt Rinehart, 1972.
Leaping Clear. New York, Viking Press, 1976.
New and Selected Poems. New York, Viking Press, 1979.
Teach Me, Dear Sister, and Other Poems. New York, Viking Press, 1983.
All of Us Here and Other Poems. New York, Viking, 1986.
The Life and Letters. Chicago, University of Chicago Press, 1994.
Beautiful False Things. New York, Grove Press, 2000.

*

Critical Studies: *The Poetry of Irving Feldman: Nine Essays,* Lewisburg, Pennsylvania, Bucknell University Press, 1992; ''Lyric Suffering in Auden and Feldman'' by Harold Schweizer, in *English Language Notes* (Boulder, Colorado), 31(2), December 1993; '''So There Were These Two Jews . . .': The Poetry of Irving Feldman'' by David R. Slavitt, in *Hollins Critic* (Hollins College, Virginia), 34(1), 1997.

* * *

Irving Feldman's poetry strives, as one critic has said, ''to infuse the tangible word with numinous significance.'' While such an attempt at transcendence is more or less doomed to failure—as Feldman himself seems aware—he has pursued it with wit, humility, and a refreshingly varied and agile poetry. ''Life is unhappy, life is sweet!'' concludes his newly born Gingerbread Man, ecstatic at the ''thrilling absolute of original breath'' (''As Fast As You Can,'' in *Lost Originals*), and Feldman's work is inspired throughout by this sense of tragic optimism.

The tragic heroes of his first book, *Works and Days,* are figures like Cato and Prometheus, overwhelmed by their fate and yet ultimately revenged, in the latter's case by humor: "the rictus of cosmic spite. / Then nothing really mattered—as his mirth bubbled off in a mist. / / O come to the mountain and see a suit of clothes on a nail" ("Non-being," *Works and Days*). Feldman examines the fates of heroes of all types, from the mythic Prometheus and the Gingerbread Man, to Charles Olson and the passengers on the *Titanic,* to the fictional Antonio, the inept Spanish *botones,* or bellboy (of "Antonio, Botones," in *Leaping Clear*), who becomes a paradigm of innocence and humanity passed over by progress.

Family and friends, Jewish society and customs, politics, religion, painting, and philosophy all take equal weight in Feldman's work, and as frustrating as this puckish diversity can sometimes be, it is welded together by his search for a transcendent knowledge—or at least a transcendent joy in the continuity and identity of life's faceted brilliance. As he says of the fat, balding athletes in "Handball Players at Brighton Beach,"

So what! the sun does not snub.
does not overlook them, shines.

and the fair day flares,
the blue universe booms and blooms

Amid life's coruscating reality there looms always a brighter ideal.

Like his subject matter, Feldman's technique is highly varied and his forms diverse. Although he often adopts or adapts the ballad, elegy, or other established forms, his writing has frequently turned to the vernacular line, and many of his later works are set in paragraphs. Even earlier, for instance in the title poem of *The Pripet Marshes,* he began to use prose stanzas:

Often I think of my Jewish friends and seize them as they are
and transport them in my mind to the *shtetlach* and ghettos.

And set them walking the streets, visiting, praying in *shul,*
feasting and dancing. The men I set to arguing, because I love
dia   lectic and song . . .

"Dialectic and song" is an ensign of Feldman's diversity, and many influences are present in his work, from the classical references of *Works and Days* to Whitmanesque songs or a bit of Olson's objectivism. Feldman has rarely rested in a single influence, and his real poetic kin are meditative poets like John Ashbery and Richard Howard.

Transmuting personal and intellectual experience in his highly dense, thoughtful poetry, Feldman clearly identifies the writing of poetry itself (in "Colloquy") with the project of transcendence, as even the titles *Magic Papers* and *Lost Originals* indicate:

I have long wanted to confess
but do not know to whom
I must speak, and cannot
spend a life on my knees.
Nonetheless, I have always
wanted to save the world

Through his dialectic and song Feldman tries to save the world not only in the political and religious senses but also in the sense of

reclamation. "We wake to poetry from a deeper dream, a purer meditation—expanse of light in water pressing unquenched on our eyes" (second elegy in "New Poems," in *New and Selected Poems*), and he rejoices in the writing of poetry itself for its revivifying of the senses, its assertion of time's ineluctable continuity, and its appreciation of a moment's glorious effulgence:

And the light
        (everywhere
off ridge, rock, window, deep
drop) says,
        I leap clear.

—Walter Bode

FENTON, James (Martin)

Nationality: British. **Born:** Lincoln, 25 April 1949. **Education:** Durham Choristers School; Repton School, Derbyshire; British Institute, Florence; Magdalen College, Oxford (Newdigate prize, 1968), 1967–70, B.A. 1970, M.A. **Career:** Assistant literary editor, 1971, editorial assistant, 1972, and political columnist 1976–78, *New Statesman,* London; freelance journalist, Indo-China, 1973–75; German correspondent, *Guardian,* London, 1978–79; theater critic, *Sunday Times,* London, 1979–84; chief literary critic, *The Times,* London, 1984–86; Far East correspondent, *Independent,* 1986–88. Since 1990 columnist, Arts, *Sunday Independent.* **Awards:** Eric Gregory award, 1969; Geoffrey Faber memorial prize, 1984; Cholmondeley award, 1986. Fellow, Royal Society of Literature, 1983. **Agent:** A.D. Peters, 10 Buckingham Street, London WC2N 6BU. **Address:** Peters Fraser & Dunlop, 5th Floor, The Chambers, Chelsea Harbour, Lots Road, London SW10 OXF.

PUBLICATIONS

Poetry

Our Western Furniture. Oxford, Sycamore Press, 1968.
Put Thou Thy Tears into My Bottle. Oxford, Sycamore Press, 1969.
Terminal Moraine. London, Secker and Warburg, 1972.
A Vacant Possession. London, TNR, 1978.
Dead Soldiers. Oxford, Sycamore Press, 1981.
A German Requiem. Edinburgh, Salamander Press, 1981.
The Memory of War. Edinburgh, Salamander Press, 1982.
Children in Exile. Edinburgh, Salamander Press, 1983; New York, Vintage, 1984.
The Memory of War and Children in Exile: Poems 1968–83. London, Penguin, 1983, as *Children in Exile,* New York, Random House, 1984.
Partingtime Hall, with John Fuller. London, Viking Salamander, 1987.
Manila Envelope. Privately printed, 1989.
Out of Danger. London and New York, Penguin, 1993.
Children in Exile: Poems 1968–1984. New York, Noonday Press, 1994.

Plays

Rigoletto, adaptation of a libretto by F.M. Piave from a play by Hugo, music by Verdi (produced London, 1982; New York, 1984). London, Calder, and New York, Riverrun Press, 1982.

Simon Boccanegra, adaptation of a libretto by Francesco Maria Piave from a play by Antonio García Gutíerrez, music by Verdi. London, Calder, and New York, Riverrun Press, 1985.

Television Documentary: *Burton: A Portrait of a Superstar,* 1983.

Other

You Were Marvellous (theater reviews). London, Cape, 1983.

All the Wrong Places: Adrift in the Politics of the Pacific Rim. Boston, Atlantic Monthly Press, 1988; as *All the Wrong Places: Adrift in the Politics of Asia,* London, Viking, 1989.

Leonardo's Nephew: Essays on Art and Artists. London, Penguin, and New York, Farrar Straus, 1998.

The Hamely Tongue: A Personal Record of Ulster-Scots in County Antrim. Newtonards, Ulster-Scots Academic Press, 1995.

Editor, *The Original Michael Frayn: Satirical Essays.* Edinburgh, Salamander Press, 1983.

Editor, *Cambodian Witness. The Autobiography of Someth May.* London, Faber, 1986; New York, Random House, 1987.

Editor, *Underground in Japan* by Rey Ventura. London, Jonathan Cape, 1992.

*

Critical Studies: "The Poetry of James Fenton" by Michael Hulse, in *Antigonish Review* (Antigonish, Nova Scotia), 58, summer 1984; "The Voice of History in British Poetry, 1970–1984" by Damian Grant, in *Etudes Anglaises* (Paris, France), 38(2), April-June 1985; "James Fenton's 'Narratives': Some Reflections on Postmodernism" by Alan Robinson, in *Critical Quarterly* (Oxford, England), 29(1), spring 1987; "An American's Confession: On Reading James Fenton's 'Out of Danger'" by Ellen Krieger Stark, in *Critical Quarterly* (Oxford, England), 36(2), summer 1994; "Auden's Heir" by Ian Parker, in *New Yorker,* 25 July 1994; "Orientations: James Fenton and Indochina" by Douglas Kerr, in *Contemporary Literature* (Madison, Wisconsin), 35(3), fall 1994.

*   *   *

The British writer James Fenton publishes rarely and collects his poetic work infrequently into exceptionally slim volumes. "A parsimonious brilliance," John Mole has said of Fenton, "is its own reward." Certainly the brilliance of his individual poems, which seem to surround themselves with an exceptional silence to create a very generous space for themselves in the crowded world of contemporary poetry, has earned Fenton a commensurate critical acclaim. This parsimony, however, is clearly not the result of a planned strategy of self-publicity. On the contrary, his poems, which differ so markedly from one another as to seem the products of several distinct kinds of imagination, convey a powerful sense of the single thing uniquely done, of the single matter and the single form uniquely exhausted. The individual Fenton poem embodies within itself a sense of how boring it would be to have anything like it done again.

Still, Fenton's poems do have their influences and analogues. Of the former Auden is certainly the strongest, and of Fenton's analogues the clearest are the new English narrative poets. The conception of the poem as a compressed fiction is central to some of his work. In addition, he shares with the so-called Martian school, which Fenton actually named, a feeling for the strangeness and alienness of the apparently ordinary world.

When the poem is denied an authentic, recognizable lyric voice, something vitally sustaining can be discovered in Fenton. The impression his poems most profoundly convey is that what can be learned about the world is infinitely more important than what can be learned about the self, and the world for Fenton is broader than for many contemporary English poets. His work as a journalist took him to Vietnam and Germany during the 1970s and again to the Far East in the 1980s, and these experiences inform, or undermine perhaps, a great deal of his work. Fenton's objectivity-his penchant for the found poem, his desire for the poem in which the reader notices only the subject matter—might perhaps be regarded as the reticence of a man appalled before some of the facts of his own experience. If the reticence began as an aesthetic choice, it has continued as a moral necessity.

To write directly of some of his subjects—Cambodia in "Cambodia," "In a Notebook," and "Dead Soldiers"; the Third Reich in "A German Requiem"; nuclear holocaust (probably) in "Wind"— would be to risk banality or sentimentality. He does perhaps run this risk in the poem in which he most clearly articulates his own feelings, "Children in Exile," about Cambodian refugees coming to terms with a new life in Italy. But even here the personal feeling seems less important than the creation of a tone through which this very reticent poet can solicit, or cajole, the feelings of the reader. The apparent naïveté of the poem's palpable design upon us is an earnest of the significance of the subject:

From five years of punishment for an offence
    It took America five years to commit
These victim-children have been released on parole.
    They will remember all of it.

Elsewhere in Fenton's poems the self-effacement is more complete, and the absence of moralizing is the clear reward in pieces that address themselves to the greatest modern themes. In "A German Requiem," for instance, the eerie final section creates an unforgettable muted image for the enormous suffering and suggests the way Fenton's own reticent imagination has found its most impressive expression. At some level the image here owes something not to Auden but to T.S. Eliot, the master of the eerie, the sinister, and the inexplicit:

His wife nods, and a secret smile,
Like a breeze with enough strength to carry one dry leaf
Over two pavingstones, passes from chair to chair.
Even the enquirer is charmed.
He forgets to pursue the point.
It is not what he wants to know.

It is what he wants not to know.
It is not what they say.
It is what they do not say.

—Neil Corcoran

FERLINGHETTI, Lawrence (Mendes-Monsanto)

Nationality: American. **Born:** Yonkers, New York, 24 March 1919; lived in France, 1920–24. **Education:** Attended Riverdale Country School, 1927–28, and Bronxville Public School, 1929–33, both New York; Mount Hermon School, Greenfield, Massachusetts, 1933–37; University of North Carolina, Chapel Hill, B.A. in journalism 1941; Columbia University, New York, 1947–48, M.A. 1948; Sorbonne, Paris, 1948–50, Doctorat de l'Université 1950. **Military Service:** U.S. Naval Reserve, 1941–45: lieutenant commander. **Family:** Married Selden Kirby-Smith in 1951 (divorced 1976); one daughter and one son. **Career:** Worked for *Time* magazine, New York, 1945–46; French teacher, San Francisco, 1951–53; cofounder, 1953, with Peter D. Martin, and since 1955 owner, City Lights Bookstore, and editor in chief, City Lights Books, San Francisco. Delegate, Pan American Cultural Conference, Concepción, Chile, 1960; participant in international literary festivals in Italy, France, England, Spain, Australia, and elsewhere. Also a painter: individual shows include Butler Institute of American Art, Youngstown, Ohio, 1993. **Awards:** Etna-Taormina prize (Italy), 1968; Camaiori prize (Italy), 1998; Ostia prize (Italy), 1998; Flaiano prize (Italy), 1998. **Address:** City Lights Books, 261 Columbus Avenue, San Francisco, California 94133, U.S.A.

PUBLICATIONS

Poetry

Pictures of the Gone World. San Francisco, City Lights, 1955.
A Coney Island of the Mind. New York, New Directions, 1958.
Tentative Description of a Dinner Given to Promote the Impeachment of President Eisenhower. San Francisco, Golden Mountain Press, 1958.
One Thousand Fearful Words for Fidel Castro. San Francisco, City Lights, 1961.
Berlin. San Francisco, Golden Mountain Press, 1961.
Starting from San Francisco. New York, New Directions, 1961; revised edition, 1967.
Penguin Modern Poets 5, with Allen Ginsberg and Gregory Corso. London, Penguin, 1963.
Where Is Vietnam? San Francisco, City Lights, 1965.
To Fuck Is to Love Again; Kyrie Eleison Kerista; or, The Situation in the West; Followed by a Holy Proposal. New York, Fuck You Press, 1965.
Christ Climbed Down. Syracuse, New York, Syracuse University Press, 1965.
An Eye on the World: Selected Poems. London, MacGibbon and Kee, 1967.

After the Cries of the Birds. San Francisco, Dave Haselwood, 1967.
Moscow in the Wilderness, Segovia in the Snow. San Francisco, Beach, 1967.
Repeat after Me. Boston, Impressions Workshop, 1967.
Reverie Smoking Grass. Milan, East 128, 1968.
The Secret Meaning of Things. New York, New Directions, 1968.
Fuclock. London, Fire, 1968.
Tyrannus Nix? New York, New Directions, 1969; revised edition, 1973.
Back Roads to Far Towns after Basho. Privately printed, 1970.
Sometime during Eternity. Conshohocken, Pennsylvania, Poster Prints, 1970.
The World Is a Beautiful Place. Conshohocken, Pennsylvania, Poster Prints, 1970.
The Illustrated Wilfred Funk. San Francisco, City Lights, 1971.
A World Awash with Fascism and Fear. San Francisco, Cranium Press, 1971.
Back Roads to Far Places. New York, New Directions, 1971.
Love Is No Stone on the Moon: Automatic Poem. Berkeley, California, Arif Press, 1971.
Open Eye, with *Open Head,* by Allen Ginsberg. Melbourne, Sun, 1972; published separately, Cambridge, Massachusetts, Pomegranate Press, 1973.
Constantly Risking Absurdity. Brockport, New York, State University College, 1973.
Open Eye, Open Heart. New York, New Directions, 1973.
Populist Manifesto. San Francisco, Cranium Press, 1975; revised edition, San Francisco, City Lights, n.d.
Soon It Will Be Night. Privately printed, 1975.
The Jack of Hearts. San Francisco, City Lights, 1975.
Director of Alienation. San Francisco, City Lights, 1975.
The Old Italians Dying. San Francisco City Lights, 1976.
Who Are We Now? New York, New Directions, 1976.
White on White. San Francisco, City Lights, 1977.
Adieu à Charlot. San Francisco, City Lights, 1978.
Northwest Ecolog. San Francisco, City Lights, 1978.
The Sea and Ourselves at Cape Ann. Madison, Wisconsin, Red Ozier Press, 1979.
Landscapes of Living and Dying. New York, New Directions, 1979.
The Love Nut. Lincoln, Massachusetts, Penmaen Press, 1979.
Mule Mountain Dreams. Bisbee, Arizona, Bisbee Press Collective, 1980.
A Trip to Italy and France. New York, New Directions, 1981.
The Populist Manifestos, Plus an Interview with Jean-Jacques Lebel. San Francisco, Grey Fox Press, 1981.
Endless Life: The Selected Poems. New York, New Directions, 1981.
Over All the Obscene Boundaries: European Poems and Transitions. New York, New Directions, 1984.
Wild Dreams of a New Beginning. New York, New Directions, 1988.
These Are My Rivers: New & Selected Poems 1955–1993. New York, New Directions, 1993.
Pictures of the Gone World. San Francisco, City Lights, 1995.
A Far Rockaway of the Heart. New York, New Directions, 1998.

Recordings: *Poetry Readings in "The Cellar,"* with Kenneth Rexroth, Fantasy, 1958; *Tentative Description of a Dinner to Impeach President Eisenhower and Other Poems,* Fantasy, 1959; *Tyrannus*

Nix? and Assassination Raga, Fantasy, 1971; The *World's Greatest Poets 1,* with Allen Ginsberg and Gregory Corso, CMS, 1971; *Lawrence Ferlinghetti,* Everett-Edwards, 1972; *Into the Deeper Pools . . . ,* Watershed, 1984.

Plays

The Alligation (produced San Francisco, 1962; New York, 1970; London, 1989). Included in *Unfair Arguments with Existence,* 1963.

Unfair Arguments with Existence: Seven Plays for a New Theatre (includes *The Soldiers of No Country, Three Thousand Red Ants, The Alligation, The Victims of Amnesia, Motherlode, The Customs Collector in Baggy Pants, The Nose of Sisyphus*). New York, New Directions, 1963.

The Customs Collector in Baggy Pants (produced New York, 1964). Included in *Unfair Arguments with Existence,* 1963.

The Soldiers of No Country (produced London, 1969). Included in *Unfair Arguments with Existence,* 1963.

3 by Ferlinghetti: Three Thousand Red Ants, The Alligation, The Victims of Amnesia (produced New York, 1970). Included in *Unfair Arguments with Existence,* 1963.

Routines (includes thirteen short pieces). New York, New Directions, 1964.

The Victims of Amnesia (produced London, 1989). Included in *Unfair Arguments with Existence,* 1963.

Novels

Her. New York, New Directions, 1960; London, MacGibbon and Kee, 1967.

Love in the Days of Rage. New York, Dutton, and London, Bodley Head, 1988.

Other

Dear Ferlinghetti/Dear Jack: The Spicer-Ferlinghetti Correspondence. San Francisco, White Rabbit Press, 1962.

The Mexican Night: Travel Journal. New York, New Directions, 1970.

A Political Pamphlet. San Francisco, Anarchist Resistance Press, 1975.

Literary San Francisco: A Pictorial History from Its Beginnings to the Present Day, with Nancy J. Peters. San Francisco, City Lights, 1980.

An Artist's Diatribe. San Diego, Atticus Press, 1983.

Leaves of Life: Fifty Drawings from the Model. San Francisco, City Lights, 1983.

Seven Days in Nicaragua Libre, photographs by Chris Felver. San Francisco, City Lights, 1984.

Editor, *Beatitude Anthology.* San Francisco, City Lights, 1960.

Editor, with Michael McClure and David Meltzer, *Journal for the Protection of All Beings 1* and *3.* San Francisco, City Lights, 2 vols., 1961–69.

Editor, *City Lights Journal.* San Francisco, City Lights, 4 vols., 1963–78.

Editor, *Panic Grass,* by Charles Upton. San Francisco, City Lights, 1969.

Editor, *The First Third,* by Neal Cassady. San Francisco, City Lights, 1971.

Editor, *City Lights Anthology.* San Francisco, City Lights, 1974.

Editor, with Nancy J. Peters, *City Lights Review I* [3]. San Francisco, City Lights, 2 vols., 1987–89.

Editor, *City Lights Pocket Poet Anthology.* San Francisco. City Lights, 1995.

Translator, *Selections from Paroles by Jacques Prévert.* San Francisco, City Lights, 1958; London, Penguin, 1963.

Translator, with Anthony Kahn, *Flowers and Bullets, and Freedom to Kill,* by Yevgeny Yevtushenko. San Francisco, City Lights, 1970.

Translator, with Reinhard Lettau, *Love Poems,* by Karl Marx. San Francisco, City Lights, 1977.

Translator, with Francesca Valente, *Roman Poems,* by Pier Paolo Pasolini. San Francisco, City Lights, 1986.

*

Bibliography: *Lawrence Ferlinghetti: A Comprehensive Bibliography to 1980* by Bill Morgan, New York, Garland, 1982.

Manuscript Collection: Bancroft Library, University of California, Berkeley.

Critical Studies: *Ferlinghetti: A Biography* by Neeli Cherkovsky, New York, Doubleday, 1979; *Lawrence Ferlinghetti: Poet-at-Large* by Larry Smith, Carbondale, Southern Illinois University Press, 1983; *Constantly Risking Absurdity: The Writings of Lawrence Ferlinghetti* by Michael Skau, Troy, New York, Whitston, 1989; *Ferlinghetti: The Artist in His Time* by Barry Silesky, New York, Warner, 1990; ''A Hundred Harms: Poetry and the Gulf War—Ferlinghetti at Laugharne,'' by Tony Curtis, in *Poetry Review* (London), summer 1992; by James Oliver, in *Dionysos: The Literature and Addiction TriQuarterly* (Seattle, Washington), winter 1993; in *How Poets Work,* edited by Tony Curtis, Brigend, Seren, 1996.

*   *   *

Lawrence Ferlinghetti is a writer whose work remains as exciting as it was in the 1950s, when he was one of the founders and the chief impresario of the beat group of poets. While most of the other beats have died or have gradually drifted away from the literary world, Ferlinghetti remains a powerful force on the poetic scene, not only as an author but also as an editor who has encouraged and published numerous young writers and as the proprietor of the City Lights Bookstore.

Like Walt Whitman, Ferlinghetti believes that the poet should be an agitator whose message reaches the great masses of people too often ignored by more traditional poets. And like Whitman, Ferlinghetti has had great success at this. His *A Coney Island of the Mind* remains one of the all-time best-sellers for a volume of poetry. Part of its success was no doubt due to its experimental technique, which owed much to e.e. cummings, and to its use of what were for the time shocking words. Published during a period of great conventionality, Ferlinghetti's book provided a rousingly vigorous alternative view of life. The book celebrates love, sex, and freedom and attacks the crass materialism that, as these lines from "Christ Climbed Down" indicate, controls society:

> Christ climbed down
> from His bare Tree
> this year
> and ran away to where
> no intrepid Bible salesmen
> covered the territory
> in two-tone Cadillacs

Godless society is the frequent target of Ferlinghetti's satiric attacks. "Beat is the soul of beatific," Jack Kerouac said, and all of the beats had a strong concern for the spiritual side of man. Ferlinghetti's poetry stems from his intense moral concern about where "the Bosch-like world" is heading.

"When the guns are roaring the Muses have no right to be silent," writes Ferlinghetti, and during the violence-filled 1960s he continued to make his voice heard. His poetry took on a surrealistic edge, in part because of the surreal rush of events in the decade. "Some days I'm afflicted / with Observation Fever / omnivorous perception of phenomena," begins "Buckford's Buddha," and in the world of "death TV" sensory overload ensues. It was at about this time that some of Ferlinghetti's poems came to be written under the influence of LSD, a drug the poet took not because of hedonism but rather, in the words of the title of one of his volumes, to find "the secret meaning of things." The poems of this period are more fragmented than his earlier work, but their message, as expressed in "Assassination Raga," a powerful elegy for the Kennedys, remains the same: "There is no god but Life . . . love love and hate hate."

In the 1970s Ferlinghetti's technical experiments involved working with the prose poem and creating Indian chants and mantras in English. He continued to keep an "open eye, open heart" on his society and to condemn "a world awash with fascism and fear." For Ferlinghetti there was no middle-aged mellowing or watering down of his ideals. A few lines from "Overheard Conversation" indicate how little his concept of poetry changed in two decades: "And still the whole idea of poetry being / to take control of life / out of the hands of / the Terrible People." On rare occasions the terrible people Ferlinghetti attacks are hackneyed subjects, as in the long poem "Vegas Tilt," which exposes the materialism of Las Vegas. This is hardly a novel or challenging concept, but more frequently his adversaries are well chosen. With Whitman, Vachel Lindsay, and Carl Sandburg, Ferlinghetti stands in the great line of American poets who have been gadflies, yea-sayers to humanity and nay-sayers to the forces of repression. One of his finest poems, "Populist Manifesto," expresses Ferlinghetti's ideas about and hopes for poetry. It is a clarion call: "Poets, come out of your closets . . . / You have been holed-up too long / in your closed world." It continues by stating that poetry has become too stifling. Ironically echoing his friend Allen Ginsberg, Ferlinghetti writes, "We have seen the best minds of our generation / destroyed by boredom at poetry readings," and after a Whitman-like catalog of the various schools of poetry flourishing today, Ferlinghetti exhorts other writers, crying,

> Poets, descend
> to the street of the world once more
> And open your minds and eyes
> with the old visual delight
> Clear your throat and speak up,
> Poetry is dead, long live poetry
> with terrible eyes and buffalo strength.

Ferlinghetti practices what he preaches. One only wishes that more poets would write with his immediacy, power, and passion.

—Dennis Lynch

FIELD, Edward

Nationality: American. **Born:** Brooklyn, New York, 7 June 1924. **Education:** New York University. Studied acting with Vera Soloviova of Moscow Art Theatre. **Military Service:** U.S. Air Force, 1942–46. **Career:** Resided in Europe, 1946–48. Has worked as a machinist, as a clerk-typist, in a warehouse, and in art reproduction. Lecturer, YM-YWHA Poetry Center, New York. **Awards:** Lamont Poetry Selection award 1962; Guggenheim fellowship, 1963; Shelley memorial award, 1975; American Academy in Rome fellowship, 1981; Lambda literary award, 1992. **Address:** 463 West Street, Apt. A323, New York, New York 10014, U.S.A.

PUBLICATIONS

Poetry

Stand Up, Friend, with Me. New York, Grove Press, 1963.
Variety Photoplays. New York, Grove Press, 1967.
Sweet Gwendolyn and the Countess. Gulfport, Florida, Konglomerati Press, 1977.
A Full Heart. New York, Sheep Meadow Press, 1977.
Stars in My Eyes. New York, Sheep Meadow Press, 1978.
New and Selected Poems from the Book of My Life. New York, Sheep Meadow Press, 1987.
Counting Myself Lucky, Selected Poems 1963–1992. Santa Rosa, California, Black Sparrow Press, 1992.
A Frieze for a Temple of Love. Santa Rosa, California, Black Sparrow Press, 1998.
Magic Words. New York, Harcourt Brace & Company, 1998.

Novel

Village (as Bruce Elliot, with Neil Derrick). New York, Avon, 1982.

Other

Editor and translator, *Eskimo Songs and Stories, Collected by Knud Rasmussen on the Fifth Thule Expedition.* New York, Delacorte Press, 1973.
Editor, *A Geography of Poets: An Anthology of New Poetry.* New York, Bantam, 1979.

Editor, *Head of a Sad Angel: Stories 1953–1966,* by Alfred Chester. Santa Rosa. California, Black Sparrow Press, 1990.

Editor, with G. Locklin and C. Stetler, *A New Geography of Poets.* Fayetteville, Arkansas, University of Arkansas Press, 1992.

Editor, *Looking for Genet, Literary Essays & Reviews,* by Alfred Chester. Santa Rosa, California, Black Sparrow Press, 1992.

*

Manuscript Collection: Special Collections, University of Delaware Library, Newark.

Critical Studies: Review by Robert Mazzocco, in *New York Review of Books,* 1967; *Alone with America* by Richard Howard, New York, Atheneum, 1969, London, Thames and Hudson, 1970, revised edition, Atheneum, 1980; ''Poetry of Inclusion'' by Warren D. Moessner, in *American Book Review,* 15(5), 1993–94; *The Homosexual Tradition in American Poetry* by Robert K. Martin, Iowa City, University of Iowa Press, 1998.

Edward Field comments:

I've begun to feel like a survivor from the time before universities took over American poetry. Poetry then belonged to what might be called a ''bohemian'' world of artists and social misfits and eccentrics. Each poet aimed for a quite distinctive voice, his own, and technique was a lonely, hard-won struggle, not the product of a workshop or M.F.A. program. But I believe that poetry will never be totally co-opted, since the tradition (could one say the Muse?) will bring it back to its genuine spirit.

*   *   *

Edward Field writes poems for which the reader is honestly grateful. They are heartfelt. Straightforward and unadorned, they have little or no figurative language but are conversational and colloquial. The speaker may be humble, sad, funny (ribald, witty, wry), and self-deprecating. There also is unabashed sentimentality. At the same time Field manages to control and distance intensely personal material. He understates, he responds, he perceives. Finally, he joins, brings together. As he expresses those feelings of shame and frustration that characterized his childhood years, he opens the door to his private hell—''the terror and guilt / and self-loathing'' he felt in his father's house.

Field's hopes for himself and the world are centered in the triumph of love, the gifts of affection and sexuality. The freedom to feel, to be natural and uninhibited—the freedom to be—these are his concerns. And so he attempts to bring people together, to overcome distances, to bring down barriers. By inviting the reader to share intimacies, by embracing the reader, Field resembles a Jewish Walt Whitman. It is in his emphasis on companionship and sexuality, on love above all, that he is most Whitmanesque.

Gentle, yearning, believing that ''all men and women are my brothers and sisters now'' (''Visiting Home''), Field writes confessional poetry. Because it is personal, it cannot help but be confessional. It is a poetry of skepticism, of cautious hope, of the sorrow of estrangement and alienation, of the search for one's way in the world. One must be one's own guru: ''you have to trust to your heart / Which often needs more than one lifetime to make a man'' (''Union City'').

The courage of the heart is what Field's poetry is mostly about. He is not afraid to be himself, to reveal his weaknesses, his fears, his humiliations, as in ''Unwanted'':

His aliases tell his history: Dumbbell, Good-for-nothing
Jewboy, Fieldinsky, Skinny, Fierce Face, Greaseball, Sissy.

Warning: This man is not dangerous, answers to any name
Responds to love, don't call him or he will come.

Through his unassuming honesty he touches the reader with prose poetry. Field's humor is effective and genuinely funny. Laughter— as device and response—enables him to avoid falling into the slough of self-pity. Laughter is a great leveler; not surprisingly, Field's bawdiness serves a democratic function. It reminds us that we all eat, excrete, copulate: ''As the smile is to the face / the hard-on is to the body'' (''Chopped Meat'').

In *Variety Photoplays* Field uses humor to offset maudlin sentiment as he discovers in old movies the familiar and universal themes—frustrated love, alienation, loneliness, prejudice, force of circumstance. His three Frankenstein poems are especially admirable: ''He is pursued by the ignorant villagers, / Who think he is evil and dangerous because he is ugly and makes ugly noises.'' Finally the majority—the real beast—succeeds in creating a monster worse than the Baron: ''He was out to pay them back / to throw the lie of brotherly love / in their white Christian teeth.'' The poem arrives at a moment of triumph:

So he set out on his new career
his previous one being the victim,
the good man who suffers.
Now no longer the hunted by the hunter
he was in charge of his destiny.

Cinema creates and shapes the fairy tales of American culture. The gothic motifs, the soap opera, the happily-ever-after quality that deceives the audience and often the actors—all are treated by Field with wry clarity and sad-eyed humor. If there is nostalgia, a sharp realization of the brevity of youth and fame (''Whatever Happened to May Caspar''), there is also the poet's unique parable *Sweet Gwendolyn and the Countess.* This poem depicts the victimization of innocence and beauty by power and aggression. Field implies that as long as innocence refuses to see and participate in the real world, refuses to be active rather than passive, it will not only continue to be victimized but also actually be contributing to its own subjugation and demise.

A Full Heart has clear moments of joy, of exuberance. This collection is more genuinely happy, for there are the fulfillment of love and the quickening of life that accompanies it. No longer the outsider, Field has been invited to the party. When love is lost, he can console himself for his having had it. Field begins with a celebration of New York—''I live in a beautiful place, a city / . . . this is a people paradise.'' Nothing is too little or ugly to praise: ''Thank God for dogs, cats, sparrows, and roaches.''

A Full Heart shows how Field goes forward and how sometimes this first requires going backward. In ''Pasternak: In Memoriam'' Field stresses personal fulfillment as opposed to heroism:

You were right:
This real person in my arms
is who I want

not the moment of passion on the barricades
not the dream of the ideal
love in a perfect world.

Survive in this world
love as you can
and go on with your work.

This is what the poet has come to learn. In such poems as "Both My
Grandmothers" and "Visiting Home" he deals with the need for
roots, for a sense of origin. His Jewishness—tradition and culture
more than a particularized system of belief—helps him to realize his
identity in a shifting and arbitrary world. If, in the second of these
poems, he acknowledges the severe difficulties visited upon him by
his father, he can also say, "thank God I am my mother's son too / for
what she gave me / is what I survived by." Suffering and love are
wedded in this world and in Field's. He is a poet whose heart is
"full," and in sharing he fills the reader's heart as well.

In *New and Selected Poems from the Book of My Life* Field
includes a generous sampling from "The Crier," an unpublished
collection. While these pieces carry lament, there is also acceptance
both of how things are and of one's own contributions to having made
them this way. "Mirror Songs" concludes with "And what has also
to be faced / is if youth was a waste / it wasn't fate's but my own
doing." Here is the cry of confrontation with the ghosts of lost
opportunities, the anxieties, guilt and shame from the past, with the
hard fact of mortality looming ever larger. "This is an entirely
different thing than life prepares you for, / nor are there any instructions for what's ahead" ("Over Fifty"). Here, too, are acknowledgment and integration. In "Triad" man's interior woman appears, the
anima that makes one whole and potent, able to struggle and to love,
as if "only by a female principle can men unite . . . or fight." In
"Narcissus" Field sees and dramatizes in the myth one's need to care
for the inner child we all carry. Thus, the youth and the poet (one
tortured by his beauty, the other by his homeliness) together read

Unwanted Forever, the message in the sybilline waters:
No feeding, no caresses, will ever comfort the pain
or calm those giant fears of a child
who still needs more love than anyone can give
and who will never grow up
or learn anything more,
but, as the magic pool showed me, is mine
and mine to care for.

Just as Field's vulnerability is always apparent, so too is his
lifelong struggle to liberate himself. He succeeds, achieving self-
acceptance and expressing gratitude for the gifts of life, especially the
gift of poetry, whose "gentle bondage" gave to him the necessary
outlet when, as in "To Poetry,"

. . . despair
had flung me down—I was drowning in my feelings—
when unsought words came like tears, a gift of healing,
and like a rescuer you were there.

It is gratitude most of all that plays over all these painful, funny, and
open expressions of the heart:

Whatever time is left to offer homage,
there's one important thing I have learned:
No better way than accept your gentle bondage—
my least effort devoted to your service
has been a thousand fold returned.

—Carl Lindner

FINKEL, Donald

Nationality: American. **Born:** New York City, 21 October 1929.
Education: Columbia University, New York. B.S. in philosophy
1952 (Phi Beta Kappa), M.A. in literature 1953. **Family:** Married
Constance Urdang in 1956 (died 1996); two daughters and one son.
Career: Instructor, University of Iowa, Iowa City, 1957–58, and
Bard College, Annandale-on-Hudson, New York, 1958–60. Member
of the department of English, 1960–92, since 1965 poet-in-residence,
and since 1992 poet-in-residence emeritus, Washington University,
St. Louis, Missouri. Visiting lecturer, Bennington College, Vermont,
1966–67, Princeton University, New Jersey, spring 1985, University
of Missouri, St. Louis, 1998–99, and Webster University, St. Louis,
Missouri, spring 2000. Visited Antarctica, 1969–70, at invitation of
National Science Foundation. **Awards:** Helen Bullis prize (*Poetry
Northwest*), 1964; Guggenheim fellowship, 1967; National Endow-
ment for the Arts grant, 1969, 1973; Ingram Merrill Foundation grant,
1972; Theodore Roethke Memorial prize, 1974; American Academy
Morton Dauwen Zabel award, 1980; Dictionary of Literary Biogra-
phy Yearbook award, 1994, for *Beyond Despair*; Elizabeth Matchett
Stover award, 1995. **Address:** 2051 Park Avenue, Apt. D, St. Louis,
Missouri 63104, U.S.A.

PUBLICATIONS

Poetry

The Clothing's New Emperor and Other Poems. New York, Scribner,
    1959.
Simeon. New York, Atheneum, 1964.
A Joyful Noise. New York, Atheneum, 1966.
Answer Back. New York, Atheneum, 1968.
The Garbage Wars. New York, Atheneum, 1970.
Adequate Earth. New York, Atheneum, 1972.
A Mote in Heaven's Eye. New York, Atheneum, 1975.
Going Under, and Endurance: An Arctic Idyll: Two Poems. New
    York, Atheneum, 1978.
What Manner of Beast. New York, Atheneum, 1981.
The Detachable Man. New York, Atheneum, 1984.
Selected Shorter Poems. New York, Atheneum, 1987.
The Wake of the Electron. New York, Atheneum, 1987.
Beyond Despair. St Louis, Garlic Press, 1994.
A Question of Seeing. Little Rock, University of Arkansas Press,
    1998.

Play

The Jar (produced Boston, 1961).

Other

Translator, *A Splintered Mirror: Chinese Poetry from the Democracy Movement.* San Francisco, North Point Press, 1991.

*

Manuscript Collection: Washington University Library, St. Louis, Missouri.

Critical Studies: "Donald Finkel: 'There Is No Perfection Possible. But There Is Tomorrow'" by Richard Howard, in Perspective (St. Louis, Missouri), 16, 1969; The *Critic's Credentials,* by Stanley Edgar Hyman, New York, Atheneum, 1978; *Alone with America,* by Richard Howard, New York, Atheneum, 1969, London, Thames and Hudson, 1970, revised edition, Atheneum, 1980; "Finkel, Stallworthy, and Stevenson" by Harry Marten, in *Contemporary Literature* (Madison, Wisconsin), 21, 1980.

*   *   *

"Plain speech is out of place in the pulpit, / poetry is out of place in the square," writes Donald Finkel, who in his works has attempted to combine prose and poetry and the religious and the secular worlds. As an early poem like "Hands" indicates, Finkel is a strong believer in the power of poetry, even though he is not totally happy with its present condition:

> The poem makes truth a little more disturbing
> like a good bra, lifts it and holds it out
> in both hands. (In some of the flashier stores
> there's a model with the hands stitched on, in red or black.)
>
> Lately the world you wed, for want of such hands,
> sags in the bed beside you like a tired wife.
> For want of such hands, the face of the moon is bored,
> the tree does not stretch and yearn, nor the groin tighten.
>
> Devious or frank, in any case,
> the poem is calculated to arouse.
> Lean back and let its hands play freely on you:
> there comes a moment, lifted and aroused,
> when the two of you are equally beautiful.

The struggle to make poetry once again a force capable of arousing and disturbing us has led Finkel in his later work to increased experimentation. This began with the use of the collage technique in his long sequence "Three for Robert Rauschenberg" *(A Joyful Noise),* but the innovation seems pale next to what Finkel attempts in later books. In these amazing volumes Finkel manages to develop a voice and a technique uniquely his own.

Answer Back is an astonishing book arranged around the metaphor of cave exploration. It has six sections, each of which is named after a particular part of Mammoth Cave. Speleology, however, is only one of Finkel's concerns, and other topics include Vietnam, the relation of the sexes, the nature of religion, the function of poetry, and the origins of the universe. His voice modulates from biblical to satiric tones, and his verse ranges from lyrics to doggerel. Interspersed among the bits of poetry are passages of prose, roughly two per page, from such varied sources as Lenny Bruce, Admiral Richard Byrd, Camus, Heraclitus, Hoyle, the *I Ching,* Jesus, Kafka, the *Kama Sutra,* the Missouri State Penitentiary, *Playboy,* Pound, and Lord Raglan. Needless to say, the whole effect is rather staggering. While Finkel's erudition is impressive and the clever juxtaposition he creates amusing, he also seems too unrestrained and has produced a poem that is too fragmented.

Like *Answer Back,* the long poem "Water Music" in *The Garbage Wars* has a controlling metaphor (experimentation on dolphins), and it, too, uses many prose borrowings. Yet here Finkel has refined his technique and uses it more subtly. His next book, *Adequate Earth,* is a masterpiece. Once again Finkel is daring in his choice of subject, for this book is a series of seven long poems about Antarctica. Finkel spent a month on the continent in 1969, and his experiences form the basis of some of the sections. Other parts have as a narrative frame the explorations of Amundsen, Byrd, and others. As usual, Finkel interpolates prose passages from various authors, but here the practice is more tightly focused than previously. And as usual, Finkel tries to bring everything into his poetry, from science to theology to politics to psychology. Here, however, he has finally chosen a subject that can stand the weight and at the same time offer great narrative potentiality. As a result, *Adequate Earth* is one of the few fine contemporary epic poems. It has a vast sweep: part of it is mythmaking, as Finkel "takes the liberty of quoting at length throughout from the gospels of the Emperor Penguins," a remarkably allegorical document; part of it is devastating satire, such as the section "Pole Business," which is a bitter attack on the commercialism encroaching on our planet's last wilderness; part of it is tragedy in its accounts of ill-fated attempts to explore the polar regions; and all of it is a tribute to man's ability to endure in even the harshest of worlds:

> We'll get used to that bite in the air
> soon enough; we'll get used to
> everything. It's what we do:
> the adaptable animal, whelped in the time
> of ice, we adapt to anything.

Full justice cannot be done to Finkel's work by brief quotations from it; as with a collage, its power comes not from any one part alone but from the interaction of all the parts. Finkel's collages are daring attempts to bring unity to the world's chaos through art. At his worst he can be obscure and pedantic; at his best he can produce works of startling resonance.

It is interesting that Finkel returns to the metaphors of exploring caves and Antarctica in his 1978 *Going Under, and Endurance,* a volume that is two books in one. Finkel, who has constantly confounded expectations about the proper subjects for poetry, here confounds expectations about the very way a book is printed and presented. The result is a bibliographer's nightmare but a reader's delight. Fortunately, the poems give the reader none of the disappointment one often feels in reading sequels. Indeed, each work is in some way superior to its predecessor, because each has a much sharper narrative focus; *Going Under* centers on the strange lives of two Mammoth Cave explorers, *Endurance* on a doomed polar expedition. It is no surprise that Finkel is so intrigued by the stories of adventures; few writers are as ambitious and daring as he.

—Dennis Lynch

FINKELSTEIN, Caroline

Nationality: American. **Born:** New York City. **Education:** Goddard College, Plainfield Vermont, 1976–78, M.F.A. 1978. **Family:** Three sons. **Awards:** Vermont Council on the Arts award, 1979; Massachusetts Artist fellowship, 1981; National Endowment for the Arts grant, 1984; Duncan Lawrie prize, Arvon Foundation, 1989; Anna Davidson Rosenberg award, Judah L. Magnus Museum, 1992; Amy Lowell Travelling fellowship, 1997–98. **Address:** Box 402, Westport Point, Massachusetts 02791, U.S.A.

PUBLICATIONS

Poetry

Windows Facing East. Port Townsend, Washington, Dragon Gate, 1986.
Germany. Pittsburgh, Pennsylvania, Carnegie Mellon University Press, 1995.
Justice. Pittsburgh, Pennsylvania, Carnegie Mellon University Press, 1999.

*

Critical Studies: In *Virginia Quarterly Review,* 69(3), summer 1993; by Stephen C. Behrendt, in *Prairie Schooner* (Lincoln, Nebraska), 70(3), fall 1996.

*   *   *

"Everything is something else," writes Caroline Finkelstein in the opening of the poem "Relatives," and she continues, "grit once bone and flesh, dog and master / a lover and his bride / wishing that the sky be night forever." Throughout her collections the poet amplifies this concept, that everything is something else, and the connections between the "thing" and the "something else" are for the reader to create. In a deft but often mystifying sort of "word-slinging" (to use beat poet Gregory Corso's term from the late 1950s), Finkelstein in some earlier poems offsets contrasting images and ideas, juxtaposing them in a way that seems not to fit, and, then, in the reading they suddenly come together to create a flowing new image or idea. Consider the following lines from "With Fox Eyes":

the weather was lousy in New York
in Berlin Nanking Rio someone swallowed whiskey
while the convoys idled leaking oil
then the shaky trains bled and there was crazy surgery
but the lindens anyway bloomed the chromy marigolds

Poems like this one gain their strength from the significance of what is not said as well as from what is. The poems leave a lot out, hence lending themselves to deconstructionist criticism. It is as if the poet were creating the skeleton, asking the reader to supply the flesh, as if she had perhaps written many intervening lines between two lines and then erased them.

In other poems the continuity is strict and organized, as in this segment from "The Dwelling":

And in the bedroom, so many times,
I was sure you didn't hear me because I couldn't read
    your looks

But listen, I was like that then, even the dog resting
    on the rug
Worried me; maybe he was a sick dog.

Here and elsewhere Finkelstein reflects upon the inevitability of misunderstandings, of missed connections, of the oversensitivities that can muddle a marriage.

In much of Finkelstein's 1995 collection *Germany* she sees with a childlike innocence, reflected in the flow of her words and in the vivid pictures she paints, the scars of the Holocaust on Jews everywhere. In "1950" she writes of a nine-year-old in Riverside Park in New York City:

I skate after school; it is four o'clock on any afternoon
Of traffic and slight shadows and the tailor on the corner;
These are small, sober hours where I move and I
    stand still.
I have no name for the passion in the air like smoke.
And the defenselessness (don't stare)
Of the human traffic and the repetition of pledges of
    allegiance
Left and right and the spies, spies everywhere . . .

Finkelstein's descriptions of sounds are uncanny, for example, ": . . . women / braiding bread: the hushed thud of that dough—" ("You Must Not Mix Milk with Meat"), and the visuals she creates are like still life paintings: "and the clams on the plate are cooling / and the fork beside the plate is absolutely clean / and pronged like a silver trident" ("To Fairy Godmother").

Some poets have difficulties with endings, but not Finkelstein. The final lines of her poems are strong and emphatic, and they often move the poem in a new direction. The poem "The Soul in the Bowl" ends this way:

when I look into my child's
face, I see
fine lines like writing
and like fracture.

Finkelstein's 1999 book *Justice* contains her strongest work. The language she employs is lyrical, forceful, tormented, and ultimately optimistic. Much of it is born of the distress of a bitter divorce, the agonized disappointment that arises from the failure of a once flourishing relationship. In the central section of the volume is a series of poems (curiously interspersed with poems seemingly unrelated to, or perhaps footnotes to, the series itself) with legal-sounding titles such as "Brief," "The Collusion," "An Opinion," and "Argument." They are poems that explore animatedly the tragic movement of love to disillusionment and outright dislike. In "Confused Figures" we read, "I colluded once with you / to become the absolute same body," and in "Her Testimony,"

for instance, I don't remember the exact
moment of betrayal when I learned
faithlessness was the silence
he called blessed

solitude and I called silence
like when children are awake in rooms
all night alone.

In "Statement" the speaker says, "I flung you hard / from my outstretched hand." It sounds as if, from Finkelstein's perspective, justice was ultimately served.

Then, in an expression of the spirit of ambivalence that follows broken relationships, the poet glances back with a bit of nostalgia at the failed marriage in a poem called "I Have His Look": "never mind what happened later; / I have his look inside my body, his eyes // like agate blue, shattered vases his poor hands."

Finkelstein's poetry is richly present, alive in the moment, and fresh in its use of language, even though, especially in the earlier works, it is occasionally terse. She is a talented writer whose work appears to grow and develop into greater coherence with each volume.

—Judy Clarence

FINLAY, Ian Hamilton

Nationality: British. **Born:** Nassau, Bahamas, 28 October 1925. Left school at age 13. **Family:** Married Susan Finlay; two children. **Career:** Concrete Poetry exhibited at Axiom Gallery, London, 1968, Scottish National Gallery of Modern Art, Edinburgh, 1972, National Maritime Museum, Greenwich, 1973, Southampton Art Gallery, 1976, Graeme Murray Gallery, Edinburgh, 1976, Kettle's Yard, Cambridge, 1977, Serpentine Gallery, London, 1977, Victoria Miro Gallery, London, 1990; Sundials: University of Kent, Canterbury, in Biggar, Lanarkshire, Royal Botanic Garden, Edinburgh; Poems designed for Max Planck Institute, Stuttgart. Editor, *Poor. Old. Tired. Horse,* Dunsyre, Lanarkshire, 1962–67; publisher, with Sue Finlay, Wild Hawthorn Press, Edinburgh, 1961–66, Easter Ross, 1966, and since 1969 Dunsyre, Lanarkshire. **Awards:** Scottish Arts Council bursary, 1966, 1967, 1968; Atlantic-Richfield award (USA), 1968. **Address:** Stonypath, Dunsyre, Carnwath, Lanarkshire, Scotland.

PUBLICATIONS

Poetry

The Dancers Inherit the Party. Worcester, Migrant Press, 1960.
Glasgow Beasts, an a Burd. Edinburgh, Wild Hawthorn Press, 1961.
Concertina. Edinburgh, Wild Hawthorn Press, 1962.
Rapel. Edinburgh, Wild Hawthorn Press, 1963.
Canal Stripe Series 3 and *4.* Edinburgh, Wild Hawthorn Press, 1964.
Telegrams from My Windmill. Edinburgh, Wild Hawthorn Press, 1964.
Ocean Stripe Series 2 to *5.* Edinburgh, Wild Hawthorn Press, 1965–67.
Cythera. Edinburgh, Wild Hawthorn Press, 1965.
Autumn Poem. Edinburgh, Wild Hawthorn Press, 1966.
6 Small Pears for Eugen Gomringer. Edinburgh, Wild Hawthorn Press, 1966.
6 Small Songs in 3's. Edinburgh, Wild Hawthorn Press, 1966.
Tea-Leaves and Fishes. Edinburgh, Wild Hawthorn Press, 1966.
4 Sails. Edinburgh, Wild Hawthorn Press, 1966.

Headlines Eavelines. Corsham, Wiltshire, Openings Press, 1967.
Stonechats. Edinburgh, Wild Hawthorn Press, 1967.
Canal Game. London, Fulcrum Press, 1967.
The Collected Coaltown of Callange Tri-kai. Newport, Monmouthshire, Screwpacket Press, 1968.
Air Letters. Nottingham, Tarasque Press, 1968.
The Blue and The Brown Poems. New York, Atlantic Richfield-Jargon Press, 1968.
After the Russian. Corsham, Wiltshire, Openings Press, 1969.
3/3's. Edinburgh, Wild Hawthorn Press, 1969.
A Boatyard. Edinburgh, Wild Hawthorn Press, 1969.
Lanes. Edinburgh, Wild Hawthorn Press, 1969.
Wave. Edinburgh, Wild Hawthorn Press, 1969.
Rhymes for Lemons. Edinburgh, Wild Hawthorn Press, 1970.
"Fishing News" News. Edinburgh, Wild Hawthorn Press, 1970.
30 Signatures to Silver Catches. Nottingham, Tarasque Press, 1971.
Poems to Hear and See. New York, Macmillan, 1971.
A Sailor's Calendar. New York, Something Else Press, 1971.
The Olsen Excerpts. Göttingen, Verlag Udo Breger, 1971.
A Memory of Summer. Edinburgh, Wild Hawthorn Press, 1971.
From "An Inland Garden." Edinburgh, Wild Hawthorn Press, 1971.
Evening/Sail 2. Edinburgh, Wild Hawthorn Press, 1971.
The Weed Boat Masters Ticket, Preliminary Text (Part Two). Edinburgh, Wild Hawthorn Press, 1971.
Sail/Sundial. Edinburgh, Wild Hawthorn Press, 1972.
Jibs. Edinburgh, Wild Hawthorn Press, 1972.
Honey by the Water. Los Angeles, Black Sparrow Press, 1973.
Butterflies. Edinburgh, Wild Hawthorn Press, 1973.
A Family. Edinburgh, Wild Hawthorn Press, 1973.
Straiks. Edinburgh, Wild Hawthorn Press, 1973.
Homage to Robert Lax. Edinburgh, Wild Hawthorn Press, 1974.
A Pretty Kettle of Fish. Edinburgh, Wild Hawthorn Press, 1974.
Silhouettes. Edinburgh, Wild Hawthorn Press, 1974.
Exercise X. Edinburgh, Wild Hawthorn Press, 1974.
So You Want to Be a Panzer Leader. Edinburgh, Wild Hawthorn Press, 1975.
Airs Waters Graces. Edinburgh, Wild Hawthorn Press, 1975.
The Wild Hawthorn Wonder Book of Boats. Edinburgh, Wild Hawthorn Press, 1975.
A Mast of Hankies. Edinburgh, Wild Hawthorn Press, 1975.
The Axis. Edinburgh, Wild Hawthorn Press, 1975.
Trombone Carrier. Edinburgh, Wild Hawthorn Press, 1975.
Homage to Watteau. Edinburgh, Wild Hawthorn Press, 1975.
Three Sundials. Exeter, Rougemont Press, 1975.
Imitations, Variations, Reflections, Copies. Edinburgh, Wild Hawthorn Press, 1976.
The Wild Hawthorn Art Test. Edinburgh, Wild Hawthorn Press, 1977.
Heroic Emblems. Calais, Vermont, Z Press, 1977.
The Boy's Alphabet Book. Toronto, Coach House Press, 1977.
The Wartime Garden. Edinburgh, Wild Hawthorn Press, 1977.
Trailblazers. Edinburgh, Wild Hawthorn Press, 1978.
Homage to Poussin. Edinburgh, Wild Hawthorn Press, 1978.
Peterhead Fragments. Edinburgh, Wild Hawthorn Press, 1979.
"SS." Edinburgh, Wild Hawthorn Press, 1979.
Dzaezl. Edinburgh, Wild Hawthorn Press, 1979.
Woods and Seas. Edinburgh, Wild Hawthorn Press, 1979.
Two Billows. Edinburgh, Wild Hawthorn Press, 1979.
Romances, Emblems, Enigmas. Edinburgh, Wild Hawthorn Press, 1981.
A Litany, A Requiem. Edinburgh, Wild Hawthorn Press, 1981.

2 Epicurean Poems and an Epicurean Paradox. Edinburgh, Wild Hawthorn Press, 1981.

The Anaximander Fragment. Edinburgh, Wild Hawthorn Press, 1981.

An Improved Classical Dictionary. Edinburgh, Wild Hawthorn Press, 1981.

3 Developments. Edinburgh, Wild Hawthorn Press, 1982.

Little Sermons Series: Cherries. Edinburgh, Wild Hawthorn Press, 1982.

The Mailed Pinkie, with Gary Hinks. Alsbach, West Germany, Verlaggalerie Leaman, 1982.

Midway 3. Edinburgh, Wild Hawthorn Press, 1982.

A Mixed Exhibition. Mission, British Columbia, Barbarian Press, 1983.

The Errata of Ovid. Edinburgh, Wild Hawthorn Press, 1983.

Talismans and Signifiers; with, Sphere into Cube. Edinburgh, Graeme Murry Gallery, 1984.

A Celebration of the Grove: Proposal for Villa Celle, with Nicholas Sloan. N.p., Parrett Press, 1984.

Interpolations in Hegel. Edinburgh, Wild Hawthorn Press, 1984.

A Country Lane with Stiles. Edinburgh, Wild Hawthorn Press, 1988.

A Shaded Path. Edinburgh, Wild Hawthorn Press, 1988.

Lidylle des Cerises. Edinburgh, Wild Hawthorn Press, 1988.

A Concise Classical Dictionary. Edinburgh, Wild Hawthorn Press, 1988.

A Proposal for Arne. Edinburgh, Wild Hawthorn Press, 1989.

Five Proverbs for Jacobins. Edinburgh, Wild Hawthorn Press, 1989.

For Simon Cutts. Edinburgh, Wild Hawthorn Press, 1989.

Sundial. Edinburgh, Wild Hawthorn Press, 1989.

A Memory of the '90s: Exquisite Bloater. Edinburgh, Wild Hawthorn Press, 1989.

I Have Seen that Death Is a Reaper. Edinburgh, Wild Hawthorn Press, 1990.

Woodpaths. Edinburgh, Wild Hawthorn Press, 1990.

Golden Age. Edinburgh, Wild Hawthorn Press, 1990.

1794. Edinburgh, Wild Hawthorn Press, 1990.

The Revolution. Edinburgh, Wild Hawthorn Press, 1990.

Mystic. Edinburgh, Wild Hawthorn Press, 1990.

Autumn. Edinburgh, Wild Hawthorn Press, 1990.

King. Edinburgh, Wild Hawthorn Press, 1990.

Sackcloth. Edinburgh, Wild Hawthorn Press, 1990.

Avenue Studios, Fulham Road: Rose Pettigrew, Pettigrew Rose. Edinburgh, Wild Hawthorn Press, 1990.

4 Baskets. Edinburgh, Wild Hawthorn Press, 1990.

Two Adaptations Edinburgh, Wild Hawthorn Press, 1990.

Flakes. Edinburgh, Wild Hawthorn Press, 1990.

3 Spaces. Edinburgh, Wild Hawthorn Press, 1990.

Detached Sentences on Friendship. Edinburgh, Wild Hawthorn Press, 1991.

Jacobin Definitions. Edinburgh, Wild Hawthorn Press, 1991.

Heraclitean Variations. Edinburgh, Wild Hawthorn Press, 1991.

The Old Stonypath Hoy. Edinburgh, Wild Hawthorn Press, 1991.

For Kalus Werner. Edinburgh, Wild Hawthorn Press, 1991.

Scud. Edinburgh, Wild Hawthorn Press, 1991.

I Sing for the Muses and Myself. Green River, Vermont, Longhouse, 1991.

A Proposal for a Garden Built on a Slope. Edinburgh, Morning Star, 1991.

Four Monostichs. Edinburgh, Wild Hawthorn Press, 1992.

Six Milestones: A Proposal for Floriade. Edinburgh, Wild Hawthorn Press, 1992.

Instruments of Revolution and Other Works. Edinburgh, Wild Hawthorn Press, 1992.

Loaves: After Paul Cezanne. Edinburgh, Wild Hawthorn Press, 1993.

Short Stories

The Sea-Bed and Other Stories. Edinburgh, Alna Press, 1958.

Other

The Bicentennial Proposal: The French War: The War of the Letter. Toronto, Art Metropole, 1989.

A Wartime Garden. Edinburgh, Graeme Murray, 1990.

Ian Hamilton Finlay & The Wild Hawthorn Press. Edinburgh, Graeme Murray, 1991.

The Poor Fisherman by Puvis de Chavannes: Reflections on a Masterpiece. Edinburgh, Talbot Rice Gallery, 1991.

The Dancers Inherit the Party, and *Glasgow Beasts.* Edinburgh, Polygon, 1996.

Ian Hamilton Finlay: Prints 1963–1997, Druckgrafik. Ostfildern, Cantz, 1997.

*

Manuscript Collection: Lilly Library, University of Indiana, Bloomington.

Critical Studies: ''Ian Hamilton Finlay Issue'' of *Extra Verse 15* (London), spring 1965; by Bryan Robertson, in *Spectator* (London), 6 September 1968; *Ian Hamilton Finlay* by Francis Edeline, Paris, Atelier de l'Agneau, 1978; *Ian Hamilton Finlay: A Visual Primer* by Yves Abrioux, Edinburgh, Reaktion, 1985; exhibition catalogues by Stephen Bann, Scottish National Gallery of Modern Art, Edinburgh, 1972, Stephen Scobie, Southampton Art Gallery, 1976, Stephen Bann and others, Kettle's Yard, Cambridge, 1977, and Stephen Bann, Serpentine Gallery, London, 1977; ''Three 'Neo-Moderns': Ian Hamilton Finlay, Edwin Morgan, Christopher Middleton'' by Alan Young, in *British Poetry since 1970: A Critical Survey,* edited by Peter Jones and Michael Schmidt, New York, Persea, 1980; ''Ian Hamilton Finlay: (De)Signing the Landscape'' by Peter Davidson, in *In Black and Gold: Contiguous Traditions in Post-War British and Irish Poetry,* edited by C.C. Barfoot, Amsterdam, Rodopi, 1994; ''A Revolutionary Arcadia: Reading Ian Hamilton Finlay's 'Un Jardin Revolutionnaire''' by Gavin Keeney, in *Word & Image* (Philadelphia, Pennsylvania), 11(3), July-September 1995.

Ian Hamilton Finlay comments:

(1970) As a concrete poet I am interested in poetry as ''the best words, in the best possible order'' . . . in the best materials, i.e., such as glass or stone for interiors or gardens. I have been described as ''the leading concrete poet now writing in English.'' But ''concrete'' has no meaning nowadays. What is concrete?

My verse is not a single thing since it has changed over the years. On the other hand, I have usually tried for the same ends—lucidity, clarity, a resolved complexity. I have used many forms, from traditional rhymed verse to poems designed as entire gardens, such as the poem I prepared for the American architect John Johansen. I consider that the seasons, nature, inland waterways, and oceans are proper themes for poetry. I do not expect poems to solve my problems. I do not believe in "the new man." Possibly A. Alvarez is the stupidest writer I have ever come across. I admire the poems of George Herbert. In the context of this time, it is not the job of poetry to "expand consciousness" but to offer a modest example of a decent sort of order.

(1980) The subject of my work is culture, without any undemocratic distinction between past and present. Besides, though one knows the past is past, one may experience it as present, as Nietzsche, for example, did when he was writing on the Greek pre-Socratics. Recently I have taken to publishing the bibliographies of my seemingly graphic works, in part to categorize them as poetry, in part to alert the viewer (reader?) to the subject beyond the object—to Plutarch in the case of the "E" (aircraft carrier) series or to the European emblem tradition (see Praz, *Studies in Seventeenth Century Imagery)* in such reliefs as "Woodland Is Pleasing to the Muses" (see my *Heroic Emblems).* It is relevant to note that the old emblematists used bibliography less as a particular illumination than as a means of "splicing" the emblem to a concept of classical culture as a whole.

(1979) To my original list of proper themes for poetry I should now add culture, not excluding warships, aircraft carriers, and warplanes. Increasingly, as our culture abandons its own traditional perspectives, the idea of a poet's statement (of his intentions?) becomes a perplexing one. To whom is such a statement actually addressed? To the public—as was peremptorily demanded of me by the Scottish Arts Council—though even in 1800 Friedrich Schlegel was unable to believe in a "public" except as an "idea"? (Today the public would be 50,000 ideas.) Or is one expected to communicate with our secularizing Arts Council art bureaucrats, public art gallery "keepers," and publishers, as if they had some essential (actual) concern with culture, history, and truth? "Only through the relationship to the infinite do content and utility rise"—Schlegel once again. Where truth has ceased to be an aspiration and has become a synonym for "the convenient" (as "nice" for "pure," "depression" for "despair," and so on), statements become a matter of dramatic allegory. The life is not the work, but it is the only possible commentary on the work; the commentary "neither uttered nor hidden" is revealed by biography event as "Event."

*　　*　　*

Ian Hamilton Finlay's poetry has undergone a considerable evolution, but the movements in the evolution are not random or, in the wrong sense, "experimental." The main driving force behind his work may be called classical, if classicism implies a deliberate search for order, form, and economy. Yet Finlay's classicism is accompanied by obviously romantic and playful elements. He indicated something of this in subtitling his 1963 collection *Rapel* "10 fauve and supremacist poems." The fauve element preserves his work from frigidity, as the supremacist element preserves it from clutter and indulgence.

His first book, *The Dancers Inherit the Party,* contains short poems of much charm and humor—in traditional rhyming verse—about love, people, fishing, Orkney. The brevity of many of these poems is taken a step further in his next two works, *Glasgow Beasts* and *Concertina,* both of which contain illustrations closely tied to the text. As well as the enhanced visual presentation, there is again a strong infusion of humor in both books.

The visual element and the movement toward verbal economy both predisposed Finlay to react with enthusiasm to the international development known as "concrete" poetry, which he learned about in 1962. Most of his work from *Rapel* onward has been received and discussed under the concrete label, unsatisfactory and amorphous as that term may be. Essentially it should signify, to quote the Brazilian Poets' "Pilot-Plan for Concrete Poetry" of 1958, a poetry that "begins by being aware of graphic space as structural agent" and is "against a poetry of expression, subjective and hedonistic." To Finlay it is a poetry with links to the purity and harmony of artists like Malevich and Mondrian and in general to those constructivist ideals of the first half of the twentieth century that had been sterilized by a new wave of expressionism. Painter as well as poet, Finlay found no difficulty in seeing and accepting this formal extension of a verbal art into a visual domain. But whether his work is to be called poetry or something else, it wins over most unprejudiced eyes by its beauty and complete integrity.

"Little Calendar" can be quoted as representing his concrete approach at its most transparent:

april	light	light	light	light
may	light	trees	light	trees
June	trees	light	trees	light
July	trees	trees	trees	trees
August	trees'	light	trees'	light
September	lights	trees	lights	trees

But from this basis, which is still that of the poem printed on the page, Finlay evolved a range of ancillary conceptions: standing poems, printed on specially folded cards; poster poems; "kinetic" poems that release a serial meaning through the act of turning over the pages of a book; and three-dimensional poem-objects and poem-environments that involve the use of metal or stone or glass and that are produced in cooperation with craftsmen in these materials. Such meticulously designed and striking objects (especially successful are *Autumn Poem* and *Ocean Stripe 5* among the kinetic books, and "Wave/Rock" and "Seas/Ease" among the three-dimensional poems) have the characteristic distinction of using the simplest of means and often a very Scottish and homely simplicity—rocks and water, boats and fishnets, canals and tugs, stars and potato fields—to bring out patterns, harmonies, analogies, and meanings that transcend their strongly local and native roots.

Much of Finlay's effort has gone into making his own home environment at Stonypath in Lanarkshire, Scotland, a garden of emblems and symbols. Trees and water along with plants and flowers are brought into intimate relationship with inscribed slabs, benches, sundials, and other objects in such a way as to suggest new perspectives and to restore old echoes of the relation between man and nature. A slab inscribed with Albrecht Dürer's monogram is placed in a setting reminiscent of an actual Dürer watercolor; an aircraft carrier carved out of stone and set on a base becomes a birdbath, with real birds as imaginary airplanes; the slate conning tower of a nuclear submarine stands black and sinister at the edge of a pond; the network of lines on a stone sundial suggests fishermen's nets on the sea. The recurrent use Finlay makes in some of these works and in other works of the 1970s—of formalized and emblematic military images, generally from World War II—raises questions of response, about which much remains to be written.

In the 1980s Finlay continued to produce books and posters and other printed material, often aphoristic and highly thought-provoking ("That of which we cannot speak, we must construct"; "Reverence is the Dada of the 1980's as irreverence was the Dada of 1918''). But he became better known for his open-air installations, where the range and fertility of his inventiveness can be gauged by comparing three works: the ''View to a Temple,'' in which a classical temple is seen through an avenue of guillotines, evidence of his great interest in the French Revolution; ''Lane with Stiles,'' done for Glasgow's 1988 Garden Festival; and the ''Man of Letters,'' a memorial to Robert Louis Stevenson. As a poet-artist sending out ideas in every direction, Finlay presents a unique challenge to received wisdom.

—Edwin Morgan

FINNIGAN, Joan

Nationality: Canadian. **Born:** Ottawa, Ontario, 23 November 1925. **Education:** Lisgar Collegiate, graduated 1944; Carleton University, Ottawa; Queen's University, Kingston, Ontario, B.A. in English, history, and economics 1967. **Family:** Married Charles Grant Mac-Kenzie in 1949 (died 1965); two sons and one daughter. **Career:** Teacher in Beechgrove, Quebec, 1945–46; reporter, Ottawa *Journal,* and freelance journalist, 1949–67; public relations, promotion, and special events director, Kingston and District United Way, 1969–74. Freelance writer, for the National Film Board of Canada, 1966–71, and the Canadian Broadcasting Corporation, Toronto. Writer-in-residence, Ottawa Public Library, 1987. Also photographer: individual shows—Upstairs Gallery, Renfrew, Ontario, 1982; Gallery Cafe, Pembroke, Ontario, 1982; Octogan Gallery Show, Calabogie, Ontario, 1986; Ottawa Public Library, 1988. **Awards:** Borestone Mountain poetry prize, 1959, 1961, 1963; Canada Council grant, 1965, 1967, 1968, 1969, 1973, 1977; Centennial prize, 1967; President's Medal, University of Western Ontario, 1969; Genie award, for screenplay, 1969; Ottawa-Carleton literary award, 1986; Pat Lowther award, 1988. **Address:** Moore Farm, Hambly Lake, Hartington, Ontario K0H 1W0, Canada.

PUBLICATIONS

Poetry

Through the Glass, Darkly. Toronto, Ryerson Press, 1963.
A Dream of Lilies. Fredericton, New Brunswick, Fiddlehead, 1965.
Entrance to the Green-house. Toronto, Ryerson Press, 1968.
It Was Warm and Sunny When We Set out. Toronto, Ryerson Press, 1970.
In the Brown Cottage on Loughborough Lake. Toronto, CBC Learning Systems, 1970.
Living Together. Fredericton, New Brunswick, Fiddlehead, 1976.
A Reminder of Familiar Faces. Toronto, NC Press, 1978.
This Series Has Been Discontinued. Fredericton, New Brunswick, Fiddlehead, 1981.
The Watershed Collection, edited by Robert Weaver. Kingston, Ontario, Quarry Press, 1988.
Wintering Over. Kingston, Ontario, Quarry Press, 1992.
Second Wind; Second Sight. Windsor, Ontario, Black Moss Press, 1998.

Plays

Up the Vallee! (produced Toronto, 1978).
Songs from Both Sides of the River (produced Ottawa, 1987–92).

Screenplay: *The Best Damn Fiddler from Calabogie to Kaladar,* 1969.

Radio Plays: *Songs for the Bible Belt; May Day Rounds: Renfrew County; In the Brown Cottage on Loughborough Lake; Children of the Shadows; There's No Good Times Left—None at All; Coming over a Country of No Lights,* 1976; *The Lakers,* 1977; *Valley of the Outaouais,* 1979; *Poems from Pontiac County,* 1984.

Other

Canada in Bed (as Michelle Bedard). Toronto, Pagurian Press, 1967.
Kingston: Celebrate This City. Toronto, McClelland and Stewart, 1976.
I Come from the Valley. Toronto, NC Press, 1976.
Canadian Colonial Cooking. Toronto, NC Press, 1976.
Giants of Canada's Ottawa Valley. Burnstown, Ontario, General Store, 1981.
Some of the Stories I Told You Were True. Ottawa, Deneau, 1981.
Look! The Land Is Growing Giants: A Very Canadian Legend (for children). Montreal, Tundra, 1983.
Laughing All the Way Home. Ottawa, Deneau, 1984.
Legacies, Legends, and Lies. Toronto, Deneau, 1985.
Finnigan's Guide to the Ottawa Valley. Kingston, Ontario, Quarry Press, 1988.
Tell Me Another Story. Toronto, McGraw Hill-Ryerson, 1988.
The Dog Who Wouldn't Be Left Behind (for children). Toronto, Groundwood 1989.
Old Scores, New Goals. Kingston, Ontario, Quarry Press, 1992.
Lisgar Collegiate, 1843–1993. Ottawa, Ontario, Lisgar Alumni Association, 1993.
Witches, Ghosts and Loups-Garous. Kingston, Ontario, Quarry Press, 1994.
Dancing at the Crossroads. Kingston, Ontario, Quarry Press, 1995.
Down the Unmarked Roads. Burnstown, Ontario, General Store, 1996.
Tallying the Tales of the Old-Timers. Burnstown, Ontario, General Store, 1999.

*

Bibliography: by Catherine Carroll (thesis), Carleton University, Ottawa, 1999.

Manuscript Collections: Queen's University Archives, Kingston, Ontario; National Library, National Archives of Canada, Ottawa.

Joan Finnigan comments:

Since the age of seven I have been writing poetry. At forty I came to creative film scripts and so began to write long poems. My poetry had always veered towards the dramatic, and my film scripts are strongly poetic: done with intensity, a boiling down to the quintessence, a search for ultimate essence. At forty I had matured enough to move from the short form—the poem—to the one requiring greater sustaining power—the screenplay. At sixty *The Watershed Collection,* a collection of the best of all my long poems, edited and with an introduction by Robert Weaver of CBC Anthology, was a milestone in my movement in the poetic direction; *Songs from Both Sides of the River,* my 1987 play at the National Arts Centre, Ottawa, was a high-water mark in the dramatic course of my work. I am working seriously on fiction now, but I know that, when I grow older and wiser, I will be able to return to my poetry.

*   *   *

That "poetry is not a turning loose of emotion but an escape from emotion" has become axiomatic in the criticism and the writing of modern poetry. Such a statement finds support in the general scientific and philosophic evolution of the age, and it informs the modern poetical canon's skepticism toward the perception of nature as a paradigm for benevolent humanism or the articulation of traditional themes (love, birth, death, marriage) through the filter of sensibility removed from the conditioning factors of the man-made environment. In Canada this consciousness is central to the work of E.J. Pratt and the poets of the McGill movement, and it is emblematized in the wilderness-garden mythos of the Frye school of poets from D.G. Jones to Margaret Atwood. The rejection of the facile romanticism at the core of Eliot's pronouncement was germane to the poetics initiated in the 1920s in Canada as a reaction against the nineteenth-century Confederation poets. At any rate, it is a commonplace now that the eternal verities can be improved upon by being expressed in diction and vision attuned to the age.

With these considerations in mind, it is no small surprise to encounter the poetry of Joan Finnigan celebrating a domestic world revolving around family life, the family cottage, family friends, love, and nature rendered in language free from sophistication. An openness toward self and others characterizes an outlook whose subjective correlative is the operations of benevolent nature. The world is Edenic and pristine in her first three books, dominated by radiant colors and cheerful sounds controlled by the key symbol of the sun shining at the height of summer. The poetry exudes a feeling of oneness with the elements that culminates in transcendental intimations of immortality, no doubt sincerely felt by the poet. Eve-like, but unlike Eve since her boundless innocence cannot precipitate any Fall of Man, she celebrates a garden whose paradisiacal emoluments she has no reason to suspect. To be sure, a few queries are raised ("Oh, who in all of heathendom, / Is half so sad as I?"), but they pose no threat of disruption to this Arcadia, where no vital concerns are entertained.

Finnigan's two favorite themes—love and nature—recur in her books. The related feelings of nostalgia, flight of time, and urbanophobia convey an undercurrent of sweet melancholy and are accentuated with the intrusion of death. In *It Was Warm and Sunny When We Set Out,* the theme is at first embarrassingly stated—"And I think perpetually now of your dead HEART (for no one could get directions to that place, not even yourself) . . ."—in the not surprising, ingenuous confessional style—"Who, who could ever believe our private murders or the possibility of this revenge?"—Finnigan delights in. It finds a more felicitous expression, however, in the contrasting use of symbols. The sun that hitherto glowed on a bountiful world presently reflects the destruction of the Covenant: it is blinding, bleeding, mocking, scorching. Though the diction falters—"If people really love one another, / snow, why do they die?"—one nonetheless finds interesting the substitution of the symbolic winter grip for the vision of warmth generated by summer. The intensity of personal suffering finally yields through visceral apprehension a sober consciousness structured by a lucid polarization of the universals in *In the Brown*

Cottage on Loughborough Lake. In a book markedly contrasting with her earlier work, the weaving of alternating polarities (light and dark, summer and autumn, outer life and inner life, life and death, happiness and sorrow) germinates in the mature expression of pain endured, challenged, and possibly conquered. Her beloved nature is still there, as anthropomorphic as ever, and the language is still mined with clichés, the world as restricted as usual. But this elegy, which can all too easily be assigned to the Wordsworthian canon, is quite moving in its expression of emotions barely recovering from the trauma of exposure to the existence of pain and cruelty. Even fractionally, Finnigan has been able to master and contain pain and bear witness to this control over emotion by finding a structure of objective correlatives. Maybe Eliot was not wrong after all.

—Max Dorsinville

FISHER, Roy

Nationality: British. **Born:** Handsworth, Birmingham, Warwickshire, 11 June 1930. **Education:** Wattville Road Elementary School; Handsworth Grammar School; Birmingham University, B.A. in English 1951, M.A. 1970. **Family:** Married 1) Barbara Venables in 1953 (divorced 1987), two sons; 2) Joyce Holliday in 1987. **Career:** Pianist with jazz groups since 1946. Lecturer, then senior lecturer, Dudley College of Education, 1958–63; principal lecturer and head of the department of English and drama, Bordesley College of Education, Birmingham, 1963–71; lecturer, then senior lecturer in American studies, University of Keele, 1972–82. Since 1982 freelance writer and musician. Director, Migrant Press, Worcester. **Awards:** Kelus prize, 1970; Cholmondeley award, 1981; Arts Council bursary, 1983; Hamlyn Foundation poetry award, 1997. D.Litt.: Keele, 1999. **Address:** Four Ways, Earl Sterndale, Near Buxton, Derbyshire SK17 OEP, England.

PUBLICATIONS

Poetry

City. Worcester, Migrant Press, 1961.
Ten Interiors with Various Figures. Nottingham, Tarasque Press, 1966.
The Memorial Fountain. Newcastle upon Tyne, Northern House, 1967.
Collected Poems 1968: The Ghost of a Paper Bag. London, Fulcrum Press, 1969.
Correspondence, with Tom Phillips. London, Tetrad Press, 1970.
Matrix. London, Fulcrum Press. 1971.
Three Early Pieces. London, Transgravity Advertiser, 1971.
Also There, with Derrick Greaves. London, Tetrad Press, 1972.
Bluebeard's Castle, with Ronald King. Guildford, Surrey, Circle Press, 1973.
Cultures, with Ian Tyson. London, Tetrad Press, 1975.
Nineteen Poems and an Interview. Pensnett, Staffordshire, Grosseteste, 1975.
Neighbours—We'll Not Part Tonight! Guildford, Surrey, Circle Press, 1976.
Four Poems. Newcastle upon Tyne, Pig Press, 1976.

Widening Circles: Five Black Country Poets, with others, edited by Edward Lowbury. Stafford, West Midland Arts, 1976.
Barnardine's Reply. Knotting, Bedfordshire, Sceptre Press, 1977.
Scenes from the Alphabet. Guildford, Surrey, Circle Press, 1978.
The Thing about Joe Sullivan: Poems 1971–1977. Manchester, Carcanet, 1978.
Comedies. Newcastle upon Tyne, Pig Press, 1979.
Wonders of Obligation. Bretenoux, France, Braad, 1979.
Poems 1955–1980. Oxford, Oxford University Press, 1980.
Consolidated Comedies. Durham, Pig Press, 1981.
Running Changes. Colchester, Essex, Ampersand Press, 1983.
A Furnace. Oxford, Oxford University Press, 1986.
Poems 1955–1987. Oxford, Oxford University Press, 1988.
Near Garmsley Camp. Madley, Hereford, Five Seasons Press, 1988.
Top Down Bottom Up. London, Circle Press, 1990.
Birmingham River. Oxford, Oxford University Press, 1994.
It Follows That. Durham, Pig, 1994.
The Dow Low Drop: New and Selected Poems. Newcastle-upon-Tyne, Bloodaxe, 1996.
Roller, with Ian Tyson. London, Circle Press, 1999.

Other

Then Hallucinations: City 2. Worcester, Migrant Press, 1962.
The Ship's Orchestra (prose poem). London, Fulcrum Press, 1966.
Titles. Nottingham, Tarasque Press, 1969.
Metamorphoses (prose poems), with Tom Phillips. London, Tetrad Press, 1970.
The Cut Pages (prose poems). London, Fulcrum Press, 1971.
Talks for Words. Cardiff, Blackweir, 1980.
The Half-Year Letters: An Alphabet Book, with Ronald King. Guildford, Surrey, Circle Press, 1983.
A Birmingham Dialogue, with Paul Lester. Birmingham, Protean, 1986.
The Left-Handed Punch, with Ronald King. Guildford, Surrey, Circle Press, 1987.
Anansi Company, with Ronald King. London, Circle Press, 1993.

*

Bibliography: *Roy Fisher: A Bibliography* by Derek Slade, London, D. Slade, 1987.

Critical Studies: "Resonances and Speculations upon Reading Roy Fisher's *City*" by Gael Turnbull, in *Kulchur 7* (New York), 1962; Stuart Mills and Simon Cutts, in *Tarasque 5* (Nottingham), 1967; "Roy Fisher's Work" by Eric Mottram, in *Stand* (Newcastle upon Tyne), xi, 1, 1969; "Roy Fisher: An Appreciation" in *Thomas Hardy and British Poetry* by Donald Davie, New York, Oxford University Press, 1972, London, Routledge, 1973; Preface by Jon Silkin to *Poetry of the Committed Individual,* London, Gollancz-Penguin, 1973; "Metal or Stone" by David Punter in *Delta 62* (Ely), 1981; "A City of the Mind" by Philip Gardner, in *Times Literary Supplement* (London), 20 March 1981; *The British Dissonance* by A. Kingsley Weatherhead, Columbia, University of Missouri Press, 1983; *Paul Lester and Roy Fisher: A Birmingham Dialogue* by Paul Lester, Birmingham, Protean, 1986; "'Music of the Generous Eye': Roy Fisher's Poems 1955–1980" by Ian Gregson, in *Bete Noire* (Hull, England), 6, winter 1988; "'If I Didn't Dislike Mentioning Works of Art': Roy Fisher's Poems on Poetics" by Bert Almon, in *ARIEL*

(Calgary, Alberta, Canada), 22(3), July 1991; "De-Anglicizing the Midlands: The European Context of Roy Fisher's *City*" by Robert Sheppard, in *English* (Leicester, England), 41(169), spring 1992; "Jazz in the Poetry of Amiri Baraka and Roy Fisher" by Mary Ellison, in *Yearbook of English Studies* (London), 24, 1994; *The Thing about Roy Fisher: Critical Essays on the Poetry of Roy Fisher* edited by Peter Robinson and John Kerrigan, Liverpool, Liverpool University Press, 2000.

Roy Fisher comments:

My work is grounded in the assumption that the human imagination creates and transacts the world and must, in view of its record, be treated with the utmost vigilance so that its operations may be intimately understood and its malfunctions predicted. As a poet, I work mostly in the zone where all the senses, with their inherent limitations, interact with the mild but tenacious restrictions of my man-made native language. Where I spot something that seems to me remarkable, I go in and follow it with language as far as I can without making unwarrantable rhetorical or metaphysical leaps. For relaxation, and to indulge the sociable side of my nature, I'm a satirist and unashamedly sarcastic.

*   *   *

Roy Fisher's poems are a triumph of conveying without saying. There are three distinct movements in reading Fisher: first, intensely objective "language," both verbal and perceptual; second, intensely subjective awareness of a state of mind—the "meaning" of the riddle; finally, a joyful, objective recognition of the meeting of separate minds.

A good poem is a riddle whose meaning has been incarnated in the reader but eludes paraphrase. Fisher is not often explicit about his intentions: "What kind of man / comes in a message?" he muses in one verse. The source of joy in art is precisely that: following the "dry track" left by the artist, we become aware simultaneously of his and our own struggle for clean, attentive life, issuing in the success of the work as direct experience.

The core of Fisher's writing, whether in prose or verse, is in this sense positive, though never brashly optimistic. There is sadness, even bitterness, concerning the attitudes our culture induces: "What's now only disproved / was once imagined." But "a genuine poet," as Goethe said, "always feels a call to fill himself with the glory of the world," and, in his 1961 volume *City,* Fisher writes, "Once I wanted to prove the world was sick. Now I want to prove it healthy." He seems tempted to "go mad after the things which are not" and yet determined not to be "able to feel only vertically, like a blind wall, or thickly, like the tyres of a bus." Fisher inhabits a ground of perceptual precision made taut by a heartrending, though quiet, sense of inexplicable significance beyond. The more one reads him, the more one wants to read. As he once wrote, "If you take a poem / you must take another / and another / till you have a poet." When one does so, one's moral and aesthetic response is increasingly to a man, an approach to living, rather than to isolated utterances.

Fisher's fineness lies in the extraordinary, intimate communication he achieves. He accomplishes this through the medium of a sophisticated, well-mannered art whose illusory coldness is the sign of a real respect for his own and his reader's individuality.

—Anne Cluysenaar

FITZGERALD, Judith (Adriana)

Nationality: Canadian. **Born:** Toronto, 11 November 1952. **Education:** York University, Toronto, 1972–77, B.A. (honors) 1976, M.A. 1977; University of Toronto, Toronto, 1978–83, Ph.D./ABD 1983. **Career:** Poetry acquisitions editor, Black Moss Press, Windsor, Ontario, 1980–86; assistant professor, Laurentian University, Sudbury, Ontario, 1981–83; entertainment critic and literary journalist, *The Globe and Mail,* 1983–84; poetry critic and literary journalist, *Toronto Star,* 1984–88; editor, General Publishing, Toronto, 1985; columnist for *Windsor Star* and *Innings,* 1985–86; literary correspondent and columnist, *Ottawa Citizen,* 1985–87; senior writer and contributing editor, *Country,* 1990–91; syndicated columnist, *Toronto Star,* 1992–93; creator and features editor and writer, *Today's Country,* 1992–98; professor and on-campus counselor, Universite Canadienne en France, Villefranche-sur-mer, France, 1994–95; editor, *Country Wave,* 1995–96; poetry columnist, *Toronto Star,* 1997–99. Senior lecturer, Glendon College, York University, Toronto, fall 1983, and Algoma University College, Ontario, spring 1984; writer-in-residence, Algoma University College, spring 1984, Hamilton Public Library, fall 1984, Laurentian University, fall 1992, and University of Windsor, 1993–94. **Awards:** Fiona Mee award, 1983; Writers' Choice award, 1986, for *Given Names: New and Selected Poems 1972–1985.*

PUBLICATIONS

Poetry

Victory. Toronto, Coach House Press, 1975.
Lacerating Heartwood. Toronto, Coach House Press, 1977.
Easy Over. Black Moss, Windsor, Ontario, 1981.
Split/Levels. Toronto, Coach House Press, 1983.
Beneath the Skin of Paradise: The Piaf Poems. Black Moss, Windsor, Ontario, 1984.
My Orange Gorange. Black Moss, Windsor, Ontario, 1985.
Given Names: New and Selected Poems, 1972–1985. Black Moss, Windsor, Ontario, 1985.
Whale Waddleby. Black Moss, Windsor, Ontario, 1986.
Diary of Desire. Black Moss, Windsor, Ontario, 1987.
Rapturous Chronicles. Stratford, Ontario, Mercury, 1991.
Ultimate Midnight. Black Moss, Windsor, Ontario, 1992.
walkin' wounded. Black Moss, Windsor, Ontario, 1993.
River. Toronto, ECW, 1995.
Twenty-Six Ways out of This World. Ottawa, Ontario, Oberon, 1999.

Other

Rapturous Chronicles II: Habit of Blues. Stratford, Ontario, Mercury, 1993.
Building a Mystery: The Story of Sarah McLachlan and Lilith Fair. Kingston, Ontario, Quarry Music, 1997.
Sarah McLachlan: Building a Mystery. Kingston, Ontario, Quarry Music, 2000.

Editor, *Un Dozen: Thirteen Canadian Poets.* Black Moss, Windsor, Ontario, 1982.

Editor, *SP/ELLES: Poetry by Canadian Women.* Black Moss, Windsor, Ontario, 1986.
Editor, *First Person Plural.* Black Moss, Windsor, Ontario, 1987.

*

Manuscript Collection: McGill University, Montreal, Canada.

Critical Studies: "Casting SP/Elles" by Lorraine York, in *Essays on Canadian Writing* (Toronto), 1991; "Dinysus between Windsor and Detroit" by A.F. Moritz, in *Books in Canada* (Toronto), 1996; "Finding the Perfect Seamless" by Rob McLennan, in *Missing Jacket* (Ottawa, Ontario), 1996; "Beyond the Blue Neon: The Lyric Authority of Judith Fitzgerald" by M. Travis Lane, in *Fiddlehead* (Fredericton, New Brunswick), 1993; interview with Wanda Campbell, in *Windsor Review* (Windsor, Ontario), 1993.

*   *   *

Judith Fitzgerald is a poet, songwriter, and journalist who writes intensely personal poems. The reader is invited to come face-to-face with the emotional existence of the author. Her poems speak from the heart and of the heart. They craft narratives with the beauty and complexity of language to tell stories of love, loss, and longing.

Fitzgerald is clearly in possession of her own intense and individual voice, and hence her poems convey ardent emotion. Her concerns run from the domestic to the anecdotal. *Rapturous Chronicles* is a long prose poem written as a tribute to the novelist Juan Butler, who committed suicide. In "Women, Language Made Me," the prefatory section of *Rapturous Chronicles,* Fitzgerald gives a biographical account: "Where I come from, I learn myself into existence by reading words in newspapers. We own no books . . . Names and origins and etymology all add up to the same thing for me . . . I believe in the power of language, of names, of etymology, of origin." Her technique of layered and resonating lyric is a move away from lyric to the narrative and a move away from the depersonalization of Olson's poetry.

In *Rapturous Chronicles II: Habit of Blues,* a prose poem novella, Fitzgerald completes her narrative of love and loss through a passionate engagement with language. She is concerned with the state of contemporary language and is fearful of the damage that the deconstruction theories of Jacques Derrida have on literature. She says in "indigo" that "Derrida crushes the right hand" and claims that "I find my self / fracture, splintered," yet in a paradoxical mode she uses every deconstructionist technique: "reaches through all sill and sash / ill and ash to untie logical progressions."

Given Names is an autobiographical work in which Fitzgerald disperses her drama, fiction, verse, polemic, and history in the form of a subversive genre ranging from one-word lines to sequences. Her unorthodox philosophical independence defamiliarizes words like "person," "names," and "syntax" and makes them come to life unaffected by gender and tradition. Her nongeneric texts play hand in hand with her lyric and emotional expressiveness, as in this sequence from "The Syntax of Things":

> heresy
> you say
> hersay
> I say
> here there

hear there
hersy
see hear
see here
hearsay
you say
heresy
heretic
come quick
you say
daresay
heresy
you say
hearsay
I say

The collection offers us a personal history of the author through the features of her life, yet these features develop into symbols of every woman's life. In the introduction Frank Davey brings to our attention the central fact of Fitzgerald's writing, the absent father. Fitzgerald's struggle has been to identify herself in the unspoken and nonpatriarchal system by claiming a new alphabet after "burning, vowels turning towards, into. / In. I. But not me. Not language, not / the combustion of self."

In *Victory* and *Beneath the Skin of Paradise* Fitzgerald has exposed her struggle with the lyric. The protagonists of both works are women who took on the lyric role in order to win acknowledgment in a male-dominated culture. The woman in *Victory*, Hazel, is a burlesque dancer who "wanted / to bring the perfect / poem home." Fitzgerald also shares this lyric dependency with Hazel: "both of us / grovel / in words we choose / worms / on fishing lines / of parasites." *Beneath the Skin of Paradise* is a tribute to the French singer Edith Piaf, who fought for everything she achieved by surmounting her struggles and proclaiming herself into public fame. Fitzgerald engages in an impressionistic treatment of aspects of Piaf's life and death and of her music. Fitzgerald's theme of an ever absent father echoes through Piaf's lyric "I can't stand / being alone / being abandoned / being suckered / being betrayed / just the sweet / love words / love . . . ."

Ultimate Midnight is a stylistically different book composed of thirteen shorter poems and the title poem, a longer piece in twelve sections, or "hours." It is a serious and powerful book in which Fitzgerald, in an elegiac tone, explores a postapocalyptic world from the perspective of the victim and survivor. She places demands on the reader by using references such as *imago mundi* and by using parentheses for puns in words like "mor(t)al." In the narrative there are many colloquial twists and literary and scientific allusions that echo the chaos of contemporary urban life. The work is postmodern in an architectural sense, for it alludes to various genres, exotic language, and satire and displaces them with a reinvented structure. Fitzgerald's complex layering uses concepts and phrases of a world in which culture, information, and artificial surroundings are the annihilation of the self and also the unavoidable traits of being human.

In reading Fitzgerald's poetry, one cannot ignore the biographical details of her past that resonate through the works. Fitzgerald's individuality and strength have developed in the works, which are efforts to come to terms with her father's absence, a fact that forced her to face a childhood of uncertainty. The anxiety about her own worth and the search for a patriarchal figure have produced in her a parallel struggle to transcend the lyric poem by discovering a new language of selfhood. The "I" of Fitzgerald's poetry can be seen as the preserver of the true voice of women through years of repression. Her poetry is passionate, and her linguistic virtuosity is free-flowing. Structural innovation is her forte.

—Renu Barrett

FLINT, Roland (Henry)

Nationality: American. **Born:** Park River, North Dakota, 27 February 1934. **Education:** University of North Dakota, Grand Forks, 1952–58, B.A. 1958; Marquette University, Milwaukee, Wisconsin, 1958–60, M.A. 1960; University of Minnesota, Minneapolis, 1960–68, Ph.D. 1968. **Military Service:** U.S. Marine Corps, 1954–56: Corporal; National Service medal. **Family:** Married 1) Janet Altic in 1962 (divorced 1973), two daughters and one son; 2) Rosalind Cowie in 1979. **Career:** Teaching assistant, Marquette University, Milwaukee, Wisconsin, 1959–60; teaching assistant and instructor, University of Minnesota, Minneapolis, 1960–68. Assistant professor, 1968–75, associate professor, 1975–81, and professor of English, 1981–86, Georgetown University, Washington, D.C. Since 1997 retired. Member, Board of Directors, Poetry Society of America, 1984–86. **Awards:** National Endowment for the Arts Discovery grant, 1970, fellowship, 1981; Corcoran Gallery award in poetry, 1976; Stanley Young fellow in poetry, Bread Loaf Writer's Conference, 1981; Silver Medalist, Council for Advancement and Support of Education's National Professor of the Year award, 1987; Maryland State Arts Council grant, 1989, 1993; National Poetry Series selection, 1989, for *Stubborn;* Maxwell Anderson award, University of North Dakota, 1993; Poet Laureate of Maryland Designate, 1995. Honorary Doctorates: North Carolina Wesleyan College, Rocky Mount, 1986; University of North Dakota, 1996. **Address:** 9819 Haverhill Drive, Kensington, Maryland 20895, U.S.A.

PUBLICATIONS

Poetry

And Morning. Washington, D.C., Dryad Press, 1975.
The Honey and Other Poems for Rosalind (chapbook). Huntington, West Virginia, Unicorn, 1976.
Say It. Washington, D.C., Dryad Press, 1979.
Resuming Green: Selected Poems, 1965–1982. New York, Dial Press, 1983.
Sicily (chapbook). Rocky Mount, North Carolina, North Carolina Wesleyan College Press, 1987.
Stubborn. Urbana, University of Illinois Press, 1990.
Hearing Voices, with William Stafford. Salem, Oregon, Willamette University Press, 1991.
Pigeon. Rocky Mount, North Carolina, North Carolina Wesleyan College Press, 1991.
Pigeon in the Night (in Bulgarian and English). Sofia, Fakel Press, 1994.
Easy. Baton Rouge, Louisiana State University, 1999.

Other

Translator, with Betty Grinburg, *Words and Graphite* by Boris
    Christov. Varna, Andina Publishing House, 1991.
Translator, with Betty Grinburg and Lyubomir Nikolov, *Wings of the
    Messenger* by Boris Christov. Sofia, Petrikoff Publications, 1991.
Translator, with Vyara Tcholakova, *Pagan* by Lyubomir Nikolov.
    Pittsburgh, Carnegie-Mellon Press, 1992.

*   *   *

Roland Flint's poetry is the sort a reader returns to, peeling back
layer after layer, to reach the heart of the work, which also often turns
out to be the heart of the matter. These are affecting poems, ones that
stubbornly persist in having their way with the reader.

Although Flint taught for many years at Georgetown University,
his poems, as represented in the collection *Stubborn,* are not academic
exercises. For instance, even "Late September, Early Morning,"
which seems at first to fit into a conventional mode—the academic
poet gently spoofing himself, writing poetry with a look over his
shoulder at his reputation—becomes more than that. Here the collection's title resurfaces like a motif: "But something stubborn wants
him scribbling daily, / even if *it* is the only thing to write about." The
italicized "it" seems at this point, early in the book, to refer to the
process of writing poetry. In retrospect, "it" also seems to refer to the
wound that persists in opening time and again in these poems: the
death of a son.

At times even the syntax of the poems appears to mirror the
title's theme of stubbornness. Flint begins a thought, interrupts it, and
then returns abruptly to the first thought, as in the ending of "Black
Sea, Mother and Son":

as if she were beginning
a morning summers and summers
ago in Sicily or Greece or
Mesopotamia,
                hung with olive and
lemon and pepper and grape
and blood orange,
 but it is
ordinary hillside
on the Balkan peninsula
north of Varna and south of
Zlatni Pyasetsi,
as it was a thousand
years ago or yesterday.

Like most good poets, he twists and reshapes language to his own
needs. What happens to his heart and mind happens to the language as
both wrestle with the loss of his son.

Although he addresses the process of writing poetry, his poems
do not step back to distance themselves from the reader. The shifts in
focus are to get a sharper view. The poet is after dangerous, raw stuff,
returning to earlier memories that ground the poems in a dual sense of
love and loss, not merely recovering the past but also re-creating it to
see what wisdom has come with time and reflection.

The grouping of the poems suggests a reaching for emotional
roots. The first section, entitled "Home," contains the poem "Nocturne," in which the poet as a boy overhears his parents making love
in the middle of the night and as the man writing the poem considers

what this event meant then and means in the present. Further into the
book, the various poems cut a passage through time, with other
section titles like "Measures" and "Anniversaries" underscoring
this technique. On the journey Flint stops often to check his pulse, that
constant wrist chronometer, with a poem to measure where he is at a
particular age compared to others he remembers who have passed that
point and gone through that opening in time before him. The following three excerpts, from "Nocturne," "Rosemary," and "Pamela,
on February 8, 1982," respectively, illustrate this:

When he hears for sure, awake,
though he's never heard it before,
he knows at once: his parents making love.
He's 14 or 15, his father 44 or 45,
his mother a year younger,
and now, when he remembers it,
he's older than they all were—50.

And what have we become—in 1989?
If I'm fifty-five you're fifty-three!
But memory still fixes your
small hands and avid mouth on me.

And she bears him with her still
on her birthday, feeling as I do
how old the boy is too this year . . .
To wish her uncomplicated happy birthdays
would be to wish the boy alive or out of thought . . .

This is strong stuff, poetry that sometimes used to be called
"confessional," drawing its strength from the sort of pain that
nourishes W.D. Snodgrass's *Heart's Needle* or Robert Lowell's *Life
Studies.* It is also like the work of the fine writer Flint celebrates in
"Jim," James Wright. The central wound, the pain the poems keep
returning to, is the death, at age ten, of the poet's son. Through his
poetry Flint seeks a way of accepting, of living with, this terrible loss,
as in "What I Have Tried to Say to You":

Our lives are what they have been: unrevisable,
changed only in our responses,
if we are still ready, somehow,
for the next day, the next
person, poem, chance, even prepared,
however unready, for the next death.
Can we permanently grieve the boy
without hating what has become of him?
What *has* become of him?
He has returned to mystery,
the same one that is our life.

—Duane Ackerson

FORCHÉ, Carolyn (Louise)

Nationality: American. **Born:** Detroit, Michigan, 28 April 1950.
Education: Michigan State University, East Lansing, B.A. in interna-
tional relations and creative writing 1972; Bowling Green State
University, Ohio, M.F.A. 1975. **Family:** Married Harry E. Mattison

in 1984; one son. **Career:** Visiting lecturer, Michigan State University, 1974; visiting lecturer, 1975, and assistant professor, 1976–78, San Diego State University; visiting lecturer, University of Virginia, Charlottesville, 1979, 1982–83; assistant professor, 1980, and associate professor, 1981, University of Arkansas, Fayetteville; visiting lecturer, New York University, 1983, 1985, and Vassar College, Poughkeepsie, New York, 1984; adjunct associate professor, Columbia University, New York, 1984–85; writer-in-residence, State University of New York, Albany, 1985; visiting associate professor, University of Minnesota, Minneapolis, summer 1985. Since 1994 associate professor, George Mason University, Fairfax, Virginia. Poetry editor, *New Virginia Review,* Norfolk, 1981; editor, *Tendril,* Green Harbor, Massachusetts. Journalist for Amnesty International in El Salvador, 1978–80, and Beirut correspondent, "All Things Considered" radio program, 1983. **Awards:** Yale Series of Younger Poets award 1975; *Chicago Review* award, 1975; Devine Memorial prize, 1975, Bread Loaf Writers Conference Tennessee Williams fellowship, 1976; National Endowment for the Arts fellowship, 1977, 1984; Guggenheim fellowship, 1978; Emily Clark Balch prize (*Virginia Quarterly Review*), 1979; Lamont Poetry Selection award, 1981; Poetry Society of America Alice Fay di Castagnola award, 1981; *Los Angeles Times* book award, 1994, for *The Angel of History;* Edita and Ira Morris Award for Peace and Culture (Stockholm), 1988. H.D.L.: Russell Sage College, Troy, New York, 1985. **Agent:** Virginia Barber Literary Agency, 101 5th Avenue, 11th Floor, New York, New York 10003, U.S.A. **Address:** George Mason University, Department of English, 4400 University Drive, Fairfax, Virginia 22030–4444, U.S.A.

PUBLICATIONS

Poetry

Gathering the Tribes. New Haven, Connecticut, Yale University Press, 1976.
The Country between Us. Port Townsend, Washington, Copper Canyon Press, 1981; London, Cape, 1983.
The Angel of History. New York, HarperCollins, and Newcastle upon Tyne, Bloodaxe, 1994.

Recording: *Ourselves, or Nothing,* Watershed, 1982.

Other

Women in American Labor History 1825–1935: An Annotated Bibliography, with Martha Jane Soltow. East Lansing, Michigan State University School of Labor and Industrial Relations, 1972.
El Salvador: The Work of Thirty Photographers, edited by Harry Mattison, Susan Meiselas, and Fae Rubenstein. New York and London, Writers and Readers, 1983.
Fever Dreams: Contemporary Arizona Poetry. Tucson, University of Arizona Press, 1997.

Editor, *Women and War in El Salvador.* New York, Women's International Resource Exchange, 1980.
Editor, *Against Forgetting: Twentieth-Century Poetry of Witness.* New York, Norton, 1993.
Editor, with Marilyn Sewell, *Claiming the Spirit Within: A Sourcebook of Women's Poetry.* Boston, Beacon Press, 1996.

Editor, *The New Intimacy,* by Barbara Cully. New York, Penguin, 1997.
Editor, with George Trakl and translator Daniel Simko, *Autumn Sonata.* N.p., Moyer Bell, 1998.

Translator, *Flowers from the Volcano,* by Claribel Alegria. Pittsburgh, University of Pittsburgh Press, 1982.
Translator, *Sorrow,* by Claribel Alegria. Willimantic, Connecticut, Curbstone Press, 1999.

*

Critical Studies: By Terrence Diggory, in *Salmagundi* (Saratoga Springs, New York), spring 1984; "Politicizing the Modern: Carolyn Forche in El Salvador and America" by Michael Greer, in *Centennial Review* (East Lansing, Michigan), 30(2), spring 1986; "Carolyn Forche: Poetry and Survival" by John Mann, in *American Poetry* (Jefferson, North Carolina), 3(3), spring 1986; "The Poet as Witness: Carolyn Forche's Powerful Pleas from El Salvador" by Paul Rea, in *Confluencia* (Greeley, Colorado), 2(2), spring 1987; "Secrets Left to Tell: Creativity and Continuity in the Mother/Daughter Dyad" by Martha M. Vertreace, in *Mother Puzzles: Daughters and Mothers in Contemporary American Literature,* edited by Mickey Pearlman, Westport, Connecticut, Greenwood, 1989; *Imaging the Body in Contemporary Women's Poetry: Helga Novak, Ursula Krechel, Carolyn Forche, Nikki Giovanni* (dissertation) by Amy Jo Kepple, Ohio State University, 1991; "Elegy As Political Expression in Women's Poetry: Akhmatova, Levertov, Forche" by Carole Stone, in *College Literature* (West Chester, Pennsylvania), 18(1), February 1991; "Protocols of Power: Performance, Pleasure and the Textual Economy" by Mary S. Strine, in *Text and Performance Quarterly* (Annandale, Virginia), 12(1), January 1992; "Carolyn Forche: Poet of Witness" by Leonora Smith, in *Still the Frame Holds: Essays on Women Poets and Writers,* edited by Sheila Roberts and Yvonne Tevis, San Bernardino, Borgo, 1993; "History, Death, Politics, Despair" by Nora Mitchell and Emily Skoler, in *New England Review* (Hanover, New Hampshire), 17(2), spring 1995; "Elegy As History: Three Women Poets 'By the Century's Deathbed'" by Anita Helle, in *South Atlantic Review* (Atlanta, Georgia), 61(2), spring 1996.

*　　*　　*

Since the publication of Carolyn Forché's second collection of poems, *The Country between Us,* she has become visible as a political poet as well as a poet of consummate craft. (The latter is attested to by the fact that her first book won the Yale Series of Younger Poets award; the second, the Lamont Poetry Selection award.) But there are dangers in all such categorizations, for to call Forché "political" is to deny the excellence of all of her poems, not only those that deal with life in El Salvador or with the political concerns of both America and the world. Forché, who received the Edita and Ira Morris Award for Peace and Culture in 1998, is political in the broadest, healthiest possible sense, in that her poems grow from the genuine, intense concerns of the poet as a living person. They bespeak her age, her craft, her education, her origins, her sex, and her intellectual persuasions. They also reflect the fact that she spent a number of years living in El Salvador, becoming a translator of several poets (she is known particularly as a translator of Claribel Alegria), a friend of many others, and a keen observer of life in that country. But her Salvadoran experience is no more important to her development as a poet than was her experience in the desert of the American Southwest or in the Midwest. Forché is a poet who uses whatever she has experienced, transmuting her material regardless of its source into sharply defined images that reach far past the personal or local.

Forché's roots are clearly in the Williams and Roethke schools of American poetry, but she has moved past their sometimes academic limitations to a free expression of all of her concerns. She is an impassioned poet, whether she writes about a girlhood friend she has lost track of, a dying idealist, or a brutal military man. Whatever subject Forché chooses, the shape and movement of the poem evokes the appropriate mood.

Forché is a poet of great versatility. What unifies the poems in her collections is not style but rather the repetition of images. Images of loss, absence, muted or stilled voices, broken lives, the simple and often tawdry objects of poverty, and—in contrast—touch appear in poems that range from stark external description to implicit dramatic monologue to letter to confession.

When Forché writes in "The Visitor," a short, image-centered poem, "In Spanish he whispers there is no time left," she establishes the pattern of language forestalled, forbidden. This whisper is amplified in other of the Salvadoran poems. "The Memory of Elena" gives us apparent language ("We find a table, ask for *paella* . . . As she talks, the hollow / clopping of a horse, the sound / of bones touched together"), but the central image, of the dark tongues of bells, ends in perversion. "The Island" also re-creates language, a dialogue between the poet persona and a worn Salvadoran woman who insistently demands, "Carolina, do you know how long it takes / any one voice to reach another?" "San Onofre, California" sets up another ironic dialogue between the living and the missing. Ironically, the only successful communication in *The Country between Us* occurs in "The Colonel" when the military figure pours a sackful of human ears on the dinner table where the poet has been dining. Speech has been realized, but instead of saving it desecrates everything human. *The Country between Us* becomes Forché's "epistemology of loss," just as *Gathering the Tribes* is her more positive statement of human endurance. As she writes in "Message," where voices are "sprayed over the walls / dry to the touch of morning" and patriots are sent off to be killed as the poet pledges,

> I will live
> and living cry out until my voice is gone
> to its hollow of earth, where with our
> hands and by the lives we have chosen
> we will dig deep into our deaths.

For all the variety of Forché's forms, for all the somber stain of her Salvadoran experience, for all the poignancy of her personal fabric of recollection, *The Country between Us* succeeds in creating a sense of joy. "Because One Is Always Forgotten," "Poem for Maya," "Ourselves or Nothing," "For the Stranger"—each poem embodies images and tones of hope: "all things human take time"; "We have, each of us, nothing. / We will give it to each other."

Forché's poems are meditative and lyrical, narrative and songlike. They draw from dream and myth both directly and subtly. They escape categorization as they lace together images of terrain and language, touch and separation, and brutality and love that are so closely related as to fuse through metaphor. The unity of Forché's collections is achieved through a singleness of vision, a finely expressed, various vision that is delightful in its chameleon-like

trappings despite the seriousness of its intention. She has become a major poet.

—Linda W. Wagner-Martin

FORD, Charles Henri

Nationality: American. **Born:** Hazlehurst, Mississippi, 10 February 1913. **Career:** Editor, *Blues,* Columbus, Mississippi, 1929–30; *View,* New York, 1940–47. Lived in Paris, 1931, 1933–34; Morocco, 1932, the United States, 1940–51, Italy, 1952–57, and since 1958 Kathmandu, Nepal. Photographer and painter: individual shows—Institute of Contemporary Arts, London, 1955; Galerie Marforen, Paris, 1956; Galerie du Dragon, Paris, 1957, 1958; Cordier and Ekstrom Gallery, New York, 1965; New York Cultural Center, 1975; Carlton Gallery, New York, 1975; Iolas Gallery, 1976; Robert Samuel Gallery, New York, 1980. **Address:** 1 West 72nd Street, New York, New York 10023, U.S.A.

PUBLICATIONS

Poetry

A Pamphlet of Sonnets. Mallorca, Caravel Press, 1936.
The Garden of Disorder and Other Poems. New York, New Directions, and London, Europa, 1938.
ABC's. Prairie City, Illinois, James A. Decker, 1940.
The Overturned Lake. Cincinnati, Little Man Press, 1941.
Poems for Painters. New York, View, 1945.
The Half-Thoughts, The Distances of Pain. New York, Prospero Pamphlets, 1947.
Sleep in a Nest of Flames. New York, New Directions, 1949.
Spare Parts. New York, New View, 1966.
Silver Flower Coo. New York, Kulchur, 1968.
Flag of Ecstasy: Selected Poems, edited by Edward B. Germain. Los Angeles, Black Sparrow Press, 1972.
7 Poems. Kathmandu, Bardo Matrix, 1974.
Om Krishna: Special Effects. Cherry Valley, New York, Cherry Valley Editions, 1979.
Om Krishna 11: From the Sick Room of the Walking Eagles. Cherry Valley, New York, Cherry Valley Editions, 1981.
Secret Haiku: Om Krishna 111. New York, Red Ozier Press, 1982.
Haiku and Imprints I [II]. Kathmandu, Operation Minotaur, 2 vols., 1984–85.
Handshakes from Heaven. Paris, Handshake, 1985.
Emblems of Arachne. New York, Catchword Papers, 1986.
Out of the Labyrinth: Selected Poems. San Francisco, City Lights, 1990.

Plays

Screenplays: *Poem Posters,* 1966; *Johnny Minotaur,* 1971.

Novel

The Young and Evil, with Parker Tyler. Paris, Obelisk Press, 1933; New York, Arno Press, 1973; London, Gay Men's Press, 1989.

Other

Editor and Translator, *The Mirror of Baudelaire.* New York, New Directions, 1942.

Editor, *A Night with Jupiter and Other Fantastic Stories.* New York, Vanguard Press, 1945; London, Dobson, 1947.

*

Manuscript Collections: University of Texas, Austin; Yale University, New Haven, Connecticut.

Critical Studies: Introduction by William Carlos Williams to *The Garden of Disorder and Other Poems,* 1938; Introduction by Edith Sitwell to *Sleep in a Nest of Flames,* 1949; introduction by Stephen Watson to *The Young and Evil,* London, Gay Men's Press, 1989.

*   *   *

When he began publishing in 1929, Charles Henri Ford was unique. He was America's surrealist poet. In retrospect he was seminal. His first two books created American surrealism. *The Garden of Disorder* welds radio jazz and iambic pentameter, surreal conceits and the sonnet form. *The Overturned Lake* shows Ford as influenced by Whitman, Poe, and Mother Goose as by Breton, Reverdy, and Éluard, employing a freer line and lyric forms. It also demonstrates Ford's forte—the surrealist image. In one poem Ford transforms the day from a poem into a horse. He turns the sky into an arm, a mouth, a man, a thief, and then an enormous face. He makes the sun into a wound, a jewel, an equation, an eye, a tear. Night is a ditch. He does all of this in eight lines and with obvious ease and clarity.

The New York school centered around Frank O'Hara and John Ashbery owes something to these early surrealist lyrics. During World War II Ford encouraged young poets like Philip Lamantia in the pages of his influential surrealist magazine, *View,* which also was the first literary magazine to publish Allen Ginsberg. Ford himself began writing longer poems at this time, typically part dream or ghost story, part amoral allegory, filled with convulsive imagery and sexual themes. Parts of these poems are often greater than their wholes. The self-conscious mannerism implicit in many of them surfaces in Ford's next two books, *Spare Parts* and *Silver Flower Coo,* collage poems that are exercises in gratuitous eroticism. Another, far more interesting series, written but not published during this period, is Ford's prose poems and found poetry, represented in the "Drawings" section of *Flag of Ecstasy.*

Out of the Labyrinth: Selected Poems, published nearly twenty years later, includes selections from *Om Krishna I* and *II,* long, frequently vivid meditations with wit and loads of what have become surrealist formulas. Ford often combines surreal juxtapositions to make a kind of allegory, in this case for passions, pain, and an immortal goddess in midflight:

Metaphysical weasel may your firstborn inherit
The gift of escapades
Hallowed Hermaphrodite stymied in a unique progression

This reader finds lines likes these a struggle, and the long poems of *Om Krishna* often seem a sequence of one- or two-liners. But they

have an honesty too, and despite the surrealist inflatus the poems do not lack integrity. Further, an individual image can revolt and astonish:

The King murdered in his castle was buried privately his
  eyes like
            piss holes in the snow.

Nevertheless, Ford's best work lies predominantly with the focused lyric form expressed most fully in his early books (poems like "Plaint" or "The Overturned Lake," for example) and with the surrealist humor of "There's No Place to Sleep in This Bed, Tanguy" or "Baby's in Jail, The Animal Day Plays Alone." In these poems Ford creates wonder, wit, and a sensuous beauty that were new to American poetry and that remain a landmark.

—Edward B. Germain

FORD, Mark (Nicholas)

Nationality: British. **Born:** Nairobi, Kenya, 24 June 1962. **Education:** Oxford University, Oxford, 1980–83, 1984–87, B.A. 1983, D.Phil. 1991; Harvard University, Cambridge, Massachusetts, 1983–84. **Family:** Married 1) Xantue Gresham in 1986 (divorced 1990); Kate Bomford in 1994. **Career:** Lecturer in English, University College, London, 1988–90, and Kyoto University, Japan, 1991–93. Since 1995 lecturer in English, University College, London. **Address:** 89b Highbury Hill, London N5 1SX, England.

PUBLICATIONS

Poetry

Landlocked. London, Chatto and Windus, 1992.

Other

Raymond Roussel and the Republic of Dreams. London, Faber, 2000.

*

Critical Studies: "Post-Modernism and Its Discontents" by Steve Clark, in *The View from Kyoto,* edited by Shoichiro Sakurai, Kyoto, Japan, Rinzen Press, 1998; "Scoops from the Tide Pools" by Helen Vendler, in *Times Literary Supplement* (London), 1 January 1999.

*   *   *

Mark Ford's poetic voice is transatlantic, cool, self-aware, and often funny. In his accomplished collection *Landlocked* the quality of play in the language brings contemporary American poets to mind, especially John Ashbery, without seeming derivative. As with Ashbery, Ford likes to mime the processes of sequential thought while tantalizingly departing from them in the interests of his poetry's "most peculiar almost whimsical shapes," as he puts it in "Funny Peculiar." Transitions behave as though advancing a poetic argument, but they actually draw attention to gaps, so that the poem invites the reader to detect a more orderly ghost of itself just behind the verbal skeleton. Thus,''Invisible Assets'' opens,

> After he threw her through a
> plate-glass window, nature seemed that much closer.
> Even the dastardly divisions in society
> might be healed by a first-rate glazier.

Although the Auden of ''Consider'' is briefly recalled here, and might even be a candidate for the ''first-rate glazier,'' Ford sends up any possible engagement with ''dastardly divisions in society'' through the jokey woodenness of the phrasing. In place of Auden's antimodernist wish to ''make action urgent and its nature clear,'' Ford entertains a postmodernist blur of possible meanings, delighting in the sheer daftness of language (''threw'' passing into ''through,'' for instance), his details tempting the reader into interpretations they simultaneously resist. He is more than content to encourage his reader to ''wander'' through a ''literary-critical / Conundrum.''

Above all Ford is a master of the intonational quotation mark, to borrow Bakhtin's term. His lines continually presuppose a sophisticated, negatively capable poet assuming the accents of a naive or blinkered speaker. In ''Street Violence,'' for instance, a macho voice overcompensates for emotional ''disappointment'': ''Too bad, I thought, for her sake, / That she didn't remember me like she should have.'' The comedy here derives from the well-caught sense of injured merit. In other places Ford allows his speaker greater self-awareness, as in the witty end of ''Night Out,'' where he turns the phrase ''couldn't care less'' on its head, making it the vehicle of a humorous competitiveness: ''I care less than any and all of you, / it's a major strength of my character, I care less / and less, and of course will never but never give that up.''

Elsewhere for Ford all the fun lies in how a person says a thing. ''Christmas'' weaves in and out of fooling around (''I very much enjoyed your latest book I lied having / NOT read it'') and parody to develop a beguiling narrative about possible death and accidental traces of a life. In ''General Knowledge'' he brilliantly captures the arbitrary weightlessness of facts in a stanza that says much about the mock-rueful persona he develops in the volume: ''It's said that every forty minutes the world is girdled / By a satellite; with a nail I trace the thin blue / Veins of the delta winding dubiously towards the sea.'' The two assertions balance received wisdom against a tentative foray into the unfamiliar, ''dubiously'' doing much to imply the speaker's attitude. Equally impressive is the sure handling of the line breaks and long line. ''A Swimming-Pool Full of Peanuts'' is the high point of *Landlocked*'s surreal capers and illustrates Ford's poker-faced ability to create just about believable yet fantastic scenarios.

Work composed after *Landlocked* shows a deepening and intensifying of Ford's concerns. In ''I Wish,'' for example, he displays his ability to write unpretentiously about the effects of his own writing in phrases such as ''an invisible host of dubious connections.'' It may be the case that in his work since *Landlocked* the poet emerges more clearly in *proprium persona* without sacrificing a shred of humor, as when he says in ''Contingency Plans,'' ''in a quandary I seized / My innate Englishness, and practised / Wrapping it around me like an old army coat,'' in which ''practised'' speaks volumes about the way Ford always looks even when he leaps.

—Michael O'Neill

FOWLER, Gene

Nationality: American. **Born:** Oakland, California, 5 October 1931. **Education:** Oakland High School, graduated 1949. **Military Service:** Served in the U.S. Army, 1950–53. **Family:** Married April Corioso in 1981; one step-daughter. **Career:** Worked as a nightclub and specialty performer, 1949–50, and as an appliance salesman and medical records clerk. Served prison sentence for armed robbery, San Quentin Prison, 1954–59. Clerk and semi-official computer programmer, University of California, Berkeley, 1959–63; poet-in-residence, University of Wisconsin, Milwaukee, summer 1970. Founder, The Re-Geniusing Project, Berkeley, 1981. **Awards:** National Endowment for the Arts grant, 1970. **Address:** 1432 Spruce Street, Berkeley, California, 94709, U.S.A.

PUBLICATIONS

Poetry

Field Studies. 24 El Cerrito, California, Dustbooks, 1965.
Quarter Tones. Grande Ronde, Oregon, GRR Press, 1966.
Shaman Songs. El Cerrito, California, Dustbooks, 1967.
Her Majesty's Ship. Sacramento, California, Grande Ronde Press, 1969.
Fires. Berkeley, California, Thorp Springs Press, 1971.
Vivisection. Berkeley, California, Thorp Springs Press, 1974.
Felon's Journal. San Francisco, Second Coming Press, 1975.
Fires: Selected Poems 1963–1976. Berkeley, California, Thorp Springs Press, 1975.
Return of the Shaman. San Francisco, Second Coming Press, 1981.
The Quiet Poems. Chapel Hill, North Carolina, Wren Press, 1982.

Other

Waking the Poet. Berkeley, California, Re-Geniusing Project, 1967.

*

Critical Study: By James K. Bell, in *Eikon* (Ogunquit, Maine), i. 1, 1967.

Gene Fowler comments:

(1980) There are no ''positions'' for nonacademic poets. Officially I am illiterate. Not qualified to teach the use of language, existing literature, or other such.

I am not and have never been a member of a school of poetry, though reviewers have tried to stuff me into one or another. I battle against such entities.

Whitman wrote critical analysis of his own work—but under other names. I've done what amounts to c.a. in letters. But here I'll say only what I believe I'm up to. I want to write poems that when recalled are confused with the reader's own experiences, not recalled—at first—as ''something read'' but as ''something that happened.'' Fighting against myth perpetuated by both outlaws and academics that craft is the same thing as academic tone. I take the Orphic myth literally. Believe words can induce and manipulate perceptions. Intend in my poems to prove this.

(1985) Beyond entertaining, informing, or even transforming the listener or reader with the shaped contents of poems, it's possible, in the making of the poem in the recipient's awareness, to rouse the experience-making faculties, the poet, in that listener or reader. And by guiding that poet through the shaping of my poem, to stir it to life, to ''waken'' it. While I teach this waking in seminar-workshops and in my ''seminar in a book,'' *Waking the Poet,* the main work in my poems, too, is this waking of the active or working poet in my listener . . . or listening reader.

(1995) I continue to cultivate the deep-seated crafts usually called ''talents'' and thought to result from a throw of the genetic dice. And to function as a ''village explainer'' regarding those crafts. There'll be a third *Fires* in a year or two and some gathered letters. I've boxes of *Waking* on my porch and will send on to anybody who buys pack room on the U.S. Mule. Beyond A.D. 2000 and beyond, or through, the poems, I'm working on language, even word birthing . . . nudging at the Amerish that'll be spoken in, say, 2094.

*   *   *

American prisons, as in the case of Gene Fowler, can be a school for poets. Prison is self-education, but Fowler's *Felon's Journal* can educate the hopelessly honest. Fowler sees himself, however, not as an outlaw but as a shaman, writing insightful poems of everyday life.

Fowler is a contemporary symbolist, a maker of surprising equations. In poems like ''The Lover'' these equations develop dramatically and become revelations: the body of the beloved is the earth. ''The Words'' is a little allegory about writing:

I carry boulders across the day
From the field to the ridge,
and my back grows tired . . .
I take a drop of sweat
Onto my thumb
Watch the wind furrow its surface,
Dream of a morning
When my furrows will shape this field,
When these rocks will form my house.
Alone, with heavy arms,
I listen through the night to older farms.

Fowler finds writing a heavy labor. His rhythms, in poems like ''Venus Returns to the Sea,'' are heavy. He likes Venus and Adonis in Roman mythology, and, like Gregory Corso, who also served time in prison, Fowler likes Greece. But what happens to words transmuted into poems? They grow hot, like coals or fires:

i come upon stones
in the wind shoved grasses
they wait
tensed
curled in on themselves

i reach out to touch
sun warmed quiet and flame
jumps to scorch my fingers.

Fires is Fowler's first major collection. *Shaman Songs,* a chapbook collected and edited in *Fires,* compares society to an Indian tribe and the poet to a neglected shaman. The songs go behind symbol and allegory to ritual and magic, as in ''On Taking Coal from the Fire in Naked Fingers'':

The word
is in the hand.
Under the moon
in the hand.
At the head of the valley
in the hand.
It glows in the hand.
Here!
Look here
in the hand.
Look at the word
in the hand.
It glows.
A great translucence
in the hand.
Go thru the translucence
in the hand.
Into the world
in the hand.

The repetition of ''in the hand'' creates chant and suggests power: the future is not in the hand of God but in the hand of the shaman. Fowler discovered the shaman at about the time another, more famous West Coast poet, Gary Snyder, did so.

The Quiet Poems, a later collection, is sophisticated, polished, and relaxed. But my favorite collection has the mock-Hollywood title *Return of the Shaman.*

—Michael Andre

FRASER, Kathleen

Nationality: American. **Born:** Tulsa, Oklahoma, 22 March 1937. **Education:** Occidental College, Los Angeles, B.A. in English 1959; Columbia University and New School for Social Research, both New York, 1960–61; San Francisco State University, 1976–77, Doctoral Equivalency in creative writing. **Family:** Married Jack Marshall, *q.v.,* in 1961 (divorced 1970); one son. **Career:** Visiting professor, Writers Workshop, University of Iowa, Iowa City, 1969–71; writer-in-residence, Reed College, Portland, Oregon, 1971–72. Director of the Poetry Center, 1972–75, associate professor of creative writing, 1975–78, and since 1978 professor, San Francisco State University. Founding editor, *HOW(ever).* **Awards:** YMYWHA Discovery award, 1964; National Endowment for the Arts grant, 1969, and fellowship, 1978. **Address:** 554 Jersey Street, San Francisco, California 94114, U.S.A.

PUBLICATIONS

Poetry

Change of Address and Other Poems. San Francisco, Kayak, 1966.
In Defiance of the Rains. Santa Cruz, California, Kayak, 1969.
Little Notes to You from Lucas Street. Iowa City, Penumbra Press, 1972.

What I Want. New York, Harper, 1974.
Magritte Series. Willits, California, Tuumba Press, 1978.
New Shoes. New York, Harper, 1978.
Each Next. Great Barrington, Massachusetts, Figures, 1980.
Something (Even Human Voices) in the Foreground, A Lake. Berkeley, California, Kelsey State Press, 1984.
Notes Preceding Trust. Venice, California, Lapis Press, 1987.
Boundary. Santa Monica, California, Lapis Press, 1988.
Giotto, Arena. Elmwood, Connecticut, Abacus, 1991.
when new time folds up. Minneapolis, Chax Press, 1993.
Il Cuore: The Heart: Selected Poems, 1970–1995. Hanover, New Hampshire, University Press of New England, 1997.

Recordings: *The Poetry of Kathleen Fraser,* McGraw Hill, n.d.; *Even Human Voices,* Watershed, 1986.

Other (for children)

Stilts, Somersaults, and Headstands: Game Poems Based on a Painting by Peter Breughel. New York, Atheneum, 1968.
Adam's World: San Francisco, with Miriam F. Levy. Chicago, Whitman. 1971.

Other

Editor, *Feminist Poetics: A Consideration of the Female Construction of Language.* San Francisco, San Francisco State University, 1984.

*

Critical Studies: *Poetics of the Feminine: Authority and Literary Tradition in William Carlos Williams, Mina Loy, Denise Levertov, and Kathleen Fraser* by Linda A. Kinnahan, Cambridge, England, Cambridge University Press, 1994; interview, in *Contemporary Literature* (Madison, Wisconsin), 39(1), spring 1998, and "Infectious Ecstasy: Toward a Poetics of Performative Transformation," in *Women Poets of the Americas: Toward a Pan-American Gathering,* edited by Jacqueline Vaught Brogan and Cordelia Chavez Candelaria, Notre Dame, Indiana, University of Notre Dame Press, 1999, both by Cynthia Hogue.

Kathleen Fraser comments:

My poetry has moved from girlish, Plath-fed lyrics, first published in the mid-1960s, toward a recognition—inside the poem—of life as a more undecided and precarious process. Language is, for me, exploratory—the fluid and changing record of daily risk taking. I use my writing to locate myself in particulars, to catch the multiplicity, the layering of thoughts, feelings, visual impressions experienced simultaneously. Writing is, in a sense, taking a reading on what has thus far transpired and what my attitude toward it is. There is, hopefully, a movement back and forth. I use my poetry as my most serious way of paying attention to the world outside of my own interior struggle. The poems begin as acts of attention and try to allow in whatever is there waiting to make itself heard. And seen. I regard the ability to write as a gift that must be honored with the utmost seriousness. My great permission giver, in learning to use that gift, was Frank O'Hara. He still appears in my dreams as a guide and

friend. I am also deeply indebted to Virginia Woolf and Gertrude Stein for complexity. American jazz (particularly Eddie Jefferson's lyrics and Betty Carter's scat) has made a much greater range of tonalities and movements available to me. Painting has always been important and often provides paths to unconscious material that I bring into the poetry. Surely my father's early chanting of limericks and lyrics from *Alice* and *Through the Looking-Glass* will always be there as playful resonance in my work. And my mother's singing. To catch the exact angle of light as two planes shift. To catch the unbroken moment between two people and speak it.

*   *   *

Kathleen Fraser's early poetry bears the imprint of the New York school, especially of Kenneth Koch, with whom she studied in the 1960s. The tone is one of playful self-mockery, as in

But over here, where it's dark out,
   I'm just me
          feeling uneasy in these nights
cold and black.
         I turn the heat up
   higher
    thinking other people's lives
are warmer

In "Because You Aren't Here to Be What I Can't Think Of" Fraser invents a dazzling inventory reminiscent of Koch's "Sleeping with Women" or Frank O'Hara's "Having a Coke with You." In this catalog poem the speaker blithely tries to convince herself that she is not going to care about her lover's involvement with someone else, all the while doing everything in her power to conjure up his presence. The distance between the lovers takes on fantastic proportions: "Because the moon's another streetlight and your lights are off, and on in someone else's" or "Because there's a saxophone playing between our telephones but you can't pick it up." Yet, injured party that she is, the speaker wryly and wisely concludes that, life being what it is, things could be worse: "because I'm not on a dancefloor with you, but here, / hanging out with my shadow over a city of windows, / lit-up, imagining another kind of life almost like this one." The lover's absence is irritating but not, finally, tragic. The same rueful comedy and witty analysis are found in "The Fault," in which the poet watches another woman make the wrong moves toward a man she herself has not hitherto paid much notice to but whom she now suddenly finds an attractive challenge:

I felt myself in love with him watching his tongue run over
  his lips

and remembered Fredericka

    always keeping the tube of vaseline in her purse

always gliding it over her mouth should there be someone
  to kiss

and thought how I liked space and long unending lines,

> how my life
> was that way, without visible connections or obvious
>   explanations
>   how I was glad
> I'd washed my hair

From this early, jaunty poetry Fraser has moved on to compose a much more serious and ambitious lyric. The confluence of the feminist movement, in which Fraser has been extremely active—she was the founding editor of *HOW(ever)*, an important journal of women's avant-garde poetry and poetics—and the language school, together with a strong sense of the visual arts already latent in her New York period, gave birth to the series of prose poems and complex phenomenological lyrics collected in *New Shoes, Each Next,* and *Notes Preceding Trust.* For example, "L'Invention Collective/Collective Invention," one of the *Magritte Series,* is based on the painter's grotesque and haunting image of a sort of reverse mermaid, a fish with human legs, slender and feminine, and with pubic hair. In Magritte's painting the fish-woman is oddly erotic and repulsive, and the single blank fish eye confronts the beholder, whose eye is drawn downward to her (its?) lower parts. She lies on the edge of the beach, the whitecaps of a picture-book blue ocean beating pointlessly behind her. Fraser invents a narrative that can incorporate this image. Her story is of a tacky domestic heroine, part comic book, part fairy tale, whose role in life is to keep things "neat and tidy" so that she is quite unable to "see / her seducers in a line and shaking their fingers." Only in her dreams does she see herself lying "at the edge of the waters," the sand scratching her body, and watch herself turn into a fish—"a face cut deep with gills and the sad eyes panting / and the absolute quiet of something about to arrive." What this something is we do not know, but it is frightening in the poem as well as in Magritte's painting. The pose of the figure invites rape, but what would that mean in this context? Fraser is playing with notions of smugness and self-deception, exploring the fantasy life of the little woman who wanted life for herself and her boy to be "as fresh as Watermelon slice."

The prose poems in *Each Next* carry on the painterly motive of the *Magritte Series,* but Fraser now fragments her texts, shifting from one pronoun to another and collaging snatches of conversation (remarks by Grace [Paley] and Francie [Shaw]) with images of green and blue (the swimming pool setting) and memories of previous swims, so as to create a taut "field of action" where words become the actors. The poet's drive toward greater density and ellipsis reaches its height in *Notes Preceding Trust,* many of whose poems are dark dreamscapes like "Everything You Ever Wanted," which begins with

> I do not trust these glaring invitations to break into green. An apple, viewed as a journey: have a bite, another bite. A red and yellow street, all dashes and splashing. Or white teeth moving in, just under the skin. First comes the comma, then the period. Walking on water, then stepping into a long breath trying to catch up. I am having trouble finding where to take the first step.

The narrative begins in a fairy-tale vein but is broken by "commonsense" observations like "first comes the comma, then the period." The ensuing dream creates a curious doubling; the poet is aware of her legs, tucked up under her, but sees them "swinging up and out over the edge to the floor." She starts to eat, but "there is nothing to eat but a small dish of buttons." Even when she awakes

and finds "a key in my wine glass," put there by a "person I desire," she cannot respond. Rather, she is recalled to routine, to "the list of necessary distractions," where "each task has a check mark next to it, a little gesture on the map's white silence." "Everything you wanted," this delicate prose poem implies, is nevertheless not within "your" grasp, for women are conditioned to be practical, to take care of others, to put "check marks" where they belong. Hence the difficulty of "break[ing] into green," a difficulty subtly dramatized in this and related poems in *Each Next.*

In her book *when new time folds up* Fraser moves into more public spaces. The lead poem, "Etruscan Places," alternates meditative free verse, pictograms, and documentary prose (for example, the letters to a friend named Annalisa) so as to probe the marks and traces of Etruscan culture as it continues to animate our lives today. Fraser's *einfühlung* into the artifacts of ancient Rome, into the "narrow walkway wide enough for territorial smuggle," is masterly on all counts. The "remorse" of the city becomes hers in these spare and delicate poems, poems that "include history" in new and subtle ways.

At one point Fraser wrote, "Love has always been the motivating force in my life." She has always written with the assertion that language and form have the capability to surmount grief and loss. *Il Cuore: The Heart: Selected Poems, 1970–1995,* a collection from her previous twelve books of poetry, spans the thematic, formal, and philosophical ways in which she has addressed loss, love, and writing poetry. In one of the earlier poems included in the volume, "The History of My Feeling" from *What I Want,* she accounts for personal emotional weight:

> I knew clearly that I hated you for entering me profoundly, for taking me inside you, for husbanding me, claiming all that I knew and did not know, you letting me go from you into this unpredictable and loneliest of weathers.

Clear language and image mark these earlier poems and evoke considerable emotional depth. Pushing toward identification in the form of a shared language, however socially acceptable, is what Fraser terms an "osmosis of rubbing up." When she utilizes this pressure in the sphere of a wider social landscape, her poetry gains even more force. She addresses notions of the present that lie buried in the past as well as ideological and cultural tensions. A deeper personal context becomes contingent on a deeper cultural context. Personal indeterminacy finds its origins outside the self. History gains as a critical lens through which to centralize the self.

"Etruscan Pages," from *when new time folds up,* marks this turn to an equation between the cultural and the personal, between history and memory. The meditation on a trip to Etruscan burial sites includes the statement "we know what each mark [of Etruscan writing] is equal to / but not, in retrospect, what was intended." Ultimately the desire for a language outside the personal so that one might avoid the eclipsing power of history seems to be at the core of these poems. She writes in the poem, "Medusa's hair was snakes. Was thought, split inward," "Historical continuity / accounts for knowing what dead words point to." The apparently personal concerns become laced with the significance and permanence of history:

> Grief is simple and dark
> as this bridge or hidden field where something did
>   exist once
> and may again, or your face receding behind the window
> a possible emptying

Loss is part of the circumscribed self—"your face receding behind the window"—but the subjective and the historical are contingent on one another. For Fraser the poem is the site of such a conflation:

> Writing is, in part, a record of our struggle to be human, as well as our delight in reimagining/reconstructing the formal designs and boundaries of what we've been given. If we don't make our claim, the world is simply that which others have described for us.

Fraser's world is lush with the power of language and its vigorous forms. For her the infusion of the personal in the historical is the concern at the "heart" of her generous and brilliant life of poetry and letters.

—Marjorie Perloff and Martha Sutro

FRENCH, Anne

Nationality: New Zealander. **Born:** Wellington, New Zealand, 5 March 1956. **Education:** Victoria University of Wellington, 1973–79, B.A. 1976, B.A. (honors) 1976; M.A. 1980; Auckland Secondary Teachers' College, Diploma in Teaching 1977. **Family:** Married to Gary Alfred James Boire; one son. **Career:** Teaching assistant, Victoria University of Wellington, 1979; editor, 1980–82, Oxford University Press, Wellington, managing editor, 1982–89, and publisher, 1990–93, Oxford University Press, Auckland. Since 1995 managing editor, Museums of New Zealand, Wellington. Since 1994 managing editor, *New Zealand Strategic Management,* Auckland. Writer-in-residence, Massey University, 1993. **Awards:** New Zealand Book award for poetry, 1988; PEN Best First Book of Poetry, 1988. **Address:** P.O. Box 1799, Wellington, New Zealand.

PUBLICATIONS

Poetry

All Cretans Are Liars. Auckland, Auckland University Press, 1987.
The Male As Evader. Auckland, Auckland University Press, 1988.
Cabin Fever. Auckland, Auckland University Press, 1990.
Seven Days on Mykonos. Auckland, Auckland University Press, 1993.
Boys' Night Out. Auckland, Auckland University Press, 1998.

Other

Editor, *Elsdon Best - Maori Religion and Mythology, Part II.* Wellington, Government Printing Office, 1980.

*

Critical Study: "French Fishes: Evasions and Tensions in the Poetry of Anne French" by Jane Stafford, in *CRNLE Reviews Journal,* 1, 1993.

*   *   *

One of the feminist writers who emerged in the 1980s, Anne French won the 1988 New Zealand Book award for poetry with her collection *All Cretans Are Liars* (1987). Its three parts move from personal disclosures to relationships with a lover to a nationalistic emphasis. The poetic comprehends both a modernist emphasis on form and diction and an intertextuality that verges on the postmodern, as in the pivotal "Eucalypts Greenlane," with its references to James Baxter, Allen Curnow, Ian Wedde, and T.S. Eliot. The earlier poems tend to be occasional, building a sense of immediacy as the narrator records an incident and then reflects on it. "Cricket," for example, begins with glimpses of a wet, desolate weekend, but by the second verse it moves to something more abstract:

> That was how it appeared. The difference
> between inventing something, and not
> is imperceptible . . .

French's second collection, *The Male as Evader* (1988), pursues this relatively simple poetic in a vigorous series of poems about men's relationships to women. Many of the poems' titles, as well as the titles of the first two of the book's three sections ("A catalogue of evaders," "The language and literature of evasion"), reflect the collection's interest in males' possession of language and the problem of women in achieving some kind of status in relation to it. "The Dangers of Literature" begins,

> So I ended up in your book? That's
> Marvellous to see myself undressed
> and systematically examined in the clear
>
> unblinking light of your malice.

Most of the poems maintain this tone and directness, but they have difficulty in solving the problem of female subjugation by language, which is at the center of the collection, as well as in dealing with the more basic entrapment by language that is represented by the traditional paradox of the title of her first collection. Only the last of the forty-four poems, "Catullus's answer book," deals with the problem and gestures beyond itself at a possibility of seeing a face reflected back that is "not, necessarily, a man."

The claustrophobic feel of the second collection provides the title of French's third, *Cabin Fever* (1990), and its theme of journeying by sea. "In a North Harbour" begins,

> There's no room
>
> for attitudes of renunciation or despair—not here,
> not today, while sky waits to be filled with spinnaker . . .

In general the collection proceeds away from the earlier aggression. In fact, the collection is informed by the imagery of a male writer, Stéphane Mallarmé. Like him, French identifies with the voyager and sailor in order to escape constriction by exploring possible identities. In "The Words" the narrator learns the masculine world of sailing terms ("The leading edge of a sail is called the luff"), and more generally in the collection the boat represents some kind of continuing entrapment in male constructions, as well, paradoxically, as offering a dexterous maneuverability. But French's narrator, as a woman, must leave the boat and enter the traditionally female element around it: "I—who have always been / incautious—swim out into the deep water" ("Motaketekete").

Seven Days on Mykonos (1993) gives a sense that the journey is completed, that territories have been mapped and boundaries fixed. The first section, "Postcards from Hamilton," represents a journey in poetry throughout the world. But there is also a sense of uncertainty once the boundaries have been reached. The remaining sections, "Stories from the Blue Chair" and "The Anthropology of New Zealand Literature," hark back to the themes of the earlier collections rather than pushing forward. In some of these poems French's customarily ironic tone is revealed as limited, particularly in those referring to the world of New Zealand literature, in which the tone may become edgy or even paranoiac, as in "New Zealanders at Home":

    . . . while above their heads the admonitory
    pohutukawa points its blood-red sta-
    mens at nobody in particular.

—Anna Smith

FRY, Christopher

Nationality: British. **Born:** Christopher Fry Harris, Bristol, 18 December 1907. **Education:** Bedford Modern School, 1918–26. **Military Service:** Non-Combatant Corps, 1940–44. **Family:** Married Phyllis Marjorie Hart in 1936 (died 1987); one son. **Career:** Teacher, Bedford Froebel Kindergarten, 1926–27; actor and office worker, Citizen House, Bath, 1927; schoolmaster, Hazelwood School, Limpsfield, Surrey, 1928–31; secretary to H. Rodney Bennett, 1931–32; founding director, Tunbridge Wells Repertory Players, 1932–35; lecturer and editor of schools magazine, Dr. Barnardo's Homes, 1934–39; director, 1939–40, and visiting director, 1945–46, Oxford Playhouse; visiting director, 1946, and staff dramatist, 1947, Arts Theatre Club, London. Also composer. **Awards:** Shaw Prize Fund award, 1948; Foyle poetry prize, 1951; New York Drama Critics Circle award, 1951, 1952, 1956; Queen's Gold Medal, 1962; Royal Society of Literature Heinemann award, 1962. D.A.: Manchester Metropolitan University, 1966; D.Litt.: Lambeth 1988; Oxford University, 1988; University of Sussex, 1994; De Montfort, 1994. Honorary Fellow, Manchester Metropolitan University, 1988. Fellow, Royal Society of Literature. **Agent:** ACTAC Ltd., 15 High Street, Ramsbury, Wiltshire SN8 2PA. **Address:** The Toft, East Dean, near Chichester, West Sussex PO18 0JA, England.

PUBLICATIONS

Poetry

Root and Sky: Poetry from the Plays of Christopher Fry, edited by Charles E. and Jean G. Wadsworth. Cambridge, Rampant Lions Press, and Boston, Godine, 1975.

Plays

Youth and the Peregrines (produced Tunbridge Wells, Kent, 1934).
She Shall Have Music (lyrics only, with Ronald Frankau), book by Frank Eyton, music by Fry and Monte Crick (produced London, 1934).
To Sea in a Sieve (as Christopher Harris) (revue; produced Reading, 1935).

Open Door (produced London, 1936). Goldings, Hertfordshire, Printed by the Boys at the Press of Dr. Barnardo's Homes, n.d.
The Boy with a Cart: Cuthman, Saint of Sussex (produced Coleman's Hatch, Sussex, 1938; London, 1950; New York, 1953). London, Oxford University Press, 1939; New York, Oxford University Press, 1951.
The Tower (produced Tewkesbury, Gloucestershire, 1939).
Thursday's Child: A Pageant, music by Martin Shaw (produced London, 1939). London, Girls' Friendly Society, 1939.
A Phoenix Too Frequent (produced London, 1946; Cambridge, Massachusetts, 1948; New York, 1950). London, Hollis and Carter, 1946; New York, Oxford University Press, 1949.
The Firstborn (broadcast 1947; produced Edinburgh, 1948). Cambridge, University Press, 1946; New York, Oxford University Press, 1950; revised version (produced London, 1952; New York, 1958), London and New York, Oxford University Press, 1952, 1958.
The Lady's Not for Burning (produced London, 1948; New York, 1950). London and New York, Oxford University Press, 1949; revised version, 1950, 1958.
Thor, With Angels (produced Canterbury, 1948; Washington, D.C., 1950; London, 1951). Canterbury, Goulden, 1948; New York, Oxford University Press, 1949.
Venus Observed (produced London, 1950; New York, 1952). London and New York, Oxford University Press, 1950.
Ring round the Moon: A Charade with Music, adaptation of a play by Jean Anouilh (produced London and New York, 1950). London and New York, Oxford University Press, 1950.
A Sleep of Prisoners (produced Oxford, London, and New York, 1951). London and New York, Oxford University Press, 1951.
The Dark Is Light Enough: A Winter Comedy (produced Edinburgh and London, 1954; New York, 1955). London and New York, Oxford University Press, 1954.
The Lark, adaptation of a play by Jean Anouilh (produced London, 1955). London, Methuen, 1955; New York, Oxford University Press, 1956.
Tiger at the Gates, adaptation of a play by Jean Giraudoux (produced London and New York, 1955). London, Methuen, 1955; New York, Oxford University Press, 1956; as *The Trojan War Will Not Take Place* (produced London, 1983), Methuen, 1983.
Duel of Angels, adaptation of a play by Jean Giraudoux (produced London, 1958; New York, 1960). London, Methuen, 1958; New York, Oxford University Press, 1959.
Curtmantle (produced in Dutch, Tilburg, Netherlands, 1961; Edinburgh and London, 1962). London and New York, Oxford University Press, 1961.
Judith, adaptation of a play by Jean Giraudoux (produced London, 1962). London, Methuen, 1962.
The Bible: Original Screenplay, assisted by Jonathan Griffin. New York, Pocket Books, 1966.
Peer Gynt, adaptation of the play by Ibsen (produced Chichester, 1970). London and New York, Oxford University Press, 1970.
A Yard of Sun: A Summer Comedy (produced Nottingham and London, 1970; Cleveland, 1972). London and New York, Oxford University Press, 1970.
The Brontës of Haworth (televised 1973). London, Davis Poynter, 2 vols., 1974.
Cyrano de Bergerac, adaptation of the play by Edmond Rostand (produced Chichester, 1975). London and New York, Oxford University Press, 1975.

Paradise Lost, music by Penderecki, adaptation of the poem by Milton (produced Chicago, 1978). London, Schott, 1978.

Selected Plays (includes *The Boy with a Cart, A Phoenix Too Frequent, The Lady's Not for Burning, A Sleep of Prisoners, Curtmantle*). Oxford and New York, Oxford University Press, 1985.

One Thing More; or, Caedmon Construed (produced Chelmsford, Essex, 1986; London, 1988). New York, London, King's College, and New York, Dramatists Play Service, 1987.

Screenplays: *The Beggar's Opera,* with Denis Cannan, 1953; *A Queen Is Crowned* (documentary), 1953; *Ben Hur,* 1959; *Barabbas,* 1962; *The Bible: In the Beginning,* 1966.

Radio Plays: for *Children's Hour* series, 1939–40; *The Firstborn,* 1947; *Rhineland Journey,* 1948.

Television Plays: *The Canary,* 1950; *The Tenant of Wildfell Hall,* 1968; *The Brontës of Haworth* (four plays), 1973; *The Best of Enemies,* 1976; *Sister Dora,* from the book by Jo Manton, 1977.

Other

An Experience of Critics, with *The Approach to Dramatic Criticism* by W.A. Darlington and others, edited by Kaye Webb. London, Perpetua Press, 1952; New York, Oxford University Press, 1953.

The Boat That Mooed (for children). New York, Macmillan, 1966.

Can You Find Me: A Family History. London, Oxford University Press, 1978; New York, Oxford University Press, 1979.

Death Is a Kind of Love (lecture). Cranberry Isles, Maine, Tidal Press, 1979.

Genius, Talent and Failure (lecture). London, King's College, 1987.

Looking for a Language (lecture). London, King's College, 1992.

The Early Days (lecture). London, Society for Theatre Research, 1997.

Editor, *Charlie Hammond's Sketchbook.* Oxford, Oxford University Press, 1980.

Editor, *A Sprinkle of Nutmeg* (wartime letters by Phyllis Fry). London, Enitharmon Press, 1993.

Editor, *Cyrano de Bergerac: A Heroic Comedy in Five Acts.* New York, Oxford University Press, 1996.

Translator, *The Boy and the Magic,* by Colette. London, Dobson, 1964.

Incidental Music: *A Winter's Tale,* London, 1951; recorded by Caedmon.

*

Bibliography: By B.L. Schear and E.G. Prater, in *Tulane Drama Review 4* (New Orleans), March 1960.

Manuscript Collection: Harvard University Theatre Collection, Cambridge, Massachusetts.

Critical Studies: *Christopher Fry: An Appreciation,* London, Nevill, 1950, and *Christopher Fry,* London, Longman, 1954, revised edition, 1962, both by Derek Stanford; *The Drama of Comedy: Victim and Victor* by Nelson Vos, Richmond, Virginia, John Knox Press,1965; *Creed and Drama* by W.M. Merchant, London, SPCK, 1965; *The Christian Tradition in Modern British Verse Drama* by William V. Spanos, New Brunswick, New Jersey, Rutgers University Press, 1967; *Christopher Fry* by Emil Roy, Carbondale, Southern Illinois University Press, 1968; *Christopher Fry: A Critical Essay,* Grand Rapids, Michigan, Eerdmans, 1970, and *More Than the Ear Discovers: God in the Plays of Christopher Fry,* Chicago, Loyola University Press, 1983, both by Stanley M. Wiersma; *Poetic Drama,* London, Macmillan, 1989, and *Christopher Fry,* Boston, Twayne Publishers, 1990, both by Glenda Leeming; "'Little Death-Watch Beetle': Nicholas Devize As the Devil in Christopher Fry's *The Lady's Not For Burning*" by John S. Bak, in *Notes on Contemporary Literature* (Carrollton, Georgia), 23(5), November 1993; by Jackie Tucker, in *British Playwrights, 1860–1956: A Research and Production Sourcebook,* edited by William Demastes and Katherine E. Kelly, Westport, Connecticut, Greenwood, 1996.

Theatrical Activities: Director: **Plays**—*How-Do, Princess?* by Ivor Novello, toured, 1936, *The Circle of Chalk* by James Laver, London, 1945; *The School for Scandal* by Sheridan, London, 1946; *A Phoenix Too Frequent,* Brighton, 1950; *The Lady's Not for Burning,* toured, 1971; and others. Actor: **Plays**—in repertory, Bath, 1937.

Christopher Fry comments:

Influences are difficult to pinpoint. Certainly, as it must be with anyone of my generation, T.S. Eliot was a releasing factor. In the plays I have tried to work toward an end that I broadly expressed in a lecture: "No event is understandable in a prose sense alone. Its ultimate meaning (that is to say, the complete life of the event, seen in its eternal context) is a poetic meaning." I have tried to shape a verse form (a metrical system) that could contain both the "theatrical" elements (rhetoric, broad colors, etc.) and the rhythms and tone of the colloquial, which would work for the "artificial comedy," or the historical, or the conversation of the present time.

*   *   *

It was Christopher Fry, and later T.S. Eliot, who led the short revival of interest in the poetic drama during the decade or so after World War II, an interest that now seems completely dead. *A Phoenix Too Frequent,* an imperfect sentimental farce, attracted some attention in 1946, and with *The Lady's Not for Burning* Fry captured the imagination of the critics and of a potentially large audience. The most obviously brilliant of Fry's plays, it was fortunate to have an impeccable production by John Gielgud and a fine cast headed by Pamela Brown, Claire Bloom, Richard Burton, and Gielgud himself. Its amusing plot and the natural yet highly decorated language, finely characterized and supremely dramatic (Fry himself was for some time an actor), were a revelation after the dryness and aridity of the language of wartime drama. Oversucculent on the page, the verse—especially when delivered in the romantic style of acting still predominant in the late 1940s—seemed irresistible in performance.

But as Fry's technical assurance grew, so critical and public interest waned. *Venus Observed,* written for Laurence Olivier, was a critical and to some extent public failure. The play was a graver comedy of autumn, and its language was more disciplined and restrained; it was still often witty, but it was quieter and without the obvious verbal fireworks of its predecessor. In *A Sleep of Prisoners,* perhaps his most entirely successful piece, Fry turned to wholly serious matters, most obviously to his perennial theme of "the growth of vision: the increased perception of what makes for life and what makes for death." Prisoners of war penned up in a church explore one another's personalities in their dreams. It is a moving and totally realized poetic drama. *The Dark Is Light Enough,* a winter play based on Fabre's parable of the butterfly making its way through storm and profound darkness to arrive brightly inviolate at its destination, was written for Edith Evans and staged in 1954. It was disliked both by critics and by the public. Since its production Fry has concentrated for the most part on translation—from Anouilh and Giraudoux, for instance—and on film scripting. He has, however, written a play that completes the quartet of plays of the seasons, a comedy of high summer.

Fry's place in the theater is perhaps ephemeral, and he has been compared, damagingly, to the Victorian poetic dramatist Stephen Phillips, whose *Paolo and Francesca* seemed at the beginning of the twentieth century to be a masterpiece but is now almost totally forgotten. The comparison seems unfair, for Fry is more accomplished both as poet and dramatist than Phillips. On the page his language is overblown and seems lacking in muscle and discipline, but in performance it is always amusing and dramatically viable, and its sentiment is at worst harmlessly touching. It is strange now to remember that many critics found Fry difficult in the 1940s and 1950s. Whatever he is, he is not that. Accused of overwriting ("Too many words!"), Fry replied in *An Experience of Critics* (1952), "It means, I think, that I don't use the same words often enough; or else, or as well, that the words are an ornament on the meaning and not the meaning itself. That is certainly sometimes—perhaps often—true in the comedies, though almost as often I have meant the ornament to be, dramatically or comedically, an essential part of the meaning; and in my more sanguine moments I think the words are as exact to my purpose as I could make them at the time of writing."

Posterity may find this claim to be true. It is unlikely that Fry is in any sense a major writer, but within his own set limits he is a craftsman of considerable accomplishment, and where Fry is most successful, he is memorable.

—Derek Parker

FULLER, John (Leopold)

Nationality: British. **Born:** Ashford, Kent, 1 January 1937; son of Roy Fuller. **Education:** Attended St. Paul's School; New College, Oxford (editor, *Isis,* 1959; Newdigate prize, 1960), B.A. 1960, M.A. 1964, B.Litt. 1965. **Military Service:** Royal Air Force, 1955–57. **Family:** Married Cicely Prudence Martin in 1960; three daughters. **Career:** Visiting lecturer, State University of New York, Buffalo, 1962–63; assistant lecturer, Manchester University, 1963–66. Since 1966 fellow, Magdalen College, Oxford. Co-founder, *Review* magazine, 1962; publisher, Sycamore Press, Oxford. **Awards:** Newigate prize, 1960; Richard Hillary memorial prize, 1961; Eric Gregory award, 1965; Faber memorial prize, 1974; Prudence Farmer prize (*New Statesman*), 1975; Southern Arts prize, 1980; Cholmondeley award, 1983; Whitbread award, 1983; Forward prize, 1996. Fellow, Royal Society of Literature. **Agent:** Patricia Kavanagh, Peters Fraser and Dunlop, Drury House, 34–43 Russell Street, London WC2B 5HA, England. **Address:** 4 Benson Place. Oxford, England.

PUBLICATIONS

Poetry

Fairground Music. London, Chatto and Windus-Hogarth Press, 1961.
The Tree That Walked. London, Chatto and Windus-Hogarth Press, 1967.
The Art of Love. Oxford, The Review, 1968.
The Labours of Hercules: A Sonnet Sequence. Manchester, Manchester Institute of Contemporary Arts, 1969.
Three London Songs, music by Bryan Kelly. London, Novello, 1969.
Annotations of Giant's Town. London, Poem-of-the-Month Club, 1970.
The Wreck. London, Turret, 1970.
Cannibals and Missionaries. London, Secker and Warburg, 1972.
Boys in a Pie. London, Steam Press, 1972.
Hut Groups. Hitchin, Hertfordshire, Cellar Press, 1973.
Penguin Modern Poets 22, with Adrian Mitchell and Peter Levi. London, Penguin, 1973.
Epistles to Several Persons. London, Secker and Warburg, 1973.
Poems and Epistles. Boston, Godine, 1974.
Squeaking Crust (for children). London, Chatto and Windus, 1974.
A Bestiary. Oxford, Sycamore Press, 1974.
The Mountain in the Sea. London, Secker and Warburg, 1975.
Bel and the Dragon. Oxford, Sycamore Press, 1977.
The Wilderness. Buffalo, Lockwood Memorial Library, 1977.
Lies and Secrets. London, Secker and Warburg, 1979.
The Illusionists: A Tale. London, Secker and Warburg, 1980.
The January Divan. Hitchin, Hertfordshire, Mandeville Press, 1980.
The Ship of Sounds. Sidcot, Somerset, Gruffyground, 1981.
Waiting for the Music. Edinburgh, Salamander Press, 1982.
The Beautiful Inventions. London, Secker and Warburg, 1983.
Come Aboard and Sail Away (for children). Edinburgh, Salamander Press, 1983.
Selected Poems 1954–1982. London, Secker and Warburg, 1985.
Partingtime Hall, with James Fenton. London, Viking Salamander, 1987.
The Grey among the Green. London, Chatto and Windus, 1988.
The Mechanical Body. London, Chatto and Windus, 1991.
Stones and Fires. London, Chatto and Windus, 1996.
Collected Poems. London, Chatto and Windus, 1996.

Plays

Herod Do Your Worst, music by Bryan Kelly (produced Thame, Oxfordshire, 1967). London, Novello, 1968.
Half a Fortnight, music by Bryan Kelly (produced Leicester, 1970). London, Novello, 1973.
The Spider Monkey Uncle King, music by Bryan Kelly (produced Cookham, Berkshire, 1971). London, Novello, 1979.
Fox-Trot, music by Bryan Kelly (produced Leicester, 1972).
The Queen in the Golden Tree, music by Bryan Kelly (produced Edinburgh, 1974).
How Did You Get Here, Jonno? music by Bryan Kelly (produced Wolverhampton, 1975).
The Ship of Sounds, music by Bryan Kelly (produced Leicester, 1975). London, Barry Brunton, 1986.
Adam's Apple, music by Bryan Kelly (produced Abingdon, Oxfordshire, 1975).

Linda, music by Bryan Kelly (produced Reading, 1975). Published as *Biscuit Girl,* London, Barry Brunton, 1986.

St. Francis of Assisi, music by Bryan Kelly (produced London, 1981). London, Barry Brunton, 1986.

Novels

Flying to Nowhere. Edinburgh, Salamander Press, 1983; New York, Braziller, 1984.

Tell It Me Again. London, Chatto and Windus, 1988.

The Burning Boys. London, Chatto and Windus, 1989.

Look Twice. London, Chatto and Windus, 1991.

A Skin Diary. London, Chatto and Windus, 1997.

Short Stories

The Adventures of Speedfall. Edinburgh, Salamander Press, 1985.

The Worm and the Star. London, Chatto and Windus, 1993.

Other

A Reader's Guide to W.H. Auden. London, Thames and Hudson, and New York, Farrar Straus, 1970.

The Sonnet. London, Methuen, 1972.

The Last Bid (for children). London, Deutsch. 1975.

Carving Trifles: William King's Imitation of Horace (lecture). London, Oxford University Press, 1976.

The Extraordinary Wool Mill and Other Stories (for children). London, Deutsch, 1980.

W.H. Auden: A Commentary. London, Faber and Faber, and Princeton, New Jersey, Princeton University Press, 1998.

Editor, with others, *Light Blue Dark Blue: An Anthology of Recent Writings from Oxford and Cambridge Universities.* London, Macdonald, 1960.

Editor, *Oxford Poetry 1960.* Oxford, Fantasy Press, 1960.

Editor, *Poetry Supplement.* London, Poetry Book Society, 1962.

Editor, with Harold Pinter and Peter Redgrove, *New Poems 1967.* London, Hutchinson, 1968.

Editor, *Poetry Supplement.* London, Poetry Book Society, 1970.

Editor, *Nemo's Almanac.* Oxford, Sycamore Press, 1971.

Editor, *New Poetry 8.* London, Hutchinson, 1982.

Editor, *Dramatic Works,* by John Gay. Oxford, Clarendon Press, 2 vols., 1983.

Editor, with Howard Sergeant, *The Gregory Poets 1983–84.* Edinburgh, Salamander Press, 1984.

Editor, *The Chatto Book of Love Poetry.* London, Chatto and Windus, 1990.

*

Critical Studies: "The Poetry of John Fuller" by Edward Mendelson, in *New Republic* (Washington, D.C.), 28 May 1977; *John Fuller: The Mountain in the Sea* by Claudio Natale, Tesi di Laurea, Universita Degli Studi di Palermo, 1983; "An Interview with John Fuller" by Mick Imlah, in *Poetry Review* (London), 72(4), January 1983; "The Poetry of John Fuller," *Antigonish Review* (Antigonish, Canada), 57, spring 1984, and "The New Zest in British Poetry: The Influence of John Fuller," in *Quadrant* (Victoria, Australia), 30(11), November 1986, both by Michael Hulse; "Coming to Life-The Poetry of John

Fuller" by Brian Hinton, in *Jellyfish Cupful: Writings in Honour of John Fuller,* edited by Barney Cokeliss and James Fenton, London, Ulysses, 1997; "John Fuller's Lines of Flight" by David Pascoe, in *Essays in Criticism* (England), 48(4), October 1998; "Mapping the Margins: Translation, Invasion and Celtic Islands in Brian Moore and John Fuller" by Sophie Gilmartin, in *An Introduction to Contemporary Fiction: International Writing in English since 1970,* edited by Rod Mengham, Cambridge, England, Polity, 1999.

*   *   *

Though appreciating John Fuller's technical control, skilled craftsmanship, and intelligence, reviewers have also noted "a seriousness lacking at the heart of his work," "the impression of a rooted reticence," and a "sense of uneasiness." *Selected Poems 1954–1982* traces his progress and, indeed, his versatility from the wit of *Fairground Music* to the depth of feeling of *The Beautiful Inventions,* illustrating along the way his ability to be entertaining, lyrical, provocative, discerning, philosophical, and continually surprising. His succeeding books have continued to show this, with Fuller's comic voice blending with James Fenton's games playing in *Partingtime Hall* and a diversity of themes and moods emerging in *The Grey among the Green.*

Despite the variety of subject and stance, all of Fuller's poems are accomplished, elegant, and technically sophisticated. His control of language and of form—concern with technique, structure, and order and with the manipulation of words—produces a detachment that moderates the immediate impact of the ideas expressed by the poems, rather than the poet, but makes them no less powerful. Indeed, the power of the poetry lies in the artfulness with which meanings are implied rather than directly stated, whether through jokes, riddles, and games (as in *Lies and Secrets* or *The Illusionists*) or through the astonishing, unexpected imagery that Fuller frequently employs, as in the sea associations of "Girl with Coffee Tray" (*Fairground Music*), the speaking hedges in "Hedge Tutor" (*The Tree That Walked*), or the little boy with the toy tank in "Galata Bridge" (*The Beautiful Inventions*).

The relationship between poetry and reality has always concerned Fuller. In "A Dialogue between Caliban and Ariel" (*Fairground Music*) he notes the limitations of language in contemplating, mirroring, or determining truth or reality: "For all their declaration / And complexity, / Words cannot see . . ." and are mere tokens ("Words are but counters in a childish game . . .") rather than agents or effective tools ("Words would not help the channeled sea to prove / It was not ocean-free, nor pine no fuel . . ."). This concern is still very much with him twenty-seven years later in *The Grey among the Green,* where we are told that

A mountain is a mountain is
Itself, lasting, indifferent, proud.
The poet on his human throne
Has often wished that he were stone,
Or fluid, or a cloud.

The similarities often seen between Fuller's poetry and Auden's make the "rooted reticence" noted above less a criticism perhaps than a reminder of Auden's lines "truth in any serious sense, / Like orthodoxy, is a reticence" ("The Truest Poetry Is the Most Feigning"). At the same time the alleged "sense of uneasiness" may arise from Fuller's overriding dependence on the order and structure of a poem rather than on the words themselves. There are limits to what can be articulated or directly stated in poetry. For Fuller "similes should make you see / What otherwise is just asserted" (*The Illusionists*), while for Auden the success of a poem is achieved by the "luck of verbal playing"—at which Fuller unquestionably continues to be very clever indeed—rather than by assertion or declaration.

—B.T. Kugler

FULTON, Alice

Nationality: American. **Born:** Troy, New York, 25 January 1952. **Education:** Empire State College, Albany, New York, B.A. in creative writing 1978; Cornell University, Ithaca, New York, M.F.A. in creative writing 1982. **Family:** Married Hank De Leo in 1980. **Career:** Assistant professor, 1983–86, William Wilhartz Professor, 1986–89, associate professor, 1990–92, and since 1992 professor of English, University of Michigan, Ann Arbor. Visiting professor of creative writing, Vermont College, Montpelier, 1987, and University of California, Los Angeles, 1991. **Awards:** MacDowell Colony fellowship, 1978, 1979; Millay Colony fellowship, 1980; Emily Dickinson award, 1980; Academy of American Poets prize, 1982; Consuelo Ford award, 1984; Rainer Maria Rilke award, 1984; Michigan Council for the Arts grant, 1986, 1991; Yaddo Colony fellowship, 1987; Guggenheim fellowship, 1986–87; Bess Hokin prize (*Poetry,* Chicago), 1989; Ingram Merrill Foundation award, 1990; Elizabeth Matchett Stover award, *The Southwest Review,* 1994. Fellow, John D. and Catherine T. MacArthur Foundation, 1991–96. D.Litt: State University of New York, 1994. **Address:** 2730 Le Forge Road, R.R. 2, Ypsilanti, Michigan 48198, U.S.A.

PUBLICATIONS

Poetry

Anchors of Light. Oneonta, New York, Swamp Press, 1979.
Dance Script with Electric Ballerina. Philadelphia, University of Pennsylvania Press, 1983.
Palladium. Urbana, University of Illinois Press, 1986.
Powers of Congress. Boston, Godine, 1990.
Sensual Math. New York, Norton, 1995.

Other

Feeling As a Foreign Language: The Good Strangeness of Poetry. Saint Paul, Minnesota, Graywolf, 1999.

*

Critical Studies: By David Lehman, in *Epoch* (Ithaca, New York), 36(3), 1986–87; "Bright Sources" by Stephen Yenser, in *Yale Review* (New Haven, Connecticut), 77(1), autumn 1987; "A Poet Who Ventures Where Others Are Reluctant to Tread" by Matthew Gilbert, in *Sunday Boston Herald,* 8 March 1987; "'The Erogenous Cusp' or Intersections of Science and Gender in Alice Fulton's Poetry" by Christanne Miller, in *Feminist Measures: Soundings in Poetry and Theory,* edited by Lynn Keller and Christanne Miller, Ann Arbor, University of Michigan Press, 1994; "The 'Then Some Inbetween': Alice Fulton's Feminist Experimentalism" by Lynn Keller, in *American Literature* (Durham, North Carolina), 71(2), June 1999.

Alice Fulton comments:

My first book, *Dance Script with Electric Ballerina,* was published when plain style was the prevailing poetic mode. I think the language of my poetry appeared dense and rather baroque in the context of the flat, unadorned expression that constituted the mainstream. Sincerity was equated with plainness of style, and any manipulations of language that deviated from spoken norms were accused of artificiality, even glibness. I have made a strong effort to incorporate contemporary American speech, culture, and ideas in my work rather than write exclusively about nature or high culture. I mix varying registers of diction in order to create rich, perhaps subversive, subtexts. And my use of the line questions equilibrium and linguistic singleness by means of syntactic doubling on enjambed words.

My second book, *Palladium,* underscored my commitment to textured, energized language. Its formal strategies are more wide-ranging. The book includes dramatic monologues and meditative or narrative poems that tend to be longer, more digressive, and intellectually more ambitious than my earlier work. I continued to explore some of the subjects touched upon in *Dance Script.* These include the search for faith (by "faith" I mean the assumptions that allow us to live in the world), the struggle between engagement and estrangement, the balance of risk and convention, the meanings of popular culture, and familial legacies and loves. I also expanded my subjects in poems that perceive and value peripheral aspects of our culture, question the assumptions surrounding gender, and explore the wayward forms classicism and mythology take in America. The word "palladium" is capacious enough to include all of these meanings. Each of the six sections of the book relate to a denotation or connotation of the title.

My third book, *Powers of Congress,* is structurally very different from *Palladium.* There are no part openings, and the movement of the book is something of a cascade. One poem is intended to trigger the next, so that the book's large scheme has more in common with waterfalls than with compartmentalized plots. The title suggests merging and transformation through government, discourse, assemblage, and sexuality. It implies both hierarchy ("powers" indicating dominance) and a disintegration of hierarchy by means of "congress." The book's undivided structure enacts the enmeshed union and removal of boundaries implicit in the title. The poems in this book are sometimes in argument with various philosophical first principles: What, if anything, can be known with certainty? Is there any evidence to indicate that consciousness does or does not persist after death? What is the nature of God? How might I redefine God? Why do we feel that mind and body are separate entities despite all scientific evidence to the contrary? In the broadest sense, the poems question assumptions and emphasize the interconnectedness of seemingly disparate things.

My interest in American culture continues in poems that explore the rift between private and public domains, the objectifying of the self as product, and our national obsession with aerobics and body building. The latter theme leads to the human fascination with unattainable perfection and the realization that one cannot be both conscious and durable. Other threads include the intrinsic pain of consciousness, the impermanence of memory, the cultural nihilism of greed, confining gender roles, the relativity of seemingly objective facts, and dual heroic spheres of war and childbirth.

*   *   *

Upon a first reading, Alice Fulton's poetry has the neon appeal of an arcade. It is filled with Jacuzzis and Tilt-a-Whirls, escalators and guitars. It is peopled with strippers, studs, steel plant owners, and nuns. While these figures of popular culture are attractive in their own right, they are not responsible for W.D. Snodgrass's introduction to Fulton's book *Dance Script with Electric Ballerina* or for the selection of *Palladium,* published in 1986, for the National Poetry Series. As Fulton writes in "Semaphores and Hemispheres," "everything . . . [is] / rich in metaphor," including the changes technology and science have brought to the world. Fulton's poetry is concerned both with these changes and their metaphorical possibility. In *Palladium,* for example, palladium in all of its forms—as metallic element, music hall, and talisman, among others—provides a structure for the book. In part 1, which is introduced by the definitions of palladium in its elemental form, Fulton places "Babies"—

born gorgeous with nerves, with brains
the pink of silver polish or
jellyfish wafting ornately
through the body below

—and "Nugget and Dust," a poem about her father's death. Birth and death are elemental subjects. Other sections of the book, introduced by palladium in its other forms, are concerned with subjects that, if less elemental, are equally complex in their embodiment of the human experience.

Faith is one of the themes central to Fulton's poetry. Religious faith, especially Roman Catholicism, plays a part in such poems as "The Great Aunts of My Childhood" in *Dance Script with Electric Ballerina* and "Sister Madeleine Pleads for Our Mary" in *Palladium.* "Orientation Day in Hades" even depicts hell as "a vat, / a barrel slatted with darkness / contained by hoops of energy" where sinners pick peppers all day, while heaven looks like a salt mine in the distance, "all grayish hills and gooey lights, / as if seen through Vaseline." In "The Perpetual Light" the speaker suggests that the dead "no longer wait with heavy patience / . . . at some ever-open gate" but rather "hotfoot it through the universe / like supple disco stars."

Fulton's poems have less to do with a faith in the afterlife, however, than with the faith that enables humans to live with hope in a world that seems increasingly chaotic. The speaker in "603 West Liberty St.," when handed words like "faith," "sin," and "penance," questions "futures inlaid with *forever*" and instead believes in "the quantum world's array of random / without chaos, its multiplicity . . . alone seemed moral." In "Fables from the Random" the human impulse to create order from chaos attracts the speaker to her lover despite his "insistent rejection / of what is / and shouldn't be" and her knowledge that he just "make[s] fables / from the random." Science is one fable through which humans impose order on chaos; chemistry, for example, "locates elements in order / to control them." Fulton turns to science again and again in her poetry. Through the metaphorical possibility of science and technology, faith increases rather than diminishes. In "The Wreckage Entrepreneur" a woman, aided by wrecking balls and "carborundum-bladed saws,"

sifts through junk. When she glimpses herself in the art deco mirrors of an abandoned warehouse, she looks dirty and small. Ultimately, however, she is in the business of salvation:

It takes faith—this tripping through the mixed blessings
of debris with eyes peeled for the toxic
toothpaste green of copper keystones . . .
. . . she wants
a shower and lather of pumice
to melt the gritty casing of her
nakedness. How small she looks
beside what she has saved.

While the usefulness of the goods she saves is dubious, the fact of her work, of activity, saves her from hopelessness.

Poetry itself is one means by which we can enter into faith. Fulton writes in "In the Beginning," the introductory poem of *Dance Script with Electric Ballerina,* that our lives carry "unknowable cargo":

The wild green groans
by which I lived before language
now gesture and have at me
only in dreams . . .

Yet the meaning of those "green groans," the dreamworld of memory, can begin to be named through poetry, as Fulton suggests in "Everyone Knows the World Is Ending":

. . . So long as we keep chanting the words
those worlds will live, but just
so long, so long, so long. Each instant waves
through our nature and is nothing.
But in the love, the grief, under and above
the mother tongue, a permanence
hums: the steady mysterious
the coherent starlight.

Thus poetry, a chant, a humming of grief and love "under and above / the mother tongue," allows permanence in a world where "each instant waves" through us and is gone. Fulton's poetry allows us to enter that mysterious permanence.

—Julie Miller

FULTON, Robin

Nationality: British. **Born:** Isle of Arran, Scotland, 6 May 1937. **Education:** Edinburgh University, M.A. 1959, Ph.D. 1972. **Career:** Schoolmaster in Scotland in the 1960s. From 1973 senior lecturer in English, Stavanger College, Norway. Editor, *Lines Review,* Edinburgh, 1967–76. **Awards:** Eric Gregory award, 1966; Edinburgh University writer's fellowship, 1969–71; Arts Council bursary, 1972; Swedish Authors' Fund bursary, 1973, 1976; Artur Lundkvist award, for translation, 1977; Swedish Academy award, for translation, 1978. **Address:** Postboks 467, N-4001 Stavanger, Norway.

PUBLICATIONS

Poetry

A Matter of Definition. Edinburgh, Giles Gordon, 1963.
Instances. Edinburgh, Macdonald, 1967.
Inventories. Thurso, Caithness Books, 1969.
The Spaces Between the Stones. New York, New Rivers Press, 1971.
Quarters. West Linton, Peeblesshire, Castlelaw Press, 1971.
The Man with the Surbahar. Edinburgh, Macdonald, 1971.
Tree-Lines. New York, New Rivers Press, 1974.
Music and Flight. Knotting, Bedfordshire, Sceptre Press, 1975.
Between Flights: Eighteen Poems. Egham, Surrey, Interim Press, 1976.
Places to Stay In. Knotting, Bedfordshire, Sceptre Press, 1978.
Following a Mirror. London, Oasis, 1980.
Selected Poems 1963–1978. Edinburgh, Macdonald, 1980.
Fields of Focus. London, Anvil Press Poetry, 1982.
Coming Down to Earth and Spring Is Soon. Plymouth, Devon, Shearsman. 1990.

Other

Contemporary Scottish Poetry: Individuals and Context. Edinburgh, Macdonald, 1974.
The Way Words Are Taken: Selected Essays. Edinburgh, Macdonald. 1989.

Editor, *Trio: New Poets from Edinburgh.* New York, New Rivers Press, 1971.
Editor, *Selected Poems 1955–1980,* by Iain Crichton Smith. Edinburgh, Macdonald, 1982.
Editor, *Complete Poetical Works,* by Robert Garioch. Edinburgh, Macdonald, 1983.
Editor, *A Garioch Miscellany: Selected Prose and Letters,* by Robert Garioch. Edinburgh, Macdonald, 1986.

Translator, *An Italian Quartet: Versions after Saba, Ungaretti, Montale, Quasimodo.* London, Alan Ross, 1966.
Translator, *Blok's Twelve.* Preston, Lancashire, Akros, 1968.
Translator, *Selected Poems,* by Lars Gustafsson. New York, New Rivers Press, 1972.
Translator, *Five Swedish Poets.* South Orange, New Jersey, Seton Hall University Press, 1972.
Translator, *They Killed Sitting Bull and Other Poems,* by Gunnar Harding. London, London Magazine Editions, 1973.
Translator, *Selected Poems,* by Tomas Tranströmer. London, Penguin, 1974; augmented edition, Ann Arbor, Michigan, Ardis, 1980.
Translator, *Citoyens,* by Tomas Tranströmer. Rushden, Northamptonshire, Sceptre Press, 1974.
Translator, *The Hidden Music and Other Poems,* by Östen Sjöstrand. Cambridge, Oleander Press, 1975.
Translator, *Selected Poems,* by Werner Aspenström. London, Oasis, 1976.
Translator, *Mary Poppins and Myth,* by Staffan Bergsten. Stockhom, Almqvist & Wiksell, 1978.
Translator, *How the Late Autumn Night Novel Begins,* by Tomas Tranströmer. Knotting, Bedfordshire, Sceptre Press, 1980.
Translator, *Baltics,* by Tomas Tranströmer. London, Oasis, 1980.

Translator, *Family Tree: Thirteen Prose Poems,* by Johannes Edfelt. London, Oasis, 1981.
Translator, *The Blue Whale and Other Prose Pieces,* by Werner Aspenström. London, Oasis, 1981.
Translator, *Starnberger See,* by Gunnar Harding. London, Oasis, 1983.
Translator, *The Wild Square,* by Tomas Tranströmer. London, Oasis, 1984.
Translator, *The Truth Barrier,* by Tomas Tranströmer. London, Oasis, 1984.
Translator, *Béla Bartók Against the Third Reich,* by Kjell Espmark. Stockholm, Norstedts, and London, Oasis, 1985.
Translator, with James Greene and Siv Hennum, *Don't Give Me the Whole Truth: Selected Poems,* by Olav Hauge. London, Anvil Press Poetry, 1985; Buffalo, New York, White Pine Press, 1990.
Translator, *Collected Poems,* by Tomas Tranströmer. Newcastle upon Tyne, Bloodaxe, 1987.
Translator, with others, *Selected Poems 1954–1986,* by Tomas Tranströmer, edited by Robert Hass. New York, Ecco Press, 1987.
Translator, *German Autumn,* by Stig Dagerman. London, Quartet, 1988.
Translator, with others, *The Stillness of the World Before Bach: New Selected Poems,* by Lars Gustafsson, edited by Christopher Middleton. New York, New Directions, 1988.
Translator, with others, *Toward the Solitary Star: Selected Poetry and Prose,* by Osten Sjöstrand, edited by Steven P. Sondrup. Provo, Utah, Brigham Young University, 1988.
Translator, *Guest of Reality,* by Par Lagerkvist. London, Quartet, 1989.
Translator, *Four Swedish Poets: Tranströmer, Ström, Sjögren, Espmark.* Buffalo, New York, White Pine Press, 1990.
Translator, *Selected Poems,* by Olav Hauge. Buffalo, New York, White Pine Press, 1990.
Translator, *One Summer Night in Sweden,* radio-play by Erland Josephson, produced BBC, 1990.
Translator, *Stone-Shadows,* by Hermann Starheimster. Oslo, Norway, Det Norske Samlaget, 1991.
Translator, *Five Swedish Poets: Kjell Espmark, Lennart Sjögren, Eva Ström, Staffan Söderblom, Werner Aspenström.* Norwich, Norvik Press, 1997.
Translator, *New Collected Poems,* by Tomas Tranströmer. Newcastle upon Tyne, Bloodaxe, and Chester Springs, Pennsylvania, Dufour Editions, 1997.
Translator, *Sorgegondolen: The Sorrow Gondola,* by Tomas Tranströmer. Dublin, Dedalus Press, 1997.

*

Critical Studies: By Colin Donati, in *Lines Review* (Edinburgh), 115, Decemeber 1990; by Mario Relich, in *The Scottish Poetry Library Newsletter* (Edinburgh), 21, July 1993; by Richard Price in *Lines Review* (Edinburgh), 131, December 1994.

*   *   *

Robin Fulton was a fastidious craftsman early in his profession as poet, the craftsmanship showing itself not in conventional verse forms but in the controlled response to the exacting objectives of his art. In ''A Lifework'' he writes,

to say what you mean is hazardous
to sort out and plainly describe
one mere subdivision
of a minor species takes more
than a home made poet with a simple lens.

At his simplest he is a meticulous observer, and in the poem of this title, ''A Meticulous Observer,'' he writes,

he watched the boys with almost pre-
hensile feet on high walls
where they risked their short lives
for reasons no-one else would appreciate

he watched girls with newly-shaped
bodies advertising themselves
without guile in the summery light
and without needing a reason to guide them

The reader is not permitted to participate in the physical sensations of these just and sensitive recordings of physiological facts. To Fulton all is seen in the mind's eye. In the progression of his poetry he uses meticulous observations as means of going beyond them, much as he can use a light, witty touch as an entry to the area of humane concern, as in ''Forecast for a Quiet Night'':

By dawn too a generation of mice
will have been sniped by a night-shift of owls
working separately and almost in silence

and the mild local disturbance behind the eyes
of the invalid
will have been noted by the next of kin.

Fulton's detached, inquisitorial mind allows him to make a critical scrutiny of events that generally have evoked passionate rhetoric from poets. He reports the Vietnam War as seen on the television screen:

the images are true because the actors are bad
the president knows how to raise an eyebrow and smile
but his victim burns clumsily unconvincingly

Fulton observes the reversal of natural expectation and leaves the reader with the questions, Where is truth and where is reality? The danger of this clinical approach is that the natural free response to the actual is inhibited, but Fulton's detachment does not go as far as aloofness. In his verse he puts his own self under inspection, and on his settling in Norway his poetry came to reflect the change in the

symbolic statements the landscape made to him. In ''In Memorian Antonius Blok,'' which is charged with memories of Bergman's *The Seventh Seal,* the Swedish scene is both threatening and beautiful:

Perched like ornaments on dim shelves
owls wait for the bewildering sky to darken
and from the wood's edge you can see the birches
silver and standing at ease before the shadowy
straight ranks . . .

The wood is also identified as Dante's, and, like Dante at the beginning of the *Inferno,* Fulton is in middle age:

It has taken you half a lifetime to reach
an understanding with the black shadow of the pine.
In the middle of life the dark wood darkens.

Fulton's poems have increasingly become concerned with identifying an elusive self that is nearly always on a journey. As early as 1976, in ''Visingo'' (*Between Flights*), he images his precariousness:

Like a blind man I hold on to railings
and
. . . my mind gropes for the next wet stepping stone.

In 1982, in ''Museums and Journeys'' (*Fields of Focus*), he says,

Our view of the present is clear
but the landscapes go on sliding past

The risk of preoccupation with the self is the loss of the independent object, but in his 1991 collection *Coming Down to Earth and Spring Is Soon* Fulton counterpoises his subjective perception with ''the . . . living wood'' of the tree outside his bedroom:

On good nights I saw
my hands young middle-
aged and old at once.
The still-living wood
of the sycamore that creaked
nursed me back to sleep.

His refining definitions are given new life by allowing the play of sensation that comes from ''creaked,'' hinting at the substantiality of the tree and its continuing life. Although Fulton never deserted images from nature, earlier having used them in a light, witty way, the deepening tone of certain of his poems is now matched by their warmth.

—George Bruce

G

GALLAGHER, Tess

Nationality: American. **Born:** Tess Bond, Port Angeles, Washington, 21 July 1943. **Education:** University of Washington, Seattle, B.A. 1963, M.A. 1970; University of Iowa, Iowa City, M.F.A. 1974. **Family:** Married 1) Lawrence Gallagher in 1963 (divorced 1968); 2) Michael Burkard in 1973 (divorced 1977); 3) the writer Raymond Carver in 1988 (companion 1979–88; died 1988). **Career:** Instructor, St. Lawrence University, Canton, New York, 1974–75; assistant professor, Kirkland College, Clinton, New York, 1975–77; visiting lecturer, University of Montana, Missoula, 1977–78; assistant professor, University of Arizona, Tucson, 1978–80; professor of English, Syracuse University, New York, 1980–90. Visiting fellow, Willamette University, Salem, Oregon, 1981. Taught inner-city high school and college students, Trinity College, Hartford, Connecticut, 1993. Since 1992 instructor of poetry aboard the *Crusader,* Seattle Resource Institute Seminars Afloat. Participant, London International Poetry Festival and European Poetry Festival, Sibiu, Romania, 1992. **Awards:** Creative Artists Public Service grant, 1976; Elliston award, 1976; National Endowment for the Arts grant, 1977, 1981, 1987; Guggenheim fellowship, 1978; *American Poetry Review* award, 1981; Washington State Governor's award 1984, 1986, 1987, 1993; New York State Arts grant, 1988; Maxime Cushing Gray Foundation award, 1990; American Library Association's Most Notable Book List, 1993; Lyndhurst prize, 1993–95. **Address:** Sky House, 119 Vista Lane, Port Angeles, Washington 98363, U.S.A.

PUBLICATIONS

Poetry

Stepping Outside. Lisbon, Iowa, Penumbra Press, 1974.
Instructions to the Double. Port Townsend, Washington, Graywolf Press, 1976.
Under Stars. Port Townsend, Washington, Graywolf Press, 1978.
Portable Kisses. Seattle, Sea Pen Press, 1978.
On Your Own. Port Townsend, Washington, Graywolf Press, 1978.
Willingly. Port Townsend, Washington, Graywolf Press, 1984.
Amplitude: New and Selected Poems. St. Paul, Minnesota, Graywolf Press. 1987.
Portable Kisses: Love Poems. Santa Barbara, California, Capra Press, 1992.
Moon Crossing Bridge. St. Paul, Minnesota, Graywolf Press, 1992.
Portable Kisses Expanded. Santa Barbara, California, Capra Press, 1994.
My Black Horse: New & Selected Poems. Newcastle upon Tyne, Bloodaxe, 1995.

Recordings: *Some with Wings, Some with Manes,* Watershed, 1982; *Lunch Poems, Tess Gallagher, 10/30/97,* University of California, Berkeley, 1997.

Plays

Screenplay: *The Night Belongs to the Police,* 1982; *Dostoevsky,* with Raymond Carver, Santa Barbara, California, Capra Press, 1985.

Television Play: *The Wheel,* 1970.

Short Stories

The Lover of Horses and Other Stories. New York, Harper, 1986; London, Hamish Hamilton, 1989.

Other

A Concert of Tenses: Essays on Poetry. Ann Arbor, University of Michigan Press, 1986.
At the Owl Woman Saloon. New York, Scribner, 1997.

Editor, *A Guide to Forgetting,* by Jeffrey Skinner. St. Paul, Minnesota, Graywolf Press, 1988.

*

Critical Studies: Reviews by Hayden Carruth in *Harper's* (New York), April 1979, and Peter Davison, in *Atlantic Monthly* (New York), May 1979; interview in *Ironwood* (Tucson), October 1979; by Harold Schweizer, in *CEA Critic* (Lewisburg, Pennsylvania), 1987; by William Doreski, in *Harvard Review* (Cambridge, Massachusetts), November 1992; "To Speak Aloud at a Grave" by Jeanne Heuving, in *Northwest Review* (Eugene, Oregon), 32(1), 1994; *Tess Gallagher* by Ron McFarland, Boise, Idaho, Boise State University, 1995; "On Disproportion" by Tony Hoagland, in *Poets Teaching Poets: Self and the World,* edited by Gregory Orr and Ellen Bryant Voigt, Ann Arbor, University of Michigan Press, 1996.

Tess Gallagher comments:

When I was a young girl salmon fishing with my father in the Strait of Juan de Fuca in Washington State, I used to lean out over the water and try to look past my own face, past the reflection of the boat, past the sun and the darkness, down to where the fish were surely swimming. I made up charm songs and word hopes to tempt the fish, to cause them to mean biting my hook. I believed they would do it if I asked them well and patiently enough and with the right hope. I am writing my poems like this. I have used the fabric and the people of my life as the bait. More and more I have learned how to speak for the others, the ones who do not speak in poetry, though their lives are of it. What do I write about? The murder of my uncle by thieves in the night, the psychic death of my husband in the Vietnam War, walking through Belfast in 1976, a horse with snow on its back circling a house where the dancers have fallen to the floor by daybreak. I have wanted the words to go deep. I have wanted music and passion and human tenderness in the poems. Intelligence and loss. Only in the language I have made for myself in the poems am I in touch with all the past, present, and future moments of my consciousness. The poem is the moment of all possibilities, where I try to speak in a concert of tenses. I do not want to disappear into the present tense, the awful now. I want to survive it and take others with me. I am more concerned about the kind of writing that allows "with" than I was in the beginning. Not just "to" or "for" or "at." The Irish have no word for "mine" or for "wife," only "he or she who goes along with me." My poetry. I cannot say that. Only "that which goes along with me."

(1990) I am presently feeling American poetry suffers from too much light and am concentrating on a certain density that allows mystery without making the poem too obscure. For instruction I am thinking a lot about Emily Dickinson and John Donne and Lorca, learning ghost songs from the Irish, oriental folktales, reading books about our relationship through history to horses (a preoccupation), pursuing friendships with "pattern painters" in Seattle, and living more consistently near the Strait of Juan de Fuca, where I was born at Port Angeles, Washington.

(1995) In *Moon Crossing Bridge* I attempted to create a psychic and emotional space in language that had not perhaps existed formerly toward the subject of mourning and grief in American heterosexual love poetry. In Roland Barthes's terms, which indicate that while pleasure may be spoken bliss may not, I have been engaged in writing the "untenable text" that occurs in the silent space between what is actually said. The density of language and image have hopefully extended areas of thought and feeling, partly through transgressional means of taking on subject matter formerly forbidden, as in poems such as "Red Poppy," "Wake," and "I Don't Know You," among others, poems that attempt to renegotiate temporal and spiritual dimensions. I consider *MCB* my best book to date, although several of the poems in *Portable Kisses* (1992, Capra Press) could actually stand within *MCB,* such as "Black Violets," "Anatomy of a Kiss," "Black Pearl," "White Kiss," and 'Like the Sigh of Women's Hair." *Portable Kisses Expanded* (1994, Capra) continues the lyrical assuagement, postmourning, that I began in the 1992 edition, developing wit and irony in the persona of the "Kiss." My present poetic involvement, besides poems for my next volume, involves the translation of the Romanian poet Liliana Ursu's book *The Sky behind the Forest,* translated with Adam Sorkin and the author. From 1991 to 1993 I worked on the film *Short Cuts* with Robert Altman, using nine stories by my late husband, Raymond Carver. I have now entered a period of concentration on the short story during the very welcome Lyndhurst grant that has allowed me time to return to this form I rediscovered during my time with Raymond Carver. I am writing toward the proverb "If you contemplate revenge, dig two graves." I hope to complete the volume by 1996 before I return to my teaching, this time at Whitman College in Walla Walla, Washington.

*   *   *

Born in the Pacific Northwest, the oldest of five children of a logger turned longshoreman, Tess Gallagher was a member of the last class taught by Theodore Roethke at the University of Washington and was also a student there of David Wagoner. This is not to say that her work bears much resemblance to theirs beyond great vitality and an obsessive desire to make words count.

Instructions to the Double is full of doubles of two sorts: people with whom the speaker closely identifies—father, mother, uncle, husband—and likenesses—reflections in a mirror, water or eyes, resemblances, shadows, ghosts, photographs. Whichever the kind, the poems that disappoint are those whose subjects remain generalized, such as "When You Speak to Me," "The Perfect Sky," and "Instructions to the Double." The most successful are concrete, rooted in intimate and intimately felt family experience: "Two

Stories," about an uncle murdered by thieves, "Coming Home," "The Woman Who Raised Goats," "Black Money," and "Time Lapse with Tulips." This last is one of Gallagher's best; it brilliantly considers and rejects illusion and fixes on reality. The wedding photograph that is the occasion for the poem is illusory in at least two senses: a photographic image is an illusion, and the particular image "preserves / a symmetry of doubt with us / at the center." The poem has its own symmetry of statement. The first stanza retrospectively denies the impact of a marital kiss and the prospects of living in connubial bliss into old age. The second stanza denies the assumption that tulips will be accepted by the bride, while the third voices the uncertainties of the wedding guests, the "symmetry of doubt." The turn suggested in stanza two ("But they are wrong") is declared at the beginning of stanza four: "Whatever the picture says, it is wrong." The real picture is something more certain. Instead of what the photograph portrayed—passion suppressed—is passion ready to be released, passion comprehending love and death:

> Inside, the rare bone of my hand and that harp
> seen through a window suddenly so tempting
>
> you must rush into that closed room, you must
> tear your fingers across it.

Symmetry and harmony are about to be achieved.

After *Instructions to the Double, Under Stars* is a letdown. The first half of the book, "The Ireland Poems," derives from Gallagher's travels in Ireland in 1976. A traveler's impressions, even those of a sensitive poet with ethnic affinities for the land visited, almost inevitably disappoint. After reading Seamus Heaney, say, with his profoundly apprehended vision of the Irelands, one is tempted to characterize Gallagher's poems, especially "Disappearances in the Guarded Sector" and "The Ballad of Ballymote," with their eternal notes of sadness, as simply more news from that unhappy land. The second half of the book, "Start Again Somewhere," is not so much a second start as a return to subjects explored in *Instructions to the Double,* as in "My Mother Remembers That She Was Beautiful." Yet even these less successful poems indicate that Gallagher has a strong voice—passionate, elegant, passionate, painstaking.

Willingly, the next major book after *Under Stars,* is much better. Dedicated to Raymond Carver, with whom she lived from 1979 and whom she married six weeks before his death in 1988 from cancer, it is full of the passion of a highly successful love affair between artists. In the several poems to Carver, various in their subject matter, we get a clear picture of an admirable man, as in "I Save Your Coat, But You Lose It Later," "Skylights," "The Hug," and "Each Bird Walking." Other poems are to Gallagher's father—"Boat Ride," "Accomplishment," and "Candle, Lamp, Firefly." There are also four fine poems to horses—"From Dread in the Eyes of Horses," "Death of the Horses by Fire," "The Cloudy Shoulders of the Horses," and "Legacy." They capture the mysteriousness of that noble beast, so much desired by her maternal Cherokee grandfather, who wanted more horses, as Gallagher tells us in "If Poetry Were Not a Morality," the first of the new poems in *Amplitude.* "Bonfire," another new poem from *Amplitude,* is about Carver and ends with the doctor's news, which "flushed us through with dread." When the dying Carver is thrown into her arms, the poet is reminded of a violin:

> It wasn't for music
>   you came to me, but

for daring—mine and yours.
When they have to, they will write in the Book
   of Welcome:
                  Two darings, two darlings.

The last two words may seem at first reading merely cutesy, but on later readings they seem daring.

The title *Amplitude* is either a bit presumptuous (*The American Heritage Dictionary* defines ''amplitude'' as (1) ''greatness of size; magnitude;'' (2) ''fullness; copiousness;'' and (3) ''breadth of range, as of intelligence'') or ironical. The book is indeed copious and varied, but it is not great of size or magnitude.

Gallagher's relationship with Carver again foregrounds her collection *Moon Crossing Bridge,* which she dedicates to her late husband. Some of the poems in the book move primarily on the strength and depth of the subject behind them instead of on what shows through. When she addresses the ambiguities and paradoxes of the survivor's life, her poems find success. ''My love's early death has scraped away my future,'' and yet life persists, even as it becomes a ''chaotic laboratory of broken approaches.'' Some of the poems work by bringing the power of remembering and the peril of grief into the study of ordinary moments and objects: ''Some griefs are sent / only to haunt.'' One of the collection's most powerful poems is ''Wake,'' which claims, ''We were dead / a little while together then, serene / and afloat on the strange broad canopy / of the abandoned world.''

Twenty-three new poems, plus the entire contents of *Moon Crossing Bridge,* are included in *My Black Horse: New & Selected Poems.* Dedicated to her mother and Carver, the volume is introduced by an essay of the poet's, titled ''My Father's Love Letters,'' in which she accounts for her parents, her childhood, and the possible origins of her life as a writer. She cites Louise Bogan as an example of her idea ''that important time junctures of past with present events via memory, with actual presences, are always inviting new meanings, revisions of old meanings, and speculation about things still in the future.''

In this spirit the poems in the collection confirm Gallagher's growing interest in attaining metaphors for the most complex and immutable thoughts. The later poems in the collection illustrate the difficulty of this endcavor; in trying to speak of the unspeakable, expression can lose its potency and intelligibility.

Gallagher's true strength is storytelling, and the best poems in *My Black Horse* demonstrate this strength. A fishing boat on a lake serves as the setting of ''Boat Ride,'' a lengthy tribute (some two hundred lines long) to both the poet's father and ''good memory, if you are such a boat.'' ''Black Silk,'' a poem that exposes a daughter's apathy toward her mother after her father's death, is one of the collection's best and works off of one of Gallagher's enduring traits, that of finding simplicity and truth amidst the archetypal.

—James K. Robinson and Martha Sutro

GALVIN, Brendan

Nationality: American. **Born:** Everett, Massachusetts, 20 October 1938. **Education:** Malden Catholic High School; Boston College, 1956–60, B.S. in natural sciences 1960; Northeastern University, Boston, 1962–64, M.A. in English 1964; University of Massachusetts, Amherst, 1965–70, M.F.A. 1967, Ph.D. in English 1970. **Family:** Married Ellen Baer in 1968; one son and two daughters. **Career:** Instructor in English, Northeastern University, 1964–65; assistant professor of English, Slippery Rock State College, Pennsylvania, 1968–69. Assistant professor, 1969–74, associate professor, 1974–80, and since 1980 professor of English, Central Connecticut State University, New Britain. Visiting professor, Connecticut College, New London, 1975–76; Coal Royalty Chairholder in Creative Writing, University of Alabama, Tuscaloosa, spring 1993. Since 1981 editor, with George Garrett, *Poultry: A Magazine of Voice,* Truro, Massachusetts. Founder and director, Connecticut Writers Conference. **Awards:** Fine Arts Work Center fellowship, 1971; National Endowment for the Arts fellowship, 1974, 1988; Artists' Foundation grant, 1978; Connecticut Commission on the Arts fellowship, 1981, 1984; Guggenheim Fellowship, 1988; Sotheby prize, Arvon International Foundation, 1988; Levinson prize, *Poetry* (Chicago) magazine, 1989; O B Hardison Jr. Poetry prize, Folger Shakespeare Library, 1991; Charity Randall Citation, International Poetry Forum, 1994. **Address:** P.O. Box 54, Durham, Connecticut 06422, U.S.A.

PUBLICATIONS

Poetry

The Narrow Land. Boston, Northeastern University Press, 1971.
The Salt Farm. Fredericton, New Brunswick, Fiddlehead, 1972.
No Time for Good Reasons. Pittsburgh, University of Pittsburgh Press, 1974.
The Minutes No One Owns. Pittsburgh, University of Pittsburgh Press, 1977.
Atlantic Flyway. Athens, University of Georgia Press, 1980.
Winter Oysters. Athens, University of Georgia Press, 1983.
A Birder's Dozen. Bristol, Rhode Island, Ampersand Press, 1984.
Seals in the Inner Harbor. Pittsburgh, Carnegie-Mellon University Press, 1985.
Wampanoag Traveler. Baton Rouge, Louisiana State University Press, 1989.
Raising Irish Walls. Bristol, Rhode Island, Ampersand Press, 1989.
Great Blue: New and Selected Poems. Champaign, University of Illinois Press, 1990.
Early Returns. Pittsburgh, Pennsylvania, Carnegie Mellon University Press, 1992.
Saints in their Ox-Hide Boat. Baton Rouge, Louisiana State University, 1992.
Islands. Tuscaloosa, Alabama, Druid Press, 1993.
Sky and Island Light: Poems. Baton Rouge, Louisiana State University Press, 1996.
Hotel Malabar: A Narrative Poem. Iowa City, University of Iowa Press, 1998.
The Strength of a Named Thing: Poems. Baton Rouge, Louisiana State University Press, 1999.

Play

Screenplay: *Massachusetts Story,* 1978.

*

Critical Studies: Article in *American Poets Since World War II* edited by Donald J. Greiner, Detroit, Gale, 1980, and ''This Business of Getting the World Right: The Poetry of Brendan Galvin,'' in *Three Rivers Poetry Journal 19–20* (Pittsburgh), 1982, both by George Garrett; by Philip Jason, in *Critical Survey of Poetry* edited by Frank N. Magill, Englewood Cliffs, New Jersey, Salem Press, 1982; ''Galvin's Outer Reaches'' by Peter Makuck, in *Texas Review* (Huntsville, Texas), 8(3–4), 1987; ''Singing What's out There'' by Mary Calahan, in *Boston College Magazine,* winter 1988; *Outer Life: The Poetry of Brendan Galvin,* edited by Martha Christina, Bristol, Rhode Island, Ampersand Press, 1991; ''The Masked Muse'' by David Barber, in *Parnassus,* 17(2), 18(1), 1992; by Philip Paradis, in *Prairie Schooner,* 67(1), spring 1993.

Brendan Galvin comments:

Critics have noted a rural-urban conflict in my work, where Cape Cod and its austere landscape, and particularly its bird life, are seen in positive terms and cities are seen as destructive to the possibility of community. Where rural and urban themes overlap, the poems sometimes point up how development and ''city values'' corrupt the environment. I have also been identified as having a quick sense of the comic, of having my attention always on the rhythm of the experience at hand, of having language and imagery always organically functional in the immediate scene and emotion. For better or worse, my poems are often compared with those of Theodore Roethke, D.H. Lawrence, Frost, William Stafford, James Dickey, and James Wright. The main thrust of my work is topical, and I tend to use catalogues, reveal my subjects immediately, and try to leave plenty of clues that will admit the reader without straining his credibility. ''Clarity'' is a key word here, and I abhor much of the recent neosurrealist verse. Trained in the natural sciences originally, I have tried to maintain accurate scientific description as much as possible, and the psychic center of my work continues to be Cape Cod, where I live part of each year and which is the ''natural bed'' out of which my poems grow. The journey motif is also strong in much of my work, and recently I have been experimenting with voices other than my own in narrative poems, trying to extend my range into longer poems.

*   *   *

''There are times when you see / farthest,'' to the ''outskirts / of awareness,'' writes Brendan Galvin in ''Those Times,'' from *Seals in the Inner Harbor,* and the poet, as in the poem ''The Mockingbird,'' ''must bring it all back / alive as the repertoire / of [his] inner ear . . . to someone awake on the outskirts . . .''

Short-lined, crowding the left margin, Galvin's poems speak the rich vocabulary of an authentic New England voice, puritanism mixing with sensuality under the watchful eye of irony, sometimes spiked with a dry sense of humor. Galvin's poems tend to be located on Cape Cod, where he has a home, and he is at his best giving witness to the abundance of nature that he sharply and shrewdly observes there. In the varied lives of birds, trees, raccoons, vegetables, oysters, and scallops Galvin finds metaphors for the human condition.

Birds hold a special affinity for Galvin. He knows birds in great detail—their habits, movements, markings—and his work is studded with fine passages about them. Associating birds with the freedom of instinct and the mystery of the life force, Galvin writes about them with wonder, as in ''The Birds,'' from *Atlantic Flyway:*

Seeing them corner above fields,
black stars across the morning,
sometimes you'd gladly relinquish
weight of your self-possession
to hover three feet from anything
and be classified rare-to-occasional . . .

The presence of birds is almost always salutary, leading Galvin's reader to the ''outskirts / of awareness'' and often to a renewed sense of priorities, a process that—Thoreau-like—may take place in one's backyard. Addressing an owl, for instance, Galvin observes, ''you drag me / home to the poetry under my nose.'' In ''The Migrants'' a man turns from trivial conversation to recall that the birds ''would be coming on'': ''Thinking of them, he thought how a man / / can turn back to the world of men, as though / the blue book of fall had opened in his hands.'' Similarly, the great blue heron of the title poem of Galvin's *Great Blue: New and Selected Poems* becomes totemic; it is guide, protector, and condition to be aspired to:

Reason, that chain-store item,
can deny this forever, but that bird
shadows us, at key moments is there,
its gumped-up look guarding justice,
longevity, the journey
of the good and diligent soul.

It is appropriate that Galvin choose the shy, ''gumped-up'' heron as his totem, for, ''loving / the nerve of a common place / that's holy,'' he locates many of his poems in such out-of-the-way places as marshes, fields, dumps, compost heaps, and tidal pools, noticing in their myriad changing forms and systems the constant surge of life, ''the urgency / we can't explain.'' ''On the still life of the mulch'' in ''A Triptych for Snowlight,'' for instance, ''sun ignites citrus and apple skins,'' readying them to burst forth into new life. Like the naturalist Henry Beston, Galvin reads ''in de-creation / creation's pretext.'' In a number of the poems, admiring ''an economy I don't understand,'' Galvin comes close to the Whitman of ''This Compost'' in his affirmation of reincorporation. Life lived out contributes to new life, as in ''Transmigration,'' where a newly ''changed'' soul begins ''to see from above / how a breeze / ignites marsh grass every-which-way / to new greens . . .''

One way of seeking to comprehend these processes is by approaching them in reverse, and Galvin occasionally uses a technique analogous to reverse-motion photography, forcing the reader to imagine backwards from effect to cause. Thus, in ''Fall Squashes'' the final squash of the season prompts Galvin to reflect back to leaf, to vine, and finally ''to the flat seed / with its journey packed in, / as deep as anything.'' In ''Glass'' the flight of a warbler into a window provokes a meditation upon how ''in our last seconds, / we are swung round / to live ourselves back through each particular'':

whole snows lifting skyward
becoming autumn leaves lifting
back into green trees,
the dead stepping out of
crumbling loam,

at the last, seed and egg
unraveling, falling away.

The natural world is to be observed, learned from, its lessons appropriated to the sphere of human activities. Galvin writes with similar acumen about small town and family life, the thrill of early romance, and the hardscrabble lives of the working class. He shows particular insight into childhood, as in ''A Green Evening,'' which employs the pattern of reversal noted above to strip away layers of complex experience as the speaker attempts to reexperience a particular evening from his childhood, realizing that he would have to

> . . . be able to erase
> acres of asphalt slots
> until scrub pine
> reappeared, and the ancient clock
> in an Esso station window,
>
> to hold that central moment,
> green and unbreakable, until
> this fraying twist comes undone
> and that evening
> spreads everywhere, and I follow
> the others over that fence
> into the orchard again.

Wampanoag Traveler, drawing upon the surviving correspondence of the eighteenth-century American natural historian Loranzo Newcomb, extends Galvin's range, providing an innovative framework upon which to exercise his interest in biology and human character as well as his facility for unusual words. Newcomb's dispatches to Europe regarding his discoveries in the New World (''pilfering / this New World for the Old'') are always passionate, by turns boastful, humorous, and often breathtakingly lyrical, as in his evocation of an apple that, he writes, he ''robbed of such wine / the northern lights swam in my eyes.'' The poems of this sequence are among Galvin's most generous, and Newcomb's concerns and self-revelations seem remarkably close to Galvin's own. Newcomb's reasons for gardening, for instance, resemble those of Galvin's for writing:

> For the surety
> of plenty, or the images such growth
> alone provides, or because I do better
> with vegetable kind than human,
> no easy admission . . .

Clearly ''gaffed by the hook'' of Cape Cod but not confined to it, Galvin writes intelligent, well-crafted poems. Convinced of the amplitude of this world, which ''sends from its least places . . . a heron flying in, just blue enough / to be separate from fog,'' Galvin has a voice that serves as a bracing tonic for these commercialized, overstimulated, ecologically troubled times.

—Robert Gaspar

GALVIN, Patrick (Joseph)

Nationality: Irish. **Born:** Cork in 1927. **Military Service:** Royal Air Force, 1940; French Foreign Legion, 1945. **Family:** Married Diana Ferrier; two sons. **Career:** Bookseller, 1947; war correspondent in Korea in the 1950s; ballad singer in England and the United States, 1955–60; film critic, 1961; editor, Tone Press, Brighton, Sussex, 1972–74; resident dramatist, Lyric Theatre, Belfast, 1974–77; writer-in-residence, West Midlands Arts Association, 1979–80. **Awards:** Leverhulme fellowship, 1974–76. **Address:** c/o Patrick Newley, 46 Arthur Court, London SW11 5JA, England.

PUBLICATIONS

Poetry

Heart of Grace. London, Linden Press, 1957.
Christ in London. London, Linden Press, 1960.
Two Summers, Parts 1–3. Brighton, Sussex, Unicorn, 1970.
On the Murder of David Gleeson, Bailiff and Citizen of This Parish. Brighton, Sussex, Tone Press, 1971.
By Nature Diffident. Brighton, Tone Press, 1971.
Lon Chaney. Brighton, Unicorn, 1971(?).
The Woodburners. Dublin, New Writers Press, 1973.
Man on the Porch. London, Martin Brian and O'Keeffe, 1980.
Collected Poems and Letters. Cork, University of Cork, 1985.
Let the Seahorse Take Me Home and Other Poems. London, Martin Brian and O'Keeffe, 1986.
Folk Tales for the General. Dublin, Raven Arts Press, 1989.
The Madwoman of Cork: Poems. Cork City, The Three Spires, 1991.
New and Selected Poems of Patrick Galvin, edited by Greg Delanty and Robert Welch. Cork, Cork University Press, 1996.

Recordings: *Irish Humour [Drinking, Love, Street] Songs,* Riverside, 4 discs, 1960; *The Madwoman of Cork: Poems,* 1960–1980 Audio Arts, 1980.

Plays

And Him Stretched (produced Dublin, 1960; London, 1961).
Cry the Believers (produced Dublin and London, 1961).
Nightfall to Belfast (produced Belfast, 1973). Included in *Three Plays,* 1976.
The Last Burning (produced Belfast, 1974). Included in *Three Plays,* 1976.
We Do It for Love (produced Belfast, London, and New York, 1976). Included in *Three Plays,* 1976.
Three Plays (includes *The Last Burning, Nightfall to Belfast,* and *We Do It for Love*). Belfast, Threshold, 1976.
The Devil's Own People (produced Dublin, 1976).
Collected Plays and Letters. London, British Theatre Association Library of Plays, 1986.

Radio Plays: *City Childe Come Trailing Home,* 1985; *The Class of '39,* 1985.

Television Play: *Boy in the Smoke,* 1965.

Novels

Song for a Poor Boy: A Cork Childhood. Dublin, Raven Arts Press, 1990.
Song for a Raggy Boy: A Cork Boyhood. Dublin, Raven Arts Press, 1991.

Other

Irish Songs of Resistance. London, Workers' Music Association, 1955; New York, Folklore Press, 1956(?).
Letter to a British Soldier on Irish Soil. Highland Park, Michigan, Red Hanrahan Press, 1972.

Editor, *Beg to Report the Following "Good News from Ireland," As Expressed in a Letter from Ensign Jones.* Brighton, Sussex, Tone Press, 1971.

*

Bibliography: By Patrick Newley, Brighton, Tone Press, 1980.

Critical Studies: *The Poems of Patrick Galvin* by Sean Lucy, Cork, University of Cork, 1974; *Patrick Galvin and the Lady Devil* by Augustus Young, N.p., Lace Curtain Press, 1974; "Circles Radiating: The Poetry of Patrick Galvin" by Greg Delanty, in *Eire-Ireland* (St. Paul, Minnesota), 29(1), spring 1994.

*   *   *

With the exception of Brian Coffey, Patrick Galvin has plowed the loneliest furrow among the mid-twentieth-century Irish poets. His work is exceptionally eccentric and violent yet full of tender insights, especially when the persona of the poem is a woman. Only Paul Durcan has created a similar body of dramatic monologues. In many ways the success of the younger Durcan, his sheer audacity, has allowed us to appreciate the achievement of Galvin more clearly. "The Madwoman of Cork" is Galvin's best-known work:

Yesterday
In Castle Street
I saw two goblins at my feet
I saw a horse without a head
Carrying the dead
To the graveyard
Near Turner's Cross.

The poem contains all of the elements that have become recognizable as the Galvin style—a female narrator, a persecuted individual, a specific, named locale, a surreal event, and a simple, inconsistent rhyme scheme. The madwoman is only one of a group of lost souls who fall from the companionship of the dead to walk the streets. There also are the "stonemother" of "The Wood-Burners," Miss Cecily Finch, the aunt on All Souls' Night, Sister Mary, and the mother who washed linen. Despite the unreality of many events, Galvin makes his poems effective by using short lines, brief phrases, and a dry tone of voice. The tone is often that of translation. Galvin was undoubtedly influenced by the writing of Lorca, but more so— and at a crucial time—by the style of fellow Corkman Frank O'Connor. Poems like "The Bard" and "Lochan" have all the violent energy of an O'Connor translation:

I am Aideen without blessing
Since I tasted my own child
Should I live to see the morrow
Christ blind me and conceal my mouth.

Galvin has published many autobiographical essays under the byline "Rainbows in Evergreen" in the *Cork Examiner*. His prose can be as unreal and evasive as his poems, charting an interior world, a subjective geography of the past both lived and imagined. The prose works, like the plays written while he was the resident dramatist at Belfast's Lyric Theatre, amplify rather than clarify the effect of such autobiographical poems as "Plaisir D'Amour":

When summer came
My father left the house
He tied a ribbon in his hair
And wore a Kaftan dress,
My mother watched him walking down the street
"He'll break his neck in that," she said—
"As if I care."

Humor is the dynamo that powers much of Galvin's narrative. Sometimes he uses the humor of situation, its potential drama, to make a serious point. In "Advice to a Poet" and "Message to the Editor," for example, he uses the awkwardness of living with an ambitious elder and the awkwardness of writing in a coffin to convey attitudes about poetry: "And when I was finally removed / To the mortuary / I was abused by a medical student / Who couldn't open a bag of chips / Let alone the body of your greatest poet." In a review of Paul Durcan's *Teresa's Bar* in 1981, Galvin said that "a poet without humour is a poet without sense."

Drama has always been a crucial element in Galvin's work, creating a counterbalance to his constant drift into unreality. Drama depends upon character, and Galvin has shown how the theater can deepen a poet's humanity. The dramatic monologue has always been one of his strengths. "The Neglected Wife" and "By Nature Diffident" are perfect examples of untrustworthy sexual narrators. Theater teaches us that characters tell lies, and the drama arises in Galvin's poems because we do not trust the personae. But theater work also forces poets to communicate, and in his poems, as in his plays, Galvin communicates through humor, monologue, and music. His unique contribution to Irish poetry is a character-filled surrealism and a teeming life of working-class Cork, a life that sings and screams with the energy of Behan and Lorca.

—Thomas McCarthy

GANDER, (James) Forrest

Nationality: American. **Born:** James Forrest Cockerille (later changed by adoption to Gander), Barstow, California, 21 January 1956. **Education:** College of William and Mary, Williamsburg, Virginia, 1974–78, B.S. and B.A. 1978; San Francisco State University, California, 1980–81, M.A. 1981; Brown University, Providence, Rhode Island, 1983–84; Massachusetts Institute of Technology, Cambridge, 1984. **Family:** Married C.D. Wright in 1982; one son. **Career:** Special lecturer, Rhode Island School of Design, Providence, 1984–86; assistant professor, 1989, associate professor, 1993–95, and professor of English literature, 1996–98, Providence College, Rhode Island; since 1999 Briggs-Copeland fellow in poetry, Harvard University, Cambridge, Massachusetts. Visiting writer, the Burren School of Art, Ireland, 1996, Writer's Workshop, University of Iowa, Iowa City, 1997, and Brown University, Providence, Rhode Island,

1998–99. **Awards:** Yaddo fellowship, 1988; National Endowment for the Arts fellowship, 1989; Gertrude Stein Award in Innovative North American Poetry, 1993, 1997; Fund for Poetry award, 1994; Whiting Writer's award, 1997; Jessica Nobel Maxwell memorial prize, *American Poetry Review,* 1998. **Address:** 351 Nayatt Road, Barrington, Rhode Island 02806–4336, U.S.A.

PUBLICATIONS

Poetry

Rush to the Lake. Cambridge, Massachusetts, Alice James Books, 1988.

Eggplants and Lotus Root. Providence, Rhode Island, Burning Deck Press, 1991.

Lynchburg. Pittsburgh, University of Pittsburgh Press, 1993.

Deeds of Utmost Kindness. Middletown, Connecticut, Wesleyan University Press, 1994.

Science & Steepleflower. New York, New Directions, 1998.

Other

Editor and translator, *Mouth to Mouth: Poems by 12 Contemporary Mexican Women.* Minneapolis, Minnesota, Milkweed, 1993.

*

Forrest Gander comments:

> Face
> What lasts in thinking is not
> So much the way
> As its horizon, the plum side
> Not facing us but richer
> In contingency
>   a lateral
> Sheer rock face
> From which hiero-
> Glyphs wave what
> Lasts comes after
> The red flash
> The negative Commemoration outside of
> Syntax, human
> Recognition turned away
> From finally itself
>   to pinions one seed
> Junipers scree
> Blasted like rusty cans
> The prehistoric wind blinds
> Us with dust a cactus
> Spine goes through our shoe
> But we are bent
> Upon not that

*   *   *

Forrest Gander draws on all of the resources of language and contemporary poetic technique in his writing. He uses space on the page, gives close attention to detail, favors the striking image, and experiments with form, and his strategies range from the lyric to the narrative. The versatile and responsive style that results is perhaps his most important contribution to contemporary poetry.

The most experimental of Gander's works is his chapbook *Eggplants and Lotus Root,* which consists of five titled sections and a coda. Each section contains three poems—"Geometric Losses," "Violence's Narrative Continued," and "Meditative"—and each of the three poems maintains a similar form and subject matter across the sections. By creating these parallels, Gander forms a book in which the poems have a subtle and complex relationship to one another, similar to recurring themes in a musical composition or to the layering of paint in abstract art. Even his less obviously experimental collections are carefully organized so that, in addition to the strength of individual poems, the collection itself assumes significance.

No matter what the overall strategy, all of Gander's poems are filled with carefully observed detail, and although the speaker may preserve emotional distance from the subject, the poems are filled with visual close-ups, as in this example from "Life of Johnson upside Your Head": "Sweat washing all of them / night sweat, clothing soaked sterno sweat, blind / face glowing like a new shoe shine." When detail is in the service of narrative, the poems become small scenes, as in "The Man Who Wouldn't Pay His Dues." Other poems are like photographs, capturing moments of insight: "Suddenly I recognize / my own face / in the waitress's eye" ("breakfast, dinner"). "Soundtracks and Color Tints" is a list poem that is almost Whitmanesque in its range, while the poems that comprise "The Second Presence" are short and imagistic, reminiscent of haiku, as in this excerpt: "Woodpecker: a sound / Wobbling / The wet trunk around." Gander's poems occasionally wander before they focus, as if the true subject were the movement of the mind itself. "The Provinces of Saturn," for example, begins with the mention of blue paper and then proceeds through loosely related statements to its conclusion: "I am unmanned without you / In this inconstant dark." Gander is also capable of powerful lyrics, as in the title poem of *Rush to the Lake,* which describes a crowd's reaction to a drowning and ends with these lines:

> The impassive water
> has slipped her
> its cold tongue.
> The nuns hold back the children
> who are straining to the edge
> of their faith
> for the dead to be like the wonderful
> dead in stories.

His images dramatize the familiar: "He hurls his tenor past the moon / while the night goes pale as teeth" ("Parable in Wolves' Clothing").

Place and longing are important subjects throughout Gander's work, and both highlight a sense of displacement. *Rush to the Lake* contains many poems concerned with Japan and Japanese culture. *Lynchberg* takes a place-name as its title. *Deeds of Utmost Kindness* contains three sections—"Roasted Gingko," "Ozark Log," and "The Faculty for Hearing the Silence of Jesus"—of poems about travel or specific locations. The images and fragmented consciousness of "Figures of Travel" approximate the dislocation of being a tourist: "Corollary to the phenomenon of looking familiar to strangers: / the language which escapes you in one country haunts you in / another." Similar to travel, erotic longing can make the self seem both singular and transformed, and it appears to be allied with what threatens as well as with what satisfies: "Emptying itself of mouthlight / Mostly I am thinking about your body / Or your pubic hair twisting into a braid / / No ease from its molten glow, no music whatsoever" ("Prelude").

Gander uses whatever technique or form an individual poem calls for. What unites his varied stylistic devices is his precise and unsentimental eye.

—Kathleen Aguero

GARFITT, Roger

Nationality: British. **Born:** Melksham, Wiltshire, 12 April 1944. **Education:** Tiffin School, Kingston upon Thames, Surrey, 1955–62; Merton College, Oxford, 1963–68, B.A. (honors) 1968. **Family:** Married 1) Sylvia Jerden-Cooke (divorced 1971); 2) Priscilla Eckhard (divorced 1979); 3) the poet Frances Horovitz (died 1983); 4) Margaret Hawke. **Career:** Secretary, Oxford Community Workshop, 1969–70; English teacher, Ousedale School, Newport Pagnell, Buckinghamshire, 1970–71, and Bicester School, Oxfordshire, 1971–72; Arts Council Creative Writing Fellow, University College of North Wales, Bangor, 1975–77; writer-in-residence, Sunderland Polytechnic, Tyne and Wear, 1978–80; Northern Arts writer, Durham County Library, 1980; Welsh Arts Council poet-in-residence, Ebbw Vale, 1984; poet-in-residence, Monmouth Comprehensive School, 1986, and Pilgrim College, Boston, 1986–87; writer-in-residence, Blyth Valley Disabled Forum, 1992. Commissioned to write a poem on glass for new County Records and Research Centre, Shrewsbury, 1994; commissioned to write a long poem for the Web site of the Poetry Society, 1999; Arts Council commission for a poetry and jazz collaboration work with composer Nikki Iles, 1999. Member, Arts Council Literature Panel, 1986–90. Poetry critic, *London Magazine,* 1973–76; editor, *Poetry Review,* London, 1978–81. **Awards:** Guinness award, 1973; Eric Gregory award, 1974; Arts Council bursary, 1983, **Agent:** Jane Turnbull, 13 Wendell Road, London W12 9RS. **Address:** c/o Carcanet Press, 4th Floor, Conavon Court, 12–16 Blackfriars Street, Manchester M3 5BQ, England.

PUBLICATIONS

Poetry

Caught on Blue. Oxford, Carcanet, 1970.
West of Elm. Cheadle, Cheshire, Carcanet, 1974.
Wall, with others, edited by Noel Connor. Brampton, Cumbria, LYC Press, 1981.
Rowlstone Haiku, with Frances Horovitz and Alan Halsey. Madley, Herefordshire, Five Seasons Press, 1982.
The Broken Road. Newcastle upon Tyne, Northern House, 1982.
Given Ground. Manchester, Carcanet, 1989.
Border Songs. Stoke Prior, Herefordshire, Five Seasons Press, 1996.
Along the Line. Bishop's Castle, England, Community College, 1996.
Leaves at the World's Edge. Bishop's Castle, England, Community College, 1997.
The Path from the Year's Height. Bishop's Castle, England, Border Poets, 1999.
Selected Poems. Manchester, Carcanet, 2000.

Other

Travelling on Sunshine. Newcastle upon Tyne, Artists' Agency, 1996.

Editor, *Collected Poems,* by Frances Horovitz. Newcastle upon Tyne, Bloodaxe, 1985.

*

Roger Garfitt comments:

My early poems began as a direct response to landscape and especially to the play of light on a landscape. I tried to re-create in language the quality and intensity of that light. Recently I have become more interested in the landscapes as a register of the lives lived there and in particular the unacknowledged lives of the majority of us. History, as it has generally been written, is the business of kings and ministers, of manufacturers and merchants. If we look instead at the unwritten histories, at the lives of the working people, our perspective is completely changed. To write those unwritten histories is to unwrite the official histories.

*   *   *

It would be too easy to slip Roger Garfitt's poetry into place somewhere in the long tradition of English pastoral poetry and leave it at that. He can certainly write skillfully and feelingly of the countryside, of the world of cattle in "Spring Grazing"—"The bullocks back and churn in a mill by the gate / Their breath hangs in snarls in the unravelling mist. / They balk at the open field"—and he has a fine eye for the landscape of agriculture—"The harvest field shelved away, a bare shelf / set with a trap: white-rimmed stumps, pebbles and cracked soil" ("Out of a Clear Blue Sky")—or for the dunes and the sea—"Sand gathers grass. Mud grows samphire. / The seven silences of water / turn to the one silence of earth" ("Titchwell").

But the urban poems "Equinox," "Born 1940," and "The Hitch-Hiker" and the group of poems written for Shelter are all equally as well observed and as sensitively written. Can these two aspects of Garfitt's works be reconciled? Is there a common factor besides that of authorship? Indeed there is, and it is that most English of preoccupations, the seasons, the aspect of external nature that affects the lives of country and town dweller alike. The shorter poem written for Shelter titled "Spring Greens" illustrates this clearly when the climate is related to the keenest of urban images:

> Whiskers on the moss. Rust
> burns beneath the overflow. In the tenements
> the damp is changing seasons.
> And all the tins in Tesco's sharpen their colours

Here the movement of the seasons is as essential to the town dweller as to the cattle in "Spring Grazing." There is winter in the city—"Dropping over the roofs a husk of twilight / caught neatly up by magnesium fans / into circle and black"—or summer at Bablock Hyth—"Out of hours, the road is warm stone / a basking place beside the stream." The titles too reveal this essential pivot on which the world of Garfitt's poetry turns: "Winter Economy," "September Morning," and "Trees in City Winter" as well as the others already mentioned. It is the element in which we are all caught and involved, the climatic environment that shapes our lives, our moods, and our outlook.

Garfitt's poetry is quietly voiced. It eschews verbal fireworks but is the more effective for that, working gently as it does toward atmosphere and significance.

In his collection *Given Ground* a stronger expression of feeling can be detected. "Homage to James K. Baxter" is a case in point, as are all the poems that celebrate those living in what he calls "the underside of History"—that majority of us who lead unchronicled and certainly uncelebrated lives yet who make the very fabric of society. Examples of such poems are the young soldier in "In Transit" and the "anonymous" man in "Freebooter." In "Blue" Garfitt expresses that delicate and peculiar sadness that accompanies happy memories: "Memory on a peg / behind the door . . ." "Blue" is one of those poems that are complete in themselves, one that a person would want on a desert island and that makes other practitioners envious.

Garfitt's poetry can be seen gaining in strength while still retaining its verbal felicities. "Culvert," which catches sharply a spirit of place, ends with the lines "Here is a Roman thread, / A forethought of stone." Another superb example is to be found in "Lower Lumb Mill," in which one of those perfect coincidences of time and place and mood is caught in the brilliantly visual: "Sunlight mullioned through branches."

—John Cotton

GARLICK, Raymond

Nationality: British. **Born:** London, 21 September 1926. **Education:** University College of North Wales, Bangor, 1944–48, B.A. (honors) in philosophy and English literature 1948. **Family:** Married Elin Jane Hughes in 1948; one son and one daughter. **Career:** Taught in Wales, 1948–59, and the Netherlands, 1960–67. Senior lecturer in English, 1967–72, and director of Welsh Studies and principal lecturer, 1972–86, Trinity College, Carmarthen. Founding editor, *Dock Leaves,* later *The Anglo-Welsh Review,* Pembroke Dock, 1949–60. **Awards:** Welsh Arts Council prize, 1969, 1973, 1977. D.Litt.: Central College, 1998. Honorary fellow of Trinity College, Carmarthen; fellow of the Welsh Academy. **Address:** 26 Glannant House, College Road, Carmarthen SA31 3EF, Wales.

PUBLICATIONS

Poetry

Poems from the Mountain-House. London, Fortune Press, 1950.
Requiem for a Poet. Pembroke Dock, Dock Leaves Press, 1954.
Poems from Pembrokeshire. Pembroke Dock, Dock Leaves Press, 1954.
The Welsh-Speaking Sea. Pembroke Dock, Dock Leaves Press, 1954.
Blaenau Observed. Pembroke Dock, Dock Leaves Press, 1957.
Landscapes and Figures: Selected Poems 1949–63. London, Merrythought Press, 1964.
A Sense of Europe: Collected Poems 1954–1968. Llandysul, Dyfed, Gomer, 1968.
A Sense of Time: Poems and Antipoems 1969–1972. Llandysul, Dyfed, Gomer, 1972.

Incense: Poems 1972–1975. Llandysul, Dyfed, Gomer, 1976.
Collected Poems 1946–1986. Llandysul, Dyfed, Gomer, 1987.
Travel Notes: New Poems. Llandysul, Dyfed, Gomer, 1992.

Recording: *Poets of Wales* series, Argo.

Other

An Introduction to Anglo-Welsh Literature. Cardiff, University of Wales Press, 1970; revised edition, 1972.
Anglo-Welsh Literature. Port Talbot, Alun, 1979.

Editor, *Poetry from Wales.* Brooklyn, Poetry Book Magazine, 1954.
Editor, with Roland Mathias, *Anglo-Welsh Poetry 1480–1980.* Bridgend, Glamorgan, Poetry Wales Press, 1984; Chester Springs, Pennsylvania, Dufour, 1985.
Editor, *The Hymn to the Virgin.* Newtown, Powys, Gwasg Gregynog, 1985.

*

Bibliography: In *A Bibliography of Anglo-Welsh Literature, 1900-1965* by Brynmor Jones, Swansea, Library Association, 1970.

Manuscript Collection: National Library of Wales, Aberystwyth.

Critical Studies: "The Poetry of Raymond Garlick" by John Hill, in *The Anglo-Welsh Review* (Pembroke Dock), summer 1972; statement by the author, in *Artists in Wales 2,* edited by Meic Stephens, Llandysul, Dyfed, Gomer, 1973; Anthony Conran, in *Poetry Wales* (Swansea), winter 1977, and *The Cost of Strangeness* by Conran, Llandysul, Dyfed, Gomer, 1982; Tony Bianchi, in *Planet* (Llangeitho, Dyfed), November 1977; *Raymond Garlick,* The Writers of Wales series, by Don Dale Jones, Cardiff, University of Wales Press, 1995.

Raymond Garlick comments:

Major themes: Wales and Europe, landscapes and figures, justice and nonviolence, art and time. Preoccupation with English as a language of Wales, clarity of communication, poetry as structure and shape. General influence: Anglo-Welsh poetry from the late fifteenth century onwards. Since 1988 a preoccupation with travel and with making poems out of it, especially out of sites of Greek antiquity.

*   *   *

Raymond Garlick is a central figure in Anglo-Welsh literature. In 1949 he founded *Dock Leaves,* later *The Anglo-Welsh Review,* a magazine that was to present the best writing from Wales. He is committed to the concept of Anglo-Welsh literature, and through his editorship and other critical writings he has been a major contributor to the growth of interest and debate about the Welsh tradition of writing in English. His *Introduction to Anglo-Welsh Literature* is a useful survey of the tradition.

Garlick's *Collected Poems 1954–1968* carries the title *A Sense of Europe,* and the book emphasizes both the poet's seven years of teaching in Holland and his commitment to Europe as an entity, expressing real values and underlying unities. That said, for Garlick his adopted country of Wales is the focus of his ideas and their expression in poetry. He has learned Welsh and lives in the Welsh-speaking town of Carmarthen. His has been one of the strongest literary voices in promoting Welsh nationalism, and he castigates the old enemy England at every opportunity, as in "Waterloo":

> I didn't know before
> that any Dutch were near the place.
> I'd always thought it was
> just French and Prussians face to face—
> and the English of course,
> that other violent race.

As Garlick says at the end of A *Sense of Europe,* "My poems / are speeches, / clumsy speeches for Wales" ("Clues"). The implications of this self-proclamation are profound: the political poet is invariably more political than poet. Certainly there are "poems and antipoems" in *A Sense of Europe* that fail as pieces of writing because the poetic structure and invention are swamped by the anger of the politics. In one such poem, "Passion 72," the Welsh Language Society protesters are spoken of in terms of Christ: "The police / are always with us, / Roman, Dyfed-Powys, / and the Passion / unfolds before us / in unchanging fashion." Many readers would find such extremity in the writing to be ludicrous. How much more controlled and effective are poems such as "View from Llansteffan" and "Agincourt." This is the dilemma facing the politically committed writer. Whether or not one is carried along by his anger, however, Garlick is clearly to be viewed as one of the most interesting of poets in Wales.

—Tony Curtis

GARRETT, George (Palmer, Jr.)

Nationality: American. **Born:** Orlando, Florida, 11 June 1929. **Education:** Sewanee Military Academy; The Hill School, graduated 1947; Princeton University, Princeton, New Jersey, 1947–48, 1949–52, B.A. 1952, M.A. 1956, Ph.D. 1985; Columbia University, New York, 1948–49. **Military Service:** U.S. Army Field Artillery, 1950–56. **Family:** Married Susan Parrish Jackson in 1952; two sons and one daughter. **Career:** Assistant professor, Wesleyan University, Middletown, Connecticut, 1957–60; visiting lecturer, Rice University, Houston, 1961–62; associate professor, University of Virginia, Charlottesville, 1962–67; writer-in-residence, Princeton University, 1964–65; professor of English, Hollins College, Hollins, Virginia, 1967–71; professor of English and writer-in-residence, University of South Carolina, Columbia, 1971–73; senior fellow, Council of the Humanities, Princeton University, 1974–78; adjunct professor, Columbia University, 1977–78; writer-in-residence, Bennington College, Bennington, Vermont, 1979, and University of Michigan, Ann Arbor, 1979–80 and 1983–84. Since 1984 Hoyns Professor of English, University of Virginia, Charlottesville. Coal Royalty Visiting Professor, University of Alabama, 1994. President of Associated Writing Programs, 1971–73. U.S. poetry editor, *Transatlantic Review,* Rome (later London), 1958–71; Contemporary Poetry Series editor, University of North Carolina Press, Chapel Hill, 1962–68; co-editor, *Hollins Critic,* Hollins, Virginia, 1965–71; short story series editor, Louisiana State University Press, Baton Rouge, 1966–69. Since 1970 contributing editor, *Contempora,* Atlanta; since 1971 assistant editor, *Film Journal,* Hollins College, Virginia; since 1972 co-editor, *Worksheet,* Columbia, South Carolina; since 1981 editor,

with Brendan Galvin, *Poultry: A Magazine of Voice,* Truro, Massachusetts. Vice-chancellor, 1987–93, and 1993–97, chancellor of Fellowship of Southern Letters. **Awards:** *Sewanee Review* fellowship, 1958; American Academy in Rome fellowship, 1958; Ford grant, for drama, 1960; National Endowment for the Arts grant, 1967; *Contempora* award, 1971; Guggenheim fellowship, 1974; American Academy award, 1985; T.S. Eliot award, 1989. Cultural Laureate of Virginia, 1986. Pen/Malamud Award for Short Fiction, 1990; Hollins College Medal, 1992; Aiken/Taylor Award, 1999. **Agent:** Jane Gelfman, John Farquharson Ltd., 250 West 57th Street, New York, New York 10107, U.S.A. **Address:** 1845 Wayside Place, Charlottesville, Virginia 22903, U.S.A.

PUBLICATIONS

Poetry

The Reverend Ghost. New York, Scribner, 1957.

The Sleeping Gypsy and Other Poems. Austin, University of Texas Press, 1958.

Abraham's Knife and Other Poems. Chapel Hill, University of North Carolina Press, 1961.

For a Bitter Season: New and Selected Poems. Columbia, University of Missouri Press, 1967.

Welcome to the Medicine Show: Postcards, Flashcards, Snapshots. Winston-Salem, North Carolina, Palaemon Press, 1978.

Luck's Shining Child: A Miscellany of Poems and Verses. Winston-Salem, North Carolina, Palaemon Press, 1981.

The Collected Poems of George Garrett. Fayetteville, University of Arkansas Press, 1984.

Days of Our Lives in Fragments: New & Old Poems. Baton Rouge, Louisianna State University Press, 1998.

Plays

Sir Slob and the Princess: A Play for Children. New York, French, 1962.

Garden Spot, U.S.A. (produced Houston, 1962).

Enchanted Ground. York, Maine, Old Gaol Museum Press, 1981.

Screenplays: *The Young Lovers,* 1964; *The Playground,* 1965; *Frankenstein Meets the Space Monster,* with R.H.W. Dillard and John Rodenbeck, 1966.

Television Plays: *Suspense* series, 1958.

Novels

The Finished Man. New York, Scribner, 1959; London, Eyre and Spottiswoode, 1960.

Which Ones Are the Enemy? Boston, Little Brown, 1961; London, W.H. Allen, 1962.

Do, Lord, Remember Me. New York, Doubleday, and London, Chapman and Hall, 1965.

Death of the Fox. New York, Doubleday, 1971; London, Barrie and Jenkins, 1972.

The Succession: A Novel of Elizabeth and James. New York, Doubleday, 1983.

Poison Pen, or, Live Now and Pay Later. Winston-Salem, North
     Carolina, Wright, 1986.
Entered from the Sun. New York. Doubleday, 1990.
The Old Army Game. Dallas, Texas, Southern Methodist University
     Press, 1994.
The King of Babylon Shall Not Come against You. New York,
     Harcourt Brace, 1996.

Short Stories

King of the Mountain. New York, Scribner, 1958; London, Eyre and
     Spottiswoode, 1959.
In the Briar Patch. Austin, University of Texas Press, 1961.
Cold Ground Was My Bed Last Night. Columbia, University of
     Missouri Press, 1964.
A Wreath for Garibaldi and Other Stories. London, Hart Davis, 1969.
The Magic Striptease. New York, Doubleday, 1973.
To Recollect a Cloud of Ghosts: Christmas in England. Winston-
     Salem, North Carolina, Palaemon Press, 1979.
An Evening Performance: New and Selected Short Stories. New
     York, Doubleday, 1985.
Bad Man Blues: A Portable George Garrett. Dallas, Texas, Southern
     Methodist University Press, 1998.

Other

James Jones. New York, Harcourt Brace, 1984.
Understanding Mary Lee Settle. Columbia, University of South
     Carolina Press, 1988.
The Sorrows of Fat City. Columbia, South Carolina, University of
     South Carolina Press, 1992.
Whistling in the Dark. New York, Harcourt Brace, 1992.
My Silk Purse and Yours. Columbia, Missouri, University of Missouri
     Press, 1993.

Editor, *New Writing from Virginia.* Charlottesville, Virginia, New
     Writing Associates, 1963.
Editor, *The Girl in the Black Raincoat.* New York, Duell, 1966.
Editor, with W.R. Robinson, *Man and the Movies.* Baton Rouge,
     Louisiana State University Press, 1967.
Editor, with R.H.W. Dillard and John Moore, *The Sounder Few:
     Essays from "The Hollins Critic."* Athens, University of Georgia
     Press, 1971.
Editor, with O.B. Hardison, Jr., and Jane Gelfman, *Film Scripts 14.*
     New York, Appleton Century Crofts, 4 vols., 1971–72.
Editor, with William Peden, *New Writing in South Carolina.* Colum-
     bia, University of South Carolina Press, 1971.
Editor, with John Graham, *Craft So Hard to Learn.* New York,
     Morrow, 1972.
Editor, with John Graham, *The Writer's Voice.* New York, Morrow,
     1973.
Editor, with Walton Beacham, *Intro 5.* Charlottesville, University
     Press of Virginia, 1974.
Editor, with Katherine Garrison Biddle, *The Botteghe Oscure Reader.*
     Middletown, Connecticut, Wesleyan University Press, 1974.
Editor, *Intro 6: Life As We Know It.* New York, Doubleday, 1974.
Editor, *Intro 7: All of Us and None of You.* New York, Doubleday,
     1975.
Editor, *Intro 8: The Liar's Craft.* New York, Doubleday, 1977.

Editor, with Michael Mewshaw, *Intro 9.* Austin, Texas, Hendel and
     Reinke, 1979.
Editor, with Sheila McMillen, *Eric Clapton's Lover: Stories from the
     Virginia Quarterly Review.* Charlottesville, University Press of
     Virginia, 1990.
Editor, with Paul Ruffin, *Contemporary Southern Short Fiction: A
     Sampler.* Huntsville, Texas, Texas Review Press, 1991.
Editor, with Mary Flinn, *Elvis in Oz.* Charlottesville, Virginia,
     University Press of Virginia, 1992.
Editor, with Susan Stamberg, *The Wedding Cake in the Middle of the
     Road.* New York, Norton, 1992.
Editor, with Paul Ruffin, *That's What I Like About the South.*
     Columbia, South Carolina, University of South Carolina Press,
     1993.
Editor, with Matthew Bruccoli, *Dictionary of Literary Biography
     Yearbook.* Detroit, Gale Research, 1997, 1998, 1999.
Editor, *The Yellow Shoe Poets.* Baton Rouge, Louisianna State
     University Press, 1999.

*

Bibliography: In *Seven Princeton Poets,* Princeton University Library, 1963; "George Garrett: A Checklist of His Writings" by
R.H.W. Dillard, in *Mill Mountain Review* (Roanoke, Virginia),
summer 1971; "George Garrett: A Bibliographical Chronicle
1947–1980," in *Bulletin of Bibliography* (Boston), January–March
1981; and *George Garrett: A Bibliography, 1947–1988,* Huntsville,
Texas Review Press, 1989, both by Stuart Wright.

Manuscript Collection: Duke University, Durham, North Carolina.

Critical Studies: By James B. Meriwether, in *The Princeton University Library Chronicle* (Princeton, New Jersey), 25(1), 1963; "The
Poetry of George Garrett" by Henry Taylor, in *Latitudes* (Houston),
2, 1968; "The Poetry of Garrett," in *Masterpieces of World Litera-
ture 6,* New York, Salem Press, 1968, and *Understanding George
Garrett,* Columbia, University of South Carolina Press, 1988, both by
R.H.W. Dillard; "George Garrett Issue" of *Mill Mountain Review*
(Roanoke, Virginia), summer 1971; *To Come Up Grinning: A Tribute
to George Garrett* edited by Paul Ruffin and Stuart Wright, Huntsville,
Texas Review Press, 1989; interview by Richard Easton, in *New
Orleans Review* (New Orleans, Louisiana), winter 1990; "Fictional
Characterizaion As Infinite Regressive Series" by Fred Chappell,
Universtiy of Georgia Press, 1990; *The Writer's Mind: Interviews
with American Authors* (Volume 2), Fayetteville, University of
Arkansas Press, 1990; by Richard A. Betts, in *Mississippi Quarterly*
(Mississippi State), winter 1991–92; by Richard Tillinghast, in *South
Carolina Review* (Clemson, South Carolina), fall 1992; "George
Garrett: The Brutal Rush of Grace" by Henry Taylor, in *Compulsory
Figures: Essays on Recent American Poets,* Baton Rouge, Louisianna
State University Press, 1992; "Just for the Fun and Games of It: The
Dramatic Writing of George Garrett" by Deborah Sussman and
Richard Dillard, in *Southern Quarterly* (Hattiesburg, Mississippi),
winter-spring 1995–96.

George Garrett comments:
     Now that I have been writing and publishing poetry for more
than fifty years, I think it is more or less safe to be a little self-
conscious without being, I hope, boringly self-reflexive. Inevitably I
have noticed a few things, both bad habits and good, about the ways I

write poems and the kinds of poems I write. One of the things I have noticed is that there is an oddly reciprocal relationship between the kinds of prose I have been working on and the poems. I meant it when I wrote earlier for this publication that "all of my work in all forms, including the verse, is part and parcel of the same voice. I make no distinction in the voice only the forms." I meant it, but it is not quite true. I should have said "voices." Plural. And I should have allowed for change. The voices are always changing. And as they change, so do the forms. My earlier stories and novels were realistic and vernacular. I see that the poetry I wrote then was formal, stylized, only intermittently colloquial. Then, some years later, as I busied myself with some novels set in the Elizabethan Age, toying with some high styles and complex forms in prose, the poetry became more informal, assertively quotidian. What I suppose I am trying to say is that my poetry and my prose seem to have gone along, hand in hand, brother and sister. I have not, I find, gone along hand in hand with the literary fashions in America. Partly because as a teacher I have to know what other poets are up to and doing, I have found a little freedom for myself by deliberately doing something different, which can be a kind of curse even as it is a blessing. I hope to continue writing poems and to try new and different things in the future.

*   *   *

George Garrett's poetry shares much of the character of his fiction. His language is free and colloquial, but it is always strictly under control and serves the larger ends of his thought and feeling. He is personal without being confessional, and his vision is Christian without being pietistic. His work is composed upon a framework of contradictions, of polarities. The sinner who is a saint, the wounding truth that finds its only anodyne in a lie, the spirit trapped in the cage of flesh that discovers moral freedom in physical action, the cruel and painful joy (and mystery) of love—these are some of the enigmas upon which Garrett builds the lively textures of his poems.

The world of Garrett's seeing and saying is a fallen one of clenched fists and dark bruises, where we all still suffer the consequences of Adam's fall in bone and flesh and where we act out that fall again and again each passing day. His Salome describes this world in the important poem bearing her name:

A bad marriage from the beginning,
you say, a complete mismatch.
Flesh and spirit wrestle
and we call it love.

We couple like dogs in heat.
We shudder and are sundered.
We pursue ourselves,
sniffing, nose to tail
a comic parade of appetites.

That is the truth,
but not the whole truth.
Do me a little justice.
I had a dream of purity
and I have lived in the desert ever since.

In the desert a person holds to what he has and to what he had, learning like Adam and Eve after they were cast out of the Garden of Eden "to lie a little and to live together." That learning is not always serious, and Garrett is capable of writing comic poems, some of which satirize our vice and folly and others of which celebrate our vital foolishness, particularly as it expresses itself in the relationships between men and women. But the tone and substance of his poetry are perhaps best expressed by the closing stanza of "For My Sons," a poem that figures importantly in the novel *Death of the Fox:*

Nothing of earned wisdom I can give you,
nothing save the old words like rock candy
to kill the taste of dust on the tongue.
Nothing stings like the serpent, no pain greater.
Bear it. If a bush should burn and cry out,
bow down. If a stranger wrestles, learn his name.
And if after long tossing and sickness you find
a continent, plant your flags, send forth a dove.
Rarely the fruit you reach for returns your love.

—R.H.W. Dillard

GASCOYNE, David (Emery)

Nationality: British. **Born:** Harrow, Middlesex, 10 October 1916. **Education:** Salisbury Cathedral Choir School; Regent Street Polytechnic, London. **Family:** Married Judy Tyler Lewis in 1975. **Career:** Lived in France, 1937–39, 1947–48, 1953–64. **Awards:** Rockefeller-Atlantic award, 1949; Biella European Poetry prize, 1983. Fellow, Royal Society of Literature, 1951; Chevalier dans l'Ordre des Arts et Lettres, 1996. **Agent:** Stephen Stuart-Smith, Enitharmon Press, 35 St. George's Avenue, London N7 0HD. **Address:** 48 Oxford Street, Northwood, Cowes, Isle of Wight PO31 8PT, England.

PUBLICATIONS

Poetry

Roman Balcony and Other Poems. London, Lincoln Williams, 1932.
Man's Life Is This Meat. London, Parton Press, 1936.
Hölderlin's Madness. London, Dent, 1938.
Poems 1937–1942. London, Editions Poetry London, 1943.
A Vagrant and Other Poems. London, Lehmann, 1950.
Night Thoughts. London, Deutsch, and New York, Grove Press, 1956.
Collected Poems, edited by Robin Skelton. London, Oxford University Press-Deutsch, 1965.
Penguin Modern Poets 17, with Kathleen Raine and W.S. Graham. London, Penguin, 1970.
The Sun at Midnight: Poems and Aphorisms. London, Enitharmon Press, 1970.
Collected Verse Translations, edited by Robin Skelton and Alan Clodd. London, Oxford University Press-Deutsch, 1970.
Three Poems. London, Enitharmon Press, 1976.
Early Poems. Warwick, Greville Press, 1980.
La Mano del Poeta, edited by Francesca Romani Paci. Genoa, Edizione S. Marco dei Giustiniani, 1982.
Five Early Uncollected Poems. Leamington Spa, Other Branch Readings, 1984.
Collected Poems 1988. Oxford, Oxford University Press. 1988.
Miserere: Poemes 1937–1942. Paris, Granit, 1989.
Selected Poems. London, Enitharmon Press, 1994.

Three Remanences. London, privately printed, 1994.
Selected Verse Translations, edited by Robin Skelton and Alan
  Clodd. London, Enitharmon Press, 1996.
Encounter with Silence: Poems, 1950. London, Enitharmon Press,
  1998.

Play

The Hole in the Fourth Wall; or, Talk, Talk, Talk (produced London,
  1950).

Novels

Opening Day. London, Cobden Sanderson, 1933.
April. London, Enitharmon Press, 2000.

Other

A Short Survey of Surrealism. London, Cobden Sanderson, 1935; San
  Francisco, City Lights, 1982.
Thomas Carlyle. London, Longman, 1952.
Paris Journal 1937–1939. London, Enitharmon Press, 1978.
Journal 1936–37. London, Enitharmon Press, 1980.
Journal de paris et d'ailleurs, 1936–1942. Paris, Flammarion, 1984.
Novalis: Hymns to the Night. Petersfield, Enitharmon Press, 1989.
The Collected Journals, 1936–1942. London, Skoob, 1991.
Lawrence Durrell. London, privately printed, 1993.
The Fire of Vision: David Gascoyne and George Barker, edited by
  Roger Scott. London, privately printed, 1996.
Selected Prose 1934–1996, edited by Roger Scott with an introduc-
  tion by Kathleen Raine. London, Enitharmon Press, 1998.
A Short Survey of Surrealism. London, Enitharmon Press, 2000.

Editor, *Outlaw of the Lowest Planet,* by Kenneth Patchen. London,
  Grey Walls Press, 1946.

Translator, *Conquest of the Irrational,* by Salvador Dali. New York,
  Levy, 1935.
Translator, with Humphrey Jennings, *A Bunch of Carrots: Twenty
  Poems,* by Benjamin Peret. London, Roger Roughton, 1936;
  revised edition, as *Remove Your Hat,* 1936.
Translator, *What is Surrealism?,* by André Breton. London, Faber,
  1936.
Translator, *The Magnetic Fields,* by André Breton and Philippe
  Soupault. London, Atlas, 1985.
Translator, with Martin Sorrell, *Remove Your Hat and Other Works,*
  by Benjamin Péret. London, Atlas, 1985.
Translator, *The Unconscious, Spirituality, Catastrophe,* by Pierre
  Jean Jouve. Child Okeford, Dorset, Words Press, 1988.
Translator, *Three Translations.* Child Okeford, Dorset, Words Press,
  1988.
Translator, *Poems of Milosz.* London, Enitharmon, 1993.
Translator, *The Present Greatness of Mozart,* by Pierre Jean Jouve.
  Birmingham, Delos Press, 1996.

*

Bibliography: "David Gascoyne: A Checklist" by A. Atkinson, in
Twentieth-Century Literature 6 (Los Angeles), 1961; *David Gascoyne:*

A Bibliography of His Works (1929–1985) by Colin Benford, n.p.,
Heritage, 1986.

Manuscript Collections: British Library, London; University of
Tulsa, Oklahoma; State University of New York, Buffalo; New York
Public Library; Brotherton Collection, University of Leeds.

Critical Studies: By Edwin Muir, in *The Observer* (London), De-
cember 1950; "Poetry and Ideas II: David Gascoyne" by Anthony
Cronin, in *London Magazine,* July 1957; "The Restoration of Sym-
bols," in *Every Changing Shape* by Elizabeth Jennings, London,
Deutsch, 1961; "A Voice from the Darkness" by Gavin Ewart, in
London Magazine, November 1965; "David Gascoyne and the
Prophetic Role," in *Defending Ancient Springs* by Kathleen Raine,
London and New York, Oxford University Press, 1967, and "Eng-
land's Last Great Poet" by Raine, in *Tenemos 10* (London), 1989;
The Ironic Harvest by Geoffrey Thurley, London, Arnold, 1974; *An
Introduction to Fifty Modern British Poets* by Michael Schmidt,
London, Pan, 1979, as *A Reader's Guide to Fifty Modern British
Poets,* London, Heinemann, 1979, New York, Barnes and Noble,
1982; *David Gascoyne, ou l'urgence de l'inexprimé* by Michel Rémy,
Nancy, France, Presses Universitaires de Nancy, 1984; by Healther
Buck, in *Agenda* (London), 26(4), Winter 1988; "David Gascoyne:
Confessional Novelist" by Peter Christensen, in *Deus Loci* (Bronx,
New York), 1, 1992; "Emblems of Friendship: Lawrence Durrell and
David Gascoyne" by Ian S. MacNiven, in *Deus Loci* (Bronx, New
York), 2, 1993.

*   *   *

In the introduction to his *Collected Poems 1988* David Gascoyne
suggests that in most of his mature work there is a constant theme:
"the intolerable nature of human reality when devoid of all spiritual,
metaphysical dimension." This sense underlies the best of Gascoyne's
early surrealist poems, giving a significance to the otherwise factitious excitement of their imagery. It was in the years immediately
before World War II that Gascoyne's poetry reached maturity,
attaining the fusion of personal and universal that is one of the
hallmarks of poetic achievement. The progress through surrealism
was a necessary liberation for Gascoyne; it was the path by which he
came to realize the hollowness of reason's claim to an all-embracing
superiority and the insufficiency of a materialist view of the universe.
His early adventures in surrealism—and no English poet was more
thorough and intimate in his knowledge of that movement, no
Englishman a better translator of the French surrealists—were deepened by a growing familiarity with the German romantic movement
and its philosophical-theological background, with the works of such
writers as Hölderlin and Novalis, Swedenborg and Böhme. This
steeping in both French and German traditions, without a loss of his
native Englishness, gave to Gascoyne a voice unique in modern
English poetry.

Gascoyne is a poet of night and music. *Night Thoughts,*
"Noctambules" or the magnificent "The Sacred Hearth" (addressed
to George Barker) are eloquent testimony to one dimension of his
sensibility:

I wandered out across the briar-bound garden, spell-
  bound. Most
Mysterious and unrecapturable moment, when I stood

There staring back at the dark white nocturnal house,
And saw gleam through the lattices a light more pure
    than gold
Made sanguine with crushed roses, from the fire-
    light that all
    night
Stayed flickering about the sacred hearth . . .
        George, in the wood
Of wandering among wood-hiding trees, where poets' art
Is how to whistle in the dark, where pockets all have holes,
All roofs for refugees have rents, we ought to know
That there can be for us no place quite alien and unknown,
No situation wholly hostile, if somewhere there burn
The faithful fire of vision still awaiting our return.

Musical imagery permeates poem after poem. Several poems are structured on musical models, and in "Mozart: Sursum Corda" Gascoyne has written one of the best of modern poems on a musical subject, celebrating that moment when

Supernal voices flood the ear of clay
And transpierce the dense skull: Reveal
The immaterial world concealed
By mortal deafness and the screen of sense,
World of transparency and last release
And world within the world. Beyond our speech
To tell what equinoxes of the infinite
The spirit ranges in its rare utmost flight.

The clay-like nature of the human body and the astronomical infinities of the spirit's range are recurrent symbols in Gascoyne's poetic language as it mediates between mud and stars.

    The very finest of Gascoyne's work was probably written in the years on either side of 1940. A series of "metaphysical poems" contains religious poetry of the highest order, though of a thoroughly individual, noninstitutional kind. In "The Gravel-Pit Field" Gascoyne has written a glorious poem in which a ravaged wartime landscape is transformed by the redemptive power of an imagination fed by spiritual awareness:

Beside the stolid opaque flow
Of rain-gorged Thames; beneath a thin
Layer of early evening light
Which seems to drift, a ragged veil,
Upon the chilly March air's tide:
Upwards in shallow shapeless tiers
A stretch of scurfy pock-marked waste
Sprawls laggardly its acres till
They touch a raw brick-villa'd rim.

Amidst this nondescript terrain
Haphazardly the gravel-pits'
Rough-hewn rust-coloured hollows yawn,
Their steep declivities away
From the field-surface dropping down
Towards the depths below where rain-
Water in turbid pools stagnates
Like scraps of sky decaying in
The sockets of a dead man's stare . . .

As I stand musing, overhead
The zenith's stark light thrusts a ray
Down through dusk's rolling vapours, casts
A last lucidity of day

Across the scene: and in a flash
Of insight I behold the field's
Apotheosis: No-man's-land
Between this world and the beyond,
Remote from men and yet more real
Than any human dwelling-place:
A tabernacle where one stands
As though within the empty space
Round which revolves the Sage's Wheel.

It is a poem that ought to be in every anthology of modern verse.

    Gascoyne was largely silent as a poet during the 1950s. The work he has written since is of considerable interest and deserves attention, but it lacks the intensity of the best of the earlier poems. Ideas previously made incarnate in the symbolic language of poetry are presented in later works in an idiom a little closer to intellectual statement. It continues to be apt, however, to apply to Gascoyne himself some words he once wrote about Carlyle, when he said that Carlyle was always aware of the need "to bear witness to the Divine nature of the true man." It is Gascoyne's conviction of that divine nature, and his simultaneously pained awareness of human weakness, that gives his best work access to a genuine sense of the tragic. The seriousness of purpose governing Gascoyne's poetic intelligence puts to shame the trivialities too common in contemporary poetry.

—Glyn Pursglove

GATENBY, Greg

Nationality: Canadian. **Born:** Toronto, Ontario, 5 May 1950. **Education:** York University, Toronto, 1968–72, B.A. in English 1972. **Career:** Editor, McClelland and Stewart, publishers, Toronto, 1973–75. Since 1975 literary coordinator, Harbourfront, and since 1980 artistic director, Harbourfront International Festival of Authors, Toronto. **Awards:** Ontario Arts Council grants, 1975–84; Canada Council grant, 1975, 1977; City of Toronto Arts award (literature), 1989; League of Canadian Poets Honorary Lifetime Member, 1991; Jack award for lifetime promotion of Canadian books, 1994. **Agent:** Lucinda Vardey Agency, 36 Maitland Street, Suite H-2, Toronto, Ontario M4Y 1C5, Canada. **Address:** c/o Harbourfront Reading Series, 417 Queen's Quay West, Toronto, Ontario M5V 1A2, Canada.

PUBLICATIONS

Poetry

Rondeaus for Erica. Toronto, Missing Link Press, 1976.
Adrienne's Blessing. Toronto, Missing Link Press, 1976.
The Brown Stealer. Oxford, Avalon, 1977.
The Salmon Country. Windsor, Ontario, Black Moss Press, 1978.
Growing Still. Windsor, Ontario, Black Moss Press, 1981.

Other

Toronto: A Literary Guide. Toronto, McArthur, 1999.

Editor, *52 Pickup.* Toronto, Dreadnaught Press, 1976.
Editor, *Whale Sound: An Anthology of Poems about Whales and Dolphins.* Toronto, Dreadnaught Press, 1977.
Editor, *Whales: A Celebration.* Toronto, Lester and Orpen Dennys, and Boston, Little Brown, 1983.
Editor, *The Definitive Notes.* Toronto, Montblanc, 1991.
Editor, *The Wild Is Always There.* Toronto, Knopf Canada, 1993.
Editor, *The Very Richness of That Past.* Toronto, Knopf Canada, 1995.

Translator, with Irving Layton and Francesca Valente, *Selected Poems,* by Giorgio Bassani. Toronto, Aya Press, 1980.

*

Critical Studies: Reviews by John Bemrose, in *Globe and Mail* (Toronto), 20 February 1982; Chris Hume, in *Toronto Star,* 2 October 1983; in *New York Times Book Review,* 20 November 1983; Bernard Levin, in *The Observer* (London), 11 December 1983; Maclean's (Toronto), 12 December 1983; *The Weekend Australian* (Sydney), 3–4 March 1984.

*   *   *

Greg Gatenby is, after Margaret Atwood and Robertson Davies, possibly the best-known Canadian writer abroad. It is certainly a fact that he is on a friendly and informal basis with innumerable influential authors from almost all the countries of the world. It is a sad fact, however, that he is recognized not for the individuality of his own body of writing but rather for his unselfish promotion of the work and careers of fellow writers in Canada and around the world.

Gatenby has directed the literary reading program of Toronto's Harbourfront cultural complex since 1975. At first he worked to bring nationally important poets and fiction writers to that reading venue. He then branched out and began to introduce visiting foreign writers, especially those on book promotion junkets. Almost single-handedly, he sought funding from corporate, commercial, and cultural bodies for what is now the prestigious Wang International Authors Festival. The festival is held in the fall, in the spring there is the International Poetry Festival, and throughout the year there are nightly group readings.

All of this activity has taken time and attention away from Gatenby's other interests. Indeed, he once admitted to a journalist at the *Toronto Globe and Mail* that he regards himself as a poet who works as an artistic director rather than as an artistic director who writes poems.

Gatenby is also a controversialist. In print and in public forums he has decried the heavy hand of the academy on the literary and publishing scene, the arbitrariness of national literary awards programs, the lack of generosity of public funding organizations, the failure of the federal government to further the country's arts on a global basis, and the grants programs of arts organizations.

Given the outspokenness of the man, it is not surprising that his poetry is strong and vigorous. Wit is one of the characteristics of his work, which has appeared in five volumes of poetry published over a five-year period beginning in 1976. Gatenby's best-known poem is the loud and amusing satire called "Academic Report on Literature III," an extended comparison of Canadian literature with the stock market: "Major U.S. indicators continue to outstrip Canadian futures . . . the interest rate in academic continued to decline . . . ."

Urbanity is another quality of the man and his métier. Stanzas in "The Sophisticates" suggest a metropolitan temperament ill at ease with local, provincial, and intellectual pieties:

. . . and outside I take a deep breath
of the dirty smog of the city
and note for the first time
how much I need to enjoy it.

It was Northrop Frye who observed that Canadians live in a land that just seems to be emerging from prehistory. Gatenby's work occasionally suggests the coexistence of the unhistoric past with the unheroic present. He wrote in "The Salmon Country,"

May Sisyphus stay a European visitor;
these stupid fish make a tale primeval
are endemic to this land, this nation, us.

This perspective has been employed with great success by the poet Al Purdy. Gatenby uses it effectively in "The Narwhal," which describes an Inuit, or Eskimo, village and its chief product, sculptures:

Each village of 300 kills a thousand
and you can smell the extinction
in every sculpture the city dwellers buy
for the primitive art, for the natives,
for nature.

There is evidence in his later poetry of a trying truce between the hard-nosed poems that satirize cultural and national concerns and the melodious lyric poems about life and love. "Reunion" presents love as "what once was intimate, / cedilla soft." This last phrase echoes throughout the poem, even to its ending: "Is now a furtive child, cynic hardened, lonely."

One of Gatenby's happiest poems, "Screen Siren," recounts how by chance he encountered his favorite movie star, the Quebec actress Carole Laure, in New York:

I made her

hear my love for dolphins, talked of books still to come—
any nonsense to protract her present, to let me
repose fluid kite tail dancing and happy.

Gatenby has a poetic voice that is characteristically his own. Whether his poems are by turn gritty and gruff or graceful and giving, characteristic of all of them is the sense that life is "once forever" and that the world as we know it does not measure up to the world as we could remake it.

—John Robert Colombo

GEDDES, Gary

Nationality: Canadian. **Born:** Vancouver, British Columbia, 9 June 1940. **Education:** King Edward High School, Vancouver 1956–58; University of British Columbia, Vancouver, 1958–62, B.A. in English and philosophy 1962; Reading University, Berkshire, 1963–64, Dip.Ed. 1964; University of Toronto, 1964–68, M.A. and Ph.D. **Family:** Married 1) Norma Fugler in 1963 (divorced 1969), one daughter; 2) Jan Macht in 1973, two daughters. **Career:** High school teacher, Texada Island, British Columbia, 1962–63; visiting assistant professor, Trent University, Peterborough, Ontario, 1968–69; lecturer, Carleton University, Ottawa, 1971–72, and University of Victoria, British Columbia, 1972–74; writer-in-residence, 1976–77, and visiting associate professor, 1977–78, University of Alberta, Edmonton. Visiting associate professor, 1978–79, and since 1979 associate professor of English, Concordia University, Montreal. General editor, Studies in Canadian Literature series, Douglas and McIntyre publishers, Vancouver. **Awards:** E.J. Pratt Medal, 1970; Canadian Authors Association prize, 1982; Commonwealth poetry prize, 1985; National Magazine Gold award, 1987; Writers' Choice award, 1988. **Address:** Department of English, Concordia University, 1455 de Maisonneuve Boulevard West, Montreal, Quebec H3G 1M8, Canada.

PUBLICATIONS

Poetry

Poems. Waterloo, Ontario, Waterloo Lutheran University, 1971.
Rivers Inlet. Vancouver, Talonbooks, 1972.
Snakeroot. Vancouver, Talonbooks, 1973.
Letter of the Master of Horse. Ottawa, Oberon Press, 1973.
War and Other Measures. Toronto, Anansi, 1976.
The Acid Test. Winnipeg, Turnstone Press, 1981.
The Terracotta Army. Ottawa, Oberon Press, 1984.
Changes of State. Moose Jaw, Saskatchewan, Coteau, 1986.
Hong Kong Poems. Ottawa, Oberon Press, 1987.
No Easy Exit. Lantzville, British Columbia, Oolichan, 1989.
Light of Burning Towers: Poems, New and Selected. Montreal, Vehicule Press, 1990.
Girl by the Water. Winnipeg, Turnstone Press, 1993.
The Perfect Cold Warrior. Kingston, Ontario, Quarry Press, 1995.
Active Trading: Selected Poems, 1970–1995. Fredericton, New Brunswick, Goose Lane, 1996.
Flying Blind. London, Enitharmon, 1998.

Plays

Les Maudits Anglais, with the Theatre Passe Muraille (produced Montreal, 1978). Toronto, Playwrights Canada, 1984.
Hong Kong (produced Winnipeg, 1986).

Radio Play: *The Inheritors,* 1983.

Short Stories

The Unsettling of the West. Ottawa, Oberon Press, 1986.

Other

Conrad's Later Novels. Montreal, McGill-Queen's University Press, 1980.
Letters from Managua: Meditations on Politics and Art. Kingston, Ontario, Quarry Press, 1990.

Editor, *20th-Century Poetry and Poetics.* Toronto, Oxford University Press, 1969; revised edition, 1973, 1985.
Editor, with Phyllis Bruce, *15 Canadian Poets.* Toronto, Oxford University Press, 1970; revised edition, as *15 Canadian Poets Plus Five, 1978;* revised edition, as *15 Canadian Poets Times 2,* 1988.
Editor, *Skookum Wawa: Writings of the Canadian Northwest.* Toronto, Oxford University Press, 1975.
Editor, *Divided We Stand.* Toronto, Martin Associates, 1977.
Editor, *The Inner Ear: An Anthology of New Canadian Poets.* Montreal, Quadrant, 1983.
Editor, *Chinada: Memoirs of the Gang of Seven.* Dunvegan, Ontario, Quadrant, 1983.
Editor, *Vancouver: Soul of a City.* Vancouver, Douglas and McIntyre, 1986.
Editor, with Hugh Hazelton, *Compañeros: Writings about Latin America.* Dunvegan, Ontario, Cormorant Books, 1990.
Editor, *The Art of Short Fiction: An International Anthology.* Toronto, HarperCollins, 1993.

Translator, with George Liang, *I Didn't Notice the Mountain Growing Dark,* by Li Pai and Tu Fu. Dunvegan, Ontario, Cormorant, 1986.

*

Critical Study: "Gary Geddes' War and Other Measures: An Analysis" by Donald R. Bartlett, in *Canadian Poetry* (London, Ontario), 8, spring-summer 1981.

Gary Geddes comments:

(1980) My poetry begins as an effort to come to terms with the influence of family and place in my life. Eventually it broadens out to include history generally, moving from lyric to narrative in order to accommodate anecdote and story. Unformed historical fragments (the Spanish conquests, the fall of Hong Kong, a reported journey of Chinese Buddhists to North America centuries ago, etc.) seem to give my imagination all it needs to work on. At the moment I am moving back and forth between poetry and fiction, writing short stories and exploring the fruitful ground between the two genres in longer forms, trying perhaps to write an epic for our times. Robert Kroetsch has said of *War and Other Measures* that it "builds, incredibly builds, it's the kind of long poem poets are only supposed to be able to dream." The trick is to combine the intensity of the lyric with the comprehensiveness of the epic. The lyrics continue to come, though the recent poem on the killings at Kent State, "Sandra Lee Scheuer," shows where my voice goes. Al Purdy has said of this poem that it is the kind of piece poets wait a lifetime for and some never achieve.

*   *   *

Somewhere en route to a mystical "new world," in a time of laughter and flowers, fifty horses were cast into a boiling ocean. They were sacrificed for the lives of God's soldiers, the men who would create a new, golden kingdom. This genesis, as reconstructed by the Canadian poet Gary Geddes, is inhabited by lustful Spanish explorers, brown-bodied natives, and shimmering islands and forests. This was the beginning of things, the foggy, bloody dawn from which emerged contemporary understandings of life and time. It was an age of power and plunder, the absolute truth of men.

Then Armageddon, World War II, clawed its way into the consciousness of the world, and time and truth triumphantly concluded with the ceremonial bombing of two cities in Japan. At the end of things shell-shocked children are frightened animals, desperate men bayonet the sick and wounded in an army hospital, and rats eat human flesh nightly in screaming, terrible dreams. Existence, identity, and perception are fragmented and anarchic, and self-reflection creates a vacuum.

Through his works Geddes explores the uses of poetry. In his meta-World War II imagination the poem is a patchwork of obliterated, chaotic codes, a document of cataclysm, as in ''Word'' from his 1981 volume *The Acid Test:*

I became flesh. I swam,
impatient, in placental
waters. Rubber gloves
guided my lethal skull
into the breach, launched
me into thinner seas.

A quart of good champagne
splashed down my sides,
a tiny motor propelled
me forward.

Ship after ship went
down, the screams
of men meant nothing.
I sang in the air, my song
shattered a child's thought.

They planted me in fields,
under bridges, no one
collected the pieces.
They dropped me on cities,
the charred flesh stuck
in my throat.

They updated me, made me
streamlined and beautiful.
I grew vain. My lust could
not be glutted. I turned on them.
They spoke of god, of honour.

I wiped my mouth
on my sleeve.

The poetry ultimately functions to provide a context for an isolated, jagged, and perplexing existence. From the periphery of accepted histories, a place sometimes arrived at by shock and revulsion, Geddes's poems resurrect fallen dreams and attitudes of mind and state, the psyche of our uncomfortable past. These fragments of previous lives still vibrate in the fractured present. We still institutionalize the unknown, arrogantly detach ourselves from death and life, and respond to conquerors with awe.

A pragmatic, angry voice inhabits Geddes's poetry. It is a voice weary under the weight of a murderous human consciousness, of the granite-clad institutions that deny its existence. Shimmering, transcending echoes are rarely heard. Geddes dislodges illusions of freedom, justice, and absolute truth with dynamite. He says in ''Time Out for Coca Cola,''

Marlon Mendizabel turns on the television
to relax after a hard day of bargaining,
his children playing on the floor at his feet.
There's an international football match
in progress on the American channel.
All morning he has met with Company officials
at the Coca Cola plant, trying to resolve items,
wages principally, that will end the strike.
The Company has hired three army lieutenants
to direct warehousing, personnel and security.
Six eyes want him gone, six new laser eyes
negotiate his disappearance piece by piece . . .

His children watch the soft drink commercial
on television, cheering on the Coke truck
as it falls behind that of its rival.
He wants to tell them it's not a matter of taste,
that the truck contains the bones of 100,000
murdered Guatemalans, killed by the death-squads
financed by government and large corporations.
Instead he lays his invisible hands on their heads
and offers up a silent prayer for their safety.
Marlon's heart grows so large it fills the room
until even those on the television notice
and stop what they're doing to watch and listen
to the voice of that heart as it communes
with God. The football players take off their helmets
and stand with heads bowed; the announcers,
for once, are at a loss for words.
Somewhere, outside Dallas, the Coke truck
pulls over, lights flashing, a door opens
and those bones form a vast bridge
that stretches from Texas all the way
to Guatemala City. Children are crossing
over that bridge, their hands joined,
singing. Nothing can stop them.

This is the quintessential use of poetry as Geddes seeks to inform the process of contemporary mythmaking.

—Doug Ekelund

GERVAIS, C(harles) H(enry)

Nationality: Canadian. **Born:** Windsor, Ontario, 20 October 1946. **Education:** University of Guelph, Ontario, B.A. 1971; University of Windsor, M.A. in English 1972. **Family:** Married Donna Wright in 1968; one daughter and two sons. **Career:** Staff member *Toronto*

Globe and Mail, 1966, and Canadian Press, Toronto, 1967; reporter, Daily Commercial News, Toronto, 1967; teacher of creative writing, St. Clair College, Windsor, 1969–71; editor, Sunday Standard, Windsor, 1972; reporter, *Chatham Daily News,* 1972–73; general news reporter, 1973–74 and 1976–81, bureau chief, 1974–76, religion editor, 1979–80, since 1980 book editor, and since 1990 entertainment writer, *Windsor Star.* Since 1969 publisher, Black Moss Press, Windsor. Since 1983 contributing editor, Oberon Press, Ottawa. Contributing guest, Morningside, Canadian Broadcasting Corporation Radio, Toronto, 1988–90. **Awards:** Western Ontario Newspaper award, 1983, 1984, 1987; Western Ontario Newspaper award, 1987. **Address:** 1939 Alsace Avenue, Windsor, Ontario N8W 1M5, Canada.

PUBLICATIONS

Poetry

Sister Saint Anne. Toronto, Bandit Press, 1968.
Something. Toronto, Bandit Press, 1969.
Other Marriage Vows. Windsor, Ontario, Sun Parlor Press, 1969.
A Sympathy Orchestra. Fredericton, New Brunswick, Fiddlehead, 1970.
Bittersweet. Guelph, Ontario, Alive Press, 1972.
Poems for American Daughters. Erin, Ontario, Porcupine's Quill, 1976.
The Believable Body. Fredericton, New Brunswick, Fiddlehead, 1979.
Up Country Lines. Moonbeam, Ontario, Penumbra Press, 1979.
Silence Comes with Lake Voices. Toronto, League of Canadian Poets, 1980.
Into a Blue Morning: Selected Poems. Toronto, Hounslow Press, 1982.
Public Fantasy: The Maggie T Poems. Guelph, Ontario, Sequel Press, 1983.
Letters from the Equator. Moonbeam, Ontario, Penumbra Press, 1986.
Autobiographies. Moonbeam, Ontario, Penumbra Press, 1989.
Playing God: New Poems. Oakville, Ontario, Mosaic Press, 1994.
Tearing into a Summer Day: Prose Poems. Buffalo, New York, Mosaic Press, 1996.

Plays

Baldoon, with James Reaney (produced Toronto, 1976). Erin, Ontario, Porcupine's Quill, 1976.
Northern Calamities. Cobalt, Ontario, Highway Book Shop, 1976.
The Fighting Parson (produced Windsor, Ontario, 1979). Erin, Ontario, Porcupine's Quill, 1983.

Other

How Bruises Lost His Secret (for children). Windsor, Ontario, Black Moss Press, 1975.
Doctor Troyer and the Secret in the Moonstone (for children). Windsor, Ontario, Black Moss Press, 1976.
The Rumrunners: A Prohibition Scrapbook. Thornhill, Ontario, Firefly, 1980.
If I Had a Birthday Everyday (for children). Windsor, Ontario, Black Moss Press, 1983.

Voices Like Thunder. N.p., Third World Resource Centre, 1984.
The Border Police: One Hundred and Twenty-Five Years of Policing in Windsor. Waterloo, Ontario, Penumbra Press, 1992.
Seeds in the Wilderness: Profiles of World Religious Leaders. Kingston, Ontario, Quarry Press, 1994.
From America Sent: Letters to Henry Miller. Kingston, Ontario, Quarry Press, 1995.

Editor, *The Writing Life: Historical and Critical Views of the Tish Movement.* Windsor, Ontario, Black Moss Press, 1976.

*

Critical Studies: "Memories of Marty As a Virginal Romantic" by Ted Plantos, and "WQ Interview with C. H. Gervais" by Judith Fitzgerald, both in *Writers Quarterly* (Toronto), spring 1986.

C. H. Gervais comments:

I have this belief that poetry communicates before it is even understood. In other words, it is not necessary for one to take apart the poem limb by limb to get at its heart or soul, but rather it is important for the reader to be absorbed into the language and music and magic of the writing. And this occurs at the outset. Sometimes the process is not understood by the poet. At times the poet is the last to recognize the authority he has, and when this takes place, you realize the power of language and music. That is why, when I write poetry, I look for these coincidences of human nature, the small accidents, knowing that the rhythms and words of my own experience will emerge. The process of writing, as one can see, is a matter of trust, of learning to be patient, of waiting for the muse to strike. Naturally, it can be frustrating; it is not easy or even satisfying to sit back. But the process can be fulfilling . . . . One needs to be patient, ready, willing.

*   *   *

The poetry of C. H. "Marty" Gervais is that of a secular man in search of the spiritual world. In the roles of the father, the husband, the traveler, the chronicler, and the storyteller, he writes poems that bridge the distance between the spiritual concerns of Thomas Merton or of Saint Martin de Porres and the relationships within his own family life and daily routines. Gervais accomplishes this with a journalistic specificity (when he is not writing poetry, he is a journalist for the *Windsor Star*), an exactness in image, and a love of detail.

Building on the reputation of his earlier works, his volumes *Letters from the Equator* and *Autobiographies* established Gervais as a voice that speaks for the family man devoted to his wife, his children, and his career, though one who is both perplexed and fascinated by the world and in need of answers. Having reached a point in his life and his literary work where he has achieved a modicum of comfortable accomplishment, Gervais weighs and acknowledges those elements he feels he can trust, such as family life and the joy he has experienced in being a father. In "Moons Still Dancing" in *Autobiographies,* Gervais pays homage to his three children by marking their respective birthdays with the phases of the moon and recalls intimate moments of parental love that have passed between them. The captured moment, the quiet, almost commonplace instant from daily life, is the currency of his poetry, and it is Gervais's ability to capture that moment that gives his work its eloquence. For example, in "The Commonplace," also from *Autobiographies,* Gervais laments the failure of life to capture as many of these moments as he would wish:

We recognize so little
of what is common
caring nothing for
identities, simply
waking each day
to accept everything
at face value,
asking nothing,
wishing no
names, no past
no future, no truth,
no record of any kind.

Yet the very act of writing poetry, of preserving the details and the richness of a passing moment, is in itself a record, a chronicle of the commonplace preserved. In this respect Gervais has maintained the focus he shares with his mentor Al Purdy in the earlier volumes of his opus. (His other important mentor, at least from the aspect of poetic problem solving, has been James Reaney.) Like Purdy, who noted in his introduction to *Into a Blue Morning* that Gervais was a "man pushing against his limitations, trying to shove the barriers in his mind a little farther ahead; snatching spare moments from being a husband and father and wage-earner to write poems," Gervais has sought to enrich and elevate minor, almost insignificant, details of daily life simply by honoring them with his attention. In "Blackberries," from *Into a Blue Morning,* Gervais recalls meeting a female acquaintance after years apart. He concludes, after noting the changes that have transpired in their lives, that

I remember a time when only eyes
sustained this, penetrating
& warm. Such is the evolution
of art—separating from
the body in a blur of motion,
trailing & faint, but alive.

For Gervais the focus of a poem is not only its purpose but also an investiture of the subject with a spirituality, a transcendence that goes beyond the mere imagistic surveillance of his early work in *Poems for American Daughters.* Like his poetic model Merton, Gervais believes in the sanctity of the spirit of the world, though not necessarily in the world itself.

The shift in Gervais's work from the early imagism to a kind of meditative spiritual writing is marked in the theme and the tone of *Letters from the Equator.* As Gervais noted in an interview, *Letters from the Equator* marked the crossing of a spiritual demarcation in his poetry, in which the perspectives and tensions of his own experience suddenly came into harmony: "I see this balance in terms of the equator. There are obvious connections. I did a lot of wandering around South America near the equator. I see the equator as a kind of dividing point between spiritual chaos in one's life and order." In the tradition of early Canadian literature such as the Jesuit Relations of the seventeenth century, Gervais has chronicled his experiences, his feelings, and his perceptions in letters. The epistolary prose poems that form the crux of *Letters from the Equator* are spiritual documents addressed to those figures who have had a bearing on his spiritual and literary life and who themselves reflect that balanced order: Proust,

Apollinaire, Georges Simenon, Goethe, Keats, Cocteau, and, of course, the Peruvian Saint Martin de Porres, whose name he adopted in place of his own Christian names of Charles Henry. After faithfully describing the details of a street scene in Lima in "First Letter to Martin in Lima," Gervais concludes, "But here your feet slide in shadows beneath eyes & hands that yearn for more than words," a recognition that poetry itself must exceed its bounds by recognizing its own limitations. In "Postcards from Gethsemani, Kentucky," a long suite of poems about a visit to Merton's monastery, Gervais concludes that "the world is one of opposites" and "extremes," in which the contemporary man of the spirit and of the world finds himself walking a tenuous line between the encumbering details of his daily existence and the profound yet static haunts of the soul.

In *Autobiographies* this dichotomy is translated into simpler metafictional terms, in which the act of making a poem or of telling a story from a singular and therefore questionable standpoint becomes the blurred distinction between truth and lies. The answer, as the earlier argument between world and spirit in *Letters from the Equator* suggested, is the realm of possibility, where one must accept what one wants to accept and believe what one wants to believe as long as that belief is held passionately. In this context Gervais becomes a love poet, with the uncertainty of love, of knowing and not knowing whether one is loved and being loved, becoming a metaphor for the male/female relationship. In "Confessions & Conclusions" he critiques his passion and that of his lover:

I reveal too much about myself; you too little.
I ought to have held back: you, to have been more
    generous.
Perhaps I have been too vulnerable. Perhaps it's too late.

Although such doubts, such uncertainties, cannot be resolved to satisfaction, one can settle for faith, faith in experience, in the moments of resolution and clarity, and in the joy one finds in his own situation. In "Little League Ball Park," which concludes *Autobiographies,* Gervais finds his equilibrium, his point of harmony, as he loses himself in his youngest son's baseball game:

But for the moment we hang on each
pitch, each movement as these players move
with ease & grace, as they time each hit, each throw,
each run, as they wait on each movement from
us, knowing we are always there, always cheering.

It is the shape of innocence that keeps
them alive, affords them confidence, drives
them to limits, careless & reckless, ignoring
the coming storm, the invading chaos
for they know we are there, always alive,
as they go through each new turn around the bases.

Regardless of their importance to others, the commonplace experiences, the certainties of life such as a child's baseball game and the beauty of seemingly insignificant lost moments, are for Gervais reliable. As a journalist whose passion is poetry, Gervais aims to tell the story as he sees it, with the facts "nailed down," the life lived, and the moments recorded.

—Bruce Meyer

GHISELIN, Brewster

Nationality: American. **Born:** Webster Groves, Missouri, 13 June 1903. **Education:** University of California, Los Angeles, A.B. 1927, and Berkeley, M.A. 1928, 1931–33; Oxford University, 1928–29. **Family:** Married Olive F. Franks in 1929; two sons. **Career:** Instructor in English, University of Utah, Salt Lake City, 1929–31; assistant in English, University of California, Berkeley, 1931–33. Instructor, 1934–38, lecturer, 1938–39, assistant professor, 1939–46, associate professor, 1946–50, director of the Writers' Conference, 1947–66, professor of English, 1950–71, Distinguished Research Professor, 1967–68, and since 1971 professor emeritus, University of Utah. Poetry editor, 1937–46, and associate editor, 1946–49, *Rocky Mountain Review,* later *Western Review,* Salt Lake City, and Lawrence, Kansas. *Member* of the editorial advisory board, *Concerning Poetry,* from 1968. **Awards:** Ford fellowship, 1952; Ben and Abby Grey Foundation award, 1965; American Academy award, 1970; Oscar Blumenthal prize, 1973, and Levinson prize, 1978 (*Poetry,* Chicago); William Carlos Williams award, 1981; Utah Arts Council Governor's award, 1982; D.H.L.: University of Utah, 1994. **Address:** 1747 Princeton Avenue, Salt Lake City, Utah 84108, U.S.A.

PUBLICATIONS

Poetry

Against the Circle. New York, Dutton, 1946.
The Nets. New York, Dutton, 1955.
Images and Impressions, with Edward Lueders and Clarice Short. Salt Lake City, University of Utah Printmaking Department, 1969.
Country of the Minotaur. Salt Lake City, University of Utah Press, 1970.
Light. Omaha, Abattoir, 1978.
Windrose: Poems 1929–1979. Salt Lake City, University of Utah Press, 1980.
The Dreamers. Winston-Salem, North Carolina, Palaemon Press, 1981.
Flame. Salt Lake City, University of Utah Press, 1991.

Other

Writing. Washington, D.C., American Association of University Women, 1959.

Editor, *The Creative Process: A Symposium.* Berkeley, University of California Press, 1952; revised edition, New York, Penguin, 1985.

*

Manuscript Collection: Lockwood Memorial Library, State University of New York, Buffalo; Princeton University Libraries, Princeton, New Jersey.

Critical Studies: *Spinning the Crystal Ball* by James Dickey, Washington, D.C., Library of Congress, 1967; "An Earthen Vessel" by William Ralston, in *Sewanee Review* (Tennessee), summer 1969; by Radcliffe Squires, in *Concerning Poetry* (Bellingham, Washington), fall 1970; by Kathleen Raine, in *Sewanee Review* (Tennessee), spring 1971; by Samuel French Morse, in *Michigan Quarterly Review* (Ann Arbor), fall 1971; by Henry Taylor, in *Masterplots: 1971 Annual and Magill's Literary Annual 1981,* New York, Salem Press, 1971, 1981; "The Long and Short of It" by Robert B. Shaw, in *Poetry* (Chicago), March 1972; "The Needle and the Garment" by X.J. Kennedy, in *Counter/Measures 3* (Bedford, Massachusetts), 1974; *The Water of Light: A Miscellany in Honor of Brewster Ghiselin,* edited by Henry Taylor, Salt Lake City, University of Utah Press, 1976; "Brewster Ghiselin Issue" of *The Blue Hotel I* (Lincoln, Nebraska), 1980; "The Poetry of Brewster Ghiselin" by Dave Smith, in *Western Humanities Review* (Salt Lake City), summer 1981; "Brewster Ghiselin: The Gift of the Waters," by Henry Taylor, in *Compulsory Figures: Essays on Recent American Poets,* Baton Rouge and London, Louisiana State University Press, 1992.

Brewster Ghiselin comments:

Like almost every poet, I feel that my poetry can live only in being heard, that it must be given the body of life as sensation of sound and of vibration and movement of the articulating voice. Though I have used a great variety of forms and measures, I have never written free verse. The measure I have most often found right is accentual, a strongly stressed and syllabically various flow that I first heard clearly when I read *Beowulf* in Old English and turned to my own freer use long before I read any of Gerard Manley Hopkins.

In my writing of poetry all considerations of verse form arise from the fact that the shaping of verse is the shaping of breath, the breath of life in every sense. If a poet says, "The poetry does not matter," as T.S. Eliot did in one context, meaning I suppose that nothing matters except what has been called "the ground of being," he simply reminds me of the vast importance of poetry, which only through accord with that inexhaustible attains whatever life it has. In the degree that poetry is realization and communion, it is false to say that it does not matter. The poetry matters. Whom the wind scatters Breath makes one again.

My central subject is men's struggle for breath, for being and light. Under the universal necessity of change, which sweeps away all form, man can have integrity and wholeness only through ceaseless shaping and reshaping of himself and his course and of those perspectives of vision that direct it. What draws my interest most and gives me matter and theme is the passion of living creatures to transcend the limits that choke them and to find and enjoy the limits that, each in changing succession, are the freeing form of a moment of breath.

(1995) A poem can be like a font. (Anglo Saxon-Old English: font, fant, from Latin *fons, fontis,* spring, fountain.) Cf. Heracleitus: "Other and other the waters flow."

*   *   *

Brewster Ghiselin's two early collections offered many poems whose parts were so polished that it was difficult to grasp the whole. The effect was that of Byzantine mosaics seen close, an effect of brilliant yet disparate atomies rather than of anatomy. Yet in a later collection, *Country of the Minotaur,* the opposite is true. The parts are still burnished, but the confluence of a tidal rhythm, an audacious language, and important themes distances the poems so that one sees their integrity and strength, as Yeats saw the integrity and strength of the lofty mosaics at Ravenna. This virtuous distance has come because Ghiselin has developed into one of the few contemporary poets whose faith rests in universals. Because his quandaries are eternal, they remain pure as they remain unresolved. Because his passions are conceived as parallels of the passions of vast energies, like sea and land, they remain at peace, most at peace when most violent.

Passion and peace define the boundaries of his poems, and the field within the boundaries is the nature that modern science has made both more heartless and more mysteriously beautiful than the nature Wordsworth knew. It is a nature that can be understood only as a broad order that barely superintends random movement or fluctuation. Except for Saint-John Perse, I can think of no one who is so majestically at home in this nomadic driftland. In some ways Ghiselin is the better poet, for he varies his focus while Saint-John Perse does not.

—Radcliffe Squires

GHOSE, Zulfikar

Nationality: British. **Born:** Sialkot, Pakistan, 13 March 1935. **Education:** Keele University, England, B.A. in English and philosophy 1959. **Family:** Married in 1964. **Career:** Cricket correspondent, *The Observer,* London, 1960–65; teacher in London, 1963–69. Since 1969 professor of English, University of Texas, Austin. **Awards:** Arts Council of Great Britain bursary, 1967. **Agent:** Sheila Land Associates, 43 Doughty Street, London WC1 2LF, England. **Address:** Department of English, University of Texas, Austin, Texas 78712, U.S.A.

PUBLICATIONS

Poetry

The Loss of India. London, Routledge, 1964.
Jets from Orange. London, Macmillan, 1967.
The Violent West. London. Macmillan. 1972.
Penguin Modern Poets 25, with Gavin Ewart and B.S. Johnson. London, Penguin, 1974.
A Memory of Asia. Austin, Texas, Curbstone Press, 1984.
Selected Poems. Karachi, Oxford University Press, 1991.

Novels

The Contradictions. London, Macmillan, 1966.
The Murder of Aziz Khan. London, Macmillan, 1967; New York, Day, 1969.
The Incredible Brazilian: The Native. London, Macmillan, and New York, Holt Rinehart, 1972.
The Beautiful Empire. London, Macmillan, 1975; Woodstock, New York, Overlook Press, 1984.
A Different World. London, Macmillan, 1978; Woodstock, New York, Overlook Press, 1985.
Crump's Terms. London, Macmillan, 1975.
The Texas Inheritance (as William Strang). London, Macmillan, 1980.
Hulme's Investigations into the Bogart Script. Austin, Texas, Curbstone Press, 1981.
A New History of Torments. New York, Holt Rinehart, and London, Hutchinson, 1982.

Don Bueno. London, Hutchinson, 1983; New York, Holt Rinehart, 1984.
Figures of Enchantment. London, Hutchinson, and New York, Harper, 1986.
The Triple Mirror of the Self. London, Bloomsbury, 1992.

Short Stories

Statement against Corpses, with B.S. Johnson. London, Constable, 1964.
Veronica and the Gongóra Passion. Toronto, TSAR, 1998.

Other

Confessions of a Native-Alien (autobiography). London, Routledge, 1965.
Hamlet, Prufrock, and Language. London, Macmillan, and New York, St. Martin's Press, 1978.
The Fiction of Reality. London, Macmillan, 1983.
The Art of Creating Fiction. Basingstoke and London, MacMillan, 1991.
Shakespeare's Mortal Knowledge. Basingstoke and London, Mac-Millan, and New York, St. Martin's Press, 1993.

Critical Studies: *Structures of Negation—The Writings of Zulfikar Ghose* by Chelva Kanaganayakam, Toronto, University of Toronto Press, 1993; ''Beyond Personal History: Zulfikar Ghose's Confessions of a Native Alien'' by June Gaur, in *Literary Criterion* (India), 31(1–2), 1996.

*   *   *

Like several of his distinguished contemporaries from the commonwealth, the Pakistani poet Zulfikar Ghose combines sophistication of technique with a sense of deracination. His gift for the rendering of minutiae is considerable, as in ''Getting to Know Fish'':

> Bombay's famous fish is called Bombay Duck.
> Slim and lazy-eyed like English haddock,
> it is a small fish, dried in the sun,
> hanging, hooked to string, among coconut trees.
> It stinks. When dry, it is boiled and eaten
> with rice; through the hollows of its eyes
> its bone-juice is pressed out, salted and spiced . . .

For a Western reader such particularity has an attraction beyond its grip on circumstance. What is matter-of-fact for Ghose is, for his audience in the West, exotic. Thus, in speaking realistically of his childhood, Ghose commands a color and romance over and above his ostensible subject. It would be deprecating Ghose's intelligence to assume that he is unaware of the fascination of his subject matter. He appears himself in his careful verses as an alien presence, where he calls attention, for example, to his crooked nose, his ''morose-Ghose face.'' But the point about Ghose is that he is alien everywhere. He looks for his roots (''To My Ancestors''), he loses India (''The Loss of India''), and he falls in love with England (''This Landscape, These People''). Yet he is not at home there. English tolerance permits an air of drought between himself and the natives (''The Alien''), and he cries, ''I belong to this landscape but not to these people'' (''Marriages''). Ghose is a poet, not of love, but of distance, not of belonging, but of alienation.

This indicates the presence of a dichotomy deep down in the plasma of Ghose's verse. He has adopted a language so completely that he must be regarded as one of its modern masters, yet his precision of detail is a pattern about a void. This is seen quite clearly when Ghose attempts a major theme, as in ''War in India'':

> In Delhi I saw this:
>   a man, yes a man and not a reptile,
>   crawl from the bank of the pavement to defile
> the streamlined river of traffic with his
>
> blood . . .

There is a disparity between the theme and its expression. The technique, adequate for tourist sketches and domestic settings, unintentionally reduces its subject matter. It is as though the eye, unsteadied by what it perceives, slides from the battle to the peripheries. An immobilized tank is seen as a crab upside down; the valleys, policed with airstrips, seem to Ghose like bowls scoured of ice. Restricted by sensibility or by technique, Ghose seems unable to rise far beyond the recording of minutiae.

All of the poems quoted so far occur in Ghose's first collection, *The Loss of India*. It is a fine book, but it has the limitations of its fineness. Deracination seems to have set limits to Ghose's imaginative horizons, and the subsequent collections extend those horizons only nominally. *Jets from Orange* brings in France (''Choosing a Language,'' ''Of Animate and Inanimate Matter'') but does so in much the same externalizing way as the first book brought in Britain. *The Violent West* evokes America, but it is an America of the yellow butterflies of Lake Travis, the brown earth of Texas. In both books there are Indian poems, and it is they that act as the real attraction. ''The Attack on Sialkot,'' ''The Kleptomaniac,'' and ''In the Desert'' have something of the intensity and the nostalgia of the poems about India in the first collection. Thus Ghose's considerable distinction depends largely on one book. Nonetheless, he has done extraordinary well in pitting an alien background against a metropolitan technique and has done so with a degree of wisdom, balance, and fusion.

—Philip Hobsbaum

GIBBONS, (William) Reginald (Jr.)

Nationality: American. **Born:** Houston, Texas, 7 January 1947. **Education:** Princeton University, New Jersey, 1965–69, B.A. in Spanish 1969; Stanford University, Palo Alto, California, 1969–74, M.A in English and creative writing 1971, Ph.D. in comparative literature 1974. **Family:** Married 1) Virginia M. Harris in 1968 (divorced 1983); 2) Cornelia M. Spelman in 1983; one stepdaughter and one stepson. **Career:** Instructor, Livingston College, Rutgers University, New Brunswick, New Jersey, 1975–76; lecturer, Princeton University, New Jersey, 1976–80, and Columbia University, New York, 1980–81. Since 1981 lecturer, then professor, Northwestern University, Evanston, Illinois. Since 1989 member of the core faculty, M.F.A. Program for Writers, Warren Wilson College, Swannanoa, North Carolina. Editor, *TriQuarterly* magazine, Evanston, Illinois,

1981–97. Co-founder of TriQuarterly Books. **Awards:** Woodrow Wilson Foundation fellowship, 1969; Guggenheim fellowship, 1984; National Endowment for the Arts fellowship, 1984; John Masefield Memorial award, 1991; Carl Sandburg award, 1992; Jesse Jones award, Texas Institute of Letters, 1995; Anisfield-Wolf Book award, 1995; Balcones poetry prize, 1998. **Member:** Texas Institute of Letters; Society of Midland Authors; Poetry Society of America; The Guild Complex, 1989. **Address:** Department of English, 215 University Hall, Northwestern University, Evanston, Illinois, 60208, U.S.A.

PUBLICATIONS

Poetry

Roofs Voices Roads. Princeton, New Jersey, Quarterly Review of Literature, 1979.
The Ruined Motel. Boston, Houghton Mifflin, 1981.
Saints. New York, Persea Books, 1986.
Maybe It Was So. Chicago, University of Chicago Press, 1991.
Sparrow: New and Selected Poems. Baton Rouge, Louisiana State University Press, 1997.
Homage to Longshot O'Leary. Duluth, Minnesota, Holy Cow! Press, 1999.

Novel

Sweetbitter. Seattle, Broken Moon Press, 1994.

Short Stories

Five Pears or Peaches. Seattle, Broken Moon Press, 1991.

Other

William Goyen: A Study of the Short Fiction. Boston, Twayne, 1991.

Editor and translator, *Selected Poems of Luis Cernuda.* Berkeley, University of California Press, 1977.
Editor, *The Poet's Work: 29 Masters of Modern Poetry on the Origins and Practice of Their Art.* Boston, Houghton Mifflin, 1979.
Editor and translator, with A.L. Geist, *Guillén on Guillén: The Poetry and the Poet.* Princeton, New Jersey, Princeton University Press, 1979.
Editor, with Gerald Graff, *Criticism in the University.* Evanston, Illinois, Northwestern University Press, 1985.
Editor, *The Writer in Our World.* New York, Atlantic Monthly Press, 1986.
Editor, *Writers from South Africa.* Evanston, Illinois, TriQuarterly Books, 1988.
Editor, with Terrence Des Pres, *Thomas McGrath: Life and the Poem.* Chicago, University of Illinois Press, 1991.
Editor and translator, *New Writing from Mexico.* Evanston, Illinois, TriQuarterly Books, 1992.
Translator, *Bakkhai,* by Euripides. New York, Oxford University Press, 2000.

*

Critical Studies: ''An Interview with Reginald Gibbons'' by Sharon Darrow, in *The Writer's Chronicle,* 32(2), October/November 1999.

*   *   *

Through his editorship of the publication *Triquarterly* from 1981 to 1997, Reginald Gibbons made a significant contribution to the development of contemporary poetry. In an age in which there are far fewer outlets for book publishing than there are poetry manuscripts, Gibbons some years ago converted what was a traditional journal into a publication of new books of poetry. Under his editorship each issue of *Triquarterly* came to contain three or four complete manuscripts rather than small selections of works by dozens of poets. It was a brilliant innovation in a field in which practices usually are set in stone.

But Gibbons's contributions to the art of poetry do not end with his work at *Triquarterly.* In fact, a good case can be built to support the assertion that his own writing eclipses his achievements at the journal. Gibbons has written award-winning short stories, edited *The Poet's Work,* translated the poems of Luis Cernuda, and produced collections of his own verse, including *Roofs Voices Roads* and *The Ruined Motel.* Gibbons's thoughtful poems, deceptively quiet in tone, contain a complexity that is absent in the work of a majority of his peers. Unlike many other poets, Gibbons is able to make palpable for readers the connection between personal revelation and experience in the larger world. If it can be said of any contemporary poet that the author's personality is truly invisible in the field of the works themselves, it can be said of Gibbons's poetry. This is no small achievement and is difficult to gauge, but after a time, even on occasions when Gibbons uses the first-person pronoun, the reader is likely to realize that the usual accompanying voice and persona of the poet are completely submerged in the characters and speakers of the poem itself:

I was thinking, This was where we had brought
the nation, to neighboring new tries
either abandoned or shuddering inward with extreme—
till you said to me, The ghosts in this place
are unhappy. Then I too could hear them—
couple revenging the hours they had
together under ceilings
that never fell on them, the too-loud talk
at dinner and the hedging, hopeful
postcards in the morning.
We stepped away from them, from the boards
and slats of their collapsed beds,
from their fatigue, from musty air and dead wires,
we went back into the salt wind
and the noisy swaying pines, out
of that heap of winter-storm
tide-wrack.

This deceptively loose passage from ''The Ruined Motel'' illustrates the point well. Whereas most poets would not expand their efforts beyond the stark autobiographical commentary springing from a discovery of a dilapidated building on a car trip, for Gibbons it marks only a beginning, the point of departure. Thus, the poem opens up to the nation itself, to the troubled people who populate it (and who trouble it, too). As they come into focus, the couple we set off with

settle into the crowd. This is appropriate, the height of fictive invention. It is a method—and a talent—all too rare in our poetry.

Winner of the National Poetry Series award for 1985, Gibbons's third collection, *Saints,* deals mainly with characters, most of whom are in search of sainthood. Whether in moments of tender vulnerability, as in the prose poem ''Five Peaches or Pears,'' or in the middle of extreme violence, as in ''The Blue Dress,'' Gibbons maintains that humanity is born of every kind of character. Sainthood, in fact, is possible everywhere, even in the most unlikely place. Searching for redemption in every corner of life and in every relationship is Gibbons's enduring quest.

The later *Maybe It Was So* contains only five love poems, but each resonates with the careful investment of a voice that expects to find transformation within its speech. In one of the poems, ''Hark,'' love is the experience that not only transforms but also deepens receptivity and cleanses the soul:

Stars in the clear night sky more silent than any other
    silence,
even a cave's; and yet at each star the noise of fusion
blasts to beggar rockets massed in the millions, a roaring
multiplied to futile infinity out there, in the silent sky
over us, as we lie close listening to each other breathe,
hearing each other's heartbeats, sensing the smallest
candle wick of each other's noiseless warming desire.

Sentimental at its heart, *Maybe It Was So* seems an attempt to validate sentimentality in love poems, even with its complex yearning to account for things so good the poet wishes they would stay forever.

Gibbons's later work stretches out into looser, more expansive forms. Mixing narrative and lyric modes in *Sparrow: New and Selected Poems,* he writes about a man remembering the dead, a woman's retaliation against a violent lover, a kiss that comes by surprise, trees in winter, and the flight of small birds he wishes he could see with no symbolic strings attached. Whether haunted by loss or striving to make involvement in a subject really matter, Gibbons proves again and again that he is capable of hearing the difficult and bringing it to poems with conviction and honesty.

—Robert McDowell and Martha Sutro

GILBERT, Jack

Nationality: American. **Born:** Pittsburgh, Pennsylvania, 17 February 1925. **Education:** University of Pittsburgh, B.A.; University of California, Berkeley, 1958–59; San Francisco State College (now University), M.A. 1962. **Career:** Associated with San Francisco State College (now University), 1956–71, University of California, Berkeley, 1958–59, Humboldt State College (now University), Juniata College, Rikkyo University, Tokyo, 1974–75, and Syracuse University, 1982–83. **Awards:** Yale Younger Poets award, Yale University, and Pulitzer prize nomination, 1962, for *Views of Jeopardy;* Guggenheim fellow in poetry, 1964; Stanley Kunitz prize, American Poetry Review prize, Pulitzer prize nomination, and National Book Critics Circle nomination for best book of poetry, 1982, for *Monolithos: Poems, 1962 and 1982;* Borestone Mountain Poetry award. **Address:** 136 Montana Street, San Francisco, California 94112, U.S.A.

PUBLICATIONS

Poetry

Views of Jeopardy. New Haven, Connecticut, Yale University Press, 1962.
Monolithos: Poems, 1962 and 1982. New York, Knopf, 1982.
Kochan, with Four Poems by Michiko Nogami. Syracuse, New York: Tamarack Editions, 1984.
The Great Fires: Poems, 1982–1992. New York, Knopf, 1994.

*

Critical Studies: Interview with Ralph Adamo and John Biguenet, in *New Orleans Review* (New Orleans), 22(3–4), fall-winter 1996; "Between Truth and Meaning" by Allen Hoey, in *American Poetry Review* (Philadelphia), 26(1), January-February 1997; "Jack Gilbert: Noh Getting Overview" by Janet C. Moore, in *Hollins Critic* (Hollins College, Virginia), 35(1), February 1998.

*   *   *

Throughout a career spanning half a century, Jack Gilbert has scrupulously avoided career moves and the collective movements that make careers. In San Francisco during the 1950s, he attended evenings at Kenneth Rexroth's home, helped to arrange one of the first performances of Allen Ginsberg's "Howl," and participated in Jack Spicer's "Magic" workshop, yet he cast himself ironically as the title character in "Malvolio in San Francisco," more self-critical than Shakespeare's character yet just as contemptuous of the drunken revelers who surrounded him: "The first rate seems unknown / In this city of easy fame." Later, amid the counterculture movement of Haight-Ashbury—"no rules for the arts, let the kids educate themselves," he recalled in an interview—Gilbert attempted to teach the rules of art to the "kids" at San Francisco State College. While his respect for the passion that moved the counterculture aligns him with the antiacademic new American poetry, in his insistence on craft Gilbert retains an allegiance to the great modernists of the early twentieth century. "The craft of the invisible," as he calls it, to distinguish it from the cosmetic formalism of midcentury academic poetry, is form in the service of content. The content includes passion, but there is a greater "fire," which differs from passion as adolescent sexuality differs from mature romantic love:

Love does not last, but it is different
from the passions that do not last.
Love lasts by not lasting.
Isaiah said each man walks in his own fire
for his sins. Love allows us to walk
in the sweet music of our particular heart.

For Gilbert the impossible challenge facing the poet is not merely to commit himself to the fires of passion, as the hero does in "Don Giovanni on His Way to Hell," but also to return from that mysterious hell and sing about it, as Orpheus does in the story Gilbert retells throughout his career. For the poet the story implies a choice between two modes of responding to the central experience of losing what one loves, as Orpheus lost Eurydice the first time. "He might have grieved / Easily," as "Malvolio in San Francisco" recognizes. The emotion alone would justify his song, the "Orphic Fallacy" that

Dudley Fitts sought to oppose by conferring the Yale Younger Poets award on Gilbert's *Views of Jeopardy.* Jeopardizing his relation to his audience, Gilbert opts for "the difficult journey," following Orpheus to hell and back in an attempt to recover in loss what is never lost, the "love [that] lasts by not lasting."

This timeless point of view establishes the terms on which the details of Gilbert's life enter his poetry. His volumes memorialize a series of love affairs: with Gianna Gelmetti (*Views of Jeopardy*), Linda Gregg (*Monolithos*), and Michiko Nogami (*Kochan* and *The Great Fires*). Although the series unfolds in time, each love is viewed retrospectively, as an instance of loss. Thus each woman is a type of Orpheus's Eurydice, while at the same time she is celebrated for "all her fresh particularity of difference," the knowledge sought by Gilbert's Don Giovanni. Ironically, the more Gilbert seeks to hold onto the particularity, the more alien his language must sound to an audience, as he himself acknowledges in "The Forgotten Dialect of the Heart." His almost ritualized recital of his lovers' names— "Gelmetti and Gregg / and Nogami lasted"—leaves the reader with nothing but names, instead of a sense of persons. Still, while failing to recover Eurydice, Gilbert manages to capture a world transformed by the experience of love. When Orpheus makes the fatal decision to look back at Eurydice, in "County Musician," it is

to have at least the face
seen freshly with loss
forever. A landscape.

Particular landscapes are associated with particular lovers in Gilbert's work—Italy with Gianna Gelmetti, the Aegean islands with Linda Gregg—but the world that emerges most powerfully in the late work, as if in contrast to the exotic homeland of his dead wife Michiko Nogami, is the Pittsburgh of Gilbert's own childhood. In "Threshing the Fire," a sequence at the conclusion of *Monolithos,* and throughout *The Great Fires* images of Pittsburgh evoke a nightmare of industry, as if Orpheus, having failed to rescue Eurydice from hell, succeeded in retrieving the landscape of hell itself. But this is the hell of Blake as much as of Orpheus, for it burns with the creative fires of imagination as well as of desire:

He does not understand, but he knew the wanting.
Remembers working in the mill, the titanic shear
Cleaving the slabs into sections. Halfway
To something. Smell of Pittsburgh after rain.

This is "the smell of journey" that "Malvolio in San Francisco" attaches to Orpheus. Unable to name the destination, Gilbert persists in that journey, "halfway / to something."

—Terence Diggory

GILBERT, Sandra M.

Pseudonym: Rosette Lewis. Also has written as Sandra Ellen Mortola and S.M. Gilbert. **Nationality:** American. **Born:** Sandra Ellen Mortola, New York City, 27 December 1936. **Education:** Cornell University, Ithaca, New York, B.A. (high honors) in English 1957; New York University, M.A. 1961; Columbia University, New York, Ph.D. 1968. **Family:** Married Elliot Lewis Gilbert in 1957 (died 1991); one son, two daughters. **Career:** Associate professor and professor of English, University of California, Davis, 1975–85; professor of English, Princeton University, New Jersey, 1985–89. Since 1989 professor of English, University of California, Davis. **Awards:** Eunice Tietjens memorial prize, *Poetry,* 1980; NEH fellowship, 1980–81, 1999; Rockefeller Foundation Humanities fellowship, 1982; Guggenheim fellowship, 1983; fellow, School of Criticism and Theory, 1984–96; Charity Randall award, International Poetry Foundation, 1990; Rockefeller Foundation Bellagio Study Center residency, 1991; University of California President's fellowship, 1991–92; Union League prize, *Poetry,* 1995; Paterson prize, 1996, for *Ghost Volcano;* Bogliasco Foundation residency, 2000; Soros fellowship, 2000. D.Litt.: Wesleyan University, 1988. **Member:** American Academy of Arts & Sciences, 1997. **Agent:** Ellen Levine Agency, 15 East 26th Street, Suite 1801, New York, New York 10010, U.S.A. **Address:** 53 Menlo Place, Berkeley, California 94707, U.S.A.

PUBLICATIONS

Poetry

In the Fourth World: Poems. University, University of Alabama Press, 1979.
The Summer Kitchen: Poems. Woodside, California, Heyeck, 1983.
Emily's Bread: Poems. New York, Norton, 1984.
Blood Pressure: Poems. New York, Norton, 1988.
Ghost Volcano: Poems. New York and London, Norton, 1995.
Kissing the Bread: New and Selected Poems, 1969–1999. New York, Norton, 2000.

Other

Acts of Attention: The Poems of D.H. Lawrence. Ithaca, New York, Cornell University Press, 1973; revised edition, Carbondale, Southern Illinois University Press, 1990.
The Madwoman in the Attic: The Woman Writer and the Nineteenth-Century Literary Imagination, with Susan Gubar. New Haven, Connecticut, Yale University Press, 1979.
No Man's Land: The Place of the Woman Writer in the Twentieth-Century, vol. I, The War of the Words, with Susan Gubar. New Haven, Connecticut, Yale University Press, 1987.
No Man's Land: The Place of the Woman Writer in the Twentieth Century, vol. II, Sexchanges, with Susan Gubar. New Haven, Connecticut, Yale University Press, 1989.
No Man's Land: The Place of the Woman Writer in the Twentieth Century, vol. III, Letters from the Front, with Susan Gubar. New Haven, Connecticut, Yale University Press, 1994.
Wrongful Death: A Medical Tragedy. New York, Norton, 1995.
Masterpiece Theatre: An Academic Melodrama, with Susan Gubar. New Brunswick, New Jersey, Rutgers University Press, 1995.
Inventions of Farewell: A Millennial Book of Elegies. New York, Norton, 2000.

Editor, with Susan Gubar, *Shakespeare's Sisters: Feminist Essays on Women Poets.* Bloomington, Indiana University Press, 1979.
Editor, *Kate Chopin's The Awakening and Selected Stories.* New York, Penguin, 1984.
Editor, with Susan Gubar, *Norton Anthology of Literature by Women: The Tradition in English.* New York, Norton, 1985.

Editor, with Susan Gubar, *A Guide to the Norton Anthology of Literature by Women.* New York, Norton, 1985.
Editor, *Orlando: A Biography,* by Virginia Woolf. London and New York, Penguin, 1993.
Editor, with Susan Gubar and Diana O'Hehir, *Mothersongs: Poems for, by and about Mothers.* New York, Norton, 1995.
Editor, with Wendy Barker, *The House Is Made of Poetry: Essays on the Art of Ruth Stone.* Carbondale, Souther Illinois University Press, 1996.

*

Critical Studies: By Chandra Mukerji, in *Contemporary Sociology,* 19(4), July 1990; by Beth Williams Baldwin, in *English Literature in Transition, 1880–1920,* 33(2), 1990; by Marilyn May, in *D.H. Lawrence Review,* 23(1), spring 1991; by Margot Norris, in *Comparative Literature,* 43(2), spring 1991; ''Learning to Read the Mother Tongue: On Sandra Gilbert's Blood Pressure'' by Kevin Clark, in *Iowa Review* (Iowa City, Iowa), 22(1), winter 1992; ''The Textual Mother As Unmothered Daughter'' by Elizabeth L. MacNabb, in *West Virginia University Philological Papers* (Morgantown, West Virginia), 38, 1992; ''Blindspots of an Old Dream of Equality: Liberal Feminism As Exclusionary Practice in 'No Man's Land''' by Vara Neverow-Turk, in *Studies in 20th Century Literature,* 17(1), winter 1993; by Elaine Showalter, in *London Review of Books* (London), 16(20), 20 October 1994; by Diane Wakoski and by Lisa Alther, both in *Women's Review of Books,* 12(10–11), July 1995; ''Fighting for Herland: The Sex Wars of Gilbert & Gubar'' by Paul Dean, in *New Criterion* (New York), 13(3), April 1995; ''Sentences of Self and Blood and Sea: The Poetry of Sandra M. Gilbert'' by Diane Raptosh, in *RLA* (West Lafayette, Indiana), 8, 1996.

Sandra Gilbert comments:

I am both a poet and a critic: in fact, though I started my writing life as a poet, I would have to confess that I achieved my earliest widespread recognition as a critic and specifically as a feminist critic. Yet in many ways, despite my intense commitment to verse, I think my career as a feminist literary critic has reflected my aesthetic ambitions as well as my political and theoretical interests. After all, I don't just believe that, as we used to say in the Women's Movement in the seventies, 'the personal is the political.' I also believe that 'the personal is the poetical.' At the same time, I want in poetry to find what visionary poets have always sought: the extraordinary in the ordinary, the numinous and luminous in the quotidian.

Where such a desire will lead me is something I am still struggling to understand.

*   *   *

Sandra M. Gilbert's reputation as a feminist in the fields of English literature and in women's and gender studies knows almost no equal in the United States, acknowledging, of course, the equally indispensable role played by her coauthor, Susan Gubar. The wonderful scholarly books of Gilbert and Gubar—*Shakespeare's Sisters* and *The Madwoman in the Attic: The Woman Writer and the Nineteenth-Century Literary Imagination,* along with their trilogy *No Man's Land: The Place of the Woman Writer in the Twentieth Century*—are required reading in many literature courses these days. Most feminists growing up in the academy during the late 1960s treasure the works of these two important women.

Given her established reputation as a feminist literary scholar, I do not envy Gilbert the task of launching herself as a poet. The public's expectations for her achievement are probably much too high. The ambition to excel in a line of creative work in a manner akin to her scholarly achievements may well have given her pause. As she knows all too well, women writers only lately have come to think of themselves as "conscious subjects in the world." They need to be possessed by their poems, and, to borrow from Mary Kinzie, it is necessary to remember that writing poetry is risk taking, a precarious venture of discovery in which very often the poet is still unfolding meaning as she parts from the poem. Until her fifth volume of poetry, Gilbert's poetic accomplishments benefit from being considered as provisional and still in the making. Poets, Kinzie writes in *A Poet's Guide to Poetry*, "stand upon the given in order to peer over into the unshaped but unfolding present." A close reading of the forms of their verse can help to fill out the partial presence they struggle to materialize in verse, something that is especially true in the case of Gilbert.

Gilbert has been writing and publishing poetry since the late 1960s. Her poetic accomplishments inevitably invite comparison to those of the best American women poets of the period and to her literary ancestors—Sylvia Plath, Amy Clampitt, Rita Dove, Adrienne Rich, Marianne Moore, and Elizabeth Bishop. Compared to the poems of these writers, her poetry is pale. She has less technical command and a considerably more limited range, and she wants the genius that marks their imaginations. Her poems lack the precision of language that distinguishes the verse of Moore, Bishop, or Plath, nor do they have these poets' particularity of image. Although she has a love of music and writes movingly of her husband's devotion to Wagner, she does not possess the sense of rhythm and music that pervades Plath and Bishop's poetry. If readers expect to find a strong feminist bent in her verse similar to that of Adrienne Rich, they will again be disappointed. She is not a writer of political advocacy, nor does she share the lesbian agenda that is characteristic of Rich's poetry at its best. Gilbert certainly calls on her feminist traditions, even naming one of her five volumes of poetry *Emily's Bread,* thus evoking the two nineteenth-century poets, Emily Brontë and Emily Dickinson, whom she greatly admires. She has crafted a volume of poetry, *The Summer Kitchen: Poems,* set in women's space and capturing a woman's voice and perceptions as well as experience. Christina Rossetti's brilliance found in "Goblin Market" has opened a vein of poetry to Gilbert, who similarly creates a grotesque and eerie mood in her book *In the Fourth World* as she catalogues the night creatures who appear to her in dreams and seem to hover just under appearances in her daylight world.

Gilbert's finest volume to date is *Ghost Volcano,* which demonstrates a much grater command of the poetic medium. In it she chronicles her mourning as she writes with an astonishing honesty and acute sense of loss about the wrongful death of her husband at the hands of surgeons, which left her a widow in 1991. In the collection she takes her place alongside the great male writers of elegies and numbers with Emily Dickinson in her ability to treat death and mourning in a singular fashion.

Gilbert is at her best when she sets forth familiar domestic subjects and offers a fresh understanding of them, at once both personal and universal. It is the candor behind her expressions of feeling that are memorable. Most of her poetry is written in a free verse that is almost prosaic. Throughout her career she plays with stanzaic form and gains her emotional effect by the play of enjambment and hard stops created by the way form and syntax strain against each

other or coincide. She uses figurative language and conceits but does so only lightly. Similarly, her reliance on alliteration or onomatopoeia or even on unusual diction or demotic speech is limited.

Gilbert's are poems of intimacy and feeling, as shown by titles like "The Dream Kitchen," "The Dressmaker's Dummy," "Daguerreotype," and "'Fallen Woman.'" Her subjects are drawn from painting or music, and she also selects more unlikely and fresher subjects—the cocktail hour or a traffic jam or that of "Getting Fired, or 'Not Being Retained.'" Other poems are drawn from nature or call up occasional moments imbued with feeling, lyrical impulses hidden just beneath the surface of things. A sense of terror or uncertainty predominates her world in the early volumes *In the Fourth World* and *Emily's Bread.* She often opens a poem with a declaration of the hour or with a title that captures the place. Familiar figures from her personal and professional life are named in her poems, and their importance to her is evident and their place in the scheme of things is assumed but not demonstrated through her evocations of them. When Gubar or her husband, Elliot Lewis Gilbert, or one of her daughters is mentioned in a poem, there is, before *Ghost Volcano,* little effort to capture the person, to make the person real to the reader.

In *Ghost Volcano,* however, something different and utterly life changing has occurred, enabling Gilbert to write with an urgency and depth of feeling largely missing from her earlier poems. Her husband of more than thirty years has died, and his death, at age sixty-one, is obscene in her eyes. She uses memory and desire to recall and evoke him again and again so that she can recover him in some manner, making her feel less remote from him and less lost than she felt when he began to die abruptly on an operating table while she and her daughter were out shopping, at the surgeon's orders, in order to "distract themselves" during what should have been an ordinary surgery. Gilbert spent more than three years writing a memoir, *Wrongful Death,* detailing with brutal realism her husband's death at the hands of the medical profession.

In *Ghost Volcano,* amid formal elegiac poems, she interweaves in five sections the "Widow's Walk" poems, which appear throughout the volume, forming what she calls "a narrative of the stages of grief" that she was struggling through during the period. The volume also contains more formal elegies. One series of meditations, "Kissing the Bread," celebrates a custom practiced in the household of her mother but passed on to her from her Sicilian relatives and linking Christian and Jewish customs that celebrate life and death. Another poem sequence reflects on her husband's Jewish heritage and commemorates the 1,000 Jewish zealots who killed themselves at Massada rather than face conquest by the Romans. Two other sections, "Water Music" and "Calla Lilies," broaden the scope of the collection with musings on nature, water, and symbolic flowers, mining them for their mythopoetic elements and placing the death of her husband in a larger context. The lyrical poems carry personal significance but also universal feelings about the temporariness of life, the uncertainty of religion, and the desire to understand and know. Hovering behind Gilbert's elegies are Tennyson's *In Memoriam* and other elegies or elegiac sequences by Walt Whitman, John Milton, Matthew Arnold, and Robert Browning. Dylan Thomas, John Crowe Ransom, Robert Lowell, Theodore Roethke, and James Dickey, to name but a few, have all written poems memorializing someone they deeply loved, be it a father, daughter, student, or child killed by a firebombing in London, but women writers have traveled this terrain less frequently.

Gilbert's volume is unmistakably the elegy of a woman, and the great force and influence behind it is Dickinson, a poet so accustomed to visitations to deathbeds that her poems breathe and speak these visits. Gilbert's poems are those of a woman who is at once a wife, a companion to her husband, the mother of three children, and a teacher who practiced the same profession as her husband. She will not accept what she sees as the false comfort of religion; her world is a dangerous one with dark forebodings, a world in which religious zealots practice mass suicides and Halloween comes around yearly, spooking children with the idea of ghosts. Gilbert does not believe in ghosts, and she cannot be certain that there is a metaphysical sphere holding her loved husband. She does not share her husband's Jewish faith, for which she will not make an apology, and she refuses to believe that had she shared his religion she could have found greater comfort. He was scared at the thought of dying, she and he had their share of quarrels, and she is honest enough to acknowledge them. She fears that he has traveled so far from her—farther than the farthest star—that she does not know any other way of finding consolation and affirming his life than to keep him alive by the force of her memory and the power of her words and her chronicle.

Gilbert thus continues her imaginary conversations with her husband, and she revisits the places they have been. She looks down on one of the rock faces on Mount Rainer as she flies over it with a friend and sees in it the cold and implacable death mask of her husband. One of the most vivid and memorable poems in the collection is ''February ll, 1992: At the Art Institute of Chicago,'' in which she calls forth her visit with her husband to see Seurat's *Sunday Afternoon on the Island of La Grande Jatte,* in near proximity in the Art Institute to van Gogh's painting of his screaming yellow bed and of the anguished ''bloodied eyes'' depicted in his self-portrait. Another equally brilliant poem incorporating the world of painting is ''December 1, 1993: Paris, Looking at Monet,'' a poem about Monet's yellow irises and water lilies and their place in the life of Gilbert and her husband over the course of their marriage and during its aftermath.

I opened by suggesting that Gilbert's poetry is provisional, requiring an active reader who can enter into her poems, inhabit them, and keep working to complete the meanings she hints at on those occasions when her ultimate meaning is still unknown to her. *Ghost Volcano* leaves fewer moments undecided and succeeds by making the reader complicit in the poet's quest. The stakes are high. On Gilbert's part, her very life depends on keeping alive the man who is dead; on the reader's part, anyone who has lost someone vital to his being has a stake in her success.

—Carol Simpson Stern

GILDNER, Gary

Nationality: American. **Born:** West Branch, Michigan, 22 August 1938. **Education:** Michigan State University, East Lansing, B.A. 1960, M.A. 1961. **Family:** Married 1) Judy McKibben in 1963 (divorced 1980), one daughter; 2) Elizabeth Mary Sloan in 1991, one daughter. **Career:** Writer in university relations department, Wayne State University, Detroit, 1961–62; instructor, Northern Michigan University, Marquette, 1963–65. Since 1966 member of the department, now professor of English, Drake University, Des Moines, Iowa. Visiting professor and writer-in-residence, Reed College, Portland, Oregon, 1983–85; writer-in-residence, Michigan State University,

1987; Senior Fulbright Professor, University of Warsaw, Poland, 1987–88; McGee Professor of writing, Davidson College, 1992; Senior Fulbright Lecturer, Safarik University, Slovakia, 1992–93. **Awards:** Bread Loaf Writers Conference Robert Frost fellowship, 1970; National Endowment for the Arts fellowship, 1971, 1976; Yaddo fellowship, 1972, 1973, 1975, 1976, 1978; MacDowell Colony fellowship, 1974; Theodore Roethke prize, 1976, and Helen Bullis prize, 1979 (*Poetry Northwest*); William Carlos Williams prize (*New Letters*), 1977; National Magazine award, for fiction, 1986. **Agent:** Nat Sobel Associates, 146 East 19th Street, New York, New York 10003. **Address:** RR 2, Box 219, Grangeville, Idaho 83530–9615, U.S.A.

PUBLICATIONS

Poetry

First Practice. Pittsburgh, University of Pittsburgh Press, 1969.
Digging for Indians. Pittsburgh, University of Pittsburgh Press, 1971.
Eight Poems. Denver, Bredahl, 1973.
Nails. Pittsburgh, University of Pittsburgh Press, 1975.
Letters from Vicksburg. Greensboro, North Carolina, Unicorn Press, 1976.
The Runner. Pittsburgh, University of Pittsburgh Press, 1978.
Jabón. Portland, Oregon, Breitenbush, 1981.
Blue Like the Heavens: New and Selected Poems. Pittsburgh, University of Pittsburgh Press, 1984.
Clackamas: Poems. Pittsburgh, Carnegie Mellon Press, 1991.
The Swing. Boise, Idaho, Limberlost Press, 1996.
The Bunker in the Parsley Fields: Poems. Iowa City, University of Iowa Press, 1997.

Novel

The Second Bridge. Chapel Hill, North Carolina, Algonquin, 1987.

Short Stories

The Crush. New York, Ecco Press, 1983.
A Week in South Dakota. Chapel Hill, North Carolina, Algonquin, 1987.

Other

Toads in the Greenhouse. Des Moines, Iowa, Perfection Form, 1978.
The Warsaw Sparks (memoir). Iowa City, University of Iowa Press, 1990.

Editor, with Judith Gildner, *Out of This World: Poems from the Hawkeye State.* Ames, Iowa State University Press, 1975.
Editor, with David Ray, *Since Feeling Is First: An Anthology of New American Poetry.* Kansas City, University of Missouri, 1976.

*

Manuscript Collection: University of Pittsburgh.

Critical Study: "'Eat Everything!' A Consideration of the Work of Gary Gildner" by James Coleman, in *Centennial Review* (East Lansing, Michigan), 30(2), spring 1986.

Gary Gildner comments:

My poems are narrative mainly. Little fictions. I am fond of the persona and have among my characters a Mexican innocent named Soap; a boy at his first football practice in a school basement that doubles as a bomb shelter; a woman who has lost part of her hand; a Civil War soldier writing cocky letters, which become less so, home to his young wife; a German youth drafted by Napoleon to help him take Russia who ends up, warm at last, in Iowa; a former pro athlete speaking from his wheelchair at a pig roast; an old man lost in a retirement home; a young man in love with a goshawk in his attic; a man and his daughter making angels in the snow . . .

Clarity, setting, story, engagement, promise, conflict, music (gathering sound), mystery, resolution—I am fond of these elements as well. Nouns and verbs. Names. And respect for the line.

I started late. I was almost twenty-eight when I wrote my first poem. I wrote it out of frustration I think, because the story I wanted to write would not grow beyond the single sheet of paper it occupied. Thinking one page not enough for a short story, I decided that the stubborn text wanted to be a poem. Not much is shorter, is it?

I was not eager to try poetry. What did I know about it? The first and last "poems" I had written were in college, moonstruck and stealing from Whitman, trying to win a stunning girl whose legs were long and sleek and whose sea green eyes troubled me everywhere, in darkness and in light. (She later had her nose bobbed and became a fashion model.)

But I played with those sentences anyway, working them into lines I thought interesting. In truth I had six short stories like that, one-pagers, all of them facing me on a humid summer's day in the middle of America when what I really wanted to be writing was a novel—a man's work!—for which the six short story notions were to be warm-up exercises. (I had just abandoned a novel I had worked five years on; with every annual rewrite it got better, but it would never sing and I knew it.) I was almost twenty-eight. I was in a hurry. I turned the six short stories into six poems and sent them off, one each, to six magazines, mainly to be rid of them, the bastards. But they were all accepted. And that changed everything.

* * *

Since publishing his debut poetry volume, *First Practice,* in 1969, Gary Gildner has displayed a strong sense of narrative, character, voice, and situation. His poems are rich in prose virtues, and his ear is quick to hear the ways in which American speech rhythms can fruitfully play with the rhythms of verse in English. In this regard he is solidly in the poetic line of Emerson and Frost.

Gildner's earliest poems contain memorable snapshots of family life and adolescence that reverberate in the reader's memory, as in "Geisha" from *Digging for Indians:*

The boxer bitch is pregnant
puffed up like an Oriental wrestler!

The boys stand back,
aloof, embarrassed
or unsure of their hands.

But the girls, their cheeks aflame,
are down on shiny knees
praising all the nipples.

The title of *Digging for Indians* and of Gildner's next book, *Nails,* along with the resonances and depths of his earlier anecdotal poems, suggested a broadening concern. In 1976 Gildner published *Letters from Vicksburg*. Working from actual letters, he constructed a sonnet sequence of letters from a Civil War soldier to his wife. His continuing concern for family life and domestic continuity was a part of larger meditations on the disruptions and recurring themes of American history.

The Vicksburg poems appear in *The Runner* along with other poems that begin in Gildner's recognizable voice but that treat characters and situations new to his work. One of them begins, "In the blue winter of 1812 / Johann Gaertner, a bag of bones, / followed Napoleon home," and "When the Retarded Swim" continues in its first lines the sentence begun by the title—"at the Y on Fridays / a lot of time is taken up / with holding them, so they do not drown." Another poem is a 133-line monologue by a young athlete paralyzed from the waist down in a motorcycle accident. Yet another is spoken by a mad gardener who brings toads into his greenhouse to control the ladybugs he brought in to control the scale attacking his orchids; he winds up neglecting the plants to feed the toads, which desert him at the onset of frost. There are also poems of marital despair. The poems in *The Runner* are longer and more resourceful than Gildner's earlier vignettes, as if they had sought and found abilities to include the rush of pain and confusion held somewhat at bay by shorter forms.

In 1981 Gildner published *Jabón*. The title character is a kind of wise fool, a crazy Mexican who washes and blesses the taxis in a small village and who, because he cannot understand in rational, adult terms the life that swirls around him, comes to understand and accept life in more immediate and intuitive terms. The character of Jabón is remarkably unsentimentalized and is buffeted fiercely for not having conventional worldly skills, but by blessing taxis and the yellow pail in which he keeps the water to wash them, he is in some way in tune with life rather than in desperate contest with it. Late in the sequence Jabón joins forces with a precocious eight-year-old boy, and two American traveling opportunists, as they sit over lunch, discuss philosophically the alliance between Jabón and the boy:

. . . You know what
flashed in my head? It's some kind of cult.
Fifty years from now, a hundred, they'll dance
in the streets to those two, and put up a statue—
and guys like us will be nowhere, eating the special.

Blue like the Heavens: New and Selected Poems has an emotional equilibrium in sharp contrast to the tumults of *The Runner,* though the dark strains of the earlier fine book are not missing. Memory, and thus by extension the imagination itself, is the central preoccupation in these poems. One begins with a saleswoman on the telephone trying to sell the speaker insulation and ends like this:

"Are your children safe? Your loved ones?" she said.
Oh dear lady beyond these cold hands,
nothing is safe in my presence. I am a small hog
with a sore throat. A frog, the last egg

from the nest of a swan, even the puny squeal
of a porcupine—I will steal anything for a song.
Even your timid voice, dear lady,
lost at the other end for a way to make me warm.

Gildner's confrontation with nostalgia, memory, and his own imaginative impulses is an interesting development from a poet who has consistently grown in skill and stature, proposing in each step of the way more complex formal and imaginative tasks for himself. It may be that he is speaking to the possibilities of further development in a poem like "Always in Late Summer Now, in the City":

I think of how the gulls hang
lightly over the lake's edge,
and how a small perch slips to the surface, tiger-striped,
and how the white birch, in places, can look at you all day
—and I think of pushing away
from the dock, pulling forward into the farther dark,
the line of pine and fir on the far shore black,
a cut moon, a few stars to lighten my cupped hands,
wondering what's under my heart
that could take me deeper.

—William Matthews

GILLIES, Valerie

Nationality: Scottish. **Born:** Valerie Simmons, Edmonton, Alberta, Canada, 4 June 1948. **Career:** Writer-in-residence, Boroughmuir High School, Edinburgh, 1978, Edinburgh Academy, 1983, Duncan of Jordanstone College of Art, Dundee, 1988–90, Dundee District Libraries, 1988–90, Mid and East Lothian, 1991–93, and University of Edinburgh, 1995–97. **Address:** 67 Braid Avenue, Edinburgh EH10 6ED, Scotland.

PUBLICATIONS

Poetry

Trio: New Poets from Edinburgh, with Roderick Watson and Paul Mills. New York, New Rivers, 1971.
Each Bright Eye: Selected Poems. Edinburgh, Canongate, 1977.
Notes on Kim. New York, Longman, 1981.
Bed of Stone. Edinburgh, Canongate, 1984.
Leopardi: A Scottis Quair. Edinburgh, Edinburgh University Press, 1987.
Tweed Journey. Edinburgh, Canongate, 1989.
The Chanter's Tune. Edinburgh, Canongate, 1990.
The Jordanstone Folio. N.p., Tay Press, 1990.
The Ringing Rock. Edinburgh, Scottish Cultural Press, 1995.
St. Kilda Waulking Song. N.p., Morning Star, 1998.

*   *   *

Although Valerie Gillies was born in Canada, where her father was a Royal Air Force officer, the family moved to Scotland when she was six months old. She began writing when she was fourteen, but none of her early efforts are included in her later collections. A major influence on her development was Norman MacCaig, who lectured at Edinburgh University, where she was educated, and who organized lunchtime readings by other poets. (He is reported to have advised her to "mind her punctuation.") She has represented Scotland at international festivals in Ireland and Wales (the Beaumaris Arts Festival) and has given poetry readings throughout Scotland. She is represented in many anthologies.

Iain Crichton Smith hailed *Each Bright Eye,* which was published in 1977 and which was Gillies's first collection, as "the most interesting and fresh book of poems to come out of Scotland for a very long time." In it she staked out her territory—birds and other animals, exotic places, and weather—in words set down with vivid, zestful imagery. These qualities are even more accomplished in her volume *Bed of Stone* (1984). There is, for example, a remarkable sequence titled "Rabbit Voices" that seems to capture the very essence of rabbitness. Consider, for example, these lines from the fifth section:

The wind blows, the rain pelts,
It patters the earth.
It is good to sleep underground,
To sleep and sleep.

But at the dry hour,
The hard trail before us,
We will take our fill:
Corn, parsley, furze,
Stems, carrots, berries.
We look all around
And see the world,
Glad to taste so many things.
Not one of us can see
When his life will give way,
Teeth marks upon it.

There are touching human portraits, too, as in "We Meet Again," in which "Your son says to my daughter/'I hate girls—go away.'" The girl seeks the boy out nonetheless, and the speaker asks,

Who will remember to-day
when they discover
their own surprising eden?
As, in the pretty far back,
once it was you and me.

Gillies has become best known in Scotland as a poet of the country's rivers. As she followed two great rivers, the Tweed and the Tay, on their journeys from their sources to the sea, she invented her own form of "Strath poetics." The river poems are found in two collections, *Tweed Journey* (1989) and *The Ringing Rock* (1995). The latter is in two sequences, one carrying the title of the volume and the other "Tay Journey." Again, the poems show fresh, searching imagery, as in "Estuary," the penultimate poem in *The Ringing Rock:*

The tide's on the turn here,
opening the pilot's chart
a man is steering out to sea,

the tiller and the light hand on it

that smells of seawater:
his hand confirms the stars.

Gillies is also interested in multimedia activities and works with musicians and visual artists. In 1996–97 a selection of her poems accompanied the paintings in the exhibition *Two Scottish Artists* on a tour of cities in Texas. With the photographer Rebecca Marr she was awarded a cross-media grant to create text and images for an exhibition on ''the wild men and domestic animals of Scotland'' and entitled *Men and Beasts*. She has written both for films and television, notably the five-part documentary *Caledonians and Romans*. She also has served as a writer-in-residence at libraries and schools in Scotland, including Edinburgh University, and she has worked with Artlink, which facilitates the production of hospital patients' work in books and exhibitions.

—Maurice Lindsay

GIOIA, (Michael) Dana

Nationality: American. **Born:** Los Angeles, California, 24 December 1950. **Education:** Stanford University, Palo Alto, California, 1969–73, 1975–77, B.A. (summa cum laude) 1973, M.B.A. 1977; Harvard University, Cambridge, Massachusetts, 1973–75, M.A. 1975. **Family:** Married Mary Hiecke in 1980; three sons (one deceased). **Career:** Worked at General Foods, White Plains, New York, 1977–92 (last title vice president). Editor, 1971–73, and poetry editor, 1975–77, *Sequoia* magazine; literary editor, 1977–79, and poetry editor, 1979–83, *Inquiry* magazine. Since 1992 independent writer, since 1995 co-director, West Chester Writers Conference, and since 1997 music critic, *San Francisco* magazine. Contributing editor, *The Hudson Review.* **Awards:** Best of the New Generation award, *Esquire,* 1984; Poetry Book Society (London) main selection, 1991; Poet's prize, 1992; Publisher's Weekly Best Books award, 1992; American Literary Translator's award, 1992. **Address:** 7190 Faught Road, Santa Rosa, California 95403–7835, U.S.A.

PUBLICATIONS

Poetry

Daily Horoscope. St. Paul, Minnesota, Graywolf, 1986.
The Gods of Winter. St. Paul, Minnesota, Graywolf, and Calstock, Cornwall, Peterloo, 1991.
The Diviners: A Book Length Poem, with Robert McDowell. Brownsville, Oregon, Story Line Press, 1995.

Other

Can Poetry Matter? Essays on Poetry and American Culture. St. Paul, Minnesota, Graywolf, 1992.

Editor, *The Ceremony and Other Stories* by Weldon Kees. Omaha, Nebraska, Abattoir Editions, 1983; expanded edition, St. Paul, Minnesota, Graywolf, 1984.

Editor, with William Jay Smith, *Poems from Italy.* St. Paul, Minnesota, New Rivers Press, 1985.
Editor, with Michael Palma, *New Italian Poets.* Brownsville, Oregon, Story Line Press, 1991.
Editor, with William Logan, *Certain Solitudes: On the Poetry of Donald Justice.* Fayetteville, University of Arkansas Press, 1997.
Editor, with X.J. Kennedy, *An Introduction to Poetry* (ninth edition). New York, Longman, 1998.
Editor, with X.J. Kennedy, *An Introduction to Fiction* (seventh edition). New York, and London, Longman, 1999.
Editor, with X.J. Kennedy, *Literature: An Introduction to Fiction, Poetry, and Drama* (seventh edition). New York, Longman, 1999.

Translator, *Mottetti: Poems of Love,* by Eugenio Montale. St. Paul, Minnesota, Graywolf, 1990.
Translator, *The Madness of Hercules*, by Seneca. Baltimore, Johns Hopkins University Press, 1995.

*

Manuscript Collection: New York Public Library, Berg Collection, New York, New York.

Critical Studies: ''The Poet in the Gray Flannel Suit'' by Bruce Bawer, in *Connoisseur* (New York), March 1989; ''Reading the New Formalists'' by Robert McPhillips, in *Poetry after Modernism,* edited by Robert McDowell, Brownsville, Oregon, Story Line Press, 1991; ''Dana Gioia and the New Formalism'' by Peter Russell, in *The Edge City Review #2* (Reston, Virginia), 1994; ''Dana Gioia and Expansive Poetry'' by Kevin Walzer, in *Italian Americana* (Providence, Rhode Island), 16(1), winter 1998.

*   *   *

Dana Gioia is probably the most interesting poet to have emerged in the United States since the 1980s. He clearly thinks about the craft and role of the poet, and because he thinks critically, he has become a highly controversial figure. He writes about poetry and his fellow poets with both sympathy and clarity. Nonetheless, American letters—especially poetry—is heavily academic, wedded to the theory of free verse, and populated largely by professionals in higher education. Gioia, who comes from the world of commerce and who, like Poe, believes strongly in formal metrics, has been forced into the role of outsider.

In his poetry Gioia often reminds me of the Italian painter Giorgio de Chirico—the melancholia of frozen seasons, the chiaroscuro framed, and the metaphysicality:

The architecture of each station still preserves
its fantasy beside the sordid tracks—
defiant pergolas, a shuttered summer lodge,
a shadowy pavilion framed by high-arched windows
in this land of northern sun and lingering winter.

Is it a deep-seated memory of Gioia's distant Italian background coming through, a touch of the baroque in modern American functionalism? I do not know. But ''In Cheever Country,'' which begins with ''Half an hour north of Grand Central'' and from which these lines are taken, is a marvelous poem that exactly captures the feel the city worker experiences when he is commuting home by train ''to the modest places which contain our lives.''

Donald Justice describes Gioia's poetry as being ''work—in which dream and reality keep intersecting most beautifully,'' and as Eliot would have said, ''that's a way of putting it.'' But there is more to be said than this, for Gioia is no mere dreamy fantast but rather a true poet of the imagination. He is one who operates not through strained metaphors of the fancy but by focusing on real particulars, and he knows it:

> Look for smaller signs instead, the fine
> disturbances of ordered things when suddenly
> the rhythms of your expectation break
> and in a moment's pause another world
> reveals itself behind the ordinary.

This is the heart of his art, for its program is to make transcendent reality accessible through the commonplace. His poetry is calmly and unobtrusively measured, and whereas Pound endeavored to make poetry concrete, Gioia keeps it simple, hence his accessibility. If I may be forgiven a pun, he makes the subtle and the complex simply accessible, and this is because in part, as with Donne, thought is its own experience—is experience.

In Gioia's volume *Daily Horoscope* there are many poems whose ostensible settings are old ruins, museums, neglected mansions, chapels, and so forth, and at first one thinks, ''Ah, another poet playing with the past . . . a poet with a strong historical sense.'' But very quickly one perceives not merely the historical sense but also the religious or, more properly, the metaphysical sense at work and sees that it is preponderant. True, ''the bankrupt palace still remains / beyond the wall that summer builds, / doors bolted shut, the roof caved in . . . ,'' yet it is not merely a poetry to evoke spent or derelict feeling but rather one to question and, as it were, reenvision such dead places:

> wasn't this the purpose of our listening:
> to sit in the same place with our eyes open
> and know that we have moved? That finally
> we've woken up into the place from which
> we've always woken up out of, that strange place
> that's always changing, constantly drifting
> between the visible and invisible,
> that place that we must stumble onto, now
> as an unkempt garden.

How marvelously he has grafted Rilke onto the tree of contemporary American poetry and regrafted the Eliot of ''Little Gidding'' back onto his American roots.

But I would not wish to mislead and to misrepresent Gioia and his style as that of only a new metaphysical poet. There are a number of highly contemporary, self-expressive, even ''social'' poems scattered throughout his books as well. I am thinking of poems like ''Cruising with the Beachboys'' or ''Bix Beiderbecke.'' In the former the poet, ''travelling on business in a rented car,'' listens nostalgically to a pop record of the 1960s; in the latter the poet works through the persona of the jazz musician who died in 1931, creating a miniature life story in twenty-five lines and concluding with

> He lit a cigarette and closed his eyes.
> The best years of his life! The Boring 'Twenties.
> He watched the morning break across the snow.
> Would heaven be as white as Iowa?

Thus, Gioia also is a very contemporary poet, down to his marvelous particularity of detail: ''Another sleepless night, when every wrinkle in the bedsheet scratches / like a dry razor on a sunburned cheek.'' But it is contemporaneity not for its own sake but only as the grist of fact awaiting his unique poetic interpretation. Gioia knows and in his poetry shows, as Robert Graves said, that ''fact and truth are not the same thing''; truth is the conclusion drawn from fact. Gioia has a great eye for fact and a mind set on telling truth, which is to say that he has vision.

Gioia's poems, as I have suggested, are a consequence of thought—even thought about thought—not ''the spontaneous overflow of powerful feelings'' but rather ''emotion recollected in tranquillity.'' This is possibly why there is here and there a movement into narrative, as, for example, in ''The Journey, the Arrival and the Dream,'' from *Daily Horoscope,* or in the desperately sad and faintly unpleasant ''The Homecoming,'' from *The Gods of Winter.* Both poems are characteristic of the soliloquy, that is, are imbued with memory. The reflective disposition, as with Philip Larkin, shows up in the perusing of old mementos, such as photographs that evoke the poet's past. I am thinking especially of ''Photograph of My Mother as a Young Girl'' and ''The Sunday News,'' both of which reveal an obsession with the past, a subliminal wish to stop the passage of time and its consequences—''and watched, as I do / years later, / too distantly to interfere''—and, similarly, the desire to find a way of resisting loss through time—''A scrap I knew I wouldn't read again / But couldn't bear to lose.'' In his own words, it is the being of ''an eternal witness trapped in time.''

A personal tragedy, the death of an infant son, brought about a shift in Gioia's poetic impulse in his second volume, *The Gods of Winter.* In this collection there is a touch of anguish, a darkening of tone, an intensification of feeling, which bring his poetry closer to lyrical spontaneity:

> Storm on storm, snow on drifting snowfall,
> shifting its shape, flurrying in moonlight,
> bright and ubiquitous,
> profligate March squanders its wealth.

Gradually, however, after writing the strange, perhaps therapeutic poem ''Counting the Children''—a poem motivated at bottom by the fear of sudden infant death syndrome, I would guess, but one that also incorporates an examination of questions of mortality and immortality—Gioia gets back into his more normal urbane stride. Measured reflection takes over again, leading from time to time to poems like ''My Confessional Sestina,'' ''Money,'' or ''News from Nineteen Eighty Four,'' all of which have something of the odor of the occasional poem about them. He has also moved into the field of translation, often a worrying sign in all but the most prolific of poets, for it can indicate a diminishing of original impulse and a conscious searching for themes.

Between Gioia's two principal volumes of poetry, however, there are a fair number of different themes, a couple of which deserve mention. One that appears early in *Daily Horoscope* is that of the suppressed nature poet, which every poet is at heart: ''suddenly I realize the obvious: / that even this parking lot / was once a field.'' It is a conflict that shades off into another theme—or variant thereof—in his later poem "Rough Country," a quiet paean to the wide-open spaces where the poet seeks "a sign that there is still / one piece of property that won't be owned." It is an interesting thought coming from a poet with a background in business and from one who has written one of the few respectable poems—albeit ironically toned—to money, beginning with an approving epigraph from Wallace Stevens—"money is a kind of poetry."

Apart from translation, there has been another interesting development in Gioia's work. He has collaborated with the composer Alva Henderson on an opera, *Nosferatu,* based on F.W. Murnau's silent movie. Asked in an interview why he, "a serious poet," would want to write an opera libretto, Gioia answered laconically, "to grow." He then added, "It is exciting to explore a new form." The results should be interesting not only for opera but also for his own poetry. If the songs—some of which this writer has seen—are anything to go by, an impressive lyricism is being birthed through the demands of music. Gioia is often panned for being in the vanguard of the so-called New Formalist movement. It is more true, however, to observe of his work, as Charles Causley wrote in the early 1990s, "These lucid, varied and beautifully-crafted poems are the work of one of the most accomplished and compelling poets to have emerged on either side of the Atlantic over the past decade."

—William Oxley

GIOVANNI, Nikki

Nationality: American. **Born:** Yolande Cornelia Giovanni, in Knoxville, Tennessee, 7 June 1943. **Education:** Fisk University, Nashville, Tennessee, 1960–61, 1964–67, B.A. (magna cum laude) in history 1967; University of Pennsylvania School of Social Work, Philadelphia, 1967; Columbia University, New York, 1968. **Family:** Has one son. **Career:** Assistant professor of Black Studies, Queens College, Flushing, New York, 1968; associate professor of English, Livingston College, Rutgers University, New Brunswick, New Jersey, 1968–72; visiting professor of English, Ohio State University, Columbus, 1984; professor of creative writing, Mt. St. Joseph on the Ohio, 1985–87. Since 1987 professor, Virginia Polytechnic Institute and State University, Blacksburg, Virginia. Founder, Niktom Publishers, New York, 1970–74. Editorial consultant, *Encore* magazine, Albuquerque, New Mexico. **Awards:** Ford grant, 1968; National Endowment for the Arts grant, 1969; Harlem Cultural Council grant, 1969; outstanding achievement award, *Mademoiselle,* 1971; Omega Psi Phi Fraternity award, 1971; National Association of Radio and Television Announcers award, 1972, for *Truth Is on Its Way;* Ohioana Book award, 1988; Jeanine Rae Award for the Advancement of Women's Culture, 1995; Langston Hughes award, 1996; inducted into Literary Hall of Fame for Writers of African Descent, Chicago State University, 1998. D.H.L.: Wilberforce University, Ohio 1972; Fisk University, 1988. D.Lit.: University of Maryland, Princess Anne, 1974; Ripon University, Wisconsin, 1974; Smith College, Northampton, Massachusetts, 1975. D.Litt.: Mt. St. Joseph on the Ohio, 1983; Indiana University, 1991; Otterbein College, 1992; Widener University, 1993; Albright College, 1995; Cabrini College, 1995; and Allegheny College, 1997. **Address:** English Department,

Virginia Polytechnic Institute and State University, Blacksburg, Virginia 24061, U.S.A.

PUBLICATIONS

Poetry

Black Judgement. Detroit, Broadside Press, 1968.
Black Feeling, Black Talk. Privately printed, 1968.
Re: Creation. Detroit, Broadside Press, 1970.
Black Feeling Black Talk/Black Judgment. New York, Morrow, 1970.
Poem of Angela Yvonne Davis. New York, Afro Arts, 1970.
My House. New York, Morrow, 1972.
The Women and the Men. New York, Morrow, 1975.
Cotton Candy on a Rainy Day. New York, Morrow, 1978.
Those Who Ride the Night Winds. New York, Morrow, 1983.
The Genie in the Jar. New York, Holt, 1996.
The Selected Poems of Nikki Giovanni. New York, Morrow, 1996.
Love Poems. New York, Morrow, 1997.
Blues: For All the Changes: New Poems. New York, Morrow, 1999.

Recordings: *Truth Is on Its Way,* Right On, 1971; *Like a Ripple on a Pond,* Niktom, 1973; *The Way I Feel,* Niktom, 1975; *Legacies,* Folkways, 1976; *The Reason I Like Chocolate,* Folkways, 1976; *Cotton Candy on a Rainy Day,* Folkways, 1978; *Nikki Giovanni in Philadelphia,* Collectables Records, 1997; *The Sun Is So Quiet,* Recorded Books, 1997.

Verse (for children)

Spin a Soft Black Song. New York, Hill and Wang, 1971; revised edition, 1985.
Ego Tripping and Other Poems for Young Readers. Westport, Connecticut, Lawrence Hill, 1973.
Vacation Time. New York, Morrow, 1980.
Knoxville, Tennessee. New York, Scholastic, 1994.
The Sun Is So Quiet. New York, Holt, 1996.

Other

Gemini: An Extended Autobiographical Statement on My First Twenty-Five Years of Being a Black Poet. Indianapolis, Bobbs Merrill, 1971; London, Penguin, 1976.
A Dialogue: James Baldwin and Nikki Giovanni. Philadelphia Lippincott, 1973.
A Poetic Equation: Conversations Between Nikki Giovanni and Margaret Walker. Washington, D.C. Howard University Press, 1974.
Sacred Cows . . . and Other Edibles (essays). New York, Morrow, 1988.
Conversations with Nikki Giovanni. Jackson, University Press of Mississippi, 1992.
Racism 101. New York, Quill, 1994.
Shimmy Shimmy Shimmy Like My Sister Kate: Looking at the Harlem Renaissance through Poems. New York, Holt, 1996.

Editor, *Night Comes Softly: An Anthology of Black Female Voices.* Newark. New Jersey. Medic Press. 1970.

Editor, with Cathee Dennison, *Appalachian Elders: A Warm Hearth Sampler.* Blacksburg, Virginia, Pocahantas Press, 1991.

Editor, *Grandmothers: Poems, Reminiscences, and Short Stories about the Keepers of Our Traditions.* New York, Holt, 1994.

Editor, *Grandfathers: Reminiscences, Poems, Recipes, and Photos of the Keepers of Our Traditions.* New York, Holt, 1999.

*

Manuscript Collection: Mugar Memorial Library, Boston University.

Critical Studies: *Nikki Giovanni,* by Virginia C. Fowler, New York, Twayne, 1992; "The Black Arts Poets" by William W. Cook, in *The Columbia History of American Poetry,* edited by Jay Parini and Brett C. Millier, New York, Columbia University Press, 1993; "Windmills or Giants? The Quixotic Motif and Vision in the Poetry of Nikki Giovanni" by Effie J. Boldridge, in *Griot* (Houston, Texas), 14(1), spring 1995; "Nikki Giovanni: The Poet As Explorer of Outer and Inner Space" by Ekaterini Georgoudaki, in *Women, Creators of Culture,* edited by Georgoudaki and Domna Pastourmatzi, Thessaloniki, Greece, Hellenic Association of American Studies, 1997.

*   *   *

After awaking to "the possibility of / Blackness / and the inevitability of / Revolution"; after dispensing with refined language for colloquial talk ("Can a nigger kill the Man / Can you kill nigger / Huh?"); after using that power to deal with social issues and at the same time whispering a desire to do something "counterrevolutionary" like making love ("Seduction"); after committing herself to a life encounter, abandoning bourgeois ways to become "a for real black person who must now feel / and inflict / pain," and admonishing all blacks to do the same; after celebrating blackness in poems like "Nikki-Rosa," "Beautiful Black Men," and "Ego Tripping," Nikki Giovanni published an autobiography, *Gemini.* Then, in 1972 she conducted a poetic tour through *My House,* a place rich with family remembrance, distinctive personalities, and prevailing love, where

the old man said my time is getting near
the old man said my time
is getting near
he looked at his dusty cracked boots to say
sister my time is getting near
and when I'm gone remember i smiled
when I'm gone remember
i smiled
I'm glad my time is getting near

A later look into the author's private life, *Cotton Candy on a Rainy Day,* revealed discouragement and fatigue. Giovanni likened herself to "the unrealized dream of an idea unborn," thinking, "I should write a poem / but there's almost nothing / that hasn't been said / and said and said," and finally stating in "Being and Nothingness," "i don't want to exert anything."

In *The Women and the Men,* her richest collection of poems, the women can "sit and wait" for love, or resent one another, or keep their integrity into old age, or aspire to greatness, or be assertive to men. "The Women Gather" shows their effectuality. Preparing for a funeral in a time when "we are no longer surprised / that the unfaithful pray loudest," the women leave off being selfish to be merciful and loving. Despite the tendency to forgive "because we have trespassed" and comfort "because we need comforting,"

The women gather
with cloth and ointment
their busy hands bowing to laws that decree
willows shall stand swaying but unbroken
against even the determined wind of death.

"Because it is not unusual to know [a man] through those who love him," we judge, but by being merciful we make a more generous accounting of "dreams" and "deeds," of "intent" and "shortcomings." The women "sift / through ashes / and find an unburnt picture."

For Giovanni a poem—"pure energy / horizontally contained / between the mind / of the poet and the ear of the reader"—is vital for touching others and preparing the young for their lives. As Paula Giddings put it in her introduction to *Cotton Candy,* Giovanni is "a witness" whose poems are "souvenirs extracted from the site of a precious moment" rather than "flawless gems." Power prevails in Giovanni's world, but she sustains the hope for love having an effect: "i dream of black men and women walking / together side by side into a new world."

—Jay S. Paul

GIZZI, Peter

Nationality: American. **Born:** Massachusetts, 1959. **Career:** Since 1995 assistant professor of literature, University of California, Santa Cruz. **Awards:** Gertrude Stein Award in Innovative North American Poetry, 1993–94, 1994–95; Lavan Younger Poets award, 1994.

PUBLICATIONS

Poetry

Periplum. Penngrove, California, Avec Books, 1992.
Music for Films. Providence, Rhode Island, Paradigm Press, 1992.
Hours of the Book. Gran Canaria, Zasterle Press, 1994.
Champ. Great Barrington, Massachusetts, The Figures, 1994.
New Picnic Time. Buffalo, New York, Meow Press, 1995.
Artificial Heart. Providence, Rhode Island, Burning Deck, 1998.
Add This to the House. Cambridge, England, Equipage, 1999.

Other

The House That Jack Built: The Collected Lectures of Jack Spicer. Hanover, New Hampshire, University Press of New England, 1998.

*

Critical Study: By Alan Gilbert, in *Denver Quarterly* (Denver), 28(4), spring 1994.

*   *   *

Peter Gizzi relies on disparate thoughts and images to reveal the paradoxical aspects of life, particularly within the context of a postmodern world. His poems seem to be a reaction to the feeling of disorientation produced by a world devoid of intrinsic meaning, one in which the traditional idea of truth is questioned. In other words, Gizzi experiences and uses poetry as a means of recapturing a feeling of meaningful participation in life.

According to Gizzi, however, life is not free of paradox. As the title of his book *Artificial Heart* suggests, existence implies stark incongruities, exemplified by the juxtaposition of the organic and inorganic. Furthermore, in Gizzi's poetic discourse the experience of incongruity is often expressed through such juxtapositions as memory and the present or subject versus object. The poet and critic Alan Gilbert has compared *Artificial Heart* to Don DeLillo's *Underworld,* suggesting that both works attempt to describe and explain the loss of a better world and that what remains is essentially a more violent world whose destructive capabilities have been cultivated and have increased.

Gizzi's call for compassion, reason, and understanding is best shown by his poem "How to Care for a Small Bird":

> Given the baby bird crisis, what if
> each child were delivered a bird
>
> having tumbled from its nest
>
> Two major problems evolve
> One is feeding it
>
> another preparing it for the wild
>
> But before you build a home of newsprint and yarn
>
> try putting it back where it came
> Remember its feat, think of its shock
> to not be dead
>
> beset in a hand not yet full grown
>
> moving through space
> doing the best it can

Gizzi's poems reflect his affinity for the work of other poets and artists, particularly Jack Spicer. Critic Andrew Joron has made a distinction between the two poets, however: "Spicer wanted to make poems out of real objects and to make a poem that has no sound in it but the pointing of a finger, Gizzi's poems point toward an object memory that is empty."

In his lengthy poem "Pierced" Gizzi reflects on poetry:

> The heart of poetry is a hollow man
> a heteronym, a forensic test, & casino chip
> a long distance call
>
> The heart of poetry is fatigue . . .
>
> The heart of poetry is an empty lot . . .
>
> The heart of poetry is fatigue . . .

In "Locket" we read the disturbing sentences

> And here is the known world. As fingers duplicate the
> event of hunger.

In his poem "Life Continues" Gizzi begins with a helpless situation-

> Life continues while the telephone intersects continuity
> with another party

—and later expresses a sense of betrayal:

> This place once marked an exit. Today it is a wall.

The poem ends with Machiavellian images:

> you of the pandering smile, you with the greasy heart, you
> lacking denouement . . .

> Even Gizzi's more optimistic expressions are disconcerting:

> A forecast of hope has provided excitement this afternoon.
> No, a forecast of excitement has provided hope this
> afternoon.

In "Rewriting the Other and the Others" readers are smothered by the prospect that

> An atmosphere becomes indelible ink.

References to classical Greek and Roman literature and to historical events reflect Gizzi's effort to make sense of a chaotic world, but even with this effort the images come across as somewhat absurd. For example, in "Rewriting the Other and the Others" Gizzi makes reference to Alcestis, whose story has been a favorite among classical and contemporary writers, artists, and composers. Euripides, Jean-Paul Sartre, T.S. Eliot, and Thornton Wilder have written plays about her, and she is the main character in operas by Handel and Gluck. Alcestis is a mythological character who sacrifices herself to save her husband, Admetus, from Zeus's wrath, yet in Gizzi's poem she is flying a kite:

> I wanted to model the morning light
> Too difficult to impasto the sky
>
> You are Alcestis with a kite
> The years whip by and tears cover answers

In a note accompanying his poem "Ode: Salute to the New York School," Gizzi explains that his poems are "performing bibliographies." His work shows that literary works "survive primarily in the ruins of the texts they leave behind."

Gizzi has received favorable criticism from several American critics as well as from critics in Britain and Australia. Overall, he is considered one of the most talented poets of his generation, one who has reintroduced tradition, beauty, and form into poetry.

—Christine Miner Minderovic

GLEN, Duncan (Munro)

Pseudonym: Ronald Eadie Munro. **Nationality:** British. **Born:** Cambuslang, Lanarkshire, 11 January 1933. **Education:** West Coats School, Cambuslang, 1938–46; Rutherglen Academy, 1946–49; Heriot-Watt College, Edinburgh, 1950–53; Edinburgh College of Art, 1953–56. **Military Service:** Royal Air Force, 1956–58. **Family:** Married Margaret Eadie in 1957; one son and one daughter. **Career:** Typographic designer, Her Majesty's Stationery Office, London, 1958–60; lecturer in typographic design, Watford College of Technology, 1960–63; editor, Robert Gibson and Sons Ltd., publishers, Glasgow, 1963–65; lecturer in graphic design, Preston Polytechnic, Lancashire, 1965–78; professor of visual communications, 1978–86, and since 1986 emeritus professor, Nottingham Trent University. Owner, Akros Publications, and editor, *Akros,* Preston, later Nottingham, 1965–83; editor, *Knowe,* 1971, and *Graphic Lines,* 1975–78, both Preston, and *Aynd,* Nottingham, 1983–86. Since 1988 editor, SPLA (Scottish Poetry Library Newsletter), Edinburgh. Fellow, Chartered Society of Designers. **Address:** 25 Johns Road, Radcliffe-on-Trent, Nottingham, England.

PUBLICATIONS

Poetry

Stanes: A Twalsome of Poems (as Ronald Eadie Munro). Kinglassie, Fife, Duncan Glen, 1966.
Idols: When Alexander Our King Was Dead. Preston, Lancashire, Akros, 1967.
Kythings and Other Poems (as Ronald Eadie Munro). Thurso, Caithness Books, 1969.
Sunny Summer Sunday Afternoon in the Park? Preston, Lancashire, Akros, 1969.
Unnerneath the Bed. Preston, Lancashire, Akros, 1970.
In Appearances. Preston, Lancashire, Akros, 1971.
Clydesdale: A Sequence o Poems. Preston, Lancashire, Akros, 1971.
Feres. Preston, Lancashire, Akros, 1971.
A Journey Past: A Sequence o Poems. Preston, Lancashire, Akros, 1972.
A Cled Score. Preston, Lancashire, Akros, 1974.
Mr. and Mrs. J.L. Stoddart at Home. Preston, Lancashire, Akros, 1975.
Buits and Wellies; or, Sui Generis. Preston, Lancashire, Akros, 1975.
Follow! Follow! Follow! and Other Poems. Preston, Lancashire, Akros, 1976.
Spoiled for Choice. Preston, Lancashire, Akros, 1976.
Weddercock. Privately printed, 1976.
Gaitherings: Poems in Scots. Preston, Lancashire, Akros, 1977.
Traivellin Man. Preston, Lancashire, Harris Press, 1977.
In Place of Wark; or, Man of Art. Preston, Lancashire, Akros, 1977.
Of Philosophers and Tinks. Preston, Lancashire, Akros, 1977.
The Inextinguishable. Preston, Lancashire, Harris Press, 1977.
My Preston. Preston, Lancashire, Herbert, 1977.
Ten Sangs. Preston, Lancashire, Akros, 1978.
Ither Sangs. Preston, Lancashire, Akros, 1978.
Ten Bird Sangs. Preston, Lancashire, Akros, 1978.
Ten Sangs of Luve. Preston, Lancashire, Akros, 1978.
Poet at Wark. Nottingham, Bonington Press, 1979.
Realities Poems. Nottingham, Akros, 1980.
On Midsummer Evenin Merriest of Nichts? Nottingham, Akros, 1981.
Facts Are Chiels. Privately printed, 1983.
The State of Scotland. Nottingham, Duncan Glen, 1983.
Portraits. Nottingham, Trent Polytechnic, 1983.
The Stones of Time. Nottingham, Duncan Glen, 1984.
Situations. Nottingham, Trent Polytechnic, 1984.
In the Small Hours: Or, To Be About to Be. Nottingham, Akros, 1984.
The Turn of the Earth. Nottingham, Akros, 1985.
Geeze!: A Sequence of Poems. Leeds, John Henderson, 1985.
Tales to Be Told. Edinburgh, Akros, 1987.
Out to the Calf of Man, September 1989: A Poem and Etchings. Edinburgh, Akros, 1990.
A Journey Into Scotland: Poems. Edinburgh, Akros, 1991.
Selected Poems 1965–1990. Edinburgh, Akros, 1991.
Echoes. Frae Classical and Italian Poetry. Edinburgh, Akros, 1992.
Seventeen Poems. Kirkcaldy, Scotland, Akros, 1997.
Selected New Poems: Nineteen-Eighty-Seven to Nineteen-Ninety-Six. Kirkcaldy, Scotland, Akros, 1998.

Other

Hugh MacDiarmid: Rebel Poet and Prophet, A Short Note on His Seventieth Birthday. Hemel Hempstead, Hertfordshire, Drumalban Press, 1962.
Hugh MacDiarmid and the Scottish Renaissance. Edinburgh, Chambers, 1964.
The Literary Mask of Hugh MacDiarmid. Glasgow, Drumalban Press, 1964.
Scottish Poetry Now. Preston, Lancashire, Akros, 1966.
An Afternoon with Hugh MacDiarmid. Privately printed, 1969.
A Small Press and Hugh MacDiarmid: With a Checklist of Akros Publications 1962–1970. Preston, Lancashire, Akros, 1970.
The MacDiarmids: A Conversation Between Hugh MacDiarmid and Duncan Glen with Valda Crieve and Arthur Thompson. Preston, Lancashire, Akros, 1970.
The Individual and the Twentieth-Century Scottish Literary Tradition. Preston, Lancashire, Akros, 1971.
A Bibliography of Scottish Poets from Stevenson to 1974. Preston, Lancashire, Akros, 1974.
Preston's New Buildings, with John Brook. Preston, Lancashire, Harris Press, 1975.
Five Literati. Preston, Lancashire, Harris Press, 1976.
Forward from Hugh MacDiarmid; or, Mostly Out of Scotland, Being Fifteen Years of Duncan Glen/Akros Publications, with a Check-List of Publications August 1962-August 1977. Preston, Lancashire, Akros, 1977.
Hugh MacDiarmid: An Essay for 11th August 1977. Preston, Lancashire, Akros, 1977.
The Autobiography of a Poet. Edinburgh, Ramsay Head Press, 1986.
Makars' Walk: Three Literary Walks in the Old Town of Edinburgh, with an Anthology of Poetry. Edinburgh, Scottish Poetry Library Association, 1990.
The Poetry of the Scots. An Introduction and Bibliographical Guide to Poetry in Gaelic, Scots, Latin and English. Edinburgh, Edinburgh University Press, 1991.
Hugh MacDiarmid: Out of Langholm and Into the World. Edinburgh, Akros, 1992.
A Nation in a Parish: A New Historical Prospect of Scotland from the Parish of Cambuslang. Edinburgh, Akros, 1995.

Splendid Lanarkshire: Past and Present: A Rediscovery and Anthology of Prose & Verse. Kirkcaldy, Scotland, Akros, 1997.

Hugh MacDiarmid & Duncan Glen: A Prospect from Brownsbank: Poems, Biographical Notes and a Bibliography. Kirkcaldy, Scotland, Akros, 1998.

Illustrious Fife: Literary, Historical & Architectural Pathways & Walks. Kirkcaldy, Scotland, Akros, 1998.

A New History of Cambuslang. Kirkcaldy, Scotland, Akros, 1998.

Editor, *Poems Addressed to Hugh MacDiarmid and Presented to Him on His Seventy-Fifth Birthday.* Preston, Lancashire, Akros, 1967.

Editor, *Selected Essays of Hugh MacDiarmid.* London, Cape, 1969; Berkeley, University of California Press, 1970.

Editor, *The Akros Anthology of Scottish Poetry 1965–1970.* Preston, Lancashire, Akros, 1970.

Editor, *Whither Scotland? A Prejudiced Look at the Future of a Nation.* London,, 1971.

Editor, *Hugh MacDiarmid: A Critical Survey.* Edinburgh, Scottish Academic Press, and New York, Barnes and Noble, 1972.

Editor, with Nat Scammacca, *La Nuova Poesia Scozzese.* Palermo, Celebes, 1976.

Editor, *Preston Polytechnic Poets.* Preston, Lancashire, Harris Press, 1977.

Editor, *Graphic Designers as Poets.* Preston, Lancashire, Harris Press, 1977.

Editor, *Typoems.* Preston, Lancashire, Harris Press, 1977.

Editor, *Akros Verse 1965–1982.* Nottingham, Akros, 1982.

Editor, with Peter France, *European Poetry in Scotland: An Anthology of Translations.* Edinburgh, Edinburgh University Press, 1989.

Editor, *Twenty of the Best: A Galliard Anthology of Contemporary Scottish Poetry.* Edinburgh, Galliard, 1990.

Editor, *A Keepsake Anthology of Anonymous Scottish Verse.* Kirkcaldy, Scotland, Akros, 1996.

Editor, *Seasons of Delight: An Anthology of Poems on Gardens, Flowers, Greenwoods & the Sea.* Kirkcaldy, Scotland, Akros, 1998.

Editor, *Scottish Literature: A New History from 1299 to 1999.* Kirkcaldy, Scotland, Akros, 1999.

Editor, *Selected Scottish and Other Essays.* Kirkcaldy, Scotland, Akros, 1999.

Editor, *'This Is No Can of Beans': A Prospect from the Window of a Small-Press Publisher.* Kirkcaldy, Scotland, Akros, 1999.

*

Bibliography: *A Duncan Glen Bibliography,* privately printed, 1980.

Manuscript Collections: National Library of Scotland, Edinburgh; Edinburgh University Library.

Critical Studies: By Paul Duncan, in *Sou' Wester* (Carbondale, Illinois), summer 1970; Sam Adams, in *Anglo-Welsh Review* (Pembroke Dock, Wales), autumn 1970; John C. Weston, in *Akros* (Preston, Lancashire), April 1971; Anne Cluysenaar, in *Stand* (Newcastle upon Tyne), 12(4), 1971; "Meaning and Self" by Walter Perrie, in *Chapman* (Hamilton, Lanarkshire), spring 1972; "The Progress of Scots" by John Herdman, in *Akros* (Preston, Lancashire), December 1972; *Two Younger Poets: Duncan Glen and Donald Campbell: A Study of Their Scots Poetry* by Leonard Mason, Preston, Lancashire,

Akros, 1976; *Our Duncan, Who Art in Trent: A Festschrift for Duncan Glen* edited by Philip Pacey, Preston, Lancashire, Harris Press, 1978; *The Dialect Muse* by Ken Edward Smith, Wetherby, Ruined Cottage, 1979; George Bruce, in *Lines Review* (Edinburgh), 74, September 1980, and in *Studies in Scottish Literature* (South Carolina), 22, 1988; W.N. Herbert, in *Edinburgh Review,* 77, 1987; by W.R. Aitken in *Lines Review* (Edinburgh), 119, 1991.

*   *   *

Duncan Glen belongs to that important community of Scottish writers who have developed a style in Scots (or Lallans-the fashionable term) on a prose base. One feels that Glen, or his people, might speak with the same calculated understatement or with the not unkindly irony of his poetry. His idiom allows him to sketch the picture of his dead father in his poem "My Faither" with a sense of truth, respect, and manliness. The poem begins,

Staunin noo aside his bress-haunled coffin
I mind him fine aside the black shinin range
In his grey strippit troosers, galluses and nae collar
For the flannel shirt. My faither.

(Standing now beside his brass handled coffin
I remember him well beside the black shining range
In his grey striped trousers, braces and no collar
For the flannel shirt. My father.)

This honest, modest achievement is characteristic of a deal of the rather better writing in Scots, but Glen goes beyond this in his finer poems. In the last verse of "My Faither" the writer looks down on the body, "laid oot in the best / Black suitin . . ." This father ("My father")—he uses the English spelling—he does not know. The solid, known person becomes dramatically unknowable.

The domestic imagery in Scots is Glen's point of beginning. His poem "Progress" begins from naive statement, bouncing along like a nursery rhyme, but there is a remorseless logic in it. It proceeds thus: "Is not nature wonderful / We cam oot heid first-get a slap / and oor mither toungue." By the end one is aware that Glen is applying a kind of Socratic dialogue to the argument. The bright tone darkens. He takes this development further in "Bacchae in Suburbia." This work is written in a homely Scots ("You are feart son?"), and one hears, as it were, behind the words the knock on the door that might mean death or torture, as it has for many in Europe in our time.

Despite the success of the concentrated moments in Glen's short poems the idiom of colloquial Scots/English speech, which comes naturally from his pen, lends itself more readily to his reflective longer poems. These have frequently suffered from diffuseness and flatness of tone, but in 1980 the publication of *Realities Poems,* a book-length sequence, marked a new achievement. Much of the subject matter is, characteristically, domestic-autobiographical, but the enjoyment of family life—and how freshly and affectionately done are all these passages—is set within a wider framework, partly philosophical and partly drawn from aspects of existence today seen as a threat to the caring family and to the aspirations that stem from the confidence such living breeds. Glen achieves this presentation in poetic terms by setting one type of experience against the other. On the one hand he tells of the happiness of, when young, chasing with Margaret, now his wife:

My breath comin quick as yours,
we race doun to the lochside house
and warmth by the rug by the fire
—and wunnerin what Mrs MacDonald thocht,

as she served us our tea.

Against this human warmth is life in "The House at Half-Way Point," "the new seat / of civilisation," where the proprietors of the hotel control those who would climb to the mountaintop by experiment and daring:

The routes hae built-in plastic railweys
and guides in uniform like railwey
porters walk the paths. There are
cassettes to be hired
gien a commentary on the set weys.

In such passages through particular experiences, couched in Glen's modest, skeptical tongue, large issues are implicit. No writer in Scots has taken this way to these issues. Consequently, it may be claimed that in doing this Glen has extended a Scots literary sensibility.

"A Divine Comedy," from *Selected New Poems,* is set on a coach tour in Italy. The speaker is enthralled by a view of Tuscany:

And a woman whispers to naebody in particular,
'Io sono Scotto,'
'Io sono Scotto.'

'Lo sono Scotto.'

The Scottish resonance heard in the voice is heard in all of Glen's poetry, and this is the basis of his achievement.

—George Bruce

GLOVER, Jon(athan Martin)

Nationality: British. **Born:** Sheffield, Yorkshire, 13 May 1943. **Education:** Leeds University, 1962–68, B.A. (honors) 1965, M.Phil. 1969. **Family:** Married Elaine Alice Shaver in 1965; two daughters. **Career:** Lecturer, Elmira College, Elmira, New York, 1966–67, Leeds College of Technology, 1967–68. Since 1968 lecturer, senior lecturer, principal lecturer, and then professor, Bolton Institute. **Address:** 3 Lightburne Avenue, Bolton, Lancashire BL1 4PL, England.

PUBLICATIONS

Poetry

The Grass's Time. Newcastle upon Tyne, Northern House, 1970.
The Wall and the Candle. Newcastle upon Tyne, Northern House, 1983.
Our Photographs. Manchester, Carcanet, 1986.
To the Niagara Frontier. Manchester, Carcanet, 1994.

Other

Editor, with Jon Silkin, *The Penguin Book of First World War Prose.* London and New York, Penguin, 1989.

Translator, *Notes for a Survivor* by Emanuel Litvinoff. Newcastle upon Tyne, Northern House, 1973.

*

Jon Glover comments:

I started to write at Leeds University. There were many important poets living and working in Leeds at the time, including Jon Silkin, Geoffrey Hill, Tony Harrison, Peter Redgrove, Ken Smith, Jeffrey Wainwright, and David Wright. We met in seminars, lectures, and poetry readings and joined in the business of writing for and helping to produce a number of magazines, including the unique weekly *Poetry and Audience* and, later, *Stand,* which has been very much part of my life ever since, both as an influence on my thought and poems and as a practical activity (helping to edit, parcel, and invoice). Jon Silkin has been a continuing source of insight and inspiration not only through his poetry and criticism but through his editorial work on the poets of the Great War. We have worked together on *The Penguin Book of First World War Prose.*

Dominant ideas derived from this period included the notion of poetry as part of a chain of communication linking evaluation and response to the events of the past with a sense of the unsteady narratives of the present. There may be some sense of political analysis and commitment mediated through the fractured pictures that bring many of the poems into being, although this is tempered and ironized through a sense of the slipperiness of language. There is also a commitment to find meanings and gifts of love in the imagery of landscape, the constructions and deconstructions of our places of habitation.

*   *   *

Jon Glover's poems are characterized by two complementary forces—the need to mistrust and the desire to let go. These forces find themselves linguistically and ideologically in the gulf between two worlds of intimate experience: an England of childhood values, questions, and irrecoverable loss, and an America (mainly the landscape of upstate New York) of discovery and of precious, small identities. In between are a number of lost worlds. These are presented as mid-Atlantic dislocations, though there are poems of "flight," perhaps in both senses, but as an attempt to review cultural origins as the artifacts and occasions of movement between cultures, histories, and futures that erupt and establish identity in the business of exchange.

The poems of *The Grass's Time* grew from Glover's first stay in the United States, where he lived as an immigrant with his American wife during the height of the Vietnam War. It was a time of disillusionment on the one hand and affirmation on the other. The intense awareness of political failure and personal powerlessness mixed with the realities of protest offered a test bed for identity, the never again certainties of growing up in a socialist family in the bomb-scarred cities of England thrown into confusion by the bomb-happy world of independent and innocent America. Poems became tokens in the cross fire, in the exchange of worlds that seemed angry with each other.

Glover later began to explore this process of exchange in which no identity was true and no single language offered accurate description. His method was to use a form of the multivoiced narrative poem sequence in which a nameless emigrant from a Scottish island explores the United States and his own memories. In *Our Photographs* mistrust is set free through poems that move from prose to verse and back again and that explore alternative languages for the same circumstance. "Pure" and "Nature" both "set up" in fairly clear prose the grounds for a linguistically richer "poem." The following quotation from "Nature" concerns the beauty of butterflies and the strange motives of the collector:

Still I have nowhere for this. And, finally, to set things in a
house would create a stillness shut from the sun, a
    civilisation
that I go on trying to leave.

 From earth colours and its skin
of thin dry crystal,
its fragile liquids snap out and are gone.

. . . These human qualities
want them collected, row upon row,
preserving each as a separate
kingdom of man's desire?
Like cold, pinned galaxies?

Based on a photograph by the New York artist Nancy Shaver, "Our Photographs" is one of Glover's most important poems of the many that interact between the pictorial "claim" (in the sense of establishing the rights—whatever they may be—to ownership) and the pictorial "legacy" (in which the rights are remade or lost to the processes of history). The poems mark their awareness of the disappearing claim by contributing further to the means of destruction, although there are poems that celebrate the attempts to preserve as well as those which lament the hopeless energies of art.

Later work by Glover, for example "Risk," which appeared in *Stand* in 1995, seems to be taking a new direction. The very title "Risk," which celebrates the latent energy of a horse being groomed, perhaps indicates a way out of the disorientation that stemmed from a desire for total mistrust and total freedom:

. . . Out there
the light so far away, it's cross; moving
away to a jump, momentarily.

It's in the middle of a bridge, a tear,
a value, splitting hairs, a parting. What's
lamented is all that's present. Gifted.

—Jon Silkin

GLÜCK, Louise (Elisabeth)

Nationality: American. **Born:** New York City, 22 April 1943. **Education:** Sarah Lawrence College, Bronxville, New York, 1962; Columbia University, New York, 1963–65. **Family:** Married 1) Charles Hertz, Jr., in 1967 (divorced); 2) John Dranow in 1977 (divorced), one son. **Career:** Taught at Goddard College, Plainfield, Vermont, 1971–72, 1973–74, 1976–80, University of Virginia, Charlottesville, 1973, University of North Carolina, Greensboro, 1973, University of Iowa, Iowa City, University of Cincinnati, 1978, Columbia University, 1979, Warren Wilson College, Swannanoa, North Carolina, 1978–80, University of California at Berkeley, 1982, at Davis, 1983, and at Irvine, 1984. Scott Professor of poetry, 1993, and since 1984 member of the faculty, Williams College, Williamstown, Massachusetts. Regents Professor, University of California, Los Angeles, 1985–87; visiting professor, Harvard University, 1995; Hurst Professor of Poetry, Brandeis University, 1996. **Awards:** Academy of American Poets prize, 1966; Rockefeller fellowship, 1967; National Endowment for the Arts grant, 1969, 1979; fellowship, 1988–89; Eunice Tietjens memorial prize (*Poetry,* Chicago), 1971; Guggenheim fellowship, 1975; 1987–88; American Academy award, 1981; National Book Critics Circle prize, 1985; Melville Cane award, 1986; Sara Teasdale memorial prize, 1986; Phi Beta Kappa Poet, Harvard University, 1990; Bobbitt National prize (with Mark Strand), Library of Congress, 1992; Pulitzer prize, 1993; William Carlos Williams award, 1993; poet laureate of Vermont, 1994; PEN/Martha Albrand award for nonfiction, 1995. Fellow, American Academy of Arts and Sciences, 1993. Honorary D.Litt.: Williams College, Williamstown, Massachusetts, 1993; Skidmore College, 1995; Middlebury College, 1996. **Address:** Creamery Road, Plainfield, Vermont 05667, U.S.A.

PUBLICATIONS

Poetry

Firstborn. New York, New American Library, 1968; London, Anvil Press Poetry, 1969.
The House on Marshland. New York, Ecco Press, 1975; London, Anvil Press Poetry, 1976.
The Garden. New York, Antaeus, 1976.
Descending Figure. New York, Ecco Press, 1980.
The Triumph of Achilles. New York, Ecco Press, 1985.
Ararat. New York, Ecco Press, 1990.
The Wild Iris. New York, Ecco Press, 1992.
The First Four Books of Poems. Hopewell, New Jersey, Ecco Press, 1995.
The First Five Books of Poems. Manchester, Carcanet, 1997.
Meadowlands. Hopewell, New Jersey, Ecco Press, 1996; Manchester, Carcanet, 1998.
Vita Nova. Manchester, Carcanet, 1999.

Other

Editor, *The Best American Poetry 1993,* with David Lehman. New York, Collier Books, 1993.
Editor, *Proofs and Theories: Essays on Poetry.* New York, Ecco Press, 1994; Manchester, Carcanet, 1999.

*

Critical Studies: By Calvin Bedient, in *Sewanee Review* (Tennessee), winter 1976, and in *Parnassus* (New York), spring-summer 1981; Joan Hutton Landis, in *Salmagundi* (Saratoga Springs, New York), winter 1977; Helen Vendler in *New Republic* (Washington,

D.C.), 17 June 1978; "The Poetry of Louise Glück" by Burton Raffel, in *The Literary Review: An International Journal of Contemporary Writing* (Madison, New Jersey), 31(3), spring 1988; "'Free/of Blossom and Subterfuge': Louise Glück and the Language of Renunciation" by Lynn Keller, in *World, Self, Poem: Essays on Contemporary Poetry from the "Jubilation of Poets,"* edited by Leonard M. Trawick, Kent, Ohio, Kent State University Press, 1990; "The 'Harsher Figure' of Descending Figure: Louise Glück's 'Dive into the Wreck'" by Laurie E. George, in *Women's Studies,* 17(3/4), 1990; *The Veiled Mirror and the Woman Poet: H.D., Louise Bogan, Elizabeth Bishop, and Louise Glück* by Elizabeth Caroline Dodd, Columbia, University of Missouri Press, 1992; "'It Meant I Loved': Louise Glück's Ararat" by Eric Selinger, in *Postmodern Culture: An Electronic Journal of Interdisciplinary Criticism* (Cary, North Carolina), 3(3), May 1993; "Without Relation: Family and Freedom in the Poetry of Louise Glück" by Suzanne Matson, in *Mid-American Review* (Bowling Green, Ohio), 14(2), 1994; "The Problem of Sincerity: The Lyric Plain Style of George Herbert and Louise Glück" by Ann Townsend, in *Shenandoah* (Lexington, Virginia), 46(4), winter 1996; *The Love of Form Is a Love of Endings: Poetic Hunger and the Aesthetic Body in Louise Glück* (dissertation) by Melissa Lee Brown, University of Iowa, 1997; "Between Truth and Meaning" by Allen Hoey, in *American Poetry Review* (Philadelphia), 26(1), January-February 1997.

*   *   *

Louise Glück's first volume, *Firstborn,* does not lack for influences, as discerning critics have been quick to remark. Most obvious are the traces of Stanley Kunitz, with whom she studied at Columbia University, and of early Robert Lowell. There are also indications that she has looked to Plath and Sexton, Crane, Jarrell, and Dugan. "My Life before Dawn," with its emphasis on sexual violence and male mental cruelty, may well represent such influences. The poem begins,

> Sometimes at night I think of how we did
> It, me nailed to her like steel, her
> Over-eager on the striped contour
> Sheet (I later burned it) and she makes me glad
> I told her—in the kitchen cutting bread—
> She always did too much—I told her Sorry baby
>   you have had
> Your share (I found her stain had dried into my hair).

There already is a subtle command of a basically five-beat line, of slant rhyme, of a character sharply conceived and convincingly rendered.

One experiences a great leap, however, with the collection that comes seven years later, for *The House on Marshland* is decisively Glück's own. Its pervasive theme is loss, and the obsessive feeling is pain in relationships with men. The triumphant achievement is the balancing of an almost bitter attitude with an undeterred hopefulness. Most of the poems are in the confessional tradition, though there is no reason to assume that they are autobiographical. Paradoxically, Glück, like Tennyson and others, writes most powerfully when she turns away from presumably private or personally apprehended experience. The less personal the experience, the more intense is the feeling with which the expression is charged. "All Hallows" seems to derive from a landscape painting, with a scene of "barrenness / of harvest or pestilence" pointing to a wife leaning out of a window.

Amid all this barrenness can she be fertile? "Brennende Liebe-1904" is a poetized love letter from an aristocratic woman in which the mood of longing is elegantly conveyed. If the supposed writer was an ancestor, one can understand why Glück has retained the umlaut in her name.

The most psychologically penetrating poem is "Abishag." The account in 1 Kings of the young woman taken to King David's bed is told from David's perspective, as are treatments by Rilke, the Hebrew Fichman, and the French Spire. Glück, however, offers Abishag's voice and perspective in a dreamlike recollection. Only a single mark of punctuation impedes the flow of the opening stanza, but the concluding stanza of the first section is firmly end-stopped, staccato, and bitter:

> They took me as I was.
> Not one among the kinsmen touched me,
> No one among the slaves.
> No one will touch me now.

Abishag has a classical Electra fantasy. She rages at her father for letting her be taken by someone other than himself.

The final section deserves quotation in full:

> In the recurring dream my father
> stands at the doorway in his black cassock
> telling me to choose
> among my suitors, each of whom
> will speak my name once
> until I lift my hand in signal.
> On my father's arm I listen
> for not three sounds: *Abishag.*
> but two: *my love-*
>
> I tell you if it is my own will
> binding me I cannot be saved.
> And yet in the dream, in the half-light
> of the stone house, they looked
> so much alike. Sometimes I think
> the voices were themselves
> identical, and that I raised my hand
> chiefly in weariness. I hear my father saying
> *Choose, choose.* But they were not alike
> and to select death, O yes I can
> believe that of my body.

Rage at her father has become hatred of self for feeling that she has been used.

In *The Garden* Glück seems to be signaling a new phase. As she has written, "The impulse to write is usually spent in a brief lyric." (The forty-nine lines of "Abishag" make it by far the longest poem in *The House on Marshland.*) Consisting of five almost independent lyrics about fear, *The Garden* is a coherent, powerful whole, perhaps Glück's highest achievement.

Descending Figure reminds one in its title of Duchamp's *Nude Descending a Staircase,* for it, too, takes descents as a subject. Beginning with the first section, "The Garden," it gives us the conversationally triumphant "The Drowned Children" and then proceeds to incorporate the previous book. "Descending Figure" is a child's view, in three parts, of a dead sister—a figure descending, a sick child in a painting in the Rijksmuseum, and the speaker's dead sister. Collectively, the three lyrics deal vividly with the fear of death. The second part of *Descending Figure*, "The Mirror," begins with "Epithalamium," a lyric ode to a bride and bridegroom that suggests an end to descending-

> the terrible charity of marriage
> husband and wife
> climbing the green hill in gold light

—and then refutes the suggestion.

Descending Figure has as its final sequence "Lamentations," reminding us of the biblical book. The five chapters of the Old Testament book are a lamentation for Jerusalem, like a widow bitterly mourning loss. Glück's poem, however, has four parts: "The Logos," "Nocturne," "The Covenant," and "The Clearing." "The Logos" speaks of the Creation, God's withdrawal from the universe, and man and woman alone. "Nocturne" details God's abandonment of the vegetable, animal, and human. "The Covenant" describes parenthood. "The Clearing" presents the evolution of beauty as "seen from the air," that is, distantly.

Glück's poetry is intimate, familial, and what Edwin Muir has called the fable, the archetypal. She often goes to the source of things—to the Old Testament, as in "Abishag" and in "Lamentations," or to Greek myth as in "Aphrodite" and "The Triumph of Achilles." This last, the title poem of a volume, moves from fable to story, for the great hero becomes humanized in lamenting the death of his friend Patroclus.

In *The Triumph of Achilles* Glück sticks with her perennial subject, that of human loss, but she experiments with new types of poems, from narratives and extended, mixed sequences to songs and orientalist attempts at capturing the immediate. "Mock Orange," the severe, often anthologized poem that initiates the collection, is spare, intense, and nonnegotiable in its stance:

> It is not the moon, I tell you.
> It is these flowers
> lighting the yard.
> I hate them.
> I hate them as I hate sex,
> the man's mouth sealing my mouth, the man's
> paralyzing body—
> and the cry that always escapes,
> the low, humiliating
> premise of union-

Erotic life has long been one of Glück's obsessions. "Marathon," a group of nine poems tracing the phases of erotic life, works as a long-lined song, gaining in lucidity as it proceeds. Although she maintains her mistrust of simple transcendence, the sequence looks closely at the legitimate ecstasies sex can provide. For Glück desire ultimately renders one isolated as much as, if not more than, it unifies one with another. In "Night Song" she states, "the bond with any one soul / is meaningless; you throw it away." *The Triumph of Achilles* is the great range of characters, stances, and worlds collected in it.

Ararat is the twin-peaked mountain in present-day Turkey that was the biblical site of Noah's landing of the ark. In titling her 1990 collection *Ararat*, Glück uses the reference to the biblical myth to illustrate the great human subjects that all art must touch on, what Glück calls "time which breeds loss, desire, the world's beauty." Not as prophetic and solemn as her previous work, the poems in *Ararat*

work in a lighter, more popularly accessible style that attempts to flesh out experience almost as prose would. Although the book tells the story of a family's dissolution, it situates it in recognizably Glückian mythic terms. In "A Novel" she writes,

> No one could write a novel about
>   this family:
> too many similar characters. Besides,
>   they're all women;
> there was only one hero.
> Now the hero's dead. Like echoes,
>   the women last longer;
> they're all too tough for their own good.

The poems in *Ararat* address a father's death, the widow's resulting crises, and the dilemmas between sisters. The poems seem to foresee, in their own way, the poems in the later collection *Meadowlands,* which gives voice to both members of a marriage locked in its own patterns of quarrel and worry. A once precious intimacy erodes between the man and woman as they discover the degree to which they "flew under different banners," as Glück says of a male and female swan in "Parable of the Swans." Not as mythic as her previous works, *Meadowlands* works in a tragicomic, highly personal style and ultimately suggests that the unforeseeable and unsympathetic forces of change are as great as the forces that drive one to austere, anorexic solitude.

When single life begins to bring a newness after a marriage has dissolved, it has, for Glück, another and profound mythic resonance. In *Vita Nova* two poems, both titled "Vita Nova," frame the collection. One is spoken by Persephone, and the other is an ironized treatment of a dream, a divorce, and a dog by the name of Blizzard: "Blizzard / Daddy needs you / . . . the kind of love he wants Mommy / doesn't have, Mommy's / too ironic—Mommy wouldn't do / the rhumba in the driveway." The myth of Orpheus, the substance of dreams, and the shards of memory are the material for these poems, and they proceed with Glück's raw, highly crafted, careful, remarkably self-knowing style: "Surely spring has been returned to me, this time / not as a lover but a messenger of death, yet / it is still spring, it is still meant tenderly."

—James K. Robinson and Martha Sutro

GOEDICKE, Patricia

Nationality: American. **Born:** Patricia McKenna, Boston, Massachusetts, 21 June 1931. **Education:** Middlebury College, Vermont, B.A. (cum laude) 1953 (Phi Beta Kappa, 1952); Ohio University, Athens, M.A. 1965. **Family:** Married 1) Victor Goedicke in 1956 (divorced 1968); 2) Leonard Wallace Robinson in 1971. **Career:** Editorial assistant, Harcourt Brace and World publishers, New York, 1953–54, and T.Y. Crowell publishers, New York, 1955–56. Instructor in English, Ohio University, 1963–68, and Hunter College, New York, 1969–71; reader-writer, Book-of-the-Month Club, 1968–69; associate professor of creative writing, Instituto Allende, San Miguel de Allende, Guanajuato, Mexico, 1972–79; writer-in-residence, Kalamazoo College, Michigan, 1977; guest faculty member of the writing program, Sarah Lawrence College, Bronxville, New York,

1980–81. Poet-in-residence, 1981–83, associate professor, 1983–90, and since 1990 professor of creative writing, University of Montana, Missoula. Co-editor, *Page,* 1961–66. **Awards:** National Endowment for the Arts award, 1969, fellowship, 1976–77; William Carlos Williams award (*New Letters*), 1977; Duncan Frazier prize (*Loon*), 1976; *Quarterly West* prize, 1977; Carolyn Kizer award, 1987; Strousse award (*Prairie Schooner*), 1987; Vi Gale award honorable mention (*Hubbub*), 1987; Arvon International Poetry Competition special commendation, 1987; Hohenberg award (*The Memphis State Review*), 1988; University of Montana research grant, 1989; *New York Times* Notable Book of the Year 1990, for *The Tongues We Speak: New and Selected Poems;* University of Montana Distinguished Scholar award, 1991; Edward Stanley award (*Prairie Schooner*), 1992; Rockefeller Foundation residency at Villa Serbelloni on Lake Como, Bellagio, Italy, 1992. **Address:** Department of English, University of Montana, Missoula, Montana 59812, U.S.A.

PUBLICATIONS

Poetry

Between Oceans. New York, Harcourt Brace, 1968.
For the Four Corners. Ithaca, New York, Ithaca House, 1976.
The Trail That Turns on Itself. Ithaca, New York, Ithaca House, 1978.
The Dog That Was Barking Yesterday. Amherst, Massachusetts, Lynx House Press, 1980.
Crossing the Same River. Amherst, University of Massachusetts Press, 1980.
The King of Childhood. Lewiston, Idaho, Confluence Press, 1984.
The Wind of Our Going. Port Townsend, Washington, Copper Canyon Press, 1985.
Listen, Love. Muncie, Indiana, Barnwood Press, 1986.
The Tongues We Speak: New and Selected Poems. Minneapolis, Milkweed, 1989.
Paul Bunyan's Bearskin. Minneapolis, Milkweed, 1992.
Invisible Horses. Minneapolis, Milkweed, 1996.
As Earth Begins to End. Port Townsend, Washington, Copper Canyon Press, 2000.

*

Critical Studies: ''The Fruit of Her Orchard'' by Tom O'Grady and Shirley Bossert, in *New Letters* (Kansas City), fall 1977; ''A Bow to Women for Poetic Providing Wealth'' by G.E. Murray, in *Sun-Times* (Chicago), 9 July 1978; ''The Trail That Turns on Itself'' by Peter Schjedahl, in *New York Times Book Review,* 17 December 1978; ''The Desperate Tongue'' by Ron Slate, in *Three Rivers Poetry Journal* (Pittsburgh), March 1979; by Rochelle Ratner, in *Library Journal* (New York), March 1980; by David Clothier, in *Los Angeles Times Book Review,* 27 April 1980; by David Kirby, in *Times Literary Supplement* (London), 13 June 1980; in *Virginia Quarterly Review* (Charlottesville), summer 1980; by Robert Phillips, in *New Letters* (Kansas City), summer 1980; by Hayden Carruth, in *Harper's* (New York), December 1980; by Donald M. Hassler, in *Tar River Poetry Review* (Greenville, North Carolina), spring 1981; ''Intellect, Grit, and a Chance to Sing in Our Chains'' by Douglas Myers, in *The Missoulian* (Missoula, Montana), 31 May 1985; ''Poetry: Changes and Channels'' by Robert McDowell, in *The Hudson Review* (New York), summer/fall 1985; in *Virginia Review,* 61(4), autumn 1985; by

Betty Thiebes, in *Cutbank,* 1985; ''Lion'' by Richard Simpson, in *Tar River Poetry Review,* fall 1985; by Hans Ostrum, in *Small Press Review,* November 1985; in *Bloomsbury Review,* November 1985; ''Disc Jockeys, Eggplants, and Despesparacidos'' by Carol Muske, in *New York Times Book Review,* 9 February 1986; by Lex Runciman, in *Western American Literature,* 11(3); by Bette Tomlinson, in *The Missoulian,* 12 December 1986; by Floyd Skloot, in *Calapooya Collage* (Monmouth, Oregon), 11, summer 1987; ''Poetry in Moments,'' in *The Missoulian* (Missoula, Montana), 28 July-3 August 1989; ''Wordsworth and Four Americans'' by Richard Simpson, in *Tar River Poetry Review,* fall 1989; ''Giving in to the Passions'' by Stephen Dobyns, in *New York Times Book Review,* 28 January 1990; ''Giving Voice to Vision'' by Kay Marie Porterfield, in *Bloomsbury Review* (Denver), March/April 1990; ''Kent State: A Gathering of Poets'' by David Shevin, in *People's Daily World Magazine,* 19 May 1990; ''Taking Nothing for Granted'' by Bette Tomlinson, in *New Letters* (Kansas City), spring 1990; by Gennie Nord, in *The Missoulian,* 29 March 1992; by Carolyn Kuebler, in *Hot Dish,* March/April 1992; by Janet Homer, in *Cutbank,* 38, summer 1992; by John Bradley, in *Calapooya Collage,* 16, August 1992; by Alice Derry, in *Hubbub,* 2(1), fall 1992; ''Emblems of Authenticity'' by Frank Allen, in *Poet Lore* (Bethesda, Maryland), spring 1993; ''Parody, Passion, and Communion'' by Richard Simpson, in *Tar River Poetry Review,* 32(2), spring 1993; ''American Latitudes'' by Calvin Bedient, in *The Southern Review* (Baton Rouge, Louisiana), 29(4), October 1993; by James Finn Cotter, in *The Hudson Review* (New York), summer 1994; ''Patricia Goedicke, Jorie Graham, and Mary Kinzie'' by Jonathan Holden, in *Prairie Schooner* (Lincoln, Nebraska), fall 1997.

Patricia Goedicke comments:

I write to set myself and perhaps a few others free: free politically in the sense that the process of ''sharing'' the private views of reality each of us sees from the separate hotel room windows of our lives is part and parcel of the assertion—indeed even a validation—of the very idea of community; and free spiritually in the sense that the intensity of poetry's concentration on the already deeply metaphorical character of language is chiefly important for the way it enables the individual, apparently incorporeal psyche to move back and forth between the material world of exterior reality and the invisible, eternally isolated interior world of the self.

Also, trusting in poetry's fierce insistence on the—at least—double-edged, continually punning nature of language to keep us true to the many-folded complexities of ''the real story'' of whatever experience brings us, I write to keep myself honest. And finally I write for pleasure, not only for the sheer delight—familiar to everyone—of rolling words around in the mouth but also for rhythm's sake, in a prosy world of walkers to evoke the liberating power of the dance, of poetry's great, healing ability to move us, as we say, ''beyond ourselves.''

*   *   *

In her first volume, *Between Oceans,* Patricia Goedicke treated with spasmodic power the chief themes that have haunted her since—myth and dreams, childhood fantasies, the I-Thou relationship wherever it is found (be it in marriage, friendship, or the larger community), and the issue of paradise and hell in human experience. She has spoken powerfully of the experience of death. Her first book has a poem about a suicide (''Priscilla'') and a loved one's death in a hospital (''The Gift''), and a sense of death pervades poems like

431

''The World Draped in White Sheets,'' which treats the miracle of childhood, when the capacity for perceiving even tragedy and accident as beautiful has not yet been lost:

> No one ever remembers how it rained when we were
>   children.
> There may have been bucketfuls more than now
> bigger
>   better
>   sluicing down over the hills
> Great wet gallons of it spilling down the streets
> but no, it is the snow, the snow we remember
>   the scabbed corpse covered up
>   the world draped in white sheets.

The poet moves with the eyes of the children who are inventing myth, learning to abstract the unacceptable into the acceptable, and continuing their survivors' duty to marvel:

> The couple that smothered in the car
>   and the cold, the cold
>   the turnip-white fingers and toes
>   the old feet stumbling, stumbling

In her later books Goedicke copes as bravely as any poet of our time with her own mortality; her poems sometimes describe the fight against a life-threatening illness, and she uses all of the resources of wit and metaphor to hold onto poetry's sustaining power and to the people whose love can be crucial. Yet she acknowledges the loneliness and alienation of her struggles:

> Slipping out of the sleeping bag of our love
> Only for a little, to try it
> In the warm bedroom, in the city
>
> I am astonished, at first
> The air is empty, I am naked
> None of your arms enfold me
>
> Nevertheless I must walk
> Once in awhile by myself

At every turn she reminds the beloved addressed and the reader (sometimes the reader is her beloved addressed) that it is essential, even a duty, to grasp the beauty of every moment. Yet ''. . . the future is lying in wait / with sad eyes looking back / like a huge slaughtered mountain.''

Goedicke is a romantic, and her love poems are always intense and willing to take a risk:

> I'm drinking nothing but rain these days
> Thinking how much I love you
>
> I still pour tears
> Even in brilliant sunshine,
> Even in snow

She is also alert to the need for change and social responsibility:

> Each day's a hot potato, let me see
> How to say it . . .
> Between the milk and the orange juice
> I think of the night before, the knife
> Edge of my own tongue—
> But the soldier never intended
> To murder the women and children—

Goedicke's poems often express a startled awareness of the I-Thou fellowship of those who have loved and suffered:

> What faces we hold out to each other! See
> We take off our glasses,
> At meetings our startled smiles
>
> Shine in the lamplight like such good children
> Nobody believes us, nobody
> Believes anybody

Her concern with what is wrong with the world pervades both personal grief and everyday mundanity:

> While we're out there standing beside a general doing
>   nothing,
> Standing beside the latest rocket doing nothing,
> While we're standing beside the cash registers doing
>   nothing.

Goedicke's search clearly is for serenity: ''For the shape of self pity is a real swamp, finally.'' There also is comfort in a relationship even with the dead: ''I put my arms around you / My last sight of you / For I am about to be killed, too.'' She has documented the familiar but unavoidable stages of grief and concluded, ''In the courtyard of my ears / Everyone's death comes whispering.'' Yet she bravely, even wisely, asserts hope: ''We must build more on less.''

In her mature poetry, showcased in *Paul Bunyan's Bearskin*, Goedicke moves through themes already familiar to her readers to a grander vision, one more objective, as if she were observing earth from a spaceship. The title poem is itself a dazzler, reminding one of Ginsberg's discursive poems on a troubled America. The arrogance that has threatened the very existence of the nation, not only a betrayal of its ideals, seems to both poets a manifestation observable at every turn. Men meddle impiously with nature; their technology gives them ''claws / to pull down Ursa Major.'' They wish, like the fools Shakespeare depicted in the days of Henry IV, to change the course of rivers, to make their impression on the heavens. As if from an airship, Goedicke inspects with a worrying compassion a nation that seems to have cancer: ''the corpse pinned to coordinates . . . one-of-a-kind cells breathing / the live rippling spirit of a bear taking up his bed / and walking, no one can predict how or when or where.'' The Native American bear is trying to survive, and the poet sings of her bond with him and the earth, not with those who have created the stone monuments of Washington, D.C., and Salt Lake City (''dazzling white bone''), showcases of death. A cancer survivor herself, Goedicke has made of her own odyssey through life-threatening illness a journey that has given her much to share with the world, especially a sense of the sacred and how precious the world was before men began their Faustian gambles, staking life on their new discoveries or the inventions of new weaponry, which are their toys.

In "Weight Bearing" an obese Native American seems to bear his caloric burden like the weight of his sufferings. A handsomer image of his isolation strikes the poet as she observes his landscape: "Out there on the mesa he is a lone cottonwood / Muttering to itself in the wind." In fact, Goedicke's poetry is almost entirely the voicing of an equally painful isolation. Even at a cocktail party (depicted in "The Periscope of the Eye"), while others are numbing themselves, angst is intrusive and commands attention, the posing of questions, an obligation to acknowledge that "there's never enough time / to think about how trapped we are, how terrified / Of drowning, of losing ourselves in the ocean / Out there with all those others . . . My friend says to be able to bear it / We must put on our blinders." This is the dilemma, but for being concerned the speaker is merely further alienated, even punished, a payoff hardly to be desired.

Yet complacency and indifference seem as elusive to Goedicke's speakers as they are easy to the people who surround her at cocktail parties. "But now all we have is our own life jackets" seems a pathetic wail, a cry for help that is answered only by "steamy saunas of self help . . ." and some joy of the body: "Cruising along in the one body / That keeps me and my family safe." Her ramblings—philosophical and provocatively near theology with their questioning about life's ultimate meaning—never seem far from a nostalgia for Eden, a simpler world, a praise of poverty and simplicity, lost to intellectuals of every ilk: "My friend says Poetry blooms best / On bread and water, even slipped through the barred / Metal hatchways of prisons." Goedicke's work affirms the old truth that only the outsider sees through shame and pretense and can offer the truth needed to confront the world's evil. "But here," she says of the unreal "real world" (this reader suspects that she includes the academic as well as the military-industrial and the political establishment, bureaucratic power structures of every description, not exempting religion), "Poetry is invisible: / As strange silos thrust themselves up . . ." The silos come not just from under the earth but also from those haunted caverns where the designs first formed themselves, the aggressive mind of man, "out of the troughs of the unconscious." The poet survives by "pretending I don't care, hurling myself into the statistics / In the land of instant gratification . . ." Yet that is no gratification at all, she confesses. Such complacency and me-tooism offer as temporary a fix as ice cream on the tongue.

Goedicke does not seem to think that technology has helped. In "Coin of the Realm" all money seems tainted by the weapons industry that endangers the lives of all, most poignantly the children. The worst-case scenario that the cold war's end promised to resolve—beneath the sham and false promises—is a continuing and terrible cause for anxiety. The doomsday scenario is kept active as a possibility and an option. Goedicke's poem seems to see purported progress as a tease and a torture. The threat is still present, and we still bankrupt ourselves to keep humanity terrified. The "missile silo near Great Falls / Montana" is still manned.

We share a planet, then, with those who are aware, terrified, and concerned—and also with the indifferent who prowl about them. Unfortunately, as Goedicke maintains in "Beyond the Mountains," our compassion is limited to what we can identify with, what we have ourselves suffered. "Pain has no shape" so long as it is known only through photographs. Only when we have walked in another's shoes can we get outside ourselves enough to care what that person has been through. We are left, therefore, with a terrible vulnerability, an inadequate sense of what we need to protect ourselves and others from. In many poems Goedicke explores the ramifications of these dilemmas and paradoxes. Her people seem to be caught in a vise of

suffering yet are too concerned for the world to beg for release, for that would make them the equals of those who do not care, whose indifference helps perpetuate suffering.

Goedicke's particular confluence of formal, intellectual, and imagistic acuity is the marker of her poems. Language as the expression of the self and the terms of the relationship between body and mind are the continuing concerns of her later work. In *Invisible Horses,* Goedicke's 1996 collection, the physical body's intelligence and consciousness—"crows falling from a brain sky / full of holes"—tells us about ourselves and physicalizes our thinking. In "The Danger of Falling" the voice tells us that what is "extraordinary" is "being-here / / or anywhere," because the body, a mere "collection of cells," goes about its business unhindered, both conscious and somehow severed from consciousness. In "Recipe," the first poem in the book, Goedicke states that "the flesh you live in is an anchor / of damp stones, you cannot move with or without it." This duality—and sometimes contradiction—of experience is the poet's hallmark as well as her particular bravery. Gratitude and devastating loss, loneliness and companionship are all equally defining for her, as "Because We Are Not Separate" states, "frantic / as crabs" at one moment, "exquisite / as a hummingbird" the next. Goedicke's astounding technical limberness and agility are reasserted again in *Invisible Horses.* Long-lined and short-lined poems, heavily and lightly punctuated poems, dense and looser verse—all reflect the poet's playfulness and love for poetic expression.

It is interesting that the subject of *Invisible Horses* is linked so closely to that of the deterioration of both the mind and body in old age, the subject of *As Earth Begins to End,* Goedicke's collection published in 2000. Here the earth itself is treated as a dissolving body, as the title poem asserts—"I've never been able to tell, where we end and earth begins beyond us"—and the pressures of last chances play through almost every poem—"the random cha-cha of cells hacked / into smaller metaphysical tatters." Electric leaps and tones mark the poems and play into the abstractions that always charge the poet. The titles of the poems—"What Holds Us Together," "What the Dust Does," "The Things I May Not Say"—can create a blurry sense of the book's concerns. Life for all of us ends too quickly, and Goedicke, in her resilient, life-affirming, and complex way, has pulled together the energies required to face these endings.

—David Ray and Martha Sutro

GOHORRY, John

Nationality: British. **Born:** Don Smith, 1943. **Address:** 17 Bedford Road, Letchworth, Hertfordshire SG6 4D1, England.

PUBLICATIONS

Poetry

A Galanty Show: Poems. Letchworth, Fearnhill School Press, 1979.
A Voyage Round the Moon. Liskeard, Harry Chambers/Peterloo Poets, 1985.
Talk into the Evening. Calstock, Cornwall, Peterloo Poets, 1992.

*

Critical Study: By Roger Garfitt, in *Poetry Review*, 84(2), summer 1994.

*   *   *

Reading John Gohorry's poetry gives one the picture of a man who either seizes on ideas or who is seized by them. He is a man who delights in the exploration and amplification of ideas and who is erudite, puzzling, and probing but never dull.

Gohorry often pursues his ideas obliquely. For example, the moon landings must have excited the imagination of many people. But to Gohorry it was not the *Eagle* landing itself, when Neil Armstrong and Edwin "Buzz" Aldrin, "inflatable Michelin men in their fat suits," performed before the cameras, that fired his imagination, but rather Michael Collins circling the moon in the command module *Columbus* waiting to pick the men up to take them home. It was Collins as the ultimate taxi man, who spent half his time cut off from light and any form of communication, that exercised Gohorry's wonder:

> Only he, circling her
> immense black back in the star silence, knows
> the true meaning of loneliness.

The art of Gohorry is to make his reader enter the situation too, to share his wonder. It is his probing imagination that seizes ours so that we share the experience of the lovers in the garden on "The Coast of Bohemia" or can imagine Sherlock Holmes interviewing five cloned Dr. Watsons, "men of identical build, age and character." And Gohorry can also engage our imagination in simple everyday experiences, as he does in "Coming Home":

> Coming back to the empty house,
> we do not ask what it has done.

But we are prompted to probe this idea for ourselves.

There also can be a delicious sensuality in Gohorry's work, as in "Yogis," in which a woman finds herself "in a tangle of knotted limbs she cannot free":

> She is rescued by the man from the flat below
> who walked up the stairs to her, naked, on two
> hands made sudden and explosive love, and then
> afterwards brought her the peace only true love

And in "Touching" we are shown two girls:

> Sixteen is an age of experiment, and there is
> something not quite innocent of the equality of
> caresses

Yet for the common reader Gohorry can perhaps sometimes go a step too far in his imaginative excursions. The remarkable longish poem, written in "authentic Chaucerian style," in which Gohorry imagines a letter written by Lewis Chaucer to his father Geoffrey, or the long poem exploring the *Leviathan* of the seventeenth-century philosopher Thomas Hobbes could leave us far behind. But the attempt to keep up can be rewarding and is worth the effort. And when

Gohorry engages us directly, we are left intrigued by the sheer enjoyment of his imaginative excursions and the way in which his quite esoteric images are sometimes brought close for us to enjoy. As George Szirtes has said, "Gohorry ought to be much better known than he is."

—John Cotton

GOLDBARTH, Albert

Nationality: American. **Born:** Chicago, Illinois, 31 January 1948. **Education:** University of Illinois, Chicago, B.A. 1969; University of Iowa, Iowa City, M.F.A. 1971; University of Utah, Salt Lake City, 1973–74. **Career:** Instructor, Elgin Community College, Illinois, 1971–72, Central YMCA Community College, Chicago, 1971–73, and University of Utah, Salt Lake City, 1973–74; assistant professor, Cornell University, Ithaca, New York, 1974–76; visiting professor, Syracuse University, New York, 1976. Since 1977 professor of creative writing, University of Texas, Austin. Advisory editor, *Seneca Review,* Geneva, New York. **Awards:** Theodore Roethke prize (*Poetry Northwest*), 1972, *Ark River Review* prize, 1973, 1975; National Endowment for the Arts grant, 1974, 1979; Guggenheim fellowship, 1983. **Address:** Department of English, University of Texas, Austin, Texas 78712, U.S.A.

PUBLICATIONS

Poetry

Under Cover. Crete, Nebraska, Best Cellar Press, 1973.
Coprolites. New York, New Rivers Press, 1973.
Opticks: A Poem in Seven Sections. New York, Seven Woods Press, 1974.
Jan. 31. New York, Doubleday, 1974.
Keeping. Ithaca, New York, Ithaca House, 1975.
A Year of Happy. Raleigh, North Carolina Review Press, 1976.
Comings Back: A Sequence of Poems. New York, Doubleday, 1976.
Curve: Overlapping Narratives. New York, New Rivers Press, 1977.
Different Fleshes. Geneva, New York, Hobart and William Smith Colleges Press, 1979.
Eurekas. Memphis, St. Luke's Press, 1980.
Ink Blood Semen. Cleveland, Bits Press, 1980.
The Smugglers Handbook. Wollaston, Massachusetts, Chowder Chapbooks, 1980.
Faith. New York, New Rivers Press, 1981.
Who Gathered and Whispered Behind Me. Seattle, L'Epervier Press, 1981.
Eurekas. Memphis, Tennessee, Raccoon, 1981.
Goldbarth's Book of Occult Phenomena. Des Moines, Iowa, Blue Buildings Press, 1982.
Original Light: New and Selected Poems 1973–1983. Princeton, New Jersey, Ontario Review Press, 1983.
Albert's Horoscope Almanac. Minneapolis, Bieler, 1986.
Arts and Sciences. Princeton, New Jersey, Ontario Review Press, 1986.
Popular Culture. Columbus, Ohio State University Press, 1989.

Delft: An Essay Poem. Maryville, Missouri, GreenTower Press, 1990.

Heaven and Earth: A Cosmology. Athens, University of Georgia Press, 1991.

Across the Layers: Poems Old and New. Athens and London, University of Georgia Press, 1993.

The Gods. Columbus, Ohio State University Press, 1993.

Ancient Musics: A Poetry Sequence. Kansas City, Missouri, Helicon Nine Editions, 1995.

A Lineage of Ragpickers, Songpluckers, Elegiasts & Jewelers: Selected Poems of Jewish Family Life, 1973–1995. St. Louis, Missouri, Time Being Books, 1996.

Adventures in Ancient Egypt: Poems. Columbus, Ohio State University Press, 1996.

Beyond: New Poems. Boston, Godine, 1998.

Troubled Lovers in History: A Sequence of Poems. Columbus, Ohio State University Press, 1999.

Novel

Marriage and Other Science Fiction. Columbus, Ohio State University Press, 1994.

Other

A Sympathy of Souls (essays). Minneapolis, Coffee House Press, 1990

Great Topics of the World: Essays. Boston, Godine, 1994.

Dark Waves and Light Matter: Essays. Athens, University of Georgia Press, 1999.

Editor, *Every Pleasure: The "Seneca Review" Long Poem Anthology.* Geneva, New York, Seneca Review Press, 1979.

*

Critical Studies: By the author, in *The Generation of 2000* edited by William Heyen, Princeton, New Jersey, Ontario Review Press, 1984; "Riddle of Being: Goldbarth's 'The Importance of Artists' Biographies'" by Thomas Lavazzi, in *Midwest Quarterly* (Pittsburg, Kansas), 27(4), summer 1986; interview with Barry Silesky, in *Aligarh Critical Miscellany* (Aligarh, India), 24, 1992.

Albert Goldbarth comments:

(1980) I do not much care to turn my poems over and study their undersides—motives, influences, psychic needs filled. I would rather go on to a new poem instead. What can be said briefly, and I think truly, is that my interest in the long poem and its possibilities grows stronger. By this I do not mean to turn my back on the shorter poem. *Comings Back,* though it included the fifteen-page "Letter to Tony," included a six-line poem I like as well. But the extended poem that includes narrative, or has scope enough to play with large bodies of time, or that finds room for dialogue or quoted source materials, that can build up litany or weave motifs in and out with the huge sweep a suite has—*Different Fleshes,* for instance—is a "novel/poem" and is one book-length piece of alternating prose and poetry sections that is able—happily, I think—to allow moments of pure lyric visionary intensity to take place within a novel-like framework—plot, historic and invented characters, quoted conversation. My hope is that some of its best moments have learned from, even include, the concentration and connotation one expects from a brief poem but that those

moments accumulate toward, and then take place within, an even richer context. In any case, that is the challenge I feel right now, and I suspect my next few efforts will record how well or poorly I have faced it.

(1985) I grow, if anything, more wary of statements of poetics. I believe my work asks to be self-sufficient. It is not a script requiring public performance, not a set of lyrics requiring musical accompaniment, not an arcane puzzle requiring for its fullest understanding prose commentary, not even, perhaps not especially, my own. All my poetry asks for is a few people who will, in solitude, care to enter the world of its pages.

* * *

Albert Goldbarth is bent on restoring useful clutter to the American lyric. For years the tendency has been to keep stripping down language to an ultimate essence, a vital center where all the truth may be put down in a phrase or a word. Most lyric language since World War II has been as gaunt as winter branches. Charles Olson stretched the line longer and freighted it with more content, Robert Lowell crabbed syntax and meter, and other poets have managed to spread language more thickly along the line, but Goldbarth has about him a certain genius to patter on indefinitely and keep it interesting.

Goldbarth's poems open any subject and become pretexts for labyrinthine monologues; his logic is a bramble bush of interconnections. Goldbarth's poetic, if one may hazard discerning it, is to pull everything around him into the form at hand. In one way his mode is high parody of our universal lust to consume, to own, to put it all into the shopping cart even if the money runs out. The poem comes back to its premise eventually, but the means is primary for a Goldbarth poem. The joy is in watching him drown in chatter and float back up again with a point.

Jan. 31 departs somewhat from this florid verse style, but the leaner lyric has some advantage for Goldbarth as he shows himself a moving, tensely emotional observer of the cold weather of Chicago, which he makes his vortex for a close commentary on love, lovemaking, survival, friendship, urban squalor, isolation, thinking, and finally hopefulness. Much of the book is written at half his range, however, and as a journal of poetic notations and some fully fledged poems, it lacks the delirious variety of his more exuberant free-form explosions.

Goldbarth renews poetic discourse by dropping back in time into the grandiloquent style of Elizabethan verse—Shakespeare's and Jonson's-and he does it shamelessly, lavishing on his verse all of the naive punning and wordplay, sonorous embellishment, exaggeration, and polysyllables that geysered up at the birth of English dialect. Laid over this older baroque is Goldbarth's sure touch with American slang, and the pastiche works, as in "A Week on the Show":

> CORRECT-O! The Lung is the Foot on the Breath-Stop!
>   Gwendolyn
> Halverstrom, clovequeen and fingerwhorls etched with spittle
>   turning Newark's alley-cobbles to delta with life electrode
>   in you
> as in cue-chalk, skewering, shewering, NOW
> for the slats are down and the scent of muff of Gazelle,
>   as the hand
> prongs five in the fifth of the gift and Luck the gland

the Lord forgot:
What astronomical body circles the earth and has phases?

But there is more to Goldbarth than mere verbal performance. His poems are nearly desperate about language and the need to keep talking, the need to explain the slightest facet of personal history with all of the terminological armament of science and philosophy. His fully conceived book *Comings Back* is also the clearest instance of how Goldbarth intends his poetry to be a point of convergence between the individual and the immense culture heaped around him. Perhaps Goldbarth intends us to see that we are again at a birth of language, a dawning of new technological speech that he dares to use as his own personal utterance. *Comings Back* is charged with scientific lore, with facts of all sorts, with statistical junk and heaps of otherwise useless information, all put to lyric use.

Goldbarth's persona is chameleon-like, dropping into other periods and other voices at whim, and he seems to suggest that the poet may no longer have a culture to possess personally. The poet may plunder the world's codes and some of its lesser secrets in swashbuckling verse, but he too is a drifter in a much larger and increasingly impersonal human realm. Unlike the vast majority of other poets now writing, Goldbarth is not interested in staking out some part of the human realm as his own, and his attention wanders from old lovers to friends, to the deep past, to fragments of experience belonging to all of human experience.

A poetic vision more in the making than fully formed lies below the verbal froth of Goldbarth's later books. He has been doggedly pursuing a certainty that life is a Moebius strip. "History repeats itself," he blandly declares at one point in *Jan. 31,* but the theme is pervasive in *Comings Back* and is the whole point of the 1977 chapbook *Curve: Overlapping Narratives.* Goldbarth later turned toward an earlier preoccupation, his own family history, from Chicago, to which the family had immigrated, back to Poland. Other Jewish poets have done accordingly in their efforts to get to the sources of their own personal myths and, by inference, the roots of imagination.

For a poet of ironic, sometimes impenetrable masks, the turn to sentimental history is buoyed up by incursions into general mythology. In *The Gods,* for example, plain living is shot through with the divine; gods inhabit the ordinary world as Goldbarth's considerable expository powers begin to mix fable with facts. In *Heaven and Earth* the two worlds become one in the poet's vivid attention to surfaces and their elusive mythical depths. Experience is a tapestry of rhymes between the sacred and profane.

Goldbarth's rash, impetuous style of writing conceals an evolving vision of the world. If he began with irony and satire, it was aimed at Cartesian certainty. In his later work satire gives way to faith, belief in spirit, and a growing seriousness about the values at stake in poetry and the literary imagination.

—Paul Christensen

GOLDSMITH, Kenneth (Paul)

Nationality: American. **Born:** Freeport, New York, 4 June 1961. **Education:** New York University, New York, 1979–80; Parsons School of Design, New York, 1980–81; Rhode Island School of Design, Providence, 1981–84, B.F.A. in sculpture 1984. **Family:** Married Cheryl Donegan in 1989; one son. **Career:** Has lectured at numerous universities, including Brown University, Stanford University, Ohio State University, University of Oregon, Princeton University, and Rhode Island School of Design. Since 1985 artist and writer. Artist-in-residence, Chateau de Bionnay, Lacenas, France, 1996, and Wexner Center, Ohio State University, 1998. **Awards:** Residency fellowship, Banff Center for the Arts, Canada, 1985; Artist grant, Artist Space, New York, 1988; National Endowment for the Arts/Mid Atlantic Visual Arts fellowship, sculpture, 1991. **Address:** 38 West 26th Street, 3B, New York, New York 10010, U.S.A.

PUBLICATIONS

Poetry

73 Poems. Brooklyn, New York, Permanent Press, 1994.
No. 111 2.7.93–10.20.96. Great Barrington, Massachusetts, The Figures, 1997.
6799. New York, zingmagazine, 2000.
Fidget. Toronto, Coach House Books, 2000.
Soliloquy. New York, Granary Books, 2000.

Recording: *73 Poems,* with composer/vocalist Joan LaBarbara, Lovely Music, Ltd., 1994.

*

Manuscript Collections: Poetry/Rare Books Collection, State University of New York, Buffalo; Ruth and Marvin Sackner Archive of Visual Poetry, Miami, Florida.

Critical Studies: "Visual Voices—Written Language Is Central to the Art of Sean Landers, Kenneth Goldsmith and Joseph Grigely" by Raphael Rubinstein, in *Art in America,* 84(4), 1996; by George Condo, in *Speak Art!: The Best of Bomb Magazine's Interviews with Artists,* New York, New Art, 1997.

*   *   *

What immediately distinguishes Kenneth Goldsmith from most other poets is that he took his degree in sculpture at an arts college and that he has since mounted one-person exhibitions at SoHo galleries. He was also included in *Heights of the Marvelous* (2000), Todd Colby's anthology of New York poets who do art in addition to poetry. Goldsmith's writing reflects a key aesthetic difference between the art world and the literary world, especially the world of graduate writing students. His poetry is extreme in its originality, as distinct from the slight deviances from acceptable styles more typical of the work of students in creative writing programs.

The premise of Goldsmith's book *Fidget* (2000) is, as he explains in the preface, "to record every move my body made on June 16, 1997 (Bloomsday)." He continues:

I attached a microphone to my body and spoke every movement from 10:00 AM, when I woke up, to 11:00 PM, when I went to sleep. I was alone all day in my apartment and didn't answer the phone, go on errands, etc. I just observed my body and spoke.

The hazards encountered in writing this long prose poem are incorporated into the work itself, as Goldsmith speaks of getting out of bed and interacting with objects in his space. There is a description of masturbation that verges on the classic. He notes that he "began to go crazy," in contrast to the tradition of poets who write about insanity that existed before they set pen to paper.

Given Goldsmith's background, it is indicative that *Fidget* was first published—that is, made public—as an exhibition at Printed Matter, a SoHo store devoted to artists' books. A year later, on 16 June 1998, it was incorporated into a performance at the Whitney Museum of American Art at Philip Morris, in which the singer Theo Bleckman "stood high on a balcony in the museum and dropped sheets of paper printed with each word as he sang them." Goldsmith then produced an electronic version, and it was not until 2000 that *Fidget* became a book.

Marjorie Perloff, who has been Goldsmith's most significant critic, commends the following passage from chapter 2 (11:00):

Walks. Left foot. Head raises. Walk. Forward. Forward. Forward. Bend at knees. Forward. Right foot. Left foot. Right foot. Stop. Left hand tucks at pubic area. Extracts testicles and penis using thumb and forefinger. Left hand grasps penis. Pelvis pushes on bladder, releasing urine. Stream emerges from within buttocks. Stomach and buttocks push outward. Stream of urine increases. Buttocks push. Sphincter tightens. Buttocks tighten. Thumb and forefinger shake penis. Thumb pulls. Left hand reaches. Tip of forefinger and index finger extend to grasp as body sways to left. Feet pigeon-toed. Move to left. Hand raises to hairline and pushes hair. Arm raises above head. Four fingers comb hair away from hairline toward back of head. Eyes see face. Mouth moves. Small bits of saliva cling to inside of lips. Swallow. Lips form words.

As Perloff observes, "In breaking down bodily functions into their smallest components, Goldsmith defamiliarizes the everyday in ways that recall such Wittgensteinian questions as 'Why can't the right hand give the left hand money?'" Aesthetically adventurous, Goldsmith works on the borders between poetry and prose and, more courageously, between poetry and what is not poetry, not to mention the borders between literature and art.

Not content with an exhibition, a performance, and publication in book form, Goldsmith also has collaborated in producing an electronic version of *Fidget* in Java applet. Here the text of the work is reconfigured by substituting the computer for the human body. As Goldsmith explains,

The Java applet contains the text reduced further into its constituent elements, a word or a phrase. The relationship between these elements is structured by a dynamic mapping system that is organized visually and spatially instead of grammatically. In addition, the Java applet invokes duration and presence. Each time the applet is downloaded it begins at the same time as set in the user's computer and every mouse click or drag that the user initiates is reflected in the visual mapping system. The different hours are represented in differing font sizes, background colors and degree of "fidgetness,"

however, these parameters may be altered by the user. The sense of time is reinforced by the diminishing contrast and eventual fading away of each phrase as each second passes.

While the scheme reflects aesthetic expressionism, the art depends upon observing severe constraints.

Fidget reflects Goldsmith's earlier *No. 111 2.7.93–10.20.96* (1997), a 606-page encyclopedic text based on words ending in the sound *ah* (what phoneticians call the "schwa"). It is a collection of words drawn from conversations, books, phone calls, radio shows, newspapers, television, and especially the Internet. The words are arranged alphabetically and by syllable count starting with single-syllable words beginning with Aù"A, a, aar, aas, aer, agh, ah air." Toward the end, in a kind of update of Raymond Queneau's classic *Exercise de Style* (1947), Goldsmith draws the texts from individual pages from unacknowledged sources. Earlier he had produced visual poems of overlapping letters, some of which were performed by the singer Joan La Barbara and collected on a CD.

It is safe to say that few other published poets are working in Goldsmithian ways.

—Richard Kostelanetz

GOLDSWORTHY, Peter

Nationality: Australian. **Born:** Minlaton, South Australia, 12 October 1951. **Education:** University of Adelaide, South Australia, B.Med. and B.Surg. 1974. **Family:** Married Helen Louise Wharldall in 1972; two daughters and one son. **Career:** Since 1974 medical practitioner in Adelaide. **Awards:** Commonwealth Poetry prize, 1982; Anne Elder prize, 1983; South Australia Biennial literary award, 1984, and poetry prize, 1988; Australia Council fellowship, 1984, 1986, 1990–91. **Agent:** Curtis Brown (Australia), P.O. Box 19, Paddington, Sydney, New South Wales 2021. **Address:** 28 Burwood Avenue, Nailsworth, South Australia 5083, Australia.

PUBLICATIONS

Poetry

Readings from Ecclesiastes. Sydney, Angus and Robertson, 1982.
This Goes with This. Crows Nest, New South Wales, ABC, 1988.
This Goes with That. Sydney, Angus and Robertson, 1991.
Wish. Sydney, Angus and Robertson, 1995.
If, Then: Poems and Songs. Sydney, Angus and Robertson, 1996.
Keep It Simple, Stupid. Pymble, New South Wales, HarperCollins, 1996.

Novels

Maestro. Sydney, Angus and Robertson, 1989; London, Bloomsbury, 1990.
Honk If You Are Jesus. Sydney, Angus and Robertson, 1992.
Magpie, with Brian Matthews. Adelaide, Wakefield Press, 1992.
Jesus Wants Me for a Sunbeam. Pymble, New South Wales, HarperCollins, 1999.

Short Stories

Archipelagoes. Sydney, Angus and Robertson, 1982.
Zooing. Sydney, Angus and Robertson, 1986.
Bleak Rooms. Adelaide, Wakefield Press, 1988.
Little Deaths. Sydney, Angus and Robertson, 1993.
Selected Stories. Pymble, New South Wales, Flamingo, 1997.

Other

Navel Gazing: Essays, Half-Truths, and Mystery Flights. Ringwood, Victoria, and New York, Penguin, 1998.

Editor, with Larry Buttrose, *Number Three Friendly Street: Poetry Reader.* Adelaide, Adelaide University Union Press, 1979.

*

Manuscript Collection: Australian Defense Forces Academy Library, Canberra.

Critical Study: *The Ironic Eye* by Andrew Reimer, Sydney, Angus and Robertson, 1994.

Peter Goldsworthy comments:

Poetry to me is the nearest words can approximate to thought and to "the mixture of the world and ourselves" (Merleau-Ponty) that we inhabit.

*   *   *

For a poet with a sparse output, Peter Goldsworthy made an impressive contribution to Australian poetry beginning in the 1980s. His first collection, *Readings from Ecclesiastes,* was published in 1982 and received several major prizes, and it is easy to see why. In a period when the last excesses of 1970s rhetoric and gesture still troubled the air with defiance and self-consciousness, Goldsworthy's poems were taut, disciplined, and sharp as a scalpel. Their wit implied an observant mind, yet they were powerful in a way that outpaced mere cleverness. Goldsworthy was not to be classified with any prevailing groups or coteries, though it might be possible to perceive antecedents in certain poems of Peter Porter or some of the Melbourne poets of the 1960s and 1970s.

Publication of Goldsworthy's second collection, *This Goes with This,* during the Australian bicentenary year in 1988 marked a return to verse after several years of writing short fiction. The short poems in the new book certainly consolidated Goldsworthy's name as an incisive writer and a skilled dissector of human (and other) foibles. "A sparkling volume," Les Murray called it, and that it is, but as the title poem also suggests, even though "this goes with this goes with this / and always will," the mature analyst discovers that "knowledge is no cure, or escape."

A volume of selected poems, titled mischievously *This Goes with That,* was published in 1991 and included work composed in the previous twenty years, though the total selection in effect reprinted the two earlier books. In 1992 the National Library of Australia issued the pamphlet *After the Ball.* Goldsworthy's knowledge of classical

music reinforces some of the later poems, which therefore act as a sort of counterpoint to his acclaimed novel *Maestro.*

—Thomas W. Shapcott

GOODISON, Lorna (Gaye)

Nationality: Jamaican. **Born:** Kingston, 1 August 1947. **Education:** St. Hugh's High School, Kingston, 1959–66; Jamaica School of Art, Kingston, 1967–68; School of the Art Students League, New York, 1968–69. **Family:** Divorced; one son. **Career:** Art teacher, Jamaica College, 1969–70; copy chief, McCann Erickson advertising, Jamaica, 1970–72; assistant creative director, LNCK Advertising, Jamaica, 1972–74; creative director, Don Miller Advertising, Jamaica, 1974–76; public relations officer, Jamaica Broadcasting Corporation, 1976; creative consultant, CARIFESTA '76, Jamaica, 1976. Since 1977 freelance writer and painter. Writer-in-residence, University of the West Indies, Kingston; 1973; Fellow, Bunting Institute, Radcliffe College, Cambridge, Massachusetts, 1986–87; visiting professor, University of Michigan, Ann Arbor, 1992, 1993, 1995. Editor, CARIFESTA 76 magazine, 1976. **Awards:** Institute of Jamaica Centenary Medal, 1981, and Musgrave Medal, 1987; Commonwealth Poetry prize, 1986. **Agent:** New Beacon Books, 76 Stroud Green Road, London N4 3EN, England. **Address:** 8 Marley Close, Kingston 6, Jamaica.

PUBLICATIONS

Poetry

Poems. Privately printed, 1974.
Tamarind Season. Kingston, Institute of Jamaica Press, 1980.
I Am Becoming My Mother. London, New Beacon, 1986.
Heartease. London, New Beacon, 1988.
Lorna Goodison. New York, Research Institute for the Study of Man, 1989.
To Us All Flowers Are Roses. London, New Beacon, 1990; Urbana, University of Illinois Press, 1995.
Selected Poems. Ann Arbor, University of Michigan Press, 1992.
Turn Thanks: Poems. Urbana, University of Illinois Press, 1999.

Play

Pepper, with Trevor Rhone and Sonia Mills (produced 1989).

Short Stories

Baby Mother and the King of Swords. London, Longman, 1990.

*

Critical Studies: "Wooing with Words: Some Comments on the Poetry of Lorna Goodison" by Pamela Mordecai, in *Jamaica Journal* (Kingston), 45, 1981; "Goodison on the Road to Heartease" and "On Becoming One's Mother: Goodison in the Context of Feminist Criticism," both by Edward Baugh, in *Journal of West Indian Literature,* 1(1), October 1986, and 4(1), 1990; "Overlapping Systems: Language in the Poetry of Lorna Goodison" by Velma Pollard, in *Carib,* 5, 1989; "Pilgrimage out of Dispossession" by Christine Pagnoulle, in *Commonwealth Essays and Studies* (Dijon, France), 17(1), autumn 1994; "Lorna Goodison: Heartease" by Frank Birbalsingh, in his *Frontiers of Caribbean Literatures in English,* New York, St. Martin's Press, 1996; *Apocrypha of Nanny's Secrets: The Rhetoric of Recovery in Africaribbean Women's Poetry* (dissertation) by Dannabang Kuwabong, McMaster University, 1997; "Language and Identity: The Use of Different Codes in Jamaican Poetry" by Velma Pollard, in *Winds of Change: The Transforming Voice of Caribbean Women Writers and Scholars,* edited by Adele S. Newson and Linda Strong-Leek, New York, Peter Lang, 1998; "Gender and Hybridity in Contemporary Caribbean Poetry" by Jana Gohrisch, in *Anglistentag 1997 Giessen,* edited by Raimund Bormeier and others, Trier, Germany, Wissenschaftlicher Verlag Trier, 1998.

Lorna Goodison comments:

(1984) I have spent a great deal of time trying to avoid writing poetry because, really, I would like to live a less difficult life. But it (poetry) keeps intruding on everything. It comes in dreams, in the middle of ordinary conversations, while trying to talk to God, when I am cooking or going about woman's business. So I surrendered. It is more powerful than all the other less difficult things I would rather be doing.

(1990) I now feel very blessed to be called poet.

*   *   *

Lorna Goodison is among the most vibrant and original poets to emerge from the Caribbean. While demonstrating tremendous sympathy for the oppressed, she neither patronizes nor sentimentalizes her subjects, and she writes with an easy, colloquial style that wears its truths lightly.

Her first published collection, *Tamarind Season,* is her most overtly political. Although it encompasses tributes to the writer Jean Rhys and the musician Miles Davis as well as poems about Toronto and New York, its major preoccupations are with race and class. "England Seen," written, as many of her poems are, in an effective combination of Creole patois and educated English, describes the disillusionment of the chief hair presser of Catherine Commonwealth Hairdressers:

. . . Icylyn's accents embrace all of Great Britain
and she does not like England.
"I tell them white people that England is
nowhere, at least I can't starve at home
if is even a breadfruit tree I can stone."

More subtle are the poems describing characters who deny their own heritage. In "My Late Friend" the speaker explains, ". . . She's fled the tropics / because the sun darkens her / my friend wants to be one with the snow . . ." "Ocho Rios" cleverly reveals layers of compromise as the poet modulates her language in a local market:

. . . "how much for the curry goat?"
"Three dolla"
"Fi wan curry goat"
"A four dolla fi tourist sista."

I beat her down to a dollar fifty,

she says I am clearly roots.
I tell her the curry goat irie . . .

The poem's message is neatly underlined in the final stanzas:

The sign in the square says "Tourism, not socialism"
and though I eat this curry sitting on a feed bag from
    Florida . . .
which Colonizer is winning in Ocho Rios?

Goodison writes with a strong sense of community. Indeed some of her most effective poems, like "Bridge Views," draw on her own family:

. . . My mother did not forget to tell us
we did not really belong there.
Her family gave their name to rivers
her children should not play in gullies
we were always on our way back to where
she originally petite bourgeoisie came from . . .

Moving to "concrete suburbia / acquiring the first weapons for / committing class suicide," the boys slowly succumb to "the schizoid waters," becoming thieves, alcoholics, and hit men: ". . . and what is now a curfew zone / was then just, Home."

Goodison's second collection, *I Am Becoming My Mother,* moves increasingly from the political to the personal. The poems in this volume are wonderfully lyrical and assured. Many of them celebrate women's lives, as does the title poem ("Yellow / brown woman / fingers always smelling of onions . . .") or "For My Mother (May I Inherit Half Her Strength)," which begins,

My mother loved my father
I write this as an absolute
in this my thirtieth year
the year to discard absolutes . . .

Describing her mother's acceptance of her father's infidelity, the poem ends,

When he died, she sewed dark dresses for the
    women among us
and she summoned that walk, straight-backed, that she
    gave to us
and buried him dry-eyed . . .

and she fell down a note to the realization that she did
not have to be brave, just this once
and she cried.

For her hands grown coarse with raising nine children
for her body for twenty years permanently fat
for the time she pawned her machine for my sister's
Senior Cambridge fees
and for the pain she bore with the eyes of a queen

and she cried also because she loved him.

In this prizewinning volume Goodison writes mostly about relationships, though politics appears in "For Rosa Parks," written to the woman who unwittingly started America's civil rights movement by refusing to give up her bus seat to a white person: "And how was this soft-voiced woman to know / that this 'No' / in answer to the command to rise / would signal the beginning / of the time for walking? . . ." Another political poem is the delightful "Bedspread," based on a real incident in which the South African police raided Winnie Mandela's home and arrested a bedspread in the colors of the African National Congress: ". . . It was woven by women with slender / capable hands / accustomed to binding wounds / hands that closed the eyes of / dead children, / that fought for the right to / speak in their own tongues . . . They wove the bedspread / and knotted notes of hope / in each strand / and selvedged the edges with / ancient blessings / older than any white man's coming . . ." As always in Goodison's work the potential anger is tempered by wisdom and hope.

Goodison's third collection, *Heartease,* seems to be searching for a new direction. Though the rhythms of reggae are still found, hymns and incantations prevail. In many of the poems the vivid language, memorable personalities, and wry politics of her earlier work seem to have been sacrificed to a vague spirituality. "A Rosary of Your Names (II)," for example, is merely an uninspiring catalog: "The Merciful / The Peace / The Source / The Hidden / The All Strivings Cease . . ." But in poems like "Blue Peace Incantation" Goodison's lyricism and rich visual descriptions are still evident: "Within blue of peace, / the azure of calm, / beat soft now bright heart, / beat soft, sound calm . . ." This volume suggests a period of transition in the work of a poet whose enduring quality is optimism.

—Katie Campbell

GOULD, Alan (David)

Nationality: Australian (emigrated from England, 1966; granted Australian citizenship, 1986). **Born:** London, England, 22 March 1949. **Education:** Woolverstone Hall, Suffolk, 1960–66, Canberra Grammar, Canberra, Australia, 1966–67; Australian National University, Canberra, 1968–71, B.A. (honors) 1971; Canberra College of Advanced Education, 1974, Diploma of Education 1974. **Family:** Married Anne Langridge in 1984; two sons. **Career:** Driver handyman, Canberra, 1972–74; relief teacher, Canberra, 1975–90. Since 1975 writer, Canberra. **Awards:** New South Wales Premier's prize for poetry, 1981; Best Book of the Year, Foundation of Australian Literary Studies, 1984; Banjo award for fiction, Australian National Book Council, 1992; Phillip Hodgins memorial medal, 1999; Royal Blind Society Audio Book of the Year, 1999, for *The Tazyrik Year.* **Agent:** Margaret Connolly, 37 Ormond Street, Paddington, New South Wales 2021, Australia. **Address:** 6 Mulga Street, O'Connor, Australian Capital Territory 2601, Australia.

PUBLICATIONS

Poetry

The Skald Mosaic. Canberra, Open Door Press, 1975.
Icelandic Solitaries. Brisbane, Queensland University Press, 1978.
Astral Sea. Sydney, Angus and Robertson, 1981.
The Pausing of the Hours. Sydney, Angus and Robertson, 1984.

The Twofold Place. Sydney, Angus and Robertson, 1986.
Years Found in Likeness. Sydney, Angus and Robertson, 1988.
Formerlight (Selected Poems). Sydney, Angus and Robertson, 1992.
Momentum. Melbourne, Heinemann, 1992.
Mermaid. Melbourne, Heinemann, 1996.
Dalliance and Scorn. Canberra, Indigo, 1999.

Novels

The Man Who Stayed Below. Sydney, Angus and Robertson, 1984.
The Enduring Disguises. Sydney, Angus and Robertson, 1988.
To the Burning City. Melbourne, Heinemann, 1991.
Close-ups. Melbourne, Heinemann, 1994.
The Tazyrik Year. Sydney, Hodder Headline, 1998.
The Schoonermaster's Dance. Sydney, HarperCollins, 2000.

Other

The Totem Ship. Sydney, Duffy and Snellgrove, 1996.

*

Manuscript Collection: National Library, Canberra.

Critical Study: "The Canberra Poets: The New Australian Poetry" by Kevin F. Pearson, in *Poetry of the Pacific Region: Proceedings of the CRNLE/SPACLALS Conference,* edited by Paul Sharrad, Adelaide, Centre for Research in the New Literature in English, 1984.

Alan Gould comments:

As might be expected from a poet who also writes novels, a good deal of my poetry is novelistic in character, presenting a setting, an interaction of people, an era, a story.

I have been interested in those moments where a person gains an overview of their own time, is able to place it within the context of a larger time. Thus many of my poems have historical settings—the Norse explorations of Greenland and North America, the period of the last sailing ships, and so on.

The idea of character intrigues me, that which makes an individual distinct and, at death, irrecoverable, that which makes a stranger act but an acquaintance unfold.

*   *   *

Alan Gould's early chapbook *The Skald Mosaic* not only used the heroic history and skaldic tradition of his mother's Iceland but also signaled his involvement with a significant 1970s Canberra group. Assembled loosely at various times around the magazine *Canberra Poetry* and the hand-set Open Door Press were David Brooks, Mark O'Connor, Kevin Hart, Philip Mead, and Gould. All have made their mark as writers, and three are academics with critical influence. O'Connor weds biology with verse. Gould alone, however, a successful novelist for the young and for the general reader as well as a poet, has achieved the versatility of the full-time writer.

The Skald Mosaic forms a substantial middle section of Gould's *Icelandic Solitaries.* The work's elemental, sometimes violent spareness is thrown into relief by the longer-breathed lines and rich vocabulary of other poems celebrating places (Bangkok, Belfast, the

Australian Monaro) and the past, with a leaning to the Viking past (''Rus ship-burial on the Volga,'' ''Akureyri''). (For many years Gould's hobby has been building models of sailing ships.) The intersection of place and history is Gould's subject, and he moves from early characters' loves and rages to honoring a literary figure in ''Homage to Joseph Conrad'' and to different locations for canvases, as in ''Wagram 1809'' and ''News of the Surrender.'' Less classifiable in context, though pointing both to an influence and to a later direction, is ''Prayer,'' whose short lines, skillful rhyming, and gliding motion recall Auden's lyric mode (for example, ''Lay your sleeping head . . . .'').

Astral Sea develops early themes, with a powerful series characterizing the lives of known Viking explorers and settlers. Here, in a further group on ports, wrecks, and exiles, and in ''The Songs of Emyr,'' which includes ghazels and the particularly fine sestina ''Marco Polo Remembers the Province of Kamul,'' Gould uses a new freedom with language to explore and interpret the informed interest that underlies many of his best poems. The following lines are from ''Leif Eriksson'':

So he sailed on hearsay, brought home the New World . . .
   those hills

enclosed him in sweet arms, exquisite hills
clothed in birch and tamarack, though world
trembled grape and whortleberry, and in
the river salmon fat as the thigh of a man
swam to the finger. That he did not fail
to see advantage there is known. Less known

what sent him back to father's and the known
acreage, turned him Christian to win bare hills
for God, why five years on from that he fails
all further notice. A son; who into Dad's world
of grudged approvals, leapt like a warning, a man
'shrewd and vigorous', at Reykjavik striding in
concrete, horizon-owner. Perhaps. But in
the gaze of his headstrong elder that stride is known.
I see them circling warily, man
and child and man and man. It is not hills
prompt their loyal quarrel, but moment, the world
tugging weakening roots . . . .

Gould's fascination with the high seas and with great marine exploration continues with the sequences ''The History of Shipping'' and ''The Great Circle,'' which work ambitiously in a lofty vein in a variety of forms. The following is from ''The Atlantic'':

. . . flying fish that leap from the sea-dazzle onto the   white
paper where Parkinson's pen moves like a lure,
to this high south, where the far peaks of the Tierra del
Fuego stream their white sub-zero scarves . . .
We are present, you are present, for presence is increase
and increase of horizons in a time and across all
times; it is our human difference.
The Pacific attends you, the first shimmer of a vast
idea, enclosing its mesh of systems and
populations; sail to the southward, toward our
consciousness.

At the same time Gould cultivates a private, quieter, questioning vein for his ''Five Verse Letters'' (one each to Hart, the Meads, and Murray) and even a roistering playfulness for talk of school days and for the bucolic ''Chatting up the bottle'' and ''Getting the old man home.''

The most impressive of Gould's later work seems to assume the cloak of Les Murray without, so to speak, the nobbling and gnarling. He conceives new company and geographies: realizations of life in the context of race and time (''The Observed Observer'') and the earth's aspect from above and clouds (''Flying over the Australian Alps,'' ''High Cloud Conversation''). Several of his poems on workers take a Murray-like delight in the jargon of jobs (''Electrician,'' ''South Coast Mechanic''). Gould is capable of biting satire, as in ''Darling I run them like a smart boutique; / surprising the profits that accrue from their chic,'' from ''Her Stable of Poets,'' and of poems that grindingly cow or capitalize on popular fears (''Pliers,'' ''Wisdom Teeth'').

In its final sequence, ''The Calms,'' the 1996 volume *Mermaid* reinforces Gould's preoccupation with the age of sail. Subtitled ''An Illustrated Sequence,'' it has fourteen lovingly drawn black-and-white illustrations, by the poet, of sails, rigging, masts, and almost unpeopled decks. The poems themselves provide the portrait studies.

An all-arounder with reserve powers, Gould has to a degree been saved by his novel writing from the touting of the poetry scene. His craftsmanship and thoughtfulness exact more than just respect, and a touch of coldness in his rhetoric cannot conceal a writer of unusual purpose, sensibility, and intelligence.

—Judith Rodriguez

GRAHAM, Henry

Nationality: British. **Born:** Liverpool, Lancashire, 1 December 1930. **Education:** Liverpool College of Art. **Career:** Painter; exhibitions in London and Northern England; gave up painting for poetry at the age of 30. Beginning 1969 lecturer in art history, Liverpool Polytechnic; now retired. Poetry editor, *Ambit* magazine, London. **Awards:** *Ambit* prize, 1968; Arts Council award, 1969, 1971. **Address:** c/o Ambit, 17 Priory Gardens, Highgate, London N6 5QY, England.

PUBLICATIONS

Poetry

Soup City Zoo, with Jim Mangnall. London, Anima Press, 1968.
Good Luck to You Kafka/You'll Need It Boss. London, Rapp and Whiting, 1969.
Passport to Earth. London, Rapp and Whiting-Deutsch, 1971.
Poker in Paradise Lost, with Jim Mangnall. Liverpool, Glasshouse Press, 1977.
Europe after Rain. West Kirby, Wirral, Headland Publications, 1981.
The Very Fragrant Death of Paul Gauguin. Hungerford, Berkshire, Rivelin Grapheme Press, 1987.
Jardin Gobe Avions. Hungerford, Berkshire, Rivelin Grapheme Press, 1991.

The Eye of the Beholder. Merseyside, Sefton Arts, 1997.
Bar Room Ballads. London, Ambit, 1999.

*

Critical Study: "A Quote and a Comment" by the author, in *Ambit 92* (London), 1983.

Henry Graham comments:

(1974) My early influences in writing were the modern American poets—Pound, Olson, Duncan, etc. But now the Englishness of all the English arts interests me more; Auden, for instance, is one of the poets I admire most. The arts, and especially poetry, are not an attempt on my part to communicate but are a way of looking into myself and the universe. If, as sometimes seems to happen, others are interested in and find in me what lies outside themselves, good; if not, good.

(1985) Today my writing is concerned principally with an international philosophy of modernism, i.e., expressionism, surrealism, and abstraction, and not with any parochial literary stance.

*   *   *

Henry Graham deals in images. His work as a painter and art historian often informs both the subjects of his verse—de Chirico, Magritte, Klee, and Samuel Palmer are mentioned with affection—and its techniques, which are visual and painterly. His better poems combine with this a sense of the special resources of poetic language.

Graham's early verse dates from the late 1960s and early 1970s, when jokiness and whimsical fantasy became a political duty and the grubby hustlings of businessman and politician were seen as emanations of death, enemies of the poet-dreamer. Though this scheme occasionally surfaces in his work, he keeps language, material, and attitudes under better control than do some of the Liverpool poets, with whom his name was at one time, perhaps misleadingly, coupled. A sense of social justice helps rescue his verse from shallowness.

Recurrent in *Good Luck to You Kafka/You'll Need It Boss* are poems about discontent, loneliness, and resentment and the way in which everyday sights and events are altered by such emotions. Verse wryly recording the bathos of Graham's own ordinary responses to living is more impressive for its humanity than for its tension or energy. His imaginative engagement is stronger when his subject is the already achieved work of art. Ten poems on paintings by Palmer derive their force from the same images as the paintings. But Palmer's distorted landscapes and figures, for example, his monstrous moons, which show the kinship of all created things and reveal God and the spiritual via the real, are reinterpreted here. Palmer's pastorals become nightmares, his symbols of fecundity threats. By contemplating symbols as pure images, Graham reveals them as exaggerated, grotesque, surreal.

Palmer's moons become Graham's own. In *Passport to Earth* he looks at "the pitted face of the moon / and think[s] of the bodies in the pits / at Belsen." This is the moon's public, "pitted" face, but it stands for personal horror too: "The huge million watt / bulb of the moon / crushes me against its face." Cold, bright, and unearthly, the moons illuminate, but in doing so they reveal the monstrosities that darkness would conceal. With these and other images Graham makes an interesting attempt to structure a book of verse by primarily visual means.

But language, too, is a mode of power, pointing away from the forlorn isolations of art and self, the sad prisoners of canvas and frame, toward the bigger world. The seven poems of *Poker in Paradise Lost*, written with Jim Mangnall and made from cut-up photo captions from *Time* magazine, offer surrealist glimpses of the United States. Lacking in focus and structure, arbitrarily scattering effects, these pieces are nevertheless successful in the coupling of occasional images: "a young Eisenhower after sophomore / year at San Quentin."

In later work Graham claims to have turned away from an interest in English writing toward European movements, in particular surrealism and expressionism. *The Very Fragrant Death of Paul Gauguin* consists largely of experiments in these modes: "Floating headless foetal teddybears ejaculate blackberries." Though still informed by a strong sense of the parallels between poetry and painting, too many of the poems in this book are pretentious, linguistically unsubtle, and lacking in authentic feeling: "I the progenitive of the biggest bang / celebrate my entropic relativistic existence."

Graham's poetry succeeds when he gives play to his sense of the power of juxtaposed images mysteriously to conjure emotion, in which the tiny formalized marks that are the artist's and the writer's stock-in-trade can gesture toward the greatest meanings:

> The sun a crescent moon
> a brown line; the cosmos. The tiny
> square and circle, peace.

—R.J.C. Watt

GRAHAM, Jorie

Nationality: American. **Born:** New York City, 9 May 1951. **Education:** Sorbonne, Paris; New York University, B.A. 1973; University of Iowa, Iowa City, M.F.A. 1978. **Family:** Married James Galvin in 1983; one daughter. **Career:** Assistant professor of English, Murray State University, Kentucky, 1978–79, and California State University, Humboldt, 1979–81; workshop instructor, Columbia University, New York, 1981–83. Since 1983 staff member, University of Iowa. Poetry editor, *Crazy Horse,* 1978–81; Bayelston chair, Harvard University, 1998–99. **Awards:** Academy of American Poets prize, 1977; Ingram Merrill Foundation grant, 1981; Bunting fellowship, 1982; Guggenheim fellowship, 1983; National Endowment for the Arts grant, 1985; Whiting award, 1985; John D. and Catherine T. MacArthur Foundation fellowship, 1990; Lavan award, Academy of American Poets, 1991; Martin Zabel award, Academy and Institute of Arts and Letters, 1992; Pulitzer prize for poetry, 1995, for *The Dream of the Unified Field: Poems, 1974–1994.* **Address:** University of Iowa, 102 Dey House, 507 North Clinton Street, Iowa City, Iowa 52245, U.S.A.

PUBLICATIONS

Poetry

Hybrids of Plants and Ghosts. Princeton, New Jersey, Princeton University Press, 1980.
Erosion. Princeton, New Jersey, Princeton University Press, 1983.

The End of Beauty. New York, Ecco Press, 1987.
Region of Unlikeness. Hopewell, New Jersey, Ecco Press, 1991.
Materialism: Poems. Hopewell, New Jersey, Ecco Press, 1993.
The Dream of the Unified Field: Poems, 1974–1994. Hopewell, New Jersey, Ecco Press, 1995; Manchester, Carcanet, 1996.
The Errancy: Poems. Manchester, Carcanet, and Hopewell, New Jersey, Ecco Press, 1997.
Swarm. New York, Ecco Press, 2000.

Recordings: *The Hiding Place,* Archive of Recorded Poetry and Literature, Library of Congress, 1995; *Lunch Poems, Jorie Graham, 9/11/97,* University of California, Berkeley.

Other

Editor, with David Lehman, *The Best American Poetry 1990.* New York, Scribners, 1991.
Editor, *Earth Took of Earth: A Golden Ecco Anthology.* Hopewell, New Jersey, Ecco Press, 1996.

*

Critical Studies: By Peter Stitt, in *Georgia Review* (Athens), spring 1984; ''Accurate Failures: The Work of Jorie Graham'' by Thomas Gardner, in *Hollins Critic* (Hollins College, Virginia), 24(4), October 1987; ''Air and Earth: Recent Books by Jorie Graham and Ellen Bryant Voigt'' by James Ulmer, in *Black Warrior Review* (Tuscaloosa, Alabama), 15(2), spring 1989; ''Jorie Graham's Hybrids of Plants and of Ghosts: Nature as Matrix'' by Gerri Reaves, in *Carrell* (Coral Gables, Florida), 27, 1989; ''The Grammar of Glamour: The Poetry of Jorie Graham'' by Mark Jarman, in *New England Review* (Hanover, New Hampshire), 14(4), fall 1992; ''Jorie Graham: Art and Erosion'' by Bonnie Costello, in *Contemporary Literature* (Madison, Wisconsin), 33(2), summer 1992; ''Fin-de-Siecle Lyric: W.B. Yeats and Jorie Graham'' by Helen Vendler, in *Fins de Siecle: English Poetry in 1590, 1690, 1790, 1890, 1990,* edited by Elaine Scarry, Baltimore, Johns Hopkins University Press, 1994; ''Ad Interim: 2000—A Delayed Reading Lightly Attended'' by Lisa Issacson, in *Denver Quarterly* (Denver), 28(4), spring 1994; ''Iconoclasm in the Poetry of Jorie Graham'' by Anne Shifrer, in *Colby Quarterly* (Waterville, Maine), 31(2), June 1995; *The Breaking of Style: Hopkins, Heaney, Graham,* Cambridge, Massachusetts, Harvard University Press, 1995, and *The Given and the Made: Strategies of Poetic Definition,* Cambridge, Massachusetts, Harvard University Press, 1995, both by Helen Vendler; *Political Poetics: Revisionist Form in Adrienne Rich, John Ashbery, Charles Wright, and Jorie Graham* (dissertation) by Phyllis Jean Franzek, University of Southern California, 1995; '''The Honest Work of the Body': Jorie Graham's Erosion,'' in *Shenandoah* (Lexington, Virginia), 46(2), summer 1996, and *The Glass Anvil,* Ann Arbor, University of Michigan Press, 1997, both by Andrew Hudgins; ''Jorie Graham: Living in the World'' by Charles Molesworth, in *Salmagundi* (Saratoga Springs, New York), 120, fall 1998; ''Critical Mass: Jorie Graham and James Tate'' by Bin Ramke, in *Denver Quarterly* (Denver), 33(3), fall 1998.

*   *   *

American poet Jorie Graham's ''Flooding,'' from *Hybrids of Plants and Ghosts,* begins,

Just rain for days and everywhere it goes it fits,
like a desire become too accurate
to be of use, the water
a skirt the world
is lifting and
lifting

like a debt ceiling . . .

For Graham the world is like a vast text deserted by its author late in the process of composition. One can almost read it fully. ''The clues are everywhere,'' says one poem, and in another starlings make ''a regular syntax on wings.'' In yet another poem we read, ''Indeed the tulips / change tense / too quickly.'' She sees ''small building materials / awaiting an idea.'' Her characteristic *explication du monde* is evident in ''One in the Hand''—

A bird re-entering a bush,
like an idea regaining
its intention, seeks
the missed discoveries
before attempting
flight again.

—and in ''The Mind''—

The leaves,
pressed against the dark
window of November
soil, remain unwelcome
till transformed, parts
of a puzzle unsolvable
till the edges give a bit
and soften. See how
then the picture becomes clear,
the mind entering the ground
more easily in pieces,
and all the richer for it.

Graham's work is sustained by continuous associative activity. Her poems seem almost to be woven, and into her raw material go ideas, visual images, abstract and very concrete nouns, and, again and again, figures for language itself. The play of perception over the waters of the perceivable world make a kind of continual reference to Genesis and remind us what an important poet Wallace Stevens is for Graham. Occasionally, as in ''Flooding,'' her associative urgency causes a skein to ravel, but her intellectual abilities and ambitions give her work gravity and free her from anecdote and occasion.

For the volume *Erosion* Graham developed some new formal strategies. One is a short-line stanza, usually of six lines, with indentations, as in this one from ''Love'':

Here it's harvest. Dust
coarsens
the light. In the heat
in the distance
the men burn
their fields

to heal them . . .

The stanzas swirl down the page in long, complex sentences, resembling the other stanza form Graham uses frequently in *Erosion,* a long single-strophed poem with all of the lines, of carefully varied lengths, printed flush left. Thus, "Mother of Vinegar" begins like this:

> Because contained damage makes for beauty, it shines
>   like a brain at the bottom of each vat, the sand
> in the shell,
>   a simple animal.

Graham has spent a lot of time in Italy, much of it looking at paintings. Works by Piero della Francesca, Luca Signorelli, Masaccio, Goya, and Gustav Klimt are central to the poems in *Erosion.* One poem in the book is titled "Still Life with Window and Fish." By such means her poems refer not to a body of knowledge—art history—but to a live tradition, a palpable continuity in the present of the longer sense of history Italy gives in comparison to the American landscape. Graham's sense that culture is an organism rather than an artifact distinguishes her work and keeps it free from cultural tourism.

The closing lines of "San Sepolcro" suggest the reach and amplitude her best poems attain:

>   . . . It is this girl
>   by Piero
> della Francesca, unbuttoning
>   her blue dress,
> her mantle of weather,
>   to go into
>
> labor. Come, we can go in.
>   It is before
> the birth of god. No-one
>   has risen yet
> to the museums, to the assembly
>   line—bodies
>
> and wings—to the open air
>   market. This is
> what the living do: go in.
>   It's a long way.
> And the dress keeps opening
>   from eternity
> to privacy, quickening.
>   Inside, at the heart,
> is tragedy, the present moment
>   forever stillborn,
> but going in, each breath
>   is a button
> coming undone, something terribly
>   nimble-fingered
> finding all the stops.

If *Erosion* is, on a certain level, concerned with the role of human beings within the animal world, Graham's *The End of Beauty* examines our human relationships from a mythic origin. Many poems in the collection feel like replications of the braided process of thought, with long, unpunctuated lines that explore, as much of her work does, the process of intellectual and imaginative work. The stunning "What the End Is For" explores both the erosive quality of dusk into evening as well as that of an emotional and physical state:

> . . . The last time I saw you,
>   we stood facing each other as dusk came on.
> I leaned against the refrigerator, you leaned against
>   the door.
> The picture window behind you was slowly extinguished,
>   the tree went out, the two birdfeeders, the metal
>   braces on them.
> The light itself took a long time,
>   bits in puddles stuck like the useless splinters of memory,
>   the chips
> of history, hopes, laws handed down.
> . . . We stood there. Your face went out a long time
>   before the rest of it. Can't see you anymore I said. Nor I,
> you, whatever you still were replied.
> When I asked you to hold me you refused.
> When I asked you to cross the six feet of room to hold me
> you refused.

In the collection *Materialism* Graham turns to another kind of dramatic poetry, one that involves conversation and philosophy. Long passages selected from the works of thinkers such as Wittgenstein, Francis Bacon, Brecht, Plato, and Walter Benjamin implore the speaker to search for the bedrock of Western culture's philosophical assumptions, and they create an especially challenging terrain in the book. The abstract language of metaphysics feels like Graham's true obsession in this collection, but when she diverges, she finds the world in its integrally shaped wholeness, its directness, its simplicity. One closing passage includes an address to dust: "oh, but tell me, morning dust, dust of the green in things, on things, dust of water / whirling up off matter, mist, hoarfrost, dust over the / fiddlehead . . ."

Making sense and, by turn, unmaking sense are the constant processes of Graham's Pulitzer prizewinning *The Dream of the Unified Field.* In this collection she persists in a constant impulse to untangle the relationship between the physical world and the nature of metaphor. In "Chaos Eve" a charge of matter instigates transformation in a moral atmosphere:

> There's the god that locked herself in the tower,
> there's the
> one cast out into the hissing open,
> the white pushing out,
> the white flaring and pushing,
> until the whole thing steps out, opening and
> shuddering, thousands
> of wings,
> into the early morning, into the late twentieth
> century.

Somehow the synapses of the mind are charted in this poetry. Simultaneity, which we understand largely as an event or events of timing and externality, is something Graham manages to track and locate on the interior. In "Easter Morning Aubade," from her collection *The Errancy,* a woman tries to "clench the first dawnlight inside her skull," but the world will not be clenched. Within her view, past sleeping soldiers, there is a boy dropping a pebble in a river. The stone passes through the surface of the water just as the scene enters the mind of the woman:

> . . . as he stares I can see
> that the place of disappearance has

disappeared,
it cannot be recovered, his eyes darting
over the moving waters,
and how a life cannot be lived therefore,
as there is no place,
in which the possibility of shapeliness
begins to rave,
and the soldiers, awakening, of course, to
the blazing not-there,
and the 30,000 mph of the sun's going,
rubbing its disappearance now all over
this,
and the hand going back into the dirt at
one's feet, fingers feeling around
for another perfect stone, wanting to see
it once again, that opening.

For Graham the external world is critical to the imaginative vitality of the interior. She has a term, "intractable thereness," that alludes to the way we comprehend physical spaces and accuracies and yet continually yearn for a completion that eludes us. The poetry of this state is both lushly sensuous and persistently fleeting. "The Guardian Angel of Self-Knowledge" depicts an angel considering people on earth scraping off superficial characteristics in attempts to find their inner selves, their core truths. Self-revelation is transformed into self-extermination: "who will they be when they get to the bottom of It? . . . Who will they resemble when they're done with resemblance?"

Graham's collection *Swarm* is intended as a book-length sequence of poems. Several poems in the volume, titled "Underneath," address suppression and restraint—via text, violence, sex, and history—and assert that our inquiries and problems are the same ones our ancestors raised. Reformation is the sustaining hope, expressed in the metaphor of a swarm of bees gathering for migration to a new home. As invested in masks and personae as Graham has always been, she takes on Eurydice, Calypso, Daphne, and Eve as voices through which she questions the possibilities of morality: "To be told best not to touch. / To touch. / For the farewell of it. / And the further replication. / And the atom / saturated with situation."

—William Matthews and Martha Sutro

GRAHN, Judy

Nationality: American. **Born:** Judith Rae Grahn, Evergreen, Illinois, 28 July 1940. **Education:** New Mexico State University, Las Cruces, 1958–59; Raton Community College, New Mexico, 1959; Washington School of Medical Techniques, Washington, D.C., 1961; Montgomery Junior College, Takoma Park, Maryland, 1962–63; Howard University, Washington, D.C., 1963–65; San Francisco State University, B.A. in women's studies 1984; California Institute of Integral Studies, San Francisco, 1994–99, Ph.D. in integral studies 1999. **Family:** Has lived with Kristine Brandenburger since 1986. **Career:** Since 1985 instructor, and since 1998 co-director and professor, M.A. programs, New College of California, San Francisco. Taught at Stanford University, Stanford, California, spring 1986, and at California Institute of Integral Studies, San Francisco, 1995–96. Conducts writing and spirituality workshops. **Awards:** Poem of the Year award, *American Poetry Review,* 1979, for *A Woman Is Talking to Death;* National Endowment for the Arts grant, 1980; American Book award, Before Columbus Foundation, 1983, for *The Queen of Wands;* Gay Book of the Year award, American Library Association, 1985, for *Another Mother Tongue;* Women of Words award, Women's Foundation, San Francisco, 1985; Lambda Book award for nonfiction, 1988, for *Really Reading Gertrude Stein;* Pioneer Gay Writer award, Outlook Foundation, 1989; Lifetime Achievement in Lesbian Letters, Bill Whitehead award, *Publisher's Triangle,* 1995; Thanks Be to Grandmother Winifred Foundation grant, 1996. **Address:** c/o Beacon Press, 25 Beacon Street, Boston, Massachusetts, U.S.A.

PUBLICATIONS

Poetry

The Common Woman Poems. Privately printed, 1969.
Edward the Dyke: And Other Poems. Oakland, California, Women's Press Collective, 1971.
She Who. Oakland, California, Women's Press Collective, 1973.
A Woman Is Talking to Death. Oakland, California, Women's Press Collective, 1974.
The Work of a Common Woman. Oakland, California, Diana Press, 1978.
The Queen of Wands. Freedom, California, The Crossing Press, 1982.
Descent to the Roses of the Family. Iowa City, Iowa, Iowa City Women's Press, 1986.
The Queen of Swords. Boston, Beacon Press, 1987.

Recordings: *Where Would I Be without You, The Poetry of Pat Parker and Judy Grahn,* Olivia Records, 1975; *Lesbian Concentrate,* Olivia Records, 1978; *March to the Mother Sea: Healing Poems for Baby Girls Raped at Home,* LavenderRose Productions, 1990; *A Woman Is Talking to Death and Other Poems by Judy Grahn,* Watershed, 1991; *A Menarche Ritual, Kerala, South India,* Serpentina Productions, 1998; *Green Toads of the High Desert,* WIND, 1999.

Plays

The Cell (produced Antioch College, Ohio, 1968).
She Who (produced Los Angeles and San Francisco, 1974).
Queen of Wands (produced Ithaca, New York, 1985; London, 1986).
Queen of Swords (produced San Francisco, 1988).
March to the Mother Sea (produced Michigan Womyn's Music Festival, 1989).

Novel

Mundane's World. Freedom, California, The Crossing Press, 1989.

Other

Another Mother Tongue: Gay Words, Gay Worlds. Boston, Beacon Press, 1983; revised edition, 1990.
The Highest Apple: Sappho and the Lesbian Poetic Tradition. San Francisco, Spinster's Ink, 1985.

Really Reading Gertrude Stein. Freedom, California, The Crossing Press, 1989.
Blood, Bread, and Roses: How Menstruation Created the World. Boston, Beacon Press, 1993.

*

Critical Studies: "The Re-Vision of the Muse: Adrienne Rich, Audre Lorde, Judy Grahn, Olga Broumas" by Mary Carruthers, in *Hudson Review,* summer 1983; "Judy Grahn: Creating a Gay and Lesbian Mythology" by Steve Abbott, in *Advocate,* September 1984; *Stealing the Language: The Emergence of Women's Poetry in America* by Alice Suskin Ostriker, Boston, Beacon Press, 1986; "Judy Grahn's Gynopoetics: 'The Queen of Swords'" by Sue-Ellen Case, in *Studies in the Literary Imagination,* fall 1988; *The Safe Sea of Women* by Bonnie Zimmerman, Boston, Beacon Press, 1990; "Judy Grahn and the Lesbian Invocational Elegy: Testimonial and Prophetic Responses to Social Death in 'A Woman Is Talking to Death'" by Margot Gayle Backus, in *Signs,* summer 1993; in *Forms of Expansion: Recent Long Poems by Women* by Lynn Keller, Chicago, University of Chicago Press, 1997; *Lesbian Identity Poetics* by Linda Garber, New York, Columbia University Press, 2000.

*   *   *

When critic Margaret Cruikshank notes that Judy Grahn's poetic language has "a rhetorical drive [that] draws on oral traditions of poetry—biblical, Black, beat, and protesting . . . ," she implicitly connects Grahn with that long tradition of American poetry written by outsiders. In this case Grahn is a lesbian feminist outsider interested in writing about her own experiences in language direct, unabashed, and celebratory. By reworking familiar sexual categories and histories, by rewriting etymology and mythology, and by reclaiming women's experiences as a subject fit for poetry, Grahn ultimately succeeds in revising the American poetic tradition as a whole.

In Grahn's book *Edward the Dyke,* Edward enters a women's bathroom at a department store and shocks three housewives there who mistake her for a man. Laying the groundwork for Grahn's lifelong poetic project of familiarizing readers with outsiders like herself by reinventing the categories of sex, gender, sexual identity, and class so that they are more inclusive, *Edward the Dyke* introduces the central preoccupation of Grahn's subsequent poems—making visible the wide variety of lesbian experience. By talking about lesbian experience in a voice so accessible, candid, and matter of fact, Grahn widens the scope of American poetry to include the voices and experiences of working-class lesbians like herself.

In "Beauty, sleeping (who shall wake us)" Grahn writes of the importance of women writers claiming their own voices and topics:

Who shall wake us
if we don't ourselves
shake loose the sleep
of ages, animate the doll
at last and bid her
rise, and move and rule.

In her introductory remarks to *The Queen of Wands,* a book of poetry whose title derives from tarot cards and whose subject is Helen of Troy and other lost queens of history, Grahn explains that she was "just going somewhere with the idea of using lyric poetry to express

herstoric narration: women's stories." In *The Common Woman Poems, Edward the Dyke, She Who,* and *A Woman Is Talking to Death* Grahn imagines a woman's alternative poetic tradition.

All of Grahn's work—poetry, fiction, and nonfiction alike—articulates women's experiences (from menstruation to lesbian lovemaking) and explores traditional myths and tales so that they encompass contemporary experience. She is preoccupied with the metaphors of weaving, websters, spinsters, and spiders, and her poetic vocabulary and figurative language invite comparison with the best of those poets who write from outside the margins about unlikely survival. Grahn says, "For language is a form of weaving too, a clothing our ideas wear, a glowing flesh they are made of, a heart that beats in them."

As Grahn explains in her nonfiction prose work *Another Mother Tongue,* by familiarizing readers with words like "dyke" she "defuses the terror people have of the word." By rewriting literary traditions, contriving new etymologies, and inventing new terms, Grahn fosters a lesbian aesthetic also employed by other writers like Mary Daly, who likewise invents a diction that serves as an alternative to the traditional tongue of the father. Grahn writes in a language that is largely simple and plain and that in works like *The Common Woman Poems* celebrates the experiences of working-class women, including mothers, lesbians, prostitutes, and waitresses. When Grahn's work is read in the context of other lesbian writers of the 1970s, 1980s, and 1990s, we can see a shared project of excavation (as in Adrienne Rich's *Diving into the Wreck*), reinvention of language (Daly's *Gyn/Ecology*), and manifesto against silence (Marilyn Hacker's *Going Back to the River* and Audre Lourde's *Cancer Journal Poems*). Grahn writes in *The Queen of Wands,*

. . . Oh womb, cell Spinster,
as you know
the only real production is love.
I mean the ties between all unlike beings,
minute connections on
the message line, the one continuous knotty cord
(oh spider webster) wrapping us together.

—Sarah Sloane

GRAY, Robert

Nationality: Australian. **Born:** 23 February 1945. **Career:** Writer-in-residence, Tokyo, 1985. **Awards:** Literature Board of Australia Senior fellowships; Marten Bequest traveling scholarship, 1982; Adelaide Arts Festival National Poetry award, 1986; New South Wales Premier's award, 1986; Grace Leven prize, 1986. **Address:** c/o Angus and Robertson, P.O. Box 290, North Ryde, New South Wales 2113, Australia.

PUBLICATIONS

Poetry

Introspect, Retrospect. Normanhurst, New South Wales, Lyre-Bird Writers, 1970.
Creekwater Journal. Brisbane, University of Queensland Press 1974.

Grass Script. Sydney, Angus and Robertson, 1978.
The Skylight. Sydney, Angus and Robertson, 1983.
Selected Poems 1963–1983. Sydney, Angus and Robertson 1985; revised and enlarged edition, 1990.
Piano. Sydney, Angus and Robertson, 1988.
Selected Poems. North Ryde, New South Wales, Angus and Robertson, 1990.
Certain Things. Port Melbourne, Victoria, William Heinemann Australia, 1993.
New and Selected Poems. Port Melbourne, Victoria, William Heinemann Australia, 1995.
Lineations. Potts Point, New South Wales, Duffy and Snellgrove, 1996.
New Selected Poems. Sydney, Duffy and Snellgrove, 1998.

Recordings: *Some Poems of Robert Gray,* ABC, 1981.

Other

Alun Leach-Jones, with Graeme Sturgeon and Christopher Gentle. Roseville, New South Wales, Craftsman House. 1988.

Editor, with Geoffrey Lehmann, *The Younger Australian Poets.* Sydney, Hale and Iremonger, 1983.
Editor, with Geoffrey Lehmann, *Australian Poetry in the Twentieth Century.* Port Melbourne, Victoria, W. Heinemann Australia, 1991.
Editor, *Selected Poems,* by John Shaw Neilson. Pymble, New South Wales, Angus and Robertson, 1993.

*

Critical Studies: Interview in *Southerly* (Sydney), March 1990; "O Claritas" by Jamie Grant, in *Quadrant* (Sydney), July 1990; "The Tendency of Metaphor: Subject and Predicate in the Imagery of an Australian Poet" by R.J. Chadwick, in *Semiotica* (Hawthorne, New York), 109(3–4), 1996; "Robert Gray and the Vitalist Tradition" by John Hawke, in *Southerly* (Sydney), 55(4), summer 1995–96; "Robert Gray and Robert Adamson—A Dialectical Study of Late Australian Romanticism" by Angus Nicholls, in *Antipodes* (Austin, Texas), 11(2), December 1997; by Barbara Williams, in her *In Other Words: Interviews with Australian Poets,* Amsterdam, Netherlands, Rodopi, 1998.

*　　*　　*

Robert Gray is among the most influential and highly regarded contemporary Australian poets, and he serves as a model for a number of younger writers. His poetry is attractive and accessible to the common reader, but the beauty of his work is the result of internal, not external, imperatives. He is fairly indifferent about the publication of his writings—particularly in magazines—and prefers to withhold a poem, often for years, revising it before releasing it in book form.

The image is central to Gray's poetic method. Sometimes the image exists in itself, unassisted by metaphor or simile, as in this short poem: "The station master / looking across the wide, hot flats, / empties tea-leaves on the tracks." Frequently the use of simile or metaphor intensifies the image, as in this poem from the same series: "This torch beam / I feel with, through the pouring night, / is smoke."

Implicit correspondences among images and the accurate transfer of physical and visual sensations into words become ends in themselves in many poems. Sometimes this concern turns extreme and strains normal syntax and logic. The opening lines of "A Labourer" are an example:

He goes out early, before work, half asleep,
webs of frost on the grass; wading
paspalum to the wood-heap,
a bone-smooth axe handle pointing at him. It lifts the block
on a corner of beetled, black
earth. The logs are like rolled roasts,
they tear apart on red-fibred meat. The axe squeaks out.

The skepticism of Taoist and Buddhist philosophy—and also socialism—inform Gray's poetry. In his 1983 volume *The Skylight,* some of his arguably less successful poems are the political aphorisms. His political concerns express themselves more memorably when he writes about social underdogs.

Gray's interest in Eastern religions is embodied in poems written directly about historical figures, including "To the Master Dogen Zenji," which opens, "Dogen came in and sat on the wood platform, / all the people had gathered / like birds upon the lake." The simplicity of this opening recalls Arthur Waley's translations from the Chinese. Other poems infuse Buddhism and Taoism into the Australian landscape. An example is the long poem "Dharma Vehicle" from *Grass Script,* in which episodes of landscapes merge with quotations or incidents from the lives of sages. The statement that for the sage "there is nothing in the world that is greater / than the tip of a hair / that grows in spring" is also a manifesto of Gray's own poetic.

Gray's subject matter ranges from country landscape to cityscape. Poems about family and lovers are important but less frequent. Gray uses mainly free verse forms. Each of his books has marked an advance in technique, with the language becoming more complex and musical, the lines longer, the syntax more orchestral and less abrupt.

Gray uses humor, occasional informality, and deliberate awkwardness to ensure intimacy of tone. A humanity and relaxed warmth pervade his writings. Anecdote seems to have become important as imagery in some later poems, perhaps as a raison d'être to support structures longer and more sustained than the pointillistic insights for which Gray was previously known.

—Geoffrey Lehmann

GRAY, Stephen

Nationality: South African. **Born:** Cape Town, 30 November 1941. **Education:** Cambridge University, B.A. in English (honors) 1964, M.A. in English 1969; University of Iowa, M.F.A. in creative writing 1969; R.A.U., Johannesburg, D. Litt. et Phil. in English 1978. **Family:** Divorced. **Career:** Lecturer in English, Aix-Marseilles, France, 1965–66; graduate assistant, University of Iowa, 1966–68; junior lecturer, University of Cape Town, 1969; lecturer, 1970–74, senior lecturer, 1974–82, full professor, 1982–92, and head of department, 1982–84, 1988–89, 1991, Rand Afrikaans University, Johannesburg. Guest professor, University of Venice and of Trento, Italy, spring 1994. Councillor, National English Literary Museum,

Grahamstown, 1980–93; board member, Federated Union of Black Arts, Johannesburg, 1992–94. **Awards:** Gold medal of the English Academy of Southern Africa, 1993. Fellow, Hawthornden Castle International Retreat for Writers, Edinburgh, 1992; fellow, Rockefeller Foundation Bellagio Study and Conference Center, Italy, 1994. **Address:** P.O. Box 86, Crown Mines 2025, South Africa.

PUBLICATIONS

Poetry

It's About Time. Cape Town, David Philip, 1974.
Hottentot Venus. London, Rex Collings, and Cape Town, David Philip, 1979.
Love Poems, Hate Poems. London, Rex Collings, and Cape Town, David Philip, 1982.
Apollo Café. Cape Town, David Philip, 1990.
Season of Violence. Aarhus, Denmark, Dangaroo Press, 1992.
Selected Poems (1960–92). Cape Town, David Philip, 1994.
Gabriel's Exhibition. Cape Town, Mayibuye, 1998.

Plays

An Evening at the Vernes. Johannesburg, Ravan, 1977.
Herman Charles Bosman's 'Cold Stone Jug:' The Play. Cape Town, Human and Rousseau, 1982.
Schreiner: A One-Woman Play. Cape Town, Philip, 1983.
Accident of Birth. Johannesburg, Congress of South African Writers, 1993.

Novels

John Ross: The True Story. Johannesburg, Penguin, 1987.
Time of Our Darkness. London, Random-Century, 1988.
Born of Man. London, GMP, 1989.
War Child. Johannesburg, Justified, 1991; London, Serif, 1993.
Drakenstein. Johannesburg, Justified, 1994.

Short Stories

Human Interest. Johannesburg, Justified, 1993.

Other

Southern African Literature: An Introduction. Cape Town, David Philip, London, Collings, and New York, Barnes and Noble, 1979.
Douglas Blackburn. Boston, G.K. Hall, 1984.

Editor, *Mhudi* by Sol T. Plaatje. London, Heinemann African Writers Series, 1978.
Editor, *Theatre One: New South African Drama.* Johannesburg, Donker, 1979.
Editor, *Tsotsi* by Athol Fugard. New York, Random, 1980.
Editor *Theatre Two: New South African Drama.* Johannesburg, Donker, 1981.
Editor, *The Penguin Book of Southern African Stories.* London and New York, Penguin, 1985.

Editor, *Market Plays.* Johannesburg, Donker, 1986.
Editor, *Makapan's Caves and Other Stories* by Herman Charles. London, Penguin, 1987.
Editor, *The Penguin Book of Southern African Verse.* London, Penguin, 1989.
Editor, *File on Fugard.* London, Methuen, 1991.
Editor, *The Penguin Book of Contemporary South African Short Stories.* Johannesburg, Penguin, 1993.
Editor, *South Africa Plays.* London, Nick Hern, and Johannesburg, Heinemann, 1993.

*

Manuscript Collection: National English Library Museum, Grahamstown, South Africa.

Critical Studies: ''The National Neurosis: A Critical Study of Stephen Gray's Local Colour'' by Michael Rice, in *English in Africa* (Grahamstown, South Africa), 4(1), 1977; ''Reply to Stephen Gray'' by Lloyd Spencer, in *African Perspective* (Johannesburg), 9, 1978; ''The Theatre, the Artist and Soweto'' by Anne Fuchs, in *Commonwealth Essays and Studies* (Dijon, France), 7(2), spring 1985; ''Fictions of Anticipation: Perspectives on Some Recent South African Short Stories in English'' by Andres Water Oliphant, in *World Literature Today* (Norman, Oklahoma), 70(1), winter 1996; '''Under the Proteatree, at Daggaboersnek': Stephen Gray, Literary Historiography and the Limit Trope of the Local'' by Louise Shabat Bethlehem, in *English in Africa* (Grahamstown, South Africa), 24(2), November 1997.

*   *   *

Of all those active on the South African literary scene no one has done more to earn the title man of letters than has Stephen Gray. From a broad background in universities in South Africa, England, the United States, and France, he has directed his versatile talents and creative energies into every form of literary activity. A poet first and foremost but also a novelist, playwright, literary historian, newspaper critic, professor of English, and anthologist, his is an astonishing achievement. But to range as widely as this is to run risks, and what is significant in his work has to be searched for and identified in a wide field that is not always even in quality.

It is as a poet that Gray's voice is at its best, moving, as one critic has put it, over ''the variegated landscapes of the past and present.'' The contemporary scene, the passing parade, is acutely, almost journalistically observed. What he sees is seldom seen with approval and is often mockingly described; he uses his talent for humor to entertain, and he sometimes gives the impression that he is taking himself for a ride. ''Apollo Café,'' for example, a poem that gives its title to one of his collections of verse, strongly evokes urban South Africa, where the ubiquitous café has a place on every corner:

Its yellow framed door is always open
For pawpaws and lichees and watermelons
For catfood and iced suckers and Marmite
And drinking yoghurt and bubblegum and lard
And cheddar cheese and mousetraps and brooms
Tuna peas bacon butter carrots chops
Matches candles fittings jelly Doom

One suspects that the often tough, no-nonsense quality in the language Gray uses may hide the deeper, more personal feeling revealed by his love poems. No longer in love, he records poignantly how "my feelings damaged and scarred":

The wound now's a trench a gutter a wrinkle
Being out of love it has healed and grown over

Though Gray has produced stimulating and disturbing writing about the South African scene of the 1960s, 1970s, and 1980s, he also has written about the past. "Because I am not personally courageous," he claims, "I prefer to retreat into the past but then merely as a strategy to use as a predictive device." On the contrary, he has never given any evidence of not being courageous and has never hesitated to adopt unfashionable or unpopular attitudes, even if doing so has aroused hostility among his contemporaries. His collection *Season of Violence,* published after the emergence of the new South Africa, is a strong antidote to the euphoria that marked this development. There was, among other things, no end to violence, and one is struck by the stark realism of "Letter," for instance:

I go to make my complaint at Union Building
Get mugged on the lawn left for dead

Dead me do not speak so what can I say?
This letter will have to do:

I go out to post a letter get gunned down
Get gunned down.

We too are gunned down by the short, sharp staccato lines.

In 1992, at the age of fifty, Gray gave up his university professorship to devote himself entirely to writing.

—Roy Macnab

GREENE, Jonathan (Edward)

Nationality: American. **Born:** New York City, 19 April 1943. **Education:** Bard College, Annandale-on-Hudson, New York, B.A. 1965. **Family:** Married 1) Alice-Anne Kingston in 1963 (divorced 1968), two daughters (one deceased); 2) Dobree Adams in 1974, one step-daughter and one step-son. **Career:** Since 1965 founding editor, Gnomon Press, Lexington, later Frankfort, Kentucky. Apprentice printer, 1966, Printing Department, University of Kentucky, and assistant production manager, production manager, and designer, 1967–75, University of Kentucky Press, Lexington. **Awards:** National Endowment for the Arts grant, 1969, 1978. **Address:** P.O. Box 475, Frankfort, Kentucky 40602–0475, U.S.A.

PUBLICATIONS

Poetry

The Reckoning. Annandale-on-Hudson, New York, Matter, 1966.
Instance. Lexington, Kentucky, Buttonwood Press, 1968.
The Lapidary. Los Angeles, Black Sparrow Press, 1969.
A 17th Century Garner. Lexington, Kentucky, Buttonwood Press, 1969.
An Unspoken Complaint. Santa Barbara, California, Unicorn Press, 1970.
Scaling the Walls. Lexington, Kentucky, Gnomon Press, 1974.
Glossary of the Everyday. Toronto, Coach House Press, 1974.
Peripatetics. St. Paul, Minnesota, Truck Press, 1978.
Once a Kingdom Again. Berkeley, California, Sand Dollar, 1979.
Quiet Goods. Monterey, Kentucky, Larkspur Press, 1980.
Idylls. Emory, Virginia, Iron Mountain Press, 1983; revised and enlarged edition, Rocky Mount, North Carolina Wesleyan College Press, 1990.
Small Change for the Long Haul. Barrytown, New York, Station Hill Press, 1984.
Trickster Tales. St. Paul, Minnesota, Coffee House Press, 1985.
Les Chambres des Poètes. Asheville, North Carolina, French Road Press, 1990.
Inventions of Necessity: The Selected Poems of Jonathan Greene. Frankfort, Kentucky, Gnomon Press, 1998.
Of Moment. Frankfort, Kentucky, Gnomon Press, 1998.

Other

Editor, *Kentucky Renaissance: An Anthology of Contemporary Writings.* Frankfort, Kentucky, Gnomon Press, 1976.
Editor, *Fiftieth Birthday Celebration for Jonathan Williams.* Frankfort, Kentucky, Truck-Gnomon Press, 1979.

Translator, *The Poor in Church,* by Arthur Rimbaud. Lexington, Kentucky, Polyglot Press, 1973.

*

Bibliography: "Gnomon Press and Jonathan Greene: Two Bibliographies" by James D. Birchfield, in *The Kentucky Review,* XI(2), spring 1992.

Manuscript Collection: State University of New York, Buffalo.

Jonathan Greene comments:

(1970) Friendships early on with deep image poets important; close ties with Robert Kelly, Robert Duncan, and Robin Blaser.

No school, but a tradition involving individual poets felt strongly: Blake, Yeats, and more recent incarnations.

(1980) My recent work has delved into psychological/philosophical ruminations as well as being concerned with living in a rural setting.

*   *   *

Jonathan Greene may be placed among the group of writers affiliated (through shared concerns rather than influence) with Robert Kelly. (Others include Charles Stein and Harvey Bialy and the prose writer Richard Grossinger.) Kelly published and wrote the introduction for Greene's first book and was his teacher and friend at Bard College.

The hermetic tradition as mediated through such writers as Blake, H.D., and Robert Duncan is a major informing presence in

Greene's work. One consequence is a frequently baffling abstractness and allusiveness, but even in the most obscure poems there is evident a care for the weight and sound of each syllable. Greene speaks of "the work, / which is / love / persistent" and of how "the *care- / takers* / portion out / their harvests, / the bounty." The bounty for us, in the most successful poems, is a delicate but tough lyricism; see, for example, "The Definition" from *The Lapidary.* Much influenced by Jung, Greene writes out of a sense of poetry as "given" from a source "beyond" and thus inevitably dealing in archetypal material. "A Palimpsest" opens with

> The old story keeps writing itself.
> Dark woods & the turn of the road
> again. I do not write it. A *turn
> of the road,* writes itself. *A
> changed life,* interpolates from
> an unknown source. Underneath,
> the writing still goes on.
> The true writing.

A haikulike poem from *Instance* puts it more imagistically: "the old tales are told, /migratory birds / come home to / the heart."

Greene's later work shows a welcome inclusion of more directly personal subject matter. At the same time, however, it retains the qualities of ear and of access to depth evidenced in his earlier books.

—Seamus Cooney

GREENLAW, Lavinia (Elaine)

Nationality: British. **Born:** London, 30 July 1962. **Education:** Kingston Polytechnic, Surrey, 1980–83, B.A. in English (honors) 1983; London College of Printing, 1984–85, diploma in publishing/ production 1985. **Family:** One daughter. **Career:** Publications editor, Imperial College of Science and Technology, London, 1985–86; desk editor, Allison and Busby, London, 1986–87; managing editor, Earthscan, London, 1988–90; assistant literature officer, Southbank Centre, London, 1990–91; principal literature officer, London Arts Board, 1991–94. Since 1994 freelance writer and reviewer. Writer-in-residence, Science Museum in London, 1994–95; British Council Fellow in Writing, Amherst College, fall 1995; writer-in-residence, Mishcon de Reya (law firm), London, 1997–98; reader-in-residence, South Bank Centre, London, 2000. **Awards:** Eric Gregory award, 1990; Arts Council of England Writers' award, 1995; Wingate scholarship, 1996–98; Forward prize for best single poem, 1997. **Agent:** Derek Johns, A.P. Watt, 20 John Street, London WC1N 2DR, England. **Address:** c/o Faber and Faber, 3 Queen Square, London WC1N 3AU, England.

PUBLICATIONS

Poetry

The Cost of Getting Lost in Space. London, Turret Books, 1991.
Love from a Foreign City. London, Slowdancer Press, 1992.
Night Photograph. London, Faber, 1993.
A World Where News Travelled Slowly. London, Faber, 1997.

Novel

Mary George of Allnorthover. N.p., 2001.

*

Critical Studies: By Ian Gregson, in *Jacaranda Review* (Los Angeles), 1994; by Pat Barker, in *The New Republic* (New York), 29 April 1996.

*   *   *

The earlier poems of Lavinia Greenlaw tend to begin decisively: "With a head full of Swiss clockmakers / she took a job at a New York factory." These lines come from "The Innocence of Radium," which tells of a girl employed to inscribe figures on dials with paint that proves to be radioactive. The product was invented by a chemist who is proud of his product, but it has deleterious effects on those who come into proximity with it:

> Over the years he watched her grow dull.
> The doctors gave up, removed half her jaw,
> and blamed syphilis when her thighbone snapped
> as she struggled up a flight of steps.
> Diagnosing infidelity, the chemist pronounced
> the innocence of radium, a kind of radiance
> that could not be held by the body of a woman,
> only caught between her teeth. He was proud
> of his paint and made public speeches
> on how it could be used by artists to convey
>
> the quality of moonlight . . .

Though much of the interest resides in the facts that Greenlaw retails, one should not underestimate her craftsmanship. She seeks, for example, to surmise the nature of the suspension bridge at Clifton: "I curl over the railings, unable to grasp / the push-and-pull dynamics of Brunel's success . . ." But a tithe of mental struggle gives her a clue, and her hint about the design is self-reflexive. It is, indeed, almost a description of her own poetic process: "then I start to accept Brunel's equation, / the simplicity holding it all in place . . . ." In this instance simplicity is the result of a linguistic and rhythmic control that is far from simple. The medium through which Greenlaw's meditations come to us is an elegantly inflected free verse, the real thing, not chopped-up prose or loosened pentameters. True free verse has a pattern that is quite scannable, with a line that thrusts, so to speak, and a line (or lines) accepting the thrust. Greenlaw thoroughly comprehends the pattern, as shown in these lines from "Suspension":

> Now it looks too easy, I can't go on,
> my sense of balance is suddenly lost
> along with my ignorance, the framework of
> the physics of what keeps us from falling.

The poem is not only about the physics of the suspension bridge but also about the art of writing verse. In effect, it reinterprets the dictum of Alexander Pope: "Those move easiest who have learned to dance."

The topics Greenlaw chooses for her poems are unusual. For example, in ''The Man Whose Smile Made Medical History'' the man in question was the subject of an experiment in the pioneer stages of plastic surgery who succumbed to viral pneumonia because of medical ignorance concerning antibiotics. Reviewers have commented on the scientific basis of Greenlaw's poetry, and indeed she was for a time the resident poet at the Science Museum in South Kensington. What she shows is that science is part of life, not some entity removed from it. Her poetry, so far from being cerebral, is touchingly human.

Greenlaw's *A World Where News Travelled Slowly* builds on the distinction of the earlier *Night Photograph*. The later collection is more colorful, more metaphorical, and more fanciful, with a greater extent of play upon words and perhaps a more self-conscious dedication to style. It includes a poem called ''Reading Akhmatova in Midwinter'' that re-creates encountering the work of the legendary Soviet poet by the Delaware River, a setting thousands of miles away from her habitat. The verse displays a kind of metaphysical yoking together of heterogeneous images:

> The revelations of ice, exactly:
> each leaf carries itself in glass,
> each stem is a fuse in a transparent flex,
>
> each blade, for once, truly metallic.
> Trees on the hill explode like fireworks
> for the minute the sun hits.

There is not only linguistic invention here but also originality of vision. An astonishing sense of identity links the tragic Russian poet, waiting in the Leningrad winter of 1935 outside the prison where her son was being held, and the young Englishwoman musing some sixty years later in a landscape equally alien. It is, in effect, a dramatic monologue and one of singular skill and scope.

Not every piece in *A World Where News Travelled Slowly* is so directly narrated. Some of the writing, especially when it approaches what would normally be thought of as human emotion, can be tantalizingly elliptical. Elizabeth Lowry, Greenlaw's best reviewer, wrote in the *Times Literary Supplement* that there is ''a heightened sense of perception restrained by a pared syntax, the suggestion of powerful forces at play.'' The suggestion can be found in a sequence of what are almost love poems, from ''Landscape'' to ''The Shape of Things'': ''Somebody has left a shadow on the carpet / as if, blinded by champagne and erotic waltzes, / they had made a grand unsteady staircase exit . . .''

—Philip Hobsbaum

GREGG, Linda (Alouise)

Nationality: American. **Born:** Suffern, New York, 9 September 1942. **Education:** San Francisco State College (now University), B.A. 1967, M.A. 1972. **Career:** Faculty member, Pippa Passes College and Humboldt State College (now University), 1967, Indian Valley College, 1975–76, University of Tucson and Louisiana State University, 1981, College of Marin, Napa State College, and Lafayette College, 1982; instructor, Iowa writing program, 1984. Since 1975 writer. **Awards:** First prize for best poems, Poetry Society of America, 1966, 1967, Frank Stanford memorial prize, *Ironwood* magazine, 1978; Guggenheim fellowship, 1983. **Address:** 165 Tamal Road, Forest Knolls, California 94933, U.S.A.

PUBLICATIONS

Poetry

Too Bright to See. Saint Paul, Minnesota, Graywolf Press, 1981.
Eight Poems. Saint Paul, Minnesota, Graywolf Press, 1983.
Alma. New York, Random House, 1985.
The Sacraments of Desire. Saint Paul, Minnesota, Graywolf Press, 1991.
Chosen by the Lion: Poems. Saint Paul, Minnesota, Graywolf Press, 1994.
Things and Flesh: Poems. Saint Paul, Minnesota, Graywolf Press, 1999.

*

Critical Studies: ''Does Poetas de U.S.A.: Linda Gregg, Noel M. Valis'' by Noel M. Valis, in *Pena Libra* (Santander, Spain), 61, spring 1987; by Richard Tillinghast, in *Partisan Review* (New York), LXI(4), fall 1994.

* * *

Linda Gregg writes a terse, lean poetry devoted to essences. Her typical sentences are short, usually declarative, and most often isolated, without transitional markers; their music consists of individual sounds, sometimes repeated, rather than continuous rhythms. Nouns predominate over verbs, and they name things by category rather than by particular quality. Mountain, tree, sky compose an emblematic landscape, idealizing ''the flatness where things are broken down / to the clearest form.'' What animates this poetry, instills it with drama, is the pain involved in the process of breaking down. Although Gregg confesses that ''it is the rising I love, from no matter what element / to the one above,'' she acknowledges, ''I must live in the suffering and desire of what / rises and falls.'' The ''reason for this poetry'' resides in the double motion, in the failure as well as the act of idealization.

Beginning with Gregg's first collection, *Too Bright to See,* an implied narrative framework endows the themes of love and desire with some degree of particularity. The second part of *Too Bright to See* is entitled ''The Marriage and After.'' Gregg's failed marriage to ''Jack'' (the poet Jack Gilbert) is the story underlying this and the subsequent volume *Alma,* and the landscape of ''clearest form'' is localized through references to the Aegean islands, where Gregg and Gilbert lived for a time. *The Sacraments of Desire* momentarily posits an autonomous, nonrelational mode of being, in which ''there is no one to see me glistening.'' A corresponding revision of landscape (''Greece When Nobody's Looking'') points toward the possibility of ''a poetry / of stars and stone and the ordinary,'' but the extraordinary power of desire ultimately reasserts itself in the act of looking: ''I look at you with eyes of a lion.'' *Chosen by the Lion,* Gregg's next collection, returns the speaker to her former position as an object of desire. Here and in *Things and Flesh* repeated references to a second love affair stand in ironic contrast to the narrative based on Gregg's marriage to Gilbert. Rather than clear Grecian melodies, the discords of American cities, particularly Chicago, now set the tone, and Gregg herself plays the role of the other woman who tempts a husband to infidelity, as Gregg had earlier suffered her own husband's infidelity. Yet in "I Thought on His Desire for Three Days" she claims no regret:

> I was strong. I knew where
> I was. I knew what I had achieved. When the wife
> called and said I was a whore, I was quiet,
> but inside I said "perhaps." It has been raining
> all night. Summer rain. The liveliness of it keeps
> me awake. I am so happy to have lived.

The perfect infinitive, "to have lived," signals a distinctive subordination of the narrative element in Gregg's work to a more metaphysical or perhaps spiritual dimension. The lived experience is always distanced, either by time or point of view. Appropriately, *Too Bright to See* appeared a full decade after the breakup of the marriage it records. The title of *Alma* names a persona onto whom Gregg projects her experience so that she can stand at a distance, watching herself watching. (Compare "Alma Watching Her Husband" in *Too Bright to See* and "Marriage and Midsummer's Night" in *Alma.*) Separation thus has broader implications in Gregg's work than the specific separation between man and woman; in fact, the plot of romantic separation is a means of evoking the ultimate separation between the visible and the invisible. "The resonance of romance brightens / the invisible so it can be seen," Gregg writes in *Alma*.

What Gregg means by "the invisible" is a question that resonates with many voices in the tradition of modern poetry, reduced to "making songs from the bones of belief," as Gregg puts it in "Alma in the Woods." She pays special homage to Blake's unrepentant joy in *Too Bright to See* and to "George Oppen's stubborn clarity" in *Things and Flesh*. In the tone she has maintained with remarkable consistency throughout her career, Gregg sides with Oppen. The meaning of her lines does not arise from the flow of imagination but rather from the fixity of consciousness. As Gregg implies in "The Heart Flowing Out," "consciousness" may be the most accurate term to represent her understanding of the invisible, the blank space of separation that confers on things their distinctness yet articulates them—in the literal sense of the term—as parts of a whole:

> Our hearts flow out through
> the consciousness, focused.
> The more it looks, the more it sees the hard
> thing shaking with its own energy
> in relation to the whole scene and its meaning.
> Making that meaning, whatever it means.

—Terence Diggory

GREGOR, Arthur

Nationality: American. **Born:** Vienna, Austria, 18 November 1923; immigrated to the United States in 1939, naturalized 1945. **Education:** Newark College of Engineering, New Jersey, B.S. in electrical engineering 1945. **Career:** Engineer, Electronic Transformer Corporation, New York, 1947–54; editor, Whitney Publications, New York, 1956–61; senior editor, Macmillan publishers, New York, 1962–70; visiting professor, California State University, Hayward, 1972–73. Professor and director of the Creative Writing Center, 1974–88, and since 1988 poet-in-residence, Hofstra University, Hempstead, New York. **Awards:** First Appearance prize (*Poetry,* Chicago), 1948; Palmer award, 1962. **Address:** Department of English, Hofstra University, Hempstead, New York 11550, U.S.A.

PUBLICATIONS

Poetry

Octavian Shooting Targets. New York, Dodd Mead, 1954.
Declensions of a Refrain. New York, Poetry London-New York Books, 1957.
Basic Movements. New York, Gyre Press, 1966.
Figure in the Door. New York, Doubleday, 1968.
A Bed by the Sea. New York, Doubleday, 1970.
Selected Poems. New York, Doubleday, 1971.
The Past Now: New Poems. New York, Doubleday, 1975.
Embodiment and Other Poems. New York, Sheep Meadow Press, 1982.
Secret Citizen. New York, Sheep Meadow Press, 1989.
The River Serpent and Other Poems. New York, Sheep Meadow Press, 1994.

Plays

Continued Departure (produced New York, 1968). Published in *Accent* (Urbana, Illinois), 1951.
Fire (produced Urbana, Illinois, 1952).
The Door Is Open (produced New York, 1970).

Other

A Longing in the Land: Memoir of a Quest. New York, Schocken. 1983.

Other (for children)

1 2 3 4 5. Philadelphia, Lippincott, 1956.
The Little Elephant. New York, Harper, 1956.
Animal Babies. New York, Harper, 1959.

*

Manuscript Collection: Mugar Memorial Library, Boston University.

Critical Studies: Reviews by Laurence Lieberman, in *Yale Review* (New Haven, Connecticut), spring 1968; by Hayden Carruth, in *Hudson Review* (New York), spring 1968; by Robert A. Carter, in Modern *Poetry Studies* (Buffalo, New York), autumn 1971; by Thomas Lask, in *New York Times,* 9 December 1971; by Christopher Collins, in *Nation* (New York), 15 February 1972; by F.D. Reeve, in *Poetry* (Chicago), January 1973; by Josephine Jacobsen, in *Nation* (New York), 9 October 1976; by Grace Schulman, in *Twentieth Century Literature* (Hempstead, New York), October 1977; by James Finn Cotter, in *Hudson Review* (New York), spring 1978.

Arthur Gregor comments:

I have tried to explore and to articulate what I consider the poetic reality in myself, a reality that lies in all. My influences have been art, nature, and those in whom throb powerfully the magic, the mystery of life.

* * *

During a time when the evolution of American poetry has been defined by large movements with clearly directed aims, Arthur Gregor has followed a decidedly independent, sometimes contrary course. In part it is a question of his European origin. He was born and raised in Vienna and has traveled extensively in the Old World, and his poetry relies upon images and allusions drawn from European history and culture. But the distinction is more basic than this. If we agree that the great movement of American poetry in the past three decades has been away from the symbolist tradition and the dominance of such poets as Eliot and Yeats and toward a poetry based not only on native themes and idioms but also on an objectivist view of reality (which does not preclude mythic values), then Gregor has clearly stood against the mainstream with his insistence upon the continuing human validity of symbolist modes of perception. It has not been an argued insistence. Though Gregor has been a journalist and editor, as well as an engineer, he has rarely resorted to theoretical statements about his own work. But in his poetry his philosophical affinities are clear. They are with the great symbolists of the European tradition and particularly with such poets of the richly colored central European imagination as Rilke and Hofmannsthal.

It is easy to overemphasize the programmatic importance of these distinctions, however, and Gregor fits comfortably enough in the American literary scene. In tone and verbal texture his verse resembles the contemporary free-form writing of most American poets. In fact, from his first poems in the 1940s Gregor used a freer, more flexible line than the formalist conventions of the period sanctioned. He could never have been classed with the academics. On the other hand, his early work showed an ornateness of diction and figure that seemed baroque at the time, as if this European poet had taken the manner of Wallace Stevens and converted it to foreign ends, though the actual influence of Stevens, if it existed at all, was superficial. From these beginnings Gregor moved toward quieter, gentler poems that reached ever further into his mystical view of experience. An evocation of unseen presences, a realization of history or of the minds of ancestors, a glimpse of the ''elsewhere'' that lies somehow within the defined particulars of each new place—these and similar themes occupied him more and more. It is difficult to say precisely what his religious orientation may be, for his poems are always written obliquely, as if alongside the standard forms of spiritual evolution, not within them. Allusions can be detected to Hebrew, Christian, Gnostic, and Vedantic motifs, but they are allusions of feeling, not form, of spirit, not substance. His vision is clearly his own. In his poems about people, though they are often richly erotic, it is the essential mystery of the person toward which the vision aspires.

The danger of Gregor's vision is that words will fail its mysteriousness and turn into mere talk, talking about what cannot be sufficiently embodied, the failure of symbolism. It is a danger that Gregor has not always surmounted, but in his best poems—some of those about his parents and his travels—his vision is conveyed intact. It is a private vision, hence in some sense exclusive or even elitist, at odds with the prevailing temper of the age. Yet Gregor's work has a

gentleness and seriousness that have won it considerable popularity, especially among young people, and his somewhat alien voice has become a distinct and useful element in the American literary sensibility of the time.

—Hayden Carruth

GROSS, Philip (John)

Nationality: British. **Born:** Delabole, Cornwall, 27 February 1952. **Education:** University of Sussex, 1970–73 B.A. (honors) 1973; Polytechnic of North London, diploma in librarianship 1977. **Family:** Married Helen Gamsa in 1976; one daughter and one son. **Career:** Editorial assistant, Collier Macmillan, London, 1973–76; librarian, Croydon Public Libraries, 1977–84. Since 1984 freelance writer and writing tutor. Since 1989 lecturer, Bath College of Higher Education. **Awards:** Eric Gregory award, Society of Authors, 1981; National Poetry Competition first prize, 1982, for *The Ice Factory;* British Broadcasting Corporation's West of England Playwriting Competition, 1986, for radio play *Internal Affairs;* Arts Council bursary, 1990, for writing for young people; Signal award for poetry, 1994; first prize, Peterloo Open Poetry Competition, 1998. **Address:** 40 York Road, Montepelier, Bristol BS6 4QF, England.

PUBLICATIONS

Poetry

Familiars. Upton Cross, Peterloo, 1983.
The Ice Factory. London and Boston, Faber, 1984.
Cat's Whisker. London and Boston, Faber, 1987.
The Air Mines of Mistila (for children). Newcastle upon Tyne, Bloodaxe, 1988.
Manifold Manor (for children). London, Faber, 1989.
The Son of the Duke of Nowhere. London and Boston, Faber, 1991.
The All-Nite Café (for children). London and Boston, Faber, 1993.
I.D. London and Boston, Faber, 1994.
Scratch City (for children). London, Faber, 1995.
A Cast of Stones. Marlborough, Digging Deeper, 1996.
The Wasting Game. Newcastle upon Tyne, Bloodaxe, 1998.
Facetaker (for children). London, Scholastic, 1999.

Novels

The Song of Gail and Fludd (for children). London, Faber, 1991.
Plex (for children). London, Scholastic, 1994.
The Wind Gate (for children). London, Scholastic, 1995.
Transformer (for children). London, Scholastic, 1996.
Psylicon Beach (for children). London, Scholastic, 1998.

*

Critical Study: By Ian McMilan, in *Poetry Review,* 85(2), summer 1995.

* * *

A reviewer in the *Times Literary Supplement* once took Philip Gross to task for writing different kinds of poetry. This, it was suggested, indicated a lack of poetic unity, as if concern for the human condition—for love, sorrow, despair, loneliness, or joy—was somehow not relevant. Perhaps the complaint was that Gross's poetry lacks a stylistic unity from the standpoint too prevalent today, that style is more important than content, when, of course, they should be complementary. The fact is that the joy of Gross's poetry lies in its variety, that some poems are actually different from others, with variety being the source of the strength of his work.

With its pyrotechnic displays of simile and metaphor, Gross's poetry can be distinctly Martian, as in "A Guest of the Atlantic":

the surf was mixing concrete

But it is not the merely decorative Martianism favored by its progenitors. It is Martianism with depth, with purpose. Gross's poem "Flits" is a superb example of this. A poem about a taxi cab—

with its meter alive
like a sanctuary lamp:
red numbers twitch
in their sleep like dogs;
at after-midnight rates
they dream quick

—it moves on to embrace profoundly dark and deep implications:

          Black cab
are you waiting for me?

Elsewhere, however, Gross's poetry can be rhyming and traditional, as in "Him":

He's the great I AM.
He's a pushy little jerk.
He's a bloke who rolls his sleeves up
when he gets to work.

But the reader of his poems also encounters the most telling of visual imagery, the imagery of the poetic eye. Here are two examples, from "Out There" and from "This Train Does Not Stop Here":

     —A strand of smoke
spooled up like milk in water.

The faces reeling past
like a photo booth strip.

The poem can then explode in delicious humor, all the more so for being dead accurate. This happens, for example, in "Walkman" in a description of two lovers in a room upstairs:

it's like a woodwork-
for-beginners class

knocking up a pig pen
with a pig already in it.

It is in Gross's first collection for young people, *Manifold Manor,* that his variety of styles and techniques comes into its own. The work is a tour de force, an amalgam of styles and modes. There are Old English poetry, riddles, hints of Ted Hughes's "Crow," Walter de la Mare's mystery, and traditional verses of all sorts. The second of Gross's collections for young people, *The All-Nite Café,* is another explosion of versatility, with wordplay ("A Bad Case of Fish"), fantasy ("The Iron Sweep"), and sentiment ("Growler"). His poetry for children is written by a poet and not by a so-called children's writer.

Gross's collection *The Wasting Game,* published in 1998, begins with a sequence of poems about his daughter's struggle with near fatal anorexia. Some of the poems are harrowing, and one can only empathize with his feelings:

I could hate
those frail maids fading beautifully
in books—

But Gross's triumph is to make poetry out of the situation. To be able to transmute his anxieties, heartrending pain, and deep concern into poetry, as he does, shows great skill. It is, I suspect, the result of the use of a disciplined and moderated language under which the reader is conscious of the smouldering heat of a passionate and emotional engagement.

Gross is a modest possessor of a remarkable and complex poetic talent.

—John Cotton

GUEST, Barbara

Nationality: American. **Born:** Wilmington, North Carolina, 6 September 1920. **Education:** University of California, Berkeley, A.B. 1943. **Family:** Married 1) Lord Stephen Haden-Guest in 1948 (divorced 1954), one daughter; 2) Trumbull Higgins in 1954, one son. **Career:** Editorial associate, *Art News,* New York, 1951–54. **Awards:** Yaddo fellowship, 1958; Longview Foundation award, 1960; Fund for Poetry prize, 1978, 1994, 1996; National Endowment for the Arts grant, 1980; Laurence Lipton award for literature, 1989; San Francisco State award for poetry, 1994; America award for literature, Contemporary Arts Council, 1995, and Josephine Miles award for poetry, P.E.N., 1996, both for *Selected Poems;* America award for literature, Contemporary Arts Council, 1996, for *Quill, Solitary, Apparition;* Foundation for Poetry award, 1998; Robert Frost medal, Poetry Society of America, 1998; Robert Frost Medal for Distinguished Lifetime Work, Poetry Society of America, 1999. **Address:** 1301 Milvia Street, Berkeley, California 94709, U.S.A.

PUBLICATIONS

Poetry

The Location of Things. New York, Tibor de Nagy, 1960.
Poems: The Location of Things, Archaics, The Open Skies. New York, Doubleday, 1962.
The Blue Stairs. New York, Corinth, 1968.

I Ching: Poems and Lithographs, with Sheila Isham. Paris, Mourlot, 1969.
Moscow Mansions. New York, Viking Press, 1973.
The Countess from Minneapolis. Providence, Rhode Island, Burning Deck, 1976.
The Türler Losses. Montreal, Mansfield, 1979.
Biography. Providence, Rhode Island, Burning Deck, 1980.
Quilts. New York, Vehicle Press, 1980.
The Nude, lithographs by Warren Brandt. New York, Art Editions, 1986.
Musicality. Berkeley, California, Kelsey Street Press, 1988.
Fair Realism. Los Angeles, Sun and Moon Press, 1989.
Defensive Rapture. Los Angeles, Sun and Moon Press, 1994.
Stripped Tales, art by Ann Dunn. Berkeley, California, Kelsey St. Press, 1995.
Selected Poems. Los Angeles, Sun and Moon Press, 1995; Manchester, Carcanet.
Quill, Solitary, Apparition. Sausalito, California, Post-Apollo Press, 1996.
The Luminous, with Jane Moorman, Palo Alto, California, Handmade, 1999.
Strings, with Ann Slacik, St. Denis, France, Handmade, 1999.
Outside of This, That Is. Calais and Vermont, Z Press, Kenward Elmslie, 1999.
If So, Tell Me. London, Reality Street Editions, 1999.
The Confetti Trees. Los Angeles, Sun and Moon Press, 1999.

Recording: *The Location of Things,* Watershed, 1984.

Plays

The Ladies Choice (produced New York, 1953).
The Office (produced New York, 1963).
Port (produced New York, 1965).

Novel

Seeking Air. Santa Barbara, California, Black Sparrow Press, 1978

Other

Robert Goodnough, with B.H. Friedmann. Paris, G. Fall, 1962.
Herself Defined: The Poet H.D. and Her World. New York, Doubleday, 1984; London, Collins, 1985.
The Altos, with Richard Tuttle. San Francisco, Hawk Hine Editions, 1991.
Rocks on A Platter. Middletown, Connecticut, Wesleyan University Press, 1999.

*

Manuscript Collections: University of Kentucky, Lexington; Lockwood Memorial Library, State University of New York, Buffalo; New York University; Yale University Beinecke Library.

Critical Studies: ''One Hundred and Three Chapters of Little Times: Collapsed and Transfigured Moments in the Fiction of Barbara Guest'' by Kathleen Fraser, in *Breaking the Sequence: Women's Experimental Fiction,* edited by Ellen G. Friedman and Miriam Fuchs, Princeton, New Jersey, Princeton University Press, 1989;

''The Artful Dare: Barbara Guest's Selected Poems'' by Brenda Hillman, in *Talisman* (Jersey City, New Jersey), 16, fall 1996; ''The Surface As Object: Barbara Guest's Selected Poems'' by Barbara Einzig, in *American Poetry Review* (Philadelphia), 25(1), January-February 1996; ''Reverence and Resistance: Barbara Guest, Ekphrasis, and the Female Gaze'' by Sara Lundquist, in *Contemporary Literature* (Madison, Wisconsin), 38(2), summer 1997.

Barbara Guest comments:
The poem gathers itself (becomes embodied) the way a narrative diffuses and is sustained by movements, auditory and visual.

*   *   *

Barbara Guest was originally associated with the so-called New York school of poets, which included Frank O'Hara, John Ashbery, Kenneth Koch, and James Schuyler. Throughout her career her work has retained contact with the visual arts and music, the tendency toward ''painterly'' abstraction, and with the notable formal experimentation that characterized the writing of all of these poets. Guest's work, however, embodies a tension between two opposed impulses: a lyric, or purely musical, impulse; and a graphic impulse that emphasizes the materiality and arrangement of words in the poem. Both elements vie for dominance in her individual poems and determine their character.

A key aspect of Guest's work, in keeping with her interest in the arts in general, is its self-reflexiveness. She often considers the problem of artistic composition and consciousness itself, and it is within this context that the interartistic metaphor of poetry as painting or music functions in her work. In the poems ''Roses'' and ''The Poetess,'' from *Moscow Mansions,* or in ''Dora Maar'' and ''The Screen of Distance,'' from *Fair Realism,* for example, Guest explores the tension between the black-and-white, depthless sense of words and the dimensional, coloristic sensuality of painting. ''The Poetess'' (after Miró) employs a Gertrude Stein-like literary cubism to dramatize the difference and interaction between figure and discourse:

A dollop is dolloping
her a scoop is pursuing
flee vain ingots   Ho
coriander darks   thimble blues
red okays adorn her
buzz green circles in flight
or submergence?   Giddy
mishaps of blackness make
stinging clouds what!

Analogously, in ''Expectation'' (*Defensive Rapture*), which makes reference to Arnold Schoenberg's atonal composition *Erwartung,* Guest explores the sonorous qualities of poetic language and the expressive possibilities of form and variation:

masked throat—

gradual broken ascent
—means intensify

through an aperture—the tilt

grave—
ropings.

This dichotomy of coloristic effect and musicality is not considered only thematically, however; it is also formally enacted by the poems in Guest's handling of syntax and form. In its symbolistic luxuriance, her coloristic use of the line recalls the late work of Wallace Stevens. This can be seen, for example, in "The Rose Marble Table," from *Fair Realism:*

Sea whose translucence disturbs inferior atoms,
that passage from ice to shallow removes familiars
as glass changes to foam, the parallel lake diminished,
combs drop into fur.

But elsewhere Guest stresses the musical qualities of language, mobilizing its latent capacities for pulse, rhythm, volume, euphony, and notation. Here, as in "Musicality," from *Fair Realism,* her poetry takes on a performative quality:

Hanging apples half notes
in the rhythmic ceiling red flagged
rag clefs

notational margins

the unfinished

cloudburst

For the early Wittgenstein the syntax of propositions, the hierarchy of their relations, and their order of succession gave a "logical picture" of the world. In an analogous way Guest explores the world-picturing or world-making—she leaves the question open—properties of the language of poetry. In her exploration of "what is the case," she is deeply concerned with syntax and with other modes of connection between words, including spatial form, lineation, and typography. Two antipodal features of Guest's poetry follow from this concern. One is her use of parataxis and typographical fragmentation, illustrated by these lines from "Ilex" (*Fair Realism*):

we lost him. he disappeared.

rinds of gold stitched to his aura—
at the entrance armed with blocks—
the stylus blunt—
mood of helmeted star light

The second is her use of a self-consuming, self-enfolding syntax, as seen in "Prairie Houses" (*The Countess from Minneapolis*):

Unreasonable lenses refract the
sensitive rabbit holes, mole dwellings and snake
climes where twist burrow and sneeze
a native species

into houses

corresponding to hemispheric requests
of flatness

euphemistically, sentimentally
termed prairie.

Guest conceives of poetry as open-ended, contingent, and risky. Poetry is suspended in a space between the world of perception and the world of imagination. Again, this is a Stevens-like view of poetry that is illustrated by lines from "Heavy Violets" (*Fair Realism*):

The world makes this division
copied by words each with a leaf
attached to images it makes of this
half in air and half out
like haloes or wrists

But Stevens's supreme fiction of a world "revolving in crystal," the utopia of imagination, may unexpectedly shatter, again reopening the question of reality in the ambiguous movement of liberation and pain ("'Look now forwards and let the backwards be,'" from *Fair Realism*):

A wrist for every watch
releasing doves

In the blown haze
a search for crystal

Broken glass

—Tyrus Miller

GUEST, Harry

Nationality: British. **Born:** Henry Bayly Guest, Penarth, Glamorganshire, Wales, 6 October 1932. **Education:** Malvern College, Worcestershire, 1946–50; Trinity Hall, Cambridge, 1951–54, B.A. in modern languages 1954; Sorbonne, Paris, 1954–55, D.E.S. 1955 (thesis on Mallarmé). **Family:** Married Lynn Dunbar in 1963; one daughter and one son. **Career:** Assistant master, Felsted School, Essex, 1955–61; head of modern languages department, Lancing College, Sussex, 1961–66; assistant lecturer, Yokohama National University, Japan, 1966–72; head of modern languages department, Exeter School 1972–91; Japanese teacher, 1979–99, Exeter University. **Awards:** Hawthornden fellowship, 1993. D.Litt.: University of Plymouth, 1998. Honorary research fellow, Exeter University, 1994. **Address:** 1 Alexandra Terrace, Exeter, Devon EX4 6SY, England.

PUBLICATIONS

Poetry

Private View. London, Outposts, 1962.
A Different Darkness. London, Outposts, 1964.
Arrangements. London, Anvil Press Poetry, 1968.
The Cutting-Room. London, Anvil Press Poetry, 1970.
Penguin Modern Poets 16, with Jack Beeching and Matthew Mead. London, Penguin, 1970.
The Place. Rushden, Northamptonshire, Sceptre Press, 1971.

Text and Fragment, The Inheritance, Miniatures. Southampton, Hampshire, Earth Ship 13, 1972.

The Achievements of Memory. Rushden, Northamptonshire, Sceptre Press, 1974.

The Enchanted Acres. Knotting, Bedfordshire, Sceptre Press, 1975.

Mountain Journal. Sheffield, Rivelin Press, 1975.

A House against the Night. London, Anvil Press Poetry, 1976.

English Poems. London, Words Press, 1976.

Two Poems. Knotting, Bedfordshire, Sceptre Press, 1977.

The Hidden Change. Higham Ferrers, Northamptonshire, Grey-lag Press, 1978.

Zeami in Exile. Knotting, Bedfordshire, Sceptre Press, 1978.

Elegies. Durham, Pig Press, 1980.

Lost and Found: Poems 1975–1982. London, Anvil Press Poetry, 1983.

The Emperor of Outer Space. Durham, Pig Press, 1983.

Dealings with the Real World. Huddersfield, Yorkshire, Smith/Doorstep Press, 1987.

Coming to Terms. London, Anvil Press, 1994.

Visit to an Unknown Suburb. Dunfermline, Fife, Raunchland, 1996.

So Far. Exeter, Stride, 1998.

Plays

The Inheritance (broadcast, 1973). Included in *Text and Fragment, The Inheritance, Miniatures,* 1972.

Radio Plays: *Beware of Pity,* from a play by Stefan Zweig, 1961; *Trial of Strength,* from a play by G.A. Golfar, 1964; *The Emperor of Outer Space* (broadcast, 1976).

Novels

Days. London, Anvil Press Poetry, 1978.

Lost Pictures. Exeter, Albertine Press, 1991.

Other

Another Island Country (essays). Tokyo, Eikôsha, 1970.

Mastering Japanese. London, Macmillan, 1989; New York, Hippocrene, 1991.

Traveller's Literary Companion to Japan. Brighton, In Print, and Chicago, Passport, 1994.

Versions. Nether Stowey, Somerset, Odyssey, 1999.

Editor and Translator, with Lynn Guest and Kajima Shozo, *Post-War Japanese Poetry.* London, Penguin, 1972.

Editor, with others, *The Elek Book of Oriental Verse.* London, Elek, 1979.

Editor and Translator, *The Distance, The Shadows: Selected Poems,* by Victor Hugo. London, Anvil Press Poetry, 1981.

*

Harry Guest comments:

(1970) Lyrical analysis of personal relationships, bisexual love, landscapes, etc. Certain amount of intellectual demand; European rather than transatlantic; syllabics or stress-length lines; high premium on musicality.

I admire Klee, the early Godard, Debussy's piano music.

(1974) *Private View* is a poem in fourteen sections dealing with the relationships between art and reality, imagination and love. "Matsushima" (1967) examines the shadow line crossed when death is felt in the marrow as inevitable. "Metamorphoses" (1968) uses a highly condensed, elliptical language for its "Six Poems on Related Themes." *The Place* is fifteen connected meditations about a holiday on the west coast of Japan, and *Miniatures* is thirty-six brief poems recording a visit with the poet's daughter to a volcanic island.

The short poems in various structural forms are primarily lyrical or narrative—love poems like "The Summers of Nowhere" or "At Shoreham"; problems of perception like "Allegories," "Autumns," or "Nocturnes for the Dead of Winter"; or of art—"The Painter . . . ," "Cinema."

The kind of poetry that most appeals to me has music and density, appeals to the senses as much as to the mind and spirit.

(1985) The six *Elegies* come as near as anything I have yet written to a statement of poetic faith—the role of memory, the mysterious commands of religion, the problem of meaning in the heart of language, this last reinforced by my experience in translating a selection of Victor Hugo's work.

English Poems celebrates a return to familiarity after six bewildered and thrilling years in Japan. The tantalizing clues of prehistory inspired several poems about Avebury, sites in northern Arizona and Brittany.

The attempt is always to show the surprise latent in the everyday, as well as to display the relevance of the extraordinary.

(1994) *Coming To Terms* collects the poems written between 1983 and 1990; *Trans-Siberian* records a journey taken across Europe and Asia by train in order to attend a poetry conference in Japan. There are poems inspired by paintings by Poussin, Boecklin, William Dyce, Sickert, and Klee; poems celebrating marriage and parenthood; poems in strict form; landscapes; dramatic monologues; legends; problems; analyses of past loves.

Apologia pro Vita Sua is a wry definition of my aims—to avoid catchpenny themes, to ignore fashionable and temporary trends, to stick to originality, to write as a member of the late twentieth century yet remain aware of the poetic tradition in earlier cultures.

As poetry is a different language from prose, a successful poem should have an idiosyncratic shape, be more than a three-dimensional focus on experience, though never less than this, by using the sound and look of words so as to communicate to reader and listener the excitement or wonder or rage that went into the writing.

To concentrate only on performing a poem in public, as many now do, seems to me to be dealing with merely one-half of the poetic potential, as a poem which only makes its impact aurally and for the moment is perilously close to journalism. Craftsmanship—professional technique—although present in the service of meaning, ought never to be discounted. The poems by others I most value are those I reread.

*   *   *

Harry Guest was first introduced to the reading public with two booklet collections in the Outposts Modern Poets Series—*Private View* and *A Different Darkness. Private View* is a series of reflective poems arising out of a visit to an art exhibition; it is largely concerned with the relationship between the artist and his subject, as well as the part played by the artist himself:

If I could catch his eye, we'd bolt for the pub
And over Guinness alternate the old crude gags
With laments for oh the brevity of beauty,
The change within a year of the expression on flesh,
The slender moving to the coarse,
Metamorphoses of the delicate.

Although he treats his theme with respect, Guest's sense of humor does not allow him to become unduly earnest.

Like much of Guest's poetry, *Private View* makes its impact by means of skillfully manipulated images and association of ideas. In *Arrangements* the poems are grouped under such headings as "Problems," "Relationships," "Criticisms," "Narratives," and "Techniques," but this classification tends to obscure Guest's real strengths and virtues as a poet. One might remark upon his skill and note the interest he displays in the techniques of other writers, reflected in such poems as "Statement," "About Baudelaire," and "Elegy for Jean Cocteau." "Sterility and regret are the only muse," he says in one of the poems, which would seem to be true for Guest, for he writes most effectively about his regrets over lost opportunities, situations not grasped, failures of communication and response. Some critics have praised his "travel" poems, but he has a style all his own and rarely writes a simple descriptive piece. "Matsushima" and "A Bar in Lerici" demonstrate his use of the environment to effect new insights into the human situation:

We talk of love,
Balanced as always between the recollection—
The afternoon spent across the bay in sunlight—
And anticipation of the stars
Tending to disappoint.
Darkness
After being born should be familiar
And natural as the scenery of the Milky Way.

Perhaps best of all are his poems celebrating the relationship between men and women, the marital relationship in particular, on which he can be lyrical and tender without losing control over his material.

In *The Cutting-Room,* written in Japan, Guest extended his range of subjects and treatment and produced the "Metamorphoses" sequence of six poems, his most ambitious work to that time, but again the more personal references to lover, wife, and daughter show his capacity for dealing with intimate relationships. In continuing his experiments with form and diction, however, Guest in later work adopts a much shorter line and exercises far tighter control of both diction and imagery, and, except for "Anniversary," he seems deliberately to avoid the warmer aspects of human relationships. "I am a man for whom the external world exists," he says in an earlier poem, and he would appear to be exploring the external world at much greater depth than before in order to find himself and to define his own psychological limits, as in "Lacunae":

These distant images bring pain.
The tors stood out,
first greyness on the silence.
If there was laughter
the echoes carried isolation,
companionship
struck stone.

All this adds up to an unusual austerity reflected to a lesser extent in the later pamphlets.

—Howard Sergeant

GUNN, Thom(son William)

Nationality: British. **Born:** Gravesend, Kent, 29 August 1929. **Education:** University College School, London; Trinity College, Cambridge, B.A. 1953, M.A. 1958; Stanford University, California, 1954–55, 1956–58. **Military Service:** British Army, 1948–50. **Career:** Member of the English department, 1958–66, visiting/senior lecturer, University of California, Berkeley, 1975–99. Poetry reviewer, *Yale Review,* New Haven, Connecticut, 1958–64. **Awards:** Levinson Prize (*Poetry,* Chicago), 1955; Maugham Award, 1959; Arts Council of Great Britain award, 1959; American Academy grant, 1964; Rockefeller award, 1966; Guggenheim Fellowship, 1971; W.H. Smith Award, 1980; Sara Teasdale prize, 1988; *Los Angeles Times* Kirsch award, 1988; Lila Wallace/Reader's Digest Writer's award, 1990; Forward Prize, 1992; MacArthur fellowship, 1993; Lenore Marshall prize, 1993. **Address:** 1216 Cole Street, San Francisco, California 94117, U.S.A.

PUBLICATIONS

Poetry

(Poems). Oxford, Fantasy Press, 1953.
Fighting Terms. Oxford, Fantasy Press, 1954; revised edition, New York, Hawk's Well Press, 1958; London, Faber, 1962.
The Sense of Movement. London, Faber, 1957; Chicago, University of Chicago Press, 1959.
My Sad Captains and Other Poems. London, Faber, and Chicago, University of Chicago Press, 1961.
Selected Poems, with Ted Hughes. London, Faber, 1962.
A Geography. Iowa City, Stone Wall Press, 1966.
Positives, photographs by Ander Gunn. London, Faber, 1966; Chicago, University of Chicago Press, 1967.
Touch. London, Faber, 1967; Chicago, University of Chicago Press, 1968.
The Garden of the Gods. Cambridge, Massachusetts, Pym Randall Press, 1968.
The Explorers. Crediton, Devon, Gilbertson, 1969.
The Fair in the Woods. Oxford, Sycamore Press, 1969.
Poems 1950–1966: A Selection. London, Faber, 1969.
Sunlight. New York, Albondocani Press, 1969.
Last Days at Teddington. London, Poem-of-the-Month Club, 1971.
Moly. London, Faber, 1971.
Corgi Modern Poets in Focus 5, with others, edited by Dannie Abse. London, Corgi, 1971.
Poem after Chaucer. New York, Albondocani Press, 1971.
Moly, and My Sad Captains. New York, Farrar Straus, 1971.
Mandrakes. London, Rainbow Press, 1973.
Songbook. New York, Albondocani Press, 1973.
To the Air. Boston, Godine, 1974.
Jack Straw's Castle. New York, F. Hallman, 1975.
Jack Straw's Castle (collection). London, Faber, and New York, Farrar Straus, 1976.

The Missed Beat. Sidcot, Somerset, Gruffyground Press, and West Burke, Vermont, Janus Press, 1976.

Games of Chance. Omaha, Abattoir, 1979.

Selected Poems 1950–1975. London, Faber, and New York, Farrar Straus, 1979.

Bally Power Play. Toronto, Massey Press, 1979.

Talbot Road. New York, Helikon Press, 1981.

The Menace. San Francisco, ManRoot, 1982.

The Passages of Joy. London, Faber, 1982; New York, Farrar Straus, 1983.

Sidewalks. New York, Albondocani Press, 1985.

Lament. Champaign, Illinois, Doe Press, 1985.

The Hurtless Trees. Privately printed, 1986.

Night Sweats. Florence, Kentucky, R.L. Barth, 1987.

Undesirables. Durham, Pig Press, 1988.

At the Barriers. New York, NADJA, 1989.

Death's Door. N.p., Red Hydra, 1989.

The Man with Night Sweats. London, Faber, and New York, Farrar Straus, 1992.

Collected Poems. London, Faber, 1993; New York, Farrar Straus, 1994.

Boss Cupid. London, Faber, and New York, Farrar Straus, 2000.

Other

The Occasions of Poetry: Essays in Criticism and Autobiography, edited by Clive Wilmer. London, Faber, and New York, Farrar Straus, 1982; revised edition, Berkeley, California, North Point Press, 1985.

Shelf Life, Essays, Memoirs, and an Interview. Ann Arbor, University of Michigan Press, and London, Faber, 1993.

Thom Gunn in Conversation with James Campbell. London, Between the Lines, 2000.

Editor, *Poetry from Cambridge 1951–52: A Selection of Verse by Members of the University.* London, Fortune Press, 1952.

Editor, with Ted Hughes, *Five American Poets.* London, Faber, 1963.

Editor, *Selected Poems of Fulke Greville.* London, Faber, and Chicago, University of Chicago Press, 1968.

Editor, *Ben Jonson.* London, Penguin, 1974.

Editor, *Erza Pound.* London, Faber, 2000.

*

Bibliography: *Thom Gunn: A Bibliography 1940–1978* by Jack W.C. Hagstrom and George Bixby, London, Rota, 1979.

Manuscript Collections: University of Maryland, College Park; Amherst College, Massachusetts; University of California, Berkeley.

Critical Studies: By the author, in *Occasions of Poetry,* 1982; "Landscapes of Repetition" by Paul Giles, in *Critical Quarterly* (Manchester), 29(2), summer 1987; in *Articulate Flesh: Male Homo-Eroticism Modern Poetry* by Gregory Woods, New Haven, Connecticut, Yale University Press, 1987; in "Thom Gunn at Sixty," supplement edited by Clive Wilmer, in *PN Review* (Manchester), 16(2), 1989; in *Three Contemporary Poets: Thom Gunn, Ted Hughes, and R.S. Thomas* edited by A.E. Dyson, London, Macmillan, 1990;

"Sense of Movement" by Wendy Lesser in *Los Angeles Times Magazine,* 14 August 1994; in *Contemporary British Poetry: Essays in Theory and Criticism* edited by James Acheson and Romana Huk, State University of New York Press, 1996; "How to Live,What to Do," by Deborah Landau in *American Literature: A Journal of Literary History* (Durham, North Carolina), March 1996; in *The Mortal Limits of Poetry and Criticism* edited by Robyn Wiegman, Durham, North Carolina, Duke University Press, 1997; in *Reclaiming the Sacred: The Bible in Gay and Lesbian Culture* edited by Raymond-Jean Frontain, New York, Haworth, 1997; "Thom Gunn at Seventy," in *Agenda,* 37(2–3), autumn/winter 1999.

*   *   *

In one of his early poems Thom Gunn observes, famously, that Elvis Presley "turns revolt into a style." Elaborating this in the poem's final stanza, Gunn provides a peg on which we can, if we like, hang the immense variety of his own work:

> Whether he poses or is real, no cat
> Bothers to say: the pose held is a stance,
> Which, generation of the very chance
> It wars on, may be posture for combat.

A "pose"—apparently superficial, possibly a matter of advertising, of presenting the self for sale—solidifies into a "stance," a relation between the self and the world that has a more achieved and focused integrity. And this, as a "posture for combat," may embrace a political or philosophical relation.

The title of Gunn's collection *Moly* takes its name from the herb that Hermes offered Ulysses to keep him proof against transformation into one of Circe's pigs. And while Gunn has not, of course, transformed himself into a pig, he has certainly never protected himself against the processes of metamorphosis. Geographically, he has moved from England to America, more specifically from 1950s Cambridge to 1960s San Francisco; metrically, he has moved from highly disciplined traditional forms, through syllabics, to a very loose kind of free form; and thematically, he has made use of such widely varied influences as French existentialist thought and American lysergic acid. And even emotionally and sexually, Gunn has moved from poems overtly addressed to women to openly frank homosexual poems. He is, altogether, a poet difficult to get clear and difficult to get whole.

There is also the further difficulty that, if one appreciates the strenuous energy under control, the formal stanzaic grandeur of poems like "On the Move" or "In Santa Maria del Popolo," it is difficult not to feel that the later work is often sentimental or downright silly. (The latter criticism seems almost mild against the poem "Listening to Jefferson Airplane," which reads in its entirety, "The music comes and goes on the wind, / Comes and goes on the brain.") But one can be generous even about these poems perhaps, if one sees Gunn's whole enterprise as a series of poses creating a stance of combative self-definition in relation to society and to the world. The poems' posturing may then be seen as a kind of moral assertion. Gunn's ultimate "carnal knowledge," in the well-known poem of that title, is that "even in bed I pose." And knowledge of oneself, as well as of others, is an infinitely recessive series ("You know I know you know I know you know," contained only by its pentameter bounds) in which one is what one presents oneself as. Gunn's poems are, as he has himself described some of them, "a debate between the passion for definition and the passion for flow."

Some of Gunn's later poems are an explicit examination of these processes and passions. The sequence "The Geysers," for instance, situates Gunn in a state between sleep and waking, between water and air, in the bathhouse of the geysers in Sonoma County, California. The poem mimics the processes occurring on the frontiers of consciousness:

> I am part of all
>   hands take
> hands tear and twine
>
> I yielded
>   oh, the yield
>   what have I slept?
> my blood is yours the hands that take accept . . .
>
> torn from the self
>   in which I breathed and trod
> I am
>   I am raw meat
>
>   I am a god

Some of Gunn's best effects are achieved, as they are here, when language, still disciplined and restrained, spreads and spills to accommodate the phases of "definition" and "flow." In the act of love and in sleep these processes are at their most immediate, for one is both defined in one's own being and involved in the being of others. The act of love and the moment of sleep are returned to again and again in Gunn's work, and they come together at the conclusion of the marvelous poem "Touch":

> What is more, the place is
> not found but seeps
> from our touch in
> continuous creation, dark
> enclosing cocoon round
> ourselves alone, dark
> wide realm where we
> walk with everyone.

In *The Passages of Joy* the clearest new note is that of nostalgia, as the poet growing older in America remembers his past in England. The sequence "Talbot Road" is that and is also an elegy for his friend Tony White. It crosses the experiences of childhood with a maturing sexuality in a way that brings together again in Gunn's work the processes of definition and flow, of innocence and experience, as when, for instance, Hampstead Heath is viewed as both the theater of childhood games and of homosexual sex:

> In a Forest of Arden, in a summer night's dream
> I forgave everybody his teens.

—Neil Corcoran

GUNNARS, Kristjana

Nationality: Canadian. **Born:** Reykjavik, Iceland, 19 March 1948. **Education:** Oregon State University, B.A. 1973; University of Regina, Saskatchewan, M.A. 1978. **Family:** Married Charles Kang in 1967 (separated 1980); one son. **Career:** High school teacher, Althyduskolinn, Eidum, Iceland, 1974–75; instructor of twentieth-century literature, University of Regina, Saskatchewan, 1979; editorial assistant, *Iceland Review,* Reykjavik, 1980–81. Since 1981 freelance writer, editor, and translator. **Awards:** Ontario Arts Council awards, 1981, 1984; Manitoba Arts Council awards, 1983, 1985; Alberta Foundation for the Literary Arts award, 1986, 1987; McNally Robinson prize, 1989, and Manitoba Book of the Year, 1989, for *The Prowler.* **Address:** Turnstone Press, 607–100 Arthur Street, Winnipeg, Manitoba R3B 1H3, Canada.

PUBLICATIONS

Poetry

One-Eyed Moon Maps. Toronto, Press Porcepic, 1980.
Settlement Poems. Winnipeg, Turnstone Press, 1980.
Wake-Pick Poems. Toronto, Anansi, 1981.
The Night Workers of Ragnarok. Toronto, Press Porcepic, 1985.
Carnival of Longing. Winnipeg, Turnstone Press, 1989.
Exiles among You. Regina, Saskatchewan, Coteau Books, 1996.

Novels

The Prowler: A Novel. Red Deer, Alberta, Red Deer College, 1989.
The Substance of Forgetting. Red Deer, Alberta, Red Deer College Press, 1992.

Short Stories

The Axe's Edge. Toronto, Press Porcepic, 1983.
The Guest House, and Other Stories. Concord, Ontario, Anansi, 1992.

Other

Zero Hour. Red Deer, Alberta, Red Deer College Press, 1991.
The Rose Garden: Reading Marcel Proust. Red Deer, Alberta, Red Deer College Press, 1996.
Night Train to Nykøbing. Red Deer, Alberta, Red Deer College Press, 1998.

*

Critical Studies: "Icelandic Rhythms" by George Johnson, in *Canadian Literature* (Vancouver), 92, spring 1982; "Troll Turning: Poetic Voice in the Poetry of Kristjana Gunnars," in *Canadian Literature* (Vancouver), 105, summer 1985, and "Ground of Being," in *Canadian Literature* (Vancouver), 111, winter 1986, both by M. Travis Lane; "Arctic Miracles, Dethroned Fables" by Patricia Keeney Smith, in *The Canadian Forum,* LXVI(758), April 1986; "Transformation of the "I": Self and Community in the Poetry of Kristjana Gunnars" by Paul Hjartarson, in *Canada and the Nordic Countries,* edited by Jorn Carlsen and Bengt Streijffert, Lund, Lund University Press, 1988; "The White Inuit Speaks: Contamination As Literary

Strategy'' by Diana Brydon, in *Past the Last Post: Theorizing Post-Colonialism and Post-Modernism,* edited by Ian Adam and Helen Tiffin, Calgary, University of Calgary Press, 1990; ''Staring into Snow: Subjectivity and Design in Kirstjana Gunnars' the Prowler'' by John Lent, in *Recherches Anglaises et Nord-Americaines* (Strasbourg, France), 24, 1991; ''Intertextual Notes in a Metafictional Autobiography: The Prowler by Kristjana Gunnars'' by Cristina Gheorghe, in *Scandinavian-Canadian Studies* (North York, Ontario), 4, 1991; ''Gender, Narrative, and Desire in The Prowler'' by Daniel Coleman, in *Textual Studies in Canada,* 4, 1994; by Janice Kulyk Keefer, in *Brick,* 51, winter 1995; ''Kristjana Gunnars and the Book of Small'' by J.S. Porter, in *Antigonish Review,* 113, spring 1998; ''Icelandic-Canadian Literature and Anglophone Minority'' by Daisy Neijmann, in *World Literature Today* (Norman, Oklahoma), 73(2), spring 1999.

Kristjana Gunnars comments:

Since we are living in a world wherein change takes place faster than our ability to absorb it, the writer's task is more urgent than ever. Writers are there to absorb new realities and examine how our lives are impacted by shifts in consciousness and understanding. A careful writer will allow the forms of literature to respond to changing needs of readers. Rather than adhering to centuries-old divisions between genres, new writers are better off interrelating prose and poetry, fiction and nonfiction, in ways that allow the reader's imagination to be open to new realities. It is worth remembering that the categories of ''novel'' and ''poetry'' and ''nonfiction'' are market-driven terms. It is up to the writer to make the market respond to the work, rather than the other way around.

*   *   *

If there is a key to Kristjana Gunnars's writing, both poetry and prose, it is the following sentence: ''I am enamoured of . . . the rediscovery of life'' (from the chapbook *Water, Waiting,* issued in 1987). Many poets have expressed their love of life, and some have lamented its loss, but few have given expression to their love of its rediscovery. For Gunnars the past is there to be brought back to life through the act of remembering those who went before. This is the act of turning one's predecessors into one's ancestors, and it is an important act for this poet because she has staked her poetry and prose on the act of remembering the lives of the hardy pioneers from Iceland who settled along the shores of the lakes of Manitoba in the second half of the nineteenth century. Gunnars herself is a latter-day immigrant from Iceland. Along with the story writer W.D. Valgardson, she has made it her mission to draw to the attention of Canadian readers this square in the country's multicultural patchwork quilt.

Gunnars's poetry seems to reverberate with the heavy stresses of Old Norse. The poet George Bowering has written that ''Gunnars's poems sound and feel as if they have lasted a few thousand years, they are that careful.'' Her early work, found in the two volumes of *Settlement Poems* (1980), makes use of documentary technique and the so-called found manner to bring back to life the early pioneer settlers. Some of the poems reproduce lines from settlers' journals and other documents, as in the following:

> july 1, 1877: the first
> rain may 5, grass
> sprouts, leaves burst

Other poems are more expressive of the poet than they are of the lot of the settler. In ''From Memory II'' Gunnars wrote,

> You want to know the trick of fertility
> want to know the trick of infertility
> to know how to stay together
> know if the other is faithful
>
> I'm forgetting fast
> it's a long trip from glasgow to Quebec
> this is the last story I'll tell

At times Gunnars's poems recall the first-person narratives of Edgar Lee Masters's *Spoon River Anthology.* The thirty poems that comprise *One-Eyed Moon Maps* (1980) are ''shaped by ancient Norse myth, the mystery of runes, and the magic of modern technology.'' Rather in the manner of a meditation on the tarot cards, Gunnars free-associates on rune stones. The results are enigmatic, inconclusive. Here are some lines from ''Wall'':

> the grave of rest
> the doors that open
> i don't want to look at earth
> but up, at moon
> . . .
> in the north, up there
> you can't die

A grim and remorseless humor is expressed in *Wake-Pick Poems* (1981), where in ''Changeling XV'' Gunnars writes that

> it isn't easy to be troll
> trolls take everything you've got
> take your innocence
> throw it away

The poem ''The Silent Hand'' from *The Night Workers of Ragnarök* (1985) seems to imply a shift in the author's concern from the past and even the present to the future:

> we cannot be sure where
> we come from. all
> that matters is
>
> where we long to go
> the silent hand that draws us
> in

Later books offer more personal poems. One example is ''Gullfoss'' in *Carnival of Longing* (1989), with its contemporary sentiments about the danger that lurks in apparently harmless words:

> I have written words to you
> and I imagine they have become knives
> that my words injure

In the journal-like contents of *Zero Hour* (1991) there is a sense of looking ahead to a future fraught with the threat of global or even celestial conflagration:

461

I have come to that place in life where
there is nothing below. There are no
lower numbers.

In her writing Gunnars has embraced the distant past, the difficult present, and the unforeseeable future. She has celebrated nearly forgotten heroes of the nineteenth century and contrasted their almost mythic lives with the ironic lives of denizens of the late twentieth century. She writes with an intensity that, given her spare, lean style, is surprising. Her achievement lies in her willingness and ability to imbue Canadian poetry with a sense of the passing of generations.

—John Robert Colombo

GUTTERIDGE, Don(ald George)

Nationality: Canadian. **Born:** Sarnia, Ontario, 30 September 1937. **Education:** Chatham Collegiate Institute, Ontario, 1956; University of Western Ontario, London, 1956–60, 1962–63, B.A. (honors) 1960. **Family:** Married Anne Barnett in 1961; one daughter and one son. **Career:** English teacher, Elmira School Board, Ontario, 1960–62; teaching fellow, University of Western Ontario, 1962–63; head of the department of English, Ingersoll School Board, Ontario, 1963–64, and London Board of Education, Ontario, 1964–68; assistant professor, 1968–74, associate professor, 1975–77, and since 1977 professor of English methods, then professor emeritus, University of Western Ontario. **Awards:** President's Medal, University of Western Ontario, 1971; Canada Council travel grant, 1973. **Address:** 114 Victoria Street, London, Ontario N6A 2B5, Canada.

PUBLICATIONS

Poetry

The Brooding Sky. Privately printed, 1960.
New Poems 1964. Privately printed, 1965.
Other Wood: New Poems. Privately printed, 1966.
Intimations of Winter: Poems for the Latter Half of 1966. New York, Bitterroot Press, 1967.
Riel: A Poem for Voices. Fredericton, New Brunswick, Fiddlehead, 1968; revised edition, Toronto, Van Nostrand Reinhold, 1972.
The Village Within: Poems Towards a Biography. Fredericton, New Brunswick, Fiddlehead, 1970.
Death at Quebec and Other Poems. Fredericton, New Brunswick, Fiddlehead, 1971.
Perspectives. London, Ontario, Pennywise Press, 1971.
Saying Grace: An Elegy. Fredericton, New Brunswick, Fiddlehead, 1972.
Coppermine: The Quest for North. Ottawa, Oberon Press, 1973.
Borderlands. Ottawa, Oberon Press, and London, Dobson, 1975.
Tecumseh. Ottawa, Oberon Press, 1976.
A True History of Lambton County. Ottawa, Oberon Press, 1977; London, Dobson, 1978.
God's Geography. Ilderton, Ontario, Brick, 1982.
The Exiled Heart: Selected Narratives, 1968–1982. Ottawa, Oberon Press, 1986.

Love in the Wintertime. Ottawa, Oberon Press, 1990.
Flute Music in the Cello's Belly. London, Ontario, Moonstone Press, 1997.

Novels

Bus-Ride. Nairn, Ontario, Nairn Publications, 1974.
All in Good Time. Windsor, Ontario, Black Moss Press, 1980.
St. Vitus Dance. London, Ontario, Drumlin, 1987.
Shaman's Ground. London, Ontario, Drumlin, 1988.
How the World Began: A Parable of 1812. Goderich, Ontario, Moonstone Press, 1991.
Summer's Idyll. Ottawa, Oberon Press, 1993.
Winter's Descent. Ottawa, Oberon Press, 1996.

Other

Language and Expression: A Modern Approach (textbook). Toronto, McClelland and Stewart, 1970.
The Country of the Young. London, Ontario, University of Western Ontario, 1978.
Brave Season: Reading and the Language Arts in Grades Seven to Ten. London, Ontario, Althouse Press, 1983.
Incredible Journeys: New Approaches to the Novel in Grades 7–10 (handbook). London, Ontario, Althouse Press, 1986; revised edition, 1990.
The Dimension of Delight: A Study of Children's Verse-Writing, Ages 11–13. London, Ontario, Althouse Press, 1988.
Stubborn Pilgrimage: Resistance and Transformation in Ontario English Teaching, 1960–1993. Toronto, Our Schools/Our Selves Education Foundation, 1994.
Teaching English: Theory and Practice from Kindergarten to Grade Twelve. Toronto, James Lorimer, 1999.

Editor, *Rites of Passage.* Toronto, McClelland and Stewart, 1979.
Editor, *Mountain and Plain.* Toronto, McClelland and Stewart, 1998.

*

Manuscript Collection: D. B. Weldon Library, University of Western Ontario, London.

Critical Studies: *Survival: Themes in Canadian Literature* by Margaret Atwood, Toronto, Anansi, 1971; ''Rivering of Vision'' by David Cavanagh, in *Alive* (Guelph, Ontario), August 1973; ''Tecumseh'' by D.H. Sullivan, in *West Coast Review* (Burnaby, British Columbia), January 1978; *A Native Heritage: Images of the Indian in English-Canadian Literature* by Leslie Monkman, Toronto, University of Toronto Press, 1981; ''Don Gutteridge's Mythic Tetralogy'' by Keith Garebian, in *Canadian Literature* (Vancouver), winter 1981; interview with Dennis Cooley, in *CV 2* (Winnipeg), August 1982; ''Places in Time: Poetry of Historical Roots'' by Peter Baltensberger, in *CV 2* (Winnipeg), September 1983; R.G. Moyle, in *Journal of Canadian Poetry* (Ottawa), 1986; *The Native in Literature: Canadian and Comparative Perspectives* by Thomas King, Cheryl Calver and Helen Hoy, Toronto, ECW Press, 1987.

Don Gutteridge comments:

One of our poets has called Canada a ''country without a mythology''; little wonder, then, that my work—like that of many

Canadian writers—is concerned with the sense of place and the perspective of time, with roots into the past and what myths can be made in the face of such vast geography and empty stretches of history. My work takes two forms: personal poems about my childhood village and narrative poems on Canadian historical figures (real and imagined). Though quite different in content and form, these two types are related in that they share my concern for making something of my own past as well as that of my country and my belief, however naive, that the two are somehow connected. Since 1978 I have turned more and more to fiction as a vehicle to continue this dual exploration of personal and public history.

*   *   *

I sometimes think that there is a dramatist lurking within Don Gutteridge and that had the poet been born in a society with a stronger sense of drama he might be writing for the stage rather than for the page. Having said that, let me backtrack by adding that inside the man there is, as well as the dramatist, the lyricist who increasingly finds expression in a lyrical rather than a dramatic manner. Certainly Gutteridge's own work has oscillated between the poles of dramatic, historical works and private, personal lyrics.

Like so many Canadian poets, Gutteridge feels close to historical movements of the often slighted past. *Death at Quebec and Other Poems* offers monologues by early Jesuit missionaries from France. *Riel: A Poem for Voices* is the first of a number of volumes of free verse devoted to the difficult relationship between the Indian inhabitants of the land and the white European settlers. It is possible to see these poems as well as poems in subsequent volumes as collections of dramatic monologues, even *pensées,* some written in contemporary idiom, some derived from the idiom of the times in question. A sense of the style and substance may be gleaned from this passage attributed to the métis leader and martyr Louis Riel:

When my body
swings like a
dead tongue
from the white—man's
scaffolding,
will there be
an eloquence
to tell . . .

Rather like the historian Francis Parkman, Gutteridge has attempted to make into his own the history of the northern half of the North American continent. It is safe to say that if these historical periods are of interest then the book-length poem is of interest.

The regional poetry of Gutteridge is somewhat similar and appears in collections that form a loose series called ''Time Is the Metaphor.'' These poems are somewhat less adventurous, which is curious since such book-length collections of poems as *A True History of Lambton County* and *God's Geography* employ many of the same methods as do the historical works in their attempt to make the overall point that history is another word for human passion. The past runs into the present, and any consideration of the present requires a reconsideration of the past. The author composes the regional poems in the same way that he does the historical works, mainly through counterpointing public and private worlds, with found and original materials interspersed with lyrical asides.

Gutteridge's personal poems are less grand, more quiet than the somewhat impersonal historical works. In such autobiographical collections as *The Village Within* the poet finds significance and perhaps solace in statements that are at once personal and powerful. In the long impressionistic poem ''Saying Grace: An Elegy'' the poet writes moving lines that are at once moody and quirky yet above all effective:

Death does not
''take us,'' it
moves into the
waiting spaces
is welcome.

The sprightly style and spirit are welcome additions to the somewhat sobering personal poems that make up *Love in the Wintertime.* ''Say Uncle'' ends with an evocation of death:

May you prosper
here among those you love
and there
amid the vast village
of stars and fostering suns.

''Said and Done'' concludes on a human note:

After all is said,
a simple hello
how are you
I love you
would have done.

—John Robert Colombo

H

HACKER, Marilyn

Nationality: American. **Born:** New York City, 27 November 1942. **Education:** Bronx High School of Science, New York; Washington Square College, New York University, B.A. 1964; Art Students League, New York. **Family:** Married the writer Samuel R. Delany in 1961 (divorced 1980); one daughter. **Career:** Worked as a teacher, mail sorter, and editor of books, magazines, and trade journals; antiquarian bookseller, London, 1971–76; lecturer, George Washington University, Washington, D.C., 1976; adjunct professor of creative writing, Columbia University, New York, 1979–81; professor of English and creative writing, Hofstra University, 1997–99. Since 1999 director of M.A. program in creative writing and literature, City College of New York. Editor, *City Magazine*, 1967–70, *Quark*, 1969–70, *Little Magazine*, 1977–80, *13th Moon*, 1982–86, all New York, and *The Kenyon Review*, Gambier, Ohio. Writer-in-residence, State University of New York, Albany, spring 1988, and Columbia University, fall 1988; George Elliston poet-in-residence, University of Cincinnati, Ohio, fall 1988; distinguished writer-in-residence, American University, Washington, D.C., spring 1989; visiting professor of creative writing, State University of New York, Binghamton, spring 1990, University of Utah, Salt Lake City, spring 1995, and Barnard College, New York, fall 1995; Fannie Hurst poet-in-residence, Brandeis University, Waltham, Massachusetts, fall 1996. **Awards:** YM-YWHA Discovery award, 1973; Lamont Poetry Selection award, 1973; National Endowment for the Arts grant, 1974, 1985, 1995; National Book award, 1975; Guggenheim fellowship, 1980; New York State Council on the Arts grant, 1980; Ingram Merrill Foundation fellowship, 1984; Co-ordinating Council of Little Magazines Editor's fellowship, 1984; Robert H. Winner award, The Poetry Society of America, 1987, 1989; Lambda literary award, 1991, for *Going Back to the River*, and 1995, for *Winter Numbers*; John Masefield Memorial award, The Poetry Society of America, 1994; B.F. Conners award, *The Paris Review*, 1994; Readers' Choice award, *Prairie Schooner*, 1995; Lenore Marshall prize, 1995, for *Winter Numbers*; Poets' prize, 1996, for *Selected Poems, 1965–1990*; Strousse award, *Prairie Schooner*, 1998, 1999; Crossing Boundaries award, *International Quarterly*, for translation, 1999; New York Foundation for the Arts grant, 1999–2000. **Address:** 230 West 105 Street, #10A, New York, New York 10025, U.S.A.

PUBLICATIONS

Poetry

The Terrible Children. Privately printed, 1967.
Highway Sandwiches, with Thomas M. Disch and Charles Platt. Privately printed, 1970.
Presentation Piece. New York, Viking Press, 1974.
Separations. New York, Knopf, 1976.
Taking Notice. New York, Knopf, 1980.
Assumptions. New York, Knopf, 1985.
Love, Death, and the Changing of the Seasons. New York, Arbor House, 1986; London, Onlywomen Press, 1987.
Going Back to the River. New York, Random House, 1990.

The Hang-Glider's Daughter: Selected Poems. London, Onlywomen Press, 1990.
Selected Poems, 1965–1990. New York, Norton, 1994.
Winter Numbers: Poems. New York, Norton, 1994.
Squares and Courtyards. New York, Norton, 2000.

Recording: *The Poetry and Voice of Marilyn Hacker,* Caedmon, 1976.

Other

Editor, with Samuel R. Delany, *Quark 1–4*. New York, Paperback Library, 4 vols., 1970–71.
Editor, *Woman Poet: The East*. Reno, Nevada, Women in Literature. 1982.

Translator, *Edge,* by Claire Malroux, Winston-Salem, North Carolina, Wake Forest University Press, 1996.
Translator, *A Long-Gone Sun,* by Claire Malroux. New York, Sheep Meadow Press, 2000.

*

Bibliography: By Suzanne Gardinier, in *Contemporary Lesbian Writers of the United States: A Bio-Bibliographical Critical Sourcebook,* edited by Sandra Pollack and Denise D. Knight, Westport, Connecticut, Greenwood, 1993.

Critical Studies: "Studying Interior Architecture by Keyhole: Four Poets" by Reg Saner, in *Denver Quarterly,* 20(1), summer 1985; Marilyn Hacker issue of *13th Moon,* 9(1–2), 1991; by John Weir, in *Advocate,* 664, 20 September 1994; interview with Annie Finch, in *American Poetry Review* (Philadelphia), 25(3), May-June 1996; "Measured Feet 'in Gender-Bender Shoes': The Politics of Poetic Form in Marilyn Hacker's 'Love, Death, and the Changing of the Seasons'" by Lynn Keller, in *Feminist Measures: Soundings in Poetry and Theory,* edited by Keller and Cristanne Miller, Ann Arbor, University of Michigan Press, 1994; *The Sonnet As the Temple of Sound and 'Gray's Anatomy'* (dissertation) by Pamela Ardith McClure, University of Missouri, Columbia, 1997.

*   *   *

From the beginning of Marilyn Hacker's career her poems have established a unique counterpoint between classical rhyming forms—sestina, sonnet, villanelle—and blunt declarative sentences to display the deranged obsessiveness of contemporary minds. Her hard-edged language in the 1970s is darkly jewel-encrusted, redolent of a devastated inner world of difficult loving, tangled sexuality, and convoluted relationships. Semiprecious gems—onyx, amethyst, alexandrite—express the hardness, mystery, and richness of experience. Lured by the foreign and strange, Hacker invents "imaginary translations," playing with exotic locales and overblown emotions. Tours de force, these poems lead into her central concern, the elucidation of her own intense passions, whether sexual, moral, or political.

Love is the premier passion that runs as a continuing strand from the earlier to the later work. Because the poem sequence "Separations," from the volume of this title, is written in sonnet form, it de-emphasizes obsession and becomes a graceful, almost Shakespearean delineation of the aspects of love, which always springs up lively and ubiquitous despite the poet's difficulties. But love arouses thoughts of death, as in the opening poem of *Presentation Piece* (1974), in which she speaks to "the skull of the beloved" as a brooding nobleman in a Jacobean play addresses the skull of his dead mistress. "The Naviga-tors" foreshadows the heartbroken elegy "Geographer" in *Separations* (1976), a poem that unites in formal, sestina-like word repetition her continuing themes of death, cities, gems, language, and painful but persisting love.

As a descriptive phrase, "persisting love" grossly understates the obsession with a young lover that besieges Hacker for a year in *Love, Death, and the Changing of the Seasons* (1986). This "verse novel," as she calls it, is a book-length sonnet sequence that empha-sizes physical love almost exclusively as the poet waits in various situations to be united with Rachel, called Ray. The poems perform in explicit, masculinized language a *Kama-Sutra* of fantasized ways of making love. When Ray breaks off the affair, the poet plunges into the utter bleakness, without perspective, of the coda's final poems. But the poems clarify an underlying motif: her lust arose from the foredoomed but irresistible wish to be young again. By 1990, in *Going Back to the River,* Hacker is on a more even keel, enjoying good food, drink, and the landscapes of two continents and appreciat-ing quotidian objects. All is not pleasure, however, and the unassimilable horrors of wartime experience and the persecution of the Jews in France are evoked in "Days of 1944: Three Friends." Thus reminded of her Jewishness, Hacker meditates further on her ethnic background and her parents' lives in the title poem of the volume, as the rivers she goes back to—Thames, Hudson, Seine—are seen not as destinations but as reminders of the flux and uncertainties of experience.

In a sense, however, by the time Hacker wrote *Winter Numbers* (1994) flux had become a way of life. (She has homes in both New York and Paris.) Here the incorporation of French words renders her forms more supple and varied while also enriching the poems' sense of place. Her internationalism lessens the pain of change, making it a modus vivendi, a respite from narrow American prejudices. But her consciousness of painful change escalates as personal losses through AIDS and cancer assail her. Death is the ultimate change that everyone fears. The word "numbers" in the book's title has multiple associations: with the metrics of poetry, with mileage, with dates and time periods, the length of time, for instance, between the diagnosis of an illness and surgery or death. In the book's last section, "Cancer Winter," meditation on her own uncertain fate after breast cancer is enlarged to include history and the fates of those dead in the Holocaust.

Hacker's delight in French culture and language led to her 1996 volume, *Edge,* translations of the poems of Claire Malroux, who is herself a translator of H. D., Derek Walcott, and other modern writers into French. The French poet's themes align with the American's: a consicousness of aging, "prescience of death," and effort to connect this tangible world in its quirky sounds and flavors with the eternal world. These preoccupations—particularly a sharp and tender sense of mortality—also pervade Hacker's 2000 collection, *Squares and Courtyards.* Here her favored form is the sonnet sequence, although she also likes the terse, imagistic three-line stanza characteristic of William Carlos Williams. In one section, "Paragraphs from a Day-book," she employs an interesting 15-line stanza invented by the poet

Hayden Caruth, to whom the volume is dedicated. Close to a book-length unified narrative, it interweaves elegiac recording of deaths—youthful, accidental, elderly, inevitable—with direct notation of survivors' lives. The settings shuttle between two continents, as Hacker herself does. Her travels provide a metaphor for the passage between life and death:

New passport stamps mark
the week of my, Ellen's and Zenka's border
crossings, unplotted flight-paths toward the dark

Haunted by death-consciousness, this work thematically builds on her earlier books. She has continued her commitment to make poetic intercession for women, blacks, homosexuals, Jews, whoever is ill and suffering. Her skilled use of form to serve candid observation, the ability to register ephemeral beauty, the strength to face loss and death for herself, for everyone—those powers infuse Hacker's poems and serve as markers of their profundity and accomplishment. Her long career continues to enrich the high tradition of English lyric.

—Jane Augustine

HADAS, Rachel (Chamberlayne)

Nationality: American. **Born:** New York, New York, 8 November 1948. **Education:** Radcliffe College, Cambridge, Massachusetts, 1965–69, B.A. 1969; John Hopkins University, Baltimore, Maryland, 1976–77, M.A. 1977; Princeton University, New Jersey, 1977–82, Ph.D. 1982. **Family:** Married 1) Stavros Kondylis in 1970 (divorced 1978); 2) George Edwards in 1978; one son. **Career:** Assistant professor, 1981–87, associate professor, 1987–92, and since 1992 professor, Rutgers University, Newark, New Jersey. **Awards:** Isobel M. Briggs traveling fellowship, 1969–70; Vermont Council on the Arts Writers grant, 1975–76; Bread Loaf Writers Conference scholar-ship, 1976; Guggenheim fellowship, 1988–89; Literature award, American Academy and Institute of Arts and Letters, 1990; McGinnis award, *Southwest Review,* 1990; Elizabeth Matchett Stover Poetry award, *Southwest Review,* 1991; Hellas award, *Hellas Magazine,* 1993; Ingram Merrill Foundation fellowship, 1977, 1994. **Member:** National Book Critics Circle (Board member), 1994; American Academy of Arts and Sciences, 1995. **Address:** 838 West End Avenue, #3A, New York, New York 10025, U.S.A.

PUBLICATIONS

Poetry

Starting from Troy. Boston, Godine, 1975.
Slow Transparency. Middletown, Connecticut, Wesleyan University Press, 1983.
A Son from Sleep. Middletown, Connecticut, Wesleyan University Press, 1987.
Pass It On. Princeton, New Jersey, Princeton University Press, 1989.
Unending Dialogues: Voices from an AIDS Poetry Workshop. Boston, Faber, 1991.
Mirrors of Astonishment. New Brunswick, New Jersey, Rutgers University Press, 1993.

The Empty Bed. Middletown, Connecticut, Wesleyan University Press, 1995.

Halfway Down the Hall: New & Selected Poems. Middletown, Connecticut, Wesleyan University Press, 1998.

Other

Form, Cycle, Infinity. Cranbury, New Jersey, Associated University Presses, 1983.

Living in Time (essays and poem). New Brunswick, New Jersey, Rutgers University Press, 1990.

The Double Legacy. Boston, Faber, 1995.

Merrill, Cavafy, Poems, and Dreams. Ann Arbor, Michigan, University of Michigan Press, 2000.

Translator, *Other Worlds Than This: Translations from Latin, French, & Modern Greek Poetry.* New Brunswick, New Jersey, Rutgers University Press, 1994.

Translator, *Oedipus the King,* by Seneca. Baltimore, Maryland, Johns Hopkins University Press Roman Drama Series, 1994.

Translator, *Helen,* by Euripedes. Philadelphia, Pennsylvania, University of Pennsylvania Press Greek Drama Series, 1997.

*

Manuscript Collection: Special Collections and Archives, Alexander Library, Rutgers University, New Brunswick, New Jersey.

Critical Studies: "Women's Creation Stories" by Lee Upton, in *Denver Quarterly* (Denver), 23(2), fall 1988; "From the Greek" by Christopher Benfey, in *Parnassus* (New York), 16(2), 1991; "Rachel Hadas, Poet and Essayist: A Bibliography, 1965–1993" by Ann Vreeland Watkins, in *Bulletin of Bibliography* (Westport, Connecticut), 51(2), June 1994; "Elegy As History: Three Women Poets 'By the Century's Deathbed'" by Anita Helle, in *South Atlantic Review* (Atlanta, Georgia), 61(2), spring 1996.

Rachel Hadas comments:

My writing seems more various than it really is: I've translated Seneca and Tibullus, Karyotakis and Baudelaire; have written a scholarly study and personal essays and poems about subjects ranging from motherhood to classical mythology to teaching to AIDS. Throughout my work, though, a personal approach tends to be balanced by a technically formal, decorous manner. The personal voice, withheld by formal technique, talks about education, books, love, teaching, death, elegy. To be a bit more logical about it, love is linked to loss, but loss is healed or redeemed by language, which expresses and fosters love, which is linked to loss. And so on.

My recent work in New York City with people with AIDS has received more journalistic attention than my previous poetry. I ran a poetry workshop at Gay Men's Health Crisis for some six years, and my experiences there continue to nourish my imagination. But then so do my happy childhood, my classical education, my years in Greece or life in New York, my career as a teacher, my being wife and mother, or my rural summers.

The titles of some of my books attest to the sense of loving, losing, giving back, carrying on: *A Son from Sleep, The Empty Bed, Pass It On, Unending Dialogues, The Double Legacy.*

* * *

Rachel Hadas is a poet whose fine sense of technique matches her sensitivity to both the universal constants and the particular variables of human experience. She is also a poet whose work reflects a profound awareness of the goals and implications of her art. These concerns coalesce in *Living in Time,* a work that consists of a long poem surrounded by prose essays. The volume's mixed form reflects Hadas's consciousness that she shares a commitment with such writers as Frost and Merrill "to mend the rift between fact and fiction, prose and poetry." Its contents point to three of the central concerns of her work over the years: an awareness of the past and of how it impinges on and merits attention from the present, a sense of the importance and the depth of what is often dismissed as "everyday" experience, and a keen effort to explore the workings of imagination as it simultaneously shapes and guides us through the webs of memory and immediate experience.

The title of her first collection, *Starting from Troy,* bears out Hadas's consistent belief that "the attempt to write as if writing were an unprecedented action is doomed to failure." Throughout her career her poems have acknowledged precedents both in their richly allusive texture (attempting to make connections with, and not merely allude to, such predecessors as Homer, Sappho, Keats, Beaudelaire, Karyotakis, and Stevens) and in their masterful handling and variation of traditional poetic forms. Thus, a fruitful dialogue between present circumstances and past forms, with their attendant values, unfolds through her use of the sestina for "The Colours of the Place" and of terza rima for "The Lesson of the Elements" and through her "Pantoum on Pumpkin Hill" (all from *Slow Transparency*). The dialogue continues through the different frameworks offered by the villanelle of "Fix It (Winter)" and by the epistolary style of "Hortus Conclusus" (both from *Pass It On*).

Hadas has been overly critical of her early work. Characterizing its spirit as one of "distinct powerlessness" ignores too much of its wit and intellectual energy, yet her observations that these poems are "skimpy on connections, whether of narrative or argument," and that "they attempt to capture complex states of mind by excluding a great deal and disguising the rest" show typically sharp critical self-awareness. Poems such as "Village Triptych" (*Starting from Troy*) and "Alien Corn" (*Slow Transparency*) achieve a terseness that borders on obscurity by following Auden's early practice of dropping articles and connectives, and Hadas's observation in "Kaleidoscope" (*Slow Transparency*) that distinct parts "die / to form a pattern" is self-descriptive of the affective cost of such hard-edged poetry. Other early poems, however, also point toward the two means by which Hadas has overcome these limitations: the commitment to everyday experience, and the exploration of the dialogical workings of the imagination, both mentioned above as keystones in her work.

A commitment to everyday experience may be viewed simply as a broadening of the concern for provenance found in Hadas's respect for the past. It is a further way of "stationing oneself in time, at a particular moment," and so one is not surprised to find signs of it in the descriptive fullness of such early poems as "Landlady" (*Starting from Troy*) and "Siesta in the Summer House" (*Slow Transparency*). But this emphasis becomes central to the success of Hadas's later collections. The birth of her child, the focus of *A Son from Sleep,* fundamentally changed her sense of herself and her place in the world, and since her art is so vitally attuned to its maker, the event changed the nature of her art. The sense of connectedness between mother and newborn caught so fully and unsentimentally in "Amnesia, Changes" is embodied in such poems as "In Lieu of Lullaby" with a new wholeness, a directness achieved without loss of lyric concision. Six short lines from "Up and Down" demonstrate both the solid detail and the metaphoric power of Hadas's later work, and their overlapping sounds also embody the interconnectedness of these traits: "Still night sweats / and bleeding still, / its bleachy smell. / Your bleat softly / shears the thick / fleece of dark."

This more broadly responsive style also has roots in the third central feature of Hadas's work, its preoccupation with the imagination's shaping power in the dialogue between inner and outer experience, past and present. It is appropriate that this concern supplies the title for the long poem "The Dream Machine," which is at the center of *Living in Time*. As with Hadas's focus on everyday experience, one can find anticipations of this emphasis in her early work. "Two Sleepers" (*Starting from Troy*) and "Dry Season" (*Slow Transparency*), for example, both depict the rapid changes of inner and outer weather that proceed from the dream machine. Yet it is in Hadas's later poetry that the subtle, shaping continuities (as well as the distortions and limitations) of the imagination receive their most probing and powerful treatment. Thus, "Generations" (*Pass It On*) turns into poetry a series of close observations on the acquisition and use of language by pursuing the threads of implications through various times and places—what "the baby / points to," what "you / look at," what "we talk of"—with amazed awareness that "the link between imagination and event" can be at once "so weak" and so necessary. The troubling ambiguity of a world "that lasts / because it never was" ("Art") gives a double edge to the title of her volume *Mirrors of Astonishment,* and yet the heft and brilliance of the blade make the reader echo her response to the rainbow in "Cupfuls of Summer"—"Look! the light!"—and eagerly await more.

—Julia Reibetanz

HALL, Donald (Andrew, Jr.)

Nationality: American. **Born:** New Haven, Connecticut, 20 September 1928. **Education:** Phillips Exeter Academy, New Hampshire; Harvard University, Cambridge, Massachusetts (Garrison and Sergeant prizes, 1951), B.A. 1951; Oxford University (Henry Fellow; Newdigate prize, 1952), B.Litt. 1953; Stanford University, California (creative writing fellow), 1953–54. **Family:** Married first wife in 1952 (divorced 1969), one son and one daughter; married Jane Kenyon in 1972 (died 1995). **Career:** Junior fellow, Society of Fellows, Harvard University, 1954–57; assistant professor, 1957–61, associate professor, 1961–66, and professor of English, 1966–75, University of Michigan, Ann Arbor. Poetry editor, *Paris Review,* Paris and New York, 1953–62; member of the editorial board for poetry, Wesleyan University Press, 1958–64. Consultant, Harper and Row publishers, 1964–81. Lived in England, 1959–60, 1963–64. Deacon, South Danbury Church, New Hampshire. **Awards:** Lamont Poetry Selection award, 1955; Edna St. Vincent Millay memorial prize, 1956; Longview Foundation award, 1960; Guggenheim fellowship, 1963, 1972; Sarah Josepha Hale award, 1983; Lenore Marshall award, 1987; N.B.C.C. award, 1989; *Los Angeles Times* award and National Book Critics Circle award, 1989, for *The One Day;* Robert Frost Silver medal, Poetry Society of America, 1991; Lifetime Achievement award, New Hampshire Writers and Publisher Project, 1992; New England Book award for nonfiction, 1993; Lily prize for poetry, 1994. Honorary Degrees: Presbyterian College, Colby-Sawyer College, Daniel Webster College; New England College, State University of New York, Bates College, University of New Hampshire, University of Michigan, Plymouth State College. Poet Laureate of New Hampshire, 1984–89. American Academy and Institute of Arts and Letters, 1989. **Agent:** Gerard McCauley Agency Inc., P.O. Box AE, Katonah, New York 10536. **Address:** Eagle Pond Farm, Danbury, New Hampshire 03230–9599, U.S.A.

PUBLICATIONS

Poetry

(Poems). Oxford, Fantasy Press, 1952.
Exile. Privately printed, 1952.
To the Loud Wind and Other Poems. Cambridge, Massachusetts, Harvard Advocate, 1955.
Exiles and Marriages. New York, Viking Press, 1955.
The Dark Houses. New York, Viking Press, 1958.
A Roof of Tiger Lilies. New York, Viking Press, and London, Deutsch, 1964.
The Alligator Bride. Menomonie, Wisconsin, Ox Head Press, 1968.
The Alligator Bride: Poems New and Selected. New York, Harper, 1969.
The Yellow Room: Love Poems. New York, Harper, 1971.
A Blue Tit Tilts at the Edge of the Sea: Selected Poems 1964–1974. London, Secker and Warburg, 1975.
The Town of Hill. Boston, Godine, 1975.
Kicking the Leaves. Mount Horeb, Wisconsin, Perishable Press, 1975.
Kicking the Leaves (collection). New York, Harper, 1978; London, Secker and Warburg, 1979.
The Toy Bone. Brockport, New York, Boa, 1979.
The Twelve Seasons. Deerfield, Massachusetts, Deerfield Press, and Dublin, Gallery Press, 1983.
Brief Lives. Concord, New Hampshire, William B. Ewert, 1983.
Great Day in the Cows' House. Mt. Carmel, Connecticut, Ives Street Press, 1984.
The Happy Man. New York, Random House, and London, Secker and Warburg, 1986.
The One Day: A Poem in Three Parts. New York, Ticknor and Fields, 1988.
Old and New Poems. New York, Ticknor and Fields, 1990.
The One Day and Poems (1947–1990). Manchester, Carcanet, 1991.
The Museum of Clear Ideas. New York, Ticknor & Fields, 1993.
The Old Life. New York, Houghton Mifflin, 1996.
Without. New York, Houghton Mifflin, 1998.

Recordings: *Today's Poets 1,* with others, Folkways, 1967; *Names of Horses,* Watershed, 1985; *Donald Hall Prose and Poetry,* Audio Bookshelf, 1997.

Plays

An Evening's Frost (produced New York, 1965).
Bread and Roses (produced Ann Arbor, Michigan, 1975).
Ragged Mountain Elegies (produced Peterborough, New Hampshire, 1983).
The Bone Ring (produced New York, 1986). Santa Cruz, California, Story Line Press. 1987.

Short Stories

The Ideal Bakery. Berkeley, California, North Point Press, 1987.

Other

Andrew the Lion Farmer (for children). New York, Watts, 1959; London, Methuen, 1961.

String Too Short to Be Saved. New York, Viking Press, 1961; London, Deutsch, 1962.

Henry Moore: The Life and Work of a Great Sculptor. New York, Harper, and London, Gollancz, 1966.

Marianne Moore: The Cage and the Animal. New York, Pegasus, 1970.

As the Eye Moves: A Sculpture by Henry Moore. New York, Abrams, 1970.

The Gentleman's Alphabet Book. New York, Dutton, 1972.

Writing Well. Boston, Little Brown, 1973; revised edition, 1976, 1979, 1982, 1985; revised edition, Glenview, Illinois, Scott Foresman, 1988; revised edition, with Sven Birkerts, New York, HarperCollins, 1991.

Playing Around: The Million-Dollar Infield Goes to Florida, with others. Boston, Little Brown, 1974.

Dock Ellis in the Country of Baseball, with Dock Ellis. New York, Coward McCann, 1976.

Riddle Rat (for children). New York, Warne, 1977.

Remembering Poets: Reminiscences and Opinions—Dylan Thomas, Robert Frost, T.S. Eliot, Ezra Pound. New York, Harper, 1978.

Goatfoot Milktongue Twinbird: Interviews, Essays, and Notes on Poetry 1970–76. Ann Arbor, University of Michigan Press, 1978.

Ox-Cart Man (for children). New York, Viking Press, 1979; London, MacRae, 1980.

To Keep Moving. Geneva, New York, Seneca, 1980.

To Read Literature: Fiction, Poetry, Drama. New York, Holt Rinehart, 1981; revised edition, 1983, 1987.

The Weather for Poetry: Essays, Reviews, and Notes on Poetry 1977–81. Ann Arbor, University of Michigan Press, 1982.

The Man Who Lived Alone (for children). Boston, Godine, 1984.

Fathers Playing Catch with Sons: Essays on Sport (Mostly Baseball). Berkeley, California, North Point Press, 1985.

Winter (essays), with Clifton C. Olds. Hanover, New Hampshire, University Press of New England, 1986.

Seasons at Eagle Pond. New York, Ticknor and Fields, 1987.

Poetry and Ambition: Essays 1982–1988. Ann Arbor, University of Michigan Press, 1988.

Anecdotes of Modern Art, with Pat Corrigan Wykes. New York and Oxford, Oxford University Press, 1990.

Here at Eagle Pond. New York, Ticknor & Fields, 1990.

Their Ancient Glittering Eyes. New York, Ticknor & Fields, 1992.

Life Work. New York, Beacon Press, 1993.

Death to Death of Poetry. Ann Arbor, University of Michigan Press, 1994.

Farm Summer 1942 (for children). New York, Dial Press, 1994.

I Am the Dog, I Am the Cat (for children). New York, Dial Press, 1994.

Lucy's Christmas (for children). New York, Harcourt Brace, 1994.

Lucy's Summer (for children). New York, Harcourt Brace, 1995.

Principal Products of Portugal. Boston, Beacon Press, 1995.

When Willard Met Babe Ruth (for children). New York, Harcourt Brace, 1996.

Old Home Day (for children). New York, Harcourt Brace, 1996.

The Milkman's Boy. N.p., Walker and Co., 1997.

Editor, *The Harvard Advocate Anthology.* New York, Twayne, 1950.

Editor, with Robert Pack and Louis Simpson, *New Poets of England and America.* Cleveland, Meridian, 1957; London, New English Library, 1974; *Second Selection,* with Pack, 1962.

Editor, *Whittier.* New York, Dell, 1961.

Editor, *Contemporary American Poetry.* London, Penguin, 1962; revised edition, 1971.

Editor, *A Poetry Sampler.* New York, Watts, 1962.

Editor, with Stephen Spender, *The Concise Encyclopedia of English and American Poets and Poetry.* London, Hutchinson, and New York, Hawthorn, 1963; revised edition, 1970.

Editor, with Warren Taylor, *Poetry in English.* New York, Macmillan, 1963; revised edition, 1970.

Editor, *The Faber Book of Modern Verse,* revised edition. London, Faber, 1965.

Editor, *A Choice of Whitman's Verse.* London, Faber, 1968.

Editor, *The Modern Stylists: Writers on the Art of Writing.* New York, Free Press, 1968.

Editor, *Man and Boy: An Anthology.* New York, Watts, 1968.

Editor, *American Poetry: An Introductory Anthology.* London, Faber, 1969.

Editor, *The Pleasures of Poetry.* New York, Harper, 1971.

Editor, with D.L. Emblen, *A Writer's Reader.* Boston, Little Brown, 1976; revised edition, 1979, 1982, 1985; revised edition, Glenview, Illinois, Scott Foresman, 1988.

Editor, *To Read Literature.* New York, Holt, 1980.

Editor, *To Read Poetry.* New York, Holt, 1981.

Editor, *The Oxford Book of American Literary Anecdotes.* New York and Oxford, Oxford University Press, 1981.

Editor, *Claims for Poetry.* Ann Arbor, University of Michigan Press, 1982.

Editor, *The Contemporary Essay.* Boston, Bedford, 1984.

Editor, *The Oxford Book of Children's Verse in America.* New York and Oxford, Oxford University Press, 1985.

Editor, *To Read Fiction.* New York, Holt, 1987.

Editor, with David Lehman, *The Best American Poetry.* New York, Scribner, 1989.

Editor, *The Essential Andrew Marvell.* New York, Ecco Press, 1991.

Editor, *The Essential E.A. Robinson.* New York, Ecco Press, 1993.

*

Critical Studies: By Ralph J. Mills, Jr., in *Iowa Review* (Iowa City), Winter 1971; "Donald Hall Issue" of *Tennessee Poetry Journal* (Martin), Winter 1971; *The Day I Was Older: Collected Writings on the Poetry of Donald Hall,* edited by Liam Rector, Santa Cruz, California, Story Line Press, 1989; "Donald Hall: Elegies from Eagle Pond" by Michael Scharf, in *Publishers Weekly,* 245(12), 23 March 1998; "'Building the House of Dying': Donald Hall's Claim for Poetry" by Chris Walsh, in *Agni,* 47, 1998.

*　　*　　*

The publication in 1988 of *The One Day,* a book-length lyric sequence, marked Donald Hall's most significant contribution to an

American poetry steadily moving away from the solipsistic popular verse of the 1960s and 1970s. More and more American poetry is opening up both to acknowledge and to tell the stories of our larger human community. In its potent and diverse characters and in its three-part structure of compelling monologues, witty dialogues, and omniscient narration, *The One Day* both continues American poetry's expansive movement to a wider range of styles and subjects and raises the stakes for any long poem to come after:

> . . . We are one cell perpetually
> dying and being born, led by a single day that presides
> over our passage through the thirty thousand days
> from highchair past work and love to suffering death.
> We plant; we store the seed corn. Our sons and daughters
> topdress old trees. Two chimneys require:
> Work, love, build a house, and die. But build a house.

The artist in the poem's first section, recalling repressed early years and then resignedly looking out at the poem's end from a life of fame and accomplishment; the middle-aged man sitting alone in nervous melancholia, meditating on his father's tragedy and his own lifelong attempt to match it; the bathetic yuppie couple of the poem's middle section; and Senex, the mad philosopher—these characters raise their voices in a vatic splendor, the roots of which are found in Whitman and Pound.

The message these witnesses have to offer is an aggressive one. Our late twentieth-century greed, they tell us, will prove to be our doom. Only generations survive, they warn us, and then only by actively remembering. That humble, sustaining act of historical witnessing is our highest and most urgent responsibility. We will be defined as a nation and culture according to how we take it up.

Hall's labors have always aimed at taking this responsibility in hand, but he struggled hard to achieve the sharp focus of his mature point of view. By the time *Kicking the Leaves* was published in 1978, Hall had six full-length poetry collections to his credit and enjoyed a respected reputation in both England and the United States as a poet, editor, and literary journalist. The books preceding *Kicking the Leaves* showcased, more than anything else, Hall's restlessness and versatility. The formal elegies and meditations in *Exiles and Marriages,* his first book and the Lamont Poetry Selection for 1955, contrast sharply with the relaxed, deep image-inspired poems found in *The Alligator Bride: Poems New and Selected.* When Hall's least successful books, *The Yellow Room: Love Poems* and *The Town of Hill,* appeared by the mid-1970s, it was apparent that the poet had been victimized by his own versatility. This is a trap from which most poets never emerge.

Hall, recognizing the need for a profound change in his life as well as in his poetry, proved to be the exception. It was then that he left the academy after twenty years of teaching and moved back to the ancestral farmhouse in New Hampshire, the place where he had spent childhood summers with his grandparents and the locale he wrote so eloquently about in the prose memoir *String Too Short to Be Saved* and later adapted as the verse play *The Bone Ring.* The move rejuvenated both the life and the poetry, returning the mature man to the peopled landscapes and seasons that were most in the man to begin with:

> Now I leap and fall, exultant, recovering
> from death, on account of death, in accord with the dead,

> the smell and taste of leaves again,
> and the pleasure, the only long pleasure, of taking a place
> in the story of leaves.

This homecoming and the work it required has its essential documents in *Kicking the Leaves* and in volumes Hall followed it up with: *The Happy Man*; the selected *Old and New Poems,* with a closing section of new poems written between 1987 and 1990; *The Museum of Clear Ideas,* an ambitious collection that includes a sequence imitating the *Odes* of Horace with great wit and the epic "Baseball," a poem written in nine "innings," with each inning composed of nine stanzas, each stanza composed of nine lines, and each line composed of nine syllables; and the aforementioned *The One Day.* If these collections were combined into "The One Book," their consistency in vision, and arguably in style, would be readily recognizable, and we would better understand David Shapiro's claim, made in a review of *The Happy Man* in the journal *Poetry,* that the poems "give us a kind of rural antidote to the conventional urban Waste Land."

In a country like the United States that eschews aging and casts an amnesiac's eye on its past and traditions, in a country that increasingly focuses on the right now and the self at the expense of historical perspective and compassion for neighbors, Hall's poetry, and especially his verse since 1978, reminds us of what is most enduring in our culture. As Liam Rector put it in the introduction to *The Day I Was Older* (1989), his critical anthology dealing with Hall's poetry, "The word *old* is something of a key to Hall's work and thinking as he has, as much as any American poet ever has, looked to find what is good, worthwhile . . . about what is old."

A poet is ultimately judged on his ability to tell the true stories of his tribe. In late middle age Hall transcended the pack of popular academic plodders all around him to become a solitary singer whose remarkable vision has included us all.

—Robert McDowell

HALL, J(ohn) C(live)

Nationality: British. **Born:** London, 12 September 1920. **Education:** Leighton Park, Reading, Berkshire; Oriel College, Oxford. **Family:** Two children. **Career:** Formerly a book and magazine publisher; trustee of the Kevin Douglas estate. **Address:** 9 Warwick Road, Mount Sion, Tunbridge Wells, Kent TN1 1YL, England.

PUBLICATIONS

Poetry

Selected Poems, with Keith Douglas and Norman Nicholson. London, Bale and Staples, 1943.
The Summer Dance and Other Poems. London, Lehmann, 1951.
The Burning Hare. London, Chatto and Windus-Hogarth Press, 1966.
A House of Voices. London, Chatto and Windus-Hogarth Press, 1973.
Selected and New Poems 1939–1984. London, Secker and Warburg, 1985.

Other

Edwin Muir. London, Longman, 1956.

Editor, *Collected Poems of Edwin Muir 1921–1951.* London, Faber, 1952; New York, Grove Press, 1957; revised edition, Faber, 1960; New York, Oxford University Press, 1965.

Editor, with Patric Dickinson and Erica Marx, *New Poems 1955.* London, Joseph, 1955.

Editor, with G.S. Fraser and John Waller, *The Collected Poems of Keith Douglas,* revised edition. London, Faber, 1966.

Editor, with G.S. Fraser and John Waller, *Alamein to Zem Zem,* by Keith Douglas. London, Faber, 1966; New York, Chilmark Press, 1967.

*   *   *

J.C. Hall's early poems, collected in *The Summer Dance,* though reflective and carefully formed, lack any strongly individual quality. As he himself acknowledged, ''All these long years I've pondered how to make / A poetry I could truly call my own.'' In the next volume, *The Burning Hare,* the influence of Edwin Muir is all-pervasive. ''Before This Journeying Began'' and ''The Double Span'' are dedicated to him, and ''The Island'' reads like a pastiche of Muir. Hall is a conservative poet, conscious of his debt to literary tradition, and ''The Playground by the Church,'' with its allusions to Valéry, is typical of his meditative poetry, which questions and explores the world of ideas and of philosophical apprehensions.

A House of Voices relies less than the previous collections on myth and symbol, although Hall remains aware of their potency. The tone of the verse is more relaxed, and the poems are more firmly rooted in the world of everyday experience. In ''The Double'' Hall ends on a note of metaphysical speculation, but the first three stanzas are more humorous and colloquial than anything in his earlier work:

I often wonder what he was really like,
That identical boy—whether he knew of me
Taking the rap, riding round on my bike
Secretly proud of the devil I dared not be.

Hall's patient search for a poetry truly his own appears finally to have been successful.

—John Press

HALL, Rodney

Nationality: Australian. **Born:** Solihull, Warwickshire, England, 18 November 1935; immigrated to Australia during his childhood. **Education:** City of Bath Boys' School; Brisbane Boys' College; University of Queensland, Brisbane, B.A. 1971. **Family:** Married Maureen Elizabeth MacPhail in 1962; three daughters. **Career:** Freelance scriptwriter and actor, 1957–67, and film critic, 1966–67, Australian Broadcasting Corporation, Brisbane. Tutor, New England University School of Music, Armidale, New South Wales, summers 1967–71 and 1977–80; youth officer, Australian Council for the Arts, 1971–73; lecturer in recorder, Canberra School of Music, 1979–83. Since 1962 advisory editor, *Overland* magazine, Melbourne; since 1967 poetry editor, *The Australian* daily newspaper, Sydney. Traveled in Europe, 1958–60, 1963–64, 1965, and the United States, 1974. Australian Department of Foreign Affairs Lecturer in India, 1970, 1981, Malaysia, 1972, 1980, and Europe, 1981, 1983, 1984. **Awards:** Australian National University Creative Arts fellowship, Canberra, 1968; Commonwealth Literary Fund fellowship, 1970; Literature Board fellowship, 1973, 1976, 1982, 1986, 1990; Grace Leven prize, 1974; Miles Franklin award, Australian Natives Association award, and Barbara Ramsden award, all for novel, 1982; Victorian Premier's literary award, for novel, 1989. **Address:** c/o Penguin Books, P.O. Box 257, Ringwood, Victoria 3134, Australia.

PUBLICATIONS

Poetry

Penniless till Doomsday. London, Outposts, 1962.
Four Poets, with others. Melbourne, Cheshire, 1962.
Forty Beads on a Hangman's Rope: Fragments of Memory. Newnham, Tasmania, Wattle Grove Press, 1963.
Eyewitness. Sydney, South Head Press, 1967.
The Autobiography of a Gorgon. Melbourne, Cheshire, 1968.
The Law of Karma: A Progression of Poems. Canberra, Australian National University Press, 1968.
Heaven, In a Way. St. Lucia, University of Queensland Press, 1970.
A Soapbox Omnibus. St. Lucia, University of Queensland Press, 1973.
Selected Poems. St. Lucia, University of Queensland Press, 1975.
Black Bagatelles. St. Lucia, University of Queensland Press, 1978.
The Most Beautiful World: Fictions and Sermons. St. Lucia, University of Queensland Press, 1981.

Recording: *Romulus and Remus,* University of Queensland Press, 1971

Play

A Return to the Brink. Sydney, Currency Press, 1999.

Novels

The Ship on the Coin: A Fable of the Bourgeoisie. St. Lucia, University of Queensland Press, 1972.
A Place among People. St. Lucia, University of Queensland Press, 1975.
Just Relations. Ringwood, Victoria, Penguin, 1982; London, Allen Lane, and New York, Viking Press, 1983.
Kisses of the Enemy. Ringwood, Victoria, Penguin, 1987; New York, Farrar Straus, 1988; London, Faber, 1989.
Captivity Captive. Melbourne, McPhee Gribble, New York, Farrar Straus, and London, Faber, 1988.
Just Relations. London and Boston, Faber, 1990.
The Second Bridegroom. Ringwood, Victoria, McPhee Gribble, and London, Faber, 1991.
The Grisly Wife. Sydney, Macmillan, and London, Faber, 1993.
A Dream More Luminous than Love: The Yandilli Trilogy. Sydney, Picador Australia, 1994; New York, Noonday Press, 1995.

Other

Social Services and the Aborigines, with Shirley Andrews. Canberra, Federal Council for Aboriginal Advancement, 1963.

Focus on Andrew Sibley. Brisbane, University of Queensland Press, 1968.

J.S. Manifold: An Introduction to the Man and His Work. Brisbane, University of Queensland Press, 1978.

Australia, Image of a Nation, 1850–1950, with David Moore. Sydney, Collins, 1983.

Journey through Australia. Richmond, Victoria, Heinemann, and London, Murray, 1989; as *Home, A Journey through Australia.* Port Melbourne, Minerva, 1990.

The Island in the Mind. Sydney, Macmillan, 1996.

Abolish the States!: Australia's Future and a $30 Billion Answer to Our Tax Problem. Sydney, Pan Macmillan Australia, 1998.

Editor, with Thomas W. Shapcott, *New Impulses in Australian Poetry.* Brisbane, University of Queensland Press, 1968.

Editor, *Australian Poetry 1970.* Sydney, Angus and Robertson, 1970.

Editor, *Poems from Prison.* Brisbane, University of Queensland Press, 1973.

Editor, *Australians Aware: Poems and Paintings.* Sydney, Ure Smith, 1975.

Editor, *Voyage into Solitude,* by Michael Dransfield. Brisbane, University of Queensland Press, 1978.

Editor, *The Second Month of Spring,* by Michael Dransfield. Brisbane, University of Queensland Press, 1980.

Editor, *The Collins Book of Australian Poetry.* Sydney, Collins, 1981; London, Collins, 1983.

Editor, *Collected Poems* by Michael Dransfield. St. Lucia, University of Queensland Press, 1987.

*

Critical Studies: ''Three Australian Poets'' by Margaret Diesendorf, in *Creative Moment* (Sumter, South Carolina), 1(2), 1972; by Jim Davidson, in *Meanjin* (Parkville, Victoria), 40(3), October 1981; '''The Parables of Life Are Life': Rodney Hall, Poet and Novelist'' by Heimo Ertl, in *Voices from Distant Lands: Poetry in the Commonwealth,* edited by Konrad Gross and Wolfgang Klooss, Wurzburg, Konigshausen and Neumann, 1983; interview with Felicity Plunkett, in *Australian and New Zealand Studies in Canada* (Prince George, British Columbia), 11, June 1994; by Susanne Braun-Bau, in *Anglistik* (Wurzburg, Germany), 8(2), September 1997; in *In Other Words: Interviews with Australian Poets* edited by Barbara Williams, Amsterdam, Netherlands, Rodopi, 1998.

Rodney Hall comments:

I suppose the only way I would be prepared to describe my own work is to say that it is basically nonconfessional. It is my hope that each poem may take on an independent life of its own. If this is possible, the emotional experience, it would seem to me, becomes available to the reader in a far more pure and direct form than is generally possible with confessional poetry, where the poet as a person perpetually obtrudes and everything is limited to his vision of himself. My experiences are nearly always projected into imaginary situations, often in an attempt to relate them back to that skeleton of our worldview, legends and myths.

I have also concentrated on a special form, which I call a progression. This consists of many short poems, each capable of standing alone, tightly interrelated so that they become something akin to a single long poem with all the peaks left in and the discursive passages cut. I have published five of these progressions so far. The average length is forty poems, the largest is sixty-six.

*　　*　　*

Of the Australian poets who came to prominence in the early 1960s, only Rodney Hall and Bruce Beaver have achieved a fully creative integration in their work of the two opposed cultural stress points of the 1960s and the 1970s. Further, the work of Beaver in the 1960s is more peripheral to its period than is Hall's output of early maturity.

Penniless till Doomsday, published in England in 1962, aroused immediate attention in Hall's adopted country of Australia. Its qualities of wit, wry appraisal, and implicit social involvement were exactly what Australia was seeking in the new decade—a way out of the cultural impasse of tired regionalism and provincial introversion that was the thinning out of the energies of the so-called new *Bulletin* school in the 1940s and the caution and intellectual sloth of the 1950s. Hall was one of the contributors to *Four Poets* (1962), the collection that made an important claim for a new group of Brisbane poets at a time when Sydney was being challenged by Melbourne as the center of Australian poetry. Hall's regional, or Brisbane, associations were essentially peripheral to his real poetic concerns, however, which were ambitiously developed in his succeeding volumes.

Hall has been a prolific writer, and his collections reveal a restless and sometimes strenuously alert intelligence preoccupied by the allure of invention. *Eyewitness* holds on to models of detachment and observation, and some of its individual poems still attack the reader with their terse exactitude and surprise. But the two extended sequences *The Autobiography of a Gorgon* and *The Law of Karma* present, in a very real way, the culmination of the 1960s in Australian poetry. *The Autobiography of a Gorgon,* shorter, encapsuled in a tight case of irony and deliberate self-regard, is, I contend, the masterpiece of its decade. *The Law of Karma* is a deliberate attempt at a schematic poem, but its self-conscious virtuosity mitigates against its final effect, substituting the power to impress for the power to move. Yet it remains a minefield of expressive force. The 1970s emphasized the impromptu and the immediate in poetry, but *The Law of Karma* is deliberate, terrifyingly insistent upon inexorable processes. In a sense it codifies the very order that was, in the year of its composition and publication, to be overthrown by a new generation.

It is interesting to note that Hall, as poetry editor for the national newspaper the *Australian,* was to become central in recognizing the emerging forces of the succeeding generation of poets and in making their work available. *The Law of Karma* is built upon a premise of social observation and indeed responsibility, something the oncoming Generation of '68 (as it has retrospectively been termed) was to make central in its concerns, tightened by the commitment of the Australian government of the day to conscription for Vietnam. Hall's next two books, *Heaven, In a Way* and *A Soapbox Omnibus,* can now be seen as transition pieces, in which the poet is acutely sensitive to the dynamics of life around him and is finally bounded by his very virtuosity of technical accomplishment. Although many of the pieces here are almost rigid in their cleverness, many are acutely moving in their interplay of tensions, and the poet tries out various structures and forms to weld together his intellectual and his responsive abilities in confrontation with this turning point in the culture's history. "Folk Tales," the concluding sequence of *A Soapbox Omnibus,* points decisively to a pedal point in Hall's work.

Selected Poems is perhaps the most remarkable of its kind in Australian literary history, for nearly half of it is given over to a long new sequence ("The Owner of My Face") that would seem almost entirely unprepared for in any of the earlier work. Hall had very early on developed what he called a "progression" of poems, *The Law of Karma* being the most fully extended of these. But "The Owner of My Face" broke radical new ground in that it explored states of subjective being and intuitive response in almost direct opposition to his prior command of authorial irony and interplay of controlled nuances ("walking the tightrope of passion and detachment," he once called it). *Black Bagatelles* expands further this area of subjective vulnerability in Hall's work but with important modifications. His sense of theater, of event, is given free play (the work is a series of dialogues with death), and his sense of irony is counterpointed, often brilliantly, with the very willingness to be "open" that is at the heart of the 1970s exploration. It is a work that allows Hall's brilliance and deep humanity full play and interplay. It is also a work of deep pain, one of the high points of the decade in Australian poetry.

Since *Black Bagatelles,* Hall has concentrated on writing fiction, and even his 1981 collection, *The Most Beautiful World,* is subtitled *Fictions and Sermons.* It is, in fact, what many readers would consider to fall into the admittedly unsatisfactory genre of prose poems. Certainly the short, lyrical prose invention seems a logical extension of the long lines and elastic cadence of his previous collection, and Hall's characteristic wit and satiric twist of phrase often have a lacerating effect in these short, sometimes energetic, sometimes theatrical essays in brevity and manipulation. In a sense they look forward to the remarkable lyrical prose of his acclaimed novel *Captivity Captive,* a work that seems much closer to poetry than to mere narrative.

—Thomas W. Shapcott

HALPERN, Daniel

Nationality: American. **Born:** Syracuse, New York, 11 September 1945. **Education:** San Francisco State College, 1963–64; California State University, Northridge, 1966–69, B.A. in psychology 1969; Columbia University, New York (Woolrich Fellow), 1970–72, M.F.A. 1972. **Family:** Married Jeanne Catherine Carter in 1982. **Career:** Since 1969 editor, *Antaeus* magazine, New York; since 1971 editor-in-chief, and since the 1990s editorial director, Ecco Press, New York; since 1978 founder and director, National Poetry Series, New York. Freelance editor, Bobbs-Merrill publishers, New York, 1971–81; founding editor, *The Pushcart Prize: Best of the Small Presses.* Teacher, American School, and Spanish School, both Tangier, Morocco, 1969; instructor, New School for Social Research, New York, 1971–76; visiting professor, Princeton University, New Jersey, 1975–76, 1987–88, 1995–96. Since 1976 associate professor, and since 1978 chair, Columbia University School of the Arts. **Awards:** Rehder award (*Southern Poetry Review*), 1971; YM-YWHA Discovery award, 1971; National Endowment for the Arts fellowship, 1974, 1975, 1987; Bread Loaf Writers Conference Robert Frost fellowship, 1974; Creative Artists Public Service grant, 1978; Guggenheim

fellowship, 1988–89. **Address:** The Ecco Press, 10 East 53ʳᵈ Street, New York, New York 10022, U.S.A.

PUBLICATIONS

Poetry

Traveling on Credit. New York, Viking Press, 1972.
The Keeper of Height (as Angela McCabe). New York, Barlenmir House, 1974.
The Lady Knife-Thrower. Binghamton, New York, Bellevue Press, 1975.
Treble Poets 2, with Gerda Mayer and Florence Elon. London, Chatto and Windus, 1975.
Street Fire. New York, Viking Press, 1975.
Life among Others. New York, Viking Press, 1978.
Seasonal Rights. New York, Viking Press, 1982.
Tango. New York, Viking, 1987.
Foreign Neon. New York, Knopf, 1991.
Selected Poems. New York, Knopf, 1994.
Something Shining. New York, Knopf, 1999.

Recordings: *Louise Gluck and Daniel Halpern Reading Their Poems,* Gertrude Clarke Whittal Poetry and Literature Fund, Library of Congress, 1990.

Other

The Good Food: Soups, Stews, and Pasta, with Julie Strand. New York, Viking, 1985.
Halpern's Guide to the Essential Restaurants of Italy. Reading, Massachusetts, Addison-Wesley, 1990.

Editor, with Norman Thomas di Giovanni and Frank MacShane, *Borges on Writing.* New York, Dutton, 1973; London, Allen Lane, 1974.
Editor, *The American Poetry Anthology.* Boulder, Colorado, Westview Press, 1975.
Editor, *The Art of the Tale: An International Anthology of Short Stories 1945–1985.* New York, Viking, 1986; as *The Penguin Book of International Short Stories 1945–1985,* London, Penguin, 1989.
Editor, *The Antaeus Anthology.* New York, Bantam, 1986.
Editor, *On Nature: Nature, Landscape, and Natural History.* Berkeley, California, North Point Press, 1987; as *On Nature,* London, Collins, 1989.
Editor, *On Reading.* New York, Ecco Press, 1987; London, Collins, 1989.
Editor, *Literature as Pleasure.* New York, Ecco Press, 1987; London, Collins, 1990.
Editor, with Joyce Carol Oates, *Reading the Fights.* New York, Holt Rinehart, 1988.
Editor, *Writers on Artists.* Berkeley, California, North Point Press, 1988.
Editor, *Our Private Lives: Journals, Notebooks, and Diaries.* New York, Vintage, 1989; as *Journals, Notebooks, and Diaries,* London. Collins. 1989.
Editor, *Plays in One Act.* Hopewell, New Jersey, Ecco Press, 1991.

Editor, with Joyce Carol Oates, *Sophisticated Cat: A Gathering of Stories, Poems, and Miscellaneous Writings about Cats.* New York, Dutton, 1992.

Editor, *The Autobiographical Eye,* with illustrations by John Sokol. Hopewell, New Jersey, Ecco Press, 1993.

Editor, *Too Far from Home: The Selected Writings of Paul Bowles.* Hopewell, New Jersey, Ecco Press, 1993.

Editor, *Dante's Inferno: Translations by Twenty Contemporary Poets.* Hopewell, New Jersey, Ecco Press, 1993.

Editor, *Not for Bread Alone: Writers on Food, Wine, and the Art of Eating.* Hopewell, New Jersey, Ecco Press, 1993.

Editor, *Nine Visionary Poets and the Quest for Enlightenment.* New York, HarperCollins, 1994.

Editor, with Jeanne Wilmot Carter, *On Music.* Hopewell, New Jersey, Ecco Press, 1994.

Editor, *Who's Writing This?: Notations on the Authorial I, with Self Portraits.* Hopewell, New Jersey, Ecco Press, 1994.

Translator, *Songs of Mririda, Courtesan of the High Atlas,* by Mririda n' Ait Attik. Greensboro, North Carolina, Unicorn Press, 1974.

*

Critical Study: ''The Elegies of Style'' by Richard Jackson, in *Georgia Review* (Athens, Georgia), 42(4), winter 1988.

*   *   *

Highly educated, moderately successful as an author, editor, and translator, Daniel Halpern is caught in the alienation, isolation, and yearning for spontaneous feeling that incites much contemporary poetry. ''The Ethnic Life,'' the first poem in his first book of poetry, *Traveling on Credit,* begins, ''I've been after the exotic / For years,'' and ends, ''For years I've lived simply / Without luxury— / With the soundness of the backward / Where the senses can be heard.'' The headlong rush to identify the ethnic and exotic with the simple leaves Halpern stranded between objective sensations and subjective feelings.

Traveling on Credit and *Street Fire* are carefully arranged into sections by topic: places are seen with a fine precision of mood; the vagaries of affection between men and women rise up out of stillness; and the small rituals of daily life and social gatherings ward off larger fears. The language of both books hews to a clear speech neither too idiomatic nor too elevated, set in lines of regular length. Throughout, Halpern aims at a middle road, oscillating between melancholy lyricism and bemused objectivity.

Wary of extremes in emotional life and of the norms of accepted tradition, Halpern concentrates on the seductive pull of the imagination. ''Aubade,'' from *Life among Others,* modifies its traditional form by being neither particularly joyous, wholly of the morning, nor precisely of lovers parting. It begins at night with the lovers going to bed: ''It is when I fall to dream in your arms / that I climb into the arms of another: / . . . until I am back again beside you / in the first light, the morning of the different day.'' The protagonist of Halpern's poems is a man to whom life has come easily; this ease, however, has spawned a restless investigation into the ambiguities and difficulties of communication.

Life among Others focuses directly on the dimensions of these difficulties, addressing openly the isolation that was held at arm's length in his earlier work. The first section puts into service the delicate atmospheric descriptions of *Traveling on Credit* to present the loneliness of the traveler's rooms:

> I sit in front of my window, I tempt
> the solitary lights that go on and off
> on the water: lights of boats, cape lights,
> the lights across the water. They pile up
> in darkness here. It is a collection, a pastime.
> Now I have the chance to speak—not to explain
> but to return everything—your bright lives
> rooted to nothing more than a light seen at a distance
> that diminishes as it moves closer and closer.

The desire for speech comes in such moments, but its consummation escapes him. The others remain nameless and faceless. The poems of the second section spring from memories and images, moments of pain and loss when the protagonist tries to accept his isolation or at least to understand it. The final four interconnected poems—''White Tent,'' ''White Train,'' ''White Contact,'' and ''I Am a Dancer''—envelope his isolation in a series of images:

> White, the color of clarity
> where nothing has to live.
> It matches everything and can go
> anywhere. It fits in and is nothing.
> White contact in a house where nothing
> is said.
>   The tent of dream
> is a privacy, the bird a way out,
> the train, power to keep on. I'm
> not really unpleasant, and there is no crime
> committed against others.

But this neat summary belies the strength of the attempt, and the sentences are too coolly structured to give us the feeling of a break in the protagonist's intellectual reserve. Despite this, the book is a clear step forward. Halpern seems a patient poet, and his patience may yet be further rewarded.

—Walter Bode

HAMBURGER, Michael (Peter Leopold)

Nationality: British. **Born:** Berlin, 22 March 1924; immigrated to England in 1933. **Education:** Attended schools in Germany; George Watson's School, Edinburgh; The Hall, Hampstead, London; Westminster School, London; Christ Church, Oxford, B.A. in modern languages, M.A. 1948. **Military Service:** Royal West Kent Regiment, then Royal Army Educational Corps, 1943–47: infantryman, non-commissioned officer, and lieutenant. **Family:** Married Ann File (the poet Anne Beresford, *q.v.*) in 1951 (divorced 1970, and remarried 1974); one son and two daughters. **Career:** Assistant lecturer in German, University College, London, 1952–55; lecturer, then reader in German, University of Reading, Berkshire, 1955–64; Florence Purington Lecturer, Mount Holyoke College, South Hadley,

Massachusetts, 1966–67; visiting professor, State University of New York, Buffalo, 1969, and Stony Brook, 1970, Wesleyan University, Connecticut, 1971, University of Connecticut, Storrs, 1972, University of California, San Diego, 1973, University of South Carolina, Columbia, 1973, Boston University, 1975, 1977, and University of Essex, Wivenhoe, 1978. **Awards:** Bollingen fellowship, 1959, 1965; German Academy Voss prize, for translation, 1964; Schlegel-Tieck prize, for translation, 1967, 1978, 1981; Arts Council translation prize, 1969; Levinson prize (Poetry, Chicago), 1972; Institute of Linguists Gold medal, 1977; Wilhelm-Heinse prize, 1978; European Poetry translation award, 1985; Goethe medal, 1986; Austrian State prize, for translation, 1988; European Translation prize, 1990; Holderlin prize, 1991; Petrarca prize, 1992. D.Litt.: University of East Anglia, Norwich, 1988. Honorary doctorate: Technische Universitat, Berlin, 1995. Fellow, Royal Society of Literature, 1972 (resigned 1986). O.B.E., 1992. **Address:** Marsh Acres, Middleton, Saxmundham, Suffolk IP17 3NH, England.

PUBLICATIONS

Poetry

Later Hogarth. London, Cope and Fenwick, 1945.
Flowering Cactus: Poems 1942–49. Aldington, Kent, Hand and Flower Press, 1950.
Poems 1950–1951. Aldington, Kent, Hand and Flower Press, 1952.
The Dual Site. New York, Poetry London-New York, 1957; London, Routledge, 1958.
Weather and Season: New Poems. London, Longman, and New York, Atheneum, 1963.
In Flashlight. Leeds, Northern House, 1965.
In Massachusetts. Menomonie, Wisconsin, Ox Head Press, 1967.
Feeding the Chickadees. London, Turret, 1968.
Travelling: Poems 1963–68. London, Fulcrum Press, 1969.
Penguin Modern Poets 14, with Alan Brownjohn and Charles Tomlinson. London, Penguin, 1969.
Home. Frensham, Surrey, Sceptre Press, 1969.
In Memoriam Friedrich Hölderlin. London, Menard Press, 1970.
Travelling I-V. London, Agenda, 1972.
Ownerless Earth: New and Selected Poems 1950–1972. Cheadle, Cheshire, Carcanet, and New York, Dutton, 1973.
Conversations with Charwomen. Rushden, Northamptonshire, Sceptre Press, 1973.
Babes in the Wood. Knotting, Bedfordshire, Sceptre Press, 1974.
Travelling VI. London, I.M., 1975.
Travelling VII. Luxembourg, Club 80, 1976.
Real Estate. London, Anvil Press Poetry, 1977.
Real Estate (collection). Manchester, Carcanet, 1977.
Palinode: A Poet's Progress. Knotting, Bedfordshire, Sceptre Press, 1977.
Moralities. Newcastle upon Tyne, Morden Tower, 1977.
Variations in Suffolk IV. Knotting, Bedfordshire, Sceptre Press 1980.
Variations. Manchester, Carcanet, 1981; Redding Ridge, Connecticut, Black Swan, 1983.
In Suffolk. Madley, Herefordshire, Five Seasons Press, 1982.
Collected Poems 1941–1983. Manchester, Carcanet, 1984.
Selected Poems. Manchester, Carcanet, 1988.
Trees. Llangynog, Embers Handpress, 1988.
Roots in the Air. London, Anvil Press, 1991.

Collected Poems 1941–1994. London, Anvil Press, 1995.
Late. London, Anvil Press, 1997.
Mr. Littlejoy: Rattlebag for the New Millennium. London, Katabasis, 1999.
Intersections: Shorter Poems 1994–1999. London, Anvil Press, 2000.

Plays

The Tower, adaptation of a play by Peter Weiss (produced New York, 1974).
Out of Estrangement, adaptation of a play by Ernst Jandl (produced Edinburgh, 1985). Published in *Comparative Criticism* (Cambridge), vol. 9, 1987.

Radio Play: *Struck by Apollo,* with Anne Beresford, 1965.

Other

Reason and Energy: Studies in German Literature. London, Routledge, and New York, Grove Press, 1957; revised edition, London, Weidenfeld and Nicolson, 1971; as *Contraries: Studies in German Literature,* New York, Dutton, 1971.
Hugo von Hofmannsthal: Zwei Studien. Göttingen, Sachse & Pohl, 1964; *Hofmannsthal:* Three Essays, Princeton, New Jersey, Princeton University Press, 1970; Cheadle, Cheshire, Carcanet, 1974.
From Prophecy to Exorcism: The Premises of Modern German Literature. London, Longman, 1965.
Zwischen den Sprachen: Essays und Gedichte. Frankfurt, Fischer, 1966.
The Truth of Poetry: Tensions in Modern Poetry from Baudelaire to the 1960's. London, Weidenfeld and Nicolson, 1969; New York, Harcourt Brace, 1970.
A Mug's Game: Intermittent Memoirs 1924–1954. Cheadle, Cheshire, Carcanet, 1973.
Art as Second Nature: Occasional Pieces 1950–1974. Manchester, Carcanet, 1975.
Literarische Erfahrungen: Aufsätze (essays). Darmstadt, Luchterhand, 1981.
A Proliferation of Prophets: Essays on German Writers from Nietzsche to Brecht. Manchester, Carcanet, 1983; New York, St. Martin's Press, 1984.
After the Second Flood: Essays on Post-War German Literature. Manchester, Carcanet, and New York, St. Martin's Press, 1986.
Testimonies: Selected Shorter Prose 1950–1987. Manchester, Carcanet. 1989.
String of Beginnings: Intermittent Memoirs 1924–1954. London, Skoob Books, 1991.
M.H. in Conversation with Peter Dale. London, Between the Lines, 1998.

Editor and Translator, *Beethoven: Letters, Journals, and Conversations.* London, Thames and Hudson, and New York, Pantheon, 1951; revised edition, London, Cape, 1966; revised edition, Thames and Hudson, 1984.
Editor, and Translator with others, *Poems and Verse Plays,* by Hugo von Hofmannsthal. New York, Pantheon, and London, Routledge, 1961.
Editor and Translator, with Christopher Middleton, *Modern German Poetry, 1910–1960: An Anthology with Verse Translations.* London, MacGibbon and Kee, and New York, Grove Press, 1962.

Editor, and Translator with others, *Selected Plays and Libretti,* by Hugo von Hofmannsthal. New York, Pantheon, and London, Routledge, 1963.

Editor, *Das Werk: Sonette, Lieder, Erzählungen,* by Jesse Thoor. Frankfurt, Europäische Verlagsanstalt, 1965.

Editor and Translator, *East German Poetry: An Anthology in German and English.* Oxford, Carcanet, and New York, Dutton, 1972.

Editor, *Selected Poems,* by Thomas Good. London, St. George's Press, 1973.

Translator, *Poems,* by Hölderlin. London, Nicholson and Watson, 1943; revised edition, as *Hölderlin: His Poems,* London, Harvill Press, 1952; New York, Pantheon, 1953; revised edition, as *Selected Verse,* London, Penguin, 1961; revised edition, as *Poems and Fragments,* London, Routledge, 1966; Ann Arbor, University of Michigan Press, 1967; revised edition, Cambridge, Cambridge University Press, 1980; revised edition, as *Hölderlin: Selected Verse,* London, Anvil Press Poetry, 1986; enlarged and revised edition, 1994.

Translator, *Twenty Prose Poems of Baudelaire.* London, Editions Poetry London, 1946; revised edition, London, Cape, 1968; San Francisco, City Lights, 1988.

Translator, *Decline: 12 Poems,* by Georg Trakl. St. Ives, Cornwall, Latin Press, 1952.

Translator, *The Burnt Offering,* by Albrecht Goes. New York, Pantheon, and London, Gollancz, 1956.

Translator, *Egmont,* by Goethe, in Classic Theatre 2, edited by Eric Bentley. New York, Doubleday, 1959.

Translator, with Yvonne Kapp, *Tales from the Calendar,* by Bertolt Brecht. London, Methuen, 1961.

Translator, with Christopher Middleton, *Selected Poems,* by Günter Grass. London, Secker and Warburg, and New York, Harcourt Brace, 1966.

Translator, *Poems,* by Hans Magnus Enzensberger. Newcastle upon Tyne, Northern House, 1966.

Translator, *Lenz,* by Georg Büchner, with *Immensee* by Theodor Storm and *A Village Romeo and Juliet* by Gottfried Keller. London, Calder and Boyars, 1966; in *Leonce and Lena, Lenz, Woyzeck,* 1972.

Translator, with others, *O the Chimneys,* by Nelly Sachs. New York, Farrar Straus, 1967; as *Selected Poems, Including the Verse Play "Eli,"* London, Cape, 1968.

Translator, with Jerome Rothenberg and the author, *Poems for People Who Don't Read Poems* by Hans Magnus Enzensberger. New York, Atheneum, and London, Secker and Warburg, 1968; as *Poems,* London, Penguin, 1968.

Translator, *And Really Frau Blum Would Very Much Like to Meet the Milkman: 21 Short Stories,* by Peter Bichsel. London, Calder and Boyars, 1968.

Translator, *Journeys: Two Radio Plays: The Rolling Sea at Setubal, The Year Lacertis,* by Günter Eich. London, Cape, 1968.

Translator, with Christopher Middleton, *Poems,* by Günter Grass. London, Penguin, 1969.

Translator, with Matthew Mead, *The Seeker and Other Poems,* by Nelly Sachs. New York, Farrar Straus, 1970.

Translator, *Stories for Children,* by Peter Bichsel. London, Calder and Boyars, 1971.

Translator, with Christopher Middleton, *Selected Poems,* by Paul Celan. London, Penguin, 1972.

Translator, *Lenz, Leonce and Lena, Woyzeck,* by Georg Büchner. Chicago, University of Chicago Press, 1972.

Translator, *Selected Poems,* by Peter Huchel. Manchester, Carcanet, 1974.

Translator, *German Poetry 1910–1975.* Manchester, Carcanet, 1977; New York, Persea, 1981.

Translator, with Christopher Middleton, *In the Egg and Other Poems,* by Günter Grass. New York Harcourt Brace, 1977; London, Secker and Warburg, 1978.

Translator, *Texts,* by Helmut Heissenbüttel. London, Boyars, 1977.

Translator, with André Lefevere, *Seedtime (La Semaison): Extracts from the Notebooks 1954–1967,* by Philippe Jaccottet. New York, New Directions, 1977.

Translator, *Poems,* by Franco Fortini. Todmorden, Lancashire, Art, 1978.

Translator, *Poems,* by Paul Celan. Manchester, Carcanet, and New York, Persea, 1980.

Translator, *An Unofficial Rilke: Poems 1912–1926.* London, Anvil Press Poetry, 1981; as *Poems 1912–1926,* Redding Ridge, Connecticut, Black Swan, 1982.

Translator, *Urworte Orphisch: Five Poems,* by Goethe. London, Klaus Meyer, 1982.

Translator, *Selected Poems,* by Marin Sorescu. Newcastle upon Tyne, Bloodaxe, 1983.

Translator, *Poems and Epigrams,* by Goethe. London, Anvil Press Poetry, 1983; as *Roman Elegies and Other Poems,* Redding Ridge, Connecticut, Black Swan, 1983.

Translator, *The Garden of Theophrastus and Other Poems,* by Peter Huchel. Manchester, Carcanet, 1983.

Translator, with Marlis Zeller Cambon, *The Blue Man and Other Stories,* by Adolf Muschg. New York, Braziller, 1985.

Translator, *Thirty-two Poems,* by Paul Celan. Norwich, Embers Handpress, 1985.

Translator, *Poems of Paul Célan.* London, Anvil Press Poetry, 1988; New York, Persea, 1989; enlarged and revised edition, 1994.

Translator, *Pigeons and Moles. Selected Writings of Günter Eich.* London, Skoob Books, 1991.

Translator, with Hans Magnus Enzensberger, *Selected Poems: Hans Magnus Enzensberger.* Newcastle upon Tyne, Bloodaxe, 1994.

Translator, *Wolf's-Bean,* by Paul Celan. Birmingham, Delis Press, and New York, William Dienttel, 1997.

Translator, *Novemberland: Selected Poems 1956–1993,* by Günter Grass. New York, Harcourt Brace, 1996.

Translator, *Selected Poems,* by Günter Grass. London, Faber, 1998.

Translator, *Kiosk,* by Hans Magnus Enzensberger. Newcastle upon Tyne, Bloodaxe, 1998; New York, Sheep Meadow Press, 1999.

Translator, *Selected Poems and Fragments,* by Friedrich Hölderlin. London, Penguin, 1998.

*

Manuscript Collections: University of Texas, Austin; Lockwood Memorial Library, State University of New York, Buffalo; University of Reading, Berkshire; Brotherton Library, University of Leeds.

Critical Studies: "The Subject beneath the Subject" by the author, in *Christian Science Monitor* (Boston), 31 January 1967; "Across Frontiers: Michael Hamburger as Poet and Critic" by Jon Glover, in *Stand* (Newcastle upon Tyne), 1970; "Rhythm" by the author, in *Agenda* (London), 10(4)-11(1), 1972–1973; "More New Poetry" by

Terry Eagleton, in *Stand* (Newcastle upon Tyne), 1973; "Forward, Ay, and Backward" by Martin Dodsworth, in *The Guardian* (London), 5 April 1973; "Ownerless Earth" by Donald Davie, in *New York Times Book Review,* 28 April 1974; "Travellers" by John Matthias, in *Poetry* (Chicago), April 1974; "The Chronicler and the Poet: Michael Hamburger at 50" by Joyce Crick, in *Poetry Nation 3* (Manchester), 1974; chapter on Michael Hamburger, in *An Introduction to Fifty Modern British Poets,* edited by Michael Schmidt, London, Pan, 1979; Michael Hamburger issue of *Agenda* (London), 35(3), 1997.

* * *

Michael Hamburger's is a poetry of ideas made as sensuous as possible by being passed through images of nature, tinged frequently with a decent, uncloying melancholy. The turning point in his poetry is made in *Weather and Season,* in which the traditionally metrical and rhyming forms have almost entirely been disbanded. As he stated in a reading he gave at the University of Iowa in 1969 (and I paraphrase), "In my previous books I used the traditional forms to protect myself from the pressure and intensity of my feelings; whereas I subsequently came to feel that, in writing the later poems, I no longer wished to evade or mask these feelings." This frank, direct criticism of an earlier stance, together with his decision to shuck off the incrustations of such forms, has brought rewards.

The poetry has two contexts. One is that of men socialized into a dilemma that may be resolved only by using the charged moral conscience ("In a Cold Season"); the other context is nature. Although one critic has justly pointed to some affinity with Edward Thomas, I suggest that Hamburger is no more a nature poet than Thomas is. In *New Bearings* Leavis indicated that for Thomas nature was used as the arena of delicate and scrupulous psychological reenactments, and for Hamburger this is also valid. Many of the poems in his pamphlet *In Flashlight* cohere to form an exploration of the use and stamina of memory. A capacity for valuation, issuing directly from responsive memory that absorbs the two nodes of experience, seen here as change through exploration and settled recurrence, is examined in "Tides" and "The Road" (*Weather and Season).* In the latter memory is the recognizing faculty by which the conscious mind penetrates its unconscious to find natural images built there into an ideal country—an absolute, alluring and unattainable—and one that the teller does "not look for . . . when awake."

The question of identity, subsumed in the role of the poet in "Man of the World" *(Weather and Season),* is more inclusively embodied in "The Search" *(Weather and Season).* In the search, "as commanded," the familiar country of the man's origins is discovered as alien, and when, through tracts of nature, he reaches the village, the symbolic ideal is released to him, to be discovered as actual, in its quality as "Why, Mors, need we tell you, mors, MORS." As expected, this is the last poem of *Weather and Season.*

The extrapolation from biography to criticism is dubious, but I think it is relevant here to indicate that Hamburger is a Jew of German birth and that with most of his family he emigrated to England in the year of Hitler's rise to power, thus averting the Nazi Holocaust. Hamburger is acutely fitted to write such a poem as "The Search," with all of its narrower, more defined implications. It is the Jewish component of this poet that hiddenly but with integrated power explores the landscape of nature and village and finds that the searcher discovers his origins and death to be identical. The same qualification permits him to write of the issues of conscience in relation to Adolf Eichmann.

Eliot has declared in another context that "humankind cannot bear very much reality," but it is Hamburger's alert and intelligent contention that it is the burden of humanity as well as its necessary precondition for survival that it use language as searchingly as possible, with a faithful rendering of the referents in experience and interpretation of them. Mercy, honesty, and perception are in this context integral: "Dare break one word and words may yet be whole." Hamburger's language is quiet and naturally spoken, even when he speaks of violence. The intensity of the poetry is in the unextraordinary and seemingly nonmanipulative but exact use of ordinary language—"the sea, that basher of dumb rock"—and its unassumingly painful exploration of painful experience ("For a Family Album"). Metaphoric imagery is used rarely. The images are visually referential, or else the metaphors live in consideration of the metaphysical data as if the data were actual or physically tangible. They are fed through hovering, tentative but persistent rhythms fitted to their unrhymed, speech-molded cadences.

Hamburger has shown a preference for the comforting rural (or even cultivated) natural phenomena of creature and plant. This desire for their presence has continued. It is this poet's matrix on which everything else is sounded and often judged. Perhaps such a preference accounts in part for the slow-moving rhythms of much of his verse.

With the possible exception of "In a Cold Season," the title poem of *Travelling* is the seed of Hamburger's most interesting, ambitious, and sustained poem. In this early version the poem is in two sections. In *Real Estate* the poem has a third section, and the whole has become the first of a suite of eleven poems under the same title. In the "Envoi" to *Travelling* Hamburger wrote, "Goodbye, words . . . / Go out and lose yourselves in a jabbering world, / Be less than nothing." The injunction is only half true for Hamburger. The "jabbering world" of which he complains has in the full version of "Travelling" become more acutely judged, an earth committed to human acquisition and possession. It is a human world that must give up what it possesses in order to enter into what cannot be possessed although supremely desired—love given to and received from another: "The place that, holding you still, / Could fill and affirm your name." "Still" means both unmoving and a condition continuous in time. Travelling involves the need for a fixed point of return, as with the compasses image in Donne's "A Valediction: Forbidding Mourning." At this point one realizes that to be in this "place" is not to possess it ("Ownerless Earth"): "Last of my needs, you / I'll unlearn, relinquish / If that was love. Too late, / Let you go, return, stay / And move on."

The close-grained, almost possessed energy of Hamburger's earlier poems tends in "Travelling" to become something other. There is an almost invariably direct syntax and a greater rhythmical assurance both in line length and enjambments. Some of this assurance is obtained by a "likeable" repetition; there are pairs or triads of things—"sand, pebble, rock"; "On cobbles, on brick, on slabs"—or of verbs—"Propel, transmute; and create / again." In the last example development is described, not enacted. This triadic formation also tends to occur in the rhythmic structure of a line, producing a wavering, wavelike movement at once "tentative and persistent," and therein lies Hamburger's enacted argument with himself. Linguistically, the argument tends to get dissolved in a resolute search for and an achievement of clarity. The clarity sometimes irons out, or expunges, what one senses as greater tensions or antagonisms beneath the surface. The achievement of "Travelling," and its version in *Real Estate,* is, nevertheless, high and consistent. The long poem, a risk these days, sustains itself around the paradox of going and staying, of being fixed and moving, where abnegation and love form the field of the drama. Even the determination to be plain and understandable has for the reader a moving vulnerability; it may not be a central part of the poem, but it is a bonus, although surely not what the poet had meant us to observe—a struggling to "get it right."

In response to the 1995 poem "Surgical Ward" I would like to suggest three things. First, it is a poem of open sympathy for people confined, those who suffer disability, face long-term illness, or are near death. (There are possible analogies with these sufferers and the inmates of the camps.) Second, the tenacity implicit in Hamburger's work, but which is sometimes in danger of being diffused, emerges in exemplary fashion and more strongly than ever in this poem. It is a personal poem expressed with such compassionate drive as to make its localized experience widely applicable and to give the effect of distributing its care. It is also a personal expression of an impersonal apprehension and thereby acquires unusual strength. Third, this tenacity is expressed in the instinctual drive of the rhythms in the form of a norm of mixed trochaic and anapestic pentameter. Although the length of line is variable, the overall effect is of a metrical not a free verse poem.

Thus, the experience of others' suffering appears to have urged out lines of greater length than had earlier been the case with Hamburger, indicating a new range of possibilities for the poet:

That's inmate small-talk when histories are exchanged,
Men drink again from the mouth, risen again from their
    shackles.

One ventures out in quest of a cigarette
Grown monstrous, mythical here, like spirit, like fire,
In celebration of freedom, not health, regained
After the dead meat of thighs trussed for knife or laser . . . .

That "Men drink again from the mouth" is an exact notation of personal response to others' predicament, yet the definite article "the" against "mouth," rather than "their mouths," makes the single orifice into synecdoche, representative and sympathetic in the registering of its living operation.

—Jon Silkin

HAMILTON, (Robert) Ian

Nationality: British. **Born:** King's Lynn, Norfolk, 24 March 1938. **Education:** Darlington Grammar School; Keble College, Oxford (editor, *Tomorrow,* 1959–60), B.A. (honors) 1962. **Family:** Married 1) Gisela Dietzel in 1963, one son; 2) Ahdaf Soueif in 1981, two sons. **Career:** Co-founder and editor, *Review,* 1962–72, and *New Review,* 1974–79, London; poetry reviewer, *London Magazine,* 1962–64, and *The Observer,* London, 1965–70; poetry and fiction editor, *Times Literary Supplement,* London, 1965–73; lecturer in poetry, University of Hull, Yorkshire, 1972–73; presenter, *Bookmark* program, BBC Television, 1984–87. **Awards:** Eric Gregory award, 1963; Poetry Society of America Melville Cane award, 1983; English-Speaking

Union award, 1984. **Address:** 54 Queen's Road, London S.W.19, England.

PUBLICATIONS

Poetry

Pretending Not to Sleep. London, The Review, 1964.
The Visit. London, Faber, 1970.
Anniversary and Vigil. London, Poem-of-the-Month Club, 1971.
Returning. Privately printed, 1976.
Fifty Poems. London, Faber, 1988.
Steps: Poems. Tregarne, Manaccan, Cornwall, Cargo Press, 1997.
Sixty Poems. London, Faber, 1998.

Other

A Poetry Chronicle: Essays and Reviews. London, Faber, and New York, Barnes and Noble, 1973.
The Little Magazines: A Study of Six Editors. London, Weidenfeld and Nicolson, 1976.
Robert Lowell: A Biography. New York, Random House, 1982; London, Faber, 1983.
In Search of J.D. Salinger. London, Heinemann, and New York, Random House, 1988.
Writers in Hollywood 1915–1951. London, Heinemann, and New York, Harper, 1990.
Keepers of the Flame: Literary Estates and the Rise of Biography. London, Hutchinson, 1992; New York, Faber, 1994.
Gazza Italia. London, Granta Books, 1994.
Walking Possession: Essays & Reviews 1968–1983. London, Bloomsbury, 1994.
Gazza Agonistes. London, Bloomsbury, 1998.
The Trouble with Money and Other Essays. London, Bloomsbury, 1998.
A Gift Imprisoned: The Poetic Life of Matthew Arnold. London, Bloomsbury, 1998; New York, Basic Books, 1999.

Editor, *The Poetry of War, 1939–45.* London, Alan Ross, 1965.
Editor, *Selected Poetry and Prose,* by Alun Lewis. London, Allen and Unwin, 1966.
Editor, *The Modern Poet: Essays from "The Review."* London, Macdonald, 1968; New York, Horizon Press, 1969.
Editor, *Eight Poets.* London, Poetry Book Society, 1968.
Editor, *Selected Poems,* by Robert Frost. London, Penguin, 1973.
Editor, with Colin Falck, *Poems since 1900: An Anthology of British and American Verse in the Twentieth Century.* London, Macdonald and Jane's, 1975.
Editor, *Yorkshire in Verse.* London, Secker and Warburg, 1984.
Editor, *The "New Review" Anthology.* London, Heinemann, 1985.
Editor, *Soho Square (2).* London, Bloomsbury, 1989.
Editor, *Oxford Companion to Twentieth-Century Poetry in English.* New York and Oxford, Oxford University Press, 1994.
Editor, *Robert Herrick: Selected Poems.* London, Bloomsbury, 1996.
Editor, *John Milton: Selected Poems.* London, Bloomsbury, 1996.
Editor, *John Clare: Selected Poems.* London, Bloomsbury, 1996.
Editor, *Love Sonnets.* London, Bloomsbury, 1997.
Editor, *Elegies.* London, Bloomsbury, 1997.
Editor, *Odes.* London, Bloomsbury, 1997.

Editor, *George Herbert: Selected Poems*. London, Bloomsbury, 1997.
Editor, *Edward Lear: Selected Poems*. London, Bloomsbury, 1997.
Editor, *Charlotte Mew*. London, Bloomsbury, 1999.
Editor, *Edgar Allan Poe*. London, Bloomsbury, 1999.
Editor, *Henry Wadsworth Longfellow*. London, Bloomsbury, 1999.
Editor, *Algernon Charles Swinburne*. London, Bloomsbury, 1999.
Editor, *Geoffrey Chaucer*. London, Bloomsbury, 1999.
Editor, *The Penguin Book of Twentieth-Century Essays*. London, Allen Lane, 1999.

*

Critical Studies: By Peter Firchow, in *The Writer's Place: Interviews on the Literary Situation in Contemporary Britain,* Minneapolis, University of Minnesota Press, 1974; ''A Glimpse at Modern English Poetry'' by Thilo von Bremen, in *Fu Jen Studies* (Taipei, Taiwan), 14, 1981; ''Pity the Monster? Reflections on a Biography of Robert Lowell'' by Edward Neill, in *Critical Quarterly* (Oxford), 27(3), autumn 1985.

*   *   *

Ian Hamilton seemed, in the days when his poetry got as close to flourishing as it ever has, to be two contrasting individuals. On the one hand, he was a reviewer with a fearsome reputation, the inheritor of the Grigson billhook; did he not, after all, rumor said, once end a catchall review with ''Mr. —'s new book has a nice title''? On the other hand, he was a poet of such vulnerability that one wondered what would have happened had he reviewed his own ''Scent of Old Roses,'' a work that reminded many readers of Dowson and early Yeats, at least in the diction—all those hands, petals, and darkening rooms, all that blood and breath.

Hamilton himself recognizes the dichotomy:

I decided . . . to keep the whole business of 'my poetry'
quite separate from the rest of my so-called literary life: a
life of book reviews, biographies, anthologies and magazines . . .

Some said that when *The Visit* appeared in 1970 the generous reviewing that greeted it had something to do with fear of Hamilton—one might get reviewed in the next issue by this man—which was surely nonsense in a world as honorable as the London literary scene!

It also has to be said at the start that under the occasionally Dowsonesque surface there is a rhythmical sensitivity in Hamilton's poems, a rigorous commitment to emotional accuracy, a dynamic sense of learning going on within the choice of words. Like Michael Fried, whose *Powers* had made a deep impression on him, Hamilton explored the frighteningly intense moments of lives with a kind of glum courage. *The Visit* was a powerful book that had, and still has, an extraordinary influence.

At a time when reactions to the perception of the pain of being human were still recovering from Dylan Thomas's occasional facetiousness (''Isn't life a terrible thing, thank God''), various options were in use: whimsy in Liverpool and a system of destruction by drugs and alcohol in America. The most important talent of the time, Geoffrey Hill, chose to look at the world through history. Hamilton, however, who is thoroughly contemporary, offered something neither

self-regarding nor jokey nor obscure, and he did not suggest that long-term suicide with whiskey or heroin was the way of the writer.

In the poem ''The Recruits,'' for example, the poet watches himself and a mental patient, who is clearly someone loved, and the details—cats, dead flies, birds—all contribute to an evocation of a terrible calm before the next onslaught:

Birds line the gutters, and from our window
We see cats file across five gardens
To the shade and stand there, tense and sullen,
Watching the sky. You cry again: 'They know'.

The dead flies pile up on the window sill . . .

(I quote here from the version published in *The Visit.*)

Other poems in the book concern the death of the poet's father. In ''Father, Dying'' the white roses, while reminiscent of earlier writers, represent the man's fading life, and the effect is overpowering. The strength comes from brevity and reticence. The technique lets Hamilton down only occasionally, when a poem is perhaps only partly penetrable and frankly sentimental (''Epitaph'') or less than usually empathetic (''Complaint'').

With their air of having had much plotting and narrative cut away, it is always the shortest poems that are the most effective. They give the sense that what is here is what seriously counts and that if we want to be in touch with what it is like to be human we had better listen. This can be seen, for example, in ''Awakening'':

Your head, so sick, is leaning against mine,
So sensible. You can't remember
Why you're here, nor do you recognize
These helping hands.
My love,
The world encircles us. We're losing ground.

Hamilton is dismissive about the poems that came after *The Visit.* He describes them in the brief introduction to *Fifty Poems* as ''bruised rewrites of what I'd done before.'' To me, however, ''Bedtime Story,'' ''Ghosts,'' and ''In Dreams'' at least have irony and power, as well as the rhythmic tact and lyrical tenderness we have become used to. Other poems were a shock when they first appeared in the *Times Literary Supplement* and in *Review,* for they seemed decadent in a different sense from the fin de siècle one. They were poems in which Hamilton seemed anxious still to be writing poems but in which his reticence had dissolved into vagueness, his use of symbols—like green branches and red coats—having become self-parodying. The poems had the decadence, in other words, of a talent that had little to say.

The poem ''Larkinesque,'' for example, seems to have only superficial homage to pay to Larkin. It is an unsuccessful attempt to take material that had earlier been movingly personal and to place it in the public domain of a divorce court. The officialese, the slang, the vulgarity—none of this finds its place in Hamilton's more customary register, and the last line (''Now clutching a slim volume of dead writs'') seems a sad return to an earlier manner that no longer has any relevance.

The very arrival of *Fifty Poems* was thus a surprise to many of Hamilton's admirers, who had assumed that poetry had deserted him. This might have been expected because of his work in the field of biography, both utterly successful (in the case of Robert Lowell) and frustrated yet absorbing (J.D. Salinger). Indeed, much of Hamilton's energy during the past few years has been spent on biography and on writing and its implications generally, for example, the experience of authorship in Hollywood. His *Keepers of the Flame* explores issues of literary estates and sheds light on many issues of interest to the reader of modern poetry, including, obliquely, Hamilton's own verse.

Although Hamilton's poetic talent may be slender, he can be deeply moving when he is sure of his ground. One hopes for something to shove the work in a new direction so that in 2010 there might be a volume titled ''A Hundred Poems,'' the last part of which is evidence of new preoccupations.

—Fred Sedgwick

HAQ, Kaiser

Nationality: Bangladeshi. **Born:** Kaiser Mohamed Hamidul Haq, Dhaka, 7 December 1950. **Education:** University of Dhaka, Bangladesh, B.A. (honors) in English 1972, M.A. in English 1973; University of Warwick, England, Ph.D. in English literature 1981. **Military Service:** Bangladesh Liberation Army, 1971–72: 2nd lieutenant; War Medal, Campaign Star, Victory Medal. **Family:** Married Dipa Haq in 1976 (died 1999). **Career:** Lecturer, 1975–82, assistant professor, 1982–85, associate professor, 1985–91, and since 1991 professor, Department of English, University of Dhaka. Member, editorial board, *Form,* Dhaka, 1982–86, and *Art,* Dhaka, 1993–95; editor, *Dhaka University Studies,* 1999–2001. Judge, Commonwealth Writers prize, 1994, and biannual short story contest in English, Singapore National Arts Council, 1995; regional chairperson, Commonwealth Writers prize, 1996, 1997. **Awards:** Senior Fulbright scholarship, 1986–87; Vilas fellowship, 1987. **Address:** Department of English, University of Dhaka, Dhaka 1000, Bangladesh.

PUBLICATIONS

Poetry

Starting Lines. Dhaka, Liberty, 1978.
A Little Ado. Dhaka, Granthabithi, 1978.
A Happy Farewell. Dhaka, University Press Ltd., 1994.
Black Orchid. London, Aark Arts, 1996.

Other

Editor, *Contemporary Indian Poetry.* Ohio State University Press, 1990.

Translator, *Selected Poems of Shamsur Rahman.* Dhaka, BRAC, 1985.
Translator, *Quartet,* by Tagore. London, Heinemann, 1993.
Translator, *The Wonders of Vilayet.* Leeds, Peepal Tree Books, 1997.

*

Critical Studies: ''A Bard from Bangladesh'' by Khushwant Singh, in *Sunday* (Calcutta), November 1990; ''Kaiser Haq: Between Western Know-How and Eastern Wisdom'' by Niaz Zaman, in *Holiday* (Dhaka), 29 November 1991; ''Scholar Sees Cultural and Literary Possibilities in Change'' by Asad Latif, in *The Straits Times* (Singapore),

16 September 1995; ''On a Road Less Travelled By: Kaiser Haq's Poetry'' by Fakrul Alam, in *Daily Star* (Dhaka), December 1995; in *Journal of Commonwealth Literature,* 32(1), 1997.

*   *   *

While a significant number of Indian poets writing in English have achieved international reputations, their counterparts in neighboring Bangladesh are significantly fewer. Among them, Kaiser Haq is the only poet who has gained worldwide acclaim. A professor of English at the University of Dhaka, Haq came of age during one of the most tumultuous periods of modern South Asian history—the 1971 civil war between the two sections of Pakistan (East and West) and the emergence of Bangladesh from the former East Pakistan. Twenty-one at the time, Haq served as an officer in the Bangladesh Liberation Army, as did other young poets writing in Bengali, who later used the event as the mainspring of their patriotic and political verse. The only poem in Haq's first collection, *Starting Lines* (1978), to treat the event directly is ''Bangladesh '71.'' Startled by the brutality he has witnessed and perhaps even participated in, the speaker asks as ''smoky dusk falls like fear / Over stone and human heart / How, and with what, shall one create art?''

Otherwise, the poems in the collection show Haq as a spirited, self-assured observer of the urban landscape. Dhaka, the capital of Bangladesh, serves as the aesthetic focus of many of the poems, which depict the beauty but more often the squalor of this unmanageable sprawl of a metropolis. His images are always striking, especially the similes, and some are even profane to South Asian sensibilities; if they were written today, they might provoke the powerful orthodox to ban his works and perhaps even call for his arrest. In ''Two Trees and Time,'' for example, he writes, ''A minaret gleams in the distance / like a condom in full bloom.''

The collection *A Little Ado,* published simultaneously with the first, contains newer and, in many ways, more mature poems. Here Haq continues his romance with the city of Dhaka, especially with its cacophony and its pungent, even revolting, smells. The poems speak of the ''reek / of masses'' (''Street Incident''), of the call of children playing hide-and-seek at night, of birds and vehicles, of beggars and vendors, and of a couple pondering with fright the prospect of returning to the city after a brief respite in the peaceful countryside. Many of the poems also reveal a more political cast. Here irony abounds in the disparities between the rich and the poor and the beautiful—sometimes, but not always, the former—and the ugly. ''Fringe Benefit,'' for example, addresses the poverty of children, who seem to be more at ease with their plight than the putatively guilty middle-class man who gives them both his apologies and money. In ''Street Incident'' adult beggars ''thrill . . . / at the divine, imported fragrance'' of a pampered wealthy woman complaining of the heat as she dashes from an air-conditioned limousine to an air-conditioned store; the beggars ''loudly chant . . . / their praises of heaven'' in the wake she leaves.

A Happy Farewell (1994) offers poems from 1978 through 1993 as well as selected verses from Haq's first two collections. While some poems have as their traditional subject the monsoons, the rivers of Bangladesh, snake charmers, and yogis, the best are centered on the quotidian life of the extended family. In ''Moon,'' for example, ''Aunts in orgies of gossip / plough through mountains of betel, / outchewing a flock of goats,'' and the excitement of witnessing an infant nephew's first words in ''Baby Talk'' prompts the conclusion that ''language / is a / life-sentence.'' Some of the most unusual poems in the collection are written in what the author calls "subcontinental English," the variety of language used by South Asians whose command of idiom and vocabulary are, by textbook standards, nonstandard, a trend started by the Indian poet Nissim Ezekiel in the 1970s. "Civil Service Romance," in the style of a memo, is a love letter cluttered with office jargon and written to a woman new in an office by a veteran who invites her friendship. Sadly amusing, it expresses the desires and attraction of a lonely man unused to approaching women as equals, especially in the workplace, and attempting to stave off his ineptness and inexperience through the objectivity and force of officialese. Poems of this type have caused considerable negative reactions in academic and critical circles, although, in fact, such language is often used and even sanctioned.

Haq's published oeuvre is small, but it is possessed of an overall excellence that places him among his peers not only in South Asia but also in the contemporary world of letters. His poems are thoughtful, well-constructed works, frequently sinewy, often delicate, in which sensibility is matched by notable imagery and poignancy, and they are always reflective of the human condition in a part of the world where, even without civil war, it is not easy to make art.

—Carlo Coppola

HARJO, Joy

Nationality: American (Native American: Muscogee [Creek]). **Born:** Tulsa, Oklahoma, 9 May 1951. **Education:** University of New Mexico, Albuquerque, 1971–76, B.A. 1976; University of Iowa, Iowa City, 1976–78, M.F.A. 1978; Anthropology Film Center, Santa Fe, New Mexico, 1982. **Family:** One son and one daughter. **Career:** Instructor, Institute of American Indian Arts, Santa Fe, New Mexico, 1978–79, 1983–84; lecturer, Arizona State University, Tempe, 1980–81; assistant professor, University of Colorado, Boulder, 1985–88; associate professor, University of Arizona, Tucson, 1988–90; professor, University of New Mexico, Albuquerque, 1991–97. Since 1992 president, Two Red Horses, Inc., Albuquerque. Editor, *Americans before Columbus,* 1979–80; contributing editor since 1984, *Contact II,* and since 1985, *Tyuonyi;* poetry editor, 1986–89, and since 1989 poetry advisor, *High Plains Literary Review.* Writer-in-residence, New Mexico Poetry in the Schools Program, 1974–76, 1979, 1980; Navajo Community College, 1978; Flaming Rainbow University, Tahlequah, Oklahoma, 1978; State Arts Council of Oklahoma, 1980–81; Sacaton Public Schools, Gila Indian Reservation, 1981; University of Alaska Prison Project, Anchorage, 1981; Arizona Commission on the Arts, Paradise Valley Public School, 1981; Institute of Alaska Native Arts, Nome, 1984; Richard Hugo Chair, University of Montana, 1985; State University of New York, Stonybrook, 1987. Plays saxophone and performs poetry with her band, Poetic Justice. **Awards:** National Endowment of the Arts fellow, 1978, 1992; first place in poetry, Santa Fe Festival for the Arts, 1980; Arizona Commission on the Arts Creative Writing fellow, 1989; American Indian Distinguished Achievement award, 1990; William Carlos Williams award, Poetry Society of America, 1991; American Book award, Before Columbus Foundation, 1991; Josephine Miles Poetry award, 1991; Native Writers' Circle of American Lifetime Achievement award, 1995; Oklahoma Book Arts award, 1995, for *The Woman Who Fell from the Sky;* Delmore Schwartz

Memorial award, 1995, for *In Mad Love and War;* Mountains and Plains Booksellers award, 1995; Bravo award, Albuquerque Arts Alliance, 1996; Lila Wallace Readers' Digest Writers' award, 1998; Governor's award for excellence in arts, 1998. Honorary Doctorate: Benedictine College, 1992. Woodrow Wilson fellowship, Green Mountain College, 1993; Witter Bynner Poetry fellowship, 1994. **Agent:** Charlotte Sheedy, Sheedy Agency, New York, New York 10012, U.S.A. **Address:** Two Red Horses Inc., 1140 Alewa Drive, Apartment D, Honolulu, Hawaii 96817–1462, U.S.A.

PUBLICATIONS

Poetry

The Last Song. Las Cruces, New Mexico, Puerto del Sol Press, 1975.
What Moon Drove Me to This. New York, I. Reed Books, 1979.
She Had Some Horses. New York, Thunder's Mouth Press, 1985.
Secrets from the Center of the World (with prose and photographs). Tucson, University of Arizona Press, 1989.
In Mad Love and War. Middletown, Connecticut, Wesleyan University Press, 1990.
Fishing. Oxhead Press, 1992.
The Woman Who Fell from the Sky. New York, Norton, 1994.
A Map to the Next World: Poetry and Tales. New York, Norton, 2000.

Recordings: *Power of the Word* series, with Bill Moyers (videotape), 1989; *Furious Light,* Watershed, 1986; *The Woman Who Fell from the Sky,* Norton, 1994; *Letter from the End of the Twentieth Century,* Red Horses Records, 1996.

Screenplays: *The Gaan Story,* with Henry Greenberg, 1984; *The Beginning,* with Henry Greenberg, 1984.

Television Plays: *We Are One, Umonho,* 1984; *Maiden of Deception Pass,* 1985; *I Am Different from My Brother,* 1986; *The Runaway,* 1986.

Novel

The Good Luck Cat. San Diego, California, Harcourt Brace, 2000.

Other

Editor, with Laura Coltelli, *Spiral of Memory.* Ann Arbor, University of Michigan Press, 1995.
Editor, with Gloria Bird, *Reinventing the Enemy's Language: Contemporary Native Women's Writing of North America.* New York, Norton, 1997.

*

Critical Studies: "Paula Gunn Allen and Joy Harjo: Closing the Distance between Personal and Mythic Space" by Jim Ruppert, in *American Indian Quarterly* (Lincoln, Nebraska), 7(1), spring 1983; interview by Joseph Bruchac, in *North Dakota Quarterly* (Grand Forks, North Dakota), 53(2), spring 1985; "Earthly Relations, Carnal Knowledge: Southwestern American Indian Women Writers and Landscape" by Patricia Clark Smith and Paula Gunn Allen, in *The*

Desert Is No Lady: Southwestern Landscapes in Women's Writing and Art, edited by Vera Norwood and Janice Monk, New Haven, Connecticut, Yale University Press, 1987; "Notes toward a New Multicultural Criticism: Three Works by Women of Color" by John F. Crawford, in *A Gift of Tongues: Critical Challenges in Contemporary American Poetry,* edited by Marie Harris and Kathleen Aguero, Athens, University of Georgia Press, 1987; "Nightriding with Noni Daylight: The Many Horse Songs of Joy Harjo" by Andrew Wiget, in *Native American Literatures* (Pisa), 1, 1989; *Through Landscape toward Story/Through Story toward Landscape: A Study of Four Native American Women Poets* (dissertation) by Nancy Helene Lang, Indiana University of Pennsylvania, 1991; "Representing Real Worlds: The Evolving Poetry of Joy Harjo" by John Scarry, in *World Literature Today* (Norman, Oklahoma), 66(2), spring 1992; "'Twin Gods Bending Over': Joy Harjo and Poetic Memory" by Nancy Lang, in *MELIUS* (Amherst, Massachusetts), 18(3), fall 1993; "Dark Continent/Dark Woman: Transformation and Healing in the Work of Helene Cixous and Joy Harjo" by Kathleen McNerney Donovan, in *Native American Literatures,* edited by Laura Coltelli, Pisa, SEU, 1994; "Politics and the Personal Lyric in the Poetry of Joy Harjo and C.D. Wright" by Jenny Goodman, in *MELIUS* (Amherst, Massachusetts), 19(2), summer 1994; "New Dreaming: Joy Harjo, Wendy Rose, Leslie Marmon Silko" by Jeanne Perreault, in *Deferring a Dream: Literary Sub-Versions of the American Columbiad,* edited by Gert Buelens and Ernst Rudin, Basel, Switzerland, Birkhauser, 1994; "Knowing All the Way Down to Fire" by Elaine A. Jahner, in *Feminist Measures: Soundings in Poetry and Theory,* edited by Lynn Keller and Cristanne Miller, Ann Arbor, University of Michigan Press, 1994; "'This Woman Can Cross Any Line': Feminist Tricksters in the Works of Nora Naranjo-Morse and Joy Harjo" by Kristine Holmes, in *Studies in American Indian Literatures* (Richmond, Virginia), 7(1), spring 1995; "Castings for a (New) New World: The Poetry of Joy Harjo" by Janet McAdams, in *Women Poets of the Americas: Toward a Pan-American Gathering,* edited by Jacqueline Vaught Brogan and Cordelia Chavez Candelaria, Notre Dame, Indiana, University of Notre Dame Press, 1999.

*   *   *

Joy Harjo has continued to develop as a writer, having moved from the competent, though occasionally predictable, language of the early poems ("I give you, my beautiful and terrible / fear") to work that resembles some of the best poetry in American English since Whitman. "Eagle Poem," a later work, for example, speaks of similarities between prayer and life in this way:

We are truly blessed because we
Were born, and die soon within a
True circle of motion,
Like eagle rounding out the morning
Inside us.

In interviews Harjo has identified herself with currents in modern American writing, particularly with the regional depth of Meridel LeSueur and Flannery O'Connor and the strong voices of Audre Lorde and Alice Walker. As with LeSueur and O'Connor, Harjo exploits the genius of landscapes (the wide open spaces of her native Oklahoma and the deserts and mountains of the West) and cityscapes (Albuquerque, Cheyenne, Okemah, Gallup, Okmulgee) that are relatively unfamiliar in the national literature. She also makes valuable use of and builds upon oral traditions that allow room for suppressed memories, silences, and dreams.

A Creek in background, Harjo often wonders aloud about her own survival and how it happened, when most of her people have disappeared and continue to disappear. In "Night Out" she talks about people who, like herself, "fought to get out, fought to get in," fearful, even after paying "the cover charge thousands of times over with your lives" that they "can never get out." In such poems Harjo speaks of herself and the Native Americans who people her poems—Navajo, Shawnee, Cherokee, Kiowa—as survivors.

"Anchorage," from the same period, speaks about "the fantastic and terrible" stories of persistence among people regarded by many as "those who were never meant / to survive." There, as in "For Alva Benson, and for Those Who Have Learned to Speak," Harjo identifies herself with those who

go on, keep giving birth and watch
ourselves die, over and over.
And the ground spinning beneath us
goes on talking.

Although forces have chipped away at her world, as "white soldiers" chipped away at Native American culture from the beginning, Harjo remains determined "to turn the earth / around" in a cooperative effort to save memories, histories, and dreams.

As her body of work unfolds, Harjo speaks with increasing confidence, more certain of the value of her own voice and the authority of the voices she makes room for in her poems. That voice has become, in fact,

memory alive
not just a name
but an intricate part
of this web of motion,
meaning: earth, sky
stars circling
my heart
centrifugal.

From the beginning Harjo not only has celebrated what was destroyed or lost but also has worked to reclaim it through prayer ("One Cedar Tree"), active resistance ("The Black Room"), and imagination ("Vision"). Beginning with *In Mad Love and War,* her work has suggested new strength, insight, and direction. Although it continues to reflect anger, regret, and anguish over what she and the people she identifies with have endured, it also carries a powerful sense—in "Transformations," for example—"that hatred can be turned into something else, if you have the right words, the right meanings, buried in the tender place in your heart where the most precious animals live."

—Michael True

HARPER, Michael S(teven)

Nationality: American. **Born:** Brooklyn, New York, 18 March 1938. **Education:** Susan Miller Dorsey High School, Los Angeles, graduated 1955; City College of Los Angeles, A.A. 1959; California State

University, Los Angeles, B.A. 1961, M.A. in English 1963; University of Iowa, Iowa City, M.F.A. 1963; University of Illinois, Urbana, 1970–71. **Family:** Married Shirley Ann Buffington in 1965; one daughter and two sons. **Career:** Statistics teacher, Pasadena City College, California, 1962; instructor in English, Contra Costa College, San Pablo, California, 1964–68; poet-in-residence, Reed College and Lewis and Clark College, Portland, Oregon, 1968–69; associate professor, California State University, Hayward, 1970. Associate professor, 1971–73, since 1973 professor of English, and since 1983 Kapstein Professor, Brown University, Providence, Rhode Island. Visiting professor, Harvard University, Cambridge, Massachusetts, 1974, 1977, and Yale University, New Haven, Connecticut, 1976; Benedict Distinguished Professor of English, Carleton College, Northfield, Minnesota, 1979; Elliston poet, University of Cincinnati, Ohio, 1979; National Humanities Distinguished Professor, Colgate University, Hamilton, New York, 1985. American specialist, International Congress of Africanists, State Department tour of Africa, 1977; council member Massachusetts Council on Arts and Humanities, 1977–80; board member, Yaddo Artists Colony; original founding member, African Continuum, St. Louis. **Awards:** American Academy award, 1972; Black Academy of Arts and Letters award, 1972; Guggenheim fellowship, 1976; National Endowment for the Arts grant, 1977; Melville Cane award, 1977; Poet Laureate, Rhode Island, 1988–93; Robert Hayden Memorial poetry award, United Negro College Fund, 1990; George Kent poetry award, 1996; Claiborne Pell award for excellence in the arts, 1997. D.Litt.: Trinity College, Connecticut, 1987. D.H.L.: Coe College, 1990. **Address:** Box 1852, Brown University, Providence, Rhode Island 02912, U.S.A.

PUBLICATIONS

Poetry

Dear John, Dear Coltrane. Pittsburgh, University of Pittsburgh Press, 1970.
History Is Your Own Heartbeat. Urbana, University of Illinois Press, 1971.
Photographs: Negatives: History as Apple Tree. San Francisco, Scarab Press, 1972.
Song. I Want a Witness. Pittsburgh, University of Pittsburgh Press, 1972.
Debridement. New York, Doubleday, 1973.
Nightmare Begins Responsibility. Urbana, University of Illinois Press, 1974.
Images of Kin: New and Selected Poems. Urbana, University of Illinois Press, 1977.
Rhode Island: Eight Poems. Roslindale, Massachusetts, Pym Randall Press, 1981.
Healing Song for the Inner Ear. Urbana, University of Illinois Press, 1985.
Songlines: Mosaics. Providence, Rhode Island, Brown/Ziggurat Press, 1991.
Honorable Amendments: Poems. Urbana, University of Illinois Press, 1995.
Songlines in Michaeltree: New and Collected Poems. Urbana, University of Illinois Press, 2000.

Recording: *Hear Where Coltrane Is,* Watershed, 1971; *Michael S. Harper and Quincy Troupe Reading Their Poems,* Gertrude

Clarke Whittal Poetry and Literature Fund, Library of Congress, 1994.

Other

Editor, *Heartblow: Black Veils* (anthology). Urbana, University of Illinois Press, 1975.
Editor, with Robert B. Stepto, *Chant of Saints: A Gathering of Afro-American Literature, Art, and Scholarship.* Urbana, University of Illinois Press, 1979.
Editor, *The Collected Poems of Sterling A. Brown.* New York, Harper, 1980.
Editor, with Anthony Walton, *Every Shut Eye Ain't Asleep: An Anthology of African Americans since 1945.* Boston, Little Brown, 1994.
Editor, with Anthony Walton, *The Vintage Book of African American Poetry.* New York, Vintage, 2000.

*

Critical Studies: *Nightmare Begins Responsibility: A Study of Michael S. Harper's Poetry* (dissertation) by Joseph Raffa, Columbia University, New York, 1985; ''Their Long Scars Touch Ours: A Reflection on the Poetry of Michael Harper'' by Joseph A. Brown, in *Callaloo* (Baltimore, Maryland), 9(1), Winter 1986; Michael Harper issue of *Callaloo* (Baltimore, Maryland), 13(4), Fall 1990; ''Robert Hayden and Michael S. Harper: A Literary Friendship,'' in *Callaloo* (Baltimore, Maryland), 17(4), Fall 1994; ''Another Version: Michael S. Harper, William Clark, and the Problem of Historical Blindness'' by Elizabeth Dodd, in *Western American Literature* (Logan, Utah), 33(1), Spring 1998.

* * *

Michael S. Harper's poetry collections reveal a broad diversity of themes and disparate interests, ranging from music (jazz and blues), to nature (birth and death), to history and myth. His writings are the manifestations of a highly sensitized black witness, and within him all of these themes coalesce and then are transposed into emotional and spiritual expressions. Harper states that ''relationships between speech and body, between men, between men and cosmology are central to my poetry.''

In certain respects Harper's poetry defies characterization, for it is controlled by intensely personal rhythms emanating from his deeply rooted jazz and blues impulses. (He tells us, for example, that ''Billie Holiday played piano in my family's house when I was twelve).'' At the same time the scope of his writing is attuned to a historical sense of moment, something of what T.S. Eliot called a perception not only of the pastness of the past but also of its presence. Harper sets out to affirm his conviction that man must not allow himself to be dislocated from his historical continuum: ''When there is no history there is no metaphor.'' It is with such conviction that his poetry at once synthesizes and articulates this sensibility. And it is out of his own blackness as well as his own humanness that Africa is viewed as the ''potent ancestor,'' providing ''a strong ancestral base that reflects the African spirit wherever it is located'':

And we go back to the well: Africa,
the first mode, and man, modally,

touches the land of the continent,
modality: we are one; a man is another
man's face, modality, in continuum,
from man, to man, contact-high, to man . . .

Out of this spiritual and historical consciousness Harper defines relationships between people and the cosmos and generates metaphor:

This suture is race
as it is blood,
long as the frozen
lake building messages
on typewritten paper,
faces of my ancestors,
warm in winter only
as their long scars touch ours.

Conviction, of course, means responsibility. Harper's responsibility as a poet is to take on "'"the very tenuous business' of operating on historical legacies," creating a "clinical imagery to draw attention, to shock a reader with a detailed, medical closeness and approximation." Thus, when surgeon is poet and flesh is landscape with its history, tradition, and myth, debridement becomes metaphor and restoration becomes image. In this sense Harper's poems may be perceived as "healing songs":

Ragboned Bob Hayden, shingled in slime,
reaches for his cereus ladder of midnight flight,
his seismographic heartbeats
sphinctered in rhiney polygraphs of light:
Dee-troit born and half-blind
in diction of arena and paradise,
his ambient nightmare-dreams streak his tongue;
mementos of his mother, of Erma, he image-makes
peopling the human family of God's mirror,
mingling realities, this creature of transcendence
a love-filled shadow, congealed and clarified.

—Charles L. James

HARRIS, Michael

Nationality: Scottish. **Born:** Glasgow, 1944. **Education:** Attended McGill University and Concordia University, Canada, M.A. in literature and creative writing. **Career:** Faculty member, Dawson College, Montreal; part-time lecturer, McGill and Concordia universities. Since 1981 poetry editor, Signal Editions, Véhicule Press. **Awards:** CBC Literary Competition, 1988; Canada Council Senior Arts award, 1990.

PUBLICATIONS

Poetry

Sparks. Lasalle, Quebec, New Delta, 1976.
Grace. Montreal, New Delta, 1978.
Miss Emily et la Mort. Montreal, VLB, 1984.

In Transit. Montreal, Véhicule Press, 1985.
New and Selected Poems. Montreal, Signal Editions, 1992.

Other

Editor, *The Signal Anthology: Contemporary Canadian Poetry.* Montreal, Véhicule Press, 1993.

Translator, *Veiled Countries/Lives,* by Marie-Claire Blais. Montreal, Véhicule Press, 1985.

*   *   *

The two linchpins of Michael Harris's considerable achievement are the sequences "Death and Miss Emily" and "Turning Out the Light" in, respectively, *Grace* and *In Transit.* Both illustrate Harris's characteristic duologue between swarming action and stillness and between inner and outer rooms. Often Harris's work depicts vulnerable confinement, indoors or outdoors: a claustrophobic interior, an agoraphobic exterior.

Miss Emily (based on Emily Dickinson) has a calculating, quietly ardent suitor in Death and lives trapped in a small room, imagined at one point as an aquarium. Inside her imprisoning house, a bell jar, Miss Emily senses another space of breadth, depth, and ecstacy. Yet when she ventures out to pick berries, the blueberries seem "like mute dead planets" or "the shadowed eyes of children / in an orphanage." She observes a scene of desolation, "a battlefield of green shoots and brittle canes, / the canes brown as bone, with air for marrow." Miss Emily is Death's accomplice, his fiancée soon to become his bride. In the climactic moment of her last day, images of an outer, untraveled room enter her chamber. So does Death.

"Death and Miss Emily" unfolds in graceful, almost serene couplets. "Turning Out the Light" is no less controlled, though the artfulness is more understated, and the stanzaic forms more flexibly structured. In it the poet's brother is confined to a room in a terminal cancer ward that becomes a grave or casket:

These walls are white doors
without handles. The surfaces
are mirrors that won't work.

Harris is unsparing in depicting the filthy minutiae of a slow death, but there is no masochistic wallowing, only intensely involved clinical accuracy. Chemotherapy, the putative cure whose excruciating effects may be worse than the disease, is thematically linked to "Some Ways of Dying," in *New and Selected Poems,* in which Elizabethan tortures and executions are compared to the ordeals undergone by a modern medical martyr.

Harris often ends such a poem with bleak humor. In "Some Ways of Dying" the patient shrieking in pain invokes the Virgin, who "allows her martyrdom, but evidently from a great distance. / Her immediate neighbours wish her dead." The poet, desperately willing his brother to health, is implicated in the processes of death by his very presence. Deathwatch poems are practically a genre in themselves, but seldom have they been controlled so powerfully and with so little self-indulgence.

"Turning Out the Light" is not the only witness to loss. Although the memorial quality of some poems in the "Family Album" section of *New and Selected Poems* (many of the pieces here are untitled, suggesting that the poet may regard them not as separate entities but as interlocked parts of a larger body of work) is relieved by glimpses of a new baby, the poet's brother haunts them, and he is joined by other deceased family members.

Another aspect of Harris's work is a special interest in *ekphraseis,* descriptive poems about works of art. Many poems are full of aqueous or insectivorous imagery, and often winter and spring are contrasted. But the poet keeps returning to rooms. ''Bearskin Rug,'' in *Grace,* shows the outer, wild room of nature tamed and subsumed within the inner, domestic one, with a bear killed to make a rug. The dualism of interior and exterior is sustained in ''The Hunting-Cabin in November.'' Inside the cabin ''the twelve-gauge glistens / with bluing and rests frozen on its rack.'' Outside ''the white-tail keeps her blood warm in the woods.'' The potential for death lurks within and without.

At the very least, adjourning to the outer room is ambiguous. ''Spring Descending,'' in *New and Selected Poems,* consists of untitled quasi-sonnets composed with an almost Shakespearean density. The mise-en-scène involves a couple secreting themselves in the countryside, nature's complexity paralleling the tensions of requited or unrequited desire.

''The Force of Love'' concerns the complications of marriage. One poem here is the wickedly satirical ''Epithalamion'' (''Warthogs shuffled up truffles for boutonnieres. / Goats handled the giving of the rings''). In ''The Saints'' Harris says,

We have confined them to small rooms
and narrow beds. They have to live in silence, but with
mice breeding hourly in their walls. Though our furnaces
steam fullbore through the night, we keep

the rooms of the saints very cold.

Harris implies that a fertile imaginative life is possible only in confinement and solitude. Elsewhere he mocks poets' egomania and monomania, perhaps even his own. But he is also saying that lyric poets introject everyone and everything in order to create a distinct, individual, and undivided voice. Harris has such a voice.

—Fraser Sutherland

HARRIS, (Theodore) Wilson

Nationality: British. **Born:** New Amsterdam, British Guiana, now Guyana, 24 March 1921. **Education:** Queen's College, Georgetown, 1934–39. **Family:** Married 1) Cecily Carew in 1945; 2) Margaret Whitaker in 1959. **Career:** Government surveyor, 1942–54, and senior surveyor, 1955–58, Government of British Guiana; moved to London in 1959. Visiting lecturer, State University of New York, Buffalo, 1970; writer-in-residence, University of the West Indies, Kingston, Jamaica, and Scarborough College, University of Toronto, 1970; Commonwealth Fellow in Caribbean Literature, Leeds University, Yorkshire, 1971; visiting professor, University of Texas, Austin, 1972, and 1981–82, 1983; guest lecturer, University of Mysore, 1978; visiting lecturer, Yale University, New Haven, Connecticut, 1979; writer-in-residence, University of Newcastle, New South Wales, Australia, 1979; Regents Lecturer, University of California, Santa Cruz, 1983; writer-in-residence, University of Queensland, St. Lucia,

Australia, 1986. Delegate to the National Identity Conference, Brisbane, 1968, and Unesco Symposium on Caribbean Literature, Cuba, 1968. **Awards:** Arts Council grant, 1968, 1970; Guggenheim fellowship, 1973; Henfield Writing fellowship, UEA, 1974; Southern Arts Writing fellowship, 1976; Guyana prize, for fiction, 1985–87; Premio Mondello Five Continents award, 1992. D.Litt.: University of the West Indies, 1984; University of Kent, Canterbury, 1988; University of Essex, 1996; University of Macerata, Italy, 1999. **Address:** c/o Faber and Faber Ltd., 3 Queen Square, London WClN 3AU, England.

PUBLICATIONS

Poetry

Fetish (as Kona Waruk). Privately printed, 1951.
The Well and the Land. Georgetown, Magnet, 1952.
Eternity to Season. Privately printed, 1954; revised edition, London, New Beacon, 1979.

Novels

The Guiana Quartet. London, Faber, 1985.
Palace of the Peacock. London, Faber, 1960.
The Far Journey of Oudin. London, Faber, 1961.
The Whole Armour. London, Faber, 1962.
The Secret Ladder. London, Faber, 1963.
Heartland. London, Faber, 1964.
The Eye of the Scarecrow. London, Faber, 1965.
The Waiting Room. London, Faber, 1967.
Tumatumari. London, Faber, 1968.
Ascent to Omai. London, Faber, 1970.
Black Marsden: A Tabula Rasa Comedy. London, Faber, 1972.
Companions of the Day and Night. London, Faber, 1975.
Da Silva da Silva's Cultivated Wilderness, and Genesis of the Clowns. London, Faber, 1977.
The Tree of the Sun. London, Faber, 1978.
The Angel at the Gate. London, Faber, 1982.
Carnival. London, Faber, 1985.
The Infinite Rehearsal. London, Faber, 1987.
The Four Banks of the River of Space. London, Faber, 1990.
Resurrection at Sorrow Hill. London, Faber, 1993.
Jonestown. London, Faber, 1996.

Short Stories

The Sleepers of Roraima. London, Faber, 1970.
The Age of the Rainmakers. London, Faber, 1971.

Other

Tradition, The Writer, and Society: Critical Essays. London, New Beacon, 1967.
History, Fable, and Myth in the Caribbean and Guianas. Georgetown, National History and Arts Council, 1970.
Fossil and Psyche (lecture on Patrick White). Austin, University of Texas, 1974.
Explorations: A Selection of Talks and Articles, edited by Hena Maes-Jelinek. Aarhus, Denmark, Dangaroo Press, 1981.

The Womb of Space: The Cross-Cultural Imagination. Westport, Connecticut, Greenwood Press, 1983.
The Radical Imagination. Liège, Belgium, University of Liège, 1992.
Selected Essays. London, Routledge, 1999.

*

Theatrical Activities: Actor: **Television**—*Da Silva da Silva,* 1987.

Bibliography: By Reinhard Sander, in *Commonwealth Literature and the Modern World,* edited by Hena Maes-Jelinek, Brussels, Didier, 1975; Sidney Singh, in *World Literature Written in English* (Guelph, Ontario), 22(1), spring 1983.

Manuscript Collections: University of the West Indies, Mona, Kingston, Jamaica; University of Texas, Austin; University of Indiana, Bloomington; University of Guyana, Georgetown.

Critical Studies: ''The Necessity of Poetry'' by Louis James, and ''Kyk-over-AI and the Radicals'' by Edward Brathwaite, in *New World* (Georgetown), 1966; *The Naked Design,* Aarhus, Denmark, Dangaroo Press, 1976, *Wilson Harris,* Boston, Twayne, 1982, *Wilson Harris, The Uncompromising Imagination,* Aarhus, Denmark, Dangaroo Press, 1991, and '''Tricksters of Heaven': Visions of Holocaust in Fred D'Aguiar's Bill of Rights and Wilson Harris's Jonestown,'' in *'Union in Partition': Essays in Honour of Jeanne Delbaere,* edited by Gilbert Debusscher, Liege, Belgium, L3-Liege Language and Literature, 1997, all by Hena Maes-Jelinek; *Wilson Harris* and the *Modern Tradition: A New Architecture of the World* by Sandra E. Drake, New York, Greenwood, 1986; *Myth and History in Caribbean Fiction: Alejo Carpentier, Wilson Harris, and Edouard Glissant,* Amherst, University of Massachusetts Press, 1992; *Caribbean Literature in English* by Lewis James, London and New York, Longman, 1999.

Wilson Harris comments:

(1970) *Fetish* and *Eternity to Season,* along with other miscellaneous poems of the early 1950s, stand at the beginning of an exploration which extends deeper and further at a later stage in my work in the novel over the 1960s. The development of the novels is foreshadowed, to some extent, in the earlier poems. Constant to that exploration within poem and novel is the use I continue to make of the brooding continental landscape of Guiana as a gateway to memory between races and cultures, Amerindian, European, African, Asian.

*   *   *

The poetry of Wilson Harris, like his contribution to the art of the novel after 1960 (he has published no poetry since then), is outside the present mainstream of Caribbean writing in English. Like Martin Carter, also of Guyana, his metaphorical perception and expression are more akin to that of the Martinican poet Aimé Césaire and the Cuban writer Alejo Carpentier. One does not find in Harris's work the clear air of the poets of the Anglophone islands. His sensibility has been formed by the world of the Guyanese forest and its rivers, with its complexities and contradictions (''Amazons''):

The world-creating jungle
travels eternity to season. Not an individual artifice
this living movement

this tide
this paradoxical stream and stillness rousing reflection.

Harris's most important poems are found in the privately published *Eternity to Season.* He does not concern himself with social conditions, individual problems, the colonial past, or a possible or impossible future. His themes are time (into which he subsumes history), creation, separation, and unity. His burden is not the Faustian ego but the environmental collective. There is some evidence of the operation of a Hegelian and Marxist dialectic in his poems. When individuals appear in his poetry, they are gigantic mythologized figures like Hector (''hero of time''), Agamemnon, Achilles (the great runner), and Teiresias.

Harris uses these figures and simple material existences like rice, water, and charcoal to initiate journeys into both cosmic space and human time, often simultaneously. Because of the nature of Harris's perception, some of his poetry is obscure, although most of it deposits its meaning after repeated reading, and sometimes, perhaps through the need to make his meaning clear, Harris eschews metaphor for a proselike statement (''Amazon''):

But earth cannot simply be
a cosmic and arbitrary discovery! what of its changing
    roots
and purposive vitality? External and internal
forces are separate illusions that move
beyond the glitter and the gloom with a knife to cut inner
    and outer times from each other
as they weave and interweave in the tapestry of life . . .

Earlier in the poem the same statement is almost magically expressed:

Branches against the sky smuggle to heaven the extreme
    beauty
of the world: the store-house of that very heaven
breaks walls to drop tall streams like falls.

The green islands of the world
and the bright leaves lift their tender blossom of sunrise
to offset arenas of sunset
and wear a wild rosette like blood.

This self same blossom burns the clouds . . .

Nor is Harris alone in this paradoxical riverine and arboreal continuum. In *Notes on the West Indies* (1806) George Pinckard, an English army doctor traveling on Guyanese waters, received and recorded the same kind of environmental breakdown and unification that Harris has transmuted into poetry:

The watery medium made no impression upon the eye, but the open azure expanse was seen the same, whether we looked upwards or downwards. We seemed suspended in the centre of a hollow globe, having the same concave arch above and below, with an inverted and an upright forest on either hand. At one spot we met a huge mass of earth resembling a small island, floating down the silent river, with a variety of plants and shrubs growing upon it; and from the water being invisible, the perfect reflection of this little plantation gave it the appearance of a clump of young trees calmly moving in a wide vacuum, with each plant growing perpendicularly upward and downward, in precise resemblance. If we held out a hand or an oar ... the same was seen below, without discovering the limpid medium between them. In short we seemed to move, like our globe itself, in ethereal space.

It is from this world that Harris has derived his sensibility. His achievement has been the creation of this sensibility in poetry. At its best his poetry moves even beyond re-creation into enactment, so that often we are able to participate in the creation (out of elements of space, time, and material) of the poet's vision (''Vision at the Well''):

Touched by vision
the light fingertips of rain pass softly
to change the stone and burden of her perfection
into rapt walls that house joy and pain and living
    imperfection.
Her cheeks are the dark glow of blood
beneath the frail temper of space and eternity, the history
of her flesh and blood is strange and new.

—Edward Kamau Brathwaite

HARRISON, Jim

Nationality: American. **Born:** James Thomas Harrison, in Grayling, Michigan, 11 December 1937. **Education:** Michigan State University, East Lansing, B.A. in comparative literature 1960, M.A. in comparative literature 1964. **Family:** Married Linda King in 1960; two daughters. **Career:** Assistant professor of English, State University of New York, Stony Brook, 1965–66. Lives on a farm in Michigan. **Awards:** National Endowment for the Arts grant, 1967, 1968, 1969; Guggenheim fellowship, 1969. **Agent:** Robert Datilla, 233 East 8th Street, New York, 10028. **Address:** RR 1, Box 135, Lake Leelanau, Michigan 49653, U.S.A.

PUBLICATIONS

Poetry

Plain Song. New York, Norton, 1965.
Locations. New York, Norton, 1968.
Walking. Cambridge, Massachusetts, Pym Randall Press, 1969.
Outlyer and Ghazals. New York, Simon and Schuster, 1971.
Letters to Yesenin. Fremont, Michigan, Sumac Press, 1973.
Returning to Earth. Ithaca, New York, Ithaca House, 1977.
Selected and New Poems 1961–1981. New York, Delacorte Press, 1982.
The Theory and Practice of Rivers. Seattle, Winn, 1986.
The Theory and Practice of Rivers and New Poems. Livingston, Montana, Clark City Press, 1989.
After Ikkyu and Other Poems. Boston, Shambhala, 1996.
The Shape of the Journey: New and Collected Poems. Port Townsend, Washington, Copper Canyon Press, 1998.

Screenplays: *Revenge,* 1988; *Castledge,* 1990; *Wolf,* 1992.

Novels

Wolf. New York, Simon and Schuster, 1971; as *Wolf: A False Memoir,* New York, Delta, 1989; London, Flamingo, 1993.
A Good Day to Die. New York, Simon and Schuster, 1973.
Farmer. New York, Viking Press, 1976.
Legends of the Fall (novellas). New York, Delacorte Press, 1979; London, Collins, 1980.
Warlock. New York, Delacorte Press, and London, Collins, 1981.
Sundog. New York, Dutton, 1984; London, Heinemann, 1985.
Dalva. New York, Dutton, 1988; London, Cape, 1989.
The Woman Lit by Fireflies. Boston, Houghton Mifflin, 1990; London, Weidenfeld and Nicolson, 1991.
Sunset Limited (three novellas). Boston, Houghton Mifflin, 1990.
A Good Day to Die. London, Flamingo, 1993.
Julip. New York, Washington Square Press, 1994.
The Road Home. New York, Washington Square Press, 1998; London, Picador, 1999.

Other

Natural World, with Diana Guest. Barrytown, New York, Open Book. 1983.
Confusion Reigns: A Quick-and-Easy Guide to the Most Easily Mixed-Up Words, with illustrations by Kimble Mead. New York, St. Martin's Press, 1987.
Just before Dark: Collected Nonfiction. Boston, Houghton Mifflin, 1991.
Raw and the Cooked. New York, Dim Gray Bar, 1992.

*

Critical Studies: ''Poets from East and West'' by Syed Amanuddin, in *Creative Moment* (Sumter, South Carolina), 1(2), 1972; ''Jim Harrison: A Checklist'' by Tom Colonnese, in *Bulletin of Bibliography* (Westport, Connecticut), 39(3), September 1982; '''Natty Bumpo Wants Tobacco': Jim Harrison's Wilderness'' by John Rohrkemper, and '''A Good Day to Live': The Prose Works of Jim Harrison'' by William H. Roberson, both in *Great Lakes Review* (Mt. Pleasant, Michigan), 8–9(2–1), Fall 1982; ''Myth and Reality in Jim Harrison's Warlock'' by Thomas Maher Gilligan, in *Critique* (Washington, D.C.), 25(3), Spring 1984; ''The Man Whose Soul Is Not for Sale: Jim Harrison'' by Hank Nuwer, in *Rendezvous* (Pocatello, Idaho), 21(1), Fall 1985; '''Macho Mistake': The Misrepresentation of Jim Harrison's Fiction'' by William H. Roberson, in *Critique* (Washington, D.C.) 29(4), Summer 1988; ''Brown Dog's Insight: The Fiction of Jim Harrison'' by Robert Johnson, in *Notes on Contemporary Literature* (Carrollton, Georgia), 27(1), January 1997; ''E.M. Cioran and 'The Man Who Gave Up His Name' by Jim Harrison'' by Aleksandra Gruzinska, in her *Essays on E.M. Cioran,* Costa Mesa, California, ARA, 1999.

Jim Harrison comments:

I write free verse, which is absurdly indefinite as a name for what any poet writes. I consider myself an internationalist and my main influences to be Neruda, Rilke, Yeats, Bunting, Lorca, and, in my own country, Whitman, Hart Crane, Robert Duncan, and Ezra Pound. Not that this helps much other than to name those I esteem and, perhaps vacantly, wish to emulate. Most of my poems seem rural, vaguely surrealistic, though after the Spanish rather than the French. My sympathies run hotly to the impure, the inclusive, as the realm of poetry. A poet at best speaks in the "out loud speech of his tribe," deals in essences whether political, social, or personal. All of world literature is his province, though he sees it as a guild only to be learned from, as he must speak in his own voice.

*   *   *

The work of Jim Harrison is imbued with a deeply rooted sense of place, and that place is in the middle of America in northern Michigan, "the only locus I know." In "Ghazals" he writes, "And I want to judge the poetry table at the County Fair. / A new form, poems stacked in pyramids like prize potatoes," and with their stark, simple images of rural life, his volumes comprise a county fair of delights. Poems such as "Young Bull," "Lisle's River," and "Dead Deer" are Harrison's songs of the plains.

From the poet's sense of place comes an understanding of nature's way. "I insist on a one-to-one relationship with nature," he says at one point, later adding, "I want to have my life / in cloud shapes, water shapes, wind shapes, / crow call, marsh hawk swooping over grass and weed tips." In poems such as "Cold August," "Natural World," and "February Swans," the shapes of nature are quietly celebrated. Consider "Dusk":

Dusk over the lake,
clouds floating
heat lightning
a nightmare behind branches;
from the swamps
the odor of cedar and fern,
the long circular
wail of the loon—
the plump bird aches for fish
for night to come down.

Then it becomes so dark
and still
that I shatter the moon with an oar.

At the end of the sequence called "A Year's Changes," looking into a pool of black water, the speaker thinks that

It appears bottomless,
An oracle I should worship at; I want
some part of me to be lost in it and return
again from the darkness, changing the creature,
or return to draw me back to a home.

In the reflections of nature Harrison looks into his own soul. His work is shallow, though, when nature is not there to provide a mirror or a muse. *Outlyer and Ghazals* is a disjointed and dispirited volume that includes poems praising whiskey and women "pliant as marshmellows." "All my poems are born dead," Harrison writes here. "I'm a bad poet." But he also writes, "If I clean up my brain . . . the Sibyl will return as an undiscovered lover."

The prophetess does indeed return with the 1973 *Letters to Yesenin,* a profoundly powerful and affecting work. Harrison's long prose poem sequence is not only an homage to the Soviet poet Sergei

Yesenin but also a meditation on such topics as life, love, freedom, the poet's craft, and, of course, nature. This "suicide note to a suicide" is a "record of agony" in which Yesenin's sufferings in totalitarian Russia are juxtaposed with Harrison's pains in rural America. The self-pitying and egocentric tone of *Outlyer* is replaced here with compassion for all humanity. "A good poet is only a sorcerer bored with magic who has turned his attention elsewhere," Harrison writes, and here is a subject worthy of attention.

With this volume and those that followed, Harrison "returned to earth," finding the sure ground that is his proper subject. The example of Yesenin gives Harrison the power to shake off the suicidal musings of *Outlyer* and to choose life, with all of its elaborate sufferings and simple joys. Harrison closes his collected poems with "After Reading Takahashi," and he closes that poem with a characteristic passage in which by looking at nature he is able to look past himself:

I've been warned by a snowy night, an owl,
the infinite black above and below me to look
at all creatures and things with a billion eyes,
not struggling with the single heartbeat
that is my life.

—Dennis Lynch

HARRISON, Tony

Nationality: British. **Born:** Leeds, Yorkshire, 30 April 1937. **Education:** Cross Flatts County Primary, Leeds, 1942–48; Leeds Grammar School, 1948–55; University of Leeds, 1955–60, B.A. in classics 1958, postgraduate diploma in linguistics. **Family:** Married 1) Rosemarie Crossfield in 1962, one daughter and one son; 2) Teresa Stratas in 1984. **Career:** Schoolmaster, Dewsbury, Yorkshire, 1960–62; lecturer in English, Ahmadu Bello University, Zaria, Northern Nigeria, 1962–66, and Charles University, Prague, 1966–67; editor, with Jon Silkin and Ken Smith, *Stand,* Newcastle upon Tyne, 1968–69; resident dramatist, National Theatre, London, 1977–79. U.K.-U.S. Bi-Centennial Fellow, New York, 1979–80. President, Classical Association of Great Britain, 1987–88. **Awards:** Northern Arts fellowship, 1967, 1976; Cholmondeley award, 1969; Unesco fellowship, 1969; Faber memorial award, 1972; Gregynog fellowship, 1973; U.S. Bicentennial fellowship, 1979; European Poetry translation prize, 1983; Whitbread prize for poetry, 1993, for *The Gaze of the Gorgon*; William Heinemann prize, 1996, for *Shadow of Hiroshima and Other Film/Poems.* Fellow, Royal Society of Literature, 1984. **Agent:** Gordon Dickerson, 2, Crescent Grove, London SW4 7AM, England.

PUBLICATIONS

Poetry

Earthworks. Leeds, Northern House, 1964.
Newcastle Is Peru. Newcastle upon Tyne, Eagle Press, 1969.
The Loiners. London, London Magazine Editions, 1970.

Corgi Modern Poets in Focus 4, with others, edited by Jeremy Robson. London, Corgi, 1971.

Ten Poems from the School of Eloquence. London, Rex Collings, 1976.

From the School of Eloquence and Other Poems. London, Rex Collings, 1978.

Looking Up, with Phillip Sharpe. West Malvern, Worcestershire, Migrant Press, 1979.

Continuous: 50 Sonnets from the School of Eloquence. London, Rex Collings, 1981.

A Kumquat for John Keats. Newcastle upon Tyne, Bloodaxe, 1981.

U.S. Martial. Newcastle upon Tyne, Bloodaxe, 1981.

Selected Poems. London, Viking Press, 1984.

The Fire-Gap: A Poem with Two Tails. Newcastle upon Tyne, Bloodaxe, 1985.

V. (single poem). Newcastle upon Tyne, Bloodaxe, 1985; with press articles, 1989.

Anno 42. N.p., Michael C. Caine, 1987.

Ten Sonnets from the School of Eloquence. London, Anvil Press Poetry, 1987.

V. and Other Poems. New York, Farrar Straus, 1989.

A Cold Coming (Gulf War poems). Newcastle upon Tyne, Bloodaxe, 1991.

Laureate's Block and Other Occasional Poems. London, Penguin, 2000.

Plays

Aikin Mata, with James Simmons, adaptation of *Lysistrata* by Aristophanes (produced Zaria, Nigeria, 1965). Ibadan, Oxford University Press, 1965.

The Misanthrope, adaptation of a play by Moléire (produced London, 1973; Washington, D.C., and New York, 197). London, Rex Collings, 1973; New York, Third Press, 1975.

Phaedra Britannica, adaptation of a play by Racine (produced London, 1975; New York, 1988). London, Rex Collings, 1975.

Bow Down, music by Harrison Birtwistle (produced London, 1977). London, Rex Collings, 1977.

The Passion, from the York Mystery Plays (produced London, 1977). London, Rex Collings, 1977.

The Bartered Bride, adaptation of an opera by Sabina, music by Smetana (produced New York, 1978). New York, Schirmer, 1978; in Dramatic Verse, 1985.

The Oresteia, music by Harrison Birtwistle, adaptation of the plays by Aeschylus (produced London, 1981). London, Rex Collings, 1981.

Yan Tan Tethera, music by Harrison Birtwistle (produced London, 1983).

The Big H, music by Dominic Muldowney (televised, 1984). Included in *Dramatic Verse,* 1985.

Dramatic Verse 1973–1985 (includes *The Misanthrope, The Bartered Bride, Phaedra Britannica, Bow Down, Medea: A Sex-War Opera, The Big H*). Newcastle upon Tyne, Bloodaxe, 1985; as *Theatre Works 1973–1985,* London, Penguin, 1986.

The Mysteries, adaptation of the Medieval Mystery Plays (produced London, 1985). London, Faber, 1985.

The Trackers of Oxyrhynchus: The Delphi Text 1988, adaptation of a play by Sophocles (produced Delphi, 1988; London, 1990). London, Faber, 1990.

The Common Chorus. London, Faber, 1992.

Square Rounds (produced London, 1992). London, Faber, 1992.

Poetry or Bust (produced Saltaire, Salt Estates, 1993). London, Faber, 1996.

The Shadow of Hiroshima and Other Film/Poems (television play). London, Faber, 1995.

The Prince's Play, adaptation of a play by Victor Hugo (produced London, 1996). London, Faber, 1996.

Prometheus (screenplay). London, Faber, 1998.

Screenplay: *Prometheus,* 1998.

Television Plays: *The Big H,* music by Dominic Muldowney, 1984; *Loving Memory* series, 1987; *The Blasphemers' Banquet,* 1989; *The Gaze of the Gorgon,* 1992; *Black Daisies for the Bride,* 1993; *A Maybe Day in Kazakhstan,* 1994; *The Shadow of Hiroshima,* 1995.

Other

Translator, *Poems,* by Palladas. London, Anvil Press Poetry, 1975.

*

Bibliography: *Tony Harrison: A Bibliography 1957–1987* by John R. Kaiser, London, Mansell, 1989.

Manuscript Collections: University of Newcastle upon Tyne; Newcastle Literary and Philosophical Society.

Critical Studies: *Essays on Tony Harrison* edited by Neil Astley, Newcastle upon Tyne, Bloodaxe, 1990; *Orpheus with His Lute: Poetry & the Renewal of Life* by Elizabeth Henry, Bristol, Bristol Classical Press, 1992; *Ancient Sun, Modern Light: Greek Drama on the Modern Stage* by Marianne McDonald, New York, Columbia University Press, 1992; *A Theatre Workbook* by Cathy Courtney, London, Art Books International, 1993; ''Home-Made Englands: History and Nostalgia in the Poetry of Geoffrey Hill and Tony Harrison'' by David Gervais, in *In Black and Gold: Continuous Traditions in Post-War British and Irish Poetry,* edited by C.C. Barfoot, Amsterdam, Rodopi, 1994; ''Repetition and Parallelism in Tony Harrison's Poetry'' by Hans Osterwalder, in *Repetition,* edited by Andreas Fischer, Tubingen, Narr, 1994; ''Tony Harrison and the Poetry of Leeds'' by Raymond Hargreaves, in *Poetry in the British Isles: Non-Metropolitan Perspectives,* edited by Hans-Werner Ludwig and Lothar Fietz, Cardiff, University of Wales Press, 1995; ''The Poet and the Geldshark: War and the Theatre of Tony Harrison'' by Carol Chillington-Rutter, in *Acts of War: The Representation of Military Conflict on the British Stage and Television since 1945,* edited by Tony Howard and John Stokes, Hants, England, Scolar, 1996; ''Poetic Subjects: Tony Harrison and Peter Reading'' by Neil Roberts, in *British Poetry from the 1950s to the 1990s: Politics and Art,* edited by Gary Day and Brian Docherty, London, Macmillan, and New York, St. Martin's Press, 1997; *Tony Harrison: Loiner* edited by Sandie Byrne, Oxford, England, Clarendon, 1997, and *H, v. and O: The Poetry of Tony Harrison* by Byrne, Manchester, England, Manchester University Press, 1998.

*   *   *

Tony Harrison is very much his own man in contemporary British poetry, having little in common with any recognizable school or movement. This detachment is reflected in the fact that he has usually been published by small or out-of-the-way presses. It is reflected more integrally, however, in his subject matter, which has consistently had to do with the tensions and pressures of having been born into the northern English working class but then having been educated away from that life by a university degree in classics, the most deeply traditional and conservative of all English liberal educations. The desire to speak in poetry for those who have had no voice in literature for themselves informs a great deal of Harrison's work. He goes to sources in the history of Europe for exemplary instances of power and political and religious oppression, as in his terrifying poem on the Inquisition, ''The Nuptial Torches,'' a monologue by Queen Isabella. He derives a kind of aesthetic, and certainly a rationale, from the way such things are central in his conception of his own family:

How you became a poet's a mystery!
Wherever did you get your talent from?

I say, I had two uncles, Joe and Harry—
one was a stammerer, the other dumb.

As these lines suggest, Harrison's material necessarily makes him profoundly self-conscious about his own role as a poet. He is, in fact, more public in his writing than many poets, having worked on translations and versions for the National Theatre—notably his highly controversial version of the Oresteia—and on librettos for international opera companies. The cosmopolitan glamour of the life such work gives him, when it features in poems juxtaposed with poems on his origins, has occasionally, I think, an element of the overinsistent. The tone in which he tells us, for instance, about receiving a gift of guavas—a fruit shaped like the female pudendum—from Jane Fonda is altogether uncertain and distasteful.

In general, however, Harrison is a highly intelligent poet, very much in control of his effects. His forms are highly ingenious, and the most telling ironies in his work derive from form itself. His iambics, his couplets, his octosyllabics—when combined with Harrison's demotic and colloquial—subvert the aristocratic and bourgeois traditions that fostered them. His sixteen-line Meredithian sonnet sequence The School of Eloquence makes this plain enough. In ''Turns,'' for instance, we read that

I thought it made me look more ''working class''
(as if a bit of chequered cloth could bridge that gap!)
I did a turn in it before the glass.
My mother said: It suits you, your dad's cap.
(She preferred me to wear suits and part my hair:
You're every bit as good as that lot are!)

All the pension crew came out to stare.
Dad was sprawled beside the postbox (still VR),
his cap turned inside up beside his head,
smudged H A H in purple Indian ink
and Brylcreem slicks displayed so folk might think
he wanted charity for dropping dead.

He never begged. For nowt! Death's reticence

Crowns his life's, and me, I'm opening my trap
to busk the class that broke him for the pence
that splash like brackish tears into our cap.

The plangency here, as in many poems in the sequence, runs the severe risk of mawkishness. Christopher Reid has suggested that the mawkishness may be deliberate, that it is a sort of awkwardness of emotion to parallel the undoubted awkwardnesses of rhythm and metaphor in the sequence—both dedicated to revising the middle-class reader's notions of the poetically acceptable. This may be true. There is certainly the sense that the poem has earned its plangencies, and the familiar tenderness is close to class despair, admitting that anything subversive in Harrison must do battle with every poet's complicity, in some ways, with the owners of the language he uses. There remains, however, the awkward fact, an awkwardness presumably not intended, that not all of these poems are at all as effective on a second reading as they are on the first; there sometimes can seem an element of the factitious or the histrionic in them.

Perhaps the best of Harrison will, in the end, turn out to be the work in which he achieves a greater measure of release for his wit and humor, his sensuousness, and his delighted eroticism, such as, for instance, the long poem in couplets A Kumquat for John Keats. Despite my own reservations about the procedures of some poems in The School of Eloquence, there is no doubt that Harrison is one of the most important and challenging poets writing in English. He is one of the few whose every new poem can be awaited with real expectation.

—Neil Corcoran

HARRY, J.S.

Nationality: Australian. Born: Adelaide, South Australia, in 1939. Career: Writer-in-residence, Australian National University, Canberra, 1989. Awards: Harri Jones memorial prize, 1971; P.E.N. International Lynne Phillips prize, 1987; Kenneth Slessor poetry prize, 1996. Address: P.O. Box 184, Randwick, New South Wales 2031, Australia.

PUBLICATIONS

Poetry

The Deer under the Skin. St. Lucia, University of Queensland Press, 1970.
Hold, for a Little While, and Turn Gently. Sydney, Island Press, 1979.
A Dandelion for Van Gogh. Sydney, Island Press, 1985.
The Life on Water and the Life Beneath. Sydney, Angus and Robertson, 1995.
J.S. Harry-Selected Poems. Ringwood, Victoria, and New York, Penguin, 1995.

*

Critical Studies: By Martin Duwell, in Overland Magazine (Mt. Eliza, Victoria), 106, March 1987; by Rose Lucas, in Poetry and Gender, edited by David Brooks and Brenda Walker, St. Lucia,

University of Queensland Press, 1989; "When Worlds Collide: A Brief Response to One Aspect of the Work of J.S. Harry" by Jennifer Maiden, in *Southerly,* 52(3), September 1992; "Looking for Some Tracks: Hunting with J.S. Harry" by Marie-Louise Ayres, and "A Parrot and a Fox: Rereading J.S. Harry" by Martin Duwell, both in *Southerly,* 56(3), Spring 1996.

*   *   *

The poetry of J.S. Harry encompasses a wide range of conflicting and competing impulses on both stylistic and thematic levels. Hers is a poetic that revels in this array of contradiction, allowing the shifting faces of incongruity, uncertainty, possibility, negation, stasis, and change to coexist in an ever turning linguistic and imagistic prism. This refusal to reduce differences and contradictions to a synthesizing homogeneity is mirrored in the forms and structures of the poems themselves, in their oscillations between the metaphysical and the concrete, the delicately aesthetic or painterly, the deliberately abrasive and subversive. In this context Harry's poetry challenges the boundaries and assumptions constructed about the interaction of life and art, the nature and role of poetry, what it means to be a poet (and in particular a woman poet), and how it might be possible with the available tools of language and imagination to weave together the threads of experience and impression to form a coherent and at least transiently meaningful poetic or life pattern.

Much of the poetry reveals itself to be caught on the horns of a metaphysical dilemma. On the one hand, Harry's work seems to yearn toward notions of a stable identity for the self and the speaking voice in the poems, which would concomitantly imply a point of ontological meaning or presence that might be clung to in the face of change and uncertainty. On the other hand, there is evident an equally strong impulse to expose the naïveté of positing such fixed or transcendent points of meaning, which leaves the poems free to engage in a philosophically destabilized jouissance. While there is an inevitable ricocheting movement between these diametrically opposed positions, I would argue that Harry's poetry seeks out a new and potentially deconstructive mode of understanding, and hence of expression, that is able to sustain generatively—albeit not to reconcile—such differences. In the imaginative spaces evoked between and beyond the formal structures of language, the poet evolves styles and strategies of perception designed to maintain the multiplicities of experience in such a way as to confront on a fundamental level the suffocating linearity and fixity of hegemonic ways of reading and seeing.

Harry most conspicuously seeks to disrupt prevailing assumptions about identity and meaning by a challenge to the codes and structures of punctuation, syntax, and the graphic presentation of the words on the page. To sever her poetic phraseology from the assumed formulations of logical thought progression, she utilizes a range of devices—dashes, dots, additional colons, extra spacing between words, altered margins, typescript symbols and abbreviations, and unconventional uses of upper- and lowercase. All of these function as strategies to disturb the surface of linear narrative, thereby creating "added space" or serving as a means of levering open latent contradictions within the finitude of the text. Such strategies thus make a clearing for other voices within the poetic text, be they the voices of philosophical difference, the unconscious, the emotions, the imagination, or an emerging female-centered consciousness.

In the poem "Parts towards a Meaning," from *The Deer under the Skin,* Harry juxtaposes a seemingly random and unlikely accumulation of impressions—the "sewers . . . under victoria street," "the

four thousand year old dead," "Soul Pattinson's baskets," "a two-foot boy in red sandals," etc.—in an apparent attempt to generate by the sheer accretion of detail a cohering significance in what might be otherwise overwhelmingly anarchic. The poet also realizes that she herself may "grow four thousand years old / looking" for this probably mythic unifying significance, the "secret name" of the gods, or the ultimate "birthbook of myth and language." Perhaps, however, with the power and talisman of language she can construct, if not discover, a dike wall of meaning to prevent a landslide into chaos and negation. Confronted with the looming depths and uncertainties that puncture the surface of the poem as "eyes press against the edges of things" to reveal the "shadows [which] go back like pansies black black deep into the sun," Harry explicitly takes on the role or responsibility of the poet and asserts,

> I have to work to find nails . . .
> the purpose of grass is the purpose of nails is the purpose
>   of words . . .
> I have to work to feel shaped sharpness grip like grass . . .

In this poem the desire to see beyond the suffocating weight of accumulated detail is imaged in the conventional terms of a descent, an underwater or chthonic exploration of what may be either knowledge or despair. This movement is echoed by the layout of the words on the page:

> onto
>   /
>   downfrom
>   /
>   grass
>   b
>   l
>   a
>   d
>   e
>   s
>   : the wrists the ankles know

It is at this point of juncture or gap—"the wrists the ankles"—that the knowledge the poem seeks can be found. Paradoxically, uncertainty, or the point of nonarrival, is the poem's discovery at these moments of support and transition, substance and hollowness. The only words and the only lives "to be believed" must come "shaped as a question," as it is only the question that prizes open the heart of the flower to uncover the risks and the promises of the shadows within and beyond.

Harry's use of the initials J.S. as a writing signature might be seen as a device to defuse or even deny her gender specificity. While some of her earlier poems, such as "How Old Pity Left the Poem" and "The Little Grenade," use neuter or even masculine pronouns, Harry's work seems to gain an increasing awareness of the complex subject position of the woman who writes within an essentially patriarchal social and linguistic system. For instance, the poem "The Baby, with the Bath-Water, Thrown Out," from *Hold for a Little While, and Turn Gently,* likens the struggle of the poet to find the language to allude to or to shape experiences to her biological capacity and choice to carry a child. Formulations that prove somehow ineffective, worn out, or clichéd are "dropped . . . by accident" by the poet in the same way as the lost fetus slides from her body and battles its doom-laden way "through the grid / at the bottom of the shower-alcove / . . . resistant / to being broken up." Not only does Harry liken the poet's struggle to conceive meaning and form in language to the woman's ability to produce independent life, but she also aligns herself with this intensely private experience in direct opposition to an unspecified "them" who would understand neither the experience of the woman nor that of the poet. Perhaps it is "they" who would trivialize such intensely felt loss with the use of clichés such as the title. Harry's poem, however, emerges out of and away from the cliché. Beginning with a colon, it suggests the unfinished or inadequate business that preceded it:

> : it will not seem
> a meaningful exercise, to them,
> to hunt new life

This hunt for new life takes on mythic proportions in the later poem "The Gulf of Bothnia" (in *A Dandelion for Van Gogh*), itself a distillation of some of the central issues within Harry's poetry. In this unique place "flounder and pike . . . / . . . seaweed and freshwater plants" live side by side, thus suggesting an environment or a philosophical framework that will nourish elements that are otherwise antithetical. The gulf, however, has a shifting significance within the poem; "cows [who] drink the sea" can exist there, yet it is also subject to its own tides and to the subtlest pulsations of change in the land or continental shelves that underpin it. It may also be suggestive of the historical or psychological origin of human life as it gives birth to "our imaginary relatives" who "grow tails to rise" in the dimmest regions of collective memory. The possible rigidity of such an equation of the sea with the matrix of life is, however, disrupted by the matter-of-fact tone that reminds us that "we are unable to breathe / in the gulf of bothnia." If there is an anesthetizing nostalgia for this apparent place of origins, or "birthbook of myth and language," where opposites can be maintained without tension, it is undercut by the realization that such a region is no longer accessible or indeed supportive of generative life and thought. Within Harry's personal and poetic terms therefore, the recalcitrant prospect of life within such a place, with its mythic stasis and resolutions, must remain an impossibly utopian, if inevitably powerful and informing, dream.

—Rose Lucas

HARSENT, David

Nationality: British. **Born:** Devonshire, 9 December 1942. **Family:** Married to Julia Watson; two sons and one daughter by a previous marriage, one daughter by present marriage. **Career:** Fiction critic, *Times Literary Supplement,* London, 1965–73, and poetry critic, *Spectator,* London, 1970–73; editorial director, Arrow Books, London, 1977–79. Since 1979 editor-in-chief and director, Andre Deutsch, London. **Awards:** Eric Gregory award, 1967; Cheltenham Festival prize, 1968; Arts Council bursary, 1969, 1983; Faber memorial award, 1978; Society of Authors travel fellowship, 1989. **Agent:** Jonathan Clowes Agency, 22 Prince Albert Drive, London NWI 7ST, England. **Address:** Andre Deutsch, 105 Great Russell Street, London WC1B 3LJ, England.

PUBLICATIONS

Poetry

Tonight's Lover. London, The Review, 1968.
A Violent Country. London, Oxford University Press, 1969.
Ashridge. Oxford, Sycamore Press, 1970.
After Dark. London, Oxford University Press, 1973.
Truce. Oxford, Sycamore Press, 1973.
Dreams of the Dead. London, Oxford University Press, 1977.
Mister Punch. Oxford, Oxford University Press, 1984.
Playback, illustrated by Ralph Steadman. London, Greenpeace, 1987.
Selected Poems. Oxford, Oxford University Press, 1989.
Storybook Hero. Oxford, Sycamore Press, 1992.
News from the Front. Oxford, Oxford University Press, 1993.
A Bird's Idea of Flight. London, Faber, 1998.

Play

Gawain, A Libretto. London, Universal Edition, 1991.

Novel

From an Inland Sea. London, Viking Press, 1985.

Other

Editor, *New Poetry 7.* London, Hutchinson, 1981.
Editor, with Mario Susko, *Savremena Britanska Poezije.* Sarajevo, Writers' Union, n.d.
Editor, with Ian Hamilton, *Another Round at the Pillars: Essays, Poems, and Reflections on Ian Hamilton.* Manaccan, Cornwall, Cargo, 1999.

Translator, *The Sorrow of Sarajevo: Poems,* by Goran Simic. Manaccan, Cornwall, Cargo, 1996.
Translator, *Sprinting from the Graveyard,* by Goran Simic. Oxford, Oxford University Press, 1997.

*

Critical Studies: By Shaun McCarthy, in *Agenda* (London), 31(2), Summer 1993; by Martyn Crucefix, in *Poetry Review,* 85(1), Spring 1995.

*   *   *

Pain, frustration, madness, and death are enduring themes in David Harsent's poetry. In *A Violent Country* he writes with intensity and directness, often relying heavily on descriptive detail and perhaps showing greater concern with the projection of experience than with the perfection of poetic form. Both in this volume and in *After Dark* many of the poems gravitate to the confessional, focusing on personal experience either directly observed (as in "Going Back" or "The Visit" in *A Violent Country*) or recovered through backward glances at formative childhood events (as in "Old Photographs" or "Home-coming" in *After Dark*).

Often Harsent's subject is women, a clearly identifiable theme in his *Selected Poems,* and his vehicle of expression animal imagery. For Harsent, ''All we know of love / is pain and the response to pain'' (''Fishbowl'' in *Dreams of the Dead*), and tenderness is balanced with the harshness, if compassion, of his madness and death poems, sometimes by vivid juxtaposition. ''A girl, I dream you as / a kind of fable: Keats, / Orlando, Abelard,'' for example, is set against the actuality of ''a rutting beast, / mad cells, / a cup of blood'' (''The Love-Match'' in *A Violent Country*).

In the later poems of *After Dark* personal experience becomes anchored in landscape and places, ''Figures in a Landscape,'' for example, ending with

Too tired to sleep and knowing of no way
to quieten you, I've walked to this cold bench.

Above the fields
mountains of purple cloud lumber through drizzle.

Between your open window and this place
the land is dark and wringing wet.

The images in the poem sequences of *Dreams of the Dead* are linked in a similar way, with personal experience placed in a larger perspective and events in themselves becoming less important.

The first Punch poems come in *Dreams of the Dead,* consolidating Harsent's move from the personal, idiosyncratic point of view to the universality of all human experience. The interest is in primitive, irrational, internalized images. Punch himself ''feels so old, something primordial . . .'' (''Punch and Judy''), and *Mister Punch* introduces him as Trickster, a spirit of disorder undermining and disrupting order and reality yet reinstating a sense of proportion. From poem to poem Punch progresses from his traditional dissipation, violence, and cunning (''He could taste blood / at the back of his throat''—''Punch in the Ancient World'') to contemplation of ''his sickness and sin'' (''Punch the Anchorite'') to penitence and pleas of ''Virgin intercede'' (''Punch at His Devotions'').

Selected Poems places the archetypes Mister Punch and The Woman, as in ''Windhound,'' for example, side by side, the real issues perhaps centering on a search for male identity in relation to The Woman. Punch tries to reconcile *puer aeternus* aspects of the Trickster archetype—indulging in fantasies, living out experiences for their own sake, and engaging in casual, promiscuous relationships—with aspects of the *senex* such as the wisdom born of experience, the exercise of judgment, and a respect for tradition. And he does so without undermining the energy, enthusiasm, and innovative skill of the *puer aeternus* or, indeed, of Harsent himself and his poetry. Certainly in ''Punch at His Devotions'' he justifies himself to the Virgin in a novel way:

Loved One, Flawless Mirror,
Tamer of Unicorns, Dove,
Star of the Sea, I enter
A plea of diminished laughter.

Harsent's style remains essentially unchanged, but his vision has enlarged considerably.

—B.T. Kugler

HART, Kevin

Nationality: Australian. **Born:** London, England, 5 July 1954; moved to Australia in 1966. **Education:** Australian National University, Canberra (Tillyard award, 1976), 1973–76, B.A. (honors) 1977; Stanford University, California (Stegner fellow), 1977–78; University of Melbourne, 1983–86, Ph.D. 1987. **Family:** Married; two children. **Career:** Coordinator, Department of Philosophy and Religious Studies, Geelong College, Victoria, 1979–83; part-time lecturer in philosophy, 1984–85, and lecturer in English, 1986–87, Melbourne University; lecturer in literary studies, Deakin University, Victoria, 1987–90. Associate professor of English, 1991–94, and since 1994 professor of English and comparative literature, Monash University, Victoria. Visiting professor, Georgetown University, Washington, D.C., 1996–97. **Awards:** Neilson prize, 1977; Australian Literature Board fellowship, 1977; Fulbright award, 1977; Harri Jones award, 1983; Wesley Michael Wright award, 1984; Victorian Premier's award, 1985; New South Wales Premier's award, 1985; Grace Leven award, 1991. Fellow, Australian Academy of the Humanities, 1994. **Agent:** Colin Golvan, 21a Mary Street, Hawthorn, Victoria 3122, Australia. **Address:** 247 Richardson Street, North Carlton, Victoria 3054, Australia.

PUBLICATIONS

Poetry

Nebuchadnezzar. Canberra, Open Door Press, 1976.
The Departure. Brisbane, University of Queensland Press, 1978.
The Lines of the Hand: Poems 1976–1979. Sydney, Angus and Robertson, 1981.
Your Shadow. Sydney, Angus and Robertson, 1984.
Peniel. Melbourne, Golvan Arts, 1990.
The Buried Harbour: Selected Poems of Giuseppe Ungaretti. Canberra, Leros, 1990.
New and Selected Poems. Sydney, Angus and Robertson, 1995.
Dark Angel. Dublin, Dedalus Press, 1996.
Nineteen Songs. Sydney, Vagabond Press, 1999.
Wicked Heat. Sydney, Paperbark Press, 1999.

Other

The Trespass of the Sign: Deconstruction, Theology, and Philosophy. Cambridge, Cambridge University Press, 1989.
A.D. Hope. Melbourne, Oxford University Press, 1992.
Samuel Johnson and the Culture of Property. Cambridge, Cambridge University Press, 1999.

Editor, *Shifting Frames: English/Literature/Writing.* Waurn Ponds, Victoria, Deakin University, 1988.
Editor, *The Oxford Book of Australian Religious Verse.* Melbourne, Oxford University Press, 1994.

*

Manuscript Collection: National Library, Canberra.

Critical Studies: "The Canberra Poets: The New Australian Poetry" by Kevin F. Pearson, in *Poetry of the Pacific Region,* edited by Paul Sharrad, Adelaide, Centre for Research in the New Literatures in English, 1984; "Reading the Signs" by Philip Mead, in *The Adelaide Review* (Adelaide), 25, 1986; "The Weight of Things" by Gary Catalano, in *Overland* (Melbourne), 104, 1986; "Secret Truths: The Poetry of Kevin Hart" by David McCooey, in *Southerly* (Southerly, Australia), 55(4), 1995; "Horizons of the Name" by Martin Harrison, in *Ulitarra,* 10, 1996; "What Bliss to Be Her Slave!: Discipline, Silence and Death in the *Symboliste* Project" by Michael Brennan, in *Masochism: Disciplines of Desire, Aesthetics of Cruelty, Politics of Danger,* edited by Natalya Lusty and Ruth Walker, Sydney, PG ARC Publications, 1998; "In the Mirror: On the Poetic Identify of Kevin Hart" by Gary Catalano, in *Imago,* 10(3), 1999.

*   *   *

Kevin Hart is an accomplished poet in a variety of forms, ranging from the prose poem to the sonnet and sestina. His early book *The Departure* perhaps leaned too heavily on an empty formalism deriving from the Movement poets of the 1950s and ultimately from the much richer formalism of Auden. This formalism produced a number of tired lines such as these: "Those years rise up and peel away. I see / I cannot exempt myself from history." But already in this book Hart was capable of the tough precision and brilliance of the sonnet "Lovers," which concludes,

> I stroke you slowly
> downwards, then kiss and sip the chalice

> between your thighs. I shift again,
> closer, and push into your body
> hard, until you close around me—
> immediate, suffuse. Your eyes
> are jammed open with joy and strain
> as all about us darkness dies.

His next two books, *The Lines of the Hand* and *Your Shadow,* demonstrate an increasing emancipation of verse form that coincided with his conversion to the Anglican and later the Roman Catholic Church. It seems likely that the formalized passion of Christianity provided a channel for the genuine religious emotion of these books, freeing language as well as feeling.

His devotional poems look back to the Metaphysical poets of the seventeenth century, particularly George Herbert, for their inspiration. This affectionate pietism can be heard in the opening lines of "To Christ Our Lord":

> My only friend,
> whose face I could not recognize in a
>   crowd,
> whose voice would not make me turn,
> forgive me for thinking such things important,
> for trusting in only what I can touch.

But it is also a tone of voice that is typically twentieth-century European, as distinct from Anglo-Saxon, and abstract in its sensibility, employing symbols such as clocks, fields, the wind, and trees as objects in a dream landscape having no reference to a particular time or place. Both volumes include a number of translations from modern European poets. Perhaps his most successful translation is "The Flies" from the Spanish of Antonio Machado.

Your Shadow presents itself as a spiritual *livre composé,* a pilgrimage from darkness into light. The volume contains a number of poems called "Your Shadow." These "shadow" poems, with their invocation of "your body's very own black flower," tend to be too genteel and morbid in their introversion. The dualism and belief in original sin that permeate the poems are difficult for the non-Christian to appreciate, although Hart's poems of religious affirmation and celebration will be enjoyed by most readers. "Easter Psalm" is an affectionate and controlled poem with a classic simplicity and restraint. The book concludes with "Poem to the Sun," which is an exultation in Christ and is equally fine.

These two later volumes include a different vein of poetry that is just as successful as the devotional poems. "The Members of the Orchestra" and "Nadia Comanechi" are successful this-worldly poems with great energy and control of language. These lines from "The Hammer" demonstrate equal power:

> This is the sanctus, the pause for preparation, for

> screwing the mind's energies tightly into muscle;
> this is the archer's erasure of himself from his tense
> matrix of forces, the moment of conditioned release
> when the mind delights in its freedom to step outside
> and adore the body, a perfected instrument of will.
> And so the instant comes, intense and blurred, the head

> strikes the nail through the knotted grain, jumping
> back as though appalled by such precise violence and
> for a moment containing the man's mind, pure energy.

—Geoffrey Lehmann

HARWOOD, Lee

Nationality: British. **Born:** Leicester, 6 June 1939. **Education:** St. George's College, Weybridge; Queen Mary College, London, B.A. (honors) in English 1961. **Family:** Married 1) Jenny Goodgame in 1961 (dissolved 1967), one son; 2) Judith Walker in 1974 (divorced 1984), one son and one daughter. **Career:** Monumental mason's mate, 1961; library and museum assistant, 1962–64, 1965–66; packer, 1964; assistant, 1966–67, and manager of the poetry department, 1971, Better Books, London; bus conductor, Brighton, 1969; lived in the United States, 1970, 1972–73; 1983–84; writer-in-residence, Aegean School of Fine Arts, Paros, Greece, Summer 1971, 1972; post office worker, Brighton, 1973–77, 1979–83, and since 1985; occasional lecturer, New College, San Francisco, 1983–84. Editor, *Night Scene* magazine, London, 1963; co-editor, *Night Train* magazine, London, 1963; editor, with Johnny Byrne, *Horde* magazine, London, 1964; editor, with Claude Royet-Journoud, *Soho* magazine, London and Paris, 1964; editor, *Tzarad* magazine, London and Brighton, 1965–69; co-editor, *Boston Eagle,* 1973–74. Chair, Poetry Society, London (resigned); Labour candidate for Sussex County Council,

1977. **Awards:** Poets Foundation award (USA), 1966; Alice Hunt Bartlett award, 1976. **Address:** 21 Chatsworth Road, Brighton, Sussex, England.

PUBLICATIONS

Poetry

Title Illegible. London, Writers Forum, 1965.
The Man with Blue Eyes. New York, Angel Hair, 1966.
The White Room. London, Fulcrum Press, 1968.
The Beautiful Atlas. Brighton, Kavanagh, 1969.
Landscapes. London, Fulcrum Press, 1969.
The Sinking Colony. London, Fulcrum Press, 1970.
Penguin Modern Poets 19, with John Ashbery and Tom Raworth. London, Penguin, 1971.
The First Poem. Brighton, Unicorn Bookshop, 1971.
New Year. London, Wallrich, 1971.
Captain Harwood's Log of Stern Statements and Stout Sayings. London, Writers Forum, 1973.
Freighters. Newcastle upon Tyne, Pig Press, 1975.
H.M.S. Little Fox. London, Oasis, 1975.
Notes of a Post Office Clerk. Gloucester, Massachusetts, Bezoar, 1976.
Boston—Brighton. London, Oasis, 1977.
Old Bosham Bird Watch and Other Stories. Newcastle upon Tyne, Pig Press, 1977; revised edition, 1978.
Wish You Were Here, with Antony Lopez. Deal, Kent, Transgravity Press, 1979.
All the Wrong Notes. Durham, Pig Press, 1981.
Faded Ribbons. Leamington Spa, Warwickshire, Other Branch, 1982.
Wine Tales (includes prose), with Richard Caddel. Newcastle upon Tyne, Galloping Dog Press, 1984.
Monster Masks: Poems 1977–83. Durham, Pig Press, 1985.
Rope Boy to the Rescue. Twickenham, Middlesex, North and South, 1988.
Crossing the Frozen River: Selected Poems. London, Paladin, 1988.
In the Mists: Mountain Poems. West Bridgford, Nottingham, Slow Dancer, 1993.
Morning Light. London, Slow Dancer, 1998.

Recording: *Landscapes,* Stream, 1968.

Short Stories

Assorted Stories. Durham, Pig Press/Staple Diet, 1985; as *Assorted Stories: Prose Works,* Minneapolis, Coffee House Press, 1987.
Dream Quilt: 30 Assorted Stories. Nottingham, Slow Dancer Press, 1985.

Other

Tristan Tzara: A Bibliography. London, Aloes, 1974.

Editor, with William Corbett and Lewis Warsh, *The Boston Eagle at Home.* Privately printed, 1973.
Editor, with Peter Bailey, *The Empty Hill: Memories and Praises of Paul Evans (1945–1991).* N.p., Skylark Press, 1992.

Translator, *A Poem Sequence,* by Tristan Tzara. Gillingham, Kent, Arc, 1969; revised edition, as *Cosmic Realities Vanilla Tobacco Dawnings,* 1975.
Translator, *Destroyed Days,* by Tristan Tzara. Colchester, Essex, Voice print, 1971.
Translator, *Selected Poems,* by Tristan Tzara. London, Trigram Press, 1975; revised and enlarged edition, as *Chanson Dada: Selected Poems,* Toronto. Coach House Press, 1987.

*

Critical Studies: In *Records and Recording* (London), April 1969; by Raymond Gardiner, in *The Guardian* (London), 8 July 1970; interview with Victor Bockris, in *Pennsylvania Review 1* (Philadelphia), 1970; *The Ironic Harvest: English Poetry in the 20th Century* by Geoffrey Thurley, London, Amold, 1974; interview with Eric Mottram, in *Poetry Information 14* (London), Winter 1975–76; "The Illusions of Freedom: The Poetry of Lee Harwood" by Paul Selby, in *Poetry Information 15* (London), 1976; *The British Dissonance: Essays on Ten Contemporary Poets* by A. Kingsley Weatherhead, Columbia, University of Missouri Press, 1983; *Some Aspects of Contemporary British Poetry with Particular Reference to the Work of Roy Fisher and Lee Harwood* (dissertation), n.p., 1989, and "Lee Harwood and the Poetics of the Open Work," in *New British Poetries: The Scope of the Possible,* edited by Robert Hampson and Peter Barry, both by Robert Sheppard; "Some British Beat History: 10—No Longer Wailing" by Dave Cunliffe, in *Kerouac Connection,* 20, Autumn 1990.

Lee Harwood comments:

I like to think of my writing as a form of collage that tries to present and create a balanced world, a four-dimensional whole. My poems work with a mixture of fragments, of stories, direct talk, suggestions, and at times quotations from other artists. They jump about, like most minds and imaginations do, and hope the reader or listener is willing to make the effort to follow, to work a bit and to collaborate in the making of the text. No writer wants to be obscure or difficult, but one cannot always talk in simplistic terms. Sometimes the nature of a subject, if it is to be expressed with any clarity and precision, must allow for complexity.

*   *   *

"I just want to tell you the truth," says Lee Harwood's voice in *Boston-Brighton.* Whereas another poet, Robert Frost, for example, might set watch at the ocean's edge for people to peer metaphysically yet not see clearly, as in "Neither Out Far nor in Deep," Harwood sees precisely what might be there:

a lone freighter
silhouetted
maybe three freighters
with crews and cooks and captains
are silhouetted
are even clear out to sea
        there
I point in front of my face.

Harwood's first two books, consciously aware of Charles Olson's *Maximus Poems,* are "mappings" of reality. They include poems,

495

photographs, historical notes, geological sketches, and photocopied advertisements. They are more collage than the *Maximus Poems,* less intense, more modestly personal. In place of Olson's grand "monstrance" of a national "Republic," Harwood looks for "a list of simple, practical and just acts" that move "towards a real 'socialism.'" Like Olson—and Joyce, too, for that matter—Harwood sees our world formed on the edge of the "ghost" world of the past. We must exist with the dead,

> not denying the ghosts
> but banding with them
> their existence our gravity
> the dead surround us,
> hold us up, that is support us,
> lovingly
> in the progress

Charting perception has been Harwood's love from the beginning. He is interested in how seeing "rows of white houses" might evolve into a song title and how hearing the song then brings, or does not bring, the houses back into view. He is interested in how reality is what we compose out of fragments and how within it everyone goes about, or does not go about. Harwood writes like a painter; life is "a bare canvas, but not empty— / all there under the surface." Poems happen when he rubs a pencil over the grain he did not know was there. The reality forms continuously at the edge of his syllables. If he is not invested in the next word, it will come in quotation marks, for in these poems language makes reality. Hence the fragments, the sudden spaces, the poems that end without periods or with a line sliced by diagonal space, or the poem that does not end at all:

> The curtains are once again opened
> and the opera continues
>
> for there is much that language does not yet know:
>
> All the books and maps and knowledge give us too little,
> leave large blank spaces, 'terra incognita'.

Reading Harwood is exploration; his world is transformed as his mind adjusts its focal length, just as the reader's is in reading. You cannot be quite sure when you turn the page that the same words will be where you remembered them to be, or that you will be, or that the reality you were watching will survive:

> the film breaks at this point. Crackling noises and smoke
> pour from the improvised projection room.

Harwood has an offbeat wit, and he is a marvelous storyteller. His poems invite us in. It is charming to be presented with open space or to be given ambiguity so economically constructed that we must enter the poem, participate, do what he would that we do, embrace our carefully chosen ghosts. The poet will even give us a quiz after reading to help:

QUESTIONS

i) Does the man go mad?

Does he even commit suicide? (hence a well-rounded drama) or continue a life of quiet suburban despair? (so a well-rounded 'Modern' drama) . . .

vi) Are we denied peace?
Not the peace of answers, set ideas and realized hopes,(stagnation), but the peace to do things we want to do for ourselves. To push on, unhindered by jobs, exhaustion, and 'the treacle of fears and evasions'!!??

Are we? See "The Beginning of the Story" in *Monster Masks.*

Social commentary has a place, but Harwood's heart touches people and love. In his lyrical poems his voice is modest, unassuming, and gentle. He writes with an impressionist's eye. Reading "The Final Painting" or "Soft White" is to sense the subtlest change of hue as a cloud shifts in the sky:

> When the sea is as grey as her eyes
> On these days for sure the soft white
> mist blown in from the ocean the town dissolving
> It all adds up her bare shoulders
>
> Nakedness rolling in from the sea
> on winter afternoons . . .

Harwood can move gracefully to prose and to collaboration. In *Wine Tales* he and Richard Caddel each inhabit a dozen wine labels in strange, marvelous vignettes. In *All the Wrong Notes* he joins photographer Judith Walker to augment dissonances in a paralyzed London, soon turning toward poetry, toward dreams, and toward the false dreams in which we struggle to disbelieve:

> It's those dreams of perfection, 'the man of your dreams', 'woman of your dreams', 'the budgie of your dreams', 'your dreams come true' to a jarring chorus of cash registers and half-stifled moans.

Against this the final poem, "The Fern Cabinet," sets an alternative. Based on quotations from writers and visionaries that unite past, present, and future, it has a lyrical reality that comes into focus as "a faint cloud passes and / the distant landscape is precise in every detail."

In his years of writing Harwood has progressed beyond his mapped world that threatened to become a hieroglyph for himself to become a lyricist for whom delicate sensuality is not a dream but a better way. He thus brought to the late twentieth century a gentleness and plausibility it sorely needed.

—Edward B. Germain

HASHMI, (Aurangzeb) Alamgir

Nationality: Pakistani. **Born:** Lahore, 15 November 1951. **Education:** University of the Punjab, Lahore, M.A. 1972; University of Louisville, Kentucky, M.A. 1977. **Military Service:** Civil Defense,

Multan Cantonment, 1965–66: Certificate of Merit 1966. **Family:** Married Béatrice Störk in 1978; one daughter and two sons. **Career:** Instructor in English, 1971–72, and tutor of English as a second language, 1972–73, Government College, Lahore; lecturer in English, Forman Christian College, Lahore, 1973–74; visiting lecturer in South Asian languages and literatures, University of North Carolina, Chapel Hill, 1974–75; lecturer in English, University of Louisville, Kentucky, 1975–78; assistant professor of English, University of Bahawalpur, 1979–80; visiting lecturer, lecturer in English, English instructor, and visiting professor of English, Universities of Zurich, Fribourg, Bern, and Basel, Klubschule Migros, Berlitz School of Languages, and Volkshochschule Zurich, all Switzerland, 1980–85; associate professor of English, International Islamic University, Islamabad, 1985–86; visiting professor of English literature, Federal Government Post-graduate College for Men, Islamabad, Spring 1986; visiting professor of American and African literature, Quaid-i-Azam University, Islamabad, Autumn 1986. Since 1986 professor and head of the department of English, University of Azad Jammu and Kashmir, Muzaffarabad. Since 1988 research professor of English and comparative literature and literary editor, PIDE, Quaid-i-Azam University, Islamabad. Since 1988 course director, Foreign Service Training Institute, Pakistan Ministry of Foreign Affairs, Islamabad. Assistant editor, *The Ravi,* Lahore, 1970–71; faculty adviser, *Folio,* Lahore, 1973–74; editor and broadcaster, *English Magazine,* Lahore, 1973–74; since 1978 foreign and consulting editor, *Explorations,* Lahore; guest editor, *The New Quarterly,* New York, 1977–78; corresponding and associate editor, *Helix,* Ivanhoe and Canberra, 1978–85; since 1979 regional representative, *Journal of Commonwealth Literature,* Oxford; since 1981 staff reviewer, *World Literature Today,* Norman, Oklahoma; since 1981 editorial adviser, *Kunapipi,* Aarhus, Denmark; since 1981 staff contributor, *Annual Bibliography of English Language and Literature,* Cambridge, England; member, editorial board, *Crosscurrent,* Hamilton, New Zealand, 1980–89; since 1982 associate editor and member of editorial board, *Commonwealth Novel in English,* Austin, Texas; contributing editor, *Pacific Quarterly,* Hamilton, New Zealand, 1982–85; member of the editorial board, *Poetry Europe,* Madras, India, 1982; since 1990 adviser, *Journal of English Studies,* Lahore; since 1990 editor, *The Routledge Encyclopaedia of Commonwealth Literature;* guest editor, *Pakistani Literature,* Islamabad, 1993. Founder, Townsend Poetry Prize, 1986. Since 1989 adviser, National Book Council of Pakistan, and chair, Standing International Conference Committee on English in South Asia. Since 1968 broadcaster, compere, commentator, lecturer, translator, and literary editor, Radio Pakistan; since 1988 compere, Pakistan Television. **Awards:** The University of the Punjab (Lahore) Scholar, 1970–72, and Certificate of Academic Merit, 1973; first prize, All-Pakistan Creative Writing Contest, 1972; Pakistan Academy of Letters Patras Bokhari award, 1985; Rockefeller Fellow, 1994; Roberto Celli Memorial award (Italy), 1994. D.Litt.: University of Luxembourg, 1984; San Francisco State University, 1984. **Address:** c/o Indus Books, P.O. Box 2905, Islamabad, GPO, Pakistan.

PUBLICATIONS

Poetry

The Oath and Amen. Philadelphia, Dorrance, 1976.
America Is a Punjabi Word. Lahore, Karakorum Range, 1979.
An Old Chair. Bristol, Xenia Press, 1979.

My Second in Kentucky. Lahore, Vision Press, 1981.
This Time in Lahore. Lahore, Vision Press, 1983.
Neither This Time/Nor That Place. Lahore, Vision Press, 1984.
Inland and Other Poems. Islamabad, Gulmohar Press, 1984.
The Poems of Alamgir Hashmi. Islamabad, National Book Foundation, 1992.
Sun and Moon and Other Poems. Islamabad, Indus Books, 1992.
A Choice of Hashmi's Verse. Karachi and New York, Oxford University Press, 1997.

Other

Commonwealth Literature: An Essay Towards the Re-Definition of a Popular/Counter Culture. Lahore, Vision Press, 1983.
The Commonwealth, Comparative Literature and the World. Islamabad, Gulmohar Press, 1988.

Editor, *Pakistani Literature: The Contemporary English Writers.* New York, World University Service, 2 vols., 1978; revised edition, Islamabad, Gulmohar Press, 1 vol., 1987.
Editor, with Les Harrop and others, *Ezra Pound in Melbourne.* Ivanhoe, Australia, Helix, 1983.
Editor, *The Worlds of Muslim Imagination.* Islamabad, Gulmohar Press, 1986.
Editor, *Encyclopedia of Post-Colonial Literatures in English.* London, Routledge, 1994.

*

Critical Studies: "Hashmi's Poetry of Double Roots" by Janet Powers Gemmill, in *Explorations* (Lahore), 1980; "Is America a Punjabi Word?: An Assessment of Alamgir Hashmi's Poetry" by Kaleem Omar, in *The Star* (Karachi), 4 July 1985; "Alamgir Hashmi's Wandering Soul" by Hina Babar Ali, in *Journal of South Asian Literature* (East Lansing, Michigan), 23(1), 1988; "Alamgir Hashmi's Poetry: Pakistan, Modernity and Language" by Bruce King, in *Journal of Indian Writing in English* (Gulbarga, India), 16(2), July 1988; "'Let's Celebrate': Alamgir Hashmi's *My Second in Kentucky*" by Michael Sharkey, in *New Literature Review* (Wollongong, Australia), 15, 1988; "A New Vision for Commonwealth Literature" by Eric Cyprian, in *The Nation* (Lahore), 23 November 1990; "New Literatures in English" by John Thieme, in *The Year's Work in English Studies* (Oxford), 69, 1991; "A Cross-Cultural Experience" by Muneeza Shamsie, in *Dawn Magazine* (Karachi), 2 October 1992; "Holding Language to Feeling" by Shaista Sonnu Sirajuddin, in *Friday Muslim* (Islamabad), 16 October 1992; "The Poems of Alamgir Hashmi" by Burton Raffel, in *The Literary Review* (Madison, New Jersey), 37(4), 1994.

Alamgir Hashmi comments:

I started writing around 1962 and began to show my work to friends around 1964–65. My first book, *The Oath and Amen,* was a thematic collection subtitled *Love Poems,* though it contained a countermovement, "Distractions," in the last section, and I had indeed written by then at least as many poems that would be described differently. Love, nevertheless, is a theme and a quality that runs through my work as a question or an answer or the distance between them, the role and the play that it must have in personal relations and the world formed so. *America Is a Punjabi* Word followed several years' residence in the United States, which had increasingly become a second home. It is a lyric-narrative, a long poem on a short scale, and it explores the same concerns in a stretchable form and a new setting, language, and feeling being a further equation of relevance. *My Second in Kentucky,* containing much of my best work done till the end of 1977 (I moved the following year), has three divisions by setting, corresponding to three different movements in my life as in my book: poems in America, poems in Pakistan, and poems in America/Pakistan. My formal and thematic preoccupations are both represented well in this volume, as they were announced in the very first book. I have been interested in Eastern and Western verse forms, terms of speech, and details of reference that could deal adequately with my particular experience and the shape of my desire.

Moving to Europe in the late 1970s, necessitated by the martial law in Pakistan, proved to be a mixed blessing; one had to adjust now, additionally, to the appearance of freedom. I began to reexamine my Swiss existence and the overall human issues involved in light of my commitments and values. Two major books are from this period: *This Time in Lahore* and *Neither This Time/Nor That Place.* In both these I have generally dropped the traditional verse forms and tried to develop a vers libre drawing on the poetic resources of natural speech as far as my linguistic access would allow. Physical culture is, paradoxically, more limited than language; almost anyone may live in the latter. As I have personally moved house several times, many of my poems have been seen to be set in here, or there, or nowhere in particular, leading to appropriate observations and generalizations. Some of the poems in the books, in fact, have omissions and deletions of lines or whole stanzas so that the poetry could be kept in circulation in the face of censorship. Only the earlier published versions in the magazines and journals, or the author's own records in such cases, could help retrieve the objective text, which has been supplied in most cases by my collected poems, *The Poems of Alamgir Hashmi.* While I feel the particular facts of composition in all such cases would be crucial to interpretation, I blame only myself for foisting my own lifestyle on my poems. All these features—of form, language, theme, and setting—can also be seen in *Inland and Other Poems,* the last poetry book completed in Switzerland. My latest book, *Sun and Moon and Other Poems,* contains poems written in Pakistan, and I believe this work represents a turning point of a life in art in such forms as will not defeat the experience. One kind of exile has led to another and found its home in the only words and rhythms possible for it.

To sum up, I must say that I do not necessarily speak in my own voice, though the poems always do, that I use my own language but I am not (always) shy of fancying my neighbor's pretty idiom, that I have compromised my poetry's weight in gold to sustain its intrinsic value, and that I have searched for a place to belong to and tried to delineate its exact relations.

I have published several books since returning to Pakistan in 1988, and my work appears regularly in journals and anthologies and in the national press. It is important to me as a writer that my work is read in this country, while it is also gratifying to see the interest from abroad, because language must connect us. I continue to see man/woman in nature, in the world, and in the society with as much wonder as the fun of the world will elicit, though touched by a sense of the tragic, which is too personal—and, I feel, cosmic—to have a long span in any narrative. With the benefit of hindsight, I can say that I write out of experience, that to live one needs more beauty than even truth. My work is one of celebration, analysis, and integration,

looking out for possibility and seeking the joy that comes from the discovery of the common natural and human element across each Berlin Wall that has been built upon the foundation of our own inhibitions or fears.

I was trained as a scholar, and I have taught English and comparative literature for the past twenty-five years in North America, Europe, and Asia. My scholarly and critical work is part of my total experience as a writer. I find the practice of poetry enriches the critical understanding of literature, which I teach as a form of knowledge about being human and as a language to understand with pleasure.

*   *   *

Although the philosophical and psychological themes of Alamgir Hashmi's mature poetry are universal, their development, form of expression, symbolism, and setting owe much to his years of study abroad, exile, and travel. Having been uprooted from Pakistan and displaced heighten his awareness of time and change, of the self isolated from others, and of alienation from the past. While his verse reveals the heritage of both the Urdu ghazel and of English poetry, Hashmi at first sought forms and language that translated and blended the two traditions into a personal style and manner. The attempt at following a bilingual muse was somewhat awkward and contrived in his first book, *The Oath and Amen,* published two years after he had traveled to the United States. *America Is a Punjabi Word* is concerned with language and the conventions of poetry in different societies. It amusingly juxtaposes clichés of the Orient with the stereotypes of the West. Such good-natured joking belongs to a period of youthful liberation and travel before rootlessness results in the sadness of being foreign, exiled, or deeply alienated. A comic surrealism parodies the American stereotype of being on the road as he travels throughout the United States with the perspective of a Pakistani journeying with a camel (his muse and foreignness). The United States is an alien country, and the essentially American is seen in a humorous analogy to the Islamic world: ''I was in New York. // I went up an / updated pyramid.'' Language becomes a theme as both poetry and foreign lands make one aware of clichés, puns, loosely expressed thoughts, symbolism, emblems, language as arbitrary signs. Hashmi brings to the language and the nakedness of American poetry his own sensibility. He feels, like language, arbitrary, exiled from reality, a camel in America.

By the time of *My Second in Kentucky* the comic mask is often dropped to reveal memories and a quiet sadness; the poet is nostalgic for Lahore and his family but no longer at home in any place. ''Of First Things,'' in its concern with the fragility of origins, growth, uncertainty of purpose, the difficulty of interpreting the flux of life, and the role of poetry in creating significance, can be read as an introduction to the volume. There is increasing obliqueness as modernist juxtaposition and the compression of the ghazel meet to create a highly poetic leaping sort of logic. Unusual expressions and purposely non-American English contribute to the feeling of exile and the ways in which language is associated with society and environment: ''Shredded in the cold / winds of Kentucky for days, / women pass around incentive: / make bold.'' But the poems set in Pakistan also reveal a sense of distance. The four ghazels, although written in couplets, are neither classically rhymed nor poems of love. Their mood is autumnal and associated with Lahore, and they conclude with rejection: ''This place is too old for me. / This sun is too old for me.''

In contrast to the heroism of exile there is the temptation to return, to make peace, to give up the quest, to settle for the possible rewards of the prodigal son. The title poem of *This Time in Lahore* treats of such tensions and temptations during a visit home. But the poet notices that his father is unshaved, his mother greying, his own books worm-eaten and wet from the last monsoon, while the military is now in command. Unlike the earlier youthful joyfulness, *This Time in Lahore* has poems that celebrate the normality of failure, the impossibility of harmony. The poems are quiet, determined, with the calm, knowing voice of experience. The pleasures of life are not utopian or a return to the flock; they are, rather, the small joys of living and of domestic comforts under cloudy skies. The feeling that emerges is that, while it is confusing, life offers pleasures, and at the end of the day the poem itself is what is important. Such themes are the subject of ''Poem in Pakistan'': ''I forget now what it was. / The poem is nevertheless.''

The tensions of exile settle into locating the self at whatever place Hashmi happens to be. Many poems in *This Time in Lahore* refer to locations: ''An Oriental Poet Dotes over Tuscany,'' ''Khyber Pass,'' ''Swans in the Lake,'' ''Going to La Chute,'' ''In the Hill Country.'' Hashmi's manner and style now seem at his command, and the writing flows naturally in a continuous movement as part of the thought. The concern with time and place, influenced by traveling and living for long periods outside Pakistan, is shown in the titles of several of his books: *America Is a Punjabi Word, My Second in Kentucky, This Time in Lahore,* and *Neither This Time/Nor That Place.* To live, to mature, to be conscious is to be alone. Love should help, but poetry is as much of an answer to the loneliness of existence as life offers. The muse incarnated as poem gives the comforts that women are expected to give. Being in the woods, hearing a quail, seeing attractive, strange flowers and animals, fantasizing about others, the poet can share the experience only with himself: ''I had no one by me / to whisper the anticipation, / to say Yes, now I have seen one, / when I had seen; / but that was just as well. / I took my hand in my own hand.''

Although later poems reveal religious desire, there is only the skeptical doubt of someone who knows that life is, to use the symbolism of ''Prayer,'' a ''dust-storm.'' Travel, age, time, storms, observing women, many cities and countries, foreigners, writing poetry—there is a pattern in the mosaic, a jigsaw puzzle that is found to have a coherent if somewhat centrifugal design. No place is the right place and no time the right time for wholeness, unity, continuity, Eden, but all places are the right place and time for experience, for consciousness, for poetry. The seven-part ''Bahawalpurlog'' brings together the vision scattered throughout these poems. The first four lines include the recurring themes, symbols, and motifs of ''doubt,'' ''dust-storm,'' ''gray,'' and writing found in his later volumes. Even at Panjnad, where Pakistan's five main rivers come together and a place that should be a symbol for a new unity, a new national language, the dust storm blows, time silts the river, and the poet feels alienated from whatever unity Arabic might have offered. Language, like reality, exiles him from the unity of oneness, of belonging. The Christ story is treated in ''A Life,'' the final poem of *Neither This Time/Nor That Place,* as having a rather different, skeptical symbolism from that common to Christianity: ''And, when two faithful women looked to heaven, / only birds' casual droppings / seemed to waft through air / the signal of his death.'' History is filled with examples of those abandoned by both humanity and the divine.

In *Inland and Other Poems* such despondency is connected with the breakup of Hashmi's marriage and with the prospect of returning to Pakistan. He is alone in these poems, feeling a further isolation, usually in a romantic, picturesque place. He reads letters, comments wryly on books, and indulges in punning. There are fantasies about people discovered in newspaper stories, reflections on love and marriage, self-mockery about celibacy, memories of Switzerland. While the volume begins with dejection and the oddments of a life without purpose, it builds toward renewal as the stories become comic and playful again and the poet begins to identify with places in Pakistan and considers the possibility of falling in love once more. Still, one is left with a feeling of a life in a stage of transition, of going back to a homeland that is no longer home.

Actually, however, Hashmi's return to live in Pakistan proved to be a real homecoming not only to Pakistan but also to the world. Renewal of the connection with his homeland also brought with it a sense of belonging to the larger world characteristically absent in the earlier work. *Sun and Moon and Other Poems,* completed during the years after his return to Pakistan, thus ushers in a decisive new phase in Hashmi's poetry. He is no longer a poet of exile, writing as an outsider. Instead, he now writes from the inside, whatever the setting of his subjects, Pakistan, the rest of Asia, or the West. Accompanying this new sense of belonging, however, is a sadness, deeper than ever, that permeates the poetry. The sadness comes from personal grief or concerns about the state of affairs in Pakistan and in the world. ''Sun and Moon,'' for example, expresses the loss of the happy time when his son, for whom the poem was written, was little and the family was together: ''tears come down like a rain that strings all instruments / making new channels of grief in this poem / and across that continent of pain.'' Several poems, ''For B'' most poignant among them, recall a woman's love, now lost. Poems such as ''Pro Bono Publico—in Pakistani English'' and ''Off the Wall'' satirize the corruption and hypocrisy of the country's leaders. Many poems deal with problems of a universal scale, especially the destructive role of colonialism in Asia, Africa, and Latin America, as conveyed in ''The Game Called Tripoly,'' ''They Are Waltzing,'' ''Napoleon's Clock,'' ''Crusoe's Island,'' and ''Winter Flight.''

Despite the pervasive sadness, Hashmi's poetry here is free from bitterness about personal hurts or utter despair about the circumstances of the world. An awareness that happiness does not last and that history throughout has been an endless recurrence of human suffering gives Hashmi's outlook a tempered, stoic quality. He is, however, also aware that sorrow is often interspersed with periods of unalloyed happiness. In poem after poem, therefore, he sets his sights on the future, on ''the interminable deltas of hope'' for happiness to come: ''Future is the only flower worth tending in this earth, / where I sow my words daily . . .'' Hashmi's poetry, his mastery over its forms having grown hand in hand with its content, is at its lyrical best in these calls to happiness. For long an exile, Hashmi has thus come to have an assured home in a common bond with the world and its future and in the world of poetry.

—Bruce King and Surjit S. Dulai

HASS, Robert

Nationality: American. **Born:** San Francisco, California, 1 March 1941. **Education:** St. Mary's College, Moraga, California, B.A. 1963; Stanford University, California (Woodrow Wilson Fellow;

Danforth Fellow), 1964–67, M.A. 1965, Ph.D. 1976. **Family:** Married Earlene Leif in 1962; three children. **Career:** Has taught at the State University of New York, Buffalo, 1967–71, St. Mary's College, Moraga, California, 1971–74, 1975–89, and University of Virginia, Charlottesville, 1974. Since 1989 professor of English, University of California, Berkeley. Poet-in-residence, The Frost Place, Franconia, New Hampshire, 1978. U.S. Poet Laureate/Consultant in Poetry, Library of Congress, 1995–97. **Awards:** Yale Series of Younger Poets award, 1972; US-UK Bicentennial Exchange fellowship, 1976; William Carlos Williams award, 1979; Guggenheim fellowship, 1980; American Academy award, 1984; MacArthur Foundation fellowship, 1984–89; NBCC award, for criticism, 1985; P.E.N./ B.A.B.R.A. award, for translation, 1986. U.S. Poet Laureate/Consultant in Poetry, Library of Congress, 1995–97. **Address:** c/o Ecco Press, 100 West Broad Street, Hopewell, New Jersey 08525, U.S.A.

PUBLICATIONS

Poetry

Field Guide. New Haven, Connecticut, Yale University Press, 1973.
Winter Morning in Charlottesville. Knotting, Bedfordshire, Sceptre Press, 1977.
Praise. New York, Ecco Press, 1979; Manchester, Carcanet, 1981.
Five American Poets, with others. Manchester, Carcanet, 1979.
Spring Drawing. New York, Dia Art Foundation, 1988.
Human Wishes. New York, Ecco Press, 1989.
Sun under Wood: New Poems. Hopewell, New Jersey, Ecco Press, 1996.

Recording: *A Story about the Body,* Watershed, 1988; *Sounding Lines the Art of Translating Poetry,* University of California Office of Media Services, 1999.

Other

Twentieth Century Pleasures: Prose on Poetry. New York, Ecco Press, 1984.
Poet's Choice: Poems for Everyday Life. Hopewell, New Jersey, Ecco Press, 1998.
An Unnamed Flowing: The Cultures of American Poetry. Washington, D.C., Counterpoint, 2000.

Editor, *Rock and Hawk: A Selection of Shorter Poems,* by Robinson Jeffers. New York, Random House, 1987.
Editor, *Selected Poems 1954–1986,* by Tomas Tranströmer. New York, Ecco Press, 1987.
Editor, with Stephen Mitchell, *Into the Garden: A Wedding Anthology: Poetry and Prose on Love and Marriage.* New York, HarperCollins, 1993.
Editor, *The Essential Haiku: Versions of Basho, Buson, and Issa.* Hopewell, New Jersey, Ecco Press, 1994.
Editor, with others, *Back Roads to Far Towns: Basho's Oku-no-hosomichi.* Hopewell, New Jersey, Ecco Press, 1996.

Translator, with Robert Pinsky, *The Separate Notebooks,* by Czeslaw Milosz. New York, Ecco Press, 1984.

Translator, with Czeslaw Milosz, *Unattainable Earth,* by Milosz. New York, Ecco Press, 1986.
Translator, with others, *Collected Poems,* by Czeslaw Milosz. New York, Ecco Press, 1988.
Translator, with Czeslaw Milosz, *Provinces* by Milosz. Hopewell, New Jersey, Ecco Press, 1993.
Translator, *Facing the River: New Poems,* by Czeslaw Milosz. Hopewell, New Jersey, Ecco Press, and Manchester, Carcanet, 1995.
Translator, *Road-Side Dog,* by Czeslaw Milosz. New York, Farrar Straus, 1998.

*

Critical Studies: ''Praise: The Poetry of Robert Hass'' by Robert Miklitsch, in *The Hollins Critic* (Hollins College, Virginia), 17(1), 1980; ''The Letter-Poem'' by Hank Lazer, in *Northwest Review* (Eugene, Oregon), 19(1–2), 1981; ''I and Ideology: Demystifying the Self of Contemporary Poetry'' by Gary Waller, in *Denver Quarterly* (Denver), 18(3), autumn 1983; '''And There Are Always Melons,' Some Thoughts on Robert Hass'' by Alan Shapiro, in *Chicago Review* (Chicago), 33(3), winter 1983; ''Poetry Chronicle: Don Pagis and Robert Hass'' by Charles Berger, in *Raritan* (New Brunswick, New Jersey), 10(1), summer 1990; ''Opposed Sensibilities: Hass and Gluck'' by Lee Upton, in *Northwest Review* (Eugene, Oregon), 28–29(3), 1990; ''Holding Out against Loss and Jacques Lacan: Some Reflections on Robert Hass's 'Sensuous Line''' by Gunilla Florby, in *Studia Neophilologica* (Oslo, Norway), 63(2), 1991; ''Robert Hass: Bard on the National Stage'' by Michael Coffey, in *Publishers Weekly,* 243(44), 28 October 1996; by Grace Cavalieri, and ''From Image to Sentence: The Spiritual Development of Robert Hass'' by Terrence Doody, both in *American Poetry Review* (Philadelphia), 26(2), March-April 1997; ''Poetry and Masculinity on the Anglo/ Chicano Border: Gary Soto, Robert Frost, and Robert Hass'' by Michael Tomasek Manson, in *The Calvinist Roots of the Modern Era,* edited by Manson, Aliki Barnstone, and Carol J. Singley, Hanover, New Hampshire, University Press of New England, 1997; by Gerald Haslam, in *Updating the Literary West,* Forth Worth, Texas, Western Literature Association, 1997.

*   *   *

Robert Hass, as he puts it in an essay in his *Twentieth Century Pleasures,* is a poet concerned with ''the pure activity of being consciously alive.'' Convinced that it is possible to turn outward, away from ''our inner emptiness . . . which mutilates the world and turns it into badly handled objects'' (''Looking for Rilke''), Hass has throughout his career worked out a number of important approaches to the problem of creating a poetry that simply says of the world, ''this is.'' The goal is most forcefully presented in another essay from the collection, in which Hass describes the way certain images ''marry the world, but . . . do not claim to possess it, and in this they have the power and the limitations of intimate knowledge. As someone can own a piece of land and have the power to change it or dispose of it as he pleases, and someone else can use that land, walk on it, work it, know the color of it changed in gray light, when the wild radish flowers, where the deer leave imprints of their bedding down, and not own it, have no external claim to it.'' Such images—using the world but relinquishing any guarantee of ownership—become for Hass "figures for that clear, deep act of acceptance and relinquishment which human beings are capable of" ("Images").

Hass's *Field Guide,* as its title suggests, is a book about "the sudden feel of life" ("On the Coast near Sausalito") involved in the act of naming. Its poems consistently contrast two different ways of handling language—an often brutal confidence in its ability to possess the world and a more tentative awareness of limits—in order to put into play a tension within Hass himself. As he puts it in "Fall," a poem about gathering mushrooms, Hass would place himself on the side of linguistic "amateurs"—gathering and naming and using the "aromatic fungi" of the world with a constant awareness of tension and limits:

> Death shook us more than once
> those days and floating back
> it felt like life. Earth-wet, slithery,
> we drifted toward the names of things.

Such amateurs, Hass suggests in "Spring," might agree with Wittgenstein that "the limits of my language / are the limits of my world," but they would also go on from there to explore the sense of flexibility and intimacy generated by speaking a language that may not hold: "We spoke all night in tongues, / in fingertips, in teeth." At the same time, however, Hass makes it clear how often his words would have it otherwise, calling him away from life and back to that drive to possess and perfect, what one poem calls "the lobotomy of description" ("Palo Alto: The Marshes").

Hass's collection *Praise* not only sets this tension going but also addresses it forcefully. This can be seen most clearly in "Meditation at Lagunitas," in which he confronts our contemporary awareness of the "loss" built into all language use: the "notion that, / because there is in this world no one thing / to which the bramble of *blackberry* corresponds, / a word is elegy to what it signifies." Focusing on such a failure to master the world, Hass realizes, rightly means that "everything dissolves: *justice, / pine, hair, woman, you,* and *I.*" Though he acknowledges giving into that inevitably frustrated desire himself, Hass counters this sense of dissolution by also remembering another, a more "tender" and limited, use of words that involves itself with the world without ever raising the question of mastery. Other poems in the book propose examples of what such a use of language might look like. "Weed," for example, notices the way the common name of a plant, absurdly "marrying the words" *horse* and *parsnips,* creates not a version of desire but something "durable and unimaginative." A drifting letter to a friend about "an odd terror in my memory" ("Not Going to New York: A Letter") suggests that its merely explanatory limits—it is a letter, "not poetry where decay and a created / radiance lie hidden inside words"—"make life seem more commonplace and—at a certain angle— / more intense." "Songs to Survive the Summer" offers his grief-stricken daughter a series of "curiously shaped" images and stories, none of which will "save" her but all of which touch the dying world "casually / . . . lustered / by the steady thoughtlessness / of human use."

In the collection *Human Wishes* Hass continues to search for ways to present by relinquishing but adds to that task an acute awareness that our "lustered," commonplace gatherings are often not as durable as we let ourselves think. "Things change," one poem wryly admits: marriages break apart, children grow up, readers gather and then splinter, a man is of two minds about something. Hass's later

poems, then, realize that there are "many visions / intersecting at what we call the crystal / of a common world, all the growing and shearing, / all the violent breaks" ("Santa Barbara Road"). Though he continues to search out common rather than poetic ways of shaping and praising the world, his forms in this book also strive to incorporate a sense of breaking and scattering. The description in "Late Spring," for example, is presented in a series of peeled-apart clauses, each of which touches some aspect of the season's shifting, intensifying rhythm but none of which holds it. A paragraph about a couple in a museum restaurant juxtaposes Hass's response to their sleepy but sure rhythms ("I have fallen in love with this equitable arrangement, and with the baby who cooperates by sleeping") with the carved faces ("suffering the numbest kind of pain") exhibited around them. The durable, commonplace gesture still remains for Hass, but now it drifts in a more broken, violent realm:

> And the man is not hurt exactly,
> he understands that life has limits, that people
> die young, fail at love,
> fail of their ambitions. He runs beside her, he thinks
> of the sadness they have gasped and crooned their
>   way out of
> coming, clutching each other with odd, invented
> forms of grace and clumsy gratitude, ready
> to be alone again, or dissatisfied, or merely
> companionable

Hass also has occupied himself with translation. His longtime collaboration with Czeslaw Milosz has resulted in several volumes, including portions of Milosz's *Collected Poems* and all of *Provinces.* If Milosz seems more determinedly political than his American translator, they meet in their concern with the problem of language and referentiality. "In Milan," from Milosz's *Collected Poems,* demonstrates the crucial difference. Accused by a friend of being "too politicized," Milosz concludes an eloquent response with

> Yes, I would like to be a poet of the five senses,
> That's why I don't allow myself to become one.
> Yes, thought has less weight than the word *lemon*
> That's why in my words I do not reach for fruit.

In contrast, in "Meditation at Lagunitas" Hass tries, despite awareness that language "is elegy to what it signifies," desperately to reach for fruit through words. The poem concludes,

> There are moments when the body is as numinous
> as words, days that are the good flesh continuing.
> Such tenderness, those afternoons and evenings,
> saying *blackberry, blackberry, blackberry.*

In what is in many ways a more obvious meshing of sensibilities, Hass's translations in *The Essential Haiku* of the three masters of the Japanese form—Basho, Buson, and Issa—are the culmination of twenty years of slow and steady work. Basho, in particular, with his closely seen and compassionate but somewhat detached sense of the world, seems to be a poetic soul mate. Apart from the value of gathering so many able and thoughtful versions of haiku in a single volume, *The Essential Haiku* also provides samplings of longer works by the three poets and some of Basho's pithy insights on poetry, as well as an informative apparatus that includes introductions for each of the poets, notes on individual pieces, and Hass's useful essay clarifying elements of haiku. The breadth of his scholarship evident in these translations, coupled with his intelligent essays on poetry and his own poems, made him one of the most exemplary choices for U.S. poet laureate and consultant in poetry to the Library of Congress, a position he held in 1995–97.

In *Sun under Wood,* published in 1996, Hass confronts his personal life with greater honesty and openness than in earlier collections. For all the naming of names in earlier poems, the reader is left with little sense, other than generally, of the turbulence of the life out of which those forcibly moderated poems emerged. Two of the personal circumstances brought into poetic light represent conflicts from childhood and from his adult life, the first with his mother's alcoholism and the second with his separation and divorce. Both experiences are traumatic enough that indirection and nondisclosure are understandable strategies, but the force they exert also seems to require release, the shapes of which are long, mixed formal sequences occurring toward the beginning and the end of the volume. The earlier conflict is first raised in the second poem, "Our Lady of the Snows," in which the speaker recalls "slip[ping]" into church "when [his] mother was in a hospital drying out" to light a candle "and bargain for [them] both." She appears again and is seen more directly in the next poem, "Dragonflies Mating," in which the poet confesses his humiliation when she appeared at basketball practice

> with her bright, confident eyes,
> and slurred, though carefully pronounced words, and the
>   appalling
> impromptu sets of mismatched clothes she was given to
> when she had the dim idea of making a good impression in
>   that state.

Hass explores this painful topic more directly and at even greater length in the following sequence, "My Mother's Nipples." Writing about this poem, Hass comments that, when the topic was first proposed to a friend, "My first idea was to make fun of the idea, my second was the painfulness of it. These suggested a form." The "form" includes long-lined, meditative poetry; brief, parodic lyrics; and prose passages that circle the subject at times and that at other times narrow it to a harrowing directness. From its opening lines the poem announces the tendency against which it will struggle:

> They're where all displacement begins.
> They bulldozed the upper meadow at Squaw Valley,
> where horses from the stable, two chestnuts, one white,
> grazed in the mist and the scent of wet grass on summer
>   mornings
> and moonrise threw the owl's shadow on voles and
>   wood rats
> crouched in the sage scent the earth gave back after dark
> with the day's heat to the night air.

We may wonder what all of this has to with the theme announced by the poem's title until we realize that the lyricism demonstrates the very evasiveness of displacement. Not until the first of the prose sections does the poem approach the pain more directly, with two memories of the mother's institutionalization. Evasion and approach represent the poles between which Hass struggles with this demonic angel.

Hass seems more than passingly acquainted with his shortfalls as elaborated in the volume's final poem, the tellingly titled "Interrupted Meditation." The poem opens with the kind of lyrical description of nature at which he excels:

> Little green involute fronds of fern at creek side.
> And the sinewy clear water rushing over creek stone
> of the palest amber, veined with a darker gold,
> thinnest lines of gold rivering through the amber
> like—ah, now we come to it.

Just what "we come to" will take another two pages of dialogue between the poet and an unnamed Polish survivor of the Nazi occupation of Warsaw that treats the relation between experience and language in the context of extreme suffering. This leads to the remembered referent of the opening, in which the unnamed interlocutor speaks:

> *Of course, here,* gesturing out the window, pines,
>   ragged green
> of a winter lawn, the bay, *you can express what you like,*
> *enumerate the vegetation. And you! you have to, I'm*
>   *afraid,*
> *since you don't excel at metaphor.* A shrewd, quick glance
> to see how I have taken this thrust. *You write well, clearly.*
> *You are an intelligent man. But*—finger in the air—
> *silence is waiting. Milosz believes there is a Word*
> *at the end that explains. There is silence at the end,*
> *and it doesn't explain, it doesn't even ask.*

Notice how what could be taken as self-congratulation on Hass's part—praise of his skill at writing, his intelligence—is rendered as a left-handed compliment, the way in which it was offered. If Hass cannot completely rise above his flaws, he at least can recognize the truth when it is articulated. The exponential growth in self-awareness evidenced in *Sun under Wood,* along with Hass's demonstrable lyrical skill and intelligence, mark his movement from one of the best poets of his generation to one of the best poets working in America today. We could all afford to learn from his penetrating self-criticism, doubtless a consequence of his refusal to publish too much and too soon, and follow as he continues this slow but sure growth to poetic majority.

—Thomas Gardner and Allen Hoey

HAZO, Samuel (John)

Nationality: American. **Born:** Pittsburgh, Pennsylvania, 19 July 1928. **Education:** Notre Dame University, Indiana (Mitchell Award, 1948), B.A. (magna cum laude) 1948; Duquesne University, Pittsburgh, M.A. 1955; University of Pittsburgh, Ph.D. 1957. **Military Service:** U.S. Marine Corps, 1950–53: Captain. **Family:** Married Mary Anne Sarkis in 1955; one son. **Career:** Instructor, Shady Side Academy, 1953–55. Instructor, 1955–58, assistant professor, 1958–60, associate professor, 1960–61, associate dean, 1961–66, and since 1964 professor of English, Duquesne University, Pittsburgh. Visiting professor, University of Detroit, 1968. Since 1966 director, International Poetry Forum, Pittsburgh. Contributing editor, *Mundus Artium* magazine, Athens, Ohio; poetry editor, *America,* Washington, D.C. U.S. State Department Lecturer in the Middle East and Greece, 1965, in Jamaica, 1966. Since 1976 editor, Byblos Editions, Pittsburgh. Commentator, National Public Radio, *Performance Today,* 1989–90. **Awards:** Pro Helvetia Foundation grant (Switzerland), 1971; Governor's award for excellence in the arts, Commonwealth of Pennsylvania, 1986; Forbes medal, Fort Pitt Museum, 1987; Elizabeth Kray award, Creative Writing Program at New York University, 1993; State Poet of the Commonwealth of Pennsylvania, 1993–96; Pittsburgh Center for the Arts Cultural award, 1995. D.Litt.: Seton Hill College, Greensburg, Pennsylvania, 1965; D.Hum.: Theil College, Greenville, Pennsylvania, 1981; Wilkes College, Wilkes-Barre, Pennsylvania, 1987; H.D.L.: Marquette University, Milwaukee, Wisconsin, 1989. **Address:** 785 Somerville Drive, Pittsburgh, Pennsylvania 15213, U.S.A.

PUBLICATIONS

Poetry

Discovery and Other Poems. New York, Sheed and Ward, 1959.
The Quiet Wars. New York, Sheed and Ward, 1962.
Listen with the Eye, photographs by James P. Blair. Pittsburgh, University of Pittsburgh Press, 1964.
My Sons in God: Selected and New Poems. Pittsburgh, University of Pittsburgh Press, 1965.
Blood Rights. Pittsburgh, University of Pittsburgh Press, 1968.
The Blood of Adonis, with Adonis (Ali Ahmed Said). Pittsburgh, University of Pittsburgh Press, 1971.
Twelve Poems, with George Nama. Pittsburgh, Byblos Press, 1972.
Seascript: A Mediterranean Logbook. Pittsburgh, Byblos Press, 1972.
Once for the Last Bandit: New and Previous Poems. Pittsburgh, University of Pittsburgh Press, 1972.
Quartered. Pittsburgh, University of Pittsburgh Press, 1974.
Inscripts. Athens, Ohio University Press, 1975.
Shuffle, Cut, and Look. Derry, Pennsylvania, Rook Press, 1977.
To Paris. New York, New Directions, 1981.
Thank a Bored Angel: Selected Poems. New York, New Directions, 1983.
The Color of Reluctance. Story, Wyoming, Dooryard Press, 1986.
Nightwords. New York, Sheep Meadow Press, 1987.
Silence Spoken Here. Marlboro, Vermont, Marlboro Press, 1988.
The Past Won't Stay behind You. Fayetteville, University of Arkansas Press, 1993.
The Holy Surprise of Right Now: Selected & New Poems. Fayetteville, University of Arkansas Press, 1996.
Latching the Fist. Pittsburgh, Byblos Press, 1996.
As They Sail. Fayetteville, University of Arkansas Press, 1999.

Plays

Until I'm Not Here Anymore (produced Pittsburgh, 1992).
Solos (produced Pittsburgh, 1994). Pittsburgh, Byblos Press, 1994.

Radio Play: *Feather,* 1996.

Novels

The Very Fall of the Sun. New York, Popular Library, 1978.
The Wanton Summer Air. Berkeley, California, North Point Press, 1982.
Stills. New York, Atheneum, 1989.

Other

Hart Crane: An Introduction and Interpretation. New York, Barnes and Noble, 1963; revised edition, as *Smithereened Apart: A Critique of Hart Crane,* Athens, Ohio University Press, 1978.
The Feast of Icarus: Lyrical Essays. Winston-Salem, North Carolina, Palaemon Press, 1984.
The Pittsburgh That Stays Within You. Pittsburgh, Byblos Press, 1986.
The Rest Is Prose. Pittsburgh, Duquesne University Press, 1990.

Editor, *The Christian Intellectual: Studies in the Relation of Catholicism to the Human Sciences.* Pittsburgh, Duquesne University Press, 1963.
Editor, *A Selection of Contemporary Religious Poetry.* Glen Rock, New Jersey, Paulist Press, 1963.

Translator, with Beth Luey, *The Growl of Deep Waters: Essays,* by Denis de Rougemont. Pittsburgh, University of Pittsburgh Press, 1976.
Translator, *Transformation of the Lover,* by Adonis. Athens, Swallow Press-Ohio University Press, 1983.
Translator, *Lebanon: Twenty Poems for One Love,* by Nadia Tueni. Pittsburgh, Byblos Press, 1990.
Translator, *The Pages of Day and Night.* Marlboro, Vermont, Marlboro Press, 1994.

*

Critical Studies: "Swimming in Sharkwater: The Poetry of Samuel Hazo" by R.H.W. Dillard, in *Hollins Critic* (Hollins College, Virginia), February, 1969; *Samuel Hazo: The Poetry of Resistance* (dissertation) by David Paul Sokolowski, Marquette University, 1992.

Samuel Hazo comments:

Suffice to say that I regard poetry as the best form of conversation with largely unknown readers or hearers whose answer is hopefully their attention and assent. The rest is for critics to discover and evaluate.

*   *   *

Samuel Hazo's first two collections, *Discovery* and *The Quiet Wars,* introduced a meditative Christian poet concerned with the tough and enduring realities of suffering and death. He displays the technical mastery necessary to avoid portentousness and unearned statement, and his style is at once traditional and colloquial, that of a modern thinking man's believable metrical utterance.

Listen with the Eye, a small collection of poems with accompanying photographs by James Blair, involves a technical departure of some importance, for many of the poems are cast in a strongly iambic free verse. The result is not so much rhythmic freedom as it is a stronger sense of the weight of each line. This quality distinguishes the new poems of *My Sons in God,* a collection of new and selected earlier poems in which the union of style and theme marks the arrival of an important American poet. Among the new poems is a group of "transpositions" from the Arabic of Ali Ahmed Said, the contemporary Lebanese poet, and here again a fresh technical influence brings to Hazo's own poems an additional firmness of line. A larger selection of Said's poems, *The Blood of Adonis,* appeared in 1971.

Once for the Last Bandit: New and Previous Poems hones the selection of early poems that appeared in *My Sons in God,* and it includes generous selections from that book and from *Blood Rights.* Nearly half of the book is given over to the title sequence, a group of poems having some of the qualities of a journal, or as Hazo calls it, "an almanac of a penman in transit." The sinuous, heavily iambic free verse is a genuinely new direction for Hazo, and while his themes of loss, God, and persistence are still central, a larger variety of starting points and tones has become available to this very resourceful poet.

—Henry Taylor

HEANEY, Seamus (Justin)

Nationality: Irish. **Born:** Castledawson, County Derry, Northern Ireland, 13 April 1939. **Education:** Anahorish School; St. Columb's College, Londonderry, 1951–57; Queen's University, Belfast, 1957–61, B.A. (honors) in English 1961; St. Joseph's College of Education, Belfast, 1961–62, Cert. Ed. 1962. **Family:** Married Marie Delvin in 1965; two sons and one daughter. **Career:** Teacher, St. Thomas's Secondary School, Belfast, 1962–63; lecturer, St. Joseph's College of Education, Belfast, 1963–66; lecturer in English, Queen's University, 1966–72; guest lecturer, University of California, Berkeley, 1970–71; moved to County Wicklow, Republic of Ireland, 1972; did regular radio work, and teaching at American universities; teacher, Carysfort Training College, Dublin, 1975–81; Allott Lecturer, University of Liverpool, 1978; professor of poetry, Oxford University, 1989–94. Visiting professor, 1982–84, and since 1984 Bovlston Professor of Rhetoric and Oratory, Harvard University, Cambridge, Massachusetts. **Awards:** Eric Gregory award, 1966; Cholmondeley award, 1967; Faber memorial prize, 1968; Maugham award, 1968; Irish Academy of Letters award, 1971; Denis Devlin memorial award, 1973, 1980; American-Irish Foundation award, 1975; American Academy E.M. Forster award, 1975; Duff Cooper memorial award, 1976; Smith literary award, 1976; Bennett award, 1982; P.E.N. prize, for translation, 1985; Whitbread award, 1987, 1997; *Sunday Times* Mont Blanc award, 1988; Premio Mondello, Mondello Foundation, Palermo, Sicily, 1993; Nobel prize for literature, 1995. D.H.L.: Fordham University, Bronx, New York, and Queen's University, Belfast, both 1982. **Memberships:** Irish Academy of Letters; American Academy of Arts and Sciences; American Academy of Arts and Letters; Royal Dublin Society. **Address:** Department of English and American Literature and Language, Harvard University, Warren House, 11 Prescott Street, Cambridge, Massachusetts 02138, U.S.A.

PUBLICATIONS

Poetry

Eleven Poems. Belfast, Festival, 1965.

Death of a Naturalist. London, Faber, and New York, Oxford University Press, 1966; revised edition, London and Boston, Faber, 1991.

Room to Rhyme, with Dairo Hammond and Michael Longley. Belfast, Arts Council of Northern Ireland, 1968.

A Lough Neagh Sequence. Manchester, Phoenix Pamphlet Poets Press, 1969.

Door into the Dark. London, Faber, and New York, Oxford University Press, 1969.

Night Drive. Crediton, Devon, Gilbertson, 1970.

Boy Driving His Father to Confession. Frensham, Surrey, Sceptre Press, 1970.

Servant Boy. Detroit, Red Hanrahan Press, 1971.

Land. London, Poem-of-the-Month Club, 1971.

Wintering Out. London, Faber, 1972; New York, Oxford University Press, 1973.

North. London, Faber, 1975; New York, Oxford University Press, 1976.

Bog Poems. London, Rainbow Press, 1975.

Stations. Belfast, Ulstemman, 1975.

In Their Element: A Selection of Poems, with Derek Mahon. Belfast, Arts Council of Northern Ireland, 1977.

After Summer. Old Deerfield, Massachusetts, Deerfield Press, 1978.

Hedge School (Sonnets from Glanmore). Newark, Vermont, Janus Press, 1979.

Field Work. London, Faber, and New York, Farrar Straus, 1979.

Ugolino. Dublin, Andrew Carpenter, 1979.

Selected Poems 1965–1975. London, Faber, 1980.

Poems 1965–1975. New York, Farrar Straus, 1980.

Sweeney Praises the Trees. Privately printed, 1981.

An Open Letter. Londonderry, Field Day Theatre Company, 1983.

Sweeney Astray: A Version from the Irish (includes prose). Londonderry, Field Day Theatre Company, 1983; London, Faber, and New York, Farrar Straus, 1984; revised edition as *Sweeney's Flight,* 1992.

Station Island. London, Faber, 1984; New York, Farrar Straus, 1985.

Hailstones. Dublin, Gallery Press, 1984.

From the Republic of Conscience. Dublin, Amnesty International, 1985.

The Haw Lantern. London, Faber, and New York, Farrar Straus, 1987.

Conlan. Baile Atha Cliath, Ireland, Coisceim, 1989.

New Selected Poems 1966–1987. London, Faber, and New York, Farrar Straus, 1990.

The Tree Clock. Belfast, Linen Hall Library, 1990.

Sweeney's Flight. London, Faber, and New York, Farrar Straus, 1992.

Seeing Things. New York, Noonday Press, 1993.

The Spirit Level. New York, Farrar Straus, 1996.

Opened Ground: Selected Poems, 1966–1996. New York, Farrar Straus, 1998.

Recording: *The Northern Muse,* with John Montague, Claddagh, 1968.

Play

The Cure at Troy: A Version of Sophocles' Philoctetes. London, Faber, 1990.

Other

The Fire i' the Flint: Reflections on the Poetry of Gerard Manley Hopkins (lecture). London, Oxford University Press, 1975.
Robert Lowell: A Memorial Lecture and an Eulogy. Privately printed, 1978.
The Making of a Music: Reflections on the Poetry of Wordsworth and Yeats. Liverpool, University of Liverpool Press, 1978.
Preoccupations: Selected Prose 1968–1978. London, Faber, and New York, Farrar Straus, 1980.
Among Schoolchildren. Belfast, John Malone Memorial Committee, 1983.
Verses for a Fordham Commencement (address in verse). New York, Nadja, 1984.
Place and Displacement: Recent Poetry of Northern Ireland. Grasmere, Trustees of Dove Cottage, 1984.
The Government of the Tongue: The 1986 T.S. Eliot Memorial Lectures and Other Critical Writings. London, Faber, 1988; as *The Government of the Tongue: Selected Prose 1978–1987,* New York, Farrar Straus, 1988.
The Place of Writing. Atlanta, Georgia, Scholars Press, 1989.
Dylan the Durable? Bennington, Vermont, Bennington College, 1992.
Joy or Night: Last Things in the Poetry of W.B. Yeats and Philip Larkin. Swansea, University College of Swansea, 1993.
The Redress of Poetry. New York, Farrar Straus, 1995.
Homage to Frost, with Joseph Brodsky and Derek Walcott. New York, Farrar Straus, 1996.
Crediting Poetry: The Nobel Lecture. New York, Farrar Straus, 1996.
Diary of One Who Vanished: A Song Cycle by Leoš Janácek in a New Version. London, Faber, 1999.

Editor, with Alan Brownjohn and Jon Stallworthy, *New Poems 1970–1971.* London, Hutchinson, 1971.
Editor, *Soundings 2.* Belfast, Blackstaff Press, 1974.
Editor, with Ted Hughes, *1980 Anthology: Arvon Foundation Poetry Competition.* Todmorden, Lancashire, Kilnhurst, 1982.
Editor, with Ted Hughes, *The Rattle Bag: An Anthology.* London, Faber, 1982.
Editor, *The Essential Wordsworth.* New York, Ecco Press, 1988.

Translator, *The Midnight Verdict.* Loughcrew, Old Castle, Gallery, 1993.
Translator, *Beowulf.* London, Faber, 1999; New York, Farrar Straus, 2000.

*

Critical Studies: *Seamus Heaney* by Robert Buttel, Lewisburg, Pennsylvania, Bucknell University Press, 1975; *Seamus Heaney* by Blake Morrison, London, Methuen, 1982; *The Art of Seamus Heaney* edited by Tony Curtis, Bridgend, Poetry Wales Press, 1982, and Chester Springs, Pennsylvania, Dufour Editions, 1993; *Seamus Heaney: A Student's Guide to the Selected Poems 1965–1975* by Nicholas McGuinn, Leeds, Arnold Wheaton, 1986; *Seamus Heaney: A Student's Guide* by Neil Corcoran, London, Faber, 1986; *Seamus Heaney* edited by Harold Bloom, New Haven, Connecticut, Chelsea House, 1986; *The Poetry of Seamus Heaney: All the Realms of Whisper* by Elmer Andrews, London, Macmillan, 1988; *Seamus Heaney* by Ronald Tamplin, Milton Keynes, Open University Press, 1989; *Seamus Heaney* by Thomas C. Foster, Boston, Twayne, 1989; *The Poetry of Resistance: Seamus Heaney and the Pastoral Tradition* by Sidney Burris, Athens, Ohio University Press, 1990; *Whatever You Say, Say Nothing: Why Seamus Heaney is No. 1* by Desmond Fennell, Dublin, ELO Publications, 1991; *Out of Step: Pursuing Seamus Heaney to Purgatory,* with drawings, by Catherine Byron, Bristol, Loxwood Stoneleigh, 1992; *Seamus Heaney: Poet and Critic* by Arthur E. McGuinness, New York, P. Lang, 1993; *Seamus Heaney: The Making of the Poet* by Michael Parker, Dublin, Gill and Macmillan, 1993; *Questioning Tradition, Language, and Myth: The Poetry of Seamus Heaney* by Michael R. Molino, Washington D.C., Catholic University of America Press, 1994; *The Achievement of Seamus Heaney* by John Wilson Foster, Dublin, Lilliput Press, 1995; *The Breaking of Style: Hopkins, Heaney, Graham,* Cambridge, Massachusetts, Harvard University Press, 1995, and *Seamus Heaney,* Cambridge, Massachusetts, Harvard University Press, 1998, both by Helen Vendler; *Seamus Heaney* edited by Michael Allen, New York, St Martin's Press, 1997; *The Poetry of Seamus Heaney* edited by Elmer Andrews, Duxford, England, Icon Books, 1998, and New York, Columbia University Press, 2000.

*   *   *

As an Ulster Catholic, Seamus Heaney has always been aware of the complex and violent history that has gone to shape modern Ireland. In "Shoreline" (*Door into the Dark*) he hears in the tide, "rummaging in / At the foot of all fields," echoes of successive waves of invaders—Celts, Danes, Normans; in *North* he writes of "those fabulous raiders," the Vikings, "ocean-deafened voices / warning me, lifted again / in violence and epiphany." Elsewhere in the same volume "Ocean's Love to Ireland" recalls, in a sinister compounding of copulation and murder that is a recurring motif, the complicity of the courtier-poet Raleigh in the Irish massacres, while "Bog Oak" (*Wintering Out*) insinuates with a cool obliqueness, into the "dreaming sunlight" of Edmund Spenser's pastoral, hints of the atrocities he supervised. "For the Commander of the 'Eliza'" and "At a Potato Digging" evoke the Great Hunger and the ruthless expediencies of British rule in 1845. "Docker," with a forced but urgent understanding, depicts the Northern Protestant not only to recall past bigotry but also to offer, in 1966, prophetic anticipation of its renewal ("That fist would drop a hammer on a Catholic— / Oh yes, that kind of thing could start again").

From his first volume onward, Heaney has written extensively of the strenuous, unremitting life of rural labor in County Derry and beyond. Many of the poems celebrate the people, crafts, and skills that sustain communal life; others, such as "The Wool Trade" or "Traditions," explore the linguistic and commercial nexus that "beds us down into / the British isles." In many poems Heaney effects a remarkable transition between manual and mental labor, the currencies of material life and of language. In "Digging," the first poem of his first volume, this theme is already enunciated; the poet digs with his pen as his father and grandfather dug with their spades the rich peat of Ireland. Violence is hinted at by the simile that adds a third implement to the human repertoire ("The squat pen rest; snug as a gun''). The title poem of *Death of a Naturalist* extends this menace, recalling the poet as a boy sickened by the pools of frog spawn that tell of a repulsive world beyond the human: "The great slime kings / Were gathered there for vengeance and I knew / That if I dipped my hand the spawn would clutch it." Throughout the volume the water rat recurs as the image of an alien yet terrifyingly familiar world, a world finally admitted in "Personal Helicon" to be close to the poet's own creative springs, as, "pry[ing] into roots . . . finger[ing] slime," this "big-eyed Narcissus" is startled by a rat that "slapped across my reflection."

Poetry itself is a "door into the dark," where we seek our own carnal origins, and "Bogland" and "Bann Clay" stress this symbolic digging for a lost, primordial center of being: "Under the humus and roots / This smooth weight. I labour / towards it still. It holds and gluts." The very language in which Heaney writes partakes of this glutinous physical presence. There is a tactile, viscous quality to his words, speaking of "the sucking clabber" of water, the "soft gradient / of consonant, vowel-meadow," or "the tawny guttural water" that "spells itself." "Anahorish," "Toome," and "Broagh" (*Wintering Out*) explore the very sounds of the old Irish words, stressing their status as material utterance, the muscular effort of a "guttural muse" whose "uvula grows / vestigial" ("Traditions"). In poems such as "Gifts of Rain" or "Oracle" the human organs of communication are in turn transferred to nature ("small mouth and ear / in a woody cleft, / lobe and larynx / of the mossy places"). Throughout *North* language is equated with the rich, secretive loam of the Irish bog, which engulfs and preserves but which can be kindled over and over into meaning, as the title poem indicates: "Lie down / in the word-hoard, burrow / the coil and gleam / of your furrowed brain. / Compose in darkness." The whole volume is as much about the difficulty of poetic composition as about the fratricidal decomposition of Ireland; death and love, language, poetry, and politics converge in poem after poem. Several poems, developing the insight of "Tollund Man" (*Wintering Out*), draw upon P.V. Glob's book *The Bog People* for a potent imagery of atrocity. In Glob's photographs of those ancient human sacrifices, preserved by the "dark juices" of the Danish peat bog, Heaney finds an analogy to the role of the modern Irish poet, the "artful voyeur" who is both an accomplice and helpless witness to "the exact / and tribal, intimate revenge" spoken of in a poem such as "Punishment." Superficially much influenced by Ted Hughes, Heaney in this double understanding of complicity and betrayal perhaps establishes his own distinctive moral and emotional stance. Unlike Hughes, however, he is finally concerned with the redemption, not the dismissal, of the human, its exhumation from a "mother ground / . . . sour with the blood / of her faithful."

Field Work skillfully balances the parochial and a larger world, as in "The Skunk," where in a California setting Heaney deliberately estranges the traditional glamour of the love poem. But the prevailing mood of the volume is elegiac, and in the title sequence it speaks of a world "stained / to perfection," making those local deaths of which it speaks elsewhere part of a universal loss and abandonment that is nevertheless the ground, the true field, within which human life is fulfilled. The title *Field Work* points the way to his later developments, poised equivocally between the local—the real fields and hedges of this sequence, from which the particular poetic talent emerged—and the larger field of meanings within which that life now finds itself, which, as indicated in a poem such as "A Postcard from North Antrim," is always elsewhere. Identity now is found in otherness and displacement, both in the literal and in the psychoanalytic sense, for it is only from outside the field that the pattern of

forces can be understood rather than simply suffered. This is the point of the important lecture *Place and Displacement* that Heaney delivered at Dove Cottage (Wordsworth's home in the Lake District) in 1984, seeing in the uprootedness of the returning native Wordsworth a model for all subsequent poetic displacements. Contemporary Northern Irish poetry, he says, reveals the same double displacement:

> The good place where Wordsworth's nurture happened and to which his habitual feelings are most naturally attuned has become . . . the wrong place. He is displaced from his own affection by a vision of the good that is located elsewhere. His political, utopian aspirations deracinate him from the beloved actuality of his surroundings so that his instinctive being and his appetitive intelligence are knocked out of alignment. He feels like a traitor among those he knows and loves.

The way to cope with "the strain of being in two places at once, of needing to accommodate two opposing conditions of truthfulness simultaneously," is not despair, however, but rather Jung's strategy of finding a "displaced perspective" in which the suffering individual must outgrow particularist allegiance while managing to "keep faith with . . . origins," "stretched between politics and transcendence . . . displaced from a confidence in a single position by his disposition to be affected by all positions, negatively rather than positively capable."

The echo of Keats's "negative capability" as an answer to Wordsworth's "egotistical sublime" indicates the way out Heaney was to find from the Northern Irish deadlock from *Field Work* onward. It is in the "lyric stance," in language as itself a site of displacement, "the whispering gallery of absence," "the voice from beyond," that the writer can seek the hopeful imaginary resolution of real conflicts. Heaney's poetry has pursued language as political metaphor and metonymy through to its source, to a recognition of language as both the place of necessary exile and the site of a perpetual return home. *Station Island* is the product of such a recognition, a volume full of departures and returns, its title sequence "of dream encounters with familiar ghosts" set on that island in Lough Derg that is a traditional place of penitential pilgrimage. The book explores the guilt of such meetings with the dead, returning from a remove to make peace with that which has been abandoned. Displacement is here seen not as exile but as freedom, whether in the wild blue yonder of America or the poetically licensed otherworlds of Dante's *Divine Comedy*. The loving fidelity of the émigré who is nevertheless just "visiting" that which he has left behind provides the motive force for the volume. In a poem ironically entitled "Away from It All," Heaney uses one of his most bathetic figures, a lobster taken out of its tank in a restaurant, to acknowledge that a person cannot go home again. The lobster is the "hampered one, out of water, / fortified and bewildered." But if this is a figure of the poet, always about to be devoured for someone else's alien enjoyment, he suffers as much because he cannot clear his head of all the lives he has left behind, for whom he still feels remotely responsible.

This anxiety explains the poet's identification in the third part of the book with the seventh-century Irish king Sweeney, "transformed into a bird-man and exiled to the trees by the curse of St. Ronan" and finding in madness a relief from misery. The identification is strong enough to have led Heaney to translate the medieval Irish poem *Buile Suibhne* in *Sweeney Astray*, a volume that, in combining his own inimitable style with fidelity to the original, provides an instance of the delicate relation between Heaney's aspirant talent and his native realm. "The First Gloss," which opens "Sweeney Redivivus," sums up this relation in miniature with its multiple puns: "Subscribe to the first step taken / from a justified line / into the margin." His Sweeney also finds himself, in "Sweeney Redivivus,"

> incredible to myself,
> among people far too eager to believe me
> and my story, even if it happened to be true.

But in *The Haw Lantern* Heaney has gone a step further, beyond the margins altogether, to deconstruct those blarney-laden stories, decentering and redefining a self-congratulatory Irishness. In the words of the title poem, it is not enough to bask in "a small light for small people." The modest wish to "keep / the wick of self-respect from dying out, / not having to blind them with illumination" is too limited, too easy an ambition. Now "it takes the roaming shape of Diogenes / with his lantern, seeking one just man" to be the true measure of this field, scrutinizing with a gaze that makes "you flinch . . . its blood-prick that you wish would test and clear you." The terror of being tested, assayed, and assessed, as well as the fraught yearning for clearance, runs through most of the poems in the volume. At its most literal in "From the Frontier of Writing" the fear is at once transformed into a parable in the harrowing encounter with an army roadblock, where "everything is pure interrogation / until a rifle motions and you move." "Parable Island" tells us that there are no authenticating origins, only a plethora of storytellings that push the origin further back into an original emptiness, scrawled over with too much meaning. It is in this area of secondary signification that Ireland "begins." As "The Mud Vision" indicates, there can be no final clearance, no return to an original clarity:

> What might have been origin
> We dissipated in news. The clarified place
> Had retrieved neither us nor itself—except
> You could say we survived.

Heaney, of course, has done more than survive; he has found a clear, clean space of demarcation. His images steer increasingly toward an aesthetic connotation above a religious one. In *Seeing Things* a biretta the poet remembers from his altar days has the poignancy of the immediately nostalgic instead of the weight of the religious. Heaney's deepest interior mythology is of the earth, but even if he drifts in his later work from the regimentations of traditional Catholicism, he does not drift from Catholicism's atmosphere or perspectives. Indeed, the marvelous in *Seeing Things* creates its own sense of the atmospheric:

> The annals say: when the monks of Clonmacnoise
> Were all at prayers inside the oratory
> A ship appeared above them in the air.
> The anchor dragged along behind so deep
> It hooked itself into the alter rails
> And then, as the big hull rocked to a standstill,
> A crewman shinned and grappled down the rope
> And struggled to release it. But in vain.
> 'This man can't bear our life here and will drown,'
> The abbot said, 'unless we help him.' So
> They did, the freed ship sailed, and the man climbed back
> Out of the marvellous as he had known it.

This is a world in which air and water refuse translation; otherworldly qualities overlap with the worldly.

Indeed, lyric poetry doubtlessly has no greater advocate than Heaney, a poet who carries on the important tradition of reading aloud. His 1996 collection *The Spirit Level* contains some of the language's most memorable lyric lines, as, for example, in "Postscript":

> And some time make the time to drive out west
> Into County Clare, along the Flaggy Shore,
> In September or October, when the wind
> And the light are working off each other
> So that the ocean on one side is wild
> With foam and glitter, and inland among stones
> The surface of a slate-grey lake is lit
> By the earthed lightning of a flock of swans,
> Their feathers roughed and ruffling, white on white,
> Their fully grown headstrong-looking heads
> Tucked or cresting or busy underwater.
> Useless to think you'll park and capture it
> More thoroughly. You are neither here nor there,
> A hurry through which known and strange things pass
> As big soft buffetings come at the car sideways
> And catch the heart off guard and blow it open.

—Stan Smith and Martha Sutro

HEATH-STUBBS, John (Francis Alexander)

Nationality: British. **Born:** London, 9 July 1918. **Education:** Bembridge School; Worcester College for the Blind; and privately; Queen's College, Oxford, B.A. (honors) in English 1942, M.A. 1972. **Career:** English teacher, Hall School, Hampstead, London, 1944–45; editorial assistant, Hutchinson and Company publishers, London, 1945–46. Gregory Fellow in Poetry, Leeds University, 1952–55; visiting professor of English, University of Alexandria, Egypt, 1955–58, and University of Michigan, Ann Arbor, 1960–61; lecturer in English, College of St. Mark and St. John, London, 1963–73. **Awards:** Arts Council bursary, 1965; Queen's Gold Medal for Poetry, 1973; Oscar Williams—Gene Derwood award, 1977; Cholmondeley award, 1988; Commonwealth poetry prize, 1989. Fellow, Royal Society of Literature, 1953, and English Association, 1994. O.B.E. (Officer, Order of the British Empire), 1989. Cross of St. Augustine, 1999. **Address:** 22 Artesian Road, London W2 5AR, England.

PUBLICATIONS

Poetry

Wounded Thammuz. London, Routledge, 1942.
Beauty and the Beast. London, Routledge, 1943.
The Divided Ways. London, Routledge, 1946.
The Charity of the Stars. New York, Sloane, 1949.
The Swarming of the Bees. London, Eyre and Spottiswoode, 1950.
A Charm against the Toothache. London, Methuen, 1954.
The Triumph of the Muse and Other Poems. London, Oxford University Press, 1958.

The Blue-Fly in His Head. London, Oxford University Press, 1962.
Selected Poems. London, Oxford University Press, 1965.
Satires and Epigrams. London, Turret, 1968.
(Selected Poems), with Thomas Blackburn. London, Longman, 1969.
Artorius, Book I. Providence, Rhode Island, Burning Deck, 1970; London, Enitharmon Press, 1973.
Penguin Modern Poets 20, with F.T. Prince and Stephen Spender. London, Penguin, 1971.
Four Poems in Measure. New York, Helikon Press, 1973.
The Twelve Labours of Hercules. San Francisco, Arion Press, 1974.
A Parliament of Birds (for children). London, Chatto and Windus, 1975.
The Watchman's Flute: New Poems. Manchester, Carcanet, 1978.
The Mouse, The Bird, and The Sausage. Sunderland, Ceolfrith, 1978.
Birds Reconvened. London, Enitharmon Press, 1980.
Buzz Buzz: Ten Insect Poems. Sidcot, Avon, Gruffyground, 1981.
This Is Your Poem. London, Pisces Press, 1981.
Naming the Beasts. Manchester, Carcanet, 1982.
New Poems. Leamington Spa, Warwickshire, Other Branch Readings, 1983.
Five Poems from the South. Isle of Wight, Yellowsands Press, 1984.
The Immolation of Aleph. Manchester, Carcanet, 1985.
Cats' Parnassus. London, Hearing Eye, 1987.
Time Pieces. London, Hearing Eye, 1988.
Collected Poems 1943–1987. Manchester, Carcanet, 1988.
A Partridge in a Pear Tree: Poems for the Twelve Days of Christmas. London, Hearing Eye, 1988.
A Ninefold of Charms. London, Hearing Eye, 1989.
The Game of Love and Death. Petersfield, Hampshire, Enitharmon, 1990.
The Parson's Cat. London, Hearing Eye, 1992.
Chimeras. London, Hearing Eye, 1993.
Sweetapple Earth. Manchester, Carcanet, 1993.
Torriano Sequences. London, Hearing Eye, 1994.
The Sound of Light. Manchester, Carcanet, 1999.

Plays

The Talking Ass (produced London, 1953). Included in *Helen in Egypt and Other Plays,* 1958.
Helen in Egypt and Other Plays (includes *The Talking Ass, The Harrowing of Hell*). London, Oxford University Press, 1958.
Helen in Egypt (produced London, 1988). Included in *Helen in Egypt and Other Plays,* 1958.

Other

The Darkling Plain: A Study of the Later Fortunes of Romanticism in English Poetry from George Darley to W. B. Yeats. London, Eyre and Spottiswoode, 1950.
Charles Williams. London, Longman, 1955.
The Verse Satire. London, Oxford University Press, 1969.
The Ode. London, Oxford University Press, 1969.
The Pastoral. London, Oxford University Press, 1969.
Hindsights. London, Hodder & Stoughton, 1993.
Literary Essays. Manchester, Carcanet, 1998.

Editor, *Selected Poems of Shelley.* London, Falcon Press, 1947.

Editor, *Selected Poems of Tennyson.* London, Falcon Press, 1947.
Editor, *Selected Poems of Swift.* London, Falcon Press, 1947.
Editor, with David Wright, *The Forsaken Garden: An Anthology of Poetry 1824–1909.* London, Lehmann, 1950.
Editor, *Mountains Beneath the Horizon: Selected Poems,* by William Bell. London, Faber, 1950.
Editor, *Images of Tomorrow: An Anthology of Recent Poetry.* London, SCM Press, 1953.
Editor, with David Wright, *The Faber Book of Twentieth Century Verse: An Anthology of Verse in Britain 1900–1950.* London, Faber, 1953; revised edition, 1965, 1975.
Editor, *Selected Poems of Alexander Pope.* London, Heinemann, 1964; New York, Barnes and Noble, 1966.
Editor, with Martin Green, *Homage to George Barker on His 60th Birthday.* London, Martin Brian and O'Keeffe, 1973.
Editor, *Selected Poems,* by Thomas Gray. Manchester, Carcanet, 1981.
Editor, with Phillips Salman, *Poems of Science.* London, Penguin, 1984.

Translator, *Poems from Giacomo Leopardi.* London, Lehmann, 1946.
Translator, *Aphrodite's Garland.* St. Ives, Cornwall, Latin Press, 1952
Translator, with Peter Avery, *Thirty Poems of Hafiz of Shiraz.* London, Murray, 1952.
Translator, with Iris Origo, *Selected Poetry and Prose,* by Giacomo Leopardi. London, Oxford University Press, 1966; New York, New American Library, 1967.
Translator, *The Horn/Le Cor,* by Alfred de Vigny. Richmond, Surrey, Keepsake Press, 1969.
Translator, with Shafik Megally, *Dust and Carnations: Traditional Funeral Chants and Wedding Songs from Egypt.* London, TR Press, 1977.
Translator, with Peter Avery, *The Ruba'iyat of Omar Khayyam.* London, Allen Lane, 1979.
Translator, with Carol Whiteside, *Anyte.* Warwick, Greville Press. 1979.
Translator, *8 Poems of Sulpicia.* London, Hearing Eye, 1999.

*

Bibliography: *John Heath-Stubbs: A Checklist* by John E. Van Domelen, Fontwell, Sussex, Centaur, 1987.

Manuscript Collections: Humanities Research Center, University of Texas, Austin; Claude Colleer Abbott Memorial Library, State University of New York, Buffalo.

Critical Studies: *Poetry and Personal Responsibility* by George Every, London, SCM Press, 1948; "John Heath-Stubbs: A Poet in Alexandria" by Shafik Megally, in *Cairo Bulletin of English Studies,* 1959; *The Price of an Eye* by Thomas Blackburn, London, Longman, and New York, Morrow, 1961; *Rule and Energy* by John Press, London, Oxford University Press, 1963; "John Heath-Stubbs Issue" of *Aquarius 10* (London), 1978; "Triad from Great Britain" by Tony Stoneburner, in *The Poetics of Faith,* Missoula, Montana, Scholars Press, 1978; *Hindsights* by John Heath-Stubbs, London, Headline Hodder, 1993; *The Literary Essays of John Heath-Stubbs* edited by A.T. Tolley, Manchester, Carcanet, 1998.

John Heath-Stubbs comments:

Influenced at Oxford by teaching of C.S. Lewis and Charles Williams; also by friendship with fellow undergraduate poets Sidney Keyes, Drummond Allison, and William Bell.

*   *   *

A remarkable feel for words, a fine metrical ear, a highly perceptive and sound critical intellect, a profound and retentive memory, a good imagination, plus a sense of humor—such have been clear attributes of John Heath-Stubbs's poetic genius from the beginning. From the time of his contributions to Michael Meyer's *Eight Oxford Poets* and his own first book of verse, *Wounded Thammuz,* to later works like *Collected Poems 1943–1987* or *Sweetapple Earth* and that remarkable subepic *Artorius,* Heath-Stubbs has been an accomplished craftsman and all-around poet, an Augustan with more than a touch of the Elizabethan about him. Time has matured his writing so that even the most trivial offering of his pen is in some measure a deft piece of poetic wisdom, or perhaps one should say of "poeticized wisdom." Certainly there is both the feeling and the evidence that whatever piece of esoteric lore, mythological gleaning, or practical information is thrown up from the remarkably erudite mind of this particular poet—and there is an almost unrivaled quantum of such data in Heath-Stubbs—it is touched, however lightly, by the magic of the Muse. And rightly so, for since World War II only two or three of the poets in England at most have so consistently dedicated themselves to the service of Apollo's daughter.

For many years Heath-Stubbs has been a most neglected poet and certainly one far outside the run of fashions and movements and academic acclaim in each successive decade since he began writing. But those critics who have chosen to note his work echo, in their different ways, Derek Stanford's description of the persona that the poems project: "The influence of his learning and the inborn dignity of his mind influenced me the more strongly because he himself made no effort to." Indeed, as all who know Heath-Stubbs will appreciate, he is a diffident man, a solitary person despite all the company he has kept in Fitzrovia and elsewhere. Michael Meyer has written of him, "John Heath-Stubbs is the most uninstitutionable of men, one of those towering solitaries, like Doughty and Charles Williams . . . who go their own way, contemptuous of literary fashion." Michael Hamburger has said, "I see John Heath-Stubbs as a tragic figure—the insider, by conviction and allegiance, who 'was not preferred' . . . not preferred because the Establishment to which he has always been committed was shifting all the time, and he was not; and because it has little use for poets who are neither sycophants or clowns. He has borne that affliction with . . . courage and dignity . . . for me he has changed far less than anyone else I know." And Sean Hutton has written, "His sensibility is strongly marked by that tragic feeling, compounded with stoicism, which one associates with Greek lyric poetry." The poet himself has stated his "policy," as it were, in verse—"I would emulate rather those / Who countered despair with elegance, / Emptiness with a grace"—and has never ceased to recognize the primary objective or purpose of poetry—". . . I would have you remember: / Your poetry is no good / Unless it move the heart." By way of stressing the point, he adds, ". . . And the human heart, / The heart which you must move, / Is corrupt, depraved and desperately wicked."

As a true servant of the Muse then, Heath-Stubbs has opted—despite his knowledge of corruption, depravity, and wickedness—to celebrate or, if not always to celebrate, at least to counter "despair with elegance, emptiness with a grace." And what emerges from these critical comments by the poet and by others is a sense of authority, an authority that has grown gradually as a result of his having "borne" the "affliction with courage and dignity." It is an authority that, according to Stanford, exerts its influence through "the inborn dignity of his mind" and through "learning." The constant factor that all of the critics, overtly or implicitly, recognize is this inborn dignity, as they also acknowledge an element of growth brought about by the constant expansion of the poet's erudition. As Anne Stevenson has said, "He has brought erudition out of the libraries and given it roots and leaves." As to why Hamburger finds the poet so unchanging—indeed, he must have been tempted to say "timeless"—it is because, despite all the tragic vicissitudes of time, Heath-Stubbs has retained, nay enhanced, his human integrity. Hence the sense of authority in his poetry and an explanation for his having even been described as "magisterial."

But what kind of poetry is Heath-Stubbs's? Can it reasonably be summed up? Probably the most frequent and useful epithet that has been applied to it is "classical-romantic." In fact, in *The Darkling Plain,* a prose study of poetry, the poet himself wrote, "The Classical vision is the most complete, rounded, and perfected of which the human mind is capable . . . In a sense, we must all attempt to be Classicists, but have to be Romantics first of all, before we can achieve this, and few of us in this life can hope to pass that stage." An even clearer summing up of his *ars poetica* occurs in the poem entitled "The Blue-Fly in His Head" (1962): "The intellect shapes, the emotions feed the poem, / Whose roots are in the senses, whose flower is imagination." And I cannot forbear quoting a description of Heath-Stubbs's poetry by J. Van Domelen: "There is a certain Byzantine quality in much of John Heath-Stubbs's poetry. An encyclopaedic knowledge of past cultures and a continual application of this knowledge that is reminiscent of Byzantium."

Perhaps because it is so obvious, insufficient stress has been given to one overriding quality of Heath-Stubbs's poetry, however. Like the poet himself, it is a poetry, linguistically speaking, "of as good blood as any in England." That is to say, Heath-Stubbs's poetry is supremely English in the way that Shakespeare's or the pristine Chaucer's was supremely English. It is an Anglo-Saxon language plasma imbued, even softened, by the rich Celtic blood of the west (which was how English came to be, the Latin influence being formatively peripheral in comparison). To the Celtic element Heath-Stubbs owes his gift for the mythological transformation of experience; to the English (or the Anglo-Saxon as developed via Chaucer) the capacity to embrace ideas and subtler intellectual states than Celtic perversity and magic allow for. And to the English strain he also owes his humor, something that must be emphasized because, with the exception of Dannie Abse, he is the only serious poet writing in England who also has a great sense of humor. In fact, Heath-Stubbs is both a poet and a wit, though he is one to whom I would rather apply the phrase "a visionary and humorist" in order to emphasize the unique character of his achievement.

It was Sebastian Barker who wrote of the "intelligent and fully conscious delight" that the reader "may expect from Heath-Stubbs's rhythms." In fact, the statement unintentionally directs at least this reader to the only real weakness to be found in his poetry. Not infrequently there is an overconsciousness that leads to a diminution, even an absence, of rhythm. Now rhythm is part of the essential lifeblood of the true poem, and no amount of flexing of the poet's metrical muscles, something Heath-Stubbs is particularly good at, can guarantee this vital factor. Consequently, quite a few respectable and interesting items get knocked off his virtuoso anvil that are nothing more than cerebral artifacts expressed in cautious but always competent meters. They are not shoddy goods, of course, but simply pieces that lack the luster of life, lack a living vitality, lack, in short, rhythm. Such are not really inspired or Muse-given pieces at all but are either metrical exercises or just plain failed poems. Naturally, they are of interest—as all Heath-Stubbs's work is of interest—but they do not delight, do not ''move the heart'' as Heath-Stubbs knows and says a true poem should do. Of course, in a prolific poet—indeed, in any poet—such failures are to be expected; not even Shakespeare hit the right note, thought, and rhythm at the same time and every time. But these critical remarks must be understood as intended simply to help ''round the picture,'' as it were. For it remains generally true that, by any standard, Heath-Stubbs's work-individually in *Artorius,* his remarkable epic for voices, and more generally in his positively cornucopian *Collected Poems 1943–1987*—forms one of the major poetical oeuvres in modern times. True, it is a corpus that has yet to be studied in the depth it deserves, but when it is, a major poet will have been firmly added to the somewhat exclusive canon of English literature.

To help round out Heath-Stubbs's achievement, it is worth adding that a remarkable volume of his literary essays was published to celebrate his eightieth birthday. It is a volume characterized especially by its readability, its erudition, its array of insights, and the manner in which it so compellingly illuminates the real qualities of many minor and neglected English poets as well as throwing unsentimental light upon the weaknesses of some of our more canonical authors. With this volume of literary essays a major poet has also become a true man of letters.

—William Oxley

HECHT, Anthony (Evan)

Nationality: American. **Born:** New York City, 16 January 1923. **Education:** Bard College, Annandale-on-Hudson, New York, B.A. 1944; Columbia University, New York, M.A. 1950. **Military Service:** U.S. Army during World War II. **Family:** Married 1) Patricia Harris in 1954 (divorced 1961), two sons; 2) Helen D'Alessandro in 1971, one son. **Career:** Taught at Kenyon College, Gambier, Ohio, 1947; University of Iowa, Iowa City, 1948; New York University, 1949; Smith College, Northampton, Massachusetts, 1956–59; Bard College, 1962–67; member of the department of English, Rochester University, New York, from 1967; poetry consultant, Library of Congress, Washington, D.C., 1982–84; University Professor, Georgetown University, Washington, D.C., 1985–93. Fulbright Professor in Brazil, 1971; Hurst Professor, Washington University, St. Louis, 1971; visiting professor, Harvard University, Cambridge, Massachusetts, 1973, and Yale University, New Haven, Connecticut, 1977; member of the faculty, Salzburg Seminar in American Studies, 1977. Trustee, American Academy in Rome, Italy, 1983–91. **Awards:** American Academy in Rome fellowship, 1951; Guggenheim fellowship, 1954, 1959; *Hudson Review* fellowship, 1958; Ford fellowship, for drama, 1960, for verse, 1968; Brandeis University Creative Arts award, 1964; Rockefeller fellowship, 1967; Loines award, 1968; Pulitzer prize, 1968; Academy of American Poets fellowship, 1969; Bollingen prize, 1983; Eugenio Montale award, 1983; Monroe award, 1987; Ruth Lilly prize, 1988; Tanning award for poetry, 1997. D.Litt.:

Bard College, 1970; L.H.D.: Georgetown University, 1981; Towson State University, Maryland, 1983; Rochester University, 1987. **Member:** Chancellor, Academy of American Poets, 1971; American Academy of Arts and Letters; American Academy of Arts and Sciences. **Address:** 4256 Nebraska Avenue, N.W., Washington. D.C. 20016, U.S.A.

PUBLICATIONS

Poetry

A Summoning of Stones. New York, Macmillan, 1954.
The Seven Deadly Sins. Northampton, Massachusetts, Gehenna Press, 1958.
Struwwelpeter. Northampton, Massachusetts, Gehenna Press, 1958.
A Bestiary, illustrated by Aubrey Schwartz. Los Angeles, Kanthos Press, 1962.
The Hard Hours. New York, Atheneum, and London, Oxford University Press, 1967.
Aesopic: Twenty Four Couplets. . . Northampton, Massachusetts, Gehenna Press, 1967.
Millions of Strange Shadows. New York, Atheneum, and London, Oxford University Press, 1977.
The Venetian Vespers. Boston, Godine, 1979; expanded version, New York, Atheneum, 1979; Oxford, Oxford University Press, 1980.
A Love for Four Voices: Homage to Franz Joseph Haydn. Great Barrington, Massachusetts, Penmaen Press, 1983.
Collected Earlier Poems. New York, Knopf, 1990.
The Transparent Men. New York, Knopf, 1990.
Flight among the Tombs. New York, Knopf, and London, Oxford University Press, 1996.

Other

Robert Lowell (lecture). Washington, D.C., Library of Congress, 1983.
The Pathetic Fallacy (lecture). Washington, D.C., Library of Congress, 1985.
Obbligati: Essays in Criticism. New York, Atheneum, 1986.
The Hidden Law: The Poetry of W. H. Auden. Cambridge, Massachusetts, Harvard University Press, 1993.
On the Laws of the Poetic Art. Princeton, New Jersey, Princeton University Press, 1995.

Editor, with John Hollander, *Jiggery-Pokery: A Compendium of Double Dactyls.* New York, Atheneum, 1967.
Editor, *Second Sight: Poems* by Jonathan Aaron. New York, Harper, 1982.
Editor, *Eve Names the Animals* by Susan Donnelly. Boston, Northeastern University Press, 1985.
Editor, *The Essential Herbert.* New York, Ecco Press, 1987.

Translator, with Helen Bacon, *Seven Against Thebes,* by Aeschylus. New York, Oxford University Press, 1973.
Translator, *Poem upon the Lisbon Disaster,* by Voltaire. Great Barrington, Massachusetts, Penmaen, 1977.

*

Bibliography: Anthony Hecht in Conversation with Philip Hoy by Philip Hoy, Stonington, Connecticut, Between the Lines, n.d.

Critical Studies: *The Burdens of Formality: Essays on the Poetry of Anthony Hecht* edited by Sydney Lea, Athens, University of Georgia Press, 1989; *Dramatic Strategies in the Poetry of Robert Lowell, Richard Howard, and Anthony Hecht* (dissertation), University of Toronto, 1990, and "'Laws that Stand for Other Laws': Anthony Hecht's Dramatic Strategy," in *Essays in Literature* (Macomb, Illinois), 21(2), fall 1994, both by Geoffrey Woolmer Lindsay; "Forms of Conviction" by Henry Taylor, in *Southern Review* (Baton Rouge, Louisiana), 27(1), winter 1991; "On Anthony Hecht" by John Hollander, in *Raritan* (New Brunswick, New Jersey), 17(1), summer 1997.

                                *   *   *

Anthony Hecht is a gifted craftsman who blends image, rhythm, and idea into rich and subtle music. His work shows imperial command over the energies of word, line, and stanza. Hecht's talents are on full display in early poems like "La Condition Botanique" and "The Gardens of the Villa D'Este," intricate, witty tours de force, lavish of image and allusion, filled with striking turns of thought. Witness one stanza from the latter poem:

> The intricate mesh of trees,
> Sagging beneath a lavender snow
> Of wisteria, wired by creepers, perfectly knit
> A plot to capture alive the migrant, tourist soul
> In its corporeal home with all the deft control
> And artifice of an Hephaestus' net.
> Sunlight and branch rejoice to show
> Sudden interstices.

Here the verbal music and the profusion of sound and color perfectly convey the poet's manifold delight in the garden, in its primitive hypnotic power ordered by the formal aesthetics of the artistic imagination. The allusion to Hephaestus's net, which trapped Ares and Aphrodite in flagrante delicto, gives mythological license to the garden as home of earthly pleasure and hints also at the paradox of incarnation. Such richness of texture is characteristic of Hecht, though in later works, notably in *The Hard Hours* and in *Millions of Strange Shadows,* he sometimes writes with simplicity and directness. Early and late, elegant seriousness often combines with colloquial jest to surprise and delight.

Hecht's poetry achieves its distinctive weight and eloquence by frequently recalling biblical and classical passages and motifs as well as many ancient and modern authors. Plato, Sophocles, Ronsard, du Bellay, Milton, Swift, Baudelaire, Yeats, and Stevens, for example, all contribute their voices to his polyphonous harmonies. Hecht writes in various metrical patterns and stanzaic forms—the double dactyl, sonnet, double sonnet, sestina, blank verse, to name just a few—and demonstrates time and again superb balance, discipline, and control, in a word, complete technical mastery.

Important subjects for Hecht's poetry include the love of men and women and of parents for children, the tense union of flesh and spirit, and the Holocaust. On this last topic Hecht has written a number of profound and searching poems. "More Light! More Light!" portrays victims who betray each other, thus extinguishing all hope for human dignity; "Rites and Ceremonies" meditates *de profundis* on human suffering and biblical promise; "It Out-Herods Herod. Pray You, Avoid It," features a father's rueful reflection that, despite his children's admiration of him, "Half God, half Santa Claus," he "could not, at one time, / Have saved them from the gas"; "The Feast of Stephen" sharply perceives the relations between the cults of athleticism and Nazism. In lighter moments Hecht parodies Matthew Arnold in "The Dover Bitch," humorously considers the seduction of a young admirer in "The Ghost in the Martini," and regales the Guggenheim Foundation with "Application for a Grant" (freely from Horace), which closes thus:

> As for me, the prize for poets, the simple gift
> For amphybrachs strewn by a kind Euterpe,
> With perhaps a laurel crown of the evergreen
> Imperishable of your fine endowment
> Would supply my modest wants, who dream of nothing
> But a pad on Eighth Street and your approbation.

The Venetian Vespers features several long poems and versions of Joseph Brodsky. The title poem is a lengthy monologue by an expatriate American on the decadent ruins of Venice. He meditates on the transformation of garbage into the "admirable and shatterable triumph" of Murano glassware. He ponders the processes of birth, death, and decay, the relationship between art and life, the movements of memory and aspiration. The corrupt and dirty city affords no pleasant garden to meditate in at eventide, no cure for "something profoundly soiled, pointlessly hurt," no ablution or "impossible reprieve, / Unpurchased at a scaffold, free, bequeathed / As rain upon the just and unjust, / As in the fall of mercy, unconstrained, / Upon the poor, infected place beneath." Instead he finds the neighborhood Madonna, "Sister Mary Paregoric, Comforter," and the momentary refuge of a thunderstorm wherein "one takes no thought whatever of tomorrow, / The soul being drenched in fine particulars." As the poignant statement of a man "who was never even at one time a wise child," the poem brilliantly reflects modern confusion, neurosis, and despair.

—Robert Miola

HEJINIAN, Lyn

Nationality: American. **Born:** San Francisco, California. **Career:** Faculty member, humanities department, California College of Arts and Crafts, Oakland, 1978; faculty member, New College of California, poetics program, San Francisco, 1986–87, 1990–98; adjunct faculty member, University of California, Berkeley, 1994–95. Visiting lecturer, University of California, San Diego, 1992; faculty member, Naropa Institute, summer writing program, Boulder, Colorado, 1992, 1995, 1998; Roberta Holloway lecturer in the practice of poetry, University of California, Berkeley, 1993; Coal Royalty chair in creative writing, University of Alabama, 1996; guest lecturer, University of Iowa, Iowa Writer's Workshop, Iowa City, 1998; visiting distinguished lecturer, St Mary's College, Moraga, California, 1999. Editor, Tuumba Press, Atelos, and *Poetics Journal,* all of Berkeley, California. Member, literature panel, National Endowment for the Arts, 1979–81, 1990–93; member, literature panel, California Arts Council, 1982–84; member, board of directors, Serendipity Books Distribution, 1984–89; member, board of directors, *LINES,*

Detroit Institute of Arts, 1985–90; president, board of directors, Small Press Distribution, 1987–89; member, steering committee, Oakland Strategic Plan for Cultural Development, California, 1993–94. **Awards:** James D. Phelan award in literature, San Francisco Foundation, 1974; National Endowment for the Arts, 1978, 1979, 1986 for editor's grants, and 1988 for translator's fellowship grant; California Arts Council, 1983, 1985, 1988 for editor's grants, and 1989 for individual artist's grant; Poetry Center book award, San Francisco State University, 1988; E-2nd Independent literary award, Leningrad, *Poetic Function,* 1989; Fund for Poetry grant, 1997. **Address:** 2639 Russell Street, Berkeley, California 94705, U.S.A.

PUBLICATIONS

Poetry

A Thought Is the Bride of What Thinking. Willits, California, Tuumba Press, 1976.
A Mask of Motion. Providence, Rhode Island, Burning Deck, 1977.
Writing Is an Aid to Memory. Berkeley, California, The Figures, 1978.
Gesualdo. Berkeley, California, Tuumba Press, 1978.
Redo. Grenada, Mississippi, Salt-Works Press, 1984.
The Guard. Berkeley, California, Tuumba Press, 1984.
Individuals, with Kit Robinson. Tucson, Arizona, Chax Press, 1988.
The Cell. Los Angeles, Sun and Moon Press, 1990.
The Hunt. La Laguna, Islas Canarias, Zasterle Press, 1991.
The Cold of Poetry. Los Angeles, Sun and Moon Press, 1994.
Wicker, with Jack Collom, Boulder, Colorado, Rodent Press, 1996.
The Little Book of a Thousand Eyes. Boulder, Colorado, Smoke-Proof Press, 1996.
Guide, Grammar, Watch, and The Thirty Nights. Perth, Western Australia, Folio, 1996.
The Traveler and the Hill and the Hill, with Emilie Clark. New York, Granary Books, 1998.
Sight, with Leslie Scalapino. Washington, D.C., Edge, 1999.
Happily. Sausalito, California, Post-Apollo Press, 2000.

Novels

My Life. Providence, Rhode Island, Burning Deck, 1980; revised edition, Los Angeles. Sun and Moon Press. 1987.
Oxota: A Short Russian Novel. Great Barrington, Massachusetts, The Figures, 1991.

Other

Translator, with Elena Balashova, *Description,* by Arkadii Dragomoshchenko. Los Angeles. Sun and Moon Press. 1990.
Translator, with Elena Balashova, *Xenia,* by Arkadi Dragomoschenko. Los Angeles, Sun and Moon Press, 1993.

*

Manuscript Collection: University of California-San Diego, La Jolla.

Critical Studies: "Too Clear" by Ross Feld, in *Parnassus: Poetry in Review* (New York), 8(1), 1978; "Mayer on Hejinian" by Bernadette Mayer, in *L=A=N=G=U=A=G=E* (New York), 13, December 1980;

"Notes on Lyn Hejinian" by Carla Harryman, in *American Poetry Archive News,* 1, winter 1984; "Hejinian's Notes," in *Content's Dream: Essays* 1975–1984, by Charles Bernstein, Los Angeles, Sun and Moon Press, 1986; "Her Favorite Device Is the Echo" by Emily Leider, in San Francisco *Chronicle,* 18 October 1987; "Two Hejinian Talks" by Stephen Ratcliffe, in *Temblor* 6, 1987; "What Then Is a Window?" by Marnie Parsons, in *Brick* (Toronto), 38, winter 1990; "Feminist Poetics and the Meaning of Clarity" by Rae Armantrout, in *Sagetrieb* (Orono, Maine), 11(3), winter 1992; "My Life through the Eighties: The Exemplary LANGUAGE of Lyn Hejinian" by David R. Jarraway, in *Contemporary Literature* (Madison, Wisconsin), 33(2), summer 1992; "Poetic Positionings: Stephen Dobyns and Lyn Hejinian in Cultural Context" by Christopher Beach, in *Contemporary Literature* (Madison, Wisconsin), 38(1), spring 1997; "Lyn Hejinian and the Possibilities of Postmodernism in Poetry" by Charles Altieri, in *Women Poets of the Americas: Toward a Pan-American Gathering,* edited by Jacqueline Vaught Brogan and Cordelia Chavez Candelaria, Notre Dame, Indiana, University of Notre Dame Press, 1999.

*   *   *

American practicality has always been a goad to poets to find some loophole in its philosophical plainness or to puncture it with ribald humor in an attempt to dismiss its deep-rootedness in the American psyche. As long as practicality remains an essential norm of taste, it will make poems squirm to overcome it or to find humorous alternatives. Certainly New England's poets have troubled themselves deeply to unseat the prominence of this slightly disguised puritan virtue. Robert Frost and Wallace Stevens both lavished much irony on the homely virtue; e.e. cummings mocked it tirelessly in childlike nonsense poems and love lyrics.

Lyn Hejinian, like Frost, was born in San Francisco and educated in New England. At age twenty-seven she returned to the Bay Area and began writing a hauntingly ungraspable mode of lyric in which a voice, disembodied but felt, unidentifiable and yet familiar, whispers to the reader of things that never converge to argument but that evaporate as softly as they came. She too has waged war on practicality, on the utilitarian notion of the poem as message or advice.

Also like Frost, Hejinian seems undecided between two orders of things in the mind or between two narratives or subjects, neither of which gains her attention long enough to become belief. Instead, like a double helix unwinding from a spool, two possibilities simply travel together loosely in parallel as she teases and frustrates her readers with seemingly ordered speech, but speech that defies resolution or interpretation.

Gesualdo, a prose meditation published by Hejinian's own Tuumba Press in 1978, offers this curious but typical observation on the doubleness of her poetry:

> The capacity of artists to manipulate for their own ends forms invented in a different spirit is one of the facts of life . . . was dying by artists whose passion and sensuousness essentially distinguished them . . . because they tremble, as it were, on the brink of one or the other commitment.

Gesualdo, Prince of Venosa, was a composer of late sixteenth-century Naples who took the madrigal form as far it would go musically and collaborated with the poet Tasso on numerous canzones and sonnets to create the equivalent of a pre-Baroque language poetry set to music. He whipped up complicated six-voice harmonies that even Stravinsky found overwrought but that Hejinian interprets as the multivocality of consciousness. She duplicates the technique in her prose and dazzles the reader with its overlay of continuous tracts of thought.

Gesualdo offers more admonitions than advice, with a sinister undertone stemming from the composer's murder of his first wife and her lover, a celebrated scandal for half a century. But an admonitory voice is also present in one of Hejinian's previous prose pamphlets, *A Thought Is the Bride of What Thinking,* published by the Tuumba Press in 1976. More tentative than *Gesualdo,* it nonetheless reveals the intention of all her later work—experiments in tonality, in reordering syntax, in riddling grammar with interjection and transposition. Her meditations draw heavily on older styles of eloquence, much of it coming from the Victorian and Edwardian eras, giving her poems a mood like that of old films and photographs.

The theme of these books is partly the irreality of language against the backdrop of the real world and the menacing forces that hamper human existence. Like other language poets Hejinian plumbs the sense of terror in the twentieth century, of holocaust and sinister forms of government, of authority bearing down on one's freedom to think. Only by the eruptions of unsorted or uncontrolled language can one tear free of grammatical traps and the incarceration that all language poets suffer in their mental lives.

A Mask of Motion, Hejinian's first collection of open-verse poems, was issued by Keith Waldrop's Burning Deck Press in 1977. The work is an extension of the suspended style of the other two prose books: "I'm confusing two different stories, she said; I know I'm mixing them up. But somehow, strange as it seems, completely unrelated events can intertwine in my memory and then I see they had something in common." This is as good an explanation of Hejinian's own method as can be found in her work. It indicates the nervous doubling of her thought and speaks to her indeterminate movements.

In *Writing Is an Aid to Memory,* Hejinian's preface prepares the reader for what follows:

> I am always conscious of the disquieting runs of life slipping by, that the message remains undelivered, opposed to me. Memory cannot, though the future return, and proffer raw confusions. Knowledge is part of the whole, as hope is, from which love seeks to contrast knowledge with separation.

The book is a sequence of forty-two passages, a relentlessly unpredictable discourse in monologue form that moves from one topic to another and from tone to tone without transition. But like a palimpsest the language reveals patterns and meanings buried in the flow of the text, submerged like the stones or fish forms in a swiftly flowing river. There are enough such glimpses of actual things in the discourse, as in the tour of the caves at Dordogne in *A Mask of Motion,* to make the reader grasp at them as the language moves along with its shimmering but intangible possibilities. Hejinian proves that language can do more than state explicit arguments; it can move a reader to different emotional states merely by the configurations of its words and tones, its subtle and unyielding mysteries.

In the prose book *My Life* we find Hejinian working from another source of ideas on language poetry: Gertrude Stein's animistic prose in *Tender Buttons.* Here Hejinian works in small units of prose reminiscence and description to vitalize the ordinary, inert "things" in one's landscape. "Long time lines trail behind every idea, object,

person, pet, vehicle, and event," she says of her epistemology. It is as apt a definition of her poetics as one finds in her canon.

—Paul Christensen

HELLER, Michael (D.)

Nationality: American. **Born:** New York City, 11 May 1937. **Education:** Miami Beach Senior High School, graduated 1955; Rensselaer Polytechnic Institute, Troy, New York (managing editor, *Rensselaer Engineer,* and editor, *Bachelor* magazine), B.S. in management engineering 1959; City College, New York 1961–63; New School for Social Research, New York (Coffey prize, 1964), 1963–64; New York University, 1970–71, M.A. in English 1986. **Family:** Married 1) Doris C. Whytal in 1962 (divorced 1978), one son; 2) the writer Jane Augustine in 1979. **Career:** Chief technical writer, Norelco Corporation, New York, 1963–65; part-time teacher of English in Spain, 1965–66; freelance industrial and advertising writer, 1966–67. Since 1967 member of the faculty, now master teacher and academic coordinator, American Language Institute, New York University. Since 1970 teacher and member of advisory panel, New York State Poetry in the Schools program. Poet-in-residence, Keystone College, Pennsylvania, 1979. Contributing editor, *Montemora* magazine and staff member, *Montemora* Foundation, New York. U.S. editor, *Origin* magazine; member of advisory board, *Pequod* magazine. **Awards:** Creative Artists Public Service grant, 1975; National Endowment for the Humanities grant, 1979, 1986; Poetry Society of America Alice Fay di Castagnola award, 1980; Yaddo Colony fellowship, 1989; New York Foundation for the Arts fellowship, 1989. **Address:** P.O. Box 1289, New York, 10009, U.S.A.

PUBLICATIONS

Poetry

Two Poems. Mount Horeb, Wisconsin, Perishable Press, 1970.
Accidental Center. Fremont, Michigan, Sumac Press, 1972.
Figures of Speaking. Mount Horeb, Wisconsin, Perishable Press, 1977.
Knowledge. New York, Sun Press, 1979.
In the Builded Place. Minneapolis, Coffee House Press, 1990.
Six Poems. New York, Hot Bird MFG, II(15), 1993.
Worldflow: New and Selected Poems. Jersey City, New Jersey, Talisman, 1997.

Other

Conviction's Net of Branches: Essays on the Objectivist Poets and Poetry. Carbondale, Southern Illinois University Press, 1985.
Living Root: A Memoir. Albany, State University of New York Press, 2000.

Editor, *Carl Rakosi: Man and Poet.* Orono, Maine, National Poetry Foundation, 1993.

*

Critical Studies: ''Moving Heaven and Earth'' by James Guimond, in *Parnassus* (New York), Winter 1972; ''At, Borders, Think'' by Alan Williamson, in *Parnassus* (New York), 1982; ''Of Music and Rites'' by Lucien Stryk, in *American Book Review* (New York), 4(2), 1982; ''A Review of *Knowledge*'' by Laszlo K. Gefin, in *Sagetrieb* (Orono, Maine), Spring 1984; Michael Heller issue of *Talisman* (Hoboken, New Jersey), Fall 1993; by Norman Finkelstein, in *Denver Quarterly* (Denver), 33(4), Winter 1998.

*   *   *

The publication in 1972 of *Accidental Center* announced an authentic, hard-edged, meditative poet of truly contemporary sensibility who worked in the objectivist manner, a poet who exemplified Oppen's ''sense of the poet's self among things'' and Reznikoff's detailed, literal, compassionate witnessing of the modern city dweller, a poet who knew that

> the words
> are precipitates
> —in themselves
> precipitous
> rare and expensive dust
> desperately grasped
> in the amalgam.

For Michael Heller the words represent a process of distillation; they are hard-won, to be treasured and used sparingly. At the same time there is a willingness to follow where the words lead, into darkness, mystery. This is a fundamental recognition, based on his awareness of physical principles, of ''how each / word is a shift of matter.''

Accidental Center was remarkable in that, unlike most first books, there was a complete absence of that overwriting that masks lack of assurance and control. The poems result from an intense concentration, a focusing on the objective, in Zukofsky's early formulation of objectivist poetry. In fact, the photo image is prevalent in the book—''the moment in the sense'' caught and held—almost as if objectivist principles were being given a technical underpinning. *Accidental Center* is a serious book that takes language seriously. The method of many of the poems is to proceed by means of simple, declarative constructs to form an image as proposition, a logic based on the ''thingness of things,'' on exact observation. The poems are often based on the paradoxical image, provoking us to respond to the artifact as material for a contemporary mythology. Numerous references employing the terms of astrophysics, chemistry, and biology function almost as a traditional mythic or religious gloss, amplifying and expanding the particular emotive context. This can be seen, for example, in ''Operation Cicero'':

> writing of the great light of cities
> . . . these are entropic times
> and those bright clusters
> in our lives
> in their rot
> are black bodies
> and absorb it all
> like a woman
> on one's bed
> who cannot bear the light

The paradoxical quality results also from the contrast between the precision of the scientific terms, economy of language, short lines, and spare style, on the one hand, and the genuine acceptance of a sort of negative capability, on the other. Things, ideas, and emotions—oneself in the world—are not rendered simplistically but exactly as a measure of their subtle relativity and mystery; what we know is a function of how we know.

Heller expresses throughout the poems of *Accidental Center* an explicit or implicit ontological concern, not in the form of an abstract disquisition but as speculation on the objects that relate to and define the self. The finest example of a poem given over wholly to this concern is the impressive ''Meditation on the Coral,'' in which our existence as city dwellers is explored in terms of the coral, symbolizing in its cellular structure our dependent and communal way of life but also, in its origins in the sea, our atavistic urges ''and the warm saline / —as of the birth sac / still a dream.''

In addition to the speculative poetry that characterized the earlier book, Heller's second major collection, *Knowledge,* contains poems that are more discursive, leisurely, and descriptive, though no less formal in intent. Having settled into a style, he is now able to accommodate more immediate and personal concerns without, however, sacrificing intensity. Thus, events that mark the perception of both continuity and change in family relationships—with father, mother, wife, son—become occasions for poems in which the occasion makes its own space and pace. Literalness coexists with irony in a number of these poems, producing a gentle humor. ''Bialystok Stanzas'' recalls the incisiveness, objectivity, and compassion of Reznikoff's depictions of traditional Jewish life and the Holocaust. But in even as occasional a poem as ''On the Beach'' Heller never relaxes his gaze. Although the occasion may seem commonplace—''watching square yards of such flesh / Baste itself with oil''—nevertheless, ''Even here, amid these minor increments / of peril, one is consoled. In this / Careless resort of life of beaches / Deceptions themselves are a kind of truth.''

The energy that informs Heller's poems—and the reason he is so rewarding as a poet—derives from ''the world already existing / without a name,'' in which the impulse is to question, to take nothing for granted, while perceiving what is there, in a very real sense, for all to know. The concluding section of ''At Albert's Landing (with my son)'' specifies the process of that special knowledge:

> Different as the woods are
> This is no paradise to enter or leave.
> Just the real, and a wild nesting
> Of hope in the real
> Which does not know of hope.
> Things lean and lean, and sometimes
> Words find common centers in us
> Resonating and filling speech.
> Let me know a little of you.

In the Builded Place—referring to a place of structure, the form and formlessness of self—Heller has arrived at a way of playing off several traditions against one another to achieve an impressive poetic structure. The book represents the poet at the height of his powers in his willingness to take risks and therefore to say more than he otherwise might have. The sense of urban angst is tempered and expanded by the Chinese and Japanese poetic, by Zen teachings and attitudes, by the tradition of Jewish humanism and the Jewish experience in America, by Rilke, by the classical tradition, and by the French:

> As another legatee of Mallarmé,
> I have strained against the tongue
> Until the word displaced
> The world's foreign body.

Heller alternates the plainsong of the literal, declarative image with an allusive, denser metaphysic, so as

> yet to make of this
> A blended music.

The poems locate the self with almost scientific precision, but this rigorous exactitude is simultaneously resonant with the possibilities and ambiguities of one man's existence at a given time. This is what gives the poems their peculiar tension, muscular and relaxed by turn, opening up the take of the poems beyond the literal ground.

Though many of these poems are of the city—and a number of others are built upon the technological image—they are of the heart and mind and gut; as buildings seem at first to be constructed of angles and planes, there is yet a life inside them that does not conform to such a fabricated aesthetic. In his meditative vision Heller helps us to discover the self in the effort to see himself clearly.

—Robert Vas Dias

HELWIG, David (Gordon)

Nationality: Canadian. **Born:** Toronto, Ontario, 5 April 1938. **Education:** Stamford Collegiate Institute, graduated 1956; University of Toronto, B.A. 1960; University of Liverpool, M.A. 1962. **Family:** Married Nancy Keeling in 1959; two daughters. **Career:** Member of the Department of English, Queen's University, Kingston, Ontario, 1962–80. Literary manager, television-drama department, 1974–76, and story editor, *Sidestreet* crime series, 1974–75, Canadian Broadcasting Corporation. Co-editor, *Quarry* magazine. **Awards:** CBC literary prize, 1983. **Address:** General Delivery, Belfast, PEI, COA 1AO, Canada.

PUBLICATIONS

Poetry

Figures in a Landscape. Ottawa, Oberon Press, 1967.
The Sign of the Gunman. Ottawa, Oberon Press, 1969.
The Best Name of Silence. Ottawa, Oberon Press, 1972.
Atlantic Crossings. Ottawa, Oberon Press, 1974.
A Book of the Hours. Ottawa, Oberon Press, 1979.
The Rain Falls Like Rain. Ottawa, Oberon Press, 1982.
Catchpenny Poems. Ottawa, Oberon Press, 1983.
The Hundred Old Names. Ottawa, Oberon Press, 1988.
The Beloved. Ottawa, Oberon Press, 1992.
A Random Gospel. Ottawa, Oberon Press, 1996.
This Human Day. Ottawa, Oberon Press, 2000.

Play

A Time in Winter (produced Kingston, Ontario, 1967). Included in *Figures in a Landscape,* 1967.

Novels

The Day before Tomorrow. Ottawa, Oberon Press, 1971; as *Message from a Spy,* Don Mills, Ontario, Paperjacks, 1975.
The Glass Knight. Ottawa, Oberon Press, 1976.
Jennifer. Ottawa, Oberon Press, 1979; New York, Beaufort, 1983.
The King's Evil. Ottawa, Oberon Press, 1981; New York, Beaufort, 1984.
It Is Always Summer. Toronto, Stoddart, and New York, Beaufort, 1982.
A Sound Like Laughter. Toronto, Stoddart, and New York, Beaufort, 1983.
The Only Son. Toronto, Stoddart, and New York, Beaufort, 1984; London, Penguin, 1988.
The Bishop. Markham, Ontario, New York, and London, Viking, 1986.
A Postcard from Rome. Markham, Ontario, Viking, 1988.
Old Wars. Markham, Ontario, Viking, 1989.
Of Desire. Markham, Ontario, Viking, 1990.
Blueberry Cliffs. Ottawa, Oberon Press, 1993.
Just Say the Words. Ottawa, Oberon Press, 1994.
Close to the Fire. Fredericton, Goose Lane Editions, 1999.
The Time of Her Life. Fredericton, Goose Lane Editions, 2000.

Short Stories

The Streets of Summer. Ottawa, Oberon Press, 1969.

Other

A Book about Billie (documentary). Ottawa, Oberon Press, 1972; as *Inside and Out,* Don Mills, Ontario, Paperjacks, 1975.

Editor, with Tom Marshall, *Fourteen Stories High: Best Canadian Stories of 71.* Ottawa, Oberon Press, 1971.
Editor, with Joan Harcourt, *72, 73, 74* and *75: New Canadian Stories.* Ottawa, Oberon Press, 4 vols., 1972–75.
Editor, *Words from Inside.* Kingston, Ontario, Prison Arts, 1972.
Editor, *The Human Elements: Critical Essays* (and *Second Series*). Ottawa, Oberon Press, 2 vols., 1978–81.
Editor, *Love and Money: The Politics of Culture.* Ottawa, Oberon Press, 1980.
Editor, with Sandra Martin, *83, 84, 85,* and *86: Best Canadian Stories.* Ottawa, Oberon Press, 4 vols., 1983–86; with Maggie Helwig, *87, 88, 89,* and *91,* 4 vols., 1987–91.
Editor, with Sandra Martin, *Coming Attractions 1983, 1984, 1985,* and *1986.* Ottawa, Oberon Press, 4 vols., 1983–86; with Maggie Helwig, *1987* and *1988,* 2 vols., 1987–88.

Translator, *Chekhov, Last Stories.* Ottawa, Oberon Press, 1991.

*

Manuscript Collection: McMaster University, Hamilton, Ontario.

Critical Studies: ''Spells against Chaos'' by Tom Marshall, in *Quarry* (Kingston, Ontario), Spring 1968; ''David Helwig's New Timber,'' in *Queen's Quarterly* (Kingston, Ontario), Summer 1974; '''The Progress of Illumination': The Design and Unity of David Helwig's Catchpenny Poems'' by Lorraine M. York, in *Canadian Poetry* (London, Ontario), 18, Spring/Summer 1986.

*   *   *

Over the years David Helwig's poetry has changed significantly, his later muse being less violent and political than in some of his earlier works. In *The Sign of the Gunman,* for instance, there is a curious stridency and rhetorical pose that seems artificial and labored: ''They are burning our cities / they are shooting at us with bullets.'' This goes hand in hand with an occasionally distasteful reveling in sutures and seared flesh: ''Somewhere is a photograph / of a man in two pieces / burned until he is only / two pieces of a cooked man.'' When the violence is necessary to greatness, as it is in his ''Apollo and Daphne,'' it is right and felt as a conclusion to the poem. But Helwig does not escape the fashionable Canadian taste for Frye-like mythology, in which Harlequin and the acrobat, like the Zeus of his ''Metamorphosis,'' appear to stand for more than they are, gesturing for significance.

The four poems that comprise *Atlantic Crossings,* however, are not racked by symbol. The image of the louse in the Columbus section, moving ''off the edge of my swollen brain / into a new world,'' has an appropriately Donnean quality. It is indicative of what preserves this collection from mere indulgence in the horrific world of madness through which it travels.

The strength of Helwig's earliest poetry is present again in his later work, a strength that owes much to a fine-edged description. Helwig's admiration for Andrew Wyeth is evident in his ''After Brueghel,'' where winter is a season ''of sudden long white distances / that empty the mind.'' There is something of the Pacific Northwest school (William Stafford, for instance) in Helwig's ''Still Life'' or ''Sunday Breakfast'':

Orange, one egg, tea in a cup
of blue and white, composing silences
against the hurt nerves fluttering.

Although some of the poems in *A Book of the Hours* come perilously close to McKuen, Helwig's affection for the familial and domestic is rarely sentimental. His ''A Shaker Chair'' is a classic of toughness:

I see in the Shaker rocking chair
stillness turning, stillness moving,
contemplation and silent standing,
even the denial of the body.

Occasionally one senses Helwig's debt to the impressionist transformation of simple painterly objects into a larger life, a debt that gives us echoes of Stevens: ''We swim before we walk. The tropic sea / within the caul is home.'' Certainly the inflections are Stevens's, and they are congenial to an attractive toughness in the verse that saves Helwig's taste for darkness, secrecy, and night and for their magic from being merely fantasy. Fantasy at its best, however, is present in his ''Summer Landscapes,'' where ''the house running away to the

stars / on the feet of mice'' has the quality of a Louis de Niverville painting.

Like many Canadian artists Helwig seemed to find his voice abroad. Liverpool nurtured him, and in his best poems one hears the voices of ''the old women / climbing Brownlow Hill / in the killing fog.''

In the best of Helwig's works there is a fine sense of detachment. This may be why his poems on Diefenbaker, the Orange Lodge, and American political issues are so weak; his spontaneous emotion is too close to their creation. The picture one retains of him is of a distant walker, a figure in his own landscape, above the world he deplores and celebrates, the world he describes in ''Christmas, 1965,'' in which ''silence / had overwhelmed the noise of men,'' leaving only the poet's voice.

—D.D.C. Chambers

HENDERSON, Hamish

Nationality: Scottish. **Born:** Blairgowrie, Perthshire, 11 November 1919. **Education:** Blairgowrie High School; Dulwich College, London; Downing College, Cambridge, M.A. **Military Service:** Highland Division during World War II. **Family:** Married; two daughters. **Career:** Senior lecturer and research fellow, 1951–87, and since 1987 honorary fellow, School of Scottish Studies, University of Edinburgh. **Awards:** Somerset Maugham award, 1949. LL.D.: University of Dundee. Honorary degrees: University of Dundee, Open University, University of Edinburgh. **Address:** School of Scottish Studies, 27 George Square, Edinburgh EH8 9LD, Scotland.

PUBLICATIONS

Poetry

Elegies for the Dead in Cyrenaica. London, Lehmann, 1948.
Freedom Come-All-Ye, in *Chapbook* special issue (Aberdeen), vol. 3 no. 6, 1967.

Other

Alias MacAlias. Edinburgh, Polygon, 1990.
The Armstrong Nose: Selected Letters of Hamish Henderson. Edinburgh, Polygon, 1996.

Editor, and contributor, *Ballads of World War II, Collected by Seumas Mor Maceanruig.* Glasgow, Caledonian Press, 1947.

*

Critical Studies: *The Poet Speaks* edited by Peter Orr, London, Routledge, and New York, Barnes and Noble, 1966; ''The Elegies of Rilke and Henderson: Influence and Variation'' by Richard E. Ziegfeld, in *Studies in Scottish Literature* (Columbia, South Carolina), 16, 1981; ''The Sea, the Desert, the City: Environment and Language in W.S. Graham, Hamish Henderson, and Tom Leonard'' by Edwin Morgan, in *Yearbook of English Studies* (London), 17, 1987; Hamish Henderson issue of *Tocher,* 43, 1991.

*   *   *

Hamish Henderson's first book of verse, *Elegies for the Dead in Cyrenaica,* was published in 1948 and was the product of the desert fighting that inspired so much of the best English poetry of World War II, including that of Keith Douglas. Appearing when it did, it tended to miss the tide of interest in war poetry that had been nourished by the conflict itself. The fact that the author has produced little poetry since has also not aided his reputation. Yet Henderson has always had a small band of admirers, and rereading his elegies it is easy to see why.

The book has two advantages: it can be read complete, as a whole, not just as a collection of poems written in different moods and on different occasions; and it has a comfortable relationship to the modernist tradition, something more likely to happen with Scottish poets than with English ones. Henderson was obviously much influenced by the Eliot of *The Four Quartets,* but at that period it was difficult not to be if one had not succumbed to the influences of Dylan Thomas or Edith Sitwell. But one also hears within his work the voices of Europe: Goethe and Hölderlin, who supply him with epigraphs, and the Alexandrian Greek Cavafy, whom he quotes. The poems are successful philosopical verse, a comparatively rare thing in twentieth-century English poetry.

Henderson combines his philosophical bent with a delicate naturalism and a skillful control of tone, which means that the poems, which are comparatively long, can rise up into the high style and leave it again without difficulty, just as the author requires. Here is an example from the beginning of the second elegy:

At dawn, under the concise razor-edge
of the escarpment, the laager sleeps. No petrol fires yet
blow flame for brew-up. Up on the pass a sentry
inhales his Nazionale. Horse-shoc-curve of the bay
grows visible beneath him. He smokes and yawns.
Ooo-augh,
  and the limitless
shabby lion-pelt of the desert completes and rounds
his limitless ennui.

One suspects that this is the kind of wartime verse most likely to last and be read by posterity.

—Edward Lucie-Smith

HENRI, Adrian (Maurice)

Nationality: British. **Born:** Birkenhead, Cheshire, 10 April 1932. **Education:** St. Asaph Grammar School, North Wales, 1945–51; King's College, Newcastle, 1951–55, B.A. (honors) in fine arts 1955. **Family:** Married Joyce Wilson in 1957 (divorced; died 1987). **Career:** Worked as a fairground worker, teacher, and scenic artist, 1955–61. Lecturer, Manchester College of Art and Design, 1961–64, and Liverpool College of Art, 1964–67. Member of the Liverpool Scene, poetry-rock group, 1967–70, American tour, 1969. Painter: individual shows—Institute of Contemporary Arts, London, 1968; Art Net, London, 1975; Williamson Art Gallery, Birkenhead, 1975; retrospective, Wolverhampton, 1976; Demarco Gallery, Edinburgh, 1978; retrospective, South Hill Park, Bracknell, 1986; Hanover Gallery, Liverpool, 1987; Library Centre, Skelmersdale, 1989; Poetry Society, London, 1990; Orrell Arts Centre, 1992; Acorn Gallery, Liverpool, 1992; Southport Arts Centre, 1993; The Storey Institute, Lancaster, 1994; Merkmal Gallery, Liverpool, 1994. Since 1970 full-time writer and painter, with occasional work with Grimms, Henri and Friends, and The Lawnmower groups; visiting lecturer, Bradford College, Yorkshire, 1973–76; writer-in-residence, Tattenhall Centre, Cheshire, 1980–82, and University of Liverpool, 1989; visiting lecturer, Trent Polytechnic, Nottingham, 1989. President, Liverpool Academy of Arts, 1972–81, and Merseyside Arts Association, 1978–80. **Awards:** Arts Council of Northern Ireland prize, for painting, 1964; John Moores Exhibition prize, 1972; D.Litt.: Liverpool Polytechnic, 1990. **Agent:** Rogers Coleridge and White, 20 Powis Mews, London W11 1JN. **Address:** 21 Mount Street, Liverpool L1 9HD, England.

PUBLICATIONS

Poetry

The Mersey Sound: Penguin Modern Poets 10, with Roger McGough and Brian Patten. London, Penguin, 1967; revised edition, 1974, 1983.
Tonight at Noon. London, Rapp and Whiting, 1968; New York, McKay, 1969.
City. London, Rapp and Whiting, 1969.
Talking after Christmas Blues, music by Wallace Southam. London, Turret, 1969.
Poems for Wales and Six Landscapes for Susan. Gillingham, Kent, ARC, 1970.
Autobiography. London, Cape, 1971.
America. London, Turret, 1972.
The Best of Henri: Selected Poems 1960–70. London, Cape, 1975.
One Year. Todmorden, Lancashire, ARC, 1976.
City Hedges: Poems 1970–76. London, Cape, 1977.
Beauty and the Beast, with Carol Ann Duffy. Liverpool, Glasshouse Press, 1977.
Words Without a Story. Liverpool, Glasshouse Press, 1979.
From the Loveless Motel: Poems 1976–1979. London, Cape, 1980.
Harbour. London, Ambit, 1982.
Penny Arcade: Poems 1978–1982. London, Cape, 1983.
New Volume, with Roger McGough and Brian Patten. London, Penguin, 1983.
Holiday Snaps. Liverpool, Windows, 1985.
Collected Poems 1967–1985. London, Allison and Busby, 1986.
Wish You Were Here. London, Cape, 1990.
Not Fade Away. Newcastle upon Tyne, Bloodaxe, 1994.

Verse (for children)

The Phantom Lollipop Lady and Other Poems. London, Methuen, 1986.
Rhinestone Rhino. London, Methuen, 1989.
Box and Other Poems. London, Mammoth, 1990.
Dinner with the Spratts. London, Methuen, 1993.

The World's Your Lobster, with Wendy Smith. London, Bloomsbury, 1998.
Skeleton Songs. London, Bloomsbury, 1999.

Recordings: (with Liverpool Scene) *St. Adrian Co., Broadway and 3rd,* RCA, 1970; *Heirloon,* RCA, 1970; *Recollections,* Charisma, 1972; (solo) *Adrian Henri,* Canon, 1974; *British Poets of Our Times,* with Hugo Williams, Argo; *The Blues in Rat's Alley,* Rats, 1988.

Plays

I Wonder: A Guillaume Apollinaire Show, with Michael Kustow (produced London, 1968).
I Want, with Nell Dunn, adaptation of their own novel (produced Liverpool, 1983; London, 1986).
The Wakefield Mysteries (produced Wakefield, Yorkshire, 1988). London, Methuen, 1993.
Fears and Miseries of the Third Term, with others (produced Liverpool and London, 1989).

Television Plays: *Yesterday's Girl,* 1973; *The Husband, The Wife, and the Stranger,* 1986.

Novel

I Want, with Nell Dunn. London, Cape 1972.

Other

Environments and Happenings. London, Thames and Hudson, 1974; as *Total Art: Environments, Happenings and Performances,* New York, Praeger, 1974.
Eric the Punk Cat (for children). London, Hodder and Stoughton, 1982.
The Art of Adrian Henri (exhibition catalogue). Bracknell, South Hill Park, 1986.
Eric and Frankie in Las Vegas (for children). London, Methuen, 1987.
The Postman's Palace (for children). London, Methuen, 1990.

*

Critical Studies: *Art in a City* by John Willett, London, Methuen, 1967; introduction by Edward Lucie-Smith to *The Liverpool Scene,* London, Rapp and Carroll, and New York, Doubleday, 1967; *The Society of the Poem* by Jonathan Raban, London, Harrap, 1971; ''Bathos, Schmathos'' by Michael Hulse, in *New Poetry 49* (London), 1980; ''Penny Arcade'' by Geoffrey Ward, in *Ambit 47* (London), 1984; introduction by Edward Lucie-Smith, in *The Art of Adrian Henri 1955–1985,* South Hill Park, Bracknell, 1986; ''Adrian Henri and the Dayglo Colours,'' in *Off the Cuff* (Liverpool), 8, 1994.

Adrian Henri comments:

(1970) I was trained as a painter and still paint and exhibit paintings. I make a living primarily by performing the works that I write, mostly with music. I think of myself as a maker and presenter of images in various media. Pop poet is, I think, the most common label.

My major influences are T.S. Eliot, Apollinaire, Mallarmé, Ginsberg, Olson, and recently Tennyson, Creeley, and Hugh MacDiarmid, also the prose of Joyce and William Burroughs. I am an autobiographical poet; my poems are extensions of my own life, some fact, some fantasy. For this reason I write perhaps more love poems than anything else. I am excited by new uses of language in the mass media, like TV commercials or pop songs, and am only interested in older verse forms (i.e., rhyme, etc.) as they survive in modern society, e.g., ballad and particularly blues. I would like my poems to be read by as many people as possible since I cannot see any point either personally or politically in writing for an elite minority. I think by doing readings and by working with the Liverpool Scene I am beginning to reach a bigger and largely nonliterary audience.

(1974) Since a serious heart illness in 1970 my way of life, and to some extent my way of working, has changed somewhat. At the moment my poetry is perhaps quieter and more traditional in character. Since spending some time in Somerset and Shropshire, I have become interested in the English landscape tradition, notably Wordsworth and Housman, and the Pre-Raphaelite painters. My work as a painter is similarly involved in an investigation into the possibilities of landscape.

(1980) I am still involved with landscape but have recently extended this to ''debris'' paintings, studies of urban wasteland. *City Hedges* perhaps reflects this. Current work includes a musical version of Jarry's *Ubu.* Economic problems have made musical collaborations less possible, but I still work with guitarist Andy Roberts and others when I can.

(1985) After a period of retrenchment in the 1970s, there seems to be a return to a greater freedom and wider range of idiom, and some of the concerns of the 1960s, in *From the Loveless Motel* and *Penny Arcade.* Touring in Germany, Canada, Norway, the U.S.A., etc., as well as round Britain, has generated a number of travel poems, and I am still interested in the long poem (as previously with *City, Autobiography, One Year*) and the problems (first articulated by Poe) of making it work at the same level of intensity as the lyric. I have been increasingly affected by the prose writings of Malcolm Lowry. In an increasingly fragmented and divisive society I still see my main problem as trying to reach as wide an audience as possible while still writing what I feel to be valid modern poetry.

(1990) Writing poems for children, and more recently for teenagers, has opened up new areas of writing for me, and I relish the challenge of communicating with a very different age group. Working more on the theater, particularly on an extended scale in *The Wakefield Mysteries,* has helped me develop a flexible free verse form for voices other than my own.

*   *   *

Adrian Henri is one of a number of contemporary artists who have forsaken conventional roles in favor of broader activity that includes public performance. Not only a poet, Henri has at various times been a painter, novelist, critic, and singer as well as an actor-out of his own poetic creations. There is in his work a strong affinity with the American artist Allan Kaprow, pioneer of the ''environment'' and the ''happening.'' Henri has written on the subject, and it is significant that his collection of poems *Penny Arcade* shares its title with one of Kaprow's assemblages. The element of ''action collage'' is constant in his writings, evident early on in the barrage of images in ''I Want to Paint'' and in the nightmare Bosch landscape of ''The Triumph of Death'' and still present years later in ''Death in the Suburbs'' and ''Annunciation.''

An intensely serious writer, Henri often displays a sly humor, and the apparent simplicity of some of his poems is deceptive. Much of his work in the 1960s is reminiscent of pop song lyrics, hardly surprising for one who has performed with rock musicians and who once led his own group, Liverpool Scene. This explains the direct, acid lines of "Batpoem" or the gentler, childlike "Love Is": "Love is feeling cold in the backs of vans / Love is a fanclub with only two fans." Lyrics of this kind cannot disguise the verbal skill and the structural grasp that underlie Henri's most freewheeling flights, akin to those of jazzmen like Parker or Coltrane. "Adrian Henri's Talking after Christmas Blues" and his later "Talking Toxteth Blues" are examples both of a biting wit and of a parodist's measure of the form. The same humor is found in "Red Card," with football imagery applied to seduction and its aftermath, while in "Any Prince to Any Princess" fairy-tale themes are hilariously revamped in government jargon. Aware of most poetic styles, Henri has throughout his career attempted several homages to bards of the past—some more serious than others—including Blake, Byron, and Housman. "Tonight at Noon," his tribute to the jazz musician Charles Mingus, in turn inspired a record album by the Jam, while in "New York City Blues" Henri mourns the passing of John Lennon.

As is inevitable with an artist whose poetry is drawn from his own experience, much of Henri's writing is devoted to love and its memories. More than most, he is able to fix in a handful of words the transitory nature of human relationships, the sense of desolation that loss of love so often brings: "The sea has carefully mislaid the beach / beyond our reach. It looks like rain / Over the boardwalk bridge we trace in vain / your lost shell earring—remembered image / of harbour, swans and rainbow—gone perhaps / back to its watery element."

Autobiography is Henri's masterpiece, a self-portrait from birth to the year 1970. From the first vivid childhood recollections through the loves and influences of youth, Henri captures superbly the flavor of his time, its scents and colors. Darting from one clutch of memories to the next, seizing with what seems like total recall the essence of each, he involves the reader in his past and brings a vanished world alive. His personality pervades the work ("sad / boy-to-be-poet / head full of words / understood by no one"), lending its unique voice to what is throughout an individual testament. *Autobiography* marks the beginning of an increased preoccupation with landscapes in subsequent poems, whether idyllic country scenes or bleak inner cities and motorways. Though love remains, and humor flickers occasionally, the overall tone is somber.

Whatever the prevailing mood, Henri's gifts remain undiminished. His most ambitious undertaking, *The Wakefield Mysteries,* recreates the original sequence of medieval religious verse dramas in modern form, effectively rendering the biblical scenes of the Creation, Flood, Nativity, and Last Judgment into current vernacular speech. Tragedy is blended neatly with bawdy humor, the action enlivened by musical interludes in which plainsong alternates with "Go Down, Moses." A mammoth task, it is also an impressive achievement.

The Collected Poems 1967–1985 draws from Henri's many works to capture the essential core of his vision in a single, coherent statement, while in *Not Fade Away* his writings display a comparable range and imagination. Whether exploring the death of fairy tales in "The Grandmothers" or erotic love in "Harvest Festival" or constructing a comic poem entirely from familiar clichés, as in "The Life of Riley," Henri offers images drawn directly from life and scattered like life into random insights. His is an individual voice that defies the transience of poetic fashion and, at its best, is too good to be missed.

—Geoff Sadler

HESKETH, Phoebe

Nationality: British. **Born:** Phoebe Rayner in Preston, Lancashire, 29 January 1909. **Education:** Preston High School, 1914–16; Dagfield Birkdale School, 1918–24; Cheltenham Ladies' College, Gloucestershire, 1924–26. **Family:** Married William Aubrey Martin Hesketh in 1931; two sons and one daughter. **Career:** Woman's Page editor, Bolton *Evening News,* 1942–45; lecturer, Bolton Women's College, 1967–69; teacher of creative writing, Bolton School, 1976–78. Member, Arts Council Poets Reading Poems and Writers in the Schools panels. **Awards:** Poetry Society Greenwood prize, 1947, 1966; Arts Council grant, 1965. Fellow, Royal Society of Literature, 1971. **Address:** 10 The Green, Heath Charnock, Chorley, Lancashire PR6 9JH, England.

PUBLICATIONS

Poetry

Poems. Manchester, Sherratt and Hughes, 1939.
Lean Forward, Spring! London, Sidgwick and Jackson, 1948.
No Time for Cowards. London, Heinemann, 1952.
Out of the Dark: New Poems, edited by Richard Church. London, Heinemann, 1954.
Between Wheels and Stars. London, Heinemann, 1956.
The Buttercup Children. London, Hart Davis, 1958.
Prayer for Sun. London, Hart Davis, 1966.
A Song of Sunlight (for children). London, Chatto and Windus, 1974.
Preparing to Leave. London, Enitharmon Press, 1977.
The Eighth Day: Selected Poems 1948–1978. London, Enitharmon Press, 1980.
A Ring of Leaves. Birmingham, Hayloft, 1985.
Over the Brook. Leicester, Taxus Press, 1986.
Netting the Sun: New and Collected Poems. Petersfield, Hampshire, Enitharmon Press, 1989.
Sundowner. London, Enitharmon Press, 1992.
The Leave Train: New and Selected Poems. London, Enitharmon Press, 1994.
A Box of Silver Birch. London, Enitharmon Press, 1997.

Plays

Radio: many documentaries, and the plays *One Pair of Eyes* and *What Can the Matter Be?*, 1979.

Other

My Aunt Edith (biography of Edith Rigby). London, Davies, 1966.
Rivington: The Story of a Village. London, Davies, 1972.

519

What Can the Matter Be? (autobiography). Penzance, Cornwall, United Writers, 1985.

Rivington: Village of the Mountain Ash. Chorley, Lancashire, Countryside, 1990.

*

Manuscript Collection: Lockwood Memorial Library, State University of New York, Buffalo.

Phoebe Hesketh comments:

I've never belonged to any literary circle and was amazed when Sidgwick and Jackson's poetry reader said they'd like to publish a collection (1948). After the early influences of border ballads, R.L. Stevenson, and de la Mare, I fell, in my teens, under the spell of the romantics, which undoubtedly colored my first published work. Gradually, through rare strokes of fortune and the common blows of fate, I began to cast off the lyrical, romantic garments for sparser, bleaker material. Writing for me now is the process of stripping to the bone—with rare bursts of lyricism. I never seem able to write the poem I want to write: when I get the germ of an idea—as soon as it takes form—the poem gets hold of me and takes me where it wills, not where I will. I never know how a poem is to end. There are longer and longer periods between poems when I'm certain I'll never write again. I can't sustain a poem from "the top half of the brain"; it comes, unbidden, from a deeper level. It is the poem, not I, that achieves the initial creation. The hard labor comes in the next stages of actual composition and revision. I feel with Robert Frost, "A poem may be labored over once it is in being; it may not be labored into being."

(1995) Though I am essentially a lyric poet, influenced by the romantics and, later, the Georgians and poets of the thirties, I have, as critics say, developed in tune with the present age, writing poems that are "stripped to the bone," witnessed by the many magazines in which I appear and my fourteenth collection, published in 1994.

*   *   *

Some of British poet Phoebe Hesketh's most effective imagery springs from her native northern landscape of "heather-shouldered fells," "grey thin-fingered wind," and "stormy solitudes . . . where reluctant spring / Retards the leaf." As she says in "Northern Stone,"

Sap of the sullen moor is blood of my blood.
The whale-back ridge and whiplash of the wind
Stripping the branches in a rocking wood—
All these are of my life-stream, scoured and thinned.

Hesketh's moors are Brontëan. So too is the visionary quest "to find the Unknown through the known," as expressed in many other evocations of this stark and stubborn country, including "Bleasdale: On Fairsnape," "Mountain Top," and "Winter Journey," with its symbolism of a solitary search bereft of consoling certainties. Her depiction of nature is never merely descriptive; its moods and seasons serve always as metaphor to communicate the experience of the human spirit and a pervasive apprehension of "what is hidden and yet near / And intimate as breath." Emily Brontë is again irresistibly recalled in poems like "Revelation," "In Praise of Darkness," and "Vision": "The air grows luminous and light takes hold / Of

darkness till my searching eyes are filled, / I see, beyond the Seen, new worlds unfold."

Yet Hesketh also delights in the world of sense: the "beer-bubble stream," the winter sun "muffled in a wool of sullen cloud," the autumn hill where the wind "with iron-fisted blows / Hammers the colours bleeding to the ground." Like Edward Thomas she celebrates the everyday simplicities of rural sights and pursuits—plowing or gathering sticks, coltsfoot on a slag heap, midsummer smoke "pale blue as lupin spires." Animals and birds—the pent-up rage of the solitary bull, the melancholy chestnut mare "with drooping underlip . . . / Tail-in to the wind," the alertly quivering fox "the colour of last year's beech-leaves," the mallard and her brood surprised by a stoat, the heron "with elegiac wings"—are captured with sharp and vivid immediacy.

The same loving precision informs Hesketh's portraits of country people: village children tumbling out of school, their days "wide open as a daisy to the sun," the classroom dunce grown wise in his hedgerow truancies, an old man "withered as a gaunt sun-wrinkled tree." It is characteristic that several of these human cameos should explore the theme of spiritual riches implicit in physical deprivation. For the blind not only the other senses but also inward vision is miraculously heightened; the cripple's intuition of the intense life in flowers, rooted like himself, enables him "to travel though I may not rise and go." A similar paradox of liberation through captivity is expressed in "Rescue" in the image of the bird finally returning to the falconer: "Thus chained and hooded, I am free at last."

Hesketh's deeply felt conviction that modern man, his life "caged with steel" and "moulded into rods by the machine," has betrayed and desecrated his natural heritage is conveyed with telling impact through poems like "Born between the Wheels," "The Invading Spring," and "No Pause for Death," and her bleak vision of the future in "The Dark Side of the Moon." On all sides she sees "devastation in the unsacred name / Of science mock the cratered human heart." Yet however fiercely "stoned with doubt," her faith ultimately reasserts itself. Walking in the city, she discovers in "one weak spire" of grass in a broken paving stone "strength enough to break / The angled world of concrete."

Seldom unconscious of "the ache of living—beauty spiked with pain" or that "even upon a peak of joy the flint comes piercing through," Hesketh has continued to affirm her hard-won belief in the attainment of inward growth through such griefs as bereavement, love renounced, and loneliness. Her poems depict both the sadness of old age and the spectacle of childhood's unsuspecting innocence overshadowed by the future. As she declares in "Reflection," "Through temporal loss of light we learn to find / The substance of a Sun that makes no shadow." In later works such as the symbolically titled *Preparing to Leave,* she has largely forsaken her earlier lyrical cadences and romantic imagery for a spare austerity that echoes her prevailing mood of "wintering in the dark."

—Margaret Willy

HEWETT, Dorothy (Coade)

Nationality: Australian. **Born:** Perth, Western Australia, 21 May 1923. **Education:** Perth College; University of Western Australia, Perth, 1941–42, 1959–63, B.A. 1961. **Family:** Married 1) Lloyd

Davies in 1944 (marriage dissolved 1949), one son (deceased); 2) lived with Les Flood, 1949–58, three sons; 3) married Merv Lilley in 1960, two daughters. **Career:** Millworker, 1950–52; advertising copywriter, Sydney, 1956–58; senior tutor in English, University of Western Australia, 1964–73. Writer-in-residence, Monash University, Melbourne, 1975, University of Newcastle, New South Wales, 1977, Griffith University, Nathan, Queensland, 1980, La Trobe University, Bundoora, Victoria, 1981, Magpie Theatre Company, Adelaide, 1982, Rollins College, Florida, 1988, and Edith Cowan University, Western Australia, 1990. Member of the editorial board, *Westerly* magazine, Nedlands, Western Australia, 1972–73, and *Overland* magazine, Melbourne, since 1970. Member of the Communist Party, 1943–68. **Awards:** Australian Broadcasting Commission prize, 1945, 1965; Australia Council grant, 1973, 1976, 1979, 1981, 1983, 1984, 1985; Australian Writers Guild award, 1974, 1982; International Women's Year grant, 1976; Nettie Palmer award for nonfiction, 1991; Australian Artists Creative fellowship, 1993; Poetry award, National Book Council, Australia, 1994; Western Australia Premier's awards, 1994, 1996; Christopher Brennan award, 1996; Lifetime Emeritus grant, Australia Council, 1997. D.Litt.: University of Western Australia, 1995. A.O. (Member, Order of Australia), 1986. **Agent:** Hilary Linstead and Associates, Suite 302, "Easts Tower," 9–13 Bronte Road, Bondi Junction, New South Wales 2022. **Address:** 496 Great Western Highway, Faulconbridge, New South Wales, 2776, Australia.

PUBLICATIONS

Poetry

What about the People, with Merv Lilley. Sydney, Realist Writers, 1962.
Windmill Country. Sydney, Edwards and Shaw, 1968.
The Hidden Journey. Newnham, Tasmania, Wattle Grove Press, 1969.
Late Night Bulletin. Newnham, Tasmania, Wattle Grove Press, 1970.
Rapunzel in Suburbia. Sydney, New Poetry, 1975.
Greenhouse. Sydney, Big Smoke, 1979.
Journeys, with others, edited by Fay Zwicky. Melbourne, Sisters, 1982.
Alice in Wormland. Paddington, New South Wales, Paper Bark Press, 1987; as *Alice in Wormland: Selected Poems.* Newcastle upon Tyne, Bloodaxe, 1990.
A Tremendous World in Her Head: Selected Poems. Sydney, Dangaroo Press, 1989.
Selected Poems. Newcastle upon Tyne, Bloodaxe, 1990; South Fremantle, Western Australia, Fremantle Arts Centre Press, 1991.
Peninsula. South Fremantle, Western Australia, Fremantle Arts Centre Press, 1994.
Collected Poems, 1940–1995. South Fremantle, Western Australia, Fremantle Arts Centre Press, 1995.
Neap Tide. Ringwood, Victoria, Penguin, 1999.

Plays

Time Flits Away, Lady (produced 1941).
This Old Man Comes Rolling Home (produced Perth, 1966; revised version produced Sydney, 1968). Sydney, Currency Press, 1976.
Mrs. Porter and the Angel (produced Sydney, 1969).
The Chapel Perilous; or, The Perilous Adventures of Sally Banner, music by Frank Amdt and Michael Leyden (produced Perth, 1971). Sydney, Currency Press, 1972; London, Eyre Methuen, 1974.
Bon-Bons and Roses for Dolly (produced Perth, 1972). With *The Tatty Hollow Story,* Sydney, Currency Press, 1976.
Catspaw (produced Perth, 1974).
Miss Hewett's Shenanigans (produced Canberra, 1975).
Joan, music by Patrick Flynn (produced Canberra, 1975). Montmorency, Victoria, Yackandandah, 1984.
The Tatty Hollow Story (produced Sydney, 1976). With *Bon-Bons and Roses for Dolly,* Sydney, Currency Press, 1976.
The Beautiful Miss Portland, published in *Theatre Australia* (Sydney). November/December and Christmas 1976.
The Golden Oldies (produced Melbourne, 1976; London, 1978). With *Susannah's Dreaming,* Sydney, Currency Press, 1981.
Pandora's Cross (produced Sydney, 1978). Published in *Theatre Australia* (Sydney), September/October 1978.
The Man from Mukinupin (produced Perth, 1979). Sydney, Currency Press, 1980.
Susannah's Dreaming (broadcast 1980). With *The Golden Oldies,* Sydney, Currency Press, 1981.
Golden Valley (for children; produced Adelaide, 1981). With *Song of the Seals,* Sydney, Currency Press, 1985.
The Fields of Heaven (produced Perth, 1982).
Song of the Seals (for children), music by Jim Cotter (produced Adelaide, 1983). With *Golden Valley,* Sydney, Currency Press, 1985.
Christina's World (opera libretto; produced Sydney, 1983).
The Rising of Pete Marsh (produced Perth, 1988).
Collected Plays. Volume 1. Sydney, Currency Press, 1992.

Screenplays: *For the First Time,* with others, 1976; *Journey among Women,* with others, 1977; *The Planter of Malata,* with Cecil Holmes, 1983; *Song of the Seals,* 1984; *Catch the Wild Fish,* with Robert Adamson, 1985.

Radio Plays: *Frost at Midnight,* 1973; *He Used to Notice Such Things,* 1974; *Susannah's Dreaming,* 1980.

Novels

Bobbin Up. Sydney, Australasian Book Society, 1959; revised edition, London, Virago Press, 1985; revised edition, New York, Penguin, 1987.
The Toucher. Ringwood, Victoria, McPhee Gribble, and New York, Penguin, 1993.

Short Stories

The Australians Have a Word for It. Berlin, Seven Seas, 1964.
Women/Love/Sex. New York, Random House, 1996.

Other

Wild Card (autobiography). Melbourne, McPhee and Gribble, and London, Virago Press, 1990.

Editor, *Sandgropers: A Western Australian Anthology.* Nedlands, University of Western Australia Press, 1973.

*

Bibliography: *Dorothy Hewett: A Bibliography* by Anne Casey, Sydney, Australian Library and Information Association Press, 1989.

Manuscript Collections: Australian National Library, Canberra; Fisher Library, University of Sydney; Flinders University, Adelaide, South Australia; University of Queensland, St. Lucia; University of Western Australia, Nedlands.

Critical Studies: "Confession and Beyond" by Bruce Williams, in *Overland* (Melbourne), 1977; interview with Jim Davidson, in *Meanjin* (Melbourne), 1979; "On a Lonely Beach" by Paul Kavanagh, in *Southerly* (Sydney), 1984; "Dorothy Hewett As Poet," in *Southerly* (Sydney), 44(4), 1984; "Jean Devanny, Katharine Susannah Prichard, and the 'Really Proletarian Novel'" by Carole Ferrier, in *Gender, Politics, and Fiction: Twentieth Century Australian Women's Novels,* edited by Carole Ferrier, St. Lucia, University of Queensland Press, 1985; "Working the Self: Issues of Form and Gender in Australian Fiction" by Paul Salzman, in *Meanjin* (Parkville, Victoria, Australia), 46(4), December 1987; *Setting the Stage: A Semiotic Re-Reading of Selected Australian Plays by Dorothy Hewett, Jack Hibbard, Louis Nowra, and Stephen Sewell* (dissertation) by Joanne Elizabeth Tompkins, York University, 1993; "Representations of Female Identity in the Poetry of Dorothy Hewett" by Jenny Digby, in *Southerly* (Sydney), 53(2), June 1993; *Dorothy Hewett: Selected Critical Essays* edited by Bruce Bennett, Canberra, Fremantle Arts Centre, 1995.

Dorothy Hewett comments:

(1980) My first collection, *Windmill Country,* was long delayed and therefore incorporated much that I had already outgrown. The locale of the book is firmly Western Australian, with consequent emphasis on landscape and ancestor worship. There is also a strong strain of politicizing in the book, influenced by regionalism and the Australian poets of my own generation, particularly Judith Wright. The book is uneven, romantic, and didactic. *Rapunzel in Suburbia,* my second collection, covers my time as an academic. It is strongly confessional, obviously influenced by Lowell and Plath, and romantic in style and subject. Fantasy is a central element in the book; there is also an introverted imagination linked with a sense of the dramatic. *Greenhouse* is an even more radical departure. The book covers my last three years in Sydney and is influenced by the city and by younger Australian city poets. There is a wider range of experimentation, a firmer control, and more substantial intellectual content. The lyrical, the fantastic, and the analytical predominate.

(1990) *Alice in Wormland* covers the last five years and, using a persona and a clipped contemporary shorthand, is the poetic biography of an Australian woman from childhood to death and after it.

*   *   *

Dorothy Hewett is a writer of extraordinary versatility whose work as a dramatist and novelist is reflected in the theatricality and strong narrative sense of her poetry. Combined with her sure lyrical

voice, these are the elements that extend her poetic range. Each book sustains continuity with those before but gathers enduring themes and symbols into fresh shapes.

Although she continues to write in many genres, Hewett's first publications were poems, and some of her most enduring work is to be found in *Windmill Country.* The romantic lyric "Legend of the Green Country," for example, engagingly captures her own and her forebearers' relationships with the wheat country of Western Australia, beginning with a flourish reminiscent of Dylan Thomas: "September is the spring month bringing tides, swilling green in the harbor mouth, / Turnabout dolphins rolling-backed in the rip and run, the king waves, / Swinging the coast." It then settles into a more individual voice—"this was my country, here I go back for nurture, / To the dry soaks, to the creeks running salt through the timber"—and concludes, once parents, grandparents, and landscape have been explored, with

I will pay this debt, go back and find my place,
Pick windfalls out of the grass like a mendicant.
The little sour apples still grow in my heart's orchard,
Bitter with grief, coming up out of the dead country.
Here I will eat their salt and speak my truth.

Hewett's 1970s poetry is unrelentingly and flamboyantly theatrical, reflecting her intense dramatic output during this period. *Rapunzel in Suburbia* and *Greenhouse* include poems of fantasy, erotically assertive, with a high level of role playing, as in "Miss Hewett's Shenanigans"—"They call, 'The Prince has come,' / & I swan down in astrakan & fur, / the lemon curtains blown against the light"—or as in "Coming to You"—"I ride across the flat land / like General Gabler's daughter." "Grave Fairytale" retells the Rapunzel legend—"Three times I lent my hair to the glowing prince"—but the object of the prince's lust is the black witch, "the beasts unsatisfied / roll in their sweat, their guttural cries / made the night thick with sound." The poem continues, "Each time I saw the framed-faced bully boy / sick with his triumph. / The third time I hid the shears . . . / Three seasons he stank at the tower's base."

In *Alice in Wormland* these roles are concentrated in the persona of Alice, and the autobiographical references take on a different form through the detachment this affords as well as by having been worked out in earlier, shorter poems. The extent of change may be perceived by comparing the lines on Hewett's grandfather in "Legend of the Green Country" with the highly dissimilar treatment of the same character in *Alice:*

He mended the gates, once a month he drove into town to
    his "lodge",
A white carnation picked at dusk from my grandmother's garden,
A dress suit with a gold watch, a chain looped over his belly,
Magnificent! ("Legend of the Green Country")

her grandfather was a window dresser
at the Bon Marche
he swaggered to Lodge to ride the goat
naked a gold watch bounced on his belly (*Alice*)

The landscape is still recognizably Australian, but it is overlaid with mythic references that serve to unite the poem:

The ocean of yellow wheat
turns green in winter
& waves like the sea . . .
This was Eden perfect circular
the candid temples of her innocence
the homestead in the clearing
ringed with hills
the paddocks pollened deep in dandelions
the magic forest dark & beckoning . . .
Alice was driven howling from the garden.

The sexual energy of the poems finds its place in a voice unmistakably Hewett's, but there is a poignant restlessness running like a tracer throughout *Alice*. Nim, an elusive figure representative of male sexuality, appears after Alice is driven out of Eden into her "secret garden / under the hump of the hill," and his "changing face / laid waste her garden." Their final meeting is described in an intensely erotic sequence ("Japan"), but Nim's refusal to stay leads in "The Infernal Grove" to a second Fall and the destruction of this new, erotic Eden—"the garden's soft with fruit fly / the black snake coils / across the path to spring":

But I would rather
live in hell she said
& forfeit heaven
to have been with him.

". . . She'd wait for him . . . till hell froze over . . . Hell froze over / the night came down / as Nim betrayed her." In the final section of the poem Alice and Nim, as owl and falcon, are reunited after her death: "it is the beast fable / it is the myth of ourselves / & only just beginning"; "that was the time / when they made friends with death."

Alice in Wormland is also a tale of political beliefs fought for and then lost ("Socialism with a human face was dead . . . she reinstated Art as her religion") and of an artist's journey to her sources. Alice's travels take her on a literary pilgrimage in which the most striking figure is Emily Brontë "coughing up blood and *Gondal*," but there are echoes of Yeats, Lawrence, and Byron. In focusing on the myth of the Fall and the quest for love, *Alice in Wormland* states more poignantly and consistently than any of Hewett's earlier poetry the paradox of the unattainable Eden.

Hewett's book *Peninsula* is set in a naturalistic garden lapped by the waves. (Ebb and flow are also important in her novel *The Toucher*.) This is a "silent garden / furred with frost / remote and still / where no one comes / where time itself is lost" ("Return to the Peninsula"). The waiting silence is not resigned but characteristically vital and questioning, captured in a striking natural image in "Return to the Peninsula":

the dry cough
of the foxes on the cliff
sitting together
their sparkling eyes
reflected off the sea

Interspersed with three peninsula poems—the first is "On the Peninsula" and the last is "The Last Peninsula"—are revisions of earlier images and childhood scenes. Australian landscape and Tennysonian myth are combined in "Lines to the Dark Tower":

Across the water meadows
on the grey sky
the dark tower stood alone
my father said
you can't live in a wheat silo
stinking of mouldy straw
and blood and bone
but he couldn't see
the plumes nodding above the hedges

In "Lady's Choice" the Lady of Shalott refuses to take the three paces to her death, and the knight is "pontificating / on God and mercy and grace and faces." Instead, "tomorrow I'll get up early / work on my poems and thread my loom."

The world of *Windmill Country* returns in "Still Lives," poems of "uncles and aunts and country cousins . . . they sift the dark fields / of my mind." But *Peninsula* always returns to the growing shadows of the garden by the sea, asking "what is the distance / between / bone and infinity? / bliss pain solitude / a breath of air" ("The Last Peninsula"). Spare, direct, and honest, the dramatic gesture remains possible. *Peninsula* celebrates the mystery at the heart of the familiar:

and shall I too
eventually disappear
in a garden hat and cloak
possibly accompanied by
a Platonic angel
leaving a note
I have been called away
from the dark cottage
but on what errand
and for what purpose?

—Nan Bowman Albinski

HEYEN, William (Helmuth)

Nationality: American. **Born:** Brooklyn, New York, 1 November 1940. **Education:** State University of New York, Brockport, 1957–61, B.S. 1961; Ohio University, Athens, 1961–67, M.A. 1963, Ph.D. 1967. **Family:** Married Hannelore Greiner in 1962; one son and one daughter. **Career:** English teacher, Springville High School, New York, 1961–62; instructor in English, State University of New York, Cortland, 1963–65. Since 1967 member of the department of English, professor and poet-in-residence, State University of New York, Brockport. Senior Fulbright-Hays Lecturer in American Literature, Germany, 1971–72; visiting professor, University of Hawaii, Honolulu, spring 1985. **Awards:** Borestone Mountain award, 1966; National Endowment for the Arts fellowship, 1974, 1984; Guggenheim fellowship, 1977; *Ontario Review* award, 1977; Eunice Tietjens memorial prize (*Poetry,* Chicago), 1978; American Academy Witter Bynner prize, 1982; Lillian Fairchild Memorial award, 1996; National Small Press Book Award for Poetry, 1997. **Address:** 142 Frazier Street, Brockport, New York 14420, U.S.A.

PUBLICATIONS

Poetry

The Mower. Privately printed, 1970.

Depth of Field. Baton Rouge, Louisiana State University Press, 1970.

The Fireman Next Door. Buffalo, Slow Loris Press, 1971.

The Train. Rochester, New York, Valley Press, 1972.

The Trail Beside the River Platte. Rushden, Northamptonshire, Sceptre Press, 1973.

The Pigeons. Mount Horeb, Wisconsin, Perishable Press, 1973.

Noise in the Trees: Poems and a Memoir. New York, Vanguard Press, 1974.

Mermaid. Derry, Pennsylvania, Rook Press, 1975.

Cardinals. Derry, Pennsylvania, Rook Press, 1976.

Cardinals/The Cardinal. Derry, Pennsylvania, Rook Press, 1976.

The Pearl. Pittsburgh, Slow Loris Press, 1976.

Of Palestine. A Meditation. Omaha, Abattoir. 1976.

Pickerel. Derry, Pennsylvania, Rook Press, 1976.

Dusk. Derry, Pennsylvania, Rook Press, 1976.

Eighteen Poems and a Story. Derry, Pennsylvania, Rook Press, 1976.

The Trench. Derry, Pennsylvania, Rook Press, 1976.

The Carrie White Auction at Brockport, May 1974. Derry, Pennsylvania, Rook Society, 1976.

XVII Machines. Pittsburgh, Sisyphus, 1976.

Ars Poetica. Derry, Pennsylvania, Rook Press, 1976.

Mare. Derry, Pennsylvania, Rook Press, 1976.

Darkness. Derry, Pennsylvania, Rook Society, 1977.

The Swastika Poems. New York, Vanguard Press, 1977.

Fires. Athens, Ohio, Croissant, 1977.

The Elm's Home. Derry, Pennsylvania, Scrimshaw, 1977.

Son Dream/Daughter Dream. Ruffsdale, Pennsylvania, Rook Press, 1978.

The Ash. Potsdam, New York, Banjo Press, 1978.

Witness. Madison, Wisconsin, Rara Avis Press, 1978.

Lord Dragonfly. Ruffsdale, Pennsylvania, Scrimshaw, 1978.

Brockport's Poems. Brockport, New York, Challenger Press, 1978.

The Children. Knotting, Bedfordshire, Sceptre Press, 1979.

Long Island Light: Poems and a Memoir. New York, Vanguard Press, 1979.

The City Parables. Athens, Ohio, Croissant, 1979.

Evening Dawning. Concord, New Hampshire, Ewert, 1979.

The Snow Hen. Concord, New Hampshire, Ewert, 1979.

Abortion. Ruffsdale, Pennsylvania, Stefanik, 1979.

Mantle. Concord, New Hampshire, Ewert, 1979.

The Descent. Knotting, Bedfordshire, Sceptre Press, 1979.

The Shy Bird. Concord, New Hampshire, Rosemary Duggan, 1980.

Our Light. Syracuse, Tamarack, 1980.

My Holocaust Songs. Concord, New Hampshire, Ewert, 1980.

1829–1979: The Bells. Brockport, New York, Challenger Press, 1980.

December 31, 1979: The Candle. Knotting, Bedfordshire, Sceptre Press, 1980.

The Ewe's Song. Concord, New Hampshire, Ewert, 1980.

Auction. Concord, New Hampshire, Ewert, 1981.

Bean. Concord, New Hampshire, South Congregational Church, 1981.

The Eternal Ash. Syracuse, Tamarack, 1981.

Lord Dragonfly: Five Sequences. New York, Vanguard Press, 1981.

The Bees. Syracuse, Tamarack, 1981.

The Trains. Worcester, Massachusetts, Metacom Press, 1981.

Blackberry Light. Concord, New Hampshire, Ewert, 1981.

The Berries. Concord, New Hampshire, Ewert, 1982.

Jesus. Syracuse, Tamarack, 1983.

Along This Water. Syracuse, Tamarack, 1983.

Ram Time. Roslyn, New York, Stone House Press 1983.

Ensoulment. Concord, New Hampshire, Ewert, 1983.

The Numinous. Salisbury, Maryland, Scarab Press, 1983.

Erika: Poems of the Holocaust. New York, Vanguard Press, 1984.

Wenzel/The Ghost. Concord, New Hampshire, Ewert, 1984.

Winter Letter to Dave Smith. Winston-Salem, North Carolina, Palaemon Press, 1984.

The Cabin. Concord, New Hampshire, Ewert, 1985.

The Spruce in Winter. Concord, New Hampshire, Ewert, 1985.

At West Hills, Long Island. Roslyn, New York, Stone House Press, 1985.

Eight Poems for Saint Walt. Roslyn, New York, Stone House Press, 1985.

The Trophy. Concord, New Hampshire, Ewert, 1986.

The Chestnut Rain. New York, Ballantine/Available Press, 1986.

Brockport Sunflowers. Concord, New Hampshire, Ewert, 1986.

The Amber. Manchester, New Hampshire, New England Reading Association, 1986.

The Bells. Concord, New Hampshire, Ewert, 1987.

Mother and Son. Dallas, Texas, Northouse and Northouse, 1987.

What Do You Have to Lose? Concord, New Hampshire, Ewert, 1987.

Four from Brockport. Dallas, Texas, Northouse and Northouse, 1988.

Brockport, New York: Beginning with ''And''. Dallas, Texas, Northouse and Northouse, 1988.

Americans. Concord, New Hampshire, Ewert, 1989.

Falling from Heaven: Holocaust Poems of a Jew and a Gentile, with L.D. Brodsky. St. Louis, Timeless Press, 1991.

The Shore. Roslyn, New York, Stone House Press, 1991.

Pterodactyl Rose: Poems of Ecology. St. Louis, Time Being Books, 1991.

Two Poems of Ecology (broadside). Concord, New Hampshire, Ewert, 1991.

Brockport Milkweed (broadside). Brockport, New York, Challenger Press, 1992.

Brockport Snow (broadside). Concord, New Hampshire, Ewert, 1992.

Ribbons: The Gulf War. St Louis, Time Being Books, 1992.

The Tower. Drayton, England, Magpie Press, 1993.

The Host: Selected Poems 1965–1990. St Louis, Time Being Books, 1994.

Owl Winter (broadside). Concord, New Hampshire, Ewert, 1994.

Blackberries (broadside). Concord, New Hampshire, Ewert, 1996.

Crazy Horse in Stillness: Poems. Rochester, New York, BOA Editions, 1996.

Windfall (broadside). Concord, New Hampshire, Ewert, 1997.

Diana, Charles, & the Queen. Rochester, New York, BOA Editions, 1998.

Novel

Vic Holyfield and the Class of 1957. New York, Ballantine/Available Press, 1986.

Other

From This Book of Praise: Poems and a Conversation with William Heyen, edited by Vince Clemente. Port Jefferson, New York, Street Press, 1978.

With Me Far Away: A Memoir. Roslyn, New York, Stone House Press, 1994.

Pig Notes & Dumb Music: Prose on Poetry. Rochester, New York, BOA Editions, 1998.

Editor, *Profile of Theodore Roethke.* Columbus, Ohio, Charles E. Merrill, 1971.

Editor, *American Poets in 1976.* Indianapolis, Bobbs Merrill, 1976.

Editor, *I Would Also Like to Mention Aluminum: A Conversation with William Stafford.* Pittsburgh, Slow Loris Press, 1976.

Editor, *The Generation of 2000: Contemporary American Poets.* Princeton, New Jersey, Ontario Review Press, 1984.

Editor, with Elizabeth Spires, *The Pushcart Prize 15, 1990–1991: Best of the Small Presses.* Wainscott, New York, Pushcart Press. 1990.

Editor, *Dumb, Beautiful Monsters: Long Island Poets.* Northport, Birnham Wood Graphics, 1996.

*

Bibliography: "Nothing We Do Is Ever Lost to the Light: William Heyen, A Preliminary Bibliography" by Ernest Stefanik, in *Bulletin of Bibliography* (Boston), summer 1979.

Manuscript Collections: Mugar Memorial Library, Boston University; University of Rochester Library, New York.

Critical Studies: *"The Swastika Poems"* by Sandra McPherson, November-December 1977, "Chapter and Verse" by Stanley Plumly, January-February 1978, and "One Man's Music" by Dave Smith, March-April 1980, all in *American Poetry Review* (Philadelphia); "The Harvest of a Quiet Eye" by Michael McFee, in *Parnassus* (New York), spring-summer 1982; John Drury, in *Critical Survey of Poetry* edited by Frank N. Magill, Englewood Cliffs, New Jersey, Salem Press, 1983; "William Heyen" by Patrick Bizzaro, in *Critical Survey of Literature* edited by Frank Magill, Pasadena, California, Salem Books, 1992.

William Heyen comments:

Often when I was a boy, alone at ponds or in the woods of Long Island, I seemed to fall into a sleeping wakefulness, into trances within which I felt an all-encompassing sense of the beauty of reality and the "impalpable sustenance of me from all things at all hours of the day," as Whitman says, that poets of primal consciousness sometimes embody in their poems. I of course had no language for these states of trance, and had not read any poetry, and feel only slightly more able to express them now, but they were times of mystical duration, and I sometimes still experience them. Maybe because I had no special awareness that such experiences were extraordinary (and I did not impoverish them with phrases like "mystical illumination" that have become clichés), I was not split from the natural world, observing it, but was part of its being, its essence and spirit. Far from the Nesconset kitchen where my mother was fixing dinner, far from the Smithtown woodworking shop where my father was operating his ripsaw, far from them and at Gibbs Pond

and other ponds in a trance, I lived the life of primal mind, if only for a few minutes at a time, that the Lakota boy who would later receive the name Crazy Horse lived. A lily pad trembled; a black head poked up in the stem notch. The mud was warm to up over my ankles, the water to my genitals. I was completely there, wordlessly, part of place and eternity. This, I think, was full consciousness in the truest sense, the life lived without the qualifications and diminishments of language. The Lakota boy must have known instinctively that words were at once sacred and helpless. Crazy Horse apparently spoke less than others. He sought visions more often than others. In my best poems, it may be, I approach the reverberations of those trance states. How to use words and story to get beyond words and story? Sometimes, somehow, maybe by way of the fusion of rhythm-music-image-idea, it can still happen. And once we are there, and not before, our world means.

* * *

When William Heyen began to explore his Long Island past in *Noise in the Trees,* later expanded into *Long Island Light,* he became a visionary poet. In his Long Island poems he balances formal control with emotional openness. Ever in dialogue with his spiritual father, the great Long Island poet Walt Whitman, Heyen goes on his own version of the journey outlined in "Song of Myself." In the spirit of Thoreau, who "travelled much in Concord," Heyen stays at home and descends within himself into various layers of the past. The spirits of American literary forefathers, above all Whitman, accompany him. Heyen ascends with fragments of his local, regional, and national heritage. He suffers pain over the loss of the land, which he dares to equate with the loss of young love, but he grows spiritually as a result.

The emotional openness of *Noise* is paralleled by an experiment in form. Between the two sequences of poems, Heyen places a prose memoir, "Noise in the Trees," a series of twenty-five vignettes from his youth, sketches, prose poems, dreams, fantasies, legends, excerpts from histories, journals, even a geological dictionary. The poems and prose are fused by the author's obsessive retrieval of what he calls his "island of the mind."

Long Island Light is an expansion and deepening of *Noise.* Some thirty-one new poems and ten prose pieces, written with increased authority, intensify the return to origins, extend the search for heritage into the present, and clarify the timelessness of the vision. The new poems about his life as a husband and father in his "second home," Brockport, New York, add a maturity and progression that suggest that Heyen has the resources and dedication to enlarge this ambitious collection.

Heyen's continuing obsession with his Long Island past and the poems it produces remind one of Whitman's ever expanding *Leaves of Grass.* The depth of Heyen's emotional and spiritual commitment, the steady growth of his technical skills, and the intensification of his vision have elevated the people and places of his Long Island—the farmer Wenzel, Gibbs Pond, Lake Ronkonkoma, Short Beach, St. James Harbor, Nesconset, even the Jericho Turnpike—to the status of myth. To quote a line from his first book, Heyen has indeed found in his Long Island past "detail that deepens to fond symbol."

Heyen's deepening rootedness in Brockport has also yielded the superb poems in *Brockport, New York: Beginning with "And."* In the spirit of the great Chinese poet Li Po, evoked in several poems, Heyen lifts his "local" Brockport, on the Erie Canal, to the cosmos beyond and connects his life and that of his small town contemporaries to the continuities of life in any place and time. From within his cabin, located behind his Brockport house, he discovers that ''all the ground is window.'' The universe pulsates in the backyard.

Heyen's obsession with family heritage drives him into the darkness of the Holocaust in *The Swastika Poems,* later expanded into *Erika: Poems of the Holocaust.* Poems addressed to his German uncles, both of whom died in World War II, emerge as part of Heyen's dialogue with the darker side of himself. When he tells his Nazi father-in-law, ''I have a stake in this,'' he speaks for all moral beings. The first five poems in the book establish Heyen's personal ''stake'' in the subject as he confronts the ghosts of his family's past and retells their stories, which intersect with the larger and darker stories of the war and the Holocaust. In the central prose piece, and in the best poems in the collection, the simple but powerful language compels us to revisit and reflect on the tragic dimensions of the Holocaust. This is a difficult, courageous, and redeeming collection. Such poems as ''Simple Truths,'' ''The Riddle,'' and ''The Children'' will outlast the age in which they were written.

Nowhere is Heyen's affection for Whitman more evident than in the book-length *The Chestnut Rain.* Like ''Song of Myself,'' it contains fifty-two sections that tenderly carry the reader along on a journey that flashes back and forth from past to present as it spirals in and out of the self, incorporating and documenting the age in which it was written and both lamenting and celebrating the poet's America, past and present. And like ''Song of Myself,'' it is a love poem, but it is filled with more darkness and sorrow. In the outstanding ''At West Hills, Long Island,'' Heyen re-creates the sacramental moment of the birth of American's greatest poet and, in an image that echoes ''Crossing Brooklyn Ferry,'' consecrates ''the float forever held in suspension.'' No poet of our time has demonstrated more profoundly than Heyen how essential Whitman's vision is to our spiritual survival and salvation.

—Norbert Krapf

HILL, Geoffrey

Nationality: British. **Born:** Bromsgrove, Worcestershire, 18 June 1932. **Education:** Fairfield Junior School; County High School, Bromsgrove; Keble College, Oxford, B.A. 1953, M.A. 1959. **Family:** Married 1) Nancy Whittaker in 1956 (marriage dissolved), three sons and one daughter; 2) Alice Goodman in 1987, one daughter. **Career:** Member of the department of English from 1954, and professor of English literature, 1976–80, University of Leeds; university lecturer in English, and fellow of Emmanuel College, 1981–88. Since 1988 university professor and professor of literature and religion, Boston University. Visiting lecturer, University of Michigan, Ann Arbor, 1959–60, and University of Ibadan, Nigeria, 1967; Churchill fellow, University of Bristol, 1980; Clark Lecturer, Trinity College, Cambridge University, 1986. **Awards:** Eric Gregory award, 1961; Hawthornden Prize, 1969; Faber memorial prize, 1970; Whitbread award, 1971; Alice Hunt Bartlett award, 1971; Heinemann award, 1971; Duff Cooper memorial prize, 1979; American Academy Russell Loines award, 1983; Ingram Merrill Foundation award, 1985. D.Litt.: University of Leeds, 1988. Honorary fellow, Keble College, 1981, and Emmanuel College, Cambridge, 1990. Fellow, Royal Society of Literature, 1972. **Address:** Emmanuel College, Cambridge, England.

PUBLICATIONS

Poetry

(Poems). Oxford, Fantasy Press, 1952.
For the Unfallen: Poems 1952–1958. London, Deutsch, 1959; Chester Springs, Pennsylvania, Dufour, 1960.
Preghiere. Leeds, Northern House, 1964.
Penguin Modern Poets 8, with Edwin Brock and Stevie Smith. London, Penguin, 1966.
King Log. London, Deutsch, and Chester Springs, Pennsylvania, Dufour, 1968.
Mercian Hymns. London, Deutsch, 1971.
Somewhere Is Such a Kingdom: Poems 1952–1971. Boston, Houghton Mifflin, 1975.
Tenebrae. London, Deutsch, 1978; Boston, Houghton Mifflin, 1979.
The Mystery of the Charity of Charles Péguy. London, Agenda, 1983; New York, Oxford University Press, 1984.
Collected Poems. London, Penguin, 1985; New York, Oxford University Press, 1986.
New and Collected Poems, 1952–1992. Boston, Houghton Mifflin, 1994.
Canaan. Boston, Houghton Mifflin, 1997.
The Triumph of Love. Boston, Houghton Mifflin, 1998; London, Penguin, 1999.

Recording: *The Poetry and Voice of Geoffrey Hill,* Caedmon, 1979.

Play

Brand, adaptation of the play by Ibsen (produced London, 1978). London, Heinemann, 1978; revised version, Minneapolis, University of Minnesota Press, 1981.

Other

The Lords of Limit: Essays on Literature and Ideas. London, Deutsch, and New York, Oxford University Press, 1984.
The Enemy's Country: Words, Contexture, and Other Circumstances of Language. Oxford, Clarendon Press, and Stanford, California, Stanford University Press, 1991.

*

Critical Studies: *Geoffrey Hill and ''The Tongue's Atrocities,''* Swansea, University College, 1978, and *The Force of Poetry,* Oxford, Clarendon Press, 1984, both by Christopher Ricks; *An Introduction to 50 Modern British Poets* by Michael Schmidt, London, Pan, 1979, as *A Reader's Guide to Fifty Modern British Poets,* London, Heinemann, 1979, New York, Barnes and Noble, 1982; *Double Lyric* by Merle E. Brown, London, Routledge, 1980; ''The Poetry of Geoffrey Hill'' by Andrew Waterman, in *British Poetry since 1970,* edited by Peter Jones and Michael Schmidt, Manchester, Carcanet and New York, Persea, 1980; by the author, in *Viewpoints: Poets in Conversation with John Haffenden,* London, Faber, 1981; *Inhabited Voices: Myth and History in the Poetry of Geoffrey Hill, Seamus Heaney and George Mackay Brown* by David Annwn Frome, Somerset, Bran's

Head, 1984; *Geoffrey Hill: Essays on His Work* (includes bibliography) edited by Peter Robinson, Milton Keynes, Buckinghamshire, Open University Press, 1985; *The Poetry of Geoffrey Hill* by Henry Hart, Carbondale, Southern Illinois University Press, 1986; *The Uncommon Tongue: The Poetry and Criticism of Geoffrey Hill* by Vincent Sherry, Ann Arbor, University of Michigan Press, 1987; *Passionate Intelligence: The Poetry of Geoffrey Hill* by E.M. Knottenbelt, Amsterdam, Rodopi, 1990; Geoffrey Hill Sixtieth Birthday issue of *Agenda* (London), 30(1–2), 1992; "Variation and False Relation in Geoffrey Hill's Tenebrae" by Andrew Michael Roberts, in *Essays in Criticism* (Oxford), 43(2), April 1993; "The 'Intelligence at Bay': Ezra Pound and Geoffrey Hill," in *Paideuma* (Orono, Maine), 22(1–2), Spring/Fall, 1993, and "'The Poet's True Commitment': Geoffrey Hill, the Computer, and Original Sin," in *Literature and Theology at Century's End,* edited by Gregory Salyer and Robert Detweiler, Atlanta, Georgia, Scholars, 1995, both by Avril Horner; "Home-Made Englands: History and Nostalgia in the Poetry of Geoffrey Hill and Tony Harrison" by David Gervais, and "Semiotics and the Poetry of David Jones and Geoffrey Hill" by Kathleen O'Gorman, both in *In Black and Gold: Contiguous Traditions in Post-War British and Irish Poetry,* edited by C.C. Barfoot, Amsterdam, Rodopi, 1994; "The Fallen World of Geoffrey Hill" by William Logan, in *New Criterion* (New York), 12(7), March 1994; "The Treacherous Years of Postmodern Poetry in English" by William A. Johnsen, in *Forked Tongues? Comparing Twentieth-Century British and American Literature,* edited by Ann Massa and Alistair Stead, London, Longman, 1994; "'The Resonances of Words': Lope de Vega and Geoffrey Hill" by Colin Thompson, in *Modern Language Review* (Leeds), 90(1), January 1995; "Music Alone Survives? Collapsing Faith in Some Sonnets by G.M. Hopkins and Geoffrey Hill" by Christine Pagnoulle, in *Cahiers Victoriens et Edouardiens,* 42, November 1995; "'Fatness' in Pound and Hill" by Lennard Nyberg, in *Studia Neophilologica* (Uppsala, Sweden), 69(2), 1997; "Poets and Prophets: Geoffrey Hill in America" by Philip Horne, in *Symbiosis,* 2(2), October 1998.

*   *   *

Geoffrey Hill's poems are poems of extremity. Their thematic poles are the extremes of sex and of death, the body's proximate cravings and terrors and its remotest cravings and terrors. Their manner of proceeding—costive, densely allusive, highly polished—is the self-protective stylistic shield of a man appalled before his experience and by what he understands to be the experience of his race in history. The poems ironically deflect their subject matter through dramatic contexts and fictionalized locations. "The Songbook of Sebastian Arrurruz," for instance, is a poem about sexual despair, but the heartrending poignancy of some of its moments is undermined by the elaborate literary deceit of the poem's form. If there is personal utterance behind the "Songbook," its tracks are well covered by the artifice in which Hill creates a fictional poet—Arrurruz himself—and then "translates" his work into English. The deliberated wit of this is entirely characteristic, as is its modernist cult of impersonality.

If such procedures occasionally have the effect of making Hill's poetry hermetic to the point of a reader's despair, they are also the signals of an intensely dramatic, historically empathetic imagination. Hill's best poems attempt to dissolve the self into history, legend, and myth and to find a meeting point between personal and communal meaning. I am thinking especially of his poem sequences "Of Commerce and Society," "Funeral Music," *Mercian Hymns,* "An Apology for the Revival of Christian Architecture in England," and *The Mystery of the Charity of Charles Péguy.* In these poems, in very different ways, Hill's essential commerce is with what he calls "the speechless dead," reimagining the occasions of their suffering and finding in it paradigms for the ways in which we all necessarily live and die.

It will perhaps be obvious from this that Hill is a poet immensely self-conscious about language itself and a poet whose moral and political preoccupations deepen everywhere into preoccupations that may properly be called religious. In the sequences "The Pentecost Castle" and "Lachrimae" these themes are focused through an attempt to come to some kind of terms with the figure of Christ as it has been presented by the mystical tradition of European Christianity. They are sequences of dark paradox that combine longing, rejection, self-abasement, and a kind of grim hope, what Hill elsewhere calls "cries of rapture and despair."

In *The Mystery of the Charity of Charles Péguy* the politico-religious interest is newly concentrated into a lengthy meditation on the figure of Péguy, whom Hill describes in a note as "one of the great souls, one of the great prophetic intelligences of our century." A French Catholic nationalist whose *Le Mystère de la Charité de Jeanne d'Arc* embodies a kind of mystical patriotism, Péguy, it must be said, is on the face of it an unlikely candidate for such celebration.

Hill's ambition in the poem is to probe, as he also probes in his essay "Our Word Is Our Bond," some of the questions about the relationship between poetic language and political action that also fascinated Yeats, a poet clearly centrally important to him. The poem's procedures, however, are oracular and hermetic, for Hill depends to a large degree on various kinds of wordplay and pun and on some use of the French language. Perhaps as a result, there has been considerable disagreement over what exactly is involved in Hill's conception of the "patria." John Lucas has also found—as I find myself—something disconcertingly "schoolmasterly" about the poem's tone in places, a tendency to "advertise its seriousness." But although it has been impossible to come to any final judgment on this worrying, complicated, resonant poem, in one respect at least it clearly brings to a climax something central to Hill's work. There is an extreme sensuousness of evocation in which the natural world and human thought are seen to interpenetrate each other in a way reminiscent of some of Eliot's *Four Quartets:*

> Yours is their dream of France, militant-pastoral:
> musky red gillyvors, the wicker bark
> of clematis braided across old brick
> and the slow chain that cranks into the well
>
> morning and evening. It is Domrémy
> restored; the mystic strategy of Foch
> and Bergson with its time-scent, dour panache
> deserving of martyrdom. It is an army
>
> of poets, converts, vine-dressers, men skilled
> in wood or metal, peasants from the Beauce,
> terse teachers of Latin and those unschooled
> in all but the hard rudiments of grace.

—Neil Corcoran

HILL, Selima

Nationality: British. **Born:** Selima Wood in London, 13 October 1945. **Education:** New Hall College, Cambridge, special degree 1966. **Family:** Married Roderic Hill in 1968; one daughter and two sons. **Career:** Writing fellow, University of East Anglia, 1991; writer-in-residence, Royal Festival Hall Dance Festival, 1992. Judge, T.S. Eliot prize, 1999. **Awards:** Cholmondeley prize, 1986; Arvon/*Observer* Poetry Competition prize, 1988. **Address:** c/o Bloodaxe Books, The Old Signal Box, Falstone, Hexham, Northumberland NE48 1AB, England.

PUBLICATIONS

Poetry

Saying Hello at the Station. London, Chatto and Windus, 1984.
My Darling Camel. London, Chatto and Windus, 1988.
The Accumulation of Small Acts of Kindness. London, Chatto and Windus, 1989.
A Little Book of Meat. Newcastle upon Tyne, Bloodaxe, 1993.
Trembling Hearts in the Bodies of Dogs: New & Selected Poems. Newcastle upon Tyne, Bloodaxe, 1994.
My Sister's Horse. Westgate, Smith/Doorstop Books, 1996.
Violet. Newcastle upon Tyne, Bloodaxe, and Chester Springs, Pennsylvania, Dufour, 1997.

Other

Editor, *Paradise for Sale.* Newcastle upon Tyne, Bloodaxe, 1996.

*

Critical Study: By Philip Gross, in *Poetry Review,* 83(4), Winter 1994.

Selima Hill comments:

"All that is personal soon rots: it must be packed in ice." I have this quotation from W.B. Yeats copied into my notebook. I do not know where I first came across it, but I often remind myself, and the people I work with, of it. I also like Bonnard's "It's what I live by." And he goes on: "I feed the picture as one feeds a large animal." So my work is a combination of rot, ice, and animal food, it sounds like.

*   *   *

Selima Hill's art is one of extreme sensitivity to the reverberation of memory (both personal and cultural) in the everyday, to speech (particularly the rhythms of suppressed anxiety), and to the subtleties of the craft itself. A deceptively relaxed iambic pace masks an intensity that can be both disturbing and disturbed. A poet who can recall Larkin at his most detached and Plath at her most stressed—sometimes in the same poem—can hardly be regarded as derivative of either. Hill can lure, lull, surprise, and scare, and she has superb timing.

In Hill's first book, *Saying Hello at the Station,* moments are both spotlighted by her observational skill and given shape and depth by the way she lets chinks of light (or shards of darkness) from the infant or distant past fall upon her subjects. The disquieting deities of ancient Egypt are often featured, haunting contemporary voices with their estranging names and the sheer potency of their myths. Not surprisingly, the most striking of these poems, "Inshallah-God Willing," sees a white man of the twentieth century menaced by these forces in their very heartland, the Valley of the Kings. One world seems to slide into another as Howard Carter's assistant ("O Pecky Callendar . . . you have disturbed / the King's long night") is addressed:

> After the gold was discovered,
> and you came back late
> to the rest house, over the sound
> of your donkey padding on the sand,
> you heard someone call
> for a light, and the door
> of your room stood open.

The lines are beautifully subtle on two levels. Hill shows a storyteller's gift for the quiet mention ("came back late," "on the sand") that expands to fill the reader's inner screen, and she has a poet's unmistakable power to fill a single word—"stood"—with more significance than would be thought possible. The particular chill engendered by that word alone is beyond the scope of visual art.

Hill combines the common sense of knowing how much eye- or ear-catching detail one poem can hold with a true sense for single words, a sense existing somewhere between the true eye and the true ear and encompassing both. In a childhood memory, for example, a girl recalls the innate menace of sharing a swimming pool with an older boy: "His hands in the moving water / seemed to float between my legs." Here the subdued "moving" is another quietly perfect option.

Hill is a natural and flexible enough poet to employ images so fused with one another that they easily avoid the relentless hiccup of clever simile that lesser writers stick and are stuck with. The following image cannot be broken down but streams in several ways: "You imagine soldiers' blood / trickling down Europe's / ice-cream-coloured map / like syrup." Elsewhere, Hill relishes clusters of suggestive consonants. We hear Flaubert in the Koseir Desert imagining eating lemon sherbet, and the fact that the recollection is being refracted through a writer's thirsty imagination gives Hill the perfect license to enjoy the description: "You dip the spoon into the frosted glass, / you crush the little mound and lift the splinters / gently to your lips, you swoon with snowy joy." The ability to describe the outlines as well as the daydreamed essences of painful wants serves the poet well as she begins to turn her attention to disintegrating states of mind.

The voices and characters of *My Darling Camel* are much troubled by limitations, surfaces, and barriers, and they often break to admit menacing figures, Plath-like disturbers of sleep or repose: the Umbrella Man, the Ptarmigan Hunter, or Father John, holding the hand of whom "was like holding a helping of trifle." They tend to be male and demonic, transfigurations of childhood memory either responsible for past distress or symbolizing it. Whatever the connection, the voices tug us through the nightmare fairground of schizophrenia, paranoia, and dense memory loss: "Little feathers / journey past my cheeks / like boats. / I'm bubbling diamonds. / I'm just a head." Structurally, the poems often zigzag to a costly mental peace or at least to a balance.

Hill has the gift of stringing together apparently fragmented details so that they not only portray a state of mind but also create a tableau, a glimpsed scene. The tiny poem "Plums," for example, explodes outwards and is more than suggestive in its plot, scenery, costumes, and props:

> The music rises like a party dress.
> Nocturnal marriages are always best.
>
> Parrot feathers. Ancient seas. Soft plums.
> *Shelter in my bedroom when she comes.*

In "The Culmination of All Her Secret Longings" voices of Laura, a mental patient, visiting friends, and letters from home are mixed up with camels, set free after the Civil War, roaming the Arizona desert, copulating, out on the rim of Laura's sanity. Other voices intrude. These incongruous splinters and the fracturing of narrative into disembodied quotation, menacing italic, and lonely, disturbed self prefigure Hill's third book, *The Accumulation of Small Acts of Kindness,* which charts the mental illness and slow recovery of a girl in a psychiatric ward.

For much of this work Hill employs an incantatory iambic pentameter, though she often splits the five feet over two or three lines. This has the effect of accentuating the rhythm and jailing the girl in it, just as she is penned in with memories, fantasies, and outer and inner voices that are barely distinct. When rhythms knock so metronomically, the reader is conditioned to expect strong rhyme, half rhyme, or no rhyme at all, but by alternating strong rhyme with none Hill voices a disturbed, frustrated inner life in which the tragedy takes trivial forms and the comedy is awful. Notice how disconcertingly close to each other "kindness" and "kind" are said in what is a blithe, distracted voice:

> 'Afternoons of fruit and acts of kindness.'
> 'I treasure every word I think he said.'
> 'His hand is lying on my lap like liver.
> Wiping up the blood. He's very kind.'

Few poets know as unflinchingly as Hill how to hit these right "wrong" notes. *The Accumulation of Small Acts of Kindness* is a risk that absolutely comes off because its poet, having long abandoned the appearance of narrative reasons for the rich and dangerous field of the troubled psyche, couples an exposing eye for the subterranean life of the mind with a magnificent gift for harnessing poetic form to depict it.

—Glyn Maxwell

HILLMAN, Brenda

Nationality: American. **Born:** Tucson, Arizona, 27 March 1951. **Education:** Pomona College, California, B.A. 1973; University of Iowa, M.F.A. 1975. **Family:** Married 1) Leonard Michaels in 1976 (divorced 1985), one daughter; 2) Robert Hass, *q.v.* **Career:** Salesperson, University Press Books, Berkeley, California, 1975–84. Since 1984 instructor in English, St. Mary's College, Moraga, California. **Awards:** Delmore Schwartz Memorial Poetry award, College of Arts and Science, New York University, and Norma Farber First Book award, Poetry Society of America, both 1986, both for *White Dress.*

PUBLICATIONS

Poetry

Coffee, 3 A.M. Lisbon, Iowa, Penumbra Press, 1981.
White Dress. Middletown, Connecticut, Wesleyan University Press, 1985.
Fortress. Middletown, Connecticut, Wesleyan University Press, 1989.
Death Tractates. Middletown, Connecticut, Wesleyan University Press, 1992.
Bright Existence. Middletown, Connecticut, Wesleyan University Press, 1993.
Loose Sugar. Middletown, Connecticut, Wesleyan University Press, 1997.

*

Critical Studies: "Dark Turtles and Bright Eyes" by the author, in *Where We Stand: Women Poets on Literary Tradition,* edited by Sharon Bryan, New York, Norton, 1993; "Splendid Investigations" by Gail Wronsky, in *Antioch Review* (Yellow Springs, Ohio), 52(1), winter 1994; by Terri Brown-Davidson, in *Prairie Schooner,* 68(2), summer 1994; "Active Magic" by Laura Mullen, in *Denver Quarterly* (Denver), 34(1), spring 1999.

*   *   *

A poet whose work has been associated both with some of the most experimental work coming out of the San Francisco area and a more traditional lyrical strain in American poetry, Brenda Hillman defies easy classification. Although she is profoundly interested in gnosticism, she is also a poet very much involved with the mundanities of contemporary life; that is, her work does not shirk an attachment to the material world in its plummeting of gnosis. Her methods for uncovering the "secret knowledge" (mystical apprehension of the godhead) are as varied as the subject matter of her poetry. Hypnosis, radical formal experimentation, and even an attempt to render the transformative processes of the alchemists in a textual representation on the page have all been part of her poetics. Certainly her engagement in the Berkeley literary scene in the 1980s and early 1990s has helped invigorate this dynamic experimental range in her work, although her vision and poetry are her own. Hillman's books of poetry constitute an important late twentieth-century exploration of poetics and the spirit, an exploration compelled by aesthetic, political, and spiritual obsessions.

Hillman's first two books, *Coffee 3 A.M.* and *White Dress,* although possessed of a blossoming lyrical voice, were certainly neither as innovative nor as realized as her work in *Fortress.* Coming of age when the canonical tradition tended to marginalize women writers, Hillman in her early work seems to grapple with what it is to be a woman poet in the late twentieth century, what modulations of voice seem appropriate. If *Fortress* established Hillman's abilities, then the following two volumes, *Death Tractates* and *Bright Existence,* announced her mature and incisive voice.

They are a paired set of books, with the poems of *Death Tractates* revolving around the loss of a dear friend. Parting and separation are recurring threads, and although the book is elegiac, the poems explore more than the depressive depths of such loss. The relationship between the spiritual and the material, existence and nonexistence, and male and female otherness are also central threads.

Bright Existence continues these explorations, adding the trope of lightness and darkness. These dualisms obsess and compel Hillman, and certainly one way to think of both of the books is as dualistic poles of expression. *Death Tractates* articulates the dark side of the soul's search for connection with its divine origin, while *Bright Existence* articulates the interconnectedness of all divisions and offers a more hopeful vision of the possibility of finding the gnosis.

This is not to imply that Hillman's vision ever reaches any conclusions. Instead, her poetry is a poetry of exploration, provisionality, and possibility. In her following book, *Loose Sugar,* she continues to explore how identity is created, and perhaps it is with this volume that she begins to articulate a more concise version of how the shaped identity under consideration in her work is more explicitly feminine. She explores the process through a variety of tropes, many of them connected to colonization and marginalization, as well as to the emergence of sexuality. For instance, consider these lines from "Orion's Belt":

When you think of those
you will not touch again
in this lifetime

You own a few points on the one body.
Some made you happy.
Everything else-

The pale sword of the hunter,
the uplifted sandal,

everything else mostly fades
in the folds of heaven-

The bodies of the men with whom the speaker interacts become a way in which her bodily nature and theirs are connected to the greater body of the cosmos. Other poems that focus on South America and the exploitations of Chevron are far less optimistic.

One of the most engaging formal aspects of *Loose Sugar* is Hillman's attempt in several of the poems to represent alchemical processes on the page. She uses a "pretextual" and "posttextual" arrangement of detritus that sifts into and from the creative process of the making of the poem, a method that is difficult to describe without extended quotation. Formal experiments of this kind also appear to be a part of Hillman's later writing. In the poem "Geology," for instance, she arranges "trigger" words in the corners of the page that almost gravitationally compel the textual development of the work. Probably one of America's foremost experimental religious poets, Hillman offers an exciting engagement with both the archaic and the contemporary worlds.

—Tod Marshall

HINE, (William) Daryl

Nationality: Canadian. **Born:** Burnaby, British Columbia, 24 February 1936. **Education:** McGill University, Montreal, 1954–58; University of Chicago, M.A. 1965, Ph.D. in comparative literature 1967.

Career: Lived in Europe 1958–62. Assistant professor of English, University of Chicago, 1967–69. Editor, *Poetry,* Chicago, 1968–78. **Awards:** Canada Foundation-Rockefeller fellowship, 1958; Canada Council grant, 1959, 1979; Ingram Merrill Foundation grant, 1962, 1963, 1983; Guggenheim fellowship, 1980; American Academy award, 1982; MacArthur Foundation fellowship, 1986. **Address:** 2740 Ridge Avenue, Evanston, Illinois 60201, U.S.A.

PUBLICATIONS

Poetry

Five Poems 1954. Toronto, Emblem, 1955.
The Carnal and the Crane. Toronto, Contact Press, 1957.
The Devil's Picture Book. London and New York, Abelard Schuman, 1960.
Heroics. Fontainebleau, France, Gosswiller, 1961.
The Wooden Horse. New York, Atheneum, 1965.
Minutes. New York, Atheneum, 1968.
Resident Alien. New York, Atheneum, 1975.
In and Out: A Confessional Poem. Privately printed, 1975; New York, Knopf, 1989.
Daylight Saving. New York, Atheneum, 1978.
Selected Poems. Toronto, Oxford University Press, 1980; New York, Atheneum, 1981.
Academic Festival Overtures. New York, Atheneum, 1985.
   Arrondissements. Erin, Ontario, Porcupine's Quill, 1988.
Postscripts. New York, Knopf, 1992.
Flotsam & Jetsam. New York, Knopf, 2000.

Plays

Defunctive Music (broadcast, 1961). Published in *Tamarack Review* (Toronto), Winter 1966.
The Death of Seneca (produced Chicago, 1968). Published in *Chicago Review,* November 1970.

Radio Plays: *Defunctive Music,* 1961 (Canada); *A Mutual Flame* (UK); *Alcestis,* 1972 (UK).

Novel

The Prince of Darkness & Co. London and New York, Abelard Schuman, 1961.

Other

Polish Subtitles: Impressions from a Journey. London and New York, Abelard Schuman, 1962.

Editor, with Joseph Parisi, The *"Poetry" Anthology 1912–1977.* Boston, Houghton Mifflin, 1978.

Translator, *The Homeric Hymns and The Battle of the Frogs and the Mice.* New York, Atheneum, 1972.

Translator, *Idylls and Epigrams,* by Theocritus. New York, Atheneum. 1982.

Translator, *Ovid's Heroines: A Verse Translation of the Heroides.* New Haven, Connecticut, Yale University Press, 1991.

Translator, *Works & Days & Theogony of Hesiod.* Chicago, University of Chicago Press, 2000.

*

Critical Studies: *Alone with America* by Richard Howard, New York, Atheneum, 1969, London, Thames and Hudson, 1970, revised edition, Atheneum, 1980; "Coming Full Circle" by Robert Martin, in *Modern Poetry Studies 7* (New York), no. 1, 1977; "Fabulous Traveller" by John Hollander, in *Canto 3* (Andover, Massachusetts), no. 1, 1979; "Parody, Pastiche, and Allusion" by David Bromwich, in *Lyric Poetry: Beyond New Criticism,* edited by Chavia Hosek and Patricia Parker, Ithaca, New York, Cornell University Press, 1985.

Daryl Hine comments:

To the degree that conscious intent plays any part in creation, which is debatable but variable surely according to genre, I strive for a certain opacity, even solidity of effect not incompatible often with apparent clarity. For me a poem is not a means of communication but an end, an object of contemplation. Meaning, almost inevitable in the medium of language, and reference, irresistible to human beings, figure for me as purely syntactical, a matter of good manners, indispensable to the symmetry and unity that constitute the structural principles of all art. I like my poetry not merely cooked but fermented and distilled. While this ideal is only rarely and partially achieved, whether in my own work or in the history of literature, it remains my only motive for writing at all, apart from amusement. The process is engaging, but the product is the thing.

* * *

When Daryl Hine's first full-length book of poems, *The Carnal and the Crane,* appeared in 1957, Northrop Frye described it as "a brilliant series of phrases" moving "across a mysteriously dark background." More than ten books of poetry, a novel, and a travel book later, the phrases retain their brilliance and the background its mystery. Elegance is characteristic of all of Hine's writing, which may be appreciated for its formal qualities if not for its expressiveness. His work resembles nothing more than an excellent, clear, but very dry wine.

The poet has called his first book "rhapsodic" and surreal in imagery and structure. *The Carnal and the Crane* was followed by *The Devil's Picture Book,* a more crafted work. *The Wooden Horse,* which explored the possibilities of dramatic monologues, led Hine to the intimate 1968 publication *Minutes.* This gave way to a technical tour de force, *The Homeric Hymns,* translations from once oral Greek poems written anonymously in the Homeric manner. With these noble-sounding praises the worlds of poetry and classical scholarship merge for Hine, as in the dactylic hexameters of the first line of "To Apollo": "How should I hymn you, Apollo, so handsomely sung of already?"

Hine's classical learning, far from being confined to *The Homeric Hymns,* reverberates rather than echoes with Greek, Roman, Christian, and even Celtic references throughout all of his poetry. It is an attractive characteristic of his work that he can capture an image with crystal clarity in a symbolist fashion, as in "Les Yeux de la tête" from *Minutes:*

> A tiny palace and a formal garden
> In miniature, lawns, flowers, jewelled trees
> By Fabergé, and in the midst a fountain
> Whose precious drops like tear drops fill the eyes.

Hine's poems proceed from image to image, building on the principle of polarity, finding in the irreconcilability of opposites proof of the inability of people to merge, the impossibility of history, in a world in which "all our wisdom is unwillingness."

—John Robert Colombo

HIRSCH, Edward (Mark)

Nationality: American. **Born:** Chicago, Illinois, 20 January 1950. **Education:** Grinnell College, Grinnell, Iowa, 1968–72, B.A. 1972; University of Pennsylvania, Philadelphia, 1975–79, Ph.D. in folklore 1979. **Family:** Married Janet Landay; one son. **Career:** Assistant professor of English, 1978–82, and associate professor of English, 1982–85, Wayne State University, Detroit; since 1985 professor of English, University of Houston, Texas. **Awards:** Seldon L. Whitcomb Poetry prize, Grinnell College, 1970–72; Academy of American Poets First Place award, 1975–77; Gustav Davidson Poetry award, New York Poetry Society, 1977; Amy Lowell Traveling fellowship, 1978; Ingram Merrill Foundation award, 1978; National Endowment for the Arts fellowship, 1982; I.B. Lavan Younger Poets award, 1983; Delmore Schwartz Memorial award, 1985; Guggenheim fellowship, 1985; Texas Institute of Arts and Letters award, 1987; Stover poetry prize, *Southwest Review,* 1987; Rome prize, American Academy in Rome, 1988; Robert and Hazel Ferguson Memorial award in poetry, 1990; Lila Wallace-Reader's Digest Writing fellow, 1993; Lyndhurst prize, 1994–96; award in literature, American Academy of Arts and Letters, 1998; MacArthur fellowship, 1998. D.H.L.: Grinnell College, 1989, Elon College, 1994. **Agent:** Liz Darhansoff, Daransoff and Verrill, 179 Franklin Street, New York, New York 10013, U.S.A. **Address:** 1528 Sul Ross, Houston, Texas 77006, U.S.A.

PUBLICATIONS

Poetry

For the Sleepwalkers. New York, Knopf, 1981.
Wild Gratitude. New York, Knopf, 1986.
The Night Parade. New York, Knopf, 1989.
Earthly Measures. New York, Knopf, 1994.
On Love. New York, Knopf, 1998.

Other

How to Read a Poem and Fall in Love with Poetry. New York, Harcourt Brace, 1999.
Responsive Reading. Ann Arbor, Michigan, University of Michigan Press, 1999.

Editor, *Transforming Vision.* Boston, Bullfinch Press, 1994.

*

Critical Studies: "'Spots of Time': Representation of Narrative in Modern Poems and Paintings" by Suzanne Ferguson, in *Word & Image* (Basingstoke, Hants, England), 4(1), January-March 1988; "Artful Dodge Interviews: Stuart Dybek and Edward Hirsch" by Benjamin Seaman, in *Artful Dodge,* 14–15, fall 1988; "'Emotional Temperature': A Conversation with Edward Hirsch" by Stan Sanvel Rubin and Judith Kitchen, in *The Post-Confessionals: Conversations with American Poets of the Eighties,* edited by Earl Ingersoll, Judith Kitchen, and Stan Sanvel Rubin, Rutherford, Fairleigh Dickinson University Press, 1989; interview with Edward Hirsch by Kevin Boyle, in *Chicago Review,* 41(1), 1995.

*   *   *

Edward Hirsch is a very likable figure in his poems; he levels with the reader about his emotions, tells stories that are everyone's experience, and has dark things to say about life in general that go directly to the heart. If one were to distill the quality that makes him so popular with critics and the general reader, it would be his youthful sincerity. Hirsch writes from the feelings of a young man of sensitivity and with the soul of a poet growing up in cold, slushy Chicago. He relives the shocks of puberty and manhood in language that lifts the merely personal to the level of myth. Therein lies both his power and his warmth.

Hirsch's poetry descends from very old sources in America. The lofty rhetoric comes from Poe, as does some of his somberness and brooding on death. Hirsch is a symbolist and writes about the landscape and his daily life as if it were a dense, brilliant metaphor of his psychological life. This can be seen, for example, in "Dusk" from his first book, *For the Sleepwalkers:*

The sun is going down tonight
like a wounded stag staggering through the brush
with an enormous spike in its heart
and a single moan in its lungs. There

is light the color of tarnished metal
galloping at its side, and fresh blood
is steaming through its thrust. Listen!
The waves, too, sound like the plunging

of hooves, or a wild hart simply
crumpling on the ground.

Hirsch owes much to T.S. Eliot in the way of irony, self-detachment, and quick shifts of logic. If there is something essentially Hirschean about him, however, it is the moderated, tightly controlled surrealism he applies to his details:

Look for the spangled scar of a crayfish
Crawling backwards, always crawling backwards

Over the veined map and dried parchment
of Apollinaire's shaved head. See how it

Creeps out of the pale blue chapel of his skin
Into the deep trenches and dry riverbeds

Curving all the way from the occupied bank
Of his damaged ear to the eastern front

Of his forehead.

Hirsch's picture of the world involves a certain amount of dislocation of the ordinary through exaggeration, repetition, and reversals. To some extent he is the beneficiary of two decades of translation of Spanish, French, and Central American poetry, which expanded the vocabulary of American poetry and gave writers a freedom to express more of the dream logic of imagination.

Hirsch brings to the Catholic imagination, which W.S. Merwin, Robert Bly, and Mark Strand translated so effectively, something of the Jewish mind in America, the burden of sorrow from a long history of persecution. The pain Hirsch describes in lyric effusions brings the Jewish past to life, filtered through the complex political worlds of Mexico, Franco's Spain, and imperial French colonies—a rich layering of thought and history that has earned Hirsch his wide reputation as a master of lyric confession.

Hirsch has matured over the years from a one-poem-per-page format to longer, bolder meditative poems engaging in literary subjects and taking on the masks of other poets, a voice-projecting form of tribute at which he is particularly adept. He has parodied many voices, including those of Rimbaud, Gérard de Nerval, Marianne Moore, Isaak Babel, Paul Celan, Matisse, Rilke, Vallejo, Lorca, Pound, Eliot, and others. Witness the specificity of the following language from "At the Grave of Marianne Moore," a canny imitation of the subject's famous style, even to the plumb-centered stanza:

This was a woman who paid dazzling attention
    to all the minor nuances of motion;
    the bobbing heads of birds, the strict tension

of snakes slithering through the weeds,

    the marvelous quickness of badgers
    who raced through their cages like perfect athletes,
    almost as artful as her beloved Dodgers.

The later book *The Night Parade* continues the theme of insomnia established in *For the Sleepwalkers.* The night parade contains the chimeras, monsters, and ghostly haunters of the night hours, when most of us are asleep. The poems brood on the more Poe-like extremities of the verse landscape, the creatures who lurk in memory or fantasy and are grasped only by lyric means. Hirsch's prefatory poem, "Memorandums," describes the book as a sort of journey into the underworld:

We will be lifted up and carried a far distance
On invisible wings
And then set down in an empty field.
We will carry our hearts in our bodies
Over shadowy tunnels and bridges.
Someday we will let them go again, like kites.

The journey is harrowing and includes visits to dead grandmothers, other relations, friends, and the unborn. "The Abortion" tells a story of young love that ends on the abortionist's table, where a girl is worked on who is not even pregnant. *"I'll never forgive you. Nothing is forgiven,"* the lover says years later to the speaker.

In Hirsch's award-winning *Earthly Measures* the persona goes in search of God and finds only the shadows, dust, and flimsy memories of spirit in the world. It is at once a very dark book and a tour de force of lyric energies. Hirsch has found his tune here, and he sings large, complex oratorios in perfect pitch.

—Paul Christensen

HIRSCHMAN, Jack

Nationality: American. **Born:** New York City, 13 December 1933. **Education:** Long Island University, New York, 1952; City College of New York, 1951–55, B.A. 1955; Indiana University, Bloomington, M.A. 1957, Ph.D. 1959. **Family:** Married Ruth Epstein in 1954 (divorced 1974); one son (deceased) and one daughter; lived with Kristen Wetterhahn, 1975–83; lived with Sarah Menefee, 1983–98; married Agneta Falk in 1999. **Career:** Instructor, Dartmouth College, Hanover, New Hampshire, 1959–61; assistant professor, University of California, Los Angeles, 1961- 66. Lived in Venice, California, 1967–71, and since 1973 in San Francisco. Painter and collage maker: exhibitions in Venice, California, 1972, and Los Angeles, 1972. Editor, *Compages: International Translations,* 1982–89; editor, *Poetry USA,* 1996. Associated with *Tree* magazine, Bolinas, California; associated with League of Revolutionaries for a New America in the 1990s. **Address:** P.O. Box 26517, San Francisco, California 94126, U.S.A.

PUBLICATIONS

Poetry

Fragments. Privately printed, 1952.
A Correspondence of Americans. Bloomington, Indiana University Press, 1960.
Two, lithographs by Arnold Belkin. Los Angeles, Zora Gallery, 1963.
Interchange. Los Angeles, Zora Gallery, 1964.
Kline Sky. Privately printed, 1965.
Yod. London, Trigram Press, 1966.
London Seen Directly. London, Goliard Press, 1967.
Wasn't It Like This in the Woodcut. London, Cape Goliard Press, 1967.
William Blake. Topanga, California, Love Press, 1967.
A Word in Your Season, with Asa Benveniste. London, Trigram Press, 1967.
Ltd. Interchangeable in Eternity: Poems of Jackruthdavidcelia Hirschman. Privately printed, 1967.
Jerusalem: A Three Part Poem. Topanga, California, Love Press, 1968.
Aleph, Benoni and Zaddik. Los Angeles, Tenfingers Press, 1968.
Jerusalem, Ltd. London, Trigram Press, 1968.
Shekinah. Mill Valley, California, Maya, 1969.
Broadside Golem. Venice, California, Box Zero, 1969.
Black Alephs: Poems 1960–1968. New York, Phoenix Book Shop, and London, Trigram Press, 1969.

NHR. Goleta, California, Christopher's, 1970.
Scintilla. Bolinas, California, Tree, 1970.
Soledeth. Venice, California, Q Press, 1971.
DT. Santa Barbara, California, Yes Press, 1971.
The Burning of Los Angeles. Venice, California, J'Ose Press, 1971.
HNYC. Topanga, California, Skyline Press, 1971.
Les Vidanges. Venice, California, Beyond Baroque Press, 1972.
The R of the Ari's Raziel. Los Angeles, Press of the Pegacycle Lady, 1972.
Adamnan. Santa Barbara, California, Christopher's, 1972.
K'wai Sing: The Origin of the Dragon. Venice, California, Beyond Baroque Press, 1973.
Cantillations. Santa Barbara, California, Yes/Capra Press, 1973.
Aur Sea. Bolinas, California, Tree, 1974.
Djackson. Salt Lake City, Rainbow Resin Press, 1974.
Cockroach Street. San Francisco, Street, 1975.
The Cool Boyetz Cycle. San Francisco, Golden Mountain Press, 1975.
Kashtaniyah Segodnyah. San Francisco, Beatitude Press, 1976.
Lyripol. San Francisco, City Lights, 1976.
The Arcanes of Le Comte de St. Germain. San Francisco, Amerus Press, 1977.
The Proletarian Arcane. San Francisco, Amerus Press, 1978.
The Jonestown Arcane. San Francisco, Poetry for the People, 1979.
The Cagliostro Arcane. San Francisco, Michael Hargreaves, 1981.
The David Arcane. San Francisco, Amerus Press, 1982.
Class Questions. N.p., Retribution Press, 1982.
Kallatumba. Fremont, California, Ruddy Duck Press, 1984.
The Necessary Is. San Francisco, Fishy Afoot Press, 1984.
The Bottom Line. Willimantic, Connecticut, Curbstone Press, 1988.
Sunsong. San Francisco, Fishy Afoot Press, 1988.
The Tirana Arcane. San Francisco, Deep Forest Press, 1991.
The Jonestown Arcane. San Diego, Parenthesis Writing Series, 1991.
The Satin Arcane. Oakland, Zeitgeist Press, 1991.
Endless Threshold. Willimantic, Connecticut, Curbstone Press, 1992.
The Back of a Spoon. San Francisco, Manic D Press, 1992.
The Heartbeat Arcane. Farmington, New Mexico, Yoo Hoo Press, 1993.
The Xibalba Arcane. Washington D.C., Azul Editions, 1994.
The Arcane on a Stick. San Francisco, Roadkill Press, 1995.
The Grafitti Arcane. San Francisco, Deliriodendron Press, 1996.
The Grit Arcane. West Yorkshire, England, Spout, 1997.
Kallatumba. Osnago, Italy, Edizioni Pulcinoelefante, 1998.
The Open Gate. San Francisco, Express Press, 1998.

Verbo-Visual Works: Verbo-visual art works, Marvin and Ruth Sackner Archive of Verbo-Visual Art, 1967–89.

Other

Editor, *Artaud Anthology.* San Francisco, City Lights, 1965.
Editor, *Amerus Anthology.* San Francisco, Amerus Press, 1978.
Editor, with Jack Mueller, *Frammis.* Berkeley, California, Artaud's Elbow, 1979.
Editor, *Would You Wear My Eyes: A Tribute to Bob Kaufman.* San Francisco, Bob Kaufman Cultural Brigade, 1989.
Editor, *Partisans.* San Francisco, Deliriodendron Press, 1995.

Translator, with Victor Erlich, *Electric Iron,* by Vladimir Mayakovsky. Mill Valley, California, Maya, 1970.

Translator, *Love Is a Tree,* by Antonin Artaud. Fairfax, California, Red Hill Press, 1972.

Translator, *A Rainbow for the Christian West,* by René Depestre. Fairfax, California, Red Hill Press, 1972.

Translator, *The Exiled Angel,* by Luisa Pasamanik. Fairfax, California, Red Hill Press, 1973.

Translator, *Igitur,* by Stéphane Mallarmé. Los Angeles, Press of the Pegacycle Lady, 1973.

Translator, *Wail for the Arab Beggars of the Casbah,* by Ait Djafer. Los Angeles, Papa Bach, 1973.

Translator, *The Crucifixion,* by Jean Cocteau. Bethlehem, Pennsylvania, Quarter Press, 1975.

Translator, *The Book of Noah,* by Johann Maier. Berkeley, California, Tree, 1975.

Translator, with Alexander Altmann, *Three Tracts,* by Eleazer of Worms. San Francisco, Beatitude Press, 1976.

Translator, *Orange Voice,* by Alexander Kohav. San Francisco, Beatitude Press, 1976.

Translator, *Four Angels in Profile, Four Bears in Fullface,* by Alexander Kohav. San Francisco, Beatitude Press, 1976.

Translator, *Requiem,* by Robert Rodzhdestvensky. San Francisco, Beatitude Press, 1977.

Translator, *Hunger,* by Natasha Belyaeva. Mill Valley, California, D'Aurora Press, 1977.

Translator, *Emigroarium,* by Alexander Kohav. San Francisco, Amerus Press, 1977.

Translator, *Dove Rose,* by Eliphas Levi. N.p., Viscerally Press, 1979.

Translator, *Vegetations of Splendor,* by René Depestre. New York, Vanguard Press, 1980.

Translator, *Yossiph Shyryn,* by Santo Cali. Trapani, Sicily, Antigruppo, 1981.

Translator, *Jabixshak: Poems and Songs of Socialist Albania.* San Francisco, Amerus Press, 1982.

Translator, *Elegies,* by Pablo Neruda. San Francisco, David Books, 1983.

Translator, *Poems,* by Sarah Kirsch. Santa Cruz, California, Alcatraz Press, 1983.

Translator, *Three Clicks Left,* by Katerina Gogou. San Francisco, Night Horn, 1983.

Translator, *Communist,* by Agim Gjakova. San Francisco, Fishy Afoot Press, 1984.

Translator, *Clandestine Poems,* by Roque Dalton. San Francisco, Solidarity 1984.

Translator, *Fistibal/Slingshot,* by Paul Laraque. Washington, D.C., Seaworthy Press/Editions Samba, 1989.

Translator, *In Memory of the Children Fallen,* by Dorou Lefteria. San Francisco, Deliriodendron Press, 1994.

Translator, *The Sea on Its Side,* by Ambar Past. Sausalito, Post-Apollo Press, 1994.

Translator, *Seven Poems,* by Rocco Scotellaro. San Francisco, Deliriodendron Press, 1994.

Translator, with Angela Beske, *Light-Force,* by Paul Celan. San Francisco, Deliriodendron Press, 1995.

Translator, *The Plain Inside,* by Claudio Galuzzi. San Francisco, Deliriodendron Press, 1997.

Translator, *Fist of Sun,* by Ferruccio Brugnaro. Willmantic, Connecticut, Curbstone Press, 1998.

Translator, *A Fling of Two Die,* by Stéphane Mallarmé. San Francisco, Deliriodendron Press, 1998.

Translator, *The Month of the Frozen Grapes,* by Katerina Gogou. San Francisco, Deliriodendron Press, 1999.

Translator, *Suicide Circus,* by Alexei Kruchenych. Los Angeles, Green Integer, 1999.

*

Manuscript Collections: University of California, Irvine and Riverside.

Jack Hirschman comments:

(1970) Poetry is man at his most complete state of consciousness. As I write this, in March of 1969, I am conscious of whirling bodies of Vietnamese women and children in the long process of death and aware that "poetry does nothing" is truth; I reject that truth for the poem I am now going to plunge into. Long live the creative act! May the overlords of the world learn the real meaning of death.

(1974) Putting my poems, my visual works, and my kabbalistic interests together, my poetry may be seen more and more to reflect—through the amuletic/hieroglyphic tradition—a politically left position which sees Hanoi as the extension of the idea of Blake's *Jerusalem.* Free to translate from many languages and moreover to broadcast such works, as well as my own, on Pacifica Radio in Los Angeles, I believe my works reveal all that is beautifully decayed in Western capitalistic societies in the hope that the interchange between the West and the future Asia and Africa takes place, so to speak, across the arc of rainbows rather than the broken backs of those who still have not forfeited the earth to machinery.

(1980) For the past six years I've been living and writing in San Francisco, especially in North Beach, as a propagandist for communism as the poetic energy of revolution itself. I've learned how to translate and to write in Russian and have worked with different cadres on the street, i.e., the Beatitude group and then the Amerus group. Poems are written in American and Russian and daily read. Since 1974 I have given away some 50,000 handmade poster-poems in the tradition of Mayakovsky—the genuine poet-painter of the Russian Revolution—and William Blake. Early Jewish kabbalism has given way to the kabbalistic Soviet, rooted in the Cyrillic language. This extension of work represents the foremost affirmation of my creative life and is an ongoing process. The latest development is the Union of Street Poets, which provides handout texts of poems to the people of San Francisco. Long life to the revolutionary poets everywhere.

(1989) For the past nine years I've been working as a cultural worker for the Communist Labor Party of North America. All texts published in the 1980s should therefore be seen in that light. Gone are esotericisms and mystical idealisms. My work is about and in relation to the working class and its struggles here and elsewhere. The highest form of art, to my mind, is an enduring agitation-propaganda.

(1995) For the past five years my works have reflected the shift from ideology to struggles from the poorest segments of society. I have mainly concentrated on my longer poems, which I call "Arcanes," which reflect my revolutionary concerns in a so-to-speak large canvas. At the same time I've continued as an agitprop writer and artist, working as a correspondent for the revolutionary newspaper *People's Tribune* as well as with cultural groupings in a collective way. Two large collections, *The Bottom Line* and *Endless Threshold,* have been translated and published in Italy, and I've twice toured that country—in 1992 and again in 1993.

(1999) For the past four years I've worked with and for the League of Revolutionaries for a New America, which developed out of the dissolution of the Communist Labor Party as a nonparty organization of militant revolutionary educators and propagandists. At the same time, because my last five books have appeared in Italy, Great Britain, and France, I have been in Europe touring a great deal during this period. When I am in San Francisco, I continue reading my works at demonstrations around issues of the new class of poor people (vis-à-vis homelessness, police brutality, and neocapitalist wars).

*   *   *

Jack Hirschman's work as a poet, translator, and radical theorist is wide-ranging, prolific, energetic, and crackling with passionate alertness and utopian zeal. He is one of the left's most prolific and consistent poetic voices, and his work resonates with an insistent reminder of the American and international radical continuum. An amazing polyglot, he has produced translations that range from German, French, Greek, Italian, Spanish, and Russian to less well represented languages like Albanian, Creole, Vietnamese, and Yiddish. The poets he has translated are dizzyingly diverse, from Artaud, Mallarmé, Célan, and Cocteau to René Depestre, Rocque Dalton, Luisa Pasamanik, and Neruda. (During the 1980s Hirschman participated in a translation collective producing *Compages,* an irregularly issued journal focusing on world literature of resistance and engagement.) In his radical internationalism Hirschman has continued an American tradition most notably practiced by Kenneth Rexroth.

Hirschman's ease with languages allows for a multilingual Joycean weave of wordplay and layered references already evident in his first collection, *A Correspondence of Americans,* and in full display in *Black Alephs: Poems 1960-1968,* published in London by the Trigram Press (with cover art and interior collages by Wallace Berman). In later publications like *The Bottom Line* the work still sings its linguistic virtuosity, but it is trimmed down, compressed, more direct, and speech-based. Hirschman's unique relation with languages has, over the decades, moved him away from an academic literary career into a pariah realm as an avowed left-wing poet-activist and agitprop artist and performer. Although he is celebrated abroad, he is marginalized in America. Thus, his works are translated into Italian and French, but, outside of those published by Curbstone Press, they are circulated in the United States mainly through samizdat-like photocopied editions self-published or published by radical friends.

The cultural politics of American modernist poetry has been ill at ease with radical libertarian poetries. The major periods of tolerance—the Great Depression of the 1930s, the beat movement of the 1950s, and the upsurge in the late 1960s—have retreated into embarrassment, erased from the record in academia. Hirschman's unabashedly overt, fully committed communist poetry has been critically neglected by mainstream literary networks, while radicals and former radicals criticize what they read as an idiosyncratic and romanticized version of Marxist-Leninist doctrine in complete disregard of its postrevolutionary history. Hirschman practices an intuitive radicalism, grounded in a long-standing sympathy for outcast heresies, millenarian rhapsodies, and the subversive spirit and its encrypted vocabularies. Despite the occasional use of jargon, his compassionate devotion to the oppressed and broken populace is stirring and often deeply effective.

Hirschman's attempts at imagining and writing so-called proletarian poetry or socialist realism yield mixed results, however. Unable to conceal his rich affiliations with the high culture (and middle-class ground) of modernism, Hirschman cannot honestly numb himself to any party line despite his devotion to an increasingly devalued international communism. These contradictions add an unintentional difficulty to his work, even though, through conscious effort, he has trimmed out literary excess to produce short-lined poems of "everyday" clarity:

> You see them
>   round about
>   midnight, in Chinatown
> sidestreets or in doorways
>   directly on Kearney
> in the shadow of the great
>   bank pyramid:
> not simply dead drunk,
> but as if dead, drunk,
> on their back sprawled,
> open-mouthed
> or on their faces, or
> so beggarly in their wine,
> they sit in doorways
> asking change
> from anything that moves:
> a blown piece of newspaper,
> the shadow of a pigeon
> in the moonlight.

Since the 1970s Hirschman has been issuing fascicles of his ongoing epic *The Arcanes* through small presses, periodicals, and homemade giveaways. It is his most sustained and important work, marking another entry into the uneasy archives of the modernist American serial poem initiated by Pound, Williams, and H.D. and later practiced by Charles Olson and Thomas McGrath, with whom Hirschman shares certain affinities. (In the postmodern realm Ron Silliman carries on the gesture.)

Worth noting also is Hirschman's generosity not only to political causes but also to the consistent furthering, both as advocate and translator, of works by radical poets and artists in the United States and elsewhere. He is a tireless presence at rallies, demonstrations, and benefits, and he remains one of the most galvanizing readers of poetry performing today.

—David Meltzer

HIRSHFIELD, Jane (B.)

Nationality: American. **Born:** New York, New York, 24 February 1953. **Education:** Princeton University, New Jersey, A.B. (magna cum laude) 1973. **Career:** Visiting poet, Wyoming Poets in the Schools, 1987; master artist, Chevron Foundation Artist in the Schools Program, 1982–84; California Poets in the Schools, 1980–85; faculty, Napa Valley Poetry Conference, 1984, 1985, 1993, 1994, 1996, 1997, 1999; faculty, Port Townsend Writers Conference, 1987, 1988, 1991, 1994; faculty member, Foothills College Writers Conference, 1989–97; lecturer, University of San Francisco, 1991–98; Truckee Meadows Writers Conference, Reno, Nevada, 1991, 1994; faculty, Squaw Valley Art of the Wild Writers Conference, 1992, 1993, 1995, 1996, 1997; visiting poet, University of Alaska, Fairbanks, 1993; adjunct professor, Northern Michigan University, 1994;

faculty, University of Minnesota Split Rock Summer Arts Seminars, 1995, 1998; visiting associate professor, University of California, Berkeley, 1995; Elliston Visiting Poet, University of Cincinnati, 2000. Since 1983 freelance editor and assistant to literary agent Michael Katz. Associate faculty, 1995, and since 1999 faculty, Bennington College Writing Seminars. **Awards:** Poetry Competition prize (later named The Discovery award), *The Nation,* 1973; Poetry prize, *Quarterly Review of Literature,* 1982; Yaddo fellowship, 1983, 1985, 1987, 1989, 1992, 1996; Guggenheim fellowship, 1985; The Joseph Henry Jackson award, The San Francisco Foundation, 1986; Gordon Barber award, Poetry Society of America, 1987; Columbia University Translation Center award, 1987, for *The Ink Dark Moon;* Djerassi Foundation artist-in-residence, 1987, 1988, 1989, 1990; Commonwealth Club of California Poetry medal, 1988, for *Of Gravity & Angels;* Cecil Hemley award, Poetry Society of America, 1988; Pushcart prize, 1988; Dewar's Young Artist Recognition award in poetry, 1990; MacDowell Colony fellowship, 1994; Rockefeller Foundation fellowship, Bellagio Study Center, 1995; Bay Area Book Reviewers award in poetry, 1995, for *The October Palace;* Best American Poems selection, 1999. **Address:** c/o HarperCollins, 10 East 53rd Street, New York, New York 10022, U.S.A.

PUBLICATIONS

Poetry

Alaya. Princeton, New Jersey, Quarterly Review of Literature, 1982.
Of Gravity & Angels. Middletown, Connecticut, Wesleyan University Press, 1988.
The October Palace. New York, HarperCollins, 1994.
The Lives of the Heart. New York, HarperCollins, 1997.

Other

Nine Gates: Entering the Mind of Poetry. New York, HarperCollins, 1997.

Editor and translator, with Mariko Aratani, *The Ink Dark Moon: Love Poems,* by Ono no Komachi and Izumi Shikibu. New York, Vintage Classics, 1990.
Editor and translator, *Women in Praise of the Sacred: 43 Centuries of Spiritual Poetry by Women.* New York, HarperCollins, 1994.

*

Critical Studies: "The World Is Large and Full of Noises: Thoughts on Translation" by the author, in *Georgia Review* (Athens, Georgia), 45(1), spring 1991; "Necessary Angels: Jane Hirshfield and Karen Fish" by Jo Brantley Berryman, in *Antioch Review* (Yellow Springs, Ohio), 48(3), summer 1990.

Jane Hirshfield comments:

My primary reason for writing has always been the attempt to understand and deepen experience by bringing it into words. Poetry, for me, is an instrument of investigation and a mode of perception, a way of knowing and feeling both self and world, and I believe that a good poem not only holds experience but creates it by allowing reader or writer to step into that place at the center where all things rise newly into being. I write, then, as a way to attend with deeper accuracy to the difficult business of being a human being in the world. But poetry is also a mode of being in which subjective and objective can approach and become each other; outer description holds inner being, and the most seemingly subjective expression touches universal experiences of passion, grief, love, loss, and the subtler experiences of both daily life and what, for lack of any better term, I will call metaphysical inquiry.

The speaking voice of a poem during its composition is intensely private for me, but the finished work is nonetheless a way of bringing fruit of inner thinking to others. Technically I am interested in making poems that find a clarity without simplicity, in a way of thinking and speaking that does not exclude complexity but also does not obscure, in poems that know the world in many ways at once—heart, mind, voice, and body. There are many kinds of poem making that seem like valid roads to me, but all encompass both word and world.

My "lineage" as a poet includes both the Western and Eastern traditions. Greek and Roman lyrics, the English sonnet, those foundation stones of American poetry Whitman and Dickinson, modern poets from Eliot to Akhmatova to Cavafy to Neruda—all have added something to my knowledge of what is possible in poetry. But equally important to me have been the classical Chinese poets such as Tu Fu, Li Po, Wang Wei, and Han Shan and the classical Japanese poets, particularly the two foremost women poets of the Heian era, Ono no Komachi and Izumi Shikibu, whom I translated in *The Ink Dark Moon.* I am also interested in the lesser known traditions—Eskimo poetry, Nahuatl poetry. I believe that full realizations of the lyric impulse can be found in every tradition and culture, and I have tried to draw on as wide a range as possible in the various essays and craft lectures I have written. The two books I have edited, *The Ink Dark Moon: Love Poems* and *Women in Praise of the Sacred: 43 Centuries of Spiritual Poetry by Women,* were each undertaken in the effort to make more widely known the work of historical women poets whose words I found both memorable and moving, able to enlarge our understanding of what it is to be human as well as to counteract the lingering myth that there were no historical women writers of significance.

*   *   *

In the afterword to *Alaya,* her first collection of poems, Jane Hirshfield notes that her intent is "to find the level of truth in a situation which is incontrovertible, as a dream is, by reason of its particularity." What emerges most clearly in this volume, which collects poems written between the poet's eighteenth and twenty-seventh years, is the first appearance of themes to be developed at greater length and with greater individual style and skill in later volumes. That she regards poetry as a kind of gift of perception and sensibility distilled into language is clear from the first poem, "How To Give," which suggests that ordinary moments can compensate for the loss of monuments of greater cultural or historical magnitude:

The only life to be had starts here:
without seams,
this daily life a coming ordinariness,
a mine to replace the chameleon history of power,
a power to replace that other power—
things shining, & things growing dark,

loud with crickets,
with bees,
the patina of use,
the habit of care.

James Wright's influence on Hirshfield can be detected in the opening poem of her second collection, the title of which, *Of Gravity & Angels,* aptly encapsulates the twin pulls in her work. "After Work" echoes the imagery and flow of Wright's "A Blessing"; like Wright, Hirshfield stops by a pasture at evening and, in this case, whistles the horses close to accept her gift of corncobs:

They come, deepened and muscular movements
conjured out of sleep: each small noise and scent
heavy with earth, simple beyond communion . . .
. . . and in the night, their mares' eyes shine, reflect-
      ing stars,
the entire, outer light of the world here.

The second section of the book, however, presents a clear departure, gathering poems often explicit in their erotic imagery. The title poem begins with the speaker telling her lover that she "want[s] the long road of your thigh / under my hand, your well-traveled thigh, / your salt-slicked & come-slicked thigh . . . ." Yet this sexual situation opens to a sense of erotic joining in a larger sense:

. . . all fontanel, all desire, the whole thing beginning
for the first time again, the first,
until I wonder then how is it
we even know which part we are,
even know the ground that lifts us, raucous,
out of ourselves,
as the rising sound of a summer dawn
when all of it joins in.

If an erection signals a kind of rising counter to the ordinary heaviness of things, it also reflects the intrinsic impulse to rise against the tug of other forces.

In *The October Palace* Hirshfield widens her net to gather Zen monks, Cycladic figures, modernist painters, Praxilla, Grant's *Common Birds and How To Know Them,* and a car named Big Mama Tomato. Such references allow her, as she writes in "The Wedding," to "think of world / in which nothing is lost, its heaped paintings, / the studded statues keeping their jewels."

Her knowledge never seems donned like a valedictory robe, however, but serves to illuminate recesses of thought. It does not rest on elegant surfaces, for, as she begins "Perceptibility Is a Kind of Attentiveness,"

It is not enough
to see only the beauty,
this light
that pools aluminum
in the winter branches of apple—
it is only a sign
of the tree looking out
from the tree,
of the light looking

back at the light,
the long-called attention.

But the things of this world do not serve only to "distract / in their sweetness and rustling." The body is also a "net," "the one / we willingly give ourselves to . . . / each knot so carefully made, the curved / plate of the sternum tied to the shape of breath, / the perfect hinge of knee . . ." ("Of the Body"). What Hirshfield hopes to help us see is a way of, as she titles one poem, "Meeting the Light Completely." The goal of Zen practice is to see the world as it is, just as it is, not other than an ideal world of enlightened experience, not quite the same. "Not one, not two," a Zen saying insists. But in the details, banal as "the chipped lip / of a blue-glazed cup," we see the beauty of "the found world," which surprises as profoundly as being able, in those odd moments when we are truly present, to recognize the former "unrecognized stranger" in "the long beloved," leading us to say with "all lovers," "What fools we were, not to have seen."

Hirshfield's collection of essays, *Nine Gates: Entering the Mind of Poetry,* provides insight into her process as a writer. Of particular note is "The World Is Large and Full of Noises: Thoughts on Translation," in which Hirshfield argues that translation "play[s] an essential role in the innumerable conversations between familiar and strange, native and import, past and future, by which history and culture are made." Given the erotic (in the fullest sense) nature of the act, the poet/translator bears considerable responsibility, not the least of which is "to convey each poem's particular strength." This challenge increases in proportion to the poem's distance across culture or time:

An older poem's increasing strangeness of language is
part of its beauty, in the same way that the cracks and
darkening of an old painting become part of its luminosity in
the viewer's mind: they enter not only the physical painting,
but our vision of it as well. This is why seeing an old painting
suddenly "restored" can be unnerving & shy; we recognize a
tampering with its relationship to time, miss the scented smoke
of the centuries' passage.

The second half of the essay details the ways in which her own process in bringing the works of Ono no Komachi and Izumi Shikibu (in *The Ink Dark Moon,* with Mariko Aratani) reveal the challenges and rewards of this labor.

Hirshfield concurrently published her collection of poems *The Lives of the Heart.* While these poems show a maturation of craft, the specificity and delicacy of focus, particularly on the natural world, remain consistent. If the poems display a little less erudition than those in *The October Palace,* the gain is an intensified presence and increased acuity of metaphor. Hirshfield's poems, however, too often leave out the shared quotidian, the hallmark of Issa's haiku. As with a still life painter who includes fruit and flowers—not necessarily rare beauties; day lilies and asters will do—the sense of the disarray of human use is often lost. Hirshfield articulates an awareness of this in "Letter to Hugo from Later," a form appropriate to her recognition:

I envy the way you managed to pack so many parts of
      the world
in such a little space, the way you'd go from pour-
      ing a glass

537

of beer to something American and huge. I don't
   write much
about America, or even people. For you, people were what
   there was:
you talked with and about them and stayed up late
to love those high-lobbed lives. I'd often enough rather
talk to horses.

It is interesting that, in using the shape of Hugo's letter poems, Hirshfield imitates as well the too often dull prosody, the lapse into prose energized, when at all, by sentiment rather than emotion. The danger for Hirshfield if, as this poem suggests, she hopes to find a way to incorporate more of this world within her poems, is to get the force of contingency without the slackening of acuity.

—Allen Hoey

HOAGLAND, Tony

Nationality: American. **Born:** Anthony Dey Hoagland, Fort Bragg, North Carolina, 19 November 1953. **Education:** Williams College, Williamstown, Massachusetts, 1971–73; University of Iowa, Iowa City, 1974–77, B.G.S. 1977; University of Arizona, Tucson, 1979–83, M.F.A. 1983. **Family:** Married Betty Sasaki in 1995. **Career:** Instructor, Arizona Western College, Yuma, 1986, College of the Holy Names, Oakland, California, 1989–90, St. Mary's College, Moraga, California, 1990–91, and University of Maine, Farmington, 1992. Writer-in-residence, Kalamazoo College, Michigan, Summer 1991. Since 1993 faculty member, writing program, Warren Wilson College, Asheville, North Carolina, and instructor, Colby College, Waterville, Maine. **Awards:** National Endowment for the Arts fellowship, 1987, 1994; Pushcart prize in poetry, 1991, 1993; Brittingham prize, University of Wisconsin Press, 1992; John C. Zacharis prize, Emerson College, 1994. Fine Arts Work Center in Provincetown fellow, 1986. **Member:** Academy of American Poets. **Address:** 47 Redington Street, Waterville, Maine 04901, U.S.A.

PUBLICATIONS

Poetry

A Change in Plans (chapbook). Sierra Vista, Arizona, San Pedro Press, 1985.
Talking to Stay Warm (chapbook). Minneapolis, Minnesota, Coffee Cup Press, 1986.
History of Desire (chapbook). Tucson, Arizona, Moon Pony Press, 1990.
Sweet Ruin. Madison, University of Wisconsin Press, 1992.
Donkey Gospel: Poems. Saint Paul, Minnesota, Graywolf Press, 1998.

Recording: *Lunch Poems, Tony Hoagland, 10/7/99,* University of California, Berkeley, 1999.

*

Critical Study: "Poetry Chronicle: An Extravagant Three: New Poetry by Mitchell, Hoagland, and Gallagher" by Peter Harris, in *Virginia Quarterly Review* (Charlottesville, Virginia), 69(4), Fall 1993.

*   *   *

The total quantity of Tony Hoagland's poetry is relatively small. Three slim chapbooks were incorporated in large part into the full-length book *Sweet Ruin,* selected by Donald Justice as the 1992 winner of the Brittingham prize. In addition, he has published other poems in various magazines. But the body of Hoagland's work is fine honed, and it has won considerable admiration not only from Justice but also from critics like Carl Dennis and Carolyn Kizer. Hoagland's poems characteristically open with dramatic flair: "When I think of what I know about America, / I think of kissing my best friend's wife / in the parking lot of the zoo one afternoon . . ." or "That was the summer my best friend / called me a faggot on the telephone, / hung up, and vanished from the earth . . ." These openings suggest the narrative mode in which Hoagland likes to work, and the need to find out what happens draws the reader into the poem. Hoagland develops his narratives in longish poems, almost always more than a page and sometimes as long as three pages, that normally resolve themselves in a wry, epigrammatic twist that implicitly acknowledges the insolubility of the initial premise; after you kiss your best friend's wife or after your best friend calls you a faggot, there is no going back.

The geography of Hoagland's poetry is white, middle-class, suburban, post-1960s. Hoagland explores this region with a pervasive irony, a bravura wit, and sometimes a probing self-awareness. Many of the poems seem to be autobiographical, edging toward the confessional. Hoagland, or his invented persona, tells us not only about his best friends but also about how his father deliberately ruined (thus the title of the book) his own marriage and was then struck down by a heart attack; about how, at age seventeen, the young poet watched his mother shrivel away with cancer; about his grandmother Bernice, who believed that "people with good manners / naturally had yachts, knew how to waltz / and dribbled French into their sentences / like salad dressing"; about "that architect, my brother," who "lost his voice, and then his wife / because he was too proud to say, 'Please, don't go'"; about the rock concerts that filled his ears and those of his friends with scar tissue; and about many, many girlfriends. Sometimes the "I" becomes a "you" to imply that these experiences are typical of a generation and a particular social group. Thus, in one poem we read of "the night your girlfriend / first disappeared beneath the sheets / to take you in her red, wet mouth / with an amethystine sweetness / and a surprising expertise, / then came up for a kiss / as her reward . . ."

In the most resonant of Hoagland's poems the thin and somewhat brittle social surface opens up to reveal unexpected depths. Sometimes the depths are religious, for God, it seems, is keeping an eye on us. In one marvelously delicate poem the poet shares a late-night cigarette with God, and in this moment "things"—the clutter of American middle-class life, not only the cars and the microwaves but all the responsibilities and human entanglements too—fall away, and we find ourselves in the presence of a great and blessed emptiness:

One does so much
   building up, so much feverish
     acquiring,
but really, it is all aimed

at a condition of exhausted
   simplicity, isn't it?
We don't love things.

The poet realizes that, at least in our sleep, we can escape the tyranny of things. All about him (and God) are ''bodies / falling from the precipice / of sleep,'' who for a few hours do not

      remember how to suffer
or how to run from it.
   They are like the stars,
      or potted plants, or salty oceanic waves.

It seems that even in American suburbia getting and having can sometimes fade away to allow a few moments of simple being, although the reference to potted plants seems to twist the poem back toward irony.

    In a few of his later poems Hoagland chooses to probe beneath the surface of American middle-class life in quest not of spiritual depths but of the social and economic underpinnings of this way of life. In ''From This Height,'' for example, we are invited to observe a seduction scene that takes place beside a hot tub in an eighth-floor condominium. The speaker, caught up in the elegance of his surroundings, suddenly finds himself looking through this veneer as he recognizes that

      we are on top of a pyramid
of all the facts
that make this possible:
the furnace that heats the water,
the truck that hauled the fuel,
the artery of highway
blasted through the mountains . . .

At the bottom, the speaker realizes, down there ''inside history's body / the slaves are still singing in the dark.'' The speaker cannot think of anything to do with this knowledge except to kiss the girl and eat another mouthful of the ''high calorie paté . . . / which, considering the price, / would be a sin / not to enjoy.'' But while the speaker of the poem seeks to deflect his new awareness with cynical wit, the poem seems to ask another kind of response from us—to move beyond cynicism and to act on this new and bitter knowledge.

—Burton Hatlen

HOBSBAUM, Philip (Dennis)

Nationality: British. **Born:** London, 29 June 1932. **Education:** Belle Vue Grammar School, Bradford, Yorkshire; Downing College, Cambridge, 1952–55, B.A. 1955, M.A. 1961; Royal Academy of Music, London, licentiate 1956; University of Sheffield, 1959–62, Ph.D. 1968. **Family:** Married 1) Hannah Kelly in 1957 (marriage dissolved 1968); 2) Rosemary Singleton in 1976. **Career:** Lecturer in English, Queen's University, Belfast, 1962–66. Lecturer, 1966–72, senior lecturer, 1972–79, and reader, 1979–85, and since 1985 Titular Professor of English, University of Glasgow. Professional research fellow, 1997. Editor, *Delta,* Cambridge, 1954–55; co-editor, *Poetry from Sheffield,* 1959–61. **Address:** 10 Oran Drive, Glasgow G20 6AF, United Kingdom.

PUBLICATIONS

Poetry

The Place's Fault and Other Poems. London, Macmillan, and New York, St. Martin's Press, 1964.
Snapshots. Belfast, Festival, 1965.
In Retreat and Other Poems. London, Macmillan, 1966; Chester Springs, Pennsylvania, Dufour, 1968.
Coming Out Fighting. London, Macmillan, and Chester Springs, Pennsylvania, Dufour, 1969.
Some Lovely Glorious Nothing. Frensham, Surrey, Sceptre Press, 1969.
Women and Animals. London. Macmillan, 1972.

Plays

Radio Plays: *Children in the Woods,* 1974; *Round the Square,* music by Nick Bicât, 1976.

Other

A Theory of Communication: A Study of Value in Literature. London, Macmillan, 1970; as *Theory of Criticism,* Bloomington, Indiana University Press, 1970.
A Reader's Guide to Charles Dickens. London, Thames and Hudson, 1972; New York, Farrar Straus, 1973.
Tradition and Experiment in English Poetry. London, Macmillan, and Totowa, New Jersey, Rowman and Littlefield, 1979.
A Reader's Guide to D.H. Lawrence. London, Thames and Hudson, 1981.
Essentials of Literary Criticism. London, Thames and Hudson, 1983.
A Reader's Guide to Robert Lowell. London, Thames and Hudson, 1988.
Metre, Rhythm, and Verse Form. London and New York, Routledge, 1996.
Metre, Rhythm, and Verse Form, London, Routledtge, 1996.

Editor, with Edward Lucie-Smith, *A Group Anthology.* London, Oxford University Press, 1963.
Editor, *Ten Elizabethan Poets.* London, Longman, 1969.
Editor, *William Wordsworth: Selected Poetry and Prose.* London, Routledge, 1989.
Editor, with Puddy Lyons and Jim McGhee, *Channels of Communication,* Glasgow, University of Glasgow, 1992.

*

Manuscript Collection: University of Texas, Austin.

Critical Studies: Reviews by P.N. Furbank, in *The Listener* (London), May 1964, and by G.S. Fraser, in *The New York Review of Books,* 1964; *The Modern Writer and His World* by G.S. Fraser, London, Deutsch, 1964, New York, Praeger, 1965; *British Poetry* *since 1960* edited by Michael Schmidt and Grevel Lindop, Oxford, Carcanet, 1972; *The Group* edited by Ian Fletcher and John Pilling, Reading, University of Reading Library, 1974; ''The Belfast Group'' edited by Frank Ormsby, in *Honest Ulsterman* (Belfast), November-December 1976; special feature in ''The Belfast Group,'' in *Honest Ulsterman,* Spring 1994.

Philip Hobsbaum comments:

I have been associated, as founder of the Group in 1955, with Lucie-Smith, MacBeth, Porter, Bell, and Redgrove. But I must emphasize that this is a process of teaching creative writing, not a movement in verse. Other groups were started in Belfast in 1963 and in Glasgow in 1967. In recent years I have divided my time between writing a history of English poetry and a series of pieces, some of which have been broadcast, that I call ''Poems for Several Voices.'' I hope to collect these, and eventually to get down on paper a sequence of poems that has been long in my mind concerning autumnal and twilight themes. It is to be called ''North Kelvin.''

*   *   *

Critics and criticism have exercised an enormous influence on the creative work of Philip Hobsbaum, and some might maintain that the impact has not always been supportive of his initial poetic impulse. At Cambridge he worked under F.R. Leavis, edited the magazine *Delta,* and founded the so-called Group, a number of poets who met regularly, first in Cambridge and later in London, for the purpose of critically examining one another's efforts. In 1959 Hobsbaum went to Sheffield University to do research under William Empson, and his first volume, *The Place's Fault,* contains the poems written while he was there. These works were the first after a silence of several years, and ''Testimony'' celebrates the return of his poetic gifts, using the analogy of Sarah's conception of a child in her period of barrenness—''Should I not rejoice / After these barren years being given a voice?''

If the title of his book and the epigraph from Philip Larkin (''waking at the fumes / And furnace-glares of Sheffield, where I changed . . .'') acknowledge his debt to Larkin and if there is a similarity in tone, Hobsbaum, unlike Larkin (who tends to observe human behavior as if from a safe distance), is not afraid to commit himself to active participation. Indeed, most of his poems are about this involvement and its effects. In the title poem he says,

> We left (it was a temporary halt)
> The knots of ragged kids, the wired-off beach,
> Faces behind the blinds. I'll not return;
> There's nothing there I haven't had to learn,
> And I've learned nothing that I'd care to teach—
> Except that I know it was the place's fault.

But more often than not Hobsbaum is concerned with his own faults rather than those of the place or situation, and he is so anxious to be frank about himself, ''warts and all,'' that he tends to lay undue emphasis upon physical defects in his wry, self-deprecating manner. He throws ridicule upon his fatness, his shortsightedness, and his decaying teeth (as in ''A Journey round the Inside of My Mouth''). At times he can be very impressive, as in ''Household Gods,'' ''Old Flame,'' and ''Testimony,'' and even in his weakest poems he retains a craftsmanlike control over his materials. In the long ''Man without

God,'' his most ambitious poem, he attempts to trace the development of his religious doubts from the superstitious rites of childhood to the intellectual questionings of maturity, but what comes across with greatest force is not so much his doubt in God as the strength of his belief in the invincibility of life.

A phrase from Larkin—''Lonely in Ireland, since it was not home''—provides the keynote to *In Retreat.* Hobsbaum's loneliness (one suspects that he would be lonely anywhere) and the threat of losing his eyesight lend a plangent tone to the volume. Yet if there is a certain amount of self-pity, there is something effectively human and communicative, for in the present situation do not most poets experience this sense of exile and this groping in the half-light for certainties? Much of his writing is mock serious, of course. He mocks himself as he remembers falling down the pub stairs (due to his defective sight) or acting like ''a balding, stout morose invigilator,'' and there is a satirical touch in his ''Interview with the Professor.'' But apart from such poems as ''The Rock Pool'' and ''For a Young Nun,'' the best things in the collection, and those that indicate a new development for Hobsbaum, are the fine monologues on Chopin and Newman, in which, turning his attention away from himself, he has a more balanced perspective and can define more clearly the predicaments of others.

In *Coming Out Fighting* Hobsbaum concentrates largely upon the personal situation. Linked together, the poems describe a married man's unsatisfactory love affair with a younger girl, his pain and disillusionment, the breakup of his marriage, and his reflections upon the girl's own marriage later. Despite the energy, humor, and immediacy of the poems, he seems able to write better when he can stand at a distance from the experience recorded, as in ''The Ice Skaters'':

> You
> Venture to catch them up, reach out, and
> Find yourself struggling in dirty water. Call,
>
> Ice in your mouth, spluttering blindly, down,
> Down into the mud, entangling with weed you go.
> Their laughter tinkles prettily over the ice.

Coming Out Fighting sets the scene for *Women and Animals,* which studies ''the nightmare of a divorce.''

—Howard Sergeant

HOFFMAN, Daniel (Gerard)

Nationality: American. **Born:** New York City, 3 April 1923. **Education:** Columbia University, New York, A.B. 1947 (Phi Beta Kappa), M.A. 1949, Ph.D. 1956. **Military Service:** U.S. Army Air Force, 1943–46: Legion of Merit. **Family:** Married Elizabeth McFarland in 1948; two children. **Career:** Instructor in English, Columbia University, 1952–56; visiting professor, University of Dijon, 1956–57; assistant professor, 1957–60, associate professor, 1960–65, and professor of English, 1965–66, Swarthmore College, Pennsylvania. Since 1966 professor of English, since 1978 poet-in-residence, Felix E. Schelling Professor of English, 1983–93, and since 1993 Felix E. Schelling Professor of English Emeritus, University of Pennsylvania, Philadelphia. Fellow of the School of Letters, Indiana University,

Bloomington, 1959; Elliston Lecturer, University of Cincinnati, 1964; lecturer, International School of Yeats Studies, Sligo, Ireland, 1965. Consultant in poetry, 1973–74, and honorary consultant in American letters, 1974–77, Library of Congress, Washington, D.C. Since 1988 poet in residence, Cathedral of St. John the Divine, New York. Visiting professor of English, King's College London, 1991–92. **Awards:** YMHA Introductions award, 1951; Yale Series of Younger Poets award, 1954; Ansley prize, 1957; American Council of Learned Societies fellowship, 1961–62, 1966–67; Columbia University Medal for Excellence, 1964; American Academy grant, 1967; Ingram Merrill Foundation grant, 1971; National Endowment for the Humanities fellowship, 1975–76; Hungarian P.E.N. Medal, 1980; Guggenheim fellowship, 1983; Hazlett memorial award, 1984; Paterson Poetry prize, 1989. Since 1972 chancellor, Academy of American Poets. **Address:** Department of English, University of Pennsylvania, Philadelphia, 19104, U.S.A.

PUBLICATIONS

Poetry

An Armada of Thirty Whales. New Haven, Connecticut, Yale University Press, 1954.
A Little Geste and Other Poems. New York and London, Oxford University Press, 1960.
The City of Satisfactions. New York and London, Oxford University Press, 1963.
Striking the Stones. New York and London, Oxford University Press, 1968.
Broken Laws. New York and London, Oxford University Press, 1970.
Corgi Modern Poets in Focus 4, with others, edited by Jeremy Robson. London, Corgi, 1971.
The Center of Attention. New York, Random House, 1974.
Able Was I Ere I Saw Elba: Selected Poems 1954–1974. London, Hutchinson, 1977.
Brotherly Love. New York, Random House, 1981.
Hang-Gliding from Helicon: New and Selected Poems 1948–1988. Baton Rouge, Louisiana State University Press, 1988.
Middens of the Tribe. Baton Rouge, Louisiana State University Press, 1995.

Other

Paul Bunyan: Last of the Frontier Demigods. Philadelphia, University of Pennsylvania Press-Temple University, 1952.
The Poetry of Stephen Crane. New York, Columbia University Press, 1957.
Form and Fable in American Fiction. New York and London, Oxford University Press, 1961.
Barbarous Knowledge: Myth in the Poetry of Yeats, Graves, and Muir. New York and London, Oxford University Press, 1967.
Poe Poe Poe Poe Poe Poe Poe. New York, Doubleday, 1972; London, Robson, 1973. "Poetry since 1945," in *Literary History of the United States,* revised edition, edited by R.E. Spiller and others. New York, Macmillan, 1974.
Others: Shock Troops of Stylistic Change (lecture). Philadelphia, University of Pennsylvania, 1975.
"Moonlight Dries No Mittens": Carl Sandburg Reconsidered. Washington, D.C., Library of Congress, 1979.

Faulkner's Country Matters: Folklore and Fable in Yoknapatawpha. Baton Rouge, Louisiana State University Press, 1989.
Words to Create a World: Interviews, Essays, and Reviews of Contemporary Poetry. Ann Arbor, University of Michigan Press, 1993.

Editor, *The Red Badge of Courage and Other Stories,* by Stephen Crane. New York, Harper, 1957.
Editor, *American Poetry and Poetics: Poems and Critical Documents from the Puritans to Robert Frost.* New York, Doubleday, 1962.
Editor, with Samuel Hynes, *English Literary Criticism: Romantic and Victorian.* New York, Appleton Century Crofts, 1963; London, Owen, 1966.
Editor, *New Poets 1970.* Philadelphia, University of Pennsylvania, 1970.
Editor, *University and College Prizes 1967–72.* New York, Academy of American Poets, 1974.
Editor, *Harvard Guide to Contemporary American Writing.* Cambridge, Massachusetts, Harvard University Press, 1979.
Editor, *Ezra Pound and William Carlos Williams: The University of Pennsylvania Conference Papers.* Philadelphia, University of Pennsylvania Press, 1983.

*

Bibliography: *Daniel Hoffman: A Comprehensive Bibliography* by Michael Lowe, Norwood, Pennsylvania, Norwood Editions, 1973.

Critical Studies: "Daniel Hoffman's Poetry of Affection" by William Sylvester, in *Voyages* (Washington, D.C.), Winter 1970; "Daniel Hoffman" by Jeremy Robson, in *Corgi Modern Poets in Focus 4,* 1971; interview with W.B. Patrick, in *Daniel Hoffman: A Comprehensive Bibliography,* 1973; "Another Country: The Poetry of Daniel Hoffman" by John Alexander Allen, in *Hollins Critic* (Hollins College, Virginia), October 1978; "An Interview with Daniel Hoffman" by Edward Hirsch, in *Shenandoah 32* (Lexington, Virginia), 4, 1981; "The Philadelphia Story" by James Finn Cotter, in *Hudson Review* (New York), Autumn 1981; "Using the Long Form" by Paul Mariani, in *Parnassus* (New York), Spring/Summer 1982; "The Objective Mode in Contemporary Lyric Poetry" by Peter Stitt, in *Georgia Review* (Athens), Summer 1982; "Hoffman's 'As I Was Going to St. Ives'" by Lewis Turco, in *Poesis* (Bryn Mawr, Pennsylvania), 1985; *"Hang-Gliding from Helicon"* by Leon V. Driskell, in *Magill's Literary Annual,* 1989; review by Ben Howard, in *Poetry* (Chicago), May 1989; "A Conversation with Daniel Hoffman" by Vincent Sherry, in *Boulevard,* Fall 1989; "A Poet's Quest: Daniel Hoffman's *Hang-Gliding from Helicon*" by J.P. White, in *Shenandoah* (Lexington, Virginia), 1990.

Daniel Hoffman comments:

I would want imagination to be free to tell the truths of feeling and to discover and reveal the shapes, the patterns, and purposes of life of which we are not aware. In a poem called "Essay on Style" I explore the innumerable possibilities for poetry and the poet's search for a fit style to express them. This is an alliterative abecedary. I will pick up a few lines from the letter *C,* in which the poet rejects cracked reproductions of chunks of the Chaos as though imitation Comprised creation . . . and the poem goes on to propose for the poet that his Destiny directs that he now Discover the drift of his difference. What in these Days of disjunction endures? A Diction to say Desire, dawn,

541

death, despair, descant . . . Devour, depart, dig, digress, discard and discord—Doggone, it is a domain here a man can or die in, go Daft with the delicacy and the daring, the Dazzle of dew in the darkness—let his Doodlings disclose new delights, for this dialect Defies desolation . . . That is what poetry ultimately gives us. It defies desolation. The world is always going to hell in a handbasket, but the poet's imagination, his vision, can find what holds "desire," "dawn," "death," "despair," and "descant" in one pattern, the articulation of which, if he is successful, will give delight.

And how to do this? You have to be open to all kinds of knowledge and experience; you have to sink an artesian well into your own consciousness to reach the depths of your being that are the heights of your being. Arriving at such a place, when I do, what I find speaks to the continuities of our experience, the recurrence of what is numinous at the center of life, as well as descriptions of the violence and sufferings we think peculiar to our time. If the resulting poems succeed in defying desolation, I hope they will give pleasure to others.

*   *   *

Daniel Hoffman's scansion is modern insofar as he frequently resorts to a shifting visual pattern of spacing, a line of varying length for rhetorical purposes of either reinforcement or of counterpoint. He both demonstrates and denotes his practice in the conclusion of *The Center of Attention:*

The Poem

Arriving at last,

It has stumbled across the harsh
Stones, the black marshes.

The appearance on the page is modern but actually evokes traditional rhythms. The first line has two unmistakably strong beats, and the isolation of the first line invites a pause, so that the first word of the next line cannot be slighted. The distinction between stressed and unstressed is sharp and consistent. Later on in the poem—"Carved on memory's staff / The legend is nearly decipherable"—one finds a line that echoes a trochaic and choriambic, followed by a line with three primary stresses and a secondary. His lines are like a steady shifting of traditional meters, but they never move into the cadences of unmistakable prose. His diction is consistently generic; he prefers to evoke a sense of swerving rather than the precisely classificatory hyperbole. The "stones" and "marshes" do not indicate a world out there, one to be photographed, but are emblematic of an inner struggle, the "harsh, black" struggle of writing. The legend, what is read, what is available to all, like a scroll or a saint's life, is "nearly decipherable," "casting its message / In a sort of singing." "A sort of" is used in the sense of "approximate," but the phrase also has the decipherably older meaning of "a particular kind," as when Swift writes about "a sort of jabber." Hoffman's use of rhyme, however sparing and occasional, however attenuated semantically or prosodically, brings him close to a tradition that bypasses Whitman and that assumes a correlation between literary and social decorum. In "The Sonnet" he contrasts his memory of Louise Bogan's faith in the sacredness of form to the formlessness of bearded youths and rumpled girls.

Hoffman's province is conservative, a poetry that indirectly evokes, without imitating them, the worlds of Yeats and Edwin Muir, a "sort of singing" to make older ways of feeling accessible today.

He is less interested in discovering new perceptions than in finding new ways of expressing feelings common to people now and in the past. He is chary of assuming a common knowledge and is sparing in specific literary references. When he quotes Mallarmé, "donner un sens plus pur aux mots de la tribu," the allusion to his own interest in Poe is decipherable, but the central meaning of the quotation expresses his own aim. (Actually his poetry should be seen as one aspect of his total literary production).

With Hoffman's concern for *bon sens,* his development has been a shift of emphasis rather than an experimentation with new assumptions. He has put successively rigorous restraints upon his lines. The title "City of Satisfactions" has ironic overtones, whereas the multiple meanings of "Broken Laws"—legal or natural identity papers or

The broken laws
Almost deciphered on
This air we breathe

—occurred in a collection that was considerably less ironic than its predecessors. Irony implies a commonly held set of social assumptions and has, perhaps, inevitably hierarchical implications of shared values. In the increasing pluralism of assumptions, Hoffman has brought the center of his attention to what can be shared. Each line has a sharply delimited focus, so that overtones emerge from the sequence of lines and from the sequence of poems.

Hoffman is capable of a wide range of tones: the "hang-gliding" of young people out in the sun and air and the classical "Helicon" of the study. The meditative mood of the poem "Himself" in *Hudson Review* ("The one most like himself is not this mirror's / Dishonest representation . . .") is sustained to the end:

The blessing given him at last

Across the alien years
Is that he now may judge his actions
By what that one most like himself would do

Whose ease with the world shames his unease,
Whose delight exceeds the joys he's known,
Whose gifts are greater than his own.

He is also capable of a certain playfulness, as the title of his 1977 book, *Able Was I Ere I Saw Elba,* suggests. The last, intense words of this book deserve particular attention because in one way or another Hoffman's poems move toward a coping with order/disorder, unease/delight, dishonesty/blessing, barbarousness/knowledge:

It's our life that's burning.
Is it ever too late to thrust
Ourselves into the ruins,
Into the tempering flame?

An awareness of living among ruins pervades Hoffman's 1995 *Middens of the Tribe,* a book-length poem evoking a range of people, rich, poor, old, young, men, women, a doctor, a stockbroker, the "magician" who "saws a woman in half," and the woman in the box who nearly gets nicked by the saw.

The poem has a "decorum" in the sense that the diction and lingo of an imagined speaker should be appropriate to the speaker's "place"—social, linguistic, geographical. Through allusiveness, irony,

542

paradox—tendencies with a faint and remote family resemblance to the New Criticism—the poem searches for place and through a fictive world attempts to probe our own. One needs the whole tribe but winds up alone on a private midden, a ''pit of manure'' or ''dunghill.''

A ''kitchen midden'' is the name for a pile of ancient refuse, shells, and bones produced by humans living in a literal kitchen—''Fact is, except for you calling on me here in the kitchen. / there's nobody in this house . . .''—or it may be a metaphorical kitchen midden of beautiful, expensive refuse:

> . . . marble columns, urns brought back from
> Italy, curtains and tapestries from France

The past seems to have more order:

> Characteristic of the Cromlech People
> is the evident arrangement of their tombs,
> the sons beside their fathers and grandfathers,
> each with tools in flint or bone of the same trade.
> We find no evidence of adolescent
> rebellion against the ascription of fixed
> roles

But passions are stronger than the pressures of the tribe:

> Their sexual pleasure releases them to
> the rejoicings spawned tadpoles stir in still ponds

The tension has no resolution, as the

> study of a culture at a distance
> must, so little known of its inner life, be
> fiction

We cannot help writing our own fiction, Hoffman implies, and will take the poem to our own purposes, as the last line indicates:

> look into my notes and write.

As the saying goes, ''any cock can crow on his own midden,'' so crow we must, as best we can, with whatever voice we have. Daniel Hoffman has many voices.

—William Sylvester

HOFMANN, Michael

Nationality: German. **Born:** Freiburg, 25 August 1957; immigrated to England in 1961. **Education:** Attended schools in Bristol, Edinburgh, and Winchester; Magdalene College, Cambridge, 1976–79, B.A. (honors) in English 1979; graduate study at University of Regensburg and Trinity College, Cambridge, 1980–83. **Career:** Since 1983 freelance writer, London. Since 1993 teacher in Creative Writing Department, University of Florida, Gainesville. Visiting associate professor, University of Michigan, Ann Arbor, fall 1994. **Awards:** Cholmondeley award, 1984; Faber memorial prize, 1988; Schlegel-Tieck prize, 1988, 1993; Foreign Fiction prize, *Independent,* 1995, for *The Film Explainer;* Arts Council bursary, 1997, for

Approximately Nowhere. **Address:** c/o Faber and Faber, 3 Queen Square, London WCIN 3AU, England.

PUBLICATIONS

Poetry

Nights in the Iron Hotel. London, Faber, 1983. Acrimony. London, Faber, 1986.
Acrimony. London, Faber, 1986.
K.S. in Lakeland: New and Selected Poems. New York, Ecco Press, 1990.
Corona, Corona. London, Faber, 1993.
Approximately Nowhere. London, Faber, 1999.

Plays

The Double-Bass, adaptation of a play by Patrick Süskind (produced London, 1989). London, Hamish Hamilton, 1987.
The Good Person of Sichuan, adaptation of a play by Bertolt Brecht (produced London, 1989). London, Methuen. 1989.

Other

Editor, with James Lasdun, *After Ovid: New Metamorphoses.* London, Faber, 1994; New York, Farrar, Straus, 1995.

Translator, *Castle Gripsholm,* by Kurt Tucholsky. London, Chatto and Windus, 1985; New York, Overlook Press, 1988.
Translator, *Blösch,* by Beat Sterchi. London, Faber, 1988; as *Cow,* New York, Pantheon, 1990.
Translator, with Christopher Middleton, *Balzac's Horse and Other Stories,* by Gert Hofmann. New York, From 1988; London, Secker and Warburg, 1989.
Translator, *The Legend of the Holy Drinker,* by Joseph Roth. London, Chatto and Windus, 1989; New York, Overlook Press, 1990.
Translator, with Shaun Whiteside, *Emotion Pictures: Reflections on the Cinema,* by Wim Wenders. London, Faber, 1990.
Translator, *The Logic of Images,* by Wim Wenders. London, Faber, 1991.
Translator, *Right and Left,* by Joseph Roth. London, Chatto and Windus, 1992.
Translator, *The Story of Mr. Sommer,* by Patrick Suskind. London, Bloomsbury, 1992.
Translator, *Death in Rome,* by Wolfgang Koeppen. London and New York, Penguin, 1993.
Translator, *The Film Explainer,* by Gert Hofmann. London, Secker & Warburg, 1994.
Translator, *The Lord Chandos Letter,* by Hugo von Hofmannsthol. New York, Penguin, 1995.
Translator, *The Man Who Disappeared (Amerika),* by Franz Kafka. London, Penguin, 1996.
Translator, *The Land of Green Plums: A Novel,* by Herta Müller. New York, Holt/Metropolitan, 1996.
Translator, *The Act of Seeing,* by Wim Wenders. London, Faber, 1997.
Translator, *The Tale of the 1002nd Night,* by Joseph Roth. New York, Picador, 1998.

Translator, *The String of Pearls,* by Joseph Roth. London, Granta, 1998.

Translator, *Rebellion,* by Joseph Roth. New York, St. Martin's Press, 1999.

*

Critical Studies: Chapter on Hofmann in *Instabilities in Contemporary British Poetry,* by Alan Robinson, London, Macmillan, 1989; *Robin Robertson, Michael Hofmann, Michael Longley,* London and New York, Penguin, 1998.

* * *

In "Withdrawn from Circulation," from *Acrimony,* Michael Hofmann says of a past self, "Nothing quite touched me." The flip, restless detachment is typical of his poetry's original dealings with personal identity. Hofmann frequently occupies and yet undercuts the privileged position offered by the word "I." "Withdrawn from Circulation" sees how conditioned a supposedly unitary self was: "the slick, witless phrases I used about girls / were a mixture of my father's and those I remembered // from *Mädchen* or *Bravo.*" In this poem, as in others, Hofmann's deadpan fooling with the inanimate hints at a larger dislocation. The poem brings the lyric "I" and the mess of history into a connection that is unnervingly (and in this case literally) contingent:

> A few doors down
> was the cellar where the RAF kept the Berlin Senator
> they had kidnapped and were holding to ransom.

Casual yet tense, close to the movement of prose but not without a certain frayed music, the lines illustrate the distinctiveness of Hofmann's poetic voice.

At the heart of Hofmann's already impressive achievement lies his management of detail, rhythm, and tone. His first collection, *Nights in the Iron Hotel,* shows a poet alert to the otherness of others. "You move the fifty-seven muscles it takes to smile. / It's strange to see you again," he writes in "First Night." The opening line makes strange a familiar action, but the second expresses a feeling of strangeness in a familiar way. The juxtaposition is sharp and troubling, the poem refusing to let itself or its reader settle. In "White Noise" the poet's awareness of his fellow lodger's routines and isolation is expressed with laconic brio:

> . . . Trailing cigarette smoke and suspicion,
> you prowl through the house, accident-prone
> and painfully thin in your sepulchral clothes.
> Reality filters through your tinted spectacles.

The opening suspension points are a signature of Hofmann's, implying trailings off, new starts, changed angles. Judgment, the lines suggest, would be impertinent, involvement impossible, for to render the "reality" of the "you," whose existence consists of fearing reality, demands that the poet observe. But observation in Hofmann is not afraid of metaphoric verve, and the poem ends with the "you" described as "delirious, trembling, / a pile of leaves." These phrases are suggestively anticipated by the opening line and a half of "Myopia in Rupert Brooke Country," the collection's preceding piece: "Birds, feathers, a few leaves, flakes of soot— / things start to

fall." This poem handles its ironies about England in the 1980s lightly and questioningly:

> A hot-air balloon sinks towards the horizon—
> the amateur spirit or an advertising gimmick?

Hofmann's poetry is highly politicized, yet it does not express opinions so much as attend to the signs through which a culture expresses (or disguises) itself. "Shapes of Things" avoids exhortation or protest. Such impulses are potent absences in what ends up as an impassively offbeat footnote to the fact that "we are living in the long shadow of the Bomb."

Acrimony, Hofmann's second collection, is among the most significant volumes to have been published by a contemporary poet writing in English. The collection is divided into two halves. The first consists of poems that often deal with being, as one title has it, "On the Margins." Some explore issues of gender, and others move between related, if apparently separated, worlds. "Aerial Perspective" half recalls the Auden of the hawk's or the helmeted airman's vision as it focuses on places "where the picturesque collides with the strategically / important." But the poem's air of aloof authority is undercut by its feeling for the vulnerability of "us blips" observed by "the big AWACS aircraft." Emotional difficulties and political tensions rub shoulders in "Impotence." Two of the most striking poems in this section are "From Kensal Rise to Heaven," which records with teasing inventiveness signs of "change and decay" in contemporary London, and "Albion Market," whose appositional details compose a picture of England that crackles with level-toned, satiric disgust.

The book's second section shows Hofmann on territory more familiar in British poetry—the domestic. But few poems about families have the ruthless perceptiveness or feeling for wider implications of Hofmann's poems about his relationship with his father, the writer Gert Hofmann. For all its greater intimacy, the second section shares with the first a concern with patriarchy, authority, the construction of masculinity. In "Day of Reckoning," for example, Hofmann notes that "I kept a tough diary, owned a blunt knife, / and my mother sat in the back with the girls." What makes the poems impressive is their verbal precision and their emotional range; they include and link feelings of accusation, rage, insecurity, physical disgust, frustrated love, and not wholly stifled admiration with the respect of one professional for another. The sustained, unrhymed, long-lined couplets of "Author, Author," for example, drive toward a conclusion that achieves cathartic release in the act of denying the possibility of "consummation":

> I ask myself what sort of consummation is available?
> Fight; talk literature and politics; get drunk together?
>
> Kiss him goodnight, as though half my life had never
> happened?

Hofmann's collection *K.S. in Lakeland: New and Selected Poems* introduced his work to an American audience. The volume draws together poems from his first two volumes and includes work previously uncollected. The new poems are crisp and deft, and the book is cannily organized. In the first part, for instance, which is largely made up of analyses of love or "unlove," "Nights in the Iron Hotel" (originally in the poet's first collection) is followed by "Between Bed and Wastepaper Basket" (originally in his second).

The literal and emotional territory they occupy is similar yet not the same, the first poem fascinated by "anaesthesia," the second inching its way to a minimal staving off of "failure": "We failed to betray / whatever trust was placed in us."

The second part consists of more political pieces. Among the new poems "Summer '87," a coded account of the aftermath of Chernobyl, is especially striking; the lines "Every Friday, the newspapers gave fresh readings, / and put Turkish hazelnuts on the index" show the poet's observant eye and sardonic humor. The third part incorporates the "father" poems from *Acrimony*. Another new poem, "The Late Richard Dadd, 1817–1886," about the "fairy-painter, father-slayer," supplies a wry coda to the intensities of "Author, Author." In the fourth part "the autobiography draws out, lengthens / towards the end" ("By Forced Marches"), and the concern with ends—personal and cultural—finds elegiac expression in what is possibly the best of the book's new poems, "A Minute's Silence." This piece, written in memory of Michael Heffernan, reveals how well Hofmann's manner can adapt itself to the articulation of straightforward feeling, not that the poem sacrifices a jot of the poet's typically angular self-awareness, which is used here to convey a previous absence of awareness:

I'm sitting coiled over my letter of condolence,
head down, left elbow out, the verbs tramping stiffly
into the furthest corners of mood and tense, closed
conditionals, Latin and peculiar pluperfects,
like Hofmannsthal's . . . . "I had had no idea . . . ."

Many of the new poems in *K.S. in Lakeland* appear in Hofmann's later collection *Corona, Corona*. This volume is marked by great rhetorical assurance, the phrasing often possessing "an air / of having been given a spin" ("Kurt Schwitters in Lakeland"). The linguistic freshness covertly celebrated here runs through the book, forming a zestful counterpoint to Hofmann's penchant for ironies and deflations as he plays the private against the public. One example is the opening of "'50s Cuba": "It was the farcical fast fast slow world / of dancing, miscegenation and cigars." Another is the close of "On the Beach at Thorpeness":

Roaring waves of fighters headed back to Bentwaters.
The tide advanced in blunt codshead curves,
ebbed through the chattering teeth of the pebbles.
Jaw jaw. War war.

In the final line "chattering" speech sardonically glimpses an undesirable alternative.

Although the poems overlapping with *K.S. in Lakeland* may be the best things in *Corona, Corona*, the whole volume is a confident restatement and development of Hofmann's themes and styles. Among the most fascinating new poems are the final section's responses to Mexico. Hofmann deftly avoids the temptation to show us his holiday snapshots, though occasionally he is too content with a syntax of deadpan enumeration. In "Aerogrammes, 1–5" and "Guanajuato Two Times" the poet comes at an old sense of estrangement with a new power of invention. In the latter poem repetition as a stylistic device is Hofmann's means of exploring repetition as a seemingly possible and yet finally impossible imaginative state: "I could stand and sway like a palm, / or rooted like a companile, crumbling slightly / each time the bells tolled, not real bells / but recordings of former bells / and never for me."

The best poems in Hofmann's next volume, *Approximately Nowhere*, are elegies for the poet's father and tense celebrations of a new relationship, and the dominant technique is that of the adroitly handled list, which is ideally suited to associative swirls of memory and to stabs of observation. Such stabs have as their target less the symptoms of late capitalist England, as in Hofmann's earlier poems, than the poet's own newly exposed and self-lacerated heart. In "For Gert Hofmann, Died 1 July 1993," the poet's eye touchingly notes "the blinds at half-mast" and "my father / for once not at his post," where the fact of death is negotiated by the line ending. When elsewhere he notes "the alarmingly long screws" taken from the coffin by an undertaker, his jokiness ("as though someone would try very hard / to get out or—you would have said—in") is offbeat and yet unexpectedly warm in its evident affection for the now dead father.

The volume contrives to be at once confessional and detached in its account of the poet's private life. The poem "Fucking" describes and provides a motive for this complicated emotional balancing act, which takes on physical form in the poem's conclusion as the lovers become "a seesaw at rest":

A zero sum game, our extravagant happiness,
matched or cancelled
by the equal and opposite unhappiness of others.

The poetry works by finding a language adequate to "a zero sum game." The balance tips in favor of "extravagant happiness" in the final poem, where the volume's characteristic listing turns into a "litany." Throughout the collection Hofmann quietly challenges himself and his readers as, with an artistry so understated that it becomes almost exhibitionist, he persuades us to experience with him category-defying states of feeling.

—Michael O'Neill

HOLBROOK, David (Kenneth)

Nationality: British. **Born:** Norwich, Norfolk, 9 January 1923. **Education:** Colman Road Primary School; City of Norwich School; Downing College, Cambridge (Exhibitioner), 1941–42, 1945–47, B.A. 1946. **Military Service:** Tank Troop Officer, and Explosives and Intelligence Officer, in the East Riding of Yorkshire Yeomanry, 1942–45: Lieutenant. **Family:** Married Margot Davies-Jones in 1949; two sons and two daughters. **Career:** Assistant editor, *Our Time* magazine, London, 1947–48; assistant editor, Bureau of Current Affairs, London, 1948–51; tutor organizer, Workers' Educational Association, 1952–53; tutor and teacher, 1953–61: at Bassingbourn Village College, Cambridgeshire, 1954–61; fellow, King's College, Cambridge, 1961–65; college lecturer in English, Jesus College, Cambridge, 1968–70; Compton Poetry Lecturer, University of Hull, 1969 (resigned); writer-in-residence, Dartington Hall, Devon (Elmgrant Trust grant), 1970–72. Assistant director of studies, 1973–75, fellow and director of English studies, 1981–88, and since 1988 emeritus fellow, Downing College, Cambridge. British Council Lecturer in Germany, 1969, and grantee in Australia, 1970; Hooker Visiting Professor, McMaster University, Hamilton, Ontario, 1984. Former president, Forum for the Advancement of Educational Therapy. Cofounder, *Use of English* magazine, 1948; member of the editorial board, *New Universities Quarterly,* 1976–86. **Awards:** King's College and Cambridge University Press grant, 1961; Leverhulme fellowship, 1964–65 and 1988–90; Arts Council grant, 1970, 1976, 1979; World Education fellowship prize, 1976. **Address:** c/o Downing College, Cambridge CB2 1DQ, England.

PUBLICATIONS

Poetry

Imaginings. London, Putnam, 1961.
Against the Cruel Frost. London, Putnam, 1963.
Penguin Modern Poets 4, with Christopher Middleton and David Wevill. London, Penguin, 1963.
Object Relations. London, Methuen, 1967.
Old World, New World. London, Rapp and Whiting, 1969.
Moments in Italy: Poems and Sketches. Richmond, Surrey, Keepsake Press, 1976.
Chance of a Lifetime. London, Anvil Press Poetry, 1978.
Selected Poems 1961–1978. London, Anvil Press Poetry, 1980.
Bringing Everything Home. Hull, Yorks, Halfacrown Press, 1999.

Plays (operas for children)

The Borderline, music by Wilfrid Mellers (produced London, 1959).
The Quarry, music by John Joubert. London, Novello, 1967.
The Wild Swans, music by John Paynter (produced Cambridge, 1979).

Novels

Flesh Wounds. London, Methuen, 1966.
A Play of Passion. London, W.H. Allen, 1978.
Nothing Larger than Life. London, Hale, 1987.
Worlds Apart. London, Hale, 1988.
A Little Athens. London, Hale, 1990.
Jennifer. London, Hale, 1990.
The Gold in Father's Heart. London, Hale, 1992.
Even If They Fail. London, Martin Breese, 1994.
Getting It Wrong with Uncle Tom. Norwich, Mousehold Press, 1998.

Short Stories

Lights in the Sky Country. London, Putnam, 1962.

Other

English for Maturity. London, Cambridge University Press, 1961.
Llareggub Revisited (on Dylan Thomas). London, Bowes and Bowes, 1962; as *Dylan Thomas and Poetic Dissociation,* Carbondale, Southern Illinois University Press, 1964.
The Secret Places: Essays on Imaginative Work in English Teaching and on the Culture of the Child. London, Methuen, 1964.
English for the Rejected. London, Cambridge University Press, 1964.
The Quest for Love. London, Methuen, 1964.
The Flowers Shake Themselves Free (songs set by Wilfrid Mellers). London, Novello, 1966.
The Exploring Word. London, Cambridge University Press, 1967.

Human Hope and the Death Instinct. Oxford, Pergamon Press, 1971.
Sex and Dehumanisation in Art, Thought and Life in Our Time. London, Pitman, 1972.
The Masks of Hate: The Problem of False Solutions in the Culture of an Acquisitive Society. Oxford, Pergamon Press, 1972.
Dylan Thomas and the Code of Night. London, Athlone Press, 1972.
The Pseudo-Revolution: A Critical Study of Extremist "Liberation" in Sex. London, Stacey, 1972.
English in Australia Now. London, Cambridge University Press, 1972.
Changing Attitudes to the Nature of Man: A Working Bibliography. Hatfield, Hertfordshire, Hertis, 1973.
Gustav Mahler and the Courage to Be. London, Vision Press, 1975; New York, Da Capo Press, 1982.
Sylvia Plath: Poetry and Existence. London, Athlone Press, 1976.
Lost Bearings in English Poetry. London, Vision Press, and New York, Barnes and Noble, 1977.
Education, Nihilism, and Survival. London, Darton Longman and Todd, 1977; Greenwood, South Carolina, Attic Press, 1978.
English for Meaning. Windsor, NFER, 1980.
John Newton, Blasphemy, and Poetic Taste. Retford, Brynmill, 1984.
Education and Philosophical Anthropology. Cranbury, New Jersey, Associated University Presses, 1987.
Evolution and the Humanities. Aldershot, Hampshire, Gower Press, 1987.
The Novel and Authenticity. London, Vision Press, 1987.
Further Studies in Philosophical Anthropology. Aldershot, Hampshire, Gower Press, 1988.
Images of Woman in Literature. New York, New York University Press, 1990.
The Skeleton in the Wardrobe. Cranbury, New Jersey, Associated University Presses, 1990.
Charles Dickens and Woman. London, Vision Press, 1990.
Wuthering Heights: Far Beyond Realism. London, Vision Press, 1990.
What Is It To Be Human? Aldershot, Hampshire, Gower Press, 1990.
Edith Wharton and the Unsatisfactory Man. London, Vision Press, 1991.
Where D. H. Lawrence Was Wrong About Woman. Cranbury, New Jersey, Associated University Presses, 1992.
Charles Dickens and the Image of Woman. New York, New York University Press, 1993.
Creativity and Popular Culture. Cranbury, New Jersey, Associated University Presses, 1994.
Tolstoy, Woman and Death. Cranbury, New Jersey, Associated University Presses, 1997.
Geroge MacDonald and the Phantom Woman. Lampeter, Wales, Edwin Mellen Press, 2000.

Editor, *Children's Games.* Bedford, Gordon Fraser, 1957.
Editor, *Iron Honey Gold* (anthology of verse). London, Cambridge University Press, 1961.
Editor, *People and Diamonds* (anthology of stories). London, Cambridge University Press, 1962.
Editor, *Thieves and Angels* (anthology of drama). London, Cambridge University Press, 1963.
Editor, *Visions of Life* (anthology of prose). London, Cambridge University Press, 1964.
Editor, with Elizabeth Poston, *The Cambridge Hymnal.* London, Cambridge University Press, 1967.

Editor, *Children's Writing.* London, Cambridge University Press, 1967.

Editor, *Plucking the Rushes* (anthology of Chinese poetry). London, Heinemann, 1968.

Editor, *I've Got to Use Words* (course for less-abled children). London, Cambridge University Press, 1969.

Editor, *The Case Against Pornography.* London, Stacey, 1972.

Editor, with Christine Mackenzie, *The Honey of Man.* Melbourne, Nelson, 1973.

Editor, with Elizabeth Poston, *The Apple Tree.* Cambridge, Cambridge University Press, 1976.

*

Critical Studies: *Toward a Moral Approach to English: A Study of the Writings of F.R. Leavis and David Holbrook* by Gordon Pradl (unpublished dissertation), Harvard University, Cambridge, Massachusetts, 1971; "Philosophical Anthropology: Two Views of Recent Work by David Holbrook," in *Human World* (Swansea), May 1973; "David Holbrook's Humanities" by Roger Poole, in *Books and Bookmen* (London), September 1973, Martin Hayden and Duke Maskell, in *Haltwhistle Quarterly,* spring 1979; "Broad Wisdom of 'Being There'" by David Hamilton Eddy, in *The Times Higher Educational Supplement,* 30 April 1993; *The Educational Imperative* by Peter Abbs. London, Falmer Press, 1994; *Powers of Being: The Work of David Holbrook,* edited by Edwin Webb, Cranbury, New Jersey, Associated University Presses, 1995.

David Holbrook comments:

A few people have seen that all my work is of a piece—Dr. Gordon Pradl, for instance, in his dissertation at Harvard (1971). In my poetry and prose fiction I am trying to find what meaning there might be in normal, everyday existence—assuming that it should be possible, there, to find a sense of having existed meaningfully. I have kept deliberately to domestic, quotidian living, searching for significance in that, since I believe we are doomed if we cannot. In my books for teachers and my anthologies I have tried to encourage those in education to cherish creativity in children, in the sense of helping to explore their existence as beings through symbolism.

To this exploration of authenticity, searching for what Maslow calls "peak-moments" in ordinary life, the hollow postures of hate are the greatest enemy. I have therefore tried to diagnose the schizoid trends in contemporary culture to show that they are false and a bluff, from James Bond myths to the literature of mental rage and pornography. At the same time I have tried to show how genuine artists may be engaged with being and problems of identity and of not knowing where to find a sense of the meaning in life, namely Dylan Thomas, Sylvia Plath, and Gustav Mahler. In doing so I have come to find the prevalent "model" of man unsatisfactory, the belief of those from Freud to Lorenz who seem to think instincts of aggression and sex are primary. I believe that culture and symbolism are man's primary needs, and I am trying to apply this view in educational books, in criticism, and in my own writing. This revolution in thought about man I believe to be part of a widespread change encompassing psychoanalysis, phenomenology, post-Kantian philosophy, and philosophical anthropology. I find more interest in this revolution in Europe and America, while at home in England the educated minority have betrayed "the people" into a new barbarism which is destroying values and making a more creative future impossible. Intellectuals slavishly follow the falsities of commercial promotion, the superficial sensationalism of "pop" and television, and proclaim their right to indulge in pornography and other vices. The onslaught of this new barbarism will make all our efforts toward a more creative education, toward new and more visionary works of the imagination, and even toward good community life futile unless there is a change of heart. But meanwhile, all one can do is to go on as best one can, in creative writing and teaching, while trying to discriminate against the culture of hate.

*   *   *

The subject matter of David Holbrook's poetry is, for the most part, domestic, personal, and everyday; it is of the "real world," of which he is an advocate in so much of his critical and educational writing. The poetry is of a world that is explored with feeling and compassion and from which morals are drawn or implied. If the poetry is not directly didactic, there is usually an undertow of didacticism detectable. His poetry can be personal to the point of being candid. Thus, in the poem "To His Wife Going to Bed" (the title itself is point enough) it is gooseflesh that is exposed "drawing your petticoat off—showing your husband what he after clings to in bed." Mind you, it is gooseflesh transfigured by being "like wind-touched-on-water." Sometimes the poems are personal to the point of embarrassment, as when in "Fingers in the Door" the poet's emotion on seeing the pain caused by closing his child's fingers in a doorjamb makes him wish "myself dispersed in hundred thousand pieces" when it was "for her I cast seed into her mother's womb."

But it is this sympathy for the pain and distress of others, and the ability to express it, that informs Holbrook's best poems. In "Unholy Marriage," a poem about the death of a young passenger on a motorcycle who lies "anointed only by the punctured oil" while her parents wait worrying because "she's late tonight," the simple, unemphasized ending—"Some news? They hear the gate / A man comes: not the best"—gives strength to the direct emotion of what has gone before.

The language employed in most of Holbrook's poems is straightforward and unadorned: "This is the sort of evening on which to write a poem." It is a reaction, one imagines, against the verbosity of the 1940s, which he castigates in his critical works. Sometimes, however, when combined with the long, freely written lines he employs, the poetry tends toward a looseness of form that can compromise the strength of the feelings expressed. If there is a weakness in his verse, it is this, along with the influence of a romanticism deriving from what would seem to be an idiosyncratic interpretation of the work of D.H. Lawrence and other literary heroes. The strength of his verse is its obvious and direct honesty, despite the pitfalls of naïveté into which it sometimes leads him.

—John Cotton

HOLLANDER, John

Nationality: American. **Born:** New York City, 28 October 1929. **Education:** Columbia University, New York, A.B. 1950 (Phi Beta Kappa), M.A. 1952; Indiana University, Bloomington, Ph.D. 1959. **Family:** Married 1) Anne Loesser in 1953 (divorced 1977), two daughters; 2) Natalie Charkow in 1981. **Career:** Junior fellow,

Society of Fellows, Harvard University, Cambridge, Massachusetts, 1954–57; lecturer, Connecticut College, New London, 1957–59; instructor, 1959–61, assistant professor, 1961–64, and associate professor of English, 1964–66, Yale University, New Haven, Connecticut; professor of English, Hunter College, City University of New York, 1966–77. Professor of English, 1977–86, since 1986 A. Bartlett Giamatti Professor of English, and since 1995 Sterling Professor, Yale University. Gauss Lecturer, Princeton University, New Jersey, 1962, 1965; visiting professor, Indiana University, 1964; lecturer, Salzburg Seminar in American Studies, 1965; Overseas Fellow, Churchill College, Cambridge, 1967–68. Since 1977 fellow, Ezra Stiles College, Yale University. Member of the poetry board, Wesleyan University Press, 1959–62; editorial assistant for poetry, *Partisan Review,* New Brunswick, New Jersey, 1959–65; contributing editor, *Harper's* magazine, New York, 1969–71. **Awards:** Yale Series of Younger Poets award, 1958; American Academy grant, 1963; National Endowment for the Arts fellowship, 1973; Levinson prize (*Poetry,* Chicago), 1974; Guggenheim fellowship, 1979; Modern Language Association Shaughnessy medal, 1982; Bolingen prize, 1983; MacArthur Foundation fellow, 1990–95; Melville Cane award, 1990; Ambassador Book award, 1994; Governor's Arts award, State of Connecticut, 1997; Robert Penn Warren-Cleanth Brooks award, 1998. D. Litt.: Marietta College, Ohio, 1982; D.H.L.:Indiana University, 1990; D.F.A.: Maine College of Art, 1993. **Member:** Chancellor, Academy of American Poets; American Academy of Arts and Letters; American Academy of Arts and Sciences. **Address:** Department of English, Box 208302, Yale University, New Haven, Connecticut 06520–8302, U.S.A.

PUBLICATIONS

Poetry

A Crackling of Thorns. New Haven, Connecticut, Yale University Press, 1958.
Movie-Going and Other Poems. New York, Atheneum, 1962.
A Beach Vision. Privately printed, 1962.
A Book of Various Owls (for children). New York, Norton, 1963.
Visions from the Ramble. New York, Atheneum, 1965.
The Quest of the Gole (for children). New York, Atheneum, 1966.
Philomel. London, Turret, 1968.
Types of Shape. New York, Atheneum, 1969.
The Night Mirror. New York, Atheneum, 1971.
Town and Country Matters: Erotica and Satirica. Boston, Godine, 1972.
Selected Poems. London, Secker and Warburg, 1972.
The Head of the Bed. Boston, Godine, 1974.
Tales Told of the Fathers. New York, Atheneum, 1975.
Reflections on Espionage: The Question of Cupcake. New York, Atheneum, 1976.
Spectral Emanations: New and Selected Poems. New York, Atheneum, 1978.
In Place. Omaha, Abattoir, 1978.
Blue Wine and Other Poems. Baltimore, Maryland, Johns Hopkins University Press, 1979.
Looking Ahead. New York, Nadja, 1982.
Powers of Thirteen. New York, Atheneum, 1983; London, Secker and Warburg, 1984.
A Hollander Garland. Newton, Iowa, Tamazunchale Press, 1985.

In Time and Place. Baltimore, Maryland, Johns Hopkins University Press, 1986.
Some Fugitives Take Cover. New York, Sea Cliff, 1988.
Harp Lake. New York, Knopf, 1988.
Tesserae. New York, Knopf, 1993.
Selected Poetry. New York, Knopf, 1993.
The Gazer's Spirit: Poems Speaking to Silent Works of Art. Chicago, University of Chicago Press, 1995.
Figurehead & Other Poems. New York, Knopf, 1999.

Play

An Entertainment for Elizabeth, Being a Masque of the Seven Motions; or, Terpsichore Unchained (produced New York, 1969). Published in *English Renaissance Monographs 1* (Amherst, Massachusetts), 1972.

Other

The Untuning of the Sky: Ideas of Music in English Poetry 1500–1700. Princeton, New Jersey, Princeton University Press, 1961.
Images of Voice: Music and Sound in Romantic Poetry. Cambridge, Heffer, and New York, Chelsea House, 1970.
The Immense Parade on Supererogation Day (for children). New York, Atheneum, 1972.
Vision and Resonance: Two Senses of Poetic Form. New York and London, Oxford University Press, 1975; revised edition, New Haven, Connecticut, Yale University Press, 1985.
Rhyme's Reason: A Guide to English Verse. New Haven, Connecticut, Yale University Press, 1981; revised edition, 1989.
The Figure of Echo: A Mode of Allusion in Milton and After. Berkeley, University of California Press, 1981.
Dal Vero, with Saul Steinberg. New York, Whitney Museum of Art, 1983.
Melodious Guile: Fictive Pattern in Poetic Language. New Haven, Connecticut, Yale University Press, 1988.
The Work of Poetry. New York, Columbia University Press, 1997.
The Poetry of Everyday Life. Ann Arbor, University of Michigan Press, 1998.

Editor, *Selected Poems,* by Ben Jonson. New York, Dell, 1961.
Editor, with Harold Bloom, *The Wind and the Rain: An Anthology of Poems for Young People.* New York, Doubleday, 1961.
Editor, with Anthony Hecht, *Jiggery-Pokery: A Compendium of Double Dactyls.* New York, Atheneum, 1967.
Editor, *Poems of Our Moment.* New York, Pegasus, 1968.
Editor, *Modern Poetry: Essays in Criticism.* London, Oxford University Press, 1968.
Editor, *American Short Stories since 1945.* New York, Harper, 1968.
Editor, with others, *The Oxford Anthology of English Literature.* New York and London, Oxford University Press, 2 vols., 1973.
Editor, with Reuben Brower and Helen Vendler, *I.A. Richards: Essays in His Honor.* New York, Oxford University Press, 1973.
Editor, with Irving Howe and David Bromwich, *Literature as Experience.* New York, Harcourt Brace, 1979.
Editor, *Poetics of Influence,* by Harold Bloom. New Haven, Connecticut, Schwab, 1988.
Editor, *The Essential Rossetti.* New York, Ecco Press, 1990.
Editor, *Edgar Lee Masters, Spoon River Anthology.* New York, Signet, 1992.

Editor, *Animal Poems.* New York, Knopf, 1994.

Editor, *Committed to Memory: 100 Best Poems to Memorize.* New York, Academy of American Poets, 1996.

Editor, *Garden Poems.* New York, Knopf, 1996.

Editor, *Frost,* by Robert Frost. New York, Knopf, 1997.

Editor, *Marriage Poems.* New York, Knopf, 1997.

Editor, with Eric L. Haralson, *Encyclopedia of American Poetry. The Nineteenth Century.* Chicago, Fitzroy Dearborn, 1998.

Editor, with David Lehman, *The Best American Poetry, 1998.* New York, Scribner, 1998.

Editor, *War Poems.* London, Everyman's Library, 1999.

Editor, with J.D. McClatchy, *Christmas Poems.* New York, Knopf, 1999.

*

Manuscript Collections: Beinecke Library, Yale University, New Haven, Connecticut; Lockwood Memorial Library, State University of New York, Buffalo.

Critical Studies: *Alone with America* by Richard Howard, New York, Atheneum, 1969, London, Thames and Hudson, 1970, revised edition, Atheneum, 1980; "The Poem As Silhouette: A Conversation with John Hollander" by Philip L. Gerber and Robert J. Gemmett, in *Michigan Quarterly Review* (Ann Arbor), vol. 9, 1970; "The Sorrows of American Jewish Poetry," in *Commentary* (New York), March 1972, *Figures of Capable Imagination,* New York, Seabury Press, 1976, and "The White Light of Trope," in *Kenyon Review* (Gambier, Ohio), new series 1, 1979, all by Harold Bloom; "'I Carmina Figurata' di John Hollander" by Cristina Giorcelli, in *Scritti in Ricordo di Gabriele Baldini,* Rome, Edizione di Storia e Letteratura, 1972; "Some American Masks" by David Bromwich, in *Dissent* (New York), winter 1973; interview with Richard Jackson, in *The Poetry Miscellany 8* (Chattanooga), 1978; "Speaking of Hollander," in *American Poetry Review* (Philadelphia), September-October 1982, and "John Hollander's *In Time and Place,*" in *White Paper,* New York, Columbia University Press, 1989, both by J.D. McClatchy; "Virtuosity and Virtue: A Profile of John Hollander" by David Lehman, in *Columbia College Today* (New York), spring 1983; "God's Spies" by Alfred Corn, in *The Metamorphoses of Metaphor,* New York, Viking, 1987; Chapter 5 of *Fallen from the Symboled World,* by Wyatt Prunty, Oxford and New York, Oxford University Press, 1990; "'The Old Refrains All Come Down to This': Dorenlot in the Pastourelle XLVIII of the Chansonnier U and Hollander's 'Notes on the Refrain'" by Anna Roberts, in *RLA* (West Lafayette, Indiana), 7, 1995; "Working through Poems" by Langdon Hammer, in *Southwest Review* (Dallas), 80(4), autumn 1995; "On John Hollander's 'Owl'" by Eleanor Cook, in *Philosophy and Literature* (Baltimore, Maryland), 20(1), April 1996; "The Dream of the Trumpeter" by the author, in *Night Errands: How Poets Use Dreams,* edited by Roderick Townley, Pittsburgh, Pennsylvania, University of Pittsburgh Press, 1998.

*   *   *

John Hollander is perhaps the most consummately sophisticated poet currently writing in English. His command of traditional forms and meters seems total (a command well evidenced in the delightful example of his *Rhyme's Reason,* simultaneously in and about a great range of verse forms), and he has invented a number of intriguing new forms. His erudition and his wit have raised allusion and imitation to new heights. He is, in short, a virtuoso.

It is perhaps not surprising that in much of Hollander's earliest work, and even occasionally in his mature work, this virtuoso facility should appear to be an end in itself. Even then the results can be immensely entertaining, as in the Dick Dongworth poems of "Fragments of a Picaresque Romance":

> Say that she was never brave
> But only greedy for the grave;
> Say Dongworth's rusty armor
> Served only to alarm her,
> Then write this of me:
> "Were she alive and free,
>   With lips like wine,
> John Thomas, my English cousin,
> Could pluck her like a raisin."
>   Waly O for Roseblush
> That she was never mine.

Gradually, however, Hollander's relation to the traditions of poetry and his use of that tradition's resources have deepened beyond parody and pastiche, and the poetry itself, while never forfeiting Hollander's individual sense of humor, has grown able to carry a far greater charge of emotion.

Hollander's mature work weds virtuosity and formal invention to philosophical wit and emotional gravity. Many of the resulting poems are dense and demanding (Richmond Lattimore has justly spoken of the frequent experience of "pleased incomprehension" in reading Hollander) but ceaselessly stimulating. *The Head of the Bed,* for instance, is a complex sequence involving a highly personal use of Hebraic myth in a visionary exploration of nightmare through a chiaroscuro of light and dark, and it is richly symbolic and provocative. Hollander's work is not always difficult of approach, though, and a doubtful reader might try the sequence "In Time" from *In Time and Place.*

Hollander's work is too various for a brief essay such as this to do anything more than point to a few areas of achievement and interest. He has written some lyrics of a neoclassical grace that would have been admired in the seventeenth century, as in "Last Echo" from *Blue Wine and Other Poems:*

> Echo has the last word,
> But she loses the rest,
> Giving in to silence
> After too little time.
> And, after all, what is
> A last word, then? After
> All the truth has been told—
> No more than a cold rhyme.

He has written poems as epistemologically teasing as Stevens (e.g., "Blue Wine," "The Altarpiece Finished"). In *Town and Country Matters* (its titular allusions to Juvenal and to *Hamlet* are entirely characteristic) there are "imitations" of Latin poetry that, while undeniably of America and of the twentieth century, have the kind of intertextual purposefulness one thinks of as eighteenth-century Augustan. Hollander's "New York," in its marvelously assured heroic couplets, views its subject through Dr. Johnson's "London: A Poem" and its original in Juvenal's Third Satire. The result is an exhilarating affirmation of what poetic tradition actually means and a work that ranges from devastating satiric wit to poised tenderness.

Much that is best in Hollander comes from his sense of poetry as ceremony. An early poem such as ''For Both of You, the Divorce Being Final'' seeks an appropriate kind of antiepithalamic ceremony. On a much larger scale the first sequence of poems in *In Time and Place* enacts a poetic ceremony for a marriage lost, though Milton is by no means the only poetic ghost in attendance. The formality of the poems—tetrameter quatrains rhymed *abba*—is crucial to the sense of the ceremonial and to the quasi-magical ritual as the poet tells us that he seeks to ''rhyme'' his lost partner ''back to bed again.'' The mirror pattern of the rhyme scheme articulates the many images of reflection, as in the beautiful and moving ''The Looking-Glass of Grief.''

Hollander is a highly self-conscious poet, and the mirror has its role here too. The inherited literary tradition is another mirror, in front of which Hollander can place himself and discern, inviting his readers to make the same observation, both what is individual about himself and what he shares with that tradition. In *Powers of Thirteen* it is the sonnet sequence that serves this purpose. Hollander's sequence is both generic and sui generis. *Rhyme's Reason* contains a typically adroit exemplum of this new form:

One final recent variant of sonnet form works
Its way purely syllabically, in unrhymed lines
Of thirteen syllables, and then squares these off with one
Less line in the whole poem—a thirteener—by thirteen.
But hidden in its unstressed trees there can lurk rhyming
Lines like these (for instance); as in all syllabic verse
Moments of audible accent pass across the face
Of meditation, summoning old themes to the fair
Courtroom of revision, flowing into parts of eight
And five lines, seven and six, or unrhymed quatrains,
Or triplets, that like this one with unaligned accents
Never jingles in its threes or imbecilities,
Then the final line, uncoupled, can have the last word.

The poems of the sequence are disposed with an attention to numerological pattern that would have delighted any Renaissance or mannerist poet. The mathematics are exact: there are 169 stanzas (13^2) and 2,197 lines (13^3). The Elizabethan sonnet sequence, Hollander implies, cannot simply be reproduced. Yet it cannot be ignored, and it is effectively redesigned here by a different consciousness.

Hollander is one of the masters of our time. When he is at his best, his technical skill and his intelligence are active in the service of subjects of the highest interest, and at every turn his work suggests ways in which the inherited tradition (not always it seems, pace Harold Bloom, felt as a burden) can continue to exert a liberating and creative influence.

—Glyn Pursglove

HOLLO, Anselm (Paul Alexis)

Also wrote as Anton Hofman and Sergei Bielyi. **Nationality:** Finnish. **Born:** Helsinki, Finland, 12 April 1934. **Education:** Attended schools in Helsinki, and in Cedar Rapids, Iowa; Helsinki University; University of Tübingen, Germany, 1952–56. **Family:** Married 1) Josephine Wirkus in 1957; one son and two daughters; 2) Jane Dalrymple in 1985. **Career:** Commercial correspondent for a Finnish lumber export company, and interpreter, United Nations Atomic Energy Agency, Vienna, both 1950s; translator and book reviewer for German and Finnish periodicals, and secretary to grandfather, Professor Paul Walden, University of Tübingen, Germany, 1955–58; program assistant and coordinator, BBC, London, 1958–66. Visiting lecturer, State University of New York, Buffalo, Summers 1967, 1969; visiting lecturer, 1968–69, lecturer in English and music, 1970–71, and head of the translation workshop, 1971–72, University of Iowa, Iowa City; visiting professor and/or poet, Bowling Green University, Ohio, 1972–73, Hobart and William Smith Colleges, Geneva, New York, 1973–74, Michigan State University, East Lansing, 1975, University of Maryland, Baltimore, 1975–77, and Southwest State University, Marshall, Minnesota, 1977–78, Sweet Briar College, Virginia, 1978–81, Naropa Institute, Boulder, Colorado, 1981–84; lecturer, New College of California, San Francisco, 1981–83. Since 1989 associate professor, writing and poetics, Naropa Institute. Former contributing editor, *Modern Poetry in Translation,* London, and *New Letters,* Kansas City, Missouri; poetry editor, *Iowa Review,* Iowa City, 1971–72. **Awards:** Creative Artists Public Service award, 1976; Yaddo fellowship, 1978; National Endowment for the Arts fellowship, 1979; Witter Bynner fellowship, 1979; American-Scandinavian Foundation award, for translation, 1980, 1989. **Address:** c/o Writing and Poetics, The Naropa Institute, 2130 Arapahoe Avenue, Boulder, Colorado 80302, U.S.A.

PUBLICATIONS

Poetry

Sateiden Valilla (Rainpause). Helsinki, Otava, 1956.
St. Texts and Finnpoems. Birmingham, Migrant Press, 1961.
Loverman. New York, Dead Language Press, 1961.
We Just Wanted to Tell You. London, Writers Forum, 1963.
And What Else Is New. Chatham, Kent, New Voice, 1963.
History. London, Matrix Press, 1964.
Trobar: Loytaa (Trobar: To Find). Helsinki, Otava, 1964.
Here We Go. Newcastle upon Tyne, Strangers Press, 1965.
And It Is a Song. Birmingham, Migrant Press, 1965.
Faces and Forms. London, Ambit, 1965.
The Claim. London, Goliard Press, 1966.
For the Sea: Sons and Daughters We All Are. Privately printed, 1966.
The Going-On Poem. London, Writers Forum, 1966.
Poems/Runoja (bilingual edition). Helsinki, Otava, 1967.
Isadora and Other Poems. London, Writers Forum, 1967.
Leaf Times. Exeter, Exeter Books, 1967.
Buffalo-Isle of Wight Power Cable. Buffalo, State University of New York, 1967.
The Man in the Tree-Top Hat. London, Turret, 1968.
The Coherences. London, Trigram Press, 1968.
Tumbleweed. Toronto, Weed/Flower Press, 1968.
Haiku, with John Esam and Tom Raworth. London, Trigram Press, 1968.
Waiting for a Beautiful Bather: Ten Poems. Milwaukee, Morgan Press, 1969.
Maya: Works 1959–1969. London, Cape Goliard Press, and New York, Grossman, 1970.
America del Norte and Other Peace Herb Poems. Toronto, Weed/Flower Press, 1970.

Message. Santa Barbara, California, Unicorn Press, 1970.

Gee Apollinaire. Iowa City, Nomad Press, 1970.

Sensation 27. Canton, New York, Institute of Further Studies, 1972.

Alembic. London, Trigram Press, 1972.

Smoke Writing. Storrs, University of Connecticut Library, 1973.

Spring Cleaning Greens, from Notebooks 1967–1973. Bowling Green, Ohio, Doones Press, 1973.

Surviving with America, with Jack Marshall and Sam Hamod. Iowa City, Cedar Creek Press, 1974.

Some Worlds. New Rochelle, New York, Elizabeth Press, 1974.

Black Book 1. Bowling Green, Ohio, Bowling Green State University, 1975.

Sojourner Microcosms: New and Selected Poems 1959–1977. Berkeley, California, Blue Wind Press, 1977.

Heavy Jars. West Branch, Iowa, Toothpaste Press, 1977.

Phantom Pod, with Joe Cardarelli and Kirby Malone. Baltimore, pod, n.d.

Lingering Tangos. Baltimore, Tropos Press, 1977.

Lunch in Fur. St. Paul, Minnesota, Aquila Rose, 1978.

Curious Data. Buffalo, White Pine Press, 1978.

With Ruth in Mind. Barrytown, New York, Station Hill Press, 1979.

Finite Continued: New Poems 1977–1980. Berkeley, California, Blue Wind Press, 1980.

No Complaints. West Branch, Iowa, Toothpaste Press, 1983.

Pick Up the House. Minneapolis, Coffee House Press, 1986.

Outlying Districts. Minneapolis, Coffee House Press, 1990.

Near Miss Haiku. Chicago, Yellow Press, 1990.

Space Baltic. Mountain View, California, Ocean View Press, 1991.

Blue Ceiling. Lawrence, Kansas, Tansy Press, 1992.

High Beam. Riverdale, Maryland, Pyramid Atlantic, 1993.

West Is Left on the Map, with Jane Dalrymple-Hollo. Boulder, Colorado, Dead Metaphor Press, 1993.

Corvus: Poems. Minneapolis, Minnesota, Coffee House Press, 1995.

Survival Dancing. Boulder, Colorado, Rodent Press, 1995.

Ahoe: (And How on Earth). Erie, Colorado, Smokeproof Press, 1997.

Polemics. Brooklyn, New York, Autonomedia, 1998.

Caws and Causeries around Poetry and Poets. Albuquerque, New Mexico, La Alameda Press, 1999.

Recording: *The Coherences,* Stream Records, 1969.

Play

In the Jungle of Cities, adaptation of a play by Brecht (produced New York, 1977). New York, Grove Press, 1966.

Other

The Minicab War (parodies), with Gregory Corso and Tom Raworth. London, Matrix Press, 1961.

Editor and Translator, *Kaddisch,* by Allen Ginsberg. Wiesbaden, Limes, 1962.

Editor and Translator, *Red Cats: Selections from the Russian Poets.* San Francisco, City Lights, 1962.

Editor, *Jazz Poems.* London, Vista, 1963.

Editor and Translator, *In der Fluchtigen Hand der Zeit,* by Gregory Corso. Wiesbaden, Limes, 1963.

Editor and Translator, *Huuto ja Muita Runoja,* by Allen Ginsberg. Turku, Finland, Tajo, 1963.

Editor and Translator, *Kuolema van Goghin Korvalle,* by Allen Ginsberg. Turku, Finland, Tajo, 1963.

Editor, *Negro Verse.* London, Vista, 1964.

Editor and Translator, *Selected Poems,* by Andrei Voznesensky. New York, Grove Press, 1964.

Editor and Translator, *Word from the North: New Poetry from Finland.* Blackburn, Lancashire, Screeches Press, 1965.

Editor and Translator, *Helsinki: Selected Poems,* by Pentti Saarikoski. London, Rapp and Whiting, 1967.

Editor and Translator, *Selected Poems,* by Paavo Haavikko. London, Cape Goliard Press, and New York, Grossman, 1968.

Editor and Translator, *The Twelve and Other Poems,* by Aleksandr Blok. Lexington, Kentucky, Gnomon Press, 1971.

Editor and Translator, with Gunnar Harding, *Modern Swedish Poetry in Translation.* Minneapolis, University of Minnesota Press, 1979.

Translator, *Some Poems,* by Paul Klee. Lowestoft, Suffolk, Scorpion Press, 1962.

Translator, *Hispanjalainen Jakovainaa,* by John Lennon. Helsinki, Otava, 1966.

Translator, *491,* by Lars Görling. New York, Grove Press, 1966.

Translator, *In the Dark, Move Slowly: Poems,* by Tuomas Anhava. London, Cape Goliard Press, and New York, Grossman, 1969.

Translator, with Sidney Berger, *Thrymskvitha* (Icelandic Skald). Iowa City, Windhover Press, 1970.

Translator, with Josephine Clare, *Paterson,* by W.C. Williams. Stuttgart, Goverts, 1970.

Translator, with Elliott Anderson, *Turbines: Twenty One Poems,* by Tomaz Salamun. Iowa City, Windhover Press, 1973.

Translator, *Querelle,* by Jean Genet. New York, Grove Press, 1974.

Translator, *Beautiful Days,* by Franz Innerhofer. New York, Urizen, 1976.

Translator, *Small Change,* by François Truffaut. New York, Grove Press, 1976.

Translator, *Years of Apprenticeship on the Couch,* by Tillman Moser. New York, Urizen, 1977.

Translator, *The Industrialized Traveller,* by Wolfgang Schivelbusch. New York, Urizen, 1979.

Translator, *The Railway Journey,* by Wolfgang Schivelbusch. New York, Urizen, 1980.

Translator, *August Strindberg,* by Olof Lagerkrantz. New York, Farrar Straus, and London, Faber, 1984.

Translator, *Poems 1958–1980,* by Pentti Saarikoski. West Branch, Iowa, Toothpaste Press, 1984.

Translator, *Women's Rites: Scenes from the Erotic Imagination,* by Jeanne de Berg. New York, Grove Press, 1987.

Translator, *Au Revoir les Enfants* (Goodbye, Children), by Louis Malle. New York, Grove Press, 1988.

Translator, *The Road to Ein Harod,* by Amos Kenan. New York, Grove Press, 1988.

Translator, *I, Eternal Child: Paintings and Poems,* by Egon Schiele. New York, Grove Press, 1988.

Translator, *The Whales in Lake Tanganyika,* by Lennart Hagertors. New York, Grove Press, and London, Deutsch, 1989.

Translator, *A Life Torn by History: Franz Werfel 1890–1945.* London, Weidenfeld and Nicolson, 1990.

Translator, *The Czar's Madman,* by Jaan Kross. London, Harvill, 1991; New York, Pantheon, 1993.

Translator, *The Rocket Mountain,* by Udo Breger. Ostheim, Germany, Verlag Peter Engstler, 1992.

Translator, *One Night Stands,* by Rosa Liksom. London, Serpent's
   Tail, 1993.

Translator, *Happy Birthday, Turk!,* by Jakob Arjouni. New York,
   Fromm International, 1993.

Translator, *Sarajevo: A War Journal,* by Zlatko Dizdarevic. New
   York, Fromm International, 1993.

Translator, *Professor Marten's Departure,* by Jaan Kross. London,
   Harvill, and New York, The New Press, 1994

Translator, *And Still Drink More!,* Jakob Arjouni. New York, Fromm
   International, 1994.

Translator, *The Poems,* by Hipponax of Ephesus. Baltimore, Tropos
   Press, 1994.

Translator, *One Man, One Murder,* by Jakob Arjouni. Harpenden, No
   Exit, 1997.

Translator, *Starfall: A Triptych,* by Lars Kleberg. Evanston, Illinois,
   Northwestern University Press, 1997.

Translator, *One Death to Die: A Kayankaya Mystery,* by Jakob
   Arjouni. New York, Fromm International, 1997.

Translator, *20 Poems,* by Lauri Otonkoski. Sausalito, California,
   Duration Press, 1999.

Other translations from German, French, and Swedish published.

*

Manuscript Collection: State University of New York, Buffalo.

Critical Studies: Interview with Barry Alpert, in *Vort* (Silver Spring,
Maryland), 2, 1972; "On Translation" by Edward Foster, in *Talis-
man* (Jersey City, New Jersey), 6, Spring 1991; "Exiles" by Pekka
Tarkka, in *Books from Finland* (Helsinki), 1, 1997.

Anselm Hollo comments:

(1970) Poems are given. They are also "graphs of a mind
moving" (Philip Whalen). Each poem, if and when it works, is a
singular, at times even unique, formal, emotional, intellectual entity,
posing no problems to the poet beyond those contained in itself. The
sources are in the poet's life, and that includes his reading, his given
"place" at any given "time," his awareness of all animate and
inanimate objects (and subjects) around him.

(1974) One way or another, most of us poets tend to aim for the
"direct hit," that deeply satisfying "ouch!" of the inner gunfighter
toppling over on the dusty little main street of the Reader's Heart. The
temper of that hit is various. Inflated reputations are proposed on what
in another medium, say painting or sculpture, would be instantly
recognized and rejected as tearjerkers. However, no poet ever was, is,
or will ever be in total control of his or her radar installation.

(1990) See you at our next event.

(1995) Ditto—but perhaps I should amplify that a little. The
"events" I had in mind are the ones that occur between reader and
writer (not "poetry slams" and such). ". . . For those of us," says
Charles Olson in his *Maximus Letter 5,* "who do live our life quite
properly in print / as properly, say, as Gloucester people live in
Gloucester / you do meet someone / as I met you / on a printed page."
My life in print has been lived, these past thirty-five years, in the
world of the small press and the little magazine. By their very nature,
their existence in a twilight zone between the truly mass-produced
and the limited (intentional or unintentional) collector's item, the
products of that world are eccentric, ephemeral, fugitive, and, at their
best, carriers of the kind of transmission letters exchanged between

artists and poets used to be in past centuries. As long as we believe
that the life of words on a page exists in a realm different from the life
of words on the phone, or on television or magnetic tape, we need the
page, pages, books.

*   *   *

The poetry of Anselm Hollo is fun. Furthermore, in his later
verse we come to expect the unexpected with every turn of the page,
almost with every new line, and we are seldom disappointed. Of late
years, too, his diction has become less "English" (meaning decorous) and more "American" (meaning slangy and colloquial). But
his poetry always has been unadorned and keyed to the rhythms of
common speech. He speaks, that is, as "one of us," not from a
platform, and this is surprising in view of the years he spent as a
program director with the BBC. Perhaps in his diction he is compensating for the fact that his father was an eminent professor of
philosophy and theory of education at the University of Helsinki.

Hollo's career as a translator also began at the University of
Helsinki, where he translated many European classics, including
Cervantes, Dostoyevsky, and Henry James, into Finnish. I mention
this because Hollo is still better known as a translator (especially for
his magnificent translations into English of Aleksandr Blok and
Andrey Voznesensky) than he is as a poet. Another fact delaying such
recognition may be that Hollo is primarily a comic poet. (What is he
laughing at? people ask themselves uneasily. Himself? Me? The
world? The nature of things? T.S. Eliot never behaved like that). Can
it be that people have been conditioned to expect poets to be serious
and are at a loss with one who has an overmastering sense of the
ridiculous, the absurd?

One of the recurrent themes in *Sensation* is the science fiction
dream, which, it turns out, is only the old romantic pursuit of the blue
flower in disguise:

Let me tell you, the captain knew
exactly what he would do
soon as he reached the destination
he would fuse with her
plumulous essence
& they would become a fine furry plant
later travelers would run their sensors over
to hear it hum
"call me up in dreamland"
by the old minstrel known as "the van"
ultimate consummation of long ethereal affair
he knew he would miss
certain small addictions
acquired in the colonies
visual images baloney sandwiches
but those would be minor deprivations
hardly bothersome in the vita nuova
he was flying high
he was almost there
& that is where
we leave him to go hurtling through the great warp
& at our own ineffable goals

A second recurrent theme is the goddess Maya, who is, the poet
explains, "the energy / put forth in producing / the performance of the
world." It follows, of course, that Hollo himself is an aspect of this

goddess. It bucks a man up when he is eating out alone to think of himself as part of the cosmic force that makes possible "the performances of the world." Like the science fiction theme, the Maya theme is comic and cheerful, with romantic overtones.

On occasion Hollo pokes fun at a somber romantic classic, here Verlaine's "Il Pleur dans Mon Coeur": "after Verlaine / right now / it is raining in Iowa City / but it ain't rainin in my heart / nor on my head / because my head / it wears a big floppy heart, ha ha / it wears a big floppy heart." The tragic note enters Hollo's poetry only rarely and does so usually in his translations, and even then, as in this brief poem from the Finnish ("Tumbleweeds"), with an element of comic surprise: "go to the lakeshore go / throw in a feather and a stone / the stone floats / it is the day your son comes home." A quieter, more intimate tone prevails in some of his earlier lyrics, as in "Webern":

switch off the light
the trees stand together
easier then
to he in our bodies

growing quietly
"dem tode entgegen"

slow it is
a slow business

to grow a few words
to say love.

A traveler through many countries and languages, Hollo has a slightly off-planet slant on human affairs. Like Puck he is convinced of our absurdity, but like Oberon, beneficent. Of his diction Peter Schjedahl has commented, "His slight verbal hesitance succeeds in communicating the sense of a man anxious lest his words misrepresent his feelings." It is very important to this poet that such misunderstandings never occur. Verbal finery and decoration might get in the way of the laughter, the cheerfulness, the outgoing spirit.

—E.L. Mayo

HONGO, Garrett (Kaoru)

Nationality: American. **Born:** Volcano, Hawaii, 30 May 1951. **Education:** Pomona College, Claremont, California, 1969–73, B.A. (honors) 1973; University of Michigan, Ann Arbor, 1974–75; University of California, Irvine, 1978–82, M.F.A. 1980. **Family:** Married Cynthia Anne Thiessen in 1982; two sons. **Career:** Director, Asian Exclusion Act, Seattle, Washington, 1976–78; poet-in-residence, Seattle Arts Commission, 1977–78; teaching assistant, 1980–82, and visiting instructor, 1983–84, University of California, Irvine; visiting assistant professor, University of Southern California, Los Angeles, 1982–83; assistant professor, University of Missouri, Columbia, 1984–89; visiting associate professor, University of Houston, Texas, 1988. Associate professor and director of creative writing, 1989–93, professor of English, 1992–93, and since 1993 professor of creative writing, University of Oregon, Eugene. Poetry editor, *The Missouri Review,* 1984–89. Jury member, Pulitzer prize poetry committee, 1990, *Los Angeles Times* Book award poetry committee, 1990, and

chair, 1991; National Book award, 1994; Kingsley Tufts Poetry award, 1995. **Awards:** National Endowment for the Arts fellowship, 1982, 1988; Lamont prize, 1987; Guggenheim fellowship, 1990; Rockefeller Foundation Residency fellowship, Bellagio Study and Conference Center, Lake Como, Italy, 1992; Iphigene Ochs Sulzburger Residency fellowship, Yaddo Corporation, 1993. **Agent:** Liz Darhansoff Literary Agency, 1220 Park Avenue, New York, 10128. **Address:** Department of Creative Writing, 144 Columbia Hall, University of Oregon, Eugene, 97403, U.S.A.

PUBLICATIONS

Poetry

The Buddha Bandits down Highway 99, with Alan Chong Lau and Lawson Fusao Inada. Mountain View, California, Buddhahead Press, 1978.
Yellow Light. Middletown, Connecticut, Wesleyan University Press, 1982.
The River of Heaven. New York, Knopf, 1988.

Play

Nisei Bar and Grill (produced Seattle, 1976).

Other

Volcano: A Memoir of Hawai'i. New York, Knopf, 1995.

Editor, *The Open Boat: Poems from Asian America.* New York, Anchor Books, 1993.
Editor, *Songs My Mother Taught Me: Stories, Plays, and Memoir by Wakako Yamauchi.* New York, The Feminist Press, 1994.
Editor, *Under Western Eyes: Personal Essays from Asian America.* New York, Anchor Books, 1995.

*

Critical Studies: "A Vicious Kind of Tenderness: An Interview with Garrett Hongo" by Alice Evans, in *Poets & Writers Magazine,* September/October 1992; "Who You Are: Japanese American Poet Garrett Hongo's Search for Identity Reveals a World to Us All" by Anna Ganahl, in *The Pitzer Participant,* Summer 1994; by Mark Jarman, in *Southern Review* (Baton Rouge, Louisiana), 32(2), Spring 1996; *Garrett Hongo* by Laurie Filipelli, Boise, Idaho, Boise State University Press, 1997.

Garrett Hongo comments:

My project as a poet has been motivated by a search for origins of various kinds, quests for ethnic and familial roots, cultural identity, and poetic inspiration, all ultimately somehow connected with my need for an active imaginative and spiritual life. One might get at these through the practice of formal religion or the contemplation of moral and even socioeconomic problems, but for me the way has led to the study and the desire to contact, through the writing of poetry, those places and peoples from which I have been separated either by force of history or of personality. I find the landscapes, folkways, and societies of Japan, Hawaii, and even southern California to continually charm and compel me to write about them and inform myself of their specificities. But this obsession with origin is more than a nostalgia or even a semilearned atavism, though these things certainly play their parts. It is rather a way to isolate and to uphold cultural and moral value in a confusing time and environment, accommodating what I know of tradition and history to contemporary circumstances. Still, it is not ultimately cultural archaeology that I want to undertake, but to produce something of traditional learning, spiritual value, and personal experience out of the cultural whirlwind I live in.

Historically I have been occupying an extremely privileged position that has allowed me the leisure to become somewhat educated and to indulge my instincts in creative writing. Two generations of my family labored as field hands on the Hawaiian sugar plantations and another at absurdly paralyzing occupations in the city in order to buy my way out. The 1960s boom in higher education, liberal federal loan and state scholarship programs, and the enlightened, equal opportunity-minded administration of California's then Governor Pat Brown got me to a fine private college where I learned good humanistic lessons alongside the children of the monied elite. Reagan and harder times ended those programs, but I had gotten my studies in by the time the corporate wolves took power. Had it not been so, I do not think I would have had the confidence and the background to go on to try and develop myself as a writer.

The encouragement of certain teachers was also vital. I owe enormous debts to those who taught me languages, history, oriental religions, and literature. But if I had not met the poets Bert Meyers, Donald Hall, C.K. Williams, and Charles Wright when I did, I am certain no poems would have ever come from me. Likewise, if Philip Levine had not been an example to me as a teacher and a poet, I doubt if I would have tried to become either.

My concerns as a poet have to do not so much with emotional authenticity—a murderer and a terrorist have that—but with emotional nobility of some kind, the idea that poems might help produce and reveal our "better nature," as Sidney once said in his *Apology*. It is an idea present in oriental philosophy too, the *jen* of Confucianism that was a notion of the innate moral and spiritual good in people that impressed Ezra Pound as one of the highest poetic values, and the idea of *samadhi,* or sensate and sentient calm, that we get from Buddhism. I do want things to be better somehow, if not in the world then at least within myself, though not only within myself, so that I might be more like the stillness that smooths the surface of a pond rather than the bullfrog that jumps into it.

And whom do I write for? It changes all the time and stays the same too. I write for the ambition I have for myself—to be a voice that I can listen to, that makes sense and raises my own bereft and mundane consciousness, that speaks to me as if it were the elder I have always wanted. And I write for all the people who might want the same thing, no matter what race, class background, or nation. And yet I write for certain "first" readers as well—my wife Cynthia Thiessen, the Nisei playwright and painter Wakako Yamauchi, the folks who raised me and whom I grew up with, and the company of the fine poets in my generation like Greg Pape, Edward Hirsch, Mark Jarman, and Arthur Smith.

Asians do read my work and I want them to as much as I ever did, as I am trying to write about us, the world we come from and live in, our histories and our spiritual ambitions.

Finally, I think I must say that I write for my father, Albert Kazuyoshi Hongo, in a very personal way. I want to be his witness, to testify to his great and noble life in struggle against anger, in struggle

against his own loneliness and isolation for being a Hawaiian Japanese who emigrated to Los Angeles without much family or community. He was a great example to me of a man who refused to hate or, being different himself, to be afraid of difference, who accepted the friendship of all the strange and underprivileged ostracized by the rest of "normal" society—Vietnamese, Mexicans, southern blacks, reservation Indians relocated to the city—and I want my poems to be equal to his heart.

(1995) *Volcano* is a book of retreat and return, meditation on going home to a home I never knew, which is this volcano. And coming back to it, to the history of my family, coming back to that culture, the biology, the biota (the animal and plant life of a particular region considered as a total ecological entity), the rainforest, the volcano itself. It is nonfiction, not like John McPhee, more like Thoreau. In writing this book, the poetic form needed to expand for me. What I found to be the form was the Japanese *nikki*. It is a travel diary, poetic prose. We have examples in American literature in *Moby Dick* and *Walden*. In that vein I wrote this book.

*   *   *

Garrett Hongo's voice is among a group of Asian-American poets who are increasingly making others in the literary community sit up and take note and to rethink what constitutes American literature. Growing up in Hawaii and Los Angeles as a Japanese-American in a predominately Euro-American culture, Hongo sees his work as a quest for history and an identity that allows him to feel that he belongs in his own country. His unique background, the precision of his perception, and his lyrical gift mark his growing oeuvre, which includes the editorship of anthologies as well as the prose work *Volcano: A Memoir of Hawai'i* (1995). *The River of Heaven* was the Lamont Poetry Selection for 1987.

Hongo's poetry, which is a search for "the strange syllables that healed desire," heard in the Buddhist mantras of his youth, draws upon the rich tapestry of his Japanese-American ancestry as well as the landscapes of Hawaii and California, where he was raised. His poems are an investigation of cultural roots and their meaning for a poet of Japanese heritage in contemporary America. His work, in a plain style punctuated by bursts of lyricism, engages the difficulty of acculturation for urban immigrants—their poverty, boredom, and alienation—as well as such omnipresent features of contemporary American culture as television, movies, and Top 40 radio.

Hongo's tone is often one of supplication, his poems acts of communion with departed ancestors. "I want the dead beside me when I dance, to help me / flesh the notes of my song, to tell me it's all right," he explains in "O-Bon: Dance for the Dead." Hongo's determination to keep the past alive suggests a method for his poems, which often employ family history or the oral history of immigrants to create memorable personal narratives, as in "Cloud Catch":

And that's about all I do,
   piecing the lives together,
getting the stories folks will tell me,
   dust in the gleam of light
swirled with a cupped hand,
   finding a few words.

Our shame, according to the poet, lies in our complicity in the "effacement" of the past, "the rough calligraphy / on rotting wood / Worm smooth and illegible" ("Ancestral Graves, Kahuku"), as in the conspiracy of silence surrounding the relocation and internment of Japanese-Americans during World War II.

"Stepchild," in order to preserve and clarify, relates bitter tales of this disgraceful episode in American history, both general and specific. While the speaker observes that "the sun blonds nothing / but the sands outside my window," rage finally gives way to acceptance and determination:

> Revenge blisters my tongue
> works in these words, says,
> "Teach a Blessingway."

Among Hongo's gallery of colorfully drawn personae, two stand out. "Pinoy at the Coming World" presents the testimony of an enterprising shopkeeper, one who has worked his way to a position of prosperity and respect within his community, attempting to cope with a flu epidemic that has devastated his town and threatens his family. After boasting about the esteem in which his customers hold him, the stunned Pinoy admits, "But none of us was ready for the flu that hit, / first the Mainland and all the reports of dead / on newspapers wrapped around the canned meats I stocked . . ." By the end of the poem, as his daughter nears "her time," Pinoy says, "I wanted to walk completely off plantation grounds / and get all the way out of town to where / sugar cane can't grow and no moon or stars / rose over pineapple fields." It soon becomes clear that Pinoy realizes his own life to be in danger:

> I wanted the roar from the sea, from falling water,
> and from the wind over mounds and stones
> to be the echo of my own grief, keening within,
> making pure my heart for the world I know is to come.

"Jigoku: On the Glamour of Self-Hate" is the extended reverie of self-purgation of an older man who, looking back on his life, loathes the trail of scheming and deception he has left behind. He imagines betraying his family identity to a nephew, who would himself imagine his uncle

> discovered, finally, by some fishermen,
> sliced from my clothes and under six fathoms
> in the boat channel of Hilo Bay,
> fused in a posture of supplication
> and folded, as a fan is folded,
> tucked to fit the trunk of my car,
> tattoos at last flailed from my skin,
> and, cut away from bone, the white threads of flesh
> a gossamer I pass through from this world to the next.

Hongo's writing traces his identity not only to his Japanese heritage but also to contemporary American popular culture. "96 Tears" uses a memorable song as the sound track for a rumination upon adolescence that considers B movies and pornographic playing cards before concluding with an impassioned denunciation of prejudice. "The Cadence of Silk" shows a charming and promising side of Hongo, "hooked on the undulant ballet / of the pattern offence," as he applies his lyricism to basketball.

Hongo is at his best in two poems that attempt to understand his father's compulsive gambling. In "Winnings" he remembers that there would sometimes be money beyond the "grocery money and money to fix / the washer," and father and son would find the world bathed "in a brief symphony of candied light." "The Pier," one of his finest poems, sifts the reasons for his father's gambling:

> For splendor, for his cheap fun, my father
> would go to the track, lose himself in the crowd
> milling around the paddock, weighing the odds
> against the look of the horse, handicapping,
> exchanging tips, rushing the window just before post-time
> and rising to his feet for the stretch run,
> beating cadence and whipping a gabardine pants leg
> in rhythm and chant to the jockey's ride.

In *Volcano: A Memoir of Hawai'i,* Hongo presents a different father—silent, morose, a reader of philosophy. He identifies with the elder man's feelings of alienation and dislocation, and like others of his own generation he finds himself through the telling of his father's tortured story. The mature writer now realizes that his father had locked himself behind a psychic prison marked by half-spoken whispers about the "Camps," prejudice, and hostile coworkers—the crime of being Japanese-American. In *Volcano* Hongo passionately re-creates the Hawaii and California of not just his father but also his grandfather in an attempt to give them voice, to reclaim these lost generations in a new history of America. In the course of doing so Hongo stakes his own claim to the past and the land. He finds his love for the natural life of Hawaii, his creative and personal inspiration in the primal, pulsating force of the living volcano.

Hongo's writing demonstrates a steady progression. *The River of Heaven* is less self-absorbed than its predecessor, *Yellow Light*. His poems enact the dramas the poet has envisaged as necessary for the imaginative life of his father, becoming for the reader a "sequence of splendid events." As Maxine Hong Kingston has put it, "To read his poems is to know one's own ordinary secret world worthy of song."

—Robert Gaspar and Ruth Y. Hsu

HONIG, Edwin

Nationality: American. **Born:** New York City, 3 September 1919. **Education:** Attended public schools in New York; University of Wisconsin, Madison, B.A. 1941, M.A. 1947. **Military Service:** U.S. Army, 1943–46. **Family:** Married 1) Charlotte Gilchrist in 1940 (died 1963); 2) Margot S. Dennes in 1963 (divorced 1978); two sons. **Career:** Library assistant, Library of Congress, Washington, D.C., 1941–42; instructor in English, Purdue University, Lafayette, Indiana, 1942–43, New York University and Illinois Institute of Technology, Chicago, 1946–47, University of New Mexico, Albuquerque, 1947–49, and Claremont College, California, summer 1949; instructor, 1949–52, and Briggs Copeland Assistant Professor 1952–57, Harvard University, Cambridge, Massachusetts. Associate professor, 1957–60, professor of English, 1960–83, professor of comparative literature, 1962–83, and since 1983 professor emeritus, Brown University, Providence, Rhode Island. Visiting professor, University of California, Davis, 1964–65; Mellon Professor, Boston University, 1977. Poetry editor, *New Mexico Quarterly,* Albuquerque, 1948–52. Director, Rhode Island Poetry in the Schools Program, 1968–72. **Awards:** Guggenheim fellowship, 1948, 1962; *Saturday Review* prize, 1957; New England Poetry Club Golden Rose, 1961; Bollingen grant, for translation, 1962; American Academy grant, 1966; Amy Lowell traveling fellowship, 1968; National Endowment for the Arts grant, 1975, 1977; National Endowment for the Arts/P.E.N. fiction project award, 1983; Poetry Society of America translation award, 1984; Columbia University Translation Center award, 1985. Decoration by the President of Portugal: Knight of the Military Order of Saint James of the Sword, 1987. Decoration by King Juan Carlos of Spain: Knight of the Cross of Isabel the Catholic, 1996. **Address:** Box 1852, Brown University, Providence, Rhode Island 02912, U.S.A.

PUBLICATIONS

Poetry

The Moral Circus. Baltimore, Contemporary Poetry, 1955.
The Gazabos: Forty-One Poems. New York, Clarke and Way 1959; augmented edition, as The Gazabos: *Forty-One Poems, and The Widow,* 1961.
Poems for Charlotte. Privately printed, 1963.
Survivals. New York, October House, 1965.
Spring Journal. Providence, Rhode Island, Hellcoal Press, 1968.
Spring Journal: Poems. Middletown, Connecticut, Wesleyan University Press, 1968.
Four Springs. Chicago, Swallow Press, 1972.
Shake a Spear with Me, John Berryman: New Poems (includes the play *Orpheus Below*). Providence, Rhode Island, Copper Beech Press, 1974; augmented edition, as *The Affinities of Orpheus,* 1976.
At Sixes. Providence, Rhode Island, Burning Deck, 1974.
Selected Poems 1955–1976. Dallas, Center for Writers Press, 1979.
Interrupted Praise: New and Selected Poems. Metuchen, New Jersey, Scarecrow Press, 1983.
Gifts of Light. Isla Vista, California, Turkey Press, 1983.
The Imminence of Love: Poems 1962–1992. Dallas, Texas Center for Writers Press, 1993.

Plays

The Widow (produced Chicago, 1953). Included in *The Gazabos,* 1961.
The Phantom Lady, translation of a play by Calderón (produced Washington, D.C., 1965). Included in *Calderón: Four Plays,* 1961.
Calderón: Four Plays, translations by Honig. New York, Hill and Wang, 1961.
Cervantes: Eight Interludes, translations by Honig. New York, New American Library, 1964.
Calisto and Melibea (produced Stanford, California, 1966). Providence, Rhode Island, Hellcoal Press, 1972; opera version (produced Davis, California, 1979).
Life Is a Dream, translation of a play by Calderón (broadcast BBC London, 1970; produced Providence, Rhode Island, 1971). New York, Hill and Wang, 1970.
Ends of the World and Other Plays. Providence, Rhode Island, Copper Beech Press, 1983.

Radio Play: *Life Is a Dream,* 1970 (UK).

Other

García Lorca. New York, New Directions, 1944; London, Editions Poetry London, 1945; revised edition, New Directions 1963; London, Cape, 1968; New York, Octagon, 1980.
Dark Conceit: The Making of Allegory. Evanston, Illinois, Northwestern University Press, 1959; London, Faber, 1960; New York, Oxford University Press, 1966; Providence Rhode Island, Brown University Press, 1973.
Calderón and the Seizures of Honor. Cambridge, Massachusetts, Harvard University Press, 1972.
The Foibles and Fables of an Abstract Man. Providence, Rhode Island, Copper Beech Press, 1979.
The Poet's Other Voice: Conversations on Literary Translation. Amherst, University of Massachusetts Press, 1985.

Editor, with Oscar Williams, *The Mentor Book of Major American Poets.* New York, New American Library, 1961.
Editor, with Oscar Williams, *The Major Metaphysical Poets.* New York, Washington Square Press, 1968.
Editor, *Spenser.* New York, Dell, 1968.
Editor and Translator, with Susan M. Brown, *The Poems of Fernando Pessoa.* New York, Ecco Press, 1986.
Editor and Translator, *Always Astonished,* by Fernando Pessoa. San Francisco, City Lights, 1988.

Translator, *The Cave of Salamanca,* by Cervantes. Boston, Chrysalis, 1960.
Translator, *Four Plays,* by Pedro Calderón. New York, Hill and Wang, 1961.
Translator, *Eight Interludes,* by Cervantes. New York, New American Library, 1964.
Translator, *Life Is a Dream,* by Pedro Calderón. New York, Hill and Wang, 1970.
Translator, *Selected Poems of Fernando Pessoa.* Chicago, Swallow Press, 1971.
Translator, *Divan and Other Writings,* by García Lorca. Providence, Rhode Island, Bonewhistle Press, 1974.
Translator, with A.S. Trueblood, *La Dorotea,* by Lope de Vega. Cambridge, Massachusetts, Harvard University Press, 1985.
Translator, with S.M. Brown, *The Keeper of Sheep,* by Fernando Pessoa. Riverdale-on-Hudson, New York, Sheep Meadow Press, 1986.
Translator, *The Unending Lightning: Selected Poems of Miguel Hernàndez.* New York, Sheep Meadow Press, 1990.
Translator, *Four Puppet Plays; Diván Poems and Other Poems; Prose Poems and Dramatic Pieces; Play without a Title,* by Federico García Lorca. Riverdale-on-Hudson, New York, Sheep Meadow Press, 1990.
Translator, *Calderón de la Barca: Six Plays.* New York, Fordham University Press, 1993.

*

Bibliography: In *Books and Articles by Members of the Department: A Bibliography* by George K. Anderson, Providence, Rhode Island, Brown University Department of English, 1967.

Manuscript Collection: John Hay Library, Brown University, Providence, Rhode Island.

Critical Studies: "The Voice of Edwin Honig" by John Hawkes, in *Voices* (Vinalhaven, Maine), January-April 1961; "To Seize Truth Assault Dogmas" by Robert Taylor, in *Providence Sunday Journal* (Rhode Island), 4 March 1962; "'Spring' Breakthrough in the New Poetry" by James Schevill, in *San Francisco Examiner-Chronicle,* 5 January 1969; "Double Exposure" by L. Alan Goldstein, in *The Nation* (New York), 19 May 1969; interviews with H.J. Cargas, in *Webster Review* (Webster Groves, Missouri), fall 1977, and with Richard Jackson, in *Poetry Miscellany 8* (Chattanooga), 1978; in *American Poets since World War II* edited by Donald J. Greiner, Detroit, Gale, 1980; "Through the Aftermath: Mythical Transformation in the Poetry of Edwin Honig" by Barbara L. Estrin, in *Salmagundi* (Saratoga Springs, New York), 52–53, spring-summer 1981; A *Glass of Green Tea-with Honig* edited by Susan Brown, Thomas Epstein, and Henry Gould, Providence, Rhode Island, Alephoe, 1994.

Edwin Honig comments:

Matters that may have influenced my becoming a writer (though perhaps this is only a nice rationalization) were an early sense of exclusion owing to my being blamed for my younger brother's accidental death when I was five and a severe, nearly fatal bout with nephritis when I was nine. A positive influence was my illiterate grandmother who spoke Spanish, Arabic, and Yiddish (but no English); I lived with her and my grandfather for a few years after my parents were divorced when I was twelve. Experiences of this sort urged certain necessities upon me: one was to write instead of choking; another, to make sense of the world around me, but sense that would not exclude my own fantasy. Both my poetry and my criticism seem to rise out of such a mixed need: the criticism that creates—Spain (Calderòn and García Lorca) as well as allegory—and the poetry that criticizes persons and places I have loved and distrusted—the "moral circuses" where the "gazabos" live.

My best poems are either unfinished or still merely notes in a notebook. Some poems got away (were printed) but have since been excluded from my books because they did not seem substantial enough or true. In the same way I quarrel constantly with the poems written by contemporaries old and young. No poet writing in English in the last sixty years has mastered his art or has resisted the nervous need to keep changing his style, and so none has been able to write as a complete human being. Perhaps Rilke and Lorca succeeded in a few poems. (I find, now that I have written the penultimate sentence, that I am echoing an opinion of Gottfried Benn.) I have taken to translating and to writing plays out of impatience with poetry and criticism, but I go on writing poetry—to stop would be a self-betrayal.

(1974)(This was written in 1966 and might just as well stand for what I feel today, though I think the statement bleaker than need be. There are probably more than two poets, for instance, who have done a service to the language or their language in the last sixty years, and I am almost willing to admit that Pound is one.)

*   *   *

Edwin Honig points out that some literary critics, idealizing a golden age of the near or distant past, "speak and write about the poetry of the past 150 years like a keeper fleaing an underbred dog that is only half the dog its sire was." Not only does Honig disagree with that critical judgment, but he has also made his own substantial contribution to the healthy state of contemporary American poetry through his work as poet, teacher, critic, anthologist, translator, and

playwright. Like the modernist poetry of a previous generation, much of Honig's poetry makes rigorous demands on the reader and thus has to find its own audience gradually—limited in size but appreciative of the depth, range, and skill they discover in the poems. It is a poetry of careful craftsmanship, breadth, learning, sharp perceptions, and deep, authentic feeling.

In the earlier volumes, obviously influenced by Eliot and the prevailing standards of modernism, the feeling is often, though not always, insulated by technical virtuosity and layers of erudition. For a time Honig moved away from the poem as carefully constructed artifact to a looser, though by no means formless, open-ended poem (*Four Springs*). The new form did not diminish any of his technique or learning, nor did it suddenly transform him into a poet easily accessible to the casual reader, but it did more readily release depths of personal emotion: "One wants to tell / how the memory rushes hungrily back to the remembered / life of the dead / beloved, until at a touch, of themselves, the episodes / rush on unreeling, / speed up beyond one's grasping; imagined again, / retelling themselves, / great hunks of life that plead again to be real!"

A headnote to *Four Springs,* observing that "in 1966 or so I began writing a poem that very soon went beyond my conception of when or where it would end" and that the book's three concluding sections "continue the story to the present date, my fiftieth birthday," gave some evidence of an intention to explore further potentiality in this new form. Later volumes, however, are reminiscent of Honig's earlier style, with a strong added interest in myth. With the conviction that, "though we can't live without myths, we find it hard to re-define and adapt them to our experience," Honig has, in *The Affinities of Orpheus,* dramatically reworded the Orpheus-Eurydice myth and has also included two sections of poems that develop further the significant experiences, emotions, and issues raised by the myth.

Honig's critical study of García Lorca calls attention to "his problematical forcing of the door of the constant enemy, death." The comment sheds as much light on Honig himself as it does on García Lorca. His book titles (*Survivals, Spring Journal, Four Springs, Gifts of Light*)—and indeed the poet's work as a whole—affirm life, but the affirmation is wrested, often fiercely and explicitly, from the omnipresent threat of death: "Death with its cup of hopefulness / needs nourishment / but won't be fed by leftovers— / tired grief, / bewilderment of life's exhaust." Honig is a fine exemplar of his own concept of the function of the poet, "that voice which celebrates the difficult, joyous, imaginative process by which the individual man discovers and enacts his selfhood."

—Rudolph L. Nelson

HOOKER, Jeremy

Nationality: British. **Born:** Warsash, Hampshire, 23 March 1941. **Education:** St. Peter's, Southbourne, 1954–59; University of Southampton, 1959–65, B.A. 1963, M.A. 1965. **Family:** Married 1) Susan Hope Gill in 1968 (divorced 1984), one son and one daughter; 2) Mieke Davies in 1986. **Career:** Lecturer in English, University College of Wales, Aberystwyth, 1965–84; Arts Council Creative Writing Fellow, Winchester School of Art, 1981–83; docent, Rijksuniversiteit, Groningen, Netherlands 1987–88. Since 1988 lecturer in English and creative studies, director, M.A. in creative writing, 1992, and professor, 1994, Bath College of Higher Education (now Bath Spa University College). Writer-in-residence, Kibbutz Gezer, Israel, 1985. Visiting professor, LeMoyne College, New York, 1994–95. **Awards:** Eric Gregory award, 1969; Welsh Arts Council prize, 1975, and bursary, 1976. **Address:** Old School House, 7 Sunnyside, Frome, Somerset BA11 1LD, England.

PUBLICATIONS

Poetry

The Elements. Llandybie, Dyfed, Christopher Davies, 1972.
Soliloquies of a Chalk Giant. London, Enitharmon Press, 1974.
Solent Shore: New Poems. Manchester, Carcanet, 1978.
Landscape of the Daylight Moon. London, Enitharmon Press, 1978.
Englishman's Road. Manchester, Carcanet, 1980.
A View from the Source: Selected Poems. Manchester, Carcanet, 1982.
Itchen Water. Winchester, Winchester School of Art Press, 1982.
Master of the Leaping Figures. Petersfield, Hampshire, Enitharmon Press, 1987.
Their Silence A Language, with Lee Grandjean. London, Enitharmon Press, 1994.
Our Lady of Europe. London, Enitharmon Press, 1997.
Groundwork, with Lee Grandjean. Nottingham, Djanogly Art Gallery, 1998.

Other

John Cowper Powys. Cardiff, University of Wales Press, 1973.
David Jones: An Exploratory Study of the Writings. London, Enitharmon Press, 1975.
John Cowper Powys and David Jones: A Comparative Study. London, Enitharmon Press, 1979.
Poetry of Place: Essays and Reviews 1970–1981. Manchester, Carcanet, 1982.
The Presence of the Past: Essays on Modern British and American Poetry. Bridgend, Glamorgan, Poetry Wales Press, 1987.
Writers in a Landscape. Cardiff, University of Wales Press, 1996.

Editor, with Gweno Lewis, *Selected Poems of Alun Lewis.* London, Allen and Unwin, 1981.
Editor, *Selected Stories,* by Frances Bellerby. London, Enitharmon Press, 1986.

*

Critical Studies: By Donald Davie, in *Poetry Nation 9* (Manchester), March 1979; by Dick Davis, in *Agenda* (London), winter-spring 1982; *David Jones and Other Wonder Voyagers* by Philip Pacey, Bridgend, Glamorgan, Poetry Wales Press, 1982; by Brian Hinton, in *Poetry Wales 18* (Bridgend), 3, 1983; by Wynn Thomas, in *Anglo-Welsh Review* (Tenby), no. 74, 1983; "Giants in the Earth: Recent Myths for British Poets" by Avrom Fleishman, in *ELH* (Baltimore, Maryland), 51(1), spring 1984; *Reading Old Friends* by John Matthias, Albany, State University of New York Press, 1992.

Jeremy Hooker comments:

My poetry is influenced by a strong physical and historical sense of place, initially as I experienced it in the south of England, where I was brought up, and as I learned to see it anew while living in Wales. I have subsequently written poems set in Wales, in continental Europe, and in Israel. I think of place as "ground," as the continuing creation of interacting natural and cultural forces, and as the meeting point of unique and common experience and of the living and the dead. I feel affinities with the Welsh tradition of praise poetry, especially as interpreted by David Jones, with his awareness of both the necessity and the difficulty of praise in a world that has largely lost a sense of the sacred. A literary and artistic tradition I particularly value is that of Wordsworth and John Constable, who said he found his art "under every hedge and in every lane," and of the American objectivists, who found their poetry in the streets of New York. Having begun as a poet of belonging, I have become increasingly concerned with strangeness and otherness and with exploring the possibility of new relationships between male and female elements of the psyche, nature and culture, and matter and spirit.

*   *   *

Five of the eight poems by Jeremy Hooker in *Introduction One* (1969) include references to other poets—Hardy, Alun Lewis, Edward Thomas, and Dafydd ap Gwilym. It has always been clear that Hooker is a poet consciously rooting himself in traditions. He is acutely aware of the traditions of writing in the south of England, his birthplace, and his adopted home, Wales.

Hooker's commitment is to an exploration of structure—historical and metaphorical. His pamphlet *The Elements* includes the notable "Elegy for the Labouring Poor":

No man's lonelier than James Mould
As he wakes with stubble-scored legs
In a rat's refuge of wattle and daub . . .
But James Mould seeing the ocean
Sees only flint acres
Fought inch by inch, chalkdust rising,
And hears only his ghostly kin
Telling their names in the stunned brain.

This gives a clear indication of the method that Hooker was to employ in his subsequent collections: the power of imagination to inhabit another's mind over the centuries.

Soliloquies of a Chalk Giant is a sequence of thirty-eight short poems dealing with the significance in myth and history of the Cerne Abbas phallic man. The cumulative effect is impressive. Hooker uses the persona of the mysterious chalk figure to explore pre-Christian and Christian psyches while creating a credible being: "And beneath me / I feel the grass rise / And fall, like the slow, / Deep breaths of a giantess." The implicit danger of such an extended work is that the poet is eventually drawn into poetic exercises. *Soliloquies of a Chalk Giant* stops short of this, but *Solent Shore* is not as exciting, not as tightly controlled, as one would have wished from this talented poet. The book focuses on the poet's personal archetypes and can be seen as a natural sequel to the previous collection.

Too often the poems in *Solent Shore* rest on images that are competent but not exciting. The poet's aim is, to be fair, ambitious: to relate his life, the person he has become, to his background, the landscape and seascape of his heritage. The book's second section, "The Witnesses," is powerful. These related poems turn around the rich sixteenth-century history of the Solent Waters. This has the necessary force to hold the poet to the core of his theme: "The very last souls I seen / was that man's father / and that man's / Drowned like rattens, / drowned like rattens" ("Mary Rose, 1545").

Hooker is an accomplished writer and critic with a vision that can only intensify and come into a compelling focus: "Wires still buzz with messages / from the *Titanic.* / A seance breaks up / when a cabin-boy screams."

—Tony Curtis

HOOVER, Paul (Andrew)

Nationality: American. **Born:** Harrisonburg, Virginia, 30 April 1946. **Education:** Manchester College, North Manchester, Indiana, 1964–68, B.A. 1968; University of Illinois, Chicago, 1971–73, M.A. 1973. **Military Service:** Conscientious objector, 1968–70: worked at Northwestern Memorial Hospital, Chicago. **Family:** Married Maxine Chernoff, *q.v.,* in 1974; one daughter, two sons. **Career:** Since 1974 poet-in-residence, Columbia College, Chicago. Founding member and former president, the Poetry Center at the School of the Art Institute of Chicago, 1974–87. Since 1986 editor, *New American Writing,* Chicago, and Mill Valley, California. **Awards:** National Endowment for the Arts fellowship, 1980; General Electric Foundation award for younger writers, 1984; Carl Sandburg award, Friends of the Chicago Public Library, 1987; Editors grant, Council of Literary Magazines and Presses, 1988; winner, Contemporary Poetry Series Competition, University of Georgia Press, 1997; Artist's grant, Marin Arts Council, California, 1999. **Member:** Modern Language Association. **Address:** 369 Molino Avenue, Mill Valley, California 94941, U.S.A.

PUBLICATIONS

Poetry

Letter to Einstein Beginning Dear Albert. Chicago, The Yellow Press, 1979.
Nervous Songs. Seattle, L'Epervier Press, 1986.
Idea. Great Barrington, Massachusetts, The Figures, 1987.
The Novel: A Poem. New York, New Directions, 1990.
Viridian. Athens, University of Georgia Press, 1997.
Totem and Shadow: New and Selected Poems. Jersey City, New Jersey, Talisman House, 1999.

Novel

Saigon, Illinois. New York, Vintage, 1988.

Other

Editor, *Postmodern American Poetry.* New York, Norton, 1994.

*

Film Adaptations: *Viridian,* independent film directed and produced by Joseph Ramirez, 1994.

Theatrical Activities: Actor: **Play**—*Rimbaud in Abyssinia,* New York, 1987.

Critical Studies: "Bridging London: Chicagoans Stretch from Midwest to West End" by Kurt Jacobsen, in *Chicago Tribune* (Chicago), 12 August 1990; "Maxine Chernoff and Paul Hoover: Avant-garde Bards" by Penelope Mesic, in *Chicago Magazine* (Chicago), September 1990; "Servitude et Grandeur Litteraires" by Paul West, in *Parnassus* (New York), 17(2), 1991; in *Writing Illinois,* by James Hurt, Urbana, University of Illinois Press, 1993; interview with Vittorio Carli, in *Letter Ex,* 93, April/May 1994; "Without a City Wall" by Mark Ford, in *Times Literary Supplement* (London), 17 March 1995; by J. Haines, in *New Criterion* (New York), 13(10), 1995; "Ambiguity Isn't What It Used to Be—Or Is It?" by Fred Muratori, in *Georgia Review,* spring 1998.

Paul Hoover comments:

The work of William Carlos Williams and Frank O'Hara was especially important to me as a young poet in the 1970s and 1980s, and they continue to be a presence. But my influences are diverse and include Wallace Stevens and John Ashbery for their use of the romantic sublime, Emily Dickinson and George Herbert for their devoutness and metaphysical compression, Cesar Vallejo for his daring and disjunctive use of the lyric, and in general the so-called New Americans, including the New York school, projectivism (especially Creeley for the tension in his voice and the beauty of his line), and beat poetry for its urgency and accessibility. Since the mid-1980s I have been alert to the theoretical position taking of the language poets. But I am not a language poet despite the assertions of the *New York Times Magazine* in 1995.

A meeting of thought and lyricism, my poetry can be described as abstract (or critical) lyric. The poems are organized less by narrative than by concept. They also are very active in language and ask to be read word by word as much as sentence by sentence. But they can also be read for the nature of their comment. All poetry, even disjunctive postmodern poetry, can be read for its argumentative, theoretical, or observational statement, as in Williams's lines "so much *depends* / upon / a red wheel / barrow." My work is never fully narrative, as is common to realist poems and their personal concerns. I prefer a poetry of quick association and the cold fusion of the metaphysical ("Zero at the Bone," Emily Dickinson). The poet Gillian Conoley once reviewed my long poem *The Novel: A Poem* as "appetitive." Like the Pac-Man video figure, I am an avid consumer and organizer of disparate materials. While I have edited a leading anthology of postmodern poetry and am associated with its practice, I see myself in the tradition of romantic metaphysics: I think, therefore I write. Like Wallace Stevens, many of my poems are concerned with poetry ("not the thing itself / but a diagram of the harvest"). But they are not without reference to events in the real world. "Desire" ends with Tiananmen Square, and "Impossible Object" comments on the murder of Nicole Brown Simpson ("the present / moment's knife / writing blind / in space"). Both complexity and the direct approach are features of my writing.

As early as the poem "The Orphanage Florist," published in the 1987 volume *Idea* (the title taken from Michael Drayton's sixteenth-century sonnet sequence), I was interested in poetic form. Like many poems in *Viridian* and *Totem and Shadow,* "The Orphanage Florist" was written in counted verse, which requires a certain number of words per line. In counted verse I prefer a two-by-two or three-by-three stanza, the number of words in the line dictating the number of lines in the stanza. The mathematical approach to composition—counting—is of course traditional. But I am also interested in the experiments of the Parisian group Oulipo, who are nontraditional as formalists. An example of Oulipian form is the Lipogram, which requires the elimination of certain letters from a piece of writing. Thus Georges Perec wrote an entire novel, "A Void," that contained no letter *e.* My recent poem "American Gestures" is a cento, a form that requires each of the poem's one hundred lines to be borrowed from other poems. Working in form provides for me emotional access unguarded by irony. Thus lyricism has become a stronger force in my poetry.

*   *   *

Paul Hoover's considerable presence in the world of "alternative" American poetry is equaled by few poets and critics. As an editor/critic as well as a poet, he has been a much admired figure for more than a generation, coediting with his wife, the writer Maxine Chernoff, the journal *New American Writing* and editing the anthology *Postmodern American Poetry,* which has since its publication in 1994 been the chief textbook through which university students have been introduced to the complex diversity of recent American poetry and poetics outside the mainstream.

While most reviews and discussion of American poetry have centered on conventional lyricism, especially as filtered through the kind of confessional work promoted by poetry workshops, Hoover has drawn attention to a wide range of experimental work from second-generation New York school writers like Alice Notley and Maureen Owen to language writers like Bruce Andrews and Charles Bernstein. A poet-in-residence at Chicago's Columbia College, Hoover has the academic credentials to present a credible case for innovative and experimental writing, and *Postmodern American Poetry,* offering selections from Charles Olson to Bernstein, may be the most admired successor, among many candidates, to Donald Allen's *The New American Poetry,* the anthology published in 1960 that first mapped out the traditions alternative American poetry has, for the most part, followed since.

Hoover wrote in the introduction to his anthology that the book "shows that avant-garde poetry endures in its resistence to mainstream ideology; it is the avant-garde that renews poetry as a whole through new, but initially shocking, artistic strategies." At the time he said this, one could find critics and at times even poets arguing that the avant-garde was dead, that it had perhaps been merely a phenomenon specific to the late nineteenth and early twentieth centuries. But by presenting works by poets as radically innovative (and radically different from one another) as Gustaf Sobin, Robert Grenier, and Michael Palmer, Hoover showed that the obituaries were somewhat premature. In the succeeding years, as enthusiasm for workshop poetry has faded while the attention given to Palmer, Notley, Susan Howe, and others recognized by Hoover has expanded, both his anthology and his journal have emerged as key entry points to American writing at the end of the century.

Hoover's influence as a critic and editor is due in part to his own accomplished work as a writer. His first book, *Letter to Einstein Beginning Dear Albert* (1979), was received by John Ashbery as "exciting and important," and the later work in his book *Totem and*

Shadow: New and Selected Poems (1999) appears to search, said *Publishers Weekly,* "for a way to articulate a more positivist poetic, whether it be through affirmative eros . . . or beauty"; the poems, the reviewer noted, are characterized by questioning that is "genuine." Between these two books Hoover published other collections of poetry and a novel, all of which earned high marks from reviewers and critics. *Viridian* (1997) won the Contemporary Poetry Series competition of the University of Georgia Press. A section of his novel, *Saigon, Illinois* (1988), appeared in the *New Yorker,* and the book itself was issued in the Vintage Contemporaries series.

Hoover's work is distinguished by an allegiance to a diversity of aesthetic tendencies. Like his anthology and his journal, his poetry responds to traditions as different as the lyricism of the New York school and the linguistic interrogations of language writing. His poetry is marked as well by a strong surrealist element and by narrative control, the latter at a time when many poets were, at least briefly, avoiding narrative as too restrictive. He is also a humorous poet—one of the few truly humorous poets of his generation—as suggested by an early work, "We've Decided" from *Nervous Songs* (1986):

> I can be myself today, tall space ape
> in a garden where other space apes play.
> What a nice time this will be! and I
> can roll on the sides of my balled feet
> like a hairy barrel loaded, swinging arms
> that scratch the ground like leaves. I'm
> an ape today, headed for my pulpit of joy
> in sunshine by the window.

But he can equally master a darker and meditative tone, as in these lines from "Stationary Journey," collected in *Viridian:*

> At the outskirts of everyplace else,
> the afternoon grows tall then leans back in its window.
> Isadora's scarf catches in Sylvia's wheel.
> The traffic is calm as a locked museum.
> Silence wakes with red leaves on its lips.

The range of Hoover's work is as unusually broad as the range of his critical and editorial tastes. He is capable of doing so much, and doing it so well, that one who is looking for a point of entry to the intricate and various currents of the contemporary American avant-garde would do well to start with him.

—Edward Foster

HOVE, Chenjerai

Nationality: Zimbabwean. **Born:** 1956. **Education:** Attended the Catholic Marist Brothers schools, Kutama and Dete, 1970s; trained as a teacher, Gweru; studied literature and education, University of South Africa; University of Zimbabwe, 1984. **Career:** Has worked as a teacher and also as editor for several publishers, including Mambo Press, Gweru, 1984. Writer-in-residence, University of Zimbabwe. Founding member, and chairman, 1984–92, Zimbabwe Writers Union. **Awards:** Zimbabwe Book Publishers Literary award, and Noma Award for Publishing in Africa, both 1989, both for *Bones.*

PUBLICATIONS

Poetry

Up in Arms. Harare, Zimbabwe, Zimbabwe Publishing House, 1982.
Red Hills of Home. Gweru, Zimbabwe, Mambo Press, 1985.
Shadows. Harare, Zimbabwe, Baobab Books, and London, Heinemann, 1991.
Rainbows in the Dust. Harare, Zimbabwe, Baobab Books, 1998.

Play

Radio Play: *Sister Sing Again Someday,* 1989.

Novels

Masimba Avanhu? Gweru, Zimbabwe, Mambo Press, 1986.
Bones. Harare, Zimbabwe, Baobab Books, and Cape Town, David Philip, 1988; Oxford and Portsmouth, New Hampshire, Heinemann, 1990.
Ancestors. Harare, Zimbabwe, College Press, and London, Picador, 1996.

Other

Guardians of the Soil: Meeting Zimbabwe's Elders. Harare, Zimbabwe, Baobab Books, and Munich, Germany, Frederking and Thaler Verlag, 1996.
Shebeen Tales: Messages from Harare. Harare, Zimbabwe, Baobab Books, 1994; London, Serif, 1997.

*

Critical Studies: "Power, Popular Consciousness, and the Fictions of War: Hove's 'Bones' and Chinodya's 'Harvest of Thorns'" by Liz Gunner, in *African Languages and Cultures* (Oxford, England), 4(1), 1991; "Language Thieves: English-Language Strategies in Two Zimbabwean Novellas" by Dan Wylie, in *English in Africa* (Grahamstown, South Africa), 18(2), October 1991; "'I Do Not Know Her, but Someone Ought to Know Her': Chenjerai Hove's 'Bones'" by Annie Gagiano, in *World Literature Written in English* (Singapore), 32–33(2–1), 1992–93; "'Dances with Bones': Hove's Romanticized Africa" by Flora Veit-Wild, in *Research in African Literatures* (Bloomington, Indiana), 24(3), fall 1993; "Self-Definition As a Catalyst for Resistance in Hove's 'Bones'" by Pauline Kaldas, in *Alif* (Cairo), 13, 1993; "'The Fading Songs of Chimurenga': Chenjerai Hove and the Subversion of Nationalist Politics in Zimbabwean Literature" by Mxolisi R. Sibanyoni, in *African Studies* (Wits, South Africa), 54(2), 1995; "The New Zimbabwe Writing and Chimurenga" by Angus Calder, in *Wasafiri* (England), 22, autumn 1995; "Thinking about Nativism in Chenjerai Hove's Work" by Matthew Engelke, in *Research in African Literatures* (Columbus, Ohio), 29(2), summer 1998.

*   *   *

Chenjerai Hove is a writer who grew up acutely conscious of the injustices imposed upon Africans during the colonial era. The year 1980 was of historical importance to Hove and Zimbabwe, as it was the year of independence from colonial rule. His voice is Zimbabwean, speaking of the Zimbabwean experience yesterday and today and perhaps implicitly warning us of tomorrow. It is born out of Zimbabwe's short, painful history, impartial to oppressor or oppressed. In the 1970s Hove attended Catholic schools and then trained as a teacher in Gweru and pursued degree studies in literature and education. It was during this time that some of his love poems and stories in Shona were published. Fourteen of his poems in English were particularly inspired by the war of liberation that he witnessed as a secondary school teacher and were published in 1980 in *And Now the Poets Speak*. Hove's status as a serious writer was confirmed with the publication of *Up in Arms* and *Red Hills of Home*. He has continued to distinguish himself in his writings in English and in Shona, the latter being used mostly in love poems, as it was the traditional form he grew up with. In his works he is haunted by the plight of the weak and vulnerable members of society who are powerless to defend themselves against the dominant historical and social forces.

In an interview conducted by Flora Wild, Hove revealed many intimate aspects of his writing. He shares the vision of Wilfred Owen, who also wrote about the absurdity of the war and the universality of human experience. In addition, Hove was influenced by two Africans writing in English: Okot p'Bitek, whose imagery Hove found to be particularly African, and Chinua Achebe, whose writings were expressive of an African experience. Regarding *Up in Arms*, Hove has said, "I question a lot of what we do in the name of civilization, for example the sophisticated methods of killing and things like that. So I do that deliberately to look at our society and shock our society into looking at itself more critically because it has destroyed itself to a point where, as I say, it is making mince-meat out of the human body." By implication he concedes that life is essentially painful, yet he has seen enough to know that without pain there is no pleasure and vice versa. *Up in Arms* is a commentary on the Zimbabwean struggle, treating such themes as dying in the bush and in the village and supporting the freedom fighters. The compactness of the work is illustrated by the fusion of the two parallel ideas of the anxious waiting of a pregnant woman and of a wife for the return of her husband from battle; both involve pain, pleasure, and resentment. In *Up in Arms* Hove creates paradoxical expressions by juxtaposing seemingly incompatible words or lines to force the reader to focus on something beyond, beneath, or in between the words. This can be seen, for example, in "A War-Time Wife," where the woman is

> Torpedoed with bulging wars
> and swelling with fragrant hope . . .
> Till one day, may be night,
> raids rupture hope and expectancy.

In "Death of a Soldier" Hove uses words in new combinations to enable us to experience directly through the various levels of his poetic medium:

> flooded with a christened hate . . .
> He died to haunt the soulless
> and to cleanse the earth he manured;
> Praise the living
> With well-nourished greens.

Another technique employed by Hove is the use of silence. By allowing silence to speak for him, he forces the reader to be still. Once the reader is still, he is aware of the poem as an energy force and of the life-death struggle of flesh and blood. In the poem ''To Father at Home,'' for example, one can almost touch the unspoken loneliness and despair that exist in the space between the lines. The horror of the Zimbabwean drought is evoked in these lines:

> If it doesn't fall
> The droplets roam the sky
> and the clouds swell with us.
> If it doesn't fall,
> then, father,
> it's we
> Who have to fall.

Hove's language is simple, and the intention is to express the Zimbabwean experience in an everyday language by referring to the village people's struggle for independence without direct mention of the war. Through his poems, Hove is trying to restore man to himself as he was when he was still free, before he was in the situation of the oppressor and the oppressed.

In *Red Hills of Home* Hove again uses the themes of pain, wounds, and scars. His images are arbitrary, and the vague feeling of despair makes the reader ponder the cause of suffering. Hove leaves this out of his poems, however, letting the physical reality remain a mystery. In *Rainbows in the Dust* we hear the same voice, passionate, gentle, strong, and haunted by shadows and visions and often by quiet despair. The poems to Ken Saro-Wiwa are compassionate, flowing from what Hove describes as a bank of memories where treasured tales are kept.

Hove is a leading figure in postcolonial Zimbabwean literature. He reveals a romanticized notion of Africa in re-creating a usable past. He has not, however, necessarily abandoned realist strategies of writing and feels no need to abandon a glorification of African history. Hove's poetry addresses itself to the human heart. He uses descriptive language to evoke powerful images and metaphors in re-creating how it was or how it is, yet he never explains why it is.

—Renu Barrett

HOWARD, Richard (Joseph)

Nationality: American. **Born:** Cleveland, Ohio, 13 October 1929. **Education:** Shaker Heights High School, Ohio; Columbia University, New York (editor, *Columbia Review*), B.A. 1951, M.A. 1952; Sorbonne, Paris, 1953–54. **Career:** Lexicographer, World Publishing Company, Cleveland, 1954–56, and Funk & Wagnalls, New York, 1956–58. Since 1958 freelance literary and art critic, and translator. Since 1988 Rhodes Professor of comparative literature, University of Cincinnati. Poetry editor, *American Review,* New York, *Shenandoah,* Virginia, *New Republic, Paris Review,* and *Western Humanities Review;* director, Braziller Poetry Series. President, P.E.N. American Center, 1977–79. Professor of English, University of Houston, 1987–97; since 1998 professor of practice, School of the Arts, Columbia University. **Awards:** Guggenheim fellowship, 1966; Harriet Monroe memorial prize, 1969, and Levinson prize, 1973 (*Poetry,* Chicago); American Academy grant, 1970, and award of merit medal, 1980; Pulitzer Prize, 1970; American Book award, for translation, 1983;

P.E.N. medal for translation, 1986; National Endowment for the Arts fellowship, 1987; France-America Foundation award, for translation, 1987; Academy of American Poets fellowship, 1989. Fellow, Morse College, Yale University, New Haven, Connecticut. MacArthur fellow, beginning 1996. Member, American Academy, 1983. **Address:** 23 Waverly Place, New York, New York 10011, U.S.A.

PUBLICATIONS

Poetry

Quantities. Middletown, Connecticut, Wesleyan University Press, 1962.
The Damages. Middletown, Connecticut, Wesleyan University Press, 1967.
Untitled Subjects. New York, Atheneum, 1969.
Findings. New York, Atheneum, 1971.
Two-Part Inventions (includes radio play *The Lesson of the Master*). New York, Atheneum, 1974.
Fellow Feelings. New York, Atheneum, 1976.
Misgivings. New York, Atheneum, 1979.
Lining Up. New York, Atheneum, 1984.
Helenistics. New York, Red Ozier Press, 1984.
No Traveller. New York, Knopf, 1989.
Selected Poems. London, Penguin, 1991.
Like Most Revelations: New Poems. New York, Pantheon Books, 1994.
Trappings: New Poems. Turtle Point Books, 1999.

Plays

Wildflowers & the Lesson of the Master (produced New York, 1976).
A Phenomenon of Nature (produced Massachussetts, 1977).
Two-Part Inventions (produced Chicago, 1979).

Other

Alone with America: Essays on the Art of Poetry in the United States since 1950. New York, Atheneum, 1969; London, Thames and Hudson, 1970; revised edition, Atheneum, 1980.
Michel Delacroix's Paris. New York, International Archive of Art, 1990.

Editor, *Preferences: 51 American Poets Choose Poems from Their Own Work and from the Past.* New York, Viking Press, 1974.

Translator, *The Immoralist,* by André Gide. New York, Random House, 1954.
Translator, *The Voyeur,* by Alain Robbe-Grillet. New York, Grove Press, 1958; London, Calder, 1959.
Translator, *The Wind,* by Claude Simon. New York, Braziller, 1959.
Translator, *The Automobile Graveyard,* a play by Fernando Arrabal (produced New York, 1961). Published with *The Two Executioners,* 1960.
Translator, *The Grass,* by Claude Simon. New York, Braziller, 1960; London, Cape, 1961.
Translator, *Two Novels (Jealousy and In the Labyrinth),* by Alain Robbe-Grillet. New York, Grove Press, 1960.

Translator, *Najda,* by André Breton. New York, Grove Press, 1961.

Translator, *Last Year at Marienbad,* by Alain Robbe-Grillet. New York, Grove Press, and London, Calder and Boyars, 1962.

Translator, *Mobile,* by Michel Butor. New York, Simon and Schuster, 1963.

Translator, *Manhood,* by Michel Leiris. New York, Grossman, 1963; London, Cape, 1968.

Translator, *Force of Circumstance,* by Simone de Beauvoir. New York, Simon and Schuster, 1963; London, Deutsch-Weidenfeld and Nicolson, 1965.

Translator, *Erasers,* by Alain Robbe-Grillet. New York, Grove Press, 1964; London, Calder and Boyars, 1966.

Translator, *For a New Novel: Essays on Fiction,* by Alain Robbe-Grillet. New York, Grove Press, 1966.

Translator, *The Poetics of Paul Valéry,* by Jean Hytier. New York, Doubleday, 1966.

Translator, *Natural Histories,* by Jules Renard. New York, Horizon Press, 1966.

Translator, *History of Surrealism,* by Maurice Nadeau. New York, Macmillan, 1967; London, Cape, 1968.

Translator, *Histoire,* by Claude Simon. New York, Braziller, 1968; London, Cape, 1969.

Translator, *May Day Speech,* by Jean Genet. San Francisco, City Lights, 1970.

Translator, *Professional Secrets: An Autobiography,* by Jean Cocteau. New York, Farrar Straus, 1970; London, Vision Press, 1972.

Translator, *The Fall into Time,* by E.M. Cioran. Chicago, Quadrangle, 1970.

Translator, *The Battle of Pharsalus,* by Claude Simon. New York, Braziller, and London, Cape, 1971.

Translator, *Dramatic Personages,* by Denis De Rougement. N.p., Kennikat, 1971.

Translator, *A Happy Death,* by Albert Camus. New York, Knopf, and London, Hamish Hamilton, 1972.

Translator, *Critical Essays,* by Roland Barthes. Evanston, Illinois, Northwestern University Press, 1972.

Translator, *Rosa,* by Maurice Pons. New York, Dial Press, 1972; London, New English Library, 1973.

Translator, *Project for a Revolution in New York,* by Alain Robbe-Grillet. New York, Grove Press, 1972; London, Calder and Boyars, 1973.

Translator, *The Fantastic,* by Tzvetan Todorov. Cleveland, Case Western Reserve University Press, 1973.

Translator, *Quebec versus Ottawa: The Struggle for Self-Government 1960–1972,* by Claude Morin. Toronto, University of Toronto Press, 1976.

Translator, *France and Algeria,* by Germaine Tillion. Westport, Connecticut, Greenwood Press, 1976.

Translator, *The Motorcycle,* by André Pieyre De Mandiargues. Westport, Connecticut, Greenwood Press, 1977.

Translator, *The Poetics of Prose,* by Tzvetan Todorov. Ithaca, New York, Cornell University Press, 1977.

Translator, *Roland Barthes,* by Barthes. New York, Hill and Wang, 1977.

Translator, *Song for an Equinox,* by St.-John Perse. Princeton, New Jersey, Princeton University Press, 1977.

Translator, *A Lover's Discourse: Fragments,* by Roland Barthes. New York, Hill and Wang, 1978; London, Cape, 1979.

Translator, *The Eiffel Tower and Other Mythologies,* by Roland Barthes. New York, Hill and Wang, 1979.

Translator, *The One Pig with Horn,* by Laurent de Brunhoff. New York, Pantheon, 1979.

Translator, *The Girl Beneath the Lion,* by André Pieyre De Mandiargues. New York, Riverrun Press, 1980.

Translator, *New Critical Essays,* by Roland Barthes. New York, Hill and Wang, 1980.

Translator, *Camera Lucida: Reflections on Photography,* by Roland Barthes. New York, Hill and Wang, 1981; London, Cape, 1982.

Translator, *The Girl on the Motorcycle,* by André Pieyre De Mandiargues. New York, Riverrun Press, 1981.

Translator, *The Trouble with Being Born,* by E.M. Cioran. New York, Seaver, 1981.

Translator, *An Introduction to Poetics,* by Tzvetan Todorov. Minneapolis, University of Minnesota Press, 1981.

Translator, *The Margin,* by André Pieyre De Mandiargues. New York, Riverrun Press, 1981.

Translator, *Ideologies in Quebec: The Historical Development,* by Denis Monière. Toronto, University of Toronto Press, 1981.

Translator, *Les Fleurs du Mal,* by Baudelaire. Brighton, Sussex, Harvester Press, 1982; Boston, Godine, 1983.

Translator, *Witches' Sabbath,* by Maurice Sachs. Chelsea, Michigan, Scarborough House, 1982.

Translator, *Empire of Signs,* by Roland Barthes. New York, Hill and Wang, 1982; London, Cape, 1983.

Translator, *Corydon,* by André Gide. New York, Farrar Straus, 1983.

Translator, with Matthew Ward, *The Fashion System,* by Roland Barthes. New York, Hill and Wang, 1983; London, Cape, 1985.

Translator, *Drawn and Quartered,* by E.M. Cioran. New York, Seaver, 1983.

Translator, *The Complete War Memoirs of Charles De Gaulle, 1940–1946.* New York, Da Capo Press, 1984.

Translator, *The Dark Brain of Piranesi and Other Essays,* by Marguerite Yourcenar. New York, Farrar Straus, 1984.

Translator, *The Grain of His Voice 1962–1980* (interviews), by Roland Barthes. New York, Hill and Wang, 1984.

Translator, *The Conquest of America,* by Tzetvan Todorov. New York, Harper, 1984.

Translator, *The Responsibility of Forms,* by Roland Barthes. New York, Hill and Wang, 1985.

Translator, *William Marshal: The Flower of Chivalry,* by Georges Duby. New York, Pantheon, 1985; London, Faber, 1986.

Translator, *A Strange Virus of Unknown Origin. A.I.D.S.,* by Jacques Leibowitch. New York, Ballantine, 1985.

Translator, *The Flanders Road,* by Claude Simon. New York, Riverrun Press, 1986.

Translator, *The Last Flowers of Manet,* by Robert Gordon and Andrew Forge. New York, Abrams, 1986.

Translator, *The Opposing Shore,* by Julien Gracq. New York, Columbia University Press, 1986.

Translator, *The Temptation to Exist,* by E.M. Cioran. New York, Seaver, 1986.

Translator, *The Rustle of Language,* by Roland Barthes. New York, Hill and Wang, 1986.

Translator, *Michelet,* by Roland Barthes. New York, Hill and Wang, and London, Blackwell, 1987.

Translator, *Past Tense: The Cocteau Diaries,* vols. 1 and 2, by Jean Cocteau. San Diego, Harcourt Brace, 2 vols., 1987–88.

Translator, *Balcony in the Forest,* by Julien Gracq. New York, Columbia University Press, 1987.

Translator, *History and Utopia,* by E.M. Cioran. New York, Seaver, 1987.

Translator, *The Traitor,* by André Gorz. New York, Routledge, 1988.

Translator, *Amyntas: North African Journals,* by André Gide. New York, Ecco Press, 1988.

Translator, *The Semiotic Challenge,* by Roland Barthes. New York, Hill and Wang, 1988.

Translator, *The Pink and the Green, and Mina de Vanghel,* by Stendhal. New York, New Directions, and London, Hamish Hamilton, 1988.

Translator, *Love in Two Languages,* by Abdelkebir Khatibi. Minneapolis, University of Minnesota Press, 1990.

More than 100 other translations of French works published.

*

Critical Studies: "Cleaving and Burning: An Essay on Richard Howard's Poetry" by Henry Sloss, in *Shenandoah* (Lexington, Virginia), 29(1), 1977; "A Conversation with Richard Howard" by Paul H. Gray, in *Literature in Performance: A Journal of Literary and Performing Art* (Chico, California), November 1981; in *Salmagundi* (Saratoga Springs, New York), fall-winter 1987; "A Chronicle of Vanishings," by Robert Richman, in *The New Criterion* (New York), December 1989; "Choosing Our Fathers: Gender and Identity in Whitman, Ashbery, and Richard Howard," by David Bergman, in *American Literary History* (Cary, North Carolina), summer 1989; "Physical Measures," by Jeffrey Donaldson, in *Salmagundi,* fall-winter 1991; "The Figure of Edith Wharton in Richard Howard's Poem *The Lesson of the Master,*" by Adeline Tintner, in *Edith Wharton Review* (Brooklyn), fall 1992; "Reading Off the Wall: Recent Books by Richard Howard," by Bin Ramke, in *Denver Quarterly,* fall 1995.

*   *   *

Since the appearance of his first book, *Quantities,* in 1962, Richard Howard's distinguished career has firmly established him as one of our most prolific poets, critics, editors, and translators. The course of his poetic development seems to me to represent the difficult and treacherous job of surmounting and transforming his learning, sophistication, and brilliance instead of simply displaying them. As with Auden, for example, an acknowledged model for Howard, he is so good at writing interesting and skillful poems that he tends to be taken in by his own cleverness.

In *Quantities,* with its variety of subjects, flexibility and power of language and structure, and penetrating insight, Howard has much to say, coupled with a virtuoso ability to say it. "The Return from Montauk," for example, presents a beautifully balanced moment in terms of a natural yet complex and ambiguous symbol. The speaker is riding a train at nightfall, and, looking to the east, he sees an image of the setting sun reflected in a window. The double perspective is completed when he turns toward the west and sees through the train window the actual setting sun, imagining, however, in line with the logic of his previously established conception, that it is the rising sun. Thus, at the moment of sunset he can envision out of the literal structure of the perception itself the sunrise, and at the moment of despair, the rebirth of hope. It is a clear and delicate poem, intricately wrought, suggesting implications that go far below its pellucid surface. It also is a thematically central poem in the book as a whole,

for Howard characteristically deals with the knife-edge upon which opposites are balanced. His vision of the abyss that falls between them is neither deep nor powerful, however, and hence the tension in his poems is sometimes not strong.

With *The Damages* we find an increased assurance and depth coupled with an increasing prolixity and confirmation of his glib knowingness. In "For Hephaistos" there is the inevitable and moving confrontation with Auden, who "taught me, taught us all a way / To speak our minds," and the speaker's grateful sense of being free of his master: "only now, at last / Free of you, my old ventriloquist, / Have I suspected what I have to say / Without hearing you say it for me first." In "The Encounter" we find a marvelously erotic and mysterious confrontation between the nameless Hero and The Female that rises convincingly to the level of myth. There are, on the other hand, Jamesian and Proustian vignettes of childhood ("Seeing Cousin Phyllis Off," "Intimation of Mortality," "Private Drive"); poems of friends, literature, and travel ("Seferiades," "Even the Most Beautiful Sunset"); and clever poems such as "To Aegidius Cantor," "Eusebius to Florestan," and "Bonnard: A Novel" that continue Howard's own line of literary ventriloquism and that anticipate the extended fascination he was to develop for the dramatic monologue in subsequent volumes.

Untitled Subjects, which won a Pulitzer, consists entirely of fifteen such monologues (mostly in the form of letters), spoken by such nineteenth-century worthies as Scott, Ruskin, Thackeray, and Mrs. William Morris and arranged chronologically from 1801 to 1915. Howard alludes to Browning in his dedication, "the great poet of otherness," and quotes the poet's saying that "I'll tell my state as though 'twere none of mine." This clearly implies that Browning was writing about himself while pretending to be speaking in the voices of others, which I think was true. But I do not think that this makes him simply a poet of otherness or that Howard's dramatic monologues are similar to his master's. What Howard's poems do, in fact, is "to bring history alive," as the jacket blurb for a historical novel or costume drama might say. They bring the past closer to us, first, by treating it as if it were present and, second, by making it personal and intimate, putting back in, as it were, what the official histories leave out. What they do not accomplish often enough, however, is catch the character in a moment of crisis, confrontation, and self-revelation, as Browning's usually do.

Similar poems make up the first part of *Findings,* and in the fourteen-page poem "November, 1889" Browning himself speaks as he nears the moment of death. It is revealing that Howard puts these words into the master's mouth:

> what is dead or dying
> is more readily apprehended by us
>   than what is part of life.
>   Nothing in writing is
> easier than to raise the dead.

Perhaps this is more Howard than Browning, and so he moves on in the second part to personal poems of love and friendship.

Two-Part Inventions varies the form by expanding the monologue to the dialogue and by broadening Howard's range of subjects to include Hölderlin, Wilde's visit to Whitman, Ibsen at Capri, Edith Wharton, Rodin, and Di Fiore. *Fellow Feelings* returns to the more usual lyric mode but deals, nevertheless, in its first section with Hart Crane, Randall Jarrell, Valery Larbaud, Auden, and Goethe. Although the second section occupies more personal ground, poets, as

Howard himself says, make "themselves public / without making themselves known." In the third section he characteristically comes back to beloved objets d'art by Donatello, Simone Martini, Bellini, and others. *Misgivings* contains commentaries on the subjects photographed by Nadar, poems about people from the Renaissance to the present, and a series of love poems.

With *Lining Up,* however, we find an increasing self-awareness and hence an increasing depth of feeling and insight. Although Howard continues to employ his intricate Marianne Moore-like syllabic stanzas and although he still favors the ventriloquist's and the connoisseur's approach, he nevertheless penetrates to deeper levels of intensity. Indeed, it almost seems as if he is acknowledging earlier criticisms of his dandified and objective manner when he writes, "I go round on the back of that other life / my reading relinquishes / like the little Egyptian heron that lives / on the backs of cows. The shoe fits perfectly" ("Homage"). Elsewhere he says, *"Figures / speak,* that is the assumption: / we receive our riches only when they come / to meet us on another's voice" ("Attic Red-Figure Calyx"). In the context of this volume the remarks are more than a mere apologia; they signify, rather, the achievement of an enriched *ars poetica,* an indication of Howard's developed ability to raise the objective to the level of the subjective. In defending Jane Austen against Charlotte Brontë's characterization of her as passionless, he says, "Wisdom's secret is detachment, not / withdrawal" ("On Lately Looking in Chapman's Jane Austen").

"Move Still, Still So," as an example, is an astonishingly brilliant erotic poem. Gladys, one of Lewis Carroll's nymphet photography models, now grown up, is talking in 1925 to her psychiatrist. Interspersed are Carroll's directions to her in 1895 as she poses in the nude. The gist, something that is not quite stated and so must be inferred from the dramatic context, is that she has a way of becoming immobile in order to release her orgasm, a curious passivity that she learned from the pleasure she felt when she held still as Carroll prepared to snap her picture but that confuses her husband into thinking that she is unresponsive during sex. The implications are delicate and pornographic at one and the same time, and the Browningesque moment of self-revelation is brilliantly managed.

Howard's volume *No Traveller* begins with a thirty-page series of letters about a strange encounter with Wallace Stevens in 1953 ("Even in Paris"), and it ends with an even stranger twenty-two-page monologue spoken by Vera Lachman ("Oracles"), an aged and sibylline professor living out her days at a scholar's retreat in Greece. Especially in the latter Howard verges on the mystical, a rite for "the discovery / of a god reborn." In between are shorter poems dealing with Loie Fuller, Proust, Rodin, Wordsworth, Fuseli, Kafka, and Woolf and with several domestic and family situations. Howard shows in this volume that he has become not only one of our most skillful but also one of our more significant poets.

Howard confronts the theme of feeling and art directly in the title poem of the volume *Like Most Revelations,* in which he rings the changes in a tightly organized lyric on the puzzling, intricate, and mutually destructive and creative relationships between the "movement" of a poem and its "form." The remainder of the volume opens up a rich display of dramatic and semidramatic monologues, lyrics, and elegies, all done in his characteristically low-keyed style— sometimes deliberately prosaic—and arranged in what seem like intricate syllabic stanzas. Thus we have the expected gallery of historical and more modern personages, including Henry James, Matisse, Isadora Duncan, Gertrude and Leo Stein, Disraeli, Mozart, Beckett, Frost, and Stevens, as well as many less specifically located

poems about art, writers, and artists. There is also an increasingly gnomic strain emerging, in which Howard includes epigrammatic sayings in his poems. Examples include "Humanity has always been the story-telling animal / that must lie to itself in order to believe"; "Unnatural acts are assigned to many, but it is always / nature which has shown—even by concealing—the way"; and "Love is / not love until it is vulnerable." Evident here also is the emergence of a new and difficult subject—the death of friends from AIDS. In addition to elegies for Donald Barthelme, Robert Phelps, James Boatwright, and others, there are specific mentions of the plague in the elegies for Matthew Ward and David Kalstone and in the long poem that concludes the book, "Man Who Beat Up Homosexuals Reported to Have AIDS Virus."

—Norman Friedman

HOWE, Fanny (Quincy)

Nationality: American. **Born:** Buffalo, New York, 15 October 1940. **Education:** Stanford University, Stanford, California, 1958–61. **Family:** Married 1) Frederick Delafield in 1961 (divorced 1963); 2) Carl Senna in 1968 (divorced in 1975); two daughters and one son. **Career:** Lecturer, Tufts University, Boston, 1968–71, Emerson College, Boston, 1974, Columbia University, New York, 1975–78, Yale University, New Haven, Connecticut, 1976, Harvard Extension, Cambridge, Massachusetts, 1977, Massachusetts Institute of Technology, Cambridge, Massachusetts, 1978–87. Since 1987 professor, University of California, San Diego. Associate director, University of California Study Center, London, England, 1993–95; distinguished visiting writer in residence, Mills College, 1996–97. **Awards:** MacDowell Colony fellowship, 1965, 1990; National Endowment for the Arts fellowship, 1969, 1991; Bunting Institute fellow, 1974; St. Botolph award for fiction, 1976; Writer's Choice award for fiction, 1984; *Village Voice* award for fiction, 1988; guest poet, Fondation Royaumont, Translations Center, France, 1990, Cambridge Conference on Poetry, Cambridge University, England, 1993, Southampton Conference on Poetry, Southampton University, England, 1993, Conference on New Poetry, Cork, Ireland, 1999, and Library of Congress, 1999; National Poetry Foundation Award, 1998; America Award, 1999. **Address:** 5580 La Jolla Blvd., #31, La Jolla, California 92037, U.S.A..

PUBLICATIONS

Poetry

Eggs. Boston, Houghton Mifflin, 1970.
The Amerindian Coastline Poem. New York, Telephone Books, 1976.
Alsace Lorraine. New York, Telephone Books, 1982.
For Erato. Berkeley, California, Tuumba Press, 1984.
Introduction to the World. New York, The Figures, 1985.
Robeson Street. Boston, Alice James Books, 1985.
The Lives of a Spirit. Los Angeles, Sun and Moon, 1986.
The Vineyard. Providence, Lost Roads, 1988.
The End. Los Angeles, Littoral Books, 1992.
The Quietist. Oakland, California, O Books, 1992.

O'Clock. London, Reality Street Editions, 1995.
One Crossed Out. Minnesota, Graywolf Press, 1997.
Q. England, Paul Green Press, 1998.
Forged. Sausalito, California, Post Apollo Press, 1999.
Selected Poems. Berkeley, University of California Press, 2000.

Novels

First Marriage. New York, Avon Equinox, 1975.
Bronte Wilde. New York, Avon Equinox, 1976.
Holy Smoke. New York, Fiction Collective, 1979.
The White Slave. New York, Avon Books, 1980.
The Blue Hills (for children). New York, Avon Books, 1981.
Yeah, But (for children). New York, Avon Books, 1982.
Radio City (for children). New York, Avon Books, 1984.
In the Middle of Nowhere. New York, Fiction Collective, 1984.
The Race of the Radical (for children). New York, Viking, 1985.
Taking Care. New York, Avon Books, 1985.
The Deep North. Los Angeles, Sun and Moon, 1988.
Famous Questions. New York, Ballantine, 1989.
Saving History. Los Angeles, Sun and Moon, 1992.
Nod. Los Angeles, Sun and Moon, 1998.

Short Stories

Forty Whacks. Boston, Houghton Mifflin, 1969.

*

Manuscript Collection: Stanford University Libraries, Stanford, California.

Critical Studies: In *Writing/Talks* by Bob Perelman, Carbondale, Southern Illinois University Press, 1985; in *Letters from Nowhere: Fanny Howe's Forty Whacks and Feminine Identity* edited by Carol J. Singley and Susan Elizabeth Sweeney, Albany, State University of New York Press, 1993.

Fanny Howe comments:

My whole effort as a novelist has been to study the imaginary, invisible, and utopian trend of each character alongside their active (political) social business. This terrible stress is expressed for me in fictional forms that separate thought from enterprise. That is what I do when I write a story—attempt to clarify the boundaries and turn them into escapes, as in the rubbery walls of an amoeba there is the ingredient for fusion.

My poetry has continued to work as a response to the daily world and how strange it is in every aspect, and I think the Arabic poetic form the ghazel is closest to the paths my own poems take. Translating a line from one of Ghalib's ghazels, Adrienne Rich wrote, "The lightning-stroke of the vision was meant for us, not for Sinai."

*   *   *

Fanny Howe has established herself as a prolific and innovative craftsperson both in poetry and in fiction. Besides several collections of poetry, she has also published a number of works of fiction. But such a distinction may be misleading, for in Howe's work the boundary between poetry and fiction is blurred. Howe began her career with two books from the major commercial publisher Houghton Mifflin: a collection of relatively traditional short stories, *Forty Whacks* (1969), and a collection of shapely lyric poems, *Eggs* (1970). In the 1970s Avon Books, a mass-circulation paperback house, began publishing Howe's novels. But the trajectory of Howe's career since then has carried her away from commercial publishers toward more avant-garde venues: the Fiction Collective, various small poetry presses, and Sun & Moon, an important publisher of experimental writing. As Howe has moved away from commercial presses, her work has increasingly been located on the shifting boundary between poetry and fiction.

Howe's later novels, such as *The Deep North* and *Saving History,* intermittently move from narrative into extended poetic riffs, in which the focus shifts from such traditional fictional concerns as character and action to the pleasures and the perils of verbal play. At the same time, in her poetry Howe has moved away from self-contained lyrics to sequences that often include a distinct narrative dimension, and the most dazzling of these sequences, *The Lives of a Spirit,* is a long prose poem. In significant measure, then, Howe has invented her own forms, and any adequate survey of her work must take into account the interplay between her poetry and her fiction.

Howe has often been grouped with the so-called language poets, an avant-garde group that since the 1970s has dedicated itself to an analytic deconstruction of the semantic and syntactic texture of language. One of Howe's sequences, "Alsace-Lorraine," is included in the principal anthology of language poetry, Ron Silliman's *In the American Tree,* and the publisher Sun & Moon is best known as the publisher of such language poets as Charles Bernstein, Lyn Hejinian, and Clark Coolidge. Howe is also linked to this movement through her sister, Susan Howe, who is generally seen as one of the major figures among the language poets.

Like the work of other writers in this movement, Howe's poetry is assertively difficult. She eschews the fragmentary syntax of some language poets and instead normally writes in sentences. But the logical connections among her sentences are often radically attenuated, so that we are forced to puzzle out the linkages for ourselves. Her longer sequences in particular work with subtle and muted patterns of recurrence that emerge only with repeated rereadings. Despite these stylistic links to language poetry, however, Howe returns again and again to certain themes that make her work atypical of the movement. First, Howe's work presents itself under the sign of Eros. Both in her poetry and her fiction she gives voice to the longings that draw human beings together—woman and man, parent and child. Second, for Howe these fundamental human relationships always have both political and spiritual dimensions. In Howe's world human beings always hunger not only for love but also for justice and righteousness. Her fiction regularly has its climax in a moment of ethical choice in which her characters, even if they are not themselves believers, act as if G-d (to use her own spelling) were watching. Her poetry, too, is consistently haunted by the possibility of G-d's presence, often envisioned in explicitly Christian—indeed, Roman Catholic—terms.

Howe's most significant poetic achievement is *The Lives of a Spirit,* which locates itself within the tradition of Rilke's *Duino Elegies.* In this book-length sequence the openness of the text, the sometimes dizzying abysses between the sentences, invite the reader to embark on a spiritual pilgrimage parallel to the author's. Howe avoids Rilke's ostentatiously high rhetoric, emphasizing not the potentially transformative power of the angelic visitation but the everyday discipline of spiritual preparation, a stance underscored by the use of thickly textured prose rather than verse. Her sequence of nine elegies begins in a cemetery by the sea and with a baby who is insistently physical—"Her damp skin, soft as a rose petal, was sweet to the cheek"—but who also seems miraculous:

> They surmised that she had floated from the stars in the navy blue sky. Like rain at sea and no one to see, the coherence of these events and conjectures was never going to be accounted for. Now nested in sea heather, the baby will, later, learn her tens and alphabets on a pillow in bed. And will sometimes wonder: Little word, who said me? Am I owned or free?

In the elegies that follow, this spirit, sometimes "she" and sometimes "I," does indeed live multiple lives, as the title of the book suggests. The presence of the mother hovers over the second and third elegies as the child begins to explore her world; the third elegy ends with "I would have said, Mother, stay at the window, but don't call me in." Later the father-as-rule-maker and sister-as-companion move to center stage, and with her lover the spirit comes to know "every level of being . . . from bone to bare skin; and why love is so close to G-d and d—th." But at the end of the ninth elegy the spirit is still—in the words of Simone Weil, Howe's alter ego in this book and throughout her career—"waiting for God":

> If I could just get my little cell in order, they would let me out again. I'm ready to go out. Through my open window, I can see the stone bank along the pond, its serpentine curve beside the path, and beyond the path, the trees. My bench is there, where I sit with folded hands.

Quietly but eloquently, *The Lives of a Spirit* invites us—with mother watching from the window perhaps—to join her waiting on the bench in the park.

—Burton Hatlen

HOWE, Susan

Nationality: American. **Born:** 1937. **Education:** Museum of Fine Arts, Boston, B.F.A. in painting 1961. **Family:** Married David von Schlegell (died 1992); one daughter and one son. **Career:** Butler Fellow in English, 1988, visiting professor of English, 1989, and since 1992 professor of English, State University of New York, Buffalo. Visiting scholar and professor of English, Temple University, Philadelphia, Spring 1990, 1991; visiting poet and Leo Block Professor at University of Denver, 1993–94; visiting Brittingham Scholar, University of Wisconsin, Madison, 1994; visiting poet, University of Arizona, 1994, Oberlin College, Ohio, 1995, and St. Joseph's College, Hartford, Connecticut, 1996; visiting professor, Stanford University, California, 1998. **Awards:** Before Columbus Foundation award, 1980, for *Secret History of the Dividing Line,* and 1986, for *My Emily Dickinson*; New York State Council of the Arts residency, 1987; Fund for Poetry award, 1987, 1989; Roy Harvey Pearce Award for Work by a Poet and Critic, 1996, for *The Birth-mark: Unsettling the Wilderness in American Literary History;* John Simon Guggenheim memorial fellowship, 1996; distinguished fellow, Stanford Humanities Center, 1998. **Address:** 115 New Quarry Road, Guilford, Connecticut 06437, U.S.A.

PUBLICATIONS

Poetry

Hinge Picture. New York, Telephone, 1974.
The Western Borders. Berkeley, California, Tuumba Press, 1976.
Secret History of the Dividing Line. New York, Telephone, 1978.
Cabbage Gardens. Chicago, Fathom Press, 1979.
The Liberties. Guilford, Connecticut, Loon, 1980.
Pythagorean Silence. New York, Montemora, 1982.
Defenestration of Prague. New York, Kulchur, 1983.
Articulation of Sound Forms in Time. Windsor, Vermont, Awede, 1987.
A Bibliography of the King's Book or, Eikon Basilike. Providence, Rhode Island, Paradigm Press, 1989.
The Europe of Trusts: Selected Poems. Los Angeles, Sun and Moon Press, 1990.
Singularities. Middletown, Connecticut, Wesleyan University Press, 1990.
The Nonconformist's Memorial. New York, New Directions, 1993.
Frame Structures. Early Poems, 1974–1978. New York, New Directions, 1996.
Pierce-Arrow. New York, New Directions, 1999.

Other

My Emily Dickinson. Berkeley, California, North Atlantic, 1985.
Incloser. Santa Fe, New Mexico, Weasel Sleeves Press, 1990.
The Birth-mark: Unsettling the Wilderness in American Literary History. Middletown, Connecticut, Wesleyan University Press, 1993.

*

Critical Studies: Susan Howe issue of *Abacus 30* (Elmwood, Connecticut), 15 November 1987, and *The Difficulties,* 3(2), 1989; "Howe's Hope: Impossible Crossings" by Linda Reinfeld, in *Tremblor,* 6, 1987; "The Mysterious Vision of Susan Howe" by George Butterick, in *North Dakota Quarterly* (Grand Forks), 55(4), Fall 1987; "Whowe: An Essay on Work by Susan Howe" by Rachel Blau Du Plessis, in *Sulfur* (Ypsilanti, Michigan), 20, Fall 1987; "Susan Howe: The Book of Cordelia" by Stephen-Paul Martin, in *Open Form and the Feminine Imagination, Postmodern Positions,* vol. 2, Washington, D.C., Maisonneuve Press, 1988; essays by Kathleen Fraser, and Charles Bernstein and Bruce Andrews, in *Postmodern Line in Poetry,* edited by Robert Frank and Henry Sayre, Urbana, University of Illinois Press, 1988; "Collision or Collusion with History: The Lyric of Susan Howe" by Marjorie Perloff, in *Contemporary Literature* (Madison, Wisconsin), 1989; Susan Howe issue of *Talisman* (Hoboken, New Jersey), 4, Spring 1990; *The Pink Guitar: Writing as Feminist Practice* by Rachel Blau DuPlessis, New York and London, Routledge, 1990; *Language Poetry: Writing as Rescue* by Linda Reinfel, Baton Rouge and London, Louisiana State University Press, 1992; *Disjunctive Poetics: From Gertrude Stein and Louis Zukovsky to Susan Howe* by Peter Quatermain, Cambridge and London, Cambridge University Press, 1992; "Susan Howe's Poetics of the Bibliography" by Kent Lewis, in *West Coast Line,* 27(1), Spring 1993; "Between Ourself and the Story: On Susan Howe" by Bin Ramke, in *Denver Quarterly,* 28(3), Winter 1994; "An End of Abstraction: An Essay on Susan Howe's Historicism" by John

Palattella, in *Denver Quarterly*, 29(3), Winter 1995; "Articulating the Inarticulate: Singularities and the Counter-Method in Susan Howe" by Ming-qian Ma, in *Contemporary Literature* (Madison, Wisconsin), 36(3), Fall 1995; "Writing History Poetically: Walter Benjamin and Susan Howe" by Paul Naylor, in *Genre: Forms of Discourse and Culture,* 28(3), fall 1995; *The Marginalization of Poetry: Language Writing and Literary History* by Bob Perelman, Princeton, New Jersey, Princeton University Press, 1996; *Paradise & Method: Poetics and Praxis* by Bruce Andrews, Evanston, Illinois, Northwestern University Press, 1996; "Waging Political Babble: Susan Howe's Visual Prosody and the Politics of Noise" by Craig Douglas Dworkin, in *Word & Image* (Philadelphia, Pennsylvania), 12(4), October-December 1996; "Susan Howe: Language/Writing/ History-notes around a Resistant Articulation" by Douglas Barbour, in *Boxkite,* 1, 1997; "Two at the Gap: Jorie Graham and Susan Howe" by John Peck, in *Partisan Review,* 1997; "'Out of My Texts I Am Not What I Play': Politics and Self in the Poetry of Susan Howe" by Nicky Marsh, in *College Literature* (West Chester, Pennsylvania), 24(3), October 1997; "Infectious Ecstacy: Toward a Poetics of Performative Transformation" by Cynthia Hogue, in *Women Poets of the Americas: Toward a Pan-American Gathering,* edited by Jacqueline Vaught Brogan and Cordelia Chavez Candelaria, Notre Dame, Indiana, University of Notre Dame Press, 1999.

*   *   *

Susan Howe, one of America's covert triumphs of poetry, began as a visual artist whose canvases gradually became sites for the written. Her first books of poetry were published in the 1970s, unfolding into the singular and significant works *The Liberties, Pythagorean Silence,* and *Defenestration of Prague.* Her manifold brilliance is grounded in a deeply webbed sense of self in history and history in self, and her lyric and bold linguistic experimentation serves only to layer each line with a rich profusion of references both public and private. In her work, as she writes of Emily Dickinson's work, "Poetry is affirmation in negation, ammunition in the yellow eye of a gun that an allegorical pilgrim will shoot straight into the quiet of Night's frame." In the preface to *The Europe of Trusts: Selected Poems* she says, "I write to break out into perfect primeval Consent. I wish I could tenderly lift from the dark side of history, voices that are anonymous, slighted—inarticulate."

Howe's work with words begins in midlife. In *Pythagorean Silence* she reworks formative memories of World War II perceived as a child and addressed as an adult; formed in the newsreel fires of film, it is a perception and reception of war as ancient male praxis in a Jacob-wrestling tension (and torment) of female questioning. "For me there was no silence before armies," she writes in "There Are Not Leaves Enough to Crown to Cover to Crown to Cover": "Malice dominates the history of Power and Progress. History is the record of winners. Documents were written by the Masters. But fright is formed by what we see not by what they say. / From 1939 until 1946 in news photographs, day after I saw signs of culture exploding into murder. Shots of children being herded into trucks by hideous helmeted conquerors—shots of children who were orphaned and lost—shots of the emaciated bodies of Jews dumped into mass graves on top of more emaciated bodies—nameless numberless men women and children, uprooted world almost demented. God had abandoned them to history's sovereign Necessity."

Howe's interrogation of history, and subsequently its official and marginal languages, commingles with both experimental and

high lyric richness in *Defenestration of Prague* and *The Liberties.* The latter awakens out of Swift's allegorical name, Stella, for Esther Johnson. Her voice completes the unheard other that *Journal to Stella* was addressed to. Howe interweaves rich Gaelic sensitivity with serious play, entangling Shakespeare's Lear as seen through Cordelia's eyes.

A poet of original intelligence, Howe has offered critical revelations on Emily Dickinson—*My Emily Dickinson*-that represent a landmark in creative scholarship, showing once again the possibility of poets being invariably the most potentially profound readers of poetry. The book is a marvel of feminist criticism that disrupts many normative feminist assumptions of Dickinson. Howe's grasp and use of historical texts enable her to fuse Calvinist and Indian captivity texts into influences, entering into the languages of early American rhetorics of spiritual and material ideologies. Howe writes that "categories and hierarchies suggest property. My voice formed from my life belongs to no one else. What I put into words is no longer my possession. Possibility has opened. The future will forget, erase, or recollect and deconstruct every poem. There is a mystic separation between poetic vision and ordinary living. The conditions for poetry rest outside each life at a miraculous reach indifferent to worldly chronology."

—David Meltzer

HUFANA, Alejandrino G.

Nationality: Filipino. **Born:** San Fernando, La Union, Philippines, 22 October 1926. **Education:** University of the Philippines, Quezon City, A.B. in English 1952, M.A. in comparative literature 1961; University of California, Berkeley (Rockefeller fellowship, 1961–62), 1957–58, 1961–62; Columbia University, New York (John D. Rockefeller III Fund fellowship, 1968–70), M.S. in library science 1969. **Military Service:** North Luzon guerrillas, 1944. **Family:** Married Julita Quiming in 1957; four daughters. **Career:** Secretary and English teacher, Cebu Chinese High School, 1952–54. Research assistant in social science, 1954–56, from 1956 member of the department, and since 1975 professor of English and comparative literature, and associate director, 1979–82, and director, 1982–85, Creative Writing Center, University of the Philippines. Since 1970 director of the library, since 1971 editor, *Pamana* magazine, and since 1979 editor, *Lahi* magazine, Cultural Center of the Philippines, Manila. Co-founding editor, *Signatures* magazine, 1955, *Comment* magazine, 1956–67, *Pamana* magazine, 1959–61, *University College Journal,* later *General Education Journal,* 1961–72, and *Heritage* magazine, 1967–68, managing editor, University of the Philippines Press, 1965–66. Artist: exhibitions in Elmira, New York, 1957, and Manila, to 1978. **Awards:** Republic Cultural Heritage award, 1965. **Address:** 22 Casanova Street, B. Culiat, Tandang Sora Avenue, Quezon City, Philippines.

PUBLICATIONS

Poetry

13 Kalisud. Quezon City, Collegian New Review, 1955.
Sickle Season: Poems of a First Decade 1948–1958. Quezon City, Kuwan, 1959.

Poro Point: An Anthology of Lives: Poems 1955–1960. Quezon City, University of the Philippines, 1961.
The Wife of Lot and Other New Poems. Quezon City, Diliman Review, 1971.
Sieg Heil: An Epic on the Third Reich. Quezon City, Tala, 1975.
Imelda Romualdez Marcos: A Tonal Epic. Manila, Konsensus, 1975.
Obligations: Cheers of Conscience. Quezon City, Diliman Review, 1975.
Dumanon: Dandaniw Iluko. Quezon City, University of Philippines Press, 1994.

Plays

Man in the Moon (produced La Union, 1956, Manila, 1970; revised version, produced Quezon City, 1972). Published in *Panorama* (Quezon City), December 1960.
Curtain-Raisers: First Five Plays (includes *Gull in the Wind, Honeymoon, Ivory Tower, Terra Firma, View from Origin*). Quezon City, University of the Philippines Social Science Research Council, 1964.
The Unicorn, in Pamana 1 (Manila), June 1971.
Salidom-ay, in Pamana 2 (Manila), September 1971.

Other

Mena Pecson Crisologo and Iloko Drama. Quezon City, Diliman Review, 1963.
Notes on Poetry. Quezon City, Diliman Review, 1973.

Editor, *Aspects of Philippine Literature.* Quezon City, University of the Philippines, 1967.
Editor, *A Philippine Cultural Miscellany, Parts I and II.* Quezon City, University of the Philippines, 1968–70.
Editor, with others, *Introduction to Literature.* Quezon City, Alemar Phoenix, 1974.
Editor, *Philippine Writings: Short Stories, Essays, Poetry.* Manila, Regal, 1977.

*

Manuscript Collections: University of the Philippines Library, Quezon City; University of Syracuse Library, New York; University of California Library, Berkeley; Cultural Center of the Philippines Library, Manila.

Critical Studies: "The Poetry So Far of A.G. Hufana" by Jean Edwardson, in *Collegian New Review* (Quezon City), January 1954; "Mutineer, Sight Ascending" by Leonard Casper, in *The Wayward Horizon: Essays on Modern Philippine Literature,* Manila, Community Publishers, 1961; "Poet's Portrait Gallery" by Andres Cristobal Cruz, in *Sunday Times* (Manila), 26 November 1961; "Dive in a Hypnosis: The Poetry of Alejandrino G. Hufana" by Albert Casuga, in Philippine Writing 2 (Manila), 1963; *New Writing from the Philippines: A Critique and Anthology* by Leonard Casper, Syracuse, New York, Syracuse University Press, 1966; "Hufana: Rebellious Poet" by Florentino S. Dauz, in *Graphic* (Manila), 8 September 1966; "A Poet's Romance with Art" by Jolico Cuadra, in *Chronicle Magazine* (Manila), 1 July 1967; *Poetry in the Plays of A.G. Hufana* by Bernardita Castillo, University of Bohol, unpublished thesis, 1973.

Alejandrino G. Hufana comments:

The prepublication discipline of any poet should be like the preperformance training of the athlete or prizefighter. All flaws considered in public must, as such, turn the performer back to this grind. Only birds or such creatures are born to the grace of what they do, which also happens to excuse their plunder.

*   *   *

Alejandrino G. Hufana is a fascinating and highly original poet. He studied in the United States and has absorbed much from American poetry, in particular from that neglected master of the epigram, Edwin Arlington Robinson. Deeply rooted in the complex culture of his native country, Hufana employs an ambitiously idiosyncratic diction that some non-Filipino readers have taken as evincing a lack of mastery of the English language-

Unclothing so the Zambul Bali Dag
May for her dead infanta deep be soft
The black she-parent grieving on the crag
A lullaby invokes: "Arrow aloft
Time for your sleep, piece-of-my-thigh,
The fletcher is not false, time for your dream,
Meat will be yours . . ."

—but this is a serious error. One of Hufana's main aims is to discover and to express what is authentically Filipino. Doing this, given so complicated and foreign-influenced a culture (there are Filipinos writing in the national language, which is an artifact, and in Spanish as well as in English), is bound to yield results that have an odd appearance to the outside world.

Hufana has been called the most successful "anthropological" poet writing in the English language. It is high time that both a British and an American publisher put out a comprehensive selection of his poetry.

—Martin Seymour-Smith

HUGHES, Glyn

Nationality: British. **Born:** Middlewich, Cheshire, 25 May 1935. **Education:** Altrincham Grammar School, Cheshire, 1946–52; Regional College of Art, Manchester, 1952–56, 1958–59, National Diploma in Design 1956, Art Teacher's Diploma 1959. **Family:** 1) Wendy Slater in 1959 (marriage dissolved), one son; 2) Roya Liakopoulos in 1974; 3) Jane Mackay in 1990 (marriage dissolved). **Career:** Art teacher in secondary schools in Lancashire and Yorkshire, 1956–65, and in H.M. Prison, Manchester, 1969–71; extra-mural lecturer in art, University of Manchester, 1971–73. Since 1973 full-time writer. **Awards:** Welsh Arts Council prize, 1969; Arts Council bursary, 1970, 1973; Guardian Fiction prize, 1982; David Higham prize, for novel, 1982. **Member:** Manchester Institute of Contemporary Arts Committee, 1966–69; Arts Council Fellow, Bishop Grosseteste College, Lincoln, 1979–81, and Southern Arts Fellow, Hampshire, 1982–84. **Agent:** Mic Cheetham Agency, 11–12 Dover Street, London W1X 3PH, England. **Address:** Mor's House, 1 Mill Bank Road, Sowerby Bridge, West Yorkshire HX6 3DY, England.

PUBLICATIONS

Poetry

The Stanedge Bull and Other Poems. Manchester, Manchester Institute of Contemporary Arts, 1966.
Almost-Love Poems. Oxford, Sycamore Press, 1968.
Love on the Moor: Poems 1965–1968. Manchester, Phoenix Pamphlet Poets Press, 1968.
Neighbours: Poems 1965–1969. London, Macmillan, and Chester Springs, Pennsylvania, Dufour, 1970.
Presence. London, Poem-of-the-Month Club, 1971.
Towards the Sun: Poems/Photographs. Manchester, Phoenix Pamphlet Poets Press, 1971.
Rest the Poor Struggler: Poems 1969–71. London, Macmillan, 1972.
The Breast. Richmond, Surrey, Keepsake Press, 1973.
Alibis and Convictions. Sunderland, Ceolfrith, 1978.
Best of Neighbours: New and Selected Poems. Sunderland, Ceolfrith, 1979.

Plays

Mary Hepton's Heaven, adaptation of his novel *Where I Used to Play on the Green* (produced Oldham, 1984).

Radio Plays: *The Yorkshirewomen,* 1978; *Dreamers,* 1979; *The Stranger,* 1979; *Pursuit,* 1999.

Television Plays: *Alone on the Moors,* 1975; *One Man Alone,* 1976.

Novels

Where I Used to Play on the Green. London, Gollancz, 1982.
The Hawthorn Goddess. London, Chatto and Windus, 1984.
The Rape of the Rose. London, Chatto and Windus, 1987.
The Antique Collector. New York, Simon & Schuster, 1990
Roth. New York, Simon & Schuster, 1993.
Bronte. N.p., Transworld, 1996; New York, St. Martin's Press, 1997.

Other

Millstone Grit (on Yorkshire and Lancashire). London, Gollancz, 1975; as *Glyn Hughes's Yorkshire: Millstone Grit Revisited,* London, Chatto and Windus, 1985.
Fair Prospects: Journeys in Greece. London, Gollancz, 1976.

Editor, *Selected Poems,* by Samuel Laycock. Sunderland, Ceolfrith, 1981.

*

Manuscript Collection: West Yorkshire Archive Service, Bradford; Brotherton Library, University of Leeds.

Critical Study: "Glyn Hughes and the Pennine Goddess" by Keith Sagar, in *Critical Survey* (Oxford, England), 4(1), 1992.

Glyn Hughes comments:
During the last decade I have published novels mostly, keeping verses in a private notebook to revise and publish them or not, according to what I think later. I certainly hope to return to writing more fully in verse forms. History teaches us that the chance of writing true poetry does seem to increase with age.

The link between my published verse and my novels is for others to analyze, but to me it has seemed an easy passage from one to the other and a development of the narratives I employed in verse anyway. Often I miss the Muse, sometimes with a physical pain, but I also know that the novel has at times provided an exotic and fulfilling bed for us, one in which we have made love many times.

*   *   *

One of the purposes of art is to bring order to the complexity of our experiences so that the truth behind them can be explored and revealed, and one aspect of this truth is to be discovered in the observation of man both against and as part of the terrain he inhabits. In the visual arts the Chinese do this superbly, and so does Hardy in his novels, where a sense of values and proportion, which is a truth in itself, is revealed. It is such an exploration of how the nature and quality of life are shaped and influenced by the environment, a sort of poetic ecology, that marks out Glyn Hughes's poems in *Love on the Moor* and in his first full collection, *Neighbours.* As Hughes said in his introduction to *Love on the Moor,* "My idealism about how people ought to live is implicit in every poem." This has been maintained in his later collections.

The terrain of Hughes's poems is one of those harsh, unrelenting, inbred bits of countryside that still endure in twentieth-century England, as described in "Rock Bottom":

> the last place of rickets and bow legs
> aching from their grip of iced roads.
> Where the stranger's stared-at smile is unreturned,
> the stranger's house is shunned.

Even the joys of spring sunshine are hard-won, as in these lines from "Toward the Sun":

> The fractured land bursts into grass.
> A farmer, woken by the sun and us,
> yaps like a terrier at the field's edge
> to defend his growth. We laugh,
> point, joke. Old walls glow
> like unripe apples as we cross his field
> to see the coltsfoot flowers.

Hughes's approach is as equally uncompromising and well suited to his subject matter. Unsentimental, his poetry is not without compassion, as illustrated in "Love on the Moor," where the farmer's wife, stirred for a moment by the smile of a visiting salesman— "What might / have been that trickle of light / to the cinders of her heart / stopped at a scowling grate"—calls her man, who shambles out "from his kitchen doze / fly open, feet in oven— / not that he'd ever lied / he would be different." Hughes's ability to touch on just the right nuance of feeling, and in situations where the slightness of its manifestation belies its depth, is quite remarkable.

The life described is harsh, but harshness is not indulged for the sake of it; rather it is allied to the quality of life portrayed, as in "Neighbours":

We communicate
in other ways: we poke the grate,
and whether we rise early or rise late
is boasted from the roof. Each broods alone
with a false air of no-one at home.

It is life withdrawn, pulled into itself—like a snail into its shell—in order to render it bearable. It is Hughes's achievement not only to have described his terrain with economy and accuracy but also to have expressed the spirit of it with a sensitivity that is masterly.

—John Cotton

HULL, Coral

Nationality: Australian. **Born:** Paddington, New South Wales, 1965. **Education:** University of Wollongong, B.A. in creative writing 1987, Doctor of Creative Arts 1998; Deakin University, M.A. 1994. **Career:** Works as an Animal rights advocate and full-time writer; director, animal Watch Australia. Editor, *Thylazine* electronic literary journal. **Agent:** Clive Newman, PO Box 2112, Kardinya, Western Australia 6163, Australia.

PUBLICATIONS

Poetry

Broken Land. N.p., Five Islands Press, 1997.
How Do Detectives Make Love? Ringwood, Victoria, Penguin Books Australia, 1998.

*

Critical Study: "Working with Coral Hull on Zoo" by John Kinsella, in *Overland,* 154, fall 1999.

*   *   *

Coral Hull came to prominence as a poet in Australia in the mid-1990s and has been a poetry editor of the important magazine *MEANJIN.* Although there is a lyrical edge to her work, which shows itself to advantage in the way her metaphors superimpose themselves over her narrative voice and in the often sharply vivid endings to her poems, Hull's natural tone is narrative-reflexive, and it achieves its effects by accretion and the use of often immensely long, flowing sentences that express streams of thoughts or associations. In this sense she carries echoes of an older poet in Australia, Bruce Beaver, especially as they both have achieved some of their most memorable work in long autobiographical sequences drenched in old childhood disturbances that come to focus through often small and particular images.

Beaver's memorable sequence "As It Was" takes as its starting point the memory of his first bee sting. Hull's book *How Do Detectives Make Love?* (1998) is most remarkable when she is delving into a childhood dominated by her ex-detective father's brutalized profession. The poem "The Black Gun," for instance, is eleven pages long, and the slow unrolling of its impact depends on the way it circles and recircles around the image of her father's hidden revolver in the living room. The long, rambling sentence structure, with its internal slash marks, has the effect of suggesting almost an alternative set of line divisions and does much to keep the reader alert to cadential tensions and tightenings within the general rhythmic flow. In some of the long pieces in the book, such as "Royal Park Stalker Sequence" and "Ex-Cop on the River Bank," there is a danger of becoming prosy, but the former—in keeping with the idea of stalkers themselves—actually gains from the lack of pace. It relies upon an almost mesmeric slowness to build upon the corner-of-the-eye sense of hunter and quarry. In an autobiographical sense Hull's father emerges over the span of the book as a memorable literary creation, even if the poet herself remains the chief protagonist.

Dorothy Porter is one of the few other contemporary women poets in Australia to have tackled with individuality the challenges of the longer poem, but she has honed her style to a clipped and almost cryptic café talk. Hull, on the other hand, takes a different tack. It has something of the Western Australia spaces in it but also the confined backyards of suburbia, which in childhood seem full of treasures but all too often contain claustrophobic defensiveness and dysfunctional families. Despite all the bleakness in these poems, however, there is quite a surge of spiritedness and even delight in the possibilities of language, so that the final effect is more generous than disgruntled. And as a notable animal liberationist, Hull has an unerring quickness of response to creatures. Nevertheless, she is a long way removed from the misanthropy of Robinson Jeffers, who once wrote, "I would rather kill a man than a hawk."

Hull's determinedly nonlyrical style has challenged many readers, but its rugged individuality is impressive.

—Thomas W. Shapcott

HULME, Keri

Nationality: New Zealander. **Born:** Christchurch, 9 March 1947. **Education:** North Beach primary school; Aranui High School; Canterbury University, Christchurch. **Career:** Formerly, senior postwoman, Greymouth, and director for New Zealand television; writer-in-residence, Canterbury University, 1985. **Awards:** New Zealand Literary Fund grant, 1975, 1977, 1979, and scholarship in letters, 1990; Katherine Mansfield Memorial award, for short story, 1975; Maori Trust Fund prize, 1978; East-West Centre award, 1979; ICI bursary, 1982; New Zealand writing bursary, 1984; Book of the Year award, 1984; Mobil Pegasus prize, 1985; Booker prize, 1985; Chianti Ruffino Antico Fattor award, 1987. **Address:** P.O. Box 1, Whataroa, South Westland, Aotearoa, New Zealand.

PUBLICATIONS

Poetry

The Silences Between: (Moeraki Conversation). Auckland, Auckland University Press, 1982.
Strands. Auckland, Auckland University Press, 1991; Sydney, Hale and Iremonger, 1992.

Novels

The Bone People. Wellington, Spiral, 1983; London, Hodder and
Stoughton, and Baton Rouge, Louisiana State University Press,
1985.
Lost Possessions (novella). Wellington, Victoria University Press,
1985.
Bait. New York, Viking, 1999.

Short Stories

The Windeater/Te Kaihau. Wellington, Victoria University Press,
1986; London, Hodder and Stoughton, and New York, Braziller,
1987.

Other

Homeplaces: Three Coasts of the South Island of New Zealand,
photographs by Robin Morrison. Auckland, Hodder and Stoughton,
1989; London, Hodder and Stoughton, 1990.

*

Critical Studies: "In My Spiral Fashion" by Peter Simpson, in
Australian Book Review (Kensington Park), August 1984; "Spiraling
to Success" by Elizabeth Webby, in *Meanjin* (Melbourne), January
1985; "Keri Hulme's 'The Bone People' and the Pegasus Award for
Maori Literature" by C.K. Stead, in *Ariel* (Calgary, Alberta), 16,
October 1985; *Leaving the Highway: Six Contemporary New Zealand
Novelists* by Mark Williams, Auckland, Auckland University Press,
1990; "Hu(l)man Medi(t)ations: Inter-Cultural Explorations in Keri
Hulme's 'The Windeater'/Te Kaihau" by Otto Heim and Anne
Zimmerman, in *Australian and New Zealand Studies in Canada*
(London, Ontario), 8, December 1992; "The Reawakening of the
Gods: Realism and the Supernatural in Silko and Hulme" by Thomas
E. Benediktson, in *Critique* (Atlanta, Georgia), 33, Winter 1992;
"The Quest for Archetypal Self-Truth in Keri Hulme's 'The Bone
People': Towards a Western Re-Definition of Maori Culture?" by
Georges-Goulven Le Cam, in *Commonwealth Essays and Studies*
(Dijon, France), 15(2), Spring 1993; "Keri Hulme's 'The Bone
People' and 'Te Kaihau': Postmodern Heteroglossia and Pre-Textual
Play" by Suzette Hanke, in *New Zealand Literature Today,* edited by
R.K. Dhawan and Walter Tonetto, New Delhi, Indian Society for
Commonwealth Studies, 1993; "Toni Morrison's 'Beloved' and
Other Unspeakable Texts from Different Margins by Keri Hulme and
Lindiwe Mabuza" by Miki Flockemann, in *Journal of Literary
Studies* (Pretoria, South Africa), 9(2), June 1993; *Unsettling the
Empire: Postcolonialism and the Troubled Identities of Settler Na-
tions* (dissertation) by Phillip Raymond O'Neill, New York Univer-
sity, 1993; "Disappearance through Integration: Three Maori Writers
Retaliate" by Patrick D. Morrow, in *Journal of Commonwealth and
Postcolonial Studies* (Statesboro, Georgia), 1(1), Fall 1993; "Keri
Hulme's 'The Bone People': A Critique of Gender" by Giovanna
Covi, in *Imagination and the Creative Impulse in the New Literatures
in English,* edited by M.T. Bindella and G.V. Davis, Amsterdam,
Rodopi, 1993; "Gendered Writing and the Writer's Stylistic Identi-
ty" by Marion Lomax, in *Essays and Studies* (Leicester, England),
47, 1994; "Transgressing Boundaries" by Mary Ann Hughes, in
SPAN (Hamilton, New Zealand), 39, October 1994; "On Women's
Writing in Aotearoa/New Zealand: Patricia Grace, Keri Hulme,

Cathie Dunsford" by Sigrid Markmann, in *English Postcoloniality:
Literatures from around the World,* edited by Radhika Mohanram and
Gita Rajan, Westport, Connecticut, Greenwood, 1996; "Conflict and
Continuity: The Family As Emblem of the Postcolonial Society" by
Pamela Dunbar, and "Godwits and Cuckoos: (Dis)Guises of the
Cultural Self in the Work of Robin Hyde and Keri Hulme" by Anne
Zimmermann, both in *Nationalism vs. Internationalism: (Inter)Na-
tional Dimensions of Literatures in English,* edited by Wolfgang Zach
and Ken Goodwin, Tubingen, Germany, Stauffenburg, 1996; *Writing
the Pacific: Imagining Communities of Difference in the Fiction of
Jessica Hagedorn, Keri Hulme, Rodney Morales, and Gary Pak*
(dissertation) by Charlene Setsue Gima, Cornell University, 1997;
"Looking Awry: Tropes of Disability in Post-Colonial Writing" by
Ato Quayson, in *An Introduction to Contemporary Fiction: International Writing in English since 1970,* edited by Rod Mengham,
Cambridge, England, Polity, 1999.

*   *   *

Born in Christchurch, the New Zealand poet Keri Hulme has
chosen to identify with her Maori heritage as a writer, and much of her
work constructs Maori identity through explorations of the *tangata
whenua* (people of the land or, more specifically, people of the
placenta). The female quality of the land and of nature and themes of
connectedness dominate much of her poetry, as in "Pa mai to reo
aroha" (Reach me your speech of love) in her first collection, *The
Silences Between (Moeraki Conversations):*

Every morning the shags stretch their
necks and slip off Maukiekie. Every
evening they return in a wavering
line.
Sometimes we have seen the living
black wheels of caa'ing whales out in
the woman sea.
Once I found an earwig big as my
thumb in the cliffs, moulding her
body round her pale brood.

The moments of joy experienced at the fusion of inner and outer
worlds can give way, however, to the opposite, experiences of loss
and absence and the longing that results. The elegiac and plangent
tone with which Hulme expresses such moments haunts her verse and
often overwhelms the more celebratory passages. Clearly the emotional center of her writing, the passages of lamentation also give it a
stronger sense of structure. The repeated questions of "E nga iwi o
ngai tahu" (By the bones [people] of the Ngai Tahu) give the poem
force and direction, driving it to a typically powerful conclusion:

Mihi. Greeting. Weeping hello.
And to me, standing out as though
I'm the cripple in a company of runners;
to me, pale and bluegrey-eyed,
skin like a ghost, eyes like stones;
to me, always the manuhiri when away from home—
the weeping rings louder than the greeting.

Hulme's first collection expresses variety and amorphousness
through variations of typeface and typographical arrangement It is

given a dialogic form through the interactions of six "Conversations" and the five "Silences" that lie between them, the latter expressing experiences in which the narrator is far from her *turangawaewae* (place to stand) and is forced to question her identity and the nature of her relationship to her home: "And on what shore does the wandering / fragment of seaweed finally ground?"

Many of the poems in Hulme's later collection, *Strands* (1992), verge on the arena that is ordinarily occupied by prose, pushing against the boundaries of both genres, with some loss of the evocative power of her more lyrical verse. The long opening poem, "Fishing the Olearia Tree," is spoken by a sardonic narrator who describes and maps a local terrain invested with the numinous:

> o my love, there are lean hammer-headed clouds
> menacing us from the horizon
> and red-eyed moths beating on the doors
>
> and the kettle, snoring away on the hob . . .

This work appeals to an older oral tradition, both European (as in the medieval ballad) and Maori (as in the *waiata*, or song), and frequently involves the use of repetition, or anaphora, which in its better moments lends Hulme's writing a distinctive momentum. These influences and qualities persist in the occasional poems that make up the second section, "Against the Small Evil Voices," and the ten slight but delightful wine songs, some written considerably earlier than the rest of the collection, that make up the third. Here Hulme shows the full range of her poetic repertoire with the lightness and deftness of skill that turns the English medieval ballad form toward an expression of the vernacular.

—Anna Smith

HULSE, Michael (William)

Nationality: British. **Born:** Stoke-on-Trent, Staffordshire, 12 June 1955. **Education:** Hanley High School, 1966–71; University of St. Andrews, 1973–77, M.A. (honors) in German 1977. **Career:** Lecturer, University of Erlangen/Nürnberg, 1977–79, Catholic University of Eichstätt, 1981–83, and since 1985 University of Cologne, all Germany. Since 1986 translator, Deutsche Welle, Cologne. Since 1987 English editor, Benedikt Taschen Verlag, Cologne. **Awards:** Poetry Society prize, 1978; West Midlands Arts grant, 1979; Eric Gregory award, 1980; Bridport Poetry Competition prize, 1988; Hawthornden Castle fellowship, 1991; Cholmondeley award, 1991. **Address:** c/o Collins Harvill, 77–85 Fulham Palace Road, Hammersmith, London W6 8JB, England.

PUBLICATIONS

Poetry

Monochrome Blood. London, Oasis, 1980.
Dole Queue. Coventry, White Friar Press, 1981.
Knowing and Forgetting. London, Secker and Warburg, 1981.
Propaganda. London, Secker and Warburg, 1985.
Eating Strawberries in the Necropolis. London, Collins Harvill, 1991.
Mother of Battles. Todmorden, Littlewood Arc, 1991.
Monteverdi's Photographs: Nine Poems on Aesthetics. Applecross, Washington, Folio, 1993.

Other

Editor, with David Kennedy and David Morley, *The New Poetry.* Newcastle upon Tyne, Bloodaxe, 1993.

Translator, *Tumult*, by Botho Strauss. Manchester, Carcanet Press, 1984.
Translator, *Essays in Honor of Elias Canetti.* New York, Farrar Straus, and London, Deutsch, 1987.
Translator, *Prison Journal*, by Luise Rinser. London, Macmillan, 1987; as *A Woman's Prison Journal: Germany, 1944*, New York, Schocken, 1988.
Translator, *Matisse,* by Volkmar Essers. Cologne, Benedikt Taschen Verlag, 1987.
Translator, *Toulouse-Lautrec*, by Matthias Arnold. Cologne, Benedikt Taschen Verlag, 1987.
Translator, *Chagall,* by Ingo F. Walther and Rainer Metzger. Cologne, Benedikt Taschen Verlag, 1987.
Translator, *Gauguin,* by Ingo F. Walther. Cologne, Benedikt Taschen Verlag, 1988.
Translator, *Munch,* by Ulrich Bischoff. Cologne, Benedikt Taschen Verlag, 1989.
Translator, *The Sorrows of Young Werther,* by Johann Wolfgang Goethe. London, Penguin, 1989.
Translator, *Cézanne,* by Hajo Duchting. Cologne, Benedikt Taschen Verlag, 1989.
Translator, *The Complete Paintings of van Gogh,* by Ingo F. Walther and Rainer Metzger. Cologne, Benedikt Taschen Verlag, 2 vols., 1990.
Translator, *Wonderful Wonderful Times,* by Elfriede Jelinek. London, Serpent's Tail, 1990.
Translator, *Jan Lobel from Warsaw,* by Luise Rinser. Edinburgh, Polygon, 1990.
Translator, *Edward Hopper,* by Rulf Guenter Renner. Cologne, Benedikt Taschen Verlag, 1991.
Translator, *Egon Schiele,* by Reinhard Steiner. Cologne, Benedikt Taschen Verlag, 1991.
Translator, *Degas,* by Bernd Growe, Cologne, Benedikt Taschen Verlag, 1992.
Translator, *Picasso,* by Ingo F. Walther. Cologne, Benedikt Taschen Verlag, 2 vols., 1992.
Translator, *Gauguin in Tahiti,* by Guenter Metken. New York, Norton, 1992.
Translator, *Helnwein,* by Andreas Maeckler. Cologne, Benedikt Taschen Verlag, 1992.
Translator, *Caspar Hauser,* by Jakob Wassermann. London, Penguin, 1992.
Translator, *Lust,* by Elfriede Jelinek. London, Serpent's Tail, 1992.
Translator, *Selected Poems of Rainer Maria Rilke.* London, Anvil Press, 1993.
Translator, *The Emigrants,* by Winfried Georg Sebald. London, Harvill Press, and New York, New Directions, 1996.

Translator, *The Rings of Saturn,* by Winfried Georg Sebald. London, Harvill Press, 1998; New York, New Directions, 1999.

Translator, *Vertigo,* by Winfried Georg Sebald. New York, New Directions, 2000.

*

Critical Studies: "Distinctions of Obvious Presences" by Bruce Meyer, *Poetry Canada Review* (Toronto), 7(1), Autumn 1985; interview with Annie Greet, in *CRNLE Reviews Journal,* 2, 1992; "Poetry and the Gulf War: On the Use of Myth in Michael Hulse's 'Mother of Battles'" by Goran Nieragden, in *Anglia* (Tubingen, Germany), 113(1), 1995.

Michael Hulse comments:

When I was a teenager, I would discover Wordsworth's poetry and spend weeks trying to write like Wordsworth, then Swift's, then Byron's, and so on. It took a long time for me to acquire any real interest in twentieth-century poetry. Finally at university, where my main interest, studies aside, was in theater, I found my sense of image and rhythm possessed by Rilke, by Eliot, by Wilbur, and Plath. It was not until 1976 that these presences had become second nature to the point where I could write poems that were altogether my own, and the earliest of my published work dates from that year. If I still have touchstones, they are Chaucer and Goethe and the New Zealander Allen Curnow, whom I consider the great poet of the English language in our time. Among the critics of any interest my touchstones are George Steiner, Matthew Arnold, and the Coleridge who wrote the closing paragraph of chapter 14 in the *Biographia Literaria.* Poetry is a pluralist art, and I dislike the proscriptive attitudes that litter the shop. Dictates on form are nonsense. I consider that every form that has been used, by poets anywhere, is available to me. Dictates on content do not interest me either; my poetry can be about whatever it pleases, though I find my work tends to return to historical matters, to Germany, to South East Asia, and to sexual, social, and religious concerns. Above all, it matters that words are not only prettily arranged but have meaning. The games-playing aesthetics widely touted today strike me as obscene in their implication that human answerability can be dispensed with in the poem. Thought through to its logical conclusion, this position implies that poets can run the trains to the camps if they wish.

I should add that I believe my poetry to articulate my atheism, my liberal humanism, my Anglo-German background, and my various interests, and I hope it does so in a way that can give pleasure to a reader who shares neither my background nor my preoccupations.

*   *   *

Michael Hulse is a poet needed at the end of the twentieth century. His resolute internationalism, his intellectual curiosity, and his concern with metaphysical issues are to be rejoiced in. Some of the poems collected in *Eating Strawberries in the Necropolis* and *Mother of Battles,* both published in 1991, show how earlier work in mastering basic techniques—syllabics and alliteration—has paid off.

For example, in "The Country of Pain and Revelation," the syllabic count cools to chilling effect the picture of the aftermath of a road accident:

The woman sitting on the glinting barrier
watching a stir of air relentlessly uplift

the silver undersides of leaves
is breathing very carefully, as if

afraid that she might be too tender for breathing.
Her hand is resting in the dusty hair of the
man lying jack-knifed on the grass . . .

And looking at the imagery here, we note how the health of the "glinting" barrier and the "silver undersides of leaves" is contrasted grimly with the "dusty" hair of the man. The lack of bombast heightens the effect.

In the same volume the sequence of poems after the painter Winslow Homer movingly depicts the sad spiritual honesty of the atheist and suggests how the metaphysicality of such a writer goes deeper than that of one or two triumphalist Christians. He may well yearn for

a statement of belief
said like a charm against the night

but "we are," he bleakly concludes, "on a godless tide / rowing home."

In his earlier work Hulse had worn his German learning rather too brashly. Once, in a review in the little magazine *Acumen* (April 1987), he rubbished the

prettier kind pastoral which . . . seems to have fallen
short of grasping the implications of the act of writing

that characterizes much English verse. He had a good point and made it well. But his impressive litany of cosmopolitan influences occasionally embarrasses even the most Europhiliac reader: "For Gustav Klimt . . . To Franz Kafka . . . After Vladimir Bukovsky . . ." There is a certain clubbish exclusivity in some of the work.

The other problem concerns technique, for example, the overvisibility of his syllabics and his reliance on alliteration and assonance. In "Fornicating and Reading the Papers" there are groups of lines that are banal in their effect, and Margaret Thatcher, one of the presumed targets of "Nine Points of the Nation" deserves fiercer than this. In "Snakes" (the poem reads to me like an early draft of what might become a fine piece) we find an undigested line of ordinary prose that will remind British readers of *Private Eye's* resident poet E.J. Thribb.

But Hulse can write about sexual love, spiritual loss, and the sense of living in a violent period of history with a strange tact and verve that makes me, for one, envious. The main elements in Hulse's work come together in "At Avila," a meditation on charity, Eros, and the muse of history.

Mother of Battles fuses ancient myth and modern history—the Persian Gulf War—in the manner of Geoffrey Hill in *Mercian Hymns,* though in more melodramatic tones. This is, as Hulse says, "a noncombatant's poem," speaking for all in Britain under sixty who have not gone to war but merely suffered it by proxy on television and in print from afar. In places it can move to tears, bringing together all of Hulse's obsessions—love, death, religion, politics, and history—although, as he might say, what else is there?

let me survive let me
go home alive and be
thrown out again of Tocqueville's

Bistro back in Dayton
oh I
want to know the flesh
the body and the blood . . .

—Fred Sedgwick

HUMMER, T(erry) R(andolph)

Nationality: American. **Born:** Noxobee County, Mississippi, 7 August 1950. **Education:** University of Southern Mississippi, B.A., M.A. 1974; University of Utah, Ph.D. 1980. **Family:** One son. **Career:** Assistant professor of English, Oklahoma State University, Stillwater, 1980–84; assistant professor of English, Middlebury College, Vermont, and since 1984 Kenyon College, Gambier, Ohio. Visiting professor, Exeter College, England; writer-in-residence, University of California, Irvine. Former senior editor of *Kenyon Review* and *New England Review.* Professor and director of creative writing, University of Oregon, Eugene. **Awards:** National Endowment for the Arts fellowship, 1987, 1992–93; Guggenheim fellowship, 1992–93. **Address:** *Kenyon Review,* Kenyon College, Gambier, Ohio 43022, U.S.A.

PUBLICATIONS

Poetry

Translation of Light. Stillwater, Oklahoma, Cedar Creek Press, 1976.
The Angelic Orders. Baton Rouge and London, Louisiana State University, 1982.
The Passion of the Right-Angled Man. Urbana, University of Illinois Press, 1984.
Lower-Class Heresy. Urbana, University of Illinois Press, 1987.
The 18,000-Ton Olympic Dream. New York, Quill/Morrow, 1990.
Walt Whitman in Hell: Poems. Baton Rouge, Louisiana State University Press, 1996.

Other

Editor, with Bruce Weigl, *The Imagination as Glory: Essays on the Poetry of James Dickey.* Urbana, University of Illinois Press, 1984.
Editor, with Devon Jersild, *The Unfeigned Word: Fifteen Years of New England Review.* Hanover, New Hampshire, University Press of New England, 1993.

*

Critical Studies: By Ronald Baughman, in *James Dickey Newsletter,* 1(1), Fall 1984; interview with Phil Paradis, in *Cimarron Review* (Stillwater, Oklahoma), 71, April 1985.

*   *   *

Southern writing in Faulkner's day could draw on the mythology of farming life, its rituals of male passage into manhood through hunting, the deflowering of girls white or black under the full moon, the death of grandparents, and the burial of family relations. All these were fresh in the age of nearly universal agriculture. By the time James Dickey came to write about these myths, they were at one remove from a southerner's daily life. They were remembered, but at a distance, as places and events outside Atlanta and other cities, as a part of the disappearing past.

With T.R. Hummer and his generation southern rural life and its folklore are now almost gone. Hummer makes good use of his own experience growing up on a Mississippi farm, but the act of reliving it is self-conscious, rhetorical. He is at his best when narrating an exciting moment in a boy's life, as in "Calf," from his 1982 book *The Angelic Orders,* where his father pulls the shattered parts of a half-born calf from the mother cow. The details are frightening and vivid, and the boy's soul is shaped by the terrifying ordeal of death, birth, and a father's authority:

the calf's back legs tear off
Like rubber boots pulled out of mud.
My brother turns away,
But I can't take
My eyes from the place
Where the calf was, and now
Is not, or cannot be seen.
My father shakes his head.
We only got half.
Rolls up his sleeves.
It's going to be mean.
Hold her head.

Contemporary southern poetry is influenced by the work of Dickey and Dave Smith. Hummer coedited a book of essays about the former, called *Imagination as Glory,* and studied under Smith at the University of Utah. He carries the mark of both writers, who fashioned a lush, sonorous rhetorical style in which the labors of growing up male in the South are sung variously in laments, love songs, and dirges over lost innocence. The style was originally minted by Faulkner's prose, with its trademark inner voices set in italics, a technique imported into Hummer's dialogical meditations with the self. Throw in the musical narratives of James Wright and you have nearly the whole pantheon of giants marking the southern style.

Hummer is more quintessentially southern in his sense of poetry as the exploration of pain, suffering, and regret. The argument of his poetry is that we are shaped by our losses. What we lose becomes our emotional heritage:

the real
Boundary between hypothesis and truth
Is pain.

In Hummer's psychology memory is the imagination, and pain is what we remember best. The poetry seems once removed from an older Christian reading of life as a pilgrim's journey toward redemption. Hummer's pilgrims suffer without religious consolation, but a form of religious faith appears in the beauty of the language, the lyric inspiration that rises from their sorrows. In "Inner Ear," from *Lower-Class Heresy,* the balance mechanism of the inner ear is ambiguously described as "*A small sealed chamber with a fine dust inside,*" a tomb, in other words, with the past inside it giving us our orientation in the world:

The dust is always settling, always falling.
Your body knows. That's how it tells up from down.

In the closing poem of *Lower-Class Heresy* we get this telling observation:

The fact is, the world is the same as yesterday,

Only colder, that's all, and what I want to see
As a visionary difference is only a difference in vision,
In light that makes me focus on the boundaries between
    things,
Their dark and believable presences in the air of almost-
    night.

Hummer is more articulate and penetrating in *Lower-Class Heresy* than in earlier books about his methods. "Solitude," he tells us in the poem "Cold," "is the laboratory of the heart." Consciousness is a result of growing up into adulthood; one wakes up into manhood to find oneself stranded in a difficult place, shorn of the usual supports of parents, grandparents, a usable past. In "The Moon and Constellations," the only place from which his language arises, Hummer says, is from the adamant principle of the body, which "appropriates everything." The hand he holds up to "whatever shatter of moon there is" confirms only "the one great law of the physical, / The body."

Hummer's capacities for lyric music and self-analysis are large. If his voice seems a little indistinct from his contemporaries, it is not for reasons of talent or skill but rather the region that raised him. The South demands that its body of myths be articulated according to certain laws of psychology and language. Although writers tend to lose something of their precise selves in the process, what they give us to read is a unique descent into the American psyche in which the sexes are drawn in vivid opposing colors and the ceremonies of coming-of-age are written in high operatic registers.

—Paul Christensen

HUNT, Sam

Nationality: New Zealander. **Born:** New Zealand, 4 July 1946. **Family:** Has one son. **Awards:** Young Poets award, 1971; Burns fellowship, 1976; New Zealand Literary Fund award, 1979; Queen's Service Medal. **Agent:** Ray Richards, Richards Literary Agency, P.O. Box 31240, Milford, Auckland, New Zealand.

PUBLICATIONS

Poetry

Between Islands. Privately printed, 1964.
A Fat Flat Blues (When Morning Comes). Wellington, Bottle Press, 1969.
Selected Poems 1965–1969. Wellington, Wellington Training College, 1970.
A Song about Her. Wellington, Bottle Press, 1970.
Postcard of a Cabbage Tree. Wellington, Bottle Press, 1970.
Bracken Country. Wellington, Glenburvie Press, 1971.

Letter to Jerusalem. Wellington, Bottle Press, 1971.
Bottle Creek Blues. Wellington, Bottle Press, 1971.
Bottle Creek. Wellington, Alister Taylor, 1972.
Beware the Man. Wellington, Triple P Press, 1972.
Birth on Bottle Creek. Wellington, Triple P Press, 1972.
From Bottle Zone (parts I-IV). Wellington, Alister Taylor, 1972.
    South into Winter. Wellington, Alister Taylor, 1973.
Roadsong Paekakariki. Wellington, Triple P Press, 1973.
Time to Ride. Wellington, Alister Taylor, 1975.
Drunkard's Garden. Wellington, Hampson Hunt, 1978.
Sailor's Morning: 100 Selected Poems, 1966–1979. Wellington, Hampson Hunt, 1979.
Collected Poems 1963–1980. Auckland, Penguin, 1980; London, Penguin, 1983.
Running Scared. Christchurch, Whitcoulls, 1982.
Selected Poems, edited by Michael Richards. Auckland, Penguin, 1987.
Making Tracks: A Selected 50 Poems. Christchurch, Hazard Press, 1991.
Down the Backbone. Auckland, Hodder Moa Beckett, 1995.

Recordings: *Beware the Man,* with Mammal; *Bottle to Battle to Death,* Jayrem, 1983.

Other (for children)

Bow-Wow. Wellington, Alister Taylor, 1974.

Other

Roaring Forties, with Gary McCormick and John McDermott. Glenfield, Auckland, Hodder Moa Beckett, 1995.

*

Critical Studies: *Introducing Sam Hunt* by Peter Smart, Auckland, Longman Paul, 1981; *Angel Gear: On the Road with Sam Hunt* by Colin Hogg, Auckland, Heinemann Reed, 1989.

Sam Hunt comments:
    Lyric tradition.

*   *   *

Sam Hunt established himself long ago as New Zealand's popular poet, barroom bard, and poet on the road. He bought himself a shack on an estuary called Bottle Creek and an old ambulance in which to travel and sleep, and he took to the roads, offering readings in schools and pubs, at literary festivals, anywhere there was an audience willing to listen and pay. His dog Minstrel, the subject of a number of his poems, went with him. From time to time Hunt had women friends, and he was married for a time and fathered a child, which provided new subjects for poems. Then he went out on the road again, the family left behind.

Hunt's literary models, at least for his mode of life, were surely Kerouac and the beat generation; beyond literature there was the whole ambience of the 1960s, the decade that saw him come to maturity. But in form Hunt's poetry was rather conservative and certainly restricted in scope. His persona was Whitmanesque, but the poetry owed more to the formal tradition of Yeats and Auden, as this reached him through the filters of the New Zealand poets James K. Baxter and Alistair Campbell, than to any American "barbaric yawp." He was a modestly but genuinely gifted lyric poet—romantic, nostalgic, sentimental—with a penchant for confessing regrets at love lost through folly, hard drinking, and his own feckless Muse.

This person has gradually become a public figure in New Zealand. For some he is a figure of fun, forever caught in the fashions of his youth; for others he is the only notion they have of what makes a poet. He has a sort of gabbling charm, somewhat patrician despite the road persona, and a gravelly and stammering but curiously resonant delivery. Schoolteachers, worried about the difficulty of making poetry acceptable to classes with no aptitude for it, bring him along to show that poetry is not difficult but has a human face. Pubs engage him because he has a following, even if there are people who cannot always be relied on to stop talking when he reads.

Some will argue that anything that makes poetry more widely known and enjoyed is to be applauded; others feel that Hunt's traveling circus debases poetry. It remains to be seen what this mode of life has done to Hunt or, more precisely, to his poetry. He talks on the radio (whether tongue in cheek or not is not clear) about his "road manager." Sometimes he seems to want to give the impression that he is making a lot of money by his trade, though that seems unlikely. He frequently expresses his disdain for critics who favor obscurity and intellectual pretensions over the poetry of the heart. But his own poetry neither grows nor develops. By the 1990s Hunt appeared to be stuck in a groove of sentiment and a lack of technical range.

—C.K. Stead

HUTCHINSON, (William Patrick Henry) Pearse

Nationality: Irish. **Born:** Glasgow, Scotland, 16 February 1927. **Education:** Christian Brothers School, Dublin; University College, Dublin; Salzburg Seminar in American Studies, 1952. **Career:** Translator, International Labor Organization, Geneva, Switzerland, 1951–53; drama critic, Radio Eireann, 1957–61, and Telefis Eireann, 1968. Gregory Fellow, University of Leeds, 1971–73. Lived in Barcelona, 1954–57, 1961–67. **Awards:** Butler award, for Gaelic writing, 1969. **Address:** School of English, University of Leeds, LS2 9JT, England.

PUBLICATIONS

Poetry

Tongue without Hands. Dublin, Dolmen Press, 1963.
Faoistin Bhacach (Imperfect Confession). Dublin, Clóchomhar, 1968.
Expansions. Dublin, Dolmen Press, 1969.
Watching the Morning Grow. Dublin, Gallery Press, 1973.
The Frost Is All Over. Dublin, Gallery Press, 1975.
Selected Poems. Dublin, Gallery Press, 1982.
Climbing the Light. Dublin, Gallery Press, 1985
Le Cead Na Gréine. Baile Atha Cliath, An Clóchamar Tta, 1989.
The Soul That Kissed the Body. Oldcastle, Gallery Press, 1990.
Barnsley Main Seam. Oldcastle, Gallery Books, 1995.

Other

Translator, *Poems,* by Josep Carner. Oxford, Dolphin, 1962.
Translator, *Friend Songs: Medieval Love-Songs from Galaico-Portuguese.* Dublin, New Writers Press, 1970.

*

Critical Studies: By Gabriel Rosenstock, in *Comhar* (Baile Atha Cliath, Ireland), 44(1), 1985; by Michael Davitt, in *Innti,* 11, 1988.

Pearse Hutchinson comments:
Themes: Growing up. Near madness. Near despair. The color bar. The horrors of puritanical Irish Catholicity. Xenophobia and Xenophilia. Travel (especially Spain). The built-in dangers (to truth) of all revolt. The difficulty, tenuous possibility, and utter necessity of love. Friendship. Social injustice. God. Pity.
Forms: Free verse and strictly rhyming metros.
Influences: Hard to say, but I suppose Auden, Cavafy, the seventeenth-century Gaelic poet Pierce Ferriter, and the contemporary Catalans Salvador Espriu (especially as to cadence) and Pere Quart.

* * *

The Irish poet Pearse Hutchinson lived for many years in Spain, and his first published work consisted of verse translations from the work of the Catalan poet Josep Carner. The effect of his experiences abroad can be seen in his first two original collections of poems, *Tongue without Hands* and *Expansions*. His delight in Mediterranean color is shown in "Málaga":

The scent of unseen jasmine on the warm night beach.

The tram along the sea road all the way from town
through its wide open sides drank unseen jasmine down.
Living was nothing all those nights but that strong flower.

Equally lighthearted is the lyrical "Fireworks in Córdoba":

Cocks and coins and golden lupins,
parachutes and parasols and shawls,
pamplinas, maltrantos, and glass lawyers,
giant spermatozoa, dwarf giants,
greengage palms, and flying goldfish . . .

Hutchinson often writes of political oppression and bad social conditions. In "Questions" he describes attempts to suppress the use of the Catalan language by imprisonment and violence: "Where one fine day, the gun smiles, and everyone rumours a thaw, / but next night, the gun kills, and all remember the law."

The poems Hutchinson has written on Irish life, both in city and country, are brisk, satiric, and ironic, as in "Men's Mission":

Some Lenten evening sharp, at five to eight,
pick a suburban road both long and straight
and leading—which do not?—to a Catholic church:
you'll see, whisked out through every creaking gate,
men only, walking all at the same brisk rate.

"Fleadh Cheoil" (the name of a popular musical festival) is a lively
account of a country town *en fête:*

> each other door in a mean twisting main street,
> flute-player, fiddler and penny-whistler
> concentrating on one sense only
> such a wild elegance of energy gay and sad
> few clouds of lust or vanity could form:
> the mind kept cool, the heart kept warm:
> therein the miracle, three days and nights
> so many dances played and so much drinking done,
> so many voices raised in singing but none
> in anger nor any fist in harm.

From the manufacturing centers of England and Scotland, exiles "in
flashy ties and frumpish hats" return for a few days to hear "an
ancient music." "Friday in a Branch Post-Office" tells of the weekly
queue of septuagenarians waiting patiently for their meager pension
and ends with the ironic comment "We don't need a statue of Cú
Chulainn / in our Branch Post-Office." The reference reminds us of
Yeats's tribute to the statue of the ancient Irish hero in the general post
office in Dublin.

—Austin Clarke

I-J

IMLAH, Mick

Nationality: Scottish. **Born:** 1956. **Education:** Magdalen College, Oxford. **Career:** Founding editor, *Oxford Poetry*, 1983; editor, *Poetry Review*, 1983–86; poetry editor, Chatto and Windus, 1989–93.

PUBLICATIONS

Poetry

The Zoologist's Bath and Other Adventures. Oxford, Sycamore Press, 1982.
Birthmarks. London, Chatto and Windus, 1988.

Other

Editor, *Dr. Wortle's School,* by Anthony Trollope. London, Penguin, 1999.

*

Critical Study: By Robert Potts, in *Times Literary Supplement* (London), 4814, 1995.

*　　*　　*

There is a feeling conveyed by many of Mick Imlah's poems of listening to a skilled if quirky saloon raconteur. The poem "Goldilocks," for example, begins with "This is a story about the possession of beds" and goes on to tell how the narrator enters a room in Oxford to find a tramp already occupying the bed. The story chats on to embrace a jokey mention of the narrator's earlier having read a paper at the "Annual Excuse for Genetics to let down its ringlets," extending the reference to the poem's title and the tramp's hair. The poem ends with the clincher "Och, if he'd known I was Scottish! Then I'd have got it," which would get the beer sippers rocking appreciatively.

Some of the other stories, such as "Lee Ho Fook's," seem a might inconsequential. It is as if the narrator himself had lost his way momentarily in the labyrinth of his story, all of which only adds to the verisimilitude of the genre. The essential difference is, of course, Imlah's narrative skills in making pointed asides. Also important are the qualities of his language and metaphor, as in these lines from "Goldilocks":

Whose snore, like the rattle of bronchial stones in a bucket,
Resounded the length and depth and breadth of the
　　problem.

One has the sense in reading these poems of being buttonholed by an Ancient Mariner, one who prevents escape from the story. "Till hush!" the reader is exhorted in "Secrets":

she let her dress
Unbutton to the locket
And parted secrets.

This uses all of the poet's economy of language and ambiguity.

From time to time a less relaxed Imlah appears, as in "Silver" and "Starter's Orders," where, no longer softened by rhetoric, the poems hit straight and hard. The following lines are from "Silver":

Wherever the ship may steer
They face the rear;
　　What lies in store
　　Is untransmuted ore.

Imlah's poetry also can be intricately imaginative, as in his long extravaganza "The Zoologist's Bath," based on the evolutionary theory of the Victorian Arthur Woolmer, whose thesis was that life would strive to return to the seas from which it had evolved:

—when I feel
My bottom buoyed, and start to think of fish.
I am at one with them;

Yes, Imlah can be both witty and sharp.

—John Cotton

IRELAND, Kevin (Mark)

Nationality: New Zealander. **Born:** Auckland, 18 July 1933. **Family:** Married Phoebe Caroline Ireland. **Career:** Founding editor, *Mate* magazine, Auckland; assistant editor, *Quote* magazine, Auckland. Writer-in-residence, Canterbury University, 1986; Sargeson fellow, Auckland, 1987; literary fellow, Auckland University, 1988, 1990. **Awards:** Commemoration medal, 1990; OBE, 1993. **Address:** 8 Domain Street, Devonport, New Zealand.

PUBLICATIONS

Poetry

Face to Face. Christchurch, Pegasus Press, 1963.
Educating the Body. Christchurch, Caxton Press, 1968.
A Letter from Amsterdam. London, Amphadesma Press, 1972.
Orchids, Hummingbirds, and Other Poems. Auckland, Auckland University Press-Oxford University Press, 1974; London, Oxford University Press, 1975.
A Grammar of Dreams. Wellington, Wai-te-ata Press, 1975.
Literary Cartoons. Auckland, Island-Hurricane Press, 1978.
The Dangers of Art: Poems 1975–1980. Auckland, Cicada Press, 1980.

Practice Night in the Drill Hall. Auckland and Oxford, Oxford University Press, 1984.

The Year of the Comet: Twenty-six 1986 Sonnets. Auckland, Islands Press, 1986.

Selected Poems. Auckland and Oxford, Oxford University Press, 1987.

Tiberius at the Beehive. Auckland and Oxford, Oxford University Press. 1990.

Skinning a Fish. Christchurch, Hazard Press, 1994.

Selected Poems. Christchurch, Hazard Press, 1997.

Short Stories

Sleeping with Angels. Auckland, Penguin, 1995.

Other

Blowing My Top. Auckland, Penguin, 1996.

The Man Who Never Lived. Auckland, Random House, 1997.

Under the Bridge and over the Moon. Auckland, Random House, 1999.

Editor, *The New Zealand Collection: A Celebration of the New Zealand Novel.* Auckland, Random House, 1989.

Translator, *Poems,* by Hristo Botev. Sofia, Bulgaria, Sofia Press, 1974.

*　　*　　*

"Thin men / write gaunt poems / and each word / sticks out / like a rib." Kevin Ireland's lines from the early poem "Deposition" also describe his own style at the time. His witty, whimsical conceits and explorations of metaphor found apt expression in poems using short lines, complex rhyme schemes, and patterns of words and phrases recurring from stanza to stanza.

Such writing relies for its success on the accurate selection and placement of individual words to hold the reader's attention and patience while the poet works out the implications of his metaphor. At times the central notion fails to sustain the poem, but Ireland's wit and sense of humor help to keep the reader's interest alive; often, indeed, it is these asides that make the slighter poems worth reading. Occasionally, Ireland's writing can fall lamentably flat, as in these lines from the late poem "A Birthday Card for Sixty": "I suppose I must have done an awful lot / of breathing, without thinking, mind / uninvolved in the mechanics of what / was going on . . .''

In "A Shrinking World" Ireland writes of New Zealand as remembered from childhood and of the homeland rediscovered on returning:

Rangitoto just yesterday
seemed a mile high
and stretched right across the sea
now it is near enough
to throw stones at
and small enough to miss

He also writes of poetry and of love; he celebrates friendships, as the roll call of dedicatees attests; and he pillories weasel words and

hypocrisy, especially from the lips of politicians, as in these lines from "Forgetting" (*Tiberius at the Beehive*):

Forgetting leads
the way: it straightens out the kinks,
sweeps away the clutter of technicalities.
It leads the assault on the treacheries
of the archives. It demolishes doubt,

obliterates contradiction, blots out disrespect.
Forgetting is the entrance to the new order.

The more open, relaxed style evident in *A Letter from Amsterdam* also characterizes the love poems of *Orchids, Hummingbirds, and Other Poems,* with their wry, affectionate humor. In the conversational (and uneven) "broken sonnets" of *The Year of the Comet* Ireland celebrates his return to New Zealand. Whatever style he essays, however, he knows that

there are some poems that work
and some that don't
in the end there is just the one difference

The title poem "Skinning a Fish" is an extended meditation on the practice of disciplined action that moves from detailed instructions for skinning (or perhaps boning) a fish, through military drill (once compulsory for New Zealand schoolboys), to the chance that flicks a fish scale into the eye. It concludes with a résumé of its themes, stated with a precision and cogency that marks a new feature of Ireland's writing:

Getting the knife in.
Doing it all by the book. Detaching
the skin from the flesh. The mathematics

of uncertainty. The way to survive.
Luckily you forget these things
by experience until you no longer

remember forgetting. Loving then returns
as second nature. Like skinning
a fish. A feeling for flesh.

—Alan Roddick

JACKSON, Michael (Derek)

Nationality: New Zealander. **Born:** Nelson in 1940. **Education:** University of Auckland, M.A. (honors) in anthropology; Cambridge University, Ph.D. **Family:** Married Pauline Harris (died 1983); one daughter. **Career:** Since 1973 senior lecturer, department of social anthropology and Maori studies, Massey University, Palmerston North. Professor of social anthropology and English studies, Indiana

University, Bloomington. **Awards:** Commonwealth poetry prize, 1976; New Zealand Book award, 1981; Katherine Mansfield writing fellowship, 1982. **Address:** Massey University, Department of Social Anthropology, Palmerston North, New Zealand.

PUBLICATIONS

Poetry

Latitudes of Exile: Poems 1965–1975. Dunedin, McIndoe, 1976.
Wall. Dunedin, McIndoe, 1980.
Going On. Dunedin, McIndoe, 1985.
Rainshadow. Dunedin, McIndoe, 1987.
Duty Free: Selected Poems 1965–1988. Dunedin, McIndoe, 1989.
Antipodes. Auckland, Auckland University Press, 1996.

Novels

Barawa and the Ways Birds Fly in the Sky. Washington, D.C., Smithsonian Institution Press, 1986.
Rainshadow. Dunedin. McIndoe. 1987.

Short Stories

Pieces of Music. Auckland, Vintage, 1994.

Other

The Kuranko: Dimensions of Social Reality in a West African Society. London, Hurst, 1977.
Allegories of the Wilderness: Ethics and Ambiguity in Kuranko Narratives. Bloomington, Indiana University Press, 1982.
Paths Towards a Clearing: Radical Empiricism and Ethnographic Inquiry. Bloomington, Indiana University Press, 1989.
At Home in the World. Durham, Duke University Press, 1995.
The Blind Impress. Palmerston North, Dunmore, 1997.
Minima Ethnographica: Intersubjectivity and the Anthropological Project. Chicago, University of Chicago Press, 1998.

Editor, with Ivan Karp, *Personhood and Agency: The Experience of Self and Other in African Cultures.* Uppsala, Uppsala University Press, 1990; Washington, D.C., Smithsonian Institution Press, 1990.
Editor, *Things As They Are: New Directions in Phenomenological Anthropology.* Bloomington, Indiana University Press, 1996.

*   *   *

Michael Jackson's poetic reputation among his New Zealand contemporaries was secured when Vincent O'Sullivan included three of the poems from Jackson's experience in Africa in the first (1970) edition of the Oxford University Press's *Anthology of Twentieth-Century New Zealand Verse.* At the time Jackson, unlike most of the older contributors to the anthology, had not published a collection of poems. But it was his first book, *Latitudes of Exile,* that brought him to a wider audience, and the book's acclaim was enhanced by its winning the 1976 Commonwealth poetry prize. With this accolade Jackson became the first of three New Zealanders to win the prize, the others being Lauris Edmond in 1985 and Allen Curnow in 1989.

Latitudes of Exile is a selection of work from 1965 to 1975, and the acknowledgments show that most of the poems that had previously been published had their first printing in New Zealand periodicals. Jackson organized his first volume, as he did his fourth book, more by theme and subject than by chronology. The first ten of the thirty pieces are drawn from African experiences, the worlds the young poet observed first in the Congo (later Zaire and now the Democratic Republic of the Congo) and later in Sierra Leone. The subjects of the remaining score range from the recollection and celebration of Jackson's childhood and ancestral associations with Taranaki-a rural province of New Zealand, even now slightly remote from the metropolitan centers, that is dominated by its great mountain and by the coastline of the Tasman Sea—to scenes and situations in Auckland and metropolitan Europe.

Although the poems seem almost invariably personal, with the ''I'' of the poem being a character, narrator, or persona close to the poet himself, they are, nevertheless, not simply leaves in a verse diary or autobiography. The title poem, dedicated to Jackson's friend and fellow poet O'Sullivan, is less about any physical exile the poet might have described or celebrated in the first ten poems and more about the alienation of spirit that comes to the poet through a recognition of the commonplaces of inhumanity and the way in which these dislocate what we would wish to regard as natural human relationships.

Jackson's second volume, *Wall,* appeared in 1980 and won the poetry section of the New Zealand Book awards in 1981. Compared with the previous volume, *Wall* shows the poet's stylistic evolution toward a more terse imagery, with short lines and staccato phrases giving emphasis to an idiomatic style and vernacular rhythms. Many of the poems speak of a lyrical response to the rural landscape of North Island:

> Mountains by day blue
> and clouds like stone
> sinking into the ridge . . .
>
>   all night and far away
> the yelping of farm dogs
> strangled on the wind.

Like their predecessors, these poems are always personal. Jackson seldom fabricates a poetic situation, nor does he often create fictitious characters or dramatic tableaux within his verse. The chief exception to this can be found in those poems that themselves speak of the poet's craft and in those that tell again stories the poet as traveler or anthropologist has heard. Sometimes these two themes blend together as the poet speaks of the mystery of language, describing it through metaphor rather than through analysis, as in the African poems ''Mask-Maker'' and ''Her.''

More and more in these poems Jackson seems to be seeking to mythologize the landscape, not only in obvious examples like ''The Old Gods'' but also more subtly in three poems—''The Skinning,'' ''The Moths,'' and ''Macrocarpas''—that are strong evocations of a now passing New Zealand farming scene:

They claw the north west gales.
In macrocarpas there is no delight,
only the blown fleece
on a broken fence
magpies scatter

With the publication and success of *Wall,* Jackson had established himself as a wholly confident poet, breaking new ground for himself in both form and imagery in a way that was seldom truly experimental but always ongoing.

Jackson's third volume, *Going On,* was published in 1985 and is certainly the most directly autobiographical work in his oeuvre. In 1982 the poet and his family lived in Menton in the south of France while Jackson held the Katherine Mansfield writing fellowship (awarded to a New Zealand writer) at the Villa Isola Bella. Soon after the family returned to New Zealand, Pauline Jackson died. The prefatory note speaks of the poems of *Going On* as making up "a kind of logbook kept during the year before and six months after" her death. The volume records events and memories as a diary or logbook would, but the poems are seldom conventional acts of grieving, remembering, or exorcising, although grief is always immanent. The poems are intensely personal but often cryptic in their private references. Unlike many of Jackson's earlier love poems, these pieces do not readily include the reader in their discourse but rather allude to places and events that are part of a private memory. Perhaps they can be called minor, both in key and in stature, yet they have moments of intense poignancy that the reader is permitted to intrude upon. Their sense of grief is sustained by an expression of animism that declares the poet's awareness of the continuing presence of his lost wife. The volume concludes with the prizewinning poem "Stone," which is composed of renderings of three myths familiar to the poet. It is as substantial a piece as anything else in the book, its lines sparse but lyrical:

The scored bark of pines
bleeds resin
for wine

A mason's mallet echoing

Rain water collects
in a stone bowl.

"Stone" is a strongly made and original poem, movingly and appropriately described in the dedication and providing an image of a source of strength for the poet as he seeks to go on.

It is becoming a practice increasingly common among New Zealand poets of Jackson's generation to present a retrospective collection in midcareer. *Duty Free: Selected Poems 1965–1988* draws from the previous three volumes and adds eleven new poems. The poems are grouped "according to subject and theme, not chronology." Three of the new poems augment the grouping that speaks of the African experiences. The second group of nineteen poems is with one exception taken from Jackson's first two books. The third group selects from *Going On,* and the fourth group contains the other eight new poems.

The last of these new poems are a mixture of pieces that recall events in a personal past, a staple of Jackson's poetry, and a mythologizing of that past, culminating in the long emblematic

poem "Magdalene of the Black Rose." Jackson is a poet of places and of the recollection of loves and affections. In speaking of these essentially private things, he affects a language that is simultaneously austere and musical.

Since leaving New Zealand in 1983 Jackson has focused on prose fiction and has continued to publish extensively in his academic field of ethnography. His two novels of the late 1980s were followed by a collection of fourteen short stories, evidently semiautobiographical, entitled *Pieces of Music,* which was published in New Zealand in 1994.

—W.S. Broughton

JACOBSEN, Josephine (Winder)

Nationality: American. **Born:** Josephine Winder Boylan, in Coburg, Ontario, Canada, 19 August 1908. **Education:** Privately, and at Roland Park Country School, Baltimore, graduated 1926. **Family:** Married Eric Jacobsen in 1932; one son. **Career:** Poetry consultant, 1971–73, and honorary consultant in American letters, Library of Congress, Washington, D.C., 1973–79. Vice president, Poetry Society of America, 1979. Member of the literary panel, National Endowment for the Arts, 1979–83. **Awards:** Borestone Mountain award, 1961, 1964, 1968, 1972; MacDowell Colony grant, 1973, 1974, 1976, 1978, 1981, 1983; *Prairie Schooner* award, for fiction, 1974, 1986; Yaddo grant, 1975, 1977, 1980, 1982, 1984; American Academy award, 1982, 1984; Academy of American Poets fellowship, 1987. L.H.D.: College of Notre Dame, Baltimore, 1974; Goucher College, Baltimore, 1974; Towson State University, Baltimore, 1983. M.Div.: St. Mary's Seminary College, 1988. Honorary degree: Johns Hopkins University, Baltimore, 1993. **Address:** 13801 York Road, Cockeysville Hunt Valley, Maryland 21030–1825, U.S.A.

PUBLICATIONS

Poetry

Let Each Man Remember. Dallas, Kaleidograph Press, 1940.
For the Unlost. Baltimore, Contemporary Poetry, 1946.
The Human Climate: New Poems. Baltimore, Contemporary Poetry, 1953.
The Animal Inside. Athens, Ohio University Press, 1966.
The Shade-Seller: New and Selected Poems. New York, Doubleday, 1974.
The Chinese Insomniacs. Philadelphia, University of Pennsylvania Press, 1981.
Adios, Mr. Moxley. Winston-Salem, North Carolina, Jackpine Press, 1986.
The Sisters: New and Selected Poems. Columbia, South Carolina, Bench Press, 1987.
Distances. Lewisburg, Pennsylvania, Bucknell University & The Press of Appletree Alley, 1991.
Collected Poems. Baltimore, Johns Hopkins University Press, 1995.
In the Crevice of Time: New and Collected Poems. Baltimore, Johns Hopkins University Press, 1995.

Recording: *Selected Poems,* Watershed, 1977; *The Poet and the Poem,* Library of Congress, 1990.

Short Stories

A Walk with Raschid and Other Stories. Winston-Salem, North Carolina, Jackpine Press, 1978.
On the Island: New and Selected Stories. Princeton, New Jersey, Ontario Review Press, 1989.
What Goes without Saying: Collected Stories of Josephine Jacobsen. Baltimore, Johns Hopkins University Press, 1996.

Other

The Testament of Samuel Beckett, with William Randolph Mueller. New York, Hill and Wang, 1964; London, Faber, 1966.
Ionesco and Genet: Playwrights of Silence, with William Randolph Mueller. New York, Hill and Wang, 1968.
From Anne to Marianne: Some American Women Poets (lecture). Washington, D.C., Library of Congress, 1973.
The Instant of Knowing (lecture). Washington, D.C., Library of Congress, 1974; as *The Instant of Knowing: Lectures, Criticism, and Occasional Prose,* Ann Arbor, University of Michigan Press, 1997.
One Poet's Poetry (lecture). Decatur, Georgia, Agnes Scott College, 1975.

*

Manuscript Collection: Mugar Memorial Library, Boston University.

Critical Studies: "Poetry and Preaching" by Hugh Kerr, in *Theology Today* (Princeton, New Jersey), October 1964; by Richard Ohmann, in *Wisconsin Studies in Contemporary Literature* (Madison), Autumn 1965; "The Matter and Manner of Beckett" by David Helsa, in *Christian Scholar* (New York), Winter 1965; "Enduring Saturday" by Anthony Burgess, in *Spectator* (London), 29 April 1966; "The Human Condition," in *Irish Press* (Dublin), 11 June 1966; "The Essential Q," in *Times Literary Supplement* (London), 30 June 1966; by John Logan, in *Epoch* (Ithaca, New York), Autumn 1966; "Art in Transition" by Laurence Lieberman, in *Poetry* (Chicago), March 1967; by Rosemary Dee, in *Commonwealth* (New York), 20 December 1968; "The Mystery of Faith: An Interview with Josephine Jacobsen" by Evelyn Prettyman, in *New Letters* (Kansas City, Missouri), 1975; in *Library Journal* (New York), 16 October 1981; in *Epoch 32* (Ithaca, New York), 1, 1982; *Commonweal* (New York), 24 September 1982; in *Nation* (New York), 16 October 1982; "The Melody of the Quotidian" by Sandra M. Gilbert, in *Parnassus* (New York), 11(1), Spring/Summer 1983; "Power As Virtue: The Achievement of Josephine Jacobsen" by Nancy Sullivan, in *Hollins Critic* (Hollins College, Virginia), 22(2), April 1985; *Josephine Jacobsen: Commitment to Wonder* (dissertation) by Evelyn Savage Prettyman, n.p. 1986; "The 'Terrible Naive' and Others: Anatomy of Evil in Josephine Jacobsen's Work" by Nancy R. Norris, in *Maryland Poetry Review,* 11, Spring/Summer 1992; "Josephine Jacobsen, Archeologist of Metaphor" by Rosemary Deen, in *13th Moon,* 10(1–2), 1992; "Joy & Terror: The Poems of Josephine Jacobsen" by Elizabeth Spires, in *New Criterion* (New York), 14(3), November 1995; "Josephine Jacobsen: An American Classic" by Grace Cavalieri, in *Pembroke* (Pembroke, North Carolina), 30, 1998; interview with A.V. Christie, in *Image* (Kennett Square, Pennsylvania), 23, Summer 1999.

Josephine Jacobsen comments:

I do not really value very highly statements from a poet in regard to her work. I can perhaps best introduce my own poetry by saying what I have not done rather than defining what I have done. I have not involved my work with any clique, school, or other group. I have tried not to force any poem into an overall concept of "how I write poetry" when it should be left to create organically its own individual style. I have not been content to repeat what I have already accomplished or to establish any stance that would limit the flexibility of discovery. I have not confused technical innovation, however desirable, with poetic originality or intensity. I have not utilized poetry as a social or political lever. I have not conceded that any subject matter, any vocabulary, any approach, or any form is in itself necessarily unsuitable to the uses of poetry. I have not tried to establish a reputation as poet on any grounds but those of my poetry.

*   *   *

Josephine Jacobsen's publication career spans more than fifty years and encompasses poetry, short fiction, and literary criticism. Despite her critical acclaim as a short story writer, Jacobsen has said, "There is nothing that compares to poetry." Poetry attempts to articulate that which cannot be articulated. Throughout her books of poetry, which range from traditional forms to free verse, Jacobsen's works evoke the mystery of being human. In an interview with Evelyn Prettyman in 1975, Jacobsen said, "As I get older and life gets more complex and more confusing, the expression of it has to get simple. You can't be diverse and wander; you have to take the gist, the seed, the one vital core." The "simple" expression of her poetry is not in any way easy or reductive; rather, its concern is the essential in subject and language, in tone and form.

A key element of Jacobsen's poetry is the relationship between the physical and the spiritual, which she sees not in opposition but in symbiosis: "I believe in the inexplicable tangle of body and spirit; the spirit is encased in the physical." This mysterious tangle becomes the subject of many of her poems, as in "The Edge" from her 1987 book *The Sisters:*

The edge? The edge is:
lie by the breath you cannot
do without; while
the breather sleeps.

Precious, subtle, that air
comes, goes, comes.
The heart propels it. It has
its thousands of hours, but

it will not last as long
as the sun, the moon's subservient
tides. It will stop, go back
to the air's great surround.

But now, subtle, precious,
regular as tide and sun
it moves in the warm body, lifts
the chest, says yes.

Listen to it, through the night.

If you wish to know the extent
to which you are vulnerable
only listen.

This is called the breath
of life. But it continues
saving your life
through the dark,

since this engine that drives your joy
is unrenounceable.
Listen, listen. Say, Love, love
breathe so. breathe so.

The breath of the sleeper, the life source for both the beloved and the lover, becomes a metaphor for the spirit that enables us to love, the spirit that makes us human. The physical act of breathing, "regular as tide and sun," affirms the eternal at the same time it reminds us that time is passing. The spirit endures; the body does not.

While this essential mystery, or "one vital core," can be written about in essays and in fiction, poetry attempts not just to write about the mystery but to become it. Jacobsen's poetry gives a physical presence to an intangible; mystery breathes in her poems. "It moves in the warm body, lifts / the chest, says yes." The language of these lines is deceptively simple. We read and understand them rationally. Yet they quietly assert their physical presence in the comfort of their vowels and soft consonants, through the shapes our mouths make in saying them and through their quiet control of our breath. These are the doors through which the mystery arrives.

Jacobsen's poetry rejoices in words for their own sake, not for the sake of the objects or ideas to which they refer. Words themselves become metaphors for the "inexplicable tangle of body and spirit." They are tangible as we sound them on our tongues; they are intangible in their complex roles as symbols. In a poem titled "Arrival of My Cousin" from *The Animal Inside,* Jacobsen writes,

But I speak of the token, the image
I was given for identity;
that word of flesh, like a name, a sound,
is what I speak of.

Through words we are identified. They allow us to recognize and name the human experience. In Jacobsen's poetry words are both flesh and names, and they constantly assert the mystery of themselves.

—Julie Miller

JAFFIN, David

Nationality: American. **Born:** New York City, 14 September 1937. **Education:** University of Michigan, Ann Arbor (Hopwood award, 1956; Oreon E. Scott award), 1955–56; New York University (Penfield Fellow), 1956–66, B.A. 1959 (Phi Beta Kappa), M.A. 1961, Ph.D. in history 1966. **Family:** Married Rosemarie Kraft-Lange in 1961; two sons. **Career:** Graduate assistant, New York University, 1961–62; lecturer in European history, University of Maryland European Division, Munich and Augsburg, Germany, 1966–69. Studied theology at the University of Tübingen, 1971–74: vicar, Tübingen, 1974–75; minister, Magstadt, 1975–78. Since 1978 minister, Evangelische Kirche, Malmsheim. **Address:** 85521 Ottobrunn bei München, Prinz Alfons Str. 13, Germany.

PUBLICATIONS

Poetry

Conformed to Stone. New York, Abelard Schuman, 1968; London, Abelard Schuman, 1970.
Emptied Spaces. London, Abelard Schuman, 1972.
Opened. Sheffield, Headlands, 1973.
Late March. Rushden, Northamptonshire, Sceptre Press, 1973.
At the Gate. New Zealand, Edge Press, 1974.
Of. Knotting, Bedfordshire, Sceptre Press, 1974.
As One. New Rochelle, New York, Elizabeth Press, 1975.
In the Glass of Winter. London, Abelard Schuman, 1975.
Changes. Godalming, Surrey, Words, 1975.
The Half of a Circle. New Rochelle, New York, Elizabeth Press, 1977.
Space Of. New Rochelle, New York, Elizabeth Press, 1978.
Preceptions. New Rochelle, New York, Elizabeth Press, 1979.
The Density for Color. Plymouth, Shearsman, 1982.
For the Finger's Want of Sound. Plymouth, Shearsman, 1982.
Selected Poems (English and Hebrew). Givatayim, Israel, Massada, 1982.
74 New Poems. Plymouth, Shearsman, 1994.
The Telling of Time: Poems 1989–1997. Lahr, Germany, Johannis, 2000.

*

Critical Studies: In *Library Journal* (New York), 15 September 1968, and 1 September 1977; *Yorkshire Post* (Leeds), 9 September 1972; *Bristol Evening Post,* 9 November 1972; by Edward Lucie-Smith, in *Emptied Spaces,* 1972, and *In the Glass of Winter,* 1975; *Workshop New Poetry 18* (London), 1973; *Samphire* (Bromsgrove, Worcestershire), ii, 4, 1973; *Poet Lore* (Boston), summer 1974; "David Jaffin: An Introduction" by Tony Frazer, in *Imprint 1* (Hong Kong), 1980; *Sewanee Review* (Tennessee), fall 1980; interview, in *Shearsman 3* (Plymouth), 1981.

David Jaffin comments:

My art is one of intense compression, both of form and meaning. I seek to create a world at once visually alive, tangible/explicit and yet abstract, inward and restrained. I feel the poetic process as an intensification of consciousness. I break through/break down those words inspired in my mind (revising over and over again while I'm writing) to derive their intrinsic form and relation. Jacques Lipchitz told me that my poems were sculpted as from stone. There must never be a word too many, no decoration, ornament, rhetoric. The craft involves the unity of image, sound, sense, tone, and idea. The poem itself is a state of being, not a theme to be developed with the "poetic trimming." The poem simply is, is not about. But craftsmanship itself is only the prerequisite for the spiritual process. A "state of being" means for me a personal and new definition of reality. All meaningful art must be this. I often describe this via tangible objects, thereby actualizing the senses. My aesthetic moves on two levels, the one being physically alive, so vivid as to be almost touched, and yet when these poems succeed, they create an absolute stillness and control. I am told my poems gain by constant rereading. I always present them at least twice at public readings.

*　　*　　*

David Jaffin's *Conformed to Stone* and *Emptied Spaces* have a sculptural quality; the poems are spare, chiseled down to the essentials. The title of each is appropriate. The first collection contains more people among its statuary—''Creatures of Stone,'' ''The Idiot,'' ''Woodcarver,'' ''Self Portrait''—while the second moves away from human models to still lifes more remote from humans, though the artistic, and particularly the sculptural, motif remains. In the latter book Jaffin seems to be hollowing out his previous forms, trying for a sort of negative space to complement the positive space the previous book had occupied. Things are defined by their absence, as in ''Door Partly Opened'':

> You let the light
> in,
> Angled-off,
>
> Your hands closed as a
> Shadow hanging there
> You let the light
> in
> As far as your face
> could allow.

Poems like this, with their sense of moments of time mysteriously arrested, remind one of French poets such as Valéry. The poet seems to be inviting us to study the scene closely and at the same time be denying total entrance.

Jaffin's poems are restrained, dignified, pictorial, and superficially simple, but they turn frequently on the ambiguities inherent in language. Reading them is bracing, like stepping through ice that is not as thick as one thought. The poem cited above, like a number of others, turns on such ambiguities and on the suggestion of deeper, more philosophical ambiguities beneath the ice. The observed person in this poem is the one who has opened the door and shed light on the speaker, and yet the light becomes merely a mask for the observed, himself no more than a shadow silhouette. The last two lines suggest a deliberate act of will as well as physical obstruction of the light, and they remind us of the different disguises we wear, that openness and shedding light on things, illuminating others, can be a mask too. Such subtleties make Jaffin's poetry rewarding.

—Duane Ackerson

JAMIE, Kathleen

Nationality: Scottish. **Born:** Johnston, Renfrewshire, 13 May 1962. **Education:** University of Edinburgh, M.A. (honors) in philosophy. **Career:** Writer-in-residence, Midlothian District Libraries, 1987–89, Dundee University, 1990–93, and University of Western Ontario, 1995–96. Since 1996 lecturer in creative writing, University of St. Andrews. Fellow, Hawthornden International Retreat for Writers, 1989. **Awards:** Eric Gregory award, 1980; Scottish Arts Council bursary, 1985, 1997; K. Blundell Trust Fund grant, 1989; Compton Fund grant, 1989; Somerset Maugham award, 1995; G. Faber memorial award, 1996; Paul Hamlyn Foundation award, 1997. **Agent:** David Fletcher Associates, 58 John Street. Penicuik, Midlothian, Scotland. **Address:** 217 High Street, Newburgh, Fife KY14 6DY, Scotland.

PUBLICATIONS

Poetry

Black Spiders. Edinburgh, Salamander Press, 1982.
A Flame in Your Heart, with Andrew Greig. Newcastle upon Tyne, Bloodaxe, 1986.
The Way We Live. Newcastle upon Tyne, Bloodaxe, 1987.
The Autonomous Region: Poems & Photographs from Tibet. Newcastle upon Tyne, Bloodaxe, 1993.
The Queen of Sheba. Newcastle upon Tyne, Bloodaxe, 1994.
Jizzen. London, Picador, 1999.

Plays

Radio plays: *Rumours of Guns,* with Andrew Greig, 1985; *The Whitsun Weddings,* 1999.

Other

The Golden Peak: Travels in Northern Pakistan. New Delhi, Penguin, 1992.

*

Manuscript Collections: University College, University of New South Wales, Canberra, Australia; National Library of Scotland.

Critical Study: In *Poetry Review,* 84(1), spring 1994.

*　　*　　*

Kathleen Jamie's first verse collection, *Black Spiders,* was published when she was only twenty years old. It shows an impressive confidence in the handling of both lyric and narrative pieces. The love poem ''November'' typifies the book's boldness, shifting the focus from an unsettled lover longing to be abroad—''He can touch me with a look / As thoughtless as afternoon / And think as much of hindering me / As he would of sailing away''—to the statement ''. . . I am left to tell him in a voice that / Seems as casual as his thought of travel: / I think as much of leaving as / Of forcing him to stay.'' The combination of clarity and ambiguity is a persistent strength in Jamie's work. So is the cryptic economy of the title poem, whose three brief sections imply both conflict and attraction between a man and a woman in an Aegean setting of sea, rocks, and a ruined convent, closing on a note at once erotic and sinister:

> She caught sight of him later, below, brushing salt from the hair of his nipples. She wanted them to tickle; black spiders on her lips.

The book is dominated by estrangement, whether in travel pieces such as "Women in Jerusalem," which tackles problems of identity through a meeting of cultures, or in the big house narrative "The Barometer," or in "Permanent Cabaret," where circus performers signal their identities via costumes. As a whole, *Black Spiders* marks a talent on the verge of discovering its purpose.

Jamie's second book, *A Flame in Your Heart,* was written in collaboration with her fellow Scots poet Andrew Greig. Originally broadcast on the radio, it tells by means of monologues and linking passages the story of a love affair between Len, a Spitfire pilot, and Katie, a nurse, during the Battle of Britain in the spring and summer of 1940. While the subject seems ripe for mawkishness and ventriloquism, Jamie seizes the chance to create a character. Katie is by turns passionate, ironical, observant, and humorous; a young woman whose appetite for life is sharpened by the circumstances of war, only to be denied by Len's death in combat.

In "Karakoram Highway," the central section of Jamie's 1987 collection *The Way We Live,* the author instructs herself—"Stop thinking now, and put on your shoes"—as a plane prepares to land. "Karakoram Highway" is a sequence in the present tense, resisting the temptation to dwell on and interpret landscape and people. Fittingly, the poem breaks off halfway across a rope bridge. It clarifies a tension in Jamie's work between interpretation and experience, which is in fact more satisfyingly handled elsewhere in the book. "Peter the Rock" is a debate between a climber who insists that "there is nothing / but rock and the climbing of rock under the sun" and the authorial voice's equally forceful pursuit of meaning, while "Bosegran" finds that "'why?' is just salt blown in the mind's eye. / The sea delights. The sun climbs higher as the world goes about." Drawn to consider a resolution of the debate in religious experience, Jamie responds with "Julian of Norwich," a monologue at once wry and exultant by an anchoress longing for the restoration of mystical insight: "Everything I do I do for you. / Brute. You inform the dark / inside of stones, the winds draughting in // from this world and that to come, / but never touch me. // ... // (And yet, and yet, I am suspended / in his joy, huge and helpless / as the harvest moon in a summer sky.)" The title poem ends the book on a note of determined celebration: "Pass the tambourine: let me bash out praises," whose subjects must include "misery and elation, mixed, / the sod and caprice of landlords / . . . the way it fits, the way it is, the way it seems / to be . . ."

Jamie's work betrays only marginal influences, Sylvia Plath to begin with and, perhaps from time to time, Elizabeth Bishop. To an unusual degree her work seems to be made from the quick of experience, her poetry seeming almost more of a mode of inquiry than an end in itself. Yet her writings are the product of a sophisticated dramatic imagination and an increasing formal assurance. She is undoubtedly one of the most intriguing poets of her generation.

—Sean O'Brien

JARMAN, Mark (Foster)

Nationality: American. **Born:** Mount Sterling, Kentucky, 5 June 1952. **Education:** University of California, Santa Cruz, B.A. 1974; University of Iowa, Iowa City, 1974–76, M.F.A. 1976. **Family:** Married Amy Kane Jarman in 1974; two daughters. **Career:** Teacher/writing fellow, University of Iowa, Iowa City, 1974–76; instructor of English, Indiana State University, Evansville, 1976–78; visiting lecturer of English, University of California, Irvine, 1979–80; assistant professor of English, Murray State University, Kentucky, 1980–83. Assistant professor, 1983–86, associate professor, 1986–92, and since 1992 professor of English, Vanderbilt University, Nashville. Poetry editor, *Intro 13,* Associated Writing Programs, Norfolk, 1982; co-publisher, 1985–87, Story Line Press, and co-editor, 1981–89, *The Reaper,* both with Robert McDowell; advisory editor, Story Line Press, 1987–89. **Awards:** Academy of American Poets prize, 1974; National Endowment for the Arts fellowship, 1977, 1983, 1992; Robert Frost fellowship, Bread Loaf Writers Conference, 1985; Guggenheim fellowship, 1991; The Poets' prize, 1991, for *The Black Riviera;* Lila Wallace-*Reader's Digest* grant, 1992; Lenore Marshall Poetry prize, 1998. **Address:** 509 Broadwell Drive, Nashville, Tennessee 37220, U.S.A.

PUBLICATIONS

Poetry

North Sea. Cleveland, Ohio, Cleveland State Poetry Center, 1978.
The Rote Walker. Pittsburgh, Carnegie-Mellon University Press, 1981.
Far and Away. Pittsburgh, Carnegie-Mellon University Press, 1985.
The Black Riviera. Middletown, Connecitcut, Wesleyan University Press, 1990.
Iris. Brownsville, Oregon, Story Line Press, 1992.
Questions for Ecclesiastes. Brownsville, Oregon, Story Line Press, 1997.

*

Critical Studies: In *Contemporary Poetry and Poetics* (Oberlin, Ohio), spring 1982.

*   *   *

Mark Jarman's poems, more than those of any other poet of his generation, effectively combine the difficult Audenesque virtues of versatility, precision, and lyric resonance. The key word behind Jarman's poetry is "recovery," reclaiming the past in a society intent on erasing the past as soon as its currency fades and in healing the wounds of painful experience. This double-edged pursuit must often lead to the exploration of elusive private memory. In Jarman's poetry the search evokes a deftly balanced tension, a decision made over and over, from poem to poem, about what can and cannot be revealed and in what settings those revelations must truthfully appear.

Jarman, long a believer in the poet's responsibility to root poems in the landscape of a particular region, often returns to Scottish and southern California settings, his personal landscapes of childhood and adolescence, and to Kentucky and Tennessee, where he has lived and taught for a number of years. In ''The Supremes,'' from his 1985 collection *Far and Away,* Jarman brings back a long-ago morning of surfing as it ends in Ball's Market for sweet rolls. On the store's television set the boys watch the famous Motown group:

> Gloved up to their elbows, their hands raised
> toward us palm out, they sing,
> 'Stop! In the Name of Love' and don't stop . . .

''Every day of a summer,'' the poet realizes, ''can turn, from one moment, into a single day.'' The poem moves on, recalling a scene in Diana Ross's first film and ''the summer it brought back,'' its minute details carefully laid out, adding up to . . . what? Unexpectedly, the poem opens up to speculate on the singers' very different memories of that summer and then winds back to the boys in the market:

> But what could we know, tanned white boys,
> wiping sugar and salt from our mouths
> and leaning forward to feel their song?
> Not much, except to feel it
> ravel us up like a wave
> in the silk of white water,
> simply, sweetly, repeatedly,
> and just as quickly let go.

A moment passes, but memory's durable capacity for haunting, for staying with those who live and feel experience rather than sleepwalking through life, can provoke a personal breakthrough, a revelation that may prove relevant to all. ''The Supremes'' leads us to the discovery that the remembered day and summer, the surfing boys, the local market that would not last, and the famous singing group combine in the poet's memory to form an experience the essence of which was ''full of simple sweetness and repetition.'' Jarman's poems thrive on such breakthroughs, in which ordinary vision, focusing intently, becomes something more penetrating, more revealing, and in which key words, such as ''sweetness'' and ''repetition,'' take on more than their usual weight, acting both as summaries of the past and as signposts indicating future experience.

In *Iris,* the seminal book-length narrative poem published in 1992, Jarman adapts the challenging double pentameter of Robinson Jeffers to tell the story of a lower-middle-class Kentucky woman's search for meaning. Iris is a single mother running from an abusive marriage and drug-related violence in her home, and her most compelling constant in a twenty-year odyssey, aside from caring for her daughter and invalid mother, is the poetry of Jeffers. When a community college English teacher asks her why she reads such a poet, Iris gives him a thoughtful answer:

> She put her hand across her mouth and spoke through
>   parted fingers. ''I don't think I can tell you.
> I have to. I love the poetry. I think there's something
>   else that he's not telling.''

It is this conviction that ultimately leads her to California and then, years later, to a car trip north to see Jeffers's rugged home, Tor House, located on a windy precipice overlooking Monterey Bay. It is there, in the shadow of ''the house where pain and pleasure had turned to poetry and stone, and a family had been happy,'' that the truth of Jeffers's experience and her own life click into place. Because the evidence of Jeffers's domestic life contradicts his stern philosophy, Iris taps into her own capacity to interpret life's complexity. She realizes at last that what we live and how we interpret complex experience may in fact amount to more than a seamless life. This is the key she has been searching for, and it unlocks the point of view that validates her many compromises and difficult decisions.

For Jarman poetry fails if it does not provide the key to such elusive discoveries. A minister's son, he forever pushes against inherited faith, testing both its truthfulness and his own capacity to believe. This effort finds its most distilled expression in the 1997 collection *Questions for Ecclesiastes* and in a related series of sonnets. In ''In Via Est Cisterna'' the poet watches as his mother is able to recall only one phrase from a Latin class she took as a girl. Once again, the suggestive significance of the phrase transcends the literal and mundane:

> A well is in the road. It is profound,
> I'm sure, it is a phrase with many levels.
> And then, I see one: the woman with five husbands
> Met Jesus there. But my mother had only one—
> Unless now having lost him she understands
> That he was never who she thought, but someone
> Who was different men with different women through
>   the years.
> In the road is a well. It fills with tears.

Making the leap from a fragment of ancient personal experience—the Latin phrase—to the ramifications of infidelity is typical of the territory one might expect to cover in Jarman's poems. These brief, varied examples verify this poet's technical virtuosity and his storytelling and lyric preeminence among his peers.

—Robert McDowell

JENNINGS, Elizabeth (Joan)

Nationality: British. **Born:** Boston, Lincolnshire, 18 July 1926. **Education:** Oxford High School; St. Anne's College, Oxford, M.A. in English language and literature. **Career:** Assistant, Oxford City Library, 1950–58; reader, Chatto and Windus Ltd., publishers, London, 1958–60. Since 1961 freelance writer. Guildersleeve Lecturer, Barnard College, New York, 1974. **Awards:** Arts Council award, 1953, bursary, 1965, 1968, 1981, grant, 1972; Maugham award, 1956; Richard Hillary memorial prize, 1966; W.H. Smith award, 1987. **Agent:** David Higham Associates Ltd., 5–8 Lower John Street, London W1R 4HA. **Address:** 11 Winchester Road, Oxford OX2 6NA, England.

PUBLICATIONS

Poetry

(Poems). Oxford, Fantasy Press, 1953.
A Way of Looking. London, Deutsch, 1955; New York, Rinehart, 1956.

The Child and the Seashell. San Francisco, Poems in Folio, 1957.

A Sense of the World. London, Deutsch, 1958; New York, Rinehart, 1959.

Song for a Birth or a Death and Other Poems. London, Deutsch, 1961; Philadelphia, Dufour, 1962.

Penguin Modern Poets 1, with Lawrence Durrell and R.S. Thomas. London, Penguin, 1962.

Recoveries. London, Deutsch, and Philadelphia, Dufour, 1964.

The Mind Has Mountains. London, Macmillan, and New York, St. Martin's Press, 1966.

The Secret Brother and Other Poems for Children. London, Macmillan, and New York, St. Martin's Press, 1966.

Collected Poems 1967. London, Macmillan, and Chester Springs, Pennsylvania, Dufour, 1967.

The Animals' Arrival. London, Macmillan, and Chester Springs, Pennsylvania, Dufour, 1969.

Lucidities. London, Macmillan, 1970.

Hurt. London, Poem-of-the-Month Club, 1970.

Folio, with others. Frensham, Surrey, Sceptre Press, 1971.

Relationships. London, Macmillan, 1972.

Growing-Points: New Poems. Manchester, Carcanet, 1975.

Consequently I Rejoice. Manchester, Carcanet, 1977.

After the Ark (for children). London, Oxford University Press, 1978.

Moments of Grace: New Poems. Manchester, Carcanet, 1979.

Selected Poems. Manchester, Carcanet, 1979.

Winter Wind. Sidcot, Somerset, Gruffyground Press, and Newark, Vermont, Janus Press, 1979.

A Dream of Spring. Stratford-upon-Avon, Celandine, 1980.

Celebrations and Elegies. Manchester, Carcanet, 1982.

Extending the Territory. Manchester, Carcanet, 1985.

In Shakespeare's Company. Shipston-on-Stour, Warwickshire, Celandine Press, 1985.

Collected Poems 1953–1985. Manchester, Carcanet, 1986.

Tributes. Manchester, Carcanet. 1989.

Times and Seasons. Manchester, Carcanet, 1992.

Familiar Spirits. Manchester, Carcanet, 1994.

In the Meantime. Manchester, Carcanet, 1996.

A Spell of Words: Selected Poems for Children. London, Macmillan, 1997.

Praises. Manchester, Carcanet, 1998.

Other

Let's Have Some Poetry. London, Museum Press, 1960.

Every Changing Shape (religion and poetry). London, Deutsch, 1961.

Poetry Today 1957–60. London, Longman, 1961.

Frost. Edinburgh, Oliver and Boyd, 1964; New York, Barnes and Noble, 1966.

Christianity and Poetry. London, Burns Oates, 1965; as *Christian Poetry,* New York, Hawthorn, 1965.

Seven Men of Vision: An Appreciation. London, Vision Press, and New York. Barnes and Noble. 1976.

Editor, with Dannie Abse and Stephen Spender, *New Poems 1956.* London, Joseph, 1956.

Editor, *The Batsford Book of Children's Verse.* London, Batsford, 1958.

Editor, *An Anthology of Modern Verse 1940–1960.* London, Methuen, 1961.

Editor, *A Choice of Christina Rossetti's Verse.* London, Faber, 1970.

Editor, *The Batsford Book of Religious Verse.* London, Batsford, 1981.

Editor, *In Praise of Our Lady.* London, Batsford, 1982.

Editor, *Collected Poems,* by Ruth Pitter. London, Enitharmon, 1996.

Translator, *The Sonnets of Michelangelo.* London, Folio Society, 1961; revised edition, London, Allison and Busby, 1969; New York, Doubleday, 1970.

*

Manuscript Collections: Oxford City Library; University of Washington, Seattle.

Critical Studies: By Margaret Byers, in *British Poetry since 1960,* edited by Michael Schmidt and Grevel Lindop, Oxford, Carcanet, 1972; "Symbolic Situations: The Shrimp and the Anemone" by W.D. Maxwell-Mahon, in *CRUX* (Pretoria, South Africa), 12(2), 1978; *A Parallel Study of Two British Women Poets: Ruth Pitter and Elizabeth Jennings* (dissertation), n.p., 1981; "Rage for Order: The Poetic Heroism of Elizabeth Jennings" by Mary Anne Schofield, in *Notes on Contemporary Literature* (Carrollton, Georgia), 13(3), May 1983; "'Here Is a Humility at One with Craft': The Thematic Content of the Poetry of Elizabeth Jennings" by Erwin A. Sturzl, in *On Poets and Poetry: Fifth Series,* edited by James Hogg, Salzburg, University of Salzburg, 1983; "Elizabeth Jennings and Gerard Manley Hopkins" by Michael Wheeler, in *Hopkins among the Poets: Studies in Modern Responses to Gerard Manley Hopkins,* edited by Richard F. Giles, Hamilton, Ontario, International Hopkins Association, 1985; "Elizabeth Jennings: 'Against the Dark'" by Sabine Foisner, in *English Language and Literature: Positions and Dispositions,* edited by James Hogg and others, Salzburg, University of Salzburg, 1990; *The Poetry and Poetics of Elizabeth Jennings* (dissertation) by Mary Brodkorb, University of New Brunswick, 1993.

Elizabeth Jennings comments:

I do not much care for writing about my own poems. The main reason for this is, I believe, that it makes one too self-conscious. However, I would like to say that I am always interested in what I am writing at present and hope to write in the future. I like to experiment with different poetic forms, and at this time I am constantly seeking for more and more clarity. I am working on a series of prose poems about paintings (painting is my second favorite art) and a series of poems, in various forms and from several viewpoints, on religious themes. I have also been writing poems about craftsmen and various aspects of nature, particularly skyscapes. For me poetry is always a search for order. I started writing at the age of thirteen and wrote only one four-line poem I now wish to preserve from childhood. My Roman Catholic religion and my poems are the most important things in my life.

*   *   *

Elizabeth Jennings was the only woman to be included in Robert Conquest's anthology *New Lines.* In her lucid diction, her use of traditional meters, and the keen and subtle intelligence in her exploration of ideas, she shares with the other so-called Movement poets a "coolness which is worked for," to quote her own description of a Chinese painter.

Jennings's absorption in the processes of "art with its largesse and its own restraint" has led to many poems that attempt to enter the experience of fellow writers and artists in other media: the sculptor, the composer, the dancer, and painters ranging in time from Rembrandt to Rouault and from Botticelli to Cézanne, van Gogh (recurringly), and Bonnard. She is also especially interested in childhood and aging. Her portraits of children are based on personal recollections of a timeless peace and safety from adult ambiguities but still more on the distresses that ultimately "built a compassion that I need to share." In addition, she writes about the feelings of the very old with a tender, intuitive sympathy. The poet's insight into contemplative states of being has resulted in intense imaginative projections into the lives of such personalities as St. John of the Cross, St. Teresa of Avila, St. Catherine, and St. Augustine. She has pondered the nature of the Virgin in fine poems like "Annunciation" and "The Visitation" and has even explored the loneliness and human conflicts of Christ. Jennings's prose poems and dramatic monologues, her translations of Michelangelo's sonnets, and an increasingly adventurous freedom and flexibility in her rhythms and verse patterns demonstrate the versatility of her gifts.

Italy, where Jennings has traveled extensively, is the background for a number of poems that epitomize her great difference from the rest of the Movement group. A profound religious conviction colors her vision of life and permeates all of her work. As a foreigner at confession, at a Roman mass, or at Assisi "where silence is so wide you hear it," she communicates the quietism most vividly realized in the magnificent "San Paolo Fuori le Mura," where the cool stillness of stone engenders an interior calm that functions as "a kind of coming home." In "Song for a Birth or a Death" the mystic's apprehensions of reality are as eloquently articulated as anywhere in contemporary poetry. "Notes for a Book of Hours" conjures the raptness of the visionary and his struggle for the elusive language capable of expressing the numinous. "A World of Light" re-creates "A mood the senses cannot touch or damage, / A sense of peace beyond the breathing word," which grows in "a dazzling dark" as reminiscent of Vaughan as later poems like "Winter Night" and "Let there be dark for us to contemplate."

Jennings is, however, equally and bitterly familiar with another kind of darkness, one of doubt, desolation, and despair, the abysses of Hopkins's "winter world" as implied in her title "The Mind Has Mountains." Recurrent breakdowns led to spells in a mental hospital, and the guilt, bewilderment, frustrations of unfulfilled love, and "very absolute of fear," which culminated in a state "clothed in confusion," are conveyed with poignant directness in many poems of her middle period. Yet this agonized experience of "climates of terror" and compassionate vulnerability to the sufferings of her fellow patients led to a recognition that "perhaps to know no desert is a lack" and an acceptance of the necessity of "the painful breaking / Which brings to birth."

The recovery chronicled in "Growing-Points" and "Consequently I Rejoice" shows a greater maturity of acceptance, a full repossession of her lost capacity for contemplative stillness, and a renewed receptivity to moments of mystical revelation. The notable broadening of range in her choice of subject and a more objective awareness of the contemporary world and of problems and predicaments other than her own are matched by a new assurance and virtuosity in the handling of language. Jennings's words describing a disabled countryman apply with equal aptness to her own impressive testimony, courage, and spiritual resilience: "gentleness / Concealing toughness," which takes "pain as birds take buffets from / The wind, then gather strength and fly and fly."

—Margaret Willy

JOE, Rita

Nationality: Canadian (Mi'kmaq). **Born:** Whycocomagh, Cape Breton, Nova Scotia, 15 March 1932. **Education:** Shubenacadie Indian Residential School, Shubenacadie, Nova Scotia, 1944–48. **Family:** Married Frank Joe in 1954 (died 1989); ten children. **Awards:** Nova Scotia Writers' Federation Competition, 1974. Member, Order of Canada, 1989.

PUBLICATIONS

Poetry

Poems of Rita Joe. Halifax, Nova Scotia, Abanaki Press, 1978.
Song of Eskasoni: More Poems of Rita Joe. Charlottetown, Prince Edward Island, Ragweed Press, 1988.
Lnu and Indians We're Called. Charlottetown, Prince Edward Island, Ragweed Press, 1991.
We Are the Dreamers: Recent and Early Poetry. Wreck Cove, Nova Scotia, Breton Books, 1999.

Other

Song of Rita Joe: Autobiography of a Mi'kmaq Poet. Charlottetown, Prince Edward Island, Ragweed Press, and Lincoln, University of Nebraska Press, 1996.

Editor, with Lesley Choyce, *The Mi'kmaq Anthology.* Lawrencetown Beach, Nova Scotia, Pottersfield Press, 1997.

*   *   *

Rita Joe was born in 1931 on the Whycocomagh reserve on Cape Breton Island in Nova Scotia. Orphaned at the age of six, she was shunted from home to home and from reservation to reservation. Joe attended school in Shubenacadie and subsequently made her home on the Eskasoni reserve. The mother of eight children, she adopted two more children and has cared for two grandchildren.

Joe began to write poems about her Micmac heritage in the late 1960s. At first her work attracted only local interest. National interest came in 1990, when she was made a member of the prestigious Order of Canada. Her collections of loosely written poems are, in their own way, as eloquent as the oratory of the late Chief Dan George, author of *My Heart Soars.*

Poems of Rita Joe (1978) has as its epigraph the following lines: "I am the Indian, / And the burden / Lies yet with me." All of the poems are untitled and, indeed, can be seen as one long poem. There is observation ("While skyscrapers hide the heavens, / They can fall"), and there is statement ("The lore and legends / Are not to be lost. / To say they are vanishing is / Not true.").

Song of Eskasoni: More Poems of Rita Joe (1988) is a collection that explores many moods. Joe asserts native pride in "Legacy": "Abandon my country? / For sale my heritage? / I do not see the need. / My birthright began / This country's history." She keeps a watchful eye for transgressions in "The Art of Communication": "I was only a child yesterday / But I am expected to be mature and brave / On the battlefield of assimilation. / Please help me." In the same poem she is quite lyrical: "Eskasoni is my home, a place of peace and harmony / Where bannock and tea are served / To anyone who is kind enough to visit." The sole false note sounded in the collection is the ascription to her of the authorship of "The Song of the Stars," a traditional Passamaquoddy lyric that predates Joe's book by a century.

Lnu and Indians We're Called (1991) offers numerous subjects for poems: a reflection on receiving the Order of Canada, a description of a royal visit, attendance at aboriginal conferences, a consideration of the trickster hero Klu'skap, thoughts on prejudice, and the poet's surprising identification with the Beothuk Indians, long thought to be extinct. Whether she calls herself a Beothuk or a Micmac, Joe has received a wide readership.

—John Robert Colombo

JOHNSON, Judith (Emlyn)

Pseudonyms: Judith Johnson Sherwin. **Nationality:** American. **Born:** New York City, 3 October 1936. **Education:** The Dalton Schools, New York, 1954; Radcliffe College, Cambridge, Massachusetts, 1954–55; Barnard College, New York, B.A. (cum laude) 1958 (Phi Beta Kappa); Columbia University, New York (Woodrow Wilson fellow, 1958), 1958–59. **Family:** Married James T. Sherwin in 1955 (divorced); three children. **Career:** Promotion manager, Arrow Press, New York, 1961; instructor, Poetry Center, New York, 1976, 1978, 1981; poet-in-residence, Wake Forest University, Winston-Salem, North Carolina, 1980. Poet-in-residence, 1980–81, assistant professor of English, 1981–87, associate professor, 1988–91, since 1992 professor of English and women's studies, and chair of department of Women's Studies, 1995–96, State University of New York, Albany; president, 1975–78, and chairman of the Executive Committee, 1979–80, Poetry Society of America; member of Board of Directors, 1994–97, and president, 1995–96, Associated Writing Programs. **Awards:** Academy of American Poets prize, 1958; Yaddo fellowship, 1964; Poetry Society of America fellowship, 1964; Aspen Writers Workshop Rose fellowship, 1967; Yale Series of Younger Poets award, 1968; *St. Andrews Review* prize, 1975; *Playboy* award, for fiction, 1977; National Endowment for the Arts fellowship, 1981; Poetry Society of America Alice Fay Di Castagnola award, 1992; D. Litt Honoris Causa, St. Andrew's College, Laurinburg, N.C., 1992. **Address:** Department of English, State University of New York, Albany, New York 12222, U.S.A.

PUBLICATIONS

Poetry

Uranium Poems. New Haven, Connecticut, Yale University Press, 1969.
Impossible Buildings. New York, Doubleday, 1973.
Waste: The Town Scold, Transparencies, Dead's Good Company. Taftsville, Vermont, Countryman Press, 3 vols., 1977–79.
How the Dead Count. New York, Norton, 1978.
The Ice Lizard. New York, Sheep Meadow Press, 1992.

Plays

Belisa's Love (produced New York, 1959).
En Avant, Coco (produced New York, 1961). two untitled multimedia works (produced Brussels, 1971, 1972).
Waste (multimedia; produced London, 1972).

Short Stories

The Life of Riot. New York, Atheneum, 1970.

Other

Editor, with Brenda S. Webster, *Hungry for Light: The Journal of Ethel Schwabacher.* Webster, Indiana, Indiana University Press, 1993.

*

Critical Studies: By Hayden Carruth, in *Harper's* (New York), June 1978, and *The Nation* (New York), January 1979; in *Choice* (Middletown, Connecticut), July-August and December 1978; by Rochelle Ratner, in *Soho Weekly News* (New York), 7 September 1978; by Carol Saltus, in *The Women's Review of Books* (Massachusetts), December 1992; by Mimi Albert, in *Poetry Flash* (San Francisco), November 1992; by Leslie Ullman, in *The Kenyon Review* (Gambier, Ohio), summer 1993; by Dianne Blakely Shoaf, in *American Book Review,* October-November 1993; "Healing Our Wounds: The Direction of Difference in the Poetry of Lucille Clifton and Judith Johnson" by Jean Anaporte-Easton, in *Mid-American Review* (Bowling Green, Ohio), 14(2), 1994.

Judith Johnson comments:

My poetry comes across in readings as drama or music more than as text. I enjoy reading with cool jazz or with quiet electronic music that provides spaces in the sound and between the sounds. Much of my poetry is meant to be sung or chanted or belted out in the shower.

All my life I have refused to let myself be limited to any theory of what poetry should be, either in form or in content. I write traditional sonnet sequences, and I write surreal poems and sound poems. Every form, every technique is of equal interest. I should feel dissatisfied with my mind if there were any approach to poetry that did not excite me to see if I could go out and do likewise.

My writing, poetry, fiction, and drama, is both feminist and political, but it is neither didactic nor hortatory. I write about my life as a woman and as a political animal because that is where my life is, those are the questions I have to face. However, I do not know the answers; any answer I examine is hypothesis, not conclusion.

I try to make a rough music, a dance of the mind, a calculus of the emotions, a driving beat of praise out of the pain and mystery that surround me and become me. My poems are meant to make your mind get up and shout.

(1995) What I have been fashioning is a poetics of generosity to replace the poetics of parsimony that governs public life and art. As with many women writers, whatever I write has seemed to take its place in the mainstream poetic culture as "other" and as "excess." The critical reaction has often been some form of "You're something else!" or "You're too much!"—some uneasy blend of admiration and condemnation. To transform feminine excess and alterity from perceived weaknesses to strengths requires rethinking both literary norms and my location within or outside them. I have chosen to consider the energy in my work a form of generosity rather than a form of excess; to consider my poetics as normative rather than marginal; to imagine transformative poetics in metaphors other than the militaristic ones associated with terms like "avant-garde"; to phrase my changing locations within life and literature in terms of what they are rather than of what they are not; to enunciate plenitude rather than lack.

What I have been fashioning, like many contemporary poets whose theoretical vocabularies differ, is a poetics of transformation rather than a poetics of representation. Aristotelian poetics valued the mimetic qualities of art, the imitation of an action rather than the action itself, holding the mirror up to nature rather than inventing and transforming and acting within nature. But just as contemporary scientific and mathematical theory seems to suggest the action of the observer within the experiment, so the poetics in which I participate stresses the poem as transformative act across a range of practices, varying from pure play, analogous to the sciences' pure research, to Marxist, feminist, or postcolonialist political activisms.

What I have been fashioning is a poetics of multiplicity, in which the capaciousness and porosity of meaning take on their own life within language. This requires a recasting of vocabulary. The idea of indeterminacy allows me to do some things, but multideterminacy or infinite determinacy allows me to do very different things. Uncertainty in physics allows us to recognize that we can know location or velocity but not both. But a point whose location we cannot determine may have multiple locations rather than no location, and this latter terminology with regard to how meaning moves allows me to work more dynamically within the text. Zeno demonstrated the shortcomings of analytic processes when he used them to prove that the arrow did not move. A magical or transformative poetics restores motion by accepting the principles of simultaneity and of multiple location.

*　　*　　*

Judith Johnson, originally introduced to the poetry world as Judith Johnson Sherwin, is not only a poet but also a mixed-media artist, fiction writer, playwright, and critic. Her poems first appeared in the 1960s and introduced major themes—technology and the devastating effects of modern politics and the difficulty and necessity of loving in the modern world—that continue into her present work. Her poems both elucidate these problems and constitute a weapon to defy them. Her style is characterized by incantatory repetitions and a skewed, tense diction that strains the limits of conventional grammar and syntax, though she often incorporates these within the classic forms of the sonnet and quatrain, updated with slant rhyme. Her similes and metaphors are extended and bizarre, drawn from the absurd artifacts of contemporary plastic culture but often also reminiscent of the seventeenth-century Metaphysical conceit. Yet her sensibility is ultramodern, influenced by and reflective of jazz, radio ads, and technological innovations.

In her first book, *Uranium Poems,* words pile up and hammer on one other without breath break, reinforcing the metaphor and message that uranium mining destroys the earth to procure ores to make bombs that destroy the world. This theme begets another, how the consciousness of various deaths permeates our lives, especially the death that haunts love, Marilyn Monroe's suicide, and the bitter political deaths of our time, murder by Adolf Eichmann. In her second collection, *Impossible Buildings,* Johnson is still hardheaded, but her language and forms are less rough-hewn. In "Materials," a sequence of ten sonnets, each poem focuses on a natural substance such as ice, wood, or water, and each is made an elegant symbol for an aspect of sexual love. The prevailing theme is larger than love, however, as the title poem makes clear. As in M.C. Escher's drawings, "impossible buildings" are constructed by the artist's mind in its creative work: "the construction is / the information."

The poems of *How the Dead Count,* while often elegiac in tone (as in the long title poem), are also often angry and satiric. The stock exchange mentality, Henry Kissinger, capitalist and technological abuses—all receive Johnson's contempt. Love returns in this book, too, as a freighted theme, a sometimes ebullient emotion but frequently bereft and sad in severance from the loved one, as in the section entitled "From Brussels." The pain rises out of conflict with, and seems to be the price of, the poet's life as an independent woman and artist. The independence, however, is an elemental source of power, not destructive to her life or to any other. In "Three Power Dances" she pits against technology the Native American mythic viewpoint, out of which she creates a totem of herself, "a great Female Bear / wide as a house sings / out of Her dark cave." The emphasis is on female being over male doing: "I hold back your day / your death dance, your night of war / This is My Power dance." This defiant yet compassionate sensibility profoundly animates the title poem, an elegy for the young dead of the civil rights movement and the Vietnam War, which continues the theme of death intermingled with our lives. These dead "count"—they matter—because they bring creative richness to birth in us by the very extremity of their situation.

No creativity or contemporary emotion can disentangle itself from our technologized milieu, however, as is made clear in Johnson's book "Cities of Mathematics and Desire," the title poem of her book manuscript that won the Poetry Society of America's Alice Fay Di Castagnola award in 1992. Here language experiments loop even higher in the imaginative air, but they serve compassion as they imitate speech impaired by stroke and collage stories, exclamations, and rude fragments to convey a multilayered sense of deracinated yet exuberant modern urban life. The title poem is an epic taking off from William Carlos Williams's mythic theme of *Paterson* (a man is a city) to dramatize the interpenetration of impersonal forces, "mathematics," and personal passion, a condition that extends from the submicroscopic collision of particles to marriage to mysterious explosions in intergalactic space. It is an exalted theme orchestrated by Johnson's impressive gift for laser-sharp, bejeweled language.

Johnson's subsequent work expands on the themes of *Cities of Mathematics and Desire.* Her unconventional creative process uses improvisation to generate performance/ritual/mythic poems that eventually appear on the page. These poems embody a large vision that unites science, philosophy, and feminism. Chaos theory in physics and shamanistic trance experiences are major influences on both Johnson's intellect and her intuition. She has made important contributions to literary theory in a generically radical verse essay, "A Poetics of Generosity: A WoManifesto," which she presented as a paper at the Modern Language Association meeting in 1997. Here she challenges the Lacanian notion that the symbolic order—that is, language and art—proceeds from "lack." It comes, she says, from surplus, from the fecundity of the universe to which the multiplicity of appearances testifies. Desire is the spark that "would now flame / this world alive / for all time." The possessor of the spark, that is, the "maker"—her term, which is preferable to "poet"—therefore has power:

> . . . the act of speech
> is always more than symbolic. It is solid,
>> actual
>> transformative
>> *the hammer of words at the lip*
>> *of the well*

Johnson is a writer to watch. She embraces both the postmodern and the archaic in a beneficent "machinery of connection" that arouses confidence in the human ability to elicit order out of chaos.

—Jane Augustine

JOHNSON, Linton Kwesi

Nationality: Jamaican and British. **Born:** Chapeltown, Jamaica, in 1952. Immigrated to England in 1963. **Education:** Tulse Hill Comprehensive School, London; Goldsmith's College, University of London, B.A. in sociology 1973. **Career:** Founding member, Race Today Collective, London. Arts editor, *Race Today* magazine. Formerly library resource and education officer, Keskidee Arts Centre. Writer-in-residence, London Borough of Lambeth. Fellow, University of Warwick, Coventry. Producer, 10-part program about Jamaican music, BBC Television. **Awards:** C. Day Lewis fellowship, 1977. **Address:** c/o Island Records Ltd., 22 St. Peters Square, London W6 9NW, England.

PUBLICATIONS

Poetry

Voices of the Living and the Dead (includes play). London, Towards Racial Justice, 1974.
Dread, Beat, and Blood. London, Bogle L'Ouverture, 1975.
Inglan Is a Bitch. London, Race Today, 1980.
Tings an' Times: Selected Poems. Newcastle upon Tyne, Bloodaxe, 1991.

Recordings: *Poet and the Roots,* Virgin, 1977; *Dread, Beat, and Blood,* Virgin, 1978; *Forces of Victory,* Island, 1979; *Bass Culture,* Island, 1980; *Making History,* Island, 1984; *In Concert with the Dub Band,* Rough Trade, 1985; *Dread Beat an' Blood,* Heartbeat, 1989; *LKJ: A Cappella Live,* LKJ Records, 1996; *More Time,* LKJ Records, 1998.

Play

Voices of the Living and the Dead (produced London, 1973). Included in *Voices of the Living and the Dead,* 1974.

*

Critical Studies: By Sarah Lawson Welsh, in *Bete Noire* (Hull, England), 12–13, autumn 1991-spring 1992; interview with Burt Caesar, in *Critical Quarterly* (Oxford), 38(4), winter 1996.

*   *   *

Linton Kwesi Johnson is the most prominent of Britain's younger black poets. Like his contemporaries, he has drawn upon the linguistic and musical resources of his West Indian heritage to create a poetry that is at once politically radical and rhythmically compelling. In the early 1970s Johnson began forging the rhythms of black music—jazz, soul, calypso, and especially Jamaican reggae—with the rich idioms of West Indian and black British English. The result has been a distinguished body of work that mixes compelling narratives of black British life, sophisticated political analysis, and passionate demands for racial justice and cultural autonomy. In becoming one of Britain's most exciting and distinctive poetic voices, Johnson has demonstrated how contemporary poetry can be both politically engaged and genuinely popular without sacrificing linguistic and thematic complexity.

Although written in Standard English, Johnson's first book, *Voices of the Living and the Dead,* displays both the passionate political commitment and the remarkable rhythmic drive that characterizes his poetry:

> Sing a song for the sawn-off shotgun
> Sing a song for the blood-stained
> blade
> Sing a song for the stones sticks
> and teeth
> Sing a song for knuckles and for feet.

Crossing the apocalyptic revolutionary theory of Frantz Fanon with the incantatory delivery of Jamaican toasters like Big Youth and I-Roy, these poems offer an eloquent call to resist oppression, if necessary through violent means. Yet the poems also recognize the disastrous effects violence has played in turning members of the black community against one another:

> madness . . . madness . . .
> madness tight on the heads of the rebels;
> the bitterness erupts like a hot-blast,
>> broke glass,
> rituals of blood and of burning
> served by a cruel in-fighting;
> five nights of horror and of bleeding,
>> broke glass,
> cold blades as sharp as the eyes of hate.
>> and the stabbings.
> It's war amongst the rebels;
> madness, madness, war.

By the time of his second collection, *Dread, Beat, and Blood* (1975), Johnson had wedded his rhythmic sophistication to an idiomatic vocabulary drawn from the dialects of black street language and Rastafarianism. It is a dark, brooding language in which the chanted repetition of key words ("dread," "war," "fire," "blood") reflects the anxiety, suffering, and anger that British blacks have experienced at the hands of a white racist society. Choosing to write in such an idiom is a political act in itself, for such language is habitually attacked by social conservatives as "substandard" and "primitive." But for Johnson such language not only expresses cultural defiance but also proves a dynamic means of expression:

Shock-black bubble-doun-beat bouncing
rock-wise tumble-doun sound music;
foot-drop find drum, blood story,
bass history is a moving
           is a hurting black story . . .

Rhythm of a tropical electrical storm
(cooled down to the pace of the struggle),
flame-rhythm of historically yearning
flame-rhythm of the time of turning,
measuring the time for bombs and for burning.

The sheer technical accomplishment of this verse—its percussive alliteration, propulsive rhythm, and sophisticated use of internal rhymes—should belie any claim that dialect poetry is necessarily facile and artless.

Johnson's later poetry, while maintaining its ties to reggae culture, has somewhat de-emphasized its Rastafarian affiliations. (In fact, in "Reality Poem" Johnson gently mocks those who "leggo wi clarity" and "start preach religion" rather than face the struggle.) Reflecting Johnson's longtime involvement with Britain's Race Today Collective, his poetry has increasingly become a chronicle of the political struggles of black Britons and a record of both triumphs ("Forces of Victory," "Di Great Insohreckshan") and setbacks ("Reggae Fi Peach," "New Craas Massahkah"). These poems bristle with place-names, political acronyms, and the specificity of historical events without forfeiting any of their linguistic power:

well doun in Southall
where Peach did get fall
di Asians de faam-up a human wall
gense di fashist an dem police shiel
an dem show dat di Asians gat plenty zeal
it is noh mistri
wi mekkin histri
it is noh mistri
wi winnin victri

In his 1984 album *Making History* there are attempts to place the black British struggle in an international context, as in "Di Eagle an' di Bear," with its mordant suggestion that the peoples of the third world have little leisure to share the nuclear anxiety of the first:

di Eagle an' di Bear
are people livin' in fear
of impendin' nuclear warfear
but as a matter of fac
b'lieve it or not
plenty people don care wedder it imminent or not
first one ta atack destry di human race
but survivin for dose whom is aware
dem life already comin' like a nightmare.

As its themes and language suggest, Johnson's work is first and foremost an oral poetry, designed to be read aloud within a community. Impressive enough on the page, his writing grows exponentially in power when intoned in its author's deep, mellifluous voice, especially when that voice is borne on the crackling rhythms of the reggae ensembles that often accompany Johnson at his readings and concerts. These gatherings inevitably attract a larger and more diverse audience than one finds at the average poetry reading, and this genuinely popular element in Johnson's work points to what is perhaps his greatest achievement. In taking poetry out of the classroom and placing it squarely in the street, the political demonstration, and the dance hall, he has shown how poetry can both reflect and dynamically contribute to the political struggles of its time. At a time when poetry often appears as an increasingly academic and circumscribed diversion, such an accomplishment deserves the greatest critical interest.

—Anthony G. Stocks

JOHNSON, Ronald

Nationality: American. **Born:** Ashland, Kansas, 25 November 1935. **Education:** Columbia University, New York, B.A. 1960. **Military Service:** U.S. Army, 1954–56. **Career:** Poet-in-residence, University of Kentucky, Lexington, 1970–71, University of Washington, Seattle, 1972; the Wallace Stegner Advanced Writing Workshop, Stanford University, 1991, and Roberta Holloway Poet, University of California at Berkeley, 1994. **Awards:** Inez Boulton award (*Poetry*, Chicago), 1964; National Endowment for the Arts grant, 1969, 1974; National Poetry Series prize, 1984. **Address:** 1490 Prince Street, Berkeley, California 94702, U.S.A. **Died:** 4 March 1998.

PUBLICATIONS

Poetry

A Line of Poetry, A Row of Trees. Highlands, North Carolina, Jargon, 1964.
Assorted Jungles: Rousseau. San Francisco, Auerhahn Press, 1966.
Gorse/Goose/Rose and Other Poems. Bloomington, Indiana University Fine Arts Department, 1966.
Sunflowers. Woodchester, Gloucestershire, John Furnival, 1966.
Io and the Ox-Eye Daisy. Dunsyre, Lanarkshire, Wild Hawthorn Press, 1966.
The Book of the Green Man. New York, Norton, and London, Longman, 1967.
The Round Earth on Flat Paper. Urbana, Illinois, Finial Press, 1968.
Reading 1 and 2. Urbana, Illinois, Finial Press, 2 vols., 1968.
Valley of the Many-Colored Grasses. New York, Norton, 1969.
Balloons for Moonless Nights. Urbana, Illinois, Finial Press, 1969.
The Spirit Walks, The Rocks Will Talk. Highlands, North Carolina, Jargon, 1969.
Songs of the Earth. San Francisco, Grabhorn Hoyem, 1970.
Maze/Mane/Wane. Cambridge, Massachusetts, Pomegranate Press, 1973.

Eyes and Objects. Highlands, North Carolina, Jargon, 1976.
RADI OS I-IV: San Francisco, Sand Dollar, 1977.
ARK: The Foundations 1–33. Berkeley, California, North Point Press, 1980.
ARK 50: Spires 34–50. New York, Dutton, 1984.

Other

The Aficionado's Southwestern Cooking. Albuquerque, University of New Mexico Press, 1968.
The American Table. New York, Morrow, 1984.
Southwestern Cooking, New and Old. Albuquerque, University of New Mexico Press, 1985; revised edition, as *The Aficionado's Southwestern Cooking,* Albuquerque, Living Batch Press, 1993.
Simple Fare: Rediscovering the Pleasures of Real Food. New York, Simon and Schuster, 1989.
Company Fare. New York, Simon and Schuster, 1991.

Translator, *Sports and Divertissments,* by Erik Satie. Edinburgh, Wild Hawthorn Press, 1965; Urbana, Illinois, Finial press, 1969

*

Manuscript Collection: University of Kansas, Lawrence.

Critical Study: In *Vort 9* (Bloomington, Indiana).

Ronald Johnson comments:

(1970) I have been primarily influenced by the Black Mountain school of poetry, i.e., Charles Olson out of Ezra Pound, Louis Zukofsky, and Williams.

To see the world in a grain of sand, to see the word in a grain of sand, this is where the poem begins. Thoreau questioned, "Who placed us with eyes between a microscopic and a telescopic world?" All is built from this position, a solid construct in the apparently invisible, exact words illuminating the ineffable. A grain of sand if looked at long enough waxes first as glowing, then as large as a moon. The architects tell us that large and small are a matter of placement and that galactic and atomic are simply hummingbirds within hummingbirds, etc. To write a poem is to begin with words, and is it not where word becomes wor(l)d the primal poem exists? And it is only an arc from there to whirled and "the push of numerous hummingbirds from a superior bush."

(1974) After ten years of writing and walking out there in the trees, I have found, as William Blake knew all along, that the trees are in the head.

(1980) I am at present at work on a three-book work titled *ARK.*

(1995) After twenty years work, *ARK* is at last completed and is soon to be published by Living Batch Press in Albuquerque, New Mexico.

*   *   *

To encounter Ronald Johnson's work, whether for the first or the hundredth time, is to slam against the universe and fall back dazed and changed. Intelligence is its foundation, but mystery plays an equal role. Indeed, Johnson is at home with opposites, and striking one against another is his chief technique.

Johnson's erudition, obvious throughout his work but especially so in the experimental *ARK* books, may occasionally intimidate. More often, however, it inspires awe. The opening of the early poem "The Different Musics," the title of which serves as the first line, exemplifies his more accessible work:

come simultaneously
across water,
accumulating fume, spray, the flex of ripple.

As fume, from the Latin *fumus,* Greek

thymos: spirit, mind. "See

DUST, THEISM: cf.
FEBRUARY, FURY, PERFUME, THYME."

(Cf. means "compare" &
"leads to useful, interesting, or related material that is not, however, essential to an understanding of the meaning.")

Opposites abound here: lyricism and epistemology, list and sentence, concrete image and abstraction, word and abbreviation, and statement, poetry, and prose.

"Stereopticon" may serve as an *ars poetica* of sorts:

What we wanted

was both words and worlds
you could put your foot through. To be

eye-deep in air,

and the inside of all things
clear

to the horizon. Clear

to the core.

Johnson desires the abstract ("words") and the physical ("worlds") simultaneously and to be at once within "all things" at the farthest reach ("the horizon") and at the heart of the universe ("the core"). In essence he wishes to become the point at which opposites are united into one, and he has achieved his wish. He is able, for example, to weld seamlessly the scientific to the poetic so that one becomes dependent upon, even invigorates, the other, as in "Four Orphic Poems and a Song":

Newton
—it is said—did not show the cause of an apple falling,

only the similitude between the apple

& the stars.

In Johnson's work, however, words and space are equally important. In *RADI OS*—based on *Paradise Lost,* from which Johnson "erased" most of Milton's first four books, leaving only the words suiting his vision—word and wordlessness (i.e., space on the page) create both tension and meaning. Johnson's title is Milton's with six letters erased—P*aradis*e L*ost*—extracting the highly technological world (''radios'') from the prelapsarian while juxtaposing them. Johnson erased all but thirteen words of Milton's first thirteen lines:

O
tree
into the World,
Man
the chosen
Rose out of Chaos:
song.

RADI OS beguiles, making sense despite occasionally odd syntax, capitalization, or punctuation, as in

we
build up
dream,
this place
Beyond
height or depth, still first and last
sit we then projecting
another World, called Man.

The epic grandeur of *Paradise Lost* has been absorbed by *RADI OS* and continues in Johnson's *ARK* books.

When, in ''Beam 28,'' ''voices'' tell Johnson ''TO GO INTO THE WORDS TO EXPAND THEM,'' his *ARK* volumes seem less elusive. The lushness of earlier volumes is evident throughout the *ARK* collections and is often counterpointed by scientific, historical, or sociological data or by found materials that force readers to expand their imaginations, as in ''Beam 1'':

Clouds loom below. Pocked moon fills half the sky. Stars

comb out its lumen
horizon
in a gone-to-seed dandelion
as of snowflakes hitting dark waters, time, and again,

then dot the plain
186, 282 cooped up angels tall as appletrees . . .

His wordplay also transforms the ordinary, often with humorous results: ''*daimon* diamond Monad I / Adam Kadmon in the sky'' (''Beam 10''). Johnson even challenges our concept of poetry. ''Ark 38,'' for example, is not a poem in the traditional sense of the word but ''just over six minutes of . . . songs of . . . birds'' taped by Johnson and broadcast by a radio station. The ''poem'' that we read in *ARK 50* consists of the section titles Johnson has given to the birds' songs. In the mid-1990s, after two decades of working on the *ARK* project, Johnson finally completed it.

Regardless of his experimentalism, erudition, and reliance on—even reverence of—other texts, Johnson has a lyric voice, at once unique and common, strange and familiar, whose subjects are as old as that of ''Adam Kadmon'':

I sing
the one wherein
all colors of this whirling world begin
and end.

—Jim Elledge

JOHNSTON, Andrew (Grahame)

Nationality: New Zealander (resident in France since 1997). **Born:** Upper Hutt, New Zealand, 7 September 1963. **Education:** Victoria University, Wellington, New Zealand, 1981; Otago University, Dunedin, New Zealand, 1982–85, B.A. in English Literature 1985; Auckland University, New Zealand, 1986, M.A. (honors) in English Literature 1986. **Family:** Married Christine Lorre in 1998. **Career:** Sub-editor, *Otago Daily Times,* Dunedin, New Zealand, 1987, *The Evening Post,* Wellington, New Zealand, 1988–89, *The Dominion,* Wellington, New Zealand, 1989–91, and *The Observer,* London, 1997–99; tutor, Otago University, Department of English, Dunedin, 1987, and Whitireia Polytechnic, Porirua, New Zealand, 1994–95; literary editor, *The Evening Post,* Wellington, New Zealand, 1991–96. Since 1999 copy editor, *International Herald Tribune,* Paris. **Awards:** Arts Council of New Zealand Toi Aotearoa, Louis Johnson New Writer's Bursary, 1991, Established Writers Bursary, 1994; PEN-Stout Centre fellowship, Victoria University of Wellington, 1993; Jessie McKay Award for Best First Book of Poetry, 1994, and New Zealand Book award for poetry, 1994, both for *How to Talk.* **Address:** *International Herald Tribune,* 181 Avenue Charles-de-Gaulle, 92521 Neuilly-sur-Seine, France.

PUBLICATIONS

Poetry

How to Talk. Wellington, New Zealand, Victoria University Press, 1993.
The Sounds. Wellington, New Zealand, Victoria University Press, 1996.
The Open Window: New and Selected Poems. Todmorden, England, Arc Publications, 1999.
Birds of Europe. Wellington, New Zealand, Victoria University Press, 2000.

*

Manuscript Collection: National Library of New Zealand, Wellington.

*   *   *

Andrew Johnston's constant attention is to the word that, as in Saint John's surprisingly emphatic declaration about what there was ''in the beginning,'' comes before what it refers to and calls it into existence. ''Being'' is there already in ''begin,'' needing only a slight rearrangement of the letters. The word, then, must be God, and when a person grants it such precedence, it works hard for him. It seems to reverse Allen Curnow's insistence on ''the reality prior to the poem,'' but the difference is more apparent than real. It is a matter of where the two poets start, from opposite poles but each working toward the same center, a world of words but one as near to ''reality'' as we can ever hope to be authors of.

In Johnston's sequence ''Fool Heart'' the Dwarf Conifer Collection is ''whistling I wish / IwishIwish.'' A dead, or dormant, phrase like ''sensible shoes'' suddenly springs to life as footprints reveal ''a toehold on the real.'' ''New leaves / put themselves out for you.'' A man whose heart, like the conifers, goes, ''I wish IwishIwish,'' ''might need a new frame of mind.'' A shag ''dives—for its other name / and comes up with *cormorant*.'' ''Old magnolias burst into Latin.'' It is to have their being arrested, confirmed, attested that the conifers and magnolias, the shoes and the shag, are wanting, and this is a miracle that only language can perform for them. There are two aspects to this approach—the word as meaning and the word as sound—and in Johnston's poetry the two have to work unusually closely together. When one is speaking by phone across continents, ''there's an echo, / it's you, it's euphony, it's funny.'' The title of his second collection, *The Sounds* (both place and aural quantity), catches this doubleness perfectly.

Reflecting on his poems at large, one feels that there is a characteristic temperamental movement in them that is an escape from an inner darkness into the neutral light of particulars. There is wit, and there is even comedy, but who ever supposed that these cannot—and commonly do not—flourish in a sad soil? The poet alone in New York, trying to remember the names of the Seven Dwarfs, remembers Happy last. In London, where the sun ''fades from star to rumour,'' he tells himself, ''Kneel and pray to the fire instead: / your wishes will be granted, as wishes are, / little by little.'' In parting from a lover, loss and grief are there but pressed down, disciplined to wit:

When I leave I leave
a lot to be desired.

There are two forms Johnston especially favors: one a poem in five, or more latterly six, loose unrhymed couplets, and the other the sestina. The poems in couplets seem in various ways to spring from, or attach themselves to, occasions. The sestinas have, instead, the appearance of generating something out of nothing. They reveal hard graft and great technical accomplishment, but not even a master of the form can make any but the first stanza sound inevitable. In ''The Singer,'' however, Johnston gets close. He also likes to use haiku, not singly but as a stanza form, and its economy suits his temperament:

along the beach road
River Glade, Park Avenue
Oak Bay, Walnut Close

fences and glimpses
architectural finish
magazine gardens

gap for the golf course
Toledo Park Motel, keep
your options open

Johnston's work has been likened to that of John Ashbery. He is one of several influences, and it may be Ashbery's example that has

encouraged Johnston's fascination with the sestina, but the temperamental difference is huge. With Johnston one does not have to take so much on trust, and he requires his words, wherever they start from, to make their way toward something we can recognize and begin to understand. Ashbery, however, prefers to stay well clear of meaning, while signaling excitedly that it is there somewhere, just out of sight.

—C.K. Stead

JOHNSTON, George (Benson)

Nationality: Canadian. **Born:** Hamilton, Ontario, 7 October 1913. **Education:** University of Toronto, B.A. 1936, M.A. 1945. **Military Service:** Royal Canadian Air Force: flight lieutenant. **Family:** Married Jeanne McRae in 1944; three sons and three daughters. **Career:** Assistant professor, Mount Allison University, Sackville, New Brunswick, 1946–49; lecturer, then professor, 1950–79, and since 1979 professor emeritus, Carleton University, Ottawa, Ontario. **Awards:** LL D: Queen's University, 1972. D.Litt.: Carleton University, 1978. **Address:** 2590 Cook's Line, R.R. 1, Athelstan, Quebec J0S 1A0, Canada.

PUBLICATIONS

Poetry

The Cruising Auk. Toronto, Oxford University Press, 1959.
Home Free. Toronto, Oxford University Press, 1966.
Happy Enough. Toronto, Oxford University Press, 1972.
Taking a Grip. Ottawa, Golden Dog, 1978.
Auk Redivivus. Ottawa, Golden Dog, 1981.
Ask Again. Moonbeam, Ontario, Penumbra, 1984.
Carl, Portrait of a Painter. Moonbeam, Ontario, Penumbra, 1986.
Endeared by Dark: The Collected Poems. Erin, Ontario, Porcupine's Quill, 1990.
What Is to Come: Selected and New Poems. Toronto, St. Thomas Poetry Series, 1996.

Other

Editor, *The Collected Poems of George Whalley.* Kingston, Ontario, Quarry, 1986.

Translator, *The Saga of Gisli, the Outlaw.* Toronto, University of Toronto Press/Dent, 1963.
Translator, *The Faroe Islanders' Saga.* Ottawa, Oberon, 1975.
Translator, *The Greenlanders' Saga.* Ottawa, Oberon, 1976.
Translator, *Rocky Shores.* Paisley, Scotland, Wilfion Books, 1981.
Translator, *Wind over Romsdal.* Moonbeam, Ontario, Penumbra, 1982.
Translator, *Pastor Bodvar's Letter.* Moonbeam, Ontario, Penumbra, 1986.
Translator, *Barba.* Kingston, Ontario, Quarry, 1986.
Translator, *Seeing and Remembering: Verse.* Newcastle upon Tyne, Bloodaxe, 1986.

Translator, *Barbara,* by Jorgen-Frantz Jacobsen. Norwich, England, Norvik, 1993.

Translator, *Thrand of Gotu: Two Icelandic Sagas from the Flat Island Book.* Erin, Ontario, Porcupine's Quill, 1994.

*

Critical Studies: By D.G. Jones, in *Canadian Literature* (Vancouver), 59, 1974; George Johnston issue of *MHRev,* 78, March 1987; ''The Later Poetry of George Johnston'' by W.J. Keith, in *Canadian Poetry* (London, Ontario), 31, fall-winter 1992.

*   *   *

In his author's introduction to *Endeared by Dark,* George Johnston indulges in a rare moment of self-defense, noting that Canadians have overemphasized the ''what'' of poetry (sentiment, clarity, observation) at the expense of the ''how'' (technique). From the time *The Cruising Auk* revealed him to be a practitioner of what critics liked to call ''serious light verse,'' Johnston has been a master of superbly unforced craftsmanship. But content is present, too, and the accumulation of delightful verbal surprises is evidenced, for example, in the early poem ''Night Noises'':

Late at night in night's neglected places
The busy diesel shunter thumps and grinds
As to and fro he singles out and chases
The helpless cars, whose businesses he minds.

The Cruising Auk brought onstage a cast of characters—Mr. Murple, Mrs. McGonigle, Miss Belaney—that Johnston treats satirically yet tenderly. In ''Queens and Duchesses,'' for example,

Miss Belaney's pleasure is vast,
   Indeed it fills the night;
She doesn't remember who kissed her last
   But he did it good, all right.

In ''Love in High Places,'' one of two long poems in *Home Free,* Johnston assembles his dramatis personae, telling the story of how Stan, the son of Edward and Sadie, rose to high political rank from humble beginnings:

And if you ask yourself where all this comes from
   And answer true
You will have to admit that his father contributed nothing
But good nature
   And a nervous tic or two.

Johnston is superb, not just in narrating Stan's background and family history, but also in depicting the anxieties of office, even as his character is shaken by the onslaught of romantic infatuation:

There were times when his trouble would come back
   And he would shake:
A wistful evening when the urgency had gone off
   And a warm breeze come on

Beside a lake,
Gert there next him behaving like a delicious
Irrecoverable
   Mistake.

''Under the Tree,'' the other long poem in *Home Free,* also mediates between the private and public spheres, powerfully tracing individual and collective complicity in the ritual of capital punishment. But Johnston is far too skilled to make the poem a diatribe against the death penalty. In any case he is dealing with humanity's guilty or oblivious relationship toward ''God's suffering ugly cunning beautiful / Wounded creature of earth . . .'' The alliterative last line, ''Darkened earth, tell our deeds to the dark,'' also reminds us that Johnston is an accomplished translator from the Old Norse, as well as from modern Scandinavian languages.

From the 1960s onward Johnston has turned away from the end rhymes and graceful scansion of his first poems to seek out more complex rhythms and to make some sacrifice in melody in favor of imagistic compression, as in ''Catpath'' in Happy *Enough:*

Black on Mrs. Crowder's porch
   watching
tabby on Mr. Moir's post
   watching
Mrs. Osborne's bullhead marmalade tom
footing along the catpath in the snow.

The comedy here resides in the photographic clarity of the scene, the simplicity and aptness of the diction, and the strategically perfect placement of ''footing.''

''Come Through,'' in *Ask Again,* plays with singular and plural and puts a new spin on anthropomorphism:

All the white brook
   takes his walk
woodlot to woodlot
   talking
among his alders.

Ask Again includes a section called ''Friends and Occasions,'' and in fact many poems are elegies, commemorations, or epithalamiums, a taking stock of a long and productive life. ''Cold Comfort,'' in *What Is to Come,* notes,

A benefit of age:
leisure to remember
the different kinds of skunk
one has been,
given occasion—

with apologies
to that gentlemanly animal.

Johnston's innate modesty and gentle irony—echoed in titles like *Happy Enough* and *Taking a Grip*—have fallen out of favor, though his work has not so much been disparaged as simply ignored. This is a considerable pity, because Johnston's subtle and lightly carried perceptions are timeless.

—Fraser Sutherland

JONES, Brian

Nationality: British. **Born:** London in 1938. **Family:** Married; two children. **Career:** English teacher at British grammar and secondary schools. **Awards:** Cholmondeley award, 1967; Eric Gregory award, 1968. **Address:** c/o Carcanet Press, 4th Floor, Conavon Court, 12–16 Blackfriars Street, Manchester M3 5BQ, England.

PUBLICATIONS

Poetry

Poems. London, Alan Ross, 1966.
A Family Album. London, Alan Ross, 1968.
Interior. London, Alan Ross, 1969.
The Mantis Hand and Other Poems. Gillingham, Kent, Arc, 1970.
For Mad Mary. London, London Magazine Editions, 1974.
The Spitfire on the Northern Line (for children). London, Chatto and Windus, 1975.
The Island Normal. Manchester. Carcanet. 1980.
The Children of Separation. Manchester, Carcanet, 1985.
Freeborn John. Manchester, Carcanet, 1990.

Play

Radio Play: *The Lady with a Little Dog,* from a story by Chekhov, 1962.

*   *   *

Brian Jones's poetry explores a world of remembered landscapes and family routines, of household tasks and passing seasons. History is traced directly through the writer's own ancestors and the drama of their humdrum lives or culled from headstones in country villages and anonymous rustic plays. The colloquial style he adopts is a conscious achievement, veiling as it does a mastery of structure and an astute deployment of half rhyme. Jones's early work recalls that of Edward Thomas in such poems as "The Unlikely Stubborn Patch" and "Stripping Walls," with their self-deprecating humor. He shares with Thomas a clear, unsentimental knowledge of country life and a pleasure in simple manual tasks. His account of cutting grass in "The Garden of a London House" shares similarities with the older poet's "Digging."

Unlike some of his contemporaries, Jones is convinced of the narrative possibilities of poetry that he feels have yet to be developed. Some of his most ambitious efforts in this form, like "The Courtenay Play," fail to satisfy completely. While one concedes the validity of his intentions, the result in this case seems fragmented and diverse, its images overemphasized. Similarly, the unity of *The Island Normal,* his most dense and concentrated collection, is not immediately apparent to the reader. This said, Jones's insistence on the extended foray justifies itself in *A Family Album,* an impressive sequence of individual portraits, each of which casts fresh light on the others. Here his narrative skill blends with an acute insight into the characters of his relatives, the mass of frailties and contradictions that render a person unique. Aunt Emily is especially memorable, not only dominating *A Family Album* but also pervading several other works,

among them the long title poem of *For Mad Mary.* The same power to compel striking portrayals from domestic life is evident in *The Spitfire on the Northern Line,* an excellent volume aimed at the younger reader. But it is in *A Family Album* and a number of shorter poems that home in on a single central incident or image that Jones is at his best. Examples of the latter include "Chopping Wood," where the passing years are seen as leading to a momentarily focused act, and the later "Church," with its contemplation of a country graveyard: "Here is the cliff-face of arrest / where good and mild and profligate / founder to a name and date / The chill comes off the stone like breath and not the cross / or altar spread / white, or words declaimed and sung / engender awe like those who once / were human, and are simply dead."

Aware of the false glamour of the countryside, which often screens an inner desolation, Jones nevertheless deplores the advance of the urban wasteland. Poems like "End of Pier" and "Return to Wasteground" note bleakly a world where piers and fairgrounds have given way to Volvo showrooms and office blocks, while "Summer Slides" depicts a Britain reduced by tourism to something between a museum and a zoo. Commercialization, it seems, is universal, encountered equally in the French town of Arles: "Angling a quick kill, mayfly tourist shops / stock sunflower prints and Gauguin-labelled beers / and endless shelves of bonsai chaises Van Gogh. / We half-search for a stall of plastic ears."

Art, Jones informs us, has always been under threat, whether from the power of the purse or the sword. In previous ages Virgil and Andrew Marvell faced the same dilemma and survived. Salvation is found in the continued struggle of the poet with his craft and in the perfecting of individual relationships, given that none of us may fully know the other. Thus, in "Andrew Marvell Awaits His Charge" the poet is shown as seeing future hope in the child he educates. Similarly, Jones himself finds time to wonder at the vulnerability of his sleeping daughter, the trust embodied in her undefended bedroom: "You scatter / dreams through the world and let them take their chance. / You sleep now, with the bedside lamp still glaring, / knowing your dolls still read, your gold shoes dance."

With his collection *Freeborn John,* Jones questions the "cold vision" that took over Britain during the 1980s, the crushing of dissent, the cultural barbarism, and the essential denial of basic humanity by the brutal "monologue" of the country's rulers. *Freeborn John* depicts modern Britain as a latter-day mirror image of Caesar's Gaul, its inhabitants cowed and coarsened by the callous worship of "market forces" as the Gauls were subjugated and depersonalized by their Roman conquerors. His own resistance takes a variety of forms in poems ranging from the subversive "leaking" of information by a rebellious civil servant to the counterimage of the Jones clan, whose close-knit tribal kinship is in itself a rejection of the cold values imposed from above. The image of Lilburne's rebellion that opens the book is a fitting one, but Jones's response is more positive and does not confine itself to confrontation alone. His examination of his relationship with father and son in "A View from the Boundary" and with his wife in "Snowstorm Viewed from Love" present a calmer and ultimately more lasting vision. In his clarity of utterance, his evocation of the ordinary, Jones draws continually from the past while speaking directly—and often bluntly—to the reader of today. His poems lend eloquence to a common speech as he explores the familiar and makes it memorable.

—Geoff Sadler

JONES, D(ouglas) G(ordon)

Nationality: Canadian. **Born:** Bancroft Ontario, 1 January 1929. **Education:** Grove School, Lakefield, Ontario; McGill University, Montreal, B.A. (honors) in English 1952; Queen's University, Kingston, Ontario, M.A. 1954. **Family:** Married 1) Betty Jane Kimbark in 1950 (divorced), three sons and one daughter; 2) Sheila Fischman in 1969; 3) Monique Baril in 1976. **Career:** Lecturer, Royal Military College, Kingston, Ontario, 1954–55, Guelph Agricultural College, Ontario, 1955–61, and Bishop's University, Lennoxville, Quebec, 1961–63. Professeur Titulaire, English Department, University of Sherbrooke, Quebec, 1963–94. Co-founder, *Ellipse* journal, 1969. **Awards:** President's medal, University of Western Ontario, 1976; Governor-General's award for poetry, 1977, and 1993, for translation; A.J.M. Smith prize, 1978; Quebec Society for the Promotion of English Language and Literature prize, 1989, 1995. D.Litt.: Guelph University, Ontario, 1982. **Address:** P.O. Box 356, North Hatley, Quebec JOB 2CO, Canada.

PUBLICATIONS

Poetry

Frost on the Sun. Toronto, Contact Press, 1957.
The Sun Is Axeman. Toronto, University of Toronto Press, 1961.
Phrases from Orpheus. Toronto, Oxford University Press, 1967.
Under the Thunder the Flowers Light Up the Earth. Toronto, Coach House Press, 1977.
A Throw of Particles: Selected and New Poems. Toronto, General, 1983.
Balthazar and Other Poems. Toronto, Coach House Press, 1988.
A Thousand Hooded Eyes, with wood engravings by Lucie Lambert. Vancouver, Les Editions Lambert, 1991.
The Floating Garden. Toronto, Coach House Press, 1995.
Wild Asterisks in Cloud. Montreal, Empyreal Press, 1997.

Other

Butterfly on Rock: A Study of Themes and Images in Canadian Literature. Toronto, University of Toronto Press, 1970.

Editor, *The March to Love: Selected Poems,* by Gaston Miron. Pittsburgh, Inter-National Poetry Forum, 1986.

Translator, *The Terror of the Snows,* by Paul-Marie Lapointe. Pittsburgh, University of Pittsburgh Press, 1976; revised and enlarged edition, as *The Fifth Season,* Toronto, Exile, 1985.
Translator, with Marc Plourde, *Embers and Earth,* by Gaston Miron. Montreal, Guernica, 1983.
Translator, *Categorics, One, Two, and Three, Poems by Normand de Bellefevuille.* Toronto, Coach House Press, 1993.
Translator, *For Orchestra and Solo Poet,* by Emile Martel. Montreal, The Muses, 1996.

*

Critical Studies: "D.G. Jones: Etre chez soi dans le monde" by George Bowering, in *Ellipse 13* (Sherbrooke, Quebec), 1973; "The Masks of D.G. Jones," in *Canadian Literature 60* (Vancouver), spring 1974, "D.G. Jones," in *Canadian Writers and Their Works: Poetry Series,* Toronto, ECW Press, 1985, and "D.G. Jones," in *ECW's Biographical Guide to Canadian Poets,* edited by Robert Lecker, Jack David, and Ellen Quigley, Toronto, ECW, 1993, all by E.D. Blodgett.

*   *   *

Verbal clarity, economy, precision, and a purity of imagery characterize the poetry of D.G. Jones. These aesthetic qualities are related to a philosophical state of mind and a quality of emotion that give the poetry an unusual consistency of tone and meaning. The relation between an "emptiness" or "barrenness" perceived in nature, on the philosophical plane (recurrent images in Jones), and an aesthetic of purity in poetry is familiar, especially in Mallarmé, and Jones can be usefully compared to the French master. Jones derives more directly from the imagists, however, from H.D. and from Ezra Pound as critical mentor; later affinities are with Wallace Stevens and Marianne Moore. He is also authentic in himself, and he does not resemble so much as parallel these poets in general ways.

Jones's first book, *Frost on the Sun,* already showed the taint of philosophic disenchantment and affected the shine of purity. *The Sun Is Axeman* revealed a marked advance in control and assurance and a full development of these features. Themes of silence, alienation, and emptiness recur—"a string of notes / limned on the stillness of a void" . . . "skeletons of trees" . . . "And silence like a snow is everywhere." A number of poems, with a patina of perfection, deal with lighter subject matter—"Clotheslines," "Schoolgirls"—and remind one of Gautier, the father of the aesthetes. A cosmic pessimism—"the universe bleeds into darkness"—underlies these poems.

Phrases from Orpheus is marked by personal suffering not unlike that of W.D. Snodgrass in *Heart's Needle,* but there is no further resemblance. Jones is not confessional; his book gives expression to pain and passion through the indirections of poetry, through the myth of Orpheus, through images and the incantations of symbolism, and through irony. Here "stars are not polite, and / even plants are / violent"; there is comfort in "that relatively immortal blue gas / the sky . . ." The poetry transcends the personal, and at its best it achieves a noble indifference or stoicism that touches on the heroic without rhetoric or mannerism.

Phrases from Orpheus is a deeply moving book and one of the most important to appear in Canada in the 1950s and 1960s. It has, unfortunately, been neglected in the hubbub created by numerous young poets appearing on the scene and by the phenomenon of popularity affecting poetry, but the book will no doubt take its place as one of the finest of its time.

—Louis Dudek

JONES, (Morgan) Glyn

Nationality: British. **Born:** Merthyr Tydfil, Glamorgan, 28 February 1905. **Education:** Castle Grammar School, Merthyr Tydfil; St. Paul's College, Cheltenham. **Family:** Married Phyllis Doreen Jones in 1935. **Career:** Formerly a schoolmaster in Glamorgan; retired. First chair,

Yr Academi Gymreig (English Section). **Awards:** Welsh Arts Council prize, for nonfiction, 1969, and Premier award, 1972. D.Litt.: University of Wales, Cardiff, 1974. **Agent:** Laurence Pollinger Ltd., 18 Maddox Street, London W1R OEU, England. **Address:** 158 Manor Way, Whitchurch, Cardiff CF4 1RN, Wales.

PUBLICATIONS

Poetry

Poems. London, Fortune Press, 1939.
The Dream of Jake Hopkins. London, Fortune Press, 1954.
Selected Poems. Llandysul, Dyfed, Gomer, 1975.
The Meaning of Fuchsias. Newtown, Gwasg Gregynog Press, 1987.
Selected Poems, Fragments, and Fictions. Bridgend, Glamorgan, Poetry Wales Press, 1988.
The Collected Poems of Glyn Jones. Cardiff, University of Wales Press, 1996.

Play

The Beach of Falesá (verse libretto), music by Alun Hoddinott (produced Cardiff, 1974). London, Oxford University Press, 1974.

Novels

The Valley, The City, The Village. London, Dent, 1956.
The Learning Lark. London, Dent, 1960.
The Island of Apples. London, Dent, and New York, Day, 1965.

Short Stories

The Blue Bed. London, Cape, 1937; New York, Dutton, 1938.
The Water Music. London, Routledge, 1944.
Selected Short Stories. London, Dent, 1971.
Welsh Heirs. Llandysul, Dyfed, Gomer, 1977.
The Collected Stories of Glyn Jones. Cardiff, University of Wales Press, 1997.

Other

The Dragon Has Two Tongues: Essays on Anglo-Welsh Writers and Writing. London, Dent, 1968.
Profiles: A Visitor's Guide to Writing in Twentieth Century Wales, with John Rowlands. Llandysul, Dyfed, Gomer, 1980.
Setting Out: A Memoir of Literary Life in Wales. Cardiff, University College Department of Extra Mural Studies, 1982.
Random Entrances to Gwyn Thomas. Cardiff, University College Press, 1982.
Goodbye, What Were You? Llandysul, Dyfed, Gomer, 1994.

Editor, *Poems '76.* Llandysul, Dyfed, Gomer, 1976.

Translator, with T.J. Morgan, *The Saga of Llywarch the Old. London,* Golden Cockerel Press, 1955.
Translator, *What Is Worship?,* by E. Stanley John. Swansea, Wales for Christ Movement, 1978.
Translator, *When the Rose-bush Brings Forth Apples* (Welsh folk poetry). Gregynog, Powys, Gregynog Press, 1980.

Translator, *Honeydew on the Wormwood* (Welsh folk poetry). Gregynog, Powys, Gregynog Press, 1984.
Translator, with T.J. Morgan, *The Story of Helodd,* Newton, Powys, Wales, Gwasg Gregynog, 1994.
Translator, *A People's Poetry: Hen Benillion.* Bridgend, Wales, Seren, 1997.

*

Bibliography: By John and Sylvia Harris, in *Poetry Wales 19* (Bridgend, Glamorgan), 3–4, 1984; *A Bibliographical Guide to Twenty-four Modern Anglo Welsh Writers,* Cardiff, University of Wales Press, 1994.

Manuscript Collection: National Library of Wales, Aberystwyth.

Critical Studies: *Glyn Jones* by Leslie Norris, Cardiff, University of Wales Press, 1973, and article by Norris in *British Novelists 1930–1959,* edited by Bernard Oldsey, Detroit, Gale, 1983; interview with Robert Minhinnick, in *New Welsh Review* (Cardiff, Wales), 1(1), summer 1988.

Glyn Jones comments:

I began my literary career as a poet, and I hope to end it in the same way.

I think of myself as belonging to the Anglo-Welsh group of poets, poets who are Welsh but who write in English.

The modern poets who have meant most to me are G.M. Hopkins, D.H. Lawrence, Walt Whitman, Dylan Thomas, plus some of the poets of my own country—I mean writers of poems in the Welsh language. I admire poets who are word- and language-conscious, but that does not mean I am indifferent to what the poet says. Hopkins appeals to me so much because I am in sympathy with his agonizing over language, and I also find acceptable his subject matter and what he has to say about it.

(1995) A volume of my stories, *The Complete Short Stories of Glyn Jones,* is to be published by the University of Wales Press within the next year or two.

I am a Welsh-speaking Welshman, but all my education has been in English. I have written very little in Welsh—no books, only a few reviews and articles.

*   *   *

Glyn Jones is essentially a lyric poet, a celebrant of the concrete more often than not. The prevailing idiom of his early poetry is a compound of influences: the traditions and (loosely adapted) the forms of Welsh poetry, the most "musical" aspects of the English tradition (Herrick, Morris, Tennyson, and Swinburne, for example), and, most obviously, Gerard Manley Hopkins. Indeed, at times the influence of Hopkins results in work one might take to be a conscious imitation of the externals of that poet's style:

> Not kiting over-white against torn winds,
> Milkily wheeling on brim-tilt wings, or heaping up
> Burnt breeze behind, with cutting air in ovals,
> The long slant cornering, his steep-sloped, pointed wings
> Speed-canted, speed-heeled over, leaned like
> > skidding wheels.

The hyphenated compounds, the pronounced alliteration and assonance, and the internal rhyme, while they obviously owe much to the influence of Hopkins (and to his example of how Welsh meter and music might be adapted to English poetry), also speak of Jones's own deeply felt love of word music, of verbal pattern.

In the early work this goes with a painter's sense of the visual (Jones is himself a painter) and a fertility of figurative language to produce a heady mixture of sound and imagination. How well rhyme is used, for example, to control the sensory and imaginative fecundity of metaphor and simile in these lines from ''Merthyr'':

> All that sensational news
> The heart hears, before she starts to bruise
> Herself against the universe's rocky rind,
> Is what she treasures most—the sight of wind
> Fretting a great beech like an anchored breaker;
> The vale, pink-roofed at sunset, a heavenly acre
> Of tufted and irradiated toothpaste; the moon
> Glistening sticky as snail-slime in the afternoon,
> Street-papers hurdling, like some frantic foal,
> The crystal barriers of squalls; the liquid coal
> Of rivers; the hooters loud liturgic boom;
> Pit-clothes and rosin fragrant in a warm room.

It is as a poet of such ''sensational news'' that Jones has remained, through a long writing career, most consistently successful. His manner has become more individual, less obviously influenced, and the concern with verbal fireworks less violent. The same sensory and imaginative energy is there, however, more exactly disciplined in such outstanding poems as ''Dawn Trees'' and ''Nant Ceri'' or in the beautiful and extraordinary ''The Meaning of Fuschias,'' where such qualities are married to a grave thoughtfulness. The enduring Celtic tradition speaks with exquisite directness in a short poem such as ''Swifts'':

> Shut-winged fish, brown as mushroom,
> The sweet, hedge-hurdling swifts, zoom
> Over waterfalls of wind.
> I salute all those lick-finned,
> Dusky-bladed air-cutters.
> Could you weave words as taut, sirs,
> As those swifts', great cywydd kings,
> Swart basketry of swoopings?

Jones was slower to find a poetic idiom in which he might successfully write of man in society. That he should feel the need to do so is hardly surprising, for those aspects of his sensibility that found more obvious expression in his fiction naturally sought a place in his poetry too. An early poem such as ''Marwnad'' comes as close to a pastiche of Lawrence as ''Gull'' to a parody of Hopkins. Gradually, however, Jones evolved a ''human'' verse idiom of his own. The seeds of it are apparent in ''Esyllt,'' though the human is still very much subordinate to the world of external nature. ''Easter'' holds these elements in a more perfect balance, each fully expressive of the other, and perceptions of human psychology begin to take their place as fully developed parts of Jones's work. The process was not without its difficulties, however. ''Profile of Rose,'' for example, fails to find a plausible idiom for narrative verse and breaks down into an overly dense kind of telegraphese. More and more, however, Jones's mature work displays his novelist's eye for social pattern and behavior. ''Where All Were Good to Me, God Knows'' or ''Goodbye, What Were You?'' are fine poems of social change, warm and generous in their sympathy but never merely sentimental. In poems like ''Another Country'' and, especially, ''The Common Path'' Jones's ability to annotate and celebrate the richness of the natural world is counterpointed by a depth of human tenderness absent from his earlier work. ''The Common Path'' is a moving account of isolation, of human contact unestablished, even avoided.

''Seven Keys to Shaderdom,'' a darker successor to the earlier series ''The Dream of Jake Hopkins,'' is an incomplete sequence of poems, with prose interludes, on an elderly artist who is looking back from a drunken old age to a bohemian youth and examining the conflicting demands of life and art as responded to in his own life. These late poems, first published in 1988 in *Selected Poems, Fragments, and Fictions,* provide clear evidence not only that Jones's creative power as a poet endured into his eighties but also that he has triumphantly brought together here his fictional imagination and his poetic technique. Gaiety and grimness, humor and despair—''that despairing radiance''—coexist in these powerful late works. Bleakness is transfigured, but an embracing sense of darkness counterpoises the earlier epiphanies of sense and vision. In an interview published in *New Welsh Review* in 1988, Jones defined poetry's purpose as delight: ''Poetry for me is for delight, like painting, like music . . . As far as we know, only human beings on this planet produce consciously, or aim at producing, what we call works of art, and only other human beings find delight in looking at these works or listening to them.'' It would be a rare and insensitive reader who could not discover such delight in generous proportions in reading Jones's own poetry.

—Glyn Pursglove

JONES, Rodney

Nationality: American. **Born:** Falkville, Alabama, 11 February 1950. **Education:** University of Alabama, B.A. in English 1971; University of North Carolina, Greensboro, M.F.A. 1973. **Family:** Married 1) Virginia Kremza in 1972 (divorced 1979), one daughter; 2) Gloria Nixon de Zepeda Jones in 1981, one son. **Career:** Copywriter, Frost & Frost Inc., Gadsden, Alabama, 1973–74; poet-in-residence, Poetry-in-the-Schools Programs, Tennessee, Alabama, and Virginia, 1974–76; poet-in-residence, Knoxville City Schools, 1977–78; writer-in-residence, Virginia Intermont College, Bristol, 1978–84. Since 1984, professor, Department of English, Southern Illinois University, Carbondale. **Awards:** Lavan Younger Poets award, Academy of American Poets, 1986, for *The Unborn;* National Endowment for the Arts fellowship; Guggenheim fellowship, 1985; General Electric Foundation Younger Writers award, 1986; Jean Stein prize, American Academy and Institute of Arts and Letters, 1989; National Book Critics Circle award, 1989, for *Transparent Gestures.* **Address:** Department of English, Southern Illinois University, Carbondale, Illinois 62901, U.S.A.

PUBLICATIONS

Poetry

Going Ahead, Looking Back. Knoxville, Southbound Books, 1977.
The Story They Told Us of Light. Birmingham, University of Alabama, 1980.
The Unborn. Boston, Atlantic Monthly Press, 1985.
Transparent Gestures. Boston, Houghton Mifflin, 1989.
Apocalyptic Narrative and Other Poems. Boston, Houghton Mifflin, 1993.
Things That Happen Once: New Poems. Boston, Houghton Mifflin, 1996.
Elegy for the Southern Drawl. Boston, Houghton Mifflin, 1999.

*

Critical Studies: "The One Clear Upspoken Sign: Four Young Poets" by Louie Skipper, in *Black Warrior Review* (Tuscaloosa, Alabama), 12(2), spring 1986; by Bill Caton, in his *Fighting Words: Words on Writing from 21 of the Heart of Dixie's Best Contemporary Authors,* Montgomery, Alabama, Black Belt, 1995; "Ghostlier Demarcations, Taller Tales: Humor of the Old Southwest in the Poetry of Rodney Jones and Leon Stokesbury" by R.S. Gwynn, in *Lamar Journal of the Humanities* (Beaumont, Texas), 23(1), spring 1997.

*   *   *

Rodney Jones's poems are anchored in the rural South, but they are the work of the smart kid who left for the big world. A number of his poems are full of a deep respect for the poor of both races struggling in the world, but he feels no need to make their dignity mythic or aristocratic. There also are many poems of the wise guy, failure, lover, father, striver, goofball, earnest student, professor, artist, and horny hippie kid. The range is impressive. His irony is habitual, stemming from a delightful sense of the absurd and with high-handed comic riffs, and it serves as a corrective to the sentiment of his elegiac sensibility.

Jones's first full book, *The Story They Told Us of Light,* was chosen by Elizabeth Bishop for the Associated Writing Programs Award Series. Although many of its poems are marred by the fashionable surrealism of the 1970s, the strengths are apparent. Some poets, like Donne, begin poems with extravagant gestures, but Jones has a characteristic intellectual and emotional leap at the end of his poems, where he flings himself into the search for meaning. This is illustrated in the following excerpts from, respectively, "Adam's Apple," "Goiter," and "for adults only":

> But how shyly
> you bowed your head. You knew
> why dogs and kisses went for the throat.

> But who will look the right way now
> out of such a past? If I remember:
> the last prayer was to be made whole;
> the first was to be beautiful.

You wanted to see her, to know where it was,
You wanted the camera inside the heart.

The power of the last example is that the poem puts the camera where it belongs and not inside the cunt, where the pornographic imagination appears to want it. The poem surprises us with what at first seems to be only the ordinary, not an easy trick. It also points to the central theme of the book, put in "Micro Journey" as "trying to get inside." Here the phrase refers to women, the heart, the place, the culture, the mind.

In his following two books, *The Unborn* and *Transparent Gestures,* Jones continues to refine the characteristic flinging of himself toward meaning at the end of the poems. Other poets do this, but, unlike Philip Levine's practice, for example, where the poem rises from a flat style to eloquence, Jones's poems simply intensify an eloquence sustained throughout. His later style, freed of affectation, is strongly marked by intense eloquence, and Jones echoes Dylan Thomas ("the field mouse / turned back from the least kernel of the spindliest cob"), Hart Crane ("floating altars in the synagogues of the hummingbirds"), or Walt Whitman, with long lines in an elegiac mood. Unlike Crane or Thomas, however, he is never unclear. His syntax has the urgency of passionate speech that needs to make itself understood. Unlike Whitman, his music derives not from the recirculation and repetition of parallel structures and an incantatory drumming syntax but rather from the forward movement of complex, far-reaching, inclusive sentences that drive to an urgent conclusion.

As these two books move toward an aphoristic clarity, at the same time Jones's work becomes more analytic and elegiac. He is a smart observer of cultural and intellectual mores. "Winter Retreat: Homage to Martin Luther King, Jr.," for example, offers a grimly comic vision of a polite conference in praise of politically correct goals as a failure of vision. With its companion piece, "Pussy," it should become a classic of its kind—a venture into political incorrectness.

Jones's next book, *Apocalyptic Narrative,* plays against its title to become a cycle of praise, even in the title poem, about the love of apocalypse that we manage to survive with our more mundane calls to faith and love. The book is filled with elegies for the dying balanced against the birth of the poet's son. The praise we find here is not the less passionate for being full of sharp discriminations, as in "The Work of Poets":

> Up here in the unforgivable amnesia of libraries,
> Where many poems lie dying of first-person omniscience,
> The footnotes are doing their effete dance, as always.

In this book the poems are more inclusive. The themes are amplified with variations, the meaning of clothes is widely illustrated, and the notion of apocalypse runs through political, erotic, and military changes. To this end Jones's long sentences driving toward an ample notion of meaning—not to simplicity but to complexity and abundance—serve their subjects brilliantly.

The ordering mind is passionately engaged here, even in its memorable comedy. There is a serious pursuit of wisdom in this richly musical poetry.

—Barry Goldensohn

JONG, Erica

Nationality: American. **Born:** Erica Mann, in New York City, 26 March 1942. **Education:** High School of Music and Art, New York; Barnard College, New York (George Weldwood Murray fellow, 1963), 1959–63, B.A. 1963 (Phi Beta Kappa); Columbia University, New York (Woodrow Wilson fellow, 1964), M.A. 1965; Columbia School of Fine Arts, 1969–70. **Family:** Married 1) Michael Werthman (divorced); 2) Allan Jong in 1966 (divorced 1975); 3) the writer Jonathan Fast in 1977 (divorced 1983), one daughter; 4) Kenneth David Burrows in 1989. **Career:** Lecturer in English, City College of New York, 1964–66, 1969–70, and University of Maryland European Division, Heidelberg, Germany, 1967–68; instructor in English, Manhattan Community College, New York, 1969–70. Since 1971 instructor in Poetry, YM-YWHA Poetry Center, New York. Member of the literary panel, New York State Council on the Arts, 1972–74. **Awards:** Academy of American Poets award, 1963; Bess Hokin prize (*Poetry,* Chicago), 1971; New York State Council on the Arts grant, 1971; Madeline Sadin award (*New York Quarterly*), 1972; Alice Fay di Castagnola award, 1972; National Endowment for the Arts grant, 1973; CAPS award, 1973; International Sigmund Freud prize, 1979. **Agent:** Ed Victor, 6 Bayley Street, Bedford Square, London WC1, England. **Address:** Erica Jong Productions, c/o Kenneth David Burrows, 425 Park Avenue, New York, New York 10022–3506, U.S.A.

PUBLICATIONS

Poetry

Fruits and Vegetables. New York, Holt Rinehart, 1971; London, Secker and Warburg, 1973.

Half-Lives. New York, Holt Rinehart, 1973; London, Secker and Warburg, 1974.

Here Comes and Other Poems. New York, New American Library, 1975.

Loveroot. New York, Holt Rinehart, 1975; London, Secker and Warburg, 1977.

The Poetry of Erica Jong. New York, Holt Rinehart, 1976.

Selected Poems 1–2. London, Panther, 2 vols., 1977–80.

At the Edge of the Body. New York, Holt Rinehart, 1979; London, Granada, 1981.

Ordinary Miracles: New Poems. New York, New American Library, 1983; London, Granada, 1984.

Becoming Light: Poems, New and Selected. New York, HarperCollins, 1991.

Novels

Fear of Flying. New York, Holt Rinehart, 1973; London, Secker and Warburg, 1974.

How to Save Your Own Life. New York, Holt Rinehart, and London, Secker and Warburg, 1977.

Fanny, Being the True History of the Adventures of Fanny Hackabout-Jones. New York, New American Library, and London, Granada, 1980.

Parachutes and Kisses. New York, New American Library, and London, Granada, 1984.

Serenissima: A Novel of Venice. Boston, Houghton Mifflin, and London, Bantam, 1987; as *Shylock's Daughter,* New York, HarperCollins, 1995.

Any Woman's Blues. New York, Harper, and London, Chatto and Windus, 1990.

Megan's Two Houses: A Story of Adjustment (for children). West Hollywood, California, Dove Kids, 1996.

Inventing Memory: A Novel of Mothers and Daughters. New York, HarperCollins, 1997.

Other

Four Visions of America, with others. Santa Barbara, California, Capra Press, 1977.

Witches (miscellany). New York, Abrams, 1981; London, Granada, 1982.

Megan's Book of Divorce: A Kid's Book for Adults. New York, New American Library, 1984; London, Granada, 1985.

Fear of Fifty: A Midlife Memoir. London, Chatto & Windus, 1994.

Erica Jong on Henry Miller: The Devil at Large. London, Vintage, 1994.

What Do Women Want?: Power, Sex, Bread & Roses. London, Bloomsbury, 1999.

*

Critical Studies: Interviews in *New York Quarterly 16,* 1974, *Playboy* (Chicago), September 1975, and *Viva* (New York), September 1977; article by Emily Toth, in *Twentieth-Century American-Jewish Fiction Writers,* edited by Daniel Walden, Detroit, Gale, 1984; "Erica Jong Revisited (or) No Wonder We Men Had Trouble Understanding Feminism" by Francis Baumli, in *University of Dayton Review* (Dayton, Ohio), 17(3), winter 1985–86; "Sexus, Nexus and Taboos versus Female Humor: The Case of Erica Jong" by Rolande Diot, in *Revue Francaise d'Etudes Americaines* (Paris), 11(30), November 1986; *Sexuality in Discourse: Feminine Models in Recent Fiction by American Women* (dissertation) by Judith Briggs Coker, n.p., 1986; "Questions of Genre and Gender: Contemporary American Versions of the Feminine Picaresque" by James Mandrell, in *Novel* (Providence, Rhode Island), 20(2), winter 1987; "The Woman Writer As American Picaro: Open Journeying in Erica Jong's 'Fear of Flying'" by Robert J. Butler, in *Centennial Review* (East Lansing, Michigan), 31(3), summer 1987; *Rewriting the American Picaresque: Patterns of Movement in the Novels of Erica Jong, Toni Morrison, and Marilynne Robinson* (dissertation) by Daniel Wayne Schmidt, Southern Illinois University, Carbondale, 1993; *Feminism and the Politics of Literary Reputation: The Example of Erica Jong,* Lawrence, University Press of Kansas, 1995, "Can One Read Literature Objectively?," in *The Practice and Theory of Ethics,* edited by Terry Kent and Marshall Bruce Gentry, Indianapolis, Indiana, University of Indianapolis Press, 1996, and "Erica Jong: Becoming a Jewish Writer," in *Daughters of Valor: Contemporary Jewish American Women Writers,* edited by Jay L. Halio and Ben Siegel, Newark, University of Delaware Press, 1997, all by Charlotte Templin; "Games with Names: Erica Jong's Juggling of Fiction and Autobiography" by Guy Stern, in *Tangenten: Literatur & Geschichte,* edited by Martin Meyer and others, Munster, Germany, Lit, 1996.

Erica Jong comments:

(1974) Though I have been writing since childhood, my first formal training in poetry came at Barnard College, where I studied from 1959 to 1963. At that time I loved the poetry of Auden, Yeats, Keats, Byron, and Alexander Pope, cultivated the command of formal verse, and developed an abiding interest in satire. My early university poems were mostly expert, satirical, and somewhat academic. I went on to do a thesis on Alexander Pope in Columbia's graduate English Department. In my early and mid-twenties, however, I became much more interested in French surrealist poetry and its South American derivatives. I came to love the poetry of Neruda and Alberti, and I learned the value of poetry that delved deep into the unconscious and relied on the association of images. It seems to me that these two influences—crisp satire and an abiding belief in the importance of unconscious material—have shaped my voice as a poet. I believe that poetry can be serious and comic at the same time, formal yet free. I think I was also liberated to write out of a frankly female persona by reading the work of such poets as Anne Sexton, Sylvia Plath, Muriel Rukeyser, Carolyn Kizer, Adrienne Rich. It has been very important to me—both in poetry and fiction—to write freely about women and women's sexuality. Throughout much of history, women writers have capitulated to male standards and have paid too much heed to what Virginia Woolf calls "the angel in the house." She is that little ghost who sits on one's shoulder while one writes and whispers, "Be nice, don't say anything that will embarrass the family, don't say anything your man would disapprove of . . ." The "angel in the house" castrates one's creativity because it deprives one of essential honesty, and many women writers have yet to win the freedom to be honest with themselves. But once the right to honesty has been established, we can go on to write about anything that interests us. We need not only write about childbirth, menstruation, and other feminist topics. I resist the subject matter fallacy in any of its forms. Writing should not be judged on the basis of its subject but on the artistry with which that subject is treated. It seems to me that all three of my published books (*Fruits and Vegetables, Half-Lives,* and *Fear of Flying*) have certain themes in common: the search for honesty within oneself, the difficulty of resolving the conflicting needs for security and adventure, the necessity of seeing the world both sensuously and intelligently at the same time. Having said all that, I should add that my views about my writing will probably be entirely different by the time this is printed.

* * *

Erica Jong has long claimed that she is first and foremost a poet. Believing, however, the culture of the United States to be a hostile place for poets, she early turned to novels to secure fame and earn a living. Although poetry actually preceded her fiction and gave her a way to express and know her feelings and heart, she found it difficult at first to forge her own voice in poetry, and once having found that voice, she disowned a goodly portion of her more formal verse. Her *Becoming Light: Poems New and Selected,* published in 1991, reflects a more forgiving attitude toward her writing, however. It offers the reader a chance to examine how Jong continually reinvents herself in language and how she forges a woman's voice while also honoring the Western traditions in poetry.

Spanning more than thirty years of Jong's writings, *Becoming Light* offers new poems, hitherto unpublished poems—many penned when she was in her late teens and early twenties—and selections from her earlier books of poetry. The book allows the reader to trace the evolution of her poetry, mark her movement from metered formal verse to free verse, and observe her changing taste as she excises some of the juicier and some of the more painful confessional poems. It also includes many poems about her fourth marriage and her all-important relationship with her daughter, Molly.

Two other works by Jong help contextualize and explain her poetry: *Erica Jong on Henry Miller: The Devil at Large* and *Fear of Fifty: A Midlife Memoir.* Each relies heavily on self-portraiture mingled with cultural commentary and literary criticism, and each probes the themes that figure so prominently in her verse as well as the lived experiences that are the basis of all of her writing. The works attest to Jong's importance as a contemporary woman writer who belongs in the traditions of the great creative writers who pushed the boundaries of poetry and fiction, opening still more bedroom and household doors and celebrating eros.

In the early poetry Jong struggles to perfect metered verse, imitating the great male masters and relishing the sheer delight of writing rhymed couplets, sonnets, and limericks. A number of the poems come from the period of her troubled marriage to her first husband, a wild man/child of fantasy, verbally brilliant and the object of Jong's lust. He suffered from schizophrenia, however, which led to his institutionalization and the annulment of their marriage. Other poems were written during her stay in Germany with her second husband, Allan Jong, the man whose name she bears. In some of these poems she is under the spell of Sylvia Plath as well as her husband and Germany, and she probes her own Jewishness and female identity. "A woman poet is a hunted Jew, eternally the outsider," Jong writes in her midlife memoir. This discovery, she confides, drove her to teach herself to write and plant her roots in a woman's tradition with H.D., Edna St. Vincent Millay, and Laura Riding, poets she was not taught about when she studied at Barnard College. The poetry of Plath and Anne Sexton then liberated her from her slavish imitations of Alexander Pope, and she discovered a writerly voice that is irreverent in its treatment of men, every bit as raunchy as that of Henry Miller, Philip Roth, or John Updike, and full of sex, women, and eating. In "The Teacher" (quoted in *Fear of Fifty*), "Flying You Home," and "The Heidelberg Landlady," she writes a visceral, erotic poetry, some of it self-mocking and deliberately provocative. She has come to want poems not merely to exist in print or to be read but to be eaten and taken in whole.

The early collections *Fruits & Vegetables* and *Half-Lives* are Jong's contemporary feminist versions of William Blake's *The Marriage of Heaven and Hell.* She offers her equivalent of Blake's fancies, parables, and commandments, and in many poems she depicts woman's consciousness as ravenous, frustrated, in heat, and oversexed. Under the spell of the confessional poets and feverish with sexual desire and "yearning," as she calls it, Jong uses poetry as the vehicle to express her primal hungers. Sex is her muse and poetry her source of comfort.

In making selections for *Becoming Light,* Jong chose from *How to Save Your Own Life* and *Witches* those poems that write of women in the kitchen or bedroom or in the disguise of the bitch-goddess or witch. Love's red wound, be it in the womb or the gaping mouth, is her subject here. From *Loveroot,* a volume that followed the publication of *Fear of Flying,* she included the poems that pay homage to Neruda, Keats, Sexton, Plath, Donne, and Miller; she places her two Sexton poems back-to-back, whereas before they had been widely separated. Although the original volume contained fifty poems, for

Becoming Light she selected only nineteen, omitting the more derivative poems as well as bitter, painful works such as "Sexual Soup" and "Colder." She retained the poems that capture her distinctively exuberant, affectionate, and frolicking voice.

Jong credits poetry for enabling her to find herself in the painful times when loss, death, divorce, broken relationships, and the pains of motherhood have threatened to overwhelm her. *Becoming Light* reflects a mature Jong. She reclaims earlier poetry that originally embarrassed her, and she includes poems that she had once refused to publish because they failed to perpetuate the myth of herself as the inventor of the "zipless fuck." Her fascination with Miller, issues of censorship and feminism, and witchcraft permeate the volume. She resists political correctness, defends her Whitmanesque bravado, and lustily, and sometimes vulgarly, sings the world of "crazy cock" and cunt and sexual yearning. She is also a poet invested in fierce mothering and loving who has become willing to wrestle with aging and another marriage. The volume rehearses the cultural history of America since the 1960s. Poignantly, it also reveals how difficult it is to be a poet in this country.

—Carol Simpson Stern

JORDAN, June

Nationality: American. **Born:** New York City, 9 July 1936. **Education:** Midwood High School, Brooklyn, New York; Northfield School for Girls, Massachusetts, 1950–53; Barnard College, New York, 1953–55, 1956–57; University of Chicago, 1955–56. **Family:** Married Michael Meyer in 1955 (divorced 1966); one son. **Career:** Assistant to the producer of the film *The Cool World,* 1964; research associate, Mobilization for Youth Inc., New York, 1965–66; director, Voice of the Children, 1967–70; member of the English Department, City College, New York, 1967–70, 1972–75, and 1977–78, Connecticut College, New London, 1968, Sarah Lawrence College, Bronxville, New York, 1971–75, and Yale University, New Haven, Connecticut, 1974–75; associate professor, 1978–82, professor of English, 1982–89, and director of the Poetry Center and the Creative Writing Program, 1986–89, State University of New York, Stony Brook. Chancellor's Lecturer, 1986. Since 1991 founder and director, Poetry for the People, and since 1994 professor of African American studies, University of California, Berkeley. Poet-in-residence, Teachers and Writers Collaborative, New York, 1966–68, MacAlester College, St. Paul, Minnesota, 1980, Loft Mentor Series, Minneapolis, 1983, and Walt Whitman Birthplace, Huntington, New York, 1988; Reid Lecturer, Barnard College, 1976; playwright-in-residence, New Dramatists, New York, 1987–88; visiting professor, Department of Afro-American Studies, University of Wisconsin, Madison, summer 1988. Member of the executive board, Teachers and Writers Collaborative, since 1978, PEN American Center, 1980–84, Poets and Writers Inc. since 1979, American Writers Congress since 1981, Center for Constitutional Rights since 1984, and Authors Guild since 1986. Political columnist, *The Progressive* magazine, since 1989, and *City Limits,* London, since 1990. **Awards:** Rockefeller grant, 1969; American Academy in Rome Environmental Design prize, 1970; New York Council of the Humanities award, 1977; Creative Artists Public Service grant, 1978; Yaddo fellowship, 1979, 1980; National Endowment for the Arts fellowship, 1982; National Association of Black Journalists award, 1984; New York Foundation for the Arts fellowship, 1985; Massachusetts Council on the Arts award, 1985; MacDowell Colony fellowship, 1987; Nora Astorga Leadership award, 1989; Freedom to Write award, PEN Center U.S.A. West, 1991; Distinguished Service award, Northfield Mount Herman School, 1993; Ground Breakers-Dream Makers award, the Women's Foundation, San Francisco, 1994; Critics award and the Herald Angel award, Edinburgh Arts Festival, 1995, for *I Was Looking at the Ceiling and then I Saw the Sky.* **Address:** Department of African-American Studies, 694 Barrows Hall #2527, University of California, Berkeley, California 94720, U.S.A.

PUBLICATIONS

Poetry

Some Changes. New York, Dutton, 1971.
Poem: On Moral Leadership as a Political Dilemma (Watergate, 1973). Detroit, Broadside Press, 1973.
New Days: Poems of Exile and Return. New York, Emerson Hall, 1974.
Things That I Do in the Dark: Selected Poetry. New York, Random House, 1977; revised edition, Boston, Beacon Press, 1981.
Passion: New Poems 1977–80. Boston, Beacon Press, 1980.
Living Room: New Poems 1980–1984. New York, Thunder's Mouth Press, 1985.
Lyrical Campaigns: Selected Poems. London, Virago Press, 1989.
Naming Our Destiny: New and Selected Poems. New York, Thunder's Mouth Press, 1989.
HARUKO/Love Poems, New and Selected Love Poetry. New York, Serpent's Tail/High Risk, 1994.
Kissing God Good-bye. New York, Doubleday, 1997.

Recordings: *Things That I Do in the Dark and Other Poems,* Spoken Arts, 1978; *For Somebody to Start Singing,* with Bernice Reagon, Black Box-Watershed, 1979.

Plays

Freedom Now Suite, music by Adrienne B. Torf (produced New York, 1984).
The Break, music by Adrienne B . Torf (produced New York,1984).
The Music of Poetry and the Poetry of Music, music by Adrienne B. Torf (produced Washington, D.C., and New York, 1984).
Bang Bang Über Alles, music by Adrienne B . Torf, lyrics by Jordan (produced Atlanta, 1986).
I Was Looking at the Ceiling and then I Saw the Sky (opera libretto), music by John Adams. New York, Scribner, 1995.

Other (for children)

Who Look at Me? New York, Crowell, 1969.
His Own Where—. New York, Crowell, 1971.
Dry Victories. New York, Holt Rinehart, 1972.
Fannie Lou Hamer (biography). New York, Crowell, 1972.

New Life, New Room. New York, Crowell, 1975.
Kimako's story. Boston, Houghton Mifflin, 1981.

Other

Civil Wars: Selected Essays 1963–1980. Boston, Beacon Press, 1981;
new edition, with a new introductory essay, New York, Scribner,
1996.
On Call: New Political Essays 1981–1985. Boston, South End Press,
1985; London, Pluto Press, 1986.
Bobo Goetz a Gun. Willimantic, Connecticut, Curbstone Press, 1985.
Moving Towards Home: Political Essays. London, Virago Press,
1989.
Technical Difficulties, New Political Essays. New York, Pantheon,
1994.
June Jordan's Poetry for the People: A Revolutionary Blueprint. New
York, Routledge, 1995.
Affirmative Acts: New Political Essays. New York, Doubleday, 1998.
Soldier: A Poet's Childhood. N.p., Basic Books, 2000.

Editor, with Terri Bush, *The Voice of the Children.* New York, Holt
Rinehart, 1970.
Editor, *Soulscript: Afro-American Poetry.* New York, Doubleday,
1970.

Manuscript Collection: Radcliffe Schlesinger Archives, Harvard
University, Cambridge, Massachusetts.

Critical Studies: "This Wheel's on Fire" by Sara Miles, in *Woman
Poet: The East,* edited by Marilyn Hacker, Reno, Nevada, Women in
Literature, 1982; "Black Poet Sees Politics as the Duty of an Artist"
by Penelope Moffet, in *Los Angeles Times,* 3 September 1986; "The
Love Poetry of June Jordan" by Peter Erickson, in *Callaloo* (Charlottesville, Virginia), 9(1), 1986; *Four Contemporary Black Women
Poets: Lucille Clifton, June Jordan, Audre Lorde, & Sherley Anne
Williams* (dissertation) by Doris Davenport, n.p., 1987; interview
with Joy Harjo, in *High Plains Literary Review* (Denver), 3(2), fall
1988; "Revolution by Search Committee" by Richard Abowitz, in
New Criterion (New York), 7(8), April 1989; "Putting Her Life on
the Line—The Poetry of June Jordan" by Peter Erickson, in *Hurri-
cane Alice,* 7(1–2), winter-spring 1990; "Naming Her Destiny: June
Jordan Speaks on Bisexuality" by Zelie Pollon, in *Deneuve,* 4(1),
February 1994; "The Lover: June Jordan's Revolution" by Michelle
Cliff, in *Village Voice Literary Supplement,* 126, June 1994; "Planets
on the Table: From Wallace Stevens and Elizabeth Bishop to Adrienne
Rich and June Jordan," in *Wallace Stevens Journal* (Potsdam, New
York), 19(2), fall 1995, and "From Warrior to Womanist: The
Development of June Jordan's Poetry," in *Speaking the Other Self:
American Women Writers,* edited by Jeanne Campbell Reesman,
Athens, University of Georgia Press, 1997, both by by Jacqueline
Vaught Brogan; "New World Consciousness in the Poetry of Ntozake
Shange and June Jordan: Two African-American Women's Response
to Expansionism in the Third World" by P. Jane Splawn, in *College
Language Association Journal* (Atlanta), 39(4), June 1996; "June
Jordan and The New Black Intellectuals" by Scott MacPhail, in
African American Review, 33(1), 1999.

*   *   *

Poet, essayist, and author of children's fiction, June Jordan is
among the most varied and prolific of contemporary black writers.
Her works chart the artistic concerns of a poet who successfully
maintains a sense of spiritual wholeness and the vision of a shared
humanity, while relentlessly engaging a brutal and often brutalizing
reality. The resultant combination—of courage and vulnerability—is
suggested by the poem "Things That I Do in the Dark," in which the
poet describes herself as a "stranger / learning to worship the
strangers / around me / whoever you are / whoever I may become."

Artistically, Jordan's work shows the influences of two radically
different aesthetic criteria. She has clearly been influenced by the
black arts movement, the cultural arm of the black power movement
of the 1970s, whose tenets require the work of art to address itself to a
black audience, explore the complexities of black life, and work
toward the building of an autonomous, vital black culture. In subject
matter, theme, and idiom, many of Jordan's poems evidence these
tendencies. In others, however, she seems at one with trends in
mainstream American poetry. These poems are intensely personal,
syntactically experimental, and thematically elusive.

The underlying unity of Jordan's work lies in its uncompromising humanism, eloquently expressed in the historically allusive
chronicle *Who Look at Me?,* in which the speaker, sometimes a single
black, sometimes blacks as a group, characterizes the search of
African-Americans for visibility as "the search to find / a fatherhood
a mothering of mind / a multimillion multi-colored mirror / of an
honest humankind" and their militance as, ultimately, a rejection of
"a carnival run by freaks / who take a life / and tie it terrible / behind
my back." The poet's own militance does not end with the political
and social struggles of blacks. She is keenly aware of the dehumaniz-
ing effects of economic exploitation ("Nowadays the Heroes" and
"47,000 Windows"), as well as of the abuses of power too easily
committed by government ("To My Sister Ethel Ennis" and "Poem
against the State [Of Things]").

Feminist concerns are poignantly expressed in the lyrical "Getting Down to Get Over," which celebrates the unique and often
solitary role of the black woman, who is "a full / Black / glorious / a
purple rose . . . a shell with the moanin / of ages inside her / a hungry
one feedin the folk / what they need." In the anguished "From an
Uprooted Condition" the speaker, with quiet frenzy, ponders "the
right way the womanly expression / of the infinitive that fights /
infinity / *to abort*?" And, finally, the precarious position of all women
in a world dominated by men is effectively portrayed in "On
Declining Values."

Despite their profusion, there is an underlying pessimism to
Jordan's love poems. The central problem is not the inherent
transitoriness of romantic love, a fact the poet quietly acknowledges
in "On a New Year's Eve." Rather, she seems to suggest that love's
true enemy is a harsh and merciless reality. Thus, in "The Wedding,"
"the early wed Tyrone / and his Dizzella" are doomed before their
life together begins, for they are "brave enough / but only two." And
in poems such as "Shortsong from My Heart," "West Coast Episode," and "On Your Love" relationships are deemed to be only
temporary havens, brief respites. Reality, in the form of an impersonal, troubling, often hostile world, always hovers in the background. It is this larger world that inevitably reclaims the individual,
and perhaps this poet, as its own.

—Saundra Towns

JOSEPH, Jenny

Nationality: British. **Born:** Birmingham, Warwickshire, 7 May 1932. **Education:** St. Hilda's College, Oxford, 1950–53, B.A. (honors) in English 1953. **Career:** Reporter, Westminster Press Provincial Newspapers, mid-1950s; lived in South Africa, 1957–59; pub landlady, London, 1969–72; language teacher, 1972–74; lecturer in extramural and adult education departments. **Awards:** Eric Gregory award, 1961; Cholmondeley award, 1975; Arts Council grant, 1976; James Tait Black memorial award, for fiction, 1986; traveling fellowship, British Society of Authors, 1995. Fellow, Royal Society of Literature. **Agent:** John Johnson, 45–47 Clerkenwell Green, London EC1R OHT. **Address:** 17 Windmill Road, Minchinhampton, Near Stroud, Gloucestershire GL6 9DX, England.

PUBLICATIONS

Poetry

The Unlooked-for Season. Northwood, Middlesex, Scorpion Press, 1960.
Rose in the Afternoon and Other Poems. London, Dent, 1974.
The Thinking Heart. London, Secker and Warburg, 1978.
Beyond Descartes. London, Secker and Warburg, 1983.
The Inland Sea. Watsonville, California, Papier-Maché Press, 1989.
Selected Poems. Newcastle upon Tyne, Bloodaxe, 1992.
Ghosts and Other Company. Newcastle upon Tyne, Bloodaxe, 1995.
All the Things I See. London, Macmillan Children's Books, 2000.

Fiction

Excerpt from *Persephone.* Oxford, Argo Magazine, 1985.
Persephone. Newcastle upon Tyne, Bloodaxe, 1986.
Extended Similes. Newcastle upon Tyne, Bloodaxe, 1997.

Other

Nursery Series (Boots, Wheels, Water, Wind, Tea, Sunday; for children). London, Constable, 6 vols., 1966–68.
Beached Boats, photographs by Robert Mitchell. Petersfield, Hampshire, Enitharmon Press, 1991.
Warning. London, Souvenir Press, 1997.

*

Jenny Joseph comments:

It is usually easier for a writer to talk about what he or she is interested in doing now or next than about what has been done. Work already published is there for all to see and off the writer's hands. However there are things I can say have interested me in other writers, not that I would claim to be like them.

I am interested in the use of the speaking voice, not merely to provide a realistic character for dramatic monologues but as material, recognizable straightaway on one level to the reader, in the musical use of language, and I enjoy a singing quality in poetry. Poetry, it seems to me, is not a novel manqué or a play manqué or a piece of music manqué or a line of philosophic enquiry manqué or political statement, but it should be able to deal with the material that goes into all these.

I think my poetry is fairly full of references to the surfaces of the world, but you could say that of anything that uses language, and it still contains a certain amount of enquiry into questions of reality, i.e., how things work. "Art" and "artificial" are words that to me are closely allied. Art forms a separate world that to have any point must always feed through roots in nonart, just as language must depend on something that is not language for its life.

The fiction I wrote between 1972 and 1979 and that was published in 1986 (*Persephone*) uses prose and verse. My interest in the structure for this book came out of my attempt in "The Life and Turgid Times of A. Citizen," a long poem in *The Thinking Heart,* to do a narrative poem where the thread was a consciousness rather than a conventional protagonist, the different verse forms representing different shifts of that consciousness. A work I wrote in the '80s and '90s—*Extended Similes*—which is also fiction, not discursive writing, is composed of short prose pieces. For these I wanted to use prose rhythms in service to poetic mode, metaphor and simile being at the heart of the poetic method to my mind, and my interest in this came about through attention to Samuel Johnson's prose style. Some of my more recent verse has been in the form of songs and shorter lyrical pieces.

Ghosts and Other Company (1995) includes songs, tales, and longer pieces using perhaps rougher language rhythms, a mixture to be found in earlier volumes.

*   *   *

Jenny Joseph's poetry tends to be philosophical in tone; there is an air of detachment about her work. As she stated in *The Bloodaxe Book of Contemporary Women Poets,* through her writing she attempts to explore the outside world, not the labyrinth of her own mind. Her ideal is to write something that becomes part of the currency of common language, like ballads or sayings. Her past as a scholar and a journalist are revealed in a meticulous attention to detail. She has a fine ear for dialogue and frequently incorporates direct speech into her poetry, and she also makes effective use of dramatic monologues.

The Unlooked-for Season, which won a Gregory award, is rather hermetic; the poet is constantly testing the line between reality and imagination, between fiction and truth. Death and loss permeate the collection; winter prevails, and summer, "the unlooked-for season," is an "amnesty." Such poems as "Lazarus," "Danae," "Persephone Returns," and "Euridyce to Orpheus" suggest a preference for classical myth over contemporary life.

Joseph's second collection, *Rose in the Afternoon,* contains her best-loved and most often anthologized poem, "Warning," which begins,

> When I am an old woman I shall wear purple
> With a red hat which doesn't go, and doesn't suit me . . .
> I shall sit down on the pavement when I'm tired
> And gobble up samples in shops and press alarm bells
> And run my stick along the public railings
> And make up for the sobriety of my youth . . .

This delicious streak of rebellion reappears throughout the collection, as does the more relaxed, colloquial language. Her tone is still largely objective, but there is more warmth, more empathy than in her earlier work; she is concerned with human characters rather than archetypes.

The poems are full of striking images, as in "Women at Streatham Hill":

> They stand like monuments or trees, not women . . .
> Nobody asks what they have done all day
> For who asks trees or stones what they have done?
> They root, they gather moss, they spread they are.
> The busyness is in the birds about them . . .

This collection contains some of Joseph's best dramatic monologues, including "Old Man Going." There is also an extremely effective long narrative poem, "Thoughts on Oxford Street from Provence and Elsewhere," that in its interweaving of verse and prose anticipates her fictional work in *Persephone*. The poem assembles a vivid cast of outspoken characters, from the abusive old man who assaults the reader with such statements as "Don't waste my time thinking that I think / That you're of any interest— / Don't waste my time if you've fucking nothing for me . . ." to the equivocal liberal who asks, "Can you accept the man who accepts you neither at your own estimate nor his? . . . Can you play a game if there not only are no rules but no one to play with?"

Joseph's third collection, *The Thinking Heart,* demonstrates a move toward lyricism and celebration in such poems as "Chorale" and "Not Able to Resist the Spring," which begins exuberantly, "There is too much stuff here: / Everything crowded, duplicated and far too many words . . ." The hint of subversiveness that revealed itself in the previous volume hovers just beneath the surface of many of these poems. When it breaks free, Joseph produces wonderful, witty pieces, and when it does not, there is a tenseness that is sometimes dramatic, though sometimes it is simply solemn. In this collection the poet frequently eschews dramatic monologue to address her reader directly. Though she does not deal overtly with women's issues, such poems as "Modern Witches" or "There Are More Accidents in the Home Than on the Roads" reveal a delightful, sly streak of feminist indignation.

In her fourth collection, *Beyond Descartes,* Joseph experiments with short imagistic poems. There is an air of compression and mystery about these works, the poems like parables or icons. She also exhibits a new sense of social conscience, as though her earlier philosophical musings have been honed down and anchored to the real world. Her characteristic wryness and use of colloquial speech combine well in a poem like "Collection for Cripples," which ends, "Did the poor crippled lady ever get home, I wonder? / Sure, somebody better equipped than I will have helped her home."

Although she has written children's books, Joseph's first venture into adult fiction was *Persephone*. As a tale of lost innocence, the book demonstrates a continuing concern for women's lives and gender politics as the young Persephone loses her illusions and gains the wisdom to tame the betrayer Hades. Joseph has said that *Persephone* is the work that has most satisfied her as a writer, and, with its integration of poetry, prose, parody, and myth, it combines the best of her narrative and poetic talents.

—Katie Campbell

JUSSAWALLA, Adil (Jehangir)

Nationality: Indian. **Born:** Bombay, 8 April 1940. **Education:** Cathedral School, Bombay, 1947–56; Architectural Association School of Architecture, London, 1957–58; Felsham House, Sussex, 1958–60; University College, Oxford, 1960–64, M.A. in 1964. **Family:** Married Veronik Jussawalla in 1971; one stepdaughter. **Career:** Supply teacher, Greater London Council, 1965; language teacher, International Language Centre, London, 1965–69, and at various colleges in Bombay, 1970–72; lecturer in English language and literature, St. Xavier's College, Bombay, 1972–75; member, International Writing Program, University of Iowa, Iowa City, 1976; book reviews editor, *Indian Express,* Bombay, 1980–81; literary editor, *Express Magazine,* 1980–82, and *Science Age,* 1983–87, both Bombay. Literary editor, 1987–89, and since 1989 editor, *Debonair,* Bombay. **Address:** Palm Springs, Flat R2, Cuffe Parade, Bombay 400 005, India.

PUBLICATIONS

Poetry

Land's End. Calcutta, Writers Workshop, 1962.
Missing Person. Bombay, Clearing House, 1976.

Plays

Television Scripts: *Train to Calcutta,* 1970; *War,* 1989.

Other

Editor, *New Writing in India.* London, Penguin, 1974.
Editor, with Eunice de Souza, *Statements: An Anthology of Indian Prose in English.* Bombay, Orient Longman, 1976.

*

Critical Studies: "Four New Voices" by Brijraj Singh, in *Chandrabhaga* (Orissa, India), 1, 1979; "The Poetry of Exile: An Introduction to Adil Jussawalla" by G.S. Amur, in *Osmania Journal of English Studies* (Huderabad, India), 13, 1977; "The Poetry of Adil Jussawalla" by N.M. Rao, in *Living Indian English Poets,* edited by Madhusudan Prasad, New Delhi, Sterling, 1989.

Adil Jussawalla comments:

It is difficult for me to talk about my own work, except that I feel that the poems I am writing now have more to do with restrictions of various kinds than the ones I wrote before. The restrictions need not always be traps. Ways are to be found to deal with them.

*   *   *

Adil Jussawalla, like most contemporary Indian poets writing in English, is an urban poet. Alienation and the unreality of the city are recurrent themes in his works. Sometimes overlapping with these themes is the unreality of the definitions of identity and experience.

Jussawalla is not a prolific poet (he published only two books of poems, *Land's End* and *Missing Person,* between 1962 and 1976), but his is a significant voice that has assimilated the influence of Ezra Pound and T.S. Eliot—''Webbed in English ironies, I cough.''

Jussawalla's harsh lyricism ''sings'' of cacophony and of the alienation of an Indian middle-class intellectual in foreign lands (*Land's End*) and in postindependence India (*Missing Person*). ''I see things in quite a different light,'' he claims. ''Fog,'' from *Land's End,* sums up this difference:

> My songs, like charred paper
> Over the fuming stoke
> Furnaces, fall to the invisible river, but the world
> Flesh and devil crowd in my skull like smoke.

Land's End comprises poems written abroad and explores the torments of being in exile. Many portray the unease of an expatriate, whether with the social and cultural context or with the landscape. ''A Prospect of Oxford'' perceives ''the city made unreal by the height,'' and ''smudged Derbyshire'' in ''Halt X'' breathes ''danger and disquietude only.'' ''November Day'' and ''Westmoreland'' are also critiques of nineteenth-century English romanticism. The former, which recalls the image of falling leaves so central to Shelley's ''Ode to the West Wind,'' is an ironic assertion of the need for human endeavor, despite its underlying futility: ''Cleaned of all my deaths / Once more [I] stand firm against / A lifeless sky.'' ''Westmoreland'' is a self-conscious evocation of the ''strange remoteness'' the poet perceives in the English countryside that ''Wordsworth and Coleridge, and God know who'' once inhabited.

''Seventeen,'' dated 1957, when Jussawalla was only seventeen, and the first poem in *Land's End,* speaks of the early replacing of a sensuously alive sensibility with ''a cold assumption of arrogance''; now ''things talk no more / though I listen.'' Neither *Land's End* nor *Missing Person,* however, explores the personal causes of this early loss. We learn only that Jussawalla's habit of detachment runs concurrently with the ''moral of silence and exile'' and is enriched by an increasing social and political concern. His anguish is more immediate in ''Missing Person,'' a poem sequence in two sections written in an impersonal style using several unidentified personae. ''Missing Person'' deals with the struggle to come to terms with the effects of colonialism and a bewildered sense of the marginalization of the middle-class intellectual in contemporary India. In a general way one senses the influence of Pound's *Mauberley* and Eliot's *The Waste Land.* The passivity of the Indian middle-class intellectual in a decadent setting and a recognition of the need for self-assertion or for change through renewal are evident in Jussawalla's verse:

> For years we prompted his first
> words, scolding the servants for theirs:
> 'Sweetie, say:
> Let there be light, let there be us.'
> We heard:
>
> 'Let there be dung.'

The shifts are cinematic and skillful, the phrases chiseled, and the images echoic, and the overall effect is of a sensibility that is essentially auditory. Jussawalla has said, ''I do tend to feel the sound of words and base my poems on them,'' and ''I cannot get away from rhymes, internal or end.'' ''Missing Person'' sometimes results in attitudinizing, however, and lacks the complete vision that makes *Mauberley* and *The Waste Land* two of the greatest poems of the twentieth century. Jussawalla's defense of his fragmentary lines (''Perhaps 'Missing Person' can only be looked at in bits and pieces'') sounds like his admission of the trap of the fallacy of imitative form into which he has willingly fallen.

Poems such as ''Sea Breeze, Bombay,'' ''The Exile's Story,'' ''Approaching Santa Cruz Airport, Bombay,'' ''A Letter from Bombay,'' or ''Nine Poems on Arrival,'' though lesser poems than ''Missing Person,'' are more accessible and have a more cohesive structure. ''Sea Breeze, Bombay'' is effective in portraying Bombay as a gatherer of refugees but is marred by a rather pat ending in which the spirit of the city, symbolized by the cool sea breeze, is so detached that it ''settles no one adrift of the mainland's histories.'' Its strength, however, is in Jussawalla's method to ''connect with myth and history.'' It is a method even more profitably applied in ''The Exile's Story'' and with heightened political overtones in ''Karate,'' ''Song of a Hired Man,'' ''Immigrant Song,'' and ''Freedom Song.''

It is another manifestation of Jussawalla's alienation that, whereas in *Land's End* he fumbles with Anglo-Catholicism, in *Missing Person* his lingering religious feelings give way to a Marxist revolutionary ideology. The change is first hinted at in ''Poppies for Marx'' in *Land's End.* It is again alluded to in the subtitle of a film, ''Missing Jack: A Slave's Revolt and Fall,'' and in the epigraph from Frantz Fanon's *The Wretched of the Earth.*

—Devindra Kohli

JUSTICE, Donald (Rodney)

Nationality: American. **Born:** Miami, Florida, 12 August 1925. **Education:** University of Miami, B.A. 1945; University of North Carolina, Chapel Hill, M.A. 1947; Stanford University, Palo Alto, California, 1948–49; University of Iowa, Iowa City, Ph.D. 1954. **Family:** Married Jean Ross in 1947; one son. **Career:** Visiting assistant professor, University of Missouri, Columbia, 1955–56; assistant professor, Hamline University, St. Paul, Minnesota, 1956–57; lecturer, 1957–60, assistant professor, 1960–63, and associate professor, 1963–66, University of Iowa; associate professor, 1966–67, and professor, 1967–70, Syracuse University, New York; visiting professor, University of California, Irvine, 1970–71; professor of English, University of Iowa, 1971–82; professor of English, University of Florida, Gainesville, 1982–92. Poet-in-residence, Reed College, Portland, Oregon, 1962; Bain-Swiggett Lecturer, Princeton University, New Jersey, 1976; visiting professor, University of Virginia, Charlottesville, 1980. **Awards:** Rockefeller grant, 1954; Lamont Poetry Selection award, 1959; Inez Boulton prize, 1960, and Harriet Monroe memorial prize, 1965 (*Poetry,* Chicago); Ford fellowship, in theater, 1964; National Endowment for the Arts grant, 1967, 1973, 1980; American Academy award, 1974; Guggenheim fellowship, 1976; Pulitzer prize, 1980; Bollingen award, 1991; Lannan literary award, 1996. Fellow, Academy of American Poets, 1988. **Member:** American Academy of Arts and Sciences, 1992; National Institute of Arts and Letters, 1992. **Address:** 338 Rocky Shore Drive, Iowa City, Iowa 52246, U.S.A.

PUBLICATIONS

Poetry

The Summer Anniversaries. Middletown, Connecticut, Wesleyan University Press, 1960.
A Local Storm. Iowa City, Stone Wall Press, 1963.
Night Light. Middletown, Connecticut, Wesleyan University Press, 1967.
Four Poets, with others. Pella, Iowa, C.U.I. Press, 1967.
Sixteen Poems. Iowa City, Stone Wall Press, 1970.
From a Notebook. Iowa City, Seamark Press, 1972.
Departures. New York, Atheneum, 1973.
Selected Poems. New York, Atheneum, 1979; London, Anvil Press Poetry, 1980.
Tremayne. Iowa City, Windhover Press, 1984.
The Sunset Maker: Poems/Stories/A Memoir. New York, Atheneum, and London, Anvil Press Poetry, 1987.
A Donald Justice Reader. Hanover, New Hampshire, University Press of New England, 1991.
Poems to Go. New York, Knopf, 1995.
New & Selected Poems. New York, Knopf, 1995.

Recording: *Childhood and Other Poems,* Watershed, 1983.

Play

The Death of Lincoln (libretto). N.p., A. Thomas Taylor, 1988.

Other

Platonic Scripts. Ann Arbor, University of Michigan Press, 1984.
Oblivion: On Writers & Writing. Ashland, Oregon, Story Line Press, 1998.

Editor, *The Collected Poems of Weldon Kees.* Iowa City, Stone Wall Press, 1960; revised edition, Lincoln, University of Nebraska Press, 1975.
Editor, with Paul Engle and Henri Coulette, *Midland.* New York, Random House, 1961.
Editor, with Alexander Aspel, *Contemporary French Poetry.* Ann Arbor, University of Michigan Press, 1965.
Editor, *Syracuse Poems 1968.* Syracuse, New York, Syracuse University Department of English, 1968.
Editor, with Robert Mezey, *The Collected Poems of Henri Coulette.* Fayetteville, University of Arkansas Press, 1990.
Editor, with Cooper R. Mackin and Richard D. Olson, *The Comma after Love: Selected Poems of Raeburn Miller.* Akron, Ohio, University of Akron Press, 1994.
Editor, *The Last Nostalgia: Poems, 1982–1990,* by Joe Bolton. Fayetteville, University of Arkansas Press, 1999.

Translator, *L'Homme qui se ferme/The Man Closing Up,* by Guillevic. Iowa City, Stone Wall Press, 1973.

*

Manuscript Collection: University of Delaware Library, Dover.

Critical Studies: *Alone with America* by Richard Howard, New York, Atheneum, 1969, London, Thames and Hudson, 1970, revised edition, Atheneum, 1980; ''On Donald Justice'' by Greg Simon, in *American Poetry Review 5* (Philadelphia), no. 2, 1976; ''Flaubert in Florida: On Donald Justice'' by Michael Ryan, in *New England Review and Breadloaf Quarterly,* 7(2), winter 1984; ''Donald Justice Special Issue'' edited by Dana Gioia and William Logan, in *Verse,* 8(3), winter/spring 1992; ''The Progress of Donald Justice'' by Lewis Turco, in *The Hollins Critic* (Hollins College, Virginia), 29(4), October 1992; ''Some Reflections on Donald Justice's Poem 'After a Phrase Abandoned by Wallace Stevens''' by Clive Watkins, in *Wallace Stevens Journal* (Potsdam, New York), 17(2), fall 1993; ''Homage to the Thin Man'' by Charles Wright, in *Southern Review* (Baton Rouge, Louisiana), 30(4), autumn 1994; interview with Dana Gioia, in *American Poetry Review* (Philadelphia), 25(1), January-February 1996; '''Black Flowers, Black Flowers': Meta-Criticism in Donald Justice's 'Bus Stop''' by James A. McCoy, in *Notes on Contemporary Literature* (Carrollton, Georgia), 26(5), November 1996.

*   *   *

Donald Justice's modest, almost cautious, output sets him apart from many of his contemporaries. It is a conscious demonstration of the care taken in the making of his elegant and craftsmanlike poems. The achievement of his first three books of poems, *The Summer Anniversaries, Night Light,* and *Departures,* became clearer when gathered in the single volume of *Selected Poems* with later, uncollected work. The book was awarded the 1980 Pulitzer Prize in poetry. Since then Justice has published additional volumes, including *The Sunset Maker,* which have further added to his stature.

Justice is one of America's most subtle and sure poets, an artist whose care with and respect for language (he has a near faultless ear) enables him to achieve effects beyond the reach of all but a few of his contemporaries. His emotional and technical range is far wider than his modest output would have us believe, and his chief tool is a transparent technique always at the service of thought and feeling.

The early, celebrated ''Counting the Mad'' is a bizarre parody on the children's nursery rhyme ''This Little Piggy'' transposed to a lunatic asylum:

> This one was put in a jacket,
> This one was sent home,
> This one was given bread and meat
> But would eat none,
> And this one cried No No No No
> All day long.

Justice's formal skill and stylishness enable him to be at ease in complex verse forms and to perform small masterpieces such as his ''Sestina: Here in Katmandu'' or ''Variations for Two Pianos,'' the latter for the pianist Thomas Higgins, which is itself a variation on the villanelle:

> There is no music now in all Arkansas.
> Higgins is gone, taking both his pianos.
>
> Movers dismantled the instruments, away
> Sped the vans. The first detour untuned the strings.
> There is no music now in all Arkansas.

Justice is a noted translator from the French, and it may be that his work has been influenced by French literature as much as by his shared American and British traditions. He owes something to Wallace Stevens (an early poem is titled ''After a Phrase Abandoned by Wallace Stevens'' and a later one, ''Homage to the Memory of Wallace Stevens''), and if he belongs with any group of contemporary American poets, it is with such diverse writers as Anthony Hecht, Richard Wilbur, and X.J. Kennedy, all masters of prosody that gives shape to emotion though the frame of traditional forms. Justice's own ''Early Poems'' ironically comments on the skilled early five-finger exercises of formalist poets such as himself. The poem takes the central metaphor of a small town seen as a poem:

How fashionably sad those early poems are!
On their clipped lawns and hedges the snows fall.
Rains beat against the tarpaulins of their porches,
Where, Sunday mornings, the bored children sprawl,
Reading the comics before their parents rise.
—The rhymes, the meters, how they paralyze.

It is characteristic that Justice, a poet whose skill is clearly demonstrated in the poem, should be so self-deprecating about his early prosodic talent. He is without pretension and is possessed of a rare humility before the craft of poetry, which has allowed his gifts to develop and broaden. The riddlingly titled ''Poem'' might also be addressed to himself as well as his readers:

This poem is not addressed to you.
You may come into it briefly,
But no one will find you here, no one.
You will have changed before the poem will.

Quite different again is ''First Death,'' a sequence of poems on the death of a grandmother that, far from indulging emotion in the way of a confessional poet, instead clearly defines feeling for the reader by recording specific memories at the time of the death. In fact, Justice writes consistently well on memory and expresses it through a wide range of sensory perceptions. For example, his poem ''Memory of a Porch'' accommodates the ''thin, skeletal music'' of a wind chime and also the ''sighing of ferns / Half asleep in their boxes.'' The sensuous collage of ''Thinking about the Past'' is moving because the personal memories are free from egotism, so that they somehow exist as concrete images of relevance to all:

Certain moments will never change, nor stop being—
My mother's face all smiles, all wrinkles soon;
The rock wall building, built, collapsed then, fallen;
Our upright loosening downward slowly out of tune—

The Sunset Maker is a volume of both poems and prose, including short stories and ''Piano Lessons: Notes on a Provincial Culture,'' an autobiographical prose essay recollecting early music lessons. A memorable group of occasional poems center on the lugubrious character of Tremayne, perhaps reminiscent of Weldon Kees's occasional protagonist ''Robinson,'' with titles such as ''The Mild Despair of Tremayne,'' ''The Insomnia of Tremayne,'' and ''Tremayne Autumnal.'' There are elegies, memories, poems on music, and others after Baudelaire, Rilke, and Kafka. A sense of melancholy and nostalgia permeates the volume in titles such as ''Nostalgia of the Lakefronts,'' ''Psalm and Lament,'' and ''Villanelle at Sundown,'' the last a poem seeking to accept aging and the passing of time:

How frail our generation has got, how sallow
And pinched with just surviving! We all go off
  the deep end
Finally, gold beaten thinly out to yellow.
And why this is, I'll never be able to tell you.

When many a larger name of today has slipped permanently from view, we shall still read Justice, who has produced many fine, enduring poems.

—Jonathan Barker

K

KANTARIS, Sylvia

Nationality: British. **Born:** Sylvia Mosley, Grindleford, Derbyshire, 9 January 1936. **Education:** University of Bristol, 1954–58, B.A. (honors) 1957, Cert.Ed. 1958; Sorbonne, Paris, 1955, diploma in French studies 1955; University of Queensland, St. Lucia, 1964–71, M.A. 1967, Ph.D. 1972. **Family:** Married Emmanuel Kantaris in 1958; one son and one daughter. **Career:** English teacher, Withywood School, Bristol, 1958–59; English and French teacher, St. Paul's Way School, London, 1960–62; tutor in French, University of Queensland, 1963–66; Open University tutor, Southwest England, 1974–84; extra-mural lecturer, Exeter University, Devon, 1974–92; writer-in-the-community, Cornwall, 1986. **Awards:** *Poetry Magazine* award (Australia), 1969; Poetry Society Competition award, 1982; Major Arts Council Literature award, 1991; Society of Authors award, 1992. D.Litt.: University of Exeter, 1989 **Address:** 14 Osborne Parc, Helston, Cornwall TR13 8PB, England.

PUBLICATIONS

Poetry

Time and Motion (as Sylvia Kantarizis). Sydney, Poetry Society of Australia, 1975; (as Sylvia Kantaris), Helston, Cornwall, Menhir, 1986.
Stocking Up. Helston, Cornwall, Menhir, 1981.
The Tenth Muse. Liskeard, Cornwall, Peterloo, 1983.
News from the Front, with D.M. Thomas. Todmorden, Yorkshire, Arc, 1983.
The Sea at the Door. London, Secker and Warburg, 1985.
The Air Mines of Mistila, with Philip Gross. Newcastle upon Tyne, Bloodaxe, 1988.
Dirty Washing: New and Selected Poems. Newcastle upon Tyne, Bloodaxe, 1989; Chester Springs, Pennsylvania, Dufour, 1990.
Lad's Love. Newcastle upon Tyne, Bloodaxe, 1993.
Lost Property. Chester Springs, Pennsylvania, Dufour, 1998.

*

Critical Studies: In *Outposts Poetry Quarterly* (Sutton, Surrey), Spring 1989; "Terpsichore and the Incredible Hulk: Sylvia Kantaris—An Accessible Contemporary" by David Wilkinson, in *In Black and Gold: Contiguous Traditions in Post-war British and Irish Poetry,* edited by C.C. Barfoot. Amsterdam and Atlanta, Georgia, DQR Studies in Literature 13, 1994.

Sylvia Kantaris comments:

With regard to form, I agree with Christina Rossetti: "In the poet, the ear dictates and the mouth listens." What fascinates me most is to discover the curious and humorous within the everyday, and I enjoy the sheer fun of mixing dictions outrageously.

(1995) I think the poet has one skin too few and that it hurts.

*   *   *

The publication of Sylvia Kantaris's *Dirty Washing,* which contains a substantial selection of her previous work together with a generous supplement of new poems, provides a fine opportunity to assess her achievement. It is a pleasant collection to read, mainly because of Kantaris's gentle conversational style, which relies on the subtle rhythms of the speaking voice. Because the style is difficult to maintain, it is not surprising that there are lapses into the prosaic from time to time. But at her best Kantaris is very good, her poems exerting a strong hold on the reader. When she starts a poem, as she often does, with a direct statement—

It takes a certain savoir-faire to give a paper on
some area of deconstructionism when
I don't know what it means

—or—

I don't put the clock back. I just stop it
for an hour and let time do the catching up

—then the hold is exerted straightaway. The extended metaphor in "Genesis" is a case in point:

May I scream? I asked
but they said no,
so I held it between my teeth
where it slowly spread.

Kantaris's style suits her brief narratives and certainly her probing reflections and descriptions. Her eye for detail often intrigues the reader:

My grandmother's kitchen looks almost normal
on the surface, though a bit too bare.
Nobody really cooks there. The drawer
contains two knives and forks which don't match;
there are two pans in the cupboard and a few
old mugs and plates. Nothing accumulates.

The poem gives not so much a picture of the kitchen as a character study of a grandmother. It is a characteristic of Kantaris's best poems that under the deceptively unassuming ordinariness of her vocabulary and syntax lie deep layers of metaphor and feeling.

Humor enlightens Kantaris's poetry too. "The Big One" and "O Little Star" are gems. While "Fairy Tales" is another example, here something deeper is revealed when Beauty

Never stopped tormenting him
until the beast emerged again
from underneath the skin.

I am of two minds about the work Kantaris has written in collaboration with others. *The Air Mines of Mistila,* with Philip Gross, is successful enough, but in *News from the Front,* with D.M. Thomas, the two voices and stances are too disparate. Besides, Kantaris's own powers of expressing the emotional and the sensual are intense enough in themselves. "Parting," for example, with its extended symbolism of the railway, is beautifully done:

> So many partings glance away ahead of us
> to where the rain slants on an empty track.

Other examples are "Some Untidy Spot" and the impressive "An Innocent Adultery," all the more powerful for its gentleness:

> . . . the day before was just the kind
> of day for touching breasts, as he had said
> casually, as if words had no fingers.

—John Cotton

KAVANAGH, P(atrick) J(oseph Gregory)

Nationality: British. **Born:** Worthing, Sussex, 6 January 1931. **Education:** Douai School; Lycée Jaccard, Lausanne; Merton College, Oxford, M.A. **Military Service:** National Service, 1949–51. **Family:** Married 1) Sally Philipps in 1956 (died 1958); 2) Catherine Ward in 1965; two sons. **Career:** Assistant floor manager, BBC Television, 1954; lecturer, British Institute, Barcelona, 1954–55, and University of Indonesia, Jakarta; staff member, British Council, 1957–59; actor, 1959–70; columnist, *Spectator,* London, 1983–96. Since 1996 columnist, *Times Literary Supplement,* London. **Awards:** Richard Hillary memorial prize, 1966; *Guardian* fiction prize, 1969; Cholmondely prize, 1992. Fellow, Royal Society of Literature, 1986. **Address:** c/o A.D. Peters, The Chambers, Chelsea Harbour, Lots Road, London SW10 OXF, England.

PUBLICATIONS

Poetry

One and One. London, Heinemann, 1960.
On the Way to the Depot. London, Chatto and Windus-Hogarth Press, 1967.
About Time. London, Chatto and Windus-Hogarth Press, 1970.
Edward Thomas in Heaven. London, Chatto and Windus-Hogarth Press, 1974.
Life before Death. London, Chatto and Windus-Hogarth Press, 1979.
Real Sky. Andoversford, Berkshire, Whittington Press, 1980.
Selected Poems. London, Chatto and Windus, 1982.
Presences: New and Selected Poems. London, Chatto and Windus, 1987.
An Enchantment. Manchester, Carcanet, 1991.
Collected Poems. Manchester, Carcanet, 1992.

Plays

Television Plays: *William Cowper Lived Here* (documentary), 1971; *Journey Through Summer* (documentary), 1973; *Paradise in a Dream* (documentary), 1981; Scarf Jack, from his own story, 1981.

Novels

A Song and Dance. London, Chatto and Windus, 1968.
A Happy Man. London, Chatto and Windus, 1972.
People and Weather. London, Calder, 1978; New York, Riverrun, 1980.
Only by Mistake. London, Calder, and New York, Riverrun, 1986.

Other

The Perfect Stranger (autobiography). London, Chatto and Windus, 1966; Minneapolis, Graywolf Press, 1988.
Scarf Jack (for children). London, Bodley Head, 1978; as *The Irish Captain,* New York, Doubleday, 1979.
Rebel for Good (for children). London, Bodley Head, 1980.
People and Places: Essays 1975–1987. Manchester, Carcanet, 1988.
Finding Connections (travel). London, Century Hutchinson, 1990.
A Book of Consolations. London, HarperCollins, 1992.
Voices in Ireland, a Literary Companion. London, John Murray, 1994.

Editor, *Collected Poems of Ivor Gurney.* Oxford, Oxford University Press, 1982; New York, Oxford University Press, 1983.
Editor, with James Michie, *The Oxford Book of Short Poems.* Oxford, Oxford University Press, 1985.
Editor, *The Bodley Head G.K. Chesterton.* London, Bodley Head, 1985; as *The Essential Chesterton,* Oxford, Oxford University Press, 1987.
Editor, *Selected Poems of Ivor Gurney.* Oxford, Oxford University Press, 1990.

*

Critical Studies: By Philip Gross, in *Poetry Review,* 83(2), summer 1993; by Robert Kee, in *The Spectator* (London), 273(8665), 6 August 1994.

*   *   *

P.J. Kavanagh's rhythms are dangerously close to prose at times; nor is he strict enough with the logic of his syntax. In the excellent and otherwise evocative poem "The Temperance Billiards Room" there is some atrociously impacted versifying halfway through that quite ruins the piece. A simple example of carelessness and lack of attention to the actualities of meaning can be seen in a couple of lines from "Birthday," from his early collection *On the Way to the Depot:*

> Who's got there before you waving like mad
> And calling hello like a wartime railway station?

The insertion of the monosyllabic "on" before "a wartime" would have avoided the obvious criticism that railway stations, whether in wartime or not, do not call out greetings. It is no use for a poet to answer, "Well, you know what I mean," for the syntactical logic of a poem must be impeccable.

That cavil past, Kavanagh is an interesting poet with a fine eye for detail and an engaging personal voice. Though his syntax can be a mess sometimes, even to the point of obscurity, he is mostly an accessible poet. He gives one the feeling of a nice, slightly lugubrious nature pushing ever hopefully through this slough of despond that is life. One knows that he is aware of all of the temptations and pitfalls, as we all are, but he unostentatiously buttonholes the reader into joining in the struggle with him. His real niceness, his greatness of spirit even, shows in a quietly dogged determination to eschew self-pity and to endeavor to celebrate. While he cannot sing like a Keats or a Dylan Thomas (he cannot sing his praises, only think them), there is a warm, quiet, ruminative tone underpinning a great many of his poems, summed up best in a single line from one of his most memorable: "I think often of the time I was perfectly happy." Indeed, the title of this poem, "Perfection Isn't like a Perfect Story," somehow captures the philosophical tone of this hopeful pragmatist among poets. In an age of so much dismal poetry the sanity of a poet like Kavanagh, who always keeps both sides of the coin as much in view as possible, is much needed.

Metaphysically speaking, Kavanagh's poetry, which tries sometimes too hard to be au courant, exists in an anxious no-man's-land between belief and nonbelief. As a man with Irish ancestry ("Ancestor-hunting: an interest as sudden / As middle-age . . ." "Borris House, Co. Carlow"), somewhere at the back of his mind there looms the presence of Saint Peter's, with all its centuries of creed and devotion. Like most modern poets, however, he finds it very difficult to live anymore within a handed-down faith. Yet the wanting of God and the craving for the angelic orders are always there. The impulse sometimes produces a half-facetious, slightly silly poem, like "Consolations," which does nothing to increase our, or his, sense of the real presence of God. But then, as it were, out of the blue comes a poem of breathtakingly simple seriousness, unmannered and true, like "Real Sky." This is a Blakean poem in which "eternity loves time, I hear it blow," and through the poem we do too. It is a poem of singular and simple beauty in which divinity is as much in its invisible rhythms as in its images or saying:

> And I remember briefly how they feel,
> My bones supported by the wind's round hand.
> A life-long love affair—I wooed the real;
> At last I see the real world exposed,
> And real sky come plucking for my hand.

This is better than a hundred wooden psalms praising conventional belief because it is a kind of proof, proof of the eternal real. It is good metaphysical poetry, and though such is rare in any poet's career, when it appears it is the best and most important kind of poetry. Its presence here and there in Kavanagh's oeuvre amply justifies Christopher Hope's comment on the poems that "they begin and end with God, though they deal with affectionate relish with the human journey that spans these poles."

The increasing subtlety of both Kavanagh's mind and its conception of his personal quest for understanding (and perhaps solid faith in) the world, wherein he feels so much "a sojourner," becomes even more apparent in the 1991 volume *An Enchantment*. His gritty praise of nature is still strong, but the grudging intrusion of philosophical ideas, hedged with irony, continues and often brilliantly:

> God without image (your masterstroke) our feeding, our
> starvation, in whom I believe as I believe in air
> stacked with potency queuing to come in,

cleanse our VDUs, our personal screens
foxed beyond reading with traffic of images.

In an interview Clive Wilmer described Kavanagh as "a nature poet," albeit a "modernised" one like Edward Thomas. But in the same interview Kavanagh himself enlarged that perception when he said, "I feel that there is another world and we have a connection with it . . . a language that is just out of earshot." Some sense of "another world" and its language comes ever nearer in his later poems.

Because Kavanagh became interested in the sad, mad, and unbearably tragic case of the poet Ivor Gurney, his own work was influenced by that writer's rugged, sometimes tortured convolutions. Kavanagh not only edited the *Collected Poems of Ivor Gurney,* but he also wrote a great and moving tribute to the poet that no report on Kavanagh's own work can, or should, ignore. The tribute shows Kavanagh at his most controlled and moving and reveals the sympathy he is capable of for another's "hurt as great as any man / Has had." It also underlines, as the best exemplum, what Martin Dodsworth justly observed of Kavanagh's work, that it presents "the vulnerable human face of poetry, domestic, unaffected, equal to its human occasions." This is about as solid an achievement as any poet in these times of confusion and insincerity can hope for.

—William Oxley

KAY, Jackie

Nationality: Scottish. **Born:** Jacqueline Margaret Kay, Edinburgh, 9 November 1961. **Education:** University of Stirling, 1979–83, B.A. (honors) in English 1983. **Family:** One son. **Career:** Writer-in-residence, Hammersmith, London, 1989–91. **Awards:** Eric Gregory award, 1991; Scottish Arts Council Book award, 1991, Saltire First Book of the Year award, 1991, and Forward prize, 1992, all for *The Adoption Papers;* Signal Poetry award, 1993, for *Two's Company;* Somerset Maugham award for *Other Lovers.* **Agent:** Pat Kavanagh, Peters Fraser & Dunlop, 503/4 The Chambers, Chelsea Harbour, London SW10 0XF, England. **Address:** 20 Townsend Road, London N15 4NT, England.

PUBLICATIONS

Poetry

The Adoption Papers. Newcastle upon Tyne, Bloodaxe, 1991.
That Distance Apart (chapbook). London, Turret, 1991.
Two's Company (for children). London, Puffin, 1992.
Three Has Gone (for children). London, Blackie Children's, 1994.
Other Lovers. Newcastle upon Tyne, Bloodaxe, 1993.
The Frog Who Dreamed She Was an Opera Singer (for children).
    London, Bloomsbury Children's, 1998.
Off Colour. Newcastle upon Tyne, Bloodaxe, 1998.

Novel

Trumpet. London, Picador, and New York, Pantheon, 1998.

*

Critical Studies: By Peter Forbes, in *Poetry Review,* 82(4), winter 1993; by C. Beeston, in *Critical Survey* (Oxford), 6(3), 1994.

*   *   *

Jackie Kay's position in English poetry is perhaps unique, and this is so first of all for external reasons that some of her most forceful poems turn into compelling motifs. She is a Scots poet who speaks and writes with a Scots accent, and she is a black poet who, as a girl growing up in an almost all-white community, had her all too visible difference thrust upon her in a number of wounding remarks. "In my country," for instance, presents through a few carefully chosen phrases the common misgivings of honest local people whose fear of difference is so deep that they would readily burn her as a witch ("her words spliced into bars / of an old wheel"). When she points out that she belongs to the place as much as they do ("*Where do you come from?* / 'Here', I said, 'Here. These parts'."), she further unsettles the natives, since they cannot safely dismiss her as a stray creature from some distant country. Similarly, the reference by the tight-mouthed, white-uniformed nurse to her "thick lip"—while she cries for her mother's "soft lips"—compounds the bodily pain of an open fracture with the worse wound of insulting dismissal.

These poems are from Kay's second collection, *Other Lovers,* and they echo chapter 7 ("Black Bottom") in the earlier *The Adoption Papers,* in which the daughter and her adoptive mother recall instances of patent unfairness and racialism, such as other children's jeering or the teacher's teasing when the girl cannot dance in step ("I thought / you people had it in your blood"). The sequence, which is fairly straightforwardly autobiographical, is a long poem printed in different types for three voices—adoptive mother, daughter, and birth mother. It is remarkable for dramatic vividness and humor, particularly in those parts in which we listen to the adoptive mother, the one the girl would call "Mum," the one whose inflections and idiosyncrasies the poet knows. The birth mother's voice, however, is more a reconstructed synthesis and does not have the same ring of intimate acquaintance.

There is great openness, at times even a certain stridency, in the seventeen poems attached to *The Adoption Papers* sequence. A number of them are about dying, at least one about dying of AIDS; some are about homosexual love, at least one about the love binding a white girl to a black girl, both of whom grew up in Africa and now live in London. The opening poem, "Severe Gale 8," is a five-part sequence about the Thatcher years in Britain, an era of increasingly unshackled private capitalism. It is also a terrible and yet hopeful fairy tale and in its way a protest song in the tradition of "We Shall Overcome" or of the nineteenth-century French weavers' song "Les Canuts." Four of the poem's five parts begin with the clause "There was no bread" and proceed to describe aspects of the extreme and only slightly exaggerated impoverishment of the many who live in cardboard cities, who wait "perhaps one year" for an urgent medical appointment, and who face irretrievable overdrafts thanks to easy credit. In the final stanza the children, whom their mothers have had to "throw out into the wind," float away to places (some now unlikely) where they find a sense of justice that they bring back to the triumphantly marching people. "I try my absolute best" is a hilarious piece on a mother's helpless and foundering attempts at feeding her children properly. As she discovers that the various healthful procedures she had trusted to be foolproof are actually flawed in one way or another, she eventually gives in, is "back on Valium," and lets her kids "[stuff] Monster Munch / and Mars bars down them":

I says it's your pocket money.
Do what you want with it.

On the whole I find that there is greater confidence both in Kay's skill at impersonation and in her use of rhythm and sounds in the later *Other Lovers.* Occasionally her handling of rhymes is brilliant, sometimes underscored by the haunting repetition of lines. In the short poem "Inside" first the lines "Inside I'd say don't please" and "Grit my teeth. Bite the pillow" and then the line "My own heart, broken like bones" are repeated. The bones sadly chime with the impossible wish that sorrow should leave her alone, and sorrow numbly echoes in the bitten pillow, the threatening shadow on the wall, and the deepening hollow in her heart.

The physical anguish of absence is prominent in a number of poems, such as "The Day," "This Long Night," "The Keeper," "Away from You," "The Crossing," and, for me probably the best, "Dusting the Phone." The last is conversational and witty while torn with longing ("Your voice / disappears into my lonely cotton sheets. / / I am trapped in it. I can't move . . . Come on, damn you, ring me. Or else. what? / / I don't know what"). The six sections of the poem called "Other Lovers" take the addressee, who is "I" only in the first section, when "you" and "I" were still "we," through the heartbreak of separating until she emerges to "a whole new life."

A poem like "Watching People Sing," shot through with the yearning of a sixteen-year-old, is a tribute to communal conviviality. "Colouring In," by contrast, is the disillusioned attempt to retrieve a lost genuineness in a place where the flames of the fire are "now [turned] down by numbers" and the protest marches—as well as the several known shops of her childhood—are smothered by McDonald's "garish red and yellow." The last line of the poem awkwardly, almost despairingly, insists on the reality of a remembered experience when a painted egg rolled to the bottom of a hill, "where it did smash, it did, and you were happy, you were."

Broken bones and broken hearts are a recurring theme sounded in the first poem of the collection, "Even the trees." This piece, which takes the whipping to death of a slave as its starting point, launches a sequence on Bessie Smith and blues singing: "In the early / light, the delicate bone-light / / that broke hearts, a song swept from field to field," "a blue song in the beat of her heart." At the end of this first poem, as indeed at the end of the last one, which also is set on a plantation, we find the anguished statement that "everything that's happened once could happen again." Horror repeats itself, albeit on a small scale, in present-day Germany with the torching of guest workers' settlements. In "Gastarbeiter" the image of a shroud is suggested by the woman's job in a textile factory ("the long swathes / of material long enough to wrap / twice around the dead; a close family"). Here, ominously, the stars are "the shapes of swastika."

"Sign" is one of the poems in which Kay protests against the erasing of other people's severalty, in this case of the right of a girl to use sign language. Along with all dissident, discordant, minority languages, her way of expressing herself, branded as "no language at all," is steamrolled by "the big one, better tongue":

They say her voice is very strange.
They tie her hands behind her back.
They say repeat after me until
she has *no language at all.*

Kay will not be reduced to the common tongue. She holds on to her particular English and her way of using it. She, too, is "a songster, making music,'' and through most of her writing she joins in songs of remembrance and commemoration.

—Christine Pagnoulle

KAZANTZIS, Judith

Nationality: British. **Born:** Oxford, 14 August 1940. **Education:** Oxford University, Somerville College, 1958–61, B.A. in modern history. **Family:** Married Alec Kazantzis in 1982 (divorced); one daughter and one son. **Career:** Home tutor for the Inner London Education Authority during 1970s; poetry reviewer, *Spare Rib* magazine, six years; member Women's Literature Collective, 1970s; committee member and panelist, South-East Arts, 1978–79. Poetry editor, *The PEN Broadsheet.* Also artist: individual shows—Poetry Society Gallery, London, 1987; Combined Harvest Gallery, London, 1989. **Address:** 32 Ladbroke Grove, London W11 3BQ, England.

PUBLICATIONS

Poetry

Minefield. London, Sidgwick and Jackson, 1977.
The Wicked Queen. London, Sidgwick and Jackson, 1980.
Touch Papers, with Michèle Roberts and Michelene Wandor. London, Allison and Busby, 1982.
Let's Pretend. London, Virago, 1984.
A Poem for Guatemala. Leamington Spa, Yorkshire, Bedlam Press, 1986.
Judith Kazantzis. Leamington Spa, Leamington Poetry Society, 1987.
Flame Tree. London, Methuen, 1988.
The Florida Swamps. London, Oasis, 1990.
The Rabbit Magician Plate. London, Sinclair-Stevenson, 1992.
Selected Poems: 1977–1992. London, Sinclair-Stevenson, 1995.
Swimming through the Grand Hotel: Poems 1993–1996. London, Enitharmon, and Chester Springs, Pennsylvania, Dufour, 1997.
The Odysseus Poems: Fictions on The Odyssey of Homer. Manaccan, Cornwall, Cargo, 1999.

Other

Editor, *The Gordon Riots: A Collection of Contemporary Documents.* London, Cape, 1966.
Editor, *Women in Revolt: The Fight for Emancipation: A Collection of Contemporary Documents.* London, Cape, 1968.

*

Critical Study: By David Herd, in *Bete Noire* (Hull, England), 14–15, 1992.

Judith Kazantzis comments:

I wrote poems all during my childhood and adolescence. Then there was a complete break until 1973 when reading Plath's *The Colossus* suddenly broke the resolution I had made not to be a writer; she offered a language I could understand emotionally and as a poet technically. It was painting, psychoanalysis, and feminism that set off my poetry in the 1970s, but underneath all was the simple experience

of marrying and having two young children. So my first book makes reference to the claustrophobia and anger I was feeling then and was consciously woman centered, and my second book, more so, and it was wider in range and more confident. I reused Greek myth and also fairy tale. Contemporary issues were coming in more explicit forms.

In 1982 I collaborated in a feminist trilogy, and my next publications have ranged from consideration of public issues, including a special interest in Latin America and U.S. relations with Latin America, to love poems and to considerations of mother-daughter, mother-son relationships. Exile and distance, my relationship to countryside and nature and to city, time—all these were growing as themes. My *Selected Poems* illustrates this wide-ranging kind of development over fifteen years, influenced by much time spent in Key West and other parts of America, though my base is very definitely English.

*   *   *

Judith Kazantzis is a poet who speaks with an intensely personal, informal voice about matters of general public concern. What is remarkable is her ability to manage such a combination without the need to resort either to full-blown rhetoric or to the confessional mode that seemed to proclaim itself as the quintessential voice of modern poetry in the late 1960s.

Kazantzis's first major collection, *The Wicked Queen,* was published in 1980, and the dominant characteristics of her work are already present in it in their full maturity: a wit that can be savage but that is deployed in the service of a quite justifiable rage at injustice, and a feminism that may at times be strident but with a stridency that is often necessary if one is to draw attention to what much of the world may choose to ignore. The themes range widely, from the stoning of an adulteress in Jeddah to a savage retelling of the tale of Little Red Riding Hood and from an imaginative reconstruction of the world of Queen Clytemnestra to the joyful, tender poem addressed to the poet's pregnant sister. There is a prickly restlessness about much of the writing, a willful, rebellious refusal to let go of a theme until all of its possibilities are exposed for all the world to see, appraise, or even jeer at if necessary. If the absurd posturings of men are often mocked, they are mocked deservedly, as in ''Those Upright Men'':

> I heard of a tribe where the men
>   held their erections all their lives,
> like rhino horns: each
> his own mascot before the main regiment of the body,
> gorgeous trophies
>   painful to bump . . .

Kazantzis's next major work was the long *A Poem for Guatemala.* Here poetry is deployed in the service of popular protest, a time-honored tradition, of course. The poem itself is divided into such sections as ''Duty,'' ''The Morning Star,'' and ''The Clinic,'' each chronicling particular instances of deprivation, injustice, and cruelty. Its rhetorical flights are gently persuasive:

> When will this land be free?
> And the villages be uncovered from the tractor tread and
> the flattened ranges of the loosened bull?
> When will the Indians sow their seed corn
> And the children grow tall in their parents' houses?

The poem represents a significant move forward for Kazantzis, from the imaginative exploration of particular acts of injustice, whether they be offenses of one kind or another against her own sex, often seen through the medium of myth, historical example, or biblical precept, to a new, more extended mode of political realism, which in this instance includes a profound concern for the ramifications of American foreign policy in Central America. As she explained, ''This poem comes of a wish to honour the life-force and courage of Guatemalans living and dying in the current unnatural conditions. These conditions are not widely known. But among those of the Americas who live in exile either as refugees abroad or in their own land, the peoples of Guatemala, especially the indigenous peoples, figure in hundreds of thousands.'' Harold Pinter described it as ''a major political poem . . . beautifully wrought, concrete, passionate . . . a most impressive achievement.''

Kazantzis's later collection *Flame Tree* is also firmly rooted in the political realities of these turbulent times. Themes of individual poems include the threat to the world's rainforests, criticism of the Thatcher government, the miners' strike of 1984, and the Falkland Islands War. ''His Little Girl Feeds Daddy'' deals with the government budget. It begins,

> Here's
> a sight of the boar
> head in closeup, mounted
> Stuffed on a wall, relaxed
> before his tusking of
> widows, disabled, geriatrics . . .

The wit is savage, mordant, rollicking. The movement of the verse, as is the case with much of Kazantzis's poetry, depends upon the rhythms of the words chosen and the way they accumulate as the words are spoken; the formal patterning depends upon the spoken impact of the piece. It is free verse of a kind, but discipline has been imposed from the start by the choice and disposition of the words themselves, which means that the poetry is never slack, never lacking in taut control. What is admirable about her use of language is the imaginative pressure behind the words, the sense of urgency that comes from having one's subject matter sharply, unflinchingly in focus:

> Cop cars squeal, howl and gasp
> Across the grid pattern. In my sleep
> Huge worms fight at intersections,
> Clapping and batting their brazen wings . . .

Flame Tree swings from Europe to the Americas and back again, from childhood to maturity, from politics to the intensely personal concerns of friends and family, and all of this is achieved without force, fuss, or gratuitous rhetorical flourish.

—Michael Glover

KEFALÁ, Antigone

Nationality: Australian. **Born:** Braila, Romania, 28 May 1935. **Education:** Primary school in Braila, high schools in Pireus and Lavrion, Greece, and New Zealand; Victoria University, Wellington, B.A. 1958, M.A. 1960. **Family:** Married 1) Robert Kerr in 1959 (divorced 1963); 2) Usher Weinrauch in 1964 (divorced 1976). **Career:** Teacher of English, New South Wales Department of Education, Sydney, 1961–68; administrative assistant, University of New South Wales, 1968–69; arts administrator, Australia Council for the Arts, Sydney, 1971–87. **Address:** 12 Rose Street, Annandale, New South Wales 2038, Australia.

PUBLICATIONS

Poetry

The Alien. Brisbane, Makar Press, 1973.
Thirsty Weather. Melbourne, Outback Press, 1978.
European Notebook. Sydney, Hale and Iremonger, 1988.
Absence: New and Selected Poems. Sydney, Hale and Iremonger, 1992.

Novels

The First Journey. Sydney, Wild and Woolley, 1975.
The Island. Sydney, Hale and Iremonger, 1984.

Other

Alexia: A Tale of Two Cultures, illustrated by Warwick Hatton (for children). Sydney, John Ferguson, 1984.

*

Bibliography: In *Bibliography of Australian Multicultural Writers* by Gunew and Mahyuddin, Melbourne, Deakin University, 1992; in *Oxford Companion to Australian Literature,* Wilde, Hooton and Andrews, 1994.

Critical Studies: ''Migrant Women Writers,'' in *Meanjin* (Melbourne), 1983, and *Framing Marginality,* Melbourne, Melbourne University Press, 1994, both by Sneja Gunew; ''The Process of Becoming'' by Judith Brett, in *Meanjin* (Melbourne), 1985; *Coming Out from Under* by Pam Gilbert, Sydney, Pandora Press, 1988; ''The Politics of Nostalgia'' by Efi Hatzimanolis, in *Hecate* (Brisbane) 6(1/2), 1990; *The Journeys Within—Striking Chords* by Nikos Papastergiadis, Sydney, Allen and Unwin, 1992; *Migrant Daughters: The Female Voice in Greek-Australian Prose Fiction* by Helen Nickas, Melbourne, Owl, 1992; ''Memory and Absence'' by Michelle Tsokos, in *Westerly* (Perth), 39(4), 1994; ''Antigone Kefala'' by Geoff Page, in his *A Reader's Guide to Contemporary Australian Poetry,* St. Lucia, U.Q.P., 1995; ''Antigone Kefala: Translating the Migratory Self'' by Saadi Nikro, in *Southerly* (Southerly, Australia), 58(1), autumn 1998.

*   *   *

In an interview published in *Poetry and Gender,* Antigone Kefala refers to her childhood writing in Romania, her learning Greek (but not writing) in Greece, and her finally starting to write in English in her last year at an Australian university. She quotes Derek Walcott: ''To change your language you must change your life.'' Her initially musical concept of poetry has slowly ''acquired more architectural form, became a tool through which some perceived truth could come alive.''

Despite the success of the children of non-English-speaking migrants in school and their increasing success in business and science, writers for whom English was a second language rarely had serious books published in Australia in the mid-1970s. *The Alien* and then *Thirsty Weather* were pioneers, and readers found that they had to acquire a new taste. The bitterness was not hostile, but readers hesitated to call the mordant accuracy funny, even if it was sometimes about faceless migration authorities or New Zealanders. An example is found in ''The Place'':

> The ships, we had heard, had sunk
> weighted with the charity of the new world
> that kept on feeding us with toys . . .

The same quality can be seen in ''The Promised Land'':

> I
> The roads were of candy
> the houses of ice cream
> the cattle of liquorice.
> Pretty, we said,
> drinking the green air,
> as in a fairy tale, we said,
> eating the green water, brackish,
> breathing the smoke that rose
> from the greenstone hills . . .

> II
> The people carved in wood
> the mark of the knife still on them
> a nordic dream whittled to knick-knacks
> with glass beads in their sockets
> which they washed every night
> in detergents . . .

Taking in images as light as skeletal leaves and yet invested with symbolic weight, readers in fact learn a new language for themselves and their places: ''the girl with the cropped hair, / nervous lips, tortured fingers . . .'' (''The Lunch''); or ''. . . soot raining on warehouses, railyards, the hotel / where we were waiting for the fixer . . . / The gutters full of onions, / blue dusted porcelain the sky, / above the railway clock / the new translucent moon was flying'' (''Ultimo Bridge'').

Kefalá's *European Notebook* maintains her bleak and brooding outlook: ''The hero came quite late / sniffing the air / his face like a skinned animal / eaten by maggots with ice heads / a musty smell about him / as he danced / his hollow eyes turned inward, / bleak tunnels with no end'' (''The Party''). Greek tradition, local social occasions, memory, return—indeed the poet finds ''fatality at the heart of each thing'' (''The Wanderer''). ''Suicide'' is a poem of great beauty:

> This timelessness
> that rises out of the earth . . .
> This silence,
> the ease that fills the trees,
> a promise of such bliss
> of self forgetfulness.

''The core of the experience I am trying to express,'' says Kefalá, ''is essentially a fatalistic one, my Greekness, I assume.'' This aspect shows in her scrupulous language and pacing and in a brevity that has nothing to do with ''having nothing to say.''

Kefalá writes sparingly, and selections of earlier work fill out later books. Her prose works also are slim, refined narratives, distillations of intense experience. In *Absence,* the title sequence of her 1992 volume of new and selected poems, ''Growing Old'' is ''gathering this knowledge one / does not want, one can not use, / a useless knowledge that / repeats itself.'' Nights are menacing experiences of absence and degradation, spoken in a soft, even voice.

''What I am searching for now, is for a balance that will allow meaning and language to hold each other in a unity in which the weight of each is not visible.'' Kefalá's limpid language somehow carries nuanced meanings, but apathy and despair lurk behind the lines, even those positively titled ''Freedom Fighter'' and ''Thanksgiving.'' No reader experiences Kefalá's poems as simple delight; equally, no reader can miss their stripped-back power.

—Judith Rodriguez

KELL, Richard (Alexander)

Nationality: British. **Born:** Youghal, County Cork, Ireland, 1 November 1927. **Education:** Methodist College, Belfast; Wesley College, Dublin, 1944–46; Trinity College, Dublin, B.A. (honors) in English and French literature 1952. **Family:** Married Muriel Adelaide Nairn in 1953 (died 1975); two sons (one deceased) and two daughters. Assistant teacher, Kilkenny College, Ireland, and Whinney Bank School, Middlesborough, Cleveland; assistant librarian, Luton Public Library, Bedfordshire, 1954–56, and Brunel College of Technology, Acton, Middlesex, 1956–59; assistant lecturer, 1960–65, and lecturer in English, 1966–70, Isleworth Polytechnic, London; senior lecturer in English, Newcastle upon Tyne Polytechnic, 1970–83. **Address:** 18 Rectory Grove, Gosforth, Newcastle upon Tyne NE3 1AL, England.

PUBLICATIONS

Poetry

(Poems). Oxford, Fantasy Press, 1957.
Control Tower. London, Chatto and Windus-Hogarth Press, 1962.
Six Irish Poets, with others, edited by Robin Skelton. London, Oxford University Press, 1962.
Differences. London, Chatto and Windus-Hogarth Press, 1969.
Humours. Sunderland, Ceolfrith, 1978.
Heartwood. Newcastle upon Tyne, Northern House, 1978.
The Broken Circle. Sunderland, Ceolfrith, 1981.
Wall, with others, edited by Noel Connor. Brampton, Cumbria, LYC Press, 1981.
In Praise of Warmth. Dublin, Dedalus, 1987.
Five Irish Poets, with others, edited by David Lampe and Dennis Maloney. Fredonia, New York, White Pine Press, and Dublin, Dedalus, 1990.
Rock and Water. Dublin, Dedalus, 1993.

*

Manuscript Collection: Literary and Philosophical Society Library, Newcastle upon Tyne.

Critical Study: ''Being Finite'' by Chris Agee, in *Books Ireland* (Kilkenny), February 1988.

Richard Kell comments:

(1970) The poems in *Control Tower,* largely reflective and descriptive, were written without any awareness of a predominant theme. In retrospect, however, it appears that one of my main concerns was the opposition between negative and positive states (restraint and freedom, deprivation and fulfillment, apathy and love, skepticism and faith, inner blindness and vision), often with a note of regret for the elusiveness of the second. Though some aspect of the theme itself was implied fairly frequently, the experiences that represented it were varied, ranging from the sight of some empty coal carts to a meditation focused on the image of a Buddhist goddess. In *Differences* the same kind of dichotomy emerges, but with an emphasis on harmony and conflict as concomitants of diversity. As for technique, I like to combine fairly well-defined verse forms—of many types and not necessarily traditional—with rhythmic flexibility. In the choice and syntactic ordering of words, I aim at intelligibility as well as imaginative precision, which does not preclude double meanings when these are useful. In general my poetry tends to be quiet and controlled rather than effusive; I love freedom but am distrustful of excess.

(1980) The poems in *Humours,* written in 1964 and 1965 and printed with accompanying pictures by Dick Ward, are concerned with familiar human dispositions, states of mind, beliefs, practices. These are often presented symbolically, and the style is dry and witty, broadly speaking, rather than lyrical. By contrast, the poems in *Heartwood* express personal feeling in a fairly direct way. They were written in memory of my wife, who died in a swimming accident in 1975.

(1985) *The Broken Circle* contains several poems of disenchantment in which the ''negative and positive states'' referred to above are associated with religious themes. ''The Dancers'' explores the possibility that aesthetic experience and artistic creation may be more meaningful witnesses to the Logos than formal religion. This poem is in five parts, not four, as a printer's error suggests; the last part begins ''May they rest in peace.''

(1990) *In Praise of Warmth* adds twenty-four new poems, on both personal and public themes, to a selection from previous books.

(1995) *Rock and Water* contains seventy new poems arranged in six thematic sections.

*   *   *

At the heart of Richard Kell's poetry is a metaphysical paradox of heart and head, clearly stated in the early poem ''The Balance'':

> Always the one that will not let me be—
> when I would overflow (the mind free,
> the heart ready to love, the voice to sing),
> reminds me with its prudent nagging tongue
>
> that life is such and such: the free mind,
> the loving heart and singing voice are kind;
> so plan, cherish, be provident, pay the bills:
> *the horses lumber, but the tiger kills.*

> Always the one that will not let me change—
> when I'd be careful, sympathize, arrange
> (the voice level, the mind about to freeze),
> recalls what goodness tamed no longer sees,
>
> that life is such and such: the frozen mind
> and level voice are to themselves unkind;
> then play, be prodigal, give joy its head:
> *the fountain's reckless, but the cistern's dead.*

Between Blakean metaphors of fountain and cistern, tigers and horses, Kell chisels a poetry of controlled moral passion. His theme recurs, with seventeen Stevens-like variations, in the title poem of *In Praise of Warmth:* ''Right and left will not make middle, / but hot and cold make warm.'' For Kell the notion of balance conspires with the nature of experience, and indeed the nature of emotional man and the uncompromising nature of ''things'' are everywhere contrasted in his work: ''Identity of opposites? Out of this world! / Being finite, I'm content with the tug-of-war.''

Kell's apparent acceptance of struggle bespeaks his torment, too, of not being able to survive at the pitch of extremes. In poems of passion or sorrow he checks himself with language persistently, sometimes humorously, calling upon his intelligence for succor. If ''violence breeds in every natural thing,'' then human beings must have recourse to discipline. In a poem aptly called ''Decorum'' he invokes the brave, austere ''far-off voice'' on the telephone bearing (in two senses) its bad news.

What is most moving about Kell's poetry is its unstated motif of human fortitude. The stoic poems of *Heartwood,* a sequence dedicated to his drowned wife, make a disciplined bid for understanding through sustained metaphor. In ''Marriage Is like a Tree'' he celebrates the sound heartwood of a marriage, ''twenty-two rings of tough growth'' that no flood could destroy: ''It could be a kind of luck, being left / the ghost of a scarred tree / still healthy when it toppled: / leaves whispering through all the mind's seasons, / a root safe in the ground for ever.''

Always a technician, a man in love with the musical scope of his art, Kell has been drawn to prosodic experiment, and a long meditation on traveling, both physical and metaphysical, has extended his considerable range. He also has had much to say in free verse about man's foolish, fearful destruction of the planet. Kell is most at home, however, in verse forms in which a play of intelligence gives shape to the complex feelings of a soul ''charged with the gloomed / benignity of green pastures,'' facing with regretful patience ''the furies of the motorway.''

—Anne Stevenson

KELLMAN, Anthony

Also has written as Tony Kellman. **Nationality:** Barbadian (naturalized U.S. citizen 1996). **Born:** Lewen Anthony Kellman, White Hall, St. Michael, Barbados, 24 April 1955. **Education:** University of the West Indies, Cave Hill, Barbados, 1982–86, B.A. (honors) in English 1986; Louisiana State University, Baton Rouge, 1987–89, M.F.A. in creative writing 1989. **Family:** Married 1) Pamela Emptage in 1981 (divorced 1987), one daughter; 2) Malaika Favorite in 1988. **Career:** Troubadour, various clubs and pubs, England, 1975–77, and various clubs and establishments, Barbados, 1977–79; reporter, *Barbados Advocate,* Barbados, 1980–82; editor, De Mattos Advertising, Barbados, 1982–84. Assistant professor of English and creative writing, 1989–93, and since 1993 associate professor of English and creative writing, Augusta State University, Georgia. Public relations officer, Central Bank, Barbados, 1985–86, and National Cultural Foundation, Barbados, 1987. Founder and coordinator, Summerville Reading Series, Augusta, Georgia, 1989–94; since 1989 director, Sandhills Writers' Conference, Augusta State University, and since 1990 founder and director, Winter Gathering of Writers, Augusta State University. **Awards:** Georgia Council for the Arts award, for fiction, 1992, for poetry, 1995; National Endowment for the Arts poetry award, 1993; Frank Collymore Literary Endowment award, 2000, for *Wings of a Stranger.* **Address:** 796 Palatine Avenue, Atlanta, Georgia 30316, U.S.A.

PUBLICATIONS

Poetry

In Depths of Burning Light. Leeds, England, Peepal Tree Press, 1982.
The Broken Sun. Leeds, England, Peepal Tree Press, 1984.
Watercourse. Leeds, England, Peepal Tree Press, 1990.
The Long Gap. Leeds, England, Peepal Tree Press, 1996.
Wings of a Stranger. Leeds, England, Peepal Tree Press, 2000.

Recordings: *Surf Poems,* Studio South, 1993; *Surf Poems II,* Studio South, 1994.

Novel

The Coral Rooms. Leeds, England, Peepal Tree Press, 1994.

Other

Editor, *Crossing Water: Contemporary Poetry of the English-Speaking Caribbean.* Greenfield Center, New York, Greenfield Review Press, 1992.

*

Critical Studies: *Come Back to Me, My Language* by J. Edward Chamberlin, Urbana, University of Illinois Press, 1993; "World Literature in Review: Barbadian" by Sasenarine Persaud, in *World Literature Today,* 69(3), summer 1995; "From Ancestral to Creole: Humans and Animals in a West Indian Scale of Values" by Jeremy Poynting, in *American Identities,* Charlottesville, University Press of Virginia, 1996; "World Literature in Review: Africa & the West Indies" by Cyril Dabydeen, in *World Literature Today,* 72(1), winter 1998.

Anthony Kellman comments:

For me poetry almost always starts with an image that I must explain to myself. This begins my journey. My aim then is to try to successfully marry language and landscape, as I follow the image, to communicate ideas. I try to allow my subconscious to rule an early draft, for I feel it is the magic of the subconscious that shapes a work and gives it its mystery and force. Then, as many other drafts as are necessary will follow in order to find *le mot juste* and the right

arrangement of syllables and cadences in the line. These choices all relate to the goal of most effectively communicating one's ideas; so form (the formal impulses of the poem) must be chosen in a way that meaning will be reinforced, made clearer, and, ultimately, have more impact on the reader. I strive to have a strong sense of music in my poetry, not necessarily traditional sound patterns (although I have written in most of the traditional forms, most of my work is in exploratory form) but the literature-as-performance idea that Frost spoke of. One should feel like dancing on hearing a poem read or on reading the poem.

Among my earlier influences were Derek Walcott, Kamau Brathwaite, Eliot, Auden, Tennyson; later Seamus Heaney, Robert Lowell, Ted Hughes, Adrienne Rich. I read a lot of African English-language poets in undergraduate school as well as Dennis Brutus and African-American poets like Amiri Baraka and Langston Hughes.

*   *   *

There have been many twists and turns in Anthony Kellman's life. Born in Barbados, he left the island for Britain at age eighteen to play Caribbean pop and folk music in pubs and folk clubs. Upon his return he worked as a reporter and, after earning a degree in English and history from the University of the West Indies, for the Central Bank of Barbados. Subsequently, in the late 1980s, he received a master's degree in creative writing from Louisiana State University and began teaching at Augusta State University in Georgia.

Also in the 1980s Kellman began his literary endeavors with two early publications: *In Depths of Burning Light* in 1982 and *The Broken Sun* two years later. They reveal the potential of his poetic craftsmanship and hint at the raw but not yet polished quality of Kellman's poetry, which started to come to full bloom with his collection *Watercourse* (1990). Vivid imagination, anecdotal storytelling, and a cosmopolitanism shaped by the centuries-long influx of peoples to Barbados are typical characteristics in his writing about the island's tumultuous history and the lush beauty of its land- and seascape. Kellman's fresh figurative language is evident in "Flight" when he writes, "On the south-east coast / where metal birds, although sensed and seen / surprise the skyscrape with ogre-like rumblings: / sudden as orange bougainvillaea or palm fronds / to the sunbather's waking eyes— / are the remains of a mansion." Another striking element of *Watercourse* is the use of the Barbadian vernacular in almost all of the poems and its juxtaposition to Standard English, which creates conflicts such as these from "Sprat": "When yuh weak, yuh humble yuhself, / When yuh weak, yuh humble yuhself, / Islands, touching, are shining shields / in the dark void of the world."

Landscapes are also significant in the novel *The Coral Rooms* (1994). A slim volume, it tells the story of Percival Veer, whose success is manifest in the executive position he holds in a bank, his large house, and his young, attentive wife. He is troubled, however, by recurring dreams of caves and by guilt over a past wrong. The more his inner world is upset, the more he feels the need to explore the limestone caves of his island, an adventure that will eventually take him back to his childhood. Realistic and dreamlike at once, the account Kellman gives is of a mythical Caribbean landscape in which the materialism of a postcolonial elite is countered by a man's search for his roots and identity.

The Long Gap, published in 1996, takes its title from the name of a street in Barbados on which Kellman walked to school, and it gives evidence of the gap that both separates Kellman from and ties him to his Caribbean home. The poems in the volume reflect the kaleidoscope of themes and multitude of aspects found in the Caribbean archipelago. Kellman enriches them with episodes honoring Barbadian artists, reflecting on politicians ("Island Lover," "Calypso Island," "Sea Horse, Pass By," "Conversations with a Dead Politician"), and giving impressions of the lifestyle of the U.S. south ("Hinckson," "A Churn in the South"). Drawing on popular and folk traditions, he intertwines dialect and standard forms to create a musical and metaphorically rich tapestry of language. Kellman is never polite in describing Barbados's development, and he is always on the lookout for the authentic in his political and social statements. Thereby he presents himself as an islander, rooted in Barbados and believing that a remembered past and the surrounding "salt water / heals all manner of illness," especially the wounds of the island's history ("Isle Man"). More than in his previous works, the fact that Barbados has shaped and still shapes Kellman's worldview runs like a thread through *The Long Gap*.

Though by profession an academic in the United States, Kellman has not lost touch with the sea, the Barbadian people, and the places of his childhood on the island, which he describes as "a sunwashed island / wrapped with lucid blue bandages" ("Isle Man"). He never tires of celebrating the natural beauty of Barbados and lists for his readers the ingredients that make up this particular place: coconut and mahogany trees, blood red ixoras, sand dunes, fossils, coral reefs, cliff edges, blue eggshell skies, khuskhus hedges, breadfruits. With *The Long Gap* Kellman has established himself as a major voice of the younger generation of Caribbean writers.

—Harald Leusmann

KELLY, Robert

Nationality: American. **Born:** Brooklyn, New York, 24 September 1935. **Education:** City College of New York, A.B. 1955; Columbia University, New York, 1955–58. **Family:** Married 1) Joan Elizabeth Laskin in 1955 (divorced 1969); 2) Helen Belinky in 1969 (divorced 1978); 3) Charlotte Mandell in 1993. **Career:** Translator, Continental Translation Service, New York, 1956–58; lecturer in English, Wagner College, New York, 1960–61. Instructor in German, 1961–62, instructor in English, 1962–64, assistant professor, 1964–69, associate professor, 1969–74, professor of English, 1974–86, director of Writing Program, 1980–93, and since 1986 Asher B. Edelman Professor of literature, Avery Graduate School of the Arts, Bard College, Annandale-on-Hudson, New York. Assistant professor of English, State University of New York, Buffalo, summer 1964; visiting lecturer, Tufts University, Medford, Massachusetts, 1966–67; poet-in-residence, California Institute of Technology, Pasadena, 1971–72, University of Kansas, Lawrence, 1975, and Dickinson College, Carlisle, Pennsylvania, 1976. Editor, *Chelsea Review,* New York, 1957–60; founding editor, with George Economou, Trobar magazine, 1960–64, and *Trobar* Books, 1962–65, New York; contributing editor, *Caterpillar,* New York, 1969–72; editor, *Los 1,* 1977. Since 1964 editor, *Matter* magazine and Matter publishing company, New York, later Annandale-on-Hudson; contributing editor, *Alcheringa: Ethnopoetics,* New York, since 1977, and *Sulfur,* Pasadena, 1981–82. **Awards:** New York City Writers Conference fellowship, 1967; *Los Angeles Times* book prize, 1980; American Academy award, 1986. D.Litt.: State University of New York, Oneonta, 1994.

Address: Department of English, Bard College, Annandale-on-Hudson, New York 12504, U.S.A.

PUBLICATIONS

Poetry

Armed Descent. New York, Hawks Well Press, 1961.

Her Body Against Time (bilingual edition). Mexico City, El Corno Emplumado, 1963.

Round Dances. New York, Trobar, 1964.

Tabula. Lawrence, Kansas, Dialogue Press, 1964.

Enstasy. Annandale-on-Hudson, New York, Matter, 1964.

Matter/Fact/Sheet/1. Buffalo, New York, Matter, 1964.

Matter/Fact/Sheet/2. Annandale-on-Hudson, New York, Matter, 1964.

Lunes, with *Sightings* by Jerome Rothenberg. New York, Hawks Well Press, 1964.

Lectiones. Placitas, New Mexico, Duende Press, 1965.

Words in Service. New Haven, Connecticut, Robert Lamberton, 1966.

Weeks. Mexico City, El Corno Emplumado, 1966.

Songs XXIV. Cambridge, Massachusetts, Pym Randall Press, 1967.

Twenty Poems. Annandale-on-Hudson, New York, Matter, 1967.

Devotions. Annandale-on-Hudson, New York, Salitter, 1967.

Axon Dendron Tree. Annandale-on-Hudson, New York, Matter, 1967.

Crooked Bridge Love Society. Annandale-on-Hudson, New York, Salitter, 1967.

A Joining: A Sequence for H.D. Los Angeles, Black Sparrow Press, 1967.

Alpha. Gambier, Ohio, Pothanger Press, 1968.

Finding the Measure. Los Angeles, Black Sparrow Press, 1968.

From the Common Shore, Book 5. Great Neck, New York, George Robert Minkoff, 1968.

Songs I-XXX. Cambridge, Massachusetts, Pym Randall Press, 1969.

Sonnets. Los Angeles, Black Sparrow Press, 1969.

We Are the Arbiters of Beast Desire. Berkeley, California, MBVL, 1969.

A California Journal. London, Big Venus, 1969.

The Common Shore, Books I-V: A Long Poem about America in Time. Los Angeles, Black Sparrow Press, 1969.

Kali Yuga. London, Cape Goliard Press, 1970; New York, Grossman, 1971.

Flesh: Dream: Book. Los Angeles, Black Sparrow Press, 1971.

Ralegh. Los Angeles, Black Sparrow Press, 1972.

The Pastorals. Los Angeles, Black Sparrow Press, 1972.

Reading Her Notes. Privately printed, 1972.

The Tears of Edmund Burke. Annandale-on-Hudson, New York, Printed by Helen, 1973.

Whaler Frigate Clippership. Lawrence, Kansas, Tansy, 1973.

The Mill of Particulars. Los Angeles, Black Sparrow Press, 1973.

The Belt. Storrs, University of Connecticut Library, 1974.

The Loom. Los Angeles, Black Sparrow Press, 1975.

Sixteen Odes. Santa Barbara, California, Black Sparrow Press, 1976.

The Lady of. Santa Barbara, California, Black Sparrow Press, 1977.

The Convections. Santa Barbara, California, Black Sparrow Press, 1978.

The Book of Persephone. New Paltz, New York, Treacle Press, 1978; revised edition, New Paltz, New York, McPherson, 1983.

The Cruise of the Pnyx. Barrytown, New York, Station Hill Press, 1979.

Kill the Messenger Who Brings Bad News. Santa Barbara, California, Black Sparrow Press, 1979.

Sentence. Barrytown, New York, Station Hill Press, 1980.

The Alchemist to Mercury, edited by Jed Rasula. Richmond, California, North Atlantic, 1981.

Spiritual Exercises. Santa Barbara, California, Black Sparrow Press, 1981.

Mulberry Women. Berkeley, California, Hiersoux Powers Thomas, 1982.

Under Words. Santa Barbara, California, Black Sparrow Press, 1983.

Thor's Thrush. Oakland, California, Coincidence Press, 1984.

Not This Island Music. Santa Rosa, California, Black Sparrow Press, 1987.

The Flowers of Unceasing Coincidence. Barrytown, New York, Station Hill, 1988.

Oahu. Rhinebeck. St. Lazaire Press, 1988.

A Strange Market. Santa Rosa, California, Black Sparrow Press, 1992.

Mont Blanc. Ann Arbor, Michigan, OtherWind Press, 1994.

Red Actions: Selected Poems, 1960–1993. Santa Rosa, California, Black Sparrow Press, 1995.

The Time of Voice: Poems, 1994–1996. Santa Rosa, California, Black Sparrow Press, 1998.

The Garden of Distances: Drawings and Poems. Kingston, New York, Documentext/McPherson and Co., 1999.

Runes. Ann Arbor, Michigan, OtherWind Press, 1999.

Recording: *Finding the Measure,* Black Sparrow Press, 1968.

Plays

The Well Wherein a Deer's Head Bleeds (produced New York, 1964). Published in *A Play and Two Poems,* with Diane Wakoski and Ron Loewinsohn, Los Angeles, Black Sparrow Press, 1968.

Eros and Psyche, music by Elie Yarden (produced New Paltz, New York, 1971). Privately printed, 1971.

Novels

The Scorpions. New York, Doubleday, 1967; London, Calder and Boyars, 1969.

Cities. West Newbury, Massachusetts, Frontier Press, 1971.

Short Stories

Wheres. Santa Barbara, California, Black Sparrow Press, 1978.

A Transparent Tree: Ten Fictions. New Paltz, New York, McPherson, 1985.

Doctor of Silence. Kingston, New York, McPherson, 1988.

Cat Scratch Fever: Fictions. Kingston, New York, 1990.

Queen of Terrors: Fictions. Kingston, New York, McPherson, 1994.

Other

Statement. Los Angeles, Black Sparrow Press, 1968.

In Time (essays). West Newbury, Massachusetts, Frontier Press, 1971.

Sulphur. Privately printed, 1972.

A Line of Sight. Los Angeles, Black Sparrow Press, 1974.

How Do I Make Up My Mind, Lord? (for children). Minneapolis, Augsburg, 1982.

Under Words. Santa Barbara, California, Black Sparrow Press, 1983.

Editor, with Paris Leary, *A Controversy of Poets: An Anthology of Contemporary American Poetry.* New York, Doubleday, 1965.

Editor, *The Journals,* by Paul Blackburn. Los Angeles, Black Sparrow Press, 1975.

*

Bibliography: By Jed Rasula and Robert Bertholf, in *Credences* (Buffalo, New York), winter 1984/85.

Manuscript Collections: State University of New York, Buffalo; Kent State University, Ohio.

Critical Studies: By Paul Blackburn, in *Kulchur* (New York), 1962; *American Poetry from the Puritans to the Present* by Hyatt Waggoner, Boston, Houghton Mifflin, 1968; review by Diane Wakoski, in *Poetry* (Chicago), 1972; Robert Kelly issue of *Vort* (Bloomington, Indiana), 1974, and *Credences* (Buffalo, New York), winter 1984/85; "The Resurrection of Pan" by Paul Christensen, in *Southwest Review* (Dallas), 78(4), autumn 1993; "The Charred Heart of Polyphemus: Tantric Ecstasy and Shamanic Violence in Robert Kelly's 'The Loom'" by Edward Schelb, in *Contemporary Literature* (Madison, Wisconsin), 36(2), summer 1995; "A Rose to Look At: An Interview with Robert Kelly" by Larry McCaffery, in his *Some Other Fluency: Interviews with Innovative American Authors,* Philadelphia, University of Pennsylvania Press, 1996; *The Persuit of Persephone: The Healing Image of Robert Kelley* (dissertation) by Robert Kevin Gaither, Texas A&M University, 1996.

Robert Kelly comments:

What help can I give the reader who would come to my work? First, tell him it is not my work, only work itself, somehow arisen through (or in spite of) my instrumentality. My personality is its enemy, only distracts. But what is there for the reader who reads to find the man? He will find the man. The man is always there, the stink of him, the hope and fear he confuses with himself, the beauty of him, struggle, dim intuitions of a glory that is not personal but that only persons can inhabit and share. That we are human in the world and share our thoughts.

And this sharing of thought, perception, is what becomes the world. The world is our shared thought.

But in language the unperceived or newly perceived can arise to break the fabric of the ordinary consensus of our lives. News from nowhere, a new handle for an old day.

Invited to introduce my work to the general reader, never! The specific reader, I rehearse for our mutual benefit two answers my work has given, and I here transcribe. 1967. Prefix to *Finding the Measure:* Finding the measure is finding the mantram, is finding the moon, as index of measure, is finding the moon's source; if that source is Sun, finding the measure is finding the natural articulation of ideas. The organism of the macrocosm, the organism of language, the organism of I combine in ceaseless naturing to propagate a fourth, the poem, from their trinity. Style is death. Finding the measure is finding a freedom from that death, a way out, a movement forward. Finding the measure is finding the specific music of the hour, the synchronous consequence of the motion of the whole world. (Measure as distinct from meter, from any precompositional grid or matrix super-imposed upon the fact of the poem's own growth "under hand.") 1973. Prefix to *The Mill of Particulars:* Language is the only genetics. Field "in which a man is understood & understands" & becomes what he thinks, becomes what he says following the argument. When it is written that Hermes or Thoth invented language, it is meant that language is itself the psychopomp, who leads the Individuality out of Eternity into the conditioned world of Time, a world that language makes by discussing it. So the hasty road & path of arrow must lead up from language again & in language the work be done, work of light, beyond. Through manipulation and derangement of ordinary language (*parole*), the conditioned world is changed, weakened in its associative links, its power to hold an unconscious world-view (consensus) together. Eternity, which is always there, looms beyond the grid of speech. I have spoken a little about my motives and my intentions. I have not presumed to speak about the work itself, which must, true to its name, do its own work and try to lure the reader to dance with it.

*　　*　　*

Robert Kelly is an extraordinarily prolific poet. By the 1990s, when he had reached his mid-fifties, he had already published some fifty volumes, many of them quite substantial. Kelly's work is densely allusive, frequently compressed in style and expression, unconventional in syntax. His poems present particular difficulties to the reader, yet it must be asserted that more often than not they reward the reader's efforts. In a poet so prolific, though, there are areas of weakness: *The Common Shore,* for example, lacks the organic coherence of his best work, and for once Kelly's learning seems less than fully absorbed and rearticulated. He has, however, also produced a series of volumes that claim a significant place in the American poetry of the 1960s, 1970s, and 1980s, including *Finding the Measure, Songs I-XXX, Axon Dendron Tree, The Loom, The Mill of Particulars, The Alchemist to Mercury, Spiritual Exercises, Under Words,* and *Not This Island Music.*

For Kelly the poem is a process of search conducted through image and idea, an act of discovery that seeks its proper and natural form. At the center of his work is a vision of wholeness, and in terms of form his best poems are exemplary enactments of Coleridgean organic (as opposed to mechanic) form. The vision and the form are joined:

the shape of a man proceeds from all sides to center
and he is the star whose body is called movement
and in his hand the sun puts out branches
leaves and petals break out of silver
the corn is eaten, the animal howls, the sun flowers.

In the endnote to the 1971 collection *Flesh: Dream: Book,* Kelly explicates "the three great sources of human information" named in the book's title: the flesh—the universe as accessible to sensory experience; the dream—the associations and fusions of vision and dream; the book—human learning. The excitement of Kelly's work, at its best, is the effectiveness with which he integrates all of these sources of "information," the way in which the poetry refuses to exclude any of the three and finds language and form for all. Kelly is a learned poet who is never merely bookish, an erotic poet who thinks at all times of the spirit, a visionary poet rooted in the sensual.

Many of Kelly's central concerns as a poet are set out in his book of essays titled *In Time,* a good preparation for an exploration of the poems themselves. For Kelly the poet is "a scientist of holistic understanding / a scholar to whom all data whatsoever are of use" and "the DISCOVERER OF RELATION / redintigrator, / explorer of ultimate connection / & connectedness in among & all." In this quest for "relation," Kelly's major tools and processes include the mental and symbolic activities of alchemy and the Hermetic tradition, geography, history, and etymology. Alchemy is a model of transformation and perception, as is the recording of dreams. Kelly's work is fired by a sense of curiosity that is both intellectual and erotic. A declaration such as the following is far from casual in its employment of symbolic language: "Since we are men, in the human scale of time & space relationships, the discovery is of ourselves through the visible, of the visible through ourselves. The gateway is the visible; but we must go in." The "entrance" is pursued and effected through an enormously wide-ranging examination of human culture and through a ruthlessly honest process of self-analysis, the two being articulated in flexible verse possessed of an individual grace.

Kelly's work constitutes a particularly American extension of the romantic poetry of the "egotistical sublime":

. . . the subjective alone
has the value
of transcending time. And by a paradox
of being utterly personal
it transcends the limitations
of cultural presupposition . . .

In the precision and fullness with which it records the movements (and the ecstasies) of a particular and perceptive mind, there resides the "utterly personal," yet transcendent, quality of Kelly's poetry. God and sexuality, human emotion and cosmic motions, flesh and spirit dance together to and in an embracing music. The dance is perceived and articulated when its measure (and the poem's) is found: the "prefix" of *Finding the Measure* tells us that "finding the measure is finding the mantram / is finding the moon . . . / . . . is finding the specific music of the hour, / the synchronous / consequence of the motion of the whole world." Kelly's longer poems are sustained inquiries after that measure, and occasionally it is also found, perfected as it were, in his shorter poems, as in "A Measure":

Some nights the moon straight overhead is not far
it is a node in the spine, a woman
could easily reach it combing her hair.

—Glyn Pursglove

KENNEDY, X.J.

Pseudonym for Joseph Charles Kennedy. **Nationality:** American. **Born:** Dover, New Jersey, 21 August 1929. **Education:** Seton Hall College, South Orange, New Jersey, B.Sc. 1950; Columbia University, New York, M.A. 1951; Sorbonne, Paris, Cert. Litt. 1956. **Military Service:** U.S. Navy, 1951–55. **Family:** Married Dorothy Mintzlaff in 1962; one daughter and four sons. **Career:** Teaching fellow, 1956–60, and instructor, 1960–62, University of Michigan,

Ann Arbor; lecturer, University of North Carolina, Greensboro, 1962–63; assistant professor, 1963–67, associate professor, 1967–73, and professor of English, 1973–79, Tufts University, Medford, Massachusetts. Visiting lecturer, Wellesley College, Massachusetts, 1964, and University of California, Irvine, 1966–67; Bruern Fellow in American Literature, University of Leeds, 1974–75. Poetry editor, *Paris Review,* Paris and New York, 1962–64; editor, with Dorothy M. Kennedy, *Counter/Measures* magazine, 1972–74. **Awards:** Hopwood award, 1959; Bread Loaf Writers Conference fellowship, 1960; Lamont Poetry Selection award, 1961; Bess Hokin prize (*Poetry,* Chicago), 1961; National Endowment for the Arts grant, 1967; Shelley memorial award, 1970; Guggenheim fellowship, 1973; New England Poetry Club Golden Rose award, 1974; *Los Angeles Times* poetry book award, 1985; American Academy Braude award, 1989; Aiken Taylor award, University of the South, 1999. D.H.L.: Lawrence University, Appleton, Wisconsin, 1989. Honorary degrees: Adelphi University, Garden City, New York, 1998. **Agent:** Curtis Brown, 10 Astor Place, New York, New York 10003. **Address:** 22 Revere Street, Lexington, Massachusetts 02420, U.S.A.

PUBLICATIONS

Poetry

Nude Descending a Staircase: Poems, Song, A Ballad. New York, Doubleday, 1961.
Growing into Love. New York, Doubleday, 1969.
Bulsh. Providence, Rhode Island, Burning Deck, 1970.
Breaking and Entering. London, Oxford University Press, 1972.
Emily Dickinson in Southern California. Boston, Godine, 1974.
Celebrations after the Death of John Brennan. Lincoln, Massachusetts, Penmaen Press, 1974.
Three Tenors, One Vehicle: A Book of Songs, with James E. Camp and Keith Waldrop. Columbia, Missouri, Open Places, 1975.
French Leave: Translations. Florence, Kentucky, Barth, 1983.
Missing Link. Bedford, Massachusetts, Scheidt Head, 1983.
Hangover Mass. Cleveland, Ohio, Bits Press, 1984.
Cross Ties: Selected Poems. Athens, University of Georgia Press, 1985.
Winter Thunder. Florence, Kentucky, Barth, 1990.
Dark Horses: New Poems. Baltimore, Johns Hopkins University Press, 1992.
Jimmy Harlow. Anchorage, Alaska, Salmon Run Press, 1994.

Verse (for children)

One Winter Night in August and Other Nonsense Jingles. New York, Atheneum, 1975.
The Phantom Ice Cream Man: More Nonsense Jingles. New York, Atheneum, 1979.
Did Adam Name the Vinegarroon?. Boston, Godine, 1982.
The Forgetful Wishing-Well. New York, Atheneum, 1985.
Brats. New York, Atheneum, 1986.
Ghastlies, Goops, and Pincushions: Nonsense Verse. New York, McElderry, 1989.
Fresh Brats. New York, McElderry, 1990.
The Kite that Braved Old Orchard Beach. New York, McElderry, 1990.
The Beasts of Bethlehem. New York, McElderry, 1992.

Drat These Brats! New York, McElderry, 1993.
Uncle Switch. New York, McElderry, 1997.
Elympics. New York, Philomel, 1999.

Other

An Introduction to Poetry (textbook). Boston, Little Brown, 1966; revised edition, 1971, 1974, 1978, 1982, 1986; revised edition, Glenview, Illinois, Scott Foresman/Little Brown, 1991; revised edition, with Dana Gioia, New York, HarperCollins, 1994, New York, Longman, 1997.
An Introduction to Fiction. Boston, Little Brown, 1976; revised edition, 1979, 1983, 1987; revised edition, New York, HarperCollins, 1991, and with Dana Gioia, 1995, New York, Longman, 1997.
Literature: An Introduction to Fiction, Poetry, and Drama. Boston, Little Brown, 1976; revised edition, 1979, 1983, 1987; revised edition, New York, HarperCollins, 1991, and with Dana Gioia, 1995, New York, Longman, 1998.
Knock at a Star: A Child's Introduction to Poetry, with Dorothy M. Kennedy. Boston, Little Brown, 1982; revised edition, 1999.
The Owlstone Crown (for children). New York, McElderry, 1983.
The Bedford Guide for College Writers (textbook), with Dorothy M. Kennedy. New York, St. Martin's Press, 1987; revised edition, 1990; revised edition, with Dorothy M. Kennedy and Sylvia A. Holladay, 1993, 1996, 1999.

Editor, with James E. Camp, *Mark Twain's Frontier.* New York, Holt Rinehart, 1963.
Editor, with Keith Waldrop and James E. Camp, *Pegasus Descending: A Book of the Best Bad Verse.* New York, Macmillan, and London, Collier Macmillan, 1971.
Editor, *Messages: A Thematic Anthology of Poetry.* Boston, Little Brown, 1973.
Editor, *Tygers of Wrath: Poems of Hate, Anger, and Invective.* Athens, University of Georgia Press, 1981.
Editor, with Dorothy M. Kennedy, *The Bedford Reader.* Boston, Bedford Books, 1982; revised edition, New York, St. Martin's Press, 1985, 1988; revised edition, with Dorothy M. Kennedy and Jane E. Aaron, 1991, 1994, 1997, 2000.
Editor, with Dorothy M. Kennedy, *Talking Like the Rain: A Read-to-me Book of Poems.* Boston, Little, Brown, 1992.
Editor, *The Eagle As Wide As the World* (for children). New York, McElderry, 1997.

Translator, *Lysistrata* by Aristophanes. Philadelphia, Penn Greek Drama Series, University of Pennsylvania Press, 1999.

*

Critical Studies: ''Squibs'' by Bernard Waldrop, in *Burning Deck* 2 (Providence, Rhode Island), spring 1963; ''Recent Poetry: The End of an Era'' by Louis L. Martz, in *Yale Review* (New Haven, Connecticut), winter 1970; Stephen Tudor, in *Spirit* (South Orange, New Jersey), spring 1970; Henry Taylor, in *Masterplots Annual,* New York, Salem Press, 1970; in *Times Literary Supplement* (London), 24 December 1971; M.L. Rosenthal, in *Shenandoah* (Lexington, Virginia), fall 1972; David Shapiro, in *Poetry* (Chicago), July 1976; Jeffrey D. Hoeper, in *Critical Survey of Poetry* edited by Frank N.

Magill, Englewood Cliffs, New Jersey, Salem Press, 1983; *Fallen from the Symboled World* by Wyatt Prundy, New York, Oxford University Press, 1990; "The Decline of Satire and the Specialist Society: Some Thoughts on the Poetry of X.J. Kennedy" by Richard Moore, in *Light* (Chicago), autumn 1992; by Emily Grosholz, in *The Hudson Review* (New York), autumn 1993; by Robert B. Shaw, in *Poetry* (Chicago), October 1993; by William Matthews, in *Shenandoah* (Lexington, Kentucky), winter 1993; "Rich in Discipline" by Ghita Orth, in *New England Review* (Middlebury, Vermont), spring 1994; X.J. Kennedy issue of *Paintbrush* (Kirksville, Missouri), autumn 1998.

X.J. Kennedy comments:

[I belong to] the Wolgamot school, a group of young poets including Donald Hall, W.D. Snodgrass, and Keith Waldrop, centering around the literary historian John Barton Wolgamot and begun at the University of Michigan in the 1950s.

Nearly always write in rhyme and meter. Favor narratives, lyrics to be sung.

(1995)Over the years I have labored under two curses, both of them labels pinned on me by early reviewers. The first is that I am a trivial light versifier. True enough, I am that sometimes but would hold that there is also such a thing as light poetry. Moreover, it seems to me that poetry can be, as W.H. Auden put it, a clear expression of mixed feelings, and so in some of my writing I have tried to blend laughter with compassion or grief.

The second curse is the label of bookish or scholarly poet, one who writes for full professors only. That label puzzles me, for I would be hard pressed to find in my work more than a handful of things that might call for footnotes. On the contrary, I have always addressed a popular audience, regardless of the fact that the popular audience has usually turned a deaf ear or gone to the dog races instead.

Since 1975 I have had the immense joy and good fortune to have written ten books of verse for children, nine of them for Margaret McElderry, a sympathetic editor-publisher. Writing verse for children calls for just as much work as writing verse for adults. The nice thing about children is that they do not give a hoot about literary fashion. You can write for them in rhymed and rhythmic stanzas if you like, and they will not mind a bit.

*   *   *

Although he occasionally writes in free verse, X.J. Kennedy has been an insistent rhymer from the beginning, and for several years he coedited a journal that catered to poets similarly inclined. In midcareer he issued this "warning to possible consumers": "Kennedy tends to write in strict riming stanza patterns, which old-fangled structures most poets have junked these days ... What I like is song and balladry; the freedom of not having to express myself, not being obliged to write what the top of my head thinks ought to be written."

Although his work is generally well known and frequently anthologized, Kennedy is seldom regarded as one of the more influential poets of his time. My wager is, nonetheless, that several of his poems, including "In a Prominent Bar on Secaucus One Day" and "Nude Descending a Staircase," will be read and, more importantly, recited from memory long after the "influential" names have disappeared in the dust.

The latter poem, inspired by a Marcel Duchamp painting that scandalized New York's Armory Show art crowd in 1913, opens with this near perfect stanza:

Toe upon toe, a snowing flesh
A gold of lemon, root and rind,
She sifts in sunlight down the stairs
With nothing on, nor on her mind

The combination of wit, precise language, and song, unexcelled by almost any American poet past or present, stays in one's memory in a way that more studiously "profound," but ultimately more ephemeral, verses seldom do.

Originally from a Roman Catholic background, Kennedy has written several poems that convey the elemental character of his place and time (before Vatican II, that is), such as "Hangover Mass" and "First Confession," which begins,

Blood thudded in my ears. I scuffed,
Steps stubborn, to the telltale booth
Beyond whose curtained portal coughed
The robed repositor of truth.

Kennedy's early poems, including the one just mentioned, resemble the best work of Karl Shapiro—"Drug Store," "Auto Wreck," or "University"—and of others who give back the exact dimension and character of particular moments in history. In such renderings of a world gone by all unnecessary commentary is stripped away. "Pottery Class," one of Kennedy's incisive portraits of middle-class suburban life circa 1960, begins, for example,

On Wednesday nights, the children rinsed and stacked,
The wives, their husbands closeted with *Time,*
From Lexington and Concord motor in
To travail in this elemental slime.

Like any good comic artist, Kennedy writes about serious matters—death, violence, suicide, our decline and fall—and always with a knowledge of earlier writers in that sometimes irreverent, sometimes bawdy tradition. Occasionally he parodies an earlier versifier—Robert Herrick, Lewis Carroll, or Robert Frost—or appropriates a Greek myth to his own purposes, as in "Narcissus Suitor":

He touched her face and gooseflesh crept—
He loved her as it were
Not for her look though it lay deep
But what he saw in her.

Another time, as in "Creation Morning," where he appropriates a theme from Genesis and Milton, Kennedy makes a philosophical or theological point in an offhand way about elemental concerns:

Needing nothing, not lonely nor bored,
Why should He have let there be light!
We can only guess.

In every case Kennedy's art is exacting; he takes language and form seriously, so that even when a poem falters, it does so because too much, rather than too little, effort shows through.

A traditionalist, Kennedy is a clever imitator of many forms, as in "Great Chain of Being" and "Talking Dust Bowl." A similar intelligence and skill are evident in the appropriately adolescent, raucous, or jaded poems about sex, including "The Flagellant's

Song,'' ''Onan's Soliloquy,'' and ''The Aged Wino's Counsel to a Young Man on the Brink of Marriage.'' In ''The Self-Exposed,'' a wicked parody of the confessional poet's lament, the speaker understands his impulse to ''bare all'' as an effort at communication, a search for community:

> What gets into me?
> I'm not one to be peter-proud,
> But my bird-out-of-hand longs to take its stand
> On the farther side from what's allowed . . .
>
> Oh, I've been to psychiatrist and priest,
> I've read an uplifting book
> But it's cold, and I hunger to walk forth dressed
> In the quilt of the world's warm look.

Kennedy's carefully arranged *Cross Ties: Selected Poems* organizes itself around the longer poems of the period 1956–84 and his songs, light verse, epigrams, and children's verses, including the characteristically irreverent ''Mother's Nerves'':

> My mother said, ''If just once more
> I hear you slam that old screen door
> I'll tear out my hair! I'll dive in the stove!''
> I gave it a bang, and in she dove.

In his selection the author unfortunately omits some serious lyrics from the 1960s, but he includes previously uncollected works. He concludes appropriately with ''Envio,'' saying, ''Go, slothful book. Just go.''

—Michael True

KENNELLY, (Timothy) Brendan

Nationality: Irish. **Born:** Ballylongford, County Kerry; 17 April 1936. **Education:** St. Ita's College, Tarbert, County Kerry; 1948–53; Trinity College, Dublin, B.A. (honors) in English and French, 1961, M.A. 1963, Ph.D. 1967; Leeds University. **Family:** Married Margaret O'Brien in 1969; one daughter. **Career:** Junior lecturer, 1963–66, lecturer, 1966–69, associate professor, 1969–73, and since 1973 professor of modern literature, Trinity College, Dublin. Guildersleeve Professor, Barnard College, New York, 1971; Cornell Professor of English Literature, Swarthmore College, Pennsylvania, 1971–72. **Awards:** AE Memorial award, 1967; the Ireland Funds literary award, 1999. **Address:** Trinity College, Dublin, Ireland.

PUBLICATIONS

Poetry

Cast a Cold Eye, with Rudi Holzapfel. Dublin, Dolmen Press, 1959.
The Rain, The Moon, with Rudi Holzapfel. Dublin, Dolmen Press, 1961.

The Dark about Our Loves, with Rudi Holzapfel. Dublin, John Augustine, 1962.
Green Townlands, with Rudi Holzapfel. Leeds, Bibliographical Press, 1963.
Let Fall No Burning Leaf. Dublin, New Square, 1963.
My Dark Fathers. Dublin, New Square, 1964.
Up and At It. Dublin, New Square, 1965.
Collection One: Getting Up Early. Dublin, Allen Figgis, 1966.
Good Souls to Survive. Dublin, Allen Figgis, 1967.
Dream of a Black Fox. Dublin, Allen Figgis, 1968.
Selected Poems. Dublin, Allen Figgis, 1969; New York, Dutton, 1971.
A Drinking Cup: Poems from the Irish. Dublin, Allen Figgis, 1970.
Bread. Dublin, Tara Telephone, 1971.
Love-Cry. Dublin, Allen Figgis, 1972.
Salvation, The Stranger. Dublin, Tara Telephone, 1972.
The Voices: A Sequence of Poems. Dublin, Gallery Press, 1973.
Shelley in Dublin. Dublin, Dublin Magazine Press, 1974; revised edition, Dublin, Beaver Row Press, 1982.
A Kind of Trust. Dublin, Gallery Press, 1975.
New and Selected Poems, edited by Peter Fallon. Dublin, Gallery Press, 1976.
Islandman. Dublin, Profile Press, 1977.
The Visitor. Dublin, St. Beuno's Press, 1978.
A Small Light. Dublin, Gallery Press, 1979.
In Spite of the Wise. Dublin, Trinity Closet Press, 1979.
The Boats Are Home. Dublin, Gallery Press, 1980.
The House That Jack Didn't Build. Dublin, Beaver Row Press, 1982.
Cromwell. Dublin, Beaver Row Press, 1983; Newcastle upon Tyne, Bloodaxe, 1987.
Moloney Up and At It. Dublin, Mercier Press, 1984.
A Time for Voices: Selected Poems 1960–1990. Newcastle upon Tyne, Bloodaxe, 1990.
The Book of Judas: A Poem. Newcastle upon Tyne, Bloodaxe, 1991.
Breathing Spaces: Early Poems. Newcastle upon Tyne, Bloodaxe, 1992.
Poetry My Arse. Newcastle upon Tyne, Bloodaxe, 1995.
The Man Made of Rain. Newcastle upon Tyne, Bloodaxe, 1998.
The Singing Tree. Newry, Abbey Press, 1998.
Begin. Newcastle upon Tyne, Bloodaxe, 1999.

Recording: *Living Ghosts: Poems by Brendan Kennelly,* Livia, 1982.

Play

Medea, adaptation of a play by Euripides (produced London, 1989). As *Euripedes' Medea: A New Version.* Newcastle upon Tyne, Bloodaxe, 1991.
Euripedes' The Trojan Women: A New Version. Newcastle upon Tyne, Bloodaxe, 1993.
Antigone, adaptation of a play by Sophocles (produced 1996).
Blood Wedding, adaptation of a play by Lorca (produced 1996).

Novels

The Crooked Cross. Dublin, Allen Figgis, 1963; Boston, Little Brown, 1964.
The Florentines. Dublin, Allen Figgis, 1967.

Other

Real Ireland, photographs by Liam Blake. Belfast, Appletree, 1984; San Francisco, Chronicle, 1988.

Myth, History, and Literary Tradition, with Thomas Kinsella and John Montague. Dundalk, Dundalk Arts Publications, 1989.

Journey into Joy: Selected Prose. Newcastle upon Tyne, Bloodaxe, 1994.

Editor, *The Penguin Book of Irish Verse.* London, Penguin, 1970; revised edition, 1972, 1981.

Editor, *Ireland Past and Present.* Dublin, Gallery Press, and London, Macmillan, 1986.

Editor, *Landmarks of Irish Drama.* London. Methuen, 1988.

Editor, with A. Norman Jeffares, *JoyceChoyce: The Poems in Verse and Prose of James Joyce.* London, Kyle Cathie Limited, 1992.

*

Critical Studies: B.A. thesis by Antonella Ceoletta, University of Venice, 1973; M.Litt. thesis by Frances Gwynn, Trinity College, Dublin, 1974; ''Poetry and Social Perspectives: Brendan Kennelly's Shelley in Dublin'' by Erwin Otto, in *Etudes Irlandaises* (Villeneuve d'Ascq, France), 1, 1976; ''Ireland's Antigones: Tragedy North and South'' by Anthony Roche, in *Cultural Contexts and Literary Idioms in Contemporary Irish Literature,* edited by Michael Kenneally, Totowa, New Jersey, Barnes and Noble, 1988; ''Poetic Forms and Social Malformations'' by Edna Longley, in *Tradition and Influence in Anglo-Irish Poetry,* edited by Terence Brown and Nicholas Grene, Totowa, New Jersey, Barnes and Noble, 1989; ''Brendan Kennelly, Instrument of Peace'' by Bernetta Quinn, in *Antigonish Review* (Antigonish, Nova Scotia), 83, Autumn 1990; ''Brendan Kennelly: Victors and Victims'' by Gerard Quinn, in *Irish Review,* 9, Fall 1990; *Dark Fathers into Light* edited by Richard Pine, Newcastle upon Tyne, Bloodaxe, 1994; ''Betraying the Age: Brendan Kennelly's Mission'' by Ake Persson, in *Irish University Review,* 26(1), Spring/ Summer 1996.

Brendan Kennelly comments:

I used to divide my poetry into rather facile categories, such as poems written about the countryside, poems written about the city, and poems that tried to express some sort of personal philosophy. I think now that such categories are false, and I believe instead that I select appropriate images from aspects of my experience and try to use them in such a way that they express what goes on within. This involves a continued struggle to discover and develop a proper language, carefully selected from the words of the world in which I live. There is this continual battle between civilized sluggishness and sharp seeing, seeing into. The poem is born the moment one sees into and through one's world and when one expresses that seeing into in a totally appropriate language. By totally appropriate, I mean a language of complete alertness. As I try to write, I know that I am involved in an activity that is a deliberate assertion of energy over indifference, of vitality over deadness, of excitement and ecstasy over dullness and cynicism. Yet the poem must take account of all these negatives. In fact, it must often use them as its raw material but, by a sort of dynamic, inner alchemy of language, rhythm, and image, transform those negatives into living forms.

*   *   *

Irish poet Brendan Kennelly's work is characterized by a great assurance of voice, by a certainty of rhythmic form, and by a wide range of subject matter, His craftsmanship is impeccable. A poem such as ''The Feeding Dark'' is an object lesson in the creative counterpointing of sentence and stanza structures. ''Six of One'' and ''Law and Order'' demonstrate two very different, but equally accomplished, uses of the sonnet. ''The Singing Girl Is Easy in Her Skill'' shows him using the villanelle for effects of great beauty and poignancy, and, to very different effect, the same form is employed in ''And Who Will Judge the Judges in Their Time.'' Elsewhere his free verse is vigorous and controlled.

Among his characteristic subjects are the inevitability and variety of human failure (''The Cherrytrees,'' *Shelley in Dublin,* ''In Spite of the Wise''), his Irish childhood (''The Brightest of All,'' ''The Kiss''), Irish rural landscape and life (''The Pig-killer,'' ''Killybegs,'' ''Carrig''), the energy of animal life (''Dream of a Black Fox,'' ''The Feeding Dark,'' ''Outside the Church''), and the nature of invasion and colonization (''Six of One'' and ''The House That Jack Didn't Build''). *Shelley in Dublin* is not entirely successful as a public poem on, among other things, the relation of England and Ireland. (It deals with Shelley's revolutionary mission to Dublin in 1812). Unusually for Kennelly, there is some flatness of rhythm and a failure to vivify the personalities involved. ''The House That Jack Didn't Build,'' on the other hand, is altogether more convincing. The two voices (''a man convinced of his own indisputable superiority and a man capable of being conquered, but also capable of resisting his conquerors'') are dramatically alive, humorous, and moving by turns-

> I changed all the rooms.
> This took me quite a while.
> Visitors comment on their style.
> It's simple. I do everything well,
> Not exactly, to be fair, in a spirit of love
> But with a genuine desire to improve
> Others, particularly

and:

> I have lost touch with my own language.
> Nothing is stranger to me than what is my own.
> I am an exile from myself.
> Words are stones in my mouth.
> The bones of my head are trampled on.

The capacity for the dramatic assumption of other voices, evidenced in ''The House That Jack Didn't Build,'' lies behind the success of Kennelly's ''Moloney'' poems and sequences such as *Islandman.* He has spoken of the use of persona as ''a method of extending the self by driving out the demons of embarrassment and inhibition.'' Both by this means and in more purely ''personal'' poems, Kennelly has produced telling, and frequently very beautiful, analyses of both the specifically Irish and the universal human experience.

—Glyn Pursglove

KHAIR, Tabish

Nationality: Indian (permanent resident of Denmark). **Born:** Ranchi, Bihar, India, 21 March 1966. **Education:** Magadh University, Gaya, Bihar, India, B.A. in English (honors), sociology, and history, 1986, M.A. 1990; University of Copenhagen, Denmark (Ph.D. Merit Scholarship), Ph.D. 1999. **Family:** Married Trine O. Jensen in 1993. **Career:** Teacher, Nazareth Academy, Gaya Bihar, India, 1986; district reporter, *The Times of India*, Patna, Bihar, India, 1986–87; staff reporter, *The Times of India,* Delhi, India, 1990–93; editor, European Telecommunications Office, Copenhagen, 1996–97; external lecturer, 1998–99, and lecturer, 1999–2001, Copenhagen University. **Awards:** National Essay Competition prize, Indian Council of Philosophical Research, Delhi, India, 1986–87; Essay Competition prize, League of Arab States Mission, Delhi, India, 1989–90; Travel award, Idella Foundation, Denmark, 1994; first prize, All India Poetry Competition, 1995–96. **Address:** Roarsvej 14 st. tv., 2000 Frederiksberg, Denmark.

PUBLICATIONS

Poetry

My World. Delhi, India, Rupa, 1991.
A Reporter's Diary. Delhi, India, Rupa, 1993.
The Book of Heroes: A Collection of Light Verse and Much Worse. Delhi, India, Rupa, 1995.
Where Parallel Lines Meet. Delhi, India, Penguin, 2000.

Novel

An Angel in Pyjamas. Delhi, India, HarperCollins, 1996.

Other

Baby Fictions. Delhi, India, Oxford University Press, 2000.

*   *   *

Tabish Khair is one of a number of Indian poets from Muslim backgrounds who live and teach abroad. Such poets are from the liberal, modernizing, secular side of Islam that includes ideas of social justice. In "The Streets of My Poems" he says,

In all my poems I simply walk the streets of my town
    once again;
Unable to leave behind men and women pitching tar
On the hot roads, muscles straining in the sun;
Unable to forget that old beggar sleeping in the shade.

My World mostly concerns home and homes, the world Khair knew and that returns in his imagination. The ugliness in the poems is a projection of the speaker's dissatisfaction with his society. Images of the morning (it feels like mourning) enter his consciousness "like water from the dry, sputtering tap outside." An aged former sailor has been drinking all night "and still lies huddled in the ordure." And "Old Mr. Rao comes out into his patched and peeling porch / With a brush between toothless gums / And stands lost in memories of lost passion."

Khair has thought about the kinds of English and rhythms appropriate for writing about Bihar. There is the slightly older diction of "ordure" and "whilst" that suggests a place lost in time; the poem's conclusion speaks of "yesterday and the days before." There is the implication of such diction that English is a literary language to these people, a language likely to be learned from books rather than spoken. The poetry is formal, with each of the five lines of each stanza conforming to normal syntactical units, and there is repetition of words and alliteration. The rhythms are unusual, as if purposefully departing from Anglo-Indian speech. Khair's poetry often has an off-centered tone and manner, as if he were aiming more for a nuanced regional or class characteristic than for the usual ways of representing Indian English.

The India of decay and of a past in which nothing happens is not always bad; in contrast to the modern world, it has a rootedness. In "House with the Grey Gate" the gate is useless, being "off one hinge and always open," while an old woman on the porch looks up whenever the gate creaks in the wind, "expecting someone; though no one comes, nor has for years." In the garden "shrubbery has spread, refusing to be weeded out," which serves as an analogy for "the old man and the old woman and an old pattern of life— / refusing to be weeded out from this skyscraping street." This is in contrast with the next poem, where, after the speaker and his friend have sat in a café discussing Durkheim's *Le Suicide,* that night his friend commits suicide. Suicide results from the anomie of modern urban life, a condition shown in the next poem, "After Work," in which the speaker has "nothing to look forward to," the streets seem "endless," the faces are those of strangers, and his apartment and heart are empty.

Other poems in *My World* speak of recurring communal tensions and proclaim a private world of the "weak" that exists alongside the road "as you drive to office, five days a week":

The walls of my world are made of clay and straw.
Water trickles in from a rent in its roof, mixing
    with my food;
But, on clear and calm nights, the stars come visiting me.
(I know all my little stars, each by its name,
Though you have probably never heard of them—
They are so small, they would be lost in your world.)

This world of the weak and poor who are close to nature will last, like those weeds of an older way of life, after the ruins of the regimented, impersonal, "prouder worlds, larger worlds" are gone.

Many of the short poems in "My India Diary" concern memories of the pains, limitations, and continuing influence of home: "to tear away your roots / wrench free / i will have to take myself apart / brick by brick." The villages are places from which "all roads lead out / / except during elections," but for those who leave such communities "where did the aloneness end / and loneliness start"?

Khair sees life as a short period of existence before nothingness. As reality causes us to be fearful, we need to make something of life, and Khair's solution is writing. *A Reporter's Diary* takes up the idea of a diary from *My World* but has death rather than home as its central theme. In "To Gyanendara" the poet recalls his dead friend: "I shall be true to us. I shall believe your death. / We knew heads are shaven in vain, graves contain emptiness, / That there is no soul to start with and no flesh after a month." The common poetic trope of returning to nature, a view consistent with Hinduism and Buddhism, is treated with irony: "The dead will live in bits and pieces scattered over the land. / The living will die in bits and pieces in the slush and sand.'' The next poem, ''The Young and the Old,'' continues the theme. Life is found to be like an onion peeled to the core: ''At the end, there was nothing to hold, to show . . . / Except, of course, the inevitable tears in the eyes.''

Many of the poems are small narrative allegories of life as seen from a materialist perspective: ''Only the dead stay in one place. / The living are condemned to movement''; ''This, perhaps, was the curse of Adam and Eve— / Having left home once, never to find home again.'' Life consists of anxieties. ''Fear'' is a recurring word, and there are two sonnets on fear. Writing is a way to seek refuge from the fear of nothingness, where we are ''hurled / from sense to senselessness.'' There are no peaceful deaths; there is always ''blood and screaming inside the head.'' The concluding poem claims that ''happiness is a word scribbled on sand,'' but if you can ignore the way the tide erases happiness, there are blue skies and a wide beach on which to write a future. Khair's imagery can be seen as ironic, or perhaps he is suggesting a revolutionary future.

Khair's vocabulary is simple and easy to follow, yet there is a coherent intellectual vision. He also has an instinct for light verse, the subjects of which are sometimes, but not always, related to his serious poetry. In the ironically titled *The Book of Heroes: A Collection of Light Verse and Much Worse* the subjects include the politician of ''The Caangrassman,'' whose ''men adore him; they are paid to, / And if you don't agree they'll 'convince' you!'' Many poems make fun of the pretenses of the professional classes. There is the paradox in ''The Dentist, Ah!'' of a man who ''tortures you like no one can, / and gets a hefty fee.'' And there is the newspaper editor who ''just a week after each tragedy . . . warned against it prophetically.''

—Bruce King

KHALVATI, Mimi

Nationality: Iranian. **Born:** Tehran, 28 April 1944. **Education:** University of Neuchatel and Drama Centre, London. **Family:** Married 1970 (divorced 1985); two children. **Career:** Actress and director, Theatre Workshop, Tehran; co-founder, Theatre in Exile. Coordinator, the Poetry School, London. **Address:** 2 North Hill Avenue, London N6 4RJ, England.

PUBLICATIONS

Poetry

I Know a Place (for children). London, Dent, 1985.
Persian Miniatures/A Belfast Kiss. Huddersfield, England, 1990.
In White Ink. Manchester, Carcanet, 1991.
Mirrorwork. Manchester, Carcanet, 1995.
Entries on Light. Manchester, Carcanet, 1997.
Selected Poems. Manchester, Carcanet, 2000.

*

Critical Study: By John Killick, in *Poetry Review,* 85(2), summer 1995.

*   *   *

Mimi Khalvati's poetry takes as its material a life spent between two countries: Iran and England. She is one of a growing number of poets writing in English for whom the English language is more than a poetic medium; it is also an adopted mother tongue. Educated in England, Khalvati did not speak Farsi as a young woman. Yet in her poems she attempts to infuse English with the inflections and richness of the other language, just as she infuses her experiences in England with her memories of another place.

Khalvati is a poet whose work follows the multiple strands of identity. ''Woman, Stone, Book,'' the first poem in *In White Ink,* focuses on a woman's attempt to define and comprehend herself and is based on a serious of symbols that appear in dreams. The symbols, the stone in particular, reappear in the course of the book, and the poem itself seems to state its project: to ''pick up / threads going every which way knowing / it can't matter much which thread / I choose to follow.'' In this poem the midrhythm line breaks create a sense of breathlessness, evoking the confusion inherent in such a complex search for identity.

Khalvati can also create a sense of coherence and calm in her poems. While fragmentation remains her subject, her form puts the pieces together in poems such as ''Amanuensis.'' Here smartly rhyming quatrains frame the poet's address to ''Mirza'' (Farsi for ''scribe''). In the course of the poem the speaking scribe (Khalvati herself) and the scribe she addresses seem to become one and the same. The poet commands,

So leave your sacks of grain

my Mirza, your ledgers and your abacus. Turn back
to brighter skills than these:
your mirrors and mosaics. From each trapezium,
polygon, each small isosceles

face, extract me, entwine me. Be my double
helix! My polestar! My asterisks!

Khalvati plays on the concept of ''Mirza'' as both poet and astrologer. The lovely rhyme between ''these'' and ''isosceles'' suggests that the speaker is attracted to the neatness of geometry, and the line break after the word ''double'' establishes the mirror relationship between the speaker and the person spoken to. Of course, Khalvati has prepared us for this firm, formal gesture with the command that precedes it. Her insistence that the scribe ''turn back'' reflects both aesthetic and cultural longing. Just as the speaker longs for a bright, reflective art (poetry, we might assume), she also seems to be recalling and reimagining her homeland of Iran.

These subjects—art and national identity—while broad on the face of things, occupy Khalvati's poems in an intensely personal way. Some of the longer poems in *In White Ink* traverse the past with greater depth, taking ''Amanuensis'' up on its challenge. In ''Plant Care: A Poem for the Change'' Khalvati juxtaposes individual aging (menopause) with shifts in the speaker's perception of home. The poem unfolds in fourteen vignettes in which memory proceeds from multiple versions of Proust's madeleines: a wasp, a cactus. These triggers lead to lyrical meditations on maternal love—and the loss of it—and memories of childhood, until it seems at last that what has been lost is the mother country. What is this homeland? ''It is a dispossession,'' we are finally told; ''I hear no footfall, see no change.''

Mirrorwork, Khalvati's second collection, continues to explore personal, familial, and cultural dispossession as its central themes. The book consists of three long sequences—at the beginning, middle, and end—with brief lyrics interspersed. *Mirrorwork*'s title poem, the first of the long sequences, is perhaps most representative of the book's themes and structures. Here the art of mirror mosaics, that same "brighter skill" alluded to in "Amanuensis," returns as a metaphor for cultural difference and internal fractures. Wholeness and singularity escape the viewer (and the reader) when she faces, even becomes, "the mirrorwork in which not even Kings / can see themselves." Everything in the poem has a double, a reflection, yet no two things are exactly the same. One of the predominant pairs of opposites is nature and artifice. As she seeks to understand the difference between English and Persian mirrorwork, the speaker is pressed to determine what is real and what is reflection. Focusing on the image of a cherry tree, the poem's complex figure for childhood, Khalvati curtails our modern attachment to "the thing itself":

> I've curtained off the tree today,
> pretending that her half of the sky is
> greyer, wetter, more opaque. The
> half I see through, where no tree is,
> is lighter actual.

Here Khalvati finds the "actual" in what is not there, emphasizing again that dispossession is the most real thing. Yet Khalvati's poems do not despair regarding "severance, / a loss of context." Rather, the poet seems to perceive a special beauty in this fragmentation, as when "willow branches bifurcate into angels' wings, epaulettes amassing, dripping silver," even when she sees "voices thrown, disowned."

Khalvati maintains a cohesive and powerful voice even as she allows that same voice to splinter before our eyes. Through her careful command of language and line she creates a poetic landscape in which memory of the actual and imagination of the possible peacefully, if not calmly, coexist.

—Sonya B. Posmentier

KINNELL, Galway

Nationality: American. **Born:** Providence, Rhode Island, 1 February 1927. **Education:** Princeton University, New Jersey, A.B. 1948; University of Rochester, New York, M.A. 1949. **Military Service:** U.S. Navy, 1945–46. **Family:** Married 1) Inés Delgado de Torres in 1965 (divorced 1984), one daughter and one son, 2) Barbara K. Bristol in 1998. **Career:** Instructor in English, Alfred University, New York, 1949–51; supervisor of liberal arts program, University of Chicago, 1951–55; American Lecturer, University of Grenoble, 1956–57; Summer session lecturer, University of Nice, 1957; Fulbright Lecturer, University of Iran, Tehran, 1959–60; poet-in-residence/visiting writer, Juniata College, Huntingdon, Pennsylvania, 1964, Reed College, Portland, Oregon, 1966–67, Colorado State University, Fort Collins, 1968, University of Washington, Seattle, 1968, University of California, Irvine, 1968–69, Deya Institute, Mallorca, 1969–70, University of Iowa, Iowa City, 1970, Sarah Lawrence College, Bronxville, New York, 1972–78, Princeton University, New Jersey, 1976, Holy Cross College, 1977, and Macquarie University, Sydney, 1979; visiting professor, Pittsburgh Poetry Forum, 1971, Queens College, New York, 1971, Columbia University, New York, 1972, 1974, 1976, Brandeis University, Waltham, Massachusetts, 1974, Skidmore College, Saratoga Springs, New York, 1975, University of Delaware, Newark, 1978, and University of Hawaii, Manoa, Honolulu, 1979–80; DeRoy Honors Professor, University of Michigan, Ann Arbor, 1987. Since 1979 director, Squaw Valley Community of Writers. Erich Maria Remarque Professor of creative writing, New York University. **Awards:** Ford grant, 1955; Fulbright scholarship, 1955; Longview Foundation award, 1962; American Academy grant, 1962, and Medal of Merit, 1976; Guggenheim fellowship, 1963, 1974; Bess Hokin prize, 1965, and Eunice Tietjens memorial prize, 1966 (*Poetry,* Chicago); Rockefeller grant, 1967; Cecil Hemley prize, 1968; Brandeis University Creative Arts award, 1968; National Endowment for the Arts grant, 1969; Ingram Merrill Foundation award, 1969; Amy Lowell traveling fellowship, 1969; Shelley memorial award, 1972; Academy of American Poets Landon translation award, 1978; American Book award, 1983; Pulitzer Prize, 1983; MacArthur fellowship, 1984. Member, American Academy, 1981. **Address:** Sheffield, Vermont 05866, U.S.A.

PUBLICATIONS

Poetry

What a Kingdom It Was. Boston, Houghton Mifflin, 1960.

Flower Herding on Mount Monadnock. Boston, Houghton Mifflin, 1964.

Poems of Night. London, Rapp and Carroll, 1968.

Body Rags. Boston, Houghton Mifflin, 1968; London, Rapp and Whiting, 1969.

Far Behind Me on the Trail. New York, Profile Press, 1969.

The Hen Flower. Frensham, Surrey, Sceptre Press, 1970.

First Poems 1946–1954. Mount Horeb, Wisconsin, Perishable Press, 1970.

The Book of Nightmares. Boston, Houghton Mifflin, 1971; London, J. Jay, 1978.

The Shoes of Wandering. Mount Horeb, Wisconsin, Perishable Press, 1971.

The Avenue Bearing the Initial of Christ into the New World: Poems 1946–1964. Boston, Houghton Mifflin, 1974.

Three Poems. New York, Phoenix Book Shop, 1976.

Brother of My Heart. Canberra, Open Door Press, 1977.

Fergus Falling. Newark, Vermont, Janus Press, 1979.

There Are Things I Tell to No One. New York, Nadja, 1979.

Two Poems. Newark, Vermont, Janus Press, 1979.

Mortal Acts, Mortal Words. Boston, Houghton Mifflin, 1980.

The Last Hiding Places of Snow. New York, Red Ozier Press, 1980.

Angling, A Day, and Other Poems. Concord, New Hampshire, William B. Ewert, 1980.

Selected Poems. Boston, Houghton Mifflin, 1982; London, Secker and Warburg, 1984.

Woodsmen. Riverside, California, Rara Avis Press, 1982.

The Fundamental Project of Technology. Concord, New Hampshire, Ewert, 1983.

The Seekonk Woods. Concord, New Hampshire, Ewert, 1985.

The Past. Boston, Houghton Mifflin, 1985; London, Secker and Warburg, 1986.

When One Has Lived a Long Time Alone. New York, Alfred A. Knopf, 1990.

Three Books. Boston, Houghton Mifflin, 1993.

Imperfect Thirst. Boston, Houghton Mifflin, 1994.

A New Selected Poems. Boston, Houghton Mifflin, 2000.

Recordings: *Today's Poets 5,* with others, Folkways; *The Poetry and Voice of Galway Kinnell,* Caedmon, 1976.

Novel

Black Light. Boston, Houghton Mifflin, 1966; London, Hart Davis, 1967; revised edition, Berkeley, California, North Point Press, 1980; Paris, Mercure de France, 1994.

Other

3 Self-Evaluations, with Anthony Ostroff and Winfield Townley Scott. Beloit, Wisconsin, Beloit Poetry Journal, 1953.

The Poetics of the Physical World. Fort Collins, Colorado State University, 1969.

Walking Down the Stairs: Selections from Interviews. Ann Arbor, University of Michigan Press, 1978.

How the Alligator Missed Breakfast (for children). Boston, Houghton Mifflin, 1982.

Thoughts Occasioned by the Most Insignificant of Human Events. Concord, New Hampshire, Ewert, 1982.

The Fundamental Project of Technology. Concord, New Hampshire, Ewert, 1983.

Remarks on Accepting the American Book Award. Concord, New Hampshire, Ewert, 1984.

Editor, *The Essential Whitman.* New York, Ecco Press, 1987.

Translator, *Bitter Victory,* by Réne Hardy. New York, Doubleday, and London, Hamish Hamilton, 1956.

Translator, *Pre-Columbian Ceramics,* by Henri Lehmann. London, Elek, 1962.

Translator, *The Poems of François Villon.* New York, New American Library, 1965.

Translator, *On the Motion and Immobility of Douve,* by Yves Bonnefoy. Athens, Ohio University Press, 1968.

Translator, *The Lackawanna Elegy,* by Yvan Goll. Fremont, Michigan, Sumac Press, 1970.

Translator, *The Poems of François Villon.* Boston, Houghton Mifflin, 1977.

Translator, *Poems,* by Villon. Hanover, New Hampshire, University Press of New England, 1982.

Translator, with Hannah Liebmann, *The Essential Rilke.* New Jersey, Ecco Press, 1999.

*

Bibliography: *Galway Kinnell: A Bibliography and Index of His Published Works and Criticism of Them,* Potsdam, New York, State University College Frederick W. Crumb Memorial Library, 1968; by William B. Ewert and Barbara A. White, in *American Book Collector* (Arlington Heights, Illinois), July/August 1984.

Manuscript Collections: Lilly Library, Indiana University, Bloomington; Dimond Library, University of New Hampshire, Durham.

Critical Studies: *Intricate and Simple Things: The Poetry of Galway Kinnell* by Lee Zimmerman, Urbana, University of Illinois Press, 1987; *On the Poetry of Galway Kinnell* edited by Howard Nelson, Ann Arbor, University of Michigan Press, 1988; *Galway Kinnell* by Richard J. Calhoun, New York, Twayne, 1992; ''Galway Kinnell: A Voice to Lead Us'' by Karen Maceira, in *Hollins Critic* (Hollins College, Virginia), 32(4), October 1995; *Critical Essays on Galway Kinnell* edited by Nancy Lewis Tuten, New York, Hall, 1996, and ''The Language of Sexuality: Walt Whitman and Galway Kinnell'' by Tuten, in *Walt Whitman Quarterly Review* (Iowa City, Iowa), 9(3), Winter 1992; ''Poetry, Personality and Wholeness: A Response to Galway Kinnell'' by Adrienne Rich, in *A Field Guide to Contemporary Poetry and Poetics,* edited by Stuart Friebert, David Walker, and David Young, Oberlin, Ohio, Oberlin College, 1997; ''Thoreau and Galway Kinnell: Self-Exile and the Need for Human Interaction'' by Anne E. Van Dyke, in *The Image of Class in Literature, Media, and Society,* edited by Will Wright and Steven Kaplan, Pueblo, Colorado, University of Southern Colorado Press, 1998; *On the Poetry of Galway Kinnell: The Wages of Dying,* Ann Arbor, University of Michigan Press, 1999.

*   *   *

Galway Kinnell's poems attempt to strike a delicate and unique balance among the urge to express the emotions of the private self, the need to identify with the creatures of the natural world, the wish to take a stance on public issues, and the obligation to discover a means of understanding the mortality of all creatures. Kinnell has been able to maintain this balance by developing an idiom that is carefully controlled. Precise language and spare, exact imagery characterize his poems.

Like many of his contemporaries, Kinnell has attempted to develop the poetic explorations of Robert Lowell and Theodore Roethke in order to learn how the breakthroughs of these poets could form a basis for a poetry that served the needs of the final third of the twentieth century. His own innovations have led him to abandon the intricate, allusive, and sometimes dense structures that characterized the works of the school of Eliot and Pound. His poems have avoided studied ambiguity, and he has risked directness of address, precision of imagery, and experiments with surrealistic situations and images.

The first two collections, *First Poems, 1946–1954* and *What a Kingdom It Was,* employed intricate, traditional rhyme schemes, a practice Kinnell increasingly abandoned in subsequent works. Like most of the later poems, these works exhibit a narrative impulse and a preference for simple, uncluttered diction. Two of the best early poems, ''First Song'' and ''To Christ Our Lord,'' employ the objectivity of narrative enhanced by rhyme to brilliant effects. Both are initiation poems. ''First Song'' tells the story of an Illinois farm boy who, after a day's demeaning labor, hears the frogs sing in a nearby pond. Joined by two neighbors, the boy accompanies the frogs' song with a primitive homemade instrument. The music they make, accompanying the natural creatures, becomes for the boy his first intimation of the connectedness of the human and the natural world, a theme Kinnell continues to explore in all of his poetry:

And into the dark in spite of a shoulder's ache
A boy's hunched body loved out of a stalk

The first song of his happiness, and the song woke
His heart into the darkness and into the sadness of joy.

This awakening, presented simply and directly, initiates the youth into the ambiguity that for Kinnell characterizes the human condition. The darkness becomes symbolic of our being surrounded by death, and the joy the youth learns depends on its opposite, sadness. The paradox is elementary, but it promises the thematic richness Kinnell's poems develop.

A more extended and rewarding treatment of the theme energizes "To Christ Our Lord." This brief narrative deals with the tension between a Christian and a Darwinian perception of the world as experienced by a young boy. Obliged to kill a bird for Christmas dinner, the boy cannot resolve his feeling of the sacredness of the life of the bird with his animal need to kill in order to live. The snow yields tracks of elk and wolves, and so the message of nature is that we must kill in order to survive. After the bird has been cooked, his family approves his action: "Now the grace praised his wicked act." The boy cannot reconcile this praise from his family with the guilt he felt when he shot the creature:

He had not wanted to shoot. The sound
Of wings beating into the hushed air
Had stirred his love, and his fingers
Froze in his gloves, and he wondered,
Famishing, could he fire? Then he fired.

The poem ends on an ambivalent note. The boy goes out after dinner and experiences a vision in which the constellation Swan becomes an emblem for the bird he killed and the Savior whose birth the day celebrates: "Then the Swan spread her wings, cross of the cold north, / The pattern and mirror of the acts of earth." The boy feels the intuition of the spiritual presence in creation, but this intuition does not cancel out the need to prey on the creatures so that man may survive.

Kinnell's work does not provide easy answers, because his work has led him to distrust simple answers to complex problems. He writes effective poems about animals in order to explore the complex relations we form with creation. Two of his frequently anthologized poems, "The Bear" and "The Porcupine," employ a flexible narrative form to deal with the same theme. Of these animals, Kinnell once told an interviewer, "I've wanted to see them in themselves and also to see their closeness to us." Each poem is organized around a movement from violence on the animal to identification with the animal as the victim of human cruelty. "The Porcupine" vividly describes the shooting of the creature and its painful, prolonged death. As the poem ends, the speaker experiences imaginative empathy with the porcupine's suffering and recognizes that it is a "blank / template of myself."

"The Bear" treats even more directly the process by which the killer becomes empathic with his victim. The speaker, an Eskimo, tells of his deliberate and brutal strategy to kill a bear. He sharpened a wolf's rib and hid it in blubber; when the bear ate the blubber, the rib punctured the lining of its stomach. Thus began a death that lasted seven days. The hunter follows the bear these seven days, "living by now on bear blood alone," finds the dead bear, and disembowels it. To protect himself against the cold, he crawls inside the carcass, where he has a dream of total identification with the sufferings of this bear, a predicament the speaker has himself created. Awakening, the

Eskimo is changed by the experience of his cruelty to nature and is therefore able to sympathize with the life cycle of man's victims.

Kinnell's longer poems address the problem of finding personal integrity in a world torn by secularism, war, and the loss of the ideal of human justice. These poems, beginning with "The Avenue Bearing the Initial of Christ into the New World" and continuing through the book-length *The Book of Nightmares,* employ a distinctive meditational structure composed of a variety of spatially or sequentially superimposed images. "The Avenue" contains fourteen unequal sections, most of which are images and impressions of the despair of the old, blacks, Puerto Ricans, Jews, bag ladies, and vendors who inhabit Avenue C in New York City. The background for these impressions is the Holocaust. The epigraph, which is in German, recalls the gas ovens, and section 11 contains a form letter mailed by the commandant of one of the death camps. The point of the association of the death camps with Avenue C is that each represents the failed promise of human society. The camps were intentional violations of that promise, whereas Avenue C represents an accidental violation. The poor and despairing on Avenue C suffer and die because of neglect: "The promise was broken too freely / To them and their fathers, for them to care."

Effective imagery communicates directly the frustrations of these forgotten citizens, whose only deliverance is death. Even death is denied the metaphysical consolation it held for Walt Whitman, but the poem echoes "Out of the Cradle Endlessly Rocking" to remind us that in the comprehensive world Whitman loved death was completion and deliverance:

Maybe it is as the poet said,
And the soul turns to thee
O vast and well-veiled Death
And the body gratefully nestles close to thee—

The consolation is less convincing than it was to Whitman, and for the victims of "this God-forsaken Avenue bearing the initial of Christ / Through the haste and carelessness of the ages," death is less a transcendence than an escape.

Mortality is also the concern of *The Book of Nightmares,* a work composed of ten related poems, each in turn containing seven sections. This carefully crafted work addresses the poet's children and constitutes an inspiring effort to explain human mortality to those we bring into this world of suffering and death. Echoing Wordsworth ironically, the poet explains his infant daughter's waking fears:

And yet perhaps this is the reason you cry,
this is the nightmare you wake from:
being forever
in the pre-trembling of a house that falls.

The child's intimations of mortality cannot be answered, and they actually intensify the poet's own anxiety. The dilemma of existence cannot be resolved, but the book is an effort to provide at least an alternative. Love is Kinnell's answer to mortality, but love means confronting the facts of physical existence directly and honestly. To his daughter he offers the legacy of honest modern parents: "And then [when she is reminded of her mortality] / you shall open / this book, even if it is the book of nightmares." The mortal, loving parent cannot offer answers, but he can leave behind a legacy of love and an attempt to explain the world as it is.

At his best Kinnell is a poet who confronts the dilemma of mortality directly. His poetry communicates the urgency of love in the face of our mortality. As Kinnell says in "Good-bye," a poem addressed to his dying mother, "It is written in our hearts, the emptiness is all. / That is how we have learned, the embrace is all."

—David C. Dougherty

KINSELLA, John

Has written as John Heywood. **Nationality:** Australian. **Born:** Perth, Western Australia, 1963. **Education:** University of Western Australia. **Career:** Writer-in-residence, Churchill College, Cambridge, 1997. Founding editor, *Salt.* **Awards:** Creative Artists fellowship, Australia Council, 1989; Western Australian Premier's prize for poetry, 1993; Harri Jones Memorial award, University of Newcastle, 1994; Furphy award, Fellowship of Australian Writers, 1995; John Bray Poetry prize, Adelaide Festival, 1996. **Address:** Fremantle Arts Centre Press, PO Box 320, South Fremantle 6160, Australia.

PUBLICATIONS

Poetry

The Frozen Sea (as John Heywood). N.p., Zeppelin Press, 1983.
Night Parrots. South Fremantle, Fremantle Arts Centre Press, 1989.
The Book of Two Faces. Perth, Western Australia, Perth Institute of Contemporary Art, 1989.
Eschatologies. South Fremantle, Fremantle Arts Centre Press, 1991.
Full Fathom Five. South Fremantle, Fremantle Arts Centre Press, 1993.
Syzygy. South Fremantle, Fremantle Arts Centre Press, 1993.
The Silo: A Pastoral Symphony. South Fremantle, Fremantle Arts Centre Press, 1995.
Erratum/Frame(d). South Fremantle, Fremantle Arts Centre Press, 1995.
The Radnoti Poems. N.p., Equipage, 1996.
The Undertow: New and Selected Poems. Todmorden, Arc, 1996.
Lightning Tree. South Fremantle, Fremantle Arts Centre Press, 1996.
Poems 1980–1994. South Fremantle, Fremantle Arts Centre Press, 1997; Newcastle upon Tyne, Bloodaxe, 1998.
Graphology. N.p., Equipage, 1997.
Authenticities. South Fremantle, Fremantle Arts Centre Press, 1998.
The Hunt. Newcastle upon Tyne, Bloodaxe, 1998.
Kangaroo Virus: Poetry. South Fremantle, Fremantle Arts Centre Press, 1998.
Visitants. Newcastle upon Tyne, Bloodaxe, 1999.

Novels

Genre. South Fremantle, Fremantle Arts Centre Press, 1997.
Grappling Eros. South Fremantle, Fremantle Arts Centre Press, 1998.

Other

Editor, *The Bird Catcher's Song.* Applecross, Western Australia, Salt, 1992.
Editor, *A Salt Reader.* Applecross, Western Australia, Salt, 1995.

Editor, *The May Anthologies 1999: Poetry.* Cambridge, Varsity, 1999.
Editor, *Landbridge: Contemporary Australian Poetry.* Todmorden, Arc, 1999.

*

Critical Studies: In *Overland,* 128, 1992; by Fay Zwicky, in *Westerly,* 38(3), spring 1993; "John Kinsella's Poetry—Some Reflections" by Xavier Pons, in *Antipodes* (Austin, Texas), 12(2), December 1998.

*   *   *

John Kinsella was awarded a major Creative Artists fellowship from the Australia Council in 1989, which enabled him to go to Cambridge, where he has lived much of the time since. He has continued, however, to be an energetic and enthusiastic spokesman for his own poetry and for Australian poetry generally, and he has been amazing prolific.

As editor of the Western Australian journal *Salt,* Kinsella has expanded both his editorial and publishing activities, but it is as a poet that he has most importantly demonstrated a striking consistency and talent. Although he has published more than a dozen books since his first volume, *The Frozen Sea* (as John Heywood) in 1983, including two collections of selected poems (in 1996 and 1997), it is probably his award-winning *The Silo* (1995) and *The Hunt* (1998) that demonstrate most tellingly his remarkable affinity for the Western Australian environment as a spiritual and metaphorical landscape. This is something he shares with Anthony Lawrence, though perhaps with the greater authority of someone who was born there. These books also show Kinsella's lively awareness of international currents in poetry, something his Cambridge residency has afforded him, although earlier collections such as *Eschatologies* (1991) and *Syzygy* (1993) indicate a strong cosmopolitan awareness. He writes within a distinctive Australian tradition, however, and is in many ways a direct link with earlier Western Australia poets such as Kenneth Mackenzie, Randolph Stow, and Dorothy Hewett. (Kinsella has coedited a regional anthology with Hewett.).

Something of Kinsella's delicate manipulation of regional overtones and universal resonances can be observed in "Courtship and Country Towns," from his collection *Visitants:*

Without really knowing why
they found themselves
getting away to the city
or neighbouring towns

whenever the opportunity
arose. It wasn't that they
disliked the girls they'd
grown up with, rather

that they were almost sisters . . .
Their mums all said it's a pity
it would be nice to see our
families wed, but the wind

disperses the seeds of a dandelion

so that they spread and find room
to prosper in fertile earth.
This town has a constant

thirst for new blood,
despite the papers, claiming
it's slowly dying, and, in any case,
dandelions were introduced.

—Thomas W. Shapcott

KINSELLA, Thomas

Nationality: Irish. **Born:** Dublin, 4 May 1928. **Education:** O'Connells, Dublin; University College, Dublin, diploma in public administration 1949. **Family:** Married Eleanor Walsh in 1955; two daughters and one son. **Career:** Worked in the Irish Civil Service, 1946–65, retired from the Department of Finance as assistant principal officer. Writer-in-residence, 1965–67, and professor of English, 1967–70, Southern Illinois University, Carbondale. Since 1970 professor of English, Temple University, Philadelphia; founder and director, Temple-in-Dublin Irish tradition program, 1976–90. Director, Dolmen Press, Dublin, and Cuala Press, Dublin; founder, Peppercanister, Dublin, 1972. **Awards:** Guinness award, 1958; Irish Arts Council award, 1961; Denis Devlin memorial award, 1967, 1970, 1988, 1994; Guggenheim fellowship, 1968, 1971; Before Columbus Foundation award, 1983. D.Litt.: National University of Ireland, Dublin, 1984. Member, Irish Academy of Letters, 1965. **Address:** Killalane, Laragh, County Wicklow, Ireland.

PUBLICATIONS

Poetry

The Starlit Eye. Dublin, Dolmen Press, 1952.
Three Legendary Sonnets. Dublin, Dolmen Press, 1952.
Per Imaginem. Dublin, Dolmen Press, 1953.
The Death of a Queen. Dublin, Dolmen Press, 1956.
Poems. Dublin, Dolmen Press, 1956.
Another September. Dublin, Dolmen Press, and Philadelphia, Dufour, 1958; revised edition, Dolmen Press, and London, Oxford University Press, 1962.
Moralities. Dublin, Dolmen Press, 1960.
Poems and Translations. New York, Atheneum, 1961.
Three Irish Poets, with John Montague and Richard Murphy. Dublin, Dolmen Press, 1961.
Downstream. Dublin, Dolmen Press, 1962.
Six Irish Poets, with others, edited by Robin Skelton. London and New York, Oxford University Press, 1962.
Wormwood. Dublin, Dolmen Press, 1966.
Nightwalker. Dublin, Dolmen Press, 1967.
Nightwalker and Other Poems. Dublin, Dolmen Press, London, Oxford University Press, and New York, Knopf, 1968.
Poems, with Douglas Livingstone and Anne Sexton. London and New York, Oxford University Press, 1968.
Tear. Cambridge, Massachusetts, Pym Randall Press, 1969.
Butcher's Dozen. Dublin, Peppercanister, 1972.
A Selected Life. Dublin, Peppercanister, 1972.

Finistere. Dublin, Dolmen Press, 1972.
Notes from the Land of the Dead and Other Poems. Dublin, Cuala Press, 1972; New York, Random House, 1973.
New Poems 1973. Dublin, Dolmen Press, 1973; London, Oxford University Press, 1976.
Selected Poems 1956–1968. Dublin, Dolmen Press, and London, Oxford University Press, 1973.
Vertical Man. Dublin, Peppercanister, 1973.
The Good Fight. Dublin, Peppercanister, 1973.
One. Dublin, Peppercanister, 1974.
A Technical Supplement. Dublin, Peppercanister, 1976.
Song of the Night and Other Poems. Dublin, Peppercanister, 1978.
The Messenger. Dublin, Peppercanister, 1978.
Fifteen Dead. Dublin, Dolmen Press, and London, Oxford University Press, 1979.
One and Other Poems. Dublin, Dolmen Press, and London, Oxford University Press, 1979.
Peppercanister Poems 1972–1978. Winston-Salem, North Carolina, Wake Forest University Press, 1979.
Poems 1956–1973. Winston-Salem, North Carolina, Wake Forest University Press, 1979.
One Fond Embrace. Dublin, Gallery Press, and Hatfield, Massachusetts, Deerfield Press, 1981.
Songs of the Psyche. Dublin, Peppercanister, 1985.
Her Vertical Smile. Dublin, Peppercanister, 1985.
Out of Ireland. Dublin, Peppercanister, 1987.
St. Catherine's Clock. Dublin, Peppercanister, 1987.
Blood and Family. Oxford and New York, Oxford University Press, 1988.
Poems from Centre City. Dublin, Peppercanister, 1990.
Personal Places. Dublin, Peppercanister, 1990.
Madonna. Dublin, Peppercanister, 1991.
Open Court. Dublin, Peppercanister, 1991.
From Centre City (Poems from 1988). Oxford, Oxford University Press, 1994.
Collected Poems. Oxford, Oxford University Press, 1996.
The Pen Shop. Dublin, Peppercanister, 1997.
The Familiar. Dublin, Peppercanister, 1999.
Godhead. Dublin, Peppercanister, 1999.

Other

Davis, Mangan, Ferguson? Tradition and the Irish Writer, with W.B. Yeats. Dublin, Dolmen Press. 1970.
The Dual Tradition: An Essay on Poetry and Politics in Ireland. Manchester, Carcanet, 1995.

Editor, *Selected Poems of Austin Clarke.* Dublin, Dolmen Press 1976.
Editor, *Our Musical Heritage,* by Seàn O Riada. Dublin, Dolmen Press, 1982.
Editor, *The New Oxford Book of Irish Verse.* Oxford and New York, Oxford University Press, 1986.

Translator, *The Breastplate of St. Patrick.* Dublin, Dolmen Press, 1954; as *Faeth Fiadha: The Breastplate of St. Patrick,* 1957.
Translator, *Longes mac n-Usnig, Being The Exile and Death of the Sons of Usnech.* Dublin, Dolmen Press, 1954.
Translator, *Thirty Three Triads, Translated from the XII Century Irish.* Dublin, Dolmen Press, 1955.

Translator, *The Tain.* Dublin, Dolmen Press, 1969; London and New York, Oxford University Press, 1970.

Translator, with Sean O Tuama, *An Duanaire: 1600–1900: Poems of the Dispossessed.* Dublin, Dolmen Press, and Philadelphia, University of Pennsylvania Press, 1981.

*

Bibliography: By Hensley Woodbridge, in *Eire-Ireland* (St. Paul, Minnesota), 1966; *The Whole Matter: The Poetic Evolution of Thomas Kinsella* by Thomas H. Jackson, Syracuse, New York, Syracuse University Press, 1995; *Thomas Kinsella* by Donatella Abbate Badin, New York, Twayne, 1996.

Critical Studies: *The New Poets: American and British Poetry since World War II* by M.L. Rosenthal, New York and London, Oxford University Press, 1967; "Thomas Kinsella Issue" of *The Hollins Critic* (Hollins College, Virginia), 4(4), 1968, and *Tracks* (Dublin), 1987; "The Poetry of Thomas Kinsella" by Robin Skelton, in *Eire-Ireland* (St. Paul, Minnesota), 4(1), 1968; *Eight Contemporary Poets* by Calvin Bedient, London and New York, Oxford University Press, 1974; *The Poetry of Thomas Kinsella* by Maurice Harmon, Dublin, Wolfhound Press, 1974, Atlantic Highlands, New Jersey, Humanities Press, 1975; "Fragments of Identity: Thomas Kinsella's Modernist Imperative" by Arthur E. McGuinness, in *Colby Library Quarterly* (Waterville, Maine), 23(4), December 1987; "Thomas Kinsella Special Issue" of *Tracks 7,* 1987; "Irelands of the Mind: The Poetry of Thomas Kinsella and Seamus Heaney," in *Canadian Journal of Irish Studies* (Saskatoon, Canada), 15(2), December 1989, and *Reading the Ground: The Poetry of Thomas Kinsella*, Washington, D.C., Catholic University of America Press, 1996, both by Brian John; "The Song of Thomas Kinsella," in *The New Criterion* (New York), 8(7), March 1990, and "The Evolving Poetry of Thomas Kinsella," in *New England Review* (Middlebury, Vermont), 18(4), Fall 1997, both by Floyd Skloot; "Kinsella and Eriugena: 'Out of Ireland'" by Mary Anderson, in *Canadian Journal of Irish Studies* (Saskatoon, Canada), 17(2), December 1991; *The Celtic Otherworld and Contemporary Irish Poetry* (dissertation) by Thomas Royster Howerton, University of North Carolina, Chapel Hill, 1993; "Kinsella, Geography, History" by David Kellogg, in *South Atlantic Quarterly* (Durham, North Carolina), 95(1), Winter 1996; *The Lady, the Land, the Hag: Irish Goddess Imagery and Male Perception in the Works by Joyce, Kavanagh, and Kinsella* (dissertation) by John Brook Alexander, University of North Carolina, Chapel Hill, 1997.

* * *

The early Thomas Kinsella might be described as an intellectual troubadour, his desire to sing increasingly crossed by a need to explain. In his first book, *Poems,* traditional love lyrics like "Soft to Your Places" and "Midsummer" were balanced by others like "Ulysses," in which a dense vocabulary was pressed into the service of a still emerging vision. It was the elegant world of Richard Wilbur but with a metaphysical twist and an Irish music.

Another September represented a more thorough cultivation of the same private garden. The romantic dandy is still in evidence ("Fifth Sunday after Easter"), but his presence does not impede Kinsella's clarification of his main theme—an obsession with time.

Its expression varies from the conventional ballad stanzas of "In the Ringwood," based on the Irish *aisling,* or vision poem—

Dread, a grey devourer,
Stalks in the shade of love.
The dark that dogs our feet
Eats what is sickened of.
The End that stalks Beginning
Hurries home its drove

—to the more analytic pose of "Baggot Street Deserta," with the poet, against his favorite backdrop of nocturnal Dublin, declaring that we must "endure and let the present punish."

The principal reproach that might be leveled against *Another September* is that the poems were not sufficiently anchored in time and place. But a less remote quality was evident toward the end of the collection, especially in the somber "Thinking of Mr. D." In his second major collection Kinsella emerges clearly as a persona, with the "pious clerkly" hand of "Priest and Emperor" now leading to the dejected face that gazes into a mirror in "A Mirror in February":

Now plainly in the mirror of my soul
I read that I have looked my last on youth
And little more; for they are not made whole
That reach the age of Christ.

Downstream can be said to mark Kinsella's change of gear from lyric to meditative. As he says in "Time's Mischief," "He must progress / Who fabricates a path, though all about / Death, Woman, Spring, repeat their first success." The most noticeable change is his determination to grapple with public themes, from the local history and politics of "A Country Walk" to the problem of Hiroshima in "Old Harry." Perhaps he does this too deliberately, for in the latter poem Harry Truman is dignified with a moral complexity alien to his character, while the most striking effects are lavished on the atom bomb's destruction of "the notorious cities of the plain."

The same determination flows over into *Nightwalker,* the title poem of which exposes the moral vacuum of modern Ireland. The monologue technique and diction are still close to early Eliot, and, as in "Chrysalides" and "Dick King" in *Downstream,* it is the more private poems that catch Kinsella's distinctive quality. The sequence on marital love, "Wormwood," is heavy with portentousness and contains at least one poem, "First Light," in which despair is crystallized drop by terrible drop. There also are some moving attempts to face the problem of physical suffering, for example, in "Our Mother":

The girl whimpers in bed, remote
Under the anaesthetic still.
She sleeps on her new knowledge, a bride
With bowels burning and disarrayed.

This vision of life as ordeal is more fully enunciated in the magnificently romantic intimacies of the long poem "Phoenix Park." As well as a celebration of married love, it is also a farewell to Kinsella's native Dublin, and one waited to see how America would affect his work. With his seriousness of purpose and strength of intellect there was a Parnassian quality that could only benefit from a more experimental poetic climate. His translation of the early Irish epic *The Tain* did not wholly succeed in "making it new," but "A Hand of Solo" and "Hen Woman," parts of a new poetic sequence, show a relaxing of technique that augured well. "Notes from the Land of the Dead" was incorporated into *New Poems 1973,* which, with *Selected Poems 1956–1968,* amounted to a new definition of Kinsella's career. But he also established a private press, Peppercanister, for broadsides like *Butcher's Dozen* and his meditation on John F. Kennedy, *The Good Fight.* Thus, his career presents the paradox of definitive achievement and increasing adventurousness, a strong combination. The private and public life, love and waste, these were the antimonies that engaged Kinsella's intensely serious gaze, but the way he extended his territory again in *One* and *Fifteen Dead* made the later Kinsella one of the darkest, strongest, least accommodating poets around, one with a rare integrity.

The same process is evident in *Blood and Family,* which again gathers his Peppercanister publications of a decade. With all its hesitations and affirmations, the volume has the feel of a major enterprise. The tone may often be dark, the language dense, and the themes seemingly disparate, but then for Kinsella "waste [is] a part of the process, / implying life." While keeping all one's reservations as to whether some of the sequences do not show "the will doing the work of the imagination," as Coleridge said of Wordsworth, or betray a leaning toward the imagination of death and disaster rather than delight in life, one must still salute Kinsella's implacable progress, which makes him the heir of his child self who declared, "I am going to know / everything."

From Centre City (1994) gathers five more Peppercanister publications in the same rigorous manner. The book opens with "One Fond Embrace," an acerbic roll call of contemporaries, and almost ends with an evening in an infamous Dublin literary pub, where Kavanagh is surrounded by acolytes. It should be clear by now that Kinsella has assumed the mantle of Austin Clarke as the conscience of his city. The destruction of the old Viking town at Wood Quay and the erection of "concrete piss-towers" at Ballymun arouse his ire—"We were the generation / of positive disgrace." At the very end of the book he leaves the city for his ancestral county, Wicklow:

On a fragrant slope descending into the fog
Over our foul ascending city
I turned away in refusal . . .

This will not be the last salvo from this Hibernian lyricist crossed with an Hebraic prophet.

—John Montague

KIRKUP, James (Falconer)

Nationality: British. **Born:** South Shields, County Durham, 23 April 1918. **Education:** South Shields High School; Durham University, B.A. 1941. **Career:** Gregory Fellow in Poetry, Leeds University, 1950–52; visiting poet and head of the Department of English, Bath Academy of Art, Corsham, Wiltshire, 1953–56; traveling lecturer, Swedish Ministry of Education, Stockholm, 1956–57; professor of English, University of Salamanca, Spain, 1957–58, and Tohoku

University, Sendai, Japan, 1959–61; lecturer in English literature, University of Malaya, Kuala Lumpur, 1961–62; professor of English literature, Nagoya University, Japan, 1969–72. Since 1963 professor of English literature, Japan Women's University, Tokyo; professor of English literature and poet-in-residence, Amherst College, Massachusetts, 1968; Arts Council creative writer, University of Sheffield, 1974–75; Morton Visiting Professor, Ohio University, Athens, 1975–76; dramatist-in-residence, Sherman Theatre, Cardiff, 1976–77. Since 1977 professor of English literature, Kyoto University of Foreign Studies. Literary editor, *Orient/West Magazine,* Tokyo, 1963–64; founder, *Poetry Nippon,* Nagoya, 1966. Since 1969 president, Poets' Society of Japan, and since 1991 president and co-founder, The British Haiku Society. **Awards:** Atlantic-Rockefeller award, 1950; Japan P.E.N. Club International literary prize, 1965; Batchelder award, for translation, 1968; Keats prize, 1974; Scott-Moncrieff prize for translation, 1993. Fellow, Royal Society of Literature, 1962. **Address:** BM-Box 2870, British Monomarks, London WC1N 3XX, England.

PUBLICATIONS

Poetry

Indications, with John Ormond and John Bayliss. London, Grey Walls Press, 1942.
The Cosmic Shape: An Interpretation of Myth and Legend with Three Poems and Lyrics, with Ross Nichols. London, Forge Press, 1946.
The Drowned Sailor and Other Poems. London, Grey Walls Press, 1947.
The Submerged Village and Other Poems. London, Oxford University Press, 1951.
The Creation. Hull, Lotus Press, 1951.
A Correct Compassion and Other Poems. London, Oxford University Press, 1952.
A Spring Journey and Other Poems of 1952–1953. London, Oxford University Press, 1954.
The Descent into the Cave and Other Poems. London, Oxford University Press, 1957.
The Prodigal Son: Poems 1956–1959. London, Oxford University Press, 1959.
The Refusal to Conform: Last and First Poems. London, Oxford University Press, 1963.
Japan Marine. Tokyo, Japan P.E.N. Club, 1965.
Paper Windows: Poems from Japan. London, Dent, 1968.
Japan Physical: A Selection, with Japanese translations by Fumiko Miura. Tokyo, Kenkyusha, 1969.
White Shadows, Black Shadows: Poems of Peace and War. London, Dent, 1970.
The Body Servant: Poems of Exile. London, Dent, 1971.
Broad Daylight. Frensham, Surrey, Sceptre Press, 1971.
A Bewick Bestiary. Ashington, Northumberland, MidNAG, 1971.
Transmental Vibrations. London, Covent Garden Press, 1971.
Zen Garden. Guildford, Surrey, Circle Press, 1973.
Many-Lined Poem. Sheffield, Headland Poetry, 1973.
Enlightenment. Osaka, Kyoto Editions, 1978.
Scenes from Sesshu. London, Pimlico Press, 1978.
Prick Prints. Privately printed, 1978.
Steps to the Temple. Osaka, Kyoto Editions, 1979.

Zen Contemplations. Osaka, Kyoto Editions, 1979.

The Tao of Water, with Birgit Skiöld. Guildford, Surrey, Circle Press, 1980.

Cold Mountain Poems. Osaka, Kyoto Editions, 1980.

Dengonban Messages. Osaka, Kyoto Editions, 1981.

Ecce Homo—My Pasolini. Osaka, Kyoto Editions, 1981.

No More Hiroshimas. Osaka, Kyoto Editions, 1982.

To the Ancestral North: Poems for an Autobiography. Tokyo, Asahi, 1983.

The Sense of the Visit. Knotting, Bedfordshire, Sceptre Press, 1984.

The Guitar Player of Zuiganji. Kyoto and London, Kyoto Editions 1985.

So Long Desired, with John McRae. London, Gay Men's Press, 1986.

Fellow Feelings. London, Gay Men's Press, 1987.

Three Poems. Child Okeford, Dorset, Words Press, 1988.

Words for Contemplation. Newcastle upon Tyne, Cloud Editions, 1992.

Shooting Stars. Flitwick, Bedforshire, Hub Editions, 1992.

First Fireworks. Flitwick, Bedfordshire, Hub Editions, 1993.

Short Takes. Flitwick, Bedfordshire, Hub Editions, 1993.

Throwback-Poems towards an Autobiography. Ware, England, Rockingham Press, 1993.

Blue Bamboo. Flitwick, Bedfordshire, Hub Editions, 1994.

Formulas for Chaos. Flitwick, Bedfordshire, Hub Editions, 1994.

Look at It This Way: Poems for Young People. Ware, England, Rockingham Press, 1994.

Omens of Disaster: Collected Shorter Poems Vol. 1. Salzburg, Austria, University of Salzburg Press, n.d.

Once and for All: Collected Shorter Poems Vol. 2. Salzburg, Austria, University of Salzburg Press, n.d.

An Extended Breath: Collected Longer Poems Vol. 1. Salzburg, Austria, University of Salzburg Press, 1996.

Strange Attractors: New Poems. Salzburg, Austria, University of Salzburg Press, 1996.

The Patient Obituarist. Salzburg, Austria, University of Salzburg Press, 1996.

Broad Daylight: Poems East and West. Salzburg, Austria, University of Salzburg Press, 1996.

Measures of Time: Collected Longer Poems Vol. 2. Salzburg, Austria, University of Salzburg Press, 1997.

Counting to 9,999. Flitwick, Bedfordshire, Hub Editions, 1997.

He Dreamed He Was a Butterfly. Flitwick, Bedfordshire, Hub Editions, 1998.

Pikadon: An Epic Poem of Hiroshima and Nagasaki. Salzburg, Austria, University of Salzburg Press, 1998.

One Man Band: Poems without Words. Flitwick, Bedfordshire, Hub Editions, 1999.

Plays

Upon This Rock: A Dramatic Chronicle of Peterborough Cathedral (produced Peterborough, 1955). London, Oxford University Press, 1955.

Masque: The Triumph of Harmony (produced London, 1955).

The True Mistery of the Nativity (televised, 1960). London and New York, Oxford University Press, 1956.

The Prince of Homburg, adaptation of a play by Heinrich von Kleist (produced New York, 1976). Published in Classic Theatre 2, edited by Eric Bentley, New York, Doubleday, 1959.

The True Mistery of the Passion: Adapted and Translated from French Medieval Mystery Cycle of Arnoul and Simon Grélan (televised, 1960; produced Bristol, 1960). London and New York, Oxford University Press, 1962.

The Physicists, adaptation of a play by Dürrenmatt (produced London and New York, 1963). London, Cape, and New York, Grove Press, 1964.

The Meteor, adaptation of a play by Dürrenmatt (produced London, 1966). London, Cape, 1973; New York, Grove Press, 1974.

Play Strindberg, adaptation of a play by Dürrenmatt (produced New York, 1971; London, 1973). Chicago, Dramatic Publishing Company, n.d.

Portrait of a Planet, adaptation of a play by Dürrenmatt (produced London, 1972). London, Cape, 1972.

The Magic Drum (for children; produced Newcastle upon Tyne, 1974; London, 1977). New York, Knopf, 1972.

Peer Gynt, adaptation of the play by Ibsen (produced Cardiff, 1973).

The Conformer, adaptation of a play by Dürrenmatt (produced Sheffield, 1974).

Cyrano de Bergerac, adaptation of the play by Rostand (produced Newcastle upon Tyne, 1975).

The Anabaptists, Period of Grace, and Frank the Fifth, adaptations of plays by Dürrenmatt (produced Cardiff, 1976).

An Actor's Revenge, music by Minoru Miki (produced London, 1978). London, Faber, 1979.

Friends in Arms (produced Cardiff, 1980).

The Damask Drum, music by Paavo Heininen (produced Helsinki, 1984). Helsinki, Pan, 1984.

An Actor's Revenge: A Kabuki Opera. London, Faber Music, 1989.

True Misteries and a Chronicle Play of Peterborough Cathedral. Salzburg, Austria, University of Salzburg Press, 1997.

Radio Play: Ghost Mother, 1978.

Television Plays: The Peach Garden, 1954; Two Pigeons Flying High, 1955; The True Mistery of the Passion, 1960; The True Mistery of the Nativity, 1960.

Novels

The Love of Others. London, Collins, 1962.

The Bad Boy's Bedside Book of Do-It-Yourself Sex. Privately printed, 1978.

Gaijin on the Ginza. London, Peter Owen, 1992.

Queens Have Died Young and Fair. London, Peter Owen, 1994.

Other

The Only Child: An Autobiography of Infancy. London, Collins, 1957.

Sorrows, Passions, and Alarms: An Autobiography of Childhood. London, Collins, 1959.

These Horned Islands: A Journal of Japan. London, Collins, and New York, Macmillan, 1962.

Tropic Temper: A Memoir of Malaya. London, Collins, 1963.

England, Now. Tokyo, Seibido, 1964.

Japan Industrial: Some Impressions of Japanese Industries. Osaka, PEP, 2 vols., 1964–65.

Japan Now. Tokyo, Seibido, 1966.

Frankly Speaking. Tokyo, Eichosha, 1966.

Tokyo. London, Phoenix House, and South Brunswick, New Jersey, A.S. Barnes, 1966.

Filipinescas: Travels Through the Philippine Islands. London, Phoenix House, 1968.

Bangkok. London, Phoenix House, and South Brunswick, New Jersey, A.S. Barnes, 1968.

One Man's Russia. London, Phoenix House, 1968.

Aspects of the Short Story: Six Modern Short Stories with Commentary. Tokyo, Kaibunsha, 1969.

Streets of Asia. London, Dent, 1969.

Hong Kong and Macao. London, Dent, and South Brunswick, New Jersey, A.S. Barnes, 1970.

Japan Behind the Fan. London, Dent, 1970.

Insect Summer (for children). New York, Knopf, 1971.

The Magic Drum (for children). New York, Knopf, 1973.

Nihon Bungaku Eiyaku No Yuga Na Gijutsu (The Elegant Art of Literary Translation from Japanese to English). Tokyo, Kenkyusha, 1973.

Heaven, Hell, and Hara-Kiri: The Rise and Fall of the Japanese Superstate. London, Angus and Robertson, 1974.

America Yesterday and Today. Tokyo, Seibido, 1977.

Mother Goose's Britain. Tokyo, Asahi, 1977.

The Britishness of the British. Tokyo, Seibido, 1978.

Eibungaku Saiken (Discovery of English Literature). Tokyo, Taishukan, 1980.

Scenes from Sutcliffe: Twelve Meditations upon Photographs by Frank Meadow Sutcliffe. Osaka, Kyoto Editions, 1981.

Folktales Japanesque. Tokyo, Kenkyusha, 1982.

I Am Count Dracula. Tokyo, Asahi, 1982.

Modern American Myths. Tokyo, New Currents International, 1982.

I Am Frankenstein's Monster. Tokyo, Asahi, 1983.

When I Was a Child: A Study of Nursery Rhymes. Tokyo, Taibundo, 1983.

My Way-USA. Tokyo, Asahi, 1984.

The Glory That Was Greece. Tokyo, Seibido, 1984.

The Joys of Japan. Tokyo, Gaku Shobo, 1985.

Lafcadio Hearn. Tokyo, Kirihara Shoten, 1985.

James Kirkup's International Movie Theatre. Tokyo, Nan-UnDo, 1985.

Trends and Traditions. Tokyo, Seibido, 1986.

Portraits and Souvenirs. Tokyo, Asahi, 1987.

The Mystery and Magic of Symbols. Tokyo, Seibido, 1987.

The Cry of the Owl: Native Folktales and Legends. Tokyo, Takumi Shoten, 1987.

Sorrows, Passions, and Alarms (autobiography). London, Collins, 1987.

I, of All People: An Autobiography of Youth. London, Weidenfeld and Nicolson, and New York, St. Martin's Press, 1988.

The Best of Britain. Tokyo, Seibido, 1989.

It's a Small World. Tokyo, Seibido, 1990.

I, of All People. London, Weidenfeld and Nicholson, 1990.

A Poet could not But be Gay. London, Peter Owen, 1992.

Me All Over: Memoirs of a Misfit. London, Peter Owen, 1992.

A Certain State of Mind: An Anthology of Classic, Modern and Contemporary Japanese Haiku in Translation with Essays and Reviews. Salzburg, Austria, University of Salzburg Press, 1995.

Burning Giraffes: An Anthology of Japanese Poetry. Salzburg, Austria, University of Salzburg Press, 1996.

Child of the Tyne: Autobiographies. Salzburg, Austria, University of Salzburg Press, 1996.

A Book of Tanka. Salzburg, Austria, University of Salzburg Press, 1996.

Tanka Tales. Salzburg, Austria, University of Salzburg Press, n.d.

Editor, *Shepherding Winds: An Anthology of Poetry from East and West.* London, Blackie, 1969.

Editor, *Songs and Dreams: An Anthology of Poetry from East and West.* London, Blackie, 1970.

Translator, with Leopold Sirombo, *The Vision and Other Poems,* by Todja Tartschoff. London, Newman and Harris, 1953.

Translator, *The Dark Child,* by Camara Laye. London, Collins, 1955.

Translator, *The Radiance of the King,* by Camara Laye. London, Collins, 1956.

Translator, *Ancestral Voices,* by Doan-Vinh-Thal. London, Collins, 1956.

Translator, *The Girl from Nowhere,* by Hertha von Gebhardt. London, University of London Press, 1958.

Translator, *Memoirs of a Dutiful Daughter,* by Simone de Beauvoir. Cleveland, World, and London, Weidenfeld and Nicolson-Deutsch, 1959.

Translator, *Don Carlo,* by Schiller, in Classic Theatre 2, edited by Eric Bentley. New York, Doubleday, 1959.

Translator, *It Began in Babel,* by Herbert Wendt. London, Weidenfeld and Nicolson, 1961.

Translator, *Sins of the Fathers,* by Christian Geissler. London, Weidenfeld and Nicolson, 1962.

Translator, *The Captive,* by Ernst von Salamon. London, Weidenfeld and Nicolson, 1962.

Translator, *The Gates of Paradise,* by Jerzy Andrzejewski. London, Weidenfeld and Nicolson, 1962.

Translator, with Oliver Rice and Abdullah Majid, *Modern Malay Verse.* London, Oxford University Press, 1963.

Translator, *My Great-Grandfather and I,* by James Krüss. London, English Universities Press, 1964.

Translator, *The Heavenly Mandate,* by Erwin Wickert. London, Collins, 1964.

Translator, *Daily Life of the Etruscans,* by Jacques Heurgon. London, Weidenfeld and Nicolson, 1964.

Translator, *Daily Life in the French Revolution,* by Jean Robiquet. London, Weidenfeld and Nicolson, 1964.

Translator, *Immensee,* by Theodor Storm. London, Blackie, 1965.

Translator, *Tales of Hoffmann.* London, Blackie, 1966.

Translator, *The Little Man,* by Erich Kästner London, Cape, and New York, Knopf, 1966.

Translator, *Michael Kohlhaas: From an Old Chronicle.* London, Blackie, 1967.

Translator, *A Dream of Africa,* by Camara Laye. London, Collins, 1967.

Translator, *The Little Man and the Little Miss,* by Erich Kästner. London, Cape, and New York, Knopf, 1969.

Translator, *The Eternal Virgin,* by Paul Valéry. Tokyo, Orient Editions, 1970.

Translator, *Brand, by Ibsen,* in The Oxford Ibsen, edited by James Walter McFarlane. London, Oxford University Press, 1972.

Translator, with Michio Nakano, *Selected Poems of Takagi Kyozo.* Cheadle, Cheshire, Carcanet, 1973.

Translator, *Modern Japanese Poetry.* Brisbane, University of Queensland Press, 1978; edited by A.R. Davis, Milton Keynes, Buckinghamshire, Open University, 1979.

Translator, *The Guardian of the World,* by Camara Laye. London, Collins, 1980; New York, Random House, 1984.

Translator, *The Bush Toads.* London, Longman, 1982.

Translator, *To the Unknown God,* by Petru Dimitriu. London, Collins, and New York, Seabury Press, 1982.

Translator, *An African in Greenland,* by Tété-Michel Kpomassie. London, Secker and Warburg, and New York, Harcourt Brace, 1983.

Translator, *Miniature Masterpieces of Kawabata Yasunari.* Tokyo, Taishukan, 1983.

Translator, *Black Letters.* London, Atlas Press, 1990.

Translator, *The Guardian of the Word,* by Camara Laye. London, Fontana Books, 1984.

Translator, *This Little Measure,* by Margherita Guidacci. Nagoya, Ko Poetry Association, 1989.

Translator, *Painted Shadows,* Jean-Baptiste Neil. London, Quartet Books, 1991.

Translator, *A Room in the Woods,* by Patrick Drevet. London, Quartet Books, 1991.

Translator, *Vagabond Winter,* by Jean-Noël Pancrazi. London, Quartet Books, 1992.

Translator, *All the World's Mornings,* by Pascal Quignard. London, Quartet Books, 1992.

Translator, *Worlds of Difference,* by Georges-Arthur Goldschmidt. London, Quartet Books, 1993.

Translator, *My Micheline,* by Patrick Drevet. London, Quartet Books, 1993.

Translator, *The Man in the Red Hat,* by Hervé Guibert. London, Quartet Books, 1993.

Translator, *The Compassion Protocol,* by Hervé Guibert. London, Quartet Books, 1993.

Translator, *State of Absence,* by Tahar Ben Jelloun. London, Quartet Books, 1994.

Translator, *Isabelle,* by Marcelle Lagesse. London, Quartet Books, 1995.

Translator, *Blindsight,* by Hervé Guibert. New York, Braziller, 1996.

Translator, *Paradise,* by Hervé Guibert. London, Quartet Books, 1996.

Translator, with Michio Nakano, *How to Cook Women: Poems and Prose of Takagi Kyozo.* Salzburg, Austria, University of Salzburg Press, 1997.

*

Manuscript Collections: Brotherton Library, University of Leeds; South Shields and Newcastle upon Tyne public libraries; Labadie Collection, University of Michigan, Ann Arbor; Library of Congress, Washington, D.C.; Harvard University, Cambridge, Massachusetts; University of Durham; Yale University, Beineke Rare Books and Manuscript Library.

Critical Study: ''James Kirkup As Haiku Poet'' by A.W. Sadler, in *Literature East and West* (Austin, Texas), 9, 1965.

James Kirkup comments:

Characterized by a very wide variety of themes and verse forms, including many oriental subjects and techniques. Most deeply influenced by Japanese and Chinese poetry, as well as by French. No English or American influences. Major themes: the sea, loneliness, music, painting, photography, sport, travel, the Orient, peace and war, science and space exploration, UFOs, legend, people, psychical research, medicine, satire, social criticism.

In my poetry I have attempted always to express an essence both of myself and of experience, a crystallization of my personal awareness of this world and worlds beyond. I feel I am slowly developing, after nearly fifty years of writing poetry, a voice that is only my own and illuminating areas of experience and technique untouched by other poets. I am original, so I do not strive for originality for its own sake or experiment with form unless the subject demands it. My aim is to be perfectly lucid, yet to provide my candor with serious and mysterious undertones of sound and meaning.

The following quote, from Constantin Brancusi, the Romanian sculptor, has influenced me in my search for essences in poetry: ''Reality is not the outer form but the idea, the essence of things.''

(1995) Finding it increasingly difficult to get serious work published by British firms, I am more and more choosing excellent small publishers like Hub Editions and Rockingham Press. I have recently concentrated on translations and on the writing of haiku, senryu, and tanka, as well as obituaries for the *Independent.* I am also writing a lot for Japanese publishers and magazines and preparing a new collection of recent poems, *A Certain Chaos.*

*   *   *

The blurb on the dust wrapper of James Kirkup's collection *The Body Servant* includes this statement by the American poet and novelist James Dickey: ''With Kirkup's work I don't feel that facility is the problem, as it is with many writers.'' Certainly Kirkup sometimes gives the impression of being able to knock off a passable poem at the drop of a hat. Subject matter is never lacking; his trash can, photographs in a railway compartment, the New Year, a pet cat— all have suggested poems. Kirkup's first collection, *The Drowned Sailor,* was published in 1947 and was very much a book of its time in style and language. A determined poeticism may be the best way of describing it, with its peppering of enormous abstractions such as ''memory's mountain'' or ''the candelabra of the soul.'' The other poets of the time (see Wrey Gardiner's *Poetry Quarterly*) were full of such stuff, as if there were an urgency to plump out otherwise flat poems, a sort of poetic padded bra, but Kirkup was too adept at this for his own good.

It was in Kirkup's second collection, *The Submerged Village,* that something distinctive was to be observed. There were still oddly old-fashioned pieces (''The Ship,'' ''Music at Night,'' and ''Poem for a New Year'') that read like those poems the leisured gentlemen of previous centuries were so adept at ''turning,'' as they would put it— competent, agreeable, but strangely impersonal. But among these were poems such as the title poem itself, in which it was as if the poet had taken a cool, hard look at his subject and determined to deny himself the indulgence of his particular facility:

Calm, the surrounding mountains look upon
the steeple's golden cross, that still
emerges from the centre of the rising lake.
Like a sinking raft's bare mast and spar
anchored to earth by chains of stone.

The facility is still there, of course, but it is used to the purpose of the poem and not as a merely decorative addition.

The progress toward an individual voice and style was to flower in the next collection, *A Correct Compassion,* in which the title poem can stand with the finest poems written since World War II. Here, in a poem written after watching the performance of an operation at the General Infirmary in Leeds, Kirkup combines keenly observed detail—

> The glistening theatre swarms with eyes, and hands,
>   and eyes.
> On green-clothed tables, ranks of instruments transmit
>   a sterile
> gleam.
> The masks are on, and no unnecessary smile betrays
> A certain tension. true concomitant of calm

while using the whole as a prolonged and deftly handled metaphor:

> —For this is imagination's other place,
> Where only necessary things are done, with the su-
>   preme the
> grave
> Dexterity that ignores technique; with proper grace
> Informing a correct compassion, that performs its love, and
> makes it live.

It is as if from the controlled skill of the surgeon Kirkup has, as the poem makes clear, not only learned something concerning the nature of art but also has found a parallel for his own technique. Another poem in the collection, ''Matthew Smith,'' begins, ''Yours, brother, is a masculine art, / The business of doing what you see.'' In a sense, with *A Correct Compassion* Kirkup's also becomes a masculine art.

It is true that the old temptations remain, and ''Rhapsody on a Bead Curtain'' sees the facility at work wringing out to the last drop the metaphor of a bead curtain as a shower. But firmness prevails almost to the point of harshness in ''Medusa''—''those frog-like legs / Seem barely able to support / That sad, amorphous bum''— where Kirkup is in danger of overbalancing the other way. Poems such as ''The Ventriloquist,'' ''A Visit to Brontë Land,'' ''Photographs in a Railway Compartment,'' and ''Summertime in Leeds'' reassure us, however, that Kirkup has found his true voice—

> No idle toy would have tempted Branwell
> From the ''Bull,'' and brandy; or kept that sister
> From her tragic poems. They knew they had nothing
>   but the moor
> And themselves. It is we, who want all, who are poor

—and that he will stick to it, even though, like Branwell, he may be tempted by the ''bull,'' as he sometimes is.

Kirkup has published numerous collections. Some have been serious volumes, some, like *The Body Servant,* with its journey over the body's parts and old chestnuts such as the part without a bone, rather more playful. The trend of his later work would seem to be toward a more direct, almost haiku-like simplicity. It probably says more about the writer of this essay than Kirkup himself if I voice a definite preference for the poetry of *A Correct Compassion* and *The Submerged Village.* Here I am saying no more than that a poet, rightly, should be remembered by his or her best work. For this reason

a selected poems as a showcase for Kirkup's best work is long overdue and would do the poet the justice he deserves.

—John Cotton

KIZER, Carolyn (Ashley)

Nationality: American. **Born:** Spokane, Washington, 10 December 1925. **Education:** Sarah Lawrence College, Bronxville, New York, B.A. 1945; Columbia University, New York, 1945–46; University of Washington, Seattle, 1946–47, 1953–54. **Family:** Married 1) Charles Stimson Bullitt in 1948 (divorced 1954), two daughters and one son; 2) John Marshall Woodbridge in 1975. **Career:** Founding editor, *Poetry Northwest,* Seattle, 1959–65; State Department specialist in Pakistan, 1964–65; director of literary programs, National Endowment for the Arts, 1966–70; lecturer or poet-in-residence, University of North Carolina, Chapel Hill, 1970–74, Washington University, St. Louis, 1971, Barnard College, New York, 1972, Ohio University, Athens, 1974, University of Iowa, Iowa City, 1975, Centre College, Danville, Kentucky, 1979, Eastern Washington University, Cheney, 1980, University of Cincinnati, Ohio, 1981, University of Louisville, Kentucky, 1982, State University of New York, Albany, 1982, Columbia School of Arts, New York, 1982, and Bucknell University, Lewisburg, Pennsylvania, 1983; acting director of the graduate writing program, Columbia University, New York, 1972; professor, University of Maryland, College Park, 1976–77; professor of poetry, Stanford University, California, 1986; senior fellow in the humanities, Princeton University, New Jersey, 1986; professor, University of Arizona, Tucson, 1989, 1990; visiting professor, University of California, Davis, 1991; Coal Royalty chair, University of Alabama, 1995. **Awards:** Governor's award, State of Washington, 1965, 1985, 1995, 1998; Masefield prize, Poetry Society of America, 1983; American Academy award, 1985; Pulitzer prize, 1985; Theodore Roethke prize; Poetry Society of America Frost Medal, 1988; Silver medal, Commonwealth Club, 1997; Aiken Taylor prize, *Sewanee Review,* 1998. D.Litt.: Whitman College, Walla Walla, Washington, 1986; Mills College, Oakland, California, 1989; St. Andrews College, Laurinberg, North Carolina; Washington State University, Pullman. **Address:** 19772 8th Street East, Sonoma, California 95476, U.S.A.

PUBLICATIONS

Poetry

Poems. Portland, Oregon, Portland Art Museum, 1959.
The Ungrateful Garden. Bloomington, Indiana University Press, 1961.
Five Poets of the Pacific Northwest, with others, edited by Robin Skelton. Seattle, University of Washington Press, 1964.
Knock upon Silence. New York, Doubleday, 1965.
Midnight Was My Cry: New and Selected Poems. New York, Doubleday, 1971.
Mermaids in the Basement: Poems for Women. Port Townsend, Washington, Copper Canyon Press, 1984.
Yin. Brockport, New York, Boa, 1984.
The Nearness of You: Poems for Men. Port Townsend, Washington, Copper Canyon Press, 1986.

Harping On: Poems 1985–1995. Port Townsend, Washington, Copper Canyon Press, 1996.

Great Poems by Women. Cheney, Washington, Eastern Washington University Press, 1997.

Pro Femina. Kansas City, Missouri, BkMk Press, 1999.

The Ungrateful Garden. Pittsburgh, Carnegie Mellon University Press, 1999.

Recording: *An Ear to the Earth,* Watershed, 1977.

Other

Proses: Essays on Poets & Poetry. Port Townsend, Washington, Copper Canyon Press, 1994.

Editor, with Elaine Dallman and Barbara Gelpi, *Woman Poet—The West.* Reno, Nevada, Women-in-Literature, 1980.

Editor, *The Essential John Clare.* Hopewell, New Jersey, Ecco Press, 1993.

Editor, *100 Great Poems by Women: A Golden Ecco Anthology.* Hopewell, New Jersey, Ecco Press, 1995.

Editor, *Picking and Choosing: Essays on Prose.* Cheney, Washington, Eastern Washington University Press, 1995.

Editor, *American Spirituals,* by Jeffrey Greene. Boston, Northeastern University Press, 1998.

Translator, *Carrying Over.* Port Townsend, Washington, Copper Canyon Press, 1988.

*

Manuscript Collection: Abbott Library, Buffalo, New York.

Critical Studies: *An Answering Music—On the Poetry of Carolyn Kizer* edited by David Rigsbee, Boston, Ford Brown & Co., 1990; "Franklin Street Days: Carolyn Kizer in North Carolina, 1970–1974" by Ronald H. Bayes, in *Pembroke* (Pembroke, North Carolina), 23, 1991; "Passwords at the Boundary: Carolyn Kizer's Poetry" by Henry Taylor, in *Hollins Critic* (Hollins College, Virginia), 34(3), 1997; "Kizer's 'The Great Blue Heron'" by Derek T. Leuenberger, in *Explicator* (Washington, D.C.), 57(2), winter 1999.

*   *   *

Carolyn Kizer works in terms of the twinned tensions of life, those central paradoxes so directly felt by women. She poses the problem of the woman poet boldly in her remarkable "A Muse of Water":

We who must act as handmaidens
To our own goddess, turn too fast,
Trip on our hems, to glimpse the muse
Gliding below her lake or sea,
Are left, long-staring after her
Narcissists by necessity . . .

Mother and muse, Kizer can write tenderly of her own mother, who taught her to love nature even at its most loathsome, "a whole, wild, lost, betrayed and secret life / Among its dens and burrows."

Although she has a poem titled "Not Writing Poetry about Children," such poems are everywhere in her work. So are cats, symbols of the female condition, as in "A Widow in Wintertime":

trying
To live well enough alone, and not to dream
Of grappling in the snow, claws plunged in fur,

Or waken in a caterwaul of dying.

The daring and diffidence of womanhood are celebrated in poems of companionship like "For Jan, In Bar Maria." But Kizer's most constant, resonant theme is love and loss, analyzed in detail in the sequence "A Month in Summer." The work ends with a quotation from Bashō, and it is in the fatalism of Japanese civilization that Kizer finds a refuge and an artistic remedy for her womanly woes: "'O love long gone, it is raining in our room.' / So I memorize these lines, without salutation, without close." One of the best woman poets around, she is profoundly committed to the process of life, however painful.

The twinned tensions of male and female are explored systematically in later volumes, including *Mermaids in the Basement,* subtitled *Poems for Women,* and its complement, *The Nearness of You: Poems for Men.* Here old and new commingle, while between the works is *Yin,* which includes two wonderful autobiographical reveries, "Running Away from Home" and "Exodus." In an era when a shrill feminism threatens to tilt the scales of past injustice, Kizer's view of the sexual universe contains polarity without hostility.

With like thrift Kizer has gathered her translations in *Carrying Over.* Urdu, Macedonian, and Yiddish testify to the diversity of her interests, but there also are translations from the great Tang poet Tu Fu, as well as of the passionate love poems of the Chinese woman poet Shu Ting, born in 1952. Old and young, past and present, yin and yang—Kizer has kept faith with her interests over several decades, and she can say with Chaucer's Criseyde that "I am my owne woman, wel at ese" in the dance of the dualities.

—John Montague

KNOEPFLE, John

Nationality: American. **Born:** Cincinnati, Ohio, 4 February 1923. **Education:** Xavier University, Cincinnati, Ph.B. 1949, M.A. 1951; St. Louis University, Ph.D. 1967. **Military Service:** U.S. Navy, 1942–46: Purple Heart. **Family:** Married Margaret Sower in 1956; one daughter and four sons (one deceased). **Career:** Producer-director, WCET Educational Television, Cincinnati, 1953–55; assistant instructor, Ohio State University, Columbus, 1956–57; instructor, Southern Illinois University, East St. Louis, 1957–61, St. Louis University High School, 1961–62, and Mark Twain Institute, Clayton, Missouri, summers 1962–64; assistant professor, Maryville College, St. Louis, 1962–66, and Washington University, St. Louis, 1963–66; associate professor, St. Louis University, 1966–72; consultant, Project Upward Bound, Washington, D.C., 1967–70; professor of literature, Sangamon State University, Springfield, Illinois, 1972–91. **Awards:** Rockefeller fellowship, 1967; National Endowment for the Arts grant, 1980; Illinois Arts Council award, 1986; Mark Twain award for distinguished contributions to Midwestern literature, Michigan State University, 1986; Illinois Author of the Year award, Illinois Association of Teachers of English, 1986; fellow, Springfield Area Arts Council, 1994; Illinois Literary Heritage award, Center for the Book, 1995. D.H.L.: Maryville University, 1996. **Address:** 1008 West Adams, Auburn, Illinois 62615, U.S.A.

PUBLICATIONS

Poetry

Poets at the Gate, with others. St. Louis, Arts Festival of Washington University, 1965.

Rivers into Islands. Chicago, University of Chicago Press, 1965.

Songs for Gail Guidry's Guitar. New York, New Rivers Press, 1969.

An Affair of Culture and Other Poems. La Crosse, Wisconsin, Northeast-Juniper, 1969.

After Gray Days and Other Poems. Prairie Village, Kansas, Crabgrass Press, 1970.

The Intricate Land. New York, New Rivers Press, 1970.

The Ten-Fifteen Community Poems. Poquoson, Virginia, Back Door Press, 1971.

Whetstone. Shawnee Mission, Kansas, Bk Mk Press, 1972.

Deep Winter Poems. Lincoln, Nebraska, Three Sheets, 1972.

Thinking of Offerings. Poems 1970–1973. La Crosse, Wisconsin, Juniper Press, 1975.

A Gathering of Voices. Ruffsdale, Pennsylvania, Rook Press, 1978.

Five Missouri Poets, with others, edited by Jim Barnes. Kirksville, Missouri, Chariton Review Press, 1979.

Poems for the Hours. Menomonie, Wisconsin, Uzzano, 1979.

A Box of Sandalwood: Love Poems. La Crosse, Wisconsin, Juniper Press, 1979.

Selected Poems. Kansas City, Missouri, University of Missouri, 1985.

Poems from the Sangamon. Urbana, University of Illinois Press, 1985.

Begging an Amnesty. Birmingham, Alabama, Druid Press, 1994.

The Chinkapin Oak: Poems 1993–1995. Springfield, Illinois, Rosehill Press, 1995.

Other

Voyages to the Inland Sea: Essays and Poems, with Lisel Mueller and David Etter. La Crosse, Wisconsin Center for Contemporary Poetry, 1971.

Dogs and Cats and Things Like That: A Book of Poems for Children. New York, McGraw Hill, 1971.

Our Street Feels Good: A Book of Poems for Children. New York, McGraw Hill, 1972.

Regional Perspectives: An Examination of America's Literary Heritage, with others, edited by John Gordon Burke. Chicago, American Library Association, 1973.

Dim Tales. Urbana, Illinois, Stormline Press, 1989.

Editor, with Dan Jaffe, *Frontier Literature: Images of the American West.* New York, McGraw Hill, 1979.

Translator, with Robert Bly and James Wright, *Twenty Poems of César Vallejo.* Madison, Minnesota, Sixties Press, 1962.

Translator, with Robert Bly and James Wright, *Neruda and Vallejo: Selected Poems.* Boston, Beacon Press, 1971.

Translator, with Wang Shouyi, *Song [T'ang] Dynasty Poems.* Peoria, Illinois, Spoon River Poetry Press, 1985.

*

Critical Studies: "Masks of Self-Deception" by Lloyd Goldman, and "The Reflective Art of John Knoepfle" by Raymond Benoit, both in *Minnesota Review 8* (St. Paul), 1968; "The Poetry of John Knoepfle" by Norman D. Hinton, in *Western Illinois Regional Studies* (Macomb, Illinois), 8(2), fall 1985; "John Knoepfle's Historical Consciousness and the Renaming of America" by Theodore Haddin, in *Chariton Review,* 12(2), fall 1986.

John Knoepfle comments:

(1970) I consider myself a poet of the American Middle West but aware of the same cosmic problems that beset everyone anywhere.

Poems written since the publication of *Rivers into Islands* are less nostalgic. They show bias toward events—often surrealistic ones—that occur in such moments when public and private experience overlap. The poetry does not attempt to analyze the content of these two kinds of experience so much as it tries to reproduce the dynamics of their encounter. This has not been particularly intentional on my part; it is simply the way the poems have been moving, perhaps in an effort to get away from a propagandist/fatalist dilemma that seems at the moment largely irrelevant. The past in these poems and the midcontinent as place are there, then, not so much as subject matter outside of the poet as they are a part of a community of experience that I feel deeply involved in.

(1974) I am more and more concerned with the nature of a voice that is adequate, that can articulate the overlapping of public and private experience, some voice that is neither totally egocentric nor totally masked speech—how to capture such a voice.

(1995) In *Begging an Amnesty* there was an attempt to honor a generous luminosity in decent human beings by presenting them against the background of a depraved time. Not that I do not witness a grudging admiration for survivors, even those who gamble away their Social Security checks by the third of the month. At the same time, because I am positing myself against perfection, I have to acknowledge my own coming up short. But this is sociology and theology. To be able to express these ideas there has to be a resonance in the language. I always want to capture this, the lucky chance that may come if I can just keep writing doggedly despite a personal sense of failure.

*   *   *

John Knoepfle was forty-three when *Rivers into Islands* was published. Its first poem, a farewell to "rebel rabble-rousing banjos," acknowledges the unusual age of this lyric poet's debut: "Welcome to the peaceful country, / delicate notes of bamboo flutes, / darkness of strummed guitars." A reverent man, longing for the deep truths of love and community and speaking quietly, even prayerfully, Knoepfle writes his disappointment—the failure of love, the loss of a heroic past, the inhumanity of contemporary America—without losing hope of consolation.

Even in a bleak hour "nothing is wasted / not even pain." In his meditations he seeks the source of affirmation ("it has to be any yes"), knowing that the effort secures his own well-being:

what does a man do
turning away
from the lines of his face
arrogance
a broken board
a door covered with snow

When love fails, Knoepfle admits that he is "drained / like a shadow like / sunlight dancing on a / sacred river." But longing overcomes hostility ("I will build / a next in your ribs"), and his aggrieved memory provides solace: "there will be some yesterday / when we will be stunned with joy."

Knoepfle's nostalgia extends to his entire country, the American Midwest, with its legacy of common folk, hard work, and settlements recent enough to be the subject of the recollections of living relatives. A heroic mood characterizes poems about miners, settlers, and laborers in *Rivers into Islands*. Knoepfle longs for the "pile driving" locomotives of his boyhood, whose whistles seemed "home-hungry sighs" and "made my heart sad," but he can lash out at reminders of his grief, as in "Keelboatman's horn": "Why do you wake up the valley? / Put down your horn. We know / of others the rivers bruised."

Knoepfle turns indignant when he writes of the present "travail of the race." The middle portion of *Rivers into Islands* tells of wrecking balls disrupting lives, a refinery flame "flaring and con- tracting / among the millionaires," the hypocrisy of a desolated generation who "pretend that if someone came with bread / we would not destroy each other for the broken crumbs." Hostility disrupts "old recollections of providence" during the Thanksgiving dinner in "pilgrims day," from *The Intricate Land*. When a daughter opines that the man her mother has shouted away may be truth, the mother smooths her skirt and cries, "truth hell . . . / that was your father." The same bitter humor characterizes "labor day this hundred years" in *the chinkapin oak,* a poem that eloquently champions the cause of workers worldwide: ". . . I know what those / stalled bargaining sessions mean oh yes / so many open graves." In "beneath kennesaw mountain" an encounter with men "overworked on good wages / too much overtime and then / the job folding" becomes the impetus for a frightening portrayal of the frenzy of turn-of-the-millennium Amer- ica. In the time of betrayal, injustice, self-interest, violence, and bigotry, even religion, Knoepfle rages in *Thinking of Offerings,* is compromised, the authority of "messengers of elohim" reduced to "what they were themselves / singing in the cavity / of his skull." *Poems from the Sangamon,* Knoepfle's most substantial book, still emphasizes the ominous—"some damn odin / eats us up don't you think"—but embeds human histories in a mythic perspective stretch- ing from the Ice Age. He elegizes lost peoples and their ways and expresses wonder in poems like "owl in the capitol dome" and "man looking for his wife" (poems presumably descended from efforts in translating Vallejo and Neruda), and his characters tell quintessentially American tall tales in "lunch room, new berlin" and "bulldog crossing." Set in a "country of moraines," the Sangamon Valley of central Illinois, the collection—Koepfle's most comprehensive— gives us a world both living and senescent:

no gold now no winning
all that melted down
hidden under loess
america of ten thousand years
taking its own back
all gone golden and gold

The gnomic poems Knoepfle wrote in the late 1970s comprise a kind of phenomenology, identifying essential human qualities to be attentiveness, passion, and affirmation. A superior world surrounds us—a natural world, more integral, perhaps more moral, certainly enigmatic. Knoepfle may rage and grieve, but he is no nihilist. He portrays himself in "poet in a small place" as one who "farms" mystery from what he finds around him, "where death is a stone in a pond / and each house defines / the solitude of every window." But it is a mistake to reduce Knoepfle to a pastoral poet or a protester. He responds eagerly to the array of this world, bringing considerable knowledge of the past to bear. And the versatility of his spirit permits him, as he writes in *the chinkapin oak,* to be "prophet or outlaw with [his] words."

—Jay S. Paul

KNOTT, Bill

Nationality: American. **Born:** William Kilborn Knott, Gratiot County, Michigan, 17 February 1940. **Education:** Carson City High School, Michigan. **Military Service:** U.S. Army. **Career:** Poet-in-residence, Emerson College, Boston, 1976. **Awards:** National Endowment for the Arts grant, 1968. **Address:** c/o WLP, Emerson College, 100 Beacon Street, Boston, Massachusetts 02116, U.S.A.

PUBLICATIONS

Poetry

The Naomi Poems, Book One: Corpse and Beans. Chicago, Follett, 1968.
Aurealism: A Study. Syracuse, New York, Salt Mound Press, 1970.
Are You Ready Mary Baker Eddy?, with James Tate. San Francisco, Cloud Marauder Press, 1970.
Auto-Necrophilia: The Bill Knott Poems, Book 2. Chicago, Follett, 1971.
Nights of Naomi. Somerville, Massachusetts, Barn Dream Press, 1971.
Love Poems to Myself. Boston, Barn Dream Press, 1974.
Rome in Rome. New York, Release Press, 1974.
Selected and Collected Poems. New York, Sun, 1977.
For Anne and Other Poems. Waban, Massachusetts, Munich Editions from Shell, 1977.
Destinations. Walton-on-Thames, Surrey, Outposts, 1978.
Becos. New York, Random House, 1983.
Poems 1963–1988. Pittsburgh, University of Pittsburgh Press, 1989.
Outremer. Iowa City, University of Iowa Press, 1989.
The Quicken Tree: Poems. Brockport, New York, BOA Editions, 1995.

Novel

Lucky Daryll, with James Tate. New York, Release Press, 1977.

*

Critical Studies: Interview with James Randall, and "For Bill Knott: In Celebration and Anticipation of His Selected/Collected Poems" by

Thomas Lux, both in *Ploughshares* (Cambridge, Massachusetts), 4(1), 1977.

Bill Knott comments:

I consider my work to fall within the minimalist or imagist tradition. My poems are rarely longer than ten-twenty lines. The hermeticist poets—Mallarmé, Ungaretti, Bonnefoy, etc.—have been lasting influences. The Greek anthology and Japanese haikuists, like Issa and Bashō are sources for me. In English I revere Milton, Matthew Arnold, and Hardy. Larkin is better than any of his American contemporaries, and I admire poets like Carol Ann Duffy and Robert Wells. I would rather be British. I loathe what Harold Bloom calls the American religion, that is, the Emersonian quest.

*   *   *

Among the passionate love lyrics and equally passionate rants against the war in Vietnam in Bill Knott's first book were a number of short neoimagist poems like this one, entitled ''Goodbye'':

If you are still alive when you read this,
close your eyes. I am
under the lids, growing black.

It was for these pieces, which caught the eye of the anthologizers, that Knott first became known. Such poems, while set apart by an admirable compression, still conformed to the contemporary poetic ideal of a unified surface and nearly transparent language. It is to his credit that Knott, with his instinct for doing the unexpected, subsequently took a less traveled path.

Many of the poems in *Auto-Necrophilia* and *Nights of Naomi* seem to have been written according to the throw of the dice, as in the one-line ''Poem'' from the first of the two volumes: ''The spinal-fusion taps at the window of blank pennies.'' Yet by fracturing the poem's surface, such experiments allowed Knott to develop a faceted verbal mirror that, while not giving the reader a complete picture of anything, portrayed the realities of consciousness from infinitely more angles than did the smooth lenses of his fellow poets. In his work of the 1970s, culminating in the *Selected and Collected Poems* and especially in *Becos,* Knott developed an idiom more expressive of human complexities and contradictions:

Like a burglar who arrives before the apartmenthouse
is even half built
Look at him catwalking the skeletal girders at one a m
like him
Misjudging every erection I am
Pockmark not interested in masks

In his pursuit of emotional honesty Knott has borrowed from the speech habits of children and adolescents. His language is typically jagged, cramped, and unwashed. He flings four-letter words about with a schoolboy's gusto. At other times, especially in *Becos,* the reader seems to be eavesdropping on the mumbled fantasy life of a gifted child:

at last comes total blindness:
touch-awkward I feel like an ogre, a clumsy giant

tripping over some ruins,
rubble of the town he's just smashed.
Tower-cursing as I bang my knee. Or no:
I'm tiny. I can see again! I see the giant walk off
favoring his one leg . . .

The voice in these poems is intimate and poignant as it deals with issues of identity, such as sexual ambiguity, that the adult mind normally sweeps under the rugs of convention and style:

I walk
On human stilts.
To my right lower leg a man is locked rigid
To the left a woman, lifelessly strapped.

Language in this transitional world is still a somewhat mysterious and plastic thing of unknown powers and uncertain properties. If part of Knott's enterprise has been to map out the contours and boundaries of the self, it has also been to uncover potentials in language that go beyond the conventions of accepted discourse, thus the solecisms, Joycean coinages, and resonant dyslexias that give his work its nervously energetic surface.

At the same time, because of the crucial role language plays in his tentative definitions of self, Knott is constantly aware—and makes his reader aware—of the slipperiness of his medium, the self-deception it all too often countenances. In a poem from *Becos* he talks about

the faith I live with, that
custodying lipserver [that] sticks
me near any old name-niche,
teeters me on
every pedestal of mislabeled
personae . . .

To counter the trickery of thought and language, Knott engages in an ongoing act of poetic revision, of ''correcting misprints in the word 'I.''' This may occur in the body of the poem, as in ''October,'' also from *Becos:*

. . . hell, money is not a good
example, it's not mechanic, I'm sorry.   Damn.
Back on the track: . . .

It also occurs more literally, from book to book, as he retitles, excerpts, and reconceives his poems.

For Knott the best insurance against the falsity of a set style is a poetry that is off balance, unbuttoned, with frequent sprung rhythms to keep readers on their toes: ''I groan up, and walk, ouch, / soft-putty self-pity patched.'' Its very unpredictability—the sense of not knowing where one is going, where one will end up—is one of the immediate attractions of Knott's work. Other pleasures include his ever present if dark humor, that determination to ''laugh it up, show pain a good time''; his fine ear for the vernacular—''Mrs. Knott was leanin over me / With this kind of eek-like look she / Was peeking at a freak or something . . .''; and his surprising, up-to-the-moment metaphors. Such effects tend to function in isolation rather than cumulatively, and even in his longer poems Knott is something of a miniaturist. Yet in *Becos* in particular there are poems conceived along more extended lines, including "The Closet," a poem about his mother's death, and "Mitts and Gloves," a meditation on baseball paraphernalia.

At a time of what seems increasing polarization in American poetry between those writing with an unqualified regard for the illusionist surface of language and those bent on the labored, ultimately retrogressive dismantling of language, Knott, by holding to his own path, may well have come upon a much needed middle ground.

—Martin McKinsey

KOCH, Kenneth

Nationality: American. **Born:** Cincinnati, Ohio, 27 February 1925. **Education:** Harvard University, Cambridge, Massachusetts, A.B. 1948; Columbia University, New York, M.A. 1953, Ph.D. 1959. **Military Service:** U.S. Army, 1943–46. **Family:** Married 1) Mary Janice Elwood in 1955 (died 1981), one daughter; 2) Karen Culler in 1994. **Career:** Lecturer in English, Rutgers University, New Brunswick, New Jersey, 1953–54, 1955–56, 1957–58, and Brooklyn College, 1957–59; director of the Poetry Workshop, New School for Social Research, New York, 1958–66. Lecturer, 1959–61, assistant professor, 1962–66, associate professor, 1966–71, and since 1971 professor of English, Columbia University. Associated with *Locus Solus* magazine, Lans-en-Vercors, France, 1960–62. **Awards:** Fulbright fellowship, 1950, 1978; Guggenheim fellowship, 1961; National Endowment for the Arts grant, 1966; Ingram Merrill Foundation fellowship, 1969; Harbison award, for teaching, 1970; Frank O'Hara prize (*Poetry,* Chicago), 1973; American Academy award, 1976; Bollingen prize for poetry, 1995; Bobbitt prize for poetry, Library of Congress, 1996; chevalier dans l'ordre des arts et des lettres, 1998. **Member:** American Academy of Arts and Letters, 1996. **Address:** Department of English, 414 Hamilton Hall, Columbia University, New York, New York 10027, U.S.A.

PUBLICATIONS

Poetry

Poems. New York, Tibor de Nagy, 1953.
Ko; or, A Season on Earth. New York, Grove Press, 1960.
Permanently. New York, Tiber Press, 1960.
Thank You and Other Poems. New York, Grove Press, 1962.
Poems from 1952 and 1953. Los Angeles, Black Sparrow Press, 1968.
When the Sun Tries to Go On. Los Angeles, Black Sparrow Press, 1969.
Sleeping with Women. Los Angeles, Black Sparrow Press, 1969.
The Pleasures of Peace and Other Poems. New York, Grove Press, 1969.
Penguin Modern Poets 24, with Kenward Elmslie and James Schuyler. London, Penguin, 1973.
The Art of Love. New York, Random House, 1975.
The Duplications. New York, Random House, 1977.

The Burning Mystery of Anna in 1951. New York, Random House, 1979.
From the Air. London, Taranman, 1979.
Days and Nights. New York, Random House, 1982.
Selected Poems 1950–1982. New York, Random House, 1985.
On the Edge. New York, Viking, 1986.
Seasons on Earth. New York, Viking, 1987.
One Train. New York, Knopf, 1994.
On the Great Atlantic Rainway, Selected Poems 1950–1988. New York, Knopf, 1994.
Straits. New York, Knopf, 1998.
New Addresses. New York, Knopf, 2000.

Plays

Bertha (produced New York, 1959). Included in *Bertha and Other Plays,* 1966.
The Election (also director: produced New York, 1960). Included in *A Change of Hearts,* 1973.
Pericles (produced New York, 1960). Included in *Bertha and Other Plays,* 1966.
George Washington Crossing the Delaware (in *3 x 3,* produced New York, 1962; produced separately, London, 1983). Included in *Bertha and Other Plays,* 1966.
The Construction of Boston (produced New York, 1962). Included in *Bertha and Other Plays,* 1966.
Guinevere; or, The Death of the Kangaroo (produced New York, 1964). Included in *Bertha and Other Plays,* 1966.
The Tinguely Machine Mystery; or, The Love Suicides at Kaluka (also co-director: produced New York, 1965). Included in *A Change of Hearts,* 1973.
Bertha and Other Plays (includes Pericles, *George Washington Crossing the Delaware, The Construction of Boston, Guinevere; or, The Death of the Kangaroo, The Gold Standard, The Return of Yellowmay, The Revolt of the Giant Animals, The Building of Florence, Angelica, The Merry Stones, The Academic Murders, Easter, The Lost Feed, Mexico, Coil Supreme*). New York, Grove Press, 1966.
The Gold Standard (produced New York, 1969). Included in *Bertha and Other Plays,* 1966.
The Moon Balloon (produced New York, 1969). Included in *A Change of Hearts,* 1973.
The Artist, music by Paul Reif, adaptation of the poem "The Artist" by Koch (produced New York, 1972). Poem included in *Thank You and Other Poems,* 1962.
A Little Light (produced Amagansett, New York, 1972).
A Change of Hearts: Plays, Films, and Other Dramatic Works 1951–1971 (includes the contents of *Bertha and Other Plays,* and *A Change of Hearts; E. Kology; The Election; The Tinguely Machine Mystery; The Moon Balloon; Without Kinship; Ten Films: Because, The Color Game, Mountains and Electricity, Sheep Harbor, Oval Gold, Moby Dick, L'Ecole Normale, The Cemetery, The Scotty Dog,* and *The Apple; Youth;* and *The Enchantment*). New York, Random House, 1973.
A Change of Hearts, music by David Hollister (produced New York, 1985). Included in *A Change of Hearts* (collection), 1973.
Rooster Redivivus (produced Garnerville, New York, 1975).
The Art of Love, adaptation of his own poem (produced Chicago, 1976).

The Red Robins, adaptation of his own novel (produced New York, 1978). New York, Performing Arts Journal Publications, 1979.
The New Diana (produced New York, 1984).
Popeye among the Polar Bears (produced New York, 1986).
One Thousand Avant-Garde Plays. New York, Knopf, 1988.
The Construction of Boston, music by Scott Wheeler (produced Boston, 1990).
The Banquet, opera with music by Marcello Panni (produced Bremen, Germany, 1998).

Screenplays: *The Scotty Dog,* 1967; *The Apple,* 1968.

Novel

The Red Robins. New York, Random House, 1975.

Short Stories

Interlocking Lives, with Alex Katz. New York, Kulchur Press, 1970.
Hotel Lambosa. Minneapolis, Coffee House Press, 1993.

Other

John Ashbery and Kenneth Koch (A Conversation). Tucson, Interview Press, 1965(?).
Wishes, Lies, and Dreams: Teaching Children to Write Poetry. New York, Random House, 1970.
Rose, Where Did You Get That Red? Teaching Great Poetry to Children. New York, Random House, 1973.
I Never Told Anybody: Teaching Poetry Writing in a Nursing Home. New York, Random House, 1977.
Making Your Own Days: The Pleasures of Reading and Writing Poetry. New York, Scribner, 1998.

Editor, with Kate Farrell, *Sleeping on the Wing: An Anthology of Modern Poetry, with Essays on Reading and Writing.* New York, Random House, 1981.
Editor, with Kate Farrell, *Talking to the Sun: An Illustrated Anthology of Poems for Young People.* New York, Holt Rinehart, 1985; London, Viking Kestrel, 1986.

*

Theatrical Activities: Director: **Plays:** *The Election,* New York, 1960; *The Tinguely Machine Mystery* (co-director, with Remy Charlip), New York, 1965.

Bibliography: ''Kenneth Koch: An Analytic List of Bibliographies'' by Vincent Prestianni, in *Sagetrieb* (Orono, Maine), 12(1), spring 1993.

Critical Studies: Interview with Kenneth Koch by David Spurr, in *Contemporary Poetry* (Bryn Mawr, Pennsylvania), 3(4), 1978; ''Beyond Irony'' by David Spurr, in *American Poetry Review* (Philadelphia), 12(2), March-April 1983; ''Kenneth Koch Revisited'' by Robert DiYanni, in *Children's Literature Association Quarterly* (Battle Creek, Michigan), 9(1), spring 1984; ''Marianne Moore and the New York School: O'Harra, Ashbery, Koch'' by Rosanne

Wasserman, in *Sagetrieb* (Orono, Maine), 6(3), winter 1987; ''Why, It's Right There in the Proces Verbal': The New York School of Poets'' by Geoff Ward, in *Cambridge Quarterly* (Oxford), 21(3), 1992; ''Dr. Fun'' by David Lehman, in *American Poetry Review* (Philadelphia), 24(6), November-December 1995; ''Kenneth Koch'' by Jordan Davis, in *American Poetry Review* (Philadelphia), 25(6), November-December 1996.

*   *   *

Kenneth Koch was one of the three principal poets of the New York school in the middle and late 1950s, a somewhat amorphous and short-lived group that also included John Ashbery and Frank O'Hara. The three had joined forces while students at Harvard before transferring their activities to New York, where they became associated with the painters who were then ascendant in the American art world, a group known as abstract expressionists. To a certain extent the poets seemed to be bringing to verbal constructs the principles of abstract expressionism; that is, they used words totally abstractly and evocatively. At the same time their prosodic practice was in revolt against the academic austerity of mid-century American poetry, and their use of syntax and measure resembled that of the contemporaneous beat movement. What distinguished the two groups, if anything, was the New York poets' retention of an earlier idea of art as in some sense a puristic activity, not socially amenable, and of the art object as distinct from and perhaps superior to the objects of ''ordinary reality.'' In addition, Koch was, during a period of residence abroad, deeply influenced by French poetry of the time, with its emphasis on psychological particularism.

These groupings and distinctions have long since broken down, of course. Koch's association with New York poetry was, in effect, his apprenticeship. Much of his early work was very far out indeed; some was frankly incomprehensible, even to the poet. Since then Koch has elevated his lyric view to another level, not in the least realistic but better organized and more simplified than his earlier view, with the result that some of his later work has been extremely effective. The freedom of his earlier verbal technique has given him a felicity that occasionally still descends to surrealistic glibness but that at its best is remarkably inventive and accurate. At the same time, substantially fixed in his poems is a depth of metaphysical concern that gives them the drive and intensity of genuinely serious experiments.

One distinction of the New York poets was their devotion to the lyric theater. Their connection with off-Broadway and off-off-Broadway gave them opportunities for experiments with dramatic writing that were open to few poets elsewhere in the country. Some of Koch's best writing occurs in the several books of plays he has published, books that have been generally neglected, however, by American poetry readers and critics.

—Hayden Carruth

KOLATKAR, Arun (Balkrishna)

Nationality: Indian. **Born:** Kolhapur, Bombay, 1 November 1932. **Career:** Works as a graphic artist in an advertising agency, Bombay. **Awards:** Commonwealth Poetry prize, 1977. **Address:** c/o Clearing House, Palm Springs, Cusse Parade, Bombay 400 005, India.

PUBLICATIONS

Poetry

Jejuri. Bombay, Clearing House, 1976.

*

Critical Studies: "Arun Kolatkar: A Bilingual Poet" by Vrinda Nabar, in *World Literature Written in English* (Canada), 16, 1977; "Four New Voices" by Brijraj Singh, in *Chandrabhaga* (Orissa, India), 1, 1979; "A Study of Arun Kolatkar's 'Jejuri'" by Karen Smith, in *Commonwealth Quarterly* (Karnataka State, India), 3(12), 1979; "'Jejuri': Arun Kolatkar's Waste Land" by M.R. Satyanarayana, in *Indian Poetry in English: A Critical Assessment*, edited by Vasant A. Shahane and M. Sivaramkrishna, Atlantic Highlands, Humanities, 1981; "A Critical Approach to Indo-English Poetry" by Syd C. Harrex, in *Only Connect: Literary Perspectives East and West*, edited by Harrex and Guy Amirthanayagam, Adelaide and Honolulu, Centre for Research in the New Literature, 1981; "Correspondence through Gestures: The Poetry of Arun Kolatkar" by Madhusudan Prasad, in *Literary Half-Yearly* (Mysore, India), 24(1), January 1983; "Arun Kolatkar and Bilingual Poetry" by Bhalchandra Nemade, in *Indian Readings in Commonwealth Literature*, edited by G.S. Amur and others, New York and New Delhi, Sterling, 1985; "Arun Kolatkar's Poetry: An Exile's Pilgrimage" by V.R. Kanadey, in *Modern Studies and Other Essays in Honour of Dr. R.K. Sinha*, edited by R.C. Prasad and A.K. Sharma, New Delhi, Vikas, 1987; "Arun Kolatkar's 'Jejuri': An Atheist's Pilgrimage," in *New Quest* (Pune, India), 79, January/February 1990; "Arun Kolatkar's 'Jejuri': Quest As Stasis" by Sudesh Mishra, in *Commonwealth Review* (New Delhi), 2(1–2), 1990–91.

*   *   *

A bilingual (Marathi and English) poet, Arun Kolatkar burst upon the Indo-English poetic scene when his *Jejuri* won the Commonwealth Poetry prize for 1977. Although his poems had appeared since 1955 in poetry magazines and anthologies, *Jejuri* was his first book. Kolatkar does not show any solipsistic uneasiness in using a foreign linguistic medium, as do A.K. Ramanujan and R. Parthasarathy. Even though his poetic idiom is objectivist, it does not surrender to the pulls of the past—cultural or linguistic—and is, indeed, characterized by an engaging "alfresco individualism."

Jejuri, comprising thirty-one titled sections, stands out as a personal epic like William Carlos Williams's *Paterson*. It dramatizes a Jungian passage to contemporary Hinduism, symbolized by the shrine at Jejuri, where one has only "to scratch a rock / and a legend springs." Ironically, the rational-minded and irreverent protagonist Manohar ("God is the word / and I know it backwards"), who regards mythmaking as characteristic of decadent Hinduism, himself succumbs to it as his "pilgrimage" nears its end. The train indicator appears to Manohar as "a wooden saint in need of paint," and in sheer desperation he is prepared to "slaughter a goat before the clock / smash a coconut on the railway track . . . / bathe the station master in milk . . . / If only some one would tell . . . / when the next train is due." Indeed, Kolatkar's easy, informal, though laconic, tone, which is suggestive of a postromantic expressionism, belies his capacity to transfigure the world with his iconoclastic cast of thought. His awareness of the shrine of Khandoba at Jejuri and its railway station,

being mythical correlatives of the postulates of a purgatory, could perhaps alone redeem his pilgrimage.

Kolatkar's subtle use of the montage technique in *Jejuri* to achieve the effect of a symbolist aesthetic (indeed, his first impulse was to make a movie) is characteristic of modern poetry. So also is his avoidance of the mixing of "an abstraction with the concrete" (Ezra Pound's dictum). He uses images instinct with the criticism of the unfolding scene—of a wasteland—that do not lessen the vibrancy of the perceiving self: "he doesn't reply / . . . and happens to notice / a quick wink of a movement / in a scanty patch of scruffy dry grass / burnt brown in the sun / and says / look / there's a butterfly / there." *Jejuri* is a virtuoso performance that exemplifies a movement toward a freer form of verse, which is what is most promising in Kolatkar's poetry.

—K. Venkatachari

KOLLER, James

Nationality: American. **Born:** Oak Park, Illinois, 30 May 1936. **Education:** North Central College, Naperville, Illinois, B.A. 1958. **Family:** Has four daughters and two sons. **Career:** Editor, *Otherwise*, 1994–97. Since 1964 editor, *Coyote's Journal* and Coyote Books, San Francisco, then New Mexico and Maine. Also painter: individual shows—Dean Velentgas Gallery, Portland, Maine, 1989; Casa Sin Nombre, Santa Fe, New Mexico, 1989; Alleycat Gallery, New York City, 1993. Since 1989 performer, combining painting, reading, and music. **Awards:** National Endowment for the Arts grant, 1968, 1973. **Address:** c/o Coyote Books, P.O. Box 629, Brunswick, Maine 04011, U.S.A.

PUBLICATIONS

Poetry

Two Hands: Poems 1959–1961. Seattle, James B. Smith, 1965.
Brainard and Washington Street Poems. Eugene, Oregon, Toad Press, 1965.
Some Cows: Poems of Civilization and Domestic Life. San Francisco, Coyote, 1966.
The Dogs and Other Dark Woods. San Francisco, Four Seasons, 1966.
I Went to See My True Love. Buffalo, Audit East/West, 1967.
California Poems. Los Angeles, Black Sparrow Press, 1971.
Messages. Canton, New York, Institute of Further Studies, 1972.
Dark Woman, Who Lay with the Sun. San Francisco, Tenth Muse, 1972.
Bureau Creek. Brunswick, Maine, Blackberry, 1975.
Poems for the Blue Sky. Santa Barbara, California, Black Sparrow Press, 1976.
Messages/Botschaften (bilingual edition). Munich, Köhler, 1977.
Andiamo, with Franco Beltrametti and Harry Hoogstraten. Fort Kent, Maine, Great Raven Press, 1978.
O Didn't He Ramble (bilingual edition). Schwetzingen, Germany, and Brunswick, Maine, Bussard-Coyote, 1980.
One Day at a Time. Markesan, Wisconsin, Pentagram, 1981.
Back River. Brunswick, Maine, Blackberry, 1981.

Great Things Are Happening (bilingual edition). Schwetzingen, Germany, Bussard, 1984.

Give the Dog a Bone. Brunswick, Maine, Blackberry, 1986.

Graffiti Lyriques, with Franco Beltrametti. Milan, Avida Dollars, 1987.

Openings. Green River, Vermont, Longhouse, 1987.

Fortune (bilingual edition). Venezia, Italia, Supernova, 1987.

Begin with the Women Sitting. Richmond, Massachusetts, Mad River, 1988.

Roses Love Sunshine. Richmond, Massachusetts, Mad River, 1989.

A Gang of 4, with Franco Beltrametti, Julian Blaine, and Tom Raworth. Brunswick, Maine, Coyote, 1989.

This Is What He Said. Weymouth, England, Stingy Artist & Last Straw, 1991.

Grandfather Had Come A Long Way. Green River, Vermont, Longhouse, 1993.

A Dream, Starring Bill Brown. Green River, Vermont, Longhouse, 1994.

In the Wolf's Mouth: Poems 1972–88. Saint-Etienne-Valle-Francaise, France, AIOU, 1995.

Road Work. Green River, Vermont, Longhouse, 1997.

The Bone Show. Rete Bioregionale Italiana, Portiolo, Italy, 1999.

Iron Bells. Espinassounel, France, AIOU, 1999.

Novels

Shannon Who Was Lost Before. Pensnett, Staffordshire, Grosseteste Review, 1974.

If You Don't Like Me You Can Leave Me Alone. Pensnett, Staffordshire, Grosseteste Review, 1974; Brunswick, Maine, Blackberry, 1977.

The Possible Movie, with Franco Beltrametti. Saint-Etienne-Vallee-Francaise, France, COYOTAIOU, 1997.

Other

Working Notes 1960–1982. Odisheim, Germany, Falk, 1985.

Gebt Dem Alten Hund'nen Knochen (Essays, Gedichte, and Prosa 1959–1985). Odisheim, Germany, Falk, 1986.

The Natural Order (essay & graphics). Green River, Vermont, Longhouse, 1990.

Like It Was. Nobleboro, Maine, Blackberry, 1999.

Editor, with others, *Coyote's Journal* (anthology). Berkeley, California, Wingbow Press, 1982.

*

Manuscript Collections: University of Connecticut, Storrs; Simon Fraser University, Burnaby, British Columbia.

Critical Studies: "Eyes and 'I'" by Richard Duerden, in *Poetry* (Chicago), May 1966; "James Koller Issue" of *Savage 2* (Chicago), 1972; Paul Kahn, in *Montemora* (New York), spring 1977, and *Poetry Information* (London), winter 1979–80.

*   *   *

It is not surprising to learn that James Koller discovered contemporary poetry by reading Jack Kerouac in 1957, for his autobiography reads like a personal version of *On the Road.* There are many landscapes in his life—Illinois, the Pacific Northwest, the Southwest, Maine—and there are many women in his life, but most of them are wives, and there are many children by the different wives. There are also many houses, simple and usually at least partly built by Koller, and even the poems range and seem to wander, looking for a voice, or perhaps they are looking for a tradition that could adequately ground and root his wandering voice. Yet there is an odd counterpoint between Koller's rooted connection to land and an ability in his life just to pack up and wander gypsylike, which makes one wonder if it was his early encounter with Zen and the beats that offered him a philosophy of paradoxes to live by, or if this comes from some purer American, Midwestern heritage. Whatever its source, Koller has the gift of a pioneer, accepting any landscape and finding it beautiful, as in the conclusion of this 1967 poem "Snow on Mt. Helena":

> a whole world
> & nothing ever dies, it's all here
> on every road, behind every tree
> growing out of the ground, a beautiful
> fire, flames
> I'm grinning
>
> exhaust, carbon
> diamonds & threads
> my mind is filled with diamonds & threads
>
> we go off in all directions, thru intersections &
> crossed roads
>
> a necklace to live in

In his essay "Message in My Poems" Koller says, "I see poetry as a celebration—a celebration of everything that exists, is alive, or has been alive (in any sense of the word)." It is easy for any poet to say this, but Koller does not mouth this Whitmanesque doctrine without a body of work to back it up. Seen through this manifesto, Koller's work is much more than a 1960s drug-inspired, sex-obsessed lyric. Perhaps because his work has seemed so bound to the lifestyle of the 1960s, critics have ignored the possible breadth and significance of this very American writer.

Certainly, trying to track down Koller's work itself and any writing about it is rather like looking for Bigfoot. Every reference work says that his magazine, *Coyote's Journal,* has existed since 1964, yet it seems to have been published only sporadically. Still, it has left a strong impression, a kind of whisper in the Grand Canyon effect. The importance of this journal to Koller's reputation is that it locates his sphere of influence. He is a poet who is almost purely the product of small presses and whose aesthetics and personal lifestyle are not congruent with a materialistic or institutionalized world. Writing programs and the idea of professional poets probably would not so much seem evil to Koller as silly or irrelevant. In the best sense he is a poet who has never sold out, though perhaps it would never have occurred to him that he could have done so.

Two slightly older contemporaries, both friendly acquaintances of his, Gary Snyder and Robert Creeley, are poets who come to mind for comparison with this elusive writer. Yet what Snyder has that grounds his work—the Zen philosophy and tradition—and what Creeley's work is grounded in—the Cavalier love lyric—are neither, at least in specifics, very important to Koller. There was a period in the 1970s when much of his imagery came from Native American sources, yet as important as this is to Koller, it is not a grounding for him. Rather, it is a familiarity, something with which he feels comfortable, at home. His work certainly expresses a feeling for animals. But Koller, if he is grounded, is grounded in people. He travels, one might guess, to meet people, not to get away from them. His autobiography is a bewildering array of names and names and more names. The events are important because of whom they were shared with. A place was important because of the people who lived there with him. In fact, Douglas MacDonald, in his introduction to the 1973 gathering of Koller's writing published in *The Savage: A Chicago Magazine,* quotes him as saying, "To me much more valuable than the poem is the man who wrote it."

The greatest paradox one might find in Koller's poetry is precisely that he believes in the man, the voice behind the poem, not the literary artifact itself. In spite of this he has a craft that moves him toward condensed, passionate lyric and revelation, such as this moment in the poem "Sitting Alone One Cold June Night before an Empty Whiskey Bottle, a Coffee Pot, & an Oil Stove with a Window through Which I Watched the Flames":

> THERE IS NO KNOWLEDGE
> THAT'S ANY KNOWLEDGE
> THERE ARE LOTS OF PEOPLE
>   THAT ARE PEOPLE

—Diane Wakoski

KOMUNYAKAA, Yusef

Also known as James Willie Brown. Nationality: American. **Born:** Bogalusa, Louisiana, 29 April 1947. **Education:** University of Colorado, B.A. (magna cum laude) in English/Sociology 1975; Colorado State University, M.A. in Creative Writing 1978; University of California, Irvine, M.F.A. in creative writing 1980. **Military Service:** Served in Vietnam as a correspondent and editor of *The Southern Cross:* Bronze Star. **Family:** Married Mandy Sayer in 1985. **Career:** Associate instructor of English composition, Colorado State University, 1976–78; teaching assistant in poetry, and writing instructor for remedial English composition program, 1980, University of California, Irvine; instructor in English composition and American literature, University of New Orleans, 1982–84; poet-in-the-schools, New Orleans, 1984–85; visiting assistant professor of English, 1985–86, associate professor of English and African-American Studies, 1986–93, professor of English and African-American Studies, 1993–98, Indiana University, Bloomington. Since 1997 professor of creative writing, Princeton University, New Jersey. Visiting associate professor of English, fall 1991, Holloway Lecturer, spring 1992, University of California, Berkeley. Production editor, *The Southern Cross* (newspaper), American Division in Chu Lai, South Vietnam, 1970; editor, *UCCA News* and *Riverrun,* University of Colorado, 1973–75; co-editor and publisher, *Gumbo: A Magazine for the Arts,* 1976–79; administrative consultant, *Indiana Review;* advisor, *Callaloo,* Johns Hopkins University. **Awards:** First Place Poetry award, Rocky Mountain Writers Forum, 1974, 1977; Fine Arts Work Center Writing fellowship, Provincetown, 1980–81; National Endowment for the Arts Creative Writing fellowship, 1981–82, 1987–88; Louisiana Arts fellowship, 1985; San Francisco Poetry award, 1986, for *I Apologize*

for the Eyes in My Head; The Dark Room Poetry prize, 1989, for *Dien Cai Dau;* Best Books for Young Adults selection, American Library Association, 1988, for *Dien Cai Dau;* Thomas Forcade award, University of Massachusetts, Boston, 1990; *Kenyon Review* award for literary excellence, 1991; *The Village Voice* Twenty-five Best Books selection, 1992, for *Magic City;* Kingsley Tufts Poetry award, 1994; Pulitzer prize for poetry, 1994. **Address:** Princeton University, Creative Writing Program, 185 Nassau Street, Princeton, New Jersey 08544, U.S.A.

PUBLICATIONS

Poetry

Dedications and Other Dark Horses. N.p., Rocky Mountain Creative Arts Journal, 1977.
Lost in the Bonewheel Factory. Amherst, Massachusetts, Lynx House Press, 1979.
Copacetic. Middletown, Connecticut, Wesleyan University Press, 1984.
Toys in a Field. N.p., Black River Press, 1986.
I Apologize for the Eyes in My Head. Middletown, Connecticut, Wesleyan University Press, 1986.
Dien Cai Dau. Middletown, Connecticut, Wesleyan University Press, 1988.
February in Sydney (chapbook). N.p., Matchbooks, 1989.
Magic City. Middletown, Connecticut, Wesleyan University Press, 1992.
Neon Vernacular (New & Selected Poems 1977–1989). Middletown, Connecticut, Wesleyan University Press, 1994.
Thieves of Paradise. Middletown, Connecticut, Wesleyan University Press, 1998.
Talking Dirty to the Gods: Poems. New York, Farrar Straus, 2000.

Other

Blue Notes: Essays, Interviews and Commentaries. Ann Arbor, University of Michigan Press, 1999.

Editor, with J.A. Sascha Feinstein, *The Jazz Poetry Anthology.* Bloomington, Indiana University Press, 1991.
Editor, with J.A. Sascha Feinstein, *The Second Set: The Jazz Poetry Anthology, Volume 2.* Bloomington, Indiana University Press, 1996.

Translator, with Martha Collins, *The Insomnia of Fire* by Nguyen Quang Thieu. Amherst, University of Massachusetts Press, 1995.

*

Critical Studies: "'Depending on the Light': Yusef Komunyakaa's 'Dien Cai Dau'" by Vicente F. Gotera, in *America Rediscovered: Critical Essays on Literature and Film of the Vietnam War,* edited by Owen W. Gilman and Lorrie Smith, New York, Garland, 1990; "Folk Idiom in the Literary Expression of Two African American Authors: Rita Dove and Yusef Komunyakaa" by Kirkland C. Jones, in *Language and Literature in the African American Imagination,* edited by Carol Aisha Blackshire-Belay, Westport, Connecticut,

Greenwood, 1992; ''Yusef Komunyakaa: The Unified Vision—Canonization and Humanity'' by Alvin Aubert, in *African American Review* (Terre Haute, Indiana), 27(1), spring 1993; ''On Yusef Komunyakaa'' by Michael Fabre, in *Southern Quarterly* (Hattiesburg, Mississippi), 34(2), winter 1996; interview with Thomas C. Johnson, in *Worcester Review* (Worcester, Massachusetts), 19(1–2), 1998.

*   *   *

Yusef Komunyakaa was awarded the Bronze Star for serving in Vietnam, where he edited the *Southern Cross*. The poems of his first full-length book, *Copacetic* (1984), are often set in the rural South of the early twentieth century. It is here that Komunyakaa establishes a historical preoccupation—his determination to understand his own time and his role in the culture by exploring the lives of his ancestors and every packed detail of his personal life. Thus, the poems of his second collection, *I Apologize for the Eyes in My Head* (1986), form a logical progression, following the great post-Civil War migration of African-Americans to the cities of the North. Komunyakaa chronicles the sad struggles of a people displaced and oppressed by those who fear the color of their skin and the economic competition they bring with them.

From the rural South to the urban North, Komunyakaa's odyssey in life and poetry moved next to Southeast Asia, where his tour of duty inspired *Dien Cai Dau,* one of the most important books about the war. In this volume Komunyakaa memorably adapts his vibrant, clipped, and jazzy style to the dramatic occasions of war. It is here that the poet's talent for storytelling flowers, and it is here that he fully confronts, although he is staggered by it, the world's extraordinary capacity for injustice and violence. Not surprisingly in *Magic City* (1992), his next book, Komunyakaa returns home from the war to Bogalusa, Louisiana, the setting of his childhood and once a center of both Ku Klux Klan activity and the civil rights movement. This evocative landscape of voodoo and Mardi Gras strikingly resembles that in the Louisiana poem cycles of Brenda Marie Osbey, and it inspires poems of tough vulnerability and astonishment. In ''Butterfly-Toed Shoes'' the narrator attends a dance:

The place smelled of catfish
& rotgut. ''Honey Hush''
Pulled us into its pulsebeat,
& somehow I had the prettiest woman
In the room. Her dress whirled
A surge of blue, & my butterfly-toes
Were copacetic & demonic . . .
She'd loop out till our fingertips
Touched & then was back in my arms;
The hem of her dress snapped
Like a boy's shoeshine rag.

The moment becomes one of seductive potential—''We were hot colors rushing toward / The darkest corner, about to kiss''—when another man cuts in. The narrator, intoxicated by ''her breath, her body,'' does not see what happens next:

The flash when her husband burst in.
Someone knocked the back door off its hinges,
& for a moment the shuffle of feet
Were on the deck of a Dutch man of War.

I'm still backing away
From the scene, a scintilla
Of love & murder.

This reaction, the backing away from yet the facing of the danger and horror, defines Komunyakaa's wholly believable stance in a challenging world.

Komunyakaa's collection *Neon Vernacular* (1994) gathers representative poems from four limited (and no longer available) editions and from three of the four volumes mentioned above (poems from *Magic City* are not included) and combines them with twelve new poems. The work continues the personal, home-based explorations familiar to readers of *Magic City,* but the perspective is that of an older observer still open to the world's experiences yet often weary of the tensions of race and economic injustice. ''The whole town smells / Like the world's oldest anger,'' says the speaker in ''Fog Galleon'' as he rides in a cab through his hometown. There are also the recurrent nightmares of the Vietnam veteran to contend with, as in the poem ''At the Screen Door.'' Coming home to what he hopes will be the woman (mother or lover) who is ''. . . the only one / I couldn't have surprised,'' he wonders if he will not meet again the story of a fellow vet:

Is this the same story
That sent him to a padded cell?
After all the men he'd killed in Korea
& on his first tour in Vietnam,
Someone tracked him down.
The Spec 4 he ordered
Into a tunnel in Cu Chi
Now waited for him behind
The screen door, a sunset
In his eyes, a dead man
Wearing his teenage son's face.

Haunting visions like this one fill these new poems, and a variety of characters bear their crosses with what hard-earned dignity they have salvaged, ''Like a man drunk on the rage / Of being alive.'' *Neon Vernacular* received the Kingsley-Tufts award in poetry and the 1994 Pulitzer.

—Robert McDowell

KOOSER, Ted

Nationality: American. **Born:** Theodore Kooser, Ames, Iowa, 25 April 1939. **Education:** Iowa State University, Ames, B.S. 1962; University of Nebraska, Lincoln, M.A. in English 1968. **Family:** Married 1) Diana Tressler in 1962 (divorced 1969), one son; 2) Kathleen Rutledge in 1977. **Career:** High school teacher, Madrid, Iowa, 1962–63; correspondent, 1964–65, and underwriter, 1965–73, Bankers Life Nebraska, Lincoln; senior underwriter, 1973–84, and vice president, 1984–98, Lincoln Benefit Life. Since 1970 part-time instructor and visiting professor in creative writing, University of Nebraska. Since 1967 publisher, Windflower Press. **Awards:** Prairie Schooner prize, 1975, 1978; National Endowment for the Arts fellowship, 1976, 1984; Society for Midland Author's poetry award,

1980; Stanley Kunitz prize, 1984; Governor's Art award, 1988; Richard Hugo prize, 1994. **Address:** 1820 Branched Oak Road, Garland, Nebraska 68360, U.S.A.

PUBLICATIONS

Poetry

Official Entry Blank. Lincoln, University of Nebraska Press, 1969.
Grass County. Lincoln, Nebraska, Windflower Press, 1971.
Twenty Poems. Crete, Nebraska, Best Cellar Press, 1973.
A Local Habitation, and A Name. San Luis Obispo, California, Solo Press, 1974.
Shooting a Farmhouse; So This Is Nebraska. Denver, Ally Press, 1975.
Not Coming to Be Barked At. Milwaukee, Pentagram Press, 1976.
Hatcher. Lincoln, Nebraska, Windflower Press, 1978.
Old Marriage and New. Austin, Texas, Cold Mountain Press, 1978.
Cottonwood County, with William Kloefkorn. Lincoln, Nebraska, Windflower Press, 1979.
Sure Signs: New and Selected Poems. Pittsburgh, University of Pittsburgh Press, 1980.
One World at a Time. Pittsburgh, University of Pittsburgh Press, 1985.
The Blizzard Voices. St. Paul, Minnesota, Bieler Press, 1986.
Weather Central. Pittsburgh, University of Pittsburgh Press, 1994.
A Book of Things. Lincoln, Nebraska, Lyra Press, 1995.
A Decade of Ted Kooser Valentines. Omaha, Nebraska, Penumbra Press, 1996.
Winter Morning Walks: 100 Postcards to Jim Harrison. Pittsburgh, Carnegie Mellon University Press, 2001.

Other

Editor, *The Windflower Home Almanac of Poetry.* Lincoln, Nebraska, Windflower Press, 1980.
Editor, *As Far As I Can See; Contemporary Writers of the Middle Plains.* Lincoln, Nebraska, Windflower Press, 1989.

*

Critical Studies: In *Can Poetry Matter?: Essays on Poetry and American Culture* by Dana Gioia, St. Paul, Minnesota, Graywolf Press, 1992; by Tom Hansen, in *North Dakota Quarterly,* 61(3), Summer 1993; by Jean Johnson, in *Poet Lore,* 90(1), Spring 1995.

Ted Kooser comments:

(1995) I have been writing poetry for thirty-five years. For the first fifteen of those years I was trying to get through to myself, and for the last twenty I have been trying to get through to my readers. Looking back over my poems of all those years, I can see my work becoming more and more accessible to a reader whose interests are more general than literary. I would like to be a popular poet without having to compromise my artistic standards to any degree, and that is a difficult task. I like nothing so much as to have letters of praise from people who ordinarily do not read poetry, and I am also very pleased when my work gets included in anthologies for use in the public school classroom. I feel like a useful person when I can contribute

something to the lives of people who may be otherwise intimidated by art and artists. My poems are very often centered about single figures of speech, conceits, and I like to provide people with these new ways of seeing the associations between things. Several years ago, after reading a poem of mine in which I describe a little family of mice moving their nest up out of a field at spring plowing time, someone wrote me to say that he would never again look at a freshly plowed field in the same way. That was the highest compliment I have ever been paid, and my goal as a poet is to offer those moments to others for as long as I am able to.

*   *   *

Ted Kooser is a genuinely popular poet. This is not to say that he commands a mass public. No contemporary poet does, at least not in America. Kooser is popular in that, unlike most of his peers, he writes naturally for a nonliterary public. His style is accomplished but extremely simple, his diction drawn from common speech, his syntax conversational. His subjects are chosen from the everyday world of the Great Plains, and his sensibility, though more subtle and articulate, is that of the average Midwesterner. He never makes an allusion that an intelligent but unbookish reader will not immediately grasp. There is to my knowledge no poet of equal stature who writes so convincingly in a manner the average American can understand and appreciate.

But to describe Kooser merely as a poet who writes plainly about the ordinary world is misleading insofar as it makes his work sound dull. For here, too, the comparison with popular art holds true. Kooser's work is uncommonly entertaining. His poems are usually short and perfectly paced; his subjects, relevant and engaging. Finishing one poem, the reader instinctively wants to proceed to another. It has been Kooser's particular genius to develop a genuine poetic style that accommodates the average reader and that portrays a vision providing unexpected moments of illuminations from the seemingly threadbare details of everyday life.

If Kooser's work is visionary, however, it is on a decidedly human scale. He offers no blinding flashes of inspiration, no mystic moments of transcendence. He creates no private mythologies or fantasy worlds. Instead he provides small but genuine insights into the world of everyday experience. His work strikes the difficult balance between profundity and accessibility, just as his style manages to be distinctively personal without being idiosyncratic. It is simple without becoming shallow, striking without going to extremes. He has achieved the most difficult kind of originality. He has transformed the common idiom and experience into fresh and distinctive poetry.

Kooser does have significant limitations as a poet. Looking across his mature work, one sees a narrow range of technical means, an avoidance of stylistic or thematic complexity, little interest in ideas, and an unwillingness to work in longer forms. In his weaker poems one sometimes notices a tendency to sentimentalize his subjects and too strong a need to be liked by his readers, which often expresses itself in a self-deprecatory attitude toward himself and his poetry. In short, Kooser's major limitation is a deep-seated conservatism that keeps him working in areas he knows he can master and that please his audience.

Significantly, however, Kooser's limitations derive directly from his strengths. His narrow technical range reflects his insistence on perfecting the forms he uses. If Kooser has concentrated on a few types of poems, he has made each of these forms unmistakably his own. If he has avoided longer forms, what member of his generation has written so many unforgettable short poems? If he has avoided complexity in his work, he has also developed a distinctive and highly-charged kind of simplicity. What his poems lack in intellectuality they more than make up for in concrete detail. If he occasionally lapses into sentimentality, it is because he invests his poems with real emotion. Even Kooser's self-deprecatory manner betrays a consistent concern for the communal role of the poet. He will not strike superior bardic poses to bully or impress his audience.

Kooser has written more perfect poems than any American poet of his generation. In a quiet way he is also one of its most original poets. His technical and intellectual interests may be narrow (indeed in terms of limited techniques he shares a common fault of his generation), but his work shows an impressive emotional range all handled in a distinctively personal way. Finally, his work does coalesce into an impressive whole. Read individually, his poems sparkle with insight. Read together, they provide one of the few broad and believable portraits of contemporary America in our poetry.

—Dana Gioia

KOPS, Bernard

Nationality: British. **Born:** London, 28 November 1926. **Education:** London elementary schools to age 13. **Family:** Married Erica Gordon in 1956; four children. **Career:** Has worked as a docker, chef, salesman, waiter, lift man, and barrow boy. Writer-in-residence, London Borough of Hounslow, 1980–82; lecturer in Drama, Spiro Institute, 1985–86, and various educational authorities, 1989–90. **Awards:** Arts Council bursary 1957, 1979, 1985; C. Day Lewis fellowship, 1981–83; London Fringe awards for *Dreams of Anne Frank,* 1993. **Agent:** Dina Lom, 6a Maddox Street, London, W.1, England. **Address:** 58 Compayne Gardens, Hampstead, London N.W.6, England.

PUBLICATIONS

Poetry

Poems. London, Bell and Baker Press, 1955.
Poems and Songs. Northwood, Middlesex, Scorpion Press, 1958.
An Anemone for Antigone. Lowestoft, Suffolk, Scorpion Press, 1959.
Erica, I Want to Read You Something. Lowestoft, Suffolk, Scorpion Press, and New York, Walker, 1967.
For the Record. London, Secker and Warburg, 1971.
Barricades in West Hampstead. London, Hearing Eye, 1988.

Plays

The Hamlet of Stepney Green (produced Oxford, London, and New York, 1958). London, Evans, 1959.
Goodbye World (produced Guildford, Surrey, 1959).
Change for the Angel (produced London, 1960).
The Dream of Peter Mann (produced Edinburgh, 1960). London, Penguin, 1960.
Stray Cats and Empty Bottles (produced Cambridge, 1961; London, 1967).

Enter Solly Gold, music by Stanley Myers (produced Wellingborough, Northamptonshire, and Los Angeles, 1962; London, 1970). Published in *Satan, Socialites, and Solly Gold: Three New Plays from England,* New York, Coward McCann, 1961; in *Four Plays,* 1964.
Home Sweet Honeycomb (broadcast 1962). Included in *Four Plays,* 1964.
The Lemmings (broadcast 1963). Included in *Four Plays,* 1964.
Four Plays (includes *The Hamlet of Stepney Green, Enter Solly Gold, Home Sweet Honeycomb, The Lemmings*). London, MacGibbon and Kee, 1964.
The Boy Who Wouldn't Play Jesus (for children; produced London, 1965). Published in *Eight Plays: Book 1,* edited by Malcolm Stuart Fellows, London, Cassell, 1965.
David, It Is Getting Dark (produced Rennes, France, 1970). Paris, Gallimard, 1970.
It's a Lovely Day Tomorrow, with John Goldschmidt (televised 1975; produced London, 1976).
More Out Than In (produced on tour and London, 1980).
Ezra (produced London, 1981).
Simon at Midnight (broadcast 1982; produced London, 1985).
Some of These Days (produced England and abroad, 1990).
Kafe Kropotkin (produced England and abroad, 1988).
Sophie: The Last of the Red Hot Mamas (produced England and abroad, 1990).
Moss (produced England and abroad, 1991).
Playing Sinatra (produced England and abroad, 1991–92). London and New York, Samuel French, 1992.
Androcles and the Lion (produced England and abroad, 1992).
Dreams of Anne Frank (produced England and abroad, 1992). London and New York, Samuel French, 1993.
Who Shall I Be Tomorrow (produced England and abroad, 1992).
Call in the Night (produced England and abroad, 1995). Included in *Plays Two,* 2000.
Plays One (includes *Playing Sinatra, The Hamlet of Stepney Green*). London, Oberon, 1999.
Plays Two (includes *Café Zeitgeist, Dreams of Anne Frank, Call in the Night*). London, Oberon, 2000.

Radio Plays: *Home Sweet Honeycomb,* 1962; *The Lemmings,* 1963; *Born in Israel,* 1963; *The Dark Ages,* 1964; *Israel: The Immigrant,* 1964; *Bournemouth Nights,* 1979; *I Grow Old, I Grow Old,* 1979; *Over the Rainbow,* 1980; *Simon at Midnight,* 1982; *Trotsky Was My Father,* 1984; *More Out Than In,* 1985; *Kafe Kropotkin,* 1988; *Colour Blind,* 1989; *Congress in Manchester,* 1990; *The Ghost Child,* 1990; *Soho Nights,* 1990; *Sailing with Homer,* 1994.

Television Plays: *I Want to Go Home,* 1963; *The Lost Years of Brian Hooper,* 1967; *Alexander the Greatest,* 1971; *Just One Kid,* 1974; *Why the Geese Shrieked,* and *The Boy Philosopher,* from stories by Isaac Bashevis Singer, 1974; *It's a Lovely Day Tomorrow,* with John Goldschmidt, 1975; *Moss,* 1975; *Rocky Marciano Is Dead,* 1976; *Night Kids,* 1983; *The Survivor,* 1991.

Novels

Awake for Mourning. London, MacGibbon and Kee, 1958.
Motorbike. London, New English Library, 1962.
Yes from No-Man's Land. London, MacGibbon and Kee, 1965; New York, Coward McCann, 1966.

The Dissent of Dominick Shapiro. London, MacGibbon and Kee, 1966; New York, Coward McCann, 1967.

By the Waters of Whitechapel. London, Bodley Head, 1969; New York, Norton, 1970.

The Passionate Past of Gloria Gaye. London, Secker and Warburg, 1971; New York, Norton, 1972.

Settle Down Simon Katz. London, Secker and Warburg, 1973.

Partners. London, Secker and Warburg, 1975.

On Margate Sands. London, Secker and Warburg, 1978.

Other

The World Is a Wedding (autobiography). London, MacGibbon and Kee, 1963; New York, Coward McCann, 1964.

Neither Your Honey nor Your Sting: An Offbeat History of the Jews. London. Robson. 1985.

Shalom Bomb: The Autobiography of Bernard Kops. London, Oberon, 2000.

Editor, *Poetry Hounslow.* London, Hounslow Civic Centre, 1981.

*

Manuscript Collections: University of Texas, Austin; Indiana University, Bloomington.

Critical Studies: "Bernard Kops" by Colin MacInnes, in *Encounter* (London), May 1960; "The Kitchen Sink" by G. Wilson Knight, in *Encounter* (London), December 1963; "Deep Waters of Whitechapel" by Nina Sutton, in *The Guardian* (London), 6 September 1969; by William Baker, in *British Playwrights since 1956: A Resource and Production Sourcebook,* edited by William W. Demastes, Greenwood, 1996.

Bernard Kops comments:

Kops creates specific relationships in order that they might relate universally. He writes compulsively, for himself, and even if his work is acceptable to others, this is a secondary process. Nevertheless, he is pleased that he can sell his work and be able to live by writing. Kops is obsessed by family themes; this runs throughout his work. The relationships are of people bound up together in an intense emotional and intellectual involvement. He believes that the great themes of Shakespeare, Racine, Sophocles, O'Neill have lasted and will last because they deal with themes common to every human being. *King Lear* and its dream and despair live for us because it lives through us; it is us. We give it life and constantly renew it. Kops is also obsessed with death, but only because he is obsessed with life. He believes motives are impossible to define ultimately, but actions are not subjective, and one must judge a man by his actions. He likes ambiguity. But he also believes in strict discipline and thinks that the writer must know exactly what he is doing even if he has shown the subjectivity and complexity of human relationships. He writes constantly about the backgrounds and the people and things he knows, or thinks he knows. The only things that he is really certain about are the existence of love, the need for it, and that "they" no longer exist. There are only us left on this earth. Kops writes about this.

*   *   *

Bernard Kops's reputation stands on his plays and novels, yet these very substantial writings can be said to arise from the wellsprings of a talent and an approach to literature that is entirely that of a poet. Further, it is that of a special sort of poet, the sort contained in the familiar quotation about "the poet's eye in a fine frenzy rolling." Kops's poems usually exhibit a tendency to the frenetic—a freewheeling fantasy, an extravagance of language and gesture, an explosive celebration of the things that he loves or that excite him, and an apocalyptic rejection of things that he hates or that appall him. He draws a great deal of his poetry from his fervent Jewishness, but not merely in the form of his sense of racial difference or his horror at the Holocaust. Many of his most successful poems grow out of his family's presence in the foreground of his experience, from which he can create universalized images for what he sees as the sad, proud, lonely, laughable continuity of human life. "Somewhere upon these impossible stairs," he wrote in a poem entitled "Prayer at Forty," "we are attempting love."

Though his poetic output has never been large, Kops's assertion in it of the need to go on "attempting love" has been unflagging and has figured equally large throughout his considerable oeuvre of plays, novels, and that splendid poet's autobiography, *The World Is a Wedding.* This determined assertion has been his poetry's source of power and its most lasting quality.

—Douglas Hill

KOSTELANETZ, Richard (Cory)

Nationality: American. **Born:** New York City, 14 May 1940. **Education:** Brown University, Providence, Rhode Island, A.B. 1962 (Phi Beta Kappa); Columbia University, New York (Woodrow Wilson Fellow, 1962–63, and International Fellow, 1963–64), M.A. 1966; King's College, London (Fulbright Fellow, 1964–65). **Career:** Program associate, John Jay College, New York, 1972–73; guest artist, WXXI-FM radio, Rochester, New York, 1975, 1976, Syracuse University, New York, 1975, Cabin Creek Center for Work and Environmental Studies, 1978, Electronic Music Studio, Stockholm, 1981, 1983, 1984, 1986, 1988, Brooklyn College Center for Computer Music, New York, 1984, Dennis Gabor Laboratory Museum of Holography, 1985, 1989, and Experimental Television Laboratory, Oswego, New York, 1985, 1986, 1987, 1989, 1990; visiting professor, University of Texas, Austin, 1977; artist-in-residence, Mishkenot Sha'ananim, Jerusalem, 1979, and DAAD Kunstler-program, Berlin, 1981–83. Co-founder, Assembling Press, 1970–82; contributing editor, *Lotfa Poetica,* Villa Nuova, Italy, 1970–71, *Arts in Society,* Madison, Wisconsin, 1970–75, *The Humanist,* Buffalo, 1970–78, *New York Arts Journal,* 1980–82, *Rampike Magazine,* Toronto, since 1987, and *Liberty,* since 1989 proprietor, Future Press, since 1976, and Words and Music, since 1982; since 1977 co-editor and publisher, *Precisely.* Visual poetry and related language art exhibited at galleries and universities since 1975, including *Wordsand,* a retrospective of work with words, numbers, and lines, which was exhibited at Simon Fraser University, University of Alberta, Cornell College (Iowa), California State College (Bakersfield), University of North Dakota, Miami-Dade Community College, and Vassar College. **Awards:** New York State Regents fellowship, 1963–64; Pulitzer fellowship, 1965; Guggenheim fellowship, 1967; National Endowment for the Arts grant, 1976, 1978, 1979, 1980, 1981, 1982, 1985,

1986, 1990, 1991; Vogelstein Foundation fellowship, 1980. **Address:** P.O. Box 444, Prince Street Station, New York, New York 10012–0008, U.S.A.

PUBLICATIONS

Poetry

Visual Language. New York, Assembling Press, 1970.
I Articulations, with *Short Fictions.* New York, Kulchur, 1974.
Portraits from Memory. Ann Arbor, Ardis, 1975.
Word Prints. Privately printed, 1975.
Rain Rains Rain. New York, Assembling Press, 1976.
Numbers: Poems and Stories. New York, Assembling Press, 1976.
Illuminations. Woodinville, Washington, and New York, Laughing Bear-Future Press, 1977.
Numbers Two. Columbus, Ohio, Luna Bisonte, 1977.
Richard Kostelanetz. New York, RK Editions, 1980.
Turfs Arenas Fields Pitches. Battleground, Indiana, High/Coo Press, 1980.
Arenas Fields Pitches Turfs. Kansas City, Bk Mk-University of Missouri, 1982.
Solo, Duets, Trios & Choruses. Kenosha, Wisconsin, and New York, Membrane-Future, 1991.
Repartitions-IV. Port Charlotte, Florida, Runaway Spoon, 1992.
Wordworks: Poems New & Selected. Rochester, New York, BOA Editions, 1993.
MoRepartitions. Port Charlotte, Florida, Runaway Spoon, 1994.
Transimations. Jim Thorpe, Pennsylvania, Black & White Press, 1998.

Recordings: *Experimental Prose,* Assembling Press, 1976; *Audio Art,* RK Editions, 1977; *Asdescent* and Anacatabasis, RK Editions, 1978; *Audio Writing,* RK Editions, 1984; *Complete Audio Writing,* RK Editions, 1985; *The Drunken Boat,* RK Editions, 1986; *Turfs Arenas Fields Pitches,* RK Editions, 1988.

lograms: *Antitheses,* RK Editions, 1985; *Abracadabra,* RK Editions, 1987; *Ambiguity,* RK Editions, 1987; *Hell/Elle,* with Eduardo Kac, RK Editions, 1987; *IIo/Log/Rup/Her,* RK Editions, 1987; *Ho/Log/Rap/Hy,* RK Editions, 1987; *Madam/Adam,* RK Editions. 1987.

Plays

Epiphanies (produced Grand Forks, North Dakota, 1980).
Lovings (produced New York, New York, 1991).

Screenplays and Video Scripts: *Openings and Closings,* with Bart Weiss, 1975; *Three Prose Pieces,* 1975; *Declaration of Independence,* 1979; *Constructivist Fictions,* with Peter Longauer, 1979; *Epiphanies,* 1980; *A Berlin Lost,* with Martin Koerber, 1985; *Partitions,* 1986; *Home Movies Reconsidered: My First Twenty-Seven Years,* 1987; *Seductions,* 1987; *Relationships,* 1987; *Video Writing,* 1987; *Video Fictions,* 1988; *Video Poems,* 1988; *Video Strings,* 1989; *Kinetic Writings,* 1989; *Turfs/Grounds/Lawns,* 1989.

Radio Scripts: *Audio Art,* 1978; *Text-Sound North America,* 1981; *Invitations,* 1981; *The Gospels/Die Evangelien,* 1982; *Glenn Gould as a Radio Artist,* 1983; *Hörspiel USA,* 1983; *Audio Writing,* 1984; *Nach Weisseneee,* with Martin Koerber and Michael Maassen, 1984; *A Special Time, the 1960s,* 1985; *Radio Comedy Made in America Today,* 1986; *Hörspielmaschmer Tony Schwartz,* 1987; *New York City Radio,* 1988; *Orson Welles as an Audio Artist,* 1988; *Kaddish,* 1990; *Norman Corwin,* 1991.

Novels

In the Beginning. Somerville, Massachusetts, Abyss, 1971.
One Night Stood. New York, Future Press, 1977.
Exhaustive Parallel Intervals. New York. Future Press. 1979.

Short Stories

Accounting. Brescia, Italy, Amodulo, 1972; Sacramento, California, Poetry Newsletter, 1973.
Ad Infinitum. Friedrichsfehn, Germany, International Artists' Cooperation, 1973.
Modulations. Brooklyn, New York, Assembling Press, 1975.
Openings and Closings. New York, D'Arc, 1975.
Constructs. Reno, Nevada, West Coast Poetry Review, 1975.
Come Here. New York, Assembling Press, 1975.
Extrapolate. New York, Assembling Press, 1975.
Three Places in New Inkland, with others. New York, Zartscorp, 1977.
Constructs Two. Milwaukee, Membrane, 1978.
Foreshortenings and Other Stories. Willits, California, Tuumba Press, 1978.
Tabula Rasa. New York, RK Editions, 1978.
Inexistences. New York, RK Editions, 1978.
And So Forth. New York, Future Press, 1979.
More Short Fictions. New York, Assembling Press, 1980.
Epiphanies. West Berlin, Literarisches Colloquium Berlin, and New York, RK Editions, 1983.
Minimal Fictions. Santa Maria, California, Asylum Arts, 1994.
Openings. Evanston, Illinois, Depth Charge, 1995.

Other

The Theatre of Mixed-Means: An Introduction to Happenings, Kinetic Environments, and Other Mixed-Means Performances. New York, Dial Press, 1968; London, Pitman, 1970.
Master Minds: Portraits of Contemporary American Artists and Intellectuals. New York, Macmillan, 1969.
The End of Intelligent Writing: Literary Politics in America. New York, Sheed and Ward, 1974.
Recyclings: A Literary Autobiography. New York, Assembling Press, 1974; augmented edition, New York, Future Press, 1984.
Grants and the Future of Literature. New York, RK Editions, 1978.
Wordsand. Burnaby, British Columbia, Simon Fraser Gallery, 1978.
Twenties in the Sixties: Previously Uncollected Critical Essays. Westport, Connecticut, Greenwood Press, 1979.
''The End'' Essentials, ''The End'' Appendix. Metuchen, New Jersey, Scarecrow Press, 1979.
Metamorphosis in the Arts. New York, Assembling Press, 1980.
Autobiographies. Santa Barbara, California, Mudborn, 1981.
The Old Poetries and the New. Ann Arbor, University of Michigan Press, 1981.

Reincarnations. New York, Future Press, 1981.

American Imaginations. West Berlin, Merve, and New York, RK Editions, 1983.

Autobiographien New York Berlin. West Berlin, Merve, 1986.

The Grants-Fix: Publicly Literary Granting in America. New York, RK Editions, 1987.

The Old Fictions and the New. Jefferson, North Carolina and London, McFarland, 1987.

Prose Pieces/Aftertexts. Calexico, California, Atticus Press, 1987.

Conversing with Cage. New York, Limelight, 1988.

On Innovative Music(ian)s. New York, Limelight, 1989.

Unfinished Business: An Intellectual Non-history, 1963–1989. New York, RK Editions, 1989.

The New Poetries and Some Old. Carbondale, Southern Illinois University Press, 1991.

Politics in the African-American Novel. N.p., Greenwood, 1991.

On Innovative Art(ists)s. Jefferson, North Carolina, McFarland, 1992.

A Dictionary of the Avant-Gardes. Flemington, New Jersey, A Cappella, 1993.

On Innovative Performance(s). Jefferson, North Carolina, McFarland, 1994.

The Fillmore East: Recollections of Rock Theater. New York, Schirmer Books, 1995.

An ABC of Contemporary Reading. San Diego, California, San Diego State University Press, 1995.

Radio Writings. Union City, New Jersey, Further State(s) of the Art, 1995.

Crimes of Culture: Three Decades of Citizen's Arrests. New York, Autonomedia, 1995.

One Million Words of Book Notes, 1958–1993. Troy, New York, Whitston, 1996.

John Cage (Ex)plain(ed). New York, Schirmer Books, 1996.

Thirty Years of Critical Engagements with John Cage. New York, Archae, 1997.

Editor, *On Contemporary Literature: An Anthology of Critical Essays on Major Movements and Writers of Contemporary Literature.* New York, Avon, 1964; revised edition, 1969.

Editor, *The New American Arts.* New York, Horizon Press, 1965; London, Collier Macmillan, 1968.

Editor, *Twelve from the Sixties.* New York, Dell, 1967.

Editor, *The Young American Writers: Fiction, Poetry, Drama, and Criticism.* New York, Funk and Wagnalls, 1967.

Editor, *Beyond Left and Right: Radical Thought for Our Time.* New York, Morrow, 1968.

Editor, *Imaged Words and Worded Images.* New York, Outer-bridge and Dienstfrey, 1970.

Editor, *Possibilities of Poetry: An Anthology of American Contemporaries.* New York, Dell, 1970.

Editor, *John Cage.* New York, Praeger, 1970; London, Allen Lane, 1971.

Editor, *Moholy-Nagy.* New York, Praeger, 1970; London, Allen Lane, 1972.

Editor, *Assembling, and Second through Eleventh Assembling.* New York, Assembling Press, 12 vols., 1970–81.

Editor, *Future's Fictions.* New York, Panache, 1971.

Editor, *Human Alternatives: Visions for Our Time.* New York, Morrow, 1971.

Editor, *Social Speculations: Visions for Us Now.* New York, Morrow, 1971.

Editor, *In Youth.* New York, Ballantine, 1972.

Editor, *Seeing Through Shuck.* New York, Ballantine, 1972.

Editor, *Breakthrough Fictioneers: An Anthology.* New York, Something Else Press, 1973.

Editor, *The Edge of Adaptation: Man and the Emerging Society.* Englewood Cliffs, New Jersey, Prentice Hall, 1973.

Editor, *Essaying Essays.* New York, OOLP, 1975.

Editor, *Language and Structure.* New York, Kensington Arts, 1975.

Editor, *Younger Critics of North America: Essays on Literature and the Arts.* Fair Water, Wisconsin, Margins, 1977.

Editor, *Esthetic Contemporary.* New York, Prometheus, 1977.

Editor, *Assembling Assembling.* New York, Assembling Press, 1978.

Editor, *Visual Literature Criticism: A New Collection.* Carbondale, Southern Illinois University Press, and London, Feffer and Simons, 1979.

Editor, *Text-Sound Texts.* New York, Morrow, 1980.

Editor, *The Yale Gertrude Stein* (selection). New Haven, Connecticut, Yale University Press, 1980.

Editor, *Scenarios.* New York, Assembling Press, 1980.

Editor, *Aural Literature Criticism.* New York, Precisely-RK Editions, 1981.

Editor, *American Writing Today.* Washington, D.C., Voice of America Forum Series, 2 vols., 1981.

Editor, *The Avant-Garde Tradition in Literature.* Buffalo, New York, Prometheus, 1982.

Editor, *The Literature of SoHo.* New York, Shantih, 1983.

Editor, with Benjamin Hrushovski, *The Poetics of the New Poetries.* New York, RK Editions, 1983.

Editor, with Stephen Scobie, *Precisely Complete.* New York, RK Editions, 6 vols., 1985.

Editor, *Esthetics Contemporary.* Buffalo, New York, Prometheus, 1989.

Editor, *Gertrude Stein Advanced.* Jefferson, North Carolina, McFarland, 1991.

Editor, *Merce Cunningham: Dancing in Time and Space.* Flemington, New Jersey, A Cappella, 1992.

Editor, *John Cage, Writer.* New York, Limelight, 1993.

Editor, *Writings about John Cage.* Ann Arbor, Michigan, University of Michigan Press, 1993.

Editor, with John Rocco, *Another E.E. Cummings.* New York, Norton, 1995.

Editor, with Joseph Darby, *Nicolas Slonimsky: The First Hundred Years.* New York, Schirmer Books, 1995.

Editor, with Joseph Darby and Matthew Santa, *Classic Essays on Twentieth-Century Music: A Continuing Symposium.* New York, Schirmer Books, and London, Prentice Hall International, 1996.

Editor, with Anson John Pope, *The B.B. King Companion: Five Decades of Commentary.* London, Omnibus, 1997.

Editor, with John Rocco, *The Frank Zappa Companion: Four Decades of Commentary.* London and New York, Omnibus, 1997.

Editor, with Robert Flemming, *Writings on Glass: Essays, Interviews, Criticism.* New York, Schirmer Books, and London, Prentice Hall International, 1997.

*

Critical Studies: *Once Again,* edited by Jean-François Bory, New York, New Directions 1968; ''Poetry and Space'' by Carolo Alberto Sitta, in *The Gazette* (Modena, Italy), 4 November 1970; ''Figured Verse and Calligrams'' by Massin, in *Letter and Image,* Paris,

Gallimard and New York, Van Nostrand, 1970; *Text-Bilder/Visuelle Poési International* edited by Klaus Peter Dencker, Cologne, Dumont Schauberg, 1972; by L.J. Davis, in *New York Times Book Review,* 21 October 1973; ''Richard Kostelanetz'' by Hugh Fox, in *West Coast Poetry Review 12* (Reno, Nevada), summer 1974; by Thomas Powers in *Harper's* (New York), November 1974; by John W. Aldridge, in *Michigan Quarterly Review* (Ann Arbor), summer 1975; by Michael Joseph Phillips, in *Small Press Review* (Paradise, California), June-July 1976; ''Just Plain Video and Video-Plus'' by Davidson Gigliotti, in *Soho Weekly News* (New York), 30 December 1976; ''Scavenger Art and Richard Kostelanetz'' by George Myers, Jr., in An *Introduction to Modern Times,* Grosse Pointe Farms, Michigan, Lunchroom Press, 1982; ''Intermedia Today: William Hellerman and Richard Kostelanetz'' by Tom Johnson, in *The Voice of New Music,* Eindhoven, NL, 1989; ''Toward a Critical Understanding of Richard Kostelanetz's Single-Sentence Stories'' by Raymond Gomez, in *Critique,* XXXV/ 4, summer 1994; ''Kostelanetz's 'Tribute to Henry Ford''' by Hildy Coleman, in *Explicator* (Washington, D.C.), 53(2), winter 1995; ''Alternative, Possibility, and Essence: An Interview with Richard Kostelanetz'' by Harry Polkinhorn and Larry McCaffery, in *Some Other Fluency: Interviews with Innovative American Authors,* edited by McCaffery, Philadelphia, University of Pennsylvania Press, 1996.

Richard Kostelanetz comments:

Though I once said that my creative work made me a ''poet,'' I now speak of myself as an ''artist and writer,'' nonetheless wishing that there were in English a single term that combined the two. ''Maker'' might be more appropriate, its modesty notwithstanding. The variousness of the work confuses not only the art public but also those critics who still expect someone to be just a poet or just a composer or just a visual artist, rather than all of those things and much else besides. The principal problem with person-centered epithets such as ''painter'' and ''writer'' is that they become not descriptions but jails, either restricting one's creative activity or defining one's creative adventure in terms of one's initial professional category (e.g., ''artist's books''). As Ad Reinhardt warned, ''Art disease is caused by a hardening of the categories.'' In truth, anyone realizing a radically different kind of poetry will probably have a radically different kind of poetry career as well. Even so, it should be possible for any of us to make poems or photographs or music as we wish and, better yet, to have these works regarded plainly as poems or photographs or music. Perhaps the sum of my artworks, including poetry, is ultimately about the discovery of possibilities, initially in the exploitation of available media and then in art and, by extension, in oneself as a creative initiator.

*   *   *

The appropriate term for most of Richard Kostelanetz's creative work is ''visual poetry.'' Although the implied definition of ''poetry'' here is radical, the label essentially designates a subgenre or intermedium of nonlinear and nonsyntactic black word forms arranged on a white page and reprintable. These forms are akin to but greatly extended from so-called shape poems, whose ancestry is traceable back through Apollinaire and George Herbert to the illuminated manuscript and Chinese ideogram. Kostelanetz's visual poems deliberately contravene current literary practice, but they also employ such specifically literary devices as punning, wit, allusion, alliteration, parallelism, and contrast. Constructivism and minimalism in the visual art tradition have also influenced him. His early poems in *Visual Language,* composed around 1967, are usually mimetic, often employing only one letter or word, and are often erotic in content. An example is found in ''Disintegration,'' in which the word increasingly fragments in repetitions down the page until it disappears entirely. *I Articulations* presents more complex structures that involve synonyms, multiple repetitions, and philosophical concerns about the nature of language.

In the 1970s Kostelanetz moved from this style and its ramifications into ''fictions,'' defined as ''sequential forms that still eschew the prosaic form of expository sentences,'' and into poems consisting entirely of numbers, thus emphasizing that formal pattern and relationship are at the heart of his aesthetic. In his work of the 1980s he carried this aesthetic into video, adding the dimension of sound correlated with moving forms on a screen and thus giving his work a dramatic potential. The early videos sometimes worked from print pieces; for instance, ''Recyclings,'' a print work that took every other word out of something previously written, was filmed with a pair of isolated lips (his own) reading in one corner of the screen and then added a second set of lips in another corner, with a voice superimposed, until at the climax many lips and words coincided indecipherably. In *Kinetic Writings* vibrating word forms appear and disappear, being transmuted from one word to another; ''lascivious,'' for example, swiftly evolves through intermittent words into ''civilized.'' On the tape entitled *Video Strings* words containing identical letters traverse the screen without break, each containing part of the following word. For example, a scrap such as ''microphonemesis'' contains ''microphone,'' ''phonemes,'' and ''nemesis.'' The ''string'' of many hundreds of words moves so rapidly that the viewer perceives only about one combination in five or six overlaps. This defiance of conventional ''reading'' is consistent with Kostelanetz's overall disregard for ''meaning'' in art. For him the experience of art is purely and entirely an experience of form.

Video attracts Kostelanetz because it is an intimate form that can be engaged in quietly at home, just as books are read. He therefore considers his enhancement of language by video and visual components to be a literary development. He is virtually alone in the poetry world in making his own videos (with technical assistance), as distinct from having them taped by others. His video work has led to experiments with holograms, in which the laser projection permits four layers of word permutations to come out of the picture plane. Film technique also influenced his 1998 book *Transimations,* created in collaboration with the designer Eun-Ha Paek. The title is arranged so that the *s* of the prefix ''trans'' overlies the *i* of ''animations,'' producing an unpronounceable coinage. Further, the letters *a* and *n* exist in both verbal formations but slide into one image, as in the old-fashioned technique used in animated cartoons. The subtitle, ''a poetry-film storyboard,'' establishes this concept, which is generally maintained throughout the book. A three-, four-, or five-letter word is modified through successive frames in which one letter is changed by a second letter superimposed on it; in the next frame the underlying letter is dropped to form a new word. Rigorous formalism remains Kostelanetz's focus, and the word changes and the juxtaposition of grids do not generate meaning. One poem is a tour de force that contains 204 frames and that mutates through shades of lighter and darker print, resembling the slats of a venetian blind, to produce thirty-five words, from ''nape'' to ''nope'' to ''hope'' and so forth, ending up at ''dial.''

Whether such language games can be categorized as visual poetry remains an open question. In any case, through his extension of the formal uses of language into new contexts, Kostelanetz breaks down preconceived barriers between media and extends the avant-garde theories that he has promulgated over the years.

—Jane Augustine

KRAMER, Lotte (Karoline)

Nationality: British. **Born:** Lotte Karoline Wertheimer, in Mainz, Germany, 22 October 1923. **Family:** Married Frederic Kramer in 1943; one son. **Career:** Laundry hand, Berkhamsted, Hertfordshire, 1939–40, and Hampton, Middlesex, 1943–47; lady's companion, Oxford, 1940–43; dress shop assistant, Richmond, Surrey, 1953–57. Since 1977 voluntary worker, Peterborough Museum. Since 1982 member of Writers in Schools, East Anglia. Also a painter; several individual exhibitions. **Awards:** Eastern Arts Board bursary, 1999. **Address:** 4 Apsley Way, Longthorpe, Peterborough, Cambridgeshire PE3 9NE, England.

PUBLICATIONS

Poetry

Scrolls. Richmond, Surrey, Keepsake Press, 1979.
Ice-Break. Peterborough, Cambridgeshire, Annakinn, 1980.
Family Arrivals. Hatch End, Middlesex, Poet and Printer, 1981.
A Lifelong House. Frome, Somerset, Hippopotamus Press, 1983.
The Shoemaker's Wife and Other Poems. Frome, Somerset, Hippopotamus Press, 1987.
The Desecration of Trees. Frome, Somerset, Hippopotamus Press, 1994.
Earthquake and Other Poems. Ware, Hertfordshire, Rockingham Press, 1994.
Selected and New Poems 1980–1997. Ware, Hertfordshire, Rockingham Press, 1997.

*

Critical Studies: "The Poetry of Lotte Kramer" by Karin Andrews, in *Agenda* (London), 22(2), summer 1984, and *Outposts* (Frome, Somerset), 155, winter 1987; "Lotte Kramer" by George Szirtes, in *Eastword,* 13(4), April 1984; "The Dark Side of History" by Carol Rumens, in *Jewish Chronicle* (London), 14 September 1984; "Rallying Calls and Laments" by Ruth Fainlight, in *Jewish Quarterly* (London), 34(4), 1987; "Lotte Kramer" by Laurence Sail, in *Stand* (London), 29(2), spring 1988; "Heavy with Baggage from Home" by Gerda Cohen, in *Jewish Chronicle* (London), 12 March 1993; "Singer of Our Song" by Gerda Mayer, in *AJR* (London), February 1993; "Remember Us" by Stella Stoker, in *Orbis,* 94, autumn 1994; "How Shall We Sing the Lord's Song in a Strange Land" by Edward Storey, in *The Month* (London), September/October 1994; "Lotte Kramer" by Wanda Barford, in *Jewish Chronicle* (London), 28 October 1994; "When Falling into Pits" by Janet Montefiore, in *Times Literary Supplement,* 1998; "The Aloes of Love" by Gillian Allnut, in *Poetry Review,* winter 1998–99.

Lotte Kramer comments:

I began to write poetry rather late in life, facing up to traumatic childhood experiences in Nazi Germany after thirty-five years. Much of my work deals with that subject and its aftermath, with the dualism inevitably connected with it. But I also write about other subjects, with the world around me as immediate and in a wider sense. I also translate some German poetry, especially Rilke, some of which is published in my books.

*   *   *

I encountered Lotte Kramer's poetry in her collection *Ice-Break,* in a batch of publications for review, and remember how it shone out like a bright beacon among the others. *Ice-Break* contained some beautifully observed poems. There was "Sunday Morning," in which her painter's eye was exercised with telling effect. In other poems lines such as "the old town ached in buckled houses" and "Land falls from us / In long stiff tongues that grip the sky" were evidence of the same eye. But Kramer's talent was not confined to the visual. In *Ice-Break* she captured mood and atmosphere just as acutely, as demonstrated in "Aspects of Home," where she writes of "this quietness that confiscates all else."

Since then Kramer has published additional collections in which she has consolidated her achievement. In *The Shoemaker's Wife* she demonstrates sharp perception and pursues her ability to produce meticulously crafted poems. In "Pavement Café" we find her observing a couple: "She pours / The rhythm of her talk through wrists / and finger tips." Another poem conjures November with a fine choice of detail: "This auburn change of tired leaves / When light turns inward." A bag of cherries or the contents of an old shoe box may evoke memories.

Kramer's is a gentle talent that succeeds by its meticulousness in the choice and ordering of detail. At its best it can conjure a vignette in which the visual clarity is informed by mood and emotion, as, for example, in "Winter Appeasement," where

She moves
In her own rhythm, her doubt
Bruising the silence,

Rehearsing
The ghosts of her winter
Appeasement.

With Kramer, as with her contemporary Gerda Mayer (who also went to England as a child refugee in 1939), it is as if the passing years have gradually unlocked memories that had been quietly held in abeyance as too painful or too deep. Thus, in Kramer's collection *Family Arrivals* we find poems with titles such as "Invocation of My Father," "The Red Cross Telegram," "Jewish Cemetery in Prague," and "Deportation" that convey powerful and remarkably disciplined expressions of deep-rooted memories and emotions:

I want to lie with them in unknown graves
And bury freedom of indulgent years.
There is no judge
To hear and end their cause.

It is as if Kramer had been waiting to perfect her art until she was able to cope with such profoundly disturbing subject matter. The beautifully controlled expression of these poems makes them the more potent.

Or is it that time loosens the inhibitions of memory? So we now see Kramer not only as the author of neatly accomplished rural poetry, tending toward the Wordsworthian, but also as the custodian of the deep and anguished memories of a refugee from Nazi Germany. They are memories from which she has forced memorable and superbly mastered poems of exile, as in ''Dreams'':

> You asked me: 'Do you dream?'
> Too quickly I agreed.
> But then plead forgetfulness
>
> Because there is this ruthlessness in dreams:
> I see the queues of death,
> Their last relentless walk.

—John Cotton

KROETSCH, Robert (Paul)

Nationality: Canadian. **Born:** Heisler, Alberta, 26 June 1927. **Education:** Schools in Heisler and Red Deer, Alberta; University of Alberta, Edmonton, B.A. 1948; McGill University, Montreal, 1954–55; Middlebury College, Vermont, M.A. 1956; University of Iowa, Iowa City, Ph.D. 1961. **Family:** Married 1) Mary Jane Lewis in 1956 (divorced 1979), two daughters; 2) Smaro Kamboureli in 1982. **Career:** Laborer and purser, Yellowknife Transportation Company, Northwest Territories, 1948–50; information specialist (civilian), U.S. Air Force Base, Goose Bay, Labrador, 1951–54; assistant professor, 1961–65, associate professor, 1965–68, and professor of English, 1968–78, State University of New York, Binghamton. Professor of English, 1978–85, and since 1985 distinguished professor, University of Manitoba, Winnipeg. Artist-in-residence, Calgary University, Alberta, fall 1975, University of Lethbridge, Alberta, spring 1976, and University of Manitoba, 1976–78. Co-founder, *Boundary 2* magazine, Binghamton, 1972. **Awards:** Bread Loaf Writers Conference grant, 1966; Governor-General's award, 1970; Killam award, 1986. Fellow, Royal Society of Canada, 1986. **Agent:** Sterling Lord, 10 St. Mary Street, Suite 510, Toronto M4Y 1P9. **Address:** Department of English, University of Manitoba, Winnipeg, Manitoba R3T 2N2, Canada.

PUBLICATIONS

Poetry

The Stone Hammer Poems, 1960–1975. Nanaimo, British Columbia, Oolichan, 1975.
The Ledger. London, Ontario, Applegarth Follies, 1975.
Seed Catalogue. Winnipeg, Turnstone Press, 1977.
The Sad Phoenician. Toronto, Coach House Press, 1979.
The Criminal Intensities of Love As Paradise. Lantzville, British Columbia, Oolichan, 1981.
Field Notes: Collected Poems. Toronto, General, and New York, Beaufort, 1981.
Advice to My Friends. Toronto, Stoddart, 1985.
Excerpts from the Real World: A Prose Poem in Ten Parts. Lantzville, British Columbia, Oolichan, 1986.
Completed Field Notes: The Long Poems of Robert Kroetsch. Toronto, McClelland and Stewart, 1989.

Play

The Studhorse Man, adaptation of his own novel (produced Toronto, 1981).

Novels

But We Are Exiles. Toronto, Macmillan, 1965; London, Macmillan, and New York, St. Martin's Press, 1966.
The Words of My Roaring. Toronto and London. Macmillan, and New York, St. Martin's Press, 1966.
The Studhorse Man. Toronto, Macmillan, and London, Macdonald, 1969; New York, Simon and Schuster, 1970.
Gone Indian. Toronto, New Press, 1973.
Badlands. Toronto, New Press, 1975; New York, Beaufort, 1983.
What the Crow Said. Toronto, General, 1978.
Alibi. Toronto, Stoddart, and New York, Beaufort, 1983.
The Puppeteer. Toronto, Random House, 1993.
The Man from the Creeks: A Novel. Toronto, Random House, 1998.

Other

Alberta. Toronto, Macmillan, and New York, St. Martin's Press, 1968.
The Crow Journals. Edmonton, Alberta, NeWest Press, 1980.
Labyrinths of Voice: Conversations with Robert Kroetsch, with Shirley Neuman and Robert Wilson. Edmonton, Alberta, NeWest Press, 1982.
Letters to Salonika. Toronto, Grand Union, 1983.
The Lovely Treachery of Words: Essays Selected and New. Toronto, Oxford University Press, 1989.
A Likely Story: The Writing Life. Red Deer, Alberta, Red Deer College Press, 1995.

Editor, with James Bacque and Pierre Gravel, *Creation* (interviews). Toronto, New Press, 1970.
Editor, *Sundogs: Stories from Saskatchewan.* Moose Jaw, Saskatchewan, Thunder Creek, 1980.
Editor, with Smaro Kamboureli, *Visible Visions: The Selected Poems of Douglas Barbour.* Edmonton, Alberta, NeWest Press, 1984.
Editor, with Reingard M. Nischik, *Gaining Ground: European Critics on Canadian Literature.* Edmonton, Alberta, NeWest Press, 1985.

*

Bibliography: ''An Annotated Bibliography of Works by and about Robert Kroetsch'' by Robert Leeker, in *Essays on Canadian Writing* (Toronto), fall 1977.

Manuscript Collection: University of Calgary Library, Alberta.

Critical Studies: ''Reinventing the Word: Kroetsch's Poetry'' by Susan Wood, in *Canadian Literature* (Vancouver), 77, 1978; ''The Border League: American 'West' and Canadian 'Region' by Eli Mandel and W.H. New, in *Crossing Frontiers: Papers in American and Canadian Western Literature,* edited by Dick Harrison and others, Edmonton, University of Alberta Press, 1979; *Robert Kroetsch* by Peter Thomas, Vancouver, Douglas and McIntyre, 1980; Robert

Kroetsch issue of *Open Letter* (Toronto), spring 1983 and summer-fall 1984; ''The Structural Horizons of Prairie Poetics: The Long Poem'' by Ann Munton, in *Dalhousie Review* (Halifax, Nova Scotia), 63(1), spring 1983; *Robert Kroetsch* by Robert Leeker, Boston, Twayne, 1986; ''Robert Kroetsch's Seed Catalogue: The Deconstruction of the Meta-Narrative of the Cowboy'' by David Arnason, in *Contemporary Manitoba Writers: New Critical Studies,* edited by Kenneth James Hughes, Winnipeg, Turnstone, 1990; *Women, Reading, Kroetsch: Telling the Difference* by Rudy Dorscht and Susan Arlene, Waterloo, Ontario, Wilfrid Laurier University Press, 1991; *Robert Kroetsch and His Works* by Ann Munton, Toronto, ECW Press, 1992; ''The Double Guide: Through the Labyrinth with Robert Kroetsch'' by Richard Land, in *The Journal of Commonwealth Literature* (London), 29(2), 1993; ''Heideggerian Elements in Robert Kroetsch's 'Seed Catalogue''' by Douglas Reimer, in *Canadian Literature* (Vancouver), 136, spring 1993; *'The Old Dualities': Deconstructing Robert Kroetsch and His Critics* by Dianne Tiefensee, Montreal, McGill-Queen's University Press, 1994; *Wordsworth after Empire: Three Postcolonial Appropriations* (dissertation) by Robert Thomas Archambeau, University of Notre Dame, 1996; ''Strange Plantings: Robert Kroetsch's 'Seed Catalogue''' by Wanda Campbell, in *Studies in Canadian Literature,* 21(1), 1996; ''The Birds, the Bees, and Kristeva: An Examination of Sexual Desire in the Nature Poetry of Daphne Marlatt, Robert Kroetsch, and Tim Lilburn'' by Darryl Whetter, in *Studies in Canadian Literature,* 21(2), 1996.

*　　*　　*

Robert Kroetsch is a writer of considerable energy, ingenuity, and ability. In the manner of the novelist Rudy Wiebe and rather like fellow poet Andrew Suknaski, Kroetsch has made it his aim to tell the tale of the Canadian prairies and, equally if not more importantly, ''to tell it like it was.'' He is an inspired teacher. His fiction is deservedly popular. His poems are characteristic of his fiction—direct, energetic, well organized—but they often seem to be ''chips off the old block,'' lesser works, somewhat interesting in themselves, but more impressive as a body of work, what the author calls in this context ''a continuing statement.''

The only way to come to terms with the past is to repossess it, and this Kroetsch does in *The Ledger* (1975). His ancestors operated a sawmill in Bruce County, Ontario, and their business ledgers from the 1850s survived. The ledgers offer the poet a springboard for business, personal, and poetical observations about his ancestors' lives and our lives today. It seems that ''the ledger survived / / because it was neither / human nor useful.'' Survival is a concomitant of existence, and so it is necessary that whatever has existed deserves to be celebrated because, like the earth itself, it will presumably outlast us all.

Kroetsch is perhaps best known for *The Stone Hammer: Poems 1960–1975,* which includes the ''Old Man Stories.'' In these he retells the tall tales of the trickster storytellers of the original inhabitants of the prairies. The title poem gives the hardheaded feeling of the poems that comprise the rest of the book:

The poem
is the stone
chipped and hammered
until it is shaped
like the stone
hammer, the maul.

Invention is characteristic of *The Sad Phoenician* (1979), a book that has more to do with the Canadian prairies than with Phoenicia. It is not what the poems say or do that is important; what is peculiar about them is that the first word in the lines of each poem is either ''and'' or ''but.'' The work was prepared for the spoken voice, not the printed word.

In his introduction to *The Crow Journals* (1980) critic Douglas Barbour talks about the ''catch-as-catch-can'' quality of Kroetsch's poetry. Barbour is right, for it seems that Kroetsch wants to include anything and everything in a poem, from anecdotes of everyday life to random thoughts occasioned by human experience. This is possible because the so-called poems are actually ''journal entries'' (Kroetsch's words) covering the years from 1973 to 1978 in the writer's life. They are a mixed bag, and they probably benefit from oral presentation.

In the preface to *Field Notes 1–8: A Continuing Poem* (1981) Eli Mandel discusses Kroetsch's sense of structure, characteristic voice, and use of parody. Randomness lies behind the structure; the voice is by turns brusque, conspiratorial, and confessional; and parody is used in the sense of allusions and quotations, oblique references to other voices once heard, and subtexts. Mandel writes that these features may be found in the following three lines:

I have to / I want
to know (now know)
? WHAT HAPPENED

It is not surprising that one characteristic of Kroetsch's poetry is the author's penchant for paradox. He is ready to take refuge in its light and enlightening demands. Here is the last poem, ''envoi (to begin with),'' in *Advice to My Friends: A Continuing Poem* (1985):

There is no real
world, my friends.
Why not, then,
let the stars
shine in our bones?

The style is at once conversational and lyrical, meditative and ironic. The collection also includes long chapbook-length sequences inspired by foreign travel, including ''Letters to Salonika,'' ''Postcards from China,'' and ''Delphi: Commentary.'' As Kroetsch explains in the first of these works, ''We write books to avoid / writing books.''

Kroetsch's poems verge on prose, and those in *Excerpts from the Real World* (1986) are prose poems. Here is one that shows the author's audaciously inventive manner:

[Of whom] do shoes dream? At night I hear them, under
your bed, dreaming they will carry me away to mysterious
places where I'll have to learn all over again how to walk,
stepping first from a slippery rock ledge onto a wet log.

In the same year Kroetsch published *Seed Catalogue,* which is described as ''part of a lifelong poem.'' In its pages the author says, ''I can no longer keep a journal. My life erases / everything I write.'' A year earlier, in *Advice to My Friends,* Kroetsch includes the following author's note:

Since the eloquence of failure may be the only eloquence
remaining in our time, I let these poems stand as the
enunciation of how I came to a poet's silence. And I

like to believe that the sequence of poems, announced in medias res as continuing, is, in its acceptance of its own impossibilities, completed.

It is difficult imagining Kroetsch's work ever being "completed" as long as he has a story to tell and the desire to share with his readers "the way it is."

—John Robert Colombo

KUMAR, Shiv K(umar)

Nationality: Indian. **Born:** Lahore, Punjab, 16 August 1921. **Education:** Fomman Christian College, Punjab University, Lahore, 1941–43, B.A. 1941, M.A. 1943; Fitzwilliam College, Cambridge, 1953–56, Ph.D. 1956. **Family:** Married Madhu Kumar in 1967; two sons and two daughters. **Career:** Lecturer, D.A.V. College, Lahore, 1945–47, and Hansraj College, Delhi, 1948–49; program executive, All India Radio, Delhi, 1949; broadcaster, BBC, 1951–53; senior lecturer and chair of the department of English, Government College, Chandigarh, 1953–56; reader in English, Punjab University, Hoshiarpur, 1956–59; professor and chair of the department of English, 1959–76, and UGC Emeritus Professor of English, 1984–86, Osmania University, Hyderabad; professor and chair of the department of English, and dean of the School of Humanities, 1976–79, and acting vice chancellor, 1979–80, University of Hyderabad; consultant, Indira Gandhi National University, New Delhi, 1986–91. Visiting professor, Elmira College, New York, 1965–67, Marshall University, Huntington, West Virginia, 1968, and University of Northern Iowa, Cedar Falls, 1969; cultural award visitor, Australia, summer 1971; visiting professor, Drake University, Des Moines, Iowa, 1971–72, Hofstra University, Hempstead, New York, 1972, University of Kent, Canterbury, 1977–78, Oklahoma University, Norman, 1980–82, and Franklin and Marshall College, Lancaster, Pennsylvania, 1982–84. President, All India English Teachers Conference, 1975. **Awards:** Smith-Mundt fellowship, 1962; Charles Holmer prize, 1984; Sahitya Akademy award, National Akademy of Letters, 1988. Fellow, Royal Society of Literature, 1978. **Member:** Advisory Board (English), Sahitya Akademy, 1978–83. **Address:** 2-F/Kakatiya Nagar, P.O. Jamia Osmania, Hyderabad 500 007, India.

PUBLICATIONS

Poetry

Articulate Silences. Calcutta, Writers Workshop, 1970.
Cobwebs in the Sun. New Delhi, Tata-McGraw Hill, 1974.
Subterfuges. New Delhi, Oxford University Press, 1976.
Woodpeckers. London, Sidgwick and Jackson, 1979.
Trapfalls in the Sky. Madras, Macmillan, 1986.
Woolgathering. Hyderabad, Orient Longman, 1998.

Play

The Last Wedding Anniversary (produced Hyderabad, 1974). New Delhi, Macmillan, 1975.

Novels

The Bone's Prayer. New Delhi, Arnold-Heinemann, 1979.
Nude before God. New York, Vanguard Press, 1983; New Delhi, Penguin, 1987.
A River with Three Banks. New Delhi, UBSPD, 1998.
Infatuation. New Delhi, UBSPD, 2000.

Short Stories

Beyond Love and Other Stories. New Delhi, Vikas, 1980.

Other

Virginia Woolf and Intuition. Hoshiarpur, Vishveshvaranand, 1957.
Virginia Woolf and Bergson's Durée Hoshiarpur, Vishveshvaranand, 1957.
Bergson and the Stream of Consciousness Novel. London, Blackie, 1962; New York, New York University Press, 1963.
Examine Your English, with M.M. Maison. New Delhi, Orient Longman, 1964.
Contemporary Indian Literature in English. Simla, Indian Institute of Advanced Study, 1992.

Editor, *Modern Short Stories.* Madras, Macmillan, 1958.
Editor, *Leaves of Grass,* by Walt Whitman. New Delhi, Eurasia, 1962.
Editor, *Apollo's Lyre.* Madras, Macmillan, 1962.
Editor, *The Red Badge of Courage,* by Stephen Crane. New Delhi, Eurasia, 1964.
Editor, *British Romantic Poets: Recent Revaluations.* New York, New York University Press, and London, University of London Press, 1966.
Editor, with Keith McKean, *Critical Approaches to Fiction.* New York, McGraw Hill, 1968.
Editor, *British Victorian Literature: Recent Revaluations.* New York, New York University Press, and London, University of London Press, 1969.
Editor, *The Life, Adventures, and Pyracies of the Famous Captain Singleton,* by Daniel Defoe. London, Oxford University Press, 1969.
Editor, *Indian Verse in English 1970.* Calcutta, Writers Workshop, 1971.
Editor, *Short Stories of Yesterday and Today.* New Delhi, Oxford University Press, 1978.
Editor, with R.K. Tongue, *English Miscellany.* New Delhi, Oxford University Press, 1980.
Editor, with Saros Cowasjee, *Modern Indian Short Stories.* New Delhi and Oxford, Oxford University Press, 1983.
Editor, *A Portrait of India: A Selection of Short Stories.* New Delhi, Vikas, 1983.
Editor, *Contemporary Indian Short Stories in English.* New Delhi, Sahitya Akademi, 1991.

Translator, *Selected Poems of Faiz Ahmed Faiz,* by Faiz Ahmed Faiz. New Delhi, Penguin Books, 1993.

*

Critical Studies: "An Essay on the Poems of Shiv K. Kumar" by R.K. Kaul, in *Osmania Journal of English Studies 11* (Hyderabad), 1, 1974; "Beyond the Empiric Point" by M. Sivaramkrishna, in *World Literature Written in English* (Arlington, Texas), November 1975; "Towards an Idiom of Sincerity" by K. Venkatachari, in *Journal of Indian Writing in English* (Gulbarga, Mysore), July 1976; "Between Kali and Cordelia" by T.G. Vaidyanathan, in *Osmania Journal of English Studies 13* (Hyderabad), 1, 1977; "Resonant Bones" by J. Birje-Patil, in *World Literature Today* (Norman, Oklahoma), autumn 1977; Shiv K. Kumar issue of *Journal of South Asian Literature* (East Lansing, Michigan), 25, fall 1990; "Modes of Self-Knowledge in Shiv K. Kumar's Poetry" by C. Sengupta, in *Creative Forum* (New Delhi), 5(1–4), January 1992.

Shiv K. Kumar comments:

Although I scribbled some verse during my undergraduate days, it was only at the age of forty-nine or so that I wrote my first serious poem. Since then poetry has been one of my most continual sources of joy.

A poem comes to me as a phrase, a line, or a nebulous image that then gets crystallized into a cluster of words. An idea never starts it off; I seem to have an innate distrust of statement. I believe that a poem achieves its most effective articulation when it emerges from the intensity of a writer's lived experience. It may not be "a kind of locked trunk of confessions," as Gabriel Pearson puts it, but it acquires its sharp identity from the poet as a private person.

Of course a poet must never forsake the artistic distance and control that mold the disparate elements of experience into a pattern. Nor should he allow any kind of intellectual discipline to ossify his sensibility. My dual role as critic and writer has made me particularly conscious of this dilemma, but I agree with Anthony Thwaite that one's activity may "fall into different compartments and that the one doesn't influence the other."

I do not think I have been influenced by any poet, though I greatly admire the work of Robert Lowell, Sylvia Plath, and Anne Sexton. Ultimately each poet has to work out his own credo of life and imagination—"we perish each alone."

Do I consider the use of a language I am not born to a serious impediment to my creativity? No. I feel that it is as much the language that chooses its writer as the writer who selects his medium. In any case, I have grown up with the English language and cannot write in any other, so I have no alternative.

It has sometimes been remarked that one of the recurring themes in my poetry is cultural interaction, a preoccupation with the polarities of East and West. But this preoccupation must be unconscious. Maybe I have stayed too long in the West, and my Indian sensibility keeps assessing my Western experience. Fundamentally, I guess, I am something of a "primitivist" who may never overcome his nostalgia for prelapsarian innocence and simplicity. What hurts me most is any kind of regimentation—political, social, intellectual, or religious. I feel that poetry is an impassioned testament to man's inner freedom. I have done other kinds of creative writing, but it is the poem that satisfies me most because it summons forth my imagination in its intensest form. In the beginning was the word, and that word was the poem, man's profoundest experience articulated through cadence and harmony.

* * *

Shiv K. Kumar's poetry is vibrantly about everyday life, felt on the tips of his senses but undercut by an ironic and sometimes satirical sense of humor. Uniting the strands of the confessional, the natural and urban landscape, and social satire is Kumar's ebullient celebration of the life principle, which is often revealed in his constructs of his "gutsy" sexuality. At his best the poems may be seen symbolically as a bursting of creativity at the seams of the repressive conventions and rituals of Indian society that are forever pressing in upon him. "Renunciation is a mere chimera," declares an early poem and is, therefore, ruled out even as a temptation; "the river of time" is "sullied by ritual and dogma—ashes and bones," laments one of his later poems. Thus, the temptations, tensions, and limited rewards of this world are Kumar's constant preoccupations.

With some exceptions Kumar's poems in *Articulate Silences* are characterized by a rather fanciful use of hyperbole, pun, and erotic imagery: "Those scythed curls . . . enact the Hegelian dialectic"; the salesgirls at Paris International Airport are "duty free"; "the girls in their minis—the thigh is the limit:— / flourishing their maxi breasts / bursting to frank exposure." Other poems such as "Genesis," "Karma," "Revelation," and "Buddha at a Night Club" play upon traditional religious concepts in order to focus on what are, in effect, aspects of an adolescent romanticism. "Sounds of Hunger," for example, spends fourteen lines describing, through a series of metaphors, the sounds of physical hunger, only to draw attention in the last four lines to "the other hunger" that "forages for silken thighs / swishing past / beyond accessibility."

"An Encounter with Death" and "Rickshaw-Wallah," both reprinted in *Subterfuges* but with the former cut down by eleven lines, anticipate Kumar's more mature style. "An Encounter with Death" recalls how on a "gutsy afternoon," sharing a boisterous joke with his old mother, he overlooked the forebodings of her sudden death and how for thirteen days, as the Hindus say, he "communed with her spirit." It is significant, however, that Kumar leaves the question of his own belief in the superstition ambiguous. "Rickshaw-Wallah," in its compression of satire and compassion, achieves an aesthetic effect that is absent from "Sounds of Hunger":

Pulling his cross
on a bellyful of questions,
with obesity belching complacency
on the cushioned seat behind.
> he computes the patches
> on the street's tattered shirt.
> Beyond the municipal precincts,
> in a slummed roost,
the mother-hen is gagging
her chicks full-throated cries
for a few grains of rice—
their last supper.

"Broken Columns," a twelve-part sequence in *Woodpeckers,* comprises vignettes of the poet's journey from the age of four, when he "plunged into precocity," through the "fuzzy yearnings" of adolescence, his visit to Cambridge, his return to India, and his marriage to "a woman I had only half known." In a sense it is the typical journey of a Hindu boy in India, but the reconstructions of memories suggests a wholly modern, skeptical, and irreverent sensibility, forever aware of the hidden ironies of life. In capturing the sensuous and the incongruous moment, ''Broken Columns'' encapsulates some of the range of Kumar's thematic concerns and the resilience of his style.

Examples of Kumar's tendency to project his sexuality into a social or natural scene around him abound in his poetry. For example, in ''Broken Columns'' a concerned father, suspecting his son's propensities, sends him to the priest in a Shiva temple for counseling; the priest, instead, takes him into a dark chamber, only to caress his neck until ''my nerves tingle like a horse's flanks.'' As he leaves the temple, he is redeemed by his revived memory of the ''aroma of deodar'' and ''the cluster of mynahs'' on the skirt of his playmate Shiela, whom he had at the age of ten once ''transfixed'' in a timber shop in order to ''plumb the bay of Bengal.''

Kumar, however, is equally deft at evoking, through cross-cultural associations, the atmosphere of a place, city, or historic monument. He is at his best when he takes up an object, a routine scene, or an incident from everyday life and sculpts it into a poem. In ''Clouds'' Kumar humanizes the clouds only to focus on the cosmic link between their peripatetic versatility and the mundane world. His clouds, like his poetry, do not simply float high over vales and hills but are involved in life on the earth. They are dexterous, friendly, and reliable, and

> Above all, it's their discernment—
> they'd let the sun break through when
> a child is on the zebra crossing,
> or drop a veil when a woman steals
> out for a rendezvous.
> Not even saints, limited in their choice,
> even pause to look about.

> But if you've once mated on this thistle-down
> beds of clouds, their mirrors
> will never betray you.

—Devindra Kohli

KUMIN, Maxine

Nationality: American. **Born:** Maxine Winokur, in Philadelphia, Pennsylvania, June 1925. **Education:** Radcliffe College, Cambridge, Massachusetts, A.B. 1946, M.A. 1948. **Family:** Married Victor M. Kumin in 1946; two daughters and one son. **Career:** Instructor, 1958–61, and lecturer in English, 1965–68, Tufts University, Medford, Massachusetts; lecturer, Newton College of the Sacred Heart, Massachusetts, 1971; visiting lecturer/professor/writer, University of Massachusetts, Amherst, 1972; Columbia University, New York, spring 1975; Brandeis University, Waltham, Massachusetts, fall 1975; Princeton University, New Jersey, spring 1977, 1979, 1982; Washington University, St. Louis, 1977; Randolph-Macon Women's College, Lynchburg, Virginia, 1978; Bucknell University, Lewisburg, Pennsylvania, 1983; Massachusetts Institute of Technology, Cambridge, 1984; Atlantic Center for the Arts, New Smyrna Beach, Florida, winter 1984; and University of Miami (Florida), spring 1995. Member of Bread Loaf Writers Conference staff, 1969–71, 1973, 1975, 1977; The Sewanee Writers' Conference staff, 1993 and 1994.

Awards: Lowell Mason Palmer award, 1960; National Endowment for the Arts grant, 1966; National Council on the Arts fellowship, 1967; William Marion Reedy award, 1968; Eunice Tietjens memorial prize (*Poetry,* Chicago), 1972; Pulitzer prize, 1973; Radcliffe College award, 1978; American Academy award, 1980; Academy of American Poets fellowship, 1985; Levinson award, 1987; Sarah Josepha Hale award, 1992; The Poets' Prize for *Looking for Luck,* 1994; Aiken Taylor Poetry prize for *Looking for Luck,* 1995; Centennial award, 1996; New Hampshire Writers Project Lifetime Achievement award, 1998; Ruth Lilly Poetry prize, 1999. Honorary degrees: Centre College, Danville, Kentucky, 1976; Davis and Elkins College, Elkins, West Virginia, 1977; Regis College, Weston, Massachusetts, 1979; New England College, Henniker, New Hampshire, 1982; Claremont Graduate School, California, 1983; University of New Hampshire, Durham, 1984; Keene State College, 1995. Poetry consultant, Library of Congress, Washington, D.C., 1981–82. Since 1979 Woodrow Wilson Visiting Fellow. Scholar, 1961–63, and since 1972 officer, Society of Fellows, Radcliffe Institute, Cambridge, Massachusetts. **Agent:** Scott Waxman Agency, 1650 Broadway, Suite 1011, New York, New York 10019. **Address:** 40 Harriman Lane, Warner, New Hampshire 03278, U.S A.

PUBLICATIONS

Poetry

Halfway. New York, Holt Rinehart, 1961.
The Privilege. New York, Harper, 1965.
The Nightmare Factory. New York, Harper, 1970.
Up Country: Poems of New England, New and Selected. New York, Harper, 1972.
House, Bridge, Fountain, Gate. New York, Viking Press, 1975.
The Retrieval System. New York, Viking Press, 1978; London, Penguin, 1979.
Our Ground Time Here Will Be Brief. New York, Viking Press, 1982.
Closing the Ring. Lewisburg, Pennsylvania, Press of Appletree Alley, 1984.
The Long Approach. New York, Viking, 1985.
Nurture. New York, Viking, 1989.
Looking for Luck. New York, W.W. Norton & Co., 1992.
Connecting the Dots. New York, W.W. Norton & Co., 1996.
Selected Poems 1960–1990. New York, W.W. Norton & Co., 1997.

Recording: *Progress Report,* Watershed, 1976.

Novels

Through Dooms of Love. New York, Harper, 1965; as *A Daughter and Her Loves,* London, Gollancz, 1965.
The Passions of Uxport. New York, Harper, 1968.
The Abduction. New York, Harper, 1971.
The Designated Heir. New York, Viking Press, 1974.
Quit Monks or Die. Ashland, Oregon, Story Line Press, 1999.

Short Stories

Why Can't We Live Together Like Civilized Human Beings? New York, Viking Press, 1982.

Other

To Make a Prairie: Essays on Poets, Poetry, and Country Living. Ann Arbor, University of Michigan Press, 1979.

In Deep: Country Essays. New York, Viking, 1987.

Women, Animals, and Vegetables: Essays and Stories. New York, W.W. Norton & Co., 1994.

Always Beginning: Prose Essays, Port Townsend, Washington, Copper Canyon Press, 2000.

Inside the Halo and the Journey Beyond, New York, W.W. Norton & Co., 2000.

Editor, *Rain*, by William Carpenter. Boston, Northeastern University Press, 1985.

Other (for children)

Sebastian and the Dragon. New York, Putnam, 1960.

Spring Things. New York, Putnam, 1961.

Summer Story. New York, Putnam, 1961.

Follow the Fall. New York, Putnam, 1961.

A Winter Friend. New York, Putnam, 1961.

Mittens in May. New York, Putnam, 1962.

No One Writes a Letter to the Snail. New York, Putnam, 1962.

Archibald the Traveling Poodle. New York, Putnam, 1963.

Eggs of Things, with Anne Sexton. New York, Putnam, 1963.

More Eggs of Things, with Anne Sexton. New York, Putnam, 1964.

Speedy Digs Downside Up. New York, Putnam, 1964.

The Beach Before Breakfast. New York, Putnam, 1964.

Paul Bunyan. New York, Putnam, 1966.

Faraway Farm. New York, Norton, 1967.

The Wonderful Babies of 1809 and Other Years. New York, Putnam, 1968.

When Grandmother Was Young. New York, Putnam, 1969.

When Mother Was Young. New York, Putnam, 1970.

When Great Grandmother Was Young. New York, Putnam, 1971.

Joey and the Birthday Present, with Anne Sexton. New York, McGraw Hill, 1971.

The Wizard's Tears, with Anne Sexton. New York, McGraw Hill, 1975.

What Color Is Caesar? New York, McGraw Hill, 1978.

The Microscope. New York, Haroer, 1984.

*

Manuscript Collection: Bienecke Library, Yale University, New Haven, Connecticut.

Critical Studies: "The Art of Maxine Kumin" by John Ciardi, in *Saturday Review* (Washington, D.C.), 25 March 1972; "Past *Halfway: The Retrieval System* by Maxine Kumin" by Sybil Estess, in *Iowa Review* (Iowa City), 10(4), 1979; "Maxine Kumin's Survival" by Philip Booth, in *American Poetry Review* (Philadelphia), 7(6), November-December 1981; "Kumin on Kumin and Sexton: An Interview" by Diana Hume George, in *Poesis: A Journal of Criticism* (Bryn Mawr, Pennsylvania), 6(2), 1985; "Courage to Survive: Maxine Kumin" by Jean B. Gearhart, *Pembroke Magazine,* 1988; "Keeping Our Working Distance: Maxine Kumin's Poetry of Loss and

Survival" by Diane Hume George, in *Aging and Gender in Literature: Studies in Creativity,* Charlottesville, University Press of Virginia, 1993; *Telling the Barn Swallow: Poets on the Poetry of Maxine Kumin,* edited by Emily Grosholz, Hanover, New Hampshire, University Press of New England, 1997.

*   *   *

Maxine Kumin, who jokingly has referred to herself, the earth motherly nature poet, as "Roberta Frost," at first may seem to possess a very simple sense of the physical world. But she is a metaphysician too. Her best collection of poems, *The Retrieval System,* explores ideas that make the notion of death acceptable. Much has been made of her close friendship with Anne Sexton, but its literary importance probably resides in forcing Kumin to leap out of her comfortable physical world of family and benevolent nature into a craggier world and personality, more like that of the curmudgeonly Robert Frost.

Earth mythology is always about use and misuse. Thus, the concerns of Kumin as a person become central to the concerns of any twentieth-century citizen of the world: how can we survive the autumn, the "fall," of our misused earth? In "Grappling in the Central Blue" Kumin offers this ongoing theme in her poetry:

Let us eat of the inland oyster.
Let its fragrance intoxicate us
into almost believing
that staying on is possible
again this year in
benevolent blue October.

Over the years some of Kumin's best poems have concerned her children and her Demeter-like role, grieving the loss of them as they grow up, but what is most compelling is that she never accepts the impossibility of return, even if it be through magic or metaphysics. Body is as transformable as any other matter. She shows in "Seeing the Bones" her willingness to accept the pain of evolution—

This year again the bruise-colored oak
hangs on eating my heart out
with its slow change

—but she insists on the myth and magic that make return, retrieval, and reincarnation possible. She concludes the poem with the ritual of reconstructing her lost daughter from old artifacts:

I do the same things day by day.
They steady me against the wrong turn,
. . . Working backward I reconstruct
you.

The charm with which Kumin works out her belief in worldly return is captured in many poems, including "The Retrieval System" ("It begins with my dog, now dead, who all his long life / carried about in his head the brown eyes of my father"). In "On Reading an Old Baedeker in Schloss Leopoldskron," a typical and lovely Kumin poem ("Soft as beetpulp, the cover / of this ancient Baedeker"), she speaks of the ongoingness of the world, with both people and "swans / in their ninetieth generation" returning often. In "Primtivism Exhibit" she returns to the theme of a retrieval system:

> Longest l look at the dread
> dog fetish, whose spiky back
> is built of rusty razorblades
> that World War II GI's let drop
> on atolls in the South Pacific
> they were securing from the Japs
> who did not shave, but only plucked
> stray hairs from chin and jaw.
> I like the way he makes a funk-
> y art out of cosmetic junk
> standing the cutting edge of old steel
> up straight to say, *World, get off my back.*

Kumin believes in animal species and sees the human animal as having a chance for survival, as in "In the Park":

> You have forty-nine days between
> death and rebirth if you're a Buddhist.
> Even the smallest soul could swim
> the English Channel in that time

The best of Kumin's poems, like this one, maintain a cool humor and charm. In addition to her rich and smooth wit, Kumin's greatest skill is to make images, wonderful images, that turn into big metaphors. Playing with dualities and manipulating everyday language so that it works with the complexities of ideas and patterns, she invokes the irony that comes out of Dionysian tragedy. A few lines from "Marianne, My Mother, and Me" define Kumin's poetry and her life: "We / must be as clear as our natural reticence / will allow." The one thing that is clear throughout her substantial body of work is that she believes survival to be possible, if only through the proper use of the imagination to retrieve those things that are loved well enough.

—Diane Wakoski

KUNENE, (Raymond) Mazisi

Nationality: South African. **Born:** Mazisi kaMdabuli Kunene, in Durban, Natal, 12 May 1930. **Education:** Natal University, B.A.(honors) in Zulu and history, M.A. in Zulu Poetry; attended School of Oriental and African Studies, London, 1959. **Family:** Married Mabowe Mathabo in 1973; four children. **Career:** Head of department of African Studies, University College of Roma, Lesotho; director of education for South African United Front; member of Anti-Apartheid and Boycott movement in Britain, 1959–68; chief representative, African National Congress in Europe and United States, 1962, and director of finance, 1972; visiting professor of African literature, Stanford University, Palo Alto, California; head of African Studies, University of Iowa; associate professor, then professor of African literature and languages, University of California, Los Angeles. Member, Faculty of Humanities, University of Natal, Durban. Has held positions in the Pan-African Youth movement and the Committee of African Organizations. **Awards:** Winner, Bantu Literary Competition, 1956. **Address:** Department of African Literature and Language, University of California, 405 Hilgard, Los Angeles, California 90024, U.S.A.

PUBLICATIONS

Poetry

Zulu Poems. New York, Africana Publishing Corporation, 1970.
Emperor Shaka the Great: A Zulu Epic. London, Heinemann, 1979.
Anthem of the Decades: A Zulu Epic Dedicated to the Women of Africa. London, Heinemann, 1981.
The Ancestors and the Sacred Mountain: Poems. London, Heinemann, 1982.

*

Critical Studies: "Contemporary Samples of English-Speaking African Poetry" by Kofi Awoonor, in *The Breast of the Earth: A Survey of the History, Culture, and Literature of Africa South of the Sahara,* New York, Anchor Press/Doubleday, 1975; "Past, Present, and Future in African Poetry" by Ken Goodwin, in *SPAN* (Murdoch, Australia), 13, October 1981; "Effects of Exile" by Anthony Delius, in *The Times Literary Supplement* (London), 4128, 14 May 1982; "Mazisi Kunene" by K.L. Goodwin, in *Understanding African Poetry: A Study of Ten Poets,* London, Heinemann, 1982; "Poetry" by Ursula A. Barnett, in *A Vision of Order: A Study of Black South African Literature in English (1940–1980),* Amherst, University of Massachusetts Press, 1983; "Vernacular Poetry" by Jacques Alvarez-Pereyre, in *The Poetry of Commitment in South Africa,* London, Heinemann, 1984; "Poetry, Humanism and Apartheid: A Study of Mazisi Kunene's Zulu Poems" by Chidi Maduka, in *Griot: Official Journal of the Southern Conference on Afro-American Studies* (Berea, Kentucky), 4(1–2), Winter/Summer 1985; "Kunene's Shaka and the Idea of the Poet As Teacher" by John Haynes, in *Ariel: A Review of International English Literature* (Calgary, Alberta), 18(1), January 1987; "Super-Shaka: Mazisi Kunene's Emperor Shaka the Great" by Z. Mbongeni Malaba, in *Research in African Literatures* (Columbus), 19(4), Winter 1988; "Patterns of Oral Poetic Trends in West and South African Poetry: Atukwei Okai and Mazisi Kunene" by Ohaeto Ezenwa, in *The Literary Griot: International Journal of Black Oral and Literary Studies* (Wayne, New Jersey), 8(1), Spring 1989; "'Sacred Geography' in Poems by Mazisi Kunene," in *Literature, Nature and the Land: Collected AUETSA Papers,* edited by Nigel Bell and Meg Cowper-Lewis, Kwa-Dlangezwa, Natal, University of Zululand, 1993; "The Writer As Philosopher: Interview with Mazisi Kunene" by Vasu Reddy, in *South African Journal of African Languages,* 16(4), November 1996.

* * *

Noteworthy features of Mazisi Kunene's poetry are that all his published work is composed in Zulu and translated into English by the author and that everything he writes is centered in the traditional beliefs, practices, and conventions of the Zulu people. An authority on Nguni literature, he is well equipped to convey to English readers the qualities of what is essentially an oral literature, with its rich cultural heritage and strong national pride. Consequently, his epic poetry is performance oriented and rhetorical, with a powerful narrative impetus. In an introduction to each volume Kunene explains to the reader relevant aspects of Zulu thought and literary conventions, such as the place of the individual in relation to ancestors and the function of the praise poem. At the same time he makes clear his rejection of Eurocentric models in favor of an African worldview.

Kunene's first volume, *Zulu Poems* (1970), reflects a wide variety of experiences and subject matter, ranging from love to war and from moral reflection to political commentary. It is given a sense of unity by a Blakean simplicity of vision expressed in African imagery. The following lines are from "Mother Earth, or the Folly of National Boundaries":

Why should those at the end of the earth
Not drink from the same calabash
And build their homes in the valley of the earth
And together grow with our children?

Emperor Shaka the Great (1979) is a monumental epic of some seventeen thousand lines. It has been attacked for its seemingly uncritical portrayal of Shaka, but a careful reading shows that Kunene is less concerned with the glorification of the Zulu monarch than with the extent to which he represents and gives expression to the communal values, history, and philosophical vision of the Zulu people. Shaka's destruction results from his flouting of traditions rooted in the natural forces governing earth and man.

Kunene's next major work, *Anthem of the Decades* (1981), which is dedicated to the "women of Africa," real and legendary, celebrates the complementary cycles of creation and destruction and of conflict and reconciliation that govern human history as reflected in the oral heritage of the African people. Made up of fifteen cycles, *Anthem* tends to lapse into didactic rhetoric, though there are passages of lyrical intensity.

Kunene's second collection of poems, *The Ancestors and the Sacred Mountain* (1982), achieves a resonance and sureness of touch absent from its predecessor. Sociopolitical concerns ("Police Raid," "Death of the Miners," "The Rise of the Angry Generation") are integrated into an overarching vision or dream of peace, of communal life lived in unity with the earth and in the light of ancestral wisdom. The imagery is elemental, striking, and free from cliché:

You are born of the mist and the dream.
Do not move, do not disturb the eternal cycles
But weave into them the sacred knots of the rainbow
And the generations that are to come must sing.

—Ernest Pereira

KUNITZ, Stanley (Jasspon)

Nationality: American. **Born:** Worcester, Massachusetts, 29 July 1905. **Education:** Worcester Classical High School; Harvard University, Cambridge, Massachusetts (Garrison Medal, 1926), A.B. (summa cum laude) 1926 (Phi Beta Kappa), A.M. 1927. **Military Service:** U.S. Army, 1943–45. **Family:** Married 1) Helen Pearce in 1930 (divorced 1937); 2) Eleanor Evans in 1939 (divorced 1958), one daughter; 3) Elise Asher in 1958. **Career:** Editor, *Wilson Library Bulletin,* New York, 1928–43. Member of the faculty, Bennington

College, Vermont, 1946–49; professor of English, Potsdam State Teachers College (now State University of New York), 1949–50, and summers, 1949–53; lecturer, New School for Social Research, New York, 1950–57; visiting professor, University of Washington, Seattle, 1955–56, Queens College, Flushing, New York, 1956–57, Brandeis University, Waltham, Massachusetts, 1958–59, Yale University, New Haven, Connecticut, 1970–72, Rutgers University, New Brunswick, New Jersey, 1974, Princeton University, New Jersey, 1978, and Vassar College, Poughkeepsie, New York, 1981; director, YM-YWHA Poetry Workshop, New York, 1958–62. Danforth Visiting Lecturer, United States, 1961–63; lecturer, 1963–67, and adjunct professor of writing, 1967–85, Columbia University, New York. Since 1968 associated with the Fine Arts Work Center, Provincetown, Massachusetts. Editor, Yale Series of Younger Poets, Yale University Press, New Haven, Connecticut, 1969–77. Consultant in poetry, Library of Congress, Washington, D.C., 1974–76. Former Cultural Exchange Lecturer, U.S.S.R., Poland, Senegal, Ghana, Israel, and Egypt. Senior Fellow in Humanities, Princeton University, 1978. Since 1969 Fellow, Yale University. Since 1985 president, Poets House, New York. **Awards:** Oscar Blumenthal prize, 1941, and Levinson prize, 1956 (*Poetry,* Chicago); Guggenheim fellowship, 1945; Amy Lowell traveling fellowship, 1953; Harriet Monroe award, 1958; Pulitzer prize, 1959; Ford grant, 1959; American Academy grant, 1959; Brandeis University Creative Arts award, 1964; Academy of American Poets fellowship, 1968; Lenore Marshall award, 1980; National Endowment for the Arts Senior fellowship, 1984; Bollingen prize, 1987; Walt Whitman award, 1987; Montgomery fellow, Dartmouth College, 1991; Centennial medal, Harvard University, 1992; National Medal of Arts, 1993; Shelly Memorial award, 1995; National Book award, 1995; St. Botolph Club Foundation award, 1996; Robert Frost medal, Poetry Society of America, 1998; Courage Conscience award, Peace Abbey, 1998. Litt.D.: Clark University, Worcester, Massachusetts, 1961; Anna Maria College, Paxton, Massachusetts, 1977. L.H.D.: Worcester State College, Massachusetts, 1980; State University of New York, Brockport, 1987. **Member:** American Academy, and since 1985 secretary; Chancellor, Academy of American Poets, 1970. **Address:** 37 West 12th Street, New York, New York, 10011, U.S.A.

PUBLICATIONS

Poetry

Intellectual Things. New York, Doubleday, 1930.
Passport to the War: A Selection of Poems. New York, Holt, 1944.
Selected Poems 1928–1958. Boston, Little Brown, 1958; London, Dent, 1959.
The Testing-Tree. Boston, Little Brown, 1971.
The Terrible Threshold: Selected Poems 1940–1970. London, Secker and Warburg, 1974.
The Coat without a Seam: Sixty Poems 1930–1972. Northampton, Massachusetts, Gehenna Press, 1974.
The Lincoln Relics. Port Townsend, Washington, Graywolf Press, 1978.
The Poems of Stanley Kunitz 1928–1978. Boston, Little Brown, and London, Secker and Warburg, 1979.
The Wellfleet Whale and Companion Poems. New York, Sheep Meadow Press, 1983.

Next-to-Last Things (includes essays). Boston, Atlantic Monthly Press, 1985.
Passing Through: The Later Poems, New and Selected. New York, Norton, 1995.

Recording: *The Only Dance,* Watershed, 1981.

Other

Robert Lowell, Poet of Terribilità lecture. New York, Pierpont Morgan Library, 1974.
A Kind of Order, A Kind of Folly: Essays and Conversations. Boston, Little Brown, 1975.
From Feathers to Iron (lecture). Washington, D.C., Library of Congress, 1976.
Interviews and Encounters with Stanley Kunitz. Riverdale-on-Hudson, New York, Sheep Meadow Press, 1993.

Editor (as Dilly Tante), *Living Authors: A Book of Biographies.* New York, Wilson, 1931.
Editor, with Howard Haycraft and Wilbur C. Hadden, *Authors Today and Yesterday: A Companion Volume to "Living Authors."* New York, Wilson, 1933.
Editor, with others, *The Junior Book of Authors.* New York, Wilson, 1934; revised edition, 1961.
Editor, with Howard Haycraft, *British Authors of the Nineteenth Century.* New York, Wilson, 1936.
Editor, with Howard Haycraft, *American Authors 1600–1900: A Biographical Dictionary of American Literature.* New York, Wilson, 1938.
Editor, with Howard Haycraft, *Twentieth Century Authors: A Biographical Dictionary of Modern Literature.* New York, Wilson, 1942; First Supplement, with Vineta Colby, 1955.
Editor, with Howard Haycraft, *British Authors Before 1800: A Biographical Dictionary.* New York, Wilson, 1952.
Editor, *Poems,* by John Keats. New York, Crowell, 1964.
Editor, with Vineta Colby, *European Authors 1000–1900: A Biographical Dictionary of European Literature.* New York, Wilson, 1967.
Editor and Translator, with Max Hayward, *Poems of Akhmatova.* Boston, Little Brown, 1973; London, Harvill Press, 1974.
Editor and Co-Translator, *Orchard Lamps,* by Ivan Drach. New York, Sheep Meadow Press, 1978; Toronto, Exile Editions, 1989.
Editor, *The Essential Blake.* New York, Ecco Press, 1987.
Editor and Co-Translator, with Max Hayward, *Poems of Akhmatova/Izbrannye Stikhi.* New York, Houghton Mifflin, 1997.
Editor, with David Ignatow, *The Wild Card: Selected Poems, Early and Late, of Karl Shapiro.* N.p., University of Illinois Press, 1998.

Translator, with others, *Stolen Apples,* by Yevgeny Yevtushenko. New York, Doubleday, 1971; London, W.H. Allen, 1972.
Translator, with others, *Story under Full Sail,* by Andrei Voznesensky. New York, Doubleday, 1974.

*

Critical Studies: "The Poetry of Stanley Kunitz" by James Hagstrum, in *Poets in Progress,* edited by Edward Hungerford, Evanston, Illinois, Northwestern University Press, 1962; *The Contemporary Poet As Artist and Critic* edited by Anthony Ostroff, Boston, Little Brown, 1964; "Man with a Leaf in His Head," in *The Nation* (New York), 20 September 1971, and "The Darkness of the Self," in *Times Literary Supplement* (London), 30 May 1980, both by Stanley Moss; "Voznesensky and Kunitz on Poetry," in *The New York Times Book Review,* 16 April 1972; *The Craft of Poetry* edited by William Packard, New York, Doubleday, 1974; "Imagine Wrestling with an Angel," in *Contemporary Poetry in America,* edited by Robert Boyers, New York, Schocken, 1975; "The Language That Saves" by Richard Vine, in *Salmagundi* (Saratoga Springs, New York), winter 1977; *Stanley Kunitz* by Marie Hénault, Boston, Twayne, 1978; Stanley Kunitz issue of *Antaeus* (New York), spring 1980; interview with Chris Busa, in *Paris Review,* spring 1982; *Stanley Kunitz: An Introduction to the Poetry* by Gregory Orr, New York, Columbia University Press, 1985; *A Celebration for Stanley Kunitz on His Eightieth Birthday,* Riverdale-on-Hudson, New York, Sheep Meadow Press, 1986; *The Art of Poetry: Interviews with Stanley Kunitz,* edited by Stanley Moss, Riverdale-on-Hudson, New York, Sheep Meadow Press, 1989; interview with Gary Pacernick, in *Michigan Quarterly Review* (Ann Arbor, Michigan), 36(4), fall 1997; interview with Leslie Kelen, in *American Poetry Review* (Philadelphia), 27(2), March-April 1998.

Stanley Kunitz comments:

Since my *Selected Poems*, I have been moving toward a more open style based on natural speech rhythms. *The Testing-Tree* (1971) embodied my search for a transparency of language and vision. Maybe age itself compels me to embrace the great simplicities as I struggle to free myself from the knots and complications, the hang-ups, of my youth. I keep trying to improve my controls over language so that I will not have to tell lies. And I keep reading the masters because they infect me with human possibility. I am no more reconciled than I ever was to the world's wrongs and the injustice of time. The poetry I admire most is innocent, luminous, and true.

*　　*　　*

The poems of Stanley Kunitz have always been carefully made (crafted, one might say) and meticulously attentive to subtleties of sound and sense. For this reason contemporary critics and poets, Theodore Roethke and Robert Lowell among them, have rightfully regarded Kunitz as "a subtly powerful presence in the poetic word of his day," according to the citation for his 1987 Bollingen prize. After an impressive start and a relatively quiet midcareer, Kunitz not only retained but also strengthened his inventiveness and skills as a major artist in his later years. What other writer, aside from his beloved Yeats, has written so well in his seventies and eighties, as in poems like "The Layers"?

I have walked through many lives,
    some of them my own,
    and I am not who I was,
    though some principle of being
    abides, from which I struggle
    not to stray.

In the early poems the argument and tone tended to be highly intellectual, almost metaphysical, with echoes of Donne and Marvell as well as their twentieth-century American admirers John Crowe Ransom and Allen Tate. For example, "Men's Creatrix," formal in style and modernist in theme, speaks of the conflict between intellect and feeling. "Benediction," an early poem in couplets, and "Grammar Lesson," a later poem in quatrains, exhibit a gift for rhyme that characterized Kunitz's first three collections. In his youth, Kunitz has said, he willed himself into being rather closed to outside influences, but since the late 1960s he has tried to make his work more open and accessible, in the manner of William Carlos Williams, "without sacrificing its more complex inner tissue."

Kunitz's vision is essentially tragic, particularly in poems retracing the myth of the lost father—"Father and Son," "The Portrait," and "Quinnapoxet." "The Testing Tree," a major work and one of several poems and essays inspired by his early years in Worcester, Massachusetts, argues that "in a murderous time / the heart breaks and breaks / and lives by breaking." Chastened by circumstance, the poetic voice remains undaunted, nonetheless, resembling the speaker Solomon Levi in "An Old Cracked Tune":

> I dance, for the joy of surviving,
> on the edge of the road.

"The Magic Curtain," also from Kunitz's later period, is, by contrast, a nostalgic love poem to his mother's housekeeper, beautiful, yellow-haired Frieda, his ally in skipping school for a day at the picture show:

> Downtown at the Front St. Bi-jo (spelt Bijou)
>   we were, as always, the first in line,
>   with a hot nickel clutched in hand,
>   impatient for *The Perils of Pauline* . . .

The love poems are among the most memorable of Kunitz's works, beginning with the early "So Intricately Is This World Resolved," through "Foreign Affairs" and "The Science of the Night," to a witty parody of the traditional love lyric, "After the Last Dynasty." In the last poem one partner compares the other to Chairman Mao:

> Loving you was a kind
> of Chinese guerilla war.
> Thanks to your lightfoot genius
> no Eighth Route Army
> kept its lines more fluid,
> traveled with less baggage,
> so nibbled the advantage.

Kunitz's remarkable collection of essays *A Kind of Order, A Kind of Folly* includes "Poet and State," perhaps the best essay on the relationship between art and politics in contemporary literature. In *Next-to-Last Things* he has added an insightful essay on Lowell, a telling note on Whitman, a moving memoir of his mother—a Luthanian immigrant—and a beautiful reflection titled "The Wisdom of the Body."

Through his devotion to art and an insistence upon a high standard of performance, Kunitz has produced a body of work that has increased in stature over the years. A selected poems, *Passing Through* (1995), marking his ninetieth birthday, gathers most of the work since *The Testing Tree* (1971), including "The Snakes of Summer," "Raccoon Journal," and the major poem "The Wellfleet Whale," set near the poet's longtime Cape Cod summer residence:

> While empires rose and fell on land
>   your nation breasted the open main,

> rocked in the consoling rhythm
>   of the tides.

Wounded, the great voyager whale, "chief of the pelagic world," dies "where the lovers lie belly to belly / in the rub and nuzzle of their sporting," where, the speaker says in a final lament,

> You have become like us,
>   disgraced and mortal.

—Michael True

KUPPNER, Frank

Nationality: British. **Born:** Glasgow, 1951. **Education:** University of Glasgow. Qualified electronics engineer. **Address:** c/o Carcanet Press Ltd., 4th Floor, Conavon Court, 12–16 Blackfriars Street, Manchester M3 5BQ, England.

PUBLICATIONS

Poetry

A Bad Day for the Sung Dynasty. Manchester, Carcanet, 1984.
The Intelligent Observation of Naked Women. Manchester, Carcanet, 1987.
Everything Is Strange. Manchester, Carcanet, 1994.

Novels

Ridiculous! Absurd! Disgusting! Manchester, Carcanet, 1989.
A Very Quiet Street. Edinburgh, Polygon, 1989.
A Concussed History of Scotland. Edinburgh, Polygon, 1990.
Something Very Like Murder. Edinburgh, Polygon, 1994.
Second Best Moments in Chinese History. Manchester, Carcanet, 1997.

*

Critical Study: By Robert Crawford, in *London Review of Books,* 17(4), 23 Feburary 1995.

*   *   *

Frank Kuppner, a native Glaswegian writer of German and Polish ancestry, came quite suddenly to notice during the 1980s as part of the upsurge in Scottish poetry, an upsurge that opposed the Scottish renaissance movement of the 1920s through the 1970s. Kuppner's first book, *A Bad Day for the Sung Dynasty,* consists of five hundred unrhymed quatrain stanzas presenting a succession of Chinese-like cameos. Some of them are very funny, for example, number 354:

> There are forty-three poets here travelling in a ferry
> Designed to carry six passengers safely across the river;
> One cannot help wondering whether this administration
> Is as sympathetic to literature as it claims to be.

Kuppner's refusal to settle for certainties was elaborated upon in a revealing interview (with an anonymous interviewer) in the magazine *Verse*. When Kuppner was asked, "How would you describe your politics, by the way?" he replied, "I wouldn't. How would *you* describe my politics?" "What?" asked the interviewer. "Well, that's accurate enough, I suppose," Kuppner responded.

A further exploration of this deliberate ambivalence is provided by Kuppner's poem in the same magazine, "Eclipsing Binaries," in which he provides what might be alternatives from the poet's worksheet. Consider, for example, a stanza from section 1, "The Net":

Who lives, for instance, through *that wall there*?
                              this
wall here?
Is it not interesting that you *do not know*?
                    can answer this?
Who is it who is in the room with *me*?
                    you?
Surely that ought to be at least a simple question?
Who is that raving lunatic on the television?

Kuppner's second collection, *The Intelligent Observation of Naked Women,* again written in unrhymed quatrains, consists of a short introductory poem and four long poems. "An Old Guide Book to Prague" achieves its remarkable effect partly by the many detailed images accurately observed with almost photographic detachment and partly by the fact that so many of his lines mark off their own word picture. The effect becomes curiously compelling, as the poem's concluding lines show:

Every twilight, the city has departed;
It has crept away into the tourists' memories,
And its quieter sister has slipped into its place;
The next day it returns, with a slight hangover.

Lights are on the statues, lights are on the porticoes,
Lights are on the monuments, lights are in the towers;
Lights show at most of the windows in the street;
But it is the lights in the street that go out first.

In the "Five Quartet" sequence, the chronicle of casual moments in a day in the life of a relationship, there are no doubt deliberate echoes of Eliot, as in the following-

Those unconvincing people, who confused
A time for arriving with a time for leaving

or:

It appears that we are neither working nor sleeping;
We are caught somewhere between the two; we are caught
At a friendly, unscheduled stop; the normal behaviour
Of our compatriots has been left behind.

If here the sequence of unrhymed quatrains begins to become a little monotonous, the imagery is always sharp and brisk, as when the poet remembers how he

. . . had removed from the top of the cooker
Yet another mountainous heap of spent matches,

And was amazed again, as every few months,
At so many lost arm-movements collected there.

Kuppner's 1989 book, *Ridiculous! Absurd! Disgusting!,* a mixture of prose and poetry, produces another set of intimately subjective variations on contemporary concerns, confirming chaos rather than making sense of it, as one critic put it, and concentrating on content rather than on style. But the chaos has its decidedly funny moments.

—Maurice Lindsay

KYGER, Joanne (Elizabeth)

Nationality: American. **Born:** Vallejo, California, 19 November 1934. **Education:** Santa Barbara College (now University of California, Santa Barbara), 1952–56. **Family:** Married 1) Gary Snyder, *q.v.,* in 1960 (divorced 1965); 2) John Boyce in 1966 (died 1972). **Career:** Lived in Japan, 1960–64; performer and poet in experimental television project, 1967–68. **Awards:** National Endowment for the Arts grant, 1968. **Address:** P.O. Box 688, Bolinas, California 94924, U.S.A.

PUBLICATIONS

Poetry

The Tapestry and the Web. San Francisco, Four Seasons, 1965.
The Fool in April. San Francisco, Coyote, 1966.
Places to Go. Los Angeles, Black Sparrow Press, 1970.
Joanne. New York, Angel Hair, 1970.
Desecheo Notebook. Berkeley, California, Arif Press, 1971.
Trip Out and Fall Back. Berkeley, California, Arif Press, 1974.
All This Every Day. Bolinas, California, Big Sky, 1975.
Up My Coast/Sulla mia costa. Melano, Switzerland, Caos Press, 1978; Point Reyes, California, Floating Island, 1981.
The Wonderful Focus of You. Calais, Vermont, Z Press, 1980.
Mexico Blondé. Bolinas, California, Evergreen Press, 1981.
Going On: Selected Poems 1958–1980, edited by Robert Creeley. New York, Dutton, 1983.
Man: Two Poems (broadside). Pacifica, California, Big Bridge Press, 1988.
The Phone Is Constantly Busy to You (broadside). Lawrence, Kansas, Tansy Press, 1989.
Just Space: Poems 1979–1989. Santa Rosa, Black Sparrow Press, 1991.
Some Sketches from the Life of Helena Petrovna Blavatsky. Boulder, Colorado, Rodent Press, 1996.

Other

The Japan and India Journals 1960–1964. Bolinas, California, Tombouctou, 1981; as *Strange Big Moon: The Japan and India Journals, 1960–1964,* Berkeley, California, North Atlantic Books, 2000.
Phenomonological. Canton, New York, Glover Publishing, 1989.

*

Manuscript Collection: University of California, San Diego.

Joanne Kyger comments:

I myself am a West Coast poet, but I also feel an affinity for much of the work of the younger New York poets.

My vision of the poet changes so I can stay alive and the muse can stay alive. I report on my states of consciousness and the story I am telling.

*　　*　　*

Joanne Kyger is not the enchantress Circe, but she has admired her. Kyger's first book, *The Tapestry and the Web,* exhibits great mythic propensities. In it she reactivates the Odysseus myth, but unlike Pound and Joyce and Olson she enlarges the feminine aspect of the *Odyssey.* She is not Penelope, however, waiting on a man (or anyone else) for her fate. Her Penelope is not domesticated patience; rather, she is the mother of Pan. Kyger's destiny as poet is her own responsibility, and she has borne it as Pan, free spirited and ranging. Her web is metaphoric of the poem itself—patterned freely and self-supporting—the isolated narrative strands that, when bound together, capture the reader and bring meaning.

Kyger's gifts as a narrator are extraordinary. In fact, it is this technique that characterizes almost all of her poems, a pattern marked by sudden cuts of consciousness, the narrative abruptly shifting in flight, not relying on startling imagery to signal changes of direction. A significant early poem is "The Maze," in which there are several entrances but only a single exit from bewilderment.

Overall, Kyger's early poems deliberately hold back personality. They are populated by disembodied presences, an unmoored "he" or "she," various "figures" engaged in vague but effective drama. Her "I" is a nonconfessional, impersonal, automatic speaker, perhaps showing the influence of Jack Spicer. In the late 1960s and in the 1970s she keeps a greater account of herself, reporting directly in such books as *Joanne* and *All This Every Day* that it is "Joanne" who is interesting, wonderful to behold, making her sense out of the world. She has kept close to what she knows, absorbed by the day's contents and contentments while rejecting paper plate, disposable America, as in "Don't Hope to Gain by What Has Preceded."

The turning point comes with "August 18" in *Places to Go,* where a new personality arises in phases like a moon over the mesa. By the time of *All This Every Day* the "I" becomes more obviously the poet's own personality and steps out into quotidian daylight, where there are sharper outlines. Dates become titles—"October 29, Wednesday," "October 31"—and poems are entries in imagination's almanac, records of the day as lived a little closer to understanding, a catalogue of motives, concordances, and accords. The daily brings with it a new ambition for *samadhi,* total consciousness, like what Little Neural Annie attains in "Soon," with what has become characteristic humor for the poet:

Little Neural Annie was fined $65 in the Oakland
Traffic Court this season for "driving while in

a state of samadhi." California secular law requires
that all drivers of motor vehicles remain firmly seated
within their bodies while the vehicle is in motion.
This applies to both greater vehicles and lesser
vehicles.

Kyger puts the comic back in the cosmic. Relationships, too, yield attainment, as in these lovely lines: "She makes / herself, decorative, agreeable, for him. They nod / inside a flower, a wonderful room." It is a leisurely, drifting poetry, stirring in the breeze, absorbing the occasional muffled chaos, a day's small panics. Only in such a relaxed state, without the uneconomical expense of willful pressure, do the lines work so effectively.

Kyger's work is generally characterized by eagerness, even in the face of a disaster such as the plundering of a camp cabin by a bear. "Destruction" may well become her best-known poem. It is a great chuckle of a poem, although a more formal analysis might speak of its excellent dramatic device. The speaker follows the bear's path of destruction, pad and pencil in hand, as if for a police report or insurance claim:

He eats all the apples, limes, dates, bottled decaffeinated
coffee, and 35 pounds of granola. The asparagus soup cans
fall to the floor. Yum! . . . Rips open the water bed, eats
　　the incense
　　and
drinks the perfume . . . Knocks *Shelter, Whole Earth
　　Catalogue,
Planet, Drum, Northern Mists, Truck Tracks, and
Women's Sports* into the oozing water bed mess.
　　　　　　　　He goes
　　down stairs and out the back wall. He keeps on going
for a long way and finds a good cave to sleep it all off.
Luckily he ate the whole medicine cabinet, including stash
of LSD, Peyote, Psilocybin, Amanita, Benzedrine,
　　Valium and
　aspirin.

Kyger's images are few; puns not essential; devices, tricks, and syncopations unintended; diction comfortable. Her lines are biomorphic, ever adjusting to what they seek to accomplish, not to hold the world at bay or shore up ruined traditions but extending out to join the oncoming freshened world. The value of her work lies in its openness, its whimsy, the acceptance of daily change. Her poems are attentive to a spirit's needs, a deeply drawn aim within aimlessness. She has never been less than autonomous and thus is beyond the futile eddies of taste. Always a free spirit, she has rarely spoken for any group larger than her thoughts. It amounts to a style to which she has faithfully adhered.

—George F. Butterick

L

LAING, Kojo

Also wrote as Bernard Kojo Laing. **Nationality:** Ghanaian. **Born:** Bernard Ebenezer Laing, Kumasi, 7 January 1946. **Education:** Glasgow University, Scotland, 1964–68, M.A. 1968; College of Management, Ghana, 1969–70, diploma in management 1970; Birmingham University, England, 1975, certificate in rural management 1975. **Family:** Married 1) Josephine Laing in 1965 (separated), five sons and three daughters; 2) Naana Anaman, one son and two daughters. **Career:** Headmaster, Cluster of Schools, Accra, 1969; district administration officer, 1969–72, district chief executive, 1972–78, Ashanti; deputy secretary, government "think tank," Accra, 1978–79; secretary, Institute of African Studies, University of Ghana, 1980–84. Since 1984 chief executive, Family Schools, Accra. **Awards:** National Poetry prize, Valco award, 1976; National Novel prize, Ghana Association of Writers, 1985. **Member:** Ghana Association of Writers, 1984. **Address:** Box 2642, Accra, Ghana.

PUBLICATIONS

Poetry

Woman of the Aeroplanes. Oxford, Heinemann, 1987; New York, Morrow, 1989.
Godhorse. Oxford, Heinemann, 1989.

Novels

Search Sweet Country. London, Heinemann, and Boston, Faber, 1986.
Major Gentl and the Achimota Wars. Oxford, Heinemann, 1992.

*

Critical Studies: "Search Sweet Country and the Language of Authentic Being" by M.E. Kropp Dakubu, in *Research in African Literatures* (Bloomington, Indiana), 24(1), spring 1993; "Culture Wars in Cyberspace: A Note on Kojo Laing's 'Major Gentl and the Achimota Wars'" by Derek Wright, in *International Fiction Review* (Canada), 23(1–2), 1996; "Science and the Re-Presentation of African Identity in 'Major Gentl and the Achimota Wars'" by Francis Ngaboh-Smart, in *Connotations* (Munster, Germany), 7(1), 1997–98; "'History Never Walks Here, It Runs in Any Direction': Carnival and Magic in the Fiction of Kojo Laing and Mia Couto" by Pietro Deandrea, in *Coterminous Worlds: Magical Realism and Contemporary Post-Colonial Literature in English,* edited by Elsa Linguanti, Francesco Casotti, and Carmen Concilio, Amsterdam, Netherlands, Rodopi, 1999.

Kojo Laing comments:

Whether poetry or prose, seeks the whole, either philosophically or psychologically, in ironic combinations of both the spiritual and the physical, the body being the base, in tragic mortality, of the spirit. Authentic living, which both mixes and transcends cultures, is linked with a modernity that—provided it is universalistic rather than purely Western—will move Africa forward without breaking the consciousness, without Western fragmentation of the mind. The theological ironies of seeking the ultimate spiritual/physical experiences while condemning institutions of worship and culture. Interested in how the African fits into space with an inclusive rather than an exclusive perspective, with informed magic. Set out first to destroy then transcend the pastoral African motif, making use of my schooling both in Ghana and in Scotland. The writing enjoys the concept of the rebel as well as the synthesizer of cultures, even though these may seem to be mutually exclusive.

*   *   *

Kojo Laing may be as prolific in fiction as in poetry, but his style is unique in both genres. Born in Ghana, he was educated in Scotland, where he received an M.A. degree, and in Ghana. He served as secretary of the Institute of African Studies at the University of Ghana and has headed private schools in his native country. He has published two volumes of poetry, and his work appears in anthologies such as *The Heinemann Book of African Poetry in English* (1990) and *The New African Poetry: An Anthology* (1999).

Laing's poetry carries a unique voice and is praised for its poetic evocation and linguistic inventiveness. On the other hand, his poetry is often riddling and playful, sometimes to the extent of detracting from its meaning. While it seemingly follows the verbal fireworks of fellow poet Atukwei Okai, Laing's poetry goes against the grain of modern Ghanaian poetry as seen in Kofi Anyidoho and Kobena Eyi-Acquah, whose simple works are generally indebted to the African oral tradition. While Akan words are interspersed among the lines, which bristle with a quaint musicality and other sound effects, Laing's poetic style is difficult to relate to the African oral tradition. Rather, it is an individualized modernist voice that cynically reflects on subjects ranging from portraits of daily life like a woman selling garden eggs in the rain to love, religion, and death.

Thus, Laing's poetic voice carries dry humor, irony, and sarcasm. In "Steps," for example, he attacks a so-called big man for his vanity. The poet often wears a strange mask. In "I am the freshly dead husband," the speaker, who has been killed in an accident, watches his fashionable wife pretending grief while "hurrying to bury" him; she bursts out laughing within as the dust covers him. In "Godsdoor" the poet addresses complaints about Christianity.

It appears, however, that for Laing, as with the Nigerian Christopher Okigbo, meaning is not a priority. Laing's poetry seems to be more concerned with communicating feeling and energy. His poems are thus of great formal and technical interest. The pictorial form of poems like "Festival" and "Wall" is eye-catching. He uses highly figurative language, especially metaphors, similes, and personification. His metaphors can be striking, for example, "The kente is the orchestra of colours" or "The Tamale man is an Accra cat." Similarly, he uses pointed similes, as in "The rain slants like the thighs / of a tall woman dancing." Personification is common in his poetry. He writes, for example, of the "huge car with a sad voice." One also reads of the "sun's tongue" and of a church door wanting to grow a mustache. Often the figures are mixed, as when he describes doors as "Muslims in Anglican churches." His poetry is filled with wit, for example, "Door sees woman whose sorrow / is larger than her breasts." There is also copious use of repetition, which may be varied, as in "Festival," "The rain slants," "Senior lady sells garden eggs," "Black girl, white girl," and "The bush."

Laing exploits the sound potential of words, hence the many instances of alliteration and assonance, as in "Omen after the last Amen," "saint selling sin at street corner," and "the bad and bitter biter." There is frequent playfulness, even when he is reflecting on serious issues. There is also a certain secular, if not sacrilegious or profane, angle to Laing's poetic voice, as in "Godsdoor." In this poem the poet speaks of the male organ, long sermons that kill birds, saints who sell sin, and priests who dance with "ecumenical lovers." There is so much about death that one gets an inkling of morbidity in a poet "lost between bitter and sweet" and who feels that "the living will use death for joy."

Laing is a unique poet whose poetic subjects, form, and techniques are inimitable. His linguistic dexterity and unusual images are bound to charm the reader.

—Tanure Ojaide

LANE, Patrick

Nationality: Canadian. **Born:** Nelson, British Columbia, 26 March 1939. **Education:** Attended Vernon High School, British Columbia. **Family:** Married 1) Mary Hayden in 1958 (divorced 1967), two sons and one daughter; 2) Carol Beale in 1973 (divorced 1978), two sons; lives with the poet Lorna Crozier, *q.v.* **Career:** Worked in sawmills and logging camps, as a house builder and field worker. Since 1966 editor, Very Stone House, later Very Stone House in Transit, Vancouver. Writer-in-residence, University of Manitoba, Winnipeg, 1978–79, University of Ottawa, 1980, University of Alberta, Edmonton, 1981–82, Saskatoon Public Library, 1982–83, and Globe Theatre Company, Regina, Saskatchewan, 1984–85. Special lecturer, University of Saskatchewan, Saskatoon, 1988–89. Also an artist and illustrator. **Awards:** Canada Council grant, 1973–74, 1976–78, 1983–84; Ontario Arts Council grant, 1975, 1978; Governor-General's award, 1978; Manitoba Arts Council grant, 1979; Saskatchewan Arts Council grant, 1983; National Magazine award, 1985; CAA award for poetry, 1988; Dorothy Livesay poetry prize, 1996. **Address:** c/o Oxford University Press, 70 Wynford Drive, Don Mills, Ontario, Canada.

PUBLICATIONS

Poetry

Letters from the Savage Mind. Vancouver, Very Stone House, 1966.
For Rita—In Asylum. Vancouver, Very Stone House, 1969.
Calgary City Jail. Vancouver, Very Stone House, 1969.
Separations. Trumansburg, New York, Crossing Press, 1969.
Sunflower Seeds. Vancouver, Western Press, 1969.
On the Street. Vancouver, Very Stone House, 1970.
Mountain Oysters. Vancouver, Very Stone House, 1971.
Hiway 401 Rhapsody. Vancouver, Very Stone House, 1972.

The Sun Has Begun to Eat the Mountain. Montreal, Ingluvin, 1972.
Passing into Storm. Vernon, British Columbia, Traumerei, 1973.
Beware the Months of Fire. Toronto, Anansi, 1974.
Certs. Prince George, British Columbia, College of New Caledonia, 1974.
Unborn Things: South American Poems. Madeira Park, British Columbia, Harbour, 1975.
For Riel in That Gawdam Prison. White Rock, British Columbia, Blackfish Press, 1975.
Albino Pheasants. Madeira Park, British Columbia, Harbour, 1977.
If. Toronto, Dreadnaught Press, 1977.
Poems, New and Selected. Toronto, Oxford University Press, 1978; London, Oxford University Press, 1979; New York, Oxford University Press, 1980.
No Longer Two People, with Lorna Uher. Winnipeg, Turnstone Press, 1979.
There Are Still the Mountains. Vancouver, Very Stone House, 1979.
The Measure. Windsor, Ontario, Black Moss Press, 1980.
The Garden. Toronto, League of Canadian Poets, 1980.
Old Mother. Toronto, Oxford University Press, 1982.
Woman in the Dust. Oakville, Ontario, Mosaic Press, 1983.
A Linen Crow, A Caftan Magpie. Saskatoon, Saskatchewan, Thistledown Press, 1984.
Selected Poems. Toronto, Oxford University Press, 1987; Oxford, Oxford University Press, 1988.
Winter. Regina, Saskatchewan, Coteau Books, 1990.
Mortal Remains. Toronto, Exile Editions, 1992.
Too Spare, Too Fierce. Madeira Park, British Columbia, Harbour, 1995.
Selected Poems, 1977–1997. Madeira Park, British Columbia, Harbour, 1997.
Conception: 17 Poems. Victoria, British Columbia, Outlaw Editions, 1997.

Short Stories

How Do You Spell Beautiful. Saskatoon, Saskatchewan, Fifth House, 1993.

Other

(Drawings). Whitehorse, Yukon, Tundra Graphics, 1981.
The Liberal Vision and the Death of Culture (lecture). Regina, Saskatchewan, Library Association, 1983.
Milford and Me (for children). Regina, Saskatchewan, Coteau, 1989.

Editor, *Blue Windows,* by Catherine M. Buckaway. Regina, Saskatchewan, Coteau, 1988.
Editor, with Lorna Crozier, *Breathing Fire: Canada's New Poets.* Madeira Park, British Columbia, Harbour, 1995.
Editor, with Lorna Crozier, *Selected Poems,* by Alden Nowlan, Concord, Ontario, Anansi, 1996.
Editor, *A Community of Monsters.* Victoria, British Columbia, Outlaw Editions, 1998.
Editor, *Blindfolds.* Victoria, British Columbia, Outlaw Editions, 1999.

*

Manuscript Collections: McMaster University, Hamilton, Ontario; University of British Columbia, Vancouver.

Critical Studies: ''Pine Boughs and Apple Trees'' by Marilyn Bowering, in *Malahat Review* (Victoria, British Columbia), January 1978; *Patrick Lane and His Works,* Toronto, ECW Press, 1984, and in *ECW's Biographical Guide to Canadian Poets,* edited by Robert Lecker and others, Toronto, ECW, 1993, both by George Woodcock; ''The Poetry of Patrick Lane'' by Dermot McCarthy, in *Essays on Canadian Writing* (Toronto), 39, fall 1989; ''How Do You Read a Riddle? Patrick Lane's 'Winter''' by Nathalie Cooke, in *Inside the Poem: Essays and Poems in Honour of Donald Stephens,* edited by W.H. New, Toronto, Oxford University Press, 1992.

*   *   *

Patrick Lane was born in the interior of British Columbia. The essential center of his poetry is its consciousness of this landscape and mythology: ''Because I never learned how / to be gentle and the country / I lived in was hard with dead / animals and men, I didn't question . . .'' If, as Lawrence Durrell says, landscape is character, Lane is a kind of Proteus taking on the shapes of his place, at once fierce and uncompromising in response to its violence and terrible beauty. He writes of logging camps and forests, of bush farming, hunting, and herding cattle, all of which he knows firsthand. Whatever the private complex out of which he writes, he understands violence. He writes of people who survive by manipulating violence—the hustlers, religious bigots, even his father—and of those who have been smashed by it—the derelicts, prostitutes, the murdered child. He speaks without judgment, knowing the cannibal impulse in himself, ''that brutal anger that cannot be relieved except on things.'' Perhaps the most exciting aspect of his work is his ability to write without sentimentality about ordinary cruelty. He also understands the traps of victimization. His poem ''What Does Not Change,'' a long piece about a prostitute, is the frankest and yet most compassionate poem I know about that world. Its language is tough and colloquial, and yet the literary allusions the poet has managed to weave into the anecdotes give the whole a larger reference that makes it a remarkable creation.

Lane has a fine gift for image and writes of the tragic not histrionically but in understatement, deflecting attention to some small detail that is made to carry the full horror of a situation. He has an empathy for all of life that is pained and vulnerable—for the young woman dead from an abortion in a dingy hotel room, for the boy who blows his mother's arm off with a bomb, for the old man who shoves pins into his dead arm trying to cadge drinks.

Lane's talent is multifaceted. He has often illustrated his poetry with his own drawings—stark, haunting images that seem to proceed from a nightmare vision. He has also published a collection of stories, *How Do You Spell Beautiful?,* most of which are located in the working-class communities of small company towns. He captures the dying towns and their impoverished inhabitants with a precise realism, but it is his lyric images that stay in the mind, as with the young woman wringing diapers at the sink, the ''seven-month foetus high up against her heart,'' who could be the presiding muse of the stories.

In 1990 Lane published perhaps his most powerful sequence, forty-five poems on the theme of winter. It begins, ''The generosity of snow, the way it forgives / transgression, filling in the many betrayals.'' The poems show the mature Lane, still haunted by loss and violence, but with a uncanny gentleness and grace located in the desolate landscapes. Ready to exorcise some of his ghosts, in 1992 he wrote *Mortal Remains,* poems about the death of his brother and about his father's murder, twenty-five years after the fact. ''Poetry cannot save us,'' he explains, ''but it can provide us with some small redemption:'' ''The wind blows, the branches move / inconsequential, fragile and forgiven.''

In his thirty-odd years of writing, Lane's work has made him central to the Canadian writing community. His talent for the memorable encounter led the poet Susan Musgrave, on the occasion of his fifty-fifth birthday, to collect the poems dedicated to him over the years. An extensive collection, it is an extraordinarily moving tribute to one of Canada's most gifted poets.

—Rosemary Sullivan

LAWRENCE, Anthony

Nationality: Australian. **Born:** Tamworth, New South Wales, 1957. **Career:** Has worked as a jackeroo. Taught and wrote in Wagga Wagga before moving to Western Australia. **Awards:** Harri Jones prize, for *Dreaming in Stone;* Gwen Harwood memorial prize, 1996; Newcastle Poetry prize, 1997; Kenneth Slessor prize, 1997, for *The Viewfinder.* **Address:** P.O. Box 75, Sandy Bay, Tasmania 7006, Australia.

PUBLICATIONS

Poetry

Dreaming in Stone. North Ryde, New South Wales, Angus and Robertson, 1989.
Three Days out of Tidal Town. Sydney, Hale and Iremonger, 1992.
The Darkwood Aquarium. London, Penguin, 1993.
Cold Wires of Rain. Ringwood, Victoria and New York, Penguin, 1995.
The Viewfinder. St. Lucia, University of Queensland Press, 1996.
New and Selected Poems. St. Lucia, University of Queensland Press, 1998.

*

Critical Studies: In *Overland,* 117, February 1990; ''Singing in Their Chairs: A Conversation between Anthony Lawrence & Brian Henry,'' in *Island Magazine,* 75, winter 1998.

*   *   *

There is a robust sensitivity in Anthony Lawrence's poetry that is imprinted on his graphic depictions of place and atmosphere. His world is filled with birds and creatures as well as with the experiences of a free-ranging lifestyle that has taken him to the outreaches of his country, from the seascapes of Western Australia to the wildernesses of Tasmania. Lawrence is also a well-traveled writer internationally, and he has the capacity to inform his poems with personal and observational detail. Technically, he has not hesitated to use various verse forms as well as the distinctively rich blank verse that is his usual means of expression.

Lawrence published his first book, *Dreaming in Stone,* which won the Harri Jones prize, in 1989. Since then he has published further collections, of which *The Viewfinder* won the 1997 Kenneth Slessor prize for poetry in the New South Wales Premier's awards. *New and Selected Poems,* which came out in 1998, is a substantial book and confirms that Lawrence is both a prolific and striking writer who has made rich use of his reading in contemporary Australian poetry as well as his personal experiences.

Perhaps the writer who has had the most enduring influence on Lawrence's work and his direction has been Robert Adamson, who has honed the metaphor of landscape into a personal statement. Lawrence has a greater flexibility and natural exuberance than his mentor, and there is in his writing a narrative quality as well as a pervading lyrical cadence. The result can be refreshing and idiosyncratic. If the range of references in Lawrence's poetry is often wide and reflects the catholicity of his reading, in a sense it always comes back to the precision of observation and experience, as in his poem ''The Sapphic Stanza'':

> You can sit through all night music television
> waiting for one song that contains a Sapphic stanza,
> but you'll go to bed or out for the morning
> papers disappointed. Though perhaps, in some
> independent label's low-budget video showing
> four women parting a wave of chest-high fennel
> by a thin industrial river, you could hear
> the natural world's equivalent of that poetic form:
> a woman unslings a semi-acoustic guitar
> as a large waterbird labours over, its wings going
> trochee trochee dactyl trochee trochee . . .
> But by then you'll be so numb from hours
> of streetwise chic and barren warehouse theatrics,
> you'll most likely fail to recognise the connection,
> and so be driven to play a Randy Newman record,
> or lie down in silence, with just enough hall light
> to keep you safe and awake until the cars start up
> and go.

—Thomas W. Shapcott

LAYTON, Irving

Nationality: Canadian. **Born:** Israel Lazarovitch in Neamtz, Romania, 12 March 1912; immigrated to Canada in 1913. **Education:** Baron Byng High School, Montreal, 1925–30; MacDonald College, Sainte Anne de Bellevue, Quebec, B.S. in agriculture 1939; McGill University, Montreal, M.A. 1946. **Military Service:** Canadian Army, 1942–43: artillery officer. **Family:** Married 1) Faye Lynch in 1938 (divorced 1946); 2) Betty Francis Sutherland in 1946, one son and one daughter; 3) the writer Aviva Cantor in 1961, one son; 4) Harriet Bernstein in 1978 (divorced 1984); one daughter; 5) Anna Pottier in 1984. **Career:** Lecturer, Jewish Public Library, Montreal, 1943–59;

high school teacher, Montreal, 1954–60; part-time lecturer, 1949–65, and poet-in-residence, 1965–66, Sir George Williams University, Montreal; writer-in-residence, University of Guelph, Ontario, 1968–69; professor of English Literature, York University, Toronto, 1970–78; poet-in-residence, University of Ottawa, 1978, Concordia University, Montreal, 1978–81, and University of Toronto, 1981; adjunct professor, Concordia University, 1988; adjunct professor and writer-in-residence, Concordia University, 1989. Co-founding editor, *First Statement,* later *Northern Review,* Montreal, 1941–43; associate editor, *Contact,* Toronto, and *Black Mountain Review,* North Carolina. **Awards:** Canadian Foundation fellowship, 1957; Canada Council award, 1959, 1963, 1967, 1968, 1973, 1979; Governor-General's award, 1959; President's Medal, University of Western Ontario, 1961; Centennial Medal, 1967; The Francesco Petrarca Premio Letterario Nazionale, 1993. D.C.L.: Bishop's University, Lennoxville, Quebec, 1970; D.Litt.: Concordia University, 1976; York University, 1979. Officer, Order of Canada, 1976. **Agent:** Lucinda Vardey Agency, 297 Seaton Street, Toronto, Ontario M5A 2T6. **Address:** 6879 Monkland Avenue, Montreal, Quebec H4B 1J5, Canada.

PUBLICATIONS

Poetry

Here and Now. Montreal, First Statement Press, 1945.
Now Is the Place: Poems and Stories. Montreal, First Statement Press, 1948.
The Black Huntsman. Privately printed, 1951.
Cerberus, with Raymond Souster and Louis Dudek. Toronto, Contact Press, 1952.
Love the Conqueror Worm. Toronto, Contact Press, 1953.
The Long Pea-Shooter. Montreal, Laocöon Press, 1954.
In the Midst of My Fever. Palma, Mallorca, Divers Press, 1954.
The Cold Green Element. Toronto, Contact Press, 1955.
The Blue Propeller. Toronto, Contact Press, 1955.
The Bull Calf and Other Poems. Toronto, Contact Press, 1956.
Music on a Kazoo. Toronto, Contact Press, 1956.
The Improved Binoculars: Selected Poems. Highlands, North Carolina, Jargon, 1956; augmented edition, 1956.
A Laughter in the Mind. Highlands, North Carolina, Jargon, 1958; augmented edition, Montreal, Editions d'Orphée, 1959.
A Red Carpet for the Sun: Collected Poems. Toronto, McClelland and Stewart, and Highlands, North Carolina, Jargon, 1959.
The Swinging Flesh (poems and stories). Toronto, McClelland and Stewart, 1961.
Balls for a One-Armed Juggler. Toronto, McClelland and Stewart, 1963.
The Laughing Rooster. Toronto, McClelland and Stewart, 1964.
Collected Poems. Toronto, McClelland and Stewart, 1965.
Periods of the Moon. Toronto, McClelland and Stewart, 1967.
The Shattered Plinths. Toronto, McClelland and Stewart, 1968.
The Whole Bloody Bird (obs, aphs, and pomes). Toronto, McClelland and Stewart, 1969.
Selected Poems, edited by Wynne Francis. Toronto, McClelland and Stewart, 1969.
Five Modern Canadian Poets, with others, edited by Eli Mandel. Toronto, Holt Rinehart, 1970.
Collected Poems. Toronto, McClelland and Stewart, 1971.

Nail Polish. Toronto, McClelland and Stewart, 1971.

Lovers and Lesser Men. Toronto, McClelland and Stewart, 1973.

The Pole-Vaulter. Toronto, McClelland and Stewart, 1974.

Seventy-Five Greek Poems 1951–1974. Athens, Hermias, 1974.

Selected Poems: The Darkening Fire 1945–1968, The Unwavering Eye 1969–1975. Toronto, McClelland and Stewart, 2 vols., 1975.

For My Brother Jesus. Toronto, McClelland and Stewart, 1976.

The Uncollected Poems 1936–1959. Oakville, Ontario, Mosaic Press, 1976.

The Poems of Irving Layton, edited by Eli Mandel. Toronto, McClelland and Stewart, 1977.

Selected Poems. New York, New Directions, 1977.

The Covenant. Toronto, McClelland and Stewart, 1977.

Selected Poems, edited by Wynne Francis. London, Charisma, 1977.

The Tightrope Dancer. Toronto, McClelland and Stewart, 1978.

The Love Poems. Toronto, Canadian Fine Editions, 1978.

Il Puma Ammansito [The Tamed Puma], illustrated by Carlo Mattioli. Milan, Trentadue, 1978; Toronto, Virgo Press, 1979.

Droppings from Heaven. Toronto, McClelland and Stewart, 1979.

There Were No Signs, illustrated by Sassu. Toronto, Madison Art Gallery, 1979.

The Love Poems of Irving Layton. Toronto, McClelland and Stewart, 1980; as *With Reverence and Delight: The Love Poems of Irving Layton,* Oakville, Ontario, Mosaic Press, 1984.

For My Neighbours in Hell. Oakville, Ontario, Mosaic Press, 1980.

Europe and Other Bad News. Toronto, McClelland and Stewart, 1981.

A Wild Peculiar Joy: Selected Poems 1945–1982. Toronto, McClelland and Stewart, 1982; revised edition, *1945–1989,* 1989.

Shadows on the Ground. Oakville. Ontario. Mosaic Press. 1982.

The Gucci Bag. Oakville, Ontario, Mosaic Press, 1983.

A Spider Danced a Cozy Jig, edited by Elspeth Cameron. Toronto, Stoddart, 1984.

Where Burning Sappho Loved. Athens, Greece, Libro, 1985.

Love Poems (portfolio), illustrated by Salvatore Fiume. Milan, Teodorani, 1985.

Dance with Desire: Love Poems. Toronto, McClelland and Stewart, 1986.

Final Reckoning: Poems 1982–1986. Oakville, Ontario, Mosaic Press, 1987.

Fortunate Exile. Toronto, McClelland and Stewart, 1987.

Fornalutx: Selected Poems, 1928–1990. Montreal, McGill-Queen's University Press, 1992.

Il Cacciatore Sconcertato [The Baffled Hunter], translated by Francesca Valente. Ravenna, Italy, Longo Editore, 1993.

Play

A Man Was Killed, with Leonard Cohen, in *Canadian Theatre Review 14* (Downsview, Ontario), Spring 1977.

Other

Engagements: The Prose of Irving Layton, edited by Seymour Mayne. Toronto, McClelland and Stewart, 1972.

Taking Sides: The Collected Social and Political Writings, edited by Howard Aster. Oakville, Ontario, Mosaic Press, 1977.

An Unlikely Affair: The Irving Layton-Dorothy Rath Correspondence. Oakville, Ontario, Mosaic Press, 1980.

Waiting for the Messiah (autobiography). Toronto, McClelland and Stewart, 1985.

Wild Gooseberries: The Selected Letters of Irving Layton. Toronto, Macmillan, 1989.

Irving Layton/Robert Creeley: The Complete Correspondence. Kingston, Ontario, McGill-Queen's University Press, 1990.

Editor, with Louis Dudek, *Canadian Poems 1850–1952.* Toronto, Contact Press, 1952; revised edition, 1953.

Editor, *Pan-ic: A Selection of Contemporary Canadian Poems.* New York, Alan Brilliant, 1958.

Editor, *Poems for 27 Cents.* Privately printed, 1961.

Editor, *Love Where the Nights Are Long: Canadian Love Poems.* Toronto, McClelland and Stewart, 1962.

Editor, *Anvil: A Selection of Workshop Poems.* Privately printed, 1966.

Editor, *Poems to Colour: A Selection of Workshop Poems.* Privately printed, 1970.

Editor, *I Side Up.* Toronto, York University Poetry Workshop, 1971.

Editor, *Anvil Blood: A Selection of Workshop Poems.* Privately printed, 1973.

Editor, *New Holes in the Wall.* Toronto, York University Poetry Workshop, 1975.

Editor, *Shark Tank.* Toronto, York University Poetry Workshop, 1977.

Editor, *Handouts from the Mountain.* Toronto, York University Poetry Workshop, 1978.

Editor, *Rawprint: Concordia Poetry Workshop Collection, 1989.* Montreal, Concordia Poetry Workshop, 1989.

Translator, with Greg Gatenby and Francesca Valente, *Selected Poems,* by Giorgio Bassani. Toronto, Aya Press, 1980.

*

Bibliography: *Irving Layton: A Bibliography 1935–1977* by Joy Bennett and James Polson, Montreal, Concordia University Libraries, 1979; by Francis Mansbridge, Toronto, ECW Press, 1994.

Manuscript Collections: University of Saskatchewan, Saskatoon; University of Toronto; Concordia University, Montreal; Brown University, Providence, Rhode Island; University of Texas, Austin; McGill University, Montreal.

Critical Studies: "Layton on the Carpet" by Louis Dudek, in *Delta 9* (Montreal), October/December 1959; "The Man Who Copyrighted Passion" by A. Ross, in *Macleans* (Toronto), 15 November 1965; "Personal Heresy" by Robin Skelton, in *Canadian Literature* (Vancouver), Winter 1965; "A Grab at Proteus: Notes on Irving Layton" by George Woodcock, in *Canadian Literature* (Vancouver), Spring 1966; "That Heaven-Sent Lively Ropewalker, Irving Layton" by Hayden Carruth, in *Tamarack Review* (Toronto), Spring 1966; "Satyric Layton" by K.A. Lund, in *Canadian Author and Bookman* (Toronto), Spring 1967; "The Occasions of Irving Layton" by Mike Doyle, in *Canadian Literature* (Vancouver), Autumn 1972; *Irving Layton: The Poet and His Critics* edited by Seymour Mayne, Toronto, McGraw Hill Ryerson, 1978; *The Poetry of Irving Layton* by Eli Mandel, Toronto, Coles, 1981; *Irving Layton: A Portrait* by Elspeth

Cameron, Toronto, Stoddart, 1985; *Irving Layton and His Works* by Wynne Francis, Toronto, ECW Press, 1985; *Italian Critics on Irving Layton* edited by Alfredo Rizzardi, Padova, Piovan, 1988; *The Place of American Poets in the Development of Irving Layton, Louis Dudek and Raymond Souster* (dissertation) by Sabrina Lee Reed, n.p. 1989; *Irving Layton & Robert Creeley: The Complete Correspondence, 1953–1978* edited by Ekbert Faas and Sabrina Reed, Montreal & Kingston, McGill-Queen's University Press, 1990; "Usurpations: A Poetics of Catastrophe and the Language of Jewish History" by Michael Andre Bernstein, in *TriQuarterly* (Evanston, Illinois), 79, Fall 1990; "'Scanned and Scorned': Freedom and Fame in Layton" by Brian Trehearne, in *Inside the Poem: Essays and Poems in Honour of Donald Stephens,* edited by W.H. New, Toronto, Oxford University Press, 1992; by Wynne Francis, in *ECW's Biographical Guide to Canadian Poets,* edited by Robert Lecker, Jack David, and Ellen Quigley, Toronto, ECW, 1993; *Irving Layton: God's Recording Angel* by Francis Mansbridge, Toronto, ECW, 1995; *An Unexpected Alliance: The Layton-Pacey Correspondence* (dissertation) by John David Michael Pacey, University of British Columbia, 1994; "Neurotic Affiliations: Klein, Layton, Cohen, and the Properties of Influence" by Michael Q. Abraham, in *Canadian Poetry* (London, Ontario), 38, Spring/Summer 1996; "Irving Layton, Leonard Cohen, and Other Recurring Nightmares" by David Layton, in *Saturday Night,* 111(2), March 1996; "Nor Are the Winged Insects Better Off: Nature, Imagery, and Reflection in Archibald Lampman and Irving Layton" by Rowland Smith, in *World Literature Today* (Norman, Oklahoma), 73(2), Spring 1999.

Irving Layton comments:

I believe the poet, at his best, is a prophet and a descendant of prophets. Once he allows himself to forget that, he becomes a mere tinkerer. He ends up making pillows and pillowcases for old fogies to go to sleep on. These love nothing better than ecstatically to snore out their veneration for beauty and order in the old rhythms they have learned so well. The poet's job is to disturb and discomfort. He's an iconoclast, a smasher of cruel idols, even when he accomplishes their destruction with the quietest of lyrics. He speaks to all men, not only to the cultivated and sensitive. Now, more than ever, he must strive to keep alive the spirit of rebellion and dissent. In a world that reveres facts and details, the poet must insist on a complex, imaginative awareness and remain the sworn enemy of all dogmas and dogmatists. Whatever else, poetry is freedom—freedom to experience, to live fully and vitally. For the doctrinaire pedant, as for the doctrinaire politician and ideologist, the poet will always have an abiding contempt. Nothing less than perfect freedom and joy will ever content him. But until that time arrives, he will continue to look into the hearts of all and with the dark ambivalences he finds there move them through terror and beauty. As long as the poet is alive and flourishing, mankind still has a future.

*   *   *

Irving Layton's expanded *Selected Poems 1945–1989* is appropriately entitled *A Wild Peculiar Joy.* The title reflects the passionate nature of Layton's poetry. His work is provocative, prophetic, and extravagant and by turns romantic, cynical, erotic, angry, joyful, and despairing. His poems convey tremendous emotional energy, and their effect can be both inspirational and infuriating.

The emotional power of Layton's poetry resides in the strongly defined persona who speaks through his verse. Layton constructs the poet as visionary, one whose role is to awaken and enlighten. "There are brightest apples on those trees," he proclaims in "The Fertile Muck," "but until I, fabulist, have spoken / they do not know their significance." Later in the same poem he poses and answers what seems to be the central question of his work: "How to dominate reality? Love is one way; / imagination another." In "Whatever Else Poetry Is Freedom" Layton presents the poet as buffoon or clown, as the wise fool who sees what others do not. Elsewhere he defines the poet as a prophet, placing himself in "The Search" in the line of "iconoclasts, dreamers, men who stood alone," with Freud and Marx, Maimonides and Spinoza:

In my veins runs their rebellious blood.
I tread with them the selfsame antique road
and seek everywhere the faintest scent of God.

In several poems he claims kinship as poet with Jesus, whom he describes in "For My Brother Jesus" as a "crucified poet" and addresses in "Xianity" as "brother and fellow poet." "Xianity" goes on to ask,

Is this what you wanted:
the grey suburban church and the greyer people
shambling into it each Sunday
you who openly consorted with whores and drunkards
and so loved laughter and joy
that you were willing to be crucified for them?

Such deliberate insults to bourgeois Christianity are frequent in Layton's work. The son of impoverished Romanian Jewish immigrants, Layton grew up in Montreal an outsider to both French Roman Catholic and English Protestant Canadian life. As a Jew, he defines himself against the blandness of puritanical Canadian society; as a representative of the working class, he defines himself against the materialism of the capitalist middle class; as a poet, he defines himself as a spokesman for a more vital and affirmative approach to life. "A dull people, without charm / or ideas," he says of Canadians in "From Colony to Nation." Such sentiments are designed not merely to offend but also to provoke response. Layton's poetic mission is to awaken Canadian society from its torpor. He presents himself as a messiah figure who seeks to invigorate his countrymen through his passionate, virile, provocative, and sometimes shocking verse.

Virility is a central aspect of Layton's persona. His writing is aggressively male in its vision of life and poetry. In "Ithaca" he compares the moment of the completion of a poem to the moment of orgasm. Metaphors of male sexuality pervade his writing, and Layton's celebration of masculinity carries with it a distinct strain of misogyny that has not endeared him to feminist readers. In "Signs and Portents," for instance, he writes, "not being handicapped in the least by vision or creativity, / women are by far the stronger sex." Layton portrays women almost exclusively as objects of male sexual desire, often praising the female body in extravagant terms, as in "The Day Aviva Came to Paris." The proper role of woman, according to Layton's poetic persona, is to serve as an object of desire and thereby as inspiration for the male poet. In "Out of Pure Lust" he scolds a young woman for her casual attitude toward sex. What, he asks, if Dante's Beatrice or Petrarch's Laura had refused to play the unattainable mistress: "What masterpieces would each have ripped off then?"

Outrageous as he may be in his condemnation of the dullness, conformity, and materialism of Canadian life and in his sexist portrayals of women, Layton reserves his greatest rage for the forces of hatred and racism that have deformed human history. As a Jew he is particularly sensitive to the horrors of the Holocaust, and he has written a number of powerful poems on the Nazi campaign of genocide. In "To the Victims of the Holocaust" he offers himself as spokesman for those whose suffering and death must not be forgotten:

> My murdered kin
> let me be your parched and swollen tongue
> uttering the maledictions
> bullets and gas silenced on your lips.

The depth of Layton's anger at the victimization of Jews comes through starkly in the brief poem "Recipe for a Long and Happy Life":

> Give all your nights
> to the study of Talmud
> By day practise
> shooting from the hip

Although there is a great deal of anger in Layton's work, there is also a great deal of joy. Just as energetically as he condemns all that he perceives as life denying, he celebrates all that is life affirming. There is a strong current of romanticism running through his work, both in his heroic portrayal of the poet as a misunderstood or ignored prophet who seeks to enlighten a misguided world and in his treatment of nature. Layton does not idealize the natural world; he portrays not only its beauty but also its ugliness, often focusing on its least attractive aspects. He writes as often of flies and worms as of butterflies, but even death in nature is a part of life, and nature's disinterested life-and-death cycle stands in opposition to human evil. In "Early Morning Sounds" Layton writes, "The innocence / of nature's cannibalism heals and purifies," whereas in "Nominalist" he writes of "men's despair and malice / covering the earth / like spears of grass."

Despite his contempt for the viciousness he witnesses too frequently in human life, Layton says in "Letter to a Lost Love," "I've Byron's way of seeing things / and think death even more absurd than life." He expresses his view of his poetic role concisely in "The Tightrope Dancer":

> Awareness of death's pull
> into nothingness
> begets tyrant and sadist
> but the prod, the harsh shove of love
> makes the defiant artist
> dance on his tightrope

Defiance is the defining characteristic of Layton's work and the source of its vitality. Although his later work reveals an increasingly acute awareness of mortality, there is no diminution of his lust for life or of his commitment to the role of the poet as prophet and visionary. "All poets are magicians or murderers," he declares in his "Birthday Poem for John Newlove," and "Whom the gods do not intend to destroy / they first make mad with poetry."

—Linda Lamont-Stewart

LEE, Dennis (Beynon)

Nationality: Canadian. **Born:** Toronto, Ontario, 31 August 1939. **Education:** University of Toronto, B.A. 1962, M.A. in English 1964. **Family:** Married 1) Donna Youngblut in 1961 (divorced 1972), two daughters and one son; 2) Susan Ruth Perly in 1985. **Career:** Full-time writer. Taught at Victoria College, University of Toronto, 1964–67, and Rochdale College, Toronto, 1967–69; artist-in-residence, Trent University, Peterborough, Ontario, 1975. Editor, House of Anansi Press, Toronto, 1967–72; consulting editor, Macmillan of Canada publishers, Toronto, 1973–78; poetry consultant, McClelland and Stewart publishers, Toronto, 1981–84. Songwriter, *Fraggle Rock* television program, Canadian Broadcasting Corporation, 1982–86. **Awards:** Governor-General's award, 1973; Canadian Library Association Book of the Year Medal, 1975, 1978; Ruth Schwartz award, 1978; Philips Information Systems prize, 1985; Vicky Metcalf award, 1986; Mr. Christie's Book award, 1991. Officer, Order of Canada, 1994. **Address:** c/o Sterling Lord Associates, 10 St. Mary Street, Toronto, Ontario M4Y 1P9, Canada.

PUBLICATIONS

Poetry

Kingdom of Absence. Toronto, Anansi, 1967.
Civil Elegies. Toronto, Anansi, 1968.
Civil Elegies and Other Poems. Toronto, Anansi, 1972.
Not Abstract Harmonies But. Vancouver and San Francisco, Kanchenjunga, 1974.
The Death of Harold Ladoo. Vancouver and San Francisco, Kanchenjunga, 1976.
Miscellany. Privately printed, 1977.
The Gods. Vancouver and San Francisco, Kanchenjunga, 1978.
The Gods (collection). Toronto, McClelland and Stewart, 1979.
Riffs. London, Ontario, Brick, 1993.
Nightwatch: New & Selected Poems, 1968–1996. Toronto, McClelland and Stewart, 1996.

Poetry (for children)

Wiggle to the Laundromat, illustrated by Charles Pachter. Toronto, New Press, 1970.
Alligator Pie, illustrated by Frank Newfeld. Toronto, Macmillan, 1974; Boston, Houghton Mifflin, 1975.
Nicholas Knock and Other People, illustrated by Frank Newfeld. Toronto, Macmillan, 1974; Boston, Houghton Mifflin, 1977.
Garbage Delight, illustrated by Frank Newfeld. Toronto, Macmillan, 1977; Boston, Houghton Mifflin, 1978.
Jelly Belly, illustrated by Juan Wijngaard. Toronto, Macmillan, and London, Blackie, 1983.
Lizzy's Lion, illustrated by Marie-Louise Gay. Toronto, Stoddart, and London, Hodder and Stoughton, 1984.
The Dennis Lee Big Book, illustrated by Barb Klunder. Toronto, Gage, 1985.
The Difficulty of Living on Other Planets: An Adult Entertainment. Toronto. Macmillan, 1987.
The Ice Cream Store. Toronto, HarperCollins, 1991; New York, Scholastic, 1992.

Ping and Pong. Toronto, HarperCollins, 1993.

Dinosaur Dinner with a Slice of Alligator Pie: Favorite Poems. New York, Knopf, 1997.

Recordings: *Alligator Pie and Other Poems,* music by Don Heckman, Caedmon, 1978; *Fraggle Rock,* music by Philip Balsam, Muppet Music, 1984.

Other

Savage Fields: An Essay in Literature and Cosmology. Toronto, Anansi, 1977.

The Ordinary Bath (for children). Toronto, McClelland and Stewart, 1979.

Body Music. Toronto, Anansi, 1998.

Editor, with R.A. Charlesworth, *An Anthology of Verse.* Toronto, Oxford University Press, 1964.

Editor, with R.A. Charlesworth, *The Second Century Anthologies of Verse 2.* Toronto, Oxford University Press, 1967.

Editor, with Howard Adelman, *The University Game.* Toronto, Anansi, 1968.

Editor, *T.O. Now: The Young Toronto Poets.* Toronto, Anansi, 1968.

Editor, *The New Canadian Poets 1970–85.* Toronto, McClelland and Stewart, 1985.

Editor, with Roberta Charlesworth, *A New Anthology of Verse.* Toronto, Oxford University Press, 1989.

*

Manuscript Collection: Fisher Rare Book Room, University of Toronto.

Critical Studies: *Task of Passion: Dennis Lee at Mid-Career* edited by Donna Bennett, Russell Brown, and Karen Mulhallen, Toronto, Descant, 1982; *Dennis Lee and His Works* by T.G. Middlebro, Toronto, ECW Press, 1985; in *The Annotated Bibliography of Canada's Major Authors, VIII,* edited by Robert Lecker and Jack David, Toronto, ECW, 1994; *Dennis Lee and George Grant: Technology and Reverence* (dissertation) by Margaret Joan Roffey, University of Western Ontario, 1996.

*   *   *

There is considerable commentary on the work of Dennis Lee, who has made notable contributions to children's verse, adult poetry, and literary criticism. Recognition of his importance and his influence on a generation of Canadian writers is found in *Task of Passion: Dennis Lee at Mid-Career,* a special issue of *Descant* magazine issued in book form in 1982 at a public celebration at Toronto's Harbourfront.

The editors of the volume, Karen Mulhallen, Donna Bennett, and Russell Brown, observed how modest was Lee's output. His works at the time included three collections of adult poetry, *Kingdom of Absence, Civil Elegies and Other Poems,* and *The Gods;* a book of literary criticism, *Savage Fields,* as well as influential uncollected essays; and the collections of children's verse *Alligator Pie, Nicholas*

Knock and Other People, Garbage Delight, Jelly Belly, and *The Difficulty of Living on Other Planets.* As the editors pointed out, Lee is concerned with "central traditional themes. Our interest in his work comes from his having found an approach, a diction whereby he can *detrivialize,* to repeat a word used by George Grant . . . and treat adequately the major, the critical ongoing issues of our era."

Lee played a transitional role in the evolution of literary thinking in Canada, linking the humanistic concerns of the 1950s with the nationalistic and cultural aspirations of the 1960s and 1970s. His range of awareness is wide enough to encompass the academy, the marketplace, and the antiestablishment. He has taught at several universities, he was the first editor of the influential House of Anansi Press, and he helped found Rochdale College, the controversial free university that flourished in Toronto in the 1960s.

Whatever Lee writes has a feeling of rightness to it. One senses the person in the voice, "the texture of our being here," "the grunt of prose," the "grainy sense of life." In his poetry and criticism he exposes the vestiges of colonial Canadian assumptions, both Victorian and American, and the commercialism of contemporary Western society, finding characteristics of an armed and wounded culture that has grown to global and epidemic proportions. As he writes in the meditative work *The Gods,* we must "honour the gods in their former selves, / albeit obscurely, at a distance, unable / to speak the older tongue; and to wait / till their fury is spent and they call on us again / for passionate awe in our lives, and a clean high style."

A generation of Canadians, exposed to Lee's verse as children, now take irreverent delight in pronouncing Canadian place-names and joking about eating "alligator pie" and going out for a walk with "Nicholas Knock." Lee once said with glee, "I'm the only poet with eight-year-old groupies."

Civil Elegies remains Lee's most impressive and influential volume. In a suitably elegiac tone, he defines himself in sociopolitical terms as a liberal leftist or cultural and social activist worried about the drift of opinion and world trends. He cautions himself, "There is nothing to be afraid of," but even the poet has his doubts about this. Like so many others, he takes refuge in the "excellent pleasures" of the bourgeois way of life, but even these are found to be wanting in the end.

The style, which contrasts throwaway allusions and tough talk, is a form of free verse that verges on "free prose." Lee's ruminations are inspired by discontinuities in contemporary culture as discussed by George Grant, the moral philosopher who wrote the influential study *Lament for a Nation* (1963). Grant saw Canada as a conservative country on a liberal continent trapped in the economic and electronic web of modern technology. In "Elegy 6" Lee peers into the future: "Though I do not deny technopolis I can see only the bread and circuses to come." Like so many other poets who take culture as their theme, he turns to the past for the measure of its mark. In "Elegy 2" he finds in the measure of the past a standard for the future:

Master and Lord, there was a
measure once.
There was a time when men could say
my life, my job, my home
and still feel clean.
The poets spoke of earth and heaven. There were no
   symbols.

The excellent pleasures of the bourgeois life resurface in *Riffs,* which is a sequence of eighty-eight sections devoted to tracking an adulterous love affair through its ups and downs and ring-a-rounds. Lee's title is taken from the world of jazz, where a riff is a repeated phrase underlying an improvised solo. Improvisation is certainly a good word to use to describe the tone and style of the whole suite of poems. Perhaps what Lee is doing with great skill may be sensed by quoting from the opening and closing sections:

When I lurched like a rumour of want through the network
   of plenty,
me-shaped pang on the lamp,
when I ghosted through lives like a headline, a scrap in the
   updraft,
and my mid-life wreckage was close & for keeps-
. . .

The dolphins of need be-
lie their shining traces.
Arcs in the air.

They do not mean to last. One
upward furrow, bright & the long disappearance,

as though by silver fiat of the sea.

The author's verbal resources permit him to encompass monologue, dialogue, many levels of diction, meditation, contemplation, and even swear words in a sequence of poems that capture the urban idiom of an educated literary person living in North America.

—John Robert Colombo

LEE, Li-Young

Nationality: American. **Born:** Jakarta, Indonesia, 19 August 1957, became American citizen. **Education:** University of Pittsburgh, 1975–79, B.A. 1979; University of Arizona, Tucson, 1979–80; State University of New York, Brockport, 1980–81. **Family:** Married Donna L. Lee in 1978; two sons. **Awards:** National Endowment fellowship, 1986, 1995; Guggenheim fellowship, 1987; Delmore Schwartz award, 1986, for *Rose;* I.B. Lavan award, 1986; Lamont award, 1990, for *The City in Which I Love You;* American Book award, Before Columbus Foundation, 1995, for *The Winged Seed.* **Address:** c/o Simon and Schuster, Simon and Schuster Building, 1230 Avenue of the Americas, New York, New York 10020, U.S.A.

PUBLICATIONS

Poetry

Rose. Brockport, New York, BOA Editions, 1986.
The City in Which I Love You. Brockport, New York, BOA Editions, 1990.

Other

The Winged Seed. New York, Simon and Schuster, 1995.

*

Critical Studies: By James Lee, in *BOMB,* 51, spring 1995; by Tim Engles, in *Explicator* (Washington, D.C.), 54(3), spring 1996; ''Inheritance and Invention in Li-Young Lee's Poetry'' by Zhou Xiaojing, in *MELUS* (Amherst, Massachusetts), 21(1), spring 1996; ''The City in Which I Love You: Li-Young Lee's Excellent Song'' by Walter A. Hesford, in *Christianity and Literature* (Carrollton, Georgia), 46(1), autumn 1996.

Li-Young Lee comments:

Each poem presents its own demands, its own requirements, and its own pleasures. Every encounter with the page is new. I proceed by unknowing.

Early influences include the Bible, Tang dynasty poetry my parents recited, Stevenson's *A Child's Garden of Verses.*

*   *   *

Li-Young Lee's subjects often overshadow the poetry in his two award-winning volumes, *Rose* (Delmore Schwartz Memorial Poetry award) and *The City in Which I Love You* (Lamont Poetry award), This makes sense given the dramatic aspects of Lee's family life, especially his father's. Once the personal physician to Mao Tse-tung, the elder Lee spent a year incarcerated as a political prisoner. In 1959, when his son was two, he escaped from Indonesia with his family, embarking on a long trek through Hong Kong, Macau, and Japan before landing in America five years later. After attending the University of Pittsburgh, the University of Arizona, and the State University of New York at Brockport, the son began to publish poems that drew heavily on the exotic, adventurous refugee experiences that he had both observed and heard recounted by family members in the United States. These poem-stories are tempered by a sense of transition, insecurity, and wish to be included that are unique to the immigrant experience anywhere. In that regard they achieve a degree of universality that appeals to many readers, especially to those who are willing to overlook Lee's slack rhythms and his periodic mistakes in phrasing and in making accurate connections within the poems.

Composing in a meandering free verse line, Lee appears to be forever in a hurry to pull together the endless threads of his observations and experience. Yet this patchwork quilt mainly features its creator's good intentions and enthusiasm. It is not so much how Lee writes, or even what he writes about, but what lurks inside his effort that most moves us. In ''The Cleaving'' Lee visits the butcher at the local market and sees himself in the man, the animals the man cuts up, and the world teeming (and eating) all around him. The lines are characteristically clipped, constructed in the skinny, note-taking style popular in some poetry circles since the 1960s:

In a world of shapes
of my dreams, each one here
is a shape of one of my desires, and each
is known to me and dear by virtue
of each one's unique corruption
of those texts, the face, the body . . .
The soul too
is a debasement
of a text . . .
God is the text.
The soul is a corruption
and a mnemonic.

As this example illustrates, the characters and situations in Lee's poems are usually incidental, setting the stage for the poet's meditative declarations about humanity's capacity for adaptability, friendship, and love. What Lee aims to honor best through his poetry is the past, and this is always a worthy goal.

—Robert McDowell

LEHMAN, David

Nationality: American. **Born:** New York City, 11 June 1948. **Education:** Columbia College, New York, 1966–70, B.A. (magna cum laude) 1970; Cambridge University, England, 1970–72, M.A. 1972; Columbia University, New York, 1972–78, Ph.D. in English 1978. **Family:** Married second wife, Stefanie Green, in 1978. **Career:** Assistant professor of English, Hamilton College, 1976–80; fellow, Society for Humanities, Cornell University, 1985, 1988; book critic and writer, *Newsweek,* 1982–89; visiting professor of English, Hamilton College, spring 1992. Since 1982 freelance writer. Since 1994 core faculty, Bennington Writing Seminars, Vermont, since 1995 professor, Columbia University, New York, and since 1996 professor, M.F.A. program, New School for Social Research, New York. Ellison poet-in-residence, University of Cincinnati, spring 1995. **Awards:** Consuelo Ford award, Poetry Society of America, 1988; Bernard F. Connors prize, *The Paris Review,* 1988; National Endowment for the Arts fellowship, 1987; Guggenheim fellowship, 1989–90; award in literature, American Academy of Arts and Letters, 1990; *New York Times* Notable Book, 1991, for *Signs of the Times;* Ingram Merrill Foundation award, 1993; Rodney G. Dennis fellowship, Houghton Library, Harvard University, 1994; Lila Wallace-*Reader's Digest* Writer's award, 1992–94. **Agent:** Glen Hartley, Writers' Representatives, Inc., 25 West 19th Street, New York, New York 10011. **Address:** 159 Ludlowville Road, Lansing, New York 14882, U.S.A.

PUBLICATIONS

Poetry

An Alternative to Speech. Princeton, New Jersey, Princeton University Press, 1986.
Operation Memory. Princeton, New Jersey, Princeton University Press, 1990.
Valentine Place: Poems. New York, Scribner, 1996.
The Daily Mirror: A Journal in Poetry. New York, Scribner, 2000.

Other

The Perfect Murder. New York, The Free Press, 1989.
Signs of the Times: Deconstruction and the Fall of Paul de Man. New York, Poseidon Press (Simon and Schuster), 1991.
The Line Forms Here. Ann Arbor, University of Michigan Press, 1992.
The Big Question. Ann Arbor, University of Michigan Press, 1995.
The Last Avant-Garde: The Making of the New York School of Poets. New York, Anchor Books, 1998.

Editor, *Beyond Amazement: New Essays on John Ashbery.* Ithaca, New York, Cornell University Press, 1980.
Editor, *James Merrill: Essays in Criticism.* Ithaca, New York, Cornell University Press, 1983.
Series editor, *The Best American Poetry* (annual anthology). New York, Scribner, since 1988.
Editor, *Ecstatic Occasions, Expedient Forms.* Boston, Macmillan, 1987.
Editor, *The KGB Bar Book of Poems.* New York, Quill, 2000.

*

Critical Study: "David Lehman: Lives of the Poets" by Michael Scharf, in *Publishers Weekly,* 245(39), 28 September 1998.

*   *   *

Since the mid-1980s David Lehman has become one of the notable editors of his generation. Readers may be most familiar with his name as a result of his general editorship of the annual anthology series *Best American Poetry.* He has also edited other works, including the critical anthology *Ecstatic Occasions, Expedient Forms* (1987), which contains poems and brief statements about writing in form by sixty-five contemporary poets. In addition to these projects Lehman has written and published several collections of his essays on literature, as well as a critical study of the mystery genre. He has also published volumes of poetry.

As one might expect from the résumé above, Lehman's poetry is erudite, often formal, and occasionally witty. His subjects include his own life, mythologies ancient and new, film (as in the poem "Henry James: The Movie"), and literature itself. One other major characteristic of Lehman's, and one that is rare in contemporary poetry, is humor. In "Rejection Slip," for instance, Lehman's elegant rhymed quatrains lampoon the hysterical bitterness of prize seekers: "The job with the big salary and the perks / Went to a toad of my acquaintance, a loathsome jerk / Instead of to me! I deserved it! Yet rather than resent / My fate, I praise it . . ." In "With Tenure" Lehman's free verse presents a lighthearted, honest case against the much honored, sought after, and maligned academic plum:

> If Ezra Pound were alive today
> (and he is)
> he'd be teaching
> at a small college in the Pacific Northwest
> and attending the annual convention
> of writing instructors in St. Louis
> and railing against tenure . . .

In another poem, "For I Will Consider Your Dog Molly," the dog rather than the dog's people becomes the central figure in a breakthrough religious experience: "For she does not lie awake in the dark and weep for her sins, and whine about her condition, and discuss her duty to God . . . For she knows that God is her savior."

The most complete expression of Lehman's thematic concerns, and arguably the best showcase of his impressive skill, is found in "Mythologies," the thirty-sonnet sequence in *Operation Memory.* This important contribution to the expansion of the contemporary poem of middle length moves effortlessly back and forth between autobiography and musings on the classics of ancient myth, psychology, literature, and news of the day. At the heart of the sequence are twin desires: to effect a tender reconciliation with his father (also with fathers throughout time and in doing so to honor and perpetuate the stories we pass on as they give us our identity), and to attain ever elusive wisdom in love:

> . . . It seems that new myths are needed
> And consumed all the time by folks like you. Each erases
> the last,
>
> Producing tomorrow's tabula rasa, after a night of dreams
> In which the tigers of wrath become the tigers of repose.

In the note following his poem "Amnesia," in *Ecstatic Occasions, Expedient Forms,* Lehman explains the case for one of his favorite devices and offers a compelling justification of the use of traditional form in poetry. "Repetition," he writes, "is not exclusively a device for providing emphasis; repetition, in an ever-shifting context, equals variation. You can't walk into the same river twice, and by the same logic, a line—repeated verbatim or with a slight change in punctuation or emphasis—will be both itself and something else the second time around." Lehman's ability and intelligence seem certain to advance our poetry for years to come.

—Robert McDowell

LEHMANN, Geoffrey (John)

Nationality: Australian. **Born:** Sydney, New South Wales, 20 June 1940. **Education:** Shore School, Sydney; University of Sydney, B.A. 1960, LL.B. 1963: qualified as solicitor 1963; masters in law 1982. **Career:** Practicing solicitor, Sydney, 1963–76. Lecturer in law and tax, Commerce Faculty, University of New South Wales, Kensington. Member, Australia Council Literature Board, 1981–84. **Awards:** Grace Leven prize, 1966, 1982. **Address:** 8 Highfield Road, Lindfield, New South Wales 2070, Australia.

PUBLICATIONS

Poetry

The Ilex Tree, with Les A. Murray. Canberra, Australian National University Press, 1965.
A Voyage of Lions and Other Poems. Sydney, Angus and Robertson. 1968.
Conversation with a Rider. Sydney, Angus and Robertson, 1972.
From an Australian Country Sequence. London, Poem-of-the-Month Club, 1973.
Selected Poems. Sydney, Angus and Robertson, 1976.
Ross' Poems. Sydney, Angus and Robertson, 1978.
Nero's Poems: Translations of the Public and Private Poems of the Emperor Nero. Sydney, Angus and Robertson, 1981.
Spring Forest. North Ryde, New South Wales, Collins/Angus and Robertson, 1992; London, Faber, 1994.
Collected Poems 1957–1996. Port Melbourne, William Heinemann Australia, 1996.

Novel

A Spring Day in Autumn. Melbourne, Nelson, 1974.

Other

Australian Primitive Painters. Brisbane, University of Queensland Press, 1977.
Taxation Law in Australia, with Cynthia Coleman. Sydney, Butterworths, 1989.
Children's Games. North Ryde, New South Wales, Angus and Robertson, 1990.
The Balloon Farmer (for children). Milsons Point, New South Wales, Random House Australia, 1994.
Sky Boy (for children). Milsons Point, New South Wales, Random House Australia, 1996.

Editor, *Comic Australian Verse.* Sydney, Angus and Robertson, 1972.
Editor, with Robert Gray, *The Younger Australian Poets.* Sydney, Hale and Iremonger, 1983.
Editor, *The Flight of the Emu: Contemporary Light Verse.* North Ryde, New South Wales, Angus and Robertson, 1990.
Editor, with Robert Gray, *Australian Poetry in the Twentieth Century.* Port Melbourne, Victoria, W. Heinemann, 1991.

*

Critical Studies: "A Governor, a Farmer, an Emperor: Rome and Australia in Geoffrey Lehmann" by Michele Morgan, in *Australian Literary Studies* (Hobart, Tasmania), May 1983; "Geoffrey Lehmann's Nero Poems" by Michael Sharkey, in *Quadrant* (Sydney), June 1984; by Barbara Williams, in her *In Other Words: Interviews with Australian Poets,* Amsterdam, Netherlands, Rodopi, 1998.

Geoffrey Lehmann comments:

In some of my earlier poems I tried to come to terms with my family. In others I found the voice of a Roman governor of Africa a congenial vehicle to explore the inevitable failure of each of us to control our own minds, as well as the natural and political world we inhabit. In these poems dolphins and lions symbolize the other world, the separate consciousness of other living creatures that continues to elude the romantic.

My two most recent books, *Ross's Poems* (my own, but not my publisher's spelling) and *Nero's Poems,* differ sharply in the voice of their narrator. *Ross's Poems* employs the first-person voice of a living person, Ross, an Australian farmer who lives near Cowra and uses the incidents of his life as a vehicle for a view of life that is partly his and partly mine. Where possible, actual names have been used, but some of the poems are transcribed out of my experience into Ross's life. Ross is the observer of limits, a lover of the surprises, the minutiae, and largeness of life, a conservationist who is skeptical about his own conservationism.

Nero's Poems purports to be translations from the poems of the Roman emperor and aims at historical and psychological accuracy. Nero rejects limits and conventional decency and is completely urban. A number of poems celebrate gardens, aqueducts, eating with friends, and urban life as a counterweight to the corruption and moral disintegration of his world. I have tried to preserve the contradictions of his character and rescue him from the aristocrats who detested a populist emperor and wrote the history books.

Since *Nero's Poems* I have written more poems through the voice of Ross, also personal, imagistic poems about single parenthood.

*   *   *

Though retrospective, Geoffrey Lehmann's spare, terse, deceptively simple poems are not mere exercises in nostalgia. Both the celebrations of Australian country lives in *The Ilex Tree, Conversation with a Rider,* and *Ross' Poems* and the imaginative re-creations of antiquity in *A Voyage of Lions* and *Nero's Poems* use the past as a vehicle for defamiliarizing and reflecting on the present. And it is perhaps to this temperamental need to view life with cool detachment (Lehmann is a lawyer by profession) rather than to any lack of concern that one should attribute the absence of burning contemporary issues in his poetry. In "The House" he characterizes himself as "favouring ironical minds who grasp ideas / But are not ruled by them." Wars and ideologies are incidental to the abiding vitality of the human spirit, which unites emperors, popes, painters, explorers, farmers, and gardeners in democratic fellowship across time and space.

An important group of poems with Australian settings provides brief vignettes of the lives of Lehmann's immediate family and forebears—his maternal grandfather practicing medicine in a "hard, tropical former mining town"; his paternal grandfather returning to die "a blackened ghost" after erecting a church in New Guinea; his fun-loving and "rumbustious" father "working out betting systems" or mending watches; his "ample" aunt affronted at being urged to "come on in, and help the tide to rise." An earlier tradition of poems on explorers, including Kenneth Slessor's "Five Visions of Captain Cook" or Francis Webb's "Leichardt in Theatre," is thus displaced by a more personal yet more representative mythology of unsung settler heroes. The humanizing impetus behind such celebrations is encapsulated in Lehmann's tribute to the "Welsh Australian" painter Lloyd Rees:

Europe respects the vision of old men,
But in Australia our dry heart still haunts us,
The inland rivers petering into sand,
And we forget our past and mock at ghosts.

But you have grown with age, ripened like Europe,
Giving your greatest harvest at the end,
Rich autumn of far outlines, smoky orchards, houses,
Time that remembers, landscape which is man.

There is an almost Flemish reverence for homely detail in Lehmann's portraits of a vintner "in hock-pale light" serving "bandicoot cooked in red wine" or a Chinese gardener with "handshake light as a ghost" carrying "bore water" to "parched chrysanthemums and roses."

Men are more frequently portrayed than women in these poems, country scenes take pride of place over the city, and though there are memorable interiors around glowing pressure lamps, Lehmann seems especially responsive to the outdoor world of vast expanses and "whispers inaudible to city people." In "The Trip to Bunyah" a sense of space is evoked simply by describing the "land-rover jolting and banging" through an ever changing landscape, its "lonely headlights fumbling." Ross (of *Ross' Poems*) by his ironbark fire imagines a vertical line passing through the roof and the moon's molten center to the stars. "Student Love," a psychologically perceptive retrospect on a relationship that failed, begins,

Journeys, highways, railway stations, nights
Of blue glass, highflying birds and stars and sheoaks,
Two months of journeys each week-end to meet
Love aching from three hundred miles away.

For Lehmann space, like time, puts the human struggle in perspective, and the stars are the ultimate reminders that, once deceased, "we have no message, only that we lived / And now are nothing, lights, dwindling star voices." Creeds to Lehmann are as suspect as ideologies, for "there is no absolute rose"; "space is immanent with roses" because what is miraculous is the richness and beauty of life itself. Part of Lehmann's humanist ideal, which in some respects is very Australian, seems to be embodied in the character of Ross himself as revealed in his ruminative monologues—unpretentious, self-reliant, kindly, wryly humorous, capable of compassion for the underdog, conscious that "each year we get further away / from the Spring Forest, / the original text," romantically convinced of the value of the simple things in life.

Though less popular, Lehmann's historical poems are often more imaginatively daring than his Australian sketches. Notable among the early "Meditations for Marcus Furius Camillus, Governor of Africa"—where the analogy with provincial Australia is no more than tacit—are the poems that speculate about the superior intellect of dolphins, again revealing Lehmann's interest in the natural world and the perspective it affords on human nature. Poems like "Cellini" and "Pope Alexander VI" are elegant, amusing dramatic monologues in the tradition of Robert Browning. In *Nero's Poems,* a more ambitious and not wholly successful venture, Lehmann draws on evidence from Tacitus and Suetonius of Nero's populism, philhellenism, and interest in the arts to suggest that he was a "more attractive human being beneath the scandalous surface" than usually assumed, indeed something of an "uomo universale." The imaginary portrait of the emperor as artist built up in these often witty monologues of varying length is correspondingly complex, indirectly reflecting different facets of the author's own artistic credo. Most frequently Nero wears the mask of a Nietzschean "Dionysius the Second" who "resists the moralist" and cries, "we give ourselves to change." But in his "Advice to Young Poets" the recommendation to "revise your inspirations"—as did Nero with his own poems, according to Suetonius—strikes a more Apollonian note, and in his "Advice for Emperors" the call to "single out / your true from your false wants" sounds like Lehmann's other alter ego, Ross.

As poetry, these lighthearted vignettes of Roman aqueducts, wine bars, wrestlers, and jockeys and of Nero's relations with his mother, mistresses, and homosexual lovers are not without charm, but the fact that all is seen through Nero's eyes tends, as in minor Elizabethan sonnet sequences, to make for monotony and a sense of flagging contrivance. As evocations of a bygone era they suffer in comparison with Lehmann's Australian retrospects in that, for all his scrupulous regard for historical accuracy, they rarely generate a sense of the spirit of place, of a Rome, for instance, where "lonely migrants pace." Credulity is also strained at times by the vernacular idiom: "If our Roman bakers baked bread / as fresh as her cunt, I'd eat bread all day." In his introduction Lehmann claims to be attempting to be true to Nero's psychology as he sees it, and there are certainly some chillingly insightful moments in the volume:

Down on the beachfront at night
savage hands drag
me into the shadows.

Each time I ask,
do they bring joy or the knife?

But convincing portrayals of evil genius are rare in imaginative literature, and though *Nero's Poems* returns us to the Roman historians with renewed curiosity, one also has the sense that in Lehmann's portrait the psychopath has been largely eclipsed by the larrikin.

—J.M.Q. Davies

LEITHAUSER, Brad

Nationality: American. **Born:** Detroit, Michigan, 27 February 1953. **Education:** Harvard University, Cambridge, Massachusetts, B.A. 1975, J.D. 1980. **Family:** Married Mary Jo Salter, *q.v.,* in 1980; one daughter. **Career:** Research fellow, Kyoto Comparative Law Center, Japan, 1980–83; MacArthur Foundation Research fellow, 1983–87; visiting writer, Amherst College, Massachusetts, 1984–85; Fulbright lecturer, University of Iceland, Reykjauil, 1989. Since 1991 lecturer, Mount Holyoke College, South Hadley, Massachusetts. **Awards:** Harvard University-Academy of American Poets prize, 1973, 1975; Harvard University McKim Garrison prize, 1974, 1975; Amy Lowell travel scholarship, 1981–82; Guggenheim fellowship, 1982–83; Lavan Younger Poets award, 1983; MacArthur Foundation research fellowship, 1983–87. **Address:** 9 Stanton Avenue, South Hadley, Massachusetts 01075–1515, U.S.A.

PUBLICATIONS

Poetry

Hundreds of Fireflies. New York, Knopf, 1982.
A Seaside Mountain: Eight Poems from Japan. New York, Sarabande Press, 1985.
Cats of the Temple. New York, Knopf, 1986.
Between Leaps: Poems 1972–1985. Oxford, Oxford University Press, 1987.
The Mail from Anywhere: Poems. New York, Knopf, and Oxford, Oxford University Press, 1990.
The Odd Last Thing She Did: Poems. New York, Knopf, 1998.

Novels

Equal Distance. New York, Knopf, 1985.
Hence. New York, Knopf, 1989.
Seaward. New York, Knopf, 1993.
The Friends of Freeland. New York, Knopf, 1997.

Short Stories

The Line of Ladies. Privately printed, 1975.

Other

Penchants & Places: Essays and Criticism. New York, Knopf, 1995.

Editor, *The Norton Book of Ghost Stories.* New York, Norton, 1994.
Editor, *No Other Book: Selected Essays,* by Randall Jarrell. New York, HarperCollins, 1995.

*

Critical Studies: "'Yes, but . . .': Some Thoughts on the New Formalism" by David Wojahn, in *Crazyhorse,* 32, spring 1987; "Games Computers Play" by David Gurewich, in *New Criterion* (New York), 7(9), May 1989.

*   *   *

An initial reaction to the work of Brad Leithauser might well be one of sheer delight in its technical mastery. In his counterpointing of meter and speech rhythm, in his control of the interplay between syntax and line ending, in the adroitness of his use of rhyme, in the delicacy with which he balances monosyllables against polysyllables, and in many other ways, Leithauser's is an exemplary craftsmanship, always exact and purposeful but never merely pedantic. The craftsmanship is at the service of much exact observation, especially of the small and the ephemeral. So in "A Quilled Quilt, A Needle Bed" fallen pine needles are noted and celebrated:

> Under the longleaf pines
> The curved, foot-long needles have
> Woven a thatchwork quilt-threads,
> Not patches, windfall millions
> Looped and overlapped to make
> The softest of needle beds.
>
> The day's turned hot, the air
> Coiling around the always
> Cool scent of pine. As if lit
> From below, a radiance
> Milder yet more clement than
> The sun's, the forest-carpet
>
> Glows. It's a kind of pelt:
> Thick as a bear's, tawny like
> A bobcat's, more wonderful
> Than both—a maize labyrinth
> Spiralling down through tiny
> Chinks to a caked, vegetal
>
> Ferment where the needles
> Crumble and blacken. And still
> The mazing continues . . . whorls
> Within whorls, the downscaling
> Yet-perfect intricacies
> Of lichens, seeds and crystals.

The subdued wordplay of "thatchwork quilt" or "whorls within whorls," the placing of "glows" in its emphatic position, turning the stanza break into a pause of rewarded expectation, the unforced half rhymes—all typify Leithauser's surefootedness.

Effects of light, especially light reflected in water, often bring out the very best in Leithauser. "Floating Light in Tokyo" is a sustained appreciation of "a jewelled inner city afloat / in light" where "lights on lights are overlaid in repeated / applications." How extraordinarily precise and evocative is the response to a passing duck's disruption of such reflections:

> With regret, then,
> you note an approaching duck, whose wake shivers
>
> all reflections; and it hurts a little
> to watch the neat incision being cut, the plush
> collapse begin as the first nudging ripple
> swings outwards. Yet as the duck, in passing,
>
> transforms into a swan, the shapely *S*
> of the neck lit in sudden fluorescent profile, P4 and familiar
>   designs begin to coalesce
> within the moat, which soon again will reflect
>
> composedly, you'll grant that while the static
> glaze was restful, welcome is this
> queen of birds with the sea-serpentine neck,
> who trails behind her such thrilling rubble.

Leithauser's attention to the evanescent (e.g., in "Angel" or "Hundreds of Fireflies"), whether in the life of insects or in the transience of lights, takes part of its force from a mostly unspoken sense that in their ephemerality such subjects are perhaps fitting emblems of human life. Such a sense is made explicit at the close of "Hundreds of Fireflies." The observation of the gathering fireflies closes with the anticipation of that moment when

>   the silent
> drift of summer through the trees
> signals us, drawn too by light,
>
> to another brief firefly season.

Leithauser's earlier work was perhaps least impressive in its treatment of individual human lives. "Two Summer Jobs" offers attractive autobiographical retrospects in which an earlier self can be observed at a distance. A similar detachment operates in the family poems of "A Noisy Sleeper" and in the series of poems on Japan (many of them extremely attractive), which are the work of an observer rather than a participant. In his first two collections Leithauser treats humanity most effectively in the generalization of the epigram rather than in the analysis of individuality. There are wit and formal shrewdness in such epigrams as "The Fame Train"—

> The season's major talents are
>   Roaring up the track.
> You can hear them coming: clique
>   Claque, clique claque

—or in the rueful "Anonymous' Lament"—

> Though love (it's been said) is a perilous game,
>   At times I might wish to be bolder—

> Just once to be either the moth or the flame
>   And not the candle-holder.

In the poems of the later *The Mail from Anywhere,* and especially in those of its first section, "A Peopled World," Leithauser demonstrates an increased capacity to register and articulate the individually felt human situation. Poems from family history, such as "Uncle Grant" and "The Caller," combine anecdote with psychological perceptiveness and compassion.

When large selections from Leithauser's first two American collections were republished in a single British volume in 1987, it was entitled *Between Leaps.* The title is thoroughly apt, for Leithauser's poems are products of composed observation, of a stillness and clarity of seeing and thinking that are unusually free of excess emotional clutter. The work in *The Mail from Anywhere* is characterized by the same qualities but seems also to add a greater emotional warmth and involvement. Leithauser's apprehension of the world—human and nonhuman—seems to be growing wider and deeper. He is a poet of considerable achievement.

—Glyn Pursglove

LEONARD, Tom

Nationality: Scottish. **Born:** Glasgow, Lanarkshire, 22 August 1944. **Education:** St. Monica's Primary School and Lourdes Secondary School, Glasgow; Glasgow University, M.A. in English and Scottish literature. **Family:** Married in 1971; two children. **Career:** Has worked in a variety of mainly clerical jobs; organized, with Joan Hughson, sound-poetry festivals Sound and Syntax, 1978, and Poetsound '84, both in Glasgow. Writer-in-residence, Renfrew District Libraries, 1986–1989; Glasgow University and Strathclyde University, 1991; Bell College of Technology, Hamilton, 1993–94. **Awards:** Scottish Arts Council bursary, 1971, 1974, 1978; Saltire Society Scottish Book of the Year award for *Intimate Voices,* 1984; Arts Council Autumn Book award for *Places of the Mind,* 1993. **Address:** 56 Eldon Street, Glasgow G3 6NJ, Scotland.

PUBLICATIONS

Poetry

Six Glasgow Poems. Glasgow, Midnight Press, 1969.
A Priest Came On at Merkland Street. Glasgow, Midnight Press, 1970.
Poems. Dublin, E. and T. O'Brien, 1973.
Bunnit Husslin. Glasgow, Third Eye Centre, 1975.
Three Glasgow Writers, with Alex Hamilton and James Kelman. Glasgow, Molendinar Press, 1976.
My Name Is Tom. London, Good Elf, 1978.
Ghostie Men. Newcastle upon Tyne, Galloping Dog Press, 1980.
Intimate Voices: Writing 1965–83. Newcastle upon Tyne, Galloping Dog Press, 1984.
Situations Theoretical and Contemporary. Newcastle upon Tyne. Galloping Dog Press. 1986.

Reports from the Present: Selected Poetry and Prose 1982–1994. London, Jonathan Cape, 1995.

Etruscan Reader 5, with Tom Raworth and Bill Griffiths. Devon, Etruscan, 1997.

Plays

If Only Bunty Was Here (radio play). Glasgow, Print Studio Press, 1979.

Tickly Mince (revue), with Liz Lochhead and Alasdair Gray (produced Glasgow, 1982).

The Pie of Damocles (revue), with others (produced Glasgow, 1983).

A Bunch of Fives, with Liz Lochhead and Sean Hardie (produced Glasgow, 1983).

Other

Satires and Profanities (miscellany). Glasgow, STUC, 1984.

Two Members' Monologues. N.p., Edward Polin Press, 1989.

On the Mass Bombing of Iraq and Kuwait, Commonly Known as "The Gulf War." Stirling, AK Press, 1991.

Places of the Mind: The Life and Work of James Thomson ("B.V."). London, Jonathan Cape, 1993.

Editor, *Radical Renfrew: Poetry in the West of Scotland from the French Revolution to the First World War.* Edinburgh, Polygon, 1990.

*

Critical Studies: "A Scots Quartette," in *Eboracum* (York), winter 1973, and "The Sea, the Desert, the City: Environment and Language in W.S. Graham, Hamish Henderson, and Tom Leonard," in *Yearbook of English Studies* (London), 17, 1987, both by Edwin Morgan; "Tom Leonard: Man with Two Heads" by Tom McGrath, in *Akros* (Preston, Lancashire), April 1974; "Noo Lissnty Mi Toknty Yi" by George Rosie, in *Radio Times* (Scottish edition), 12–18 February 1977; Tom Leonard, Glasgow, National Book League, 1978; *Poéstie, Sonore Internationale* by Henri Chopin, Paris, Jean-Michel Place, 1979; "Poetry for the People in Glasgow Patois" by Alasdair Gray, in *Glasgow Herald,* 17 March 1984; "Poetry in Glasgow Dialect" by Stephen Mulrine, in *Focus on Scotland,* edited by Manfred Gorlach, Amsterdam, Benjamins, 1985; "Scots, Poets, and the City" by Barry Wood, in *The History of Scottish Literature, IV: Twentieth Century,* edited by Cairns Craig, Aberdeen, Aberdeen University Press, 1987; "Urbanity in an Urban Dialect: The Poetry of Tom Leonard" by Ronald K.S. Macaulay, in *Studies in Scottish Literature* (Columbia, South Carolina), 23, 1988; "One Human Being Speaking to Another: Tom Leonard's Glasgow Poetry" by Valerie Shepherd, in her *Language Variety and the Art of the Everyday,* n.p., Pinter, 1990; "Ma Language Is Disgraceful: Tom Leonard's Glasgow Dialect Poems" by Colin Milton, in *Englishes around the World, I: General Studies, British Isles, North America,* edited by Edgar W. Schneider, Amsterdam, Benjamins, 1997.

*   *   *

Tom Leonard is one of the most interesting of the Scottish poets who emerged during the 1960s. His reputation in Scotland has tended to center on his poems in the Glasgow dialect, but in fact, as the publication of his first general collection, *Six Glasgow Poems,* made clear, he is a man of many styles, a restless, formal experimenter whose language is laid with surprises, traps, and ironies. There is a considerable element of humor, sometimes fantastic and sometimes moderately black, to attract the reader, and a recurring deadpan strangeness is characteristic. Some of the ironical effects are slight, jokey, throwaway. But in the best poems, as with "simile please / say cheese," the interlock of images and ideas forces the humor to work in unusual and meaningful ways. The Glasgow poems make use of local idiom and pronunciation for a range of effects, from the bold outspoken back talk of schoolgirls skipping their bus fares ("A Scream") to the more sophisticated meshing of religion and football in "The Good Thief." These poems take the risk of being obscure to English readers, although the book provides a translation for the sake of offering a tribute to the much attacked Glasgow environment, not that the tribute is anything but unsentimental.

Language, religion, sex, and politics continue to be explored in *Bunnit Husslin* and *Ghostie Men* in poems of great precision and compression, though sometimes with an outspokenness alarming to educational authorities, and *Intimate Voices* offers a useful collection and survey of his work from 1965 to 1983. The "voice" of the title is crucial, not only in the sense that Leonard's accurate ear allows him to make use of monologues, dialogues, parodies, casual remarks, and language games with a minimum of overlay or working up or pretension but also since it helps to suggest his growing interest in performance and in the dramatic or the semidramatic. The dramatic monologue, applied particularly to political subjects—and his political commitment, always there, has become more prominent—is developed in the slashing prose pieces of *Satires and Profanities,* a centenary tribute to James (B.V.) Thomson's book of the same title, and in *Two Members' Monologues.* The latter also contains his "A Handy Form for Artists," in which readers are invited to state their reasons for not taking part in Glasgow's so-called City of Culture events of 1990. In poetry his independence of mind slices through a range of modern cant in *Situations Theoretical and Contemporary.* Leonard is an instantly communicative poet whose work, including its "bad language," about which there will always be diverse views, nevertheless repays close attention on the printed page.

—Edwin Morgan

LePAN, Douglas (Valentine)

Nationality: Canadian. **Born:** Toronto, Ontario, 25 May 1914. **Education:** University of Toronto schools; University College, University of Toronto, B.A.; Merton College, Oxford, M.A. **Military Service:** Canadian Army, 1942–45: artillery man. **Family:** Married Sarah Katharine Chambers in 1948 (separated 1971); two sons. **Career:** Lecturer, University of Toronto, 1937–38; instructor and tutor in English Literature, Harvard University, Cambridge, Massachusetts, 1938–41. Joined Canadian Department of External Affairs, 1945: first secretary on the staff of the Canadian High Commissioner in London, 1945–48; various appointments in the Department of External Affairs, including that of special assistant to the Secretary of State, Ottawa, 1950–51; counselor and later minister counselor for

External Affairs at the Canadian Embassy, Washington, D.C., 1951–55; secretary and director of research, Royal Commission on Canada's Economic Prospects (Gordon Commission), 1955–58; assistant under-secretary of state for economic affairs, 1958–59. Professor of English Literature, Queen's University, Kingston, Ontario, 1959–64; principal, University College, 1964–70; university professor, 1970–79, and since 1979 emeritus professor, University of Toronto. **Awards:** Guggenheim fellowship, 1948; Governor-General's award, for poetry, 1954, for fiction, 1965; Oscar Blumenthal prize (*Poetry,* Chicago), 1972; Lorne Pierce Medal, 1976. D.Litt.: University of Manitoba, Winnipeg, 1964; University of Ottawa, 1972; University of Waterloo, Ontario, 1973; University of Toronto, 1990, LL.D.; Queen's University, Kingston, Ontario, 1969; York University, Toronto, 1976; Dalhousie University, Halifax, Nova Scotia, 1980. Fellow, Royal Society of Canada, 1968. **Member:** Canada Council, 1964–70. **Address:** Massey College, 4 Devonshire Place, Toronto, Ontario MSS 2EI, Canada.

PUBLICATIONS

Poetry

The Wounded Prince and Other Poems. Toronto, Clarke Irwin, and London, Chatto and Windus, 1948.
The Net and the Sword. Toronto, Clarke Irwin, and London, Chatto and Windus, 1953.
Something Still to Find: New Poems. Toronto, McClelland and Stewart, 1982.
Weathering It: Complete Poems 1948–1987. Toronto, McClelland and Stewart, 1987.
Far Voyages. Toronto, McClelland and Stewart, 1990.
Macalister, or Dying in the Dark. Kingston, Canada, Quarry Press, 1995.

Novel

The Deserter. Toronto, McClelland and Stewart, 1964.

Other

Bright Glass of Memory: A Set of Four Memoirs. Toronto, McGraw Hill Ryerson, 1979.

*

Critical Studies: "The Bird of Heavenly Airs: Thematic Strains in Douglas LePan's Poetry" by M. Davies, in *Canadian Literature* (Vancouver), 15, winter 1963; "Defeat of Egoism: A Critique of *The Deserter*" by W.C. Lougheed, in *Queen's Quarterly* (Kingston, Ontario), 72, autumn 1965; "European Emblem and Canadian Image: A Study of Douglas LePan's Poetry" by S.C. Hamilton, in *Mosaic* (Winnipeg, Manitoba), 3, winter 1970; "Man in the Maze" by D.G. Priestman, in *Canadian Literature* (Vancouver), 64, spring 1975; "The Wounded Eye: The Poetry of Douglas LePan" by J.M. Kertzer, in *Studies in Canadian Literature* (Fredericton, New Brunswick), 6(1), 1981; "Wild Hamlet with the Features of Horatio: Canadian Content in the work of Douglas LePan" by D.J.B. Smith, in

Regionalism and National Identity, edited by Berry and Acheson, Katoomba, Australia, ACSANZ, 1985; "The Moon, the Heron, and the *Thrush,* George Seferis, Douglas LePan, and Greek Myth" by George Thaniel, in *Classical and Modern Literature* (Terre Haute, Indiana), 1989.

*   *   *

I once asked Douglas LePan about the proper spelling of his surname. "Are 'Le' and 'Pan' one word or two? Should there be a space between them or not?" The poet considered the question for some time, as if it was being asked of him for the first time, and said, "I think the proper way to spell the name is to insert a half-space between the 'Le' and the 'Pan.'"

"A half-space!" This anecdote summarizes, at least for me, a number of LePan's essential characteristics. When faced with a new or even an old situation, he considers it on its own terms. He ponders it carefully, and then he responds in a measured, meaningful, somewhat surprising, yet authoritative way. These are some of the characteristics of the man, and they are certainly characteristics of his writing.

LePan is a very accomplished person. In addition to writing poems of merit, he has served as a distinguished diplomat and influential academic. His carefully written memoirs touch on experiences in the diplomatic corps and in academic life and on friendships with the painter Wyndham Lewis and the economist John Maynard Keynes. Reading his poems, one has the feeling that his words and themes have been chosen with one eye fixed on their fitness as responsible utterances and with the other open to their literary associations.

LePan's first two books of poems were largely concerned with the experience of war. In their sleek lines he expressed an open-mouthed admiration for the muscular man of action. He composed notable poems about dying soldiers and the *coureurs de bois* who roamed the woods of New France. As he wrote in *The Net and the Sword,*

> Thinking of you, I think of the *coureur de bois.*
> Swarthy men grown almost to savage size
> Who put their brown wrists through the arras of the woods.
> And were lost—sometimes for months.

But LePan was also concerned with the repercussions of actions, not with those whose "care is how they fall, not why." This consideration has led him to theorize about Canadian experience over the centuries. "A Country without a Mythology" is the title of a major poem in the collection *The Wounded Prince* and a catchphrase close to the hearts of those Canadian artists who in the 1960s and 1970s were engaged in the mythologizing, and in some cases the remythologizing, of the landscape of the country. As LePan saw him, the quintessential Canadian was "Wild Hamlet with the features of Horatio," an insight and image worthy of the pen of a political poet like Zbigniew Herbert.

With the years LePan has acquired an uncharacteristic forthrightness and an unabashed vigor of expression. As the critic Malcolm Ross once noted, the strong poems in *Something Still to Find* depict a world "at peace" that seems more terrifying than the world at war as described in *The Net and the Sword.* The poems that make up *Far Voyages* go much further and express a gentle love, addressed to a young man, that has come late to a lonely life. The language of the late poems, for all their passion, remains as graceful and dignified as ever. Here is the opening of ''Greetings'':

> If I were coming to greet you out of antiquity
> I would have in my hand a pomegranate for you, or a
>   cockerell,
> or a red-figured wine-cup with your name on it.

Every so often the poet offers the reader a colorful surprise, as in ''Flames, at the Beginning'':

> I am burning your letter, as you asked me to.
> In the light through the window it flames up like a great
>   gold chrysanthemum.
> Our love will flourish like that, extravagant and secret.

The final two words convey the essence of LePan.

These are certainly characteristics of LePan's book *Macalister, or Dying in the Dark,* described as a verse drama and published to mark the fiftieth anniversary of the end of the World War II. The columnist John Fraser called the work ''a conspicuous act of remembrance,'' for it recalls the life and death of a college friend, John Kenneth Macalister, who served as a member of the Allied wartime intelligence service until his death at Buchenwald. LePan asks such questions as ''without a core of courage / how can anything be achieved, can anything be built?''

The poet Tom Marshall has effectively summarized LePan's achievement: ''Throughout his work the poet is haunted by moments of beauty or violence, sometimes by the two together. Lost innocence and paradise is a recurrent theme but so, more happily, is paradise occasionally regained.''

—John Robert Colombo

LERNER, Laurence (David)

Nationality: British. **Born:** Cape Town, South Africa, 12 December 1925. **Education:** University of Cape Town, B.A. 1944, M.A. 1945; Pembroke College, Cambridge. B.A. 1949. **Family:** Married Natalie Winch in 1948; four sons. **Career:** Schoolmaster, St. George's Grammar School, Cape Town, 1946–47; assistant lecturer, then lecturer in English, University College of the Gold Coast, Legon, Ghana, 1949–53; extra-mural tutor, then lecturer in English, Queen's University of Belfast, 1953–62; lecturer, then reader, 1962–70, and professor of English, 1970–84, University of Sussex, Brighton; Kenan Professor of English, Vanderbilt University, Nashville, Tennessee, 1985–95. Visiting professor, Earlham College, Richmond, Indiana, University of Connecticut, Storrs, 1960–61, University of Illinois, Urbana, 1964, University of Dijon, 1967, University of Munich, 1968–69, 1974–75, University of Paris III 1982, University of Ottawa, 1983, University of Würzburg, 1989–90, and University of Vienna, 1994. **Awards:** Prudence Farmer prize (*New Statesman*), 1975; South-East Arts prize, 1979. Fellow, Royal Society of Literature, 1986. **Address:** Abinger, 1B Gundreda Road, Lewes, East Sussex BN7 1PT, England.

PUBLICATIONS

Poetry

(Poems). Oxford, Fantasy Press, 1955.
Domestic Interior and Other Poems. London, Hutchinson, 1959.
The Directions of Memory: Poems 1958–1963. London, Chatto and Windus, 1963.
Selves. London, Routledge, 1969.
Folio, with others. Frensham, Surrey, Sceptre Press, 1971.
A.R.T.H.U.R.: The Life and Opinions of a Digital Computer. Hassocks, Sussex, Harvester Press, 1974; Amherst, University of Massachusetts Press, 1975.
The Man I Killed. London, Secker and Warburg, 1980.
A.R.T.H.U.R. & M.A.R.T.H.A.; or, The Loves of the Computers. London, Secker and Warburg, 1980.
A Dialogue. Oxford, Pisces Press, 1983.
Chapter and Verse: Bible Poems. London, Secker and Warburg, 1984.
Selected Poems. London, Secker and Warburg, 1984.
Rembrandt's Mirror. London, Secker and Warburg, and Nashville, Tennessee, Vanderbilt University Press, 1987.

Play

The Experiment (produced Brighton, 1980).

Novels

The Englishmen. London, Hamish Hamilton, 1959.
A Free Man. London, Chatto and Windus, 1968.
My Grandfather's Grandfather. London, Secker and Warburg, 1985.

Other

English Literature: An Interpretation for Students Abroad. London, Oxford University Press, 1954.
The Truest Poetry: An Essay on the Question: What is Literature? London, Hamish Hamilton, 1960; New York, Horizon Press, 1964.
The Truthtellers: Jane Austen, George Eliot, and D.H. Lawrence. London, Chatto and Windus, and New York, Schocken, 1967.
The Uses of Nostalgia: Studies in Pastoral Poetry. London, Chatto and Windus, and New York, Schocken, 1972.
Thomas Hardy's ''The Mayor of Casterbridge'': Tragedy or Social History? London, Chatto and Windus, 1975.
An Introduction to English Poetry: Fifteen Poems Discussed. London, Arnold, 1975.
Love and Marriage: Literature and Its Social Context. London, Arnold, 1979.
The Literary Imagination: Essays on Literature and Society. Brighton, Harvester, and New York, Barnes and Noble, 1982.
The Two Cinnas: Quakerism, Revolution and Poetry: A Dialogue. London, Quaker Home Service, 1984.
The Frontiers of Literature. London, Blackwell, 1988.
Philip Larkin. Plymouth, Northcote House for the British Council, 1997.
Angels & Absences: Child Deaths in the 19th Century. Nashville, Tennessee, and London, Vanderbilt University Press, 1997.
Wandering Professor. London, Caliban, 1999.

Editor, *Poems,* by Milton. London, Penguin, 1953.

Editor, *Shakespeare's Tragedies: A Selection of Modern Criticism.* London, Penguin, 1963.

Editor, with John Holmstrom, *George Eliot and Her Readers: A Selection of Contemporary Reviews.* London, Bodley Head, 1966.

Editor, *Shakespeare's Comedies: A Selection of Modern Criticism.* London, Penguin, 1967.

Editor, with John Holmstrom, *Thomas Hardy and His Readers: A Selection of Contemporary Reviews.* London, Bodley Head, 1968.

Editor, *Poetry South East 2: An Anthology of New Poetry.* Tunbridge Wells, Kent, South East Arts Association, 1977.

Editor, *The Victorians.* London, Methuen, and New York, Holmes and Meier, 1978.

Editor, *Reconstructing Literature.* Oxford, Blackwell, 1983.

Editor, with Vereen Bell, *On Modern Poetry: Essays Presented to Donald Davie.* Nashville, Tennessee, Vanderbilt University Press, 1988.

Editor and translator, *Baudelaire.* London, Everyman's Poetry, 1999.

Translator, *Spleen,* by Baudelaire. Belfast, Festival, 1966.

*

Laurence Lerner comments:

My poems are comprehensible, sad, modern in subject matter rather than form. Some are lyrical and personal; many are dramatic and represent the attempt to enter a variety of selves. In *Chapter and Verse* I tried to perform the perhaps incompatible tasks of introducing the Bible to the modern secular reader for whom it is no longer culturally central and subverting the traditional stories by means of an unusual viewpoint or unorthodox judgement. If I could write half a dozen more poems as good as "The Merman" or "Raspberries," I would be satisfied. *Rembrandt's Mirror* deals largely with my family (ancestors and descendants) and their role in the poet's emotional life. It contains a poem in which Rembrandt addresses his mirror, but the title also indicates the intimate and domestic subject matter. My next (and possibly final) project, which may never be completed, is to write a series of poems about philosophers. I love the idea of using poetry to support and subvert reason simultaneously.

*   *   *

Like the best of his criticism, Laurence Lerner's poetry is sensible, direct, and aware of the complexities of human behavior. Many of the poems in his first collection, *Domestic Interior,* are reactions to different environments. Their strength lies not so much in description as in the way they establish a mental rapport with the external world, in which closely observed incidentals find their place in a wider pattern of experience:

While shaping eyes stare from the moving train:
Or else a water-colour landscape glows
Grey-green and tawny under a wash of rain,
Or blue with blobs of cabbages in rows.

Most of these poems are "efficient" and well argued in a sense that reminds one of the best poetry of the 1930s, though occasionally the argument only partly conceals a certain diffuseness of detail. In the more successful ones, however, like the title poem and "Meditation on the Toothache" (in actual fact a meditation on the imagination), a

powerful social concern is firmly rooted in the trivia of the individual life and in the means by which these may be absorbed into artistic creation. The dramatic sense is evident in "Domestic Interior" and "Mimesis," both poems in which the subject is approached through a number of protagonists.

Lerner's second collection, *The Directions of Memory,* is more adventurous in technique and shows a willingness to handle more difficult kinds of experience. Though one still occasionally feels that a poem has not found its ideal form, there is a more subtle sense of construction and a growing skill in the use of imagery. Several of the most striking poems deal with sexual relationships, sometimes from the woman's point of view. These range from the dream of aggression ("Housewife as Judith") to qualified celebration, as in "The Anatomy of Love." In the fine poem "Midnight Swim" a profoundly disturbing situation is conveyed through a brilliantly controlled central metaphor. The same can be said of the most moving poem in the volume, "Years Later," the monologue of an unborn Jewish child, the victim (with its mother) of a Nazi atrocity. These poems show a determination to face up to the more disturbing aspects of life with honesty, intelligence, and, at times, wit.

The same combination of qualities persists, with increasing verbal power, in *Selves.* The central section of the collection includes a group of monologues in which various victims of human cruelty—a laboratory rat, a monkey involved in a feeding experiment, a battery-reared cockerel—comment on their situations with grimly humorous logic. Though in one sense such poems are a natural extension of Lerner's interest in contemporary psychological theory, their real originality comes from the skill with which they render essentially inarticulate suffering in terms of a recognizable human idiom. In other poems ("The Merman," "Adam Names the Creatures," "Information Theory") the concern with communication extends to the nature of language itself. Here, as in "The Merman," the deliberate assumption of inarticulateness becomes a powerful device for exploring the gap between words and reality:

When humans talk they split their say in bits
And bit by bit they step on what they feel.
They talk in bits, they never talk in all.

So live in wetness swimming they call "sea";
And stand on dry and watch the wet waves call
They still call "sea".
    Only their waves don't call.

Lerner's continued questioning of the basis of language and perception lies at the root of *A.R.T.H.U.R.* It would be wrong to dismiss this as a jeu d'esprit. Certainly the poems are ingenious, entertaining, and wittier than anything else he has written, though none of this should blind one to their underlying seriousness. As the introductory poem makes clear, the world of *A.R.T.H.U.R.* ("Automatic Record Tabulator but Heuristically Unreliable Reasoner") is divided between "metal people" and "movers," in other words, between computers and human beings. This leads to some unusual perspectives: "Movers are constantly bending and running / Through a world of edges and obstacles. Cunning / Their reflexes, but cannot eliminate mourning." From the human point of view the effect is one of "making strange," a process that is carried still further in poems like "Literary Criticism" and "Arthur takes a test for divergent thinking," which are concerned with the properties of language itself. Here the game seems innocent enough. Elsewhere, however, as in certain stories by Borges, there are hints of more frightening possibilities, the sense, for example, that new objects can be brought into existence by the mere fact that it is possible to name them. Hence the ending of "Arthur's reply," with its brilliant final pun: "We can try anything: just turn me on, / Feed me the facts, and wait for trial and terror."

The possibilities of such poems are extended in *A.R.T.H.U.R. & M.A.R.T.H.A.; or, The Loves of the Computers,* an equally engaging collection in which human sexual relationships are tested almost to destruction by the witty application of scientific metaphor. Both sequences are impressive evidence of Lerner's inventiveness in a mode that few British poets have attempted and that represents, in Edwin Morgan's phrase, "a natural extension of the imagination in an age of science."

Lerner's collections *The Man I Killed* and *Chapter and Verse: Bible Poems* mark a partial return to earlier allegiances, though the directness of the best poems may owe something to the pointed simplicity and sureness of rhythm he had been compelled to practice in the "scientific" poems. The former takes its title from "The Experiment," one of Lerner's most powerful poems, in which his earlier preoccupation with the scientific treatment of animals is brought to a head in the imagined victimization of man at his own hands. Here and elsewhere the tone varies between humor, irony, and the deliberately flat statement of the horrific, with notable gains in economy of language and skill in counterpointing conversational rhythms against carefully controlled patterns of repetition. Less spectacularly, though no less forcefully, the spaciousness and verbal richness of the earlier dramatic monologues give way, as in the two Rembrandt poems ("Saskia" and "Youthful Self-Portrait"), to a greater incisiveness in which the heaviest burden falls on the simplest words ("then," "now," "selves") carefully spaced within a verse pattern created largely by natural phrasing and the skillful use of eye rhymes and line breaks.

Though *The Man I Killed* is the stronger collection, *Chapter and Verse* (published at the same time as the excellent *Selected Poems*) brings together and intensifies many of Lerner's earlier preoccupations in the course of re-creating a series of biblical episodes from Genesis to Apocalypse. Though occasionally the commentary becomes a little predictable, the general effect is shrewd, entertaining, and at times (as in the fine poem on Poussin's painting of Saint Matthew) deeply moving. Again, in a poem like "Ishmael" one admires the economy with which scattered hints from Genesis are taken up and welded into a coherent discourse that compels the reader to enter the speaker's subversive mentality and to see things from what, in his own terms, is a legitimate point of view. The deepest irony is that, at certain crucial moments, this point of view is made to overlap with the reader's own. By opening a channel between the present time and that of the speaker, phrases like "God's first Jew" and "What does the future cost?" emphasize both the relevance of the biblical narrative and its power to disturb.

Lerner's volume *Rembrandt's Mirror* is one of his best. Though the virtues of his earlier collections are very much in evidence—above all the quizzical, critical mind that continues to offer new perspectives on experience—there is an increasing assurance in the use of formal techniques and in the ability to play comic variations on some of his most serious themes. Several poems of this type, like "Starting" and the splendid "A Short Guide to Academic Life," are genuinely funny, and the whole volume shows a fascination with the incongruities of human life that is never allowed to become condescending. Many of the more serious poems enact what at one point

Lerner calls "Touching the past of others, testing it / Into existence" ("In Fifteen Years"). It is this that links the accomplished dramatic monologues and the series of poems on painters and their subjects that make up the second part of the book. More important, it accounts for the group of poems on family relationships opening the collection, in which Lerner projects his own personal history into both the past and the imminent future. Though none of these poems is quite as poignant as the marvelous "Raspberries" (from *The Man I Killed*), the kind of detailed exploration they represent, with its delicate balancing of distance and intimacy, is an impressive achievement, the poetic counterpart to the process recorded in fictional terms in his novel *My Grandfather's Grandfather.*

Such poems seem to come from a firm and individual center of experience that Lerner has come to take for granted. For some time he has given the impression of a poet who is working hard on himself and who has a great deal of resourcefulness. His publication in 1999 of a substantial selection of Baudelaire in English verse translation is among the most effective versions to have appeared. Lerner's own poetic idiom, with its combination of clarity and passion, seems an ideal vehicle for the older poet. Conversely, one is made aware of the frequent presence of Baudelaire in Lerner's own original poetry, a major source, one would guess, of its particular strengths.

—Arthur Terry

LEVENSON, Christopher

Nationality: Canadian. **Born:** London, England, 13 February 1934; naturalized Canadian citizen, 1973. **Education:** Harrow Grammar School for Boys, graduated 1952; Downing College, Cambridge, 1954–57, B.A. 1957; University of Bristol, Dip.Ed. 1962; University of Iowa, Iowa City, M.A. 1970. **Military Service:** Conscientious Objector: worked with the Friends Ambulance Unit International Service, 1952–54. **Family:** Married Ursula Frieda Lina Fischer in 1958, four sons (divorced, then remarried in 1977, 1986). **Career:** Taught at the International Quaker School, Eerde, Holland, 1957–58; English Lektor, University of Munster, West Germany, 1958–61; taught at Rodway Technical High School, Mangotsfield, Gloucestershire, 1962–64. Since 1968 member of the department of English, currently associate professor, Carleton University, Ottawa. Editor, *Delta* magazine, two years; editor and co-founder, *ARC* magazine. **Awards:** Eric Gregory award, 1960. **Address:** Department of English, Carleton University, Ottawa, Ontario K1S 5B6, Canada.

PUBLICATIONS

Poetry

New Poets 1959, with Iain Crichton Smith and Karen Gershon. London, Eyre and Spottiswoode, 1959.
Cairns. London, Chatto and Windus/Hogarth Press, 1969.
Stills. London, Chatto and Windus/Hogarth Press, 1972.
Into the Open. Ottawa, Golden Dog Press, 1977.
The Journey Back and Other Poems. Windsor, Ontario, Sesame Press, 1978.
No-Man's-Land. Toronto, League of Canadian Poets, 1980.
Arriving at Night. Oakville, Ontario, Mosaic Press, 1986.

The Return. Hitchin, Hertfordshire, Mandeville Press, 1986.
Half-Truths. Don Mills, Ontario, Wolsak and Wynn, 1990.
Duplicities: New and Selected Poems. Oakville, Ontario, Mosaic Press, 1993.

Other

Editor, *Poetry from Cambridge.* London, Fortune Press, 1958.
Editor and translator, *Seeking Heart's Solace: An Anthology of 16th- and 17th-Century Dutch Love Poems.* Toronto, Aliquando Press, 1981.
Editor, *Light of the World: An Anthology of Seventeenth-Century Dutch Religious and Occasional Poetry.* Windsor, Ontario, Netherlandic Press, 1982.
Editor, *Coming to Canada: Poems,* by Carol Shields. Ottawa, Carleton University Press, 1992.
Editor, *Reconcilable Differences: The Changing Face of Poetry by Canadian Men Since 1970: An Anthology.* Calgary, Bayeux Arts, 1994.

Translator, *Van Gogh,* by Abraham M.W.J. Hammacher. London, Spring, 1961.
Translator, *The Leavetaking,* by Peter Weiss. New York, Harcourt Brace, 1962; with *Vanishing Point,* London, Calder and Boyars, 1966.
Translator, *The Golden Casket: Chinese Novellas of Two Millennia* (translation from the German version by Wolfgang Bauer). London, Allen and Unwin, 1965; Westport, Connecticut, Greenwood Press, 1978.

*

Critical Study: "Four Poets" by Ivan Boldizsar, in *New Hungarian Quarterly* (Budapest), 22(82), summer 1981.

*   *   *

A considerable body of verse by the British-born Canadian poet Christopher Levenson was published in volume form as long ago as 1959. His works may be found in Edwin Muir's compilation *New Poets.* But nobody took sufficient notice of his distinctive voice at the time:

Exiled ambassadors of their heart's country, refugees
Carry their futures in one attache case . . .

In the distorting mirrors of my travels,
Where is tomorrow, now that yesterday
Is bartered for snapshots . . . ?

Past the last city, on to the great plain,
The fevered air grows still, the lights behind us,
Thrown from a thousand scattered windows, blur:
We are alone . . .

It was no accident that the author called this early collection "In Transit," and the word "transit" recurs throughout his work. The characteristic persona is that of an exile observing the scenes through which he passes:

They came here in transit, would not learn the language
Their children gabble, had not meant to stay,
But gradually drained of will, subsided into
The institutional gray . . .

This is a later poem—"Transit Camp"—and the rhymes, though rather insistent, seem an attempt to variegate the Audenism of Levenson's basic verse structure.

There is, in other words, a characteristic cadence in these poems, and it is evoked mainly when the author considers the plight of the wanderer. The cadence is a genuine contribution to contemporary poetry:

I stand, tenebral, gazing down on a city
lost under smoke but luminous, to overhear
its many baffled night sounds, catch its drift
of hasty farewells, and sift through memory
a half-heard language I no longer know
in a remote country . . .

This is a strain dominant in Levenson's later poetry. *Into the Open,* published in 1977, shows the characteristic style, but it is quarrying a deeper vein. The central facts of topography are being allegorized. "Domestic Flight" begins,

From above, the imposed civility
of maps, undeflected straight lines
of concession roads, and farms'
Foursquare geometry excised from wilderness . . .

But the poem dilates on that wilderness—"great gashes of the wolfish dark, / snow-muzzled tundra." The allegory continues through the book. A patient is wired to an encephalograph, and his dreams are explored—"the frenzied writing on the drum descends / to a scrawl of slow valleys."

Most ambitious of all is "The Journey Back," in the book of the same name, which is a long poem of some twenty pages related to the Hungarian composer Béla Bartók's native terrain. It is particularly moving on the subject of Bartók collecting folk songs. An old woman refuses to sing to order:

but he was no sooner gone,
not yet out of earshot, than she started, the melodies
bubbling back like a salt flat spring that the tides had
covered,
restored, woven from silence, for herself only . . .

Levenson does not forget the regime that, at least until the political transformations of the early 1990s in eastern Europe, was hostile to Bartók and, by implication, to all art. The artist cannot sing to order, whether the order is issued by a collector or by the "dark-suited commissars / at the Ministry of Culture."

The poem is a more impressive performance than could have been predicted from the earlier work. In this union of geography, art, and compassion, Levenson seems to have reached a greater linguistic richness and a surer understanding of human motivation in what turned out to be his unexpectedly fertile middle age.

—Philip Hobsbaum

LEVI, Peter (Chad Tigar)

Nationality: British. **Born:** Ruislip, Middlesex, 16 May 1931. **Education:** Prior Park College, Bath; Beaumont College, Berkshire, 1946–48; Campion Hall, Oxford, M.A. 1961; British School of Archaeology, Athens, 1965–68. **Family:** Married Deirdre Craig in 1977. **Career:** Member of the Society of Jesus, 1948–77: ordained priest, 1964; resigned priesthood, 1977. Tutor and lecturer in classics, Campion Hall, 1965–77; lecturer in classics, Christ Church, Oxford, 1979–82. Fellow, St. Catherine's College, Oxford, 1977–2000; professor of poetry, Oxford University, 1984–89. Archaeology correspondent, *The Times,* London, 1977–78. Has also worked as a schoolteacher, archaeologist, and prison chaplain. Member, Kingman Committee on English Literature, 1987–88. **Awards:** Southern Arts literature prize, 1984. Fellow, Society of Antiquaries. Fellow, Royal Society of Literature, 1985. **Agent:** John Johnson, 45 Clerkenwell Green, London EC1, England. **Address:** Prospect Cottage, The Green, Frampton on Severn, Glos GL2 7DY, England. **Died:** 1 February 2000.

PUBLICATIONS

Poetry

Earthly Paradise. Privately printed, 1958.
The Gravel Ponds. London, Deutsch, and New York, Macmillan, 1960.
Orpheus Head. Privately printed, 1962.
Water, Rock, and Sand. London, Deutsch, and Philadelphia, Dufour, 1962.
The Shearwaters. Oxford, Allison, 1965.
Fresh Water, Sea Water. Llandeilo, Carmarthen, and London, Black Raven Press-Deutsch, 1966.
Pancakes for the Queen of Babylon: Ten Poems for Nikos Gatsos. London, Anvil Press Poetry, 1968.
Ruined Abbeys. London, Anvil Press Poetry, 1968.
Life Is a Platform. London, Anvil Press Poetry, 1971.
Death 15 a Pulpit. London, Anvil Press Poetry, 1971.
Penguin Modern Poets 22, with Adrian Mitchell and John Fuller. London, Penguin, 1973.
Collected Poems 1955–1975. London, Anvil Press Poetry, 1976.
Five Ages. London, Anvil Press Poetry, 1978.
Private Ground. London, Anvil Press Poetry, 1981.
The Echoing Green: Three Elegies. London, Anvil Press Poetry, 1983.
The Lamentation of the Dead. London, Anvil Press Poetry, 1984.
Shakespeare's Birthday. London, Anvil Press Poetry, 1985.
Shadow and Bone. London, Anvil Press Poetry, 1989.
Goodbye to the Art of Poetry (lecture in verse). London, Anvil Press Poetry, 1989.
The Marches. London, Merrievale, 1989.
The Rags of Time. London, Anvil Press Poetry, 1994.
Reed Music. London, Anvil Press Poetry, 1997.

Plays

Screenplays: *Ruined Abbeys,* 1966; *Foxes Have Holes,* 1967;

Seven Black Years, 1975; *Art, Faith, and Vision,* 1989.

Novels

The Head in the Soup. London, Constable, 1979.
Grave Witness. London, Quartet, and New York, St. Martin's Press, 1985.
Knit One, Drop One. London, Quartet, 1986; New York, Walker, 1988.
To the Goat (novella). London, Hutchinson, 1988.
Shade Those Laurels by Cyril Connolly, completed by Levi. London, Bellew, 1990.

Other

Beaumont 1861–1961. London, Deutsch, 1961.
The Light Garden of the Angel King: Journeys in Afghanistan. London, Collins, and Indianapolis, Bobbs Merrill, 1972.
John Clare and Thomas Hardy (lecture). London, Athlone Press, 1975.
In Memory of David Jones (sermon). London, The Tablet, 1975.
The Noise Made by Poems. London, Anvil Press Poetry, 1977.
Atlas of the Greek World. Oxford, Phaidon Press, 1980; New York, Facts on File, 1981.
The Hill of Kronos. London, Collins, 1980; New York, Dutton, 1981; as *The Hill of Kronos: A Personal Discovery of Greece.* London, HarperCollins, 1991.
The Greek World, photographs by Eliot Porter. New York, Dutton, 1980; London, Aurum Press, 1981.
The Flutes of Autumn. London, Harvill Press, 1983.
A History of Greek Literature. London and New York, Viking, 1985.
The Frontiers of Paradise: A Study of Monks and Monasteries. London, Collins, 1987; New York, Weidenfeld and Nicolson, 1988.
The Life and Times of William Shakespeare. London, Macmillan 1988; New York, Holt Rinehart, 1989.
Goodbye to the Art of Poetry. London, Anvil Press Poetry, 1989.
Boris Pasternak. London, Century Hutchinson, 1990.
The Art of Poetry: the Oxford Lectures, 1984–1989. New Haven, Yale University Press, 1991.
Atlas of the Greek World. New York, Facts on File, 1991.
Tennyson. London, Macmillan, 1993.
Edward Lear: A Biography. New York, Scribner, 1995.
Eden Renewed: The Public and Private Life of John Milton. New York, St. Martin's Press, 1997.
Horace: A Life. Boston, Routledge and Kegan, 1998.
Virgil: His Life and Times. New York, St. Martin's Press, 1999.

Editor, *The English Bible 1534–1859.* London, Constable, and Grand Rapids, Michigan, Eerdmans, 1974.
Editor, *Pope.* London, Penguin, 1974.
Editor, *A Journey to the Western Isles of Scotland, and The Journal of a Tour to the Hebrides,* by Johnson and Boswell. London, Penguin, 1984.
Editor, *The Penguin Book of Christian Verse.* London, Penguin, 1984.
Editor, *Just So Stories,* by Rudyard Kipling. London, Penguin, 1987.

Translator, with Robin Milner-Gulland, *Selected Poems of Yevtushenko.* London, Penguin, and New York, Dutton, 1962; as *Poems Chosen*

691

by the Author, London, Collins-Harvill Press, 1966; New York, Hill and Wang, 1967.

Translator, *Guide to Greece,* by Pausanias. London, Penguin, 2 vols., 1971.

Translator, *The Psalms.* London, Penguin, 1977.

Translator, *The Cellar,* by George Pavlopoulos. London, Anvil Press Poetry, 1977.

Translator, *The Murderess,* by Alexandros Papadiamantis. London and New York, Writers and Readers, 1983.

Translator, *Marko the Prince* (Serbo-Croat epic poetry). London, Duckworth, and New York, St. Martin's Press, 1984.

Translator, *The Holy Gospel of John.* Worthing, Churchman, 1985; Wilton, Connecticut, Morehouse-Barlow, 1988.

Translator, *Heroic Lament for the Young Lieutenant Lost in Albania,* O. Elytis. Privately printed, 1990.

Translator, *The Revelation of John.* London, Kyle Cathie Ltd., 1992.

*

Manuscript Collection: Boston College, Chestnut Hill, Massachusetts.

Critical Studies: ''Poems without Excuses: Some Notes on Peter Levi'' by Neil Corcoran, in *Agenda* (London), 17(2), 1979; interview with John Haffenden, in *Poetry Review* (London), 74(3), September 1984; Peter Levi Special Issue of *Agenda* (London), 24(3), autumn 1986.

*   *   *

Peter Levi's poetry—like that of Wallace Stevens, with which it sometimes enters into a kind of dialogue—is often concerned with its own procedures. In the early poem ''The Tractor in Spring,'' Levi establishes the connection between language and theme that he has maintained throughout his work:

I want words whose existence is this,
the rough soil and the root work in them,
praising heaven I ever took for theme
this planet, its unnatural wishes,
common reason and human justice,
and growth of life, the last increase of time.

The words he finds for the abstractions of ''reason'' and ''justice'' often create a complex kind of interior landscape in which a mood is evoked or a scene described in order to prompt some defining relation between the human consciousness and its embracing contingencies of nature and of history. In establishing this definition, Levi characteristically uses the mode of elegy.

His favored landscapes are seen through rain, wind, and mist; he imagines himself ''counting the pigeons in the snow-cold air, / listening to small voices of the other birds, / walking in the wind that sweeps this poem bare.'' His sense of history is darkened by a central awareness of what he calls ''the class divisions built into the language'' and by the certainty that the humanist values represented by the language are in decay, that ''in our lives Europe is saying goodnight.'' The poems, then, move ambivalently but honestly between lament and gestures of encouragement. The long poem ''Canticum,'' for instance, arguably one of Levi's major achievements, oscillates between exactly these poles when it attempts to feel

out in language what a world radically different from the one we must live in might be like:

Not one by one but everyone breaks in,
we shall come back with armfuls of lilac
and the crooked trees behind our kitchens
will blossom again. It is the future
which says death to us and which we love.

The desire to discover alternatives to what Levi sees as the debilitation of middle-class English has prompted experimentation with kinds of writing—especially with a kind of gentle surrealism inherited largely from modern Greek poetry—not normally handled by serious contemporary writers in the English tradition. Levi has described this element in the work of George Pavlopoulos, which he has translated, as ''a glitter on the skin of his poems.'' It might also be said of Levi himself. The surrealism of his poetic sequence *Pancakes for the Queen of Babylon,* for example, never entirely loses touch with the real and avoids the more obvious dottinesses of the tradition as it has previously manifested itself in English. This sequence and several others, such as ''Thirty Ways of Drowning in the Sea,'' ''Rivers,'' and ''Five Ages of a Poet,'' are among Levi's most important works.

Levi's later poetry displays a deepened strength and authority, a sureness in his own voice and strategies. But it also reflects a striking out in some interesting new directions. There is a collection of vignettes, like ''Officers and Gentlemen,'' that set a particular social class in the ironic perspectives of history. There also is a handful of finely achieved, tenderly dignified love poems, and the grotesquerie of the ''Pigs'' sequence strikes an altogether different note:

Pigs refuse pork sausages
coated in chocolate. They do sniff them.
Sows murder piglets.
What has some smell of incest
is not sheer cold horror.
Who write this, an old silver-bristle.
I am brutish enough.
They are brutish enough.

Levi's is a unique voice in contemporary English poetry; there is absolutely no one remotely like him. His sadness, his humor, and his preposterously resilient assertiveness (''An easy smell blowing about a hill / is the beginning of the truth about life,'' for instance) are intoxicating. His achievement is remarkable.

—Neil Corcoran

LEVINE, Philip

Nationality: American. **Born:** Detroit, Michigan, 10 January 1928. **Education:** Wayne State University, Detroit, B.A. 1950, M.A. 1955; University of Iowa, Iowa City, M.F.A. 1957; Stanford University, California (fellowship in poetry, 1957). **Family:** Married Frances Artley in 1954; three sons. **Career:** Instructor, University of Iowa, 1955–57. Member of the faculty since 1958, and professor of English, California State University, Fresno, 1969–92. Taught fall semester at

Tufts University, Medford, Massachusetts, 1981–88; Elliston Professor of Poetry, University of Cincinnati, 1976; poet-in-residence, National University of Australia, Canberra, summer 1978; visiting professor, Princeton University, New Jersey, 1978, Columbia University, New York, 1978, 1981, 1984, University of California, Berkeley, 1980, and Brown University, Providence, Rhode Island, 1984; adjunct professor, New York University, 1984; University Professor, Brown University, 1985; visiting professor, Vanderbilt University, spring 1995. **Awards:** San Francisco Foundation Joseph Henry Jackson award, 1961; Chapelbrook award, 1968; National Endowment for the Arts grant, 1969, 1970 (refused), 1976, 1982; Frank O'Hara prize, 1972, and Harriet Monroe memorial prize, 1976 (Poetry, Chicago); American Academy grant, 1973; Guggenheim fellowship, 1973, 1980 (twice); Lenore Marshall prize, 1976; National Book Critics Circle award, 1980; American Book award, 1980; New England Poetry Society Golden Rose, 1987; Ruth Lilly award, 1987; B.A.B.R. award, 1989; *Los Angeles Times* Book prize, and National Book award, 1992, for *What Work Is;* Pulitzer prize, 1995, for *The Simple Truth.* **Address:** 4549 North Van Ness Avenue, Fresno, California 93704, U.S.A.

PUBLICATIONS

Poetry

On the Edge. Iowa City, Stone Wall Press, 1963.
Silent in America: Vivas for Those Who Failed. Iowa City, Shaw Avenue Press, 1965.
Not This Pig. Middletown, Connecticut, Wesleyan University Press, 1968.
Five Detroits. Santa Barbara, California, Unicorn Press, 1970.
Thistles: A Poem Sequence. London, Turret, 1970.
Pili's Wall. Santa Barbara, California, Unicorn Press, 1971.
Red Dust. Santa Cruz, California, Kayak, 1971.
They Feed They Lion. New York, Atheneum, 1972.
1933. New York, Atheneum, 1974.
New Season. Port Townsend, Washington, Graywolf Press, 1975.
On the Edge and Over: Poems Old, Lost, and New. Oakland, Cloud Marauder Press, 1976.
The Names of the Lost. New York, Atheneum, 1976; with *They Feed They Lion,* New York, Knopf, 1999.
7 Years from Somewhere. New York, Atheneum, 1979.
Ashes: Poems New and Old. New York, Atheneum, 1979.
One for the Rose. New York, Atheneum, 1981.
Selected Poems. New York, Atheneum, and London, Secker and Warburg, 1984.
Sweet Will. New York, Atheneum, 1985.
A Walk with Tom Jefferson. New York, Knopf, 1988.
What Work Is. New York, Knopf, 1991.
New Selected Poems. New York, Knopf, 1991.
The Simple Truth. New York, Knopf, 1994.
Smoke. Toledo, Ohio, Aureole Press, 1997.
Unselected Poems. Santa Cruz, California, Greenhouse Review Press, 1997.
The Mercy: Poems. New York, Knopf, 1999.

Recording: *The Poetry and Voice of Philip Levine,* Caedmon, 1976; *Hear Me,* Watershed, 1977.

Other

Don't Ask (interviews). Ann Arbor, University of Michigan Press, 1981.
The Bread of Time: Toward an Autobiography. New York, Knopf, 1994.

Editor, with Henri Coulette, *Character and Crisis: A Contemporary Reader.* New York, McGraw Hill, 1966.
Editor, and Translator, with Ernesto Trejo, *Tarumba: The Selected Poems of Jaime Sabines.* San Francisco, Twin Peaks Press, 1979.
Editor and Translator, with Ada Long, *Off the Map: Selected Poems of Gloria Fuertes.* Middletown, Connecticut, Wesleyan University Press, 1984.
Editor, *The Essential Keats.* New York, Ecco Press, 1987.

*

Critical Studies: By X.J. Kennedy, in *Poetry* (Chicago), 1964; by Robert Dana, in *North American Review* (Mt. Vernon, Iowa), 1964; by Hayden Carruth, in *Hudson Review* (New York), 1968; "Personally, I'd Rather Be in Fresno" by Stuart Peterfreund, in *New: American and Canadian Poetry 15* (Trumansburg, New York), May 1971; "Borges and Strand, Weak Henry, Philip Levine" by James McMichael, in *Southern Review* (Baton Rouge, Louisiana), winter 1972; "Interview with Philip Levine," in *American Poetry Review* (Philadelphia), 1(1), 1972; "'The True and Earthly Prayer': Philip Levine's Poetry," in *American Poetry Review* (Philadelphia), 3(2), 1974, and "Back to This Life," in *New England Review* (Hanover, New Hampshire), winter 1979–80, both by Ralph J. Mills, Jr.; "The Burned Essential Oil: The Poetry of Philip Levine" by Charles Molesworth, in *Hollins Critic* (Virginia), December 1975; "Philip Levine" by Calvin Bedient, in *Sewanee Review* (Tennessee), spring 1976; "New Poems" by Jay Parini, in *Poetry* (Chicago), August 1977; "Bringing It Home" by Stephen Yenser, in *Parnassus* (New York), fall-winter 1977; "The Poetry of Anarchism" by Paul Bernard, in *Marxist Perspectives,* summer 1979; "The Politics of Philip Levine" by Phoebe Pettingen, in *New Leader* (New York), 13 August 1979; "The Second Self" by Dave Smith, in *American Poetry Review* (Philadelphia), November-December 1979; William Matthews, in *Ohio Review* 26 (Athens), 1981; *On the Poetry of Philip Levine: Stranger to Nothing* edited by Christopher Buckley, Ann Arbor, University of Michigan Press, 1989; "In the Tradition of American Jewish Poetry: Philip Levine's Turning" by Richard Chess, in *Studies in American Jewish Literature* (University Park, Pennsylvania), 9(2), fall 1990; "Philip Levine on Teaching Poetry: An Interview" by Sally A. Jacobsen, in *Poets' Perspectives: Reading, Writing, and Teaching Poetry,* edited by Jacobsen and Charles R. Duke, Portsmouth, New Hampshire, Boynton/Cook, 1992; "The Visionary Poetics of Philip Levine and Charles Wright" by Edward Hirsch, in *The Columbia History of American Poetry,* edited by Jay Parini and Brett C. Millier, New York, Columbia University Press, 1993; *Tapinosis in the Poetry of Frank O'Hara and Philip Levine* (dissertation) by Ellen Anne Ferguson, Washington University, 1996; interview with Paul Mariani, in *Image* (Kennett Square, Pennsylvania), 14, summer 1996; "New Jerusalems: Contemporary Jewish American Poets and the Puritan Tradition" by Jonathan N. Barron, in *The Calvinist Roots of the Modern Era,* edited by Aliki Barnstone and Michael Tomasek Manson, Hanover, New Hampshire, University Press of New England, 1997.

Philip Levine comments:

I have said elsewhere that I tried to write poetry for people for whom there is no poetry, and I believe that is true even though I said it twenty years ago. Those were the people of Detroit, the people I grew up with who brothered, sistered, fathered, and mothered me and lived and worked beside me. Their presence seemed utterly lacking in the poetry I inherited at age twenty, so I have spent the last forty-some years trying to add to our poetry what was not there.

*　　*　　*

The poetry of Philip Levine is somber, reflective, and honest. It is spare in form, taut in expression, simple in idiom. Levine has turned away from conventional metrical form and rhyme to write largely in blank or free verse, often in flexible three- or four-beat lines. He employs the image, hard, clean, and concrete, stripped of effusive sentiment, free from intellectual editorials. Levine protests against the evils of the modern world and searches for personal freedom and fulfillment. At its best his poetry, highly personal and nostalgic, is stark, restrained, and powerful.

Levine often indicts modern urban life, exposing its joyless futility and ugliness. Witness these lines from "Clouds":

Morning is exhaustion, tranquilizers, gasoline,
the screamings of frozen bearings,
the failures of will, the TV talking to itself.

The clouds go on eating oil, cigars,
housewives, sighing letters,
the breath of lies. In their great silent pockets
they carry off all our dead.

For their silence and acquiescence the poet concludes that clouds "should be punished every morning, / they should be bitten and boiled like spoons." The anger here frequently modulates into lament over the eternally gray cityscapes, the meaningless motions, the endless Mondays "shrill with the smells of garbage / and gasoline." The poet's struggle to find a place in such a world often provokes confrontation with the past, present, and future. Most things valuable and precious, he uneasily realizes, are subject to time, to the power that turns all to ash. "New Season" meditates on the poet's mother turning seventy and concludes with striking and direct imagery:

the woman
is 70 now—the willow is burning,
the rhododendrons shrivel
like paper under water, all
the small secret mouths are feeding
on the green heart of the plum.

"Starlight" recalls the lost embrace of the poet's father and the lost world of childhood. Evident here is Levine's preoccupation with domestic life. In his darker moments he articulates the disappointments and pains of family relations. In "Father" the poet hisses, "Don't come back"; in "My Son and I" he portrays the huge and silent spaces between himself and his son.

Yet, despite sensitivity to the assault on civilized life and to the pang of existential isolation, Levine sometimes finds cause for hope and joy. On such occasions his poems are hard-won affirmations, not facile celebrations. The poet draws inspiration from the earth and elemental things. In "Holding On," for example, he observes "green fingers / holding the hillside, / mustard whipping in / the sea winds, one blood-bright / poppy breathing in / and out," and he declares, "40 miles from Málaga / half the world away / from home, I am home and / nowhere, a man who envies / grass." In "A Sleepless Night," after noticing plum blossoms, sycamores, limes, poppies, and a mockingbird, he concludes, "A man has every place to lay his head." Levine also finds pleasure in old friends and acquaintances, especially those who are colorful outcasts. There are Uncle Joe, rough and salacious, who tenderly held up the newborn poet so that he could see the winter sun ("No One Remembers"); blind Tatum, who "can't hardly wait" to "see" Willie Mays ("On the Corner"); Cal, "short for Calla, the lily," who sleeps on the job, at peace in the rain ("Making It New"). The most serious affirmations are poignantly imperfect victories of love over loneliness. In "Lost and Found" "father and child / hand in hand, the living and / the dead" enter the world; in "The Rains" the poet promises that he and his wife, also "hand in hand," will one day transcend the world, "soured / with years of never / giving enough, darkened / with oils and fire," to go forward "while our clothes darken / and our faces stream / with the sweet waters / of heaven." As the poet says in "Sources," we do have each other.

For the most part Levine is an introspective poet. His later volumes, however, show serious concern with the Spanish Civil War, the setting for several moving tributes to fallen soldiers ("On the Murder of Lieutenant José Del Castillo by the Falangist Bravo Martinez, July 12, 1936," "For the Fallen," "Montjuich," "Francisco, I'll Bring You Red Carnations"). Though limited in range and overreliant on minor chords, Levine's music is distinctive and intelligently modern.

—Robert Miola

LIEBERMAN, Laurence (James)

Nationality: American. **Born:** Detroit, Michigan, 16 February 1935. **Education:** University of Michigan, Ann Arbor (Hopwood award, 1958), B.A. 1956, M.A. in English 1958; University of California, Berkeley. **Family:** Married Bernice Braun in 1956; one son and two daughters. **Career:** Former poetry editor, *Orange County Illustrated and Orange County Sun,* California. Taught at Orange Coast College, Costa Mesa, California, 1960–64, and College of the Virgin Islands, St. Thomas, 1964–68. Associate professor of English, 1968–70, and since 1970 professor of English, University of Illinois, Urbana. Creative Writing Fellow, University of Illinois Center for Advanced Studies, Japan, 1971–72. Poetry reviewer, *Yale Review,* 1968–74. Since 1971 poetry editor, University of Illinois Press. **Awards:** Yaddo fellowship, 1963, 1967; Huntington Hartford Foundation fellowship, 1964; National Endowment for the Arts grant, 1969, 1986; University of Illinois Center for Advanced Study grant, 1971, 1981; Illinois Arts Council fellowship, 1982, 1990–91, 1994; Jerome Shestack award, *American Poetry Review,* 1986; University of Illinois Center for Advanced Study grant, 1991, 2000; Arnold Beckman fellowship in creative writing, 1993. **Address:** Department of English, University of Illinois, Urbana, Illinois 61801, U.S.A.

PUBLICATIONS

Poetry

The Unblinding. New York, Macmillan, 1968.

The Osprey Suicides. New York, Macmillan, and London, Collier Macmillan, 1973.

God's Measurements. New York, Macmillan, 1980.

Eros at the World Kite Pageant: Poems 1979–1982. New York, Macmillan, 1983.

The Mural of Wakeful Sleep. New York, Macmillan, 1985.

The Creole Mephistopheles. New York, Scribner, 1989.

New and Selected Poems: 1962–92. Urbana, University of Illinois Press, 1993.

The St. Kitts Monkey Funds. Omaha, Nebraska, The Cummington Press, 1995.

Dark Songs: Slave House and Synagogue. Fayetteville, University of Arkansas Press, 1996.

Compass of the Dying. Fayetteville, University of Arkansas Press, 1998.

The Regatta in the Skies: Selected Long Poems. Athens, University of Georgia Press, 1999.

Flight from the Mother Stone. Fayetteville, University of Arkansas Press, 2000.

Other

Unassigned Frequencies: American Poetry in Review 1964–77. Urbana, University of Illinois Press, 1977.

Beyond the Muse of Memory: Essays on Contemporary American Poets. Columbia, University of Missouri Press, 1995.

Editor, *The Achievement of James Dickey: A Comprehensive Selection of His Poems with a Critical Introduction.* Chicago, Scott Foresman, 1968.

*

Critical Studies: "Fool, Thou Poet" by Vernon Young, in *Hudson Review* (New York), winter 1973–74; "Tough Scarskins" by John R. Cooley, in *Modern Poetry Studies* (Buffalo), winter 1974; "All's a Mirroring," in *Mississippi Valley Review* (Macomb, Illinois), spring 1974, and "The Expansional Muse of Laurence Lieberman," in *Chariton Review* (Kirksville, Missouri), fall 1996, both by James Ballowe; "Generous Props," in *Counter/Measures 3,* 1974, and "Castles, Elephants, Budhas...," in *American Poetry Review* (Philadelphia), May-June 1981, both by Dave Smith; "Actions Undone" by Richard Johnson, in *Parnassus* (New York), fall-winter 1974; "Poems and Pictures" by David Quemada, in *New Letters* (Kansas City), March 1975; "Bending and Unbending into Beatitudes" by Ronald Wallace, in *Chowder Review* (Amherst, Massachusetts), summer 1980; Leonard Neufeldt, in *New England Review* (Hanover, New Hampshire), summer 1980; "Radiance beyond Measure" by Peter Mackuck, in *Tar River Poetry* (Greenville, North Carolina), fall 1980; "Acts of Grace: About One of Laurence Lieberman's Poems," in *Chariton Review* (Kirksville, Missouri), fall 1980, "Convergences," in *Sewanee Review* (Tennessee), summer 1984, and "Another Life Lurking," *Southern Review,* 33(2), spring 1997, all by Thomas Swiss; "Dimensions of Reality" by Peter Stitt, in *Georgia Review*

(Athens), winter 1980–81; "Confessions of Travelers and Pilgrims" by Peter Serchuk, in *Sewanee Review* (Tennessee), spring 1981; "Poets and Peddlers" by Harry Thomas, in *Michigan Quarterly Review* (Ann Arbor), winter 1982; by G.E. Murray, in *Quarterly West* (Salt Lake City), fall-winter 1982–83; by Robert Hill, in *South Carolina Review* (Clemson), fall 1983; "Gaijin's Measurements," in *Parnassus* (New York), winter 1984–85; "Poetry Changes & Channels" by Robert McDowell, in *The Hudson Review* (New York), winter 1986; "Poetry Travels" by James Finn Cotter, in *Hudson Review* (New York), autumn 1989, "The Wider World Dimension: The Carib Chronicle of Laurence Lieberman" by Michael Bujega, in *Chariton Review* (Kirksville, Missouri), spring 1990; "Innocent Abroad" by Brendan Galvin, in *Tar River Poetry* (Greenville, North Carolina), fall 1990; "Poetry Preserves" by James Finn Cotter, in *The Hudson Review* (New York), summer 1994; "Travelogue Poetry: The Narrative Vision of Laurence Lieberman" by Samuel Maio, in *Chariton Review* (Kirksville, Missouri), spring 1994; "Who Can Resist the Stories? Narrative and Witness in the Cross-Cultural Poetry of Laurence Lieberman" by Sandra Meek, in *Denver Quarterly,* 31(3), winter 1997; "The Guest of History" by David Kirby, in *Parnassus* (New York), 22, 1997.

Laurence Lieberman comments:

(1975) My first and second volumes of poetry, *The Unblinding* and *The Osprey Suicides,* dealt principally with the four years I spent in St. Thomas (1964–68), exploring life in the Caribbean and the underwater world of the coral reefs as their primary subject. The underwater cycle of poems spanned two books, much as I expect my cycle of poems in progress about Japan to span the next two books. *God's Measurements* was completed this year, and it contains roughly half of the poems I plan to write about Japan, where I spent a year on a traveling fellowship (1971–72).

*　　*　　*

For more than three decades Laurence Lieberman has been creating his own brand of poetry. His effort to create a world of discovered beauty based almost entirely on travel to rich and exotic lands and to the bottom of the sea is unique. Since his first book, published in 1968, he has taken us with him on journeys to southern California, Hawaii, Japan, and various islands in the Caribbean. At first the poetry was a kind of novelty, a unique excursion of a talented poet into the exquisite moments of discovery of the relationship of being and things. The poems in *The Unblinding, The Osprey Suicides,* and *God's Measurements* tend to be wonderful epiphanies of inspired moments of relatedness with nature. In two later volumes, *The Mural of Wakeful Sleep* and *The Creole Mephistopheles,* however, he repeats the pattern of the long free verse narrative travelogue but without the same intensity of the earlier verse. Too frequently poems bog down in banalities such as "flippered feet," "rubbery ice skates," "the adjacent cow's wriggly orbit," "the one six letter verb which best expresses the freakish displacement of liquid and solid bodies in air—SPLASH."

Nonetheless, when Lieberman makes the best use of language, he achieves a kind of baroque or Elizabethan eloquence that transforms his experience into art. Lieberman's first volume, *The Unblinding,* reveals his attempt to find his subject and medium. In the remarkable poem "The Family Tree" he finds it; he discovers a felt—not thought—relationship between his life and the life of things, which grow together as one. The development of his work over the years may be seen as a continual effort to capture this fundamental oneness of inner and outer. Unlike so many of his contemporaries who deal with the problems of self in a decadent modern world, he discovers a world he can embrace that secures him from the sickness of the age.

In the title poem of *The Unblinding* Lieberman speaks of the "tough, unknown, real images that burn his senses and mind," "incandescent moments that fall into his hands unsought, undeservedly given or lent . . . visions . . . that can—and do on occasion—sweep me off into their own orbits." No alienated poet here, but rather a voice, a vehicle through which the power of "incandescent moments" sing. His travels to Japan, Hawaii, and the Caribbean provide him a locale and subject matter for the force that illuminates his imaginative life. In *The Unblinding* he had already discovered the stark and beautiful power of the sea as a medium for his poetic exploration, but in *The Osprey Suicides, God's Measurements,* and *Eros at the World Kite Pageant* he reaches out to this world with the poise and dexterity of a poet who has found his voice and subject. So committed to this world is Lieberman that *The Osprey Suicides* might be subtitled "the underwater world of Laurence Lieberman." No poet before him has written so devotedly and with such knowledge of this world. In these poems he searches the depths of faraway oceans, tides, and bays, seeking in coral and sea creatures a vision of an ultimate truth. Lurking in underwater caverns, in subterranean darkness, strange life-forms challenge his senses, confound his mind. Lieberman, however, is not merely a spectator in this underwater world but also often an intruder. He hunts with a spear gun and kills for sport. Although such a relationship with this world suggests a fundamental alienation, the events of the poems are much like a Faulkner or Hemingway encounter with nature. Not only is there the moment of self-discovery and affirmation in the act of the hunt but also an experience of ultimate power; the hunt becomes a search for God. In the final section of *The Osprey Suicides* Lieberman describes the danger of the hunt: the predator may become victim, may in fact become his own death wish.

In *Eros at the World Kite Pageant* Lieberman breaks new metaphysical ground. The poem "Psychodrama: Tokyo Mime Film" pushes his quasi-mystical passion for relationship or quest for life to new heights. In this poem the poet provides us with a vision of a profound psychic energy that pushes outward into the vacancy of the nonself to embrace and incorporate it as part of the oneness that he has sought throughout his work. This oneness is like that of the Buber I-Thou relationship: being is achieved only through a relationship that allows each partner to be both itself and affirmed. Such is Lieberman's relationship with the world. Sometimes fraught with violence, sometimes threatening to destroy the poet himself, this relationship is the hard-fought battle to overcome the alienation of a century and to establish a renewed covenant with things.

In *The Mural of Wakeful Sleep* and *The Creole Mephistopheles* Lieberman continues his search in the Caribbean for that essence of relationship between inner and outer, between himself and things. His effort seems not to succeed, however, as his insistence on returning to the same format and style of his previous poetry works against him. One reads with the sense of having been here before. The language lacks the eloquence and precision of the earlier work, and the form of long narrative is overworked. Even so, there are moments when the poems—such as "Banana Dwarf" or parts of "The Mural of Wakeful Sleep"—achieve a lyrical beauty that reminds us of the best of Lieberman.

—Richard Damashek

LIFSHIN, Lyn (Diane)

Nationality: American. **Born:** Lyn Diane Lipman, Burlington, Vermont, 12 July 1946. **Education:** Syracuse University, New York, B.A. 1961; University of Vermont, Burlington, M.A. 1963; Brandeis University, Waltham, Massachusetts; State University of New York, Albany, 1964–66; Bread Loaf School of English, Vermont. **Family:** Married Eric Lifshin in 1966. **Career:** Teaching Fellow, State University of New York, Albany, 1964–66; educational television writer, Schenectady, New York, 1966; instructor, State University of New York, Cobleskill, 1968, 1970; writing consultant, Mental Health Department, 1970, and Empire State College, 1973, both Albany; poet-in-residence, Mansfield State College, Pennsylvania, 1974, University of Rochester, New York, 1986, and Antioch Writers Conference, 1987. **Awards:** Hart Crane award; Yaddo fellowship, 1970, 1971, 1975, 1979, 1980; MacDowell fellowship, 1973; Millay Colony fellowship, 1975, 1979; Creative Artists Public Service award, 1976; Cherry Valley Editions Jack Kerouac award, 1984; Madelin Sadin award, 1989. **Address:** 2142 Apple Tree Lane, Niskayuna, New York 12309, U.S.A.

PUBLICATIONS

Poetry

Why Is the House Dissolving. San Francisco, Open Skull Press, 1968.
Femina 2. Oshkosh, Wisconsin, Abraxas Press, 1970.
Leaves and Night Things. West Lafayette, Indiana, Baby John Press, 1970.
Black Apples. Trumansburg, New York, Crossing Press, 1971; revised edition, 1973.
Tentacles, Leaves. Belmont, Massachusetts, Hellric Press, 1972.
Moving by Touch. Traverse City, Michigan, Cotyledon Press, 1972.
Lady Lyn. Milwaukee, Morgan Press, 1972.
Mercurochrome Sun Poems. Tacoma, Washington, Charis Press, 1972.
I'd Be Jeanne Moreau. Milwaukee, Morgan Press, 1972.
Love Poems. Durham, New Hampshire, Zahir Press, 1972.
Undressed. Traverse City, Michigan, Cotyledon Press, 1972.
Lyn Lifshin. Durham, New Hampshire, Zahir Press, 1972.
Poems by Suramm and Lyn Lifshin. Madison, Wisconsin, Union Literary Committee, 1972.
Forty Days, Apple Nights. Milwaukee, Morgan Press, 1973.
Audley End Poems. Long Beach, California, MAG Press, 1973.
The First Week Poems. Plum Island, Massachusetts, Zahir Press, 1973.
Museum. Albany, New York, Conspiracy Press, 1973.
All the Women Poets I Ever Liked Didn't Hate Their Fathers. St. Petersburg, Florida, Konglomerati, 1973.
The Old House on the Croton. San Lorenzo, California, Shameless Hussy Press, 1973.
Poems. Minneapolis, Northstone, 1974.
Selected Poems. Trumansburg, New York, Crossing Press, 1974.
Upstate Madonna: Poems 1970–1974. Trumansburg, New York, Crossing Press, 1974.
Shaker House. Tannersville, New York, Tideline Press, 1974.
Blue Fingers. Milwaukee, Shelter Press, 1974.
Plymouth Women. Milwaukee, Morgan Press, 1974.
Shaker House Poems. Chatham, New York, Sagarin Press, 1974.

Mountain Moving Day. Trumansburg, New York, Crossing Press, 1974.

Walking thru Audley End Mansion Late Afternoon and Drifting into Certain Faces. Long Beach, California, MAG Press, 1974.

Blue Madonna. Milwaukee, Shelter Press, 1974.

Poems. Gulfport, Florida, Konglomerati, 1974.

Green Bandages. Genesco, New York, Hidden Springs, 1975.

Old House Poems. Santa Barbara, California, Capra Press, 1975.

North Poems. Milwaukee, Morgan Press, 1976.

Naked Charm. N.p., Fireweed Press, 1976.

Paper Apples. Stockton, California, Wormwood, 1976.

Some Madonna Poems. Buffalo, White Pine Press, 1976.

More Waters. Cincinnati, Waters, 1977.

The January Poems. Cincinnati, More Waters, 1977.

Pantagonia. Stockton, California, Wormwood, 1977.

Mad Girl Poems. Wichita, Kansas, Caprice Out of Sight Press, 1977.

Lifshin & Richmond. Oakland, California, Bombay Duck, 1977.

Poems, with John Elsberg. Filey, Yorkshire, Fiasco, 1978.

Offered by Owner. Cambridge, New York, Natalie Slohm, 1978.

Leaning South. New York, Red Dust, 1978.

Glass. Milwaukee, Morgan Press, 1978.

Early Plymouth Women. Milwaukee, Morgan Press, 1978.

Crazy Arms. Chicago, Ommation Press, 1978.

Doctors. Santa Barbara, California, Mudborn, 1979.

35 Sundays. Chicago, Ommation Press, 1979.

Men and Cars. Ware, Massachusetts, Four Zoas Press, 1979.

More Naked Charm. Los Angeles, Illuminati Press, 1979.

Madonna. Stockton, California, Wormwood, 1980.

Lips on That Blue Rail. San Francisco, Lion's Breath, 1980.

Colors of Cooper Black. Milwaukee, Morgan Press, 1981.

Leaving the Bough. New York, New World Press, 1982.

Blue Dust, New Mexico. Fredonia, New York, Basilisk Press, 1982.

Finger Prints. Stockton, California, Wormwood, 1982.

In the Dark with Just One Star. Milwaukee, Morgan Press, 1982.

Want Ads. Milwaukee, Morgan Press, 1982.

Lobster and Oatmeal. Sacramento, California, Pinch Penny, 1982.

Reading Lips. Milwaukee, Morgan Press, 1982.

Hotel Lifshin. Eureka, California, Poetry Now, 1982.

Blue Horses Nuzzle Tuesday. Burlingame, California, Minotaur Press, 1983.

Madonna Who Shifts for Herself. Long Beach, California, Applezaba, 1983.

Naked Charm (collection). Los Angeles, Illuminati Press, 1984.

The Radio Psychic Is Shaving Her Legs. Detroit, Planet Detroit, 1984.

Matinee. Chicago, Ommation Press, 1984.

Kiss the Skin Off. Cherry Valley, New York, Cherry Valley, Editions, 1985.

Remember the Ladies. East Lansing, Michigan, Ghost Dance Press, 1985.

Camping Madonna. Portlandville, New York, MAF Press, 1986.

Vergin' Mary and Madonna. El Paso, Texas, Vergin Press, 1986.

Raw Opals. Los Angeles, Illuminati Press, 1987.

The Daughter May Be Let Go. Harbor Beach, Florida, Clock Radio Press, 1987.

Red Hair and the Jesuit. Parkdale, Oregon, Trout Creek Press, 1988.

Many Madonnas, edited by Virginia I. Long. St. John, Kansas, Kindred Spirit Press, 1988.

Rubbed Silk. Los Angeles, Illuminati Press, 1988.

Dance Poems. Chicago, Ommation Press, 1988.

The Doctor. Los Angeles, Applezaba, 1990.

Blood Road. Los Angeles, Illuminati Press, 1989.

Reading Lips. Milwaukee, Morgan Press, 1989.

Skin Divers, with Belinda Subraman. Leeds, Yorkshire, Krax, 1989.

Under Velvet Pillows. Middletown Springs, Vermont, Four Zoas Press, 1989.

Not Made of Glass. Saratoga Springs, New York, Karista, 1990.

Reading Lips. Milwaukee, Morgan Press, 1992.

Marilyn Monroe. Portland, Oregon, Quiet Lion, 1994.

Appleblossoms. East Lansing, Michigan, Ghostdance, 1994.

Parade. Stockton, California, Wormwood, 1994.

Shooting Kodachromes in the Dark. Manotick, Ontario, Penumbra Press, 1994.

Blue Tattoo. Desert Hot Springs, California, Event Horizon Press, 1995.

Cold Comfort. Santa Rosa, California, Black Sparrow Press, 1997.

Before It's Light. Santa Rosa, California, Black Sparrow Press, 1999.

Recordings: *Lyn Lifshin Reads Her Poems,* Women's Audio Exchange, 1977; *Offered by Owner,* Slohm, 1978.

Play

Screenplay: *Not Made of Glass,* 1989.

Other

Editor, *Tangled Vines: A Collection of Mother and Daughter Poems.* Boston, Beacon Press, 1978.

Editor, *Ariadne's Thread: A Collection of Contemporary Women's Journals.* New York, Harper, 1982.

Editor, *Lips Unsealed.* Santa Barbara, California, Capra Press, 1990.

*

Bibliography: By Marvin Malone, in *Wormwood Review* (Stockton, California), 12(3), 1971.

Manuscript Collection: University of Texas, Austin; Temple University, Philadelphia, Pennsylvania.

Critical Studies: By Bill Katz, in *Library Journal* (New York), June 1971, and December 1972; Carol Rainey, in *Road Apple Review* (Albuquerque, New Mexico), summer-fall 1971; Victor Contoski, in *Northeast* (La Crosse, Wisconsin), fall-winter 1971–72; James Naiden, in *Minneapolis Star,* 18 April 1972; Dave Etter, in *December* (West Springs, Illinois), 1972; ''Lyn Lifshin'' by Jim Evans in *Windless Orchard* (Fort Wayne, Indiana), summer 1972; Eric Mottram, in *Little Magazine* (New York), summer-fall 1972; *New York Times Book Review,* 18 December 1978; ''Lyn Lifshin Issue'' of *Poetry Now* (Eureka, California), 1980, and *Greenfield Review* (Greenfield Center, New York), 1983; ''Breathing Poems: An Interview with Lyn Lifshin'' by Jay Dougherty, in *BOGG,* 60, 1988.

Lyn Lifshin comments:

I'm usually better at doing something than talking about how and why I do it. One time I spent days trying to say how I wanted the words to be connected to touch the reader's body. Somehow. Except that sounded strange, and so I tore it up . . . It seems to me that the poem has to be sensual (not necessarily sexual, tho that's OK too) before it can be anything else. So rhythm matters a lot to me, most, or at least first. Before images even. I want whoever looks at, whoever eats, the poem to feel the way old ebony feels at four o'clock in a cold Van Cortlandt mansion, or the smell of lemons in a strange place, or skin.

Words that I like to hear other people say the poems are are strong, tight, real, startling, tough, tender, sexy, physical, controlled—that they celebrate (Carol Rainey), reflect joy in every aspect of being a woman (James Naiden).

I always steal things I like from people, other poets, especially from blues, old black and country blues rhythms (after most readings people come and ask how, where I started reading the way I do; another mystery really). So I was glad to have Dave Etter say that *Black Apples* "comes on like a stack of Cannonball Adderley records, blowing cool, blowing hot, sometimes lyrical and sweet, sometimes hard bop, terse and tough."

*   *   *

Perhaps no other contemporary American poet has been as widely published as Lyn Lifshin, whose prolific production has sometimes overshadowed the true range and significance of her work. From her early poems—written soon after her departure from the academic world, to which, unlike many other poets, she has never returned—in which she presents with painful accuracy the shallowness and insincerity of a world where one may "fail to understand the requirements," to her later work, in which she enters the lives of such diverse people as women in early Plymouth and Indians on exhibit in museums and deals straightforwardly with her own family, especially the relationship between mother and daughter, she has been a risk taker. The risk has been most obvious, perhaps, in her poems on sexuality, in which both the emotional and the physical relationships between men and women are laid bare. One would be hard-pressed to find another writer who has done as thorough a job of evoking the despair of a woman caught in the traps that social restrictions and marriage create for Americans. She is far more than a poet with only one subject, however, even though her voice is one that is always recognizable.

Lifshin's poetry is characterized by a breathless quality, a voice reflected by pages of short lines, incomplete sentences, pauses, and sudden revelations. Until the moment of explosion, her poems can be disarmingly simple. At times her candor, especially about sex, is as hard and cold as the sound of feet on the pavement of a red-light district late at night. Few have written more bitingly or more tenderly about modern sexual mores, especially as reflected in the lives of women. At other times, in her so-called Madonna poems, for example, she explores worlds in which the line between physical experience and imagination blurs. Lifshin's many Madonnas are both modern and widely archetypal, both funny and sad, as shown by titles such as "Parachute Madonna" and "Shifting for Herself Madonna."

Although Lifshin's poems are the result of an almost religious devotion to her craft, she seems to reach many of the final versions not so much by rewriting and reworking a single poem as by producing series that gradually—or even cumulatively—reach the desired effect. The result is a body of work that is impressive in its size, almost epic in proportion, an irony when one considers that few individual Lifshin poems are more than thirty lines in length. Her work might be seen, in fact, as a journey through her own life and through time, through the lives of other women (her work as an anthologist is an indication of her interest in the writing of women in general), creating a poetic collage of the latter part of the twentieth century, its optimism and its depressions. In the midst of all this she has placed herself,

continually searching for meaning and identity as a woman, as a poet, as one of Jewish heritage, as a threatened member of the human species in the confusing landscape of history, personal liberty, and social reality.

Whereas the writers of classical times wrote long, connected epics, Lifshin has ventured forth with short lyrics. Her voice is that of a female Odysseus, sometimes confused, often innocent, but always tenacious, one whose journey takes us along and teaches us as we go.

—Joseph Bruchac

LINDSAY, (John) Maurice

Nationality: Scottish. **Born:** Glasgow, 21 July 1918. **Education:** Glasgow Academy, 1928–36; Scottish National Academy of Music, now the Royal Scottish Academy of Music, Glasgow, 1936–39. **Military Service:** Cameronians (Scottish Rifles) at the Staff College, Camberley, Surrey, and in the War Office during World War II. **Family:** Married Aileen Joyce Gordon in 1946; one son and three daughters. **Career:** Drama critic, *Scottish Daily Mail,* Edinburgh, 1946–47; music critic, *The Bulletin,* Glasgow, 1946–60; editor, *Scots Review,* 1949–50; program controller, 1961–62, production controller, 1962–64, and features executive and chief interviewer, 1964–67, Border Television, Carlisle. Director, 1967–83, and since 1983 consultant, Scottish Civic Trust, Glasgow. Editor, with Douglas Young, Saltire Modern Poets series, 1964; editor, 1976–80, and editor, with Alexander Scott, 1980–89, *Scottish Review.* Honorary secretary-general, Europa Nostra, 1983–90. Honorary Fellow, Royal Incorporation of Architects in Scotland, 1985. **Awards:** Atlantic Rockefeller award, 1946. D.Litt.: University of Glasgow, 1982. C.B.E. (Commander, Order of the British Empire), 1979. **Address:** Park House, 104 Dumbarton Road, Bowling G60 4BB, Scotland.

PUBLICATIONS

Poetry

The Advancing Day. Privately printed, 1940.
Perhaps To-morrow. Oxford, Blackwell, 1941.
Predicament. Oxford, Alden Press, 1942.
No Crown for Laughter. London, Fortune Press, 1943.
The Enemies of Love: Poems 1941–1945. Glasgow, Maclellan, 1946.
Selected Poems. Edinburgh, Oliver and Boyd, 1947.
Hurlygush: Poems in Scots. Edinburgh, Serif, 1948.
At the Wood's Edge. Edinburgh, Serif, 1950.
Ode for St. Andrews Night and Other Poems. Edinburgh, New Alliance, 1951.
The Exiled Heart: Poems 1941–1956, edited by George Bruce. London, Hale, 1957.
Snow Warning and Other Poems. Arundel, Sussex, Linden Press, 1962.
One Later Day and Other Poems. London, Brookside Press, 1964.
This Business of Living. Preston, Lancashire, Akros, 1971.
Comings and Goings. Preston, Lancashire, Akros, 1971.
Selected Poems 1942–1972. London, Hale, 1973.
The Run from Life: More Poems 1942–1972. Burford, Oxfordshire, Cygnet Press, 1975.
Walking without an Overcoat: Poems 1972–76. London, Hale, 1977.

Collected Poems, edited by Alexander Scott. Edinburgh, Paul Harris, 1979.

A Net to Catch the Winds and Other Poems. London, Hale, 1981.

The French Mosquitoes' Woman and Other Diversions. London, Hale, 1985.

Requiem for a Sexual Athlete and Other Poems and Diversions. London, Hale, 1988.

Collected Poems 1940–90. Aberdeen, Aberdeen University Press, 1990.

On the Face of It: Collected Poems Volume 2. London, Hale, 1993.

News of the World: Last Poems. Edinburgh, Scottish Cultural Press, 1994.

Speaking Likenesses. Edinburgh, Scottish Cultural Press, 1998.

Worlds Apart. Edinburgh, Diehard, 2000.

Plays

Fingal and Comala (produced Braemar, 1953; London, 1958).

The Abbot of Drimock, music by Thea Musgrave (produced London, 1958).

The Decision, music by Thea Musgrave (produced London, 1967). London, Chester, 1967.

Other

A Pocket Guide to Scottish Culture. Glasgow, Maclellan, 1947.

The Scottish Renaissance. Edinburgh, Serif, 1949.

The Lowlands of Scotland: Glasgow and the North, Edinburgh and the South. London, Hale, 2 vols., 1953–56; revised edition, 1973–77.

Robert Burns. The Man, His Work, The Legend. London, MacGibbon and Kee, 1954; revised edition, 1968, 1978; New York, St. Martin's Press, 1979.

Dunoon: The Gem of the Clyde Coast. Dunoon, Town Council of Dunoon, 1954.

Clyde Waters: Variations and Diversions on a Theme of Pleasure. London, Hale, 1958.

The Burns Encyclopaedia. London, Hutchinson, 1959; revised edition, 1970; London, Hale, and New York, St. Martin's Press, 1980.

Killochan Castle, with David Somervell. Derby, Pilgrim Press, 1960.

By Yon Bonnie Banks: A Gallimaufry. London, Hutchinson, 1961.

The Discovery of Scotland: Based on Accounts of Foreign Travelers from the Thirteenth to the Eighteenth Centuries. London, Hale, and New York, Roy, 1964.

Environment: A Basic Human Right. Glasgow, Scottish Civic Trust, 1968.

The Eye Is Delighted: Some Romantic Travellers in Scotland. London, Muller, 1970.

Portrait of Glasgow. London, Hale, 1972; revised edition, 1981; revised edition, as *Glasgow,* 1989.

Robin Philipson. Edinburgh, Edinburgh University Press, 1976.

History of Scottish Literature. London, Hale, 1977; revised edition, 1992.

Lowland Scottish Villages. London, Hale, 1980.

Francis George Scott and the Scottish Renaissance. Edinburgh, Paul Harris, 1980.

The Buildings of Edinburgh, with Anthony F. Kersting. London, Batsford, 1981; revised edition, 1987.

Thank You for Having Me (autobiography). London, Hale, 1983.

Unknown Scotland, with Dennis Hardley London, Batsford, 1984.

The Castles of Scotland. London, Constable, 1986; revised edition, 1994.

Victorian and Edwardian Glasgow from Old Photographs. London, Batsford, 1987.

Count All Men Mortal: The History of the Scottish Provident. Edinburgh, Canongate, 1987.

An Illustrated Guide to Glasgow 1837. London, Hale, 1989.

Edinburgh, Past and Present, with David Bruce. London, Hale, 1990.

A Mini Guide to Scottish Gardens, with Joyce Lindsay. Edinburgh, Chambers, 1994.

Chambers Guide to Good Scottish Garden, with Joyce Lindsay. Edinburgh, Chambers, 1995.

Editor, *Sailing To-morrow's Seas: An Anthology of New Poems.* London, Fortune Press, 1944.

Editor, *Poetry Scotland One, Two, Three, Four.* Glasgow, Maclellan, 4 vols., 1945–53.

Editor, *Modern Scottish Poetry: An Anthology of the Scottish Renaissance 1920–1945.* London, Faber, 1946; revised edition, 1966; revised edition, as *Modern Scottish Poetry 1925–1985,* London, Hale, 1986.

Editor, *Pocket Guide to Scottish Culture.* Glasgow, Maclellan, 1947.

Editor, with Fred Urquhart, *No Scottish Twilight: New Scottish Stories.* Glasgow, Maclellan, 1947.

Editor, *Selected Poems of Sir Alexander Gray.* Glasgow, Maclellan, 1948.

Editor, *Poems,* by Sir David Lyndsay. Edinburgh, Oliver and Boyd, 1948.

Editor, with Hugh MacDiarmid, *Poetry Scotland Four.* Edinburgh, Serif, 1949.

Editor, with Helen Cruickshank, *Selected Poems of Marion Angus.* Edinburgh, Serif, 1950.

Editor, *John Davidson: A Selection of His Poems.* London, Hutchinson, 1961.

Editor, with others, *Scottish Poetry One to Nine.* Edinburgh, Edinburgh University Press, 6 vols., 1966–72; Glasgow, University of Glasgow Press, 1 vol., 1974; Manchester, Carcanet, 2 vols., 1975–76.

Editor, *A Book of Scottish Verse,* revised edition. London, Oxford University Press, 1967; revised edition, with R.L. Mackie, London, Hale, 1983.

Editor, *Scotland: An Anthology.* London, Hale, 1974; New York, St. Martin's Press, 1975.

Editor, *Modern Scottish Poetry: An Anthology of the Scottish Renaissance 1925–1975.* Manchester, Carcanet, 1976.

Editor, *As I Remember: Ten Scottish Authors Recall How Writing Began for Them.* London, Hale, 1979.

Editor, *Scottish Comic Verse: An Anthology.* London, Hale, 1981.

Editor, with Alexander Scott, *The Comic Poems of William Tennant.* Edinburgh, Scottish Academy Press, 1990.

Editor, with Joyce Lindsay, *The Scottish Dog.* Aberdeen, Aberdeen University Press, 1989

Editor, *The Youth and Manhood of Cyril Thornton,* by Thomas Hamilton. Aberdeen, The Association for Scottish Literary Studies, 1990.

Editor, with Joyce Lindsay, *A Pleasure of Gardens.* Aberdeen, Aberdeen University Press, 1991.

Editor, with Joyce Lindsay, *The Scottish Quotation Book.* London, Hale, 1991.

Editor, with Joyce Lindsay, *The Music Quotation Book.* London, Hale, 1992.

Editor, with Joyce Lindsay, *The Theatre and Opera-Lover's Quotation Book.* London, Hale, 1993.

Editor, with Joyce Lindsay, *The Burns Quotation Book.* London, Hale, 1994.

*

Manuscript Collections: National Library of Scotland, Edinburgh; Edinburgh University Library; Mitchell Library, Glasgow.

Critical Studies: By Alexander Scott, in *Whither Scotland?,* edited by Duncan Glen, London, Gollancz, 1971; *Studies in Scottish Literature 1971,* Columbia, University of South Carolina Press, 1973; ''A Different Way of Being Right: The Poetry of Maurice Lindsay'' by Donald Campbell, in *Akros* (Preston, Lancashire), April 1974; by Christopher Rush, in *Scottish Literary Journal* (Aberdeen), summer 1980; by Douglas Gifford, in *The Scottish Bookseller,* summer 1991; ''Collective Consciousness'' by Ian Crichton Smith, in *The Weekend Scotsman,* 6 January 1991; by Carol Gow, in *Supplement, Scottish Literary Journal,* summer 1991; ''Dear Maurice, a Tribute to Maurice Lindsay on His Eightieth Birthday'' by John Sutherland and Lester Borley, *Times Literary Supplement* (London), 4976, 1998.

Maurice Lindsay comments:

I suppose I began writing at an early age because I wanted to preserve and share some tangible aspects of my own experience, to capture the flavor of the fleeting moment, or, as Alexander Scott once put it, ''to catch the lyric cry.'' In my early writing days, under the pressure of the 1939–45 war (the second half of which I spent as a staff officer in the British War Office in London), I wrote too quickly—one never knew how long one might be alive! All the poems from 1939 to about 1950 have therefore been substantially revised in my *Collected Poems 1940–90.* (Fortunately, until fairly recently I have never had any difficulty in conjuring back the force of early experiences.)

These early poems dealt with love, the sights and sounds of wartime life in London, nostalgia for Scotland, from which I was temporarily exiled, and what George Bruce described as sketches of my ''gallery of ancient Tories.'' They also included the outcome of my brief flirtation with Lallans, or Scots, some examples of which are included in my *Collected Poems.* Efforts to express the full range of modern experience in a language that survives only in dialect forms, none of which I ever spoke, however, eventually made me move over to Scoto-English, the language I and the majority of late twentieth-century Scots do, in fact, speak.

My middle-period poems reflect the growing up of my family, the sense of place, which I have sought after in many countries, and my passionate interest in music, the discipline in which I was first trained. This indeed perhaps also explains my interest and delight in fixed forms and my frequent use of rhyme, the sense and aptness of which come easily to me. (This concern with the musicality of verse, however, has undoubtedly led to the rejection of my work in some quarters by certain younger academic anthology editors, though I have no doubt that when fashion is no longer a factor in such matters

there will be a reconsideration of it!) In America poetry has become very much a campus affair and seems likely to become so too in Scotland. This is not a healthy state of affairs. Poetry should be for people, not just for academics!

In my old age I have been much concerned, on the one hand, with the human comedy and, on the other, with the enormous waste of life that wars over man-made religions, as they all are—inflexible dogmas and false certainties—continually bring about. I have been especially interested in the range of feeling, even of satirical anger, that the sonnet form is capable of sustaining.

The Scottish renaissance movement, of which in my early days I supposed I formed a part, like all other movements, loosens its adherents into their own individualities as they mature. It is quite clear to me that for those who speak a Scots dialect Scots is a proper tongue, as is Gaelic to a Gaelic speaker, even if both languages have increasingly to defend their fringe corners under the assault of English and Americanese issuing from television, now the strongest cultural influence on the majority in the affluent countries of the world.

I have indicated my dislike of dogmatic literary ''schools'' of this or that, of claques and cliques (both favored groupings easily assumed by the frequently contentious Scot), and my conviction that balanced and dispassionate assessments can only be retrospectively, when the clamors and the credos of such groupings have been silenced by history.

When I was young, the radio producer, novelist, and dramatist Robert Kemp once said to me, ''If you want to be a poet in Scotland, you have to possess the stamina of a prizefighter and the hide of a rhinoceros.'' I can now endorse that diagnosis made more than half a century ago, having recently sent off to the publisher my final collection, *News of the World: Last Poems,* and, after more than fifty-five years spent in the service of poetry, I think I can understand the puzzlement of the good Glaswegian who recognized my physiog as we stood side-by-side having a pee in the underground lavatory of Glasgow's St. Vincent Place and that subsequently became the quatrain in my *Collected Poems 1940–90,* in a poem entitled ''In a Glasgow Loo'':

I hope yuh dinna mind me speakin tae yi, sur, but ahve seen youse on the telly? Whit dyuh dae for a livan? Yuv retired? Yuh wrote? A po-it? Micht yuh no jist as weel hae peed inti thuh wund?

*   *   *

The publication of Maurice Lindsay's *Collected Poems 1940–90* confirmed his position as one of the most consistently satisfying and accomplished poets writing in Britain today. His range of subject and form extends from the barbed fables of *Bairnsangs* in the 1940s to the astringent satires of his later work, from his fully realized portraits and landscapes of the 1960s to the boisterous and bawdy comedies of the 1980s, and from tender love poems to a poetry of ideas in the autobiographical *A Net to Catch the Winds* and the finely controlled nostalgia of another autobiographical sequence, ''Fifty Years On: Variations on a Glasgow Theme.''

The lyric impulse, a celebration of the natural world and peopled landscapes, has been a continuous thread in Lindsay's poetry since the 1940s. The lyrics in *On the Face of It* and *News of the World,* two collections published in the 1990s, show him writing at the height of his powers, with the same keen eye for detail and the same robust sensitivity that leave the best of the lyrics, for example, "Highland Waterfall" and the sequence "On Milton Hill," finely poised between the physical and the mystical.

Another constant factor, and one that adds a sense of urgency to Lindsay's work, is his openness to new forms of experience. Apart from satires of religion and politics Lindsay has never colonized specific areas of experience. Instead, he constantly moves on to explore new territories, both thematically and geographically, and the overall effect of these explorations is to convey a sense of restless creative energy. "A Rough Day," from *On the Face of It,* and, more explicitly, "Directions for a Funeral," from *News of the World,* show the poet considering his own advancing years and the approach of the ultimate experience—death. But through the creative paradox of his art—the combination of humility and boldness of spirit with which he speaks of final things—Lindsay transforms his poems of mortality into affirmations of life.

The most distinctive development in Lindsay's later work is the increasing clarity and compassion of his moral vision. There are glimpses of this in his poetry of the 1960s and 1970s, and with the publication of the sequence "On Trial," in the 1988 collection *Requiem for a Sexual Athlete,* the vision begins to be expressed in more forceful and sustained ways. "On Trial" is a "Scottish" poem in the sense that the characters who people the sequence belong to Glasgow or to west-central Scotland; two sequences in *On the Face of It,* "The Gulf War" and "Making Wars," are, as their titles indicate, international in their scope. The cycle of sonnets that forms the title sequence for *News of the World* is both local and international. The cycle shows simple human values being betrayed by the manipulators of power and childhood innocence corrupted by the atrocities of war.

These sonnets also suggest that Lindsay is more acutely aware than most of his contemporaries of the vast forces—political, military, economic, religious—that are shaping and distorting the modern world. "News of the World" is a rare achievement; it is a public poetry, a poetry of fiercely conflicting ideas, a disturbing expression of the terrors of violence, and ultimately a poetry of profound tenderness. Lindsay's voice in *News of the World* remains identifiably Scottish, but the vision is of the universal human condition. Throughout this wide-ranging, deeply satisfying collection, Lindsay's assured technique confirms that he remains as true to the craft of poetry as he does to the experience that prompts the poems.

Lindsay is essentially a poet, but he has made an outstanding contribution to Scottish literature as an editor of several anthologies and of the journal *Scottish Review.* He also is the author of *The Burns Encyclopaedia* and the *History of Scottish Literature* and of critical biographies of Robert Burns and Francis George Scott.

—James Aitchison

LIVINGSTONE, Douglas (James)

Nationality: South African. **Born:** Kuala Lumpur, Malaysia, 5 January 1932. **Education:** Schools in Malaysia, Australia, and South Africa; Kearney College, Natal, South Africa; qualified in pathogenic bacteriology, Pasteur Institute, Salisbury, Rhodesia; University of Natal, Ph.D. in biological science, 1989. **Career:** Officer in charge, Pathological Laboratory, Broken Hill (Kabwe) General Hospital, Zambia,

1959–63. Since 1964 bacteriologist in charge of marine work, Natal. **Awards:** Guinness prize, 1965; Cholmondeley award, 1970; Olive Schreiner prize, 1975; English Association prize, 1978; C.N.A. literary award, 1985; Thomas Pringle award, 1989. D.Litt.: University of Natal, 1982; Rhodes University, 1990. **Address:** c/o Council of Scientific and Industrial Research, P.O. Box 17001, Congella, 4013 Natal, South Africa.

PUBLICATIONS

Poetry

The Skull in the Mud. London, Outposts, 1960.
Sjambok and Other Poems from Africa. London and New York, Oxford University Press, 1964.
Poems, with Thomas Kinsella and Anne Sexton. London and New York, Oxford University Press, 1968.
Eyes Closed against the Sun. London and New York, Oxford University Press, 1970.
The Sea My Winding Sheet and Other Poems. Durban, Theatre Workshop, 1971.
A Rosary of Bone, edited by Jack Cope. Cape Town, David Philip, 1975; revised edition, 1983.
The Anvil's Undertone. Johannesburg, Donker, 1978.
Selected Poems. Johannesburg, Donker, 1984.

Plays

The Sea My Winding Sheet (broadcast, 1964; produced Durban, 1971). Included in *The Sea My Winding Sheet and Other Poems,* 1971.
A Rhino for the Boardroom (broadcast, 1974). Published in *Contemporary South African Plays,* edited by E. Pereira, Johannesburg, Ravan Press, 1977.
The Semblance of the Real (produced Durban, 1976). Published in *Modern Stage Directions,* edited by Stephen Gray and David Schalwyk, London, Longman, 1984.

Radio Plays: *The Sea My Winding Sheet,* 1963 (Rhodesia); *A Rhino for the Boardroom,* 1974.

Other

The Distribution and Occurrence of Coliforms and Pathogenic Indicators of Pollution within the Surf-Zone and Near-Shore Waters of the Natal Coast, with J.W. de Goede and B.A. Warren-Hansen. Natal, Council of Scientific and Industrial Research, 1968.
Microbial Studies on Seawater Quality off Durban: 1964–1988. Natal, Council of Scientific and Industrial Research, 1990.
A Littoral Zone. Cape Town, Carrefour Press, 1991.

*

Bibliography: *Douglas Livingstone: A Bibliography* by A.G. Ullyatt, Pretoria, University of South Africa, 1979.

Critical Studies: *Douglas Livingstone: A Critical Study of His Poetry,* Johannesburg, Donker, 1981, and ''Douglas Livingstone,'' in *South African English Poetry: A Modern Perspective,* Johannesburg, Donker, 1984, both by Michael Chapman; ''Livingstone's Poems in 'The Wild Wave''' by David Levey, in *CRUX* (Pretoria), 20(3), August 1986; '''Moon-Rites and Rain-Dances': The Malaysian Connection in Douglas Livingstone's Poetry'' by Stephen Gray, in *ACLALS Bulletin,* 7(6), 1986; ''The Politics of Tolerance in South African Literature,'' in *Annali di Ca' Foscari* (Padua, Italy), 30(1–2), 1991, and ''The Poetry of Moral Commitment in South Africa: The Life and Work of Douglas Livingstone,'' in *Annali di Ca' Foscari* (Padua, Italy), 31(1–2), 1992, both by Marco Fazzini; ''Littorally: A Note on Douglas Livingstone'' by Tony Morphet, in *Pretexts* (South Africa), 6(2), November 1997.

Douglas Livingstone comments:

Some African themes, especially animals, to reflect the nature of man. Happier with form. Attempts to shape poem to subject. Influences unknown, but favorite poets: Chaucer, John Clare, Catullus, Shelley, Marvell, Donne, Cavafy, E.A. Robinson, Wilfred Owen, and Sylvia Plath among the dead.

*   *   *

Douglas Livingstone is perhaps the outstanding voice of white South African poetry, yet the poet with whom he is most readily linked comes from another continent altogether—Miroslav Holub of the Czech Republic. In the work of both poets, each a major voice of his respective culture, there is a fascinating link between their writing life, an act undertaken in privacy, and their profession. Livingstone, who has spent much of his life in Natal, is a diver and marine biologist by profession; Holub is an immunologist. For both their respective scientific disciplines have nurtured and enriched their perceptions of the world. For Livingstone it is the visible, tangible world: ''I guess I have a fairly intense inner life that is not religious in the conventional sense, which is focused on the planet, its seas, the sun, moon, night sky . . .'' For Holub it is the invisible world as perceived through the microscope that has shaped his poetic vision.

Livingstone's ''Lake Morning in Autumn'' offers an example of the degree of precision that we have come to expect from his dispassionate observing eye:

Before sunrise the stork was there
resting the pillow of his body
on stick legs growing from the water.

A flickering gust of pencil-slanted rain
swept over the chill autumn morning;
and he, too tired to arrange

his wind-buffeted plumage,
perched swaying a little,
neck flattened, ruminative . . .

That poem was published in a collection entitled *Sjambok and Other Poems from Africa,* and a number of other items in the same book were written in celebration of particular birds and animals—the puff adder, the jackal, the vulture—the poet often reflecting poignantly upon the impact of human intruders. A once proud, now moth-eaten, lion has ''a balding monk's tonsure, / and his fluid thigh muscles flop / slack as an exhausted boxer's . . .''

The verse play entitled *The Sea My Winding Sheet* is a retelling of the myth of the Titans who besieged Mount Olympus, citadel of the gods. The gods brought to their aid Heracles, who succeeded in repulsing them with his club. The Titans in their death throes turned to stone, becoming the continents, including, of course, the continent of Africa. The play is in essence a tribute to the earth in all its superb physicality, but it is also a celebration of the ability of humankind to preside over and shape its seemingly intractable terrain, success, of course, depending ultimately upon a happy compact between the two. The following lines are from ''New Men Will Clump About'':

The tracks and prefabs will scar her seas
With tracks and alloys; diamond-booted drills
Inject and measure her by tall degrees.
Her temperature, soaring upon the hills

As sunlight blindly edges on her face,
Will shepherd them, melting, to the cold cubes
Prepared below the needle peaks that lace
The songs of constant stars in shortwave tubes.

There is an unspoken assumption among many readers of poetry that science and poetry are somehow incompatible, a product of the romantic fallacy. In Livingstone's work the two go hand in hand, and it is as natural for him to incorporate the reference to ''shortwave tubes'' into the poem as it is to celebrate sunlight and the ''needle peaks.''

In his translations from the Zimbabwean Shona, Livingstone has made available to us a range of local voices that might otherwise have gone unheard. The best of these have an immediacy, a vividness, a freshness of perception, and an affectionate attention to local detail that feel totally authentic. Wil Chivaura has this to say of love, for example, in a poem of that title:

Love, my sister-in-law, has to be fried
like a mealie cob in the pan of courtship,
sides reddening from the incessant turning
—the only love-philtre tempting to men.

Another poem is written in praise of an object of great value to the author, a small beer pot:

You're good as gold,
made from real earth
—earth that shines even when
uncooked—the rich earth.
Precious before you were moulded,
an egg in the hands of women,
baked in the fire's red embers,
your brown crimsoned with pride.

Livingstone's versatility as a translator is in evidence in his renderings from the Hungarian of Gyula Illyés and the French of José María de Heredia.

The poet's professional concern for the earth's flora and fauna accompanies a deep-rooted belief that there is something indomitable about life itself (''If you threaten a cell, even a nonsentient one, it will retreat if it can, or fight back . . .''), and we can read his poetry in a somewhat similar light. ''Fighting words in the form of poems'' is essentially an act of commitment and affirmation and a testimony to the belief that what can be transmitted by language, and from one language to another, humanizes, enriches, and bonds us.

—Michael Glover

LLEWELLYN, Kate

Nationality: Australian. **Born:** Katherine Jill Sky Brinkwath, Tumby Bay, South Australia, 1940. **Education:** Bush schools in South Australia; University of Adelaide, 1975–78, B.A. 1978. **Family:** Married Richard Dutton Llewellyn in 1960 (divorced 1975); one son and one daughter. **Career:** Trainee nurse, Royal Adelaide Hospital, South Australia, 1954–58; registered nurse, Adelaide, 1958–60; co-owner and director, Llewellyn Galleries, Dulwich, 1968–75. **Agent:** Tim Curnow, Curtis Brown Literary Agents, 7 Union Street, Paddington 2021, New South Wales, Australia. **Address:** 300 The Mall, Laura 2780, New South Wales, Australia.

PUBLICATIONS

Poetry

Trader Kate and the Elephants. Adelaide, Friendly Street Poets, 1983.
Luxury. Sydney, Redress Press, 1985.
Honey. Hudson, Hawthorn, 1988.
Figs. Hudson, Hawthorn, 1989.
Selected Poems. Hudson, Hawthorn, 1992.
Crosshatched. N.p., 1994.
Sofala, and Other Poems. Kew, Victoria, Hudson, Hawthorn, 1999.

Recordings: *The Waterlily,* Bolinda Audio Books, 1987.

Other

The Waterlily. Hudson, Hawthorn, 1986.
Dear You. Hudson, Hawthorn, 1987.
The Mountain. Hudson, Hawthorn, 1990.
Angels and Dark Madonnas—Travels in Italy and India. Hudson, Hawthorn, 1991.
Lilies Feathers and Frangipani. Sydney, HarperCollins, 1993.
The Floral Mother and Other Essays. Sydney, HarperCollins, 1995.
Gorillas Tea & Coffee (Travels in East Africa). Sydney, HarperCollins, 1995.
Burning: A Journal. Hawthorn, Victoria, Hudson, 1997.
Stardust. Hawthorn, Victoria, Hudson, 1997.

Editor, *The Penguin Book of Australian Women Poets.* Penguin, Melbourne, 1986.

*

Manuscript Collection: A.D.F.A. Library, Duntoon, Canberra, Australia.

Critical Studies: In *Overland Magazine* (Mt. Eliza, Victoria), 1989; ''A.D. Hope's 'Ulysses' and Kate Llewellyn's 'Penelope': Two Modern Voices from the Past'' by Malati Mathur, in *Commonwealth Review* (New Delhi, India), 2(1–2), 1990–91; ''Mapping the Unpredictable: The Art of Kate Llewellyn'' by Anne Gunter, in *Overland* (Melbourne, Australia), 127, winter 1992.

*   *   *

Kate Llewellyn first attracted notice as a poet when she contributed work to *Sisters Poets No 1* (1979), a pioneering collection of women's poetry. In 1986, with Susan Hampton, she edited *The Penguin Book of Australian Women Poets,* an even more important anthology that was to help redefine the achievement of Australian women in poetry from the colonial period to the present day.

Llewellyn's own first collection, *Trader Kate and the Elephants,* was joint winner of the Anne Elder award for a first volume of poetry. It established her tone of sensuous directness, a combination of earthiness and often playful associative juxtapositions. Her second collection, *Luxury,* more closely defined her increasing command of a direct, colloquial voice to express the confidence of her feminine explorations of self and of relationships. Later collections such as *Honey* and *Figs,* as well as *Selected Poems,* continued to explore this rich vein of sensuous intimacy, but the processes of aging and of an underlying rueful acceptance have moved more into the foreground of her writing.

Although Llewellyn has been prolific as a poet, she has perhaps gained greater readership through a series of three diarylike prose volumes (though distinctions between prose and poetry are frequently lost in these books). *The Waterlily* traces the author's move from Sydney up to the mountain resort of Leura, noting everything from daily gardening life to isolation and the vagaries of human relationships. *Dear You,* written as a series of letters to an absent lover, is notable for its honesty to experience. The third volume of this poetic prose trilogy, *The Mountain,* is addressed to her daughter.

Crosshatched, a verse collection published in 1994, reconciles the diary-note form of the autobiographical trilogy with the more clipped cadences of Llewellyn's earlier poetry, notably in the work based on the disastrous bushfires in the Blue Mountains of New South Wales in January 1994. Other poems revisit classical myths in the well-established feminist tradition. *Sofala* (1999) has the sort of easy authority Llewellyn has now made her own in both prose and poetry. If there is a new wistful quality, there is never any sense of resignation.

—Thomas W. Shapcott

LOCHHEAD, Liz

Nationality: Scottish. **Born:** Motherwell, Lanarkshire, 26 December 1947. **Education:** Glasgow School of Art, 1965–70, diploma 1970. **Career:** Teacher of art at schools in Glasgow, Scotland, and Bristol, England; lecturer, University of Glasgow. **Awards:** Scotland prize, British Broadcasting Corporation, 1971; new writing award, Scottish

Arts Council, 1972, for *Memo for Spring;* Scottish Arts Council fellowship, 1978. **Address:** 11 Kersland Street, Glasgow G12 8BW, Scotland.

PUBLICATIONS

Poetry

Memo for Spring. Edinburgh, University of Edinburgh Press, 1972.
The Grimm Sisters. London, Next Editions, 1981.
Dreaming Frankenstein and Collected Poems. Edinburgh, University of Edinburgh Press, 1984; as *Dreaming Frankenstein and Other Poems,* Edinburgh, Polygon, 1999.
True Confessions and New Clichés. Edinburgh, University of Edinburgh Press, 1985; revised edition, Edinburgh, Polygon, 1993.
Bagpipe Muzak. London, Penguin, 1991.

Plays

Blood and Ice (produced Edinburgh, 1982; revised version, produced London, 1984). Edinburgh, Salamander Press, 1982; New York, Methuen, 1983.
Tickly Mince (revue), with Tom Leonard and Alisdair Gray (produced Glasgow, 1982).
The Pie of Damocles (revue), with others (produced Glasgow, 1983).
A Bunch of Fives, with Tom Leonard and Sean Hardie (produced Glasgow, 1983).
Silver Service. Edinburgh, Salamander Press, 1984.
Dracula, adaptation of the novel by Bram Stoker (produced Edinburgh, 1985). With *Mary Queen of Scots Got Her Head Chopped Off,* London, Penguin 1989.
Tartuffe, adaptation of the play by Moliére (produced Edinburgh, 1985). Edinburgh, Polygon, 1985.
Mary Queen of Scots Got Her Head Chopped Off (produced Edinburgh and London, 1987). With *Dracula,* London, Penguin, 1989.
The Big Picture (produced Glasgow, 1988).
Patter Merchant (produced Edinburgh, 1989).
Jock Tamson's Bairns, with Gerry Mulgrew (produced Glasgow, 1990).
Quelques Fleurs (produced Edinburgh and London, 1991).
Perfect Days (produced Edinburgh,1998). London, Nick Hern Books, 1998; revised edition, London, Nick Hern, 1999.

Screenplay: *Now and Then,* 1972.

Radio Play: *Blood and Ice,* 1990.

Television Play: *Sweet Nothings* in *End of the Line* series, 1984.

                                        *

Critical Studies: "Past Lives in Present Drama: Feminist Theatre and Intertextuality" by Beate Neumeier, in *Frauen und Frauendarstellung in der englischen and amerikanischen,* edited by Therese Fischer-Seidel, Tubingen, Germany, Narr, 1991; "Feminist Nationalism in Scotland: 'Mary Queen of Scots Got Her Head Chopped Off'" by Ilona S. Koren-Deutsch, in *Modern Drama* (Downsview, Ontario), 35(3), September 1992; "'The Devil Is Beautiful': Dracula: Freudian Novel and Feminist Drama" by Jan McDonald, in *Novel Images: Literature in Performance,* edited by Peter Reynolds, London, Routledge, 1993; "Desire and Difference in Liz Lochhead's 'Dracula'" by Jennifer Harvie, in *Essays in Theatre,* 11(2), May 1993; in *British Playwrights, 1956–1995: A Research and Production Sourcebook* edited by William W. Demastes, Westport, Connecticut, Greenwood, 1996; "The Mirror and the Vamp: Liz Lochhead" by Anne Varty, in *A History of Scottish Women's Writing,* edited by Douglas Gifford and Dorothy McMillan, Edinburgh, Edinburgh University Press, 1997.

                        *   *   *

The Scottish writer Liz Lochhead's 1972 verse collection *Memo for Spring* made an immediate impact with its freshness and truth to experience. The appeal was direct, and yet the writing used more verbal devices than might appear at a glance or on a first hearing. An ability to talk about very ordinary things—her young sister trying on her shoes, a trip from Glasgow to Edinburgh, her grandmother knitting, the clang of steelworks, a child carrying a jug of milk, the end of a love affair—is in a few poems flattened out toward triviality or the prosaic, but for the most part the warmly observing eye and ear are convincingly on target. The experience has a Glasgow and Lanarkshire background, but one attractive poem, "Letter from New England"—where elements of ironical comment on small-town life are entertainingly presented through the persona of a surprised visitor—shows an encouraging ability to move into a wider world.

The author's subsequent books of poetry have confirmed her promise and extended her range. *The Grimm Sisters* takes up themes from ballads and fairy tales and retells the stories either from a new angle or with a modern perspective. *Dreaming Frankenstein,* a collection of her earlier volumes with a substantial and impressive addition of new poems, shows both a development of her storytelling gift and a deepening of her psychological probing of human relationships, especially as seen from a woman's point of view. The extension of Lochhead's work into the theater, with plays on the Frankenstein and Dracula stories and an interest in cabaret-type monologues, gives further evidence of a productive and confident talent. Her dramatic monologues, songs, and performance pieces were collected in 1985 in *True Confessions and New Clichés,* a sparkling and witty book to read, even though its contents are meant to be heard. Prose and verse and song and action come together in her extremely effective play *Mary Queen of Scots Got Her Head Chopped Off,* which takes a fresh and moving look at Scottish history and the myths that run through it.

—Edwin Morgan

LOGUE, Christopher

Nationality: British. **Born:** Portsmouth, Hampshire, 23 November 1926. **Education:** Prior Park College, Bath; Portsmouth Grammar School. **Military Service:** British Army, 1944–48. **Family:** Married Rosemary Hill in 1985. **Career:** Lived in France, 1951–56. Contributor, *Private Eye,* London, until 1993. **Address:** 41 Camberwell Grove, London SE5 8JA, England.

Publications

Poetry

Wand and Quadrant. Paris, Olympia Press, 1953.
The Weekdream Sonnets. Paris, Jack Straw, 1955.
First Testament. Rome, Botteghe Oscure, 1955.
Devil, Maggot, and Son. Amsterdam, Stols, and Tunbridge Wells, Kent, Peter Russell, 1956.
She Sings, He Sings. Rome, Botteghe Oscure, 1957.
A Song for Kathleen. London, Villiers, 1958.
The Man Who Told His Love: Twenty Poems Based on Pablo Neruda's "Los Cantos d'Amores." London, Scorpion Press, 1958.
The Song of the Dead Soldier, To the Tune of McCafferty: One Killed in the Interests of Certain Tory Senators in Cyprus. London, Villiers, 1959.
Memoranda for Marchers. Privately printed, 1959.
Songs. London, Hutchinson, 1959; New York, McDowell Obolensky, 1960.
Songs from "The Lily-White Boys." London, Scorpion Press, 1960.
Patrocleia. An Account of Book 16 of Homer's *Iliad.* London, Scorpion Press, 1962; Ann Arbor, University of Michigan Press, 1963.
Logue's A.B.C. London, Scorpion Press, 1966.
I Shall Vote Labour. London, Turret, 1966.
The Words of Christopher Logue's Establishment Songs, Etcetera. London, Poet and Printer, 1966.
Selections from a Correspondence Between an Irishman and a Rat. London, Goliard Press, 1966.
Pax. An Account of Book 14 of Homer's *Iliad.* London, Turret, 1967.
Gone Ladies, music by Wallace Southam. London, Turret, 1968.
Rat, Oh Rat. Privately printed, 1968.
Hermes Flew to Olympus. Privately printed, 1968.
SL. Privately printed, 1969.
The Girls. Privately printed, 1969.
New Numbers. London, Cape, 1969; New York, Knopf, 1970.
For Talitha. London, Steam Press, 1971.
What. Richmond, Surrey, Keepsake Press, 1972.
Twelve Cards. London, Lorrimer, 1972.
Singles. London, John Roberts Press, 1973.
Mixed Rushes. London, John Roberts Press, 1974.
The Crocodile (for children). London, Cape, 1976.
Abecedary. London, Cape, 1977.
Red Bird: Love Poems. Guildford, Surrey, Circle Press, 1979.
Ode to the Dodo: Poems from 1953 to 1978. London, Cape, 1981.
War Music. An Account of Books 16 to 19 of Homer's *Iliad.* London, Cape, 1981; New York, Farrar Straus, 1987.
Kings. An Account of Books 1 and 2 of Homer's *Iliad.* London, Faber, and New York, Farrar Straus, 1991.
The Husbands. An Account of Books 3 and 4 of Homer's *Iliad.* London, Faber, and New York, Farrar Straus, 1994.
Selected Poems, edited by Christopher Reid. London, Faber, 1997.

Recordings: *Christopher Logue Reading His Own Poetry,* with Laurie Lee, Jupiter, 1960; *Red Bird,* with Tony Kinsey and Bill Le Sage, 1960; *Songs from the Establishment,* with Annie Ross, 1962; *The Death of Patroclus,* with Vanessa Redgrave, Alan Dobie, and others, Spoken Arts, 1963.

Plays

The Trial of Cob and Leach: A News Play (produced London, 1959).
The Lily-White Boys (lyrics only), book by Henry Cookson, music by Tony Kinsey and Bill LeSage (produced London, 1960).
Trials by Logue (Antigone and Cob and Leach) (produced London, 1960).
Friday, adaptation of a work by Hugo Klaus (produced London, 1971). London, Davis Poynter, 1972.
War Music, music by Donald Fraser, adaptation of *The Iliad* (produced London, 1977).
The Arrival of the Poet, music by George Nicholson (produced Newcastle, 1985).
The Seven Deadly Sins, songs for a ballet with music by Kurt Weill, adaptation of a work by Bertolt Brecht (produced Bath, 1986).

Screenplays: *Savage Messiah,* 1972; *Crusoe,* with Walon Green, 1989.

Radio Play: *Strings,* music by Jason Osborn, 1989.

Television Play: *The End of Arthur's Marriage,* with Stanley Myers, 1965.

Novel

Lust (as Count Palmiro Vicarion). Paris, Olympia Press, 1959.

Other

The Arrival of the Poet in the City: A Treatment for a Film. Amsterdam, Yellow Press, and London, Mandarin, 1963; revised edition, music by George Nicholson, Mainz, Germany, Schott, 1983.
Ratsmagic (for children). London, Cape, and New York, Pantheon, 1976.
Puss-in-Boots Pop-Up (for children). London, Cape, 1976; New York, Greenwillow, 1977.
The Magic Circus (for children). London, Cape, and New York, Viking Press, 1979.
Bumper Book of True Stories. London, Private Eye-Deutsch, 1980.
Prince Charming—A Memoir. London, Faber, 1999.

Editor, *Count Palmiro Vicarion's Book of Limericks.* Paris, Olympia Press, 1955.
Editor, *Count Palmiro Vicarion's Book of Bawdy Ballads.* Paris, Olympia Press, 1956.
Editor, *True Stories.* London, New English Library, 1966.
Editor, *True Stories from "Private Eye."* London, Deutsch, 1973.
Editor, *The Children's Book of Comic Verse.* London, Batsford, 1979.
Editor, *London in Verse.* London, Secker and Warburg, 1982.
Editor, *Sweet and Sour: An Anthology of Comic Verse.* London, Batsford, 1983.
Editor, *The Oxford Book of Pseuds.* London, Private Eye-Deutsch, 1983.
Editor, *The Children's Book of Children's Rhymes.* London, Batsford, 1986.

Translator, *Baal,* by Bertolt Brecht (produced Leicester, 1986).

*

Bibliography: *Christopher Logue, A Bibliography 1952–1997* by George Ramsdeu, Yorkshire, Stone Trough Books, 1997.

Critical Study: ''Enforced Aphasia: Language and Violence in Christopher Logue's Homeric Poetry'' by James Campbell, in *Lit* (Storrs, Connecticut), 7(4), March 1997.

Theatrical Activities: Actor: **Play**—First Player and Player King, in Hamlet, 1982; London 1980. **Films**—*Dante's Inferno,* 1966; *The Peasants' Revolt,* 1970; *The Devils,* 1970; *Moonlighting,* 1982. **Television**—*The Gadfly,* 1977; *Bird of Prey,* 1982.

*   *   *

A powerful and original stylist, Christopher Logue displays an impressive array of talents, and it seems unlikely that any poet can match his range of ''starring roles.'' Logue has played Cardinal Richelieu in Ken Russell's classic film *The Devils,* written a pornographic novel for the Olympia Press of Maurice Girodias, and been imprisoned as a CND activist and member of the Committee of 100, sharing a cell with playwrights Arnold Wesker and Robert Bolt. These and other (often outrageous) adventures are detailed in his entertaining autobiography *Prince Charming.* Perhaps more remarkable still is the fact that none of his ''off-page'' activities manages to overshadow his considerable skills as a poet.

During the 1960s Logue and Adrian Mitchell enjoyed something of a cult status as leaders of the poetry-reading movement that was associated with protests against the Vietnam War. Like Mitchell, Logue holds radical opinions, but he controls his anger to a greater degree in his poems. His bitter attacks on imperialism, capital punishment, and nuclear warfare are sheathed in a flawless, elegant verse often reminiscent of the Augustan age. Nor is he confined merely to political topics, showing himself equally adept as a social satirist, writer of comic children's verse, translator, and reteller of fairy tales. Logue's formidable gifts are evident from his earliest work in the 1950s. The descriptive landscapes and the songlike ''Airs and Graces'' of his first collection have a dream vision quality exploited in later writings, while the charged sexuality of ''Six Sonnets'' reveals the poet as already an assured master of his craft. These poems display a marked awareness of poetry's origins in music and the spoken word.

Significantly, Logue's most consistently impressive collection is called *Songs,* and his Homeric retellings—themselves an interpretation of what was once oral poetry—have been adapted as a musical performance. *Songs* contains some of Logue's most enduring verses, their political message tempered by a poet's perception and distance. In ''Song of the Dead Soldier'' he attacks the idea of empires established by force and in ''Lullaby'' the institution of capital punishment. ''The Busker's Song'' debunks the symbols of British imperial power as actors in a fairground sideshow, while poems like ''Professor Tuholsky's Facts'' and ''Loyal to the King'' ridicule mankind's delusions of grandeur, our vaunted battles and slaughters derided on a cosmic scale as the efforts of fleas on a ball of dung. Most memorable is ''The Story of the Road,'' where in a skillfully matter-of-fact style Logue describes the attempt of downtrodden third world peasants to build a neglected inland road in defiance of the authorities.

Logue's later collections show a change of emphasis, the poet's attention shifting during the 1960s from revolutionaries to pop stars

and criminals and his verse reflecting the permissive and somewhat unreal atmosphere of the time. To one with such a sure grasp of style, there is always a dangerous tendency to appear glib, and certainly an element of slick facility creeps into satirical pieces like ''Private Eye's True Stories'' and ''The Oxford Book of Pseuds,'' while in *The Arrival of the Poet in the City* Logue's surreal treatment of everyday London transformed into nightmare seems deliberately to provoke the reader with its account of ''forbidden'' sexual and sadistic acts. All the same, to accuse Logue of triviality in his later work is less than the truth. Rather, he accurately portrays a world intent on trivializing itself through its own mass media: ''Twilight in autumn. Late birds shake their wings. / Terrorists laugh among the chimneytops. / Yard rises through a skylight. Crack. One drops. / Voices complain about the state of things.''

War Music, Logue's version of books 16–19 of the *Iliad,* ranks with *Songs* as his finest achievement. It seems ironic that so antiwar a writer as Logue should so brilliantly capture the feeling of this ancient conflict, depicting with unforgettable skill the intrigues of gods and men and bringing home to the reader the shockingly brutal nature of hand-to-hand combat between Trojan and Greek. Logue later returned to this earliest and greatest of epic poems, bringing his personal interpretation to the first four books of the *Iliad.* In *Kings* and *The Husbands* he explores the origins of the conflict in Helen's seduction by Paris, the resulting confrontation between Priam and Agamemnon, and the quarrels, combats, and challenges that precede the wholesale slaughter of the later books. Here, as in *War Music,* he brings the ancient time alive on the page in powerful modern English.

Logue's eye remains keen, the strength and poise of his verse as assured as ever. The varied nature of his writing continues to impress, from the comic verse of *The Crocodile* to the ''psychedelic Lewis Carroll'' vision of ''The Isles of Jessamy.'' ''The Girls'' ranks among the finest of his later works, its potentially sensational subject matter—lesbian lovemaking, incest, and murder—evoked with a lyrical, sensuous restraint. The pattern of the story progresses through a succession of brief, fragmented images and interior monologues to its violent climax, the innermost thoughts of the characters matched by passages of inspired description: ''Leaves mute the weir. Its waters sound / like cola seething in a paper cup.'' Whether he is recounting the gradual corruption of a rock idol or the downfall of affluent criminals or producing the witty capsule masterpieces of *Abecedary* and *Singles,* Logue's ability is undeniable. ''Urbanal,'' his bitter lament for a beloved tree felled by his neighbor, contains all of the old anger in its neatly measured lines. ''Urbanal'' and ''The Girls'' are both included in *Selected Poems,* which brings together these and other poems in a concise summary of Logue's writing to date and once again displays the multifaceted nature of his talent. Logue's ability to wring balance, precision, and strength from the messy business of everyday life—both his and our own—remains undiminished and continues to astound.

—Geoff Sadler

LOMAS, Herbert

Nationality: British. **Born:** Todmorden, Yorks, 7 February 1924. **Education:** King George V School, Southport, 1935–42; University of Liverpool, 1946–49, post-graduate studentship, 1949–50, B.A.

(honors) in English language and literature 1949, M.A. 1952. **Military Service:** King's Liverpool Regiment, 1943–44: Lance-corporal; Indian Army, Royal Garhwal Rifles, 1944–46: Second-lieutenant and Lieutenant. **Family:** Married 1) Marie Yvonne Wright in 1951 (divorced 1956), one son; 2) Annukka Partanen in 1956 (divorced 1967); 3) Mary Marshall Phelps in 1968 (died 1994), one daughter and one son. **Career:** English teacher, Anargyrios School, Spetsai, Greece, 1950–51; lecturer, 1952–64, and senior lecturer, 1965, University of Helsinki, Finland; lecturer, 1966–67, permanent lecturer, 1967–68, and senior lecturer, 1968–72, Borough Road College, Isleworth, Middlesex; principal lecturer, West London Institute of Higher Education, 1972–82. President, Suffolk Poetry Society, 1999. **Awards:** Poetry prize, Guinness Poetry Competition, 1961; Cholmondeley award, 1982; *Observer* Book of the Year award, 1986, for *Letters in the Dark;* Finnish Best Translation of the Year award, 1991; Poetry Book Society Biennial Translation award, 1991; Finnish State prize for translation, 1992. Knight First Class, Order of the White Rose of Finland, 1991. **Member:** Finnish Literature Society, 1992. **Address:** North Gable, 30 Crag Path, Aldeburgh, Suffolk 1P15 5BS, England.

PUBLICATIONS

Poetry

Chimpanzees Are Blameless Creatures. London, Mandarin Books, 1969.
Who Needs Money? London, Blond and Briggs, 1972.
Private and Confidential. London, London Magazine Editions, 1974.
Public Footpath. London, Anvil Press, 1981.
Fire in the Garden. Oxford, Oxford University Press, 1984.
Letters in the Dark. Oxford, Oxford University Press, 1986.
Trouble. London, Sinclair-Stevenson, 1992.
Selected Poems. London, Sinclair-Stevenson, 1995.
A Useless Passion. London, London Magazine Editions, 1998.

Other

A Handbook of Modern English for Finnish Students (part-author). Helsinki, Werner Söderström OY, 1957.
Editor and translator, *Contemporary Finnish Poetry.* Newcastle upon Tyne, Bloodaxe Books, 1991.

Translator, *Territorial Song.* London, London Magazine Editions, 1981.
Translator, *Wings of Hope and Daring* by Eira Stenberg. Newcastle upon Tyne, Bloodaxe Books, 1992.
Translator, *Fugue* by Kai Nieminen. Helsinki, Musta Taide, 1992.
Translator, *Black and Red* by Ilpo Tiihonen. Guildford, Surrey, Making Waves, 1993.
Translator, *The Eyes of the Fingertips Are Opening* by Leena Krohn. Helsinki, Musta Taide, 1993.
Translator, *Narcissus in Winter* by Risto Ahti. Guildford, Surrey, Making Waves, 1994.
Translator, *Two Sequences for Kuhmo* by Lauri Otonkoski. Kuhmo, Kamaramusikin Kannatusyhdistys, 1994.
Translator, *The Year of the Hare* by Arto Paasilinna. London, Peter Owen, 1995.
Translator, *Selected Poems of Eeva-Liisa Manner.* Guildford, Surrey, Making Waves, 1997.

Translator, *Three Finnish Poets.* London, London Magazine Editions, 1999.
Translator, *A Tenant Here: Selected Poems of Pentti Holappa.* Dublin, Dedalus Press, 1999.

*

Herbert Lomas comments:

Why be a poet, since poetry can look like a minor art (such as making reproduction furniture) in the twentieth century? One does not choose to be a poet; one is chosen, probably by one's passions. Poems have pestered me all my life; they are my form of speech.

Shelley's *A Defence of Poetry* convinced me that poetry was worth devoting a life to, and Shelley's thesis is not so easily dismissed as some would like to think. I lost my Christian faith during the war but was helped to become an existentialist through Sartre and a Christian existentialist through Berdyaev. Simplifying as much as I can, it seems to me that the world has preferred Nietzsche to Christ, in various degrees of virulence, and that is what is wrong with it.

The art of poetry should first please and perhaps exalt the reader but then be a civilizing force by reminding people of their feelings, their imperfections, their humanity, their need to love and be loved, and their right to be themselves. Nevertheless, it is impossible to state one's aims shortly without sounding pretentious.

*　　*　　*

The quiet but distinctive voice of Herbert Lomas has been slower to gain the hearing it deserves than might have been expected. This may be partly explained by the fact that on returning to England in 1965, after some thirteen years in Finland, he decided to discard what he had written up to then and to make a fresh start. But despite the decision to turn his back on his early work, he was eventually to resurrect some of it. What he had put aside included an extended sequence of short poems recording his youthful experiences as an infantryman with the British army from 1943 to 1946. A selection of these appeared in the *London Magazine* in February 1995 and the whole series three years later in the volume *A Useless Passion.* This volume also included two new sequences, one of them "Death of a Horsewoman," in which the poet mourns the loss of his wife in lines that fix moments of grief as if in amber.

The early poems of army life show that at nineteen or twenty, and with a volume of Auden in his kit bag, Lomas already possessed a sharply observant and often sardonic eye, a disconcerting candor, and an incisive style of his own. The deaths of two men, set to guard an air-sea rescue plane parked on the promenade at Dover and killed by a German shell from Calais that also destroyed the aircraft, elicit a biting comment:

> Someone in authority
> ought to have realised
>
> that people
> are a poor protection
> against high explosives.

That Lomas, though intent on reshaping himself, would remain very much his own man was indicated by the first small collection of his maturity, *Chimpanzees Are Blameless Creatures* (1969). By turns conversational and conventionally formal and employing imagery that veers between the urbane and the surreal, the poems discuss subjects as diverse as childhood terrors, sex, political and social issues, and religious belief. In later volumes Lomas has continued to examine these and other themes, such as music and family history, as well as to offer versions of Finnish poems (of which he is a notable translator) and of Horace and Valéry. There is in Lomas something of an amiable anarchist, dissatisfied as he is with current social structures and values, but he is honest enough to admit that he cannot confidently identify any clear means of improvement. What he does find clear, although it makes him uncomfortable, is that the architecture of society can seem at once ''so solid'' and yet be ''so unaccountably deceiving.''

These contradictions and perplexities lie at the core of much of Lomas's work. He is not, as he describes Jane Austen, ''one of those happy authors / Who've no history or self.'' He speculates on the elusive nature of perception—

Is it you I love or myself?
Are roses red in the dark?

—and he sees mice glowing in the eyes of an owl as it hunts by infrared or perceives invisible, eerie strands of communication:

On a night like this
Dead people
Can use the moonlight
Like a telephone.

A moral pilgrimage, or in Lomas's eloquent phrase the pursuit of ''the absconded divine,'' is the subject of his most powerfully sustained and cohesive work, *Letters in the Dark* (1986). This is a sequence of fifty-two poems inspired by visits to Southwark Cathedral in London. The poems discuss many of the uncertainties and dilemmas that attend the question of faith, and they do so in language that is often inspired and sometimes idiosyncratic but of consistent technical composure. This technical assurance is particularly evident in Lomas's handling of traditional stanza forms, in which rhyme is deployed with a casual deftness that conceals rather than advertises its use.

Chronologically on either side of *Letters in the Dark* are *Fire in the Garden* (1984) and *Trouble* (1992). The spiritual dimension is also apparent in these collections, but both, especially *Trouble,* are shot through with humor and paradox, reminding the reader at times of Larkin in a lighter mood. Hardy is another poet whose shade lurks somewhere at the back of Lomas's poetic persona, as, for example, in these lines on the men who dug Britain's canals:

The navvies are all dead, and what they left is a clear
stretch of almost stillness that's always been there.

Yeats's ghost, appropriately enough for a poet who asserted a firm belief in them, is here too. In what seems at first glance an act of temerity, Lomas has even paraphrased ''The Wild Swans at Coole''— and gotten away with it—an astonishing tour de force. This is not to say that Lomas's voice is anything but his own; in fact, it is always resolutely and often captivatingly individual:

Grief makes holes in a face
and so does laughter. The womb's
a hole, the soul's a hole

and Felicity's the name of a cat
going through a hole
just wide enough for her whiskers.

To summarize Lomas's work in a sentence, it could be said that his poems have been written for the love of people, of life, and of God. He might say, echoing Dylan Thomas, that he would be a damn fool if they were not.

—Rivers Carew

LONGLEY, Michael

Nationality: Irish. **Born:** Belfast, Northern Ireland, 27 July 1939. **Education:** Malone Primary School, 1946–51; Royal Belfast Academical Institution, 1951–58; Trinity College, Dublin, B.A. (honors) in classics 1963. **Family:** Married Edna Broderick in 1964; two daughters and one son. **Career:** Assistant master, Avoca School, Blackrock, 1962–63, Belfast High School and Erith Secondary School, 1963–64, and Royal Belfast Academical Institution, 1964–69. Director for literature and the traditional arts, Arts Council of Northern Ireland, Belfast, 1970–91. **Awards:** Eric Gregory award, 1965; Commonwealth Poetry prize, 1985; Whitbread prize for poetry, 1991; Cholmondeley award, 1992; Ireland Funds of America literary award, 1996. **Address:** 32 Osborne Gardens, Malone, Belfast 9, Northern Ireland.

PUBLICATIONS

Poetry

Ten Poems. Belfast, Festival, 1965.
Room to Rhyme, with Seamus Heaney and David Hammond. Belfast, Arts Council of Northern Ireland, 1968.
Secret Marriages: Nine Short Poems. Manchester, Phoenix Pamphlet Poets Press, 1968.
Three Regional Voices, with Barry Tebb and Iain Crichton Smith. London, Poet and Printer, 1968.
No Continuing City: Poems 1963–1968. London, Macmillan, and Chester Springs, Pennsylvania, Dufour, 1969.
Lares. London, Poet and Printer, 1972.
An Exploded View: Poems 1968–1972. London, Gollancz, 1973.
Fishing in the Sky: Love Poems. London, Poet and Printer, 1975.
Penguin Modern Poets 26, with Dannie Abse and D.J. Enright. London, Penguin, 1975.
Man Lying on a Wall: Poems 1972–1975. London, Gollancz, 1976.
The Echo Gate: Poems 1975–1978. London, Secker and Warburg, 1979.
Selected Poems 1963–1980. Winston-Salem, North Carolina, Wake Forest University Press, 1980.
Patchwork. Dublin, Gallery Press, 1981.
Poems 1963–1983. Edinburgh, Salamander Press, 1985.
Gorse Fires. London, Secker and Warburg, and Winston-Salem, North Carolina, Wake Forest University Press, 1991.
Baucis & Philemon. London, Poet and Printer, 1993.
Birds & Flowers. Edinburgh, Morning Star, 1994.
The Ghost Orchid. London, Cape, 1995.
Broken Dishes. Newry, Abbey Press, 1998.

Selected Poems. London, Cape, 1998.
Out of the Cold. Newry, Abbey Press, 1998.
The Weather in Japan. London, Cape, 2000.

Other

Tupenny Stung: Autobiographical Chapters. Belfast, Lagan Press, 1994.

Editor, *Causeway: The Arts in Ulster.* Belfast, Arts Council of Northern Ireland, and Dublin, Gill and Macmillan, 1971.
Editor, *Under the Moon, Over the Stars: Young People's Writing from Ulster.* Belfast, Arts Council of Northern Ireland, 1971.
Editor, *Selected Poems,* by Louis MacNeice. London, Faber, 1988.
Editor, *Poems by W.R. Rodgers.* Oldcastle, Gallery Press, 1993.

*

Critical Studies: ''Options: The Poetry of Michael Longley'' by Michael Allen, in *Eire-Ireland* (St. Paul, Minnesota), 10(4), 1975; ''A Question of Balance'' by John Mole, in *Times Literary Supplement* (London), 8, Feb 1980; ''‘Singing the Darkness into the Light’: Reflections on Recent Irish Poetry'' by Harry Marten, in *New England Review* (Hanover, New Hampshire), 3, 1980; ''Semantic Scruples: A Rhetoric for Politics in the North'' by D.E.S. Maxwell, in *Literature and the Changing Ireland,* edited by Peter Connelly, Corrards Cross, England, Colin Smythe, and Totowa, New Jersey, Barnes and Noble, 1982; ''Three Irish Voices'' by Charles O'Neill, in *Spirit* (South Orange, New Jersey), fall-winter 1989; ''Poetry Imagery As Political Fetishism: The Example of Michael Longley'' by Brian McIlroy, in *Canadian Journal of Irish Studies* (Saskatoon, Canada), 16(1), July 1990; ''Michael Longley's Homes'' by Peter McDonald, in *The Chosen Ground: Essays on the Contemporary Poetry of Northern Ireland,* edited by Neil Corcoran, Bridgend, Ireland, Seren, 1992; ''Michael Longley's List'' by John Lyon, in *English* (Leicester, England), 45(183), autumn 1996.

*   *   *

Michael Longley is one of several interesting Irish poets who made their debut during the 1960s. His first collection, *No Continuing City,* was already quite mature, although a number of the poems it contained dated from Longley's undergraduate years. His second collection, *An Exploded View,* showed that he had acquired greater technical assurance and had further humanized and extended his thematic range. Subsequent collections have consolidated his position as a poet of considerable importance.

Longley has consistently maintained a careful and disciplined attitude toward his craft, whether writing free verse or using rhyme and meter. He has successfully accommodated contemporary idiom within a wide variety of traditional forms, ranging from terza rima and the sonnet to octosyllabic eight-line stanzas. This skill owes much to a profound study of the metaphysical poets. Without having assimilated John Donne, Longley could hardly have written as he has of moths (''Epithalamion''):

Who hazard all to be
Where we, the only two it seems,

Inhabit so delightfully
A room it bursts its seams
And spills onto the lawn in beams . . .

In these early poems Longley demonstrated how effectively he could use various resonant words, such as ''brainstorm,'' ''histories,'' and ''anthem,'' although he tended to overexploit them. Greater maturity has brought a more finely honed technique, enabling him to discard such props. At the same time his ability to suggest the mysteries that underlie the appearances of life has been retained and developed. ''Casualty,'' a poem about a decaying sheep, exhibits this kind of awareness, although the earlier poeticisms have disappeared:

For the ribs began to scatter
The wool to move outward
As though hunger still worked there

As though something that had followed
Fox and crow was desperate for
A last morsel and was
Other than the wind or rain.

A deep sympathy with the animal world is very apparent in Longley's output. The variety of creatures in his poems is so large that there is a feeling at times of having wandered into a nature reserve. Longley looks on animals with an essentially kindly eye, with something of a city dweller's view perhaps. Sometimes they suggest the working of elemental forces; thus, the badger ''manages the earth with his paws.'' But the red in tooth and claw has at most no more than an implied presence in this poet's vision of nature; his animals are not offered as images of cruelty or menace.

To draw attention to Longley's interest in the animal world is not to imply that his creative scope is narrow. On the contrary, his imagination finds stimulus in areas as diverse as jazz, Ireland's prehistory, or the ancient literatures of Greece and Rome, in which he was immersed as a student, and of China. Thus, one encounters lines on a Sheela-na-gig (an ancient Irish female fertility figure) rubbing shoulders with glosses on passages from Ovid and from the *Odyssey* and the *Iliad,* as well as a poem on a water lily that celebrates the flower in lines as delicate and luminous as those of a Chinese lyric:

As if Venus and Betelgeuse had wings
And instead of mountainside or tree-top

Had found the right place for falling stars
And glided to a standstill on the lake . . .

Many poems, among them some of Longley's most compassionate, confront the horrors of the world wars, the Nazi concentration camps, and the troubles in Northern Ireland, where he lives. One of these links the delayed effects on his father of wounds sustained in World War I with the murders in Belfast of three British soldiers and a bus conductor. Despite living in an environment of such conflict, Longley has not rejected the fractured and psychically scarred society to which he is heir, as many Irish writers have done. In fact, he has made a point of claiming Ireland as his country, ''though today / *Timor mortis conturbat me.*'' Longley's sense of attachment to his Irish identity is indeed, like the standing stone of which he writes, firmly set to help him

To record the distances
Between islands of sunlight
And, as hub of the breezes,
To administer the scene . . .

—Rivers Carew

LOWBURY, Edward (Joseph Lister)

Nationality: British. **Born:** London, 6 December 1913. **Education:** St. Paul's School, London, 1927–33; University College, Oxford (Newdigate prize, 1934, Matthew Arnold memorial prize, 1937), 1933–37, B.A. (honors) 1936, B.M., B.Ch. 1939; London Hospital, University of Oxford Medical School, 1937–39, M.A. 1940, D.M. 1957. **Military Service:** Specialist in pathology, Royal Army Medical Corps, 1943–47: Major. **Family:** Married Alison Young, daughter of the poet Andrew Young, in 1954; three daughters. **Career:** Bacteriologist, 1946–79, and member, Medical Research Council Scientific Staff, Birmingham Accident Hospital; consultant adviser in bacteriology, Birmingham Regional Hospital Board, and founder and honorary director, Hospital Infection Research Laboratory, Birmingham, 1964–79. Editor, *Equator* magazine, Nairobi, Kenya, 1945–46. Visited the United States as a World Health Organization consultant in hospital infection in 1965; John Keats Memorial Lecturer, Guy's Hospital, London, 1973; visiting professor of medical microbiology, University of Aston, Birmingham, 1979. **Awards:** University of Birmingham research fellowship, 1957. Hon. D.Sc.: University of Aston, Birmingham, 1977; LL.D.: University of Birmingham, 1980. Fellow, Royal College of Pathologists, 1963; honorary fellow, Royal College of Physicians, 1977, and Royal College of Surgeons, 1978. Fellow, Royal Society of Literature, 1974. O.B.E. (Officer, Order of the British Empire), 1979. **Address:** 79 Vernon Road, Birmingham B16 9SQ, England.

PUBLICATIONS

Poetry

Fire: A Symphonic Ode. Oxford, Blackwell, 1934.
Port Meadow. Oxford, Blackwell, 1936.
Crossing the Line. London, Hutchinson, 1947.
Metamorphoses. Privately printed, 1955.
Time for Sale. London, Chatto and Windus-Hogarth Press, 1961.
New Poems. Richmond, Surrey, Keepsake Press, 1965.
Daylight Astronomy. London, Chatto and Windus-Hogarth Press, and Middletown, Connecticut, Wesleyan University Press, 1968.
Figures of Eight. Richmond, Surrey, Keepsake Press, 1969.
Green Magic (for children). London, Chatto and Windus, 1972.
Two Confessions. Richmond, Surrey, Keepsake Press, 1973.
The Night Watchman. London, Chatto and Windus-Hogarth Press, 1974.
Poetry and Paradox: An Essay, with Nineteen Relevant Poems. Richmond, Surrey, Keepsake Press, 1976.
Troika, with John Press and Michael Riviere. Stoke Ferry, Norfolk, Daedalus Press, 1977.
Selected Poems. Aberystwyth, Celtion Press, 1978.
The Ring. Birmingham, Pardoe, 1979.
A Letter from Masada. Richmond, Surrey, Keepsake Press, 1982.

Goldrush. Shipston-on-Stour, Warwickshire, Celandine Press, 1983.
Masada; Byzantium; Celle: Apocryphal Letters. Bristol, Sceptre Press, 1985.
Birmingham! Birmingham! Richmond, Surrey, Keepsake Press, 1985.
Flowering Cyprus. Hereford, Pointing Finger Press, 1986.
Variations on Aldeburgh. Hitchin, Hertfordshire, Mandeville Press, 1987.
A Letter from Hampstead: A Doctor Remembers His Patient, Bernard van Dieren. Richmond, Surrey, Keepsake Press, 1987.
Selected and New Poems. Frome, Somerset, Hippopotamus Press, 1990.
First Light: Eleven Poems. Richmond, Surrey, Keepsake Press, 1991.
Collected Poems. Salzburg, University of Salzburg Press, 1993.

Recording: *The Poet Speaks 2,* Argo.

Other

Facing North (miscellany), with Terence Heywood. London, Mitre Press, 1960.
Thomas Campion: Poet, Composer, Physician, with Timothy Salter and Alison Young. London, Chatto and Windus, and New York, Barnes and Noble, 1970.
Drug Resistance in Antimicrobial Therapy, with G.A.J. Ayliffe. Springfield, Illinois, Thomas, 1974.
Physic Meet and Metaphysic: A Celebration For Edward Lowbury, edited by Yann Lovelock. Salzburg, University of Salzburg, 1993.
Hallmarks of Poetry: Reflections on a Theme. Salzburg, University of Salzburg, 1994.

Editor, with others, *Control of Hospital Infection: A Practical Handbook.* London, Chapman and Hall, 1975.
Editor, *Widening Circles: Five Black Country Poets.* Stafford, West Midland Arts, 1976.
Editor, *Night Ride and Sunrise: An Anthology of New Poems.* Aberystwyth, Celtion Press, 1978.
Editor, with Alison Young, *The Poetical Works of Andrew Young.* London, Secker and Warburg, 1985.
Editor, with Alison Young, *To Shirk No Idleness: A Critical Biography of the Poet Andrew Young.* Salzburg, University of Salzburg Press, 1997.
Editor, with Alison Young, *Selected Poems of Andrew Young.* Manchester, Carcanet, 1998.

*

Manuscript Collections: University of Birmingham Library; State University of New York Library, Buffalo.

Critical Studies: ''Edward Lowbury,'' in *Southern Review* (Baton Rouge, Louisiana), spring 1970, and ''The Poetry of Edward Lowbury,'' in *Agenda* (London), 26(4), winter 1988, both by John Press; ''Edward Lowbury Issue'' of *Outposts* (Frome, Somerset), 164, spring 1990; by Anthony Selbourne, in *Agenda* (London), 31(3), fall 1993.

Edward Lowbury comments:

Poetry is an obsessional activity through which, at intervals in my medical life, I have been able to work off accumulated tension. It is for me an exploration through words of various experiences and in particular of painfully or pleasurably exciting or disturbing or conflicting experiences—love, hardship and loss, the attritions of time, childhood and age, nature and the unknown, experiences in my medical work. Situations that cause laughter as well as those that cause emotional responses seem to me suitable material for poetry. In the poem I discover verbal, visual, and metrical equivalents to represent the conflicts and ambiguities of the world about which I write. When the components shape themselves into structures, i.e., poems, with an inner tension, with what I judge to be the correct balance of thought and feeling, of harmony and discord, and when the structures give me—and others—a simultaneous feeling of surprise and inevitability, I feel I have found whatever it was I was looking for in my exploration. I usually take many wrong turnings before I find, if I ever do find, the right one. I think I can recognize when I have struck the right path and the place where I should stop, but I realize that neither the writer nor any individual critic can make categorical judgments.

*   *   *

Edward Lowbury's first collection of poems, *Port Meadow*, published when he was twenty-two, is graceful and pleasing but no more. His next collection, *Crossing the Line,* appeared in 1947, having won a competition organized by Hutchinson and judged by Edmund Blunden and Louis MacNeice. It represents a considerable advance on Lowbury's earlier work, two of the most interesting poems being "Tapiola," dedicated to Sibelius, and "The Dark Languages," written in Basic English, an early example of Lowbury's delight in tackling a technical problem.

It was not until 1961 that Lowbury brought out *Time for Sale.* During the war he had spent three years in East Africa as an officer in the Royal Army Medical Corps, and some of the poems in this collection take as their theme various aspects of East African life. "The Huntsman," for example, recounts a Swahili legend, and "Mua Hills" evokes with power and unsentimental sympathy the realities of tribal life:

> Black eyes, black heads—Kamba, Kikuyu, Nandi
> Sprout like grapes, expert at hanging round
> And doing nothing; were they warriors once,
>   Now gone to seed?

The remaining poems in *Time for Sale* display Lowbury's delight in the visible world, delicacy of perception, and compassion for men and women, especially for those who suffer the extremes of pain.

The sequence *Metamorphoses,* written in terza rima with lines of six syllables (Lowbury's own invention), explores with precision and wit a variety of objects: windmills, bombed buildings, a nightingale, and, most exquisite of all, a swan:

> From bill to breast a snake,
> From nape to tail a cloud
> Resting upon the lake,
>
> Puffed up rather than proud
> The swan in any place
> Attracts a little crowd.

One poem, "Surgery of a Burn," draws on Lowbury's experience of the operating theater. He not only describes the operation with clinical accuracy but also portrays the shock and agony experienced by those who return after surgery to the world of consciousness:

> Now sutures, bandages—the amen;
>   A spider in the brain
> Tugs at its web; returning light
>   Is flanked by fear and pain.

"Night Train" shows Lowbury's art at its finest. The setting is the carriage of a train in which the travelers are transfigured by the light of the moon. Lowbury sets great store by paradox, believing it to be not an ingenious verbal trick but rather a means of penetrating into the heart of the ambiguity and mystery in which our lives are shrouded. In Greek mythology the Gorgon turned men to stone, but in Lowbury's poem the moonlight that whitens and petrifies also reveals the soul. The poet's wit and acute observation are raised to the power of lyrical delight, and the poetic imagination is, like the moon, a source of illumination:

> The prosperous upstart, insolent
>   To those less certain of their goal,
> Becomes a statue, shares the fate
> Of Lot's wife, draws the Gordon's eye
>   And, petrified, reveals a soul.

Since *Time for Sale* there has been no revolutionary change of direction in Lowbury's verse, but the range and depth of his imagination have steadily increased. We may note the entrance of new themes: married love, the world of childhood, the majesty of nature, the sickness of our society, the death of men and women dear to the poet. In some of his later poems Lowbury commands a grave music appropriate to the prevailing mood of sadness, nowhere more eloquently than in "Departure," one of the most impressive poems in *The Night Watchman.* The mourners at the funeral of a friend and colleague

> take away
> More of you than we leave: a restless memory
> Of sentences unfinished, kindnesses
> Never requited, moments in the sun
> Or the green valley; these rather than ashes
> And something more remote than outer space
> Compel my tears, require my requiem.

In the 1980s Lowbury published two collections inspired by places and by those associated with their history. *Birmingham! Birmingham!,* a celebration of the city that has been Lowbury's home for half a century, is marked by dry humor and an easy, colloquial intimacy. "Mr Hansom's Pantheon" (the Town Hall where concerts have been held for more than one hundred years) is an example of Lowbury's deftness. This is the place

> Where spring-water Sibelius conducted
> *The Swan* and, in the Interval,
>   Asked for his double-Scotch to be topped-up—
> With whisky.

The anecdote, while not invalidating Lowbury's earlier "Tapiola," does set it in a wider perspective.

The second collection, *Variations on Aldeburgh*, portrays diverse facets of this small Suffolk fishing port and the surrounding countryside: buildings such as the Moot Hall, Snape Maltings, and the churches of Aldeburgh and of Blythburgh; inhabitants past and present—George Crabbe, for example, who told the story of Peter Grimes, the protagonist of Britten's opera; and some of those who created and sustained the Aldeburgh Festival. More romantic than *Birmingham! Birmingham!*, this volume combines the formal and the conversational with unobtrusive skill.

Another venture is a series of what Lowbury called *Apocryphal Letters,* the first three of which were published under the title *Masada; Byzantium; Celle.* They describe, respectively, the siege of Masada by the Romans in A.D. 72, the blinding of fifteen hundred Bulgar prisoners in 1014 by Byzantine Emperor Basil II, and the fate of Caroline Matilda, the youngest sister of King George III and the former queen of Denmark, who was imprisoned in a castle in Jutland. Lowbury's powers of narration and his ability to depict historical dramas and those who took part in them are equally impressive.

Lowbury's *Collected Poems* (1993) reprints all of the poems in the volumes published between 1961 and 1991, together with a selection from four volumes published between 1934 and 1957. The book ends with thirty-eight uncollected poems written in every decade from the 1930s to the 1990s. The final poem in the book, "79 Vernon Road," is one of Lowbury's finest achievements. In a celebration of love and a contemplation of death the poet asks,

> do I see
> A snowman we once made
> For the children? Today it looks
> Translucent, seems to move inscrutably
>
> Towards the window, but can't quite decide
> When it will tap the glass
> And beckon one of us to follow
> Through to the spaceless, timeless world outside.

Lowbury's devotion to his art for well over half a century has produced a substantial body of work distinguished by technical accomplishment and imaginative richness. Although his narrative and philosophical poems are of high quality, it is perhaps his lyrics and his meditations on personal themes that constitute his finest achievements.

—John Press

LUCIE-SMITH, (John) Edward (McKenzie)

Nationality: British. **Born:** Kingston, Jamaica, 27 February 1933. Settled in England in 1946. **Education:** King's School, Canterbury; Merton College, Oxford, B.A. 1954. **Military Service:** Education officer, Royal Air Force, 1954–56. **Career:** Worked in advertising, 1956–66. Freelance journalist. Co-founder, Turret Books, London, 1965. **Awards:** Rhys memorial prize, 1962; Arts Council Triennial poetry prize, 1962. Fellow, Royal Society of Literature. **Agent:** Rogers Coleridge and White Ltd., 20 Powis Mews, London W11 1JN, England.

PUBLICATIONS

Poetry

(Poems). Oxford, Fantasy Press, 1954.
A Tropical Childhood and Other Poems. London and New York, Oxford University Press, 1961.
Penguin Modern Poets 6, with Jack Clemo and George MacBeth. London, Penguin, 1964.
Confessions and Histories. London and New York, Oxford University Press, 1964.
Fir-Tree Song. London, Turret, 1965.
Jazz for the N.U.F. London, Turret, 1965.
A Game of French and English. London, Turret, 1965.
Three Experiments. London, Turret, 1965.
Gallipoli—Fifty Years After. London, Turret, 1966.
Cloud Sun Fountain Statue. Cologne, Hansjörg Mayer, 1966.
Silence, music by Wallace Southam, London, Turret, 1967.
"Heureux Qui, Comme Ulysse. . ." London, Turret, 1967.
Borrowed Emblems. London, Turret, 1967.
Towards Silence. London, Oxford University Press, 1968.
Teeth and Bones. London, Pebble Press, 1968.
Six Kinds of Creature. London, Turret, 1968.
Snow Poems. London, Turret, 1969.
Egyptian Ode. Stoke Ferry, Norfolk, Daedalus Press, 1969.
Six More Beasts. London, Turret, 1970.
Lovers. Frensham, Surrey, Sceptre Press, 1970.
The Rhino. London, Steam Press, 1971.
A Girl Surveyed. London, Hanover Gallery, 1971.
The Yak, The Polar Bear, The Dodo, The Goldfish, The Dinosaur, The Parrot (posters). London, Turret, 1971.
Two Poems of Night. London, Turret, 1972.
The Rabbit. London, Turret, 1973.
The Well-Wishers. London and New York, Oxford University Press, 1974.
Seven Colours. Cambridge, Rampant Lions Press, 1974.
Inscriptions/Inscripciones. Mexico City, Ainle Press, 1975.
Beasts with Bad Morals. London, Leinster Fine Books, 1984.

Novel

The Dark Pageant. London, Blond and Briggs, 1977.

Other

Mystery in the Universe: Notes on an Interview with Allen Ginsberg. London, Turret, 1965.
Op Art, edited by Duncan Taylor. London, BBC, 1966.
What Is a Painting? London, Macdonald, 1966.
Thinking about Art: Critical Essays. London, Calder and Boyars, 1968.
A Beginner's Guide to Auctions (as Peter Kershaw). London, Rapp and Whiting, 1968.
Movements in Art since 1945. London, Thames and Hudson, 1969; revised edition, 1975, 1984; as *Late Modern: The Visual Arts since 1945,* New York, Praeger, 1969; revised edition, 1976; revised edition, Thames and Hudson, 1984.
A Concise History of French Painting. London, Thames and Hudson, and New York, Praeger, 1971.

Eroticism in Western Art. London, Thames and Hudson, and New York, Praeger, 1972; as *Sexuality in Western Art,* London, Thames and Hudson, 1991.

Symbolist Art. London, Thames and Hudson, and New York, Praeger, 1972.

Movements in Modern Art, with Donald Carroll. New York, Horizon Press, 1973.

The First London Catalogue: All the Appurtenances of a Civilized, Amusing, and Comfortable Life. London, Paddington Press, and New York, Two Continents, 1974.

World of the Makers: Today's Master Craftsmen and Craftswomen. London, Paddington Press, and New York, Two Continents, 1975.

The Waking Dream: Fantasy and the Surreal in Graphic Art 1450–1900, with Aline Jacquiot. London, Thames and Hudson, and New York, Knopf, 1975.

The Invented Eye: Masterpieces of Photography 1839–1914. London, Paddington Press, and New York, Two Continents, 1975.

The Burnt Child: An Autobiography. London, Gollancz, 1975.

Joan of Arc. London, Allen Lane, 1976; New York, Norton, 1977.

How the Rich Lived, and *Work and Struggle: The Painter as Witness 1870–1914,* with Celestine Dars. London and New York, Paddington Press, 2 vols., 1976–77.

Henri Fantin-Latour. Oxford, Phaidon, and New York, Rizzoli, 1977.

Art Today: From Abstract Expressionism to Superrealism. Oxford, Phaidon, and New York, Morrow, 1977; revised edition, as *Art Now: From Abstract Expressionism to Superrealism,* Morrow, 1981; revised edition, Phaidon, 1983.

Tóulouse-Lautrec. Oxford, Phaidon, 1977; New York, Dutton, 1978; revised edition, Phaidon, 1983.

Work and Struggle: The Painter As Witness 1870–1914. New York and London, Paddington Press, 1977.

Outcasts of the Sea: Pirates and Piracy. London and New York, Paddington Press, 1978.

A Concise History of French Painting. London, Thames and Hudson, and New York, Oxford University Press, 1978.

Super Realism. Oxford, Phaidon, 1979.

Furniture: A Concise History. London, Thames and Hudson, and New York, Oxford University Press, 1979.

Cultural Calendar of the Twentieth Century. Oxford, Phaidon, 1979.

Art in the Seventies. Oxford, Phaidon, and Ithaca, New York, Cornell University Press, 1980.

The Story of Craft: A History of the Craftsman's Role. Oxford, Phaidon, and Ithaca, New York, Cornell University Press, 1981.

The Art of Caricature. London, Orbis, and Ithaca, New York, Cornell University Press, 1981.

The Body: Images of the Nude. London, Thames and Hudson, 1981.

The Sculpture of Helaine Blumenfeld. London, Sinclair Browne, 1982.

Bertie and the Big Red Ball (for children). London, Murray-Gallery Five, 1982.

Jan Vanriet. Amsterdam, Van Gennep, 1982.

A History of Industrial Design. Oxford, Phaidon, and New York, Van Nostrand, 1983.

The Thames and Hudson Dictionary of Art Terms. London and New York, Thames and Hudson, 1984.

American Art Now. Oxford, Phaidon Press, and New York, Morrow, 1985.

Art of the 1930's: The Age of Anxiety. London, Weidenfeld and Nicolson, and New York, Rizzoli, 1985.

Lives of the Great Twentieth-Century Artists. London, Weidenfeld and Nicolson, and New York, Rizzoli, 1986.

Sculpture Since 1945. Oxford, Phaidon, and New York, Universe, 1987.

The Self-Portrait: A Modern View, with Sean Kelly. London, Sarema Press, 1987.

The New British Painting, with Carolyn Cohen and Judith Higgins. Oxford, Phaidon, 1988.

Impressionist Women. London, Weidenfeld and Nicolson, and New York, Crown, 1989.

Art Today. Oxford, Phaidon, 1989.

Art in the Eighties. Oxford, Phaidon, 1990.

Art Deco Painting. Oxford, Phaidon, 1990.

Outcasts of the Sea: Pirates and Piracy. Norwalk, Connecticut, Easton Press, 1990.

Richard Lippold, Sculpture, with Curtis L. Carter and Jack W. Burnham. Milwaukee, Wisconsin, Patrick and Beatrice Haggerty Museum of Art, Marquette University, 1990.

Fletcher Benton. New York, H.N. Abrams, 1990.

Alexander. London, Art Books International, 1992.

Rustin: Drawings. London, T. Heneage, 1991.

Harry Holland: The Painter and Reality. London, Art Books International, 1991.

Art & Civilization. Englewood Cliffs, New Jersey, Prentice Hall, 1992.

Wendy Taylor. London, Art Books International, 1992.

Andres Nagel. Barcelona, Ediciones Poligrafa, S.A., 1992.

Elizabeth Fritsch: Vessels from Another World, Metaphysical Pots in Painted Stoneware. London, Bellew-Northern Centre for Contemporary Art, 1993.

Art and Civilization. New York, H.N. Abrams, 1993.

Latin American Art of the Twentieth Century. New York, Thames and Hudson, 1993.

Frink: A Portrait. London, Bloomsbury, 1994.

Race, Sex, and Gender in Contemporary Art: The Rise of Minority Culture. London, Art Books International, 1994.

American Realism. London, Thames and Hudson, 1994.

John Kirby: The Company of Strangers. Edinburgh, Mainstream Publishing, 1994.

Elisabeth Frink: Sculpture since 1984 and Drawings. London, Art Books International, 1994.

Chadwick. Stroud, Gloucestershire, Lypiatt Studio, 1997.

Ars Erotica: An Arousing History of Erotic Art. London, Weidenfeld and Nicolson, and New York, Rizzoli, 1997.

Zoo: Animals in Art. London, Aurum Press, and New York, Watson-Guptill, 1998.

Adam: The Male Figure in Art. London, Weidenfeld and Nicolson, and New York, Rizzoli, 1998.

Judy Chicago: An American Vision. New York, Watson-Guptill, 2000.

Editor, *Rubens.* London, Spring, 1961.

Editor, *Raphael.* London, Batchworth Press, 1961.

Editor, with Philip Hobsbaum, *A Group Anthology.* London, Oxford University Press, 1963.

Editor, *The Penguin Book of Elizabethan Verse.* London, Penguin, 1965.

Editor, *The Liverpool Scene.* London, Rapp and Carroll, and New York, Doubleday, 1967.

Editor, *A Choice of Browning's Verse.* London, Faber, 1967.

Editor, *The Penguin Book of Satirical Verse.* London, Penguin, 1967.

Editor, *Holding Your Eight Hands: A Book of Science Fiction Verse.* New York, Doubleday, 1969; London, Rapp and Whiting, 1970.

Editor, with Patricia White, *Art in Britain 1969–70.* London, Dent, 1970.

Editor, *British Poetry since 1945.* London, Penguin, 1970; revised edition, 1985.

Editor, with Simon Watson-Taylor, *French Poetry Today: A Bilingual Anthology.* London, Rapp and Whiting-Deutsch, 1971.

Editor, *Primer of Experimental Poetry 1870–1922.* London, Rapp and Whiting-Deutsch, 1971.

Editor, *A Garland from the Greek: Poems from the Greek Anthology.* London, Trigram Press, 1971.

Editor, *Masterpieces from the Pompidou Centre.* Paris, Centre Georges Pompidou, 1982; London, Thames and Hudson, 1983.

Editor, *The Male Nude: A Modern View.* Oxford, Phaidon, and New York, Rizzoli, 1985.

Editor, with Paul J. Smith, *Craft Today: Poetry of the Physical.* New York, Weidenfeld and Nicolson, 1986; as *American Craft Today,* London, Weidenfeld and Nicolson, 1987.

Editor, *The Essential Osbert Lancaster: An Anthology in Brush and Pen.* London, Barrie and Jenkins, 1988.

Editor, *Women and Art: Contested Territory,* by Judy Chicago. New York, Watson-Guptill, 1999.

Translator, *Manet,* by Robert Rey. Milan, Uffici Press, 1962.

Translator, *Jonah: Selected Poems of Jean-Paul de Dadelsen.* London, Rapp and Carroll, 1967.

Translator, *Five Great Odes,* by Paul Claudel. London, Rapp and Whiting, 1967; Chester Springs, Pennsylvania, Dufour, 1970.

Translator, *The Muses,* by Paul Claudel. London, Turret, 1967.

*

Manuscript Collections: Humanities Research Center, University of Texas, Austin; Pennsylvania State University, University Park.

Edward Lucie-Smith comments:

(1970) My activities, though various, seem to revolve about poetry and the modern arts in general. I hate the term "poet." I am simply a man who tries to react honestly to the world.

Since I was one of the founder-members of the Group and for some years chairman of its discussions, I am in that sense a Group poet. Nowadays I cannot think of anyone who writes much like me.

I think my development as a poet could be described roughly as follows: I began in the wake of the Movement, among a group of undergraduate poets at Oxford that included Anthony Thwaite, George MacBeth, Adrian Mitchell, and Geoffrey Hill. I was then a poet of tight conventional forms, and my chief subject was childhood experience. Under the influence of the sessions of the Group, I began to write longer poems, often dramatic monologues, which were greatly influenced by Browning. Poems of this sort appear in my second volume, *Confessions and Histories.* At this period I gradually became dissatisfied with conventional verse forms and especially with their lack of real flexibility. I began to look for forms that would give (a) greater colloquialism, (b) greater simplicity, and (c) greater concision. The results of these experiments can be seen in my third book, *Towards Silence,* and I have continued them in my more recent work. The metrical principle in most of my recent poetry is twofold: a strict syllabic "ground," and a melody of strong and light stresses. I use the syllabic pattern to syncopate the meter I have chosen, which is usually mismatched to it, e.g., dactyls and a seven- or an eleven-syllable line. The effect is, I think, very like that of Greek or Latin poetry, without strictly copying Greek or Latin forms. The influences are various: Catullus, the Elizabethan experiments with classical meter and especially Campion, Rochester for his colloquial directness, French medieval poetry, and Pound. I am very concerned to preserve strict prose order of words. A common criticism of my recent work is that it is too "thin," not complex enough. My translators, on the other hand, tend to complain of simplicity that conceals difficulty.

I am interested in extending the scope of poetry, in writing poster poems and poems to be set to music, for example.

My themes are, I think, commonly erotic (poems about love), historical, and aesthetic (poems about artists and works of art, etc.) and occasionally religious.

*   *   *

Edward Lucie-Smith's poetry has ranged over the years from the neatly turned and rhymed Movement verses of his Fantasy Press pamphlet of 1954 to the experimentation and freedom of syllabics in, for example, his collection *Towards Silence,* published in 1968. Together with this variety and development goes an impression of a conscious artistry, not only in individual poems but also in the compilation of the collections themselves. The poems in *Towards Silence* gain from being read as a collection, though each poem stands in its own right. There also is the influence of Lucie-Smith's knowledge of and occupation with the visual arts. The carefully juxtaposed visual images are often starkly clear, and the poems themselves have frequently been prompted by paintings or sculpture: "An unstrung bow. The white, slack / Body collapsing. Mourners / Like mountains / Pieta."

The danger with such poetry can be that the artistry too finely applied tends to exclude feeling, but in the best of Lucie-Smith's poetry this is not so. In early personal poems about his boyhood, such as "A Tropical Childhood" or "The Lesson," the feeling is to be clearly felt: "I cried for knowledge which was bitterer / Than any grief. For there and then I knew / That grief has uses." In the group of poems about artists in the collection *Confessions and Histories,* for example, the popular "Caravaggio Dying" and, to my mind, the much better "Soliloquy in the Dark," he succeeds in expressing an empathy not only with the situation he takes as his subject matter but also with the feelings of the characters involved:

> —how I used to stumble
> From frame to frame and rap upon the glass
> And scratch the canvas with my old man's nails,
> Tears smarting useless eyes with salt and gum.
> Flat is not round. And dankness is not colour.

In later poems, while they use much freer forms, the earlier note of personal feeling comes through strongly:

> Don't wonder what it was
> that filled the space between
> thinking and thinking.
>   Gone.
> My day is like a staircase
> with one step missing.

It was the collection *Towards Silence* that signaled a movement into a more markedly direct simplicity of statement and form, though the implications and overtones may be far from being simple, as in the nearly perfect poem "Silence" that rounds off the book: "Hear / Your own noisy machine, which / Is moving towards silence." From the same period comes the remarkable translation of Paul Claudel in *Five Great Odes*, in which Lucie-Smith captures the quality and feelings of this high, near baroque poetry. To set this translation beside the simple directness of his own poetry is to illustrate Lucie-Smith's versatility and the range of his accomplishment.

—John Cotton

LUX, Thomas

Nationality: American. **Born:** Northampton, Massachusetts, 10 December 1946. **Education:** Emerson College, Boston, B.A. 1970; University of Iowa, Iowa City, 1971. **Family:** Married Jean Kilbourne in 1983 (divorced); one daughter. **Career:** Poet-in-residence, Emerson College, 1972–75; since 1975 member of the faculty, Sarah Lawrence College, Bronxville, New York; since 1975, Warren Wilson College; since 1980, Columbia University, New York; University of Houston, 1981; Boston University, 1981; Cooper Union, New York, 1987. Co-founder and editor, Born Dream Press; managing editor, *Iowa Review*, Iowa City, 1971–72, and *Ploughshares*, Cambridge, Massachusetts, 1973. **Awards:** Bread Loaf scholarship, 1970; MacDowell Colony fellowship, 1973, 1974, 1976, 1978, 1980, 1982; National Endowment for the Arts grant, 1976, 1981, 1988; Guggenheim fellowship, 1988; Kingsley Tufts Poetry award, 1995, for *Split Horizon*. **Address:** Department of English, Sarah Lawrence College, One Mead Way, Bronxville, New York 10708–5999, U.S.A.

PUBLICATIONS

Poetry

The Land Sighted. Cambridge, Massachusetts, Pym Randall, 1970.
Memory's Handgrenade. Cambridge, Massachusetts, Pym Randall, 1972.
The Glassblower's Breath. Cleveland, Ohio, Cleveland State University, 1976.
Sunday. Boston, Houghton Mifflin, 1979.
Like a Wide Anvil from the Moon the Light. New York, Black Market, 1980.
Massachusetts. Roslindale, Massachusetts, Pym Randall, 1981.
Tarantulas on the Lifebuoy. Bristol, Rhode Island, Ampersand Press, 1983.
Half Promised Land. Boston, Houghton Mifflin, 1986.
Sunday: Poems. Pittsburgh, Carnegie Mellon, 1989.
The Drowned River. Boston, Houghton Mifflin, 1990.
A Boat in the Forest. Easthampton, Massachusetts, Adastra Press, 1992.
Pecked to Death by Swans. Easthampton, Massachusetts, Adastra Press, 1993.
Split Horizon. Boston, Houghton Mifflin, 1994.

The Blind Swimmer: Selected Early Poems, 1970–1975. Easthampton, Massachusetts, Adastra Press, 1996.
New and Selected Poems, 1975–1995. Boston, Houghton Mifflin, 1997.

Other

Editor, with Jane Cooper and Sylvia Winner, *The Sanity of Earth and Grass.* Gardiner, Maine, Tilbury House, 1994.

*

Critical Study: "A Shelter, a Kingdom, a Half Promised Land: Three Poets in Mid-Career" by Peter Harris, in *Virginia Quarterly Review* (Charlottesville, Virginia), 63(3), summer 1987.

* * *

Intensely personal, the poetry of Thomas Lux is tormented and tortured, full of complex and disjointed images reflecting an insane and inhospitable world. The sense of personal pain is strongest in his early poetry, where he seems to be wrestling with his own private hell. Part of his growth as a poet has been to move out of the strictly personal into a more public realm, where private grievances and personal difficulties are projected against the background of contemporary history and events and against a background of metaphysical despair. From his first collection in 1972 Lux has been hard at work grappling with what he calls life's "facts," a term too banal and neutral to convey the harshness of meaning he gives it in his poetry.

Memory's Handgrenade, published in 1972, immediately established Lux as a new poet capable of providing astonishing and shocking insights in a variety of powerful poetic forms. Lux turned out poems in which the sane and the insane, the real and the surreal, interpenetrate in juxtapositions of images that create shocking and original insights into the nature of the human condition. Ever on the edge of madness, and sometimes seemingly over that edge, Lux writes with an intensity of personal psychological distress that reminds us of the work of Roethke and Plath. In the poem "Five Men I Know" Lux provides brief "portraits" (more like snapshots) of five men in such extraordinary, nightmarish, and personal circumstances that they seem to be in some sense part of Lux and represent aspects of his personality. Yet the poem is so highly symbolized that understanding the meaning of the men's circumstances or of their dreams is difficult. Although hard to decode, the images are startling and original and suggest an entirely new voice in American poetry.

In his next volume, *The Glassblower's Breath*, Lux's preoccupation with a nightmarish and ego-centered world takes on a new dimension. In addition to the poems in which there is no reference beyond the self, he has written many poems in which he seeks to place himself in historical time and, in the process, to establish a point of external reference. The book is a successful effort to achieve relationship with the world. The book's title comes from the poem "History and Abstraction," in which Lux considers the idea of the passage of time as an abstraction for which he has complete disdain. Rather, he sees historical truth bound up in significant achievements or events. Characteristic of Lux is the fact that these events are "dark" moments in human history such as the development of the electric chair. For him "technology reached its peak / with the electric chair." The most fascinating dimension of his idea of history is bound up in his image "of the dead / glassblower's breath still caught / in the red vase . . .," an image that suggests a condition of intense isolation as well as entrapment. The world of the creator is a closed world that in some sense stands outside history. The image is a metaphor for Lux's sense of his own creativity; he sees himself trapped in the words of his poems.

Lux's next volume, *Sunday,* contains forty new poems in the vein of the previous book. For the moment Lux seems to be trapped in writing about death and loss, subjects he pursues with a vengeance. If anything, the volume is devoted to revealing more of the terrible facts about life—its pain, its suffering, and its ultimate emptiness and meanness. In "Solo Native" he projects an image of the utter desolation of existence: "You're alone and you know / a few things: the stars are pinholes, / slits in the hangman's mask." In "Gold on Mule" he provides a metaphor for nature's inhospitality: "the sun slams / on the wing of a fly / seeking moisture around the eye / of a mule . . ." In "Miserable Time" he presents the Italian poet Dino Campana, in an adaptation from his poems *Orphic Songs,* speaking casually of his longing for death as if it meant nothing to him: "I hope the Pale One comes to me and says: / Let's go, Pal." Throughout the entire volume there is hardly a moment of relief from such concerns.

In the later volume *Half Promised Land* Lux collects many of the poems that had appeared in earlier volumes. There is a noticeable shift in this volume from poems that have little objective reference to poems that have a great deal to say about the external world. Lux demonstrates concern for social problems, for the poor, the hungry, and the homeless, for a society based on money, class, and privilege, and for the inequality and injustice of such a society. Historical movements, events, and persons become his subject matter, as in "Dr. Goebbel's Novels," a poem about the lies and deceits perpetrated by the notorious Nazi propagandist Joseph Goebbels. In "A Tenth of a Cent a Stitch" Lux deplores the condition of homelessness, which he sees as a crime against humanity. He contrasts the plight of the homeless living in cardboard boxes to the sumptuous lifestyle of the rich.

Lux's volume *The Drowned River* breaks new ground. From his first volume, *Memory's Handgrenade,* it was apparent that Lux was a master of direct statement. His rhythms and syntax imitate speech that is hard and precise, one in which no word is superfluous. The words are like sand or small stones stuck in the mouth or hurled at the eyes. In this direct speech Lux forces us to see life as meager, unpromising, and finally disastrous. In *The Drowned River* he has become so adept at presenting these "truths" that he is now able to appear almost relaxed, conversational, casual. Understatement becomes a powerful poetic tool for him to hammer home once more his view of the futility of human existence. Of course, it is possible to acknowledge a kind of courage in his continuous effort to sound the dirge of life in his songs and to remain uncompromising in his vision.

Such it is in the world of Lux. There is no place here for the fainthearted, the weak, or the hopeful. Life, it seems, is not to be lived but rather endured.

—Richard Damashek

M

MACKEY, Nathaniel (Ernest)

Nationality: American. **Born:** Miami, Florida, 25 October 1947.
Education: Princeton University, Princeton, New Jersey, 1965–69,
A.B. 1969; Stanford University, Stanford, California, 1970–74, Ph.D.
1975. **Family:** Married Pascale Gaitet in 1990; one daughter and one
stepson. **Career:** Professor, University of Wisconsin, Madison,
1974–76; professor, University of Southern California, Los Angeles,
1976–79. Since 1979 professor, University of California, Santa Cruz.
Editor, *Hambone.* **Awards:** Woodrow Wilson fellowship, 1969;
National Poetry Series selection, 1985, for *Eroding Witness;* Whiting
Writer's award, 1993. **Address:** c/o Moving Parts Press, 70 Cathedral
Drive, Santa Cruz, California 95060, U.S.A.

PUBLICATIONS

Poetry

Four for Trane. Los Angeles, Golemics, 1978.
Septet for the End of Time. Santa Cruz, California, Boneset Press,
    1983.
Eroding Witness. Urbana, University of Illinois Press, 1985.
Outlantish. Tucson, Chax Press, 1992.
School of Udhra. San Francisco, City Lights Books, 1993.
Song of the Andoumboulou: 18–20. Santa Cruz, California, Moving
    Parts Press, 1994.
Whatsaid Serif. San Francisco, City Lights Books, 1998.

Recording: *Strick: Song of the Andoumboulou 16–25,* Spoken En-
    gine, 1995.

Novels

Bedouin Hornbook. Lexington, Kentucky, Callaloo Fiction Series,
    1986.
Djbot Baghostus's Run. Los Angeles, Sun and Moon Press, 1993.

Other

*Discrepant Engagement: Dissonance, Cross-Culturality and Experi-
    mental Writing.* New York, Cambridge University Press, 1993.

Editor, with Art Lange, *Moment's Notice: Jazz in Poetry and Prose.*
    Minneapolis, Minnesota, Coffee House Press, 1993.

*

Critical Studies: "Let's Call This: Race, Writing, and Difference in
Jazz" by Winston Smith, in *Public* (Toronto), 1990/91; Nathaniel
Mackey issue of *Talisman* (Hoboken, New Jersey), 1992; "The
'Mired Sublime' of Nathaniel Mackey's *Song of Andoumboulou*" by
Paul Naylor, in *Postmodern Culture* (Raleigh, North Carolina), 1995;
interview with Christopher Funkhouser, in *Callaloo* (Baltimore),
18(2), spring 1995; "On Nathaniel Mackey," in *Chicago Review,*
43(1), winter 1997; *Scenes of Intent: Community, Lyric Subjectivity,*

*and the Formation of Poetic Career: Robert Duncan, Robin Blaser,
Charles Olson, and Nathaniel Mackey* (dissertation) by Andrew
Richard Mossin, Temple University, 1998.

*　　*　　*

Nathaniel Mackey's work describes and inhabits a pluralistic
universe of spirits. Divinities from Africa and the Middle East weave
through his prose and poetry like a root system, creating what might
be described as a New World spirit culture of jazz.

Eroding Witness (1985), Mackey's first full-length collection,
serves as a pantheon and map for his unique series *From a Broken
Bottle Traces of Perfume Still Emanate,* of which *Bedouin Hornbook*
(1986) is the first volume. Though classified as a novel, the book can
equally be viewed as a prose poem in epistolary form. In the work N.,
a postbebopper, postmodern poet-musician, who is the book's main
character, carries on a conversation with the Angel of Dust about the
deeper nature of the priesthood and practice of jazz on both an
everyday and a cosmic level. In part through language itself, these two
levels are conflated in a way that seems both natural and tinged with
yearning. N. doubles on saxello and contrabass clarinet in a jazz band
first called the Deconstructive Woodwind Chorus, then named the
East Bay Dread Ensemble, and finally, and appropriately, known as
the Mystic Horn Society, and he reports to the Angel of Dust about the
band's various jobs. For example, just as the band is renamed Mystic
Horn Society, he writes, "We haven't done any actual playing yet but
we've had an interesting series of discussions on the idea of *duende,*
some of them quite heated at times." The world through which N.
moves is surrounded by polycultural presences and signs from
African religions transformed through slavery, colonization, exile,
containment, and resistance.

Bedouin Hornbook is the most profoundly well realized work of
poetic writing to emerge out of the American free jazz movement,
which began in the late 1960s and was identified with the political and
social black power movement in the United States. The book's
heterodox play crunches anthropology (texts and numbers), critical
theory, poetic ethnography (Hurston, Deren), and musicology into a
continuum that has no end to its delights and surprises. It is an
extraordinary project.

Mackey also edits *Hambone,* a vigorous literary periodical. It
includes a broad, yet precise range of poetry and poetics, in which Sun
Ra can be read in the same company as Leslie Scalapino. With Art
Lange he coedited *Moment's Notice,* an outstanding anthology of
poetic and creative writing on jazz that is notable for its intelligence,
inclusiveness, and scope.

—David Meltzer

MACLEAN, Alasdair

Nationality: Scottish. **Born:** Glasgow,16 March 1926. **Awards:**
Cholmondeley award, 1974; Heinemann award, 1974. **Address:** c/o
Victor Gollancz Ltd., 14 Henrietta Street, London WC2E 8QJ,
England.

PUBLICATIONS

Poetry

From the Wilderness. London, Gollancz, 1973; New York, Harper, 1975.
Waking the Dead. London, Gollancz, 1976.

Other

Night Falls on Ardnamurchan: The Twilight of a Crofting Family. London, Gollancz, 1984.
A MacDonald for the Prince: The Story of Neil MacEachen. Sornoway, Isle of Lewis, Acair, 1982; revised edition, 1990.
Summer Hunting a Prince: The Escape of Charles Edward Stuart. Sornoway, Isle of Lewis, Acair, 1992.

*   *   *

The attempt to come to grips with the fundamental questions about life with which serious literature ought to be concerned need not of itself be related to the physical location of the writer. Alasdair Maclean left university studies to work a croft near Ardnamurchan in Argyll. *From the Wilderness* did not appear before the public until he was into his forties, although something of his quality could be seen from anthologized poems in the annual *Scottish Poetry* and elsewhere. He is, therefore, a late starter, at any rate so far as publication is concerned. All to the good, since it means that for the most part he wants to say things, not merely to gyrate like some youthful virtuoso for the sake of attracting fashionable attention. He also has an assured and personal voice.

Maclean tells his reader bluntly what to expect from him:

I leave the foothills of the images
and climb, What I pursue's not means but ends.
You may come, if you've a mind to travelling.
Meet me at the point where the language bends.

At his best Maclean writes with a hard, direct economy, drawing his imagery and the strength of his thought from the way of life he loves and with which he is familiar. For instance, there is the countryman's unsentimental approach to matters of life and death, as in "Hen Dying":

The other hens have cast her out.
They batter her with their beaks
Whenever they come across her.
Most of them are her daughters.
Hens are inhuman.

Maclean's poem "Rams" uses the same terse, short-sentence style to build up a powerful apprehension of nature's sexual prodigality and mindless directorial force, a fact that the ingenuity of Homo sapiens often contrives to fudge for comfort:

I found a ram dead once.
It was trapped by the forefeet

in the dark waters of a peatbog,
drowned before help could arrive
by the sheer weight of its skull.
Maiden ewes were grazing near it,
immune to its clangerous lust.
It knelt on the bank, hunched over its own image
its great head buried in the great head facing it.
Its horns, going forward in the old way,
had battered through at last to the other side.

Not a word, not a rhythm is false here, and Maclean has many poems with this quality in his first collection. There is also some harsh satire apparently arising, though not always admitting such origin, out of the unconfessed awareness of the Gael that his way of life and his culture are now peripheral and that, rant as he may against the urban-dwelling Lowlander, the Gael himself has been his own worst enemy. Not all of these outbursts are entirely plausible, as in "Eagles":

An eagle of that breed once, for a joke,
picked up a stunted Highlander
and flew him south, witless from the journey
but fertile still,
Hence your race of Lowlands Scots.

Inevitably, as in every collection, there are some filler pieces in which there is evident the metaphysical influence of the later, and poetically drier, Norman MacCaig. Such a poem is "Sea and Sky," its feyly sentimental conclusion so out of keeping with the firmness of this poet's best texture and direct sounding voice. Fanciful trifling of this sort is far below the level of a poet who can ring fierce, rough honesty out of the stony fields of Ardnamurchan and the hard life their isolation demands. To me Maclean is certainly the most interesting Scottish poet to make his appearance for at least a couple of decades.

—Maurice Lindsay

MAC LOW, Jackson

Nationality: American. **Born:** Chicago, Illinois, 12 September 1922. **Education:** University of Chicago, 1939–43, A.A. 1941; Brooklyn College, New York, 1955–58, A.B. (cum laude) in Greek 1958. **Family:** Married 1) painter Iris Lezak (divorced 1973), one son and one daughter; 2) Anne Tardos in 1990. **Career:** Freelance music teacher, English teacher, translator, and editor, 1950–66; reference book editor, Funk and Wagnalls, 1957–58, 1961–62, and Unicorn Books, 1958–59; copy editor, Alfred A. Knopf, 1965–66, all in New York; instructor of English, Mannes College of Music, New York, 1966; instructor, American Language Institute, New York University, 1966–73; instructor, Naropa Institute, Boulder, Colorado, 1975, State University of New York, Albany, 1984, State University of New York, Binghamton, 1989, State University of New York, Buffalo, 1989, Temple University, Philadelphia, 1989, Schule fur Dichtung in Wien, Vienna, Austria, 1992, Bard College, Annandale-on-Hudson, New York, 1994, Brown University, Providence, Rhode Island, 1994,

University of California, San Diego, 1990, and University of Pennsylvania, Philadelphia, 1997. Member of the editorial staff, and poetry editor, 1950–54, *Why?* (later *Resistance*), a pacifist-anarchist magazine; poetry editor, *WIN* magazine, New York, 1966–75. **Awards:** Creative Artists Public Service grant, 1973, 1976; PEN grant, 1974; National Endowment for the Arts fellowship, 1979; Guggenheim fellowship for poetry, 1985; book award, San Francisco State University Poetry Center, 1985; Fulbright Travel grant New Zealand, 1986; Composer's grant, Queen Elizabeth II Arts Council of New Zealand, 1986; fellowship in poetry, New York Foundation for Arts, 1988; Fund for Poetry grant, New York, 1988, 1991, 1998. **Address:** 42 North Moore Street, New York, New York 10013, U.S.A.

PUBLICATIONS

Poetry

The Pronouns: A Collection of 40 Dances—for the Dancers—6 February-22 March 1964. New York, Mac Low, 1964; London, Tetrad Press, 1970.

August Light Poems. New York, Caterpillar, 1967.

22 Light Poems. Los Angeles, Black Sparrow Press, 1968.

23rd Light Poem: For Larry Eigner. London, Tetrad Press, 1969.

Stanzas for Iris Lezak. Barton, Vermont, Something Else Press, 1972.

4 Trains, 4–5 December 1964. Providence, Rhode Island, Burning Deck, 1974.

36th Light Poem: In Memoriam Buster Keaton. London, Permanent Press, 1975.

21 Matched Asymmetries. London, Aloes, 1978.

54th Light Poem: For Ian Tyson. Milwaukee, Membrane Press, 1978.

A Dozen Douzains for Eve Rosenthal. Toronto, Gronk, 1978.

Phone. New York, Printed Editions, 1978.

Asymmetries 1–260: The First Section of a Series of 501 Performance Poems. New York, Printed Editions, 1980.

Antic Quatrains. Minneapolis, Bookslinger, 1980.

From Pearl Harbor Day to FDR's Birthday. College Park, Maryland, Sun and Moon, 1982.

"Is That Wool Hat My Hat?" Milwaukee, Membrane Press, 1983.

Bloomsday. Barrytown, New York, Station Hill Press, 1984.

French Sonnets, Composed Between January 1955 and April 1983. Tucson, Black Mesa Press, 1984.

The Virginia Woolf Poems. Providence, Rhode Island, Burning Deck, 1985.

Representative Works 1938–1985. New York, Roof, 1986.

Words nd Ends from Ez. Bolinas, California, Avenue B, 1989.

Twenties: 100 Poems, 24 February 1989–3 June 1990. New York, Roof Books, 1991.

Pieces o' Six: Thirty-three Poems in Prose, 1983–1987. Los Angeles, Sun and Moon Press, 1992.

42 Merzgedichte in Memoriam Kurt Schwitters: February 1987-September 1989. Barrytown, New York, Station Hill, 1994.

Barnesbook, from works by Djuna Barnes, cover art by Anne Tardos. Los Angeles, Sun and Moon Press, 1996.

20 Forties: 20 Poems from the Series "154 Forties" Written and Revised 1990–1999. Gran Canaria, Zasterle Press, 1999.

Recordings: *A Reading of Primitive and Archaic Poems,* with others, Broadside; *From a Shaman's Notebook,* with others, Broadside.

Plays

The Marrying Maiden: A Play of Changes, music by John Cage (produced New York, 1960). Los Angeles, Sun and Moon Press, 1999.

Verdurous Sanguinaria (produced New York, 1961). Baton Rouge, Louisiana, Southern University, 1967; Los Angeles, Sun and Moon Press, 1999.

Thanks: A Simultaneity for People (produced Wiesbaden, 1962).

Letters for Iris, Numbers for Silence (produced Wiesbaden, 1962).

A Piece for Sari Dienes (produced Wiesbaden, 1962).

Thanks II (produced Paris, 1962).

The Twin Plays: Port-au-Prince, and Adams County, Illinois (produced New York, 1963). New York, Mac Low and Bloedow, 1963.

Questions and Answers . . . A Topical Play (produced New York, 1963). New York, Mac Low and Bloedow, 1963.

Asymmetries No. 408, 410, 485 (produced New York, 1965).

Asymmetries, Gathas and Sounds from Everywhere (produced New York, 1966).

A Vocabulary for Carl Fernbach-Flarsheim (produced New York, 1977). New York, Mac Low, 1968.

Two Plays (includes *The Marrying Maiden* and *Verdurous Sanguinaria*). Los Angeles, Sun and Moon Press, 1999.

Performance Scores and Broadsides (published New York, Mac Low): *A Vocabulary for Sharon Belle Mattlin [Vera Regina Lachman, Peter Innisfree Moore],* 1974–75; *Guru-Guru Gatha,* 1975; *1st Milarepa Gatha,* 1976; *1st Sharon Belle Mattlin Vocabulary Crossword Gatha,* 1976; *Homage to Leona Bleiweiss,* 1976; *The WBAI Vocabulary Gatha,* 1977, revised edition, 1979; *A Vocabulary Gatha for Pete Rose,* 1978; *A Notated Vocabulary for Eve Rosenthal,* 1978; *Musicwords (for Phill Niblock), 1978; A Vocabulary Gatha for Anne Tardos,* 1980; *Dream Meditation,* 1980; *A Vocabulary Gatha for Malcolm Goldstein,* 1981; *1st [2nd] Happy Birthday, Anne, Vocabulary Gatha,* 1982; *Unstructured Meditative Improvisation for Vocalists and Instrumentalists on the Word "Nucleus,"* 1982; *Pauline Meditation,* 1982; *Milarepa Quartet for Four Like Instruments,* 1982; *The Summer Solstice Vocabulary Gatha,* 1983; *Two Heterophonics from Hereford Bosons 1 and 2,* 1984; *Phonemicon from Hereford Bosons 1,* 1984.

Radio Writing: *Dialog unter Dichtern/Dialog among Poets,* 1981, *Thanks/Danke,* 1983, *Reisen/Traveling,* 1984 (all Germany); *Locks,* 1984.

Composer: Incidental music for *The Age of Anxiety* by W.H. Auden, produced New York, 1954; for *The Heroes* by John Ashbery, produced New York, 1955; for his *Words nd Ends from Ez; The Ten Bluebird Asymmetries,* 1967; *Tranverse Flute Mime Piece,* 1981; *A Bean Phenomenon for Alison Knowles,* 1984; *The Birds of New Zealand,* 1986; *Iran-Contra Hearings,* 1987; *Ezra Pound and 99 Anagrams,* 1989; *Fieldpiece,* 1996; *Dream Other People Different,* 1997.

*

Critical Studies: Jackson Mac Low issue of *Vort* 8 (Silver Spring, Maryland), 1975, and *Paper Air* (Blue Bell, Pennsylvania), 2(3), 1980; "Jackson Mac Low: The Limits of Formalism" by Ellen

Zweig, in *Poetics Today* (Durham, North Carolina), 3(3), summer 1982; "Jackson MacLow: Samasara in Lagado" by Steve McCaffery, in *North Dakota Quarterly* (Grand Forks, North Dakota), 55(4), fall 1987; "Poetics of 'Systematic Chance' and 'Instructions': 'Gatha' Series by Jackson Mac Low" by Nasashi Nosaka, in *Language and Culture* (Sapporo, Japan), 21, 1991.

Theatrical Activities: Actor: **Plays**—in *Tonight We Improvise* by Pirandello, New York, 1959, and other plays.

Jackson Mac Low comments:

I consider myself a composer of poetry, music, and theater works.

I do not think that I belong to any particular school of poetry, but my work, especially that of 1954–80, is closely related to that of such composers as John Cage, Morton Feldman, Earle Brown, Christian Wolff, and La Monte Young, and it has close affinities with the work of such concrete poets as Emmett Williams.

While my earliest work (1937–40) uses mostly free verse and experimental forms, the poems between 1940 and 1954 tend to alternate between traditional metrical forms (and variations on them) and experimental forms, most of which are varieties of free verse. From 1954, however, the poems, plays, and "simultaneities" incorporate methods, processes, and devices from modern music, including the use of chance operations in composition and/or performance, silences ranging in duration from breath pauses to several minutes, and various degrees of improvisation by performers. Many of the works are simultaneities—works performed by several speakers and/or producers of musical sounds and noises at once. These range from completely instrumental pieces (e.g., "Chamber Music for Barney Childs," 1963; "Winds/Instruments," 1980) through works combining speech and other sounds (e.g., *Stanzas for Iris Lezak* as simultaneity, 1960), to ones involving only speech (e.g., "Peaks and Lamas," 1959). Other features include indeterminacy (the quality of a work that is in many ways different at every performance) and various degrees of "syntacticalness," ranging from structures that are essentially strings of unrelated words to ones that are partially or fully syntactical in the ordinary sense of the word. Works after 1960 use various proportions of chance and choice in composition and performance. Some performance poems (e.g., "Velikovsky Dice-Song," 1968; "A Vocabulary for Annie Brigitte Gilles Tardos," 1979) incorporate multiple slide projections or films.

After November 1981 most of my poems and prose works have been written directly (without use of chance operations or similar systems), although some chance operations have been employed in composing performance works. Performers' choices usually figure largely in performances of the latter. I have also written and recorded four radio works—three for Westdeutscher Rundfunk, Cologne (1981, 1983, and 1984) and one for a production group in New York (1984).

*   *   *

Jackson Mac Low's multifarious activities as an artist are all directed toward the exploration of limits and boundaries, the boundaries between poetry and music, poetry and drama, even poetry and dance, or, taken differently, the limits of the ego, of will, of meaning, of significant order. Although he has written in traditional metrical forms and continues to write in an uninhibited variety of free verse that he calls "spontaneous expression," his most characteristic work is an investigation of indeterminacy, chance, and improvisation. His

language frequently breaks down to the phonemic level and becomes pure sound. Its meaning derives directly from its structure rather than—like traditional poetry—from its semantic content. In a world in which all meaning appears to become increasingly statistical, the evidence of Mac Low's poetry is of central importance.

The sources of Mac Low's work are diverse. He was educated as a neo-Aristotelian at the University of Chicago, and in a sense he remains a classical formalist. He is, however, also a self-proclaimed anarchist and, like John Cage, has been heavily influenced by Buddhist thought. His practice embodies these ideas in microcosm with remarkable consistency by creating works, as he says, "wherein both other human beings & their environments & the world 'in general' (as represented by such objectively hazardous means as random digits) are all able to act within the general framework & set of 'rules' given by the poet 'the maker of plots or fables' as Aristotle insists—not necessarily of everything that takes place within that framework!"

At its simplest Mac Low's theory produces work like "The Phone Poems," a suite of randomly generated variations on one of his spontaneous poems. Mac Low, however, is primarily a performance poet, and many of his most characteristic works—the gathas and other similar pieces written on graph paper, for example—are not well published. ("5th Gatha" in *America: A Prophecy,* edited by Jerome Rothenberg and George Quasha, 1973, is one of the most widely available examples of these works.) In the grid poems he typically selects words or phrases at random from a vocabulary source and arranges them on the grid by predetermined rules. In performance this "score" becomes the basis for rule-governed improvisation. Although the rules vary from piece to piece, Mac Low always insists that it is an exercise in listening, and the performers are asked to give careful attention to the overall form as it develops and to try to contribute to the dynamics of the whole. The performance, in other words, becomes an exploration of group psychology and social order.

In *22 Light Poems,* which is perhaps Mac Low's most beautifully conceived book, the central device is a more or less randomly prepared chart that is keyed to playing cards. "1st Light Poem" is purely a result of random selections from the chart. Others admit "coincidental" input from the environment in which the poem is written (a radio, for example), allow concrete events to stand in place of poems, or freely mix the poet's own spontaneous expression with random material. In one of the light poems written after the publication of the book Mac Low allows his numerous typing errors to stand. Despite the indeterminacy, however, *22 Light Poems,* as well as imaginative realizations of the dances in *The Pronouns,* withstand rigorous formal analysis. Order, given an opportunity, thrives.

Since the early 1980s Mac Low has written increasingly without the employment of the chance methods that had earlier been a primary feature of his work. The effect of the change is not as dramatic as one might expect. The newer work is as startlingly abrupt and surprising as the old. The random and the chosen converge on a space of language that seems to be itself a powerful source of creative production. The poem entitled "Various Meanings" begins,

The bottom of a green arras extends a vocabulary
whose rest is deep and boundless moving through space
and the stars. From time to time we lost the noise
   of an edge
where we were plagued by nocuous effects and
      then moved on
toward a dominant object.

At once self-reflexive and completely unpredictable, the poem unfolds by finding its cues for continuation from its own vocabulary and rhythm.

Mac Low's work adduces cogent evidence that the classic Western attitudes toward meaning derive from categorical distinctions that result alternatively in the radical isolation of consciousness and in ruthless exploitation of the external world. As Mac Low conceives it, the act of the poem, rather than isolating the poet in his vision, opens free and useful intercourse between the poet and the external world.

—Don Byrd

MACNAB, Roy (Martin)

Nationality: South African. **Born:** Durban, 17 September 1923. **Education:** Hilton College, Natal; Jesus College, Oxford, M.A. **Military Service:** Naval Officer, 1942–45. **Family:** Married Rachel Mary Heron-Maxwell; one son and one daughter. **Career:** Cultural attaché, South African High Commission, London, 1955–59; counselor for cultural and press affairs, South African Embassy, Paris, 1959–67; director, South Africa Foundation, London, 1968–84. **Awards:** Fellow, Royal Society of Arts (UK). D.Litt. and D.Phil.: University of South Africa, Pretoria. **Address:** South Africa Foundation, 7 Buckingham Gate, London S.W.1, England.

PUBLICATIONS

Poetry

Testament of a South African. London, Fortune Press, 1947.
The Man of Grass and Other Poems. London, St. Catherine Press, 1960.
Winged Quagga, with *Reassembling World,* by Douglas Reid Skinner. Cape Town, David Philip, 1981.

Novel

The Cherbourg Circles. London, Hale, 1994.

Other

South and Central Africa. New York, McGraw Hill, 1954.
Journey into Yesterday: South African Milestones in Europe. Cape Town, H. Timmins, and London, Bailey Brothers and Swinfen, 1962.
The Youngest Literary Language: The Story of Afrikaans. Johannesburg, South African Broadcasting Corporation, 1973.
The French Colonel: Villebois-Mareuil and the Boers 1899–1900. Cape Town and London, Oxford University Press, 1975.
The English-Speaking South Africans. Johannesburg, South African Broadcasting Corporation, 1975.
The Story of South Africa House. Johannesburg, Jonathan Ball, 1983.
Gold, Their Touchstone: Goldfields of South Africa 1887–1987. Johannesburg, Jonathan Ball, 1987.
For Honour Alone: The Cadets of Saumur in the Defence of the Cavalry School, France, June 1940. London, Hale, 1988.

Editor, with Martin Starkie, *Oxford Poetry 1947.* Oxford, Blackwell, 1947.
Editor, with Charles Gulston, *South African Poetry: A New Anthology.* London, Collins, 1948.
Editor, *Towards the Sun: A Miscellany of South Africa.* London, Collins, 1950.
Editor, *Poets in South Africa: An Anthology.* Cape Town, Maskew Miller, 1958.
Editor, *George Seferis: South African Diaries, Poems & Letters.* Cape Town, Casseform Press, 1990.

*

Manuscript Collection: Thomas Pringle Collection, Rhodes University, Grahamstown.

Critical Studies: By Anthony Delius, in *Books Abroad* (Norman, Oklahoma), summer 1955; Guy Butler, in *Listener* (London), 24 May 1956; William Plomer, in *London Magazine,* February 1957; *A Critical Survey of South African Poetry in English,* by G.M. Miller and Howard Sergeant, Cape Town, Balkema, 1957; *South African Poetry,* Pretoria, University of South Africa, 1966; *Momentum: On Recent South African Writing* edited by M.J. Daymond and others, Pietermaritzburg, South Africa, University of Natal Press, 1984.

*   *   *

Roy Macnab's first book of poetry, *Testament of a South African,* strikes the reader as a sincere attempt to convey the poet's thoughts and feelings, but the result unfortunately is somewhat obscured by his struggle with words, which he himself refers to as "a faithless flirt, / Not a lover of your art." Behind this struggle one senses the poet's genuine feeling for the African landscape, but the main subject of the collection is the poet's participation in World War II. This experience left him with a feeling of restless discontent, and like the soldiers of Erich Maria Remarque's books he is constantly searching for a meaning or a purpose in his present life that is noble enough to merit the sacrifice of the war. He is, however, invariably disappointed. His heroes come back from the war "battered but unbroken in the time of test," and they find "only the inevitable dullness of Friday's wages / And further occasion for being bored." Even those soldiers who died on the battlefield are not allowed to rest in peace, and Macnab is haunted by the knowledge that consequent ages may change their attitude to his heroes, a theme he explores in poems like "El-Alamein Revisited." In his disgust with urban life Macnab turns to the pioneers and the settlers, for it is in these people that he finds the spirit of exploration that so obviously appeals to him.

In *The Man of Grass* Macnab continues to explore the themes of ugly, boring city life versus the courage of soldiers and pioneers exemplified by Cecil Rhodes, who had "bold schemes" and "thoughts of fire." With the epic title poem he adds a religious dimension. The man of grass is the first Christian martyr in South Africa, a Jesuit priest killed in 1560, and Macnab tells his story in regular, often rhymed stanzas, alternating between first-person narrative, conveying the priest's dedication, and third-person narrative, setting the scene. The collection has some unfortunate phrases. "The bark of my faith / Bent to the tide of infidel bays" seems somewhat out of tune with the state of thinking in 1960, as does the following thought about "savages" from the poem "Stages": "sometimes the tom-tom beat a single thought to his numbness."

With the next collection, *Winged Quagga,* Macnab takes a logical step back to the time before the world was polluted by civilization. The quagga is an extinct animal, associated with the landscape of the African past. The poet glimpsed this in his childhood, and now he longs for it. The wings are the wings of the imagination, in an analogy with Pegasus, and the collection is about re-creating in the imagination the lost magnificence of the primeval African landscape, untouched by human beings. The three-part division reflects a classical approach to the subject. The first part re-creates the land from the beginning (the cosmic theme), the second part describes the poet's development from birth and innocence to awareness and loss of innocence (the ontogenetic theme), and the third part returns to the poet's present situation, with a final poem wondering about approaching death.

In the first part the poet creates his world of rock, ice, mountains, reptiles, flora, and fauna, and he reaches a point of perfection in the poem "Anni Mirabili," in which nature exists in perfect balance and harmony with itself, beautifully evoked in the image of "Birds from a bowl of sky / To fall in patterns on the running backs of herds." The form is a classic eight-line stanza, sometimes rhymed, and it is combined with carefully constructed imagery that occasionally moves into fully developed conceits, as in the poem "Amphitheatre," where the whole of Africa is seen in terms of an amphitheater, with the animals as dramatis personae. There is, however, a deliberate attempt to break the classical severity by mixing in modern (anachronistic) terms with the purpose of undercutting the seriousness and creating a lighter, more humorous mood. An example of this is found in the poem "The Animals," where the migration of herds of animals is described as "from motels of the water-holes." The section ends with a reminder that this world is unfolded in the poet's mind, like "paper gardens of Japan uncurled / To life in a glass of water," a companion image to the winged quagga.

The second part, set in the landscape created in the first section, charts the growing awareness of the poet's young self. It discusses his loss of innocence, when he first sees a springbok caught in a trap, and the enlargement of his horizon in terms of meeting the train that carries the newspapers and has access to the wider world. Nature is still an important presence, but in poems like "The Storm" and "Aftermath" it is discussed in domesticated, rather than cosmic, terms, emphasizing the fall into civilization: the dying storm is "haunting the chimney like a snatch of gossip." In this section the presence or nonpresence of people becomes problematic. "Brown people" are seen, much as the animals, to belong to the landscape and to be voiceless. One exception to this is the poem "Dark Stranger," in which the poet describes a sinister black figure who wants to "create New Yorks" in the "Pepperpots of towns" and whom the poet sees as plotting a dark future "where once white empires wore their crowns." Macnab seems to be in the tradition of the last of the great white hunters who care passionately about wildlife but who are less compassionate when it comes to human beings.

The third part does not live up to the expectations of the genre, failing to create a synthesis of the first two parts. It starts well with a childhood tale about a migrating hippopotamus, which combines humor and mourning for the loss of the wonderful world of such tales. But it then falls apart into individual poems about separate and unrelated topics concerned with the poet's present-day London world, and it ends with a melancholic but brave view of old age and death.

—Kirsten Holst Petersen

MACPHERSON, (Jean) Jay

Nationality: Canadian. **Born:** London, England, 13 June 1931. **Education:** Carleton University, Ottawa, B.A. 1951; University College, London, 1951–52; University of Toronto, M.A. 1955; Ph.D. 1964. **Career:** Member of the English department, Victoria College, University of Toronto, 1957–96. **Awards:** *Contemporary Verse* prize, 1949; Levinson prize, *Poetry* magazine, Chicago, 1957; President's medal, University of Western Ontario, 1957; Governor-General's award, 1958.

PUBLICATIONS

Poetry

Nineteen Poems. Deyá, Mallorca, Seizin Press, 1952.
O Earth Return. Toronto, Emblem, 1954.
The Boatman. Toronto, Oxford University Press, 1957.
Welcoming Disaster: Poems 1970–1974. Toronto, Saannes, 1974.
Poems Twice Told: Collected Poems. Toronto, Oxford University Press, 1981; New York, Oxford University Press, 1982.

Other

Four Ages of Man: The Classical Myths (textbook). Toronto, Macmillan, and New York, St. Martin's Press, 1962.
Pratt's Romantic Mythology: The Witches' Brew. St. John's Newfoundland, Memorial University, 1972.
The Spirit of Solitude: Conventions and Continuities in Late Romance. New Haven, Connecticut, Yale University Press, 1982.

*

Critical Studies: By Kildare Dobbs, in *Canadian Forum* (Toronto), XXXVII, 438; "Poetry" by Northrop Frye, in "Letters in Canada: 1957," in *University of Toronto Quarterly,* XXVII; "The Third Eye" by James Reaney, in *Canadian Literature 3* (Vancouver); Milton Wilson, in *Fiddlehead 34* (Fredericton, New Brunswick); Munro Beattie, in *Literary History of Canada* (Toronto), University of Toronto Press, 1965; "Poetry" by Michael Gnarowski, in "Letters in Canada: 1974," in *University of Toronto Quarterly,* XLIV, 1974; "In the Whale's Belly: Jay Macpherson's Poetry" by Suniti Namjoshi, in *Canadian Literature* (Vancouver), 79, 1978; "The 'Unicorn' Poems of Jay Macpherson" by Audrey Berner, in *Journal of Canadian Literature* (Ottawa), 3(1), winter 1980; *Second Words: Selected Critical Prose* by Margaret Atwood, Toronto, Anansi, 1982, and Boston, Beacon Press, 1984; "Toward a Feminist Hermeneutics: Jay Macpherson's Welcoming Disaster" by Lorraine Weir, in *Gynocritics: Feminist Approaches to Canadian and Quebec Women's Writing,* Toronto, ECW, 1987; *Jay Macpherson and Her Works,* Toronto, ECW Press, 1989, and "Jay Macpherson," in *ECW's Biographical Guide to Canadian Poets,* edited by Robert Lecker, Jack David, and Ellen Quigley, Toronto, ECW, 1993, both by Lorraine Weir; "Jay Macpherson's Welcoming Disaster: A Reconsideration" by W.J. Keith, in *Canadian Poetry* (London, Ontario), 36, spring-summer 1995.

*   *   *

Jay Macpherson's *The Boatman* has been accepted with enthusiasm by academic critics as well as the general public and has been reprinted many times since its first publication in 1957. The book is a subtly organized suite of lyrics—elegiac, pastoral, epigrammatic, and symbolist-that utilize the traditional forms of quatrain and couplet with great metrical virtuosity. It also shows a remarkable flair for the presentation of serious philosophical and, indeed, religious themes in verse that is sometimes beautifully lyrical and sometimes comic in the tradition of Lear or Gilbert or of nursery rhymes—and sometimes both at once.

The book has as its unifying theme the transmutation of time—bound physical reality into the eternal and the spiritual through the magical intermediary of man's imagination. Symbol and myth are the instruments, and the drama of man's Fall and Redemption is worked out in terms derived from the Bible, Milton, Blake, and such modern poets and scholars as Robert Graves and Northrop Frye. Among the protagonists whose fables supply the seeds of the mystical drama unifying the book are Noah, Leviathan, the Queen of Sheba, Mary of Egypt, Eurynome, Merlin, Helen, and such symbolic figures as The Plowman, The Fisherman, The Shepherd, and Angels. One of the reasons for the success of these poems is that they take the reader into the world of childhood faith through the unquestionable truth of fairy tale and legend. The elegance and grace of the writing and the authority with which wit and a sense of comedy are conveyed in verse that is both timeless and temporary also give the book an appeal to the most sophisticated of readers.

The Boatman and *Welcoming Disaster* (1974) complete Macpherson's poetical oeuvre. In 1981 the two books were published together, along with other poems, as *Poems Twice Told.* Macpherson is also the author of a scholarly study, *The Spirit of Solitude: Conventions and Continuities in Late Romance* (1982), that includes a remarkable essay about the Canadian achievement in romance literature titled "This Swan Neck of the Woods." Here she explains that "Canadian literature is without strong individual characters on the whole, being much more forceful in its presentation of settings. Man appears rather generalized: what has character is the wilderness, the city, the snow, the sea."

Macpherson taught for many years at Victoria College in the University of Toronto, where, influenced by the literary critic Northrop Frye, she in turn influenced the poet and writer Margaret Atwood. For some years Macpherson was grouped with the poet and dramatist James Reaney and the poet Daryl Hine and was considered to be a leading member of a so-called mythopoeic school of writers led by Frye. The association did not win readers, but at least it drew attention to her work in respectable places. For instance, Macpherson and Hine are the only two Canadian poets listed by Harold Bloom in his influential *Western Canon.*

—A.J.M. Smith and John Robert Colombo

MacSWEENEY, Barry

Nationality: British. **Born:** Newcastle upon Tyne, Northumberland, 17 July 1948. **Education:** Rutherford Grammar School; Harlow Technical College, 1966–67. **Family:** Married Elaine Randell in 1972. **Career:** Formerly freelance journalist; director, Blacksuede Boot Press; editor, with Elaine Randell, *Harvest* and *The Blacksuede Boot,* Barnet, Hertfordshire. **Awards:** *Stand* prize, 1967; Arts Council grant, 1971. **Address:** 55 Haydon Place, Denton Burn, Newcastle upon Tyne, England. **Died:** 9 May 2000.

PUBLICATIONS

Poetry

Poems 1965–1968: The Boy from the Green Cabaret Tells of His Mother. Hastings, Sussex, The English Intelligencer, 1967; New York, McKay, 1969.
The Last Bud. Newcastle upon Tyne, Blacksuede Boot Press, 1969.
Six Sonnets for Nathaniel Swift. Newcastle upon Tyne, Blacksuede Boot Press, 1969.
Lost Is the Day. London, Ted Cavanagh, 1970.
Joint Effort, with Peter Bland. Barnet, Hertfordshire, Blacksuede Boot Press, 1970.
Flames on the Beach at Viareggio. Barnet, Hertfordshire, Blacksuede Boot Press, 1970.
Our Mutual Scarlet Boulevard. London, Fulcrum Press, 1971.
Just 22 and Don't Mind Dyin': The Official Biography of Jim Morrison, Rock Idol. London, Curiously Strong, 1971.
Fools Gold. Newcastle upon Tyne, Blacksuede Boot Press, 1972.
The Elevated Horse. London, Hutchinson, n.d.
Brother Wolf. London, Turret, 1972.
5 Odes. London, Transgravity Advertiser, 1972.
Dance Steps. London, Joe DiMaggio Press, 1972.
Fog Eye. London, Ted Cavanagh, 1973.
6 Odes. London, Ted Cavanagh, 1973.
Pelt Feather Log. London, Grosseteste Press, 1975.
Black Torch. London, New London Pride, 1978.
Odes. London, Trigram Press, 1978.
Blackbird: Elegy for William Gordon Calvert, Being Book Two of Black Torch. Durham, Pig Press, 1980.
Starry Messenger. Ashford, Kent, Secret Books, 1980.
Ranter. Lenton, Nottinghamshire, Slow Dancer Press, 1985.
Hellhound Memos. London, The Many Press, 1993.
Pearl. Cambridge, Equipage, 1995.
The Book of Demons. Newcastle upon Tyne, Bloodaxe, 1997.

Other

Elegy for January: An Essay Commemorating the Bi-Centenary of Chatterton's Death. London, Menard Press, 1970.
The Tempers of Hazard, with Thomas A. Clark and Chris Torrance. London, Paladin, 1993.

*   *   *

The diversification of British poetry in the 1960s meant that attention was frequently focused on poets operating from, or at least with their roots in, the provinces. Liverpool was a breeding ground for the so-called pop poets, but an equally lively, and in many ways more fertile, scene developed in and around Newcastle, where Barry MacSweeney was an important member of the local poetry community.

MacSweeney's early work, as represented in *Poems 1965–1968: The Boy from the Green Cabaret Tells of His Mother,* has a strong sense of the geography of his locality, and there are numerous references to its physical appearance. But more important, the rhythm of the poems and their structure seem to be shaped by the twin influences of the city and the country. It would be wrong to call MacSweeney a purely urban poet because, like many provincials, he is obviously aware of often being on the edge of the moors or close to the coast. The land and the sea spill into his poems, balancing them and keeping them from settling into bright exercises in urban playfulness. At the same time he has a sharp eye for the hard side of the city:

> They stood smoking damp and salvaged
> cigarettes mourning their lost bundles,
> each man tagged OF NO FIXED ABODE.

> Mattresses dried in the early sunshine
> blankets hung over railings and gravestones
> water and ashes floated across the cobbled hill.

MacSweeney may have had roots in the northeast, but when the necessities of work took him away from the area, likewise his writing changed. He seems to have been affected by aspects of the 1960s mood, and he began to produce poems, as in *Our Mutual Scarlet Boulevard,* that, in his own words, "had to do with dreams; either sleep, fantasy, or the luxurious influence of various hallucinogens." They were perhaps a worthwhile experiment and certainly displayed skill in construction, but they lacked the concern and directness of the earlier work, leading one to wonder if MacSweeney had lost his way in a fashionable maze. But he soon demonstrated that the experience was something he had learned from rather than been changed by, and *Brother Wolf* proved that he was still his own man. It had a tautness that seemingly came from a desire to discard the unnecessary and was rich in form and content.

Most of MacSweeney's work after 1970 or so appeared in little magazines or was published by small presses and may have been overlooked because of that fact. But he continued to write powerfully, and his poetry benefited from a return to his original concerns. *Black Torch,* a long poem sequence building on the events of a nineteenth-century miners' strike in the northeast, brought in the poet's links to the area, referred to its landscape and traditions, and touched on twentieth-century problems facing an idealist in an imperfect world. It is an ambitious work and, although flawed, has much to recommend it. The language jabs at the reader's consciousness:

> no requiem no hymn no journey song
> stopping to drink from a broken stream
> ghosts of miners on the fell
> shadowy poachers armed with snares
> melt & make no noise

Odes, another sequence from the 1970s, goes off in a different direction and is almost mystical at times, with MacSweeney aiming to milk words for the meaning derived from their rhythms and sounds rather than their dictionary definitions. Not all of the pieces succeed, but they are never boring and at their best are slightly mysterious and provocative, with some lines lingering in the mind as if to tease with their play on the subconscious.

It is clear that MacSweeney devoted most of his poetic energies in the 1970s and 1980s to longer works, and *Ranter* is probably his major achievement. In it he mixes memory—his own and the historical—so that the poem moves in and out of time. It blends images of a long tradition of English dissent—

> Ranter: Leveller, Lollard,
> Luddite, Man of Kent, Tyneside
> broadsheet printer,
> whisperer of sedition,
> wrecker of looms

—with evocations of the landscape and life of the northeast of England:

> Mill chimneys and derelict sites,
> burning rubbish in back lanes,
> high moors of mist and snowdrifts,
> to the land of Bloodaxe and Bede
> you fetched me from the city I loved.
> Kiln-bricks piled high in a yard.
> Men with flushed faces and women alone,
> children scratting from door to door.

It also hints at separation and loss and of the pain of regret:

> I wouldn't go with you
> down that road. Now
> we are both alone
> by rivers we love.

Ranter combines the personal and the political, and it is difficult to extract from it and still be fair to MacSweeney's overall intentions. The effect very much depends on the poem's being read in its entirety. The rhythms and the language play an important part throughout, and although individual phrases have beauty ("shivering primrose / and the wind's dark beat"), their movement is best understood in context. The poem is effectively an accumulation of all of MacSweeney's ideas over the years.

—Jim Burns

MADHUBUTI, Haki R.

Pseudonyms: Don L. Lee. **Nationality:** American. **Born:** Little Rock, Arkansas, 23 February 1942. **Education:** Dunbar Vocational High School, Chicago; Wilson Junior College; University of Illinois, Chicago Circle; Chicago City College, A.A. 1966; Roosevelt University, Chicago, 1966–67; University of Iowa, Iowa City, M.F.A. 1984. **Military Service:** U.S. Army, 1960–63. **Family:** Married Johari Amini; two children. **Career:** Apprentice curator, DuSable Museum of African American History, Chicago, 1963–67; stock department clerk, Montgomery Ward, Chicago, 1963–64; post office clerk, Chicago, 1964–65; junior executive, Spiegel's, Chicago, 1965–66. Taught at Columbia College, Chicago, 1968; writer-in-residence, Cornell University, Ithaca, New York, 1968–69; poet-in-residence, Northeastern Illinois State College, Chicago, 1969–70; lecturer, University of Illinois, Chicago, 1969–71; writer-in-residence, Morgan State College, Baltimore, 1972–73, Howard University, Washington, D.C., 1970–75, and Central State University, Wilberforce, Ohio, 1979–80. Since 1984 associate professor of English, Chicago

State University. Founding member, Organization of Black American Culture Writers Workshop, 1967–75. Since 1969 director, Institute of Positive Education, Chicago. Since 1967 editor and publisher, Third World Press, Chicago; since 1972 editor, *Black Books Bulletin,* Chicago. **Awards:** National Endowment for the Arts grant, 1969, 1982; Kuumba Workshop Black Liberation award, 1973. **Address:** Third World Press, 7524 South Cottage Grove Avenue, Chicago, Illinois 60619, U.S.A.

PUBLICATIONS (earlier works as Don L. Lee)

Poetry

Think Black. Detroit, Broadside Press, 1967; revised edition, 1968, 1969.
Black Pride. Detroit, Broadside Press, 1968.
Back Again, Home. Detroit, Broadside Press, 1968.
One Sided Shoot-Out. Detroit, Broadside Press, 1968.
For Black People (And Negroes Too). Chicago, Third World Press, 1968.
Don't Cry, Scream. Detroit, Broadside Press, 1969.
We Walk the Way of the New World. Detroit, Broadside Press, 1970.
Directionscore: Selected and New Poems. Detroit, Broadside Press, 1971.
Book of Life. Detroit, Broadside Press, 1973.
Earthquakes and Sunrise Missions: Poetry and Essays of Black Renewal 1973–1983. Chicago, Third World Press, 1984.
Killing Memory, Seeking Ancestors. Detroit, Lotus, 1987.
GroundWork: New and Selected Poems of Don L. Lee/Haki R. Madhubuti from 1966–1996. Chicago, Third World Press, 1996.
Heartlove: Wedding and Love Poems. Chicago, Third World Press, 1998.

Recording: *Rappin' and Readin',* Broadside Press, 1971.

Other

Dynamite Voices: Black Poets of the 1960's. Detroit, Broadside Press, 1971.
From Plan to Planet: Life Studies: The Need for Afrikan Minds and Institutions. Detroit, Broadside Press, 1973.
A Capsule Course in Black Poetry Writing, with others. Detroit, Broadside Press, 1975.
Enemies: The Clash of Races. Chicago, Third World Press, 1978.
Say That the River Turns: The Impact of Gwendolyn Brooks. Chicago, Third World Press, 1987.
Black Men: Obsolete, Single, Dangerous?: African American Families in Transition: Essays in Discovery, Solution, and Hope. Chicago, Third World Press, 1990.
Africa-Centered Education: Its Value, Importance, and Necessity in the Development of Black Children. Chicago, Third World Press, 1994.
Claiming Earth: Race, Rage, Rape, Redemption: Blacks Seeking a Culture of Enlightened Empowerment. Chicago, Third World Press, 1994.

Editor, with Patricia L. Brown and Francis Ward, *To Gwen with Love.* Chicago, Johnson, 1971.

Editor, with Maulana Karenga, *Million Man March/Day of Absence: A Commemorative Anthology.* Chicago, Third World Press, 1996.
Editor, with Gwendolyn Mitchell, *Releasing the Spirit: A Collection of Literary Works from Gallery 37.* Chicago, Third World Press, 1998.
Editor, with Gwendolyn Mitchell, *Describe the Moment: A Collection of Literary Works from Gallery 37.* Chicago, Third World Press, 2000.

*

Critical Studies: "Black Poetry's Welcome Critic" by Hollie I. West, in *The Washington Post* (Washington, D.C.), 6 June 1971; "A Black Poet Faces Reality" by Vernon Jarrett, in *Chicago Tribune,* 23 July 1971; "The Relevancy of Don L. Lee As a Contemporary Black Poet" by Annette Sands, in *Black World* (Chicago), June 1972; "Some Black Thoughts on Don L. Lee's *Think Black:* Thanks by a Frustrated White Academic Thinker" by Eugene E. Miller, in *College English* (Champaign, Illinois), May 1973; *New Directions from Don L. Lee* by Marlene Mosher, Hicksville, New York, Exposition, 1975; *An Analysis of the Poetry of Three Revolutionary Poets: Don L. Lee, Nikki Giovanni, and Sonia Sanchez* (dissertation) by Elaine Marie Shouse, n.p., 1976; *The Black Idiom, African-American Poetry and Haki R. Madhubuti: A Stylistic Analysis* (dissertation) by John Thomas Wolfe, n.p., 1977; *Objectism in the Poetics of Haki R. Madhubuti and Some Contemporary Black Poets* (dissertation) by Lizzie Mae Golden, n.p., 1978; "'Ain'ts,' 'Us'ens,' and 'Mother-Dear': Issues in the Language of Madhubuti, Jones, and Reed" by Lemuel Johnson, in *Journal of Black Studies,* 10, 1979; "Militant Singers: Baraka, Cultural Nationalism and Madhubuti" by William J. Harris, in *Minority Voices* (University Park, Pennsylvania), 2(2), 1979; "The Public Response to Haki R. Madhubuti, 1968–1988" by Julius E. Thompson, in *Literary Griot* (Wayne, New Jersey), 4(1–2), spring-fall 1992; *The X-Factor Influence on the Transformed Image of Africa in the Poetry of Haki Madhubuti and Sonia Sanchez: Issues of Renaming and Inversion* (dissertation) by Regina Belvex Jennings, Temple University, 1993.

*   *   *

Looking at the continuum of his writing, one is impressed by Haki R. Madhubuti's matured technical independence, worldview, awareness of the social implications of technology, and abiding love for his people. The result is poetry that successfully conveys spontaneity and emotional compulsion as well as thoughtful ideological commitment. Beginning as one of the young African-American poets who emerged during the black arts movement in the late 1960s, Madhubuti (known at the start of his career as Don L. Lee) proved to be one of the most powerful in content and one of the most creative and influential in technique. Earlier perceptions of him as brash, irreverent, or almost fanatical served to divert attention from certain qualities and habits that underlie his revolutionary stance—intellectual thirst, broad and intense reading and study, high seriousness, thoughtful reflection, and a predilection for both analysis and synthesis.

Madhubuti's artistic outlook has always been consciously utilitarian and informed by sociopolitical concerns centering on black people's self-definition, self-determination, self-help through collective and institutional efforts, and humanness. Examples include "In the Interest of Black Salvation," which shows disillusionment with orthodox Euro-American religion; "Back Home Again," an account of an excursion into an alien (white) "establishment" world and a subsequent return to blackness; "But He Was Cool," a satire on the vapid, faddish, and showy lifestyles affected by some African-Americans; and "Re-Act for Action," a cry for aggression against racism.

While his focus is socioethnic, Madhubuti's thematic concerns may be considered universally relevant. A people's needs, he asserts, are food, clothing, shelter, and education. In the context of this worldview, he believes that the miseducation of African Americans has conditioned them to "do what / they / have been taught to do." Thus, because African-American men find themselves "walking the borders / between / smiles and outrage," they must see clearly and act responsibly and morally. He writes that "conscious men do not make excuses / do not expect their women to carry their water, / harvest the food and prepare it too. / world over it is known that / breast sucking is only guaranteed for babies." As a corollary he points out the inherent power of women: "if black women do not love, / there is no love." Of their inherent beauty, he writes that "dark women are music / some complicated well worked / rhythms / others simple melodies." To both men and women, he advises, ". . . be what you want your children to be."

An example of Madhubuti's particular interest in the African diaspora is shown by the dedication of the title poem in his collection *Killing Memory, Seeking Ancestors* to Nelson and Winnie Mandela. Thinking in international terms, he foresees in "The End of White World Supremacy" "The day, hour, minute / and / second that the / chinese / and / japanese / sign / a / joint / industrial / and / military / pact."

Madhubuti prefers the speech of the African-American urban masses, much of it well suited for oral delivery. (He is in demand for public appearances.) Particularly in his earlier poetry, he frequently achieves the desired aural effects through extra vowels or consonants, phonetic spellings, and elisions. In his earlier work he is also partial to spatial arrangements, broken words, unconventional syntax and punctuation, and the ampersand and diagonal. Throughout his corpus he is fond of playing with words, particularly syntactic reversals and the breaking of words into components, which he uses for irony, purposeful double meaning, emphasis of discreet components of meaning, aural effects, and other reasons. His imagery is strong, concrete, and specific. Occasionally his late poetry, most noticeable in *Killing Memory, Seeking Ancestors,* moves toward prose poetry, as in "Poet: Whatever Happened to Luther." Frequently he builds a poem's tension incrementally, withholding its point or resolution until the end, at which time the poem's logic or impact is made manifest.

Madhubuti illustrates the office of the poet as shaman, griot, priest, prophet, and seer.

—Theodore R. Hudson

MAGEE, Wes

Nationality: British. **Born:** Greenock, Renfrew, 20 July 1939. **Education:** Ilford County High School, Essex, 1951–56; Goldsmiths' College, University of London, 1964–67, teaching certificate 1967. **Military Service:** British Army Intelligence Corps, 1960–62. **Family:** Married Janet Parkhouse in 1968; one son and one daughter. **Career:** Worked as a bank clerk in the 1950s; head teacher, Blackthorn Junior School, Welwyn Garden City, Hertfordshire, 1978–81; and Brough County Primary School, North Humberside, 1981–90. Since 1990 full-time writer and lecturer. Editor, *Prism* magazine, London, 1964–67. **Awards:** Leeds University New Poets award, 1973. **Address:** Santone House, Low Street, Sancton, Yorkshire YO4 3QZ, England.

PUBLICATIONS

Poetry

Postcard from a Long Way Off. Portrush, County Antrim, Ulsterman, 1969.
The Radish. Frensham, Surrey, Sceptre Press, 1970.
Urban Gorilla. Leeds, School of English Press, 1972.
Proust in a Crowded Store. Rushden, Northamptonshire, Sceptre Press, 1974.
No Man's Land. Richmond, Surrey, Keepsake Press, 1976.
Creature of the Bay: A Set of Poems. Kingston upon Thames, Surrey, Court Poetry Press, 1977.
Headland Graffiti. Knotting, Bedfordshire, Sceptre Press, 1978.
No Surrender! Liverpool, Headland, 1978.
The Dream Spectres. Nottingham, Byron Press, 1978.
No Man's Land (collection). Belfast, Blackstaff Press, 1978.
Aberllefenni: At the Slate Quarry. Bristol, Xenia Press, 1979.
Wrecks. Bristol, Xenia Press, 1980.
Poems for a Course [2], with John Cotton. Hitchin, Hertfordshire, Priapus, 2 vols., 1980–84.
The Football Replays. Higham Ferrers, Northamptonshire, Greylag Press, 1980.
A Dark Age. Belfast, Blackstaff Press, 1981.
Flesh, or Money. Todmorden, Yorkshire, Littlewood Arc Press, 1991.

Verse (for children)

Reptile Rhymes. Bristol, Xenia Press, 1977.
The Space Beasts. Maidstone, Kent Library Service, 1979.
The Witch's Brew and Other Poems. Cambridge, Cambridge University Press, 1988.
Morning Break and Other Poems. Cambridge, Cambridge University Press, 1988.
The Legend of the Ragged Boy. London, Andersen Press, 1992; New York, Arcade, 1993.
Surprise, Surprise! Harlow, Longman, 1994.
Amanda and the Pot of Gold. Loughborough, Ladybird, 1998.

Plays

The Real Spirit of Christmas (for children; produced Swindon, Wiltshire, 1976). London, French, 1978.
The Working Children (for children). Aylesbury, Buckinghamshire, Ginn, 1993.

Other (for children)

Oliver, The Daring Birdman. London, Longman, 1978.
Don't Do That! series. Aylesbury, Buckinghamshire, Ginn, 6 vols., 1987.
Story Starters series. Aylesbury, Buckinghamshire, Ginn, 4 vols., 1987.

The Scribblers of Scumbagg School. London, Orchard Books, 1993.
The Scumbagg School Scorpion. London, Orchard Books, 1995.
Sports Day at Scumbagg School. London, Orchard Books, 1996.
The Spook Spotters of Scumbagg School. London, Orchard Books, 1996.
The Emperor and the Nightingale: A Story from China. Oxford, Ginn, 1999.
John's Birthday Party. Harlow, Addison Wesley Longman, 1999.
The Fantastic Four at the Seaside. Oxford, Oxford University Press, 1999.
Poets Writing in a Variety of Forms. Harlow, Longman, 1999.

Other

Imaginative Writing. Leamington Spa, Scholastic, 1994.

Editor, *All the Day Through.* London, Evans, 1982.
Editor, *Dragon's Smoke.* Oxford, Blackwell, 1985.
Editor, *A Shooting Star.* Oxford, Blackwell, 1985.
Editor, *A Calendar of Poems.* London, Bell and Hyman, 1986.
Editor, *A Christmas Stocking.* London, Cassell, 1988.
Editor, *A Big Poetry Book.* Oxford, Blackwell, 1989.
Editor, *Madtail, Mimiwhale and Other Shape Poems.* London, Viking Kestrel, 1989.
Editor, *Matt, Wes and Pete.* London, Macmillan Children's, 1995; as *Lost Property Box,* Macmillan Children's, 1998.

*

Manuscript Collection: Colin Huggett (private collector), Tregarth, Gwynedd, North Wales.

Wes Magee comments:

Tough and muscular language appropriate to the experiences of our age has always been of central interest to me in poetry. Principally I have used personal experience in the poems in an attempt to make wider and even universal gestures. Underlying my interest in human and animal violence has been a concern to record the compassionate, the need for humans to stand together. Such a paradox lies within many of the poems, and it is the need to resolve, for myself, such an issue that makes me produce poems even though an awakening and increasing activity in the world of writing for children tend to consume more and more of my writing time.

*　　*　　*

Wes Magee's poetry explores the dark side of the human psyche. Its author searches a hard, unpitying universe, examines the signs, and draws a stony conclusion from what he finds. Death, cruelty, and suffering, whether inflicted by mankind upon itself or encountered in the animal kingdom, serve Magee as central themes that recur constantly in his work. From the early poems of *Postcard from a Long Way Off,* through *Urban Gorilla,* to the mature, assured expression of *A Dark Age,* the reader is assailed by images of a continual, unrelenting violence. Exposed as a young farm worker to the appalling conditions of battery production systems and a nature "red in tooth and claw," Magee writes from an experience that confirms his worst forebodings. Seen through his eyes, the universe itself becomes a threat, taking on malevolent life to attack the poet and with him the

rest of the human race: "Night comes jackbooting through the wood / And the sky roars at trees and a dying light. / Pregnant, the river is gulped into darkness / While sheep, like town lights, blot out one by one."

This grim, comfortless vision of man and his environment dominates Magee's writing, with musings on the inevitability of cosmic entropy and human decay. With a keen, merciless eye, the poet documents man's innate propensity for violence—schoolboys stoning a dead rat, the scientist experimenting on laboratory animals. Scanning the packed, sweating cattle in their trucks, the pigs awaiting slaughter in their steel cages, Magee draws a chilling parallel with the death convoys of Belsen. Genocide, whether of pigs or persons, reveals man as a habitual and an instinctive killer who is himself destined for extinction. At all times the poet senses that he too is under observation from other nonhuman intelligences, galactic onlookers who may well judge his race and find it wanting. Man's savagery, it seems, is matched only by his insignificance in the face of creation.

Magee's writing fits perfectly with the bleak desolation of his themes. His poems achieve a powerful and imaginative reworking of language, abounding with unexpected images that startle with a visual, almost a tactile, force. Words convey the feel of rough surfaces, bringing to the reader the hard touch of stone, the sharpness of metal. Using a style that blends subtlety with aggression and adopting a deliberate starkness of expression, Magee creates a poetry whose perceptions are both deep and readily understood. Through this medium he presents the play of murderous natural forces and the cruelties of the animal world. "Pig Poems," from the collection *No Man's Land,* are a disturbing example of his ability, not least the horrific "Fairy Tale," in which a hen and her chicks are devoured by the pigs: "But her bowels are lead. The old sow has her / in the trough, thin bones crunching like wafers. / Crazed, her head shrieks from the pig's champing jaws. // Beak, feathers, feet, sucked to a terror world / where heat lies packed and light has never struck. / The thick dust whirls. / Blood's licked from lips like wine."

Shocking as these images are, Magee forces the reader to acknowledge the unpalatable truth that the pig's vicious instincts are surpassed by the humans who fatten beasts in cages to make them ready for the knife. All are part of the same uncertain, threatening world that may at any moment alter shape and turn on its unsuspecting victims, as in "Discovering a Sea Cave," where the poet emerges to find "the seascape oddly changed, the rocks restructured." Magee returns continually to death as the central reality of his poems. Whether comic-macabre reflections on human and animal skulls, memories of dead creatures trapped in suburban attics, or Magee's own visit to Belsen as a drunken National Serviceman, the message remains constant. Life is dogged by violence and brutality and brings us to the same final destination: "All ending up . . . in hushed places / Where only scrap-metal gypsies come / Or detectives with bright spades."

Thankfully, Magee ensures that the gloom is not unrelieved. Most of his darkest poems are lit by a gallows humor, a sly wordplay leavening the overall menace, as in "Mineshaft," where the black mouth of a slate quarry swallows "a stoned Welshman," or in "Cattle Trucks," where the poet visualizes the doomed prisoners standing "cowed" in the darkness. A handful of works evade the doom and horror. In "Love on a Mountain Top" Magee recalls an afternoon's eroticism with wistful sadness. The gentler side of his writing surfaces more frequently in his collection *Flesh or Money,* whose poems reflect on the pains and joys of adolescent love, the stolen idyll of a writers' weekend retreat, and poignant obituaries to

Elvis and John F. Kennedy. In "State" an attractive female canvassing for his vote sets him musing on the dangerous blend of politics and lust, the "flesh or money" of the volume's title. Magee's memories of the 1970s love culture are analyzed in "Imagine," the peaceful hopes of that past age contrasting sadly with a bleak, merciless present that is tellingly depicted in "Cries of London" and "Incident on the Housing Estate." In today's grim world, where the stars gleam coldly as "studs on a leather jacket," there is little enough to be had in the way of love.

Magee's talent for humorous writing surfaces more openly in his collections for children, evident in such poems as "The Silent Teacher" in *Morning Break,* and it runs the gamut from shapes to counting and skipping rhymes in *The Witch's Brew.* In adult and juvenile works alike, his images stun with their visual power: a ship "claws grimly / up the horizon's steel rim," firelight "reels" off the walls "like a Christmas Eve drunk," while a bathroom cockroach "steals across the carpet like a hearse." Magee sees his poems as "shedding light down the white page's darkness," and the strength of his writing justifies the claim. In the end, however, it is the vision of darkness, so superbly lit by his words, that returns to haunt the reader, the cruelty and violence embodied by the waiting pigs in their cage: "their endless day filled tight with screaming. / Knives are ground on stones. And it's going on now."

—Geoff Sadler

MAGUIRE, Sarah

Nationality: British. **Born:** West London, 1957. **Education:** University of East Anglia, B.A. in English; studied at Cambridge University. **Career:** Teacher of creative writing, London Lighthouse; writer-in-residence at an English prison, 1992–93; creative writing fellow, University of Leeds, 1996; poetry reader, British Council, Palestine, 1996. Since 1990 tutor, Arvon Foundation. Writer, teacher, broadcaster, and contributor to periodicals. **Address:** Notting Hill, London, England.

PUBLICATIONS

Poetry

Spilt Milk. London, Secker and Warburg, 1991.
The Invisible Mender. London, Cape, 1997.

*

Critical Studies: In *Poetry Review,* 84(1), spring 1994, and 84(2), summer 1994.

*		*		*

Sarah Maguire is one of a number of young women poets emerging in the late twentieth century (Lavinia Greenlaw and Kate Clanchy also come to mind) who combine acute powers of observation and metaphysical wit together with flexuous technique in the writing of free verse. In Maguire's case, she was a gardener before reading English at the University of East Anglia, notable for its school of writing supervised by Malcolm Bradbury. The school may have helped her verse technique, and undoubtedly her practice in gardening encouraged the minute observation of detail that is a notable feature of her poems.

Maguire's first book, *Spilt Milk,* made a great impression and caused her to be chosen as one of twenty *New Generation* poets. "Wit and lyricism, precision and suggestiveness," commented Tim Dooley in the *Times Literary Supplement,* "her poems attend to wider issues—sexual politics, nationality, exploitation—without losing their primary sense of physical presence." Two of these early poems have become familiar in anthologies: "Uisge Beatha" and "What Is Transparent." The first dwells on the pleasures of love in terms of whisky (the title is Irish for "water of life"): "the hot sweet smoked malt / that I burned of and for you." "What Is Transparent" makes a quite startling use of light and translucence to get across two phases of the speaker's life, each marked by a coal miners' strike:

> I find two candles,
> Turn out all the lights and watch the news:
> The bluish screen tricking the faces of these men
> Who work with darkness, underground.

Unusual for a young poet, Maguire's second book, *The Invisible Mender,* is even better than her first. The gardener's eye comes wonderfully into play in a series of poems called "Nursery Practices." These feature "The Grafting Knife," with the tool's cherry wood clasp finished with brass; "The Greenhouse," with unopened air heady with the odor of cloves and roses; "The Growing Room," with walls of loam shelved in green trays; the "Year-Round Chrysanthemums," with the flowers' magenta and saffron faces "phototropic with desire"; and the whole, personalized in "Watershed," the shrewdly observed chronicle of a dry summer. In subject as well as style the poems make for uncommonly pleasant reading.

In a darker vein "The Hearing Cure," quite an ambitious poem, makes temporary deafness the occasion for a tender elegy on the protagonist's mother:

> your wasted
> beautiful hands
> slim messengers of fear.
> Weeks on
>
> you start to tell me things
> I've never heard before,
> all that silence
> frozen in your limbs . . .

What might seem a tone oversubdued is ratified by the continuing theme of hearing and deafness: "a litany," "we've hardly talked," "you'd not complain," "their sight is sound," this last spoken of the bats whose high-pitched cries are the first thing the speaker hears after her period of occlusion.

Since then Maguire has embarked on a sequence called "The Florists at Midnight." Most of the poems in the sequence are written in a stepped verse composed of triads (three-line stanzas) feminized from the usage of William Carlos Williams and mediated by Elizabeth Bishop and Adrienne Rich, the latter of whom has exerted a vast subterranean influence on British women poets many years her junior. To learn from her elders in this way, as Maguire certainly has done, is to be subtly original. Her subjects are her own, and her special knowledge of gardening once more comes into play. She mourns the flowers cut and packed in cellophane and, in doing so, comments upon our deracinated and sanitized civilization:

> Packed buckets
> of tulips, of lilies, of dahlias
>   spill down from tiered shelving
>
> nailed to the wall.
> Lifted at dawn,
>   torn up from their roots
>
> then cloistered in cellophane,
> they are cargoed across continents
>   to fade far from home . . .

The strength is in the fact that Maguire knows exactly what these transit sheds look like. The depth is that she might almost have been writing about asylum seekers.

As in the published volumes, there are poems about travel. Maguire finds herself lost in the suburbs of Marrakech or looped by jasmine in Yemen or, in Aden, listening to the distant, heated voices intermingling with the scratching of the cicadas. And again there is the core of personal feeling, the sense of loss voiced in pieces based on the ghazel, an Arabic form in which the poem is constructed of discrete couplets and a form she has made curiously her own.

There can be few projects envisaged by a contemporary poet that offer so much of interest. This writer is an individual, an unmistakable voice among the young women who form so notable an element in the poetry of our time. They have brought into consciousness matters hitherto unexplored. Much of the hope for the future lies with Maguire and her near contemporaries.

—Philip Hobsbaum

MAHAPATRA, Jayanta

Nationality: Indian. **Born:** Cuttack, Orissa, 22 October 1928. **Education:** Stewart European School, Cuttack, 1933–41; Ravenshaw College, Cuttack, B.Sc. (honors) 1946; Patna University, M.Sc. (honors) in physics 1949. **Family:** Married Jyotsna Rani Das in 1951; one son. **Career:** Sub-editor, *Eastern Times,* Cuttack, 1949; lecturer in physics, Ravenshaw College, 1950–58, G.M. College, Sambalpur, 1958–61 and 1962–65, Regional Engineering College, Rourkela, 1961–62, and B.J.B. College, Bhubaneswar, 1965–69, all in Orissa; reader in Physics, F.M. College, Balasore, 1969–70, Ravenshaw College, 1970–81, and Shailabala Women's College, Cuttack, 1981–86. Visiting writer, University of Iowa, Iowa City, 1976–77, in Australia, 1978, Japan, 1980, University of Malaysia, Kuala Lumpur, 1988, Universitas Indonesia, Jakarta, 1988, and University of the Phillipines, Manila City, 1988; visiting fellow, Shivaji University, Kolhapur, 1983; invited poet, Asian Poets Conference, Tokyo, 1984, Singapore Festival of Arts, Singapore, 1988, New Literatures in English Conference, Giessen, West Germany, 1989, Cuirt International Poetry Festival, Galway, Ireland, 1992, Poetry International, The South

Bank Centre, London, 1992, El Consejo Nacional Para la Cultura y las Artes, Mexico, 1994, and Mingei International Museum of World Folk Art, La Jolla, California, 1994; Indo-Soviet Cultural Exchange writer, U.S.S.R., 1985. Associate editor, *Gray Book,* Cuttack, 1972–73; guest editor, *South and West,* Fort Smith, Arkansas, 1973; editor, *Chandrabhaga,* Cuttack, 1979–85; poetry editor, *Telegraph* (Calcutta), 1985–89 and 1994–96. Since 2000 editor, *Chandrabhaga: A Magazine of World Writing.* **Awards:** Jacob Glatstein memorial award (*Poetry,* Chicago), 1975; Sahitya Akademi (National Academy of Letters) award, New Delhi, 1981; Rockefeller Foundation award, 1986; First Prize (International), Scottish International Open Poetry Competition, 1990; Gangadhar National award for poetry, Sambalpur University, 1994; Ramakrishna Jaidayal Harmony award, 1994. **Address:** Tinkonia Bagicha, Cuttack 753001, Orissa, India.

PUBLICATIONS

Poetry

Close the Sky, Ten by Ten. Calcutta, Dialogue, 1971.
Svayamvara and Other Poems. Calcutta, Writers Workshop, 1971.
A Rain of Rites. Athens, University of Georgia Press, 1976.
Father's Hours. Calcutta, United Writers, 1976.
Waiting. New Delhi, Samkaleen, 1979.
The False Start. Bombay, Clearing House, 1980.
Relationship. Greenfield, New York, Greenfield Review Press, 1980.
Life Signs. New Delhi, Oxford University Press, 1983.
Dispossessed Nests: The 1984 Poems. New Delhi and Jaipur, Nirala, 1986.
Selected Poems. New Delhi and Oxford, Oxford University Press, 1987.
Burden of Waves and Fruit. Washington, D.C., Three Continents Press, 1988.
Temple. Mundelstrup, Denmark, Dangaroo Press, 1989.
A Whiteness of Bone. New Delhi, Viking Penguin, 1992.
Bali. Cuttack, Vidyapuri, 1993.
The Best of Jayanta Mahapatra. Kozhikode, Bodhi, 1995.
Kahibi Gotie Katha. Cuttack, Arya Prakashan, 1995.
Shadow Space. Kottayam, D.C. Books, 1997.
Baya Raja. Cuttack, Vidyapuri, 1997.

Other

Tales from Fakirmohan (for children). Cuttack, Orissa, Students' Store, 1969.
True Tales of Travel and Adventure (for children). Cuttack, Orissa, Students' Store, 1969.
Orissa. New Delhi, Lustre Press, 1987.
Poemas. Mexico, Instituto de Cultura de Campeche, 1994.
The Green Gardener. Hyderabad, Orient Longman, 1997.

Translator, *Countermeasures: Poems,* by Soubhagya Kumar Misra. Calcutta, Dialogue, 1973.
Translator, *Wings of the Past: Poems,* by Jadunath Das Mohapatra. Calcutta, Rajasree, 1976.
Translator, *Song of Kubja and Other Poems,* by Sitakant Mahapatra. New Delhi, Samkaleen, 1981.

Translator, *I Can, But Why Should I Go: Poems,* by Shakti Chattopadhyaya. New Delhi, Sahitya Akademi, 1994.

Translator, *Verticals of Life: Poems.* New Delhi, Sahitya Akademi, 1996.

Translator, *Tapaswini: A Poem.* Bhubaneswar, Orissa Sahitya Akademi, 1998.

*

Manuscript Collection: All India Poetry Centre, Bhopal.

Critical Studies: By K. Ayyappa Paniker, in *Osmania Journal of English Studies* (Hyderabad), 13(1), 1977; "Crisis of Belief" by Frank Allen, in *Parnassus* (New York), spring-summer 1981; "Jayanta Mahapatra: A Poetry of Decreation" by Meena Alexander, in *Journal of Commonwealth Literature* (Oxford), 18(1), 1983; "Vision of a Reconciliator" by Gary Corseri, in *Fiction, Literature, and the Arts Review* (Brookline, Massachusetts), spring 1983; "Neither Alien Nor Postmodern: Jayanta Mahapatra's Poetry from India" by John Oliver Perry, in *Kenyon Review* (Gambier, Ohio), 8(4), 1986; *The Poetry of Jayanta Mahapatra: A Critical Study* edited by Madhusudan Prasad, New Delhi, Sterling, 1986; *Jayant Mahapatra* by Devinder Mohan, New Delhi, Arnold-Heinemann, 1987; "Experimentalists II: Mehrotra and Mahapatra," in *Modern Indian Poetry in English,* by Bruce King, New Delhi, Oxford University Press, 1987; "Rites and Signs: A Note on Jayanta Mahapatra's Poetic Sensibility" by G.N. Devy, in *Living Indian-English Poets: An Anthology of Critical Essays,* edited by Madhusudan Prasad, New Delhi, Sterling, 1989; "Silence As a Mode of Transcendence in the Poetry of Jayanta Mahapatra" by D.R. Pattanaik, in *Journal of Commonwealth Literature,* 16(1), 1991; "Telephone Message for Mr. Jayanta Mahapatra: A Memoir" by Cyril Dabydeen, in *World Literature Written in English* (Singapore), 32(1), spring 1992; "Quest for Roots: Poetry of Jayanta Mahapatra" by Niranjan Mohanty, in *Creative Forum* (New Delhi), 5(1–4), 1992; "The Abstraction of Language: Jayanta Mahapatra and A.K. Mehrotra As Indian 'Postmodernists'" by Joseph Swann, in *Fusion of Cultures?,* edited by Peter O. Stummer and Christopher Balme, Amsterdam, Netherlands, Rodopi, 1996; *The Poetry of Jayanta Mahapatra* by Rabindra K. Swain, New Delhi, Prestige, 1999.

Jayanta Mahapatra comments:

Mystery has always fascinated me—a sense of the unknown, of things unexplainable, even in those areas which appear so very familiar in our lives—and so it is with poetry. All poetry that touches, arousing a tremor in the heart, should have this element of the unknown in it; a manner of silence which suddenly stops the reader, as it were, expanding the horizon in which the reader finds himself. I suppose not many people believe in this kind of poetry, although, judging from the traditionally built-in sense of mysticism an Indian has, such poetry should have had a wide readership.

Mystery is like the rain, falling like false jewels in the sky, which catch the light as they fall, like the trail of a rainbow; and perhaps it is these bits of a rainbow which a poem should catch to be able to move the reader and instill in his or her mind a "stirring" of some kind.

I should call this stirring in the mind a madness, which might border on irrationality; but it is exactly this quality of the unknown and ununderstandable which go to make the beauty of a poem. And this is how I feel: that one must try somehow to reach the border between things understandable and ununderstandable in a poem, between life and death, between a straight line and a circle.

Perhaps this paucity of our knowledge about death, about the nowhere which exists in the mind about the knowledge of death and of our future, and about this boundary when flesh disappears and time enters, holds an unusual power that drives one to create the flow in a poem. And so, the unknown, the mysterious which one can never fully fathom, leads to an unending questioning in my own poetry.

In a poem I wrote some 16 years ago, titled "A Rain of Rites," I found myself once again at the border between two separate regions of the mind—between what, perhaps, I understood and what I did not, using "rain" as a symbol for that substance which makes up my life, those blurs of vague light that pulsate with the days, making me ask at the end of the poem:

What still stale air sits on an angel's wings?
What holds my rain so it's hard to overcome?

I suppose such questionings come from somewhere deep within oneself, and that there is no reason or rationale for these things. But such questions and such searching move me, and I am unable to resist them in my poetry. For poetry is voice—*vaak* — and it is a voice which is forged from those elements which constitute the world both within and without—a voice which carries with it its unusual power of survival.

I think I have always been in love with silence, and its destruction is, to me, as perhaps to everyone else, a matter of concern. Silence is a word which comes back over and over again into my life and, consequently, to the poetry I write. And silence exerts an air of mystery that makes me reach into the unknown, to sense things I had never felt before.

So, for me, a poem is knit together by an inconceivable silence. Silence which is an intangible substance, of which words are but manifestations, words which can build the poem from a silence and to which the poem must eventually return. Does this silence lie within the heart? Maybe it does, as it waits to burst out of one with a child-like pang of pain on its way to becoming the idiom of the poem. For this silence is a sound I will always remember, as it appears to move through my days, and I feel it like an armor I sheathe myself in, to protect myself from the outside world.

And at times perhaps, not having exactly understood this silence I experience within myself, I let it open out for me a thousand memories, a thousand longings, as these, in turn, come into being in a poem I write. For there is no doubt that a poem is always made in the field of one's imagination. So somehow poem after poem comes to *be,* as I use this silence I feel as a myth, using different symbols and metaphors as they suit my own experience.

When one writes in this way, maybe poetry enters the country of dream and the meaning of the poem becomes unclear, difficult to emerge from the poem itself. This is what some critics have said about my poetry: that it becomes obscure, not giving up its meaning easily to the reader after one reading. But I ask myself: What use is a poem if it is easily understood, if there is a straightforward working of the words, more in the manner of a statement? True poetry, perhaps, has always lent itself to an indirect approach, and where one wants to return to an overwhelming silence. It becomes difficult to explain such processes which take place in the mind.

So because the poem happens in the mind, the poem itself becomes the idea. When I write a poem around the idea of silence, then perhaps the whole poem is my silence; not the words which contain the idea and which might not be apparent at all to the reader of the poem.

As I write this, I know it becomes harder and harder to explain the idea of silence and its mystery. And I do realize that a poem is made in isolation: although once it is made, it should reach out to the reader. In my poetry, I have measured this silence of mine with symbols like "rain" or "sleep" or "stone"—which are, once again, very private symbols. Born as we are to fundamental thoughts of doubt and uncertainty, it is not easy to predict anything in this world we live in, least of all the outcome of a poem. But the workings of the mind go on, even as I realize that the fact of observation of an object is uncertain, because it is linked with the passage of time and with the fact that we are always moving, as pointed out so aptly by the German physicist, Werner Karl Heisenberg. So also, I know of nothing for certain in our world.

The pattern of understanding has not appeared to change with the poems I have written and it shall probably remain so. For me, poetry shall only be the flash of light which one sees when one is nearing the end of a tunnel. The poem itself, the process which goes to make it, will ever remain a mystery. All knowledge is provisional, so why should a poem be otherwise?

The mind in one's being is shaped by all one sees and all that one has failed to see. From this mind, the poem. Once the poem is done, I can feel its power stir in me, perhaps in a way of consolation for things I have not been able to do. Perhaps it brings me back to reality, while a mixture of pain and satisfaction fills the senses—it is difficult to know.

And yet, our sense of what a poem is, is formed out of the very fact of assimilation of those many poems we have encountered through the years, and it is no use denying that these links have not been made in one's poetry. I should like to think that this has happened in the poetry I have written. If the quality of mystery appeals to me, then this has come from the value I have learnt to place on how such words and ideas have gone on to become poetry. And this poetry, like all other art perhaps, alternated between deception and revelation.

Finally, I'd like to admit that studying physics and then going on to teach it for years has made me aware, intensely in some ways, of this world we inhabit; it tells me where I am. Does it help me in some way to find my bearings? I cannot say. Most of us Indians are grounded to the regions of our existence with our quality of fatalistic consciousness, and so help us to be on better terms with the unconscious. Physics has revealed to me that there is a presence of this unconscious in even inert matter; maybe this has fairly well integrated the conscious and the unconscious in me. But in the beginning I never wanted to write poems to suit my readers, keeping my thoughts to the reader's limits and never going *beyond* the reader. Perhaps this restricted my readership in India, and it was painful, but I didn't want to make any literary concessions.

One cannot deny that such poetry is mysterious, touching the abstract at times. Whether such poetry fails or succeeds is a different matter. But it is the kind of poetry I like to write. Words like "silence," "darkness," "sleep," or "absence" are indeed unknowns in the world of ours; and, used in poems, may be scorned by critics, but often engage the reader's sympathies.

Ruled by the unconscious, it seems but natural that one comes out with the mysterious in a poem. I am not insisting that this unconscious is a god, or a computer gone haywire. But it dictates. It makes me imagine. It makes me speak in different ways to satisfy the need to say what I feel. And that is all I can truthfully say.

(1995) After years of continuous writing, one feels today that one should perhaps give up the notion of writing poetry altogether, because this is all we know; that they, the words, the makers of poetry, will forever remain beyond us in spite of our painstaking attempts to let the poems we have made tell us we are content with them. And perhaps at some point of time there is an inexplicable urge to build a sort of wall, which could well mean the feeling not to write at all; or perhaps the breaking down of some hazy dream, not any reality—like watching the flesh of the knife the poet holds slice into the heads of this double-headed snake called poetry. And yet, if neither is real, what difference does it truly make?

At times I ask myself: Is this because, time and again one is appalled by the debilitating poverty I am exposed to as an Indian, living by the slums in the heart of this old, congested city? And about which one has been able to do nothing?

Poetry has always been responsible to life. By this, I mean that a poet is first of all responsible to his own heart, otherwise he cannot be called a poet. And maybe those other factors which are necessary to the makings of a good poet will come only later. And so, if the poet's conscience matters, it seems but natural that he would write about those things which appear unfair to him. It is the poet again who will talk about injustice and cruelty and greed in the society in which he lives, hoping in his heart of hearts that these would be taken care of. Certainly one cannot place the poet in the role of a social reformer; but there can be no denying the fact that he would like to see a just and fair society come into existence, to see the smile appear on the face of every destitute child on the street, on every man, woman, and animal on this earth he inhabits.

But these are tall orders. History has always proved otherwise. The outcome is that the poet uses his "bad heart" to go on writing his poems until he comes to a stage when he would perhaps make the ultimate decision in his life: *not* to write. This comes about through years of painful work, through countless words which he had supposed would get the attention they deserved. It is the Wall he faces at this moment. . . .

*   *   *

Many of Jayanta Mahapatra's poems are hermetic. They refer obliquely to unspecified desires, guilts, and memories which haunt the "inner world of his own making—a world spaced by his own life, of secret allusions, of desire and agony, of a constantly changing alignment between dream and reality," as Mahapatra put it in "The Inaudible Resonance in English Poetry in India" (*Literary Criterion* 1980). It is the creation of an inner world, evolving in complexity and richness from poem to poem, volume to volume, that makes Mahapatra a postmodernist constructing his own realm of silence, solitude, memory, and desire, while remaining haunted by the Indian environment, with its rituals and myths, from which he feels separated by his Christian upbringing, skepticism, and scientific education.

Mahapatra early developed a unique style in which multiplicity of significances, dislocated, often baffling syntax, and disruption of grammar are held together rather by rich patterns of imagery and sound than by any clarity of argument or narrative. In the poem "Love," in *Close the Sky, Ten by Ten,* we are warned, "leave thought alone/to find the meaning/. . . it will not turn/to/a sentence." The title *Close the Sky, Ten by Ten* comes from "Sanctuary," a statement of withdrawal into the self (possibly from extramarital pleasures): "now i close the sky/with a square ten by ten." The obscurity results from a complexity of themes presented obliquely within short lyrics built from contrasts, contradictory statements, and other techniques that tend to oppose or deconstruct what at first appears to be claimed.

Mahapatra first pulled his fragmented themes together into a more unified vision in *A Rain of Rites,* where meditation on the local landscape is a starting place for the articulation of emotions felt at the edge of awareness. In such poems as "Dawn," "Village," "Old Palaces," and "Samsara" the imagination acknowledges the external world, then de-creates it, finding a possible alternative reality within the self passively awaiting illumination and renewal. Some poems, such as "The Whorehouse in a Calcutta Street," reveal a new interest in social content, while others, such as "Indian Summer Poem," obliquely allude to traditional Indian symbols and myths. The volume is unified by its recurrence of themes and images and by a constancy of tone and mood, with the rain, sky, dawn, river, flowers, roots, shadows, stones, trees, and sun becoming symbols in the poet's quest for significance: "What is there in ceremony, in a ritual's deeply hidden meaning?/The familiar words are roots, and out of place."

Mahapatra's titles seem part of a continuing private autobiography—*Waiting, The False Start, Relationship, Life Signs.* The evolving body of poetry alludes to false starts, hopes, disillusionments, anxieties, and contradictions as Mahapatra gropes "from poem to poem for the key to human understanding." While the lyrics are rich in the atmosphere of the Indian landscape, its legends, and the historical past of Orissa, their main concern is what Mahapatra has called "the essentiality of his being." He often returns to the problem of what he is, the truth of what he sees and feels, and his sense of being distinct from the traditional India of his surroundings. In "Waiting" he contrasts the "deadened dust," "soiled three-year-old children," and "luckless widows shuffling up and down/the fractured temple steps" with his observation of them: "You hardly know the vision isolates you"; "Every day I see them debase themselves/and am afraid, understanding nothing."

Relationship is a twelve-part dream epic, a psychic quest into the poet's roots as represented by the past and symbolism of Orissa. It is an attempt to go beyond the self, to give classical poetic status to the locality, while unburdening the sense of guilt that results from the poet's alienation from the culture in which he lives: "I know I can never come alive/if I refuse to consecrate at the altar of my origins."

In *Life Signs* Mahapatra's vision is his main theme: "the song that reaches our ears is just our own"; "It is the silence which says the world is not ours"; "So we drag meanings/from what we see"; "Or is it only desire, hoping to resume its inner light." The magnificent "The Lost Children of America" is as much about the poet's own relationship to India as it is about those foreigners drawn to the myths of his country. While it is easy to become impatient with his mannerisms, obscurity, private symbols, and long, incantatory lines, Mahapatra has developed the unique vision, style, and poetic mode of a major writer.

While Mahapatra's subsequent volumes appear uneven in quality, with slack rhythms and odd associations, that was often true of the earlier books until they became familiar and could be seen in perspective. The later volumes increasingly are concerned with death and focus more on the social problems of contemporary India as the poet attempts to go beyond his own isolation to write of a nation of hunger, poverty, injustice, violence, and fanaticism. The two parts of *Dispossessed Nests: The 1984 Poems* include somber, disillusioned, somewhat obscure meditations on the deaths caused by Punjabi terrorists and the horrors of the Bhopal disaster in which thousands were injured or killed by chemical fumes. The poems in *Burden of*

Waves and Fruit, selected from a period after the late 1970s, are linked by such recurring images and themes as rain, the sun, dreams, memory, the past, and fear of death. There is more use of rhyme, line closure, and other formal structures than in the earlier books. The sources of poetry—desire, memory, life, and death—are related, as in "Song of the Bones," which asks, "Does one find death/in an act which comes out of love?" The movement is from the volume's opening poem, with its rain, expressionless sky, and "old fireflies" (the sparks of memories; see the "Fireflies" of Manohar Shetty's *A Guarded Space* [1981]), to the concluding "The Year's Last Evening," where the speaker thinks of "walking past a fear,/turning away as though it did not exist here."

Temple is a lyric sequence mixing Indian legend, mythology, and ideas about illusion, reality, and self-referentiality (the poet, the sources of his imagination, and his poem) in a dream about women in Indian history, culture, and contemporary society. Horror at the gang rape and murder of a twelve-year-old girl is juxtaposed with the suicide of an eighty-year-old woman, the exemplary purity of Sita, bloody sacrificial offerings to goddesses, and the Hindu belief that women's orgasm (*shakti*) is the divine force and ultimate consciousness. The Hindu notion of existence as suffering is central to the vision. Is reincarnation the source of the sufferings with which women are burdened?

The patterns of experience and style as established in Mahapatra's previous works continue and evolve along similar lines in *A Whiteness of Bone.* Most of the same themes as before—the inner and the outer worlds, the quest for significance, pain and suffering, love, truth, poetry, memories, dreams, silence, old age, childhood, myths and rituals, social and political circumstances, time, and death—and the same images—rain, the sky, night, day, the sun and moon, stars, river, water, wind, roots, stones, rocks, sand, flowers, trees, birds, fishes—proliferate here again and are handled with an increased sureness of touch. Language, too, has gained further fluency and control. The syntax is less convoluted, with frequent use of end-stopped lines and of rhyme. Although Mahapatra's poetry is still suffused with mysterious meanings, it has become easier than before to trace the lines of thought and feeling in it.

The main themes of *A Whiteness of Bone* are death and time. The bone of the title symbolizes the loss of life's significance and the decay that the passage of time brings. Published in the sixty-fourth year of Mahapatra's life, the book has an ominously somber quality about it. An experience of continuous pain and a tragic sense of despair permeate the poems. A dichotomy between the eternity of the physical world and the evanescence of human existence, as in "Unreal Country" ("Only the world/is left, and the rain/that hangs from the branches") and in "Dawn" ("The foothills survive./Footsteps of a few who walked on them/are silent"), runs throughout *A Whiteness of Bone.* Only a spontaneous engagement with the present, like a child's, as in "The Waiting," brings a happiness that transcends the limits of the ephemeral: "To wait for purpose is to be devoid of meaning./But the child does not wait any more./He leaves no tears,/no tales or marks." As before in Mahapatra, poetry is the subject of several poems, which connects one with an eternal reality, as in "A Sound of Flutes": "Through your notes/you would let my death live,/a heartbeat of hooves/tame sheep leave over devious slopes." In "All the Poetry There Is" Mahapatra says that poetry "appears to rise out of the ashes" of suffering: "And the ashes turn and wheel through the dance/like birds of prey in awesome grace in the skies."

In *A Whiteness of Bone* the focus of Mahapatra's poetry tilts further away from an absorption in the self toward social reality. He seeks wisdom and expansion of his poetic vision from involvement with the poor and the simple. "In An Orissa Village" recalls the advice of an old villager: "'Look at the sky,' you had said,/'not why you came here nor/what you try to see.'... Someday, if I keep recalling you,/maybe understanding will go out/into the world with me." In "Evening Ritual" (after a visit to a Koraput village) the poet remembers another "old man saying if I wanted to help them,/if I had seen anything there that mocked my world/Here was the light that stumbled on my words"; the poem concludes, "Now perhaps, I'll wait for morning,/my sleep nourished from people/who had caught the moon in their tears,/the shadows thick with the ashes of burnt stars..." Numerous poems, such as "Deaths in Orissa," "The Rage in Those Young Eyes," "The Fifteenth of August," "Of Independence Day," "A Sullen Balance," "Another Love Poem," and "Red Roses for Gandhi," lament the conditions prevailing in contemporary India and call for redress. "A Sullen Balance" captures the feeling of utter helplessness and decay a person living in India experiences: "Like a patient crocodile/she leaves her prey to rot into softness/fastened beneath the roots/of some banyan of our heritage/ that overhangs the river of our time." "Red Roses for Gandhi" describes how a number of students chose to immolate themselves by fire in protest against the government's unjust policies: "They are dying, dancers in the air, like birds, almost human,/adorned with the sunshine of youth,/their hearts consumed with purpose,/their hands folding their flame like festive ritual lamps,/gathering wings..." Like the previous collections *A Whiteness of Bone* also contains poems about the gas disaster of Bhopal. "The Hill" delineates the suffering caused by the tragedy: "Even the palms hide their high heads/in the bare sky, like all resolves./For somewhere either children have died/or have not died."

Mahapatra continues to translate poetry of other writers from Indian languages into English. His translation of Bengali poems by Sakti Chattopadhyay, who has a love of life, in *I Can, But Why Should I Go* is of a piece with his own poetry. His book of poems in Oriya, *Bali* ("The Victim"), represents an aspect of Mahapatra's rootedness in his native culture different from his English poetry.

—Bruce King and Surjit Dulai

MAHON, Derek

Nationality: British. **Born:** Belfast, Northern Ireland, 23 November 1941. **Education:** Belfast Institute, 1953–60; Trinity College, Dublin, 1960–65, B.A. in French 1965. **Family:** Married Doreen Douglas in 1972; two children. **Career:** English teacher, Belfast High School, 1967–68, and Language Centre of Ireland, Dublin, 1968–70; writer-in-residence, University of East Anglia, Norwich, 1975, Emerson College, Boston, 1976–77, and New University of Ulster, Coleraine, 1977–79. Co-editor, *Atlantis,* Dublin, 1970–74; drama critic *The Listener,* 1971–72, features editor of *Vogue,* 1974–75, and poetry editor, *New Statesman,* since 1981, all London. **Awards:** Eric Gregory award, 1965; Arts Council bursary, 1981; Scott Moncrieff prize, for translation, 1989. **Agent:** Deborah Rogers, Ltd., 49 Blenheim Crescent, London W11 2EF, England. **Address:** c/o Oxford University Press, Ely House, 37 Dover Street, London W1X 4AH, England.

PUBLICATIONS

Poetry

Twelve Poems. Belfast, Festival, 1965.
Design for a Grecian Urn. Cambridge, Massachusetts, Erato, 1967.
Night-Crossing. London, Oxford University Press, 1968.
Ecclesiastes. Manchester, Phoenix Pamphlet Poets Press, 1970.
Beyond Howth Head. Dublin, Dolmen Press, 1970.
Lives. London, Oxford University Press, 1972.
The Man Who Built His City in Snow. London, Poem-of-the-Month Club, 1972.
The Snow Party. London and New York, Oxford University Press, 1975.
Light Music. Belfast, Ulsterman, 1977.
In Their Element: A Selection of Poems, with Seamus Heaney. Belfast, Arts Council of Northern Ireland, 1977.
The Sea in Winter. Dublin, Gallery Press, and Old Deerfield, Massachusetts, Deerfield Press, 1979.
Poems 1962–1978. London, Oxford University Press, 1979.
Courtyards in Delft. Dublin, Gallery Press, 1981.
The Hunt by Night. Oxford, Oxford University Press, 1982; Winston-Salem, North Carolina, Wake Forest University Press, 1983.
A Kensington Notebook. London, Anvil Press Poetry, 1984.
Antarctica. Dublin, Gallery Press, 1986.
Selected Poems. Oldcastle, Gallery Press, 1990; New York, Penguin, 1993.
The Yaddo Letter. Oldcastle, Gallery Press, 1992.
The Hudson Letter. Oldcastle, Gallery Books, 1995; Winston-Salem, North Carolina, Wake Forest University Press, 1996.
The Yellow Book. Oldcastle, Gallery Press, 1997; Winston-Salem, North Carolina, Wake Forest University Press, 1998.
Collected Poems. Oldcastle, Gallery Books, 1999.

Recording: *Adam Zagajewski and Derek Mahon Reading Their Poems,* Gertrude Clarke Whittall Poetry and Literature Fund, Library of Congress, 1992.

Plays

High Time, adaptation of a play by Molière (produced Derry, 1984). Dublin, Gallery Press, 1985.
The School for Wives, adaptation of a play by Molière. Dublin, Gallery Press, 1986.
The Bacchae: After Euripedes. Oldcastle, Gallery, Press, 1991.

Radio Features: on Brain Moore, 1975, J.G. Farrell, 1980, Olivia Manning, 1981, John Montague, 1982, and Robert Lowell, 1984.

Television Adaptations: *Shadows on Our Skin,* 1980, and *How Many Miles to Babylon?* 1981, both by Jennifer Johnston; *First Love,* by Turgenev, 1982; *The Demon Lover,* by Elizabeth Bowen, 1983; *A Moment of Love,* by Brian Moore, 1984; *The Cry,* with Chris Menaul, by John Montague, 1984.

Other

Journalism: Selected Prose 1970–1995. Oldcastle, Gallery Press, and Chester Springs, Pennsylvania, Dufour, 1996.

Editor, *Modern Irish Poetry.* London, Sphere, 1972.

Editor, with Peter Fallon, *The Penguin Book of Contemporary Irish Poetry.* London, Penguin, 1990.

Translator, *The Chimeras,* by Nerval. Dublin, Gallery Press, 1982.

Translator, *Selected Poems* by Philippe Jaccottet. London, Viking, 1987; Winston-Salem, North Carolina, Wake Forest University, 1988.

Translator, *Phaedra,* by Jean Racine. Oldcastle, Gallery Books, 1996.

Translator, *Words in the Air: A Selection of Poems,* by Philippe Jaccottet. Oldcastle, Gallery Books, 1998.

*

Critical Studies: "The Poetry of Derek Mahon" by Brian Donnelly, in *English Studies* (Nijmegen, Netherlands), 60, 1979; "'Singing the Darkness into the Light': Reflections on Recent Irish Poetry" by Harry Marten, in *New England Review* (Hanover, New Hampshire), 3, 1980; by Arthur E. McGuinness, in *Eire-Ireland* (St. Paul, Minnesota), 16(1), spring 1981; "Somewhere, Out There, Beyond: The Poetry of Seamus Heaney and Derek Mahon" by Andrew Waterman, in *PN Review* (Manchester, England), 8(1), 1981; "Semantic Scruples: A Rhetoric for Politics in the North" by D.E.S. Maxwell, in *Literature and the Changing Ireland,* edited by Peter Connolly, Gerrards Cross, England, Colin Smythe, and Totowa, New Jersey, Barnes and Noble, 1982; "'To the Point of Speech': The Poetry of Derek Mahon" by Eamon Grennan, in *Contemporary Irish Writing,* edited by James D. Brophy and Raymond J. Porter, Boston, Twayne, 1983; "Poetry and Politics: Response to the Northern Ireland Crisis in the Poetry of John Montague, Derek Mahon, and Seamus Heaney" by Conor Johnston, in *Poesis* (Bryn Mawr, Pennsylvania), 5(4), 1984; *The Significance of Landscape and History in the Poetry of Seamus Heaney, Derek Mahon and John Montague* by John M. Byrne, Newcastle upon Tyne, University of Newcastle upon Tyne, 1984; "Derek Mahon's Development" by John Constable, in *Agenda* (London), 22(3–4), autumn-winter 1984–85; "An Urbane Perspective: The Poetry of Derek Mahon" by Maurice Riordan, in *The Irish Writer and the City,* edited by Maurice Harmon, Gerrards Cross, England, Colin Smythe, and Totowa, New Jersey, Barnes and Noble, 1984; "The Poetry of Derek Mahon" by David E. William, in *Journal of Irish Literature* (Newark, Delaware), 13(3), September 1984; "Derek Mahon: The Lute and the Stars" by Robert Taylor, in *Massachusetts Review* (Amherst), 28(3), autumn 1987; "Cast a Wary Eye: Derek Mahon's Classical Perspective" by Arthur E. McGuinness, in *Yearbook of English Studies* (London), 17, 1987; "History in the Poetry of Derek Mahon" by Joris Duytschaever, in *History and Violence in Anglo-Irish Literature,* edited by Duytschaever and Geert Lernout, Amsterdam, Rodopi, 1988; "Derek Mahon's Humane Perspective" by Brendan Kennelly, in *Tradition and Influence in Anglo-Irish Poetry,* edited by Terence Brown and Nicholas Grene, Totowa, New Jersey, Barnes and Noble, 1989; "International Perspectives in the Poetry of Derek Mahon" by Bill Tinley, in *Irish University Review* (Dublin), 21(1), spring-summer 1991; "History and Poetry: Derek Mahon and Tom Paulin" by Peter McDonald, in *The Poet's Place: Ulster Literature and Society,* edited by Gerald Dawe and John Wilson Foster, Belfast, Institute of Irish Studies, 1991; "'Even Now There Are Places Where a Thought Might Grow': Place and Displacement in the Poetry of Derek Mahon" by Hugh Houghton, in *The Chosen Ground: Essays on the Contemporary Poetry of Northern Ireland,* edited by Neil Corcoran, Bridgend, Ireland, Seren, 1992;

Derek Mahon issue of *Irish University Review* (Dublin), 24(1), spring-summer 1994; "A Residual Poetry: Heaney, Mahon and Hedgehog History" by Scott Brewster, in *Irish University Review* (Dublin), 28(1), spring-summer 1998.

*   *   *

What one initially notices in the poetry of Derek Mahon is a strong sense of place. On first reading, some of his best poems appear to be topographical. They have titles such as "Day Trip to Donegal," "April on Toronto Island," and "Teaching in Belfast." In poem after poem local properties are assiduously assembled. "A Garage in Co. Cork" speaks of "building materials, fruit boxes, scrap iron, / Dust-laden shrubs and coils of rusty wire . . ." Always clearly signaled, however, is the possibility of release, in this instance, "Beyond, a swoop of mountain where you heard, / Disconsolate in the haze, a single blackbird."

The idea of an individual gesture dissolving the present clutter is highly characteristic of Mahon. In the dawn after the late-night hubbub described in "Rock Music" the speaker hears "a single bird / Drown with a whistle that residual roar . . ." A similar signal suggests the positive quality Mahon finds in the work of a distinguished predecessor. "In Carrowdore Churchyard" is an elegy on Louis MacNeice: "Maguire, I believe, suggested a blackbird / And over your grave a phrase from Euripides . . ."

The quality Mahon admires in MacNeice is manifested in his own work by a characteristic so insistent as to justify employing the term "poetic touchstone":

> From the pneumonia of the ditch, from the ague
> Of the blind poet and the bombed-out town you bring
> The all-clear to the empty holes of spring;
> Rinsing the choked mud, keeping the colours new.

Detritus is associated with death, and death is represented as physical occlusion. Set against this is a sense of release evoked in a series of images that suggest an individual mode of *claritas.* In "Consolations of Philosophy" a few of the dead, immured in rotten boards and broken urns, "remember with delight / the dust gyrating in a shaft of light . . ." This contrast between detritus and release is found in "A Refusal to Mourn." An old man's house—"Cinders moved in the grate, / And a warm briar gurgled"—is set against the old man's deliverance. It is a deliverance not to a graveyard but to the oblivion conferred by the seasons: "In time the astringent rain / Of those parts will clean / The words from his gravestone . . ."

The imprisoned masses referred to in "A Disused Shed in Co. Wexford" wait for "light meter and relaxed itinerary." The exiled proprietor in "The Chinese Restaurant in Portrush" sees "the light / Of heaven upon the mountains of Donegal." Much of "The Poet in Residence" consists of a letter to the lover of the imprisoned Tristan Corbière that is written and then torn up. The words of the letter escape, as their author cannot: "The little bits of white / Looked, in the mist, like gulls in flight."

These touchstones all involve a sense of release and deploy a characteristic vocabulary: "the *glittering* west," "a *swoop* of mountains," "the *all-clear,*" "a shaft of *light,*" "*clean* / The words," "the *light* of heaven," and this last, "gulls in *flight.*" The examples could be multiplied, but the drift is clear and is subsumed in the poem called, punningly, "Light Music": "A land of cumulus / seen from above / is the life to come . . ."

The places that throng Mahon's poetry seem to have been created as a means of providing the launching pad for release. It could be said that he has been half in love with death and that death has not been, in Keats's phrase, "easeful." The mood of Mahon's late collection *The Yellow Book* is elegiac. It is dedicated to the memory of the poet's friend Eugene Lambe, and the elegy "To Eugene Lambe in Heaven" forms its centerpiece.

Here Mahon breaks all the rules. He has gone back to a mode of rambling meditation, familiar in the nineteenth century, with a discursive rhyme scheme that, though it hovers about the elegiac quatrain, rhymes, so to speak, where it touches:

It's after closing-time on a winter's night
in Smokey Joe's café a generation ago—
rain and smoke, and the table are packed tight
with drunken students kicking up a racket,
exchanging insults, looking for a fight
since there's nothing to do and nowhere else to go;
and the sad Italians (parents, daughter, son)
who own the place and serve these savages
of the harsh north their chips and sausages
look up and grin with relief as you come in,
their baffled faces lighting up at once
at your quaint "whisker" and velvet smoking jacket . . .

The reader has to wait for the rhyme for "racket," evinced in line four, to be completed, in line twelve, with "jacket." The "racket"/ "jacket" rhyme is a species of intruder, for without it we would have a straightforward "night"/"ago"/"tight"/"fight"/"go" scheme, that is to say, *abaab*.

This is typical of late Mahon, the rhythm slightly sprung, the rhyme scheme seemingly casual but, in fact, interfered with to release a flood of reminiscences emanating from a definite place. Here it is Smokey Joe's, the university café abutting on Queen's University. It proves, however, to be a base for taking off into what is at once an exploration of a period and of the places that make it up: University Road, Belfast, "Dublin in the '60s," "Covent Garden . . . living above the market." The destination is death, entered into with a quiet dignity—"philosophical with your dwindling flow of visitors"— somehow a consummation to be wished.

In the late poems of Mahon the wish for release is actualized in a manner more earthy than that previously entertained. The personae look back to "the treetops of Fitzwilliam Square," with its "famous Georgian doors"("Axel's Castle"), to the "nobler poetry" of the time "when the gutters bubbled, the drains stank" ("shiver in your tenement"), to "the big-game trophies and lion skins" ("The World of J.G. Farrell"). This last is yet another elegy, almost a companion piece to the grimmest poem of all, that in memory of the poet's mother: "Oh I can love you now that you're dead and gone / to the many mansions in your mother's house."

"The spirit unappeasable and peregrine"—Eliot's great invocation—might almost apply to Mahon. Whatever he holds and wherever he is, the spirit yearns to be somewhere else. The sense of place and the sense of occlusion assert themselves simultaneously, only to be dissolved into *claritas*. The linguistic mastery with which he seems to achieve the unachievable gathers this most restless of poets into the society of his masters.

—Philip Hobsbaum

MAIDEN, Jennifer

Nationality: Australian. **Born:** Penrith, New South Wales, 7 April 1949. **Education:** Macquarie University, North Ryde, New South Wales, B.A. 1974. **Family:** Married David Toohey in 1984; one daughter. **Career:** Tutor in creative writing, Outreach, Evening College Movement, and Blacktown City Council, all New South Wales, Fellowship of Australian Writers, and University of Western Sydney, 1976–91. Writer-in-residence, Australian National University, Canberra, New South Wales, State Torture and Trauma Rehabilitation Unit, and University of Western Sydney, all 1989. **Awards:** Australia Council grant or fellowship, 1974, 1975, 1977, 1978, 1983, 1984, 1986. Harri Jones memorial prize; Butterly-Hooper award. **Address:** P.O. Box 4, Penrith, New South Wales 2750, Australia.

PUBLICATIONS

Poetry

Tactics. St. Lucia, University of Queensland Press, 1974.
The Occupying Forces. St. Lucia, Makar Press, 1975.
The Problem of Evil. Sydney, Poetry Society of Australia, 1975.
Birthstones. Sydney, Angus and Robertson, 1978.
The Border Loss. Sydney, Angus and Robertson, 1979.
For the Left Hand. Sydney, South Head Press, 1981.
The Trust. Wentworth Falls, New South Wales, Black Lightning Press, 1988.
The Winter Baby. Sydney, Angus and Robertson, 1990.
Bastille Day. Canberra, National Library of Australia, 1990.
Selected Poems of Jennifer Maiden. Ringwood, Victoria, and New York, Penguin, 1990.
Acoustic Shadow. Ringwood, Victoria, and New York, Penguin, 1993.

Novels

The Terms. Sydney, Hale and Iremonger, 1982.
Play with Knives. Sydney, Allen and Unwin, 1990.

Short Stories

Mortal Details. Melbourne, Rigamarole, 1977.

*

Critical Studies: By Elizabeth Perkins, in *Linq* (Townsville, Queensland), 16(3), 1989; in *Overland,* 128, 1992, and 138, fall 1995.

*   *   *

"Ambivalent, ambidextrous, ambiguous, androgynous, amorous, ironic"—so Jennifer Maiden characterizes her poetry. "Teasing, intellectual irony, too, has always seemed to me a humane new channel toward pensive seduction for what otherwise, in more direct poetry, can be a jealous urge for power over the reader." Such poetic intent suggests demanding work, resistant to easy interpretation. It also promises, in its fruition, accomplished, complex poetry that is controlled, cerebral, and yet sensuous. Maiden's assured role as an

Australian poet of significance attests that these promises have been kept.

The properties Maiden lists, and to which might be added wit, are at work in her eight-part poem "The Trust." In a footnote she cautions that, while the poem is "about" the reader-writer relationship, this is just one aspect of a work that "concentrates on all forms of intimacy." The first part begins in midconversation but soon warns the reader to maintain critical distance, while simultaneously beckoning us into the poem:

> . . . Don't trust
> me yet: I don't know what I will still
> require of you, and you don't know
> as yet the depth and danger in your trust.
> There is no room here to run, and none
> in you that I can run from. Here she is!
> . . . We can wake her.
> When you do, you clasp her shoulders, fear
> that somehow your hands don't look right.

Three characters—a woman, a man, and an antelope (unicorn?)—are brought to life within an enclosed garden. The resonant images undergo several transformations, with the writer inviting the reader into a series of carefully staged scenes: "just do / what you like to the oyster-woman, but / note that 'to' not 'with', / and save some fear for later"; "He's / alive and you are quite free to explore. Yes, / ignore that first ignoble moral scruple." The reader is cajoled into erotic experiences with the "characters," the writer standing guard and assuring privacy. In the fourth part the writer becomes an actor:

> It isn't to escape that I have come, but
> your other's body's thin enough to hold,
> is artefactually fragile . . .
> and every pulse is subtle, is a watch
> to tell me time and date and where and this,
> exclusive as a dream.

Within this enclosure the "others" change shape, dying, with the antelope as a sacrifice, and being resurrected in different forms, while the garden freezes over and disappears.

Like the garden, the poem is enclosed. Its end is its beginning, for its last line is also the first ("here it is. As it is always said / we-begin-here-at-the-end and anything which comes / after that is what we will discuss"). Indeed, within this circularity there is "no room to run." The transitional lines repeated to link sections of the poem often hinge on the impossibility of the escape routes of the real world: "If all things here were penetrably live, / you would trust in an escape by promises."

The poet's voice is sometimes hospitable: "flood the glass / and we will drink to you— / who'll never now be stranger to / our gates, which you must soon accept are gone"; "I have only / come to empty ashtrays, to clean / cages. Take your meal." Sometimes, however, it is admonitory: "and who and why / are these poor creatures married in our arms? / You have no right to pity. It is mine. / I own this army."

The true characters of "The Trust" are the reader and the writer. They manipulate the others like marionettes, an androgynous two in a collusion of mind, offering and enjoying bodies within the garden while dogs howl at the gates. The staged scenes increasingly reveal themselves as synonyms for intimate relationships in which roles are forever changing and that which is eaten later consumes. For instance,

the sacrificed antelope becomes a guest at a ceremonial meal: "The woman converts simply to a chair. / The man becomes a table, well. The small / antelope sits feeding now. / It is clovenly exquisite, / picking softly at smoked entrails." The ritual dance in the garden continues through sacrifice, death, resurrection, and cyclic change (winter), impermanence within a cycle of renewal through change. "The Trust" is at once an exercise in the examination of the illusions of poetry ("The lyrical vulture / flexes his wings a little, on the ground / with her, you and no drama: and I wait") and in the exchanges of intimacy. The interplay of themes and adroit precision of language is illustrative of Maiden's work at its most accomplished.

Maiden's career has been extraordinarily prolific, and her collections are carefully shaped. *The Trust* and *The Problem of Evil* balance their complex long poems with shorter, lighter selections. "Falling to Prettiness," "Celebration," and "Language" ("I need to learn a language but not english / or at present any further maidenese. / I know some anglo-saxon but it is / a lonely language") contrast with "The Trust." "The Problem of Evil" is a poetic novella of guerrilla warfare that has received several interpretations, for example, the incursion of poetry into the domain of prose or the war between the sexes. The poems that follow it—"Mobiles," "The Sponge"—are set in recognizably domestic worlds. *For the Left Hand* is a volume on a single theme, a woman who has lived "thirty years in a house with the boxes, gentling." Longer poems "For the Left Hand" (1, 11, and 111) enclose a series of short "boxes," with a segment of her life in each compartment.

Birthstones reaches beyond the jewels of each month. January has five lines on the garnet and "the myriad redness of birth." It is followed by "Truce," on the child within the womb: "You are as beautiful / as blood underwater . . . Our shadows fuse & melt / & swim a dark survival / that panicked to be felt." "Seal Pup" twists these gentle images of birth and blood; a mother seal is killed by hunters, and her pup "suckles from the dead." The September sapphire, "One chill of mary-blue . . . defying tenderness between / wearer & worn," precedes the brittle "Serenade" of "mutilated fondness" and "Mars & Venus," dominated by cool tones of blue and white, of "icy perfumes." One of the distinctive touches of "maidenese" is most surely felt in the imaginative pairings of Maiden's poetry.

—Nan Bowman Albinski

MAJOR, Clarence

Nationality: American. **Born:** Atlanta, Georgia, 31 December 1936. **Education:** Art Institute, Chicago (James Nelson Raymond Scholar), 1952–54; Armed Forces Institute, 1955–56; New School for Social Research, New York, 1972; Norwalk College, Connecticut; State University of New York, Albany, B.S. 1976; Union Graduate School, Yellow Springs and Cincinnati, Ohio, Ph.D. 1978. **Military Service:** U.S. Air Force, 1955–57. **Family:** Married 1) Joyce Sparrow in 1958 (divorced 1964); 2) Pamela Ritter. **Career:** Research analyst, Simulmatics, New York, 1966–67; director of creative writing program, Harlem Education Program, New Lincoln School, New York, 1967–68; writer-in-residence, Center for Urban Education, New York, 1967–68, and Teachers and Writers Collaborative-Teachers College, Columbia University, 1967–71; lecturer, Brooklyn College, City University of New York, 1968–69, spring 1973, 1974–75,

Cazenovia College, New York, summer 1969, Wisconsin State University, Eau Claire, fall 1969, Queens College, City University of New York, springs 1972, 1973, and 1975, and fall 1973, Sarah Lawrence College, Bronxville, New York, 1972–75, and School for Continuing Education, New York University, spring 1975; writer-in-residence, Aurora College, Illinois, spring 1974; assistant professor, Howard University, Washington, D.C., 1974–76, and University of Washington, Seattle, 1976–77; visiting assistant professor, University of Maryland, College Park, spring 1976, and State University of New York, Buffalo, summer 1976; associate professor, 1977–81, and professor, 1981–89, University of Colorado, Boulder. Professor since 1989, and since 1991 director of creative writing, University of California, Davis. Visiting professor, University of Nice, France, 1981–82, fall 1983, University of California, San Diego, spring 1984, and State University of New York, Binghamton, spring 1988; writer-in-residence, Albany State College, Georgia, 1984, and Clayton College, Denver, Colorado, 1986, 1987; distinguished visiting writer, Temple University, Philadelphia, fall 1988; guest writer, Warren Wilson College, 1988. Editor, *Coercion Review,* Chicago, 1958–66; staff writer, *Proof and Anagogic and Paideumic Review,* Chicago, 1960–61; associate editor, *Caw,* New York, 1967–70, and *Journal of Black Poetry,* San Francisco, 1967–70; reviewer, *Essence* magazine, 1970–73; columnist, 1973–76, and contributing editor, 1976–86, *American Poetry Review,* Philadelphia; editor, 1977–78, and since 1978 associate editor, *American Book Review,* New York; associate editor, *Bopp,* Providence, Rhode Island, 1977–78, *Gumbo,* 1978, *Departures,* 1979, and *par rapport,* 1979–82; member of the editorial board, *Umojo,* Boulder, Colorado, 1979–80; editorial consultant, Wesleyan University Press, Middletown, Connecticut, 1984, and University of Georgia Press, Athens, 1987; since 1986 fiction editor, *High Plains Literary Review.* Also artist: individual shows—Sarah Lawrence College, 1974; First National Bank Gallery, Boulder, Colorado, 1986. **Awards:** National Council on the Arts award, 1970; National Endowment for the Arts grant, 1970, 1975, 1979; Creative Artists Public Service grant, 1971; Fulbright-Hays Exchange award, 1981–83; Western States Book award, 1986, for *My Amputations;* Pushcart prize, 1989, for ''My Mother and Mitch.'' **Address:** Department of English, 1 Shields Avenue, University of California, Davis, California 95616, U.S.A.

PUBLICATIONS

Poetry

The Fires That Burn in Heaven. Privately printed, 1954.
Love Poems of a Black Man. Omaha, Nebraska, Coercion Press, 1965.
Human Juices. Omaha, Nebraska, Coercion Press, 1965.
Swallow the Lake. Middletown, Connecticut, Wesleyan University Press, 1970.
Symptoms and Madness. New York, Corinth, 1971.
Private Line. London, Paul Breman, 1971.
The Cotton Club: New Poems. Detroit, Broadside Press, 1972.
The Syncopated Cakewalk. New York, Barlenmir House, 1974.
Inside Diameter: The France Poems. Sag Harbor, New York and London, Permanent Press, 1985.
Surfaces and Masks. Minneapolis, Coffee House Press, 1988.
Some Observations of a Stranger in the Latter Part of the Century. Los Angeles, Sun and Moon Press, 1989.

Parking Lots. Mount Horeb, Wisconsin, Perishable Press, 1992.
Configurations: New and Selected Poems 1958–1998. Port Townsend, Washington, Copper Canyon Press, 1998.

Novels

All-Night Visitors. New York, Olympia Press, 1969.
Private Line. London, Paul Breman, Ltd., 1971.
NO. New York, Emerson Hall, 1973.
Reflex and Bone Structure. New York, Fiction Collective, 1975.
Emergency Exit. New York, Fiction Collective, 1979.
My Amputations. New York, Fiction Collective, 1986.
Such Was the Season. San Francisco, Mercury House, 1987.
Painted Turtle: Woman with Guitar. Los Angeles, Sun and Moon Press, 1988.

Short Stories

Fun and Games. Duluth, Minnesota, Holy Cow! Press, 1990.

Other

Dictionary of Afro-American Slang. New York, International, 1970; as *Black Slang: A Dictionary of Afro-American Talk,* London, Routledge, 1971.
The Dark and Feeling: Black American Writers and Their Work. New York, Third Press, 1974.
Juba to Jive: A Dictionary of African-American Slang. New York, Viking, 1994.

Editor, *Writers Workshop Anthology.* New York, Harlem Education Project, 1967.
Editor, *Man Is Like a Child: An Anthology of Creative Writing by Students.* New York, Macomb's Junior High School, 1968.
Editor, *The New Black Poetry.* New York, International, 1969.
Editor, *Calling the Wind: Twentieth Century African-American Short Stories.* New York, HarperCollins, 1993.
Editor, *The Garden Thrives: Twentieth Century African-American Poetry.* New York, HarperCollins, 1995.

*

Bibliograpies: ''Clarence Major: A Checklist of Criticism'' by Joe Weixlmann, in *Obsidian* (Fredonia, New York), 4(2), 1978; ''Toward a Primary Bibliography of Clarence Major'' by Joe Weixlmann and Clarence Major, in *Black American Literature Forum* (Terre Haute, Indiana), 12(2), summer 1979.

Critical Studies: In *New York Times,* 7 April 1969; *Quarterly Journal of Speech* (New York), April 1971; *Saturday Review* (New York), 3 April 1971; *Chicago Sun-Times,* 28 April 1971; *Poetry* (Chicago), August 1971; *Virginia Quarterly Review* (Charlottesville), winter 1971; *New York Times Book Review,* 1 July 1973; *Interviews with Black Writers* edited by John O'Brien, New York, Liveright, 1973; ''Five Black Poets: History, Consciousness, Love and Harshness,'' in *Parnassus* (New York), 3, spring-summer 1975, and *Drumvoices: The Mission of Afro-American Poetry—A Critical History,* New York, Doubleday, 1976, both by Eugene B. Redmond; *The Life: The Lore and Folk Poetry of the Black Hustler* by Dennis

Wepman, Ronald B. Newman, and Murray B. Binderman, Philadelphia, University of Pennsylvania Press, 1976; "Clarence Major: Persephone in Fragments," in *Open Form and the Feminine Imagination,* by Stephen-Paul Martin, Washington, D.C., Maisonneuve Press, 1988; "Against Commodification: Zuni Culture in Clarence Major's Native American Texts" by Steve Hayward, in *African American Review* (Terre Haute, Indiana), 28(1), spring 1994.

*   *   *

In an epigraph to his novel *Reflex and Bone Structure,* Clarence Major announces that the book "is an extension of, not a duplication of reality. The characters and events are happening for the first time." The statement describes equally well the poetry, in which Major's deliberate opacity discourages our attempt to track his language as references to an empirical world. Even when reading verse, we expect words readily to demonstrate a correspondence to outside things or events, for our linguistic competency develops through the code of usage. Like other postmodern writers, however, Major uses language as a newly constructed code.

Major's poems are cast subjectively as dramas of feelings, sometimes in conflict, at other times with their complexities resolved by time. Always, however, the dynamic comes from a logic of emotional knowledge that, more often than not, conceals the subject—what the poem is about. Such verse holds that the structures of feeling have been shaped uniquely, and it follows that the patterns of expression must be intrinsic to poetic execution. In "Overbreak" he writes,

> there is a remarkable verb of
> things
> here: a remarkable sensation of
> infected spirits feeling
> & pushing bravely like nurtured waves in
> the machines of
> the sensation, the tremor of water as it
> surrounds the heart beat

The absence of conventional punctuation makes "Overbreak" an uninterrupted utterance that is intensely felt. Yet the original stimulus has been absorbed into abstractions, the currency of mental constructions that nevertheless stop short of concept.

Major's code regularly employs eccentric punctuation and unusual typographical arrangement so that the poems must be seen as well as heard. Clotted lines such as "O supreme sledgehammer of reposing verbal stacks of / nouns verbs adjectives charming" insist upon the primary sensation of words as sounds. These and other eccentricities then reinforce the premise implied by such fused syntax, as in this passage from "The Design":

> I am tired of the
> apartment is dull a place but it comes
> to this each
> item you left, a few belongings . . .

If conventional syntax asserts the dominance of rational order, then this disruption argues the existence of an extension of reality, its integrity requiring designation of a new, arbitrary system of signs.

Because it stakes all on the tone conveyed by a linguistic code we can never entirely decipher, Major's verse risks obscurity. Of course,

the risk is well taken. The discontinuities between his verse and the patterns of conventional usage become an experiment in poetics as well as poems.

—John M. Reilly

MALOUF, David

Nationality: Australian. **Born:** Brisbane, Queensland, 20 March 1934. **Education:** Brisbane Grammar School, 1947–50; University of Queensland, Brisbane, 1951–54, B.A. (honors) in English 1954. **Career:** Lecturer, University of Sydney, 1968–77. **Awards:** Australian Literature Society Gold Medal, 1974, 1983; Grace Leven prize, 1975; James Cook award, 1975; Australia Council fellowship, 1978; New South Wales Premier's Prize, for fiction, 1979; Melbourne *Age* Book of the Year award, 1982; Miles Franklin prize, 1991; Prix Femina Etranger (France), 1991, for *The Great World;* Adelaide Festival prize, 1991; *Los Angeles Times* Fiction award, 1994, for *Remembering Babylon*; IMPAC International Dublin literary award, 1996. **Agent:** Rogers Coleridge and White, 20 Powis Mews, London W11 1JN, England. **Address:** 242 Kingsford Smith Drive, Hamilton, Brisbane, Queensland 4007, Australia.

PUBLICATIONS

Poetry

Four Poets, with others. Melbourne, Cheshire, 1962.
Bicycle and Other Poems. St. Lucia, University of Queensland Press, 1970; as *The Year of the Foxes and Other Poems,* New York, Braziller, 1979.
Neighbours in a Thicket. St. Lucia, University of Queensland Press, 1974.
Poems 1975–76. Sydney, Prism, 1976.
Selected Poems. Sydney, Angus and Robertson, 1980.
Wild Lemons. Sydney, Angus and Robertson, 1980.
First Things Last. St. Lucia, University of Queensland Press, 1980; London, Chatto and Windus, 1981.
Selected Poems. Sydney, Angus and Robertson, 1991.
Poems, 1959–89. St. Lucia, University of Queensland Press, 1992; as *Selected Poems, 1959–89.* London, Chatto and Windus, 1994.

Plays

Voss (opera libretto), music by Richard Meale, adaptation of the novel by Patrick White (produced Sydney, 1986).
Blood Relations. Sydney, Currency Press, 1988.
Baa Baa Black Sheep, A Jungle Tale (opera libretto). London, Chatto and Windus, 1993.

Novels

Johnno. St. Lucia, University of Queensland Press, 1975; New York, Braziller, 1978.
An Imaginary Life. New York, Braziller, and London, Chatto and Windus, 1978.

Child's Play, with Eustace and the Prowler. London, Chatto and
Windus, 1982; as *Child's Play, The Bread of Time to Come: Two
Novellas,* New York, Braziller, 1982.
Fly Away Peter. London, Chatto and Windus, 1982.
Harland's Half Acre. London, Chatto and Windus, and New York,
Knopf, 1984.
The Great World. London, Chatto and Windus, and New York,
Pantheon, 1990.
Remembering Babylon. London, Chatto and Windus, and New York,
Pantheon, 1993.
Conversations at Curlow Creek. London, Chatto and Windus, and
New York, Pantheon, 1996.

Short Stories

Antipodes. London, Chatto and Windus, 1985.

Other

New Currents in Australian Writing, with Katharine Brisbane and
R.F. Brissenden. Sydney and London, Angus and Robertson,
1978.
12 Edmondstone Street (essays). London, Chatto and Windus, 1985.

Editor, with others, *We Took Their Orders and Are Dead: An Anti-
War Anthology.* Sydney, Ure Smith, 1971.
Editor, *Gesture of a Hand* (anthology of Australian poetry). Artarmon,
New South Wales, Holt Rinehart, 1975.

*

Manuscript Collections: University of Queensland, St. Lucia; Australian National University Library, Canberra.

Critical Studies: Interviews in *Commonwealth 4* (Rodez, France),
1979–80, *Meanjin 39* (Melbourne), and *Australian Literary Studies*
(Hobart, Tasmania), October 1982; "David Malouf As Humane
Allegorist" by James Tulip, in *Southerly* (Sydney), 1981; "David
Malouf and the Language of Exile" by Peter Bishop, in *Australian
Literary Studies* (Hobart, Tasmania), October 1982; *Sheer Edge,
Aspects of Identity in David Malouf* by Karin Hansson, Lund,
Sweden, Lund University Press, 1991; *Provisional Maps, Critical
Essays on David Malouf,* edited by Amanda Nettelbeck, Center for
Studies in Australian Literature, 1994; "On Frontiers: The 'National-
ism' of David Malouf's Poetry and Its Implications for a Definition of
'Commonwealth Literature'" by Barnard Turner, in *Nationalism vs.
Internationalism: (Inter)National Dimensions of Literatures in Eng-
lish,* Tubingen, Germany, Stauffenburg, 1996; by Barbara Williams,
in *In Other Words: Interviews with Australian Poets,* Amsterdam,
Netherlands, Rodopi, 1998.

David Malouf comments:

I like to think of poetry as work done at a place of concordance:
where the past and future meet in visible present, where change is
celebrated but continuity established, where the actual is open to the
fabulous, where the individual stands as the point of connection
between a single life and the totality of things. Language also belongs
to two worlds: the world of communication and of our mysterious
naming to ourselves of what surrounds us. Standing as it does at this
crossing point between adjacent, and perhaps rival, zones, it seems
like an ideal vehicle for the "passages" I have in mind. Poems are
acts of reconciliation.

*   *   *

Although relatively unprolific as a poet, David Malouf has
attained a high degree of achievement in the poetry he has published.
He first appeared as one of a Brisbane-based group of new poets in
Four Poets, and in that selection he laid out many of his ongoing
preoccupations: childhood incidents and resonances, expressed with
considerable delight in small, concrete details; a cosmopolitan familiarity with European history and culture as something intrinsic to his
vision; and a sharp, ironic view of contemporary man's social and
political milieu, most deftly expressed in "Epitaph for a Monster of
Our Times," about Adolf Eichmann:

> an organization man
> *par excellence,* whom we
> need only convict at last
> of gross efficiency.

Bicycle and Other Poems followed after a long period of apparent
silence, and it immediately placed Malouf in the forefront of his
generation. The work confirmed his mature, ironic, yet sympathetic
view of life and events, but it added a capacity to blend elements of
quiet fantasy with more subterranean urgencies of wonder, loss, and
the precariousness of living. The Brisbane poems in this volume have
the extraordinary richness of observation and sensuous focus that
characterize his first novel, *Johnno,* but the book is perhaps most
notable for its wide-ranging resources of reference, something pursued even further in his next collection, *Neighbours in a Thicket.*

Although it contains some striking poems of childhood remembrance, with a perspective that is now richer and darker, in *Neighbours in
a Thicket* Malouf explores a strong vein of cultural and personal
association, a sort of cross-hatching of reflective—and reflexive—
emblems of recall. These are essentially meditative poems, poems of
exploration rather than arrival, and their starting point is always a fine
awareness of the past as being something as immediate and contemporaneous as the present. This capacity to respond to time laterally
rather than chronologically makes Malouf unique among Australian
poets in that it enables him to transcend issues of cultural identity and
assertion, issues that have been of dominant concern in so much
Australian writing. Malouf's sense of region is intense and sharply
visual. He is thus the most European, yet one of the most regional, of
contemporary Australian poets.

Poems 1975–76 can be seen as a lyrical interlude in Malouf's
output. It is a short book that is dominated by two love sequences of
unusual resonance, mainly through their recognition that it is by way
of the word that all avenues of perception may be opened up.
Malouf's exploration of language is here heightened by an overtly
celebratory intent. In the poems published since this book, elements
of pure invention have increasingly concerned the poet, and he often
achieves a sense of almost breathtaking virtuosity. Malouf's second
novel, *An Imaginary Life,* which is virtually a prose poem of great
lyric power, has achieved international acclaim since it was first
published in New York. His first American collection, *The Year of the
Foxes,* though it is essentially a reprint of *Bicycle and Other Poems,* is
a further sign of international recognition of this most elegant and
cosmopolitan of Australian poets.

Even if in some ways it may be seen as a volume of consolidation, *First Things Last* contains a number of important poems. A gentle surrealism pervades some of the poems, though the most memorable individual works are a superb elegy for Igor Stravinsky, which is also a meditation upon art, and those poems based upon Malouf's Tuscany, a world of sharp perceptions, and an increasingly mature understanding of the human condition. Yet Malouf's youthful capacity for joy and celebration has not been lost.

Malouf's international career as a novelist has revived interest in his poetry. Publication in 1992 of the reasonably comprehensive *Poems 1959–89* by the University of Queensland Press was preceded in the previous year by *Selected Poems,* from Angus and Robertson, in an edition clearly aimed at the educational market. The 1992 selection includes thirty-three previously unpublished poems written in the 1980s. They are drawn mainly from Malouf's semipermanent residence in Tuscany and enhance the sense of mature meditative power exemplified earlier in *First Things Last.*

—Thomas W. Shapcott

MANHIRE, Bill

Nationality: New Zealander. **Born:** William Manhire, Invercargill, 27 December 1946. **Education:** Otago Boys High School; University of Otago, Dunedin, B.A. 1967, M.A. (honors) 1968, M.Litt. 1970; University College, London, 1970–73, M.Phil. 1973. **Family:** Married Marion McLeod in 1970; one daughter and one son. **Career:** Lecturer, 1973–78, senior lecturer in English, 1978–87, reader, 1987–98, since 1998 professor of English and creative writing, and since 2000 director of the Centre for Creative Writing, Victoria University, Wellington. Editor, Amphedesma Press, Dunedin, 1971–75; General Editor, New Zealand Stories series, Victoria University Press. **Awards:** New Zealand Book award, 1977, 1985, 1992; Nuffield fellowship, 1980; New Zealand Arts Council scholarship, 1989, and award for achievement, 1992; Buckland award, 1990; Montana book award, 1994, 1996; Fulbright Senior Scholar, 1999; inaugural New Zealand poet laureate, 1997–99. **Address:** Centre for Creative Writing, Victoria University of Wellington. P.O. Box 600, Wellington 1, New Zealand.

PUBLICATIONS

Poetry

Malady. Dunedin, Amphedesma Press, 1970.
The Elaboration. Wellington, Square and Circle, 1972.
Song Cycle. Wellington, Sound-Movement Theatre, 1975.
How to Take Off Your Clothes at the Picnic. Wellington, Waite-ata Press, 1977.
Dawn/Water. Eastbourne, New Zealand, Hawk Press, 1980.
Good Looks. Auckland, Auckland University Press-Oxford University Press, 1982.
Locating the Beloved and Other Stories. Wellington, Single Title Press, 1983.
Zoetropes: Poems 1972–82. Sydney and Wellington, Allen and Unwin-Port Nicholson Press, 1984; Manchester, Carcanet, 1985.
The Old Man's Example. Wellington, Wrist and Anchor Press, 1990.
Milky Way Bar. Manchester, Carcanet, 1991.

Hoosh. Wellington, Anxious Husky Press, 1995.
My Sunshine. Wellington, Victoria University Press, 1996.
Sheet Music: Poems 1967–1982. Wellington, Victoria University Press, 1996.
What to Call Your Child. Auckland, Godwit/Random, 1999.

Other

Maurice Gee. Auckland and Oxford, Oxford University Press, 1986.
The Brain of Katherine Mansfield. Auckland, Auckland University Press, 1988.
The New Land: A Picture Book. Auckland, Heinemann Reed, 1990.
South Pacific. Manchester, Carcanet, 1994.
Songs of My Life. Auckland, Godwit, 1996.
Doubtful Sounds: Essays and Interviews. Wellington, Victoria University Press, 2000.

Editor, *New Zealand Universities Arts Festival Yearbook 1969.* Dunedin, Arts Festival Committee, 1969.
Editor, *N.Z. Listener Short Stories 1–2.* Wellington, Methuen, 2 vols., 1977–78.
Editor, with Marion McLeod, *Some Other Country: New Zealand's Best Short Stories.* Wellington, Unwin, 1984.
Editor, *Six by Six: Short Stories by New Zealand's Best Writers.* Wellington, Victoria University Press, 1989.
Editor, *Soho Square.* London, Bloomsbury, 1991.
Editor, *100 New Zealand Poems.* Auckland, Godwit, 1993.
Editor, *Mutes & Earthquakes: Bill Manhire's Writing Course at Victoria.* Wellington, Victoria University Press, 1997.

*

Critical Studies: "Pavlova and Wrists: The Poetry of Bill Manhire" by Peter Crisp, in *Islands 24* (Auckland), November 1978; "The Poetry of Bill Manhire" by Hugh Lauder, in *Landfall* (Christchurch), September 1983; "Joker: Playing Poetry in the Eighties: Manhire, Curnow, Stead, Horrocks" by Michele Leggott, in *World Literature Written in English* (Singapore), 23(1), winter 1984; "Writing through the Margins: Sharon Thesen's and Bill Manhire's Apparently Lyrical Poetry" by Douglas Barbour, in *Australian and New Zealand Studies in Canada* (Prince George, British Columbia, Canada), 4, fall 1990; "The Old Man's Example: Manhire in the Seventies" by John Newton, in *Opening the Book,* edited by Mark Williams and Michele Leggott, Auckland, Auckland University Press, 1995; "Beyond the Brain of Katherine Mansfield: The Radical Potentials and Recuperations of Second-Person Narrative" by Dennis Schofield, in *Style* (DeKalb, Illinois), 31(1), spring 1997; by Antonella Sarti, in *Spiritcarvers: Interviews with Eighteen Writers from New Zealand,* Amsterdam, Netherlands, Rodopi, 1998.

*   *   *

From his early prominence as a student poet in *The Elaboration* (1972), Bill Manhire has been an ironic lyricist wryly if self-consciously poised between playfulness and nostalgia. He elaborates the formula with considerable adroitness. Characteristically, the effect is attained by setting up an expectation of conventional lyric romanticism and then disappointing it. Thus, in "Summer" the romantic connotations of the subject are subverted by a casual conversational tone—"See? / And occasionally, one supposes, /

some marriage may be celebrated''—and by an intrusive self-referentiality—''. . . the poet sits, somewhat alone, / saying, 'Hell, another masterpiece.'''

Along with conventional poetic language, wistfulness, loss, and the dying fall recur, identified by Ken Arvidson as ''a rather sad diminuendo.'' Manhire's pose is often that of a reluctant romantic writing of stars, moon, clouds, light, love, children, and solitude but hoping that no one will notice. The connotations are knowingly interspersed with whimsy, inconsequentiality, puns, jokes on grammar, and scraps of pop culture and New Zealand vernacular. The mix has become so familiar as to set something of a local fashion, as has the mannered tone of shy tentativeness, an apologetic hesitancy about both language and emotion. As Macdonald P. Jackson has noted in his overview of Manhire in the *Oxford Companion to New Zealand Literature* (1998), these ''hesitancies are subsumed within an elegant music, marked by artfully sliding cadences.''

Although this approach can become mannered and coy, in Manhire's middle, and best, period it produced poignant insights and a poetry that was both playful and felt. ''Zoetropes,'' for instance, purports to be a jest about the frustration often felt by exiled New Zealanders on glimpsing the letter *z* in a foreign newspaper, but it develops into a wistful statement of nostalgia and evocation of New Zealand's remote and fragile place in the world:

> The land itself is only
> smoke at anchor, drifting above
> Antarctica's white flower,
>
> tied by a thin red line
> (5000 miles) to Valparaiso.

There is a fineness of small effect in this that commentators frequently identify as Manhire's greatest strength. The ''fizz of flowers in a vase'' (''A Scottish Bride''), ''the modest glow / of a radio at night'' (''The Voyeur''), or ''watching the small explosions / under your wrists'' (''The Song'') are often cited as evidence.

If Manhire's later work has become more consciously portentous, that may be through the pressures of the poet's public role and the prescription that ''playfulness'' must be mixed with ''deep seriousness.'' At his best he attends with fine care to language, placing weight in unexpected places, seeking to give value to the trivial or banal. He fills his poems with clichés and catchphrases, giving them resonance by repetition or incantation and sometimes turning them over and over so that they catch new light: ''But what a day! The favourite lost / by a neck''; ''Loosen up, chum''; ''Weary, stale, flat, unprofitable / World . . .'' Sometimes whole poems— ''The Pickpocket,'' ''The Poetry Reading,'' ''Vanessa's Song''—are only the slightest step from total parody or pastiche. When the formula works, Manhire can surprise and shift gears and tone, as in ''The Swallow'':

> John Keats,
> what is he counting on,
> his fingers? No
>
> John Keats is counting on
> the morning—the clouds rise
> skyward one by one
> from all his fingers

The procedure, of course, involves risk. Evasions and puzzles can frustrate, for the reader must submit to the implication that the reward is greater than the game. The surrealistic shifts in reference and idiom are often puzzling, but perhaps only that: ''Music is this task you undertake. / It is not painful, more like eating crayons / while you lie in bed with the children.''

Manhire draws his ''lyrical foliage'' from many sources and models, often American, as the mock gangster story ''On Originality'' acknowledges. He commonly gives a literary-intellectual spin to an item of popular culture or vernacular idiom, a habit that some find problematic. Interests in horse racing and slang or grammatical errors (''Declining the Naked Horse'') are mocked in a way uncomfortable to readers less sensitive to what used to be called ''vulgarity.'' ''Visiting Mr Shackleton,'' for instance, compiles a poem from a collage of phrases written by enthusiastic Antarctic tourists in a visitors' book:

> Cool! Wow! Beautiful! Awesome!
> Like going back in time.
> Amazing! Historic! Finally
> I am truly blessed.

Implying as this does the poet's intellectual and verbal superiority, if only in arranging the phrases into poetic form, it seems supercilious as well as revealing of an ear less well attuned to American than to New Zealand idiom. The same element of patronizing mockery detracts from the treatment of such popular celebrities as Billy Graham (''An Amazing Week in New Zealand'') or the explorers of the Antarctic that have become a well-publicized interest (''The Adventures of Hillary,'' among others).

Manhire's later work has often become more expansive, with a narrative or dramatic dynamic and a concern for topical events that may reflect his experiments since the late 1980s with short fiction. His most successful and characteristic form is still the enigmatic miniaturist lyric, and there are good examples in his 1999 volume *What to Call Your Child.* After an almost untainted early career, critical opinion in New Zealand has moved against him, perhaps because of his public prominence as New Zealand's first poet laureate, although the title has no official status and was conferred by an enterprising commercial sponsor. Nicholas Reid criticized the formula of approaching ''the big themes apologetically, with puns and wordplay and colloquial jokes and pop-culture allusions,'' and Luke Strongman found the later work ''superficial'' and expressive mainly of ''the literary machine that he's patiently helped construct.'' Arvidson similarly wrote of ''a Manhire species of poetry to which he is of course still the main generic contributor,'' comparing the ''somewhat diaristic'' Antarctic poems unfavorably with those of a younger poet, Chris Orsman.

—Roger Robinson

MANN, Chris(topher Michael Zithulele)

Nationality: South African. **Born:** Port Elizabeth, 6 April 1948. **Education:** University of the Witwatersrand, Johannesburg, B.A. 1970; Oxford University (Rhodes scholar; Newdigate prize, 1973) B.A. (honors) 1973; University of London, M.A. 1975. **Family:** Married Julia G. St. John Skeen in 1980; one daughter and one son.

Career: Teacher, Baring High School, Nhlangano, Swaziland, 1975–76; lecturer, Rhodes University, Grahamstown, 1977–79; director, Valley Trust medical and agricultural project, near Durban, 1980–92; director, Grahamstown Foundation, 1993–98. Since 1998 research associate, Institute for Study of English in Africa. Founder and member, *Zabalaza* band, 1981–86. **Awards:** Olive Schreiner prize, 1983. **Agent:** David Philip Publishers Pty. Ltd., Box 23408, Claremont, Cape Province 7735, South Africa. **Address:** Institute for Study of English in Africa, Rhodes University, Grahamstown 6140, South Africa.

PUBLICATIONS

Poetry

First Poems. Johannesburg, Bateleur Press, 1977.
New Shades. Cape Town, David Philip, 1982.
Kites and Other Poems. Cape Town, David Philip, 1990.
Mann Alive!: Poems. Cape Town, David Philip, 1992.
South Africans: A Set of Portrait-Poems. Pietermaritzburg, University of Natal Press, 1996.

Plays

The Sand Labyrinth (produced Grahamstown, 1980).
The Magic Toaster, with Doris Hilliard. Halstead, Theatre Scripts, 1990.

Other

Chris Mann and Grammar. N.p., Lingua Press Publishers, 1990.

Editor, with Guy Butler, *A New Book of South African Verse in English.* Cape Town, Oxford University Press, 1979; Oxford, Oxford University Press, 1980.

*   *   *

Chris Mann's *First Poems* exhibited many of the faults common to a debut volume: mawkish naïveté ("Kneeling in moonlight, / with all your kissable crinkles," from a poem titled "Darkness, Ivory, and Clay"); uncertainty of touch and tone, particularly evident in tacked-on and contrived conclusions to poems that deserved better, as in "Summer Evening at the Kowie," with its bizarrely irrelevant close ("as the foam begins to gleam, / paddle between the devil / and the deep, receptive sea"); and self-conscious poeticisms and unconscious echoes ("the well-doved day"; "halfway to heaven on a reapripe day"; "Two women on a beach at evening, / who murmur of this and that"). Yet despite its uneven quality, there is much of interest in Mann's first collection, not least its exuberant variety of styles and modes, ranging from ballad stanzas adapted to a South African voice and setting ("Bennie and Anna," based on Hood's "Ben Battle") to social satire, in which the targets are disappointingly predictable, and from the alliterative "View from the Edge," an exercise in the style of Swinburne, to the formal lyricism of "Words of the Overseas Missionary." There are the promising "Poems of

Place," and Mann is clearly interested in the oral potential of verse, with one section comprising "Poems to Be Said Aloud." Few of the "Love Poems" are altogether successful, a notable exception being the brief but finely realized "A Few Initial Words":

> What is there
> to say
> when the girl
> who walks ahead of you
> turns,
> and knee-deep
> in a sea of green barley
> opens out her arms?

New Shades, Mann's second volume, is a much more assured and rounded achievement. Themes and modes attempted in the preceding volume recur but are more sparingly indulged and more subtly developed, as in the ballad rhythms of "To Lucky with His Guitar":

> So here's Lucky, Coolhand Lucky the Tall;
> Sunday afternoon, easing into town;
> hasn't a word (drifting over New Street);
> nothing to tell us (tapping the pavement);
> but Coolhand riffs; zig-zag bass; stringshine chords.

Evocations of persons and places in this volume are more thoughtful in tone, more substantial in content. Examples include "Nightscapes" and "The Pupil and Teacher's Reunion," in which the self-conscious awkwardness experienced on such occasions is sympathetically explored rather than cleverly hit off:

> We grope onwards (retired Matrons, famous
> tries and expulsions, nicknames and googlies)
> trudging upstream like anxious sangomas
> for bonds, for kinships which eddy and shift
> like shapes in the water but will not show.

The use of "sangomas" (from the Zulu word for a diviner) in the stanza points to Mann's increasing use of words and phrases from indigenous languages, beside the more pointed South Africanisms of his colloquial poems.

New Shades is also characterized by a larger proportion of poems for performance, which may be more effective in presentation or with musical accompaniment than they appear to be in print. Although Mann on occasion lapses into pseudoprofundities (as in "Bush and Sky") and mere imitation (the Laurentian note is unmistakable in "Napes"), his second volume is a distinct advance on the first.

—Ernest Pereira

MAPANJE, Jack

Nationality: Malawian. **Born:** Kadango Village, Mangochi District, c. March 25, 1944. **Education:** Zomba Catholic Secondary School; University of Malawi, Zomba, B.A., Dip.Ed.; University of London,

M.Phil.; University College, London. **Family:** Married Mercy Mapanje; two daughters, one son. **Career:** Since 1975 lecturer in English, then head of department of English, Chancellor College, University of Malawi. In political detention, Mikuyu Prison, near Zomba, 1987–91; research fellow, Exeter College, Oxford, 1992–93; Greater North International Writer in Residence, 1993; visiting professor, University of Leeds, 1993–94. Returned to Malawi July 1995. Chair, Linguistics Association, Southern African Development Coordination Conference. **Awards:** Poetry International award (The Netherlands), 1988. **Address:** c/o William Heinemann Ltd., Michelin House, 81 Fulham Road, London SW3 6RB, England.

PUBLICATIONS

Poetry

Of Chameleons and Gods. London, Heinemann, 1981.
The Chattering Wagtails of Mikuyu Prison. Jordan Hill, Oxford, and Portsmouth, New Hampshire, Heinemann, 1993.
Skipping without Ropes. Newcastle upon Tyne, Bloodaxe, and Chester Springs, Pennsylvania, Dufour, 1998.

Recording: *Jack Mapanje of Malawi,* Voice of America, 1979(?).

Other

Editor, with Landeg White, *Oral Poetry from Africa: An Anthology.* London, Longman, 1983.
Editor, with Angus Calder and Cosmo Pieterse, *Summer Fires: New Poetry of Africa.* London, Heinemann, 1983.
Editor, with James Gibbs, *The African Writers' Handbook.* Oxford, African Books Collective, 1999.

*

Critical Studies: "Jack Mapanje, Malawian Poet: Some Personal Reactions" by Angus Calder, in *ACLAS Bulletin,* 5(3), December 1980; "'Whiskers Alberto' and 'The Township Lambs': Towards an Interpretation of Jack Mapanje's 'We Wondered about the Mellow Peaches,'" in *The Journal of Commonwealth Literature* (Leeds), 22(1), 1987, and "'Singing in the Dark Rain': Malawian Poets and Censorship," in *Index on Censorship* (London), 17(2), February 1988, both by James Gibbs; "Of Chameleons and Paramount Chiefs: The Case of the Malawian Poet Jack Mapanje" by Leroy Vail and Landeg White, in *Review of African Political Economy,* 48, 1990; by the author, in *The Word behind Bard and the Paradox of Exile,* edited by Kofi Anyidoho, Evanston, Illinois, Northwestern University Press, 1997; "Being Aplace" by Angela Smith, in *Yearbook of English Studies,* 27, 1997.

*   *   *

When the poet Jack Mapanje was arrested on 25 September 1987, a protest movement that focused the energies of friends, colleagues, and human rights activists was quickly set in motion. The pressure was substantial and insistent, testimony to the way Mapanje had impressed other people and to the way public opinion could be mobilized in support of an imprisoned poet.

In addition to being a poet, Mapanje has long been an administrator and a scholar, linguist, literary critic, university lecturer, student of folklore, husband, father, and Catholic. More recently he has become an exile. He is best known, however, as a prison poet, and although prison doors actually closed behind him for only a limited period, there are dimensions of his life that indicate that he became a prisoner in 1963 and that he remains one to this day.

Hastings Kamuzu Banda made the whole of Malawi into a prison by the draconian laws his parliament passed from about 1963 onward. In the introduction to his first volume of poems, *Of Chameleons and Gods* (1981), Mapanje described the struggle he had long been involved in. He referred to verses spanning "some ten turbulent years," in which he had attempted "to find a voice or voices as a way of preserving some sanity." For part of those ten years he was a student at the University of Malawi, where he wrote poems reflecting his engagement with a tradition of poetry that was being distorted by Banda's supporters. He also showed an awareness of developments throughout the continent, and he was determined to provide a literary personality for the new nation. In this he was supported by those who formed the Malawi Writers' Group.

After graduation Mapanje went to London to begin a postgraduate degree with a thesis titled "The Use of Traditional Literary Forms in Modern Malawian Writing in English." At the same time he responded in verse to experiences in England and to news reaching him from Malawi. He developed a conversational, critical, coded, apparently innocuous style that drew strength from the conventions of riddling and from carefully directed questioning.

Some years later the poems written in London were joined with those written during the Soche years in *Of Chameleons and Gods,* where they were followed by a section entitled "Re-Entering Chingwe's Hole." In this latter section Mapanje charts his experiences on returning to Malawi to take up a lectureship at the University of Malawi, an institution scarred by detentions and deportations. Having convinced the university authorities that he was "sound," Mapanje returned to London and, while doing research for a doctorate in linguistics, began to publish work prompted by Banda's tyrannical rule. Although the poems employed relatively subtle codes and conventions, they were disaffected, critical, and subversive.

Mapanje submitted some forty-seven poems to Heinemann, and in 1981 *Of Chameleons of Gods* was published in London. Exploiting a loophole in the regulations, it also, to the surprise of many, went on sale in Malawi. Mapanje himself returned home in April 1983 with, as he put it, "a PhD, three books, a baby-boy." He soon discovered that he had returned at a particularly tense time. Out of concern for what was happening around him and anxious to retain links with the international community, Mapanje continued to seek outlets for his work. He may have been encouraged by indications that censorship had been relaxed somewhat and by evidence of local and international esteem. He was still vulnerable, however, as became clear in June 1985 when *Of Chameleons and Gods* was banned.

Mapanje's response was to try to find out why the Censorship Board had taken action. He bravely wrote up his findings for a conference of writers in April 1986. Versions of the account may have been among the documents taken from his home and office when, in September 1987, he was "picked" from the Zomba Gymkhana Club by security officers. Just why the security forces moved in on Mapanje remains open to speculation. What is not in doubt is the fact that he was held for more than three and a half years in Mikuyu Prison, a time of extreme deprivation spent in appalling conditions. Paradoxically, however, the period was marked by considerable intellectual freedom.

The Chattering Wagtails of Mikuyu Prison, published in 1993, includes reflections on experiences from 1983 onward, along with oblique questionings of the glaring discrepancies in attitude encountered through the early 1980s. The prison poems give the feeling that, because the poet is suffering the extreme sanction of the state, he can write with a new openness. Mapanje has since begun to publish a prose account that provides further glimpses of his experiences in prison, and he has also looked at prison literature in a broad academic context.

Although Chattering Wagtails concludes with a section entitled "The Release and Other Curious Sights," Mapanje returned to prison experiences for the material in the first section of his third volume of poetry, Skipping without Ropes. In the helpful explanatory notes to the collection, he observes, "Skipping without rope was the most harmless form of exercise tolerated." Although the collection contains many poems written since the poet left Mikuyu Prison, there is a sense in which he remains bound by his experiences of Malawi itself as a prison. When he emerged from Mikuyu, Mapanje was anxious to reengage with the world, but images of dependence and detention pursued him. The reluctance of the University of Malawi to take him back led him to move with his family to York to begin a life in exile, which is another kind of detention. The postprison and the exile poems indicate a degree of accommodation to altered circumstances, including the changes that have taken place in Malawi, but the shadow of the detention camp is long.

The poem that closes the collection offers an image of Africa with "weeping scars" caused by silence on important issues. It ends with a statement of commitment to continuing the "struggle." The writing inevitably prompts the recognition that for Mapanje poets, who are the custodians of yesterday, remain trapped in a dialogue with their homelands, with their todays and their tomorrows.

—James Gibbs

MARKHAM, E(dward) A(rchibald)

Pseudonyms: Paul St. Vincent; Sally Goodman. **Nationality:** British. **Born:** Montserrat, West Indies, 1 October 1939. Immigrated to England in 1956. **Education:** Montserrat Secondary, until 1956; Kilburn Polytechnic, London, 1960–62; University of Wales, Lampeter, 1962–65, B.A. in philosophy and English; University of East Anglia, Norwich, 1966–67; University of London, 1967. **Career:** Lecturer, Kilburn Polytechnic, London, 1968–70, and Abraham Moss Centre, Manchester, 1976–78; director, Caribbean Theatre Workshop, Eastern Caribbean, 1970–71; creative writing fellow, Hull College of Higher Education, Yorkshire, 1979–80; media coordinator, Enga Provincial Government, Wabag, Papua New Guinea, 1983–85; editor, Artrage magazine, London, 1985–87; writer-in-residence, University of Ulster, Coleraine, 1988–91. Since 1980 assistant editor, Ambit magazine, London; editor, Enga Nius magazine, Papua New Guinea, 1983–85; editor, Writing Ulster. **Member:** Member of the general council, Poetry Society, 1976–77; member, GLA New Writing and Distribution Committee, 1986–87; director, Minorities Arts Advisory Service, London, 1987–90; member of the managing committee, Poetry Book Society, London, 1987–90. **Awards:** C. Day Lewis fellowship, 1980–81. **Address:** c/o Bloodaxe Books Ltd., P.O. Box 1SN, Newcastle upon Tyne NE99 1SN, England.

PUBLICATIONS

Poetry

Cross-Fire. Walton-on-Thames, Surrey, Outposts, 1972.
Mad and Other Poems. Solihull, Warwickshire, Phaeton Press, 1973.
Lambchops (as Paul St. Vincent). Leicester, Omens, 1976.
Philpot in the City (as Paul St. Vincent). Yorkshire, Curlew, 1976.
Lambchops in Disguise (as Paul St. Vincent). London, Share, 1976.
Master Class. Yorkshire, Curlew, 1977.
The Lamp. Knotting, Bedfordshire, Sceptre Press, 1978.
Love Poems. Cambridge, Lobby Press, 1978.
Games and Penalties. Hatch End, Poet and Printer, 1980.
Love, Politics, and Food. Cambridge, Massachusetts, Von Hallett, 1982.
Family Matters. Stafford, Warwickshire, Sow's Ear, 1984.
Human Rites: Selected Poems 1970–1982. London, Anvil Press Poetry, 1984.
Lambchops in Papua New Guinea. Port Moresby, Papua New Guinea, IPNGS, 1985; Stafford, Warwickshire, Sow's Ear, 1986.
Living in Disguise. London, Anvil Press Poetry, 1986.
Towards the End of a Century. London, Anvil Press Poetry, 1989.
Maurice V.'s Dido. London, Hearing Eye, 1991.
Letter from Ulster & The Hugo Poems. Todmorden, Lancashire, Littlewood Arc, 1993.
Misapprehensions. London, Anvil Press Poetry, 1995.

Plays

The Masterpiece (produced Lampeter, 1964).
The Private Life of the Public Man (produced St. Vincent, West Indies, 1970).
Dropping Out Is Violence (produced Montserrat, West Indies, 1971).

Novel

Making Time. Leeds, Peepal Tree, 1999.

Short Stories

Something Unusual. London, Ambit, 1986.
Ten Stories. N.p., Sheffield Hallam University, School of Cultural Studies, 1994.

Other

A Papua New Guinea Sojourn: More Pleasures of Exile. Manchester, Carcanet, 1998.

Editor, with Arnold Kingston, Merely a Matter of Colour. London, Q, 1973.

Editor, *Hinterland: Caribbean Poetry from the West Indies and Britain.* Newcastle upon Tyne, Bloodaxe, 1989; Chester Springs, Pennsylvania, Dufour, 1990.

Editor, with Howard Fergus, *Hugo Versus Montserrat.* London, Linda Lee, 1989.

Editor, *The Penguin Book of Caribbean Short Stories.* London and New York, Penguin, 1996.

*

Critical Studies: ''Bold Survivor'' by Carol Rumens, in *Times Literary Supplement* (London), 24 October 1986; ''Caribbean Lines'' by Robert Welch, in *Yorkshire Post* (Leeds), 17 May 1990; ''White Words on a Black Ground'' by Giles Foden, in *Times Literary Supplement* (London), 2 March 1990; ''E. Archie Markham: A Poet of Many Voices'' by Bruno Gallo, in *Caribana* (Milan, Italy), 5, 1996; *A Fertschrift for EA Markham* edited by Freda Vollaus and Tracey O'Rourke, Leeds and Sheffield, Linda Lee Books, 1999.

*   *   *

''We are multi-national; cosmopolitan,'' E.A. Markham says in the introduction to a volume of Caribbean poetry he edited. His own poetry roams among Montserrat, Britain, Papua New Guinea, and Albania, takes on different identities—Sally Goodman, Paul St. Vincent—and speaks in the voice of a housewife or a character called Lambchops, but it nevertheless maintains an identifiable style. It is interesting that it was his Pessoa-like adoption of two alter egos that seems to have helped give force and confidence to a voice that in his first publications hardly stood out from the crowd.

Among Markham's early pamphlet collections, *Mad* contains just two poems that might be worthy of a place in a collected edition. ''The Early Years of a Tyrant'' is a telling thumbnail sketch of a rebel manqué who ''after an unfinished / novel, a dab at teaching, and / a mini-tour of foreign / parts (returning to mourn / a much-loved dog) joined the local / library, bored with politics.'' Here the quiet but lethal derision and the smooth enjambment of the lines give promise of Markham's mature voice. ''Anonymous'' establishes the mood of much of the poet's intimate work, a poetry of departure, reunion, and communication by letter that is shot through with moving observations of a transience that so many contemporary poets seem to eliminate from their work (and perhaps their lives). The language here is less specific than in later poems, but it avoids the adolescent use of metaphor that weakens the worst of Markham's early verse, as in ''I am the recurring pause / that you envy.''

The high point of Markham's small press publications came with *Love, Politics, and Food,* important for the reprinting of a BBC radio talk in which he explained the conception and birth of the Lambchops character. As a reviewer of a later volume has remarked, Markham has ''forged for himself a fresh, original voice out of Standard English'' without recourse to dialect. The reference to Standard English is contentious, but Markham's eschewal of broad dialect has been made possible by his adoption of fictional personae, beginning in the 1970s with the Sally Goodman housewife poems and continuing in the 1980s with Lambchops. His own name and identity seem to have become ''an affliction contracted under some insidious Victorian dispensation.'' It is characteristic of the writer's good humor and lack of pretension that he can make such a statement

without raising hackles. His work can be aggressive, and it is always committed but never polemical. The Lambchops persona is intended as an everyman figure:

> Lambchops are classless like the old mini was said to be:
> both the Swiss and the Albanians eat Lambchops
> . . . We can
> conceive of a fat man as well as a thin man tucking into a
> Lambchop. Aesthetically too, lamb chops are about right—
> somewhere between the Diner's card and the breadfruit.

By this time the different strands in Markham's work had become clearly identifiable: (1) the pseudonymous poems, (2) poems about sex, politics, and travel, combining what blurb writers, for once, correctly identify as acute observation and trenchant humor, and (3) intensely personal poems, often epistolary in form, about love, friendship, and family.

On the surface ''Life after Speracedes,'' a long poem written as a sequence of letters to a distant intimate, speaks evocatively of a love interrupted by distance but held together by memory:

> These are not attempts to nudge memory,
> not straws that friends glance at, guardedly.
> They are yours, without this letter. They speak
> of shared address, a suitcase left, a plan for home.

But there is a playful undertow to the poem that gives it its force— ''You do not recall last year in Speracedes, in Cabris . . . It was not last year, you're growing literal''—and enables Markham to speak both as the romantic and restless poet who is afraid to put down roots and as a lover keen to hold on to a relationship. This is a strain that can never tire of expression, and it is good to find a modern poet giving it contemporary utterance:

> But for the drug which lures me to the more perfect, more
> remote place from which to say, 'Come home', I would not
> still bother you . . .

Figurative writing was still not a strength in this book—two poems make use of an identical, and not very brilliant, image (''In Albtown's carless 'Lowry' Squares'')—but it prepared the way for the major collections of the 1980s, *Human Rites* and *Living in Disguise,* which, together with Markham's editorial and performance work, have secured his position as one of the more important writers of modern English-language poetry.

Living in Disguise organizes its poems into their constituent groups, the final section, ''Four Letters and a Sermon,'' containing work of a richness and compassion that is immensely satisfying to read. ''Letter to Mauritius,'' written in rhyming couplets, is representative of Markham's finest work, and he glosses a reference to Gracchus at the back of the book in a manner that is worth quoting, since it can give new readers a sense of the flavor of the man:

> Tiberius Gracchus and Gaius Gracchus, tribunes of the
> plebs, and their agricultural reforms, were as passionately
> discussed as, say, the recent political independence of
> Jamaica, or anticipation of Worrell's cricket team to
>   England,
> after having destroyed India (five-nil) in the West
> Indies in 1962. Everyone seemed to believe that a new era

of possibility was opening up (even across the Atlantic) and
that we were poised to participate in it. Ah well, even the
Gracchi brothers died violently.

Markham's later collection, *Towards the End of a Century,* has
confirmed the growing stature of a poet who can write with equal
brilliance in several different guises and registers.

—Michael Thorn

MARLATT, Daphne

Nationality: Canadian. **Born:** Daphne Buckle, Melbourne, Victoria,
11 July 1942. **Education:** University of British Columbia, Vancouver,
B.A. 1964; Indiana University, Bloomington, M.A. 1968. **Family:**
Married Alan Marlatt (divorced); one son. **Career:** Instructor in
English, Capilano College, North Vancouver, 1968, 1973–76. Writer-in-residence, University of Manitoba, Winnipeg, 1982, University
of Alberta, Edmonton, 1985–86, and University of Western Ontario,
1993. Visiting lecturer, University of Saskatchewan, 1998–99. Poetry
editor, *Capilano Review,* Vancouver, 1973–76; editor, with Paul de
Barros, *Periodics,* Vancouver, 1977–81; associate editor, *Island,*
1980–83; member of the editorial collective, *Tessera,* 1983–91.
Awards: Canada Council grant, 1969, 1973, 1985, 1996. **Address:**
c/o Writers' Union of Canada, 24 Ryerson Avenue, Toronto, Ontario
M5T 2P3, Canada.

PUBLICATIONS

Poetry

Frames of a Story. Toronto, Ryerson Press, 1968.
Leaf Leaf/s. Los Angeles, Black Sparrow Press, 1969.
Vancouver Poems. Toronto, Coach House Press, 1972.
Steveston. Vancouver, Talonbooks, 1974; revised edition, Edmonton,
Alberta, Longspoon, 1984.
Our Lives. Carrboro, North Carolina, Truck Press, 1975; revised
edition, Lantzville, British Columbia, Oolichan, 1979.
Solstice: Lunade. Buffalo, State University of New York, 1980.
Here and There. Lantzville, British Columbia, Island, 1981.
How Hug a Stone. Winnipeg, Turnstone Press, 1983.
Touch to My Tongue. Edmonton, Alberta, Longspoon, 1984.
Double Negative. Charlottetown, Prince Edward Island, Gynergy,
1988.
Salvage. Red Deer, Red Deer College Press, 1991.
Two Women in a Birth, with Betshy Warland. Toronto and New York,
Guernica, 1994.

Novels

Zócalo. Toronto, Coach House Press, 1977.
Ana Historic. Toronto, Coach House Press, 1988; London, Women's
Press, 1990.
Taken. Toronto, House of Anansi, 1996.

Other

Rings (miscellany). Toronto, York Street Commune, 1971.
Selected Writing: Net Work, edited by Fred Wah. Vancouver,
Talonbooks, 1980.
What Matters: Writing 1968–1970. Toronto, Coach House Press,
1980.
Mauve, text in French by Nicole Brossard. Montreal, nbj/writing,
1985.
Character, text in French by Nicole Brossard. Montreal, nbj/writing,
1986.
Ghost Works. Edmonton, NeWest, 1993.
Readings from the Labyrinth. Edmonton, NeWest Press, 1998.

Editor, *Steveston Recollected: A Japanese-Canadian History.* Victo-
ria, Provincial Archives of British Columbia, 1975.
Co-editor, *Opening Doors: Vancouver's East End.* Victoria, Provin-
cial Archives of British Columbia, 1979.
Editor, *Mothertalk: Life Stories of Mary Kiyoshic Kiyooka,* by Roy
Kiyooka. Edmonton, NeWest Press. 1997.

*

Bibliography: *Daphne Marlatt and her Works* by Douglas Barbour,
Toronto, ECW Press, 1992; *Contemporary Canadian and U.S. Women
of Letters* by Thomas M.F. Gerry, New York and London, Gale, 1993.

Critical Studies: "Daphne Marlatt's Poetry" by Robert Lecker, in
Canadian Literature (Vancouver, British Columbia), 76, 1978; "'Body
I': Daphne Marlatt's Feminist Poetics" by Barbara Godard, in
American Review of Canadian Studies, 15(4), 1985; "Phyllis Webb,
Daphne Marlatt and Simultitude" by Laurie Ricou, in *A Mazing
Space: Writing,* edited by Shirley Neuman and Smaro Kamboureli,
Edmonton, Longspoon, 1986; Daphne Marlatt issue of *Line,* 13,
spring 1989; "No Tongue in Cheek: Recent Work by English
Canadian Poets Daphne Marlatt, Lola Lemire Tostevin and Margaret
Atwood" by Christl Verduyn, in *Canadian Woman Studies,* 8(3), fall
1987; *Translation Poetics: Composing the Body Canadian* (disserta-
tion) by Pamela Banting, University of Alberta, 1992; *The Feminist
Romantic: The Revisionary Rhetoric of "Double Negative," "Naked
Poems," and "Gyno-Text"* (dissertation) by Susan Lee Drodge,
Memorial University of Newfoundland, 1996; "The Birds, the Bees,
and Kristeva: An Examination of Sexual Desire in the Nature Poetry
of Daphne Marlatt, Robert Kroetsch, and Tim Lilburn" by Darryl
Whetter, in *Studies in Canadian LIterature,* 21(2), 1996; *Narrative in
the Feminine: Daphne Marlatt and Nicole Brossard* by Susan Lynne
Knutson, Waterloo, Ontario, Wilfrid Laurier University Press, 1999.

*   *   *

In "Musing with Mothertongue" (in *Tessera*) Daphne Marlatt
notes that "language is first of all for us a body of sound." It is this
sense of poetry and, indeed, of all language as sound that gives
Marlatt's work its characteristic rhythms and that explains as well the
other quality that marks her writing—its meticulous attention to detail
and form. The images that Marlatt selects are exact renderings of the
environment she is describing, but their appropriateness extends
beyond the mimetic; they fragment and rejoin to form impressions

governed by the sounds they make in combination. These new relationships of word elements and phrases, sometimes created by spontaneous association and sometimes by carefully crafted quibbles, punctuation, or postmodern doubling—''this body my (d)welling place''—create in the poems and even in her prose criticism a series of new and deeper meanings as the writing progresses. It is as process then that the poems must be read and, in fact, that the whole of Marlatt's work should be seen. The later work interrogates the process even more strongly, questioning the relationship of female sexuality, mothering, and language within an *écriture féminine,* a concern for language as body. The novel *Ana Historic* overlays personal and social history onto the process of language, creating a biography as historiography. The later *Ghost Works* continues the layering of memory, autobiography, and narrative, though in a more straightforward diction and with less conscious wordplay.

The early poems in *Frames of a Story* establish Marlatt's desire for an escape into a literary process that will free her two protagonists from the framing influence of their grandmother's strict past, even as it frees Marlatt from the framing strictures of traditional literary expression. To some extent the dilemma is autobiographical in that Marlatt is the child of colonial British parents, a background she later explores in ''In the Month of Hungry Ghosts.'' More important, the struggle of the two girls to see themselves and each other through new frames, to create a world out of their own perceptions, becomes the central aim of the poems. The two girls—each an extension of one aspect of Marlatt's own struggle toward commitment and self—do not succeed in finding freedom, nor does Marlatt find her independent voice.

In *Leaf Leaf/s,* however, Marlatt begins to assemble experience from the disparate images around her and to create poetry from the sounds these images evoke in words. The curious amalgam of visual and aural images that mark her writing from this point forms a series of complex photographs that simultaneously present a picture, its sounds, the effect of the image on the perceiver, and the resonance of that perception in the reader's ear. These four sets of stimuli for every impression, each one independent but all necessary for the total effect, force a process in reading that renders the poetry not only amazingly precise but also experiential. One does not observe the world Marlatt reports, but rather one enters it and, in fact, creates it with her.

Marlatt's vision has been called ''phenomenological'' by Douglas Barbour, Robert Lecker, and others, and certainly by the time of the *Steveston* poems it is clear that her universe has become one of sense perceptions. It is important, however, to observe the role of sound as one of these sensations, in itself a separate aspect of the world and an equal building block with other influences in which the poet finds herself immersed. This composite universe does not follow a sequential, conscious intellectual analysis in its groupings of phenomena, yet, in the relationship of sound to meaning and of personal experience to poetic moment, a strict relationship of cause and effect emerges. The layering of perception is perhaps most clearly seen in *Double Negative,* in which a train trip across Australia links visual documents with memories of lovemaking between two women, with concepts of the desert, with the train as umbilical cord linking the earth as mother to the ''cyclical nature of female orgasm'' (37). Nowhere is Marlatt's a linear construct, however, not even aboard a train. She seeks in a central metaphor of birth for an explanation of the writing impulse and a feminine vision of causality. Indeed, in *Rings* the entrances of the husband into the private world of mother and child mark a shift from a soft and creative language to one of more

complex, but less felt, ideas and of direct connections. The experiences that fill Marlatt's world become more and more fragments of feminine process: blood, water, a letting go, mouths as sucking. Again, in *Tessera* she suggests that ''like the mother's body, language is larger than us and carries us along with it. It bears us, it births us, insofar as we bear with it.''

The work since *How Hug a Stone* develops these concerns from a more overtly theoretical perspective. In retrospect, however, one can see in the earliest poems the clear roots of the poet's identification with language as an extension of the female body and the process of writing as linked to the processes of female sexuality, to menstrual blood, to flowing. The sounds become more gentle as they are freed of what Marlatt calls ''terms for dominance tied up with male experience,'' such as those she employs in the angry sociological statements of *Steveston. Salvage* rewrites the experience of the *Steveston* poems and other early work, removing the discourse of dominance and bringing forward the feminist concerns that Marlatt feels were always in the background of the work. The pun of its title echoes the aim of *Double Negative* to ''[im]print'' the negative term ''women'' with the positive. All of the work retains astonishing clarity, and the precise patterns her work forms create the multiple and overlapping impressions that are the core of Marlatt's poetry.

—Reid Gilbert

MARSHALL, Jack

Nationality: American. **Born:** Brooklyn, New York, 25 February 1937. **Education:** Lafayette High School, Brooklyn. **Family:** Married Kathleen Fraser, *q.v.,* in 1961 (divorced 1970); two sons. **Career:** Worked as a shipping clerk, salesman, farmhand, steel mill hand, and deck hand; copywriter, J.C. Penney, New York; longshoreman, San Francisco. Taught poetry workshops at the University of Iowa, Iowa City, 1969–71, California Western College, San Diego, 1972–74, San Francisco State University, 1975, and United States International University, San Diego. **Awards:** Bay Area Book Reviewers award, 1984; PEN West Center award, 1993, for *Sesame.* **Address:** c/o Coffee House Press, 27 North Fourth Street, Suite 400, Minneapolis, Minnesota 55401, U.S.A.

PUBLICATIONS

Poetry

The Darkest Continent. New York, For Now Press, 1967.
Bearings. New York, Harper, 1969.
Floats. Iowa City, Cedar Creek Press, 1971.
Surviving in America, with Anselm Hollo and Sam Hamod. Iowa City, Cedar Creek Press, 1972.
Bits of Thirst. Iowa City, Cedar Creek Press, 1972.
Bits of Thirst and Other Poems and Translations. Berkeley, California, Blue Wind Press, 1976.
Arriving on the Playing Fields of Paradise. Santa Cruz, California, Jazz Press, 1983.
Arabian Nights. Minneapolis, Coffee House Press, 1986.

Sesame. Minneapolis, Coffee House Press, 1993.
Chaos Comics. Tesuque, New Mexico, Pennywhistle Press, 1994.
Millennium Fever. Minneapolis, Coffee House Press, 1997.

*

Critical Study: By James Gurley, in *Poet Lore,* 89(2), summer 1994.

Jack Marshall comments:
Poetry for me is precise emotion and perception propelled.

*   *   *

A reviewer has called Jack Marshall ''an original voice at a time when many American poets are doing imitations of each other.'' This statement reflects a central bias of our time: throughout our culture we equate difference with worth. There is a mainstream practice in today's poetry, as indeed there has been in every period; each poet cannot be different from every other poet. It is true that Marshall's poetry is unusual, but it is not unique; others depart from the norm in similar ways. To consider his work, we need to define the ways in which it is distinct and try to evaluate them, rather than to assign merit to difference in itself.

One of the features of Marshall's poetry, especially in his early work, is a refusal of consistency, a lack of connection between words, images, and ideas, and a lack of narrative progression. The tendency is hard to illustrate without lengthy quotation, but it can be seen in a typically surreal stanza like this from *Bearings:*

Everywhere, the air priming.
Huns happen
in streetclothes, listen.
Goodbye, wheelchair,
smooth wings play the sound of
home.

The rejection of relationships between events in the poem is a refusal of movement; we are encouraged not to follow a thread through the work but to inhabit each dispossessed image, each word even, as a thing-in-itself. In this sense such writing is related to the contemporary mode called language poetry.

Marshall does not always write in this style. In the same volume he gives us more traditional poems like ''Hitch-hiker,'' about a wandering poet who passes through ''the festooned, blazing towns,'' wondering whether they are dreams. This statement, with its gorgeous image, might be taken as a metaphor for his less accessible work: a hitchhiker's passage through towns that blur into dreams.

Disconnectedness is still seen in Marshall's later poems, though not as urgently and not as often. ''Dawn Notes,'' from the 1986 volume *Arabian Nights,* is a series of impressions that are internally consistent but only loosely related. Their separateness is emphasized by lines drawn between them in the text; they are like jottings in a writer's notebook. The influence here is oriental rather than surreal:

What leaves in the light
show red and gold
are in the dark
black
and blue

Each work-
day of the weak
feels like hauling
a whole unfucking week

Caw caw caw-high
in the trees, hooting
birds mimic
a train horn's far
bending
echo

Juxtaposition of apparently unrelated items can provide an exhilarating release from the drag of lineality and predictability, but for some readers deflected meanings and incongruities are a facile way to imply profundity. They suggest, as hallucination does, that because a thing is strange it provides clues to the unfathomable. Incoherence alone, however, does not guarantee hidden truth, and for some at least the truly profound rests within a meaningful universe.

Another feature of Marshall's work is the tendency toward rambling abstraction. He often employs a peculiar, clumsy syntax in stanza-long sentences that stumble forward and break off as if overwhelmed:

It's weird, that time—or gap in time—
midwinter seclusion, unending or starting
over, yourself nearly over-
dosed on cutting loose ego,
when more than ever in confusion comes hastening
doubt that from the start what you took up doing
was needed done, matters, that what you inherit
being alive needs realized desire to keep on
being alive and move you
              on your way . . .

As it staggers into an ellipsis, this stanza from a poem in *Arabian Nights* is an attempt to reveal the process of poetry and of life, struggling forward in bewilderment and longing. The title, ''Make, Not Have,'' suggests this, and the next stanza confirms it:

            Now amnesia, aphasia, the break-
down of brain cells all hoot
as you can no more hold
in sequence your last thought, next
move, how long since
in-breath, long drawn, long held,
let go, or bare skin felt mild
warm air bringing the far spring-
cleanings of childhood near, bringing you,
without a step, there . . .

There is a brave integrity here, a groping recognition that plays against the seamless assurance of polished poems. In this case the singular style is a necessity of the poem.

The valorization of idiosyncrasy is a symptom of the divorce between poetry and the community: the idiosyncratic vision is not the shared, public vision. Originality excites us because it is alien, like a foreign country. The question is whether an oddity is merely exotic or whether, like "Make, Not Have," it recovers something in our origins, a reality denied in the public version of truth.

—Jane Somerville

MATHIAS, Roland (Glyn)

Nationality: British. **Born:** Near Talybont-on-Usk, Breconshire, 4 September 1915. **Education:** Caterham School; Jesus College, Oxford (Meyricke Exhibitioner, 1934; Honorary scholar, 1936), B.A. (honors) in modern history 1936, B.Litt. 1939, M.A. 1944. **Family:** Married Mary (Molly) Hawes in 1944; one son and two daughters. **Career:** Senior history master, Cowley School, St. Helens, Lancashire, 1938–41; resident master, Blue Coat School, Reading, Berkshire, 1941–45; assistant history master, Carlisle Grammar School, 1945–46; senior history master, St. Clement Danes Grammar School, London, 1946–48; headmaster, Pembroke Dock (later Pembroke) Grammar School, Wales, 1948–58, Herbert Strutt School, Belper, Derbyshire, 1958–64, and King Edward's Five Ways School, Birmingham, 1964–69. Since 1969 full-time writer. School-master-Fellow, Balliol College, Oxford, 1961, and University College, Swansea, 1967; part-time extramural lecturer, University College, Cardiff, 1970–77; visiting lecturer, University of Rennes, France, 1970, University of Brest, France, 1970, and University of Alabama, Birmingham, 1971. Editor, *The Anglo-Welsh Review*, 1961–76. Chair, English Section, Yr Academi Gymreig, 1975–78, and Literature Committee, Welsh Arts Council, 1976–79. **Awards:** Welsh Arts Council bursary, 1968, award, 1969, and prize, 1972, 1980. D.H.L.: Georgetown University, Washington, D.C., 1985. **Address:** Deffrobani, 5 Maescelyn, Brecon, Powys LD3 7NL, Wales.

PUBLICATIONS

Poetry

Days Enduring and Other Poems. Ilfracombe, Devon, Stockwell, 1943.
Break in Harvest and Other Poems. London, Routledge, 1946.
The Roses of Tretower. Pembroke Dock, Dock Leaves Press, 1952.
The Flooded Valley. London, Putnam, 1960.
Absalom in the Tree and Other Poems. Llandybie, Dyfed, Gomer, 1971.
Snipe's Castle. Llandysul, Dyfed, Gomer, 1979.
Burning Brambles: Selected Poems 1944–1979. Llandysul, Dyfed, Gomer, 1983.
A Field at Vallorcines. Llandysul, Ceredigion, Gomer, 1996.

Short Stories

The Eleven Men of Eppynt and Other Stories. Pembroke Dock, Dock Leaves Press, 1956.

Other

Whitsun Riot: An Account of a Commotion Amongst Catholics in Herefordshire and Monmouthshire in 1605. Cambridge, Bowes, 1963.
Vernon Watkins. Cardiff, University of Wales Press, 1974.

The Hollowed-Out Elder Stalk: John Cowper Powys as Poet. London, Enitharmon Press, 1979; Chester Springs, Pennsylvania, Dufour, 1985.
A Ride Through the Woods: Essays on Anglo-Welsh Literature. Bridgend, Glamorgan, Poetry Wales Press, 1985.
Anglo-Welsh Literature: An Illustrated History. Bridgend, Glamorgan, Poetry Wales Press, 1986.

Editor, with Sam Adams, *The Shining Pyramid and Other Stories by Welsh Authors.* Llandysul, Dyfed, Gomer, 1970.
Editor, *David Jones: Eight Essays on His Work as Writer and Artist.* Llandysul, Dyfed, Gomer, 1976.
Editor, with Sam Adams, *The Collected Short Stories of Geraint Goodwin.* Tenby, H.G. Walters, 1976.
Editor, with Raymond Garlick, *Anglo-Welsh Poetry 1480–1980.* Bridgend, Glamorgan, Poetry Wales Press, 1984.

*

Critical Studies: "The Poetry of Roland Mathias," in *Poetry Wales* (Llandybie), summer 1971, and "Profile: Roland Mathias," in *New Welsh Review* (Lampeter), 4, spring 1989, both by Jeremy Hooker; interview in *Poetry Wales* (Llandybie), 18(4), 1983; *'Texts against Chaos': Anglo-Welsh Identity in the Poetry of R.S. Thomas, Raymond Garlick, and Roland Mathias* (dissertation) by Megan Sue Lloyd, University of Kentucky, 1993; *Roland Mathias* by Sam Adams, Cardiff, University of Wales Press, 1995.

Roland Mathias comments:

In my earlier poetry the sense of place was very strong. Even love poems used the place or history symbol.

Of recent years the process has changed. The secret place is always Wales, but since my return to it physically there has been a blurring of the remembered image by the present reality. In consequence I have become slightly more personal in my poetry in an overt sense, but there are more people about, more predicaments than mine. I think of history still, of my stock, my parents, family love, and my own insufficiency in the line of descent. For me the old nonconformist sense of guilt is not inhibiting and useless; it gives me a particular vision of the present through the past, a measurement. Out of it I can write.

I would add, however, that I continue to find significance in the parochial and believe that poetry is often weakened and diluted by being devoted to situations in which the element of the personal is small. My vision begins with Wales, and the rest of the world merely adheres to it.

*   *   *

Such joy as there is in Roland Mathias's work is far from unconfined. There is an essential gravity to most of his work, a seriousness of theme and a weightiness of language that cohere in a distinctive view of the world. In an interview published in 1983 Mathias said of his work and his outlook, "I'm certainly suspicious of beauty. It isn't merely that my Puritan upbringing has always made me feel that Keats' dictum about beauty and truth was horribly wrong. My first response is always one of suspicion of anything that intends a large gesture particularly when it is a large gesture which is intended to exemplify beauty. Beauty in itself doesn't save." In the same interview Mathias spoke of the theme of guilt as a recurrent one in his work. The sense of sin and the mistrust of beauty and rhetoric have inevitable consequences. The poetry is often tortuous and knotted in both sound and syntax, clotted with a consonantal music that eschews conventional melodies and intricate in structure as one clause qualifies another in the single-minded pursuit of honest statement. Truth here is quite distinct from beauty (or at any rate from any conventional idea of beauty) and certainly ranks a great deal higher than beauty as a poetic aim. Mathias never writes merely to please his readers or even to make life comfortable or easy for them. Stylistically he has always been true to himself and has remained largely uninfluenced by the fashionable voices of Anglo-Welsh poetry, his own idiom appearing closer to Browning and Hopkins than to any of his contemporaries.

The characteristic tone is evident, for example, in the opening lines of "Solway" (*The Roses of Tretower*):

Off the low fields the lagging pools
Slip. The anomalous privet droops. Saliva spills
From the beaks of the huts towards
The restless claw-marks on the shore of birds.

Wall holds the cropped farm up.

The natural world is not a source of renewal or comfort for Mathias. It remains largely indifferent to human suffering, to the individual's sense of his own (and man's) inadequacy. In "Searching Spring," from the same collection, the season offers no kind of renewal. There is no revelatory abundance in nature:

Gravelgreat are the hills and perching
Walls are haggard over pitted ground:
In the red manner of a gash the lurching
Streams collide, leaving shoulders ragged
And sudden like the edge
Of our disaster and grave wound. Boulders
Like roofs are lifted off our talk:
Bushes that ruff the hedge and clothe our seeming
Crack in the night and the strained teeming
Multitude of roots sticks in the sight.
No measure now of things that stalk
And vein the sick flayed province under boots:
I had no notion till the fork dug in
My chiefest covenant was with my skin.

The density of the language is typical, and the "gash" and the "grave wound" are characteristic of a repeated pattern of images. In "The Path to Dinas," "the bird's eye wanders / Back to the wound half-healed." In "Testament" we are told that

I was the child
Of belief, aching pitifully
In the unready hours
At the wounds I must suffer
When I walked out weaponless
And grown.

Nature and man alike carry their scars in poem after poem. "The Lurking Ancestor" (*The Roses of Tretower*) carries as an epigraph

words from Donne: "Man hath no centre, but misery; there and only there, he is fixed and sure to find himself." Finding oneself through one's pain has been a recurrent theme in Mathias's work. At the heart of this process of self-discovery is the recognition of

Man that is God and ghost, fuel and fire,
Factor and master, ephemeral, crossed
Peccator maximus stirring to desire.

For Mathias the landscapes to value are those without "secondary forms / Pretty distractions," territories that "lay the action bare," where there is no evading "the bull-nosed rushes of a wrong / On right" ("Freshwater West Revisited"). His historical subjects, too, are chosen for much the same reason. There is no facile pretense at any kind of objective, or even national, history. Rather, as he says in the last line of "Memling," one of the best of his historical poems, "the history we choose speaks largely of ourselves."

As poet, critic, and editor, Mathias has been a major influence on the evolution of the very idea of Anglo-Welsh literature in our time. Jeremy Hooker has rightly observed that "he has taken his Anglo-Welsh situation far more seriously than all but a few writers with whom he shares it, and he has done so partly out of his humble sense of himself as an outsider who cannot claim to be fully Welsh, and who must earn his place in Wales by the quality of his effort and understanding." The poems in the sequence "Tide-Reach" (*Snipe's Castle*) bring together many of Mathias's familiar themes, and they succeed in doing so in language that has a greater lyricism and clarity than is often the case in his work. They are affirmatory poems freed to a great extent from the insistent doubt and suspicion of most of his earlier work. In the first poem, "The Green Chapel," the "woundhole" is unambiguously the "mark of where God is." The last poem of the sequence, "Laus Deo," closes with lines to which we may surely apply the terms "beauty" and (quite unpejoratively) "large gesture":

It is one
Coherent work, this Wales
And the seaway of Wales, its Maker
As careful of strength as
Of weakness, its quirk and cognomen
And trumpet allowed for
This whole peninsula's length.
It is one affirmative work, this Wales
And the seaway of Wales.

To read these lines, which close Mathias's collection of selected poems, *Burning Brambles,* is to recognize a joy hard earned.

—Glyn Pursglove

MATTHIAS, John (Edward)

Nationality: American. **Born:** Columbus, Ohio, 5 September 1941. **Education:** Ohio State University, Columbus, 1959–63, B.A. 1963; Stanford University, California, 1963–65, M.A. 1966; University of

London (Fulbright Fellow), 1966–67. **Family:** Married Diana Adams in 1967; two children. **Career:** Assistant professor, 1967–73, associate professor, 1973–80, and since 1980 professor of English, University of Notre Dame, Indiana. Visiting professor, Clare Hall, Cambridge, 1976–77, Skidmore College, Saratoga Springs, New York, summer 1978, and University of Chicago, spring 1980. **Awards:** Columbia University Translation Center award, 1979; Ingram-Merrill Foundation award, 1984, 1990; Society of Midland Authors poetry award, 1984; Society for the Study of Midwestern Literature poetry prize, 1986; Slobadan Jovanovic literary prize, 1989; George Bogin memorial award, Poetry Society of America, 1990; Lily Endowment grant, 1991–92; Ohio Library Association poetry award, 1996. **Address:** Department of English, University of Notre Dame, Notre Dame, Indiana 46556–0368, U.S.A.

PUBLICATIONS

Poetry

Herman's Poems. Rushden, Northamptonshire, Sceptre Press, 1973.
Turns. Chicago, Swallow Press, and London, Anvil Press Poetry, 1975.
Double Derivation, Association and Cliché: From the Great Tournament Roll of Westminster. Chicago, Wine Press, 1975.
Two Poems. Knotting, Bedfordshire, Sceptre Press, 1976.
Crossing. Chicago, Swallow Press, and London, Anvil Press Poetry, 1979.
Rostropovich at Aldeburgh. Knotting, Bedfordshire, Sceptre Press, 1979.
Bathory and Lermontov. Ahus, Sweden, Kalejdoskop, 1980.
Northern Summer: New and Selected Poems 1963–1983. Athens, Swallow Press/Ohio University Press, and London, Anvil Press Poetry, 1984.
Tva Dikter. Lund, Sweden, Ellerstroms, 1989.
A Gathering of Ways. Athens, Swallow Press/Ohio University Press, 1991.
Swimming at Midnight: Selected Shorter Poems. Athens, Swallow Press/Ohio University Press, 1995.
Beltane at Aphelion: Collected Longer Poems. Athens, Swallow Press/Ohio University Press, 1995.
Pages: New Poems and Cuttings. Athens, Swallow Press/Ohio University Press, 2000.

Other

Reading Old Friends: Reviews, Essays, and Poems on Poetics. Albany, State University of New York Press, 1992.

Editor, *23 Modern British Poets.* Chicago, Swallow Press, 1971.
Editor, *Five American Poets.* Manchester, Carcanet, 1979.
Editor, *Introducing David Jones.* London, Faber, 1980.
Editor and Translator, with Göran Printz-Påhlson, *Contemporary Swedish Poetry.* Chicago, Swallow Press, and London, Anvil Press Poetry, 1980.
Editor, *David Jones: Man and Poet.* Orono, Maine, National Poetry Foundation, 1989.
Editor, *Selected Works of David Jones.* Orono, Maine, National Poetry Foundation, 1993.

Translator, with Göran Printz-Påhlson, *Rainmaker,* by Jan Östergren. Athens, Ohio University Press, 1983.
Translator, with Vladeta Vuckovic, *The Battle of Kosovo.* Athens, Swallow Press/Ohio University Press, and Buxton, Derbyshire, Aquila, 1987.

*

Critical Studies: ''John Matthias: Crossing'' by William Sylvester, in *Credences* (Buffalo, New York), spring 1981; ''The Poetry of John Matthias: Between the Castle and the Mine'' by Vincent Sherry, in *Salmagundi* (Saratoga Springs, New York), fall 1984; ''Crossings and Turns: The Poetry of John Matthias,'' in *The Presence of the Past,* by Jeremy Hooker, Bridgend, Glamorgan, Poetry Wales Press, 1987; ''The Poems As Quest'' by Willard Spiegelman, in *Parnassus* (New York, New York), 17(2) and 18(1), 1992; *World Play Place: Essays on the Poetry of John Matthias* edited by Robert Archambeau, Athens, Swallow Press/Ohio University Press, 1998.

John Matthias comments:

It is probably best not to say very much about one's own work. The background to mine includes a brief, early, but intense period of study with John Berryman and three years at Stanford University in the middle 1960s when I first became acquainted with a group of poets—all at that time students of Yvor Winters—whose work is now well known: Robert Hass, John Peck, Robert Pinsky, and James McMichael. I still feel a considerable affinity with these four poets. In the late 1960s I began spending long periods of time in England. The prehistory, history, and geography of East Anglia have been crucial for my writing, both as background and foreground, during more than fifteen years. More recently the direction of my work has been shaped by a short but very significant period of time spent in Fife, Scotland, and by several years of collaboration with Göran Printz-Påhlson translating contemporary Swedish poetry. Though I am an American poet, most of what seems to me my best work has been written in Britain, often about British subjects. Stylistically I consider myself an eclectic and would defend eclecticism. Like Robert Duncan, I can say that much of my work is derivative without feeling unhappy about it. I, too, then would be glad to ''emulate, imitate, reconstrue, approximate.'' My deepest, and in some ways contradictory, enthusiasms among English-language poets of our century are for Pound, David Jones, early Auden, middle Lowell, middle Berryman, and Geoffrey Hill. The fictions of Guy Davenport have also meant much to me.

*   *   *

The essential oddity and eccentricity of John Matthias's sensibility, and of his always interesting and inventive poetry, can be most easily suggested by pointing out that he is clearly influenced by two odd and eccentric poets who are also quite exceptionally different from each other, John Berryman and David Jones, on both of whom Matthias has written excellent critical essays. From the former he takes a proud, performing—perhaps even self-regarding—poetic self and a readiness to be painfully personal, and from the latter he takes a penetrating interest in the recovery of a history and a tradition from a particular landscape—in Matthias's case primarily the Fens—and a magpie hoarding of out-of-the-way information and anecdotes, which form the kernel of a number of ruminative poems. The combination of the American and the British influence seems a necessary one for Matthias who, American by birth, has strong British connections and family and who has lived in both countries, and the relationship between the two is signaled in the title of his book *Crossing.*

It is probably clear that any poet who feels himself capable of absorbing and assimilating two such potently individual voices must have a strong poetic personality and constitution, and this is indeed the case with Matthias, who rarely actually sounds like Berryman or Jones but who profitably turns their influences in his own work into an original kind of linguistic playfulness and daring. Through a number of very different kinds of poems, Matthias manages to establish and maintain a recognizable voice of his own: high-pitched and excitable; sometimes showily displaying its range of cultural references, but usually with a genuinely Berrymanic kind of urgency and enthusiasm that save it from the merely boastful; but often undermined by a distinct sadness, a profound sense of the transience of earthly delights, whether those of history and culture or those of the personal life, those of the world, or those of the flesh.

It is extremely difficult to quote from Matthias's work, since many of his best poems are lengthy sequences that explore a particular theme and worry about a particular set of circumstances or a historical occasion with an expansive experimental or exploratory breadth and energy. Music is obviously important to him. Composers and musical pieces are mentioned quite frequently in the poems, and some of the separate parts of his sequences have a kind of musical interrelatedness. Matthias speaks about the activity of writing these poems as "assembling certain kinds of structure." For example, "Turns: Towards a Provisional Aesthetic and a Discipline," the poem that gives its name to his volume *Turns,* provides an elaborate descant on the extraordinary "theme" of its opening part, a "translation" into Middle English of the opening sentences of *Jude the Obscure.* This zany toying and tinkering with different epochs and cultures are among the essential signatures of Matthias and are apparent in many of his most innovative sequences, for instance, "The Stefan Batory Poems" and "The Mihail Lermontov Poems."

Personally, however, I like most the long reflective poems, often addressed to friends or to members of his family, in which important personal memories or sensations are evoked and set in the larger contexts of the public and political worlds. In some of these poems the America of the 1960s, and especially the experience of Vietnam, is given an exceptionally vivid poetic presence. These immediacies and realities ground a poetry that is, perhaps, sometimes in danger of overelaboration and oversophistication and thus ripe for parody. But usually the extraordinarily recondite learning and allusiveness, complete with considerable annotation, function as genuine elements of style and vision and not as mere parade or decoration. Some of the excitement of reading Matthias comes from being kept on one's toes, but it is when the sophistication is firmly at the service of human emotion that his work gains its most remarkable effects. This is undoubtedly the case in one of his finest poems, "Epilogue from a New Home: For Toby Barkan," which is an apology to the wife of a dead friend for not being able to write an elegy. In apologizing, of course, a marvelous elegy does get written. This is the final stanza:

> Oh, I remember you that day: the terror in
> your face, the irony and love. And I remember
> What you wanted me to do. That ancient charge: to
> read whatever evidence in lives or lies appears,
> In stones or bells—transform, transfigure then whatever
> comedy, catastrophe or crime, and thus

Return the earth, thus redeem the time. And this:
> to leave it all alone (unspoken always: look, I have
> This moment and this place): *Cum on, cum on my owyn*
> *swet chyld; goo we hom and take owr rest . . .*
> *Sing we to the oldest harpe, and playe . . .* Old friend,
> old debt: I'm welcoming at last your presence now.
> I'm but half oriented here. I'm digging down.

—Neil Corcoran

MAXWELL, Glyn

Nationality: British. **Born:** Welwyn Garden City, England, 1962. **Education:** Oxford University; Boston University. **Career:** Freelance writer and editor. **Awards:** Eric Gregory award, 1991; Poetry Book Society Choice for *Tale of the Mayor's Son,* and Recommendation for *Out of the Rain;* Somerset Maugham award for *Out of the Rain.* **Address:** c/o Bloodaxe Books, P.O. 1SN, Newcastle upon Tyne NE99 1SN, England.

PUBLICATIONS

Poetry

Tale of the Mayor's Son. Newcastle upon Tyne, Bloodaxe, 1990.
Out of the Rain. Newcastle upon Tyne, Bloodaxe, 1992.
Rest for the Wicked. Newcastle upon Tyne, Bloodaxe, 1995.
The Breakage: Poems. London, Faber, 1998; Boston, Houghton Mifflin, 1999.

Plays

Gnyss the Magnificent: Three Verse Plays. London, Chatto and Windus, 1993.
Wolfpit: The Tale of the Green Children of Suffolk. Todmorden, ARC, 1996.

Novel

Blue Burneau. London, Chatto and Windus, 1994.

Other

Editor, with Michael Dobbs, *The Bridport Prize: Poetry and Short Stories.* Bristol, England, Sansom and Company, 1996.
Editor, *Moon Country: Further Reports from Iceland,* by Simon Armitage. London and Boston, Faber, 1996.

*

Critical Studies: "Glyn Maxwell's 'Out of the Rain'" by Scott Anderson, in *Agni* (Boston), 37, 1993; in *Poetry Review,* 84(1), spring 1994; by Nick Hornby, in *Poetry Review,* 85(2), summer 1995; by A.

Topping, in *Critical Survey* (Oxford), 8(2), 1996; "Glyn Maxwell: Aestheticising Place-Myth" by D. Brown, in *Critical Survey* (Oxford), 9(1), 1997.

*   *   *

Glyn Maxwell is one of the most prolific and immediately impressive of the new wave of contemporary British poets. His work is marked by a confidence of address and an ability to create an immediate excitement in the reader. He writes naturally in a wide range of traditional prosodic forms and gives them energetic new life. Form is not a restraint into which he fits but a creative release that lends his work edge and wit. Furthermore, he experiments with form and can often undermine prosodic form with the syntax of loosely structured demotic speech. His work first came to prominence in the British journal *Poetry Review* in 1987, and it has been praised by Derek Walcott, Joseph Brodsky, Peter Porter, and Peter Forbes.

Maxwell writes poems from the point of view of many different individuals and expresses himself in many voices. His facility is great, but the reader is led to feel that Maxwell needs to set himself a range of technical challenges in order to be himself in verse. He is a prolific writer and can write at length. His sequence "Out of the Rain" is twenty pages long, and many poems run from between two to three pages.

Maxwell's gift is essentially protean, enabling him to write a range of types of poem, be it lyric, narrative, or dramatic. This makes it difficult to pinpoint one or two poems that are representative of the best in each of his books. He is a poet who needs to be read entire. His poems reward close reading, but the sheer diversity of voices and subjects encountered in them make reading Maxwell a demanding experience. The challenging nature of the work is offset, however, by a lively sense of humor that entertains the reader. The titles of Maxwell poems are often playful and puzzling: "Actress-as-Cat," "Tale of a Chocolate Egg," "We Are Off to See the Wizard."

In a *Poetry Review* questionnaire Maxwell mentioned W.H. Auden, Robert Frost, and the early music of Bob Dylan as influences on his work. At time he can be reminiscent of all three, and he can remind us of formal poets a generation earlier than his own, such as John Fuller or James Fenton. Maxwell has said that his main reading is of dead poets, and his work provides evidence of a wide reading of poetry written in English.

The world of Maxwell's poems is essentially contemporary, recognizably postsurrealist, post-Paul Muldoon, and expressive of images of a shared modern reality through traditional forms. His narratives tend to be tangential rather than linear. The poems often start with an arresting line that places the reader in an unclear situation that then becomes clearer during the reading. (In this, and in his writing of verse drama, the reader is tempted to add Robert Browning as another influence.) The title poem from Maxwell's dazzling first book, *Tale of the Mayor's Son,* effectively buttonholes the reader through a number of direct and initially enigmatic pointers to the story to come:

The Mayor's son had options. One was death,
and one a black and stylish trilby hat
he wore instead, when thinking this: I Love.

The town was not elaborate. The sky

was white collisions of no special interest
but look at the Mayor's son, at the bazaar!

In its evocation of two young women at a swimming pool, the later poem "Helene and Heloise" brings together a number of Maxwell traits:

So swim in the embassy pool in a tinkling breeze
The sisters, *mes cousines*, they are blonde-haired
Helene and Heloise,
One for the fifth time up to the diving board,
The other, in her quiet shut-eye sidestroke
Slowly away from me though I sip and look.

Maxwell writes lyric poems too, such as "Poem in Blank Rhyme," which employs only one rhyme and which begins, "This isn't very difficult to do." The poem ends with these lines:

Now over there, I'm standing in the dew,
Remembering and hoping. But it's true:

Days are very many. Days are few.
I want to be with someone and you're who.

Maxwell's book *Rest for the Wicked* contains "New Year Song," a dramatic lyric from a play:

The apple's eaten, the year is died,
The sun is climbing over the side,
The sparrow's flown the ocean wide,
Remembering me, forget me.

Other poems in *Rest for the Wicked* tackle serious public events, as in "The Sarajevo Zoo," where the strangulation of the besieged Bosnian city is presented through the effect on the unfed zoo animals. Despite the efforts of the two zookeepers, the animals are driven to eat one another. The poem is public, somber, and plain in form, and it steers clear of cleverness. When armed troops arrive,

Trees were what you could not see the starving
beasts behind, or see there were now no beasts,
only the keepers crouching with their two lives,
Then winter howled a command and the sorry branches
shed their leaves.

The Breakage, published in 1998, shows equally the continuing need to come to terms with the mainstream modern English verse tradition in which Maxwell's work is firmly based and a further deepening of themes in his poetry. The impressive sequence of fourteen poems titled "Letters to Edward Thomas" is an act of homage to a poet who developed an existing meditative and fluid English verse line (which Maxwell adapts in the sequence) as an alternative to modernism's clearer break with tradition. The poem also aims to come to terms with World War I, which remains the greatest trauma of twentieth-century Britain and in which Thomas died. Other poems in the book add a further, more personal connection to the experience of Thomas. Poems such as "My Grandfather at the Pool" and "June 31st, the Somme" tell us that Maxwell's own grandfather fought in the war and survived. In "Letters to Edward Thomas" Maxwell confesses to the older poet, "Whom do I write for? Anybody? Yes, / You.'' In its pages *The Breakage* demonstrates once again the virtuoso range of Maxwell's talent, from occasional poems, hard-edged lyrics, and conversational pieces to ''Under These Lights,'' a fine elegy for Brodsky.

Given his undeniable gifts, his ambition to express things clearly, and his energetic springing line, there is little doubt that Maxwell is a key figure in British poetry today.

—Jonathan Barker

MAYER, Gerda (Kamilla)

Nationality: British. **Born:** Gerda Kamilla Stein, Carlsbad, Czechoslovakia, 9 June 1927; immigrated to Britain in 1939; became citizen in 1949. **Education:** Attended schools in Czechoslovakia and England, 1933–44; Bedford College, London, 1960–63, B.A. 1963. **Family:** Married Adolf Mayer in 1949. **Career:** Worked on farms in Worcestershire and Surrey, 1945–46; office worker in London, 1946–52. **Address:** 12 Margaret Avenue, London E4 7NP, England.

PUBLICATIONS

Poetry

Oddments. Privately printed, 1970.
Gerda Mayer's Library Folder. Kettering, Northamptonshire, All-In, 1972.
Treble Poets 2, with Florence Elon and Daniel Halpern. London, Chatto and Windus, 1975.
The Knockabout Show (for children). London, Chatto and Windus, 1978.
Monkey on the Analyst's Couch. Sunderland, Ceolfrith Press, 1980.
The Candy-Floss Tree (for children), with Norman Nicholson and Frank Flynn. Oxford, Oxford University Press, 1984.
March Postman. Berkhamsted, Hertfordshire, Priapus, 1985.
A Heartache of Grass. Calstock, Cornwall, Peterloo Poets, 1988.
Time Watching. London, Hearing Eye, 1995.
Bernini's Cat: New and Selected Poems. North Shields, Northumberland, Iron Press, 1999.

Other

Editor, *Poet Tree Centaur: A Walthamstow Group Anthology.* London, Oddments, 1973.

*

Gerda Mayer comments:

I have written square poems, pointed poems; my poems have been around.

*   *   *

Gerda Mayer's poems have that direct simplicity of approach that gives them an air of timelessness, something of the atmosphere of

folktales that address God or the universe as if it were as casual as speaking over the fence to a next-door neighbor. I do not know if this has anything to with Mayer's Czechoslovakian origins and memories, but I suspect that it has, and the fact is that her poems are like that: ''Save the world God, save your creatures save us for a rainy day.'' Even when she is taking on current subjects and concerns such as the environment, the same approach comes to the fore, and ''Consumer'' assumes a fabulosity:

> The Great Consumer
> crops the ground bare
> where are the flowers?
> where the sweet parsnips?

It is the same quality that enables her to invest the everyday with the surreal clarity of dreams:

> The waiter licks the tablecloth clean
> he licks clean the plates the glasses the
> flowers his tongue
> moves between the prongs of the forks

It is a superb talent that is Mayer's own, and it makes her a fine creator of poems for young people. Like all the best poems for young people, hers are not written down to them but are a natural extension of the rest of her work, with the same sharp humor and directness of approach:

> In childhood I took it for granted
> that Adam and Eve were Jews:
> though implied rather than stated
> it was Good News.

Mayer's collection *Monkey on the Analyst's Couch* confirms her place alongside the other poets of a sharp-eyed sparkling wit such as Stevie Smith. But at the back of Mayer's poetry is a depth of dark experience that makes her balanced and wry view of the world the more remarkable and worthy of our attention.

In *A Heartache of Grass* Mayer confronts the depth of dark experience more directly to produce a moving and chastening collection of poems. The book is dedicated to Muriel and Trevor Chadwick, to whom, she says, ''I owe my preservation.'' Behind the dedication is a story of physical and emotional survival, of heartrending experiences, and of the downright savagery of the Nazi regime. It is not that Mayer forgives, for who could forgive such mindless barbarity? It is not that she reconciles us to the horrors of the time; that would be asking the impossible. It is not that she lashes out in anger, which could be understood. What she does is to confront these outrages against common humanity with a dignity and intelligence that is the opposite of what her enemies and her race's enemies stood for. That she can do this with humor is an even greater measure of her spirit. In this she is a model to those of us who strive toward Christian values and to many of her own coreligionists. The poem quoted above ends,

> The swastikas of my childhood,
> chalked up on the wall,
> the rain and the years have washed away
> And the Bible survives them all.

In *A Heartache of Grass* it is as if Mayer has been working toward this confrontation all the time. In her poem ''Make Believe,'' addressed to her father Arnold Stein, who disappeared in the maelstrom that was Europe in 1940, she triumphantly and movingly succeeds:

> That is why at sixty
> when some publisher asks me
> for biographical details,
> I still carefully give
> the year of my birth,
> the name of my hometown:
> GERDA MAYER born '27, in Karlsbad,
> Czechoslovakia . . . write to me, father.

A Heartache of Grass is a book to be read as a testament to the dignity of the human spirit and as a lesson in the use of poetry.

Eminently readable and deceptively simple, Mayer's poetry is penetrating stuff. It should be read with care, as readers can suddenly find themselves falling unexpectedly into great wells of meaning and emotion.

—John Cotton

MAYNE, Seymour

Nationality: Canadian. **Born:** Montreal, Quebec, 18 May 1944. **Education:** McGill University, Montreal (Chester Macnaghten Prize, 1962), B.A. (honors) 1965; University of British Columbia, Vancouver, M.A. 1966, Ph.D. 1972. **Career:** Lecturer, Jewish Institute, Montreal, 1964, and University of British Columbia, 1972. Lecturer, 1972, assistant professor 1973–78, associate professor, 1978–85, and since 1985 professor of English, University of Ottawa. Visiting professor, Hebrew University of Jerusalem, 1979–80, 1983–84, and Concordia University, Montreal, 1982–83; writer-in-residence, Hebrew University, Jerusalem, winter 1987–88; visiting professor, University of La Laguna, Spain, spring 1993. Co-editor, *Cataract,* Montreal, 1961–62; poetry editor, *Forge,* Montreal, 1961–62; editor, *The Page,* 1962–63, and *Catapult,* Montreal, 1964; managing editor, Very Stone House, Vancouver, 1966–69; poetry editor, *Ingluvin,* 1970–71, and managing editor, Ingluvin Publications, 1970–73, Montreal; editor, Mosaic Press, Oakville, Ontario, 1974–82, *Jewish Dialog,* Toronto, 1974–81, and *Stoney Monday,* Ottawa, 1978. Contributing editor, 1982–90, and poetry editor, 1990–95, *Viewpoints,* Montreal; contributing editor, *Tel Aviv Review,* 1989–96; founder and consulting editor, *Bywords,* Ottawa, since 1990; founder and editorial board member, *Parchment,* London, Ontario, since 1992; consulting editor, *Poet Lore,* Bethesda, Maryland, since 1992; founder and consulting editor, *Graffito,* Ottawa, since 1994; and contributing editor, *Jerusalem Review,* Jerusalem and Tel Aviv, since 1997. **Awards:** Canada Council bursary, 1969, and grant, 1973, 1977, 1979, 1984; Ontario Arts Council grant, 1974, 1976, 1983, 1985, 1987, 1992, 1994; Segal prize, 1974; York Poetry Workshop award, 1975; American Literary Translators Association Poetry Translation award, 1990; Jewish Book Committee prize, 1994; Louis L. Lockshin memorial award, 1997. **Address:** Department of English, University of Ottawa, Ottawa K1N 6N5, Canada.

PUBLICATIONS

Poetry

That Monocycle the Moon. Montreal, Catapult, 1964.
Tiptoeing on the Mount. Montreal, McGill, 1965; revised edition, Montreal, Catapult, 1965.
From the Portals of Mouseholes. Vancouver, Very Stone House, 1966.
I Am Still the Boy. Vancouver, Western Press, 1967.
Ticklish Ticlicorice. Vancouver, Very Stone House, 1969.
The Gigolo Teaspoon. Vancouver, Very Stone House, 1969.
Earseed. Vancouver, Very Stone House, 1969.
Anewd. Vancouver, Very Stone House, 1969.
Mutetations. Vancouver, Very Stone House, 1969.
Manimals (includes prose). Vancouver, Very Stone House, 1969.
Mouth. Kingston, Ontario, Quarry Press, 1970.
For Stems of Light. Vernon, British Columbia, Very Stone House, 1971; revised edition, Ottawa, Valley, 1974.
Face. Burnaby, British Columbia, Blackfish, 1971.
Name. Erin, Ontario, Press Porcépic, 1975; revised edition, Oakville, Ontario, Mosaic Press, 1976.
Diasporas. Oakville, Ontario, Mosaic Press, 1977.
Begging. Oakville, Ontario, Mosaic Press, 1977.
Racoon. Ottawa, Valley, 1979.
Abel and Cain. Jerusalem, Sifrei HaEmek, 1980.
The Impossible Promised Land: Poems New and Selected. Oakville, Ontario, Mosaic Press, 1981.
Seven Poems. Toronto, League of Canadian Poets, 1983.
Neighbour Praying. Jerusalem, Sifrei HaEmek, 1984.
Vanguard of Dreams: New and Selected Poems. Tel Aviv, Sifriat Poalim, 1984.
Crazy Leonithas. Ottawa, Valley, 1985.
Two Poems. Privately printed, 1985.
Children of Abel (includes prose). Oakville, Ontario, Mosaic Press, 1986.
Diversions. Ottawa, Noovo Masheen Press, 1987.
Down Here. Ottawa, Tree, 1990.
Six Ottawa Poets, with others. Oakville, Ontario, Mosaic Press, 1990.
Simple Ceremony. Tel Aviv, Hakibbutz Hameuchad, 1990.
Killing Time. Oakville, Ontario, Mosaic Press, 1992.
Locust of Silence: New and Selected Poems. Tel Aviv, Iton 77, 1993.
The Song of Moses and Other Poems. Ottawa, Concertina, and London, Menard Press, 1995.
Five-O'Clock Shadows, with others. Toronto, Letters Bookshop, 1996.
Dragon Trees. Ottawa, Friday Circle Chapbook Series, 1997.
City of the Hidden. Tel Aviv, Gjanim, 1998.
Carbon Filter: Poems in Dedication. Toronto, Paris, and New York, Mosaic Press, 1999.

Other

Editor, with Patrick Lane, *Collected Poems of Red Lane.* Vancouver, Very Stone House, 1968.
Editor, with Victor Coleman, *Poetry of Canada.* Buffalo, Intrepid Press, 1969.
Editor, with Dorothy Livesay, *Forty Women Poets of Canada.* Montreal, Ingluvin, 1971.

Editor, *Engagements: The Prose of Irving Layton.* Toronto, McClelland and Stewart, 1972.

Editor, *Cutting the Keys.* Ottawa, University of Ottawa, 1975.

Editor, *Splices.* Ottawa, University of Ottawa, 1975.

Editor, *The A.M. Klein Symposium.* Ottawa, University of Ottawa, 1975.

Editor, *Choice Parts.* Ottawa, University of Ottawa, 1976.

Editor, *Irving Layton: The Poet and His Critics.* Toronto, McGraw Hill Ryerson, 1978.

Editor and Co-Translator, *Generations: Selected Poems,* by Rachel Korn. Oakville, Ontario, Mosaic Press, 1982.

Editor, *Essential Words: An Anthology of Jewish Canadian Poetry.* Ottawa, Oberon Press, 1985.

Editor and Co-Translator, *Crossing the River: Selected Poems,* by Moshe Dor. Oakville, Mosaic Press, 1989.

Co-editor, *At the Edge: Canadian Literature and Culture at Century's End.* Jerusalem, Magnes Press, 1995.

Co-editor, *Jerusalem: An Anthology of Jewish Canadian Poetry.* Montreal, Véhicule Press, 1996.

Co-editor, *A.M. Klein, Selected Poems.* Toronto, Buffalo, New York, and London, University of Toronto Press, 1997.

Co-editor, *A Rich Garland: Poems for A.M. Klein.* Montreal, Véhicule Press, 1999.

Translator, with Catherine Leach, *Genealogy of Instruments,* by Jerzy Harasymowicz. Oakville, Ontario, Mosaic Press, 1974.

Translator, *Burnt Pearls: Ghetto Poems of Abraham Sutzkever.* Oakville, Ontario, Mosaic Press, 1982.

Translator, with Laya Firestone-Seghi and Howard Schwartz, *Jerusalem as She Is: New and Selected Poems,* by Schlomo Vinner. Kansas City, BkMk Press, 1991.

Translator, with Rivka Augenfeld, *Night Prayer and Other Poems* by Melech Ravitch. Oakville, Mosaic Press, 1993.

Translator, with Jaroslaw Sokol, *I Live on a Raft,* by Jerzy Harasymowicz. Ottawa, Concertina, 1994.

*

Manuscript Collections: National Archives of Canada, Ottawa; University of Ottawa; Canadiana Collection, Jewish Public Library, Montreal; Jewish National and University Library, Jerusalem.

Critical Studies: By Peter Stevens, in *Canadian Forum* (Toronto), March 1968; "Other Vancouverites" by A.W. Purdy, in *Canadian Literature 35* (Vancouver), winter 1968; "New Poetry of the East" by Tom Marshall, in *New: American and Canadian Poetry 15* (Trumansburg, New York), April-May 1971; by Greg Gatenby, in *English Quarterly* (Waterloo, Ontario), winter 1975–76; by Aviva Layton, in *Quill and Quire* (Toronto), December 1978; by Kenneth Sherman, in *Canadian Literature 80* (Vancouver), spring 1979; by Mervin Butovsky, in *Jewish Book Annual,* New York, Jewish Book Council, 1982; by Anita Norich, in *Shdemot 18* (Tel Aviv), 1982; by John Oughton, in *Books in Canada* (Toronto), March 1982; by Bert Almon, in *Choice* (Middletown, Connecticut), July-August 1982; by Michael Thorpe, in *Canadian Literature 95* (Vancouver), winter 1982; by Tony Cosier, in *Canadian Materials,* March 1986; by Marya Fiamengo, in *Canadian Literature 112* (Vancouver), spring 1987; by Harry Prest, in *University of Windsor Review* (Ontario), 20(1), fall-winter 1987; by Shloime Perel, in *Small Press Review* (Paradise,

California), November 1987; by Roslyn Lester and Adam G. Fuerstenberg, both in *Canadian Ethnic Studies* (Montreal), 21(1), 1989; by Aloma Halter, in *The Jerusalem Post Magazine* (Jerusalem), June 1990; by Michael Greenstein, in *Ariel: A Review of International English Literature* (Calgary), 23(2), April 1992; by Shmuel Shatal, in *Al Hamishmar* (Tel Aviv), June 1993, and *Hadoar* (New York), January 1994; by Y. Ben-David, in *Iton 77* (Tel Aviv), May-June 1993; by Adam G. Fuerstenberg, in *Journal of Canadian Poetry* (Ottawa), 9, 1994; "Seymour Mayne: A Modernist Bard" by Tibor Krausz, in *Canadian Jewish News,* 16 July 1998; "Citizen of Two Worlds" by Mark Elliott Shapiro, in *Ha'Aretz Magazine,* 13 November 1998.

Seymour Mayne comments:

What I have to say about poetry is written into the poems and titles of my books. I have learned from Hebrew liturgy and prayer and the early study of biblical poetry.

*   *   *

In "Seymour's Similies," a section of his book *Craft Slices* (1985), George Bowering caught in one line an essential characteristic of the life and work of Seymour Mayne: "The writer is pleading for the poetical." Bowering did not use the word "poet," but rather the word "writer." Behind that choice of words there may lurk the sense that, while Mayne writes respectable and responsible poems, he is not a natural, lyrical poet in the sense that Irving Layton or Leonard Cohen, two bards from Mayne's Montreal, are lyrical poets. Bowering also used the verb "pleading." One senses that there lurks behind many of the poems the figure of a man beseeching, sometimes hectoring, the reader to agree with him. Someone is trying very hard because the stakes are so high. Finally, there are Bowering's words "the poetical." In his writings Mayne yearns for an epiphany, for the advent of the poetical as an experience that is perhaps above and beyond the poem.

Mayne has indeed been very busy. He has edited several little magazines and founded two private presses, Very Stone House and Ingluvin Press, and he helped as well to establish Mosaic Press— Valley Editions. He is a recognized commentator on the work of A.M. Klein and Irving Layton, he has taken an active part in drawing attention to Jewish writing in Canada, and he has translated the writings of Jewish writers from eastern and central Europe.

Mayne's principal publication is *Mouth,* a full—length collection of miscellaneous poems, some of which chart the relationship of various bodily orifices and, in a Freudian fashion, find a link between or among them. He writes in "Fang of Light," "and make the mouth / one vibrating hoop / of his whole / orificial self." The mood and image are there, but the language, especially the diction, is mixed and not always specific or emotional.

Contradictory themes emerge in Mayne's poetry, and these include human desire as against bodily guilt and human transcendence as against whimsical reasonableness or ironic insight. Perhaps his poetry will pass through a religious or spiritual reconciliation of these opposites. The necessary drive is there, for the poet writes in "You Don't Scream,"

Tear yourself away.
Bleed, if you must.

A fever will rise in your eyes
and burn like a need.

—John Robert Colombo

McAULEY, James J(ohn)

Nationality: Irish. **Born:** Dublin, 8 January 1936. **Education:** Clongowes Wood College, 1948–53; University College, Dublin, 1960–62, B.A. 1962; University of Arkansas, Fayetteville, 1966–68, M.F.A. 1971. **Family:** Married 1) Joan McNally in 1958 (divorced 1968), three children; 2) Almut R. Nierentz in 1968, two children; 3) Deirdre O'Sullivan in 1982, one son. **Career:** Journalist, Electricity Supply Board, Dublin, 1954–66; lecturer, Municipal Gallery of Modern Art, Dublin, 1965–66; graduate assistant, University of Arkansas, 1966–68; assistant professor and director of the creative writing program, Lycoming College, Williamsport, Pennsylvania, 1968–70. Assistant professor, 1970–73, associate professor, 1973–78, director of the creative writing program, 1972–76, 1978–80, 1984–86, 1990–92, and professor of English, 1978–98, Eastern Washington University, Cheney. Since 1978 director, Summer Writing Workshop, Dublin, Ireland. Art critic, *Kilkenny Magazine,* Dublin, 1960–66; associate editor, *Poetry Ireland,* Dublin, 1962–66; arts consultant, *Hibernia National Review,* Dublin, 1964–66; book reviewer, *Irish Times,* Dublin, 1964–66; reporter, *North West Arkansas Times,* Fayetteville, 1967. Since 1978 editor, Dolmen Press, Dublin. Since 1993 director, Eastern Washington University Press. **Awards:** National Endowment for the Arts grant, 1972. **Address:** Department of English, Eastern Washington State University, Cheney, Washington, 99004, U.S.A.

PUBLICATIONS

Poetry

Observations. Blackrock, Ireland, Mount Salus Press, 1960.
A New Address. Dublin, Dolmen Press, London, Oxford University Press, and Chester Springs, Pennsylvania, Dufour, 1965.
Draft Balance Sheet: Poems 1963–1969. Dublin, Dolmen Press, London, Oxford University Press, and Chester Springs, Pennsylvania, Dufour, 1970.
Home and Away. Privately printed, 1974.
After the Blizzard. Columbia, University of Missouri Press, 1975.
The Exile's Recurring Nightmare. San Francisco, Aisling Press, 1975.
Recital: Poems 1975–1980. Portlaoise, County Laoighis, Dolmen Press, 1982.
The Exile's Book of Hours. Lewiston, Idaho, Confluence Press, 1982.
Coming and Going: New and Selected Poems 1968–1988. Fayetteville, University of Arkansas Press, 1989.

Play

The Revolution (produced Dublin, 1966).

*

Critical Studies: Review in *Hibernia* (Dublin), 1970; *Choice* edited by Michael Hartnett and Desmond Egan, Dublin, Goldsmith Press, 1970, revised edition, 1979.

James J. McAuley comments:

My first book, *Observations,* consists of sixteen confessional lyrics, very young poems, imitative, private. *A New Address* is the offspring of my two-year love affair with *Roget's Thesaurus:* poems resulting from my preoccupation with words, their sounds and associations. *Draft Balance Sheet* resulted from my two-year study of poetry and poetics under James Whitehead at Arkansas. *After the Blizzard* is a collection of love poems, satires, narratives, and monologues. *The Revolution* is a satire on Easter 1916 and its end result, the modern Irish state. *Recital* is a collection of varied work over five years. *The Exile's Book of Hours* follows the pattern of the medieval prayer books.

(1995) *Coming and Going* attempts a reprieve of my preoccupations with language and technique over twenty years and of my obsession with revision. It is not always very helpful for authors to comment on the subjects of their poems, but a new and selected volume tends to reveal, even to the poet, a recurrent pattern to do with the tension between the life of the spirit and life in the world.

* * *

Although James J. McAuley has lived as long in the United States as in his native Ireland, there is about his poetry, despite notable forays into American politics, popular culture, and vernacular, a consistent and recognizably Irish timbre. The basso continuo of his poetry, to use another musical term (for McAuley himself is exultantly appreciative of Brahms, Handel, and Dvořák), sounds a speculative, scholastic tone appropriate to one who, like that most famous of Irish schoolboys, attended Clongowes Wood. In *Coming and Going: New and Selected Poems 1968–1988,* for example, McAuley writes a number of *aor*s, poems that are derived from an old Gaelic form for lampoon, satire, or personal attack. The invective expressed in ''Against the Ingrate, Who Abused Our Hospitality'' unmasks the all-too-familiar unwelcome guest who masquerades as a lost soul:

Now you lean over suicide's precipice
Till a few murmurs reach you: *Ah, don't*
This you take for applause.

Now the Wronged Artist—what an act!
What a go-boy you are—what a chancer!
Every favor you accept as your due;
You judged us all in the fixed
Lens of your own condition,
Immured in trickery, neck-deep
In bad luck and cosmic sorrow.

The demystifying attitude is a consistent feature of McAuley's poetry, one familiar to readers of Irish literature, who can detect similar tones of sly appraisal, comic debunking, or cautious suspicion in writers from Joyce to Trevor. McAuley is obviously conscious of the sense of remove that imprints his poetry. He often writes of himself as the exile and has two collections (*The Exile's Recurring Nightmare* and *The Exile's Book of Hours*) that chronicle a prevailing sense of dispossession. At times in McAuley's poetry the object of evaluation is reversed so that what is debunked are the poet's own initial desires. In "Examination," for example, the conventional scenario of the lust-ridden professor and the pliant student is comically interrupted by the sardonic realization that for the straining young woman "this easy test / on Medea brings you grief. / With all these treasures blessed, / You still will make an F."

In many respects McAuley's chief skill is to depict a scene that is commonplace enough but then to use the course of the poem to darken incrementally, and often imperceptibly, the original. In "Love & Death in the Flowershop" the grinning plaster elf is transformed into a menacing death god as the poem turns from an erotic, Renaissance romp of love among the seeds into an inverted myth of rape, in which, at the denouement,

> I'll tackle her in the azaleas, hey nonny no.
> I'll plant, she'll scream, I'll dig, she'll squirm, I'll sow;
> & just then the Elf in his quaint nightcap will arrive
> To turn me into a climbing vine, whose leaves
> Are evergreen, but darken when I grieve.

Both "Examination" and "Love & Death in the Flowershop" are from McAuley's 1975 publication *After the Blizzard,* which won for the poet the Washington Governor's award and is perhaps the strongest collection of his poetry. Part of what is most impressive about the collection is McAuley's skillful and revitalizing use of traditional forms, particularly the sonnet, terza rima, monologue, and rondel. Many of the finest poems in the collection are not satiric *aors* but rather contribute in registers of different tones to the sense that McAuley is always writing against something.

In the opening and closing poems of the collection, as well as in "After the Blizzard," McAuley writes around the unnameable: the forces of momentary disintegration, of frightening disorientation, and of the fearsome, hidden beasts that menace. In the collection's first poem, "Oh, Bad: or, Morning Song," rituals of careless kindness guard against the daily futilities that themselves threaten to become habitual. In "After the Blizzard" the insomniac's dismay is similarly alleviated through the child's sleeping breath and a remembered half line of poetry. In the collection's last poem, "The Path," the narrative describes an unidentified beast whose "black form on the long ridge" becomes a snarling, leaping attack. The journey of the tracking party that sets out but does not find the beast becomes a metaphysical lesson on what will "always be there" and cannot be lived without. McAuley's poems are always eloquently vigilant of the "dark beyond our lights."

—Jeanne Colleran

McCAFFERY, Steve

Nationality: Canadian. **Born:** Sheffield, England, 24 January 1947. **Education:** Hull University, England, 1965–68, B.A. (honors) 1968; York University, Toronto, 1968–69, M.A. 1969; State University of New York, Buffalo, 1997–98, Ph.D. 1998. **Family:** Married 1) Margaret McCaffery in 1968 (divorced 1983); 2) Karen MacCormack in 1998. **Career:** Lecturer, University of California, San Diego, 1989; lecturer in English, Queen's University, Kingston, Ontario, 1993–95, and California Institute of the Arts, Valencia, 1997. Since 1998 assistant professor in English, York University, Toronto. **Address:** 1086 Bathurst Street, 2nd Floor, Toronto, Ontario M5R 3G9, Canada.

PUBLICATIONS

Poetry

Dr. Sadhu's Muffins. Victoria, Press Porcépic, 1974.
'Ow's Waif. Toronto, Coach House Press, 1975.
Intimate Distortions. Erin, Ontario, Porcupine's Quill, 1978.
Knowledge Never Knew. Montreal, n.p., 1983.
Evoba. Toronto, Coach House Press, 1987.
The Black Debt. London, Ontario, Nightwood Editions, 1989.
Theory of Sediment. Vancouver, Talonbooks, 1991.
The Cheat of Words. Toronto, ECW Press, 1996.

Novel

Panopticon. Toronto, blewointment press, 1984.

Other

North of Intention. New York, Root Books, 1986.
Rational Geomancy, with bpNichol. Vancouver, Talonbooks, 1992.
Imagining Language, with Jed Rasula. Cambridge, Massachusetts, MIT Press, 1998.
Prior to Meaning: The Protosemantic and Poetics. Evanston, Illinois, Northwestern University Press, 2000.

Editor, with bpNichol, *The Story So Four.* Toronto, Coach House Press, 1976.

*

Manuscript Collections: Getty Museum, Malibu, California; Simon Fraser University, Burnaby, British Columbia.

Critical Studies: In *Textual Politics and the Language Poets* by George Hartley, Bloomington, Indiana University Press, 1989; in *The New Poetics in Canada and Quebec: From Concretism to Post-Modern* by Caroline Bayard, Toronto, University of Toronto Press, 1989; in *Poetic License,* Evanston, Illinois, Northwestern University Press, 1990, and *Radical Artifice,* Chicago, University of Chicago Press, 1991, both by Marjorie Perloff; in *Art Discourse/Discourse in Art* by Jessica Prinz, New Brunswick, New Jersey, Rutgers University Press, 1991; in *Touch Monkeys: Nonsense Strategies for Reading Twentieth Century Poetry,* Toronto, University of Toronto Press, 1994; *Steve McCaffery and His Work* by Clint Burnham, Toronto, ECW Press, 1995; *Repositionings: Readings of Contemporary Poetry, Photography, and Performance Art* by Frederick Garber, Pennsylvania State University Press, 1995; *A Primer for the Gradual Understanding of Steve McCaffery* (dissertation) by Kent Richard Arthur Lewis, University of Victoria, 1997; *ABC of Reading TRG: Steve McCaffery, bpNichol, and Critical Desire* by Peter Cyril Jaeger, Vancouver, Talonbooks, 1999.

*   *   *

For many years Steve McCaffery was principally known as one of the Four Horsemen, a group of experimental poets who performed their sound poems publicly. The group consisted of bpNichol, Rafael Barreto-Rivera, and Paul Dutton. Formed in Toronto in 1970, it disbanded with the death of bpNichol in 1989. McCaffery has also been active in the Toronto Research Group, which experiments with the innovative uses of language in a way somewhat similar to New York's language poets.

One problem with writing about McCaffery's work is that the texts, such as they are, are actually scores for rehearsed or improvised performances. Any meanings that may be gleaned from them are necessarily secondary in importance to the pure sounds of the words or syllables, and the aesthetic achievement lies in—and rises from— the performance itself, not in the words of the script. There are features both contemporary and traditional (dadaists and objectivists are part of the tradition) in McCaffery's work. It is work, not writing.

In England Now That Spring (1979) is a collaboration with bpNichol that offers scripts of performances and collaborations presented in the United Kingdom. The reader can see that the audiences had good reason to be amused, for humor is part of the poets' approach. *Knowledge Never Knew* (1983) is a collection of aphorisms, what the author refers to as ''condensed ruins.'' Here are four of them:

to plan ahead is to punish yourself
to not plan ahead is to punish others

you can find many excuses for a poem
but only one reason for a word

never read
never write
always continue to learn

unthink the thinkable

Of these, perhaps the last could serve as McCaffery's motto. *Panopticon* (1984) divides the pages horizontally and vertically into columns and presents texts, both found and original, as channels: ''If men are silent, books will find a voice.''

The difficulty of writing about McCaffery's work is a problem that faces every commentator. In *Dictionary of the Avant-Gardes* (1993) the poet and critic Richard Kostelanetz devoted an appreciative entry to the work of the Four Horsemen. He identified three of its members, adding, ''and Steve McCaffery (1948), a London-born writer who deserves a separate entry here, if I could figure out how to summarize his difficult, perhaps excessively obscure work (and so refer curious readers to Marjorie Perloff's 1991 book *Radical Artifice*).''

—John Robert Colombo

McCARTHY, Thomas

Nationality: Irish. **Born:** Cappoquin, Waterford, 1954. **Education:** University College, Cork, B.A. 1975, higher diploma in education 1986. **Family:** Married Catherine Coakley in 1982; one daughter and one son. **Career:** Since 1978 librarian, Cork Corporation, Cork. Visiting professor, Macalester College, Minnesota, 1994–95. Editor, *Poetry Ireland Review,* 1984–85. **Awards:** Patrick Kavanagh award, 1977; Irish Arts Council bursary, 1978, 1983; International Writing Program fellow, State University of Iowa, 1978–79; Alice Hunt Bartlett prize, Poetry Society, 1981; annual literary award, American-Irish Foundation, 1984. **Address:** Cork City Libraries, Grand Parade, Cork, Ireland.

PUBLICATIONS

Poetry

The First Convention. Dublin, Dolmen, 1978.
The Sorrow Garden. London, Anvil, 1981.
The Non-Aligned Storyteller. London, Anvil, 1984.
Seven Winters in Paris. Dublin, Dedalus Press, 1989.
The Lost Province. London, Anvil Press Poetry, 1996.
Mr. Dineen's Careful Parade: New and Selected Poems. London, Anvil Press Poetry, 1999.

Novel

Without Power. Swords, Dublin, Poolbeg, 1991.
Asya and Christine. Swords, Dublin, Poolbeg Press, 1992.

Other

Gardens of Remembrance. Dublin, New Island Books, 1998.

*

Critical Study: ''''Orphaned Like Us': Memory in the Poetry of Thomas McCarthy'' by James Naiden, in *Eire-Ireland* (St. Paul, Minnesota), 26(2), summer 1991.

*   *   *

Thomas McCarthy's work can be seen as an exploration of politics, society, and the self in contemporary Ireland. For McCarthy reality is linked with the politics of the Fianna Fáil Party, formed by Eamon de Valera in the 1920s. McCarthy was born in the 1950s into the republic of Ireland only a few years after the final ties with the United Kingdom had been severed. Therefore, his heroes are not so much the heroes of revolutionary change as the men of a more recent past and a modern era. His heroes are the makers of Ireland such as de Valera.

The poems in *The First Convention* reflect a young man's concerns in present-day Ireland. The themes are stated in an idiom that reveals an interest in political identity, an identity the poet regards with a certain disenchantment but one that provides him with a sounding board for the diverse subjects of his work. The Irish past and its traditions, his background in a small provincial town, and the isolation of the creative mind are all reflected in the collection. It reveals a poet capable of writing in a thoughtful elegiac mode with a appraisal of the political colorations of Ireland in the 1950s.

In *Seven Winters in Paris* McCarthy writes tenderly about private affections and acutely about public figures and events. The title sequence is a series of brief poems reflecting on Ireland and Paris in the past and the present. This sequence evolves into another dealing with the joy and trouble of parenthood in a time of menace and bombs. Other poems are set in London and Cork, their starting points including library work, being in a hospital, railway stations, and family life. The moving and eloquent moments of the volume are best seen in quiet poems that are full of detail, such as ''The Gathering of Waves'':

> You are always heading for the ocean,
> Unhappy until you can eavesdrop on water
> And the waves' conversations.
> The sea must be an adequate listener
> Or an expansive, avuncular teller of tales.
> Happy with your feet in water,
> You are always calling to me at the shore,
> Telling me what the sea is,
> What a lover can't miss, what the ocean tells you.

McCarthy also writes with a political voice that is deeply rooted in his own country:

> There was no Thomas MacGreevy waiting
> With a stroke of orange in his morning-dress
> But undiplomatic Paris:
> Fireflies on the rosewood spinet.

Reality for McCarthy is linked with the internal workings of the Fianna Fáil Party. His work is as much an exploration of the constituency politics of the Dáil, a house of the Irish Parliament, as of idealism. He achieves his aims by applying a lyric impulse to a mundane world of disappointments and animosities. His characters are often party members and senior officials of the government or heroes of the past. In the sequence ''A Neutral State, 1944'' on de Valera, in *The Sorrow Garden,* he writes in a mood of regretful, measured, and mature evaluation:

> There would be the neutral yawning of the sea
> Above immediate memory; troubles in the black
> City of war would move across their night eye
> Like the wash of a periscope causing an ache
>
> Of fear. But they would look across the bow
> Beyond the wash of sorrow, over the war-sea
> To the naked lights of Ireland: (the soft glow
> Of De Valera's land, and her bog neutrality).

Other poems look at figures who combined politics and writing, such as Vladimir Nabokov, André Gide, and Arthur Koestler.

Though McCarthy's political themes dominate his poetry, he is also a love poet and an elegist. The title poem of *The Sorrow Garden* is an emotional poem for his late father:

> It is an image of irreversible loss,
> This hole in my father's grave that needs
> Continuous filling. Monthly now, my
> Uncle comes to shovel a heap of earth
> From the spare mound. Tear-filled, he
> Compensates the collapse of his brother's
> Frame. I arrive on my motor-bike to help
> But he will not share the weight of grief.

The Non-Aligned Storyteller is a volume that focuses mainly on the theme of postwar Ireland, its long Sunday afternoons and its population depleted by emigration.

The main influences on the poetry of the republic have been older poets such as Thomas Kinsella and Richard Murphy and, more distantly, Yeats. An exception to the divisions between the poets of Northern Ireland and of the republic of Ireland has been the cross-border work of John Montague, who has powered the work of many young poets from the republic. There are other poets of both Northern Ireland and of the republic who have had an influence on McCarthy— Derek Mahon, Anthony Cronin, Desmond O'Grady, and Paul Durcan. McCarthy also celebrates a number of figures in his poems: Francis Stuart, Bashevis Singer, AE, and Parnell. He tends to side with men who were victims of convention yet were the protectors of it.

McCarthy is a poet with a strong social awareness of the humiliations suffered by his family in an Ireland marked by poverty and emigration. He is a voice for the emergent middle-class in a country with a long history of struggle for freedom.

—Renu Barrett

McCLURE, Michael (Thomas)

Nationality: American. **Born:** Marysville, Kansas, 20 October 1932. **Education:** University of Wichita, Kansas, 1951–53; University of Arizona, Tucson, 1953–54; San Francisco State University, B.A. 1955. **Family:** Married Joanna Kinnison in 1954 (divorced); one daughter. **Career:** Assistant professor, 1962–77, associate professor, 1977, and since 1978 professor, California College of Arts and Crafts, Oakland. Playwright-in-residence, American Conservatory Theatre, San Francisco, 1975; associate fellow, Pierson College, Yale University, New Haven, Connecticut, 1982. Editor, with James Harmon, *Ark II/Moby I,* San Francisco, 1957. **Awards:** National Endowment for the Arts grant, 1967, 1974; Guggenheim fellowship, 1971; Magic Theatre Alfred Jarry award, 1974; Rockefeller fellowship, for drama, 1975; Obie award, for drama, 1978; Pushcart prize for poetry, 1991; Lifetime Achievement award in poetry, National Poetry Association, 1993. **Agent:** Helen Merrill Ltd., 361 West 17th Street, New York, New York 10011. **Address:** c/o New Directions, 80 8ᵗʰ Avenue, New York, New York 10011–5126, U.S.A.

PUBLICATIONS

Poetry

Passage. Big Sur, California, Jonathan Williams, 1956.
Peyote Poem. San Francisco, Wallace Berman, 1958.
For Artaud. New York, Totem Press, 1959.
Hymns to St. Geryon and Other Poems. San Francisco, Auerhahn Press, 1959.
The New Book: A Book of Torture. New York, Grove Press, 1961.
Dark Brown. San Francisco, Auerhahn Press, 1961.
Two for Bruce Conner. San Francisco, Oyez, 1964.
Ghost Tantras. Privately printed, 1964.
Double Murder! Vahroooooooohr! Los Angeles, Wallace Berman, 1964.
Love Lion, Lioness. Privately printed, 1964.
13 Mad Sonnets. Milan, East 128, 1964.
Poisoned Wheat. Privately printed, 1965.
Unto Caesar. San Francisco, Dave Haselwood, 1965.

Mandalas. San Francisco, Dave Haselwood, 1965.

Dream Table. San Francisco, Dave Haselwood, 1966.

Love Lion Book. San Francisco, Four Seasons, 1966.

Hail Thee Who Play. Los Angeles, Black Sparrow Press, 1968; revised edition, Berkeley, California, Sand Dollar, 1974.

Muscled Apple Swift. Topanga, California, Love Press, 1968.

Plane Pomes. New York, Phoenix Book Shop, 1969.

Oh Christ God Love Cry of Love Stifled Furred Wall Smoking Burning. San Francisco, Auerhahn Press, 1969(?).

The Sermons of Jean Harlow and the Curses of Billy the Kid. San Francisco, Four Seasons, 1969.

The Surge. Columbus, Ohio, Frontier Press, 1969.

Hymns to St. Geryon, and Dark Brown. London, Cape Goliard Press, 1969; San Francisco, Grey Fox Press, 1980.

Lion Fight. New York, Pierrepont Press, 1969.

Star. New York, Grove Press, 1971.

99 Theses. Lawrence, Kansas, Tansy Press, 1972.

The Book of Joanna. Berkeley, California, Sand Dollar, 1973.

Transfiguration. Cambridge, Massachusetts, Pomegranate Press, 1973.

Rare Angel (writ with raven's blood). Los Angeles, Black Sparrow Press, 1974.

September Blackberries. New York, New Directions, 1974.

Solstice Blossom. Berkeley, California, Arif Press, 1974.

Fleas 189–195. New York, Aloes, 1974.

A Fist Full (1956–1957). Los Angeles, Black Sparrow Press, 1974.

On Organism. Canton, New York, Institute of Further Studies, 1974.

Jaguar Skies. New York, New Directions, 1975.

Man of Moderation. New York, Hallman, 1975.

Flea 100. New York, Hallman, 1975.

Antechamber. Berkeley, California, Poythress Press, 1977.

Antechamber and Other Poems. New York, New Directions, 1978.

Fragments of Perseus. New York, Jordan Davies, 1978.

Letters. New York, Jordan Davies, 1978.

The Book of Benjamin, with Wesley B. Tanner. Berkeley, California, Arif, 1982.

Fragments of Perseus (collection). New York, New Directions, 1983.

Fleas 180–186. Berkeley, California, Les Ferriss, 1985.

Selected Poems. New York, New Directions, 1986.

Rebel Lions. New York, New Directions, 1991.

Simple Eyes & Other Poems. New York, New Directions, 1994.

Three Poems. New York, Penguin, 1995.

Rain Mirror: New Poems. New York, New Directions, 1999.

Plays

!The Feast! (produced San Francisco, 1960). Included in *The Mammals,* 1972.

Pillow (produced New York, 1961). Included in *The Mammals,* 1972.

The Growl, in Four in Hand (produced Berkeley, California, 1970; produced separately New York, 1976). Published in *Evergreen Review* (New York), April-May 1964.

The Blossom; or, Billy the Kid (produced New York, 1964). Milwaukee, Great Lakes Books, 1967.

The Beard (produced San Francisco, 1965; New York, 1967; London, 1968). Privately printed, 1965; revised version, New York, Grove Press, 1967.

The Shell (produced San Francisco, 1970; London, 1975). London, Cape Goliard Press, 1968; in *Gargoyle Cartoons,* 1971.

The Cherub (produced Berkeley, California, 1969). Los Angeles, Black Sparrow Press, 1970.

The Charbroiled Chinchilla: The Pansy, The Meatball, Spider Rabbit (produced Berkeley, California, 1969). Included in *Gargoyle Cartoons,* 1971.

Little Odes, Poems, and a Play, The Raptors. Los Angeles, Black Sparrow Press, 1969.

The Brutal Brontosaurus: Spider Rabbit, The Meatball, The Shell, Apple Glove, The Authentic Radio Life of Bruce Conner and Snoutburbler (produced San Francisco, 1970; *The Meatball* and *Spider Rabbit* produced London, 1971, New York, 1976; *The Authentic Radio Life of Bruce Conner and Snoutburbler* produced London, 1975). Included in *Gargoyle Cartoons,* 1971.

Gargoyle Cartoons (includes *The Shell, The Pansy, The Meatball, The Bow, Spider Rabbit, Apple Glove, The Sail, The Dear, The Authentic Radio Life of Bruce Conner and Snoutburbler, The Feather, The Cherub*). New York, Delacorte Press, 1971.

The Pansy (produced London, 1972). Included in *Gargoyle Cartoons,* 1971.

Polymorphous Pirates: The Pussy, The Button, The Feather (produced Berkeley, California, 1972). *The Feather* included in *Gargoyle Cartoons,* 1971.

The Mammals (includes *The Blossom, !The Feast!, Pillow*). San Francisco, Cranium Press, 1972.

The Grabbing of the Fairy (produced Los Angeles, 1973). St. Paul, Truck Press, 1978.

The Pussy, The Button, and Chekhov's Grandmother; or, The Sugar Wolves (produced New York, 1973).

McClure on Toast (produced Los Angeles, 1973).

Gorf (produced San Francisco, 1974). New York, New Directions, 1976.

Music Peace (produced San Francisco, 1974).

The Derby (produced Los Angeles, 1974; revised version produced New York, 1981).

General Gorgeous (produced San Francisco, 1975; Edinburgh, 1976). New York, Dramatists Play Service, 1982.

Two Plays. Privately printed, 1975.

Sunny-Side Up (includes *The Pink Helmet* and *The Masked Choir*) (produced Los Angeles, 1976). *The Pink Helmet* included in *Two Plays,* 1975; *The Masked Choir* published in *Performing Arts Journal* (New York), August 1976.

Minnie Mouse and the Tap-Dancing Buddha (produced San Francisco, 1978). Included in *Two Plays,* 1975.

Two for the Tricentennial (included *The Pink Helmet* and *The Grabbing of the Fairy*) (produced San Francisco, 1976).

Range War (produced Tucson, 1976).

Goethe: Ein Fragment (produced San Francisco, 1977). Published in *West Coast Plays 2* (Berkeley, California), Spring 1978.

Josephine the Mouse Singer, adaptation of a story by Kafka (produced New York, 1978). New York, New Directions, 1980.

The Red Snake (produced San Francisco, 1979).

The Mirror (produced Los Angeles, 1979).

Coyote in Chains (produced San Francisco, 1980).

The Velvet Edge. Privately printed, 1982(?).

The Beard, and VKTMS: Two Plays. New York, Grove Press, 1985.

Television Play: *The Maze* (documentary), 1967.

Novels

The Mad Cub. New York, Bantam, 1970.

The Adept. New York, Delacorte Press, 1971.

Other

Meat Science Essays. San Francisco, City Lights, 1963; revised edition, San Francisco, Dave Haselwood, 1967.

Freewheelin' Frank, Secretary of the Angels, as Told to Michael McClure by Frank Reynolds. New York, Grove Press, 1967; London, New English Library, 1974.

Scratching the Beat Surface. Berkeley, California, North Point Press, 1982.

Specks (essays). Vancouver, Talonbooks, 1985.

Lighting the Corners: On Art, Nature, and the Visionary: Essays and Interviews. Albuquerque, New Mexico, University of New Mexico, 1993.

Acorn Alone: A Story for Children. Virginia Beach, Virginia, A.R.E. Press, 1994.

Huge Dreams: San Francisco and Beat Poems. New York, Penguin, 1999.

Touching the Edge: Dharma Devotions from the Hummingbird Sangha. Boston, Shambhala, 1999.

Editor, with David Meltzer and Lawrence Ferlinghetti, *Journal for the Protection of All Beings 1 and 3.* San Francisco, City Lights, 2 vols., 1961–69.

*

Bibliography: *A Catalogue of Works by Michael McClure 1956–1965* by Marshall Clements, New York, Phoenix Book Shop, 1965.

Manuscript Collections: Simon Fraser University, Burnaby, British Columbia; University of California, Berkeley.

Critical Studies: ''This Is Geryon,'' in *Times Literary Supplement* (London), 25 March 1965; interview in *San Francisco Poets* edited by David Meltzer, New York, Ballantine, 1971, revised edition, as *Golden Gate,* San Francisco, Wingbow Press, 1976; ''Michael McClure Symposium'' in *Margins 18* (Milwaukee), March 1975; *Two Playwrights of the San Francisco Renaissance: Lawrence Ferlinghetti and Michael McClure* (dissertation) by Thomas Whiteford Boeker, n.p., 1979; ''Post Modernist Poetics: Four Views'' by Kevin Power, in *Revista Canaria de Estudios Ingleses* (Tenerife, Spain), 2, March 1981; interview with Mitchell Smith, in *Kerouac Connection,* 26, spring 1994.

Theatrical Activities: Actor: Films—*Beyond the Law,* 1968; *Maidstone,* 1971.

Michael McClure comments:

Poetry is a muscular principle, an athletic song or whisper of fleshly thought. We can be as serious as blue black gloom or bright as a buttercup in the dawn. The spirit of poetry is loops we send out from the expanding helix of our lives. With poetry we can meet an old perception on a mountaintop or in a subway or view a new perception loping in the distance like a wolf or glimmering like an opal in the twilight.

*   *   *

In *A Catalogue of Works by Michael McClure 1956–1965* Marshall Clements lists translations into French, German, Spanish, and Italian. More than three decades ago people recognized Michael McClure's high seriousness. His purpose was not to *épater le bourgeois* but rather to present, without any moralizing, *épatement* itself as a process. Postcards, pictures, plays, and poems break through ''the preconception of poem and stanzas,'' as in the 1959 picture of a horse's head and above it a horse with the words ''Fuck Death.'' In ''Double Murder! VAHROOOOM!'' Jack Ruby shoots Lee Harvey Oswald. At the zoo McClure recorded the lion's roar and his own ''beast language'' from *Ghost Tantras.* His play *The Beard* has actors take roles about real people, Jean Harlow and Billy the Kid, who had become actors in roles in history.

In one play, *The Cherub,* a bed is an actor and snores, wakes up, speaks, and has a missile countdown while Jesus and Camus ''are at it again upstairs.'' The explosive exuberance leads to a sweetly innocent and still moving conclusion: a naked man and a naked woman repeat ''good morning'' to each other. A movie of clouds becomes a cluster of grapes. They repeat ''yes'' to each other. The light flares up and dies out and leaves a cluster of grapes.

The force of the play comes from the interwoven ''topologies of reality,'' as McClure phrases it in a preface to his *Rare Angel.* The meanings of ''topology'' cluster around *topos* (place) and *logos* (word). A word finds place, ''gives birth to itself from the substrate by writing out muscular and body sensations which are the source of thought.'' His sense of the body-cave, cave-body, the body with open pores, open to the world, and an open system appears in most of his works and in particular in *Meat Science Essays.* He involves the reader with typographical disjunctions and a vertical tracking down the page. The typography sometimes seems to shape the voice:

> LET'S STOP! LET'S STOP
> THIS ENDLESS MURDER BY POLITICS!
> LET
> US
> DO WHAT
> WE CAN TO STOP
> so very much useless pain!

A highly varied length of line ventilates an otherwise strict sestina (*Antechamber*). Capitals sometimes seem to draw attention to a *discordia concors:*

> LITTLE ODE
>
> *for Joanna*
>
> AND DEATH SHALL HAVE NO TERROR WHEN LOVE
> MAY BALANCE THEE, MADONNA, IN MY HEART.
> I shall die with the wrinkled lines
> around thy eyes upon my shield
> of consciousness,
> I confess
> I worship thee
> and all material things.
>
> Rose petals falling!
>
> The secret loves of wolves!

Deer mice trembling in the snow!

Turquoise set in worn and darkended silver!

This poem, written for Joanna McClure, herself a poet, seems to echo McClure's early sonnets and villanelles in tone and affinity, but the motion remains his own, as in well-established volumes like *September Blackberries* or *Jaguar Skies.* All of his poems move. The term "Logos" also implies order and sequence. E-motion is from *emovere*. The motion of perception is at least as important as the particulars of what is perceived.

One reads on page 9 in McClure's *The Daily Vision*, "COMING / BACK / THROUGH / THE / SKY"; on page 18, "COMING / BACK / THROUGH / THE / SKY: / COMING / BACK / WITH / OBSESSIONS; / COMING BACK THROUGH THE SKY"; on page 23, "COMING / BACK / THROUGH / THE / SKY / TO THE SUBSTRATE"; on page 30, "THE HOP OF A SILVERFISH / / THE AWKWARD HOP OF A SILVERFISH / is perfect!"; on page 31, "COMING / BACK / THROUGH / THE / SKY, / THE / AWKWARD / HOP / OF / A / SILVERFISH / IS / PERFECT." The disparate elements meet, or separate, in the kinetics of perception. The typography and the words create a "flicker of interacting," the effects of will and of luck. The visual image of the conclusion of "The Cherub," a cluster of grapes, has an analogous statement in *The Daily Vision:* "WE ARE GRAPES. We are aggregates in bunches. BLACK GRAPES."

In *Scratching the Beat Surface,* a book of poems and prose or, perhaps more accurately, a work in which the words shift in emphasis from the presentational to the discursive, McClure sets forth his broadly expansive affiliations: Creeley and Olson, with openings to Asian sensitivities and also to science, a range best epitomized by a broadside from Slug Press that begins in bold black type with

IT IS THE INTERPENETRATION

and concludes with bold type followed by a comment in lowercase:

THAT'S WHAT
sense is

—William Sylvester

McDONALD, Ian (A.)

Nationality: Guyanese. **Born:** St. Augustine, Trinidad, 18 April 1933. Immigrated to Guyana in 1955. **Education:** Queen's Royal College, Trinidad, 1942–51; Cambridge University, 1951–55, B.A. (honors) in history, M.A. **Family:** Married Mary Angela Callender in 1984; three sons. **Career:** Chair, Demerara Publishers, Georgetown, 1988–94. Director of marketing and administration, 1976–99, and since 2000 chief executive officer, Sugar Association of the Caribbean. Since 1972 chair, Demerara Sugar Terminals, Georgetown; since 1981 director, Theatre Company of Guyana, Georgetown; joint editor, with A.J. Seymour, 1984–89, and since 1989 editor, *Kyk-over-Al* magazine. Director, Hand-in-Hand Fire and Life Insurance Company Ltd. Captain, West Indies Davis Cup Tennis Team, 1960s. **Awards:** Royal Society of Literature prize, for novel, 1969; Guyana National award, 1987. Fellow, Royal Society of Literature, 1970;

Guyana prize for literature (poetry), 1992, for *Essequibo.* D.Litt.: University of the West Indies, 1997. **Address:** c/o Sugar Association of the Caribbean, Demerara Sugar Terminal, River View Ruimveldt, Georgetown, Guyana.

PUBLICATIONS

Poetry

Selected Poems. Georgetown, Labour Advocate, 1983.
Mercy Ward. Calstock, Cornwall, Peterloo, 1988.
Essequibo. Calstock, Cornwall, Peterloo, 1992.
Jaffo the Calypsonian. Leeds, Peepal Tree, 1994.

Plays

The Tramping Man (produced Georgetown, 1969). Included in *A Time and a Season,* edited by Errol Hill, Kingston, Jamaica, University of the West Indies, 1976.

Television Play: *The Hummingbird Tree,* adaptation of his own novel, 1992.

Novel

The Humming-Bird Tree. London, Heinemann, 1969.

Other

Editor, *AJS at 70: A Celebration on His 70th Birthday of the Life, Work, and Art of A.J. Seymour.* Georgetown, Autoprint, 1984.
Editor, with Stewart Brown, *Heinemann Book of Caribbean Poetry.* London, Heinemann, 1992.
Editor, with others, *They Came in Ships.* Leeds, Peepal Tree, 1998.

*

Bibliography: In *Bibliography of Literature from Guyana* by Robert E. McDowell, Arlington, Texas, Sable, 1975.

Ian McDonald comments:

Formal poetry is not just a minority taste; it is a miniminority indulgence in Caribbean society. There is no conception of what Pushkin was talking about when he wrote, "That hour is blessed when we meet a poet . . . he stands on a basis of equality with the powerful of the earth and the people bow down before him."

We inherited a society in which poetry was viewed with noncomprehension if not with scorn. It was the most discredited of the arts. As Arnold Bennett said, in English-speaking countries the word "poetry" disperses a crowd quicker than a fire hose. The breach between formal poetry and ordinary people widened until the divorce came to be accepted as a sort of law of nature.

And yet there can never be any doubt about the deep and abiding importance of poetry. Language is the most potent force in any society, and poetry is the purest form of language. When language in this purest form is neglected, soon language itself will be corrupted and perverted. When societies descend into such a condition, true poets find it hard to exist and, in despair, go into exile. Soon a vicious circle of corrupted society and poetry in exile begins to spin. Such a phenomenon is well known. What is less measurable is the incidence of internal exile arising from a cultural indifference to native creativity and contempt specifically for the art of writing poetry.

In this context of poetry endangered a way to get through to the ordinary person had to be discovered or rediscovered. Verse in ''nation language,'' folk ballad, calypso, dub poetry, performance poems have accordingly emerged, and thank God for them all and their growing influence.

But as a ''formal'' poet myself I am uneasy in this realm of newly popular poetry. I desperately want Caribbean poets to close the gap between ordinary people and poetry. I hate the idea of poets in their ivory towers. I loathe the thought that nobody should learn and love poetry except poets themselves and teachers of poetry. But I am very doubtful that I myself can ever join the performance poetry bandwagon. So I hope my own poetry can somehow fit in somewhere between the ''formal, unread'' and the ''fashionable, dub.''

I want poetry to gain influence by telling truth, giving pleasure, and creating fascination. Like all art, poetry must be inextricably bound up with giving pleasure and stimulating the ordinary imagination. If a poet loses his pleasure-seeking audience, he has lost the audience most worth having. I believe that profoundly. I cannot get out of my mind some lines written by Osip Mandelstam, that great poet who lived and died in difficult times:

> The people need poetry that will be their own secret To
>   keep them awake forever And bathe them in the bright-
>   haired wave Of its breathing.

*   *   *

Ian McDonald's creative work, which began while he was at Cambridge University in the 1950s, may be divided into his Trinidad phase (including *Selected Poems* and his novel, *The Humming-Bird Tree*) and his Guyana phase (he has worked there since leaving Cambridge in 1955). From the outset McDonald's poetry has revealed a remarkable consistency of style, a long-line conversational lyric, carrying along with it and expressing a sensibility of Matisse-like color and elegance of decor, under which there has always resided an intense appreciation for the outsider, the underperson, the psychological exile, and, in his second major book of poems, *Mercy Ward,* a compassionate concern for those who suffer in hospitals, hospices, and asylums. In 1984 he became joint editor—along with its founder, A.J. Seymour—of the literary periodical *Kyk-over-Al,* becoming the sole editor after Seymour's death in 1989.

Selected Poems contains most of the early classics—''Jaffo, the Calypsonian,'' ''Yusman Ali, the Charcoal Seller,'' ''Pineapple Woman,'' ''Pelting Bees,'' ''The Stick Fighters,'' and ''Indian Love Statement'':

> Tassim loves her like an idiot, makes himself a saga boy,
> Puts green cedar leaves to scent his clothes, sweetens his
>   hair with bay rum.
> He makes sweet eyes at her all day and praises her
>   green eyes.
> He does nothing practical and his only gift is sentiment.
> I on the other hand am determined to make less brittle
>   love to her.

> Though I am as I will be overall gentle I bring her not a
>   little pride and confidence.
> Also I bring her faults: she knows the smell of my sweaty
>   armpits if I work hard
> I do not hide it: cane-field sweat is good water.
> Nor do I hide some roughness in my manners, being
>   unused to Tassim and his like.
> Yet I bring her also gifts and assurances of love, a basket
>   of oranges,
> A chaplet made of jumby beads, boxes of mother-of-pearl,
> A parasol of rough blue cotton stemmed and ribbed
>   with bamboo,
> Beads, candied shaddocks, rings, everything I bring her in
>   shrewd love.

But there are also relatively new poems, such as ''Mais of Jamaica,'' ''Son Asleep, Aged Six Months,'' ''Colour Poem,'' ''My Father's Prayer Book, Page 44,'' and a blind, hushed, inspired poem of great courtesy and love for Seymour, one of the great-grandfathers of Caribbean literature:

> One night your poems were in my hands
> And sudden as blindness in the room
> The lamplight in the dark went out:
> I was sightless in the poem's heart.
> I sat there in the deepening night,
> A half-moon slowly etched the trees,
> The sea-wind slowly made its quiet sound.
> I held your poems on my knee
> And in my mind their cadence grew.
> Gradually I heard them like waves that run
> Driven by the wind against a far-off shore:
> That restless whisper from when the world began,
> That eternal sound that men have hungered for.

When Seymour died in December 1989, McDonald was with him almost to the end, and he concluded a memorial he wrote for him with these words (I recall part of it here since it is as much a poem as McDonald or any of us has ever written):

> The last time I visited there was no recognition. I sat by his bed and called his name but there was nothing. He slept, his breathing laboured, his head wet with perspiration, an old, good man going to his death. I sat by him and held his hand for a long time. Sometimes there was life in his fingers and I looked to see if he would wake but he did not wake. I sat holding his hand with my memories of him until it was dark and I felt it was time to go. At first he had been like a father to me and later I had been like a son to him. I closed my eyes and dreamed and said a confused prayer . . . Now, half-dreaming, hand in hand, beside the old man who could not any longer speak his clear and shining lines, I sensed the greatness of his spirit come near enough to touch and move me one last time as the greater silence gathered like welcoming.

Mercy Ward, which appeared a year before this affecting song of praise, is one of the most moving documents produced by any writer of the Caribbean. Here are some fifty men and women facing death with fear, patience, panache, ache, and often courage—''The few deep breaths she takes / Seem precious things to do.'' The Essequibo River, sky, and mango trees and breathless memories run by outside their brilliant, ordinary, ended/ending lives:

> The stroke stuns him into just a stare:
> Mouth screams without a scream being there.
> Neck muscles tighten, throat-apple thrums.
> Plucks with fingers at his lips and tongue
> To rip out songs or words or anything,
> He strains and sweats to say a single word.
> Paradise would be to let out half a cry . . .

More softly now,

> On the brown, iron bedside table
> She's dropped an old fan delicate as fern.
> Ivory stems pinned with silver pins:
> Torn yellow silk opening in between
> Shows red plums on a tree with birds.
> Lace gone black tatters on the spray of bone.
> Sweetheart's gift now nearly all used up,
> It lies abandoned, heirloom at its end.
> Framed beyond all further composition
> She'll never pick it up again it seems.
> Glossy grape-skin once, now so raisin-withered,
> Blue-veined, liver-freckled hand
> Plucks weakly at the congealed sheet.

> A nurse in passing senses what is wanted:
> An ancient grace is reasserted.
> How honourable are simple, well-learned ways!
> A practised gesture with a lovely thing
> At once transforms the gesturer:
> What gathered round this death's defeated,
> What is brutal falls away,
> Momentarily all's not lost.
> Life's pattern knits up anew:
> What's to come has been before,
> What has gone may re-appear.
> All's not settled, all's unsure:
> The picture can be drawn again.
> If only briefly, she fans the breathless air.

—Edward Kamau Brathwaite

McFADDEN, David

Nationality: Canadian. **Born:** Hamilton, Ontario, 11 October 1940. **Family:** Married Joan Pearce in 1963 (divorced 1979); two daughters. **Career:** Night proofreader, 1962–70, and reporter, 1970–76, Hamilton *Spectator;* freelance journalist and editor, 1976–79; writer-in-residence, Simon Fraser University, Burnaby, British Columbia, 1978; instructor in writing, David Thompson University Centre, Nelson, British Columbia, 1979–82; taught creative writing, Victoria Park and Don Mills schools, Toronto, 1982–83; writer-in-residence, University of Western Ontario, London, 1983–84, Metropolitan Toronto Public Library, 1985–86, and Hamilton Public Library,

1987–88. Founding editor, *Mountain Magazine,* Hamilton, 1960–63, and *Writing Magazine,* Nelson, British Columbia, 1979–82; member of editorial board, *Swift Current,* 1983–84; contributing editor, *Quill and Quire,* Toronto, 1983–84. **Awards:** Canada Council bursary, 1968, and fellowship, 1976, 1982; Mickey award, 1975; Nebula award, 1977; Canadian Broadcasting Corporation prize, 1979; National Magazine award, 1981, 1982. **Address:** David Thompson University Center, Nelson, British Columbia V1L 3C7, Canada.

PUBLICATIONS

Poetry

The Poem Poem. Toronto, Weed/Flower Press, 1967.
The Saladmaker: A Humility Cycle. Montreal, Imago, 1968; revised edition, Montreal, Cross Country, 1977.
Letters from the Earth to the Earth. Toronto, Coach House Press, 1968.
Poems Worth Knowing. Toronto, Coach House Press, 1971.
Intense Pleasure. Toronto, McClelland and Stewart, 1972.
The Ova Yogas. Toronto, Weed/Flower Press, 1972.
A Knight in Dried Plums. Toronto, McClelland and Stewart, 1975.
The Poet's Progress. Toronto, Coach House Press, 1977.
On the Road Again. Toronto, McClelland and Stewart, 1978.
I Don't Know. Montreal, Véhicule Press, 1978.
A New Romance. Montreal, Cross Country Press, 1979.
My Body Was Eaten by Dogs: Selected Poems, edited by George Bowering. Toronto, McClelland and Stewart, and Flushing, New York, Cross Country, 1981.
Country of the Open Heart. Edmonton, Longspoon Press, 1982.
A Pair of Baby Lambs. Toronto, Front Press, 1983.
The Art of Darkness. Toronto, McClelland and Stewart, 1984.
Gypsy Guitar: One Hundred Poems of Romance and Betrayal. Vancouver, Talonbooks, 1987.
Anonymity Suite. Toronto, McClelland and Stewart, 1992.
There'll Be Another. Vancouver, Talonbooks, 1995.

Plays

The Collected World of David McFadden (produced Hamilton, Ontario, 1977).
Nirvana at Twilight (produced Toronto, 1982).
At the Corner of King and Kenilworth (produced Toronto, 1983).

Novels

The Great Canadian Sonnet. Toronto, Coach House Press, 2 vols., 1970.
A Trip around Lake Huron. Toronto, Coach House Press, 1980.
A Trip around Lake Erie. Toronto, Coach House Press, 1981.
Canadian Sunset. Windsor, Ontario, Black Moss Press, 1986.
A Trip around Lake Ontario. Toronto, Coach House Press, 1988; with *A Trip around Lake Huron* and *A Trip around Lake Erie,* as *Great Lakes Suite,* Burnaby, British Columbia, Talonbooks, 1997.

Short Stories

Three Stories and Ten Poems. Toronto, Prototype, 1982.
Animal Spirits: Stories to Live By. Toronto, Coach House Press, 1983.

Other

An Innocent in Ireland: Curious Rambles and Singular Encounters.
Toronto, McClelland and Stewart, 1995.
*An Innocent in Scotland: More Curious Rambles and Singular
Encounters.* Toronto, McClelland and Stewart, 1999.

*

Critical Study: "Proofing the World: The Poems of David McFadden"
by George Bowering, in *Canadian Poetry* (London, Ontario), 7, fall-
winter 1980.

*   *   *

"I'm particularly pleased to inhabit the same world as McFadden,"
wrote Al Purdy when he read the manuscript of *Intense Pleasure,*
"even if he's crazy as a bedbug." Although David McFadden—at the
time a poet and newspaperman who lived and wrote in Hamilton,
Ontario, a community not celebrated for its artists—had been publishing short collections of his poems and Richard Brautigan-like prose
since 1967, it was not until 1972, with the appearance of *Intense
Pleasure,* that his work reached a wide public and the nature of his
singular talent became clear.

McFadden is not as "crazy as a bedbug," for he is as "crazy as a
fox" and as witty and often as irrelevant as any number of stand-up
comics who specialize in witty one-liners and put-downs and one-
upmanships. Many of his poems are nightclub routines with fast lines
like "He knew he was pregnant," "I'm addicted to toothpicks," and
"Now I'm middle-aged I want to be an alligator." The poems are
amusing, lively, and light and often exhausting to read.

In the poem "Ova Yoga," McFadden wrote, "Inside every
chicken is a human being trying to get out." Inside McFadden there is
another poet beginning to be heard. This is the observer of modern
society beset, but not swallowed up, by the incongruities and
irrationalities of contemporary life. This is the poet who in one poem
presents a midget's-eye view of the world and who in another
discovers that Adolf Hitler is alive and well in Hamilton and arranges
an interview. This is the poet who is attracted to the pop and kitsch
characteristics of Canadian advertising: "This is Bruce Marsh speaking / for Kraft Foods in Canada."

But McFadden the poet is more than the stand-up comic, the
entertainer. He is an artist who like Apollinaire seeks to celebrate
"the heroic of the everyday," who tries to grant a modicum of
immortality to such things as "three Motorcycles parked diagonally
at the curb / in front of 111 Brucedale Avenue." One looks at
Liverpudlian poets like Roger McGough for an approximation of
McFadden's tone. More to the point perhaps are the long dead but
ever useful dadaists, with their nostalgia for the evanescent. McFadden is
a dadaist prophet of the ephemeral present.

McFadden's later poems are as funny as ever. In one poem Lord
Vishnu speaks in a Scots accent. In another the astrophysicist Edwin
Hubble "discovered the universe was a bubble." In "Moonkat" the
poet writes about "the moon, / Chubby as a checker, as a billionaire,"
taking the reader on a number of little mental trips. The later poems
are rather more philosophical than the early ones. "Pictograms by
Starlight" offers a few quasi-philosophical quips of the low caliber of
"Why am I Here? So I won't have to be / Elsewhere." Yet the poem

itself explores new terrain, the psychological rather than the social
landscape, as informed by lucid dreaming:

Some invent what they write but there's no dream
Like the dream of whatever happens to be transpiring
In your mind in the moment. Impossible to capture
In all its thrilling brilliance.

"Impossible to capture" by anyone but David McFadden.

—John Robert Colombo

McGOUGH, Roger

Nationality: British. **Born:** Liverpool, Lancashire, 9 November
1937. **Education:** St. Mary's College, Crosby, Lancashire; Hull
University, Yorkshire, B.A. in French and geography 1957, Cert. Ed.
1960. **Family:** Married 1) Thelma Monaghan in 1970 (dissolved
1980), two sons; 2) Hilary Clough in 1986, one son and one daughter.
Career: Schoolteacher, Liverpool, 1960–64; lecturer, Liverpool College of Art, 1969–70; poetry fellow, University of Loughborough,
Leicestershire, 1973–75. Formerly member of the performing group
The Scaffold. Freelance writer and performer. **Awards:** *Signal* award,
1984, 1998; BAFTA award, for television play, 1985; Royal Television Society award, 1992; Cholmondeley award, 1998. Honorary
professor, Thames Valley University, 1993. Fellow, John Moores
University, 1999. O.B.E. (Officer, Order of the British Empire), 1997.
Agent: Peters, Fraser & Dunlop, Drury House, 34–43 Russell Street,
London WC2B 5HA, England.

PUBLICATIONS

Poetry

The Mersey Sound: Penguin Modern Poets 10, with Adrian Henri and
Brian Pattern. London, Penguin, 1967; revised edition, 1974,
1983.
Frinck, A Life in the Day of, and *Summer with Monika: Poems* (novel
and verse). London, Joseph, and New York, Ballantine, 1967;
revised edition of *Summer with Monika,* London, Deutsch, 1978.
Watchwords. London, Cape, 1969.
After the Merrymaking. London, Cape, 1971.
Out of Sequence. London, Turret, 1973.
Gig. London, Cape, 1973.
Sporting Relations. London, Eyre Methuen, 1974.
In the Glassroom. London, Cape, 1976.
Holiday on Death Row. London, Cape, 1979.
Unlucky for Some. London, Bernard Stone, 1980.
Waving at Trains. London, Cape, 1982.
New Volume, with Adrian Henri and Brian Patten. London, Penguin,
1983.
Crocodile Puddles. London, Pyramid, 1984.
Melting into the Foreground. London, Viking, 1986.
Selected Poems. London, Cape, 1989.
Blazing Fruit. London, Penguin, 1990.

You at the Back. London, Puffin, 1991.
Defying Gravity. London, Penguin, 1993.
The Way Things Are. London, Viking, 1999.

Recordings: *The Incredible New Liverpool Scene,* CBS, 1967; *McGough McGear,* Parlophone; *"Scaffold" Live at Queen Elizabeth Hall,* Parlophone; *"Scaffold" L. The P.,* Parlophone; *Grimms,* Island; *Fresh Liver,* Island; *Sleepers,* DJM; *McGough/Patten,* Argo; *Summer with Monika,* Island, 1978; *Gifted Wreckage,* with Brian Patten and Adrian Henri, Talking Tape, 1984; *Jelly Pie,* with Brian Patten, Puffin, 1987.

Plays

Birds, Marriages and Deaths, with others (produced London, 1964).
The Chauffeur-Driven Rolls (produced Liverpool, 1966).
The Commission (produced Liverpool, 1967).
The Puny Little Life Show (produced London, 1969). Published in *Open Space Plays,* edited by Charles Marowitz, London, Penguin, 1974.
Zones (produced Edinburgh, 1969).
Stuff (produced London, 1970).
P.C. Plod (produced London, 1971).
Wordplay (produced London, 1975).
Summer with Monika, music by Andy Roberts (produced London, 1978).
Watchwords (produced Nottingham, 1979).
Like Father, Like Son, Like (produced Nottingham, 1980).
Lifeswappers (produced Edinburgh and London, 1980).
All the Trimmings, music by Peter Brewis (produced London, 1980).
Golden Nights and Golden Days (produced on tour, 1980).
Behind the Lines (revue), with Brian Patten (produced London, 1982).
The Mouthtrap, with Brian Patten (produced Edinburgh and London, 1982).
Wind in the Willows (lyrics only, with William Perry), book by Jane Iredale, music by Perry, adaptation of the story by Kenneth Grahame (produced Washington, D.C., 1984; New York, 1985).
A Matter of Chance, adaptation of a story by Nabokov (produced Edinburgh and London, 1988).

Screenplay: *Plod,* 1972.

Radio Plays: *Gruff: A TV Commercial,* 1977; *Walking the Dog,* 1981; *The Narrator,* 1985; *FX,* 1989.

Television Plays: *The Lifeswappers,* 1976; *Kurt, B.P. Mungo, and Me,* 1983; *Fast Forward* (for children), 1986; *Mistaken Identity,* 1990; *Little Red Riding Hood,* 1991; *The Elements,* 1992; *The Curse of the Methuselah Tree,* 2000.

Other (for children)

Mr. Noselighter. London, G. Whizzard, 1976.
You Tell Me, with Michael Rosen. London, Kestrel, 1979.
The Great Smile Robbery. London, Kestrel, 1982.
Sky in the Pie. London, Kestrel, 1983.
The Stowaways. London, Viking Kestrel, 1986.
Noah's Ark. London, Dinosaur, 1986.
Nailing the Shadow. London, Viking Kestrel, 1987.

An Imaginary Menagerie. London, Viking Kestrel, 1988.
Helen Highwater. London, Viking, 1989.
Counting by Numbers. London, Viking Kestrel, 1989.
Pillow Talk. London, Viking, 1990.
The Lighthouse That Ran Away. London, Bodley Head, 1990.
My Dad's a Fire Eater. London, Puffin, 1992.
Another Custard Pie. London, Collins, 1993.
Lucky. London, Puffin, 1994.
The Magic Fountain. London, Bodley Head, 1995.
Stinkers Ahoy! London, Viking, 1995.
The Kite and Caitlin. London, Bodley Head, 1996.
Until I Met Dudley. N.p., Francis Lincoln, 1997.
Bad, Bad Cats. London, Puffin, 1997.

Other

Editor, *Strictly Private: An Anthology of Poetry.* London, Kestrel, 1981.
Editor, *The Kingfisher Book of Comic Verse.* London, Kingfisher, 1986.
Editor, *The Kingfisher Book of Poems about Love.* London, Kingfisher, 1997.
Editor, *The Ring of Words.* London, Faber, 1998.

*

Manuscript Collection: University of Hull.

Critical Study: "Roger McGough: The Popstar Poet" by John Gough, in *Children's Literature Association Quarterly* (Battle Creek, Michigan), 10(4), winter 1986.

*   *   *

Of the three original Liverpool poets, it is Roger McGough who most obviously combines the roles of writer and performer in his work. From his collaborations with Adrian Henri and Brian Patten through brief pop stardom with The Scaffold and beyond, the performance element is present in virtually all of his poems, bringing with it the familiar echoes of circus, pantomime, and old-time music hall. The wit and verbal mastery that are his main gifts find straightforward expression in a style whose apparent simplicity often hides the skill behind it. This ability allows McGough to write equally well for children and adults without condescending or altering his approach. *Sky in the Pie,* for instance, shows the same quirky humor and sly wordplay that distinguish the adult collections, not only in its surreal title poem but also in the more down-to-earth "Snowman" and "Pantomime Poem," the latter revealing an important source of inspiration. Measured beside Henri and Patten, McGough is the natural comic of the trio, although his humor is frequently underpinned with serious intentions. His writing tends more to amusement than to bitter anger, and polemics from him are few and far between and are usually made from a humanitarian rather than a political standpoint. The antiwar "A Square Dance," in which the poet addresses the doomed troops in the style of a hoedown caller, and the antiracist "I'm Dreaming of a White Smethwick" ("May your days be merry and bright / And may all your citizens be white") are typical examples.

McGough's main concern is with the flaws and frailties of human nature and the joys and vicissitudes of love. These he regards with a wry detachment, aided by his skill in making the real seem strange: "for in the morning / when a policeman / disguised as the sun / creeps into your room / and your mother / disguised as birds / calls from the trees / you will put on a dress of guilt / and shoes with broken high ideals." With McGough the actual blurs into the world of dream, with inanimate objects taking on human characteristics while people metamorphose into pets or programmed robots. The horror he introduces is of a semicomic kind found in certain fairy stories or on the pantomime stage. "The Scarecrow" and the man-eating pigs of "The Lake" belong to such a genre.

All the same, McGough's involvement with the human race is real enough, and at times his laughter is tinged with sympathy and compassion. "Head Injury" portrays the nightmare world of the damaged victim ("I feel a colour coming, mottled, mainly black") by one who has clearly taken the trouble to live inside his mind. More touching is the poignant scene in "The Identification" in which a distraught father, faced with the charred body of his son, struggles to explain why the boy was carrying cigarettes when he had been forbidden to smoke. In such moments as these McGough's matter-of-fact delivery and avoidance of sentimentality bring home the meaning of the tragedy to those concerned. Poems like "The Identification" are proof of a talent that in his case is too often overlooked.

Human tragedy apart, there are few subjects on which McGough cannot raise a smile. He makes frequent jibes at poetry itself in works like "I Don't Like the Poems" or "Take a Poem, Miss Smith," in which various stock clichés are dictated by the bored poet to his all-too-compliant secretary. His ability to laugh at himself has never been in question, from the early amused resignation of "Aren't We All" to his tongue-in-cheek assessment of McGough the rock star: "I was somebody then (the one on the right / with glasses singing Lily the Pink)." His penchant for punning and wordplay reemerges in "Nottingham," where he rejects the thought of seducing an English lit student, not wishing to be "laid / alongside our literary heritage / allocated my place in her / golden treasury of flesh." Guilty at all times of "poetic licentiousness," McGough sees his poetry as a subversive act, a flying in the face of the canons of respectable taste: "May they [your poems] break and enter, assault and batter / and loiter in the mind with intent . . . / may they bushwhack bandwagons / then take to the hills / may they break new wind . . ."

Later collections show a deepening concern with flawed humanity, a more evident compassion, while losing none of the keen perception found in McGough's earlier work. The wry, tragicomic family portraits of *Melting into the Foreground,* sharply but affectionately drawn from life, rank with the best of McGough's writing. So, too, for different reasons, does his presentation of the mindless rapist in "The Jogger's Song," where the true horror of the act is laid bare in the attacker's own excuses.

McGough's later collections also continue to reveal his wit and invention, his flair for putting an unusual slant on the commonplace and his skill in expressing the full range of emotions through his verse. In the title poem of *Defying Gravity* he is forced to contemplate the death of a close friend, while "Cinders" recalls his meeting his young daughter after a school pantomime, a meeting that brings awareness of his own mortality and of his vulnerability as a father. *The Way Things Are* sees the poet firing off wickedly amusing salvos in all directions, the sad and the comic blended as they so often are in real life. McGough presents wry pictures of suburbia ("Posh") and of inner-city deprivation ("Shite"), satirizes Hollywood imagery in "Casablanca" with his story of a Scouser uncle's exotic girlfriend,

and mocks rose-tinted nostalgia in "Old-Fashioned Values." "The Heath Forecast" is a hilarious application of BBC speak to the human body, while self-mockery surfaces in "Trust Me, I'm a Poet," in which McGough presents himself as a smooth-talking con artist in search of funds. In "Coach and Horses" he comments that "writing, like skinning beermats, is a displacement activity," and in "The Wrong Beds" he comes to the sad conclusion that "life is a hospital ward, and the beds we are put in / are the ones we don't want to be in . . ." "What Happened to Dorothy" once more presents life's tragic side, an old photograph bringing back the memory of a child scalded to death: "There's Dorothy, still seven." In the meantime works such as *Pillow Talk* and *Stinkers Ahoy!* maintain his appeal to a younger audience, while two excellent selections—You at the Back and *Blazing Fruit*—bring together the pick of his adult poetry from the previous twenty years and provide a useful perspective on his highly individual talent.

McGough's seriousness is real, if not always immediately apparent. His insights are keen, his touch deft and assured and never unduly labored. These light-fingered but winning ways continue to draw readers to him whatever the fluctuations of poetic fashion.

—Geoff Sadler

McGUCKIAN, Medbh

Nationality: Irish. **Born:** Medbh McCaughan, Belfast, Northern Ireland, 12 August 1950. **Education:** Dominican Convent, Fortwilliam Park, Belfast, 1961–68; Queen's University, Belfast, 1968–74, B.A. 1972, M.A. in English and Dip.Ed. 1974. **Family:** Married John McGuckian in 1977; three sons and one daughter. **Career:** Since 1975 English teacher, St. Patrick's College, Knock, Belfast. Writer-in-residence, Queen's University, 1986–88. **Awards:** Eric Gregory award, 1980; Rooney prize, 1982; Arts Council award, 1982; Alice Hunt Bartlett award, 1983; Cheltenham prize, 1989. Lives in Belfast. **Address:** c/o Gallery Press, Oldcastle, County Meath, Ireland.

PUBLICATIONS

Poetry

Single Ladies: Sixteen Poems. Budleigh Salterton, Devon, Interim Press, 1980.
Portrait of Joanna. Belfast, Honest Ulsterman Press, 1980.
Trio Poetry, with Damian Gorman and Douglas Marshall. Belfast, Blackstaff Press, 1981.
The Flower Master. Oxford and New York, Oxford University Press, 1982.
The Greenhouse. Oxford, Steane, 1983(?).
Venus and the Rain. Oxford and New York, Oxford University Press, 1984; revised edition, Oldcastle, Gallery Press, 1994.
On Ballycastle Beach. Oxford, Oxford University Press, and Winston-Salem, North Carolina, Wake Forest University Press, 1988; revised edition, Oldcastle, Gallery Books, 1995.
Two Women, Two Shores, with Nuala Archer. Baltimore, New Poets, 1989.

Marconi's Cottage. Oldcastle, Gallery Press, 1991.
The Flower Master, and Other Poems. Oldcastle, Gallery Press, 1993.
Captain Lavender. Oldcastle, Gallery Press, and Winston-Salem, North Carolina, Wake Forest University Press, 1994.
Selected Poems: 1978–1994. Oldcastle, Gallery Press, and Winston-Salem, North Carolina, Wake Forest University Press, 1997.
Shelmalier. Oldcastle, Gallery Press, and Winston-Salem, North Carolina, Wake Forest University Press, 1998.

Other

Editor, *The Big Striped Golfing Umbrella: Poems by Young People from Northern Ireland.* Belfast, Arts Council of Northern Ireland, 1985.

Translator, *The Water Horse: Poems in Irish,* by Nuala Ní Dhomhnaill. Oldcastle, Gallery Books, 1999.

*

Critical Studies: "Contemporary Women Poets in Ireland" by Robert H. Henigan, in *Concerning Poetry* (Bellingham, Washington), 18(1–2), 1985; "Two Poems by Medbh McGuckian: Symbol and Interpretation" by Ingrid Melander, in *Anglo-Irish and Irish Literature: Aspects of Language and Culture,* edited by Birgit Bramsback and Martin Croghan, Uppsala, Sweden, Uppsala University, 1988; "The Perfect Mother: Authority in the Poetry of Medbh McGuckian" by Clair Wills, in *Text & Context* (Beaconside, Stafford), 3, autumn 1988; "Threaders of Double-Stranded Words: News from the North of Ireland" by John Drexel, in *New England Review* (Middlebury, Vermont), 12(2), winter 1989; "The 'Imaginative Space' of Medbh McGuckian" by Susan Porter, in *Canadian Journal of Irish Studies* (Saskatoon, Canada), 15(2), December 1989; "Flower Logic: The Poems of Medbh McGuckian" by Molly Bendall, in *The Antioch Review* (Yellow Springs, Ohio), 48(3), summer 1990; "Medbh McGuckian's Poetry: Maternal Thinking and a Politics of Peace" by Ann Beer, in *Canadian Journal of Irish Studies* (Saskatoon, Canada), 18(1), July 1992; "Initiations, Tempers, Seductions: Postmodern McGuckian" by Thomas Docherty, in *The Chosen Ground: Essays on the Contemporary Poetry of Northern Ireland,* edited by Neil Corcoran, Bridgend, Ireland, Seren, 1992; "Reading Medbh McGuckian: Admiring What We Cannot Understand" by Peggy O'Brien, in *Colby Quarterly* (Waterville, Maine), 28(4), December 1992; *Through the Cracked Looking Glass: The Irish Woman Poet Imagines Subjecthood* (dissertation), University of California, Los Angeles, 1993, and "'Rising Out': Medbh McGuckian's Destabilizing Poetics," in *Eire-Ireland* (St. Paul, Minnesota), 30(4), winter 1996, both by Mary O'Connor; *The Celtic Otherworld and Contemporary Irish Poetry* (dissertation) by Thomas Royster Howerton, University of North Carolina, Chapel Hill, 1993; "Medbh McGuckian: Imagery Wrought to Its Uttermost" by Cecile Gray, in *Learning the Trade: Essays on W.B. Yeats and Contemporary Poetry,* edited by Deborah Fleming, West Cornwall, Connecticut, Locust Hill, 1993; "'The Book of Myths in Which Our Names Do Not Appear'": A Study of the Struggle of Irish Women Poets with the Tradition of Modern Irish Poetry* (dissertation) by Eileen Marie Thompson, University of Oregon, 1994; "'How Things Begin to Happen': Notes on Eilean Ni Chuilleanain and Medbh McGuckian" by Peter Sirr, in *Southern Review* (Baton Rouge, Louisiana), 31(3), summer 1995; "Obliquity in the Poetry of Paul Muldoon and Medbh McGuckian," in *Eire-Ireland* (St. Paul, Minnesota), 31(3–4), fall-winter 1996, and "'You Took Away My Biography': The Poetry of Medbh McGuckian," in *Irish University Review,* 28(1), spring-summer 1998, both by Shane Murphy; *Women Creating Women: Contemporary Irish Women Poets* edited by Patricia Boyle Haberstroh, Syracuse, New York, Syracuse University Press, 1996; "'The More with Which We Are Connected': The Muse of the Minus in the Poetry of McGuckian and Kinsella" by Guinn Batten, in *Gender and Sexuality in Modern Ireland,* edited by Maryann Valiulis and Anthony Bradley, Amherst, University of Massachusetts Press, 1997; "'Some Sweet Disorder'—The Poetry of Subversion: Paul Muldoon, Tom Paulin and Medbh McGuckian" by Elmer Andrews, in *British Poetry from the 1950s to the 1990s: Politics and Art,* edited by Gary Day and Brian Docherty, London, Macmillan, and New York, St. Martin's Press, 1997.

Medbh McGuckian comments:

I do not really feel established enough to be of interest to the general reader. My work is usually regarded as esoteric or exotic, but that is only because its territory is the feminine subconscious, or semiconscious, which many men will or do not recognize and many women will or cannot admit. My poems do not seek to chart real experience but to tap the sensual realms of dream or daydream for their spiritual value, which enhances and makes bearable the real. Through suffering, emotion, illness, people achieve order, art, strength. I believe wholly in the beauty and power of language, the music of words, the intensity of images to shadow paint the inner life of the soul. I believe life is a journey upward, beyond, inward, a ripening process. As the body wearies, the spirit is born. My themes are as old as the hills and out-of-date—love, nature, the seasons, children—but I hope what is new is the voice binding them all, sophisticating itself into something eventually simple.

*   *   *

It quickly became a commonplace to criticize Medbh McGuckian's poetry for obscurity, lack of focus, and a plethora of images. It was ever thus, for the Irish, like the Scots and the Welsh, have long experienced and understood the tyranny of English lucidity, which seeks to control the very ways in which it is permissible to create meaning. McGuckian's poetry recognizes that one mode of resistance is obliquity, the refusal to be bullied into proprietorial, "acceptable" meaning. The same conflict lies behind such diverse works as Robert Graves's "Welsh Incident" and Seamus Heaney's *North.* Being Irish and female combines to place McGuckian at a double remove from the dominant powers. She responds with a power of her own, one born of awareness, for she has anticipated her English critics when, in *Venus and the Rain,* she declares that "this oblique trance is my natural / Way of speaking." She also can expose the connections between language and domination in lines like "my longer and longer sentences / Prove me wholly female," where what at first appears to be submissiveness and self-mockery turns out to subvert the reader's hasty assumptions.

McGuckian's poems revel in their imaginative and elaborate qualities. It is not just a matter of dense imagery and difficult metaphor. Meaning is constantly deferred, and sometimes, by a careful twist, the meaning is placed out of reach after the reader thinks it has been grasped. Even her syntax questions the ways of dominance, for her long, accretive sentences deny us the easy passage that can come only when one clause is ruthlessly subordinated to another.

Yet all of this is achieved with elegant wit, for the challenges to the unself-aware custodians of power and meaning are delivered implicitly, even in disguise. Sometimes the disguise is of a person innocent of most things beyond domesticity, certainly eschewing polemic or overtly political language, apparently engaged only in "a little ladylike sewing." But McGuckian's domestic subjects are saved from coziness by placing them near bold images of desire and sexuality. Woven like a sampler, *The Flower Master* is a deliberately florid book, structured with innumerable flower images. Likewise, *Venus and the Rain* is conceived as a coherent whole, an attempt to map out a distinctively female mythology and eroticism. There are many other signs of McGuckian's talent, such as her ability to be extravagant and careful, modest and ambitious at the same time or the way in which the "I" enters and leaves even her earliest poems in *Single Ladies* with complete naturalness and assurance of tone.

These poems call forth from the reader a patient, slow approach, willingly given after one begins to understand McGuckian's aims. The contract between poem and reader is like that between lovers, with the poem rejecting whatever smacks of brusque violation. Secretive, the poems nevertheless yield up a charge of authentic emotion each time. Sexual approach or rejection, indeed, is their paradigm for the approach to meaning:

> Yours is the readership
> Of the rough places where I make
> My sweet refusals of you, your
> Natural violence.

There is, of course, a risk inherent in subversive obliquity. It is not the risk that a certain readership will be baffled but that the impulse to translate everything into something else can lead to involutions that divert one from one's own purposes, as McGuckian is aware when she writes of "my tenable / Emotions largely playing with themselves." Much of the language of *On Ballycastle Beach* remains figurative and interior to the point of difficulty ("lightning arranges the logarithms / Of ferns, equates the radius / Of the moon to the number of breaths / We draw in an hour"), but she has also always had another linguistic register of disarming simplicity:

> As a child cries, all over, I kept insisting
> On robin's egg blue tiles around the fireplace,
> Which gives a room a kind of flying-heartedness.

The domestic, the unconscious, and the erotic are still predominant preoccupations, but the later part of the book suggests a widening of scope.

In its blending of the native and the exotic and in its strivings with language, McGuckian's talent sometimes suggests the Yeats of "Crossways" and "The Rose." But her voice is quite distinctively her own. An almost feverish richness of vocabulary and image is set off against a calmness of tone that is generated by the meditative or descriptive statements and the leisurely syntax. At their best her poems leave the reader with the feeling that a new language, exhilarating and mysterious, is being found in which to treat of emotion.

—R.J.C. Watt

McHUGH, Heather

Nationality: American. **Born:** California, 20 August 1948. **Education:** Radcliffe College, Cambridge, Massachusetts, 1965–69, B.A. 1970; Denver University, M.A. 1972. **Family:** Married in 1968 (divorced); 2) Niko Boris in 1987. **Career:** Visiting lecturer, Antioch College, Yellow Springs, Ohio, 1971–72; poet-in-residence, Stephens College, Columbia, Missouri, 1974–76; assistant, then associate professor of English, State University of New York, Binghamton, 1976–84. Since 1984 Milliman writer-in-residence, University of Washington, Seattle. Visiting professor, Warren Wilson College, M.F.A. Program for Writers, Swannanoa, North Carolina, 1980–85, Columbia University, New York, 1980 and 1981, and University of California, Irvine, 1982; Holloway Lecturer, University of California, Berkeley, 1987; Coal-Royalty Chair, University of Alabama, 1991; Elliston Poet, University of Cincinnati, 1992; visiting professor, University of California, Los Angeles, 1994, and University of Iowa, 1991, 1995. Member, Board of Directors, Associated Writing Programs, 1981–83, and Literature Panel, National Endowment for the Arts, 1983–86. **Awards:** Academy of American Poets prize, 1972; MacDowell Colony fellowship, 1973, 1974, 1976; National Endowment for the Arts grant, 1974, 1981; Houghton Mifflin New Poetry Series award, 1977; Creative Artists Public Service grant, 1980; Rockefeller Foundation Bellagio Residency, 1984; Guggenheim fellowship, 1989; finalist, National Book award, 1994. **Address:** Department of English, Box 354330, University of Washington, Seattle, Washington 98195–4330, U.S.A.

PUBLICATIONS

Poetry

Dangers. Boston, Houghton Mifflin, 1977.
A World of Difference. Boston, Houghton Mifflin, 1981.
To the Quick. Middletown, Connecticut, Wesleyan University Press, 1987.
Shades. Middletown, Connecticut, Wesleyan University Press, 1988.
Hinge & Sign: Poems 1968–1993. Middletown, Connecticut, Wesleyan University Press, 1994.
The Father of the Predicaments. Midletown, Connecticut, Wesleyan University Press, 1999.

Other

Broken English: Poetry and Partiality, Middletown, Connecticut, Wesleyan University Press, 1993.

Translator, *D'aprés tout: Poems,* by Jean Follain. Princeton, New Jersey, Princeton University Press, 1981.

Translator, with Niko Boris, *Because the Sea Is Black: Poems of Blaga Dimitrova.* Middletown, Connecticut, Wesleyan University Press, 1989.

Translator, with Nikolai Papov, *101 Poems by Paul Ceran.* Middletown, Connecticut, Wesleyan University Press, 2000.

*

Critical Studies: By Mary Karr, in *Harvard Book Review* (Cambridge, Massachusetts), 5 & 6, summer & fall, 1987; ''Poetry Chronicle. Four Salvers Salvaging: New Work by Voigt, Olds, Dove, and McHugh'' by Peter Harris, in *The Virginia Quarterly Review* (Charlottesville), 64, spring 1988; ''Killing Joke'' by Joshua Weiner, in *The Threepenny Review* (Berkeley, California), spring 1989; ''COMMENT: No Perimeters'' by Marianne Boruch, in *American Poetry Review* (Philadelphia), March/April 1989; by Joshua Clover in *Colorado Review* (Fort Collins), spring 1994; ''Among the Wordstruck: A Review of the Poems of John Ashbery and Heather McHugh'' by Linda Gregerson, in *New York Times Book Review* (New York), 23 October 1994; by Marion K. Stocking, in *Beloit Review,* fall 1994; ''Brokenglish'' by John Palatella, in *Denver Quarterly,* 31(1), summer 1996.

*   *   *

Heather McHugh took Browning's line ''Our interest's on the dangerous edge of things'' as the epigraph of *Dangers,* in which she contrives to ''drive / together argument and matter till you know / not what the matter is but how it shouts.'' Even though she sounds solitary and defiant, choosing ''the artifice of hate'' through which ''the face / refuses to shine,'' she seeks to know, and thus sustain, connections. For her ''the sweetness / is of paradox.'' In the nine small dramas of singleness and interaction that comprise the book's middle, the characters are always endangered, always persistent. The coast, where water can threaten, is her favorite vehicle to show that, even though life comprises ''little / gross and no net / worth,'' ''you know you can't / live anywhere else.''

McHugh's interest in *A World of Difference* is less social than spiritual. She assigns herself responsibility for comprehending. She repudiates confessionalism, caricaturing such writers as ''gunning / their electrics, going / IIIII,'' and insists that ''vision isn't insight, / buried at last in the first / person's eyes.'' She accepts a world in which ''the form of life / is a motion'' and color is the frequency and not the object.'' In such a context human importance is dubious. Take the lovers in ''When the Future Is Black,'' who regard themselves as only a presence ''designed to keep / / the past and future from forever / meeting.'' Although we like to insist that ''we make / a world of difference,'' McHugh craves selfless transcendence. Unlike those who would name—that is, possess—God and try to ''read / themselves / into his will'' (note the pun), she wants to forget ''all names / / for worship'' and ''our history of longing'' and be God's ''great blue breath, / his ghost and only song.''

A formidable task, presumptuous perhaps, even inviting madness, but she maintains vigilance, scouring her language for misleading and distracting meaning. ''Always I have to resist / the language I have / to love,'' she says in ''Like.'' But unlike the discursive, frequently rhymed and metrical poems of *Dangers,* the spareness and eccentricity of *A World of Difference* produce remarkable clarity. ''Language Lesson, 1976,'' for instance, after seeming to satirize sayings like ''hold the relish'' (meaning ''forget'' it) and ''love'' (meaning, in tennis, ''nothing''), becomes a powerful love lyric:

> I'm saying go so far
> the customs are untold,
>
> make nothing without words
> and let me be
> the one you never hold.

Personal crises enter the poems of McHugh's third and fourth books. ''I / / have lost my certainty,'' she writers in *To the Quick,* ''and spent my spirit in a waste / of one romance.'' Likewise, in *Shades* she rebounds from the death of a friend from AIDS. ''Day and die are cast together,'' yet she remains affirmative: ''It's not / when, what or how we are / that makes one wonder / without end. It's *that.''*

The fundamental problem renews itself: ''The ends / of life are rich, it's only / explanation that grows poor . . .'' Poetry, McHugh declares in *Broken English,* ''does not give itself as evidence, as inscription.'' Rather, ''it is the place that suffers inscription. It bears the mark or scar of what was seen and what was grasped.'' A remarkable consistency—of vision and language— marks her entire work. Through language echoing Joyce, cummings, Berryman, and most of all Beckett, her tenacity of thought approaches radical watching.

The poems newly collected in *Hinge & Sign* contain riveting examples. In ''Circus'' ''the elephant on pain / / of punishment, five times upon / the shovels of its toenails, kneels for peanuts.'' By observing the pauses, construing phrases in each phase of their gathering, one finds the nuances of McHugh's vision. Paradoxically, while suggestions are multiple, the syntax plays with certainty. ''Does darkness fail?'' she asks in ''Scenes from a Death''; ''or does the moviehouse of our mentality / just open . . . ?''

This persistence to know and express precisely does not fail McHugh, even when she is confronted, as in *The Father of the Predicaments,* with the agonizing death of a loved one and the end of her second marriage. In the long collage poem ''Not a Prayer'' she disrupts chronology in an effort to present the disorienting final days in the life of her mother-in-law. This project requires a new modulation of language—some passages as raw as a journal entry, others as dramatic as a carefully shaped story, and poetry in various cadences and formats. A remarkable fusion emerges: the portrayal of persons in physical and emotional extremity and a meditation on the inadequacy of language.

For all of McHugh's intelligence and inventiveness, one may be most struck by her courage. Defiant or sympathetic, pained or joyous, she has the intuition and wit—the emotional equilibrium—to face the full mystery of experience. She can examine, for example, hilarity (see ''Past All Understanding'') or admit that love may be a ''history of strangleholds.'' She may have mellowed since *Danger,* at least toward individuals, but she does not compromise her art. In ''Not a Prayer'' she remembers that ''the father of the predicaments, wrote Aristotle's translator, is being.'' In the title poem, however, the father is a merciless mentor who ''train[s] us in the virtues we most lacked'' and requires that she

. . . return his stare
Correctly, without fear. Unless I could,
Unblinking, more and more incline
Toward a deep unblinkingness of his,
He would not let me rest.

—Jay S. Paul

McKAY, Don

Nationality: Canadian. **Born:** Owen Sound, Ontario, 1942. **Education:** University of Western Ontario, B.A., M.A.; University of Wales, Ph.D. **Career:** Has taught creative writing at the University of New Brunswick, University of Victoria, and University of Western Ontario. **Awards:** Canadian Authors Association literary award, 1983; National Magazine award, 1991; Governor General's award for poetry, 1991. **Agent:** McClelland and Stewart, Inc., 481 University Avenue, Suite 900, Toronto, Ontario M5G 2E9, Canada.

PUBLICATIONS

Poetry

Moccassins on Concrete: Poems. Montreal, Content, 1972.
Long Sault. London, Ontario, Applegarth Follies, 1975.
Lightning Ball Bait. Toronto, Coach House Press, 1980.
Birding, or Desire: Poems. Toronto, McClelland and Stewart, 1983.
Sanding Down This Rocking Chair on a Windy Night. Toronto, McClelland and Stewart, 1987.
Night Field: Poems. Toronto, McClelland and Stewart, 1991.
Apparatus. Toronto, McClelland and Stewart, 1997.
The Book of Moonlight: Poems. Victoria, British Columbia, Outlaw Editions, 2000.
Another Gravity. Toronto, McClelland and Stewart, 2000.

*

Critical Studies: By Alanna F. Bondar, in *Studies in Canadian Literature* (Fredericton, New Brunswick), 19(2), 1994; ''Don McKay and Metaphor: Stretching Language toward Wilderness'' by Kevin Bushell, in *Studies in Canadian Literature* (Fredericton, New Brunswick), 21(1), 1995; '''Got to Meander If You Want to Get to Town': Excursion and Excursionist Figures in Don McKay'' by Susan Elmslie, in *Wascana Review,* 30(1), spring 1995.

*   *   *

Don McKay can appropriately be called a ''nature poet.'' The recurring themes in his poetry are his fascination with wildlife, especially birds, and the relationship of the poet to the natural world. McKay uses poetry as his instrument in conveying the essential consciousness of nature. In retrospect one can see from the earliest poems the foundation of McKay's identification with the use of language to fulfill this goal. He writes with honesty and directness, and his seriousness about the terrain around him is immediately apparent. He is demanding of his readers, who are drawn into his contemplative use of poetic metaphors and ornithological knowledge. To McKay nature poetry is a discovery or recovery of ''wilderness'' within language. In the process of demonstrating what it means to be a nature poet, McKay has developed a new language that helps to explain his poetry and its place in language.

McKay's collection *Sanding Down This Rocking Chair on a Windy Night* contains distinct themes, many of which are summarized in the last poem, ''A Mouth.'' The range of subjects is broad, and the scattered images of natural and human life evoke an impressionistic treatment in the format and sequences. Many poems are concerned with the limits of language, and McKay inventively explores the nature of expression by using the metaphor of his rocking chair in the title prose poem. Written as a narrative in the first person, it is the longest work in the collection. It has as its theme the recovery and renewal of energy, which is expressed through McKay's metaphorical use of the chair as the Muse who is invoked by the poet and re-creator through his sanding, shaping, and aligning. McKay has informally linked poignant passages of past and present to create a rich syntactical ambiguity of form and content:

Rocking on the porch, easing the shriek,
prying open places for the oven bird and nuthatch softly
honking from the dead limb on the big soft maple
(sawed up and burnt two years ago, remember, solid
yet)
or if you are you'll rock
tautly as though winding up a watch,
still thinking grimly how the wheel of claws runs
everything
the next next next of embryo and oven bird,
the mouth.

Another collection, *Birding, or Desire,* consists of eighty-two poems arranged in four sections by season. Here the motif of flight is the central metaphor for the poetic process. Just as birds migrate to warmer and exotic climates, the poet follows his vision to dreamlike and surreal states beyond the realm of the mundane. The four sections are representative of ''movements'' in which McKay addresses the nature of poets, the poetic process, and the poet-reader dynamic. When birding, the poet observes the birds' markings, sounds, and movements with the precision of a biologist. His interest in oral traditions includes vernacular and poetic languages and foreign bird chirps. The book looks at the process of meaning and of language making.

Night Field is a contemplative book that demands attention from its readers. It is replete with metaphors that provide the reader with insights into the similarities between things. Migrating butterflies are seen as flaying hankies, the nest of the Baltimore oriole as a ''sturdy fragile woven scrotum.'' The opening lines of ''Waking at the Mouth of the Willow River,'' the first poem in the collection, contain striking images in a weaving pattern that is descriptive of the fraying of an old shirt, interspersed with the pauses of punctuation, like the break in the continuity of thread around holes: ''Sleep, my favourite flannel shirt, wears thin, and shreds, and / birdsong happens in the holes. In thirty seconds the naming / of species will begin.''

Apparatus is a contemplative work, at times written in the form of stream of consciousness, in which the reader is actively involved in the poet's mental process of classifying the natural order of things. To McKay objects not only have a surface identity but also an eternal purpose of being. He takes us on a spiritual journey but explains the spiritual in physical terms by alluding to the literary and the biological. The quality of his work is rhapsodic, and it must be read aloud.

The cover shows a drum pedal in a circle centered on a red background. The reader is immediately led to anticipate a contraption that will present itself for further exploration, and in *Apparatus* we come to be engaged in reexamining the apparatuses that characterize modern Western society: cars, dryers, the blades of helicopters, baseball gloves, and atom counters. McKay writes about musical instruments such as the piano, saxophone, and drums, and in each the precision of the keys, strings, and pedals are like "the animal in the instrument" in order to stay "in touch with clutter" ("Setting Up the Drums"). He compares the precision of a crafted tool to that of a poem, as each points toward clutter, toward that which has not been ordered. Poetic rhythms are similar to those of drums. The same "grab, give / grab," the naming and leaps of letting go, are instinctual characteristics of both. The reader ponders the nature of our relationship to the tools we have fashioned.

The nature of these relationships is the subject of McKay's "Baler Twine: Thoughts on Ravens, Home, and Nature Poetry," first published in 1995 in *Studies in Canadian Literature/Études en littérature canadienne*. In the essay he speaks of "materiel" (the title he gives to the third section of *Apparatus*), which he defines as a kind of appropriation that can be of a first order, in which things are addressed in the mode of utility. The making of tools falls under this category. Or it can be of a second order, which is either the colonization of another's death or the absolute denial of death: "things made permanent and denied access to decomposition, then return to elements." This second order of appropriation is what McKay calls "materiel."

The venue for McKay's performance is the natural Canadian world of pine trees, goldfinches, mountains, lakes, and grizzly bears. He is a poet who is thoroughly engaged in re-creating the world through language, and, in the process of clarifying and demonstrating what it means to be a nature poet, McKay has developed a new language that replaces nature, or wilderness, to extend the understanding of nature poetry far beyond a linear terrain.

—Renu Barrett

McKENDRICK, Jamie

Nationality: British. **Born:** James Stewart McKendrick, Liverpool, 27 October 1955. **Education:** Nottingham University, 1973–76, B.A. (honors) 1976; Oxford University, 1976–79. **Family:** Married Xon de Ros in 1992. **Career:** Lecturer, Universita di Salerno, Italy, 1984–88. Since 1991 part-time instructor, Sarah Lawrence Program, Wadham College, Oxford, and since 1999 poet-in-residence, Hertford College, Oxford University. **Awards:** Eric Gregory award, 1983; Southern Arts Literature award, 1992, for *The Kiosk on the Brink;* Forward-Poetry prize and Poetry Book Society Choice, 1997, for *The Marble Fly.*

PUBLICATIONS

Poetry

The Sirocco Room. Oxford and New York, Oxford University Press, 1991.
The Kiosk on the Brink. Oxford and New York, Oxford University Press, 1993.

The Marble Fly. Oxford and New York, Oxford University Press, 1997.
Sky Nails: Poems 1979–1997. London, Faber, 2000.

*

Critical Studies: By Roger Garfitt, in *Poetry Review,* 84(1), spring 1994; by Lavinia Greenlaw, in *New Statesman* (London), 13 March 2000.

*   *   *

Jamie McKendrick's first volume of poems, *The Sirocco Room,* which appeared in 1991, received that rarest of things in poetry, a reprint prompted by the critical enthusiasm with which it was greeted. McKendrick's immediate success was due to the fact that years of diligent application to the craft of verse had filled his first book with fully achieved poems rather than journeyman work. His undoubted skill has not led to a slick technique that presents a calculated face to the reader; rather, it has enabled him to express himself in a subtly original way.

The Sirocco Room introduced a number of key themes to be found in McKendrick's work: an interest in science, history, language, and everyday life and an ironic sense of humor that undercuts what has appeared to some as a perhaps rather unhopeful feeling in the poems. The book was praised by Tom Paulin for its "haunting sense of displacement, a fineness of aesthetic perception combined with a strangely laid-back despair." It is filled with knowledge. "A Petrified Zoo," for example, contains references to the Silurian age and to fossil ammonites and trilobites. In "Ill Wind" we meet McKendrick's characteristically edgy tone of voice:

To talk of the weather was a morbid sign.
The winds blew wherever they wanted to
raining their freight of dust.

The Kiosk on the Brink appeared in the same year McKendrick was selected to appear in *Poetry Review*'s influential 1993 New Generation Poets promotion. The book was praised by the novelist William Boyd, who identified a "cool, complex intelligence, a wry worldly lyricism." It contains the sequence "Mountain," on various phenomena of the natural world. "The Crystal Sky" juggles complicated concepts in an entertaining way—"The city of glass was throwing stones / of glass at the neighbouring city of stone"—and follows the concept through to the ending lines:

Then in the brittle hour before dawn
it occurred to me there might might there not
still be time to set my house in order.

The tentative sense of a possible hope in the face of an apparently impossible situation is made clear in the language of the poem, which repeats itself in "there might might there not," demonstrating the mind changing direction from hopelessness to hope within half a line. McKendrick's effects are often as subtle and as intelligent as this, providing a tenuous sense of the possibility of discovering the good life while living on the brink of a volcano. The memorable image of "the kiosk on the brink / vending cans of molten sugar" appears in

"On the Volcano," part of the "Mountain" sequence. The poem, which has the feeling of a fable, ends with the memorable lines

with those chunks of pyrite, fool's gold, fire
cooled, cast and cubed in the dire forge.

McKendrick's third volume, *The Marble Fly,* received both the Poetry Book Society Choice and the prestigious Forward-Poetry prize for the best collection of 1997. "Gainful Employment" is a good example of the tentative but very real sense of spiritual advance and meticulous self-honesty to be found in his work. The poet sits at his oak desk "putting the house / I haven't got in order." The thought in the poem is subtly expressed and unfolds a sense of poetry as "an unconsolable / joy," ending with

No one can say it's wasting time, my time, the time
    I've got,
to enter the very thread of the helix,
to live always expecting the unheard of.

Again we meet a careful repetition, here of the "wasting time, my time, the time I've got," which wins through from an almost Thomas Hardy-like "waiting in unhope" to "expecting the unheard of" with its modest but nonetheless clear affirmation.

McKendrick's poems can appear as riddling as the novels of Philip K. Dick or the fable poems of Norman Cameron, yet they are usually rooted in a reality, sometimes learned, sometimes reflecting the basic things of everyday life, in which we can share. McKendrick has also produced memorable versions of poems by Montale, Machado, and Carlos Drummond de Andrade and a remarkable poem, "Galatea and Polyphemus," after Ovid.

Sky Nails: Poems 1979–1997 contains a generous selection from all three of McKendrick's previous volumes and makes a welcome addition to the collection of anyone who cares about poetry today. It is telling that McKendrick took the title of the book from the poem "Sky Nails," on the imaginary nails his workmates teased him about but that he then turns into a positive definition of his poems:

that will nail anything
to nothing
and make it stay.

—Jonathan Barker

McKEOWN, Tom

Nationality: American. **Born:** Thomas Shanks McKeown, Evanston, Illinois, 29 September 1937. **Education:** University of Michigan, Ann Arbor, 1957–62, A.B. 1961, A.M. 1962; Northwestern University, Evanston, Illinois, summer 1961. **Career:** Instructor, Alpena College, Michigan, 1962–64, and Wisconsin State University, Oshkosh, 1964–68; poet-in-residence, Stephens College, Columbia, Missouri, 1968–74, and University of Wisconsin, Stevens Point, 1976–81; professor of English, Savannah College of Art and Design, 1982–83, and University of Wisconsin, Oshkosh, 1983–87; poet-in-residence, University of Wisconsin, Madison, 1989–94. Since 1994 involved with poetry tutorials correspondence schools. **Awards:** Hopwood award, University of Michigan, 1968; Wurlitzer Foundation grant, 1972, 1975; Yaddo grant, 1973, 1975; Wisconsin Arts Council fellowship, 1980. **Address:** 1220 North Gammon Road, Middleton, Wisconsin 53562–3806, U.S.A.

PUBLICATIONS

Poetry

Alewife Summer. Albuquerque, New Mexico, Road Runner Press, 1967.
Last Thoughts. Madison, Wisconsin, Abraxas Press, 1969.
The Winds of the Calendar. Albuquerque, New Mexico, Road Runner Press, 1969.
Drunk All Afternoon. Madison, Wisconsin, Abraxas Press, 1969.
The Milk of the Wolf. Columbia, Missouri, Asari Press, 1970.
The Cloud Keeper. Dublin, Seafront Press, 1972.
The House of Water. Fredonia, New York, Basilisk Press, 1974.
The Luminous Revolver. Fremont, Michigan, Sumac Press, 1974.
Driving to New Mexico. Santa Fe, New Mexico, Sunstone Press, 1974.
Maya/Dreams. Stevens Point, University of Wisconsin Press, 1977.
Certain Minutes. Stevens Point, Wisconsin, Scopcraeft Press, 1978.
Circle of the Eye. New York, Columbia University Press Music Publications, 1982.
Invitation of the Mirrors. Oshkosh, Wisconsin Review Press, 1985.
Three Hundred Tigers. Bruce, Wisconsin, Zephyr, 1994.

*

Critical Studies: "Contemporary Poetic Statements," in *Road Apple Review* (Oshkosh, Wisconsin), 1971; in *December Magazine* (Western Springs, Illinois), December 1971; in *Back Door* (Poquoson, Virginia), 1971; in *New Voices in American Poetry: An Anthology* edited by David Allan Evans, Cambridge, Massachusetts, Winthrop, 1973.

Tom McKeown comments:

Have several unfinished novels, but I have little interest in them now. Poetry is my full-time obsession.

I lean toward the surreal in poetry. Like experimentation rather than the tired, heavy academic stuff.

Write in free verse almost entirely. No major themes really other than the usual ones: love, death, separation, alienation, war, etc. I am mainly concerned with the dream and poetic possibilities that arise out of the dream. This is the area of the surreal where a non sequitur progression of images or image clusters are drawn from the unconscious mind. The surreal deals with the landscapes of dreams, and thus there are infinite possibilities for new and startling creations. Always there is a possibility for a satori, or sudden illumination. Have been influenced perhaps by Neruda, Breton, and Trakl.

Recently my poems have been reaching more toward the mystical and supernatural.

*   *   *

Tom McKeown is a poet who is able to be both concrete and surreal in his poetry. He admits to the influence of various Spanish and Latin American poets. He shares with one of these writers, Neruda, a surrealism that keeps a strong grip on the landscape—in McKeown's case the Midwest—in which he lives. His work manages a particularly skillful synthesis of English nature poetry and Spanish and French surrealism.

In an essay he contributed to *Their Place in the Heat,* McKeown notes that he is attracted to both the nature/mythic/archetypal and the surreal approaches in his writing. For him the poet strives to be a shaman, or visionary, as in the poem "The Buffalo, Our Sacred Beast" from *Drunk All Afternoon.* Here he becomes a medicine man leading the buffalo back to trample on the civilization that has crushed them: "I carry a flag with a buffalo on it / and on my staff I spin a human skull." Another of his poems, "Aztec Dream," also evokes ancient rites, again involving human sacrifice.

Many of McKeown's poems are meditations, existing at a point where nature and the author intersect, and images can move swiftly from clearly observed scenes into dream states in which something transcending both the observer and the observed makes itself felt. In longer collections such as *Certain Minutes* this meditative quality is especially strong. Throughout these poems there is a feeling for stillness, for capturing isolated scenes and moments, coexisting with considerable movement. Sudden leaps of imagery take place within poems as scenes taken in by the outer eye yield to those caught by the inner eye. But the leaping takes place between poems as well, with locales switching abruptly from McKeown's familiar American heartland to exotic places such as New Mexico or semitropical coastlines. The collection concludes with the most exotic locale of all in "Lost in Yucatan," in which the author takes the plunge into the totally fantastic:

> There is a face, a woman's face, coming up
> Out of a green pool in Yucatan, the one
> That has always been speaking, speaking
> Among lush fern. This blossoming, this woman,
> Who may have been waiting a thousand years,
> Reaches the surface, makes no sound, locks
> Her deep emerald eyes into the sun and vanishes.
> There are no ripples where she parted the water.

McKeown is a compassionate writer, and his poetry does not lack for feeling. Some poems in *Certain Minutes,* such as "The Last Drunken Friday in Missouri" and "Driving after Midnight," deal with losses only obliquely suggested, but a sense of mourning lost connections or relationships informs the poems. At other times the loss may be more explicitly spelled out, as in "The Lady on Black Oak Road," about a woman's suicide. (Even the collection's dedication to three friends underscores this theme.) An elegiac note touches his earlier work too. One short collection, *Last Thoughts,* contains four elegies, including the powerful "Body En Route":

> A twenty year old boy
> is en route home. Killed
> in Viet Nam . . .
> Nothing stirs in the gray houses.
> Silence from his metal box.
> The park is without voices.
> The wind blows a terrible darkness.

Other poets dart through *Certain Minutes* like tropical birds flashing by, barely glimpsed. In "The Lady on Black Oak Road" a woman sitting in her car in her garage, waiting for carbon monoxide to do its work, sees "Sylvia," apparently Sylvia Plath, sitting by her side. In a less specific way the poems also pay tribute to poets such as Wallace Stevens and Hart Crane. The ending of "Advice from the Glacier" suggests Stevens's "The Snowman" in its attempt to blend with what is utterly alien, reaching for a "mind of winter":

> Inside my body,
> a great peak of granite and snow
> whispers:
>> If you will learn
>> my clear eye
> will let you
> live forever.

Other poems and imagery suggest Crane, as in the beginning of "Beyond This Place, This Hour": "The white bridges by the sea / are filled with sun / Laughing gulls curve." Mostly, though, these poems find one voice, that of McKeown, speaking with quiet intensity in poems such as "Meditation on Evening." Here a leaf suggests one life among many and one hour among a multitude.

Focusing on this one point of life, we can gain a mystical affinity with all of existence:

> The light of evening floods the plain.
> Shadows of leaves shudder: the shadow
> of one leaf moves through many leaves.
> Green transparencies overlap . . .

—Duane Ackerson

McMASTER, Rhyll

Nationality: Australian. **Born:** Brisbane, Queensland, 13 August 1947. **Family:** Married Roger McDonald in 1967 (divorced 1994); three daughters. **Career:** Secretary, University of Queensland, Brisbane, 1966–71; nurse, Canberra Hospital, 1976–78; farmer, Braidwood, New South Wales, 1980–92. Poetry editor, *Canberra Times,* 1994; since 1994 manuscripts assessor, National Book Council. **Awards:** Harri Jones Memorial prize, 1971; Victorian Premier's prize, 1986, and Grace Leven prize, 1987, both for *Washing the Money;* Literature Board of the Australia Council fellowship, 1992; Grace Leven prize, 1995, for *Flying the Coop*; CAPO fellowship, Capital Arts Patrons' Organisation, A.C.T., 1997. **Address:** P.O. Box 96, Braidwood, N.S.W. 2622, Australia.

PUBLICATIONS

Poetry

The Brineshrimp. Brisbane, University of Queensland Press, 1972.
Washing the Money. Sydney, Angus and Robertson, 1986.
On My Empty Feet. Melbourne, Heinemann, 1993.
Flying the Coop (new and selected poems). Melbourne, Heinemann, 1994.
Chemical Bodies. Sydney, Brandl and Schlesinger, 1997.

Plays

Radio Play: *On My Empty Feet*, 1996.

*

Manuscript Collection: National Library of Australia, Canberra.

Critical Studies: "Recent Australian Poetry: The Ordinary and the Extraordinary: Rhyll McMaster, Andrew Taylor, Bruce Beaver, Robert Harris and Jan Owen" by Alan Gould, in *Quadrant* (Victoria, Australia), 30(10), October 1986; "'Vital Organ with Strings Attached': The Poetry of Rhyll McMaster" by Peter Alexander, in *Southerly* (Australia), 55(4), summer 1995–96.

*   *   *

Rhyll McMaster's first collection of poems, *The Brineshrimp,* was published in 1972. It immediately established her as a distinctive poet and was awarded the Harri Jones Memorial prize. Patrick White bought copies to give to his friends. David Malouf wrote of the collection, "Spare, tough, eloquent, these poems poke into corners of the ordinary and come up with discoveries that are sometimes scary, often hilarious, always enlarging of our sense of the pathos and mystery of things."

It was fourteen years before McMaster's second collection, *Washing the Money,* appeared. A tiny volume of forty pages, it is padded out with home photographs of characteristic acerbity and with an ultrasound of her third daughter, Stella, in utero at fifteen weeks. A young woman's precise observations have been overtaken in this book by a meticulous, intense will to tease out both precision and resonance from tiny domestic moments from childhood, and the second half explores with characteristically quirky imagery the neighborhood world of contemporary living.

On My Empty Feet (1993) is a more substantial volume that explores with chilling coolness and power the effects of a stroke suffered by McMaster's mother. The book also has a range of suburban voices in which the poet's ear for the rhythms of everyday speech are balanced by her always quirky and vivid sense of image.

Only a year after this volume, McMaster published *Flying the Coop,* a book of selected poems that contains a substantial selection of new work. It is clear that, after the constraints of years of domestic priorities, a changed lifestyle has released a dramatic and sometimes terrifying new flow of creativity. This new energy has been further exemplified in the collection *Chemical Bodies* (1997), though the personal here has been displaced by a more intellectual wit and curiosity.

—Thomas W. Shapcott

McNAIR, Wesley C.

Nationality: American. **Born:** Newport, New Hampshire, 19 June 1941. **Education:** Keene State College, New Hampshire, 1959–63, B.A. in English 1963; Middlebury College, Vermont, 1964–68, 1970–75, M.A. in English 1968, M.Litt. in American literature 1975;

Dartmouth College, Hanover, New Hampshire, 1970–71. **Family:** Married Diane Reed in 1962; three sons and one daughter. **Career:** Associate professor of English, Colby-Sawyer College, New London, New Hampshire, 1968–87. Since 1987 associate professor, professor of English, and director of creative writing, University of Maine, Farmington. Visiting associate professor, Dartmouth English, Hanover, New Hampshire, 1984; visiting professor, Colby College, Waterville, Maine, 2000–01. **Awards:** National Endowment for the Arts poet-in-residence at Marietta College, 1977; National Endowment for the Arts fellowship in poetry, 1980, 1990; Dennis award, University of Missouri Press, 1984; Eunice Tietjens prize, *Poetry,* 1984; Guggenheim fellowship in poetry, 1986; Robert Frost Poet-in-Residence, Tyrone Guthrie Centre for the Arts, Ireland, 1987; Rockefeller Foundation fellowship, 1993; Theodore Roethke prize, *Poetry Northwest,* 1993; first prize for best poem published in *Yankee,* 1994; Maine Arts Commission Individual Artist fellowship, 1996; Sarah Josepha Hale medal, 1997. **Address:** RFD 2, Box 790, Norridgewock, Maine, U.S.A.

PUBLICATIONS

Poetry

The Faces of Americans in 1853. Columbia, University of Missouri Press, 1983.
The Town of No. Boston, Godine, 1989; reprinted, with *My Brother Running,* 1997.
12 Journeys in Maine. Portland, Maine, Romulus Editions, 1992.
My Brother Running. Boston, Godine, 1993; reprinted, with *The Town of No,* 1997.
The Dissonant Heart. Portland, Maine, Romulus Editions, 1995.
The Town of No & My Brother Running. Boston, Godine, 1997.
Talking in the Dark. Boston, Godine, 1998.
Fire. Boston, Godine, 2001.

Other

Mapping the Heart: Reflections on Place and Poetry. Boston, Godine, 2000.
Editor, *The Quotable Moose: A Contemporary Maine Reader.* Hanover, New Hampshire, University Press of New England, 1994.

*

Critical Studies: "Giving Voice to Community" by John Repp, in *American Book Review,* 12(6), January 1991; in *Southern Review* (Baton Rouge, Louisiana), 29(4), fall 1993.

Wesley C. McNair comments:

The ultimate poetry is to connect us to our feeling self, which is the deepest self we have. The feeling self can be dangerous to us because it insists that we live real lives. So people will do almost anything to kill it—drugs, alcohol, overwork, excessive church going—there are lots of ways to do the job. What I most want to do as a poet is to remind readers of how important their intuitive, feeling self is. I have other concerns, too, as a writer, some of which I have discovered as I have written. I want to inspire compassion for those living at the periphery of our vision—the poor, the crazy, misfits, the underclass. And when I write about my home place of New England, as I often do, I do not want to portray a nostalgic world elsewhere but the place as I know it, with its dislocated culture, its poverty, its eccentrics, its broken dreams, and its hopefulness. In my regional work, moreover, I always want to find what is universal in the local, so I am not just writing about one place but in some way about all places.

*   *   *

Wesley C. McNair is a New England poet. As the poet Donald Hall has observed, McNair preserves "the speech and character of a region intimately known. Because he is a true poet, his New England is unlimited." McNair's somewhat autobiographical poems describe the environs of New Hampshire and the people he was familiar with while growing up there. His two best-known works are *The Town of No* and *My Brother Running*. In the early 1990s, as the poet Maxine Kumin has noted, McNair did not have the recognition he deserved, but after he published *12 Journeys in Maine* in 1992, his work began to become better known and his popularity to spread outside New England.

McNair's poems reflect the lives of ordinary people in rural areas, particularly those who have lived without the basic prerequisites of a comfortable life. McNair's descriptions of their lives are realistic and truly evocative. The poet's own childhood was lived in poverty. His father abandoned the family when the boy was very young, and the family experienced a great deal of financial hardship. McNair explained to Jack Barnes of Maine Books Online, "One of my earliest memories is my mother begging coal from the town manager."

McNair's poems depicting rural life tell seemingly simple stories while revealing a situation that is both dismal and complicated. Thus, in the poem "Mina Bell's Cows" a widow whose cows have died experiences more than merely a loss:

O where are Mina Bell's cows who gave no milk
and grazed on her dead husband's farm?
Each day she walked with them into the field,
loving their swayback dreaminess more
than the quickness of any dog or chicken . . .
O when the lightning struck Daisy and Bets,
her son dug such great hole in the yard
she could not bear to watch him . . .

"The Last Time Shorty Towers Fetched the Cows" concerns a smallish man who, inebriated, walked off the edge of a roof he was working on when it was time to call in the cows. In "The Bird Man" McNair uses bird metaphors to describe the meeting between a hired hand and an old and sick woman:

. . . she takes her curls away so I can see her small, shaved
head: where they opened the skull's bone to stop her
trembling. Here, she says, and Here, guiding my hand
so earnestly, so eager to help me find the pitiable, gray
skin that suddenly I am holding the poor, cracked egg
of her head in my arms and singing a song I do not
know . . .

McNair's largely autobiographical volume *My Brother Running* is replete with powerful metaphors. The poet uses his brother, a compulsive jogger who dropped dead of a heart attack while running, as a symbol of the ominous trend constantly to be in forward motion, to work harder and faster, no matter what the result or the cost. It is like a contemporary New England *Modern Times*.

In an essay written for *Ploughshares,* McNair discusses poets, poetry, and teaching poetry. He asserts that poetry is a difficult and subversive art. In comparing poetry to other literary forms, McNair states that, while an essay seeks to tell, a poem, as Robert Frost remarked, seeks to "tell how it can." The essay is a statement; the poem is a riddle. McNair describes the novelist as a carpenter, while the poet is a jeweler. In describing the process of writing poetry, McNair notes, "The process of poems is braille-like, allowing the reader entry by touch, so that what forms in the mind and heart forms first in the hand. In writing a poem, we must find the right thing—familiar and yet mysterious to the touch—to place in the reader's hand."

McNair remembers that his fifth and sixth grade teachers described him as "unconscious" while his mother called him "stubborn." He states, "Yet it was only by being both of these things that I became a poet."

—Christine Miner Minderovic

McNEIL, Florence

Nationality: Canadian. **Born:** Vancouver, British Columbia, 8 May 1940. **Education:** University of British Columbia, Vancouver, B.A. 1961, M.A. 1965. **Family:** Married David McNeil in 1973. **Career:** Instructor in English, Western Washington State College (now University), Bellingham, 1965–68; assistant professor, University of Calgary, Alberta, 1968–73, and University of British Columbia, 1973–76. Since 1976 full-time writer. **Awards:** Macmillan of Canada prize, 1965; Canada Council award, 1976, 1978, 1980, 1982; Canadian National Magazine award, 1979; Sheila Egoff prize, for children's literature, 1989. **Address:** 20 Georgia Wynd, Delta, British Columbia V4M 1A5, Canada.

PUBLICATIONS

Poetry

A Silent Green Sky. Vancouver, Klanak Press, 1967.
Walhachin. Fredericton, New Brunswick, Fiddlehead, 1972.
The Rim of the Park. Port Clements, British Columbia, Sono Nis Press, 1972.
Emily. Toronto, Clarke Irwin, 1975.
Ghost Towns. Toronto, McClelland and Stewart, 1975.
A Balancing Act. Toronto, McClelland and Stewart, 1979.
The Overlanders. Saskatoon, Saskatchewan, Thistledown Press, 1982.
Barkerville. Saskatoon, Saskatchewan, Thistledown Press, 1984.
Swimming out of History: Poems Selected and New. Parksville, British Columbia, Oolichan Press, 1991.
A Company of Angels. Victoria, British Columbia, Ekstasis Editions, 1999.

Novel

Breathing Each Other's Air. Vancouver, Polestar Press, 1994.

Play

Barkerville (produced Vancouver, 1987).

Radio Play: *Barkerville: A Play for Voices,* 1980.

Other

When Is a Poem: Creative Ideas for Teaching Poetry Collected from Canadian Poets. Toronto, League of Canadian Poets, 1980.
Miss P and Me (for children). Toronto, Clarke Irwin, 1982; New York, Harper, 1984.
All Kinds of Magic (for children). Vancouver, Douglas and McIntyre, 1984.
Catriona's Island (for children). Vancouver, Douglas and McIntyre, 1988.

Editor, *Here Is a Poem.* Toronto, League of Canadian Poets, 1983.
Editor, *Do the Whales Jump at Night: An Anthology of Canadian Poetry for Children.* Vancouver, Douglas and McIntyre, 1990.

*

Critical Studies: In *Canadian Literature* (Vancouver), autumn 1977; *CV 2* (Winnipeg), 4, spring 1979, and autumn 1982.

Florence McNeil comments:

I am interested in visual imagery and contrasts. Therefore, my poetry is often about art and visual imagery, and my imagery is mainly visual. I am also intrigued by history and the passing of time—how things remain the same and yet are different, how the past not only informs but also judges us, and how we are haunted by images of the past and the distant. I like to write about the family, an important historical link or connection to me. I come from Hebridean Scots, newly emigrated in the 1920s, bringing with them the Gaelic language and a romantic, ironic, self-effacing worldview. They have crept into much of my work; the sense of continuity with the past, with the ties of an extended family, and with a culture in many ways at odds with the North American culture provides much of my material. I am also interested in linked, connected poems; *Emily, Walhachin,* and *Barkerville* are all a series of connected poems. *The Overlanders* is a long poem based on a historical event. I am interested in the narrative, perhaps because I heard so many tales and legends as a child, but in transforming the narrative into something that speaks to us today, creating a universal situation, set of emotions. I use irony and wit in my writing to underline contrasts between reality and unreality. I have always been interested in the differences: representation of the thing and the thing itself and the various shades of truth in what is perceived. Perhaps it comes down to trying to untangle reality and illusion and ponder the unanswerable question, Is there any way to know? In my poetry I try to go below the surface of things, if not to know at least to make peace with the entanglement of fact and fiction. As I ventured into fiction, I found many of the same themes and interests emerging: the visual imagery, the contrasts, the sense of family, and of course the sense of story and narrative suggested by my linked poems.

*　　*　　*

Although Florence McNeil cannot be identified with any specific group, she is, like many other Canadian poets, a graduate of a university creative writing program, and in dedicating *A Balancing Act* she thanks Earle Birney "for his help and encouragement in the beginning." She also has a Canadian interest in the long documentary poem or linked series of poems based on historical material about a person, tribe, place, or event. In her book *Walhachin* she chose a settler's "imagined monologue" to tell the story of Walhachin, a town by the Thompson River in the British Columbian dry belt. Despite initial prosperity the town returned to sagebrush and wilderness after World War I had killed many of its men and a disastrous rainstorm had destroyed irrigation flumes. (The fascination with extinct communities is echoed in the title of another book, *Ghost Towns.*) Monologue also unifies the poems in *Emily,* based on the life and work of the great English-born West Coast painter Emily Carr (1871–1945), who is able to "find a leaf large as the coast."

In her book *Barkerville* McNeil draws on the gold rush days of an 1860s boomtown in the Cariboo Mountains country of northeastern British Columbia. Illustrated with period photographs, the book uses the metaphor of a stage set to exhibit a frenetic cast of adventurers seeking riches. Reinforcing the theatrical motif are poems and prose poems about the Barkerville Dramatic Society, Martin "the World-Renowned Wonder-Creating Magician," concerts and minstrel performances, and dance hall girls. The effect is of a photograph album filled with vivid snapshots, and the focal figure is Billy Barker, the hard-drinking Cornish sailor who struck gold but died penniless in 1894: "someone mentioned that he almost made it into the twentieth century." Appropriately, *Barkerville* was produced as a stage play in Vancouver in 1987.

The documentary impulse also extends to poems, particularly in *The Rim of the Park,* that illustrate scenes from McNeil's own life. In her most substantial work, *Ghost Towns,* she returns to her childhood, but the book also includes "Old Movies," "Montgolfier's Balloon," "Lilienthal's Glider," and a poem on the English Channel crossing of Louis Blériot. Even when the personal "I" intervenes, she is the onlooker. In "The Extra," perhaps her best poem, she says, "I am half a Roman spectator / at the cardboard coliseum," and she asks,

is there a place (beyond the corner of the screen)
to utilize
my enduring inability
to be completed?

Although sometimes at the expense of the imagistic incisiveness that marked poems like "At a Poetry Convention" ("The moon shone with transparent purpose / cutting through the lean quarrels of ice"), McNeil in later work has moved toward more fluid diction and increased openness of form. The sense of historical wonder remains, however. Her collection *Swimming out of History* gathers poems from six previous books and adds new ones. In the title poem time and timelessness merge:

Only the clear wimple of water
radiating
my arms circling
like hands on a clock
that has no numerals
And time is now.

—Fraser Sutherland

McNEILL, Anthony

Nationality: Jamaican. **Born:** St. Andrew, 17 December 1941. **Education:** Excelsior College, 1952; St. George's College, 1953–59; Nassau Community College, 1964–65; Johns Hopkins University, Baltimore, 1970–71, M.A. 1971; University of Massachusetts, Amherst, M.A. 1976. **Family:** Married Olive Samuel in 1970 (divorced); one child. **Career:** Civil service clerk, Port Maria and Kingston, 1960–64; trainee journalist and columnist, The Gleaner Company, Kingston, 1965–66; producer and scriptwriter, JIS-Radio, St. Andrew, 1966–68; trainee manager, Jamaica Playboy Club-Hotel, 1968–69; assistant to editor, *Jamaica Journal,* Kingston, 1970; teaching fellow, John Hopkins University, Baltimore, Maryland, 1970–71; teaching assistant, University of Massachusetts, 1971–75; tutor, CAC, University of the West Indies, Mona, Kingston, 1975–76, 1994–95; assistant director of Publications, Institute of Jamaica, Kingston, 1975–81; columnist, *The Gleaner,* 1981–82; lecturer, Excelsior Community College, Kingston, 1982–83; fellowship to International Writing Program, University of Iowa, 1985; teacher, Danny Williams School for the Deaf, Kingston, 1989; English teacher, Immaculate Conception High School, Kingston, 1990; English teacher, Holy Childhood High School, 1991; English teacher, St. Hugh's High School, 1992–93; freelance proofreader/copy editor, University of the West Indies, Mona, Kingston, 1994. **Awards:** Jamaica Festival prize, 1966, 1971, 1990; Silver Musgrave Medal, 1972. **Address:** c/o L. Wint, Camperdown, Linstead P.O., Jamaica, West Indies.

PUBLICATIONS

Poetry

Hello Ungod. Baltimore, Peacewood Press, 1971.
Reel from "The Life-Movie." Mona, Jamaica, Savacou, 1975.
Credences at the Altar of Cloud. Kingston, Institute of Jamaica, 1979.
Chinese Lanterns from the Blue Child. Leeds, England, Peepal Tree Press, 1998.

Other

Editor, with Neville Dawes, *The Caribbean Poem: An Anthology of 50 Caribbean Voices.* Kingston, Institute of Jamaica, 1976.

*

Critical Studies: By David Lyon, in *Contraband* (Portland, Maine), 1 May 1972; "An Extreme Vision" by Mervyn Morris, in *Sunday Gleaner* (Kingston), 28 January 1973; Wayne Brown, in *Jamaica Journal* (Kingston), March-June 1973; introduction to *Reel From "The Life-Movie,"* 1975, and "Lighting Words," in *Sunday Gleaner* (Kingston), January 1980, both by Dennis Scott; "An Invitation to Read McNeill's *Reel from "The Life-Movie"* by Bob Stewart, in *Jamaica Daily News* (Kingston), 29 June 1975; "He Writes Poetry 'of the Mindscape'" by Dorothy Pennant, in *Sunday Gleaner* (Kingston), 1975; "Our Modern Poets and Playwrights" by George Panton, in *Sunday Gleaner* (Kingston), 21 October 1979; "Please No

Labels for This Jamaican Poet" by Cuthbert Alexander, in *Trinidad Express,* 26 March 1979; "The Journey to the Light of Anthony McNeill's *Credences at the Altar of Cloud*" by Femanda Steele, in *Caribbean Quarterly* (St. Andrew, Jamaica), 30(1), March 1984; essay by Wilfred D. Samuels, in *Fifty Caribbean Writers: A Bio-Bibliographical Sourcebook* edited by Daryl C. Dance, Westport, Connecticut, Greenwood, 1986.

Anthony McNeill comments:

1. My poems are struck sorrow-lanterns.
2. My poems are village-girl simple.
3. The faster my writing comes into being the more it instructs me.
4. It's the music that comes from the floor of the sea that I'm after.
5. I'm a failed writer for money's success.
6. I kneel at one font,   Poem-and-Earth.
7. I stop at one church,   Poem-and-Earth.

*   *   *

Anthony McNeill is the first and most accomplished poet to appear out of his generation of the anglophone Caribbean. McNeill is new in the sense that, coming to maturity in the late 1960s, he is past the rhetorical colonial assertions and dramatic nationalist self-doubts of the *entre des guerres* writing that gave us Carter, Roach, and the early Derek Walcott. His work is of the present in that it deals with clairol and speed and is very much concerned with splitting, suicide, and animal identity. But there is nothing gratuitously contemporary about these energies and work. Here is a poet of patient, scrupulous craftsmanship who is concerned with rhythm, cadence, form, and the fissionable rather than fashionable qualities of his words.

McNeill's definitive collection is *Reel from "The Life-Movie."* It contains thirty poems, eighteen of which appear in his earlier twenty-poem *Hello Ungod.* The two together give a fair idea of McNeill's thematic interests and poetic development. He begins, in setting and style, as a lyrical nature poet, as in "Cliff-Walking": "and this cliff / where swallows confirm / the sooncome of rain, / of long evenings adrift / from your meaning again and again." But this is not traditional nature in which metaphors come to rest in contemplation of superordinate glories. Note the phrase "adrift / from your meaning" in the last line of the poem, which just before had said, "and my eyes ride / upward, oaring me back / to *loneliness*" (my italics). It is this modern urban problem and paradox, the concern of anglophone poetry from Auden through Lowell to Plath, that quickly comes to dominate his page.

In fact, the sense of interior loneliness so pervades McNeill's poetry that even physical love ("Mummy +," "Dermis") is vitiated by it, until the persona/victim loses his hold on the self and becomes other. This can be seen, for example, in the zoo poem "Rimbaud Jingle":

When you trip
on my skin of sickness, bruised blue,

I'll slip from my cage and into
the pure life of lions. I'm death-
sick of being two . . .

This leads to a frighteningly clear and "cool" contemplation of the antisolutions: suicide ("Who'll See He Dive?") or the use of hallucinogens ("The Lady Accepts the Needle Again"):

> The lady slips
> out to her loveliness
> lost irrevocably lost The Lady cries out
> for ships The Lady cries out for Paris . . .
>
> The Lady gets sexy & rings
> a towering eunuch into her hell

But what makes McNeill an important new voice is his comprehensive perception of this agony. The result of interior loneliness is not just personal freak but also social impasse ("Reel," "American Leader") and cultural, perhaps even cosmic, catastrophe ("Hello Ungod," "Black Space"). All of the post-Dostoyevsky archetypes gather in his poetry, suffering from the death of God. They include the mad clown, the schizophrenic, the ape, Aunt Angel, The Lady, Godot, Dracula, and the dread icons from McNeill's own formative experience of the Kingston ghetto—Brother Joe, Saint Ras, and Don Drummond, the sacred trombone man. All of them walk through a broken, shadowed wordscape "whose irradiant stop is light," whose "true country" is "both doubt and light."

It is from this double (paradoxical, sometimes schizoid) vision that McNeill's remarkable sensibility expresses itself. But his development contains its own perils. More and more the light of his poetry seems to radiate not from the sun, no matter how distant, but from an agnostic space lit only by the flicker of a (life) movie, so that the poet finds himself, as in "Flamingo," locked into the "ponderous ingot / that weights down the base of / his / box," until only a dark solar doubt (unseen ungod) is left: "At twenty-nine guru / I'm still unprepared; / one day I will shatter / / yank loose in the wind / as a man stuck together with pins. / When the god comes, I'll tell him the perfect *flamingo* he gifted is gone" (my italics). But surely for one so seriously embattled with his own talent, this can be only a temporary or apparent illumination.

—Edward Kamau Brathwaite

McPHERSON, Sandra

Nationality: American. **Born:** San Jose, California, 2 August 1943. **Education:** Westmont College, Santa Barbara, California, 1961–63; San Jose State College, B.A. in English 1965; University of Washington, Seattle, 1965–66. **Family:** Married 1) Henry Carlile in 1966 (divorced 1985), one daughter; 2) Walter Pavlich in 1995. **Career:** Technical writer, Honeywell Inc., Seattle, 1966. Member of the faculty, Writers Workshop, University of Iowa, Iowa City, 1974–76, 1978–80, and Pacific Northwest College of Art, Oregon Writers' Workshop, Portland, 1981–85; visiting faculty member, University of California, Berkeley, 1981. Since 1985 professor of English, University of California, Davis. Also runs an antiques business. Poetry editor, *Antioch Review*, Yellow Springs, Ohio, 1979–81, and *California Quarterly*, 1985–88; founder, Swan Scythe Press, 1999. **Awards:** Helen Bullis prize (*Poetry Northwest*), 1968; Bess Hokin

prize, 1972, and Oscar Blumenthal prize, 1975 (*Poetry,* Chicago); Ingram Merrill grant, 1972, 1984; Poetry Society of America Emily Dickinson prize, 1973; National Endowment for the Arts grant, 1974, 1980, 1985; Guggenheim fellowship, 1976; American Academy award, 1987; Eunice Tietjens Memorial prize (*Poetry,* Chicago), 1991. **Address:** 2052 Calaveras Avenue, Davis, California 95616–3021, U.S.A.

PUBLICATIONS

Poetry

Elegies for the Hot Season. Bloomington, University of Indiana Press, 1970.
Radiation. New York, Ecco Press, 1973.
The Year of Our Birth. New York, Ecco Press, 1978.
Sensing. San Francisco, Meadow Press, 1980.
Patron Happiness. New York, Ecco Press, 1984.
Pheasant Flower. Missoula, Montana, Owl Creek Press, 1985.
Floralia. Portland, Oregon, Trace, 1985.
Responsibility for Blue. Denton, Texas, Trilobite Press, 1985.
At the Grave of Hazel Hall. Sweden, Maine, Ives Street Press, 1988.
Streamers. New York, Ecco Press, 1988.
Designating Duet. West Burke, Vermont, Janus Press, 1989.
The God of Indeterminacy. Urbana and Chicago, University of Illinois Press, 1993.
Edge Effect: Trails and Portrayals. Middletown, Connecticut, Wesleyan University Press, 1996.
The Spaces between Birds: Mother/Daughter Poems 1967–1995. Middletown, Connecticut, Wesleyan University Press, 1996.
Beauty in Use. West Burke, Vermont, Janus Press, 1997.

Other

Editor, *Journey from Essex: Poems for John Clare.* Port Townsend, Washington, Graywolf Press, 1981.
Editor, with Bill Henderson and Laura Jensen, *The Pushcart Prize XIV: Best of the Small Presses, 1989–1990.* Wainscott, New York, Pushcart Press, 1989.

*

Critical Studies: "Let Me See That Book" by Marie Harris, in *Parnassus* (New York), 3(1), 1974; "Women Poets and the 'Northwest School'" by Carol Jane Bangs, in *Women, Women Writers, and the West,* edited by L.L. Lee and Merrill Lewis, Troy, New York, Whitston, 1979; interview with Cecelia Hagen, in *Northwest Review* (Eugene, Oregon), 20(2–3), 1982; "The Belabored Scene, The Subtlest Detail: How Craft Affects Heat in the Poetry of Sharon Olds and Sandra McPherson" by Terri Brown-Davidson, in *Hollins Critic* (Hollins College, Virginia), 29(1), February 1992; "Flowery Codes: Sandra McPherson's Poetics of Gender and Naturalism" by Suzanne Matson, in *Denver Quarterly,* 28(2), fall 1993.

*   *   *

From her first book on, Sandra McPherson has demonstrated an unusual ability to organize diverse associations and experiences into rich, complex, and deeply satisfying poems. Hers is a world in which the presence of nature—she is unusually intimate with the natural world, even for a poet—calls for an imaginative response that looks to rival the curiosities, wonders, and coincidences of natural history and taxonomy. The human presence on the planet, complicating everything by its needs and appropriations, is never ignored, but the poet, while conscious of her own human fallibility, is able to bring a kind of objectivity to her scrutiny of life that keeps her clear of sentimentality or special pleading. The reader learns to trust her: the rigor of her designs, the scope of her sympathies, the shaping power of her imagination.

One can, of course, trace influences in McPherson's work, especially those of Sylvia Plath and Elizabeth Bishop, but she is very much her own person and voice from early on. A poem like "Resigning from a Job in a Defense Industry," in her first collection, *Elegies for the Hot Season,* typifies her originality. It glances at the superficially exciting language of the technocratic world—"microhenries," "wee wee ductors," "blue beavers"—and then swerves to respond to the impoverished imaginations of fellow workers trying to preserve a sustaining relationship with the outside world. The speaker recalls the company talent show, with its "oils and sentiment / Thick on still lifes and seacoasts, / The brush strokes tortured as a child's / First script." The level gaze hovers here between judgment and sympathy in a way that satisfies the poem's and reader's best instincts: "Someone / Had studied driftwood; another man, / The spray of a wave, the mania / Of waters above torpedoes." The poem captures a large segment of modern American life in a confident, unfussy way. It is clear even at this youthful stage that the poet can transcend her ordinary self and achieve, through apparently effortless language, a visionary outlook that never loses its rooting in ordinary experience.

Subsequent collections have deepened and widened this command, displaying a steady growth of mastery and a consistent development of style. One can follow details of the poet's life—marriage, motherhood, eventual divorce, mental illness in a daughter, remarriage, relations with adoptive parents, and a midlife reunion with birth parents—but their function is that more or less impersonal grounding in experience mentioned above. One can also monitor the sustaining presence of the natural world, as in this fifth section of the ten-part poem "Studies in the Imaginary" from *The Year of Our Birth:*

> A botany class comes close
> where I am wandering the spongy ground around
> a spring. How unlikely they will identify me,
> stop and pronounce the existence of anyone
> moving faster than locust or colt's foot.
> But then, if I could even approach on foot
>
> or with an extrovert word,
> I wouldn't bow out to meditate, awkward
> as that duck, green and bronze, strolling grass-spattered
> through bamboo. Strangers
> are so fast, no slowing you, no halting the wings
> of the hummingbird.

Interesting things are being done with rhyme, sound, and form here, but it is the mystery of rhythm and encounter that is central both to the subject of the poem and the behavior of the language. The light touch and elusive control of statement might recall John Ashbery, but the expert handling of submerged drama and marshaled associations is clearly McPherson's own.

McPherson's structures can become so intricate and her associations so private that she occasionally loses her way or exhausts her reader's patience, but the time she takes with individual poems and with assembling her collections bespeaks a willingness to wait and work until she can get it right. Emotional control, Bishop's way as against Plath's, a survivor's mode, seems more and more crucial to McPherson's success. The greater the possibilities for runaway feelings, the greater the need to rein them in through understatement and exceptionally orchestration of detail. A short poem from *Patron Happiness* helps make the point:

EARTHSTARS. BIRTHPARENTS' HOUSE

> Geasters. She bent down
> At the dappled base of the tree,
> And among the brown leaves
> Geasters stood up.
>
> Oranges peel like these,
> She said. Rinds bent back.
>
> When it rains, their legs swell up
> And walk.
>   Stranger feet
> Than mine
> All those years
> Outside your door.

The final stanza is charged with the emotion of a woman meeting her mother for the first time in middle age. It is powerful not only for its understatement but also for its objectified setting. Mother and daughter are not discussing their lives and feelings but rather looking together at an unusual fungus. We sense that this is no dodge. The poet's subjective interest is as firmly fixed on the wonder of a name ("geaster" means "earthstar") and on the curious shape, texture, and behavior of a mushroom most people would pass without noticing as it is on her strange reunion. The poem's implicit claim is that there is finally no difference between fact and emotion, spirit and matter. It knits the world together again before our eyes. A reader who would fully understand the poem must be willing to take the trouble to know what a geaster is, to look it up in a book or, better still, find one in the field. This poet will not encourage us to be lazy, unobservant, ignorant, or maunderingly subjective.

She has typically informed herself exhaustively about these subjects before plunging into an imaginative relationship with them that, once again, has given rise to surprising, intricate, and moving poems. No one who reads one of her quilt poems, much less the series of them, is likely to look at a quilt with the same eyes again. Her sympathy with the unsung creators of her own culture has proved to be profound and revelatory.

—David Young

McQUEEN, Cilla

Nationality: British and New Zealander. **Born:** Birmingham, England, 22 January 1949. **Education:** Columba College, Dunedin; Otago University, M.A. (honors) in French 1970. **Family:** Married

Ralph Hotere in 1974; one daughter. **Career:** Teacher. Artist: individual shows—Bosshard Galleries, Dunedin, 1982; Red Metro Gallery, Dunedin, 1983. **Awards:** New Zealand Book award, 1983, 1989; P.E.N./Jessie Mackay award, 1983; Air New Zealand/P.E.N. travel award, 1984; Robert Bums fellowship, 1985, 1986; Fulbright Visiting Writer's fellowship, 1985; Inaugural Australian-New Zealand Writers' exchange fellowship, 1987; Goethe Institute scholarship, 1988; New Zealand Book award, 1991, for *Berlin Diary*. **Address:** P.O. Box 69, Portobello, Dunedin, New Zealand.

PUBLICATIONS

Poetry

Homing In. Dunedin, McIndoe, 1982.
Anti Gravity. Dunedin, McIndoe, 1984.
Wild Sweets. Dunedin, McIndoe, 1986.
Benzina. Dunedin, McIndoe, 1988.
Berlin Diary. Dunedin, McIndoe, 1990.
Crikey (new and selected poems 1978–1994). Dunedin, McIndoe, 1994.

Recordings: *Bad Bananas,* Strawberry Sound, 1986–87; *Otherwise,* with Alistair Macdougall, 1989.

Plays

Harlequin and Columbine (produced Dunedin, 1987).
Red Rose Café (produced Dunedin, 1990).

Radio Play: *Spacy Calcutta's Travelling Truth Show,* 1986.

*

Critical Studies: "Pilot Small's Transport across the Meniscus: The Poetry of Cilla McQueen" by Ian Wedde, in *Untold* (Christchurch), 3, autumn 1985; by Maree Brown, in *Landfall,* 45(3), September 1991.

Cilla McQueen comments:

My work is concerned with duality, the theme of the meniscus, the borderline area between subjective and objective experience.

*   *   *

Stylistic changes have taken place in Cilla McQueen's poetry. The lyricism that tended to dominate the poems in her first volume yielded first to a pared-down, energetic, pop-inspired minimalism, then reemerged in *Benzina* with "beauty in spareness. / what is & what is not" ("Some Poets"). The distinctive aspects of her poetry remain: a painter's eye for detail and color, a sense of the dramatic, and a quirky sense of humor.

McQueen describes herself as "poet, composer and intermedia artist." This versatility has been combined with performance, for example, as poet and musician with a rock group. It also plays an important role in her writing through her fondness for visual patterns, references to pop culture, and synaesthetic imagery. In *Homing In* her "Words Fail Me" gaily knocks down artificial boundaries between the arts, as the poet's desire "to put into line what / the words are not fluid enough for" cause her to start

> drafting lines on to graph paper
> & pairing coordinates. I hope
> that they can then be mass produced
> in the form of sheet music which
> can be sung anywhere.

The poem concludes with a visual pun on the inadequacies of language, paradoxical in its success:

> Words
>   fail me she says
> & proceeds to fill several more lines
> with scribbled black biro words fail me

Visual patterns, which should be seen on the page to gain their full effect—dropped lines, half lines—are important structural features of many other poems in *Homing In*. "Low Tide, Aramoana" and "Weekend Sonnets, Carey's Bay" share this mimetic approach to seascapes and emotions, as does "By the Water":

> Dark glissades to meet the
> light   on reefs of air: I find you
> dismembered in the landscape
> among indolent hills
>   You disperse & are
> gone again

The combination of sensual responses to landscape in "Words Fail Me" is the subject of "Synaesthesia," a much less visual poem in *Benzina*. Here, through the formality of rhymed iambic pentameter, the same boundaries are recrossed in a complex series of patterns and harmonies that are directed more toward the ear than the eye:

> the eyes see patterns that the brain can sing
> invisibly the music pictures sound
> draws out the music inside everything
> & sings the lines of light my hand has found

While experimenting with language and form, McQueen has also given her poetry satiric bite. "Living Here," one of her most frequently anthologized poems, pictures each New Zealander surrounded by a personal flock of sheep, "little human centres each within an outer / circle of sheep around us like a ring of / covered wagons." Gradually the human characters take on the characteristics of sheep, bleating "the safest place in the world to live," insulated but also isolated by their fleece:

> We're calling fiercely to each other
> through the muffled spaces   grateful for
> any wrist-brush
>   cut of mind or touch of music
> lightning in the intimate weather of the soul.

The transition from whimsy is highly effective, its judgment softened just enough by the inclusive "we." "Living Here" also directs attention to the frequent images of electricity and lightning in the poems that succeed it, poems that deliberately try to leap the "muffled spaces" that inhibit communication.

Anti Gravity is a move in this direction, its title signifying McQueen's growing interest in the language of physics as well as her continuing attack on conformity. Gravity in one sense is successfully defied by the playfulness of her lines; gravity in its other sense can be less easy to defy. The stuntman in "That's Incredible" catches his falling parachute "with one second to spare," a second in which the poet speculates "where the quasars drill out to infinite distance" and "while the time ripples past in numbers." "Princess Alice the Incredible Lady Gymnast" meets a different end. Having "constructed a flying machine / of surpassing grace & lightness / out of shells & feathers & fishing-line," Princess Alice meets the fate of Icarus:

> . . . a cloud of birds forced her down
> in unfamiliar country
> where a parliament of trees
> condemned her for alienation from earth
> & sentenced her forthwith
> to dissolution
>> (now you
>> see her
>> now you

Poetry also being, as it declares itself, "anti gravity," McQueen discusses its creation in terms of similar danger in "No Poem":

> I like the relationship between thought & paper
> to get faster . . .
>> the more you play around with words
> the more they frighten you with the punch
> they pack   like the images I cover my walls with
> which . . .
>> have become unfixed scraps of reality
> exploding on contact
>> which is why we seem to be picking
> our way through a minefield just a few of us anarchists
> white flags & mortars both ways across no mans land

This sense of danger pervades the shorter, sharper poems of *Wild Sweets*. "Wild Sweets" alternates conventional images of romantic love with violence and danger: "what I mean by / love? a terrorist incident / a torn artery an electric arc a / touch without fear." So too does "A Lightning Tree": "I have made of words a lightning tree / to earth my dangerous love through poetry." These and other poems carry the electrical charge of "lightning in the intimate weather of the soul." "Wink" and "Dreamscript 1" use cut-and-jump film techniques.

Benzina displays less of this kinetic energy. McQueen's voice here is generally quieter, more reflective, the lyricism that had been displaced returning with the brevity that had displaced it. *Wild Sweets* includes several poems of this kind ("Nuages," "Solstice"), *Benzina* far more. In "Under the Tree," "Silence," and "Rainlight" ("sun bows / mirrored colours / over / to join beneath us / to hold the water / calm in a bowl") their delicate stillness contrasts with a newer form of experiment, the prose poem ("Short Story, 1984") of short sentences and a dramatic use of punctuation.

But whether in pop or lyrical mode, McQueen could never be called a romantic. Even when grief and shock are her subjects, as in "Vegetable Garden Poem (1)," the emotions are buried in the middle of the poem ("a friend of ours shot himself / yesterday"), which ends with the poet "trying to write. / Trying to disappear." In "Some Poets" she sets out quite clearly what her poetry is not and, more importantly, what it is, for "Some poets,"

> they get
> shit on their shoes
> & trail it everywhere
>
> their
> ragged impossible
> tenderness
>
> ah so bloody romantic
> still I wish
>
> huh.
> fuck wishing.
>
> time for some
> naked light!
>
> beauty in spareness.
> what is & what is not.

—Nan Bowman Albinski

McWHIRTER, George

Nationality: Canadian. **Born:** Belfast, Northern Ireland, 26 September 1939. Immigrated to Canada in 1966. **Education:** Boys' Model School, Belfast, 1948–51; Grosvenor High School, Belfast, 1951–57; Queen's University, Belfast, 1957–62, B.A. (honors) in English 1961, Dip.Ed. 1962; University of British Columbia, Vancouver (Macmillan prize), 1968–70, M.A. 1970. **Family:** Married Angela Coid in 1963; one daughter and one son. **Career:** Assistant master, Kilkeel Secondary School, Northern Ireland, 1962–64, and Bangor Grammar School, Northern Ireland, 1964–65; English teacher, University of Barcelona, and Berlitz School, Barcelona, 1965–66, and Alberni Secondary School, Port Alberni, British Columbia, 1966–68. Assistant professor, 1970–76, associate professor, 1976–82, professor since 1983, and head of creative writing, University of British Columbia, 1983–93. Associate editor, 1970–76, coeditor, 1976–77, advisory editor, 1977–89, and since 1990 adviser on translation, *Prism International*, Vancouver; editor, *Words from the Inside*, Kingston, Ontario, 1974–75. **Awards:** Canada Council grant, 1969, 1975; Macmillan prize, 1969; Commonwealth poetry prize, 1972; Ethel Wilson prize, for fiction, 1988; F.R. Scott prize, for translation, 1988. **Address:** 4637 West 13th Avenue, Vancouver, British Columbia V6R 2V6, Canada.

PUBLICATIONS

Poetry

Catalan Poems. Ottawa, Oberon Press, 1971.
Columbuscade. Vancouver, Hoffer, 1974.
Bloodlight for Malachi McNair. San Francisco, Kanchenjunga, 1974.
Queen of the Sea. Ottawa, Oberon Press, 1976.
Twenty-Five. Fredericton, New Brunswick, Fiddlehead, 1978.
Ties. Toronto, League of Canadian Poets, 1980.
The Island Man. Ottawa, Oberon Press, 1981.
Fire before Dark. Ottawa, Oberon Press, 1983.
The Voyeur and the Countess Wielopolska. Vancouver, Tanks/Hoffer, 1988.
A Staircase for All Souls. Lantzville, Oolichan Books, 1993.
Incubus: The Dark Side of the Light. Ottawa, Oberon Press, 1995.
Musical Dogs. Ottawa, Oberon Press, 1996.
Ovid in Saskatchewan. Toronto, League of Canadian poets, 1998.

Plays

Radio Plays: *Suspension,* 1969; *The House on the Water, 1981; The Listeners,* 1981.

Novels

Paula Lake. Ottawa, Oberon Press, 1984.
Cage. Ottawa, Oberon Press, 1987.
The Listeners. Ottawa, Oberon, 1991.

Short Stories

Bodyworks. Ottawa, Oberon Press, 1974.
God's Eye. Ottawa, Oberon Press, 1981.
Coming to Grips with Lucy. Ottawa, Oberon Press, 1982.
A Bad Day to be Winning. Ottawa, Oberon, 1991.

Other

Editor and Translator, *The Selected Poems of José Emilio Pacheco.* New York, New Directions, 1987.
Editor and Translator, *Where Words Like Monarchs Fly: A Cross-Generational Anthology of Mexican Poets (1934–1955) in Translations from North of the 49th Parallel.* Vancouver, Anvil Press, 1998.

*

Manuscript Collection: University of British Columbia, Vancouver.

George McWhirter comments:

My work to date has been preoccupied with people and substance, people as consumers of substance and at the same time as those consumed by substance. He who eats will in turn be eaten. Such was the base of *Catalan Poems.* The family, man, woman, and child, one flesh, one substance was the central dramatic vehicle for this. *Columbuscade* uses the idea of Columbus to deal with the impossibility of escape from the flesh in terms of space; we can jump no farther than ourselves. Even if there was a new world, few would embark; the superscription of the book runs, ''All are chosen for the crew, but few

embark fearing a new world.'' This is the fundamental dilemma in *Queen of the Sea,* which is set in the Belfast shipyards. Recently I have come to regard things and substance as part of the infinite imagination of light. The unknown is the point of disembarkation, the intellect provides place-names as we pass, the real rudder in the rear of the head is the intuition. The main thing that poetry does for me is turn ideas or intimations into the properties of the five senses. This is what life itself does for us.

(1995) *Cage,* in the person of the Irish American priest Ben Carragher, deals with the conflict of faith and works. In giving the Tetelcingan Indians a cottage industry that manufactures bird cages in the churchyard, the priest dedicates himself to the tangible benefits of a religious organization, which ultimately traps his spirit and his body in the village ''for good.'' The small miracle he has wrought becomes a test of faith.

Fire before Dark, with the long poem ''Training in the Language,'' looks at immigrants being given a second life in their second tongue, a difficult way of being born again.

A Staircase for All Souls sees British Columbia as the physical paradise for which the immigrants, who have come from the Old to the New World, have forfeited the spiritual. The title is ironic. For the souls on the West Coast of Canada, they sail permanently between two shores: eternity and the flesh.

*   *   *

The poems of George McWhirter represent a playful though highly formal approach to poetic expression. While his poems feature cryptic metaphors and complicated analogues, they are linked chronologically and tend to relate a larger narrative. Each of his five major books serves to reconfirm and to reassess its immediate precursor at the levels of both versification and ideology. Individual poems do not stand independently but instead function to advance the greater argument of the volumes in which they appear. In *Queen of the Sea,* for instance, McWhirter's subjects are mainly places and things. His impressionistic approach in poems such as ''The Floating Restaurant,'' ''Keel,'' ''A Launching,'' and ''The Plate Shop'' reveals a departure from his earlier *Catalan Poems,* a closely knit series of narrative verses featuring dialogue and the intimate thoughts of a cast of recurring characters.

The McWhirter canon can be seen as a succession of converging and diverging stylistic and philosophical notions. On the one hand, his poems can be exclusively imagistic, while, on the other, they can espouse complicated, hypothetical ideas at length. In *Catalan Poems* McWhirter tells the magical story of Eduardo Valls, a citizen of dying Catalonia. The poems constitute an array of darkly intriguing and paradoxical characters, from Maria Jesus, a Madonna-prostitute figure (''a country girl / Who offers herself for hire''), to Raura, the surrealist aficionado who fancies a real dinner with Dali at a San José market. The collection anticipates the intensely Spanish flavor of McWhirter's verse and touches upon the poet's thematic preoccupation with expatriate and immigrant experience. The itinerant, exotic nature of *Catalan Poems* is an essential facet of McWhirter's style and is featured in other books such as *Twenty-Five* and *The Island Man.*

Like *Queen of the Sea, Twenty-Five* is also a series of impressionistic descriptions of places and objects. In this book of poems about Mexico, which have titles beginning with ''One'' and ending with ''Twenty-Five,'' McWhirter's subjects range from Vera Cruz to hummingbirds. Unlike *Queen of the Sea,* however, *Twenty-Five* is consistently tricky and comic, fraught with wordplay and fantastic, often sensual visions. In ''Five'' ''The dog tackles the turkey / and he gobbles.'' In ''Eighteen''

> Her tamales toddle
> fat and slimy out of their corn
> wrapper. They squat
> in the hand like weary white
> selignite waiting for an order.

The oddly integrated images continue in *The Island Man.* In ''Saturday-Morning Drag'' the author asks his readership to ''consider Fate, plain and plastic / as an old Volkswagen wheel.'' *The Island Man,* however, distinguishes itself in other ways as well, for it describes in an overtly autobiographical fashion McWhirter's dealings with linguistic duplicity and cultural dislocation. Quite a few of the poems in the collection rely on the author's experience and observations as a well-traveled Irishman turned Canadian. ''One thing that defies comprehension to the island / man is the continent,'' says the persona of ''Insular'' in speaking about Canada; nevertheless, ''he will begin the study of a nation / at his leisure.'' In fact, much of *The Island Man* is the leisurely study, as McWhirter says in ''Saturday-Morning Drag,'' ''charting the traffic / of peoples—Irish and Canadian, Indian and white.''

The charting continues in *Fire before Dark,* a volume that concerns itself primarily with Irish and western Canadian traditions. McWhirter's long poem ''Training in the Language'' articulates the dilemmas and the benefits of living in a multicultural society; as the poem says succinctly at its outset, ''And when we got there, / we couldn't understand / The half of them.'' One of McWhirter's more important poems, it analyzes cultural alienation at the level of language—''languaging'' in the multicultural vernacular of West Coast life—''Kalamari,'' ''Kitsilano,'' ''salmon from the Pacific.'' Even differences as subtle as Irish and North American English are explored. Representative of McWhirter's poetic philosophy, ''Training in the Language'' espouses mutual understanding and reconciliation. He envisions Canada as

> this great scarred glacier of a place, unable
> To snap the beam of scalding sunlight from its eye
>
> Will melt, evaporate.

Yet while the image of a commingling of cultures across the many provinces that make up Canada—of ''bald tundra, / Or badlands / Orgumbo''—appears to be a reality, McWhirter admits that Canada, like other countries, deceives itself. The great cultural ''mosaic'' of the nation, he suggests, ''isn't so, / The land up there still suffocates with snow.''

—Susan C. Hines

MEAD, Matthew

Nationality: British. **Born:** Buckinghamshire, 12 September 1924. **Military Service:** British Army, 1942–47, including three years in India, Ceylon, and Singapore. **Family:** Married Ruth Adrian. **Career:** Editor, *Satis* magazine, Edinburgh, 1960–62. Has lived in Germany since 1962, currently in Bad Godesberg. **Address:** c/o Anvil Press Poetry, 69 King George Street, London SE10 8PX, England.

PUBLICATIONS

Poetry

A Poem in Nine Parts. Worcester, Migrant Press, 1960.
Identities. Worcester, Migrant Press, 1964.
Kleinigkeiten. Newcastle upon Tyne, Satis, 1966.
Identities and Other Poems. London, Rapp and Carroll, 1967.
The Administration of Things. London, Anvil Press Poetry, 1970.
Penguin Modern Poets 16, with Harry Guest and Jack Beeching. London, Penguin, 1970.
In the Eyes of the People. Edinburgh, Satis, 1973.
Minusland. Edinburgh, Satis, 1977.
The Midday Muse. London, Anvil Press Poetry, 1979.
A Roman in Cologne. Edinburgh, Satis, 1985.
A Sestina at the End of Socialism: And Other Final Verses. Ampleforth, York, Satis, 1996.

Other

Translator, with Ruth Mead, *Shadow Land: Selected Poems of Johannes Bobrowski.* London, Carroll, 1966; revised edition, London, Donald Carroll, 1967.
Translator, with Ruth Mead, *Generation,* by Heinz Winfried Sabais. Edinburgh, Satis, 1967.
Translator, with Ruth Mead and others, *O the Chimneys,* by Nelly Sachs. New York, Farrar Straus, 1967; as *Selected Poems of Nelly Sachs,* London, Cape, 1968.
Translator, with Ruth Mead, *Generation and Other Poems,* by Heinz Winfried Sabais. London, Anvil Press Poetry, 1968.
Translator, with Ruth Mead, *Amfortiade and Other Poems,* by Max Hölzer. Edinburgh, Satis, 1968.
Translator with Ruth Mead, *Horst Bienek.* Santa Barbara, California, Unicorn Press, 1969.
Translator, with Ruth Mead, *Elisabeth Borchers.* Santa Barbara, California, Unicorn Press, 1969.
Translator, with Ruth Mead and Michael Hamburger, *The Seeker and Other Poems,* by Nelly Sachs. New York, Farrar Straus, 1970.
Translator, with Ruth Mead, *Selected Poems,* by Johannes Bobrowski and Horst Bienek. London, Penguin, 1971.
Translator, with Ruth Mead, *Mitteilungen/Communications,* by Heinz Winfried Sabais. Dammstadt, Roether, 1971.
Translator, with Ruth Mead, *Socialist Elegy,* by Heinz Winfried Sabais. Darmstadt, Roether, 1975.
Translator, with Ruth Mead, *From the Rivers,* by Johannes Bobrowski. London, Anvil Press Poetry, 1975.
Translator, with Ruth Mead, *The Tightrope Walker,* by Christa Reinig. Edinburgh, Satis, 1981.
Translator, with Ruth Mead, *The People and the Stones,* by Heinz Winfried Sabais. London, Anvil Press Poetry, 1983.
Translator, with Ruth Mead, *The Raven,* by Gunter Bruno Fuchs. Edinburgh, Satis, 1984.
Translator, with Ruth Mead, *Shadow Lands,* by Johannes Bobrowski. London, Anvil Press Poetry, 1984.

Translator, with Ruth Mead, *Songs from the Old Folk's Home,* by Christian Geissler. Edinburgh, Satis, 1988.

Translator, with Ruth Mead and Eva Hesse, *Selected Poems 1957–1987,* by Horst Bienek. Greensboro, North Carolina, Unicorn Press, 1989.

Translator, with Ruth Mead, *Doors of Smoke,* by Wolfgang Bächler. Edinburgh, Satis, 1991.

Translator, with Ruth Mead, *Flamingo Dance,* by Urs Oberlin. Edinburgh, Satis, 1991.

*

Critical Studies: By Christopher Middleton, in *London Magazine,* 1964, and in *Neue Deutsche Literatur* (Berlin), February 1965; by A. Kingsley Weatherhead, in *The British Dissonance,* Columbia, University of Missouri Press, 1983; ''The Poetry of Matthew Mead'' by Dick Davis, London, *PN Review,* #42.

*   *   *

Matthew Mead has been spoken of as a modernist, a social critic, and a poet who is proletarian and unacademic. On the contrary, his qualities are those of literary accomplishment. He can turn an epigram or a ballad as well as anyone writing today. The reader may feel his way through deliberately fragmented homages to Ezra Pound or Robert Creeley to light upon such finely tooled verse as this:

Bodies are rolled from bed to scuffed slippers
and day stiff-jointed; in sense repetition;
in spring one more spring; the figure
in a worn carpet traced with a dull eye.

And the house old, the wind's sound, each ache
lent art and length, given due weight
the dragging footfall. For this are we bent
and gnarled and wrinkled—to cross the room . . .

It is not that Mead is an escapist; his translations of Bobrowski, done in collaboration with his wife, would assure us of that. Rather, he is a Poundian in a sense deeper than that of technical allegiance, an aesthete distressed by the blood and chaos of totalitarian Europe. The poem quoted, ''To Redistort a Weltanschauung,'' comes from his retrospective collection *Identities.* Here is an extract from *The Administration of Things:*

What she herself believes
No man alive conceives

We tell the lawful tale
(All fictions else must fail)

And loyal beyond the lie
Nor daring to deny

That what we have she gave
We make of what we have

Lending it length and art
Embellishing each part

A faith to ravage noon
With phases of the moon . . .

It is clear that writing such as this resembles nothing so much as the more Elizabethan lyrics of John Donne—''But come bad chance / And we join to it our strength / And we teach it art and length / Itself o'er us to advance . . .''—or the more lapidary verse of Andrew Marvell—''Caesar's head at last / Did through his laurels blast / . . . And if we must speak true / Much to the man is due . . .'' In Mead's original work there is a gap between subject and presentation. Those who have followed his work with interest all these years hoped that he would turn this characteristic hiatus to dramatic use. Or if not that, they wished him to find a range of subject matter suited to the cool detachment of his technique.

—Philip Hobsbaum

MEAD, Philip (Stirling)

Nationality: Australian. **Born:** Brisbane, Queensland, 31 August 1953. **Education:** Australian National University, Canberra, 1972–75, B.A. 1975; La Trobe University, Melbourne, 1976–80, M.A. 1981; Melbourne University, 1986–90, Ph.D. 1990. **Family:** Married Jenna Mead in 1974; one daughter. **Career:** Lockie Lecturer in Australian Writing, University of Melbourne, 1987–95. Since 1995 senior lecturer in English, University of Tasmania, Hobart. Founder, with Alan Gould, David Brooks, and Mark O'Connor, *Canberra Poetry.* **Address:** English Department, University of Tasmania, Hobart 7000, Australia.

PUBLICATIONS

Poetry

Songs from Another Country. Canberra, Open Door Press, 1975.
Be Faithful to Go: Poems. London, Angus & Robertson, 1980.
The Spring-Mire: Poems. Canberra, Brindabella Press, 1982.
The River Is in the South. St. Lucia, University of Queensland Press, 1984.

Other

Editor, with Gerald Murnane and Jenny Lee, *The Temperament of Generations: Fifty Years of Writing in Meanjin.* Carlton, Victoria, Meanjin: Melborune University Press, 1990.
Editor, with John Tranter, *The Penguin Book of Modern Australian Poetry.* Ringwood, Victoria, Penguin Books, 1991.
Editor, with John Tranter, *The Bloodaxe Book of Modern Australian Poetry.* Newcastle upon Tyne, Bloodaxe, 1994.
Editor, *Kenneth Slessor: Critical Essays.* St. Lucia, University of Queensland Press, 1996.

*

Manuscript Collection: National Library of Australia, Parkes.

Critical Study: "Mixed Motives, Mixed Diction: Recent Australian Poetry" by Chris Wallace-Crabbe, in *Journal of Commonwealth Literature* (East Sussex, England), 19(1), 1984.

*   *   *

Philip Mead's early chapbook *Songs from Another Country,* now suppressed, announced his allegiance to the Bodalla district and his youthful enthusiasm for the romantic figures of the poet-horseman Adam Lindsay Gordon and the outlaw Ned Kelly. Its imprint, Open Door Press, recalls Mead's association with Kevin Hart and Alan Gould as youthful Canberra writers in the burgeoning poetry scene in Australia in the 1970s. Mead's editing of the magazine *Canberra Poetry* was an early demonstration of his interest in taking on an editorial role.

The poetic voice of *Be Faithful to Go* is characterized by thoughtful concentration. Mead alternates subjects from art (Bartók, Mondrian, Wallace Stevens, a *Jules and Jim* still, a Conder painting, a museum) with brief essays on passages of Australian landscape and monologues for the colonial orator Deniehy and the explorer Wills. The mode of "Chinese Graves in Beechworth Cemetery" is reflection:

> . . . walking here, aware
> to the rim of my eye, of what earth is for . . .

> For those who were quietly digested
> when the mine-shaft's yellow mud stomach caved in,
> for those who died young, unjustly or sick
> the glittering blood-crimson characters
> spattered across their stone plugs . . .

The dying Wills's monologue, on the other hand, strikes an extreme of agony, perhaps that of a new identity:

> Now . . . I am dying like an angel
> wrapped in flame, one moment this, the next
> bones knocking about the rock,
> part of the desert's cranium . . .
> . . . I am dying like the worst
> in hell, the worst in hell shall know me.
> Let the sun swing and gong against
> the moon. I am dying like my God.

The Spring-Mire, a limited edition with fine drawings, is suggestive of Mead's later direction. There are several short pieces with observations that owe their style to Stevens:

> The wind is always
> moving against the trees here,
> which is the way we move . . .

> We are learning
> to speak like the day
> with the sun through
> our words.

This River Is in the South (1984) collects poems Mead wished to preserve. The poet seems to have assessed his natural bent for a long-lined, thoughtfully paced meditation that is nonetheless tight enough to be constantly resonant with meaning and with the sensation of feeling toward meaning.

Visual reference points are used in the fine "A Photograph of Delmore Schwartz" and in "Woman at a Window" (a Degas). In poems such as "The Henty River, Western Tasmania" a new primacy is discovered in experience of the land:

> . . . you are travelling back . . . Back

> across the spring-mire you can feel is valved and
>   ascending.
> But the returning is through change not distance
> to the river. There is no distance through the forest
> now,

> only a sudden thickening of secrecy and green shade,
> the rain crowding through the leaves like applause. You
> will
> know this travelling and you will know the place. It is the

> stations of forgiveness and of reverberating silence. And
>   the return.

The impulse is to visit sacredness—"the place," "the secret place"— where earth and human being meet, as in "Magnificence":

> I am saying there is

> a declension in memory where the mind goes and is.
> Where it is magnificent; where the wildflower bends in
>   the rain.

Mead's perceptions assume even more importance in light of the fact that he has been poetry editor for *Meanjin Quarterly* for several years and also has become the joint editor of Hazard Press, which publishes Australian and New Zealand poets. Though he has been slow to write and to create his own style, he has a depth of feeling and subtlety in the course of his thought that arouses expectations.

—Judith Rodriguez

MEEHAN, Paula

Nationality: Irish. **Born:** Dublin, 25 June 1955. **Education:** Trinity College, Dublin, 1972–77, B.A. 1977; Eastern Washington University, Cheney, Washington, 1981–83, M.F.A. 1983. **Career:** Has held varioius residencies in universities, communities, prisons, and theaters. Has written for film and for contemporary dance and has frequently collaborated with musicians, from the avant-garde to folk, and with visual artists. **Awards:** Irish Arts Council bursary in literature, 1987, 1990; Martin Toonder award for literature, 1995; Butler literary award for poetry, Irish American Cultural Institute, 1998.

PUBLICATIONS

Poetry

Return and No Blame. Dublin, Beaver Row Press, 1984.
Reading the Sky. Dublin, Beaver Row Press, 1988.
The Man Who Was Marked by Winter. Oldcastle, County Meath, Gallery Press, 1991, and Cheney, Washington, Eastern Washington University Press, 1994.
Pillow Talk. Oldcastle, County Meath, Gallery Press, 1994.
Mysteries of the Home: A Selection of Poems. Newcastle upon Tyne, Bloodaxe, 1996.
Dharmakaya. Manchester, Carcanet, 2000.

Plays

Kirkle (produced Dublin, 1995).
The Voyage (produced Dublin 1997).
Mrs. Sweeney (produced Dublin 1997). Dublin, New Island, 1999.
Cell (produced Dublin 1999). Dublin, New Island, 2000.

*

Critical Studies: Interview with Theo Dorgan, in *Colby Quarterly* (Waterville, Maine), 28(4), December 1992; "Refusing the Poisoned Chalice: The Sexual Politics of Rita Ann Higgins and Paula Meehan" by Karen Steele, in *Homemaking: Women Writers and the Politics and Poetics of Home,* edited by Catherine Wiley and Fiona R. Barnes, New York, Garland, 1996; "Dry Socks and Floating Signifiers: Paula Meehan's Poems" by Tracy Brain, in *Critical Survey* (England), 8(1), 1996; "The Pressure of Humanity" by Ben Howard, in *Shenandoah* (Lexington, Virginia), 46(1), spring 1996.

*   *   *

Paula Meehan's rise has been rapid since her first collection, *Return and No Blame,* appeared in 1984 and her second, *Reading the Sky,* in 1988. The poems are jaunty and warm, seeking a full, feminine voice. She looks back to tradition, assuming the voice of Liadain or rewriting one of the few human poems from the bardic tradition as if it were a woman speaking. She also uses North Dublin street talk; indeed, she seems more involved with the city than any Irish poet since Clarke and Kinsella.

Meehan's third book, *The Man Who Was Marked by Winter* (1991), draws on the first two, but there is a new surety, as in "The Pattern," an expanded sequence for her mother. There is uneasiness as well, what Antoinette Quinn has called "a migrant restiveness," the poet as prowler, an uneasiness that also shows in the love poems. Meehan can be comic about male inefficiency, as in "My Love about His Business in the Barn," but "The Statue of the Virgin at Granard Speaks" is a poignant indictment of an Irish society that lets young women go to waste.

Athena, warrior and goddess of wisdom, is the image on the cover of *Pillow Talk* (1994), and the complex nature of woman is a recurring theme. Traditional views are rejected in "Not Your Muse," but Meehan's father is transformed into Saint Francis in the opening poem, and there is a lovely lament for a broken marriage in "Not alone the rue in my herb garden . . .":

> O my friend,
> do not turn on me in hatred,
> do not curse the day we met.

What is impressive about Meehan's later work is the increasing ease with which she deals with a variety of moods, from the gentle to the ferocious:

> From one breast
> flows the Milky Way, the starry path,
> a sluggish trickle of pus from the other.

She is one of the best younger poets around, and as Eavan Boland says, her "themes are daring and open up new areas for her own work as well as for contemporary Irish poetry."

—John Montague

MEHROTRA, Arvind Krishna

Nationality: Indian. **Born:** Lahore, Pakistan, 16 April 1947. **Education:** University of Allahabad, Uttar Pradesh, 1964–66, B.A. 1966; University of Bombay, 1966–68, M.A. 1968. **Family:** Married Vandana Jain in 1969; one son. **Career:** Lecturer in English, 1968–77, and since 1978 reader in English, University of Allahabad. Visiting writer, University of Iowa, Iowa City, 1971–73; lecturer in English, University of Hyderabad, India, 1977–78. Editor, *damn youla magazine of the arts,* Allahabad, 1965–68; founder, Ezra-Fakir Press, Bombay, 1966. **Awards:** Homi Bhabha fellowship, 1981; *Gettysburg Review* award, 1994. **Address:** Jyoti Apartments, 1 N.K. Mukerji Road, Allahabad 211001, India.

PUBLICATIONS

Poetry

Bharatmata: A Prayer. Bombay, Ezra Fakir Press, 1966.
Woodcuts on Paper. London, Gallery Number Ten, 1967.
Pomes/Poemes/Poemas. Baroda, India, Vrischik, 1971.
Nine Enclosures. Bombay, Clearing House, 1976.
Distance in Statute Miles. Bombay, Clearing House, 1982.
Middle Earth. New Delhi. Oxford University Press, 1984.
The Transfiguring Places. New Delhi, Ravi Dayal, 1998.

Other

Editor, *Twenty Indian Poems.* New Delhi, Oxford University Press, 1990.
Editor, *The Oxford India Anthology of Twelve Modern Indian Poets.* New Delhi, Oxford University Press, 1992.
Editor, with Daniel Weissbort, *Periplus: Poetry in Translation.* New Delhi, Oxford University Press, 1993.

Translator, *Three Poems,* by Bogomil Gjuzel. Allahabad and Iowa City, Ezra Fakir Press, 1973.
Translator, *The Absent Traveller: Prakrit Love Poetry from the Gathasaptasati of Satvahana Hala.* New Delhi, Ravi Dayal, 1990.

*

Critical Studies: ''Image As an Immoderate Drug'' by N.R. Shastri, in *Osmania Journal of English Studies 13* (Hyderabad), 1, 1977; ''A Wonderland of Riddles and Fantasies,'' in *Toronto South Asian Review* 2, 2, 1983, and ''Looking into the Poetry of Arvind Krishna Mehrotra,'' in *Living Indian English Poets,* edited by Madhusudan Prasad, New Delhi, Sterling, 1989, both by Bibhu Padhi; ''The Abstraction of Language: Jayanta Mahapatra and A.K. Mehrotra As Indian 'Postmodernists''' by Joseph Swann, in *Fusion of Cultures?,* edited by Peter O. Stummer and Christopher Balme, Amsterdam, Netherlands, Rodopi, 1996.

* * *

Arvind Krishna Mehrotra has said that ''a poem comprises games, riddles and accidents . . . and the poet creates as many accidents as he can.'' Mehrotra is probably the best-known Indian writer of surrealist English verse. He uses some of the characteristic techniques of surrealist writing, such as an uninhibited dependence on chance or accident in composition, the collocation of unusual words and phrases, the yoking together of heterogeneous objects and situations and contexts, broken syntax, the ascription of unusual characteristics to familiar objects, and the exaltation of the dream state. The general aim is to transform the reader's consciousness and to change his conception of reality. Mehrotra has cited Breton's first *Manifesto* (1924) as one of the influences on his work. Breton defined surrealism as ''pure psychic automatism by which it is intended to express either verbally or in writing, the true function of thought. Thought dictated in the absence of all control exerted by reason and outside all aesthetic or moral control.''

Mehrotra modified these aims of course, and not all of his poetry fits the surrealist category. For instance, poems such as ''Songs of the Ganga'' (*Nine Enclosures*) are relatively straightforward works in which experimentation is held to a minimum. Another, perhaps better known, poem that is more characteristic and not particularly difficult is ''The Sale,'' in which the language of salesmanship is exploited to suggest the sellout of the world and its impending conversion to a wasteland. It would be misleading, however, to suggest that Mehrotra's poetry is ''about'' this or that, about something external to itself. The poems are ''enclosures'' whose aims are to capture the reader within themselves. Their principal means are a haunting poetic rhythm and the disturbing image:

The widow next door
Lives off her trained
Parrot.
It reads the future
And tells you when
To avoid it.
At night
She dances in the streets
And fills the air
With abuse.
The decorated general

Is alone
In his tent;
The pyres burn
Like new volcanoes.

While the second strophe reads like a summary of World War I poetry, the first reads rather like a joke, a story, a song. Children enjoy it as it is and do not ask for its meaning. The world of the child and the world of the grown-ups are juxtaposed, and the meaning arises from this juxtaposition.

Poetry such as Mehrotra's is international, and it is not much bothered with the question of ''Indianness,'' which is such a persistent concern of some of his contemporaries. His poetry is difficult and chancy, but the chances quite often come off. His later poems, however, seem to be written in a non-European mode and with only a touch of the surrealistic technique:

Summer is at hand.
New leaves fill the branches
With sunlight, a red and green kite
Bends into the wind. It is two bits
Of thin paper joined
In the middle. It opens the sky.
I have three small rooms and a terrace
Where I sit out and read Han Shan
To my new-born son, or make
That kite. My possessions are few.
I'll stay here.

Poems such as these raise no questions, debate no issues, wave no flags. Peaceful in themselves, they also provide a moment of peace to their readers.

Middle Earth contains many new and uncollected poems. The image continues to be the mainstay of Mehrotra's style. Some of the poems, ''The World's a Printing House,'' for example, may be read as his apology for the poetry he is interested in writing. There is, however, a narrative structure in many of the poems, and they perhaps indicate a new phase in Mehrotra's career.

Mehrotra's translations, especially of Prakrit love poetry, have been justly praised for their fidelity and poetic quality. He has succeeded admirably in restoring these ancient love poems to the enjoyment of the modern reader. In general, he has a remarkable gift for intuiting the meaning of poems written in other languages—transmitted to him through a collaborator—and for rendering the poems into English.

—S. Nagarajan

MEINKE, Peter

Nationality: American. **Born:** Brooklyn, New York, 29 December 1932. **Education:** Hamilton College, Clinton, New York, A.B. 1955; University of Michigan, Ann Arbor, M.A. 1961; University of Minnesota, Minneapolis, Ph.D. in English 1965. **Military Service:** U.S. Army, 1955–57. **Family:** Married Jeanne Clark in 1957; two daughters and two sons. **Career:** English teacher, Mountain Lakes

High School, New Jersey, 1958–60; assistant professor of English, 1961–66, and poet-in-residence, 1973, Hamline University, St. Paul, Minnesota; assistant professor, 1966–68, associate professor, 1968–72, and professor of literature and director of the writing workshop, 1972–93, Florida Presbyterian College, later named Eckerd College, St. Petersburg, Florida. Visiting professor, University of Sussex, Brighton, summer 1969; director, AMFC French Program, University of Neuchâtel, Switzerland, 1971–72; Fulbright lecturer, University of Warsaw, 1978–79; poet-in-residence, Hamilton College, winter 1981; Jenny Moore Lecturer, George Washington University, Washington, D.C., 1981–82; writer-in-residence, Thurber House, Columbus, 1987, Davidson College, North Carolina, 1989, University of Hawaii, 1993, Austin Peay University, Clarksville, Tennessee, 1995, University of North Carolina, Greensboro, 1996, and Randolph-Macon Woman's College, Virginia, 1999. **Awards:** National Endowment for the Arts fellowship, 1974, 1989; Poetry Society of America Gustav Davidson award, 1976, and Lucille Medwick prize, 1984; Emily Clark Balch prize (*Virginia Quarterly Review*), for fiction, 1982; O. Henry award, for fiction, 1983; P.E.N. award, for fiction, 1984, 1987, 1988; Flannery O'Connor award, for short fiction, 1986; Emily Dickinson award, 1992, Paumanok Poetry award, 1993; Provincetown Master Artist's fellowship, 1995; Chapbook prize, Sow's Ear Press, 1996. **Address:** 147 Wildwood Lane S.E., St. Petersburg, Florida 33705, U.S.A.

PUBLICATIONS

Poetry

Lines from Neuchâtel. Gulfport, Florida, Konglomerati Press, 1974.
The Night Train, and The Golden Bird. Pittsburgh, University of Pittsburgh Press, 1977.
The Rat Poems; or, Rats Live on No Evil Star. Cleveland, Bits Press, 1978.
Trying to Surprise God. Pittsburgh, University of Pittsburgh Press, 1981.
Underneath the Lantern. Meadville, Pennsylvania, Heatherstone Press, 1986.
Night Watch on the Chesapeake. Pittsburgh, University of Pittsburgh Press, 1987.
Far from Home. Meadville, Pennsylvania, Heatherstone Press, 1988.
Liquid Paper: New & Selected Poems. Pittsburgh, University of Pittsburgh Press, 1991.
Campocorto. Abingdon, Virginia, Sow's Ear Press, 1996.
Scars. Pittsburgh, University of Pittsburgh Press, 1996.
Zinc Fingers. Pittsburgh, University of Pittsburgh Press, 2000.

Short Stories

The Piano Tuner. Athens, University of Georgia Press, 1986.

Other

Howard Nemerov. Minneapolis, University of Minnesota Press, 1968.
The Legend of Larry the Lizard (for children). Richmond, John Knox Press, 1968.

Very Seldom Animals (for children). St. Petersburg, Florida, Possum Press, 1969.
The Shape of Poetry. Boston, The Writer, Inc., 1999.

*

Manuscript Collection: University of Florida, Gainesville.

Critical Studies: "Speaking to Us All" by Philip Jason, in *Poet Lore* (Boston), 1982; *Bounds Out of Bounds* by Roberta Berke, Oxford, Oxford University Press, 1982; "Trying to Surprise God" by Eric Nelson, in *Mickle St. Review* (Philadelphia), 1983; "Poems to Embrace" by Jason Scott Bell, in the St. Petersburg *Times* (Florida), 20 September 1987; "Meinke Revisited" by Dionisio Martinez, in *Organica Quarterly* (Tampa, Florida), autumn 1992; "Easy Listening" by Henry Taylor, in *Poetry* (Chicago), May 1993; "The Illusion of Wholeness" by Dionisio Martinez, in *International Quarterly,* June 1993; "Beginning to Bloom: A Talk with Peter Meinke" by David Jasper, in *Weekly Planet* (Tampa, Florida), 1998.

Peter Meinke comments:

My poems and stories have to stand on their own, and I have little to say about them. I am a slow writer in both genres and try to write as clearly as possible. I am seldom surreal, though occasionally my dreams enter my writing in strange ways. I am interested in the formal problems of sounding contemporary in traditional forms. I do not know what I would do if I did not write; I've never tried it.

(1995) I took early retirement from Eckerd College in order to devote more time to my writing.

*   *   *

Peter Meinke's *The Night Train, and The Golden Bird* contains a variety of poems, both lyric and comic, free-form and formal. Yet all are imbued with the poet's seriousness and hardheadedness, an unmistakable tone the reader discovers in the very first poem, "The Night Train." In Meinke's train the passengers are suicides on the way to nowhere, and their misery and futility are embodied in the rhythm of the train:

> their fingers drum the drumroll of their wake
> on train compartment windows, when they take
> their lives it is the right place
> this closed anonymous world inside a train
> a nothing sort of place; for god's sake
> get on with it: there's nothing much at stake

Note the rhymes: "wake," "take," "sake," "stake." By breaking his lines where he does, by using repetitive rhymes, and by reducing punctuation to a minimum, Meinke creates a powerful and evocative poem.

What Meinke does in "The Night Train" is similar to what he does in most of his work. He seems to let the poem dictate its own form, to let the lines break where they must and to punctuate themselves. What gives his poems power is the ability to risk lines like these in the grimly comic "Vegetables":

Disemboweled peas

slide into tumbrils, dizzy
with air, beets bleed on the
sinkboard, celery wilts with its heart
in our hands.

At the same time Meinke's poems are highly controlled and show a firm understanding of conventional prosody. The second title poem, ''The Golden Bird,'' is a villanelle, and the moving antiwar poem ''The Monkey's Paw'' demonstrates his lyric gifts as well as his concern and his anger:

When the war is over the bones of the lonely dead
will knit and rise from ricefield and foxfield
like sea-things seeking the sea, and will head
toward their homes in Hanoi or Seattle
clogging the seaways, the airways, the highways
climbing the cliffs and trampling the clover
heading toward Helen, Hsueh-ying, or Mary
when the war is over

Measures like these make Meinke a rare poet in our time, one who hears music where there is mostly din.

—Cynthia Day

MELTZER, David

Nationality: American. **Born:** Rochester, New York, 17 February 1937. **Education:** Public schools in Brooklyn and Los Angeles; Los Angeles City College, 1955–56; University of California, Los Angeles, 1956–57. **Family:** Married Christina Meyer in 1958; three daughters and one son. **Career:** Manager, Discovery Bookshop, San Francisco, 1959–67; editor, *Maya,* Mill Valley, California, 1966–71; teacher, Urban School, San Francisco, 1975–76. Since 1970 editor, *Tree* magazine and Tree Books, Bolinas, later Berkeley, California. Since 1980 core faculty, Graduate Poetics program, and since 1988 chair, Undergraduate Writing and Literature program, Humanities, New College of California, San Francisco. Composer, musician, and singer: performed with Serpent Power and David and Tina, 1970–72; member of MIX, a performance ensemble, with poet Clark Coolidge and vocalist/songwriter Tina Meltzer. **Awards:** Council of Literary Magazines grant, 1972, 1981; National Endowment for the Arts grant, 1974, for publishing, 1975; Tombstone award for poetry from the James Ryan Morris Memorial Foundation, 1992. **Address:** Box 9005, Berkeley, California 94709, U.S.A.

PUBLICATIONS

Poetry

Poems, with Donald Schenker. Privately printed, 1957.
Ragas. San Francisco, Discovery, 1959.
The Clown. Larkspur, California, Semina, 1960.
Station. Privately printed, 1964.
The Blackest Rose. Berkeley, California, Oyez, 1964.
Oyez! Berkeley, California, Oyez, 1965.

The Process. Berkeley, California, Oyez, 1965.
In Hope I Offer a Fire Wheel. Berkeley, California, Oyez, 1965.
The Dark Continent. Berkeley, California, Oyez, 1967.
Nature Poem. Santa Barbara, California, Unicom Press, 1967.
Santamaya, with Jack Shoemaker. San Francisco, Maya, 1968.
Round the Poem Box: Rustic and Domestic Home Movies for Stan and Jane Brakhage. Los Angeles, Black Sparrow Press, 1969.
Yesod. London, Trigram Press, 1969.
From Eden Book. San Francisco, Cranium Press, 1969.
Abulafia Song. Santa Barbara, California, Unicorn Press, 1969.
Greenspeech. Goleta, California, Christopher, 1970.
Luna. Los Angeles, Black Sparrow Press, 1970.
Letters and Numbers. Berkeley, California, Oyez, 1970.
Bronx Lil/Head of Lillin S.A.C. Santa Barbara, California, Capra Press, 1970.
32 Beams of Light. Santa Barbara, California, Capra Press, 1970.
Knots. Bolinas, California, Tree, 1971.
Bark: A Polemic. Santa Barbara, California, Capra Press, 1973.
Hero/Lil. Los Angeles, Black Sparrow Press, 1973.
Tens: Selected Poems 1961–1971, edited by Kenneth Rexroth. New York, McGraw Hill, 1973.
The Eyes, The Blood. San Francisco, Mudra, 1973.
French Broom. Berkeley, California, Oyez, 1973.
Blue Rags. Berkeley, California, Oyez, 1974.
Harps. Berkeley, California, Oyez, 1975.
Six. Santa Barbara, California, Black Sparrow Press, 1976.
Bolero. Berkeley, California, Oyez, 1976.
The Art, The Veil. Milwaukee, Membrane Press, 1981.
The Name: Selected Poetry 1973–1983. Santa Barbara, California, Black Sparrow Press, 1984.
Arrows: Selected Poetry, 1957–1992. Santa Roas, Black Sparrow Press, 1994.

Recordings: *Serpent Power,* Vanguard, 1972; *Poet Song,* Vanguard, 1974; *David Meltzer Reading,* Membrane, 1981; *Nurse,* S-Tapes, 1982.

Novels

Orf. North Hollywood, Essex House, 1968.
The Agency. North Hollywood, Essex House, 1968.
The Agent. North Hollywood, Essex House, 1968.
How Man! Blocks in the Pile? North Hollywood, Essex House, 1968.
Lovely. North Hollywood, Essex House, 1969.
Healer. North Hollywood, Essex House, 1969.
Out. North Hollywood, Essex House, 1969.
Glue Factory. North Hollywood, Essex House, 1969.
The Martyr. North Hollywood, Essex House, 1969.
Star. North Hollywood, Brandon House, 1970.
The Agency Trilogy. New York, Richard Kasak Books, 1994.
Out. New York, Richard Kasak Books, 1994.

Other

We All Have Something to Say to Each Other: Being an Essay Entitled ''Patchen'' and Four Poems. San Francisco, Auerhahn Press, 1962.
Introduction to the Outsiders (essay on Beat Poetry). Fort Lauderdale, Florida, Rodale, 1962.

Bazascope Mother (essay on Robert Alexander). Los Angeles, Drekfesser Press, 1964.

Journal of the Birth. Berkeley, California, Oyez, 1967.

Isla Vista Notes: Fragmentary, Apocalyptic, Didactic Contradictions. Santa Barbara, California, Christopher, 1970.

Abra (for children). Berkeley, California, Hipparchia Press, 1976.

Two-way Mirror: A Poetry Note-book. Berkeley, California, Oyez, 1977.

Editor, with Lawrence Ferlinghetti and Michael McClure, *Journal for the Protection of All Beings 1 and 3.* San Francisco, City Lights, 2 vols., 1961–69.

Editor, *The San Francisco Poets.* New York, Ballantine, 1971; revised edition, as *Golden Gate,* San Francisco, Wingbow Press, 1976.

Editor, *Birth: An Anthology.* New York, Ballantine, 1973.

Editor, *The Secret Garden: an Anthology in the Kabbalah.* New York, Seabury Press, 1976.

Editor, *The Path of the Names,* by Abraham Abulafia. Berkeley, California, Tree, and London, Trigram Press, 1976.

Editor, *Birth: An Anthology of Ancient Texts, Songs, Prayers, and Stories.* Berkeley, California, North Point Press, 1981.

Editor, *Death* (anthology). Berkeley, California, North Point Press, 1984.

Editor, *Reading Jazz: The White Invention of Jazz.* San Francisco, Mercury House, 1993.

Translator, with Allen Say, *Morning Glories,* by Shiga Naoya. Berkeley, California, Oyez, 1975.

*

Manuscript Collections: Washington University, St. Louis; University of Indiana, Bloomington; University of California, Los Angeles.

Critical Studies: *David Meltzer: A Sketch from Memory and Descriptive Checklist,* Berkeley, California, Oyez, 1965, and *6 Poets of the San Francisco Renaissance,* Fresno, California, Giligia Press, 1967, both by David Kherdian; *The Secret Record: Modern Erotic Literature* by Michael Perkins, New York, Morrow, 1976; in *Vort* (Berkeley, California), 1979; *Apocalyptic Messianism and Contemporary Jewish-American Poetry* by R. Barbara Gitenstein, Albany, State University Press of New York, 1986; "A Poetics of Absence: Kabbalist Allegory in the Poetry of Paul Celan, Edmond Jabes, and David Meltzer" by Bruce Ross, in *Allegory Revisited: Ideals of Mankind,* edited by Anna-Teresa Tymieniecka, Dordrecht, Kluwer Academy, 1994.

David Meltzer comments:

A fracturing of forms and vocabularies gradually empty and/or useless in advancing the ongoing art and craft. Clear division between poetry as institution and in-house practice for a professional class and caste of practitioners and that of experimental, populist, eccentric, amateur ranters and ravers. The upward/downward spiral of cyberspace is wired expansiveness, yet with tendency toward reduction and containment framed in soothing clique speak of technocrat consumers. In a fin de siècle moment the postcolonial fusions of languages, the play and resistance of rap, radiates more energy and possibility than art zooed by any so-called dominant cultures. Epistemic earthquake, a whole lot of shaking going on, as the old waxworks gets reinvented, reclaimed, and rewritten.

*   *   *

David Meltzer's poetry is well known, as the presence of a third volume of selected poems (*Arrows,* 1994) indicates. He has said that his first poem, at age eleven, was a "trance-mission." He has indeed had a long career.

As he gratefully acknowledges, Meltzer was first made known through the efforts of Kenneth Rexroth. Some of Meltzer's affiliations are indicated by his *Golden Gate* interviews with Rexroth, William Everson, Lawrence Ferlinghetti, Lew Welch, and Michael McClure, one of the few collections of interviews in which the interviewer is also interesting. For example, Welch mentioned that he had learned how fast he could run when he was a boy beset by other boys. Meltzer then asked, "How did you become interested in language? For instance, you talk about your speed, being able to move . . . when did you realize that language was a way of moving too?" Welch responded, "That's a well-put question." Meltzer also appeared in the historically important *Floating Bear,* edited by Diane di Prima and Amiri Baraka (then LeRoi Jones). Although Meltzer's roots are with the San Francisco poets, he found that language was a way of moving in space and time.

One can scarcely sum up Meltzer's poetry. He has "home movies" and "Rustic and Domestic Home Movies for Stan and Jane Brakhage." He has "translated" a Chinese rice paper notebook containing his scrawls into poems for Jack and Ruth Hirschman. He has notes for a poem to H.P. Lovecraft, and he admonishes us that "the gods exhort us to understand the form of light." He seems to phrase the question for us: "Who is it in there. / Wiring these poems" (*Blue Rags*). (Period. No question mark. "Questions are Remarks," Wallace Stevens wrote.) But there is no obvious answer. It is not necessarily true that "the Jew in me is the ghost of me / hiding under a stairway" (*The Dark Continent*), because his poetry also has a wide range of Hebraic lore, as if we were threatened by having a golem's shapeless mass:

Without Neshamah (light of God)
the Golem's intelligence was small.
Also lacking the other two intelligences:
Chochmah (Wisdom) & *Bina* (Judgement)

His poetry coheres by consistent ways of feeling rather than by conceptually calibrated systems:

Others balance by
Kneeling to pray.
I allow them their poem

This is mine.
A patchwork poem
Pathwork.

Patchwork. Pathwork. Fragmentation provides opportunity. One perceives through fragments and finds unexpected connections, as for example in "Lamentation for Lee Harvey Oswald": "the moment they long to see, / the shattered skull, the blood / We are all spies." In an epigraph from the *Zohar* to his book *Yesod,* the twenty-two fragments, the twenty-two letters of the Hebrew alphabet, make perception possible, as the ten words (presumably the Sephiroth, the names of God) make analogies possible. (Yesod, basis, was perceived by Pico della Mirandola as analogous to the sphere of Luna.)

Meltzer has an energizing range of scholarly material. His anthologies *Birth* and *Death* collect ancient and modern myths, stories, texts, and sayings from South America, New Zealand, India, and elsewhere. In *Birth* the ten pages of sources and the checklist seem to be culled from much larger lists, because they are consistently interesting and important.

Meltzer's own mythmaking can put an amusing tone to serious purpose, as for example in his work *Bark,* a particular favorite among younger poets:

> Dog didn't know he was a dog and climbed a tree, hung
> from a branch with his tail, swinging back and forth,
> singing a song that sounded like it came out of a tenor
> saxophone.
> "Dogs don't do such things," a master said, passing by
> the tree.
> He put dog in his place and give him a name
> and a collar
> and trained him with rolled up newspaper never to sing
> again.

He can also be more immediate and with less of a parable:

> It's simple.
> One morning
> Wake up ready
> For new work
> Pet the dog,
> Dog's not there
> Rise and shine.
> Sun's not there.
> Take a deep breath
> No air
> Look for the sun.
> No sun.
>
> It's simple
> Wake up one morning
> Ready for new work
> & the animals are on strike
> With the air, the sea the
> Earth quit us
> Casts us off
> Like a sickness in the firey core.

A temporary resting place for Meltzer's poetry ("the end / Not the end") can be taken in his concluding words for the 1984 selected poems *The Name:*

> each word the word creating
> protecting life in lights of song or silence
> all else goes against it

—William Sylvester

MEREDITH, William (Morris, Jr.)

Nationality: American. **Born:** New York City, 9 January 1919. **Education:** Lenox School, Massachusetts; Princeton University, New Jersey (Woodrow Wilson fellow, 1946–47), B.A. (magna cum laude) 1940. **Military Service:** U.S. Army Air Force, 1941–42, and in the U.S. Naval Reserve, 1942–46, 1952–54; Lieutenant Commander. **Career:** Copyboy and reporter, *New York Times,* 1940–41; resident fellow in Creative Writing, Princeton University, 1947–48, 1949–50, 1965–66; assistant professor of English, University of Hawaii, Honolulu, 1950–51; member of the department, 1955, and professor of English, 1965–83, Connecticut College, New London. Taught at Bread Loaf Writers Conference, Vermont, summers 1958–62. Opera critic, *Hudson Review,* New York, 1955–56. Member, Connecticut Commission on the Arts, 1963–65; director of the humanities, Upward Bound Program, 1964–68; poetry consultant, Library of Congress, Washington, D.C., 1978–80. **Awards:** Yale Series of Younger Poets award, 1943; Harriet Monroe memorial prize, 1944, and Oscar Blumenthal prize, 1953 (*Poetry,* Chicago); Rockefeller grant, for criticism, 1948, for poetry, 1968; *Hudson Review* fellowship, 1956; American Academy grant, 1958; Ford fellowship, for drama, 1960; Loines award, 1966; Van Wyck Brooks award, 1971; National Endowment for the Arts grant, 1972, fellowship, 1984; Guggenheim fellowship, 1975; Vaptsarov prize (Bulgaria), 1979; *Los Angeles Times* prize, 1987; Pulitzer prize, 1988; Academy of American Poets fellowship, 1990. Member, American Academy; Chancellor, Academy of American Poets from 1964. **Address:** 337 Kitemaug Road, Uncasville, Connecticut 06382–2208, U.S.A.

PUBLICATIONS

Poetry

Love Letter from an Impossible Land. New Haven, Connecticut, Yale University Press, 1944.
Ships and Other Figures. Princeton, New Jersey, Princeton University Press, 1948.
The Open Sea and Other Poems. New York, Knopf, 1958.
The Wreck of the Thresher and Other Poems. New York, Knopf, 1964.
Winter Verse. Privately printed, 1964.
Earth Walk: New and Selected Poems. New York, Knopf, 1970.
Hazard, The Painter. New York, Knopf, 1975.
The Cheer. New York, Knopf, 1980.
Partial Accounts: New and Selected Poems. New York, Knopf, 1987.
Effort at Speech: New and Selected Poems. Evanston, Illinois, TriQuarterly Books/Northwestern University Press, 1997.

Recording: *Selected Poems,* Watershed, 1977; *The Poet and the Poem,* Library of Congress, 1990.

Play

The Bottle Imp (libretto), adaptation of the story by Robert Louis Stevenson, music by Peter Whiton (produced Wilton, Connecticut, 1958).

Other

Reasons for Poetry, and The Reason for Criticism (lectures). Washington, D.C., Library of Congress, 1982.
Poems Are Hard to Read. Ann Arbor, University of Michigan Press, 1991.

Editor, *Shelley.* New York, Dell, 1962.
Editor, *University and College Poetry Prizes, 1960–66, in Memory of Mrs. Fanny Fay Wood.* New York, Academy of American Poets, 1966.
Editor, with Mackie L. Jarrell, *Eighteenth Century Minor Poets.* New York, Dell, 1968.
Editor, *Poets of Bulgaria.* Greensboro, North Carolina, Unicorn Press, 1986; Chingford, Essex, Forest, 1988.
Editor, with Richard Harteis, *Window on the Black Sea: Bulgarian Poetry in Translation.* Pittsburgh, Carnegie Mellon University Press, 1992.

Translator, *Alcools: Poems 1878–1913,* by Apollinaire. New York, Doubleday, 1964.

*

Manuscript Collection: Middlebury College, Vermont.

Critical Studies: ''The Language of the Tribe'' by Neva Harrington, in *Southwest Review,* 1982; *Three Contemporary Poets of New England* by Guy Rotella, Boston, Twayne, 1983; review of *Partial Accounts* by Edward Hirsch, in *New York Times Book Review,* 31 July 1988; interview with Betty Parry, in *Plum Review,* 4, fall-winter 1992.

*   *   *

Introducing William Meredith's *Love Letter from an Impossible Land,* Archibald MacLeish observed that the poet's ''instincts are sound'' (''He seems to know, without poisoning himself in the process, which fruits are healthful and which fruits are not''). The consistencies in Meredith's subsequent volumes have proved MacLeish's observation to be true, and his success was signaled by a wider appreciation with the award of a Pulitzer in 1988 for *Partial Accounts: New and Selected Poems.* Although his meters have loosened in later books, Meredith remains a formal poet who achieves imaginative participation in his subjects by creating them at an aesthetic distance. Poise and understanding are sought and revealed in the subjection of the facts of experience to an imaginative yet rational order. If the experience in a Meredith poem begins as a brute fact or raw emotion, it is transmuted into a shapelier, more civil, and more intelligible image of itself. His work renders emotional force into forms. In a period when many poets sacrifice convention and form for force and immediacy, the risks in his aesthetic are evident. Yet the reader responsive to the legitimate demands such poetry makes will find among the resulting poems those that acknowledge the forces engendering them. In his elegy to the sailors lost in a sunken submarine, the title poem from *The Wreck of the Thresher,* Meredith writes,

Why can't our dreams be content with the terrible facts?
The only animal cursed with responsible sleep.

We trace disaster always to our own acts.
I met a monstrous self trapped in the black deep:
All these years, he smiled, *I've drilled at sea*
For this crush of water. Then he saved only me.

Confronting the inexplicable tragedy of meaningless death, Meredith characteristically concludes, ''Whether we give assent to this or rage / Is a question of temperament and does not matter.''

This poem reflects two of Meredith's abiding concerns, the threat of death and the loneliness of the sea, already enunciated in the final ten poems of his first book. Service as a naval aviator in two Pacific wars marked out for Meredith a part of his donnée. Images of oceanic space, the lonely sky, distant islands seen from vast heights, the unknown destinies of men in wartime, and the responses of an American to oriental cultures (Japan, Korea, Hawaii) recur in his poems. Characteristically, he deals with such themes pictorially, fixing his images as though in a painting, imposing upon them the designs imagination discovers and the forms and meters appropriated by a scrupulously sensitive ear. His instinct is to render such design. For example, in ''Rus in Urbe'' (from *The Open Sea*) he chooses ''in a city garden an espalliered tree,'' not nature unadorned but nature shaped by human skill and imagination. Yet in a later poem, ''Roots'' (from *The Wreck of the Thresher*), a dialogue narrative in the mode of Frost, he discovers in nature itself the pattern that in ''Rus in Urbe'' imagination had to wrest by altering the shapes of trees.

The new poems in *Earth Walk: New and Selected Poems* use a conversational, colloquial style, as in ''Walter Jenks' Bath'': ''These are my legs. I don't have to tell them, legs, / Move up or down or which leg.'' With like informality of diction Meredith explores dreams, probes memory, creates characters, and, as in the title poem, makes a wry statement about being himself at a time when almost everyone else is preoccupied by somebody else's Moon walk. The formality of the work is less a matter of surface and detail (such as regular stanza, rhythm, and rhyme) than formerly, but the design of the experience is quietly interiorized in each poem. His tone is modest rather than boisterous, his range deceptively larger than the voice whose speech provides the style.

Hazard, The Painter is a series of sixteen poems dramatizing the life not only of the artist of its title but also, by inference, of his time. For two years Hazard has been at work on a painting of a falling parachutist, ''the human figure dangling safe . . . full of half remembered instruction / but falling, and safe.'' Hazard ''is in charge of morale in a morbid time,'' the time of Richard Nixon's election as U.S. president, when the ''nation has bitterly misspoken itself.'' He measures his own modest gift against the greatness of Titian and Renoir and reflects on his relationships to his wife, children, and friends and to the earth. The tone of the poems is at once intimate and slightly distanced by third-person narration, and the effect of the suite is that of a novel in verse, a whole life economically suggested by glimpses. Its theme is no less than the artist's responsibility in a time when ''more of each day is dark'': ''Gnawed by a vision of rightness / that no one else seems to see, / what can a man do / but bear witness.''

As a result of the acquaintance made with Bulgarian poets during his year as the consultant in poetry at the Library of Congress, Meredith published *Poets of Bulgaria* (1986), with translations by himself and others. This was followed by another collection coedited with Richard Harteis, *Window on the Black Sea: Bulgarian Poetry in Translation* (1992), twenty-two contemporary poets translated by twenty-seven Americans. In recognition of his service to Bulgarian literature, Meredith was given citizenship in that country by presidential decree in 1996.

In 1983 Meredith suffered a stroke, resulting in aphasia, a particularly cruel blow to a poet. With the help of Harteis, his longtime companion who fortuitously had been a military medic, Meredith made a slow but marked recovery. His new and selected poems in 1997 has the appropriate title *Effort at Speech*. Michael Collier's appreciative foreword points out Meredith's debts to Frost, Auden, and Muriel Rukeyser. Collier writes, ''Meredith's optimism is not facile . . . It carries with it the knowledge that 'we are all relicts, wearing black' (''In Loving Memory of the Late Author of *Dream Songs*''). Meredith's belief in his own vision of things is embedded in his faith that when words are used accurately to describe experience they cannot lie or bear false witness.'' This quality of self-searching honesty pervades his poems.

In 1976 Meredith published a complete translation of *Alcools* by Apollinaire, a poet whose intuitive mode of apprehending experience would seem quite different from his own. In his poem ''For Guillaume Apollinaire'' Meredith writes, ''But these poems— / How quickly the strangeness would pass from things if it were not for them.'' The same may be said of his own best work.

—Daniel Hoffman

MERWIN, W(illiam) S(tanley)

Nationality: American. **Born:** New York City, 30 September 1927. **Education:** Princeton University, New Jersey, A.B. in English 1947. **Family:** Married 1) Diana Whalley in 1954 (separated 1968 and divorced); 2) Paula Dunaway in 1983. **Career:** Tutor in France and Portugal, 1949, and to Robert Ciraves's son in Mallorca, 1950; freelance translator, London, 1951–54; playwright-in-residence, Poet's Theatre, Cambridge, Massachusetts, 1956–57; poetry editor, *The Nation,* New York, 1962; associate, Théâtre de la Cité, Lyons, France, 1964–65. **Awards:** Yale Series of Younger Poets award, 1952; *Kenyon Review* fellowship, 1954; American Academy grant, 1957; Arts Council of Great Britain bursary, 1957; Rabinowitz research fellowship, 1961; Bess Hokin prize, 1962, and Harriet Monroe memorial prize, 1967 (*Poetry,* Chicago); Ford grant, 1964; Chapelbrook award, 1966; P.E.N. translation prize, 1969; Rockefeller grant, 1969; Pulitzer prize, 1971; Academy of American Poets fellowship, 1973; Shelley Memorial award, 1974; National Endowment for the Arts grant, 1978; Bollingen prize, 1979; Aiken Taylor award, 1990; Maurice English award, 1990; Dorothea Tanning prize, 1994; Lenore Marshall award, 1994. **Member:** American Academy of Arts and Letters, Academy of American Poets. **Agent:** The Wylie Agency, 250 West 57th Street, Suite 2114, New York, New York 10107, U.S.A.

PUBLICATIONS

Poetry

A Mask for Janus. New Haven, Connecticut, Yale University Press, 1952.

The Dancing Bears. New Haven, Connecticut, Yale University Press, 1954.

Green with Beasts. London, Hart Davis, and New York, Knopf, 1956.

The Drunk in the Furnace. New York, Macmillan, and London, Hart Davis, 1960.

The Moving Target. New York, Atheneum, 1963; London, Hart Davis, 1967.

The Lice. New York, Atheneum, 1967; London, Hart Davis, 1969.

Three Poems. New York, Phoenix Book Shop, 1968.

Animae. San Francisco, Kayak, 1969.

The Carrier of Ladders. New York, Atheneum, 1970.

Signs. Iowa City, Stone Wall Press, 1971.

Writings to an Unfinished Accompaniment. New York, Atheneum, 1973.

The First Four Books of Poems. New York, Atheneum, 1975.

Three Poems. Honolulu, Petronium Press, 1975.

The Compass Flower. New York, Atheneum, 1977.

Feathers from the Hill. Iowa City, Windhover Press, 1978.

Finding the Islands. Berkeley, California, North Point Press, 1982.

Opening the Hand. New York, Atheneum, 1983.

The Rain in the Trees. New York, Knopf, 1988.

Selected Poems. New York, Atheneum, 1988.

Travels. New York, Knopf, 1993.

The Vixen. New York, Knopf, 1996.

The Folding Cliffs. New York, Knopf, 1998.

The River Sound. New York, Knopf, 1999.

East Window. Port Townsend, Washington, Copper Canyon Press, 1999.

Plays

Darkling Child, with Dido Milroy (produced 1956).

Favor Island (produced Cambridge, Massachusetts, 1957).

Fufemia, adaptation of the play by Lope de Rueda, in *Tulane Drama Review* (New Orleans), December 1958.

The Gilded West (produced Coventry, England, 1961).

Turcaret, adaptation of the play by Alain Lesage, in *The Classic Theatre,* vol. 4, edited by Eric Bentley, New York, Doubleday, 1961.

The False Confession, adaptation of a play by Marivaux (produced New York, 1963). Published in *The Classic Theatre,* vol. 4, edited by Eric Bentley, New York, Doubleday, 1961.

Yerma, adaptation of the play by Garcia Lorca (produced New York, 1966).

Iphigenia at Aulis, with George E. Dimock, Jr., adaptation of a play by Euripides (produced Princeton, New Jersey, 1982). New York, Oxford University Press, 1982.

Other

A New Right Arm (essay). Oshkosh, Wisconsin, Road Runner Press, n.d.

Selected Translations 1948–1968. New York, Atheneum, 1968.

The Miner's Pale Children. New York, Atheneum, 1970.

Houses and Travellers. New York, Atheneum, 1977.

Selected Translations 1968–1978. New York, Atheneum, 1979.

Unframed Originals: Recollections. New York, Atheneum, 1982.

Regions of Memory: Uncollected Prose 1949–1982, edited by Ed Folsom and Cary Nelson. Urbana, University of Illinois Press, 1987.

The Lost Upland. New York, Knopf, 1993.

Editor, *West Wind: Supplement of American Poetry.* London, Poetry Book Society, 1961.

Editor, *The Essential Wyatt.* New York, Ecco Press, 1989.

Translator, *The Poem of the Cid.* New York, New American Library, and London, Dent, 1959.

Translator, *The Satires of Persius.* Bloomington, Indiana University Press, 1961; London, Anvil Press Poetry, 1981.

Translator, *Some Spanish Ballads.* London, Abelard Schuman, 1961; as *Spanish Ballads,* New York, Doubleday, 1961.

Translator, *The Life of Lazarillo de Tormes: His Fortunes and Adversities.* New York, Doubleday, 1962.

Translator, *The Song of Roland in Medieval Epics.* New York, Modern Library, 1963; published separately, New York, Random House, 1970.

Translator, *Transparence of the World: Poems of Jean Follain.* New York, Atheneum, 1969.

Translator, *Products of the Perfected Civilization: Selected Writings,* by Sebastian Chamfort. New York, Macmillan, 1969.

Translator, *Voices: Selected Writings of Antonio Porchia.* Chicago, Follett, 1969; revised edition, New York, Knopf, 1988.

Translator, *Twenty Love Poems and A Song of Despair,* by Pablo Neruda. London, Cape, 1969.

Translator, with others, *Selected Poems: A Bilingual Edition,* by Pablo Neruda, edited by Nathaniel Tarn. London, Cape, 1969; New York, Delacorte Press, 1972.

Translator, *Chinese Figures: Second Series.* Mount Horeb, Wisconsin, Perishable Press, 1971.

Translator, *Japanese Figures.* Santa Barbara, California, Unicorn Press, 1971.

Translator, *Asian Figures.* New York, Atheneum, 1973.

Translator, with Clarence Brown, *Selected Poems of Osip Mandelstam.* London, Oxford University Press, 1973; New York, Atheneum, 1974.

Translator, *Vertical Poems,* by Roberto Juarroz. Santa Cruz, California, Kayak, 1977; enlarged edition, Berkeley, California, North Point Press, 1988.

Translator, with J. Moussaieff Masson, *Sanskrit Love Poetry.* New York, Columbia University Press, 1977; as *The Peacock's Egg: Love Poems from Ancient India,* Berkeley, California, North Point Press, 1981.

Translator, *Four French Plays.* New York, Atheneum, 1985.

Translator, *From the Spanish Morning.* New York, Atheneum, 1985.

Translator, with Soiku Shigemetsu, *Sun at Midnight,* by Muso Soseki. Berkeley. California, North Point Press, 1989.

Translator, *Pieces of Shadow,* by Jaime Sabines. N.p., Marsilio, 1995.

*

Bibliography: "Seven Princeton Poets," in *Princeton Library Chronicle* (Princeton, New Jersey), autumn, 1963; *Understanding W.S. Merwin* by H.L. Hix, University of South Carolina Press, 1997.

Manuscript Collection: University of Illinois, Urbana.

Critical Studies: W.S. Merwin issue of *Hollins Critic* (Hollins College, Virginia), June 1968; "W.S. Merwin and the Nothing That Is" by Anthony Libby, in *Contemporary Literature 16* (Madison, Wisconsin), 1973; "The Continuities of W.S. Merwin" by Jarrold Ramsey, in *Massachusetts Review 14* (Amherst), 1973; *W.S. Merwin: Essays on the Poetry* edited by Ed Folsom and Cary Nelson, Urbana, University of Illinois Press, 1987; *Poetry As Labor & Privilege* by E.J. Brunner, Urbana, University of Illinois Press, 1991; *Difficult Language in the Poetry of W.S. Merwin* (dissertation), University of Toronto, 1992, and "The Riddle's Charm," in *Dalhousie Review* (Canada), 77(3), autumn 1997, both by Robert Finley; *The Still Performance: Writing, Self, and Interconnection in Five Postmodern American Poets* by James McCorkle, Charlottesville, University of Virginia Press, 1992; *From Origin to Ecology: Nature and the Poetry of W.S. Merwin* (dissertation), University of Mississippi, 1992, "W.S. Merwin and the Mysteries of Silence," in *South Dakota Review* (Vermillion, South Dakota), 32(1), spring 1994, and "Writing outside the Self: The Disembodied Narrators of W.S. Merwin," in *Style* (DeKalb, Illinois), 30(2), summer 1996, all by Jane Frazier; "Forms Open and Closed: The Poetry of W.S. Merwin," in *Gettysburg Review* (Gettysburg, Pennsylvania), 7(1), winter 1994, and "A Poetry of Transcendence," in *Gettysburg Review* (Gettysburg, Pennsylvania), 10(4), winter 1997, both by Floyd Collins; "Jeffers and Merwin: The World beyond Words" by Neal Bowers, in *Robinson Jeffers and a Galaxy of Writers: Essays in Honor of William H. Nolte,* edited by William B. Thesing, Columbia, University of South Carolina Press, 1995; *W.S. Merwin* by H.L. Hix, Columbia, University of South Carolina Press, 1997; "Metrical Inventions: Zukofsky and Merwin" by Albert Cook, in *College Literature* (West Chester, Pennsylvania), 24(3), October 1997; *W.S. Merwin and the Postmodern Environment* (dissertation) by Carl Clifton Tolier, Austin, University of Texas, 1997.

*   *   *

I imagine the writing of a poem, in whatever mode, still betrays the existence of hope, which is why poetry is more and more chary of the conscious mind in our age.

The mystery of man's condition, like the mystery of the word, is like the sea—which fills W.S. Merwin's poetry-with its attendant whales, birds, moon, tides, rocks, and bells; this is a poetry filled with silences and distances, doors and dreams. The early works are sometimes remarkable in their lyrical ease—e.g., "Song of Marvels," "Song of Three Smiles," "Song of the New Fool." Others, more formal and elegant, are long and elaborate narratives based upon folktales and myth, where story and character are of secondary importance to the poet's questions, much like Wallace Stevens's, about reality and art. In "East of the Sun and West of the Moon," an elaborate five hundred-line poem of thirty-nine thirteen-line stanzas in iambic pentameter, Merwin adapts a Norse fairy tale, itself an adaptation of Apuleius's Cupid and Psyche legend. But the story remains mere decoration, a frame within which he contemplates the relationship of art and imagination to reality. "All magic is but metaphor," he writes, and also notes the following: "All metaphor . . . is magic." Then, speculating on the perfection of art and eternity over the flux of this world, his character ponders, "Why should I / complain of such inflexible content, / Presume to shudder at such serenity, / Who walk in some ancestral fantasy." Like Yeats's Oisin, Merwin's persona is drawn to this world and would "ride a while the mortal air."

Perhaps Merwin's numerous and remarkable translations (Porchia, Neruda, Follain, René Char, Jorge Guillén, *The Song of Roland, The Poem of the Cid*) have stimulated or reinforced his own experiments with meter and form (from Yeats's and Stevens's symbolism to

Neruda's surrealism and Follain's linguistic innovations). Nevertheless, by the mid-1960s Merwin had honed the form we most often associate with him: the spare and sometimes epigrammatic line, simple language, and absence of allusion, myth, rhyme, and punctuation. His focus had turned in great part to the articulation of the "desert of the unknown," of the absurd, nothingness, silence, as in "Daybreak": "The future woke me with its silence / I join the procession / An open doorway / Speaks for me / Again." This world of the unknown, always benignly indifferent to man, beckons the poet, with his infinite imagination, for articulation; the poet begs for comprehension and consolation.

Merwin has been associated with the tradition of contemporary poets known as the oracular poets, and if his surrealistic style has been compared to that of Roethke, Bly, Wright, Dickey, Plath, Olson, and even Lowell, his apocalyptic vision is entirely his own. Death for Merwin is not an entrance into harmony with the universe; rather, it is an entrance into nothingness. In an impressive blending of form and content, Merwin's muted voice and conspicuous absence of punctuation reflect his very quest and felt experience: "I know nothing / learn of me," he writes, and "I taught them nothing. Everywhere / The eyes are returning under the stones. And over / My dry bones they built their churches, like wells" ("The Saint of the Uplands"). Like Beckett, a master in the spare articulation of nothingness, Merwin writes, "It is when I assert to nothing that I assert to all."

Merwin's attraction to nothingness, and the knowledge it inspires, is often associated with water and also with sleep, night, and even erotic experience, as in "Sailor Ashore": "the waters are / Under the earth. Now to run from them. / It is their tides you feel heaving under you, / Sucking you down, when you close your eyes with women." Such knowledge, which all men aspire to and only a few can articulate in their own limited terms, becomes their statement of personal tragedy. Of the informed sailor in "The Shipwreck" he writes, ". . . this sea, it was / Blind, yes, as they had said, and treacherous— / They had used their own traits to character it—but without / Accident in its wildness, in its rage, / Utterly and from the beginning without / Error. And to some it seemed the waves / Grew gentle, spared them, while they died of that knowledge."

At times the poet cries out for revelation: "Oh objects come and talk with us while you can." But perhaps more frequently he feels paralyzed and in intolerable pain of spiritual emptiness. Sometimes nature is forbidding and frightening: "The whole night is alive with hands / Is aflame with palms and offerings / . . . in mid-winter . . . empty gloves."

Merwin concretizes the benign indifference of the universe in his many plants and animals, which have the knowledge he seeks. In "Noah's Raven" the raven turns away from Noah and says, "Why should I have returned? / My knowledge would not fit into theirs [man's]." Again recalling Wordsworth's imagery, the poet describes his isolation in the face of an enlightened nature: "You would think the fields were something / To me, so long I stare out, looking / For their shapes or shadows through the matted gleam, seeing / Neither what is nor what was, but the flat light rising."

When the poet achieves revelation, his vision is one of "blindness," his condition that of a stone. Perhaps man is ultimately "invisible, invisible, invisible," an alien in "silence," "trying to read what the five polars are writing / On the void" ("A Scene in May"). In an utter calm of despair he writes, "Not that heaven does not exist but / That it exists without us / . . . Everything that does not need you is real" ("The Widow").

Given a world of cosmic indifference, one might hope for comfort in the world of men. Merwin's most bitter poems, however, treat man's brutality to man. Of family relationships he writes, "tell me anything more / Of every kinship than its madness . . ." ("Uncle Hess"). Man has ruined his environment, and he has destroyed nature: "Men think they are better than grass" ("The River of Bees"). But nature will avenge men who "made up their minds to be everywhere because why not / everywhere was theirs because they thought so" ("The Last One"). Man has also created a ludicrous, albeit murderous, political world. In several poems Merwin writes of contemporary atrocities in Asia as a pattern throughout history as well as his own personal act: "I / all that / has become of them / clearly all is lost." The political liberal mocks himself in "I Live Up Here": ". . . a little bit to the left / And I go down only / For the accidents." American society encourages its own collapse in "Unfinished Book of Kings." Merwin's despair for America's future resounds in "News of the Assassins": "An empty window has overtaken me / After the bees comes the smell of cigars / In the lobby of darkness."

Opening the Hand is an exquisite collection that traces the poet's childhood experiences, especially with his father, and his awakening to the world of time and change, abundance and mystery. The volume expresses Merwin's reconciliation to the facts of silence and isolation and his celebration of the occasional knowledge that all things touch and are touched by every other thing. The opening poem, "The Waters," is a beautiful evocation of the moment of finality, of what he elsewhere calls "nothingness," and it is written in a spirit of exaltation and epiphany reminiscent of Yeats's "Sailing to Byzantium." The music of the lines, also reminiscent of Frost, and the purity of his language reinforce a deeply felt affirmation toward the balance of all things: "I was the whole summer remembering / more than I knew / . . . joys and griefs I had not thought were mine / woke in this body's altering dream / knowing where they were / faces that would never die returned / toward our light through mortal waters."

A remarkable simplicity, lyricism, poise, and joy also mark *The Rain in the Trees*. Merwin again talks of his childhood and family, but he more prominently celebrates the ultimate ignorance and yet exaltation he feels for having survived a wondrous but mysterious world through the power of human love. The volume is strikingly simple in language and syntax; there is not the slightest trace of weighty metaphor or allusion, and the lines have an easy and hypnotic grace. Despite the continuing difficulties of translating experience into language, of locating or identifying himself in and through history, and of understanding his youth and middle years, the poet is grateful to his beloved for the comfort he now and at last feels in the vast universe: "we wake together and the world is here in its dew / you are here and the morning is whole / finally the light is young / . . . now we have only the age that is left / to be together / the brief air the vanishing green" ("Before Us"). Even in the face of the harshest realities, he is appreciative of whatever time and love remain for him. The spirit of the volume is underscored in a poem in which he states his need to say thank you despite the terror that remains: "the forests falling . . . / the words going out like cells of a brain / with the cities growing over us." All the same, he continues, "we are saying thank you faster and faster," even though there is "nobody listening."

Travels returns to the narrative myths of Merwin's earlier work to concentrate on a variety of historical figures, each blinded by an impossible dream given the limitations of the self and the world. As Merwin portrays his gallery of heroes, each one's goal has been ultimately to save, create, or define "living things / with no value that we know." The poet honors their quests, as he sympathetically notes the variety of motives driving them and the inevitable failure at the end of each one's journey. Of the twenty-one-year-old Rimbaud, he writes that "suddenly . . . / with his poems already . . . / fed to the flames," he traveled throughout Europe, tried his gift at the piano, but remained "useless, / unwelcomed and unloved." Merwin similarly marks the frustrated poetic activity of two Native Americans ("Lives of the Artists"). He describes the isolating and physically scarring and debilitating travels of Manuel Córdova. Most of the narratives focus on naturalists like Marini and John and William Bartram. Speaking in the voice of the "grass man"—David Douglas, the Scot for whom the fir tree was named—he says, "I could not have believed how my life would stop / all at once and slowly like some leaf in air / and still go on neither turning nor / falling any more."

Merwin is always in love with nature, and the volume includes lyrics that resound with his familiar lament about human dissolution as, at the same time, they exalt nature's nurturing qualities. "A Summer Night" conveys Merwin's enlightened appreciation of nature's dependably recurrent cycles: "The cloud brightens in the east / the moon rises out of the long evening / . . . the smell of roses waves through the stone room / . . . So long I have known this that it seems to me to be mine . . . / I have carried it with me without knowing it was there." One of the most beautiful poems is the opening "Cover Note." The poet reveals his most intimate insecurities: "I hope I make sense to / you in the shimmer of / our days while the world we / cling to in common is / burning for I have not / the ancients' confidence / in the survival of / one track of syllables / nor in some ultimate moment of insight that / supposedly will dawn / once and for all upon / a bright posterity."

Travels reveals language at new levels of purity, as though the word existed in its own right. Merwin omits punctuation entirely and enjambs both lines and stanzas; stanzaic end rhymes provide a foundation through which verse mirrors the existential condition. As such, with flawless and haunting musical cadences, Merwin's chaste forms convey the distance between the speaker and the spoken, the individual and his fate.

Ted Hughes called *The Folding Cliffs* a "truly original masterpiece, on a very big scale." This fictionalized poetic and historical narrative takes on the dimensions of an epic; at the same time the poet destroys the myth of Hawaii as a paradise. Merwin focuses on a chaotic and dangerous Hawaii in the 1870s and 1880s when leprosy, among other Western diseases, spread through the islands. He traces the vigorous official attempts—and subsequent persecutions and executions—committed by Europeans and Americans in their determination to place families in leper colonies, and he focuses on the resistance of one family in particular. His tenderness toward the victims separated from family and friends is striking, and he spares little in rendering the inhumanity of the soldiers and white settlers.

Merwin's descriptions of Hawaii's ecological abundance and peril parallel the plight of both the victims and victimizers. As the fugitives sought remote parts of the island, for example, he writes, "The wind had lashed at them here / . . . / the sky had filled with dark clouds and the rain had found them / they had leaned against the cliff / wall in the racing fog / the water spilling over them as / they crept forward / scarcely able to move but afraid of / being caught there." The volume is permeated with Merwin's descriptions of human despair in the environment in which it is experienced: "Born on the land the shore grass / hissing while the night slips / through a narrow place a man is / born for the narrows / a woman is born for where the / waters open / the passage is for a god it is not / for a human."

As its title suggests, *The River Sound* returns to one of Merwin's favorite subjects and symbols; it also returns to his recurrent reevaluation of old myths and legends. "The Stranger," as the poet tells us, is about a Guarani legend recorded by Ernesto Morales. The tour de force of the volume is the fifty-eight-page "Testimony," an autobiographical poem that lists various people to whom he would leave the treasures of a lifetime, now "the year I would be seventy." To one friend he would leave "this late spring / with its evenings in the garden / all the years of it beginning / from the moment I met her in / Fran's living room and the veiled green / leaves were young that we walked under . . ." To another he would leave "the morning as it is / clear and still with the bell from down / across the valley reaching us / to say the hour over again / so that we can pay attention . . ." Names like Galway Kinnell, Richard Howard, and Alastair Reid are on his list, but most are his closest friends with unfamiliar names. The poem concludes with the moving statement that in the vast empire of time that which we call our own is "only / as thick as one stamp that might be / on a post card but we would see / none of that where we were today / . . . I had not seen / where would the card be going to / that the stamp was to be put on / would I see what was written down / on it wherever it was sent / and the few words what would they mean / that we took with us as we went."

—Lois Gordon

MEZEY, Robert

Nationality: American. **Born:** Philadelphia, Pennsylvania, 28 February 1935. **Education:** Kenyon College, Gambier, Ohio, 1951–53; University of Iowa, Iowa City, 1956–60, B.A. 1959; Stanford University, California (poetry fellow, 1961), 1960–61. **Military Service:** U.S. Army, 1953–55. **Family:** Married Olivia Simpson in 1963; two daughters and one son. **Career:** Worked as a probation officer, psychology technician, social worker, and copywriter; instructor, Western Reserve University, Cleveland, 1963–64, and Franklin and Marshall College, Lancaster, Pennsylvania, 1965–66; assistant professor, Fresno State University, California, 1967–68; associate professor, University of Utah, Salt Lake City, 1973–76; professor of English and poet-in-residence, Pomona College, Claremont, California, 1976–99. **Awards:** Lamont Poetry Selection award, 1960; Ingram Merrill Foundation fellowship, 1972, 1989; Guggenheim fellowship, 1977; American Academy award, 1983; National Endowment for the Arts fellowship, 1986; P.E.N. poetry award, 1987, and Bassine Citation, 1988, both for *Evening Wind*. **Address:** Department of English, Pomona College, 140 West Sixth Street, Claremont, California 91711, U.S.A.

PUBLICATIONS

Poetry

Berg Goodman Mezey, with others. Philadelphia, New Ventures Press, 1957.
The Wandering Jew. Mount Vernon, Iowa, Hillside Press, 1960.
The Lovemaker. Iowa City, Cummington Press, 1961.
White Blossoms. Iowa City, Cummington Press, 1965.
Favors. Privately printed, 1968.
The Book of Dying. Santa Cruz, California, Kayak, 1970.

The Door Standing Open: New and Selected Poems 1954–1969. Boston, Houghton Mifflin, and London, Oxford University Press, 1970.

Last Words: For John Lawrence Simpson, 1896–1969. West Branch, Iowa, Cummington Press, 1970.

Couplets. Kalamazoo, Michigan, Westigan Press, 1976.

Small Song. Grand Rapids, Michigan, Humble Hills Press, 1979.

Evening Wind. Middletown, Connecticut, Wesleyan University Press 1987.

Natural Selection. Edgewood, Kentucky, Robert Barth Press, 1997.

Joe Simpson. N.p., Stone Wall Press, 1998.

The Ballad of Charles Starkweather, with Donald Justice. N.p., Peich Press, 1999.

A Joyful Noise. N.p., Stone Wall Press, 1999.

Collected Poems. Fayetteville, Arkansas, University of Arkansas Press, 2000.

Other

Selected Translations. Kalamazoo, Michigan, Westigan Press, 1981.

Editor, with Stephen Berg, *Naked Poetry: Recent American Poetry in Open Forms.* Indianapolis, Bobbs Merrill, 1969; *The New Naked Poetry,* 1976.

Editor and translator, *Poems from the Hebrew.* New York, Crowell, 1973.

Editor, with Donald Justice, *The Collected Poems of Henri Coulette.* Fayetteville, Arkansas, University of Arkansas Press, 1990.

Editor, *Thomas Hardy: Selected Poems.* New York, Penguin, 1998.

Editor, *The Poetry of E.A. Robinson.* New York, Random House, 1999.

Translator, *The Mercy of Sorrow,* by Uri Zvi Greenberg. Philadelphia, Three People Press, 1965.

Translator, *Tungsten,* by César Vallejo. Syracuse, New York, Syracuse University Press, 1988.

*

Critical Studies: By Ralph J. Mills, Jr., in *American Poetry Review* (Philadelphia), fall 1974; ''The Dying of the Light: American Jewish Self-Portrayal in Henry Roth and Robert Mezey'' by Noam Flinker, in *The Jewish Self-Portrait in European and American Literature,* edited by Hans-Jurgen Schrader, Elliott M. Simon, and Charlotte Wardi, Tubingen, Germany, Niemeyer, 1996.

Robert Mezey comments:

(1995) Pound said that poetry atrophies when it gets too far from music. That is one reason it is in its present state, for which he himself is not altogether blameless. Free verse, so called, has swept the field. Since there is so little competent metrical verse, what exactly is free verse free from? It has, merely by being inept and voluminous, obscured the norm, the only possible norm, and wanders around the field it has swept, stumbling and falling. There did not seem to be so much awful poetry thirty or forty years ago, when I was young; perhaps I was a less exacting reader. I suppose most poetry in every age is bad, but ours has grown so amateurishly bad, so aggressively or complacently bad, that it tends to drive out the good. The upshot of all our experiment is that we have found new ways to be bad, ways never seen before or even imagined. Well, all I can do at my age is to accept

my limitations and try to write as well as I possibly can. That is a poet's only social and moral obligation. (Of course, as a person and citizen he has many.)

*   *   *

Robert Mezey is a metaphysical poet not because like Donne he ransacks Scholastic philosophy for images but because like Hamlet and all true metaphysicians he is given to asking unanswerable questions about himself and the world. He is not, however, a ''philosophical'' poet. A great weight of passion accumulates behind his studied reserve, and what finally emerges over the dam is intensely felt, tightly controlled poetry.

Early in his career Mezey came under the influence of the formalist critic and poet Yvor Winters, and Mezey's book *The Lovemaker* betrays this influence clearly. Of Winters and his own subsequent development he writes wryly in a note appended to a group of his poems in *Naked Poetry,* an anthology of American poems in open forms edited by himself and Stephen Berg,

When I was quite young I came under unhealthy influences—Yvor Winters, for example, and America, and my mother, though not in that order. Yvor Winters was easy to exorcise; all I had to do was meet him. My mother and America are another story and why tell it in prose?

Once in Iowa City a friend said, ''Why do you write in think so. It is possible I'm not a poet at all. But I am a man, a Piscean, and unhappy, and therefore I make up poems.

Mezey is a poet all right and an important one, but there is no doubt that a kind of passionate melancholy underlies most of his poetry. Yeats said, ''Out of our quarrel with the world we make rhetoric; out of the quarrel with ourselves, poetry.'' Mezey is never rhetorical, but his quarrel really seems to be with the nature of things. He avoids the Hardyesque rhetoric against the universe through the adroit use of images that supply objective correlatives for his own moods. In ''There,'' for example, microcosm (the poet) and macrocosm (the world) seem to fuse:

It is deep summer. Far out
at sea the young squalls darken
and roll, plunging northward,
threatening everything. I see
the Atlantic moving in slow
contemplative fury
against the rocks, the frozen
headlands, and the towns sunk deep
in a blind northern light. Here,
far inland, in the mountains
of Mexico, it is raining
hard, battering the soft mouths
of flowers. I am sullen, dumb,
ungovernable. I taste myself
and I taste those winds, uprisings
of salt and ice, of great trees
brought down, of houses and cries
lost in the storm; and what breaks
on that black shore breaks in me.

The tone here is perhaps more Byronic than usual in his poems, where urban images have their place along with natural ones. But the poem does show quite clearly his strategy for making turbid and passionate feelings objective through the use of corresponding images from the natural world.

Mezey thinks of himself as having abandoned traditional meter and rhyme. His and Berg's anthology is exclusively concerned with poems in what he calls "open form." Yet as one reads over the poem just quoted, one becomes aware that a great measure of the force of the poem is owing to the tightly controlled rhythms employed. No line in the poem contains more than four stresses or fewer than three, a close approach to "regular" meter, yet these fluctuations in line length do much to suggest the fluctuating pressures of the storm and the sea. One senses, too, that such powerful rhythmic control had to be exerted to keep the poem from exploding all over the page, and the control over raw emotion manifests itself mainly through the poet's handling of rhythm.

Mezey obviously values clarity in a writer. Three things, I think, account for the unfailing clarity of these passionate poems. Two have already been mentioned—sharp, clear images, many of which turn out to be objective correlatives, and rhythmic control—and the third is frequent, unobtrusive, but effective employment of articulatory symbolism—the forced miming by the organs of speech of the very action or object being described. To illustrate, I quote from another of his poems about autumn, "Touch It." This is the second stanza:

> Past the thinning orchard the fields
> are on fire. A mountain of smoke
> climbs the desolate wind, and at its roots
> fire is eating dead grass with many small teeth.

The very shaping of the words in the final line here enforces upon the reader a sort of chewing action. Again, in "There"—"it is raining / hard, battering the soft mouths / of flowers"—simply shaping the words pantomimes the effect the words describe.

These three factors, and perhaps many more that have escaped me, but at least these three, make possible the shaping of raw emotion in Mezey's poems toward the extraordinary clarity they achieve.

—E.L. Mayo

MICHIE, James

Nationality: British. **Born:** Weybridge, Surrey, 24 June 1927. **Education:** Trinity College, Oxford. **Career:** Editor, then chief editor, Heinemann publishers, London, 1951–61; director, Bodley Head publishers, London, 1961–89. **Address:** c/o Jonathan Cape Ltd., 20 Vauxhall Bridge Road, London SWIV 2SA, England.

PUBLICATIONS

Poetry

Possible Laughter. London, Hart Davis, 1959.
New and Selected Poems. London, Chatto and Windus, 1983.
Aesop's Fables. London, Jonathan Cape, 1989.
Collected Poems. London, Sinclair-Stevenson, 1994.

Other

Editor, with Kingsley Amis, *Oxford Poetry 1949.* Oxford, Blackwell, 1949.
Editor, *The Bodley Head Book of Longer Short Stories.* London, Bodley Head, 1974; as *The Book of Longer Short Stories,* New York, Stein and Day, 1975.
Editor, with P.J. Kavanagh, *The Oxford Book of Short Poems.* Oxford, Oxford University Press, 1985.
Contributor, *The Folio Golden Treasury: The Best Songs and Lyrical Poems in the English Language.* London, Folio Society, 1997.

Translator, *The Odes of Horace.* New York, Orion, 1963; London, Hart Davis, 1964.
Translator, *The Poems of Catullus: A Bilingual Edition.* London, Hart Davis, and New York, Random House, 1969.
Translator, *The Epigrams of Martial.* London, Hart Davis MacGibbon, and New York, Random House, 1973.
Translator, *Selected Fables,* by La Fontaine. London, Allen Lane, and New York, Viking Press, 1979.
Translator, with Colin Leach, *Helen/Euripides.* Oxford and New York, Oxford University Press, 1981.
Translator, *Poems from the Greek Anthology.* London, Folio, 1990.
Translator, *The Art of Love* by Ovid. London, Folio, 1993.

*   *   *

James Michie is probably better known as a translator than as an original poet, which is hardly surprising considering the wit and energy of his versions of Horace, Catullus, and Martial. His translations are not "modern" in the usual sense—they have nothing in common, for example, with the free renderings and "homages" of Pound or Lowell—but are cast in the neoclassical tradition of Pope and Dryden, in which the order of English rhyme and meter offers a kind of substitute satisfaction for the unrenderable richness of the Latin. Thus Catullus's celebrated "Odi et amo. Quare id faciam, fortasse requiris? / Nescio, sed fieri sentio at excrucior" becomes, in Michie's version,

> I hate and love. If you ask me to explain
>   The contradiction,
> I can't, but I can feel it, and the pain
>   Is crucifixion.

Michie's own poetry has been collected in two volumes. The first, *Possible Laughter,* is slender, with only thirty-two poems, few of which are longer than a page. They reflect some of the qualities of the Latin verse that Michie has translated, its economy, its sophistication, and particularly its good-natured cynicism about human nature. The chief English influence seems to have been the light (but serious) black doggerel of Auden during the 1930s, with its popular ballad forms and quick, surprising imagery. In "Quiet, Child," for example, Michie observes,

> Glumly we chew on with murder
>   Long past the appetite of hate.
> Nothing but their shadows' outlines
>   Left, like grease-stains on a plate,
> People leaning over bridges
>   Quietly evaporate.

And big as a telephone directory
   His bomber's casualty list,
Gloved, the pilot leaves behind him,
   Represented by a mist,
Individuals who were furious,
   But no longer now exist.

The poems vary considerably in theme and metrical form, from the Betjeman-like "Park Concert" to the more troubled, individual voice of "Nightmare" and "At Any Rate," with their darker observations about human cruelty and helplessness. Time, with its subtle erosions, is the enemy:

The hours, pretending they do not know how to combine,
Walk up as charming freebooters, unarmed, disclaiming
Allegiance to that remote and iron-grey battle-line.

Fidelity is weak, and the lovers may

   hold like amulets
Precious hands, or go linking
Arms, but no one gets
Cleanly through without slinking.
Quite innocent,
Moving to kiss, although they hadn't meant
It, they'll find themselves archly winking.

   New and Selected Poems consists half of poems from *Possible Laughter,* some lightly revised, and half of new poems. The latter are again relatively short, formal yet varied in form and subject matter, with a similar feel about them as the earlier poems.

   The prevailing tone of Michie's verse is neither brutal nor tragic but much in the spirit of the man in "The End of the Sage" who achieves wisdom in death:

"Much wiser and much dafter,
Now that I quite agree
To become dead,
I achieve a witticism,
And I see at last," he said,
"Hazy like foothills possible laughter."

                                —Elmer Borklund

MIDDLETON, (John) Christopher

Nationality: British. **Born:** Truro, Cornwall, 10 June 1926. **Education:** Felsted School, Essex; Merton College, Oxford, B.A. 1951, D.Phil. 1954. **Military Service:** Royal Air Force, 1944–48. **Career:** Lecturer in English, Zurich University, 1952–55; lecturer in German, King's College, University of London, 1955–66. Since 1966 professor of Germanic languages and literature, University of Texas, Austin. **Awards:** Faber memorial prize, 1964; Guggenheim fellowship, 1974; DAAD Kunstlerprogramm fellowship, Berlin, 1975, 1978; National Endowment for the Arts fellowship, 1980; Camargo Foundation poetry fellow, 1999. **Address:** Department of German, University of Texas, Austin, Texas 78712, U.S.A.

PUBLICATIONS

Poetry

Torse 3: Poems 1949–1961. London, Longman, and New York, Harcourt Brace, 1962.
Penguin Modern Poets 4, with David Holbrook and David Wevill. London, Penguin, 1963.
Nonsequences: Selfpoems. London, Longman, 1965; New York, Norton, 1966.
Our Flowers and Nice Bones. London, Fulcrum Press, 1969.
Der Taschenelefant: Satire. Berlin, Neue Rabenpresse, 1969.
The Fossil Fish: 15 Micropoems. Providence, Rhode Island, Burning Deck, 1970.
Briefcase History: 9 Poems. Providence, Rhode Island, Burning Deck, 1972.
Fractions for Another Telemachus. Knotting, Bedfordshire, Sceptre Press, 1974.
Wild Horse. Knotting, Bedfordshire, Sceptre Press, 1975.
The Lonely Suppers of W. V. Balloon. Manchester, Carcanet, and Boston, Godine, 1975.
Razzmatazz. Austin, Texas, W. Thomas Taylor, 1976.
Eight Elementary Inventions. Knotting, Bedfordshire, Sceptre Press, 1977.
Pataxanadu and Other Prose. Manchester, Carcanet, 1977.
Carminalenia. Manchester, Carcanet, 1980.
Wooden Dog. Providence, Rhode Island, Burning Deck, 1982.
111 Poems. Manchester, Carcanet, 1983.
Serpentine (prose). London, Oasis, 1984.
Two Horse Wagon Going By. Manchester, Carcanet, 1986.
Selected Writings. Manchester, Carcanet, 1989.
The Balcony Tree. Manchester, Carcanet, 1992.
Intimate Chronicles. Manchester, Carcanet, and Riverdale-on-Hudson, Sheep Meadow, 1996.
In the Mirror of the Eighth King. Los Angeles, Green Integer, 1999.

Play

The Metropolitans (libretto), music by Hans Vogt. Kassel, Alkor, 1964.

Other

Bolshevism in Art and Other Expository Writings. Manchester, Carcanet, 1978.
The Pursuit of the Kingfisher: Essays. Manchester, Carcanet, 1983.
Jackdans Jiving: Selected Essays on Poetry and Translation. Manchester, Carcanet, 1998.

Editor and translator, with Michael Hamburger, *Modern German Poetry 1910–1960: An Anthology with Verse Translations.* London, MacGibbon and Kee, and New York, Grove Press, 1962.
Editor and translator, with William Burford, *The Poet's Vocation: Selections from the Letters of Holderlin, Rimbaud, and Hart Crane.* Austin, University of Texas Press, 1967.
Editor, *German Writing Today.* London, Penguin, 1967.
Editor, *Selected Poems,* by Georg Trakl. London, Cape, 1968.
Editor, and translator with others, *Selected Stories,* by Robert Walser. Manchester, Carcanet, and New York, Farrar Straus, 1982.

Editor, and translator with others, *Goethe: Selected Poems.* Cambridge, Massachusetts, Suhrkamp-Insel, and London, Calder, 1983.

Editor, and translator with others, *The Figure on the Boundary Line: Selected Prose,* by Christoph Meckel. Manchester, Carcanet, 1983.

Editor, and translator with others, *The Stillness of the World Before Bach: New Selected Poems,* by Lars Gustafsson. New York, New Directions, 1988.

Translator, *The Walk and Other Stories,* by Robert Walser. London, Calder, 1957.

Translator, with others, *Primal Vision,* by Gottfried Benn. New York, New Directions, 1960.

Translator, with others, *Poems and Verse Plays,* by Hugo von Hofmannsthal. New York, Pantheon, 1961.

Translator, with Michael Hamburger, *Selected Poems,* by Gunter Grass. London, Secker and Warburg, and New York, Harcourt Brace, 1966.

Translator, *Jakob von Gunten,* by Robert Walser. Austin, University of Texas Press, 1969.

Translator, *Selected Letters,* by Friedrich Nietzsche. Chicago, University of Chicago Press, 1969.

Translator, with Michael Hamburger, *Poems,* by Gunter Grass. London, Penguin, 1969; as *Selected Poems,* 1980.

Translator, *The Quest for Christa T.,* by Christa Wolf. New York, Farrar Straus, 1970; London, Hutchinson, 1971.

Translator, with Michael Hamburger, *Selected Poems,* by Paul Celan. London, Penguin, 1972.

Translator, *Selected Poems,* by Friedrich Holderlin and Eduard Morike. Chicago, University of Chicago Press, 1972.

Translator, *Inmarypraise,* by Gunter Grass. New York, Harcourt Brace, 1974.

Translator, *Kafka's Other Trial: The Letters to Felice,* by Elias Canetti. New York, Schocken, 1974; London, Penguin, 1978.

Translator, with Michael Hamburger, *In the Egg and Other Poems,* by Gunter Grass. New York, Harcourt Brace, 1977; London, Secker and Warburg, 1978.

Translator, *The Spectacle at the Tower,* by Gert Hofmann. New York, Fromm, 1985.

Translator, *Our Conquest,* by Gert Hofmann. New York, Fromm, 1985.

Translator, *The Parable of the Blind,* by Gert Hofmann. New York, Fromm, 1986; London, Secker and Warburg, 1988.

Translator, *Balzac's Horse and Other Stories,* by Gert Hofmann. New York, Fromm, 1988.

Translator, with Leticia Garza-Falcón, *Andalusian Poems.* Boston, Godine, 1993.

*

Critical Studies: "Shapes in Imaginary Space" by Philip Crick, in *Ninth Decade* 2, 1983; "Christopher Middleton: Journeys Broken at the Threshold" by Ian Gregson, in *Bete Noire* (Hull, Humberside, England), 10–11, autumn 1990-spring 1991.

*   *   *

In an interview in *London Magazine* in 1964, Christopher Middleton criticized his English contemporaries for a parochialism of form and content that cut them off from the great heritage of European modernism. The latter, he argued, had "at most points connected . . . a strong sense of social revolution, a catastrophic view of history," with an "interest in the radical remaking of techniques." Both in his translations, primarily from the German, and in his own poetry, Middleton has tried to keep open this connection. Middleton's "catastrophic view of history" leads him continually to those moments at which personal crisis interlocks with social crisis. Thus, in "The Arrest of Pastor Paul Schneider" the pastor is dragged reluctantly from a nightmare of arrest to its actuality; in "January 1919" history rips the "holed head" of the murdered German revolutionary Liebknecht out of context, to display it "bleeding across a heap of progressive magazines"; in "The Historian" Procopius, official historian to the tyrant Justinian, is snatched from the desk where he writes his secret exposé of the regime just as he realizes that the only authentic opposition is in deeds not words. The interrupted sentence that closes the poem reveals the fragility of men amid a history they cannot control, the witness always potentially a victim ("The thought still bothers me, that, instead of writing, I might have changed the"). Many of Middleton's poems turn Hitler's and Stalin's death camps into universal symbols of twentieth-century history, uprooting men from their own proper lives to a dream of deportation and massacre, whether it is the "figures torn from a fog," "feeding on garbage in the camp near Voronezh" ("Pavlovic Variations") or the "eclipsed / Future[s]" slid into the ovens at Treblinka ("Idiocy of Rural Life"). But terror lurks not only in the major events of a public history. Middleton's poetry also detects the threat of extinction in more mundane, trivial situations. A pair of gloves left on the floor of a lavatory (so that "it seems, you'd think, smothering a giggle, / someone has been sucked down the john") can summon up a terrifying vision of people who have disappeared.

Middleton's poetry repeatedly evokes, in his own words, "a really live sense of what it is like to live in a society where the direction of life has fallen into the hands of malevolent or ignorant functionaries, where all human values seem to be threatened by inhuman organization." Poems such as "Octobers" and "Autobiography" record how this menace inserts itself into the most idyllic and private experiences. But "history . . . isn't the past at all, it is the multitudinous new life saturating the present," and "the little significant things" it is the poet's duty to "unravel" ("Glaucus") contain promise as well as threat, renewal as well as destruction. This is perhaps why so many of Middleton's poems are concerned with children, the inheritors for whom history, the future, is always open, though it may again and again be suppressed, as for "Fania, ten / at the turn of the century," in "The Pogroms in Sebastopol," or for "Pavel's child," who "came to pieces in my hands," dug out of the snow of the camps ("Pavlovic Variations"), or for the napalmed Vietnamese children in "Mérindol Interior," whose photographed agony intrudes into the poet's comfortable middle-class world.

At its best there are a hardness, a tautness, and a lack of false color and sentimentality to Middleton's language that argue an ascetic's imagination. Yet at the same time his poetry is passionately involved in the world, "odd as it is to care," as he says in one poem, "anyhow for things / their mass & contour / & all beginnings." His world is substantial yet curiously abstract, figured and yet not personalized. He writes often in the third or second person, and even when he appears himself, attention is nearly always focused on what is out there rather than on subjective response. This classical yet human distance is maintained by a deliberate employment of the "defamiliarization" technique described by the Russian formalist

Viktor Shklovsky, whom Middleton acknowledges on several occasions. The disjunctions, dislocations, and unexpected collocations of his language, the experimental diversity of structure and theme, and a movement between extremes of abstrusity and explicitness, using the very opacity of his language to concentrate our gaze as if for the first time on familiar object and event—all enable Middleton to pursue the "defining of enigmas" that is for him the poetic vocation, exposing us to "the strangeness of being alive . . . the strangeness of living things outside oneself."

In "Oystercatchers," for example, the unexpected verb discloses a world strangely detached from man ("rocks in the bay below / Retrieved their shadows"), while "Wire Spring" turns the pun of the title into a sinister vision by reviving dead metaphors ("The first clock said: it is time we killed. / The second clock said: it is time we told"). "The simplest model for such poems is not the linguistic 'statement' but the question," Middleton notes on the dust jacket of *The Lonely Suppers of W.V. Balloon,* and indeed all of his poetry is hermeneutic, interrogative, quizzical, questioning reality with a skeptical and informed eye and perpetually reminding us that language is not an innocent carrier of meaning but itself a force for good or ill that preempts all our seeing. It is this that accounts for the range of Middleton's experiments with the resources of language, whether concrete or found poems, cut ups and grafts, or such pieces as "Computer's Karl Marx," which, starting with a joke (a history of revolution written by a computer that has only the letters of the words "production relations" to play with), goes on to show how the limits of language are the limits of the world. It is perhaps finally in this ludic sense of the ludicrous, derived from Dada and surrealism and coupled with a quite un-English seriousness, that Middleton justifies his claim to the European inheritance.

—Stan Smith

THE MIGHTY SPARROW

Nationality: Trinidadian. **Born:** Grandroy Bay, Grenada, 9 July 1935; moved to Trinidad in 1938. **Family:** Married Margaret Skinner, two daughters and two sons. **Career:** Calypso singer/performer: first public Carnival appearance in 1956; many international tours. **Awards:** Trinidad Carnival Calypso King Crown, 1956, 1960, 1962, 1963, 1972, 1973, 1974, and Road March Crown, 1956, 1958, 1960, 1961, 1966, 1969, 1972, 1984; Hummingbird Medal (Trinidad); The Chaconia Gold (Trinidad and Tobago). D.Litt.: University of the West Indies, Kingston, Jamaica.

PUBLICATIONS

Poetry

One Hundred and Twenty Calypsoes to Remember. Port of Spain, n.p., 1963.
Sparrow: The Legend: Calypso King of the World. Port of Spain, Inprint, 1986(?).

Recordings: more than 60 albums, and many singles.

*

Critical Studies: "Sparrow and the Language of the Calypso" by Gordon Rohlehr, in *Caribbean Quarterly* (Mona, Kingston), 14(1–2), March-June 1968; *The Future in the Present—Selected Writings by CLR James.* Westport, Connecticut, L. Hill, and London, Allison & Busby, 1977.

*   *   *

That the subject of this essay, along with the other practitioners of the tradition from which he comes, was not given an entry in *Contemporary Poets* until the fifth edition is indicative of the conservative tendency to define the poet, even in modern times, as an artist, separate from the traditions of the culture. Compounding this conservative stance is the fact the Caribbean and colonial literatures generally arrived on the scene apparently in full bloom as texts (mainly in the period after 1945), without that classical development from, say, the Homeric or Ljala or Vedic oral traditions that only much later appeared in written form. Without a classical tradition for his base, this category of poet suffers the lingering assumption of being somehow of a different, and lesser, breed. Yet these troubadours, griots, and calypsonians include all the elements we customarily associate with poetry: an idea growing into montage, rhythm, metrics, tone, metaphorical life supported by a wide range of language resources, sound and/or sight patterns, allusions to and from the culture of the audience.

Such is the poetry of The Mighty Sparrow, who revolutionized calypso (*kaiso*) singing in 1956 when he sang "Jean and Dinah" at the Trinidad carnival. Since then he has occupied the throne as ruler of a "kingdom" that represents one of the most fecund of the popular/traditional musical forms of Trinidad and the rest of the Caribbean. The art, vitality, and cultural vehemence of this artist is an example of the old (and also very modern alternative) oral tradition within the English-language poetry of the Caribbean.

"Jean and Dinah" concerns the presence of American forces, who established strategic military, naval, and air bases in Trinidad during World War II. Their money and technical know-how acted as a (contradictory) catalyst in what was until then a fairly slow-moving Caribbean society. In "Jean and Dinah" Sparrow's satirical concern is with the demimonde of pimps, prostitutes, "wahbeens," "glad girls," "saga," and "glamour boys" who were involved in certain aspects of the U.S. servicemen's sociosexual entertainment. The song is set at a time when the Yankees were "de-escalating" their presence after dispute with the Trinidadian government over continued occupation of some of the island's land space, with the girls feeling the pinch as the main source of their pay packets dried up. Sparrow, taking on the persona of the local boys who had been neglected by these "jamettes" during the period of the American "occupation," now sings his plessure: "Trouble in town when the price drop down / Yankees gone, Sparrow tek over now." "Jean and Dinah" consists (in the 1963 printed version) of four eight-line stanzas rhyming in the traditional *kaiso* couplets, *aabbccdd,* with a six-line chorus much more adventitiously structured, *abbcc* and a half-rhymed *d,* and a rhymed caesura: "Don't make no row . Sparrow tek over now." There is also slang ("they park up in town") and nation-language ("make style"), with a biblical touch in the last line:

Is the glamour boys again
We are going to rule Port of Spain
No more Yankees to spoil the fete
Dorothy have to take what she get

All of them who use to make style
Taking their two shillin with a smile
No more Hotel and Simmonds bed
By the sweat of thy brow thou shall eat bread

The cross-rhythms, tone, performance body language, mimesis, and other forms employed by calypsonians cannot, of course, be conveyed in the written text.

"Mango Vert," from the same occupation period, is an example of one of the chief characteristics of the *kaiso,* the sexual double entendre:

A Yankee man an a woman was in confusion
A Yankee man an a woman was in confusion
The woman give him something to eat
With stringy stringy hair but it tasting sweet
He say a rather do without
It go stick up in me teet a done wash me mout

She said if you eat it right the hair won't stick in you mout
An you bound to say how it tasting sweet sweet sweet
But if you eat it wrong don't walk in the street
Everybody go know when they see the hair in you teet . . .

The song, however, ends somewhat anticlimactically because of the rather clumsy effort, in good vaudeville style, to "disappoint" the audience with a "clean" end:

A knock on the door very boldly
When a burst the door an a enter
A see them standin up in the centre
The stupid Yankee catchin cold feet
Is a mango vert the man fraid to eat

From early in his career Sparrow became a supporter—though a very critical and sometimes quite hostile one—of the nationalist government of Trinidad and Tobago under Eric Williams. Williams became the first prime minister of independent Trinidad and Tobago in 1962 on a wave of idealism, and he instigated a number of reforms, such as a new tax system and better pay for the police in an effort to stamp out bribery and corruption. In "Police Get More Pay" Sparrow uses several formal *kaiso* devices, including first-line (verse) repetitions ("mad, mad, mad," "cheap, cheap, cheap, cheap"), increased complexity of the song's chorus, the alternation of long and short lines, an increased caesura rhyming, and the use of acceleration through (in the chorus) the first and third lines, capped each time by a short line:

They use to get a shilling here collect a shilling there
But all a dat stop

If they only say they broke   people say they
   makin joke
They pay gone up . . .

But it was with "Dan Is the Man in the Van," Sparrow's exposé of the fundamental irrelevance, escapism, and fantasy of colonial education, that most sertainly established him as a local artist making the transition from parochial limitations to wider subject matter. The title comes from one of the Royal Readers, British textbooks that for many West Indian schoolchildren were practically the only books they had access to. Memorable lines from the text like "Dan is the man in the van" are often illustrated in the song by non-Caribbean scenes such as "Dan-is-the-English-Man-in-what-looks-like-an-English-milk-Van." A "single-tone" (four-line) *kaiso* makes up the body of the text, alternating with a changing "double-tone" (eight-line) chorus that breaks up the fixed meter and allows room for improvisational intervention with, throughout the poem, caesuras of varying placement:

Ac   .   cording to the education you get when you small
You'll grow up with true ambition and respect from
   one and all
But in my days in school   .   they teach me like a fool
The things they teach me I should be a block-headed mule

Pussy has finish his work long ago
An now he restin and ting
Solomon Agundy was born on a Mondee
The Ass in the Lion Skin
Winkin, Blinkin and Nod
Sail off in a wooden shoe
How Agouti lose e tail and Alligator trying to get monkey
   liver soup

Dan is the man in the van . . .

Sparrow extends his satire to nursery rhymes and snippets from some of the pictured fables included in the Royal Readers. But his punch line and the message he communicated so brilliantly to the anglophone Caribbean on the eve of political independence was that imperial education was really a plot to keep Caliban down and that his (Sparrow's) native creativity came not from Prospero's books but from his own oral folk tradition: "If me head was bright I woulda be a damn fool . . ."

In "Ten to One Is Murder," certainly one of Sparrow's finest achievements, he returned to the folk/slave *kalinda* (a stick-fighting call-and-response song form). The form provided him with the perfect dramatic format through which to recount an incident (possibly true) in which he was attacked by a street gang on the pretext that he had "interfered" with one of their women and in which he was apparently forced to use his gun ("me wedger") in self-defense. The poem begins with the raconteur using caesura rhymed triolets followed by a "break-out" chorus and orchestra that is used as an insistent chant after each new line of disclosure; the syllabics increase in intensity until the work reaches double time in the heat of the battle, ending in a mimesis of violence. But the most remarkable feature of this *kalinda,* possible only in the flexible oral tradition, is Sparrow's rhyme scheme, based almost entirely on the letter *r:*

Well they playin bad
They have me feelin bad
Well they playin beast
Why they run for Police

Ten to one is murder!
Ten criminals attack me outside a Miramar

Ten to one is murder!
About ten in de night on the fifth of October
Ten to one is murder!
Way down Henry Street up by HGM Walker
Ten to one is murder!
The leader of the gang was a hot like a pepper
Ten to one is murder!
An every man in the gang had a white handle razor
Ten to one is murder!
They say a push the girl from Grenada
Ten to one is murder!
You could imagine my position, not a police in the area
Ten to one is murder! . . .

By the mid-1960s Sparrow's art had entered its classical phase, his characteristic artistic devices and verse forms already established in his first ten years as a performer. What we have witnessed since then is his continuing quotidian engagement with what turns out to be an increasingly imploding postcolonial society. We find Sparrow slimming, as he says, not slowing down: rearranging as necessary or requested some of the old classics; ignoring perhaps as a bad job the involuted politics of his beloved country; and growing more philosophical in the role as an adviser and statesman to younger lovers and calypsonians.

—Edward Kamau Brathwaite

MILLER, E(ugene) Ethelbert

Nationality: American. **Born:** New York City, 20 November 1950. **Education:** Howard University, Washington, D.C., 1968–72, B.A. in African American studies 1972. **Family:** Married Denise King in 1982, two children. **Career:** Since 1974 director, African American Resource Center, Howard University; visiting professor, University of Nevada, Las Vegas, 1993. Jessie Ball Dupont Scholar, Emory & Henry College, 1996; scholar-in-residence, George Mason University, 2000. Since 1974 founder and organizer, Ascension poetry reading series, Washington, D.C. **Awards:** Washington, D.C. Mayor's Art award, 1982; Public Humanities award, Washington, D.C., Community Council, 1988; Washington, D.C., Arts Commission fellowship, 1989; Columbia Merit award, 1993; O.B. Hardison, Jr., Poetry prize, 1995; Stephen Henderson Poetry award, 1997. Honorary doctorate of literature, Emory & Henry College, 1996. **Address:** P.O. Box 441, Howard University, Washington, D.C. 20059, U.S.A.

PUBLICATIONS

Poetry

The Land of Smiles/Land of No Smiles. Privately printed, 1974.
Andromeda. N.p., Chiva, 1974.
Women Surviving Massacres and Men. Washington, D.C., Anemone Press, 1977.
The Migrant Worker. Washington, D.C., Washington Writers Publishing House, 1978.

Season of Hunger/Cry of Rain: Poems 1975–1980. Detroit, Lotus Press, 1982.
Where Are the Love Poems for Dictators? Washington, D.C., Open Hand, 1986.
First Light, New and Selected Poems. Baltimore, Black Classic Press, 1994.
Whispers, Secrets & Promises. Baltimore, Black Classic Press, 1998.

Other

Editor, with Ahmos Zu-Bolton, *Synergy D.C. Anthology.* Washington, D.C., Energy Black South Press, 1975.
Editor, *In Search of Color Everywhere: A Collection of African-American Poetry.* New York, Stewart, Tabori & Chang, 1994.
Editor, *Fathering Words: The Making of an African American Writer.* New York, St. Martins Press, 2000.

*

Manuscript Collection: Howard University, Washington, D.C.

Critical Studies: ''A 60's Harvest: The Poetic Vision of E. Ethelbert Miller'' by Priscilla Ramsey, in *Freedomways* (New York), 24, 1984; ''The Aesthetic of E. Ethelbert Miller'' in *Warriors, Conjurers and Priests* by Joyce Joyce, Chicago, Third World Press, 1994; ''Letters: Wanda Coleman to E. Ethelbert Miller'' by E. Thelbert Miller, in *Callaloo,* winter 1999.

E. Ethelbert Miller comments:

Question: How long has it been legal for African-Americans to write in the United States? I think about this question and conclude that writing is still a political decision for every African-American writer. I started writing poetry in the late 1960s. I felt that I had a responsibility at that time to create something useful for my community. As I look around at the present political climate, I realize that there is a need for writers to understand where the lines are being drawn. We must stand in solidarity with everyone who desires freedom and human rights. The older I become, the more aware I am of the clock ticking. The poems come slower now than when I was in my twenties. Somehow I feel that because I am a writer I am a better human being.

*   *   *

In the poetry of E. Ethelbert Miller, the gentle wit, topicality, particularity of incident, simple language, and metaphoric references can belie a utilitarian poetry of relevant sociopolitical commentary. While he was a student at Howard University during the height of the black arts movement, Miller's poetry was already different from the assertive, declarative, and even strident writing that was not unusual at the time. He was, and is, his own poet.

Miller approaches, explores, and evaluates experiences and situations for providential meaning and significance, always with an openness, often letting the correlative suggest its subject matter. In *Andromeda,* his first collection, he is the young poet predictably concerned with values, introspection, and love. In *The Migrant Worker* he has moved from self to the world and what that world means to the communal self. *Season of Hunger/Cry of Rain: Poems*

1975–1980 is much concerned with ethos; he "... will take the / journey back / sail / the / middle passage" ("Tomorrow"). It is in this volume that he introduces a series of wryly philosophical "BoWillie" poems, for example, "bo willie shirley me / we headin for maryland / me I'm in the front seat / shirley she mad and fussin / cause she always gotta sit / in the back / i put on a cracker accent / and call her a sassy colored gal / we argue back and forth / bo willie he don't pay us no mind / he thinks we kids / he wears a beard that makes / him look like jesus / and i think to myself / maybe that's why he don't say nothin" ("Intersections: Crossing the District Line"). The collection also exhibits characteristic Miller whimsy. To a girlfriend who complains that he wears jeans every place, he prophesies that when he is "dressed / up in a coffin," he will ask her to let him "take her / somewhere / she hasn't / been" ("Dressed Up").

Miller's most overtly emotional poetry, and the works in which he comes closest to anger, is found in *Where Are the Love Poems for Dictators?* With their conscience-arresting imagery, these poems are openly political, and although their locale is South and Central America, they are worldwide in their concerns: "its close to midnight / & america wonders why michael jackson / wears one glove / while in argentina jews are missing / & the coast of nicaragua / is surrounded by mines" ("Thriller"). He is concerned about the hungry everywhere who are told, "do not worry / about food / / the dead do not starve" ("There Is a Place Where the Sea Goes When It Is Tired") and about places where "one could always find bones / growing in the fields" (untitled). In another instance he perceives a psychosocial kinship of African Americans to a Latin American peasant girl who on her wall tapes pictures of blond movie stars next to one of Jesus. The collection is not wholly grim, however, and in one section his habitual bemusement is particularly evident. For instance, he has not neglected the mysteriousness of love: "it was afterwards / when we were in the shower / that she said / / 'you're gonna write a poem about this' / 'about what?' i asked" ("Another Love Affair/ Another Poem").

First Light perhaps best illustrates the autobiographical elements of the thinking, feeling, and experiences that inform Miller's artistry. The thematic range is inclusive, as varied as, say, baseball, family, religion, and jazz. One favorite theme is love. By adolescence love's spirituality had become a reality: "the day my mother / threw away my comic books / and encouraged me to read the bible / was the day i gave up being / a superhero and started to think / of miracles / / this is how i came to love you / like moses looking over his / shoulder before he left that / mountain." The possibilities for communal love, along with its latent benefits, are consistently a factor in his perceptions of the capabilities of humankind.

Miller's lines are conversational, vernacular, and pithy, as if they are quiet spurts of thought or fragments of little whispers. The stanzaic design of his poetry is dictated by content, and his meter is subtle, free, and nonpercussive. There is no formal aural rhyme. Miller has a noticeable talent for the conceit, and he is capable of stark imagery, as when in "No Tacos for the Shah" the speaker, a poor woman whose husband is missing, to keep "from giving herself to the men" lights a small candle for him and says, "i watch it burn / like the inside of my womb / a soft wax dripping from between / my legs / the fire gone so long / the smoke of my husband / rising / across the border." His poetry's thematic impact is often suspended until there is revelatory, pointed closure that can reverberate for the reader: in South America "when they ask me questions / about communism or the government / i smile & say / / pete rose / pete rose / / sometimes

they laugh / sometimes i laugh / / we seldom / laugh together" ("Driver").

Because of his acuity of vision and thought, wit, technical subtlety, and artistic integrity, Miller has become known and respected for the authentic poet that he is. He is also known and respected for his work as an organizer and a catalyst of poetry events, an editor of collections, and a selfless promoter of established as well as fledgling poets.

—Theodore R. Hudson

MINHINNICK, Robert

Nationality: British. **Born:** Neath, Glamorgan, Wales, 12 August 1952. **Education:** Bridgend Grammar School; University College, Cardiff, 1978–82, B.A. 1981, M.A. 1982. **Family:** Married Margaret Bates in 1977; one daughter. **Career:** Has worked as a clerk, postman, salvage worker, and teacher, 1971–84; manager of Glamorgan Heritage Coast, environmental program, 1984–85; writer-in-residence in Mid-Glamorgan, 1985–86. Since 1986 environmental education worker, Friends of the Earth, Porthcawl, Mid-Glamorgan. **Awards:** Eric Gregory award, 1980; Welsh Arts Council award, 1980, 1984; John Morgan literary award, 1989. **Address:** 11 Park Avenue, Porthcawl, Mid-Glamorgan, Wales.

PUBLICATIONS

Poetry

A Thread in the Maze. Swansea, Christopher Davies, 1978.
Native Ground. Swansea, Triskele, 1979.
Life Sentences. Bridgend, Glamorgan, Poetry Wales Press, 1983.
The Dinosaur Park. Bridgend, Glamorgan, Poetry Wales Press, 1985.
The Looters. Bridgend, Glamorgan, Seren, 1989.
Hey Fatman. Bridgend, Glamorgan, Seren, 1994.
Badlands. Bridgend, Wales, Seren, and Chester Springs, Pennsylvania, Dufour, 1996.
Selected Poems. Manchester, Carcanet, 1999.

Other

Watching the Fire Eater? Bridgend, Glamorgan, Seren, 1992.
A Postcard Home: Tourism in the Mid-'Nineties. Llandysul, Gomer, 1993.

Editor, *Green Agenda: Essays on the Environment of Wales.* Bridgend, Glamorgan, Seren, 1994.
Editor, *Drawing Down the Moon: Poems and Stories 1996.* Bridgend, Glamorgan, Seren, 1995.

*

Critical Study: "Two Kinds of Poetic Thought: Robert Minhinnick and John Davies" by Richard Poole, in *Anglo-Welsh Review* (Aberystwyth, Wales), 88, 1988.

Robert Minhinnick comments:

My poems are simply the statement of a man declaring an interest. They examine the process of living, while hopefully contributing to it.

*   *   *

A sense of place and a sense of the past are the closely interrelated twin themes predominant in the work of Robert Minhinnick, and from these he patiently evolves his own mythology "on native ground." In "The Strata" excavations evoke the activity of another Welsh poet, working here six centuries earlier, and prompt the impulse "to fashion with blunt words my own design." The "rooky archaeologist" of "The Midden," "history's black / Sediment . . . under [his] nails," likewise digs for the past in quest of a shared genealogy. Minhinnick apprehends the presence of "time's hidden strata" everywhere: in the wave-battered Atlantic promontory of Sker and the primeval agelessness of rock and turbulent water that "seems to fall out of a fierce past," in "The Force," in the "medieval" cries of owl and nightjar, and in the ghosts that haunt ruined places—an abandoned quarry, locomotive yard, or even garage.

The potent spell of the past persists in the poet's own life too. Recapturing the feel and flavor of his early experience with sensuous precision, Minhinnick works the seam of boyhood memory as profitably as did Seamus Heaney in his early work. The pungency of ivy, an authentic "odour of childhood," recalls the atmosphere of that vanished world: of flight from the gamekeeper and his dogs, "fright hot as nettlerash," stealing unripe fruit from the orchard and "the sour exhilaration of that sin," hide-and-seek in the graveyard among "the dead in their dormitory," the savagery of the ritual village pig killing, the sharp grief of loss in "After a Friendship." Especially memorable and moving are several affectionately detailed cameos of his grandfather in poems like the fine "Native Ground" and "Ways of Learning" and in "Drinks after the Funeral" and "Grandfather in the Garden," with seeds "like ammunition in his hands."

Minhinnick's relish for human personality emerges from his various portraits drawn from both rural and industrial South Wales, which he knows with equal intimacy. "That axe-wielding man," Reilly the gardener, and estate workers sitting among freshly sawed logs stacked "like new loaves, the smell as sweet," keep company with the ganger, whose "sweat bursts from his skin like tar-blisters," and the tough mother of "hard-skinned miners / Kicking a pig's bladder on the coal-slip." Poems like "Old Ships," "Salvage," and "Profile in Iron" vigorously delineate the Cardiff dockworkers, for whom "the dialect / Of iron is more powerful than psalms." The loneliness of the beery racing man with a genuine love of horses is observed with sympathetic perception as well as visual vividness. So, too, are his bemused drinking companions—"pub-fixtures" like "gargoyles carved from the bar's stained wood."

This simile serves to illustrate the impact of Minhinnick's imagery, which is as strikingly individual in his observation of nature as of people: in his lovingly meticulous scrutiny of plants in "Herbals," of grasshopper and dragonfly, or of "the strange night turbulence of eels . . . / Inscribing circles on tar-black water." He watches "a crown of foam winking / Like beer-froth" on the sea, wheeling swifts "swastika the sky," and the winter constellations' "archipelagoes of light" and shadow "stamping bone-coloured frosts / And grass as stiff as canvas."

Minhinnick handles language with a controlled economy that at the same time conveys the impression of powerful energy in leash.

This blend of technical assurance with an imaginative intensity bred of his self-confessed "violent need to praise" make him one of the most interesting and accomplished poets writing in Wales today.

—Margaret Willy

MINTY, Judith M.

Nationality: American. **Born:** Detroit, Michigan, 5 August 1937. **Education:** Michigan State University of Agriculture and Applied Science (now Michigan State University), 1954–59; Ithaca College, B.S. 1957; Muskegon Community College, 1970–71; Grand Valley State College (now Grand Valley State Colleges), 1971; Western Michigan University, M.A. 1973; Michigan Technological University, Ph.D. (honors) 1997. **Family:** Married Edgar Sheldon Minty in 1957; two daughters and one son. **Career:** Assistant professor, Central Michigan University, Mount Pleasant, 1977–78; associate professor and visiting poet-in-residence, Syracuse University, New York, 1979. Professor and poet-in-residence, 1982–93, and since 1993 professor emerita, Humboldt State University, Arcata, California. Guest lecturer, English Grand Valley State University, Allendale, Michigan, 1974–77; poet-in-prison pilot project, Muskegon Correctional Facility, Michigan, 1977; visiting poet-in-residence, Interlochen Center for Arts, Michigan, 1980, University of Oregon, Eugene, 1983, and University of Nebraska, Lincoln, 1994; visiting lecturer, University of California, Santa Cruz, 1981–82. **Awards:** International Poetry Forum award, 1973, for *Lake Songs and Other Fears;* John Atherton fellow in poetry, Breadloaf Writers Conference, 1974; Yaddo fellow, 1978, 1979, 1982; Eunice Tietjens award, *Poetry,* 1974; Montalvo award, 1989; Mark Twain award, Society for the Study of Midwestern Literature, Michigan State University, 1998; Michigan Council for the Arts grant, 1981, 1983; Foundation for Women Residence grant, 1994.

PUBLICATIONS

Poetry

Lake Songs and Other Fears. Pittsburgh, University of Pennsylvania Press, 1974.
Yellow Dog Journal. Los Angeles, Central Publications, 1979.
In the Presence of Mothers. Pittsburgh, University of Pennsylvania Press, 1981.
Counting the Losses. Aptos, California, Jazz Press, 1986.
Dancing the Fault. Orlando, University of Central Florida, 1991.
Walking with the Bear. East Lansing, Michigan State University Press, 2000.

*

Critical Studies: "Mother Lore: A Sequence for Daughters" by Marilyn Zorn, in *Great Lakes Review* (Mt. Pleasant, Michigan), 6(1), 1979; "To Sustain the Bioregion: Poets of Place" by William Barillas, in *Midamerica* (East Lansing, Michigan), 17, 1990.

*   *   *

Judith M. Minty writes in archetypal images—of water, wind, and bears. Her early poems tend to be male centered, while the later ones develop the female side, merging the male and the female into a seamless journey through the North Woods of Michigan. Somewhat reminiscent of Robert Frost's self-imposed geographical limitations, Minty narrows her borders, fixing her poems specifically in time and place.

Minty's first book of poems, *Lake Songs and Other Fears* (1974) is a very uneven work; it is disjointed, with poems that seem unrelated. She does, however, introduce motifs—water, wind, the father—that continue in her later works. Her second book, *Yellow Dog Journal* (1979), is a much more complete, mature collection. The book is framed by quotes from the *Kalevala,* the national epic of Finland, reflecting the Finnish immigrant culture of Michigan's Upper Peninsula, the setting of *Yellow Dog Journal.* Divided into two seasons, fall and spring, the collection consists of a series of related poems that read like a poetic journal. Individually the poems sometimes seem small and weak, but taken as whole, they are evocative of the magic of living in the northland. The mythic symbol of the poetic voice is the bear—sometimes frightening, sometimes comforting, but always a presence. In one of the book's most powerful poems, the refrain is "When I last dreamed the bear," and in this poem the voice comes to an understanding of the bear and, perhaps, of the father: "And though we never spoke, / I knew then that he loved me, and so began / to stroke his rough back, to pull him even closer." The book is about a return to the woods and a return to the father (who also left the North Woods). Minty writes of the father's stories of Yellow Dog River: "Late nights, he'd whisper its bends / my face close to his Finnish guttural, / cheeks flushed from his beard's rough stubble." The collection is the poet's epic journey to her place of creativity, and, as with other epic heroes, much of the journey is solitary.

In Minty's 1981 collection *In the Presence of Mothers'* the individual poems are much more complex. The poet's language, again like Frost's, is simple, but there is a deeper meaning beneath the images, an exploration of the unconscious, personified by the northern nature presented in the poems. For example, the poem "Ice Storm" is in some ways a response to Frost's poem "Birches." In Minty's poem

At first, the trees accept their new skins.
But by the third day, they can't
bear the weight. They begin
to bend, bow down to the sleep, and we

hunch like stones over the breakfast table.

By the end, however, after the trees have split and broken, "we gather limbs and find / the few faint buds that exposed themselves." Like Frost's poem, Minty's is about a celebration of life even in the midst of loss.

Minty's collection *Dancing the Fault* (1991) seems to be the culmination of her earlier work. In this book she captures the sense of home. Even though many of the pieces are set in California or New York, the essence of the spirit of the North Woods of Michigan is not far away. The collection includes poems of friendship and motherhood. One of the central pieces of the book, "Christine, On Her Way to China: An Earthquake Poem," provides the title of the collection. In the poem Minty writes, "I thought, even then, how we are planted here, / how ordinary our lives are, how we must / make adventure from these briefest shifts and passings." It seems as if this is a core

theme to Minty, to learn to "dance the fault," to make a celebration of life.

Reading Minty's poetry provides lessons in the workings of the mind of a poet and in the development of a voice. At first halting and disjointed, Minty has moved on to become evocative in her exploration of deep meanings in a sense of place—in the woods and water and in the bear.

—Jenny Brantley

MISHRA, Sudesh (Raj)

Nationality: Fijian (permanent resident of Australia). **Born:** Suva, 21 November 1962. **Education:** University of Wollongon, New South Wales, 1981–84, B.A. (honors) 1984; Flinders University of South Australia, 1985–89, Ph.D. 1989. **Career:** Lecturer in English, University of the South Pacific, 1989–93; Australian Research Council Postdoctoral Research Fellow, Flinders University of South Australia, 1993–96. Member, and president since 1991, Fiji Writers' Association. **Awards:** Flinders University Postgraduate Scholarship, 1985–89; Harri Jones Memorial prize for poetry, 1988; Australian Research Council Postdoctoral fellowship, 1993–96. **Address:** CRNLE, Flinders University, Bedford Park, South Australia 5042, Australia.

PUBLICATIONS

Poetry

Rahu. Suva, Fiji, Vision International Publishers, 1987.
Tandava. Melbourne, Meanjin Press, 1991.
Memoirs of a Reluctant Traveller. Adelaide, CRNLE-Wakefield Press, 1994.

Play

Ferringhi (produced Suva, Fiji, 1993).

Other

Preparing Faces: Modernism and Indian Poetry in English. Adelaide, CRNLE-University of the South Pacific Press, 1995.

Editor, with Seona Smiles, *Trapped: A Collection of Writing from Fiji.* Suva, Fiji, Fiji Writers' Association, 1992.

*

Manuscript Collection: Centre for Research in the New Literatures in English (CRNLE), Flinders University, Bedford Park, South Australia.

Critical Studies: "Little India" by Vijay Mishra, in *Meanjin* (Parkville, Victoria, Australia), 49(4), summer 1990; interview with Annie Greet, in *CRNLE Reviews Journal,* 2, 1993.

Theatrical Activities: Actor: **Play**—*Ferringhi,* Suva, Fiji, 1993.

Sudesh Mishra comments:

If all writing is about running away from platitudes, I write to run away from that greatest of platitudes—death.

I tend to work with traditional poetic forms because I like breaking the rules that govern them, not from a sense of bloody mindedness but from a sense of the complexities of a postcolonial existence. As the descendant of indentured laborers from India, born in British Fiji and having spent my adult life in Australia, I am very much aware of the impure character of my inheritance. Outright rejection of any part of this inheritance would be, to say the least, a utopian maneuver. For how can I rid myself of the sediments of history that constitute my being as discourse? And these sediments are Indian, Fijian, English, Australian, American. I may not like the legacy of colonialism, for instance, but I cannot deny that it forms part of my discursive being. So I engage in a perpetual quarrel with myself, and the use of traditional forms is part of this quarrel. I look at it this way: if the sonnet form represents the imprisoning structures of colonial legacy, then I will attempt to implode the form itself with the intention of making room for other sediments that were denied legitimacy by the logic of colonialism. Toward this end, I smuggle into a given form vernaculars, voices, stresses that go against the grain of tradition and history. The idea is to break the rules from within, so that, while the negative of the sonnet form is always there, the prosodic laws governing it may be at odds with what is perhaps considered normative. In many ways this is the postcolonial condition par excellence: the never-ending struggle of competing positions that signals the equally never-ending search for identity.

*　　*　　*

Born and raised in Fiji, Sudesh Mishra writes poems that reflect the influence of high modernist poets, including Yeats and Eliot, and of a British colonial education. But like the Caribbean poet Derek Walcott, Mishra works both with and against his inheritance. He uses traditional poetic forms to relate untraditional stories, many of them about growing up in the South

Pacific. In "Irony," from *Tandava,* he writes, "For now, I shall be content to deploy / This compass, cause laughter or raise hackles, / And scare the freckles off politicians / And prigs." Increasingly his work is steeped in irony and is less purely lyrical in its impulse.

Mishra is self-conscious about his poetic influences. In "Confessions of a Poetaster from Fiji," the opening poem of his first book, *Rahu* (1987), Mishra reveals that "at twenty" he got "hooked on Yeats" and that he "lays strange bricks to fashion [his] own Byzantium." In "Feejee," from his second book, *Tandava* (1991), he echoes Yeats's Crazy Jane poems:

"I am of Feejee,
The bitter land of Feejee,
And hate is all we know," cried she,
"Leap down that mango tree
And dance with me
In this bitter land of Feejee."

His "Black Swans in Ballarat" hearkens back to Yeats's wild (and black) swans at Coole Park, although Mishra's swans are more politically symbolic than are Yeats's:

What history is this, unmarked by the slaver's staff,
we watch sailing across the vague municipal lake?

The poem ends with a rhetorical question, as do many of Yeats's most famous poems, but the question positions the poet as dark, like ink, not white, like prototypical swans and poets:

So we watch—colonizer and colonized, assailant
and victim—the concert of ebony swans that leave

in their wake the arrowheads of invisible tribes.
And what if we gave history to them; would they
carry our botched visions through their centuries,
slaughter their white image with a squirt of ink?

Mishra often seems to be attempting to do just that, to slaughter a dominant worldview and poetic tradition with his "squirt of ink." In poems such as "The Grand Pacific Hotel" he describes an Indian's sense of his own invisibility and desire to use his language against him: "I tire of the turban, / The looped cerements of my non-presence. / Some day I will name myself in their script."

The object of Mishra's satire is often the tradition from which his poetry emerges. His "Loving Song of R.J. Tangaya" performs a parody of Eliot's "The Love Song of J. Alfred Prufrock" and of *The Waste Land.* He substitutes for the bartender's call of "Hurry up, please, it's time," in Eliot's poem, his own "HURRY UP SAHIB ITS TIME." Mishra's awareness of his influences, then, is self-consciously ambivalent, going against his own words in "Feejee" that "ours in the simple faith in what is said." In another poem, "Confessional," Mishra writes of his sense of being out of place as a nonwhite poet from a tropical island:

By a decade or two
I missed the limbo. Louis Armstrong
And hallucinogens. A decade or two since
(I understand soundly that a decade or two
Ago there wasn't a slot in the uppity throng
For brown lads who horsed on canefences.

Mishra's allusion to American empire, particularly as represented in the music of Armstrong, is especially complicated. While Armstrong was black, he is used here to represent white privilege, just as Mishra's own work might be used to justify modernist poetry. But Mishra's work, while written in an idiom familiar to readers of white modernist poets, cannot be mistaken for theirs. Rather, it reflects the vision of a poet born closer to cane fields than to American or European cities. His career as a writer of criticism, fiction, and drama, as well as of poetry, promises to be long and accomplished.

—Susan M. Schultz

MITCHELL, Adrian

Nationality: British. **Born:** London, 24 October 1932. **Education:** Greenways School, Wiltshire; Dauntsey's School, West Lavington, Wiltshire; Christ Church, Oxford (editor, *Isis* magazine, 1954–55), 1952–55. **Military Service:** Royal Air Force, 1951–52. **Family:** Married Celia Hewitt. **Career:** Reporter, Oxford Mail, 1955–57, and *Evening Standard,* London, 1957–59; columnist and reviewer, *Daily Mail, Woman's Mirror,* the *Sun,* the *Sunday Times, Peace News,*

Black Dwarf, New Statesman, and the *Guardian,* all London. Instructor, University of Iowa, Iowa City, 1963–64; Granada Fellow in the Arts, University of Lancaster, 1967–69; fellow, Wesleyan University Center for the Humanities, Middletown, Connecticut, 1971–72; resident writer, Sherman Theatre, Cardiff, 1974–75; visiting writer, Billericay Comprehensive School, Essex, 1978–80; Judith E. Wilson Fellow, Cambridge University, 1980–81; resident writer, Unicorn Theatre for Young People, London, 1982–83. **Awards:** Eric Gregory award, 1961; P.E.N. prize for translation, 1966; Tokyo Festival award, for television, 1971; Fellow, Royal Society of Literature, 1988. **Agent:** Peters Fraser and Dunlop, Fifth Floor, The Chambers, Chelsea Harbour, Lots Road, London SW10 OXF, England.

PUBLICATIONS

Poetry

(Poems). Oxford, Fantasy Press, 1955.
Poems. London, Cape, 1964.
Peace Is Milk. London, Peace News, 1966.
Out Loud. London, Cape Goliard Press, and New York, Grossman, 1968; revised edition, as *The Annotated Out Loud,* London, Writers and Readers, 1976.
Ride the Nightmare: Verse and Prose. London, Cape, 1971.
Cease-Fire. London, Medical Aid Committee for Vietnam, 1973.
Penguin Modern Poets 22, with John Fuller and Peter Levi. London, Penguin, 1973.
The Apeman Cometh. London, Cape, 1975.
For Beauty Douglas: Collected Poems 1953–1979. London, Allison and Busby, 1982.
Nothingmas Day (for children). London, Allison and Busby, 1984.
On the Beach at Cambridge: New Poems. London, Allison and Busby, 1984.
Love Songs of World War Three (collected song lyrics). London, Allison and Busby, 1989.
Celia, Celia; Goodbye. London, Poems on the Underground, 1989.
Adrian Mitchell's Greatest Hits. Newcastle upon Tyne, Bloodaxe, 1991.
All My Own Stuff. London, Simon and Schuster, 1991.
Blue Coffee: Poems, 1985–1996. Newcastle upon Tyne, Bloodaxe, and Chester Springs, Pennsylvania, Dufour, 1996.
Balloon Lagoon and the Magic Islands of Poetry (for children). London, Orchard, 1997.
Heart on the Left: Poems, 1953–1984. Newcastle upon Tyne, Bloodaxe, and Chester Springs, Pennsylvania, Dufour, 1997.
Dancing in the Street: A Poetry Party. London, Orchard, 1999.

Recording: *Poems,* with Stevie Smith, Argo, 1974.

Plays

The Ledge (libretto), music by Richard Rodney Bennett (produced London, 1961).
The Persecution and Assassination of Jean-Paul Marat as Performed by the Inmates of the Asylum of Charenton under the Direction of the Marquis de Sade [Marat/Sade], adaptation of a play by Peter Weiss (produced London, 1964; New York, 1965). London, Calder, 1965; New York, Atheneum, 1966.

The Magic Flute, adaptation of the libretto by Schikaneder and Giesecke, music by Mozart (produced London, 1966). US, with others (produced London, 1966). Published as *US: The Book of the Royal Shakespeare Production US/Vietnam/ US/Experiment/Politics. . . ,* London, Calder and Boyars, 1968; as *Tell Me Lies,* Indianapolis, Bobbs Merrill, 1968.
The Criminals, adaptation of a play by Jose Triana (produced London, 1967; New York, 1970).
Tyger: A Celebration of the Life and Work of William Blake, music by Mike Westbrook (produced London, 1971). London, Cape, 1971.
Tamburlane the Mad Hen (for children; produced Devon, 1971).
Man Friday, music by Mike Westbrook (televised 1972; produced London, 1973). With *Mind Your Head,* London, Eyre Methuen, 1974.
Mind Your Head, music by Andy Roberts (produced Liverpool, 1973; London, 1974). With *Man Friday,* London, Eyre Methuen, 1974.
The Government Inspector (as *The Inspector General,* produced Nottingham, 1974; revised version, as *The Government Inspector,* produced London, 1985). London, Methuen, 1985.
A Seventh Man, music by Dave Brown, adaptation of the book by John Berger and Jean Mohr (produced London, 1976).
White Suit Blues, music by Mike Westbrook, adaptation of works by Mark Twain (produced Nottingham and London, 1977).
Houdini: A Circus-Opera, music by Peter Schat (produced Amsterdam, 1977; Aspen, Colorado, 1980). Amsterdam, Clowns, 1977(?).
Uppendown Mooney (produced Welwyn Garden City, Hertfordshire, 1978).
The White Deer (for children), adaptation of the story by James Thurber (produced London, 1978).
Hoagy, Bix, and Wolfgang Beethoven Bunkhaus (produced London, 1979; Indianapolis, 1980).
In the Unlikely Event of an Emergency, music by Stephen McNeff (produced Bath, 1979; London, 1988).
Peer Gynt, adaptation of the play by Ibsen (produced Oxford, 1980).
The Mayor of Zalamea; or, The Best Garrotting Ever Done, adaptation of a play by Calderon (produced London, 1981). Edinburgh, Salamander Press, 1981.
Mawgli's Jungle, adaptation of *The Jungle Book* by Kipling (pantomime; produced Manchester, 1981).
You Must Believe All This (for children), adaptation of "Holiday Romance" by Dickens, music by Nick Bicat and Andrew Dickson (televised 1981). London, Thames Television-Methuen, 1981.
The Wild Animal Song Contest (for children; produced London, 1982).
Life's a Dream, with John Barton, adaptation of a play by Calderon (produced Stratford-on-Avon, 1983; London, 1984).
A Child's Christmas in Wales, with Jeremy Brooks, adaptation of the work by Dylan Thomas (produced Cleveland, 1983).
The Great Theatre of the World, adaptation of a play by Calderon (produced Oxford, 1984).
C'mon Everybody (produced London, 1984).
Animal Farm (lyrics only), book by Peter Hall, music by Richard Peaslee, adaptation of the novel by George Orwell (for children; produced London, 1984; Baltimore, 1986). London, Methuen, 1985.
The Tragedy of King Real (screenplay), in *Peace Plays 1,* edited by Stephen Lowe. London, Methuen, 1985.
Satie Day/Night (produced London, 1986).
The Pied Piper (for children), music by Dominic Muldowney (produced London, 1986). Birmingham, Oberon, 1988.

Mirandolina, adaptation of a play by Goldoni (produced Bristol, 1987).

The Last Wild Wood in Sector 88 (produced Rugby, 1987).

Love Songs of World War Three (produced London, 1988).

Fuente Ovejuna, adaptation of the play by Lope de Vega (produced London, 1988).

Woman Overboard, adaptation of a play by Lope de Vega, music by Monty Norman (produced Watford, 1988).

The Patchwork Girl of Oz, adaptation of the story by L. Frank Baum (for children; produced Watford, 1988).

The Pied Piper. Birmingham, Oberon, 1988.

Anna on Anna (produced Edinburgh and London, 1988; Baltimore, 1990).

The Tragedy of King Real (produced Ongar, Essex, 1989).

The Wild Animal Song Contest and Mowgli's Jungle. Oxford, Heinemann Educational, 1993.

The Snow Queen: A Play with Songs (for children), adaptation of the story by Hans Christian Andersen. London, Oberon, 1996.

The Siege: A Play with Songs. London, Oberon, 1996.

Plays with Songs. London, Oberon, 1996.

The Lion, the Witch and the Wardrobe (for children), adaptation of the novel by C.S. Lewis. London, Oberon, 1998.

Tom Kitten and His Friends: A Play with Songs (for children), adaptation of stories by Beatrix Potter. London, S. French, 1998.

The Mammoth Sails Tonight! (for children). London, Oberon, 1999.

Screenplays: *Marat/Sade,* 1966; *Tell Me Lies* (lyrics only), 1968; *The Body* (commentary), 1969; *Man Friday,* 1976; *The Tragedy of King Real,* 1983.

Radio Play: *The Island* (libretto), music by William Russo, 1963.

Television Plays: *Animals Can't Laugh,* 1961; *Alive and Kicking,* 1971; *William Blake* (documentary), 1971; *Man Friday,* 1972; *Somebody Down There Is Crying,* 1974; *Daft As a Brush,* 1975; *The Fine Art of Bubble Blowing,* 1975; *Silver Giant, Wooden Dwarf,* 1975; *Glad Day,* music by Mike Westbrook, 1979; *You Must Believe All This,* 1981; *Juno and Avos,* from a libretto by Andrei Voznesensky, music by Alexei Rybnikov, 1983.

Initiated and helped write student shows: *Bradford Walk,* Bradford College of Art; *The Hotpot Saga, The Neurovision Song Contest,* and *Lash Me to the Mast,* University of Lancaster; *Move Over Jehovah,* National Association of Mental Health; *Poetry Circus,* Wesleyan University; *Mass Media Mash* and *Mud Fair,* Dartington College of the Arts, 1976 and 1977.

Novels

If You See Me Comin'. London, Cape, and New York, Macmillan, 1962.

The Bodyguard. London, Cape, 1970; New York, Doubleday, 1971.

Wartime. London, Cape, 1973.

Man Friday. London, Futura, 1975.

Other (for children)

The Adventures of Baron Munchausen. London, Walker, 1985.

The Baron Rides Out [on the Island of Cheese, All at Sea]. London, Walker, and New York, Philomel, 3 vols., 1985–87.

Leonardo, The Lion from Nowhere. London, Deutsch, 1986.

Our Mammoth [Goes to School, in the Snow]. London, Walker, 3 vols., 1987–88; San Diego, Harcourt Brace, first 2 vols., 1987–88.

Rhinestone Rhino. London, Methuen, 1989.

Our Mammoth Has a Baby. London, Walker, 1989.

The Ugly Duckling, adaptation of the story by Hans Christian Andersen, illustrated by Jonathan Hale. London and New York, D. Kindersley, 1994.

Steadfast Tin Soldier, adaptation of the story by Hans Christian Andersen, illustrated by Jonathan Hale. New York, D. Kinderseley, 1996.

Maudie and the Green Children. Vancouver, Tradewind, 1996.

Gynormous: The Ultimate Book of Giants. London, Orion Children's, 1996.

My Cat Mrs. Christmas. London, Orion Children's, 1998.

Twice My Size. London, Bloomsbury, 1998.

The Adventures of Robin Hood and Marian. London, Orchard, 1998.

Nobody Rides the Unicorn. London, Doubleday, 1999; New York, Levine, 2000.

Editor, *Strawberry Drums.* London, Macdonald, 1989.

Other

Naked in Cheltenham (miscellany). Cheltenham, Gastoday, 1978.

Tourist Snapshots of Chile. London, Chile Solidarity Campaign, 1985.

Love Songs of World War Three. London, Allison and Busby, 1989.

The Thirteen Secrets of Poetry. Hemel Hempstead, Simon and Schuster, 1993.

Who Killed Dylan Thomas? Swansea, Ty Llên, 1998.

Editor, with Richard Selig, *Oxford Poetry 1955.* Oxford, Fantasy Press, 1955.

Editor, *Jump, My Brothers, Jump: Poems from Prison,* by Tim Daly. London, Freedom Press, 1970.

*

Theatrical Activities: Actor: **Plays**—*C'mon Everybody,* London, 1984.

Critical Study: "Europe's Vicious Circle: Adrian Mitchell's 'Autobahnmotorwayautoroute'" by Karl J. Haussler, in *Anglistik & Englischunterricht* (Heidelberg, Germany), 53, 1994.

Adrian Mitchell comments:

My mind and imagination and my life have been altered by many things and many people. Other people's poetry has been among my most important experiences, and I do not just mean great poetry. Politically speaking, it was poetry as much as anything else that pushed me first in the direction of left-wing political action, in which I include committee work, demonstrating, envelope addressing, as well as poetry. To cite some of the poets who have educated and influenced me: Wilfred Owen, Walt Whitman, Kenneth Patchen, Alex Comfort, Brecht, Beckett, John Arden, Allen Ginsberg, and most of all William Blake. (But I have been influenced by hundreds of others, most of all by my close friends and my family and a teacher named Michael Bell.) I am sometimes called a committed poet. So is your old man.

There are many poets who because they turn their back on politics believe they are somehow not engaged. But their indifference or their silence contributes toward the status quo. And the status quo demands, at different periods, exploitation, starvation, poverty, mass murder, torture, vile prisons, the stunting of children's imaginations and—in some part of the world during every day of my lifetime—war. When the revolution comes, I expect some poetry to make some contribution toward it; every revolution so far has had its own songs and poems. That contribution toward changing the world may be very small, but the smallest contribution helps when it is a matter of changing the world. I do not think that poets should sit down and say, "I've got to write a political poem." But I think a poet, like any other human being, should recognize that the world is mostly controlled by political forces and should become politically active. And if a poet attempts to live his politics, his poems will become politically active too.

*   *   *

A writer whose work savages most establishment conventions, Adrian Mitchell often appears to present his poems and dramas as a series of revolutionary acts. Acknowledged as a natural precursor and kindred spirit of the Liverpool poets, he emerged as a major force in the public readings of the 1960s, with their attendant cult of protest and rebellion. To those who criticize the political involvement of his writings, Mitchell replies that poets also hold opinions. Ultimately, he feels, one cannot be neutral about injustice. He is a strong socialist, but his attacks go beyond party boundaries to denounce not merely capitalism and class privilege but also civilization itself when it becomes an excuse for genocide: "The brand name for a tribe of killer apes / Is civilization."

Having formed his style from a mass of diverse influences, Mitchell seems able to produce poems for all occasions, some of his works tightly structured while others spill out in loose, free-blowing patterns akin to the playing of jazz and blues. In these latter poems, as in most of his plays, a strong non-Western element surfaces, the process of creation seeming more important than the finished artifact. On the other hand, his mastery of the rhyming form and his penchant for humorous one-liners—"I play golf so I exist"—nod in the direction of his poetic heritage. "Sorry Bout That" and "C'mon Everybody" display a telling verbal felicity: "Truth is a diamond / A diamond is hard / You don't exist without a Barclaycard."

An obvious spiritual ancestor is William Blake, whose radical antiauthoritarian vision is echoed in much of Mitchell's writing. In his drama *Tyger* and in the television play *Glad Day* he renders tribute to Blake with "celebrations" that blend propaganda and satire with slapstick comedy. Many of Mitchell's poems invoke the author of *Songs of Innocence* and *Songs of Experience,* while in the dramas Blake is quoted directly.

Not always a humorous poet, Mitchell expresses strong feelings in his writing, and his is the rage of a man who cares. Angered at the sight of human suffering, in "Subnormal Children" and "Old Age Report" he champions the downtrodden young and old alike: "The hell with retiring / Let them advance." His antiwar tirades have produced a number of memorable poems, varying from the caustic, balanced verses of "Chile in Chains" to the gradual, cumulative imagery of "Tell Me Lies about Vietnam." "On the Beach at Cambridge" depicts the nightmare aftermath of nuclear war, a vision surpassed by the grim, restrained narrative of one of Mitchell's finest creations, "The Dust": "When the bombs fell, she was sitting with

her man / Straight and white in the family pew / While in her the bud of a child grew / The city crumbled, the deaths began."

Like his poetry readings, Mitchell's dramas are often semi-improvisatory collaborations, happenings reminiscent of the performance readings of Adrian Henri or Roger McGough. Most feature a strong element of audience participation, and through them Mitchell is able to obtain a spontaneous interaction between performers and audience. Mitchell has written, "A better thing than the human tear / is the human song," and it is his songs that bridge the gap between poems and dramas, being carried over into the latter as musical inserts that form an integral part of the plays and that lend emphasis to the characters and their actions. Mitchell has imbibed numerous musical influences—from blues singers, jazz musicians, Leiber-Stoller, music hall, and show tunes—and poems in the form of songs enliven his plays.

Greatest Hits brings together a selection of Mitchell's most requested items from live poetry readings, which he presents, not without a certain wry humor, as his "40 Golden Greats." With this collection he once more affirms his links with the world of popular entertainment (in the 1960s his performances and those of the Meryerside trio were seen as sharing affinities with the emerging stars of British pop music) and his love for some aspects of the rock scene. *Greatest Hits,* which spans four decades of his career and contains some of his best work, was later to form the basis of a "Greatest Hits" performance reading tour in the early 1990s.

The arrival of the new millennium finds Mitchell as active and committed as ever, producing interesting work in a number of different fields. He has brought out several anthologies of poetry for younger readers, contributing his own verses to *Balloon Lagoon and The Magic Islands of Poetry,* while in *Dancing in the Street* he provides an intriguing blend of verse, ranging from Shakespeare and Andrew Marvell to the lyrics of modern rock music. His adult poetry has been gathered into two significant collections, *Heart on the Left: Poems, 1953–1984* and *Blue Coffee: Poems, 1985–1996.* While both books reward the interested reader, the former collection (decorated with some rather disturbing Ralph Steadman illustrations) obviously contains the more familiar material, and it is *Blue Coffee* that holds Mitchell's latest work. Once again he acquaints us with the array of talents at his disposal. Anger with politicians and their violent "final solutions" comes to the fore with "Blood and Oil," a passionate denunciation of the Allied invasion of Iraq, which Mitchell read live on British television at the height of the Persian Gulf conflict. The same emotions fire "The Boy Who Danced with a Tank," in which the poet applauds the courage of the doomed young protestors in Tiananmen Square and condemns the brutal force brought against them.

These poems, however, show only one of many moods. Mitchell casts a comic eye over his first sexual awakenings in "A Puppy Called Puberty," indulges a penchant for scatological humor in "A Warning to Those Who Fly," and finds a new and amusing way of looking at his own craft of words: ("Every morning down the poetry pit / Cut a few tons from the verseface.") "Night Thoughts in Treorchy" contains the ultimate put-down for those tedious "write about what you know" literary commissars: "Shakespeare should have stayed in Stratford upon Avon / and written about Warwickshire / not Italian teenagers up to no good / or alien lovers in imaginary woods / or a black soldier having a hard time in the army / or a Danish prince gradually going barmy." The core of this collection is found in Mitchell's memories of childhood and his tributes to family and friends. From hatred of playground bullying and glamorous fantasies of warfare as shown in "Spitfire Daydream" he charts his awareness of war's true horror through its effect on his beloved parents. Mitchell celebrates the lives of father, wife, and children in such poems as ''Celia's Flower'' and ''A Late Tribute to Jock Mitchell.'' Most poignant of all the poems in *Blue Coffee* are those in memory of his adopted daughter, the gifted and tragically short-lived artist Boty Goodwin. Mitchell's verses in ''For Boty'' and ''Every Day'' bring home the feeling of loss and grief and at the same time an awareness of her continued presence for those whose lives she touched so profoundly: ''Every day we're going to listen to your Voice / and you Laughter like a Trumpet Break.''

In the end it is not Mitchell's righteous anger against tyranny, or even his wit or humor, that impresses us most, but the warmth and humanity that come through so constantly in his poetry. These, and his many other qualities, will continue to win him an audience in years to come.

—Geoff Sadler

MITCHELL, Elma

Nationality: Scottish. **Born:** Airdrie, Lanarkshire, 19 November 1919. **Education:** Somerville College, Oxford, B.A. (first-class honors) in English 1941; University College, London, diploma in librarianship. **Career:** Staff member, Library, British Broadcasting Company, London, 1941–43; library and information officer for various organizations, including British Employee's Confederation. **Address:** Tanlake Cottage, Buckland St. Mary, Chard, Somerset TA20 3QF, England.

PUBLICATIONS

Poetry

The Poor Man in the Flesh. Stockport, Cornwall, Peterloo Poets, 1976.
The Human Cage. Liskeard, Cornwall, Peterloo Poets, 1979.
Furnished Rooms. Liskeard, Cornwall, Peterloo Poets, 1983.
People Etcetera: Poems New and Selected. Liskeard, Cornwall, Peterloo Poets, 1987.

Recording: *U.A. Fanthorpe and Elma Mitchell,* Peterloo Poets, 1983.

*

Critical Study: ''Unauthorized Voices: U.A. Fanthorpe and Elma Mitchell'' by Marilyn Hacker, in *Grand Street* (Denville, New Jersey), 8(4), summer 1989.

* * *

In *British Book News* Shirley Toulson aptly described Elma Mitchell's strength as a poet in her having ''the rare ability of making tough, compassionate and compelling verse out of the minutiae of domestic existence.'' Whether writing about childbirth, embroidery, mining coal, or turning out mattresses, Mitchell addresses the daily, the quotidian, the rituals of ordinary existence with a keen eye and an ear sensitive to sound and rhythm. But her relationship to the rites of ordinary life is often a troubled one, in ''Thoughts after Ruskin,'' for example, puncturing Ruskin's ideal of women as reminding him of lilies and roses: ''Me they remind rather of blood and soap / Armed with a warm rag, assaulting noses, / Ears, neck, mouth and all the secret places.'' In the poem ''Hanging Out the Wash'' the most ordinary of weekly rituals becomes imbued with vague threats, the adjectives and verbs recasting laundry as a victim of the elements:

> The teeth of wooden and plastic pegs hold down
> Our woollies to be raped by a screaming north-easter.
> The sun assaults their colouring: a shirt
> Is crucified in ice: knickers distended, pregnant.

Both ''Hanging Out the Wash'' and ''Late Fall'' demonstrate Mitchell's mixed attitude toward Christianity, evident in the latter poem by the speaker's lax attitude toward the butterflies in her garden. When a butterfly lands on her hand, she remarks,

> Some warmth or texture or suspected sap
> Inveigled it into this possible trap.

Mitchell ends the poem with the line ''There is no god walking in this garden.'' In the poem ''The Crucifixion will not take place,'' from *People Etcetera,* Jesus gives a press conference, while other poems reinterpret the Gospel According to John.

Two major themes dominate Mitchell's work: an attention to the household economy managed largely by women, and the Scottish rural landscape, which is closely observed. Her rhythmic, often iambic, careful lines are inflected by colloquialisms (''wamble,'' ''bollop,'' ''shaggies,'' ''maunders'') and a shifting point of view. In ''Shepherd at Work,'' for example, we have three viewpoints, those of the shepherd, the dog, and the sheep. But whether assuming the work of women or the natural world (sheep, trees, songbirds, cows, rain, moths) as her central subject, Mitchell has an edge and a wit that cohere with an expert poetic voice, one that pays particular attention to steady rhythms, alliteration, and assonance. This edge ultimately makes Mitchell, like the speaker in the poem ''Disabilities'' who celebrates ''the romp of imperfect,'' a writer who composes while wearing ''dark spectacles against a rose-coloured sun.''

Finally, as Mitchell warns readers in ''This Poem,'' she knows as well as any poet that ''words / Can seriously affect your heart.''

—Sarah Sloane

MITCHELL, Susan

Nationality: American. **Born:** New York City, 1944. **Education:** Wellesley College, Massachusetts. **Career:** Has held teaching positions at Middlebury College, Vermont, and Northeastern Illinois University. Holds the Mary Blossom Lee Endowed Chair in Creative Writing, Florida Atlantic University. **Awards:** National Endowment for the Arts fellowship; grants from the state arts councils of Massachusetts, Illinois, Vermont, and Florida; Claire Hagler fellow, Fine Arts Work Center, Provincetown; Hoyns fellow, University of Virginia; Guggenheim Foundation fellow, 1992; Lannan Foundation fellow, 1992; Kingsley Tufts poetry award, 1993. **Address:** c/o

HarperCollins Publishers, 10 East 53rd Street, New York, New York 10022–5299, U.S.A.

PUBLICATIONS

Poetry

The Water inside the Water. Middletown, Connecticut, Wesleyan University Press, 1983.
Rapture. New York, HarperPerennial, 1992.
Erotikon: Poems. New York, HarperCollins, 2000.

*

Critical Studies: ''Underwater Pavilions'' by Tam Lin Neville, in *American Poetry Review* (Philadelphia), 23, January/February 1994; ''On Disproportion'' by Tony Hoagland, in *Poets Teaching Poets: Self and the World,* edited by Gregory Orr and Ellen Bryant Voigt, Ann Arbor, University of Michigan Press, 1996.

*   *   *

Susan Mitchell's poems, and the numerous honors they have garnered for their author, embody and reflect the world of mainstream American poetry. Her period style often begins with the pentameter line, which she expands or contracts from poem to poem, frequently transforming it into a unit that is closer to prose than to poetry. She is fond of repetition. She presents layers of detail yet leaves most connections between details largely up to the reader. On many occasions it appears that her poems have an almost aimless quality. They can seem laborious, elaborate, and self-conscious in expression: ''. . . I'm devoted / to an enormous expanse of violet / which is how the Atlantic wants to be today.'' Time and again Mitchell burrows back to the familiar business of analyzing personal experience rather than of allowing the artful presentation of experience itself to reveal the truth. What is most often lacking in this style is a fully formed individual point of view. Without one, writers who may feel deeply cannot sufficiently sort out their feelings to present them in the context that poetry requires. Thus, they have difficulty following where poetry would lead them.

For example, in ''The Child Bride,'' from *Rapture,* Mitchell's release from a hospital occasions free association that brings up the woman that Poe almost married, Poe's wife, Dante's Beatrice, and Dante's intention in writing *The Divine Comedy* (''Paradise is what Dante did with loss''), all of which comes in the first twelve lines. The method continues with a catalog of images found in the hospital and in those things in life that are a mystery to the author: pain, pleasure, water, Poe, and, most important, the self. The poem's long middle offers extended clinical speculation on death and loss. Then, suddenly, poetry happens:

> . . . Poe's child
> bride was singing when she had her first hemorrhage,
> as if music and blood flow from the same vein and the
> heart
> can pump only so much. The song split, traveling
> in two directions, and one was a foreign
> country always out of reach, a bird singing

in a forest she could not enter, though Poe described it for her, a place where strange brilliant flowers, star-shaped, burst out upon the trees where no flowers had been known before.

For a shining moment the writer disappears in poetry itself, devoid of strategies and agendas. But the moment ends, followed by another thick passage speculating on the nature and endurance of pain. This passage maneuvers the writer back to center stage, in control once more:

> . . . I forget
> the name of my own country, forget
> which language is which.

Mitchell certainly is not alone in writing in such a period style, and on occasion there are indications that she is capable of greater artistry. ''Bus Trip,'' also from *Rapture,* is one of her better poems:

> All across America children are learning to fly.
> On a bus leaving New Hampshire, on a bus
> leaving Colorado, I sat next to a child
>
> who had learned how to fly
> and she carried her flying clenched
> inside both fists. She carried her flying
>
> in a suitcase and in a stuffed dog
> made of dirt and the places where she had stood
> all night listening to the rain . . .

The simplicity here rings true. It is evocative and tender. It is enough.

—Robert McDowell

MOFFETT, Judith

Nationality: American. **Born:** Louisville, Kentucky, 30 August 1942. **Education:** Hanover College, Indiana, 1960–64, B.A. (cum laude) 1964; Colorado State University, Fort Collins, 1964–66, M.A. in English 1966; University of Wisconsin, Madison, 1966–67; University of Pennsylvania, Philadelphia, 1969–71, M.A. 1970, Ph.D. in American civilization 1971. **Family:** Married Edward B. Irving in 1983. **Career:** Fulbright Lecturer, University of Lund, Sweden, 1967–68; assistant professor, Behrend College, Pennsylvania State University, Erie, 1971–75; visiting lecturer, program in creative writing, University of Iowa, Iowa City, 1977–78; visiting lecturer, 1978–79, assistant professor of English, 1979–86, adjunct assistant professor, 1986–88, adjunct associate professor, 1988–93, and since 1993 adjunct professor of English, University of Pennsylvania. **Awards:** Fulbright grant, 1967, 1973; American Philosophical Society grant, 1973; Swedish Institute grant, 1973, 1976, 1983; Nathhorst Foundation (Sweden) grant, 1973; Eunice Tietjens memorial prize, 1973, and Levinson prize, 1976 (*Poetry,* Chicago); Borestone Mountain poetry award, 1976; Ingram Merrill grant, 1977, 1980; Columbia University translation prize, 1978; Bread Loaf Writers Conference Tennessee Williams fellowship, 1978; Swedish Academy translation prize, 1982; National Endowment for the Humanities translation fellowship, 1983; National Endowment for the Arts fellowship, 1984; Swedish Academy translation grant, 1993. **Address:** 951 East Laird Avenue, Salt Lake City, Utah 84105, U.S.A.

PUBLICATIONS

Poetry

Keeping Time. Baton Rouge, Louisiana State University Press, 1976.
Whinny Moor Crossing. Princeton, New Jersey, Princeton University Press, 1984.

Novels

Pennterra. New York, Congdon and Weed, 1987; London, New English Library, 1988.
The Ragged World. New York, St. Martin's Press. 1991.
Time, Like an Ever-Rolling Stream. New York, St. Martin's Press, 1992.

Short Stories

Two That Came True. Eugene, Oregon, Pulphouse Press, 1992.

Other

James Merrill: An Introduction to the Poetry. New York, Columbia University Press, 1984.
Homestead Year: Back to the Land in the Suburbs. New York, Lyons & Burford, 1995.

Translator, *Gentleman, Single, Refined, and Selected Poems 1937–1959* (bilingual edition), by Hjalmar Gullberg. Baton Rouge, Louisiana State University Press, 1979.

*

Critical Studies: "Studying Interior Architecture by Keyhold: Four Poets" by Reg Saner, in *Denver Quarterly* (Denver), 20(1), summer 1985; "The Profession of Science Fiction, 46: Grinding Axes" by Farah Mendlesohn, in *Foundation* (London), 62, winter 1994–95.

Judith Moffett comments:

(1985) As a child I was given no guidance or encouragement about poetry, but I was born into a family of Southern Baptists and heard the King James Bible read and quoted more or less daily throughout my early life, and it seems to me now that those biblical cadences still underlie the way I hear and use language. By the age of ten or eleven I had discovered Kipling's *Jungle Books* in the library and memorized the small poems introducing each story ("Now Chil the Kite brings home the night / That Mang the Bat set free . . .") with the purest pleasure. Later I happened upon, and was entranced by, Vachel Lindsay's "Ghost of the Buffaloes," and still later it was Stephen Vincent Benét's *John Brown's Body*. With each discovery came the urge to imitate, and that was how I started trying to write poems. From the beginning sound was valued more than sense.

Galloping tetrameters were what I responded to and therefore what I tried to write. I marvel now at my best students' intuitive understanding of what poetic language is and does, since I grew up depending almost entirely on the surge or quietness of forms to make language into poetry.

Having come thus far on my own, I stalled for a while in graduate school. Then, in graduate school I had the tremendous luck to be James Merrill's student for half a semester, and the experience of his poetry at that time had the force of a revelation. It quite literally changed my life. Merrill showed me, by his example, how to move ahead. I could see in his work the effects I cared about most in poetry (beauty, metrical skill, narrative) cranked up to a height tremendously beyond my own reach, yet as it were on the same extension ladder. Though we cared, and wrote, about quite different things, somehow the listening and controlling ear was much the same.

Because of this ear, at variance with the sensibilities of all but a handful of my own generation of poets, I learned only slowly and with difficulty to appreciate and then to write free verse, and I still find formal verse more satisfactory in a fundamental way for much of what I want to say.

Eventually I seemed to use poetry more and more often to tell a story; even short lyric stanzas add up, like beads on a string, and carry a narrative line. I have found also that nearly every poem I finished has what a friend has called a "ruminative" quality—that is, it seems appropriate to think things over in a poem—which may explain why, unlike many writers, I have never felt out of place in academe. I have consciously worked to become more restrained in emotional expression, to imply and suggest instead of serving up great shovelsful of feelings, and also to fight clear of my earlier experiments at compressing by way of linguistic density, and I have had fair success. I have also consciously tried to be briefer, but at that have done far less well. In early middle life I have settled most happily into the longish local-color-narrative-cum-philosophical-exploration on the one hand and the unabashedly formal lyric on the other, with various other odes and styles thrown in from time to time. In the impulse to this I recognize a reassertion of my early, much loved influences, but as far as I can tell, it has caused me (pace Harold Bloom) no anxiety. The family resemblance gives me pleasure, but what I have had to say and do is different.

More recently I have been writing science fiction: three novels and a story collection, with a fourth novel in the works.

*   *   *

Few poets of her generation would undertake the stylistic balances Judith Moffett attempts: an urbane, ethical, and ultimately social tone for which the modern model is Auden and the ultimate model Horace; a range of rhyme and stanza patterns that calls attention to her considerable technical skills, her master in this respect being James Merrill; and an affection for a meditative tone and for autobiographical subject matter that links her to the most interesting poets of her generation. These lines from a sonnet sequence, "Now or Never," in which the woman speaker, childless in her mid-thirties, is considering if she will ever have children, are characteristic:

> They gave me in my kindergarten year
> What seemed irrelevant, an Old Maid deck.
> Gems, wrinkled skin, strange glasses on a stick,
> Long gloves, pressed lips, and horrible orange hair,
> No child, no husband ever to be hers,

That gaunt crone wasn't anything like me!
I got her meaning fast: *ignominy*
Is being single in a game of pairs.

The benign contest between the discursive and formal tension is her favorite effect, a moral as well as technical balance. She distrusts the bardic, and the merely personal, or even the very personal unconstrained by formal considerations chosen before the poem, can be self-serving. She has the learning and literary range to strike such poise, for she has a doctorate, has written an excellent book on Merrill's work, and has translated from contemporary Swedish poetry.

Her poems err sometimes toward chattiness (''I always liked even upchucky babies''). And her ability to find poetry in daily life can lead her with cries of delight to the obvious (''Now whatever I glimpse qualifies the vast''). But she is willing to risk such lapses to arrive at lines like these from ''Bending the Twig,'' a poem about a girl who passes through puberty earlier than her peers. It builds on topics we have seldom heard discussed without smirking or melodrama, though it builds, too, on smirking and melodrama, not despising what we cling to:

Looking older than one's age required,
it dismayed me to learn, a decorum
appropriate not to the real but to the apparent.

This intelligent, skillful, and deceptively full-hearted poet is one of the most interesting and quietly ambitious of her generation.

—William Matthews

MOLE, John

Nationality: British. **Born:** Taunton, Somerset, 12 October 1941. **Education:** King's School, Bruton, Somerset; Magdalene College, Cambridge, 1961–64, B.A. (honors) in English 1964, M.A. 1969. **Family:** Married Mary Norman in 1968; two sons. **Career:** English teacher, Haberdashers' Aske's School, Elstree, Hertfordshire, 1964–73; chair of the English department, Verulam School, Hertfordshire, 1973–81; chair of the English department, St. Albans School, 1981–98. Exchange teacher, Riverdale Country School, New York, 1969–70; poet-in-residence, Magdalene College, 1996; since 1998 visiting poet, University of Hertfordshire, and ''official poet'' of the City of London. Presenter, *Poetry Now, Poetry Please,* and *Time for Verse,* BBC Radio, 1983–89; regular poetry reviewer, *Encounter,* London. Editor, with Peter Scupham, Cellar Press, and Mandeville Press, both in Hitchin, Hertfordshire. Since 1979 vice president, Ver Poets. **Awards:** Eric Gregory award, 1970; *Signal* award, for poetry for children, 1988; Cholmondeley award, 1994. **Address:** 11 Hill Street, St. Albans, Hertfordshire AL3 4QS, England.

PUBLICATIONS

Poetry

A Feather for Memory. London, Outposts, 1961.
The Instruments. Manchester, Phoenix Pamphlet Poets Press, 1970.
Something about Love. Oxford, Sycamore Press, 1972.

The Love Horse. Manchester, E.J. Morten, 1974.
Landscapes. Berkhamsted, Hertfordshire, Priapus, 1975.
A Partial Light. London, Dent, 1975.
The Mortal Room. Berkhamsted, Hertfordshire, Priapus, 1977.
The Tales of Rover. Hitchin, Hertfordshire, Mandeville Press, 1977.
Our Ship. London, Secker and Warburg, 1977.
On the Set. Richmond, Surrey, Keepsake Press, 1978.
From the House Opposite. London, Secker and Warburg, 1979.
Once There Were Dragons (for children), with Mary Norman. London, Deutsch, 1979.
Christmas Past, with Peter Scupham. Hitchin, Hertfordshire, Mandeville Press, 1981.
Feeding the Lake. London, Secker and Warburg, 1981.
Christmas Games, with Peter Scupham. Hitchin, Hertfordshire, Mandeville Press, 1983.
In and Out of the Apple. London, Secker and Warburg, 1984.
Christmas Visits, with Peter Scupham. Hitchin, Hertfordshire, Mandeville Press, 1984.
Learning the Ropes. Winscombe, Somerset, Gruffy Ground Press, 1985.
Winter Emblems, with Peter Scupham. Hitchin, Hertfordshire, Mandeville Press, 1986.
Christmas Fables, with Peter Scupham. Hitchin, Hertfordshire, Mandeville Press, 1987.
Homing. London, Secker and Warburg, 1987.
Boo to a Goose (for children). Calstock, Cornwall, Peterloo Poets, 1987.
Christmas Gifts, with Peter Scupham. Hitchin, Hertfordshire, Mandeville Press, 1988.
Christmas Books, with Peter Scupham. Hitchin, Hertfordshire, Mandeville Press, 1989.
The Mad Parrot's Countdown (for children). Calstock, Cornwall, Peterloo Poets, 1990.
Catching the Spider (for children). London, Blackie, 1990.
The Conjuror's Rabbit (for children). London, Blackie, 1992.
Depending on the Light. Calstock, Cornwall, Peterloo Poets, 1993.
Back by Midnight (for children). London, Penguin Books, 1994.
Selected Poems. London, Sinclair-Stevenson, 1995.
Hot Air (for children). London, Hodder, 1996.
Copy Cat (for children), with Bee Willey. London, Kingfisher, 1997.
The Dummy's Dilemma and Other Poems (for children). London, Hodder, 1999.
For the Moment. Calstock, Cornwall, Peterloo Poets, 2000.

Other

Understanding Children Writing, with others. London, Penguin, 1973.
Passing Judgements: Poetry in the Eighties: Essays from Encounter. Bristol, Bristol Classical Press, 1989.

Editor, *Poetry: A Selection.* Hemel Hempstead, Hertfordshire, Dacorum College, 1974.
Editor, with Anthony Thwaite, *Poetry 1945 to 1980.* London, Longman, 1983.

*

Manuscript Collection: State University of New York, Buffalo.

John Mole comments:

Apart from the routine essays, I did not write much at school. I preferred to read novels, and, as for poetry, I was more concerned to know about it than to read it. I was at least aware that there was something intellectually distinguished about claiming an interest in modern poetry, but that was as far as it went. Then, one Sunday in 1960, I picked up the "Review" section of the *Observer* and noticed a front-page spread of poems by Robert Graves called "Symptoms of Love." I began reading casually, became disconcertingly excited, and by the time I had finished the sequence I knew that I wanted to write poetry. Robert Graves was not an unfamiliar name to me; after all, he wrote novels, but what was this? So off I went and fashioned lapidary love poems with titles like "Prodigal Daughter," "Bard in Exile," etc. With all the presumptuousness of admiration, I sent them to Graves, who was at that time Oxford Professor of Poetry, and he said kind things; he even rewrote the closing lines of one of them in order to tighten up the syntax. It was important to get the shape right; mere feeling, as a later Oxford professor remarked, was too easy. I was hooked. Swinburne had blessed the baby Graves while he was still in his pram, and now Graves had corrected my syntax. The lineage was apparent.

I find poetry hard to talk about except in terms of my shifting enthusiasm for different poets and my permanent concern for patterning and craftsmanship. I enjoy what W.H. Auden calls "hanging around language," and there is usually some verbal sport going on in my most overtly "serious" poems, whether it be counting syllables or manipulating couplets. I do not believe that counting and manipulating, mathematical or geometric though they may sound, squeeze out feeling; I think they pack it in. In general, I hope that the best of my work may be memorable and capable of moving my readers. Anything else to be said about it can be said by others if they will.

(1995) Perhaps I should add a few words about a relatively recent development—that is, my work for children. I have always felt, in James Joyce's memorable phrase, that "my childhood bends beside me" and do not make an exclusive distinction between poems written for adults and those written with younger readers in mind. I was gratified when the poet Gavin Ewart wrote in the *Times Literary Supplement* of my first children's collection, "It is hard to separate the childlike from the childish; and this has always been one of Mole's strengths, as he exploits the two-way traffic between both."

*   *   *

There are special qualities about John Mole's poetry. One of them is wit, by which I mean the intellectual enjoyment of and interest in ideas and language that permeate his work. The other quality is more difficult to define but has roots in what we might call old-fashioned virtues. It is not that these virtues have disappeared or are not prized today, but they are, sadly, less current. They have a great deal to do with being straightforwardly for what is right or being on the right side as was, say, Sherlock Holmes or Miss Marple, as well as possessing a touch of undemonstrative courage. If I use examples from fiction, it is because I hope that they help to fix the period and ethos more clearly. I expect that the word I am looking for is "wholesome." As Mole himself put it in his poem "A Sunday Painter," "Unique and wholesome as a loaf of bread."

This could suggest a sort of cozy safeness that might be off-putting, but even in Mole's sequence about Victorian playthings, "Penny Toys," which is praised for its lightness of touch, the poems are not as safe as all that. Far from it. While jack-in-the-box may be

reassuringly faithful and true, he still "wants you," and there are the rumblings of time's winged chariot and the shadows of the necessary end being cast long across the nursery: "With a hey do diddle my cat Brown / The time has come to put him down."

Then there is the wit of Mole's poems. "Wit" is not a word that any longer figures much in critical writing. Perhaps it is because the word expresses a quality of sharpness of intellect that does not often occur in contemporary poetry. Yet it is a word that springs to mind when discussing Mole's work. This is not only because Mole has written humorous poetry; see, for example, his longish jazz poems and the delightful adaptations of Robert Desnos's "Chantefables," where the pleasure they give is derived from the display of technical high jinks, as in "The Owls":

> Mother owls make beau-
> tiful mothers, a few
> might brew more nourishing mouse stew
> than they do,
> but most of them muddle through

It is also because the mind behind and the intellectual pressure driving all of Mole's work are what distinguish it, the poems impinging on us through the impetus of their logical progression. In the poems contained in the collections *From the House Opposite* and *In and Out of the Apple* we find the wit and the humor progressing more and more toward penetrating observations of the human situation. The justly celebrated "The Tales of Rover" is a case in point, and even a seemingly light poem like "Bestial Homilies" ends with "Be warned by Nature not to let things go— / The animals prepare to say: We told you so." A certain menace shows through the jokey surface.

The seemingly straightforward and clearly defined everyday scenes often possess a disturbingly Magritte-like quality of mystery: "The rain of course / still falls as it should / which is not on them" ("The Mirror"). "Depths" seems to me to be a key poem in Mole's work, dealing directly with what is basic to the theme of his serious work, prophetically stated:

> Such a depth
> Is fearful, nothing moves
> But thoughts of what may start there
> Even at this moment
> Coming up.

Mole's 1987 collection *Homing* further establishes him as a poet of an assured, meticulous craftsmanship and with a sensitive ear for cadence. It is the development of his writing of poetry for young people, however, in which he displays the same technique and care to be found in his poetry for adults, that has come to be of special significance. His poetry for children can be seen as a natural development of his delight in wordplay and word games, the "Chantefables" and the "Penny Toys" poems mentioned earlier being a foretaste.

Mole's first collection for young people, *Boo to a Goose* (sensitively illustrated by Mary Norman), marked out his territory and set his standards, and it justly won the Signal award. Subsequent collections for young people-including *Catching the Spider, The Conjuror's Rabbit,* and *Back by Midnight*—have seen Mole take his rightful place in the tradition of worthy poets writing for children. He can be seen as a direct poetic successor to Walter de la Mare, James Reeves, and Charles Causley, poets who respected their young audiences and did not condescend or write down to them. If there

817

should be a Campaign for Real Poetry for Children—and a case could be made for a dire need for one—Mole and his work would be in the vanguard. Underlying the playfulness of his work is the serious respect Mole shows for young readers through the craftsmanship and the care he takes. The intricate thought and technique of ''Jig Saw Man'' is an example:

> Do you really think you can
> Keep up with the Jig Saw Man
> Who sits and thinks and thinks and sits
> Surrounded by a sea of bits
> Of every shape, of every size.
> Then suddenly with blazing eyes
> Puts this one here and that one there

The superbly crafted ''A Ghost Story'' begins with

> When you come home and it's raining
> And there's nobody in
> And the kettle's switched off but still steaming

and continues with its reverberations and thought-provoking atmosphere. ''A Ghost Story,'' among others of Mole's poems, lingers hauntingly with you after its reading, a mark of the genuine article.

The 1995 *Selected Poems* contains a weighty selection of new work, among which is a group of eleven poems, each with two six-line verses, that represent Mole at his assured best as a poet who has come into his own. These are vintage Mole poems, in the rhythm of which one can hear his authentic voice, shown, for example, in ''A Browning Version'':

> No it didn't work out and to cut a long story
> She swallowed her pride and a cold cappuccino
> Decided his kind was a probable handful
> So better press on regardless through customs
> Where the ribbon she wore in her coat was admired
> By a poet booked in on the cross-channel ferry.

The poems are urbane, with a touch of self-mockery in their confidence, and a delight.

—John Cotton

MONTAGUE, John (Patrick)

Nationality: Irish. **Born:** Brooklyn, New York, 28 February 1929. **Education:** St. Patrick's College, Armagh; University College, Dublin, B.A. in English and History 1949, M.A. 1952; Yale University, New Haven, Connecticut (Fulbright scholar), 1953–54; University of Iowa, Iowa City, M.F.A. 1955. **Family:** Married 1) Madeleine de Brauer in 1956 (divorced 1972); 2) Evelyn Robson in 1973 (separated 1993), two daughters; 3) Elizabeth Wassell in 1993. **Career:** Film critic, Dublin *Standard,* 1949–52; worked for Irish Tourist Board, 1956–59; Paris correspondent, *Irish Times,* 1961–64; taught at the Poetry Workshop, University of California, Berkeley, spring 1964 and 1965, University College, Dublin, spring and summer 1967, and spring 1968, and the Experimental University of Vincennes; lecturer in poetry, University College, Cork, 1972–88; writer-in-residence,

State University of New York, Albany, 1990; 1st Ireland Professor of Poetry, 1999. **Awards:** May Morton memorial award, 1960; Arts Council of Northern Ireland grant, 1970; Irish American Cultural Institute prize, 1976; Marten Toonder award, 1977; Alice Hunt Bartlett memorial award, 1979; Guggenheim fellowship, 1979; Hughes Irish Fiction award, 1988; Irish American Foundation award, 1995. **Member:** Irish Academy of Letters. **Agent:** Peters Fraser and Dunlop Group Ltd., 5th Floor, The Chambers, Chelsea Harbour, Lots Road, London SW10 OXF, England.

PUBLICATIONS

Poetry

Forms of Exile. Dublin, Dolmen Press, 1958.

The Old People. Dublin, Dolmen Press, 1960.

Three Irish Poets, with Thomas Kinsella and Richard Murphy. Dublin, Dolmen Press, 1961.

Poisoned Lands and Other Poems. London, MacGibbon and Kee, 1961; Chester Springs, Pennsylvania, Dufour, 1963; revised edition, Dublin, Dolmen Press, 1977.

Six Irish Poets, with others, edited by Robin Skelton. London, Oxford University Press, 1962.

Old Mythologies. Privately printed, 1965.

All Legendary Obstacles. Dublin, Dolmen Press, and London, Oxford University Press, 1966.

The Rough Field. Dublin, Dolmen Press, and London, Oxford University Press, 1972; Winston-Salem, North Carolina, Wake Forest University Press, 1979.

Patriotic Suite. Dublin, Dolmen Press, 1966.

Home Again. Belfast, Festival, 1967.

Hymn to the New Omagh Road. Dublin, Dolmen Press, 1968.

The Bread God: A Lecture, with Illustrations in Verse. Dublin, Dolmen Press, 1968.

A New Siege. Dublin, Dolmen Press, 1969.

A Chosen Light. London, MacGibbon and Kee, 1967; Chicago, Swallow Press, 1969.

The Planter and the Gael, with John Hewitt. Belfast, Arts Council of Northern Ireland, 1970.

Tides. Dublin, Dolmen Press, 1970; Chicago, Swallow Press, 1971.

Small Secrets. London, Poem-of-the-Month Club, 1972.

The Cave of Night. Cork, Golden Stone Press, 1974.

O'Riada's Farewell. Cork, Golden Stone Press, 1974.

A Slow Dance. Dublin, Dolmen Press, and Winston-Salem, North Carolina, Wake Forest University Press, 1975.

The Great Cloak. Dublin, Dolmen Press, London, Oxford University Press, and Winston-Salem, North Carolina, Wake Forest University Press, 1978.

The Leap. Dublin, Gallery, and Old Deerfield, Massachusetts, Deerfield Press, 1979.

Selected Poems. Dublin, Dolmen Press, Oxford, Oxford University Press, and Winston-Salem, North Carolina, Wake Forest University Press, 1982.

Deities. New York, At-Swim Press, 1982.

The Dead Kingdom. Dublin, Dolmen Press, Oxford, Oxford University Press, and Winston-Salem, North Carolina, Wake Forest University Press, 1984.

Mount Eagle. Oldcastle, County Meath, Gallery Press, 1988; Newcastle upon Tyne, Bloodaxe, 1989.

New Selected Poems. Newcastle upon Tyne, Bloodaxe, 1990.

Time in Armagh. Oldcastle, County Meath, Gallery Press, 1993.

About Love. Riverdale-on-Hudson, New York, The Sheepmeadow Press, 1993.

Collected Poems. Winston-Salem, North Carolina, Wake Forest University Press, and Oldcastle, County Meath, Gallery Press, 1995.

Smashing the Piano Gallery. Winston-Salem, North Carolina, Wake Forest University Press, 1999.

Recording: *The Northern Muse,* with Seamus Heaney, Claddagh, 1968.

Play

The Rough Field (produced London, 1973). Dublin, Dolmen Press, 1984.

Novel

The Lost Notebook (novella). Cork, Mercier Press, 1987.

Short Stories

Death of a Chieftain and Other Stories. London, MacGibbon and Kee, 1964; Chester Springs, Pennsylvania, Dufour, 1967.

An Occasion of Sin. Fredonia, New York, White Pine Press, 1992.

A Love Present. Dublin, Wolfhound Press, 1997.

Other

The Figure in the Cave and Other Essays, edited by Antoinette Quinn. Dublin, Lilliput, and Syracuse, New York, Syracuse University Press, 1989.

Editor, *The Dolmen Miscellany of Irish Writing.* Dublin, Dolmen Press, 1962.

Editor, with Liam Miller, *A Tribute to Austin Clarke on His Seventieth Birthday, 9 May 1966.* Dublin, Dolmen Press, and Chester Springs, Pennsylvania, Dufour, 1966.

Editor, *The Faber Book of Irish Verse.* London, Faber, 1974; as The *Book of Irish Verse,* New York, Macmillan, 1977.

Editor, *Bitter Harvest: An Anthology of Contemporary Irish Verse.* New York, Scribner, 1989.

Translator, *A Fair House: Versions of Irish Poetry.* Dublin, Cuala Press, 1973.

Translator, with Evelyn Robson, *November,* by André Frénaud. Cork, Golden Stone Press, 1977.

Translator, with C.K. Williams, *Ponge.* Winston-Salem, North Carolina, Wake Forest University Press, 1994.

Translator, *Carnac,* by Guillevic. Newcastle upon Tyne, Bloodaxe, 1999.

*

Critical Studies: *The New Poetry* by M.L. Rosenthal, New York and London, Oxford University Press, 1967, and *The Modern Poetic Sequence* by Rosenthal and Sally M. Gall, New York and Oxford, Oxford University Press, 1983; by John MacInerney, in *Hibernia* (Dublin), 15 December 1972; by D.S. Maxwell, in *Critical Quarterly* (London), summer 1973; by Derek Mahon, in *Malahat Review* (Victoria, British Columbia), July 1973; by Thomas Dillon Redshaw, in *Studies* (Dublin), spring 1974; *John Montague* by Frank Kersnowski, Lewisburg, Pennsylvania, Bucknell University Press, 1975; "John Montague, Seamus Heaney, and the Irish Past" by Graham Martin, in *The Present* (New Pelican Guide to English Literature), edited by Boris Ford, London, Penguin, 1983; *Hill Field: Poems and Memoirs for John Montague on His 60th Birthday* edited by Thomas Dillon Redshaw, Oldcastle, County Meath, Gallery Press, and Minneapolis, Coffee House Press, 1989; *Redeeming Pattern of Experience: John Montague's Text and Tradition, 1949–1989* (dissertation) by Carolyn Margaret Meyer, McMaster University, 1991; "Matriarchs, Mothergoddesses, and the Poetry of John Montague" by Elizabeth Grubgeld, in *Etudes Irlandaises* (Sainghinen en Melantois, France), 18(2), December 1993; interview with Nancy Gish, in her *Hugh MacDiarmid: Man and Poet,* Edinburgh, Edinburgh University Press, 1992; "Embodying the Past: History and Imagination in John Montague's 'The Rough Field'" by Elmar Schenkel, in *Anglistentag 1992 Stuttgart: Proceedings,* edited by Hans Ulrich Seeber and Walter Gobel, Tubingen, Niemeyer, 1993; "John Montague and William Carlos Williams: Nationalism and Poetic Construction" by Paul Bowers, in *Canadian Journal of Irish Studies,* 20(2), December 1994; "'Campaigning against Memory's Mortmain': Benjaminian Allegory in John Montague's 'The Rough Field'" by David Gardiner, in *Notes on Modern Irish Literature* (Butler, Pennsylvania), 8, 1996; *Northern Exposures: Politics, Pressure and Tradition in the Poetry of Montague, Heaney, and Muldoon* (dissertation) by Kevin Brady, Drew University, 1996; "John Montague: Passionate Contemplative" by Augustine Martin, in *Irish Writers and Their Creative Process,* edited by Jacqueline Genet and Wynne Hellegouarc'h, Gerrards Cross, England, Smythe, 1996; "Lost, Unhappy and at Home: The Robinson Crusoe Complex in Contemporary Irish Poetry" by Michael Faherty, in *The Classical World and the Mediterranean,* edited by Giuseppe Serpillo and Donatella Badin, Cagliari, Italy, Tema, 1996; "A Second Tongue" by Eamonn Wall, in *Shenandoah* (Lexington, Virginia), 46(3), fall 1996; "'Bog Queens': The Representation of Women in the Poetry of John Montague and Seamus Heaney" by Patricia Coughlan, in *Seamus Heaney,* edited by Michael Allen, New York, St. Martin's Press, 1997; "To Do Penance and Rejoice" by R.T. Smith, in *Southern Review* (Baton Rouge, Louisiana), 34(1), winter 1998.

John Montague comments:

I am usually classed as an Irish poet, and that is true insofar as I am deeply involved with the landscape and people of Ireland, particularly Ulster. In Gaelic poetry Ireland appears both as a maiden and a hag, a sort of national muse, and her hold is still strong, especially now that her distinctive culture is being submerged. But underneath these tribal preoccupations beats a more personal struggle, the effort to affirm lovingly, to salvage some order, in the face of death and change. The technique is a blend of postmodern (Williams and Pound) and old Gaelic poetry, which could also be regarded as an aspect of nationality, for an Irish poet (following Joyce, Yeats, Beckett) has a better chance of being international than an English writer. But my effort to understand as much of the modern world as possible serves only to illuminate the destruction of that small area from which I initially came, and that theme in turn is only part of the larger one of continually threatened love.

*   *   *

There is something tight-lipped about John Montague's poetry. It is revealed even in the terse titles of his volumes and in the repeated use of a short, abrupt line in which enjambment projects the reader into sudden peripeties and reversals and the shifts of pace and meaning have the effect of a clipped, curt rebuff. Yet within these constraints the poetry can flower into an unexpected lyric generosity. Not many poets, for example, could carry off successfully the Anglo-Saxon bluntness of "Love, A Greeting" (*Tides*):

> a lifetime's
> struggle to exchange
> with the strange
> thing inhabiting
> a woman—
>   face,
> breasts, buttocks,
> the honey sac
> of the cunt . . .

It is the puritanical tautness of his speech that can bring off such large gestures. Constriction is Montague's native ground, as "Home Again" admits. Narrowness runs as a theme throughout his work, an expression of the bare past and "bleak economic future" shared, as he has written, by all such peripheral and remote areas of Europe as Ulster, Brittany, and the Highlands. It is this that marks him out clearly as one of the Ulster school of poets, despite the casual displacement of his Brooklyn birth. The "narrow huckster streets" of Belfast, "all this dour, despoiled inheritance," together with the heritage of sectarian hatred in "a culture where constraint is all," have a precise economic origin: "narrow fields wrought such division." "Rough Field," which gives the title to one of his major collections, is not just a translation of the Gaelic name for his native village but, in the words of an Afghan proverb that provides his epigraph, the summary of a historical destiny: "I had never known sorrow, / Now it is a field I have inherited, and I till it." In "The Bread God" he sees this in turn reproduced in "the lean parish of my art." Deracination is a major theme for Montague from his first volume, *Forms of Exile,* through his later work.

"A Lost Tradition," in *The Rough Field,* laments the physical expropriation that goes with the loss of the Gaelic, which no amount of "school Irish" can compensate for: "The whole landscape a manuscript / We had lost the skill to read, / A part of our past disinherited." The whole volume explores the consequences of this uprooting, spanning several hundred years of Irish history, while always relating the public events to the particular lives of individual men and families, including Montague's own forebears. "A Grafted Tongue" sees the linguistic loss not just as a metaphor for this larger dispossession but also as its key event: "To grow / a second tongue, as / harsh a humiliation / as twice to be born." "Lament for the O'Neills" and "Stele for a Northern Republican" indicate that the loss is one lying close to the heart of both communities in the North. The latter poem unsentimentally, but with bitterness, acknowledges his own father's "right to choose a Brooklyn slum / rather than a half-life in this / by-passed and dying place."

In *A Slow Dance* Montague moves away from history into the shadowy realms of Celtic myth to explain the modern violence of Northern Ireland, resurrecting that ancient "black widow goddess" whose "love-making / is like a skirmish" and who wears "a harvest necklace of heads." The move brings with it a loss of precisely that kind of acute historical particularity that distinguishes his best verse,

but it remains nevertheless an impressive volume. The "slow dance" of the title unites human and elemental cycles and pagan and Christian Ireland in a ritual return to origins, where fertility and massacre are intimately linked. But it is finally the "sad awkward / dance of pain" of all the living upon the graves of all the dead, and perhaps its most moving sequence is the intense and personal elegy for his close friend the composer O'Riada, who died in 1971.

The love poems of *The Great Cloak* return to the lucid, melodic airs of *Tides* and *A Chosen Light,* but the atmosphere has been darkened by the intervening public violence, which now finds its correlative in personal life. These poems are as much concerned with loss, jealousy, marital breakdown, and its humiliation and shame as with the lyric celebration of love, "that always strange moment / when the clothes peel away / (bark from an unknown tree)" ("Do Not Disturb"). The violence spoken of as inseparable from love in such a fine early poem as "The Same Gesture" (*Tides*) is now felt more urgently and as a greater threat. Only briefly, in the sequence of poems that explore the consciousness of the estranged wife, is any connection explicitly acknowledged between personal disintegration and the larger violence of the North ("She Writes"). But throughout Montague is groping toward a new understanding of the interdependence of the personal and the political and of their common roots in a harsh and sour history. Such a quest can bring him desperately close to the unspeakable, to silence, shamefaced and appalled, as "No Music" recognizes:

> To tear up old love by the roots,
> To trample on past affections:
> There is no music for so harsh a song.

The Dead Kingdom charts a journey north along "minor roads of memory" from Cork to Fermanagh when the poet is summoned by his mother's death to traverse a landscape dense with personal, historic, and mythic associations. The volume itself is a "dead kingdom," preserving in print "things that are gone" and sardonically accepting its own ultimate disappearance like the library of Alexander before it and later "substantial things / hustled oblivion" down the maw of Spenser's "goddess Mutability, / dark lady of Process, / our devouring Queen." When individuals die, a unique "world of sense & memory" vanishes with them. Races and nations alike are "locked / in their dream of history," subjective realms as "fragile / as a wild bird's wing," bulldozer and butterfly alike ephemeral forms. Even the archaeological relics of ancient Ireland are now torn up by the mechanized peat cutters that destroy the bog wholesale. Yet as "A Flowering Absence" suggests, the poet's own childhood experience of exile and fostering compels him to fill this emptiness, urged by a "terrible thirst" for knowledge and love "to learn something of that time / Of confusion, poverty, absence." This accounts for the journey upstream to the source, which is also, as the last poem, "Back," indicates, a journey to his own death. "There is no permanence," an epigraph from *The Book of Gilgamesh* tells us. But another speaks of the need to discover the "source of lost knowledge," and in the penultimate poem it is the impulse to name that provides those "frail rope-ladders / across fuming oblivion" that offer "a new love, a new / litany of place names" and allow the poet to return home to "a flowering presence."

Return is also a motif of Montague's volume *Mount Eagle,* which opens with the image of one salmon that "returns, / a lord to his underwater kingdom" and of another dying, abdicating a polluted planet. This ecological lament runs through the volume, providing some of its most powerful writing. But the book closes in another, more hopeful return of the salmon in ''Survivor,'' where the old, bare earth reappears, promising that ''life might begin again'' after all the human poison has been purged, and where Fintan, a recurring presence, finds himself turning into a salmon that returns from the ocean bottom to reclaim its own. (The poem recalls the legendary Finn who tasted of the salmon of knowledge.) The returns of this book are not merely nostalgic trips back to the origins. On the contrary, in a volume that is shot through with the hope of renewal it is the past that returns to the present, sustaining and vivifying it. The cricket in ''Hearth Song'' strikes up again as in his childhood. A boyhood friend from across the religious divide turns up in a Belfast pub to save the embattled poet from ''a swirl of trouble'' with two off-duty men from the Ulster Defence Regiment. A childhood memory of a squat, coarse Jim Toorish caught splashing naked in a pool returns redeemed, cleansed of giggling prurience, in ''a satyr, laughing in / the spray at Florence.'' In a sequence of sensually charged love poems celebrating the conjunction of May and September, memories of youth's glad animal movements restore the aging man, disclosing ''secret wellsprings / of strength,''

those long, lovely

Leaps in the dark
returning now to steady
my mind, nourish
my courage as

No longer young
I take your hand.

''Someday I will exorcise it enough to forget and forgive, but at the age of sixty, images from that little hell on the hill haunt me, too harsh for long contemplation.'' So Montague wrote in the title essay of *The Figure in the Cave* of his time from 1941 to 1946 at Saint Patrick's in Armagh. *Time in Armagh* (1993), the title punning on the notion of imprisonment, attempts an exorcism and a contemplation of the poet's peculiarly life-denying education in a Roman Catholic boarding school. The themes—sexual repression, bullying, caning, religious zeal—are familiar in Irish writing about adolescence and schooling, but Montague makes them new and his own through an economical style capable of straight talk (''A system / without love is a crock of shite'' is the way the title poem ends), wry sarcasm (''Father Roughan, all too rightly named''), and a strain of subdued lyricism sharply refusing to make amends for the past yet implying an alternative and a better set of values. In ''Peephole'' the poet writes, ''Besides, alas, / The only opening left was our imagination,'' and the openings created by imagination are continually explored by the volume, which has something of a Dantean flavor as it reenters the ''hell'' of the Senior and Junior Rings. Montague's characteristic eye for the larger implications of his subject is evident throughout. World War II is a menacing presence at the edge of the child's existence. The prose poem ''The Bomber's Moon'' notes how ''the stain on the Eastern sky was growing, like a bloodshot eye'' as the German bombers moved over Belfast. Elsewhere Montague writes with laconic sympathy about ''the camp where German / Prisoners were kept,'' and he finds a place in the collection for a slightly revised version of the much earlier poem ''The Welcoming Party,'' about watching newsreels of the concentration camps. *Time in Armagh* is an impressive example of difficult personal experience shaped into disciplined, unsentimental poetry.

Montague's *Collected Poems* (1995) allows the reader to take the measure, within a single volume, of a major poetic achievement. The book shapes itself round what its editors, Peter Fallon and Dillon Johnston, call ''his three major 'orchestrations'''(*The Rough Field, The Great Cloak,* and *The Dead Kingdom*), followed by lyrics and concluding with *Time in Armagh* and the impressive *Border Sick Call*. In this last sequence, as he describes a journey taken by himself and his brother along the Fermanagh-Donegal border, Montague often works with a short, crisp line and an idiom alert both to the ''solid, homely detail'' of this world and to intimations ''glimpsed uneasily in dream.'' Undertaking their ''Ulster border pilgrimage / where demarcations disappear,'' the two men confront rural life and suffering and Ireland's past and present. Montague meditates on memory, poetry, history, and the possibility of an ''unexpected affirmation,'' an affirmation that does not dispel disquiet or questioning.

Affirmation is an eloquent and convincing impulse in *Smashing the Piano* (1999), a volume that is ''heart-sick for harmony.'' Acutely conscious of suffering, Montague is always on the lookout for evidence of what is finest about others, even as he refuses to idealize. If the title poem records destruction, it begins to set against destruction—rather as though it were an updated version of Hardy's ''During Wind and Rain''—a series of family memories, and ''Sunny Jim'' signs a truce with the poet's father. ''Remission'' captures the pathos but also the courage of a friend ''paralysed from the waist down'' who behaves as though ''beyond death's encroaching ruin, / there dwelt some final, lasting sweetness.'' Throughout, Montague adjudicates the rival claims of ''encroaching ruin'' and ''lasting sweetness,'' the subject of some fine love poems, with a persuasive, balancing artistry.

—Stan Smith and Michael O'Neill

MORAES, Dom(inic Frank)

Nationality: British. **Born:** Bombay, India, 19 July 1938; son of journalist and writer Frank Moraes. **Education:** Jesus College, Oxford (Editor, *Gemini,* 1958–60), B.A. in English 1959, M.A. **Military Service:** U.S. Army in Vietnam, 1971–73: Honorary Colonel. **Family:** Married 1) Judith St. John in 1963 (marriage dissolved), one son; 2) Leela Naidu in 1969. **Career:** Journalist, and scriptwriter and director, BBC and ITV; roving reporter, *New York Times Sunday Magazine,* 1968–71; managing editor, *Asia Magazine,* Hong Kong, 1971–73; chief literary consultant, United Nations Fund for Populations, 1973–77. **Awards:** Hawthornden prize, 1958; Lamont prize, 1960; Overseas Press Citation (USA), 1972; Central Literacy Academy of India award for English, 1994. **Agent:** Curtis Brown, 162–168 Regent Street, London WlR 5TA, England. **Address:** 12 Sargent House, Allana Marg, Bombay 39, India.

PUBLICATIONS

Poetry

A Beginning. London, Parton Press, 1957.
Poems. London, Eyre and Spottiswoode, 1960.
Penguin Modern Poets 2, with Kingsley Amis and Peter Porter. London, Penguin, 1962.

John Nobody. London, Eyre and Spottiswoode, 1965.
Poems 1955–1965. New York, Macmillan, 1966.
Bedlam Etcetera. London, Turret, 1966.
Absences. New Delhi, Sterling, 1983.
Collected Poems 1957–1987. New Delhi and New York, Penguin, 1987.
Serendip: Poems. New Delhi and New York, Viking, 1990.
Three Indian Poets: Nissim Ezekiel, A.K. Ramanujan, Dom Moraes. Madras, Oxford University Press, 1991.

Other

Green Is the Grass (on cricket). Bombay, Asia Publishing House, 1951.
Gone Away: An Indian Journal. London, Heinemann, and Boston, Little Brown, 1960.
My Son's Father: An Autobiography. London, Secker and Warburg, 1968; as *My Son's Father: A Poet's Autobiography,* New York, Macmillan, 1969.
The Tempest Within: An Account of East Pakistan. New York, Barnes and Noble, 1971.
From East and West: A Collection of Essays. New Delhi, Vikas, 1971.
A Matter of People. London, Deutsch, and New York, Praeger, 1974.
The Open Eyes: A Journey Through Karnataka. Bangalore, Government of Karnataka, 1976.
Mrs. Gandhi. London, Cape, 1980; as *Indira Gandhi,* Boston, Little Brown, 1980.
Bombay. New York, Time Life, 1980.
Answered by Flutes: Reflections from Madhya Pradesh. Bombay, Asia Publishing House, 1983.
Trishna. Bombay, Perennial Press, 1987.
Sunil Gavaskar: An Illustrated Biography. Madras, Macmillan, 1987.
Rajasthan, Splendour in the Wilderness. New Delhi, Himalayan Books, 1988.
Never at Home. New Delhi, Viking, 1992.

Author of introduction, *Gemini: Poems,* by Jeet Thayil. New Delhi, Viking, 1994.
Author of introduction, *Women,* by Prabuddha Das Gupta. New Delhi, Viking, 1996.

Editor, *Voices for Life: Reflections on the Human Condition.* New York, Praeger, 1975.

Translator, *The Brass Serpent,* by T. Carmi. London, Deutsch, 1964; Athens, Ohio University Press, 1965.

*

Manuscript Collections: University of Texas, Austin; State University of New York, Buffalo; University of Arizona, Tucson.

Critical Studies: *The Poetry of Encounter: Three Indo-Anglian Poets* by Emmanuel Narendra Lall, New Delhi, Sterling, 1983; article in *The Hindu* (Madras), 29 April 1990; *Three Indian Poets: Nissim Ezekiel, A.K. Ramanujan, Dom Moraes* by Bruce King, Madras, Oxford University Press, 1991.

*   *   *

Dom Moraes began to write poetry at the age of twelve, and by the age of fifteen he had attracted the attention of W.H. Auden. Stephen Spender, whom he calls his mentor, published him in *Encounter,* and Karl Shapiro in *Poetry.* Moraes published his first book of poems, *A Beginning,* when he was only nineteen. This was followed during the next nine years by additional books of poetry. But between 1966 and 1983 Moraes published no poetry at all, although prose works appeared. At last, in 1983, he broke his silence with the publication of *Absences,* and in 1987 his *Collected Poems 1957–1987* appeared.

Moraes has said that poetry haunts him, recurring in his mind as sounds, phrases, or even single words, out of which a poem eventually arises. During the years of his poetic silence he was trying to put down words that had not, he says, haunted him or come to him out of the air. In 1982, however, he found himself suddenly writing poetry again in an altogether new style without trying to master it, and he wrote eleven poems in quick succession. He hastened to publish the poems as *Absences,* fearing that the elusive muse might as suddenly vanish again. But the poems continued to come, a mystery that Moraes says he cannot explain.

Moraes has explained his methods of composition in this way: "As soon as I have an idea for a poem, I open a notebook at random and write it down. I do the same as further ideas strike me, so that pieces of the poem may be scattered throughout a notebook, interspersed with pieces of other poems. One poem may have parts of it strewn over several notebooks. When I am actually in the process of completing a poem, I work from typescripts, sometimes as many as 30 of them, anyway, too many to keep, so I throw them away." In the foreword to his *Collected Poems* Moraes says that he regards *John Nobody,* published in 1965, as a better book than earlier ones "because there was some kind of thought, rather than pure imagination, attempting to direct the poems." Still, it seemed to him that many of the poems in *John Nobody* did not convey what he had intended at the start, and he has now come to regard the poems written after 1982 as better than the early ones. The new style certainly has greater lucidity.

What distinguishes Moraes among Indian poets writing in English are a powerful organic sensibility, a skillful use of metrical and nonmetrical verse patterns, compressed but still lucid imagery ("malignant bureaucracy / Festooning sores with coloured tape"), and a remarkable ability to create an unusual mood, atmosphere, or unnameable emotion. There is plenty of variety in subject, genre, tone, feeling, and scene. The diction is wide-ranging, evocative, and sensuous. Occasionally there is an unusual word, precisely used ("The nictitation of his drunken eyes"; "the cruses of my eyes"; "vultures / Alate as angels on each corpse").

Wordsworth, on whom Moraes has written a poem, said that poems to which value can be attached are never produced on just any variety of topics but by a man who, being possessed of more than usual organic sensibility, has thought long and deeply of his subject. Of Moraes's more than usual organic sensibility there can be no doubt, but many of his poems suffer from a certain intellectual thinness that somewhat diminishes the appeal of their stylistic felicity. The thinness may be a symptom of a lack of cultural or religious conviction. In a poem called "Son," for example, which records the birth of the boy, the speaker refers to the infant as coming through "the burning bush," but the biblical allusion does not add significantly to the meaning.

Moraes has said that "myths nest inside [his] head" and that he is fascinated by history (including, we may add, archaeology), which has the quality of myth for him. (''My imaginative processes operate like this, and I cannot change them.'') The interpretative illumination of life and the world that myths have provided to many poets, however, is not conspicuous in Moraes's use of them. Thus, the poem ''Merlin'' reaches the somewhat disappointing conclusion that Merlin's magic will not work now, so that Merlin wants to die. (Compare Eliot's use of the Cumaean sibyl.) His reading of history is also somewhat lacking in vision and philosophical interpretation. Mythic perception calls for an imagination characterized by a sense of cyclic time and of tradition and for a more than usual capacity to transcend oneself and contemporary reality.

Moraes's book *Serendip* (1990) was published three years after *Collected Poems.* The first section is a collection of fourteen-line poems that give a chronological account of certain episodes in the history of Sri Lanka. (Serendip, meaning ''island of jewels,'' was an ancient name for Sri Lanka.) The poems bring out well the strong points of Moraes's poetic craft: graceful phrasing, a sure sense of rhythm, the right image, a wide knowledge of history and myth, and a rich vocabulary, The second section, ''Steles,'' contains poems based on recollections of his past life and the emotions evoked by them. Presiding over this section and the next one, ''Barrows,'' is the thought of death. The tone is one of regret and sadness for a misspent life, but the poet's gift for the right word has luckily survived. The third section also contains many poems based on remote Icelandic myth and history. Perhaps the most successful poems are in the final section, simply called ''Other Poems.'' They are on a variety of themes and in a variety of forms, with a movement that is slow and meditative and with a tone of resignation and gentle melancholy. The images create and focus the emotion precisely. The poet is aware that he is living on the past and in the past, and in ''Laureate'' there is even an intimation that his poetic powers have declined:

> The endless paper yellows down the years.
> Once his empowered words, knotted for stress,
> Drew his heart outward on a catch of breath
> As though he felt a sudden flight of birds,
> Constructed out of shreds, cohere and fly
> Up from his hands, above astonished heads.

The last poem of the collection, ''Future Plans,'' expresses the hope of a reconciliation with the way things have gone.

—S. Nagarajan

MORGAN, Edwin (George)

Nationality: Scottish. **Born:** Glasgow, 27 April 1920. **Education:** Rutherglen Academy; Glasgow High School; Glasgow University, 1937–40, 1946–47, M.A. (honors) in English 1947. **Military Service:** Royal Army Medical Corps, 1940–46. **Career:** Assistant lecturer, 1947–50, lecturer, 1950–65, senior lecturer, 1965–71, reader, 1971–75, Titular Professor in English, 1975–80, became emeritus professor, Glasgow University. Since 1987 visiting professor in English studies, University of Strathclyde, and University College of Wales, Aberystwyth. **Awards:** Cholmondeley award, 1968; Scottish Arts Council award, 1968, 1973, 1975, 1977, 1978, 1983, 1985, 1988, 1991; Hungarian P.E.N. Memorial Medal, 1972; Soros translation award, 1985; Stakis prize for Scottish Writer of the Year, 1998. D.Litt.: Loughborough University, Leicestershire, 1981, University of Glasgow, 1990, University of Edinburgh, 1991. Hon. D. Univ.: University of Stirling, 1989, University of Waikato, New Zealand, 1992. Hon. M. Univ: Open University, 1992. O.B.E. (Officer, Order of the British Empire), 1982. **Address:** 19 Whittingehame Court, Glasgow G12 0BG, Scotland.

PUBLICATIONS

Poetry

The Vision of Cathkin Braes. Glasgow, Maclellan, 1952.
The Cape of Good Hope. Tunbridge Wells, Kent, Peter Russell, 1955.
Starryveldt. Frauenfeld, Switzerland, Gomringer Press, 1965.
Scotch Mist. Cleveland, Renegade Press, 1965.
Sealwear. Glasgow, Gold Seal Press, 1966.
Emergent Poems. Stuttgart, Hansjorg Mayer, 1967.
The Second Life. Edinburgh, Edinburgh University Press, 1968.
Gnomes. Preston, Lancashire, Akros, 1968.
Proverbfolder. Corsharn, Wiltshire, Openings Press, 1969.
Penguin Modern Poets 15, with Alan Bold and Edward Kamau Brathwaite. London, Penguin, 1969.
The Horseman's Word: A Sequence of Concrete Poems. Preston, Lancashire, Akros, 1970.
Twelve Songs. West Linton, Peeblesshire, Castlelaw Press, 1970.
The Dolphin's Song. Leeds, School of English Press, 1971.
Glasgow Sonnets. West Linton, Peeblesshire, Castlelaw Press, 1972.
Instamatic Poems. London, Ian McKelvie, 1972.
The Whittrick: A Poem in Eight Dialogues. Preston, Lancashire, Akros, 1973.
From Glasgow to Saturn. Cheadle, Cheshire, Carcanet, and Chester Springs, Pennsylvania, Dufour, 1973.
The New Divan. Manchester, Carcanet, 1977.
Colour Poems. Glasgow, Third Eye Centre, 1978.
Star Gate: Science Fiction Poems. Glasgow, Third Eye Centre, 1979.
Poems of Thirty Years. Manchester, Carcanet, 1982.
Grafts/Takes. Glasgow, Mariscat Press, 1983.
4 Glasgow Subway Poems. Glasgow, National Book League, 1983.
Sonnets from Scotland. Glasgow, Mariscat Press, 1984.
Selected Poems. Manchester, Carcanet, 1985.
From the Video Box. Glasgow, Mariscat Press, 1986.
Newspoems. London, Wacy, 1987.
Themes on a Variation. Manchester, Carcanet, 1988.
Tales from Limerick Zoo. Glasgow, Mariscat Press, 1988.
Collected Poems. Manchester, Carcanet, 1990.
Hold Hands among the Atoms. Glasgow, Mariscat Press, 1991.
Sweeping Out the Dark. Manchester, Carcanet Press, 1994.
Virtual and Other Realities. Manchester, Carcanet, 1997.
Demon. Glasgow, Mariscat Press, 1999.
New Selected Poems. Manchester, Carcanet, 2000.

Recordings: *Selected Poems,* Canto, 1985; *Seventeen Poems of Edwin Morgan,* Scotsoun, 1987.

Plays

The Apple-Tree: A Medieval Dutch Play (produced Edinburgh, 1982). Glasgow, Third Eye Centre, 1982.

Master Peter Pathelin, adaptation of a medieval French farce. Glasgow, Third Eye Centre, 1983.

The Charcoal-Burner (opera libretto), 1969.

Valentine (opera libretto), 1976.

Columba (opera libretto), 1976.

Spell (opera libretto), 1979.

Cyrano de Bergerac, translated from Edmond Rostand. Manchester, Carcanet Press, 1992.

Other

Essays. Cheadle, Cheshire, Carcanet, 1974.

Rites of Passage: Translations. Manchester, Carcanet, 1976.

Hugh MacDiarmid. London, Longman, 1976.

East Europèan Poets. Milton Keynes, Buckinghamshire, Open University Press, 1976.

Provenance and Problematics of "Sublime and Alarming Images" in Poetry. London, British Academy, 1977.

Edwin Morgan: An Interview, with Marshall Walker. Preston, Lancashire, Akros, 1977.

Twentieth-Century Scottish Classics. Glasgow, Book Trust Scotland, 1987.

Nothing Not Giving Messages: Reflections on His Work and Life, edited by Hamish Whyte. Edinburgh, Polygon, 1990.

Crossing the Border (essays). Manchester, Carcanet, 1990.

Evening Will Come They Will Sew The Blue Sail. Edinburgh, Graeme Murray, 1991.

Christopher Marlowe's Dr. Faustus: In a New Version. Edinburgh, Canongate, 1999.

Editor, *Collins Albatross Book of Longer Poems: English and American Poetry from the Fourteenth Century to the Present Day.* London, Collins, 1963.

Editor, with George Bruce and Maurice Lindsay, *Scottish Poetry One to Six.* Edinburgh, Edinburgh University Press, 1966–72.

Editor, *New English Dramatists 14.* London, Penguin, 1970.

Editor, *Scottish Satirical Verse: An Anthology.* Manchester, Carcanet, 1980.

Editor, with Carl Macdougall, *New Writing Scotland 5 and 6.* Aberdeen, Association for Scottish Literary Studies, 2 vols., 1987–88; *7,* with Hamish Whyte, 1989.

Editor, *Roadworks: Song Lyrics for Wildcat,* by David Anderson and David MacLennan. Glasgow, Third Eye Centre, 1987.

Editor, *The City of Dreadful Night,* by James Thomson. Edinburgh, Canongate Press, 1993.

Translator, *Beowulf.* Aldington, Kent, Hand and Flower Press, 1952; Berkeley, University of California Press, 1962.

Translator, *Poems from Eugenio Montale.* Reading, Berkshire, University of Reading School of Art, 1959.

Translator, *Sovpoems: Brecht, Neruda, Pasternak, Tsvetayeva, Mayakovsky, Martynov, Yevtusheko.* Worcester, Migrant Press, 1961.

Translator with David Wevill, *Sándor Weöres and Ferenc juhász Selected Poems.* London, Penguin, 1970.

Translator, *Wi the Haill Voice: Poems by Mayakovsky.* Oxford, Carcanet, 1972.

Translator, *Fifty Renascence Love-Poems,* edited by Ian Fletcher. Reading, Berkshire, Whiteknights Press, 1975.

Translator, *Selected Poems,* by Platen. West Linton, Peeblesshire, Castlelaw Press, 1978.

Translator, with others, *Eternal Moment: Selected Poems,* by Sándor Weöres. Budapest, Corvina, and London, Anvil Press Poetry, 1988.

Translator, *Attila József: Fragments.* Edinburgh, Morning Star Publications, 1992.

Translator, *Cecilia Vicuna: PALABRARmas.* Edinburgh, Morning Star Publications, 1994.

Translator, *Collected Translations.* Manchester, Carcanet, 1996.

*

Bibliography: *Edwin Morgan: A Selected Bibliography 1950–1980* by Hamish Whyte, Glasgow, Mitchell Library, 1980; *About Edwin Morgan,* edited by Robert Crawford and Hamish Whyte, Edinburgh, Edinburgh University Press, 1990.

Manuscript Collections: Glasgow University Library; Mitchell Library, Glasgow; National Library of Scotland, Edinburgh.

Critical Studies: By Tom Buchan, in *Scottish International* (Edinburgh), August 1968; "Scottish Poets: Edwin Morgan and Iain Crichton Smith," in *Stand* (Newcastle upon Tyne), 10(4), 1969, and *Contemporary Scottish Poetry*, Edinburgh, M. Macdonald, 1974, both by Robin Fulton; *Worlds: Seven Modern Poets,* London, Penguin, 1974; J.A.M. Rillie, in *Lines Review* (Edinburgh), March 1976; *An Introduction to Fifty Modern British Poets* by Michael Schmidt, London, Pan, 1979, as *A Reader's Guide to Fifty Modern British Poets,* London, Heinemann, 1979, New York, Barnes and Noble, 1982; "The Poetry of Edwin Morgan: Translator of Reality," in *Akros* (Nottingham), April 1980, and *Science and Psychodrama: The Poetry of Edwin Morgan and David Black,* Frome, Somerset, Bran's Head, 1982, both by Robin Hamilton; "The Poetry of Edwin Morgan" by R.S. Edgecombe, in *Dalhousie Review* (Halifax, Nova Scotia), 62(4), winter 1982–83; The *Poetry of Edwin Morgan* by Geddes Thomson, Aberdeen, Association for Scottish Literary Studies, 1986; *About Edwin Morgan* edited by Robert Crawford and Hamish Whyte, Edinburgh, University of Edinburgh Press, 1990; "Edwin Morgan: A Celebration," in *Chapman* (Edinburgh), 64, spring/summer 1991; "The Moons of Morgan" by W.N. Herbert, in *Poetry Review* (London), 81(2), autumn 1991; "Mayakovsky in English Translation" by G.M. Hyde, in *Translation & Literature* (Edinburgh), 1, 1992; "New Lang Syne: Sonnets from Scotland and Restructured Time" by Amy Houston, in *Scottish Literary Journal* (Aberdeen), 22(1), May 1995; "Edwin Morgan: Two Interviews," in *Studies in Scottish Literature* (Columbia, South Carolina), 29, 1996, and "Playing Translation with Morgan and MacCaig," in *Forum for Modern Language Studies* (Scotland), 33(1), January 1997, both by Marco Fazzini; "Edwin Morgan: Messages and Transformations" by Roderick Watson, in *British Poetry from the 1950s to the 1990s: Politics and Art,* edited by Gary Day and Brian Docherty, London, Macmillan, and New York, St. Martin's Press, 1997.

*   *   *

"It seems this is a world of change. . ."—the extraterrestrial narrator of "Memories of Earth" speaks also for Edwin Morgan, who aims to reflect a world "continually changing and changing fast" in poems of notable variety. Yet in his first collection, *The Vision of Cathkin Braes,* some persistent features of his work are already apparent. His sense of the comic shows in the title poem, in which a wildly unlikely group—including Salome, John Knox, and Lauren Bacall—end up dancing together. Linguistic playfulness, in which words dance together, is already established in "Verses for a Christmas Card," whose word weldings ("endyir starnacht," "brookrims hoartrack") look back through Joyce and Hopkins to the Anglo-Saxon poets.

Significantly, some translations from the Anglo-Saxon were included in *Dies Irae,* a collection intended to complement *The Vision of Cathkin Braes,* although it remained unpublished until 1982. The loneliness of individuals in alien environments and the destruction of cities are recurring themes in these poems, in "Dies Irae," in the distinctly nuclear apocalypses offered by "Stanzas of the Jeopardy," and in many later poems. But recurrent too is the expression of hopefulness, of faith in humankind's ability to fight on, to continue exploring.

Still largely missing, however, was a sense of the everyday contemporary world in its many aspects. Morgan has suggested that *The Cape of Good Hope* dealt with but did not resolve "the dilemma of the . . . solitary creator and his . . . involvement with humanity." The resolution began with the so-called Glasgow poems, started around 1962–63 and appearing in *The Second Life* (1968). These poems may record moments of pure observation ("Linoleum Chocolate") or events of more personal involvement ("In the Snack-Bar"). They may be celebratory ("Trio"), partly comic ("The Starlings in George Square"), or verging on nightmare, as in "Glasgow Green": "Cut the scene. / Here there's no crying for help, / it must be acted out, again, again."

A series of love poems, adumbrated in the title poem and beginning perhaps in "The Unspoken," share a simplicity of language with the Glasgow poems; they move from joy to sadness to something more somber. But most distinctively new in *The Second Life, Emergent Poems,* and *Gnomes* are the concrete and related poems. One aim of concrete poetry, simultaneity, is attained in the single line of "Siesta of a Hungarian Snake," while other possibilities are explored in "The Chaffinch Map of Scotland," with its strongly kinetic effect, and the playful permutations of "The Computer's First Christmas Card." Related, but more serious, are the variations in "Opening the Cage" on John Cage's "I have nothing to say and I am saying it and that is poetry," including, for instance, "It is and I am and I have poetry saying say that to nothing." Such work is not, as has been suggested, "necessarily slight," as "Message Clear," one of the "emergent poems," shows. The poem's last line—

i am the resurrection and the life

—gradually emerges from the statements that can be extracted from it, such as

i am he   r   e
i am   ren   t

Morgan's belief that poets today should be more concerned with science and technology, especially space exploration, is confirmed by several poems. Yet "In Sobieski's Shield," with its Beckett-like

ending, ". . . it's hard / to go let's go," and "From the Domain of Arnheim," stressing courage, are as close to Anglo-Saxon poems as to science fiction. *Instamatic Poems* presents life through events, often bizarre or macabre, culled from newspapers. They are written in a style of apparent objectivity but often have a sharp, if barely stated, comment. The poems in the supplementary collection *Takes* have a more relaxed, more overtly authorial tone.

From Glasgow to Saturn is as wide-ranging as the title suggests. Morgan has stated that many of his poems are really dramatic monologues. Here they include attempts "to get *everything* speaking," whether an animal, an object ("The Apple's Song"), or the (perhaps) mythical ("The Loch Ness Monster's Song"). Playfulness ("Itinerary") and apocalypse ("Last Message") find many forms; love poems express estrangement and loss. A single poem, "London," for example, may move from memories, dreams, and collage to direct observation and comment, and the powerful concluding group approaches its Glasgow themes through the phantasmagoric, direct, and satiric.

This diversity is carried forward by *The New Divan* and *Star Gate,* where clichés and proverbs are multiplied dreadfully in "The Clone Poem." Dunbar is updated in "A Good Year for Death," and "emergent" poems become divergent in "Lévi-Strauss at the Lie-Detector," where "any classification is superior to chaos" yields "any class fiction is superior chaos." With Morgan travel in space or time tends to return us to the present, so that "Memories of Earth" finally celebrates "ordinary fortitude." *The New Divan,* a sequence of one hundred short poems dedicated to Hafiz, is related both to the world of the Persian poet and to the Middle East of Morgan's war service.

There are moments in this sequence that may remind us of Stevens. Morgan has consistently shown (and acknowledged) an awareness of the American modernist tradition from Whitman through Williams, Olson, Creeley, and Ginsberg to Ashbery. Yet his work is unlike that of any similarly aware English poet. His Scottishness has provided another tradition, that of Dunbar, Burns, and MacDiarmid. He has supplemented this by looking abroad, in his considerable work as a translator, to such different talents as Mayakovsky, Michaux, Gomringer, Leopardi, and Attila József.

Morgan's versatility has continued to be shown in poem sequences and separate poems. The "Grafts" in *Grafts/Takes* "are based," Morgan explains, "on fragments from abandoned poems by Michael Schmidt"—fragments that have acted as the stimuli for new and distinctive poems. A collaboration with Peter McCarey resulted in the "reconstructing" of "some fairly well-known poems." Thus, Stevens joins Shakespeare in "Not Marble: A Reconstruction": "A Sqezy bottle in Tennessee / if you want permanence, will press / a dozen jars into the wilderness." *Newspoems* represents an unwitting collaboration by "newspapers and other ephemeral material" Morgan creatively misread, finding unintended messages that he cut out and pasted down. In an austere, more minimal way, the poems parallel Tom Phillips's *A Humament.* "What results," Morgan writes, "is a series of 'inventions,' both in the old sense of 'things found' and in the more usual sense of 'things devised.'"

One device Morgan uses to generate poems is the list, as in "Nineteen Kinds of Barley," "A Trace of Wings" (a tribute to Basil Bunting), and, notably, "An Alphabet of Goddesses." In these works the range of moods and styles matches the titular subjects, from the breezy couplets of "Queen Alcyone" to the somber chanting of "Lethe" to the terrible self-referring riddle of "Sphinx." They are poems that, again, refer us to the present: ". . . why is it easier for a rich man to ride his camel into heaven than for three million unemployed to pass through the eye of a needle . . . ?" A classic formal device is used in *Sonnets from Scotland* to alternate comic invention ("Outward Bound"), apocalypse ("The Target"), and visions of some remote past or desolate future ("The Age of Heracleum") with poems referring to figures such as James Hutton, the prophet of continual geological change ("Theory of the Earth"), or presenting haunting inventions ("The Mirror": "It hangs in time and not in space").

"Right to Reply," in *From the Video Box,* is strangely inventive even though it is derived from the television series. The programs to which the video responses are given include the burning of the library at Alexandria, the world jigsaw final, "a programme for the colour-blind" (who alone saw something special), or "Giotto's O": ". . . the great / final ease of creation." The responses, on the other hand, may be of comic outrage, total irrelevance (an awfully nice person who has lost their cat), or, chillingly, the fragmentary voice of James Hogg's Justified Sinner.

Here and elsewhere Morgan is close to the surrealist tradition and to the practice of making the familiar strange, the Russian formalists' *ostranenie,* as in such short poems as "The Bear," which sees *The Winter's Tale* from the bear's viewpoint. Yet the move is toward renewed clarity, freshness of vision, and the acceptance of everyday life, including the "blessed trivia that keep us from dying." A group of poems in *Themes on a Variation* continues the exploration of intensely personal themes of love and relationship, and the third section of one of them, "Stanzas," addresses a crucial problem: "To be simple, to be clear, to be true— / the sweat and cost of it are surely such / that all must shut up shop." "Waking on a Dark Morning" tracks an emergence from an almost anonymous dream or nightmare to a positive awareness and decision: "It was an early bus that wakened me / . . . The night never wanted me to speak, did it? / But speak we will, and clearly too . . ."

The emphasis on clarity is present, though with somber under-tones, at the end of "Epilogue: Seven Decades" in the 1990 *Collected Poems:* "I want to catch whatever light is there / in full sight." The title of the 1994 book of poems and translations, *Sweeping out the Dark,* suggests, if ambivalently, a shift of emphasis. It refers most directly to the last section ("The Synthesis") of "Trajectory (Six Sonnets)": "Hell can be ahead. / In backstreet Naples, under her living cliff, / a woman vigorously sweeps out the dark." The parallel trajectories are of a spaceflight and a more earthly seeming revolution. The downfall of the communist regimes in Eastern Europe and the possible consequences are the concern of several poems, "A Warning" being one of the most direct: "Take your string bag. An orange / will appear by magic, steaks, heroin, tickets / for strippers." Elsewhere, in "A Chapter," people who had achieved "social justice" found themselves afflicted by a "malaise" that their "well-kept houses, / the well-swept streets and unpolluted highways, / . . . graffiti / buried under harmonies of paintwork" could not assuage. Perhaps, as the next poem, "A Change," seems to suggest, what they lacked was something disorderly, dishevelled, "boisterous," which a group of unidentified journeying people bring to the city.

The darkness of wars, violence, and oppression is not swept away but rather into the light in such poems as "An Elegy," "Urban Gunfire," and "Whistling," while "the lighter darkness that confounds us / the twilight of not knowing . . . / . . . the slow precipitate of phantoms" are the subject of "Twilights." But it is notable that the voice heard in "Waking on a Dark Morning" finds an answering voice in "Persuasion"—"You never thought much of the darkness,

did you?"—suggesting that love can be "tender still to backcourts and dim woodlands." This acceptance of and giving expression to another view of what "darkness" can mean typify Morgan's openness, his readiness to engage with many possibilities and experiences, ranging from the significance of memories and past moments in "Tram-Ride, 1939 (F.M.)" or "Hands On, 1937" through personal or harshly public themes to such "particulars" as, for instance, observing and praising magpies: ". . . and this page, seeing / these things, first white, now white and black, to pay its / tribute to, and lay out, thus, its pleasure" ("A Defence"). In an interview Morgan has said that, in relation to the possibilities of virtual reality for poetry, "I'm very attracted to the idea of the poet as explorer, undergoing a quest . . . maybe many quests ultimately cohering." For Morgan this involves acceptance of ". . . that / mass of change and chance and challenge" ("A Particular Country"), encounter and celebration, and the readiness to be surprised and to surprise.

—Geoffrey Soar

MORGAN, (George) Frederick

Nationality: American. **Born:** New York City, 25 April 1922. **Education:** St. Bernard's School, New York, 1927–35; St. Paul's School, Concord, New Hampshire, 1935–39; Princeton University, New Jersey, 1939–43, A.B. 1943. **Military Service:** U.S. Army Tank Destroyer Corps, 1943–45: Staff Sergeant. **Family:** Married 1) Constance Canfield in 1942 (divorced 1957), six children (two deceased); 2) Rose Fillmore in 1957 (divorced 1969); 3) Paula Deitz in 1969. **Career:** Founder, with Joseph Bennett and William Arrowsmith, and since 1947 editor, *The Hudson Review,* New York; chair of the advisory council, Department of Romance Languages and Literatures, Princeton University, 1973–90. **Awards:** Chevalier de l'Orde des Arts et des Lettres (France), 1984. **Address:** c/o *The Hudson Review,* 684 Park Avenue, New York, New York 10021, U.S.A.

PUBLICATIONS

Poetry

A Book of Change. New York, Scribner, 1972.
Poems of the Two Worlds. Urbana, University of Illinois Press, 1977.
Death Mother and Other Poems. Urbana, University of Illinois Press, 1979.
The River. New York, Nadja, 1980.
Refractions (translations). Omaha, Nebraska, Abattoir, 1981.
Northbook. Urbana, University of Illinois Press, 1982.
Eleven Poems. New York, Nadja, 1983.
Poems, New and Selected. Urbana, University of Illinois Press, 1987.
Poems for Paula. Ashland, Oregon, Story Line Press, 1995.

Other

The Tarot of Cornelius Agrippa. Sand Lake, New York, Sagarin Press, 1978.
The Fountain and Other Fables. Cumberland, Iowa, Pterodactyl Press, 1985.

Editor, *The Hudson Review Anthology.* New York, Random House 1961.

Editor, *The Modern Image: Outstanding Stories from "The Hudson Review."* New York, Norton, 1965.

Translator, *Seven Poems,* by Mallarmé. New York, Christopher Wilmarth, 1981.

Translator, *Refractions.* Omaha, Nebraska, Abattoir, 1981.

*

Critical Studies: "The Shocks of Normality" by Laurence Lieberman, in *Yale Review* (New Haven, Connecticut), spring 1974; "The Poetry of Frederick Morgan" by Hayden Carruth, in *New Republic* (Washington, D.C.), 15 May 1976; "Poet's View" by Thomas Lask, in *New York Times,* 15 April 1977; Chad Walsh, in *Washington Post,* 22 May 1977; "Recent American Poetry" by Andrew Waterman, in *PN Review 8* (Manchester), 1978; interview in *New England Review* (Hanover, New Hampshire), spring 1979; "Frederick Morgan's 'Tarot'" by Sydney Lea, in *Southern Review* (Baton Rouge, Louisiana), autumn 1979; "To Articulate Sweet Sounds Together" by Alfred Corn, in *Washington Post Book World,* 2 March 1980; James Finn Cotter, in *America* (New York), 22 March 1980; "Mother of Pain, Mother of Beauty" and untitled article, both by David Sanders, in *Tar River Poetry* (Greenville, North Carolina), spring 1980 and spring 1983; "Poems of Imagination and Fancy" by Richard Tillinghast, in *Sewanee Review* (Tennessee), summer 1980; "Three Poets in Mid-Career" by Dana Gioia, in *Southern Review* (Baton Rouge, Louisiana), summer 1981; in *The Reaper 6* (Evansville, Indiana), autumn 1982; C.B. Cox, in *Critical Quarterly* (Manchester), winter 1982; "Arms and the Muse" by Emily Grosholz, in *New England Review/Bread Loaf Quarterly* (Middlebury, Vermont), summer 1983; "Struck by Lightning: Four Distinct Modern Voices" by G.E. Murray, in *Michigan Quarterly Review* (Ann Arbor), autumn 1983; "Myth, Poetry, and Superstition" and "Varieties of Poetic Experience," both by Jerome Mazzaro, in *Sewanee Review* (Tennessee), winter 1984 and winter 1988; "Recovering Pieces of the Morgenland" by Robert Schultz, in *Virginia Quarterly Review* (Charlottesville), winter 1988; "Between Decorum and Abandon" by Robert Richman, in *New Criterion* (New York), February 1989; "Voyage to an Inner Day" by Daniel Hoffman, in *Southern Review* (Baton Rouge, Louisiana), winter 1989; interview with Frederick Morgan by Michael Peich, in *Hudson Review,* 51(2), 1998.

*   *   *

Of the various strains in Frederick Morgan's poetry, two predominate: the legendary-fabulous and the celebratory-consolatory. In addition, he has a number of fanciful and whimsical poems, personal poems in various modes—nostalgic memories, grateful love songs to his wife, companionable conversations with children—and thoughtful poems that explore the natural world and man's place in it.

In its purest form the legendary-fabulous is the mode of *The Tarot of Cornelius Agrippa,* a set of twenty-two short fables of rogues, sorceresses, magicians, kings, queens, princesses, and other animate and inanimate denizens of fairyland and the tarot pack. The fables are cast as prose poems, but they are in very loose rhythms and the unsophisticated language of children's stories. Indeed, Morgan's images for the imaginative and religious projections of adult sensibility often have the simplicity and naïveté of a child's vision:

> Child, you will die; but between that breath and this—
> now at this moment, unless you put her off—
> eternity outspreads her glittering fields
> where animals play and rivers dance in the sun:
> mostly invisible to the time-bent mind . . .

The twenty-first poem of A *Book of Change,* from which these lines are taken, is in what I am calling the celebratory-consolatory mode. In such poems Morgan is engaged with deep emotional and spiritual issues, here the paradise within, informed by the "glowing, sacred center." Further, he is committed to sharing his insights into life, death, love, time, a spiritualized natural world, eternity, and God in the commendable hope that such insights will help us with our perplexities and sorrows. Given his personal losses, he might well say with Walt Whitman, "I am the man, I suffer'd, I was there," and with D.H. Lawrence, "Look! We have come through!"

Many of these poems, however, seem to be conceived less as art than as communication, as ways of sharing joys and sorrows, of stating opinions and attitudes, of asserting faith, hope, and charity (or sexual love). An instructive comparison could be made, for example, between the glittering generalities of the passage just quoted and the poetically charged specifics of the analogous section in William Carlos Williams's "Asphodel, That Greeny Flower," where, in the opening of the "Coda," Williams meditates strenuously on the "huge gap / between the flash / and the thunderstroke." Of course Morgan cannot be faulted for not being Williams. It is just that, given the worth of the enterprise, one hopes for more of the poetic development manifested between his first and second books.

One cluster in particular in *Poems of the Two Worlds*—"The Old Days," "The Priest," "Hideyoshi," and "Maitreya"—has a spare clarity and evocativeness that demonstrate Morgan's mastery of his medium. "Hideyoshi," certainly one of Morgan's best poems, performs the unusual feat of making believable a character in whom love of violence and love of beauty are integrated in the interests of justice and spiritual wholeness. On the one hand, the Japanese warrior-hero of the poem cuts his enemy to pieces; on the other, he makes a flower arrangement out of emblems of war:

> So he took a bucket, and his horse's bit
> (which he hung by one ring from the bucket-handle)
> and rigged them into a flower-holder,
>
> then with his bloody sword
> cut wild blossoms and grasses
> and in an hour's silence
> composed a subtle and delicate combination . . .
>
> Those whom he had conquered
> he now must judge:
> he wished a mind clean-purged
> of violence and ardor.

The effect is rather as if one of Yeats's bitter and violent men who "longed" for "sweetness . . . night and day" ("Ancestral Houses") had somehow, on Morgan's page, completed himself.

—Sally M. Gall

MORGAN, (Colin) Pete(r)

Nationality: British. **Born:** Leigh, Lancashire, 7 June 1939. **Education:** Normanton School, Buxton, Derbyshire, 1950–57. **Military Service:** British Army Infantry, 1958–63. **Family:** Married Kate Smith in 1965; one daughter and one son. **Career:** Freelance writer: creative writing appointments for Northern Arts, and at Loughborough University, 1975–77; also a television writer; member of literature panel of Yorkshire Arts, 1973–76, and Northern Arts. **Awards:** Scottish Arts Council bursary, 1969; Arts Council of Great Britain award, 1973. **Agent:** David Higham Associates, 5–8 Lower John Street, London WlR 4HA. **Address:** Moorsams House, Tommy Baxter Street, Robin Hood's Bay, North Yorkshire, England.

PUBLICATIONS

Poetry

A Big Hat or What? Edinburgh, Kevin Press, 1968.
Loss of Two Anchors. Edinburgh, Kevin Press, 1970.
Poems for Shortie. Solihull, Warwickshire, Aquila, 1973.
The Grey Mare Being the Better Steed. London, Secker and Warburg, 1973.
I See You on My Arm. Todmorden, Lancashire, Arc, 1975.
Ring Song. Gulfport, Florida, Konglomerati, 1977.
The Poet's Deaths. Manchester, North West Arts, 1977.
Alpha Beta. Ilkley, Yorkshire, Scolar Press, 1979.
The Spring Collection. London, Secker and Warburg, 1979.
One Greek Alphabet. Sunderland, Ceolfrith, 1980.
Reporting Back. Leamington, Warwickshire, Other Branch, 1983.
A Winter Visitor. London, Secker and Warburg, 1984.
The Pete Morgan Poetry Pack. Ilkley, Yorkshire, Proem, 1984.

Plays

Still the Same Old Harry (produced Edinburgh, 1972).
All the Voices Going Away (produced Ilkley, Yorkshire, 1979).

Screenplay (documentary): *Gardens by the Sea,* 1973.

Television Documentaries: *Coming On Strong* series, 1974; *Here Comes Everybody* series, 1975; *Between the Heather and the Sea,* 1982; *A Voyage Between Two Seas,* 1983.

Other

The Yorkshire Ridings, paintings by John Tookey. London, Gordon Fraser, 1987.

Editor, *C'mon Everybody: Poetry of the Dance.* London, Corgi, 1969.

*   *   *

The first words in Pete Morgan's introduction to his anthology *C'mon Everybody: Poetry of the Dance* are "Plato said it—'The dance is god-like in itself. It is a gift from heaven.'" These words also describe Morgan's poetry at its best. As his poems bound along, or dance, with effortless ease and as they present their innocent pictures of knights, stallions, "the bull with the rumpus horn," and my Moll and partner Joe, the impression is of something given, not made. His poems seem to be immediately original without any special seeking after difference, yet their origins are evident. They begin in the world of nursery rhymes, which have a known audience they captivate. Morgan's poems also have an audience, or rather many audiences, which respond to his excellent readings. Some of the poems are well suited for ballad-style music settings. Yet, despite the immediacy of communication and the surface simplicity of the poems, beneath is a psychological curiosity and a sharpness of perception that reveal that the poet has not sold out his intelligence.

"The White Stallion" begins with

> There was that horse
>   that I found then
>   my white one
> big tall and lean as
>   and mean as hell

The supple movement, the momentary halt in the penultimate line, and the unexpected drive of the last line is the work of a craftsman who has learned from, among others, Auden, though the last poems of Yeats have also been caught in Morgan's ear to his advantage. More significant perhaps is the use he makes of the commonplace "mean as hell." He rejoices in the lively vernacular phrase. There is so much delight in his first book, *A Big Hat or What?,* in such poems as "My Moll and Partner Joe," "Whoops! I nearly smiled again," "Elegy for Arthur Prance," and "My enemies have sweet voices," that the subtle tones and undertones may not be regarded.

By the mid-1970s a different poet, taking off directly from his physical environment, emerges to culminate in the singular appreciation of the life about him in "A Winter Visitor." The high style has been replaced by a reflective, conversational voice: "The first thin snow of winter / Settles our differences / And that's what's good about it." This is the norm in which Morgan takes account of Robin Hood Bay, its history and geology, a few of its people, and happenings such as the birth of a calf:

> There's nothing giving! At her rump
> The folds of skin are bloody, raw.
> Her calf, still pinioned in that trap,
> Sticks out a thick tongue, clears a snout
>
> That sniffs and learns the smell of May.
> Already ancient though not born
> The brown eyes—wide intelligent—
> Look into mine for something more
>
> Than I can ever give to him.
> Then like a curded milk he comes—
> A slabby from a bottle' neck
> Shuddering across the floor.

Despite the absorption into the intimate sensations of the birth, Morgan can still suggest the more detached, professional character of Shillah:

> I start the engine, drive away,
> Bucking on the ruts of earth,
> From Shillah picking petty faults
> With what looked marvellous to me.

There is a scrupulous honesty in Morgan's dealing with the facts. The continuity of nature is projected against the precariousness of human life: "We need to know just where we stand, what odds / Are stacked against us by which gods." His work ultimately shows respect and affection for the natural world and for its people, including his son, whom he teaches not to bring down the conkers from the chestnut tree with sticks but to wait for a "garnering and gathering":

> From that ripe minute when they fell
> Into my son's good sight and he
> Comes singing home
> From gentle harvesting.

This is an impressive achievement and a very taking one.

—George Bruce

MORGAN, Robert

Nationality: American. **Born:** Hendersonville, North Carolina, 3 October 1944. **Education:** Emory College, Oxford, 1961–62; North Carolina State University, Raleigh, 1962–63; University of North Carolina, Chapel Hill, 1963–66, B.A. 1965; University of North Carolina, Greensboro, 1967–68, M.F.A. 1968. **Family:** Married Nancy K. Bullock in 1965; one son and two daughters. **Career:** Teaching assistant, University of North Carolina, Greensboro, 1967–68; instructor, Salem College, Winston-Salem, North Carolina, 1968–69; lecturer, 1971–73, assistant professor, 1973–78, associate professor, 1978–84, professor, 1982–92, and since 1992 Kappa Alpha Professor of English, Cornell University, Ithaca, New York. McGee Visiting Writer, Davidson College, 1998. **Awards:** National Endowment for the Arts fellowships, 1968, 1974, 1981, 1987; Southern Poetry Review prize, 1975; Eunice Tietjens award, 1979; Jacaranda Review fiction prize, 1988; Guggenheim fellowship, 1988–89; Amon Liner prize, 1989; James G. Hanes Poetry prize, 1991; North Carolina award in literature, 1991. **Address:** Department of English, Goldwin Smith Hall, Cornell University, Ithaca. New York 14853, U.S.A.

PUBLICATIONS

Poetry

Zirconia Poems. Northwood Narrows, New Hampshire, Lillabulero Press, 1969.
The Voice in the Crosshairs. Ithaca, New York, Angelfish Press, 1971.
Red Owl. New York, Norton, 1972.
Land Diving. Baton Rouge, Louisiana State University Press, 1976.
Trunk & Thicket. Fort Collins, Colorado, L'Epervier Press, 1978.
Groundwork. Frankfort, Kentucky, Gnomon Press, 1979.
Bronze Age. Emory, Virginia, Iron Mountain Press, 1981.
At the Edge of the Orchard Country. Middletown, Connecticut, Wesleyan University Press, 1987.
Sigodlin. Middletown, Connecticut, Wesleyan University Press, 1990.
Green River: New and Selected Poems. Hanover, New Hampshire, University Press of New England, 1991.

Wild Peavines: New Poems. Frankfort, Kentucky, Gnomon Press, 1996.
Topsoil Road: Poems. Baton Rouge, Louisiana State University Press, 2000.

Short Stories

The Blue Valleys: A Collection of Stories. Atlanta, Georgia, Peachtree, 1989.
The Mountains Won't Remember Us and Other Stories. Atlanta, Georgia, Peachtree, 1992.
The Hinterlands: A Mountain Tale in Three Parts. Chapel Hill, North Carolina, Algonquin, 1994.
The Truest Pleasure. Chapel Hill, North Carolina, Algonquin, 1995.
Gap Creek. Chapel Hill, North Carolina, Algonquin, 1999.
The Balm of Gilead Tree and Other Stories. Frankfort, Kentucky, Gnomon Press, 1999.

Other

Good Measure: Essays, Interviews and Notes on Poetry. Baton Rouge, Louisiana State University Press, 1993.

*

Bibliography: "Robert Morgan: A Bibliographical Chronicle, 1963–1981" by Stuart Wright, in *Bulletin of Bibliography* (Westport, Connecticut), 39(3).

Manuscript Collections: Emory University, Atlanta, Georgia; University of North Carolina, Chapel Hill.

Critical Studies: "*Land Diving*" by William Matthews, in *Meridian* (New York), 1980; "Robert Morgan's Pellagian Georgics: Twelve Essays" by William Harmon, in *Parnassus* (New York), fall/winter 1981; "A Conversation with Robert Morgan" by Suzanne Booker, in *Carolina Quarterly* (Chapel Hill, North Carolina), spring 1985; "Recovering Pieces of the Morgenland" by Robert Schultz, in *Virginia Quarterly Review* (Charlottesville), winter 1988; "*At the Edge of the Orchard Country*" by Ted Kooser, in *Prairie Schooner* (Lincoln, Nebraska), summer 1989; chapter in *Looking for Native Ground: Contemporary Appalachian Poetry* by Rita Sims Quillen, Boone, North Carolina, Appalachian Consortium Press, 1989; "Pieces of the Morgenland: The Recent Achievements in Robert Morgan's Poetry" by P.H. Liotta, in *Southern Literary Journal* (Chapel Hill, North Carolina), spring 1990; Robert Morgan issue of *The Iron Mountain Review,* summer 1990; "Coming Out from under Calvinism: Religious Motifs in Robert Morgan's Poetry," in *Shenandoah* (Lexington, Virginia), summer 1992, and "He Hoes Forever: Robert Morgan and the Pleasure of Work," *Pembroke* (Pembroke, North Carolina), March 1999, both by John Lang; *Robert Morgan and the American Romantic Tradition* (dissertation) by Suzanne R. Booker-Canfield, Greensboro, University of North Carolina, 1998.

Robert Morgan comments:
Since I was in college I have been writing both poetry and fiction, but all my first seven books were volumes of poetry. Like many of the poets of the 1960s, I began writing in open forms and only started experimenting with rhyme and traditional form in the mid 1970s. Many of my poems have been concerned with the Blue Ridge

Mountains of North Carolina, where I grew up, but I have also written about American history, upstate New York, where I have lived since 1971, the sciences, and about family stories and characters. I especially like to write about machines and gadgets.

No one has yet discovered a culture without poetry. Language itself was probably a discovery of the poetic imagination and only later put to use for practical ends, as pure mathematics can be used for physical description and problem solving. And while it is true poetry is a medium of the gut as well as the mind, it is also true poetry is rarely just a secular art. The subject of most poems is rediscovery of spiritual desire. Poems work by stirring memory, by unexpected connections, accuracy of naming, delight in wordplay. And the music of poetry comes as much from the quickness of what is said as from the pattern of syllables.

When I was about fifteen, I wanted to write some epic work, poem, or musical composition, as grand as the Cicero Mountain across the river from our house. But later, as I actually began writing verse, I became more interested in compression, indirection, in the use of simple language to embody complex experience. My ideal was to write poetry accessible to everyone but tough enough, and rich enough, to reveal something on each successive reading. That is an ideal I am still working toward.

*   *   *

In a period when disconnection, disaffection, and disaffiliation seem the coin of the poetry realm, it is a pleasure to read a poet as connected as Robert Morgan. His poetry is connected to a particular place, the Blue Ridge Mountains of his native North Carolina, and it explores his ties to the people of that region, to generations of family, to the earth and natural process, to animals, plants, and things, to the historic, prehistoric, and geological past. His poems, as well as his stories, reflect the strengths of these deep connections, this rootedness. Together with his fine sense of craft, his allegiance to his native area gives his writing a quiet power and universality.

The titles of Morgan's collections, along with several luminous lines and images, signal his allegiances. *At the Edge of the Orchard Country* reveals a regional tie but implies a universe beyond; *Groundwork* suggests the native soil that he works, even mines; the title poem of *Land Diving* dramatizes an important Morgan principle: "The meaning is the closeness"; the concrete *Trunk & Thicket* includes a telling prose memoir titled "Homecoming"; and *Red Owl* contains the short poem "New-Plowed Ground" that features an apt metaphor for Morgan's poetics: "You can't navigate without / getting dirt in your shoes."

In the essay "The Cubist of Memory" Morgan claims that as a southern poet he decided to reject Faulknerian rhetoric and "go off in an unknown direction . . . toward plainness, compactness, simplicity . . . . To help free myself from myself—from ego, ambition, self-consciousness—to get on with the work, I tried to be true to objects, and to the verbal objects that measured and enacted world and thought." In many of his poems, especially those collected in *At the Edge of the Orchard Country* and *Sigodlin,* he does indeed achieve a southern lushness of detail, tempered by what one might ordinarily consider a Midwestern reserve and plainness of language. In these poems there is a balance between the concrete and the abstract, the romantic and the classical, the scientific and the literary, the head and the heart. His poem about a treaty with the Cherokees, "Ninety-Six Line," ends with an image of Morgan poised standing in different worlds: "I grew up," he says, "with one foot in the English / country,

one in the high dark / hunting ranges, and felt a chill / when stepping across to either / imaginary dominion."

It is hard to think of a contemporary American poet with a deeper sense of family ties, customs, and lore than Morgan. The ordinary, everyday rural objects he looks upon constantly reveal traces and residues of former lives. He loves to tell the stories, some eccentric, that open up the lives of parents, cousins, aunts and uncles, grandparents, and great-grandparents. He is haunted by the uncle, after whom he was named, who died in England in World War II. One of his best poems, "White Autumn," a classic "portrait" poem, celebrates the life and world of his matriarchal great-grandmother. Morgan's loving detail brings to life not only the individual woman but also several generations of family, the history of a region, and layers of the collective past. We see the matriarch rocking in her chair on her mountain porch: "The cats passed through her lap and legs / and through the rungs of her seat," as "she rode that upright cradle to sleep / and through many long visits with tiers of family, / kissing the babies like different kinds of fruit." We can see the independent, strong-hearted leader of the clan "bath[ing] / in a warm river of books and black coffee." Like any fine poet, Morgan makes us enter into many lives by taking us within one individual life deeply lived: "On that creaking throne she ruled a tiny kingdom / through war, death of kin." Kinship is Morgan's major theme and deepest metaphor.

—Norbert Krapf

MORITZ, A(lbert) F(rank)

Also writes as Albert Moritz, Albert F. Moritz, or Al Moritz.
Nationality: American (naturalized Canadian citizen since 1994).
Born: Warren, Ohio, 15 April 1947. **Education:** Marquette University, Milwaukee, Wisconsin, 1965–75, B.A. 1969, M.A. 1971, Ph.D. 1975. **Family:** Married Theresa Carrothers in 1969; one son. **Career:** Since 1975 professor of English. **Awards:** Canada Council grant, 1982, 1983, 1986, 1992, 1994, 1999; Ingram Merrill Foundation fellowship, 1982; John Simon Guggenheim Foundation fellowship, 1990; literature award, American Academy and Institute of Arts and Letters, 1991; Ontario Arts Council Works-in-Progress grant, 1999. **Address:** 14 Alpha Avenue, Toronto, Ontario M4X 1J3, Canada.

PUBLICATIONS

Poetry

Here. Portland, Maine, Contraband Press, 1975.
Black Orchid. Toronto, Dreadnaught Press, 1981.
Between the Root and the Flower. Vancouver, Blackfish Press, 1982.
The Visitation. Toronto, Aya Press, 1983.
The Tradition. Princeton, New Jersey, Princeton University Press, 1986.
Song of Fear. London, Ontario, Brick Books, 1992.
Ciudad Interior. Zacatecas, Mexico, Universidad Autonóma de Zacatecas, 1993.
The Ruined Cottage. Toronto, Wolsak and Wynn, 1993.
Phantoms in the Ark. Vancouver, Ronsdale Press, 1994.
Mahoning. London, Ontario, Brick Books, 1994.
A Houseboat on the Styx. Victoria, British Columbia, Ekstasis Editions, 1998.

Rest on the Flight into Egypt. London, Ontario, Brick Books, 1999.
The End of the Age. Toronto, Watershed Books, 2000.

Other

Canada Illustrated. Toronto, Methuen Canada, 1982.
The Pocket Canada: A Complete Guide to the World's Second-Largest Country, with Theresa Moritz. Toronto, Van Nostrand Reinhold, 1982.
America the Picturesque. New York, Dodd, Mead and Company, 1983.
Leacock: A Biography, with Theresa Moritz. Toronto, Stoddart, 1985.
The Oxford Illustrated Literary Guide to Canada, with Theresa Moritz. Toronto, Oxford University Press, 1987.
Stephen Leacock: A Remarkable Life, with Theresa Moritz. Toronto, Fitzhenry and Whiteside, 2000.
The Most Dangerous Woman in the World: A New Biography of Emma Goldman, with Theresa Moritz. Toronto, Subway Books/ University of Toronto Press, 2000.

Translator, with Jane Barnard, *Children of the Quadrilateral: Selected Poems of Benjamin Péret.* Syracuse, New York, Bitter Oleander Press, 1976.

Translator, with others, *Ludwig Zeller in the Country of the Antipodes: Poems 1964–79.* Toronto, Mosaic Press, 1979.

Translator, with Theresa Moritz, *Testament for Man,* by Gilberto Meza. Toronto, Dreadnaught Press, 1982.

Translator, with Beatriz Zeller, *The Marble Head,* by Ludwig Zeller. Toronto, Mosaic Press, 1986.

Translator, with Beatriz Zeller, *The Ghost's Tattoos,* by Ludwig Zeller. Toronto, Mosaic Press, 1989.

Translator, with Theresa Moritz, *Body of Insomnia,* by Ludwig Zeller. Vancouver, Ekstasis Editions, 1996.

Translator, with Theresa Moritz, *Rio Loa: Station of Dreams,* by Ludwig Zeller. Toronto, Mosaic Press, 1999.

*

Critical Studies: In *Canadian Literature,* 131, winter 1991; *Commoneal* (New York), CXIX(19), 6 November 1992.

A.F. Moritz comments:

For me poetry is a mode of knowledge and a mode of participation, uniting these two things that often seem at odds. Its knowledge and participation are often obscure, conflicted, grasped more in faith and hope or mute going on than in fulfillment, while it registers and sings our actual ignorance and the shortcomings of our experience of nature, self, and society. This struggle, inward and outward, makes it impossible for poetry to be complacent and complaisant, necessary for it to be dynamic and gracious. I do not forget though that talk of participation and knowledge can be a self-benediction of the poet on grounds of generosity. Poetry is generous, but it is also pure self-delighting play of the self with its powers, and it is also craft, skilled shaping that seems to stand outside words and meaning and handle them with wholly unintellectual absorption. The pursuit of knowledge and participation, the investigation of their forms in the troubling here and now, the encounter between passion and duty, the demand for a perfect and living form are always together in poetry. It

leads toward the complete imagination in our own voice, where there are no gulfs between the world longed for, the world of longing, and this world. It led me to anarchist and metaphysical wantings, for justice and mercy. It led me to want above all to write a song like "'Twas on a Holy Thursday," "Michael," "Now sleeps the crimson petal," "When Lilacs Last in the Dooryard Bloom'd," or any of those of Trakl, Vallejo, Jiménez, Celan, Breton, Seferis, Quasimodo, Ungaretti, Montale, Artaud, Césaire, and many others, so many that it is wrong to name a few. I remember one summer Byron teaching me to scorn everything and William Carlos Williams teaching me to love everything with the same gust, and an earlier summer memorizing *Hamlet* and Virgil, and a still earlier summer, almost the earliest, gulping at what Isaiah had sung of the identity of failure and triumph. I would like to repeat, and solve, and remake that in my own way, as did Paz and Ritsos and Bonnefoy.

*   *   *

A.F. Moritz is active as an occasional university lecturer, creative writing instructor, cultural journalist, literary translator, and dedicated poet. Common to these activities is a respect for the spoken and written word. It could be said that Moritz and language are inseparable and that for him and his readers the world of words has replaced the real or everyday world. In *The Oxford Companion to Canadian Literature* Geoff Hancock states that Moritz is "in the tradition of the Romantics. His poems are often philosophically dense meditations on visionary states in a nature increasingly threatened by the mechanical world." That is as true as far as it goes. More likely, Moritz is not so much a nineteenth-century romantic as he is a pre-Socratic (or post-Sartrean) philosopher who postulates the principles of a whole new order of reality independent of the world as we know it.

This is a somewhat daunting task, never explicitly addressed in any one poem. Instead there is the evidence of the practice. "Loneliness," one of Moritz's earliest poems from the chapbook *Water Follies* (1978), includes lines like these: "The desertion of women composes / the black refrigerator without walls." The bland statement and the range of reference with no appeal to common sense suggest that the poet is really a surrealist. It is safe to say that surrealism is one of the motors of Moritz's writings. Image follows image in splendid array. Moritz has translated from the Spanish many volumes of the surreal poetry and prose of the Chilean-born writer and artist Ludwig Zeller.

If surrealism is one influence on the work of Moritz, philosophy is another. His poetry is an endeavor to express in words a different world order. The undertaking does not take the form of acts of charity, feelings of love, or delight in incident. It takes the form of disquisitions on metamorphoses. The collection *Black Orchid* (1981) includes an afterword in which the poet writes, "The word manifests our situation, to ourselves, and afterward to others, and in poetry the word most nearly approaches its own reality. A poem, once created, stands before us as an enigmatic being which reveals that expression is a phenomenon of presence: its nature is not so much informative as sacramental."

The esthetic approach to transfiguration finds expression in the title poem of the collection:

The fountain raises its head
and with water's passionate vengeance
loses all
to color the dry rock with these flowers.

Although Moritz seldom writes about himself directly (the first-person singular is largely absent), he does so in "Memories of a Small Town Childhood":

> The horizon always seemed to you and me
> too big a word to mean those dirty rooftops
> pasted against a grey newspaper of sky
> so wet the pain ran down all over us.

Here a world is evoked and right away revoked in "pain." More than most, Moritz's poems are rhetorical—hortatory and oratorical.

Moritz's most accessible collection is *The Tradition* (1986). The title poem has much to say about ancestors: "There is no way to know them, / unless to presume that they were much like us." Is there solipsism here? If there is, the poet is able to break or at least bend its confining bars in the moving poem "The Boy," which begins like this:

> Sometimes a man feels a boy walk out of him
> and close the door. Then, turning to a window,
> the man can watch him, always growing smaller,
> a long way down the path that gently drops
> across the steep hill.

The boy of the man walks into the sea and fishes in its waters. The poem ends with

> And it doesn't matter that he won't catch anything,
> when the suns sets he goes home.

It is a fine set piece. "The Chinese Writing Academy" offers irony:

> And we who are poets and bureaucrats
> will not ask in poems why we write—
> no question so inconsequential as that.
> For we who know the sorrows of being out of power
> know poetry is only part
> of a larger question
> which also we will ignore with all our art.
> We will only wonder silently while we sing
> why we do anything.

Moritz's later collections discuss the "larger question" with eloquence, though often as well with a hint of garrulousness. About the collection *Song of Fear* (1992) the poet P.K. Page has written, "Some of the poems are like fables; some like tableaux—motionless, full of portent, with the gravity and power of myth."

In *The Ruined Cottage* (1993) and *Mahoning* (1994) there are signs that Moritz has become more autobiographical. The latter title is a reference to the Mahoning River of the poet's childhood near Niles, Ohio. Although he has lived in Canada since 1975, he seems to be returning to his past, or perhaps transforming it into a new past is a better way of expressing it. Here is "The Five-Foot Shelf" from the 1993 collection:

> A man in middle life
> of self-regarding intellectual rigor
> and a cold, analytical curiosity
> that reduces the world and his own body
> to objects,

> a man who took himself apart
> and found nothing but the parts,

> is rescued
> by a flower, a stone, a wooden stool,
> a child doing something simple.

So if surrealism and philosophy are the motive power behind Moritz's earlier work, it is possible that to these can be added the disclosure of autobiography in an attempt to create a new order for the past as well as the present.

—John Robert Colombo

MORRIS, Mervyn

Nationality: Jamaican. **Born:** Kingston in 1937. **Education:** Munro College, Kingston; University of the West Indies, Kingston (Government Exhibitioner); St. Edmund Hall, Oxford (Rhodes scholar). **Family:** Married; two sons and one daughter. **Career:** Formerly Senior English Master, Munro College; assistant registrar, Warden of Taylor Hall, from 1966, senior lecturer in English, from 1970, and later reader in West Indian literature, University of the West Indies; visiting lecturer, University of Kent, Canterbury, 1972–73. **Award:** Institute of Jamaica Musgrave Medal, 1976. **Address:** Department of English, University of the West Indies, Mona, Kingston 7, Jamaica.

PUBLICATIONS

Poetry

The Pond. London, New Beacon, 1973; revised edition, New Beacon, 1997.
On Holy Week. Kingston, Sangster, 1976; as *On Holy Week: A Sequence of Poems for Radio.* Sydney, Dangaroo Press, 1993.
Shadowboxing. London, New Beacon, 1979.
Examination Centre: Poems. London, Beacon Books, 1992.

Other

Is English We Speaking: West Indian Literature. British Library, 1993; as *Is English We Speaking and Other Essays,* Kingston, Ian Randle, 1999.
A Study Guide to Old Story Time. San Juan, Trinidad, Longman, 1995.

Editor, *Seven Jamaican Poets: An Anthology of Recent Poetry.* Kingston, Bolivar Press, 1971.
Editor, *My Green Hills of Jamaica, and Five Jamaican Short Stories,* by Claude McKay. Kingston, Heinemann, 1979.
Editor, with Pamela Mordecai, *Jamaica Woman: An Anthology of Poems.* Kingston, Heinemann, 1980.
Editor, *Selected Poems,* by Louise Bennett. Kingston, Sangster, 1982.
Editor, *Focus 1983: An Anthology of Contemporary Jamaican Writing.* Kingston, Caribbean Authors, 1983.
Editor, *Riddym Ravings and Other Poems* by Jean Binta Breeze. London, Race Today, 1988.

Editor, *It a Come,* by Michael Smith. San Francisco, City Lights, 1989.

Editor, with Stewart Brown and Gordon Rohlehr, *Voice Print: An Anthology of Oral and Related Poetry from the Caribbean.* London and Chicago, Longman, 1990.

Editor, *The Faber Book of Contemporary Caribbean Short Stories.* London, Faber, 1990.

Editor, with Edward Baugh, *Progressions: West Indian Literature in the 1970s.* Kingston, University of West Indies, Mona, 1990.

Editor, *Aunt Roachy Seh,* by Louise Bennett. Kingston, Sangster, 1993.

Editor, with E. Kamau Brathwaite and Lorna Goodison, *Three Caribbean Poets on Their Work.* Mona, Jamaica, Institute of Caribbean Studies, 1993.

*

Critical Studies: *Modern Romance: A Study of Techniques and Themes* (dissertation) by Stacey Schlau, n.p., 1976; "'Balanced/in Pain': A Study of the Male/Female Relationship in the Poetry of Mervyn Morris" by Roydon Salick, and "Religion and Poetry: A Study of Mervyn Morris's 'On Holy Week'" by Gloria Lyn, both in *Journal of West Indian Literature* (Kingston, Jamaica), 1(1), October 1986; interview with Pam Mordecai, in *Matatu* (Main, Germany), 12, 1994.

*   *   *

Mervyn Morris's first poems, appearing from the early 1960s in the *Sunday Gleaner, Bim,* the *Jamaica Journal,* and *The Pond* and, along with his "schooldays" poems, all collected in his first published volume, quickly established him as perhaps Jamaica's leading poet of domesticity. But even here there were already gnomic tendencies lurking in the darker corners of the verse. In "Family Pictures," for instance, the apparent man-hero is also a "victim" and "master of one cage," and in "The Reassurance" we note the man-king's crown becoming a blind visor, so that he has to tap out "a peephole in his crown" that becomes, by the poem's end, "the . . . peephole in the mind." "Journey into the Interior" has a similar, almost too obvious, quality:

Stumbling down his own oesophagus
he thought he'd check his vitals out.
He found the entrails most illegible,
it wasn't clear what innards were about.

He opted to return to air and light
and certainty; but when he tried
he found the passage blocked; so now
he spends the long day groping there, inside

But it is in *Shadowboxing,* with, as Morris himself points out, the poems minimizing themselves into what he hopes will be their very essence, that he most nicely essays his sense of critical contradiction. He produces what a critic once called "boxes within boxes," some, like the following ("Dream"), perhaps a little too minimal:

I dreamt

I grabbed a pail

to dip some water up
to drink

and saw
things floating
in the murk

and then I woke up
thirsty

Morris is a bit too concerned with pointing out the moral instead of allowing these poems to be their own moral. Even at their best these "onion skin poems," as someone else has described them, often put an almost inordinate strain on manner, on implied tone, and—signally—on the last line, with sometimes a resulting sag within the middle of the strophe.

In the end it is to Morris's early poems that we return. For it is here, in his crafty "race" and Georgian schooldays poems, that we most comfortably find his characteristic generosity and sense of equanimity and that his contradictory gnomic lurking works best:

The future darkening, you thought it time
to say good-bye. It may be you were right.
It hurt to see you go; but, more,
it hurt to see you slowly going white.

Following is another example:

In 19-something X was born
in Jubilee Hospital, howling, black.

In 19- (any date plus four)
X went out to school.
They showed him pretty pictures
of his Queen.

When he was 7, in elementary school,
he asked what naygas were.
In secondary school he knew.
He asked in History one day
where slaves came from.
"Oh, Africa," the master said,
"Get on with your work."

Up at the university he didn't find himself;
and, months before he finally dropped out,
would ramble round the campus late at night
and dab his blackness on the walls.

Perhaps the best example, even if it is atypical, of Morris making a spectacular break from Georgian into nation language occurs in his poem on that mystic, troubled icon of Jamaican independence, the great ska/jazz trombonist Don Drummond. His labyrinthine solos—musical boxes within boxes within boxes—led, it is said, to his death (possibly by suicide) in a Kingston lunatic asylum:

Me one, way out in the crowd,
I blow the sounds, the pain,
but not a soul
would come inside my world

or tell me how it true.
I love a melancholy baby,
sweet, with fire in her belly;
and like a spite
the woman turn a whore.
Cool and smooth around the beat
she wake the note inside me
and I blow me mind.

Inside here, me one
in the crowd again,
and plenty people
want me blow it straight.
But straight is not the way; my world
don' go so; that is lie.
Oonu gimme me back me trombone, man:
is time to blow me mind.

—Edward Kamau Brathwaite

MORRISON, (Philip) Blake

Nationality: British. **Born:** Burnley, Lancashire, 8 October 1950.
Education: Ermysteds Grammar School, Skipton, Yorkshire, 1962–69;
University of Nottingham, 1969–72, B.A. (honors); McMaster University, Hamilton, Ontario, 1972–73, M.A.; University College, London, 1974–78, Ph.D. **Family:** Married Katherine Ann Drake in 1976; two sons and one daughter. **Career:** Fiction and poetry editor, *Times Literary Supplement,* London, 1978–81; deputy literary editor, 1981–86, and literary editor, 1987–89, *Observer,* London. Since 1990 literary editor, *Independent on Sunday,* London. **Awards:** Eric Gregory award, 1980; Somerset Maugham award, 1984; Dylan Thomas prize, 1985; E.M. Forster award, 1988. Fellow, Royal Society of Literature, 1988. **Agent:** Pat Kavanagh, Peters Fraser and Dunlop Ltd., Fifth Floor, The Chambers, Chelsea Harbour, Lots Road, London SW10 OXF. **Address:** 54 Blackheath Park, London SE3 9SQ, England.

PUBLICATIONS

Poetry

Dark Glasses. London, Chatto and Windus, 1984; revised and enlarged edition, 1989.
The Ballad of the Yorkshire Ripper and Other Poems. London, Chatto and Windus, 1987.
Selected Poems. London, Granta, 1999.

Play

The Cracked Pot: A Play, adaptation and translation of a play by Heinrich von Kleist. New York, Samuel French, 1996.

Other

The Movement: English Poetry and Fiction of the 1950's. Oxford and New York, Oxford University Press, 1980.
Seamus Heaney. London, Methuen, 1982.

The Yellow House (for children). London, Walker, and San Diego, Harcourt Brace, 1987.
And When Did You Last See Your Father?: A Son's Memoir of Love and Loss. New York, Picador, 1993.
As If: A Crime, a Trial, a Question of Childhood. London, Granta, and New York, Picador, 1997.
Too True. London, Granta, 1998.

Editor, with Andrew Motion, *The Penguin Book of Contemporary British Poetry.* London and New York, Penguin, 1982.
Editor, with Sara Dunn and Michele Roberts, *Mind Readings: Writers' Journeys through Mental States.* London, Minerva, 1996.
Editor, *The Gospel According to John: Authorised King James Version.* Edinburgh, Canongate, 1998.
Editor, *A Way of Life: Portraits from the Funeral Trade.* Manchester, Len Grant Photography, 1999.

*

Critical Study: By Michael Dirda, in *Grand Street* (Denville, New Jersey), 6(3), spring 1987.

Blake Morrison comments:

I have always resented Auden's line (or rather those who quote Auden's line) "Poetry makes nothing happen," which is not to say that my poetry is polemical but that it is concerned to combat in some small way the untruths, injustices, and imperfections of the world we inhabit. In my first book, *Dark Glasses,* I was much preoccupied with secrecy, lies, privacy, the difficulty of openness in both private and public life. In my second, *The Ballad of the Yorkshire Ripper,* the obsession was with masculinity, misogyny, the cult of the hard, which required a journey into childhood and dialect. All this sounds very grandiose. Probably my poetry is about what poetry has always been about—love, death, memory, and loss. But without some meliorist ambition, a wish that poetry could make something happen, I doubt that I would even write at all.

*   *   *

Blake Morrison's activities as editor, anthologist, and competition adjudicator in London's literary whirlpool have tended to deflect attention from his two excellent collections of verse, *Dark Glasses* and *The Ballad of the Yorkshire Ripper.* The much publicized exchanges between Morrison and Michael Horovitz have similarly removed the spotlight of attention from the poems. Not that Morrison is without a readership; he has received a Somerset Maugham award, an E.M. Forster award, and a Dylan Thomas prize. Not bad going for two slim volumes.

Dark Glasses appeared in 1984 (a revised and expanded edition was published in 1989) and included poems previously noticed in Faber's *Poetry Introduction 5. Dark Glasses* was a debut notable for its clarity of expression (the poems are immensely readable), the carefully achieved polish and finish, and the emergence of a voice, albeit with Philip Larkin looming hugely in the background. Morrison's tone was quiet, absorbed, even reticent. He could play the Martian without having to strain for effect—"Brown pups, a cow opening its sad eye, / The shine of the dining-room table" (from "Grange Boy") refers to conkers. Or consider these lines from "Meningococcus":

That night of his high fever
I held a stream against me,
his heart panicky as a netted bird,
globes of solder on his brow.

Not unlike his coanthologist Andrew Motion, Morrison develops the theme of secrecy ("English, we hoard our secrets to the end"), and observed violence—human and natural—crops up repeatedly. Morrison deals with such contemporary matters as criminality and domesticity in an unassuming, quiet manner. He comes across as writer-as-humble-joe.

The long poem "The Inquisitor" deals almost breathlessly with political and financial crimes in an episodic, filmic structure. It resembles one of those TV thriller series in which confusion is everything. The pace of the poem is hectic, yet the end product is clouded with mystery. Perhaps that is the point, that there are no easy answers.

The collection *The Ballad of the Yorkshire Ripper* is dominated by the title poem, a fourteen-page monologue in four-line rhyming stanzas. The narrator is an unnamed Yorkshireman speaking in dialect. The poem examines the secret crimes, the deviousness, and the cold criminality of Peter Sutcliffe, yet it manages a compassionate and thoughtful tone. A bleak humor, not easily discovered in *Dark Glasses,* emerges from time to time through the fog of violence and death:

Everweer in Yorkshire
were a creepin fear an thrill.
At Elland Road fans chanted
"Ripper 12 Police Nil."

and

So cops they lobbed im questions
through breakfast, dinner, tea,
till e said: "All right, you've cracked it.
Ripper, aye, it's me."

The poem works well, and it gives Morrison the opportunity to include other poems dealing with his Yorkshire background and to enlarge on family scenes with an Anglican setting. He still retains his power to astonish with imagery ("a lorry backed up in its exhaust / like a polar bear fading into snow.") and generally widens his range of subject matter to include nature, love, aspects of work, and history.

Morrison writes with a restrained power in his two collections of memorable poetry. It remains unclear, however, if his energy and potential are fully realized on the page or if his involvement in the literary world has defused his ability to write as elegantly and meaningfully as his books indicate he might do.

—Wes Magee

MOSS, Thylias (Rebecca)

Nationality: American. **Born:** Thylias Rebecca Brasier, Cleveland, Ohio, 27 February 1954. **Education:** Syracuse University, New York, 1971–73; Oberlin College, Oberlin, Ohio, 1979–81, A.B. in creative writing 1981; University of New Hampshire, Durham,

1981–83, M.A. in English/Writing 1983. **Family:** Married John L. Moss in 1973; two sons. **Career:** Drama and Reading Rehabilitation Specialist, Bellevue Elementary School, Syracuse; order checker, 1973–74, junior executive auditor, 1975–79, data entry supervisor, 1974–75, The May Company, Cleveland; graduate assistant, 1981–83, lecturer, 1983–84, University of New Hampshire, Durham; instructor, Phillips Academy, Andover, Massachusetts, 1984–92; Fannie Hurst Poet, Brandeis University, Waltham, Massachusetts, 1992; visiting professor, University of New Hampshire, Durham, 1991–92. Assistant professor, 1993–94, associate professor, 1994–98, and since 1998 professor, University of Michigan, Ann Arbor. **Awards:** Cleveland Public Library Poetry Contest Winner, 1978, for "Coming of Age in Sandusky"; Dewar's Profiles Performance Artist award in poetry, 1991; Witter Bynner prize, American Academy and Institute of Arts and Letters, 1991; Whiting Writer's award, 1991; Guggenheim fellowship, 1995; MacArthur fellowship, 1996. **Member:** Academy of American Poets. **Agent:** Faith Hamlin, Sanford J. Greenburger Associates, 55 Fifth Avenue, New York, New York 10003, U.S.A. **Address:** P.O. Box 2686, Ann Arbor, Michigan 48106, U.S.A.

PUBLICATIONS

Poetry

Hosiery Seams on a Bowlegged Woman. Cleveland, Ohio, Cleveland State University Press, 1983.
Pyramid of Bone. Charlottesville, University of Virginia Press, 1989.
At Redbones. Cleveland, Ohio, Cleveland State University Press, 1990.
Rainbow Remnants in Rock Bottom Ghetto Sky. New York, Persea, 1991.
Small Congregations: New and Selected Poems. Hopewell, New Jersey, Ecco Press, 1993.
Last Chance for the Tarzan Holler: Poems. New York, Persea, 1998.

Plays

The Dolls in the Basement (produced New England Theater Conference, 1984).
Talking to Myself (produced Durham, New Hampshire, 1984).

Other

I Want to Be (for children). New York, Dial Books, 1993.
Tale of a Sky-Blue Dress. New York, Bard, 1998.

*

Critical Studies: In *The American Religion* by Harold Bloom, New York, Simon and Schuster, 1992; in *Hudson Review,* 47(1), spring 1994; by Tim Martin, in *Prairie Schooner,* 68(2), summer 1994.

Theatrical Activities: Director and Actor: **Plays**—all her own plays; *Dolls in the Basement,* 1984; *Talking to Myself,* 1984. Actor: **Play**—Female lead in *Midnight Special* by Clifford Mason, 1973.

Thylias Moss comments:
The day, the hour are lost to me, but one day I began to write when I was not quite seven years old. Since then there has been no

stopping. But the immediate provocation and necessity of that ''then''; who knows? An odd compulsion, to begin this process of thoughts appearing from fingers as if the thoughts had been bled, but it began even as the universe began. First on heavy paper around which my mother's stockings came wrapped, stories and poems happened. She would discard the stiff paper, and I saw it in the wastebasket, saw the mistake of the discarding, realized the possibilities had been trashed, so I retrieved the paper and on it formed words for the first time. What was it that I should have been doing instead; what chore went neglected? It was silent, diligent enterprise, but I had seen the explosions on Sundays, the preacher's hands on a book, fingering words that inspired everything else that happened as the congregation huddled on its knees around the pulpit at altar call to be relieved of all human misery by a blues-dominated prayer and sermon that made the congregation swoon and that intoxicated them with the spirit of the Lord, wrenching out the misery in the healing rhythm, stripping them of everything but the Lord. Words made them shout, made them experience glory that perhaps was not actually there, their feelings providing glory with the only substance it had. How wondrous! I wanted to make such words. I wanted to make what the preacher called ''text.''

There was also the way my father could transform the world with just his words and voice, my father who established in the kitchen on Saturday nights, while he drank whiskey, a school for his young brothers-in-law, a school to which I, at six by far the youngest pupil, was also invited. He lectured mostly on the dialectics of the soul, asking the forbidden questions, giving words power over any taboo, and thereby endowing them with an affirming ability that still delights the part of me that remembers his tale at bedtime of the girl that geese surround, their feathers locked as tightly as a snow house. Around her they honk, their circle tightening, their feathers brushing against her, some of the feathers working their way into her skin until, when the circle widens, in the center is a goose princess whose new wings are a form of crown. Such words. Such influence.

*   *   *

''A visionary storyteller,'' as Charles Simic has called her, Thylias Moss is a true betokener, one who gives us signs and portents. We listen to Moss to hear how our world is doing. Each poem holds news. Rarely linear, the news is in patterns woven from observation, from myth, from analogies and not quite parallels that make us search for what the signs portend.

Few poets can be so deadly with irony, so surprising and direct, as in ''EASTER'':

> Dr. Frankenstein feeds his son voltage, juice
> fires up the hormones
>
> on the day of unkillable testosterone
>
> while Mary and Martha heed their spices,
> their urges to preserve, not dulled by the impropriety of
>   the kitchen
>   in which they slaughter lambs and chickens.

Moss can be in turn mocking, urbane, ironically self-deprecating, angry, lyrical, but always impassioned. Concerned equally with psychology and religion, she focuses more on injustice than on politics or history. She yearns to heal, but she sees the rents in the

social fabric too clearly to go farther without pointing. She shows us mythic connections between events. So the potential extinction of whole species, including our own, becomes a tale of Little Red Riding Hood in which, if only it could end happily, the baboons and the mackerel and the egrets would join ''the grandmother / and Little Red Riding Hood / walking out of a wolf named Dachau'' (from ''There Will Be Animals'').

Moss is a teacher who one day brought a flower to class and asked her students to describe it. And the next day. And every day, while the petals fell and dusted themselves away and the brute thorn stem browned and drooped. And the day after that. And the day after that. ''By the end of the term,'' she said, ''they began to know one flower.'' And to see metamorphosis, the deceptiveness of beauty, the power language has to somehow transcend death, at least for now. Her poems teach us this.

Moss is a spellbinding reader. One cannot take her voice lightly; it is a preacher's voice, amber honey on a straight razor. She sings jazz. She can build entire poems from a painting or from a chance rhyme (''Timex Remembered''), write colloquial syllabics, drop in song lyrics, children's voices, letters, drive-by shootings, fairy tales, and the life of Riley—her poetry is America; her poems can hold anything.

And Moss's canvas is enormous. She writes detailed poems about saints, biblical stories, water softeners, kings, farmers, writing, lactation, fire, and faith. Beneath many of her poems lies a deep, pure ambiguity. The opening lines of ''Glory'' lay that out straight:

> The sun does not really rise; the earth turns and leans
> into that perception as it circles a sun busy burning
> for the sake of light.
>
> That's what I'd like God to do, burn himself again
> for the sake of light. Commit to the bush instead of
>   vacating
> when it got too hot, berries burning the hands pick-
>   ing them,
> picking Him, Moses suffering heat as they suffer in a
>   Chicago August
> five hundred dropping, no rapture to sustain them, members
> of Star of Hope . . .

There is no subtlety, no aside, no coloration, no disaffection, no irony, no affection, no shading, no leap that seems beyond Moss's control of language. And she tells great jokes and laughs at them. The following is from ''Sour Milk'':

> . . . And God, don't forget that God loved him
> and loved P.T. Barnum—has to love a good hoax,
> a literality in which His being love
>
> unifies all theories :)

Excerpts cannot do Moss justice. Her news builds from the first words to the last in her search for clear vision. The following is from ''Advice'':

> *I visit shrines all over Europe and Asia; when*
> *D.C's Holocaust Memorial Museum opened, I was there*
> *feeling uneasy about my innocence for innocence*

can not actually be proven; it is becoming increasingly
difficult to prove because we are finally learning
    our hearts.

    . . . and I will not abandon this poem
that attempts to touch much of what keeps touching me
    shaping me into a woman who hopes to finish know-
        ing herself
in time to begin to know something else.

    And if what Moss knows flares before our eyes, we may realize
that our vision has been dulled for a long time. But surely there is no
irony when Moss reassures us in ''Sour Milk'' that

    . . . Every generation loses something

but as long as this loss makes it possible to gain
    something else,
to sidestep as though really traveling to galaxies
    more distant
than distance where some believe we can witness

life beginning in nutrient-laden watery primordial soup just
    starting
to diversify, mutate as we know life does because we're
    here, each one of us
the result   and it's OK to call it intelligent or miraculous
    no matter

what it really is.

Moss's poems are rooted in contemporary American awareness, and all of the effects of our daily lives are here, its sounds, its materialism, its distrust of logic and government, its agonizing awareness of race, femininity, and sexuality. So too are its surreal devices, its loosely arranged lines, casual enjambments in the service of the speaking voice, predilection for the startling truth and for a canvas mythic in breadth and intensity. Moss has a sense of humor both Horace and Juvenal would admire. There is a fierceness in her, a prophet's compassion, and a vision that pierces anything fake.

—Edward B. Germain

MOTION, Andrew

Nationality: British. **Born:** London, 26 October 1952. **Education:** Radley College, 1965–70; University College, Oxford (Newdigate prize, 1975), B.A. (honors) 1975, M.Litt. 1977. **Family:** Married 1) Joanna Jane Powell in 1973 (dissolved 1983); 2) Janet Elisabeth Dalley in 1985, two sons and one daughter. **Career:** Lecturer in English, University of Hull, 1977–81; poetry editor, 1982–84, and editorial director, 1985–89, Chatto and Windus publishers, London; editor, *Poetry Review,* London, 1980–82; editor, Faber and Faber publishers, London. Appointed poet laureate, 1999. **Awards:** Eric Gregory award, 1978, 1987; Cholmondeley award, 1979; Arvon-Observer prize, 1981; John Llewelyn Rhys prize, 1984; Dylan Thomas award, 1987; Maugham award, for biography, 1987; Whitbread

award for biography, 1993. **Agent:** Peters Fraser and Dunlop, 5th Floor, The Chambers, Chelsea Harbour, Lots Road, London SW10 OXF. **Address:** c/o Faber and Faber Ltd., 3 Queen Square, London WCIN 3AU, England.

PUBLICATIONS

Poetry

Goodnestone: A Sequence. London, Workshop Press, 1972.
Inland. Burford, Oxfordshire, Cygnet Press, 1976.
The Pleasure Steamers. Manchester, Carcanet, 1978.
Independence. Edinburgh, Salamander Press, 1981.
Secret Narratives. Edinburgh, Salamander Press, 1983.
Dangerous Play: Poems 1974–1984. Edinburgh, Salamander Press, 1984.
Natural Causes. London, Chatto and Windus, 1987.
Two Poems. Child Okeford, Dorset, Words Press, 1989.
Love in a Life. London, Faber and Faber, 1991.
The Price of Everything. London, Faber and Faber, 1994.
Salt Water. London, Faber and Faber, 1997.
Selected Poems. London, Faber and Faber, 1999.

Other

The Poetry of Edward Thomas. London, Routledge, 1980.
Philip Larkin. London, Methuen, 1982.
The Lamberts: George, Constant and Kit. London, Chatto and Windus, 1986.
Philip Larkin: A Writer's Life. London, Faber and Faber, 1993.
Keats. London, Faber and Faber, 1997.

Editor, with Blake Morrison, *The Penguin Book of Contemporary British Poetry.* London, Penguin, 1982.

*

Manuscript Collection: University of Hull.

Critical Studies: '''I Could Have Outlived Myself There': The Poetry of Andrew Motion'' by Michael Hulse, in *Critical Quarterly* (Oxford, England), 28(3), autumn 1986; '''All the Lives I've Led': The Uses of Fiction and Autobiography in the Poetry of Andrew Motion'' by Mary Conde, in *Anglistentag 1992,* edited by Hans Ulrich Seeber and Walter Gobel, Tubingen, Niemeyer, 1993.

*   *   *

Andrew Motion is one of a group of younger contemporary English poets whose work reveals a fascination with ''narrative,'' with, that is, the potential effectiveness of refracting some kind of story or plot through an essentially lyric form or sequence. His early volume *The Pleasure Steamers* contains one such lengthy sequence, ''Inland,'' which, in the character of a Fenland villager of the early seventeenth century, tells the story of the introduction of enclosures from the point of view of someone dispossessed by them. The main effort of the sequence is to point up the fragility and brittleness of the personal life when set against its controlling context in the public world:

> Tomorrow, high tides will press
> our future from us
> back into emptiness;
> so now, unpin your hair,
> open your dress.

This becomes a characteristic procedure in Motion's work. Effects of pathos are created by the attempt at some kind of interiority of empathy with the sufferings of fictionalized characters usually drawn from episodes of English history: the seventeenth-century Fenland, World War II, the end of the British Empire in India.

In selecting such episodes for his material, Motion—who has written a critical book on Edward Thomas—reveals himself as a quintessentially English poet. The word "England" echoes through some of his work. In one poem it is an England that "turns out of the sun," and the powerful sense of loss in Motion's work is intimately responsive to the experience of a nation, or a class, undergoing the anxieties and uncertainties of postimperial and postcolonial withdrawal. This sense of loss also derives, however, from the tragic experience of Motion's own adolescence, when his mother had a riding accident and suffered in a coma that lasted until her death ten years later. This grim circumstance recurs in a number of different forms in Motion's work but particularly in the third section of *The Pleasure Steamers,* where the effects of pathos are in complete consonance with those of "Inland":

> Whatever time might bring,
> all my journeys take me
> back to this dazzling dark:
> I watch my shadow ahead
> plane across open fields,
> out of my reach for ever,
> but setting towards your bed
> to find itself waiting there.

The narratives in Motion's poems, then, take their particular edge of unease from the way their predominant emotions act as some kind of filter or mask for the poet's own. Their obliquities and lacunae, features remarked on by a number of reviewers, avoid direct statement and leave a large part of the act of interpretation open to the reader. Halfway perhaps between personal lyric and dramatic monologue, such poems as "The Letters," "Resident at the Club," and the superbly complicated and inclusive "Independence"—the narrator being a retired Anglo-Indian widower whose wife has died in childbirth—return again and again to images of loss, abandonment, and estrangement and to a fundamental preoccupation with the final human loss, death, and its human response, grief. The poem "Open Secrets," which begins the volume *Secret Narratives,* explores Motion's own self-consciousness about these procedures in a way that suggests some further intensification of his own narrative strategies:

> He was never
> myself, this boy, but I know if I tell you his story
> you'll think we are one and the same: both of us hiding
> in fictions which say what we cannot admit to ourselves.

—Neil Corcoran

MOURÉ, Erin

Nationality: Canadian. **Born**: Calgary, Alberta, 17 April 1955. **Education:** University of Calgary, 1972–73; University of British Columbia, Vancouver, 1974–75. **Career:** VIA Rail Canada, Customer Services branch, Montreal, 1976–95. Since 1996 freelance editor, writer, and translator. Contributing editor, *Raddle Moon,* Vancouver, 1998. **Awards:** National Magazine award (gold), 1983; Pat Lowther Memorial award, 1985; Governor General's award for poetry, 1988; National Magazine award (silver), 1994. **Address:** c/o The Writer's Union of Canada, 24 Ryerson Avenue, Toronto M5T 2P3.

PUBLICATIONS

Poetry

Empire, York Street. Toronto, Anansi, 1979.
The Whisky Vigil. Madeira Park, British Columbia, Harbour, 1981.
Wanted Alive. Toronto, Anansi, 1983.
Domestic Fuel. Toronto, Anansi, 1985.
Furious. Toronto, Anansi, 1988.
WSW (West South West). Montreal, Vehicule Press, 1989.
Sheepish Beauty, Civilian Love. Montreal, Véhicule Press, 1992.
The Green Word: Selected Poems. Toronto, Oxford University Press, 1994.
Search Procedures. Toronto, Anansi, 1996.
A Frame of the Book. Toronto, Anansi, 1999.
Pillage Laud. Toronto, Moveable Type, 1999.

*

Manuscript Collection: National Library of Canada, Ottawa.

Critical Studies: "Changes the Surface: A Conversation with Erin Moure" by Robert Billings, in *Waves* (Richmond Hill, Ontario), 14(4), spring 1986; by Dennis Denisoff, in *Canadian Writers and Their Works,* edited by Robert Lecker, Jack David, and Ellen Quigley, Toronto, ECW, 1995; *Search Proceures: Carnivalization in Language-and Theory-Focused Texts of Four Canadian Women Writers* (dissertation) by Eugenia Sojka, Memorial University of Newfoundland, 1996; "Amen, She Said: The Language of Religion/The Religion of Language in Erin Moure and Lola Lemire Tostevin" by Karen I. Press, in *West Coast Line,* 32(25), spring 1998.

*   *   *

Erin Mouré's poetics, strongly feminist and deconstructive, work to disrupt the status quo and dismantle systems that perpetuate stasis. Although this is evident in early collections, her later poetry goes further in its subversion of the normative structure of language. By so breaking up the "surface of sense," Mouré's poetry allows previously repressed voices to come through and speak against social strongholds of racism, sexism, and homophobia. Part of the process is syntactic, whereby she questions the validity of "correct" linguistic form by privileging a previously suppressed or submissive form. In *Furious,* Mouré exemplifies this by focusing on the preposition as a central figure of syntactic construction, as, for example, in "Rolling Motion":

> Your face in my neck &
> arms dwelling upward face
> in my soft leg open
> lifted upward airborne soft
> face into under into rolling
> over every upward motion
> rolling open over your
> Face in my neck again over
> turning risen touch billows
> my mouth open enter
> dwelling upward face
> in your soft leg open
> lifted upward airborne soft
> face into under into motion
> over every upward open
> rolling open over your
> Face in my neck again
> & arms

To complement the poems in this collection, Mouré includes a final section entitled "The Acts," which serves partially to document the writing process of particular poems and to describe her technique. On "Rolling Motion" she writes,

> It is the force of the *preposition* that *alters place*! Can its displacement of the noun/verb dis-place also *naming*, displacing reality? Even momentarily. Make a fissure through which we can leak out from the "real" that is sewn into us, to utter what could not be uttered in the previous structure. Where we have not been represented, except through Dominant (in this case, patriarchal) speaking, which even we speak, even we women.

Mouré enunciates her feminist project by refusing to accept structures that either reinforce or, at the least, do not question assumptions that privilege the belief system of the dominant order. Part of this process is the reflexive questioning of the poet that focuses not just on obvious power positions but also on the reader's readily made assumptions of the act of interpretation. In *WSW (West South West)* Mouré "responds" to the poem "Tucker Drugs" with a series of possible readings in "Naming a Poem Called Tucker Drugs," printed on the page facing the poem:

> In which we don't know what weather is.
> "A poem in which the weather is not mentioned."
> "A poem with a dog, a car, a drug store, and a
>   mother in it."
> "A poem in which there is not much weather."
> "A poem in which the possible weather is limited by the
>   presence of a consumer object."
> "A poem with a dog in it."
> "Tucker Drugs."
>
> People may make a mistake if you call it this. With
>   representation &
> naming being what they are, don't confuse people.

With such a tongue-in-cheek reference—the poet wants to, if not confuse, then seriously question the singularity of vision so often brought to a text—Mouré introduces a sense of plurality to the poem. The suggestion is that under the surface is a surfeit of voices, despite the apparent rigidity of "representation & naming." This rigidity of discourse, and the concomitant hegemonic values assumed by the dominant order, is further questioned in *Furious* in a pair of poems that play off each other. In the first poem, "Pure Reason: Science," the poet narrates the story of laboratory animals protesting their treatment:

> The day the animals came on the radio, fed-up, the electrodes in
>   their hands
> beaming, small tubes leading into their brains where chemicals enter,
> & the bubbling light from that, the experiment
> of science,
> the washed fur on their faces & in their voice
>
> *The quick brown fox jumped over the lazy dog* is a comparison
>   we reject,
> they say.

Such already bleak, fantastic humor is effectively blackened, however, when Mouré turns her attention in "Pure Reason: Femininity" to the feminist project and the very real and utterly humorless situation of women in a male-dominated society:

> The day the women came on the radio, fed-up, electrodes
>   in their purses
> beaming, small tubes leading into their brains where
>   doctors enter,
> the bubbling light from that, neuronic balance, the de/
>   pression of their inner houses,
>
> washed skin on their faces & in their voice
>
> *She belongs to a certain class of women whose profession
> is to promote lust* is a comparison we reject,
> they say to the judge.

While the humor of the first poem does not completely elide the danger inherent in oppressive power, its purpose here is to act as a palimpsest for the painful issue of patriarchal dominance and misreadings. Reading this latter poem, a person is made deliberately aware of the former, and the insinuation is that control and domination are exercised by gender as well as species, perhaps in a far more insidious way.

Through her deconstructive verse Mouré rigorously questions current and accepted political structures, taking them to task for their subjugating power. By playing with polyvocality in her poetics, she sets up a reflexive dialogue with herself and her reader. Mouré's rejection and deliberate complication of conventional narrative structures enable her to create a new vision that empowers those voices traditionally silenced. Hers is a poetics that rails against the dominant in order to effect change, to validate the subjugated, and to dismantle and alter static, unreflexive, and oppressive systems.

—Ashok Mathur

MTSHALI, (Mbuyiseni) Oswald

Nationality: South African. **Born:** Oswald Joseph Mtshali (changed name), Vryheid, Natal, 17 January 1940. **Education:** Queen of the Angels Primary School and Inkamana High School, Vryheid; Columbia University, New York, M.A. in creative writing, M.Ed., Ed.D. 1998; doctoral candidate, Rhodes University, Grahamstown. **Family:** Married 1) Margaret Mntambo in 1968 (divorced 1975), four children; 2) Glaudinah Jacoba in 1983. **Career:** Driver for an engineering firm, 1963–65; briefly imprisoned, then acquitted; after 1965 messenger and general delivery man, National Growth Fund investment company, Johannesburg; deputy headmaster, Pace Commercial College, Jabulani, Soweto; worked for South African Council of Churches; columnist, *Rand Daily Mail,* Johannesburg, 1972; arts critic, *The Star,* from 1979. **Awards:** Olive Schreiner prize, 1975. **Address:** 3 Washington Square Village, Bleeker Street, New York, New York 10012, U.S.A.

PUBLICATIONS

Poetry

Sounds of a Cowhide Drum. Johannesburg, Renoster, 1971; London, Oxford University Press, and New York, Third Press, 1972.
Fireflames. Pietermaritzburg, Natal, Shuter and Shooter, 1980; Chicago, Chicago Review, 1983.

Play

Money Makes Madness, with Barney Simon and others, music by M. Davashe and others, adaptation of *Volpone* by Ben Jonson (produced Johannesburg, 1972).

Other

Editor, *Give Us a Break: Diaries of a Group of Soweto Children.* Johannesburg, Skotaville, 1988.

*

Bibliography: *Oswald Mbuyiseni Mtshali, South African Poet: An Annotated Bibliography* by Gillian Goldstein, Johannesburg, University of the Witwatersrand Department of Bibliography, 1974.

Critical Studies: "Free As a Black, Free As a Poet," in *Drum* (Johannesburg), 22, May 1975; "Three South African Poets" by John F. Povey, in *World Literature Written in English* (Arlington, Texas), 16, 1977; "Protest Poetry in South Africa and Mtshali's Refuge under 'The Cryptic Mode'" by Igbarumun Igbudu, in *Kuka* (Zaria, Nigeria), 1979; "Books in English from the Third World" by Charles R. Larson, in *World Literature Today* (Norman, Oklahoma), 58(3), summer 1984; "Landscapes of Exile in Selected Works by Samuel Beckett, Mongane Serote, and Mbuyiseni Oswald Mtshali" by Cecelia Scallan Zeiss, in *Anglo-Irish and Irish Literature: Aspects of Language and Culture,* edited by Birgit Bramsback and Martin Croghan, Uppsala, Uppsala University, 1988; "Pictures of Social Discrimination: The Poetry of Oswald Mtshali" by David Olusegun Agbaje, in *Literary Half-Yearly* (Mysore, India), 32(2), July 1991; "The Rhetoric of Violence in South African Poetry" by Stephen Watson, in *New Contrast,* 78, 1992; "Apartheid and Christianity in Oswald Mtshali's 'Sounds of a Cowhide Drum'" by Karibi T. George, in *Neohelicon* (Amsterdam), 19(1), 1992.

Oswald Mtshali comments:

I am neither a romantic nor a traditionalist. Maybe I am a socially involved poet of South Africa, as Charles Dickens was a socially involved novelist of England.

I consider Lorca, Allen Ginsberg, and Yevtushenko as some of the poets I admire. I draw my themes from my life as I live and experience it. I write in the free verse form because it allows me more freedom in expression without the restriction of meter and rhyme. I depict the life of humanity as a whole as reflected in my environment, Mofolo Village; my community, Soweto; my society, Johannesburg; my country, South Africa. As an aspirant black poet in South Africa, I have no model poet on whom to base my style.

*   *   *

No volume of poems published in South Africa has been as instantly successful as Oswald Mtshali's *Sounds of a Cowhide Drum.* It sold more than ten thousand copies in a year and paved the way for Mongane Serote, Sipho Sepamla, and other black poets of the 1970s. For probably the first time white South Africans found themselves interrogated in their own language by a black writer, and for most the experience was a revelation. As Mtshali remarked in 1972, "I think it is because people are curious and eager to know what the current of thought and feeling is between black and white . . . The gap between the races here is so wide that my book seems to have the effect of a stone thrown into a pond." This is well illustrated in "The Master of the House," in which the quiet and reasonable—and reassuring—tones of the black man ("illegally" visiting his wife in the servants' quarters) are edged with irony:

> Master, I am a stranger to you,
> but will you hear my confession?
>
> I am a faceless man
> who lives in the backyard
> of your house . . .
>
> As the rich man's to Lazarus,
> the crumbs are swept to my lap
> by my Lizzie . . .

The poem culminates, however, in an image taut with fear and menace:

> I am the nocturnal animal
> that steals through the fenced lair
> to meet my mate,
> and flees at the break of dawn
> before the hunter and the hounds
> run me to ground.

Mtshali's experience of the brutalizing effect of imprisonment was the catalyst that gave his work direction and purpose, yet compassion, irony, and a fine control of tone, rather than bitterness and anger, characterize *Sounds of a Cowhide Drum.* The free verse form makes for flexibility of tone, and he utilizes a wide range of speaking voices, from the innocent yet acute questions of a child ("Boy on a Swing")—

> Mother!
> Where did I come from?
> When will I wear long trousers?
> Why was my father jailed?

—to the mocking chant of a road gang as they work under the eyes of a white foreman ("A Roadgang's Cry")—

> It starts
> as a murmur
> from one mouth to another
> in a rhythm of ribaldry
> that rises to a crescendo
> 'Abelungu ngo' dam-Whites are damned
> Basibiza ngo Jim-they call us Jim'

The verse ranges from the descriptive to the narrative and even anecdotal and is characterized by vivid metaphors and similes drawn from everyday experience. One is constantly aware that the speaker is—can only be—a black man writing with candor and wry humor of his life as a child and an adult in apartheid South Africa. Occasionally the writing becomes self-conscious or lapses into cliché; generally, however, the pressure of felt experience gives the verse authority and force. The brutal realism of "An Abandoned Bundle," in which a newborn baby "dumped on a rubbish heap" is torn apart by scavenging township dogs, modulates without contrivance or a hint of censure into

> Its mother
> had melted into the rays of the rising sun,
> her face glittering with innocence
> hcr hcart as pure as untrampled dew.

Prompted mainly by the Soweto uprising of 1976, Mtshali's second volume, *Fireflames,* found a publisher only in 1980 and was promptly banned. Attractively illustrated by black artists from Natal and dedicated to "the brave schoolchildren of Soweto," the volume givcs ovcrt expression to what was implicit, but understated, in its predecessor. Even poems dealing with events that involved the poet personally lack the freshness of observation and sureness of touch that typify the first volume. Instead, there are an uncertainty of tone and a gaucheness of expression, as though the poet is not fully engaged with his subject matter. This is seen, for instance, in "This Poem Is for Ben":

> Some poems are conceived in the womb of pain;
> Others have their gestation in the placenta of hope;
> A few flash through the mirror of the mind in
> a sweet moment of madness;
> (Young poets begin in gladness and end in madness;
> the rest are nurtured in the plastic incubator of despair.)

Here the Wordsworthian quote is contrived, the effect banal. Equally pedestrian and lacking in urgency or individuality of expression are the poems of protest, the rallying cries and expostulations that make up the bulk of the volume. Empty rhetorical gestures, an uncomfortable melange of styles, and a shrillness of tone render these poems less than worthy of the events and persons they seek to commemorate. Occasionally Mtshali does strike a new note or come up with vividly realized images, as in "Walking in a Snowfall on Manhattan":

> The sun was a dangling button
> above the New York city skyline;
> a blob of jelly
> on the windshields of the yellow cabs,
> those ubiquitous salamanders,
> wiggling and slithering on slush-covered Broadway.

Generally, however, *Fireflames* offers little more than the embers of a talent that promised so much, an impression borne out by the dearth of new poems published since.

—Ernest Pereira

MUDROOROO

Psuedonyms: Colin Johnson; Mudrooroo Narogin. **Nationality:** Australian (Aboriginal Australian: Nyoongah). **Born:** Colin Thomas Johnson, in East Cuballing, Western Australia, 21 August 1938. **Education:** Clontarf, Boys Town, Perth, 1950s; Murdoch University, Perth; Melbourne University, Perth, 1985–87, B.A. (honors) 1987. **Family:** Lives with Janine Mary Little since 1993. **Career:** Lecturer, University of Northern Territory, Darwin, 1987; lecturer, University of Queensland, Brisbane, 1988. Since 1991 chair, Aboriginal Studies, Murdoch University, Perth; co-founder, Aboriginal Oral Literature and Dramatists Association. **Awards:** Western Australia Premier's prize for poetry and most outstanding entry, 1992. **Member:** Australian Society of Authors; Aboriginal Oral Literature and Dramatists Association. **Agent:** David Grossman Literary Agency Ltd., 118B Holland Park Avenue, London W11 4UA, England.

PUBLICATIONS

Poetry

The Song Circle of Jackie. Melbourne, Hyland House, 1986.
Dalwurra. Nedlands, University of Western Australia Press, 1988.
The Garden of Gethsemane: Poems from the Lost Decade. Melbourne, Hyland House, 1991.
Pacific Highway Boo-Blooz: Country Poems. St. Lucia, Queensland, University of Victoria Press, 1996.

Plays

The Mudrooroo/Mueller Project. Sydney, New South Wales University Press, 1993.

Novels

Wildcat Falling (as Colin Johnson). Sydney, Angus and Robertson, 1965.
Long Live Sandaware (as Colin Johnson). Melbourne, Hyland House, 1979.

Doin Wildcat. Melbourne, Hyland House, n.d.
Master of the Ghost Dreaming. Sydney, Angus and Robertson, 1991.
Wildcat Screaming. Sydney, Angus and Robertson, 1992.
The Kwinkan. Sydney, Angus and Robertson, 1993.
Undying. North Ryde, New South Wales, Angus and Robertson, 1998.
Underground. Pymble, New South Wales, Angus and Robertson, 1999.

Other

Writing from the Fringe: A Study of Modern Aboriginal Literature. Melbourne, Hyland House, 1990.
Aboriginal Mythology. London, Aquarian/HarperCollins, 1994.
Us Mob: History, Culture, Struggle: An Introduction to Indigenous Australia. Sydney, New South Wales, Angus and Robertson, 1995.
Indigenous Literature of Australia. South Melbourne, Victoria, Hyland House, 1997.

*

Manuscript Collection: The Baytte Library, Perth.

Critical Studies: *Mudrooroo: A Critical Study* by Adam Shoemaker, Sydney, Angus and Robertson, 1993; ''The Novels of Mudrooroo'' by Bill Perrett, in *Critical Survey* (Oxford), 6(1), 1994; interview with Susanne Bau, in *Antipodes* (Brooklyn, New York), 8(2), December 1994; ''Mastering Ceremonies: The Politics of Ritual and Ceremony in Eleanor Dark, Rudy Wiebe and Mudrooroo'' by Penny Van Toorn, in *ANZSC*, 12, December 1994; ''Mudrooroo: The Politics of Aboriginal Performance and Aboriginial Sovereignty'' by Bill Dunstone, in *Post-Colonial Stages: Critical and Creative Views on Drama, Theatre and Performance,* edited by Helen Gilbert, London, Dangaroo, 1999.

*　　*　　*

Mudrooroo, who previously published under the name Colin Johnson and who also has used the name Mudrooroo Narogin, first gained recognition in 1959 as a talented beginner in writing drama. Since then he has become an impressive writer of fiction, leading off with a novel of modern urban Aboriginal youth, and he has pioneered the literary expression of an Aboriginal point of view on centrally important historical events—the war against whites waged by a Western Australian Aboriginal leader and the near genocide of Tasmanian Aborigines. Always a polemicist but also the writer of a scholarly study of modern Aboriginal literature, he began to publish poetry only in the late 1980s.

Mudrooroo's first publication of poetry in book form, *The Song Circle of Jacky,* uses ''Jacky'' as a generic name (a name much applied to Aborigines by whites too imperious to bother learning Aboriginal names) for the modern, observant Aborigine, who is probably Mudrooroo himself. Jacky has views on U.S. highways and on invasive wars resisted by civil terrorism. He also witnesses Aboriginal suffering of many kinds, including death in prison, and urges land and other rights. A jaunty poem fantasizes the sale ''lock, stock and Aborigines, / Of Australia to GMH in the interests / Of all-round prosperity plus the curbing of inflation, / And the paying of an army of anti-terrorist squads / Armed to the teeth to fight an opposition yet to appear.''

Mudrooroo's shorter-lined verse recalls Oogeroo's work, but whereas she often used simple rhyming forms, he has chosen mostly to be free of such formality. The verse is pedestrian, but its straightforward and sometimes trenchant wording, with ringing or pathetic repetitions, makes it easily accessible. As in ''Song Thirty,'' Jacky the initiated, Jacky the *kurdaitcha* man, is also a teacher:

'Mummy, mummy,
What's a Naboriginal? . . .
Mummy, do you know about the Unguru?
Said it was a great big snake;
Said it strick when it was hurt;
Said that it was hurting now—
Mummy, I'm too scared to cry,
I don't want our land to die.'
Jacky smiles, he's getting through.

Dalwurra, published in 1988 (the bicentenary of white settlement in Australia), contains the map, in the idiom of an Aboriginal drawing, of a trip to Singapore, Calcutta, New Delhi, Madras, London, and other places. The traveler is the Black Bittern, Dalwurra, of the title, and the forty-four poems of the ancestral being's journey (the black bittern is a nonmigratory bird) duplicate Mudrooroo's travels and show his anguish at unwelcome encounters and reminders of racial oppression.

The tagging of exotic animals to represent outside peoples in contact with Dalwurra is interesting, but it certainly needs the explanations given in the book's introduction. Indians going to London to live are characterized as Peacock ''selling the wings, / Selling the tail feathers, / Buying the ticket, / Creating the luck, / Dyeing his tail feathers white, / Practising: / The rain in Spain falls mainly on London town.'' Blackbird is a victimized black man in London. Mole is a reflection on the Underground (''The red snouted one / Snuffles itching claws, / The red-clawed one / Tumbles red-lidded eyes / Blind to the sight, / Blind to the light . . .''). The end poems about the Black Bittern (''indigo-maroon'') in its habitat are touching and beautiful, and they use the repetitions typical of song cycles, as in ''Home'':

Wandering the beaches and creeks,
Wandering the beaches and creeks searching,
Searching for fish, searching the shoreline,
As one of a flock, as one of a flock . . .
Had there even been a time of indigo-maroon?
And then his feet stamp out the log-coffin of sweet honey
Residing, residing in the time of indigo-maroon.

Along with earlier pieces, Mudrooroo's selected poems, *The Garden of Gethsemane: Poems from the Lost Decade,* includes several extensive groups. Mudrooroo is a versatile poet, and he sees the necessity for the description of natural phenomena in the Aboriginal mode, as in ''Lightning'':

Dunno who he was, that brother with the hammer
With the mallet in his fist, just a brother . . .
Namaragan, sweep us together in your lightning flashes,
Namaragan, as my clapsticks mark out the rhythm
Your hammer crashes and in the wind spirit child-
　　ren whisper
Out the consternation of their line, of our line, of your line.

Mudrooroo writes strong political poems, including those that protest injustice against or the misery of deprived Aborigines and others of reconciliation, as well as personal and sensuous poems. He has seen the need for an exemplary writer, and he has taken on the task himself. As readers accustom themselves to Mudrooroo's view of the world and to the references in his poems, they come to admire the concept and to treasure the best poems as extensions of the Aboriginal oral tradition. Such readers can only celebrate the making of a poet in full view, for Mudrooroo is certainly one of the finest writers in Australia and arguably one of a handful of the most significant.

At the time of the publication of *Pacific Highway Boo-Blooz* in 1996, Mudrooroo's personal history received great publicity when it was revealed that his ancestry was not part Aboriginal but Jamaican Creole. His personal upbringing, however, which so greatly influenced his acceptance and understanding of Aboriginality, remained unchanged. This included his formative early experiences in school, orphanage, and prison, where his Aboriginality was unquestioned. *Pacific Highway Boo-Blooz* uses country-and-western song contours to evoke life on the margins of society and along the "dole paradise" of Queensland's Pacific beaches. Mudrooroo has probably done more to instill an Aboriginal consciousness in Australian writing than any other practitioner. Conditioning can be as powerful a formative element in a person's experience as genetics.

—Judith Rodriguez

MUELLER, Lisel

Nationality: American (emigrated from Germany in 1939). **Born:** Elisabeth Neumann, Hamburg, Germany, 8 February 1924. **Education:** University of Evansville, Indiana, 1940–44, B.A. 1944; Indiana University, Bloomington, 1950–53. **Career:** Visiting professor, Goddard College and Warren Wilson College, 1977–86. Poet-in-residence, University of Chicago, Washington University, Elmhurst College, Wichita State University, and University of Missouri-Kansas City. **Awards:** Lamont Poetry Selection, Academy of American Poets, 1975; National Book award, 1981; National Endowment for the Arts fellowship, 1990; Carl Sandburg award, 1990; Honorary Doctorate: Lake Forest College, Illinois, 1985; Pulitzer prize in poetry, 1997. **Address:** 909 West Foster, Apartment 607, Chicago, Illinois 60640, U.S.A.

PUBLICATIONS

Poetry

Dependencies. Chapel Hill, North Carolina, University of North Carolina Press, 1965.
Life of a Queen. LaCrosse, Wisconsin, Juniper Press, 1970.
The Private Life. Baton Rouge, Louisiana, Louisiana State University Press, 1976.
Voices from the Forest. LaCrosse, Wisconsin, Juniper Press, 1977.
The Need to Hold Still. Baton Rouge, Louisiana State University Press, 1980.
Second Language. Baton Rouge, Louisiana State University Press, 1986.
Waving from Shore. Baton Rouge, Louisiana State University Press, 1989.

Learning to Play by Ear (essays and selected early poems). LaCrosse, Wisconsin, 1990.
Alive Together: New and Selected Poems. Baton Rouge, Louisiana State University Press, 1996.

Other

Translator, *Selected Later Poems of Marie Louise Kaschnitz.* Princeton, New Jersey, Princeton University Press, 1980.
Translator, *Whether or Not* by Marie Louise Kaschnitz. LaCrosse, Wisconsin, Juniper Press, 1984.
Translator, *Three Daughters* by A.W. Mitgutsch. New York, Harcourt Brace, 1987.
Translator, *Circe's Mountain* by Marie Louise Kaschnitz. Minneapolis, Minnesota, Milkweed, 1990.

*

Critical Studies: "Comment on the Writer's Language: A Poem by Lisel Mueller" by Reginald Gibbons, in *Indiana Review* (Bloomington), spring 1985; "'The Steady Interior Hum': A Conversation with Lisel Mueller" by Stan Sanvel Rubin and William Heyen, in *The Post-Confessionals: Conversations with American Poets of the Eighties,* edited by Earl G. Ingersoll, Judith Kitchen, and Stan Sanvel Rubin, Rutherford, Fairleigh Dickinson University Press, 1989.

Lisel Mueller comments:

When I Am Asked
When I am asked
how I began writing poems,
I talk about the indifference of nature.

It was soon after my mother died,
a brilliant June day,
everything blooming.

I sat on a gray stone bench
in a lovingly planted garden,
but the daylilies were as deaf
as the ears of drunken sleepers
and the roses curved inward.
Nothing was black or broken
and not a leaf fell
and the sun blared endless commercials
for summer holidays.

I sat on gray stone bench
ringed with the ingenue faces
of pink and white impatiens
and placed my grief
in the mouth of language,
the only thing that would grieve with me.

*   *   *

Lisel Mueller has not only received important American prizes—the Lamont and the National Book and Carl Sandburg awards-but she has also helped to bestow them. She served with John Frederick Nims, poet and former editor of *Poetry* magazine, and with Helen Vendler, professor and critic, as a judge for the Bollingen prize when it was awarded to Stanley Kunitz in 1987. Although sometimes considered to be a Midwestern poet, Mueller has been published nationally—in the East by *The New Yorker,* in the Midwest by Juniper Press in Wisconsin, and in the South by Louisiana State University. She has also been active as a translator and a teacher. She has given notable support to former students (for example, Paulette Roeske) and to younger poets such as Deborah Pope and Nance Van Winckel.

Mueller's poems typically focus on common experiences. She favors the familiar rather than the exotic, almost as if she had asked herself, What do I know about myself that has some public significance? She has said that her immediate decision to write poetry was influenced by the unexpected death of her mother. In much of her poetry she expresses herself by means of observed details:

I sat on a gray stone bench
in a lovingly planted garden,
but the daylilies were as deaf
as the ears of drunken sleepers
and the roses curved inward.
Nothing was black or broken
and not a leaf fell
and the sun blared endless commercials

The word "clarity" is often used to describe Mueller's poetry. In "My Grandmother's Gold Pin" such details as "fleur-de-lis," "elegant braids," "ebony," "cherry soup," and "beer soup" belong to a mood of aesthetic innocence, where beautiful things are good, plain things homey, and emotions central and clear. There is a sense of loss and of joy but not of moral complexity or ambiguity. Conflicts tend to be well defined without an overlay of ideology.

Although personal, Mueller's poems do seem to favor a certain distancing, as in this excerpt from the set of short poems "Imaginary Painting":

How I would paint the future

A strip of horizon, and a figure,
seen from the back, forever approaching.

These lines also show her setting a limit:

How I would paint Love

I would not paint love.

Mueller's poems have been likened to those of William Matthews, Linda Pastan, Carl Dennis, Rita Dove, Jonathan Holden, and Michael Waters, especially in their exploration of where private and public concerns intersect. As with these poets, personal conflicts may be evoked as a condition but not as an idiosyncrasy; otherwise, the fortissimo of personal or social involvements might become literally "unspeakable." The poems are as fluent as thoughtful speech; their rhythms tend, more often than not, to have rising cadences rather than acoustically assertive iambic lines.

Mueller's poems also speak with civility. In the poem "A Story," for example, she tells "How Fire Took Water to Wife," concluding with the lines

but after a while she weeps
and says he is killing her,
he shouts that he cannot breathe
underwater—

Make up your own
ending, you say to the children
and they will, they will

—William Sylvester

MULDOON, Paul

Nationality: Irish. **Born:** County Armagh, Northern Ireland, 20 June 1951. **Education:** St. Patrick's College, Armagh; Queen's University, Belfast. **Family:** Married Jean Hanff Korelitz in 1987; one daughter. **Career:** Radio and television producer, BBC Northern Ireland, 1973–86; Judith E. Wilson Fellow, Cambridge University, 1986–87; writing fellow, University of East Anglia, Norwich, 1987; visiting professor, Columbia University, New York, 1987–88, and Princeton University, New Jersey, 1987–88; writer-in-residence, YMHA, New York, 1988; Roberta Holloway Lecturer, University of California, Berkeley, 1989; visiting professor, University of Massachusetts, Amherst, 1989–90. Since 1990 lecturer, since 1993 director of creative writing program, and since 1995 professor, Princeton University. **Awards:** Eric Gregory award, 1972; Faber memorial prize, 1982; John Simon Guggenheim Memorial fellow, 1990; Geoffrey Faber award, 1991; T.S. Eliot prize, 1994; Academy award in literature, American Academy of Arts and Letters, 1996; Irish Times prize for poetry, 1997. **Address:** Princeton University, Creative Writing Program, Princeton, New Jersey 08544, U.S.A.

PUBLICATIONS

Poetry

Knowing My Place. Belfast, Ulsterman, 1971.
New Weather. London, Faber, 1973.
Spirit of Dawn. Belfast, Ulsterman, 1975.
Mules. London, Faber, and Winston-Salem, North Carolina, Wake Forest University Press, 1977.
Names and Addresses. Belfast, Ulsterman, 1978.
Why Brownlee Left. London, Faber, and Winston-Salem, North Carolina, Wake Forest University Press, 1980.
Immram. Dublin, Gallery Press, 1980.
The O-Os' Party. Dublin, Gallery Press, 1980.
Out of Siberia. Dublin, Gallery Press, and Deerfield, Massachusetts, Deerfield Press, 1982.
Quoof. London, Faber, and Winston-Salem, North Carolina, Wake Forest University Press, 1983.
The Wishbone. Dublin, Gallery Press, 1984.
Selected Poems 1968–1983. London, Faber, 1986; New York, Ecco Press, 1987.
Meeting the British. London, Faber, and Winston-Salem, North Carolina, Wake Forest University Press, 1987.
Madoc: A Mystery. London, Faber, 1990.
Shining Brow. London, Faber, 1993.

The Annals of Chile. London, Faber, and New York, Farrar Straus, 1994.
Kerry Slides. Loughcrew, Oldcastle, Ireland, Gallery Press, 1996.
The Noctuary of Narcussus Batt. London and Boston, Faber, 1997.
Hay. London, Faber, and New York, Farrar Straus, 1998.

Play

Television Play: *Monkeys,* 1989.

Other

Editor, *The Scrake of Dawn: Poems by Young People from Northern Ireland.* Belfast, Blackstaff Press, 1979.
Editor, *The Faber Book of Contemporary Irish Poetry.* London, Faber, 1986.
Editor, *The Essential Byron.* New York, Ecco Press, 1989.
Editor, *The Faber Book of Beasts.* London and Boston, Faber, 1997.
Editor, *Bandanna: An Opera in Two Acts and a Prologue,* by Daron Hagen. London, Faber, 1999.

*

Critical Studies: By Mary DeShazer, in *Concerning Poetry* (Bellingham, Washington), 14(2), fall 1981; "Juniper, Otherwise Known: Poems by Paulin and Muldoon" by Adrian Frazier, in *Eire-Ireland* (St. Paul, Minnesota), 19(1), spring 1984; "Paul Muldoon and the Poetics of Sexual Difference," in *Contemporary Literature* (Madison, Wisconsin), 28(3), fall 1987, and "Yeats, Muldoon, and Heroic History," in *Learning the Trade: Essays on W.B. Yeats and Contemporary Poetry,* edited by Deborah Fleming, West Cornwall, Connecticut, Locust Hill, 1993, both by William A. Wilson; "'Armageddon, Armagh-geddon': Language and Crisis in the Poetry of Paul Muldoon" by John Goodby, in *Anglo-Irish and Irish Literature: Aspects of Language and Culture,* edited by Birgit Bramsback and Martin Croghan, Uppsala, Uppsala University, 1988; "Threaders of Double-Stranded Words: News from the North of Ireland" by John Drexel, in *New England Review* (Middlebury, Vermont), 12(2), winter 1989; "Poetic Forms and Social Malformations" by Edna Longley, in *Tradition and Influence in Anglo-Irish Poetry,* edited by Terence Brown and Nicholas Grene, Totowa, New Jersey, Barnes and Noble, 1989; "A Northern Perspective: Dual Vision in the Poetry of Paul Muldoon" by Kathleen McCracken, in *Canadian Journal of Irish Studies* (Saskatoon, Canada), 16(2), December 1990; "Bog Poems and Book Poems; Doubleness, Self-Translation, and Pun in Seamus Heaney and Paul Muldoon" by Richard Brown, in *The Chosen Ground: Essays on the Contemporary Poetry of Northern Ireland,* edited by Neil Corcoran, Bridgend, Seren, 1992; *The Celtic Otherworld and Contemporary Irish Poetry* (dissertation) by Thomas Royster Howerton, University of North Carolina, Chapel Hill, 1993; "Hermeneutic Hermeticism: Paul Muldoon and the Northern Irish Poetic" by John Goodby, in *In Black and Gold: Contiguous Traditions in Post-War British and Irish Poetry,* edited by C.C. Barfoot, Amsterdam, Rodopi, 1994; "'Everything Provisional': Fictive Possibility and the Poetry of Paul Muldoon and Ciaran Carson" by Jonathan Allison, in *Etudes Irlandaises* (Sainghinen en Melantois, France), 20(2), autumn 1995; *Paul Muldoon* by Tim Kendall, Bridgend, Wales, Seren, and Chester Springs, Pennsylvania, Dufour, 1996; *Northern Exposures: Politics, Pressure and Tradition in the Poetry of Montague, Heaney, and Muldoon* (dissertation) by Kevin Brady,

Drew University, 1996; "Muldoon's Humor" by Peter Robinson, in *Shiron* (Japan), 35, June 1996; "Obliquity in the Poetry of Paul Muldoon and Medbh McGuckian" by Shane Murphy, in *Eire-Ireland* (St. Paul, Minnesota), 31(3–4), fall-winter 1996; "Paul Muldoon: A Postmodern Ulysses?" by Carol Tell, in *The Classical World and the Mediterranean,* edited by Giuseppe Serpillo and Donatella Badin, Cagliari, Italy, Tema, 1996; "'Some Sweet Disorder'—The Poetry of Subversion: Paul Muldoon, Tom Paulin and Medbh McGuckian" by Elmer Andrews, in *British Poetry from the 1950s to the 1990s: Politics and Art,* edited by Gary Day and Brian Docherty, London, Macmillan, and New York, St. Martin's Press, 1997; *Reading Paul Muldoon* by Clair Wills, Newcastle upon Tyne, Bloodaxe, and Chester Springs, Pennsylvania, Dufour, 1998.

*   *   *

Paul Muldoon's poetic career made a precocious start and has sustained a prodigious pace. His first collection, *New Weather,* was well received when he was twenty-two, and in an influential and enthusiastic review of his second collection, *Mules,* Seamus Heaney concluded that Muldoon was "one of the very best." The qualities that characterized the early volumes have remained his hallmark—a lively storyteller's wit combined with a cryptic element that fascinates rather than defeats the reader. The subject matter on which these technical powers have been brought to bear has been distributed evenhandedly between the private and public domains: the privacy of sexuality and family relations, and the public area of Northern Irish violence and tension. But this is to separate off his subjects too neatly, for common to all his writing is a cool and amused eye, wryly observant. As with many writers in the Irish tradition, meaning is produced more by concern with form than with substance, and there is a delight in the suggested rather than the declamatory.

Although the writers Muldoon himself pays tribute to as influences are exponents of the lyric (Thomas, Frost, MacNeice), a striking feature of his work is the tendency to use the lyric to build toward larger units, characteristic of the major modernist-symbolist poets of the early part of the twentieth century, Yeats and Eliot. (Muldoon says that in his student days he thought the latter was God.) In particular Muldoon develops Yeats's practice of making each single volume of poetry a consistent symbolic statement. But Muldoon is a symbolist with a difference; his symbols are not received or traditional (the rose, the swan, the sword) but new: mushrooms, American Indians, mules, figures from the cinema. Sometimes these are transparent (for instance, mules as figures of the various unresolved dualities in Northern Ireland, unsuccessfully matched), but more often they are private and left open-ended ("quoof" was the family term for a hot-water bottle). What is most characteristic of him is to write in innocent, transparent language but with unclear meaning. He greatly reveres Joyce and is influenced by him in various linguistic effects, in particular the way his usage responds to the auditory as much as the semantic, but the general effect of his language is the opposite of Joyce's. Whereas *Finnegans Wake* distorts word forms by packing several meanings into a single unit, Muldoon uses traditional words, with apparently straightforward senses, to uncertain purpose.

Because of this the center of Muldoon's poetic worldview is a kind of metaphysics of doubt, not surprising perhaps in the context of Northern Ireland, where the most strongly held views are not necessarily the most worthy of credence. A typical, elegant occurrence of this comes at the end of the poem "History," in *Why Brownlee Left:*

Into the room where MacNeice wrote 'Snow',
Or the room where they say he wrote 'Snow'.

The poems that develop this open-endedness most strikingly, and that advance on the structure of a Yeats volume, are the long poems with which Muldoon ends his books. Possibly the most successful of these is ''The More a Man Has the More a Man Wants'' in *Quoof*. This brilliant, rambling narrative, corresponding to ''Immram'' in *Why Brownlee Left,* draws on details of Northern Irish violence in a series of forty-nine fourteen-line poems, playing artfully with the structure of the sonnet and ending with an item outside the sonnet-based structure (''Huh''), a negative comment, it seems, on the certainty or advisability of any such enterprise. Within this doubtful framework Muldoon runs through his repertoire of Joycean linguistic devices, including the associative runs of phonetically or semantically echoing words (Gallogly, Gollogly, Golightly, Ingoldsby, English) and his playing off of clichés against more traditionally poetic registers.

But Muldoon is by no means only a player of games. For example, few poems have expressed more eloquently the desolation of Northern Irish life than has ''Aisling'' in *Quoof*. For a poet who has been accused of evasiveness or of being ivory-towerish, he refers a great deal to such sensitive areas as ''our Protestant neighbour,'' ''the British,'' or the IRA hunger strikers. Within its formal peculiarities the poetry strongly suggests observed reality in its nonassertiveness. The universal authority of poetic judgment is declined in a way that claims to see what can be seen objectively from the outside, no more, no less.

Above all, behind the apparent whimsy and caution and formal playing, Muldoon has an exceptional lyric gift, justifying his claims of descent from MacNeice but perhaps surpassing the master. Two examples might be noted. The first is the title poem of the collection *Why Brownlee Left,* an essay in a familiar modern genre, the empty parable that waits to be invested with the reader's meaning. The question of why Brownlee left is entirely open at the end, looking to the future for an answer, no more assertive than his horses,

like man and wife,
Shifting their weight from foot to
Foot, and gazing into the future.

Another example of his lyric gift is ''The Fox,'' an elegy for his father in *Meeting the British,* outstanding even in an age of excellent elegies because of its simplicity and compassion.

What it proves is that Muldoon has the technique to turn successfully to any poetic area, even one as remote as this from his reserved and canny narrations.

—Bernard O'Donoghue

MULLEN, Harryette (Romell)

Nationality: American. Born: Florence, Alabama, 1 July 1953. Education: University of Texas, Austin, 1971–75, B.A. in English 1975; University of California, Santa Cruz, 1985–89, M.A. in literature 1988, Ph.D. in literature 1990. Career: Instructor, Austin Community College, Texas, 1975–77; temporary office worker, Manpower, Austin, Texas, 1977–79; artist in the schools, Texas Commission on Arts, Beaumont and Galveston, 1978–81; teaching assistant, University of California, Santa Cruz, 1985–89; visiting lecturer/ dissertation fellow, University of California, Santa Barbara, 1988–89; assistant professor, Cornell University, Ithaca, New York, 1989–95. Since 1995 associate professor of English and African American studies, University of California, Los Angeles. Awards: Dobie-Paisano fellowship, 1981–82; Helene Wurlitzer Foundation of New Mexico artist grant, 1982; literature award, Junior Black Arts Academy, Dallas, 1986; Rockefeller fellowship, Susan B. Anthony Center for Women's Studies, University of Rochester, New York, 1994–95; Gertrude Stein Award in Innovative American Poetry, 1994–95; first prize, Katharine Newman Award for Best Essay, *MELUS,* 1996; artist residency, Virginia Center for the Arts, 1999. Address: Department of English, University of California, Los Angeles, Box 90095–1530, 2225 Rolfe Hall, Los Angeles, California 90095, U.S.A.

PUBLICATIONS

Poetry

Tree Tall Woman. Galveston, Texas, Energy Earth Communications, 1981.
Trimmings. New York, Tender Buttons Books, 1991.
S*PERM**K*T. Philadelphia, Singing Horse Press, 1992.
Muse & Drudge. Philadelphia, Singing Horse Press, 1995.

Other

Freeing the Soul: Subjectivity, Race, and Difference in Slave Narratives. London, Cambridge University Press, 1999.

*

Media Adaptation: *Seven Cabaret Songs,* music composition by T.J. Anderson, with lyrics from *Muse & Drudge,* 2000.

Critical Studies: By Stephen Yenser, in *Partisan Review* (New York), 61(2), spring 1994; ''Signifyin(g) on Stein: The Revisionist Poetics of Harryette Mullen and Leslie Scalapino'' by Elisabeth A. Frost, in *Postmodern Culture* (Cary, North Carolina), 5(3), May 1995; by Calvin Bedient, in *Callaloo* (Baltimore, Maryland), 19(3), summer 1996; by Fred Chappell, in *Georgia Review,* 50(3), fall 1996; interview with Cynthia Hogue, in *Postmodern Culture* (Charlottesville, Virginia), 9(2), January 1999.

*   *   *

Harryette Mullen is a feminist language poet who writes from her experience and knowledge and from her desire to understand herself as an African-American woman. Although she uses language in a highly creative, symbolic, and playful way, her poems conjure up illuminating images of a woman in a patriarchal culture and of a black person in a white culture. Throughout her poetry Mullen's use of metaphors, homophones, aphorisms, allusions, blues, and jazz— particularly the woman's voice—allows her to pack a wealth of meaning into a short space. When one delves into Mullen's poetry, even reading between the lines is important.

Mullen began to write poetry as a child growing up in a middle-class family of schoolteachers and ministers in segregated Texas, and she published her first poem in high school. She was exposed to

African literature and Afro-American folklore at the University of Texas, but she heard women and black writers only at local readings, for at the time they were not studied as part of the canon. Her first book, *Tree Tall Woman,* which was published in 1981, was influenced by the black arts movement, in which black writers took as their subject the positive aspects of their culture.

In a doctoral program in the history of consciousness at the University of California, Santa Cruz, Mullen became a student of Nathaniel Mackey, a black language poet. In an interview with Cynthia Hogue in *Postmodern Culture* in 1999, Mullen cited Gwendolyn Brooks and Lorenzo Thomas as being "important" to her work. But it was reading Gertrude Stein's *Tender Buttons* that led Mullen to her second book, *Trimmings,* which was published in 1991. As Elizabeth A. Frost states in the article "Signifyin(g) on Stein: The Revisionist Poetics of Harryette Mullen and Leslie Scalapino" (*Postmodern Culture,* 1995), "Mullen marks her text with both 'mainstream' speech and the black vernacular in what she calls a 'splicing together of different lexicons' . . ." Frost adds, "Mullen appropriates cliches linked to African-American culture and forces us to ask what 'black' and 'white' culture actually consist in — where the lines are drawn." For example, one of Mullen's short evocative pieces reads, "Her red and white, white and blue banner manner. Her red and white all over black and blue. Hannah's bandanna flagging her down in the kitchen with Dinah, with Jemima. Someone in the kitchen I know." Mullen's homage to Stein thus takes the older poet's playfulness with language a step further by placing the language within a racial and gender context.

If *Trimmings* is considered to be poetry about women with clothes, Mullen's next book, *S*PERM**K*T,* which was published in 1992, can be seen as poetry about women and food. As the title indicates, *S*PERM**K*T* is a takeoff on supermarket consumerism within a male culture, on the way in which women are seen and constructed by advertising.

Muse & Drudge, published in 1995, is written in quatrains. In "'Ruses of the Lunatic Muse': Harryette Mullen and Lyric Hybridity" (*Women's Studies,* 1998), Frost calls the work "a long poem as blues: fragmented and improvisational, disjunctive in its continuities." She says that "Mullen mixes the influences of avant-garde groups too often considered in isolation: like poets of the Black Arts Movement, Mullen experiements with a speech-based idiom, but, like language-influenced writers, she launches her cultural critique by rejecting the rules of syntax and fashioning a distinctively visual, punning, and allusive play with language."

Influenced by both literary and folkloric studies, Mullen invokes Sappho, the ancient Greek lyric poet, along with the loudmouthed Sapphire from the old *Amos 'n' Andy* radio show. Sapphire, once a perjorative name, is now being reclaimed by black women. In a stanza from *Muse & Drudge,* Mullen cleverly reclaims Sapphire and further posits Sappho as a blues singer: "Sapphires's lyre styles / plucked eyebrows / bow lips and legs / whose lives are lonely too."

—Jacquelyn Marie

MURPHY, Richard

Nationality: Irish. **Born:** County Mayo, 6 August 1927. **Education:** Canterbury Cathedral Choir School (Cathedral Chorister, 1940); King's School, Canterbury (Milner scholar), 1941–42; Wellington College, Berkshire, 1943–44; Magdalen College, Oxford, 1945–48, B.A. 1948, M.A. 1955; Sorbonne, Paris, 1954–55. **Family:** Married Patricia Avis in 1955 (divorced 1959); one daughter. **Career:** Director, English School, Canea, Crete, 1953–54; writer-in-residence, University of Virginia, Charlottesville, 1965; visiting fellow, Reading University, Berkshire, 1968; Compton Lecturer in poetry, University of Hull, Yorkshire, 1969; O'Connor Professor of Literature, Colgate University, Hamilton, New York, 1971; visiting professor of poetry, Bard College, Annandale-on-Hudson, New York, 1972, 1974; Princeton University, New Jersey, 1974–75, University of Iowa, Iowa City, 1976–77, and Syracuse University, New York, 1977–78; distinguished visiting poet, Catholic University, Washington, D.C., 1984, Pacific Lutheran University, Tacoma, Washington, 1985, Wichita State University, Kansas, 1987, and University of Tulsa, Oklahoma, 1992, 1994. **Awards:** AE memorial award, 1951; Guinness award, 1962; Arts Council of Great Britain bursary, 1967, award, 1976; Marten Toonder award, 1980; American-Irish Foundation award, 1983. Fellow, Royal Society of Literature (UK), 1968; member, Aosdàna. **Address:** The New Forge, Cleggan, County Galway, Ireland.

PUBLICATIONS

Poetry

The Archaeology of Love. Dublin, Dolmen Press, 1955.
Sailing to an Island. Dublin, Dolmen Press, 1955.
The Woman of the House: An Elegy. Dublin, Dolmen Press, 1959.
Three Irish Poets, with John Montague and Thomas Kinsella. Dublin, Dolmen Press, 1961.
The Last Galway Hooker. Dublin, Dolmen Press, 1961.
Six Irish Poets, with others, edited by Robin Skelton. London and New York, Oxford University Press, 1962.
Sailing to an Island (collection). London, Faber, 1963; New York, Chilmark Press, 1964.
Penguin Modern Poets 7, with Jon Silkin and Nathaniel Tarn. London, Penguin, 1965.
The Battle of Aughrim and The God Who Eats Corn. London, Faber, and New York, Knopf, 1968.
High Island: New and Selected Poems. London, Faber, and New York, Harper, 1974.
Selected Poems. London, Faber, 1979.
Care. Amsterdam, Cornamona Press, 1983.
The Price of Stone. London, Faber, 1985.
The Price of Stone and Earlier Poems. Winston-Salem, North Carolina, Wake Forest University Press, 1985.
New Selected Poems. London, Faber, 1989.
The Mirror Wall. Newcastle upon Tyne, Bloodaxe, and Winston-Salem, North Carolina, Wake Forest University Press, 1989.

Recording: *The Battle of Aughrim,* Claddagh, 1969.

*

Manuscript Collection: McFarlin Library, University of Tulsa, Oklahoma.

Critical Studies: *Richard Murphy, Poet of Two Traditions: Interdisciplinary Studies* (includes bibliography by May Fitzgerald), edited by Maurice Harmon, Dublin, Wolfhound Press, 1978; "The Poetry of Richard Murphy" by Dennis O'Driscoll, in *Poetry Australia* (New South Wales), 71, 1979; "Perception of Roots: The Historical Dichotomy of Ireland As Reflected in Richard Murphy's 'The Battle of Aughrim' and John Montague's 'The Rough Field'" by James J. Lafferty, in *Studies in Anglo-Irish Literature*, edited by Heinz Kosok, Bonn, Bouvier, 1982; "Richard Murphy: Poet of Nostalgia or Pietas?" by James D. Brophy, in *Contemporary Irish Writing*, edited by Brophy and Raymond J. Porter, Boston, Iona College Press, 1983; "The Poet As Builder: Richard Murphy's 'The Price of Stone'" by Joseph Sendry, in *Irish University Review* (Dublin), 15(1), spring 1985; "Three Irish Voices" by Charles O'Neill, in *Spirit* (South Orange, New Jersey), fall-winter 1989; "The Historian, the Critic and the Poet: A Reading of Richard Murphy's Poetry and Some Questions of Theory" by Joseph Swann, in *Canadian Journal of Irish Studies* (Saskatoon, Canada), 16(1), July 1990; *The Historiography of Three Irish Poets: W.B. Yeats, Seamus Heaney, and Richard Murphy* (dissertation) by Robert James Clougherty, University of Tulsa, 1991.

*   *   *

In his earlier poems, collected in *Sailing to an Island,* Richard Murphy succeeds as a lyrical biographer. He has created a poetry of epitaph and biography. "Woman of the House," for example, is an elegy for his grandmother, Lucy Mary Ormsby:

Time can never relax like this again,
She in her phaeton looking for folk-lore,

He writing sermons in the library
Till lunch, then fishing all the afternoon.

But Murphy's thematic range is not limited to the Anglo-Irish world. There are early poems about Wittgenstein in Galway, fishermen, Crete, and the drowning of a novice: "Now his feet were washed / in the sluicing bilges." Murphy writes in a distinctly clear style, following traditional verse structures with great ease and breaking away from these structures only when the theme requires it. His is a mandarin style washed clean by the activity of the sea. He shares with Louis MacNeice and Elizabeth Bowen a deep architectural sense and a wonderful capacity to re-create silent interiors. He began with the interior world of the family and the home but moved outward to embrace a broader architecture of Galway folk memory and Irish history. His career has been built around three broad concerns: the seaboard folklore of the west of Ireland, the Roman Catholic-Orange conflict of the Battle of Aughrim (1691), and the activity of home building in *The Price of Stone*. He has a novelist's sense of structure and ability to make connections, as in "Gate Lodge" from *The Price of Stone:*

I face my forebear's relic, a neat sty
That hovelled with his brogue some grateful clod
Unearthed by famine; and I hear go by
Your souper choir school voice defrauding God.

Murphy's sea poems and his seal poems—"Sailing to an Island," "The Cleggan Disaster," "Seals at High Island," and "Stormpetrel"—have become classics of the Irish poetic canon. Their rhythm and vocabulary are unique. The following lines are from "Sailing to an Island":

Now she dips, and the sail hits the water.
She luffs to a squall; is stuck; and shudders.
Someone is shouting. The boom, weak as a scissors,
Has Snapped . . .

So completely has Murphy mastered the folklore and rhythms of western Ireland that one never doubts the integrity of his world. Although educated out of Ireland and brought up in the Anglican tradition, he has always spoken for the native as well as the Anglo-Irish tradition. Like Yeats, Murphy alternates between revulsion and return, but his ear never betrays him, so that he constantly repeats Catholic voices. He picks up a rosary being said in a shop or uses the technique of Catholic blessing, of benediction, in a poem like "Stormpetrel": "Gipsy of the sea . . . / Waif of the afterglow . . . / Pulse of the rock . . ."

In his book-length poem *The Battle of Aughrim* he has created a narrative in several voices, like a radio play, around the central theme of the Irish defeat near Athlone in 1691. The poem moves through a series of tight lyrics to Saint Ruth's speech: "I my self will Command you; the Church will pray for you, your Posterity will bless you . . ." The narrative juxtaposes quotes from the Reverend George Story's *Impartial History* with descriptions of Sarsfield and Luttrell, with Luttrell's murder and Sarsfield's fatal exile:

Berwick the bastard sired by James the Shit
Immortalized you with no head but grit.
He took your widow Honor for his wife,
When saving the Sun King you lost your life.

In his collection *The Price of Stone* Murphy moves from the "cool creek of traitors" that was Aughrim to a more personally haunted world of houses. In poem after poem houses speak—Letterfrack Industrial School, a rectory, Kylemore Castle, a gate lodge, a barn. All speak of human habitation, of abandonment, and of possession. "Little Barn" says,

I've been converted to increase the rent
Between us, cornered in a stable yard.

It is a curious achievement for homes to speak of human migration. Murphy sets up an anthropology based on stone. But the technical brilliance of each verse and the cool detachment that created it are in keeping with the distinctive classical tradition of the Irish Anglican community. Perhaps houses and their stonework are the only documents without prejudice in Irish history. And this has been the crucial impetus in Murphy's work—a willed bridging of two traditions, an effort to connect sensuously and emotionally with two versions of Irish history.

—Thomas McCarthy

MURRAY, Les(lie) (Allan)

Nationality: Australian. **Born:** Nabiac, New South Wales, 17 October 1938. **Education:** Taree High School; University of Sydney (co-editor, *Arna* and *Hermes;* literary editor, *Honi Soit*), 1957–60, 1962. **Military Service:** Royal Australian Naval Reserve, 1960–61. **Family:** Married Valerie Gina Maria Morelli in 1962; three sons and two daughters. **Career:** Translator, Australian National University, Canberra, 1963–67; officer in Prime Minister's Department, 1970–71; co-editor, *Poetry Australia,* Sydney, 1973–80; writer-in-residence at universities of New England, Armidale, New South Wales; Stirling; Newcastle, New South Wales; Copenhagen; New South Wales; and Sydney. Scottish-Australian Writers Exchange fellow, 1981. **Awards:** Grace Leven prize, 1965, 1980, 1990; Australian Commonwealth Literary Fund fellowship, 1968, 1971; Cook Bi-Centenary prize, 1970; Literature Board Senior fellowships, 1973–79, 1981–84; National Book Council award, 1975, 1985, 1992; C.J. Dennis memorial prize, 1976; Australian Literary Society Gold Medal, 1984; Canada-Australia prize, 1985; Australian Bicentennial prize, 1988; New South Wales Premier's prize for poetry, 1993; Victoria Premier's prize for poetry, 1993; T.S. Eliot prize, 1996; Queen's Gold Medal for Poetry, 1998. D.Litt.: University of New England, 1990; University of Stirling, 1991; Australian National University, 1994. Officer, Order of Australia, 1988. **Agent:** Mrs. Margaret Connolly, 16 Winton Street, Warrawee, New South Wales 2074, Australia. **Address:** c/o Angus and Robertson, 4/31 Waterloo Road, North Ryde, New South Wales 2111, Australia.

PUBLICATIONS (works before 1990 as Les A. Murray)

Poetry

The Ilex Tree, with Geoffrey Lehmann. Canberra, Australian National University Press, 1965.
The Weatherboard Cathedral. Sydney, Angus and Robertson, 1969.
Poems against Economics. Sydney and London, Angus and Robertson, 1972.
Lunch and Counter Lunch. Sydney, Angus and Robertson, 1974.
Selected Poems: The Vernacular Republic. Sydney, Angus and Robertson, 1976.
Ethnic Radio. Sydney, Angus and Robertson, 1979.
The Boys Who Stole the Funeral. Sydney, Angus and Robertson, 1980; New York, Farrar Straus, 1991.
The Vernacular Republic: Poems 1961–1981. Sydney, Angus and Robertson, and Edinburgh, Canongate, 1982; revised edition, New York, Persea, 1982.
Equanimities. Copenhagen, Razorback Press, 1982.
The People's Otherworld. Sydney and London, Angus and Robertson, 1985.
Selected Poems. Manchester, Carcanet, 1986.
The Daylight Moon and Other Poems. Sydney, Angus and Robertson, 1987; Manchester, Carcanet, and New York, Persea, 1988.
The Idyll Wheel: Cycle of a Year at Bunyah, New South Wales, April 1986-April 1987. Canberra, Officina Brindabella, 1989.
Dog Fox Field. Sydney, Angus and Robertson, and Manchester, Carcanet, 1990; New York, Farrar Straus, 1993.
The Vernacular Republic: Poems, 1961–1983. Sydney, Angus and Robertson, 1990.
The Rabbiter's Bounty: Collected Poems. London, Carcanet, and New York, Farrar Straus, 1991; Port Melbourne, Heinemann, 1994.
Translations from the Natural World. Paddington, Isabella Press, 1992; New York, Farrar Straus, 1994.
Subhuman Redneck Poems. Sydney, Duffy and Snellgrove, and Manchester, Carcanet, 1996; New York, Farrar Straus, 1997.
New Selected Poems. Sydney, Duffy and Snellgrove, 1998.

Collected Poems. Manchester, Carcanet, 1998.
Fredy Neptune. Manchester, Carcanet, and Sydney, Duffy and Snellgrove, 1998; New York, Farrar Straus, 1999.
Conscious and Verbal. Manchester, Carcanet, 1999.
Learning Human: Selected Poems. New York, Farrar Straus, 2000.

Other

The Peasant Mandarin: Prose Pieces. St. Lucia, University of Queensland Press, 1978.
Persistence in Folly: Selected Prose Writings. Sydney, Angus and Robertson, and London, Sirius, 1984.
The Australian Year: The Chronicle of Our Seasons and Celebrations, photographs by Peter Solness. Sydney, Angus and Robertson, 1985.
The Gravy in Images. Hobart, Tasmania, International Liturgy Assembly, 1988.
Blocks and Tackles: Articles and Essays 1982–1990. Sydney, Angus and Robertson, 1990.
The Paperbark Tree. Manchester, Carcanet, 1992.
Killing the Black Dog: Essays and Poems. Annandale Press, New South Wales, Federation Press, 1997.
A Working Forest: Selected Prose. Potts Point, New South Wales, Duffy and Snellgrove, 1997.
The Quality of Sprawl. Sydney, Duffy and Snellgrove, 1999.

Editor, *The New Book of Australian Verse.* Melbourne, Oxford, and New York, Oxford University Press, 1986.
Editor, *Anthology of Australian Religious Poetry.* Blackburn, Victoria, Collins Dove, 1986.
Editor, *Fivefathers: Five Australian Poets of the Pre-Academic Era.* Manchester, Carcanet, 1994.

Translator, *An Introduction to the Principles of Phonological Description,* by Trubetzkoy The Hague. Niihoff. 1968.

*

Manuscript Collection: National Library of Australia, Canberra.

Critical Studies: ''The Poetry of Les A. Murray'' by Dianne Ailwood, in *Southerly* (Surrey Hills, New South Wales), 3, 1971; ''An Interview with Les A. Murray,'' in *Quadrant* (Sydney), December 1976, and ''Garlands of Ilex,'' in *Poetry Australia* (Sydney), May 1979, both by Robert Gray; ''Evading the Modernities: The Poetry of Les A. Murray'' by Gary Catalano, in *Meanjin* (Melbourne), May 1977; *Study Notes on the Poetry of Les A. Murray* by Penelope Nelson, Melbourne, Methuen, 1978; Ken Goodwin, in *Australian Poems in Perspective,* Brisbane, University of Queensland Press, 1979; ''Country Poetry and Town Poetry: A Debate with Les Murray'' by Peter Porter, in *Australian Literary Studies* (Hobart, Tasmania), May 1979; ''The Frequent Image of Farms: A Profile of Les Murray'' by Graham Kinross-Smith, in *Westerly* (Nedlands, Western Australia), September 1980; ''Les Murray's Watershed'' by C.J. Koch, in *Quadrant* (Sydney), September 1980; ''The Common Dish and the Uncommon Poet'' by John Barnie, in *Kunapipi* (Aarhus, Denmark), 1, 1982; *A Vivid Steady State: Les Murray and Australian Poetry* by Laurence Bourke, Kensington, New South Wales University Press, 1992; ''This Country Is My Mind'' by Carmel Gaffney, in

Westerly (Nedlands, Australia), 39(1), autumn 1994; ''Fullness of Being in Les Murray's 'Presence: Translations from the Natural World''' by Bert Almon, in *Antipodes* (Brooklyn, New York), 8(2), December 1994; '''Countour-Line by Countour': Landscape Change As an Index of History in the Poetry of Les Murray'' by Martin Leer, in *Australian Literary Studies* (St. Lucia, Queensland), 16(3), May 1994; '''Religions Are Poems': Spirituality in Les Murray's Poetry'' by Nicholas Birns, in *'And the Birds Began to Sing': Religion and Literature in Post-Colonial Cultures,* edited by Jamie S. Scott, Amsterdam, Rodopi, 1996; ''Land and Theory'' by Martin Harrison, in *Southerly,* 57(2), winter 1997; ''Les Murray and the Tradition of the Emblem Poem'' by Rodney Stenning Edgecombe, in *Counterbalancing Light: Essays on the Poetry of Les Murray,* edited by Carmel Gaffney, Armidale, Australia, Kardoorair, 1997; by Jamie Grant, in *Southerly,* 58(2), winter 1998; by Barbara Williams, in her *In Other Words: Interviews with Australian Poets,* Amsterdam, Rodopi, 1998.

* * *

Les Murray is the Australian poet of his generation who is most clearly marked for celebrity. His work combines great force of personality, an extraordinary play of language, and masterful confrontation with—one could say a masterful dancing among—large and difficult subjects.

The poems in Murray's first book, shared with Geoffrey Lehmann, mostly treat of country places and customs, an abiding preoccupation. The exception is the much anthologized ''The Burning Truck,'' a sustained run of thirty-six lines about the truck and the fearfully delighted onlookers.

Later book titles have emphasized Murray's local and partisan temper and his uncompromising allegiances. These can be explored in the books of critical essays and reviews. The poems present a wide range of reflections on man's interactions with nature, firmly localized, for Murray of all Australian poets has most strongly celebrated small-farming districts, particularly his own Northern Rivers (of New South Wales) with its dairy industry. This interest first culminates in the magnificent sequence ''Walking to the Cattle Place'' in *Poems against Economics*. In many different forms, quirkily ranging from Sanskrit derivations to ideas of God, from bullock jumping in Australia to the salutation of a Xhosa tribesman, the poems encounter, discuss, and play with man's age-old role as a cattle herder, as in ''The Names of the Humble'':

Fence beyond fence from breakfast
I climb into my thought
and watch the slowing of herds into natural measures.

Nosedown for hours, ingesting grass, they breathe grass,
trefoil, particles, out of the soft-focus earth
dampened by nose-damp. They have breathed great
    plateaux to dust.

. . .

They concede me a wide berth at first. I go on being
    harmless
and some graze closer, gradually. It is like watching
an emergence. Person.

Where cattletracks mount
boustrophedon to the hills
I want to discern the names of all the humble.

Other human creations Murray discusses are the Lee Enfield rifle (''SMLE''), law and order (''The Police: Seven Voices''), and learning (''Sidere Mens Eadem Mutato,'' a reminiscence and discussion in nine unrhymed sonnets that is based on Murray's university experience). ''Vindaloo in Merthyr Tydfil'' is groaningly funny and ''Folklore'' not merely funny.

David Malouf, in a careful discussion (''Subjects Found and Taken Up'' in *Poetry Australia*) of *Lunch and Counter Lunch,* began by calling Murray ''perhaps the most naturally gifted poet of his generation.'' Malouf remarked on his ''almost unlimited'' verbal inventiveness, the freshness and originality of his insights, and his wit and humor but then stated his uneasiness at Murray's need for a debating stance. He said that he felt the earlier subject matter had been worked through and that new material must be found ''fully expressive'' of Murray's gifts.

The astonishing adaptation in English of the Aboriginal song cycle might be taken as Murray's reply. ''The Buledelah-Taree Holiday Song Cycle'' has thirteen long-lined sections. They look Whitmanesque on the page but actually are distinctive, and although there is some rhythmical affinity with Robinson Jeffers, Murray's lines are end-stopped:

It is the season of the Long Narrow City; it has crossed the
    Myall, it has entered the North Coast,
that big stunning snake; it is looped through the
    hills, burning all night there.
Hitching and flying on the downgrades, processionally
    balancing on the climbs,
it echoes in O'Sullivan's Gap, in the tight coats of
    the flooded-gum trees;
the tops of palms exclaim at it unmoved, there near
    Wootton.
Glowing all night behind the hills, with a north-
    shifting glare, burning behind the hills;
through Coolongolook, through Wang Wauk, across the
    Wallamba,
the booming tarred pipe of the holiday slows and
    spurts again; Nabiac chokes in glassy wind,
the forests on Kiwarrak dwindle in cheap light;
    Tuncurry and Forster swell like cooking oil.

The poems celebrate the country-bred city dweller's yearly return with his family to his childhood district, camping and picnicking, fishing, showing off accustomed things, observing change. Other popular poems that go to the native earth are ''The Broad Bean Sermon'' and ''Laconics: The Forty Acres.'' They continue Murray's earlier interest, one that is further explored in *The Daylight Moon,* published a year after Murray returned to live on the farm where he had grown up.

The enterprise and skill—and scholarly scrupulousness, for Murray is a polyglot who has worked as a translator—involved in using the song cycle also points to an urgent interest in the racial mix in Australia, first strongly signaled in ''Jószef'' in *Lunch and Counter Lunch*. This interest is carried into poems related to his Celtic origins and celebrating the arrival of his wife's family in Australia.

The verse novel *The Boys Who Stole the Funeral* has a plot characteristically expressive of Murray's allegiance to the rural community and his contempt for city folk and sophisticates, his instinct for principled rebellion, and his need for heroic presentation of a case. The hero's aim is to bury an old soldier fittingly; his destiny, an encounter in the bush with two mentors—one white and one black—is an interesting variation of a motif used by Xavier Herbert in his 1938 novel *Capricornia*. But Murray's energy in reaching toward sufficiently subtle and final-sounding truths and principles, embodied in the symbolic "Common Dish," is all his own.

Murray's achievements in the 1980s includes *The Idyll Wheel,* a calendar cycle of monthly poems for the year April 1986 to April 1987 that richly evoke his hometown of Bunyah. Filled with the lore of a district, it includes local stories ("spoken video") in kitchens in June and "Midwinter Haircut," set in July, as well as the yearly round of animal husbandry and agriculture.

Murray's influence was widely felt during the 1970s through his editorship of *Poetry Australia* and during the subsequent period when he served as the poetry series editor for the publisher Angus and Robertson. He has been involved in several controversies, including a flyting with Peter Porter over poetic values: Boeotian (rural and bardic, supported by a Gaelic background—Murray) or Athenian (urban and sophisticated—Porter). Standing on bardic tradition, he is a doughty proponent of continuous public funding for full-time poets. His poetry bears witness to his staunch and highly individual Roman Catholicism. He is a vivid and dogmatic presence at festivals and conferences, and his strongly held, sometimes reactionary opinions continue to win him polemic responses.

Murray's public position, both in Australia and internationally, grew in the later years of the 1990s. He won the T.S. Eliot prize in 1996, and in 1998 he was awarded the Queen's Gold Medal for Poetry. With the publication of the aggressively titled *Subhuman Redneck Poems* in 1996, Murray revealed for the first time a medical and mental crisis that had its origins in his mother's early death and his unhappy experiences as a bullied "fat boy." Despite brilliant individual poems in the collection, its overall aggressive stance leaves a bitter aftertaste. The poem-novel *Fredy Neptune* was published in 1998, and although the work won numerous awards and has a startlingly ambitious narrative that ranges across many of the "big" historical crises of the twentieth century and pays tribute to everything from the Hollywood epic to European masterworks, it has proved a difficult book for many of Murray's admirers to accept wholeheartedly. In some ways it is congruent with *Subhuman Redneck Poems*. In 1996 the poet suffered a serious illness and was in a coma for three weeks and was not expected to live. Murray's 1999 collection, *Conscious and Verbal,* though presenting evidence of the author's amazingly prolific output during this period, also contains some of the breathtaking inventiveness of his earlier *Translations from the Natural World*. The delight in language and life shines through the collection, as does a sense of recovery and balance.

Murray easily retains the unofficial position of national poet, for though he is firmly based in northeastern New South Wales, he has traveled throughout and written brilliantly of many parts of Australia. He has clearly attempted to articulate a personal, national, and artistic ethos ("The Vernacular Republic") that, though it may appear to be right-wing, can be seen as being affiliated with country and small-farm life, in the line of the turn-of-the-century *Sydney Bulletin*. Other poets have proved more limited in range and spirit, less spectacular in their talents, and less ready to assume a public role, and they also lack Murray's authentic connection to an undoubted rural and outback heartland.

—Judith Rodriguez

MURRAY, Rona

Nationality: Canadian. **Born:** London, England, 10 February 1924. **Education:** Queen Margaret's School, Duncan, British Columbia, 1933–41; Mills College, Oakland, California, 1941–44; Victoria College, British Columbia, 1960–61, B.A. (honors) 1960; University of British Columbia, Vancouver, 1963–65, M.A. 1965; University of Kent, Canterbury, Ph.D. 1972. **Family:** Married 1) Ernest Haddon in 1944, two sons and one daughter; 2) Walter Dexter in 1972. **Career:** Special instructor, University of Victoria, 1961–62; head of English Department, Rockland School, Victoria, 1962–63; teaching assistant/lecturer, University of British Columbia, 1963–66; associate lecturer, Selkirk College, Castlegar, British Columbia, 1968–74; instructor, Douglas College, Surrey, British Columbia, 1974–76; visiting lecturer in creative writing, 1977–79, and in English, 1981–83, University of Victoria; instructor, Open Learning Institute (now Open University), 1984–88. **Awards:** British Columbia Centennial One-Act Play award, 1958; Macmillan of Canada award, 1964; Norma Epstein award, 1965; Canada Council grant, 1976, 1979; Pat Lowther award, 1982. **Agent:** Joanna Kellock, 11017–80th Avenue, Edmonton, Alberta T6G OR2, Canada. **Address:** 3825 Duke Road, R.R.1, Victoria, British Columbia V8X 3W9, Canada.

PUBLICATIONS

Poetry

The Enchanted Adder. Vancouver, Klanak Press, 1965.
The Power of the Dog and Other Poems. Victoria, British Columbia, Morriss, 1968.
Ootischenie. Fredericton, New Brunswick, Fiddlehead, 1974.
Selected Poems. Delta, British Columbia, Sono Nis Press, 1974.
From an Autumn Journal. Toronto, League of Canadian Poets, 1980.
Journey. Victoria, British Columbia, Sono Nis Press, 1981.
Adam and Eve in Middle Age. Victoria, British Columbia, Sono Nis Press. 1984.
The Lost Garden. Victoria, British Columbia, Hawthorne Society, 1993.

Plays

Blue Ducks' Feather and Eagledown (produced Vancouver, 1958).
One, Two, Three Alary (produced Castlegar, British Columbia, 1970; Seattle, 1983).
Creatures (produced Seattle, 1980). Published in *Event 7* (New Westminister, British Columbia), no. 2, n.d.

Short Stories

The Indigo Dress and Other Stories. Victoria, British Columbia, Sono Nis Press, 1986.

Other

Journey Back to Peshawar. Victoria, British Columbia, Sono Nis
  Press, 1993.

Editor, with Walter Dexter, *The Art of Earth: An Anthology.* Victoria,
  British Columbia, Sono Nis Press, 1979.
Editor, *Threshold.* Victoria, British Columbia, Sono Nis Press, 1998.

*

Rona Murray comments:

(1985) In my poetry I attempt to record subjective, personal
experience through concrete detail and, generally, through the manner in which the material is spaced on the page rather than through
traditional forms, although recently I have been returning to the latter.
There appear to be two distinct demands from which it grows: the first
to form order, as I see it, out of chaos; the second to record certain
ecstatic, usually numinous occurrences. The poems are literal rather
than symbolic, and I have been astonished at critics who have
ascribed symbolic meanings to my reality. My last book has a
political, feminist basis, although I hope it moves beyond this to a
universal statement on the varying attitudes in our culture between the
male and female. I consider poetry a ''given'' aesthetic form, realized
in a state of excitement, with ease, and then subjected to the writer's
critical judgment. Therefore, it appears to be most successful if the
poet masters his techniques and then trusts to the mercy of inspiration.
I believe that it originates in the subconscious, or in the right side of
the brain, or in Yeats's *Spiritus Mundi* and that all the scribe can do is
to wait for its emergence when it chooses to manifest itself. Forced
poetry appears to me to be inevitably boring. Perhaps for this reason I
am now concentrating on fiction. One can be a professional fiction
writer, but not a professional poet, except in so far as one teaches, or
writes about, the craft, not in its practice. Presently I have a collection
of short fiction under consideration with a publishing house and am
working on a novel.

*   *   *

The work of Rona Murray is not well known across Canada, but
it does have a devoted following on the West Coast, where she has
lived since her eighth year, where she was educated, and where she
has taught. Her work includes poems, plays, stories, and novels. She
is a serious and thoughtful writer with a characteristic manner who
deliberately calculates her effects and then makes the most of them.
She is one of Robin Skelton's favorite poets.

It has been noted that ''white'' is a key word in Murray's work.
The word may appear as a noun or as an adjective, but it is always
used symbolically, conveying the twin notions of innocence and
death. The double meaning is apparent in the following passages,
taken from the first and the eighth poems in her *Selected Poems*
(where the poems are numbered rather than titled):

I have been into the halls of the dead;
the old man said I wore white,
and white makes the woman invulnerable,
he said.

and

The whiteness   the birches
grasp me   closer
than   can
any lover or   friend.

The collection *Adam and Eve in Middle Age* counterpoints
Murray's poems with reproductions of eleven paintings by the
Victoria artist Phyllis Serota. The poems and paintings purport to
deliver a message ''to all the daughters of Eve.'' The message is
meaningful in a postmodern fashion. Adam and Eve speak in turn,
and as the reviewer Judith Fitzgerald has observed, ''Here, in true
anachronistic fashion, Eve writes poetry and Adam broods over the
problems of state, taxes, the scarcity of jobs, and child abuse.''

In an earlier collection Murray noted: ''I explore / five-finger
exercises. / No more.'' But her poems, her probings, her attempts to
find stasis in a changing world do more than that. They journey and
return to discover the multiple significances of ''white.''

—John Robert Colombo

MUSGRAVE, Susan

Nationality: Canadian. **Born:** Santa Cruz, California, 12 March
1951. **Education:** Oak Bay High School. **Family:** Married Stephen
Douglas Reid in 1986; two daughters. **Career:** Instructor in English
and creative writing, University of Waterloo, Ontario, 1983–85,
Kootenay School of Writing, British Columbia, 1986, and Camosun
College, Victoria, British Columbia, 1988–90; writer-in-residence,
University of Waterloo, 1983–85, University of New Brunswick,
Fredericton, 1985, Vancouver Public Library, 1986, Festival of the
Written Arts, Pender Harbour, British Columbia, 1987, 1993, and
1994, Ganaraska Writer's Colony, Fiction Workshop, 1988, Sidney
Public Library, British Columbia, 1989, Ganges High School, 1989
and 1991, George P. Vanier Secondary School, 1991, Kaslo Summer
School of the Arts, 1991, University of Western Ontario, 1992–93,
University of Toronto, 1995; writer-in-electronic-residence, York
University, 1991–94. Columnist, Toronto *Star* and Vancouver *Sun.*
Awards: Canada Council grant, 1969, 1972, 1976, 1979, 1983, 1985,
1989, 1991; National Magazine award (silver), 1981; British Columbia Cultural Fund Grant, 1991, 1994; b.p. Nichol Poetry Chapbook
award, 1991; Reader's Choice award (*Prairie Schooner*), winter
1993. **Agent:** Bukowski Agency, 182 Avenue Road, Toronto, Ontario MSR 2JI. **Address:** 10301 West Saanich Road, P.O. Box 2421,
Sidney, British Columbia V8L 3Y3, Canada.

PUBLICATIONS

Poetry

Songs of the Sea-Witch. Vancouver, Sono Nis Press, 1970.
Skuld. Frensham, Surrey, Sceptre Press, 1971.
Birthstone. Frensham, Surrey, Sceptre Press, 1972.
Entrance of the Celebrant. Toronto, Macmillan, and London, Fuller
  d'Arch Smith, 1972.
Equinox. Rushden, Northamptonshire, Sceptre Press, 1973.
Kung. Rushden, Northamptonshire, Sceptre Press, 1973.

Grave-Dirt and Selected Strawberries. Toronto, Macmillan, 1973.

Gullband Thought Measles Was a Happy Ending (for children). Vancouver, J.J. Douglas, 1974.

Against. Rushden, Northamptonshire, Sceptre Press, 1974.

Two Poems. Knotting, Bedfordshire, Sceptre Press, 1975.

The Impstone. Toronto, McClelland and Stewart, 1976; London, J. Jay, 1977.

Kiskatinaw Songs, with Séan Virgo. Victoria, Pharos Press, 1977.

Selected Strawberries and Other Poems. Victoria, Sono Nis Press, 1977.

For Charlie Beaulieu . . . Knotting, Bedfordshire, Sceptre Press, 1977.

Two Poems for the Blue Moon. Knotting, Bedfordshire, Sceptre Press, 1977.

Becky Swan's Book. Erin, Ontario, Porcupine's Quill, 1978.

A Man to Marry, A Man to Bury. Toronto, McClelland and Stewart, 1979.

Conversation During the Omelette aux Fines Herbes. Knotting, Bedfordshire, Sceptre Press, 1979.

When My Boots Drive Off in a Cadillac. Toronto, League of Canadian Poets, 1980.

Taboo Man. N.p., Celia Duthie, 1981.

Tarts and Muggers: Poems New and Selected. Toronto, McClelland and Stewart, 1982.

The Plane Put Down in Sacramento. Vancouver, Hoffer, 1982.

I do not know if things that happen can be said to come to pass or only happen. Vancouver, Hoffer, 1982.

Cocktails at the Mausoleum. Toronto, McClelland and Stewart, 1985.

Desireless: Tom York (1947–1988). N.p., Celia Duthie, 1988.

Musgrave Landing. Scarborough, Ontario, Prentice Hall, 1988.

Kestrel and Leonardo (for children). N.p., Studio 123, 1990.

The Embalmer's Art: Poems New and Selected. N.p., Exile Editions, 1991.

In the Small Hours of the Rain. Victoria, British Columbia, 1991.

Forcing the Narcissus. Toronto, McClelland and Stewart, 1994.

Dreams Are More Real Than Bathtubs. Victoria, British Columbia, Orca Book, 1998.

Things That Keep and Do Not Change. Toronto, McClelland and Stewart, 1999.

What the Small Day Cannot Hold: Collected Poems 1970–1985. Vancouver, Porcepic Books, 2000.

Plays

Gullband (produced Toronto, 1976).

Radio Play: *The Wages of Love,* 1987.

Novels

The Charcoal Burners. Toronto, McClelland and Stewart, 1980.

Hag Head (for children). Toronto, Clarke Irwin, 1980.

The Dancing Chicken. Toronto, Methuen, 1987.

Other

Great Musgrave. New York, Prentice-Hall, 1989.

Musgrave Landing: Musings on the 'Writing Life. Toronto, Stoddart, 1994.

Editor, *Clearcut Words: Writers for Clayoquot.* Victoria, British Columbia, Hawthorne Society for Reference West, 1993.

Editor, *Because You Loved Being A Stranger: 55 Poets Celebrate Patrick Lane.* N.p., Harbour Publishing, 1994.

*

Manuscript Collection: McMaster University, Hamilton, Ontario.

Critical Studies: ''The White Goddess: Poetry of Susan Musgrave'' by Rosemary Sullivan, in *Contemporary Verse 2* (Winnipeg), 1975; ''Susan Musgrave: The Self and the Other'' by Dennis Brown, in *Canadian Literature* (Vancouver), 79, 1978; ''Desire and Death: Susan Musgrave'' by Jon Pearce, in *Malahat Review* (Victoria), 53, 1980; by Jeanette Lynes, in *Profiles in Canadian Literature,* edited by Jeffrey M. Heath, Toronto, Dundurn, 1986; ''An Archetype of Pain: From Plath to Atwood and Musgrave'' by Catherine Ahearn, in *Still the Frame Holds: Essays on Women Poets and Writers,* edited by Sheila Roberts and Yvonne Pacheco Tevis, San Bernardino, California, Borgo, 1993.

*   *   *

I happened to have an opportunity to speak with Susan Musgrave when I was trying to obtain her volume of poetry *Forcing the Narcissus.* Nervously identifying myself, I reminded her that I was the critic who on reading her early volumes had feared that she as well as her poetic persona might succumb to dark suicidal impulses. Her obsessive, poignant treatment of death, insanity, and blood reminded me of Sylvia Plath's poetry in *Ariel.* I recanted this judgment in the third edition of *Contemporary Poets* (1980), however, and although subsequent volumes continued to work in the starker vein of the early poetry, I knew better than quickly to confuse art with life. She laughed, saying that if I feared for her well-being then the fear would probably resurface when I read this volume. ''It is dark,'' she said, or some words to that effect, but the darkness is largely a function of the publisher's will. Her editors removed the lighter verse, choosing to give the volume tonal unity, but in doing so they denied the reader the opportunity to hear a more carefree voice. The volume is full of images that strike with the force of a lash; they bring blood and pain, but they also bring beauty, forgiveness, and transcendence.

Looking back at Musgrave's works, I can see why the comparison to Plath's writings was almost unavoidable. The feminist stances of the two poets were similar; so were their attitudes toward men, lesbianism, and sex. Musgrave's imitation of Plath's ''Daddy'' and ''Lady Lazarus'' in her poem ''Exposure'' was unmistakable. She was the celebrant of death, ''the spilled child,'' and all she looked at was transformed into death. In ''The Opened Grave'' she placed herself at the ''edge of things.'' Her poems of witchcraft read like strange and deeply disturbing myths of blood rites and sexuality pervaded with violence. The inhabitants of her witch kingdoms resembled those in Gustave Doré's illustrations—beetles, white moths, and figures with bloated heads angling out of hunched shoulders and shriveled torsos, shaking their gnarled hands, leering at their prey. These lines from ''Finding Love'' are chilling:

> From my bed I could hear
> the ripe wound open, the thick sea
> pouring in. I told you, then,

the first lie I had in my heart;
the carcass of a dull animal
slipped between our sights.

The poem "MacKenzie River, North" is another work imbued with terror.

What I failed to recognize was that, although Musgrave's range was limited in *Songs of the Sea-Witch* and *Entrance of the Celebrant* and although her themes were obsessive and derivative, her sense of the bizarre and her ability to evoke the mood of bewitched kingdoms could serve her well in an entirely different vein of poetry. In the earlier collections she used these gifts to evoke strange, disturbing worlds fraught with psychological significance. In the third section of *Grave-Dirt and Selected Strawberries,* however, she transforms them to create a high-spirited, bawdy, and wonderfully affectionate pastiche of poems and prose in celebration of the strawberry. Musgrave gleefully parodies herself and writes in the best eighteenth-century traditions of comedy, bringing some of the writings of Erica Jong to mind. In her fanciful history the strawberry is her picaresque hero. His origins are traced, his baptism marked, and his emergence in the writings of others duly recorded, and all the facts about him that every strawberry lover would like to know are cataloged. Musgrave feigns an anthropological tone and hilariously records the harvest customs of the strawberry, its method of reproduction, its behavior in captivity, its sense of fellowship. The collection is giddy, witty, and full of good fun. It could not be more unlike her other poetry.

Musgrave's writings from *Equinox* through *The Impstone* reflect continued growth in the kind of poetry that won her acclaim. "Memorial to a Lover" (*Two Poems*) imitates Plath. Others feature her interest in Indian lore and witchcraft. The moon poems, like the "Kiskatinaw Songs" (*Grave-Dirt and Selected Strawberries*), experiment with rhythms from songs, chants, and ballads. Poems like "The Firstborn" and *Equinox* represent Musgrave's best handling of the world of nightmare and demons, in which dark rituals are enacted between the self and its demon other.

The personal love poetry in *Cocktails at the Mausoleum* is softer and more mellow in its tone, some of it becoming much more loving. The shift in tone and Musgrave's widening of her range suggest that some critics were too quick to condemn her for the alleged antimale stance they detected in some of the poems published in *A Man to Marry, A Man to Bury* (1979). Many poems explore her private domain, her personal friends, and her journeys on the lecture circuit. These poems, such as "Black Morning," "We Come This Way But Once," and her Salmonberry Road poems, are reminiscent of the poetry of Frank O'Hara, in which personal material, friends, and particular geographical locations are cited to create the sense that direct personal experience is being recorded. These poems employ a colloquial idiom; they make references to private materials that mean something quite different to the poet than they can ever mean to the public. And they depict a landscape of experience in which the city or creek or street is named simply because the very act of naming prevents the named thing from finally being appropriated.

Musgrave Landing (1988) continues to combine an erotic poetry with the poetry of her dark imaginings, a poetry full of torture and dismemberment. Some of the poems are less controlled than usual, exploring almost wantonly the material of her dreams. Some of the dramatic monologues recall the humor and wit displayed in her collection of poems about the strawberry. They are fanciful, brash, and bawdy. "My Boots Drive Off in a Cadillac" is told from the point of view of a prostitute. It and other poems in *Tarts and Muggers,* particularly "Boogeying with the Queen," show us Musgrave writing a tough, cocky poetry.

Some of Musgrave's poetry is still written too much under the spell of the style as well as the subject matter of the confessional poets. Her poem about her trip to Plath's grave and another poem called "Salad Days" demonstrate that she can move beyond this mode, however. Her poem about her own father, "You Didn't Fit," has an original cast to it. Nonetheless, she remains highly indebted to John Berryman, Theodore Roethke, Joyce Carol Oates, Robert Lowell, Ted Hughes, and even Erica Jong. Her poems about environmental issues or the drug trade give voice to her social consciousness but remain too rhetorical and predictable. Only the "Requiem for Talunkwan Island," written from the point of view of a Haida ghost returning to the island, has a powerful and original voice, giving force to her complaint against a logging industry that has caused erosion of the land and made reforestation impossible.

Forcing the Narcissus is a heart-wrenching volume of poems. Many have appeared before, some are revised, and others are new. In "The Gift" the speaker foresees all of the harrowing lessons from hell that an infant born of a drug-addicted mother will come to know: "After nine months of happiness / you're learning withdrawal, what it's like to be / fully human, how your mother only gives you / all she's got to give." The poems in the section "From the Wet Heart of the Wound" chart the raw emotions of a child brutalized by her father or of a child reliving the loss of her father and the estrangement from her mother. "Family Plot" exudes the chill of the graveyard, calling forth painful memories and delving deeper into the storehouse of memory and the depths of graves. "The Spirituality of Cruelty" voices Musgrave's credo that art transfigures violence and pain. It is a restatement of Yeats's theme in "The Circus Animal's Desertion." All of the ladders start with, all beauty comes from "the foul rag-and-bone shop of the heart." Musgrave's poetry is full of terror, and from it beauty is born.

—Carol Simpson Stern

NANDY, Pritish

Nationality: Indian. **Born:** Bhagalpur, Bihar, 15 January 1947.
Education: La Martiniere, Calcutta; Presidency College, Calcutta.
Family: Married 1) Rina Mumtaz in 1966 (divorced), two children;
2) Rina Biswas in 1977, two children. **Career:** Publicity and public
relations manager, Guest Keen Williams Ltd., Calcutta, 1969–82;
since 1982 publicity director, Times of India Group, Bombay; since
1968 editor Dialogue Calcutta, later Dialogue India; poetry editor,
Illustrated Weekly of India. Named Padmashri, 1977. **Address:** 5
Pearl Road, Calcutta 17, India.

PUBLICATIONS

Poetry

Of Gods and Olives: 21 Poems. Calcutta, Writers Workshop, 1967.
I Hand You in Turn My Nebbuk Wreath: Early Poems. Calcutta,
    Dialogue, 1968.
On Either Side of Arrogance. Calcutta, Writers Workshop, 1968.
Rites for a Plebeian Statue: An Experiment in Verse Drama. Calcutta,
    Writers Workshop, 1969.
From the Outer Bank of the Brahmaputra. New York, New Rivers
    Press, 1969.
Masks to Be Interpreted As Messages. Calcutta, Dialogue, 1970; as
    Masks to Be Interpreted in Terms of Measure, Calcutta, Writers
    Workshop, 1971.
Madness Is the Second Stroke. Calcutta, Dialogue, 1971.
The Poetry of Pritish Nandy. Calcutta, Oxford University Press, 1973.
Dhritarashtra Downtown: Zero. Calcutta, Dialogue, 1974.
Riding the Midnight River: Selected Poems. New Delhi, Arnold
    Heinemann, 1975.
Lonesong Street. Calcutta, Poets Press, 1975.
Songs of Mirabai. New Delhi, Arnold Heinemann, 1975.
A Stranger Called I. Calcutta, Poets Press, 1976.
In Secret Anarchy. Calcutta, United Writers, 1976.
Nowhere Man. New Delhi, Arnold Heinemann, 1977.
Pritish Nandy, Thirty. New Delhi, Arnold Heinemann, 1978.
Anywhere Is Another Place. New Delhi, Arnold Heinemann, 1979.
*Tonight This Savage Rite: The Love Poetry of Kamala Das and
    Pritish Nandy.* New Delhi, Arnold Heinemann, 1979.
The Rainbow Last Night. New Delhi, Arnold Heinemann, 1981.

Short Stories

Some Friends. New Delhi, Arnold Heinemann, 1981.

Other

Editor, *Getting Rid of Blue Plastic: Poems Old and New,* by Margaret
    Randall. Calcutta, Dialogue, 1967.
Editor, *Poetry from India.* Calcutta, Dialogue, 1970.
Editor, *Indian Poetry in English 1947–1972.* Calcutta, Oxford Uni-
    versity Press, 1972.
Editor, *Indian Poetry in English.* New Delhi, Sterling, 1973.

Editor, *Indian Poetry in English Today.* New Delhi, Arnold Heinemann,
    1974.
Editor, *Modern Indian Poetry.* New Delhi, Arnold Heinemann, 1974;
    London, Heinemann, 1976.
Editor, *Bengali Poetry Today.* East Lansing, Michigan State Univer-
    sity Press, 1974.
Editor, *Strangertime: An Anthology of Indian Poetry in English.* New
    Delhi, Hind, 1977.
Editor, *Modern Indian Literature.* New Delhi, Arnold Heinemann,
    1978.
Editor, *The Vikas Book of Modern Indian Love Stories [Poetry].* New
    Delhi, Vikas, 2 vols., 1979.
Editor, *The Lord Is My Shepherd: Selections from the Psalms.* New
    Delhi, Vikas, 1982.
Editor, *Tales of Romance and Valour from Rajasthan.* New Delhi,
    Vika, 1982.
Editor, *Krishna, Krishna: The Devotional Songs of Mirabai.* New
    Delhi, Vikas, 1983.
Editor, *Love, The First Syllable: The Mystic Songs of Kabir.* New
    Delhi, Vikas, 1983.

Translator, *I Had You in Turn* by Nebbuk Wreath. Calcutta, Dia-
    logue, 1969.
Translator, *Some Modern Cuban Poems.* Calcutta, Satyabrata Pal,
    1969. Transcreator, *The Complete Poems of Samar Sen.* Calcutta,
    Writers Workshop, 1970.
Translator, *Subhas Mukhopadhyay: Poet of the People.* Calcutta,
    Dialogue, 1970.
Translator, *Poems from Bangladesh.* New Delhi, Perspective, 1971.
Translator, *The Prose Poems of Lokenath Bhattacharya.* Calcutta,
    Dialogue, 1971.
Translator, *Bangladesh: Voice of a New Nation.* Calcutta, Dialogue,
    1971.
Translator, *Shesh Lekha: The Last Poems of Rabindranath Tagore.*
    Calcutta, Dialogue, 1973.
Translator, *The Songs of Mirabai.* New Delhi, Arnold Heinemann,
    1975.
Translator, *The Poetry of Kaiff Azmi.* New Delhi, Arnold Heinemann,
    1976.
Translator, *The Giraffe Flames* (poems) by Sunil Gangopadhyaya.
    New Delhi, Arnold Heinemann, 1976.
Translator, *Modern Indian Stories.* New Delhi, Vikas, 1985.
Translator, *Snake and Other Stories,* by Premendra Mitra. Calcutta,
    Seagull, 1990.
Translator, *Unchained Melody.* New Delhi, Rupa, 1994.
Translator, *Untamed Heart.* New Delhi, Rupa, 1994.
Translator, *Careless Whispers: Pritish Nandy Recreates the Best of
    Sanskrit Love Poetry.* New Delhi, Rupa, 1994.

*

Critical Studies: *The Poetry of Pritish Nandy,* Calcutta, Writers Workshop, 1969, and ''Workpoints for a Study of Pritish Nandy's
'In Transit, Mind Seeks''' in *Banasthali Vidyapith Magazine,* 1969,
both by Satyabrata Pal; *Pritish Nandy,* New Delhi, Arnold Heinemann,

1975, and "Politics and the Poetry of Pritish Nandy," in *Contemporary Indian English Verse: An Evaluation,* edited by Chirantan Kulshrestha, New Delhi, Arnold Heinemann, 1980, both by Subharanjan Dasgupta; "Magic of the Midnight Mist: A Study of Pritish Nandy's Poetry" by Niranjan Mohanty, in *Living English Poets,* edited by Madhusudan Prasad, New Delhi, Sterling, 1989; "Quest for Perennial Values in Pritish Nandy" by Ashley E. Myles, and "Pritish Nandy: Quest for Being" by A.K. Awasthi, both in *Creative Forum* (New Delhi), 5(1–4), January-December 1992.

Pritish Nandy comments:

Trying to achieve an entirely new breakthrough in form and evolve a new language to characterize Indian writing in English. Feel that creative writing in English by Indians is generally imitative in both form and approach. What is required is a new language that will be characteristic and structurally powerful, with a logic of its own. It is this Indian English that must be worked out, and that is what I am trying to do. Also trying to discover/build a tradition for Indo-Anglian poetry, the fusion of a modern language with the myths and symbols we have. Indian writers in English till now have ignored this quest for a tradition, which I consider vital for a living poetry. Finally a personal quest; a secular, politically involved poet has his own peculiar problems.

*   *   *

Pritish Nandy's early poems are often in short-line free verse; others form typographical pictures or use e.e. cummings's style of spacing. Nandy skeptically mingles Indian, classic, and Christian imagery, with gentle irony toward gods who "have aged and are not aware" or toward Christ, who "came third in the contest / with death / and wrote a poem on the cross." The poet indeed pities those who have to live with him, for he "shreds their magic faith into a million assumptions." He is equally skeptical about such rationalists as a recluse found dead: "having read too much of / Salinger / he had checkmated himself in one / man chess." Indeed, "to understand by cataloguing is like / splitting hairs on a bald head."

Perhaps this is why Nandy thinks that English poetry stopped at Auden (American "never began"). He most frequently alludes to Spanish-language poets, notably Lorca. His own effort is to combine and symbolize: "What you cannot explain in terms of symbols is lost forever like blind totems and ruins in an old man's face." Words are only "masks to be interpreted in terms of messages."

Nandy was long preoccupied with the frustrations of penetrating to realities or of saying anything meaningful if he did. He praised a friend for seeking "a new level of communication" and compacted his own images so as to make surreal sense: "your eyes bled like a violet tiger / as I watched the winds strangle / whispers of the apocalypse." But certain themes are clear: death, loneliness, and suffering and the mitigations of love, sex, and friendship.

In *Masks to Be Interpreted as Messages,* Nandy changed to short statements in rhythmic prose, and in his best-known poem, "Calcutta, If You Must Exile Me," he states in brutally direct style the cruelties that revolt him. The horrors in Bangladesh then jolted him into plain, moving statements of sympathy with all victims of hate, whether in India, Vietnam, or Colombia—"the marauders changed their name but the sufferers each time were the same." At times he despairs—"blood is a country you and I have loved in vain"—but he no longer thinks of leaving—"Dark city I shall not disown you again." Though he writes for those who cannot read the language he uses, "my voice is the voice of my people, for I speak of their loves and ambitions and secret shames."

Nandy later found consolation in translating Tagore's last poems, a "devastating confrontation with death." The message, of "haunting simplicity," is that "death is but a new birth of the spirit into the great unknown." Modern Indian poetry, Nandy says, draws "strength from the bedrock of our tradition," yet it is violent, anguished, brutally contemporary." His own certainly is.

—George McElroy

NATHAN, Leonard (Edward)

Nationality: American. **Born:** Los Angeles, California, 8 November 1924. **Education:** Georgia Institute of Technology, Atlanta, 1943; University of California, Los Angeles, 1946–47; University of California, Berkeley, B.A. (summa cum laude) 1950, M.A. 1952, Ph.D. in English 1961. **Military Service:** U.S. Army, 1943–45. **Family:** Married Carol Nash in 1949; one son and two daughters. **Career:** Instructor, Modesto Junior College, California, 1954–60; since 1960 member of the department of rhetoric, chair of the department, 1968–72, professor of rhetoric until 1992, and since 1992, professor emeritus, University of California, Berkeley. **Awards:** Phelan award, 1955; Longview award, 1961; American Institute of Indian Studies fellowship, 1966; American Academy award, 1971; University of California Creative Awards fellowship, 1973; Guggenheim fellowship, 1976; University of California humanities research fellowship, 1983. **Address:** 40 Beverly Road, Kensington, California 94707–1304, U.S.A.

PUBLICATIONS

Poetry

Western Reaches. San Jose, California, Talisman Press, 1958.
The Glad and Sorry Seasons. New York, Random House, 1963.
The Matchmaker's Lament and Other Astonishments. Northampton, Massachusetts, Gehenna Press, 1967.
The Day the Perfect Speakers Left. Middletown, Connecticut, Wesleyan University Press, 1969.
Flight Plan. Berkeley, California, Cedar Hill Press, 1971.
Without Wishing. Berkeley, California, Thorp Springs Press, 1973.
Coup and Other Poems. Lincoln, Nebraska, Windflower Press, 1975.
Returning Your Call. Princeton, New Jersey, Princeton University Press, 1975.
The Likeness: Poems Out of India. Berkeley, California, Thorp Springs Press, 1975.
The Teachings of Grandfather Fox. Ithaca, New York, Ithaca House, 1976.
Lost Distance. Madison, Wisconsin, Chowder, 1978.
Dear Blood. Pittsburgh, University of Pittsburgh Press, 1980.
Holding Patterns. Pittsburgh, University of Pittsburgh Press, 1982.
Carrying On: New and Selected Poems. Pittsburgh, University of Pittsburgh Press, 1985.
The Potato Eaters. N.p., Orchises Press, 1999.

Recording: *Confessions of a Matchmaker,* 1973.

Other

The Tragic Drama of William Butler Yeats: Figures in Dance. New York, Columbia University Press, 1965.

The Poet's Work: An Introduction to Czeslaw Milosz, with Arthur Quinn. Cambridge, Massachusetts, Harvard University Press, 1991.

Diary of a Left-Handed Bird Watcher. St. Paul, Minnesota, Graywolf Press, 1996.

Editor, *Talisman Anthology.* Georgetown, California, Talisman Press, 1963.

Translator, with others, *Modern Hindi Poetry.* Bloomington, Indiana University Press, 1965.

Translator, *First Person, Second Person,* by Ageyeya. Berkeley, California, Center for South and Southeast Asia Studies, 1971.

Translator, *The Transport of Love: The Meghaduta of Kalidasa.* Berkeley, University of California Press, 1976.

Translator, *Grace and Mercy in Her Wild Hair: Selected Poems to the Mother Goddess,* by Ramprasad Sen. Boulder, Colorado, Great Eastern, 1982.

Translator, with James Larson, *Songs of Something Else: Selected Poems,* by Gunnar Ekelöf. Princeton, New Jersey, Princeton University Press, 1982.

Translator, with others, *The Indian Poetic Tradition: Select Readings from Sanskrit, Prakrit, Pali, and Apabhramsa Poetry.* Agra, Y.K., 1983.

Translator, with Czeslaw Milosz, *Happy as a Dog's Tail,* by Anna Swirszczynska. San Diego, Harcourt Brace, 1985.

Translator, with Czeslaw Milosz, *With the Skin: The Poems of Aleksander Wat.* New York, Ecco Press, 1989.

Translator, with Czeslaw Milosz, *Talking to My Body: Poems of Anna Swir.* Port Townsend, Washington, Copper Canyon Press, 1996.

*

Manuscript Collection: Syracuse University Library, New York.

Critical Studies: In *Shenandoah* (Lexington, Virginia), autumn 1969; *Malahat Review* (Victoria, British Columbia), October 1969; *Quarterly Journal of Speech* (New York), winter 1970; *Poetry* (Chicago), January 1971; *Ohio Review* (Athens), spring-summer 1976; *Advocate* (Los Angeles), 16 June 1976; *Southern Humanities Review* (Auburn, Alabama), fall 1976; *Small Press Review* (Paradise, California), March 1977; *Prairie Schooner* (Lincoln, Nebraska), fall 1980; *Northwest Review* (Eugene, Oregon), no. 3, 1981; *New Letters* (Kansas City), summer 1981; *Hudson Review* (New York), fall 1982; *Chowder Review* (Quincy, Massachusetts), summer 1983; *Salmagundi* (Saratoga Springs, New York), fall 1983; ''To Wake Up Cold in Fact: The Poetry of Leonard Nathan'' by Jonathan Holden, in *New England Review* (Hanover, New Hampshire), 16(4), fall 1994.

Leonard Nathan comments:

Nathan's poetry over the years has moved steadily toward the development of a voice that might give human conversation the form to make it memorable. He returns again and again to certain subjects: the difficult redemption possible in human relations; the pathos and courage of human purpose set adrift in an inhuman universe; and the sudden illumination that can transform experience into a meaning so intense that the only term for it is ''supernatural.''

*　　*　　*

In his review of *The Glad and Sorry Seasons,* John Woods quite rightly observed that Leonard Nathan has a ''preference for statements of revelation'' and that his demands on metaphor are relatively minor. Nathan convinces by conclusive statement, seldom by narrative or emotional persuasion. Although he inclines toward declarative and reductionist poetry, his lines are not so concentrated as, say, W.S. Merwin's, and he does not have Merwin's power to startle and amaze through revelation. Nathan employs a steady iambic meter, with frequent variation in end rhymes. His lines seldom fail; they are refined, restrained, and well polished.

The dominant tonality of *The Glad and Sorry Seasons* is autumnal. The poet is middle-aged and wise, detached and reflective:

> I sweeten by the minute, bodying
> The spirit of my seed; hear how I sing
> Inside my skin—that's blood, that growing sound,
> The psalm of mellowing . . .

The following lines from ''First Girl,'' while perhaps uncharacteristic of Nathan's lyrics, reveal the intensity he is capable of:

> As she bent, I woke, and felt a pull like water
> And saw above her head a foreign blue,
> And nothing was homely, even my heavy body,
> And what I had never learned I always knew.

This snow queen, resplendent in frosted radiance, has transformed the poet and ''crystallized the wildest flux of nature.'' But the time of ecstasy is past and ''too long ago for second thoughts.''

The Day the Perfect Speakers Left seems to bemoan the disintegration of high culture and humanistic values. Several poems strike a pose reminiscent of Ezra Pound's ''Hugh Selwyn Mauberley'' in its condemnation of our ''botched civilization,'' our ''old bitch gone in the teeth.'' In Nathan's ''The Crisis'' a shadowy figure, a Greek or Jew, has come ''to see his children's children, how they escaped / His law, his love, his unpronounceable name.'' The title poem of the volume confirms the notion and may remind one of Arnold's ''Dover Beach.'' The birds have assembled for what the poet fears is a final migration:

> And leave-taking was another,
> Sadder version of dusk we were attending,
> And as though a whole age were going out,
> Its head covered, and going out with it
> A purpose including stars and stones.

Returning Your Call is less derivative in style and subject than Nathan's earlier books. His voice is more direct, less given to cleverness and wit than previously. There are fine single achievements, such as ''Audit'' and ''Breathing Exercises.'' In the latter poem the poet cries, in fear and urgency, ''For God's sake, keep breathing.'' There is in this book more sense of tension, near disaster, and struggle against loss. ''Breathing Exercises'' also tells us that "inside Leonard / Nathan is a little spirit." While hardly confessional, his poetry now seems willing to grapple more intensely with tougher topics. We hear a voice struggling to regain contact with itself and with close friends. There is also a suggestion that Nathan recognizes the cleverness and restraint of his verse: "someday I'm going to speak / in my own voice . . . you'll have to cover my mouth with your free hand . . . ." This is precisely what is missing from Nathan's poetry: a strong, direct, and unfettered voice.

In general, the consistently polished flow of Nathan's lines is both remarkable and lamentable; one soon craves roughness in line and subject. It is Nathan's very control of his material that keeps most of his poems, while always of craft, from becoming poems of authority. By his own construct ("Mao for nightmare, Mozart for slippers"), we need to hear more of Nathan's nightmares, less about his slippers.

—John R. Cooley

NEWLOVE, John (Herbert)

Nationality: Canadian. **Born:** Regina, Saskatchewan, 13 June 1938. **Family:** Married Susan Mary Phillips in 1966; one step-son and one step-daughter. **Career:** Senior editor, McClelland and Stewart publishers, Toronto, 1970–74; writer-in-residence, Concordia University, Montreal, 1974–75, University of Western Ontario, London, 1975–76, University of Toronto, 1976–77, Regina Public Library, 1979–80, and David Thompson University Centre, Nelson, British Columbia, 1982–83. Since 1986 English editor, Office of the Commissioner of Official Languages, Ottawa. **Awards:** Koerner Foundation grant, 1964; Canada Council grant, 1965, 1967, 1977, 1983; Governor-General's award, 1973; Saskatchewan Writers' Guild Founders' award, 1984; Literary Press Group award, 1986; Archibald Lampman award, 1994. **Address:** 105 Rochester Street, Ottawa, Ontario K1R 7L9, Canada.

PUBLICATIONS

Poetry

Grave Sirs. Vancouver, Robert Reid, 1962.
Elephants, Mothers and Others. Vancouver, Periwinkle Press, 1963.
Moving In Alone. Toronto, Contact Press, 1965.
Notebook Pages. Toronto, Charles Pachter, 1966.
Four Poems. Platteville, Wisconsin, It, 1967.
What They Say. Toronto, Weed/Flower Press, 1967.
Black Night Window. Toronto, McClelland and Stewart, 1968.
The Cave. Toronto, McClelland and Stewart, 1970.
7 Diasters, 3 Theses, and Welcome Home. Click, Vancouver, Very Stone House, 1971.
Lies. Toronto, McClelland and Stewart, 1972.
The Fat Man: Selected Poems 1962–1972. Toronto, McClelland and Stewart, 1977.
Dreams Surround Us: Fiction and Poetry, with John Metcalf. Delta, Ontario, Bastard Press, 1977.
The Green Plain. Lantzville, British Columbia, Oolichan, 1981.
Three Poems. Prince George, British Columbia, Gorse Press, 1985.
The Night the Dog Smiled. Toronto, ECW Press, 1986.

La verde piana, introduced and translated by Carla Comellini. Bologna, Italy, Piovan Editore, 1990.
Apology for Absence: Selected Poems, 1962–1992. Erin, Ontario, Porcupine's Quill, 1993.

Other

Editor, *Dream Craters,* by Joe Rosenblatt. Erin, Ontario, Press Porcépic, 1974.
Editor, *The Collected Poems of Earle Birney.* Toronto, McClelland and Stewart, 2 vols., 1975.
Editor, *Canadian Poetry: The Modern Era.* Toronto, McClelland and Stewart, 1977.
Editor, *The Collected Poems of F.R. Scott.* Toronto, McClelland and Stewart, 1981.

*

Bibliography: "An Annotated Bibliography of Works by and about John Newlove" by Robert A. Lecker, in *Essays on Canadian Writing* (Downsview, Ontario), spring 1975; *John Newlove and His Works* by Douglas Barbour. Toronto, ECW Press, 1992.

Manuscript Collections: University of Toronto Library; Humanities Research Center, University of Texas, Austin; Elizabeth Dafoe Library, University of Manitoba, Winnipeg.

Critical Studies: "How Do I Get Out of Here: The Poetry of John Newlove" by Margaret Atwood, spring 1973, and "Something in Which to Believe for Once: The Poetry of John Newlove" by Jan Bartley, fall 1974, both in *Open Letter* (Toronto); "Weather Report: 'Stars, Rain, Forests'" by Douglas Barbour, and "Driving Home with John Newlove" by Susan Glickman, both in *Essays on Canadian Writing* (Toronto), 36, spring 1988; "Place in the Poetry of John Newlove" by E.F. Dyck, in *Canadian Literature* (Vancouver, British Columbia), 122–123, autumn-winter 1989; "John Newlove and His Works," in *Canadian Writers and Their Works*, edited by Robert Lecker and others, Toronto, ECW, 1992, and in *ECW's Biographical Guide to Canadian Poets,* edited by Robert Lecker and others, Toronto, ECW, 1993, both by Douglas Barbour.

John Newlove comments:

If I had a statement to make on my own work, it would consist of the fifth part of Wallace Stevens's "Thirteen Ways of Looking at a Blackbird." In any case, I would rather read than write.

*   *   *

The voice in the poetry of John Newlove is that of an individual in search of absolution, but from what, and from whom, is not always clear. At times absolution is asked of the self, as if personal scrutiny and self-criticism will lead to a better understanding of the person within the persona. At other times absolution is asked from the world, as if the persona has somehow betrayed himself, his lovers, and his better instincts. Never does the persona ask for absolution from the reader, and it is this that is at the center of the enigma, the source of strength, and the core of the truth in Newlove's poetry. Like Rilke, Newlove is a poet in search of the uncertain, if only to find in himself what cannot be betrayed or made inconstant.

In the poems about his childhood in the Canadian prairie towns of Verigin and Kamsack, including "Verigin" and "My Daddy Drowned" from *Elephants, Mothers and Others,* Newlove questions the world of his childhood, a time and place where he feels he did not belong, where violence, isolation, and separateness (the three plagues of life in his poetry) rear their absurd heads in such innocent acts as the birth of kittens and swimming with Doukhobor boys at a watering hole. In such poems details and events play against one another with a kind of cold irony. The persona is stung by his experiences, so that the only refuge from the world resides in the acknowledgment of its absurdities.

In "An Accidental Life," which prefaces *The Green Plain,* Newlove confides (although he suggests that his life has had nothing but a series of prefaces) that poetry was a way with which the absurd could become an avenue for atonement:

That paradise was broken, ruined abruptly after an eternity. Child's time. I ran home, crying, in shame: in shame, because I was the ruiner: not as Adam ruined Eden, seeking wisdom, but as Cain the spoiler disrupted a second Arcadia. I was Cain, the guilty one who did what he had to do. Is the mark on me? No. In the end, it was only, I suppose, a child's misunderstanding of the world and himself.

For Newlove the search for sin within himself, and the discovery that sin is a natural human phenomenon, is a kind of surrogate for religion, where the processes of doubt and confession imply a secular redemption for which the poet still appears to be waiting. The closest Newlove comes to such a resolution is in his sequence, or "spiritual epic," "White Philharmonic Novels" in *The Night the Dog Smiled,* where he asks, "What do you remember / after you've been happy?" Newlove argues that

The message is that there is no message. You can't live forever on resentment.

The thing is whether to stuff stuff into the middle or into the many endings.

Like a dissonant, atonal symphony, or perhaps like an orchestra tuning before a conductor takes the stage, "White Philharmonic Novels" is a pastiche of notes, anecdotes, literary references, observations, and miniature chronicles of a man slowly moving toward contentment.

As with Rilke's *Duino Elegies,* most of Newlove's work in *The Night the Dog Smiled* and *The Green Plain* is meditative, reflexive, and self-critical. Gone is the rowdy man of his early work:

I made these voices.

The arrangement is all.

It grew and grew until it was bigger than I was and it made me think that I was bigger than I was.

As Newlove suggests in the final lines of "White Philharmonic Novels," there is no use for a witness who cannot tell his tale. The choice is simple; the persona would rather be a survivor—a giver and receiver of love—than a dissipated romantic. As if to underline his new stance, Newlove concludes "The Permanent Tourist Comes Home" (possibly a play on Leonard Cohen's poem from the 1960s titled "The Only Canadian Tourist in Havana Turns His Thoughts Homeward") with the line "Awkwardly, I am in love again."

For the Newlove canon the trek toward self-realization and contentment has gradually sublimated itself into an internal monologue, and it is for this reason that Newlove's poetry stands as a touchstone for the transformation of an external vision to an internal one that has been the key development in Canadian poetry over the past quarter century or so. In an earlier statement on his work Newlove referred readers to part 5 of Wallace Stevens's "Thirteen Ways of Looking at a Blackbird," with the implication that Newlove considered his poems to be in a state of transition between a poetry of inflection and a poetry of innuendo.

Nowhere is this transition more apparent than in "Ride Off Any Horizon" from *Black Night Window.* Like "Thirteen Ways of Looking at a Blackbird," Newlove's poem examines the processes of vision: the historical, the sociological, the geographical, and the personal. The implication throughout the poem is that the external, the visible, the real can be transformed into the metaphysical by acts of memory and imagination. Like the later "White Philharmonic Novels," "Ride Off Any Horizon" is a pastiche of scenes drawn from a variety of sources—sources that coalesce in a blurring of boundaries and distinctions between genres of vision and the way one perceives through them. The resulting impression is an extension of horizons or, failing that, the amalgamation of limits. "Ride Off Any Horizon" is a benchmark poem in Canadian literature because it signals the start of an era in which there has been a conscious desire on the part of poets to blur the distinction between the internal and the external realms of perception. The "new internalization," which has become the hallmark of such poets as Bronwen Wallace and Lorna Crozier, can be attributed in large part to Newlove, a poet whose oeuvre has charted a course for others to follow between inflection and innuendo.

Newlove's sense of innuendo has a darker and almost spiritual side. His awareness of mortality, which represented a kind of "daredevil's game" in the earlier works, has metamorphosed into an urgency as both he and his vision have matured. In poems such as "Cold, Heat" and part 2 of "Syllables" in *The Night the Dog Smiled,* the proximity of death to life has sharpened the poet's appetite for love to the point that love has become the reason for existence, a recognition that is itself a form of redemption.

—Bruce Meyer

NGAI, Sianne

Nationality: American. **Born:** Washington, D.C., 3 October 1971. **Education:** Brown University, Providence, Rhode Island, M.F.A. 1995; Harvard University, Cambridge, Massachusetts, Ph.D. candidate late 1990s. **Family:** Married Daniel Farrell in 1996.

PUBLICATIONS

Poetry

My Novel. Buffalo, New York, Leave Books, 1994.
Discredit. Providence, Rhode Island, Burning Deck, 1997.
TelepromptER*. Elmwood, Connecticut, Potes and Poets Press, 1998.
Criteria. Oakland, California, O Books, 1998.

*   *   *

In work that appears linguistically subversive, Sianne Ngai distorts syntax and form in ways that question constructions of meaning. Consistently abstract, often to the point of obscurity, her poems explore dimensions, change, boundaries, and such categories as "the with" and "the about." There are distinct differences, however, between the work in Ngai's first collection, the chapbook *Discredit,* and her later volume *Criteria.* In the earlier book, which consists of six linked sections, each containing several short pieces that can be read as one coherent poem, Ngai examines themes of memory, appearance, and transmutation. Several images from the work are visually or metaphorically striking, as is this single line from the first section: "The scar is the shape of a garden named after a bird of a passing complexion." Elsewhere in the same poem the speaker observes "the way a signature follows the body as tedious stitches on a garment" or the way in which

The paper floats to meet the image in something like water
Like an expensive pencil
Drawing you under the valid pretext of fatigue.

Throughout *Discredit* Ngai presents cryptic phrases that could be bits of overheard conversation or dreams ("Very few and I'm sorry for that" or "Bright vacuum of sun, or incomprehension."). She also uses space on the page to fragment language and to create distance between or within phrases. These are techniques Ngai expands more daringly in *Criteria,* a collection of nine pieces that includes "My Novel," a prose poem in twenty-one "chapters" that is arguably the most approachable work in the book. Although "My Novel" employs relatively conventional sentence patterns, its images and associations are consistently surreal, as in this passage from chapter 19, "Scenography":

Water trapped in the brain blocks a memory of the river,
    save for the fact
that I could not see. The name said this was because
    language had cast is weather
into disparate parts. A parable or armor and orthope-
    dics kept
our attention to the slide, where metazoa and various other
    animalcules
defended themselves from the rain.

In ways that suggest the work of Jorie Graham or, less directly, Emily Dickinson, Ngai uses carefully chosen interruptions and repetitions to heighten meaning, as in "Title of With":

Take the bus to the outline————————
————
take the bus to the outline of the sign——————
where casuality [sic.]
retrieves the title of enough——————————

——————————————————————
. . . . Use fork
for pitch of right——————————-use fork
for puncture
for puncture the enough.

Such pieces achieve an almost oracular tone and force the reader to confront the reality of the plain black line. Is the reader expected to fill in the blank? Or has something been deleted? The device is both startling and ambiguous.

Among Ngai's most innovative works is "The Enemy," which opens *Criteria.* It begins with Ngai's characteristic techniques of repetitions and unfilled space on the page. Soon, however, the poet begins to insert bracketed commands such as "repeat" or "strike through," which suggest elements of both process and performance. As phrases are repeated and combined with increasing urgency, the reader experiences and participates in the act of composition:

unlike discipline
remorse [strike through] happens to need to
[repeat] "happens to need to" [strike through] claim
    instincts has to really want to

where the individual happens to need to change the
batteries or her rifle from one shoulder to the other
where discipline becomes abstract opening the door
where answering the bell and opening the door where all
are audible acts unlike the secretion of saliva where the
individual happens to need to change where the
individual has to really want to change.

Although Ngai makes thematic and stylistic choices that limit the accessibility of her work, her creative risks stretch boundaries and "puncture the enough" of how poems can mean.

—Elizabeth Shostak

NICHOLS, Grace

Nationality: Guyanese. **Born:** 18 January 1950. Moved to England in 1977. **Education:** St. Stephen's Scots School, Georgetown; Progressive and Preparatory Institute, Georgetown; University of Guyana, Georgetown, diploma in communications. **Family:** Lives with the poet John Agard, *q.v.*; two daughters (one from a previous marriage). **Career:** Teacher in Georgetown, 1967–70; reporter with national newspaper, Georgetown, 1972–73; information assistant, Government Information Services, 1973–76; freelance journalist in Guyana, until 1977. **Awards:** Commonwealth poetry prize, 1983; British Arts Council bursary, 1988. **Agent:** Anthea Morton-Saner, Curtis Brown, 162–68 Regent Street, London W1R STB, England.

PUBLICATIONS

Poetry

I Is a Long-Memoried Woman. London, Caribbean Cultural International, 1983.
The Fat Black Woman's Poems. London, Virago Press, 1984.
Come On into My Tropical Garden (for children). London, A. and C. Black, 1988.
Lazy Thoughts of a Lazy Woman, and Other Poems. London, Virago Press, 1989.
Sunris. London, Virago Press, 1996.
Asana and the Animals: A Book of Pet Poems. London, Walker, and Cambridge, Massachusetts, Candlewick, 1997.

Novel

Whole of a Morning Sky. London, Virago Press, 1989.

Other (for children)

Trust You, Wriggly. London, Hodder and Stoughton, 1980.
Baby Fish and Other Stories. Privately printed, 1983.
Leslyn in London. London, Hodder and Stoughton, 1984.
The Discovery. London, Macmillan, 1986.
No Hickory No Dickory No Dock (nursery rhymes), with John Agard. London, Viking, 1990.
Give Yourself a Hug (poems). London, A and C Black, 1994.

Editor, *Black Poetry.* London, Blackie, 1988; as *Poetry Jump Up,* London, Penguin, 1989.
Editor, *Can I Buy a Slice of Sky?* London, Blackie, 1991.
Editor, with John Agard, *A Caribbean Dozen.* N.p., Walker Books, 1994.

*

Critical Studies: "'Writing the Body': Reading Joan Riley, Grace Nichols and Ntozake Shange" by Gabriele Griffin, in *Black Women's Writing,* edited by Gina Wisker, New York, St. Martin's Press, 1993; "Grace Nichols' 'Sugar Cane': A Post-Colonial and Feminist Perspective" by Elfi Bettinger, in *Anglistik & Englischunterricht* (Heidelberg, Germany), 53, 1994; "The Body As History and 'Writing the Body': The Example of Grace Nichols" by Alison Easton, in *Journal of Gender Studies,* 3(1), 1994; "Gender and Hybridity in Contemporary Caribbean Poetry" by Jana Gohrisch, in *Anglistentag 1997 Giessen,* edited by Raimund Borgmeier, Herbert Grabes, and Andreas H. Jucker, Trier, Germany, Wissenschaftlicher Verlag Trier, 1998; "The Divine Body in Grace Nichols's 'The Fat Black Woman's Poems'" by Mara Scanlon, in *World Literature Today* (Norman, Oklahoma), 72(1), winter 1998; "On the (False) Idea of Exile: Derek Walcott and Grace Nichols" by Aleid Fokkema, in *(Un)Writing Empire,* edited by Theo D'Haen, Amsterdam, Rodopi, 1998.

*   *   *

Grace Nichols's career as a poet had a distinguished start with the collection *I Is a Long-Memoried Woman,* which won the Commonwealth poetry prize in 1983. The collection charts the slave experience from the point of view of the black woman and touches on the pain, fear, confusion, anger, and strength of slave women. The use of the first-person narrative gives the collection its intimate, lived-through, genuinely soul-searching tone, and yet Nichols is careful to point out that the "I" is every slave woman by giving her a "web of kin," a composite African ancestry, including most of the tribes who were enslaved. The collection is tightly organized, moving chronologically from "the beginning" through "the vicissitudes" of slave existence, "the sorcery" to cope with it, "the bloodling" that centers around the emotional agony of motherhood in slave conditions, and "the return," in which the slave finally rebels and is returned to herself. Cutting across this chronology is a consistent woman's point of view and frame of reference. The African ancestral world is evoked in terms of fertility goddesses, the power of traditional women, and their daily lives (cooking, farming, and child rearing), and the New World experiences refer to the martyrdom of rebel women, the heroines of the struggle, and to the hard labor and "namelessness" of the slave women.

The main strength of the collection lies in the courage with which Nichols searches out and discusses the most painful areas of the slave woman's condition: the fight to retain dignity and self-esteem in humiliating circumstances, the shame connected with the knowledge that there were black slave traders as well, and, most of all, the contradictions of motherhood, the pain that should have been joy and that led some slave women to kill their babies. Occasionally the poet/persona gives in to depression and despair, as in the poem "Sunshine," which concludes with the lines "the truth is / my life has slipped out / of my possession." The main cause for despair is not the harsh conditions but the severing of ties and the loss of tradition, roots, and rituals: "but I / armed only with / my mother's smile / must be forever gathering / my life together like scattered beads." The schizophrenic universe of this New World slave condition is convincingly and movingly described in poems like "Drum-Spell" and "Web of Kin." The latter poem also offers a possible, if hard, way out of the dilemma—"and my eyes everywhere reflecting / even in dreams I will submerge myself"—suggesting a slow gathering of strength through a period of watchfulness and suspended action.

The overall tone of the collection, however, is defiant, celebrating women's capacity for survival. Rebellion is traced in a hundred small ways. In poems like "Love Act," "Skin Teeth," and "Nanny" the traditional image of the smiling and happy female house slave is exploded, and "nanny / mistresswife" is seen to harbor self-awareness and controlled hatred until the moment is ripe and she gains her own freedom or, in the imagery of the book, she becomes "a woman / holding my beads in my hand." Form varies between free verse and ritualistic incantations and also relies on West Indian popular songs, some written in dialect and the rest in clearly marked West Indian English, styles that suit the subject perfectly.

The Fat Black Woman's Poems is a less unified collection that consists of four unlinked sections. The first section, which gives the book its title, is a lighthearted, occasionally very funny exploration of the thoughts and problems of a fat, self-assured black woman. Seriousness lurks behind the fun, however, as in the poem "The Fat Black Woman Remembers," in which the poet/persona makes sure that her image does not coincide with the image of that other fat black woman, Jemima, "tossing pancakes / to heaven / in smokes of happy hearty / murderous blue laughter . . . But this fat black woman ain't no Jemima / Sure thing Honey / Yeah." The following two sections, "In Spite of Ourselves" and "Back Home Contemplation," cover traditional themes in West Indian literature: the feeling of alienation from British society and thoughts about home and childhood, vacillating between nostalgia for the lost world of childhood and anger at present conditions of poverty and exploitation.

Lazy Thoughts of a Lazy Woman continues both the themes and the style of the previous collections. It starts off lightheartedly with poems about dust and grease and continues with a varied collection of thoughts and impressions about themes such as Eve, the Jamaican tourist industry, break dancing, and white male power. There is a greater emphasis on woman-centered or feminist themes in poems like "Ode to My Bleed" and "My Black Triangle." There is also a more extensive use of West Indian dialect. The tone is mostly light, offering sudden gifts of insight: "Even the undeserving / love floods / risking all." Despite this, Nichols's first collection remains her most substantial, with the following volumes adding the dimension of humor.

—Kirsten Holst Petersen

NÍ CHUILLEANÁIN, Eiléan

Nationality: Irish. **Born:** Cork, 28 November 1942. **Education:** University College, Cork, B.A. in English and history 1962, M.A. in English 1964; Lady Margaret Hall, Oxford, 1964–66, B.Litt. in Elizabethan prose 1969. **Family:** Married Macdara Woods in 1978; one son. **Career:** Lecturer, 1966–85, and since 1985 senior lecturer, Trinity College, Dublin. Founder, with Pearse Hutchinson, Macdara Woods and Leland Bardwell, *Cyphers* literary magazine, 1975. **Awards:** *Irish Times* prize, 1966; Patrick Kavanagh prize, 1973, for *Acts and Monuments;* Books Ireland Publishers' award, 1975, for *Site of Ambush;* O'Shaughnessy prize, Irish-American Cultural Foundation, 1992. **Address:** Trinity College, University of Dublin, Dublin 2, Ireland.

PUBLICATIONS

Poetry

Acts and Monuments. Dublin, Gallery Press, 1972.
Site of Ambush. Dublin, Gallery Press, 1975.
The Second Voyage. Dublin, Gallery Press, and Winston-Salem, North Carolina, Wake Forest University Press, 1977; Newcastle upon Tyne, Bloodaxe, 1986. Cork.
The Rose-Geranium. Dublin, Gallery Press, 1981.
The Magdalene Sermon. Dublin, Gallery Press, 1989; as *The Magdalene Sermon and Earlier Poems,* Winston-Salem, North Carolina, Wake Forest University Press, 1991.
The Brazen Serpent. Winston-Salem, North Carolina, Wake Forest University Press, 1995.

Other

Editor, *Irish Women: Image and Achievement.* Dublin, Arlen House, 1985.
Editor, *Belinda,* by Maria Edgeworth. London, J.M. Dent, 1993.
Editor, with J.D. Pheifer, *Noble and Joyous Histories: English Romances 1375–1650.* Dublin, Irish Academic Press, 1993.
Editor, *The Water Horse: Poems in Irish,* by Nuala Ní Dhomhnaill. Oldcastle, Gallery Books, 1999.

*

Critical Studies: "Contemporary Women Poets in Ireland" by Robert H. Henigan, in *Concerning Poetry* (Bellingham, Washington), 18(1–2), 1985; "'What You Have Seen Is Beyond Speech': Female Journeys in the Poetry of Eavan Boland and Eiléan Ní Chuilleanáin" by Sheila C. Conboy, in *Canadian Journal of Irish Studies* (Saskatoon, Canada), 16(1), July 1990; "'Out of Myth into History': The Poetry of Eavan Boland and Eiléan Ní Chuilleanáin" by Deborah Sarbin, in *Canadian Journal of Irish Studies* (Saskatoon, Canada), 19(1), July 1993; *'The Book of Myths in Which Our Names Do Not Appear': A Study of the Struggle of Irish Women Poets with the Tradition of Modern Irish Poetry* (dissertation) by Eileen Marie Thompson, University of Oregon, 1994; "'How Things Begin to Happen': Notes on Eiléan Ní Chuilleanáin and Medbh McGuckian" by Peter Sirr, in *Southern Review* (Baton Rouge, Louisiana), 31(3), summer 1995; "'Our Bodies' Eyes and Writing Hands': Secrecy and Sensuality in Ní Chuilleanáin's Baroque Art" by Dillon Johnston, in *Gender and Sexuality in Modern Ireland,* edited by Anthony Bradley and Maryann Gialanella Valiulis, Amherst, University of Massachusetts Press, 1997; "Hidden Ireland: Eiléan Ní Chuilleanáin and Munster Poetry" by John Kerrigan, in *Critical Quarterly,* 40(4), winter 1998.

Eiléan Ní Chuilleanáin comments:

My work issues from problems in everyday life, but it does so obliquely, via myths, folklore, and history. It draws on visual description of rooms and landscapes, on childhood memories and literary allusions, and since these are sometimes enigmatic, my poems can be so too.

*   *   *

Since 1966, when she won the *Irish Times* prize for poetry, Eiléan Ní Chuilleanáin has written with a remarkable consistency of theme and method. Her subject matter is personal, but it is seen through a strange perspective. Although the "I" of the poems has always been the personal "I," it is revealed through odd angles and amazing connections between mythical moments and moments of skewed looking. She is a poet of empty kitchens, silent, well-lit places, well-scrubbed tables. She shares with Thomas Kinsella that peculiar ability to find genius in odd corners. The drama in her poems is a reductive one. A poem often begins with a moment of insight, an epiphany, and is then reduced to a series of physical descriptions. Her geography is askew because she is highly sensitive to the play of light on objects. Her world is "ridged / Pocked and dented" with the decency of thought:

And wake again in an afternoon bed
Grey light sloping from window-ledge
To straw-seated armchair. I get up,
Walk down a silent corridor
To the Kitchen. Twilight and a long scrubbed table . . .

In "The Ropesellers" she finds "a soft corner of sunlight," and in "Atlantis" there is "light wavering in water," while in "Chrissie," a poem from *The Magdalene Sermon,* "Light fills the growing cavity / That swells her, that ripens to her ending." Her ability to notice well-lit cavities and sunlit corners is symptomatic of solitary character or at least of the flight toward solitude. But these solitudes are not aimless; they are loaded with adult perceptions and become energized with a deep unease:

What man forgets, at home
In the long noons of peace
His own imprisonment or the day of his release?

It is in the sequence *Cork* that these images of well-lit places are fully orchestrated. The sequence originally accompanied drawings of Cork City by Brian Lalor and was subsequently republished in *The Rose-Geranium*. In "Cork" Ní Chuilleanáin tries to match Lalor's lines with her own, this time the well-lit corners being mainly exterior:

The spiders are preparing for autumn.
They weave throughout the city:
Selecting the light for their traps,
They swell with darkness.

Because of its peculiar geography—all "insolent flights of steps," "gables and stacks," and "painted windowsills"—Cork City provides an ideal myth kitty for a poet with Ní Chuilleanáin's sensitivity. The success of the sequence lies in its perfect marriage of talent and material. "The Rose-Geranium" is a more sensual and human poem, with its touched textures, bodies folded, pillow, jam jar, and pear tree. The poet's presence is stronger and the descriptions more judgmental:

I seek for depths as planets fly from the sun,
What holds me in life is flowing from me and I flow
Falling, *out of true.*

Despite these silent places there is a constant movement, both physical and spiritual, in Ní Chuilleanáin's poems. She has been a voyager through the physical world in ferryboats—"Shipbuilders all believe in fate; / The moral of the ship is death"—in airplanes—"We came down above the houses / In a stiff curve, and / At the edge of Paris airport / Saw an empty tunnel"—or through ferry and ferry road to that described in "Dreaming in the Ksar Es Souk Motel." The places described are places of arrival, a half-carpeted room in Rome or a familiar bed in Oxford. In many of Ní Chuilleanáin's poems there is a displaced psyche, a much traveled and much disrupted point of view. The spirit seeks a resting place. The poet is never entirely unpacked before the psyche has to orientate itself again in "one more of your suddenly furnished houses." Her poems constantly say, "We live here now," with "now" the shifting sand upon which the poet builds a frantic, distracted foothold. Yet she does build a foothold, and the speed with which she builds has created a skeptical, edgy viewpoint. It is remarkably free from the many stultifying parishes of Irish poetry. Venturing forth, or voyaging, has provided Ní Chuilleanáin with her great intellectual context. Her world has remained passionately self-centered, but she is aware of the one voyaging pedigree:

Turn west now, turn away to sleep
And you are simultaneous with
Maelduin setting sail . . .
With Odysseus crouching again
Inside a fish-smelling sealskin,
Or Anticlus . . .

These mythical voyagers—Maelduin, Odysseus, and Anticlus—are the only pedigree Ní Chuilleanáin has acknowledged. She has chronicled the lives of various women from both a historical and personal viewpoint. In particular she has a strange empathy with Roman Catholic sisters, from convent life in "The Rose-Geranium"—"nothing is to be mine / Everything ours"—to convent life in Calais—"They handed her back her body, / its voices and its death." She has spoken of the used and subdued bodies of women and of the wife who collects the "rifled / Remains of her husband." But it is reticence rather than polemic that distinguishes her work. She is the least directly political of Irish poets, knowing that "in retrospect, it is all edge." Ní Chuilleanáin is one of the constant outsiders in Irish poetry, never staying in any one parish long enough to collect her polling card. She is free of prejudice and pretense. It is to the mythical voyagers that she owes allegiance. There is a whiff of much traveled intelligence from her work, as if she were up and going long before cow shit or bog water could cling to her boots.

—Thomas McCarthy

NORRIS, Leslie

Nationality: Welsh. **Born:** Merthyr Tydfil, Glamorgan, 21 May 1921. **Education:** Cyfthfa Castle School, 1931–38; City of Coventry College, 1947–49; University of Southampton (Ralph Morley prize, 1958), 1955–58, Dip.Ed., M. Phil., 1958. **Military Service:** Royal Air Force, 1940–42. **Family:** Married Catherine Mary Morgan in 1948. **Career:** Teacher, Grass Royal School, Yeovil, Somerset, 1948–52; deputy head, Southdown School, Bath, 1952–55; head teacher, Aldingbourne School, Chichester, 1955–58; principal lecturer in degree studies, College of Education, Bognor Regis, Sussex, 1958–73; visiting lecturer, University of Washington, Seattle, 1973, 1980, 1981; resident poet, Eton College, 1977; Arts Council writing fellow, West Sussex Institute of Higher Education, 1979–80. Since 1983 Humanities professor of creative writing, Brigham Young University; Provo, Utah. **Awards:** Welsh Arts Council award, 1967, 1968, 1980, 1989 (senior fiction award), and prize, 1978; Alice Hunt Bartlett prize, 1970; Cholmondeley prize, 1979; David Higham prize, for fiction, 1980; Katherine Mansfield award, 1981; John Hughes prize, 1991. Fellow, Royal Society of Literature, 1962, and Welsh Academy, 1990. D.Litt: University of Glamorgan, 1994. D.H.L.: Brigham Young University, 1996. **Agent:** Charles Schlessiger, Brandt and Brandt, 1501 Broadway, New York, New York 10036. **Address:** 849 South Carterville Road, Orem, Utah 84058, U.S.A.

PUBLICATIONS

Poetry

Tongue of Beauty. London, Favil Press, 1941.
Poems. London, Falcon Press, 1946.
The Ballad of Billy Rose. Leeds, Northern House, 1964.
The Loud Winter. Cardiff, Triskel Press, 1967.
Finding Gold. London, Chatto and Windus, 1967.
Curlew. St. Brelade, Jersey, Armstrong, 1969.
Ransoms. London, Chatto and Windus, 1970; Newtown, Powys, Gwasg Gregynog, 1987.
His Last Autumn. Rushden, Northamptonshire, Sceptre Press, 1972.
Mountains, Polecats, Pheasants and Other Elegies. London, Chatto and Windus, 1973.

Stone and Fern. Winchester, Southern Arts Association, 1973.
At the Publishers'. Berkhamsted, Hertfordshire, Priapus, 1976.
Ravenna Bridge. Knotting, Bedfordshire, Sceptre Press, 1977.
Islands Off Maine. Cranberry Isles, Maine, Tidal Press, 1977.
Merlin and the Snake's Egg. New York, Viking Press, 1978.
Hyperion. Knotting, Bedfordshire, Sceptre Press, 1979.
Water Voices. London, Chatto and Windus—Hogarth Press, 1980.
Walking the White Fields: Poems 1967–1980. Boston, Little Brown, 1980.
A Tree Sequence. Seattle, Spring Valley Press, 1984.
Selected Poems. Bridgend, Glamorgan, Poetry Wales Press, 1986.
Sequences. Layton, Utah, Gibbs Smith, 1988.
Norris's Ark. Portsmouth, New Hampshire, Tidal Press, 1988.
A Sea in the Desert. Bridgend, Glamorgan, Seren, 1989.
Collected Poems. Bridgend, Glamorgan, Seren, 1996.

Recording: *Poems,* with Dannie Abse, Argo, 1974.

Short Stories

Sliding. New York, Scribner, 1976; London, Dent, 1978.
The Girl from Cardigan. Bridgend, Glamorgan, Seren, and Layton, Utah, Gibbs Smith, 1988.
Collected Stories. Bridgend, Glamorgan, Seren, 1996.

Other

Glyn Jones. Cardiff, University of Wales Press, 1973.

Editor, *Vernon Watkins 1906–1967.* London, Faber, 1970.
Editor, *Andrew Young: Remembrance and Homage.* Cranberry Isles, Maine, Tidal Press, 1978.
Editor, *The Mabinogion,* translated by Lady Charlotte Guest. London, Folio Society, 1980.

Translator, with Alan Keele, *The Sonnets to Orpheus,* by Rainer Maria Rilke. Columbia, South Carolina, Camden House, 1989.
Translator, *The Duino Elegies,* Rainer Maria Rilke, Columbia, South Carolina, Camden House, 1993.

*

Manuscript Collection: National Library of Wales, Aberystwyth.

Critical Studies: By Sam Adams, in *Poetry Wales* (Cardiff), 1972; R. Jenkins, in *Anglo-Welsh Review* (Pembroke Dock), 1972; Ted Walker, in *Priapus* (Berkhamsted, Hertfordshire), 1972; Norman Rosenfeld, in *Tar River Poetry* (Greenville, North Carolina), 1983; *Leslie Norris* by James Davies, Cardiff, University of Wales Press, 1989; *An Open World: Essays on Leslie Norris* edited by Eugene England and Peter Makuck, Columbia, South Carolina, Camden House, 1994.

Leslie Norris comments:

My poetry is an attempt to re-create, not to describe. The birds or animals or people or buildings or trees existing in my poems must exist root, branch, claw, skin, and stone. The texture of my words must be made of feathers or bones, bark or whatever; the lines must move with real muscle. I think I am a Jungian poet, bringing up the images from some unknown source. The poems come unbidden, and my task is to recognize them; often I am well toward the end of a poem before I know what it is "about." But afterwards I work with unremitting labor to make sure of the poem's clarity, to make its surface perfect. I think my poems ought to be like onions, the golden outer skin flawless, the weight surprisingly heavy, solid, much more than you would expect. Then when the outer skin is peeled, there is a moist, pearly inner layer of meaning, then another and another.

Somewhere in the process you might begin to weep.

(1995) More recently I am involved in writing a long autobiographical poem.

*   *   *

Leslie Norris's birth at Wern Farm, just outside Merthyr Tydfil, Wales's Klondike of the nineteenth century, and his subsequent residence in southern England together provided the cultural tension that, after a long silence, generated his poetry of the 1960s and made it something quite different from the early work in *Tongue of Beauty.* The gap is bridged, of course, by Norris's fascination with and power over words, but the Merthyr to which he could never go back, which was, in the spirit of his youth and that of other writers his seniors, quite dead, was the source of many elegies. This was the case in *Finding Gold* in particular, which was an expression both of the irrecoverability of his own youth and of a more general irrecoverability ("And yes, those boys are gone"). It was not that he could not return to Wales— he did that, first with holidays in Cardiganshire and then by the purchase of his cottage Wthan—but what his residence in England did was to make it possible to approach the Welsh heritage in a way that would have been strange to the Merthyr-bound man. It also linked and contrasted the peaceful rurality of Sussex with the more wayward and half-tamed spirit of the countryside round Llandysul.

Perhaps Norris was always a man of the country, and his great achievement, visible more and more in books like *Mountains, Polecats, Pheasants and other Elegies,* has been to use the simple physical stimuli of a rural world to make poems no more than occasionally recondite and always couched in a language that accommodates images in the most natural manner possible and gives continuous pleasure. His syntax is rarely distorted or difficult. What he has evolved is that most difficult thing to master and obtain, a style that in its limpidity, clarity, and latent force carries the simple, the anecdotal, even the common experience and gives it an unexpected memorability. This quality is not confined to his poetry, for which he received the Cholmondeley prize in 1978; the ecstatic reception of his volume of short stories, *Sliding*—he was awarded both the David Higham prize and a Welsh Arts Council prize for the work—was the recognition of an achievement very similar.

Like Edward Thomas and, to a lesser extent, Andrew Young, Norris can conjure common observation into his own idiosyncratic mode. His recourse, even in later books, to boyhood memories of the boxing ring or of the collier's care for birds or dogs—or, more piercingly, to recollection of a classmate killed at Aberfan—provides the variety that makes his countryman's perception the more poignant. Norris is that rare poet who has made his work accessible without cheapening the experience of the poem or blunting its delicacy. In this sense he is an ambassador for poetry at the court of the general public in a generation that sorely needs one.

—Roland Mathias

NORSE, Harold (George)

Nationality: American. **Born:** New York City, 6 July 1916. **Education:** Brooklyn College, B.A. 1938; New York University, M.A. 1951. **Career:** Worked as a sheet metal worker, dancer, and proofreader, 1941–44; instructor in English, Cooper Union, New York, 1949–52, Lion School of English, Rome, 1956–57, and U.S. Information Service School, Naples, 1958; part-time teacher, San Jose State University, California, 1973–75; instructor in creative writing, New College, San Francisco; founding editor, *Bastard Angel,* San Francisco. **Awards:** Borestone Mountain Poetry award, 1968; National Endowment for the Arts fellowship, 1974; De Young Museum grant, 1974; Lifetime Achievement award for poetry, National Poetry Association, 1991. **Address:** 157 Albion Street, San Francisco, California 94110, U.S.A.

PUBLICATIONS

Poetry

The Undersea Mountain. Denver, Swallow, 1953.
The Dancing Beasts. New York, Macmillan, 1962.
Ole. Bensenville, Illinois, Open Skull, 1966.
Karma Circuit: 20 Poems and a Preface. London, Nothing Doing in London, 1967; San Francisco, Panjandrum Press, 1974.
Christmas on Earth. N.p., Minkoff Rare Editions, 1968.
Penguin Modern Poets 13, with Charles Bukowski and Philip Lamantia. London, Penguin, 1969.
Hotel Nirvana: Selected Poems 1953–1973. San Francisco, City Lights, 1974.
I See America Daily. San Francisco, Mother's Hen, 1974.
Carnivorous Saint: Gay Poems 1941–1976. San Francisco, Gay Sunshine Press, 1977.
Mysteries of Magritte. San Diego, Atticus Press, 1984.
The Love Poems, 1940–1985. Trumansburg, New York, Crossing Press, 1986.
Sniffing Keyholes. San Francisco, Synaesthesia Press, 1998.

Novel

Beat Hotel. Augsburg, Maro, 1975; San Diego, Atticus Press, 1983.

Other

Memoirs of a Bastard Angel. New York, Morrow, 1989; London, Bloomsbury, 1990; Paris, DuRocher, 1991; Hamburg, Rogner & Bernhard, 1992.
The American Idiom: A Correspondence. San Francisco, Bright Tyger Press, 1990.

Translator, *The Roman Sonnets of G.G. Belli.* Highlands, North Carolina, Jargon, 1960.

*

Manuscript Collection: Lilly Library, Indiana University, Bloomington.

Critical Studies: *Bomb Culture* by Jeff Nuttall, London, MacGibbon and Kee, 1968, New York, Delacorte Press, 1969; *Orpheus Unacclaimed: A Study of the Poetry of Harold Norse* by John A. Wood, Fayetteville, University of Arkansas unpublished thesis, 1969; "Hotel of the Carnivorous Heart: The Norse Saga Rediscovered" by Paul Grillo, in *NorthEast Rising Sun 2,* 6–7, 1977; in *Isthmus 6* (San Francisco), 1977; Nanos Valaoritis, in *Surréalisme 2,* Paris, Savelli, 1977; "An American Catullus" by W.I. Scobie, in *The Advocate* (Los Angeles), 19 October 1977; *The Great American Poetry Bake-Off* by Robert L. Peters, Metuchen, New Jersey, Scarecrow Press, 1979; *Articulate Flesh* by Gregory Woods, New Haven, Connecticut and London, Yale University Press, 1987; *Whitman's Wild Children* by Neeli Cherkovski, Venice, California, Lapis Press, 1988; by Robert Craft, in *New York Review of Books,* 38(1–2), 17 December 1991.

Harold Norse comments:

Using the American vulgate, I generally tend to record experience through a spontaneous, heart-centered, autobiographical poetry for readers, not specialists. Via a rather surrealistic approach that attempts to capture the complexity of living by means of an anagogical imagery of the absurd, contradictory, and tragicomic, I try to present the passions, feelings, and events of my own life and time, often centered in the erotic tradition of Greco-Roman poetry, secular and profane. I see the function of my poetry as a voicing of the substrata of the passional life, in both senses of strong emotion and suffering. I do not know whether I have chosen this or been chosen for it, as I have always written in this way—and God help the poor reader!

*   *   *

Harold Norse is an interesting example of a poet who started his literary career in a relatively formal manner, both from the point of view of his writing and the circles he moved in, and then decided to throw in his lot with the bohemian and often expatriate world of little magazines and small presses. His early work reflected the influence of Hart Crane, as in this brief example from the early *The Dancing Beasts:*

> The sun scattered those diamonds
> Like coruscations of castanets
> Over the sinewy blue belly
> Of the sea; while one great rock rose,
> The fat fin of a whaleshaped isle . . .

But by the time this collection appeared in print Norse was moving toward a looser, more open form of poetry, perhaps under the influence of some of the poets of the beat generation. It has also been suggested that he was much affected by the Roman dialect poems of G.G. Belli, which he translated into an engaging American idiom. As the 1960s developed, Norse began to appear in print with poems that used the language and rhythms of everyday speech to describe the facts of his life:

> the bottle of mineral water is guillotining the trees
>   i tighten my scarf

in cap & hornrimmed specs
I'm superimposed on italy

         speeding north
into rain & winter

Of course, the drawback with this kind of writing, which is fairly typical of the poems in *Karma Circuit,* is that it expects the reader to be interested in the information it offers, and its way of piling detail upon detail, short phrase upon short phrase, can become tiresome. It is true that this particular poem, written while traveling, does catch the rhythm and fragmentary nature of a long train journey, but the reader may be forgiven for wanting something more.

Norse's forays into free verse have caused him to write unevenly, sometimes bringing off a poem, sometimes letting it wander too much to hold the reader's attention. What he does do well is to portray the artistic outsider in society, and his collection *Hotel Nirvana* is almost a catalogue of literary and other references. He mentions painters such as Picasso and Braque, pays homage to the dead poet Maxwell Bodenheim, states a preference for Gershwin over Hemingway in a poem that neatly combines images of Paris and New York, and lists numerous other heroes, including Baudelaire, Rimbaud, and Artaud. The book is, in fact, a useful record of the life of an expatriate bohemian poet, though it does have flashes of humor that save it from sounding pretentious:

In November I gave a poetry reading which was so well
     advertised
     one day in advance that 5 people actually
     came, 4 of them
     drunk and cantankerous . . .

As well as opting to become a literary outsider, moving around and publishing where and when he could, Norse also involved himself with the gay community, and many of his poems reflect this fact. *Carnivorous Saint: Gay Poems 1941–1976* brings together a large selection of his work, and although it is inevitably variable in quality, it has many fine poems. It also gives the reader an opportunity to see Norse at work in a variety of styles. There is, for example, the simple formality of the 1950 poem ''Angel of Last Summer'':

''So, beat the rug. Keep your house clean.''
The angel smiled, his muscles gleamed.
He beat the rug, I read my book,
The washing flapped, and the chimneys shook.

As a stylistic contrast there is the looser 1975 poem ''The Love Song of an Old Beatnik'':

After you left I missed you so much
I began to floss my teeth wildly.
There was nothing to do.
The sunflower seeds you put in a jar—
don't worry, they'll keep
much better than me till you're back.

Carnivorous Saint can be a provocative book in some ways, but it is central to an understanding of Norse's poetry.

By deciding to move away from formal verse and a literary life linked to a major publishing center, Norse has taken chances with his work, much of which has been published in small press editions. Likewise, he has taken chances with the nature of his poems' subject matter and content. They have come to represent a way of life that runs counter to many social, political, and literary beliefs. From this point of view his work has value, despite its variable quality, for it records certain attitudes for posterity. But at their best the poems also stand on their own merits, whatever their sociological background. They retain their energy and concern, and when Norse is firmly in control of the language and rhythm, they keep the reader interested and entertained.

—Jim Burns

NOTLEY, Alice

Nationality: American. **Born:** Bisbee, Arizona, 8 November 1945. **Education:** Barnard College, New York, B.A. 1967; University of Iowa, Iowa City, M.F.A. 1969. **Family:** Married the writer Ted Berrigan in 1972 (died 1983), two sons; 2) Douglas Oliver in 1988. **Awards:** National Endowment for the Arts grant, 1980; Poetry Center award, 1982; G.E. Foundation award, 1983; Fund for Poetry grant, 1987, 1989. **Address:** 101 St. Marks Place, 12A, New York, New York 10009, U.S.A.

PUBLICATIONS

Poetry

165 Meeting House Lane. New York, ''C'' Press, 1971.
Phoebe Light. Bolinas, California, Big Sky, 1973.
Incidentals in the Day World. New York, Angel Hair, 1973.
For Frank O'Hara's Birthday. Cambridge, Street Editions, 1976.
Alice Ordered Me to Be Made: Poems 1975. Chicago, Yellow Press, 1976.
A Diamond Necklace. New York, Frontward, 1977.
Songs for the Unborn Second Baby. Lenox, Massachusetts, United Artists, 1979.
When I Was Alive. New York, Vehicle, 1980.
Waltzing Matilda. New York, Kulchur, 1981.
How Spring Comes. West Branch, Iowa, Toothpaste Press, 1981.
Three Zero, Turning Thirty, with Andrei Codrescu, edited by Keith and Jeff Wright. New York, Hard Press, 1982.
Sorrento. Los Angeles, Sherwood Press, 1984.
Margaret and Dusty. Minneapolis, Coffee House Press, 1985.
Parts of a Wedding. New York, Unimproved Editions Press, 1986.
At Night the States. Chicago, Yellow Press, 1988.
Selected Poems of Alice Notley. Hoboken, New Jersey, Talisman House, 1993.
The Descent of Alette. New York, Penguin, 1996.
Mysteries of Small Houses. New York, Penguin, 1998.

Play

Anne's White Glove (produced New York, 1985). Published in *New American Writing,* no. 1, 1987.

Other

Doctor Williams' Heiresses: A Lecture. Berkeley, California, Tuumba Press, 1980.
Tell Me Again (autobiography). Santa Barbara, California, Am Here, 1981.
Homer's "Art". Canton, New York, Institute for Further Studies, 1990.
The Scarlet Cabinet: A Compendium of Books, with Douglas Oliver. New York, Scarlet Editions, 1992.

*

Critical Studies: Interviews in *Talisman,* 1, fall 1988, and in *Onthebus,* 4–5(2–1), 1992; "Machine's Corpse: Within the City's Body" by Mark Irwin, in *Denver Quarterly* (Denver), 32(1–2), summer-fall 1997.

* * *

Alice Notley is an American poet whose expression has been shaped by a conscious indebtedness to the legacy of William Carlos Williams. Regarding herself as one of "Doctor Williams' Heiresses," Notley has realized that "you could use him to sound entirely new if you were a woman. It was all about this woman business. I thought we didn't need to read women—I mean find the hidden in the woodwork ones—so much as find the poems among whatever sex that made you feel free to say whatever you liked. Williams makes you feel that you can say anything, including your own anything."

In most of her published work "your own anything" centered around Notley's life with her first husband, the poet Ted Berrigan, and their children on New York City's Lower East Side. Her poetry reflects her intelligence, humor, and commitment to her craft, and it is perhaps strongest when she is expressing her remarkable sensitivity to the nuances of human relationships. Rather than insist on her own emotional independence as an emancipated woman in the fashion of her New York contemporaries Anne Waldman and Diane Wakoski, Notley stresses the bonds between people, savoring with great refinement the closeness and communication that result from shared feelings. With delicacy and simple wonder she describes the miracle of physical possession in "Song," from the collection *When I Was Alive:*

> Who shall have my fair lord
> Who but I who but I who but Alice
> By the black window
> Softly in November
> Who but I who but I who but Alice

In more complex poems like "Sonnet" (from *A Diamond Necklace*) Notley brilliantly explores the components of a long marriage between two famous people, the comedy team of George Burns and Gracie Allen:

> The late Gracie Allen was a very lucid comedienne,
> Especially in the way that lucid means shining and bright.
> What her husband George Burns called her illogical logic
> Made a halo around our syntax and ourselves as we laughed.
>
> George Burns most often was her artful inconspicuous
>   straight-man.

> He could move people about stage, construct skits
>   and scenes, write
> And gather jokes. They were married as long as ordinary
>   magic
> Would allow, thirty-eight years, until Gracie Allen's death.
>
> In her fifties Gracie Allen developed a heart condition.
> She would call George Burns when her heart felt funny and
>   fluttered.
> He'd give her a pill and they'd hold each other till the
>   palpitation
> Stopped—just a few minutes, many times and
>   pills. As magic fills
> Then fulfilled must leave a space, one day Gracie Allen's
>   heart fluttered
> And hurt and stopped. George Burns said unbeliev-
>   ingly to the doctor,
>   "But I still have some of the pills."

Notley responds to a broad spectrum of American culture, and her experiments with poetic forms and free verse owe as much to Gertrude Stein, Frank O'Hara, and Berrigan as they do to Williams. Like them, she believes that she is writing primarily to express her own personal tone of voice, which is her music and her breath. She understands Williams's concept of the variable foot to mean "the dominance of tone of voice over other considerations . . . I break my lines where I do, as I'm being as various as my voice should be in our intimacy." She feels that her speech sounds as the voice of "the new wife, & the new mother" in her own time, but her intent is to make a poem rather than present a platform of social reform: "I'm not all that interested in being a woman, it's just a practical problem that you deal with when you write poems. You do have to deal with the problem of who you are so that you can be a person talking."

Describing herself as an "imperfect medium," Notley insists on her own limitations as a poet. She often deliberately deflates what she senses as her own pretensions, as in "The Prophet," a long poem from the collection *How Spring Comes,* which ends with the lines "You must never / Stop making jokes. You are not great you are life." When this tone of self-depreciation is absent, however, and she concentrates on presenting her keen perceptions of her subject, her work has considerably more substance. Despite her loyalty to Williams, it would appear from the evidence of her poetry that her reflections—like Emily Dickinson's—are as sharp as her observations. Notley should trust them more, along with her heart.

—Ann Charters

NYE, Naomi Shihab

Nationality: American (Palestinian-American). **Born:** Naomi Shihab, St. Louis, Missouri, 12 March 1952. **Education:** Trinity University, San Antonio, Texas, 1970–74, B.A. 1974. **Family:** Married Michael Nye in 1978; one son. **Career:** Visiting writer, University of Hawaii, fall 1991, University of Alaska, Fairbanks, spring 1993, Texas Center for Writers, Austin, 1995. Since 1978 freelance visiting writer in schools around the country. **Awards:** Texas Institute of Letters Poetry prize, 1980, 1982; Charity Randall prize, International Poetry Forum, 1989; I.B. Lavan award, Academy of American Poets, 1989;

Jane Addams Children's Book award, 1995, 1998; John Simon Guggenheim fellowship, 1997–98; Judy Lopez memorial award for children's literature, 1998; Best Book for Young Readers award, Texas Institute of Letters, 1998; Witter Bynner fellow, 2000. **Address:** 806 South Main Avenue, San Antonio, Texas 78204, U.S.A.

PUBLICATIONS

Poetry

Different Ways to Pray. Portland, Oregon, Breitenbush Books, 1980.
Hugging the Jukebox. Portland, Oregon, Breitenbush Books, 1982.
Yellow Glove. Portland, Oregon, Breitenbush Books, 1986.
Red Suitcase. New York, BOA Editions, 1994.
Words under the Words: Selected Poems. Portland, Oregon, Far Corner Books, Eighth Mountain Press, 1995.
Fuel. New York, BOA Editions, 1998.

Recordings: *The Language of Life with Bill Moyers,* National Public Broadcasting, 1995; *The United States of Poetry,* 1996.

Other

Sitti's Secrets (for children). New York, Four Winds Press/Macmillan, and London, Hamish Hamilton, 1994.
Benito's Dream Bottle, illustrated by Yu Cha Pak. New York, Simon and Schuster, 1995.
Never in a Hurry. University of South Carolina Press, 1996.
Habibi (for teenagers). New York, Simon and Schuster, 1997.
Lullaby Raft, illustrated by Vivienne Flesher. New York, Simon and Schuster, 1997.

Editor, *This Same Sky.* New York, Four Winds Press/Macmillan, 1992.
Editor, *The Tree Is Older Than You Are.* New York, Simon and Schuster, 1995.
Editor, with Paul B. Janeczko, *I Feel a Little Jumpy around You.* New York, Simon and Schuster, 1996.
Editor, *The Space between Our Footsteps: Poems & Paintings from the Middle East.* New York, Simon and Schuster, 1998.
Editor, *What Have You Lost?,* photographs by Michael Nye. N.p., Greenwillow, 1999.

*

Critical Studies: "Loners Whose Voices Move" by Philip Booth, in *Georgia Review* (Athens, Georgia), 43(1), spring 1989; "Doomed by Our Blood to Care: The Poetry of Naomi Shihab Nye" by Gregory Orfalea, in *Paintbrush* (Kirksville, Missouri), 18(35), spring 1991; "Writing to Save Our Lives: An Interview with Naomi Shihab Nye" by Bryce Milligan, in *Paintbrush* (Kirksville, Missouri), 18(35), spring 1991.

Naomi Shihab Nye comments:

We go back and back to where it all begins. The sources, the mysterious wells. Each thing gives us something else.

It was not whether you were rich or poor, but if you had a big life, that was what mattered. A big life could be either a wide one or a deep one. It held countless possible corners and conversations. A big life did not stop at the alley or even the next street. It came from somewhere and was going somewhere, but the word "better" had no relation really. A big life was interested and wore questions easily. A big life never for one second thought it was the only life.

Something was in the closet, besides our clothes, which might or might not be friendly. A branch scratched a curious rhythm on the dark window. Our father came from Palestine, a beloved land far across the sea. Some people called it the Holy Land. Both my parents seemed holy to me. At night our father sat by our beds, curling funny stories into the air. His musical talking stitched us to places we had not been yet. And our mother, who had grown up in St. Louis, where we were growing up, stood by our beds after our father's stories, floating into sleep on a river of songs: "Now rest beneath night's shadow . . . ." She had been to art school and knew how to paint people the way they looked on the inside, not just the outside. That is what I wanted to know about too. What stories and secrets did people carry with them? What songs did they hold close in their ears?

Reading cracked the universe wide open; suddenly we had the power to understand newspapers, menus, books. I loved old signs, Margaret Wise Brown, Louisa May Alcott, Carl Sandburg, Langston Hughes, the exuberant bounce of sentences across a page. I remember shaping a single word—"city," "head"—with enormous tenderness. In second grade my class memorized William Blake's *Songs of Innocence.* Reading gave us voices of friends speaking from everywhere, so it followed that one might write down messages too. Already I wrote to find out what I knew and what connected. Sometimes writing felt like a thank-you note, a response to what had already been given.

My German-American grandmother gave me a powder puff that, when tapped thirty years later, still emits a small, mysterious cloud.

My Palestinian grandmother gave me a laugh and a tilt of the head.

My great-uncle Paul gave me a complete sewing kit a hundred years old and one inch tall.

Whenever people have asked, "Where do you get ideas to write about?" I wonder, "Where do you not?"

*   *   *

Poets have long observed that a persona is not merely the poet's mask but also a version of the writer's self from some point in the past where imagination is strongest. For many women poets it is a childhood self, a lively, perhaps sexually neutral creature free to explore the world as a self, not as a gendered person. Naomi Nye is building a reputation in her prolific canon as the voice of childhood in America, the voice of the girl at the age of daring exploration. But more importantly she animates a sense of the American girl as a mysterious priestess of nature, someone whose eyes are full of animistic landscapes crammed with Mexican ghosts, strange voices, paradox, and magic.

To make it all work Nye takes us into the ordinary world as if we were accompanying her to the corner store for sugar or a bag of flour. Instead, we are faced with a pixie with messages like this one from "Eye-to-Eye" in *Different Ways to Pray:*

We will meet at the corner,
you with your sack lunch,
me with my guitar.
We will be wearing our famous street faces,
anonymous as trees.
Suddenly you will see me,

you will blink, hesitant,
then realize I have not looked away.
For one brave second
we will stare
openly
from borderless skins.
This is my salary.
There are no days off.

Clear, limpid language is Nye's method of luring us away from
our notion of the world. We follow her out of conventional reality into
the dreamworld of a new, young Alice. She promises many adventures, some of them quaint, Pollyannaish, and simple, a few even
pointless. But what she establishes poem by poem is a rare voice of
contentment, pure female happiness with the world as it is. In a land of
so much grim confessionalism, so much lyric anger and disillusion,
Nye has the field of optimism all to herself. An example is found in
"So Much Happiness" from *Hugging the Jukebox:*

Since there is no place large enough
to contain so much happiness,
you shrug, you raise your hands, and it flows out of
                              you
into everything you touch. You are not responsible.
You take no credit, as the night sky takes no credit
for the moon, but continues to hold it, and share it,
and in that way, be known.

Nye seems to be rewriting Blake's *Book of Thel,* the voice of
innocence set down in the modern city. She does not avoid the horrors
of urban life, but she patches together the vision of simple nature
struggling up through the cracks of the city. In the title poem from
Hugging the Jukebox she describes a small boy singing with a large
voice in front of the jukebox in a Honduran bodega. It may not seem
like much to work with, but Nye makes it her personal anthem. The
boy is any child with a big voice singing to the world:

His voice carries out to the water where boats are tied
and sings for all of them, *a wave.*
For the hens, now roosting in trees,
for the mute boy next door, his second-best friend.
And for the hurricane, now brewing near Barbados . . .

The quiet, insistent argument of Nye's various books is that she
can grasp the life of ethnic minorities in America—and elsewhere—
by voicing a kind of unassuming gaiety about life. She reaches out in
her poems to hug the marginalized and the denied, to put everyone on
an equal footing with her. She declares her democratic passions in a
trance of rapturous lyricism, the kind that only children know in their
giddiest moments. It is an odd logic to spin out in half a dozen well-
respected books, but this is Nye's strategy.

Nye later began moving toward an adult vision, but she did so in
fits and starts. In *Yellow Glove* even the title suggests something of
her turn to womanly matters, and we also find the new tone in "When
the Flag Is Raised":

Today the vein of sadness pumps
its blue wisdom through this room and
you answer with curtains. A curtain lifts
and holds itself aloft.

Somewhere in Texas, a motel advertises
rooms for "A Day, Week, Month, or Forever."
The melancholia of this invitation
dogs me for miles.

But in "Who's Who in 1941" a more familiar persona resumes,

I'm being insulted in a library. The librarian thinks
                              I'm a high
school student sneaking out of class. "Who do you think
                              you are?"
she shouts. We are alone. I want to answer enigmatical
                              ly. I am the
ghost pressing against your window. I am the termite
                              feasting on the
secret boards of your house. She stands, she glares
                              at me. She has a
hairdo. The rest of the school is taking a test.

The same is found in "The Brick," which begins with

Each morning in the gray margin
between sleep and rising, I find myself
on Pershing Avenue, St. Louis, examining bricks
in buildings, looking for the one I brushed
with my mitten in 1956.

As she tells us later in the poem, "the center of memory" is "the
place where I get off and on."

Nye is important in other ways than as the voice of girlhood and
optimism in contemporary life. She has emerged as the leading figure
in Southwestern poetry and seems to articulate the female psyche of
the region after a long, trying history of pioneering on the plains and
prairies and having withstood the cramping stereotype of school-
marm, rancher's wife, and silent guardian of household realms. Nye
brings attention to the female as a humorous, wry creature with brisk,
hard intelligence and a sense of personal freedom unheard of in the
decades before.

In that sense Nye completes the work begun by her Texas
forebears Lexie Dean Robertson and Vassar Miller, both of whom
articulated the female imagination in highly disciplined lyrics. Nye
goes beyond them in skill and pixieish intelligence, however. She
continues to grow in her work and seems now to voice both sides of
the female psyche, young and old, as in the moving lyric "New
Year," also from *Yellow Glove:*

Where a street might just as easily have been
a hair ribbon in a girl's ponytail
her first day of dance class, teacher in mauve leotard
rising to say, We have much ahead of us,
and the little girls following, kick, kick, kick,
thinking what a proud sleek person she was,
how they wanted to be like her someday,
while she stared outside the window at the high wires
strung with ice, the voices inside them opening out
to every future which was not hers.

—Paul Christensen

NYE, Robert

Nationality: British. **Born:** London, 15 March 1939. **Education:** Dormans Land, Surrey; Hamlet Court, Westcliff, Essex; Southend High School, Essex. **Family:** Married 1) Judith Pratt in 1959 (divorced 1967), three sons; 2) Aileen Campbell in 1968, one daughter, one stepdaughter, and one stepson. **Career:** Since 1961 freelance writer; since 1967 poetry editor, the *Scotsman;* since 1971 poetry critic, *The Times.* Writer-in-residence, University of Edinburgh, 1976–77. **Awards:** Eric Gregory award, 1963; Scottish Arts Council bursary, 1970, 1973, and publication award, 1970, 1976; James Kennaway Memorial award, 1970; *Guardian* Fiction prize, 1976; Hawthornden prize, 1977; Society of Authors Travel Scholarship, 1991. Fellow, Royal Society of Literature, 1977. **Agent:** Anthony Sheil Associates, 43 Doughty Street, London WCIN 2LF, England; or, Wallace and Sheil Inc., 177 East 70th Street, New York, New York 10021, U.S.A. **Address:** Thornfield, Kingsland, Ballinhassig, County Cork, Ireland.

PUBLICATIONS

Poetry

Juvenilia 1. Northwood, Middlesex, Scorpion Press; 1961.
Juvenilia 2. Lowestoft, Suffolk, Scorpion Press, 1963.
Darker Ends. London, Calder and Boyars, and New York, Hill and Wang, 1969.
Agnus Dei. Rushden, Northamptonshire, Sceptre Press, 1973.
Two Prayers. Richmond, Surrey, Keepsake Press, 1974.
Five Dreams. Rushden, Northamptonshire, Sceptre Press, 1974.
Divisions on a Ground. Manchester, Carcanet, 1976.
A Collection of Poems 1955–1988. London, Hamish Hamilton, 1989.
XIV Poems. Codognan, France, Editions Ottezec, 1994.
Collected Poems. London, Sinclair-Stevenson, 1995.

Plays

Sawney Bean, with William Watson (produced Edinburgh, 1969; London, 1972; New York, 1982). London, Calder and Boyars, 1970.
Sisters (broadcast, 1969; produced Edinburgh, 1973). Included in *Penthesilea, Fugue, and Sisters,* 1975.
Penthesilea, adaptation of the play by Heinrich von Kleist (broadcast, 1971; produced London, 1983). Included in *Penthesilea, Fugue, and Sisters,* 1975.
The Seven Deadly Sins: A Mask, music by James Douglas (produced Stirling and Edinburgh, 1973). Rushden, Northamptonshire, Omphalos Press, 1974.
Mr. Poe (produced Edinburgh and London, 1974).
Penthesilea, Fugue, and Sisters. London, Calder and Boyars, 1975.

Radio Plays: *Sisters,* 1969; A Bloody Stupit Hole, 1970; *Reynolds, Reynolds,* 1971; *Penthesilea,* 1971; *The Devil's Jig,* with Humphrey Searle, from a work by Thomas Mann, 1980; *Mrs. Shakespeare,* adaptation of the novel, 1980.

Novels

Doubtfire. London, Calder and Boyars, 1967; New York, Hill and Wang, 1968.
Falstaff. London, Hamish Hamilton, and Boston, Little Brown, 1976.
Merlin. London, Hamish Hamilton, 1978; New York, Putnam, 1979.
Faust. London, Hamish Hamilton, 1980; New York, Putnam, 1981.
The Voyage of the Destiny. London, Hamish Hamilton, and New York, Putnam, 1982.
The Memoirs of Lord Byron. London, Hamish Hamilton, 1989.
The Life and Death of My Lord Gilles de Rais. London, Hamish Hamilton, 1990.
Mrs. Shakespeare: The Complete Works. London, Sinclair-Stevenson, 1993.
The Late Mr. Shakespeare. London, Chatto and Windus, 1998.

Short Stories

Tales I Told My Mother. London, Calder and Boyars, 1969; New York, Hill and Wang, 1970.
Penguin Modern Stories 6, with others. London, Penguin, 1970.
The Facts of Life and Other Fictions. London, Hamish Hamilton, 1983.

Other (for children)

Taliesin. London, Faber, 1966; New York, Hill and Wang, 1967.
March Has Horse's Ears. London, Faber, 1966; New York, Hill and Wang, 1967.
Bee Hunter: Adventures of Beowulf. London, Faber, 1968; as *Beowulf: A New Telling,* New York, Hill and Wang, 1968; as *Beowulf, The Bee Hunter,* Faber, 1972; as *Beowulf,* New York, Dell, 1982, and London, Orion, 1994.
Wishing Gold. London, Macmillan, 1970; New York, Hill and Wang, 1971.
Poor Pumpkin. London, Macmillan, 1971; as *The Mathematical Princess and Other Stories,* New York, Hill and Wang, 1972.
Cricket: Three Stories. Indianapolis, Bobbs Merrill, 1975; as *Once upon Three Times,* London, Benn, 1978.
Out of the World and Back Again. London, Collins, 1977; as *Out of This World and Back Again,* Indianapolis, Bobbs Merrill, 1978.
The Bird of the Golden Land. London, Hamish Hamilton, 1980.
Harry Pay the Pirate. London, Hamish Hamilton, 1981.
Three Tales. London, Hamish Hamilton, 1983.
Spine-Chilling Tales. London, Orion, 1995.
Lord Fox. London, Orion, 1997.

Other

Editor, *A Choice of Sir Walter Ralegh's Verse.* London, Faber, 1972.
Editor, *William Barnes, A Selection of His Poems.* Cheadle, Cheshire, Carcanet, 1972.
Editor, *A Choice of Swinburne's Verse.* London, Faber, 1973.
Editor, *The Faber Book of Sonnets.* London, Faber, 1976; as *A Book of Sonnets,* New York, Oxford University Press, 1976.
Editor, *The English Sermon 1750–1850.* Manchester, Carcanet, 1976.
Editor, *PEN New Poetry.* London, Quartet, 1986.

Editor, with Elizabeth Friedmann and Alan J. Clark, *First Awakenings: The Early Poems of Laura Riding*. Manchester, Carcanet, and New York, Persea Press, 1992.

Editor, *A Selection of the Poems of Laura Riding*. Manchester, Carcanet, 1994.

*

Manuscript Collections: University of Edinburgh; University of Texas, Austin; National Library of Scotland, Edinburgh; Colgate University, Hamilton, New York.

Critical Studies: By A. Alvarez, in *The Observer* (London), 1961, 1963; by Martin Seymour-Smith, in *The Scotsman* (Edinburgh), 1963; in *Times Literary Supplement* (London), 1963; *British Book News* (London), February 1970; *Guide to Modern World Literature* by Martin Seymour-Smith, Macmillan, 1985; "Literary Exploration: The Fictive Sea Journals of William Golding, Robert Nye, B.S. Johnson, and Malcolm Lowry" by Andrew Hassam, in *ARIEL* (Calgary, Alberta), 19(3), July 1988.

*   *   *

The career of Robert Nye has been a peculiar one. He began with some éclat, publishing poems in the *London Magazine* and in *Delta* when he was only sixteen years old. One of these lyrics, "Other Times," is almost his best. It appears, somewhat revised, in his first retrospective collection, *Darker Ends:*

Midsummer's liquid evenings linger even
And melt the wind in autumn, when bonfires
Burn books and bones, and lend us foreign faces.
At such a heart's November I might wish
For summer's heir to come, with his cruel kiss
Sealing the promises we could not keep.

One may feel that there are a few too many possessives here— "midsummer's," "heart's," "summer's." Yet the poem is purged in diction from its earlier version in his first volume, *Juvenilia 1:*

Midsummer's liquid evenings linger even
And leave four hours of autumn bonfires—
Terre Gaste of your sleevelessness; imp and scraps,
The oily rags, old bike spokes, bones and cans
And executed dolls forstitched and lax
Folding pink little arms precipitant to ash.

This, in its turn, had been altered from the very first published version, in *Delta* in the autumn of 1956, where we have "a tragedy of autumn bonfires / Raw with a gardener's rubbish, flesh and scraps . . ." The older, more austere Nye appears to have spent the intervening years weeding through several of his teenage pastures. There is no doubt that some fine lyrics are the result of the school of Graves and Riding, perhaps more Riding— whom he has edited—than Graves.

What Nye has done with "Other Times" he has also done with lyrics such as "Kingfisher," "I've Got Sixpence," and "At Last." There is a late draft of "At Last" in *Darker Ends* and an even later draft in *Collected Poems*. Here "my empty heart" is reduced to "my heart," and "a colder, harder bed," which was originally "another (warm) death-bed," is sharpened to "some graver sort of bed":

Dear, if one day you hear my heart,
Under your cheek, forget to start
Its life-long argument with my head,
Do not rejoice that I am dead
And need some graver sort of bed,
But say: "At last he's found the art
To hold his tongue and lose his heart."

What we see is the poet constantly revisiting his text over a period of some thirty-five years. He does not often alter it substantially, but he prunes, refines, purges, and, unusually for a reviser after the first flush of creation, improves the poem.

If there is a progress in the work of this lyric poet, it is to rise from the stepping-stones of his former cloudy romanticism to finer things. Nye has emerged as a poet of wit, epigram, and genuine distinction. The poems in *Divisions on a Ground,* for example, are at their best when they are most purged and spare. Nye achieves some poignant effects not so much through words themselves—his vocabulary is not elaborate—but through telling combinations of words: "The least disgust betrays the heart's persistence. / You kiss the snowscape on the windowpane; / I watch your breath shrink from it, a warm fleck / In freckled glass" ("At the Window"). It is all there— the identification of warmth, life, and the capacity to feel disgust at death, a capacity that overcomes the merely aesthetic appreciation that led the girl in the poem to kiss the windowpane in the first place. Even so, the poem is thoroughly revamped for *Collected Poems* as "Owl": "'Howlet,' she whispers, 'howlet, owlet, owl,' / Kissing the owl-light on the windowpane . . ." Somebody is going to take trouble in years to come putting together a variorum edition of this painstaking revisionist.

Consider "All Hallows," originally in the same sequence:

Once as a child I saw the willows
Across the river at All Hallows,
Each one distinct although six miles away.
What brought them close and brings them now again
Sharp to the mind's eye like an icon of it?
An orthodox theology of tears.

This poem, at least, survived without alteration, and it is a piece of which the author appears to have been uncommonly fond. In a letter on the subject he wrote, "What is it that made both the original vision and the present recollection possible, and the answer is given 'An orthodox theology of tears.' It was because I had tears in my eyes that I had the moment of unusual vision as a boy, and (in the poem's terms) for the same reason that I was blessed with clear memory of it." The poem is as austere and telling as a haiku translated by James Kirkup or Keith Bosley.

There have been two further retrospectives: *A Collection of Poems 1955–1988* and the *Collected Poems* of 1995. Both are fastidious selections rather than "collected poems" in the usual sense. Some poems have been dropped, and in many cases the process of revision has continued. There also are new poems, and by no means are all of them variations on familiar themes. There are, for example, what seem to be evocations of the author's early life, as in "Childhood Incident" and "Going to the Dogs." Both, without sacrificing a quirky humor, have an incidence of allegorical content, and both use refrain in an ingenious way that supports a singing line.

There are a dozen or so fresh lyrics included in *Collected Poems*. One of them, "Hospital Incident," is quite surprising. It is an account of a dying boy who, in a final act of defiance, musters enough strength to throw an orange he had been given at a great main window, shattering it and dying in the achievement: "'Ladies!' he shouts. 'How's that?'"

Other lyrics are more in what has been the main line of Nye's development. *Collected Poems* ends with "Hares Dancing," which could have been written by W.H. Davies except that it cuts deeper and is phrased with a greater degree of sharpness. The point is that the poet as a child saw hares dancing in the snow, and it was to him a species of epiphany or inscape. He has carried the vision through a life fraught with the usual cares and setbacks. Now, "as pain at my heart's core tears," he will dwell no more on these negative aspects but seek rest and resolution:

> I will close my eyes
> And see no more lies

But dance with the dancing hares.

The epiphany continues. Perhaps such verse, as distinct from Nye's popular novels, will never please the public at large. But superb reviewer of verse as he is, Nye has himself provided the best comment on the dedication to form and beauty that is so palpably the hallmark of his work. Characteristically, it comes from a late poem not collected, "An English Education." It recalls a teacher who beat time with a white wand as the children declaimed the Psalms:

> But most she taught me how the heart speaks best
> When it is given words of praise to say . . .
> . . . Still speaking from the heart in poetry,
> Because alas I cannot stop myself.

—Philip Hobsbaum

O

OAKES, Philip (Barlow)

Nationality: British. **Born:** Burslem, Staffordshire, 31 January 1928.
Education: Royal School, Wolverhampton; Darwen Grammar School.
Family: Married 1) Stella Fleming (dissolved 1989); 2) Gillian
Hodson in 1989; one son and two daughters. **Career:** Reporter, Sly's
Court Reporting Service, 1945–46, 1949–55; reporter and columnist
("The World I Watch"), *Daily Express,* London, 1955–56; columnist and literary editor, *Truth,* London, 1955–56; film critic, *Evening
Standard,* London, 1956–58; television scriptwriter, Granada and
BBC, London, 1958–62; film critic, *Sunday Telegraph,* London,
1963–65; assistant editor, *Sunday Times Magazine,* London, 1965–67;
arts columnist, *Sunday Times,* London, 1965–80; columnist, *Independent on Sunday,* 1990. Since 1990 columnist, *Guardian Weekend.*
Agent: Elaine Greene Ltd., 31 Newington Green, London N16 9PU,
England.

PUBLICATIONS

Poetry

Unlucky Jonah: Twenty Poems. Reading, Berkshire, University of
    Reading School of Art, 1954.
In the Affirmative. London, Deutsch, 1968.
Notes by the Provincial Governor. London, Poem-of-the-Month
    Club, 1972.
Married/Singular. London, Deutsch, 1973.
Selected Poems. London, Deutsch, 1982.

Play

Screenplay: *The Punch and Judy Man* with Tony Hancock, 1962.

Novels

Exactly What We Want. London, Joseph, 1962.
The God Botherers. London, Deutsch, 1969; as *Miracles: Genuine
    Cases Contact Box 340,* New York, Day, 1971.
Experiment at Proto. London, Deutsch, and New York, Coward
    McCann, 1973.
A Cast of Thousands. London, Gollancz, 1976.
Shopping for Women. London, Deutsch, 1994.

Other

Tony Hancock. London, Woburn Press, 1975.
From Middle England: A Memory of the Thirties. London, Deutsch,
    1980; New York, St. Martin's Press, 1983.
Dwellers All in Time and Space: A Memory of the 1940's. London,
    Deutsch, 1982; New York, St. Martin's Press, 1984.
At the Jazz Band Ball: A Memory of the 1950's. London, Deutsch,
    1983.

Editor, *The Entertainers.* London, Woburn Press, 1975.
Editor, *The Film Addict's Archive.* London, Elm Tree, 1977.

*

Manuscript Collection: State University of New York, Buffalo.

*   *   *

The poetry of Philip Oakes is a personal, almost private mode of
utterance whose style is reflective rather than declamatory. While
rejecting the critical pigeonholing that conveniently lumps him with
such poets as Kingsley Amis, John Wain, Elizabeth Jennings, and
Philip Larkin as part of the so-called Movement, he shares with these
writers a respect for the formal disciplines of the poet's craft. Oakes
parts company from the unfettered improvisation of the performance
poets, and his work reaffirms the harnessing of thought and feeling to
metrical patterns and structures. Within this framework he expresses
himself with a subtle precision, his outlook tempered by a constant
awareness of his own and mankind's essential frailties.

Oakes appears to be less than convinced about the human race,
regarding man as a flawed, tragic creature enmeshed by hostile
natural forces. "Unlucky Jonah," the title poem of his earliest
collection, presents human imperfection as personified by the unwilling prophet, whose continual impotence in the face of the universe is
shown at all stages—his vain flight from the angel, imprisonment
inside the whale, and eventual despair. Resigned to his own and
others' shortcomings, Oakes sees his fellow creatures as victims
trapped in their environments, whether the hunters frozen in the
Brueghel painting or the love-starved child of "Jean's Song." Winter
is presented as a manifestation of death, as a symbol of the destruction
that man ultimately deserves. The sentiment is pointedly expressed in
"A Country Carol," where Oakes depicts a reborn Christ child
returning to pass judgment on humankind: "a mirror for our charity. /
This time, for us to burn; for us to die." Related territory is explored in
"Dragons," with the poet achieving his own version of a myth in
which man, as the hero, slays the dragon only to find that he himself is
"the dragon's heir" and is also doomed. Human cruelty to other
species is shockingly visualized in "Live Baiting," with Oakes
revealing his abhorrence of a practice he himself once indulged in.
Political statements are rare and show a certain amount of anti-
American feeling. In "Weather" Oakes attacks the global brinkmanship of the United States during the Vietnam era, and in "Miss
America!" he ridicules what he sees as its crass commercialism.
More subtle but equally telling is "Notes by the Provincial Governor," in which the bankruptcy of colonialist attitudes is exposed in
microcosm by the stocking and eventual stagnation of a fish pond:
"Their fault, theirs. / I grant them self-determination. / Now I shall
found another colony." Oakes envisages a world out of sympathy
with its human inhabitants. In "Facing the North," for example, the
poet is forced to turn and confront the north wind, with its chilling
reminder of annihilation: "Heat is consumed by the greedy sun, / No
rain falls that will not reach the sea, / The elements proclaim their
unity / And only man denies his true relation."

Threatened by a hostile world, Oakes seeks reassurance from its dangers in family ties, humdrum domestic chores, and the physical and spiritual forms of love. This decision is particularly marked in the collections *In the Affirmative* and *Married/Singular,* where the domestic milieu is explored in a manner that, while rigorous and free of sentiment, shows a remarkable sensitivity on the part of the writer. Oakes finds cosmic verities in routine household acts, and he draws spiritual renewal from them. Love, lust, and their related complexities are viewed clearly and honestly, without euphemism. Oakes stresses the positive aspects of sexual attraction in "In the Affirmative" and "Girl on a Bus," while "Inside" hymns the beloved as a landscape to be explored afresh by the invading lover. Pornographic fantasy is gently and amusingly brought down to earth in "Dirty Pictures," with Oakes commenting on the holey socks and bad teeth of the participants as he studies the tacky, rather than titillating, postcards. While he speaks of love as "a necessary pain," he evidently finds in domesticity a force for good, which is affirmed in the chores of making a bed, lighting a fire, and baking, all of which are memorably described in his poems. The concept is perfectly represented in the moving "Guarantee," where Oakes regards his beloved with an unflattering but loving eye: "You are not for special / occasions, but for everyday. You have / The virtues of denim, wholemeal, and worsted / . . . You meet all guarantees. You are as promised."

Outside the home Oakes admits to a sneaking sympathy for misfits, for those eccentric individuals whose natures place them beyond the protection of the conformist herd. Such figures are encountered in all of his collections, including *Selected Poems,* which unites the best of each. Whether depicting the immense, genial Daniel Lambert or the nervous Mr. Valobra, lamenting the tramp in the park who chooses to die "in his own good time," or recounting the tragicomic odysseys of demented army and naval officers in pursuit of mermaids and unicorns, Oakes blends wit and irony into a judicious balance, viewing his flawed fellow humans with a wry but genuine affection.

—Geoff Sadler

OATES, Joyce Carol

Pseudonyms: Rosamond Smith; Fernandes/Oates. **Nationality:** American. **Born:** Millersport, New York, 16 June 1938. **Education:** Syracuse University, New York, 1956–60, B.A. in English 1960 (Phi Beta Kappa); University of Wisconsin, Madison, M.A. in English 1961; Rice University, Houston, 1961. **Family:** Married Raymond J. Smith in 1961. **Career:** Instructor, 1961–65, and assistant professor of English, 1965–67, University of Detroit; member of the department of English, University of Windsor, Ontario, 1967–78. Since 1978 writer-in-residence, and currently Roger S. Berlind Distinguished Professor, Princeton University, New Jersey. Since 1974 publisher, with Raymond J. Smith, *Ontario Review,* Windsor, later Princeton. **Awards:** National Endowment for the Arts grant, 1966, 1968; Guggenheim fellowship, 1967; O. Henry award, 1967, 1973, and Special Award for Continuing Achievement, 1970, 1986; Rosenthal award, 1968; National Book award, 1970; Rea award, for short story, 1990; Heideman award, for one-act plays, 1990; Bobst Lifetime Achievement award, 1990; Walt Whitman award, 1995; Fisk Fiction

prize, 1996, for *Zombie.* **Member:** American Academy, 1978. **Agent:** John Hawkins, 71 West 23rd Street, Suite 1600, New York, New York 10010. **Address:** Princeton University, Creative Writing Department, 185 Nassau Street, Princeton, New Jersey 08540, U.S.A.

PUBLICATIONS

Poetry

Women in Love and Other Poems. New York, Albondocani Press, 1968.
Anonymous Sins and Other Poems. Baton Rouge, Louisiana State University Press, 1969.
Love and Its Derangements. Baton Rouge, Louisiana State University Press, 1970.
Wooded Forms. New York, Albondocani Press, 1972.
Angel Fire. Baton Rouge, Louisiana State University Press, 1973.
Dreaming America and Other Poems. New York, Aloe Editions, 1973.
The Fabulous Beasts. Baton Rouge, Louisiana State University Press, 1975
Seasons of Peril. Santa Barbara, California, Black Sparrow Press, 1977.
Women Whose Lives Are Food, Men Whose Lives Are Money. Baton Rouge, Louisiana State University Press, 1978.
Celestial Timepiece. Dallas, Pressworks, 1980.
Nightless Nights: Nine Poems. Concord, New Hampshire, Ewert, 1981.
Invisible Woman: New and Selected Poems 1970–1982. Princeton, New Jersey, Ontario Review Press, 1982.
Luxury of Sin. Northridge, California, Lord John Press, 1984.
The Time Traveller: Poems 1983–1989. New York, Dutton, 1989.

Plays

The Sweet Enemy (produced New York, 1965).
Sunday Dinner (produced New York, 1970).
Ontological Proof of My Existence, music by George Prideaux (produced New York, 1972). Included in *Three Plays,* 1980.
Miracle Play (produced New York, 1979). Los Angeles, Black Sparrow Press, 1974.
Daisy (produced New York, 1980).
Three Plays (includes *Ontological Proof of My Existence, Miracle Play, The Triumph of the Spider Monkey*). Windsor, Ontario Review Press, 1980.
The Triumph of the Spider Monkey, from her own story (produced Los Angeles, 1985). Included in *Three Plays,* 1980.
Presque Isle, music by Paul Shapiro (produced New York, 1982).
Lechery, in *Faustus in Hell* (produced Princeton, New Jersey, 1985).
In Darkest America (Tone Clusters and The Eclipse) (produced Louisville, Kentucky, 1990; *The Eclipse* produced New York, 1990).
American Holiday (produced Los Angeles, 1990).
Twelve Plays. New York, Dutton, 1991.
I Stand Before You Naked (produced New York, 1991).
How Do You Like Your Meat? (produced New Haven, Connecticut, 1991).
Black (produced Williamstown, Massachusetts, 1992).

Gulf War (produced New York, 1992).

The Secret Mirror (produced Philadelphia, 1992).

The Rehearsal (produced New York, 1993).

The Perfectionist (produced Princeton, New Jersey, 1993). Included in *The Perfectionist and Other Plays.* Hopewell, New Jersey, Ecco Press, 1995.

The Truth-Teller (produced New York, 1995).

Here She Is! (produced Philadelphia, 1995).

New Plays. Princeton, New Jersey, Ontario Review Press, 1998.

Novels

With Shuddering Fall. New York, Vanguard Press, 1964; London, Cape, 1965.

A Garden of Earthly Delights. New York, Vanguard Press, 1967; London, Gollancz, 1970.

Expensive People. New York, Vanguard Press, 1968; London, Gollancz, 1969.

Them. New York, Vanguard Press, 1969; London, Gollancz, 1971.

Wonderland. New York, Vanguard Press, 1971; London, Gollancz, 1972.

Do with Me What You Will. New York, Vanguard Press, 1973; London, Gollancz, 1974.

The Assassins: A Book of Hours. New York, Vanguard Press, 1975.

Childwold. New York, Vanguard Press, 1976; London, Gollancz, 1977.

Son of the Morning. New York, Vanguard Press, 1978; London, Gollancz, 1979.

Unholy Loves. New York, Vanguard Press, 1979; London, Gollancz, 1980.

Cybele. Santa Barbara, California, Black Sparrow Press, 1979.

Angel of Light. New York, Dutton, and London, Cape, 1981.

Bellefleur. New York, Dutton, 1980; London, Cape, 1981.

A Bloodsmoor Romance. New York, Dutton, 1982; London, Cape, 1983.

Mysteries of Winterthurn. New York, Dutton, and London, Cape, 1984.

Solstice. New York, Dutton, and London, Cape, 1985.

Marya: A Life. New York, Dutton, 1986; London, Cape, 1987.

You Must Remember This. New York, Dutton, 1987; London, Macmillan, 1988.

Lives of the Twins (as Rosamond Smith). New York, Simon and Schuster, 1987.

Soul-Mate (as Rosamond Smith). New York, Dutton, 1989.

American Appetites. New York, Dutton, and London, Macmillan, 1989.

Because It Is Bitter, and Because It Is My Heart. New York, Dutton, 1990.

Snake Eyes (as Rosamond Smith). New York, Dutton, 1992.

Black Water. New York, Dutton, 1992.

Foxfire. New York, Dutton, 1993.

What I Lived For. New York, Dutton, 1994.

Zombie. New York, Dutton, 1995.

You Can't Catch Me (as Rosamond Smith). New York, Dutton, 1995.

First Love: A Gothic Tale. Hopewell, New Jersey, Ecco Press, 1996.

Tenderness. Princeton, New Jersey, Ontario Review Press, 1996.

We Were the Mulvaneys. New York, Dutton, 1996.

Double Delight (as Rosamond Smith). New York, Dutton, 1997.

Man Crazy. New York, Dutton, 1997; London, Virago, 1998.

My Heart Laid Bare. New York, Plume, 1998.

Broke Heart Blues: A Novel. New York, Dutton, and London, Virago, 1999.

Blonde. New York, Echo Press, 1999; London, Fourth Estate, 2000.

Short Stories

By the North Gate. New York, Vanguard Press, 1963.

Upon the Sweeping Flood and Other Stories. New York, Vanguard Press, 1966; London, Gollancz, 1973.

The Wheel of Love. New York, Vanguard Press, 1970; London, Gollancz, 1971.

Cupid and Psyche. New York, Albondocani Press, 1970.

Marriages and Infidelities. New York, Vanguard Press, 1972; London, Gollancz, 1974.

A Posthumous Sketch. Los Angeles, Black Sparrow Press, 1973.

The Girl. Cambridge, Massachusetts, Pomegranate Press, 1974.

Plagiarized Material (as Fernandes/Oates). Los Angeles, Black Sparrow Press, 1974.

The Goddess and Other Women. New York, Vanguard Press, 1974, London, Gollancz, 1975.

Where Are You Going, Where Have You Been? Stories of Young America. Greenwich, Connecticut, Fawcett, 1974.

The Hungry Ghosts: Seven Allusive Comedies. Los Angeles, Black Sparrow Press, 1974; Solihull, Warwickshire, Aquila, 1975.

The Seduction and Other Stories. Los Angeles, Black Sparrow Press, 1975.

The Poisoned Kiss and Other Stories from the Portuguese (as Fernandes/Oates). New York, Vanguard Press, 1975; London, Gollancz, 1976.

The Triumph of the Spider Monkey. Santa Barbara, California, Black Sparrow Press, 1976.

Crossing the Border. New York, Vanguard Press, 1976; London, Gollancz, 1978.

Night-Side. New York, Vanguard Press, 1977; London, Gollancz, 1979.

A Sentimental Education (single story). Los Angeles, Sylvester and Orphanos, 1978.

The Step-Father. Northridge, California, Lord John Press, 1978.

All the Good People I've Left Behind. Santa Barbara, California, Black Sparrow Press, 1979.

Queen of the Night. Northridge, California, Lord John Press, 1979.

The Lamb of Abyssalia. Cambridge, Massachusetts, Pomegranate Press, 1979.

A Middle-Class Education. New York, Albondocani Press, 1980.

A Sentimental Education (collection). New York, Dutton, 1980; London, Cape, 1981.

Last Day. New York, Dutton, 1984; London, Cape, 1985.

Wild Saturday and Other Stories. London, Dent, 1984.

Wild Nights. Athens, Ohio, Croissant, 1985.

Raven's Wing. New York, Dutton, 1986; London, Cape, 1987.

The Assignation. New York, Ecco Press, 1988.

Heat and Other Stories. New York, Dutton, 1991.

Where Is Here? Hopewell, New Jersey, Ecco Press, 1992.

Haunted Tales of the Grotesque. New York, Dutton, 1994.

Will You Always Love Me? And Other Stories. New York, Dutton, 1995.

The Collector of Hearts: New Tales of the Grotesque. New York, Dutton, 1998.

Other

The Edge of Impossibility: Tragic Forms in Literature. New York, Vanguard Press, 1972; London, Gollancz, 1976.

The Hostile Sun: The Poetry of D. H. Lawrence. Los Angeles, Black Sparrow Press, 1973; Solihull, Warwickshire, Aquila, 1975.

New Heaven, New Earth: The Visionary Experience in Literature. New York, Vanguard Press, 1974; London, Gollancz, 1976.

The Stone Orchard. Northridge, California, Lord John Press, 1980.

Contraries: Essays. New York, Oxford University Press, 1981.

The Profane Art: Essays and Reviews. New York, Dutton, 1983.

Funland. Concord, New Hampshire, Ewert, 1983.

On Boxing, photographs by John Ranard. New York, Doubleday, and London, Bloomsbury, 1987; expanded edition, Hopewell, New Jersey, Ecco Press, 1994.

(Woman) Writer: Occasions and Opportunities. New York, Dutton, 1988.

Come Meet Muffin. Hopewell, New Jersey, Ecco Press, 1998.

Where I've Been, and Where I'm Going: Essays, Reviews, and Prose. New York, Plume, 1999.

Editor, *Scenes from American Life: Contemporary Short Fiction.* New York, Vanguard Press, 1973.

Editor, with Shannon Ravenel, *The Best American Short Stories 1979.* Boston, Houghton Mifflin, 1979.

Editor, *Night Walks: A Bedside Companion.* Princeton, New Jersey, Ontario Review Press, 1982.

Editor, *First Person Singular: Writers on Their Craft.* Princeton, New Jersey, Ontario Review Press, 1983.

Editor, with Boyd Litzinger, *Story: Fictions Past and Present.* Lexington, Massachusetts, Heath, 1985.

Editor, with Daniel Halpern, *Reading the Fights* (on boxing). New York, Holt, 1988.

Editor, *The Best American Essays.* N.p., Ticknor and Fields, 1991.

Editor, with Daniel Halpern, *The Sophisticated Cat: A Gathering of Stories, poems, and Miscellaneous Writings about Cats.* New York, Dutton, 1992.

Editor, *The Oxford Book of American Short Stories.* Oxford, Oxford University Press, 1992.

Editor, *George Bellows: American Artist.* Hopewell, New Jersey, Ecco Press, 1995.

Editor, *The Essential Dickinson.* Hopewell, New Jersey, Ecco Press, 1996.

Editor, *American Gothic Tales.* New York, Plume, 1996.

Editor, *Story: The Art and the Craft of Narrative Fiction.* New York, Norton, 1997.

Editor, *The Best of H.P. Lovecraft.* Hopewell, New Jersey, Ecco Press, 1997.

Editor, with R.V. Cassill, *The Norton Anthology of Contemporary Fiction.* New York, Norton, 1997.

Editor, *Telling Stories: An Anthology for Writers.* New York, Norton, 1997.

*

Bibliography: *Joyce Carol Oates: An Annotated Bibliography* by Francine Lercangé, New York, Garland, 1986.

Manuscript Collection: Syracuse University, Syracuse, New York.

Critical Studies: *The Tragic Vision of Joyce Carol Oates* by Mary Kathryn Grant, Durham, North Carolina, Duke University Press, 1978; *Joyce Carol Oates* by Joanne V. Creighton, Boston, Twayne, 1979; *Critical Essays on Joyce Carol Oates* edited by Linda W. Wagner, Boston, Hall, 1979; *Dreaming America: Obsession and Transcendence in the Fiction of Joyce Carol Oates* by G.F. Waller, Baton Rouge, Louisiana State University Press, 1979; *Joyce Carol Oates* by Ellen G. Friedman, New York, Ungar, 1980; *Joyce Carol Oates's Short Stories: Between Tradition and Innovation* by Katherine Bastian, Bern, Switzerland, Lang, 1983; *Isolation and Contact: A Study of Character Relationships in Joyce Carol Oates's Short Stories 1963–1980* by Torborg Norman, Gothenburg, Studies in English, 1984; *Joyce Carol Oates: Artist in Residence* by Eileen Teper Bender, Bloomington, Indiana University Press, 1987; *Understanding Joyce Carol Oates* by Greg Johnson, Columbia, University of South Carolina Press, 1987; *Conversations with Joyce Carol Oates,* edited by Lee Milazzo, Jackson, University Press of Mississippi, 1989.

*   *   *

Reviewers of Joyce Carol Oates's first poetry collection called her work "apocalyptic" and "savage," adjectives that remain valid for her poetic canon. There are no lyric forms in Oates's work, and the poems do not tolerate surface readings or pregnant pauses. They evoke no tenderness or nostalgia. Each pierces the reader's sensibility, often with literal images of bodily penetration or destruction. Although they are intensely personal poems, many of which have furnished controlling metaphors or significant images in Oates's fiction, they stand independently, and the reader's struggle to understand them is like augury using one's own entrails. Almost always the persona is a victim—women, children, blue-collar males, semiliterate rural families—incapable of expressing the terrible intersection of personal and historic, public and private existence, and it is this that gives rise to the grief of the poem. There are silent voices too, for example, the autistic child and the mummified child bride in *Invisible Woman.*

Oates forges her disturbing visions through the sheer discipline of language and clarity of image, relying only on assonance and alliteration to heighten it. Even when a poem deliberately evokes the work of another poet, she shuns the poetic devices of the original and often inverts its vision, as demonstrated, for example, by the echoes of Emily Dickinson in "After Love a Formal Feeling Comes."

The isolated state of the individual is a given in Oates's poems and cuts across the thematic concerns. "Vanity," the nearly conventional poem that closes *Anonymous Sins,* adumbrates this isolation. Evoking the refrain of Ecclesiastes, the poem concludes, "The beloved is a cage / you cannot enter. Others can enter cheaply."

The vulnerability of children and the collusion of adults with the hostile forces that threaten them are frequent themes. In *Anonymous Sins* the cycle of songs "Three Dances of Death" echoes Blake's *Songs of Innocence and of Experience.* In "American Morocco" an obese child, ridiculed by her parents' guests, accompanies them on a tour of the family's bomb shelter, a replica of El Morocco so secure that "Christ could not raise us / from our safe tinkly tomb." In "Happy Song: Not for Adults" a child trying frantically to please her parents becomes "... segments of bone / strained beyond your knowledge." "Back Country," in *Invisible Woman,* begins with a drunken father shooting his children's dog, which suffers, howls, bleeds, and is at last buried by neighbors. Fearful of the man, the neighbors rationalize his violence—both to the dog and to his own family—with ''these things happen, / Dogs get in the way.'' The perceiving child understands that children do too.

The destructive quality of love between a man and a woman is a constant in Oates's poems. Rendered in images of fusion and decomposition, it is most frequently represented in *Love and Its Derangements,* where ''Growing Together'' uses a terrifying pun to present the progress of a sexual marathon that leaves the couple with hair grown into one another's bodies and with toenails ''. . . outlined in harmless old dirt [that] scrape against all our legs / for weeks.'' In ''Giving Oneself a Form Again'' a woman who has withdrawn from a period of intense sensuality seeks the Wordsworthian shape of a childhood soul, but she finds that after carnal knowledge ''the child will not be touched.'' She then retreats into autoeroticism, in which, at orgasm, ''like wasps the blood flares / and subsides'' and the outline of her isolate body is like ''. . . iron spikes of fences / beside sidewalks of ice.''

The narrative unity of *Angel Fire* compels the reader to recognize Oates's vision that all love is rooted in a desire for annihilation. ''The Still Small Voice behind the Great Romances'' charts the persona's realization that her search for romantic love has been a desire ''to see the sun slide over the edge / of the continent!—I always wanted that urgency / at the edge of satiation.'' In ''How I Became Fiction'' the female finds that even the stares of men, which once defined her, are gone—''. . . no darkness / would recover them, no alley make them male again''—and she becomes, as the males who once stared at her have become, only the character in a narration that is their hospital records. In ''Prophecies'' the long awaited lover is imagined as a devourer who cannot be tamed by physical beauty or by possessions and whose recognition as such lies just outside consciousness, at the edge of the eye. ''Iris into Eye,'' the final poem of *Angel Fire,* which is used as an epigraph in the novel *Wonderland,* brings all of the buried knowledge into consciousness as the perceiver is forced to enter her own history.

The Fabulous Beasts experiments with the inclusion of two long prose pieces, but it is the shorter and more conventional Oates poems that contribute most to achieving the stated intention of revealing the relationship between the individual and an all-inclusive whole, the fabulous beast of history and nature. There is a fine poem to Sylvia Plath, ''Mourning and Melancholia . . .'' and another that honors Plath with a turn on her own lines. ''Lies Lovingly Told'' observes that ''every man adores / the woman who adores / the Fascist.'' The title poem is a vision of Yeats's rough beast, slouching toward the newsroom, indifferent to the historical location of the carnage in the grainy photographs that will be printed and that could be scenes from North Africa in 1939 or from Southeast Asia in 1968. This closing poem and two others, ''In Case of Accidental Death'' and ''In the Air,'' suggest a transition to the more public poems that appear in *Women Whose Lives Are Food, Men Whose Lives Are Money* and in *Invisible Woman,* and they are among the finest works from Oates's hand. ''In Case of Accidental Death'' explores the insularity that sanctifies terrible events with the religious platitude that ''it is somehow good'' and because ''being local is also a tradition / in this country.'' The resigned view of random violence in the poem echoes Auden's ''Musée des Beaux Arts'':

But perhaps there will be ditchwater
and spiky tart-smelling weeds

and overhead a heavy airliner
with passengers marveling
at the landscape
and an unswervable destination.

''In the Air'' recounts the razing of an old house in images of atomic explosions: ''The cellar rises / into daylight [revealing] the earth and its undigested things / we hoped no one outside the family / would ever see.''

Women Whose Lives Are Food, Men Whose Lives Are Money continues familiar themes and techniques. Here again are the grim round of materialism and the violent embraces of lovers, devoid of any sign that they can be transcended. A number of the poems—for example, ''After Sunset,'' ''Guilt,'' ''Skyscape,'' and ''The Suicide''—pivot on the tension between a concretely recalled event and the persona's struggle to extract meaning from it, but the tendency of the previous volume to explore public events expands. ''Public Outcry'' and ''American Independence'' present the media's tendency to invite public statements from the uninformed on the insignificant and to consume in a manner that transforms everything ''. . . to human heat, human flesh / human waste.''

Invisible Woman includes an epilogue of fourteen poems previously collected but excludes any from *Anonymous Sins,* the first collection. Oates indicates here that she has chosen to reprint only those poems that best support the volume's theme of the invisibility of our deepest identity. The newly collected poems once again use familiar techniques to explore the constant themes, but there is a growth marked by the powerful distillation of the earlier treatments. The hand-to-mouth struggle and the outrageous expectations of American blue-collar life that required a dozen poems in *Women Whose Lives Are Food, Men Whose Lives Are Money* are conveyed more powerfully by a single poem, ''Jesus, Heal Me,'' a poem in which union meetings, layoffs, time clocks, and reusable brown lunch bags are juxtaposed with the redemption of a new covenant whose revelation is sought in the columns of lottery winners. The greater depth with which early themes are explored is evident in the four-line poem ''A Miniature Passion,'' where the wasp sting-orgasm of ''Giving Oneself a Form Again'' has become ''. . . so deep, / all my flesh was crater to it.''

Finally, this excellent volume provides a vision of the male and female life, the private and the historically implicated life, in coexistence. ''Celestial Timepiece,'' a quilt that provides an organizing metaphor in the novel *Bellefleur,* presents the history of quilt making as a woman creating a map of her world. While men are off fighting on a map of death, homeless and in hospitals, women produce ''. . . an entire world stitched to perfection.'' This can be hung on the wall like a conqueror's map and convey to those who touch it a history of frugal, fruitful domesticity: ''Your fingers read it like Braille.''

—Rose Marie Burwell

O'BRIEN, Gregory (Leo)

Nationality: New Zealander (also Irish citizen). **Born:** Matamata, Waikato, 9 April 1961. **Education:** University of Auckland, 1980–83, B.A. 1984. **Family:** Married Jenny Bornholdt, *q.v.,* in 1994; two sons.

Career: Since 1984 writer and artist. Writer-in-residence, 1995, and since 1997 teacher of creative writing, Victoria University, Wellington. Since 1997 part-time curator, Wellington City Gallery. **Awards:** Sargeson fellowship, 1988. **Address:** 26 Waipapa Road, Hataitai, Wellington, New Zealand.

PUBLICATIONS

Poetry

Location of the Least Person. Auckland, Auckland University Press, 1987.
Dunes & Barns. Auckland, Modern House, 1988.
Man with a Child's Violin. Christchurch, Caxton, 1990.
Great Lake. Sydney, Local Consumption, 1991.
Malachi. Adelaide, Australia, Little Esther Books, 1993.
The Long Fall from Splendour to Splendour. Auckland, Puriri Press, 1993.
Days beside Water. Auckland, Auckland University Press, 1993; Manchester, Carcanet, 1994.
Irishman & Industry. Auckland, Pear Tree Press, 1997.
Winter I Was. Wellington, Victoria University Press, 1999.

Novel

Diesel Mystic. Auckland, Auckland University Press, 1989.

Other

Moments of Invention. Auckland, Heinemann Reed, 1988.
Nigel Brown. Auckland, Random House, 1991.
Lands and Deeds. Auckland, Godwit, 1996.
Hotere-Out the Black Window. Auckland, Godwit, 1997.

Co-editor, *White Horse Black Dog.* Wellington, Sport, 1995.
Co-editor, *My Heart Goes Swimming: New Zealand Love Poems.* Auckland, Godwit, 1996.
Co-editor, *An Anthology of New Zealand Poetry.* Auckland, Oxford University Press, 1996.

*

Critical Study: By Margaret Mahy, in *Landfall,* 44(1), March 1990.

*   *   *

Gregory O'Brien is both a poet and a painter and latterly a valued, one might almost say a necessary, voice in the public presentation of the work of major New Zealand artists—notably Colin McCahon and Ralph Hotere-and in the articulation, not of a theory, but of a language and a set of reference points for talking about them. He has sometimes illustrated his own poems, and their visual elements are unusually strong.

As a poet, O'Brien has always been confident, fluent, inventive, and industrious, beginning as something like a surrealist, in which almost everything in the picture was "real," or had a recognizable foundation in "fact," but was chosen and arranged in comic or disconcerting conjunctions. It was a kind of wit that had great charm and was happy to risk the charge of whimsy. But soon the real, the natural and recognizable order of things, was being allowed predominance and authority, though still with the underlying sense that its stability was hardly more than a pact dictated by social convenience. Thus the natural order of things was seen as our necessary myth, our convention of representation, causing us to overlook the miracles of absurd conjunction that are around us all the time.

Observant, excited, always on the move, O'Brien has remained a quirky aggregator, a maker of lists and connections, a teller of tales and tallies. Loquacious and nervous, quick, clever and affectionate, amusing and engaging—*l'homme, c'est le style.* "The camera is a chatterbox / of the eyes," he writes in one poem, seeming to catch an aspect of self in the characterization.

There is also, lurking somewhere behind this life energy, the bleak knowledge that we occupy a universe that is flying apart and that any slight sense we have of controlling our own destiny is an illusion. So we must keep talking to one another and perhaps to God. O'Brien's poems all have the sound of a voice, of communication that hopes for communion, of language as the game by which we prove ourselves, the instrument with which we divert ourselves while the sun goes down.

Through the second half of the 1990s his work continued playful and the touch light, but there was a steadying of focus and a gain in ballast as life commitments (love, marriage, children) made the need for some kind of "faith" more urgent. In this sense, more than in the sense that O'Brien's Catholicism is important to him (which it is), many, perhaps all, of his poems can be seen as prayers. But they are neither solemn nor unserious, and they have, in Keats's phrase, no "palpable design" on the reader. O'Brien is a kind of priest who intones, "Let us play." And the piety is real.

O'Brien's poems are also often stories, unplotted narratives that continue to reveal, as his early work did, how unordinary the ordinary is. Deadpan astonishment is his stock-in-trade. The places we inhabit are as absurd as they are beautiful. Seeing is believing, and the surprise of it seldom wanes or wavers.

These narratives mix disparate elements without apology (but usually with explanatory notes!). He is a huge raider of history—big and small, local and family—of biography, and of locations, spaces, and landscapes, always giving his readers a sense of rapid movement through space (his poems travel) and time (things are always happening where things have happened). There is copiousness, untidiness, clutter, and jitter. There is also reflection, a reaching beyond the comic, droll, or bizarre toward the sad shadows of general truths.

Perhaps what holds this all together is the consistency with which the painter's eye pulls everything into scenes:

A woman is kneeling in a stream—
  the mist is a sponge drawing the town
up into itself. Dogs lie around the park
like battered violins
  their music scattered . . .

In the very best, the absolutely proper, sense—the sense of a great tradition—everything in O'Brien's poetry, even the eloquence, is borrowed and reused. He has made his proper connections with those who have gone before, and his lines are open to the future.

—C.K. Stead

O'BRIEN, Sean

Nationality: British. **Born:** London, 19 December 1952. **Education:** Selwyn College, Cambridge, 1971–74, B.A. in English 1974; Birmingham University, 1975–76, M.A. 1977; Hull University, 1976–79; Leeds University, 1980–81, Post-Graduate Certificate in Education, 1981. **Career:** Teacher, Beacon School, Crowborough, East Sussex, 1981–89; fellow in creative writing, University of Dundee, 1989–90; founding editor, with Stephen Plaice, *The Printer's Devil* literary magazine, Brighton, East Sussex, 1990. **Awards:** Eric Gregory award, 1979; Somerset Maugham award, 1984; Cholmondeley award, 1988. **Address:** 56 Mafeking Road, Brighton BN2 4EL, East Sussex, England.

PUBLICATIONS

Poetry

The Indoor Park. Newcastle upon Tyne, Bloodaxe, 1983.
The Frighteners. Newcastle upon Tyne, Bloodaxe, 1987.
Boundary Beach. Belfast, Ulsterman, 1989.
HMS Glasshouse. Oxford and New York, Oxford University Press, 1991.
A Rarity. Hull, Carnivorous Arpeggio Press, 1993.
Ghost Train. New York, Oxford University Press, 1995.
The Ideology. Huddersfield, Smith/Doorstop, 1997.

Other

Bloody Ambassadors: The Gruesome Stories of Irish People Tried for Murder Abroad. Dublin, Poolbeg, 1993.
The Deregulated Muse: Essays on Contemporary British and Irish Poetry. Newcastle upon Tyne, Bloodaxe, 1995.

Editor, *The Firebox: Poetry in Britain and Ireland after 1945.* London, Picador, 1998.

*

Critical Studies: *Five Irish Writers: The Errand of Keeping Alive* by John Hildebidle, Cambridge, Harvard University Press, 1989; "'Won't You Let Me Take You on a Sea Cruise?': Sean O'Brien's 'H.M.S. Glasshouse'" by Bruce Woodcock, in *Bete Noire* (Hull, Humberside, England), 12–13, autumn 1991-spring 1992.

Sean O'Brien comments:

It is extremely difficult to comment on my own work. I am particularly interested in history, politics, and place. My early poems drew heavily on Hull, the city where I grew up, and northern loyalties have continued to figure in my work since moving to the south in the early 1980s. That move, coinciding with the embedding of Thatcherism in power, has tended to emphasize the conflicts of culture and class with which Britain is afflicted. The conditions of the 1980s seem to me to have presented poets with a problem that has gone largely unaddressed, that of writing poetry which confronts moral and economic barbarism while remaining art. The successes of Douglas Dunn and Tony Harrison tend to emphasize their isolation, though the general preference for (at best) oblique relations with political realities is understandable, given the absence of precedent since Auden. In my own experience the largely implicit political concerns of my first book, *The Indoor Park,* became a good deal more vocal in its successor, *The Frighteners,* partly through satire and historical reflection but also in the effort to use the resources of fantasy and image to bind the personal and political together. At present my work (for example, in the pamphlet *Boundary Beach*) finds itself more acquainted with the south, though not reconciled to it, and seems to be pursuing a course at times more inward and less unyielding than before. I would like the poems I write to be dramatic and to work through image rather than discursiveness.

*   *   *

Sean O'Brien's talent was one of the most notable and promising to emerge in the 1980s. Nearly all of his poetry combines realism and social observation with an element of the highly imaginative, even the fantastic. The combination makes for a quite distinctive style, recognizable even in his earliest published work.

A sense of place is central to O'Brien's verse. In *The Indoor Park* many poems focus on a conservatory in Pearson Park in Hull, and Boundary Beach, which provides the title of another of his collections, is in Brighton, where he has lived. Both landscapes, however, are symbolic as well as literal. The Hull connection and O'Brien's preoccupations have led to his being called one of "the sons of Dunn." Larkin also is visible as a powerful influence, but so are the more polymorphous gifts of Auden, which show up in O'Brien's predilection for switching between the panoramic view and the telling local detail and in his ability to capture the menacing suggestiveness of something out of view waiting to happen. Like the park and the beach, his other characteristic landscapes are bounded or circumscribed, places of transition, transit, or temporary resort, such as seaside towns and ports—"The dead harbour, the pub and the station buffet."

Out of these settings O'Brien conjures a sense of baffled lives shaped by their time and place. In a belated world loaded with the weight of history and worn-out ideology, people are "condemned to live this script / Until the gestures make you retch." Yet besides this sense of repetitious fixity there is a stress on the provisionality and restlessness of human lives. Traveling stands for the potential to escape, a potential seldom realized as characters "sleep in early restaurants" and "inspect the shipping lists / Until the time is right."

O'Brien believes that poems should be models of the world. This explains his frequent references to maps and atlases seen as magical or suggestive things, for in them empirical signs meet the world of the imagination, suggesting space, scope, and possibility. His imaginative sweeps across the topography of England, with the nighttime full of "slack-jawed insomniacs" and "stoplights rehearsing in private," are strikingly evocative. The poet experiences a startled detachment from his surroundings. His is a world "guilty of itself," one that is a "residue / Of time got wrong, got lost, or not recalled, / Just looking at itself."

English by birth and residence, O'Brien is a keen, even affectionate, student of Englishness, though he has no love for many of the things that have been done in England's name. A major preoccupation is the "insult called / History, that won't pay the rent." People have "waited into age / For history to change its mind," but the personal life and even love remain shaped by a disabling past—invisible decades / Of rain, domestic love and failing mills / . . . Are fading into what we are: two young / Polite incapables." Not only the individual but language too becomes recruited to purposes beyond itself, as words finish up "strapped to the big wheel of syntax." The poems in the first section of *The Frighteners,* "In a Military Archive," use the relics of war and war's impact on the lives of children as metaphors for the inherited weight of the past that bears down upon people instructed to "try to think of history as home." But the brutalities of war are shown as continuing into the present, for these poems merge into others witty and acidic that blast the southern English Tory complacencies and hypocrisies of the 1980s and confront with real passion and authority questions such as police attitudes or the miners' strike.

Most of O'Brien's poems are as fully loaded with images as he can make them, but they often avoid top-heaviness by being conceived as living speech, which in *The Frighteners* is often fiercely demotic. At times the richness of his imagination becomes cryptic and inscrutable, but the clarity of his best images is shining. Occasionally there is something like Raine's Martian manner, in phrases such as "Chestnut trees / Are fire-damaged candelabra" or "The goldfish . . . rehearsing blasé vowels at the sun." But the resemblance is superficial. Where the Martian mode can be reactionary, inviting us to refresh a sense of wonder at, and hence to acquiesce in, things as they actually are, O'Brien evokes a convincing sense of astonishment that we could ever have allowed things to get this way. Like his character Ryan, who "was born expecting something quite different," O'Brien remarks that "all this is England, / Just left here, and what's to be done?"

—R.J.C. Watt

O'DONOGHUE, Bernard

Nationality: Irish. **Born:** James Bernard O'Donoghue, Cullen, County Cork, 14 December 1945. **Education:** St. Bede's College, Manchester; Lincoln College, Oxford, 1965–71, M.A. 1968, B.Phil. in medieval literature 1971. **Family:** Married Heather Mackinnon in 1977; two daughters, one son. **Career:** Systems analyst, IBM, Manchester, 1968–69; lecturer in English, Magdalen College, Oxford, 1971–95. Since 1975 fellow in English, Wadham College, Oxford. **Awards:** Whitbread Poetry prize, 1995, for *Gunpowder.* **Member:** Royal Society of Literature, 1999. **Address:** Wadham College, Oxford OX1 3PN, England.

PUBLICATIONS

Poetry

Poaching Rights. Oldcastle, County Meath, Gallery Press, 1987.
The Weakness. London, Chatto and Windus, 1991.
Gunpowder. London, Chatto and Windus, 1995.
Here Nor There. London, Chatto and Windus, 1999.

Other

The Courtly Love Tradition. Manchester, Manchester University Press, 1982.
Poems of Thomas Hoccleve. Manchester, Carcanet, 1982.

*

Critical Study: By John Burnside, in *Agenda* (London), 33(3–4), fall 1996.

Bernard O'Donoghue comments:

I believe strongly in the importance of the public context of writing, so I think of myself as a writer of place. Most of my poems tend to be set in the area I grew up in, in North Cork, in the 1950s and 1960s, but I do not think that means that this is the only place they apply to. I am always quoting Tom Paulin's phrase "theoretical locations" to refer to the places we write about to say what it is we want to say about the world at large. The writers I feel most consciously influenced by are Larkin (for a wry view of the world) and Richard Murphy (for a freeish but shaped Irish vernacular language). I would claim that my tendency to write elegy as a way of repaying a debt to society is a positive rather than a pessimistic impulse. And the last shaping influence I am aware of is music: both the living tradition of intricate musical forms in my native Sliabh Luachra, and my own chosen interest in classical music, my great and obsessive consolation. In literature I am a medievalist, and I like living professionally at the same tempting, provocative remove from my subjects as I am from the events of childhood.

*   *   *

"Immaturities" is the title of the opening section of Bernard O'Donoghue's collection *The Weakness.* But O'Donoghue gives little sense as a poet of not always having known that he wanted to sound quizzically aware of human idiosyncrasy, tragedy, and imperfection and to convey that awareness in verse whose blank verse movement is closer to a deliberate buzzard flap than to a lyric swallow flight. In "Bittern" he finds in the posture of the bird, "standing, kind of" and "soliciting nobody / For nothing," a self-mocking alter ego for his own artistic persona. Poetically, O'Donoghue wears self-deprecating hesitation like a cloak.

What is cloaked is an undeceived yet compassionate vision in which ordinariness and the unexpected jostle. In *The Weakness* "Coole Park or Ballylee, 1989" sets its semijokey alternatives-"the All-Ireland final" or "another tried pilgrimage"—against the elegiac plangencies of Yeats's "Coole and Ballylee, 1931." Yeats laments that "all is changed, that high horse riderless"; O'Donoghue writes as though it were better to dismount any possible Pegasus and takes a distinctly deglamorizing walk "in Coole woods, trying to distinguish seven." The art of O'Donoghue's best pieces lies in a precarious balance between the understated and the significant. It is a balance not wholly sustained by "Kindertotenlieder," in which O'Donoghue sets himself "imagining the worst that can be feared" and asserts that "the mind too is a country / Like Somalia." In fact, the wryness of poems such as "The Nth Circle," wittily addressing the all-too-human theme of "bad luck," becomes him better than the melodrama into which he is tugged by "Kindertotenlieder."

To his poetry's advantage, however, wryness is not quite all for O'Donoghue. In *Gunpowder* he treats an emotional topic in "The Great Famine" with an awareness of the fact that our knowledge of history comes to us through a veil of anecdotes. But in "Neighbourhood Watch," which admittedly is wryly titled, O'Donoghue is able to evoke with detached yet impassioned clarity how outsiders come to be outsiders. "The tinkers," opposed to "the shopkeepers" and "the people," earn our sympathy partly because O'Donoghue employs a chillingly accurate form of free indirect discourse. Thus, "the people" "used to take / the tinkers' children in service by the year, / But now they're warier and make their own beds.'' Elsewhere a residual lyricism survives, all the more welcome because of its fugitive shyness. As if commenting metaphorically on its development, ''The Rainmaker'' eschews ''the bleared weather'' in favor of ''bird-filled shores / Where ringed plover vies with lapwing / To catch your eye against the latening sun.'' *Gunpowder,* like much of O'Donoghue's work, is very much the product of a ''latening'' and knowingly belated talent, aware, as shown in ''Romantic Love,'' of debunking scientific realities (eyes are brown because of a ''superfluity / Of uric acid'') yet able in the final lines of the poem to resurrect an updated romanticism.

Here nor There contains some of O'Donoghue's finest writing, including poems such as the deeply affecting ''Ter Conatus,'' in which the Virgilian title signals an unmawkish illumination of tongue-tied love and loss and ''a lifetime of / Taking real things for shadows.'' The poem displays O'Donoghue's gifts to the full, especially his ability to suit colloquial yet weighted lines to stanzas that continually oblige the reader to pause and ponder. True to its title, much of the volume reveals a preference for oppositions that dissolve without resulting in a further synthesis. But a countertruth also manifests itself in poems such as ''Reassurance,'' which excoriates religious consolation with a sudden ferocity that is no less effective for knowing that it composes a rhetoric as it turns on ''we who have turned to the sports news, / Leaving the hanged girl from Srebenica / On the front page.'' The poem avoids the knowingness of ''Kindertotenlieder'' without forfeiting an appropriate vigilance about its status as a verbal creation. It is for such self-awareness and strength of feeling that one ultimately values O'Donoghue.

—Michael O'Neill

O'DRISCOLL, Dennis

Nationality: Irish. **Born:** Thurles, County Tipperary, 1 January 1954. **Education:** Christian Brothers' Schools, Thurles; Institute of Public Administration, Dublin, 1971–72, certificate in public administration 1972; University College, Dublin, 1972–75. **Family:** Married Julie O'Callaghan in 1985. **Career:** Executive officer, 1970–76, higher executive officer, 1976–83; since 1983, assistant principal officer, Revenue Commissioners, Dublin. Member of council, Irish United Nations Association, 1975–80; literary organizer, Dublin Arts Festival, 1977–79; editor, *Poetry Ireland Review,* Dublin, 1986–87; writer-in-residence, University College, Dublin, 1987. **Awards:** Irish Arts Council bursary, 1985, 1996. **Address:** c/o International Customs Branch, Castle House, South Great George's Street, Dublin 2, Ireland.

PUBLICATIONS

Poetry

Kist. Portlaoise, Dolmen Press, 1982.
Hidden Extras. Dublin, Dedalus Press, and London, Anvil Press Poetry, 1987.
Five Irish Poets, with others. Fredonia, White Pine Press, and Dublin, Dedalus Press, 1990.

Long Story Short. London, Anvil Press Poetry, and Dublin, Dedalus Press, 1993.
The Bottom Line. Dublin, Dedalus Press, 1994.
Quality Time. London, Anvil Press Poetry, and Chester Springs, Pennsylvania, Dufour, 1997.
Weather Permitting. London, Anvil Press Poetry, 1999.

Other

Editor, with Peter Fallon, *The First Ten Years: Dublin Arts Festival Poetry.* Dublin, Dublin Arts Festival, 1979.

*

Critical Studies: ''A Poet Hits His Stride'' by Seamus Heaney, in the *Sunday Tribune* (Dublin), 19 September 1982; ''O'Driscoll's Finest Poetry'' by Bernard O'Donoghue, in *Irish Literary Supplement* (New York), 2(2), 1983; ''Laughter from Drab Normality'' by Brendan Kennelly, in the *Sunday Tribune* (Dublin), 2 August 1987; ''The Modern Order'' by Steven Matthews, in *Times Literary Supplement* (London), 1 October 1993; ''Mortician Discovers Lyric Grace'' by Peter Sirr, in *Irish Literary Supplement* (New York), 13(1), 1994.

Dennis O'Driscoll comments:

The primary impulse behind my early poetry was a sense of bewilderment, sometimes bordering on disbelief, at the human condition: the tenuous hold we have on life, the humiliations and uncertainties experienced during that life, and the degradations of illness and death. Thematically the work has broadened; stylistically it has become less raw, with an increased irony and black humor. Themes occurring more frequently include some associated with the monotonous routines involved in earning a living. The poems are written out of—though not necessarily about—personal experiences: the early deaths of my parents; the office job I have held since I was 16.

I like to use the most economic language possible in my poetry, unless the theme prompts otherwise. In this respect I have learned a great deal from the east European poets, about whom I have written a considerable amount of critical prose. A concise style is also appropriate to a life that is dominated by nonliterary demands and that allows time only for the writing of those poems that insist forcefully on being committed to the page.

*   *   *

Dennis O'Driscoll was known in Ireland as a reviewer of poetry, particularly in the now defunct periodical *Hibernia* and in the *Sunday Tribune,* which it metamorphosed into, before his own poetry became well known. Indeed, he can claim the distinction of having preached the virtues of major cosmopolitan poets, both in eastern Europe and elsewhere, some time before they were much attended to in England: writers such as Brecht as poet, Miroslav Holub, and Les Murray, as well as neglected English and Scottish poets such as W.S. Graham, George Mackay Brown, and John Whitworth. He was a maker of reputations at a remarkably early age (before he was twenty-five), with a notably discriminating eye.

When O'Driscoll's first volume, *Kist,* was published in 1982 (the poet was twenty-eight), its virtues were to some extent those of the widely read reviewer. There were far-ranging references to modern writers—Holub, Kafka, Pasternak, Vinokurov-as well as expert poems in various genres of lyric, mostly of an imagist kind. But what was much more striking was an insistent consistency of theme, indicated by the volume's archaizing title (meaning "coffin" as well as the Elizabethan "kissed," as in "Farewell unkist!") and by the cover illustration, Munch's *The Kiss of Death*. The book is dominated by mortality, an imaginative fixation suggested by the early deaths of O'Driscoll's parents, first his mother of cancer and his father very shortly afterward. But the theme is carried with an extraordinary, paradoxical energy. Even while the insistent pathology threatens to become stifling, the immediacy of the plain language is focused on the physical elements of life while they are being lost. This is most evident in the poem "Someone," which has attained some celebrity:

> someone is dressing up for death today, a change
>   of skirt or tie . . .
> shaving his face to marble for the last laying-out
> spraying with deodorant her coarse armpit grass . . .
> someone's thighs will not be streaked with elastic in the
>   future . . .
> someone's coffin is being sanded, laminated, shined . . .

Universality is lightly suggested by the crossing of gender, and the sensual tactility of everyday life is made desirable by its ephemerality. This meeting of the quotidian and the transcendent is O'Driscoll's hallmark, seen in several short poems on death and illness, as in the title poem and in "Thalidomide," where the last word is a masterstroke of satiric protest at the President of the Immortals,

> whose hands a neighbour cannot find
> to press inside the customary shilling of luck.

O'Driscoll often reminds us with grim humor that his professional work is concerned with death duties in the Irish civil service. Perhaps it is this that enables him to make death no more than an event like any other, an Irish attitude in the tradition running from Swift to Beckett. In a review of O'Driscoll's second book, *Hidden Extras,* Brendan Kennelly made the illuminating suggestion—surprising at first blush—that "O'Driscoll has the makings of a deeply comic poet," comic, that is, in the way in which Beckett is. (We might remember that this lugubrious literature has, after all, been called "the Irish comic tradition.") The dominance of the funereal by the witty in the second book is indicated by the cover illustration, in the Irish edition, by Peter Brookes, a grim variation on Wittgenstein's duck-rabbit—a skull that is also a mouse smoking a cigarette. Although the liking for imagist conciseness is still evident, as in the series called "Breviary," for example, the typical O'Driscoll poem is now more discursive. It is a catalogue that extends on the model of "Someone," which reappears as the last poem here among a small group of poems from *Kist,* or a narrative that extends through the simple exposition of its details.

What is impressive in O'Driscoll's later work is still the evocation of the everyday with an observant, unpatronizing eye. Compassion is suggested without sentiment or irony in poems about people at work or the poet's family or locality. The range and unlabored humor of the poems are suggested by the title *"Thurles after Zbigniew Herbert,"* marrying the parochial with the cosmopolitan. O'Driscoll's admiration for Brecht is recalled frequently in the way patent and

artless narratives are invested with meaning. But he is very much of his age and country in the unflinching way he treats mortality with humor, at the furthest remove from disgust. That his view of the human condition is essentially positive is unmistakable, as in "Spoiled Child," reminiscent of Lamb's "Dream Children," or in "Declan at Twenty," to his brother:

> On blustery days, I wonder if the wind is with or against
> you as you cycle there, along unsheltered miles . . . .

—Bernard O'Donoghue

O'GRADY, Desmond (James Bernard)

Nationality: Irish. **Born:** Limerick, 27 August 1935. **Education:** St. Michael's Primary School, Limerick; Sacred Heart College, Limerick; Cistercian College, Roscrea, County Tipperary; National University of Ireland, Dublin, 1954–56; Harvard University, Cambridge, Massachusetts, M.A. 1964. Ph.D. in Celtic languages and literatures and comparative literatures 1982. **Family:** Married 1) Olga Nora Jwaideh in 1957 (divorced), one daughter; 2) Florence Tamburro (divorced), one son and two step-sons; 3) Ellen Beardsley, one daughter. **Career:** Taught at Berlitz School in Paris, 1954–56, Cambridge Institute and British Institute, Rome, St. George's English School, Rome, Roxbury Latin School, West Roxbury, Massachusetts, Harvard University, and Overseas School of Rome; visiting professor, 1971, and poet-in-residence, 1975–76, American University, Cairo; visiting professor of English, University of Tabriz, Iran, 1976–77, and University of Alexandria, Egypt, 1978–80. **Member:** Aosdána; Academy of Irish Arts and Letters. **Address:** Rincurran Hermitage, Kinsale, County Cork, Ireland.

PUBLICATIONS

Poetry

Chords and Orchestrations. Limerick, Echo Press, 1956.
Reilly. London, Phoenix Press, 1961.
Professor Kelleher and the Charles River. Cambridge, Massachusetts, Carthage Press, 1964.
Separazioni. Rome, Rapporti Europei, 1965.
The Dark Edge of Europe. London, MacGibbon and Kee, 1967.
The Dying Gaul. London, MacGibbon and Kee, 1968.
Hellas. Dublin, New Writers Press, 1971.
Separations. Dublin, Goldsmith Press, 1973.
Stations. Cairo, American University in Cairo Press, 1976.
Sing Me Creation. Dublin, Gallery Press, 1977.
His Skaldcrane's Nest. Dublin, Gallery Press, 1979.
The Headgear of the Tribe. Dublin, Gallery Press, 1979.
The Wandering Celt. Dublin, Gallery Press, 1984.
Alexandrian Notebook. Dublin, Raven Arts Press, 1989.
Tipperary. Galway, Salmon Publishing, 1991.
My Fields This Springtime. Belfast, Lapwing, 1993.
The Road Taken: Poems, 1956–1996. Salzburg, University of Salzburg Press, 1996.

Other

Translator, *Off Licence: Translations from Irish, Italian and Armenian Poetry.* Dublin, Dolmen Press, 1968.

Translator, *The Gododin,* from the Welsh of Aneirin. Dublin, Dolmen Press, 1977.

Translator, *A Limerick Rake: Versions from the Irish.* Dublin, Gallery Press, 1978.

Translator, *Grecian Glances.* Cambridge, Massachusetts, Inkling Press, 1981.

Translator, *The Seven Arab Odes.* London, Agenda, and Dublin, Raven Arts Press, 1990.

Translator, *Ten Modern Arab Poets.* Dublin, Dedalus Press, 1992.

Translator, *Alternative Manners,* by C.P. Cavafy. Alexandria, Egypt, n.p., 1993.

Translator, *Trawling Tradition: Translations 1954–1994.* Salzburg, University of Salzburg, 1994.

Translator, *The Golden Odes of Love.* Cairo, Egypt, American University in Cairo Press, 1997.

Translator, *Selected Poems of C.P. Cavafy.* Dublin, Dedalus Press, 1998.

*

Critical Studies: ''Desmond O'Grady Issue'' of *Stony Thursday Book* (Limerick), 1979; ''Re-Envisioning Yeats's 'The Second Coming': Desmond O'Grady and the Charles River'' by Karen Marguerite Moloney, in *Learning the Trade: Essays on W.B. Yeats and Contemporary Poetry,* edited by Deborah Fleming, West Cornwall, Connecticut, Locust Hill, 1993.

Desmond O'Grady comments:

My early work dealt with the experience of growing up on the west coast of Ireland, with the leaving of that place for the cities of the Continent and America and the need to connect my life there with the one I had left. My later work deals with the theme of the journey and the theme that emerges from that, separation—separation from people, places, things.

My middle work, the long poem *The Dying Gaul,* was an attempt at making a self-portrait of what it is to be a Celt. It is this persona that journeys and is separated in my later work. He is a wandering Celt who records his wanderings and experiences and attempts to connect what was left with what is found.

The prologue of my volume *Sing Me Creation* gives an attempt at condensing my purpose:

Who saw everything to the ends of the land began at the
    end of a primary road. Who saw the mysteries, knew
    secret things, went a long journey and found the whole
    story cut in stone. His purpose: praise, search, his
    appointed pain, and the countries of the world that
    housed his image. Weary, worn out with his labours, he
    returned and told what he'd seen and learned to help
    kill the winter.

When I am not writing poems of my own, I translate the poems of others. Translation is to me like drawing is to an artist. As a result there is much translated poetry collected under the general title *Trawling Tradition.* For me, however, one of the importances of translation is that it brings me closer to my own language.

*   *   *

Desmond O'Grady spent some years in Paris, but he has taught in Rome and elsewhere since 1965. In his second collection, *Reilly,* he uses a bohemian young man as a satirical persona and amusingly describes his reckless adventures in Dublin:

tables and chairs cleared of books and belongings,
the firegrate stuffed with stale fish-and-chips
and a dry whiskey bottle.
Finger-rubbed into the windowpane dust:
Reilly Rotted Here.

The Dark Edge of Europe is a selection from O'Grady's previous work. Many of the poems evoke Paris and Italy, and the imagery in them is contemporary in its unexpectedness, as in ''Girl and Widow on a Sea Park Bench'':

In this park by the sea, marvellous
As marble, under the fronded green of the palms,
The sun strafing
The stones with flat tracers of light, water like mercury
Tinnular out of the fountain.
You come to me out of the gold stained day like a word.

O'Grady spent his early years in Limerick, and many of his poems are inspired by his return visits, as in ''Homecoming'':

The familiar pull of the slow train
trundling after a sinking sun on shadowed fields.
White light splicing the broad span of the sky.
Evening deepens grass, the breeze,
like purple smoke, ruffles its surface.
Straight into herring-dark skies the great cathedral spire
is sheer Gothic.

Like Joyce and other Irish writers, O'Grady expresses in compressed lines the effect of a puritanical education:

Unwinking eyes of saints and hushed confession queue—
For one loud nervous boot
Of frightened heart.
I felt the Churcheyed, fidget fear of schooltied youth.

Sometimes he objectifies his early experiences, as in his depiction of an old man who turns ''for the safest healer / To a clean and bandaged silence of the heart.''

—Austin Clarke

OKAI, John

Nationality: Ghanaian. **Born:** Ghana. **Education:** Gorky Literary Institute, Moscow, M.A. (Litt.) 1967; University of Ghana, Accra; University of London, M. Phil. **Career:** Lived in the U.S.S.R.,

1961–67; lecturer in Russian, University of Ghana, Legon. **Awards:** Royal Society of Arts fellowship, 1968. **Address:** Department of Modern Languages, University of Ghana, P.O. Box 25, Legon, Ghana.

PUBLICATIONS

Poetry

Flowerfall. London, Writers Forum, 1969.
The Oath of Fontomirom and Other Poems. New York, Simon and Schuster, 1971.
Lorgorligi: Logarithms and Other Poems. Tema, Ghana Publishing, 1974.

*

Critical Studies: ''John Atukwei Okai: The Growth of a Poet'' by Jawa Apronti, in *Universitas* (Legon, Ghana), 2(1), 1972; ''Polyrhythmics and African Print Poetics: Guillen, Cesaire, and Atukwei Okai'' by J. Bekunuru Kubayanda, in *Interdisciplinary Dimensions of African Literature,* edited by Kofi Anyidoho and others, Washington, D.C., Three Continents, 1985; ''Patterns of Oral Poetic Trends in West and South African Poetry: Atukwei Okai and Mazisi Kunene'' by Ohaeto Ezenwa, in *Literary Griot* (Wayne, New Jersey), 8(1), spring 1989.

*   *   *

The use of musical rhythms in poetry is nothing unusual, but few contemporary writers make so great a use of the musical heritage of their culture as does John Okai. The sounds of the talking drums of Ghana figure strongly in his poems, and the titles of most of them, such as ''Fugue for Fireflies'' and ''Okponglo Concerto,'' bear witness to the musical bent of his work. The repetition and alliterative forms that are a part of traditional verse are brought by Okai into the English language, producing effects that are often close to hypnotic. This occurs, for example, in ''Modzawe,'' where the line ''Let human beings be human beings again'' is repeated six times and where Okai refers to traditional drums, allowing the musicality of their names to shape his lines:

Descend O God! descend O God!
To the echo-wail-boom and music of
The Dodonpo and the Odono
And the festive Bintim Obonu . . .

His Ghanaian background is not the only source Okai draws from, however. Having studied in England, the United States, and Russia, Okai can refer as familiarly to apple trees as to palms, and his poems often contain catalogs of people and places that reflect this catholic experience:

the swallow
    and the bougainvillea . . .
modigliani's woman with a necklace . . .
leonardo da vinci's mona lisa
the parrot
    and the bougainvillea . . .
shostakovich's leningrad symphony . . .

dvorak's new world symphony (part two) . . .
the sparrow
    and the bougainvillea
frank lloyd wright's falling water . . .
ya-na's palace at wa in ghana . . .

If there is a fault in Okai's work, it may be that some of his lines take on a singsong quality, seeming to sacrifice sense in favor of sound, for he can be more alliterative in his writing than was Old English verse. His ''Sunset Sonata'' is filled with lines such as

Still stand stubborn
    To stones that strangle the dawn,
Still stand stubborn
    To stones that maim the morn,
Still stand stubborn
    To stones that assail the sun . . .

Because of this some critics attempt to dismiss Okai, not seeing that even in his most highly alliterative passages there is still meaning.

It cannot be denied that Okai's work is assertive and, especially when read aloud, charged with vitality. His work has been a great influence in enlivening the poetry scene in Ghana, and the directions in which his poems move take advantage of a rich and, in English, relatively unexplored patrimony.

—Joseph Bruchac

OKARA, Gabriel (Imomotimi Gbaingbain)

Nationality: Nigerian. **Born:** Bumodi, Ijaw District, Rivers State, Western Nigeria, 21 April 1921. **Education:** Government College, Umuahia; trained as a bookbinder; studied journalism at Northwestern University, Evanston, Illinois, 1956. **Career:** Principal information officer, Eastern Regional Government, Enugu, until 1967; Biafran information officer, Nigerian Civil War, 1967–69. Since 1972 director of the Rivers State Publishing House, Port Harcourt. **Awards:** Nigerian Festival of the Arts award, 1953; Commonwealth Poetry prize, 1979. **Address:** 24 Nembe Road, Port Harcourt, Rivers, Nigeria.

PUBLICATIONS

Poetry

Poetry from Africa, with others edited by Howard Sergeant. Oxford, Pergamon Press, 1968.
The Fisherman's Invocation. London, Heinemann, 1978.

Novels

The Voice. London, Deutsch, 1964; New York, Africana, 1970.
An Adventure to Juju Island (for children). Ibadan, Heinemann, 1992.
Little Snake and Little Frog (for children). Ibadan, Heinemann, 1992.

*

Critical Studies: *Mother Is Gold: A Study of West African Literature* by Adrian A. Roscoe, London, Cambridge University Press, 1971; "Heterogeneous Worlds Yoked Violently Together: The Commonwealth Poetry Prize, 1979" by Kirsten Holst Petersen, in *Kunapipi,* 1(2), 1979; "The Poetry of Gabriel Okara" by Bruce King, in *Chandrabhaga* (Orissa, India), 2, 1979; by Susan Beckmann, in *World Literature Written in English* (Singapore), 20(2), autumn 1981; "The Significance of Gabriel Okara As Poet" by Samuel O. Asein, in *New Literature Review* (Wollongong, New South Wales), 11, November 1982; "His River's Complex Course: Reflections on Past, Present and Future in the Poetry of Gabriel Okara" by S.A. Gingell, in *World Literature Written in English* (Singapore), 23(2), spring 1984; "The 'Sharp and Sided Hail': Hopkins and His Nigerian Imitators and Detractors" by Emeka Okeke-Ezigbo, in *Hopkins among the Poets: Studies in Modern Responses to Gerard Manley Hopkins,* edited by Richard F. Giles, Hamilton, Ontario, International Hopkins Association, 1985; "Gabriel Okara: Poet of the Mystic Inside" by Obi Maduakor, in *World Literature Today* (Norman, Oklahoma), 61(1), winter 1987; "Okara's Poetic Landscape" by Ayo Mamudu, in *Commonwealth Essays and Studies* (Dijon, France), 10(1), autumn 1987; "Gabriel Okara: A Poet and His Seasons" by M.J.C. Echeruo, in *World Literature Today* (Norman, Oklahoma), 66(3), summer 1992; "Language and Meaning in Gabriel Okara's Poetry" by Isaac I. Elimimian, in *College Language Association Journal* (Atlanta, Georgia), 38(3), March 1995.

*   *   *

One of the most gifted, and certainly the least literary, of African poets is Gabriel Okara. He has proved to be what can only be described as a "natural" in that he is highly original in both outlook and expression and appears to have learned his craft without being influenced unduly by the stylistic mannerisms of any other poet. This, however, has not been without considerable effort on his part. "In order to capture the vivid images of African speech," he observed in an article in *Transition,* "I had to eschew the habit of expressing my thoughts first in English. It was difficult at first, but I had to learn." That he has been successful in capturing the African scene, the African color and excitement, and the changing African moods is evidenced by such poems as "The Mystic Drum," "Were I to Choose," "Adhiambo," and "Piano and Drums."

There is, in fact, an almost mystical quality about Okara's work. It seems to spring from his racial inheritance, his instincts and sensitivity rather than his intellect, and he exhibits a curious power when he draws upon the great oral traditions to release this nervous energy, as in "The Mystic Drum." In "Adhiambo" he tries to define his feelings on the subject—"Maybe I'm a medicine man / hearing talking saps / seeing behind trees"—and in "Piano and Drums" he writes of the jungle drums "telegraphing the mystic rhythm, urgent, raw like bleeding flesh." In other poems, which probably have more impact upon non-African readers, he is practical and down to earth, extremely perceptive in his judgments, and almost analytical in his approach. These qualities can be seen, for example, in "Once upon a Time"—"There was a time indeed / they used to shake hands with their hearts"—and "You Laughed and Laughed and Laughed," in which the ancient world of Africa merges with the modern world.

—Howard Sergeant

OLDS, Sharon

Nationality: American. **Born:** San Francisco, California, 19 November 1942. **Education:** Stanford University, California, B.A. (honors) 1964; Columbia University, New York, Ph.D. 1972. **Career:** Lecturer-in-residence on poetry, Theodor Herzl Institute, New York, 1976–80; visiting teacher of poetry, Manhattan Theatre Club, New York, 1982, Nathan Mayhew Seminars, Martha's Vineyard, Massachusetts, 1982, YMCA, New York, 1982, Poetry Society of America, 1983, Squaw Valley Writers' Conference, 1984–90, Sarah Lawrence College, Bronxville, New York, 1984, Goldwater Hospital, Roosevelt Island, New York, since 1985, Columbia University, New York, 1985–86, and State University of New York, Purchase, 1986–87; Fanny Hurst Chair in literature, Brandeis University, Waltham, Massachusetts, 1986–87; adjunct professor, 1983–90, director, 1988–91, and since 1990, associate professor, Graduate Program in Creative Writing, New York University. **Awards:** Creative Arts Public Service award, 1978; Madeline Sadin award, 1978; Guggenheim fellowship, 1981–82; National Endowment for the Arts fellowship, 1982–83; Lamont prize, 1984; National Book Critics Circle award, 1985; Lila Wallace/Reader's Digest fellowship grant, 1993–96; Walt Whitman Citation of Merit, New York State Writers Institute, 1998; New York State Poet, 1998. **Agent:** c/o Alfred A. Knopf, 201 East 50th Street, New York, New York 10022. **Address:** Graduate Program in Creative Writing, New York University, 19 University Place, Room 200, New York, New York 10003–4556, U.S.A.

PUBLICATIONS

Poetry

Satan Says. Pittsburgh, Pennsylvania, University of Pittsburgh Press, and London, Feffer and Simons, 1980.
The Dead and the Living. New York, Knopf, 1984.
The Gold Cell. New York, Knopf, 1987.
The Matter of This World: New and Selected Poems. Nottingham, Slow Dancer Press, 1987.
The Sign of Saturn. London, Martin Secker and Warburg, 1991.
The Father. New York, Knopf, 1992; London, Martin Secker and Warburg, 1993.
The Wellspring: Poems. New York, Knopf, 1995; London, Cape, 1996.
Blood, Tin, Straw. New York, Knopf, 1999.

Recording: *Coming Back to Life,* Watershed, 1984.

*

Critical Studies: "Sharon Olds: Painful Insights and Small Beauties" by Jonah Bornstein, in *Literary Cavalcade* (New York), January 1989; "American Visionaries: Helen Keller and the Poets Muriel Rukeyser, Denise Levertov, and Sharon Olds," in *Women against the Iron Fist: Alternatives to Militarism 1900–1989,* by Sybil Oldfield, Cambridge, Massachusetts, Blackwell, 1989; "Talking to Our Father: The Political and Mythical Appropriations of Adrienne Rich and Sharon Olds" by Suzanne Matson, in *American Poetry Review* (Philadelphia), November/December 1989; "Sharon Olds Gathers Students into Poetry Family" by Rosemary Klein, in *Kimball Mountain Observer,* April 1992; "Olds Breaks New Poetic Ground" by

Fran Fanshed in *Columbia Flier,* 5 November 1992; "'Never Having Had You, I Cannot Let You Go': Sharon Olds's Poems of a Father-Daughter Relationship" by Brian Dillon, in *Literary Review* (Madison, New Jersey), 37(1), fall 1993; "Sentencing Eros" by Calvin Bedient, in *Salmagundi* (Saratoga Springs, New York), 97, winter 1993; "I Am (Not) This: Erotic Discourse in Bishop, Olds, and Stevens" by Alicia Ostriker, in *Wallace Stevens Journal* (Potsdam, New York), 19(2), fall 1995; "A Note on Two Poems by Sharon Olds" by Martin Kich, in *Notes on Contemporary Literature* (Carrollton, Georgia), 26(2), March 1996; *'I Have Always Longed to Believe in What I Am Seeing': Sharon Olds's Revisioning of Confessional Poetry* (dissertation) by Richard Benjamin Poverny, Rutgers University, 1996; "Death-Watch: Terminal Illness and the Gaze in Sharon Olds's 'The Father'" by Laura E. Tanner, in *Mosaic* (Canada), 29(1), March 1996; "Olds's 'My Father Speaks to Me from the Dead'" by Peter C. Scheponik, in *Explicator* (Washington, D.C.), 57(1), fall 1998.

Sharon Olds comments:

I began by working in close forms and then more and more wanted a line break and a poem shape (the body of the poem on the page) that felt more alive to me.

Questions that interest me include, Is there anything that should not or cannot be written about in a poem? What has never been written about in a poem? What is the use, function, service of poetry in a society? For whom are you writing? (The dead, the unborn, the woman in front of you in the checkout line at Shop-Rite?)

I teach poetry workshops at New York University and at Goldwater Hospital, a New York City public hospital for the severely physically disabled. "If you do not bring forth that which is within you, that which is within you will destroy you. If you bring forth that which is within you, that which is within you will save you." (Heretical Gospel of Thomas)

Poets of the generation just ahead of mine whose work I have especially learned from and loved: Muriel Rukeyser, Galway Kinnell, Philip Levine, Ruth Stone.

*   *   *

Sharon Olds's poetry is intimate and personal, wrenched from her own life. Prosaic yet precise, it has a diamond-sharp clarity that makes it too hard to be confessional. It lacks the bitterness and anger so often found in contemporary women's poetry, as well as the wit and irony that tend to accompany such bitterness. Though not overtly spiritual, her work has an almost religious purity; it is cathartic. While some may find her grounding in domestic life too mundane, most readers are shocked and exhilarated by the extraordinary candor of her material and the lyricism with which she presents it. The work is strong, vibrant, and celebratory, a far cry from the neurasthenic expositions of such predecessors as Emily Dickinson.

Olds's first collection, *Satan Says,* was described by Marilyn Hacker as "daring and elegant." It dealt with the experiences of adolescence and early motherhood. Whitmanesque in its celebration of the body and the self, it spoke with a confidence and eroticism rare in first collections. Poems like "The Sisters of Sexual Treasure" are remarkably frank: "As soon as my sisters and I got out of our / mother's house, all we wanted to / do was fuck, obliterate / her tiny sparrow body and narrow / grasshopper legs. The men's bodies / were like our father's body! . . . we could have him there, the steep forbidden / buttocks, backs of the knees, the cock / in our mouth, ah

the cock in our mouth . . ." In a poem like "Prayer," which parallels the birth of a first child with a first sexual encounter, Olds contributes to the small but healthy branch of poetry that explores women's most intimate experiences. And in "The Language of the Brag," also about childbirth, she challenges the elders, placing her own work at the center of the American tradition:

> . . . I have lain down and sweated and shaken
> and passed blood and feces and water and
> slowly alone in the centre of a circle I have
> passed the new person out
> and they have lifted the new person free of the act
> and wiped the new person free of that
> language of blood like praise all over the body.
>
> I have done what you wanted to do, Walt Whitman,
> Allen Ginsberg, l have done this thing,
> I and the other women this exceptional
> act with the exceptional heroic body,
> this giving birth, this glistening verb,
> and I am putting my proud American boast
> right here with the others.

Olds's second book, *The Dead and the Living,* won awards from both the American Academy of Poets and the National Book Critics. An exquisite collection, it displays a deepening and refining of her art. The first section, "Poems for the Dead," begins with poems honoring both public and anonymous figures, from Marilyn Monroe to the starving Armenians of 1921. The chilling "Aesthetics of the Shah" begins, "The first thing you notice / is the skill / used on the ropes, the narrow close-grained / hemp against that black cloth / the bodies are wrapped in . . ." "The Issue," about racial tension in Rhodesia, gives a detailed description of a bayoneted black baby, ending with the lines "Don't speak to me about / politics. I've got eyes, man." These poems, her most overtly political, move beyond the partisan to express a general compassion for humanity. Also in this section are poems for dead relatives, among which is "Miscarriage," with its stark realization that

> . . . I never went back
> to mourn the one who came as far as the
> sill with its information: that we could
> botch something, you and I . . .

The second section, "Poems for the Living," deals with childhood, love, marriage, and children—"the tasting, and the / giving of life." Several of the poems are about a drunken, abusive father and a weak, abused mother. They reveal extraordinary pain and potential hatred, but, as always in Olds's work, the subjects are redeemed through confrontation and acceptance. As honest with herself as she is relentless with her subjects, the poet confesses in the magnificent "The Fear of Oneself" that ". . . you say you believe I would hold up under torture / for the sake of our children . . . It is all I have wanted to do, / to stand between them and pain. But I come from a / long line / of women / who put themselves / first . . ."

Olds's third collection, *The Gold Cell,* concentrates on personal relationships in poems about motherhood, love, and lust. "Greed and Aggression," for example, begins, "Someone in the Quaker meeting talks about greed and aggression / and I think of the way I lay the massive / weight of my body down on you / like a tiger lying down in gluttony and pleasure on the / elegant heavy body of the eland it eats . . .'' In this collection, as in her earlier ones, Olds celebrates the savage, fragile chaos of life with poems such as ''Summer Solstice, New York City,'' which ends after a tense, dramatic description of a man trying to jump off a building:

> . . . and they closed on him, I thought they were going to
> beat him up, as a mother whose child has been
> lost will scream at the child when it's found, they
> took him by the arms and held him up and
> leaned him against the wall of the chimney and the
> tall cop lit a cigarette
> in his mouth, and gave it to him, and
> then they all lit cigarettes, and the
> red, glowing ends burned like the
> tiny campfires we lit at night
> back at the beginning of the world.

—Katie Campbell

OLIVER, Mary

Nationality: American. **Born:** Maple Heights, Ohio, 10 September 1935. **Education:** Ohio State University, Columbus, 1955–56; Vassar College, Poughkeepsie, New York, 1956–57. **Career:** Chair of the Writing Department, 1972–73, and member of the writing committee, 1984, Fine Arts Work Center, Provincetown, Massachusetts; Mather Visiting Professor, Case Western Reserve University, Cleveland, 1980, 1982; poet-in-residence, Bucknell University, Lewisburg, Pennsylvania, 1986, and University of Cincinnati, Ohio, 1986; Banister Writer-in-Residence, Sweet Briar College, Sweet Briar, Virginia, 1991–95; William Blackburn visiting professor, Duke University, 1995. Since 1996 Catharine Osgood Foster Professor, Bennington College. **Awards:** Poetry Society of American prize, 1962, Shelley memorial award, 1970, and Alice Fay di Castagnola award, 1973; National Endowment for the Arts fellowship, 1972; Guggenheim fellowship, 1980; American Academy award, 1983; Pulitzer Prize, 1984; Christopher award for *House of Light,* 1991; L.L. Winship award for *House of Light,* 1991; National Book award for Poetry for *New and Selected Poems,* 1992. **Agent:** Molly Malone Cook Literary Agency, P.O. Box 619, Provincetown, Massachusetts 02657, U.S.A.

PUBLICATIONS

Poetry

No Voyage and Other Poems. London, Dent, 1963; revised edition, Boston, Houghton Mifflin, 1965.
The River Styx, Ohio, and Other Poems. New York, Harcourt Brace, 1972.
The Night Traveler. Cleveland, Bits Press, 1978.
Twelve Moons. Boston, Little Brown, 1979.
Sleeping in the Forest. Athens, Ohio Review Chapbook, 1979.
American Primitive. Boston, Little Brown, 1983.
Dream Work. Boston, Atlantic Monthly Press, 1986.
House of Light. Boston, Beacon Press, 1990.

New and Selected Poems. Boston, Beacon Press, 1992.
White Pine. New York, Harcourt Brace, 1994.
Blue Pastures. New York, Harcourt Brace, 1995.
West Wind: Poems and Prose Poems. Boston, Houghton Mifflin, 1997.
Winter Hours: Prose, Prose Poems, and Poems. Boston, Houghton Mifflin, 1999.

Other

A Poetry Handbook. New York, Harcourt Brace, 1994.
Rules for the Dance: A Handbook for Writing and Reading Metrical Verse. Boston, Houghton Mifflin, 1998.

*

Critical Studies: ''The Poetry of Mary Oliver: Modern Renewal through Mortal Acceptance'' by Jean B. Alford, in *Pembroke* (Pembroke, North Carolina), 20, 1988; ''Mary Oliver and the Tradition of Romantic Nature Poetry'' by Janet McNew, in *Contemporary Literature* (Madison, Wisconsin), 30(1), spring 1989; ''Dialogues between History and Dream'' by Lisa M. Steinman, in *Michigan Quarterly Review* (Ann Arbor, Michigan), 26(2), spring 1987; *'Voices the Heart Can Hear': From Silence to Voice in the Poetry of Mary Oliver* (dissertation) by Janet Lee Warman, University of Tennessee, 1991; ''The Language of Nature in the Poetry of Mary Oliver'' by Diane S. Bonds, in *Women's Studies* (New York), 21(1), 1992; ''Moore, Bishop, and Oliver: Thinking Back, Re-Seeing the Sea,'' in *Twentieth Century Literature* (Albany, New York), 39(3), fall 1993, and ''The Native American Presence in Mary Oliver's Poetry,'' in *Kentucky Review* (Lexington, Kentucky), 12(1–2), autumn 1993, both by Robin Riley Fast; ''Mary Oliver, Poetic Iconographer'' by Joan Mellard, in *Language and Literature* (San Antonio, Texas), 16, 1991; *Journeys into the Border Country: The Making of Nature and Home in the Poetry of Robinson Jeffers and Mary Oliver* (dissertation) by Kirk Dade Glaser, University of California, Berkeley, 1993; '''Into the Body of Another': Mary Oliver and the Poetics of Becoming Other'' by Vicki Graham, in *Papers on Language and Literature* (Edwardsville, Illinois), 30(4), fall 1994; ''Nature, Spirit, and Imagination in the Poetry of Mary Oliver'' by Douglas Burton-Christie, in *Cross Currents* (New Rochelle, New York), 46(1), spring 1996; ''Mary Oliver: The Poet and the Persona'' by Sue Russell, in *Harvard Gay and Lesbian Review,* 4(4), fall 1997; ''Hurry Up or Wait: Oliver's 'Going to Walden''' by John Chamberlain, in *Thoreau Society Bulletin* (Lincoln, Massachusetts), 225, fall 1998.

*   *   *

life's winners are not the rapacious but the patient:
what triumphs and takes new territory

has learned to lie for centuries in the shadows
like the shadows of the rocks.

Mary Oliver did not lie in the shadows for centuries before receiving the Pulitzer Prize for poetry in 1984. She has been a quiet, modest poet, however, one whose work reflects a pastoral life lived (first in Ohio, then in Provincetown) with plants and animals far more than with human beings. Her early work was reviewed by both Philip

Booth and Joyce Carol Oates as being influenced by Robert Frost, and, as with Frost, her first book, *No Voyage and Other Poems,* was published in England.

Like Frost, she has migrated to a home in New England, whose landscape dominates the poetry in both *Twelve Moons* and *American Primitive.* She is also like her mentor in being anything but the "primitive" that her work guilefully suggests. In fact, if one thinks of the tradition in American letters created by Thoreau—the man who talked about the value of independence, self-subsistence, and a life connected with the land while in fact, as Leon Edel points out, he lived in a cabin close enough to his mother's house to enable him to go there every day for home-baked cookies and other things he did not care to provide for himself—then we can see Oliver as part of this tradition. Her poems enrich the fantasy life of Americans who read the L.L. Bean catalogues and dress for hunting, hiking, and the outdoor life, while in fact they never face the hardships that are part of such a life.

Reading Oliver's poetry gives the same wonderful, vicarious satisfaction. Her knowledge of plants and animals is so rich that no one could question its authenticity. But it is presented in beautiful and not realistic images: (speaking of raccoons) "walking, / silvery, slumberous, / each a sharp set of teeth, / each a grey dreamer"; (hibernating snakes) "and their eyes are like jewels— / and asleep, though they cannot close. / And in each mouth the forked tongue, / sensitive as an angel's ear"; (about being in a swamp) "I feel / not so much wet as / painted and glittered / with the fat grassy / mires, the rich / and succulent marrows / of earth." She writes of egrets in this way:

> Even half-asleep they had
>   such faith in the world
> that had made them—
>   tilting through the water,
>   unruffled, sure,
>   by the laws
> of their faith not logic,
>   they opened their wings
>   softly and stepped
>   over every dark thing

Thus no one ever experiences fear, pain, frustration, or being out of control, all the miseries we urbanized creatures usually feel in the wilderness. Oliver's poetry gives each reader the illusion that the natural world is graspable, controllable, and beautiful. In addition, the reader feels that she is facing truth and reality, all of the struggles she knows are out there.

This vision of gentleness and possibility, that the natural world is obtainable and belongs to anyone who simply opens his or her eyes, comes from Thoreau through Frost, and it is one that only a few other contemporary poets have grappled with. (Perhaps Maxine Kumin would be an example of a poet who works in this mode.) Oliver's poems, however, have been compared by Robert DeMott to those of Roethke and Galway Kinnell, saying that all three poets are "sensitive to visitations by the 'dark things' of the wood." But if Oliver writes of "dark things," they are friendly, benevolent dark things. Even her vision of death is gentle, pastoral, and haunting rather than fearful and violent. What the critics seem to be pointing out is that there is alive today in American poetry a strain of writing that glorifies man's natural relationship to animals, plants, and the nonhuman world. It seems to be a necessary vision, one in which beauty and simplicity, achieved through a nonviolent portrait of nature's ecosystems, could replace nuclear holocaust. Oliver writes this vision clearly, persuasively, and with natural elegance.

—Diane Wakoski

OLSON, Toby

Nationality: American. **Born:** Merle Theodore Olson, Berwyn, Illinois, 17 August 1937. **Education:** Occidental College, Los Angeles, 1962–64, B.A. 1964; Long Island University, Brooklyn, New York, 1964–66, M.A. 1966. **Military Service:** Surgical technician in the U.S. Navy, 1957–61. **Family:** Married 1) Ann Yeomans in 1963 (divorced 1965); 2) Miriam Meltzer in 1966. **Career:** Associate director, Aspen Writers Workshop, Colorado, 1964–67; assistant professor, Long Island University, 1966–74; member of the faculty, New School for Social Research, New York, 1967–75; professor of English, Temple University, Philadelphia, 1984. Poet-in-residence, State University of New York, Cortland, 1972, and Friends Seminary, New York, 1974–75. **Awards:** Creative Artists Public Service grant, 1975; P.E.N. Faulkner award, for fiction, 1983; Pennsylvania Council on the Arts fellowship, 1983; Yaddo Colony fellowship, 1985; National Endowment for the Arts fellowship, 1985; Guggenheim fellowship, 1985; Rockefeller Foundation fellowship, 1987. **Address:** 329 South Juniper Street, Philadelphia, Pennsylvania 19107, U.S.A.

PUBLICATIONS

Poetry

The Brand: A Five-Part Poem. Mount Horeb, Wisconsin, Perishable Press, 1969.
Worms into Nails. Mount Horeb, Wisconsin, Perishable Press, 1969.
The Hawk-Foot Poems. Madison, Wisconsin, Abraxas Press, 1969.
Maps. Mount Horeb, Wisconsin, Perishable Press, 1969.
Pig/s Book. New York, Doctor Generosity Press, 1970.
Cold House. Mount Horeb, Wisconsin, Perishable Press, 1970.
Poems. Mount Horeb, Wisconsin, Perishable Press, 1970 (?).
Tools. New York, Doctor Generosity Press, 1971.
Shooting Pigeons. Mount Horeb, Wisconsin, Perishable Press, 1971.
Vectors. Milwaukee, Ziggurat-Membrane Press, 1972.
Home (broadsheet). Chicago, Wine Press, 1972.
Fishing. Mount Horeb, Wisconsin, Perishable Press, 1973.
The Wrestlers and Other Poems. New York, Barlenmir House, 1974.
City. Milwaukee, Membrane Press, 1974.
A Kind of Psychology. Milwaukee, Lionhead, 1974.
Changing Appearance: Poems 1965–1970. Milwaukee, Membrane Press, 1975.
A Moral Proposition. New York, Aviator Press, 1975.
Priorities. Milwaukee, Lionhead, 1975.
Seeds. Milwaukee, Membrane Press, 1975.
Standard-4. New York, Aviator Press, 1975.
Home. Milwaukee, Membrane Press, 1976.

Three and One. Mount Horeb, Wisconsin, Perishable Press, 1976.

Doctor Miriam: Five Poems by Her Admiring Husband. Mount Horeb, Wisconsin, Perishable Press, 1977.

Aesthetics. Milwaukee, Perishable Press, 1978.

The Florence Poems. London, Permanent Press, 1978.

Birdsongs: Eleven New Poems. Milwaukee, Perishable Press, 1980.

Two Standards. Madison, Wisconsin, Salient Seeding Press, 1982.

Still/Quiet. Madison, Wisconsin, Landlocked Press, 1982.

Sitting in Gusevik. Madison, Wisconsin, Black Mesa Press, 1983.

We Are the Fire: A Selection of Poems. New York, New Directions, 1984.

Unfinished Building. Minneapolis, Coffee House Press, 1993.

Human Nature: Poems. New York, New Directions, 2000.

Novels

The Life of Jesus. New York, New Directions, 1976.

Seaview. New York, New Directions, 1982; London, Boyars, 1985.

The Woman Who Escaped from Shame. New York, Random House, 1986.

Utah. New York, Simon and Schuster, 1987.

Dorit in Lesbos. New York, Simon and Schuster, 1990.

At Sea. New York, Simon and Schuster, 1993.

Other

Editor, *Margins 1976.* Milwaukee, Margins Press, 1976.

Editor, with Muffy E.A Siegel, *Writing Talks: Views on Teaching Writing from across the Professions.* Upper Montclair, New Jersey, Boynton/Cook, 1983.

*

Critical Study: By Robert Vas Dias, in *Poetry Information* (London), winter 1976–77; by Donald Barthelme, in the Toby Olson issue of *The Review of Contemporary Fiction* (Naperville, Illinois), summer 1991; review by James Sallis, in *Book World,* 23(25), 20 June 1993.

Toby Olson comments:

I remember receiving the impression in school that poetry was a kind of crossword/jigsaw puzzle; the student was helped to figure out meanings and fittings, and in the end he could say he "understood" the poem. Often the result did not seem worth the effort that got him to it. School talk seldom moved beyond puzzle solving to the possibilities of appreciation. Though this kind of attitude may still prevail, I am no longer able to think of poetry, that which I write and read and value, in this puzzle-solving way.

For me poetry is no less than good talk about important things, and this good talk has as its end the telling and presentation of truth. I would like it if my poems were able to fix important talk, make it in some way permanent. I would like it if when my poems were difficult it was because the things I was trying to talk about were difficult things to say; there should be no other reason for them being hard to understand.

My poems are not often very difficult in the puzzle sense of it. I am not much interested in metaphor as comparison, symbolism, or myth; I am very interested in finding structures of good talk that can

then become the fixed structures of particular poems. I feel that there is enough in the world around me and what it can recall to me from my own past to make any poem. I trust that the experience of the human tribe is enough in each of us so that if I speak out of attention and with care I will be heard by those who can give a little time for listening.

I suppose, then, that I feel that my poetry intends to be always both autobiographical and communal, that it is through writing about what I can see, hear, and feel that I can best touch the nature that I believe is common in all of us.

*   *   *

The title of Toby Olson's first major collection, *Changing Appearance: Poems 1965–1970,* should alert the reader to the poet's preoccupation with scenes of persons and objects immediately and literally given to him. In this preoccupation Olson is heir to an attitude of attention and to a certain tone—ironic but not unsympathetic—identified with Paul Blackburn. The influence of Blackburn on Olson can also be found in certain scenes, and through Blackburn he is heir to one aspect of William Carlos Williams (that there are "no ideas but in things") and, less directly, to the imagist phase of Ezra Pound. This is not an inconsiderable inheritance. Technically, it involves the sure handling of speech rhythms in varying line lengths and stanza formations and the reporting of exactly what is before one's eyes, along with a predilection for the urban, the unelevated, and the unsublime and for the ironies revealed by such reporting. Like Blackburn and Williams, Olson is also the writer of forthright, unconventional love poems.

Yet this inheritance, like any other, has its limitations. Its special appeal is that of the sharply focused but spontaneous snapshot; in a few words evocative images are constructed and entire scenes laid out. The snapshot, or—to use a phrase from Blackburn—the out-the-window poem, is limited by its very focus to the personal, the local. It has no horizon, and its emphasis on brevity allows for little if any complexity or sustained development of perception. Olson deals with the inherent limitations of his approach in a number of ways. In the early poetry of *Changing Appearance,* he most often uses thematic grouping; for example, the poems of the "Pig/s Book" section all involve the pig in relation to other animals. He later turned to the series, and in a published note on this mode of organization Olson has commented that he did so because it allows for the clarity of the individual poem and for "the a-rational quality of the poems' genesis extended over a period of time."

The most impressive treatments of series in Olson's work can be found in *Home,* a long poem of thirty-six parts that successfully enlarges upon its title's theme and that would at first appear to be the very embodiment of the restricted personal and local, and in *Aesthetics,* which seeks not simply a larger space but a constantly expanding and complex subject matter as well. As the opening lines of this latter book declare, *"Paint what you see /* is already a philosophical problem: / a blood-spot on the eye's membrane / absent in the still-life."* In another book of the same year, *The Florence Poems,* Olson returns to thematic grouping for an entire volume. This time the theme is the early death of a friend. The book begins with reflections in "Graveside," and each poem of the group then remembers past incidents of shared experience and, in the book's progression, leads toward the final commending "into the perfect / community of our isolate lives." Olson's combination here of detailed, unsentimental recollection with mythic elements such as the trickster figure and

Indian whale legends, along with the constant spiritual notion of "our secret names," is both masterful and moving.

Olson's collection *Unfinished Building* offers further evidence of a continuing affinity with his Blackburnian inheritance as well as his own unique extension of that inheritance. "Clouds," a poem dedicated to Blackburn, is representative. It begins with quotidian reality—"The cold cereal turns to mush in the bowl / and the rain comes again"—and proceeds to a direct evocation of a shared poetics: "A song is a game of Spell against Ideas . . . Values / are left to silence / unless they sing." Thereafter the poem becomes increasingly complex. The complexity is achieved by multiplying the identity of the speaker, who at times is Blackburn toward the end of his life and at other times is Olson's father in a similar position and Olson himself as the adolescent son. The multiplication is complexly musical rather than merely ambiguous. Perhaps most impressive is the poem's close, which unites all of the speaker's identities to address, collectively, "my dears," their wives (and perhaps the poem's readers). The close affirms nothing less than love between men and women even though "the sickness" of misunderstanding "always comes again." The poem thus affirms Olson's personal regard for Blackburn and love between persons generally, but it is not a sentimental poem. Using the simplest words and the most usual reality embodied by those words, the poem achieves a musical complexity that is resolved with humane generosity: "I could not die / until I died, / for living."

Since *Unfinished Building* Olson has published a further collection, *Human Nature.* Readers will find in it both continuity and change in relation to his previous work. Continuity is seen in the "standards" series, poems involving the popular American song (as treated in "In Jazz") and organized on the occasional basis of Robert Duncan's "Passages." And overall there continues to be close attention to landscape, both emotional and geographical. Change is present too, however, for these poems are more story based. They tell stories and use images as instigations for stories rather than as the climax or the "point" of each poem. They thus extend, not repudiate, the Blackburn model. The poems typically begin with immediate events in the Cape Cod locale, then branch off into the locale of memory. This branching motion is dreamlike, conjoining both past and present. "Cloud-Castle Blues" is a good example. The poem follows the progress of a baseball game, including the behavior of various members of the crowd, and recalls incidents of the speaker's own youth, and in between all of this "Larry and I talk about dying." This "harmonic extension" is comparable to the jazz pianist Bill Evans's way with a "standard" melody line: suspended, shaded, complicated, and finally returned to and restated "anew." Like Evans's music, these new poems attain moments of delicate beauty and serious emotional depth but always within the context of "everydayness." They have delicate and serious things to say about human nature even as those things are always found in the not so delicate or serious context of the everyday.

Olson also writes fiction and has published several novels. I will not attempt to summarize his fiction except to say that readers will find in it the same qualities that distinguish his poetry, although there is, of course, a significant difference in scale. Above all, the novels offer a denser, more richly musical texture. It may be that the most apt designation for this humanly attentive and technically innovative writer is prose poet.

—John Taggart

ONDAATJE, (Philip) Michael

Nationality: Canadian. **Born:** Colombo, Ceylon (now Sri Lanka), 12 September 1943. **Education:** St. Thomas' College, Colombo; Dulwich College, London; Bishop's University, Lennoxville, Quebec, 1962–64; University of Toronto, B.A. 1965; Queen's University, Kingston, Ontario, M.A. 1967. **Family:** Married 1) Betty Kimbark in 1963, one daughter and one son; 2) Kim Jones (separated). **Career:** Taught at the University of Western Ontario, London, 1967–71. Since 1971 member of the Department of English, currently professor, Glendon College, York University, Toronto. Visiting professor, University of Hawaii, Honolulu, summer 1979, Brown University, 1990; editor, Mongrel Broadsides. **Awards:** Ralph Gustafson award, 1965; Epstein award, 1966; E.J. Pratt Medal, 1966; President's Medal, University of Western Ontario, 1967; Canada Council grant, 1968, 1977; Governor-General's award, 1971, 1980; Canada-Australia prize, 1980; Booker McConnell prize, British Book Trust, and Governor General's award, 1992, for *The English Patient.* **Address:** Department of English, Glendon College, York University, 2275 Bayview Avenue, Toronto, Ontario M4N 3M6, Canada.

PUBLICATIONS

Poetry

The Dainty Monsters. Toronto, Coach House Press, 1967.
The Man with Seven Toes. Toronto, Coach House Press, 1969.
The Collected Works of Billy the Kid: Left Handed Poems. Toronto, Anansi, 1970; New York, Norton, 1974; London, Boyars, 1981.
Rat Jelly. Toronto, Coach House Press, 1973.
Elimination Dance. Ilderton, Ontario, Naim Coldstream, 1978; revised edition, Ilderton, Brick, 1980.
There's a Trick with a Knife I'm Learning to Do: Poems 1963–1978. Toronto, McClelland and Stewart, and New York, Norton, 1979; as *Rat Jelly and Other Poems 1963–1978,* London, Boyars, 1980.
Secular Love. Toronto, Coach House Press, 1984; New York, Norton, 1985.
Two Poems. Milwaukee, Woodland Pattern, 1986.
The Cinnamon Peeler: Selected Poems. London, Pan, 1989; New York, Knopf, 1992.
Handwriting. London, Bloomsbury, 1998; New York, Vintage, 2000.

Plays

The Collected Works of Billy the Kid (produced Stratford, Ontario, 1973; New York, 1974; London, 1984).
Coming through Slaughter, adaptation of his own novel (produced Toronto, 1980).

Novels

Coming through Slaughter. Toronto, Anansi, 1976; New York, Norton, 1977; London, Boyars, 1979.
In the Skin of a Lion. Toronto, McClelland and Stewart, New York, Knopf, and London, Secker and Warburg, 1987.
The English Patient. London, Picador, 1992.
Anil's Ghost. Toronto, McClelland and Stewart, New York, Knopf, and London, Bloomsbury, 2000.

Other

Leonard Cohen. Toronto, McClelland and Stewart, 1970.
Claude Glass. Toronto, Coach House Press, 1979.
Tin Roof. Lantzville, British Columbia, Island, 1982.
Running in the Family. Toronto, McClelland and Stewart, and New York, Norton, 1982; London, Gollancz, 1983.

Editor, *The Broken Ark* (animal verse). Toronto, Oberon Press, 1971; revised edition, as *A Book of Beasts,* 1979.
Editor, *Personal Fictions: Stories by Munro, Wiebe, Thomas, and Blaise.* Toronto, Oxford University Press, 1977.
Editor, *The Long Poem Anthology.* Toronto, Coach House Press, 1979.
Editor, with Russell Banks and David Young, *Brushes with Greatness: An Anthology of Chance Encounters with Greatness.* Toronto, Coach House Press, 1989.
Editor, with Linda Spalding, *The Brick Anthology.* Toronto, Coach House Press. 1989.
Editor, *The Faber Book of Contemporary Canadian Short Stories.* London, Faber, 1990.
Editor, *From Ink Lake: An Anthology of Canadian Short Stories.* New York, Viking, 1990.
Editor, with B.P. Nichol and George Bowering, *An H in the Heart: A Reader.* Toronto, McClelland and Stewart, 1994.

*

Manuscript Collection: National Archives, Ottawa; Metropolitan Toronto Library.

Critical Studies: *Spider Blues: Essays on Michael Ondaatje* edited by Sam Solecki, Montreal, Véhicule Press, 1985; *The Other Side of Dailiness: Photography in the Works of Alice Munro, Timothy Findley, Michael Ondaatje, and Margaret Laurence* by Lorraine M. York, Toronto, ECW Press, 1988; ''Outlaw and Explorer: Recent Adventurers in the English-Canadian Long Poem'' by Robert A. Kelly, in *Antigonish Review* (Antigonish, Nova Scotia), 79, autumn 1989; ''Michael Ondaatje and the Problem of History'' in *CLIO* (Fort Wayne, Indiana), 19(2), winter 1990; ''Michael Ondaatje and the Production of Myth'' by George Elliott Clarke, in *Studies in Canadian Literature* (Fredericton, New Brunswick), 16(1), 1991; '''The Widening Rise of Surprise': Containment and Transgression in the Poetry of Michael Ondaatje'' by Ajay Heble, in *Wascana Review of Contemporary Poetry and Short Fiction* (Regina, Saskatchewan), 26(1–2), spring-fall 1991; ''Coming through the Spider's Web: Ondaatje's Murderous Metaphors'' by Edward Parkinson, in *Signature,* 5, summer 1991; '''Sri Lankan' Canadian Poets: The Bourgeoisie That Fled the Revolution'' by Suwanda H.J. Sugunasiri, in *Canadian Literature* (Vancouver, British Columbia), 132, spring 1992; *Michael Ondaatje* by Douglas Barbour, New York, Twayne, 1993; *Discoveries of the Other: Alterity in the Work of Leonard Cohen, Hubert Aquin, Michael Ondaatje, and Nicole Brossard* by Winfried Siemerling, Toronto, University of Toronto Press, 1994; ''Postmodern Canadian Autobiography: Daphne Marlatt's 'How Hug a Stone' and Michael Ondaatje's 'Running in the Family''' by Annette Lonnecke, in *The Guises of Canadian Diversity: New European Perspectives,* edited by Serge Jaumain and Marc Maufort, Amsterdam, Rodopi, 1995; '''Fears of Primitive Otherness': 'Race' in Michael Ondaatje's 'The Man with Seven Toes''' by Gerry

Turcotte, in *Constructions of Colonialism: Perspectives on Eliza Fraser's Shipwreck,* edited by Ian J. McNiven and others, London, Leicester University Press, 1998.

Theatrical Activities: Director: **Films**—*Sons of Captain Poetry,* 1971; *Carry on Crime and Punishment,* 1972; *Royal Canadian Hounds,* 1973; *The Clinton Special,* 1974.

*   *   *

It is ironic that Michael Ondaatje is a writer who exemplifies every aspect of the Whitman tradition in American poetry, for he is a Canadian writer, though once removed, since he was born and spent his boyhood in Ceylon (now Sri Lanka). His exotic story is told in a work of prose, *Running in the Family,* which most people read as if it were poetry. Indeed, Ondaatje is a melting pot of techniques, and his work, as Whitman said of his own, ''contains multitudes.''

Ondaatje's writing can take the form of intense lyric poems, as in ''Kim at Half an Inch'':

Brain is numbed
is body touch
and smell, warped light

hooked so close
her left eye
is only a golden blur
her ear a vast
musical instrument of flesh

The moon spills off my shoulder
slides into her face

It also can look like prose but work as poetic language and the retelling or making of myth, as does what is perhaps his best-known book, *The Collected Works of Billy the Kid,* which won the Governor-General's award in 1971. Moving in and out of imagined landscape, portrait and documentary, and anecdote and legend, Ondaatje writes for the eye and the ear simultaneously. A critic reviewing his work for *Books in Canada* in 1982 said that ''each new book of Michael Ondaatje's seems wholly different from those that preceded it, and wholly the same ... the characters keep outgrowing the confines of fact.''

Like Whitman, Ondaatje is a writer of democratic vistas. He is fascinated by the lives of common people who do uncommon things, such as Billy the Kid, or figures from the world of jazz like Buddy Bolden, the subject of *Coming through Slaughter.* His own family seems impersonally related to him, as with Whitman's eye he sees equally both the large and the small, the close and the distant. Also like Whitman, he is fascinated by the taboos and peculiarities that combine to give him a voice that is unique but also universal.

Unlike Whitman, however, Ondaatje has a dark, witty side that makes his poetic voice irreverent, though rarely abrasive. His language alternates between the short lines of lyric verse and the long lines that actually become prose or prose poetry. His work lends itself to theater, and he has made several films as well. Yet his identity is as a poet, for it is the voice that is central in Ondaatje's work, a voice giving him control over both interiors and exteriors, as in these lines from *The Collected Works of Billy the Kid:*

I am here with the range for everything
corpuscle muscle hair
hands that need the rub of metal
those senses that
that want to crash things with an axe
that listen to deep buried veins in our palms
those who move in dreams over your women night
near you, every paw, the invisible hooves
the mind's invisible blackout the intricate never
the body's waiting rut.

What Ondaatje also possesses is a gift to draw on the myths of American culture in such a way that the reader can understand the depth of common experience. From a young outlaw of the American West to a strange, neurasthenic New Orleans jazz trumpet player to his eccentric relatives with their pet cobra warming itself on the radio in Sri Lanka, Ondaatje writes with lyric intensity about the differences we all share.

—Diane Wakoski

ORMSBY, Frank

Nationality: Irish. **Born:** Enniskillen, County Fermanagh, Northern Ireland, 30 October 1947. **Education:** Queen's University, Belfast, 1966–71, B.A. 1970, M.A. 1971. **Career:** Editor, *Honest Ulsterman* magazine, Belfast, 1969–89. Since 1971 Teacher of English, Royal Belfast Academical Institution. **Awards:** Eric Gregory award, 1974; Cultural Traditions award, 1992. **Address:** 70 Eglantine Avenue, Belfast BT9 6DY, Northern Ireland.

PUBLICATIONS

Poetry

Ripe for Company. Belfast, Ulsterman, 1971.
Business As Usual. Belfast, Ulsterman, 1973.
A Store of Candles. London, Oxford University Press, 1977.
Being Walked by a Dog. Belfast, Ulsterman, 1978.
A Northern Spring. London, Secker and Warburg, 1986.
The Ghost Train. Oldcastle, Ireland, Gallery, 1995.

Other

Editor, *Poets from the North of Ireland.* Belfast, Blackstaff Press, 1979.
Editor, *Northern Windows: An Anthology of Ulster Autobiography.* Belfast, Blackstaff Press, 1987.
Editor, *The Long Embrace: Twentieth-Century Irish Love Poems.* Belfast, Blackstaff Press, 1987; Boston, Faber, 1989.
Editor, *Thine in Storm and Calm: An Amanda McKittrick Ros Reader.* Belfast, Blackstaff Press, 1988.
Editor, *The Collected Poems of John Hewitt.* Belfast, Blackstaff Press, 1991.
Editor, *A Rage for Order: Poetry of the Northern Ireland Troubles.* Belfast, Blackstaff Press, 1992.

*

Critical Study: "The Permanent City: The Younger Irish Poets" by Gerald Dawe, in *The Irish Writer and the City,* edited by Maurice Harmon, Gerrards Cross, Buckinghamshire, Smythe, and Totowa, New Jersey, Barnes and Noble, 1984.

* * *

Frank Ormsby, like several of his Northern Irish contemporaries, cultivates the seeing eye. One cannot help but admire the precision of phrase that defines a neighbor in terms of his childless yard, that finds delight in a circular flower bed made out of an old tire, or that, as in "The Barracks," sees the official garnishing of a police station in terms of an ordinary garden:

The woman tending flowers bends her head
At work on the lupins. Elsewhere the beds
Are weeded. Turned-up soil darkens the edge
Of lawn and plastered wall. The chipped hedge
at the rear might be suburban . . .

Ormsby is at work on the lupins and also on the massage parlor, the police museum, and the air raid shelter. He is industrious in his attempts to compose a landscape with figures and not only in the poem of that name:

What haunts me is a farmhouse among trees
Seen from a bus window, a girl
With a suitcase climbing a long hill
And a woman waiting . . .

At first it seems as though the poems exist for the things seen. Certainly Ormsby has a determined faithfulness to his subjects that almost entails a rejection of what used to be called "verbal magic." Individual poems yield up their attractions reluctantly. Nevertheless, a personality emerges from the composite, certainly dour and grimly honest, but refreshingly so.

At times Ormsby can be quite moving, as in "In Memoriam":

Father, I'm forgetting you. Mind struggles
With the smudge of ten years, that shadow loitering
Off focus. Squat as a tumulus, you've gone
To ground.

Also moving are poems about his mother and about marriage, and the insight in these poems does much to mitigate what might otherwise seem an occasional gaucherie.

Ormsby certainly has the virtues of prose, especially clarity and particularity, but these also are qualities of poetry. The writer is his own best critic when he takes the title of his first collection, *A Store of Candles,* from a phrase in a poem called "Under the Stairs." Under the stairs he finds the usual jumble of a life's progress—the shaft of a broom, a tire, assorted nails. He also finds that which, however modestly, can illumine the jumble: "a store of candles for when the light fails."

Ormsby built upon this perceptiveness in his second collection, *A Northern Spring.* It is dominated by a sequence of soliloquies and lyrics feigned to be spoken by American soldiers in World War II. There are glimpses of the homeland left behind, of a death in a country lane near Argentan and of one in the "bocage," of a burial, of a padre with his big Norton pummeling the back roads, of maimed civilians on the road to Pont-l'Abbé and at Isigny, and of nearly losing the war:

> Parachuting after dark, I almost drowned
> in the Vire estuary.
> Stumbled half the night
> through woods, cornfields, clover, country lanes,
> so far off course the maps were useless . . .

It is all precise, glum, low power, very much like the Ulster poems of the first book or, indeed, like this: "My careful life says: 'No surrender. / Not an inch.'" One wonders if Ormsby is capable of instilling that essential spark of drama, turning his soliloquies into dramatic monologues, for instance, with the implied activity of an interlocutor.

Ormsby is certainly a writer of more than ordinary competence. There are moving poems about his father in his third collection, *The Ghost Train,* and, with an unexpected tenderness in so habitually stern a poet, about his honeymoon in Paris: "Your face grows secret and lovely. It is a face / of many fathoms in this time and place." He should not be categorized as a lesser Derek Mahon or Michael Longley, his elder contemporaries from Northern Ireland. As the efficient editor of the *Honest Ulsterman* and of several anthologies, Ormsby has shown himself capable of sympathies more wide-ranging than would be suggested by his oeuvre. Nonetheless, he is the author of an impressive body of work.

—Philip Hobsbaum

ORR, Gregory (Simpson)

Nationality: American. **Born:** Albany, New York, 3 February 1947. **Education:** Hamilton College, Clinton, New York, 1964–66; Antioch College, Yellow Springs, Ohio, 1966–69, B.A. 1969; Columbia University, New York, 1969–72, M.F.A. 1972. **Family:** Married Trisha Winer in 1973; two daughters. **Career:** Junior fellow, University of Michigan, Ann Arbor, 1972–75; assistant professor, 1975–80, associate professor, 1980–88, and since 1988 professor of English, University of Virginia, Charlottesville; visiting writer, University of Hawaii, Manoa, fall 1982. Since 1976 poetry consultant, *Virginia Quarterly Review,* Charlottesville. **Awards:** YM-YWHA Discovery award, 1970; Academy of American Poets prize, 1970; Bread Loaf Writers Conference *Transatlantic Review* award, 1976; Guggenheim fellowship, 1977; National Endowment for the Arts fellowship, 1978, 1989; Fulbright grant, 1983. **Address:** Department of English, University of Virginia, Charlottesville, Virginia 22903, U.S.A.

PUBLICATIONS

Poetry

Burning the Empty Nests. New York, Harper, 1973.
Gathering the Bones Together. New York, Harper, 1975.
Salt Wings. Charlottesville, Virginia, Poetry East, 1980.
The Red House. New York, Harper, 1980.

We Must Make a Kingdom of It. Middletown, Connecticut, Wesleyan University Press, 1986.
New and Selected Poems. Middletown, Connecticut, Wesleyan University Press, 1988.
City of Salt. Pittsburgh, University of Pittsburgh Press, 1995.
Orpheus and Eurydice. Port Townsend, Washington, Copper Canyon Press, 2000.

Other

Stanley Kunitz: An Introduction to the Poetry. New York, Columbia University Press, 1985.
Richer Entanglements: Essays and Notes on Poetry and Poems. Ann Arbor, Michigan, University of Michigan Press, 1993.

Editor, with Ellen Bryant Voigt, *Poets Teaching Poets.* Ann Arbor, University of Michigan Press, 1996.

*

Critical Studies: "Transparency and Prophecy" by Greg Kohl, in *American Poetry Review 4* (Philadelphia), no. 4, 1975; "Silence, Surrealism, and Allegory" by Alan Williamson, in *Kayak 40* (Santa Cruz, California), November 1975; "On Gregory Orr" by Hank Lazer, in *Iowa Review* (Iowa City), winter 1981; "Falling and Returning: The Poetry of Gregory Orr," in *Pequod 15* (New York), 1983, and *Out of the Sixties: Storytelling and the Vietnam Generation* (chapter on survival), New York, Cambridge University Press, 1993, both by David Wyatt; interview with Sean Thomas Dougherty, in *Salt Hill Journal* (Syracuse, New York), 4, 1997; interview by Alan DeNiro, in *Artful Dodge,* 32–33, 1998.

*   *   *

The poetry of Gregory Orr attempts to come to terms with the facts of death and life. When he was twelve, he accidentally shot and killed his eight-year-old brother in a hunting accident. A few years later his mother died suddenly and unexpectedly. Both are episodes with which he has had to come to terms. Peter Orr's death is exorcised in the 1975 sequence *Gathering the Bones Together.* The painful memories persist in such poems as "After a Death" and "Driving Home after a Funeral," which are collected with more pleasant and varied Wordsworthian (or Roethkean) memories of boyhood in a sequence called *The Red House.* Many other poems draw upon the fatally paired events of his youth, and he was still dealing with them in his 1988 prose poem "The Mother."

Orr's work, however, does not reflect the kind of psychological damage or obsession that we would associate with, say, Conrad Aiken or John Berryman. He has more affinities with Stanley Kunitz, about whom he has written a book-length study. His poems have a similar burning intensity, a compactness of language, and that wise placement of a striking image that mark Kunitz's most memorable poems. While Kunitz searched for his absent and elusive father, Orr seeks to confront the pain arising from the deaths of his brother and mother. But there is also what he called in an interview the question of "whether you experience the illusion of change and growth or whether there is some self that persists," what Kunitz calls a "principle of being." This sense of change versus selfhood is central to Orr's search for a way out of a potentially crippling youthful experience toward the renewed innocence of an emotionally integrated adult. Orr's poetic career thus moves from the demons of his haunted memories to a more confident and assured sense of himself as teacher, husband, and poet.

In spite of his numerous poems about death, Orr is not a grim or tragic poet. He has at least three other strings to his lyre: a gentle wit, a love of nature, and a recurring interest in sexual desire. The subject of desire is in fact woven through Orr's poems, and he explores it in reminiscences of sexual encounters with his wife, as in "Nantucket Morning/This World," "A Storm in March," and, most memorably, "Coming Down from Volcano." His settings are varied, and they understandably reflect the places of his own life—the Hudson Valley of his boyhood, Alabama of the 1965 freedom rides, Hawaii, Virginia, Italy, Yugoslavia. He also has explored the looser and freer form of the prose poem, and he included five new ones in the 1988 *New and Selected Poems*. The poems are flatly but sharply told in a voice slightly wry, slightly wondering. His taste for the surrealistic, already seen in his earlier work, is given room to flourish in a medium that invites free association, as in "Padua," where his thoughts move disconcertingly but seamlessly from the murder of Aldo Moro to the sculptures of Donatello, to the preserved tongue of Saint Anthony, to an American-style jeans boutique.

Orr's imagery is often sexually charged, as it is at the end of "Nantucket Morning/This World," a poem in which he finds a heaven on earth through sexual love: "On a bed / of needles, an upturned scallop / shell, its fluted rim lipped with dew." And he often finds the image that mingles life and physical corruption. In the dedication of the 1986 volume to Trisha, his wife, Orr writes,

> The truth's in myth not fact,
> a story fragment or an act
> that lasts and stands for all:
> how bees made honey in a skull

While he says in "Amor as a God of Death on Roman Stone Coffins" that "it's morbid to confuse the mysteries of sex and death," Orr nevertheless does so deliberately in "A Storm in March," in which he describes "man / and wife coupling / above their own dust / on the carved Etruscan tomb."

Orr once told an interviewer, "The analogue for my early work was the dream where the meaning is clear, not the dream that is misty and obscure. The kind of a dream that lets us wake up saying, 'I know that means something! There is some message in this to me.' Some crystallization of meaning." In the prose poem "Oysters" he writes, "What fascinates most, what compels imagination, can't be looked at directly, but only with averted eyes, as we gaze our fill in the mirror of art." Although one of Orr's strengths is looking at things directly, in many poems he employs the indirectness of dream, perhaps as a way to mitigate the pain of confronting reality and at the same time to plumb the psychological depths of his experience, as in "Spring Floods":

> In a muddy field
> an open coffin
> only I could see;
> it was a boat my mother
> sent to fetch me,
> just as she sent the flood.

> Water roiled so deeply
> who could calm it
> as she once did,
> laying her cool hand
> on my forehead in the dark
> room before sleep?

The most attractive things about Orr's poems are their utter honesty and directness, their refreshing lack of pretension, their flashes of humor, their occasional Roethkean flashes of mystical vision in nature, and their frank, sensitive, and circumspect treatments of sexual love, sometimes set against a background of death and dissolution.

Orr is a poet who has achieved an equilibrium. He has had to battle his childhood experiences and in order to do so has had to confront them. These traumatic events are the material, perhaps even the reason, for his poems. Yet they are not formless cries of anguish; they are finished poems. As he writes in "Oysters," "We need borders and forms to contain the terror we feel but don't understand."

—Donald Barlow Stauffer

ORTIZ, Simon J.

Nationality: American (American Indian: Acoma Pueblo). **Born:** Albuquerque, New Mexico, 27 May 1941. **Education:** Fort Lewis College, Durango, Colorado, 1962–63; University of New Mexico, Albuquerque, 1966–68; University of Iowa, Iowa City (International Writing Fellow), 1968–69. **Military Service:** U.S. Army. **Family:** Married Marlene Foster in 1981 (divorced 1984); three children. **Career:** Public relations consultant, Rough Rock Demonstration School, Arizona, 1969–70, and National Indian Youth Council, Albuquerque, 1970–73; taught at San Diego State University, California, 1974, Institute of American Arts, Santa Fe, New Mexico, 1974, Navajo Community College, Tsaile, Arizona, summers 1975–77, College of Marin, Kentfield, California, 1976–79, University of New Mexico, 1979–81, Sinte Gleska College, Mission, South Dakota, 1985–86, and Lewis and Clark College, Portland, Oregon, 1990. Editor, *Quetzal,* Chinle, Arizona, 1970–73. Since 1982 consulting editor, Pueblo of Acoma Press. **Awards:** National Endowment for the Arts grant, 1969, 1982. **Address:** 308 Sesame S.W., Albuquerque, New Mexico 87105, U.S.A.

PUBLICATIONS

Poetry

Naked in the Wind. Pembroke, North Carolina, Quetzal Vhio Press, 1970.
Going for the Rain. New York, Harper, 1976.
A Good Journey. Berkeley, California, Turtle Island Press, 1977.
Song, Poetry, Language. Tsaile, Arizona, Navajo Community College Press, 1978.

From Sand Creek: Rising in This Heart Which Is Our America. New York, Thunder's Mouth Press, 1981.

A Poem Is a Journey. Bourbanais, Illinois, Pternandon Press, 1981.

Short Stories

Howbah Indians. Tucson, Blue Moon Press, 1978.

Fightin': New and Collected Stories. New York, Thunder's Mouth Press, 1983.

Men on the Moon: Collected Short Stories. Tucson, University of Arizona Press, 1999.

Other

The People Shall Continue (for children). San Francisco, Children's Press, 1977.

Fightback: For the Sake of the People, For the Sake of the Land. Albuquerque, University of New Mexico Native American Studies, 1980.

Blue and Red (for children). Acoma, New Mexico, Pueblo of Acoma Press, 1982.

The Importance of Childhood. Acoma, New Mexico, Pueblo of Acoma Press, 1982.

The People Shall Continue. San Francisco, Children's Book Press, 1988.

Chaco Canyon: A Center and Its World, with others. Santa Fe, Museum of New Mexico Press, 1994.

Woven Stone. Tucson, University of Arizona Press, 1992.

After and Before the Lightning. Tucson, University of Arizona Press, 1994.

Editor, with Rudolfo A. Anaya, *A Ceremony of Brotherhood 1680–1980.* Albuquerque, Academia, 1981.

Editor, *Earth Power Coming.* Tsiale, Arizona, Navajo Community College Press, 1983.

Editor, *These Hearts, These Poems.* Acoma, New Mexico, Pueblo of Acoma Press, 1984.

Editor, *Speaking for the Generations: Native Writers on Writing.* Tucson, University of Arizona Press, 1998.

*

Critical Studies: By Willard Gingerich, in *Fiction International* (San Diego, California), 1983; "Common Walls: The Poetry of Simon Ortiz" by Kenneth Lincoln, in *The Colphin 9* (Aarhus, Denmark), 1984; "The Ethnic Imagination: A Case History" by Dennis Hoilman, in *Canadian Journal of Native Studies,* 5(2), 1985; *Simon Ortiz* by Andrew Wiget, Boise, Boise State University, 1986; "Simon Ortiz: The Poet and His Landscape" by William Oandasan, in *Studies in American Indian Literatures* (Richmond, Virginia), 11, 1987; "Luci Tapahonso and Simon Ortiz: Allegory, Symbol, Language, Poetry" by Dean Rader, in *Southwestern American Literature,* 22(2), spring 1997; interview with Mary Lindroth and Kathleen Anderson, in *Speaking of the Short Story: Interviews with Contemporary Writers,* edited by Farhat Iftekharuddin and others, Jackson, University Press of Mississippi, 1997; by Marie-Madeleine Schein, in *Updating the Literary West,* Fort Worth, Texas, Western Literature Association, 1997; "Toward an Ecology of Justice: Transformative Ecological Theory and Practice" by Joni Adamson Clarke, in *Reading the Earth: New Directions in the Study of Literature and Environment,* edited by Michael P. Branch and others, Moscow, University of Idaho Press, 1998.

Simon J. Ortiz comments:

My writing, mostly using the tradition of Native American oral narrative, is a stand within the storm that is America. The wind will change; there will be calm.

* * *

The poetry of Simon J. Ortiz is a powerful and moving record of a Native American who is an alien in his own land. In "A Designated National Park," he writes, "This morning, / I have to buy a permit to get back home." The preface to *A Good Journey,* the most important collection of his work, is an excerpt from an interview. Ortiz is asked, "Why do you write? Whom do you write for?" He replies, "Because Indians always tell a story. The only way to continue is to tell a story and that's what Coyote says . . . Your children will not survive unless you tell something about them—how they were born, how they came to this certain place, how they continue."

In "Notes for My Child" Ortiz tells his daughter how she was born, and in the context of his other work—in which his native tradition asserts itself most tellingly in the ritualization of significant events—it is a bemused but good-humored account of an encounter with the impersonality of a hospital. Many of his poems also are about coming to certain places. His sense of place is always precise, and even when he is in relatively unfamiliar territory, he is able to locate himself in human geography. Above all, however, his are poems of continuance. Ortiz has a confidence that things will go on, a confidence that no Euro-American, I expect, has ever been able to feel, and this assurance informs all of his work.

The fundamental strata of *A Good Journey* are storytelling and prayer. Even in the poems that deal with the confusion, ugliness, and impersonality of modern American life—"Burning River," for example—the memory of the timeless rituals serves as an orientation. In some ways, of course, the original sources are as lost to him as they are to other Americans. "The prayers of my native selfhood," he writes, "have been strangled in my throat." Some of the more self-consciously traditional poems, such as "Telling about Coyote," in which Coyote is "the existential man, Dostoevsky Coyote," suffer from the paradox inherent in any attempt to restore a lost tradition. It is, of course, the lack of self-consciousness that makes the tradition most attractive. In poems like "Earth and Rain, The Plants and Sun," "Canyon de Chelly," "Apache Love," "Vision Shadows," and "When It Was Taking Place," Ortiz gives us some of the most complete articulations to be found in English of the consciousness that swells in proximity with the eternity that ritual makes manifest.

Ortiz should not be read as a specimen Native American or as an anthropological curiosity. He is, above all, an American poet and a very good one. Neither his loss of orientation in the Los Angeles airport nor his obvious enthusiasm for the variety and drama of American geography is uniquely Native American. Lines such as these might be envied by any poet: "And the immensity of the place / settles upon me without weight. / I knew that we were near / one of the certain places / that is the center of the center."

—Don Byrd

O'SULLIVAN, Vincent (Gerard)

Nationality: New Zealander. **Born:** Auckland, 28 September 1937. **Education:** University of Auckland, M.A. 1959; Lincoln College, Oxford, B.Litt. 1962. **Family:** Married. **Career:** Formerly lecturer, Victoria University, Wellington, and reader, Waikato University, Hamilton; visiting fellow, Yale University, New Haven, Connecticut, 1976; writer-in-residence, Victoria University, 1981, University of Tasmania, Hobart, 1982, and Deakin University, Geelong, Victoria, 1982; playwright-in-residence, Downstage Theatre, Wellington, 1983; editor, *Comment,* Wellington, 1963–66; literary editor, *New Zealand Listener,* Wellington, 1978–79. **Awards:** Commonwealth scholarship, 1960; Macmillan Brown prize, 1961; Jessie MacKay award, 1965; Farmers poetry prize, 1967, 1971; Fulbright award, 176; Wattie Book award, 1979; New Zealand Book award, 1981. **Address:** Pukeroro, R.D. 3, Hamilton, New Zealand.

PUBLICATIONS

Poetry

Our Burning Time. Wellington, Prometheus, 1965.
Revenants. Wellington, Prometheus, 1969.
Bearings. Wellington and London, Oxford University Press, 1973.
From the Indian Funeral. Dunedin, McIndoe, 1976.
Butcher & Co. Wellington, Oxford University Press, 1976; London, Oxford University Press, 1978.
Brother Jonathan, Brother Kafka. Wellington and Oxford, Oxford University Press, 1980.
The Rose Ballroom and Other Poems. Dunedin, McIndoe, 1982.
The Butcher Papers. Auckland, Oxford University Press, 1982.
The Pilate Tapes. Auckland, Oxford University Press, 1986.
Selected Poems. Auckland and New York, Oxford University Press, 1992.
Houses of Sin. New York, Woodstock Books, 1995.
Seeing You Asked. Wellington, Victoria University Press, 1998.

Plays

Shuriken. Wellington, Victoria University Press, 1985.
Jones and Jones. Wellington, Victoria University Press, 1989.
Billy. Wellington, Victoria University Press, 1990.

Novel

Miracle: A Romance. Dunedin, McIndoe, 1976.

Short Stories

The Boy, the Bridge, the River. Dunedin, McIndoe, 1978.
Dandy Edison for Lunch and Other Stories. Dunedin, McIndoe, 1981.
The Nest Room. Edinburgh, Tragara Press, 1988.
Master of Fallen Years. Edinburgh, Tragara Press, 1990.
The Snow in Spain: Short Stories. Wellington, Allen and Unwin, 1990.
Palms and Minarets: Selected Stories. Wellington, Victoria University Press, 1992.
Let the River Stand. Auckland and New York, Penguin, 1993.

Other

New Zealand Poetry in the Sixties. Wellington, Department of Education, 1973.
Katherine Mansfield's New Zealand. Melbourne, Lloyd O'Neal, 1974; London, Muller, 1975.
James K. Baxter. Wellington, Oxford University Press, 1976; London, Oxford University Press, 1977.
Finding the Pattern, Solving the Problem: Katherine Mansfield the New Zealand European (lecture). Wellington, Victoria University Press, 1989.
Selected Letters/Vincent O'Sullivan. Loanhead, Tragara Press, 1993.
Believers to the Bright Coast. Aucland, Penguin, 1998.

Editor, *An Anthology of Twentieth-Century New Zealand Poetry.* London, Oxford University Press, 1970; revised edition, Wellington and London, Oxford University Press, 1976; revised edition, 1987.
Editor, *New Zealand Short Stories 3.* Wellington, Oxford University Press, 1975; London, Oxford University Press, 1976.
Editor, *The Aloe, with Prelude,* by Katherine Mansfield. Wellington, Port Nicholson Press, 1982; Manchester, Carcanet, and Atlantic Highlands, New Jersey, Humanities Press, 1983.
Editor, with M.P. Jackson, *New Zealand Writing since 1945.* Auckland, Oxford University Press, 1983.
Editor, with Margaret Scott, *The Collected Letters of Katherine Mansfield 1: 1903–1917.* Oxford and New York, Oxford University Press, 1984; 2: 1918–1919, 1987.
Editor, *Collected Poems,* by Ursula Bethell. Auckland, Oxford University Press, 1985.
Editor, *An Anthology of Twentieth Century New Zealand Poetry.* Auckland, Oxford University Press, 1987.
Editor, *Poems of Katherine Mansfield.* Auckland, Oxford University Press, 1988.
Editor, *Selected Letters,* by Katherine Mansfield. Oxford, Clarendon Press, 1989.
Editor, *New Zealand Stories,* by Katherine Mansfield. Auckland and New York, Oxford University Press, 1997.

*

Critical Studies: "Tragic Power in Vincent O'Sullivan's 'Shuriken'" by Phillip Mann, in *Australasian Drama Studies* (Queensland, Australia), 18, April 1991; "Re-Orienting Australian Drama: Staging Theatrical Irony" by Joanne Tompkins, in *ARIEL* (Calbary, Alberta), 25(4), October 1994; "Setting Allegory Adrift in John Ashbery's 'Mountains and Rivers,' James Joyce's 'Portrait of the Artist as a Young Man,' and Vincent O'Sullivan's 'Let the River Stand'" by Katrina Bachinger, in *Trends in English and American Studies: Literature and the Imagination,* edited by Sabine Coelsch-Foisner and others, Lewiston, New York, Mellen, 1996; by Antonella Sarti, in her *Spiritcarvers: Interviews with Eighteen Writers from New Zealand,* Amsterdam, Rodopi, 1998.

*   *   *

Despite the sheer gusto and figurative invention of his verse, Vincent O'Sullivan suffers on two counts—from being a New Zealander and from being an academic. As he said in his preface to a selection of New Zealand poetry, to be a New Zealander means to be burdened with the ''cultural penalty'' of dissociation from Europe and the search for self-definition. To be an academic means to know all of the skills in theory. O'Sullivan argues, however, that the gap between the uninformed heart, or reality, and the overinformed head, or technique, can be bridged in two ways: by the ''rigorous liberty'' allowed by the exiled condition, and by the adaptation of old forms, which is itself construction. O'Sullivan's occasional achievements by either avenue are memorable, but more often his poems fall into the wasteland between original autobiographical experience and borrowed or highly wrought belles lettres.

The clearest example of O'Sullivan's original success is his reworking of Greek myth: using common facts themselves for a striking image (Helen, ''who once had a town to read by''), dramatizing the characters' experience (Ulysses says, ''Lip me to silence then, true Penelope''), or twisting the story (the labyrinth is now within Theseus). At the other extreme is his beautiful lyric gift in reporting private experience, usually love (''You, your own leaven, knead perpetual myth''). When the poem is tied closely to a dramatic setting, as in ''Island Bay,'' the result is a perfect harmony of form and feeling. In this poem the poet recalls a love affair as he watches the red bus that carried him to their assignation, resolving to forget it all:

> But if the seventh, sacred wave rides higher by an inch . . .
> or the sky lightens, so much as with a match
> struck by some walker half a mile off . . .
> then all's unsaid. Reason walks the plank.
> We wait for a bus to drive out of the sea.

Too however, though, the objective correlative to the poet's emotion or imagery is insufficiently evoked, resulting in obscurity or rhetorical indulgence. The long sonnet sequence on the French engraver Charles Meryon tries to dramatize just this problem, the dangerous divorce of imagination from reality. Here reality is Meryon's vision of Paris, and his New Zealand experience is abandoned— ''Akaroa, the south, lay a hulk, a boyish error.'' Yet as O'Sullivan ably shows through his own art, New Zealand was the real ''in the way a hawk / over these hills can switch a sky to metal / for the stilled prcy.'' Thc allegorical mcaning is clear; O'Sullivan must begin with himself, ''the swan of the body,'' and not the seductive artifice of Yeats's embroidered coat—''Skin and bones are verbs, / and there's our crown.''

Masterly as O'Sullivan's gift is for the right image, the dramatic moment, and the colloquial expression, it is unfortunate that he rarely employs it. In the earlier poetry he is seduced by elegance (''Thc girl I'd talk of, she goes decked in this''); ''Limbs, Lady, Are Like Islands'' goes one ponderous title; and we find words like ''uniquest'' and ''unvintageable.'' In later work the problem is uninspired exposition, a feeling of forced writing, often redeemed only by a clever final line. A poem about archery ends with ''and when you close your eyes the bird-like drift of it,'' and a poem about a mad neighbor boarding a bus with ''the doors shut behind her like palace sluts.'' Even the title sequence from *Butcher & Co.,* featuring a Crow-like butcher who ''grizzles'' his knife on the stone, swamps his vulgar vitality with calculated images (''death, that perfect hinge'') and awkward metaphysics (''Power Sticks Says B. As the Fan Flings''). Brute Butcher reads the *Odyssey* instead of, as Bloom, being it.

Because of the gaudy juxtaposition of myth and reality in Central American life and because it is essentially a report on experience, *From the Indian Funeral* is remarkably successful. Here O'Sullivan

gives himself to his environment rather than to literature (''I am sick of the smooth ending''). As a New Zealander ''facing the world without myth,'' he borrows everyday imagery to re-create the American's world (''your next meal as planned for as a vacation'') and Aztec imagery to imply the poverty of his own (the tourists dine by a statue of an Aztec ''whose god ate time'').

When O'Sullivan simply assumes his undeniable skill at adapting other myths and symbols and like his mentor Yeats ''lies down in the foul rag and bone shop of the heart'' to take the ''rigorous liberty'' of communicating his own experience, then his words ''are out and hunting.'' Too often, however, his poetry has been impenetrably private, philosophically abstruse, or forgettably occasional, like the girls in *Revenants* who merely have ''bartered talk.''

O'Sullivan later came to concentrate on fiction and drama. His subsequent volumes of poetry include *The Butcher Papers,* which refines the character of Butcher in a series of telegraphic playlets and monologues (''*the 20th Century, sport, that's the age of the Meat Man*'') that finally prove tedious in their elliptical philosophizing. *The Rose Ballroom* contains poems that expand in more congenial terms the poet's epistemological and metaphysical bent, and *The Pilate Tapes* is a kind of latter-day version of the Christ story told mostly from the perspective of Pilate:

> *Ecce!* his fingers tinker on the cosmic
>   pulse. Mr Pilate is still
> receiving. *Ergo,* still transmits.

—David Dowling

OSUNDARE, Niyi

Nationality: Nigerian. **Born:** Oluwaniyi Osundare, Ikerri, 12 March 1947. **Education:** University of Ibadan, B.A. (honors) in English 1972; University of Leeds, England, M.A. in English 1974; York University, Toronto, Canada, Ph.D. in English 1979. **Career:** Since 1982 lecturer, University of Ibadan. Taught at the University of Wisconsin and the University of New Orleans, 1990–92. **Awards:** Commonwealth Poetry prize, and Association of Nigerian Authors Poetry prize, both 1986, both for *The Eye of the Earth;* Cadbury Poetry prize, 1989; Fulbright scholarship, 1990, 1991; Noma prize, 1991, for *Waiting Laughters: A Long Song in Many Voices.* **Agent:** Heinemann Educational Books, Ighodaro Road Jericho, PMB 5205, Ibadan, Oyo State, Nigeria.

PUBLICATIONS

Poetry

Songs of the Marketplace. Ibadan, New Horn Press, 1983.
Village Voices. Ibadan, Evans Brothers, 1984.
A Nib in the Pond. Ife, University of Ife, 1986.
The Eye of the Earth. Ibadan, Heinemann Educational Books, 1986.
Moonsongs. Ibadan, Spectrum Books, 1988.
Songs of the Season. Ibadan, Heinemann Educational Books, 1990.
Waiting Laughters: A Long Song in Many Voices. Ikeja, Lagos, Malthouse Press, 1990.

Selected Poems. Oxford, Heinemann International Literature and Textbooks, 1992.

Midlife. Ibadan, Heinemann Educational Books, 1993.

Seize the Day and Other Poems for the Junior. Ibadan, Agbo Areo Publishers, 1995.

Horses of Memory. Ibadan, Heinemann Educational Books, 1998.

Pages from the Book of the Sun: New and Selected Poems. Trenton, New Jersey, Africa World Press, 2000.

Other

The Writer As Righter: The African Literary Artist and His Social Obligations. Ife, University of Ife, 1986.

African Literature and the Crisis of Post-Structuralist Theorising. Ibadan, Options Book and Information Service, 1993.

Thread in the Loom: Essays on African Literature and Culture. Trenton, New Jersey, Africa World Press, 2000.

*

Critical Studies: "New Trends in Nigerian Poetry: The Poetry of Niyi Osundare and Chinweizu," in *Literary Criterion* (Bangalore, India), 23(1–2), 1988, and "The Development of Niyi Osundare's Poetry: A Survey of Themes and Technique," in *Research in African Literatures* (Bloomington, Indiana), 26(4), winter 1995, both by Aderemi Bamikunle; "The Praxis of Niyi Osundare, Popular Scholar-Poet," in *World Literature Written in English* (Singapore), 29(1), spring 1989, and "A Peopled Persona: Autobiography, Postmodernism and the Poetry of Niyi Osundare," in *Genres Autobiographiques en Afrique,* edited by Janos Riesz and Ulla Schild, Berlin, Reimer, 1996, both by Stephen H. Arnold; "Orality and the Craft of Modern Nigerian Poetry: Osundare's 'Waiting Laughters' and Udechukwu's 'What the Madman Said,'" in *African Languages and Cultures* (Oxford, England), 7(2), 1994, and "Survival Strategies and the New Life of Orality in Nigerian and Ghanaian Poetry: Osundare's 'Waiting Laughters' and Anyidoho's 'Earthchild,'" in *Research in African Literatures* (Columbus, Ohio), 27(2), summer 1996, both by Ezenwa-Ohaeto; "Niyi Osundare and the Materialist Vision: A Study of 'The Eye of the Earth'" by Charles Bodunde, in *Ufahamu* (Los Angeles), 25(2), spring 1997; by Richard Taylor, in *Anglistik* (Wurzburg, Germany), 8(1), March 1997; "Folklore and the Primacy of National Liberation in 'Village Voices'" by Olusegin Adekoya, in *Commonwealth Essays and Studies* (Dijon, France), 20(2), spring 1998.

*   *   *

Describing himself as "a farmer born and a peasant bred," Oluwaniyi Osundare is the son of a father who was a drummer, an oral artist, and a farmer and a mother who was a dyer and weaver. His name literally means "God has honor; the Spirit of the river has vindicated my innocence." Also a dramatist, literary critic, scholar of linguistics, and political commentator, he reigns as Africa's most prolific and popular anglophone poet of the alternative (sometimes rendered "alter-native") tradition of the generation succeeding the founders of Nigerian verse in English—Wole Soyinka, Christopher Okigbo, and Gabriel Okara. Not only is he Africa's most public and selfless poet, he is also—after Soyinka—the most translated and honored, a profoundly rooted, local poet who is also a cosmopolitan much revered by a world audience. Among the awards testifying to

this are the Commonwealth Poetry prize, two Cadbury prizes for poetry (from the Association of Nigerian Authors), the Noma award (sponsored by the Japanese and equivalent to an African Nobel prize in literature), the Fonlon-Nichols award (African Literature Association), given for excellence in contributions to aesthetics and to the struggle for human rights, and honorary doctorates from French and American universities.

The range of themes in Osundare's volumes of poetry is vast, though they are primarily centered on social and ecological concerns, which is not surprising for an avowed socialist. Among his principal preoccupations are communality, generosity, hard work, perseverance in the face of adversity, African self-esteem, justice, frugality, respect for nature and the earth, a sense of beauty, and memory, especially the imperative of historical preservation. Being a "tabloid bard" has helped establish his popularity, and in the occasional poetry in his weekly newspaper column "Songs of the Season" satire is the most frequently encountered mode, with subtle subversion peaking out from nearly all of his lines. In his other work, however, Osundare creates composed volumes rather than collections, and reading individual poems in isolation from the totality of the books that contain them vitiates their potency.

Osundare also writes for younger readers, as, for example, in *Seize the Day* (1995), thus helping keep African poetic traditions alive and exposing his audiences to poetic strategies from non-African cultures. Though not necessarily influenced by them, Osundare shows affinities with Walt Whitman (in his use of free verse and in his vision and oracular emphasis on common people), Bertolt Brecht (in his mordant, sarcastic alterations of popular expressions), and Pablo Neruda (in tender, lyrical poems celebrating humble objects from trees to trains).

Because the venom Osundare sometimes injects into the veins of the dominant culture flows from "the fang of facts," an adequate understanding of many of his poems requires at least some knowledge of colonial and contemporary, or postcolonial (to him, neocolonial or recolonial), history. His poetic function is not only to be a rememberer but more importantly "a reminder." Nevertheless, he is not dogmatic about embracing clarity. For example, *Moonsongs* (1988), written during a long convalescence from an attempted assassination in 1987 in which he suffered blows to the head from an ax and was left for dead, has been described by many critics as "surreal." Yet its symbolism, though arcane, personal, and obscure, can be grasped with study.

The simplicity of the bulk of Osundare's poetic oeuvre is an illusion. He is not an anglophone African poet; he is a Yoruba poet who writes in English. No existing theory illuminates his work, but it can be illuminated. For those willing to make efforts to gain a modicum of competence in Yoruba, at least some of the new dimensions with which he gracefully endows poetry in English can be appreciated. To readers with no understanding of Yoruba, his verse is a beautiful grisaille. To use an analogy, the Yoruba elements in Osundare's poems lie beneath what appear to be English conventions in the way artistic watermarks in banknotes remain invisible unless a person knows how to look for them, what kind of light to hold them up to. Without such knowledge African poetry in English can seem diluted, simple, and deficient, when it actually is anything but that.

The easiest way to get a glimpse of the multivalent Yoruba nature of Osundare is to keep in mind that he is above all a performance poet, one who uses drums to generate tonal and rhythmic expectations in his audience and who frequently prefaces his poems with indications of musical instrumentation and forms to accompany the words. To Osundare, in keeping with Yoruba tradition, poetry is a speech-song continuum, with the audience's participation a given. (Call and response, as seen in the relationship between African-American preachers and their congregations, is routinely assumed by this poet.) Repetition of sounds is fundamental to Yoruba poetics, though not in the English or European style of rhyme, meter, alliteration, and assonance. There is a high incidence of onomatopoeia and parallelism, and Yoruba tonal and other structural patterns prevail. These musical patterns can be appreciated without being fully understood, despite the fact that they have semantic and narrative layers that are imperceptible to the untrained ear.

Likewise, the poetic forms employed by Osundare may not be obvious. Though he occasionally writes a ballad, a sonnet, or an ode and may even employ certain elements of English prosody, he prefers the conventions of *oriki* (praise poems), *ijala* (hunters' chants and work songs), and other Yoruba forms drawn from a deep well of fables, parables, lullabies, proverbs, riddles, and similar sources. Each of these has indigenous specifications, but he often alters them in a continual effort to dereify and defossilize concepts and language in the service of cultivating fresh thought, a new inner life, provocative and entertaining expression, and social activism.

There is a common thread of perceptual and ideological consistency running throughout Osundare's work. This ranges from the youthful poems of works such as *Village Voices* and *The Eye of the Earth*—all published by the mid-1980s—to transitional works such as *Moonsongs* and his more mature works beginning in the 1990s, including *Waiting Laughters* and *Horses of Memory*. But there is also a constant of experimentation and increasing reach seen in the poet's development. Over time the specific localities of early poems have dissolved into more general African and wider settings, extending Osundare's accessibility to a more universal audience.

As the critic Biodun Jeyifo wrote in the introduction to *Songs of the Marketplace,* in Osundare ''we confront both poetry of revolution and a revolution in poetry, in terms of forms and techniques.'' In less than two decades Osundare moved from being a mighty local force in African letters to being a poet of global stature.

—Stephen Arnold

OUTRAM, Richard (Daley)

Nationality: Canadian. **Born:** 1930. **Education:** Victoria College, University of Toronto. **Career:** Worked for the Canadian Broadcasting Corporation. **Awards:** Toronto Book award, 1999, for *Benedict Abroad.*

PUBLICATIONS

Poetry

Eight Poems. Toronto, Tortoise Press, 1959.
Exsultate, Jubilate. Toronto, Macmillan Company of Canada, 1966.
Creatures. Toronto, Gauntlet Press, 1972.
Seer. Toronto, Aliquando Press, 1973.
Thresholds. Toronto, Gauntlet Press, 1973.
Locus. Toronto, Gauntlet Press, 1974.

Turns and Other Poems. London, Chatto and Windus/Hogarth Press, 1975; Toronto, Anson-Cartwright Editions, 1976.
Arbor. Toronto, Gauntlet Press, 1976.
The Promise of Light. Toronto, Anson-Cartwright Editions, 1979.
Selected Poems: 1960–1980. Toronto, Exile Editions, 1984.
Man in Love. Erin, Ontario, Porcupine's Quill, 1985.
Hiram and Jenny. Erin, Ontario, Porcupine's Quill, 1988.
Mogul Recollected. Erin, Porcupine's Quill, 1993.
Around & About the Toronto Islands. Toronto, Gauntlet Press, 1993.
Hiram and Jenny—Unpublished Poems. Ottawa, Food for Thought Books, 1994.
Peripatetics. Toronto, Gauntlet Press, 1994.
Tradecraft. Toronto, Gauntlet Press, 1994.
Eros Descending. Toronto, Gauntlet Press, 1995.
Benedict Abroad. Toronto, St. Thomas Poetry Series, 1998.

*   *   *

Richard Outram is not used to making the headlines, but he did so in 1999 when he was named the recipient of the Toronto Book award. The award, with a cash prize of $10,000, marked the publication of the book *Benedict Abroad,* a series of poems about a typical Torontonian. The award gave rare public recognition to a poet who for more than four decades has continued to write his own idiosyncratic poems while paying scant attention to the misunderstandings of the public and the demands of the media. It is good to see talent and dedication honored.

Until now Outram's poetry has been more prized than praised, but there are indications that his work could reach a wider readership than it has had in the past. Limited editions of suites of his poems, beautifully designed and illustrated with wood engravings by his wife, the artist Barbara Howard, have appeared in private editions produced by the Tortoise, Gauntlet, Martlett, and Aliquando presses. Over the years the suites have been collected and reprinted in volumes that appear to be not so much stocktakings as statements made along the way.

If a single word encapsulates Outram's poetry it is ''metaphysical,'' for like the Metaphysical poets of seventeenth-century England he composes poems that are traditional in form, mainly metered and rhymed, bright and brief, lyrical in tone, celebratory in spirit, religious in nature, philosophic in attitude, and rich in contrasts, paradox, and wit. What prevails is a sense of self and a sense of self-imposed limits.

Outram has not wavered from his concerns since the publication of his first full book, *Exultate, Jubilate,* in 1966. Two of its poems epitomize themes characteristic of his work. The first is that of the magician, the second that of the master. References to magicians and escape artists and shamans appear in many of his books. The last stanza of ''Prestidigator'' brings the curtain down:

Padlock the stage
Door; and douse
The lights: this is
A dark house.

The magician is out of business but still in possession of his powers. The last lines of ''Djinn,'' about a mischievous spirit nearly released from its bottle, suggest that the poet may be seen to be a miracle worker, releasing the spirits, but that he is certainly not a free agent: ''(I shall be his master, Master; / He must do what I must ask!)''

Especially effective is the repetition and intensification of the word ''must.'' Outram's poetry was like this in the 1960s, and it is like this at the end of the century: allusive, subtle, and suggestive, if unfashionable.

The poem ''Escape Artist'' in *Turns and Other Poems* (1975) includes these lines, indicative of the poet's power with language:

> I learned to pick handily
> Locks of all known makes;
> To shatter the strongest links;
> To slip the most cunning snare
> That one could contrive . . .

Indeed, it is difficult to imagine anyone else writing or rewriting any of Outram's poems or slipping these cunningly contrived bonds. Who is imprisoning whom? The poet the reader? The expectation the subject matter? Fate the poet? ''Riddle'' in *The Promise of Light* (1979) suggests that there are phases or levels of freedom:

> Subtle on a simple ground;
> Always lost as I am found;
> If you would discover me,
> Then surrender & be free.

In the end everyone is discovered, redeemed. In form and content, in iambic lines and rhyming verses, there are echoes of vatic poets like William Blake and Jay Macpherson and perhaps a reverberation or two from a highly mannered poet like Robert Finch.

Selected Poems: 1960–1980 (1984) reprints eighty-three poems from the first phase of Outram's life and work. The tone is lyrical and celebratory, though certainly not in the manner of Christopher Smart or Walt Whitman. Outram is too much a schoolmaster for that. Indeed, there is something of the cleric to him, as many of the poems allude to a deeply felt Christian faith. For instance, ''In Praise of Poetry'' ends with ''and praying, being prayed.''

''Conjuror with Doves'' appears in *Man in Love* (1985), an illustrated collection that resembles an emblem book. Stage magicians produce doves that fly away, but evidence of their appearance remains:

> After, a single
> White evident feather drifts, settles
> Through silence, cherished.

Outram's later book-length collections have overriding themes of their own, akin to John Berryman's collections and W.B. Yeats's ''Crazy Jane'' suite. *Hiram and Jenny* (1988), which takes an affectionate peak at friends in a small Maritime town, brings to mind Edwin Lee Masters's *Spoon River Anthology*. Also set in the Maritimes is *Mogul Recollected* (1993), a series of poems about a circus elephant that drowned in 1836. The volume elicited the praise of Alberto Manguel: ''Richard Outram is one of the finest poets in the English language.'' Finally, *Benedict Abroad* (1998) has a Bech-like subject who is not only a Torontonian but also a ''man of the world.''

Outram is a man who measures and treasures his words. With each new poem, with each new book, he conjures up contrasts and paradoxes of a metaphysical and almost mystical nature that attest to an art and a craft worthy of admiration—and many more readers.

—John Robert Colombo

OWEN, Jan

Nationality: Australian. **Born:** Adelaide, South Australia, 18 August 1940. **Education:** University of Adelaide, 1958–62, 1974, B.A. 1963. **Family:** Married 1) Balazs Bajka in 1964 (divorced 1972), one son and one daughter; 2) Anthony Brown in 1972 (separated 1995), one son. **Career:** Laboratory assistant, Waite Institute, Adelaide, 1957–60; library assistant, 1961, librarian, 1962–64, 1966, Barr Smith Library, Adelaide; librarian, South Australian Institute of Technology Library, 1969–71, Salisbury College of Advanced Education Library, 1971–75, and Technical and Further Education College, Gillies Plains, 1981–84. Since 1985 creative writing teacher in schools, colleges, and universities throughout Australia. **Awards:** Ian Mudie award, 1982; Jessie Litchfield prize, 1984, for *Boy with a Telescope;* Grenfell Henry Lawson prize, 1985; Harri Jones Memorial prize, 1986, for *Boy with a Telescope;* Anne Elder award, 1986, for *Boy with a Telescope;* Mary Gilmore prize, 1987, for *Boy with a Telescope;* Wesley Michel Wright Poetry prize, 1992. **Agent:** Margaret Connolly, 17 Ormond Street, Paddington, New South Wales, Australia. **Address:** 14 Fern Road, Crafers, South Australia 5152, Australia.

PUBLICATIONS

Poetry

Boy with a Telescope. Sydney, Angus and Robertson, 1986.
Fingerprints on Light. Sydney, Angus and Robertson, 1990.
Blackberry Season. Canberra, Molongolo Press, 1993.
Night Rainbows. Melbourne, Heinemann, 1994.

*

Manuscript Collection: Australian Defence Force Academy (University of New South Wales), Canberra.

Critical Studies: ''Being Observant, Keeping Faith'' by Alan Gould, in *Quadrant* (Sydney), April 1995; interview with Jenny Digby, in *Island Magazine*, 65, 1995–96.

Jan Owen comments:

My poetry is lyrical for the most part but often with an ironical or humorous edge. Common themes are transience and loss, contradiction, the hidden or other; I am drawn to difference, to otherness, and to the implicit rather than the explicit, what is hidden within (not beneath) appearances. I would like to be able to say, ''Nothing alien is alien to me.'' So I write about the tiny and the faraway, stars and insects, other times and places. My subject matter is fairly wide and includes modern physics, math, and grammar, as well as exploration, war, art, trees, gemstones, domesticity, relationships, childhood. Imagination and perception come before introspection for me, and other people are perhaps the most common subject of all; the human psyche seems to infiltrate even poems on carnations, tektites, zippers, etc.

My early work has been called exuberant, philosophical, funny, but more recent work is darker in tone and subject matter, though humor is still evident; I am working on a manuscript of parodies at the moment.

I write in traditional rhymed forms—a lot of sonnets—as well as free verse. Sound is very important to me, and I think Plath, Roethke, Judith Wright were influences here, as well as the rhymes taught me as a child, the early Australian ballads, and poems such as Coleridge's "Ancient Mariner" read and learned at an early age. I admire the Australian poets Gwen Harwood and Les Murray, the Americans Galway Kinnell, Randall Jarrell, Frost, Ammons, and Sharon Olds, and the Eastern European poets Zbigniew Herbert, Miroslav Holub, and Wislawa Szymborska. Yehuda Amichai is also certainly a poet I hope to learn from.

It has been said that I write poems that deliberate, that I attempt to reconcile a thing's meaning with its being. According to Alan Gould I share with Plath and Hughes "the notion that a peculiarly rich ground for poetry is that which falls between the eye's capacity for precision and focus, and the intellect's knowledge that all significances, no matter how glittering, are unstable."

*   *   *

Jan Owen made an immediate impact on many of her fellow poets and contemporaries with her first collection, *Boy with a Telescope,* published in 1986. It received two of the important honors reserved for new poets in Australia—the Anne Elder prize and the Mary Gilmore award. Even before her first book, however, she had been noticed, and during the early 1980s she won several prizes for individual poems and was published regularly in journals and, later, anthologies. Many critics felt that her work, after the larrikin decade of the 1970s, represented a return to standards of craft and poise and a concern for subtlety and nuance. In the sometimes abrasive Australian poetry scene of the 1980s her work was hailed by Chris Wallace-Crabbe and others as evidence of a new generation of poets reaching maturity and writing without ostentation or gimmickry, something always regarded as dangerous in the local cultural environment, where laconism is more highly regarded than bravado.

Owen's second collection, *Fingerprints on Light* (1990), maintains the sensitivity to detail and concreteness of image that can resonate beyond itself. These qualities can be seen, for example, in "Digging Potatoes":

My grandfather turned the earth
all morning long in the skittery autumn sun
on the weedy patch by the stable wall,
stacking unsteady pyramids
of dirty dimpled knees in the bonfire air
while the tame-tease willy wagtail
skimmed the flung-up clods
and thought me a rival for witchetty grubs.

The ten-page sequence "Write to Me at Rochefort" displays Owen's ambition and willingness to work on a larger canvas. It is within a tradition well established in Australia, what is known as the voyager poem. Early navigators and Pacific explorers have inspired many poets since Kenneth Slessor's landmark "Five Visions of Captain Cook" (1931). Owen's poem is based on early French voyagers, and although it uses the devices of diary entries, letters, and impressionistic notes, it maintains her characteristic lyric tautness and

concludes with a reference to the Aborigines and their encounter with change. The use of Aboriginal words in the last section carries allusions to the earlier Jindyworobak movement of determined Australianism, as well as to the later, environmentally inspired attempt to reclaim a wider Australian heritage. The following lines are from "Eora Tribe":

Shaking their wings like this like this
like the clan of *Gareway* shaking their wings
over the place of Sting-rays shaking their feathers
those people pale as the moon *Yenadah*
folding their wings to the place of Sitting-Down
those people pale as bone
making the horns of *Yettadah* on their boughs
following running water looking for food
calling the earth *boodjeri*
calling the fire *boodjeri*
resting by *Jujabala*
resting in the place of Making Canoes.

The influence of Les Murray's "The Buledelah-Taree Holiday Song Cycle" (1976) is also evident here. (Murray's bucolic concerns may be thought to be evident in other of Owen's poems as well, though her own impeccable lyricism and sharpness identify her work more tellingly.)

Blackberry Season (1993), which offers a greater refinement in these qualities, was quickly followed by *Night Rainbows* (1994). The latter is a rich and varied collection that can move from the eight-poem sequence "Describing Words" (more frolicsome and virtuoso than Judith Wright's earlier sequence "Some Words") to a Christian nativity sequence ("This Marriage") and a skillfully wicked set of parodies on fellow Australian poets ("Impersonations"). The impression in this book is of energy, flow, release, and an increasingly flexible and vigorous craftsmanship. In her impressive corpus of work Owen has shown every sign of increasing mastery and outreach.

—Thomas W. Shapcott

OWENS, Rochelle

Nationality: American. **Born:** Brooklyn, New York, 2 April 1936. **Education:** Lafayette High School, Brooklyn, graduated 1953. **Family:** Married George Economou, *q.v.,* in 1962. **Career:** Worked as a clerk, typist, telephone operator; founding member, New York Theatre Strategy; visiting lecturer, University of California, San Diego, 1982; adjunct professor, and host of radio program *The Writer's Mind,* University of Oklahoma, Norman, 1984; distinguished writer-in-residence, Brown University, Providence, Rhode Island, and University of Southwestern Louisiana, 1997. **Awards:** Rockefeller grant, 1965, 1975; Ford grant, 1965; Creative Artists Public Service grant, 1966, 1973; Yale University School of Drama fellowship, 1968; Obie award, 1968, 1971, 1982; Guggenheim fellowship, 1971; National Endowment for the Arts grant, 1974; Villager award, 1982; New York Drama Critics Circle award, 1983; Fellowship, Rockefeller Foundation Bellagio Stucy Center, Italy. **Agent:** Dramatists Guild, 1501 Broadway, New York, New York 10036. **Address:** 1401 Magnolia, Norman, Oklahoma 73072, U.S.A.

PUBLICATIONS

Poetry

Not Be Essence That Cannot Be. New York, Trobar Press, 1961.
Four Young Lady Poets, with others, edited by LeRoi Jones. New York, Totem-Corinth, 1962.
Salt and Core. Los Angeles, Black Sparrow Press, 1968.
I Am the Babe of Joseph Stalin's Daughter. New York, Kulchur,1972.
Poems from Joe's Garage. Providence, Rhode Island, Burning Deck, 1973.
The Joe 82 Creation Poems. Los Angeles, Black Sparrow Press, 1974.
The Joe Chronicles 2. Santa Barbara, California, Black Sparrow Press, 1979.
Shemuel. St. Paul, New Rivers Press, 1979.
French Light. Norman, Oklahoma Press with the Flexible Voice, 1984.
Constructs. Norman, Oklahoma, Poetry Around, 1985.
Anthropologists at a Dinner Party. Tucson, Arizona, Chax Press, 1985.
W.C. Fields in French Light. New York, Contact II, 1986.
How Much Paint Does the Painting Need? New York, Kulchur, 1988.
Black Chalk. Norman, Oklahoma, Texture Press, 1992.
New and Selected Poems 1961–1988. New York, Contact, 1994.
Rubbed Stones: Poems from 1960–1992. Norman, Oklahoma, Texture Press, 1994.
New and Selected Poems: 1961–1996. San Diego, California, Junction Press, 1997.
LUCA: Discourse on Life & Death. San Diego, California, Junction Press, 2000.

Recordings: *A Reading of Primitive and Archaic Poetry,* with others, Broadside; *From a Shaman's Notebook,* with others, Broadside; *The Karl Marx Play,* Kilmarnock, 1975; *Totally Corrupt,* Giorno, 1976; *Black Box 17,* Watershed Foundation, 1979.

Plays

Futz (produced Minneapolis, 1965; New York, Edinburgh, and London, 1967). New York, Hawk's Well Press, 1961; revised version in *Futz and What Came After,* 1968, in *New Short Plays 2,* London, Methuen, 1969.
The String Game (produced New York, 1965). Included in *Futz and What Came After,* 1968.
Istanboul (produced New York, 1965; London, 1982). Included in *Futz and What Came After,* 1968.
Homo (produced Stockholm and New York, 1966; London, 1969). Included in *Futz and What Came After,* 1968.
Beclch (produced Philadelphia and New York, 1968). Included in *Futz and What Came After,* 1968.
Futz and What Came After. New York, Random House, 1968.
The Karl Marx Play, music by Galt MacDermot, lyrics by Owens (produced New York, 1973). Included in *The Karl Marx Play and Others,* 1974.
The Karl Marx Play and Others (includes *Kontraption, He Wants Shih!, Farmer's Almanac, Coconut Folksinger, O.K. Certaldo*). New York, Dutton, 1974.
He Wants Shih! (produced New York, 1975). Included in *The Karl Marx Play and Others,* 1974.

Coconut Folksinger (broadcast 1976). Included in *The Karl Marx Play and Others,* 1974.
Kontraption (produced New York, 1978). Included in *The Karl Marx Play and Others,* 1974.
Emma Instigated Me, published in *Performing Arts Journal I* (New York), Spring 1976.
The Widow, and The Colonel, in The Best Short Plays 1977, edited by Stanley Richards. Radnor, Pennsylvania, Chilton, 1977.
Mountain Rites, in The Best Short Plays 1978, edited by Stanley Richards. Radnor, Pennsylvania, Chilton, 1978.
Chucky's Hunch (produced New York, 1981). Published in *Wordplays 2,* New York, Performing Arts Journal Publications, 1982.
Who Do You Want, Peire Vidal? (produced New York, 1982). With *Futz,* New York, Broadway Play Publishing, 1986.
Plays by Rochelle Owens. New York, Broadway Play Publishing, 2000.

Screenplay: *Futz* (additional dialogue), 1969.

Radio Plays: *Coconut Folksinger,* 1976 (Germany); *Sweet Potatoes,* 1977; *Three Front,* 1994 (France).

Television Plays: (video): *Oklahoma Too: Rabbits and Nuggets,* 1987; *How Much Paint Does The Painting Need?,* 1992; *Black Chalk,* 1994.

Short Stories

The Girl on the Garage Wall. Mexico City, El Corno Emplumado, 1962.
The Obscenities of Reva Cigarnik. Mexico City, El Corno Emplumado, 1963.

Other

Editor, *Spontaneous Combustion: Eight New American Plays.* New York, Winter House, 1972.

Translator, *The Passersby,* by Liliane Atlan. New York, Holt, 1993.

*

Manuscript Collections: Mugar Memorial Library, Boston University; University of California, Davis; University of Oklahoma, Norman; Lincoln Center Library of the Performing Arts, New York; Smith College, Northampton, Massachusetts; New York Public Library, Billy Rose Theatre Collection; Columbia University Rare Book & Manuscript Library, New York.

Critical Studies: In *World 29* (New York), April 1974; "Rochelle Owens Symposium," in *Margins 24–26* (Milwaukee), 1975; *Contemporary Authors Autobiography Series,* Detroit, Gale, 1985; in *Parnassus* (New York), 12(2), 1985; in *Talisman* (Hoboken, New Jersey), 12, spring 1994.

Theatrical Activities: Director and actress: several of her own plays.

Rochelle Owens comments:

As a poet I want to suggest that one must go beyond static notions of consciousness and come to terms with the fact that there are writers, creative people, who always need to seek a redefinition of aesthetic possibilities. For me the process of writing is a continuing effort to expand my resources, to participate in the act of finding new reverberations in a sensory/metaphysical language. My poetry has much to do with my personal and social identity as a woman in patriarchal culture and resists both in form and idea the absolute power of organized doctrine, principles, and procedure. My writing challenges traditional notions about the universality of expressive modes and has created new definitions of how I as a woman poet use language, create language, and subvert it. Many of these dynamics have much in common with the avant-garde in general. *LUCA: Discourse on Life & Death,* a long book-length poem that I began in 1988 and completed in 1998, creates the dynamic of process and is a continual assembly and reassembly of the subject matter—a loose personal narrative around the theme of Leonardo and the Mona Lisa. Portions of the text became the framework of a video that I made titled *Black Chalk.* It is my third video. As a young writer I was part of the early off-Broadway experimental theater movement in New York City. Concerning my poetry, I want the reader and listener to pay attention; the more knowledge, education, intuition, and savvy they possess, the more they will reap from the writing. It will paint dimensions and new boundaries. It is for an audience who seeks a new poetic idiom, a language of breath, image, sound, space, symbol, and time represented by the white pages. Poetry is an act of creation that manifests a radical engagement with language, a model of my mind shaping itself. It very well might be an essential document to the condition of our time.

* * *

Rochelle Owens is better known as a playwright than as a poet, but her poems enact her theatrical imagination and provide an essential stimulus to it. In poetry (as distinct from drama) she can concentrate exclusively on verbal invention, coining words and splashing them disjunctively on the page, disrupting grammar, and free-associating with maximum tonal contrast:

O IF I FORGET THEE O ZION
LET AMERICA'S BALLS RUST

Of Jewish background and married to a Greek, Owens relishes the interplay of deviant personae and images stolen from both "high" and "low" culture that serve as metaphors for polar conflicts—Jew versus Christian, Turk versus Greek, white versus black, male versus female, the sacred versus the secular, the powerful versus the helpless. In *The Joe 82 Creation Poems,* through the voices of the primal couple Wild-Man and Wild-Woman, Owens redesigns the myths of creation to reflect both the internal artistic energy of every mind and the external feminist struggle of women to escape the prevalent male-dominant ideas that have led to an insane and polluted world. Wild-Woman, Lilith-like and joyous, expresses the disordering that is needed to re-create a new order on the planet, "mother" earth. Wild-Woman's energy is defeated, however, in morally bankrupt American society, as the poet dolefully makes clear in a tone of protest and deep hopelessness through the acid portraits of "Anthropologists at a Dinner Party." This double-column diatribe, to be read "across and down and up," describes a racist, sexist "round-haunched anthropologist / of Pict descent" (the Picts being a mix of Scottish aborigines and Aryan invaders) who studies American Indians and is "worried that people of mixed / races were opportunists."

Owens presents an antidote to this male hegemony in *W.C. Fields in French Light,* poems meditating on the Cathedral of Sacré Coeur in Paris in "the voice of W.C. Fields" and expressing a humorous, androgynous, multinational vision. The woman artist becomes the conduit of the universal unconscious as her subjective journey to the "sacred heart" of all things has her walk "up the hill to Sacré Coeur." There, holding nothing back, "I hurl the javelin to the top." The poem ends without a period, leaving the poet in continuous upward trajectory.

French culture also influences *How Much Paint Does the Painting Need,* another formally innovative book in which color forms from cubist and modernist paintings are "translated" onto the page in rectangular blocks as if framed on canvas, thus equating poetry and painting. As in abstract expressionism, these forms are seen "tearing into the yellow rhythms into the emergency / of blue between the bubbles . . . the pigment forged / into the base of the skull the territory breaking / out of the paint between the spaces tearing through."

The paradoxes of "tearing through"—the acts of violence that create culture—are explored in Owens's series poem *LUCA: Discourse on Life & Death* and in her selected *Rubbed Stones: Poems from 1960–1992.* Here three major themes intertwine, and they are presented through three characters: the artist, represented by Leonardo da Vinci (Lenny) and his anatomy notebooks—"we murder to dissect"; the artist's object, *Mona Lisa* (Mona), who is also the female model anatomized; and Freud (Sigmund, Siggy), the analyst of the psyche, or soul. The overall premise is that the analytic Western mode of "rational" thought destroys, whereas unconscious thought creates, symbolized here by the Ur-mind of pre-Columbian cultures whose dug-up remains are not understood by "the anthropologists at the dinner party." These men also destroy the living culture, so that the poem ends with the grim image of a crucified Osage woman.

Owens's *New and Selected Poems: 1961–1996* continues the observations of Luca, who historically was Leonardo da Vinci's close friend. Owens stands in for Luca, a fellow painter in the studio who can register and comment on the artist's life. Through this device she constructs a surreal drama that plays riffs on eternal conflicts between art and science, creation and dissection, and the dominant male artist and the submissive female model. Owens's formal structure, mostly three-line stanzas all printed flush left, holds in place the staccato, highly disjunctive phrases that mimic Luca's deracinated thoughts with their contemporary overtones:

all mental disciplines have
been rewritten since something
alien extent on deviations which

A feminist undercurrent is revealed by a fragmentary phrase:

. . . in the end
of the author's century in the middle
of this middle herstory

from the child to the cultural woman

Mona Lisa, the pictorial enigma, is the "cultural woman," the woman artist, Owens herself. Shifting personae permit her free associations, thrust up from the unconscious to mix with conscious thought.

903

Owens's poetry continues to display her intelligence and accomplishment in far-reaching inventiveness that bursts boundaries to make it postmodernly new.

—Jane Augustine

OXLEY, William

Nationality: British. **Born:** Manchester, Lancashire, 29 April 1939. **Education:** College of Commerce, Manchester; qualified as Chartered Accountant. **Family:** Married Patricia Holmes in 1963; two daughters. **Career:** Office boy, Salford, Lancashire, 1955–57; articled clerk, Manchester, 1957–64; chartered accountant, Deloitte and Company, London, 1964–68, and Lazard Brothers, London, 1968–76. Since 1976 freelance writer; editor or co-editor, *New Headland,* 1969–74, *Laissez Faire,* 1971–75, *Orbis,* 1972–74, *Littack,* 1972–76, *Village Review,* 1973–74, *Poetry Newsletter,* 1976–78, *Littack Supplement,* 1976–80, and *Lapis Lazuli,* 1977–78; assistant editor, *Acumen,* 1984–94; founder, Long Poem Group. **Member:** Royal Institute of Philosophy, 1982–83, General Council of Poetry Society of Great Britain, 1990–92. **Address:** 6 The Mount, Furzeham, Brixham, South Devon TQ5 8QY, England.

PUBLICATIONS

Poetry

The Dark Structures. London, Mitre Press, 1967.
New Workings. Privately printed, 1969.
Passages from Time: Poems from a Life. Epping, Essex, Ember Press, 1971.
The Icon Poems. Epping, Essex, Ember Press, 1972.
Opera Vetera. Privately printed, 1973.
Mirrors of the Sea. London, Quarto Press, 1973.
Fightings (as Jason Hardy). Epping, Essex, Ember Press, 1974.
Eve Free. Knotting, Bedforshire, Sceptre Press, 1975.
The Mundane Shell. Egglescliffe, Cleveland, Uldale House, 1975.
Superficies. Breakish, Isle of Skye, Aquila, 1976.
Wind. Leicester, Cog Press, 1976.
The Exile. Egglescliffe, Cleveland, Uldale House, 1979.
The Notebook of Hephaestus and Other Poems. Kinross, Lomond Press, 1981.
The Vitalist Reader: A Selection of the Poetry of Anthony L. Johnson, William Oxley, and Peter Russell, edited by James Hogg. Salzburg, University of Salzburg, 1982.
A Map of Time. Salzburg, University of Salzburg, 1984.
The Triviad and Other Satires. Salzburg, University of Salzburg, 1984.
The Mansands Trilogy. Richmond, Surrey, Keepsake Press, 1988.
Mad Tom on Tower Hill. Exeter, Stride, 1989.
Forest Sequence. Bath, Mammon Press, 1991.
The Patient Reconstruction of Paradise. Brixham, Devon, Acumen Publications, 1991.
The Playboy. Salzburg, University of Salzburg, 1992.
In the Drift of Words. Ware, Rockingham Press, 1992.
Cardboard Troy. Exeter, Stride, 1993.
The Hallsands' Tragedy. Plymouth, Westwords, 1993.

Collected Longer Poems. Salzburg, University of Salzburg, 1994.
The Green Crayon Man. Ware, Rockingham Press, 1997.

Other

Sixteen Days in Autumn (travel). Privately printed, 1972.
Three in Campagna. Privately printed, 1973.
Synopthegms of a Prophet. Brixham, Devon, Ember Press, 1981.
The Idea and Its Imminence. Salzburg, University of Salzburg, 1982.
Of Human Consciousness. Salzburg, University of Salzburg, 1982.
The Cauldron of Inspiration. Salzburg, University of Salzburg, 1983.
The Inner Tapestry. Salzburg, University of Salzburg, 1985.
On Poets and Poetry: Letters Between a Father and Son, with Harry Oxley, edited by Patricia Oxley. Salzburg, University of Salzburg, 1988.
Distinguishing Poetry, edited by Glyn Pursglove. Salzburg, University of Salzburg, 1989.
Three Plays. Salzburg, University of Salzburg, 1996.
No Accounting for Paradise. Ware, Rockingham Press, 1997.

Editor, *Completing the Picture: Exiles, Outsiders & Independents.* Exeter, Devon, Stride, 1995.

Translator, *Poems of a Black Orpheus,* by Léopold S. Senghor. London, Menard Press, 1981.
Translator, *Ndesse,* by Léopold S. Senghor. London, Menard Press, 1981.
Translator, *She Chases Me Relentlessly,* by Léopold S. Senghor. London, Menard Press, 1986.

*

Bibliography: *William Oxley: A Bibliography* by James Hogg, Salzburg, University of Salzburg, 1984; *William Oxley: A Bibliography* by Wolfgang Görtschacher, Salzburg, University of Salzburg, 1992.

Critical Studies: "Poet in Profile: William Oxley" by Mike Shields, in *The Writer* (Aylesbury, Buckinghamshire), April 1975; "Littack: On the Attack" by Derek Stanford, in *The Statesman* (Karachi), 12 and 19 April 1975; "Through Littack to Vitalism" by V. Fenech, in *Bulletin and Times of Malta,* 1976; *William Oxley: A Survey of His Poetry and Philosophy* by P.H., Salzburg, University of Salzburg, 1984; *The Vitalist Seminar,* and *Vitalism and Celebration,* both edited by James Hogg, Salzburg, University of Salzburg, 1984, 1987; "William Oxley: Retrospective," in *Poets Voice* (Bath), 3(3), 1987; *The Role of Nature in William Oxley's Poetry* by Eva Mörwald, Salzburg, University of Salzburg, 1989; *Outsiders: William Oxley, II* edited by James Hogg and Holger Klein, Salzburg, University of Salzburg, 1992; *A Glass of New Made Wine: Testschrift for Willim Oxley* edited by Wolfgang Görtschacher and Glyn Pursglove, Salzburg, University of Salzburg, 1999.

William Oxley comments:

Toward the end of the 1960s I began to take an active interest in contemporary poetry. I found it a time of great confusion and in retrospect can see that much of that confusion rubbed off on me. I was most pained not just by the apparent absence of standards but also by the very real attack on all standards that was everywhere being made. Against this I reacted strongly while, at the same time, endeavoring a rational analysis of the situation as far as it affected the current poetry scene. Naturally, in such chaotic circumstances my reaction, insofar as it took printed form, tended to be something of an overreaction as well as philosophically confusing in itself.

For some time, as a consequence of my analysis of the then poetry scene, I had one basic aim, which was to contribute something toward bringing about a change in the prevailing climate of poetry and poetics in the United Kingdom: a movement away from what I considered to be the dry academic poetry on offer in certain more conservative quarters and away from the formless morass of undisciplined experimentalism and gimmickry on offer in more populist and radical quarters. Toward this end the magazine *Littack* was founded in 1972 with the aim of working out in open forum a new poetics. A more vital poetry was sought by a number of poets who have since become loosely known at the vitalist poets.

In 1976 *Littack* was replaced by the *Littack Supplement,* which endeavored to concentrate upon widening the definition of a vitalist poetry through a less polemical and more thoughtful series of editorials as well as by the careful reviewing of a wide range of poetry books and pamphlets. Also, to emphasize the importance of freeing poetry from its chains of prose literalness and formlessness, I sought to encourage in the *Littack Supplement* the printing of poems that inclined toward imaginative and symbolic values couched in lyrical, or at least rhythmical, forms, rather than either the purely literal and superficial descriptions of experience or the pseudoinnovatory poetry that, by and large, still predominated.

Even with the passing of the *Littack Supplement* in 1980, my hope remains the same: to see the revitalization of the true tradition of poetry, which works through a multidimensional and analogical use of language rather than by a one-dimensional prose discourse, giving a poetry of sufficient breadth of concern as to be variously described as "a poetry of the whole mind" and "a poetry of cosmic concern." It is a hope that I have observed slowly but surely being realized in several quarters over the last few years.

One question, however, continues to rear its head, despite the half decade that has elapsed since the cessation of the whole *Littack* venture, and that is as to the exact nature of a vitalist poem. Most of all has this arisen because of the mistaken assumption made by several critics that a vitalist poem must always be characterized by aggressivity and strong language. This is not so. For while it is true to say that the inner integrity of any poem depends upon its possessing a certain vitality, like an electric circuit, and while some poems, like some human beings, may be said to possess more vitality than others, the tone and voice of the poet, even his verbal gestures, do not determine that vitality. What determines the vitality of a poem is the particular conjunction of feeling and thought. If feeling and thought are successfully married in a given verbal pattern, which pattern they largely determine, then the whole will possess a certain vitality, a vitality that, in turn, reflects the natural vitality of whatever is the poem's particular subject. But neither an active disposition, nor a reflective disposition, nor a strong nor a weak personality on the part of the poet guarantees vitality to any particular poem. For as Keats rightly observed, the "negative capability" of the poet is the most crucial factor of all in poetic creativity. It is the life-giving or life-imparting gift of the poet. It does not matter whether a poem be classified as personal or public, epic or sonnet, cooked or raw—or any way other described—a poem must develop a life of its own, generate its own vitality, in order to live. So any good poem—no matter what its tone, mood, or subject—is a vitalist poem. Finally, it is my own view that a certain philosophical blood transfusion is needed from time to time

for good poetry to be written, and for this reason I hold that a truly vitalist poem says something of significance about the human condition.

(1995) Although, as I have suggested, there is a greater awareness now than twenty years ago of the forces inimical to the creation of the sort of genuine poetry fit to take its place in the traditional canon, the state of the art remains highly problematic. With the advance of technology and its implicit belief that anything can be made and any skill taught, through creative writing programs in the United States and the proliferation of writing workshops in the United Kingdom there is now the additional complication of the plethora of poetry "experts" and the creation of the "designer poet." So that, while the willful obscurantism and meaningless experimentalism of the sixties avant-gardism has been largely marginalized in English poetry, it has now been replaced by a technically correct product of trivial import whose proselike, streetwise tone and message, characterized by academic cleverness, dominates the marketplace. As a result, real poetry of feeling and intelligence is all too often obscured, a situation that, in addition, has led to critical appreciation becoming, in Britain at least, more and more media led. In essence, today in poetry there is an ever increasing tendency for cleverness and glitter to replace seriousness.

* * *

William Oxley has been publishing poetry since 1967 and began writing seriously some three years before that. His earliest poems, with a few exceptions, are heavily influenced by early modernism, by the example of Eliot and Pound. Yet Oxley never appears fully at home in this idiom, for all the undoubted competence of a number of the poems. His own sense of this is apparent in the "Apologia" to his *Opera Vetera,* a selection of poems written between 1964 and 1969. There he writes that "during the latter half of 1972 I called a halt deliberately to what has since 1964/65 been a very prolific period of versifying. In short, I vowed poetic celibacy. I did this because I felt I was simply not developing poetically in any consistent way; indeed, I wasn't even sure if I was developing at all." The period of "celibacy" was the beginning of a conscious redirecting of his poetical activity, the beginning of a new kind of commitment.

This commitment has found expression in a number of ways. Oxley has produced some prose works remarkable for their independence and honest thoroughness of thought and for what they betoken of a determination to analyze the very bases of creative activity as perceived and experienced by the poet himself. *Of Human Consciousness* and *The Idea and Its Imminence* are philosophical works that are, in the best and highest sense, the work of an amateur; they are, that is to say, the product of love, and they are free of the debilitations of fashionable philosophical jargon. In the same way *The Cauldron of Inspiration,* though it has unmistakable weaknesses, constitutes an exciting and perceptive account of poetry and its importance that would be well beyond most academic critics. This far-reaching reflection upon the fundamentals of his thought and his craft was accompanied by his campaigning editorship of *Littack.* There he elucidated his concept of "vitalist" poetry, gave an analysis of the limitations of much contemporary verse, and attempted to indicate some possible ways forward.

In terms of Oxley's own poetry, all of this activity has borne fruit in a quantity of work radically different from, and superior to, his earlier writing. He has, with some courage, pursued the creation of an appropriate idiom for a kind of philosophical and discursive poetry that has long been out of fashion. A series of long poems—e.g., *The*

Exile, The Mundane Shell, ''The Rose on the Tree of Time,'' *A Map of Time*—have tackled very large ideas in forms and manners of great interest and individuality. The best of these are gathered together, in whole or selection, in the *Collected Longer Poems.* Many of them are works of intelligence and beauty, and they deserve to be better known. Given the prevailing poetic climate, they might be termed experimental poems, and, like most experiments, they have their moments of failure. Taken as a whole, however, they constitute a valuable extension and development of the tradition represented by the longer poems of MacDiarmid and Russell in their fusion of lyrical, narrative, and discursive idioms.

A Map of Time is the most sustained of these poems, approaching the epic in both length and aspiration. It is a subjective epic, its focus the developing consciousness of the poet, its patterns of conflict and discovery centered upon the attempt to trace the contours of an inner world. The loss of paradise and the possibility of its being regained are at the heart of the poem's complex structure of variation and allusion. Within, and part of, that structure of argument are passages of considerable beauty, nowhere more so than in ''Hymn,'' in praise to the sea, which begins as follows:

> But in hymn of waters I now praise
> The high blue spirit here at turn of tide:
> Among the shakeless shiftless rocks of red
> The sun downpours upon this secret shapéd bay.
> O what essential glimpsed fragments!
> In torn and twisted beauty of the waves
>
> That roll forever countless into me . . .
> The streaks of subtle rust on sable stone
> The stakes of leathered weathered wood
> The pleached grief of almost human shape
> Or girl-smooth cheek of powdered slate
> And the burnt and withered necklaces of weed
> That lie among the fireworks of the spray.

The apprehension of sensual beauty and the note of veneration are both very much in character. Elsewhere, *The Playboy,* with overtones of the political thriller, is nearer to a verse novel than to an epic. Its exploration of materialism's implications, its witty dialogue, and its perceptive sketches of character make it as readable as it is thought provoking.

At their best Oxley's shorter poems display a powerful visionary lyricism. This is vividly the case in his love lyrics (e.g., the series ''To Lily,'' ''Lily Inviolate,'' and ''My Lily'') and in his intense poems of place and landscape (e.g., ''The Lane,'' ''Green Lanes,'' ''Wheat,'' ''Paradise,'' and *The Mansands Trilogy*), which make articulate the poet's intimations of eternity. Consider, for example, ''That Other Land'' from *The Mansands Trilogy*:

> The dandelion clock clouds
> of a different heaven
> seas of which this sea
> is but a small mercurial lake
> and trees of which these trees
> are but sullen gauzy tufts
> on windswept hills
> of all-too-shadowy seasons,
> are what we seek
> through all our dismayed lives.
> Nature in all its grandeur
> and minute, insect-threaded marvel,
> is but a broad hint
> of what's beyond:
> hinterland of the mind
> and paradise where all souls dwell.

Oxley's apprehension of the paradisal is located within a highly specific sense of the ''mean temporality'' of much that is most characteristic of modern society and a similarly keen sense of human mortality. The collection of short poems *In the Drift of Words* contains a number of works set in graveyards and others that contemplate the deaths of specific individuals. All, however, find in the trappings of death a paradoxically vivid affirmation of life. The infectious fun of other poems (e.g., ''Poem Written at Dannie Abse's Desk'' and ''To Elizabeth'') testifies to an exhilarating engagement with the world.

An occasional stridency of tone has sometimes marred Oxley's writing, most often in his satirical poems, both in epigram and in mock-heroic (e.g., *The Triviad*), distracting attention from the precise judgment and acute intelligence at work. In the best of his poems (e.g., ''Lucy & Her Colonel'', first published in *Encounter* in January 1989 and collected in *In the Drift of Words*) there is a striking balance of passion and stillness expressed in language of impressive composure. Oxley's range of style and subject is very wide, and his best work is marked by poetic intelligence and metaphysical understanding.

—Glyn Pursglove

P

PACK, Robert

Nationality: American. **Born:** New York City, 29 May 1929. **Education:** Dartmouth College, Hanover, New Hampshire, B.A. 1951; Columbia University, New York, M.A. 1953. **Family:** Married 1) Isabelle Miller in 1950; 2) Patricia Powell in 1961; two sons and one daughter. **Career:** Taught at Barnard College, New York, 1957–64, and Poetry Workshop of the New School for Social Research, New York. Since 1970 Abernathy Professor, Middlebury College, and since 1973 director, Bread Loaf Writers Conference, Vermont. Editor, *Discovery,* New York. **Awards:** Fulbright fellowship, 1956; American Academy grant, 1957; Borestone Mountain poetry award, 1964; National Endowment for the Arts grant, 1968. **Address:** Middlebury College, Middlebury, Vermont 05753, U.S.A.

PUBLICATIONS

Poetry

The Irony of Joy. New York, Scribner, 1955.
A Stranger's Privilege. Hessle, Yorkshire, Asphodel, and New York, Macmillan, 1959.
Guarded by Women. New York, Random House, 1963.
Selected Poems. London, Chatto and Windus, 1964.
Home from the Cemetery. New Brunswick, New Jersey, Rutgers University Press, 1969.
Nothing But Light. New Brunswick, New Jersey, Rutgers University Press, 1972.
Keeping Watch. New Brunswick, New Jersey, Rutgers University Press, 1976.
Waking to My Name: New and Selected Poems. Baltimore, Johns Hopkins University Press, 1980.
Faces in a Single Tree: A Cycle of Monologues. Boston, Godine, 1984.
Clayfeld Rejoices, Clayfeld Laments: A Sequence of Poems. Boston, Godine, 1987.
Before It Vanishes: A Packet for Professor Pagels. Boston, Godine, 1989.
Fathering the Map: New and Selected Later Poems. Chicago, University of Chicago Press, 1993.
Minding the Sun. Chicago, University of Chicago Press, 1996.
Rounding It Out: A Cycle of Sonnetelles. Chicago, University of Chicago Press, 1999.

Other

Wallace Stevens: An Approach to His Poetry and Thought. New Brunswick, New Jersey, Rutgers University Press, 1958.
The Forgotten Secret (for children). New York, Macmillan, 1959.
Then What Did You Do? (for children). New York, Macmillan, 1961.
How to Catch a Crocodile (for children). New York, Knopf, 1964.
Affirming Limits: Essays on Morality, Choice, and Poetic Form. Amherst, University of Massachusetts Press, 1985.
The Long View: Essays on the Discipline of Hope and Poetic Craft. Amherst, University of Massachusetts Press, 1991.

Editor, with Donald Hall and Louis Simpson, *The New Poets of England and America.* New York, Meridian, 1957; London, New English Library, 1974; *Second Selection,* Meridian, 1962.
Editor and Translator, with Marjorie Lelach, *Mozart' s Librettos.* Cleveland, World, 1961.
Editor, with Tom Driver, *Poems of Doubt and Belief: An Anthology of Modern Religious Poetry.* New York, Macmillan, 1964.
Editor, with Marcus Klein, *Literature for Composition on the Theme of Innocence and Experience.* Boston, Little Brown, 1966.
Editor, with Marcus Klein, *Short Stories: Classic, Modern, Contemporary.* Boston, Little Brown, 1967.
Editor, *Selected Letters,* by Keats. New York, New American Library, 1974.
Editor, with Sydney Lea and Jay Parini, *The Bread Loaf Anthology of Contemporary American Poetry.* Hanover, New Hampshire, University Press of New England, 1985.
Editor, with Jay Parini, *The Bread Loaf Anthology of Contemporary American Short Stories* [Essays]. Hanover, New Hampshire, University Press of New England, 2 vols., 1987–89.
Editor, with Jay Parini, *Poems for a Small Planet, An Anthology of Nature Poetry.* Hanover, New Hampshire, University Press of New England, 1993.
Editor, with Jay Parini, *American Identities: Contemporary Multicultural Voices.* Hanover, New Hampshire, Middlebury College Press, 1994.
Editor, with Jay Parini, *Touchstones: American Poets on a Favorite Poem.* Hanover, New Hampshire, Middlebury College Press, 1996.
Editor, with Jay Parini, *Introspections: American Poets on One of Their Own Poems.* Middlebury, Vermont, Middlebury College Press, 1997.

*

Critical Studies: "Fresh Flowers for the Urn: Reassessing Robert Pack" by Paul Mariani, in *Massachusetts Review* (Amherst), winter 1982; *At an Elevation: On the Poetry of Robert Pack* edited by David Bain, Middlebury, Vermont, Middlebury College Press, 1994.

*   *   *

From his earliest works to *Fathering the Map: New and Selected Later Poems,* which provides a fine overview of his accomplishments, Robert Pack's poetry has celebrated man's organic relationship to all levels of creation, a relationship complicated by the playful, sometimes nagging "curse of consciousness" ("Stellar Thanksgiving"). Many of his poems are awed yet ironical responses to epigraphs from books on physics and astronomy and reveal a fascination with the mysteries of the physical universe and the equally enigmatic possibilities of the human cosmos. Such poems explore the archaeological, biological, and mythic hints of man's collective past (and unimaginable future) and his private prenatal memories.

"Grieving on a Grand Scale," a representative work, ranges from the imagined death of a lover, through speculations on the inevitable demise of the whole scale of nature, to the implications of such devastations on the fate of the persona, always the crux for Pack.

907

Though the poem resolves "... to mourn softly, without hope of resurrection," the final lines comfort with the image of an unknowing yet elegiac universe: "young deer / Do not move (their loose watery lips / Slide over their gums with a sound like weeping." Pack generally avoids sentimentality by acknowledging human involvement in both "the crooked weasel's crooked chase" ("Canoe Ride") and the horror, however stylized, of "... lace / Of mouse bones in owl feces" ("The Black Ant").

Poems like "Descending" interpret the terror implicit in the universe as the real cost of exclusion from paradise, but Pack, negating traditional answers, substitutes openness to the wonders of creation, whatever their origin: "... above, no missing God / I miss; high satisfying sky though, and below, / Chrysanthemums in garb of gaiety" ("Raking Leaves"). "Prayer for Prayer," the concluding poem in *Faces in a Single Tree,* plays more seriously with religion as a wife, acknowledging the accuracy of her husband's reading of her beliefs, develops a final enigma: "Darling, I know you know something in me approves you laughing at my need to pray / ... listen to God's silences even as the wind blows through / the icicles and piles snow by our shed: / we may be in for quite a night of it." Similarly, the title poem in *Fathering the Map* concludes when a father, without making orthodoxy explicit, bequeaths his son a childhood map and the rich and comforting traditions it implies: "all blank but for a single pin / to represent an ark, / in hope another covenant to save the earth / may find words in the dark."

The key image of delight for Pack is the family. "Breakfast Cherries" celebrates the richness of ephemeral family pleasure. In "Everything Is Possible" the expectant father achieves the illusion of godhead, while the husband in "Were It To" sees daily life as a recapitulation of paradise. Though children "redeem all sorrow," such redemption never completely calms latent anxiety or ignores the inherited pain implicit in all human relationships. "The Mountain Ash Tree," with its equivocally symbolic berries, offers Pack's most complex vision of man's precarious optimism; despite the ominous appearance and bitter taste of the fruit, its unraveled meanings force the reader to share the final affirmation that "I am still alive."

Because of the relatedness of all elements in the universe, man can revert to the "hermit crab" comfort of "shell" and "tentacles" ("My House") or aspire to a level where "only his thought remains / melodious and luminous ..." ("Venus"). Such diversity parallels man's transcending of generational limits as he enacts several family roles simultaneously. A son, struggling to distinguish mother from wife and himself from his dead father, invokes the father's return and, ironically, a renewal of the whole process: "Dreaming I seek your skeleton below; / I dig the worms and find your embryo" ("Father"). "The Boat" achieves the strongest dramatization of this theme when the speaker, with deadpan earnestness, accepts both the fusion and separateness of familial roles: "I dressed my father in his little clothes. / Blue sailor suit, brass buttons on his coat. / He asked me where the running water goes. / ... He told me where all the running water goes. / And dressed me gently in his little clothes." The strict terza rima perfectly embodies the theme of freedom within the ambiguous order of family cycles.

The dramatic monologues of *Faces in a Single Tree,* reminiscent of Frost, darken this image of family life. In "Nursing and Dreaming" a husband's anger at his wife's absorption in their infant son combines with painful memories of his mother and younger brother and with speculations on his father's possible reactions to both offspring. Despite the psychological complexity of such poems, their competent iambic lines unfortunately endow the varied speakers with similarities of voice and imagery that do not allow distinct personalities to emerge.

Amplification through repetition and the varying of verb forms becomes a stylistic signature for Pack: "I grow by choosing what I choose to know" ("Song to Myself"). Among a variety of sestinas, villanelles, and free verse, Pack's strongest form is a moral nursery rhyme in which a convincingly guileless speaker agonizes, with inevitable repetitions, toward a resolution that both repels and involves the reader. "I shot an otter because I had a gun" leads, with icy detachment, to "He shot an otter because he had a gun" ("The Shooting"). While Pack can sustain a bitingly ironic or flippant voice throughout a poem, he fails at social satire in works like "Routine" and at literary satire in "Advice to Poets," achieving only modest success with "Wilt Thou Condemn Me?," which teases for fifteen stanzas on the ambiguous virtues of irony. Pack is apparently a ruthless judge of his own verse, for he deleted many fine earlier poems from *Fathering the Map* and revised others.

Clayfeld Rejoices, Clayfeld Laments uses the developing consciousness of a sculptor to dramatize the abiding concerns of Pack's poetry, perhaps most effectively in a dream vision of a Las Vegas slot machine:

> When Clayfeld pulled the lever down again,
>   three phoenixes descended
> in a row, and printed coins, like tiny suns,
>   flowed from an opening
> as when Zeus came to Danae in a shower ...

"Inheritance," a series of thematically unified poems with five-line stanzas, continues Pack's speculations on man's evolution and his ambiguous power in the present, "... standing in his garden with an eggplant / like a plant in his palm" ("Grandeur"). Like the "Clayfeld" cycle, the "Inheritance" poems often focus on the artist's response to his perceived reality but are more explicit in articulating a credo: whether "it's good to face what's bad; / that's what a poem must do or else it lies" ("The Long and the Short of What's Good and What's Bad").

Before It Vanishes is Pack's twenty-nine-poem response, sometimes skeptical, sometimes delighted, to Heinz Pagels's popularizations of theories on the origin, nature, and possible fate of the universe. Pack's polished, occasionally moving four-line stanzas, usually rhymed *abcb,* do not convey the sense of awe overcoming terror that characterizes similar speculations in Milton, who provides the epigraph to the volume as well as many verbal and thematic motifs. Rather, Packs's verse seems closer to eighteenth-century redactions of cosmological theory, though he substitutes colloquialism for formal elegance. He skillfully uses run-on lines, sometimes between stanzas, to play against his formal pattern, but these line breaks rarely achieve that enrichment of meaning resulting from an altered context. Significantly, the strongest poem is "Outlasting You," Pack's elegy for Pagels, whose death cry in a mountain accident assumes its place in a rich pattern of familial and universal grief and ultimately fuses with Pack's:

> ... your father's cry,
>   a stranger's, or perhaps

you hear my decomposing voice
come echoing unloosed from a crevasse.

Fathering the Map continues Pack's celebration of "... poets who / can find within a lily pond / their own reflections ..." ("Cherry Robbers"), a brilliant emblem of the complex relation between nature and the human creator. The best of this collection, perhaps of all Pack's work, is "Wild Turkey in Paradise," in which the speaker boasts of "two apple trees I planted years ago," so fertile that "I let them ripen unplucked on the branch / and fall, according to the rhythm of the year." "Such bounty" attracts, "strutting stupid from the woods (as if / no hunters stalked Vermont) / six turkeys," who rapidly proceed to a state of drunkenness in which "... their eyes / blazed with amazing knowledge that transported them, / within their bodies, into paradise." The speaker's capacity to absorb this experience while remaining detached enough to speculate on its significance and to re-create it as a poem is a perfect analogue to Pack's poetic practice.

Pack's obsessive themes continue to find powerful expression in his volumes *Minding the Sun* and *Rounding It Out,* though he is perhaps less vigorous than formerly in culling weaker verses and curbing a tendency toward schoolmasterish homiletics, especially when lamenting man's despoiling the planet and hastening the demise of an already doomed universe. Characteristically, some of the strongest poems in *Minding the Sun* exemplify his eclecticism, as in this passage of Keatsian intensity and lushness in "Autumn Berries":

And suddenly the field is hushed,
no crickets call, no drowsy wood doves sing,
no winds carouse among the pines,
or strum the thistle and the thorn; the dawn no longer
is reflected in the dew,
and though red berries linger on my lips, I'm left,
pale brother, here alone with you.

And a Wordsworthian moment captures a child's openness to the world of the senses "that brought such thoughtless happiness to me" ("Determination"). As in earlier volumes, Pack's best poems are witty, thoughtful responses to scientific or philosophic epigraphs, most notably in "The Loss of Estrus," "The Trees Will Die," and "Witzelsucht" (wit-seeking), whose titles suggest the range of his interests.

Sometimes the formal structure of *Rounding It Out,* a series of forty-eight "sonnetelles" (sixteen-line sonnets with villanelle-like repetitions), produces verses that sound mechanical or even glib. But generally Pack remains a master of enjambment, his best lines simultaneously undermining and enforcing their traditional meters and demonstrating the "solace in grief when grief is rhymed" ("Invitation"). He brilliantly intensifies natural details, as in the owl's "honed eyes" ("Stone Thoughts") and romanticizes natural phenomena, as in his paean to a tomato plant in "Pruden's Purple": "So leafy-thick, so languorously lush." With seeming casualness, Pack hints in "Baled Hay" at one of the enduring themes of his poetry, the possible order of the natural world: "A randomness that also seems designed." He has continued to communicate the evidence of the excited eye and meditative consciousness of the true poet.

—Burton Kendle

PADEL, Ruth

Nationality: Irish. **Born:** London, 8 May 1946. **Education:** Lady Margaret Hall, Oxford, B.A. (honors) 1969; Wolfson College, Oxford, M.A., D.Phil. 1976. **Family:** Married Myles Burnyeat in 1984; one daughter. **Career:** Research fellow and lecturer, Oxford University, 1972–80; lecturer in classics, Birkbeck College, University of London, 1980–84. Since 1984 freelance writer and lecturer. **Awards:** National Poetry Competition winner, 1996. **Address:** 50 Thurlow Road, London NW3 5PJ, England.

PUBLICATIONS

Poetry

Alibi. London, Many Press, 1985.
Summer Snow. London, Century Hutchinson, 1990.
Angel. Newcastle upon Tyne, Bloodaxe, 1995.
Fusewire. London, Chatto and Windus, 1996.
Rembrandt Would Have Loved You. London, Chatto and Windus, 1998.

Other

In and Out of the Mind: Greek Images of the Tragic Self. Princeton, New Jersey, Princeton University Press, 1992.
Whom Gods Destroy: Elements of Greek and Tragic Madness. Princeton, New Jersey, Princeton University Press, 1995.

*

Critical Studies: By Barbara Goff, in *Classical Philology,* 89(2), April 1994; by Jasper Griffin, in *The Spectator* (London), 274(8704), 6 May 1995; by Marianne McDonald, in *Theater,* 26(3), 1995.

*   *   *

Ruth Padel's poetry explores the extremes of human emotion. Drawing their subjects from a wide range of narrative situations and their language from multiple lexicons, her poems are at ease inhabiting a mental ward, fine arts museums, or the myriad abodes of lovers. But mostly Padel's poems inhabit minds: the mind of a prostitute on her way to pick up a trick, of a GI, of a mental patient, of her doctor, and, in *Rembrandt Would Have Loved You,* of a lover. In a talk called "Public Poets, Public Poems, Public Art" at the British Library, Padel began, "I want to start with what poetry does anyway when you write it—it makes public something that is private, it comes from your private mind." Indeed, this seems to be her own project, and she embraces the lyric poem as the form in which several "private minds" become audible and converse.

Angel, Padel's 1995 book, seems to be a poetic version of her diagnosis. That is, the poet renders the private minds of her characters in order to classify, comprehend, and account for them. We see here the relationship between Padel's poetry and her critical work, which traces the meaning of madness in Greek mythology. Of course, Padel does not simply replicate the diagnostic process; she questions it, turns it on its head by speaking through the subject, and essentially investigates investigation. The title poem, in the voice of an alien, offers scientific diction—the language of classification and investigation—alongside the plainest of plain speech. The "angel" describes himself as "a nest of rays, all protein, / grey velvet triangles / six metres wing to wing" and imagines his own dissection: "Suppose they clawed / one ring from my antenna-bone / up through that tunnel of sea-cow / and acetta swabs." But, he concludes, "they" still would not know him. The proof of this—and the poem's real brilliance—lies in the final gesture toward colloquialism, when the angel-alien addresses us directly: "Baby," he says, "where I come from, / we had pre-rusted pictoscopes to tell us about aliens like you."

These sorts of linguistic juxtapositions drive Padel's poems. In "The Starling" the speaker describes a bird who "looked, then, a bedraggled poisonous orchid," setting the narrative of Bedlem [sic] inmates against the lyricism of the natural world. In the final section of the book a Bedlem doctor's voice becomes remarkably imagistic and nonclinical in "Peach Tree," wondering, "How can I leave / a free-standing peach tree, / my greenfrosted waste-mould / salad of broken-glass light?" In these lines we seem to hear the voice of the poet, who, though drawn to the abstract, cannot leave the image behind.

How lucky for her readers that *Rembrandt Would Have Loved You* maintains Padel's commitment to numerous ways of storytelling. In a series of love poems Padel establishes the vulnerability and strength of her speaker. Obsessive love, the center of the book, is at once conventionally titillating ("the breeze / On your nipples"), contemporary ("lightning . . . / Imagining itself Aretha Franklin"), and warm ("the warmest small patisserie in the world"). While *Angel* is primarily voice driven, the raw imagery of the book becomes more finely wrought here, lending to *Rembrandt*'s single voice a tremendous consistency. Mythological and cultural allusions abound, from Echo and "the *Mahabarata* Bride" to the Spice Girls, but they never seem to exclude the reader from the poems.

Because of Padel's ability to traverse the earth verbally, her poems speak to concerns larger than the single mind or the single love affair. The fractures and longings of her characters' spirits are global, and in this sense Padel is a truly contemporary poet.

—Sonya B. Posmentier

PADGETT, Ron

Nationality: American. **Born:** Tulsa, Oklahoma, 17 June 1942. **Education:** Columbia University, New York (Boar's Head poetry prize and George E. Woodberry award, 1964), A.B. 1964; Fulbright fellow, Paris, 1965–66. **Family:** Married; one son. **Career:** Taught poetry workshops at St. Mark's-in-the-Bowery, New York, and poetry writing in New York public schools, 1969–76; writer in the community, South Carolina Arts Commission, 1976–78. Associate editor, *Paris Review,* 1968–70; founding editor, Full Court Press, 1973. Since 1981 director of publications, Teachers & Writers Collaborative, New York. **Awards:** Gotham Book Mart prize, 1964; Poets Foundation grant, 1965, 1968; Columbia University Translation Center award, 1976; National Endowment for the Arts fellowship, 1983; Guggenheim fellowship, 1986; New York Foundation for the Arts grant, 1990; Foundation for Contemporary Performance Arts grant, 1996; American Academy of Arts and Letters grant, 1999. **Address:** 342 East 13th Street, New York, New York 10003, U.S.A.

PUBLICATIONS

Poetry

Some Thing, with Ted Berrigan and Joe Brainard. Privately printed, 1964.
In Advance of the Broken Arm. New York, "C" Press, 1964.
Sky. London, Goliard Press, 1966.
Bean Spasms: Poems and Prose, with Ted Berrigan. New York, Kulchur, 1967.
Tone Arm. Brightlingsea, Essex, Once Press, 1967.
100,000 Fleeing Hilda, with Joe Brainard. New York, Boke, 1967.
Bun, with Tom Clark. New York, Angel Hair, 1968.
Great Balls of Fire. New York, Holt Rinehart, 1969; revised edition, Minneapolis, Coffee House Press, 1990.
Sweet Pea. New York, Aloe, 1971.
Sufferin' Succotash, with Joe Brainard, with *Kiss My Ass,* by Michael Brownstein. New York, Adventures in Poetry, 1971.
Poetry Collection. Penfield, New York, Strange Faeces Press, 1971.
Back in Boston Again, with Ted Berrigan and Tom Clark. Philadelphia, Telegraph, 1972.
Oo La La, with Jim Dine. London, Petersburg Press, 1973.
Crazy Compositions. Bolinas, California, Big Sky, 1974.
Toujours l'Amour. New York, Sun Press, 1976.
Arrive by Pullman. Paris, Generations, 1978.
Tulsa Kid. Calais, Vermont, Z Press, 1979.
Triangles in the Afternoon. New York, Sun Press, 1980.
How to Be a Woodpecker. West Branch, Iowa, Toothpaste Press, 1983.
How to Be Modern Art, with Trevor Winkfield. West Branch, Iowa, Coffee House Press, 1984.
Light as Air. Paris, Aldo Crommelynck, 1989.
The Big Something. Great Barrington, Massachusetts, Figures, 1990.
New & Selected Poems. Lincoln, Massachusetts, Godine, 1995.

Plays

Seventeen: Collected Plays, with Ted Berrigan. New York, "C" Press, 1965.
Chrononhotonthologos, with Johnny Stanton, adaptation of the play by Henry Carey. New York, Boke, 1971.

Novel

Antlers in the Treetops, with Tom Veitch. Toronto, Coach House Press, 1973.

Short Stories

2/2 Stories for Andy Warhol. New York, "C" Press, 1965.

Other

The Adventures of Mr. and Mrs. Jim and Ron, with Jim Dine. London, Cape Goliard Press, and New York, Grossman, 1970.
Among the Blacks: Two Works, with Raymond Roussel. Bolinas, California, Avenue B, 1988.
Pantoum. New York, Teachers & Writers Collaborative, 1988.

Blood Work: Selected Prose. Flint, Michigan, Bamberger Books, 1993.

Ted: A Personal Memoir of Ted Berrigan. Great Barrington, Massachusetts, The Figures, 1993.

Creative Reading. Urbana, Illinois, National Council of Teachers of English, 1997.

Albanian Diary. Great Barrington, Massachusetts, The Figures, 1999.

The Straight Line: Writings on Poetry and Poets. Ann Arbor, University of Michigan Press, 2000.

Editor, with Ted Berrigan, *Literary Days,* by Tom Veitch. New York, "C" Press, 1964.

Editor, with David Shapiro, *An Anthology of New York Poets.* New York, Random House, 1970.

Editor, with Bill Zavatsky, *The Whole Word Catalogue 2.* New York, McGraw Hill, 1976.

Editor, with Nancy Larson Shapiro, *The Point: Where Teaching and Writing Intersect.* New York, Teachers & Writers Collaborative, 1983.

Editor, *The Complete Poems,* by Edwin Denby. New York, Random House, 1986.

Editor, *Handbook of Poetic Forms.* New York, Teachers & Writers Collaborative, 1987.

Editor, *The Teachers and Writers Guide to Walt Whitman.* New York, Teachers & Writers Collaborative, 1991.

Editor, with Christopher Edgar, *Educating The Imagination.* New York, Teachers & Writers Collaborative, 1994.

Editor, *World Poets: An Encyclopedia for Students.* New York, Scribner, 2000.

Translator, *The Poet Assassinated,* by Guillaume Apollinaire. New York, Holt Rinehart, 1968; enlarged edition, as *The Poet Assassinated and Other Stories,* Berkeley, California, North Point Press, 1984; Manchester, Carcanet, 1985.

Translator, *Dialogues with Marcel Duchamp,* by Pierre Cabanne. New York, Viking Press, 1970; London, Thames and Hudson, 1971.

Translator, with David Ball, *Rldasedlrad les Dlcmhypbdf,* by Valery Larbaud. New York, Boke, 1973.

Translator, with Bill Zavatsky, *The Poems of A.O. Barnabooth,* by Valery Larbaud. Tokyo, Mushinsha, 1974.

Translator, *Kodak,* by Blaise Cendrars. New York, Boke, 1976.

Translator, *Complete Poems,* by Blaise Cendrars. Berkeley, California, University of California Press, 1992.

*

Critical Studies: "The New American Poetry" by Jonathan Cott, in *The New American Arts,* New York, Horizon Press, 1966; "Reverdy in New York" by Mortimer Guiney, in *World Literature Today* (Norman, Oklahoma), 59(4), autumn 1985; "Supernatural Diet" by Stephen Ratcliffe, in *Talisman* (Jersey City, New Jersey), 7, fall 1991; "A Night Painting of Ron Padgett" by David Shapiro, in *Talisman* (Jersey City, New Jersey), 7, fall 1991; "The Tulsa Kid" by Karen Volkman, in *The Voice Literary Supplement,* September 1996; "Padgett the Collaborator" by Clayton Eshleman, in *Chicago Review,* 43(2), spring 1997; "Ron Padgett's Visual Imagination" by Alice Notley, in *Arshile,* 9, 1998.

*   *   *

Ron Padgett writes in a loose tradition begun by Charles Henri Ford in the 1930s and carried forward by Frank O'Hara and Ted Berrigan. It is a New York school or a New York surrealism—polymorphic, a confluence of modernisms of all kinds, anticonventional in almost every way. Like his predecessors, Padgett modulates poems beyond traditional limits. In his 1969 poem "Wonderful Things," for example, he varies the diction from the language of formal elegy—"Anne, who are dead . . . ."—to that of insanity—"Seriously, I have this mental (smuh!) illness . . ." Then, taking a new direction, he retroactively wraps the whole poem in the disarmingly ingenuous diction of a storyteller ("and that's what I want to do / tell you wonderful things").

A naive world surfaces in Padgett's poetry: mysterious appearances, holes in the sky, falling clouds, ghosts, secret notes, funny animals, elvishness. These lines are from *Great Balls of Fire:*

DECEMBER

I will sleep
in my little cup.

At its purest the effect is wonder: "A child draws a man and the earth / is covered with snow." Padgett's power comes from his voice. When it speaks directly, it is the clearest voice of a child in modern poetry. (See "Buckets" in *Great Balls of Fire* as an example.) When it speaks otherwise, as in these lines from *How to Be a Woodpecker,* it is a whole other game:

I would rather not participate in this society
anymore, hello, but I must because I do not have
the money to live outside it, *on my yacht.* This
paragraph is a verbal checkerboard. It's your move.

Behind his irony Padgett grows full of Dada ("What modern poetry needs / is a good beating"), ready to parody anything established ("When I see birches / I think of nothing . . . . One could do worse than see birches"). Like the dadaists, he can pit art against life with ease, as he does in "Tone Arm":

Let's take a string quartet
Playing one of Beethoven's compositions
We may explain it as the scratching
Of a horse's hair against a cat's gut
Or we may explain it as the mind
Of a genius soaring up to an infinite
Horse's hair scratching against an infinite cat's gut.

Padgett's zany, ebullient wit often hides the intelligence and sensitivity that lie under the surface. Although he launches a bombast against intellectual history ("Tone Arm"), which, he explains,

Is now only an imitation of itself
Like a car
Driving towards itself in the rain
Only to be photographed from behind,

casual references to intellectual concepts fill his work. The rules of poetry get no attention they do not deserve, as in "Haiku" from *Tulsa Kid:*

First: five syllables
Second: seven syllables
Third: five syllables

Some modern art movements do not fare much better, as shown in "Ode to the Futurist Painters and Poets":

You, Futurists, thought the airplane and telephone so
    wonderful! Ha!

Padgett knows both poetry and painting well. Scores of artists pass through his work. Horace, Ungaretti, Max Jacob, Jim Dine, Rilke, Gris, Reverdy, John Lyly, Mallarmé, Castiglione, Jasper Johns, Fairfield Porter, and Thomas Hardy exist alongside Gabby Hayes, Carl Yazstrzemski, and Mighty Mouse. Padgett himself has translated Apollinaire, Duchamp, Cendrars, and Larbaud. Yet he wears his knowledge lightly, as if to say, "Well, doesn't everybody know this stuff?"

Padgett's poems are made out of magic words, as shown in "Cufflinks":

But you never can tell
what might happen.
Jean-Baptiste Marie Alouette Francois-Jones
might be born any minute
to Mr. and Mrs. Arturo-Torres Helen Kafka
who are riding across the night sky
on shafts of silver light. Their
spurs jangle and glint like spurs
in the immensity of space. Is space
immense? Or is it fast?
Here today to discuss the question
is Mrs. Arturo-Torres Helen Kafka.
Madame, uh
where is she? She was sitting here
in this chair
uh
who took
that chair?

He often takes the question of whether a reality can exist without language and reverses it. Who did take the chair? He pushes this inquiry to its limit in *Supernatural Overtones,* a collaboration with Clark Coolidge that explores the edges of how meaning means.

Many of Padgett's poems celebrate paintings; some are collaborations with painters or graphic artists. Other poems surrealistically evoke a mood, an attitude, a complex of emotions. His later works have become intermittently darker. There is a limit, it seems to me, to what can be expressed through Padgett's method. But he can transcend it, as he does in the poem "Dog" from *The Big Something,* a powerful lament for two dead friends that is colloquial and conversational-

New York's lost some of its rough charm

—he says of Ted Berrigan and Edwin Denby:

And there's just no getting around it
By pretending the rest of us can somehow make up for it
Or that future generations will. I hear

A dog barking in the street and it's drizzling
at 6 A.M. and there's nothing warm
Or lovable or necessary about it, it's just
Some dog barking in some street somewhere.
I hate that dog.

The zaniness, the cuteness is gone; faced with death, cuteness just does not cut it. But an underlying seriousness has been in Padgett's poetry from the beginning; it just has not surfaced frequently. It is similar in this respect to the elegiac lyricism that arises only in the final four lines of "16 November 1964" or to the intellectual honesty of the final couplet of "When I Think More of My Own Future Than of Myself" (1969) or to the eloquence in this final section from "My Room" (1990):

I can hear a brook from my window now, and I think of it running into the little spot we call Wayne Pond, named after my son, who was named after my father. All this confluence in a room I didn't feel comfortable in until a few minutes ago, a room that, broken like a mustang, becomes a friend to man, we who are so desperately in need of friends among the plants and animals of this earth, and yes, the humans too, and the rooms we build around ourselves.

Padgett's poetry has bemused us, made us smile, even laugh out loud. After such a confluence one may wonder if the reflection in this new room marks the surfacing of lyrical, elegiac, thoughtful tones in this remarkable poet, who is, as Aram Saroyan has called him, "the grand old *young* man of the New York School of poets."

—Edward B. Germain

PADHI, Bibhu

Nationality: Indian. **Born:** Cuttack, Orissa, 16 January 1951. **Education:** Christ College, Cuttack, 1965–66; Ravenshaw College, Cuttack, 1966–71, B.A. (honors) in English 1969, M.A. 1971; Utkal University, Bhubaneswar, Orissa, D.Litt. 1991. **Family:** Married Minakshi Rath in 1976; two sons. **Career:** Lecturer in English, Regional College of Education, Bhubaneswar, Orissa, 1972–74, Ravenshaw College, Cuttack, Orissa, 1974–81, and BJB College, Bhubaneswar, Orissa, 1981–85; senior lecturer in English, Ravenshaw College, Cuttack, Orissa, 1985–92. Since 1992 reader in English, SCS College, Puri, Orissa. **Awards:** Orbis Readers' award, 1985, 1989. **Agent:** Gerald Pollinger, Laurence Pollinger Ltd., 18 Maddox Street, Mayfair, London W1R OEU, England. **Address:** College Square, Cuttack 753003, Orissa, India.

PUBLICATIONS

Poetry

Guide to the Temple. New Delhi, Indus Publishing Company, 1988.
A Wound Elsewhere. New Delhi, Rupa/HarperCollins, 1992.
Lines from a Legend. Leeds, England, Peepal Tree Books, 1993.
Painting the House. New Delhi, Orient Longman, 1999.

Other

D.H. Lawrence: Modes of Fictional Style. Troy, New York, Whitston, 1989.

Indian Philosophy and Religion: A Reader's Guide, with Minakshi Padhi. Jefferson, North Carolina, and London, England, McFarland and Co., 1990.

Translator, *A Morning of Rain and Other Poems: Selected Poems of Sitakant Mahapatra.* New Delhi, Vikas, 1992.

*

Critical Study: By Elgin W. Mellown, in *D.H. Lawrence Review,* 22(3), fall 1990.

Bibhu Padhi comments:

I think I wrote my first poem in 1968, when I was an undergraduate at Ravenshaw College. Like all first poems, it was a love poem. The literary inspiration came from the Elizabethan sonneteers, Robert Frost, e.e. cummings! I wrote my first "serious" poem in 1975, "From the Extra Medical Ward." The theme was death and how it affected my youngish vision of the world. Other themes have followed—personal relationships, ancestral friendships, my own cultural identity, birds, beasts, the feeling of depression, isolation and poverty in the midst of having almost everything ... materially speaking.

I have been influenced by all the poets I have loved and admired. The senior Indian poet, Jayanta Mahapatra, then Thomas Hardy, Robert Frost, Dylan Thomas, William Stafford, James Merrill, Raymond Carver, Cesare Pavese, Quasimodo, Ungaretti, Seferis, Lorca, Rilke, Popa Neruda (and several other European and Latin American poets), and the Oriya poet Bhima Bhoi. I love poetry that is not deliberately "difficult" and has something to say. And by that I do not mean anything "moral"; what I have in mind is not something that is merely "intelligent." I hate intelligent poetry—the poetry that is purely cerebral. For me poetry must come from the heart—yes, I mean it; otherwise, you are only hastening the death of poetry. As such, the printed word is something fast dying, so why hasten that process? I think nearly 90 percent of what is being written and published today in the name of poetry comes nowhere near my idea of a good/great poem—its honesty, its overall lyrical appeal, its disarming simplicity.

Personally, I do not sit down every day to write something. I just wait for the first line to appear and stay in me for at least a day before I sit down to begin and end a poem. Normally I do not leave a poem half-finished, but then if I do, I soon return to it. And I do not believe in too much revision. I think the poem comes in its near complete form—that is, if the medium, the poet, is sincere. Poetry is not playing with words. I let the words play on me once they have "chosen" me to be their instrument. I just try to clean myself from time to time. There have been quite a few lean periods in my career. No regrets for these whatsoever.

*   *   *

In Bibhu Padhi's India little happens, and what does happen takes place slowly. Padhi occasionally admits that the main road in Cuttack is noisily crowded with cars, but otherwise he shuts out modern phenomena except, as with power failures, to indicate the unchanging, hopeless nature of his life and of that of the community. What might have been the subject matter for a novel—"Our small town has been filled with / rural migrants in search of small jobs"—is rapidly passed over for a litany of "rheumatism and migraine. / The cycle starts all over again."

Jayanta Mahapatra has also created a poetry of boredom about Orissa state, one in which he is an outsider watching the world of believers with their customs and rituals. In Mahapatra's poetry the nationalists' eternal India becomes highly localized, and it is seen through the eyes of a misplaced modern who wishes that he were one of the faithful but who instead writes poems about the difficulty of expressing perceptions and yearnings. Padhi, however, is not Mahapatra, and the Mahapatra-style lyrics of waiting and watching are not his strength. Padhi is not an outsider; he is a Brahman, an insider.

But Padhi has learned from Mahapatra how to make a poetry of waiting, of silence, of monotony, of place: "It is raining in Cuttack once again. / The rain that arrives so gently / that it can scarcely be heard." Padhi's is a poetry of the interior life, in which little is said, there is little communication between people, and much of what is felt is barely articulated, as it is somehow beyond the reach of the words that are being used to locate and define it: "Words are sometimes faintly heard, / or just remembered from a distant year / when I was small. Modest words." This is a highly subjective poetry, stripped of the pleasures of lyricism: "I write this line / I could've written another line." The manner, voice, and tone and the treatment of the subject are flat, uncolored. In Padhi's verse English is used without much change in stress or pitch, while accents fall regularly in equal time: "I could've kept my line / invisible, secret ... I admit though that such lines / do appear on the page, but only when / / I am not writing, or only planning / to remember the missing line."

In Padhi's world life drones on from day to day. This can be as bad a fate as the chaos and fears of urbanization. In the title poem of *A Wound Elsewhere,* a poem with more flare-ups of excitement than most, he addresses himself as if he were another, someone who could not understand what he feels:

> Not here, not here, not this, not here.
> It is one of so many things that
> you've failed to locate this year.
> You face questions about your
> declining health, from anxious lips;
> the answers remain ordinary, familiar.
> Not this, not here, not this, not here.

The manner is distinctive, with its contrast between the poetic (the end rhymes, the old-fashioned diction of "anxious lips," and the repetitions) and the flat clichés ("one of so many things," "failed to locate," "declining health"). There are similar contrasts between the specificity of what is denied as the subject of the poem and the vagueness of what is: "It isn't the migraine that you get ... nor the wish to lie / in bed, face in the pillow ... It isn't because ..." The poem concludes with a triumphal hopelessness: "No one knows, no one need know. / It is always some *other* place— / the hurt stealing into the night from there."

If Padhi's poems can at times appear to be a parody of his manner, so can those of any poet with a strong characteristic style and a body of work that often, and sometimes foolishly, repeats itself: "No one comes, and you celebrate / the loss of a day, every following / day, with a mere look on your face.'' A friend tells him, ''You who live in Cuttack / will never see the world. Even if you leave / for another town or choose a wife from another place.'' Someone from Cuttack will return to the crowds, filth, flies, and mosquitoes. Padhi does not reply, but he thinks,

> . . . I've been here since the time
> I was born a good thirty-five years ago,
> in this town encircled by three rivers
> and with the superstitious clouds
> of my town's forefathers
> still hanging about my eyes in a loving stupor.

A Wound Elsewhere and *Lines from a Legend* reveal a small, narrow society of close yet often strained and impoverished relationships that is almost novelistic. It is a provincial society in which the annual rise of the river, another power failure, or the coming of the rainy season is an event. A father dies, is remembered, becomes almost a ghost haunting the poet. There are memories of Padhi's grandmother, a child is born, and there are Brahman rituals. Padhi feels that he seldom speaks with his wife the way he did in the past; a friend's son moves away. He wonders why he continues to live in his father's house; he then has another house built, and they move in. Padhi and Mahapatra grow apart as Mahapatra retreats into some mood, and Padhi recalls a time when they could speak without being falsely polite. It is this society of births, deaths, anniversaries, illness, misunderstandings, wounded friendships, and the children of friends, all within the small world of Orissa, that eventually emerges from Padhi's poems and that makes his poetic world different than Mahapatra's.

Padhi has created poetry about the provinces, the places where there are no single career women and from which one's best friends and their children depart for higher education and better jobs elsewhere. It is a lower-middle-class perspective of those who stay at home and teach at the local college and for whom nothing changes, or changes slowly, while others move on to the problems of life in the big cities or abroad. As with any poet, there are the hours of waiting for the poem to come, but here the waiting for inspiration and a subject becomes analogous to life itself.

—Bruce King

PAGE, Geoff(rey Donald)

Nationality: Australian. **Born:** Grafton, New South Wales, 7 July 1940. **Education:** Armidale School, 1952–57; University of New England, Armidale, New South Wales, 1958–62, B.A. (honors), Dip.Ed. **Military Service:** National military, 1959. **Family:** Married Carolyn Anne Page in 1972; one son. **Career:** English and history teacher, Canberra high schools, 1964–74. Since 1974 senior English teacher, Narrabundah College, Canberra. Writer-in-residence, University of Wollongong, New South Wales, 1982, Australian Defence Force Academy, Canberra, 1987, Curtin University, 1990, and Edith Cowan University, 1993. **Awards:** Australian Literature Board grant, 1975, 1983, 1987, 1993. **Address:** 8 Morehead Street, Curtin, A.C.T. 2605, Australia.

PUBLICATIONS

Poetry

Two Poets, with Philip Roberts. St. Lucia, University of Queensland Press, 1971.
Smalltown Memorials. University of Queensland Press, 1975.
Collecting the Weather. Brisbane, Makar Press, 1978.
Cassandra Paddocks. Sydney, Angus and Robertson, 1980.
Clairvoyant in Autumn. Sydney, Angus and Robertson, 1983.
Collected Lives. Sydney, Angus and Robertson, 1986.
Smiling in English, Smoking in French. Deakin, A.C.T., Brindabella, 1987.
Footwork. Sydney, Angus and Robertson, 1988.
Selected Poems. Sydney, Angus and Robertson, 1991.
Grove Corners. Sydney, Angus and Robertson, 1992.
Human Interest. Sydney, William Heinemann Australia, 1994.
Mrs. Schnell Arrives in Heaven: And Other Light Verse. Cook, A.C.T., Polonius Press, 1995.
The Great Forgetting: Poems. Canberra, Aboriginal Studies Press, 1996.
The Secret. Kew, Victoria, William Heinemann Australia, 1997.
The Scarring. Alexandria, New South Wales, Hale and Iremonger, 1999.

Plays

Radio Plays: *The Line of Least Resistance,* 1976; *The Life and Death of James Lionel Michael,* 1982.

Novels

Benton's Conviction. Sydney, Angus and Robertson, 1985.
Winter Vision. St. Lucia, University of Queensland Press, 1989.

Short Stories

Invisible Histories (includes verse). Sydney, Picador, 1990.

Other

Using "The First Paperback Poets Anthology." Brisbane, University of Queensland Press, 1974.
A Reader's Guide to Contemporary Australian Poetry. St. Lucia, University of Queensland Press, 1995.

Editor, *Shadows from the Wire: Poems and Photographs of Australians in the Great War.* Ringwood, Victoria, Penguin, 1983.
Editor, *On the Move: Australian Poets in Europe.* Springwood, New South Wales, Butterfly Books, 1992.

*

Critical Study: By Alan Gould, in *Quadrant* (Victoria, Australia), 36(6), June 1992.

Geoff Page comments:
It is risky for poets to comment on their own work; that is a matter for their readers. The risks of dogmatism or self-deception are too great. I would simply say that I am happy to be part of a very

diverse poetic culture in Australia, where many different ars poeticas contend and/or coexist; happy too that Australian poetry is now being better recognized as an important part of the worldwide tradition of poetry in English. For those who wish to know more, let them buy the books!

*   *   *

Geoff Page emerged later than some of his contemporaries as a poet of importance in Australia. He is underrepresented in anthologies, but he has produced a body of honestly felt and moving work that is impressive in its totality.

His work is characterized by its clarity and succinctness of image, as in these lines from ''Flying over the Western Districts''—

Down
through five clear miles of air

the patterns of our tenure
lie strange across the ground

—or in these lines from ''Prowlers''—

A floorboard sprung
will bring a groan
vaguely down the hall.

Angles of furniture
hold them strangely.
Books along a shelf give out

their varying degrees of light
as, guiltless yet,
they slip away—

The accuracy and the deceptive plainness of Page's imagery derive from William Carlos Williams, but these combine in Page's work with an Australian concern for landscape, history, and narrative. He is perhaps the most typically Australian poet of his generation, without being in any way nationalistic in his work. His deliberately dry and low-key delivery and the celebration of survival in poems such as ''Grit,'' which praises

the country women
of my mother's generation . . .
that hard abundance year by year
mapped in a single word,

may be seen by some, particularly outsiders, as archetypally Australian. This is to simplify Australians, however, and Page, himself no simplifier, would see himself and other Australians in more complex terms.

In poem after poem Page is concerned with wastage and lost opportunities, as in these lines from ''Break-Up'':

Once, quite near the end,
we showered together.
While the soap
clung round your nipples
and the water slid

down either back,
my body
committed
yours
to memory.

This concern is also seen in his poems about World War I and the death of his grandmother and in ''Aubade.'' Memories of making love conclude on this note: ''we listen to the world / fill up with light / and with our losses.'' Page's determinedly negative stance and his painstaking understatement cumulatively spell out a passionate rhetoric of loss. He is not unaware of the decorative and filmic aspects of his subject matter, however. Thus, in ''Daguerreotype Tennis'' he writes,

The roller's hauled
one unaware last time
and left,
the game postponed.

This self-awareness includes a wry, implicit humor. And occasionally there are overtly humorous poems such as ''In Dante's Hell,'' which deals with the Australian obsession with discussing vintages.

—Geoffrey Lehmann

PAGE, P(atricia) K(athleen)

Nationality: Canadian. **Born:** Swanage, Dorset, England, 23 November 1916; immigrated to Canada in 1919. **Education:** St. Hilda's School for Girls, Calgary, Alberta; Art Students League, and Pratt Institute, New York. **Family:** Married William Arthur Irwin in 1950; two stepdaughters and one stepson. **Career:** Formerly sales clerk and radio actress, Saint John, New Brunswick; filing clerk and historical researcher, Montreal; script writer, National Film Board, Ottawa, 1946–50; conductor of writers workshops, Toronto, and University of Victoria, British Columbia, 1974–78. Painter, as P.K. Irwin: individual shows—Picture Loan Society, Toronto, 1960; Galeria de Arte Moderna, Mexico City, 1962; Art Gallery of Greater Victoria, British Columbia, 1965. **Awards:** Bertram Warr award (*Contemporary Verse*), 1940; Oscar Blumenthal award (*Poetry,* Chicago), 1944; Governor-General's award, 1955; National Magazines award, 1985; Canadian Authors Association literary award, 1986; Hubert Evans award, for nonfiction, 1987; Banff School of Fine Arts National award, 1989; Readers' Choice award (*Prairie Schooner*), 1993. D.Litt.: University of Victoria, 1985; University of Guelph, 1990. L.L.D.: University of Calgary, 1989; Simon Fraser University, 1990. Officer, Order of Canada, 1977. **Address:** 3260 Exeter Road, Victoria, British Columbia V8R 6H6, Canada.

PUBLICATIONS

Poetry

Unit of Five, with others, edited by Ronald Hambleton. Toronto, Ryerson Press, 1944.
As Ten As Twenty. Toronto, Ryerson Press, 1946.

The Metal and the Flower. Toronto, McClelland and Stewart, 1954.

Cry Ararat! Poems New and Selected. Toronto, McClelland and Stewart, 1967.

Poems, Selected and New. Toronto, Anansi, 1974.

Five Poems. Toronto, League of Canadian Poets, 1980.

Evening Dance of the Grey Flies. Toronto, Oxford University Press, 1981; New York, Oxford University Press, 1982.

The Glass Air: Poems Selected & New. Toronto and New York, Oxford University Press, 1991.

Hologram: A Book of Glosas. London, Ontario, Brick Books, 1994.

The Hidden Room: Collected Poems. Erin, Ontario, Porcupine's Quill, 1997.

Play

The Travelling Musicians (libretto), music by Murray Adaskin (produced Victoria, British Columbia, 1984).

Novel

The Sun and the Moon (as Judith Cape). Toronto, Macmillan, and New York, Creative Age Press, 1944.

Short Stories

The Sun and the Moon, and Other Fictions. Toronto, Anansi, 1973.

Unless the Eye Catch Fire. N.p., Full Spectrum Press, 1994.

Other

Brazilian Journal. Toronto, Lester and Orpen Dennys, 1987.

A Flask of Sea Water (for children). Toronto, Oxford University Press, 1989.

The Travelling Musicians. N.p., Kids Can Press, 1991.

The Goat That Flew. Victoria, British Columbia, Beach Holme Press, 1993.

Editor, *To Say the Least: Canadian Poets from A to Z.* Erin, Ontario, Press Porcépic, 1979.

*

Bibliography: "The Poetry of P.K. Page: A Checklist" by Michele Preston, in *West Coast Review* (Burnaby, British Columbia), January 1979.

Manuscript Collection: Canadian Archives, Ottawa.

Critical Studies: By Daryl Hine, in *Poetry* (Chicago), 1968; "Traveller, Conjuror, Journeyman" by the author, in *Canadian Literature* (Vancouver), autumn 1970; *The Bush Garden* by Northrop Frye, Toronto, Anansi, 1971; "The Poetry of P.K. Page" by A.J.M. Smith, in *Canadian Literature* (Vancouver), autumn 1971; "P.K. Page: The Chameleon and the Centre" by Constance Rooke, in *Malahat Review* (Victoria), January 1978; "A Size Larger Than Seeing: The Poetry of P.K. Page" by Rosemary Sullivan, in *Canadian Literature* (Vancouver); "Retrospect and Prospect: P.K. Page" by Jean Mallinson, in *West Coast Review* (Burnaby, British Columbia), January 1979; "Double Landscape" by S. Namjoshi, in *Canadian Literature* (Vancouver), 46; *P.K. Page and Her Works* by John Orange, Toronto, ECW Press, 1990; by John Orange, in *ECW's Biographical Guide to Canadian Poets,* edited by Robert Lecker, Jack David, and Ellen Quigley, Toronto, ECW, 1993; "Tracing a Terrestrial Vision in the Early Work of P.K. Page" by Diana Relke, in *Canadian Poetry* (London, Ontario), 35, fall-winter 1994; "The Multiple Self in the Poetry of P.K. Page" by Douglas Freake, in *Studies in Canadian Literature* (Fredericton, New Brunswick), 19(1), 1994; "P.K. Page's Brazilian Journal: Language Shock" by Denise Adele Heaps, in *Biography* (Honolulu), 19(4), fall 1996; P.K. Page issue of *Malahat Review* (Victoria), 117, winter 1996; "For Sure the Kittiwake: Naming, Nature, and P.K. Page" by Brian Bartlett, in *Canadian Literature* (Vancouver), 155, winter 1997; "Toward a Poetics of Dislocation: Elizabeth Bishop and P.K. Page Writing 'Brazil'" by Kevin McNeilly, in *Studies in Canadian Literature* (Fredericton, New Brunswick), 23(2), 1998.

*   *   *

P.K. Page is an artist of many aspects. She has written a romance (*The Sun and the Moon*), magic realist short stories, essays on the writer's role, and an eloquent volume of travel writing-cum-autobiography (*Brazilian Journal*). Under her married name of P.K. Irwin, she is a painter and printmaker of repute. The various arts she practices interact, and her poetry is distinguished by the strongly visual aspect of the white-and-green country of the imagination that extends before the mind's eye as one reads. The shapes in her paintings suggest underlying narratives and syntactical correspondences, and there are times when her poems read like paintings, as in the color imagery of "Stories of Snow" and "Elegy." Her poems often play with the intriguing phenomena of visual perspective—spring as seen at minuscule ground level in "Short Spring Poem" or the intermingling making and unmaking of landscape and identity found throughout "Reflection in a Train Window."

Page began to publish in the early 1940s, a seminal time in Canadian poetry, and her first pieces appeared in *Preview,* one of the most influential Canadian magazines of modern poetry, in whose editing she played a part. In 1946 she published her first independent book, *As Ten as Twenty,* which shows a strong awareness of British avant-garde trends of the 1930s and an appropriate social radicalism but which also contains visionary poems that create luminous worlds of their own, like the haunting "Stories of Snow," in which legend and dream and childhood memories are mingled in what A.J.M. Smith once called "a crystal clairvoyance." Although her political consciousness sometimes expresses itself in Audenesque generalities of social radicalism, it frequently results in an empathetic re-creation of individual plights that continue in *The Metal and the Flower.* Poems such as "The Stenographers" and "Typists" show a wonderful capacity to enter into the perspectives of other people and chart their inner landscapes. Formally, Page's work is prodigiously accomplished right from the beginning; she is equally at home in rhymed poetry and free verse, and she displays an unerring ear for slant rhyme and for the rhythmical momentum achieved by alternating between lines of various lengths. The opening stanza of "Mineral" displays all of these characteristics:

Soft and unmuscular among flowers and papers
and changed as if grown deaf or slightly lame

she writes to strangers about him as if he were a stranger,
avoids the name
which he no longer has a use for, which
he disinherited as he was leaving.
It had a different ring when he was living.

The poems that came after a decade of silence—from the mid-1950s to the mid-1960s, a period during which she traveled with her diplomat husband to Australia, Brazil, and Mexico—reflect Page's concentration on painting during that time. They are poems in which the visual evokes the visionary, and they show her turning toward physical landscapes and natural images to find means of liberation from the alienated, imprisoned self. The concluding lines of ''Cry Ararat!'' emphasize the power of the visionary conjunction between the natural world and its beholders: ''A single leaf can block a mountainside; / all Ararat be conjured by a leaf.'' This recognition involves Page in a deepened awareness—which is at the sometimes troubled heart of her finest later poetry—of the paradoxical nature of the artist's calling, entailing both a celebratory delight in visionary power and a chastening sense of the limitations of that power. The delight rings out in the opening line of ''Cook's Mountains'': ''By naming them he made them.'' Much as Wallace Stevens's singer makes the world by singing it, in ''The Idea of Order at Key West,'' Cook (''his tongue / silvered with paradox and metaphor'') glazes the Glass House Mountains with his gaze, and at the act of naming they are altered ''to become / the sum of shape and name.'' More sober and self-critical, ''After Rain'' confronts the solipsism of the enterprise (''I lift the blind / upon a woman's wardrobe of the mind'') and builds to a plea that the birds inhabiting her garden ''keep my heart a size / larger than seeing.''

In the years since it was voiced, the birds have answered Page's plea favorably. Although the poems in *Evening Dance of the Grey Flies* and *The Glass Air* are sharply and intensely visual in their sensuous evocation of color and space, and although the ordinary seems to become transfigured and translucent through Page's visionary apprehension in such poems as ''Finches Feeding'' or ''Invisible Presences Fill the Air,'' other poems manifest an unabated capacity for sympathetic identification with the ordinary. It may be the ordinary miseries of a friend growing old, as in ''Phone Call from Mexico,'' or of the ordinary shocks—inarticulate before Page gives them a voice—of a weather-wrung tree in ''Out Here: Flowering'' or of captive whales in ''Leviathan in a Pool.'' Given the intense partnership that her poetry sets up between the artist's vision and the valued independence of the objects encountered by it, it seems altogether appropriate that the following collection, *Hologram,* is a sequence of ''glosas''—acts of collaboration between her lines and those of other poets. Each of the fourteen glosas in *Hologram* consists of interweavings with, and variations on, a quatrain written by another poet. Page's comment on the first poem outlines the collection's masterful balance of creative autonomy and imaginative sympathy: ''I felt as if I were hand in hand with Seferis. A curious marriage—two sensibilities intermingling.'' In its structure the book takes us through widening circles of sympathetic identification that unfold like a flower from the artist's determination to ''un-me myself'' (''Inebriate''), attaining through its embrace of the world's human and natural otherness a realization of the goal Page sets herself in ''Planet Earth'': ''It has to be stretched and stroked. / It has to be celebrated. / O this great beloved world and all the creatures in it.'' At the same time the sequence delves into the source and center of both the world's plenitude and the self's need to embrace it, concluding in

''The Answer'' that we live ''only for love, the love that is / so focussed on its object that I die / utterly, a candle in the sun, / a drop of water in the sea.'' In her foreword Page describes the collection as ''a book of homage'' to those poets who helped her find her voice. It is also a book that calls forth and rewards homage from its readers, a deeply satisfying product of the ''marriage'' between Page's large heart and large talent.

—George Woodcock and Julia Reibetanz

PALMER, Michael

Nationality: American. **Born:** New York City, 11 May 1943. **Education:** Harvard University, Cambridge, Massachusetts, 1961–68, B.A. in French 1965, M.A. in comparative literature 1967. **Family:** Married Cathy Simon in 1972; one daughter. **Career:** Editor, *Joglars Magazine,* Providence, Rhode Island, 1964–66; contributing editor, *Sulfur* magazine, Los Angeles. **Awards:** National Endowment for the Arts fellowship, 1975. **Address:** 265 Jersey Street, San Francisco, California 94114, U.S.A.

PUBLICATIONS

Poetry

Plan of the City of O. Boston, Barn Dream Press, 1971.
Blake's Newton. Los Angeles, Black Sparrow Press, 1972.
C's Songs. Berkeley, California, Sand Dollar, 1973.
Six Poems. Los Angeles, Black Sparrow Press, 1973.
The Circular Gates. Los Angeles, Black Sparrow Press, 1974.
Without Music. Santa Barbara, California, Black Sparrow Press, 1977.
Alogon. Berkeley, California, Tuumba Press, 1980.
Notes for Echo Lake. Berkeley, California, North Point Press, 1981.
First Figure. Berkeley, California, North Point Press, 1984.
Sun. Berkeley, California, North Point Press, 1988.
For a Reading: A Selection of Poems. New York, Dia Art Foundation, 1988.
An Alphabet Underground: Poems. Viborg, Denmark, After Hand, 1993.
At Passages. New York, New Directions, 1995.
The Lion Bridge. New York, New Directions 1998.

Plays

Radio Plays: *Idem l-4,* 1979.

Dance Scenarios (collaborations with Margaret Jenkins Dance Company): *Interferences,* 1975; *Equal Time,* 1976; *Video Songs,* 1976; *About the Space in Between,* 1977; *No One But Whitington,* 1978; *Red, Yellow, Blue,* 1978; *Straight Words,* 1980; *Versions by Turns,* 1980; *Cortland Set,* 1982; *First Figure,* 1984.

Other

The Danish Notebook. N.p., Avec Books, 1999.

Editor, *Code of Signals: Recent Writings in Poetics.* Berkeley, California, North Atlantic, 1983.

Editor, with Régis Bonvicino and Nelson Ascher, *Nothing the Sun Could Not Explain: 20 Contemporary Brazilian Poets.* Los Angeles, Sun and Moon Press, 1997.

Translator, with Geoffrey Young, *Relativity of Spring: 13 Poems,* by Vicente Huidobro. Berkeley, California, Sand Dollar, 1976.

Translator, *Jonah Who Will Be 25 in the Year 2000* (screenplay), by Alain Tanner and John Berger. Berkeley, California, North Atlantic, 1983.

Translator, with Norma Cole, *The Surrealists Look at Art.* Venice, California, Lapis Press, 1990.

Translator, *Theory of Tables,* by Emmanuel Hocquard. Providence, Rhode Island, O-Blek editions, 1994.

Translator, with John High and Michael Molnar, *Blue Vitriol,* by Alexei Parshchikov. N.p., Avec Books, 1994.

Translator, *Three Moral Tales,* by Emmanuel Hocquard. N.p., Noble Rider, 1996.

*

Critical Studies: By Michael Davidson, in *Caterpillar 20* (Sherman Oaks, California), 1973; Steve McCaffery, in *Open Letter* (Toronto), fall 1975, April 1978, and fall 1978; David Chaloner, in *Poetry Information* (London), summer 1976; William Corbett, in *L=A=N=G=U=A=G=E 2* (New York), 1978; Martin Dodman, in *Montemora* 5 (New York), June 1979; George Lakoff, in *Poetics Journal 2* (Berkeley, California), 1982; Alan Soldofsky, in *Ironwood 19* (Tucson), 1982; *Language Poetry: Writing As Rescue* by Linda Reinfeld. Baton Rouge and London, Louisiana State University Press, 1992; ''Important Pleasures and Others: Michael Palmer, Ronald Johnson'' by Eric Murphy Selinger, in *Postmodern Culture* (Cary, North Carolina), 4(3), May 1994; ''Language Poetry, Language Technology, and the Fractal Dimension: Michael Palmer Prints Out a Kingdom'' by Tan Lin, in *A Poetics of Criticism,* edited by Juliana Spahr and others, Buffalo, New York, Leave, 1994; *The Poetics of Resistance: A Critical Introduction to Michael Palmer* (dissertation) by Lauri Scheyer Ramey, University of Chicago, 1996; ''Without Measure: Duration in Palmer and Willis'' by Joshua McKinney, in *Denver Quarterly* (Denver, Colorado), 31(4), spring 1997; ''Making the Dust Rise: Michael Palmer's Interrogation into Being'' by David W. Clippinger, in *Salt Hill Journal* (Syracuse, New York), 2, spring 1996.

*   *   *

It has long been a dogma of poetic criticism that it is impossible to paraphrase a poem. Most poems, of course, can be paraphrased, and it is frequently useful to do so, especially when the reader is making a first acquaintance with a work. The poetry of Michael Palmer, however, cannot be paraphrased. Its meaning is strictly a function of the complex interrelations of specific linguistic details.

A typical poem—''On the Way to Language,'' for example—is a linguistic environment in which poetic particles, phonemes, rhythms, rhymes, images, and bits and pieces of found language perform a complex dance. The present example shares its title with a translation of one of Heidegger's philosophical treatises. The reader must assume that this is no accident, and it is clear that Palmer is a reader of modern philosophy. Having made this somewhat arcane connection (it is not one of Heidegger's better-known works), however, one by no means has a key to the poem. In fact, the information seems to lead nowhere. The poem takes the form of answers and questions, upsetting normal expectations of order, and although it suggests certain Heideggerian themes, it is noncommittal. The poem closes when the abstract title produces an image of a concrete ''way''—''the valley of desire / crossed by the bridge / of frequent sighs''— but in context this is really another enigma rather than a resolution.

The theme of Palmer's work, to the extent that it may be said to have a theme, is a Heideggerian or, perhaps more to the point, Wittgensteinian astonishment at the existence of phenomena. We are presented with a world and a language that are endlessly fascinating. It is possible to trace local connections and to follow this or that line of thought to its frequently absurd conclusion, but there is no closure except for the confrontation with the inexplicable and irreducible stuff of language and the world.

It is demanding poetry. The ideal reader is one who can combine intense concentration with willingness to play—in all senses of the word—to play as a child and also, perhaps more importantly, to play as a musician. Despite the fact that Palmer's most interesting volume is entitled *Without Music,* all of his work is best read in the spirit of a musician studying a score, trying different tempos, different phrasings, and so forth.

Palmer is involved in an exploration of possibilities in language that have been largely disregarded. He takes a passage from Géza Rohéim's *Magic and Schizophrenia* as the epigraph to *Without Music,* and he also names Louis Wolfson's *Le Schizo et les langues* as one of his important sources. We are beginning to learn that traditional syntax and traditional forms of poetic organization are merely laborsaving devices that allow a vague, careless attention to language. When such simple strategies are exposed, however, and attention is brought to bear without reservation, it begins to discover possibilities for the production of meaning far more powerful than those we have previously known. One of the unexpected turns in this situation is that we learn the schizophrenic's bewilderment to be a result of wandering unaided into this difficult and exciting realm of experience.

In his later work Palmer seems to declare a significantly new direction. The objectively distanced tone of the earlier work now gives way to an intellectually denser texture, in the vein of poets as different from one another as Paul Célan and Robert Duncan. The poems, as in this one from the late 1980s, seem almost to erase themselves:

Unutterable

pages

of counterlight

in the fluid window

a dog sings songs

asking nothing

we cannot speak.

The ambiguity of these lines seems to have touched a terminus of the ironic possibility that is central to Palmer's project. His elegant and beautifully crafted work now enters the contest of visionary poetry with silence.

—Don Byrd

PAPE, Greg(ory Laurence)

Nationality: American. **Born:** Eureka, California, 17 January 1947. **Education:** Fresno State College, B.A. in English 1970; California State University, Fresno, M.A. in English 1972; University of Arizona, M.F.A. in creative writing 1974. **Family:** Married Marnie Prange in 1988; two sons. **Career:** Instructor, California State University, Fresno, 1970–72; teaching assistant, 1972–73, instructor, New Start program for minority students, 1973, and teaching associate, 1973–74, University of Arizona; instructor, Pima Community College, Tucson, Arizona, fall 1976; worked in Writers-in-Residence and Writers-in-Schools programs, Arizona Commission on the Arts and Humanities, 1977–79; assistant professor, Hollins College, Virginia, 1979–80; visiting assistant professor, University of Missouri, Columbia, fall 1980, 1981–82; visiting writer, spring 1981, and writer-in-residence, spring 1983, University of Alabama; Bingham Poet-in-Residence, University of Louisville, 1983–84; visiting assistant professor, Northern Arizona University, 1984–85; associate professor, Florida International University, 1985–87. Associate professor, 1987–93, and since 1994 professor, University of Montana, Missoula. Coal Royalty Endowed Chair in Creative Writing, University of Alabama, fall 1993. **Awards:** Discovery award for poetry, 1973; writing fellowship, Fine Arts Work Center, Provincetown, Massachusetts, 1974–76; Charles Philbrick fellowship in writing, 1976; Robert Frost fellowship in poetry, Bread Loaf Writers Conference, 1978; National Endowment for the Arts fellowship, 1978, 1984; Pushcart prize, 1988–89; Richard Hugo Memorial Poetry award, *Cutbank,* 1990–91; Edwin Ford Piper Poetry award, University of Iowa Press, 1991. **Address:** English Department, University of Montana, Missoula, Montana 59812, U.S.A.

PUBLICATIONS

Poetry

Little America. Tucson, Arizona, The Maguey Press, 1976.
Border Crossings. Pittsburgh, University of Pittsburgh Press, 1978.
Black Branches. Pittsburgh, University of Pittsburgh Press, 1984.
The Morning Horse. Lewiston, Idaho, Confluence Press, 1991.
Storm Pattern. Pittsburgh, University of Pittsburgh Press, 1992.
Sunflower Facing the Sun. Iowa City, University of Iowa Press, 1992.
Small Pleasures. Tuscaloosa, Alabama, Lagniappe Press, 1994.

*

Critical Study: "Easy Listening" by Henry Taylor, in *Poetry,* CLXII(1), April 1993.

*   *   *

Greg Pape's early collections *Border Crossings* (1978) and *Black Branches* (1984) introduced an honest, unpretentious poet with a deep affinity for wide-open spaces. His landscapes are the dry, ancient towns of the American Southwest and the long roads between them. With extraordinary sensitivity to physical details and sensations and to the sounds of Hispanic place-names, he makes the ordinary seem moving and strange, the simple observation seem heavy with import. In his later work he has developed a delicate sensitivity to the brief but intense moments of connection that occur between people, whether they are lovers, close friends, or strangers and wherever their encounters take place, from the desert to the supermarket. He appeared at first to be working with a somewhat limited array of technical resources, producing primarily a free verse whose lines tended to break where a natural pause would occur. Although this is an honorable and widely used free verse technique, many poets who use it find out only by experience that it is as easy to develop predictable rhythms in free verse as it is in meter.

Subsequent books such as *Storm Pattern* and *Sunflower Facing the Sun* are excellent collections in which any apprehensions about Pape's ability to grow into a deeper command of technique are quite firmly put to rest. He remains loyal to free verse, but his range of effects is much wider than in his earlier books. Objects, people, and episodes repay his close attention and help the poems toward tighter connections or clearer visions of particular ideas. The poems often move in ways that are at first surprising and then deeply satisfying.

"In Line at the Supermarket," for example, draws us into its situation by way of our reactions to certain stereotypes. The couple in front of the speaker at the checkout have spiked hair and threatening tattoos, but their conversation is as ordinary as anyone's:

"We don't need a ham this big," he says,
as he holds it under her nose.
"Yes we do" and she places her fingertips
on the ham and pushes it back down,
lightly, to the stalled conveyor.

"In Line at the Supermarket" is a strong reminder that we are all in this together, that the human enterprise is at the same time strong and fragile.

"Blessing at the Citadel," a superb poem at the end of *Sunflower Facing the Sun,* is set in the remote ancient home of the Hopi. Three human silhouettes loom on a rock, as if they might be gods, but one approaches the speaker and blesses him:

Go pray, he said. What for? I asked.
Pray for now, this place, all your relations.
Pray for the hostages.
Then he walked off down the trail
to join the others, not gods
but poor, living men from Moenkopi
here at the home of their ancestors
to pray for the world and bless a stranger.

Looking at lines like these, it is almost impossible to know how rarely such simple yet momentous effects are achieved. Pape's maturing craftsmanship and his deepening humanity have led him to poems of engaging wisdom, strength, and timelessness.

—Henry Taylor

PARTHASARATHY, R(ajagopal)

Nationality: Indian. **Born:** Tirupparaitturai, near Tiruchchirappalli, Tamil Nadu, 20 August 1934. **Education:** Don Bosco High School, Bombay, 1944–51; Siddharth College, Bombay University, 1951–59, B.A. in English 1956, M.A. in English 1959; Leeds University, Yorkshire (British Council scholar), 1963–64, postgraduate diploma in English studies 1964; University of Texas, Austin, 1982–86, Ph.D. in English 1987. **Family:** Married Shobhan Koppikar in 1969; two sons. **Career:** Lecturer in English, Ismail Yusuf College, Bombay, 1959–62, and Mithibai College, Bombay, 1962–63, 1964–65; lecturer in English language teaching, British Council, Bombay, 1965–66; assistant professor of English, Presidency College, Madras, 1966–67; lecturer in English, South Indian Education Society College, Bombay, 1967–71. Regional editor, Madras, 1971–78, and editor, Delhi,1978–82, Oxford University Press; member of the International Writing Program, University of Iowa, Iowa City, 1978–79; assistant instructor in English, University of Texas at Austin, 1982–86; director, program in Asian Studies, 1994–98, and currently associate professor of English, Skidmore College, Saratoga Springs, New York. Member of the advisory board for English, National Academy of Letters, New Delhi, 1978–82. **Awards:** Ulka poetry prize, *Poetry India,* 1966; runner-up for the Commonwealth poetry prize of the Commonwealth Institute, London, 1977, for *Rough Passage;* PEN/Book-of-the-Month Club translation citation of the PEN American Center, 1994, for *The Tale of an Anklet: An Epic of South India;* Sahitya Akademi (National Academy of Letters) prize for translation, 1995; Association for Asian Studies A.K. Ramanujan book prize for translation, 1996. **Address:** Department of English and Program in Asian Studies, Skidmore College, 815 North Broadway, Saratoga Springs, New York 12866–1632, U.S.A.

PUBLICATIONS

Poetry

Rough Passage. Delhi, Oxford University Press, 1977.

Other

Editor, with J.J. Healy, *Poetry from Leeds.* Calcutta, Writers Workshop, 1968.

Editor, *Ten Twentieth-Century Indian Poets.* Delhi, Oxford University Press, 1976.

Translator, *The Cilappatikaram of Ilanko Atikal: An Epic of South India.* New York, Columbia University Press, 1993.

*

Critical Studies: "Two Indian Poets" by William Walsh, in *Literary Criterion 11* (Mysore), winter 1974; "R. Parthasarathy: Images of a Poet" by Roger Iredale, in *Tenor 1* (Hyderabad), July 1978; "The Parthasarathy Passage: An Interview" by Ayyappa Paniker, in *Tenor 2* (Hyderabad), January 1979; "The Achievement of R. Parthasarathy" by Brijraj Singh, in *Chandrabhaga 2* (Cuttack), winter 1979; *The Two Faces of Alienation: The Poetry of A.K. Ramanujan and R. Parthasarathy* (M.A. thesis) by G.N. Devi, Leeds University, 1979; "The Unity of Design in *Rough Passage*" by P.D.

Chaturvedi, in *Commonwealth Quarterly 5* (Mysore), 17, 1980; "The Return of the Exile: The Poetry of R. Parthasarathy" by Vasant A. Shahane, in *Indian Poetry in English: A Critical Assessment,* Delhi, Macmillan, 1980; "The Last Refinement of Speech" by M. Sivaramakrishna, in *Contemporary Indian English Verse: An Evaluation,* New Delhi, Arnold Heinemann, 1980; *Perspectives on the Poetry of R. Parthasarathy* edited by Bijay Kumar Das, Bareilly, Parakash Book Defoot, 1983; "Tension into Poetry: R. Parthasarathy" by Ujjal Dutta, in *Indian Literature 26* (New Delhi), 1, 1983; "R. Parthasarathy: The Language of Deracination" by Sudesh Mishra, in *A Sense of Exile: Essays in the Literature of the Asia-Pacific Region,* Nedlands, Centre for Studies in Australian Literature, University of Western Australia, 1988; *Modern Indian Poetry in English,* 2nd ed., Delhi, Oxford University Press, 1989; "To the End of the Marriage: R. Parthasarathy's *Rough Passage*" by G.N. Devy, in *Living Indian English Poets: An Anthology of Critical Essays,* New Delhi, Sterling Publishers, 1989; *Contemporary Indian Poetry in English: Nissim Ezekiel, Kamala Das, A.K. Ramanujan, and R. Parthasarathy,* New Delhi, Atlantic Publishers, 1991; by Terence Diggory, in *Writers of the Indian Diaspora: A Bio-Bibliographical Critical Sourcebook,* Westport, Connecticut, Greenwood Press, 1993; by Arvind K. Mehrotra, in *The Oxford Companion to Twentieth-Century Poetry,* Oxford University Press, 1994; "The Ithacan Voyages of R. Parthasarathy and A.K. Ramanujan" by Rajeev S. Phatke, in *New Perspectives in Indian English Literature: Essays in Honour of Professor M.K. Naik,* edited by C.R. Yaravintelimath and others, New Delhi, Sterling Publishers, 1995.

R. Parthasarathy comments:

One of the realities of the literary scene in our time is that of the exile as writer who takes his language and homeland abroad with him or writes in a language other than his own. Exile is seen as a rite of passage he must go through before he earns the right to speak. *Rough Passage* is in the tradition of the literature of exile, where the English language and residence abroad are in the nature of attempts to situate myself more firmly at home. The dominance of English in India made us exiles in our own homeland, and no Indian writer of the last one hundred and fifty years has escaped the bewitchment of English. Modern Indian literature is unthinkable without the English language. *Rough Passage* states this unequivocally: "He had spent his youth whoring / after English gods." It is within the framework of exile that *Rough Passage* ought to be read. Exile, I repeat, is not a prison house; it is in exile that a writer is most at home.

One of the problems that the Indian poet writing in English faces is the problem of trying to relate himself meaningfully to a living tradition. The poet who writes only in English is unable to relate himself to any specific tradition. He cannot relate himself, for instance, to the tradition of English verse, and he should not. Nor can he relate himself to a tradition of verse in any one of the Indian languages. From the beginning I saw my task as one of acclimatizing the English language to an indigenous tradition. In fact, the tenor of *Rough Passage* is explicit: to initiate a dialogue between myself and my Tamil past. The poem attempts a redefinition of myself as a Tamil—what it means to be a Tamil after having whored after English gods. "Homecoming," in particular, tries to derive its sustenance from grafting itself on to whatever I find usable in the Tamil tradition. I was eventually able to nativize in English something that had eluded me over the years—the flavor, the essence of Tamil mores.

I am aware of the hiatus between the soil of the language I use and my own roots. Even though I am Tamil speaking and yet write in

English, there is the overwhelming difficulty of using images in a linguistic tradition that is quite other than that of my own. I believe that an Indian poet who thinks long and hard enough on his own use of language, even if it is English, sooner or later will, through the English language, try to come to terms with himself as an Indian, with his Indian past and present, and that the language will become acclimatized to the Indian environment. Further, if the poet has access to an Indian language, even though he may not write in it himself, he can gradually try to appropriate that language's tradition. This would mean reconciling ourselves to Tamil English verse, Kannada English verse, Marathi English verse, and so on—all segments of a pan-Indian mosaic that we recognize as the literatures of India. When that happens, the severed head, Indian English verse, will no longer ''choke / to speak another tongue.''

''Stanzas: A Tale of India'' (1999), a long poem as yet in typescript, is rooted in the Tamil and Sanskrit literary traditions, whose resonances it tries to convey in English verse. It dwells on the paradox of India since the Raj in an attempt to map the turbulent history of the subcontinent, striking in the process a truly epic note.

*　　*　　*

R. Parthasarathy published the collection *Rough Passage* in 1977. In the mid-1990s he prepared a second collection, *Indian Summer,* for publication. *Rough Passage* is divided into three sections—''Exile,'' ''Trial,'' and ''Homecoming.'' The preface recommends that the work be read as one poem, as an autobiographical poem in fact. The sequence is initiated by the tension felt by the poet between his Tamil heritage and the environment in which he grew up, that of the English language and of Pax Britannica, which produced a feeling of displacement in him and in many of his generation. The dilemma, simply stated, is how an Indian writer can be himself when he writes in a language that is not his mother tongue or the language of his community or his tradition. Parthasarathy's solution is to write what he calls ''colored'' English poems, poems whose outer form is English but whose inner form is Tamil.

In *Rough Passage* the attempt is only partially successful. Although there are discernible Tamil elements in many of the poems, they do not make the immediate impression that, for example, Pound's Chinese translations do. The Tamil that Parthasarathy favors is not the contemporary idiom which has been debased by the cinema but rather its ancient form. He has translated into English verse an ancient Tamil epic, the *Cilappati-karam* of Ilanko Atikal, which has been highly praised by both poets and scholars for its fidelity and its poetic qualities. One may say that the translation fulfilled a biographical need or urge.

The title of Parthasarathy's second collection, *Indian Summer,* serves to remind us of his residence in the United States and of the fact that he is now middle-aged. In a note to the collection Parthasarathy quotes dictionary meanings of the phrase ''Indian summer'' to justify the title. In the American context it calls attention to the collection as a work of his maturity, and in the Asian context it evokes India but discourages nostalgia by alluding to the oppressive heat of the summer there.

Parthasarathy speaks of his dissatisfaction with the structure of *Rough Passage* and its representation of ''the poet's'' growth. He looks upon the second collection as a spiritual exercise (Latin *exercitia spiritualia,* Sanskrit s$_d$hana). In a note Parthasarathy explains that the sequence has a circular structure and that it moves from the outer (*puram*) to the inner (*akam*) world, these being the two great categories into which poetry in Tamil is classified. *Akam* has as its focus the individual within the matrix of familial relationships, and *puram* is centered outside this matrix and explores the relationship between the individual and the world around him. Themes of exile and homecoming, central to *Rough Passage,* are thus of secondary importance in *Indian Summer.* As his note goes on to say, ''The end of the rough passage is now in sight: home (both the physical home of 8 Salem Drive, Saratoga Springs, New York, and India on the one hand, and the spiritual home of poetry and asceticism on the other).''

The antidote to the feeling of displacement recorded in *Rough Passage* consists in returning to traditional India and what it stands for. In this sense Parthasarathy claims that, although it includes many poems from *Rough Passage, Indian Summer* is a national poem embodying the spirit of India: ''Individual and national histories blend together to tell the story of a troubled land.'' Parthasarathy's claim raises the difficult question of whether there is a single spirit of India. In one of the poems, for example, the poet declares that we must escape from time and that we can do so if ''the word'' can ''absolve'' the object. (He speaks of ''the abomination of objects.'') It may be submitted, however, that the escape from time also includes escaping from the past, from tradition, and that the object can be ''absolved'' only by dissolving it, which happens when the object, or the world, is perceived as maya. (See, for example, the Indian novelist Raja Rao's *The Serpent and the Rope.*) To deabominate the object, or to sanctify it, we need the prelapsarian word, for the poetic word cannot semantically function without the object. Parthasarathy speaks of ''the domed word'' as the ''high byzantine saddle'' for this lowly donkey, the object. ''But the donkey will kick and protest: 'I carry the saddle.''' Perhaps the clue is in the word ''domed.'' The poetic word must merge and lead to the silence above, the silence into which words, after speech, reach.

In 1973 Nissim Ezekiel, himself a distinguished Indian poet writing in English and a critic and an editor of several poetry magazines, praised Parthasarathy's poetry for the meticulous use of words, controlled rhythms, careful choice of poetic images, authenticity of feelings, and relevance of concerns to contemporary India. This was high praise, but it was well deserved. In *Indian Summer* the conflicts that were the theme of the early poetry have abated, and in spite of an occasional tired figure (''cut the air with a knife'' or ''Streets unwind like cobras'') Parthasarathy's second collection provides further proof of Ezekiel's praise.

—S. Nagarajan

PASTAN, Linda

Nationality: American. **Born:** Linda Olenik, New York City, 27 May 1932. **Education:** Fieldston School, New York; Radcliffe College, Cambridge, Massachusetts, B.A. 1954; Simmons College, Boston, M.L.S. 1955; Brandeis University, Waltham, Massachusetts, M.A. 1957. **Family:** Married Ira Pastan in 1953; two sons and one daughter. **Awards:** Dylan Thomas award, 1955; Swallow Press New Poetry Series award, 1972; National Endowment for the Arts grant, 1972; Bread Loaf Writers Conference John Atherton fellowship, 1974; Alice Fay di Castagnola award, 1977; Maryland Arts Council grant, 1978; Bess Hokin prize (*Poetry*, Chicago), 1985; Maurice English award, 1986; poet laureate of Maryland. 1991–94. **Agent:** Jean V. Naggar Literary Agency, 336 East 73rd Street, New York, New York 10021. **Address:** 11710 Beall Mountain Road, Potomac, Maryland 20854, U.S.A.

PUBLICATIONS

Poetry

A Perfect Circle of Sun. Chicago, Swallow Press, 1971.
On the Way to the Zoo. Washington, D.C., Dryad Press, 1975.
Aspects of Eve. New York, Liveright, 1975.
The Five Stages of Grief. New York, Norton, 1978.
Selected Poems. London, Murray, 1979.
Setting the Table. Washington, D.C., Dryad Press, 1980.
Waiting for My Life. New York, Norton, 1981.
PM/AM: New and Selected Poems. New York, Norton, 1982.
A Fraction of Darkness. New York, Norton, 1985.
The Imperfect Paradise. New York, Norton, 1988.
Heroes in Disguise. New York, Norton, 1991.
An Early Afterlife. New York, Norton, 1995.
Carnival Evening: New and Selected Poems 1968–1998. New York, Norton, 1998.

Recording: *Mosaic,* Watershed, 1988.

*

Critical Studies: "Theme and Structure in Linda Pastan's Poetry" by Benjamin V. Franklin, in *Poet Lore,* 75(4), 1981; "'Whatever Is at Hand': A Conversation with Linda Pastan" by Stan Sanvel Rubin, in *The Post-Confessionals: Conversations with American Poets of the Eighties,* edited by Earl G. Ingersoll, Judith Kitchen, and Stan Sanvel Rubin, Rutherford, Farleigh Dickinson University Press, 1989; "Jewish Voices and Themes: Rose Drachler, Julia Vinograd and Linda Pastan" by Harriet Parmet, in *Studies in American Jewish Literature* (University Park, Pennsylvania), 13, 1994; "Family Values and the Jewishness of Linda Pastan's Poetic Vision" by Sanford Pinsker, in *Women Poets of the Americas: Toward a Pan-American Gathering,* edited by Jacqueline Vaught Brogan and Cordelia Chavez Candelaria, Notre Dame, Indiana, University of Notre Dame Press, 1999.

*   *   *

Linda Pastan has long seen herself as Eve, not the temptress but as one of the fallen. In "At Woods Hole" the bathers "learn nothing, lying / on sand hot and pliant as each other's flesh." Trapped in sensuality, they may appreciate beauty, but that is part of the cosmic deception: "waves seem to bring the water in forever / even as the tide moves surely out." Like Poe, Pastan has been conscious of the limits of the mind and the impossibility of exceeding them. In "The Last Train" she imagines one boy fascinated with disappearing buffalo and another with the vanishing long-distance passenger train, and she concludes that we all "follow sleep as well as we are able / along disintegrating paths of vapor, / high above the dreamlike shapes of clouds."

But Pastan seems more willing to abide by the limits of consciousness than does Poe. Her effort has been to clarify this humanness. In "At the Gynecologist's" her "body so carefully / contrived for pain" "gallop[s] towards death / with flowers of ether in my hair." Acutely aware of her mortality, she tries to escape it. In "Bicentennial Winter" she senses "what wildness / is left," and though she is tempted to skate the frozen Potomac, she does not partake of the "dangerous / freedom." In "Evening at Bird Island" she finds violence instead of beauty: "under my rocking floor / fish swallow other fish, / feeding / like bad dreams / under the surfaces of sleep." The problem is that the human necessarily pervades everything: "There is a figure in every landscape."

While Pastan's vision has been consistent throughout her work, *The Five Stages of Grief* is the most effective at presenting the array of her responses. There is denial, when life is made up largely of the familiar and even deaths "wait like domestic animals," "patient and loving" ("After"). In anger she would just as soon that "everything happen / off-stage" and that she stay "with the scenery" ("Exeunt Omnes"). The stage of bargaining produces only a minimum of consolations, as set forth in "Ice Age":

> We must learn
> the cold lessons
> the dinosaurs learned:
> to freeze magnified
> in someone else's history;
> to leave our bones behind.

In depression even the sun seems like a "huge stone / rolled against the door of death / to hold it shut" ("It Is Still Winter Here"). Finally, there is acceptance, when the sun is "warm amnesia" and a woman and her griefs sing back and forth ("Old Woman"). But acceptance, though "its name is in lights," seems unattainable, for as the title poem says, "Grief is a circular staircase."

In the 1980s Pastan's vulnerability intensified. "At all / the outposts of my body," she writes in "Low Tide," "the driftwood fires / burn down, / and a stranger stands / shooting a perfect / arc of urine / into the ashes." Aging, her children's leaving, and especially her parents' deaths bring disequilibrium: "There is nobody / left standing between you / and the world, to take / the first blows / on their shoulders."

But in *The Imperfect Paradise,* which concludes with new poems of Eden, Pastan approaches reconciliation. Instead of denying grief, she locates it against the possibility of the benign, as in "The Imperfect Paradise":

> If landscape were the genius of creation
> And neither man nor serpent played a role . . .
>
> Would [God] have rested on his bank of cloud
> With nothing in the universe to lose,
> Or would he hunger for the human crowd?

It is possible to know the miracle of renewal. In "Grudnow" Pastan depicts her immigrant grandfather as having willed such optimism. Just as "he always / sipped his tea through a cube of sugar / clenched in his teeth," "he sipped his life here, noisily, / through all he remembered / that might be sweet in Grudnow." This renewal manifests itself in the wit and extravagance of "In the Rearview Mirror," "The Safecracker," and "The Ordinary Weather of Summer," as well as in Pastan's success with uncharacteristically formal verse in "Turnabout" and the six-sonnet title poem. To speak in her terms, she has permitted two opposing forces—the Edenic, often humanized in her gardener husband, and the evil of death—to find equilibrium.

Heroes in Disguise is Pastan's most affirmative book. She emphasizes relaxing and forgiving and speaks often of happiness. Images of gardens, particularly of planting, abound, and she declares allegiance to the mysteries of nature. Pastan celebrates "that old song" desire as well. In short, she attests to her acceptance of the earth and the self despite their imperfections. During a plane flight ("In Midair"), as she looks out over "a kind of blueprint of earth," she sees humanity "suspended / / by an act of faith, part way / to what we think of as heaven, / and somehow alive."

—Jay S. Paul

PATEL, Gieve

Nationality: Indian. **Born:** Bombay, 18 August 1940. **Education:** St. Xavier's High School, Bombay; St. Xavier's College, Bombay, B.Sc.; Grant Medical College, Bombay, M.B.B.S. **Family:** Married Toni Diniz in 1969; one daughter. **Career:** Medical officer, Primary Health Centre, Sanjan, Gujarat, 1969–71. Currently runs a private general medical practice, Bombay Central hospital. Also a painter: individual shows—Jehangir Art Gallery, Bombay, 1966–84; Sridharani Gallery, New Delhi, 1966; Pundole Art Gallery, Bombay, 1972; Chemould Gallery, Bombay, 1975; Art Heritage Gallery, New Delhi, 1979. **Awards:** Woodrow Wilson fellowship, 1984; Rockefeller fellowship, 1992. **Address:** SE Malabar Apartments, Nepean Road, Bombay 400 036, India.

PUBLICATIONS

Poetry

Poems. Bombay, Ezekiel, 1966.
How Do You Withstand, Body. Bombay, Clearing House, 1976.
Mirrored, Mirroring. New Delhi, Oxford University Press, 1991.

Plays

Princes (produced Bombay, 1971).
Savaksa (produced Bombay, 1982). Published in *Bombay Literary Review* (Bombay), no. 2, 1989.
Mister Behram (produced Bombay, 1987). Bombay, Praxis, 1988.

*

Critical Studies: "The Ambiguous Fate of Being Human: The Poetry of Gieve Patel" by M.N. Sarma, in *Osmania Journal of English Studies* (Hyderabad), 13(1), 1977; "Gieve Patel: Poet As Clinician of Feelings" by Vrinda Nabar, in *Indian Literary Review* (New Delhi), 3(3), October 1985; "The Poetry of Gieve Patel: A Critical Scrutiny" by Vineypal Kaur Kirpal, in *An Anthology of Critical Essays,* edited by M. Prasad, New Delhi, Sterling, 1989; "Post-Colonial India As Portrayed by Two Parsi Playwrights" by Karen Smith, in *New Literatures Review* (Wollongong, New South Wales, Australia), 19, summer 1990.

Gieve Patel comments:

My first book of poems deals with a young person's confrontation with death and disease in hospital, on the streets; moral and emotional issues pertaining to living in an economically constrained country; and the attempt to stand firmly on one's feet, without despair, in this situation.

The second book goes a step further into these concerns. The human body is viewed as a target of violence; the violence is seen to emanate from the state as well as from the psyche of each individual. Hence, there are political and psychological resonances to these poems. Marginally, if I may say so, the concern is also metaphysical. In the end the attempt is to see how it is that the body survives the violence perpetrated against it.

The third book addresses God, with irony and some passion. Imagery from nature is more pronounced here than in the earlier books.

I write in free verse, the rhythm controlled strictly and varied to serve the thematic needs of the poem. I favor a lucid line of writing, not denying the occasional need for ambiguity and on rare occasions even obscurity.

The poems usually move from puzzlement and confusion to knowledge of a kind.

*   *   *

Over three decades and three volumes of poetry, Gieve Patel has acquired a distinctive voice, ranging across a scale from detached but sharp observation through tolerant skepticism to controlled vehemence. His poems are generally spare and lean of shape, gesture, and movement, their originality a matter of quick, unexpected figurative turns and complex attitudes ("the odour of genitals . . . a hair's breath from decay"!). His steady-eyed appraisal of the disorienting and the disquieting confronts experience without evasion or overinvolvement: "I am not kissing leper sores. / Merely working my way to suggest / It might have been better / Not to look away" ("In the Open"). His poems abjure facile resolutions, being generally concerned to note an honest ambivalence in their responses to people and situations. His first volume, *Poems,* is characterized by a concern expressed with an economy of restraint. Accosted on each annual return to his home village by the begging persistence of an old woman, he remarks in "Nargol,"

I am friendly, I smile, I am
No snob. Lepers don't disgust me. But also
Tough resistance: I have no money.

To give in to her importunity would be a form of entrapment in the guilt she banks on, but not giving her money is another kind of giving in. As the poet walks away, he shrugs aside insouciance for a sober recognition:

I have lost to a power too careless
And sprawling to admit battle,
And meanness no defence.
Walking to the sea I carry
A village, a city, the country,
For the moment
On my back.

"To a Coming Love" reveals an engaging disengagement from the clichéd expression and stock motif:

This silence is not
That we have nothing to say
But is an assessment
Of loss: Watch it unwind . . .

The very title of Patel's second volume, *How Do You Withstand, Body,* indicates the direction his poetry took in a decade. (The title can be read with a question mark or exclamation mark or with both). That Patel is a doctor by profession is evident from his clinical eye for detail and also from the kind of clinical detail his poems handle with familiarity and a tonic freedom from squeamishness. The metaphysical, after all, can be reached only through the physical. In this second volume the poetic self is less willing to remain a meditative or analytic voice, although much of the poetry is still written from the viewpoint of an onlooker rather than a participant. (This is clearly a choice and predilection, for he has always spared us a Patel Agonistes, never doubting, as he says in "Confessional Poet," our capacity to believe that "I too could flaunt my vices, / not being short of those.") The new passion and rhetoric are exemplified most effectively in "University," Patel's refusal to mourn the death by massacre of students and professors in Dacca. In "What's In and Out" the look at the body and the bodily is intent and intensive:

Before I die I should like
To have known me each way
All over. I know the stomach affords
A pleasure different from
The prick. And a different ache.

The same thing is expressed in "O My Very Own Cadaver":

. . . Now who would suspect
The inch to square
Inch cuticular ecstasies
Of this shameless carnal?

A steady engagement with violence finds consistently forceful expression throughout the volume. In "The Ambiguous Fate of Gieve Patel, He Being neither Muslim nor Hindu in India" (he is in fact a Parsi) the communalism that has characterized a modern secular country is placed in laconic perspective with a neat energy that does not sacrifice any of its balance: "To be no part of this hate is deprivation." The sparse, wry personal encounters have a sour relish, as, for instance, in "Just Stretch Your Neck":

The sexual odour of rejected women overpowers me.
I am called grotesquely to account

For ecstasies they may have missed.
I am a chameleon about to swallow a nauseous butterfly.
Look, I'm turning green.

The poems from Patel's third collection, *Mirrored, Mirroring,* mark an interesting shift. His first two volumes had an urban (Bombay) orientation, but now the poet has time to move out and to look around. Patel has always preferred to write in free verse. His later poems tend to be longer, more relaxed, with room for images and characters (including some memorable animals and odious humans) to interact in expansive anecdotes. The syntax and idiom are less clenched and tense, and the rhythm and flow are more like conversation or a voice overheard. Where the poet had once questioned the need for a God, preferring "to pare / My fingernails and weep profoundly / Before the crescents" ("To Make a Contract"), the need is now acknowledged and accommodated, although it is done in a typically questioning way, as in "Simpleton"—

Honest cloud
concealing nothing but the body of God,
Restore my lost assurance! . . .
What's in store now for numbskull touch?
What for simpleton sound?

—or in "Speeding"—

. . . The fate of God
Is to see His universe so,
In overview . . .
Rooting into the intoxication of His Dump

The poetry "cannot believe there could be / Living without quarry and burden" but everywhere regards the spectacle with an irony leavened by compassion. It is this sober combination that makes Patel's lively watchfulness so attractive and medicinal in the enervated hothouse of Indian poetry in English.

—Rajeev S. Patke

PATERSON, Alistair (Ian Hughes)

Nationality: New Zealander. **Born:** Nelson, 28 February 1929. **Education:** Nelson College, 1943–47; Christchurch Teachers College, 1948–49, diploma 1949; Victoria University College, Wellington, 1951–52, B.A. 1953; New Zealand Armed Services Command and Staff College, Whenuapai, 1969; University of Auckland, Dip.Ed. 1972. **Family:** Married 1) Karen Hope Edwards in 1954 (divorced 1978); three daughters and two sons; 2) Alison Jean Blaiklock in 1985. **Career:** Teacher, Auckland Point School, Nelson, 1950, and Taita North School, Wellington, 1953; Instructor Officer, rising to rank of lieutenant commander, Royal New Zealand Navy, 1954–78; dean of general studies, New Zealand Police Department, 1974–78; education officer, New Zealand Education Department, 1978–89. Consultant, American Institute of Police Science, 1977–78. Editor, *Mate*, 1973–77, and *Climate*, 1978–81, both Auckland, *Pilgrims,*

Dunedin, 1981–82, and *Poetry New Zealand*. **Awards:** Fulbright fellowship, 1977; Reid memorial award (University of Auckland), 1981; Katherine Mansfield award for fiction, 1993. **Address:** P.O. Box 9612, Newmarket, Auckland, New Zealand.

PUBLICATIONS

Poetry

Caves in the Hills: Selected Poems. Christchurch, Pegasus Press, 1965.
Birds Flying. Christchurch, Pegasus Press, 1973.
Cities and Strangers. Dunedin, Caveman Press, 1976.
The Toledo Room: A Poem for Voices. Dunedin, Pilgrims South Press, 1978.
Qu'appelle. Dunedin, Pilgrims South Press, 1982.
Odysseus Rex. Auckland, Oxford University Press, 1986.
Incantations for Warriors. Auckland, Earl of Seacliffe Art Workshop, 1987.

Novel

How to Be a Millionaire by Next Wednesday. Auckland, David Ling Publishing Ltd., 1994.

Other

The New Poetry. Dunedin, Pilgrims South Press, 1982.

Editor, *15 Contemporary New Zealand Poets.* Dunedin, Pilgrims South Press, 1980; New York, Grove Press, 1982.
Editor, *Garrett on Education.* Wellington, Tutor, 1981.
Editor, with James Laughlin, *New Directions 46* (New Zealand issue). New York, New Directions, 1983.
Editor, *Short Stories from New Zealand.* Wellington, Highgate Price Milburn, 1988.
Editor, with Stan Bell and Tim Cloudsley, *Coincidence.* Glasgow, Open Circle, 1995.

*

Alistair Paterson comments:

After commencing in the traditional New Zealand lyric/pastoral mode, I moved into a study of contemporary American verse, a study that resulted in the development of a style and technique based on open form as expounded by Pound, Creeley, and Olson. This interest led to my arranging for Robert Creeley to visit New Zealand in 1976 and assisting with the Robert Duncan visit a little later. It also led to my writing poems of the longer form (about four hundred lines) as typified by *The Toledo Room, Qu'appelle,* and *Odysseus Rex.* More recently I have been working in the short story field as well as in poetry. As an editor and reviewer I have tended to concentrate on the encouragement of postmodern writing in open forms and on its extension into the work of other New Zealand writers. My most recent interest is in the relationship between postmodernism and semiotics.

(1995) During the last few years I have become more interested in fiction and in 1993 won the Katherine Mansfield award ($5,000)

for fiction. My first novel—social commentary in the main—was published in 1994.

*   *   *

Alistair Paterson's first book, *Caves in the Hills,* was very much the conventional collection of the postwar years—thirty or so pieces more or less well made on a variety of subjects in a variety of forms, fairly impersonal, modern in tone and language (no romantic poeticizing), each poem a discrete item. There was the feeling of a man looking around for subjects on which poems might be written. But there was one item that stood apart. The sequence called ''The Metropolis'' is an early Paterson attempt, not altogether successful, at what later become characteristic of his work. The language, one feels, is struggling to gain ascendancy over the statement the poem is making, so that reference, meaning, the poem's ''subject,'' will be only one element in a total poetic structure.

In his second and third books, *Birds Flying* and *Cities and Strangers,* we can see Paterson experimenting, reaching out for freer forms. His subject remains on the whole what it was for the Wellington poets of the 1950s—a rather gloomy realism about domestic, urban, and suburban life and about human relationships. Again in the best of the poems, however, there is an attempt to make the movement of the language, the flow of syntax and grammar, more than direct statements or imagery, carry the feelings that spring from the occasion or event that is the subject. This is a distinct advance from the mode in which Paterson began, in which poets too often seem to feel that they can do the fiction writer's job in a few dozen lines, summing up a human action (and particularly human failure) in smart, well-organized images and phrases. It seems that Paterson found his way out of that mode by a close study of the postmodernist American poets, and it was from their work that he acquired his interest in open form and sequences.

The Toledo Room combines Paterson's characteristic subject with his developing interest in open form. It is a dramatic work in which a number of characters speak, none of them clearly identified. They seem to talk about their lives, their love affairs, their failures, and the political climate. They are concerned about, and caught up in, the roles their circumstances impose. But the adopting of roles, the assuming of masks, is the game of life itself, and the whole vision, though perhaps negative, is also wry and amused and is gathered into a music—the structure of the poem itself—that has beauty. This is Paterson writing at his best.

> Summer
> & the sounds of summer—
>   we should all be accustomed to it
>   but the sun throws down such heat
> it seems like dying (or death)
> fading, falling into silence
>   seizing the albatross in its flight.
> Outwards we follow the horizon
>   the sweep of the bay
>   inwards translate
> what's seen and said into another language
>   into some kind of script
>   words, phrases, pages with footnotes:
>   Marsden's weather-worn cross
>   in that far country above lonely water.

Having found his method and established his form, which he called ''double margin field form'' (using margins justified to the right and left of the page), Paterson went on to write three long poems—*Qu'appelle, Incantations for Warriors,* and *Odysseus Rex*—that were meant ultimately to form a single major work. Practical difficulties, however, resulted in their publication separately, in the wrong order, and with different publishers, so that the full force of the experiment was not seen between single covers, where certain interconnections of theme and method would be more striking. One can say, however, that the poems show a cumulative force, revealing once again that Paterson's poetry, though somewhat narrow in range and consequently repetitive in its effects, speaks with an authentic and individual voice, at once bleak, lyrical, and nostalgic.

—C.K. Stead

PATERSON, Don(ald)

Nationality: Scottish. **Born:** Dundee, 30 October 1963. **Career:** Since 1982 jazz musician, London. Writer-in-residence, Dundee University, 1993–95. Since the late 1990s poetry editor, Picador Books. **Awards:** Eric Gregory award, 1990; Forward Poetry prize for best first collection, 1993; Arvon/Observer International Poetry Competition, 1993; Scottish Arts Council Book award, 1993; T.S. Eliot prize, 1998; Geoffrey Faber prize, 1998. **Address:** c/o Faber and Faber, 3 Queen Square, London WC1N 3AU, England.

PUBLICATIONS

Poetry

Nil Nil. London, Faber, 1993.
God's Gift to Women. London, Faber, 1997.
The Eyes. London, Faber, 1999.

*

Critical Studies: By Michael Hulse, in *Poetry Review,* 83(2), summer 1993; in *Poetry Review,* 84(1), spring 1994; ''The Dilemma of the Poet'' by the author, in *How Poets Work,* edited by Tony Curtis, Bridgend, Seren, 1996.

Don Paterson comments:

I believe that the poem (a form of public art, as distinct from the practice of poetry, which is a private religion) belongs to the reader. The desire to comment on my own work is usually misplaced, as it derives from a proprietorial, not a generous instinct. So I am trying to avoid it.

*   *   *

The three published volumes of Don Paterson amount to 171 pages, and within that modest compass there are more wordplays, allusions, puns, and aporia than would serve most other poets over a

lifetime. This represents a remarkable combination of easy colloquialism and linguistic texture. Paterson seems to have solved the conflict that is likely to take place between utterance and form. ''Bird'' is one of a quartet of sonnets concerned with demise:

> The wind baffled lightly as they filled the grave
> and a queasy flutter left us, the last faint
> ripple of the peristaltic wave
> that ushered her out. In eight months, her complaint
> had whittled her down to the palsied sylph
> who filched the car-keys from her snoring spouse
> and went out to prove a point; then found herself,
> like Alice, on the wrong side of the glass.

> Later, back at the house, I overheard
> the disembodied voices in the hall
> where George, who'd only last another year,
> was trying to be philosophical:
> ''Ach, there was nothin' o' her. She was nae mair
> than a sparra, nae mair than a wee bird.''

One sign of a good poet is a dynamic use of verbs. Here we have, in the octave alone, ''baffled,'' ''ushered,'' ''whittled,'' and ''filched.'' This is a fetching reapplication of sonnet form and a characteristic of the arts that enthused reviewers and competition judges alike.

Paterson has an infectious delight in language, as evidenced by his vocabulary: ''the foaming lip *mussitates,*'' ''the best way to play the *bodhran,*'' ''you work out a *grimoire,*'' and, on a single page, ''a sackful of doves rendered up to the heavens / in private *irenicon*'' and ''made nothing of him, save for his fillings, his *tackets.*'' The *Oxford English Dictionary* defines ''mussitate'' as an obsolete form of ''mutter''; *Merriam-Webster's Collegiate* defines ''bodhran'' as an Irish drum made of goatskin; *Collins's French Dictionary* defines ''grimoire'' as ''unreadable scribble''; and, according to *Oxford,* ''irenicon,'' usually spelled ''eirenicon,'' is the term for a proposal to promote peace, most often between churches, and ''tacket'' is a small nail, a little tack. This is one of the finest examples of dictionary bashing in verse since Wallace Stevens, although, unlike Stevens, Paterson does not go on to invent a word when he cannot find one to suit his purpose.

The mixture of the colloquial and the learned can be seen in ''The Alexandrian Library,'' a kind of ode to lost books and a bibliophile's delight. One is tempted to invoke Borges as an exemplar. Certainly Borges would have known Stanyhurst's eccentric translation of the *Aeneid,* though he might not have so readily embraced *The Al Bowlly Songbook* and the back issues of *Button Collector,* let alone *16 RPM—A Selective Discography* and *Living with Alzheimer's.* The last is not only a contradiction in terms but, for obvious reasons, is repeated on the next page.

There is a sequel to ''The Alexandrian Library'' in Paterson's book *God's Gift to Women,* but, like most sequels, it does not live up to the standard of its predecessor. ''The Return of the Book'' shows Paterson's tendency in his later work to sacrifice structure to texture. The charismatic phrasing is still there, but it is harder to determine the context. The sequel rambles over nine pages, as does the title poem, and it would take considerably more narrative pressure than is evinced here to justify such discursiveness. More successful, at four pages, is ''A Private Bottling.'' Even so, the poem includes a surprising amount of heterogeneous matter. The datum is a man listening to the radio as he samples a vast profusion of whiskeys in memory of a love: "Tonight I toast her with the extinct malts / of Ardlussa, Ladyburn and Dalintober / and an ancient pledge of passionate indifference . . ." On the whole Paterson is better in shorter forms, as in "Baldovan," the name of a defunct train station, and "The Lover," which is already being anthologized: "Poor mortals, with your horoscopes and blood-tests— / what hope is there for you . . .?"

The tendency to discursiveness has been recognized and checked by recourse to the Andalusian poet Machado, whom Paterson has chosen to imitate in his collection *The Eyes*. If Paterson's versions are compared with those of a more conventional translator such as Willis Barnstone, it can be seen that the difference between the two lies in the degree of recourse to ellipsis. Barnstone writes, "Beside the black water. / A scent of sea and jasmine. / Malaguenean evening"; Paterson, "By the black lagoon / sea-smell, jasmine: / Malaga dusk."

Whether original or derived, the poetry of Paterson can charm at the same time it baffles. His is the talent of the postmodern novelist, and it is difficult to imagine this proto-Joycean talent patiently developing his gifts from one slim volume of poems to the next. He seems to need a mask or a persona through which to speak his mind. Though certainly one of the most talented of the younger British poets, there is absent from his writing a cohesion of structure sufficient to contain his effervescent phrase making.

—Philip Hobsbaum

PATRIARCA, Gianna

Nationality: Canadian (immigrated to Canada in 1960). **Born:** Ceprano, Italy. **Education:** York University, B.A. in English, B.Ed. **Career:** Works as an elementary school teacher, Metropolitan Separate School Board, Ontario. **Awards:** Nominated for the Milton Acorn Memorial People's poetry award, 1995.

PUBLICATIONS

Poetry

Italian Women and Other Tragedies. Toronto, Guernica Editions, 1994.
Daughters for Sale. Toronto and New York, Guernica Editions, 1997.
Ciao, Baby. Toronto, Guernica Editions, 1999.

*

Critical Study: "Gianna Patriarca's 'Tragic' Thought: 'Italian Women and Other Tragedies'" by Anthony Julian Tamburri, in *Canadian Journal of Italian Studies* (Hamilton, Ontario), 19(53), 1996.

*   *   *

The poetry of Gianna Patriarca is the record of a woman's attempt to put the past behind her and face the everyday life of the present. Born in rural Italy, Patriarca was taken to Canada at an early age and raised in Toronto. Today her voice is a distinct and vital one that sounds above the mumblings of the city's large Italian population.

Patriarca writes poems about her background and about her ongoing attempt to escape from it and yet to embrace it in terms of her identity and individuality. She writes about these matters in a direct and heartfelt way. Love and affection, anger and pique are characteristic emotions and moods. Expressions of these feelings are moderated by a sympathetic nature, a warmhearted humor, and a willingness to assimilate the slights and cruelties of the world.

The single subject for Patriarca is her Italian-Canadian upbringing, which in her poems is a tangled web of personal relationships with members of her family. Every poet writes about and out of the personal experience of the past, but to a greater degree than with any other Canadian poet Patriarca's subject is her life.

Each of Patriarca's books expands her world from the starting point of her childhood. *Italian Women and Other Tragedies* (1994) deals with the immigrant experience itself; this is her Italian book. *Daughters for Sale* (1997) describes her family members; it is her Italian-Canadian book. *Ciao, Baby* (1999) examines the effects of this mixed paternity on the younger generation; it is her Canadian book. The metamorphosis from an immigrant girl through a troubled young woman to a confident artist and citizen is complete.

The answer to the question of what comes next is found in the characteristics of Patriarca's poems in these collections. The title poem of the first book describes Italian women as those "who were born to give birth":

> i have seen them wrap their souls
> around their children
> and serve their own hearts
> in a meal they never
> share.

They are the immigrant women she describes in "Returning":

> in the sixties we came in swarms
> like summer bees
> smelling of something strange
> wearing the last moist kiss
> of our own sky.
> we came with heavy trunks
> empty pockets
> and a dream

She writes that the small Italian towns of her family seem in memory to be larger than metropolitan Toronto.

Four prose poems appear in the book *Daughters for Sale*. Reminiscences of Patriarca's own childhood are complemented with advice to the newborn daughter sleeping in her arms in "My Morning Child": "don't awaken too soon, my darling girl / the world can wait." Patriarca skewers religious inhibitions in "A Kiss," male pretensions and anatomy in "Ode to Balls," the inevitability of death in "The Last Season," inconstancy in "Perfect Love," constancy in "My Husband," and child rearing in "A Mother Poem":

> my baby is scared of ghosts
> and only wants stories with happy endings

sometimes i sneak a story
that makes her cry
then my baby looks like me

If the poems in Patriarca's first two books are dark, there is a quickening of spirit in *Ciao, Baby*. With the title she is in effect saying, "Good-bye to all that." In "Love Poem" she writes about enjoying breakfast in bed and then a lover's caresses: "this is something / i need to get used to." There is the celebration of marriage in "My English Love":

that i am loved at all
surprises me
that i am loved by you
mystifies me

The passage of time exacts its measure in "Notes on Aging":

i am middle aged now
something i thought
would only happen
to others
has happened to me

With its passing the poet is able to face the past and laugh. In "Two Fat Girls" Patriarca describes her youthful self and a friend sauntering along one of the city's Italian streets and catching the eyes of the boys: "maybe we were just two fat girls . . . romantic and silly, just two young girls."

Is Italy receding? In "One More Time" Patriarca writes,

my love affair with Italy
is coming to an end
the passion is just a smoldering
a small spark that sometimes ignites
but quickly cools leaving only the memory

all affairs have their time

Are there places to replace Italy? In the poem "Picasso Had Paris" Patriarca mentions Picasso's Paris and Pasolini's Rome. But Toronto is hers too:

i have Clinton and College
on a January night
with a skinny cappuccino
and a DuMaurier light

—John Robert Colombo

PATTEN, Brian

Nationality: British. **Born:** Liverpool, Lancashire, 7 February 1946. **Education:** Sefton Park Secondary School, Liverpool. **Career:** Reporter, *Bootle Times,* and editor, *Underdog,* both Liverpool. Regents Lecturer, University of California, San Diego, 1985. **Awards:** Eric Gregory award, 1967; Arts Council grant, 1969; Mystery Writers of America special award, 1976; Writers award, Arts Council of England, 1998. **Agent:** Rogers Coleridge and White, 20 Powis Mews, London W11 1JN, England.

PUBLICATIONS

Poetry

Portraits. Privately printed, 1962.
The Mersey Sound: Penguin Modern Poets 10, with Adrian Henri and Roger McGough. London, Penguin, 1967; revised edition, 1974, 1983.
Little Johnny's Confession. London, Allen and Unwin, 1967; New York, Hill and Wang, 1968.
Atomic Adam. London, Fulham Gallery, 1967.
Notes to the Hurrying Man: Poems Winter '66-Summer '68. London, Allen and Unwin, and New York, Hill and Wang, 1969.
The Homecoming. London, Turret, 1969.
The Irrelevant Song. Frensham, Surrey, Sceptre Press, 1970.
Little Johnny's Foolish Invention (bilingual edition), translated by Robert Sanesi. Milan, M'Arte, 1970.
Walking Out: The Early Poems of Brian Patten. Leicester, Transican, 1970.
At Four O'Clock in the Morning. Frensham, Surrey, Sceptre Press, 1971.
The Irrelevant Song and Other Poems. London, Allen and Unwin, 1971; revised edition, 1975.
When You Wake Tomorrow. London, Turret, 1971.
And Sometimes It Happens. London, Steam Press, 1972.
The Eminent Professors and the Nature of Poetry as Enacted Out by Members of the Poetry Seminar One Rainy Evening. London, Poem-of-the-Month Club, 1972.
Double Image, with Michael Baldwin and John Fairfax. London, Longman, 1972.
The Unreliable Nightingale. London, Rota, 1973.
Vanishing Trick. London, Allen and Unwin, 1976.
Grave Gossip. London, Allen and Unwin, 1979.
Love Poems. London, Allen and Unwin, 1981.
New Volume, with Adrian Henri and Roger McGough. London, Penguin, 1983.
Storm Damage. London, Unwin Hyman, 1988.
Grinning Jack: Selected Poems. London, Unwin Hyman, 1990.
Armada. N.p., Flamingo Books, 1997.

Recordings: *Selections from Little Johnny's Confession and Notes to the Hurrying Man and New Poems,* Caedmon, 1969; *Vanishing Trick,* Tangent, 1976; *The Sly Cormorant,* Argo, 1977; *Gifted Wreckage,* with Roger McGough and Adrian Henri, Talking Tape, 1984; *Jelly Pie,* with Roger McGough, Puffin, 1987; *Grizzelda Frizzle and Other Stories,* 1994; *Juggling with Gerbils,* Penguin Audio Books, 2000.

Plays

The Pig and the Junkle (for children; produced Nottingham, 1975; London, 1977).
The Sly Cormorant (for children; produced London, 1977).

The Ghosts of Riddle Me Heights (for children; produced Birmingham, 1980).

Behind the Lines (revue), with Roger McGough (produced London, 1982).

The Mouthtrap, with Roger McGough (produced Edinburgh and London, 1982).

Gargling with Jelly, adaptation of his own poems (for children; produced Hull, 1988).

Radio Plays: *The Hypnotic Island,* 1977; *Blind Love,* 1983.

Television Plays (for children): *The Man Who Hated Children,* 1978; Mr. Moon's Last Case, from his own story, 1983; *The Dying of the Light* (documentary), 1998.

Other (for children)

The Elephant and the Flower: Almost-Fables. London, Allen and Unwin, 1970.

Jumping Mouse. London, Allen and Unwin, 1971.

Manchild. London, Covent Garden Press, 1973.

Two Stories. London, Covent Garden Press, 1973.

Mr. Moon's Last Case. London, Allen and Unwin, 1975; New York, Scribner, 1976.

Emma's Doll. London, Allen and Unwin, 1976.

The Sly Cormorant and the Fishes: New Adaptations into Poetry of the Aesop Fables. London, Kestrel, 1977.

Gargling with Jelly. London, Viking Kestrel, 1985.

Jimmy Tag-Along. London. Viking Kestrel, 1988.

Thawing Frozen Frogs. London, Viking, 1990.

Grizzelda Frizzle and Other Stories. London, Viking, 1992.

Impossible Parents. London, Walker Books, 1994.

The Utter Nutters. London, Viking, 1994.

Beowulf and the Monster. N.p., Scholastic, 1999.

The Blue and Green Ark. N.p., Scholastic, 1999.

Juggling with Gerbils. London, Puffin, 2000.

Editor, *Gangsters, Ghosts, and Dragonflies: A Book of Story Poems.* London, Allen and Unwin, 1981.

Editor, *The Puffin Book of 20th Century Children's Verse.* London, Viking, 1991; revised edition, 1999.

Other

Editor, with Pat Krett, *The House That Jack Built: Poems for Shelter.* London, Allen and Unwin, 1973.

Editor, *Clare's Countryside: Natural History Poetry and Prose,* by John Clare. London, Heinemann, 1981.

*

Critical Studies: Interview with S. Balu Rao, in *Indian Literature* (New Delhi), 28(1), January-February 1985; ''Brian Patten: Poesie'' by Franco Nasi, in *Verri* (Bologna, Italy), 3–4, September-December 1995; *Brian Patten* by Linda Cookson, London, Northcote House, 1997; ''A Gallery to Play To'' by Phil Bowen, in *The Story of the Liverpool Poets,* Stride Publications, 1999.

*   *   *

A precociously gifted writer, Brian Patten won early fame in the 1960s, when still a teenager, as one of the three so-called Liverpool poets. The runaway success that came as a result of the live performance poetry read by himself, Roger McGough, and Adrian Henri, closely linked to the emergence of the pop scene headed by the Beatles and kindred groups, established him as part of a recognized ''school.'' With hindsight it can now be seen that, while the ''Liverpool poet'' tag was a convenient identification at the time, Patten and his colleagues were three talented artists with their own individual styles who happened to be moving in the same direction. All have since emerged as significant voices on the poetic scene, and Patten himself has not lived in Liverpool for more than thirty years.

Outwardly the most serious of the Liverpool poets, Patten creates a body of work notable for its romanticism. Love figures prominently in his writing, with recurrent images of seduction and its aftermath—the sleep of sated lovers, cast-off dresses, the sadness of parting. Another feature, akin to the poets of an earlier age, is his fondness for quiet contemplation away from the hustle of urban life, moments of solitude in deserted woods or under the rain. His precocious ability is evident in his early poems, where Patten's youth is betrayed by the number of schoolboy reminiscences and parallels. ''Little Johnny's Confession,'' for all its acid wit, suggests an author himself not long out of school, while the worldly assurance of ''Party Piece'' fails to convince entirely. In ''Where Are You Now, Batman?'' his lament for the heroes of a vanished childhood displays a real, and recent, nostalgia. These poems demonstrate the writer's potential and indicate the decisions he has already reached on the nature and purpose of his chosen form. ''Interruption at the Opera House'' and the more self-indulgent ''Prosepoem toward a Definition of Itself'' reveal his view of poetry as a natural and subversive act, at once a gift to the masses—''the rightful owners of the song''—and a rejection of the cultured elite who regard it as their property. Wary of critics, suspicious of intellectual analysis, Patten in ''A Literary Gathering'' tells of his unease among the dissectors and his relief when, once outside, he is free of ''the need / To explain away any song.''

A writer with a penchant for the hardness and clarity of the fairy tale, Patten has produced several books for children, one of them a retelling of Aesop's fables. Ironically, much of his adult poetry is less accessible than that of Henri or McGough. The style is dense and compact, with abrupt changes, short, intense lines, and potent images—''our love like a whale from its deepest ocean rises''—which sometimes threaten to overwhelm the rest of the poem. Rejecting the carefully packaged sentiments and elegant observations of conventional poetry, Patten demands a means of expression that reflects the harshness of reality: ''I want to give you something / that bleeds as it leaves my hand / and enters yours, / something that by its rawness, / that by its bleeding / demands to be called real.'' Despite the frequent complexity of his utterances, he finds inspiration from the commonest sources. Patten hears celestial music as a girl sings in the bathroom, offers his beloved a blade of grass in lieu of a poem, even finds a small dragon in his woodshed. At his best he compels the reader's acceptance, piercing a thicket of sentences with rare and startling visions.

Storm Damage combines the familiar lyricism with a darker, reflective mood. Savaged by his own intense feelings, Patten hits out at superficiality in others. Literary critics, ''God-freaks,'' media personalities, and trendy priests are dismissed with a venomous, scathing wit. In ''Dead Thick'' Patten ridicules the English teacher who does not read books—''I'm too busy for literature, that's the problem''—and later concocts his own amusing history of English lit from Chaucer to Ted Hughes. Distanced from friends whose rebellion has given way to suburban conformity, he ponders sadly on Adam's Fall and on the betrayal of 1960s idealism: "So much hoped for, so little altered." Yet in spite of his regrets, he still finds time in poems like "The Ambush" and "As She Goes Home This Evening" to celebrate the joy and pain of love.

With *Armada* Patten attempts to reassess and understand his past experiences. Inspired by the death of his mother, to whom the collection is dedicated, *Armada* gives poetic expression to thoughts and emotions hidden for many years. Patten revisits a traumatic childhood, his playground landscape of bomb sites and derelict buildings now long since vanished. In "The Betrayal" he laments this lost world and its inhabitants, which up to now he had failed to write about: "Now they have become the air I breathe, / Not to have marked their passing seems such a betrayal." "Stepfather" recalls his mother's brutal husband, who even in death is felt as a malevolent presence by the poet, while "Ghost Ship" finds Patten thinking of the sailor father he never knew. Central to the book is the image of his mother. The title poem calls back a memory of childhood, the boy Patten sailing his toy boats on a pond while his mother ("old at twenty-three, alone") watches impatiently, eager to be gone. Just as the boats are blown by the wind, so she is now "blown out of reach / by the smallest whisper of death." In "Ward Sixteen" Patten records her passing, and in "Cinders" he provides a bitter, poignant memorial to her bleak life: "You never went to a ball, ever / In all your years sweeping kitchens / No fairy godmother appeared, never. / / Life was never a fairy-tale / Cinders soon." Contemplating and transcending his past through his poems, Patten offers the healing power of love as a response, the positive message exemplified in "So Many Different Lengths of Time": "A man lives for as long as we carry him inside us / for as long as we carry the harvest of his dreams, / for as long as we ourselves live, / holding memories in common, a man lives." The most significant of Patten's collections to date, *Armada* is given detailed examination by Linda Cookson in her excellent critical study of the poet. With it Patten confirms his position as one of the leading poetic voices of our time.

—Geoff Sadler

PATTERSON, Raymond R(ichard)

Nationality: American. **Born:** New York City, 14 December 1929. **Education:** Lincoln University, Pennsylvania, 1947–51, A.B. 1951; New York University, 1954–56, M.A. 1956. **Military Service:** United States Army, 1951–53. **Family:** Married Boydie Alice Cooke in 1957; one child. **Career:** Children's supervisor, Youth House for Boys, New York, 1956–58; instructor in English, Benedict College, Columbia, South Carolina, 1958–59; English teacher in New York City public schools, 1959–68. Professor of English, 1968–92, and since 1992 professor emeritus, City College of the City University of New York. Vice President, the Poetry Society of America, 1985–88; PEN executive board, 1989–90; trustee, Walt Whitman Birthplace Association, 1985–99. **Awards:** Borestone Mountain award, 1950; National Endowment for the Arts grant, 1969, collaborative fellowship, 1989; Creative Artists Public Service grant, 1977; The City College Langston Hughes award, 1986; James Madison University Furious Flower Lifetime Achievement award in literature, 1994. **Address:** 2 Lee Court, Merrick, New York 11566, U.S.A.

PUBLICATIONS

Poetry

Twenty-Six Ways of Looking at a Black Man and Other Poems. New York, Award Books, and London, Tandem, 1969.
For K.L. Buffalo, White Pine Press, 1980.
Elemental Blues. Merrick, New York, Cross-Cultural Communications. 1983.
Three Patterson Lyrics for Soprano and Piano. Bryn Mawr, Pennsylvania, Merion Music, Inc., 1986.

*

Critical Studies: By Aaron Kramer, in *Freedomways* (New York),1970; Eugene B. Redmond, in *Drumvoices,* New York, Anchor Press. 1976.

Raymond R. Patterson comments:

For me writing poetry is an exploration of the possibilities of experience; a poem written is a poem discovered, providing useful knowledge about the territory we travel through.

*   *   *

Contemporary black poetry is rooted in the special upheaval that gripped the United States during the 1950s and 1960s, when, in a last-ditch push for full integration, black people in both the north and the south took to the streets. The result of their effort was the recognition by some that the country would cede nothing through protest. From that political truth grew the black power movement. Its cultural arm, the black arts movement, views all art as a weapon in the struggle for black liberation. In this context the aim of black literature is the total evaluation of the ideas and images by which blacks have traditionally defined themselves.

The poet Raymond R. Patterson reflects the influence of all of these forces. The result has been a body of poetry that is seminal in its explorations of black life. Concerned more with the psychological than the physical, Patterson is the poet-chronicler, capturing in verse the revolution in black thought that created the 1960s: "Come into my black hands. / Touch me. Feel the grip / And cramp of angry circumstances . . ." From the crucial admission of individual rage—a rage given force and articulation in real life by Malcolm X—the poet moves on to attack the various ploys used by blacks to navigate the American holocaust: "Black boys push carts in alligator shoes," while aspiring integrationists ". . . carry the word in Brooks Brothers suits," and those of the tiny elite, while fully convinced of their infallibility, are "thinking, sometimes . . . / Someone lied. Sometimes thinking suicide." But all is illusion and self-deception, insists the poet. Beneath the carefully controlled masks "there is enough / Grief- / Energy in / The Blackness / Of the whitest Negro / To incinerate / America."

Incineration is the key to "Riot Rimes U.S.A.," the eighty-five poem sequence that is Patterson's most popular work. The poems are humorous and ironic by turn in their first-person depictions of the Harlem riot of 1965. From the poet's perspective the event was the high point of the African experience in America: "My mama hadn't said one word / To my daddy for two whole years. / But after the riots, she was so happy / She was crying tears . . . / Nothing suits a family like a big strong male.''

—Saundra Towns

PAULIN, Tom (Neilson)

Nationality: British. **Born:** Leeds, Yorkshire, 25 January 1949. **Education:** Rosetta Primary School and Annadale Grammar School, Belfast; University of Hull, B.A. (honors) in English; Lincoln College, Oxford, B.Litt. 1973. **Career:** Since 1972 lecturer in English, University of Nottingham. **Awards:** Eric Gregory award, 1976; Somerset Maugham award, 1978; Faber memorial prize, 1982; Fulbright scholarship, 1983–84. **Address:** Department of English, University of Nottingham, University Park, Nottingham NG7 2RD, England.

PUBLICATIONS

Poetry

Theoretical Locations. Belfast, Ulsterman, 1975.
A State of Justice. London, Faber, 1977.
Personal Column. Belfast, Ulsterman, 1978.
The Strange Museum. London, Faber, 1980.
The Book of Juniper. Newcastle upon Tyne, Bloodaxe, 1981.
Liberty Tree. London, Faber, 1983.
The Argument at Great Tew. Dublin, Willbrook Press, 1985.
Fivemiletown. London, Faber, 1987.
Selected Poems 1972–1990. London, Faber, 1993.
Walking a Line. London, Faber, 1994.
The Wind Dog. London, Faber, 1999.

Plays

The Riot Act: A Version of Sophocles' Antigone (produced Belfast, 1984; London, 1986). London, Faber, 1985.
The Hillsborough Script: A Dramatic Satire. London, Faber, 1987.
Seize the Fire: A Version of Aeschylus' Prometheus Bound. London, Faber, 1990.

Other

Thomas Hardy: The Poetry of Perception. London, Macmillan, and Totowa, New Jersey, Rowman and Littlefield, 1975.
A New Look at the Language Question. Derry, Field Day Theatre, 1983.
Ireland and the English Crisis. Newcastle upon Tyne, Bloodaxe, 1984.
Ted Hughes: Laureate of the Free Market? Liverpool, Liverpool Classical Monthly, 1990.
Minotaur: Poetry and the Nation State. London, Faber, 1992.
Writing to the Moment: Selected Critical Essays: 1980–1996. London, Faber, 1996.
The Day-Star of Liberty: William Hazlitt's Radical Style. London, Faber, 1998.

Editor, with Peter Messent, *Henry James: Selected Tales.* London, Dent, 1982.
Editor, *The Faber Book of Political Verse.* London, Faber, 1986.
Editor, with Fanny Dubes and Ian Dury, *Hard Lines 3.* London, Faber, 1987.
Editor, *The Faber Book of Vernacular Verse.* London, Faber, 1990.
Editor, with David Chandler, *The Fight and Other Writings,* by William Hazlitt. London, Penguin, 2000.

*

Critical Studies: ''Juniper, Otherwise Known: Poems by Paulin and Muldoon'' by Adrian Frazier, in *Eire-Ireland* (St. Paul, Minnesota), 19(1), spring 1984; ''The Permanent City: The Younger Irish Poets'' by Gerald Dawe, in *The Irish Writer and the City,* edited by Maurice Harmon, Gerrards Cross, Buckinghamshire, Smythe, and Totowa, New Jersey, Barnes and Noble, 1984; ''Ireland's Antigones: Tragedy North and South'' by Anthony Roche, in *Cultural Contexts and Literary Idioms in Contemporary Irish Literature,* edited by Michael Kenneally, Totowa, New Jersey, Barnes and Noble, 1988, ''Songs of Battle: Some Contemporary Irish Poems and the Troubles'' by Tjebbe A. Westendorp, in *The Clash of Ireland: Literary Contrasts and Connections,* edited by C.C. Barfoot and Theo D'haen, Amsterdam, Rodopi, 1989; ''History and Poetry: Derek Mahon and Tom Paulin'' by Peter McDonald, in *The Poet's Place: Ulster Literature and Society,* edited by Gerald Dawe and John Wilson Foster, Belfast, Institute of Irish Studies, 1991; ''Involved Imaginings: Tom Paulin'' by Bernard O'Donoghue, in *The Chosen Ground: Essays on the Contemporary Poetry of Northern Ireland,* edited by Neil Corcoran, Bridgend, Seren, 1992; *Coming to Consciousness: Lyric Poetry As Social Discourse in the Work of Charles Simic, Seamus Heaney, Tom Paulin, Tony Harrison, and Rita Dove* (dissertation) by Jonathan Hufstader, Harvard University, 1993; ''A Poet's Task'' by Michael Olmert, in *Archaeology,* 48(1), January-February 1995; '''Some Sweet Disorder'—The Poetry of Subversion: Paul Muldoon, Tom Paulin and Medbh McGuckian'' by Elmer Andrews, in *British Poetry from the 1950s to the 1990s: Politics and Art,* edited by Gary Day and Brian Docherty, London, Macmillan, and New York, St. Martin's Press, 1997.

*   *   *

Tom Paulin belongs to that group of poets from Northern Ireland, including John Montague, Seamus Heaney, Michael Longley, and Derek Mahon, who have had such a great impact on contemporary British writing. Paulin is an intellectual and academic as well as a poet, and in his case the poetry seems part of a large endeavor of situating and describing the crisis in the North—as much in critical and political essays as in poetry—in a way calculated to confront blasé or unconcernedly prejudiced English attitudes. As a result the characteristic tone of his poetry is the opposite of ingratiating. It is dour, tight-lipped, and fricative in his first two books and more relaxed, oblique, and dialectically slippery in his third, *Liberty Tree.* Throughout, however, his poetry is determined to clear a space for itself, to muscle in, to intrude.

The essential procedure of much of the earlier work—on which the major influence is perhaps Auden—is to discover in nature and in earlier historical epochs, particularly revolutionary and postrevolutionary Russia, metaphors or analogous anecdotes for Paulin's own sense of history. The poetry works through probing various oppositions and confrontations with a fine analytical passion: ''stillness'' and ''history,'' poetry and political fact, ''formal elegance'' and the vindictive god who ''scatters / bodies everywhere and has broken the city.'' It is plain that these confrontations are essentially those of Paulin's own nature. The poetry longs, sometimes in a virtually dandified way, for a release from the necessity of public conscience, but it feels guilt about the longing and must labor to recover a sense of responsibility and urgency. In the earlier work Paulin is at his best with a kind of Marvellian compaction of an insistent personal lyric cadence with a clear-eyed, unsentimental public concern that weighs the difficulties a poem has in assuming a position and then goes ahead:

> Special constables train their
> machine guns on council flats;
> water cannon, fire, darkness.
> The clocks are bleeding now on
> public buildings. Their mottoes,
> emblems of failure, tell us:

> *What the wrong gods established*
> *no one can ever save.*

In the third book Paulin's language—perhaps now under the sway of Yeats and Pound—undergoes an astonishing and unpredictable transformation. He writes in much looser, much freer, and sometimes very thin forms and employs Ulster dialect as a major element in his lexicon of English possibilities. Such words as ''neapish,'' ''fremd,'' ''glubbed,'' ''biffy,'' and ''sleakit'' pepper many of the poems. This is clearly the result of Paulin's desire to invigorate what he regards as the moribund in Standard English, but it presents difficulties—in poems that already have difficulties enough—for a reader unfamiliar with the dialect. Annotation would be a great help. The dialect words, however, are only one aspect of a new, delighted sensuousness of apprehension. In some of the poems Paulin has created a kind of writing sui generis, in which he anatomizes the futility of the situation in Northern Ireland with a grim disgust (in the excellent ''Desert-martin,'' for instance) and imaginatively measures the possibilities of an eventual resolution of the conflict.

Several critics have called the politics of these poems utopian, and certainly it is difficult to see that the more prophetic of them could be in any way a valuable contribution to realistic debate. But their surely justified poetic strategy is to withhold definition or resolution and to open instead into the allusive, the suggestive, the metaphoric, and the emblematic. The best of them—and in my opinion one of the best poems written in English in recent times—is the lengthy sequence ''The Book of Juniper.'' The poem allegorizes the juniper plant, which ''wills its own survival'' in desolate places, in a series of religious, natural, historical, and culinary evocations. This richly inventive poem culminates in a vision of armies of juniper carriers from the two Irelands meeting to form

> that sweet
> equal republic
> where the juniper
> talks to the oak,
> the thistle,
> the bandaged elm,
> and the jolly jolly chestnut.

This is utopian politics perhaps, but the urgent sweetness of its imagined release also is a measure of its desperation.

Paulin is one of those poets in whom the most important matter of contemporary British politics is finding its most appropriate poetic voice.

—Neil Corcoran

PEACOCK, Molly

Nationality: American. **Born:** Buffalo, New York, 30 June 1947. **Education:** State University of New York, Binghamton, B.A. (magna cum laude) 1969; Johns Hopkins University, Baltimore, Maryland (Danforth Fellow), M.A. (honors) 1976. **Family:** Married Michael Groden. **Career:** Director of academic advising, 1970–73, and coordinator of innovational projects, 1973–75, State University of New York, Binghamton; poet-in-residence, Delaware State Arts Council, Wilmington, 1978–81; learning specialist, Friends Seminary, New York, 1981–92. Artist-in-residence, MacDowell Colony, 1975, 1976, 1979, 1982, 1985, 1989, and Yaddo Colony, 1980, 1982. Visiting lecturer, Poetry One-to-One Conferences, since 1985, YMCA Unterberg Poetry Center, New York, since 1986, Hofstra University, Hempstead, Long Island, New York, 1986, 1988, Columbia University, New York, 1987, Barnard College, 1989, 1990, and New York University, 1989. President, 1989–94, and since 1994 co-president, Poetry Society of America. Since 1992 contributing editor, *House & Garden;* spoken word editor, Oxygen Media, 1999. **Awards:** Creative Arts Public Service award, 1977; Ingram Merrill Foundation award, 1978, 1988; New York Foundation for the Arts award, 1985, 1990; National Endowment for the Arts award, 1990; Woodrow Wilson Foundation fellow, 1994–2000. **Agent:** Kathleen Anderson, Anderson Grinberg Literary Management, 226 West 23 Street, #3, New York, New York 10011. **Address:** 505 East 14th Street, #3G, New York, New York 10009, U.S.A., and 229 Emery Street East, London, Ontario N6C 2E3, Canada.

PUBLICATIONS

Poetry

And Live Apart. Columbia, University of Missouri Press, 1980.
Raw Heaven. New York, Random House, 1984.
Take Heart. New York, Random House, 1989.
Original Love: Poems. New York, Norton, 1995.

Other

Paradise, Piece by Piece (memoir). New York, Riverhead, and Toronto, McClelland and Stewart, 1998.
How to Read a Poem & Start a Poetry Circle. New York, Riverhead, and Toronto, McClelland and Stewart, 1999.

Co-editor, *Poetry in Motion: 100 Poems from the Subways and Buses.* New York, Norton, 1996.
Co-editor, *The Private I: Private Life in a Public Age. The Graywolf Forum 2000.* Minneapolis, Minnesota, Graywolf Press, 2001.

*

Critical Studies: "A Venusian Sends a Postcard Home" by Christopher Benfey, in *Parnassus* (New York), 12(2), 1985; "Traditional Form and the Living, Breathing American Poet" by Fred Muratori, in *New England Review/Breadloaf Quarterly* (Boston), 9(2), winter 1986; "Four from Prospero" by David Wojahn, in *Georgia Review* (Athens), 43(3), fall 1989; interview with Andreas Gripp, in *Afterthoughts,* 5(3), fall/winter 1998–99; in *The Ghost of Tradition: Expansive Poetry and Postmodernism,* by Kevin Walzer, Ashland, Oregon, Story Line Press, 1999.

Molly Peacock comments:

Subjects that are often explosive in nature and verse that often experiments with traditional form are some characteristics of my poetry. The main theme that has concerned me is love in all its manifestations: family love, eroticism, love of self, altruism, religious love, and hatred, of course, too. I favor honesty that sometimes shocks and temper this with the traditional music of rhyme; therefore even the most painful subjects are examined with lush language and a sense of play. The poems in *Raw Heaven* spin off from the traditional sonnet, with highly sensual points of view. In *Take Heart* I use greater dramatic tension, writing about an alcoholic father, abortion, religious faith, and nuclear war.

In *Original Love* I look at love in its making: romance, marriage, friendship, and mother love. *How to Read a Poem & Start a Poetry Circle* examines thirteen talisman poems of mine, from an anonymous lyric by a medieval woman to Gerard Manley Hopkins, John Clare, Jane Kenyon, Elizabeth Bishop, and Jane Kenyon. Each chapter tells the story of a relationship with a poem, incorporating ways to read it. *Paradise, Piece by Piece,* my literary memoir, traces the maverick sanity of the major decisions of my life—deciding to be a poet, deciding against motherhood, and taking a flying leap into marriage with a man I rediscovered after twenty years. What I enjoy about my writing is the sense of humor, the sensuous boldness, and the clear structures that display—and balance—the complexities of the world.

*   *   *

Molly Peacock is part of that generation of American poets who came of age during the Vietnam War, the largest single such generation in American history, a group that cut its aesthetic teeth on dadaism, surrealism, and the "logic of classical consummations" that modernism, perhaps erroneously, presupposed to be its inheritance and trial. Peacock's generation, much influenced by feminism, is primarily revisionary, formed by electronic American life and propelled by the apocalyptic psychoanalytical and political imperatives of a relentless questioning of what is conscious and what is unconscious, what is private and what is public, what is spirit and exactly where spirit becomes entangled with the body of matter as matters move their way. This generation has entered literature somewhat as a handheld cannon enters a push-button war, and the Freudian undergarments of such imagery are something Peacock's poetry has much explored.

Peacock's body of work is rightly identified as being an important part of the resurgence of inherited forms that took place in the poetry of America beginning in the 1980s. Her contribution, distinguished by its metaphysical idiom and approach, is marked by idiosyncrasies that call to mind Marianne Moore's work, while it was Elizabeth Bishop's poetry that released Peacock into the colloquial eloquence she has made purely—with imperfection as part of her aesthetic—her own. Peacock has found her freedom in being bound, and her signature use of rhyme, employed for dramatic effect, has been particularly inventive, amusing, and skilled. In "She Lays" (from *Raw Heaven*), one of Peacock's hallmark poems, a scene of masturbation is a poignant occasion both linguistically, sexually, and socially: ". . . revelation without astonishment, / understanding what is meant. / This is world-love. This is lost I'm."

A reader moves through Peacock's obsessive rhyme schemes, sometimes further conceptualized by use of an anagram or some other a priori warp, with both ease and inevitability. It is not so much end rhyme that gives her work a formal poise, though incessant end rhyme is characteristic, but more to the point is the deployment of endless sound chambers in her poems that render the very movement of the words inherently formal, artful, and self-conscious. At the same time the words are awash in the bravura of the meaning they go after. Her meters often form free verse, although her work has mistakenly been reviewed in America as iambic, perhaps presumed because of her use of rhyme. But the most important formal device of her poetry is the underlying dramatic form that is always driving the machine, bending the meanings in their propulsion toward closure, sculpting a lineation in which each line is both an action, a recovery, and a horizon. Her use of rhyme is akin to the uses to which James Cummins put the sestina form in his book of poems *The Whole Truth*—ebullient, exacting, rending thought and heart in a narrative of movements that are absolutely integral and inevitable to the subject matter at hand.

Peacock's work stands out among that of many in her generation by its shameless use of abstract idiom and imagery, turning, in effect, an ongoing revision of William Carlos Williams's "No ideas but in things" on its imagistic head. Williams's dictum somehow remains at the center of American phenomenology, and the concreteness it has inspired in American poetry has made for both high moments of objectivist epiphanies and low instances of materialistic listings and descriptions. In terms of rhetorical effusion Peacock's work harks back more to a Yeats and in terms of theme and tone more to the moral metaphysics we might associate with a Donne or a Landor.

In contemporary terms Peacock's work is also remarkably close in spirit and execution to W.D. Snodgrass and particularly the Snodgrass of *Heart's Needle*. Autobiographical somewhere to the side of Ginsberg's mad mouthings, Plath's spells, and Lowell's historical self-absorptions, Peacock's work advances the terrain of *Heart's Needle* both in its ingenious (and unobtrusive) use of rhyme and in its ruminations upon psychological and social states and circumstances. Her work makes much of sexuality, abortion, life in cities, life spent close to or distant from others, and life spent in response to the unaffording costs and persistently available revenues and expenses of our childhoods. Peacock has found the means to present psychological material in a context that is not solipsistic, while she delineates social states mercifully devoid of politically correct cant.

—Liam Rector

PECK, John (Frederick)

Nationality: American. **Born:** Pittsburgh, Pennsylvania, 13 January 1941. **Education:** Allegheny College, Meadville, Pennsylvania, A.B. 1962; Stanford University, California, Ph.D. in English 1973; C.G.

Jung Institute, Zurich, diploma in analytical psychology 1992. **Family:** Married Ellen Margaret McKee in 1963 (divorced 1981); one daughter. **Career:** Instructor in English, 1968–70, and visiting lecturer, 1972–75, Princeton University, New Jersey; assistant professor, 1977–79, and professor of English, 1980–82, Mount Holyoke College, South Hadley, Massachusetts; visiting professor of English, University of Zurich, 1985–92, and Skidmore College, Saratoga, New York, 1995–97. **Awards:** American Academy award, 1975; American Academy in Rome fellowship, 1978; Guggenheim fellowship, 1981; Delmore Schwartz award, New York University, 1995; Ingram Merrill fellow, 1995. **Address:** 647 Stickney Brook Road, Brattleboro, Vermont 05301–9635, U.S.A.

PUBLICATIONS

Poetry

Shagbark. Indianapolis, Bobbs Merrill, 1972.
The Broken Blockhouse Wall. Boston, Godine, 1978; Manchester, Carcanet, 1979.
Argura. Manchester, Carcanet, 1993.
Selva Morale. Manchester, Carcanet, 1995.
M and Other Poems. Evanston, Illinois, TriQuarterly Books, 1996.
Collected Shorter Poems, 1966–1996. Manchester, Carcanet, 1999.

Other

Literary Terms and Criticism: A Student's Guide. London, Macmillan, 1984.
How to Study a Poet. London, Macmillan, 1988.
The Poems and Translations of Hi-Lö. Manchester, Carcanet, 1991; Riverdale-on-Hudson, New York, Sheep Meadow Press, 1993.
How to Study a Novel. London, Macmillan, 1995.

Editor, with Sharon Libera, *Mr. Jefferson's Horses,* by Sarah Youngblood. South Hadley, Massachusetts, Mt. Holyoke College, 1985.
Editor, *Middlemarch,* by George Eliot. New York, St. Martin's Press, 1992.

*

Critical Studies: In *Trying to Explain* by Donald Davie, Ann Arbor, University of Michigan Press, 1979, Manchester, Carcanet, 1980; by James Powell, in *Occident* (Berkeley, California), 1980; "Coordinate Forces in 'The Leader of the People'" by James C. Work, in *Western American Literature* (Logan, Utah), 16(4), February 1982.

*   *   *

John Peck's *Shagbark* has rightly been called the most brilliant first book of poetry since Wallace Stevens's *Harmonium.* Difficult and encoded, it is yet recognizable at once as original and ambitious, and its forty-three poems are inscribed in a language as various as it is precise. The originality is, in part, a result of its insistently revealed ancestry, tracings that make up the heartwood of this autobiography whose main metaphor is the organic growth of a tree. If Peck's first

father has been Ezra Pound—the subject of his doctoral thesis and modernist perfector or of the hieratic moment, which Peck will flamboyantly inherit and make his own—other forebears are Browning, Hardy, H.D., Yeats, and Blake. Peck's erudition is enormous, as is the range of his reference. Painters—Cole, van Gogh, Kollwitz—the anatomist Vesalius, and philosophers such as Leibniz and Kierkegaard are passionately addressed and reimagined. Like Liebniz, the poet searches for unity in diversity; like Kierkegaard, he invents against the pull of dread and terror. I would guess that the great Polish teacher and poet Czeslaw Milosz is present here too, for Peck shares and practices his interest in the way things begin and then endure and change through time. In Peck's most beautiful and ambitious poem, "March Elegies," the centerpiece of his second volume, *The Broken Blockhouse Wall,* he writes the following:

> Circling, a man may
>   retell the story
> Lived by another because neither
>   Is in that way free.

The expressed tension between past and present, between father and son, and the passing on of fictions describe Peck's whole poetic succinctly and refer, too, to the duty, felt with chivalric ardor, of being true to a chosen other. A poet becomes himself through mimesis and breaking free.

Peck's strategies for creating a self are manifest in the structure of *Shagbark.* The first section is nearly claustrophobic, for the poet is alone in nature, beset by dreams, inventing routes of escape from solitude. An imagery of doors, sills, and thresholds underlines the desire for growth and new entrances. Human presences are distant or dreamed. In the second section poems are addressed to relatives, teachers, and friends, and their stories are listened to and retold. In "Reliquary" the poet listens to a Polish exile who has landed in his Pennsylvania hometown "trace / The history of those things he wished to share, / Tokens obscure with other time and place." The expanded awareness of time and place leads Peck to those moments of breakthrough that are at once groves or circles of light, psychic transition from one state to another, and, synonymously, the origins of poetry itself. In a Browningesque monologue, "The Factor Remembers His Lady," we find the following:

>   And when I asked her what plan
> She would follow were she to lose her way, then
>
> She said her father once learned from his father
> An oath in runes for entry into the core
>
> Of their old wood; and learned the path leading there
> And learned the look of that hid place, forever.

Peck's tracings backward have a Jungian thrust, and his poems move ambitiously toward the re-creation of both a personal and a racial unconscious.

The greatest adventure of the book is undertaken in the poems in the third section. Each of these incontestably superb poems is based on the art or account of another artist, and the geography covered extends from the English village of "Ringers" to the Holland of Vesalius to ancient China—a Poundian destination—where two hand scrolls are minutely observed. The poet enters the scrolls and, like the spectators of old, adds his own scrupulously rendered reactions and thoughts to them. Coming to the end of Chang Tse-tuan's famous scroll of the Festival at the River, he ruminates on what is "picturable / but not pictured." These studies prepare him not only for his role as poet but also as a human being continuously willing himself to grow by the highest moral and aesthetic standards. Finally, in the fourth section, like Ulysses returning home to Ithaca, Peck breaks through into a present that has been there throughout the journey but is only at this point representable. He meets, as if for the first time, the Penelope whose "sweater on the couch" now seems rich and an object allowable in his poems. A modern epic has been achieved. A poet has come into being.

In *The Broken Blockhouse Wall* Peck returns to the obdurate landscapes of his Pennsylvania childhood and the imagery of rock, mine, river, barge, and freight. Again the clear and the blurred, the hard and the yielding, and wind and land underwrite the dialectic Peck finds everywhere. In his return there is also a new freedom to ride out the drift of analogies, a riding that describes his odd genius. In "March Elegies" Peck relives moments from family history and dazzles the reader with language that moves from the "beshatted drawers" of a Civil War immigrant to the high dreams of mythological heroes. A perfect example of Peck's method—his humor, his fascination with the energy and power of poetry, and his delight in curiosity and chance—is transparent in "Letting Up." It begins with reflections and an ordinary walk through his neighborhood and moves him back to a moment in the Civil War:

> When the gray infantry broke through at Shiloh
> They found campfires, skillets over them cooking,
> Sunday breakfasts laid out, and swirls of steam still
>   Coming off coffee.
>
> Communion that seems an end, fleeting, factive,
> Must begin somewhere. They stopped, ate and drank,
>   snooped
> Through tents and read letters from girls. And they
>   were Lost to the advance.

—Joan Hutton Landis

PEERADINA, Saleem

Nationality: Indian. **Born:** Bombay, 5 October 1944. **Education:** St. Xavier's College, Bombay, 1964–67, B.A. 1967; Bombay University, 1967–69, M.A. 1969; Wake Forest University, Winston-Salem, North Carolina, 1971–73, M.A. 1973. **Family:** Married Mumtaz Peeradina in 1978; two daughters. **Career:** Lecturer, Kirti College, Bombay, 1969–71; instructor, Forsyth Country Day School, Winston-Salem, North Carolina, 1973–74; lecturer, Indian Institute of Technology, Bombay, 1974–75, St. Xavier's College, Bombay, 1976–77, Sophia College, Bombay, 1977–84; copywriter, Hindustan Thompson Associates, Bombay, 1984–87; visiting international scholar and professor, Adrian College/Alma College, Adrian, Michigan, 1988–89. Since 1989 associate professor, Siena Heights University, Adrian, Michigan. **Awards:** Fulbright Travel grant, 1971; British Council Writer's grant, 1983. **Address:** Siena Heights University, 1247 East Siena Heights Drive, Adrian, Michigan 49221–1755, U.S.A.

PUBLICATIONS

Poetry

First Offence. Bombay, Newground, 1980.
Group Portrait. Oxford, Oxford University Press, 1992.

Other

Editor, *Contemporary Indian Poetry in English.* Bombay, Macmillan, 1972.
Editor, *Multifold: A Book of Student Writings.* Winston-Salem, North Carolina, Wake Forest University, 1973.
Editor, *Cultural Forces Shaping India.* Bombay, Macmillan, 1988.

*

Critical Studies: By Bruce King, in *Modern Indian Poetry in English,* Bombay, Oxford University Press, 1987; "The Poetry of Saleem Peeradina" by Jaidev, in *Journal of South Asian Literature* (Lansing, Michigan), 1988; "The Humanism of Saleem Peeradina" by Jaidev and Sharma, in *Contemporary Indian Poetry in English,* Calcutta, Writers' Workshop, n.d.

Saleem Peeradina comments:

Whenever I have composed personal statements, I have always regretted them later. Seeing them in print produces a shock of strangeness: while the statement remains fixed, my position has often evolved. But writers are reckless creatures. So here goes one more time.

My dislocation in America is only the most visible of geographical and cultural shifts in my career. The real place of fidelity and fertility resides elsewhere. I continue to draw from the richness of my Indian origin and sources, while, at the same time, maintaining a global perspective. I should say that I have always produced out of a double consciousness, from having multiple allegiances to place, language, religion, the arts, and ideology. I was bicultural in a different way even in Bombay, my birthplace. Every place remakes itself into an environment of exile that can be an extremely stimulating condition for a writer. I live, teach, and write the conflict itself.

That, however, does not imply a perpetual state of unsettledness. In any given place you can construct a habitat to have a temporary home. Standing in the doorway, you can take your measure relative to the vistas stretching around you. Waiting at the window, you can watch for flares in the sky. The periphery is in constant motion; the center moves when you break your stillness. My writing emerges out of this condition of being.

*   *   *

Saleem Peeradina primarily writes a terse poetry of place. The scene of his early poems is most often Bombay, whose teeming developments "grew on your hands like sixth fingers" ("Bandra"). For his later work the poetic place is a generalized cityscape, against which the human subject comes into manifest being. In "Group Portrait" a scooter carries a family of four to the beach:

> A getaway vehicle
> for a clutch of kindred souls

       poised in flight
from the city's snares.

They are made whole by their brief escape: "We rise as a family /
for the city dark to reclaim us." The ironic urban triptych "Family Man"
predicts that middle-class homeowners will discover

       soon enough
as a prisoner in a cell does,
the trajectory of their paces

Between wall and wall, the floor plan's
Four corners.

From the rigid stratifications of urban space Peeradina finds an
unsentimental redemption in the freer topography of familial relations, particularly in the parent's apprehension of his children. These
lines are from "Michigan Basement II":

I am what I appear

To them: a country without borders. My space
Is their turf. I surface, with no place to hide

Except just below the skin.
Remaining whole is no longer the point.

It's staying divided, attaining equipoise.

Not unexpectedly, Peeradina's anatomies of the city are balanced by versions of the pastoral. Here, too, as in "The Purity of
Pastoral," the landscape is never unpeopled:

The river mumbles, stirs
Where the woman bends as if
the ripples were shifting circles
of some dream the pot displaced.

In "Garden" human sexual awakening takes its terms from the lush
plenitude of nature:

Under a custard-apple tree
I would wait, trusting her curiosity
Would bring my cousin to me.
And she would come, trusting me.

Then, with a single jolt, with power
From my lurking hand the tree's
Thousand leaves hurled on her
A shower of stored rain.

The landscape itself participates in the innocently incestuous act,
fittingly located in a dreamlike past, and the tentative syntax is
entirely appropriate for this rite of initiation and communion.

Peeradina's resolutely secular imagination finds comfort in the
specificity of human affiliation, substituting for religious mysteries
the daily currents of domestic affection and civic connection. In

"Differences," a rare confessional poem, an apostate speaker revisits
the seat of religion, the mosque:

Their lifted faces betrayed
a collective suspension of disbelief; and
ugh, the absurd posture of their hands . . .
The old pain raged in me as
I left the impotent walls
and stepping out

Found the sky ablaze.

Rather than the "shouldered conspiracy" of worship, the speaker
chooses to rub "shoulders with warm indifferent shoulders / In the
street alive with dung and tyres"; yet the end of the poem leads him
only to a "questioning silence." We might speculate that it is
precisely to answer this silence that Peeradina writes. Like the main
character in his long narrative poem "Beginnings," a disobedient son
who has schooled himself into a successful writer,

He has a name now
for the labour he puts into daydreaming.
He has heard the call: an agitation of the spirit
In the act of finding a resolution in words.

Peeradina's unflinchingly honest poems are offered as a principled and necessary impiety. Despite the occasional prosy awkwardness and faltering line, his skeptical intelligence is well served by his
static, tableaulike images and angular rhythms. His title for the
collection *Group Portrait,* by articulating social attachments with the
detachment of the solitary observer, accurately conveys the duality of
his poetic stance. As a poet Peeradina wishes to be both family man
and outsider. His is an austerely modernist sensibility tempered by a
genuine compassion, even a tenderness, for the middle-class life it
ironizes.

—Minnie Singh

PERELMAN, Bob

Nationality: American. **Born:** Robert Perelman, Youngstown, Ohio,
2 December 1947. **Education:** University of Michigan, Ann Arbor,
B.A. 1969 (Phi Beta Kappa), M.A. in classics 1970; University of
Iowa, Iowa City, M.F.A. in poetry 1971; University of California,
Berkeley (Chancellor's Dissertation Year fellowship), Ph.D. in Eng-
lish 1990. **Family:** Married Francie Shaw in 1975; two sons. **Career:**
Cambridge Adult Education, Massachusetts, 1973–74; lecturer, Hobart
College, Geneva, New York, 1974–75, Northeastern University,
Boston, 1975–76, California College of Arts and Crafts, Oakland,
California, 1978, Sonoma State University, California, 1979–81,
University of San Francisco, 1982–84, San Francisco State Univer-
sity, 1987. Assistant professor of English, 1990–95, and since 1995
associate professor of English and chair, creative writing program,
University of Pennsylvania, Philadelphia. Visiting poet, University of
Iowa Writer's Workshop, Iowa City, 1996; visiting professor, King's
College, London, 1997–98. Editor, *Hills* magazine, Berkeley, Cali-
fornia, 1973–80. **Awards:** Pew Disciplinary award, 1993; University

of Pennsylvania Research Foundation award, 1993. **Address:** Department of English, University of Pennsylvania, Philadelphia, Pennsylvania 19104, U.S.A.

PUBLICATIONS

Poetry

Braille. Ithaca, New York, Ithaca House Press, 1975.
Seven Works. Berkeley, California, Figures, 1978.
a.k.a. Berkeley, California, Tuumba Press, 1979; enlarged edition, Great Barrington, Massachusetts, Figures, 1984.
Primer. San Francisco, This Press, 1981.
To the Reader. Berkeley, California, Tuumba Press, 1984.
The First World. Great Barrington, Massachusetts, Figures, 1986.
Face Value. New York, Roof, 1988.
Captive Audience. Great Barrington, Massachusetts, Figures, 1988.
Virtual Reality. New York, Roof Press, 1993.
The Future of Memory. New York, Roof Press, 1998.
Ten to One: Selected Poems. Middletown, Connecticut, Wesleyan University Press, 1999.

Play

The Alps (produced San Francisco, 1980). Published in *Hills* (Berkeley, California), 9, 1980.

Other

The Trouble with Genius: Reading Pound, Joyce, Stein, and Zukofsky. Berkeley, University of California Press, 1994.
The Marginalization of Poetry: Language Writing and Literary History. Princeton, New Jersey, Princeton University Press, 1996.

Editor, *Writing/Talks.* Carbondale, Southern Illinois University Press, 1985.

*

Critical Studies: *Total Syntax* by Barrett Watten, Carbondale, Southern Illinois University Press, 1984; *The New Sentence* by Ron Silliman, New York, Roof, 1987; *Textual Politics and the Language Poets* by George Hartley, Bloomington, Indiana University Press, 1989; *A Poetics* by Charles Bernstein, Cambridge, Harvard University Press, 1992; *Double Reading: Postmodernism after Deconstruction* by Jeffrey T. Nealon, Ithaca, Cornell University Press, 1993.

*   *   *

What does a poet write about now that Western civilization is (finally) dead? I once watched newscaster Tom Brokaw with then President George Bush and his wife Barbara on TV, their interview sandwiched between a tampon ad and the Pillsbury Doughboy. The rhetoric of the three Americans formed an impermeable shield, utterly incestuous and hell-bent on selling a state product none of them could articulate; the noise simply spun without friction on its own synthetic inertia in perfect, fleshless symmetry: "the dead language everyone reads by nature / but no one gets to speak." Television now constitutes an all too digestible medium that goes down so blandly we fail to notice that we have metamorphosed into vestigial appendages of a smaller, more neutral national me: "History (present tense, all lies) is the strictest form of bondage," "a communicated disease."

Bob Perelman seeks immunization against this through language as a site for exploratory, highly political, and socially conscious poetics. He begins with grammar, the alphabet: "syntax," he writes, "is, for me, a kind of history." If community is to be achieved—sincere communion, that is, among real others, not the self-congratulatory products of workshop poets and New Formalists burping out metaphors of moral significance (and other myths) in fetishized sermons ripe for *The New Yorker*—then one might best begin with the tangible and tactile, that is, with language as the subject of its own conveyance: "Words: wind sculpture. Mouth: wet red rubber bag" and "Trying to hear the words before and after they make sense."

Not that Perelman is a romantic when it comes to defining community: "There is no such easily positable thing as a writing community. Writers are part of the larger community-which-is-not-a-community-either . . . there's no simple, single mechanism of mediation between one and many." Despite this, Perelman understands that "the sentence is an obstacle to noise," and to move beyond noise—be it the vatic homilies of smug contemporary poets or the anesthetic of the television talk shows—might be our only alternative. We now recognize the concept of the self to be at least questionable, if not ridiculously (tragically) nostalgic: "In theory the names are on tight, but when they move the bodies fall apart." In light of this, I find Perelman's urgency to write, read, and interact within a known community of individuals not so much heroic as reanimating.

Perelman has pointed out that language poetry has often been accused of being the product of soulless androids powered by literary theory. (For those unfamiliar with the works of this tribe and its associates, an effective entry point would be reading works by Perelman and friends in *In the American Tree,* edited by Ron Silliman, while a good starting point for Perelman's work might be *The First World* or *Face Value.*) This is due, in part, to the determination of writers like Perelman to "liberate language from the shackles of nominative clarity." Language poetry, from Perelman's frame, is aimed at grappling with the bankrupt notions of self, history, and other matters through reconstruction of the language, an inherently political attack: "all figures of speech are a crime against the state. Crimes against a mythical clarity."

The scenes and psychic debris of Perelman's poetry gyrate in kaleidoscopic flashes of unsettling speed, and he is one of the few contemporary poets maintaining a position several dozen steps ahead of the techno-sophisticated barrage of passionate statistics and reified commodification of our "culture." Perelman's mind is a centrifuge with the hatch left open; to walk into his poems is to get stained and splattered. These are works that scathingly, sometimes abstrusely, but more often hilariously slice through the international headline Muzak we mistake for knowledge.

Words are opaque, but vibratory, nodules; we butt our heads against them and raise welts on our temples. We read the bumps with our fingertips (our signatures), are sometimes moved to respond with further words, which in turn give rise to other transitory maps, and thus the dialectic web gets woven. Perelman is a wonderfully inventive architect unafraid to let himself be composed by his alphabet. He knows that language is an artificial intelligence and that he, like all of us, is a virus in the machine: "Seeing something continually for the first time. And it's done with *words.*"

—Derek Owens

PESEROFF, Joyce

Nationality: American. **Education:** Queens College, City University of New York, Flushing, 1964–69, B.A. 1969; University of California, Irvine, 1969–71, M.F.A. 1971. **Family:** Married; one daughter. **Career:** Visiting instructor, University of Michigan, Ann Arbor, 1974–75; instructor, Massasoit Community College, Brockton, Massachusetts, 1976–78; lecturer, Massachusetts Institute of Technology Writing Program, 1978–79; instructor, Hellenic College, Brookline, Massachusetts, 1979; visiting professor, Brandeis University, Waltham, Massachusetts, 1980; instructor, Wheelock College, Boston, 1983; adjunct professor, Emerson College, Boston, 1986–96; visiting professor and poet-in-residence, University of Massachusetts, Boston Harbor Campus, 1997–2000. **Awards:** Pushcart prize, 1978; Massachusetts Council on the Arts fellowship, 1983; National Endowment for the Arts fellowship, 1984. **Address:** 24 Balfour Street, Lexington, Massachusetts 02421, U.S.A.

PUBLICATIONS

Poetry

The Hardness Scale. Cambridge, Massachusetts, Alice James Books, 1977.
A Dog in the Lifeboat. Pittsburgh, Carnegie Mellon University Press, 1991.
Mortal Education. Pittsburgh, Carnegie Mellon University Press, 2000.

Other

Editor, *Robert Bly: When Sleepers Awake.* Ann Arbor, University of Michigan Press, 1984.
Editor, *The Ploughshares Poetry Reader.* Watertown, Massachusetts, Ploughshares Books, 1987.

*

Critical Studies: "Joyce Peseroff's 'The Hardness Scale'" by Robert Pinsky, in *Ploughshares* (Cambridge, Massachusetts), 4(3), 1978; "Feminism, Romanticism, and the New Literacy in Response Journals" by Deanne Bogdan, in *Reading and Response,* edited by Mike Hayhoe and Stephen Parker, Milton Keynes, England, Open University Press, 1990.

*   *   *

An accomplished and productive poet, Joyce Peseroff writes about relationships, family members, nature, and New England, using direct, conversational language. Many of her poems ponder the female experience and include feminist insights.

The title poem of *A Dog in the Lifeboat* relates how a dog is thrown off a lifeboat because the survivors are not willing to share water and food. It observes that, while the dog faces death, so will everyone eventually. "My Mother's Wallet" praises the poet's mother for having earned her own money by working in a department store. This was money "not taken from a man but earned." Thus the poem has a feminist slant in finding value in women's economic

independence. Other poems deal with sex and motherhood. "Fertility," for example, examines childhood musings about conception, and "Sheba's Wisdom" considers problems of motherhood, such as dealing with day care providers. Feeling torn about leaving her child in day care, the speaker talks of her "terrible milk dribbling love." Like Sheba, pregnant by Solomon, the speaker is "a woman willing to watch a child / divided," which illustrates her conflict. "Exercise," about human imperfection, describes an exercise class held in a church, with "a melancholy portrait / Of Christ staring down at us."

Poems about relationships include "The Glad Café," in which a couple sit looking out at the sea. The speaker muses that "soon will come the end of our little time together." Although life is short, the mundane "fractious life" continues in arguments about cutting the grass. In "Spring Dress" a young woman mends a dress in April. When a boy takes her on a motorcycle ride, she hopes that her dress will not need stitching, implying that it may be torn in a passionate encounter. The dress symbolizes the promise of spring and of sexual vitality.

A Dog in the Lifeboat contains poems about nature such as "Study," in which the poet speaks about winter and her work and links the creative process to the season. In "Bluebird" the speaker recalls her mother's advice, and she relates to her own daughter by choosing a song, "Bluebird at my window," and gains insight into the struggles of motherhood. "Alone—First Week of Summer," another poem that links nature and motherhood, reveals that the speaker does not know she is two weeks pregnant. After observing a phoebe who returns thrice to an empty nest, she speculates whether the bird does so because of instinct, distress, or forgetfulness. She wonders about the bird's maternal instinct and about that of a woman.

"The Red Rocker" recalls William Carlos Williams's "Red Wheelbarrow," an imagist classic. But because no one sits in Peseroff's rocker and there are no visitors, the poem evokes a sense of loneliness: "I feel the emptiness of something built for motion, stilled." In "Making a Name for Myself," from the collection *The Hardness Scale,* the poet sometimes whimsically calls herself W.C. Williams when giving her name.

The Hardness Scale deals with love and relationships and with personal experience and offers musings about life. Evoking Shakespeare, "The Dark Lady of the Sonnets" describes an attempt to change a man's head and heart in a revolutionary way. The contemporary woman wears provocative clothing and rides with guerillas, yet ironically she identifies with her role as a "dark lady." "Love Poem" takes an odd turn at the end when violence intrudes as the speaker unexpectedly remarks, "I think of you but find / the actual burglar / is beating me with sticks." "Anatomy," a witty poem about men's preference for large breasts like "melons" or small ones likes "lemons," notes that "no woman is average there." When the poet asks whether any woman would want a man without a penis, she answers that all would agree the idea to be insane. "This Poem Is for You" is addressed to a lover, but because the relationship is coming to an end, it has a sad, ironic tone. In spite of present happiness, the speaker in "Poem" realizes that all persons will die: "I remember we / will never get out / of this alive."

"The Long March," included in *The Ploughshares Poetry Reader,* has an isolated speaker whose only pet is a stuffed dog. The beginning stanza sets the stage for loneliness as the speaker describes a Torah scroll in the middle of a fence with a missing picket, like "a missing tooth / in the face of God." "The Hardness Scale" uses jewels to organize its message to a lover whose outrageous drunken episodes anger the speaker. Whereas diamonds are a ten on the hardness scale, he is an eleven. The speaker cannot give him diamonds because they are "forever," indicating the tenuousness of the relationship. In "Mortal" the poet meditates upon her own mortality, realizing that she has trusted nature instead of being aware of its dangers and the capriciousness of human survival.

Like Emily Dickinson, Peseroff uses concrete images and speech in the foreground while being concerned with the emotional effects of her juxtapositions. Her tone is conversational, direct, realistic, often provocative, and sometimes humorous. Like Williams, she adopts an American poetic line and diction. When her speaking voice examines feminine experience and conflicts, she resembles confessional poets like Sylvia Plath and Louise Glück.

—Shirley J. Paolini

PESKETT, William

Nationality: British. **Born:** 12 May 1952. **Education:** Royal Belfast Academical Institution; Christ's College, Cambridge, degree in zoology. **Family:** Married Naomi Peskett. **Career:** Has worked as a journalist and biology teacher. **Awards:** Eric Gregory award, 1976. **Address:** c/o Secker and Warburg, 81 Fulham Road, London SW3 6RB, England.

PUBLICATIONS

Poetry

Cleaning Stables. Belfast, Ulsterman, 1974.
The Nightowl's Dissection. London, Secker and Warburg, 1975.
A Killing in the Grove. Belfast, Ulsterman, 1977.
A More Suitable Terrain. Belfast, Ulsterman, 1978.
Survivors. London, Secker and Warburg, 1980.

*   *   *

A training in zoology, reinforced by years of teaching science, has afforded William Peskett a pabulum denied to most contemporary poets. He writes about the night owl, crayfish, ant, and moth and does so without the urge to gloss or prettify. In "Moths" he says,

The female moth is like the male.
When you crush it,
it doesn't bleed—
it sprinkles your hands with talcum.

Peskett sees humans as having aggrandized their position in the universe at the expense of fellow beings. He compares their posturings unfavorably with the silent practicality of vegetables and is glad that Darwin established a new cage at the zoo for Homo sapiens. Several times over he shows the human being violating the dignity of other species. In "The Nightowl's Examination," for instance, he says,

I take every cell from him
and every molecule
from each of these

and examine them.

I take everything. He gives
me nothing in return.

The pressure of Peskett's subject matter compels his verse into a certain stripped economy. What has been quoted here looks less like illustration excerpted from larger works than like independent epigram or even haiku. This is a quality of style, especially in the earlier poems. Peskett advocates appreciation as distinct from analysis, but he finds himself having to bow before the precocity of youth. As expressed in the poem "My Child," the attitude comes out thus: "my child / will slowly select a summer / and apply it firmly / to the spring."

This is a crisp way of indicating growth and disillusion. Such crispness, however, comes with negative qualities. Peskett's poems as wholes tend towards the prosaic. One misses the verbal roll and rise found in his older contemporaries from Ulster, especially Seamus Heaney and Derek Mahon. This lack would not be so noticeable if the epigrams quoted existed by themselves. But once they are read in context, as part of the poems from which they were culled, they look like precepts embedded in a tissue of explication. There is an account of Belfast courageously proceeding with business as usual that, for all its formal layout, is little better than prose—"Across the road a bar / might be open as usual, / its lounge blown out / and fenced on the pavement / as a book is pulled from the shelf . . ." This is not saved by the book metaphor. It would need more rhythmic shape and linguistic zest to be lifted out of the merely circumstantial. Yet the epigrammatic conclusion of the poem has the ictus that the poem as a whole lacks: "A man says you can cut / the tongue from an ox / but never take the shine / from its eye." Given a definitive title, this could be a self-explanatory poem standing on its own.

This point is perhaps more true of the earlier verse than of the later. There is more warmth in Peskett's second book. He wants to leave the world to the kingfisher, the blackbird, the kestrel— "these beautiful casualties," as he describes them. The elusiveness of feline identity fascinates him, as does the loss of dignity even in the demise of a mouse—"the little shame of urine."

Though more purged and dry than that of Lawrence, Peskett's vision resembles in some degree Rupert Birkin pondering in *Women in Love* "a world empty of people, just uninterrupted grass, and a hare sitting up." Epigrammatically—as ever, when at his best—Peskett phrases his version of this feeling in "Coypu":

Slowly the coypu peels a view
from the ecstatical level of the river.
The banks fall
to the landscape's climax.

—Philip Hobsbaum

PETERS, Lenrie (Leopold Wilfred)

Nationality: Gambian. **Born:** Bathurst (now Banjul), 1 September 1932. **Education:** Trinity College, Cambridge, 1953–56, B.A. (honors Science Tripos) 1955; University College Hospital, London, 1956–59, M.B. in 1959, B. Chir. **Career:** Surgical registrar, Northampton General Hospital, England, 1966–69; surgeon, Victoria Hospital, Gambia, 1969–72. Since 1972 surgeon in private practice,

Banjul. Freelance broadcaster, BBC African and World Service, 1955–68. Fellow, Royal College of Surgeons, 1967, West African College of Surgeons, and International College of Surgeons, 1992. Chair, National Library Board, 1979–87, and Gambia College Board of Governors, 1979–87; trustee, 1985–88, and chair, 1988–91, West African Examinations Council; member, Research and Scholarship Committee International of Surgeons, 1995. Judge, African Region of the Commonwealth prize for fiction, 1995. Officer of the Republic of the Gambia. **Address:** Westfield Clinic, P.O. Box 142, Banjul, Gambia.

PUBLICATIONS

Poetry

Poems. Ibadan, Nigeria, Mbari, 1964.
Satellites. London, Heinemann, 1967.
Katchikali. London, Heinemann, 1971.
Selected Poetry. London, Heinemann, 1981.

Novel

The Second Round. London, Heinemann, 1965.

*

Manuscript Collection: School of Oriental and African Studies, London.

Critical Studies: *New West African Literature* edited by Kolawole Ogungbesan, London, Heinemann, 1979; *Understanding African Poetry* by K.L. Goodwin, London, Heinemann, 1982; *West African Poetry: A Critical History* by Robert Frazer, Cambridge, Cambridge University Press, 1986.

Lenrie Peters comments:

All poetry is a search, and mine is no exception. A search for the nature of human consciousness and of the universe—its joy and despair, its passion. Its sublime nobility and its degradation—the miracles of nature. A search for the meaning of existence and of man's setting within it. My poetry attempts a medley of song and has been at different times both the tear bowl and the chalice! But always with the ecstasy of hope rising out of gloom.

*   *   *

The Gambian poet Lenrie Peters is one of the least classifiable of African poets. Although African themes and images abound in his work and there is a deep, continuing concern about the state and fate of modern Africa, he is formally the least African of his generation of writers. There is no traceable debt to the techniques of oral poetry and, with the rare exception of the abandoned Gambian fertility god in the title poem of *Katchikali,* no use of indigenous mythology. Peters writes in short, tight stanzaic structures and in slim free-verse paragraphs with sporadic rhymes, and though these appear to owe something to European modernism's dismantling of conventional metrics, they are in fact highly personal and original forms that have their own inherent and instinctive sense of structure. He is a cosmopolitan poet in both style and subject—"The universe is my book"—and includes in his work poems on international subjects in science,

music, politics, evolution, and sports (there is a poem on the Chinese nuclear bomb and an elegy on Winston Churchill). His taut, densely packed poems, which always give an impression of space beyond the words on the page, cover the broad, universal spectrum of human experience. There are meditations on aging and death, the risks of love, and the loneliness of exile; painful mental dissections of sexual passion and of the failure of even the most extreme experiences to yield meaning; and expressions of personal crisis and public anger. As Peters is a specialist surgeon working in the frustrating conditions of third world squalor and deprivation, the last two subjects often coincide, as in the poem "Waking in the Night" (*Katchikali*), where the lack of electricity prevents the physician from saving a life.

Peters's early volume *Satellites* is aptly named, for there is a sense in these poems, first, of the tough-minded but sensitive poet-doctor's double alienation from the hub of fashionable literary activity and the harsh factual world of his profession, and, second and more precisely, of the writer orbiting his subject, always distanced and detached, never abandoned and immersed. The poet inhabits his own aloof mental space, beyond relationships: "We have lived as if in vacuum cylinders." Although Peters's work has a hard, crystalline clarity and is full of startling, incisive images, it is not the doctor's surgical precision so much as his unsentimental professional detachment, discouraging intimacy, that informs and pervades it. These are agonized, spectatorial poems, about the dispassionate observer's attitude to his experience and his desperation to confront its meaning rather than the experience itself. The poet-surgeon does not probe but surveys the human, urban, and natural anatomy of a strangely anonymous world, always with a sense of bewilderment and disorientation and often in sheer wonderment at its existence. But even the ultimate experiences defraud, hemmed in and fenced off from us as they are by conditions and disappointments. In "Watching Someone Die" even death, in whose mundane presence the doctor spends much of his time, becomes unimpressive—"Everything and nothing has happened"—and it is finally only "the changing of the tide at the boundary hour." There is no revelation or insight, no enlightenment or enhanced sensitivity, but, on the contrary, "reinforced brutality to life / a rugged cliff bloodstained / with the agonising rhythm of many heads." The probing of the surgeon's scalpel "at the cutting chaotic edge of things" becomes an inverted image, or negative, of the imaginative piercing that is the real goal of the poet's quest and a compensatory substitute for this other, more spiritual penetration. The success of the first serves as an index to the failure of the second. In two poignant poems from the next volume, "You Lie There Naked" and "You Talk to Me of Pain," the patient's physical pain comes to symbolize the mental anguish of the physician. Faced with the unknowable, the latter has no surgery to get him to the heart of an experience, to extract its meaning and remove the source of his perplexity. "Steel is impotent," and the anatomist remains remote, a satellite to his own experience, "this stranger with the scalpel from outer space."

Peters's moral and intellectual position is as shifting and slippery as his subject matter. Although he is distrustful of the intellect— "The mind / Is like the desert winds / Ploughing the empty spaces"— he is the most intellectual of African poets. Ideas dictate the shape of his narrow, minimalist verse structures and orchestrate his images, and his best poems achieve a tight concentration of thought, image, and sensation. He is also capable of highly speculative, philosophical poems, such as "On a Wet September Morning," a metaphysical disquisition on nature and evolution in which the poet's physical presence expands across the whole of space and time. Although he sometimes boils over in rage at the frustrations of underdevelopment and Africa's snail-paced progress, he frowns at the encroachments of advanced technology upon the spontaneity of life, its alienating, artificial packaging of experience, and reviles all blind, unconsidered kinds of "progress" that ruin more than they remedy. The art of the true healer (here Peters is more than a diagnostician of Africa's ills) maintains continuity with tradition: "It is I who carry your past / I forbid progress / and I who measure / out your future like a potion." The poems of private crisis and dilemma pick a tortured path between attitudes of docile resignation and barren resentment and between solidarity with the downcast and, disturbing this complacency, the fear that the comparative comfort of his own elitist position amounts to complicity with their exploiters. By contrast, the more public poems gathered in the "New Poems" section of Peters's *Selected Poetry* radiate confidence and certainty about what is needed for Africa's future.

In this collection Peters, ever an inveterate enemy of tribalism and nationalism, focuses on the problems of the continent at large. There is a ruthlessly honest poem on Soweto that does not spare comparable conditions in black African countries and some angry polemics that hold up the squalid realities of the rude village and venal metropolis against the spurious idealism of pan-Africanism and negritude. The prevailing themes are Africa's political disunity and instability, the social injustice and glaring underdevelopment, and the need for original ideas and self-reliance. These are prosy, oratorical poems that seem only partially to engage the poet's sensibility and imagination; the swift movement of images under the pressure of ideas, which is a compelling feature of the private poems, is here missing. Peters's gift is essentially a lyric one, developed out of firsthand experience. When he expands to public themes, his style slackens, the tight structures of thought unravel, and the delicacy and precision of his best poems are lost.

—Derek Wright

PETERS, Robert L(ouis)

Nationality: American. **Born:** Eagle River, Wisconsin, 20 October 1924. **Education:** University of Wisconsin, Madison, B.A. 1948, M.A. 1949, Ph.D. 1952. **Military Service:** U.S. Army, 1943–46: technical sergeant. **Family:** Married Jean Louise Powell in 1950 (divorced 1972); three sons (one deceased) and one daughter. **Career:** Instructor in English, University of Idaho, Moscow, 1951–52; assistant professor of humanities, Boston University, 1952–54; assistant professor of English, Ohio Wesleyan University, Delaware, 1954–57; associate professor of English, Wayne State University, Detroit, Michigan, 1957–63; associate professor, 1963–66, and professor of Victorian literature, 1966–68, University of California, Riverside. Professor of English and comparative literature, 1968–92, and since 1993 emeritus professor, University of California, Irvine. Visiting professor, University of California, Los Angeles, summer 1965, and University of Utah, Salt Lake City, summer 1967. Bibliographer, 1958–68, and member of the editorial board, 1962–68, *English Literature in Translation;* member of the board, Wayne State University Press, Detroit, 1959–62; associate editor, *Criticism: A Quarterly of Literature and the Arts,* 1961–63; assistant editor and bibliographer, *Journal of Aesthetics and Art Criticism,* 1963–65;

contributing editor, *American Book Review,* New York, since 1978, and *Poetry Australia,* Berrima, New South Wales, since 1989; editor, *Poetry Now* Series, 1982–87; since 1985 contributing editor, *Little Magazine Review* and *Small Press Review.* **Awards:** American Council of Learned Societies grant, 1963; Guggenheim fellowship, 1966–67; Borestone Mountain award, 1967; Yaddo Colony fellowship; MacDowell Colony fellowship, 1973–74; National Endowment for the Arts fellowship, 1974; Di Castagnola prize, 1984; Larry P. Fine Criticism award, 1985, for *Black and Blue Guide #2.* **Address:** 9431 Krepp Drive, Huntington Beach, California 92646, U.S.A.

PUBLICATIONS

Poetry

Songs for a Son. New York, Norton, 1967.
The Sow's Head and Other Poems. Detroit, Michigan, Wayne State University Press, 1968.
Connections in the English Lake District. London, Anvil Press Poetry, 1972.
Eighteen Poems. Privately printed, 1973.
Red Midnight Moon. San Francisco, Empty Elevator Shaft Press, 1973.
Byron Exhumed. Fort Wayne, Indiana, Windless Orchard Press, 1973.
Cool Zebras of Light. Santa Barbara, California, Christopher Press, 1974.
Holy Cow: Parable Poems. Los Angeles, Red Hill Press, 1974.
Bronchial Tangle, Heart System. Hanover, New Hampshire, Granite, 1974.
The Gift to Be Simple: A Garland for Ann Lee. New York, Liveright, 1975.
Shaker Light. Milwaukee, Wisconsin, Pentagram Press, 1975.
The Poet as Ice-Skater. San Francisco, Manroot, 1975.
Hawthorne: Poems Adapted from The American Notebooks. Fairfax, California, Red Hill Press, 1977.
Gauguin's Chair: Selected Poems, 1967–1974. Trumansburg, New York, Crossing Press, 1977.
The Drowned Man to the Fish. St. Paul, Minnesota, New Rivers Press, 1978.
Ikagnak, the North Wind: With Dr. Kane in the Arctic, A Verse Sequence. Pasadena, California, Kenmore Press, 1978.
Love Poems for Robert Mitchum. Huntington Beach, California, Poet-Skin Press, 1981.
Celebrities: In Memory of Margaret Dumont, Dowager of the Marx Brothers Movies (1890–1965). Berkeley, California, Sombre Reptiles, 1981.
The Picnic in the Snow. St. Paul, Minnesota, New Rivers Press, 1982.
What Dillinger Meant to Me. New York, Seahorse Press, 1983.
Hawker. Greensboro, North Carolina, Unicorn Press, 1984.
Kane. Greensboro, North Carolina, Unicorn Press, 1985.
Crunching Gravel. San Francisco, Mercury House, 1988.
Haydon. Greensboro, North Carolina, Unicorn Press, 1989.
Breughel's Pig. Los Angeles, Illuminati, 1989.
Good Night, Paul. N.p., GLB Publishers, 1992.
Love Poems for Robert Mitchum: Poems. Saint John, Kansas, Chiron Review Press, 1992.
Poems: Selected and New (1967–1991). Santa Maria, California, Asylum Arts, 1992.

"Twin Peaks" Cherry Pie: New Poems. Pocatello, Idaho, The Rednec Press, 1995.
Feather, A Child's Death and Life. Madison, University of Wisconsin Press, 1997.

Plays

Fuck Mother (produced New York, 1970).
Ludwig of Bavaria. Cherry Valley, New York, Cherry Valley, 1986.
The Blood Countess. Cherry Valley, New York, Cherry Valley, 1987.

Novels

Snapshots for A Serial Killer: A Fiction and a Play. N.p., GLB Publishers, 1991.
Zapped: Two Novellas. N.p., GLB Publishers, 1993.

Other

The Crowns of Apollo: Swinburne's Principles of Criticism and Art: A Study in Victorian Criticism and Aesthetics. Detroit, Michigan, Wayne State University Press, 1965.
The Great American Poetry Bake-Off (essays). Metuchen, New Jersey, Scarecrow Press, 3 vols., 1979–87.
The Peters Black and Blue Guide to Literary Journals. Silver Spring, Maryland, Cherry Valley, vols. 1 and 2, 1983–85; Paradise, California, Dust, vol. 3, 1986.
Crunching Gravel: On Growing Up in the Thirties. N.p., Mercury House, 1988.
Hunting the Snark: A Compendium of New Poetic Terminology. New York, Paragon House, 1989; revised edition, as *Hunting the Snark: American Poetry at Century's End: Classifications and Commentary,* Greensboro, North Carolina, Avisson Press, 1997.
Where the Bee Sucks: Workers, Drones, and Queens of Contemporary American Poetry. Santa Maria, California, Asylum Arts, 1994.
For You Lili Marlene: A Memoir of World War II. Madison, University of Wisconsin, 1995.

Editor, *Victorians on Literature and Art.* New York, Appleton Crofts, 1961; London, Owen, 1964.
Editor, with David Halliburton, Edmund *Gosse's Journal of His Visit to America.* West Lafayette, Indiana, Purdue University Press, 1966.
Editor, with George Hitchcock, *Pioneers of Modern Poetry.* San Francisco, Kayak, 1967.
Editor, with Herbert M. Schueller, *The Letters of John Addington Symonds.* Detroit, Michigan, Wayne State University Press, 3 vols., 1967–69.
Editor, with Timothy D'Arch Smith, *Gabriel: A Poem,* by John Addington Symonds. London, Michael de Hartington, 1974.
Editor, *Letters to a Tutor: The Tennyson Family Letters to Henry Graham Dakyns (1861–1911),* with *The Audrey Tennyson Death-Bed Diary.* Metuchen, New Jersey, Scarecrow Press, 1988.
Editor, *Nell's Story: A Woman from Eagle River,* by Nell Peters. Madison, University of Wisconsin Press, 1995.

*

Manuscript Collection: Spencer Library, University of Kansas, Lawrence.

Critical Studies: "Literary Reputation and the Thrown Voice" by Billy Collins, in *A Gift of Tongues: Critical Challenges in Contemporary American Poetry,* edited by Marie Harris and Kathleen Aguero, Athens, University of Georgia Press, 1987; interview with Paul Trachtenberg, in *Paintbrush* (Kirksville, Missouri), 14(28), autumn 1987; "The Poetry's the Thing: An Interview with Robert Peters" by Jim Cory, in *James White Review,* 13(1), winter 1996.

*   *   *

Most of Robert L. Peters's work operates through a close attention to the concrete; for him most ideas (and emotions) are, indeed, "in things." This remains true, though less absolutely so in some of his later publications, in both major areas of his work—his "personal" poems (e.g., *Songs for a Son, The Drowned Man to the Fish, Holy Cow*) and what one might call his poems of historical ventriloquism (e.g., *Hawthorne, The Gift to Be Simple*).

One pole of Peters's somewhat Manichaean vision of humanity is the product of a kind of disgust. His volume *The Sow's Head and Other Poems,* for example, includes "Campanella 65: A Set of Explosions." In this group of poems Peters takes as his starting point Italian sonnets by the Dominican Tommaso Campanella (1568–1639); the resulting poems are, says Peters, "free improvisations . . . and should not be regarded as translations." The most powerful is *"De Dignitate Hominis":*

This beautiful world is truly God's creature,
God's image, praising God whose type it is.

And we are this creature's worms;
vile families of us sink mouths
into the pink lining of its guts,
sate ourselves, flex elastic tails,
quiver. Why should we know its
intellect or its love?

The tone is reminiscent of the medieval *De Contemptu Mundi,* and it is a tone that, in even more violently expressive manner, is frequently found in Peters's work. The tone is related to recurrent images of dismemberment and torn flesh. The quintessential poem in this line is "The Butchering: Eagle River, Wisconsin," a narrative of an apparently youthful experience that for Peters has an archetypal status, a disturbing, and quasi-religious, revelation of horror and beauty. In *The Sow's Head* and *The Drowned Man to the Fish* there are many poems of separation and lust, estrangement and pain, yet there is at times a kind of invocation of beauty, curiously echoic of Christopher Smart. The following is from "Christmas Poem 1966; Lines on an English Butcher-Shop Window":

O beautiful severed head of hog
O skewered lamb-throat, marble eye of duck, O
    meadow-freshened hare suspended . . .
O livers tumbling, O clattering jewel of
    pancreas and ligaments of stomach wall . . .
I see you all!

An intense experience of loss is approached very differently in the moving poems of *Songs for a Son,* occasioned by the death of Peters's young son. The thirty-eight poems of this sequence have an admirable control and honest exactitude of language. What is perhaps most poignant of all is the poet's realization that ''my son's image / was painted on sand,'' that there are very real limits to his capacity to restore the image mentally:

> But I am blind!
> Unable to create a brow,
> a lash, the hollow down
> the back of the neck,
> the throat!

Of Peters's less explicitly personal work, the best is perhaps found in the eighty-five poems of his sequence *The Gift to Be Simple: A Garland for Ann Lee.* Its subject is Mother Ann Lee, founder of the Shakers, and the poems provide an imaginative account of her childhood in England, her marriage, and her arrival in America, where she was ultimately beaten to death. Her bearing of witness, her imprisonment, her perception of all evil as sexual in origin, her self-mortification, her moments of vision—all are powerfully conveyed in language of deceptive simplicity. The energy of Peters's writing is self-evident, but what is perhaps not so readily appreciated is the careful craftsmanship of his best work. Consider, for example, the effective use of internal rhyme and the counterpointing of line ending and syntax in the first of the Ann Lee poems:

> Ann at twilight, Ann
> at dawn, Ann with her
>
> meager playthings on
> the lawn, a stick doll
>
> tucked into her pocket
> a polished hen bone for
>
> a locket, and on another
> string a miniature tin dog
>
> with a tin ball in his mouth.

Peters's attitude toward language and his reverence for the exactly observed presented without rhetoric are well evidenced in the poems he mined from Hawthorne's *The American Notebooks.* Consider, for example, this passage from Hawthorne: ''Remarkable characters:—a disagreeable figure, waning from middle-age, clad in a pair of tow homespun pantaloons and very dirty shirt, bare-foot, and with one of his feet maimed by an axe; also, an arm amputated two or three inches below the elbow, his beard of a week's growth, grim and grisly, with a general effect of black;—altogether a filthy and disgusting object.'' Here is Peters's adaptation:

> Dirty shirt, bare-foot
> one of his feet maimed
> by an axe. An arm
> amputated below the elbow,
> Grim and grisly, a
> general effect of black.

Elsewhere Hawthorne emerges as the author of a kind of Americanized haiku, as in ''Moonlight'':

> I bathed in the river
> which was as calm as death.
>
> I plunged down into the sky.

My own preference is for this ''quieter'' end of Peters's range rather than for the poetry of angst and despair. Still, that both should be on offer, so to speak, is a measure of the interest to be found in his work. Although Peters is not a major poet (he is more influenced than influencing), there is much genuine poetry to be found in his work, and he deserves to be read.

—Glyn Pursglove

PETRIE, Paul (James)

Nationality: American. **Born:** Detroit, Michigan, 1 July 1928. **Education:** Wayne State University, Detroit, 1946–51, B.A. 1950, M.A. 1951; University of Iowa, Iowa City, Ph.D. 1957. **Military Service:** U.S. Army, 1951–53. **Family:** Married Sylvia Spencer in 1954; two daughters and one son. **Career:** Instructor, 1959–62, assistant professor, 1962–66, associate professor, 1966–69, professor of English, 1969–90, University of Rhode Island, Kingston. **Awards:** Capricorn Book award, 1984. **Address:** 200 Dendron Road, Wakefield, Rhode Island 02879, U.S.A.

PUBLICATIONS

Poetry

Confessions of a Non-Conformist. Mount Vernon, Iowa, Hillside Press, 1963.
The Race with Time and the Devil. Francestown, New Hampshire, Golden Quill Press, 1965.
The Leader: For Martin Luther King, Jr. Providence, Rhode Island, Hellcoal Press, 1968.
From under the Hill of Night. Nashville, Tennessee, Vanderbilt University Press, 1969.
The Idol. Kingston, Rhode Island, Biscuit City Press, 1973.
The Academy of Goodbye. Hanover, New Hampshire, University Press of New England, 1974.
Light from the Furnace Rising. Providence, Rhode Island, Copper Beech Press, 1978.
Time Songs. Kingston, Rhode Island, Biscuit City Press, 1979.
Not Seeing Is Believing. Lacrosse, Wisconsin, Juniper Press, 1983.
Strange Gravity: Songs, Physical and Metaphysical. Cranberry Isles, Maine, Tidal Press, 1984.
The Runners. Pittsburgh. Slow Loris Press, 1988.

*

Critical Study: In *The Literary Review,* 38(2), winter 1995.

Paul Petrie comments:

My whole approach to poetry, both thematic and technical, is governed by a hatred of dogmatic theorizing, and since the twentieth century represents the very apotheosis of theorizing, a paradise for half-baked creeds and countercreeds, I find myself in a school of one. If there is any critical notion that I find appealing, it is Keats's idea of negative capability, but even that has its limitations. In short, I believe that there is nothing that cannot be said in poetry and that there is no limitation on the way it can or should be said. A poem need not be new or old, in free verse or meter, understated or overstated; all that it must be is a good poem.

As for my own work, I would describe it as lyrical, relatively emotional, dramatic in its inclusion of opposites and with a stronger current of movement than is common in verse today, and perhaps with an overindulgence in the doctrine of statement through images. My major strengths are rhythm and organization; my major weaknesses are a lack of exact detail and firm diction. I have a personal notion of the poem as an act of praise, be it positive or negative in theme and tone, and I tend to regard poetry as a semireligious vocation. But I do not demand that others share these attitudes, and I can think of excellent poems that would stretch these terms to the breaking point. The poems will remain; the theory will go.

*   *   *

Paul Petrie is well known to students of contemporary American poetry. For more than three decades his poems have appeared in a wide variety of literary journals and magazines and in several volumes. A sense of death in life and of fragile mortality seems to be the exclusive concern of the books. Haunted by death in his dreams and plagued by it in his waking life, Petrie, in an intense and passionate creative act, transforms his fear and dread into art. As *The Race with Time and the Devil* suggests, such an act is not an easy or an unambiguous triumph. His best poems are alive with the sense of a real person's struggle to achieve an elemental relationship with and understanding of the natural cycles of life and death.

There is in Petrie a clear movement toward concentration, sharpness, and mastery of medium. *Confessions of a Non-Conformist* is an adequate work, though not particularly original. *The Race with Time and the Devil* is a marked improvement and contains a number of fine poems, especially the five-poem sequence "Pictures of Departure"—"The Last Words of Frederick II," "Chain," "The Church of San Antonio de la Florida," "Morning Psalm," and "In Defense of Colds." *From under the Hill of Night* deserves the most praise. Poems such as "Under the Hill of Night," "The Party," "Mark Twain," "Kindertoten," and "Notes of a Would-Be Traveler" are excellent. In them Petrie has achieved fully the desire to articulate his organic sense of the world.

—Richard Damashek

PHILLIPS, Carl

Nationality: American. **Born:** Carl Phillips, Jr., Everett, Washington, 23 July 1959. **Education:** Harvard University, Cambridge, Massachusetts, 1977–81, A.B. 1981; University of Massachusetts, Amherst, 1981–83, M.A.T. 1983; Boston University, Boston, 1992–93,

M.A. 1993. **Family:** With Doug Macomber since 1991. **Career:** High school teacher, Falmouth High School, Falmouth, Massachusetts, 1985–91. Assistant professor, 1993–96, and since 1996 associate professor, Washington University, St. Louis, Missouri. **Awards:** Samuel French Morse poetry prize, 1992, for *In the Blood;* Academy of American Poets prize, 1993; Guggenheim fellowship, 1997; Witter Bynner fellowship, Library of Congress, 1997.

PUBLICATIONS

Poetry

In the Blood. Boston, Northeastern University Press, 1992.
Cortège. St. Paul, Minnesota, Graywolf Press, 1995.
From the Devotions. St. Paul, Minnesota, Graywolf Press, 1998.
Pastoral. St. Paul, Minnesota, Graywolf Press, 2000.
The Tether. New York, Farrar Straus, 2001.

Other

Translator, *Philoctetes,* by Sophocles. New York, Oxford University Press, 2001.

*

Critical Studies: "The Dark Room Collective: Thomas Sayers Ellis, Trasi Johnson, John Keene, Janice Lowe, Carl Phillips, Sharan Strange, Natasha Trethewey, Kevin Young," in *Callaloo* (Baltimore, Maryland), 16(3), summer 1993; interview with Charles H. Rowell, in *Callaloo* (Baltimore, Maryland), 21(2), spring 1998; in *New Republic* (New York), 9 March 1998; "Symbolic Changes: Karen Helfrich Talks with Carl Phillips," in *Lambda Book Report,* 6(9), 1 April 1998.

*   *   *

Carl Phillips, initially received in some quarters as a lyric writer within conventions suggested by the term "workshop poet," has emerged in his greater poems as a somewhat less traditional poet, one of the most original of his generation. Phillips's rhetorical abilities were never in doubt, but in part his early work was at times misread as, to use Harold Bloom's words, "cultural guilt" or the products of "the School of Resentment." Social afflictions that are common to gay life in America have led to powerful narrative and lyrical poems, but Phillips is concerned with more than the record or expression of personal suffering. Although he is very much a poet of eros, it is not merely a localized, personal experience that underlies his work. Autobiography enters, explicitly at times, but it does so as a source for language rather than as cause for public complaint. Unlike confessional works, his poems do not call for the reader's sympathy. As in all great poetry, the prime subject is language itself.

"Elegy," in Phillips's first book, *In the Blood* (1992), begins, "Poor Eros: sadly, as in the boning of fowl / or of angels in defeat, someone has snapped / his wings off . . ." and weaves through six syntactically complex stanzas to what might otherwise be a strictly sentimental conclusion, an older man remembering the time when "his / pink legs [worked] whole crowds into longing." But the easy sentimentality and self-indulgence of such moments are not the subject or point. Rather, Phillips controls the movement of the man's reflections in measured stanzas, the stoically ordered language moderating the tone. The man may be self-indulgent, but the poem is not. The reader is kept at arm's length, watching the words take their exact places like the bits and pieces of an enormously complex mosaic. In the end the man's feeling may be simple and direct, but the reader's interest lies in the labyrinthine process involved in expressing it.

Phillips is a mosaicist, building his poems from bits and pieces of language rather than starting with grand gestures or complaints and then letting these carry the poem. In this his temperament is classical. The orderly progression is evident, for example, in the concluding section of "Arcadia" in *From the Devotions* (1998), where he writes,

> He is not like the others, who say nothing and leave soon.
>   This one—done, but still stiff—is a dark
> weight upon him, that stays, groaning/whispering
> *baby* and *pie*.

The musically baroque twists in the second line break at exactly the right moment, after "dark," to prompt a momentary pause before the eye reaches "weight," allowing in turn the weight in the sound of the word to enforce the meaning. Phillips is musically exact, and his work is clearly the result of considerable struggle to attain the exact pitch, a degree of precision that is never easily achieved. There are few poets around who do it this well.

As both gay and African-American, Phillips is an outsider in America. While another writer might use this social identity for complaint (as if the object were to be "accepted," although if he were, the reason for poetry, at least the kind of poetry he writes, would be lost), Phillips uses it to create his own precisely measured space. He is like William Bronk, another gay poet whose response to being an outsider was not anger or resentment but a controlled understanding of what was left. And what was left proved to be everything worth knowing.

Phillips's major book *From the Devotions* tracks a route from physical desire to spiritual awareness, and it is a process of this kind that most concerned Bronk. The latter was known as a poet who saw physicality as delusive but inescapable, nor, as the poems make clear, would he have wanted to escape it if he could. Similarly, Phillips says in "In the Days of Thrown Confetti" (*From the Devotions*),

> You remember.
> Back when, I suppose,
> it could be said we didn't care
>
> about the earth, anymore
> than about the flesh, but I
> don't say it.

This is not to argue that Phillips learned from Bronk but that they have pursued parallel trajectories. Rather than be poets of complaint, protesting the injustices in being chosen as the outsider, each has carved out, with meticulous attention to language, spiritual recognitions that are at least the equal of anything reached by conventional pursuit. One finds similar trajectories in other major gay poets of the period, for instance, Gerrit Lansing, Ronald Johnson, Robert Duncan, and Jack Spicer. The end in each case is not an exploitation of one's self in the name of poetry but rather the invention of intricate linguistic worlds that can comprehend the largest kinds of understanding.

Phillips may prove to be absolutely the equal of predecessors like Bronk. He may well be one of our major poets.

—Edward Foster

PICKARD, Tom

Nationality: British. **Born:** Thomas MacKenna in Newcastle upon Tyne, Northumberland, 7 January 1946. **Education:** Newcastle secondary schools; Ruskin College, Oxford, 1977–78. **Family:** Married 1) Constance Davison in 1964 (dissolved 1978), one son and one daughter; 2) Joanna Voit in 1979, one son; 3) Svava Barker in 1999. **Career:** Worked for a seed merchant, construction company, and wine merchant, 1962–64; served an apprenticeship to Basil Bunting; co-founder and manager, Morden Tower Book Room, 1963–72, and Ultima Thule Bookshop, 1969–73, Newcastle; C. Day Lewis Fellow, Rutherford Comprehensive School, London, 1976–77; creative writing fellow, University of Warwick, Coventry, 1978–79. Director of documentary films. Occasional articles for *The Guardian, Daily Telegraph,* and *New Statesman & Society.* **Awards:** Northern Arts award, 1965; Arts Council grant, 1969, 1973. **Agent:** Judy Daish Associates, 83 Eastbourne Mews, London, W2 6LQ, England.

PUBLICATIONS

Poetry

High on the Walls. London, Fulcrum Press, 1967; New York, Horizon Press, 1968.
New Human Unisphere. Newcastle upon Tyne, Ultima Thule, 1969.
The Order of Chance. London, Fulcrum Press, 1971.
Dancing under Fire. Philadelphia, Middle Earth, 1973.
Hero Dust: New and Selected Poems. London, Allison and Busby, 1979.
O.K. Tree! Durham, Pig Press, 1980.
Domestic Art. Vancouver, Slug Press, 1981.
In Search of "Ingenuous." Vancouver, 1981.
Custom and Exile. London, Allison and Busby, 1985.
Tiepin Eros: New & Selected Poems. Newcastle upon Tyne, Bloodaxe Books, 1994.
fuckwind: poems and songs. Buckfastleigh, Devon, Etruscan Books, 1999.

Plays

Radio Documentary: *The Jarrow March,* 1976.

Television Scripts: *Squire,* 1974; *The Dragon Story,* 1983; *Lambton Worm (Everybody Here),* 1983; *We Make Ships* (also director), 1988; *Tell Them in Gdansk* (also director), 1989; *Finnegan's Wake,* 1990; *Birmingham Is What I Think With* (also director), 1991, 1997; *The Shadow & The Substance* (also director), 1994; *On the Job,* 1995.

Short Stories

Guttersnipe. San Francisco, City Lights, 1972.

Other

Serving My Time to a Trade. Orono, Maine, Paideuma, 1980.
The Jarrow March, with Joanna Voit. London, Allison and Busby,
   and New York, Schocken, 1982.
We Make Ships. London, Secker and Warburg, 1989.

*

Bibliography: In *Poetry Information 18* (London), 1978.

Manuscript Collections: Northern Arts, Newcastle upon Tyne; State
University of New York, Buffalo.

Critical Studies: ''Tom Pickard,'' in *Lip 1* (Philadelphia), 1972, and
in *Poetry Information 18* (London), 1978, both by Eric Mottram;
''Pick's Progress'' by Richard Caddell, in *Literary Review 6* (London), 1979; ''Hero Dust'' by Kenneth Cox, in *Montemora 7* (New
York), 1980; by Tony Baker, in *Sharp Study and Long Toil: Basil
Bunting Special Issue* of *A Durham University Journal Supplement*
(Durham), 1995.

Tom Pickard comments:

   Instead of a personal statement I send this poem, which says all I
want to say about writing poetry at this moment.

   in search of ''ingenuous''

   opening a dictionary
   between inflict
   and inhuman
   my eye falls
   on a flower
   placed there
   and preserved
   by you

   seeing
   it informs
   my heart
   infolds

   *

   between idolize
   and I.L.O.
   a violet
   whose moth petals
   hover on
   ignotum per ignotius

   explanation
   obscures the object

   *   *   *

''ad rather be skint than an industrial cog''

   Apparently against all the odds for a working-class Newcastle
school-leaver, a commitment to poetry and a refusal to accept the
menial life allocated to him lay behind the achievement of Tom
Pickard's first book, *High on the Walls.* His ''horror of being limited''
helped him to an early awareness of modern American writing,
fostered by contact with Dorn, Creeley, and others. The spareness of
such lyrics as ''City Summer'' certainly has affinities with Williams
and these later poets, yet Pickard sought to remain true to his own area
and language and to his working-class experience. His work is
permeated by a sense of the Northumbrian locality, whether a
countryside still close to Thomas Bewick's (''The Game Bird''), the
industrial heritage of ''Stowell Street Corporation Yard,'' or the
settings of his prose work *Guttersnipe.* The human consequences of
this heritage are set out in ''Birthplace—Bronchitis'' (''The old men
cannot walk up banks / without leaving brown cockles on the path''),
and local speech is strongly used in such poems as ''Rape'' and
''Scrap.'' Completing the work are lyrics of sexual love and involvement (''To Puberty,'' ''The Bodies Are Touching'') and the experience of parenthood (''The Bairn'').

   In his preface to *High on the Walls,* Basil Bunting (whose work
Pickard helped to rescue from neglect and who in turn offered
encouragement and continued advice) praised Pickard's ''skill to
keep the line compact and musical'' and hoped that he would learn
''to sing with a longer breath.'' This can be related to the problem of
evolving forms to embody a range of themes, from the most personal
to the social and political. A subtle merging is already apparent in as
brief a poem as ''Factory'' (''fingers of a hand / that whisper softly / at
my napes hair / / smoke blowing / in the winds of engines''). But *The
Order of Chance* begins with a poem that marks a new move forward.
An angry lament for generations of such men as his father, ''The
Devil's Destroying Angel Exploded'' is dedicated to John Martin and
has something of the Northumbrian painter's somber vision, while
referring insistently to the present:

   no colour
   but dancing black
   producers of heat
   confused in the cold
   moon full above the dole

As Eric Mottram (his most perceptive and informed critic) has
stressed, mythic and folk elements were becoming important in
Pickard's work, nourished by his reading in Jung, his own dreams,
and his direct knowledge of local folk rituals. Such elements are
notably present in ''New Body,'' with its magical transformations:
''As you felt my bear's claw / I was a snake / / As you stroked my cat's
fur / I was a fish.'' The volume ends with the prose sequence
''Warmth,'' but before that comes part of a long poem bearing the
title ''Magpie.''

   This poem became the substantial and complex ''Dancing under
Fire.'' It used varying forms to explore the possibilities of energy in,
for instance, a move from stone as defensive wall or the oppressiveness of ''city concrete'' to stone as used constructively, to walls
dissolved by love and ''stone stances'' that ''one fixed gaze / burns
into life'' or, to cite another example, the sequence from plant (in the
now separate poem ''The Order of Chance'') to coal to fire. The past,
the mythic, and the personal alternate and merge. A row of street
lamps is ''. . . a dragon coiled / in the valley'' but also is sexual love
and the flames of industrial fires, energy whose exploitation can be
damaging, both socially and personally, or revivifying. A sequence of
individual transformation, reiterating the word ''dissolve,'' precedes

the evocation of the shell-shocked victim, Marta, whose "lack of words makes us suppose so much," counterbalanced in turn by "a voice from someone's telly," which offers only "shadows / of the real event."

The final stress is on love, on active acknowledgment ("father you built the lines I travel on"), and on the assertion, perhaps central to Pickard's work, that "what is chosen / remains." A group of "Snake Poems" continues the dragon-fire-energy theme in dreamlike, often violent visions of family relationships still rooted, as in "Gateshead," in actuality. A family is more directly seen in the television play *Squire,* while the poems interspersed in his radio documentary, *The Jarrow March,* stress the human warmth, the solidarity of parents and children, in that political action by "family men / hunger dancers."

"Hero Dust," Pickard's next long poem, opposes to a bluesstyle prophecy of "bad news" a synthesis, in twenty-eight numbered but formally differing verses, of several recurrent themes. These range from industrial desolation ("moss mottled with oil / and slime") through the possibilities of chance, love, action, the entwining of pain and joy, and a fierce energy ("my fury flames furnaces") to end in lostness and betrayal counterbalanced by the quoted words "I have saved the bird in my breast." The transforming potential of love is again suggested in "Ballad" and "City Garden," while such poems as "Rat Palace" (with the unanswered "how can we help each other?") detail the evils of political control. An enhanced European awareness, aided by periods of living in Warsaw, is shown here and in *Custom and Exile.* There are no long poems in this collection, but elements and themes recur, building toward a complex unity. Sensuous perception is explored in "Signed and Dated on the Lover," one of several poems related to paintings (in this case Ingres's *La Grande Odalisque*), the concern being both what is perceived and ". . . the act/of seeing" ("Diana at Her Bath"); "We compare notes, and / they compare" ("Goya Sketching"). Other poems explore personal themes of sexuality, tenderness, pregnancy, birth, and physical separation in ways both subtle and direct: "a bird / in your bush / sings" ("Words"); "ok tree / you can bloom / Spring's arrived / with two green eyes" ("OK Tree").

The living warmth and fertility of human relationships are typically contrasted in "Blue Brood" with

        . . . a passing train
                travelling
        nuclear waste

Pickard's often angry concern with public, political events and their impingement on people continues. Such poems as "Sweet F.A." are related to the earlier years of the Thatcher administration, and "Spring Tide," his tribute to Bunting, is set in the context of "a filthy winter to have lived through, / . . . A year-long miner's strike / broken." "A Sense of History," with its pensioners scraping "the dry earth" for "small bits of coal," suggests a sad continuity with the world of his early poems and contrasts sharply with the society glimpsed in "Golden City Delivery Boy," which is inhabited by managers, directors, bankers, and their attendant servants and where "a general's daughter / prepares roast lamb / in an immaculate kitchen."

Later, a period as writer-in-residence at Austin and Pickersgill's shipyard in Sunderland led to *We Make Ships,* a documentation of Pickard's talks with workers there. The shelving of his play for BBC television, *Left Over People,* which dealt both with the 1936 Jarrow March and the situation in Sunderland in 1986, was seen by Pickard as "part of a much wider dismantling of our civil liberties." The experience gives an added retrospective edge to such poems as "My Radio, 1" ("its timing is perfect / and variable // . . . its motives / pure . . .") and "My Radio, 2" ("interprets the past / manages the present"). Yet, against this he can set his own practice as a writer: "my pen wants to manage / its own affairs, / thinking it knows best: // my pen demands / complete autonomy" ("My Pen," a poem, as it happens, with a Polish context). The vivid and playful "Recipe: Pastime for the Unemployed" ends with words that, although referring to the hazards of cookery, express the spirit of much of his work: "fight back."

This spirit is certainly present in *Tiepin Eros,* which contains both new and selected earlier poems. It is expressed in "The Double D Economy/Depravity and Deprivation," for instance, and in the angry, riddling questions of "Who Is the Whore of Armageddon?": "Whose smile is manicured money talking? / Whose arms embrace the globe?" Anger also more directly informs human concern in poems such as "Contractor Song," which deals with the harsh and dangerous life of shipyard workers, while in "The Bridge" two people become lovers in a setting of "abandoned factories / and shutdown shipyards . . . / . . . collapsed wharfs, / idle slipways, skeletal staithes." This bringing together of the individual, the personal, with social or political factors occurs in other poems, such as "A History Lesson from My Son on Hadrian's Wall," where past and present are set side by side, reinforcing and illuminating each other. "Energy" moves from observation of swallows gathering in an autumnal north to "slow flying jets under / a low lying sky" that ". . . fly south over armies assembled in the dust" to a scene of desert war, and it does this with an elliptical brevity that is also found in, for instance, "Nues (a painting by Djurdje Teodorvic)," "Dedication," and the toughly sensuous "Sea Trout." Pickard's practice of revising poems, such as "The Order of Chance," in successive printings has been perceptively discussed by Tony Baker. A further paring down, an even greater succinctness, is often involved, "Diana at Her Bath," for instance, being reduced to thirteen lines from twenty-five in *Custom and Exile,* so that the rapidity of our reading mirrors "the act / of seeing." This combination of brevity and subtlety with passionate involvement contributes much to Pickard's very distinctive voice.

The first section of *Tiepin Eros* ends with "The Sayings of Chairman Q," a satire on our obsession with queuing that prefigures the list poems in Pickard's 1999 volume *fuckwind,* a hymn of praise to physical love. The book is comprised of forty-seven new poems, divided into four sets, that span all manner of styles in an explosive, creative diversity. There is the sea shanty ("Ballad of Jamie Allen"), the blues ("Gypsy Lady"), the folk narrative ("Rope"), the song lyric (literally, with the music printed out), list poems, and permutational poems like "Satchi & Satchi" (although these may be closer to the rhythms of children's stamp-the-foot games). There are brief haikulike lyrics such as "Dark" and "Holymire," each of six telling lines. But often the elements of nature and love are combined, as in "Wroth," "Rift," and "Kip Law," for Pickard's excitement is no longer framed in urban contexts but increasingly reflects the high, morose hills around Alston in the Pennines where he lives. The introduction is contributed by Paul McCartney, and the front cover pictures Pickard's inspiration, Svava.

—Geoffrey Soar and Bill Griffiths

PIERCY, Marge

Nationality: American. **Born:** Detroit, Michigan, 31 March 1936.
Education: University of Michigan, Ann Arbor (Hopwood Award,
1956, 1957), A.B. 1957; Northwestern University, Evanston, Illinois,
M.A. 1958. **Family:** Married Ira Wood (third marriage) in 1982.
Career: Instructor, Indiana University, Gary, 1960–62; poet-in-
residence, University of Kansas, Lawrence, 1971; visiting lecturer,
Thomas Jefferson College, Grand Valley State Colleges, Allendale,
Michigan, 1975; visiting faculty, Women's Writers' Conference,
Cazenovia College, New York, 1976, 1978, 1980; staff member, Fine
Arts Work Center, Provincetown, Massachusetts, 1976–77; writer-
in-residence, College of the Holy Cross, Worcester, Massachusetts,
1976; Butler Professor of Letters, State University of New York,
Buffalo, 1977; Elliston Professor of poetry, University of Cincinnati,
1986; DeRoy Distinguished Visiting Professor, University of Michi-
gan, 1992. **Awards:** Borestone Mountain award, 1968, 1974, Na-
tional Endowment for the Arts grant, 1978; Rhode Island School of
Design Faculty Association Medal, 1985; Carolyn Kizer prize, 1986;
Sheaffer Eaton-P.E.N. New England award, 1989; Carolyn Kizer
prize, 1990; Golden Rose Poetry prize, New England Poetry Club,
1991; May Sarton award, New England Poetry Club, 1991; Brit ha-
Dorot award, The Shalom Center, 1992; Barbara Bradley award, New
England Poetry Club, 1992; Arthur C. Clarke award for Best Science
Fiction Novel Published in the United Kingdom, 1993; Notable Book
award, American Library Association, 1997, for *What Are Big Girls
Made Of?*. Honorary degree: Lesley College. **Member:** Board,
Massachusetts Cultural Council, 1990–91; board of directors, 1982–85,
and since 1985, advisory board, Coordinating Council of Literary
Magazines. **Agent:** Lois Wallace, Wallace Literary Agency, 177 East
70th Street, New York, New York 10021, U.S.A., and Sara Fisher,
A.M. Heath, 79 St. Martin's Lane, London WC2N 4AA, England.
Address: Box 1473, Wellfleet, Massachusetts 02667, U.S.A.

PUBLICATIONS

Poetry

Breaking Camp. Middletown, Connecticut, Wesleyan University
   Press, 1968.
Hard Loving. Middletown, Connecticut, Wesleyan University Press,
   1969.
A Work of Artifice. (broadside) Detroit, Red Hanrahan Press, 1970.
4-Telling, with others. Trumansburg, New York, Crossing Press,
   1971.
When the Drought Broke. (broadside) Santa Barbara, California,
   Unicorn Press, 1971.
To Be of Use. New York, Doubleday, 1973.
Living in the Open. New York, Knopf, 1976.
The Twelve-Spoked Wheel Flashing. New York, Knopf, 1978.
The Moon Is Always Female. New York, Knopf, 1980.
Circles on the Water: Selected Poems. New York, Knopf, 1982.
Stone, Paper, Knife. New York, Knopf, and London, Pandora Press,
   1983.
My Mother's Body. New York, Knopf, and London, Pandora Press,
   1985.
Available Light. New York, Knopf, and London, Pandora Press,
   1988.
Mars and Her Children. New York, Knopf, 1992.

Eight Chambers of the Heart, Selected Poems. London, Penguin,
   1995.
What Are Big Girls Made Of? New York, Knopf, 1997.
The Art of Blessing the Day. New York, Knopf, 1999.
Early Grrrl. N.p., Leapfrog Press, 1999.

Recordings: *Laying Down the Tower,* Black Box, 1973; *Reading and
   Thoughts,* Everett Edwards, 1976; *Reclaiming Ourselves,* Radio
   Free People, 1973; *At the Core,* Watershed, 1976; *be careful,
   there's a baby in the house,* Green Linnet Records, Inc., 1991.

Play

The Last White Class: A Play about Neighborhood Terror, with
   Ira Wood (produced Northampton, Massachusetts, 1978).
   Trumansburg, New York, Crossing Press, 1980.

Novels

Going Down Fast. New York, Simon and Schuster, 1969.
Dance the Eagle to Sleep. New York, Doubleday, 1970; London,
   W.H. Allen, 1971.
Small Changes. New York, Doubleday, 1973.
Woman on the Edge of Time. New York, Knopf, 1976; London,
   Women's Press, 1979.
The High Cost of Living. New York, Harper, 1978; London, Women's
   Press, 1979.
Vida. New York, Summit, and London, Women's Press, 1980.
Braided Lives. New York, Summit, and London, Allen Lane, 1982.
Fly Away Home. New York, Summit, and London, Chatto and
   Windus, 1984.
Gone to Soldiers. New York, Summit, and London, Joseph, 1987.
Summer People. New York, Summit, and London, Joseph, 1989.
He, She and It. New York, Knopf, 1991; as *Body of Glass.* London,
   Michael Joseph, 1992.
The Longings of Women. New York, Fawcett/Columbine, and Lon-
   don, Michael Joseph, 1994.
City of Darkness, City of Light. New York, Fawcett/Columbine,
   1996.
Storm Tide, with Ira Wood. New York, Fawcett/Columbine, 1998.
Three Women. New York, Morrow, 1999.

Other

The Grand Coolie Damn. Boston, New England Free Press, 1970.
Parti-Colored Blocks for a Quilt. Ann Arbor, University of Michigan
   Press, 1982.

Editor, *Early Ripening: Young Women's Poetry Now.* London and
   New York, Pandora Press, 1987.

*

Bibliography: In *Contemporary American Women Writers: Narra-
tive Strategies* edited by Catherine Rainwater and William J. Scheick,
Lexington, University Press of Kentucky, 1985; *Marge Piercy: An
Annotated Bibliography* by Patricia Doherty, Westport, Connecticut,
Greenwood, 1996.

Manuscript Collection: Harlan Hatcher Graduate Library, University of Michigan, Ann Arbor.

Critical Studies: "A Black Poet Speaks of Poetry" by June Jordan, *American Poetry Review,* July/August 1974; "Marge Piercy: A Collage" by Nancy Scholar Zee, in Oyez Review (Berkeley, California), 9(1), 1975; *Ways of Knowing: Critical Essays on Marge Piercy* edited by Sue Walker and Eugenie Hamner, Mobile, Alabama, Negative Capability Press, 1986; "You Are Your Own Magician: A Vision of Integrity in the Poetry of Marge Piercy" by Jean Rosenbaum, and "Marge Piercy: A Vision of the Peaceable Kingdom" by Victor Contoski, both in *Modern Poetry Studies,* 8, 1977; "Excellence in Poetry" by Hayden Carruth, in *Harper's Magazine* (New York), November 1978; "'Grabbing the Gusto' Marge Piercy's Poetry" by Jerome Judson, in *Writer's Digest* (Cincinnati, Ohio), 61, 1981; "Imagery of Association in the Poetry of Marge Piercy" by Edith Wynne, in *Publications of the Missouri Philological Association,* 1985; "Amber Mayflies of the Moment: A Brief Introduction to Marge Piercy and Her Poems," *Outlet,* Dubuque, Iowa, 1993; *An Alchemy of Genres: Cross Genre Writing by American Women* by Diane P. Freedman, University Press of Virginia, 1994; *The Repair of the World: The Novels of Marge Piercy* by Kerstin W. Shands, Westport, Connecticut, Greenwood, 1995; "Erotic and Existential Paradoxes of the Golem: Marge Piercy's He, She and It" by Diane Sautter, in *Journal of the Fantastic in the Arts* (Stow, Ohio), 7(2–3), 1996; "Chaos and Utopia: Social Transformation in 'Woman on the Edge of the Time'" by Elham Afnan, in *Extrapolation* (Kent, Ohio), 37(4), winter 1996; "Feminist Science Fiction: The Alternative Worlds of Piercy, Elgin, and Atwood" by Sema Kormali, in *Journal of American Studies of Turkey* (Ankara, Turkey), 4, fall 1996; *Out of the Broom Closet: The Deep Hidden Meaning of Domesticity in Postfeminist Novels by Louise Erdrich, Mary Gordon, Toni Morrison, Marge Piercy, Jane Smiley, and Amy Tan* (dissertation) by Jeannette Anne Cooperman, Saint Louis University, 1996; *Subject to Negotiation: Reading Feminist Criticism and American Women's Fictions* by Elaine Neil Orr, Charlottesville, University Press of Virginia, 1997; "Feminist Utopian Fiction and the Possibility of Social Critique" by Josephine Carubia Glorie, in *Political Science Fiction,* edited by Donald M. Hassler and Clyde Wilcox, Columbia, University of South Carolina Press, 1997; "The Ultimate America—Marge Piercy's 'Woman on the Edge of Time'" by Agnieszka Rzepa, in *Studia Anglica Posnaniensia* (Poznan, Poland), 32, 1997; "Grass-Roots Ecofeminism: Activating Utopia" by Cathleen McGuire and Colleen McGuire, in *Ecofeminist Literary Criticism: Theory, Interpretation,* edited by Greta Gaard and Patrick D. Murphy, Urbana, University of Illinois Press, 1998; "Technology As Eros's Dart: Cyborgs As Perfect (Male?) Lovers" by Anca Vlasopolos, in *Foundation* (England), 73, summer 1998.

Marge Piercy comments:

I have always worked to try to make my poems accessible and meaningful to an audience. That does not mean that the poem is necessarily simple; it is as complicated as it needs to be. A poem can speak through rich and complex imagery as long as it is emotionally coherent. I also write a type of poem with little or no ornament, just as I also work in long line, short lines, and lines that hover around iambic tetrameter or pentameter. In making the arrangement of sounds and silences that the notation of a poem on the page is supposed to create in the air or in the reader's mind, I am working in measures drawn from American speech and American prosody. However, my influences are various, ancient as well as modern, and international.

I imagine that I speak for a constituency, living and dead, and that I give utterance to energy, experience, insight, words flowing from many lives as well as my own. In truth I do not make much distinction between the sources inside and outside. What I mean by being of use is not that the poems function as agitprop or that they are didactic, although some of them are. I have no more hesitation than Pope or Hesiod did to write in that mode as well as many others. What I mean is simply that readers will find poems that speak to and for them, take those poems into their lives and say them to each other and put them up on the kitchen or bathroom or bedroom wall and remember bits of them in stressful or quiet times. That the poems may give voice to something in the experience of our lives has been my intention. For women especially to find ourselves spoken for in art gives dignity to our pain, our anger, our lust, our losses. We can hear what we hope for and what we fear in the small release of cadenced utterance.

*　　*　　*

Marge Piercy is one of the most prolific of contemporary poets. She has a large international following, and her work has been translated into a number of languages. Her poetry is informal, often prosy, and based on the rhythms of American speech. In her introduction to *Circles on the Water* she explains, "Once in a great while I do work in rhyme . . . mostly in the center of lines rather than on the end where to my ear it sticks out and chimes." Although Piercy strives to be "accessible and meaningful," her poems are studded with classical references, and she aligns herself with Pope and Hesiod in the didacticism of some of her work.

Coming to maturity in the 1960s, Piercy began writing as a political poet, drawing inspiration from her roots as an American, working-class, Jewish woman. Her first two volumes, *Breaking Camp* and *Hard Loving,* reveal her preoccupation with the civil rights, peace, and women's movements.

In the mid-1970s Piercy's poetry took on a rural focus when she moved from New York to a farmhouse on Cape Cod. The rhythms of rural life inspire many of her later poems, particularly in the volumes *Living in the Open* and *The Twelve-Spoked Wheel Flashing.* Moving from nature to mother earth in *The Moon Is Always Female,* Piercy channels her earlier feminism into an exploration of femininity. Fascinated with pagan relics and lunar myths, the poet relates the cycles of her own life to the cycles of the seasons. Love, lust, and personal commitment are prevailing concerns, and Piercy begins to confront her background in a theme that comes to fruition in her later volume *My Mother's Body.* Though written in memory of her mother, the book is really a tribute to all unacknowledged women, as shown in these lines from "They Inhabit Me":

I am pregnant with certain deaths
of women who choked before they
could speak their names
could know their names
before they had names to know . . .

In the title poem Piercy tackles her mother's death: "My father heard the crash but paid / no mind, napping after lunch, / yet fifteen hundred miles north / I heard and dropped a dish. / Your pain sunk talons in my skull / and crouched there cawing . . ." Eventually the poet reconciles herself to her lost mother: ". . . This body is your body, ashes now / and roses, but alive in my eyes, my breasts, / my throat, my thighs. You run in me / a tang of salt in the creek waters of my blood, / you sing in my mind like wine. What you / did not dare in your life you dare in mine."

In the second section life is reaffirmed through marriage, though Piercy resists any easy homilies. "Witnessing a Wedding" warns, ". . . It is not strangeness in the mate / you must fear, and not the fear / that loosens us so we lean back . . . but familiarity we must mistrust, / the word based on the family / that fogs the sight and plugs the nose . . ." The final two sections concentrate on the mundane rituals of daily living with some delightfully sensual, original poems like "Six Underrated Pleasures," which praises folding sheets, picking beans, taking hot baths, planting bulbs, canning, and sleeping with cats:

> . . . They are curled into flowers
> of fur, they are coiled
> hot seashells of flesh in my armpits, around my head
> a dark sighing halo.
> They are plastered to my side,
> a poultice fixing sore muscles
> better than a heating pad.
> They snuggle up to my sex
> purring. They embrace my feet . . .

Piercy's collection *Available Light* continues to honor vegetable love in such poems as "Morning Love Song," which begins, "I am filled with love like a melon / with seeds, I am ripe and dripping sweet juices. / If you knock gently on my belly / it will thrum ripe, ripe . . ." Strongly autobiographical, the collection displays a wry sense of humor. For example, "Something to Look Forward To" is a mischievous exposé of menopause:

> . . . How often halfway up the side of a mountain,
> during a demonstration with the tactical police
> force drawn up in tanks between me and a toilet;
> during an endless wind machine panel with four males
> I the token woman and they with iron bladders,
>
> I have felt that wetness and wanted to strangle
> my womb like a mouse . . .

One of the most moving poems in the collection, "Joy Road and Livernois," illustrates Piercy's ability to rail against injustice without ever losing sense of the individuals behind the politics. After charting a group of childhood friends through prostitution, addiction, suicide, and madness, the poet confesses that

> . . . I got out of those Detroit blocks where the air
> eats stone and melts flesh, where jobs
> dangle and you jump and jump, where there are
> more drugs than books, more ways to die
> than ways to live, because I ran fast
> ran hard, and never stopped looking back.
> It is not looking back that turned me
> to salt, no, I taste my salt from the mines
> under Detroit, the salt of our common juices.
> Girls who lacked everything except trouble,
> contempt and rough times, girls
> used like urinals, you are the salt

keeps me from rotting as the years swell.
I am the fast train you are travelling in
to a world of a different color, and the love
we cupped so clumsily in our hands to catch
rages and drives onward, an engine of light.

Beneath the politics, behind the feminist, the nature seeker, or the amused, amazed, or enraged lover, there is always a sense of reverence, an irrepressible celebration of life.

—Katie Campbell

PILLING, Christopher (Robert)

Nationality: British. **Born:** Birmingham, Warwickshire, 20 April 1936. **Education:** King Edward's School, Birmingham, 1947–54; University of Leeds, Yorkshire, 1954–57, B.A. (honors) 1957; Institute of French Studies, La Rochelle, France, 1955; Diplôme d'Études Françaises, 1955; Loughborough College, University of Nottingham, 1958–59, Cert. Ed. 1959. **Family:** Married Sylvia Pilling in 1960; one son and two daughters. **Career:** Assistant in English. École Normale, Moulins, France, 1957–58; French and athletics teacher, Wirral Grammar School, Cheshire, 1959–61, King Edward's Grammar School, Birmingham, 1961–62, and Ackworth School, Pontefract, Yorkshire, 1962–71, 1972–73; head of modern languages, Knottingley High School, Yorkshire, 1973–78; tutor in English, University of Newcastle upon Tyne Department of Adult Education, 1978–80; head of French, Keswick School, Cumbria, 1980–88. Reviewer, *Times Literary Supplement,* London, 1973–74. **Awards:** New Poets award, 1970; Arts Council grant, 1971, 1977; Kate Collingwood award, for play, 1983; Northern Arts award, 1985; Lauréat du Concours Européen de Création Littéraire, 1992; Tyrone Guthrie Centre residency, 1993; European Poetry Translation Network Residency, Tyrone Guthrie Centre, Annaghmakerrig, for the translation of Turkish poets, 1995, and for the translation of Israeli Poets, 1998; Bourse des Communautés Européennes for Residency at the Collège International des Traducteurs Littéraires, Arles, 1996; Hawthornden fellowship, 1998. **Address:** 25 High Hill, Keswick, Cumbria CA12 5NY, England.

PUBLICATIONS

Poetry

Snakes and Girls. Leeds, University of Leeds School of English Press, 1970.
Fifteen Poems. Leeds, University of Leeds School of English Press, 1970.
In All the Spaces on All the Lines. Manchester, Phoenix Pamphlet Poets Press, 1971.
Wren and Owl. Leeds, University of Leeds School of English Press, 1971.
Andrée's Bloom and the Anemones. Rush den, Northamptonshire, Sceptre Press, 1973.
Light Leaves. Hitchin, Hertfordshire, Cellar Press, 1975.
War Photographer Since the Age of 14. Hitchin, Hertfordshire, Starwheel Press. 1983.
Foreign Bodies. Newcastle upon Tyne, Flambard Press, 1992.

Cross Your Legs and Wish. Bradford, Redbeck Press, 1994.
The Lobster Can Wait. Nottingham, Shoestring Press, 1998.
In the Pink. Bradford, Redbeck Press, 1999.

Other

Translator, *Les Amours Jaunes,* by Tristan Corbière. Calstock, Cornwall, Peterloo Poets, 1995.
Translator, with David Kennedy, *The Press,* by Max Jacob. Dublin, Fishamble Press, 2000.

*

Critical Studies: By Julian MacKenney, in *Poetry and Audience* (Leeds), 1 May 1970; by Harry Guest, in *Modern Poetry in Translation,* King's College, University of London, 1998.

*   *   *

Snakes and Girls and *In All the Spaces on All the Lines* show Christopher Pilling bringing out, at his best, the subjective depths of everyday domestic moments by forming around them multiple concrete and abstract analogies. This can be seen, for example, in "Sunscape," "Old Celtic Cocoon," and "Partial Ellipse," all in *Snakes and Girls.* The opening of "Partial Ellipse" illustrates how concretely observant this poetic evocation can be:

My wife's wedding ring is no longer
Circular:

A gold curve
Is all I see on a hand-coloured

Background.
One does not think the world is

Round.

Pilling's more discursive poems tend to be less fully achieved. They do, however, suggest the poet's intellectual grasp of his life-loving orientation, as shown by this excerpt from "Crow Answers by Flight":

The world is not so sinister, such dark.
The left-handed is another turn of truth.
The poet needs an ambidextrous strain.
The words must not go to the ends of the earth.
Hammer them to the gallows of a poem
And let them cry of a spirit they have denied.

—Anne Cluysenaar

PINSKY, Robert (Neal)

Nationality: American. **Born:** Long Branch, New Jersey, 20 October 1940. **Education:** Rutgers University, New Brunswick, New Jersey, B.A. 1962; Stanford University, California (Woodrow Wilson, Stegner, and Fulbright fellow), M.A., Ph.D. 1966. **Family:** Married Ellen Bailey in 1961; three daughters. **Career:** Assistant professor of Humanities, University of Chicago, 1967–68; professor of English, Wellesley College, Massachusetts, 1968–80; professor of English, University of California, Berkeley, 1980–89. Since 1988 professor of English, Boston University. Visiting lecturer, Harvard University, Cambridge, Massachusetts, 1979–80; Hurst Professor, Washington University, St. Louis, 1981. Poetry editor, *New Republic,* Washington, D.C., 1978–87, and since 1996 *Slate.* **Awards:** Massachusetts Council on the Arts grant, 1974; Oscar Blumenthal prize (*Poetry,* Chicago), 1978; American Academy award, 1980; Saxifrage prize, 1980; Guggenheim fellowship, 1980; William Carlos Williams award, 1985; Landon prize in translation, 1995; *Los Angeles Times* book award, 1995; Shelley memorial award, 1996; Ambassador book award in poetry, 1997; Poet Laureate of the United States, since 1997; Lenore Marshall prize in poetry, 1997, for *The Figured Wheel;* Harold Washington literary award, 1999. **Address:** Department of English, Boston University, 236 Bay State Road, Boston, Massachusetts 02215, U.S.A.

PUBLICATIONS

Poetry

Sadness And Happiness. Princeton, New Jersey, Princeton University Press, 1975.
An Explanation of America. Princeton, New Jersey, Princeton University Press, and Manchester, Carcanet, 1979.
Five American Poets, with others. Manchester, Carcanet, 1979.
History of My Heart. New York, Ecco Press, 1984.
The Want Bone. New York, Ecco Press, 1990.
The Figured Wheel: New and Collected Poems 1966–1996. New York, Farrar Straus, 1995.
Jersey Rain. New York, Farrar Straus, 2000.

Novel

Mindwheel (computerized novel; Steve Hales and William Mataga, programmers). Richmond, California, Synapse Software, 1985.

Other

Landor's Poetry. Chicago, University of Chicago Press, 1968.
The Situation of Poetry: Contemporary Poetry and Its Traditions. Princeton, New Jersey, Princeton University Press, 1977.
Poetry and the World. New York, Ecco Press, 1988.
The Sounds of Poetry. New York, Farrar Straus, 1998.
The Handbook of Heartbreak. New York, Morrow, 1998.
Americans' Favorite Poems. New York, Norton, 1999.

Translator, with Robert Hass, *The Separate Notebooks,* by Czeslaw Milosz. New York, Ecco Press, 1984.
Translator, *The Inferno of Dante.* New York, Farrar Straus, 1994.

*

Manuscript Collection: Regenstein Library, University of Chicago.

951

Critical Studies: By Hugh Kenner, in *Los Angeles Times,* 11 February 1976; by Robert van Hallberg, in *Chicago Review,* spring 1976; by William Pritchard, in *Times Literary Supplement* (London), 11 June 1976; by Louis Martz, in *Yale Review* (New Haven, Connecticut), autumn 1976; *The Didactic Muse* by Willard Spiegelman, Princeton, New Jersey, Princeton University Press, 1989; ''On Robert Pinsky'' by James Longenbach, in *Salmagundi* (Saratoga Springs, New York), 103, summer 1994; ''The Horatian Poetics of Ezra Pound and Robert Pinsky'' by Lowell Bowditch, in *Classical World,* 89(6), July-August 1996; ''Story Tellers'' by Louise Gluck, in *American Poetry Review* (Philadelphia), 26(4), July-August 1997; ''Robert Pinsky: The Poet Laureate and His Poems'' by Grace Cavalieri, in *Pembroke* (Pembroke, North Carolina), 31, 1999; ''The Poet Laureate on His Land: Robert Pinsky's 'An Explanation of America''' by William E. Sheidley, in *The Image of America in Literature, Media, and Society,* edited by Will Wright and Steven Kaplan, Pueblo, Colorado, Society for the Interdisciplinary Study of Social Imagery, 1999.

*   *   *

If there is a consistent ground rule for Robert Pinsky's poems, early to late, it is that apparent simplicity is the invitation to troubling complexity. It is an attractive movement of the mind, finding exceptions to simple rules, unexpected textures to smooth surfaces, division and ambivalence to simple feelings. And the strategies are abundance, surprise, and variations on a theme. In ''Poem about People,'' the first poem in his first book, *Sadness and Happiness,* what begins as genial and compassionate people watching-

Balding young men in work shoes

And green work pants, beer belly
And white T-shirt, the porky walk
Back to the truck, polite; possible
To feel briefly like Jesus,

A gust of diffuse tenderness . . .

—turns to a friend's painful divorce and then to a movie clip that in turn leads to a burning vision of desperate personal shame-

. . . the sensitive
Young Jewish soldier nearly drowns

Trying to rescue the thrashing
Anti-semitic bully, swimming across
The river raked by nazi fire,
The awful part is the part truth:

Hate my whole kind, but me,
Love me for myself.

It is not a predictable sequence.

The most ambitious poems in the book are meditative sequences—''Tennis,'' the title poem ''Sadness and Happiness,'' and ''Essay on Psychiatrists''—that are in the form of theme and variations. The last includes comic social scenes, satire, a discussion of Pentheus and Dionysus as psychiatrists, and Yvor Winters's defense of madness in poets, and it concludes that we are all psychiatrists fumbling our way between stars. It is a poem designed to make psychiatrists uneasy, being itself uneasy about their claims to power over the secret life. Predictably, psychiatrists might say that jealousy for their mastery of the sexual secret underlies the poem.

An Explanation of America is just that. Its classical antecedent is not the Juvenal-Johnson-Lowell ''Vanity of Human Wishes'' but rather Horace's Epistle I, xvi, written from his Sabine farm, which Pinsky translates as part of his text. It is philosophical discourse, not satire. The poem is addressed to his oldest daughter, much of it quite genuinely so, for the mode of address is not merely a trope in some of the poem's very challenging passages. The daughter is often a real presence in the poem and appears to be too iconoclastic, intelligent, and searching to be satisfied with easy answers. She is a critic of ''that tyrant and sycophantic lout, the Majority,'' and the speaker says,

. . . Political Science bores you,
You prefer the truth, and with a Jesuit firmness
Return to your slogan: ''Voting *is not fair.*''

A sense of the poem's complexity and uneasiness of feeling is implicit in the following list:

I want for you to see the things I see
And more, Colonial Diners, Disney, films
Of concentration camps, the napalmed child
Trotting through famous news film in her diaper
And tattered flaps of skin, *Deep Throat,* the rest.

This is not an America free of cruelty, nor with the last entry is the monologue to the daughter easy about domesticated sexuality. The explanation is not tidy or even terribly analytic. It is impressionistic, rather, and concludes with a sense of America as dreamlike—''So large, and strangely broken, and unforseen.''

Pinsky's commitment to discursive poetry is seen in his next book, *History of My Heart,* in which he adopts his method defiantly in the face of the dominant approach to his subject, which is the shaping of his feelings. Instead of confession or epiphanies of the atomistic ego or intimations of moral instructions that thwart childhood narcissism, Pinsky offers explanations that are complex, ironic, and allusive. In the title poem of the volume history becomes family mythmaking in his mother's fantasy of meeting Fats Waller, which was drawn from a movie, in the way language creates experience in an account of a first sexual tryst (''To see eyes melting so I could think *This is it, / They're melting!*''), and in a cluster of images we are presented with the overarching erotic revery that

Makes the one who feels seem beautiful to the beholder
Witnessing the idea of the giving of desire—nothing more
  wanted
Than the little singing notes of wanting—the heart

Yearning further into giving itself into the air, breath
Strained into song emptying the golden bell it comes from,
The pure source poured altogether out and away.

It should be clear that the explanatory and discursive mode has not eliminated lyricism. It has in fact restored to the lyric the modes of discourse that have been rare in the twentieth century. The strategy is continued in the remainder of the book. In "The Unseen," set in a tour of a concentration camp, Pinsky addresses the absent God:

O discredited Lord of Hosts, your servant gapes

Obediently to swallow various doings of us, the most
Capable of all your former creatures—we have no shape,
We are poured out like water, but still

We try to take in what won't be turned from in despair.

This is not cold exposition but rather intelligent discourse about the heart's history in history. In his poem "The Cold" Pinsky retrieves this fashionable, exhausted word and moves the philosophical cold outdoors as weather, where it belongs:

Or like me, working in a room alone,

Watching out from a window . . .

   . . . not having been out in hours
I come up close idly to feel the cold,
Forgetting for a minute what I was doing.

The Want Bone refers not a phallic image but to an oral one, the dried mouth bones of a shark, an emblem of its desire to live. It is death longing for life and love, food and family. In the poems of this book pastiche and assemblage have joined the technique of variations on a theme to produce deliberate derangement of the apparent subjects and greater tension between centripetal and centrifugal forces. We find an explicit celebration and savoring of the richness of words and of their anarchic history. There is more play with language than in previous books, and Pinsky has adapted stories of Jesus' childhood from the Apocrypha and embroidered the story of the prophet Daniel. In a prose section Jesus, in the form of a ciclogriff, befriends Isolde to learn about love. Tristan is a violent bard, however, and Jesus cannot save Tristan or Isolde, who is boundlessly committed to him. We see it coming, but the charm is in the telling. This is the book of a poet approaching fifty who is determined to expand his art. Pinsky maintains his sense of the well-shaped line, stanza, and poem. He strays far from the iambic but never entirely moves out of its range. His rhymes, typically off-rhymes, are inventive and formal without being insistent. The volume shows him to be one of the most sophisticated technicians of his generation and perhaps one of its finest poets.

The new poems in *The Figured Wheel: New and Collected Poems 1966–1996* extend this mastery, and the book contains poems that may well become American classics. Particularly effective is "Avenue," a poem central to a sequence about cities, and an elegy for Elliot Gilbert called "Impossible to Tell," which is built around two jokes. This is a new and daring type of elegy, and I like to imagine the author of "Lycidas" being thrilled by its rightness. The new poems in the volume are not a random assortment. In a note to "Avenue," with reference to an explanation of Yom Kippur as the day of "at-one-ment," Pinsky says, "All, one: a play of unity and diversity that in turn makes me think of the fragmented, plural American city, held together visibly by words, by the signs and spoken or sung syllables of

its streets, where all our 'they' is somehow 'one.'" This motif is woven throughout the new poems, many of which deal with the city as the figure for the multiplicity and "numerousness" of the soul. It is the interwoven web of our humanity in which the matrix of Charlie Parker, Pushkin, Sax (the inventor of the instrument), and the sax-playing Pinsky is united in "Ginza Samba." Pinsky's vision (and it is right to speak of it using this term) has a lot of the philosophical playfulness of Borges mixed with the air of the historical menace of Milosz.

Pinsky includes "The Rhyme of Reb Nachman," a poem composed for a Halloween celebration, among his selection of translations and a poem by Milosz, "Incantation," among his own poems. The latter is explained, at least in part, by the fact that his translation of "The World" was rejected by Milosz as not being sufficiently subordinated to the Polish, as being an English poem in its own right. It is an odd situation but entirely appropriate to the overlapping boundaries Pinsky's new work celebrates.

Like all of his previous books, *Jersey Rain* reflects Pinsky's determination to expand his art. The move in this case is toward a high style, a solemnity, a high seriousness in the Arnoldian sense. It was not that Pinsky did not demonstrate this quality before, but earlier it was accompanied by a subversive metaphysical wit, for example, the jokes in his elegies and his sly satirical flashes. Such qualities are rarer in this book. The move is similar to what is seen in a number of important American writers, for example, Eliot, Faulkner, William Carlos Williams, and Hemingway, late in their careers. The poems are still rooted in Pinsky's vernacular strength that flourishes in delicate tension with his formality, which is itself subtle and not self-assertive. For this reason it can be missed by young, infatuated readers, just as they may not notice the loosened formality of Yeats, Bishop, Lowell, or Stevens. Consider the lines that conclude "Autumn Quartet," a birthday poem:

Among the epic bravos, a civic man.
The centaurs showed him truth in fabulation,
In every living city the haunted ruin.

The reach is impressive, seeing Odysseus as artist, explorer, and destroyer, the latter usually reserved for Achilles. And Odysseus takes his place in a row of heroes that include Lincoln, Washington, Leopold Bloom, and Jackie Robinson.
"Ode to Meaning" is an elegy with no jokes. Its reach is straightforwardly metaphysical, and its tone and music are elevated. The poem begins with-

Dire one and desired one,
Savior and sentencer

—and concludes with-

If I
Dare to disparage
Your harp of shadows I taste
Wormwood and motor oil, I pour
Ashes on my head. You are the wound. You
Be the medicine.

The meaning invoked here has become deeply interwoven with death and its meaning. The poem is very different from the improvisational

and digressive prose piece "An Alphabet of My Dead," one of the few works in the collection that points backward toward Pinsky's earlier work. It is nostalgic and full of a sense of real loss, but it lacks the grief-driven desperation for meaning of the "Ode to Meaning." It is this latter quality that characterizes the book.

Pinsky's translation *The Inferno of Dante* is the most idiomatic and vigorous adaptation of terza rima in English. His strategy of using consonantal rhyme in place of exact rhyme has enabled him to avoid much of the artificiality of earlier translations and to approximate Dante's famous compression. In fact, he is so successful that Dante's tercets seldom last three lines in Pinsky's English, and the direct link in Italian between syntax and stanza structure is abandoned. Unlike the original, almost all of Pinsky's tercets are enjambed.

Among Pinsky's other books is *The Sounds of Poetry,* a guide to prosody for students that focuses on accents and sound patterns without scansion or the customary classifications of accentual-syllabic poetry. The starting point is vocal reality rather than traditional prosody, although a discussion of meter and the sounds it explains runs throughout. The book is restricted, however, and gives way to a nontechnical empirical approach. In effect, Pinsky is paraphrasing technical prosody for technophobes at the same time that his sustained attention to sound reveals patterns that were not attended to before.

Someone looking for connections between Pinsky and his graduate school mentor, the important and charismatic critic-poet Yvor Winters, would strain to find them. Pinsky is a poet-critic, and the priority of poetry is important. Early in his career he lost Winters's tone of fastidious, moralistic criticism that did not suffer opposition gladly, and he has restored Williams to the Winters canon and expanded it to include all sorts of decadent New Yorkers. While there is a vivid heroic portrait of Winters in the long poem "Essay on Psychiatrists," what survives of the influence in Pinsky's poetry is a struggle with traditional forms and a diction that favors aestheticized, philosophical coldness and certitude in only a few early poems. Pinsky's criticism likewise has grown free of Winters's influence. It is urbane and international and lacks the odor of orthodoxy.

Pinsky has taken his elevation to the poet laureateship of the United States with deep seriousness, and he has taken on the task of establishing a record of the "best-loved poems" of the American people, of a fluid and dynamic vernacular canon. His approach is to exclude the customary canon shapers, the poets and scholars, in order to discover a popular, demotic consensus. This is part of a somewhat quixotic overall project of recovering or defining the historical memory of a pluralist culture of improvised traditions, one that is separable from the commercial project of pop culture. In addition, Pinsky's presence on the Public Broadcasting System's *Newshour* every week has made poetry present to a wide audience.

—Barry Goldensohn

PITT-KETHLEY, (Helen) Fiona

Nationality: British. **Born:** Edgware, Middlesex, 21 November 1954. **Education:** Haberdashers' Aske's Girls' School, 1960–71; Chelsea School of Art, London, 1972–76, B.A. (honors). **Agent:** Giles Gordon, Anthony Sheil Associates, 43 Doughty Street, London WC1N 2LF. **Address:** 11 Edward Road, St. Leonards, East Sussex TN37 6ES, England.

PUBLICATIONS

Poetry

London. Privately printed, 1984.
Rome. Bath, Mammon Press, 1985.
The Tower of Glass. Glasgow, Mariscat Press, 1985.
Sky Ray Lolly. London, Chatto and Windus, 1986.
Gesta. London, Turret, 1986.
Private Parts. London, Chatto and Windus, 1987.
The Perfect Man. London, Abacus, 1989.
Dogs. London, Sinclair-Stevenson, 1993.
Double Act. London, Arcadia Books, and Chester Springs, Pennsylvania, Dufour Editions, 1996.

Novels

The Misfortunes of Nigel. London, Peter Owen, 1991.
The Maiden's Progress. London, Turret, 1992.

Other

Journeys to the Underworld. London, Chatto and Windus, 1988.
Too Hot to Handle. London, Peter Owen, 1992.
The Pan Principle. London, Sinclair-Stevenson, 1994.

Editor, *The Literary Companion to Sex.* London, Sinclair-Stevenson, 1992; New York, Random House, 1994.
Editor, *The Literary Companion to Low Life: An Anthology of Prose and Poetry.* London, Sinclair-Stevenson, 1995.

*

Critical Studies: In the *London Review of Books,* 17(9), and 17(14), 1995.

Fiona Pitt-Kethley comments:

I am a satirist. My satire is aimed chiefly at contemporary hypocrisies. A lot of these are centered around sexuality. I think my work differs from all past satire in one respect. In order not to seem self-righteous, I satirize myself at the same time as criticizing others, using incidents from my own life to illustrate the points I am making.

(1995) I am one of the most versatile and hardworking authors on the poetic scene. Apart from poetry, my main vocation, I have produced travel books, novels, anthologies, and a massive amount of journalism. I am currently a critic for the *Times* and have worked for most of the quality newspapers. I have also traveled extensively, as I am writing a book of essays on the world's red-light districts. I have performed my poems around the country and for radio and TV. I have, to date, been considered too controversial for any major grants or awards but hope that this situation will change.

*   *   *

Readers of the *London Review of Books* have come to half expect, when scanning the classifieds, to light upon the statement "Fiona Pitt-Kethley is available." The demands of publicity are disconcerted by such compliance—whosoever compelleth her to go a mile, she goeth with him twain—and even the innuendo is astringently straightforward. She is "available" to give readings from her own poetry, whose effect is doubtless doubled, but perhaps also skewed, by the memorable name thus promoted, with its suggestion that the Roedean Rake Is Coming Clean.

For actually—an important distinction—it was the Chelsea School of Art. She has a good poem, "The Hidden Persuaders," that shows her ignoring a sixth-form book list for the Oxbridge bound ("all modern, serious but popular"):

I gave the lot up and went in for Art.
I'll wash my own brains, thank you very much.

Fair enough, but in the poems she brings to market she washes other people's dirty linen and comments with the traditional freedom of washerwomen. The subject of her satire is often that heavy inheritance of nervous hypocrisy, incompetence, and miscalculation that thwarts and inflames appetite in the sons of Adam. The pitiful instances are real, and the voice that speaks the poems, being unambiguously her own, seems in turn wide-eyed, explosively amusing, and more than a touch caddish.

Occasionally, for instance, we get a whiff of *l'esprit* (or *la revanche*) *d'escalier,* as she placards her victim by name:

Ken Roberts

Ken Roberts rings me up to ask if I
like going to the cinema alone—
and, like a fool, I stop to talk to him.

He says he bets that he could turn me on.
(I bet he cant.) I say this, but it's hard
to put his kind of bubbly pervert down.

Hard? Maybe—but that last phrase does it. The voice of female experience has him formulated, sprawling on a pin, and it is memorably funny. Sometimes, though, her tactics are truly deplorable. An earlier version of one of her better poems included a name whose owner begged her to remove it. She could have justifiably refused, but she complied, only to spell out the whole story in a footnote that effectively revealed her correspondent's identity and left the sour taste of spite mixed in with the clean one of indignation.

She can, however, write marvelously without either:

We smelt the baby oil from the back row.
The "Senior Mr. Hastings" was judged first.
The oldest held a world above his head
(invisible) to music of the spheres.

These almost Dickensian escapes from the predictable are accomplished with such ease that one puzzles at her relapses. Of these the most important occur in the seventy-line poem, central to her work as a whole, called "Prostitution." It is one of those poems ("Gents Only," the splendid "Phone Call," and, of course, her *London Review of Books* small ad are others) in which the exploitative hypocrisies of sex are linked to those of the book trade. Some lines can take your head off-

Chatto's my pimp. My cut is five percent
(well in arrears)

—or, more winsomely—

What should I do, what chances do I have?
Arvon-the poet's pools? (Yes we all try.)

Surely here she has found her major subject. And what possibilities! The ghosts of Pope and Gissing, of Pound and Aphra Behn hover near the midnight belfry. Will the iron tongue of satire sound again? Or will we hear naught but obsession, beating its leathery wings?

The under-thirties Gregory Awards?
(Twenty to women out of 144.)
I was turned down for one of those six times.
Anthony Thwaite seems guilty on that score.

What a disappointment! What thin and bitter gruel!

Of course, the Arts Council does grants . . . just three.
But '87 was Caribbean Year,
so every applicant *had to be* black.

The female Casanova is changing before our eyes into the mad victim. The bloody buggers in suits are going to get off again.

The truth is that, as with most of us, Pitt-Kethley's sense of justice is too self-centered to appeal convincingly to others. Therefore, her anecdotes (and her poems are mostly anecdotal) do not always escape the monotonies of parti pris, and, as a result, their principled hedonism and frankness seem weirdly ungenerous. She is at her best when a burst of verbal inventiveness and humor wins us into complicity. And that happens either at her most delicate ("Mr. Hastings") or at her most indelicate:

Large cocks are good for narcissism, not sex.
Their owners have this tendency to stand
as if they're waiting for a prize at Cruft's.
'What a big boy! Aren't I the lucky girl?'
we're meant to say. They're Ozymandias-like
about their things.

—Hugh Buckingham

PLUMLY, Stanley (Ross)

Nationality: American. **Born:** Barnesville, Ohio, 23 May 1939. **Education:** Wilmington College, Ohio, B.A. 1961; Ohio University, Athens, M.A. 1968. **Family:** Married Hope Plumly in 1974. **Career:** Visiting poet, Louisiana State University, Baton Rouge, 1968–70, Ohio University, 1970–73, University of Iowa, Iowa City, 1974–76, Princeton University, New Jersey, 1976–78, Columbia University, New York, 1977–79, and University of Michigan, Ann Arbor, spring 1979; professor of English, University of Houston, 1979-mid-1990s. Since the mid-1990s professor of English, University of Maryland, College Park. Poetry editor, *Ohio Review,* Athens, 1970–75, and *Iowa Review,* Iowa City, 1976–78. **Awards:** Delmore Schwartz memorial award, 1973; Guggenheim grant, 1973; National Endowment for the Arts grant, 1977, 1984. **Address:** Department of English, University of Maryland, College Park, Maryland 20742, U.S.A.

PUBLICATIONS

Poetry

In the Outer Dark. Baton Rouge, Louisiana State University Press, 1970.
Giraffe. Baton Rouge, Louisiana State University Press, 1973.
How the Plains Indians Cot Horses. Crete, Nebraska, Best Cellar Press, 1975.
Out-of-the-Body Travel. New York, Ecco Press, 1977.
Summer Celestial. New York, Ecco Press, 1983.
Boy on the Step. New York, Ecco Press, 1989.
The Marriage in the Trees. Hopewell, New Jersey, Ecco Press, 1997.
Now That My Father Lies Down Beside Me: New & Selected Poems, 1970–2000. New York, Ecco Press, 2000.

Recording: *The Poet and the Poem,* Library of Congress, 1990.

Other

Editor, with Michael Collier, *The New Bread Loaf Anthology of Contemporary American Poetry.* Hanover, New Hampshire, Middlebury College Press, 1999.

*

Manuscript Collection: State University of New York, Buffalo.

Critical Studies: "Stanley Plumly and the Mind of Summer" by Edward Hirsch, in *Crazyhorse* (Little Rock, Arkansas), fall 1983; "Out beyond Rhetoric" by David Young, in *Field* (Oberlin, Ohio), spring 1984; "Matthews on Plumly" by William Matthews, in *Ohio Review* (Athens), fall 1984; "The Discursive Muse: Robert Hass's 'Songs to Survive the Summer'" by Bo Gustavsson, in *Studia Neophilologica* (Oslo, Norway), 61(2), 1989; "'The Why of the World': A Conversation with Stanley Plumly" by Stan Sanvel Rubin and Judith Kitchen, in their *The Post-Confessionals: Conversations with American Poets of the Eighties,* Rutherford, Fairleigh Dickinson University Press, 1989; "The Crystal and the Flame" by David Young, in *Field* (Oberlin, Ohio), 42, spring 1990; interview with David Biespiel and Rose Solari, in *American Poetry Review* (Philadelphia), 24(3), May-June 1995; "Loss and Redemption" by Floyd Collins, in *Gettysburg Review* (Gettysburg, Pennsylvania), 11(4), winter 1998.

Stanley Plumly comments:

I see my poems as attempts to make something whole of the disparate and difficult parts of my experience. In that sense they are fictions—that which is made of other materials.

*　　*　　*

Stanley Plumly says, "I believe in a poetry of protagonist-antagonist relationship, in which the energy, the tension . . . is the result of what happens between the two . . . Which means that for me a poem is a problem of the trinity, father-son-ghost." The ghost is created by the friction of the father and son; it is the poem's content, born mainly through metaphor. Thus, he argues that "bringing the disparate into immediate and intimate relation . . . is the hope I have

for my poems. My father in the ground is a unifying principle." Plumly's artful use of "ground" in this apparently discursive observation is characteristically manifold.

In the Outer Dark is constructed of primal polarities, some more abstract than others. But no abstraction is simply disembodied, no object locked in specificity. Central are light-darkness, motion-stillness, speech-silence, water-stone, father-son. Sun, wind, and tongue flesh out the first three parts; consciousness and humanized Christian allusions generalize the others. The metaphors conveying these tensions are "moving toward one center," "still inside me," a prior "source," an "embryo," a "womb," an original (not this outer) dark. Moreover, they are so compact that the polarities and our senses of them, as though synesthetic, seem interchangeable: "The body tunes to a single sense . . ." Thus, just as "stillness" may be sensed both aurally and kinesthetically, the speaker listens with his hands and "warms" not the cold but "the dark."

For Plumly the antagonist and protagonist may despair, but the poem's content cannot. The poem can, however, celebrate, "art [being] first of all a moral act." It is hard to say if this book is finest in darkness, light, or shadow, but Plumly chooses man's inevitable position and in "Between Flesh and What Follows" arranges the first and penultimate lines so as to say "The Dark that lies . . . And the Light that lies." Any poem's true content is shadow.

Animal titles designate the three parts of *Giraffe.* Plumly perceives and identifies with an incipience of flight in each creature, especially as it is conceived at night or in dreams. The poems are, then, emblems of the awakening to transcendence. "Walking Out" makes the point more humanly clear: "I would be silence. Even the sleeves / of my best coat would not know me." These various, still unrealized leave-takings are, however, not only initiated by a poem about loneliness ("Since England Is an Island") but also lead back to another on the same subject ("One of Us").

While the father continues to provide tension, conflict between the desire for death and for the transformation of life is equally basic. But the poems of darkness and extinction neither dull the volume's celebratory edge nor fail in themselves to honor struggle (as in the lovely, elegiac "Jarrell") and survival (as in "Dreamsong"). Though never evasive about Jarrell's lifelong flirtation with easing himself out of life, Plumly regards him as a man who, even imaginatively, doubted his own seriousness and ultimately as "a man walking out of himself on a road at dawn" with "the dark piled up behind." Before rising and walking the water, the persona of "Dreamsong" says, "I wanted to die. / I wanted the whole / day."

Perhaps the key to the collection is in "One Line of Light," the geographical background of which is flood country:

> I think of my house as a ship
> lit up like a birthday.
> I walk around inside it
> with the page of a poem—
> the day's log,
> the night's psalm.
> The dark is my ocean.
> I know the water's rising
> in the next town.

In "Jarrell" that poet is himself, "the page of his poem filling up," which is a masterstroke of ambiguity and metonymy. In "Walking Out" and "Heron," "flight" or its "mockery" are imagined "at the edge of water."

"The Wish to Be a Red Indian," a bit of Kafka provided as a postscript to *Giraffe,* is equally a preface to *Out-of-the-Body Travel.* It involves naturalness and creature identification as conditions of pure motion and the dissolution of fetters. When the speaker says, "We lie in that other darkness, ourselves," he is, among other things, considering the truth of lives not our own. Getting out of ourselves is at once impossible and imperative. These poems realize the poet's experience only as a portion of the lives, deaths, and painful self-divisions of others, particularly the members of his family. Two poems entitled "Anothering" are about the mother's transcendence through her progeny but in conjunction with the sad vacancy the child's "out-of-the-body travel" leaves in its wake. But death is the principal battleground for transcendence. Recurrently, as in the last two poems, Plumly discovers perpetuity and new life in identification with the dead, especially the father, both as a person and an archetype:

Whatever two we were, we become
one falling body, one breath.

And whosoever be reborn in sons
so shall they be also reborn . . .
And you, my anonymous father,
be with me when I wake.

The title poem, devoid of all artiness, is perfectly apt. His "raw, red cheek / pressed against the cheek of the [violin's] wood," the father elevates his merely "sad relatives" with that mournful music Yeats knew and made through "Lapis Lazuli."

Plumly's subtle prosody continues in *Summer Celestial,* the key word being "witness." His focus shifts more strongly to the maternal nurture of youth and the natural, especially botanical, wonders of his early life in Ohio. The exploration of his past in this volume, especially his remembrance of a fecund connection to the natural environs of his home, is extended significantly in *Boy on the Step.* Whether it is deepened is, however, problematical.

Thumbing through *Boy on the Step,* a reader is at once taken by the manifest formality of the poems. Patterned and matching stanzas, many with identically repeated line indentations, are the rule. Indeed, only the prose poem, "The James Wright Annual Festival," stands apart from this ubiquitous formal practice. The last fourteen poems are virtual sonnets, but they are cast in a curious line, nearly always of eleven syllables, a line as close to blank verse as the stanza is to the sonnet. The guarded freedom of the line seems to counterpoint stanzaic formality throughout the collection. But it is formality that most lingers in the mind, giving subtlety to feeling but also somehow dampening it.

Though certainly concerned with the lost and hurt parents, these mainly melancholic pieces are in search of a recollected sense of spiritual well-being, given once by nature but undone by time and history, especially the two great wars of the twentieth century. It is really a yearning, and its elaboration suggests both Keats and Roethke, though these poems do not go as far toward metaphysical success in their enterprise as do the later works of Roethke. For now at least the poet is spiritually stalled amid an "industrial rain," his intimations of an elevated wholeness restrained by a desolate reality:

My eye, hooked like a bird's, fixes on anything, even in memory: how the black rain

washes clean, how the dry leaf opens and
is lifted whole back into the new wind.
The spirit puts its nose against the glass—
The sky is nothing, is a starved black wing.

—David M. Heaton

PORTER, Dorothy (Featherstone)

Nationality: Australian. **Born:** Sydney, 1954. **Education:** Graduated from Sydney University 1975; earned a Diploma of Education. **Career:** Has worked as a part-time teacher and lecturer in poetry and writing, University of Technology, Sydney. Since 1994 full-time writer. **Awards:** Book of the Year, *Age,* National Book of the Year for Poetry, and Braille Book of the Year, all for *The Monkey's Mask.*

PUBLICATIONS

Poetry

Little Hoodlum. Sydney, Poetry Society of Australia, 1975.
The Night Parrot. Wentworth Falls, New South Wales, Black Lightening Press, 1984.
Driving Too Fast. St. Lucia, University of Queensland Press, 1989.
Akhenaten. St. Lucia, University of Queensland Press, 1992; London, Serpent's Tail, 1999.
The Monkey's Mask. South Melbourne, Victoria, Hyland House, and New York, Arcade, 1994; London, Serpent's Tail, 1997.
Crete. South Melbourne, Victoria, Hyland House, 1996.
What a Piece of Work. Sydney, Picador, 1999.

Recordings: *Some Poems of Dorothy Featherstone Porter,* A.B.C., 1979.

Other

Rookwood (for young adults). St. Lucia, University of Queensland Press, 1991.
The Witch Number (for young adults). St. Lucia, University of Queensland Press, 1993.

*

Critical Studies: "Festive Fun and Dangerous" by Jenny Digby, in *Island,* 57, summer 1993; "Ham-Fists in Those 'Male Size Golf Gloves'" by Kathleen Mary Fallon, in *Southerly* (Sydney), 55(3), spring 1995; by Finola Moorhead, in *Southerly* (Sydney), 55(1), fall 1995; "'The Giant Octopus Is Dying': Maternal Archaeology in Dorothy Porter's 'Crete'" by Rose Lucas, in *Southerly* (Sydney), 58(1), autumn 1998.

*   *   *

Although her first book, *Little Hoodlum,* was published in 1975, when she was twenty-one, and she has continued to bring out her work regularly, it was in 1994, with the publication of her verse novel *The Monkey's Mask,* a feminist crime thriller, that Dorothy Porter achieved a remarkable literary and popular success. *The Monkey's Mask* has sold more copies in Australia than many a best-selling novel, and it has been adapted for the stage and radio as well as for film. The themes and the verse style—staccato and nervous, elliptical and sharply modulated—have contributed as much to the success of the book as has the story itself, which brilliantly portrays its main character, a lesbian detective.

There are ample precedents for *The Monkey's Mask* in Porter's earlier books, most notably in *Akhenaten,* which is also effectively a verse novel. *Akhenaten* explores the always intriguing Egyptian ruler, and it is particularly striking in its handling of the themes of incest and sexual perversion. It certainly drew attention to the increasing confidence with which the poet could handle sexually explicit subject matter, with short clipped lines and an almost startled lyricism.

After *The Monkey's Mask* Porter produced the collections *Crete* and *What a Piece of Work. Crete* includes a sequence that reflects something of the oriental fascination of *Akhenaten* but in more attenuated form. *What a Piece of Work,* which appeared in 1999, is Porter's second major verse novel and was short-listed for the prestigious Miles Franklin Fiction award. It was the first verse novel to receive this distinction, though there have been a number of efforts in the form: Les Murray's *The Boys Who Stole the Funeral* and *Fredy Neptune,* as well as Alan Wearne's *The Nightmarkets* and Jordie Albison's *The Hanging of Jean Lee.*

What a Piece of Work is told in the first-person voice of Dr. Peter Cryen, the superintendent of Callan Park Psychiatric Hospital in Sydney. One of his patients, named Frank, is a poet and is clearly a portrait of the great Australian poet Francis Webb, who spent many years incarcerated there. Frank is mad, but his madness seems curiously sane when compared with the increasingly frenetic sexual and masochistic behavior of Dr. Cyren. The verse form gains its strength from the tightly controlled and cryptic lines, and the narrative is largely implied through the sequence of brief meditations and responses of the doctor as his personal life unravels:

> sometimes mad Frank
> is the best company
>   in the world
>
> I tell him
> how much
>   I loved my mother
> his yellow teeth
> like glowing ears
>   listening
>
> ''what did she look like?''
> he asks
>   softly
>
> I close my eyes
> and let them
>   sting
>
> the dark takes her shape
> her wonderful
>   heart-hooking smell

> 'My mother'
> the night floods my throat
>   'looked like Anne Bancroft'.

—Thomas W. Shapcott

PORTER, Peter (Neville Frederick)

Nationality: Australian. **Born:** Brisbane, Queensland, 16 February 1929. **Education:** Church of England Grammar School, Brisbane; Toowoomba Grammar School. **Family:** Married 1) Jannice Henry in 1961 (died 1974), two daughters; 2) Christine Berg in 1991. **Career:** Journalist in Brisbane, 1947–48; moved to England in 1951; worked as a clerk and bookseller, and advertising writer for 10 years. Since 1968 freelance writer. Compton Lecturer in Poetry, University of Hull, Yorkshire, 1970–71; visiting lecturer in English, University of Reading, Berkshire, autumn 1972, University of Sydney, 1975, and University of New England, Armidale, New South Wales, 1977; writer-in-residence, Melbourne University, 1983, and University of Western Australia Nedlands, 1987. **Awards:** Cholmondeley award, 1976; Society of Authors traveling scholarship, 1980; Duff Cooper prize, 1984; Whitbread prize, 1988; Gold Medal, for Australian literature, 1990. D.Litt.: Melbourne University. **Address:** 42 Cleveland Square, London W2, England.

PUBLICATIONS

Poetry

Once Bitten, Twice Bitten. London, Scorpion Press, 1961.
Penguin Modern Poets 2, with Kingsley Amis and Dom Moraes. London, Penguin, 1962.
Poems, Ancient and Modern. Lowest oft, Suffolk, Scorpion Press, and New York, Walker, 1964.
Words without Music. Oxford, Sycamore Press, 1968.
Solemn Adultery at Breakfast Creek: An Australian Ballad, music by Michael Jessett. Richmond, Surrey, Keepsake Press, 1968.
A Porter Folio: New Poems. Lowest oft, Suffolk, Scorpion Press, 1969.
The Last of England. London and New York, Oxford University Press, 1970.
Epigrams by Martial. London, Poem-of-the-Month Club, 1971.
After Martial. London, Oxford University Press, 1972.
Preaching to the Converted. London, Oxford University Press, 1972.
Jonah, illustrated by Arthur Boyd. London, Secker and Warburg, 1973.
A Share of the Market. Belfast, Ulsterman, 1973.
Peter Porter Reads from His Own Work (includes recording). Brisbane, University of Queensland Press, 1974.
The Lady and the Unicorn, illustrated by Arthur Boyd. London, Secker and Warburg, 1975.
Living in a Calm Country. London, Oxford University Press, 1975.
Les Trés Riches Heures. Richmond, Surrey, Keepsake Press, 1978.
The Cost of Seriousness. London, Oxford University Press, 1978.
English Subtitles. Oxford and New York, Oxford University Press, 1981.

The Animal Programme. London, Anvil Press Poetry, 1982.
Collected Poems. Oxford, Oxford University Press, 1983.
Fast Forward. Oxford, Oxford University Press, 1984.
Narcissus, illustrated by Arthur Boyd. London, Secker and Warburg, 1984.
The Run of Your Father's Library. London, Albion Press, 1984.
Machines. Hitchin, Hertfordshire, Mandeville Press, 1986.
The Automatic Oracle. Oxford, Oxford University Press, 1987.
Mars, illustrated by Arthur Boyd. London, Deutsch, 1988.
Possible Worlds. Oxford, Oxford University Press, 1989.
A Porter Selected. Oxford, Oxford University Press, 1989.
The Chair of Babel. Oxford, Oxford University Press, 1992.
Millennial Fables. Oxford, Oxford University Press, 1994.
Collected Poems. Oxford, Oxford University Press, 1999.

Plays

Radio Plays: *The Siege of Munster,* 1971; *The Children's Crusade,* 1973; *All He Brought Back from the Dream,* 1978.

Other

Roloff Beny in Italy, with Anthony Thwaite. London, Thames and Hudson, and New York, Harper, 1974.
The Shape of Poetry and the Shape of Music. Hobart, University of Tasmania, 1980.
Sydney. New York and London, Time Life, 1980.

Editor, *A Choice of Pope's Verse.* London, Faber, 1971.
Editor, *New Poems, 1971–72.* London, Hutchinson, 1972.
Editor, with Anthony Thwaite, *The English Poets: From Chaucer to Edward Thomas.* London, Secker and Warburg, 1974.
Editor, with Charles Osborne, *New Poetry 1.* London, Arts Council, 1975.
Editor, *Poetry Supplement.* London, Poetry Book Society, 1980.
Editor, *Thomas Hardy.* London, Weidenfeld and Nicolson, 1981.
Editor, with Howard Sergeant, *The Gregory Awards Anthology 1980.* London, Secker and Warburg, 1981.
Editor, *The Faber Book of Modern Verse,* 4th edition. London, Faber, 1982.
Editor, *Christina Rossetti.* Oxford, Oxford University Press, 1986.
Editor, *William Blake.* Oxford, Oxford University Press, 1986.
Editor, *William Shakespeare.* Oxford, Oxford University Press, 1986.
Editor, *Complete Poems* by Martin Bell. Newcastle upon Tyne, Bloodaxe, 1988; Chester Springs, Pennsylvania, Dufour, 1989.
Editor, *John Donne.* London, Aurum Press, 1988.
Editor, *Lord Byron.* London, Aurum Press, 1989; as *Byron,* New York, Crown, 1989.
Editor, with Musaemura Zimunya and Kofi Anyidoho, *The Fate of Vultures: New Poetry of Africa.* London, Heinemann, 1989.
Editor, *William Butler Yeats: The Last Romantic.* London, Aurum Press, 1990.
Editor, *Elizabeth Barrett Browning.* London, Aurum Press, 1992.
Editor, *Robert Burns.* London, Aurum Press, 1992.
Editor, *Robert Browning.* London, Aurum Press, 1993.
Editor, *Coleridge.* London, Aurum Press, 1994.
Editor, with A.S. Byatt, *New Writing 6.* London, Vintage, 1997.
Editor, *The Oxford Book of Modern Australian Verse.* Melbourne, Oxford University Press, 1998.

Translator of poetry, *Michelangelo: Life, Letters, and Poetry,* edited by George Bull. Oxford, Oxford University Press, 1987.

*

Bibliography: *Peter Porter: A Bibliography 1954–1986* by John R. Kaiser, London, Mansell, 1989.

Manuscript Collections: Lockwood Memorial Library, State University of New York, Buffalo; University of Indiana, Bloomington; British Library, London; University of Reading, Berkshire; Australian National Library, Canberra.

Critical Studies: By Clive James, in *The Review 24* (Oxford); by Roger Garfitt, in *British Poetry since 1960*, edited by Michael Schmidt and Grevel Lindop, Oxford, Carcanet, 1972; *Spirit in Exile* by Bruce Bennett, Melbourne, Oxford University Press, 1991; *Peter Porter* by Peter Steele, Melbourne, Oxford University Press, 1992; interview with John Kinsella, in *Westerly* (Australia), 40(3), spring 1995; in *In Other Words: Interviews with Australian Poets* by Barbara Williams, Amsterdam, Rodopi, 1998.

*   *   *

By 1973 Peter Porter was already acclaimed. Nevertheless, he welcomed the opportunity to select two of his poems for inclusion in a compendium edited by James Gibson, *Let the Poet Choose.* "I feel, perhaps over-sensitively," Porter remarked, "that I am often misrepresented in anthologies." One of the pieces he chose, "The Great Poet Comes Here in Winter," may be found in his second collection, *Poems, Ancient and Modern.* This book, however, like its even more energetic predecessor, *Once Bitten, Twice Bitten,* was known for many years only to the cognoscenti. The two books, together with *A Porter Folio,* were first issued by a courageous backstreet publishing firm, Scorpion Press, with limited print runs and inadequate distribution. The books were difficult to acquire, and they seem to have made little difference to the reading public's awareness of Porter and his work.

This is a pity since, without necessarily disparaging the later titles that came out under the aegis of the Oxford University Press, the first two volumes are probably the best. *Once Bitten, Twice Bitten,* in particular, is not so much an initial volume as a retrospective collection. Porter was thirty-two when it was published in 1961, and he had been writing copiously since the mid-1950s. There are fifty-seven pages here and fifty-three poems, most of them very good indeed. Yet comparatively few of the poems escaped into anthologies. Though the volume was included, fortunately without alteration, in the *Collected Poems* of 1983, the critics already were far better acquainted with the later works than with the earlier.

The modest yellow dust jacket of the first Scorpion publication contrasts with the claims of its anonymous blurb writer: "This is the authentic voice of our time . . . austere, ironic, socially committed. No poet has tackled issues so central to the problems of modern living since the young Auden." With hindsight the writer could have gone even further to say, for example, that Porter was not only a satirist but also a rhetorician. With his fine ear for music he is in line not only with the young Auden but also with the Dryden of *Mac Flecknoe* and the Pope of "The Epistle to Burlington":

They can never trespass enough
Against us, who use their surly right
Of making the world hateful . . .

At the present time, after the pseudorepublics of the Eastern bloc have exposed their internal economies, this statement from the 1950s seems not only mordant but also enhanced. It is art that is the solace for ''thirty years' unhappiness on end'':

The injustice of delight! All that is made
Makes this ventriloquist's serenade—
Words to sing, beautiful impermanence . . .

How, Porter asks, can we possibly deserve Bach and Mozart?

. . . There is a practice of music which befriends
The ear—useless, impartial as rain on desert— And
    conjures the listener for a time to be happy,
Making from this love of limits what he can,
Saddled with Eden's gift, living in the reins
Of music's huge light irresponsibility.

Yet this poem, ''Walking Home on St Cecilia's Day,'' is not to be found in the anthologies. John Lucas, a genuine admirer of Porter's work, nevertheless thought that no modern poet could be compared with Solzhenitsyn or Heinrich Böll. He, and critics like him, should learn by heart this glorious poem, together with ''The Historians Call Up Pain,'' ''A Christmas Recalled,'' ''Mr Roberts,'' ''A Moral Tale Has a Moral End,'' and ''Who Gets the Pope's Nose,'' all from *Once Bitten, Twice Bitten.*

Because of the limited distribution of this volume and of its most immediate successors, however, critical comment has tended to center on ''The Workers,'' ''The Widow's Story,'' ''Applause for Death'' (*The Last of England*); ''The Old Enemy,'' ''Fossil Gathering,'' ''The Tomb of Scarlatti'' (*Preaching to the Converted*); and ''All the Difference in the World,'' ''The Werther Level,'' ''At Lake Massaciuccoli,'' ''The Unfortunate Isles,'' and ''Landscape with Orpheus'' (*English Subtitles*). These are genuine poems that would have made anyone's reputation. They are not, however, Porter at his best.

Still less so are the real anthology poems, one or two of which may be found in almost any school compendium. Most familiar is ''Your Attention Please,'' a trick poem about World War III, originally broadcast in the tones of a BBC news reader: ''The Polar DEW has just warned that / A nuclear rocket strike of / At least one thousand megatons / Has been launched by the enemy / Directly at our major cities . . .'' The shock effect diminishes on successive rereadings. This, and a number of not dissimilar poems, were probably set in motion by being included in Porter's section of *Penguin Modern Poets 2.* The poet is greater, however, than his admirers seem to recognize.

The trouble with the anthology aspect of Porter's work is that it approximates to some of the smart journalism that, from time to time, he satirizes. Throughout his career Porter has shown an increasing tendency to join up with that which he initially derogated. One can see this as early as ''The World of Simon Raven'' (1963): ''Nanny's facing Nigel with stained sheets.'' By the time *The Last of England* was produced, the habit seemed to be ingrained: ''His critical

triumphs are recorded / In the ten books Leavis lauded.'' It is with no surprise that we find *Fast Forward* (1984) dedicated to Clive James, a media person who might well have served as a model for one of the satirical portraits in the earlier books.

As Anthony Thwaite remarked in *Poetry Today,* however, Porter has also emerged in the semblance of an elegiac poet. This is seen preeminently in the collection *The Cost of Seriousness.* Thwaite refers, as one of many examples, to Porter's ''Exequy,'' written about his wife, who died tragically and young. Porter came to his subject by way of an original poem by Henry King. But the twentieth-century poet writes tetrameters that are less like those of King than like those of the Auden of *The Double Man:* ''The rooms and days we wandered through / Shrink in my mind to one—there you / Lie quite absorbed by peace—the calm / Which life could not provide is balm / In death . . .'' Auden also mediates between Porter and his putative originals in the younger poet's imitation of Marvell (''Who Needs It,'' 1987) and George Herbert (''A Chagall Postcard,'' 1989): ''From earth to sky the cry ascends, / What breaks will threaten where it mends, / Proud lovers end as pallid friends, / These feed on those.''

Indeed, Auden and Porter are very similar. A poem such as ''Europe'' could well have been written by either: ''Breathe honey looking south, the mined land over; / Tamed temples take the flash of rain / Buckets up to their gone gods, their many / Children born stinging like the horsefly . . .'' This is, in fact, by Porter. The main difference between the poets is that Porter almost totally lacks Auden's vein of lyricism. There is no equivalent in Porter to ''Oh what is that sound that so thrills the ear'' or ''Our hunting fathers.'' In comparison to Porter as a master rhetorician, however, even the Auden of ''The Shield of Achilles'' seems insubstantial. Porter triumphs in what Auden only essayed, the invocation of history. From the angry standpoint of the later 1950s, Porter looks back over six centuries and puritanically envies the certainties of a past with far worse torments than those of his own present. This is from ''The Historians Call Up Pain:''

We cannot know what John of Leyden felt
Under the Bishop's tongs—we can only
Walk in temperate London, our educated city,
Wishing to cry as freely as they did who died
In the Age of Faith. We have our loneliness
And our regret with which to build an eschatology.

This is an impressive display of rhetoric. With a degree of critical perception, Frank Kermode quoted the passage as an epigraph for his book *Sense of an Ending.* As the second millennium closed, it was in the work of Porter, if anywhere, that there was heard the echo of a grand style.

Porter's later books, however, tend to echo this echo. The verse is never less than deliberated, in the best sense of the word. This is, nevertheless, the voice of an elder statesman. Revisiting Italy, he is tormented by thoughts of his dead wife (''Bad Dreams in Venice''). The talk with his friends is of death and of those who have died (''The Blond Arm of Coincidence''). It is the poets who wrote in their old age and about old age, Hardy, Yeats and Stevens, who tend to be invoked. Gone is any feeling of ''losing a troubled innocence.'' Rather than the intellectual energy of the earlier years, the reviewers of *Millennial Fables* tend to praise the author's literary cunning. They point not to social commitment and authenticity but, as with Robert Nye, to ''literary accomplishment of a high order.''

Yet there is still an alert sense of danger behind the high rhetoric. With more appropriateness than most, Porter is able to quote Isaiah: ''The wild beasts of the islands shall cry in their desolate houses.'' Rest assured, the dragon is not dead. The title poem of Porter's 1997 collection, *Dragons in Their Pleasant Palaces,* declares, ''eyes in / the Bible Lands dilate at searing jets / and burning rigs are pillars raised by night . . .'' We do not escape the pillar of fire by night, but it does not necessarily lead us to a promised land. What one can hope for is a peaceful end. Porter has lived to see some of his most talented contemporaries—George MacBeth, Jon Silkin, Ted Hughes—die. In ''The Deaths of Poets'' he views dissolution with that most honorable of modern stances, stoicism: ''Fountains wait, unblocked / of rubbish, cypresses stand to, / and someone's coming with moist hair to bring / you to the house you've always hoped to live in.'' Why write then? In an extraordinary poem whereby John Ford is made to answer T.S. Eliot, the poet who wrote an essay about that Jacobean playwright three hundred years later, Porter says, ''The paradox is poetry, a sort of / versified cascade not requiring metaphor.''

Λ ''versified cascade not requiring metaphor'' is certainly a good description of the later verse. It may be felt that the early promise of genius has not been wholly fulfilled. Perhaps the essential Porter is the work of an angry young man of the 1950s. Yet taken as a whole, this is a massive and comprehensive oeuvre. The later verse, grave as it often is, shows that there is a positive as well as a negative side to existence. The boys may still be howling, as in the earlier pieces, to take the girls to bed. But travel, reading, and meditation serve to remind the poet of what he celebrated in the early poem ''Walking Home on St Cecilia's Day,'' perhaps the best ever written about music: ''the injustice of delight.''

—Philip Hobsbaum

POWELL, Neil

Nationality: British. **Born:** London, 11 February 1948. **Education:** Sevenoaks School, Kent, 1959–66; University of Warwick, Coventry, 1966–71, B.A. in English and American literature 1969, M. Phil. in English 1975. **Career:** Teacher of English, Kimbolton School, Huntingdon, 1971–74, and St. Christopher School, Letchworth, Hertfordshire, 1974–86; owner, Baldock Bookshop, Hertfordshire, 1986–90. Since 1990 freelance writer and editor. **Awards:** Eric Gregory award, 1969. **Address:** c/o Carcanet Press, 4th Floor, Conavon Court, 12–16 Blackfriars Street, Manchester M3 5BQ, England.

PUBLICATIONS

Poetry

At Little Gidding. Rushden, Northamptonshire, Sceptre Press, 1974.
Afternoon Dawn. Hitchin, Hertfordshire, Cellar Press, 1975.
Suffolk Poems. Hitchin, Hertfordshire, Mandeville Press, 1975.
Four Letters. Sundridge, Kent, Letter Press, 1976.
A Mandeville Troika, with Peter Scupham and George Szirtes. Hitchin, Hertfordshire, Mandeville Press, 1977.
At the Edge. Manchester, Carcanet, and Chester Springs, Pennsylvania, Dufour, 1977.

Out of Time. Hitchin, Hertfordshire, Mandeville Press, 1979.
A Season of Calm Weather. Manchester, Carcanet, 1982.
True Colours: New and Selected Poems. Manchester, Carcanet, 1991.
The Stones on Thorpeness Beach. Manchester, Carcanet, 1994.
Selected Poems. Manchester, Carcanet, 1998.

Novel

Unreal City. Brighton, Millivres, 1992.

Other

A Commentary on Henry V. Petersfield, Hampshire, Studytapes, 1973.
Carpenters of Light: Some Contemporary British Poets. Manchester, Carcanet, 1979; New York, Barnes and Noble, 1980.
Roy Fuller: Writer and Society. Manchester, Carcanet, 1995.
The Language of Jazz. Manchester, Carcanet, 1997.

Editor, *Selected Poems* by Fulke Greville. Manchester, Carcanet. 1990.
Editor, *Gay Love Poetry.* London, Robinson, and New York, Carroll and Graf, 1997.

*

Critical Studies: ''A Slight Angle'' by the author, in *Critical Quarterly* (Manchester), summer 1982; '''These Shifting Constances': Time, Place and Personality in Three New Collections of Verse'' by Bill Ruddick, in *Critical Quarterly* (Oxford, England), 26(3), autumn 1984; ''Starting Out Again'' by Conor O'Callaghan, in *Times Literary Supplement* (London), 16 October 1998.

Neil Powell comments:

I started writing poems at school because I liked making these things out of words—the ''things'' being sonnets or villanelles or anything that offered the challenge and discipline of matching sense with form—and I remain fascinated by the oddly liberating possibilities of formal poetry. But the choice between metaphysicality and romanticism, the head and the heart, seems to me one that ideally need not be made. The poets I most admire are those who balance intellect and emotion in ways that transcend the necessary imbalances of their historical moments—Greville, Marvell, Coleridge, Auden, Gunn.

My poems are rooted in love and friendship, in the random shuttlings of memory and in the sense of place. The East Anglian landscape, with its huge skies, ragged coastline, and hidden valleys, has been especially kind to me. I am fortunate in the diversity of my literary work, which at present includes a good deal of editing and reviewing as well as extended prose projects in biography, criticism, and fiction. Consequently, I am not at all surprised if I find I have not written any poetry for months, though I am immoderately grateful when a poem does begin to bubble up, pushing everything else out of the way, demanding my undivided attention.

*   *   *

Neil Powell's collection *At the Edge* carries as its epigraph a verse by Donald Davie: ''The purest hue, let only the light be sufficient / Turns colour.'' The book itself is a conscious attempt to form a poetic in accordance with this precept. A firm admiration for the controlled force found in the work of Davie and Thom Gunn has led Powell to a consciousness that to write poetry is to exercise the intelligence as well as the heart and that the disciplines of a severe formalism are those most likely to prove fruitful:

> The poem's flow—the rock pools or the bends,
> Metre or syntax, shaping its slow progress—
>
> Becomes a formal fountain as we turn
> Our private art to public artifice.

The exact and exacting patterns, accurate rhyme schemes, and clear stanzaic forms of the poems are deployed to hold up to the light episodes of time past and time present. Inside these crystals the past and the present become each other, and their relationship is celebrated with a restrained, intelligent affection and a consciousness that ends and beginnings are artful mimics of each other:

> The years are misting over. I recall
> Something I didn't say a dream ago,
> Return abruptly to the reading class.
> The weeping condensation on a window
> Becomes the image of another day,
> A conversation in a different place
> Minutely glimpsed, and very far away.

In these handy-dandyings of personal time Powell makes an easy, rueful use of a conjurer's personal box of props, and a golden world gathers its tarnish to the accompaniment of a bric-a-brac of talk, drink, jazz, and old sunlight. More subtle and striking deeper home are the meditations on time in collusion with place. These poems show a wariness of dramatic effects and grand gestures, at their happiest with the undemonstrative and hidden landscapes of East Anglia. The poet is frequently found in the role of eavesdropper, watcher, revenant, alert for the chance disclosure of some part of the secret compact that place and time have made, a compact itself under threat:

> Trespasser? Tenant? Neither will win, the sea insists,
>   in the vanished places—Dunwich, Walberswick—
> where lanes scrawl to the margin of a torn-off coastline
>   whose history is written by the tide.

Always beyond the local familiarities and the boundaries, the edges and lines formed by masons and poets, lie worlds evading circumscription. Some of Powell's most impressive poems move out toward enigmatic and uncharted areas of sea, dizzying weathers, oblivion. Roads lead endlessly and nightmarishly on

> Until ''The North'' proclaims a giant sign,
> As if the north were somewhere you could reach
> By following a disembodied line
> Which joins nowhere to nowhere, each to each,
>
> And work to home. Or will it merely end

> In featureless space, an orange void stretching
> On each side of the road, round the next bend,
> With distant amber lamps, the planets, gleaming?

The stance taken by the poet at this stage of his career is one of some ambivalence. The game is played neither at home nor away but often in some temporary ground we may provisionally call either. Metaphor is used sparingly, with Powell preferring an accurate and evocative use of detail held in place by an intellectual scaffolding. This can lead to a rather dry philosophical tone and a preponderance of abstraction in the weaker poems. His later work, however, shows a relaxed and sparer style emerging, which promises to bring a suppler tension to his forms:

> I walk through the silent town. A breeze is blowing
> Snuffed-out candles from horse-chestnut trees,
> The unknown is on the air, and I am knowing
> Something I cannot recognise, unless
>
> It is a distant prospect of the future, showing
> All that is and all that will come to be,
> As blossoms of the past are going, going.

—Peter Scupham

PRINCE, F(rank) T(empleton)

Nationality: British. **Born:** Kimberley, Cape Province, South Africa, 13 September 1912. **Education:** Christian Brothers' College, Kimberley; Balliol College, Oxford; Princeton University, New Jersey, 1935–36; Study Groups Department, Chatham House, 1937–40. **Military Service:** Intelligence Corps, 1940–46. **Family:** Married Pauline Elizabeth Bush in 1943; two daughters. **Career:** Member of the English Department, from 1946, and professor of English, 1957–74, University of Southampton. Visiting fellow, All Souls College, Oxford, 1968–69; Clark Lecturer, Cambridge University, 1972–73; professor of English, University of the West Indies, Jamaica, 1975–78; visiting professor, Brandeis University, Waltham, Massachusetts, 1978–80, Amherst College, Massachusetts, 1979, Washington University, St. Louis, 1980–81, Sana'a University, North Yemen, 1981–83, and Hollins College, Virginia, spring 1984. President, English Association, 1985–86. **Awards:** American Academy E.M. Forster award, 1982. D.Litt.: University of Southampton, 1981; D.Univ.: University of York, 1982. **Address:** 32 Brookvale Road, Southampton, Hampshire S02 IQR, England.

PUBLICATIONS

Poetry

Poems. London, Faber, and New York, New Directions, 1938.
Soldiers Bathing and Other Poems. London, Fortune Press, 1954
The Stolen Heart. San Francisco, Press of the Morning Sun, 1957
The Doors of Stone: Poems 1938–1962. London, Hart Davis, 1963.
Memoirs in Oxford. London, Fulcrum Press, 1970.

Penguin Modern Poets 20, with John Heath-Stubbs and Stephen
Spender. London, Penguin, 1971.
Drypoints of the Hasidim. London, Menard Press, 1975.
Afterword on Rupert Brooke. London, Menard Press, 1976.
Collected Poems. London, Anvil Press Poetry/Menard Press, and
New York, Sheep Meadow Press, 1979.
The Yüan Chên Variations. New York, Sheep Meadow Press, 1981.
Later On. London, Anvil Press Poetry, and New York, Sheep
Meadow Press, 1983.
Walks in Rome. London, Anvil Press Poetry and New York, Sheep
Meadow Press, 1987.
Collected Poems: 1935–1992. Manchester, Carcanet, and New York,
Sheep Meadow Press, 1993.

Other

The Italian Element in Milton's Verse. Oxford, Clarendon Press,
1954.
William Shakespeare: The Poems. London, Longman, 1963.

Editor, *Samson Agonistes,* by Milton. London, Oxford University
Press, 1957.
Editor, *The Poems,* by Shakespeare. London, Methuen, and Cam-
bridge, Massachusetts, Harvard University Press, 1960.
Editor, *Paradise Lost, Books I and II,* by Milton. London, Oxford
University Press, 1962.
Editor, *Comus and Other Poems,* by Milton. London, Oxford Univer-
sity Press, 1968.

Translator, *Sir Thomas Wyatt* by Sergio Baldi. London, Longman, 1961.

*

Critical Studies: *F.T. Prince: A Study of His Poetry* by Alka Nigam,
Salzburg, University of Salzburg, 1983; "The Later Poetry of F.T.
Prince" by W.G. Shepherd, in *Agenda* (London), 26(4), winter 1988.

*   *   *

For more than half a century, F.T. Prince has stood fast among
the tides of fashion. His verse is leisurely, eloquent, and syntactically
elaborate. It suggests the spaciousness of a bygone age:

A beautiful girl said something in your praise.
And either because in a hundred ways
I had heard of her great worth and had no doubt
To find her lovelier than I thought
And found her also cleverer . . .

"To a Friend on His Marriage" is related to modern classics
such as the Yeats of "Her Praise" and "No Second Troy" and, more
remotely, the Auden of "A Bride in the 30's." Prince's poem does
not, however, merely derive from these. Rather, what we have here is
a remarkable absorption of sources. That is to say, the eloquence of
Prince is an achievement in its own right.

Though his mode may seem essentially that of the meditative
lyric, Prince has turned it to account in several ambitious monologues.
Leonardo da Vinci informs his patron,

You should understand that I have plotted,
Being in command of all the ordinary engines
Of defence and offence and fifteen buildings
Less others less complete: complete, some are courts of
serene stone . . .

In a tone not dissimilar, Michelangelo surveys his old age elegiacally,
but with a certain detachment:

And there is always
Some victor and some vanquished, always the fierce
substance
And the divine idea, a drunkenness
Of high desire and thought, or a stern sadness . . .

This, in its turn, is related to the resigned stance imputed to Edmund Burke:

in both worlds
There is now this fistulous sore that runs
Into a thousand sinuosities; and the wound now
Opens the red west, gains new ground . . .

These voices have a family resemblance. They share a deliberate
vocabulary and slowness of movement. The tone is essentially that of
such meditative lyrics as "The Babiaantje," "The Question," and
"To a Friend on His Marriage" itself. It would seem that the oeuvre
of Prince adds up to a respectable contribution to modern literature by
a scholar-poet.

Such a characterization of Prince, however, is not complete. He
has, as most academics have not, his classic. It is a poem that lives in
the mind rather than in the study. "Soldiers Bathing" is one of the
few great poems of World War II, the only one perhaps that could
justly be said to stand beside the classics of World War I. It is a
remarkable fact that the techniques deployed in Prince's other poems
do duty here: the slow-moving line, the distilled concept, the imagery
refracted through a recollection of great art. Yet the total effect is,
unlike the Leonardo and Michelangelo poems, urgent and poignant:

The sea at evening moves across the sand.
Under a reddening sky I watch the freedom of a band
Of soldiers who belong to me. Stripped bare
For bathing in the sea, they shout and run in the warm air;
Their flesh worn by the trade of war, revives
And my mind towards the meaning of it strives . . .

The plot is direct and moving. Soldiers stripped of the
accoutrements of war show themselves thereby at once released and
vulnerable. Such a datum need not come a poet's way once in a
lifetime. The poem superbly combines story line with archetype.
Further, there is a highly characteristic vision here. We are aware of a
detached persona considering all of this. It is not Leonardo, not
Michelangelo, but it is certainly someone not unlike Prince's presentation of those figures—erudite, distanced, eloquent. The person is a
kind of ideal aesthete:

Because to love is frightening we prefer
The freedom of our crimes. Yet, as I drink the dusky air,

I feel a strange delight that fills me full,
Strange gratitude, as if evil itself were beautiful,
And kiss the wound in thought, while in the west
I watch a streak of red that might have issued from Christ's
    breast.

Prince is unlikely to thank his critics for setting "Soldiers Bathing" far above the rest of his work, intelligent and informed though that work is. Notwithstanding, it will be the specialist who analyzes "The Old Age of Michelangelo" and who will go on to peruse Prince's autumnal works—thoughtful studies of the communal life of the Hasidim, of Rupert Brooke at Cambridge, of the love life of Laurence Sterne. Those who are not aware of caring especially for poetry may, on the other hand, find that they know "Soldiers Bathing" by heart.

—Philip Hobsbaum

PRYNNE, J(eremy) H(alvard)

Nationality: British. **Born:** England, 24 June 1936. **Career:** University lecturer in English, and librarian, Gonville and Caius College, Cambridge. **Address:** Gonville and Caius College, Cambridge CB2 lTA, England.

PUBLICATIONS

Poetry

Force of Circumstance and Other Poems. London, Routledge, 1962.
Kitchen Poems. London, Cape Goliard Press, and New York, Grossman, 1968.
Day Light Songs. Pampisford, Cambridgeshire, R. Books, 1968.
Aristeas. London, Ferry Press, 1968.
The White Stones. Lincoln, Grosseteste Press, 1969.
Fire Lizard. Barnet, Hertfordshire, Blacksuede Boot Press, 1970.
Brass. London, Ferry Press, 1971.
Into the Day. Privately printed, 1972.
A Night Square. London, Albion Village Press, 1973.
Wound Response. Cambridge, Street Editions, 1974.
High Pink on Chrome. Privately printed, 1975.
News of Warring Clans. London, Trigram Press, 1977.
Down Where Changed. London, Ferry Press, 1979.
Poems. Edinburgh, Agneau 2, 1982.
The Oval Window. Privately printed, 1983.
Marzipan. Cambridge, P. Riley, 1986.
Bands Around the Throat. Privately printed, 1987.
Word Order. Kenilworth, Warwickshire, Prest Roots Press, 1989.
Jie ban mi Shi Hu, from holograph, in Chinese. Cambridge, Peter Riley Books, 1992.
Not-You. Cambridge, Equipage, 1993.
Her Weasels Wild Returning. Cambridge, Equipage, 1994.
Bands around the Throat. Boston and Manchester, Exact Change, 1995.
For the Monogram. Cambridge, Equipage, 1997.
Red D. Gypsum. Cambridge, Massachusetts, Barque, 1998.
Pearls That Were. Cambridge, privately printed, 1999.

Poems. Newcastle upon Tyne, Bloodaxe, 1999.
Triodes. Cambridge, Massachusetts, Barque, 1999.

Editor, Special edition of *Parataxis* (Brighton, England), 7, fall 1994.

*

Critical Studies: "A Note on J.H. Prynne's 'Royal Fern'" by N.H. Reeve and Richard Kerridge, in *English* (Leicester, England), 35(152), summer 1986; *Marx's Concept of Determination: Literature and Cognition* (dissertation) by Jeremy F. Points, n.p., 1989; "Nothing But Morality: Prynne and Celan" by Geoffrey Ward, in *Contemporary Poetry Meets Modern Theory,* edited by Antony Easthope, Toronto, University of Toronto Press, 1991; "Enlarging History: The Poetry of J.H. Prynne" by Andres Rodriguez, in *Sagetrieb* (Orono, Maine), 10(3), winter 1991; "Making (Non) Sense of Postmodernist Poetry" by McHale, in *Language, Text, and Context: Essays in Stylistics,* edited by Michael Toolan, London, Routledge, 1992; "Life at the Rim of Itself: J.H. Prynne's Poetry" by N.H. Reeve and Richard Kerridge, in *Durham University Journal* (New Elvet, Durham), 86(55), July 1994; *The Engineering of Being: An Ontological Approach to J.H. Prynne* (dissertation) by Birgitta Sigrid Johansson, Umea University, 1997.

*   *   *

Apart from his first and—as it were—apprentice collection, *Force of Circumstance,* J.H. Prynne's poetry has subsequently maintained an utterly singular development, paying no regard whatsoever to the recognized currency of contemporary English verse. This singularity is created and sustained through an intense but usually indirect reference to entire ranges of previous literatures and the writings of other cultures—American, European, and Middle and even Far Eastern. Prynne's poetry is to a high degree intellectually complex, and it has consistently made minimum concessions to the reader's conventional expectations. A continuous effect encountered in the close reading of his texts is the experience of being thrown back upon all of one's interpretative resources and often enough of being chastened by the limitations of one's knowledge. In this way the reader finds that he or she has to construct a meaning that can only be fragmentary, and beyond this a beguiling lure remains, indicating that there is much more still to be known in terms of the formal beauty and the ethical purchase the lines offer and withdraw. This is to say that Prynne's poetry requires its reader continuously to consider how any meaning is derived at any point during the process of interpretation and, further, whatever meaning is temporarily entertained, then to subject it to rigorous questioning. To read Prynne is to undergo an education.

How do we actually keep up with our dangerous and complex times? How does anyone avoid giving up the relentless effort of understanding, so as not to collapse into resentment or some hopeless form of nostalgia for a safely distant past? A good deal of contemporary poetry might be said to be broken in these ways, in that it is not of the moment but rather is archaic or even (terrible fate) old-fashioned. Prynne's writing, however, can be considered within the terms of many utterly pressing, absolutely current debates. References to economic pressure or to arguments within the life sciences are intrinsic to many of his poems, and the central strategy of putting into question the nature of our meanings is itself a procedure that has a good deal in common with the more interesting forms of so-called deconstruction. His poems examine the economic structures of need and the place human values such as trust, hope, or the experience of damage may occupy within them; again, these concerns have real parallels within Marxist debates. His strategic use of such specialized vocabularies, more usually thought of as exclusively scientific, attempts to propose an ethical regimen from the complexities of what are conventionally taken to be branches of technical knowledge.

Prynne's poems are not only severe. Their intransigence often rises to effects of sharp beauty, a kind of cool aesthetic that draws on imagery of ice, tundra, human extremity, and (to steal an adjective, itself beautiful, from *Into the Day*) "madrigalian" formal perfection. The angular, austere delights of these poems are themselves a virtue, but it is exactly this concentration upon what is crystalline that creates the faceted resources of the texts' meanings.

From where may a view be taken, from which point may all the information be totalized, in the system of our society where all the systems interpenetrate to a degree that is virtually physiological, as complex as a body? Do we need a view from which to take proper heed of all the variables? What would such a vantage be when we are implicated by way of terror, harm, disgust, and even joy, with all the operations of this infinitely complex world, where no one language can hope to cover all options but each language is pervaded by the values of the others? The following is from *The Oval Window:*

> Think now
> or pay now and think later, the levels
> of control nesting presume a reason
> to cut back only and keep mum.

In Prynne's poetry large-scale economic movements and closely detailed aspects of medical physiology are read into one another so that the subject—the self—is caught within the defining structures of social force and biological necessity. Between these parameters the conduct of our ethical and emotional lives, themselves mutually implicated, is explored:

> So: from now on too, or soon lost,
> the voice you hear is your own
> revoked, on a relative cyclical downturn
> imaged in latent narrow-angle glaucoma.

By virtue of this plangent scope the poem may again have become the most conscious point of its time, but this will not by any means make it the most restful locus.

—Nigel Wheale

PUGH, Sheenagh

Nationality: British. **Born:** Birmingham, 20 December 1950. **Education:** Mundella Grammar School, Nottingham; University of Bristol, 1968–71, B.A. (honors) in German and Russian. **Family:** Married Michael J.H. Burns in 1977; one son and one daughter. **Career:** Higher executive officer, Welsh Office, Cardiff, 1971–79. Branch secretary, Society of Civil Servants, Cardiff, 1974–79. Since 1993 tutor in creative writing, Glamorgan University. **Awards:** Babel translation prize, 1984; British Comparative Literature Association translation prize, 1985; Cardiff International Literature Festival prize, 1988, 1994; Forward prize for best individual poem, 1998; Cholmondeley award, 1999. **Address:** 4C Romilly Road, Canton, Cardiff CF5 1FH, Wales.

PUBLICATIONS

Poetry

Crowded by Shadows. Bridgend, Glamorgan, Poetry Wales Press, 1977.
What a Place to Grow Flowers. Swansea, Triskele, 1979.
Earth Studies and Other Voyages. Bridgend, Glamorgan, Poetry Wales Press, 1982.
Beware Falling Tortoises. Bridgend, Glamorgan, Poetry Wales Press, 1987.
Selected Poems. Bridgend, Glamorgan, Seren Books, 1990.
Sing for the Taxman. Bridgend, Glamorgan, Seren Books, 1993.
Id's Hospit. Bridgend, Glamorgan, Seren Books, 1997.
Stonelight. Bridgend, Glamorgan, Seren Books, 1999.

Other

Translator, *Prisoners of Transience.* Bridgend, Glamorgan, Poetry Wales Press, 1985.

*

Critical Studies: "The Poetry of Sheenagh Pugh" by John Whitehead, in *Babel* (Munich), 4, 1984; "Sheenagh Pugh: Interview with Richard Poole," in *Poetry Wales,* January 1995.

Sheenagh Pugh comments:

I write because I like to play with words, to record what interests me, and to sound off about what annoys—same as anyone else does. Themes I have kept going back to include death, loneliness, snooker, political tyranny, and fellow feeling. I wrote some green poems early in the 1980s, before anyone else was doing it, but not a lot of people noticed; getting on a bandwagon too early is as bad as too late. The poets I like best, and have tried to learn from, are Sorley MacLean, Andreas Gryphius, Hans-Ulrich Treichel, and above all Robert Henryson. I like poems to be crafted and literate and not written in chopped-up prose, but not written either in a language that defies the understanding of reasonably intelligent persons. And I like them to be about something that matters, not silly verbal games for bored academics. I hate being called a "woman poet" and have no time for anyone who thinks gender matters outside a bedroom. For actual enjoyment I prefer translating, especially German poetry of the Thirty Years' War period.

* * *

Sheenagh Pugh, though born in Birmingham, established her reputation in Wales, where she has lived for a number of years. She is regarded as one of the strongest and most original voices in poetry in Wales, which is no doubt due to the freshness and unconventionality of her approach. Her family roots include a Welsh grandmother, but her roots in writing are as cosmopolitan as any poet in Britain. She read Russian and German at Bristol University, and her collection of translations, *Prisoners of Transience,* which won the Babel translation prize in 1984, is perhaps her most notable achievement.

Pugh's first book, *Crowded by Shadows,* drew praise from several reviewers, most notably D.M. Thomas, who called it "the most promising first collection I have read for years . . . her poetry does not, refreshingly, try to put the world to rights, nor finger the abscess of private emotion; instead, it lays itself open to the world of others . . . ." Her collection *Earth Studies and Other Voyages* builds on that principle as its title sequence explores the feelings of space travelers who have escaped an earth that seems no longer worth inhabiting and who now live on *Terra 2.* Under titles such as "Geography 1 & 2," "History 1 & 2 & 3," and "Biology 1 & 2 & 3," Pugh allows herself the detachment to sum up ironically the character and failings of the planet as we have used and abused it. One of the astronauts remembers returning from a trip to Iceland:

> . . . When I got back
> to Heathrow, and walked out into Reading.
>
> I damn near choked on this warm gritty stuff
> I called air; also on the conjecture
> that we'd all settle for second best
> once we'd forgotten there was something more.

This represents a fall from grace in that, when asked about heaven, one of the older travelers says,

> . . . If you really want to know
> what I think about heaven, the truth is
> I think I lived there.

The nineteen poems that constitute the *Earth Studies* sequence may well be one of the earliest examples of a consciously green poetry in Britain.

The other poems in the collection, the "Other Voyages" of the title, deal with sailors and conventional sea journeys but also include "Old Widowers" and "The T.V. Hero":

> the likeness of a make-believe man
> fills our space more harmlessly than most.

It is not a feminist point that Pugh is making here. Women appear off-center in the bulk of her poetry, like the females in "St. Cuthbert and the Women" who ". . . move, / far off, in their brave colours, bright / as illuminated manuscript initials" and who water the island "with their laughter, their chat about / some small happiness." It is the male personal pronoun that predominates in her writing, which can be off-putting. She has written in *Planet* magazine and elsewhere about her stance on issues of gender in writing. She wants there to be no difference, no significance, a position that has failed to satisfy other women writers who see things in more confrontational terms. She chooses only two women poets in her selection of translations in *Prisoners of Transience,* though that is surely more indicative of the history of women's writing in Europe than any sinister predilection on the part of the poet.

These translations, from two French poets and thirteen from the German, range from the twelfth century to Stefan George, who died in the year that Hitler became chancellor of Germany. Pugh's versions respect the rhyme schemes of the originals, though she wisely recognizes that half rhymes are just as acceptable to modern readers.

She employs these rhymes and the basis of the iambic pentameter to good effect, and I wonder if her next collection of original poetry, *Beware Falling Tortoises,* published two years later, suffers from the experience. Too often in this collection the poetry lacks tautness and satisfactory resolution, and the writing, I feel, could have benefited from the sort of prosodic discipline of which *Prisoners of Transience* proved Pugh most capable. Poems such as "I Am Roerek," "Pharisees," and "He Was a Man of His Word" are thus less accomplished than "She Was Nineteen and She Was Bored," "A Short History of Cocaine Abuse," and "Memoirs of a Dutch Tulip Merchant." This last is evidence that Pugh can fashion a dramatic monologue:

> . . . I remember I sold
> a single *Semper Augustus*—in '31,
> I think it was, the year the Austrians
> burned Magdeburg—for thousands: everyone
> wanted *Augustus*. It had a white ground
> striped with crimson and iron; the more broken
> the colours were, the more it was worth.

This is much more effective than "Crusaders," the poem that follows it. In "Crusaders" the modern voice projects unconvincingly from the character of a medieval knight. Again, in the three-poem sequence "Dieppe" Pugh's attempts to capture the soldiers' voices too often slacken the lines so that the poetry is lost. These attempts to enter fully into character do work, however, to complement the dominant mode of her poetry, which is that of the author's dispassionate gaze and the wry comment. It might be assumed that Pugh's models are Philip Larkin and the Movement rather than Anne Sexton and Sylvia Plath; she maintains, however, "I was, until recently, incredibly ignorant of *all* English verse; all my models, if I had any, were mediaeval, Henryson, mainly." Certainly she is closer to Fleur Adcock than Wendy Cope, and, no matter how strongly one feels that she may be tempted by the neat rhyme and the obvious barb, she generally is in control of her verse. The problem with the poet assuming the role of wry commentator is that the reader may grow to dislike the persona and suspect smugness. Larkin is saved from this fate by the frequent revelations of his own vulnerability; he is deliberately transparent in the way that his frailty shows beneath the commentary. Pugh rarely offers the reader a glimpse of her deepest feelings. We encounter her brain but not so obviously her heart. These lines from "Cameraman" seem apposite:

> . . . Do not be tempted
> to turn the camera inward:
> your stricken looks are no concern
> of the public's. They need the word
>
> on what you saw, not how
> you felt. It is they who must feel
> they saw it; they were there; so
> involved, they condemn somewhat
> the remote like of you.

Time and the vagaries of life may well pull Pugh more centrally into her own poetry. With the appearance in 1990 of her *Selected Poems* and the culling of weaker work, Pugh would seem to have reached the middle point of her achievement as a poet. If she can successfully build on her strengths as a translator and deploy further the prosodic skills she has exhibited there in the service of her often unnerving eye, then she should establish herself as one of the more notable contemporary voices.

—Tony Curtis

PURDY, Al(fred Wellington)

Nationality: Canadian. **Born:** Wooller, Ontario, 30 December 1918. **Education:** Dufferin Public School, Trenton, Ontario; Albert College, Belleville, Ontario; Trenton Collegiate Institute, Ontario. **Military Service:** Royal Canadian Air Force during World War II. **Family:** Married Eurithe Parkhurst in 1941; one son. **Career:** Has held numerous jobs; taught at Simon Fraser University, Burnaby, British Columbia, spring 1970; poet-in-residence, Loyola College, Montreal, 1973, University of Manitoba, Winnipeg, 1975–76, and University of Western Ontario, London, 1977–78. **Awards:** Canada Council fellowship, 1960, 1965, 1968, 1971, award, 1973, and grant, 1974, 1975, 1980; President's Medal, University of Western Ontario, 1964; Governor-General's award, 1966, 1987. A.J.M. Smith prize, 1974; Jubilee Medal, 1978. Order of Canada, 1987. **Address:** Rural Route 1, Ameliasburgh, Ontario K0K 1A0, Canada. **Died:** 21 April 2000.

PUBLICATIONS

Poetry

The Enchanted Echo. Vancouver, Clarke and Stuart, 1944.
Pressed on Sand. Toronto, Ryerson Press, 1955.
Emu, Remember! Fredericton, University of New Brunswick, 1956.
The Crafte So Longe to Lerne. Toronto, Ryerson Press, 1959.
Poems for All the Annettes. Toronto, Contact Press, 1962.
The Old Woman and the Mayflowers. Ottawa, Blue R, 1962.
The Blur in Between: Poems 1960–61. Toronto, Emblem, 1962.
The Cariboo Horses. Toronto, McClelland and Stewart, 1965.
North of Summer: Poems from Baffin Land. Toronto, McClelland and Stewart, 1967.
Poems for All the Annettes (selected poems). Toronto, Anansi, 1968
Wild Grape Wine. Toronto, McClelland and Stewart, 1968.
Spring Song. Fredericton, New Brunswick, Fiddlehead, 1968.
The Winemaker's Beat-étude. Willowdale, Ontario, Fiddlehead, 1968.
Interruption. Willowdale, Ontario, Fiddlehead, n.d.
Love in a Burning Building. Toronto, McClelland and Stewart, 1970.
Five Modern Canadian Poets, with others, edited by Eli Mandel. Toronto, Holt Rinehart, 1970.
The Quest for Ouzo. Trenton, Ontario, M. Kerrigan Almey, 1970.
On Being Romantic & 5 Love Poems. Vancouver(?), Deodar Shadow Press, 197-.
Selected Poems. Toronto, McClelland and Stewart, 1972.
Hiroshima Poems. Trumansburg, New York, Crossing Press, 1972.
On the Bearpaw Sea. Burnaby, British Columbia, Blackfish Press, 1973; revised edition, Toronto, Red Maple Editions, 1994.
Sex and Death. Toronto, McClelland and Stewart, 1973.
Scott Hutcheson's Boat. Prince George, British Columbia, Caledonia, 1973.
In Search of Owen Roblin. Toronto, McClelland and Stewart, 1974.
Sundance at Dusk. Toronto, McClelland and Stewart, 1976.

The Poems of Al Purdy. Toronto, McClelland and Stewart, 1976.
At Marsport Drugstore. Sutton West, Ontario, Paget Press, 1977.
A Handful of Earth. Coatsworth, Ontario, Black Moss Press, 1977.
No Second Spring. Coatsworth, Ontario, Black Moss Press, 1977.
Moths in the Iron Curtain. Cleveland, Black Rabbit, 1977.
Being Alive: Poems 1958–78. Toronto, McClelland and Stewart, 1978.
The Stone Bird. Toronto, McClelland and Stewart, 1981.
Bursting into Song: An Al Purdy Omnibus. Willowdale, Ontario, Fiddlehead Press, 1982.
Piling Blood. Toronto, McClelland and Stewart, 1984.
Collected Poems. Toronto, McClelland and Stewart, 1986.
Two/Al Purdy. Vancouver, Colophon, 1990.
The Woman on the Shore. Toronto, McClelland and Stewart, 1989.
Naked with Summer in Your Mouth: Poems. Toronto, McClelland and Stewart, 1994.
Rooms for Rent in the Outer Planets: Selected Poems, 1962–1996. Madeira Park, British Columbia, Harbour Publishing, 1996.
To Paris Never Again: New Poems. Madeira Park, British Columbia, Harbour Publishing, 1997.

Recording: *Al Purdy,* Ontario Institute for Studies in Education, 1971.

Plays

Point of Transfer: The Selected Plays of Al Purdy. Trenton, Ontario, Harbour Publishing, 1991.

Novel

A Splinter in the Heart. Toronto, McClelland and Stewart, 1990.

Other

No Other Country. Toronto, McClelland and Stewart, 1977.
Morning and It's Summer: A Memoir. Montreal, Quandrant, 1983.
The Bukowski/Purdy Letters: A Decade of Dialogue 1964–1974, with Charles Bukowski, edited by Seamus Cooney. Sutton West, Ontario, Paget Press, 1983.
The Purdy/Woodcock Letters: Selected Correspondence 1964–1984. Toronto, ECW Press, 1988.
Yehl the Raven. Madeira Park, British Columbia, Harbour Publishing, 1991.
Cougar Hunter: A Memoir of Roderick Haig-Brown. Vancouver, Phoenix Press, 1992.
Reaching for the Beaufort Sea: An Autobiography. Madeira Park, British Columbia, Harbour Publishing, 1993.
Starting from Ameliasburgh: The Collected Prose of Al Purdy. Madeira Park, British Columbia, Harbour Publishing, 1995.
The Man Who Outlived Himself: An Appreciation of John Donne: A Dozen of His Best Poems. Madeira Park, British Columbia, Harbour Publishing, 1999.

Editor, *The New Romans: Candid Canadian Opinions of the United States.* Edmonton, Alberta, Hurtig, and New York, St. Martin's Press, 1968.
Editor, *Fifteen Winds: A Selection of Modern Canadian Poems.* Toronto, Ryerson Press, 1969.
Editor, *I've Tasted My Blood: Poems 1956–1968,* by Milton Acorn. Toronto, Ryerson Press, 1969.

Editor, *Storm Warning: The New Canadian Poets.* Toronto, McClelland and Stewart, 1971; *Storm Warning 2,* 1976.

Editor, *Wood Mountain Poems,* by Andrew Suknaski Jr. Toronto, Macmillan, 1976.

Editor, *Into a Blue Morning: Poems Selected and New 1968–1981,* by C.H. Gervais. Toronto, Hounslow Press, 1982.

Editor, with Doug Beardsley, *No One Else Is Lawrence!: A Dozen of D.H. Lawrence's Best Poems with Introduction and Commentary.* Madeira Park, British Columbia, Harbour Publishing, 1998.

*

Bibliography: By Marianne Micros, in *The Annotated Bibliography of Canada's Major Authors 2,* edited by Robert Lecker and Jack David, Downsview, Ontario, ECW Press, 1980.

Manuscript Collections: University of Saskatchewan, Saskatoon; University of British Columbia, Vancouver; Lakehead University, Thunder Bay, Ontario; Thomas Fisher Rare Book Library, University of Toronto.

Critical Studies: "In the Raw: The Poetry of A.W. Purdy" by Peter Stevens, in *Canadian Literature* (Vancouver), spring 1966; interview with Gary Geddes, in *Canadian Literature* (Vancouver), 1969; *Al Purdy* by George Bowering, Toronto, Copp Clark, 1970; *Harsh and Lovely Land* by Tom Marshall, Vancouver, University of British Columbia Press, 1979; "Al Purdy's Contemporary Pastoral" by D.G. Jones, in *Canadian Poetry* (London, Ontario), 10, spring-summer 1982; "Al Purdy and His Works" by Louis MacKendrick, in *Canadian Writers and Their Works,* edited by Robert Lecker, Jack David, and Ellen Quigley, Toronto, ECW, 1990; "The Correspondence of Margaret Laurence and Al Purdy" by John Lennox, in *Recherches Anglaises et Nord-Americaines* (Strasbourg, France), 24, 1991; *Loopholes and Catacombs: Elements of Bakhtian Dialogue in the Poetry of Al Purdy* (dissertation) by John C. Van Rys, Dalhousie University, 1993; by H.R. Percy, in *Queen's Quarterly,* 101(4), winter 1994.

Al Purdy comments:

(1970) Themes? Sex and death (which last naturally includes life). Subjects? Anything that appeals to me. Form? Pretty irregular, but generally with rhythm running somewhere, sometimes off-rhymes and assonance. Influences? Very many, including the usual big names (Pound, Eliot, Yeats); also César Vallejo, Neruda, Superveille, Charles Bukowski, Robinson Jeffers, etc., etc. Style? I have some strong prejudices against schools of any kind, including most particularly the Creeley-Olson Black Mountain bunch and their imitators. I do not dismiss these people and believe it is possible to learn much from them, but only if one remains oneself, something most of them apparently find difficult. I believe that when a poet fixes on one style or method he severely limits his present and future development. By the same token I dislike the traditional forms. But I use rhyme, meter, and (occasionally) standard forms when a poem seems to call for it. Rules tend to be exclusive of anything outside their own strictures. I think most traditional poets would agree with this, but go right on using traditional meter and rhymes; poets like prime ministers are all against war and on the side of truth and justice.

Perhaps I should say that I began to write nearly forty years ago, influenced at that time by people whom I do not appreciate very much now. For instance, I like some of G.K. Chesterton's poems, and

his influence no doubt remains with me but is, I think, difficult to discern in what I write today. At one time iambic metrics were so deeply implanted in my mind that it took me years of not trying to break out of iambics to finally break out of iambics. I suppose other people's styles were apparent in my stuff until publication of *Poems for All the Annettes* in '62, and this book (and *The Blur in Between,* also published '62 but earlier poems than *Annettes*) is the transitional period between what I was and am and change into. I have a fixation about change, which can also be regarded as a self-conscious weakness as well as strength. And yet I wrote a poem in Athens, Greece, in January 1969 ("The Time of Your Life") that is probably the best I have ever written, at least I think so now.

*　　*　　*

With some forty books of verse and several of prose to his credit, not counting anthologies he has edited, Al Purdy is one of the most prolific of Canadian writers. He is also one of the most consistently interesting Canadian poets and one who has steadily grown in stature and in the respect of readers and critics. Although he has been publishing poetry for more than a generation and writing it even longer, his first volume, *The Enchanted Echo,* appeared only in 1944, and it was not until the mid-1960s, when he was already well into middle age, that he emerged as one of Canada's leading poets. He has been vigorous in statement and energetic in traveling the land to read his poetry and in traveling the world to gather experience. He is a writer "for whom the visible world exists" palpably and directly, and the impressions gathered in travel have always played a recognizable role in shaping both the content and the mood of a great deal of his poetry. But the heart of Purdy's world, the place that gives its name to so many of his poems and appears as the symbolic omphalos of his imaginative world, is Roblin Lake, near Ameliasburgh in the heart of Loyalist Ontario, where he lives and whose traditions, transmitted in the lives of his farmer forebears, have stirred the emotions inspiring much of his best work. An example is "My Grandfather's Country":

> But the hill-red has no such violence of endings
> the woods are alive
> and gentle as well as cruel
> unlike sand and sea
> and if I must give my heart to anything
> it will be here in the red glow
> where failed farms sink back into earth
> the clearings join and fences no longer divide
> where the running animals gather their bodies together
> and pour themselves upward
> into the tips of falling leaves
> with mindless faith that presumes a future.

Purdy's lack of an academic background, unusual in the Canadian literary world, has been an advantage to him in many ways, leading him to wander far and freely, to work at many callings, and to bring to his writing a wide down-to-earth experience. On the technical side it has liberated him from formal disciplines and has enabled him to work at his own pace, apart from the literary fashions that sweep North American campuses, and to take what he wants where he wants, from Williams, from Auden and Thomas, from Pratt and Bimey and Layton. By such means he has progressed from the traditional lyricism of *The Enchanted Echo* to the open forms and personal voice of midperiod books like *The Cariboo Horses* and *Wild Grape Wine* and of later books like *The Stone Bird* and *Piling Blood.* What has struck readers about Purdy's verse since the late 1950s is its intense oral impact. It is free verse in the truest form—fluent, untrammeled by conventions, yet possessing rhythmic and grammatical forms that distinguish it from statement in prose.

Purdy's verse is always near to experience; the poem emerges from life and the concept from the poem. Pieces about his wanderings in Canada, like those in *The Cariboo Horses,* or abroad, like those in *Hiroshima Poems,* often seem to have served Purdy as a journal, so close is the interval between conception and creation, so immediate the response to experience. This does at times lead to unevenness in tone and quality, which Purdy controls to an extent by weeding out much of a voluminous production.

The Crafte So Longe to Lerne is the volume in which Purdy's special character as a poet first detaches itself from his original derivativeness. This is seen in the opening of forms and in the thematic evolution of a type of poetry that is really a philosophic continuum where the here and now, immediately perceived, becomes the Blakean grain in which, if not the world, at least universal values are reflected. Purdy himself regards a later volume, *Poems for All the Annettes,* as the point where "other people's styles" ceased to be apparent in his work. Certainly by the time he won the Governor-General's award for *The Cariboo Horses,* he was writing at the top of his individual form, having developed a long-lined and colloquially free manner as well as an ability to be intellectually direct without sacrificing the suggestive dimensions of poetic imagery. Purdy has drawn freely on the funds of miscellaneous knowledge that a generalizing and autodidactic mind accumulates; yet, though densely allusive, he is never obscure. His poems often show a remarkable ability to bring images drawn from great sweeps of time and space into a meaningful relationship with what he sees before him in the everyday contemporary setting. A fine example is "In the Caves," the concluding poem of *Being Alive.* Purdy imagines the creative passion of a Paleolithic artist and by implication relates it to the poet's modern agony:

And I do not know why
whether because I cannot hunt with the others
and they laugh
or because the things I have done are useless
as I may be useless
but there is something I must follow
into myself to find
outside myself in the mammoth
beyond the scorn of my people
who are still my people
my own pain and theirs
joining the shriek that does not end
that is inside me now

Such poetry traps with an extraordinary appearance of spontaneity the roving speculations of a highly original mind.

Being Alive includes most of Purdy's best poems to the late 1970s and perhaps shows his work in its greatest variety up to that period. Yet there is a power and a radiance about later volumes like *The Stone Bird* and *Piling Blood* and even *The Woman on the Shore* that place him securely among the major Canadian poets. Indeed, when one reads the four hundred pages of the definitive *Collected Poems,* together with the even later poems of *The Woman on the Shore,* one realizes there are not many better poets writing anywhere in English. One of the signs of his ultimate success is that, while his poetic persona was dominant in the work of his middle period, in his later work it is the poet rather than the creator who comes into the reader's vision, the artifact rather than the artificer. In his own way Purdy recognizes this—that the poet and even the poetic persona can die but the poem lives—and so in "Pre-Mortem," the last of the new pieces he includes in the *Collected Poems,* he grants that "a poem can have a soul / just as a man can / the man's soul of course is unknowable, the poem's soul may be known obliquely . . ." In the remarkable last verse he envisages the point of death, when the poet is beyond awareness but the poem survives and continues its own life:

For the dying man
the world's marvelous clichés
fade and revivify
flush into pallor
as the cancer feeds
and like little lambs in springtime
his heart skips apace
A name is spoken in the silence
and then only the soul
hears the name which is the poem's
soul and no writer
listens but the poem listens
in a coldness that obtains
at the fire's centre

Purdy's poems are likely to survive and remain among the classics of Canadian writing. Thus, the *Collected Poems* is not merely a personal document, the commemoration of a life's work, but it is also one of the milestones in the development of a nation's literary traditions.

—George Woodcock

PYBUS, Rodney

Nationality: British. **Born:** Newcastle upon Tyne, 5 June 1938. **Education:** Rossall School, Lancashire, 1951–56; Gonville and Caius College, Cambridge (exhibitioner), 1957–60, B.A. 1960, M.A. 1965. **Family:** Married Ella Johnson in 1961; two sons. **Career:** Teacher, Aiglon College, Switzerland, 1960–61, and Firfield Road Boys School, Newcastle, 1961–62; journalist, Newcastle *Journal,* 1962–64; writer and producer, Tyne Tees Television, Newcastle, 1964–76; tutor in the Adult Education Poetry Workshop, University of Newcastle, 1974–76; lecturer in English and mass communication, Macquarie University, Sydney, 1976–79; literature officer, Northern Arts, Cumbria, 1979–81; tutor, University of Liverpool Department of Extension Studies, 1981–82. Since 1982 full-time writer. Australian editor, 1976–79, deputy-editor, 1991–93, co-editor, 1993–98, and since 1999 associate editor, *Stand Magazine,* Leeds. **Awards:** Alice Hunt Bartlett prize, 1973; Arts Council fellowship, 1982, 1985; National Poetry Competition, Third prize, 1988; Hawthornden fellowship, 1989; Peterloo Poetry Competition prize, 1989; BBC Wildlife Poetry Competition prizewinner, 1997. **Address:** 21 Plough Lane, Sudbury, Suffolk CO10 2AU, England.

PUBLICATIONS

Poetry

In Memoriam Milena. London, Chatto and Windus, 1973.
Bridging Loans and Other Poems. London, Chatto and Windus, 1976.
At the Stone Junction. Newcastle upon Tyne, Northern House, 1978.
The Loveless Letters. London, Chatto and Windus, 1981.
Wall, with others, edited by Noel Connor. Brampton, Cumbria, LYC Press, 1981.
Talitha Cumi, with David Constantine. Newcastle upon Tyne, Bloodaxe, 1983.
Cicadas in Their Summers: New and Selected Poems 1965–1985. Manchester, Carcanet, 1988.
Flying Blues. Manchester, Carcanet, 1994.

Other

Editor, with William Scammell, *Adam's Dream: Poems from Cumbria and Lakeland.* Ambleside, Cumbria Literature, 1981.

*

Manuscript Collection: Literary and Philosophical Library, Newcastle upon Tyne; University of Hull Library.

Critical Studies: ''La Beauté dans l'Oeuvre de Rodney Pybus'' by Alain Suberchicot, in *Cahiers* (Pau, France), 16, 1989; ''Some Poets Now'' by Jon Silkin, in *The Life of Metrical and Free Verse in Twentieth-Century Poetry,* New York, Macmillan, 1997.

Rodney Pybus comments:

Different historical periods and characters have often given me a means of focusing on the present. Through the use of personae I have tried both to make more personal and at the same time to distance my attempts at dramatizing my response to political and moral issues. I take it as a given that the world and the word are inextricable and that poetry in its many languages should never be thought of solely as matters of aesthetic concern.

More recently I have used birds and butterflies as images of nature and emblems of human desires and feelings. And I have experimented in the second part of *Flying Blues* with a new form, a verse novella told in letters, in an attempt to combine some of the energies of an unfolding narrative with an exploration of moral and artistic themes, to reclaim, in other words, some of the ground that poetry has ceded to fiction.

*   *   *

Many of the most successful of Rodney Pybus's poems are those that confront the extremes of contrast between the world of possibilities and the horror man has made of it: ''Strange to think / The same language, the same letters / written by Hitler and Heine.'' This he manages via historical personae, sometimes ancient (Petronius or Procopius), sometimes more recent (Milena Jesenská, the friend of Kafka, or Yevgeny Zamyatin). The parallels between Nero's Rome and Hitler's Germany are telling, and the way of coping with them, enduring them, are similar. The adoption of either a carapace of stoicism or an urbane disdain is nevertheless vulnerable, for sooner or later life's acid will dissolve it or the jackboot smash it. Yet the spirit, manifest in an often oblique dignity, remains untouched: ''I am the conscience that runs out.''

This is not a cry of despair but rather a restatement of human dignity in its refusal to flinch from the truth. The language, too, especially in those poems set in ancient Rome or Constantinople, underlines this. The modern colloquialisms not only bring the situations into relation with the twentieth century but also are an expression of the sardonic intelligence that protects the mind from the horrors it encounters:

> I despair, Caius, I despair!
> Everything is in the hands
> of that trigger-happy
> paranoid lecher—
> except me, thank heaven!

The poems in which the subject is external nature, for example, ''Foxes'' and ''Stoop,'' are sharply observed and often hold the reader by means of startling images, as in ''Greenfinch'':

> Wound-up
> by hunger or habit, it jerks
> its food out in a parody
> of famine—broad bill
> bashing into nuts,
> then filching slivers
> between the strings
> as if they sizzled—
>
> cocking its head
> like that of a tiny
> galvanised parrot.

The violence of ''bashing,'' ''sizzled,'' and ''galvanised'' forces the reader's attention.

But good as they are, these poems have the air of exercises, for others have treated the subjects, and as well, before. It is when Pybus explores the emotional world of the survival of individual values in a situation in which such values have collapsed or achieves an empathy with the exceptional, as in his poem on Samuel Palmer, ''Summer's Lease,'' that he is his own man and writes poems that only he could have written.

—John Cotton

R

RAINE, Craig (Anthony)

Nationality: British. **Born:** Bishop Auckland, County Durham, 3 December 1944. **Education:** Barnard Castle School; Exeter College, Oxford, 1963–68, B.A. in English (honors) 1966, B.Phil, 1968. **Family:** Married Ann Pasternak Slater in 1972; one daughter and three sons. **Career:** Lecturer, Exeter College, 1971–72, 1975–76, Lincoln College, 1974–75, and Christ Church, 1976–79, Oxford. Since 1991 fellow of New College, Oxford University. Books editor, *New Review,* London 1977–78; editor, *Quarto,* London, 1979–80; poetry editor, *New Statesman,* London, 1981, and Faber and Faber, London, 1981–91. **Awards:** Cheltenham Literary Festival prize, 1977, 1978; Prudence Farmer award, 1978, 1980. Cholmondeley award, 1983. **Address:** c/o New College, Oxford University, Oxford OX1 3BN, England.

PUBLICATIONS

Poetry

The Onion, Memory. London, Oxford University Press, 1978.
A Martian Sends a Postcard Home. London, Oxford University Press, 1979.
A Journey to Greece. Oxford, Sycamore Press, 1979.
A Free Translation. Edinburgh, Salamander Press, 1981.
Rich. London, Faber, 1984.
History: The Home Movie. London, Penguin, and New York, Doubleday, 1994.
Clay: Whereabouts Unknown. London and New York, Penguin, 1996.
Collected Poems, 1978–1998. London, Picador, 1999.

Plays

The Electrification of the Soviet Union (libretto), adaptation of a novella by Boris Pasternak, music by Nigel Osborne (produced Glyndbourne, 1987). London, Faber, 1986.
1953: A Version of Racine's Andromaque (broadcast 1990). London, Faber, 1990.

Radio Play: *1953: A Version of Racine's Andromaque,* 1990.

Radio Documentary: *James Joyce: A Touch of the Artist,* 1982.

Other

Haydn and the Valve Trumpet: Literary Essays. London, Faber, 1990.
Editor, *A Choice of Kipling's Prose.* London, Faber, 1987.
Editor, with others, *1985 Anthology.* Beaworthy, Arvon Foundation, 1987.
Editor, *Collected Stories,* by D.H. Lawrence. New York, Knopf, 1994.
Editor, *Lolita,* by Vladimir Vladimirovich Nabokov. London, Penguin, 1995.

Translator (poetry only) with Ann Pasternak Slater, *Boris Pasternak: The Tragic Years 1930–1960,* by Eugeny Pasternak, prose translation by Michael Duncan. London, Collins, 1990.

*

Critical Studies: "The Dialectic of the Image: Notes on the Poetry of Craig Raine and Christopher Reid" by Michael Hulse, in *Malahat Review* (Victoria, British Columbia), 64, February 1983; "Martian Invasion" by Andrew Waterman, in *Helix* (Ivanhoe, Victoria, Australia), 17, 1984; "Craig Raine's Poetry of Perception: Imagery in 'A Martian Sends a Postcard Home'" by Charles Forceville, in *Dutch Quarterly Review of Anglo-American Letters* (Amsterdam), 15(2), 1985; "Telling It Like It's Not: Ted Hughes and Craig Raine" by A.D. Moody, in *Yearbook of English Studies* (London), 17, 1987; Craig Raine issue of *Ploughshares* (Boston), 13(4), 1987; "'But Who Is Speaking?': 'Novelisation' in the Poetry of Craig Raine" by Ian Gregson, in *English* (Leicester, England), 41(170), summer 1992; "Elizabeth Bishop and the 'Martian' Poetry of Craig Raine and Christopher Reid" by David G. Williams, in *English Studies* (Nijmegen, Netherlands), 78(5), September 1997; "Anonymous Deaths: A Reading of Derek Mahon's 'A Refusal to Mourn' and Craig Raine's 'In the Mortuary'" by Violeta Delgado, in *Miscelanea* (Saragossa, Spain), 18, 1997.

*　　*　　*

Craig Raine, who is usually considered the leading light in a group that has come to be known collectively as the Martians, after the title of his second book, is an immensely clever poet. His poems have always been exciting verbal performances, elaborate structures of proliferating metaphors in which an immense web of interrelationships is spun. A butcher "stands / smoking a pencil like Isambard Kingdom Brunel"; a baker "smiles like a modest quattrocento Christ"; and a college quad is "cobbled like a blackberry." A vacuum cleaner is a cow; falling bricks decline a Latin pronoun ("hic, haec, hoc"); houses in North Oxford are troops on parade; a market is a book; a breast is a blister; a marquee is "Gulliver's grimy white shirt"; and, as in the title of one poem, "Two Circuses Equal One Cricket Match." Raine writes poems that contort and gyrate through great acrobatics of perception.

The performance is extremely self-conscious in its desire to revise received opinion about the world. The poem that gave its title to the Martians, "A Martian Sends a Postcard Home," takes this perceptual revision to one extreme when it imagines how the most familiar and domesticated elements of our lives might seem to an alien from outer space:

Rain is when the earth is television.
It has the property of making colours darker.

Model T is a room with the lock inside—
a key is turned to free the world

for movement, so quick there is a film
to watch for anything missed.

But time is tied to the wrist
or kept in a box, ticking with impatience.

In homes, a haunted apparatus sleeps,
that snores when you pick it up.

If the ghost cries, they carry it
to their lips and soothe it to sleep

with sounds. And yet, they wake it up
deliberately, by tickling with a finger.

This is entirely characteristic of Raine in its delighted, self-entranced ingenuity and also in the way it seems to crave a more innocent, cleansed version of the world to be at home in. Some of the poems in this vein perhaps become overingenious and invite a certain element of self-congratulation in the reader who unravels them. It might also be said of some of his work what has been said of John Donne—a poet for whom Raine clearly has the profoundest respect—that once you have mastered it there is little else you can do with it.

It is apparent, however, in Raine's book *Rich* that he is well aware of these possible objections to some of his procedures and that he intends to go on from the more obvious Martian mannerisms into further linguistic inventions and explorations. He writes poems in forms of dialect, in pidgin English, and in "translationese." But this ingenuity, which is delightfully clever and inventive in itself, is now more clearly in the service of apprehensible emotional and moral meanings, and the dandyish element of the earlier work is completely eradicated. In *Rich* he writes a marvelously responsive poetry of childhood, not least in the long and extraordinary prose memoir about his extraordinary father titled "A Silver Plate." He writes superb poems about bereavement, political terror, and the odd universe inhabited by the mentally disordered. In an element always present in his work, but not always so successfully, he also writes a richly tender erotic poetry. In the volume's title poem Raine imagines nature as a bountiful woman who must be wooed by the poet with words. At one point in the poem she is imagined, when in flood, as "transforming the world / like the eye in love." At its best Raine's own vision operates on the world in a similarly erotic way. His delighted, sensuous evocations of ordinary human circumstances have a genuinely transforming reverence and tenderness, as when, for instance, he conjures up the mental world inhabited by his small daughter in a way that sets it in parallel with the remoteness from us of the civilization of the Incas:

How she comes, a serious face
from every corner of the garden,
cupping a secret
she wants me to see,
as if she had somehow

invented the wheel. O Inca.

—Neil Corcoran

RAINE, Kathleen (Jessie)

Nationality: British. **Born:** London, 14 June 1908. **Education:** County High School, Ilford; Girton College, Cambridge, M.A. in natural sciences 1929. **Family:** Married 1) the writer Hugh Sykes Davies (divorced); 2) Charles Madge (marriage dissolved), one daughter and one son. **Career:** Research Fellow, Girton College, Cambridge, 1955–61; Andrew Mellon Lecturer National Gallery of Art, Washington, D.C., 1962. Co-editor, *Temenos,* London, 1981–92; founded the Temenos Academy, 1992. **Awards:** Harriet Monroe memorial prize, 1952, and Oscar Blumenthal prize, 1961 (*Poetry,* Chicago); Arts Council award, 1953; Chapelbrook award; Cholmondeley award, 1970; Smith Literary award, 1972; Foreign Book prize (France), for nonfiction, 1979; Queen's Gold Medal for Poetry, 1993; Swami Vivekanand award of the International Institute of Indian Studies, 1994; D. Litt.: Leicester University, 1974; Durham University, 1979; University of Caen, France, 1987. Fellow, Royal Society of Literature; Officier de l'Ordre des Arts et des Lettres, 1994. **Address:** 47 Paultons Square, London SW3 5DT, England.

PUBLICATIONS

Poetry

Stone and Flower: Poems 1935–43. London, Nicholson and Watson, 1943.
Living in Time. London, Editions Poetry London, 1946.
The Pythoness and Other Poems. London, Hamish Hamilton, 1949; New York, Farrar Straus, 1952.
Selected Poems. New York, Weekend Press, 1952.
The Year One. London, Hamish Hamilton, 1952, New York, Farrar Straus, 1953.
The Collected Poems of Kathleen Raine. London, Hamish Hamilton, 1956; New York, Random House, 1957.
Christmas 1960: An Acrostic. Privately printed, 1960.
The Hollow Hill and Other Poems 1960–1964. London, Hamish Hamilton, 1965.
Six Dreams and Other Poems. London, Enitharmon Press, 1968.
Ninfa Revisited. London, Enitharmon Press, 1968.
Pergamon Poets 4: Kathleen Raine and Vernon Watkins, edited by Evan Owen. Oxford, Pergamon Press, 1968.
A Question of Poetry. Credition, Devon, Gilbertson, 1969.
Penguin Modern Poets 17, with David Gascoyne and W.S. Graham. London, Penguin, 1970.
The Lost Country. Dublin, Dolmen Press, and London, Hamish Hamilton, 1971.
Three Poems Written in Ireland. London, Poem-of-the-Month Club, 1973.
On a Deserted Shore. Dublin, Dolmen Press and London, Hamish Hamilton, 1973.
The Oval Portrait and Other Poems. London, Enitharmon Press-London, Hamish Hamilton, 1977.
Fifteen Short Poems. London, Enitharmon Press, 1978.
The Oracle in the Heart and Other Poems 1975–1978. Dublin, Dolmen Press, and London, Allen and Unwin, 1980.
Collected Poems 1935–1980. London, Allen and Unwin, 1981.
The Presence: Poems 1983–1987. Ipswich, Golgonooza Press, and Rochester, Vermont, Inner Traditions, 1987.

To the Sun. Child Okeford, Words Press, 1988.

Selected Poems. Ipswich, Golgonooza Press, 1988; Rochester, Vermont, Inner Traditions, 1989.

Living with Mystery. Ipswich, Golgonooza Press, 1991.

Other

William Blake. London, Longman, l951; revised edition, 1965, 1969.

Coleridge. London, Longman, 1953.

Poetry in Relation to Traditional Wisdom. London, Guild of Pastoral Psychology, 1958.

Blake and England (lecture). Cambridge, W. Heffer, 1960.

Defending Ancient Springs (essays). London and New York, Oxford University Press, 1967.

The Written Word. London, Enitharmon Press, 1967.

Blake and Tradition. Princeton, New Jersey, Princeton University Press, 1968; London, Routledge, 1969; abridged edition, as *Blake and Antiquity,* 1974.

William Blake. London, Thames and Hudson, 1971.

Faces of Day and Night (autobiography). London, Enitharmon Press, 1972.

Yeats, The Tarot and the Golden Dawn. Dublin, Dolmen Press, 1972; New York, Humanities Press, 1973; revised edition, Dolmen Press, 1976.

Hopkins, Nature, and Human Nature (lecture). London, Hopkins Society, 1972. Autobiography: 1. *Farewell Happy Fields.* London, Hamish Hamilton, 1973; New York, Braziller, 1977. 2. *The Land Unknown.* London, Hamish Hamilton, and New York, Braziller, 1975. 3. *The Lion's Mouth.* London, Hamish Hamilton, 1977; New York, Braziller, 1978.

Death-in-Life and Life-in-Death (lecture). Dublin, Dolmen Press, 1974.

David Jones: Solitary Perfectionist. Ipswich, Golgonooza Press, 1974.

A Place, A State, drawings by Julia Trevelyan. London, Enitharmon Press, 1974.

The Inner Journey of the Poet. Ipswich, Golgonooza Press, 1976.

Berkeley, Blake, and the New Age (lecture). Ipswich, Golgonooza Press, 1977.

David Jones and the Actually Loved and Known. Ipswich, Golgonooza Press, 1978.

From Blake to "A Vision." Dublin, Dolmen Press, 1979.

Blake and the New Age. London, Allen and Unwin, 1979.

Cecil Collins, Painter of Paradise. Ipswich, Golgonooza Press, 1979.

"What Is Man?" Ipswich, Golgonooza Press, 1980.

The Human Face of God: William Blake and the Book of Job. London, Thames and Hudson, 1982.

The Inner Journey of the Poet and Other Papers, edited by Brian Keeble. London, Allen and Unwin, and New York, Braziller, 1982.

Poetry and the Frontiers of Consciousness. London, Guild of Pastoral Psychology, 1985.

Yeats the Initiate: Essays on Certain Themes in the Work of W.B. Yeats. Dublin, Dolmen Press, and London, Allen and Unwin, 1986.

The English Language and the Indian Spirit: Correspondence Between Kathleen Raine and K.D. Sethna. Privately printed, 1986.

India Seen Afar. Green Books, 1990.

City of Imagination: Last Papers on William Blake. Ipswich, Golgonooza Press, 1991.

Autobiographies. Scoob Books, 1991.

W.B. Yeats and the Learning of the Imagination. Ipswich, Golgonooza Press, 1999.

Editor, with Max-Pol Fouchet, *Aspects de Littérature Anglaise, 1918–1945.* Paris, Fontaine, 1947.

Editor, *Letters of Samuel Taylor Coleridge.* London, Grey Walls Press, 1950.

Editor, *Selected Poems and Prose of Coleridge.* London, Penguin, 1957.

Editor, with George Mills Harper, *Thomas Taylor the Platonist: Selected Writings.* Princeton, New Jersey, Princeton University Press, and London, Routledge, 1969.

Editor, *A Choice of Blake's Verse.* London, Faber, 1974.

Editor, *Shelley.* London, Penguin, 1974.

Translator, *Talk of the Devil,* by Dénis de Rougemont. London, Eyre and Spottiswoode, 1945.

Translator, *Existentialism,* by Paul Foulquié. London, Dobson, 1948.

Translator, *Cousin Bette,* by Balzac. London, Hamish Hamilton, 1948.

Translator, *Lost Illusions,* by Balzac. London, Lehmann, 1951.

Translator, with R.M. Nadal, *Life's a Dream by Calderón.* London, Hamish Hamilton, 1968; New York, Theatre Arts, 1969.

*

Manuscript Collections: British Library, London; University of Texas, Austin; University of California, Irvine.

Critical Studies: *Kathleen Raine* by Ralph J. Mills, Jr., Grand Rapids, Michigan, Eerdmans, 1967; Kathleen Raine issue of *Agenda* (London), 31(4); chapter on Kathleen Raine by Christine Jordis, in *Le Paysage de l'Amour et le Roman Anglais,* Paris, Seuil, 1994; "A Note on Kathleen Raine" by Peter Russell, in *North Dakota Quarterly* (Grand Forks, North Dakota), 63(1), winter 1996.

Kathleen Raine comments:

I began as a poet of spontaneous inspirations, drawing greatly on nature and fortified by my more precise biological studies. Though I was born in London, my poetic roots were in wild Northumberland where I lived as a child. Most of my poems have been written in Cumberland or Scotland, some in Italy, Greece, or France, but very few in London, where I at present live.

I have studied the symbolic language of Blake, Shelley, Yeats, Coleridge, and other poets of the romantic tradition who employ that language of analogy inseparable from the perennial philosophy, of which Christianity is our own cultural branch, that regards man as a spiritual and immortal being. Increasingly, in a materialist society, the meaning of words and the symbolic implications of traditional poetry become changed or lost. And this makes it difficult, if not impossible, for a poet of my kind to be anthologized with writers committed to another view of the nature of things. I have much sympathy for the young generation now reacting against materialist culture, but I am too firmly rooted in the civilization of the past to speak their language. *Temenos* is an attempt to reaffirm values that we regard as essential if the arts are to recover from their present decline, which we attribute to the loss of the imaginative vision—the sacred dimension—in an increasingly secular society.

*   *   *

The work of Kathleen Raine presents a difficulty for contemporary critics, not because it is difficult but because of the difficulties they have with an overtly philosophical poetry. After her first three books, Raine does not often "tell it slant." She is no Emily Dickinson, who was perhaps her most profound female predecessor in modern times. Again, Raine's Plotinism, Neoplatonism, and universal religious beliefs, which come through often in her poetry with—as Geoffrey Grigson put it, "the smell of dogma"—do not recommend her to many critics. But it should be added that she is also a victim of the modern critical failure that persists in seeing the poetry in terms of the poet, a critical habit that has proved judgmentally disastrous for the appreciation of the work of many poets.

Raine's first three books, *Stone and Flower, Living in Time,* and *The Pythoness,* often metrically more formal than later ones, represent her increasingly conscious struggle to escape various fashionable influences of the 1920s and 1930s. She was quite blunt about it in the introduction to her *Collected Poems 1935–1980:* "I have found myself only by a process of successive rejections. I had to tear myself free of the influence of Cambridge friends and contemporaries who had adopted the scientific and political attitudes so powerfully propagated in that university, as they were in Oxford." In this tearing free, Raine has paid a number of prices, some personal, some critical. With regard to the latter, it should be noted that, even today, many poets and critics consider her best poetry to be contained in her first three books. But it has to be said that this critic does not share that view, believing her work to have grown in profundity and interest, while agreeing that the early books often show a better craftsmanship and greater concrete immediacy.

Beginning with the aptly titled *The Year One* in 1952, her fourth book, Raine's meters became far freer than before. But unlike, say, Hugh MacDiarmid—who went through a similar sea change—Raine has never really lost her rhythm. There are two reasons for this. The first is that she developed an extremely distinct and, as it were, soulfull voice, a voice, as G.S. Fraser and others have pointed out, of great "purity." And the second reason for her rhythmical maintenance derives from her reading of Milton, Wordsworth, Herrick, Gray, Shelley, Coleridge, and Blake, to mention a number of detectable influences in her *Collected Poems.* It has generally been accepted that the likes of Coleridge, Milton, and Blake have influenced her thinking, her "content," but close reading of the poetry shows that she has quietly borrowed their rhythms too and made them her own. By this process Raine has been able to sustain rhythm in the otherwise amorphous forms of her later poetry. Since her early books she has employed not so much a free verse as a freed verse, one that uses rhyme in a deliberately patchy way, just as her line lengths tend to be irregular. But mostly she finds an energy of joy or grief to power the poetically necessary rhythm.

Despite being a poet of remarkable purity and ethereal imagination, Raine has produced work very close to her experience. And it is not only experience of books. Though she has patently been influenced by a motley crew of metaphysicians and philosophers that include the pre-Socratics, Plato, Plotinus, and Berkeley and, in modern times, Henri Corbin and Carl Jung, there is a strong, underlying lived experience as well.

Somewhere around the time of *The Year One,* after two failed marriages, there came upon her a powerful sense of sin:

This person formed
For sin, by sin?
How could these hands be mine,
Shaped as they are by all the ill I have done . . .

And this, soon enough, made her an adherent of the myth of the Fall. She is no Pelagian. At most there are the desire, increasingly informing her poetry, to return to Eden and the belief that

Man acts amiss, pure only the song
That breaks from the lips of love, or the wordless cry
When grief or pain makes mock of all that is human in us?

Although grief and pain—the note of lament rather than of self-pity—informs many of Raine's poems even into old age and there is never much real serenity, she is at her best with "the song / That breaks from the lips of love." And it was a great and failed love affair, recorded in her autobiography, that gave birth to some of her finest poems, especially "The Marriage of Psyche" with its famous line "He has married me with a ring, a ring of bright water." Increasingly from that poem onward, and maturing in what is perhaps her best collection overall, *The Hollow Hill,* the "pure" voice becomes human and, therefore, more personal, though without ever losing its purity. Excellent poems include "The Wilderness," "Last Things," and "Soliloquies upon Love." Indeed, "Soliloquies" illustrates as well as any poem the features that modern critics find both acceptable and unacceptable in this poet's work. First, acceptable because concrete and immediate, with that touch of scholarship today's savants love:

Young Athenians at a café table gesturing with nimble wrists
Have those full pencilled eyes, those profiles, lacking only
            the beard of Odysseus . . .
Observed in cement-dust; a beggar girl walking like a caryatid
Alone in her misery as banished Electra,
Lingers in her exile at the 'bus terminus for Chalchis.

Then unacceptable because it is "too abstract," "too philosophical":

Love, blind to imperfection, sees only the perfect;
But from how great a distance the inviolate casts its images
Whose gleams upon our waters ignorance plunges after;
To a body a seeming that is not, whose being eludes
            passion's embrace.
No one has possessed beauty: how can we from an
            intellective dream of requited love?

Of course, both are integral parts of a single poem, and doubtless posterity's critics of greater breadth will not have the same hang-ups as those of today. They never do when a poet is safely dead.

At Cambridge Raine studied the natural sciences, and as Fraser observed, she learned "an exactness of natural observation" that often, if fleetingly, shows through in her poems, although it is mostly used only to underscore her philosophical concerns. Nature for her is not just physical placement and phenomena: "Inviolate sanctuaries of the heather and the bees, / The hair's form, the lapwing's nest, the high places of joy.'' For Raine nature is, in fact, the material incarnation of the divine ''in leaves ensphered.''

What I have described as a great failed love affair of Raine's life surfaced as a theme persistently in *The Hollow Hill* and *The Lost Country,* and it culminated in *On a Deserted Shore,* a long series of exquisitely poignant lyric poems. These are the high points of her freed form. They are so economical and intense, despite measurement more by eye than car, as to be lyrics that live on the very edge of a cry. Two lines sum up the philosophy of these poems that finally are about unrequited loving:

All truths are lies
Save love to love in love replies.

The whole sequence constitutes some of the finest and most moving love poetry published in the English language, certainly in modern times. But once again critics have largely passed these poems by in their eagerness to dispose of Raine's views or to dismiss her work as ''romanticism.''

There is neither politics nor social realism about any of her work. As Michael Hulse wrote, ''There is no hope of her noticing the litter of coke cans and cigarette butts in the Western Isles of Scotland'' or anywhere else she sets her poems. Equally, as the same critic has pointed out, she is open to the charge of ''poeticizing inversions'' and ''redeployed, tired symbols.'' But as Hulse finally admits, she ''again and again creates beautiful poetry out of [her] intuitions.'' And can one ask for more?

After *On a Deserted Shore* came *The Oval Portrait*—in which Raine's poems to her deceased mother are as fine specimens of civilized, nonsentimental feeling as one could wish for—and other volumes, with a *Collected Poems* in 1981 and a *Selected Poems* in 1988. Her later work has appeared in the magazines *Agenda* and *Acumen.* Though avowedly poems of old age, there is no diminishment of their obsessive questing, their questioning of existence, or any falling off in energy. Indeed, they bear eloquent witness to that saying of Blake's, who is Raine's most admired mentor, ''energy is eternal delight.'' True, there is much complaint of mortality and old age, but, like all of Raine's work from the beginning, the latest work continues to delight in its own special, enrhythming energy. So that like Yeats, another of her admirations, she remains poetically strong to the last.

—William Oxley

RAKOSI, Carl

Also known as Callman Rawley. **Nationality:** American. **Born:** Berlin, Germany, 6 November 1903; immigrated to the United States in 1910. **Education:** University of Wisconsin, Madison, B.A. 1924, M.A. 1926; University of Pennsylvania, Philadelphia, M.S.W. 1940; University of Chicago; University of Texas, Austin. **Family:** Married Leah Jaffe in 1939; one daughter and one son. **Career:** Instructor, University of Texas, 1928–29; social worker, Cook County Bureau of Public Welfare, Chicago, 1932–33; supervisor, Federal Transient Bureau, New Orleans, 1933–34; field work supervisor, Graduate School of Social Work, Tulane University, New Orleans, 1934–35;

caseworker, Jewish Family Welfare Society, Brooklyn, New York, 1935–40; case supervisor, Jewish Social Service Bureau, St. Louis, 1940–43; assistant director, Jewish Children's Bureau, and Bellefaire, both Cleveland, 1943–45; executive director, Jewish Family and Children's Service, Minneapolis 1945–68; writer-in-residence, Yaddo Colony, 1968–75, University of Wisconsin, 1969–70, and Michigan State University, East Lansing, 1974. In private practice of psychotherapy, Minneapolis, 1958–68. Since 1986 senior editor, *Sagetrieb,* Orono, Maine. **Awards:** National Endowment for the Arts award, 1969, fellowship, 1972, 1979; Fund for Poetry award, 1988; National Poetry Association award, 1988. **Address:** 126 Irving Street, San Francisco, California 94122, U.S.A.

PUBLICATIONS

Poetry

Two Poems. New York, Modern Editions Press, 1933.
Selected Poems. New York, New Directions, 1941.
Amulet. New York, New Directions, 1967.
Ere-VOICE. New York, New Directions, 1971.
Ex Cranium, Night. Los Angeles, Black Sparrow Press, 1975.
My Experiences in Parnassus. Santa Barbara, California, Black Sparrow Press, 1977.
Droles de Journal. West Branch, Iowa, Toothpaste Press, 1981.
History. London, Oasis, 1981.
Spiritus 1. Durham, Pig Press, 1983.
Meditation. Madison, Wisconsin, Woodland Pattern, 1985.
Collected Poems. Orono, Maine, National Poetry Foundation, 1986
Poems, 1923–1941. Los Angeles, Sun and Moon Press, 1995.
The Earth Suite. South Devonshire, England, Etruscan Books, 1997.
The Old Poet's Tale. South Devonshire, England, Etruscan Books, 1999.

Other

Collected Prose. Orono, Maine, National Poetry Foundation, 1984.

*

Manuscript Collections: University of Wisconsin, Madison; Harvard University, Cambridge, Massachusetts.

Critical Studies: ''The Objectivist Poet: Interviews with Oppen, Rakosi, Reznikoff, and Zukofsky,'' in *Contemporary Literature* (Madison, Wisconsin) 10(2), and ''The Poetry of Carl Rakosi,'' in *Iowa Review* (Iowa City), 2(1), both by L.S. Dembo; ''Carl Rakosi's Americana Poems'' (thesis), Milwaukee, University of Wisconsin, 1981, and ''Unexpected Arrangement,'' in *Wisconsin Review* (Oshkosh), 22(1), both by Martin J. Rosenblum; ''The Mindscape of Carl Rakosi'' by Lawrence Fixel, in *American Poetry* (Albuquerque, New Mexico), 10(3); ''Carl Rakosi, A Warm, Steady Presence'' by Andrei Codrescu, in the Baltimore *Sun,* 1 April 1984; *Conviction's Net of Branches,* Carbondale, Southern Illinois University Press, 1985, and ''Heaven and the Modern World,'' in the *New York Times,* 8 March 1987, both by Michael D. Heller; ''An Objectivist Speaks'' by Jack Marshall, in *Poetry Flash* (San Francisco), March 1987; *Carl Rakosi:*

Man and Poet edited by Michael Heller, Orono, Maine, National Poetry Foundation, 1993; "Looking for the Real Carl Rakosi: Collecteds and Selecteds" by Marjorie Perloff, in *Journal of American Studies* (England), 30(2), August 1996; by Gary Pacernick, in *American Poetry Review* (Philadelphia), 26(1), January-February 1997.

Carl Rakosi comments:

I am identified with the objectivists, but it is questionable whether the term has meaning any more.

*   *   *

Carl Rakosi was a member of a group of poets (Louis Zukofsky, Charles Reznikoff, George Oppen) who, in the 1930s, called themselves objectivists. He wrote under his own name, but in order to practice his profession of social work he lived under the name Callman Rawley. His early work, if not political, is a poetry of social and political awareness. In 1941 New Directions published a very slim volume of his work, called *Selected Poems,* in the multipublisher Poet of the Month series. The short, prosy poems bear titles like "Early American Chronicle," "The People," and "To an Anti-Semite."

> *The People*
>
> *O you in whom distrust lies under*
> *   like a gallstone*
> *and desire grows up aching*
>
> *   like a sharp tooth,*
> *courage rises over all*
> *   because it is your heart*
> *and knows no high airs or aloofness.*
>
> *When I was young*
> *and my moods stood between us,*
> *you made me feel lonely.*
>
> *Now I plant myself*
> *in the middle of the street*
> *and swear I shall never leave you,*
> *for you stand between me and my moods.*

By 1975, however, when Black Sparrow Press published a later selection of poems (*Ex Cranium, Night*), there are far more titles like "Nine Natures of Metaphor" and "With Age the Heart" than "The China Policy" or "Nuclear Ode." The later poetry is preoccupied with the subject of the art's place in the world or what it means to be a poet. An example of this is "The Response to Hamlet," which is one of three prose poems that make up "The History of Man":

> The response to Hamlet: Leakey, the British anthropologist, beholding for the first time the skull of Zinjanthropus, 1,500,000 years in his hand.

Most of Rakosi's poems are short and spritely and not at all meditative, though seemingly made up of conclusions about the meaning of the world. In his prose piece "Day Book" he says,

The special characteristic of the very short poem is that the reader has to be hit before he realizes he's been shot. But for this to happen, the author, in the writing of it, also has to be hit before he realizes he's been shot.

As a poet, Rakosi is a sort of gadfly, stinging and buzzing about everything, a reminder that to live intelligently is never to relax or leave unnoticed any slightly foolish thing. He assumes as his role that of the philosopher-poet, commentator on all of life, as, for instance, in "The Weight Lifter":

> When a man's
>   sweat
> is strong
>   enough to repel
> mosquitoes,
>   boy,
> that's character.

—Diane Wakoski

RANDALL, Julia

Nationality: American. **Born:** Baltimore, Maryland, 15 June 1923. **Education:** Bryn Mawr School, Baltimore; Bennington College, Vermont, A.B. 1945; Johns Hopkins University, Baltimore, M.A. 1950. **Career:** Biology laboratory technician, Harvard University, Cambridge, Massachusetts, 1946–48; instructor, Johns Hopkins University, 1949–52, and University of Maryland overseas extension, Paris, 1952–53; library assistant, Goucher College, Towson, Maryland, 1954–56; instructor, Peabody Conservatory, Baltimore, 1956–59; instructor, then assistant professor, Towson State College, Baltimore, 1958–62. Assistant professor, 1962–66, and from 1966 associate professor of English, Hollins College, Virginia. **Awards:** *Sewanee Review* fellowship, 1957; National Endowment for the Arts grant, 1966, 1982; American Academy grant, 1968. **Address:** Rt. 1, Box 64, North Bennington, Vermont 05257, U.S.A.

PUBLICATIONS

Poetry

The Solstice Tree. Baltimore, Contemporary Poetry, 1952.
Mimic August. Baltimore, Contemporary Poetry, 1960.
4 Poems. Hollins College, Virginia, Tinker Press, 1964.
The Puritan Carpenter. Chapel Hill, University of North Carolina Press, 1965.
Adam's Dream. Hollins College, Virginia, Tinker Press, 1966.
Adam's Dream: Poems. New York, Knopf, 1969.
The Farewells. Chicago, Elpenor Press, 1981.
Moving in Memory. Baton Rouge, Louisiana State University Press, 1987.
The Path to Fairview: New & Selected Poems. Baton Rouge and London, Louisiana State University Press, 1992.

*

Critical Studies: "The Double Dream of Julia Randall" by Mary Kinzie, in *Hollins Critic* (Virginia), February 1983; "The Trees Win Every Time (Julia Randall)" by Marilyn Hacker, in *Grand Street* (New York), autumn 1988; by Fred Chappell, in *The Georgia Review* (Athens, Georgia), summer 1993; by John Alexander Allen, in *The Hollins Critic* (Hollins, Virginia), fall 1993; by Lawrence Joseph, in *Kenyon Review* (Gambier, Ohio), winter 1994.

Julia Randall comments:

It seems to me quite beyond the call of duty, modesty, or even common sense to answer questions about one's own verse. Influences? The usual ones for our time: Eliot, Yeats, Rilke, Stevens, Thomas; behind them Hopkins, Wordsworth, Dickinson, the great, ambiguous ghost of Milton, and the lesser ghosts of hymn and ballad makers. Also, very importantly, musicians, painters, naturalists, novelists, philosophers, and prophets. My subjects are drawn about equally from nature, especially the Maryland-Virginia countryside, and from the arts, which is to say about half my poems are literal and half imaginary. They are personal or local, rather than dramatic or topical. My forms are frequently traditional quatrains but tend now toward something larger or looser, with either sustained or irregular use of slant rhyme. I belong to no school that I know of. I try to achieve at least an articulation of the questions that particular experience seems to pose: How do we attach ourselves to or separate ourselves from each other or from time? How do we know? Where or to whom do we most belong? How do we mean? I try to write complete poems, sensible to the eye and ear as well as to the mind.

*   *   *

The poems of Julia Randall are tough and compressed, with a complexity that demands much of the reader. They have hard lines in the traditional sense, taut and metaphysical, but they are also lyrical and musically beautiful, written in a language that sings even as it tightens into knots of fused words and ideas. The poems are highly allusive and are often witty in the fullest sense; the language leaps to imagination, and words contort themselves for the mind's delight. They are highly charged entities in which the arcane and archaic are alloyed with metaphysical passion into an active communion with the colloquial and the immediate. The times of her poems are precise and detailed, often carefully dated, but they open out, forward and back, into thought, memory, and belief, into what can best be termed imaginative mediation—the mind fully at work in the harmonies (and disharmonies) of the present, not analyzing and organizing it but rather experiencing it down to the very bone.

Randall's earliest poems were more self-consciously aesthetic, almost hermetic at times, but even in them she wrote from a commitment to the immediacy of experience, to learning from the inside out. An example can be found in the poem "Inscape I," from her first book, *The Solstice Tree:*

You

that curl the blind hand over the breast,
sing for a sign, sign for a feast,

fasten the blade, explore the vein,
learn the familiar blood.

Following poems were more openly personal, less artificially wrought, while losing none of the compressed intensity of the early work. She addresses the world and her "masters" (Stevens and Rilke, Wordsworth, Lawrence, Woolf, and Yeats); she invokes them, plant and poet, stone and artist, demanding of them and of herself "what we see clear, but clumsily half-tell." What she sees is the world of bone and blood and words, but also the power of being itself, beyond and through them all.

I walked by the stream. The hay was loud
with bugs escaping; they know
what danger is. I too
feared once the many-bladed mower.
Once, but not now.

In her late work, in *Moving in Memory* and in the new poems in *The Path to Fairview: New and Selected Poems,* Randall continues her exploration of the self and its knotty relationships with the world, but she often does so in more open forms, loosening her line without losing the intensity of her lyrical expression. She examines old age and the sure prospect of dying with the same keen, ironic, and often exultant eye with which she has always examined the passionate and painful days of her living. She bemoans with sorrow and with rage a natural world wounded by pollution and callous human indifference, but she honors her craft and the work of predecessors that has shaped her life and world. Perhaps even more importantly, she values friendship that lasts, concluding her collection with these lines from "A Winter Gallery":

Nor camel king nor pastor, I
take messages at home.
Providing friendship abide,
a rod and staff are at my side,
whatever journey I must go,
what crux of craft or character,
whatever kingdom come.

—R.H.W. Dillard

RANDALL, Margaret

Nationality: American. **Born:** New York City, 6 December 1936. **Education:** University of New Mexico, Albuquerque, 1954–55. **Family:** Married 1) Sam Jacobs in 1955 (divorced 1958); 2) Sergio Mondragon in 1962 (marriage dissolved 1967); 3) lived with Robert Cohen, 1968–75; 4) lived with Antonio Castro, 1976–79; 5) married Floyce Alexander in 1984 (divorced), four children; 6) has lived with Barbara Byers since 1986. **Career:** Assistant to director, Spanish Refugee Aid, New York, 1960–61; founder and co-editor, *El Corno Emplumado,* Mexico City, 1962–69; editor, Cuban Book Institute, Havana, 1969–75; self-employed writer and photographer, Havana, 1976–80; publicist, Nicaraguan Ministry of Culture, Managua, 1981–82; staff member, Foreign Press Center, Managua, 1983; adjunct assistant professor, University of New Mexico, 1984–87; visiting professor of English, Trinity College, Hartford, Connecticut, 1987–88, and spring 1990; visiting professor in Latin American studies, Oberlin College, Ohio, 1988; Hubert H. Humphrey Professor of international affairs, Macalester College, St. Paul, Minnesota, spring 1989; visiting professor of women's studies, University of Delaware, Newark, spring 1991; visiting professor, English department, Trinity College, Hartford, Connecticut, spring 1992, spring 1994. Managing editor, *Frontiers: A Journal of Women Studies*, University of New Mexico, 1990–91. Photographer: individual shows—Consejo Mexicano de Fotografia, Mexico City, 1982; Pro Venezuela, Caracas, 1983; Casa Fernando Gordillo, Managua, Nicaragua, 1983; Full Circle Books, Salt of the Earth Books, and Champagne Taste, all Albuquerque, 1983–87; Gallery 44, Toronto, 1984; Presentation House, Vancouver, 1984; Institute for Policy Studies, Washington, D.C., 1984; Woodland Pattern Gallery, Milwaukee, 1985; Trinity College, Hartford, Connecticut, 1986; Everhart Museum (retrospective), Scranton, Pennsylvania, 1988; House Works, Ottawa, 1989; University of New Mexico at Los Alamos Gallery, 1989. Member of board of directors, Inter-Hemispheric Education Research Center, Albuquerque, and Curbstone Press, Willimantic, Connecticut. **Awards:** American Academy grant, 1960; Carnegie Fund grant, 1960; Lillian Hellman-Dashiell Hammett award, for writers who have been victims of political persecution, 1990. **Address:** 50 Cedar Hill Road NE, Albuquerque, New Mexico 87122, U.S.A.

PUBLICATIONS

Poetry

Giant of Tears and Other Poems. New York, Tejon Press, 1959.
Ecstasy Is a Number. New York, Tejon Press, 1961.
Poems of the Glass. Cleveland, Renegade Press, 1964.
Small Sounds from the Bass Fiddle. Albuquerque, New Mexico, Duende Press, 1964.
October. Mexico City, El Corno Emplumado, 1965.
25 Stages of My Spine. New Rochelle, New York, Elizabeth Press, 1967.
Water I Slip Into at Night. Mexico City, El Corno Emplumado, 1967.
Getting Rid of Blue Plastic: Poems Old and New, edited by Pritish Nandy. Calcutta, Dialogue, 1967.
So Many Rooms Has a House But One Roof. Nyack, New York, New Rivers Press, 1968.
Part of the Solution. New York, New Directions, 1972.
Day's Coming! Privately printed, 1973.
With These Hands. Vancouver, New Star, 1974.
All My Used Parts, Shackles, Fuel, Tenderness, and Stars. Kansas City, Missouri, New Letters, 1977.
We. New York, Smyrna Press, 1978.
Carlota. Vancouver, New Star, 1978.
A Poetry of Resistance. Toronto, Participatory Research Group, 1983.
The Coming Home Poems. East Haven, Connecticut, Long River, 1986.
Albuquerque: Coming Back to the USA. Vancouver, New Star, 1986.
This Is about Incest. Ithaca, New York, Firebrand, 1987.
Memory Says Yes. Willimantic, Connecticut, Curbstone Press, 1988.
The Old Cedar Bar, with drawings by E.J. Gold. Nevada City, California, Gateways, 1992.
Dancing with the Doe. Albuquerque, New Mexico, West End Press, 1992.
Hunger's Table: Women, Food & Politics. Watsonville, California, Papier-Mache Press, 1997.

Other

Los Hippies. Mexico City, Siglo XXI, 1968.
Cuban Woman Now. Toronto, Canadian Women's Educational Press, 1974.
La Situación de la Mujer. Lima, Centro de Estudios de Participación Popular, 1974.
Spirit of the People: Vietnamese Women Two Years from the Geneva Accords. Vancouver, New Star, 1975.
Inside the Nicaraguan Revolution: The Story of Doris Tijerino. Vancouver, New Star, 1978.
No se Puede Hacer la Revolución sin Nosotras. Havana, Casa de las Américas, 1978.
El Pueblo no Sólo es Testigo. La Historia de Dominga. Rio Piedras, Puerto Rico, Huracán 1978.
Sueños y Realidades de Guajiricantor. Mexico City, Siglo XXI, 1979. *Women in Cuba: Twenty Years Later.* New York, Smyrna Press, 1981.
Sandino's Daughters: Testimonies of Nicaraguan Women in Struggle. Vancouver, New Star, and London, Zed, 1981; revised edition, New Brunswick, New Jersey, Rutgers University Press, 1995.
Testimonios. San José, Costa Rica, Alforja Centro de Estudios de Participación Popular, 1983; edition in English, Toronto, participatory Research Group, 1985.
Christians in the Nicaraguan Revolution. Vancouver, New Star, 1983.
Risking a Somersault in the Air: Conversations with Nicaraguan Writers. San Francisco, Solidarity, 1984.
Women Brave in the Face of Danger: Photographs of and Writings by Latin and North American Women (photographs). Trumansburg, New York, Crossing Press, 1985.
Nicaragua Libre! (photographs). Boston, Gritare!, 1985.
Photographs by Margaret Randall: Image and Content in Differing Cultural Contexts (exhibition catalogue). Scranton, Pennsylvania, Everhart Museum, 1988.
The Shape of Red: Insider/Outsider Reflections, with Ruth Hubbard. San Francisco, Cleis Press, 1988.
Coming Home: Peace Without Complacency. Albuquerque, West End Press, 1990.
Walking to the Edge: Essays of Resistance. Boston, South End Press, 1991.
Gathering Rage: The Failure of Twentieth Century Revolutions to Develop a Feminist Agenda. New York, Monthly Review Press, 1992.
Sandino's Daughters Revisited. New Brunswick, Rutgers University Press, 1994.
Our Voices, Our Lives: Stories of Women from Central America and the Caribbean. Monroe, Maine, Common Courage Press, 1995.
The Price You Pay: The Hidden Cost of Women's Relationship to Money. New York, Routledge, 1996.

Editor, *Las Mujeres.* Mexico City, Siglo XXI, 1970.
Editor, *Postal Beat.* Madrid, Visor, 1977.
Editor, with Elinor Randall, *Clean Slate: New and Selected Poems.* East Haven, Connecticut, Curbstone Press, 1993.

Translator, *Let's Go!,* by Otto-René Castillo. London, Cape Goliard Press, 1970; Willimantic, Connecticut, Curbstone Press, 1984.

Translator, *This Great People Has Said "Enough!" and Has Begun to Move: Poems from the Struggle in Latin America.* San Francisco, People's Press, 1972.

Translator, *These Living Songs: Fifteen New Cuban Poets.* Fort Collins, Colorado State Review Press, 1978.

Translator, *Breaking the Silences* (Cuban women poets). Vancouver, Pulp Press, 1982.

Translator, *Carlos, Dawn Is No Longer beyond Our Reach,* by Romas Borge. Vancouver, New Star, 1984.

*

Manuscript Collection: New York University Library.

Critical Studies: "The Sense of the Risk in the Coming Together" by Alvin Greenberg, in *Minnesota Review 6* (St. Paul), 2, 1966; *Women of the Mosquito Press: Louise Bryant, Agnes Smedley, and Margaret Randall As Narrative Guerillas* by Carolyn Nizzi Warmbold, Austin, University of Texas, n.d.; *El Corno Emplumado* by Alan Davidson, Salt Lake City, University of Utah, 1992; *Toward a Poetics of Conscience: Contemporary U.S. Women Poets and Their Politics* (dissertation), Bowling Green State University, 1993, and *Writers of Conscience: Meridel LeSueur and Margaret Randall*, Fort Wayne, University of Indiana, 1993, both by Gloria J. Still; "Sexual Trauma/Queer Memory: Incest, Lesbianism, and Therapeutic Culture" by Ann Cvetkovich, in *GLQ* (Langhorne, Pennsylvania), 2(4), 1995.

Margaret Randall comments:

The poem is vital to me as a life experience. In recent years I have become involved as well in photography. That, oral history, and the poem are linked to one another in my expression. Women's creativity is particularly important to me.

*   *   *

The strength of Margaret Randall's poetry comes from its position on the immediate edges of experience—experience fresh and untempered whatever its quality (loving or violent) and brought forth directly as an offering of the poet's own self. She has been consistently a poet whose major concern is to confront whatever happens—however new and however great the risks—and she is prepared to grow, as an artist and a person, from that encounter, always seeking to "create a new language for this, a new place." The dangers of such an approach are great—that the experience will be too raw, too unformulated, to become meaningful or that, particularly in areas of political or social concern, failure to find the new words may cause one to fall back on sloganizing. But as she knows, the values are well worth the risk: giving a sense of the immediacy of the poet living through a significant encounter (with self, dreams, other people, events, new places), discovering herself in the midst of that encounter, and opening up to the reader the potential for a similar discovery.

Thus, for the most part Randall's poems deal with, as she says in "Everyone Comes to a Lighted House," "people moving together" and with her own emergence, as detailed in "Eyes," through such encounters to new vision: "The dream went on but I woke up. / The bus is full my stop's coming up everyone has new eyes." The brief prose pieces included in her 1972 book *Part of the Solution* present in greater detail encounters comparable to those that take place in the poems. They are not actually stories but rather meetings, generally

bizarre and traumatic, in which the poet confronts, or has forced upon her, experiences that call her entire sense of self, society, or relationships into question. Again, as in all of her work—and in the movement of her life as well—what is preeminent is the sense of risk, particularly of risk as potential for the new, for learning and growth, as in "So Many Rooms Has a House but One Roof":

> One side a surface where the hole forms, opens,
> to persist means look through
> or change
> as water runs over the found object.

One changes, Randall indicates, not by becoming something different but by self-discovery, even in the act of writing. The encounters around which her writing centers become the potential for creativity in both her life and her poetry, and the odds she describes Fidel risking in the mountains become as well her own sense of challenge and possibility, as she concludes in "Both Dreams": "in forests we'll conquer because we have to."

—Alvin Greenberg

RAWORTH, Tom

Nationality: Irish. **Born:** Thomas Moore Raworth, South East London, England, 19 July 1938. **Education:** University of Essex, Colchester, Essex, 1967–70, M.A. 1970. **Family:** Married Margaret Valarie in 1959; four sons, one daughter. **Career:** Fiction instructor, Bowling Green State University, Ohio, 1972–73; resident poet, Northeastern Illinois University, Chicago, 1973–74; visiting lecturer, University of Texas, Austin, 1974–75; poet-in-residence and member of the English faculty, King's College, Cambridge University, 1977–78; visiting lecturer and poet-in-residence, University of Cape Town, South Africa, 1991; visiting lecturer, University of California, San Diego, 1996; visiting distinguished writer, Columbia College, Chicago, 1999. Founder, with Barry Hall, Goliard Press, 1965–67; editor and publisher, *outburst,* 1961–63, *Before Your Very Eyes!,* 1964, and *Infolio,* 1986–87. **Awards:** Alice Hunt Bartlett prize, 1969, for *The Relation Ship;* Writers' bursary, Arts Council of Great Britain, 1970, 1977; Cholmondeley award, 1972; Poetry Skipper gold medal for Services to International Poetry, Italy, 1999. **Address:** 99 Norfolk Street, Cambridge CB1 2LD, England.

PUBLICATIONS

Poetry

The Relation Ship. London, Goliard Press, 1966.
Haiku, with John Esam and Anselm Hollo. London, Trigram Press, 1968.
The Big Green Day. London, Trigram Press, 1968.
Lion Lion. London, Trigram Press, 1970.
Moving. London, Cape, and New York, Grossman, 1971.
Tracking. Bowling Green, Ohio, Doones Press, 1972.
Pleasant Butter. Paris and Northampton, Massachusetts, Blue Pig Press, 1972.
Act. London, Trigram Press, 1973.
Back to Nature. London, Joe DiMaggio, 1973.

Cloister. Paris and Northampton, Massachusetts, Blue Pig Press, 1975.

Common Sense. San Francisco, Zephyrus Image, 1976.

The Mask. Berkeley, California, Poltroon Press, 1976.

Sky Tails. Cambridge, Lobby Press, 1978.

Nicht Wahr, Rosie? Berkeley, California, Poltroon Press, 1979.

Lèvre de Poche. Durham, North Carolina, Bull City Press, 1983.

Heavy Light. London, Actual Size Press, 1984.

Tottering State: Selected and New Poems 1963–1984. Berkeley, California, The Figures, 1984; as *Tottering State: Selected Poems, 1963–1987,* London, Paladin Grafton Books, 1988; revised edition, as *Tottering State,* Oakland, California, O Books, 2000.

Lazy Left Hand. London, Actual Size Press, 1986.

Sentenced He Gives a Shape. Tenerife, Spain, Zasterle Press, 1989.

From Eternal Sections. Dublin, Hardpressed Poetry, 1990.

Eternal Sections. Los Angeles, Sun and Moon Press, 1993.

Survival. Cambridge, Equipage Press, 1994.

Silent Rows. N.p., Massachusetts, The Figures, 1995.

Frames. Riva san Vitale, Switzerland, Giona Editions, 1995.

Clean & Well Lit. New York, Roof Books, 1996.

Meadow. Sausalito, California, PostApollo Press, 1998.

Landscaping the Future. Bologna, Italy, Porto dei Santi, 1999.

Other

A Serial Biography. London, Fulcrum Press, 1969.

Betrayal. London, Trigram Press, 1972.

Logbook. Berkeley, California, Poltroon Press, 1977.

Four Door Guide (poetry and prose). Cambridge, Street Editions, 1978.

Visible Shivers (poetry and prose). Oakland, California, O Books, 1987.

Translator, *What Day Is It,* by Liliane Giraudon. Rosendale, New York, Womens' Study Workshop, 1985.

Translator, *Between the Eyelashes,* by Dario Villa. Colchester, England, Active in Airtime Press, 1993.

*

Bibliography: "Tom Raworth—An Exhibition" by K. Nolan and P. Riley, in *Cambridge Conference of Contemporary Poetry 8,* Cambridge, England, 1998.

Manuscript Collections: Special Collection, University of California at San Diego Library, La Jolla, California; Special Collection, University of Connecticut Library, Storrs, Connecticut.

Critical Studies: In *The British Dissonance: Essays on Ten Contemporary Poets* by A. Kingsley Weatherhead, Columbia, University of Missouri Press, 1983; by Kit Robinson, in *Dictionary of Literary Biographies,* Detroit, Gale, 1985; by John Higgins, in *Minnesota Review* (New York), 26, 1986; *The Flight of Syntax: Percy Bysshe Shelley and Tom Raworth,* London, Birkbeck College, 1990, and "Subject & Sentence: The Poetry of Tom Raworth," in *Critical Enquiry* (Chicago), 17(2), winter 1991, both by John Barrell; "Post-Modern Post-Poetry: Tom Raworth's Tottering State" by Peter Brooker, in *Contemporary Poetry Meets Modern Theory,* London, Harvester Press, 1992; "Difficult Poetry: Tom Raworth and the Frame of Postmodernism" by Colette Guldimann, in *Pretexts*

(Capetown, South Africa), 6(2), 1997; ". . . The Endless Deployment of Writing" by Simon Perril, in *Cambridge Conference of Contemporary Poetry 8,* Cambridge, England, 1998.

Tom Raworth comments:

My aim was and continues to be to write what I find interesting to read as, and after, I write it.

*   *   *

In 1989 Tom Raworth commented on the focus of his poetry: "At the back there is always the hope that there are other people . . . other minds, who will recognise something that they thought was to one side or not real. I hope that my poems will show them that it *is* real, that it *does* exist." That his intention has remained constant does not mean that the poetry has not changed.

Raworth was part of the growth of an experimental British poetry during the 1960s and was active as a publisher as well as a poet. His early poems follow the dictum of Charles Olson's projectivism that "ONE PERCEPTION MUST IMMEDIATELY AND DIRECTLY LEAD TO A FURTHER PERCEPTION" without reflection, qualification, or discrimination, although Raworth's effects were often comic and surreal. The presentation of sharp detail and rapid relocation of point of view created indeterminate lyrics and fictions. Throughout the decade improvisatory intuition was pitched against reductive knowledge: "imagine / being / and not / knowing."

In "Stag Skull Mounted," written in 1970, the diaristic serialism leads the perceptions toward their own deletion. The text becomes increasingly minimal until it arrives at the inevitable entry "word," a blank entry, and the entries "poem" and "poem / poem," which satisfy reductive definitions of a poem.

Raworth's own redefinition occurred in a series of long poems ("Ace," "Writing," "Catacoustics," and "West Wind") written between 1972 and 1983. The short lines, often single words, stretch down the page, at times a discrete series of perceptions or found materials, at other times part of a loose paratactic movement of meanings, with abrupt shifts and interruptions, that avoid clear thematic resolution. The analogy with edited strips of film is often made. The meaning of such work is partly the experience of reading it, which can include the experience of hearing Raworth himself. He delivers his poetry at a tremendous speed. It is as if the "film" has to be projected at a certain speed to animate the stills of each line into movement, though it is a movement best intuitively sensed rather than intellectually grasped. As one poem has it,

feeling
speed
of thought
take
it off
make
it firm
lay back
play back
cracked energy

"West Wind" turns the method to more political purposes. Raworth was resident in the United States for much of the 1970s, and the return to Thatcherite Britain ("colourless nation / sucking on grief") is rendered with qualities of anger and compassion as well as with humor.

Oddly, the series of 153 austere poems written between 1986 and 1990 and published in *Visible Shivers* (1987) and *Eternal Sections* (1993) repress these qualities and return to a challenging obliquity. Working against the constraint of fourteen lines, the poems present rearrangements of perceptions, found materials, and narratives, although the expectation of each draws the reader in. They play with this anxiety by being both empty and overdetermined, the effects of both being caused by self-interruption. An implicit utopianism is declared by such a method, since they hold the sequence open as an "eternal" saying and reading, something that cannot be reduced totally to what is said upon the page. Because no poem or line is typical, the works are difficult to quote from, but in the following excerpt the loosely hinged lines hint at the inadequacy of reductive systems of knowledge even while subjecting the expression of this doubt to the method of the sequence, which is fueled by the doubt:

> such division into subjects
> consequences of a failure
> defined by humanist criticism
> must be understood always
> with the same concern in mind
> a different style of beauty
> may appear to be a contradiction

Both of these books were published in the United States, and Raworth has been an influence upon, and has been influenced by, writers associated with the language movement. A second edition of his selected poems, *Tottering State,* was published in Britain in 1988, where it received little official recognition, although it was well received among members of the lively avant-garde, who recognize Raworth as their most important poet. *Clean & Well Lit,* which collects poems from the 1980s and 1990s, shows an extension of the methods developed in the shorter poems, particularly in the significantly entitled sequence "Emptily." A third edition of *Tottering State* was published in 2000, significantly, like the first edition, in the United States.

—Robert Sheppard

RAY, David (Eugene)

Nationality: American. **Born:** Sapulpa, Oklahoma, 20 May 1932. **Education:** University of Chicago, B.A. 1952, M.A. 1957. **Family:** Married 1) Florence (divorced), one daughter; 2) Ruth in 1964 (divorced), one son (deceased 1984) and one stepdaughter; 3) Judy Morrish in 1970, one stepdaughter. **Career:** Member of the faculty, Wright Junior College, Chicago 1957–58, Northern Illinois University, DeKalb, 1958–60, and Cornell University, Ithaca, New York, 1960–64; assistant professor of literature and humanities, Reed College, Portland, Oregon, 1964–66; lecturer in English, University of Iowa, Iowa City, 1969–70; associate professor, Bowling Green State University, Ohio, 1970–71. Professor of English, 1971–95, and since 1995 professor emeritus, University of Missouri, Kansas City. Visiting professor, Syracuse University, New York, 1978–79, University of Rajasthan, India, 1981–82, and University of Otago, Dunedin, New Zealand, 1987. Indo-U.S. fellow, 1981–82. Editor, *Chicago Review,* 1956–57; associate editor, *Epoch,* Ithaca, New York, 1960–64; editor, *New Letters,* Kansas City, Missouri, 1971–85.

Awards: *New Republic* Young Writers award, 1958; Bread Loaf Writers Conference Robert Frost fellowship, 1964; Woursell Foundation and University of Vienna fellowship, 1966; Coordinating Council of Literary Magazines fellowship, 1979; William Carlos Williams award, 1979, 1993; National Endowment for the Arts fellowship, 1983; Sotheby's Arvon prize, 1983; P.E.N. fiction award, 1983, 1984, 1985, 1986, 1987; Maurice English award, 1988; award for poetry, *Nebraska Review,* 1989; national poetry award, Passaic Community College, 1989; first prize for fiction, *Kansas City View,* 1990; first prize award, Stanley Hanks Memorial Contest, St. Louis Poetry Center, 1990, 1991; first prize in fiction and first prize in poetry, H.G. Roberts Foundation award, 1993; Kossuth award, Hungarian Freedom Fighters. **Address:** 2033 East 10th Street, Tucson, Arizona 85719–5925, U.S.A.

PUBLICATIONS

Poetry

X-Rays. Ithaca, New York, Cornell University Press, 1965.
Dragging the Main and Other Poems. Ithaca, New York, Cornell University Press, 1968.
A Hill in Oklahoma. Shawnee Mission, Kansas, Bkmk Press, 1972.
Gathering Firewood: New Poems and Selected. Middletown, Connecticut, Wesleyan University Press, 1974.
Enough of Flying: Poems Inspired by the Ghazals of Ghalib. Calcutta, Writers Workshop, 1977.
The Tramp's Cup. Kirksville, Missouri, Chariton Review Press, 1978.
Five Missouri Poets, with others, edited by Jim Barnes. Kirksville, Missouri, Chariton Review Press, 1979.
The Farm in Calabria and Other Poems, edited by Morty Sklar. Iowa City, Spirit That Moves, 1980.
The Touched Life: Poems Selected and New. Metuchen, New Jersey, Scarecrow Press, 1982.
On Wednesday I Cleaned Out My Wallet. San Francisco, Pancake Press, 1985.
Elysium in the Halls of Hell. Jaipur, India, Nirala, 1986.
Sam's Book. Middletown, Connecticut, Wesleyan University Press, 1987.
The Maharani's New Wall and Other Poems. Middletown, Connecticut, Wesleyan University Press, 1989.
Wool Highways. Kansas City, Missouri, Helicon Nine Editions, 1993.
Kangaroo Paws: Poems Written in Australia. Kirksville, Missouri, Thomas Jefferson University Press, 1994.

Recording: *An Old Nickel and Dime Store,* Watershed, 1978.

Short Stories

The Mulberries of Mingo. Austin, Texas, Cold Mountain Press, 1978.

Other

Editor, *The Chicago Review Anthology.* Chicago, University of Chicago Press, and London, Cambridge University Press, 1959.
Editor, *From the Hungarian Revolution: A Collection of Poems.* Ithaca, New York, Cornell University Press, 1966.

Editor, with Robert Bly, *A Poetry Reading against the Vietnam War.* Madison, Minnesota, American Writers Against the Vietnam War, 1966.

Editor, with Robert M. Farnsworth, *Richard Wright: Impressions and Perspectives.* Ann Arbor, University of Michigan Press, 1973.

Editor, with Gary Gildner, *Since Feeling Is First: An Anthology of New American Poetry.* Kansas City, University of Missouri, 1976.

Editor, with Judy Ray, *New Asian Writing.* Calcutta, Writers Workshop, 1979.

Editor, with Jack Salzman, *The Jack Conroy Reader.* New York, Burt Franklin, 1979.

Editor, *From A to Z: 200 Contemporary American Poets.* Athens, Swallow Press—Ohio University Press, 1981.

Editor, *Collected Poems,* by E.L. Mayo. Athens, Ohio University Press, 1981.

Editor, with Amritjit Singh, *India: An Anthology of Contemporary Writing.* Athens, Ohio University Press, 1983.

Editor, *New Letters Reader 1 and 2.* Athens, Swallow Press—Ohio University Press, 2 vols., 1983–84.

Editor, with Judy Ray, *Fathers: A Collection of Poems.* New York, St. Martin's Press, 1997.

Translator, *Not Far from the River* (from the Prakrit). Jaipur, India, Prakrit Society, 1983; enlarged edition, Port Townsend, Washington, Copper Canyon Press, 1990.

*

Critical Study: By Andy Brumer, in *New York Times Book Review* (New York), 17 January 1988.

David Ray comments:

I like comparisons that have been made of my poems to X rays or to found objects, as my poems are attempts to render verbal equivalents of what happens inside me or in persons or things I have found in the world and that have given me and sometimes them a different context through my finding them.

*   *   *

David Ray's poems are rooted in personal experience—those that have befallen him or persons he knows—and in places: his childhood homes, his hometown, various American cities and countrysides, and foreign shores. At their best, and much of Ray's work is excellent, his poems reveal their maker's deep understanding of the subject at hand while simultaneously offering the reader an elegance of expression. His work is never heavy-handed or fey but always honest, whether he is zeroing in on memories of his childhood or on his sociopolitical concerns. Speaking to his son in "At the Washing of My Son," Ray remembers when he first saw the boy, focusing on a topic most fathers would find difficult, if not impossible, to approach—the Oedipal situation—with such sharpness and candor that one is momentarily awestruck.

Ray displays a lyrical intensity that is enthralling. A boy's terror over growing old is revealed in the second part of "Two Farm Scenes." The wonderful contrast of the "grandfather / Grey in the startling sun" with the "silken curls" of corn tassels, a youthful and sexual image, shows Ray's craft at its most effective. The same thing may also be observed in "The Paseo in Irun" or in "At the Train Station in Pamplona," in which lovers break up. Ray's poems reverberate with detail. Some are of a private, lyrical nature, but other details are decidedly public in nature, evoking a particular time and place.

Many of Ray's poems offer poignant, even brutal views of rural or small town life. The "I" in one of the strongest of these, "Dragging the Main," finally speaks with the girl with whom he is infatuated and whom he has been following "round and round the / City blocks" all night. But urban life does not escape Ray's eye. In poems such as "A Midnight Diner by Edward Hopper" he reveals the loneliness of city dwellers.

Nevertheless, nowhere in Ray's work is the brutality and loneliness of life more evident and more heartfelt than in those poems, published in *Sam's Book,* that deal either overtly or covertly with the untimely death of his son. In "To Sam," for example, the loneliness, the hurt, and the numbness caused by the loss are revealed succinctly, without self-pity but with an open-eyed, almost startling objectivity. In a similar manner his exhaustion over coping with Sam's death is disclosed in "Beads, Pony, Prayer": "Dear Lord let us pray for another day / In which nothing happens, absolutely nothing."

While most of Ray's work is personal, even private, there is a public side to him, a strong social concern that rarely sinks into the pedantic or propagandistic. Whether addressing issues of international importance or those of concern in the United States, his public poetry is as deeply felt and intelligent as his more private work. In "Some Notes on Vietnam," for instance, his bitterness over U.S. involvement in that Asian country is concisely, powerfully stated:

What have they brought to the streets
of Saigon except smog
and for the kids lessons on how to suck?

Yet his social consciousness does not exclude the possibility of, or even the need for, humor in dealing with the social ills of our day. For example, "The Indians near Red Lake," which is told from a Native American's point of view, sometimes uses humor to reveal the absurdity of white chauvinism.

Elysium in the Halls of Hell and *The Maharani's New Wall* are rooted in Ray's experiences in India. The collections are filled with portraits of untouchables, purdah, starvation, and despair, but within such scenes, which are painted objectively, the reader finds glimmers of truth. In "Grapes of Wrath," for example, Ray suggests a parallel between the Okies of the United States and the untouchables of India.

A more muted, but no less heartfelt, political concern is at work in Ray's collections *Wool Highways* and *Kangaroo Paws.* Both books recount Ray's experiences during visits to, respectively, New Zealand and Australia. Relying on his keen observations and finely honed craft, the poems abound with peacocks, kangaroos, the bush, Aborigines, and the didgeridoo and with persons of literary importance who are little known, if at all, elsewhere, the poets James K. Baxter and A.D. Hope, for example. Yet these poems never succumb to the stranger-in-a-strange-land genre. Instead, what is new to Ray becomes in his capable hands uniquely his and, in turn, his reader's.

—Jim Elledge

READING, Peter

Nationality: British. **Born:** Liverpool, 27 July 1946. **Education:** Alsop High School; Liverpool College of Art, B.A. 1967. **Family:** Married Diana Gilbert in 1968; one daughter. **Career:** Schoolteacher in Liverpool, 1967–68; lecturer in art history, Liverpool College of Art, 1968–70; laborer, and worker in animal feed company, Shropshire, 1970–81; writer-in-residence, Sunderland Polytechnic, 1981–83. Since 1983 weighbridge operator at an agricultural food mill, Shropshire. **Awards:** Cholmondeley award, 1978; Dylan Thomas award, 1983; Whitbread award, 1986. Fellow, Royal Society of Literature, 1988. **Address:** 1 Ragleth View, Little Stretton, Shropshire, England.

PUBLICATIONS

Poetry

Water and Waste. Walton-on Thames, Surrey, Outposts, 1970.
For the Municipality's Elderly. London, Secker and Warburg, 1974.
The Prison Cell & Barrel Mystery. London, Secker and Warburg, 1976.
Nothing for Anyone. London, Secker and Warburg, 1981.
Fiction. London, Secker and Warburg, 1979.
Tom o'Bedlam's Beauties. London, Secker and Warburg, 1981.
Diplopic. London, Secker and Warburg, 1983.
5x5x5x5x5, with David Butler. Sunderland, Ceolfrith Press, 1981.
C. London, Secker and Warburg, 1984.
Ukelele Music. London, Secker and Warburg, 1985.
Essential Reading, edited by Alan Jenkins. London, Secker and Warburg, 1986.
Stet. London, Secker and Warburg, 1986.
Final Demands. London, Secker and Warburg, 1988.
Perduta Gente. London, Secker and Warburg, 1989; as *Ukelele Music: Perduta Gente,* Evanston, Illinois, Northwestern University Press, 1994.
Shitheads. London, Squirrelprick, 1989.
3 in 1. London, Chatto and Windus, 1992.
Evagatory. London, Chatto and Windus, 1992.
Last Poems. London, Chatto and Windus, 1994.
Collected Poems. Newcastle upon Tyne, Bloodaxe, 1995; Chester Springs, Pennsylvania, Dufour Editions, 1996.
Work in Regress. Newcastle upon Tyne, Bloodaxe, and Chester Springs, Pennsylvania, Dufour Editions, 1997.

Other

Developing Engaged Readers in School and Home Communities. Mahwah, New Hampshire, Erlbaum Associates, 1996.

*

Critical Studies: By Tom Paulin, in *Grand Street* (Denville, New Jersey), 7(4), summer 1988; "'No-God and Species Decline Stuff': The Poetry of Peter Reading" by Dennis O'Driscoll, in *In Black and Gold: Contiguous Traditions in Post-War British and Irish Poetry,* edited by C.C. Barfoot, Amsterdam, Rodopi, 1994; "Poetic Subjects: Tony Harrison and Peter Reading" by Neil Roberts, in *British Poetry from the 1950s to the 1990s: Politics and Art,* edited by Gary Day and Brian Docherty, London, Macmillan, and New York, St. Martin's Press, 1997.

*   *   *

Peter Reading's third volume begins with an Auden pastiche, and there are further outcroppings, in the primly ludic vein, as late as his sixth, e.g., "Englished." The older poet's example—the deliberately impure diction, the notion of form as a set of ground rules—has certainly set its mark even on Reading's more pungent and characteristic verse. But whereas for Auden form and theme had to come together in his mind before he could write and impurity was ecumenical (disparate vocabularies convene on surprisingly good terms), for Reading the clash is all.

To that end Reading's details are frequently offensive and tendentious. As he often manages to sound both haughtily fastidious and recklessly insensitive, it is small wonder that he has incurred reprobation:

> Muse! Sing the Rasta, who stabbed out a
> baby's eye with a Biro . . .

Despite appearances, this is not gutter press racism but rather a meditation on the old adage that the pen is mightier than the sword, a meditation that swallows its own tail:

> [Squirrelprick Press is producing my
> latest, *Blood Drops in Distich,*
>   hand-deckled limp-covered rag,
>   Special Edition of ten.]

The "uriniferous subway" where the atrocity occurred runs, we are told, "Underneath Blake St." We have not built Jerusalem, and Reading's sword sleeps in his hand. The rowdy diction admits its own complicity.

The close of the early "Chiaroscuro" married wit to formal sensitivity, but Reading increasingly went in for bravura experiments whose expressive raisons d'être were somewhat banal and obvious, as in "Nocturne" or "Trio." The next step, taken in "10x10x10," from *Nothing for Anyone,* was to eliminate the raison d'être:

> One might as well invent any kind of
> structure (ten stanzas each of ten lines each
> of ten syllables might be a good one),
> the subject matter could be anything.

We are in the realm of the put-on. If form and theme are not to be married, at least they might struggle.

But once Reading's books ceased to be mere collections, their plots brought significance to the arbitrary forms. The best is *C,* a poem of one hundred proses, each comprising one hundred words and assembled, we are to believe, by a terminally ill cancer patient. For the reader each section becomes a day in a life whose end is terrifyingly calculable, and the inventiveness within constraints seems in consequence the trace of life itself. The ninety-ninth ends dramatically in midsentence. The hundredth is within parentheses:

(The suicide is untrue. Bodily weakness prevents my moving from the bed. The dismay to my wife and child which suicide would occasion renders such a course untenable. They would interpret my self-destruction as failure on their part to nurse me properly. Conversely, the grief my daily decline causes them is difficult for me to bear. If I could only end the terrible work and unpleasantness I cause them . . . But bodily weakness prevents my moving from the bed. Shit gushes unbidden from the artificial anus on my abdomen. My wife patiently washes my faece-besmirched pyjamas, for *prosaic* love.)

Tears (or Grace) are said to "gush unbidden," and the penultimate sentence does not gainsay this, nor does the third in its choice economy hold aloof.

This tensely lucid prose, in which form and theme are as one, is, however, not typical. Reading's later work skips or flounders in the swampy and uncertain terrain where spoken English leaks into printed language and vice versa. Consider the opening distich of *Ukelele Music:*

They must have been about 17/18, possibly 19:
one, tattooed on his hand MAM; one tattooed on his arm LOVE.

In direct speech newsprint conventions have nonetheless dictated the less audible form for the youths' ages. Contrariwise, the quite inaudible slash midline should, for some readers, mark a caesarea ("In the hexameter rises / the fountain's silvery columns"). Three imperfectly compatible rhythms—of heard speech, of the eye's silent scanning, and of an alien prosody—fight it out in the reader's ear, an internalized Lebanon where capitals might mean emphasis but probably do not.

The reader, thus wrong footed, is to register this cacophony as his own culture's, while seeing, with eerie slow-motion precision, its consequence—a type of event that is usually diagnosed or deprecated from the comfortable distance of a morning paper:

Now the kid started to skrawk; one of our heroes smirked,
      spat,
fondled the empty pint bottle he had in his hand and then
      smashed it
on an adjacent brick wall, held the bits to the child's throat.

I said "Hurt me if you like but don't injure the
      innocent baby—

it can't defend itself, see? Don't do it don't do it *please!*"

He said "If I do the baby, I'll get what I want, so I'll
      cut it."
He shoved the glass in her cheek; twisted the jag-
      ged edge in.

Such writing takes nerve. The writer must not be too quick to show that his heart is in the right place, as he is here with "our heroes," as the sarcasm reassures. But in one sense these lines are easier to read, for the meter, in enforcing both the desperate rhythms of the mother's pleading and the muscular "shoving" and "twisting," temporarily

naturalizes itself. Generally, however, the appeal of Reading's verse to the ear is, though intense, intermittent.

—Hugh Buckingham

REANEY, James (Crerar)

Nationality: Canadian. **Born:** South Easthope, Ontario, 1 September 1926. **Education:** Elmhurst Public School, Easthope Township, Perth County; Central Collegiate Vocational Institute, Stratford, Ontario, 1939–44; University College, Toronto (Epstein award, 1948), B.A. 1948, M.A. 1949, graduate study, 1956–58, Ph.D. in English 1958. **Family:** Married Colleen Thibaudeau in 1951; two sons (one deceased) and one daughter. **Career:** Member of the English Department, University of Manitoba, Winnipeg, 1949–56; professor of English, Middlesex College, University of Western Ontario, London, 1960–92. Founding editor, *Alphabet* magazine, London, 1960–71. Active in theater groups in Winnipeg and London; founder, Listeners Workshop, London, 1966. **Awards:** Governor-General's award for poetry, 1950, 1959, for drama, 1963; President's Medal, University of Western Ontario, 1955, 1958; Massey award, 1960; Chalmers award, 1975, 1976. D.Litt.: Carleton University, Ottawa, 1975. Officer, Order of Canada, 1975. Fellow, Royal Society of Canada, 1978. **Agent:** Dean Cooke, 457A Danforth Avenue, Suite 201, Toronto, Ontario M4K 1P1, Canada. **Address:** Department of English, University of Western Ontario, London, Ontario N6A 3K7, Canada.

PUBLICATIONS

Poetry

The Red Heart. Toronto, McClelland and Stewart, 1949.
A Suit of Nettles. Toronto, Macmillan, 1958.
Twelve Letters to a Small Town. Toronto, Ryerson Press, 1962.
The Dance of Death at London, Ontario. London, Ontario, Alphabet, 1963.
Poems, edited by Germaine Warkentin. Toronto, New Press, 1972.
Selected Shorter [and Longer] Poems, edited by Germaine Warkentin. Erin, Ontario, Press Porcépic, 2 vols., 1975–76.
Imprecations: The Art of Swearing. Windsor, Ontario, Black Moss Press, 1984.
Performance Poems. Goderich, Ontario, Moonstone Press, 1990.

Plays

Night-Blooming Cereus music by John Beckwith (broadcast 1959; produced Toronto, 1960). Included in *The Killdeer and Other Plays,* 1962.
The Killdeer (produced Toronto, 1960; Glasgow, 1965). Included in *The Killdeer and Other Plays,* 1962; revised version (produced Vancouver, 1970), in *Masks of Childhood,* 1972.
One-Man Masque (also director: produced Toronto, 1960). Included in *The Killdeer and Other Plays,* 1962.
The Easter Egg (produced Hamilton, Ontario, 1962). Included in *Masks of Childhood,* 1972.

The Killdeer and Other Plays. Toronto, Macmillan, 1962.

The Sun and the Moon (produced London, Ontario, 1965). Included in *The Killdeer and Other Plays,* 1962.

Names and Nicknames (for children; produced Winnipeg, 1963). Rowayton, Connecticut, New Plays for Children, 1969.

Aladdin and the Magic Lamp, Apple Butter, Little Red Riding Hood (puppet plays; also director: produced London, Ontario, 1965). *Apple Butter* included in *Apple Butter and Other Plays,* 1973.

Let's Make a Carol (for children), music by Alfred Kunz. Waterloo, Ontario, Waterloo Music, 1965.

Ignoramus (for children), produced London, Ontario, 1966). Included in *Apple Butter and Other Plays,* 1973.

Listen to the Wind (also director: produced London, Ontario, 1966). Vancouver, Talonbooks, 1972.

The Canada Tree (produced Morrison Island, Ontario, 1967).

Colours in the Dark (for children; produced Stratford, Ontario, 1967). Vancouver and Toronto, Talonbooks-Macmillan, 1970.

Geography Match (for children; produced London, 1967). Included in *Apple Butter and Other Plays,* 1973.

Three Desks (produced London, Ontario, 1967). Included in *Masks of Childhood,* 1972.

Don't Sell Mr. Aesop (produced London, Ontario, 1968).

Genesis (also director: produced London, Ontario, 1968).

Masque, with Ron Cameron (produced Toronto, 1972). Toronto, Simon and Pierre, 1974.

Masks of Childhood, edited by Brian Parker. Toronto, New Press, 1972.

All the Bees and All the Keys, music by John Beckwith (for children; produced Toronto, 1972). Erin, Ontario, Press Porcépic, 1976.

Apple Butter and Other Plays for Children. Vancouver, Talonbooks, 1973.

The Donnellys: A Trilogy. Erin, Ontario, Press Porcépic, 1983. 1. *Sticks and Stones* (produced Toronto, 1973). Erin, Ontario, Press Porcépic, 1975. 2. *The St. Nicholas Hotel* (produced Toronto, 1974). Erin, Ontario, Press Porcépic, 1976. 3. *Handcuffs* (produced Toronto, 1975). Erin, Ontario, Press Porcépic, 1977. All included in *The Donnellys,* Vancouver, Beach Holme, 2000.

Baldoon, with C.H. Gervais (produced Toronto, 1976). Erin, Ontario, Porcupine's Quill, 1976.

The Dismissal; or, Twisted Beards and Tangled Whiskers (produced Toronto, 1977). Erin, Ontario, Press Porcépic, 1979.

The Death and Execution of Frank Halloway; or, The First Act of John Richardson's Wacousta (produced Timmins, Ontario, 1977). Published in *Jubilee 4* (Wingham, Ontario), 1978; complete version, as *Wacousta!* (produced Toronto, 1978), Erin, Ontario, Press Porcépic, 1979.

At the Big Carwash (puppet play; produced Armstrong, British Columbia, 1979).

King Whistle! (produced Stratford, Ontario, 1979). Published in *Brick 8* (Ilderton, Ontario), Winter 1980.

Antler River (produced London, Ontario, 1980).

Gyroscope (produced Toronto, 1981). Toronto, Playwrights, 1983.

The Shivaree (opera), music by John Beckwith (produced Toronto, 1982).

I the Parade (produced Waterloo, Ontario, 1982).

The Canadian Brothers, from a novel by John Richardson (produced Calgary, 1983). Published in *Major Plays of the Canadian Theatre 1934–1984,* edited by Richard Perkyns, Toronto, Irwin, 1984.

Crazy to Kill (detective opera), music by John Beckwith (produced Guelph, Ontario, 1989).

Serinette (opera), music by Harry Somers (produced Sharon, Ontario, 1990).

Sleigh without Bells (puppet play, produced London, Ontario, 1991).

Lewis Carroll's Alice through the Looking-Glass (produced Erin, Ontario, 1994).

The Donnellys. Vancouver, Beach Holme, 2000. Includes *Sticks and Stones, The St. Nicholas Hotel,* and *Handcuffs.* Originally published in 3 vols.

Radio Plays: *Blooming Cereus,* 1959; *Wednesday's Child,* 1962; *Canada Dash, Canada Dot* (3 parts), music by John Beckwith, 1965–67; *The Story of the Gentle Rain Food Co-Op,* 1998.

Other

The Boy with an "R" in His Hand. Toronto, Macmillan, 1965.

14 Barrels from Sea to Sea. Erin, Ontario, Press Porcépic, 1977.

Take the Big Picture. Erin, Ontario, Porcupine's Quill, 1986.

The Box Social and Other Stories. Erin, Ontario, Porcupine's Quill, 1996.

Father Bought a Tollgate Company (for children). Erin, Ontario, Porcupine's Quill, 1998.

*

Manuscript Collections: University of Toronto; Toronto Public Library; University of Western Ontario.

Critical Studies: *James Reaney* by Alvin A. Lee, New York, Twayne, 1968; *James Reaney* by Ross G. Woodman, Toronto, McClelland and Stewart, 1971; *James Reaney* by J. Stewart Reaney, Agincourt, Ontario, Gage, 1977; *Approaches to the Work of James Reaney* edited by Stan Dragland, Downsview, Ontario, ECW Press, 1983; ''James Reaney and His work'' by Richard Stingle, in *Canadian Writers and Their Works,* edited by Robert Lecker, Jack David, and Ellen Quigley, Toronto, ECW, 1990; in *Biography & Autobiography: Essays on Irish and Canadian History and Literature* by James Noonan, Ottawa, Carleton University Press, 1993; ''Alchemy in Ontario: Reaney's 'Twelve Letters to a Small Town''' by Wanda Campbell, in *Canadian Literature* (Vancouver), 151, winter 1996.

Theatrical Activities: Director: **Plays**—*One-Man Masque,* Toronto, 1960; *Aladdin and the Magic Lamp, Apple Butter,* and *Little Red Riding Hood,* London, Ontario, 1965; *Listen to the Wind,* London, Ontario, 1966; *Genesis,* London, Ontario, 1968. Actor: **Plays**—in *One-Man Masque,* Toronto, 1960.

James Reaney comments:

Stratford Festival asked me to adapt *Alice through the Looking Glass* because other attempts had failed. Adaptors were not poets; I was. My starting out as a poet seems to have something to do with the theatrical and prose activities, as if, under the tutelage of my teacher Northrop Frye, I early realized that I could graduate from lyric poems to epos, poetry for public performance. My pursuit of metaphor with a communal effect has led me to teaching young people and children how to counter the materialism of our society with metaphor; whole schools learned to play chess because of my workshops with them about *Alice* last spring. Since most of my plays are strong on metaphors and choral work backed up by workshops with young people, I have watched my poetry change bodies and minds and characters. In effect, I am after the revival of what used to be called "faith"—the ability to hold an "impossible" thing in your soul and make it transport you to a higher level of consciousness. I admire the White Queen's telling Alice that you have to practice at believing impossible things—"I've believed as many as five before breakfast." I keep trying.

* * *

At the heart of James Reaney's writing is some good old-fashioned message making. This rural Ontario poet who found himself wowed by the critical ideas of Northrop Frye and the poetry of William Blake has always been intent on hammering home his own ideas, many of which revolve around gothic themes, victimization, death, ghosts, and human folly. But in some instances he simply invites the reader to accompany him as he delves into the power and even the curiosities and eccentricities of language and myth.

Such didacticism should not surprise anyone, considering this poet's own recognition that, above all else, he is a teacher. Indeed, after 1949 he made a career as a university teacher, first at the University of Manitoba and later at the University of Western Ontario. A colleague and writer, Stan Dragland, has written that "Reaney is always a teacher, whatever he's doing, whether lecturing, writing essays, poetry or plays, or conducting drama workshops . . . Education is one of his most important themes . . ." Reaney has underlined this in interviews. In one instance he remarked that "teaching is really first."

Hence, one need not look far, for the message is right there, often just in front of the reader and surprisingly obvious. So much so that it is often overlooked, causing one to feel a little foolish in not recognizing it right away. It is not that Reaney's work is complicated or convoluted; rather, it is deceptively simple. The tendency is for critics to reach beyond to grasp something remote. In truth, Reaney's writing is entirely straightforward, accessible, easy. He sees it that way, too, arguing that much of its strength is in its narrative quality. Where readers may stray into confusion is when they come up against the predominance of symbolism and allusion, something that Reaney is the first to acknowledge.

But the symbolism and allusions all serve Reaney's greater intentions. They are part of the whole vehicle, which is to teach, to disseminate a view of the world. In some instances the objective is to turn the imagination upside down, to transform people's ideas of life and language and history. Often it is simply to advance a new consciousness of one's own roots, and Reaney has consistently been an enthusiastic promoter of regional literature. For a brief time after he had shut down his literary magazine *Alphabet,* he put out the occasional literary newsletter called *Halloween,* in which he concentrated on "souwesto" literature, or writing from southwestern Ontario, the region in which he resides. Reaney's thinking has always been that, while the writing may seem limited and provincial, it in fact takes on grander universal proportions. At the same time, however, Reaney is not interested in bogging down the reader in elaborate patterns that make little sense, which is why he turns to storytelling, although not always in the conventional sense. For example, his early book *A Suit of Nettles* is a metrical masterpiece, taking as its model Spenser's *The Shepheardes Calendar,* but it is a poem with voices, allegorical in approach and drawing upon animals for its characters.

Reaney's "Great Lakes Suite" from *The Red Heart,* his first volume, which won top literary honors in Canada, is a marvelous

work that also uses voices. Here, however, the voices are the chain of North American lakes themselves, as they boast to one another,

> I am Lake Superior,
> Cold and gray.
> I have no superior;
> All other lakes
> Haven't got what it takes:
> All are inferior.
> I am Lake Superior.

Reaney's style in this volume and throughout his work is to search for an easy-to-grasp style that tells a story and shows rather than shouts. He himself has written about this, saying, "The simpler art is—the richer it is."

To this end Reaney draws upon the familiar, turning to childhood memories, emotions, and experiences and examining them in more than a sentimental manner. He searches for the universal. Occasionally, too, he polarizes events, sometimes for shock value. In "The School Globe" the poet returns to the memory of an old and faded globe used in his boyhood classroom. Holding the artifact from his youth, he muses,

> Sometimes when I hold this
> Wrecked blue cardboard pumpkin
> I think: here in my hands
> Rest the fair fields and lands
> Of my childhood
> Where still lie or still wander
> Old games, tops and pets;
> A house where I was little
> And afraid to swear
> Because God might hear . . .

But such memories turn sour at the end, as Reaney realizes that the "husk" of the world he clasps is better than the real world. The truth is that childhood was not kind. As he stands in the classroom, he writes,

> if someone in authority
> Were here, I'd say
> Give me this old world back . . .
> And I'll give you in exchange
> The great sad real one
> That's filled
> Not with a child's remembered and pleasant skies
> But with blood, pus, horror, death,
> stepmothers, and lies.

Reaney's concern that poetry take the reader somewhere is evident in the various shifts he has made in his own style. For example, he moved from the highly structured *A Suit of Nettles,* a complex allegorical satire on Canadian life, to the much later emblematic poems, or what some might call "concrete poetry." In these latter works Reaney uses text and pictures to lead his reader closer to the themes he cares about.

But it is wrong to assume that it is only in these experimental pieces that Reaney demonstrates a more ebullient approach. For him the figurative representation takes over for the words, so that what dominates the works is simple iconography. What Reaney offers are "emblems," or unsophisticated hand-drawn pictures, of rings of a felled tree or the image of the "windlady" in a funnel cloud or the plan of a Canadian farm.

The Canadian poet B.P. Nichol described this new consciousness in Reaney's writing as presenting "real objects in the real world." The concern for style and language is approached differently in a small book called *Imprecations: The Art of Swearing.* Here Reaney studies "cursing," describing it as "a lost skill." In it the poet begins with his childhood memories of what constituted swearing. He then turns to the act of trying his own hand at cursing, not so much in stringing together obscenities but rather in finding appropriate targets to lambaste. To the giant grocery chain that plans to build a major shopping plaza across the road from the Temple of the Children of Peace, he writes, "May you swallow a penny and pass a pound." To the minister of education who remarked that "poetry was optional" in schools, Reaney incants,

> . . . when the rebirth vats
> Are wheeled out and you ask for a new body,
> May the Great Partmaker in the Garden of Adonis
> Say as you ask, "What about an eye, got any eyes?"
> "Eyes, Betty, Ears, Betty? Big toes, Betty?
> We don't stock them anymore,
> There's not the demand there once was.
> We've run out.
> They're optional."

In her introduction to Reaney's *Poems,* Germaine Warkentin says that the intention of so much of what the poet does is "to induce in his audience that act of the imagination which will make them reach from one to the other." This is evident as one sees how energetic he has been in moving people to action, both in his workshops and in his classes. It is all part of that authentic desire to teach the world, to make them appreciate its fundamentals, that poetry is or can be alive in everyone.

—Marty Gervais

REDGROVE, Peter (William)

Nationality: British. **Born:** Kingston, Surrey, 2 January 1932. **Education:** Taunton School, Somerset; Queens' College, Cambridge. **Family:** Married 1) Barbara Redgrove (marriage dissolved), two sons (one deceased) and one daughter; 2) Penelope Shuttle, *q.v.,* in 1980, one daughter. **Career:** Scientific journalist and editor, 1954–61; visiting poet, State University of New York, Buffalo, 1961–62; Gregory Fellow in poetry, Leeds University, 1962–65; poet-in-residence, Falmouth School of Art, Cornwall, 1966–83; O'Connor Professor, Colgate University, Hamilton, New York, 1974–75; Leverhulme Emeritus Fellow, 1985–87; writer-at-large, North Cornwall Arts, 1988. **Awards:** Fulbright fellowship, 1961; Arts Council grant, 1969, 1970, 1973, 1975, 1977, 1982; *Guardian* Prize, for fiction, 1973; Prudence Farmer award, 1977; Imperial Tobacco award, for radio play, 1978; Giles Cooper award, for radio play, 1981;

Italia Prize, for radio play, 1982; Cholmondeley award, 1985. Fellow, Royal Society of Literature, 1982; Queen's Gold Medal for poetry, 1997. **Agent:** David Higham Associates, 5–8 Lower John Street, London W1R 4HA, England. **Address:** One Arwyn Place, Falmouth, Cornwall TR11 4BB, England.

PUBLICATIONS

Poetry

The Collector and Other Poems. London, Routledge, 1960.
The Nature of Cold Weather and Other Poems. London, Routledge, 1961.
At the White Monument and Other Poems. London, Routledge, 1963.
The Force and Other Poems. London, Routledge, 1966.
The God-Trap. London, Turret, 1966.
The Old White Man. London, Poet and Printer, 1968.
Penguin Modern Poets II, with D.M. Black and D.M. Thomas. London, Penguin, 1968.
Works in Progress MDMLXVIII. London, Poet and Printer, 1969.
The Mother, the Daughter and the Sighing Bridge. Oxford, Sycamore Press, 1970.
The Shirt, the Skull and the Grape. Frensham, Surrey, Sceptre Press, 1970.
Love's Journeys. Cardiff, Second Aeon, 1971.
The Bedside Clock. Oxford, Sycamore Press, 1971.
Love's Journeys: A Selection. Crediton, Devon, Gilbertson, 1971.
Dr. Faust's Sea-Spiral Spirit and Other Poems. London, Routledge, 1972.
Two Poems. Rushden, Northamptonshire, Sceptre Press, 1972.
The Hermaphrodite Album, with Penelope Shuttle. London, Fuller d'Arch Smith, 1973.
Sons of My Skin: Selected Poems 1954–1974, edited by Marie Peel. London, Routledge, 1975.
Aesculapian Notes. Knotting, Bedfordshire, Sceptre Press, 1975.
Skull Event. Knotting, Bedfordshire, Sceptre Press, 1977.
Ten Poems. London, Words Press, 1977.
The Fortifiers, The Vitrifiers, and the Witches. Knotting, Bedfordshire, Sceptre Press, 1977.
From Every Chink of the Ark and Other New Poems. London, Routledge, 1977.
Happiness. Berkhamsted, Hertfordshire, Priapus, 1978.
The White, Night-Flying Moths Called "Souls." Knotting, Bedfordshire, Sceptre Press, 1978.
The Weddings at Nether Powers and Other New Poems. London, Routledge, 1979.
The First Earthquake (single poem). Knotting, Bedfordshire, Martin Booth, 1980.
The Apple-Broadcast and Other New Poems. London, Routledge, 1981.
The Working of Water. Durham, Taxus Press, 1984.
A Man Named East and Other New Poems. London, Routledge, 1985.
The Mudlark Poems and Grand Buveur. London, Rivelin Grapheme Press, 1986.
In the Hall of the Saurians. London, Secker and Warburg, 1987.
The Moon Disposes: Poems 1954–1987. London, Secker and Warburg, 1987; enlarged edition, as *Poems 1954–1987,* London, Penguin, 1989.

The First Earthquake (collection). London, Secker and Warburg, 1989.
Dressed as for a Tarot Pack. Exeter, Devon, Taxus Press, 1990.
The Laborators. Exeter, Devon, Stride, 1993.
My Father's Trapdoors. London, Cape, 1994.
Abyssophone. Exeter, Devon, Stride, 1995.
Assembling a Ghost. London, Cape, 1996.
Orchard End. Exeter, Devon, Stride, 1997.
Selected Poems. London, Cape, 1999.

Plays

The Sermon: A Prose Poem (broadcast, 1964). London, Poet and Printer, 1966.
Three Pieces for Voices. London, Poet and Printer, 1972.
In the Country of the Skin (broadcast, 1973). Rushden, Northamptonshire, Sceptre Press, 1973.
Miss Carstairs Dressed for Blooding and Other Plays. London, Boyars, 1976.
The God of Glass (broadcast, 1977). London, Routledge, 1979.
The Hypnotist (produced Plymouth, 1978).
Martyr of the Hives (broadcast, 1980). Published in *Best Radio Plays of 1980,* London, Eyre Methuen, 1981.

Radio Plays: *The Nature of Cold Weather,* 1961; *The White Monument,* 1963; *The Sermon,* 1964; *The Anniversary,* 1964; *The Case,* 1965; *Double Bill,* 1965; *In the Country of the Skin,* 1973; *The Holy Sinner,* from a novel by Thomas Mann, 1975; *Dance the Putrefact,* music by Anthony Smith-Masters, 1975; *The God of Glass,* 1977; *Martyr of the Hives,* 1980; *Florent and the Tuxedo Millions,* 1982; *The Sin-Doctor,* 1983; *Dracula in White,* 1984; *The Scientists of the Strange,* 1984; *Time for the Cat-Scene,* 1985; *The Valley of Trelamia,* 1986; *Ashiepaddle, The Three Feathers, The Juniper Tree, The One Who Set Out to Study Fear, The Master Thief,* and *The Flounder,* all from stories by the Grimm Brothers. 1987; *An Inspector Named Horse,* 1997.

Television Plays: *Mr. Waterman,* 1961; *Jack Be Nimble* (*Leap in the Dark* series), 1980.

Novels

In the Country of the Skin. Rushden, Northamptonshire, Sceptre Press, 1972.
The Terrors of Dr. Treviles, with Penelope Shuttle. London, Routledge, 1974.
The Glass Cottage: A Nautical Romance, with Penelope Shuttle. London, Routledge, 1976.
The God of Glass. London, Routledge, 1979.
The Sleep of the Great Hypnotist. London, Routledge, 1979.
The Beekeepers. London, Routledge, 1980.
The Facilitators; or, Mr. Hole-in-the-Day. London, Routledge, 1982.

Short Stories

The One Who Set Out to Study Fear. London, Bloomsbury, 1989.
What the Black Mirror Saw. Exeter, Devon, Stride, 1997.

Other

The Wise Wound: Menstruation and Everywoman, with Penelope Shuttle. London, Gollancz, 1978; as *The Wise Wound: Eve's Curse and Everywoman,* New York, Marek, 1979; revised edition, London, Grafton, 1986.
The Black Goddess and the Sixth Sense. London, Bloomsbury, 1987; as *The Black Goddess and the Unseen Real: Our Unconscious Senses and Their Uncommon Sense,* New York, Grove Press, 1988.
Alchemy for Women: Personal Transformation through Dreams and the Female Cycle, with Penelope Shuttle. N.p., Rider Books, 1995.

Editor, *Poet's Playground 1963.* Leeds, Schools Sports Association, 1963.
Editor, *Universities Poetry 7.* Keele, Universities Poetry Management Committee, 1965.
Editor, with John Fuller and Harold Pinter, *New Poems 1967.* London, Hutchinson, 1968.
Editor, with Jon Silkin, *New Poetry 5.* London, Hutchinson, 1979.
Editor, *Cornwall in Verse.* London, Secker and Warburg, 1982.

*

Manuscript Collections: Humanities Research Center, University of Texas, Austin; Brotherton Library, University of Leeds; Sheffield University Library.

Critical Studies: ''Peter Redgrove'' by Paddy Kitchen, in *Times Educational Supplement* (London), 24 March 1971; ''Peter Redgrove'' by Marie Peel, in *Books and Bookmen* (London), April 1973; ''Ways of Booming'' by Douglas Dunn, in *Encounter* (London), September 1975; interview with Jed Rasula and Mike Erwin, in *Hudson Review* (New York), autumn 1975; ''The Voice of the Green Man'' by Anne Stevenson, in *Times Literary Supplement* (London), 18 November 1977; ''Peter Redgrove Issue'' of *Poetry Review* (London), September 1981; ''Not Mad or Bad'' by George Szirtes, in *Quarto* (London), January-February 1982; ''Summer Cobwebs'' by Peter Bland, in *London Magazine,* February 1982; interview with Michelene Wandor, in *On Gender and Writing,* London, Pandora Press, 1983; ''Scientist of the Strange: An Interview with British Poet Peter Redgrove'' by Philip Fried, in *Manhattan Review,* 3(1), summer 1983; ''The Poetry of Dreams: An Interview with Peter Redgrove'' by Valerie Sinason, in *Changes* (London), 1(4), 1983; ''Interview with Peter Redgrove,'' in *Poetry Review* (London), June 1987, *The Lover, The Dreamer and The World—The Poetry of Peter Redgrove,* Sheffield, Sheffield Academic Press, 1994, and ''Dance of Being: The Poetry of Peter Redgrove,'' in *British Poetry from the 1950s to the 1990s: Politics and Art,* edited by Gary Day and Brian Docherty, London, Macmillan, and New York, St Martin's Press, 1997, all by Neil Roberts; ''Control of the Life-Sources'' by A.S. Byatt, in *Times Literary Supplement* (London), 12–18 August 1988; *Peter Redgrove—A Flood of Poems,* edited by Jeremy Robinson, N.p., Crescent Moon, 1994; ''Singing the Real: The Later Poetry of Peter Redgrove'' by Paul Bentley, in *English* (Leicester, England), 44(179), summer 1995.

*   *   *

"The most ordinary people have the most extraordinary dreams, and in them have a capacity for understanding and adaptation far beyond their waking lives," Peter Redgrove wrote in a review in the *Guardian* (12 April 1979). "Why do we so taboo the dream life when it is so plainly a continuum with the waking creative imagination?"

This continuum has always been a preoccupation of Redgrove's work, and most of his later poetry has had the free associations, the astonishing, surreal proliferation of details, and the magical transformations of plot and image we associate with dreaming. But even in his early poems Redgrove was concerned to explore that tabooed interface where the ordinary domesticated ego feels both appalled and exhilarated by the sweeping energies of an exuberant and amoral instinctual world. The house, invaded by apparently alien forces that turn out to be an essential part of its being, is a frequent symbol of this process. In the fine poem "Old House" the richly kinetic verbs and boisterous syntax record such an invasion with ambiguous enthusiasm. The man, trying to sleep but afraid of it (as in so many of these early poems), seems at first to be threatened by a dark, deathly force, suffocating in the debris of the past. It is not the past, however, but rather the future that terrifies, as the last line of each stanza indicates, speaking of a child not yet born and of the father's dread of bringing it into such a world. Only with the reassurance of the last stanza, which reduces his terror to a "silly agony" as his wife turns in her sleep and calls to him, does he learn "what children were to make a home for."

In poem after poem this theme is repeated, in "Expectant Father" and "Foundation," for example, or in "Bedtime Story for My Son," which turns in the end into a story aimed at reassuring the father as much as the child. The house seems to be haunted by the voice of a small boy. It finally becomes clear that the ghost is not the past but the future pressing into existence. The voice comes "from just underneath both our skins," and the poem concludes, like so many of these early ones, on a carefully prepared note of discovery, educating man and wife into love, procreation, and time, which carries as its obverse a grasping of the supersession latent in all fulfillment. In these early poems it is the tension between domesticity, responsibility, and the worried paternal ego in the hard-earned house and the spawning, heady, but anarchic powers of the instinct that makes for their success. The emotional strain of keeping the spiritual house in order gives the poems a linguistic resolution and vigor and a sense of contained energies. But the strain also breeds those nagging, fretful ghosts that haunt the early works, lurking in corners and unused rooms and in "Corposant" in a moldy larder. In "Ghosts" the realization to which the poem works in its last lines is that the terrace is haunted, after ten years of marriage, not by anything external but by the "bold lovers" themselves with their "hints of wrinkles. / Crows-feet and shadows," haunted, "like many places with rough mirrors now. / By estrangement, if the daylight's strong."

Later poems are more at ease, using a flamboyant and vertiginous whirl of language and imagery to communicate their sense of the vibrant energies of the natural world. "Lazarus and the Sea," in Redgrove's first volume, presages this development, initiating the theme of Orphic descent that is at times to overwhelm his poetry. Lazarus, dredged "back to my old problems and to the family" out of "the tide of my death," is resentful of his savior, feeling uprooted as if by some hostile judgment that charges him "with unfitness for this holy simplicity." An antinomian desire for return to such "holy simplicity" lies behind much of the later poetry. In *The Weddings at Nether Powers,* as the title suggests, the theme is still strong. In "Pleasing the Black Vicar" Redgrove speaks of wanting "to accept / The presence beyond the altar, beyond appearances," a wish that also

lies behind the macabre yet strangely translucent parable of the emperor who wishes to be flayed in "The Son of My Skin" (*Three Pieces for Voices*). A note to *The Weddings at Nether Powers* tells us that "the poems descend, and return with something not thought or felt before." In a sense this is not just a descent into the unconscious of nature, into dream and the lost continent of the carnal body, but it is also a descent into the unconscious language, which has always for Redgrove been corporeal, tangible, fleshly.

In Redgrove's poems we move, as in "The House in the Acorn," through a series of opening and beckoning doors, losing ourselves in a more and more mysterious world where dimension and proportion are lost, a world where, as in "Dr. Faust's Sea-Spiral Spirit," "The roses have learnt to thunder" and "The plain pinafores alert themselves / And are a hive of angry spots," passing though the ritual mysteries of language as we go through the metamorphoses of a nature in which all is flux and entropy, creation and de-creation, decomposition and renewal. In "The Case" Redgrove offers a line that sums up this double process of discovery and return, in which all changes and all remains the same: "It was like a door opening on a door of flowers that opened on flowers that were opening." In "Power" he tells us that "we rose out of magma where power put his finger, / And the lines show." In "The Force" a mill wheel that produces electricity from a mountain beck becomes a symbol of the relation of consciousness to its unconscious sources: "It trembles with stored storms / That pulse across the rim to us, as light."

In *The Apple-Broadcast* electricity and water are again linked. Water is the Heraclitean flux that "makes her way, accustomed, / Into all places." In poem after poem it assumes a multitude of forms, traveling along the food chain and infusing the cells of animal and plant and human being alike in an electrochemical transfer of energies. The "apple broadcast" of the title is revealed in "Dream Kit" by a pun that blooms into literalness. Television and radio sets are "materialising cabinets" in which a reality in flux is made manifest: "The whole / Earth's atmosphere is a pond / Of trembling waves." But television is only an artificial dreaming kit compared with the dreaming mind "that pushes its tumbler / Into the river that flows / Under the skin." From the opening poem of the volume, with its wine glass left out on the patio overflowing with "thunderwater" greedily gulped down by the poet, to the title poem, which closes the volume, the poet is a divine for whom "Water is everywhere, and I think with it, / And remember with it" ("From the Life of a Dowser"), translating its broadcasts into speech acts and poems and his own life. Thus he propagates (again in a double sense) that message inscribed in the DNA of the genetic code, in which, as in "The Eye of Dr. Horus," the child is always the apple of the parent's eye and from whose eye in turn "the next life peers," reminding him of his own supplanting, so that "I can see that I am passing through / And withering as her gaze grows." Yet Redgrove refuses to be thrown by this sense of supersession, delighting rather in its reassurance of renewal.

Poems such as "The Idea of Entropy at Maenporth Beach," in which a girl in a white dress renews herself by a baptismal immersion in "the fat, juicy, incredibly tart muck" of the beach, and studies such as *The Wise Wound,* about menstruation, insist on recovering the rejected, the spurned, and the tacky origins of our being, restoring an image of the human as a living process of ingestion, excretion, sheddings, and growth, like the nature that is all flux and exhalation—wind, water, spore, and, in the title of one poem, "Nothing but Poking." Redgrove pursues this vision with a missionary zeal, even insisting, in the review cited above, "that the Special Theory of

Relativity originated in a wet dream of the young Albert Einstein, in which he was riding through the universe astride a beam of light . . . Whether you think the story beautiful or ugly, possible or not, will depend on your knowledge of the true ways of the imagination.''

—Stan Smith

REED, Ishmael (Scott)

Nationality: American. **Born:** Chattanooga, Tennessee, 22 February 1938. **Education:** Buffalo Technical High School; East High School, Buffalo, graduated 1956; University of Buffalo, 1956–60. **Family:** Married 1) Priscilla Rose in 1960 (separated 1963, divorced 1970), one daughter; 2) Carla Blank-Reed in 1970, one daughter. **Career:** Staff writer, Empire Star Weekly, Buffalo, 1960–62; freelance writer, New York, 1962–67; co-founder, East Village Other, New York, and Advance, Newark, New Jersey, 1965. Teacher, St. Mark's in the Bowery prose workshop, New York, 1966. Since 1971 chair and president, Yardbird Publishing Company, editor, *Yardbird Reader*, 1972–76, since 1973 director, Reed Cannon and Johnson Communications, and since 1981 founder and editor, with Al Young, *Quilt* magazine, all Berkeley, California. Since 1967 Lecturer, University of California, Berkeley. Lecturer, University of Washington, Seattle, 1969–70, State University of New York, Buffalo, 1975, 1979, Sitka Community Association, summer 1982, University of Arkansas, Fayetteville, 1982, Columbia University, New York, 1983, Harvard University, Cambridge, Massachusetts, 1987, and University of California, Santa Barbara, 1988. Visiting professor, fall 1979, and since 1983 associate fellow of Calhoun House, Yale University, New Haven, Connecticut; visiting professor, Dartmouth College, Hanover, New Hampshire, 1980; since 1987 associate fellow, Harvard University Signet Society. Since 1976 president, Before Columbus Foundation. Chair, Berkeley Arts Commission, 1980, 1981. Associate editor, *American Book Review.* **Awards:** National Endowment for the Arts grant, 1974; Rosenthal Foundation award, 1975; Guggenheim fellowship, 1975; American Academy award, 1975; Michaux award, 1978; MacArthur fellow, 1998. **Agent:** Ellis J. Freedman, 415 Madison Avenue, New York, New York 10017, U.S.A. **Address:** c/o Penguin USA, 375 Hudson Street, New York, New York 10014–3658, U.S.A.

PUBLICATIONS

Poetry

Catechism of d neoamerican hoodoo church. London, Paul Breman, 1970.
Conjure: Selected Poems 1963–1970. Amherst, University of Massachusetts Press, 1972.
Chattanooga. New York, Random House, 1973.
A Secretary to the Spirits. New York, NOK, 1978.
New and Collected Poems. New York, Atheneum, 1988.

Novels

The Free-Lance Pallbearers. New York, Doubleday, 1967; London, MacGibbon and Kee, 1968.
Yellow Back Radio Broke-Down. New York, Doubleday, 1969; London, Allison and Busby, 1971.

Mumbo-Jumbo. New York, Doubleday, 1972.
The Last Days of Louisiana Red. New York, Random House, 1974.
Flight to Canada. New York, Random House, 1976.
The Terrible Twos. New York, St. Martin's Press-Marek, 1982; London, Allison and Busby, 1990.
Reckless Eyeballing. New York, St. Martin's Press, 1986.
The Terrible Threes. New York, Atheneum, 1989.
Japanese by Spring. London, Allison and Busby, 1993.

Other

The Rise, Fall and . . . ? of Adam Clayton Powell (as Emmett Coleman), with others. New York, Bee-Line, 1967.
Shrovetide in Old New Orleans (essays). New York, Doubleday, 1978.
God Made Alaska for the Indians. New York, Garland, 1982.
Cab Calloway Stands In for the Moon. Flint, Michigan, Bamberger, 1986.
Ishmael Reed: An Interview. Dallas, Contemporary Research Press, 1990.
Airin' Dirty Laundry. Reading, Massachusetts, Addison-Wesley, 1993.
The Reed Reader. New York, Basic Books, 2000.

Editor, *19 Necromancers from Now.* New York, Doubleday, 1970.
Editor, *Yardbird Reader* (annual). Berkeley, California, Yardbird, 5 vols., 1971–77.
Editor, with Al Young, *Yardbird Lives!* New York, Grove Press, 1978.
Editor, *Calafia: The California Poetry.* Berkeley, California, Yardbird, 1979.
Editor, with Al Young, *Quilt 2–3.* Berkeley, California, Reed and Young's Quilt, 2 vols., 1981–82.
Editor, *Writin' Is Fightin': Thirty-Seven Years of Boxing on Paper.* New York, Atheneum, 1988.
Editor, with Kathryn Trueblood and Shawn Wong, *The Before Columbus Foundation Fiction Anthology: Selections from the American Book Awards, 1980–1990.* New York, Norton, 1992.
Editor, with Richard Nagler, *Oakland Rhapsody: The Secret Soul of an American Downtown.* N.p., North Atlantic Books, 1995.
Editor, *MultiAmerica: Essays on Cultural Wars and Cultural Peace.* New York, Viking, 1997.

*

Bibliography: ''Mapping Out the Gumbo Works: An Ishmael Reed Bibliography'' by Joe Weixlmann, Robert Fikes, Jr., and Ishmael Reed, in *Black American Literature Forum* (Terre Haute, Indiana), spring 1978.

Critical Studies: *Conscientious Sorcerers: The Black Postmodernist Fiction of Leroi Jones, Amiri Baraka, Ishmael Reed, and Samuel R. Delany* by Robert Elliot Fox, New York, Greenwood Press, 1987; *Ishmael Reed and the New Black Aesthetic Critics* by Reginald Martin, New York, Macmillan, 1988; *Ishmael Reed* by Jay Boyer, Boise, Idaho, Boise State University, 1993; *Signifyin(g) Revisions, Pretexts, Subtexts, and Posttexts: Elements of Multiculturalism in Ishmael Reed's Writing* (dissertation) by Pierre Damien Mvuyekure, State University of New York, Buffalo, 1993; Ishmael Reed issue of

Callaloo (Baltimore, Maryland), 17(4), fall 1994; *Ishmael Reed and the Ends of Race* by Patrick McGee, New York, St. Martin's Press, 1997.

Ishmael Reed comments:

Themes—personal, magic, race, politics; no particular verse form.

*   *   *

Ishmael Reed is a satirist who is primarily a novelist, but like many other Afro-American writers he started his literary career writing poetry. *Conjure* is arguably his most important collection of poetry, and although it was not published until 1972, it is made up of renderings dating to 1963, four years before his first novel. In 1962 Reed had joined the Umbra Workshop in New York City, and he tells us that "he began to become acquainted with the techniques of the Afro-American literary style." He also spent tenureships as the editor of two newspapers he cofounded during the mid-1960s, the *East Village Other* and the *Newark Advance.* These experiences and the poignancy of the era helped to shape a political view tempered by a "certain amount of philosophical skepticism." They also shaped his method, what Reed has come to call "boxing on paper," an apt trope for one who evokes criticism from many quarters because he refuses to "pull punches." He notes, "I think it is important to maintain a prolific writing jab." But boxing, as Reed well understands, means making appropriate adjustments for each opponent, finding just the right style to attack an adversary, while realizing that a predictable manner is to court defeat. Thus, Reed's poetry is committed to no style save "The Neo-HooDoo Aesthetic," the title of one of his poems. A passage from "Neo-HooDoo Manifesto" iterates the point beyond the realm of "fightin'":

Neo-HooDoo believes that every man is an artist and every artist a priest. You can bring your own creative ideas to Neo-HooDoo. Charlie "Yardbird (Thoth)" Parker is an example of the Neo-HooDoo artist as an innovator and improvisor.

Many of Reed's poems foreshadow the subjects of his novels and point up the fact that his later preoccupations have been the result of thinking over an extended period of time. For example, in his introduction to *19 Necromancers from Now,* Reed writes that because "black writers have in the past written sonnets, iambic pentameter, ballads, [and] every possible Western gentleman's form," they have sacrificed their own originality. He further says that "sometimes I feel that the condition of the Afro-American writer in this country is so strange that one has to go to the supernatural for an analogy." It is from this feeling that Reed has developed the view that the black artist should function as a "conjuror" who employs Neo-HooDoo as a means of freeing his fellow victims from the psychic attack of their oppressors. Neo-HooDoo has come to represent Reed's notion of an Afro-American aesthetic precisely because he traces its roots to more ancient and non-Western sources.

Reed's poems are not unique in either their intent or their responsibility, but they are pungent examples of the dynamic wit and unabashed approach he demonstrates in his novels. Much of his work is scathing, uncompromising satire, but Reed is always in full control. A typical example of his thematic focus on the incompatibility of Western civilization and the cultures of Africa and Asia is illustrated in this excerpt from "Badman of the Guest Professor"—

its not my fault dat yr tradition
was knocked off wop style & let in
d alley w/pricks in its mouth, i
read abt it in d papers but it was no
        skin off my nose
wasn't me who opened d gates & allowed
d rustlers to slip thru unnoticed. u
ought to do something about yr security or
        mend yr fences partner

—and again in his prosy dictum from "The Ghost of Birmingham," a poem for which he feels impelled to apologize because it "shows the influence of people I studied in college":

There has never been in history another culture as the
Western civilization—a culture which has practiced the
belief
that the physical and social environment of man is subject
to
rational manipulation and that history is subject to the
will and
action of man; whereas central to the traditional cultures
of
the rivals of Western civilization, those of Africa and
Asia, is
a belief that it is environment dominates man.

Reed's works have been criticized by sympathizers from the left, the right, and the middle, from advocates of both black and white views, and from supporters of both sides of the gender issues. As time goes on, however, he is convinced that his ability to spar with all manners of pugilists improves.

—Charles L. James

REED, Jeremy

Nationality: British. **Born:** Jersey, Channel Islands, in 1951. **Education:** University of Essex, Colchester, B.A. (honors). **Awards:** Eric Gregory award, 1982; Somerset Maugham award, 1985. **Address:** c/o Jonathan Cape Ltd., 20 Vauxhall Bridge Road, London SW1V 2SA, England.

PUBLICATIONS

Poetry

Night Attack. Osterley, Middlesex, Open Arteries Press, n.d.
Target. Jersey, Andium Press, 1972.
Vicissitudes. London, Morgue at Zero, 1974.
Agate Paws. Osterley, Middlesex, White Dog Press, 1975.
Diseased Near Deceased. London, Caligula, 1975.
The Priapic Beatitudes: 13 Runic Epiphanies to a Jade Novella.
        Newcastle upon Tyne, Laundering Room Press, 1975.
Emerald Cat. Osterley, Middlesex, White Dog Press, 1975.
Ruby Onocentaur. Hounslow, Middlesex, Guillotine Press, 1975.
Blue Talaria. Osterley, Middlesex, White Dog Press, 1976.
Count Bluebeard. Breakish, Skye, Aquila/Phaeton Press, 1976.

The Isthmus of Samuel Greenberg. London, Trigram Press, 1976.

Jack's in His Corset. London, Many Press, 1978.

Saints and Psychotics: Poems, 1973–1974. London, Enitharmon Press, 1979.

Walk on Through. Peterborough, Spectacular Diseases, 1980.

Bleecker Street. Manchester, Carcanet, 1980.

No Refuge Here. Leaman, 1981.

A Long Shot to Heaven. London, Menard Press, 1982.

A Man Afraid. London, Enitharmon Press, 1982.

The Secret Ones. London, Enitharmon Press, 1983.

By the Fisheries. London, Cape, 1984.

Elegy for Senta. Privately printed, 1985.

Nero. London, Cape, 1985.

Skies. London, Enitharmon Press, 1985.

Border Pass. Privately printed, 1986.

Selected Poems. London, Penguin, 1987.

Engaging Form. London, Cape, 1988.

The Escaped Image. Child Okeford, Dorset, Words, 1988.

Nineties. London, Cape, 1990.

Dicing for Pearls. Petersfield, Hampshire, Enitharmon Press, 1990.

Volcano Smoke at Diamond Beach. Newcastle upon Tyne, Cloud, 1992.

Black Sugar: Trisexual Poems. London, Owen, 1992.

Bitter Blue: Tranquillizers, Creativity, Breakdown. London and Chester Springs, Pennsylvania, Owen, 1995.

Brigitte's Blue Heart. Kidderminster, Crescent Moon, 1997.

Claudia Schiffer's Red Shoes. Kidderminster, Crescent Moon, 1998.

Novels

The Lipstick Boys. London, Enitharmon Press, 1984.

Blue Rock. London, Cape, 1987.

Red Eclipse. London, Cape, 1989.

Inhabiting Shadows. London, Owen, 1989.

Isidore. London, Owen, 1991.

Red-Haired Android. San Francisco, City Lights, 1992.

When the Whip Comes Down: A Novel about de Sade. London, Owen, 1992.

Delirium: An Interpretation of Arthur Rimbaud. San Francisco, City Lights, 1994.

Diamond Nebula: A Novel. London, Owen, 1994.

Chasing Black Rainbows. London, Owen, 1994.

Pop Stars. London, Enitharmon, 1994.

Kicks. London, Creation, 1994.

Sweet Sister Lyric. London, Enitharmon Press, and Chester Springs, Pennsylvania, Dufour Editions, 1996.

Short Stories

Red Hot Lipstick: Erotic Stories. London and Chester Springs, Pennsylvania, Owen, 1996.

Other

Madness: The Price of Poetry. London, Owen, 1989.

Lipstick, Sex, and Poetry: An Autobiography. London, Owen, 1991.

Waiting for the Man. London, Picador, 1994.

The Last Star: A Study of Marc Almond. London and San Francisco, Creation, 1995; revised edition, London, Velvet, 1999.

Heart on My Sleeve. Paris and London, Alyscamps Press, 1996.

Dorian. London and Chester Springs, Pennsylvania, Owen, 1997.

Another Tear Falls: A Study of Scott Walker. London and San Francisco, Creation, 1998.

Sister Midnight. London, Velvet, 1998.

Angels, Divas and Blacklisted Heroes. London, Owen, 1999.

The Last Decadent: A Study of Brian Jones. London, Creation, 1999.

Patron Saint of Eye-Liner. London, Creation, 2000.

Translator, *Novalis Hymns to the Night,* by Georg Phillipp Friedrich von Hardenberg. Petersfield, Hampshire, Enitharmon Press, 1989.

Translator, *The Coastguard's House* (verse), by Eugenio Montale. Newcastle upon Tyne, Bloodaxe, 1990.

*

Critical Study: ''An Introduction to Reed, Lasdun, and Robertson'' by Robert Billings, in *Waves* (Richmond Hill, Ontario), 11(1), fall 1982.

*   *   *

In an era of poetry broadly characterized by understatement, austerity, or the sporadically successful association of subjects and objects normally considered to have little of interest in common, the work of Jeremy Reed is rich, charged, and more traditional in its imagery and concerns. While there is a case for saying that flora and fauna were due for an emancipation, having been for a few generations nervously evaded—as if washed out over the ages—Reed is perceived in some quarters to be an aloof, rarified poet making a bygone music. Again, on the other hand, he is seen by David Gascoyne and others as a lone and true poetic voice, an inheritor, one of the very few to sustain the work of the surrealists and imagists, to retain faith in art as art, and to keep alive an admittedly unfashionable aesthetic. The publisher Cape has advertised him with the following, which is probably fair to say: ''No other contemporary poet arouses such extremes of passion.''

Reed's first major collection was the award-winning *By the Fisheries,* in which he makes abundantly clear that the level of his eye and the richness of his palette are capable of fine discovery, that a unique and individual subject can enumerate and evoke with the objectivity of an especial science. An integrity is created simply by the depth and patience of Reed's observation. Exhaustive, he is rarely exhausting, though a poet who works like this cannot expect always to discover or deliver. This is first-phase Reed at its most enraptured, reminding diction of its resources, reveling in the scent of rare words:

> Before her stretched a plain, and asphodels
> and the mauve crocus were a coloured rain
> entrancing her to stoop, and white umbels
> of hemlock caught the breeze . . .

But it also is a world of dirt and decay, and his eye sees this with a kind of sympathetic detachment. ''Buoys,'' for instance, lie unused in a shipping yard, ''their cyclopean / eyeballs gone rusty from staring / unlidded at the ocean.'' While Reed stares likewise at nature, he is capable of fresh and delighting insight, exemplifying the duty of the poet to keep watching, even marking time, so that a few poems reach a glimpse like this one describing waves: ''and each still adamantly disbelieves / the end of summer, holds to the late sun / like birds in migration, half turning back, / unsure it's not lonelier to go on.'' He is very much a painterlike writer, a poet of studies through which he hones his style in step with the changing world around him. The words he gives the distraught poet in ''John Clare's Journal'' suggest the stylistic loneliness of Reed's chosen path: ''Better to be a botanist, and mark / each seasonal change, and what's peculiar / to one's native region . . ..''

The Clare poem and those written with the voices of ''Christopher Smart in Madness'' and ''The Person from Porlock'' are impressive departures from Reed's nature watch. The Person's encounter with the ''scholar . . . given over to verse and reverie'' is inevitably quite funny, but it is rather chilling too and might not have disgraced that scholar's famously scary ballad, for ''he . . . looked unseeingly right through my head, / as though the page was on the other side.''

The collection *Nero* heralds further departures and intensifications. In a series of violent nature poems such as ''Spider Fire'' and ''Wounded Gull,'' Reed displays growing muscularity and command. This line from the former, though decasyllabic like most of Reed's early lines, is drawn out and up by a strong beat on the word ''shock,'' which is itself just that—''What was the fire's shock through a spider's eye?'' These lines, however, make clear a watchful and joyous craft in sound: ''I watched from the hill's summit; a black hoop / ironed into the shire was a ring of ash / incinerating insects in its char.'' The poem ends with the further (and downplayed) discovery of the surviving spiders, ''too tired to hide.''

Luxuriant sound is inevitably Reed's constant temptress, and his aesthetic can seem not so much archaic or willful as overcooked and indulgent. It is the fruits of his looking hard at the natural world that always succeed best. ''Dead Weasels'' is a better poem than ''The Music of Blue,'' while the voyage through Baudelaire's back pages is not for the fainthearted, its vigor undeniable but its disgust rather forced.

Yet *Nero* also includes some vivid cover versions of Horace and Catullus, clever choices for a poetry so tactile and detailing, that stand Reed in good stead in his title poem, in which the emperor goes crazy with the ''whole deranged, effete imperial zoo / looking on . . . .'' Visions of a toppling, days-numbered civilization strengthen other poems too as ''a transistor / bubbles with its platitudinous tide / of universal misexpenditures.'' In the section ''After Montale'' in his *Selected Poems* the work of the Italian poet provides the canvas for Reed's brush. This is another good choice of master for a poet not so much concerned with conclusions and history as with the texture of the moment, of the line itself.

The poetry-reading public Reed so sharply divides is further split by two later collections, *Engaging Form* and *Nineties,* though wherever one stands, it is possible to admire this poet's restlessness, his unwillingness to stick to the single-track highway. These books mark a growing concern with the wider and contemporary world while stylistically veering into the more surreal. The nuclear threat, AIDS, drugs, and America jostle with Hölderlin, Lorca, Jean Genet, and David Bowie. Reed takes flights and risks here, too soon perhaps into the abstract: ''LOVE AND DEATH. / Are much the same; the fear of one / involves the other.'' One wonders whether fellow worshipers of the aesthetic and the stylized—Bowie, Lou Reed, Ashbery, Egon Schiele—or minor passersby in the palace of excess— voyeurs, transvestites, fetishists—make the best subjects for this kind of poet. It is not easy to outshine orioles or peacocks with words.

Reed remains his own man, however, devoted to his aesthetic in a way that can be seen either as outmoded or as too self-concerned— and certainly at times banal—or on the other hand as original, courageous in its solitude, and a reminder of poetic modes that merely happen to be neglected by the mainstream style of contemporary British poetry. What it must come down to are the best moments, and a poet who finds phrases like ''technology occludes the light,'' ''an airless, thundery panic,'' or a ''green wildfire of regenerative weeds'' and who evinces such a commitment to observation and accurate depiction is certainly an artist whose career repays following, whether or not one believes that at any one time he is finding the right tunes for his chosen instrument.

—Glyn Maxwell

REID, Alastair

Nationality: British. **Born:** Whithorn, Wigtonshire, Scotland, 22 March 1926. **Education:** University of St. Andrews, Scotland, M.A. (honors) 1949. **Military Service:** Royal Navy, 1943–46. **Family:** Has two sons. **Career:** Taught at Sarah Lawrence College, Bronxville, New York, 1950–55; fellow in writing, Columbia University, New York, 1966; visiting professor of Latin American studies, Antioch College, Yellow Springs, Ohio, 1969–70, Oxford University and St. Andrews University, 1972–73, Colorado College, Colorado Springs, 1977, 1978, Yale University, New Haven, Connecticut, 1979, and Dartmouth College, Hanover, New Hampshire, 1979. Since 1959 staff writer and correspondent, New Yorker. Lecturer, Association of American Colleges, 1966, 1969. **Awards:** Guggenheim fellowship, 1957, 1958; Scottish Arts Council award, 1979. D.H.L.: Colorado College, 1986. Lives in New York and the Dominican Republic. **Address:** c/o New Yorker, 4 Times Square, New York, New York 10036, U.S.A.

PUBLICATIONS

Poetry

To Lighten My House. Scarsdale, New York, Morgan and Morgan, 1953.
Oddments Inklings Omens Moments. Boston, Little Brown, 1959; London, Dent, 1961.
Corgi Modern Poets in Focus 3, with others, edited by Dannie Abse. London, Corgi, 1971.
Weathering: Poems and Translations. Edinburgh, Canongate, and New York. Dutton, 1978.

Other (for children)

I Will Tell You of a Town. Boston, Houghton Mifflin, 1956; London, Hutchinson, 1957.
Fairwater. Boston, Houghton Mifflin, 1957.
A Balloon for a Blunderbuss. New York, Harper, 1957.
Allth. Boston, Houghton Mifflin, 1958.
Ounce Dice Trice. Boston, Little Brown, 1958; London, Dent, 1961.
Supposing. Boston, Little Brown, 1960; London, Sidgwick and Jackson, 1973.
To Be Alive!. New York, Macmillan, 1966.
Mother Goose in Spanish, with Anthony Kerrigan. New York, Crowell, 1967.

Uncle Timothy's Traviata. New York, Delacorte Press, 1967.
La Isla Azul. Barcelona, Editorial Lumen, 1973.

Other

Passwords: Places, Poems, Preoccupations. Boston, Little Brown, 1963; London, Weidenfeld and Nicolson, 1965.
Whereabouts: Notes on Being a Foreigner. Berkeley, North Print Press and Edinburgh. Canongate, 1987.
Ariel V. Caliban. Santafe de Bogota, Colombia, Tercer Mundo Editores, 1994.
Alastair Reid Reader. Middlebury, Vermont, University Press of New England, 1994.
Oases: Poems and Prose. Edinburgh, Canongate, 1997.

Editor, with Emir Rodriguez Monegal, *Borges: A Reader.* New York, Dutton, 1981.

Translator, with others, *Ficciones,* by Jorge Luis Borges. New York, Grove Press, and London, Weidenfeld and Nicolson, 1965.
Translator, *We Are Many,* by Pablo Neruda. London, Cape Goliard Press, 1967; New York, Grossman, 1968.
Translator, with Anthony Kerrigan, *Jorge Luis Borges: A Personal Anthology.* New York, Grove Press, 1967; London, Cape, 1968.
Translator, with Ben Belitt, *A New Decade: Poems 1958–67,* by Pablo Neruda. New York, Grove Press, 1969.
Translator, with others, *Selected Poems: A Bilingual Edition,* by Pablo Neruda, edited by Nathaniel Tam. London, Cape, 1970; New York, Delacorte Press, 1972.
Translator, *Extravagaria,* by Pablo Neruda. London, Cape, 1972; New York, Farrar Straus, 1974.
Translator, with others, *Selected Poems,* by Jorge Luis Borges. New York, Delacorte Press, and London, Penguin, 1972.
Translator, *Fully Empowered,* by Pablo Neruda. New York, Farrar Straus, 1975, London, Souvenir Press, 1976.
Translator, *The Gold of the Tigers,* by Jorge Luis Borges. New York, Dutton, 1977; with The Book of Sand, London, Allen Lane, 1979.
Translator, *Don't Ask Me How the Time Goes By: Poems 1964–1968,* by José Emilio Pacheco. New York, Columbia University Press, 1978.
Translator, *Isla Negra: A Notebook,* by Pablo Neruda. New York, Farrar Straus, 1981; London, Souvenir Press, 1982.
Translator, with Andrew Hurley, *Legacies: Selected Poems,* by Heberto Padilla. New York, Farrar Straus, 1982.
Translator, *Pablo Neruda: Absence and Presence,* by Luis Poirot. New York, Norton, 1990.
Translator, with Alexander Coleman, *A Fountin, A House of Stone,* by Heberto Padilla. New York, Farrar, Straus, and Giroux, 1992.
Translator, *Amador,* by Fernando Savater. New York, Holt, 1994.
Translator, with others, *Selected Poems: Jorge Luis Borges.* New York, Viking/Penguin, 1999.

*

Manuscript Collections: State University of New York, Buffalo; National Library of Scotland, Edinburgh.

Critical Studies: "Glanville-Hicks' Nausicaa, Graves, and Reid" by Deborah Hayes, in *Focus on Robert Graves and His Contemporaries*

(Heidelberg, Germany), 1(2), May 1989; "Overdoing the Generosity" by Charles Tomlinson, in *Times Literary Supplement* (London), 4173, 25 March 1983.

*   *   *

Although *Weathering,* the 1978 collection of Alastair Reid's poems, includes a generous selection from his previous books, it also shifts the focus so that his distinctive contribution to literature becomes more evident. By contrast, in the earlier *Oddments Inklings Omens Moments* (1959) a playful interest in words themselves and in such subject matter as mirrors, magic, ghosts, cats, frogs, children, and games gives such immediate pleasure that his deeper, underlying human concerns might be overlooked. But the concern is present in the earlier poems. In "Cat-Faith," for example, Reid's gratitude for the existence of a creature secure in its individuality, beautifully adapted for survival in a hazardous life, is at bottom a confirmation of an ultimate virtue in life itself. His valuation finds explicit expression in "Amazement is the thing. / Not love, but the astonishment of loving." This affirmation is made in the recognition and acceptance for the law that "the garden is not ours." In "Mediterranean" we are tenants:

> The rent is paid in breath
> and so we freely give
> the apple tree beneath
> our unpossessive love.

It is the writer's "unpossessive love" that allows him to accept the variety of life as it presents itself, and it is his fascination with words that gives his poems their rare music, as in "The Rain in Spain": "Faces press to windows. / Strangers moon and booze. / Innkeepers doze." The poet's technique draws the ordinary scene intimately and delicately, as in "Me to You": "Tell me about the snowfalls / at night, and tell me how we'd sit in firelight / hearing dogs huff in sleep."

Affection, and generally tenderness, is written into the individual thing observed so that we are made aware of its transient nature, but unlike the more characteristic contemporary poet there is no sense of threat to identity. Consequently, there is an absence of tension or drama in the verse. If this is a limitation, one should not conclude that Reid's poetry, just in its observation and openness to impression, has been easily achieved. The later poetry shows reasons for his confidence and sense of wholeness. In "The Spiral" he writes,

> the rooted self in me
> maps out its true country.
> And, as my father found
> his own small weathered island,
> so will I come to ground

—George Bruce

REID, Christopher (John)

Nationality: British. **Born:** Hong Kong, 13 May 1949. **Education:** Kingswood House, Epsom, Surrey, 1956–62; Tonbridge School, Kent, 1962–67; Exeter College, Oxford, 1968–71, B.A. (honors),

1971. **Family:** Married Lucinda Catherine Gane in 1979. **Career:** Formerly librarian, Ashmolean Classics Library, Oxford; has also worked as an actor, filing clerk, theater flyman, and nanny/tutor. Editor, ''News and Reviews'' section of *Crafts* magazine, Crafts Council, London, 1979–81. Since 1986 publisher, and since 1991 poetry editor, Faber and Faber, London. **Awards:** Eric Gregory award, 1978; Prudence Farmer award, 1978, 1980; Somerset Maugham award, 1980; Hawthornden prize, 1981. **Address:** c/o Faber and Faber, 3 Queen Square, London WC1N 3AU, England.

PUBLICATIONS

Poetry

Arcadia. London and New York, Oxford University Press, 1979.
Pea Soup. Oxford and New York, Oxford University Press, 1982.
Katerina Brac. London, Faber, 1985.
In the Echoey Tunnel. London and Boston, Faber, 1991.
Universes. London, Ondt & Gracehopper, 1994.
Expanded Universes. London and Boston, Faber, 1996.

Other

Editor, *The Poetry Book Society Anthology 1989–1990.* London, Hutchinson, 1990.

*

Critical Studies: ''The Dialectic of the Image: Notes on the Poetry of Craig Raine and Christopher Reid,'' in *Malahat Review* (Victoria, British Columbia), 64, February 1983, and ''Craig Raine & Co.: Martians and Story-Tellers,'' in *Antigonish Review* (Antigonish, Nova Scotia), 59, autumn 1984, both by Michael Hulse; ''Martian Invasion'' by Andrew Waterman, in *Helix* (Ivanhoe, Victoria, Australia), 17, 1984; ''Elizabeth Bishop and the 'Martian' Poetry of Craig Raine and Christopher Reid'' by David G. Williams, in *English Studies* (Nijmegen, Netherlands), 78(5), September 1997.

* * *

Christopher Reid is frequently associated with Craig Raine as one of the so-called Martian school of poets, whose work is characterized above all by an extravagant or exuberant use of visual simile and metaphor in an attempt to make the familiar (frequently the domestic) seem, in fact, the theater of the richly exotic and strange. ''Douanier Rousseau had no need to travel / to paint the jungles of his paradise,'' Reid says in one of his poems, and, referring often in his work to a wide variety of painters (notably Vuillard, Vermeer, Brueghel, and Matisse), he shares with Rousseau a certain intense sharpness and immediacy of childlike vision:

Welcome to our peaceable kingdom,
where baby lies down with the tiger-rug

and bumblebees roll over like puppies
inside foxglove-bells . . .

Like some of the other writers loosely associated with the Martians, Reid can occasionally seem to produce poems that are little more than collections of special effects. I particularly like the tankards in a London pub that, ''pot-bellied, on hooks, / are lords of the air and as free / as a flight of sitting-room ducks,'' where the joke of the rhyme is in affectionately sympathetic consonance with the deflating hyperbole of the simile. I like, too, the amazing conceits of ''Baldanders,'' where a series of similes for a weight lifter culminates in this way:

Glazed, like a mantelpiece frog,
he strains to become

the World Champion (somebody, answer it!)
Human Telephone.

But Reid has larger and more profound preoccupations in his work than the mere elaboration of such visual interrelationships, his ''playground of impromptu metaphors,'' beguiling as this often is. The delighted apprehensions of his work are given their particular edge by an insistent pressure, from just outside, of everything that is not delight. What he calls ''art's oddness and justness'' is a different kind of ritual to cope with, above all, the pressure of mortality now that the consolations of religion are no longer operable.

Many of Reid's poems do actually elaborate some kind of religious imagery, making, as it were, newly domestic sacraments out of the secular, and others, like the excellent ''Magnum Opus'' and ''Charnel,'' consider, quite a way after Larkin's ''Church Going,'' the emptied meanings of a Christian cathedral and graveyard. Similarly, when visiting Japan, Reid is drawn to the traditional stamping grounds of the sacred in ''a world / lacking all reciprocity.'' The conclusion of one of these poems, ''Itsukushima,'' addresses a highly secular prayer to very secular objects but suggests, nevertheless, the impulse everywhere apparent in Reid to coax some kind of benediction out of the necessary and contingent circumstances of ordinary life: ''Green seaweed wraiths, a beer-can, drunk, / are tugged by the tide . . . You Nothings, bless / me in my next-to-nothingness!'' Reid's delight is never light-headed; it knows the nothingness it has to work hard not to be. Like his own eponymous ''Ambassador,'' visiting a planet inhabited by children's toys, Reid too no doubt adheres

to the maxim, that through a studious
reading of chaos we may
arrive at the grammar of civilisation.

—Neil Corcoran

REVELL, Donald (George)

Nationality: American. **Born:** New York City, 12 June 1954. **Education:** Harpur College, Binghamton, New York, 1971–75, B.A. in English 1975; State University of New York, Binghamton, 1977–77, M.A. in English 1977; State University of New York, Buffalo, 1977–80, Ph.D.in English 1980. **Family:** Married 1) Astrid A. Revell in 1985 (divorced 1990), one daughter; 2) Claudia Keelan in 1992, one son. **Career:** Instructor, University of Tennessee, Knoxville,

1980–82; assistant professor, Ripon College, Wisconsin, 1982–85; assistant professor, 1985–88, associate professor, 1988–93, and professor, 1993–94, University of Denver, Colorado. Since 1994 professor, University of Utah, Salt Lake City. **Awards:** National Endowment for the Arts fellowship, 1988, 1995; Ingram Merrill fellowship, 1990; PEN Center USA West medal in poetry, 1990; Guggenheim fellowship, 1992. **Address:** 7335 West Agate Avenue, Las Vegas, Nevada 89113, U.S.A.

PUBLICATIONS

Poetry

From the Abandoned Cities. New York, Harper and Row, 1983.
The Gaza of Winter. Athens, University of Georgia Press, 1988.
New Dark Ages. Hanover, New Hampshire, Wesleyan/University Press of New England, 1990.
Erasures. Hanover, New Hampshire, Wesleyan/University Press of New England, 1992.
Beautiful Shirt. Hanover, New Hampshire, Wesleyan/University Press of New England, 1994.
There Are Three. Hanover, New Hampshire, Wesleyan/University Press of New England, 1998.

Other

Translator, *Alcools,* by Guillaume Apollinaire. Hanover, New Hampshire, Wesleyan/University Press of New England, 1995.

*

Critical Studies: "The Borders of Astonishment" by David Young, in *Field,* 48, spring 1993; interview with Tod Marshall, in *American Poetry Review* (Philadelphia), 25(4), July-August 1996.

*   *   *

Donald Revell is one of America's most important contemporary poets. His work draws from a variety of traditions, including French surrealism, poststructuralist theory, musical form, and late twentieth-century political realities. Perhaps Revell's most fervent attraction is to the mystical and antinomian tradition embodied in the religiosity of Anne Hutchinson, the poetry of the likes of William Blake, and the philosophical inquiry of Wittgenstein. In a 1996 interview published in the *American Poetry Review* Revell said, "As I get older I become more and more of an antinomian. I distrust any name. I think it's the project of poetry, the project of writing, the project of reading, the project of doing almost anything to unname things."

Revell's first book, *From the Abandoned Cities,* was selected by C.K. Williams for the National Poetry series. Using a variety of formal structures, the book reveals deft control as well as a unified vision. The poems render a variety of emotional states and are frequently elegiac in measured and compelling lines. For instance, consider these lines from "Odile":

Later that night, I thought of her, and of
the bells she wore. A swan in death, she fell
into the music I had wanted love

to be, and ended there. I cannot tell
you much of her beyond that dying. It
was absolute. My lamp had been a bare
intelligence until she died, a fit
of pointless energy at which to stare
and be annihilated like a bug
in summer . . .

The rhythm is clean and the language clear. In *The Gaza of Winter* many of the poems seem to wrestle with the premises of Revell's first volume. To put it another way, if personal pain is often the grid upon which the metrics of *From the Abandoned Cities* find their beats, then *The Gaza of Winter* articulates the speaker's realization that such pain is not unique. Terrible things happen to everybody; few personal tragedies are original. The last poem in the book is perhaps a coda in that regard. "The Raft of the Medusa," based on the painting by Gericault of shipwrecked survivors who resort to cannibalism, offers these lines: "A long time / before anyone is shipwrecked, he has chosen / part of a novel or some green window / never to die, never to let him die."

Revell's next book, *New Dark Ages,* further explores the realization that "subject matter is not what poetry is made of." Once one moves beyond the particularity of one's own tragedies, the affairs of the polis, of those outside the self, are real. The book articulates several significant ideas, perhaps most importantly that the private and public are the same and that lying in either realm brings about awfulness. Revell understood the mid-1980s as a time of incredible opportunity, as a chance to move beyond the grizzly history of the early part of the century toward a way of doing things anew, "to make a new polity." Such a movement never happened, however, and instead

We put each other in camps. I crush my lover with a kiss
and then it is impossible to lover her.
What must die if we are to live without barbed wire
and bad sex is the very idea of otherness.
And to kill the idea, we have merely to find
one victim in ourselves who will die for nothing.

New Dark Ages is a powerful and pivotal collection. Combining the explorations of his first two books, this third volume articulates a vision of the changing face of the world on the order of Blake's conception of a New Jerusalem.

Erasures, which followed *New Dark Ages,* speaks to the plain fact that the opportunity for a "new polity" was unrealized. It is a book of despair. The language of the book is more opaque, as if Revell is implying that the failure to move out of a "new dark age" is profoundly connected to how tarnished language has become. Words used as expected perpetuate lies; hence, Revell tries to disrupt expectations by breaking syntactical conventions and shaping a new music to render a new vision. Radical lineation, shifts in usage, and a generalized instability of language govern the book. Consider, for example, these lines:

It is a white train
sees and makes it darker.
Oh sustain it.
I am in the wires.

The book signals a movement toward realizing the antinomian, and Revell disrupts expectations in order to make a reader think about how expectations shrink the world toward definition. For the antinomian definition is death.

Beautiful Shirt reveals a further exploration of this tradition. The long poems of this collection are complex renderings of musical form. Written out of a further dislocation of the familiar (many of the poems came out of the author's "immediate circumstances" of travel in France and elsewhere), the collection compounds the elegiac conclusions of *Erasures*. Revell's next book, *There Are Three,* is propelled by diverse energies. Motivated by both the loss of a father and renewal through the birth of a son, the poet attempts to understand a world from which "God is gone" and we are left with "only a window and a wilderness / remaining." Windows allow vision, however, and clear vision is the beginning of revelation. The title poem reads, "An hour along / the groundless tangents / of a meadow is not wasted / until it ends." The lines imply that there is no loss until we impose "the barrier" of a conceived closure upon the experience, an ordering principle. Other poems articulate similar sentiments, as, for instance, "Overthrow," in which we read, "On such a night, the stars could not consent to constellations."

In some ways Revell is a religious poet, but having declared that, I feel the need to qualify the statement. He is a religious poet in the way Kandinsky was a religious painter or in the way Thoreau was a religious writer. His aim is always toward revelations of the provisional interstices through which grace emerges. The quotations from Blake and Hutchinson and Thoreau; the emphasis on time as durational, as a musical score, like a snow-covered meadow, onto which history has not scratched its notes; the revisions of grammar and syntax—all embody Revell's dedication to searching for wilderness, a place of possibility for the Arcadian vision in which contradictions can blossom and coexist like "flowers," fisting "their beautiful / contentions without choice."

—Tod Marshall

RIACH, Alan (Scott)

Nationality: Scottish. **Born:** Airdrie, Lanarkshire, Scotland, 1 August 1957. **Education:** University of Caen, International Language Certificate, 1977; Churchill College, Cambridge, B.A. in English 1979, M.A. in English 1985; University of Glasgow, Ph.D. in Scottish Literature 1985. **Family:** Married Raewyn Maree Garton in 1992; one son. **Career:** Course director and creative writing teacher, Workers Education Association, Glasgow, 1979–80; course director and English teacher, Foreign Language Study Program, Kent, England, 1981–83; creative writing teacher, Community Education, Lanarkshire, 1982; private tutor in English literature, Lanarkshire, 1982–83. Tutor, 1986–89, senior tutor, 1990, and since 1990 lecturer, advanced lecturer, then senior lecturer in English, University of Waikato, School of Humanities, Hamilton, New Zealand. Since 1987 scriptwriter for Radio New Zealand. **Awards:** Research grant, Department of Education and Sciences, U.K. State Studentship, 1979–82; University Grants Committee fellowship New Zealand, 1986–87, 1988–90; visitor to the United States as guest of American Embassy International Visitor Programme of USIA, 1993; International Visiting fellow, Institute for Advanced Studies in the Humanities, University of Edinburgh, 1995. **Address:** c/o English Department, University of Waikato, Private Bag 3105, Hamilton, New Zealand.

PUBLICATIONS

Poetry

For What It Is, with Peter McCarey. Wellington, Untold Books, 1988.
This Folding Map. Auckland, Auckland University Press, 1990.
An Open Return. Wellington, Untold Books, 1991.
First and Last Songs. Auckland, Auckland University Press, and Edinburgh, Chapman, 1995.

Recordings: *Fixing the Focus: The Poetry of Alan Riach,* New Zealand Radio, 1992; *In Verse: Alan Riach—Poems,* Scottish Television, 1988.

Other

Hugh MacDiarmid's Epic Poetry. Edinburgh, Edinburgh University Press, 1991.

Editor, with Mark Williams, *The Radical Imagination: Lectures and Talks by Wilson Harris.* Liege, Belgium, University of Liege, 1992.
Editor, with Michael Grieve, *Selected Poetry of Hugh MacDiarmid.* Manchester, Carcanet, 1992; New York, New Directions, 1993.
Editor, *Selected Prose of Hugh MacDiarmid.* Manchester, Carcanet, 1992.
Editor, *Scottish Eccentrics.* Manchester, Carcanet, 1993.
Editor, with Michael Grieve and W. R. Aitken, *Hugh MacDiarmid: Complete Poems Volume I.* Manchester, Carcanet, 1993.
Editor, with Michael Grieve and W. R. Aitken, *Hugh MacDiarmid: Complete Poems Volume II.* Manchester, Carcanet, 1994.
Editor, *Lucky Poet: The Autobiography of Hugh MacDiarmid.* Manchester, Carcanet, 1994.
Editor, *Contemporary Scottish Studies,* by Hugh MacDiarmid. Manchester, Carcanet, 1995.
Editor, *Albyn: Shorter Books and Monographs,* by Hugh MacDiarmid. Manchester, Carcanet, 1996.
Editor, with Angus Calder and Glen Murray, *The Raucle Tongue: Hitherto Uncollected Prose. I, 1911–1926,* by Hugh MacDiarmid. Manchester, Carcnaet, 1996.
Editor, with Angus Calder and Glen Murray, *The Raucle Tongue: Hitherto Uncollected Prose. II, 1927–1936,* by Hugh MacDiarmid. Manchester, Carcanet, 1997.
Editor, with Angus Calder and Glen Murray, *The Raucle Tongue: Hitherto Uncollected Prose. III, 1937–1978,* by Hugh MacDiarmid. Manchester, Carcanet, 1998.
Editor, with Roderick Watson, *Annals of the Five Senses and Other Stories, Sketches and Plays,* by Hugh MacDiarmid. Manchester, Carcanet, 1999.

*

Theatrical Activities: Actor: **Plays**—Douglas in *Henry IV Part 1* by Shakespeare, Cambridge, England, 1977; Malvolio in *Twelfth Night* by Shakespeare, Hamilton, New Zealand, 1991; King's Officer in *Tartuffe* by Molière, Hamilton, New Zealand, 1992.

Critical Studies: "'This Folding Map,' Alan Riach" by Edwin Morgan, in *Landfall,* 45(3), September 1991; "Alan Riach, Hugh

MacDiarmid's Epic Poetry'' by Roderick Watson, in *Modern Language Review*, 88, October 1993.

* * *

The poetry of the Scottish-born, New Zealand-based writer Alan Riach represents another variation on the theme of expatriate writing. The title of his collection *This Folding Map* (1990) collapses its words one under another to remind us how a folding map collapses parts of the world it represents on top of other parts. This strategy for connecting the author's ''here'' and ''there'' seems reinforced by epigraphs quoting Wilson Harris and M.P. MacDiarmid that promise exploration of displacement and translation and by the opening of ''They dream only of Scotland'':

> The dreams they dream are only of
> Scotland to be looking for it through
> hundreds of islands and millions
> of acres of gorse . . .

But when Riach opens his map further, it becomes increasingly obvious that Scotland's and New Zealand's gorse problems provide one of only a few points of connection between the two countries. Beyond the connection made between the two countries' cities of Hamilton in ''The Miners'' and ''The Blues,'' there is little else to define him as other than a writer concerned primarily with his native country.

The titles of the four sections of *This Folding Map* promise a concern with the locations of sites, but the poems tend to suffer from a lack of specificity. The majority refer to the Northern Hemisphere and Scotland, or they are in a curious and ironical way mapless in that they have no clear, informing locale. ''North'' is representative of the former:

> —Scotland if surrounded on all sides with sea,
> Except one, to which it bears
> A proximity much like a candle
> Burning brightly in the black eye-socket
> Of a tremendous skull.

The intensity of this focus on Riach's birthplace is nearer the colonial sensibility than the postcolonial, and it is countered by a number of poems in which there is no clear sense of place at all. ''Landscape I,'' for example, gives sharp images of frozen water and ''wizened tree'' without evoking particularity, and the poem dissipates its forms before wrenching back to the image of a rabbit in a manner that seems to reflect a fear of unknown spaces. The need to focus on known detail rather than the unknown generality of landscape is a mark of colonial poetry (for example, in the early Australian poets Charles Harpur and Henry Kendall). The poem ''I don't know what you're saying, she said'' conveys this sense of deracination, as its title suggests, in the querulous voice of a woman:

> . . . so many things you hear you don't begin
> to understand what they mean why they're said
> where they come from what they do . . .

Many of the poems in *The Folding Map* address problems of attachment and authenticity by forms of translation and intertextuality.

The volume evokes a variety of other writers: the Gawain poet, Trelawny, Cervantes, Charles Olson, John Ashbery, and Paul Blackburn. In the case of the latter two poets evocation becomes almost an acknowledgment of plagiarism. For example, Ashbery's poem ''They dream only of America'' becomes in Riach's hands ''They dream only of Scotland,'' the poem urbanized sufficiently to point up both similarity and difference in a way that reminds us that Riach's map folds east to west as well as north to south.

—Anna Smith

RICH, Adrienne (Cecile)

Nationality: American. **Born:** Baltimore, Maryland, 16 May 1929. **Education:** Roland Park Country School, Baltimore, 1938–47; Radcliffe College, Cambridge, Massachusetts, A.B. (cum laude) 1951 (Phi Beta Kappa). **Family:** Married Alfred H. Conrad in 1953 (died 1970); three sons. **Career:** Lived in the Netherlands, 1961–62. Taught at the YM-YWHA Poetry Center Workshop, New York, 1966–67; visiting poet, Swarthmore College, Pennsylvania, 1966–68; adjunct professor, Graduate Writing Division, Columbia University, New York, 1967–69; lecturer, 1968–70, instructor, 1970–71, assistant professor of English, 1971–72, and professor, 1974–75, City College of New York; Fannie Hurst Visiting Professor, Brandeis University, Waltham, Massachusetts, 1972–73; professor of English, Douglass College, New Brunswick, New Jersey, 1976–78; A.D. White Professor-at-Large, Cornell University, Ithaca, New York, 1981–85; visiting professor, San José State University, California, 1985–86; professor of English and feminist studies, Stanford University, California, 1986–93. Since 1992 national director, the National Writers' Voice Project. Clark Lecturer and distinguished visiting professor, Scripps College, Claremont, California, 1983; Burgess Lecturer, Pacific Oaks College, Pasadena, California, 1986. Columnist, *American Poetry Review,* Philadelphia, 1972–73; co-editor, *Sinister Wisdom,* 1980–84; member of editorial collective, *Bridges: A Journal for Jewish Feminists and Our Friends,* 1989–93. **Awards:** Yale Series of Younger Poets award, 1951; Guggenheim fellowship, 1952, 1961; Ridgely Torrence memorial award, 1955; American Academy award, 1961; Amy Lowell traveling scholarship, 1962; Bollingen Foundation grant, for translation, 1962; Bess Hokin prize, 1963, and Eunice Tietjens memorial prize, 1968 (*Poetry,* Chicago); National Translation Center grant, 1968; National Endowment for the Arts grant, 1970; Shelley memorial award, 1971; Ingram Merrill Foundation grant, 1973; National Book award, 1974; Donnelly fellowship, Bryn Mawr College, Pennsylvania, 1975; Fund for Human Dignity award, 1981; Ruth Lilly prize, 1986; Brandeis University Creative Arts Medal, 1987; Elmer Holmes Bobst award, 1989; Commonwealth award in literature, 1991; Frost Silver medal of the Poetry Society of America, 1992; *Los Angeles Times* Book award in poetry, 1992; Lenore Marshall/*Nation* award, 1992; William Whitehead award, 1992; Lambda Book award, 1992; The Poets' prize, 1993; Fred Cody award, 1994; Harriet Monroe prize, 1994; Academy of American Poets fellowship, 1992; MacArthur fellowship, 1994–99; Dorothea Tanning award, Academy of American Poets, 1996. D.Litt.: Wheaton College, Norton, Massachusetts, 1967; Smith College, Northampton, Massachusetts, 1979; Brandeis University, 1987; City College of New York, 1990; Harvard University, 1990; Swarthmore

College, 1992. **Address:** c/o W.W. Norton, 500 Fifth Avenue, New York, New York 10110, U.S.A.

PUBLICATIONS

Poetry

A Change of World. New Haven, Connecticut, Yale University Press, 1951.
(Poems). Oxford, Fantasy Press, 1952.
The Diamond Cutters and Other Poems. New York, Harper, 1955.
Snapshots of a Daughter-in-Law: Poems 1954–1962. New York, Harper, 1963; London, Chatto and Windus, 1970.
Necessities of Life: Poems 1962–1965. New York, Norton, 1966.
Selected Poems. London, Chatto and Windus, 1967.
Leaflets: Poems 1965–1968. New York, Norton, 1969; London, Chatto and Windus, 1972.
The Will to Change: Poems 1968–1970. New York, Norton, 1971; London, Chatto and Windus, 1973.
Diving into the Wreck: Poems 1971–1972. New York, Norton, 1973.
Poems Selected and New 19S0–1974. New York, Norton, 1975.
Twenty-One Love Poems. Emeryville, California, Effie's Press, 1976.
The Dream of a Common Language: Poems 1974–1977. New York, Norton, 1978.
A Wild Patience Has Taken Me This Far: Poems 1978–1981. New York, Norton, 1981.
Sources. Woodside, California, Heyeck Press, 1983.
The Fact of a Doorframe: Poems Selected and New 1950–1984. New York, Norton, 1984.
Your Native Land, Your Life. New York, Norton, 1986.
Time's Power: Poems 1985–1988. New York, Norton, 1989.
An Atlas of the Difficult World: Poems 1988–91. New York, Norton, 1991.
Collected Early Poems, 1950–1970. New York, Norton, 1993.
Dark Fields of the Republic Poems, 1991–1995. New York, Norton, 1995.
Selected Poems, 1950–1995. Knockeven, Ireland, Salmon, 1996.
Midnight Salvage: Poems, 1995–1998. New York, Norton, 1999.

Recordings: *Today's Poets 4,* with others, Folkways; *Adrienne Rich Reading at Stanford,* Stanford, 1973; *A Sign I Was Not Alone,* with others, Out and Out, 1978; *Planetarium: A Retrospective,* Watershed, 1986; *Tracking the Contradictions: Poems 1981–1985,* Watershed, 1987.

Plays

Ariadne. Privately printed, 1939.
Not I, But Death. Privately printed, 1941.

Other

Of Woman Born: Motherhood as Experience and Institution. New York, Norton, 1976; London, Virago, 1977.
Women and Honor: Some Notes on Lying. Pittsburgh, Motheroot, 1977; London, Onlywomen Press, 1979.
On Lies, Secrets, and Silence: Selected Prose 1966–1978. New York Norton, 1979; London, Virago, 1980.

Compulsory Heterosexuality and Lesbian Existence. Denver, Antelope Press, 1980; London, Onlywomen Press, 1981.
Blood, Bread, and Poetry: Selected Prose 1979–1985. New York, Norton, 1986; London, Virago, 1987.
What Is Found There: Notebooks on Poetry and Politics. New York, Norton, 1993; London, Virago, 1995.

Editor, with David Lehman, *The Best American Poetry 1996.* New York, Scribner, 1996.

Translator, with William Stafford and Aijaz Ahmad, *Poems by Ghalib.* New York, Hudson Review, 1969.
Translator, *Reflections* by Mark Insingel. New York, Red Dust, 1973.

*

Manuscript Collection: Schlesinger Library, Radcliffe College, Cambridge, Massachusetts.

Critical Studies: *Adrienne Rich's Poetry* edited by Barbara Charlesworth Gelpi and Albert Gelpi, New York, Norton, 1975; *American Triptych: Anne Bradstreet, Emily Dickinson, Adrienne Rich* by Wendy Martin, Chapel Hill, University of North Carolina Press, 1984; *The Transforming Power of Language: The Poetry of Adrienne Rich* by Myriam Díaz-Diocaretz, Utrecht, HES, 1984; *Reading Adrienne Rich: Reviews and Re-visions 1951–1981* edited by Jane Roberta Cooper, Ann Arbor, University of Michigan Press, 1984; *Translating Poetic Discourse: Questions on Feminist Strategies in Adrienne Rich* by Díaz-Diocaretz, Amsterdam, Benjamins, 1985; *A New Tradition? The Poetry of Sylvia Plath, Anne Sexton, and Adrienne Rich* by Janice Markey, Frankfurt, Lang, 1985; *The Aesthetics of Power: The Poetry of Adrienne Rich* by Claire Keyes, Athens, University of Georgia Press, 1986; ''Adrienne Rich: North America East'' by Terrence DesPres, in *Praises and Dispraises,* New York, Viking, 1988; ''Driving to the Limits of the City of Words': The Poetry of Adrienne Rich'' by Willard Spiegelman, in *The Didactic Muse,* Princeton, New Jersey, Princeton University Press, 1989; *The Dream and the Dialogue: Adrienne Rich's Feminist Poetics* by Alice Templeton, Knoxville, University of Tennessee Press, 1994; *Lyric Trials—Lyric and Rhetoric in Contemporary Poetry: Seamus Heaney, Adrienne Rich, A.R. Ammons, John Ashbery* (dissertation) by Kevin Vincent McGuirk, University of Western Ontario, 1993; *'A House of Difference': Constructions of the Lesbian Poet in Audre Lorde, Adrienne Rich, and Paula Gunn Allen* (dissertation) by Sagari Dhairyam, University of Illinois, Urbana, 1993; *Skirting the Subject: Pursuing Language in the Works of Adrienne Rich, Susan Griffin, and Beverly Dahlen* (dissertation) by Alan Shima, Uppsala University, 1993; ''Another Look at Genre: Diving into the Wreck of Ethics with Rich and Irigaray'' by Elizabeth Hirsh, in *Feminist Measures: Soundings in Poetry and Theory,* edited by Lynn Keller and Cristanne Miller, Ann Arbor, University of Michigan Press, 1994; ''Wrestling with the Mother and the Father: 'His' and 'Her' in Adrienne Rich'' by Betty S. Flowers, in *Private Voices, Public Lives: Women Speak on the Literary Life,* edited by Nancy Owen Nelson, Denton, University of North Texas Press, 1995; ''Planets on the Table: From Wallace Stevens and Elizabeth Bishop to Adrienne Rich and June Jordan'' by Jacqueline Vaught Brogan, in *The Wallace Stevens Journal* (Potsdam, New York), 19(2), fall 1995; *Political Poetics: Revisionist Form in Adrienne Rich, John Ashbery, Charles Wright, and Jorie Graham* (dissertation) by Phyllis Jean Franzek, University of Southern California, 1995; "Women and Poetry" by Carol Muske, in *Michigan Quarterly Review* (Ann Arbor, Michigan), 35(4), fall 1996; "Body As Metaphor in the Poetry of Adrienne Rich" by Jane Caris, in *Pleiades* (Warrensburg, Missouri), 16(2), spring 1996; *Women's Stories of the Looking Glass: Autobiographical Reflections and Self-Representations in the Poetry of Sylvia Plath, Adrienne Rich, and Audre Lorde* by Carmen Birkle, Munich, Germany, Fink, 1996; "Framing Water: Historical Knowledge in Elizabeth Bishop and Adrienne Rich" by Roger Gilbert, in *Twentieth Century Literature* (Hempstead, New York), 43(2), summer 1997; *Stein, Bishop, and Rich: Lyrics of Love, War, and Place* by Margaret Dickie, Chapel Hill, University of North Carolina Press, 1997; *'A Politics of Asking Women's Questions'? Adrienne Rich's Later Career* (dissertation) by Sylvia Babette Henneberg, University of Georgia, 1997; "'Where Are We Moored?': Adrienne Rich, Women's Mourning, and the Limits of Lament" by Maeera Shreiber, in *Dwelling in Possibility: Women Poets and Critics on Poetry,* edited by Shreiber and Yopie Prins, Ithaca, New York, Cornell University Press, 1997; *Fashioning the Female Subject: The Intertextual Networking of Dickinson, Moore, and Rich* by Sabine Sielke, Ann Arbor, University of Michigan Press, 1997; *Toward an Ethics of Location: Witnessing Community in Adrienne Rich's Poetry* (dissertation) by Joshua Samuel Jacobs, Rutgers University, New Brunswick, 1997; *Adrienne Rich: Passion, Politics and the Body* by Liz Yorke, London, Sage, 1997; "Reply to Adrienne Rich" by Diane Wakoski, in *The Critical Response to Robert Lowell,* edited by Steven Gould Axelrod, Westport, Connecticut, Greenwood, 1999.

*   *   *

Adrienne Rich's earliest volume, *A Change of World,* introduces two themes that have persisted throughout her career: the pyrrhic victories of human accomplishment in the battle against time and the plight of being a woman. Many poems describe the patience and accommodation every woman must learn if she is to remain in a relationship with a man, who by nature is distant and detached, in an "estranged intensity / Where his mind forages alone" ("An Unsaid Word"). *The Diamond Cutters and Other Poems* reiterates how patience, resignation, and isolation are a woman's fate: "We had to take the world as it was given," she writes, for "[we] live in other people's houses" ("The Middle-Aged"). The title poem in *Snapshots of a Daughter-in-Law* treats the woman's "blight" in a mythic, historical, and literary context. In fact, Rich insists, the traditional and proper roles of good wife and housekeeper are a woman's funeral preparations: "Soon we'll be off. I'll pack us into parcels / stuff us in barrels, shroud us in newspapers" ("Passing On"). The perverse dependency upon men for sustenance and the isolation from other women that accompanies this lead women to self-hatred. The only real alternatives are depression or suicide: "A thinking woman sleeps with monsters / The beak that grabs her, she becomes."

Necessities of Life concentrates primarily upon erotic experience. The poet is in search of both a comfortable relationship with her own body and a relationship with a woman that will give her the childlike (and even womblike) security she has lost. To her lover she says, "Sometimes at night / you are my mother / . . . and I crawl against you, fighting / for shelter, making you / my cave" ("Like This Together"). In *Leaflets* Rich's political rage surfaces. As poet and woman, she calls for sisterhood, a new politics, and a new language. Her resistance is active: "I'd rather / taste blood, yours or mine,

flowing / from a sudden slash, than cut all day / with blunt scissors on dotted lines / like the teacher told." *The Will to Change* deals with the problems of retaining the "oppressor's language" ("The Burning of Paper instead of Children"). It is essential to return to feeling, Rich argues, and she connects erotic sexuality, poetry, and political action: "When will we lie clear headed in our flesh again?" she asks, for whenever "a feeling enters the body / [it] is political." Finally, admitting that "we have come to an edge of history when men . . . have become dangerous to children and other living things, themselves included," she commits herself to total sexual-political warfare.

Diving into the Wreck admits Rich's total antipathy toward men. "I hate you," she says to her male adversary and continues, "The only real love I have ever felt / was for children and other women." "Phenomenology of Anger" is a militantly feminist poem that rages against repressed human energy, which men handle in war and murder but which women escape only in "Madness, Suicide, Death." "The Stranger" goes beyond sexual warfare as Rich, the poet who is a prisoner of language, becomes androgynous. Perhaps love and nurturing will be restorative. She writes, "I am the androgyne / I am the living mind you fail to describe / in your dead language," and, as "mermaid" and "merman," she concludes, "We circle silently / about the wreck / we dive into the hold."

In *Your Native Land, Your Life,* Rich raises a confident and elegant political voice. She accepts her "verbal privilege" as a poet to incite her audience to action against the injustices endured by every minority—from American Indian and black to Jew and lesbian. As the title suggests, she reflects on her own experiences in order to raise larger moral issues. Many poems are intimate revelations of her experiences as a Jew, woman, and daughter ("the eldest daughter raised as a son, taught to study but not to pray"). "Sources" raises key questions about identity, choices, and helplessness: "*With whom do you believe your lot is cast? / From where does your strength come?* / I think somehow, somewhere / every poem of mine must raise those questions / . . . There is a *whom,* a *where* / that is not chosen that is given and sometimes falsely given / in the beginning we grasp whatever we can to survive." At times she worries that she is becoming self-consciously political and wonders if "everything we write / will be used against us / or against those we love." Ultimately, however, through the common pain of human relationships and survival in time, there may be a transcendent "purification." She would connect herself with the world's pain, even though "the body's pain and the pain on the streets / are not the same but you can learn / from the edges that blur / you who love clear edges / more than anything watch the edges that blur."

In *Time's Power* Rich again recalls her childhood loneliness and a life mixed "with laughter / raucousing the grief" and suggests that in the end "all we read is life. Death is invisible / . . . Only the living decide death's color" ("Living Memory"). She has been like a visitor to a foreign land, in an alien universe: "So why am I out here, trying / to read your name in the illegible air? / —vowel washed from a stone, / solitude of no absence, / forbidden face-to-face / . . . / trying to hang these wraiths / of syllables, breath / without echo, why?" Other poems recall the wounds of a painful mother-daughter relationship and Rich's special sensitivity to women's, especially lesbians', experiences as victims of a hostile, punitive culture. Several historical poems are particularly interesting, including "Letters in the Family" and "Harper's Ferry."

Rich shoulders the burdens of the world in *An Atlas of the Difficult World.* In many poems she clearly transcends the role of feminist poet, now deeply concerned with how, in any number of disenfranchised groups, various elements—history, culture, and individuals—create and impose evil upon the innocent. Her subjects range from the victims of a concentration camp to a woman beaten by her husband in a trailer to two lesbians brutally attacked while vacationing. Gays and lesbians become emblematic of the many in society scarred by injustice and indignity.

The title poem, in thirteen parts, is a devastating image of the individual lost in the American "Sea of Indifference, glazed with salt." She says of this society, "I don't want to know / wreckage, dreck and waste," but as she admits, "these are the materials" of "our fissured, cracked terrain." America is "a cemetery of the poor / who died for democracy." Among her heroes—always the more modest members of society—are Leo Frank, hung in 1915 solely because he was a Jew; the father of Anne Sullivan (Helen Keller's teacher), forced to come to America during the Irish potato famine; Latino migrant workers in California; the imprisoned George Jackson.

The volume also returns to familiar themes of feminist rage: "You were a woman walked on a leash. / And they dropped you in the end" ("Olivia"); the difficulties of childhood ("That Mouth"); age ("She"); Jewish female identity ("Eastern War Time"); and death ("Final Notations"). Some of Rich's descriptive passages, particularly of nature, are unusually beautiful. She writes of the black-eyed Susan, the flower that during "Late summers, early autumns / . . . binds / the map of this country together," that here is "the girasol, orange gold- / petalled / with her black eye / [which] laces the / roadsides from Vermont to / California / . . . her tubers the / jerusalem artichoke / that has fed the Indians, fed the hobos, could feed us all." The poet asks, "Is there anything in the soil . . . that makes for / a plant so generous?" It is what is called "humanity"—politically, socially, and ecologically—that is responsible for natural and individual "waste": "The watcher's eye put out, hands of the / builder severed, brain of the maker starved / those who could bind, join, reweave, cohere, replenish / now at risk in this segregate republic." The concept of "waste" haunts the volume.

In *Dark Fields of the Republic* Rich transforms her nostalgia for past, personal dreams into a broad compassion for all humanity in its naive or grandiose aspirations. In the poem "In Those Years" she speaks of how she once sought personal connection, "a personal life / and yes, that was the only life we could bear witness to." Now, however, her focus is the imperative of universal responsibility and, concomitantly, universal love: "The great dark birds of history screamed and plunged / into our personal weather / . . . where we stood, saying *I*." In more simplified but deeply impassioned language, the poet clearly emphasizes the beauty of personal differences:

Once we were dissimilar
yet separate   that's beauty   that's what you catch.

Particularly interesting are "Revolution in Permanence," about Ethel Rosenberg; "Food Packages: 1947," on Rich's familiar theme of post-Holocaust German-Jewish identity; and "Six Narratives," about how "the big dream strained and shifted" in a love relationship.

Midnight Salvage once again establishes Rich as one of the most distinguished poets of our time. While the specifics of political and gender issues punctuate the volume, Rich transcends these to concern herself with the most basic issues of humanity. The volume begins with an epigraph from George Oppen: "I don't know how to measure happiness. The issue is happiness . . ."

At the turn of the millennium Rich writes with a passion and assurance as though to clarify the agenda of her life. This is a poetry of exquisite lyricism filled with the poet's sense of time and self-criticism. In the title poem, in eight sections, she writes that she "could not play by the rules," that she "never expected hope would form itself / completely in my time." Nevertheless, she will still "submit to whatever poetry is" and "accept no limits." "Midnight Salvage" recapitulates old themes: "When I ate and drank liberation once I walked / arm-in-arm with someone who said she had something to teach me." Other poems return to the Holocaust: "there is the village where no villager survived" ("Char"); to war, time, and aging: "In the heart of pain where mind is broken / and consumed by body, I sit like you / on the rocky shore" ("1941"); to people of her youth, from a paraplegic Vic Greenberg to Billie Holiday and Charlie Parker ("The Night Has a Thousand Eyes").

Rich asks of herself, "How did you get here anyway?," reaffirming her commitment to the reader: "With all my fear I'm here with you, trying what it / means, to stand fast; what it means to move." In the extraordinary prose section "A Long Conversation" that concludes the volume, she writes of her human heritage:

I come from the kind of family where loss means not just grief but utter ruin—adults and children dispersed into prostitution, orphanages, juvenile prisons, emigration—never to meet again. I wanted to show those lives—designated insignificant—as beauty, as terror. They were significant to me and what they had endured terrified me. I knew such a life could have been my own. I also knew they had saved me from it. —I tried to show all this and as well to make an art as impersonal as it demanded—I have no theories. I don't know what I am being forgiven. I am my art. I make it from my body and the bodies that produced mine. I am still trying to find the pictorial language for this anger and fear rotating on an axle of love.

—Lois Gordon

RIDLER, Anne (Barbara)

Nationality: British. **Born:** Anne Barbara Bradby, Rugby, Warwickshire, 30 July 1912. **Education:** Downe House School; King's College, London, diploma in journalism 1932. **Family:** Married Vivian Ridler in 1938; two sons and two daughters. **Career:** Member of editorial department, Faber and Faber publishers, London, 1935–40. **Awards:** Oscar Blumenthal prize, 1954; Union League Civic and Arts Foundation prize, 1955 (*Poetry,* Chicago). **Address:** 14 Stanley Road, Oxford OX4 IQZ, England.

PUBLICATIONS

Poetry

Poems. London, Oxford University Press, 1939.
A Dream Observed and Other Poems. London, Editions Poetry London, 1941.
The Nine Bright Shiners. London, Faber, 1943.
The Golden Bird and Other Poems. London, Faber, 1951.
A Matter of Life and Death. London, Faber, 1959.
Selected Poems. New York, Macmillan, 1961.

Some Time After and Other Poems. London, Faber, 1972.
Italian Prospect: Six Poems. Oxford, Perpetua Press, 1976.
Dies Natalist: Poems of Birth and Infancy. Oxford, Perpetua Press, 1980.
Ten Poems, with E.J. Scovell. Leamington, Other Branch Readings, 1984.
New and Selected Poems. London, Faber, 1988.
Collected Poems. Manchester, Carcanet, 1994.

Plays

Cain (produced Letchworth, Hertfordshire, 1943; London, 1944). London, Editions Poetry London, 1943.
The Shadow Factory: A Nativity Play (produced London, 1945). London, Faber, 1946.
Henry Bly (produced London, 1947). Included in *Henry Bly and Other Plays,* 1950.
Henry Bly and Other Plays. London, Faber, 1950.
The Mask, and The Missing Bridegroom (produced London, 1951). Included in *Henry Bly and Other Plays,* 1950.
The Trial of Thomas Cranmer, music by Bryan Kelly (produced Oxford, 1956). London, Faber, 1956.
The Departure, music by Elizabeth Maconchy (produced London, 1961). Included in *Some Time After and Other Poems,* 1972.
Who Is My Neighbour? (produced Leeds, 1961). With *How Bitter the Bread,* London, Faber, 1963.
The Jesse Tree: A Masque in Verse, music by Elizabeth Maconchy (produced Dorchester, Oxfordshire, 1970). London, Lyrebird Press, 1972.
Rosinda, translation of the libretto by Faustini, music by Cavalli (produced Oxford, 1973; London, 1975).
Orfeo, translation of the libretto by Striggio, music by Monteverdi (produced Oxford, 1975; London, 1981). London, Faber Music, 1975; revised edition, 1981.
Eritrea, translation of the libretto by Faustini, music by Cavalli (produced Wexford, Ireland, 1975). London, Oxford University Press, 1975.
The King of the Golden River, music by Elizabeth Maconchy (produced Oxford, 1975).
The Return of Ulysses, translation of the libretto by Badoaro, music by Monteverdi (produced London, 1978).
The Lambton Worm, music by Robert Sherlaw Johnson (produced Oxford, 1978). London, Oxford University Press, 1979.
Orontea, translation of the libretto by Cicognini, music by Cesti (produced London, 1979).
Agrippina, translation of the libretto by Grimani, music by Handel (produced London, 1982).
La Calisto, translation of the libretto by Faustini, music by Cavalli (produced London, 1984).
Così fan Tutte, translation of the libretto by da Ponte, music by Mozart (produced London, 1986; broadcast, 1988). Oxford, Perpetua Press, 1987.
The Marriage of Figaro, translation of the libretto. Oxford, Perpetua Press, 1991.

Other

Olive Willis and Downe House: An Adventure in Education. London, Murray, 1967.
A Victorian Family Postbag. Oxford, Perpetua Press, 1988.

Profitable Wonders: Aspects of Thomas Traherne, with A.M. Allchin and Julia Smith. Oxford, Amate Press, 1989.
A Measure of English Poetry. Oxford, Perpetua Press, 1991.

Editor, *Shakespeare Criticism 1919–1935.* London and New York, Oxford University Press, 1936.
Editor, *A Little Book of Modern Verse.* London, Faber, 1941.
Editor, *Time Passes and Other Poems,* by Walter de la Mare. London, Faber, 1942.
Editor, *Best Ghost Stories.* London, Faber, 1945.
Editor, *The Faber Book of Modern Verse,* revised edition. London, Faber, 1951.
Editor, *The Image of the City and Other Essays,* by Charles Williams. London, Oxford University Press, 1958.
Editor, *Selected Writings,* by Charles Williams. London, Oxford University Press, 1961.
Editor, *Shakespeare Criticism 1935–1960.* London and New York, Oxford University Press, 1963.
Editor, *Poems and Some Letters,* by James Thomson. London, Centaur Press, and Urbana, University of Illinois Press, 1963.
Editor, *Thomas Traherne: Poems, Centuries, and Three Thanksgivings.* London, Oxford University Press, 1966.
Editor, with Christopher Bradby, *Best Stories of Church and Clergy.* London, Faber, 1966.
Editor, *Selected Poems of George Darley.* London, Merrion Press, 1979.
Editor, *The Poems of William Austin.* Oxford, Perpetua Press, 1983.

*

Manuscript Collection: Eton College Library, Buckinghamshire.

Critical Studies: *The Christian Tradition in Modern British Verse Drama* by William V. Spanos, New Brunswick, New Jersey, Rutgers University Press, 1967; ''Anne Ridler at Seventy'' by Tracey Warr, in *Poetry Review* (London), 73(1), March 1983.

*   *   *

In ''News of the World,'' a poem included in A *Matter of Life and Death,* Anne Ridler's collection of 1959, there is to be found the following line:

Love is our interest, love our capital theme.

Love in its various senses (the differences are perceived, but that which unifies them is felt and insisted upon) is indeed the recurrent theme of much of Ridler's best work. Love of individual, love of God, love of family, love of place, love of humanity—these, and the threat to them in separation and isolation, are the subjects that repeatedly lie at the heart of her most successful poems.

The early, World War II poems of *The Nine Bright Shiners* include several moving poems of lovers separated (e.g., ''At Parting'' and ''Bring Back''). ''Leaving Ringshall,'' in *A Matter of Life and Death,* addresses the complex relationships of persons and places loved:

. . . a place is loved for what we felt there,
Not for itself alone. Yet in a portrait
The setting holds the key: met out of context

A face is nameless, or if daily seen,
Confused in memory by its many frames.

So, though we treat the landscape as a background,
Without it we are—nowhere.

"On Changing Places," from the same volume, makes a related affirmation (in opposition to that which reason "affirms") in its opening lines and conveniently illustrates Ridler's skill in the interweaving of image and idea:

And is there such a word as parting?
Reason affirms it, but the heart
Denies, and risks a deal of pain
By debts of joy received and given;
While time spins on like a spider, weaves
With years for thread, with hour and season,
Twisting the figure of daily lives,
And warps it fast to the place it loves.

The metaphysical note is quite a common one in Ridler (and the adjective is used both in its philosophical-religious sense and as a term from the history of English poetry). One poem, "Risinghall Summer," is subtitled "Remembering Marvell's 'Appleton House,'" and there are quite a number of other poems in which either Donne or Herbert seems to be "remembered." Elsewhere, the presences of Eliot, Auden, or Charles Williams are easily discerned. Yet to say this is not to dismiss Ridler as slavishly derivative; like many another member of what Geoffrey Grigson has called "the long roll of good minor poets," she has been able to evolve her own distinctive voice out of the influences of intrinsically greater or more individual poets. She has been able to write poems that, while they exhibit such influences, could not be mistaken for the work of any one of these other poets. The minor poet can create a new synthesis and can breathe a personal life into it, as in "Anniversary":

This fig-tree spreads all hands toward the light,
    Five broad fingers to each, solid and still
    As those that are chiselled on pulpit or stall.
And yet the light pervades those carven leaves,
Not as my dark hands divert the sun
    If I hold them before my face—
    These invert it, let it pass,
A green effulgence that the trunk receives.

These fifteen years I have spread my hands to the light of your
    love.
Its rays should long ago have made me strong:
    Did my remorse for wrong
Or fears filter its power from the light,
Or did my darkness divert it from my heart,
    That I am still so callow and unsure,
    And cannot think to endure
Even the shortest winter out of your sight?

It would probably be a largely meaningless exercise to attempt to subdivide Ridler's poems into religious and secular. There are, of course, some specifically Christian poems, such as "Prayer in a Pestilent Time" (*The Nine Bright Shiners*) or the very beautiful "Carol to Be Set to Music" (*A Matter of Life and Death*). More often, subjects not inherently religious in nature are considered within discursive meditations in which faith and doubt exist in repeated counterpoint, e.g., in "Lyme Regis—Golden Cap" (*A Matter of Life and Death*) and "Corneal Graft" (*Some Time After*). Her poems of place and of family are at their best when they apprehend the divine in the ordinary, as in the azalea taken indoors that "speaks in a blaze, like a prophet returned from the wilderness" ("Azalea in the House" from *Some Time After*). Perhaps Ridler's best single poem is "A Matter of Life and Death," a sonata-like contemplation upon her son's development from embryo to manhood that, characteristically, explores larger themes of mutability, of the impermanence that is the pleasure and the pain of all human experience.

In 1988 there appeared Ridler's *New and Selected Poems,* her previous major collection having appeared some sixteen years earlier. The volume closes with "The Halcyons," the story of Ceyx and Alcyone from Ovid via the *Book of the Duchesse.* It is a superbly crafted poem in a variety of verse forms and ends with an affirmation of the tale's significance that is, fittingly, a recapitulation of much that is central to the work of this rewarding poet.

. . . something more is meant
    By those myths of bird-changes.
That love continues blest
    In different guises;
That immortality
    Is not mere repetition:
It is a blue flash,
    A kingfisher vision.
It is a new-feathered
    And procreant love,
Seen where the halcyon
    Nests on the wave.

—Glyn Pursglove

RÍOS, Alberto (Alvaro)

Nationality: American. **Born:** Nogales, Arizona, 18 September 1952. **Education:** University of Arizona, B.A. (honors) in English literature and creative writing 1974, B.A. (honors) in psychology 1985, M.F.A. in creative writing 1979; attended law school at University of Arizona 1975–76. **Family:** Married Maria Guadalupe Barron in 1979. **Career:** Artist, 1978–83, and since 1983 consultant, Artists-in-Education Program, Arizona Commission on the Arts, Phoenix. Assistant professor, 1982–85, associate professor, 1985–89, professor, 1989–94, and since 1995 regent's professor of English, Arizona State University, Tempe. Counselor and instructor in English and algebra, Med-Start Program, University of Arizona, summers 1977–80; writer-in-residence, Central Arizona State College, Coolidge, 1980–82; member, National Advisory Committee, National Artists-in-Education Program, 1980. **Awards:** First Place, Academy of American Poets poetry contest, 1977; writer's fellowship, Arizona Commission on the Arts, 1979; National Endowment for the Arts fellowship, 1980; Walt Whitman award, Academy of American Poets, 1981, for *Whispering to Fool the Wind;* Western States Book award, 1984, for *The Iguana Killer;* Pushcart prize for fiction, 1986, and poetry, 1988, 1989, 1993; Guggenheim fellow, 1988–89; Governor's Arts award, State of Arizona, 1991. **Address:** English Department, Arizona State University, Tempe, Arizona 85287, U.S.A.

PUBLICATIONS

Poetry

Elk Heads on the Wall (chapbook). San Jose, California, Mango Press, 1979.
Sleeping on Fists (chapbook). Story, Wyoming, Dooryard Press, 1981.
Whispering to Fool the Wind. New York, Sheep Meadow Press, 1982.
Five Indiscretions. New York, Sheep Meadow Press, 1985.
The Lime Orchard Woman: Poems. New York, Sheep Meadow Press, 1988.
Teodora Luna's Two Kisses. New York, Norton, 1990.

Short Stories

The Iguana Killer: Twelve Stories of the Heart. New York, Blue Moon Press, 1984.
Pig Cookies and Other Stories. San Francisco, Chronicle Books, 1995.
The Curtain of Trees: Stories. Albuquerque, University of New Mexico Press, 1999.

Other

Capirotada: A Nogales Memoir. Albuquerque, University of New Mexico Press, 1999.

*

Critical Studies: ''The Breathless Patience of Alberto Ríos'' by Deneen Jenks, in *Hayden's Ferry Review* (Tempe, Arizona), 11, fall/winter 1992; ''Androgyny's Whisper: 'Teodoro Luna's Two Kisses' by Alberto Ríos'' by John Jacob, in *American Book Review,* 15(4), October 1993; interview with William Barillas, in *Americas Review* (Seattle), 24(3–4), fall/winter 1996.

*   *   *

Ever since his first full book of poetry, *Whispering to Fool the Wind,* won the Walt Whitman award in 1981, Alberto Ríos has been one of our most admired and influential Hispanic authors. Born in Nogales, Arizona, and a product of public schools and later of the creative writing program at the University of Arizona, Ríos in his poetic preoccupations is anything but narrow or exclusive. In spare, often thickly symbolic lines, he may write about the trials and rewards of courtship, what it would be like to be a woman, or how it was growing up in a racially charged region like the American Southwest. Having grown up in a bilingual environment, Ríos approaches his subjects on more than one cultural level. Drawing most consistently on the oral tradition of his Hispanic heritage, Ríos is drawn to storytelling (his short stories, like his poems, are worthy of attention), to finding, declaring, and celebrating the diversity and power of community in the experience of those around him. Thus, his vision is

more outward directed, less private than might at first glance be apparent.

This subtlety can be observed in a representative poem such as ''Nogales, 1958,'' from the 1988 collection *The Lime Orchard Woman*:

> The black birds at Bank's Bridge fly
> Out from underneath at quitting time,
> 5:00 in a small town, for everyone.
> And the town makes its way home.
>
> The paperboys come out, wiry and clear.
> Everybody in a car buys a *Herald.*
> On the way home you cannot help but see
> Someone you know, who will wave . . .
>
> My mother is cutting limes for the rice
>
> And I am watching. Today I have watched
> The washing machine go around,
> And smelled it. That is best,
> Lifting its lid just a little.
>
> I have watched the girls coming
> Home from school with books held
> Against their small chests.
> They talk about boys that way
>
> Everyday, holding something in their arms.
> And that is all.
> Evening comes, and nothing else happens
> More than dinner, the news,
>
> One page in a coloring book about trees.

Arresting in its simplicity, this poem—like Ríos at his best—is most believable in expressing the wide-eyed, watchful observations of a young child. Through its inhabitants the town itself is in motion (''And the town makes its way home''). For the child the world's larger motions are contained in the movement and smell of the washing machine, just as the essence of the late day is embodied in the vision of his mother ''cutting limes for the rice'' and in the ''one page in a coloring book about trees.'' This simplicity of vision, embodied in a pared-down, sympathetic style, carves out its own secure space in our poetic landscape. It is a space reserved for the few among us whose artful, optimistic message is one of sincere hope in a frightful time.

—Robert McDowell

ROBERTSON, Robin

Nationality: British. **Born:** 1955. **Career:** Worked as an editor for Penguin Books and Secker and Warburg, 1980s. Editor, Jonathan Cape, London. **Awards:** Forward Poetry prize and First Book award, Scotland, both for *A Painted Field.*

PUBLICATIONS

Poetry

A Painted Field. London, Picador, 1997; New York, Harcourt Brace, 1998.

*

Critical Studies: Interview with Dennis Brown, in *Critical Survey,* 10(1), 1998; by W.S. Milne, in *Agenda* (London), 36(3–4), spring 1999.

*   *   *

Robin Robertson is one of the more remarkable publishers of recent times. He popularized that most cerebral of poets, Geoffrey Hill, by putting him into Penguin Books. He edited and to some extent masterminded the flow of volumes emanating from the pen of that generously copious poet Peter Redgrove. First at Secker and Warburg in the 1980s and then later at Cape, Robertson maintained a list of undeniable quality, including such poets as Sharon Olds, Michael Longley, Sarah Maguire, and John Burnside, one or two of whom he could make a fair claim to have discovered. He superintended the publication of the most controversial Booker prizewinner, James Kelman, who, like Burnside and Robertson himself, is a Scot.

Robertson's poems show, as do those of some of his protégés, that there really is a Scottish tradition. This prominent metropolitan publisher has never, in his heart, left Scotland. One could deduce his provenance, even if his book *A Painted Field* were shorn of its biographical note. The verse is exact in detail, with an almost Calvinist adherence to the truth, and the truth, also in the Calvinist tradition, brings no comfort. In "Three Ways of Looking at God"

The long trees bend to the grain of the gale,
streaming the dark valley like riverweed.
All night: thunder, torn leaves; a sheathing of wings . . .

In "Sheela-na-Gig"

The rain slows, and stops; light deepens
at the lid of the lake, the water creased
by the head of an otter, body of a bird . . .

And in "Pibroch" the speaker says,

And how I long now for the pibroch,
pibroch long and slow, lamenting all this:
all this longing for the right wave,
for the special wave that toils
behind the pilot but can never find a home . . .

In these poems night is impending, the sea is gray and uneasy, and a storm is either on its way or already upon us. The interiors are no more inviting. One is chilled by grandfather's dark parlor and frozen by his unlit kitchen; another house is abandoned, its cups thick with spoor and the mattress rolled back to the shape of the last sleeper. The people in these grim poems slash their wrists and overdose on drugs.

This is a world populated by the sick and the dying, as in "Fugue for Phantoms":

Where have they risen, the sea-dead, bobbing in effigy:
skin gone to curd, and worn now like a fragile dress,
water behind the eyes like the insides of oyster shells;
their huge heads puckered, their faces pursed like lips . . .

Such grimly dedicated recounting of exact detail.

When Robertson finds a hero, it is Marsyas, reputed in ancient Greek mythology to have taken up the flute and to have challenged the musicianship of Apollo himself. In response to the man's temerity the indignant god tied Marsyas to a tree and flayed him alive. The physical particularity renders this emphatically no poem for the squeamish. Another hero, the protagonist of the ambitious poem "Camera Obscura," is based on the life of the unsuccessful Victorian painter David Octavius Hill, whose pioneering work in photography was totally ignored. His view of life is suitably grim:

We have caught the memento mori,
the injuries of time, and coloured them
bruise-blue and sanguine. Lovers,
exposed by corpse-light . . .

The technique, indeed the verbal distinction, of Robertson's work has not been ignored. To that extent he has been more fortunate than either Marsyas or Hill. Robert Potts, a more than ordinarily discerning reviewer of contemporary verse, said of Robertson in the *Guardian,* "The maritime Scotland from which literary London has removed Robertson is evoked, sometimes brilliantly, in the chiselled pieces of description with which he tries to get to the heart of it, while perceptively stressing the failure of art to represent and not supplant ('By the time you've looked, you've missed it')."

What we have in Robertson's poetry is the chronicling, with a hard-won specificity, of failure. One is reminded of the eighteenth-century poet William Collins, whose eloquent odes reached a climax in his hypnotizing, wire-drawn "Ode to Evening," or, perhaps more pertinently, of Matthew Arnold, whose constitutional melancholy found voice in "Dover Beach," his lament for a failed civilization. There are the raw materials of a modern "Ode to Evening" or "Dover Beach" here, but the final masterpiece has not arrived, not even in "Camera Obscura," impressive though that poem certainly is. It is probably a matter of the poet recognizing what all these discrete perceptions add up to.

Robertson's senior contemporary, the illustrious Norman MacCaig, had a vision; so far Robertson has only a nightmare. But it is a powerful Calvinist nightmare, a Scot seeing through a glass darkly. It will serve, it will endure, until something more positively cohesive comes along.

—Philip Hobsbaum

ROCHE, Paul

Nationality: British. **Born:** India, 25 September 1916. **Education:** Gregorian University, Rome, Ph.B., Ph.L., S.T.L. 1949. **Family:** Married Clarissa Tanner; five children. **Career:** Instructor, Smith

College, Northampton, Massachusetts, 1957–59; poet-in-residence, California Institute of the Arts, Valencia, 1972–74, Emory and Henry College, Emory, Virginia, spring 1980, Notre Dame University, Indiana, autumn 1980, and Albion College, Michigan. Grants Ferry Distinguished Lectureship, Centenary College, New Jersey, 1990–92. Abbe Copps Judge of Poetry Contest, Olivet College, Michigan, 1994. **Awards:** Bollingen Foundation fellowship, 1958; Alice Fay di Castagnola award, 1965; Alice Hunt Bartlett prize, 1966; Vogelstein Foundation fellowship, 1978. D.Litt.: Albion College. Commander, Military and Hospilaller Order of St. Lazarus of Jerusalem. **Address:** 5 Calle de Ampurias, Soller, Mallorca, Spain.

PUBLICATIONS

Poetry

The Rank Obstinacy of Things: A Selection of Poems. New York, Sheed and Ward, 1962.

22 November 1963 (The Catharsis of Anguish). London, Adam, 1965.

Ode to the Dissolution of Mortality. New York, Madison Avenue Church Press, 1966.

All Things Considered. London, Duckworth, 1966; New York, Weybright and Talley, 1968.

To Tell the Truth. London, Duckworth, 1967.

Te Deum for J. Alfred Prufrock. New York, Madison Avenue Church Press, 1967.

Lament for Erica. Bembridge, Isle of Wight, Yellowsands Press, 1971.

Enigma Variations and. . . Gloucester, Thornhill Press, 1974.

The Kiss. Richmond, Surrey, Keepsake Press, 1974.

A Visit to India. Calcutta, Writers Workshop, 1998.

New Tales from Aesop. Calcutta, Writers Workshop, 1999.

Fifty Poems. Calcutta, Writers Workshop, 1999.

Recording: *Death at Fun City,* Mercury, 1972.

Plays

Medea, translation of the play by Euripides (produced New York, 1978). Included in *Three Plays of Euripides,* 1974.

Oedipus the King, Oedipus at Colonus, and *Antigone,* translations of plays by Sophocles (produced New York, 1980).

Screenplay: *Oedipus the King,* 1967.

Novels

O Pale Galilean. London, Harvill Press, 1954.

Vessel of Dishonour. London, Sheed and Ward, 1962; New York, New American Library, 1963.

Other

The Rat and the Convent Dove and Other Tales and Fables (for children). Aldington, Kent, Hand and Flower Press, 1952.

New Tales from Aesop for Reading Aloud. Notre Dame, Indiana, University of Notre Dame Press, and London, Honeyglen, 1982.

With Duncan Grant in Southern Turkey. London, Honeyglen, 1982.

The Bible's Greatest Stories. New York, Penguin, 1990.

Translator, *The Oedipus Plays of Sophocles.* New York, New American Library, 1958; revised edition, New York, Penguin, 1991.

Translator, *The Orestes Plays of Aeschylus.* New York, New American Library, 1963.

Translator, *Prometheus Bound, by Aeschylus.* New York, New American Library, 1964.

Translator, *The Love Songs of Sappho.* New York, New American Library, 1966; revised edition, New York, Penguin, 1991.

Translator, *3 Plays of Plautus.* New York, New American Library, 1968.

Translator, *Philoctetes, Lines 676–729,* by Sophocles. Bembridge, Isle of Wright, Yellowsands Press, 1971.

Translator, with others, *The Living Mirror: Five Young Poets from Leningrad.* London, Gollancz, and New York, Doubleday, 1972.

Translator, *Three Plays of Euripides: Alcestis, Medea, The Bacchae.* New York, Norton, 1974.

Translator, *The Complete Sophocles.* New York, Penguin Putnam, 2000.

*

Critical Studies: By John Engels, in *Minnesota Review* (St. Paul), 1963; Patricia de Joux, in *The Times* (London), 5 January 1968; John Moffitt, in *America* (New York), May 1968.

Paul Roche comments:

(1970) There is always a sufficient reason even for the worst of happenings, and it is always sufficiently human. I say in my work, "Father forgive them for they know not what they do: and forgive *me.*" Poetry is awareness heightened to the point of love. It is a way of apprehending the intensity of being. I try to re-create experience more intensely, reduce it to a luminous whole, render intuitive the meaning and metaphysics of the universe, and so feed myself and others the kernel of being. My greatest influences have been the Bible (Authorized or Douay), Shakespeare, Hopkins, Eliot, Aeschylus, Sophocles, Euripides, and Sappho.

(1974) For me poetry is an incantation of exact experience that seizes the mind and the heart; it is the orchestration of language toward maximum perception; it is condensed verbal impact. Poetry and art are the unique channels through which knowledge is humanized, enters the bloodstream, is made part of ourselves. Although I write my poems to please myself, to purge myself, I am fully aware of using myself as the exemplar for all human beings, and so ultimately I write for humanity. However embedded in the particular consciousness (even confessional) of a poet his poem is, for me it is only successful if it reaches universality, which is to say, if anyone (or almost anyone—some people are just too bovine to bother with) picking up that poem is wounded, is hit, is illuminated, and can say, "This is about me. Or it may not exactly be about me, but I now know what it is like to be that person."

(1995) As to contemporary poetry, there is no doubt that never has there been a time when so many poets have been pouring out so many poems. And we have taken to heart Ezra Pound's injunction to write our poetry at least as well as we write our prose, so much so that a great deal of contemporary poetry is prose, but very good prose.

*   *   *

Although born in India and educated in England and at the Gregorian University in Rome, where he graduated in philosophy, Paul Roche has also lived in the United States, the West Indies, and Mexico. As a result of an outlook that has never been confined by national boundaries, he has never been unduly influenced by localized coteries, though profiting from them all, and his poetry is equally enjoyed in Britain and America. His skill as a translator had been fully exploited in his own creative writing so that even what he describes as ''mere verse'' has a liveliness and command of language lacking in the work of many other poets. Whether he writes about events or personal relationships, draws upon his impressive knowledge of mythology or religion, or makes use of private experience as a starting point for reflection upon the nature of things and the behavior of his fellows, he has a flair for spotlighting major issues in a playfully ironic and often humorous vein while also coming to grips with reality. One of his methods is to approach the metaphysical through the physical, and he has written a whole series of poems—''The Brick,'' ''The Spent Matchstick,'' ''The Hairbrush,'' and ''The Nail-Scissors''—about inanimate objects.

Roche's ''Act of Love'' remains one of the most satisfactory poems ever written on such an intimate and delicate subject, and his ''Paradigm of Love'' is a remarkable example of wordplay used in a valid and effective manner:

Does love live
Only
As a mirror lives
And give
So much back
Only
As a mirror gives
Which gazes
Only
With what gazing gave
And gives
By gazing back
That only?

In *To Tell the Truth* Roche continues his somewhat hit-or-miss exploration of the significance of experience in a variety of styles, encompassing the satirical ''Spring Song of the Petroleum Board Meeting,'' the amusing commentary on Eliot's poetry, ''Te Deum for J. Alfred Prufrock,'' the lyrical ''Her Love Longs for Tears,'' and a poem of protest entitled ''The Lobotomy'':

Oh God! The explosion that shook me up so,
That series of small deadly jolts
Dislocating me for one whole desiccated year,
And the sinister cutting away of something I didn't know . . .
How I wish I had gone on a real war,
had been shredded with shrapnel
Or lost half my head.

Enigma Variations and . . . is uneven too. Everything is thrown into the pot—wordplay, literary games, light verse, satire, paradox (''The hollow in the bowl / Present by its absence''), lyrics, lively sketches, serious comment—as if to illustrate the title, yet here and there insights seep through:

Everyone is walking with an inner space
Everyone is moving with an inner time
Everyone is growing with an inner change
Everyone is being with an inner pace
Walking, moving, growing, being
Within, beside, beyond, behind
From and to and in and through
Everyone is growing
Everyone is going
Everyone is coming, coming, coming
Everyone is . . .
Becoming.

Death at Fun City is a long satirical poem concerned with what man is making of his own environment. The poem shows Roche working toward greater freedom in his choice of form.

—Howard Sergeant

RODGERS, Carolyn M(arie)

Nationality: American. **Born:** Chicago, Illinois, 14 December 1945. **Education:** University of Illinois, Navy Pier, 1960–61; Roosevelt University, Chicago, 1961–65, B.A. in English 1981; Chicago State University, 1982; University of Chicago, M.A. in English 1984. **Career:** Y.M.C.A. social worker, Chicago, 1963–68; instructor in Afro-American literature, Columbia College, Chicago, 1969, and University of Washington, Seattle, 1970; writer-in-residence, Albany State College, Georgia, 1971, Malcolm X College, Chicago, 1971–72, and Roosevelt University, 1983; visiting professor of Afro-American literature, Indiana University, Bloomington, 1973; English remediation tutor, Chicago State University, 1981; instructor, Columbia College, 1989–91. Since 1998 faculty advisor to student newspaper and instructor in English, Harold Washington College. Columnist, Milwaukee *Courier.* Formerly Midwest editor, *Black Dialogue,* New York. **Awards:** Conrad Kent Rivers award, 1968; National Endowment for the Arts grant, 1969; Gwendolyn Brooks fellowship. **Address:** 12750 South Sangamon, Chicago, Illinois 60643, U.S.A.

PUBLICATIONS

Poetry

Paper Soul. Chicago, Third World Press, 1968.
Two Love Raps. Chicago, Third World Press, 1969.
Songs of a Blackbird. Chicago, Third World Press, 1969.
Now Ain't That Love. Detroit, Broadside Press, 1969.
For H.W. Fuller. Detroit, Broadside Press, 1970.
Long Rap/Commonly Known As a Poetic Essay. Detroit, Broadside Press, 1971.
How I Got Ovah: New and Selected Poems. New York, Doubleday, 1975.
The Heart As Ever Green. New York, Doubleday, 1978.
Translation. Chicago, Eden Press, 1980.
Eden and Other Poems. Chicago, Eden Press, 1983.

Morning Glory. Chicago, Eden Press, 1989.
We're Only Human. Chicago, Eden Press, 1994.
A Train Called Judah. Chicago, Eden Press, 1996.
The Girl with Blue Hair. Chicago, Eden Press, 1996.
Salt. Chicago, Eden Press, 1998.

Novel

A Little Lower Than the Angels. Chicago, Eden Press 1984.

*

Critical Studies: "Contractions in Black Life: Recognized and Reconciled in 'How I Got Ovah'" by Estella M. Sales, in *College Language Association Journal* (Atlanta), 25(1), September 1981; "Imagery in the Women Poems: The Art of Carolyn Rodgers" by Angelene Jamison, and "Running Wild in Her Soul: The Poetry of Carolyn Rodgers" by Bettye J. Parker-Smith, both in *Black Women Writers (1950–1980): A Critical Evaluation,* edited by Mari Evans, Garden City, New York, Anchor-Doubleday, 1984; "The Poetics of Matrilineage: Mothers and Daughters in the Poetry of African American Women, 1965–1985" by Fabian Clements Worsham, in *Women of Color: Mother-Daughter Relationships in 20th-Century Literature,* edited by Elizabeth Brown-Guillory, Austin, University of Texas Press, 1996.

Carolyn M. Rodgers comments:

I seek to tell the truth. To explore the human condition, the world's condition. To illuminate the ordinary, the forgotten, the overlooked. To show that the specific me is often the general you and us. I seek to write simply, so that a child might understand, and to write profoundly, so that the educated, the intellectual may enjoy and find mental food. What is written by me is written through me as well. That is to say I am an instrument.

(1995) Reading over my first paragraph, which was written almost ten years ago, I think how noble and idealistic I was. I am sure that right now, today, I would not assign myself such a lofty, monumental task. I think I would say now I write because I love to and I do not know anything better to do except, perhaps, compose music and songs. I hope I leave a rich legacy of Afro-American literature behind, like many of my favorite Afro-American writers did.

*   *   *

Carolyn M. Rodgers's poetry is a poetry of naming. What is to be named is how the personal and the political are interwoven in our behavior, in our dreams, in our daily ideologies. The difficulty for the namer, Rodgers would have us see, is in showing how the strands come together, in making one voice represent the many threads that compose the single psyche within culture: "I've had tangled feelings lately . . . / there are several of me and / all of us fight to show up at the same time" ("Breakthrough"). In the course of her work Rodgers speaks as a militant for black unity, as a lover, as a daughter, as a devout Christian, as a self-conscious artist. These personae, both complementary and contradictory, constitute a powerful image of black womanhood fighting to define itself against the power and privilege of the white world.

Given the dynamics of racial oppression, the plurality of Rodgers's voice is perhaps less remarkable than the fact of the voice per

se. In "The Quality of Change" the poet refers to a muted past that reaches into the present:

> we have spent the years
> talking in profuse & varied
> silences to people
> who have erected walls for themselves
> to hear through.

Her poems, especially the early works, are efforts to break the silences, to break down the walls. The reader must hear the harshness of life in the streets of Chicago, as in "U Name This One":

> where pee wee cut lonnell fuh fuckin wid
> his sistuh and blood baptized the street
> at least twice ev'ry week and judy got
> kicked outa grammar school fuh bein pregnant
> and died tryin to ungrow the seed

Those things that have been hidden, hushed, or repressed in black culture must be recognized and understood, as are the forms of "high" white culture. The following is from "To the White Critics":

> my baby's tears are a three-act play, a sonnet, a novel,
> a volume of poems.
> my baby's laugh is the point and view,
> a philosophical expression of
> oppression and survival

The self that challenges the oppressor also challenges itself, and Rodgers's work makes clear the complications that arise from trying to be free of damaging constraints. Many of her most personal poems address the problem that what is wrong usually comes packaged with what is right. A slavish sexuality may be the most honest ("Now Ain't That Love?"), the least visible revolutionary strategy may be the most effective ("For H.W. Fuller"), and material possessions may provide an intensely necessary pleasure ("Things"). The poems about her mother, for example, "It Is Deep," illustrate the contradictions of maternal gifts. The woman who

> thinks that I am under the influence of
>   **communists**
> when I talk about Black as anything
> other than something ugly

is also

>   very obviously,
> a sturdy Black bridge that I
> crossed over, on

In Rodgers's aesthetic the challenge to the poet is to give form to the "consistent incongruity" ("Breakthrough") that characterizes her life. The measure of her success is our understanding that the incongruity is ours.

—Janis Butler Holm

RODRIGUEZ, Judith

Nationality: Australian. **Born:** Judith Green, Perth, Western Australia, 13 February 1936. **Education:** Brisbane Girls' Grammar School, 1950–53; University of Queensland, St. Lucia, 1954–57, B.A. (honors) 1957; Girton College, Cambridge, 1960–62, M.A. 1965; University of London, Cert. Ed. 1968. **Family:** Married 1) Fabio Rodriguez in 1964 (divorced 1981), three daughters and one son; 2) Thomas W. Shapcott, *q.v.,* in 1982. **Career:** Resident teacher, Fairholme Presbyterian Girls' College, Toowoomba, 1958; lecturer, University of Queensland Department of External Studies, 1959–60; lecturer in English, Philippa Fawcett College of Education, London, 1962–63, and University of the West Indies, Kingston, Jamaica, 1963–65; lecturer, St. Giles School of English, London, 1965–66, and St. Mary's College of Education, Twickenham, Middlesex, 1966–68; lecturer, 1969–76, and senior lecturer, 1977–85, La Trobe University, Melbourne; writer-in-residence, University of Western Australia, Nedlands, summer 1978, and Rollins College, Winter Park, Florida, 1986; lecturer on Australian literature, Macquarie University, North Ryde, New South Wales, 1985; visiting fellow, Western Australian Institute of Technology, South Bentley, 1986; lecturer in English, Macarthur Institute of Higher Education, Milperra, Sydney, 1987; lecturer in writing and writer-in-residence, Royal Melbourne Institute of Technology, 1988–89; writer-in-residence, Ormond College University of Melbourne, 1988–89. Since 1989 lecturer in writing, Victoria College; senior lecturer, Deakin University, 1993. Poetry editor, *Meanjin,* Melbourne, 1979–82; poetry columnist, Sydney *Morning Herald,* 1984–86. Since 1989 poetry consultant, Penguin Books Australia. Also artist and illustrator: individual shows in Melbourne, Brisbane, Adelaide, and Paris. **Awards:** Australia Council fellowship, 1974, 1978, 1983; South Australian Government prize, 1978; Artlook Victorian prize, 1979; P.E.N. Stuyvesant prize, 1981; Feminist Fortnight Favourite, 1989, for *New and Selected Poems;* Chistopher Brennan award, 1994. AM (Member of the Order of Australia), 1994. **Address:** P.O. Box 231, Mont Albert, Victoria 3127, Australia.

PUBLICATIONS

Poetry

Four Poets (as Judith Green), with others. Melbourne, Cheshire, 1962.
Nu-Plastik Fanfare Red and Other Poems. St. Lucia, University of Queensland Press, 1973.
Broadsheet Number Twenty-Three. Canberra, Open Door Press, 1976.
Water Life. St. Lucia, University of Queensland Press, 1976.
Shadow on Glass. Canberra, Open Door Press, 1978.
3 Poems. Melbourne, Old Metropolitan Meat Market, 1979.
Angels. Melbourne, Old Metropolitan Meat Market, 1979.
Arapede. Melbourne, Old Metropolitan Meat Market, 1979.
Mudcrab at Gambaro's. St. Lucia, University of Queensland Press, 1980.
Witch Heart. Melbourne, Sisters, 1982.
Mrs. Noah and the Minoan Queen, with others, edited by Rodriguez. Melbourne, Sisters, 1983.

Floridian Poems. Winter Park, Florida, Rollins College, 1986.
The House by the Water: New and Selected Poems. St. Lucia, University of Queensland Press, 1988.
The Cold. Canberra, National Library of Australia (Pamphlets Poets), 1992.

Plays

Poor Johanna (produced Adelaide, 1994). In *Heroines,* edited by D. Spender. Melbourne, Penguin, 1991.
Lindy, with Robyn Archer (opera libretto). Music by Moya Henderson, n.d.

Novel

Winners: A Novel. New York, Knopf, 1979.

Other

Noela Hjorth, with Vicki Pauli. Clarendon, South Australia, Granrott Press, 1984.

Editor, *Mrs. Noah and the Minoan Queen.* Melbourne, Sisters, 1983.
Editor, with Andrew Taylor, *Poems from the Australian's 20th Anniversary Competition.* Sydney, Angus and Robinson, 1985.
Editor, *I sogni cantano l'alba: poesia contemporeana,* translated by G. Englaro. Milan, Lanfranchi, 1988.
Editor, *The Collected Poems of Jennifer Rankin.* St. Lucia, University of Oueensland Press. 1990.

Translator, *Your Good Colombian Friend,* by Jairo Vanegas. Upper Ferntree Gully, Papyrus Press, 1995.

*

Manuscript Collection: Fryer Research Library, University of Queensland, Brisbane.

Critical Studies: Interviews in the Australian National Archive, 1976, *Women and Writing: Into the Eighties,* Clayton, Victoria, Monash University, 1980, *Uomini e Libri 97* (Milan), January-February 1984, *Bagdala* (Novi Sad, Yugoslavia), 1984, Sydney *Bulletin,* 1985, *The Age* (Melbourne), 3 January 1987, and *Linq* (Townsville, Queensland), 1987; "More Wow than Flutter" by Les A. Murray, in *Quadrant* (Sydney), October 1976; "Bolder Vision than Superintrospection" by P. Neilsen, in *The Age* (Melbourne), 12 March 1977; "Sea Change" by C. Treloar, in *Twenty-Four Hours* (Sydney), August 1977; "Restless, domestic. . ." by Chris Wallace-Crabbe, in *Australian Book Review* (Melbourne), December 1980; "A Positive Poetic" by Jennifer Strauss, in *Australian Book Review* (Melbourne), April 1983; "The White Witch and the Red Witch: The Poetry of Judith Rodriguez" by Delys Bird, in *Poetry and Gender: Statements and Essays in Australian Women's Poetics,* St. Lucia, University of Queensland Press, 1989; "A Lifetime Devoted to Literature: A Tribute to Judith Rodriguez" by Jennifer Strauss, in *Southerly* (Sydney), 1992; "Judith Rodriguez," in *Dialogues with Australian Poets* by R.P. Rama, Calcutta, Writers Workshop Press, 1993; "An Interview with Judith Rodriguez" by Peter Haddow, in

Famous Reporter (Kingston, Tasmania), 1993; "'By What Sign/Are You Walking?': The Poetry of Judith Rodriguez" by Lyn McCredden, in *Australian Literary Studies,* 18(2), October 1997; in *In Other Words: Interviews with Australian Poets* by Barbara Williams, Amsterdam, Rodopi, 1998.

Judith Rodriguez comments:

Three articles about my writing, by myself:

"Archimedas' platform, images of poetry, woman writing," in *Meanjin* (Melbourne), Winter 1988.

"Statements," in *Poetry and Gender: Statements and Essays in Australian Women's Poetics,* St. Lucia, University of Queensland Press, 1989.

"Out of the Dream, Voices," in *Fine Line* (Melbourne), December 1990.

I write poetry to live more fully. I dare to hope that poetry strengthens the best we can think and do. There is a delightful self-indulgence in this dialogue with readers and with those who have lived and will live.

My first close critic was the poet John Manifold.

Writing for stage and collaborating with a composer have been exciting, loosening-up, new-way adventures for me.

Establishing a poetry list for Penguin Books Australia has been a marvelous experience.

*   *   *

Judith Rodriguez first attracted attention (under her maiden name Judith Green) in 1962 as one of the contributors to *Four Poets,* a volume that presented the early work of four young writers with Brisbane affiliations and that, in effect, announced the emergence of a new force in Australian poetry. More than a decade later this force came to be tagged "the Queensland octopus" to indicate a sort of energy that was less regional than adaptive. Although each of the original four (Rodriguez, David Malouf, Rodney Hall, and Don Maynard) came to occupy important editorial positions, they did so in states other than Queensland, which is often regarded as the Deep South of Australian culture.

In her first poems Rodriguez displayed a vigorous manipulation of language, which was barely kept in check by the formal lyricism of the time, to serve the ends of immediacy and directness of expression. There is the sense of a new writer still seeking a style and a voice, though the uneven "Essay on M.K." comes closest to pushing the author into genuine self-exploration. It was not after a long period in Europe and Jamaica and an uneventful return to Australia that her second volume, *Nu-Plastik Fanfare Red,* was published. The increase in command and in certainty of direction is immediately clear in poems such as "Sojourners at Phoenix":

They are here, Svetlana, as they were there.
Men. Difficult to love. Difficult not to.

Slavers strung out in harness, iron-galled;
smiths of ideals, lining up at the anvil for thrashing.

Stalin, that fathered five-year plans and prisons.
And an architect of together. You can't say fairer.

And when you left, Svetlana, and when you left
with nothing ahead but maybe

glimmer in the jaws of the escape hatch
you could not perhaps slip through whole . . .

Her poetry had become imbued with a warm female sharpness—precisely observed moments and objects and responses, place rather than time, people through things, humanity through attitudes. Her tone had become clipped, never sloppy, and her poems were as tightly packed as a larder full of preserves. She had found a way to use language to contain her wide experience and range of interests.

Rodriguez's next full book, *Water Life,* was illustrated (or, rather, complemented) with the author's own vigorous and sensuous linocuts, and it received a major literary award. Her femininity is never embittered, though the exploration of her womanness has been increasingly fruitful for her writing and her development and has led to moments of painful honesty. *Water Life* summed up not only stages in the poet's own intellectual and emotional development but also that of a generation of women, and in ways it was directed to growth and celebratory instincts rather than rejection and self-immolation. The later small collection, *Shadow on Glass,* refines the characteristic Rodriguez energy to an almost clenched lyricism. It could be said that the lyrical mode has always exercised this poet's mind, but only in her late work has the combination of song-flow and mind-stress fully cohered, and, even then, it has done so only fitfully. She is in many ways the most exciting and explorative of the so-called Queensland octopus generation, her work providing the sense of an intellect—and a female strength—in the course of liberation and growth. In any terms her achievement and challenging way with language are apparent.

Publication of *New and Selected Poems,* nearly half of which is new work, reinforced the idea of water as a strong underlying principle used often with quite unconventional modes of approach to the idea of feminine fluidity and suppleness. What is more immediately apparent, though, in this impressive volume is the unique personal voice, quirky yet touching universal recognitions, direct and anecdotal without losing (or underlying too vehemently) the poet's apprehension of the numinous. At the first Feminist Book Fair in Melbourne in 1989 the work was regarded by many as one of the outstanding books presented.

In 1992 Rodriguez published the booklet *The Cold,* which is dominated by a long poem addressed to the older poet Barbara Giles. The poem indicates a development toward a longer, retrospective viewpoint in Rodriguez's work, something reinforced by other poems in the booklet. Rodriquez's presence during this period also has been evident in her position as poetry adviser to Penguin Books Australia, where she has invigorated the publisher's list and brought new vigor to the marketing of Australian poetry.

—Thomas W. Shapcott

ROOT, William Pitt

Nationality: American. **Born:** Austin, Minnesota, 28 December 1941. **Education:** University of Washington, Seattle, B.A. 1964; University of North Carolina, Greensboro, M.F.A. 1967; Stanford University, Stanford, California, 1968–69. **Family:** Married 1) Judy Bechtold in 1965 (divorced 1970), one daughter; 2) Pamela Uschuk in 1987. **Career:** General helper, Todd Shipyards, Seattle, Washington; stock clerk, warehouseman, and teamster, Seattle and Long Beach,

California, 1960–64; bouncer, Sweet Chariot Bar, Seattle, 1964–65. Instructor, Slippery Rock State College, Pennsylvania, 1967; assistant professor of English, Michigan State University, East Lansing, 1967–68; Stegner Creative Writing Fellow, Stanford University, California, 1968–69; visiting lecturer or writer, Mid-Peninsula Free University, 1969–70, Amherst College, Massachusetts, 1971, Wichita State University, Kansas, 1977, University of Southwestern Louisiana, Lafayette, 1977, University of Montana, Missoula, 1978, 1980–81, 1983–86, and Interlochen Arts Academy, Michigan, 1979. Since 1986 associate professor, Hunter College, New York. Since 1971 active in poets-in-schools programs in several states. **Awards:** Academy of American Poets university prize, 1966; Rockefeller grant, 1969; Guggenheim grant, 1970; National Endowment for the Arts grant, 1973; Pushcart prize for poetry, 1977, 1980, 1985; Bicentennial exchange fellowship, 1978; Stanley Kunitz award, 1981; Guy Owen prize, 1982; Poet Laureate of Tucson, 1997. **Address:** English Department, Hunter College, 195 Park Avenue, New York, New York 10021–5024, U.S.A.

PUBLICATIONS

Poetry

The Storm and Other Poems. New York, Atheneum, 1969.
Striking the Dark Air for Music. New York, Atheneum, 1973.
The Port of Galveston. Galveston, Texas, Galveston Arts Center, 1974.
A Journey South. Port Townsend, Washington, Graywolf Press, 1977.
7 Mendocino Songs. Portland, Oregon, Mississippi Mud Press, 1977.
Coot and Other Characters: Poems New and Familiar. Lewiston, Idaho, Confluence Press, 1977.
Fireclock. Boston, 4 Zoas Press, 1981.
Reasons for Going It on Foot. New York, Atheneum, 1981.
In the World's Common Grasses. Santa Cruz, California, Moving Parts, 1981.
Invisible Guests. Lewiston, Iowa, Confluence, 1984.
Faultdancing. Pittsburgh, University of Pittsburgh Press, 1986.
Trace Elements from a Recurring Kingdom. Lewiston, Idaho, Confluence Press, 1994.

Plays

Screenplays (with Ray Rice): *Song of the Woman and the Butterflyman,* 1975; *7 for a Magician,* 1976; *Faces,* 1981.

Other

The Unbroken Diamond: Nightletter to the Mujahideen. Galveston. Texas. Pipedream Press. 1983.

Editor, *What a World, What a World! Poetry by Young People in Galveston Schools.* Galveston, Texas, Pipedream Press, 1974.

Translator, *Kingdom of Quick Song: Selected Odes of Pablo Neruda.* Boston, 4 Zoas Press, 1984.

*

Manuscript Collection: University of North Carolina Library, Greensboro.

Critical Studies: By Benjamin DeMott, in *New York Times Book Review,* 10 December 1967; ''Notes on Current Books,'' in *Virginia Quarterly* (Charlottesville), August 1969; ''The Storm'' by Robin Skelton, in *Malahat* Review (Victoria, British Columbia), October 1969; ''Striking the Dark Air for Music'' by Paul Nelson, in *Carleton Miscellany* (Northfield, Minnesota), September 1974; ''An Ultimate Magician: Notes on the Work of William Pitt Root'' by Floyd Skloot, in *Chowder Review* (Wallaston, Massachusetts), winter 1978.

William Pitt Root comments:

As a counter to the proliferation of much instant poetry, I regard with respect the efforts of such men as Bly and Merwin in America or Hughes in England, who, with others, bring into English the works of writers from other cultures where the conditions for the development of the human spirit are still more trying, more essentially demanding.

Regarding my own work, I hope it reflects something of the qualities I admire most in Roethke (whose primordial consciousness is inimitable), Frost (who forged memorable work out of an inconsolable solitude), Williams (whose love of animation in people and nature was inexhaustible), García Lorca (whose passions were essential, unsummoned), and Whitman, Blake, Neruda, Lawrence, and Jeffers (who share the impulse to accomplish the mythic common bond out of the apparently commonplace)—these are men who in opening to their own experience can extend us as well. These poets are makers, not designers, and what they make is self being freed of ego, first defining, then transcending those limits. In America, now, the most exciting groundwork for such growth is being established by the waking generations of women who dare to explore their own frontiers. I should add I mean those who travel by foot, to distinguish between them and those who travel by bandwagon. No frontier has ever been approached by bandwagon.

*   *   *

William Pitt Root's book *Reasons for Going It on Foot* is so animated with the beauty and mysteries of wildlife that one is convinced that his earlier obsession with the dead and the dying has been dismissed for being only part of the story. In *Striking the Dark Air for Music,* Root exposes a vision of death as being the mean conclusion to a short and troublesome life:

> I saw the crippled tree
> crumple into colors, shedding
> their brilliant disease of leaves
> that left the branches dead.

If life must be celebrated, it must be noted that life is mostly menacing. In ''A Start'' the poet recognizes spring while holding his young daughter's ''flowersmeary hands.'' Then he feels ''the green blades cocked / in dry wood / drive free.'' The word ''cocked'' serves to undermine the poem's theme of new life with the hint that it arrives armed and dangerous.

Root's later work, however, nearly abandons these earlier worries with poems that celebrate life and the living. Everywhere in *Reasons for Going It on Foot* the living are awake with action. In one poem slugs are making love; in another it is the spiders who are amorous. Throughout the book the images of birds dancing, of men and women "diving like seals," of hands as "quick fish" appear as the sparkling rewards of the book's quest expressed in its title poem:

> . . . I may identify
> myself as a stranger
>
> eager to know
> the ways of those
>
> I beg my life from
> as I pass.

The desire is to be filled with the happenings of others' lives, to be as conspicuously alive as the slugs in "Slugs Amorous in the Air," not to feel empty and alone after the "white birds like spirits gathered for a ceremonial / dance . . . / . . . drew their long yellow legs onto the commotion of/their wings" and were gone.

Though Root's theme has changed, his style has not. His snap-to-it diction and no-frills syntax remain. Though he was already the unsung master of personification, Root's skill in this area has become even more sophisticated since he now more readily compounds metaphor with sound. This is exemplified in the contrast between the earlier line "The sun heats and robs me" and the later and more musical line "a single horse / stood beneath the single singing tree."

What has not changed is Root's continuing experimentation with the poem's form. *Reasons for Going It on Foot*, for instance, like his earlier books exhibits a variety of stanza patterns that range from the couplet, to the quatrain, to stanzas with unjustified margins, to stanzas justified like prose. Root's versatile use of form is one of his enduring traits as a craftsman. His ability to evoke the pains of life and the lushness of nature in thrifty images is his enduring trait as a poet.

—Susan Kaplan

ROSE, Peter

Nationality: Australian. **Born:** Melbourne, 8 June 1955. **Education:** Haileybury College, 1972; Monash University, Melbourne, 1973–76, B.A. 1976. **Family:** With Christopher Menz since 1998. **Career:** Academic and reference publisher, Oxford University Press, Melbourne, 1990–2000. **Awards:** St. Kilda Centenary poetry prize, 1990; Harri Jones award, 1991; Queensland Premier's prize, 1991, 1992. **Agent:** Jenny Darling & Associates, P.O. Box 235, Richmond, Victoria 3121, Australia. **Address:** 123 Brougham Place, North Adelaide, South Australia 5006, Australia.

PUBLICATIONS

Poetry

The House of Vitriol. Sydney, Picador, 1990.
The Catullan Rag. Sydney, Picador, 1993.
Donatello in Wangaratta. Sydney, Hale and Iremonger, 1998.

*

Critical Study: In *Overland,* 136, spring 1994.

*   *   *

Peter Craven has commented that Peter Rose has quickly established himself as being "in the mainstream of Australian writing, alongside such accomplished figures as Porter and Murray." Words like "elegant," "cosmopolitan," and "consummate" have been used to describe his work.

Rose spent his boyhood in Wangaratta, a country town in Victoria, and after graduating from Monash University he worked as a medical bookseller before joining Oxford University Press, where he was for a number of years involved in the publishing of general and reference works. His preoccupation with the broad spectrum of European culture is perhaps illustrated by the titles of his books: *The House of Vitriol* (1990), *The Catullan Rag* (1993), and *Donatello in Wangaratta* (1998). But though there is indeed a foreground of art, literature, and the inheritance of Western culture in his poetry, it is placed in the uncomfortable context of a man who will never shake off a lonely and private childhood. The cultural baggage is completely integrated. It is a part of the writer, and his vision is indeed enriched, not decorated, by what has become his basis for comparison and reference. This does not mean that the environment has been relegated, but it is the environment of feeling and the ironic sensibilities that mask feeling.

Rose has an accomplished capacity to weave into his poems subtle suggestions of an ordinary Australian background and an extraordinary foreground of learned reference and emotional smoke screens. This can be seen, for example, in "Greening":

> Let's not watch the main event,
> let's watch the people.
> There we shall be beautifully private,
> each lake with its own suicide,
> those grand disclosures
> aching on a beach.
> Your beauty is the last quotation,
> an available dark . . .
> So let's postpone matter for a while:
> the final caper; an auspicious turn.

It is this heightened awareness of nuance that infuses Rose's poetry with a sort of robust delicacy and assures him a position among the leading Australian poets of his generation. His debt to Peter Porter and sometimes even Hal Porter (a hint of the baroque) has been absorbed into his own distinctive tone.

—Thomas W. Shapcott

ROSENBLATT, Joe

Nationality: Canadian. **Born:** Joseph Rosenblatt, Toronto, Ontario, 26 December 1933. **Education:** Central Technical School, and George Brown College, Toronto. **Family:** Married Faye Smith in

1970; one son. **Career:** Worked as a laborer, factory worker, plumber's mate, gravedigger, and civil servant until 1958; worked for Canadian Pacific Railway, 1958–65. Visiting lecturer, University of Victoria and University of Western Ontario, 1980; writer-in-residence, University of Western Ontario, 1979–80, Universities of Rome and Bologna, 1987, and Saskatoon Public Library, 1985–86. Senior editor, *Jewish Dialogue,* Toronto, 1970–83; associate editor, *Malahat Review,* University of Victoria, 1980–82. President, League of Canadian Poets, 1983–85. Artist: individual show of drawings, Gadatsy Gallery. **Awards:** Canada Council grant, 1966, 1968, 1973, 1980, 1986, 1992; Ontario Arts Council award, 1970; Governor General's award, 1976; British Columbia Book prize, 1986; British Columbia Arts Council project grant, 1991. **Address:** 221 Elizabeth Avenue, Qualicum Beach, British Columbia V9K 1G8, Canada.

PUBLICATIONS

Poetry

Voyage of the Mood. Don Mills, Ontario, Heinrich Heine Press, 1963.
The LSD Leacock. Toronto, Coach House Press, 1966.
Winter of the Luna Moth. Toronto, Anansi, 1968.
The Bumblebee Dithyramb. Erin, Ontario, Press Porcépic, 1972.
Blind Photographer: Poems and Sketches. Erin, Ontario, Press Porcépic, 1973.
Dream Craters, edited by John Newlove. Erin, Ontario, Press Porcépic, 1974.
Virgins and Vampires. Toronto, McClelland and Stewart, 1975.
Top Soil. Erin, Ontario, Press Porcépic, 1976.
Loosely Tied Hands: An Experiment in Punk. Windsor, Ontario, Black Moss Press, 1978.
Snake Oil. Toronto, Exile, 1978.
The Sleeping Lady. Toronto, Exile, 1979.
Brides of the Stream. Lantzville, British Columbia, Oolichan Books, 1983.
Poetry Hotel: Selected Poems 1963–1985. Toronto, McClelland and Stewart, 1985.
Gridi nel Buio (Poems in Italian and English). Abano Terme, Italy, Piovan Editore, 1990.
Beds & Consenting Dreamers. Lantzville, British Columbia, Oolichan Books, 1994.
A Tentacled Mother. Toronto, Exile, 1995.
The Rosenblatt Reader. Toronto, Exile, 1995.
The Voluptuous Gardener. Vancouver, Beach Holme Press, 1996.

Recording: *Joe Rosenblatt,* High Bamet, 1971.

Play

I Get High on Butterflies (score), music by Nancy Talfer. Waterloo, Ontario, Waterloo Music, 1984.

Short Stories

Tommy Fry and the Ant Colony. Windsor, Ontario, Black Moss Press, 1979.

Other

Doctor Anaconda's Solar Fun Club: A Book of Drawings. Erin, Ontario, Press Porcépic, 1977.
Escape from the Glue Factory: A Memoir of a Paranormal Toronto Childhood in the Late Forties. Toronto, Exile, 1985.
The Kissing Goldfish of Siam: A Memoir of Adolescence in the Fifties, Toronto. Toronto, Exile, 1989.

*

Manuscript Collections: Public Archives of Canada, Ottawa; University of Toronto.

Joe Rosenblatt comments:

My own verse and prose poems basically attack the human condition and society with its crass materialism and phony value structure.

My poetry is traditional and influenced by American poets such as Hart Crane and Robert Frost. My poems are concerned with the Moloch or mammon monster of society and the insatiable appetite of the creature. The monster finds its expression in my animal poems. For example, in my bat poems the psyche of man is found in this terrestrial animal of darkness. Therefore my kinship is with Swift and misanthropes. My superhero is Ambrose Bierce. In nearly all my poems the quest of man is spiritual cannibalism—soul theft and the protein of money.

I use the traditional devices of poetry in my work such as rhyme, assonance, and metric extension.

*　　*　　*

For the most part Joe Rosenblatt "is a poet of the small presses," but he is, nevertheless, well known in Canada. At times he has seemed, superficially, more interested in the world of plants, insects, and animals than that of human beings, but this is more an aspect of his fascination with the unusual, the rare, and the minute than a lack of sympathy with the race of man. He has said, "I only deal with the bizarre," but he adds that his later poems are "more directly confessional poems, written without the intervention of imagery or my old animal disguises." Rosenblatt draws as well as writes, and in the drawings images of grotesque and curiously human, though debased, animals and reptiles abound. He has had exhibitions of his drawings in several Toronto galleries, and his 1973 book *Blind Photographer* might more properly be called a book of drawings illustrated by poems than the opposite. He has said that "drawings are the lazy man's way to writing anti-poems, poems without intellectualizing and verbalizing."

It is typical of Rosenblatt to hint that he is not much interested in thoughtful technique; in fact, in both poems and drawings he is always meticulously careful of detail. His interest in "insect and plant sexuality" is extraordinary, and Norman Snider has said rightly that "Rosenblatt is a miniaturist in his sensibility, his poems are minute and exquisite observations of the tiny phenomena of nature." It remains only to add that wit, in the true meaning of the word, is the prime mark of his work.

—John Newlove

ROSS, Alan

Nationality: British. **Born:** Calcutta, India, 6 May 1922. **Education:** Haileybury; St. John's College, Oxford. **Military Service:** Royal Naval Volunteer Reserve, 1942–47. **Family:** Married Jennifer Fry in 1949; one son. **Career:** Staff member, British Council, 1947–50; staff member, *The Observer,* London, 1950–71. Since 1961 editor, *London Magazine;* since 1965 managing director, London Magazine Editions, formerly Alan Ross Publishers, London. **Awards:** Atlantic-Rockefeller award, 1946. Fellow, Royal Society of Literature, 1971. C.B.E. (Commander, Order of the British Empire), 1982. **Address:** 4 Elm Park Lane, London S.W.3, England.

PUBLICATIONS

Poetry

Summer Thunder. Oxford, Blackwell, 1941.
The Derelict Day: Poems in Germany. London, Lehmann, 1947.
Something of the Sea: Poems 1942–1952. London, Verschoyle, 1954; Boston, Houghton Mifflin, 1955.
To Whom It May Concern: Poems 1952–57. London, Hamish Hamilton, 1958.
African Negatives. London, Eyre and Spottiswoode, 1962.
North from Sicily: Poems in Italy 1961–64. London, Eyre and Spottiswoode, 1965.
Poems 1942–67. London, Eyre and Spottiswoode, 1967.
A Calcutta Grandmother. London, Poem-of-the-Month Club, 1971.
Tropical Ice. London, Covent Garden Press, 1972.
The Taj Express: Poems 1967–1973. London, London Magazine Editions, 1973.
Open Sea. London, London Magazine Editions, 1975.
Death Valley. London, London Magazine Editions, 1980.

Other

Time Was Away: A Notebook in Corsica. London, Lehmann, 1948.
The Forties: A Period Piece. London, Weidenfeld and Nicolson, 1950.
The Gulf of Pleasure (travel). London, Weidenfeld and Nicolson, 1951.
Poetry 1945–50. London, Longman, 1951.
The Bandit on the Billiard Table: A Journey through Sardinia. London, Verschoyle, 1954; revised edition, as *South to Sardinia,* London, Hamish Hamilton, 1960.
Australia 55: A Journal of the M.C.C. Tour (cricket). London, Joseph, 1955.
Cape Summer, and The Australians in England. London, Hamish Hamilton, 1957.
The Onion Man (for children). London, Hamish Hamilton, 1959.
Danger on Glass Island (for children). London, Hamish Hamilton, 1960.
Through the Caribbean: The M.C.C. Tour of the West Indies 1959–1960 (cricket). London, Hamish Hamilton, 1960.
Australia 63 (cricket). London, Eyre and Spottiswoode, 1963.
The West Indies at Lord's (cricket). London, Eyre and Spottiswoode, 1963.
The Wreck of Moni (for children). London, Alan Ross, 1965.
A Castle in Sicily (for children). London, Alan Ross, 1966.

Colours of War: War Art 1939–45. London, Cape, 1983.
Ranji, Prince of Cricketers. London, Collins, 1983.
Blindfold Games: An Autobiography. London, Collins Harvill, 1986.
The Emissary: G.D. Birla, Gandhi and Independence. London, Collins Harvill, 1986.
West Indian Summer, with Patrick Eagar. London, Hodder and Stoughton, 1988.
Coastwise Lights (autobiography). London, Collins Harvill, 1988.
After Pusan. London, Harvill, 1995.
Winter Sea: War, Journeys, Writers. London, Harvill, 1997.
Reflections on Blue Water: Journeys in the Gulf of Naples & in the Aeolian Islands. London, Harvill, 1999.
Green Fading into Blue: A Sporting Memoir. London, Deutsch, 1999.

Editor, *Selected Poems of John Gay.* London, Grey Walls Press, 1950.
Editor, with Jennifer Ross, *Borrowed Time: Short Stories,* by F. Scott Fitzgerald. London, Grey Walls Press, 1951.
Editor, *Abroad: Travel Stories.* London, Faber, 1957.
Editor, *The Cricketer's Companion.* London, Eyre and Spottiswoode, 1960; revised edition, London, Eyre Methuen, 1979.
Editor, *Poetry Supplement.* London, Poetry Book Society, 1963.
Editor, *London Magazine Stories 1–12.* London, London Magazine Editions, 1964–80.
Editor, *Leaving School.* London, London Magazine Editions, 1966.
Editor, *Living in London.* London, London Magazine Editions, 1974.
Editor, *Selected Poems,* by Lawrence Durrell. London, Faber, 1977.
Editor, *The Turf.* Oxford, Oxford University Press, 1982.
Editor, *London Magazine 1961–1985.* London, Chatto and Windus, 1986.
Editor, *Signals: Thirty New Stories to Celebrate Thirty Years of the 'London Magazine.'* London, Constable, 1991.
Editor, with Jane Rye, *Signals-2: 25 London Magazine Stories.* London, London Magazine, 1999.

Translator, *The Undersea Adventure,* by Philippe Diolé. New York, Messner, 1953.
Translator, *The Sacred Forest,* by Pierre Gaisseau. London, Weidenfeld and Nicolson, 1954.
Translator, *Seas of Sicily,* by Philippe Diolé. London, Sidgwick and Jackson, 1955; as *Gates of the Sea,* New York, Messner, 1955.

*

Manuscript Collection: Arts Council of Great Britain, London.

*   *   *

Alan Ross began as what is vaguely called a war poet. He was in Germany during the early part of the Allied occupation, and his subjects were German gun sites and military hospitals, day and night in Hamburg, Lüneburg Heath, and the dark night of the soul that, as he saw it, was closing in on Germany. The subjects were grim, but the poet's spirit did not fully reflect them, for his awareness of the sensuous world was too strong. "Lüneburg," for instance, has as its refrain "The courtroom holds the afternoon in chains." The idea is to convey that Germany, too, is in chains, but the verse that follows might reflect a peaceful life in Oxford: "October settles on water and weeping willows. / Under stone bridges, leaves like boats / Drift golden . . .''

Many years later, when preparing his collected poems, Ross revised many of these early pieces in a remarkable way, stiffening them, making exact what had been vague. "Sengwarden" originally began and ended with the line "At Sengwarden the silence is the space in the heart." (As a young poet Ross had a weakness for this kind of romantic and not very meaningful statement.) This line was dropped, and the revised poem begins,

Something (but what) could be made of this.
Two U-boat officers turning to piss
In swastika shapes against a wall.

These revised early poems, which bear only the relationship of mood to their originals, are certainly among Ross's best work. In general he shows a love of color and gaiety that sometimes declines to mere prettiness. He has written about cricket at Brighton and the World Cup, the Grand Canal and mine dances in Johannesburg, the Autostrada del Sole and the Finchley Road. He records the scene vividly, but too often he seems content just to do this without looking beneath or outside it. His poem about the Finchley Road begins, "Beyond the window the tyre-coloured road deflates / Like a tube at night." One appreciates the ingenious aptness of the image, but it is expressive only on a superficial level. Sometimes a general moral is drawn in the last verse in an attempt to add meaningfulness to a poem that is really no more than a record of observations.

Perhaps Ross was unlucky in the period at which he began writing. His natural tendency to romantic excess was encouraged by World War II and by the poets most in favor at the time. In the 1930s or in the 1950s his tendency to see everything in terms of brightly colored pictures would have been controlled, and this in fact he has tried to do himself. The poems he wrote in Africa between 1958 and 1960 offer pictures just as clear as those in his earlier work, but some of them, like "Rock Paintings," "Sometime Never," and "Such Matters as Rape," go a good deal further by expressing involvement with the scenes described.

Death Valley, the collection of poems written in various parts of the United States, has all of the pictorial sharpness of the early work plus a keenness of observation that is never merely journalistic. This fine volume was rather impercipiently received, however.

—Julian Symons

ROTHENBERG, Jerome (Dennis)

Nationality: American. **Born:** New York City, 11 December 1931. **Education:** New York public schools, 1937–48; City College of New York, B.A. 1952; University of Michigan, Ann Arbor, M.A. 1953. **Military Service:** Served in the U.S. Army in Germany, 1954–55. **Family:** Married Diane Brodatz in 1952; one son. **Career:** Instructor, City College of New York, 1959–60; lecturer in English, Mannes College of Music, New York, 1961–70; Regents Professor, University of California, San Diego, 1971; visiting lecturer in anthropology, New School for Social Research, New York, 1971–72; visiting professor, University of Wisconsin, Milwaukee, 1974–75, San Diego State University, 1976–77, University of California, San Diego, 1977–79 and 1980–84, University of California, Riverside, 1980,

University of Oklahoma, Norman, 1985, State University of New York, Albany, 1986, and Binghamton, 1986–88. Since 1988 professor of visual arts and literature, University of California, San Diego. Distinguished Aerol Arnold Chair in English, University of Southern California, Los Angeles, 1983; distinguished writer-in-residence, New York State Writers Institute, Albany, 1986. Founding publisher, Hawk's Well Press, New York, 1958–65; editor or co-editor, *Poems from the Floating World,* 1960–64, *Some/Thing,* 1965–68, and *Alcheringa,* 1970–76, all New York, and *New Wilderness Letter,* 1976–85; contributing editor, *Stony Brook,* Stony Brook, New York, *Change International,* Paris, *Dialectical Anthropology,* Amsterdam, and *Sulfur,* Pasadena, California. **Awards:** Longview Foundation award, 1960; Wenner-Gren Foundation grant, 1968; Guggenheim grant, 1974; National Endowment for the Arts grant, 1976; American Book award, 1982. D.Litt.: State University of New York, Oneonta, 1997. **Address:** c/o New Directions, 80 Eighth Avenue, New York, New York 10011, U.S.A.

PUBLICATIONS

Poetry

White Sun, Black Sun. New York, Hawk's Well Press, 1960.
The Seven Hells of the Jigoku Zoshi. New York, Trobar, 1962.
Sightings I-IX, with *Lunes* by Robert Kelly. New York, Hawk's Well Press, 1964.
The Gorky Poems (bilingual edition). Mexico City, El Corno Emplumado, 1966.
Between: Poems 1960–1963. London, Fulcrum Press, 1967.
Conversations. Los Angeles, Black Sparrow Press, 1968.
Poems 1964–1967. Los Angeles, Black Sparrow Press, 1968.
Offering Flowers, with Ian Tyson. London, Circle Press, 1968.
Sightings I-IX & Red Easy a Color, with Ian Tyson. London, Circle Press, 1968.
Poland/1931. Santa Barbara, California, Unicorn Press, 1969.
The Directions, with Tom Phillips. London, Tetrad Press, 1969.
Polish Anecdotes. Santa Barbara, California, Unicorn Press, 1970.
Poems for the Game of Silence 1960–1970. New York, Dial Press, 1971.
A Book of Testimony. Bolinas, California, Tree, 1971.
Net of Moon, Net of Sun. Santa Barbara, California, Unicorn Press, 1971.
Poems for the Society of the Mystic Animals, with Ian Tyson and Richard Johnny John. London, Tetrad Press, 1972.
A Valentine No a Valedictory for Gertrude Stein. London. Judith Walker, 1972.
Seneca Journal I: A Poem of Beavers. Madison, Wisconsin, Perishable Press, 1973.
Three Friendly Warnings, with Ian Tyson. London, Tetrad Press, 1973.
Esther K. Comes to America, 1931. Greensboro, North Carolina, Unicorn Press, 1974.
The Cards. Los Angeles, Black Sparrow Press, 1974.
Poland/1931 (complete edition). New York, New Directions, 1974.
The Pirke and the Pearl. Berkeley, California, Tree, 1975.
Seneca Journal: Midwinter, with Philip Sultz. St. Louis, Singing Bone Press, 1975.
A Poem to Celebrate the Spring and Diane Rothenberg's Birthday. Madison, Wisconsin, Perishable Press, 1975.

Book of Palaces: The Gatekeepers. Boston, Pomegranate Press, 1975.

I Was Going through the Smoke, with Ian Tyson. London, Tetrad Press, 1975.

Rain Events. Milwaukee, Membrane Press, 1975.

The Notebooks. Milwaukee, Membrane Press, 1976.

A Vision of the Chariot in Heaven. Boston, Hundred Flowers Book Shop, 1976.

Narratives and Realtheater Pieces, with Ian Tyson. Bretenoux, France, Braad, 1977.

Seneca Journal: The Serpent, with Philip Sultz. St. Louis, Singing Bone Press, 1978.

A Seneca Journal (complete edition). New York, New Directions, 1978.

B*R*M*Tz*V*H. Madison, Wisconsin, Perishable Press, 1979.

Abulafia's Circles. Milwaukee, Membrane Press, 1979.

Letters and Numbers. Madison, Wisconsin, Salient Seedling Press, 1979.

Vienna Blood and Other Poems. New York, New Directions, 1980.

For E.W.: Two Sonnets. London, Spot Press, 1981.

Imaginal Geography 9: Landscape with Bishop. San Diego, Atticus Press, 1982.

The History of Dada as My Muse. London, Spot Press, 1982.

Altar Pieces. Barrytown, New York, Station Hill Press, 1982.

That Dada Strain. New York, New Directions, 1983.

15 Flower World Variations, with Harold Cohen. Milwaukee, Membrane Press, 1984.

A Merz Sonata. Easthampton, Massachusetts, Emanon Press, 1985.

New Selected Poems 1970–1985. New York, New Directions, 1986.

Gematria 5. Binghamton, New York, Bellevue, 1987.

Khurbn and Other Poems. New York, New Directions, 1989.

Further Sightings and Conversations. San Francisco, Pennywhistle Press, 1989.

The Lorca Variations (1–8). Tenerife, Spain, Zasterle Press, 1990; New York, New Directions, 1993.

The Gematria. Los Angeles, Sun and Moon Press, 1990.

Pictures of the Crucifixion: Poems. New York, Granary, 1995.

Seedings & Other Poems. New York, New Directions, 1996.

Paris Elegies & Improvisations. San Diego, California, Meow Press, 1998.

Recordings: *Origins and Meanings,* Folkways, 1968; *From a Shaman's Notebook,* Folkways, 1968; *Horse Songs and Other Soundings,* S-Press, 1975; *6 Horse Songs for 4 Voices,* New Wilderness, 1978; *Jerome Rothenberg Reads Poland/1931,* New Fire, 1979; *Rothenberg/Turetzky: Performing,* Blues Economique, 1984; *The Birth of the War God,* with Charlie Morrow and The Western Wind, Laurel, 1988.

Plays

The Deputy, adaptation of a play by Rolf Hochhuth (produced New York, 1964). New York, French, 1965.

That Dada Strain, music by Bertram Turetzky (produced San Diego, 1985; New York, 1987).

Poland/1931 (produced New York, 1988).

Radio Plays: *Das Hörspiel des Bibers,* 1984 (Germany); *Der Dada Ton [That Dada Strain],* 1986 (Germany).

Other

Pre-Faces and Other Writings. New York, New Directions, 1981.

The Riverside Interviews 4: Jerome Rothenberg, edited by Gavin Selerie. London, Binnacle Press, 1984.

A Paradise of Poets: New Poems & Translations. New York, New Directions, 1999.

Editor and Translator, *New Young German Poets.* San Francisco, City Lights, 1959.

Editor, *Ritual: A Book of Primitive Rites and Events* (anthology). New York, Something Else Press, 1966.

Editor, *Technicians of the Sacred: A Range of Poetries from Africa, America, Asia and Oceania.* New York, Doubleday, 1968; revised edition, Berkeley, University of California Press, 1985.

Editor, *Shaking the Pumpkin: Traditional Poetry of the Indian North Americas.* New York, Doubleday, 1972; revised edition, New York, Alfred van der Mark, 1986.

Editor, with George Quasha, *America a Prophecy: A New Reading of American Poetry from Pre-Columbian Times to the Present.* New York, Random House, 1973.

Editor, *Revolution of the Word: A New Gathering of American Avant Garde Poetry 1914–1945.* New York, Seabury Press, 1974

Editor, with Michel Benamou, *Ethnopoetics: A First International Symposium.* Boston, Alcheringa, 1976.

Editor, with Harris Lenowitz and Charles Doria, *A Big Jewish Book: Poems and Other Visions of the Jews from Tribal Times to the Present.* New York, Doubleday, 1978; revised edition, with Lenowitz, as *Exiled in the Word,* Port Townsend, Washington, Copper Canyon Press, 1989.

Editor, with Diane Rothenberg, *Symposium of the Whole: A Range of Discourse Toward an Ethnopoetics.* Berkeley, University of California Press, 1983.

Editor, with David M. Guss, *The Book, Spiritual Instrument.* New York, Granary, 1996.

Editor, with Pierre Joris, *Poems for the Millennium: The University of California Book of Modern & Postmodern Poetry, Volume One, from Fin-de-Siecle to Negritude.* Berkeley, University of California Press, 1998.

Editor, with Pierre Joris, *Poems for the Millennium: The University of California Book of Modern & Postmodern Poetry, Volume Two, from Postwar to Millennium.* Berkeley, University of California Press, 1998.

Editor, with Steven Clay, *A Book of the Book: Some Works & Projections about the Book & Writing.* New York, Granary, 2000.

Translator, *The Flight of Quetzalcoatl,* from a Spanish prose version of the original Aztec by Angel Maria Garibay. Brighton, Sussex, Unicorn Bookshop, 1967.

Translator, with Michael Hamburger and the author, *Poems for People Who Don't Read Poems,* by Hans Magnus Enzensberger. New York, Atheneum, and London, Secker and Warburg, 1968; as *Poems,* London, Penguin, 1968.

Translator, *The Book of Hours and Constellations,* by Eugen Gomringer. New York, Something Else Press, 1968.

Translator, *The 17 Horse Songs of Frank Mitchell, Nos. X-XIII.* London, Tetrad Press, 1969.

Translator, with Harris Lenowitz, *Gematria 27.* Milwaukee, Membrane Press, 1977.
Translator, *4 Lorca Suites.* Los Angeles, Sun and Moon Press, 1989.

*

Bibliography: *Jerome Rothenberg: A Descriptive Bibliography* edited by Harry Polkinhorn, Jefferson, North Carolina, McFarland, 1988.

Manuscript Collection: Archive for New Poetry, University of California, San Diego.

Critical Studies: "20th Century Music" by Diane Wakoski, in *Parnassus* (New York), fall-winter 1972; "Uniting History in a 'Biological Fellowhood'" by Paula Gunn Allen, in *Contact II* (New York), fall 1978; by Thomas Meyer, in *American Book Review* (New York),September-October 1981; by George F. Butterick, in *Sulfur 4* (Pasadena, California), 1982; by David Toolan, in *Commonwealth* (New York), 4 November 1983; *Interpreting the Indian: Twentieth Century Poets and the Native American* by Michael Castro, Albuquerque, University of New Mexico Press, 1983; "Restorative Topographies: Notes on Ethnopoetics from a Province of the Mind" by Judith Gleason, in *Parnassus* (New York), 11(2), 1984; *In Search of the Primitive: Rereading David Antin, Jerome Rothenberg and Gary Snyder* by Sherman Paul, Baton Rouge, Louisiana State University Press, 1986; *Apocalyptic Messianism and Contemporary Jewish-American Poetry* by R. Barbara Gitenstein, Albany, State University of New York Press, 1986; "Soundings: Zaum, Seriality and the Discovery of the 'Sacred'" by Marjorie Perloff, in *American Poetry Review* (Philadelphia), February 1986; "Where the Real Song Begins: The Poetry of Jerome Rothenberg" by Eric Mottram, in *Dialectical Anthropology* (Amsterdam), 2(2–4), 1986; "On Rothenberg's Revised 'Technicians of the Sacred'" by Jed Rasula, in *Poetics Journal,* 6, 1986; "Rothenberg's Continuing Revolution of the Word" by John Zalenski, in *North Dakota Quarterly* (Grand Forks), 55(4), fall 1987; "Literacy and the Roots of Poetry: A Conversation with Jerome Rothenberg" by Fred Garber, in *Forum* (Binghamton, New York), April 1987; "Jerome Rothenberg: That Dad Strain," in *Great American Poetry Bakeoff,* vol. 3, by Robert L. Peters, Metuchen, New Jersey, Scarecrow Press, 1987; "Some Bearings on Ethnopoetics" by Paul Christensen, in *Parnassus* (New York), 15(1), 1989; "Coyote Cohen: Or, the Universal Trickster in Jerome Rothenberg's Evolving Collection Poland/1931" by R. Barbara Gitenstein, in *Studies in American Jewish Literature* (University Park, Pennsylvania), 9(2), fall 1990; "Contemporary Poetics and History: Pinsky, Klepfisz and Rothenberg" by James McCorkle, in *Kenyon Review* (Syracuse, New York), 14(1), winter 1992; "Thinking Made in the Mouth: The Cultural Poetics of David Antin and Jerome Rothenberg" by Hank Lazer, in *Picturing Cultural Values in Postmodern America,* edited by William G. Doty, Tuscaloosa, University of Alabama Press, 1995; *Interactive Poetics: Native-American/European-American Encounter As a Model for Poetic Practice* (dissertation) by Molly Weigel, Princeton University, 1996; "The Messianic Ethnography of Jerome Rothenberg's Poland/1931" by Norman Finkelstein, in *Contemporary Literature* (Madison, Wisconsin), 39(3), fall 1998; *The Terror of Our Days: Sylvia Plath, William Heyen, Gerald Stern, and Jerome Rothenberg Poetically Respond to Holocaust* (dissertation) by Harriet Parmet, Lehigh University, 1998.

Jerome Rothenberg comments:

I did not know at the opening how old our work as poets was. Like others my age then—and others before and after us—I was looking for what in my own time would make a difference to that time. What is easily forgotten is the condition of the time itself that should make us want to go in that direction, to pull down and to transform. As a young child I heard people still talking about the "world" war (even the "great" war) in the singular, but by adolescence the second war had come and with it a crisis in the human capacity to reduce and stifle life.

Auschwitz and Hiroshima came to be the two events by which we speak of it—signs of an enormity that turned myth into history, metaphor into fact. The horror of those events encompassed hundreds and thousands of like disasters, joined, as we began to realize, to other, not unrelated violence against the environment/the earth and the other-than-human world. By the mid-twentieth century, in Charles Olson's words, man had been "reduced to so much fat for soap, superphosphate for soil, fillings and shoes for sale," an enormity that had robbed language (one of our "proudest acts," he said) of the power to meaningfully respond, had thus created a crisis of expression (no, of meaning, of reality), for which a poetics must be devised if we were to rise again beyond the level of a scream or of a silence more terrible than any scream.

It is in this sense that I would speak of poetry and politics (and of an avant-garde informed by such a poetry and politics). The poets who live with language and remember the need to resist and remake feel whatever moves they make to be political and charged with meaning in the political sense. Time will determine if the politics is good or bad—if, as I would see it, it contributes to our liberation or our deeper entrapment—but that it is a politics is something I would choose never to deny. As poet I am most interested in the work of those other poets and artists for whom such questions have clearly played a central role and for whom the politics has played itself out not only, or even principally, as a subject matter but in the language and structure of the poem itself.

It is in some such ways, whether ultimately viable or not, that the avant-garde of modernism challenged the traditional/ conventional art and poetry that preceded it. And it is in this way too that postmodern poets and artists, from Dada to the present, have challenged the works of the preceding modernists, not as a nostalgic return to the state-bred values of official culture but to keep open the channels of renewal that remain the central necessities behind the impulse of a poetry and art of transformations. The history of that art, that poetry (as of every other art since its separation from its people's central rites), has never been free from corruption, whether by money or by power, and the failure of most avant-gardes to address or redress that corruption must surely be their greatest failure. Nor would I want to say that every claim to change and transformation is valid on its face. But I remain equally unconvinced, as a poet, about the value of any poetry that does not have some such claim, explicit or implicit, as a central part of its agenda.

*   *   *

There is a tradition in American letters that some of the best writers must go abroad to find their true recognition. Europeans were touting Walt Whitman for his revolutionary and refreshing manner of writing himself into his poems while Americans were still hemming and hawing, and Poe had to be translated by Baudelaire to gain recognition. Charles Bukowski has found his greatest audience in

Germany, Italy, France, and Sweden. Jerome Rothenberg also is understood in Europe better than he is in the United States.

What has become apparent is the immense intellectual energy that has gone into Rothenberg's poetry and, even more, into his aesthetic explorations and other writings. Anthologies edited by Rothenberg are not merely collections of books full of poems. Each one is an exercise in studying the possibilities of poetry. Not only his selections but also his editorial writing and essays continue to show us how superficial our readings and definitions of poetry have become. In this sense he is part of that great movement in letters, created by Pound and carried on by Olson, to search for the real connections between the past and the present in art and history, life and language.

Rothenberg's later work has evolved from a personal mythology that includes his sense of himself as an American Jew, born in Brooklyn in 1931 of eastern European ancestors, and as an inheritor of the Native American traditions that he has come to revere and feel part of by study and adoption into one of the tribes of the Seneca. In *That Dada Strain* he acknowledges other origins and resonances, in particular a use of the dadaist's sense of twentieth-century language as collapsing in on itself and needing to be reconstructed by all who wish to make language serve new purposes rather than to reinforce old, often obsolete, values.

Rothenberg concluded *Vienna Blood* with a tour de force, "Abulafia's Circles," an homage to Tristan Tzara, founder of the dadaist movement. It is a poem written for performance as well as a ritual presentation of all of Rothenberg's own secret ideas about poetry, and after reading it (or, preferably, hearing him perform it) one must be overwhelmed by the wide spectrum of possibilities Rothenberg takes into the poem. He uses incantation. He uses catalogs. He uses historical perspective and narrative devices for presenting that perspective. He uses both surrealist and realist imagery. He uses ritual, song, and even analytical discussion. These techniques are used to show the complexity of any identity once we consider all of its possible origins.

In his collection *Khurbn and Other Poems* Rothenberg offers another overwhelmingly powerful dramatic poem, this one a meditation on the Holocaust during the Nazi regime. In the introduction to the book he says,

> When I was writing *Poland/1931,* at a great distance from the place, I decided deliberately that that was not to be a poem about the holocaust. There was a reason for that, I think, as there is now for allowing my uncle's khurbn to speak through me. The poems I first began to hear at Treblinka are the clearest message I have ever gotten about why I write poetry.

The various parts of the poem move through a kind of requiem for the human race, presenting the unusual combination of ferocity, black but playful or arabesque language, and dark vision that readers have come to associate with Rothenberg and his mythic treatment of big subjects. The following is from "Di Toyte Kloies":

> Let a worm the size of a small coin come out of the
> table where you're sitting
> Let it be covered with the red mucus falling from his
> nose (but only you will see it)

Because Rothenberg writes large-purposed works, never concentrating his poems into political messages, "Khurbn" is far more than a poem about this terrible episode in human history. For Rothenberg, in the tradition of Pound and Olson, political concerns and aesthetic concerns are the same or at least are interacting realities, as shown in these lines from "Der Vidershtand":

> began with this in Olson's words it was
> the pre/face so much fat for soap
> superphosphate for soil fillings & shoes for sale
> such fragmentation delivered by whatever means
> the scrolls of auschwitz buried now brought to light
> again

Rothenberg's first collection of poems, *White Sun, Black Sun,* gave little indication of the rich intellectual feast that was to follow. The early poems are small, vivid imagistic works, some of which, like the title poem, were deeply influenced by Blake's *Songs of Innocence,* but all held a surrealist promise of uncovering the dreamworld and the world of the unconscious rather than an intellectual journey. One could, however, have guessed the immense possibilities that lay ahead for him by reading his essay on the concept of "deep image," written in the early 1960s, in which he talks about poetry "as a natural structure arising at once from the act of emotive vision." He tells us that "the power of the deep image is its ability to convey a sense of two-worlds-in-one: directly: with no concept to come between the inner experience and its meaning."

It is now clear that Rothenberg, through his translations of primitive poetry, his elaborate exploration of cultural anthropology, and the extension of his deep-image poetry into the realm of ethnopoetics, is a pioneer of a new approach to poetry itself. Like Gary Snyder and other poets who wish to move away from an anthropocentric universe and his Native American brothers who wish to abolish the Eurocentric way of thinking that has abused nonwhite peoples, Rothenberg hopes to expand and diversify poetry so that it will represent this bigger vision of the world. Perhaps he is describing himself in the poem "A Flower Cantata":

> he weaves his flowers into flower words,
> a flower song beginning
> that will become a flower word song
> or will become a root song,
> song root flowers at his beckoning
> inside a house of flowers,
> a flower world,
> plumed flowers adrift
> on flower drums
> the fathers would call delicious flowers

—Diane Wakoski

ROWBOTHAM, David (Harold)

Nationality: Australian. **Born:** Toowoomba, Queensland, 27 August 1924. **Education:** Toowoomba East State Grammar School; Queensland Teachers' College; University of Sydney (Lawson prize, 1949); University of Queensland, Brisbane (Ford Medal, 1948), B.A., M.A. (Qual.) **Military Service:** Royal Australian Air Force, Southwest Pacific, 1942–45. **Family:** Married Ethel Jessie Matthews in 1952; two daughters. **Career:** Editorial staff member *The Australian Encyclopedia,* 1950–51; freelance journalist, Sydney and London,

1949–52; columnist, Toowoomba *Chronicle,* 1952–55; broadcaster, Australian Broadcasting Commission National Book Review Panel, 1957–63; literary and theater critic, 1955–64, chief book reviewer, 1964–69, arts editor, 1969–80, and literary editor, 1980–87, Brisbane *Courier-Mail.* Commonwealth Literary Fund Lecturer, University of Queensland, 1956, 1964, and University of New England, Armidale, New South Wales, 1961; senior tutor in English, University of Queensland, 1965–69. **Member:** Since 1963 foundation councillor, Australian Society of Authors; state president, Australian Fellowship of Writers, 1982; member, Commonwealth Games Literature Committee, 1982; since 1992 member, New South Wales Writers' Centre, Australian Journalists' Association, and International Federation of Journalists. **Awards:** Sydney *Morning Herald* Competition prize, 1949; Grace Leven prize, 1964; Xavier Society award, 1966; Australian Commonwealth Literary Fund travel grant, 1972; Australia Council grant, 1974, 1976, 1978, 1981, 1985. Emeritus Fellow of Australian Literature, Australia Council, 1989. AM (Member of the Order of Australia), 1991. **Address:** 28 Percival Terrace, Holland Park, Brisbane, Queensland 4121. Australia.

PUBLICATIONS

Poetry

Ploughman and Poet. Sydney, Lyre Bird Writers, 1954.
Inland. Sydney, Angus and Robertson, 1958.
All the Room. Brisbane, Jacaranda Press, 1964.
Bungalow and Hurricane: New Poems. Sydney, Angus and Robertson, 1967.
The Makers of the Ark. Sydney, Angus and Robertson, 1970.
The Pen of Feathers. Sydney, Angus and Robertson, 1971.
Selected Poems. St. Lucia, University of Queensland Press, 1975.
Mighty Like a Harp. St. Lucia, University of Queensland Press, 1975.
Maydays. St. Lucia, University of Queensland Press. 1980.
New and Selected Poems 1945–1993. Melbourne, Penguin Books Australia, 1994.
The Ebony Gates: New and Wayside Poems. Rockhampton, Central Queensland University Press, 1996.

Novel

The Man in the Jungle. Sydney and London, Angus and Robertson, 1964.

Short Stories

Town and City: Tales and Sketches. Sydney, Angus and Robertson, 1956.

Other

Brisbane: A Monograph. Sydney, University of Sydney, 1964.

Editor, *Queensland Writing.* Brisbane, Fellowship of Australian Writers. 1957.

*

Manuscript Collection: National Library of Australia, Canberra.

Critical Studies: *Australian Literature* by Cecil Hadcraft, London, Heinemann, 1960; *Creative Writing in Australia* by John K. Ewers, Melbourne, Georgian House, 1966; *Focus on David Rowbotham* by John Strugnell, Brisbane, University of Queensland Press, 1969; ''Some Recent Australian Poetry'' by Ronald Dunlop, in *Poetry Australia* (Sydney), 1972; ''Australian Poetry'' by Vernon Young, in *Parnassus 7* (New York) 1, 1978; *Modern Australian Poetry 1920–1970* by Herbert C. Jaffa, Detroit, Gale, 1979; David Malouf, in *Australian Literary Studies 10* (Brisbane), 3, 1982; ''Powerful Poetry'' by Manfred Jurgensen, in *The Courier-Mail,* 5 February 1994; ''The Self As Springboard'' by Martin Duwell, in *The Australian (National) Weekend Review,* 26 March 1994; ''The Age of Vigilance'' by David Gilbey, in *Australian Book Review,* 159, April 1994.

David Rowbotham comments:

I found when I began that I belonged with poets who contributed to the renaissance of Australian poetry in the immediate postwar years, a historical and prolific movement seldom acknowledged now. Of my postwar generation of fellows who returned from the war and started publishing verse, I am, at seventy-five and among a turbulent poetic scene, the only one still alive and practicing. This claim and perspective, this alpha and omega, now seems to be the only way of precisely advocating that, while silly yet divisive ''poetry wars'' have been waged in Australia in the midst of life's always greater issues, from people's day-to-day battles in town and city to brutality and duplicity amongst the grandeur of the world, I have preferred to keep to my own compulsions. As a returned serviceman, I wrote, in lyric, narrative, and portraiture, about what I might have lost. I did not express ''experimentation.'' The countryside and people were far more important to get down, which I did in *Ploughman and Poet* (1954) and *Inland* (1958), my first books of verse, poems from which appeared in new anthologies for decades. I was a poet instinctively drawn toward telling a story of his time, which might well become a story of himself; Lermontov said the story of a man's soul could be more interesting and instructive than the story of a whole nation. Over time change and development came in preoccupations, imagination, and technique simultaneously. They came in an emerging endeavor in the whole of my work to range. (One can not have been born on a mountain without wishing to use such an operative verb.) They came, too, with an endeavor to admit all variety as well as engage with the energy that the dimension called vision demanded. From the lifetime that went by, issued—I give as instances—poems not only about ploughmen and townsfolk but about myself as one of them and about men in space (*The Pen of Feathers,* 1971), emigration, travel, wars, death (*Maydays,* 1980), love, loyalty, belief, and their opposites such as life, peace if ever possible (''Honey Licked from a Thorn,'' 1993), and home, hates, betrayal, and the wrestle for faith (''The Ebony Gates,'' 1996), concomitant with the wrestle to continue writing. And it is here that new assessments by Shapcott, Duwell, Jurgensen, and Myers may be taken as an analysis of what, through poetry, my poetry and perhaps I have become. Here also, toward the end, my new book of verse, *The Pacific Star,* a volume largely examining war, sums up what, unknowingly, was to be the final reach of the young survivor who wrote so long ago of the home country he returned to and began to celebrate. I have always written as a survivor and have tried to do so without humbug.

*   *   *

David Rowbotham began writing and publishing after World War II as a young follower of the *Bulletin* school of nature poets, a movement that encouraged Australian writers to look more closely at and reaffirm their own regional identity and meaning. Such a coming to terms with the Australian landscape was important at the time, but it threatened poetry with an ever expanding wash of mynah bird and billabong versification. Rowbotham wrote a number of very delicate lyrics in his first book, *Ploughman and Poet,* but his second collection, *Inland,* though it contained probably his most anthologized (and one of his best) poems, "Mullabinda," did not really prepare his readers for the change in direction, to a more introverted and personal poetry, that was first displayed in the volume *All the Room.*

From this point on Rowbotham's poetry has struggled its way doggedly, and with considerable effort, into areas of response and experience far removed from the gentle, sunny Darling Downs countryside of the earlier books. It is a measure of Rowbotham's integrity that he has not paid easy court to currently fashionable styles and mannerisms, even when they have been shown to be amenable to the sort of personal self-exploration he has been struggling to realize. At its worst, then, his later work in such books as *The Makers of the Ark* and *The Pen of Feathers* is marred by a residue of quatrain-making habits not fully explored or justified. At its best the later poetry counterpoints a conservative vocabulary and rhythm with an intensely felt response to the poet's own discoveries and concerns, which have been thought through with an almost painful honesty to their own relevance in his poetic search. Rowbotham has become one of the significant loners in Australian poetry.

In 1989 a series of individual Rowbotham poems began to appear in literary journals, giving evidence of a continuing personal grappling with experience and contemplation, expressed in terms of a taut lyricism along the lines of his best earlier work. *New and Selected Poems 1945–1993,* which was published in 1994, contains fifty-one pages of previously uncollected work and, together with a tautly selected sampling of earlier poems, demonstrates the persistent integrity and individuality of his mature achievement. *The Ebony Gates* continues the strain of vigor and tautness, though the chafing tone, tinged with an old rancor, is modified and reconciled (if uncomfortably) with a warmth of recognition of his early origins and a sort of homecoming.

—Thomas W. Shapcott

RUDOLF, Anthony

Nationality: British. **Born:** London, 6 September 1942. **Education:** City of London School, 1953–60; British Institute, Paris, 1961; Trinity College, Cambridge, 1961–64, B.A. in modern languages and social anthropology 1964. **Family:** Married in 1970 (divorced 1981); one son and one daughter. **Career:** Junior executive, British Travel Association, London and Chicago, 1964–66; English and French teacher, London, 1967–68; worked in bookshops, London, 1969–71; London editor, *Stand* magazine, Newcastle upon Tyne, 1969–72; literary editor, 1970–72, and managing editor, 1972–75, *European Judaism,* London; advisory editor, *Modern Poetry in Translation,*

London, 1973–83, Heimler Foundation Publications, London, 1974–76, and *Jewish Quarterly,* London 1975–82. Since 1969 co-founder and editor, Menard Press, London. Adam Lecturer, Kings College, London University. **Awards:** H.H. Wingate/J. Quarterly prize for best nonfiction book on Jewish theme, 1991. Hawthornden fellow, 1993. **Address:** 8 The Oaks, Woodside Avenue, London N12 8AR, England.

PUBLICATIONS

Poetry

The Manifold Circle. Oxford, Carcanet, 1971.
The Same River Twice. Manchester, Carcanet, 1976.
After the Dream: Poems 1964–1979. St. Louis, Cauldron Press, 1979.
Broccoli. N.p., Culford Press, 1990.
Mandorla, illustrations by Julia Farrer. N.p., Ki Press, 1994.

Plays

The Soup Complex, adaptation of a play by Ana Novac. Newcastle upon Tyne, Northumberland, Stand, 1972.
The Storm: The Tragedy of Sinai, adaptation of a play by Eugene Heimler. London. Menard Press. 1976.

Other

Byron's Darkness: Lost Summer and Nuclear Winter (essay). London, Menard Press, 1984.
From Poetry to Politics: The Menard Press 1969–1984. London, Menard Press. 1984.
At an Uncertain Hour: Primo Levi's War against Oblivion. London, Menard Press, 1990.
Wine from Two Glasses: Trust and Mistrust in Language. London, Kings/Adam, 1991.
I'm Not Even a Grownup: The Diary of Jerzy Feliks Urman. London, Kings/Menard Press, 1991.
Engraved in Flesh: Piotr Rawicz and His Novel Blood from the Sky. London, Menard Press, 1996.
The Arithmetic of Memory. N.p., Bellew, 1999.

Editor, with Richard Burns, *An Octave for Paz.* Farnham, Surrey, Sceptre Press—Menard Press, 1972.
Editor, *Poems from Shakespeare IV.* London, Globe Playhouse Trust, 1976.
Editor, with Howard Schwartz, *Voices within the Ark: The Modern Jewish* Poets. New York, Avon, 1980.
Editor, *Spleen.* London, Menard Press, 1990.
Editor, *Sage Eye: the Aesthetic Passion of Jonathan Griffin.* London, Menard/Kings, 1992.
Editor, *Theme and Version: Plath and Ronsard.* London, Menard Press, 1995.
Editor, with J. Rety, *Collected Poems & Selected Translations of A.C. Jacobs.* London, Menard Press/Hearing Eye, 1996.

Translator, *Selected Poems, by Yves Bonnefoy.* London, Cape, 1968; New York, Grossman, 1969.

Translator, *Tyorkin, and the Stovemakers: Poetry and Prose of Alexander Tvardovsky.* Cheadle, Cheshire, Carcanet, 1974.

Translator, *Relative Creatures: Victorian Women in Society and the Novel 1837–1867,* by Françoise Basch. London, Allen Lane, 1974.

Translator, with Peter Jay and Petru Popescu, *Boxes, Stairs, and Whistle Time: Poems,* by Popescu. Knotting, Bedfordshire, Omphalos Press, 1975.

Translator, with Daniel Weissbort, *The War Is Over: Selected Poems,* by Evgeny Vinokurov. Cheadle, Cheshire, Carcanet, 1976.

Translator, *A Share of Ink,* by Edmond Jabès. London, Menard Press, 1979.

Translator, *Things Dying Things Newborn: Selected Poems,* by Yves Bonnefoy. London, Cape, 1985.

Translator, *The Unknown Masterpiece,* by Balzac. London, Menard Press, 1988.

Translator, *Flow Tide,* by Vigee. London, Menard/Kings, 1992.

Translator, *Traite du piomistre,* by Yves Bonnefoy. Birmingham, Delos, 1994.

Translator, *Striking Root,* by Ifigenija Simonovic. London, Menard Press, 1996.

Translator, with J. Naughton, *New & Selected Poems,* by Yves Bonnefoy. Chicago, Chicago University Press/Carcanet, 1996.

Translator, *On Raymond Mason,* by Yves Bonnefoy. Birmingham, Delos, 1999.

*

Critical Studies: Review by George Mackay Brown, in *The Scotsman* (Edinburgh), 21 January 1977; by Fred Beake, in *Poet's Voice,* Bath, 1995.

Anthony Rudolf comments:

After the Dream is a more or less definitive reworking of my two earlier collections. In the fifteen years since it was published, I have mainly worked on literary criticism, poetry translation, fiction, and autobiography, but lately I have returned to poetry (or poetry has returned to me) and hope to find a publisher for a new and selected poems.

*   *   *

Anthony Rudolf is a man of many parts—poet, translator (principally from French and Russian), editor, pamphleteer, and obituarist, to name but a few of them. He has not been a very prolific poet in his own right, and the best of his poems from the 1960s and 1970s were gathered together in a collection entitled *After the Dream,* published in 1980. But the finest of his pieces are memorable indeed, exquisite miniatures fresh in their detail, carefully composed, taut and spare, never lacking in reverberation. They recall some of his influences and mentors, among others Carl Rakosi and George Oppen. There is always evidence of a shrewd economy in the choice of detail, and it is in fact in the form of the short poem that he has achieved his most significant results. The title poem of the collection, for example, is a pleasing act of semantic jugglery, but it is far more than the mere exercise in wordplay that such a description might suggest:

He took my words.
     Without a word
he changed the order of my things.
Still my poem, just about.
Much water has flowed by.
      No word.
But to this day, ten years on
I write the same words.
     The end
of all my words is a beginning.

The piece is about the pressure of external influence upon the individual and the poem. It is about the influence of words and the influence of relationships. It is an exploration of how reality is grounded in the poem and of how the reality of poetry as a thing made perpetually eludes any final statement as to its meaning, in whole or as a construct made from words that belong to us all. The poem's rich ambiguities are held in careful tension, and the simplicity of the expression belies the complexity of the ideas.

In spite of his achievements as a poet, Rudolf is equally well known as a translator of poetry and as a publisher of poetry in translation through his Menard Press imprint. The poet with whom we associate his name most readily is Yves Bonnefoy, probably the most gifted French poet of his generation. Rudolf's translations of Bonnefoy were first published in book form in 1968; in 1985 there appeared a new selection, *Things Dying Things Newborn,* which was neither a reprint nor a revised edition of that earlier book, in spite of the fact that it included revised translations of many of the poems appearing in the earlier volume. Subsequent translations of Bonnefoy were published in 1994 and 1999. Essentially, it is the work of a translator who has been learning on the job, for over the years Menard and other presses have published a wide range of Rudolf's translations, including his own versions of Jabès.

Rudolf's efforts to introduce Bonnefoy to the English-speaking world have continued. He contributed a substantial supplement on the work of Bonnefoy to Anvil Press's *Poetry World,* an annual (occasionally biannual) publication devoted to poetry in translation. The supplement includes a major essay, hitherto unpublished, entitled "Poetry and Truth." This is an especially fascinating document because it was written in English by Bonnefoy and only lightly edited by Rudolf. We therefore have an opportunity to experience the sweep of Bonnefoy's thought and his particular French timbre without the mediation of a translator. The supplement concludes with a long prose explication of Bonnefoy's poetry and ideas arranged by theme and then by his successive books of poetry. This valuable exposition, an "unwriting" as Rudolf describes it, digs at the roots of Bonnefoy's thinking about the relationship between poetry, metaphysics, and the world of language and phenomena. As we read it, we are taken back into Rudolf's own work as a poet, a world in which there is always a strong sense of the poet battering at the door of language as sign, squeezing out the pith of meaning. There is a perpetual recognition that the simplest poetic act is always far from simple precisely because it issues from a thinking, sentient being who has himself undergone a double divorce—from the world of being insofar as he has the powers to reflect upon its mysterious nature without reentering it and from language itself insofar as language can never be anything other than common to us all and therefore sullied to a degree.

Mercifully, at its best poetry can serve as an act of cleansing and purification, and poetry and Bonnefoy are at one in their belief that poetry is a secular liturgy.

—Michael Glover

RUMENS, Carol (-Ann)

Nationality: British. **Born:** Carol-Ann Lumley, London, 10 December 1944. **Education:** St. Winifred's Convent School, London; Coloma Convent Grammar School, Croydon, Surrey, 1955–63; Bedford College, University of London, 1964–66. **Family:** Married David Rumens in 1965 (divorced 1985); two daughters. **Career:** Publicity assistant, 1974–77, and advertising copywriter, 1977–81, London; poetry editor, *Quarto,* London, 1981–82, and *Literary Review,* London, 1984–88; creative writing fellow, Kent University, Canterbury, 1983–85. Regular book reviewer, *The Observer,* London. **Awards:** Alice Hunt Bartlett award, 1982; Arts Council award, 1982; Cholmondeley award, 1984. Fellow, Royal Society of Literature, 1984. **Agent:** Peters, Fraser and Dunlop, 5ᵗʰ Floor, The Chambers, Lots Road, London SW10 0XF, England. **Address:** c/o Chatto and Windus, 20 Vauxhall Bridge Road, London SW1V 2SA, England.

PUBLICATIONS

Poetry

Strange Girl in Bright Colours. London, Quartet, 1973.
A Necklace of Mirrors. Belfast, Ulsterman, 1978.
Unplayed Music. London, Secker and Warburg, 1981.
Scenes from the Gingerbread House. Newcastle upon Tyne, Bloodaxe, 1982.
Star Whisper. London, Secker and Warburg, 1983.
Direct Dialing. London, Chatto and Windus, 1985.
Selected Poems. London, Chatto and Windus, 1987.
The Greening of the Snow Beach. Newcastle upon Tyne, Bloodaxe, 1988.
From Berlin to Heaven. London, Chatto and Windus. 1989.
Thinking of Skins: New & Selected Poems. Newcastle upon Tyne, Bloodaxe, 1993.
Best China Sky. Newcastle upon Tyne, Bloodaxe, and Chester Springs, Pennsylvania, Dufour, 1995.
Holding Pattern. Belfast, Blackstaff Press, 1998.
The Miracle Diet: Poems. Newcastle upon Tyne, Bloodaxe, 1998.

Play

Nearly Siberia (produced Newcastle upon Tyne and London, 1989).

Novel

Plato Park. London, Chatto and Windus, 1987.

Other

Jean Rhys: A Critical Study. London, Macmillan, 1985.

Editor, *Making for the Open: The Chatto Book of Post-Feminist Poetry 1964–1984.* London, Chatto and Windus, 1985.
Editor, *Slipping Glances: Winter Poetry Supplement.* London, Poetry Book Society, 1985.
Editor, *New Women Poets.* Newcastle upon Tyne, Bloodaxe, 1990.
Editor, *Two Women Dancing: New & Selected Poems,* by Elizabeth Bartlett. Newcastle upon Tyne, Bloodaxe, and Chester Springs, Pennsylvania, Dufour, 1995.

*

Critical Study: "Women Poets and 'Women's Poetry': Fleur Adcock, Gillian Clarke, and Carol Rumens" by Lyn Pykett, in *British Poetry from the 1950s to the 1990s: Politics and Art,* edited by Gary Day and Brian Docherty, London, Macmillan, and New York, St. Martin's Press, 1997.

*   *   *

Carol Rumens wrote in a Poetry Book Society bulletin on the occasion of the publication of her first collection, *Unplayed Music,* "Experiencing things imaginatively as an alternative for dealing with 'real' occurrences is, I suppose, an activity especially familiar to anyone who writes." Because "real" is in quotation marks, we can assume a particular meaning, which I take to be "directly experienced." It is possible (indeed it is the strength of Rumens's poetry that she does this so well) to experience imaginatively occurrences that, while not direct to the poet, were direct occurrences to others. These occurrences, while not unreal, have to be apprehended by the poet imaginatively. She goes on to say in another bulletin that "I do not belong to that school of thought which says in the face of extreme horror, suffered by others, one should be silent. On the contrary I believe that all the forces of imagination should be employed to speak of their suffering."

I labor this point because some of the most telling of Rumens's later poems have been concerned with the sufferings, horrors, persecutions, and exiles during and deriving from the history of Europe in the first half of the twentieth century, subjects that many of those who lived through the period have deliberately avoided as being too immediate in their enormity and their emotional charge for what they felt would be an adequate response. That Rumens's distance from these events allows her to experience them imaginatively, and that her use of this particular aspect of the intelligence is such that the empathy she achieves in a poem such as "Outside Osweicin" is stunning, is a source of the power of her work. In the early 1980s Rumens's interest in Eastern Europe and Russia began to predominate, and it was then that she began to dare to take on subjects of such overwhelming impact.

Most of the poems in Rumens's first collection and in *Star Whisper* that followed display an acute observation and an ability to touch the nerves underlying the domestic and the personal. This is especially true of her love poems, where her technical accomplishment makes no small contribution to their quality and effectiveness. This quality is best illustrated by quoting what is as near a perfect poem as I have encountered in recent years, "The Last Day of March":

The elms are darkened by rain
On the small, park sized hills
Sigh the ruined daffodils

As if they shared my refrain
—that when I leave here, I lose
All reason to see you again.

What's finishing was so small,
I never mentioned it.
My time, like yours, was full,
And I would have blushed to admit
How shallow the rest could seem;
How so little could be all.

Rumens's group of love poems shares this ability to give depth of meaning and emotional truth to what are common experiences. The simply named "Love Poem" is another example of this, while "The Ballad of the Morning After" makes the connection explicit:

And that's the story of our lives,
The whole damned human race

Rumens's collection *From Berlin to Heaven* is of a piece with her work as a whole. As the title conveys, the poems are related to her travels but move from the basically descriptive to the metaphysical.

—John Cotton

RUSSELL, (Irwin) Peter

Nationality: British. **Born:** Bristol, 16 September 1921. **Education:** University of London, 1946–50. **Military Service:** British and Indian Army, 1939–46. **Family:** Married; two sons and two daughters. **Career:** Owner, Pound Press, 1951–56, Grosvenor Bookshop, 1951–58, and Gallery Bookshop, London, 1959–63; lived in Venice, 1965–83. Poet-in-residence, University of Victoria, British Columbia, 1975–76, and Purdue University, West Lafayette, Indiana, 1976–77; teaching fellow, Imperial Iranian Academy of Philosophy, Tehran, 1977–79. Editor, *Nine* magazine, 1949–57. Since 1990 editor, *Marginalia.* **Awards:** International *Le Muse* prize for lyric poetry, Florence, Italy; international *Dante Alighieri* prize, for *Dante and Islam,* Accademia dantesca casentinese. **Address:** c/o *Marginalia,* La Turbina, 52026 Pian di Scò, Arezzo, Italy.

PUBLICATIONS

Poetry

Picnic to the Moon. Privately printed, 1944.
Omens and Elegies. Aldington, Kent, Hand and Flower Press, 1951.
Descent: A Poem Sequence. Privately printed, 1952.
Three Elegies of Quintilius. Tunbridge Wells, Kent, Pound Press, 1954.
The Spirit and the Body: An Orphic Poem. Privately printed, 1956.
Images of Desire. London, Gallery Bookshop, 1962.
Dreamland and Drunkenness. London, Gallery Bookshop, 1963.
Complaints to Circe. Privately printed, 1963.
Visions and Ruins: An Existentialist Poem. Aylesford, Kent, Saint Albert's Press, 1964.

Agamemnon in Hades. Aylesford, Kent, Saint Albert's Press, 1965.
The Golden Chain: Lyrical Poems 1964–1969. Privately printed, 1970.
Paysages Légendaires. London, Enitharmon Press, 1971.
The Elegies of Quintilius. London, Anvil Press Poetry, 1975.
Acts of Recognition: Four Visionary Poems. Ipswich, Suffolk, Golgonooza Press, 1978.
Theories. Tehran, Crescent Moon Press, 1978.
Elemental Discourses. Salzburg, University of Salzburg, 1981.
Malice Aforethought: Satirical Poems. Salzburg, University of Salzburg, 1981.
The Vitalist Reader: A Selection of the Poetry of Anthony L. Johnson, William Oxley, and Peter Russell, edited by James Hogg. Salzburg, University of Salzburg, 1982.
All for the Wolves: Selected Poems 1947–1975, edited by Peter Jay. London, Anvil Press Poetry, and Redding Ridge, Connecticut, Black Swan, 1984.
Quintiliiapocalypseos fragmenta. London, Agenda, 1986.
The Duller Olive; Poems 1942–1958 previously uncollected or unpublished. Salzburg, University of Salzburg, 1993.
A False Start: London Poems, 1959–1963. Salzburg, University of Salzburg, 1993.
Berlin-Tegel, 1964: Poems and Translations. Salzburg, University of Salzburg, 1994.
Venice Poems, 1965. Salzburg, University of Salzburg, 1995.
More for the Wolves. Salzburg, University of Salzburg, 1997.

Other

Africa: A Dream. Salzburg, University of Salzburg, 1981.
Teorie e Altre Liriche. Rome, C. Mancosu, 1990.
Poetic Asides, 2 volumes. Salzburg, University of Salzburg, 1992–93.
The Pound Connection. Salzburg, University of Salzburg, 1992.
The Image of Woman as a Figure of the Spirit. Salzburg, University of Salzburg, 1992.
From the Apocalypse of Quintilius. Salzburg, University of Salzburg, 1997.
Something about Poetry: Selected Lectures and Essays by Peter Russell. Salzburg, University of Salzburg, 1997.
The Global Brain Awakens: Our Next Evolutionary Leap. Shaftesbury, Element, 2000.

Editor, *Ezra Pound: A Collection of Essays to be Presented to Ezra Pound on His Sixty-Fifth Birthday.* London, Peter Nevill, 1950; as *An Examination of Ezra Pound,* New York, New Directions, 1950.
Editor, Money Pamphlets by £. London, Peter Russell, 6 vols., 1950–51.
Editor, with Khushwant Singh, *A Note . . . on G.V. Desani's "All about H. Hatterr" and "Hali."* London and Amsterdam, Szeben, 1952.
Editor, *ABC of Economics,* by Ezra Pound. Tunbridge Wells, Kent, Pound Press, 1953.
Editor, *The Consciousness Revolution: A Transatlantic Dialogue,* by Ervin Laszlo. Shaftesbury, Element, 1999.

Translator, *Landscapes,* by Camillo Pennati (bilingual edition). Richmond, Surrey, Keepsake Press, 1964.

*

Manuscript Collections: University of Buffalo, New York; Humanities Center, University of Texas, Austin.

Bibliography: *A Bibliography of the Writings of Peter Russell* by Glyn Pursglove, Salzburg, University of Salzburg, 1995.

Critical Studies: "Quintilius: Three Elegies" by Edward O'Neill, in *Comparative Literature* (Oregon), 1955; "Between the Lines" by Kathleen Raine, in *Southern Review* (Baton Rouge, Louisiana), spring 1974; "Pagan Idioms" by Peter Levi, in *Times Literary Supplement* (London), 6 February 1976; *A Servant of the Muse: A Garland for Peter Russell on His Sixtieth Birthday,* Salzburg, University of Salzburg, 1981, and *The Salzburg Peter Russell Seminar 1981–82,* University of Salzburg, 1982, both edited by James Hogg; "By What Criteria" by William Oxley, in *Salzburg Studies in English Literature* (Salzburg), 1983; *A Vitalist Seminar,* Salzburg, University of Salzburg, 1984; "The Poetry of Peter Russell" by Peter Levi, in *Agenda* (London), 22(3–4), 1985; "Cultivating Asphodel and Hemlock in the Garden" by Robert Nye, in *The Times* (London), 27 February 1985; "Peter Russell's poem 'Smoke'" by Anthony L. Johnson, and "Touchstone and His Dilemma: The Poetry of Peter Russell" by Stephen Wade, both in *Vitalism and Celebration,* edited by Hogg, Salzburg, University of Salzburg, 1987; "Agamemnon in Hades: Peter Russell's Philosophical Diary" by Wolfgang Reisinger, in *Outsiders* (Salzburg), 1, 1989; "Una Voce dimenticata: Peter Russell," in *Il Sole 24 ore* (Milan), 31 July 1991; "Ishmael among the Scriveners" by Thomas Fleming, in *Chronicles* (Rockford, Illinois), November 1991; "Peter Russell: *Teorie*" by Glyn Pursglove, in *The Swansea Review* (Swansea), 8, October 1991; *Peter Russell: Poet and Publisher* (dissertation) by Michael Wagner, University of Salzburg, 1991; "Homage to Quintilius Stultus" by W.G. Shepherd, in *Marginalia 7* (Pian di Scò, Italy), December 1992; "Peter Russell" by Gisbert Kranz, in *Inklings: Jahrbuch für Literatur und Astetik* (Aachen, Germany), 9, 1992; "La poesia di Peter Russell" by Emanuele Ocelli, in *Talentino* (Torino, Italy), March 1994; Peter Russell issue of *Agenda* (London), autumn 1994; "Peter Russell's *Selected Poems*" by Joy Hendry, in *Marginalia* (Pian di Scò, Italy), 1994; "For Love of the Muse" by Stacey Kors, in *Chronicles* (Rockford, Illinois), November 1994; *'Life Is a Celebration Not a Search for Success': Studies in the Poetry of Peter Russell* by Anthony L. Johnson, Salzburg, University of Salzburg, 1995.

*   *   *

For many years Peter Russell was perhaps the major neglected talent of our time—the author of one of the finest books of purely "English" lyrics (*The Golden Chain*) since the 1960s; the author of a gigantic, mostly unpublished epic poem, *Ephemeron,* running to some two thousand pages; and the author of *Paysages Légendaires,* a book impregnated with great wisdom and that music the Celts call *cael moer,* or "great music." In Russell one was dealing with not just the Poundian theory of the multilingual poet of the future (and Russell was Pound's greatest disciple) but also with the realization of such a poet as fact. The sheer magnitude of the job of investigating the innumerable works produced by Russell since *Picnic to the Moon* in 1944 was not a sufficient excuse for not trying. Still less was it an excuse for the wanton neglect of a poet of whom such a figure as Hugh MacDiarmid had written, "Peter Russell is, in my opinion, a writer who has so far received nothing like due recognition . . . no one in Great Britain today has rendered anything like the disinterested, many-sided and sustained service to Poetry," the latter comment referring to Russell's work as editor of *Nine* and as publisher of many of today's established figures long before they were known.

In the early 1970s Enitharmon Press published Russell, as did Anvil Press beginning later in the decade. Since that time Anvil and, later, the Salzburg University Press have endeavored to tackle the daunting task of publishing the poet. As a result, by the 1990s the true stature of the poet had become better recognized. The prestigious literary journal *Agenda* produced a handsome issue that amounts to a partial Festschrift on Russell's work, while the University of Salzburg announced a further volume of studies for the poet's seventy-fifth birthday.

Of *Paysages Légendaires,* Hugh McKinley's phrase "tribute open-eyed, yet illuminate, of life entire" is remarkably apposite. This is how the poem opens:

> Palladian villas and the changing seasons
>
> An old man digging in the shade
>
> The gold sun varnishes
> The small viridian of the elms
> And gilds the hidden cadmium of the glades.

In fact, the expression throughout is best described as an open-eyed style.

The book also is a rare work of unimpeachable seriousness and poetic wisdom. Perhaps the most interesting feature of *Paysages Légendaires,* and the explanation of its style, is the absence of a close or particularly tense (or overtense) verbal and syntactical density, which induces an unusual clarity in the verse. This goes a long way toward compensating for the major disadvantage of a modern sequential but nonnarrative long poem, namely, the breaks in continuity that so trouble the average reader. It is a poem that reads well.

The sheer intelligence of the poem commands respect, but what matters is that one feels it to be an extraordinarily "aware" poem, a poem aware of and in touch with the mainstream of human thought. This awareness of the "now" is undoubtedly achieved by a profound knowledge of the "then" and exemplifies what is, perhaps, the poem's central preoccupation:

> It will take time to build again,
> To build the soul's tall house,
> The tower of the wandering self
> Foursquare beneath the moon.

Many people, myself among them, think that poetry—the "real" part, the heart's meat of the matter—is the line or lines of words that are necklace perfect. It is something that glitters with ineffable quality, wisdom, beauty, and life, a kind of instant revelation in words, the discovery, as Russell puts it, that "every natural effect has a spiritual cause / (That which is above, is below)." Indeed, if poetry is the unshakable line, the memorable phrase, then Russell is one of the best English poets writing.

Myth is the stuff of thought, one might say, and *Paysages Légendaires* is a "thoughtful" poem. There is little concrete description, and where there is, the object tends toward the emblematic and metaphorical. There is, however, one short passage in which the descriptive element is uppermost:

> Sweet bones are growing in the earthly night

> Slow maturations in the endless dark
> Of subterranean galleries, telluric force
> That broods whole centuries upon a single grain
> That crumbles or coagulates.

One gets a sense of the tremendousness of life, its continual working. The key word is ''broods,'' which reveals brilliantly the meaning behind the description, the life within.

Apart from the practical problem of the range of Russell's work, there is another problem, which is only a ''problem'' in the framework of present-day poetry's dusty picture. This derives from the fact that the more one reads Russell's poetry, the more one realizes that it demands imagination. In poem after poem one finds the feeling transcending the flat detail of experience.

There also is a copious knowledge displayed of life both past and present, and at times there is that true linguistic metamorphosis that provides a permanent frame—be it only a single good line—in which the present is held up before our eyes to be seen in infinite terms. Therefore, parodying Pound, these poems must ''go to the imaginative'' if they are to be understood and to the serious if they are to be loved.

More and more certain and clear lines of achievement have come to be appreciated since the appearance of *Paysages Légendaires.* The first achievement became apparent with the publication in the mid-1970s of *The Elegies of Quintilius.* These are a series of meditations by a fictitious Roman poet, supposedly of the latter days of the empire. Writing in the *Times Literary Supplement* in 1976, Peter Levi said of these ''spoof'' poems, ''In *The Elegies of Quintilius* the mask, if it is one, fits so closely to Mr Russell, as the mask should in the perfect translation, that there is no useful distinction between persona and personality . . . They are readable, excellent poems, and it would be crazy to dismiss them as pastiche . . . He ought to be reviewed by the best English critics, not as a Classical joke.'' Not only have more and more critics come to appreciate these elegies, but the poet himself has considerably expanded the corpus of ''Quintilius's'' writings, so that there now exists an almost cosmic mind history of both the real and the imagined poet via the developed vehicle of the sequential poems. Further examples of these poems have appeared in the volume of selected poems published by Anvil in 1984 and elsewhere.

The second major strand to emerge stretches forward from the aforementioned *Golden Chain* volume and is composed of a seemingly endless flow of lyric poems, many of them highly formal. These culminate in, but have not ceased with, a large bilingual volume (in English and Italian) entitled *Teorie e Altre Liriche* and published in Italy. The weakness in this volume, and to some degree in the whole of Russell's lyric achievement up to this book, is a tendency to repetitiveness of rhythm and a not infrequent rhythmic awkwardness. That said, however, what cannot be denied is his frequent ability to make palpable the haunting music of the true romantic poet, and the ''great music'' present in the more impressionistic *Paysages Légendaires* appears even in his most formal lyrics.

It has to be admitted, however, as Dick Davis observed on reviewing Russell's *All for the Wolves: Selected Poems 1947–1975,* that there are a number of difficulties in getting ''at the substance of Peter Russell's achievement,'' not least of which in Davis's view is the fact that ''Russell's public *persona* is so close to Pound's as to seem almost a parody of it.'' To this I would add the too overt influence of the satirical Roy Campbell. But in the final analysis the chief difficulty that critics must experience in coming to terms with Russell's poetry is the cumbrous and inept working of so many lines in what would otherwise be very good poems, a fault almost certainly due to a lack of attention to rhythm and diction that derives from a deficiency of self-criticism by Russell of his multitudinous outpourings. Those features that Davis describes as ''less beguiling'' and that he exemplifies as ''the Wardour Street language of many of the poems . . . the woodenness of rhythm in some of the rhymed verses, and the laxness of rhythm which seems to indicate a laxness in the mind that conceived the poem . . .'' are barriers to a wider appreciation of Russell's work.

But the third strand of achievement is one that constitutes, if not a complete rebuttal of Davis's strictures on Russell's work, at least a considerable sidelining of them. The publication of *The Duller Olive, A False Start,* and *Berlin-Tegel, 1964* by the University of Salzburg, in conjunction with the two Anvil Press volumes, go a considerable way toward overcoming the difficulties in getting ''at the substance of Peter Russell's achievement.'' Not only do the three Salzburg collections have fascinating introductions by the poet—introductions that, for once, enhance the reader's view of the poems and do not detract from or overexplain them—but they also go a long way toward providing the critical focus that has hitherto been lacking on the tremendous output of this poet. It can now be safely claimed that those barriers I formerly felt were ''insuperable'' to the wider appreciation of Russell's work have begun to crumble rapidly.

—William Oxley

RUTSALA, Vern

Nationality: American. **Born:** McCall, Idaho, 5 February 1934. **Education:** Reed College, Portland, Oregon, B.A. 1956; University of Iowa, Iowa City, M.F.A. 1960. **Military Service:** U.S. Army, 1956–58. **Family:** Married Joan Colby in 1957; two sons and one daughter. **Career:** Since 1961 member of the English Department, currently professor, Lewis and Clark College, Portland, Oregon. Visiting professor, University of Minnesota, Minneapolis, 1968–69, Bowling Green State University, Ohio, 1970. Editor, *December* magazine, Western Springs, Illinois, 1959–62. **Awards:** National Endowment for the Arts grant, 1974, 1979; Northwest Poets prize, 1975; Guggenheim fellowship, 1982; Pushcart prize, 1985; Carolyn Kizer prize, 1988, 1997; Masters fellowship, Oregon Arts Commission, 1990; Oregon Book award, 1992; The Juniper prize, 1993; Duncan Lawrie prize, Arvon Foundation, 1994. **Address:** Department of English, Lewis and Clark College, Portland, Oregon, 97219, U.S.A.

PUBLICATIONS

Poetry

The Window. Middletown, Connecticut, Wesleyan University Press, 1964.
Small Songs: A Sequence of Poems. Iowa City, Stone Wall Press, 1969.

The Harmful State. Lincoln, Nebraska, Best Cellar Press, 1971.

Laments. New York, New Rivers Press, 1975.

The Journey Begins. Athens, University of Georgia Press, 1976.

Paragraphs. Middletown, Connecticut, Wesleyan University Press, 1978.

The New Life. Portland, Oregon, Trask House, 1978.

Walking Home from the Icehouse. Pittsburgh, Carnegie Mellon University Press, 1981.

The Mystery of the Lost Shoes. Amherst, Massachusetts, Lynx House Press, 1984.

Backtracking. Santa Cruz, California, Story Line Press, 1985.

Ruined Cities. Pittsburgh, Carnegie Mellon University Press, 1987.

Selected Poems. Brownsville, Oregon, Story Line Press, 1991.

Little-Known Sports. Amherst, Massachusetts, University of Massachusetts Press, 1994.

Other

Editor, *British Poetry 1972.* Phoenix, Arizona, Baleen Press, 1972.

*

Bibliography: *Vern Rutsala* by Erik Muller, Boise, Idaho, Boise State University Press, 1998.

Critical Studies: By Norman Friedman, in *Chicago Review,* June 1967; ''The Voice from over Our Shoulders: The Poetry of Vern Rutsala'' by Carol Bangs, in *Concerning Poetry* (Bellingham, Washington), 13(2), 1980; ''Vern Rutsala-en kort introduktion'' by Lars Nordstrom, in *Kulturtidskriften Horisont* (Vasa, Finland), 34(4), 1987.

Vern Rutsala comments:

(1980) Many of the poems in *The Window* are centered in and around houses—often houses in some worn suburb—and are concerned with what might be seen in such an area. The central image of the window is appropriate then, and the poems reflect both what can be observed and what happens within. More recent work follows this pattern, though its focus is usually much more inward. Though the rhythms I use are relatively free, I often like to make use of regular stanza forms. My themes are not unusual, the common obsessions of poets: How does one live? Why is the world as it is? *Paragraphs,* a collection of prose poems, explores directions that differ a good deal from my earlier work. *Laments* and *The Journey Begins* have continued my concern with contemporary life, while also beginning to explore the past and our relationship to it. *The New Life* focuses rather directly on western America. It is part of a longer work called *Walking Home from the Icehouse. Backtracking* is a book-length poem concerned with time and memory, while *Ruined Cities* continues explorations of daily life and recent history.

(1995) A poem starts with something I call a kind of buzz or hum of potential. There is rarely any explicit idea. Usually it is just a feeling that I have got hold of the very tip of something, and the first lines are an effort to uncover what that thing may be. Obviously, it has to seem worth pursuing, and the pursuit results in a draft that is open to every possibility that bears on that triggering buzz. Form, sense, the niceties of language are not concerns at this point. What is important is the block of words that form the first draft, the kitchen sink draft. The draft is usually set aside for a time—out of the need to earn a living but increasingly by preference—and looked at later with a cold eye. If the buzz is still there, then the shaping begins, which may go on for hours, weeks, months. Though we all want them to come across quickly, each poem sets its own agenda. You know the poem may not work out, but you take the chance and hope the law of averages is with you. But, as Eliot said, you write with a wastebasket. And that is the only way—every writer lives with waste, almost extravagantly so—carefulness and caution strangle the creative impulse. Staying alert and not too anxious keeps it alive.

*   *   *

Vern Rutsala has one the keenest poetic responses to contemporary middle-class society since Cummings, Auden, the earlier Karl Shapiro, and some of Louis Simpson. His special achievement in *The Window* is to have made the furniture of everyday bourgeois life in America available to the uses of serious poetry. He is thus somewhat like the better pop artists, such as Edward Kienholz, who makes assemblages out of found objects, the chassis of an old car, for example. With a few skillfully constructed figures, Rutsala can confront us with ourselves as we fumble erotically in the backseat with our dates in a doomed search for pleasure and joy (''Lovers in Summer'').

But there is here not merely a familiar world of skate keys, wagons, bicycles (''Sunday''); there is also a commanding vision that governs the shaping of that world. Rutsala hears the glacier knocking in the cupboard and the rumble of violence and despair hidden within our domestic walls. He deals card after card, building up unbearably to a remorseless climax until not a corner is left for us to hide in; nothing is spared, not a toothbrush, family album, mantelpiece clock, visit from relatives, souvenir ashtray, flushing of the toilet, garden hose. Nothing escapes his illumination of things so ordinary that we have forgotten them, so close that we have not really seen them, revealing what we thought we already knew but never quite understood.

Each aspect of our lives, each object of our mundane environment, is a badge of the numb but terrible disparity between life's possibilities and the horror of diminishment we are all suffering from. A bathroom mirror is a symbol of the abyss, which is not so much the inevitable loss of childhood as the crushing emptiness of spirit characteristic of living in an imperialistic, commercial, and technological civilization (''Gilbert and Market''). In such a society even childhood is no Eden, and children are not spared (''Playground'').

''Nightfall'' is one of the most moving poems in *The Window:*

Night settles like a damp cloth
over the houses. The houses that are shut,
that show no wear. Lawns
are patrolled by plywood flamingoes
or shrubbery clipped from magazines.

The poem develops to reveal compulsive housecleaning, sports pages, basement workshops, skills for repairing things, dinner dishes in the kitchen sink, bills, two cars, committee meetings, unused telephone appointment pads—and desperate and suicidal children. Then, as the time for sleep comes, some people lie awake in the glow of a cigarette, obsessed by disappointment and heartbreak. The poem concludes perfectly:

Dawn lies coiled in clocks.
There are no conclusions here. The dark is there.
Cigarettes burn down and are ground out
in souvenir ashtrays from vacations by the sea.

The Window does, however, suffer from an overly even stylistic tone as well as from a certain distance between its persona and the world that is seen so clearly. But these flaws are on their way to being redeemed in Rutsala's subsequent work. Although *Small Songs,* a sequence of invitations by common household objects, is a rather minor effort and seems to lack development, *Laments,* his next full volume, marks an advance in depth and variety. Decorated with etchings by James Burgess of fruits, plants, and nuts that seem more like grotesque lobsters, this book, as its title indicates, is still fascinated by the party-is-over mood, by loss, by what to make of a diminished thing. Yet the speaker moves more into the foreground, thus providing that sense of involvement lacking in *The Window,* and the situations, imagery, and rhythms are more consciously diversified, thus mitigating the threat of monotony. Nevertheless, the feeling of exasperation, even exhaustion, remains much the same, and Rutsala's grasp of its significance, or even of other possible moods, awaits further insight.

The Journey Begins and *Paragraphs* signal a shift out of this impasse. In the former volume Rutsala proclaims as usual that "here we practice the cottage / industry of the banal; here we / probe the mysteries of the commonplace" ("Like the Poets of Ancient China"), but something else is beginning to happen: "we must nurse / the deadness from the air / so we may breathe" ("Unlocking the Door"). These mysteries are beginning to yield something significant ("Beginning"):

> The past gone,
> an instant, drained like stream
> water full of clarity, light,
> ice, the flavor of mountains
> that gave you only one thing:
> a wetness on your lips, taste.

Such unaccustomed freshness of taste enables Rutsala in *Paragraphs* at last to touch the springs of neurosis itself and to find the mirror, even the cause, of the desolation in society. In other words, his sense of the abyss becomes internalized. The pieces in this book are brief prose poems but are also related, as he says, "to the fable, the aphorism, the maxim, the character, and the joke." Many are effectively epigrammatic and eminently quotable, but I will limit myself to a single characteristic example, "Demon":

> No matter how you shuffle your traits—making diligenceand order turn up regularly—he is always there, waiting. In fact, the harder you try to hide him the more often he breaks into your nights like a party-crashing drunk spilling drinks, upending tables, yelling obscenities at ancient maidens. The trick, you see, is to admit him calmly, see that he is really you—not a double, but *you,* not some actor or black sheep but simply you. He fits your skin; take him places, feed him smoked oysters and good bourbon, let him dance any time he wants to, let him sing. If you fail to do this he will kill himself.

Having found the demon, we must acknowledge him, enable him, or we are doomed to the impasse, and so we follow Rutsala on his tormented journey to the interior, where he extends his forms as he deepens his vision. In his next three full-length volumes he proceeds to explore memories of his early years and the experiences of his family. *Walking Home from the Icehouse* is centered largely on a Depression childhood in Idaho and Oregon. Immigrants from Finland, his family endured hard times, and the mood and atmosphere are cold and bleak. Written in a plain, free verse style, mainly in short lines, the poems prompt the speaker himself to admit that "there should be passion / That show of feeling / When feeling snaps / Across the page / With asterisks / But the words refuse . . . ." ("Moving West").

Accordingly, *Backtracking,* true to its title, is more about the problem of writing during past years than about the past itself. The lines and poems are a bit longer, the tones less stark, and the mood more dreamlike and surreal than harsh and naturalistic. The Proustian theme is the felt need to write about the past in order not to lose it: "Oh how we / egg our memories on, egg them back to / sources within a dream, some pool, some thick / liquid darkness, the swamp where everything / began—the swamp behind the old lost / house" ("The Jerrybuilt Dream").

Finally, *Ruined Cities* contains lovely poems about the family, especially Rutsala's own children. Talking to one of them, he writes, "some long tension, some / crimped deep fiber in me / relaxed for good when you arrived" ("Lela and Others"). Yet there remains the baffled need for "the end of dreams," that forgotten something: "We've missed the boat somehow / and wait on standby for the next . . ." ("Forgotten Dreams"). That old Ahab-like need to strike through the mask "and find what lies coiled / and raging there" haunts him still.

Little-Known Sports contains fifty-four prose poems, most less than a page and some but a single line, divided into three nearly equal sections. The first, "The Art of Photography and Other Sorrows," has to do with snapshots—of the speaker, Madame Aupick, Herr Keuner, and Vitalie Rimbaud, among others—and proceeds to pieces about a man obsessed with time, choice, academic life, and so forth. Except for the first poem these are spoken, as are most poems throughout the book, in the present tense and in the second or third person; the tone is mostly wry, epigrammatic, and ironic. The second section, "Bestiary," contains comments about one of Rutsala's favorite topics, the inanimate objects found in every household, such as the fruit bowl, dust mop, or ironing board, which he sees as animate creatures. The third, "Little-Known Sports," sees ordinary activities—such as sleeping, answering the phone, smoking—as athletic events. The most interesting of these is "Homage," about "solitary sports," the best of which "was practiced by a doctor in New Jersey who danced naked by himself late at night" (compare William Carlos Williams's "Danse Russe"); "Lying," which claims that "in order to lie successfully you quite simply must know what the truth is"; and "Being Second-Rate," which I quote here entire:

> There are people—and institutions—which quite clearly relish this activity. The pleasure is derived both from the warmth of many companions—as at the start of a marathon— and the avoidance of any pain which is—also as in a marathon— reserved for the leaders.

Although I do not find this volume as significant as the earlier *Paragraphs,* it does reveal Rutsala still busy at his craft, perhaps readying himself by means of these mordant pieces to move closer to letting his "Demon" sing and thereby to find himself at last.

—Norman Friedman

RYAN, Gig (Elizabeth)

Nationality: Australian and British. **Born:** Leicester, England, 5 November 1956. **Education:** LaTrobe University, Melbourne, 1974; Sydney University, 1983–87; University of Melbourne, 1991–93, degree in Latin and Ancient Greek 1993. **Career:** Also works as songwriter and musician. **Awards:** Australia Council Literature Board Writers grant, 1979, 1982, 1988, 1992; co-winner, Anne Elder award, 1982; C.J. Dennis Victorian Premiers award for poetry, 1999. **Address:** 1189 Burke Road, Kew, Melbourne 3101, Australia.

PUBLICATIONS

Poetry

The Division of Anger. Sydney, Transit Press, 1981.
Manners of an Astronaut. Sydney, Hale and Iremonger, 1984.
The Last Interior. Melbourne, Scripsi, 1986.
Excavation. Sydney, Picador, 1990.
Pure and Applied. N.p., PaperBark Press, 1998.

Recordings: *Six Goodbyes,* Big Home Productions, 1988; *Real Estate,* Chapter Music, 1999.

*   *   *

The publication of Gig Ryan's *The Division of Anger* in 1980 announced, with a certain frisson among audiences at readings in Sydney and Melbourne, the presence of a new enfant terrible. Ryan's harsh delivery, each phrase chopped down at the end, emphasized her preoccupation with people moving among drugs, disgust, venality, and a jeering despair.

Backed by the resolutely urban poet John Tranter, the publisher and editor of Transit Poetry, Ryan has continued to carry out his agenda for a realism under fluorescent light that favors the explicit argot of urban disillusionment. The realism is trenchant and unrelenting enough at times to get in the way of an appreciation of Ryan's brilliant ways of unsettling the reader, her constantly resourceful subjective notation, her montage technique, her deliberate banality and bad taste and pasted-on similes, her occasional sentimentality, and, finally, her ability to be very funny. The following is from "Getting it":

> He kisses, his pale guilt blowing
> like a flower. You're luxurious, unsure.
> Your eyes opening like telescopes
> on a clean brain.
> You're so silly in the kitchen, like a new
>   appliance . . .
>
> Will you buy me a dark salmon citroen
> please, with all your brilliant money,
> how it smells like a bank-clerk.

The same qualities are seen in "Dying for it"—

> He copes with the table.
> I would kill a thousand crocodiles for you.

His sincerity clacking like chain-mail,
death-hot, and your dead throat moves
one dream down

—and in "In the lovely crowd"—

> You want a man to apologise to,
> He avoids the place now like Queensland,
> as his radical politics fatten . . .

Manners of an Astronaut is described in the blurb as a "deeply coherent 'discontinuous narrative,'" though the narrative probably matters little to Ryan's fans, who enjoy the authentic mix in each poem. There is no obvious buildup of characters and situations among the monologues. *The Last Interior* continues the vein of anger and disgust, with the incitement of "bad-behaviour" opening lines, as in "Four":

> Now that my obsession's had it, I'm bored.
> You waver before me like bad television.
> and
>   Getting drunk, I insult everybody.
> and
>   They shoot up in the kitchen.
> and
>   We lay on the floor, getting speed
> and your face like an airport
> and
>   In love again like plaster . . .

Those who had been waiting for development in Ryan's art probably felt that the moment had come when *Excavation* was published. Here are poems about the media, politics ("The mind's shacks are stranded and overpopulated, South Africa," "On first looking into Fairfax's Herald"), and social problems ("Living in a vacant lot"). Sharp-edged phrases still overlap everywhere, and epigrams are up and non sequiturs down. This is clearly a controlled and varied menu and, even when cynically dismissive, near enough to good-humored, as in "Gone too":

> He says I'm a liar
> I shelve death back into my head
> The sick cells, the murder
> I figured it was a goer,
> new, and all
> Why are you so weak?
> I like him like air.
> He tells me to fuck off: what's new?
> A great girl friend vacuums and builds a temple
> Not me
> I turn the heart into a quiver,
> shoot and forget.

No one, even those such as Alan Wearne and John Forbes among the near contemporaries who support her most strongly, writes like Ryan. Her hand is immediately recognizable within a few lines. She is one of the ablest younger "established" poets in Australia, though the question stands as to a perceived sameness in her work. With her 1998 book *Pure and Applied,* Ryan's characteristic tone has become honed to biting precision, particularly in the political and socially acerbic poems, while her portrait poems and dramatic monologues bring to fierce life her passionate concerns, and her highly crafted knowledge of the range of poetic and song patterns coheres them into a unified and vivid personal expression.

—Judith Rodriguez

S

SAIL, Lawrence (Richard)

Nationality: British. **Born:** London, 29 October 1942. **Education:** Sherborne School, Dorset, 1956–61; St John's College. Oxford, 1961–64, B.A. in French and German 1964. **Family:** Married 1) Teresa Luke in 1965 (divorced 1981); one son and one daughter; 2) Helen Bird in 1994. **Career:** Administration officer, Greater London Council, 1965–66; head of modern languages, Lenana School, Nairobi, 1966–70; part-time teacher, Millfield School, Somerset, 1973–74; teacher, 1976–80, and visiting writer, 1980–81, Blundells School, Devon; teacher, Exeter School, Devon, 1982–91. Since 1991 freelance writer. Editor, *South West Review,* Exeter, 1980–85. Chair, Arvon Foundation, 1990–94. Program director, 1991, and co-director, 1999, Cheltenham Festival of Literature. **Awards:** Hawthornden Fellow, 1992; Arts Council Writer's Bursary, 1993. **Member:** Fellow, Royal Society of Literature. **Address:** Richmond Villa, 7 Wonford Road, Exeter, Devon EX2 4LF, England.

PUBLICATIONS

Poetry

Opposite Views. London, Dent, 1974.
The Drowned River. Hitchin, Hertfordshire, Mandeville Press, 1978.
The Kingdom of Atlas. London, Secker and Warburg, 1980.
Devotions. London, Secker and Warburg, 1987.
Aquamarine. Sidcot, Somerset, Gruffyground Press, 1988.
Out of Land: New & Selected Poems. Newcastle upon Tyne, Bloodaxe, 1992.
Building into Air. Newcastle upon Tyne, Bloodaxe, 1995.

Play

Radio Play: *Death of an Echo,* 1980.

Other

Children in Hospital, with Teresa Sail. Gloucester, Thornhill Press, 1976.

Editor, *South West Review: A Celebration.* Exeter, South West Arts, 1985.
Editor, *First and Always: Poems for the Great Ormond Street Children's Hospital.* London, Faber, 1988.
Editor, *100 Voices.* Exeter, Wheaton, 1989.
Editor, with Kevin Crossley-Holland, *The New Exeter Book of Riddles.* London, Enitharmon, 1999.

*

Critical Study: By John Lucas, in *Poetry Review,* 83(2), summer 1993.

Lawrence Sail comments:

Auden ("In Memory of W.B. Yeats") says it all: "In the prison of his days / Teach the free man how to praise."

* * *

Do it once more. Lob the stone
you have just chosen—a layered chip
of Siena cathedral, green and whitish,
pummelled by pressures greater than Gothic—
and see it slither, mix to the mile-long
shelf of the foreshore.

This stanza from "On Porlock Beach" is typical Lawrence Sail. Verses seem to rise like the tide or a wave and then fall or subside. The next stanza is another "breath" start. The tone of subdued elegance pervades poem after poem. Sail certainly crafts and constructs his work with precision. While his language appears robust, the rhythm of rise and fall tends to lull the reader.

Sail examines the natural world; we read about roses climbing, autumn closures, beech trees, "a vivid crescent of gorse." Only occasionally do people intrude on these pastorals, although they do appear more frequently in his collection *Devotions.* The careful approach is everywhere evident, as is a sense of genuine concern for the world and its minor inhabitants. Sail offers a variety of forms; stanzas can be three, four, five lines or more, and line lengths vary pleasingly. Yet there is still that similar rhythm whatever the shape of the poem on the page, as in "Wild Buddleia":

One gust released them
to shed the purple perfume
on facades, city traffic:
Imperial messengers, bearing
prophylactic annunciations.

Ted Hughes is a ghostly figure behind some of Sail's work. The occasional move into taut, tough language is followed by a sense of cathedral calm. He is the considered poet, intent and watching, just now and then finding a subject worthy of his attention. Like Philip Larkin, he is careful with his output, niggardly as regards quantity. The reader invariably nods with satisfaction at the end of a Sail poem. Everything is in its place, the artifact is complete, but it is less than sufficient to satisfy the hunger for greater sustenance.

—Wes Magee

ST. JOHN, Bruce (Carlisle)

Nationality: Barbadian. **Born:** Barbados, West Indies, 24 December 1923. **Education:** St. Giles' Boys' School, Combermere Secondary School, and Harrison College, 1929–42; Loughborough College, Leicestershire, England, 1945–47, External B.A. (University of London), 1953; Royal Conservatory of Music, Toronto, 1956; University of Toronto, 1962–64, M.A. in Spanish 1964. **Family:** Married Ruby

Marjorie Skeete in 1959 (divorced 1981); one daughter and one son. **Career:** Assistant master, St. Giles' Boys' School, 1942–44, and Combermere School, 1944–64; lecturer, 1964–75, and since 1976 senior lecturer in Spanish, University of the West Indies, Bridgetown, Barbados. Member, National Council for Arts and Culture, Barbados. **Awards:** Yaddo grant, 1972, 1976, 1978; Yoruba Foundation prize, 1973. **Address:** P.O. Box 64, Bridgetown, Barbados, West Indies.

PUBLICATIONS

Poetry

The Foetus Pains. Bridgetown, EP, 1972.
The Foetus Pleasures. Bridgetown, EP, 1972.
Bruce St. John at Kairi House. Port of Spain, Kairi, 1974; revised edition, 1975.
Joyce and Eros and Varia. Bridgetown, Yoruba Press, 1976.
Bumbatuk 1. Bridgetown, Cedar Press, 1982.

Play

The Vests (produced Bridgetown, 1977; Manchester, 1980).

Other

Por el Mar de las Antillas: A Spanish Course for Caribbean Secondary Schools. London, Nelson, 1978.

Editor, with Beverley A. Steele, *Tim Tim Tales: Children's Stories from Grenada, West Indies.* St. George's, Grenada, University of West Indies Extra Mural Department, 1976.
Editor, with others, *Aftermath: An Anthology.* Greenfield Center, New York, Greenfield Review Press, 1977.
Editor, *Caribanthology 1.* Bridgetown, Cedar Press, 1981.

*

Critical Studies: "The Poetry of Bruce St. John" by Michael Gitkes, in *Tapia* (Port of Spain), 15 June 1975; "Sex and Class in the Poetry of Bruce St. John" by Elaine Fido, in *Tapia* (Port of Spain), 24 August 1975; "If Barbados Could Speak" by Robert L. Morris, in *Manjak 9* and *10* (Bridgetown), 1975; introduction by Christopher David, to *Bruce St. John at Kairi House*, 1975.

Bruce St. John comments:

In my poetry in Barbadian dialect I try to express viewpoints on Barbadian human situations in the natural language of Barbadians as they actually speak it, according to my knowledge of the Barbadian dialect lexicon and its structure of thought and speech. Each poem is tested and retested in sound before, during, and after its composition. The views expressed are not always my own; they are our views as Barbadians.

In my poetry in English I tend to express my own views in Barbadian speech rhythms and in an English that is my own, in that I choose and position words in order to say effectively what I want to say. In short, I strive to develop a language of my own in order to express myself. In my English poems I give fully the whole range of my experience and draw on my exposure to other cultures. I restrict this range somewhat in my dialect poems.

*   *   *

Dialect has been used in Caribbean poetry from the beginning, as it were, when plantocratic poets and poetasters attempted to reproduce the "broken lingo" of their black servants and slaves. Although Louise Bennett began writing and reciting exclusively in dialect verse in the early 1940s, there was still, as late as the mid-1960s, a passionate debate as to whether patois could be used as the language of serious poetry. Edward Brathwaite's *Rights of Passage* (1967) appeared to settle the matter, but it was not until the poets of the 1970s, above all Bruce St. John, a former concert singer and physical education instructor and a lecturer in Spanish at the University of the West Indies, that "nation-language" came into its own.

Conceived of and used as an alternative to "bad," or "bongo," grammar, nation-language appeals to a large, increasingly culturally conscious audience to such a degree that it is practically unthinkable today for any serious Caribbean poet not to at least include it in his work. In doing so, Caribbean poets move closer and closer stylistically to the *kaiso* and reggae singers, who have always assumed the native to be the norm. The miracle of nation-language at its poetic best is that it not only reproduces the language of the people but also reaches and reechoes their inner vibrations and very bones, so that words, psyche, and sense become involved. As he should, the nation-poet expresses the total culture of his subject in word, soul, and body language.

The dialogue and dramatic monologue are natural to the culture, and Bennett always used the forms. But what St. John adds is a sense of superstructure. The dialogue forms a litany that in itself becomes a commentary on the Bajan personality, and the language is intensified not only through form but also through the investigation of contemporary political and moral issues that are juxtaposed against traditional norms expressed through proverb and riddle. This happens, for example, in "Bajan Litany":

> Follow pattern kill Cadogan. *Yes, Lord.*
> America got black power? *O Lord.*
> We got black power. *Yes, Lord.*
> Wuh sweeten goat mout bun'e tail . . . *O Lord.*
> Jamaica got industry? *O Lord.*
> We got industry. *Yes Lord.*
> Jamaica got bauxite? (Silence)
> (Louder) Jamaica got bauxite? . . . *Yes, Lord.*
> De higher monkey go, de more he show 'e tail.

St. John tackles traditional subjects such as kite flying, cricket, sea bathing, and the other woman and more modern issues such as the ambiguities of postcolonial politics and the constantly vexing question of Bajan education (contrasted with the more native *studyation*). Everything is said in a way that allows us to see and hear for the first time from the inside, as it were, through the persona of Archie. Archie/St. John are aware that education and language are intimately connected, and the respect for this connection says more about one's cultural authenticity than any politician or pedagogue ever could. Consider, for example, these lines from "Bajan Language":

> Evah language got a rhythm but Bajan
> Lick guitar drum an banjo stiff wid blows
> Imag'ry purty an sweet like a rose

Limey try fuh muck up we poor nation
But Bajan save we life so here we goes . . .

St. John is as Bajan as Miss Lou is Jamaican and as Paul Keens-Douglas is Trinidadian, and yet they all transcend territorial boundaries to capture and express the spirit of the Caribbean. It is in this both new and ancient tradition of word seers and sound poets that the future of Caribbean poetry lies. But the body of their poetry will have to be constantly enriched, as is being done, with the emerging underground resources of culture itself.

—Edward Kamau Brathwaite

ST. JOHN, David

Nationality: American. **Born:** Fresno, California, 24 July 1949. **Education:** California State University, Fresno, 1967–72, B.A. 1972; University of Iowa, Iowa City, 1972–74, M.F.A. 1974. **Family:** Married 1) Bonnie Bedford in 1968 (divorced 1974), one son; 2) Molly Bendall in 1990; one daughter. **Career:** Assistant professor, English Department, Oberlin College, Ohio, 1975–77; assistant professor, then associate professor, Johns Hopkins University, Baltimore, Maryland, 1977–87. Since 1987 professor, English Department, University of Southern California, Los Angeles. Assistant poetry editor, *Iowa Review,* 1974–75; associate editor, *Field,* 1975–77, and *Seneca Review,* 1977–81. Since 1981 poetry editor, *Antioch Review.* **Awards:** Discovery/*The Nation* prize, 1975; Great Lakes College Association New Writers award, 1976, for *Hush;* National Endowment for the Arts fellowship, 1976, 1984, 1994–95; Guggenheim fellowship, 1978–79; James D. Phelan prize, 1980, for *The Shore;* Prix de Rome fellowship in literature, 1984. **Address:** English Department, University of Southern California, Los Angeles, California 90089–0354, U.S.A.

PUBLICATIONS

Poetry

Hush. Boston, Houghton Mifflin, 1976.
The Shore. Boston, Houghton Mifflin, 1980.
No Heaven. Boston, Houghton Mifflin, 1985.
Terraces of Rain: An Italian Sketchbook, with illustrations by Antoine Predock. Santa Fe, New Mexico, Recursos Books, 1991.
Study for the World's Body: New and Selected Poems. New York, HarperCollins, 1994.
In the Pines: Lost Poems, 1972–1997. Buffalo, New York, White Pine Press, 1998.
The Red Leaves of Night. New York, Harper Flamingo, 1999.

Recording: *Black Poppy,* Watershed, 1995.

Other

Where the Angels Come toward Us: Selected Essays, Reviews, and Interviews. Fredonia, New York, White Pine Press, 1995.

Translator, with others, *God's Shadow* by Reza Baraheni. Bloomington, University of Indiana Press, 1976.

*

Critical Studies: By Norman Dubie, in *American Poetry Review* (Philadelphia), spring 1977; by Robert Hass, in *Los Angeles Times Book Review,* 27 November 1994; by Katrina Roberts, in *Agni Review* (Boston), spring 1995.

*   *   *

David St. John is a skillful poet. *Hush,* a collection of poems written by his mid-twenties, clearly establishes his talent as well as reflecting preoccupations common to younger poets. As with many young poets, there are poems modeled after the work of other writers as well as impressionistic poems inspired by paintings. Many of the poems in this collection, however, also connect quite powerfully with the author's personal history. The literary allusions and painterly approach generally work for, rather than against, the outcome. Many poems deal with the struggle to get beyond the preoccupation with self that is part of being an artist to establish the intimacy necessary to being a worthwhile human being. This theme is reflected in a quote from Paul Éluard that precedes the body of the work: "Are we two or am I all alone."

"Naming The Unborn" and "Hush," the title poem, both deal with the loss of a son, the poet's second child, who was the victim of a miscarriage. "Naming The Unborn" contains powerful images that evoke the loss:

> Afterwards,
> his face rose in our dreams
> like a planet,
>
> and we said:
>
> you,
> broken tear,
> little star of red mud,
>
> flesh-blown and milky;
> you, Joseph.

In "Hush" the poet compares mourning his son to

> The way a tired Chippewa woman
> Who's lost a child gathers up black feathers,
> Black quills and leaves
> That she wraps & swaddles in a little bale, a shag
> Cocoon . . .
> . . . As you
> Cry out, as if calling to a father you conjure
> In the paling light, the voice rises, instead in me.

In some poems the author's thoughts about other artists manage to connect forcefully with his own life and personal grief. "Six/Nine/Forty-Four" concerns Keith Douglas, a British poet killed in the

Normandy invasion of World War II. A poem in four parts, it develops in a series of short takes like scenes from a newsreel, with literary and personal themes reinforcing one another. St. John alludes to events from Douglas's life, such as his poems being censored as he writes from the front in North Africa, and imagines the deceased poet's parents in London, intercutting these events with scenes from his own life and that of his father, a flyer who was also in the service. The scenes culminate with the three mens' lives overlapping in the Shangri-La, a bar the father had visited earlier and where the poet himself gets drunk:

> These sons picking through the silences
> of abandoned Quonset huts, where they were born.
> These fathers: suddenly air. Blown from cockpits
> into the shrugs of sons, the shrugs of my friends
> & poets; all of us walking out of these pages,
> & the wars, & these fathers. I've fallen
> asleep in the same Shangri-La.
> Asleep in my father's old overcoat.

Here the poet, like a painter, applies successive layers of images, including the echo from Jarrell's "Death of the Ball Turret Gunner," until the picture is wrenchingly clear.

"Iris," another strong poem, uses the painterly approach well. It begins with the poet as a child telling his grandmother that there is a train inside an iris. The poem develops the image, less playfully, into "a darkened porthole lit by the white, angular face / Of an old woman, or perhaps the boy beside her in the stuffy, / Hot compartment." Peering deeper into the iris, he sees it become even more like a tunnel the train is moving through, making its "drive deep into the damp heart of its stem." The tunnel then becomes a corridor of elms arching like the ceiling of a "French railway pier," a place he walks through, holding an iris, to wave good-bye to his grandmother. As he watches her departure, the image shifts to that of an "empty garden," and the poem winds down toward an ominous conclusion:

> . . . a man
> Is walking toward him.
>
> Dull shears in one hand; & now believe me: The train
> Is gone. The old woman is dead, & the boy.

The collection does not conclude with an easy affirmation. Instead, there is a sense of life's always unfinished business, to be continued in future work. This is typified by the last poem, "You," in which a couple take a boat trip haunted by mutual, unspoken recriminations. But there is also a gesture the speaker sees as important. He sees the other person's life changing "because you reached far / Out of the boat, to pick a dead bird off a wave." The gesture echoes the speaker's earlier act of leaning far over a balcony railing to reach into a lime tree "because you wanted / Your gin with lime." The poem, like others in the collection, suggests the many ways we communicate, striving to reach beyond words: "The only prayer is to continue."

—Duane Ackerson

SALOM, Philip

Nationality: Australian. **Born:** Bunbury, Western Australia, 8 August 1950. **Education:** Muresk Agricultural College, 1967–68; Curtin University, Perth, 1974–76, B.A. in English, Dip.Ed. 1981. **Family:** Married 1) Helena Salom in 1978 (divorced 1993), one son; 2) Meredith Kidby in 1994, one daughter. **Career:** Agricultural technician, gardener, and house painter, 1969–73; freelance writer and illustrator, Adult Aboriginal Education, Perth, and Student Guild, Curtin University, 1977–78; extension project officer, Department of Agriculture, Perth, 1978–80; tutor and part-time lecturer, Curtin University, 1982–90; writer-in-residence, Western Australia Colleges of Advanced Education, 1988; Singapore National University, 1989; B.R. Whiting Library/Studio, Rome, 1992. Lecturer, Murdoch University, 1994. **Awards:** Commonwealth Poetry prize, 1981, 1987; Western Australian Literary award, 1984, 1988; Australia Council fellowship, 1985, 1987, 1989, 1992; Western Australian Department for the Arts fellowship, 1990; Western Australian Premiers prize for fiction, 1991; Australia/New Zealand Literary Exchange fellowship, 1992. **Address:** Lot 501, Mills Road, Glen Forrest, Western Australia 6071, Australia.

PUBLICATIONS

Poetry

The Silent Piano. Fremantle, Western Australia, Fremantle Arts Centre Press, 1980.
The Projectionist: A Sequence. Fremantle, Western Australia, Fremantle Arts Centre Press, 1983.
Sky Poems. Fremantle, Western Australia, Fremantle Arts Centre Press, 1987.
Barbecue of the Primitives. St. Lucia, University of Queensland Press. 1989.
Tremors. Canberra, National Library, 1992.
Feeding the Ghost. Melbourne, Penguin, 1993.
The Rome Air Naked. Ringwood, Victoria, Penguin, 1996.
New and Selected Poems. Fremantle, Western Australia, Fremantle Arts Centre Press, 1998.

Plays

Screenplays: *The Box,* 1977; *The Giant,* 1978; *Always Then and Now,* 1993.

Novel

Playback. Fremantle, Fremantle Arts Centre Press, 1991.

*

Manuscript Collection: University College/Australian Defence Force Academy, Canberra.

Critical Studies: "The Surreal Face of Verse" by Philip Neilsen, in *The Age* (Melbourne), 29 August 1987; "Sojourn in the Sky: Conventions of Exile in Philip Salom's *Sky Poems*" by Kirsten Holst Petersen and Anna Rutherford, in *Westerly* (Perth), June 1988; "The Self Moving" by Keith Russel, in *Quadrant* (Sydney), April 1989; by

Dennis Haskell, in *Wordhord, Contemporary Western Australian Poetry,* Fremantle, Fremantle Arts Centre Press, 1989; by Barbara Williams, in her *In Other Words: Interviews with Australian Poets,* Amsterdam, Rodopi, 1998.

Philip Salom comments:

Describing one's own poetry is not easy, especially in a few paragraphs. My work began as lyrical and representational—symbolist and very concrete in style—and yet, under the influence of the great dramatic monologues of Browning and Eliot, it moved strongly into monologue and "speech." Since then it has become increasingly described as "surrealistic," "erotic," "ontological," and "imaginative" and is noted for its exuberance, intensity, and boldness of imagery. Well, these all seem appropriate enough! (I will not add the less flattering comments, some of which are also true.) It is now often a conceptual poetry, but certainly not always.

The act of creation is central to my poems, not only as a response to poetry itself but also to human perception in general. My work is ontological, inquiring, achieving its effects by frequent re-creation of events, myths, public customs, and rituals in order to play them back upon themselves and so reveal within them (by irony, metaphor, satire) my altered layers of meaning and emotion. Often this involves creating worlds where "reality" is bent and fabulist, is teased and/or hurt into showing its less obvious aspects. I try to maintain a (difficult) balance between reaching for justice and yet developing a kind of moral open-endedness.

Many poems are about desire in the erotic sense but also the metaphysical. I use concrete and sensual language to explore being and to reach out, unexpectedly, beyond the literal, to "flash," as I call it, beyond the basic into the deeply resonant and other.

In fact, I am quite in love with metaphor and its power to defamiliarize, to see and feel, as it were, newer features of the commonplace. I seldom startle, or shock, or ornament—despite the densely imagistic character of my poems—merely for the hell of it; all my imagery has inherent sense within the poems, which still allows for the pleasures, which are shock and charm, of such usage. For the reader, as for the poet, I hope.

(1995) Recently I have been exploring with page form and have developed a multiple layering on the page that amounts to one or more poems plus prose plus fragments, all creating a composite or what I call a concurrent poem. This is for me akin to what we perceive/how we perceive and allows the poet and the reader to escape the oppression inherent in one poem's style and exclusiveness. This new poem is much more lateral and inclusive than any other.

*   *   *

As one of the more prolific, energetic, and technically self-conscious of his generation of Australian poets, Philip Salom has tended to elude easy classification. His first collection, *The Silent Piano,* seemed to promise several possible lines of development. There was the life study poet, recording his rural origins with a sensual substantiality of imagery, sometimes fresh in its regional precision, sometimes violent, sometimes charged with the melancholy of a great Australian emptiness aching for "uncertainty and change." Given that one of these desired changes was the transformation of the mundane, it was not surprising to recognize a touch of the transcendental romantic, the metaphysical quester "walking on the eyelids of God." Such imagery, however, suggested an infusion of a type then less common in Australian poetry—a paradoxical surrealist,

perhaps even a magic realist, given his professed debt to the Latin Americans, especially to Borges, and his "clash between the magic and the brutal."

This influence was more clearly dominant in Salom's next two volumes. *The Projectionist* is constantly concerned with perception, image, and reality; picture showing and picture viewing is the name of the game. We are given notice in the opening poem, "Let," with its suggestion of the fiat of Creation, that the poet as projectionist-creator will obey the injunction that "there is only to note every feature, also mention / ugliness, when necessary tell lies." The more spectacular mentions of ugliness found in "Mrs Benchley" and "The Railway Line" (with its graphically violent representation of a real or fantasized rape/murder) caused an uneasiness among some readers that culminated in an accusation of misogyny from a reviewer of *Sky Poems.* It is true that the poetic gaze of *The Projectionist* objectifies everything, including macho masculinity, which is hardly endorsed by its representation. Nonetheless, within the mythopoesis of the first two, possibly three, collections, grotesquerie is much more marked in his figuration of the female. While it can seem gratuitously hostile, it would appear in the case of the hunchbacked Mrs. Bentley that Salom is attempting something akin to the ambiguous valorization of the crippled Rhoda of Patrick White's *The Vivisector,* which Salom nominates as one impetus to his writing of poetry.

The surrealist framework of *Sky Poems* allow a wider and more exuberant range. Employing the conventions of apotheosis, Salom invites readers to share a vantage point of observation from which he comments on his place of origin (Australia) and the places of its mythology ("Seeing Gallipoli from the Sky"). But this sky is not heaven; it is "a word-processor," enabling the construction (and deconstruction) of fantasized scenarios. It contains the possibility of paradise for those who can achieve the difficult task of creating it ("Ghazals on Poets and Allegories"), but skepticism about the human capacity to do so is the more dominant effect, invoked as it is by the unreconstructed beings to be found in "Wandering in the Sky" or the witty sexual desolation of "He Sees She Sees."

The mixture of satirical commentator and lyric celebrant continues in *Barbecue of the Primitives* and *Feeding the Ghost.* Neither represents the kind of poetic leap forward of *Sky Poems,* yet each contributes to a growing poetic maturity. Despite its title, *Barbecue of the Primitives* extends the tonal and representational boundaries of Salom's work with gentler and more personal writing about his wife, child, and mother, while *Feeding the Ghost* makes a surefooted transition from regionalism to internationalism, most impressively in "In the Month of Hungry Ghosts." This long sonnet sequence plays elegant variations on the classical sonnet form while exploring not only the new geographical site of Singapore but also a new paradoxical view of the so substantial world as a hungry ghost needing to be fed by poetry but ready, like the starving cats of Singapore, to be scared off by "the wrong words."

It is *The Rome Air Naked* that marks a major development in Salom's poetics. The volume is the realization of what he had earlier announced as experimentation with a composite, or "concurrent," poem, to be achieved by a "layering on the page" of "one or more poems, plus prose plus fragments." It is also a multilayered poem of intensely intertwined erotic responses to the sensuality of (present) Rome and that of his (absent) lover. It resonates with the noisy traffic of "rip, render and ecstasy" (where else but in Rome), yet there are also eloquent moments of stillness, of listening to a silence in which thought can fly toward the absent lover "like sunlight in your glass." Altogether, it is something of a tour de force, although one finally wonders whether the hyperspace technique of the "poems of disso-ciation" will prove as durable as the more formally conventional poems. Certainly it is a problem for the more technically adventurous poet that anthologies remain probably the major form of access to an audience and thence into public memory, and it is difficult to extract a segment suitable for anthologizing from these so-called concurrent poems. In the meantime *New and Selected Poems,* published in 1998, provides a useful moment of stasis and a definition of substantial achievement.

—Jennifer Strauss

SALTER, Mary Jo

Nationality: American. **Born:** Grand Rapids, Michigan, 15 August 1954. **Education:** Harvard University, Cambridge, Massachusetts, B.A. (cum laude) 1976; New Hall, Cambridge, M.A. (with first class honors) 1978. **Family:** Married Brad Leithauser *q.v.* in 1980; two daughters. **Career:** Instructor, Harvard University, Cambridge, Massachusetts, 1978–79; staff editor, *Atlantic Monthly,* Boston, Massachusetts, 1978–80; instructor in English conversation at various institutions in Japan, 1980–83. Since 1984 lecturer, Mount Holyoke College, South Hadley, Massachusetts. Poet-in-residence, Robert Frost Place, 1981. **Awards:** Discovery (*The Nation*) prize, 1983; National Endowment for the Arts fellow, 1983–84; Lamont Poetry prize, Academy of American Poets, 1988, for *Unfinished Painting;* Ingram-Merrill Foundation fellowship, 1989; Witter Bynner Foundation Poetry prize, American Academy and Institute of Arts and Letters, 1989; Lavan award, Academy of American Poets, 1990; Guggenheim fellowship, 1993. **Address:** c/o Alfred A. Knopf, 201 East 50th Street, New York, New York 10022, U.S.A.

PUBLICATIONS

Poetry

Henry Purcell in Japan. New York, Knopf, 1985.
Unfinished Painting. New York, Knopf, 1989.
Sunday Skaters. New York, Knopf, 1994.
A Kiss in Space. New York, Knopf, 1999.

Other

The Moon Comes Home (for children). New York, Knopf, 1989.

*

Critical Study: "The Not-So-New Formalism" by David Lehman, in *Michigan Quarterly Review* (Ann Arbor, Michigan), 29(1), winter 1990.

*   *   *

Mary Jo Salter is one of the best of the younger poets now writing in traditional forms. Her work has variety, grace, humor, and

depth. Her first book, *Henry Purcell in Japan* (1985), opens with a poem that introduces many of the themes that inform much of her subsequent work. "For an Italian Cousin" recounts the speaker's reaction as her cousin shows her the Roman Catholic church she attends and describes the local observance of Good Friday. The speaker is shocked by the waxen image of Christ on the chapel's crucifix and by her cousin's naïveté:

> Tempted to joke, I'm silenced by
> the trusting expression on her face,
> flushed with the light of this stained glass
> where Christ is always about to die.

Yet the speaker thinks of another church, San Marco in Venice, where images have shown her "a world I've pieced / together with a kind of faith, at least." The mosaics there seem less stone than flesh:

> A puzzle of figures floats on the walls
> and in golden domes, and you have the feeling
> this heavenly gold is not a ceiling—
> but space itself, from which no one falls.

The voice here, as in most of Salter's poems, is controlled and plausibly conversational. The speaker's mind makes rapid connections and associations, many of them metaphorical, and the speaker brings an American sensibility self-consciously to bear upon remote surroundings. Salter and her family have spent significant stretches of time abroad, in Japan, Paris, and Iceland, and these places have provided settings for many of her poems.

Salter received the Lamont award of the Academy of American Poets for her second collection, *Unfinished Painting* (1989). Reflecting additional years of practice, the poems are more fully achieved technically, and the balance between the attractive ingenuity of slighter poems and the depth of feeling in more solemn ones is more assured. There is the wit that rhymes "umbrage" and "Cambridge" and sees in the face of Big Ben "a daily mirror of the Times," and there is the heart for elegies to the poet's mother and for Etsuko, a Japanese friend. The title poem, about a painting reproduced on the book's jacket, again confronts the tension between the passage of time and those objects that evoke single moments. The painting is by the poet's mother and portrays the poet's brother as a child.

Sunday Skaters (1994), Salter's third collection, begins with several poems evoking the joys and the trials of love and of parenthood, both experienced and observed. Here is "Lullaby for a Daughter," the shortest but not the least of these:

> Someday, when the sands of time
> invert, may you find perfect rest
> as a newborn nurses from
> the hourglass of your breast.

In these poems close but apparently effortless observation is backed by a deep moral sense that greatly enriches Salter's work, though it never makes it too solemn to be believed. Solemnity, in fact, is scarce here, even when the poems are at their most serious, for Salter is constantly alert for the small jokes the language plays upon itself.

The book ends with two longer poems of notable ambition. "Two American Lives" evokes crucial moments in the lives of Thomas Jefferson and Robert Frost and, according to notes at the back of the book, required considerable research. The poems live, however, on their own terms and bring great moments to life, free of the sound of index cards.

—Henry Taylor

SANCHEZ, Sonia

Nationality: American. **Born:** Birmingham, Alabama, 9 September 1934. **Education:** Hunter College, New York, B.A. in political science 1955; New York University, 1959–60; Wilberforce University, Ohio, Ph.D. in fine arts 1972. **Family:** Married Etheridge Knight, (divorced); one daughter and two sons. **Career:** Staff member, Downtown Community School, 1965–67, and Mission Rebels in Action, 1968–69, San Francisco; instructor, San Francisco State College, 1967–69; lecturer in black literature, University of Pittsburgh, 1969–70, Rutgers University, New Brunswick, New Jersey, 1970–71, Manhattan Community College, New York, 1971–73, and City University of New York, 1972; associate professor, Amherst College, Massachusetts, 1972–73, and University of Pennsylvania, Philadelphia, 1976–77; associate professor of English, 1977–79, since 1979 professor of English, Faculty Fellow, Provost's Office, 1986–87, Presidential Fellow, 1987–88, and Laura Carnell Chair in English, Temple University, Philadelphia. Columnist, *American Poetry Review,* 1977–78, and Philadelphia *Daily News,* 1982–83. **Awards:** P.E.N. award, 1969; American Academy grant, 1970; National Endowment for the Arts award, 1978; Smith College Tribute to Black Women award, 1982; Lucretia Mott award, 1984; Before Columbus Foundation award, 1985; PEW fellow, 1993; Legacy award, Jomandi Productions, 1994. Honorary doctorate: Baruch College, 1993. **Address:** Temple University, Women's Studies, Philadelphia, Pennsylvania 19122, U.S.A.

PUBLICATIONS

Poetry

Homecoming. Detroit, Broadside Press, 1969.
We a BaddDDD People. Detroit, Broadside Press, 1970.
Liberation Poem. Detroit, Broadside Press, 1970.
It's a New Day: Poems for Young Brothas and Sistuhs. Detroit, Broadside Press, 1971.
Ima Talken bout The Nation of Islam. Astoria, New York, Truth Del., c.1971.
Love Poems. New York, Third Press, 1973.
A Blues Book for Blue Black Magical Women. Detroit, Broadside Press, 1974.
I've Been a Woman: New and Selected Poems. Sausalito, California, Black Scholar Press, 1978; revised edition, Chicago, Third World Press, 1985.
Homegirls and Handgrenades. New York, Thunder's Mouth Press, 1984.
Under a Soprano Sky. Trenton, New Jersey, Africa World Press, 1987.
Wounded in the House of a Friend. Boston, Beacon, 1995.
Does Your House Have Lions? Boston, Beacon, 1997.

Like the Singing Coming off the Drums: Love Poems. Boston, Beacon, 1998.
Shake Loose My Skin: New and Selected Poems. Boston, Beacon, 1999.

Recordings: *Homecoming,* Broadside Voices, 1969; *We a BaddDDD People,* Broadside Voices, 1969; *A Sun Woman for All Seasons,* Folkways, 1971; *Sonia Sanchez and Robert Bly,* Black Box, 1971; *Sonia Sanchez: Selected Poems, 1974,* Watershed, 1975; *IDKT: Captivating Facts about the Heritage of Black Americans,* Ujima, 1982; *Sacred Ground,* with Sweet Honey in the Rock, EarthBeat! Records, 1995.

Plays

The Bronx Is Next (produced New York, 1970). Published in *The Drama Review* (New York), summer 1968.
Sister Son/ji (produced Evanston, Illinois, 1971; New York, 1972). Published in *New Plays from the Black Theatre,* edited by Ed Bullins, New York, Bantam, 1969.
Dirty Hearts '72, in *Break Out! In Search of New Theatrical Environments,* edited by James Schevill. Chicago, Swallow Press, 1973.
Uh, Uh: But How Do It Free Us? (produced Evanston, Illinois, 1975). Published in *The New Lafayette Theatre Presents,* edited by Ed Bullins, New York, Doubleday, 1974.
Malcolm Man/Don't Live Here No Mo' (produced Philadelphia, 1979).
I'm Black When I'm Singing, I'm Blue When I Ain't (produced Atlanta. 1982).
Black Cats Back and Uneasy Landings (produced Philadelphia, 1995).

Short Stories

A Sound Investment. Chicago, Third World Press, 1980.

Other

The Adventures of Fathead, Smallhead, and Squarehead (for children). New York, Third Press, 1973.
Crisis in Culture. N.p., Black Librarian Press, 1983.

Editor, *Three Hundred Sixty Degrees of Blackness Comin' at You.* New York, 5X, 1972.
Editor, *We Be Word Sorcerers: 25 Stories by Black Americans.* New York. Bantam. 1973.

*

Critical Studies: "Sonia Sanchez and Her Work" by S. Clarke, in *Black World* (Chicago), June 1971; "The Poetry of Three Revolutionists: Don L. Lee, Sonia Sanchez, and Nikki Giovanni" by R. Roderick Palmer, in *CLA Journal* (Baltimore), September 1971; "Sonia Sanchez Creates Poetry for the Stage" by Barbara Walker, in *Black Creation* (New York), fall 1973; "Notes on the 1974 Black Literary Scene" by George Kent, in *Phylon* (Atlanta), June 1974; *Black Women Writers at Work* edited by Claudia Tate, New York, Continuum, 1983; *Black Women Writers (1950–1980)* edited by Mari Evans, New York, Doubleday, 1984; "Pre-Feminism in the Black

Revolutionary Drama of Sonia Sanchez'' by Rosemary K. Curb, in *The Many Forms of Drama,* edited by Karelisa Hartigan, Lanham, Maryland, UPs of America, 1985; ''Sonia Sanchez: Will and Spirit'' by D.H. Melhem, in *MELUS* (Amherst, Massachusetts), 12(3), fall 1985; ''Our Lady: Sonia Sanchez and the Writing of a Black Renaissance'' by Houston A. Baker, in *Black Feminist Criticism and Critical Theory,* edited by Baker and Joe Weixlmnn, Greenwood, Florida, Penkevill, 1988; ''Sonia Sanchez's Homegirls and Handgrenades: Recalling Toomer's Cane'' by James Robert Saunders, in *MELUS* (Amherst, Massachusetts), 15(1), spring 1988; ''The Southern Imagination of Sonia Sanchez'' by Joanne Veal Gabbin, in *Southern Women Writers: The New Generation,* edited by Tonette Bond Inge and Doris Betts, Tuscaloosa, University of Alabama Press, 1990; ''Refusing to Be Boxed In: Sonia Sanchez's Transformation of the Haiku Form'' by Frenzella Elaine De Lancey, and ''The Blue/ Black Poetics of Sonia Sanchez'' by Regina B. Jennings, both in *Language and Literature in the African American Imagination,* edited by Carol Aisha Blackshire-Belay, Westport, Connecticut, Greenwood, 1992; ''The Black Arts Poets'' by William W. Cook, in *The Columbia History of American Poetry,* edited by Jay Parini and Brett C. Miller, New York, Columbia University Press, 1993; *The X-Factor Influence on the Transformed Image of Africa in the Poetry of Haki Madhubuti and Sonia Sanchez: Issues of Re-Naming and Inversion* (dissertation) by Regina B. Jennings, Temple University, 1993; *Keepers of the Oral Traditions: An Afrocentric Analysis of Representative Plays by African-American Females, 1970–1984* (dissertation) by Julyette Tamy Adams, Bowling Green State University, 1995; interview with Danielle Alyce Rome, in *Speaking of the Short Story: Interviews with Contemporary Writers,* edited by Farhat Iftekharuddin, Mary Rohrberger, and Maurice Lee, Jackson, University Press of Mississippi, 1997.

*   *   *

As a mature poet, Sonia Sanchez continues to write for political, economic, and social purposes, seeing no necessary dichotomy between cause-oriented, utilitarian writing and art. Earlier, as a leading poet of the black arts movement and believing that African-Americans were expressing thoughts that previous generations had been afraid to utter, she saw the times as propitious and urgent for black artistic militancy. ''I write because I must,'' she once declared, and ''if you write from a black experience, you're writing from a universal experience as well.''

In an early poem Sanchez writes, ''white people /ain't rt bout nothing,'' and she chastises blacks who adopt white values and lifestyles. To blacks who ''have come to / believe that we are/ not'' she gives the prescription ''inhale the ancient black breath.'' Thus, she teaches that African-Americans must know their enemies, accept themselves, demonstrate ethnic pride and unity, be moral, act communally, and go about the serious business of intelligent and courageous self-direction. In delivering such messages, then and now, much of her poetry is direct, uncompromising, demanding, militant, even abrasive. Yet it is not without tenderness, a quality openly evident in her poems for children and in her love poems, notably those dealing with love among African-Americans and between man and woman.

As her collected works show, Sanchez's poetry has not been static in substance and technique. *Homecoming* is a young poet's grappling with conceptions of self, others, and the world. *We a BaddDDD People* stresses black strength and self-love, identification

of the human and institutional enemies of black people, ''we''ness in place of the personal and subjective ''I.'' *It's a New Day,* ''poems for young brothas and sistuhs,'' warns of dangers and points out the necessity for unity, wholeness of spirit, and clearness of purpose and actions. Having by this time joined the Nation of Islam, Sanchez in *Love Poems* tones down her language as she explores the dynamics of healthy relationships among black people. The poet's still evolving technical style is apparent in *A Blues Book for Blue Black Magical Women,* an autobiographical, perhaps confessional, volume. Addressed to ''Queens of the Universe'' and divided into the sections ''Past,'' ''Present,'' ''Rebirth,'' and ''Future,'' it is not an anthology or collection but rather thematically united poetry that ironically and satirically echoes T.S. Eliot's *The Waste Land.* While Eliot is pessimistic, however, Sanchez is determinedly optimistic.

I've Been a Woman is a gathering of new and selected poems. In the evolving of her poetry Sanchez has tended not to move from exhorter to persuader, but she is always the teacher. ''C'mon yall,'' she encourages, ''on a safari / into our plantation jungle / minds / and let us catch the nigger / roamen inside of us,'' and she invites, ''Come into Black geography / you, seated like Manzu's cardinal, / come up through tongues / multiplying memories.'' *Under a Soprano Sky* continues her technical and thematic predilections. The volume especially continues the topicality and real-person subjects in her poems and demonstrates well her use of the specific in the conveying of broader philosophical positions.

In *Wounded in the House of a Friend* Sanchez's volition for entering the pain-filled corridor of human life is apparent. She supports her own contention that ''this is not a small voice / you hear,'' as she nimbly and powerfully speaks in the multiple voices of the hopeless and the hope filled. She broadens her political, social, and cultural landscape of racism and sexism to include a heightened awareness of the daily and personal traumas of infidelity, drug addiction, abuse, and rape that afflict a global humanity. Sanchez stages the title poem as an absurdist drama in which the loss of shared values destroys a marriage. The male and female speakers trudge through the emotional sludge of suspicion and hurt and of recognition and resolution, finally to understand that the husband's ''wolfdreams'' of adulterous relationships and his aspirations for a spiraling corporate career are opposed to the wife's penchant for down-to-earth activism.

Sanchez's voice resonates with the clarity of a seasoned eavesdropper as she shares the narratives of human pain. Drug abuse is the dominant theme in ''Love Song No. 3,'' in which an eighteen-year-old addict hammers her grandmother to death to gain access to insurance money, and in ''Poem for Some Women,'' in which a drug-addicted mother temporarily trades the ''prettiest little girl,'' her seven-year-old daughter, to satisfy her ''jones jones jones / habit habit habit'' for drugs. In ''Eyewitness:/Case No. 3456'' the female speaker ''nicks'' the reader with the wrenching agony of the knife she endures at the hands of a rapist. Sanchez's ability to gaze at life with an unflinching stare and to capture and manipulate the screaming and moaning voices that enter her cultural, political, and social domain is evident in both the physical and emotional scars of the victims and the psychological wounds of the perpetrators.

Sanchez seeks balance in the work by ending with a signature series of haiku and tanka that breathlessly alter the terrain with fragments of memory: ''if i had known then / what i know now, i would have / picked my own cotton.'' But it is through her tributes that Sanchez's persistent and resilient spirit soars. She weaves the trials of the past with the hopes of the future as she pays homage to *Essence* magazine, Spelman College, Bill Cosby, James Baldwin, and the singing group Sweet Honey in the Rock.

Does Your House Have Lions? is Sanchez's elegy for her half brother who died of AIDS following his youthful trek from the south to "embrace the city and the streets" of New York, where he "enslaved his body to cocaine." In complicated, yet noble rhyme royal stanzas, Sanchez imagines the poignant voices of the estranged family as they make the arduous journey through desertion, alienation, and pain to reconciliation and love. The brother's illicit engagements in New York conjure up all of the family's old hurts and angers. His terminal illness forces them to prepare him for the final journey to their ancestors, who sing out, "come here African," and the brother, who finally accepts his fate, responds, "I am coming." Sanchez tackles a difficult social issue, but, by deft handling of form, language, and tone, she invites us all to participate in restoring our loved ones to a place of dignity and rest.

In *Like the Singing Coming off the Drums: Love Poems* Sanchez forcefully extends her experimentation with form to create a volume predominantly comprised of Japanese haiku, tanka, and sonku, along with new blues haiku and tributes to notable people like Ella Fitzgerald, Bill and Camille Cosby, and Gwendolyn Brooks. Sanchez playfully redefines the ethnic culture of the haiku by using the black vernacular in "let me be yo wil / derness let me be yo wind / blowing you all day," and she shares an ironic passion in "I have caught fire from / your mouth now you want me to / swallow the ocean." Relentlessly challenged by newness, Sanchez, who has publicly embraced the controversial hip-hop poets and been hailed "an ambassador of hip-hop," includes two poems for slain rapper/poet Tupac Shakur. In "Love Poem [for Tupac]" she writes, "I will not / burp you up / I hold you close to my heart," and in "For Tupac Amaru Shakur" she asserts in a blend of African chants, "ayyee—ayyee-ayyee / I'm going to save these young niggaz / because nobody else want to save them / nobody ever came to save me . . ."

Shake Loose My Skin: New and Selected Poems is a compilation taken from Sanchez's most highly regarded works, including *I've Been a Woman, Homegirls and Handgrenades, Under a Soprano Sky, Wounded in the House of a Friend, Does Your House Have Lions?*, and *Like the Singing Coming off the Drums*, and it includes a section of new poems. Although the collection can boast of the vast landscape of Sanchez's more mature and technically honed works from 1978 to 1998, it notably excludes her most revolutionary poetry from the black arts movement, with which she first gained prominence.

Several new poems in *Shake Loose My Skin* are riveting in their urgent cry for a unified humanity. The haunting refrain of "Mrs. Benita Jones Speaks" recalls Lorraine Hansberry's award-winning play *A Raisin in the Sun*. The irony of Sanchez's contemporary monologue is its thematic similarity of racial ostracization; a single mother of three children laments the racial hostility initiated by her new community of white "Christians" that leaves her "shipwrecked by circumstances." In "Morning Song and Evening Walk" the narrator revives Martin Luther King's injunctions against a racist society: "*. . . the storm will / not abate until a just distribution of the fruits of / the earth enables men [and women] everywhere to live / in dignity and human decency.*" And in "For Sweet Honey in the Rock," the name of the singing group, the speaker merges poetry and a familiar spiritual, "I'm gonna stay on the battlefield," as she urges a divided society of brown, yellow, black, white, gay, and lesbian people to "*come to this battlefield / called life.*"

Over the years Sanchez has come to depend less on poetic statement and more on indirection, thereby requiring the reader's active participation in explication. In her later works the thematic concerns are clear: love, reconciliation, and a unified humanity. In her figurative language she favors the imagistic, metaphorical, and ironic. Many of her allusive constructs depend upon emotive and intellectual recognition by African-Americans, a recognition often reliant on what critic Stephen Henderson would call the reader's and hearer's ethnic "saturation." For example, in an ironic image reversal Sanchez writes about patriarchal poet Sterling A. Brown as the "griot of the wind / glorifying red gums smiling tom-tom teeth," and in a poem about singer Billie Holiday she says, "speak yo / strange / fruit amid these / stones." Yet it is abundantly clear in her later works that Sanchez is addressing a wider breadth of social concerns and a broader audience. "Love Conversation [AIDS day 1994 in Philadelphia, for Essex Hemphill]" is an assertive appeal of a female AIDS victim to her African gods: "... oya olukun oya sistah ... I ammmmmmm / hiv positive but I ammmm / still, woman, lover, mother, / sistah, artist, organizer, activist."

As to structure, Sanchez usually fits form to substance. Her poems are modern in their nontraditional spatial configurations, unconventional syntax and mechanics, portmanteau terms, and improvisational quality. She occasionally uses the sonnet form and rhyme royal. In her later work she has composed more haiku and tanka, and although they follow line and syllabic conventions, they tend in substance to be statements rather than suggestive evocations of fleeting experiences. Though over time her poetry has shifted from a literal to a more subtle and cerebral tone, it is still characteristically pointed.

Much of Sanchez's poetry is addressed principally to African-Americans, among whom she is highly respected. She also, however, has a sizable following among white readers, especially among those whom she characterizes as "progressive" whites. Critics' assessments of Sanchez's poetry vary. It is not unusual for academic and establishment critics and anthologists, who rely upon traditional, received criteria and canons, to pay only passing attention to her earlier work. Women critics tend to regard her poetry favorably and in fact began paying serious attention to her work well before her rediscovery by African-American critics. African-American critics and literary academicians generally consider Sanchez to be an unusually talented and significant poet.

—Theodore R. Hudson and B.J. Bolden

SANDERS, (James) Ed(ward)

Nationality: American. **Born:** Kansas City, Missouri, 17 August 1939. **Education:** University of Missouri, Columbia, 1957–58; New York University, B.A. in classics 1964. **Family:** Married Miriam Kittell in 1961; one daughter. **Career:** Editor and publisher, *Fuck You/ A Magazine of the Arts,* Fuck You Press, 1962–65; organizer of The Fugs rock satire group; owner, Peace Eye Bookstore, New York, 1964–70. Visiting professor, Bard College, Annandale-on-Hudson, New York, 1979, 1983. **Awards:** National Endowment for the Arts grant, 1966, 1970, fellowship, 1987; Frank O'Hara prize, 1967; Guggenheim fellowship, 1983; Before Columbus Foundation American Book award, 1988; New York Foundation for the Arts fellowship in nonfiction, 1993. **Address:** P.O. Box 729, Woodstock, New York 12498, U.S.A.

PUBLICATIONS

Poetry

Poem from Jail. San Francisco, City Lights, 1963.
King Lord—Queen Freak. Cleveland, Renegade Press, 1964.
The Toe-Queen. New York, Fuck You Press, 1964.
A Valorium Edition of the Entire Extant Works of Thales! New York, Fuck You Press, 1964.
Banana: An Anthology of Banana-Erotic Poems. New York, Fuck You Press, 1965.
The Complete Sex Poems of Ed Sanders. New York, Fug-Press, 1965.
Peace Eye. Buffalo, Frontier Press, 1965; revised edition, Cleveland, Frontier Press, 1967.
Fuck God in the Ass. New York, Fuck You Press, 1967.
Shards of God. New York, Grove Press, 1971.
Egyptian Hieroglyphics. Canton, New York, Institute of Further Studies, 1973.
20,000 A.D. Plainfield, Vermont, North Atlantic, 1976.
Love and the Falling Iron. Bolinas, California, Yanagi, 1977.
The Cutting Prow. Santa Barbara, California, Am Here-Immediate Editions, 1981.
Hymn to Maple Syrup and Other Poems. Woodstock, New York, PCC, 1985.
Poems for Robin. Woodstock, New York, PCC, 1987.
Thirsting for Peace in a Raging Century: Selected Poems 1960–1985. Minneapolis, Coffee House Press, 1987.
The Ocean Étude and Other Poems. Woodstock, New York, PCC, 1990.
Hymn to the Rebel Cafe. Santa Rosa, California, Black Sparrow, 1993.
1968: A History in Verse. Santa Rosa, California, Black Sparrow, 1997.
The Poetry and Life of Allen Ginsberg: A Narrative Poem. Woodstock, New York, Overlook Press, 2000.

Recordings: *Sanders Truckstop,* Reprise Records, 1970; *Beer Cans on the Moon,* Reprise Records, 1972; *Songs in Ancient Greek,* Olufsen Records, 1990.

Plays (musical dramas)

The Municipal Power Cantata, with others (produced Woodstock, New York, 1978). Woodstock, New York, Poetry Crime and Culture Press, 1978.
The Karen Silkwood Cantata (produced Woodstock, New York, 1979).
Star Peace (produced Oslo, Norway, 1986).
Cassandra (produced Woodstock, New York, 1992).

Screenplays: *Amphetamine Head; Mongolian Cluster Fuck.*

Novel

Fame and Love in New York. Berkeley, California, Turtle Island Foundation, 1980.

Short Stories

Tales of Beatnik Glory. New York, Stonehill, 1975; revised edition, as *Tales of Beatnik Glory Volumes I & II,* New York, Citadel, 1990.

Other

The Family: The Story of Charles Manson's Dune Buggy Attack Battalion. New York, Dutton, 1971; London, Hart Davis, 1972; revised edition, as *The Family: The Manson Group and Aftermath,* New York, Signet/New American Library, 1990.
Vote!, with Abbie Hoffman and Jerry Rubin. New York, Warner, 1972.
Investigative Poetry. San Francisco, City Lights, 1976.
The Party: A Chronological Perspective on a Confrontation at a Buddhist Seminary. Woodstock, New York, PCC, 1980.
The ZD Generation. Barrytown, New York, Station Hill Press, 1980.
Creativity and the Self-Fulfilled Bard. Woodstock, New York, PCC Publications, 1992.
Chekhov. Santa Rosa, California, Black Sparrow, 1995.
America: A History in Verse. Santa Rosa, California, Black Sparrow, 1999.

Editor, *Poems for Marilyn.* New York, Fuck You Press, 1962.
Editor, *Bugger: An Anthology of Buttockry.* New York, Fuck You Press, 1964.
Editor, *Despair: Poems to Come Down By.* New York, FU Press, 1964.
Editor, with Ken Weaver and Betsy Klein, *The Fugs' Song Book!* New York, Peace Eye Bookshop, 1965.
Editor, *The Party.* Woodstock, New York, Poetry Crime and Culture Press, 1980.

*

Manuscript Collection: University of Connecticut Library, Storrs.

Critical Studies: Interview with Tandy Sturgeon, in *Contemporary Literature* (Madison, Wisconsin), 31(3), fall 1990, and with Sean Thomas Dougherty, in *Long Shot,* 13, 1992.

*   *   *

In Ed Sanders's poetry the raw energy of a 1960s-style peace march, a rock concert, and an orgy impels a fine intelligence. Many of his poems can be read as political protest, and some might be read, by a reader intent upon it, as pornography. The best of his work in *Peace Eye* and *20,000 A.D.*—probably his two most interesting books— should be read, however, as representing a perhaps unexpected turn in the tradition of Pound and Olson.

"Ed Sanders' language," Olson writes, "advances in a direction of production which probably isn't even guessed at." His language is always near the breaking point, always at the verge of howl and groans. Rude, slangy, obscene, and blasphemous, it violates any remaining verbal taboos. At the same time, however, it frequently spills over into Greek, Egyptian hieroglyphs, and glyphlike drawings, giving the impression that one language, or even language itself, cannot contain Sanders's, to use one of his own terms, "Endless

Gush'' (which, it should be noted, is a translation of Anaximander's central term, *tò ápeiron*). Especially when he recites it himself, one has a sense in his language of an archaic power. At its best, however, it is more than that, for we begin to sense the relationship between the "holy" and the "accursed" as it is recorded in the etymology of "sacred." The closing section of "The Fugs," "Hymn to the Vagina of Mercy," and "Arise Garland Flame" and "Holy Was Demeter Walking the Corn Furrow" are, as it were, songs from a satyr play.

Sanders's poetry is truly outrageous; that is its beauty. It is a test of Blake's proverbs of hell. Read at length, it loses its shock value and tends to become tedious, but it is not intended for that kind of consumption. His poems are performance pieces for an athletic performer like Sanders himself, who was the lead singer with a rock group for several years.

A later turn in Sanders's work can also be seen as an outgrowth of the Pound-Olson tradition, which proposed poetry as a gathering of significant information. Sanders characteristically pushes any possibility to its literal limits. We must, Olson says, be "cooked / and ruled by information." Sanders's response to this demand is what he calls "investigative poetry." *The Family,* his careful, objective, and thorough report on the Charles Manson case, was his first investigative poem, or at least the idea of investigative poetry derived from his experience of writing the book. Manson was a sign that something had gone seriously wrong with the political movements of the 1960s. The message of investigative poetry, though it stretches traditional definitions of poetry perhaps even beyond the breaking point, is that no political movement can be effective without complete information. It is an attempt to find a fulcrum for political power at precisely the point where governments are most vulnerable—in gathering, organizing, and effectively communicating knowledge. In the manifesto "To the Z-D Generation," Sanders writes, "Never hesitate to open up a case file even upon the bloodiest of beasts or plots! We will see the day of relentless pursuit of data! Interrogate the Abyss." In *The Karen Silkwood Cantata,* first performed on May 20, 1979, Sanders combined performance with the results of investigation.

Sanders's work as a poet, performer, fiction writer, and journalist is of a piece. In all of these modes he combines outrage at greed, bigotry, and tyrannical forms of enforced morality with both an old-fashioned sense of decency and the insistence upon an ecstatic union with the other. At the same time he is able as a poet to give his attention to such utterly mundane and pragmatic matters as the hearings of the New York state legislature on telephone rates and nuclear energy.

—Don Byrd

SANDY, Stephen

Nationality: American. **Born:** Minneapolis, Minnesota, 2 August 1934. **Education:** Yale University, New Haven, Connecticut, B.A. 1955; Harvard University, Cambridge, Massachusetts (Dexter Fellow, 1961), M.A. 1959, Ph.D. in English 1963. **Military Service:** U.S. Army, 1955–57. **Family:** Married Virginia Scoville in 1969; one daughter and one son. **Career:** Instructor in English, Harvard University, 1963–67; Fulbright lecturer, University of Tokyo, 1967–68; visiting assistant professor of English, Brown University, Providence, Rhode Island, 1968–69; visiting lecturer, University of Rhode Island, Kingston, 1969. Member of the literature faculty, 1969–74, and since 1975 professor of English, Bennington College, Vermont. Director of poetry workshops at Chautauqua Institution, New York, 1975, 1977, 1996, Johnson State College, Vermont, 1976, 1977, Bennington College, 1976, 1977, and Wesleyan University, Middletown, Connecticut, 1981; poet-in-residence, Y Poetry Center, Philadelphia, 1985; visiting professor, Harvard University, summers 1986, 1987, 1988; McGee Distinguished Visiting Professor of Writing, 1994. Panelist, Arts Review Panel, Jacob J. Javits Fellowships, U.S. Department of Education, 1992; final judge, The Hopwood Awards, University of Michigan, 1999. **Awards:** Academy of American Poets award, 1955; *Harvard Monthly* prize, 1961; Huber Foundation fellowship, 1973; Vermont Council on the Arts fellowship, 1974, 1988; Ingram Merrill Foundation fellowship, 1985; National Endowment for the Arts fellowship, 1988; Chubb LifeAmerica fellow, MacDowell Colony, 1993; *Reader's Digest* Residency for Distinguished Writers, Yaddo, 1997; co-winner, *Mudfish* poetry prize, 1998; Howard Moss Residency in poetry, Yaddo, 1998; senior fellow in literature, Fine Arts Work Center, Provincetown, 1998. Phi Beta Kappa poet, Brown University, 1969. **Address:** Box 276, Shaftsbury, Vermont 05262–0276, U.S.A.

PUBLICATIONS

Poetry

Caroms. Groton, Massachusetts, Groton School Press, 1960.
Mary Baldwin. Privately printed, 1962.
The Destruction of Bulfinch's House. Cambridge, Massachusetts, Identity Press, 1963.
The Norway Spruce. Milford, New Hampshire, Ferguson Press, 1964.
Wild Ducks. Milford, New Hampshire, Ferguson Press, 1965.
Stresses in the Peaceable Kingdom. Boston, Houghton Mifflin, 1967.
Home Again, Looking Around. Milford, New Hampshire, Ferguson Press, 1968.
Spring Clear. Pascoag, Rhode Island, Delmo Press, 1969.
LVIII: To Caelius (version of poem by Catullus). Tokyo, Voyagers' Press, 1969.
Japanese Room. Providence, Rhode Island, Hellcoal Press, 1969.
A Dissolve, music by Richard Wilson. New York, Schirmer, 1970.
Light in the Spring Poplars, music by Richard Wilson. New York, Schirmer, 1970.
Jerome. North Bennington, Vermont, Grel Press, 1971.
Roofs. Boston, Houghton Mifflin, 1971.
Soaking, music by Richard Wilson. New York, Schirmer, 1971.
Elegy, music by Richard Wilson. New York, Schirmer, 1972.
Phrases, Fields, Kanda (6 P.M.). North Bennington, Vermont, Grel Press, 1972.
Can, music by Richard Wilson. New York, Fischer, 1973.
One Section from "Revolutions." San Francisco, Grabhorn Hoyem, 1973.
The Difficulty. Providence, Rhode Island, Burning Deck, 1975.
Landscapes. White Creek, New York, White Creek, 1975.
From "Freestone." Binghamton, New York, Bellevue Press, 1975.
Freestone: Sections 25 and 26. Binghamton, New York, Bellevue Press, 1977.
End of the Picaro. Pawlet, Vermont, Banyan Press, 1977.
Arch (card). Binghamton, New York, Bellevue Press, 1977.
The Hawthorne Effect. Lawrence, Kansas, Tansy Press, 1980.

After the Hunt. Brattleboro, Vermont, Moonsquilt Press, 1982.

Chapter and Verse. Brattleboro, Vermont, Moonsquilt Press, 1982.

Flight of Steps. Binghamton, New York, Bellevue Press, 1982.

Riding to Greylock. New York, Knopf, 1983.

To A Mantis (chapbook). North Hoosick, New York, Plinth Press, 1987.

Man in the Open Air. New York, Knopf, 1988.

The Epoch (chapbook). North Bennington, Vermont, Plinth Press, 1990.

Thanksgiving over the Water. New York, Knopf, 1992.

Gulf Memo (broadside). Bellows Falls, Vermont, The Bridge Press, 1993.

Vale of Academe: A Prose Poem for Bernard Malamud (chapbook). Spartanburg, Holocene Press, 1996.

The Thread, New and Selected Poems. Baton Rouge, Louisiana, and London, Louisiana State University Press, 1998.

Black Box. Baton Rouge, Louisiana, and London, Louisiana State University Press, 1999.

Recordings: *Heartbeats: New Songs from Minnesota for the AIDS Quilt Songbook* (music), Innova, 1997; *Stresses in the Peaceable Kingdom: The Choral Music of Richard Wilson* (music), Albany Records, 1999.

Other

Vita de Sancto Hieronymo: An Antiphonal Cantata, music by Henry Brant. New York, MCA Music, 1973.

The Raveling of the Novel: Studies in Romantic Fiction from Walpole to Scott. New York, Arno Press, 1980.

The Breakers Pound, music by Dan Locklair. Toronto, E.C. Kerby Ltd., 1989.

The Second Law, music by Richard Wilson, in *The Aids Quilt Songbook.* New York, Boosey & Hawkes, 1994.

Translator, *A Cloak For Hercules,* in *The Complete Roman Drama, Seneca, Vol II.* Baltimore, John Hopkins University Press, 1994.

Translator, *Seven against Thebes,* a verse translation of Aeschylus. Philadelphia, University of Pennsylvania Press, 1998.

*

Manuscript Collection: Houghton Library, Harvard University, Cambridge, Massachusetts; Beinecke Rare Book Library, Yale University, New Haven, Connecticut.

Critical Studies: "Like the Bones of Dreams" by Heather Ross Miller, in *American Scholar* (Washington, D.C.), autumn 1967; by Vernon Young, in *Hudson Review* (New York), winter 1971–72; by Richard Howard, in *American Poetry Review* (Philadelphia), May-June 1973; "The Difficulty" by Dick Higgins, in *Margins 24–26* (Milwaukee), 1975; by Kate Lewis, in *Harvard Advocate* (Cambridge, Massachusetts), June 1983; "Witnesses and Seers" by Terence Diggory, in *Salmagundi* (Saratoga Springs, New York), fall 1983; "Stafford, Sandy, and Willard" by Jerome Mazzaro, in *Michigan Quarterly Review* (Ann Arbor), summer 1984; "Stages of Growth" by Phoebe Pettingell, in *New Leader* (New York), 11–25 January 1988; "When You've Seen One Perfect Spot" by Richard Nunley, in *The Berkshire Eagle,* 30 March 1988; "The Year in Poetry, 1988" by

Kurt Heinzelman, in *The Massachusetts Review* (Amherst, Massachusetts), XXX(1), spring 1989; "Poetry in Review" by Phoebe Pettingell, in *The Yale Review* (New Haven, Connecticut), 80(4), October 1992; "The Everyday and the Transcendent" by Richard Tillinghast, in *Michigan Quarterly Review* (Ann Arbor), XXXII(3), summer 1993; "In the Divide: Skeptic Master, Stung Pilgrim" by Chard deNiord, in *The New England Review* (Middlebury, Vermont), 16(2), spring 1994; in *New Republic* (New York), 25 August 1997; by Robert J. Brophy, in *Bryn Mawr Classical Review,* 14 September 1997; by David Yezzi, in *Poetry,* CLXXIV, June 1999; "The Black Box of American Culture" by Douglas K. Currier, in *Vermont Times,* 9(25), 16 June 1999; "Sandy at 35,000 Feet" by Richard Nunley, in *Berkshire Eagle,* 11 August 1999.

*   *   *

Stephen Sandy's poems exhibit extraordinary powers of observation, technical mastery of the craft, and a distinctive way of thinking about the present and the past. For forty years he has ruminated on his experiences in America and abroad in these disquieting postmodern times. Moments from his boyhood in Minnesota when he hunted with his father or rode the trolley cars of the Minneapolis Street Railway Company with his grandmother are vividly captured. Many poems minutely describe the rural landscape of Vermont or a New England graveyard. Others have more public subjects, such as the gunman in the tower in Austin, Texas, the war in Vietnam, and the Persian Gulf War. A poet's poet, he loves language and form and moves easily from free verse and tight rhyme patterns to poems written in rhythms and language that capture the dissonances of the metropolis. In one poem, for example, he uses demotic speech and offers a poetic riff on Penn Station's madness and the "confabs of zonked homeless." He treats subjects as varied as Robert Mitchum's movies, chic Manhattan couples, four corners in Vermont, and the boy found in a taped-shut vacuum cleaner box abandoned in a field in Maryland. His poems are rich with a sense of time and its passing. His mind is keen and reflective, full of fresh discoveries and brimming with excitement. Some of his poems are wildly witty; others, deeply sad. Some are exquisite in their lyricism; others are difficult, full of dense passages and philosophical thought.

Words, often quite unpoetic ones, are Sandy's argot. He has Marianne Moore's fondness for unusual words, particularly those describing flora and fauna. "Bovine spongiform encephalopathy" appears in "Daphnis and Chloe." In "Blue Perennial Border" he lingers over "fresh lucubrations." In "Elixir" he parodies the opening lines of "Kubla Khan," writing, "On Mao Shan did Tao Hongjing a fabulous / pharmacopeia decree: of cinnabar / And orpiment, mica and malachite . . ." He writes an outrageous parody of Yeats's "Among School Children." He is a great imitator, and many poems pay homage to ancient masters as well as a host of modern poets. I.A. Richards, T.S. Eliot, W.B. Yeats, Robert Frost, Sylvia Plath, Anne Sexton, John Berryman, Allen Ginsberg, and many others figure in his verse. Sandy's poems compare well with those of James Merrill, Theodore Roethke, Amy Clampitt, and Richard Wilbur.

Sandy's poems immerse the reader, albeit briefly, in the world as he sees and experiences it. Many of his lyrical poems are autobiographical. Some offer philosophical ruminations, and others provide social commentary. His late volumes *The Thread,* a selection of poems from five earlier volumes that concludes with a section of new poems on the theme of America, and *Black Box* offer a retrospective of his work and confirm his standing as an important American poet.

The Thread opens with "Wild Ducks" from the early volume *Stresses in the Peaceable Kingdom:*

Nine mallards amiably swim
the stream's treadmill. Sedate,
intent; bills front, they form
a V unmoving as kites

Swimming the unseen wind.
Upstream they go together;
they glide as if upstream
some hand guides them there.

With button eyes not looking
they move, unmoved, in the pull
                  of taut, positioning strings,
the hand's extended will.

Yeats's "The Wild Swans at Coole" hovers behind the image, but Sandy's poem has a singular feel. In his frequently anthologized and very funny poem "The Woolworth Philodendron" Sandy spots a real plant—"a sort of proto-gewgaw, if you please"—in the Woolworth dime store and takes it home and watches it grow over five months, in its own wild way complicit with the dark plots of the sun while he labors at his "boring" tasks. In a more serious vein, in "Hiawatha" and "The Destruction of Bulfinch's House" Sandy treats the themes of the loss of innocence, past traditions, and historical landmarks. In "Home from the Range" he turns the familiar folk refrain into the lament of a soldier returning from a firing range with his hearing impaired.

The Thread continues with a series of poems from *Roofs* about Sandy's journey from New England to Japan and back again. His elegy "Charley" is both an intensely personal poem about the death of a friend killed in Vietnam's demilitarized zone and a poem of bitter protest against the war. Other poems about Japan recall some of Paul Engle's poems on the same subject. Both poets experiment with words and space them on the page to capture the delicate line and sensibility of Japan. Sandy's poems on Japan are painterly.

In the next two sections of *The Thread* Sandy selects poems that appeared earlier in *Riding to Greylock* and *Man in the Open Air*. He also culls poems from three earlier limited editions—*The Difficulty, End of the Picaro,* and *After the Hunt*—reproducing those that seem to have worn best over time and giving some of them fresh titles or a slightly altered form. In the early collections Sandy had traced the mental journey of his speaker—a thinly disguised extension of himself—and wrestled with problems of perspective, the poet's relationship to his personal and historical pasts, and his need to trace the journey of his literary counterpart and double, the Picaro, in order to know himself. His poem "The White Oak of Eagle Bridge" shows Sandy at his best, minutely describing his fields, his neighbors mowing, and the majestic oak stretching its black arms against the sky, only later to be felled and recalled nostalgically by the poet and an old farmer who recalls still another oak, its twin, that once stood beside it and lent its name to the farm Sandy now owns.

The volume concludes with poems from *Thanksgiving over the Water* and with new poems. In "The Tack" a fly stings Sandy as he prunes his pine bushes. He dwells on the welt on his arm and, later, a polished tack on the wall. Both call forth a host of images and memories in a manner akin to "the floppy discs of memory" that keep printing out feedback. He is reminded of a boyhood spanking, a homeless beggar, and another poet, Coleridge, who, like Sandy himself, found in the external world the same chasms and columns that had come from within and become the subject of his poems long before he encountered them in external reality. In "Four Corners, Vermont" Sandy, in a manner reminiscent of Marianne Moore, re-creates a "Norman-Rockwell-ish tableau" of the activities of a boy and a bellhop, a cop and a governor upstate on a Sunny October day on Vermont's Main Street, which could be any Main Street in midland America's small towns.

The poems in *Black Box* are the poetic equivalent of the snapshots glimpsed from the aperture of a black camera box. Sandy's black box is his unerring eye and unusual mind. The poems in this collection, some early, some late, offer all the pleasures one associates with reading Sandy. Some are his reflections on the end of the millennium, as in "Brain Decade," where he records the excesses of postmodernity and the horrors and marvels of the catheter lab. Various poems recall the old days and old loves, the wetlands of the world, the utter changing of the "figure-ground relationship in your life" following a scrape with life-threatening heart disease, the intimacy of listening to Chopin in Japan, and late-breaking news and other assorted reflections. For the most part the poems are lucid and less difficult to understand than usual, making *Black Box* a delicious volume to commemorate the millennium. All of Sandy's poems grapple with who we are and what we live for, and very often he startles the reader with the rightness of his wisdom.

—Carol Simpson Stern

SANER, Reg(inald Anthony)

Nationality: American. **Born:** Jacksonville, Illinois, 30 December 1931. **Education:** St. Norbert College, West De Pere, Wisconsin, B.A. 1952; University of Illinois, Urbana, M.A. 1956, Ph.D. in English 1962. **Military Service:** U.S. Army Infantry, 1952–53: Lieutenant; Bronze Star. **Family:** Married Anne Costigan in 1958; two sons. **Career:** Freelance photographer, Illinois, 1952–56; photographer and writer, Montgomery Publishing Company, Los Angeles and San Francisco, 1956; assistant instructor, 1956–60, instructor, 1961–62, assistant professor, 1962–67, associate professor, 1967–72, and since 1973 professor of English, University of Colorado, Boulder. **Awards:** Fulbright scholarship, 1961; Borestone Mountain award, 1972; Academy of American Poets Walt Whitman award, 1975; National Endowment for the Arts fellowship, 1976; Creede Repertory Theatre prize, 1981; University of Colorado Distinguished Research fellowship, 1983; Colorado Governor's award, 1983; Quarterly Review of Literature 45th Anniversary award, 1989; Colorado Center for the Book award, for nonfiction, 1993. **Address:** 1925 Vassar Drive, Boulder, Colorado 80303, U.S.A.

PUBLICATIONS

Poetry

Climbing into the Roots. New York, Harper, 1976.
So This Is the Map. New York, Random House, 1981.
Essay on Air. Athens, Ohio Review Books, 1984.
Red Letters. Princeton, New Jersey, Quarterly Review of Literature, 1989.

Other

The Four-Cornered Falcon: Essays on the Interior West and the Natural Scene. Baltimore, John Hopkins University Press, 1993.
Reaching Keet Seel: Ruin's Echo and the Anasazi. Salt Lake City, University of Utah Press, 1998.

*

Critical Studies: Interviews in *Gumbo Review* (Fort Collins, Colorado), spring 1977, *Aspen Anthology* (Colorado), fall 1978, and *Ohio Review 32* (Athens), 1984; by James Reiss, in *American Book Review,* 13(3), June 1991.

Reg Saner comments:

Living among rocks, clouds, and trees in Colorado, I tend to get my most immediate impulses from them. Nature poetry, always a crossroads where earth and air intersect. My feel for things and men is temporal. Man on the edge, the dangerous edge of things, fascinates me. I look into ways our address defines us because I believe what we are will always be where.

Being an atheist, I write poetry that is perhaps naturally religious, though mountain environment, by its potential hostility, staggers anyone's complacent sentimentalizing. Being a Catholic atheist, I have a sense of man that is historical. Wherever I look, either among Anasazi Indian ruins of Chaco Canyon or into the brickwork lining Brunelleschi's cupola over the Duomo of Florence, I hear people saying, "We were." The sound is of mayflies hitting ice.

*   *   *

Poems about mountains have a tendency to diminish into what Reg Saner calls "pure calendar art," but even as he acknowledges this risk, Saner shows how to avoid the traps in *Climbing into the Roots.* By making the mountains his "chosen place," Saner has staked out a claim that will long bear his mark, even if he eventually abandons it for some other territory. For Saner's concern is less with the grandeur of the mountains than with the perspective they allow, "this difficult magnificence / where we are most our own." In these poems he climbs into a cleaner, purer air where, feet planted firmly on rock, he can look out to look in, just as he has climbed up to get into the roots:

Under the rosy foreskin of dawn,
turned for a parting glance, I leave
and take all I can. The mountain's huge
bite of glacial cirque
hovers, a small glass square
pressed to the shape of a tent,
with, still slightly warm,

a sleep print. All summer I'll come
and go, eating spaces like these
to make sure.
My death must be a simply enormous death.

Throughout Saner's poems one feels an embracing sense of place, a blend of the physical and the spiritual, but even more impressive is the enlarged time frame within which this place—the American Rocky Mountains—is so finely realized. In a manner reminiscent of Loren Eiseley's powerful essays, Saner makes these poems compellingly human—"staring up between, guessing / how huge a dark we're in"—but the intelligence that is guessing here is quite aware that the mountains on which he stands evolved from an earlier geological state and, further, that they are now posed "under gravity's big guns," ready to wear or crash down to become the sand of the desert below. The tension such an awareness creates prevents any of the poems from being still lifes, even though they are largely unpeopled. It also establishes a rich context for Saner to confront in concrete ways a range of issues prehistoric and historic, physical and metaphysical.

Not all of Saner's poems are set in the mountains, of course, nor are all of them flawless successes. At times his usually brilliant metaphors overreach themselves, the tensions of the poems become too explicit, the imaginative leaps are forced ("At ponds / whose tundra edges seem rich / I put my hand on Miss America's muff"). Some poems in *Climbing into the Roots,* especially "One War Is All Wars," "Flag," and "Smiling at 180," appear to contribute little if anything to the otherwise unified trajectory of the book. Saner is not usually his best in small situations, and when he moves away from the mountains, his poems sometimes seem to lose vital energy and become more self-consciously rhetorical. Fortunately, such breaks are few.

One of the qualities that distinguishes *Climbing into the Roots* is that so much of it appears to be the product of mature, intelligent listening. Saner accepts the rhythms operating on the mountains ("timing / our talk to the tent's nylon whip and crackle" or, as he puts it in another poem, "To make talk, we listen"), and he channels his energy into confronting the experience and resisting facile interpretations:

Like a silence coming out of the stones,
the universe flying at terrible speeds
further into itself.
If it is not here it is nowhere.
The stillness where all words are kept.

In an age when the hard sell has become commonplace, it is a rare pleasure to find such fertile listening in so many excellent poems. And it is clearly one of the reasons the best of Saner's work has a lasting quality. He has listened with sensitivity to enrich and enlarge, rather than exploit, his experience, and thus he can now take us closer to "the place that we know / must always / be part of the distance."

—Stanley W. Lindberg

SATYAMURTI, Carole

Nationality: British. **Born:** Farnborough, Kent, 13 August 1939. **Education:** University of London, 1957–60, 1972–79, B.A. 1960, Ph.D. 1979; University of Illinois, Champaign, 1960–61, M.A. 1967; University of Birmingham, England, 1964–65, postgraduate diploma in social work 1965. **Family:** Married T.V. Satyamurti in 1963 (divorced 1986); one daughter. **Career:** Lecturer, University of

Singapore, 1963–64; social worker, Save the Children Fund, Kampala, Uganda, 1965–67; social worker, Ealing Child Guidance Clinic, London, 1967–68. Since 1968 lecturer, senior lecturer, now principal lecturer, University of East London. **Awards:** National Poetry Competition First prize, 1986; Arts Council (UK) Writers' award, 1988. **Address:** 15, Gladwell Road, London N8 9AA, England.

PUBLICATIONS

Poetry

Broken Moon. Oxford, Oxford University Press, 1987.
Changing the Subject. Oxford, Oxford University Press, 1990.
Striking Distance. Oxford, Oxford University Press, 1994.
Selected Poems. Oxford, Oxford University Press, 1998.
Love and Variations. Newcastle upon Tyne, Bloodaxe, 2000.

Other

Occupational Survival. Oxford, Basil Blackwell, 1981.

Editor, with Noel Parry and Michael Rustin, *Social Work, Welfare & The State.* London, Edward Arnold, 1979.

*

Critical Study: By Silvia Kantaris, in *Poetry Review,* 85(2), summer 1995.

Carole Satyamurti comments:

Many of the poems I write are concerned, from different points of view, with the way in which one life touches on another. By this I mean not just the influence that people have on each other but, more specifically, the otherness of others and the way we imagine them—or fail to. The other life in question may be that of a stranger or someone we think we know well, or it may be our own other lives—past, future, or potential.

The epigraph for *Striking Distance* is Elizabeth Bishop's startling question "Why should I be my aunt / or me, or anyone?" ("In the Waiting Room"), and many of the poems are an exploration of different dimensions of that existential shock. It does seem to me very strange and arbitrary that I inhabit one skin rather than another, and I often have the vertiginous illusion that by really attending to another state of being one might enter into that other person, that other life. There is a tension between the connectedness and separateness of lives, between sameness and difference, that several of the poems try to capture. The distance between people can seem striking.

Someone accused me once of writing as if I wished that language was not necessary. I do mind absolutely about language, but I want it to act as a window rather than a mirror—framing, letting light in, allowing as clear a view as possible of what lies beyond it. This is not to imply some simple equivalence between language and what it denotes; Derrida is right. Nor do I think that what the language refers to is itself straightforward. But primarily I search for a precision, a "rightness" of language, rather than an exciting inventiveness.

We go through our lives, if we are lucky, with something that feels like a self. But there are times when we do not "feel ourselves"

or when we feel we will never be the same again. Many of my poems are about turning points, real or imagined, moments that mark a shift between one way of being and another.

The voice varies. To write in a different persona, for instance, is itself an imperfectly achieved act of imagining the other, and always in the recognition that one can hardly ever get within striking distance of it.

*　*　*

The hallmark of Carole Satyamurti's poetry at its best is the clarity and precision of its language, the sharpness of its visual imagery, and its concerns. She seeks, she tells us in an article for the Poetry Book Society, "a rightness of language rather than an exciting inventiveness." She goes for substance rather than style. Nevertheless, her first collection, *Broken Moon,* displays a proper poetic concern for language and its place in our identities. The first impressive and substantial poem in the book, "Between The Lines," treats of a childhood in which "words are dust-sheets, blinds," and where "adults buried questions under bushes." It is a place where the developing child is "striving for language that would let me out" and "where people were difficult to read." A later poem, "Erdywurble," pursues the matter of language further, to the point at which a flawed child invents his own language until "his words trickled, stopped." The language and the child die together.

This concern continues in Satyamurti's later collections of poems. In *Changing the Subject,* for example, the poem "Birth Rite" explores experience beyond words to a deeper language:

To be reborn with you
I shed responsibility,
my social face,
speech, consciousness.
I reach back to the dark.

Then there are those everyday encounters with ambivalence and ambiguity in "How Are You?" or with the hierarchy of nomenclature in "Knowing Our Place."

There are, of course, other concerns in Satyamurti's poetry. It is a humane poetry in which, she tells us, she is concerned with "the otherness of others." A direct confrontation with this comes in the acceptance of the fact that her daughter has grown up and has assumed her own individuality. This is movingly expressed in the poem "Pulling Away."

There can be sharpness as well as insight in Satyamurti's observations, along with a waspish sense of humor. "Singapore 1963," a poem that is close to being perfect, illustrates not only her skill in conjuring visual imagery but also her mastery of a fierce irony. The street market is presented vividly in admirably economic images both visual and aural: its "naptha glare," the paucity of the listed offerings displayed on the spread mat, and the "cat-cries aimed at those almost as ragged as herself." The self-important commentary of the poet's companion, "rehearsing your lecture as we walked," is a counterpoint that is juxtaposed with savage irony but that also underlines the concern of the poem itself.

Another special personal quality in Satyamurti's poetry is that of sympathetic courage, which is to be found in her longish sequence of poems "Changing the Subject." As the title indicates, these poems return to the matter of language. The evasion of the subject of cancer and even the word itself is the starting point. The poems move on to a deeper consideration, rooted firmly in the life and routines of hospital life and with a deeply sympathetic concern for the other patients, which underlines her own courageous stance. If this sounds daunting, it is redeemed by Satyamurti's sureness of touch and poetic sensibility.

—John Cotton

SCALAPINO, Leslie

Nationality: American. **Born:** Santa Barbara, California, 25 July 1947. **Education:** Reed College, B.A.: University of California, Berkeley, M.A. **Family:** Married 1) Wesley St. John in 1968 (divorced 1975); 2) Tom White in 1987. **Career:** Member of English faculty, College of Marin, Kentfield, California, New College of California, San Francisco, 1982, 1983–84, San Francisco State University, 1984, University of California, San Diego, 1990, San Francisco Art Institute, 1994–2000, Mills College, Oakland, California, 1996–97, and summers since 1992 Bard College. Co-editor, *Foot,* 1979. Since 1986 publisher, O Books. **Awards:** Woodrow Wilson fellowship; National Endowment for the Arts fellowship, 1976, 1986; Before Columbus Foundation award, 1988; San Francisco State University Poetry Center award, 1988; Lawrence Lipton award, 1988. **Address:** 5729 Clover Drive, Oakland, California 94618, U.S.A.

PUBLICATIONS

Poetry

O and Other Poems. Berkeley, California, Sandollar Press, 1976.
The Woman Who Could Read the Minds of Dogs. Berkeley, California, Sandollar Press, 1976.
Instead of an Animal. Berkeley, California, Poltroon Press, 1977.
This Eating and Walking at the Same Time Is Associated Alright. Bolinas, California, Tombouctou, 1979.
Considering How Exaggerated Music Is. Berkeley, California North Point Press, 1982.
That They Were at the Beach. Berkeley, California, North Point Press, 1985.
Way. Berkeley, California, North Point Press, 1988.
Crowd and Not Evening or Light. Oakland, California, and Paris, France, O Books, 1990.
Green and Black, Selected Writings. Jersey City, New Jersey, Talisman, 1996.
New Time. Hanover, New Hampshire, Wesleyan University Press/ University Press of New England, 1999.

Plays

The Present (produced San Francisco, 1993).
The Weatherman Turns Himself In (produced San Francisco, 1993).
Goya's L.A., a play (produced San Francisco, 1995). Elmwood, Connecticut, Potes & Poets Press, 1994.
Stone Marmalade (The Dreamed Title), with Kevin Killian. N.p., Singing Horse Press, 1996.

Novels

The Return of Painting, The Pearl, and Orion/A Trilogy. Berkeley, California, North Point Press, 1991.
Defoe. Los Angeles, Sun & Moon Press, 1994.
The Front Matter, Dead Souls. Hanover, New Hampshire, Wesleyan University Press/University Press of New England, 1996.

Other

How Phenomena Appear to Unfold (essays and plays). Elmwood, Connecticut, Potes & Poets Press, 1990.
Objects in the Terrifying Tense/Longing from Taking Place (essay). New York, Roof Books, 1994.
The Public World/Syntactically Impermanence. Hanover, New Hampshire, Wesleyan University Press/University Press of New England, 1999.

*

Critical Studies: The Leslie Scalapino issue of *Talisman #8* (Hoboken, New Jersey), 1992; ''Signifyin(g) on Stein: The Revisionist Poetics of Harryette Mullen and Leslie Scalapino'' by Elisabeth A. Frost, in *Postmodern Culture* (Cary, North Carolina), 5(3), May 1995; ''Magic and Mystery in Poetic Language: A Response to the Writings of Leslie Scalapino'' by Susan Smith Nash, in *Talisman* (Jersey City, New Jersey), 14, fall 1995; ''Formalism, Feminism, and Genre Slipping in the Poetic Writings of Leslie Scalapino'' by Laura Hinton, in *Women Poets of the Americas: Toward a Pan-American Gathering,* edited by Jacqueline Vaught Brogan and Cordelia Chavez Candelaria, Notre Dame, Indiana, University of Notre Dame Press, 1999.

Leslie Scalapino comments:

I write using numerous forms, wanting to track continual change. If there were one sentence written on my work, I would like it to be ''Leslie Scalapino has made lots of changes and does not avoid reality.''

*   *   *

Leslie Scalapino is a situational poet. Like the language poets with whom she is associated, Scalapino focuses less on isolated events and heightened responses, including her own, than on the cultural matrices that produce them. To know why something happened or why she (re)acted the way she did, Scalapino looks not for the personal, mythical, symbolic, or historical ''point of origin'' but for patterned webs of circumstance. She writes series of poems or stanzas, for instance, rather than individual lyrics. Her work is elliptical like Emily Dickinson's, repetitive like Gertrude Stein's, minimally narrative like Ernest Hemingway's, and spatially exploratory like H.D.'s and Robert Duncan's. But Scalapino finds her own way to patch together her stories.

Consider these stanzas from Scalapino's prose piece ''That They Were at the Beach-Aelotropic Series'':

It'd have to be some time ago—I got cake on me, handed to me by my mother, we're in a taxi. Men in another car—

beside me, I'm somewhat immature in age—whistled and called to me customary stemming from seeing me eating the cake

(so I'm embarrassed)

Such congested narrative spurts are more customary in a Hemingway or Raymond Carver story than in a prose poem. The past is made present not by ignoring the frame, the narrative commentary, but by foregrounding it. Stein's "continuous present" is the time of narration. Comparing one of her works to a comic book, Scalapino explains that "the writing does not have actual pictures. It 'functions' as does a comic book—in being read. And read aloud to someone the picture has to be described or seen and then what the figure it says read." The situation here is complex and unusual; the mother and child, eating in lurches, are not at home, and the men whistling are not neighbors. The embarrassment, both past and retroactive, is equally situational; to the men the child is a "piece of cake," along with her mother, who cannot protect the child from seeing herself in their eyes. The "customary" origin both of the men's and of her "reaction" is given in a series of participles and gerunds. These relational words and syntactical networks are privileged in Scalapino's work over isolated verbs or nouns. The word "that" in "That they were at the beach," like "considering" in "Considering How Exaggerated Music Is," constructs the societal loom of what is taken for granted for anything to happen.

In the series "Walking By," which opens her looming booklength poem *Way,* Scalapino plays her oral history off disjunctive, reflective Dickinsonian verse. The poem and book begin with a syntactical strand:

to have
seem-
ed still—
though not
wanting to
be serene
—their—

I was in school; the bus driver seeing a girl crossing the street hadn't stopped—she'd been hit—so the other students—the boys—would hit the side of the bus everyday

when we went around that corner—our understanding the driver—and clairvoyant

their—to
simply
make
that—
having
occur-
red to me

Again, we are thrown into a situation and a syntax that is bigger than we are, even with Scalapino's advantage of hindsight. The pattern is an intricate weave of seeing and being seen (compare "serene"), homicide and prank, man and boys and girls, and pluperfect with past perfect and present infinitive. The girl is as mute and "still" (silent,

continuous) as the victim she witnesses; the accident has "occurred" and is still "occurring" ("run in the way," "happen," "think of") to her. The muted framing verses, which afford less perspective than the grim little story itself, mark an interior style in which the basic participants and grammatical elements are sorted out. These halting verses have displaced Scalapino's concluding parentheses—"(so I'm embarrassed)"—as hesitant conclusions to the "accident" and its aftermath.

Scalapino's fragmented webs of consciousness are quilts of social conscience. In "Bum Series," also from *Way,* Scalapino patches together the "bums" (to use their situational, political name) who have died from exposure on the docks, the new wave person in imported "bum-wear," the homelessness popular during the Reagan years, and the unloading freighters, adding to the trade imbalance that produces more bums:

to their
social struggle in their
whole setting, which is
abroad and its
relation to the freighter

to the person of
new wave attire—that
person's relation to
the freighter

when the bums are not
alive—at this time—though
were here, not abroad—and
not aware in being so of a
social struggle

These nonsequential, floating stanzas mime their apparently isolated incidents and individuals. But the syntactical loom, which would subordinate clauses, promotes its "main" subject and predicate and reveals deviations from proper word order, never surfaces. The class-bound global sentence remains a piece of resistance. The drama in Scalapino's vast, minimal poetry is its setting, and her settings are among the most engaging in contemporary poetry.

—John Shoptaw

SCAMMELL, William

Nationality: British. **Born:** Hythe, Hampshire, 2 January 1939. **Education:** University of Bristol, 1964–67, B.A. (honors) in English and philosophy. **Family:** Married; two sons. **Career:** Lecturer in English, University of Newcastle, 1975–91. Chair, Northern Arts Literature Panel, 1982–85; artist-in-residence, Djerassi Foundation, California, 1985; guest artist, Akademi Schloss Solitude, Stuttgart, 1991; writer-in-residence, Nottingham Polytechnic, 1991; selector, Poetry Book Society, 1990–92. **Awards:** Cholmondeley award, 1982; British Arts Council award, 1985; Arvon Poetry Competition prize, 1987; Northern Arts Writers award, 1988, 1991, 1994; Poetry Society National Poetry Competition first prize, 1989. **Address:**

Heathfield Cottage, Heathfield Farm, Aspatria, Cumbria CA5 3SP, England.

PUBLICATIONS

Poetry

Yes and No. Liskeard, Cornwall, Peterloo, 1979.
A Second Life. Liskeard, Cornwall, Peterloo, 1982.
Time Past. Liskeard, Cornwall, Treovis Press, 1982.
Jouissance. Liskeard, Cornwall, Peterloo, 1985.
Eldorado. Calstock, Cornwall, Peterloo, 1987.
Bleeding Heart Yard. Calstock, Cornwall, Peterloo Poets, 1992.
The Game: Tennis Poems. Plymouth, Peterloo Poets, 1992.
Five Easy Pieces. London, Sinclair-Stevenson, 1993.
Barnacle Bill and Other Poems. Dublin, Dedalus, 1994.
All Set to Fall Off the Edge of the World. Northumberland, Flambard Press, 1998.

Recording: *William Scammell and Elizabeth Bartlett,* Peterloo, 1984.

Other

Keith Douglas: A Study. London, Faber, 1988.

Editor, with Rodney Pybus, *Adam's Dream: Poems from Cumbria and Lakeland.* Ambleside, Cumbria Literature, 1981.
Editor, *Between Comets: For Norman Nicholson at 70.* Durham, Taxus Press, 1984.
Editor, *The New Lake Poets.* Newcastle upon Tyne, Bloodaxe, 1991.
Editor, *This Green Earth: A Celebration of Native Poetry.* Cumbria, Ellenbank Press, 1992.
Editor, *Winter Pollen: Occasional Prose by Ted Hughes.* London, Faber, 1994.

Translator, with others, *The Biggest Egg in the World,* by Marin Soresen. Newcastle upon Tyne, Bloodaxe, 1991.

*

Critical Studies: By Victoria Rothschild, in *The Spectator* (London), 270(8606), 19 June 1993; by Keith Turner, in *Poetry Review,* 83(2), summer 1993; by Roger Garfitt, in *Poetry Review,* 84(2), summer 1994.

*   *   *

In the poem "Neighbours" William Scammell writes, "Intellectual consanguinity / is deficient in roughage." The typicality of the sentence lies in the Audenesque mixing of registers, the chuff collision between abstraction and concreteness, a frequent Scammell trick. Writing about Robert Lowell in his first book, he talks about the American's "baroque wrangle with God," thereby hauling into one line enough images for a medium-sized lyric.

This is clearly related to another Audenesque feature, a highly developed sense of play with words, a hedonistic gusto revealing itself in complex verse forms that can race at length delightfully. "A Letter from Cumbria" in *Jouissance* is one of the best examples of this, a nimble, surefooted poem inclusive enough to pay homage to lambs "jump-jetting on all fours," "Callaghan, Wilson, Thatcher, Foot, / Sir Clement This, Lord Keeper That, / the whole great bumbling *apparat* / of Whitehall," several—ologies, an IUD (gratuitously glossed in otherwise helpful, non-Eliot-like notes), Paul Simon, Jane Austen, and, among many others, "Lord / ('Civilisation') Clark."

The immaculate freshness of most of the rhymes serves, unfortunately, to point up the poor ones, for example, "it's/arithmatics," "apt/tact," and "enrobes/roads." But such lapses can be forgiven in the face of one stanza that uses rhymes never dreamed of before: "ELO / Lao tse To / who (as in 'wholly') / Lo" (as in Lowell).

Scammell delights in difficult words like "topos," not in the *Shorter Oxford English Dictionary* but, oddly, in Collins. (Auden could have had Scammell in mind when he described a poet's study as containing, among other things, "dictionaries [the very / best money can buy—].") He also likes archaic usages, like "threat" as a verb, as well as familiar words rinsed of accretions by odd contexts ("Nabokov, that ilk").

To read Scammell intensively is to be aware of a rich crush of names, whole lists alliteratively and delightedly assembled. An example in *Yes and No* is "Passchendale, Ypres, the Somme, Verdun . . . ." *A Second Life* develops the mannerism by making it more inclusive and surprising, like a shopping bag that contains soap powder, engine oil, Charlie Parker LPs, and a book on Frege: "Paddington, / Tarzan, Charlie's Angels, Liverpool / ('Champions of Europe'), the Bionic Man . . . ." By the time we get to *Jouissance* a two-page spread offers us "Not Mau Mau, not Makarios, Korea . . . ," "Not Beowulf, not Kyd," and "Laurence Sterne, / Borges, Prokofiev, Arp, Stevens, Joyce . . . ." Scammell might hone his technique, one occasionally feels, with a spurt of ignorant irritation.

Scammell wears his culture everywhere, not just on his sleeve. Rereading his books intensively over one weekend feels like scanning an elegant brochure for a high-level course on European culture that takes in music, twentieth-century history, Victorian writers (especially Tennyson), modern poetry, philosophy, the Lakes crew, painters—Scammell's listing mannerism is contagious. But it is sometimes hard to penetrate a poem. I have read and reread "The Small Rain" in *A Second Life* over eight years and think that it is very beautiful. But I have not got near the center of it, despite noting the reference to "Western Wind" and all the sex it implies. Now and then one thinks of the note in Eliot (of all people!) to the effect that "obscurity is swank."

Yet all this culture is not a disguise. Scammell is clearly a presence in his work, fantasizing sexually, drinking, making love to his wife. If he has a motto, it is found in his lyric "Spring Song":

Of all the symphonies, *Jupiter* wears best.
A kitten abseils down the wicker chair.
This whisky augurs well. After tennis
my wife glows in the dusk like earthenware.

When mildly drunk, Richard Strauss will do—

Four Last Songs to polychrome the head.
Sex and death forever! One fits like a shoe,
the other, barefoot, amorously tiptoes

to
my
   bed

Later, in *Jouissance,* Scammell develops this theme in his own context and that of Tennyson's life (''Love is death! and sex is death! / and death is all around!''). The words he uses constantly enact his hedonistic delight in life, and there is at the end a unity between the poet as lover, eater, drinker, and so forth and the poet as reveler in words and rhymes. The other side of this antithesis is shown in moving elegies for friends. ''Into Our Heads,'' ''Point Blank,'' and ''The Right Distance,'' all in *Jouissance,* are fine poems.

Love and death are not the only opposites in these poems. It is clear, in fact, that Scammell's obsession is with antitheses in general, for example, the ''two dangers (that) never cease threatening the world: order and disorder'' as Valéry puts it in the epigraph to *Jouissance.* Scammell's concern is to use his highly developed formal technique to impose a kind of temporary order on a world that is messy and confusing. He is not merely displaying his knowledge but rather learning through the collision of order and disorder.

Scammell is strong when he describes nature, occasionally in the manner of Elizabeth Bishop. His description of a swan eating a frog in *Yes and No* is almost as compulsive as the event must have been to watch. Nine measured, varied, elegant sentences describe a heartlessness that is unforgettable. A later poem, ''The Tall Hedge,'' describes cows in a similar manner:

> . . . A dozen cows, heads giant
> dreamy sycamore seeds, swayed down
> to bathe in the smoking ash . . .
> For one whole week they anchored in that place
> shifting and bumping like fat rowing boats
> tied to a pier . . .

Nothing in Scammell's work has been dull. He conveys his own pleasure in language, can be vivid and suggestive, and is moving on the great matters by bringing them down to the details they really are:

> The gold watch that I brought from
> Curaçao is fastened on your speckly
> wrist, turning heirloom by the hour.

—Fred Sedgwick

SCANNELL, Vernon

Nationality: British. **Born:** Spilsby, Lincolnshire, 23 January 1922. **Education:** Queen's Park School, Aylesbury, Buckinghamshire; University of Leeds, Yorkshire, 1946–47. **Military Service:** Gordon Highlanders, 1941–45. **Family:** Married Josephine Higson in 1954; two daughters and three sons (one deceased). **Career:** Professional boxer, 1945–46; English teacher, Hazelwood School, Limpsfield, Surrey, 1955–62. Since 1962 freelance writer and broadcaster. Resident poet, village of Berinsfield, Oxfordshire, 1978; visiting poet, Shrewsbury School, Shropshire, 1978–79, and King's School, Canterbury, 1979. **Awards:** Heinemann award, 1961; Arts Council grant, 1967, 1970; Cholmondeley award, 1974; Southern Arts Writers fellowship, 1975; Society of Authors traveling scholarship, 1987. Fellow, Royal Society of Literature, 1960. Granted Civil List pension, 1981. **Address:** 51 North Street, Otley, West Yorkshire LS21 1AH, England.

PUBLICATIONS

Poetry

Graves and Resurrections. London, Fortune Press, 1948.
A Mortal Pitch. London, Villiers, 1957.
The Masks of Love. London, Putnam, 1960.
A Sense of Danger. London, Putnam, 1962.
Walking Wounded. London, Eyre and Spottiswoode, 1965.
Epithets of War: Poems 1965–1969. London, Eyre and Spottiswoode, 1969.
Pergamon Poets 8, with Jon Silkin, edited by Dennis Butts. Oxford, Pergamon Press, 1970.
Selected Poems. London, Allison and Busby, 1971.
Company of Women. Frensham, Surrey, Sceptre Press, 1971.
Corgi Modern Poets in Focus 4, with others, edited by Jeremy Robson. London, Corgi, 1971.
Incident at West Bay. Richmond, Surrey, Keepsake Press, 1972.
The Winter Man: New Poems. London, Allison and Busby, 1973.
Meeting in Manchester. Rushden, Northamptonshire, Sceptre Press, 1974.
The Loving Game. London, Robson, 1975.
An Ilkley Quintet. Privately printed, c.1975.
A Morden Tower Reading 1, with Alexis Lykiard. Newcastle upon Tyne, Morden Tower, 1976.
New and Collected Poems 1950–1980. London, Robson, 1980.
Winterlude. London, Robson, 1982.
Funeral Games and Other Poems. London, Robson, 1987.
Soldiering On: Poems of Military Life. London, Robson, 1989.
A Time for Fires. London, Robson, 1991.
Collected Poems 1950–1993. London, Robson, 1994.
The Black and White Days: Poems. London, Robson, 1996.
Views and Distances. London, Enitharmon, 2000.

Poetry (for children)

Mastering the Craft. Oxford, Pergamon Press, 1970.
The Apple-Raid and Other Poems. London, Chatto and Windus, 1974.
Catch the Light, with Gregory Harrison and Laurence Smith. Oxford, Oxford University Press, 1982; New York, Oxford University Press, 1983.
The Clever Potato. London, Century Hutchinson, 1988.
Love Shouts and Whispers. London, Century Hutchinson, 1990.
Travelling Light. London, Bodleyhead, 1991.

Plays

Radio Plays: *A Man's Game,* 1962; *A Door with One Eye,* 1963; *The Cancelling Dark,* music by Christopher Whelen, 1965.

Novels

The Fight. London, Peter Nevill, 1953.
The Wound and the Scar. London, Peter Nevill, 1953.
The Big Chance. London, Long, 1960.
The Shadowed Place. London, Long, 1961.
The Face of the Enemy. London, Putnam, 1961.
The Dividing Night. London, Putnam, 1962.
The Big Time. London, Longman, 1965.
Ring of Truth. London, Robson, 1983.

Other

Edward Thomas. London, Longman, 1963.
The Dangerous Ones (for children). Oxford, Pergamon Press, 1970.
The Tiger and the Rose: An Autobiography. London, Hamish Hamilton, 1971.
Three Poets, Two Children, with Dannie Abse and Leonard Clark, edited by Desmond Badham-Thornhill. Gloucester, Thornhill Press, 1975.
Not without Glory: Poets of the Second World War. London, Woburn Press, 1976.
A Proper Gentleman. London, Robson, 1977.
A Lonely Game (for children). Exeter, Wheaton, 1979.
How to Enjoy Poetry. Loughton, Essex, Piatkus, 1983.
How to Enjoy Novels. London, Piatkus, 1984.
Argument of Kings: An Autobiography. London, Robson, 1987.
Drums of Morning: Growing Up in the Thirties. London, Robson, 1992.

Editor, with Patricia Beer and Ted Hughes, *New Poems 1962.* London, Hutchinson, 1962.
Editor, *Your Attention Please: An Anthology from the Open University Poets.* Winchester, Hampshire, Hesperus, 1983.
Editor, *Sporting Literature.* Oxford, Oxford University Press, 1987.

*

Manuscript Collections: British Library, London; University of Texas, Austin.

Critical Studies: ''Naming the Unicorn'' by Gavin Ewart, in *Ambit* (London), 1975; ''Towards Text Typology'' by Graham C. John, in *Applied Text Linguistics: Six Contributions from Exeter,* edited by Alan J. Turney, Exeter.

Vernon Scannell comments:

Major themes: violence, the experience of war, the sense of danger that is part of the climate of our times. These are contrasted with poems of a more private nature that affirm the continuity and indestructibility of the creative spirit. Some verse satire. The work is traditional, very direct, and firmly rooted in recognizable human experience.

*   *   *

Vernon Scannell is the ordinary man as poet, yet with not an ounce of that English failing of inverted snobbery in him. Why? Because of a genuine, unparaded humility—

. . . how insolent to make
These blurred attempts when Shakespeare, Donne
     and Blake
Have done what they have done. And yet it tempts,

This longing to make wicks of words . . .

—and because of a long and intelligent experience of day-to-day life. The character projected in his verse is that of the eternal British Tommy who has seen it all, who knows what ''makes things tick'' (for example, see the poem ''Any Complaints?''), and who is downright honest—as far as it is given to any human being to be so. He is like a Roy Campbell without the bravado and that much truer to life. He is a man with guts, and Scannell's own truest character is perceived through this admiration for a certain Jack-the-lad, a quondam schoolfellow sympathetically portrayed in the poem ''A Kind of Hero.'' He is a bad but noble lad who in

The end was killed at Alamein.
He wore handcuffs on the troopship
Going out: his webbing
All scrubbed as white as rice;
And we, or others like us,
Were promoted
By his last, derisive sacrifice.

It was also in the roped-off crucible of the boxing ring that Scannell learned not only to trade with his fists but in the honesty of truth of well; he learned a humane realism through playing by the rules. In the rough experience of the ring he came to appreciate real men, those who

     . . . never knew
The failure of success . . . they were real
Members of our craft, good workmen, proud
To wear the badges of the trade, a breed
That if it dies, could surely mean the end
Of what I still believe the greatest game.

Scannell is firmly of those whom the hard school of life has taught a respect for nothing but the truth, a responsibility that the poet has to take doubly seriously, for as he says in his autobiography *The Tiger and the Rose,* ''a poet has no time for duplicity or propaganda: he is too busy trying to get his words right.''

Scannell is a workmanlike poet who uses rhyme well but not notably and whose imagery is often startling but rarely far-fetched. His principal themes are mortality, the persistent itch of love and lust, and man's inability to know the whole truth about anything. He is about as nondidactic a poet as it is possible to be without sinking completely to the level of a purely descriptive writer. From *A Mortal Pitch,* published in 1957, to *Funeral Games,* in 1987, and the later and lighthearted *Soldiering On,* Scannell has not really developed. His style, a demotic-toned, sometimes slangy brew that is sweetened from time to time with lines of almost sugary beauty, remains the same. His very unphilosophical explorations rarely break new ground, but such is his skill and accessibility that he takes one easily into the everyday world and makes the reader exclaim admiringly at each nicely balanced, perceptive observation. His is an Augustan sensibility in rough-hewn form.

Although he is more than just a descriptive poet, Scannell's powers of description are considerable:

> Endlessly the stream slides past,
> Jellies each white flat stone
> Which stares through its slithering window at
> The sky's smeared monotone.

These lines are from "The Anniversary," in the 1975 collection *The Loving Game,* a poem illustrating two of his most important stylistic features. The first is an excellent gift for surprising, but 100 percent accurate, terms; an example is "Jellies each white flat stone," which calls up precisely and freshly the effect of water passing over stones. Second, as this same poem neatly demonstrates, his ability to personalize the so-called objective or inanimate things of nature is tastefully and not incongruously analogical.

There is a great deal of gently perverse humor in Scannell's poetry too, a humor that relies not so much on situation or exaggeration as on memorably ludicrous lines like "I am not old enough to cope with age" or "Oh Christ, I'll always be too young to die" ("Two Variations on an Old Theme"). Then there are lines of excellent perception seasoned with a touch of humor, like this from "Report on Drinking Habits": "His eyes' brightness advertises / Good meals and unadventurous sleeping." One does not quite know whether to applaud these lines most for their wisdom or their fun.

Scannell's volumes *Funeral Games* and *Soldiering On* are eloquent epitomes of the character and range of his talent. The beauty and tenderness of "Candle Reflections"—

> Their tears silent, warm and lenitive
> Cooling to translucent blebs like pearls.
>
> Their element has always been religious . . .

—both contrast with and complement the earthy, half-barbaric language of "Swearing In" or "Bayonet Training":

> Be brutal, ruthless, tough.
> I want to hear you scream for blood
> As you rip out his guts . . .

This ordinary man's bard retains a verbal energy rooted very much in the common tongue, yet it rises frequently to that perfectly heightened vernacular that has always been, and will always be, the language vehicle of true poetry. Though what will endure of Scannell's work, as with that of any poet, can be only a few poems of a sufficient but inescapable brightness, perhaps his most remarkable achievement is the tactful balance he has always maintained between honest accuracy of observation and the free, unhindered play of the imagination ("Its fragrant and substantial presence . . ."). There is both body and soul in all of his poems: "Through every sense the quintessential fruit . . . / Here, domestic, familiar as a pet." Finally, there is wisdom and maturity that shows in an understanding of memory, best expressed in "The Long and Lovely Summers," from *Funeral Games:*

> And yet we still remember them—the long
> And lovely summers, never smeared or chilled—
> Like poems, by heart; like poems, never wrong,
> The idyll is intact, it's truth distilled

> From merciful fact, preserved as by the sharp
> And merciful mendacities of art.

For poetry, as the Greeks said, is a daughter of memory, and the truest poetry is memory best understood.

—William Oxley

SCHMIDT, Michael (Norton)

Nationality: Mexican. **Born:** Mexico City, 2 March 1947. **Education:** The Hill School, Pottstown, Pennsylvania; Christ's Hospital, Horsham, Sussex; Harvard University, Cambridge, Massachusetts, 1966–67; Wadham College, Oxford, B.A. in English 1969, M.A. 1977. **Family:** Married Claire Harman in 1979 (divorced); two sons and one daughter. **Career:** Since 1969 managing director, Carcanet Press, Oxford, later Cheadle, Cheshire, and Manchester. Gulbenkian Fellow, University of Manchester, 1972–75. Since 1972 fellow, Manchester Poetry Centre; co-editor, 1972–84, and since 1984 editor, *Poetry Nation,* later *PN Review,* Manchester. **Awards:** Fellow, Royal Society of Literature, 1993. **Address:** Carcanet Press, 4th Floor, Conavon Court, 12–16 Blackfriars Street, Manchester M3 5BQ, England.

PUBLICATIONS

Poetry

Black Buildings. Oxford, Carcanet, 1969.
One Eye Mirror Cold. Oxford, Sycamore Press, 1970.
Bedlam and the Oakwood: Essays on Various Fictions. Oxford, Carcanet, 1970.
Desert of the Lions. Oxford, Carcanet, 1972.
It Was My Tree. London, Anvil Press Poetry, 1972.
My Brother Gloucester: New Poems. Manchester, Carcanet, 1976.
A Change of Affairs. London, Anvil Press Poetry, 1978.
Choosing a Guest: New and Selected Poems. London, Anvil Press Poetry, 1983.
The Love of Strangers. London, Century Hutchinson, 1989.
Selected Poems, 1972–1997. Huddersfield, Smith/Doorstop Books, 1997.

Novels

The Colonist. London, Muller, 1980; as *Green Island,* New York, Vanguard Press, 1982.
The Dresden Gate. London, Century Hutchinson, 1986; New York, Vanguard Press, 1987.

Other

Reading Modern Poetry. London, Routledge, 1989.
Lives of the Poets. London, Weidenfeld and Nicolson, 1998; New York, Knopf, 1999.
Editor, with Grevel Lindop, *British Poetry since 1960: A Critical Survey.* Oxford, Carcanet, 1972.

Editor, *Ten English Poets.* Manchester, Carcanet, 1976.

Editor, *The Avoidance of Literature: Collected Essays,* by C.H. Sisson. Manchester, Carcanet, 1978.

Editor, *An Introduction to Fifty British Poets 1300–1900.* London, Pan, 1979; as *A Reader's Guide to Fifty British Poets,* London, Heinemann, and New York, Barnes and Noble, 1980.

Editor, *An Introduction to Fifty Modern British Poets.* London, Pan, 1979; as *A Reader's Guide to Fifty Modern British Poets,* London, Heinemann, 1979; New York, Barnes and Noble, 1982.

Editor, with Peter Jones, *British Poetry since 1970: A Critical Survey.* Manchester, Carcanet, and New York, Persea, 1980.

Editor, *Eleven British Poets.* London, Methuen, 1980.

Editor, *Some Contemporary Poets of Britain and Ireland.* Manchester, Carcanet, 1983.

Editor, *New Poetries,* Manchester, Carcanet, 1994.

Editor, *A Calendar of Modern Poetry,* Manchester, *PN Review,* 1994.

Editor, with Nick Rennison, *Poets on Poets.* Manchester, Carcanet, 1997.

Editor, with Alastair Niven, *Enigmas and Arrivals: An Anthology of Commonwealth Writing.* Manchester, Carcanet, 1997.

Editor, *Lyrical Ballads: With a Few Other Poems,* by William Wordsworth. London and New York, Penguin, 1999.

Editor, *A Shropshire Lad,* by A.E. Housman. London, Penguin, 1999.

Editor, *New Poetries II: An Anthology.* Manchester, Carcanet, 1999.

Editor, *The Harvill Book of Twentieth-Century Poetry in English.* London, Harvill, 1999.

Translator, with Edward Kissam, *Flower and Song: Poems of the Aztec Peoples.* London, Anvil Press Poetry, 1977.

Translator, *On Poets and Others,* by Octavio Paz. New York, Holt, 1986; London, Carcanet, 1987.

*

Critical Study: By Michael Hulse, in *Antigonish Review* (Antigonish, Nova Scotia), 85–86, spring/summer 1991.

*   *   *

Michael Schmidt's achievements as a poet cannot be separated from his work as a publisher of poetry and criticism (he founded the Carcanet Press in the 1960s while at Oxford and became its doughty helmsman) and as editor of the bimonthly journal *PN Review,* a publication whose avowed aim has always been to "set poetry and criticism back in the mainstream of cultural concern." What we have come to expect from him is a certain kind of scrupulousness, a degree of intellectual sobriety. Poetry is above everything else a serious art, seems to be his claim, and one whose decline, were that to happen, would have the most catastrophic consequences for the intellectual and emotional temper of the nation.

In practical terms this means that both the press and the magazine have often championed what one might describe as some of the more old-fashioned virtues—meter, rhyme, and syntax, for example. Formal excellence has been one of their touchstones. After all, poetry is a craft like any other. This is not to suggest, however, that Schmidt himself has not been a willing learner, a pragmatist when pragmatism has been called for. In spite of his belief in a critical approach to poetry, he has a healthy suspicion of much of the tortuous literary

theorizing that passes for critical analysis in many of our institutions of higher education. And while some of the poets in Carcanet's list in its early years may have seemed docile and green fingered in their quintessential Englishness, to the point of tedium, later authors sometimes created a flurry of atonal excitement, for example, the New York poet John Ashbery.

Schmidt himself was born in Mexico and educated at Harvard and Oxford. English is, therefore, his second language. His poetry moves restlessly from New World to Old and back again. His collection *Black Buildings* was among the first pamphlets Carcanet ever published from Pin Farm, near Oxford, when the press lacked even a telephone, let alone offices. None of these poems was reprinted when his volume of selected poems appeared in 1983, but they give us a strong indication of some of his early influences. In one an abrupt juxtaposition of telling details brings Ezra Pound to mind: "mad dog's slaver, the shore foam, / all salt-white the stone . . ." In another Sylvia Plath swims unsteadily into view, teetering on the brink of emotional implosion: "I am the porcelain clock, / touch my alarm, / stroke my polio arms. / I look through no glass. . . ." And the landscape of Mexico—its aridity, its starkness, its essential hostility to human occupation—is vividly evoked.

After Schmidt claimed England as his second home, his poetry began to be colored, understandably enough, by the tones of the English landscape, and by the late 1970s the surface details of many of his poems seemed mild mannered, decorous, and almost self-consciously English in their concern with the flowers, shrubs, birds, and other minutiae of gardens. How sharply the description in "Adam" contrasts with the stark terrain of Mexico:

I name my little trees, the oak and beech,
The willow, apple, sycamore—all planted close.
I name such blossoms as I know: the lilac,
The honeysuckle with its hint of flesh.

The almost Georgian blandness is, however, something of a feint. The self-conscious Englishness of the scene in the above poem has been evoked by no less a person than Adam, and in other poems there are similar details and events that lend the seeming tranquillity of their contexts a patina of strangeness. Savage emotions are buried here. The narrator himself is often a *promeneur solitaire,* beguiled by his own shadow or his own reflection. Another quality one is often aware of in Schmidt's poetry is the extent of his absorption in literature, and how could one expect otherwise of a man whose prime enthusiasm is poetry, who spends his days reading it and perhaps some of his evenings writing it? In the fascinating poem "Habit" Schmidt has this to say about an iris:

A Tyrian iris in a wooded place:
Give it a name, but it will not be tended;
It has frail rules of growth, its air, regardless,
A single treasure lost in a starless soil—

Or found. Stretching a hand
Towards the stem of the imagined bloom
I discover a thing tangible,
Clothed in Tyrian fabric, mine in a wooded place.

The thing found is surely not a flower but a poem, and the very way in which the matter is expressed calls up William Carlos Williams and I.A. Richards. Such is the extent of the poet's literary absorption.

Schmidt's collection *The Love of Strangers* consists of a series of autobiographical fragments in verse, often elegiac in temper, in many cases acts of "imagined reparation." The poet pays homage, begs forgiveness, and acknowledges debts to people, worlds, and particular locales he has left behind and now—as a gesture of bonding, of love—wishes to reclaim. Some of the figures are recognizable as poets, writers that by publishing he has wrested from undeserved obscurity—Sylvia Townsend Warner, for example. One of the most successful evokes a moment in his youth when he consorted with a matador, a giant of a man whose livid scar, the worst of twenty on his body, "looked like the lid / Of a dead eye." The young man yearned to be a matador himself, but his cape work was not up to it, and anyway he had not been born an Indian. The poem brings home to us almost more than any other the extraordinary contrast between Schmidt's Mexican childhood, a life lived among the most brutish simplicities, and his adult roles as editor, critic, and poet. Scant wonder that by its very nature *PN Review* has been oppositional.

—Michael Glover

SCHMITZ, Dennis (Mathew)

Nationality: American. **Born:** Dubuque, Iowa, 11 August 1937. **Education:** Loras College, Dubuque, B.A. 1959; University of Chicago, M.A. 1961. **Family:** Married Loretta D'Agostino in 1960; three daughters and two sons. **Career:** Instructor in English, Illinois Institute of Technology, Chicago, 1961–62, and University of Wisconsin, Milwaukee, 1962–66. Assistant professor, 1966–69, since 1966 poet-in-residence, associate professor, 1969–74, and since 1974, professor of English, California State University, Sacramento. **Awards:** New York Poetry Center Discovery award, 1968; Big Table award, 1969; National Endowment for the Arts fellowship 1976, 1985, 1992; Guggenheim fellowship, 1978; di Castagnola award, 1986; Shelley memorial award, 1988. **Address:** Department of English, California State University, 6000 Jay Street, Sacramento, California 95819, U.S.A.

PUBLICATIONS

Poetry

We Weep for Our Strangeness. Chicago, Follett, 1969.
Double Exposures. Oberlin, Ohio, Triskelion Press, 1971.
Goodwill, Inc. New York, Ecco Press, 1976.
String. New York, Ecco Press, 1980.
Singing. New York, Ecco Press, 1985.
Eden. Champaign, University of Illinois Press, 1989.
About Night: Selected and New Poems. Oberlin, Ohio, Oberlin College Press, 1993.

*

Critical Study: "The Crystal and the Flame" by David Young, in *Field* (Oberlin, Ohio), 42, spring 1990.

*   *   *

Dennis Schmitz's poems are wry, brilliant, and unpredictable. They explore the grotesqueness of the physical world as a means of discovering its spiritual possibilities—Flannery O'Connor's short stories come to mind as an interesting analogue—and they are not afraid to be disquieting, funny, adventurous, and difficult. Stylistically, Schmitz has found a way to embody his physical-spiritual tensions in a distinctive version of American free verse: a continually enjambed line, a preference for the lowercase and for minimal punctuation, and a cross-roughing of syntax and stanza that sets up separate ordering procedures and thus asks the reader to intensify his or her concentration. A poem from his second major collection, *Goodwill, Inc.,* serves to demonstrate characteristics of both subject and style in this unusual writer:

STAR AND GARTHER THEATER

it is always night here
faces close but never heal
only the eyes develop

scabs when we sleep & head
by head the dream is drained
into the white pool

of the screen. we go on rehearsing
THE REVENGE OF FRANKENSTEIN
my arm is sewn to your shoulder.
your father's awful hand
& an actual criminal brain

take root under the projector's
cold moon. I wanted to do
only good. I planted my mouth
& kisses grew all over skid row.
now the fat ladies of the night

are lowered into the lace
stockings & strapped into their black
apparatus. this body is grafted
to theirs. alone we are helpless,

but put together winos, whores
& ambivalent dead we walk the daytime
world charged with our beauty.

Our experience of this poem may begin in delight at the capturing of the inner-city world of run-down movie houses that show old horror films and feature striptease acts. The comparison between lust as a mechanical feature of such a world and the nightmare constructions of conglomerate monsters in the horror films is brilliant in itself, but the poem argues more seriously, as we move into a full consideration of its claims, that we are all implicated by our common humanity in the skid row subculture and its meanings. The safe distance we feel at first, a distance of superiority and judgment, disappears, leaving us with our "grafting" to the world of whores and winos and the problem of their beauty as human beings like ourselves. The poem's meanings are deeply social and penetratingly psychological, but at the same time it is light-footed and playful in its moral exploration. The poem covers its ground too nimbly and modestly to make us feel that it has doctrinaire designs upon us. In this respect Schmitz may be superior to O'Connor, whose Roman Catholic beliefs and preoccupations he largely shares.

Schmitz's range of subjects and treatments is considerable. He knows the city, the rural Midwest where he grew up, and California, where he has taught for three decades. He does psychological portraits, narratives, and fantasies. He can base a poem on a news item or a photograph. Many of his poems are rooted in mundane details of suburban family life—tree pruning, house repair, minor and major illnesses, driving. Others take up subjects as diverse as the last surviving Japanese soldier hiding on Okinawa, a boy sneaking into a zoo at night, or a stuntman character climbing a skyscraper while dressed as a cartoon character. Schmitz's upbringing tells him that this is a fallen world; its inhabitants dream of upward movement and reunion with the divine. Our bodies are our encumbrances, but they are also our only sources of transcendence. We can use art to help us face the truth of our separation from the perfect and the eternal. The poem "Kindergarten," from *Singing,* shows how effectively Schmitz can deploy such insights:

> Bee-logic: each small life
> for the hive,
> but not one of them lived out
>
> at the same speed—
> your heart thuds *fortissimo* but slow,
> my heart trots to its death.
>
> Proto-druggist pickpocket or priest
> begin as mysteries to themselves.
> Big-Head Vincent who chews his pastels
>
> & wipes spit with the blue
> over his squat trees,
> & Levonn too who wets himself
>
> is one of us.
> Our keeper Sister Agnes,
> wrinkled as a peach-nut & left-handed,
>
> sings Latin, whose inside
> is God's, she says, but we can go in
> too with our tongues & the head
>
> will follow, simplifying
> heaven. Vincent went to heaven
> in wet April. We sang a few words
>
> of "Nunc Dimittis" among the gladiolus
> & floribunda wreaths
> gripping each other's fingers
>
> as we knelt all points in a compass,
> expecting somehow to sing
> Vincent up. But we belonged
>
> to the headless Vincent
> someone crayoned on the cloakroom
> wall under his coathook,

> the feet broken
> right-angles, the heavy
> arms straining against gravity—
>
> a child's unfinished body,
> waxy & insistent.

Personal memory here is beautifully distanced and framed so that the rhythms of life and death may reveal themselves through childish understanding. The wax of the crayon that draws the effigy of the dead child echoes the wax of the beehive that is the kindergarten and the larger arena of life, a physical reality that asserts itself in the colors and textures that preoccupy the children—their teacher is fascinatingly wrinkled, for example, and the hand-holding and kneeling rival any spiritual meanings of the memorial ritual—and lock them back into life and their fallen world. Again, it seems appropriate to note that Schmitz's poems move with a spryness and wit that belie paraphrase and theology. He has made a kind of music out of it all, we realize, a strange legerity that relocates our sense of the spiritual and refreshes us with the possibilities of language and unity. This is a poet who works steadily and well, never compromising his standards, and who presumably is not better known only because his poems require a level of attentiveness that the culture at large is still laboring toward.

—David Young

SCHNACKENBERG, Gjertrud

Nationality: American. **Born:** Tacoma, Washington, 27 August 1953. **Education:** Mount Holyoke College, South Hadley, Massachusetts, B.A. (summa cum laude) 1975. **Family:** Married Robert Nozick in 1987. **Career:** Visiting fellow, St. Catherine's College, Oxford University, 1997; visiting scholar, Getty Research Institute, 2000. **Awards:** Radcliffe College Bunting Institute fellowship, 1979–80; Lavan award, 1983; American Academy-Institute of Arts and Letters Rome fellowship, 1983; National Endowment for the Arts fellowship, 1986; Guggenheim fellowship, 1987; Academy Award in literature, American Academy of Arts and Sciences, 1998. H.D.L.: Mount Holyoke College, 1985. **Member:** Fellow, American Academy of Arts and Sciences, 1996. **Address:** c/o Farrar Straus and Giroux Inc., 19 Union Square West, New York, New York 10003, U.S.A.

PUBLICATIONS

Poetry

Portraits and Elegies. Boston, Godine, 1982; revised edition, New York, Farrar Straus, 1986; London, Century Hutchinson, 1987.
The Lamplit Answer. New York, Farrar Straus, 1985; London, Century Hutchinson, 1986.
A Gilded Lapse of Time. New York, Farrar Straus, 1992; London, Harvill, 1993.
The Throne of Labdacus. New York, Farrar Straus, 2000.
Supernatural Love: Poems 1973–1992. New York, Farrar Straus, 2000.

*

Critical Study: "Return to Metaphor: From Deep Imagist to New Formalist" by Paul Lake, in *Southwest Review* (Dallas, Texas), 74(4), autumn 1989.

*   *   *

In the mid-1980s a new American formalism was signaled and discussed. By 1987 Alan Shapiro was able to declare in *Critical Inquiry,* "Open the pages of almost any national journal or magazine, and where, ten years ago, one found only one or another kind of free verse lyric one now finds well-rhymed quatrains, sestinas, villanelles, sonnets and blank verse dramatic monologues or meditations." Perhaps this New Formalism had something to do not only with a dialectical reaction to dominant modes of American poetry but also to the proliferating creative writing programs in universities. In any event, the American renaissance in formal strategies led to poems being published that were neither better nor worse than most verse available at any time. For most poetry published is, alas, tedious and unlit.

But some of the poets associated with the New Formalism demand serious attention, not least Gjertrud Schnackenberg, who has used meter and rhyme without subduing emotional currents. She has, to adapt a phrase of Richard Wilbur, employed her cadences and rhyme not as ornament but as emphasis.

Her first book, *Portraits and Elegies*—well named, for that is what the poems in it exactly are—was published in 1982. Her elegies, though corseted, are full of feeling. Through the telling of anecdotes they conjure up a once-loving father-daughter relationship. The touching memories of her father are a form of celebration as well as a requiem. In twelve separate poems she celebrates her father's piano playing; his ability to extract a significant lesson from some mundane incident, such as a bird dropping excreta on his head; his courteous behavior during a brush with a bow-tied English cyclist at Cambridge; father-and-daughter trips that involve night fishing and visits as tourists to Norway, Rome, and Germany. The total effect of these dozen beautifully composed elegies is to hear the speaking voice of a young woman in controlled mourning, rather than one displaying a "grief approaching lunacy."

There is a second notable sequence in Schnackenberg's first book, sixteen poems called "19 Hadley Street." These prove to be snapshots of the denizens of an affluent house over two centuries. The album's initial pages reveal a married couple in 1960, the husband fatally ill with cancer. We turn the pages and return to voices of the past, first to the wife as a child in 1905, then to earlier generations who have lived in that same house on Hadley Street. These sepia poems of domesticity, happy or tragic, are set against the appropriate historical background until we are led to the root, to the engendering guilt that is intrinsic to American history:

. . . Your mother lost her wits
When news came that a squaw was torn to bits
By village dogs in Hockanum . . .

After this dazzling debut, we were not disappointed by the poems in Schnackenberg's second volume, *The Lamplit Answer,* though here some of the narratives and portraits seem overlong and labored. Apart from empathetic glimpses of Chopin, Simone Weil, and Darwin, we are surprised by such grim, Grimm-like, fairy-tale variants as "Two Tales of Clumsy" that feature death's representative, a certain No-No. By the way, it is surprising that this poem contains an occasional aural error, as in the fourth line below:

To Mrs Clumsy since that happy time
She summoned Clumsy with her dinner chime.
And there is Clumsy's darling lying dead.
How like a rubber ball bounces her head
As No-No drags her feet-first from this life.
Then No-No dresses up as Clumsy's wife . . .

The humorous tone of this macabre fairy story is extended to a sequence of love poems. These, addressed to a lover who has abandoned her, though ostentatiously witty and clever, cannot be current of feeling that motors them, and thus the sequence is saved from frivolity. Moreover, Schnackenberg has the knack of being able to lift the conclusion of her poems with a striking image or simile—"window squares like Bibles closed forever, squares of black"—or with sheer eloquence, as in her first book in the ending to the elegy called "Bavaria," where she recalls how she stood outside Neuschwanstein castle, accompanied by her father, a professor of history:

We linger, for a moment, at the gates:
Here Ludwig, in his grisly innocence,
Plucked water lilies planted an hour since
By silent gardeners, hurled his dinner plates
At statue niches peopled with assassins,
And wept that Nietzsche called his love a Jew.
It is November 1962,
A siren from the village rises, spins
Itself into a planet of alarm
That hangs a moment in the wilderness,
And dusk comes through the forest with Venus,
Star of emergency, upon its arm.

Schnackenberg is at her best when her historical perspectives are personalized in this way and when emotion is recollected in tranquility. Those suspicious of the possibilities of the New Formalism should turn, for instance, to "Supernatural Love," the final impressive poem in *The Lamplit Answer.* Here the poet reinhabits a scene from childhood in which, once again, the dramatis personae are father and daughter. The poem resonates in the mind long after the book is closed because of its rhymes and meter, because of theme, feeling, and telling image, because of the evidence of an intricately organizing mind that skillfully stitches all of these together.

—Dannie Abse

SCOTT, John A.

Nationality: British. **Born:** Littlehampton, Sussex, 23 April 1948. **Education:** Monash University, Clayton, Victoria, Australia, B.A. (honors) and diploma in education, 1970; graduate study, 1975–76; doctoral study at University of Technology, Sydney, Australia, 1991. **Career:** Lecturer in media, Swinburne Institute, Melbourne, 1974–80, and Canberra College of Advanced Education, 1981–89. Since 1989 lecturer in writing, Wollongong University, New South Wales. Resident, *Cité Internationale des Arts,* Paris, 1990. **Awards:** Poetry Society of Australia award, 1970; Mattara prize, 1984; Literature Board senior writer's fellowship, 1985, 1986, 1988, 1990; University of Melbourne Wesley Michael Wright award, 1985, 1988; Victorian Premier's prize, 1986, 1994; Fellowship of Australian Writers A.N.A. award, 1990. **Address:** c/o University of Wollongong, Northfields Avenue, Wollongong, New South Wales 2500, Australia.

PUBLICATIONS

Poetry

The Barbarous Sideshow. St. Lucia. Queensland. Makar Press. 1975.
From the Flooded City. St. Lucia, Queensland, Makar Press, 1981.
Smoking. Melbourne, Scripsi, 1983.
The Quarrel with Ourselves; and Confession. Melbourne, Rigamarole, 1984.
St. Clair: Three Narratives (includes prose). St. Lucia, University of Queensland Press, 1986; revised edition, Sydney, Picador, 1990.
Singles: Shorter Works, 1981–1986. St. Lucia, University of Queensland Press, 1989.
Translation. Sydney, Picador, 1990.
Selected Poems. St. Lucia, University of Queensland Press, 1995.

Plays

Radio Scripts: *The All-Australian Show,* 1977; *Now Is the Time, If Ever There Was a Time, for the People of Australia to Rise in Anger and Start to Intervene in the Affairs of Governing This Country,* 1977; *Eleven, Eleven,* 1979; *77 km, North 63 East,* 1979.

Novels

Blair. Melbourne, McPhee Gribble, 1988; New York, New Directions, 1989.
What I Have Written. Melbourne, McPhee Gribble, 1993; New York, Norton, 1994.
Before I Wake. Ringwood, Victoria, Penguin, and New York, Viking Penguin, 1996.

Other

The Book of Rats (graphics). Sydney, Transit Press, 1981.
Dante's Political Purgatory. Philadelphia, University of Pennsylvania Press, 1996.

Editor and Translator, *Emmanuel Hocquard: Elegies and Other Works.* Plymouth, Devon, Shearsman, 1988.

*

Manuscript Collection: Australian Defence Force Academy, Canberra.

Critical Studies: "Enlarging Our Experiment with Narrative: John A. Scott's Trilogy with Annotations" by Martin Duwell, in *Australian Literary Studies* (Queensland), 15(3), May 1992; "Perversions in the Text of 'Before I Wake'" by Michael Brennan, in *Southerly,* 58(4), summer 1998–99.

John A. Scott comments:

A highly metaphoric poetry that seeks to reconcile a poetic based on ambiguity, metamorphosis, contraction, and ellipsis with extended narrative structures. Scott's oeuvre, both poetry and prose, may be seen as an extended meditation on the relationship between language, power, and sexuality.

*   *   *

Restlessly talented, John A. Scott tends to elude categorization and to flout normative criteria for inclusion in mainstream anthologies, where he nonetheless seems underrepresented given his considerable success in the realm of literary prizes. It is his technical virtuosity that commonly attracts initial praise from critics. More rare are assessments like that of Philip Mead, who considers him "one of the few Australian poets with an incipient view of society and the directions it might be taking." This may indeed prove to be what gives Scott lasting significance. Meanwhile, inventive imagery and language, seen by some as his prime strength, provoke occasional rebukes for "linguistic excess" and can cause even admirers to have trouble getting their bearings.

It is not only that Scott requires of readers the oblique responses appropriate to the literary techniques of parody and allusion. He also requires readers to bring into play habits of reception that we are more familiar with in fiction and film. Clues to his idea of the process of writing (and of reading) are provided in the appropriately named prose poem "Projection":

> Later the detective will teach him how dangerous it is to see things incorrectly, or to search for the wrong things: the seductions of order and chaos, and the way film makes detectives of us all.

The visual, along with the need to "read" it, is extremely important in Scott's work, and it is frequently linked with violence. "*Our real aggression* he thought / *is optical*" comes from the sequence "A Documentary on Gravity: Eight Sonnets on a Drawing by Rod Moss." The first of the sonnets does indeed exercise optical violence by constantly superimposing the visual attributes of one thing upon another while drawing attention to this by insistent preference for simile and analogue rather than unifying metaphors.

In the three narratives that make up *St. Clair* violence is a distinctive quality of both language and experience. "Preface" is a mythomystical evocation of ecstatic Sadean sexuality, desire's "exquisite variations" played out in a world of inadvertence where "we write our fictions in the sexual act" only to find that "at the point of emergence, love reverts to loss." The volume as a whole, however, is structurally divided into past, present, and future, and within this structure sexual excess as a past focus of our anxieties is superseded in the present of "St. Clair" and the future of "Run in the Stocking" by concerns about the use of psychiatric technology as a means of social control.

The title poem is set in a psychiatric hospital officially taken over for treatment of "a new insane," political dissidents. It is a world both phantasmagoric and appallingly prosaic. Scott's multifocused, elliptical treatment draws us into a world where, as part of truth's corruption, language degrades, disintegrating into manipulative ideological abstractions or mere noises of violence or seduction. ''Run in the Stocking'' is a murder mystery whose affinities to futuristic sci-fi are less important than those with Dürrenmatt's somber studies of uncertain fact and certain guilt. Its epigraph from Baudelaire makes explicit one of Scott's running subtexts, that violence is another face of anomie, so that we find in our own image ''an oasis of horror in a desert of tedium.''

Scott is, however, neither exclusively visual nor unremittingly somber. Sound montage, also important in his work, helped to establish his early reputation as a performance poet. He plays exuberant language games in poems such as ''Alliteration & the Rise & Fall of the New Classifieds'' and can be impishly irreverent in literary allusions. ''The Third Coming'' consists of the three lines

Nightfall in Bethlehem.
A rough beast thumbing
through the street directory.

It is Marvell's turn in ''De-Boning the Garden,'' but in its more sustained wit this becomes a sophisticated essay on the problematics of metaphor. Himself a master of the baroque metaphor, Scott nonetheless shares contemporary distrust of the figurative, as at the end of ''Changing Room'' when lover and similes depart together, leaving ''everything quite suddenly / and only like itself . . .''

''Changing Room'' comes from the 1989 volume *Singles,* where the charged eroticism of earlier work often modulates to a perplexed and sensuous tenderness of the kind experienced by the speaker in ''Breath,'' who lies awake beside a lover whose breathing is the only thing giving shape and sense to the dark. Readers hoping for new poetic developments out of this more sympathetic feeling for the texture of quotidian lives have had to accept the fact that Scott's attention is firmly fixed on experimental prose. At least the new *Selected Poems* of 1995 brings out-of-print works back into circulation, allowing something of an overview of his poetic achievements.

—Jennifer Strauss

SCULLY, James (Joseph)

Nationality: American. **Born:** New Haven, Connecticut, 23 February 1937. **Education:** Southern Connecticut State College, New Haven, 1955–57; University of Connecticut, Storrs, B.A. 1959 (Phi Beta Kappa), Ph.D. 1964. **Family:** Married Arlene Steeves in 1960; two sons (one deceased) and one daughter. **Career:** Instructor, Rutgers University, New Brunswick, New Jersey, 1963–64; teacher, Hartford Street Academy, Connecticut, 1968; associate professor, 1964–75, professor, 1973–92, and since 1992 professor emeritus, University of Massachusetts, Amherst. General editor, ''Art on the Line'' series, Curbstone Press, Willimantic, Connecticut, 1980–85. **Awards:** National Defense fellowship, 1959–62; Ingram Merrill Foundation fellowship, 1962; Lamont Poetry Selection award, 1967; Contributors' prize (*Far Point*), 1969; Jennie Tane award (*Massachusetts Review*), 1971; Guggenheim fellowship, 1973; National Endowment for the Arts grant, 1976, 1990; Islands and Continents award, for

translation, 1980; Bookbuilders of Boston award, for bookcover design, 1983. **Address:** 39 Dashiell Hammett, #301, San Francisco, California 94108, U.S.A.

PUBLICATIONS

Poetry

The Marches. New York, Holt Rinehart, 1967.
Communications, with Grandin Conover. Amherst, Massachusetts Review, 1970.
Avenue of the Americas. Amherst, University of Massachusetts Press, 1971.
Santiago Poems. Willimantic, Connecticut, Curbstone Press, 1975.
Scrap Book. Willimantic, Connecticut, Ziesing Brothers, 1977.
May Day. Corvallis, Oregon, Minnesota Review Press, 1980.
Apollo Helmet. Willimantic, Connecticut, Curbstone Press, 1983.
Raging Beauty: Selected Poems. Washington D.C., Azul Press, 1994.

Other

Line Break: Poetry as Social Practice. Seattle, Washington, Bay Press, 1988.

Editor, *Modern Poetics.* New York, McGraw Hill, 1965; as *Modern Poets on Modern Poetry,* London, Collins, 1966.
Editor, and translator with Arlene Scully, *Poetry and Militancy in Latin America,* by Roque Dalton. Willimantic, Connecticut, Curbstone Press, 1981.

Translator, with C. John Herington, *Prometheus Bound,* by Aeschylus. New York and London, Oxford University Press, 1975.
Translator, with Maria A. Proser, *Quechua Peoples Poetry,* edited by Jesús Lara. Willimantic, Connecticut, Curbstone Press, 1977.
Translator, with Maria A. Proser and Arlene Scully, *De Repente/All of a Sudden,* by Teresa de Jesús. Willimantic, Connecticut, Curbstone Press, 1979.

*   *   *

The poems in James Scully's *The Marches* are meditative, dense as the persistence of the past in the present,

as if,
rockbound, this were the kingdom come,

and the hunched fields were crystal-clear
Jerusalem, and life was judged
vibration in the summer air.

Connecticut, northern France, Slovenia's Lake Bled, Venice, Gibraltar, Lake Sunapee in New Hampshire—wherever, ''you could almost hear / lost gods breathing in the earth.'' Another noise is time passing: ''pink-pale clouds march / as far as the mind can reach, wilting, / central Jersey spread under like spilt milk.''

Avenue of the Americas is a far less scattered book, focused by loss. A child is dead at six months; a brilliant and extravagant friend is dead. Rapacious grief runs through the poems. Scully's language is less measured than before, more various—discursive, argumentative, and lyrical all in the same few lines. Organizing themes are Edenic America, friendship and family, the failure of art to console and its power to instruct, the spiritual collapse of American political life in the 1960s. The rocklike past of *The Marches* is transmogrified by history, by evolution, and seems to be spending itself as fast as the present:

> Even the beautiful are too
> > heartsick for beauty,
> astronauts will never make it to the stars
> but burn up.

The book includes translations from Joseph Brodsky, whose political themes underscore Scully's own.

Occasionally so ambitious that they fail of their own philosophical weight, Scully's later poems have the urgency and personal risk of letters to a beloved friend. (One group of poems in *Avenue of the Americas* was evidently written as a series of such letters.) But the poems are not confessional, and the poet does not set himself up in them as a representative man. They move toward the wider life that is their persistent obsession by a manifest sense that language, perhaps more than history or evolution, is our shared life: "Maybe that's what poetry is, one of the species / claiming grandeur. / It's that helpless."

—William Matthews

SCUPHAM, (John) Peter

Nationality: British. **Born:** Liverpool, Lancashire, 24 February 1933. **Education:** The Perse, Cambridge 1942–47; St. George's Harpenden, 1947–51; Emmanuel College, Cambridge, 1954–57, B.A. (honors) in English, 1957. **Military Service:** Royal Army Ordnance Corps. **Family:** Married Carola Braunholtz in 1957; one daughter and three sons. **Career:** English teacher, Skegness Grammar School, Lincolnshire, 1957–61. Since 1961 member of the English Department, St. Christopher School, Letchworth, Hertfordshire. Editor, with John Mole, Cellar Press, and since 1974 owner, Mandeville Press, both in Hitchin, Hertfordshire. **Awards:** Fellow, Royal Society of Literature. **Address:** Old Hall, Norwich Road, South Burlingham, Norwich NR13, England.

PUBLICATIONS

Poetry

The Small Containers. Stockport, Cheshire, Phoenix Pamphlet Poets Press, 1972.
The Snowing Globe. Manchester, E.J. Morten, 1972.
Children Dancing. Oxford, Sycamore Press, 1972.
The Nondescript. Stockport, Cheshire, Phoenix Pamphlet Poets Press, 1973.
The Gift: Love Poems. Richmond, Surrey, Keepsake Press, 1973.
Prehistories. London, Oxford University Press, 1975.
A Mandeville Troika, with Neil Powell and George Szirtes. Hitchin, Hertfordshire, Mandeville Press, 1977.

The Hinterland. London, Oxford University Press, 1977.
Megaliths and Water, drawings by Andy Christian. Brampton, LYC Museum, 1978.
Natura. Sidcot, Somerset, Gruffyground Press, and Iowa City, Windhover Press, 1978.
Summer Palaces. Oxford and New York, Oxford University Press, 1980.
Christmas Past, with John Mole. Hitchin, Hertfordshire, Mandeville Press, 1981.
Transformation Scenes: A Sequence of Five Poems. Hitchin, Hertfordshire, Red Gull Press, 1982.
Winter Quarters. Oxford, Oxford University Press, 1983.
Christmas Games, with John Mole. Hitchin, Hertfordshire, Mandeville Press, 1983.
Christmas Visits, with John Mole. Hitchin, Hertfordshire, Mandeville Press, 1985.
Out Late. Oxford, Oxford University Press, 1986.
Winter Emblems, with John Mole. Hitchin, Hertfordshire, Mandeville Press, 1986.
Christmas Fables, with John Mole. Hitchin, Hertfordshire, Mandeville Press, 1987.
The Air Show. Oxford, Oxford University Press, 1988.
Christmas Gifts, with John Mole. Hitchin, Hertfordshire, Mandeville Press, 1988.
Christmas Books, with John Mole. Hitchin, Hertfordshire, Mandeville Press, 1989.
Watching the Perseids. Oxford, Oxford University Press, 1990.
Selected Poems. Oxford, Oxford University Press, 1990.
The Ark. Oxford, Oxford University Press, 1994.
Night Watch. London, Anvil Press Poetry, 1999.

*

Manuscript Collection: British Library, London.

Critical Studies: In *New Statesman* (London), 29 September 1972; by Michael Longley, in *Phoenix 9* (Stockport, Cheshire), winter 1972; in *Irish Times* (Dublin), 6 January 1973; in *The Teacher* (London), 2 March 1973; in *Encounter* (London), 18 May 1973; in *Times Literary Supplement* (London), 23 May 1975 and 21 November 1977; "Lessons in Survival" (interview), in *PN Review* (Manchester), 10(5); "Mature Students: Peter Scupham and Andrew Waterman" by Neil Powell, in *British Poetry since 1970: A Critical Survey,* edited by Peter Jones and Michael Schmidt, New York, Persea, 1980; "Giants in the Earth: Recent Myths for British Poets" by Avrom Fleishman, in *ELH* (Baltimore, Maryland), 51(1), spring 1984; by Roland John, in *Agenda* (London), 26(3), autumn 1988; "Poetic Practice" by the author, in *The Poet's Voice and Craft,* edited by C.B. McCully, Manchester, Carcanet, 1994.

Peter Scupham comments:

I feel with Auden that poetry is a game of knowledge, and I enjoy the complexity of rules that make the game worth playing. I enjoy, and hope my work demonstrates, formalities, ironies, technical complexities, patterns, elegance. But since the game is a game of knowledge, I also hope my poems are about something, that they possess a strong sense of the reality of people and objects. The game should be played for someone or something else's sake, not for the poet's. I enjoy tightrope walking, cadence, clarity, celebrations; I dislike the raw, the self-absorbed, the cosmic. The poets for whom I feel particular elective affinities would include James Reeves, Norman Cameron, Louis MacNeice, Richard Wilbur, John Crowe Ransom. I would like my best poems to unite the dance of beauty with the dance of death.

*   *   *

The subject matter of Peter Scupham's poetry reflects the wide-ranging interests of an acute intelligence: archaeology in "Un Peu d'Histoire: Dordogne"; jazz in "Fats Waller"; children and family in "Small Pets," "Four Fish," and "Family Ties"; and so we could go on. The poetry itself is marked by a scrupulous care in the use of language and form, which results in a precision of expression and feeling.

Scupham is keenly aware of our vulnerability, of that incidence of tragedy that lies close to the surface of everyday domestic life: "All this dark humus / A soft compound of shared sufferings. / The earth is knit together with absences" ("At Home"). Life is not without menace even in the nursery, where "the small child tosses. It is not easy / To have wolves wished upon you. / They wait patiently beside the bed" ("Wolves"). His preoccupation with prehistory and the earth's geological and historical past is tied in, for in Scupham's world the sense of a common bond between all humanity, past and present, is never far off; our concerns and fears are shared through the ages. It is a poetry of a committed conscience, deriving depth from a historical perspective where responsibility is everyman's. This is seen clearly in the impressive poem "The Nondescript," which Scupham wrote for Friends of the Earth and in which the use of the first person manages to be strongly impersonal and yet all-embracing—"I am plural. My interests are manifold / I see through many eyes. I am fabulous"—so that the poem manages to address the reader while involving him as a participant in its tragic consequences—"I have prepared a stone inheritance / It flourishes beneath my fertile tears."

Scupham's collection *The Hinterland* marks a movement toward more recent history, and the sonnet sequence that gives the collection its title has as its central theme World War I. The dazzling technical feat of writing fifteen sonnets linked by their first and last lines, with the final sonnet composed of those lines, is such that critics have been beguiled by the quality of the work itself. But the poet has infused his historical perspective with a remarkable emotional immediacy:

Where blood and stone proclaim their unities
Under the topsoil vagaries of green
Works the slow justle of the small debris . . .

He continues the trend in the collections *Summer Palaces* and *Winter Quarters,* and there are splendidly direct and moving poems based on his father-in-law's World War I diaries and his own National Service. The latter collection's wry humor is conveyed in a series of dazzling conceits and metaphors. While it is true that Scupham's poetry can be so loaded with meaning, overtones, and allusions that it reminds one of those great summer bees freighted with rich pollen, he has done the art a service in reminding us that technical excellence and true feeling are not inimical. Indeed, his poetry recalls Jonathan Raban's concept of "The Society of the Poem," and once a reader has entered the world of a Scupham poem and accepted its perceptions and ethos, all falls into place, and the experience becomes profoundly enriching.

In later collections an increased warmth and depth of feeling break through Scupham's formidably meticulous technique. For example, his poem "Cat's Cradle" is so moving that I find it difficult to read without salty eyes. The poem, a small masterpiece, is precisely crafted with an exactness that is a means to an end and not an end in itself:

His face with its sharp look,
    His fur grown stray and dim—
For these long miles of sleep,
    Let the earth cradle him.

Humor comes to the fore too in the remarkable series of parodies in the collection *Out Late*. There is the parody of Robert Frost—

It's not that the way was hard.
    Though the rocks and the boulders there
Had guessed that another yard
    Was a step too hard to bear

—and of John Betjeman-

Blessed bells of Great St Mary's,
    Hunting through the April air,
When He speaks among your tumult,
    Grant my name may find Him there

—where the real humor lies in the exactness of the pastiche. From these poems there emerges not only a poet who demands an awed admiration but also one who can be a friend.

In the 1999 collection *Night Watch* Scupham continues the development of his style, moving from a scrupulously tight formal brilliance to a more relaxed conversational mode. Nevertheless, the reader should not be deceived by this seeming relaxation. There are a remarkable compactness and richness of language in which allusion follows allusion, reference follows reference, ideas bounce off one another, and shards of memory are recovered to build up a cumulative atmosphere and recollection of the past.

It is a world in which language and history are retrieved and "packed up in the old kit-bags" ("Terminus"). In spite of the humor, the atmosphere created is often one of a quiet, contemplative melancholy:

You played in childhood at being dead
and look, it all came true.

The collection contains at least one small poetic masterpiece, "Arras Easter 1998," about the discovery of the bodies of three British soldiers, two identified and one not, who were killed in World War I and who are given long overdue military funerals. Marked by its grim humor, the poem skillfully and sensitively recalls the ethos and the language of the time:

three Fusiliers, two metal dog-tagged,
late, but uncrimed for this last posting;
their taken names and numbers
restored for eighty years good conduct.
One, obstinate in a dumb insolence,

dispersed his syllables about the earth
and, carried in to this assize, must be
sentenced to the usual reprimand—

"The Night Kitchen" is another haunting poem in the collection. The scene superbly set in the opening lines—"Headlamps glancing away from the night ahead / glaze the room over"—it proceeds to pursue its theme of mutability—"Everything that happens happens in passing." Scupham continues to be as accomplished as ever.

—John Cotton

SEDGWICK, Fred

Nationality: British and Irish. **Born:** Dublin, 20 January 1945. **Education:** Various schools in London, 1950–63; St. Luke's College, Exeter, 1965–68, Certificate in Education; Open University, 1970–74, B.A.; University of East Anglia, Norwich, 1982–84, M.A. **Family:** Married Dawn Anne Toft in 1980; one son. **Career:** Teacher in Stevenage and Berkhamsted, Hertfordshire; head teacher, Swing Gate First School, Berkhamsted, 1975–81, Bramford Primary School, Ipswich, 1981–84, and Downing Primary School, Ipswich, 1984–90. Tutor, Open University, 1986–87. In-service education lecturer for local authorities and other organizations. Freelance lecturer and writer, publishing articles on education and other subjects in *The Guardian, The Times Educational Supplement, Art and Craft, Curriculum, Cambridge Journal of Education,* and other publications. **Address:** 52 Melbourne Road, Ipswich, Suffolk IP4 5PP, England.

PUBLICATIONS

Poetry

Really in the Dark. Berkhamsted, Hertfordshire, Priapus, 1976.
The Garden. Hitchin, Hertfordshire, Dodman, 1977.
A Berkhamsted Three, with John Cotton and Freda Downie. Berkhamsted, Hertfordshire, Priapus, 1978.
Details. Oxford, Mid-Day, 1980.
From Another Part of the Island. Berkhamsted, Hertfordshire, Priapus, 1981.
A Garland for William Cowper. Berkhamsted, Hertfordshire, Priapus, 1984.
The Living Daylights. West Kirby, Wirral, Headland, 1986. *Falernian.* Berkhamsted, Hertfordshire, Priapus, 1987.
Hey! (for children), with John Cotton. London, Mary Glasgow, 1990; with *The Biggest Riddle in the World,* as *Two by Two,* 1990.
Lies. Merseyside, Headland, 1991.
Pizza, Curry, Fish and Chips (for children). London, Longman, 1994.
Fifty. Ipswich, James Daniel Daniel John Press, 1995.

Other

Here Comes the Assembly Man: A Year in the Life of a Primary School. Basingstoke, Hampshire, Falmer, 1989.
Lighting Up Time: On Children's Writing. Stowmarket, Suffolk, Triad, 1990.

The Expressive Arts. London, David Fulton, 1993.
Drawing to Learn, with Dawn Sedgwick. London, Hodder and Stoughton, 1993.
Personal, Social, and Moral Education. London, David Fulton, 1994.
Art Across the Curriculum, with Dawn Sedgwick. London, Hodder and Stoughton, 1995.
Read My Mind: Young Children, Poetry, and Learning. London and New York, Routledge, 1997.
Shakespeare and the Young Writer. London and New York, Routledge, 1999.
Thinking about Literacy: Young Children and Their Language. London and New York, Routledge, 1999.

Editor, *This Way That Way: A Collection of Poems for Schools.* London, Mary Glasgow, and New York, McDougal Littel, 1989.
Editor, *Collins Primary Poetry.* London, HarperCollins, 1994.
Editor, *Learning Together: A Practical Guide for Parents,* by Dawn Sedgwick. London, Bloomsbury, 1996.
Editor, *Two by Two: Poems,* by John Cotton. Ipswich, James Daniel Daniel John Press, 1999.

*

Fred Sedgwick comments:

I think of writing as a learning activity: learning about myself, about the world, about the relationship, often dislocated, between the two. I see less and less a real distinction between what I write outside poetry on the one hand—about education, for example, especially children's writing and drawing—and on the other my poems. I think I am more fastidious about my verse, though, putting it through twenty or thirty drafts, discarding more than nine-tenths of what I start.

I seemed at first to be mostly concerned with domestic things, but I always relished telling lies, or making fictions, depending on how you look at it. I have written more political verse, as I have seen the systematic rubbing away of the education service in Britain from uncomfortably close up. I am using rhyme and strict forms more than before.

I do not know who has influenced me, but the poets I admire are Douglas Dunn, Heaney, Larkin, Plath, Auden, Edward Thomas, and Cowper. I write for children, and I am finding less that my work for them is somehow not so important as my mainstream work. Also, many of my poems now seem to have no obvious home as either mainstream or children's. They seem to belong to both.

The worst insult you can offer child or adult is to be dull. I try to avoid that. "For the love of Man and in praise of God" will do for me, as it did for Dylan Thomas.

*   *   *

Fred Sedgwick's earlier poems had the virtues, without the sentimentality, of what was misleadingly called the minimalist school. I say "misleadingly" since I suspect that the superficial, even banal, critical label of minimalist was applied only because the poems were not very long. At their best, in the hands of Ian Hamilton and Hugo Williams, such poems were certainly not minimal in any other sense of the word. Here is Sedgwick's "Details" to show what I mean:

Your clothes are neatly folded, your hair smooth—
even before love you get these details right.

Your arms around my neck, you close your eyes,
moving my body quickly into yours

and wonder why I take your hand, pause,
remove the gold ring, pushing lies
and your marriage just beyond the light,
sadly getting the one false detail right.

While a rather more accomplished poem than many of this genre, it is, more to the point, a poem full of narrative reverberations, overtones, and continuing ripples of meaning, with overlaying touches of angst, *tristesse,* and mutability. If poetry is about condensed language, of setting fuses in the mind, then ''Details'' is a fine example. Technically it is about getting the maximum of power with the minimum of force and the avoidance of pumped-up language. Indeed, the effect of the poem is in indirect ratio to the force used. It is a poetic economy in which words have to earn their place.

As Sedgwick's poetry began to expand both in technique and subject matter, the deep human concern and sense of ever present tragedy continued to illuminate his work. His series of poems about William Cowper are a case in point, where that sad, haunted genius, ever threatened by breakdown and mental and spiritual distress, is a symbol for the human situation, something akin to what is described in Miguel Unamuno's *The Tragic Sense Of Life:*

You know there is a storm behind this quiet.
The first big drops distort your face. You scream.

It is a milieu in which a loved one is addressed with ''This, my hopeless, is where the summer ends'' and in which life and the ghost in the machine that haunts us all are looked at directly and unflinchingly. It is what Thomas Hardy is supposed to have done, where the sentimental exits and concern enters. Yet even the sentimental can serve its turn, as in the poem ''At Exeter St David's''—''And you and I, all Brief Encounter and cheap music''—which concludes, ''It's very nice. But we can't take it home.'' There is the lurking primitive beneath the skin in ''Another Part of the Island''—''gross, and everyday, like death''—or the directly graphic, as in ''The Ballad of Darren Cullen.'' Yet Sedgwick's poetry can be tenderly compassionate, the more obviously so in the poems about the birth and progress of his son Daniel.

In Sedgwick's poetry we encounter not so much the true voice of feeling as the voice of true feeling. It may sometimes seem harsh, but it is the real thing. Nevertheless, it is not a world without humor, and it can laugh at itself, as in ''Love Story'':

The sexual telegrams were tender
But came back stamped RETURN TO SENDER.

In the collection *Lies,* published in 1991, we have the same sharp observation mellowed by Sedgwick's concern for the human condition. There is also sharp literary observation in the series of poems ''The Literary Life,'' with the homages to poets Sedgwick admires adopting the styles of the poets concerned:

The ale is thin, the valley
    We can no longer see
Is scored by car and pylon, not
    The snowy cherry tree.

There also is deeply felt social comment in the series of poems ''National Curriculum.'' It is good to see this humane poet's range and poetic skills widening in *Lies.*

I should not end without mentioning Sedgwick's poetry for young people. He is one of that honorable company of poets, which includes Kit Wright and John Mole, who succeed in writing poetry for children and not the condescendingly comic joke books or the sickeningly sentimental hearts-and-flowers stuff that threatens to replace poetry for youngsters.

—John Cotton

SEIDEL, Frederick (Lewis)

Nationality: American. **Born:** St. Louis, Missouri, 19 February 1936. **Education:** St. Louis Country Day School, 1948–53; Harvard University, Cambridge, Massachusetts, A.B. 1957. **Family:** Married Phyllis Munro Ferguson in 1960 (divorced 1969); one daughter and one son. **Career:** Paris editor, 1960–61, and since 1961 advisory editor, *Paris Review,* Paris and New York. Writer-in-residence, Rutgers University, New Brunswick, New Jersey, 1964. **Awards:** National Endowment for the Arts grant, 1968; *American Poetry Review* prize, 1979; Lamont Poetry Selection award, 1979; National Book Critics Circle award, 1981; Guggenheim fellowship, 1993. **Address:** 251 West 92nd Street, New York, New York 10028, U.S.A.

PUBLICATIONS

Poetry

Final Solutions. New York, Random House, 1963.
Sunrise. New York, Viking Press, 1980.
Men and Women: New and Selected Poems. London, Chatto and Windus, 1984.
These Days: New Poems. New York, Knopf, 1989.
Poems 1959–1979. New York, Knopf, 1989.
My Tokyo: Poems. New York, Farrar Straus, 1993.
Going Fast: Poems. New York, Farrar Straus, 1998.
The Cosmos Poems. New York, Farrar Straus, 2000.

*

Critical Study: ''On Dubie and Seidel'' by Frederick Garber, in *American Poetry Review* (Philadelphia), 11(3), May-June 1982.

*   *   *

Though largely apprentice work, Frederick Seidel's first book, *Final Solutions,* had the distinction of stirring up controversy: an award granted, then denied, and a publication offer withdrawn on the grounds of shocking and possibly libelous content. While it is difficult today to see what was found so objectionable when the book appeared, it is easy to see the promise others noted. The weaknesses of a first book—the reaching after effect, an overreliance on models (especially Robert Lowell)—are balanced by the figurative boldness of Seidel's language, his willingness to take emotional and prosodic risks. Most successful are the poems in the uncluttered confessional mode of Lowell's *Life Studies,* as in this harrowing passage about his mother's lobotomy:

> Tumbling gold whorls of hair shaved back for the incision;
> The skin, as always, Madonna-smooth,
> Without care, below the bandages;
> Greener than ever, her eyes are open—
> "How are you?" she asks, "how *are* you?"
> And starts to smile, and is wheeled past.
> My father's grief-stunned eyes clung to his face like a
>   starfish.

Sunrise, Seidel's second book, appeared seventeen years later. The volume stands out as one of the few attempts to carry forward Lowell's enterprise of forging public poetry out of intensely private material. Now, however, the voice is unmistakably Seidel's: brooding, rosined with liquor, by turns mandarin and hip. In fact, voice is one of the few things that does hold fast. Otherwise, the coordinates shift and dissolve, and the language moves in disturbing circles:

> The tan table of the desert is an empty
> Sunlit plaza by de Chirico
> That has no meaning, that is like the desert
> Rising in the windows of an Astrojet.

This is nowhere more true than in the title poem. In this stream-of-consciousness tour de force of more than 350 lines, impressions break with dizzying speed on the reader, and reference points change as fast as they are registered. The reader must ultimately decide whether the poem, as densely allusive and maddeningly elliptical as *The Cantos,* finally coheres, but the ride through is exhilarating.

The implications of sunrise here and throughout the collection are twofold. In the broadest cultural terms it conjures up the renovative energies of the 1960s that evaporated so quickly in the succeeding decades. At the same time it implies a countermovement—opening one's eyes from youthful, "wish-fulfilling dreams" to behold clearly the limitations of one's self and one's world.

Yet youth and the 1960s for Seidel were not cut of standard cloth. His were spent among glamorous politicians, famous filmmakers and chefs, and rock and art superstars, along with a dusting of nobility. ("Step one," he writes, "is to be rich.") For him the dream of the 1960s began with the inauguration of John Kennedy and ended with the assassination of Robert Kennedy seven years later:

> Shy, compassionate and fierce
> Like a figure out of Yeats;
> The only politician I have loved says *You're dream-*
>   *ing* and says
> *The gun is mightier than the word.*

A poem like "Pressed Duck," in which Seidel describes his circle as "dreaming and innocent, / Like the last Romanovs," raises the question of which side of the barricades he would have been on had there been a revolution. In the same poem he speaks of

> . . . our English clothes
> And Cartier watches, which ten years later shopgirls
> And Bloomingdale's fairies would wear,
> And the people who pronounce chic *chick.*

Elsewhere, Seidel remarks joylessly, "Women won." Yet he stands back from these positions and ironizes them. But he does not condemn them. The willingness to abide moral ambiguity, which marks the book as a genuine work of postmodernism, comes out most remarkably in "Men and Women," his hymn to a championship Italian racing motorcycle. "What definition of beauty," he muses, "can exclude / The MV Agusta racing 500–3, / From the land of Donatello . . . ?" At the same time Seidel's preference for "Jamesian gray" rather than "Jacobean black and white" allows him to see the cultural contradictions the motorcycle embodies. This work of beauty, this "phallus which was musical when it roared," was produced "by the largest helicopter manufacturer in Europe, / whose troop carriers shield junta and emir from harm . . ."

It is tempting to read Seidel's *These Days* as a follow-up volume; even its title suggests an update of sorts. *Sunrise* had closed on two poems about existential dead ends: "The Last Entries in Mayakovsky's Notebook" and "Hart Crane near the End." The new book begins with a funeral, and there is indeed a sense of being addressed from the grave: "I'm typing this with fingers of cold wax." In several poems he imagines himself buried alive in an avalanche: "I move my head from side to side. / I cannot move."

If *Sunrise* evoked the descent of innocence into history, *These Days* portrays posthistorical reality, where "every dawn is Hiroshima." Cultural decline has been overtaken by cosmic entropy: "The universe hung like a flare for a while, and went out." Unfortunately, the same entropy is evident in the poetry. The centrifugal energies of Seidel's imagination previously had been held in check, if only barely, by the harness of stanza and occasional rhyme; his later poems veer between a flatly rhyming formalism and somewhat diffuse, fuguelike improvisations. Nor is there the same attempt to yoke the personal and public. Poems about his school days and adult friends alternate with poems entitled "Empire" and "AIDS Days," yet the two spheres scarcely touch. A characteristic of our times? Perhaps, but Seidel's poetry has suffered by it.

—Martin McKinsey

SEIDMAN, Hugh

Nationality: American. **Born:** Brooklyn, New York, 1 August 1940. **Education:** At the Massachusetts Institute of Technology, Cambridge, 1957–58; Polytechnic Institute of Brooklyn, 1958–61, B.S. 1961; University of Minnesota, Minneapolis, 1961–64, M.S. 1964; Columbia University, New York, 1967–69, M.F.A. 1969. **Family:** Married Jayne Holsinger in 1990. **Career:** Member of the faculty, New School for Social Research, New York, 1976–98. Since 1984 self-employed technical documentation specialist and consultant. Visiting poet or writer, Yale University, New Haven, Connecticut, 1971, 1973, City College of City University of New York, 1972–75, Wilkes College, Wilkes-Barre, Pennsylvania, 1975, Wichita State University, Kansas, 1978, New York State Poets-in-the-Schools, 1978–81, Washington College, Chestertown, Maryland, 1979, University of Wisconsin, Madison, 1981, College of William and Mary, Williamsburg, Virginia, 1982, Columbia University, 1985, and Writer's Voice, New York, 1988. **Awards:** Yale Series of Younger Poets award, 1969; National Endowment for the Arts grant, 1970, and fellowship, 1972, 1985; Creative Artists Public Service grant, 1971; Yaddo fellowship, 1972, 1976, 1988; MacDowell Colony fellowship,

1974, 1975, 1989; *Writer's Digest* prize, 1982; New York Foundation for the Arts poetry grant, 1990. **Address:** 463 West Street, New York, New York 10014, U.S.A.

PUBLICATIONS

Poetry

Collecting Evidence. New Haven, Connecticut, Yale University Press, 1970.
Blood Lord. New York, Doubleday, 1974.
Throne/Falcon/Eye. New York, Random House, 1982.
People Live, They Have Lives. Oxford, Ohio, Miami University Press, 1992.
Selected Poems: 1965–1995. Oxford, Ohio, Miami University Press, 1995.

Recording· *The Ecstasy of Odin's Eye,* Watershed, 1984.

Other

Coeditor, *Westbeth Poets.* New York, Poetry New York, 1971.
Coeditor, *Equal Time.* New York, Equal Time, 1972.

*

Critical Studies: By Peter Davison, in *Atlantic* (New York), January 1971; by Beth Bentley, in *Seattle Times,* 10 January 1971; by Denis Donoghue, in *New York Review of Books,* 16 May 1971; by Rochelle Ratner, in *East Village Other* (New York) 18 May 1971; by Bill Zavatsky, in *New York Times Book Review,* 26 December 1971; by Theodore Enslin, in *Occurrence 3* (Mechanicsburg, Pennsylvania), 1975; by Gary Ross, in *Globe and Mail* (Toronto), 1 February 1975; by John Koethe, in *Parnassus* (New York), spring-summer 1975; by Joseph Parisi, in *Poetry* (Chicago), September 1975; by Michael Heller, in *Granite* (Hanover, New Hampshire), winter 1975–76; by Marilyn Crabtree, in *Kansas City Star,* 27 February 1983; by Richard Tillinghast, in *New York Times Book Review,* 2 May 1983; by Paul Pines, in *American Book Review* (Newark, New Jersey), July-August and September-October 1984; by Louise Glück, in *The Village Voice Literary Supplement* (New York), October 1991; by Keith Tuma, and by Ligero Smith, in *Sulfur* (Ypsilanti, Michigan), spring 1993; by Richard Silberg, in *Poetry Flash* (Berkeley, California), May/June 1993; by Calvin Bedient, in *Poetry* (Chicago), March 1994; by Gerald Burns, in *Another Chicago Magazine* (Chicago), 27, 1994; by Lawrence Joseph, in *American Book Review* (Newark, New Jersey), 1994; by Susan Shapiro, in *St. Petersburg Times* (Florida), April 1995.

Hugh Seidman comments:

One gets up in the morning and goes to the typewriter. And one continues against whatever else.

It is pleasurable to make an object, in this case with words. As the desire to make something implies, coherence is a pressure. I like to think that there is some similarity between solving a problem in mathematics or physics, the two subjects of most of my academic training, and "solving" a poem. However, while a mathematical statement is finally only a relationship between abstract symbols relative to an axiomatic context, in the poem there is the possibility of saying something true, emotionally true. This is because our poems

are smarter than we are no matter how we are ourselves struck into our own ignorance. Though truth may take a lifetime, since one's poems are never more than oneself.

At the risk of sounding ridiculous, I am interested in the ancient tasks of love, death, and rebirth. And in the ongoing tension and paradox of the private heart in the public world. And this is the great excitement, the great adventure. Yet it is also the great risk, for one may fail utterly even if to others hardly a thing seems to be happening one way or the other. Which returns us to the fact that one gets up and still writes, even so, against all that one knows.

And all of this may not be so, yet it is.

(1995)Recent poems have been formed by high contraction, as in

HOW   Keep nothing, nothing left, but a faint breath of
        nothing.

At the same time a feeling of almost physical labor:

BREATH   Bored concrete. Millions of years to drill
          through, though some drove gold chariots.

And outside?

In the media the oral. Readings; performances; slams; subway poems, like ads, like the oral; MTV; compact discs.

Elsewhere, some want common denominator poems; some want nonspeech prime number poems, divisible only by themselves and ONE.

And personally?

When the forces that brought forth the words are no longer forces? Make the telephone book emotional. Take dictation from "any (one or thing)." Nothing to know or learn but this. The séance table lifts; the spirit trumpet speaks; and not by tricks.

Meanwhile, lurking, the orders:

MALIBU, 1976 Tan, bared to the water: courtesan, sexual
        laughter. Crossing the provinces of youth toward the
        hereafter. Or I invent this—but never the roads to that
        capitol.

(2000)SOUND BITE (grrrrrrrrrrrrrrrr!)

Up Bethune, past the supermarket, where the homeless put aluminum cans in plastic sacks. Suddenly, one to another, just as I pass, something like "damn thing makes you go blind—then makes you go deaf trying to hear it." The ear registers the phrasing, though the brain needs time to catch up. And then I'm out of hearing, with no clue on the subject.

If you want, set it up:

Damn thing
Make you blind.
Make you deaf
Trying to hear.

*   *   *

Hugh Seidman's remarkable poems embody the disjunctive music of the present, a music of simultaneous dread and prophecy, of razorlike imagery and asperous beauty. In his first book of poems, *Collecting Evidence,* Seidman laid down for himself the mandate to write of "each grief, each relief / each day and everyday / in consummate craft and artistry." In the following book, *Blood Lord,* and then with *Throne/Falcon/Eye* the mandate seems to have been accomplished in a body of work of extraordinary originality and power.

The first thing to strike the reader of Seidman's poems is what marks them off from the work of his contemporaries. For unlike the bland horizontal mumbling of much contemporary American poetry, Seidman's poems have a calligraphic jaggedness, a capacity, as they work down the page, to inscribe allusively large areas of emotion and complexity. This is shown, for example, in "Zero":

> The unbroken lake creaks
> but a rat snaps in the trap
> and thumb skin cracks and bleeds
>
> And once I jabbed a fish-hole
> and the black birds
> bud oddly on the trees in the furnace cold
>
> And the cloud rim is fire
> and the ice in space freezes harder
> and the astral TV flickers

The world registers on the poet not as a series of mediated images but as acutely sharp and painful arousals, as calls to being of nearly inarticulate body and mind states in which ". . . now I touch myself / like all dumb things at the ice-hole / who do not know why they know."

Central to Seidman's work is a vision of a world in which the cultural artifact, the iconic datum, whether it be high art or high tech or the pop spillage of the media, no longer shines in an exemplary light but instead exhibits with a fascinated horror the very price of its existence. Thus in "Agent Orange," on America's Vietnam experience, every "light has a dark / like the inhaled sun over gunships that stained jungles." The poem makes material that brooding, nightmarish craziness of America in which the astronaut can "leap like a boy with a robot's fervor" and ". . . the night of the high school prom begins / to glow / like a vast angel in a coma . . ."

In such poems Seidman is both willing and able to draw on the resonances of tradition, to play off the dancing syllables of the Metaphysicals, for example, not only for effect but also for humor. His use of the traditional sounding line often becomes an instrument of black comedy, of a childlike rhythmical analogue, as in "Newton" from *Blood Lord:*

> Newton, praise Newton, his tree
> the apple is free . . .
>
> Nipple hairs tickle Newton's nose
> he feasts on cheese of toe, he cries
> Hosanna to the head

In "Couplets" from *Throne/Falcon/Eye,* a mock-heroic poem of failed love that runs together current politics, W.C. Fields, and Fidel Castro in its meditations, we are told,

> The moral was too banal that we quarrelled
> like the mainland and the island . . .
>
> And below the stars I miss you in my bed
> Till the sun comes like a warhead

> Like love that flares to solitude
> beyond the evil and the good

A mysterious and enigmatic dimension of Seidman's work is shown in the poems that allegorize the materials of Egyptian mythology, in particular Isis and the cult of the dead. These poems, even as they obliquely refer to the moral and existential dilemmas of the present, most nearly resemble a form of pure poetry or the inverted symbology of a Nerval. They are at once gorgeous in tone and impenetrable, as though structured in a time warp or black hole in which history and poetry are boiling at a critical mass, as in these stunning lines from "Hymn":

> As all are commanded to yield like the mummy when the
>   dung beetle rolls the sun
> before all the befores of the trillion nights past night
>   and day
> though I knew that the broken receding mouth of
>   the Sphinx had nothing to add
> of resurrection in the history of its grimace.

The ambitiousness of such poetry, with its wide range of subjects that includes culture, parents, and sociopolitical arenas, is matched by Seidman's impeccable ear and craft. In his poems one overhears not only a formal cleanliness of language but also a reach for larger intercommunicative ironies, for strategies by which the poem can break with the solipsism of modern verse and enter into meaningful dialogue with the world.

Such poetry is difficult and unsettling, for in a time of transposed and debased values poetry, too, must be transposed if it is to touch the modern reader. Thus, the muse in the poem "Muse" is invoked only to hail:

> Ah, good-by!
>
> Now you are like the ideal of a shadow
> like the blank metals of the dark that long to be struck
> into the coins of light

In its scale of poetic values and tones, Seidman's work incarnates a density of language and a corrosive beauty found in few modern poets in English.

Seidman's later work in *People Live, They Have Lives* and in the nearly book-length selection that concludes *Selected Poems: 1965–1995* are marked by extreme condensation and heightened musicality. They show a paring away of excess and inaccuracy until the rhythmic and denotative modes of the poem are made to coincide. This stripped-down language is well suited to invoking a dark and yet visionary measure of modern urban life, as in these lines from "E Train-8:32 AM":

> . . . And the black messenger sleeps,
> his bird's head on his chest.
> And the blond with her child sleeps,
> sitting up as we bore through the dark.
>
> For now labor must be done
> by the poor from the planets of sleep,
> from the dust blown over the statues
> to the hard terrains and facades.

But the same compression can also yield a plaintive sweetness, as in the title poem of *People Live, They Have Lives:*

> He cries to the vulnerable sun
> and the lost moon—which turn
> and turn over France
> where no parent has ever been.

Seidman's late poems, which are among his finest, so actively court brevity and silence that they are almost typographical doorways into invisibility. In ''Lift Off'' the poet meditates on his deceased parents:

> Father thought and thought.
> Mother eyes white
> ignition.

Poems like these owe as much to the epigram or Zen koan as to the modern image. Rather than presenting a picture on the page, they provoke the reader's mind to yield to the space of contemplation, to consider the nearly hidden realms of being that lie parallel to the plane of our verbalizations, as in ''End'':

> Thoughtless, we think: what is will be.

> What lives in our acts?
> Shock of touch, sky awe, dream, chromosome.

> Each gas, isotope, metal that grieves,
> like whatever it is that thinks.

Seidman's impressive body of work is a complex and thoroughly original contribution to contemporary American poetry.

—Michael Heller

SENIOR, Olive (Marjorie)

Nationality: Jamaican (immigrated to Canada in 1991). **Born:** Jamaica, 23 December 1941. **Education:** Carleton University, Ottawa, 1963–67, B.S. 1967. **Career:** Reporter and sub-editor, *Daily Gleaner* newspaper, Jamaica; information officer, Jamaica Information Service, 1967–69; public relations officer, Jamaica Chamber of Commerce and editor, *JCC Journal,* 1969–71; publications editor, Institute of Social and Economic Research, University of the West Indies, Jamaica, and editor, *Social and Economic Studies,* 1972–77; freelance writer and researcher, part-time teacher in communications, publishing consultant, and speech writer, Jamaica, 1977–82; managing editor, Institute of Jamaica Publications, and editor, *Jamaica Journal,* 1982–89; freelance teacher, writer, lecturer, internationally, 1989–94; visiting lecturer/writer-in-residence, University of the West Indies, Cave Hill, Barbados, 1990. Director of Fiction Workshop, Caribbean Writers Summer Institute, University of Miami, Florida, 1994, 1995. Dana Visiting Professor of creative writing, St. Lawrence University, Canton, New York, 1994–95. **Awards:** Commonwealth Writers' prize, 1967; Gold, Silver, and Bronze medals for poetry and fiction, Jamaica Festival Literary Competitions, 1968–70; Winner in two categories, Longman International Year of the Child Short Story

Competition, 1978; Institute of Jamaica Centenary medal for creative writing, 1979; UNESCO award for study in the Philippines, 1987; Jamaica Press Association award for editorial excellence, 1987; United States Information Service, International Visitor award, 1988; Institute of Jamaica, Silver Musgrave medal for literature, 1989; F.G. Bressani Literary prize for poetry, 1994, for *Gardening in the Tropics.* Hawthornden fellow, Scotland, 1990; International Writer-in-Residence, Arts Council of England, 1991. **Agent:** Nicole Aragi, Watkins/Loomis Agency, 133 East 35th Street, Suite 1, New York, New York 10016, U.S.A.

PUBLICATIONS

Poetry

Talking of Trees. Kingston, Calabash, 1986.
Gardening in the Tropics. Toronto, McClelland and Stewart, 1994.

Short Stories

Summer Lightning. London, Longman, 1987.
Arrival of the Snake-Woman. London, Longman, 1989.
Quartet, with others. London, Longman, 1994.
Discerner of Hearts. Toronto, McClelland and Stewart, 1995.

Other

The Message Is Change. Kingston, Jamaica, Kingston Publishers, 1972.
Pop Story Gi Mi (four booklets on Jamaican heritage for schools). Kingston, Ministry of Education, 1973.
A-Z of Jamaican Heritage. Kingston, Heinemann and Gleaner Company Ltd., 1984.
Working Miracles: Women's Lives in the English-Speaking Caribbean. London, James Currey, and Bloomington, Indiana University Press, 1991.

Editor, *The Journey Prize Anthology: Short Fiction from the Best of Canada's New Writers.* Toronto, McClelland and Stewart, 1996.
Editor, *Jamaica: Portraits, 1955–1998,* by Maria LaYacona. Marco Island, Florida, Marco Press, 1998.
Editor, *Go Tell It on the Mountain: And Related Readings,* by James Baldwin. Evanston, Illinois, McDougal Littell, 1998.

*

Critical Studies: Olive Senior issue of *Callalloo* (Baltimore), 11(3), summer 1988; in *Critical Strategies* by Malcolm Kinnery and Michael Rose, Boston, Bedford Books/St. Martin's Press, 1989; in *Out of the Kumbla: Caribbean Women and Literature,* edited by Carole Boyce Davies and Elaine Savory Fido, New York, Africa World Press, 1990; in *Caribbean Women Writers,* edited by Selwyn Cudje, Wellesley, Massachusetts, Calaloux Publications, 1990; in *Motherlands: Black Women's Writing from Africa, the Caribbean and South Asia,* edited by Susheila Nasta, London, The Women's Press, 1991; in *The Bloomsbury Guide to Women's Literature,* edited by Claire Buck, New York, Prentice Hall, 1992; in *Come Back to Me My Language: Poetry and the West Indies* by J.E. Chamberlin, Champaign, University of Illinois Press, 1993; in *Woman Version:*

Theoretical Approaches to West Indian Fiction by Women by Evelyn O'Callaghan, London, Macmillan, 1993; "The Fiction of Olive Senior" by Richard F. Patteson, in *Ariel, A Review of International English Literature* (Calgary, Alberta), 24(1), January 1993; "Jamaica in the Fiction of Olive Senior" by Mary Conde, in *Swansea Review,* 1994; "'Mixed Worlds': Olive Senior's Summer Lightning" by John Thieme, in *Kunapipi* (Aarhus, Denmark), 16(2), 1994; "The East Indian Presence in Jamaican Literature: With Reference to 'The Arrival of the Snake Woman' by Olive Senior" by Velma Pollard, in *Encountering the Other(s): Studies in Literature, History, and Culture,* edited by Gisela Brinkler-Gabler, Albany, State University of New York Press, 1995; interview with Wolfgang Binder, in *Commonwealth Essays and Studies* (Dijon, France), 18(1), autumn 1995; "Talking of Households: Olive Senior's Postcolonial Identities" by Mrak Beittel and Giovanna Covi, in *Nationalism vs. Internationalism: (Inter)National Dimensions of Literatures in English,* edited by Wolfgang Zach and Ken Goodwin, Tubingen, Germany, Stauffenburg, 1996; "Registering Woman: Senior's Zig-Zag Discourse and Code-Switching in Jamaican Narrative" by Barbara Lalla, in *ARIEL* (Canada), 29(4), October 1998.

*   *   *

In a headnote to the last section of her first book, *Talking of Trees*, Olive Senior quotes Bertolt Brecht: "What kind of period is it when to talk of trees is almost a crime because it implies silence about so many horrors?" Senior, as if to answer Brecht, writes serious and noisy poems about the natural world while little ignoring the horrors of Jamaica's colonial history. In the long title poem she writes,

> Our roots tied up the harbour
> Mangroves of resistance.

In this and other poems Senior locates Jamaica's political history in its botanical one, drawing on the historical fact that Jamaica was colonized and peopled with slaves because of its agricultural importance:

> Cane trash mi life
> Cane break mi spirit
> Cane sweeten mi bizzie
> Banana rotten mi clothes

Senior's second book, *Gardening in the Tropics,* contains a sequence of twelve poems that begin with the title phrase. But the most powerful poem of the collection may be her "Meditation on Yellow," which examines the meaning of the color in both its aesthetic and political senses. The poem is addressed to (one assumes white) tourists who are served their tea at three in the afternoon by black waiters. It begins with an apology of sorts for the blackness of the toast and the waiter's skin but then becomes a litany of angry explanation:

> but I've been travelling long
> cross the sea in the sun-hot
> I've been slaving in the cane rows
> for your sugar
> I've been ripening coffee beans
> for your morning break

The list goes on to include bananas, oranges, ginger, cocoa, and aluminum, all of which the speaker has been growing or mining from the land.

Senior recognizes that the system of colonization she so aptly describes is not limited to physical labor but also manifests itself in the educational system and in the English language itself. She addresses the issue of language in "Pineapple":

> With yayama
> fruit of the Antilles,
> we welcomed you
> to our shores,
> not knowing in
> your language
> "house warming"
> meant "to take
> possession of" and "host"
> could so easily turn hostage.

The educational system refuses to recognize the landscape in which it operates. In "Colonial Girls School" Senior writes about the "borrowed images" that "willed our skins pale" and "yoked our minds to declensions in Latin / and the language of Shakespeare." This system "told us nothing about ourselves . . . / There was nothing of our landscape there / Nothing about us at all." Like her fellow Caribbean poet Derek Walcott, however, Senior writes mostly in the Standard English of her education, even as she makes her central subject the landscape and her gardening and writing, which she obviously intends to link metaphorically.

Senior also explores the ways in which the assumptions enforced by the educational system are internalized by the family. (It is difficult to label any of her poems autobiographical, since her strongest form is dramatic monologue and she is often obviously not writing as herself.) In "Cockpit Country Dreams" the speaker quotes her mother, who had forced her to choose only one of the family's histories as her own:

> Listen child, said my mother
> whose hands plundered photo albums
> of all black ancestors: Herein
> your ancestry, your imagery, your pride.
> Choose this river, this rhythm, this road.
> Walk good in the footsteps of these fathers.

It is interesting that the last line contains a grammatical flaw assigned to the mother. It is as if her origins, likely in patois, cannot be hidden even as she tries hard not to reveal them. At her best Senior turns this contrast on its head, exploring the strengths of her place and her writing of it. In "Gardening on the Run" she again conflates the acts of writing and gardening:

> We are always there
> like some dark stain in your
> diaries and notebooks, your
> letters, your court records,
> your law books—as if we had
> ambushed your pen. Now I have
> time to read (and garden), I who
> spent so many years in disquiet,

living in fear of discovering,
am amazed to discover, Colonist,
it was you who feared me.

The poet's act of discovering her origins in the natural and historical worlds thus reverses that of Columbus discovering the New World. It proves liberating to Senior, however, as a gardener and, more importantly, as a poet.

—Susan M. Schultz

SEPAMLA, (Sydney) Sipho

Nationality: South African. **Born:** Johannesburg, 1932. **Career:** Trained as a teacher and taught in secondary schools. Personnel officer for company in East Rand. Editor, *New Classic* and *S'ketsh!* magazines. **Address:** c/o Fuba Academy, P.O. Box 4202, Johannesburg 2000, South Africa.

PUBLICATIONS

Poetry

Hurry Up to It! Johannesburg, Donker, 1975.
The Blues Is You in Me. Johannesburg, Donker, 1976.
The Soweto I Love. Cape Town, Philip, London, Rex Collings, and
     Washington, D.C., Three Continents Press, 1977.
Children of the Earth. Johannesburg, Donker, 1983.
Selected Poems, edited by Mbulelo Vizikhungo Mzamane. Johannes-
     burg, Donker, 1984.
From Goré to Soweto. Johannesburg, Skotaville Publishers, 1988.
Rainbow Journey. Florida Hills, South Africa, Vivlia, 1996.

Novels

The Root Is One. London, Rex Collings, 1979.
A Ride on the Whirlwind. Johannesburg, Donker, 1981; London,
     Heinemann, 1984.
Third Generation. Johannesburg, Skotaville, 1986.
Scattered Survival. Johannesburg, Skotaville, 1988.

*

Critical Studies: ''Sipho Sepamla: Spirit Which Refuses to Die'' by Stephen Gray, in *Index on Censorship* (London), 7(1), 1978; ''Sipho Sepamla, The Soweto I Love'' by Vernie February, in *African Literature Today* (Freetown, Sierra Leone), 10, 1979; ''The Price of Being a Writer'' by Mark Ralph-Bowman, in *Index on Censorship* (London), 11(4), August 1982; ''Black Consciousness in East and South African Poetry: Unity and Divergence in the Poetry of Taban Lo Liyong and Sipho Sepamla'' by Ezenwa-Ohaeto, in *Presence Africaine* (Paris), 140, 1986; ''The Days of Power: Depictions of Politics and Community in Four Recent South African Novels'' by Kelwyn Sole, in *Research in African Literatures* (Bloomington, Indiana), 19(1), spring 1988; ''Fictionalization, Conscientization and

the Trope of Exile in Amandla and Third Generation'' by Johan Geertsema, in *Literator* (South Africa), 14(3), November 1993; *Riot: Episodes of Racialized Violence in African and African American Culture* (dissertation) by Sheila Smith McKoy, Duke University, 1994.

*   *   *

Sipho Sepamla and Mongane Wally Serote are the two poets who started the black poetry revival in the 1970s in South Africa. They centered their poetry around life in the townships and expressed the anger and frustration of the urban, educated black, increasingly hemmed in and thwarted by the apartheid state. Both were influenced by the black consciousness movement and the new resulting self-awareness and sense of value. Sepamla is a case of a peace-loving man imbued with a generous love for humankind and a natural inclination toward gradualism, persuasion rather than violence, antiracism, and belief in the values of education and art but who is pushed into bitterness, hatred, and an increasingly radical form of protest. In his first collection, *Hurry Up to It!,* he uses humor and irony as weapons of protest, and they give the poetry an essentially private dimension despite the public nature of the subject of apartheid. An example of this is ''To Whom It May Concern,'' in which Sepamla uses apartheid officialese to criticize the inhumanity of the system:

Please note
The remains of R/N 417181
Will be laid to rest in peace
On a plot
set aside for Methodist Xhosas

Such irony is always in danger of souring into bitterness under the impact of the gross injustices of the system, something Sepamla is aware of and tries to fight. In the poem ''Nibblings'' he expresses hate for lies, bitterness, blacks who hate whites, white liberals, and people who admire him because of his education, but he is basically ''in love with mankind.'' Despite bitter poems like ''The Applicant,'' his first collection is lighter in tone than the following volumes.

The Blues Is You in Me came out in the year of the Soweto uprising, and the theme of political protest is prevalent. A poem like ''I Remember Sharpeville'' is in the mold of the classic protest poem. Dedicated to ''our dead heroes,'' it tells the story of the uprising, describes the anger and the shame at the burial of the victims, and vows to remember their names. The language has changed from private imagery to public rhetoric, and the poet uses organic imagery to convey the strength of the uprising:

like a sponge
it sucked into its core
the aged and the young . . .
it rolled over
crushing the cream
and the scum of its make-up
into a solid compound
of black oozing energy.

The more sinister aspects of the oppression are discussed in terms of silence, both a reality and an apt metaphor for a poet's greatest fear. In ''Silence'' the poet protests against enforced silence, banning, and jail (''don't kill me with silence''), and in ''Silence: 2'' the silence of jail is compounded with that of despair (''a silence I fear''). Finally, in ''Double Talk,'' a poem about broken promises of improved conditions, there is ''a huge enforced silence, but nodding of heads.''

Although living in a deteriorating political climate, Sepamla continues to express his basic wish to live and love and not to be forced to feel bitter and humiliated, something that can be seen in poems like ''The Ash Urns'' and ''The Love I Know.'' There is even room for one nonpolitical, lighthearted occasional poem, ''The Peach Tree,'' which incidentally highlights deprivation by indicating the vast areas of experience that are eclipsed by the cruelty of the system and the necessity of fighting it. In the same vein the poet feels guilty about not taking an active enough part in the uprising, as in poems like ''Tried to Say'' and ''Reaching Out,'' in which he wishes that he could be ''without apologies and unsaid insanities.''

A final theme, which points forward to the following collection, is township life, a celebration of survival skills outside white law in poems like ''Statement: the Dodger,'' ''Zoom,'' and ''The Kwela-Kwela,'' which tells the story of a boy on false crutches. The form of the poetry varies with the content, but it is all free verse and saturated with jazz rhythms, often syncopated, which lend a sense of urgency.

The Soweto I Love continues the themes of the previous collections but also expresses the new awareness and, even more radically, the altered state of being of the post-Soweto era. The poem ''At the Dawn of Another Day'' exemplifies this ontological change, with the refrain ''give me this day myself'' seen as the result of the new order. Children are taking the lead and telling their parents what to do, and students are leading the community. The last illusions about peaceful solutions and the good intentions of the system have been broken, naked violence has erupted, and a new order of consciousness has been born, carrying the poet along with it. The radicalization in this volume of what had been essentially moderate views is seen to be a result of the excessive violence of the system in putting down the uprising. Poems like ''A Child Dies'' describe the brutality: ''he was pounded and pounded / with a gun but . . . we buried the mess another day.'' Torture and murder have become part of the poet's daily reality and, in poems like ''How a Brother Died,'' his poetic vocabulary, and he monitors his own change. In ''The Late, Late Show'' he rejects all attempts at conciliation and declares, ''I can feel my grin turn to a grimace / my patience has been wearing thin.''

Sepamla's new sense of defiance is expressed in a series of confrontations with the system under its various guises. These confrontations are not violent, for the poet is not a revolutionary hero, but he is registering the new mood made possible by the schoolchildren fighting in the streets. In ''On Judgement Day'' he rejects the stereotyping of blacks as ''singers, runners and peace lovers.'' As there are only dirges to sing and no peace to love, the long and cherished tradition of peaceful resistance must be abandoned. In ''Measure for Measure'' he further distances himself from the white images of blacks:

> calculate the size of house you think is good for me
> and ensure the shape suits tribal taste . . .
> and when all that is done
> let me tell you this
> you'll never know how far I stand from you.

This defiance is hard-won, for through his education Sepamla has been exposed to a Western value system, which he cannot deny and which still informs most of his poetry. The radicalization of a basically moderate poet like Sepamla is an indication of the state of affairs under apartheid in South Africa.

—Kirsten Holst Petersen

SEROTE, Mongane Wally

Nationality: South African. **Born:** Johannesburg, 8 May 1944. **Education:** Sacred Heart High School, Leribe, Lesotho; Morris Isaacson High School, Soweto; Columbia University, New York, M.F.A. 1979. **Family:** Married Pethu Serote. **Career:** Former copywriter for advertising company, Johannesburg; staff member, Medu Arts Ensemble, Gaborone, Botswana. Since 1986 cultural attaché, Department of Arts and Culture, African National Congress, London. Imprisoned under terrorism act, 1969–70. **Awards:** Ingrid Jonker prize, 1973; Fulbright scholarship. **Agent:** Jane Gregory Agency, Riverside Studios, Crisp Road, Hammersmith, London W6 9RL. **Address:** 28 Penton Street, P.O. Box 38, London N1 9PR, England.

PUBLICATIONS

Poetry

Yakhal'inkomo. Johannesburg, Renoster, 1972.
Tsetlo. Johannesburg, Donker, 1974.
No Baby Must Weep. Johannesburg, Donker, 1975.
Behold Mama, Flowers. Johannesburg, Donker, 1978.
The Night Keeps Winking. Gaborne, Botswana, Medu Art Ensemble, 1982.
Selected Poems, edited by Mbulelo Vizikhungo Mzamane. Johannesburg, Donker, 1982.
A Tough Tale. London, Kliptown, 1987.
Third World Express. Cape Town, D. Philip, 1992.
Come and Hope with Me. Cape Town, D. Philip, 1994.
Freedom Lament and Song. Cape Town, D. Philip, 1997.

Novel

To Every Birth Its Blood. Johannesburg, Ravan Press, 1981; London, Heinemann, 1983; New York, Thunder's Mouth Press, 1989.

Other

On the Horizon. Fordsburg, South Africa, Congress of South African Writers, 1990.
Gods of Our Time. Randburg, South Africa, Ravan Press, 1999.

*

Critical Studies: ''Towards a Survey: A Reflection on South African Poetry'' by Cosmo Pieterse, in *Culture in Another South Africa,* edited by Willem Campscreur and Joost Divendal, New York, Olive Branch, 1989; ''An Author's Agenda (2)'' by the author, in *Southern African Review of Books,* 3(3–4), February-May 1990; *Orpheus in Africa: Fragmentation and Renewal in the Work of Four African*

Writers by Jane Wilkinson, Rome, Bulzoni Editore, 1990; ''Negotiating Poetry: A New Poetry for a New South Africa'' by Colin Gardner, in *Theoria* (Natal, South Africa), 77, May 1991; ''Black Man's Burden: A Conversation with Mongane Wally Serote'' by Andrew McCord, in *Transition,* 61, 1993; ''Stoking the Third World Express: The Politics of Cultural Transformation'' by Jean-Philippe Wade, in *English in Africa* (South Africa), 20(1), May 1993; ''Waiting for the Children: Coetzee and Serote across Cultural Barriers'' by Andre Viola, in *Nationalism vs. Internationalism: (Inter)National Dimensions of Literatures in English,* edited by Wolfgang Zach and Ken Goodwin, Tubingen, Germany, Stauffenburg, 1996; interview with Rolf Solberg, in *Writing South Africa: Literature, Apartheid, and Democracy, 1970–1995,* edited by Derek Attridge and Rosemary Jolly, Cambridge, England, Cambridge University Press, 1998.

Mongane Wally Serote comments:

I am primarily known as a poet. I have, though, written short stories, a novel, and plays and am preparing a manuscript of essays on culture.

* * *

Mongane Wally Serote is perhaps the foremost black South African poet of his generation, and throughout his career his poetry has consistently been a political, committed, liberation poetry. According to Serote, any writer, but especially one in a country such as South Africa, cannot separate writing from the political and cultural situation in which he or she writes. As Serote said in 1990 in the *Southern African Review of Books,*

What is the role of writing in overcoming ignorance? . . . Writing, which is a segment of culture which is life itself, cannot be divorced from economics or politics. It is how societies are organized that says how they will eradicate ignorance. It is for all these issues . . . that I can say that the first commitment of any writer is to politics; the second, which makes the writer, is in writing.

In South Africa's ''anti-life culture'' of apartheid, the role of the poet, particularly the black poet, was that of freedom fighter. Writing in English, a language for black South Africans that both represents colonialism and oppression and marks its difference from the oppressors' tongue, Afrikaans, Serote created a poetry of protest and of hope, but his writing primarily documented the suffering, hope, and struggle of his people. It was populist, accessible, and oral in mode. (Much protest writing in South Africa must be performed orally, for the adult population is about 50 percent illiterate, thus the prevalence of drama and poetry as forms of literature and oratory.) But it was nevertheless not simple, being rich in allusion, imagery, and metaphor. Like much contemporary poetry in South Africa, as Cosmo Pieterse has said, ''the lexicon of [Serote's] poetry is the experience of pain . . . Its vocabulary is militant but not militaristic, its diction various, as that of its tonalities . . . vibrate on many levels: the poem-song involves us in pain and tragedy and asks us to re-evaluate our history and our existence.'' Poems such as ''Prelude'' demonstrate his keen awareness of the contested position of writing in such cultural struggle, even as it documents his commitment:

When i take a pen,
my soul bursts to deface the paper

pus spills—
spreads
deforming a line into a figure that violates my love,
when i take a pen,
my crimson heart oozes into the ink,
dilutes it
spreads the gem of my life
makes the word i utter a gasp to the world—
my mother, when i dance your eyes won't keep pace
look into my eyes,
there, the story of my day is told.

As in much of Serote's other poetry, this poem is made up of short bursts of words and speech and of powerful, evocative metaphors. As Pieterse suggests, Serote's poetry is song. Serote relies on the rhythms and structures of song—repetition, brevity, powerful images—to create a sustained emotional intensity that pervades all of his work. Critics of Serote's work have pointed to his innovative poetic craftsmanship, often ignoring the African sources of the poetry, as Mbulelo Vizikhungo Mzamane suggests in his introduction to Serote's *Selected Poems:*

. . . making-by-naming is not an invention of a new poetic device but the use of traditional oral modes and indigenous forms of expression—which may sound ''new'' and ''fresh'' to those who are not intimately acquainted with the traditional culture and languages—but which are, in fact, the authentic evocation of the social and cultural milieu.

Serote's use of a vocabulary and syntax ''genuinely shaped by black urban life in South Africa'' and of township colloquialisms and clichés is, then, not so much innovative as hybrid, both documenting and ironically commenting on the position of the community for and to which he writes. Mzamane explains that

. . . he can also cultivate an artistic detachment through the use of expressions that are deadpan, which . . . bring out most effectively the callousness and the insensitivity of the people . . . [and] in a manner which never detracts from the gravity of the situation evoked . . . the simplicity and effective tone of his language . . . are intended to make his appeal to the black community as broadly based as possible.

Of the many European and African forms that blend in Serote's poetry the elegy and the African panegyric form are perhaps the most prominent. Poetry about place especially uses the devices of repetition and invocation to provide an almost incantatory power. Serote's Alexandra poems and his ''City Johannesburg'' are perhaps the best examples:

This way I salute you:
My hand pulsates to my back trousers pocket
Or into my inner jacket pocket
For my pass, my life,
Jo'burg City,
My hand like a starved snake rears my pockets
For my thin, ever lean wallet,
While my stomach groans a friendly smile to hunger,
Jo'burg City

My stomach also devours coppers and papers
Don't you know?
Jo'burg City, I salute you;
. . .

That, that is all you need of me,
Jo'burg City, Johannesburg
. . .

Jo'burg City, you are dry like death,
Jo'burg City, Johannesburg, Jo'burg City.

A short poem such as "For Don M.—Banned" uses repetition and consonance to a different effect. Certainly the significances of "white" in this poem, as well as the metonyms for imprisonment, demonstrate how inextricably Serote's writing is wedded to the South African context, and the poem also resonates with the sense of political hope for and the inevitability of liberation that later became pronounced in his poetry. (It is worthwhile noting, too, that this poem is the allusion in André Brink's novel *A Dry White Season*):

it is a dry white season
dark leaves don't last, their brief lives dry out
and with a broken heart they dive down gently headed for
    the earth,
not even bleeding.
it is a dry white season brother,
only the trees know the pain as they still stand erect
dry like steel, their branches dry like wire,
indeed, it is a dry white season
but seasons come to pass.

If there is a political movement or progression in Serote's poetry, it has been toward a more radical and optimistic view of the possibilities for black South Africa. Strongly informed, as Mzamane suggests, by the black consciousness movement, Serote's poetry moves from concern with and addresses to the white community, as in the poem "The Actual Dialogue," to a complete commitment to and involvement with his own community. Serote's epic poems, in particular, manifest this trend in his work, their length allowing him to combine many of his characteristic concerns, styles, and devices. *No Baby Must Weep; Behold Mama, Flowers;* and *A Tough Tale* are by turns meditative, autobiographical, and hortatory, the first in particular being a sustained treatment of the role that women, especially in their role as mothers, have had to play in the struggle in South Africa. Mzamane comments,

. . . in some of these poems he conceives of Black women—downtrodden and degraded yet long-suffering and dignified—as being the vanguard of the Black people's struggle for liberation . . . The effect of these poems is to explode the myth that women in traditional society are passive and subservient, by showing their crucial role in sustaining life, ensuring social stability and effecting change.

There are occasions when Serote's depiction of women reverts to stereotype and other uncomfortable images, in "Alexandra," for instance, where the metaphor of the town as a woman elides the lived oppression of black women. Throughout most of his work, however, he celebrates and mourns women's position respectfully and sincerely. *No Baby Must Weep* opens with an address to the mother

figure—"let me hold your hand / black mother let me hold your hand and walk with you"—moves to an address to the speaker's actual mother from childhood—"mama / you know you never let me become a caddie / or a garden-boy / let's stop here a little mama"—and then speaks from adulthood:

i'm hurt mama
my heart bleeds like the pouring sky
and my pores squeeze droplets out
alas
i wish to stop weeping
but mama
you in your hope as fat as your breast
fed me with the mild milk
you put me on your lap of hope
me a load on your back
I'm hurt mama,
my heart is a wound leaping pain like flames
I'm frightened of death
because i have never lived
mama
you grew a hollow and named it me

The poem then leaves the mother to address the mother country, Africa—"i / i am the son of this earth / . . . / let my hand go now my mama / leave me here in the street this dirty dusty muddy street /leave me here / alone in the minute of my moment"—and finally comes to rest at home—"ah / africa / is this not your child come home."

Serote has also devoted a considerable amount of his writing to the victims of apartheid, to those who were banned, tortured, and imprisoned, as well as to another representative group, children. These poems are often the focal points for his horror and outrage. Thus, "Child of the Song" assaults any sense of complacency:

yes, the day was not ours nor the night
remember how someone's baby rushed out of the
    tenth floor
and crushed on the tar
his blood splashing on the flower petals in the garden
so you heard the laughter of the law
what will you say to your son
mourn?

But children also become the hope for the future. Indeed, Serote figures all black South Africans to be "children of Soweto," and in "The Breezing Dawn of the New Day" he suggests that "yet some day has gone and left some children here / who ask and ask and so teach us how to talk and fix an eye on any other eye." In this context the Afrikaners' self-appellation as the chosen people, "god's children," is bitterly ironic—"did you hear / how some people, god's children, talk / about us"—and Serote indicates black Africans' determination to talk back and reclaim their history for their children's future:

we sing here, for we can sing still, about our national life
a life
which must grow now
like a child
a child looked after and taught well

that is our future,
we keep the record
. . .
and some child somewhere in the mist of this death
   will know
the breezing dawn of the new day—
they will put brick on brick
and build, a new country.

As the title of this poem and the subsequent long poem "There Will Be a Better Time" suggest, Serote's increasing militancy also evolved into an apocalyptic vision, a hopeful one, of the political future for South African blacks. "There Will Be a Better Time" is adamant in its denial of the situation under apartheid—"no we say / no we say in one voice / no more we say / no more of the bad time"— and concludes by avowing a better future—"ah / there *will* be a better time made by us." This is not to suggest, however, that the anger and intensity of Serote's poetry has dwindled completely or that his commitment to documenting the suffering of his community has lessened. His long poem *A Tough Tale* holds both directions in tension:

Then, I must admit—our sorrow is as red as blood
the silence comes
the quietness holds us, with its chill
it cuts then, painfully, between the mind and heart
. . .
They come young
motherless
they speak of rubber bullets and birdshots
they speak of young fresh blood spilled in the streets
these children of a restless hour.

Serote, however, ultimately refuses the despair that filled some of his earlier poetry: "This is not and must not be a sad tale / it cannot be." He imagines his country's future in a way that reflects back on his love for South Africa and for his art: "we know all this and more / and yet this time asks: *really?* / yes we do / for our future is a poem which says so."

—Aruna Srivastava

SETH, Vikram

Nationality: Indian. **Born:** Calcutta, 20 June 1952. **Education:** Corpus Christi College, Oxford, B.A. (honors) 1975, and M.A. (honors) 1978, in philosophy, politics, and economics; Stanford University, California, M.A. in economics 1979; Nanjing University, China, 1980–82, university diploma. **Career:** Senior editor, Stanford University Press, 1985–86. **Awards:** Thomas Cook Travel Book award, 1983; Ingram Merrill fellowship, 1985–86; Guggenheim fellowship, 1986–87; Commonwealth poetry prize, 1986; Sahitya Academy award, 1988; W.H. Smith award, 1994, for *A Suitable Boy*. **Agent:** Giles Gordon, Anthony Sheil Associates, 43 Doughty Street, London WC1N 2LF, England; or Irene Skolnick Agency, 121 West 27th Street, Suite 601, New York, New York 10001, U.S.A. **Address:** c/o HarperCollins, 10 East 53ʳᵈ Street, New York, New York 10022–5244, U.S.A.

PUBLICATIONS

Poetry

Mappings. Calcutta, Writers Workshop, 1981.
The Humble Administrator's Garden. Manchester, Carcanet, 1985.
All You Who Sleep Tonight. New Delhi, Penguin, New York, Knopf, and London, Faber, 1990.
Beastly Tales from Here and There, illustrated by Ravi Shankar. New Delhi and New York, Viking, 1992.
The Poems, 1981–1994. New York, Penguin, 1995.

Novels

The Golden Gate: A Novel in Verse. New York, Random House, and London, Faber, 1986.
A Suitable Boy. New York, HarperCollins, and London, Phoenix, 1993.

Other

From Heaven Lake: Travels through Sinkiang and Tibet. London, Chatto and Windus, 1983; New York, Vintage, 1987.
Arion and the Dolphin: A Libretto. New Delhi and New York, Penguin Books, 1994.
Arion and the Dolphin (for children), illustrated by Jane Ray. London, Orion Children's Books, 1994; New York, Dutton Children's Books, 1995.
An Equal Music. New Delhi, Viking, and London, Phoenix, 1999.

Translator, *Three Chinese Poets: Translations of Poems by Wang Wei, Li Bai, and Du Fu.* New Delhi, Viking, and New York, HarperPerennial, 1992.

*

Critical Studies: "Vikram Seth's 'The Golden Gate'" by Rowena Hill, in *Literary Criterion* (Bangalore, India), 21(4), 1986; "'Homeward Ho!' Silicon Valley Pushkin" by Marjorie Perloff, in *American Poetry Review* (Philadelphia), 15(6), November-December 1986; "'The Golden Gate' and the Quest for Self-Realization" by Makarand R. Paranjape, in *ACLALS Bulletin,* 8(1), 1989; "'The Golden Gate': The First Indian Novel in Verse" by Santosh Gupta, in *The New Indian Novel in English: A Study of the 1980s,* edited by Viney Kirpal, New Delhi, Allied Publishers, 1990; "Recycling the Genre: The Russian and American Novel in Verse: The Case of Pushkin's 'Evgenii Onegin' and Seth's 'The Golden Gate'" by Roumiana Deltcheva, in *Rosyjska Ruletka,* 2, 1995; "Trunks of the Banyan Tree: History, Politics & Fiction" by J.H. Walker, in *Island Magazine,* 63, winter 1995; "'The World Goes On': Narrative Structure and the Sonnet in Vikram Seth's 'The Golden Gate'" by Jay Curlin, in *Publications of the Arkansas Philological Association* (Conway, Arkansas), 22(2), fall 1996.

Vikram Seth comments:
   I write in different genres so as not to bore myself—and the reader. And I like writing that is clear, even deceptively clear.

*   *   *

Vikram Seth is another poet of exile in the postcolonial world, in which writers seemingly switch societies, cultures, and even languages with ease, yet under the poised surface are the anxieties of those without the security of home and place. *Mappings* records Seth's feelings of nostalgia for India after studying abroad for many years and his continuing attraction to the "notes of other birds, / The nightingale, the wren." For Seth the poetic traditions, other than those of India, at the time were British and, later, American and Chinese. Many of the poems are of youthful restlessness and ambivalent feelings toward family. They are also antiromantic and express a rational hedonism; life is to be enjoyed while it lasts. A game of Scrabble, travel, or an evening of sex seem equally pleasurable. The comic rhymes and conscious superficialities, pastiche, and parody deflate seriousness, mock high culture, and add up to an alternative vision.

The Humble Administrator's Garden also reports on surfaces and the trivia of life while using such forms as the sonnet, quatrain, and epigrammatic couplet. Although some poems are in free verse, Seth usually writes a regularly stressed line. A refusal to look inward, a celebration of simple pleasures and of survival, and a half-serious resort to platitude and pastiche for amusement and as defense make Seth a poet of our time, of eclecticism and self-aware artifice. *The Humble Administrator's Garden* is divided into poems about China, where Seth studied for two years, India, where he was born and raised, and California, where he then lived. China is a place to discover universal brotherhood despite cultural differences, India is a land of memories and lost relations, but America, for all its comforts and pleasures, is lonely and dangerous. The China poems are imagistic and atmospheric, but tendencies towards chinoiserie are held in check by Western stanzaic forms. Often the poems offer analogies to the poetics of their creation. In the title poem, a sonnet, unscrupulous means and administrative practicality create the satisfying art of the garden. Mr. Wang "may have got / The means by somewhat dubious means, but now / This is the loveliest of gardens. What / Do scruples know of beauty anyhow?"

The California poems refer to loneliness, former loves, and nostalgia for a foreign, European past, presumably Seth's period as a student at Oxford. Emotions are mocked by expressing them platitudinously: "The fact is, this work is as dreary as shit. / I do not like it a bit." "There is so much to do / There isn't any time for feeling blue." The language is varied to invigorate an otherwise unreverberant diction. Although some of the poems appear so offhand in subject and manner as to be close to triviality, there is often a sense of a threat to survival. "Ceasing upon the Midnight" begins with absurdity ("He stacks the dishes on the table. / He wants to die, but is unable"), moves through memories of other countries and cultures, and returns to an unromantic, nonsuicidal, alcoholic present: "The bottle lies on the ground. / He sleeps. His sleep is sound." Deftly, ironically maneuvering its way through obvious echoes, the poem imitates the structure, movement, and psychology of the typical romantic ode, but it is undermined by bland irony, part of a highly unromantic poetic: "the rules / of metre, shield him from / Himself"; consequently, "to cease upon / / The midnight under the live-oak / Seems too derisory a joke." "Unclaimed" epigrammatically comments upon a passing sexual encounter: "To make love with a stranger is the best. / There is no riddle and there is no test." The throwaway manner is like the theme. Claiming "that this is all there is," Seth deflates romantic urges. To celebrate the pleasures of the passing moment and of ordinary life is to argue for a poetic of what is as opposed to the ideal.

The Golden Gate is a 307-page verse novel written in nearly six hundred fourteen-line, sonnetlike stanzas and loosely modeled upon Pushkin's *Eugene Onegin.* It is also an amused love song to San Francisco for its beauty and as symbol of the contemporary good life. Italian coffee houses, Japanese and Chinese restaurants, all-night bookshops, ice cream parlors (with Bubble Gum and Pumpkin Pie flavors), Berkeley, Silicon Valley, Telegraph Hill, and the Oakland hills provide settings for conversations and actions by characters who are representative of the various subcultures of the San Francisco area: John, a self-controlled WASP yuppie computer designer; Phil, a warm Jewish pacifist dropout; Janet, a Japanese feminist rock musician and sculptor; Liz, a career-minded Italian corporate lawyer; and her pious brother Ed, a troubled Roman Catholic homosexual. John's conservative inhibitions, his obsession with proper forms of behavior, his homophobia, and his intolerance and rages at deviance eventually cause him to lose Liz and reject Phil, his closest male friend. Loneliness and the need for others, central themes of *The Golden Gate,* are not resolved through romantic love. Phil says, "Passion's a prelude to disaster," and Liz does not "feel sure / I can trust passion any more." When Liz breaks with John and announces her forthcoming marriage, her father asks, "You do love Phil?" She replies, "Not on your life," and she thinks, "I couldn't / Hope for a better better half: / A good kind man who makes me laugh." By contrast John lives alone in a wretched state of anger, guilt, and desire.

Seth offers the reader a 1980s version of Ariosto, Butler, or Byron in which the self-conscious act of writing narrative is made part of the fun through the author's comments upon himself and his techniques, long digressions, the interweaving of plots, deft shifts of scenes, suspended development, and unexpected events and coincidences. Outrageous rhymes ("iguana"/"sultana"; "inter alia"/"full regalia") add variety and delight to an absurd but functional stanza rhymed *ababccddeffegg.* While many stanzas have literary echoes and allusions or offer a variation in how the three quatrains and couplet are welded, the poem is equally rooted in present-day popular culture, and the contemporary idiom is beautifully employed. The wit often updates the past: ". . . Don't put things off till it's too late. / You are the DJ of your fate." Rhyming has become fun. While part of the effect of *The Golden Gate* is the brisk, clear movement of the story within its swift tetrameter lines and many feminine rhymes, the interruptions, contrasts, and unexpected twists are ingenious. When Phil attends a party to meet Sue, Liz's sister, he instead falls in love with her brother Ed. Phil confesses to Liz, who reveals that she had known since "Sunday before the equinox / You both wore the same mismatched socks." *The Golden Gate* acknowledges its origins in epic romance through witty imitations of such conventions as an invocation to the muse, allusions to its predecessors, and the use of pets as an American equivalent to epic machinery and gods. Besides Ed's five-foot green iguana named Arnold Schwarzenegger and Janet's two "Sweet Siamese of rare refulgence," there is Liz's "Magnificat" Charlemagne, who jealously urinates on John's clothes and eventually contributes to the breakdown of their engagement. Seth invests significance in ordinary life, and even his formalism has the seeming spontaneity, directness, and immediacy of free verse.

Seth's next book, *All You Who Sleep Tonight,* is a collection of poems on diverse subjects. The "sleep" of the title is a metaphor for death, loss, the evasion of feelings, including the feelings of love, and the historical past, particularly those parts of it that brought grievous suffering upon individuals or whole peoples. The poems in the book are divided into five sections. The first section, "Romantic Residues," focuses on the quality of love in today's world. Its central theme is the reluctance to make a commitment and to take the risks that come with it. Love comes to an end or is not allowed to grow from the beginning, as in ''A Style of Loving'': ''Picnic, movie, ice-cream; / Talk; to clear my head / Hot-buttered rum-coffee for you; / And so not to bed.'' Evasion of involvement, however, brings with it its own pain, and a melancholy feeling overhangs these poems. The ''lovers'' in ''The Room and the Street'' say farewell to each other after being together for a short while: ''You take my hand, / Then stand and frown awhile. / At my express demand / You undertake to smile.'' The poems in the second section, ''In Other Voices,'' show high seriousness, an element new in Seth's poetry. ''Work and Freedom'' portrays the horrors of the Holocaust indirectly by imagining the unbearable effect on the commandant of Auschwitz as a human being who is relieved to gain his freedom from his work when offered another assignment. ''A Doctor's Journal Entry for August 6, 1945'' evokes vividly the atomic destruction of Hiroshima. ''Ghalib, Two Years after the Mutiny'' gives a poignant depiction of the suffering of the great Urdu poet in the days when India was in the last throes of its conquest by the British. ''In Other Places,'' the third section of the book, is mainly a series of tender vignettes on different places, but it also includes a longer poem, ''On the Fiftieth Anniversary of the Golden Gate Bridge.'' The next section, ''Quatrains,'' reflects a further expansion of Seth's perspective on human experience. It consists of four-line poems on miscellaneous subjects that range from a flippant phone conversation with a woman who hangs up to the semiserious philosophical observation that ''your eyes, my understanding, all will rot . . .'' The perspective deepens in the last section, ''Meditations of the Heart,'' where the themes of death and a feeling of oneness with others in a common human fate dominate: ''All you who sleep tonight / . . . Know that you aren't alone. / The whole world shares your tears, / Some for two nights or one, / And some for all their years.''

In his successive writings Seth has continued to reveal ever new dimensions of his versatility. *Beastly Tales from Here and There* is a retelling of fables, two each from India, China, Greece, and Ukraine, besides two fables of his own creation. At one level these are stories for children, combining simple moral instruction with entertainment. Their strength, however, lies in their ability to entertain. Seth has mastered the art of storytelling, and his verse flows fluently and with perfect resilience. The apt use of specific and sufficient detail and a sense of both the comic and the tragic bring the characters and the situations fully alive, thus carrying the listener or the reader into the imaginary worlds of the stories. Captivating as the stories are for younger readers, like most fables they also have a level of seriousness suited to adults. For one thing, as in real life, the moral lessons are not always clear and categorical; in fact, one is often left wondering if a story contains any lesson at all. For instance, in ''The Hare and the Tortoise,'' although Ms. Hare loses the race to Teddy, she receives all of the attention from the admiring pressmen and becomes successful and rich. While she is ''pampered rotten,'' the tortoise is ''forgotten.'' Such a lifelike outcome may be beyond the comprehension of a child's innocent mind.

The story closest to life is ''The Elephant and the Tragopan,'' one of the two original fables by Seth. Its theme is the protection of the natural environment, also a subject of major concern in *The Golden Gate*. Led by an elephant and a tragopan, the wild animals of Bingle Valley march in a rally to the human town to protest against the building of a dam that would destroy their habitat. The head of the Man-Council, Bigshot, who is responsible for the decision to build the dam in order to build his vote bank and fortune, tries to manipulate the leaders into withdrawing their agitation. Failing to persuade them, he decides to hold them as prisoners. In the ensuing scuffle and confusion, he wrings the tragopan's neck and kills him, but he is stopped from going any further by his own son, who rises against him in support of the animal cause and sanity. Seth ends the story on an ambiguous note, however, leaving it ''for the world'' to decide whether or not the dam will be built.

Yet another kind of book by Seth is *Arion and the Dolphin,* a libretto for an opera. The story is based on the legend of the poet Arion of the seventh century B.C., who was associated with the court of Periander of Corinth and is credited with the invention of the dithyramb. In Seth's treatment Arion is a musician who sings to the accompaniment of the lyre and who serves as court musician to Periander, the tyrant of Corinth. He goes to Sicily to compete in a music festival and receives a large amount of gold for winning the competition. On return voyage to Corinth the sailors on the ship decide to kill him in order to take his gold. They force the captain, who had become Arion's friend on the voyage out, to agree to support them. Arion leaps overboard and is saved by dolphins, who dance and feast and sing with him. One dolphin becomes Arion's close friend, and the two together reach Corinth. Periander does not believe Arion's story, however, and orders him put in a prison cell, and the dolphin is caught by fishermen and turned into a circus act. Tortured and suffering because of its separation from Arion, the dolphin dies. Periander now realizes how much Arion and the dolphin loved each other, and he repents having doubted Arion's story and having caused the dolphin's death.

Arion and the Dolphin is a story of innocence. At one level it also is a story for children, and it is not surprising that Seth has written a version for children. Both Arion and the dolphin personify pure innocence and goodness, but the story also provides a forgiving understanding of characters who commit evil deeds. The goodness of the captain is obvious, and it is clear that he is compelled to comply with the sailors in their decision to kill Arion. The evil of the sailors is explained by their poverty, and Periander's high-handedness and cruelty are explained as being the result of his position. There is an underlying dichotomy in the story between the world of the sea and sky on the one hand and the earth on the other, the former representing unadulterated nature and goodness and the latter the human world fraught with evil. Arion derives the inspiration for his music from the sea through the sounds in a conch shell given to him by the captain. The most beautiful passages in the book are lyrical descriptions of the sea. The story ends with Arion's prayer to his muse for unity between the natural and the human worlds: ''May music bind the sky, the earth, the sea / In tune, in harmony.''

—Bruce King and Surjit Dulai

SHANGE, Ntozake

Nationality: American. **Born:** Paulette Williams, Trenton, New Jersey, 18 October 1948; took name Ntozake Shange in 1971. **Education:** Schools in St. Louis and New Jersey; Barnard College, New York, 1966–70, B.A. (cum laude) in American studies 1970; University of Southern California, Los Angeles, 1971–73, M.A. in American studies 1973. **Family:** Married David Murray in 1977 (2nd marriage; divorced); one daughter. **Career:** Faculty member Sonoma State College, Rohnert Park, California, 1973–75, Mills College,

Oakland, California, 1975, City College, New York, 1975, and Douglass College, New Brunswick, New Jersey, 1978. Since 1983 associate professor of drama, University of Houston. Artist-in-residence, Equinox Theater, Houston, from 1981, and New Jersey State Council on the Arts. **Awards:** New York Drama Critics Circle award, 1977; Obie award, 1977, 1980; Columbia University Medal of Excellence, 1981; *Los Angeles Times* award, 1981; Guggenheim fellowship, 1981; Nori Eboraci award, Bernard College, 1988; Lila Wallace-Reader's Digest Fund annual writer's award, 1992; Paul Robeson Achievement award, National Coalition of 100 Black Women, 1992; Living Legend award, National Black Theatre Festival, 1993; Claim Your Life award, 1993; Monarch Merit award; Pushcart prize. **Address:** Department of Drama, University of Houston—University Park, 4800 Calhoun Road, Houston, Texas 77004, U.S.A.

PUBLICATIONS

Poetry

Melissa and Smith. St. Paul, Bookslinger, 1976.
Natural Disasters and Other Festive Occasions. San Francisco, Heirs, 1977.
Nappy Edges. New York, St. Martin's Press, 1978; London, Methuen, 1987.
Some Men. Privately printed, 1981.
A Daughter's Geography. New York, St. Martin's Press, 1983; London, Methuen, 1985.
From Okra to Greens. St. Paul, Coffee House Press, 1984.
Ridin' the Moon in Texas: Word Paintings. New York, St. Martin's Press, 1988.
I Live in Music. New York, Welcome Enterprises, 1994.

Recording: *I Live in Music,* Watershed, 1984; *Beneath the Necessity of Talking: Performance Piece,* American Audio Prose Library, 1989.

Plays

For Colored Girls Who Have Considered Suicide When the Rainbow Is Enuf (produced New York, 1975; London, 1980). San Lorenzo, California, Shameless Hussy Press, 1976; revised version, New York, Macmillan, 1977; London, Eyre Methuen, 1978; included in *Plays: One,* 1992.
A Photograph: Lovers-in-Motion (as *A Photograph: A Still Life with Shadows, A Photograph: A Study of Cruelty* produced New York, 1977; revised version, as *A Photograph: Lovers-in-Motion,* also director: produced Houston, 1979). New York, French, 1981.
Where the Mississippi Meets the Amazon, with Thulani Nkabinda and Jessica Hagedorn (produced New York, 1977).
Spell #7 (produced New York, 1979; London, 1985). Included in *Three Pieces,* 1981, and in *Plays: One,* 1992; published separately, London, Methuen, 1985.
Black and White Two-Dimensional Planes (produced New York, 1979).
Boogie Woogie Landscapes (produced on tour, 1980). Included in *Three Pieces,* 1981.
Mother Courage and Her Children, adaptation of a play by Brecht (produced New York, 1980).

From Okra to Greens: A Different Kinda Love Story (as *Mouths* produced New York, 1981; as *From Okra to Greens in Three for a Full Moon,* produced Los Angeles, 1982). New York, French, 1983.
Three Pieces: Spell #7, A Photograph: Lovers-in-Motion, Boogie Woogie Landscape. New York, St. Martin's Press, 1981.
Three for a Full Moon, and Bocas (produced Los Angeles, 1982).
Educating Rita, adaptation of the play by Willy Russell (produced Atlanta, 1983).
From Okra to Greens: A Different Kind of Love Story: A Play with Music and Dance. New York and London, French, 1985.
Three Views of Mt. Fuji (produced New York, 1987).
Betsey Brown, adaptation of her own novel, with Emily Mann, music by Baikida Carroll, lyrics by Shange, Mann, and Carroll (also director: produced Philadelphia, 1989).
The Love Space Demands: A Continuing Saga (produced London, 1992). New York, St. Martin's Press, 1991; included in *Plays One,* 1992.
Plays: One (includes *For Colored Girls Who Have Considered Suicide When the Rainbow Is Enuf, Spell #7, I Heard Eric Dolphy in His Eyes, The Love Space Demands: A Continuing Saga).* London, Methuen, 1992.

Novels

Sassafrass: A Novella. San Lorenzo, California, Shameless Hussy Press, 1977.
Sassafrass, Cypress and Indigo. New York, St. Martin's Press, 1982; London, Methuen, 1983.
Betsey Brown. New York, St. Martin's Press, and London, Methuen, 1985.
Liliane: Resurrection of the Daughter. London, Methuen, 1995.

Other

See No Evil: Prefaces, Essays, and Accounts 1976–1983. San Francisco, Momo's Press, 1984.
Whitewash. New York, Walker and Company, 1997.
If I Can Cook, You Know God Can. Boston, Beacon Press, 1998.

Editor, *The Beacon Best of 1999: Creative Writing by Women and Men of All Colors.* Boston, Beacon Press, 2000.

*

Critical Studies: *Rites of Passage in the Writing of Ntozake Shange: The Poetry, Drama, and Novels* (dissertation), n.p., 1989, and "New World Consciousness in the Poetry of Ntozake Shange and June Jordan: Two African-American Women's Response to Expansionism in the Third World," in *College Language Association Journal* (Atlanta, Georgia), 39(4), June, 1996, both by P. Jane Splawn; "'The Poetry of a Moment': Politics and Open Form in the Drama of Ntozake Shange" by John Timpane, in *Studies in American Drama* (Columbus, Ohio), 4, 1989; "'. . . If It's a Statistic, It's Not a Woman': A Look at 'Serious Lessons Learned' by Ntozake Shange" by Helen Kidd, in *Contemporary Poetry Meets Modern Theory,* edited by Antony Easthope, Toronto, University of Toronto Press, 1991; *Ntozake Shange: A Critical Study of the Plays* by Neal A. Lester, New York, Garland, 1995; "Kozmic Reappraisals: Revising

California Insularity'' by Maria Damon, in *Women Poets of the Americas: Toward a Pan-American Gathering,* edited by Jacqueline Vaught Brogan and Cordelia Chavez Candelaria, Notre Dame, Indiana, University of Notre Dame Press, 1999.

Theatrical Activities: Director: **Plays**—*The Mighty Gents* by Richard Wesley, New York, 1979; *A Photograph: Lovers-in-Motion,* Houston, 1979. Actress: **Plays**—The Lady in Orange in *For Colored Girls Who Have Considered Suicide When the Rainbow Is Enuf,* New York, 1976; in *Where the Mississippi Meets the Amazon,* New York, 1977; in *Mouths.* New York. 1981.

*   *   *

Ntozake Shange is a poet, playwright, and novelist. Like many contemporary black writers, Shange attempts to forge a place within the literary tradition for forms, styles, and subject matter that have been excluded from it. The tradition has largely been determined by white males, and Shange's verse draws attention to the cultural and gender specificity of her concerns. Whereas the white male tradition has foregrounded sameness and universality, traditions that politically serve to support its own value systems and ideology, Shange's poetry foregrounds difference and demands that differences be allowed to make themselves felt. In poems like ''2 march 1984 (cowry shells & heart),'' from *Ridin' the Moon in Texas,* Shange voices black culture's rejection of the value system that has been imposed upon it:

    our rhythms   our guitar pulses
    are prohibited on the subway/considered déclassé
    north of 57th street/south of gramercy park
    our hearts don't beat
    they sweep us off our feet
    block the chaos & tumult the white people
    call civilization/ . . .

As Shange asserts in this passage, different cultures move to different rhythms, and the attempt to homogenize such differences inevitably leads to their repression by the dominant culture. Shange focuses on the oppression of white male culture and its literary dictates and draws attention to the fecundity of those voices it has ignored and silenced. Stylistically, her poetry is also different and signifies her rejection of white male literary forms. The lack of punctuation in Shange's writings reflects the idea that punctuation has been used to control and restrict the natural flow of language. In turn, the dialect in which she writes works in opposition to a white, ''educated'' discourse and reflects the cadence and rhythm of black speech. Poems like ''A Celebration of Black Survival'' display their roots in the black oral tradition and effect the lyrical movement of songs:

    what does it mean that blk folks cd sing n dance?
    why do we say that so much/we don't know what we mean/
    i saw what that means/good god/did i see/like i cda
    waked on the water myself/i cda clothed the naked & fed
    the hungry/with what dance i saw tonight/ . . .

While Shange's poetry attempts to forge a place for African-Americans, as well as for the oppressed people of the third world, it is also committed to forging a place for women. In works like ''Some Men'' Shange concentrates on the plight of women, emphasizing the effects of men's efforts to make women conform to male standards:

    he kept the space empty. so no one wd ever imagine
    that a woman lived there/which is what he wanted
    for no one to know.
    if she lived empty & angular as he did, she'd become
    less a woman & part of the design/where anything he
    wanted to happen/happened.

As this poem suggests, for a woman to conform to male expectations of her is to lose her feminine self, a self that differs from male conceptions of what it should be. Shange's verse rejoices in femininity and in the differences she draws between female and male. It also highlights the gifts womanhood offers, and in poems like ''torso'' Shange tries to combat the ways in which femininity has been trivialized and marginalized in patriarchal discourse:

    . . . a petal
    of a woman not knowing
    her fragrance enchanted
    men who could not bring themselves
    to call her name
    all they could do was turn away
    their eyes shut tightly
    refusing to lose the vision, the scent
    of the petal of a woman
    the flower meandering
    by the hummingbirds

Shange's prioritization of feminine traits is mirrored in the form of her poetry, which is fluid and circular rather than pointed and direct. Her verse is oriented toward the body and in particular highlights the nonrestrictive impetus of black feminine culture. The imagery of gestation and birth she frequently employs emphasizes the connection between femininity and creative fecundity. Just as her celebratory poems about black culture often resemble song, so the verse she writes in support of femininity relies on dance. Dance becomes Shange's means of drawing attention to the natural movements of the female body. In poems like ''I'm a poet who,'' from her play *For Colored Girls Who Have Considered Suicide When the Rainbow Is Enuf,* she equates dance with femininity, since dance, she suggests, provides a vehicle for the expression of feminine experience:

    hold yr head like it was ruby sapphire
    I'm a poet
    who writes in english
    come to share the worlds witchu . . .
    come to share our worlds witchu
    we come here to be dancin
    to be dancin
    to be dancin
    baya

Shange's efforts to combine poetry and dance constitute further subversion of traditional forms. She calls *For Colored Girls* a ''choreopoem,'' thus signaling its blend of poem, play, and dance. Similarly, *Ridin' the Moon in Texas* is a combination of poetry and visual art. By mingling artistic forms Shange's poetry attempts to subvert the traditional boundaries that have been erected between genres, styles, forms, and experiences. As she does this, she promises to be an important figure in forging a place for minority writings that refuse to conform to traditional white male literary expectations.

—Priscilla L. Walton

SHAPCOTT, Jo

Nationality: British. **Born:** London, 24 March 1953. **Education:** Trinity College, Dublin, B.A. (first-class honors), 1976; Dublin College of Music, 1974–76; St. Hilda's College, Oxford, B.A. 1978; Harvard University, Cambridge, Massachusetts, 1978–80; University of Bristol, diploma (with distinction) in adult and community education 1984. **Career:** Lecturer in English, Rolle College, Exmouth, 1981–84; education officer, 1984–86, and acting senior education officer, 1986, Arts Council, London; education officer, South Bank Centre, London, 1986–91; Judith E. Wilson Senior Visiting Fellow in creative writing, Cambridge University, Pembroke College, 1991. Lyricist and librettist. **Awards:** Harvard University Harkness fellowship, 1978–80; South West Arts Literature award, 1982; Poetry Society National Poetry prize, 1985, 1993; Commonwealth prize, 1989, for *Electroplating the Baby;* Prudence Farmer award, *New Statesman,* 1989. **Address:** London, England.

PUBLICATIONS

Poetry

Electroplating the Baby. Newcastle upon Tyne, Bloodaxe Books, and Chester Springs, Pennsylvania, Dufour, 1988.
Phrase Book. Oxford and New York, Oxford University Press, 1992.
Motherland. N.p., Gwaithel and Wilwern, 1996.

Other

Editor, with Matthew Sweeny, *Emergency Kit: Poems for Strange Times.* London, Faber, 1996.

*

Critical Studies: "Responses to Elizabeth Bishop: Anne Stevenson, Eavan Boland, and Jo Shapcott" by David G. Williams, in *English* (Leicester, England), 44(180), 1995; "Pavlova's Physics: The Poems of Jo Shapcott" by Jane Satterfield, in *Antioch Review,* 55(2), spring 1997; by Lavinia Greenlaw, in *New Statesman* (London), 13 March 2000.

*   *   *

That Jo Shapcott is the only person to have won the Poetry Society National Poetry prize twice should itself be a sufficient accolade. But what is the special quality of her poetry?

The word most often used to describe Shapcott's poetry is "surrealistic," not a description of which she herself is very fond. None of us likes to be neatly labeled or pigeonholed in this way; it is

too restrictive, too pat. But her prizewinning poem "The Surrealists' Summer Convention Came to Our City" probably prompted the label:

> We were as limp as the guide book
> to the city

This recalls Dali's limp watches melting in the desert sun. And here I think is a clue. What is called Shapcott's surrealism grows out of her poetic observation of her experiences, whereas Dali imposed his images on his pictures, with the result that they are often rootless and sometimes superficial, having the shelf life of a good joke. I suspect that this popular surrealism is at the bottom of Shapcott's rejection of the label. Her surrealism, if we must call it such, is organic, while that of Dali and his followers is synthetic.

"Electroplating the Baby," the title poem of Shapcott's first major collection, is an idea that would appear to have all the trappings of surrealism about it. Yet the poem derives from something that people actually believed and acted upon, however mistakenly. Thus,

> It would be impossible to say.
> It is infinitely possible.

If I were to look for a single word to describe Shapcott's poetry, it would be "protean." The subjects of many of her poems are just that. As shown in the following lines, for example, Tom of "Tom and Jerry Visit England" changes his shape and his nature:

> I banged full face into a query—
> and ended up with my front shaped
> like a question mark for hours.

Even Shapcott's sheep transform themselves. It is an important aspect of the art of poetry to transform the way we look at things, and Shapcott's poetry does just that.

Then there is Shapcott's later superb poem "Thetis." Thetis was the sea goddess with the faculty of infinitely changing her form. And here we come to the most important aspect of Shapcott's poetry, the quality of its language. In "Thetis" the sensual power of the language is such that one can enjoy the sensation with the goddess as she slips into her shapes:

> as I stretch
> my limbs for the transformation, I'm laughing
> to feel the surge of other shapes beneath my skin.

> I think
> my soul has slithered into this

> Low tremendous purrs start at the pit
> of my stomach, I'm curving through long grass,
> all sinew, in a body where tension
> is the special joy-

The skillful use of assonance and alliteration makes this poem a tour de force of voluptuous imagery in which the reader shares the physical joy of changing shape. So what we are talking about is a poet's vision beautifully expressed.

The theme of changing shapes is pursued in such poems as "Today I Am a Vogue Model" and "Elephant," as is the pursuit of appropriately sensual language in which to express the theme. And it is the language of Shapcott's poems that is the key to their excellence. A single word can reverberate in her poems, as, for example, "distance" does in "Motherland":

Distance. The word is ingrained like pain.
So much for England and so much
for my future to walk into the horizon
carrying distance in a broken suitcase.

Changing shape, expressed in such classical works as Ovid's *Metamorphoses,* is a theme that runs deep in our mythology and folklore. Thus, Shapcott is in good company. And in *Phrase Book* she pursues the metamorphosis of language as it passes from one to another, a further deep, flowing concern.

—John Cotton

SHAPCOTT, Thomas W(illiam)

Nationality: Australian. **Born:** Ipswich, Queensland, 21 March 1935. **Education:** Ipswich Grammar School, 1949–50; University of Queensland, Brisbane, B.A. 1968. **Military Service:** National Service, 1953. **Family:** Married 1) Margaret Hodge in 1960, three daughters and one son; 2) Judith Rodriguez, *q.v.,* in 1982. **Career:** Clerk, H.S. Shapcott, Public Accountant, Ipswich, 1951–63; partner, Shapcott and Shapcott, Accountant, Ipswich, 1963–72; public accountant, Sole Trader, Ipswich, 1972–78; director, Australia Council Literature Board, Sydney, 1983–90; executive director, National Book Council, 1992–97. Since 1997 inaugural professor of creative writing, University of Adelaide, South Australia. Chairman, Copyright Agency Limited, Sydney, 1998–99. Fellow, Australian Society of Accountants, 1970; Churchill fellow (U.S.A. and England), 1972. **Awards:** Grace Leven prize, 1962; Sir Thomas White memorial prize, 1967; Sydney Myer Charity Trust award, 1968, 1970; Canada-Australia prize, 1979; Struga International Poetry Festival Golden Wreath award (Yugoslavia), 1989; New South Wales Premier's special prize, 1995; Michel Wesley Wright prize, 1995. D.Litt.: Macquarie University, Sydney, 1989. Officer, Order of Australia, 1989. **Member:** Australian Arts Council Australian Literature Board, 1973–76; Copyright Agency Limited, 1991–99. **Address:** P.O. Box 231, Mont Albert, Victoria 3127, Australia.

PUBLICATIONS

Poetry

Time on Fire. Brisbane, Jacaranda Press, 1961.
Twelve Bagatelles. Adelaide, Australian Letters, 1962.
The Mankind Thing. Brisbane, Jacaranda Press, 1964.
Sonnets 1960–1963. Privately printed, 1964.
A Taste of Salt Water. Sydney, Angus and Robertson, 1967.
Inwards to the Sun. St. Lucia, University of Queensland Press, 1969.
Fingers at Air: Experimental Poems 1969. Privately printed, 1969.
Begin with Walking. St. Lucia, University of Queensland Press, 1972.
Interim Report. Privately printed, 1972.

Shabbytown Calendar. St. Lucia, University of Queensland Press, 1975.
Seventh Avenue Poems. Sydney, Angus and Robertson, 1976.
Selected Poems. St. Lucia, University of Queensland Press, 1979.
Turning Full Circle (prose poems). Sydney, Prism, 1979.
Stump and Grape and Bopple Nut (prose inventions). Brisbane, Bullion, 1981.
Welcome! St. Lucia, University of Queensland Press, 1983.
Travel Dice. St. Lucia, University of Queensland Press, 1987.
Selected Poems. St. Lucia, University of Queensland Press, 1989.
Poems. Skopje, Yugoslavia, Misla, 1989.
In the Beginning. Canberra, National Library of Australia, 1990.
The City of Home. St. Lucia, University of Queensland Press, 1995.
The Sun's Waste Is Our Energy. Cambridge, England, Salt Folio, 1998.

Play

The Seven Deadly Sins, music by Colin Brumby (produced Brisbane, 1970). Privately printed, 1970.

Novels

The Birthday Gift. St. Lucia, University of Queensland Press, 1982.
White Stag of Exile. Melbourne, Allen Lane, 1984.
Hotel Bellevue. London, Chatto and Windus, 1986.
The Search for Galina. London, Chatto and Windus, 1989.
Mona's Gift. Melbourne, Penguin Australia, 1993.
Theatre of Darkness. Sydney, Random House, 1998.

Short Stories

Limestone and Lemon Wine. London, Chatto and Windus, 1988.
What You Own. Sydney, Angus & Robertson Imprint, 1991.

Other

Focus on Charles Blackman (art monograph). St. Lucia, University of Queensland Press, 1967.
Poetry as a Creative Learning Process. Kelvin Grove, Queensland, Kelvin Grove College of Advanced Education, 1978.
Flood Children (for children). Brisbane, Jacaranda Press, 1981.
The Literature Board: A Brief History. St. Lucia, University of Queensland Press, 1988.
The Art of Charles Blackman. London, Deutsch, 1990.
Biting the Bullet: A Literary Memoir. Sydney, Simon & Schuster, 1990.
Editor, with Rodney Hall, *New Impulses in Australian Poetry.* University of Queensland Press, 1968.
Editor, *Australian Poetry Now.* Melbourne, Sun, 1969.
Editor, *Poets on Record.* University of Queensland Press, 1970–73.
Editor, *Contemporary American and Australian Poetry.* University of Queensland Press, 1976.
Editor, *Consolidation: The Second Paperback Poets Anthology.* University of Queensland Press, 1982.
Editor, *Contemporary Australian Poetry.* Stuga, Yugoslavia, Macedonian Literary Association, 1987.
Editor, *The Moment Made Marvellous: The UQP Poetry Anthology.* University of Queensland Press, 1998.

Translator, with Ilja Casule, *Katika Kulavkova: Time Difference.* Skopje, Macedonia, Zumpres, 1998.

Translator, with Ilja Casule, *An Island on Land: Anthology of Contemporary Macedonian Poetry.* Sydney, Macquarie University, 1999.

*

Manuscript Collections: Australian National Library, Canberra;Fryer Library, University of Queensland, Brisbane; Mitchell Library, Sydney.

Critical Studies: By L. Clancy, in *Meanjin* (Melbourne), 1967; by Carl Harrison-Ford, in *Meanjin* (Melbourne), 1972; by James Davidson, in *Meanjin* (Melbourne), 1975; by Michael Denholm, in *Tasmanian Review* (Hobart), 2, summer 1979; in *Westerly* (Nedlands, Western Australia), 1, 1989, and in *In Other Words: Interviews with Australian Poets,* Amsterdam, Netherlands, Rodopi, 1998, both by Barbara Williams; by Bruce Beaver, in *Scripsi* (Melbourne), 4(4), 1987; by Peter Porter, in *Australian Literary Studies* (St. Lucia), 14(4), 1990; "'What Is Gone Is Not Gone': Intimations in the Poetry of Thomas Shapcott" by David McCooey, in *Australian Literary Studies,* 18(1), May 1997.

Thomas W. Shapcott comments:

(1980) When I first began writing and publishing poetry in the 1950s, I was soaking myself eagerly in T.S. Eliot and Dylan Thomas, that decade's heroes, as well as discovering new worlds in the important Penguin anthologies of that period. When I had begun to be published, I made contact with my own contemporaries and my Australian peers. I have always been interested in experimentation, in the challenge of form (closed forms, open forms), but in the 1950s experimental writing was unfashionable—and unpublishable. My early lyricism was more immediately accepted. In recent years I have been concerned with exploring ways of balancing essentially lyrical expression with the cadence of lyric speech.

I have always been interested in expressing a sense of region, whether it be the provincial backwaters of "Shabbytown" or "Seventh Avenue" mobility. But my essential concern has always been with issues of personality and belief. I once wrote, "I believe poetry is a movement towards celebration. Art—Poetry—is to struggle toward the light, knowing the light bums all sight to blindness. We cannot outstare the sun, but it is not in our nature to endure the darkness. Thus all true poetry is in some way a form of experimentation, a groping outwards. Even the earth is moving, how can we stand still?" I still hold to that.

(1985) I still hold to that. Recent work in prose has been an attempt to integrate lyric form and tone with narrative and documentary techniques. It all becomes, in different ways, evidence.

(1995) The evidence interacts with intuition or experience, with memory as both a modifier and a trickster. To discover the impersonality of personal recall releases large energies. The task has always been to bridge distance. Distance itself is a real bridge.

*   *   *

Among the new work in Thomas W. Shapcott's *Selected Poems* is "Make the Old Man Sing," a sequence of fourteen poems providing an answer—defiant, elegiac, energetically physical—to the preceding "A Record of Flamenco Singing," which may itself serve as something of a definition of Shapcott's poetics:

In my country
old men do not sing.
We have closed off
elegy, defiance.
We will not remember
the release possible
the terrible monkeys in the voice
taunting us
haunting
holding out ripe sweet grapes
bitter lemons
in handfuls, till we gulp.

Not that we should take the notion of an old man too literally. Also within later work we find Shapcott making a witty stocktaking and, in "Turning Fifty," accepting the definition of self that comes with growing older, while the sequence "Life Taste" celebrates middle-aged lovers and bodies:

Stiff in parts, subtle,
careful of knots and the meaning of patterns
we can stay in the middle or sprawl like most people:
in the big bed we bounce and are buoyant, believable.

Perhaps the brush with death recorded in "Post-Operative" indicates an altered balance in the tonal mixture that has characterized Shapcott's work. There has always been an alert psychological and sensuous responsiveness to present particularities. In "Stuff of Myths," for example, he urges, "Never disbelieve the sensual air on your body. / That keeps you living." On the other hand, he has an elegiac sense of the past, both personal and historical, that is saved from weakening into mere nostalgia partly by intellectual curiosity about the processes and patterns of change and partly by that dramatizing power that enables him to summon up the past with a powerful illusion of substance and immediacy.

This quality makes forcefully attractive Shapcott's middle-period poems of colonial history, whether factual, as in "Macquarie as Father" or "Portrait of Captain Logan," or fictional, as in "Miss Norah Kerrin Writes to Her Betrothed." But these are more than period reconstructions. They reveal formative cultural elements, reminding us, for instance, that behind the mythical, laconic, independent men of the bush stand the urban exiles of convict life, made frantic not by imprisonment ("I got used to chains") but by silence and space, until they twisted into the fabric of Australian attitudes one implacable strand of hostility to nature: "I will cut down every tree, / every one. I will be invincible" ("The Trees: A Convict Monologue").

In such poems presences conventionally dismissed and evaded as defective or freakish claim acknowledgment as "real / and alive / among / us," as in the splendid "Litanies of Julia Pastrani (1832–1880)." "It all becomes," Shapcott has said, "in different ways, evidence." But if that search for evidence has sometimes led outward to the integration "of lyric form and tone with narrative and documentary techniques" in fictional works such as *White Stag of Exile* and *The Search for Galina,* it has also provided a stance for poetic scrutiny of personal history. "Instructions for Moving" is a sequence about "broken presents," breaking up a household, a marriage, and trying to do it with neither bitterness nor denial of loss: "We need to demonstrate, this meal, / separation does not exclude civility." It ends with an elegy both playful and poignant for the household cat, used over the years "to bind and divide":

Black cat showed us. More than any animal of ours
the death of black cat claws at our exposed parts.
Her dying was slow we were not sure,
we were dry eyed.
Black cat intended it would be that way.

More ominous evidence is found in ''Young Doctor's Kit,''
about the remembered death of a childhood pet, a dog bitten by a tick
at Christmastime in 1944:

We were saved from the War but I heard
what the Vet said: ''What's in the system stays.''
We don't know what we hoard.

But if it is death that is hoarded, it is unlikely that Shapcott will
go down silent. His has been a constant and prolific voice, and in his
development is encapsulated much of the history of contemporary
Australian poetry. He has said that his early work ''explored primarily responses to environment and a young man's apprehension of
life.'' In a poem like ''Shadow of War'' we find a rural world of
substantial images in which the intersection of landscape and human
experience is effected by building the poem around a dramatic or
narrative nexus. Its serious emotional content—the uncomprehended
anguish of the farmer whose son has been killed at war—is contained
by normative syntax and formal stanzaic structures.

''Sestina with Refrain'' (1976) offers a very different voice,
self-conscious about form, playing typographical games, fracturing
syntax and narrative sequence, as the speaker resists the ''bruising''
of his dead World War I father. In the interim Shapcott had been
involved as poet, editor, and critic with a realignment of literary
allegiances toward North America and with changes in the linguistic
and formal nature of poetry that transferred primacy from world to
word. There is a migration to New York, to Seventh Avenue and
Central Park, where trees become not natural objects to be recorded
but elements in a fragmented experience, inventions of perception.

This inventiveness Shapcott carried home with him to Bisbane
(''Shabbytown'') and can be seen in ''The City of Home,'' where
''the smell of lantana still clings to an old pullover,'' although it is a
place ''reached only in dreams'' for someone who has become much
preoccupied with names, exile, and the lively chanciness of traveling.
Nonetheless, his has become one of the voices speaking with a new
kind of noncolonial confidence, whether in looking back to an
inheritance European as well as English or in declaring in ''Taste of
Life'' of the new house that is ''the map of ancestors,''

We are in this together,—The key fits. Ours.
Nothing will keep us from stamping this place
into liver-red bricks of our own.

—Jennifer Strauss

SHAPIRO, David (Joel)

Nationality: American. **Born:** Newark, New Jersey, 2 January 1947.
Education: Columbia University, New York, B.A. (magna cum
laude) 1968, Ph.D. 1973; Clare College, Cambridge (Kellett fellow,
1968–70), B.A. (honors) 1970, M.A. 1974. **Family:** Married Lindsay

Stamm in 1970; one child. **Career:** Instructor and assistant professor
of English, Columbia University, 1972–81. Visiting professor, Brooklyn
College, 1979, and Princeton University, New Jersey, 1982–83. Since
1980 writer-in-residence and visiting adjunct professor, Cooper Union, New York. Associate professor of art history, 1980–96, and since
1996 professor, William Paterson College, Wayne, New Jersey. Since
1963 a violinist with several orchestras, including the New Jersey
Symphony and the American Symphony; since 1970 editorial associate, *Art News,* New York. Since 1980 has collaborated with the
architect John Hejduk on theatrical masques and architectural projects. **Awards:** Gotham Book Mart award, 1962; Bread Loaf Writers
Conference Robert Frost fellowship, 1965; Ingram Merrill Foundation fellowship, 1967; Book-of-the-Month Club fellowship, 1968;
Creative Artists Public Service grant, 1974; Morton Dauwen Zabel
award, 1977; National Endowment for the Arts grant, 1979, 1980, and
Humanities fellowship, 1979, 1980; Graham Foundation grantee,
1996–97; Foundation for Continuing Performance Art grantee,
1996–97. **Address:** 3001 Henry Hudson Parkway, Bronx, New York
10463–4747, U.S.A.

PUBLICATIONS

Poetry

Poems. Privately printed, 1960.
A Second Winter. Privately printed, 1961.
When Will the Bluebird. Privately printed, 1962.
January: A Book of Poems. New York, Holt Rinehart, 1965.
Poems from Deal. New York, Dutton, 1969.
A Man Holding an Acoustic Panel. New York, Dutton, 1971.
The Dance of Things. New York, Lincoln Center, 1971.
The Page-Turner. New York, Liveright, 1973.
Lateness (single poem). New York, Nobodaddy Press, 1976.
Lateness (collection). Woodstock, New York, Overlook Press, 1978.
To an Idea. New York, Overlook Press, 1983.
House, Blown Apart. Woodstock, New York, Overlook Press, 1988.
After a Lost Original. Atascadero, California, Solo Press, 1990.

Plays

New England Masque, music by Morton Feldman (produced Boston).

Screenplay: *Mobile Homes,* with Rudolph Burckhardt.

Other

John Ashbery: An Introduction to the Poetry. New York, Columbia
    University Press, 1979.
Poets and Painters (exhibition catalog). Denver, Denver Art Mu-
    seum, 1979.
Jim Dine: Painting What One Is. New York, Abrams, 1981.
Jasper Johns: Drawings 1954–1984. New York, Abrams, 1984.
Mondrian Flowers. New York, Abrams, 1990.
Alfred Leslie: The Killing Cycle, with Judith Stein. St. Louis, Mis-
    souri, Saint Louis Art Museum, 1991.
The Thunder God: A Chinese Folktale. Sydney, Harcourt Brace,
    1992.
Michael Goldberg: Goldberg Variations. Viterbo, Italy, Edizioni
    Primaprint, 1997.

Editor, with Ron Padgett, *An Anthology of New York Poets*. New York, Random House, 1970.

Editor, *Inventory: New & Selected Poems,* by Frank Lima, West Stockbridge, Massachusetts, Hard Press, 1997.

Editor, with Bill Beckley, *Uncontrollable Beauty: Toward a New Aesthetics*. New York, Allworth Press, 1998.

Translator, with Arthur A. Cohen, *The New Art of Color: The Writings of Robert and Sonia Delaunay*. New York, Viking Press, 1978.

*

Manuscript Collection: Syracuse University Library, New York.

Critical Studies: In *New York Review of Books,* Christmas 1971; unpublished master's theses by Stephen Paul Miller, City University of New York, and Michael Simon, Brown University, Providence, Rhode Island, 1977; Thomas Fink, in *American Poetry Review* (Philadelphia), January-February 1988; "The Paranoia of Postmodernism" by William Bywater, in *Philosophy and Literature* (Baltimore, Maryland), 14(1), April 1990; "Tracing David Shapiro's 'The Seasons'" by Thomas Fink, in *Contemporary Literature* (Madison, Wisconsin), 37(3), fall 1996.

Theatrical Activities: Director: **Film**—*House (Blown Apart),* 1984.

David Shapiro comments:

(1975) Simone Weil said, "The Fool, taken literally, is speaking the truth." Often, in my favorite poets, paradox and "nonsense" achieve not so much the ambiguity analyzed denotatively and connotatively by Mr. Empson but a pointing to logos by its extreme absence. As early tribes were obsessed by shadows, convinced that an animal's shadow was part of the animal, so Stein, Carroll, Borges employ the techniques of nonsense because they are convinced, like me, that the poet's task is to subdue—in Rimbaud's terms—the formless. If the task of positivism was to expunge nonsense, the work of poetry is to use it. That is "the meaning of meaninglessness," to use nonsense and uncertainty and discontinuity as the central tone and abiding metaphor of our peculiar predicament.

(1990) My early statements underlining the use of psychological and philosophical uncertainty now strike me as exactly that: the work of a young man in a decent neo-Nietzschean mode. But I have come to mistrust the massive skepticism of this epoch. My standards today are less likely to be the masters of nonsense than radical pluralists whose methods are polarized between doubt and affirmation. Sir Isaiah Berlin, Meyer Schapiro, Roman Jakobson, Gershom Scholem, and Walter Benjamin as critical models are my luminous teachers. Gilbert-Rolfe has criticized this as my "humanism," but I am unwilling to associate with the fashionable inhumanism of our day, though I have written on groups and collaboration. But the example of a Pasternak and his mistrust of the group, with his agonized celebration of the revolutionary city, still holds for me as a musical standard of imperfection. Perhaps my "maximalist" pluralism is as eristic as the minimalism of my youth. But I would like to see it as the mature reformulation of a formalism. I still associate myself with Stevens's remark: "All poetry is experimental poetry." But I am also guided by another of his adages: "There is no wing like meaning." I had the arrogant desire to make the fresh empirical impressionism of the so-called New York school into something angry, less lenient with

history and sexuality, solid as Cézanne. My musical model: the polyrhythms of Elliot Carter and the eternal example of Mozart's late divertimento. But with all of these models I would like to think of escaping the anxiety of influence by a "joys of influence." A poet is always most absurd when "speaking," and speaking of his intentions. So perhaps the worst in one will be this very ambition, as opposed to the antiheroic unpretentious lyricists without the impedimenta of tradition.

*   *   *

David Shapiro is a latter-day metaphysical poet. Although the reader is more likely to encounter the spaceship or the automobile in his poems than Donne's twin compasses, or reference to the ideas of Jacques Derrida and Gottlob Frege than to Scholasticism, the term applies nevertheless. Shapiro's poetry captures the ambiguity of the mind in motion: the logical frames of thought and their ruptures, remembrance's fitful tracing and forgetting's gentle erasure. In his later work this theme of writing, memory, and forgetting has taken on greater cultural and historical urgency as Shapiro mediates the nature of Jewish experience, which for thousands of years has been marked by the complementary antipodes of abandonment and hope. New voices have thus entered Shapiro's poetic colloquy of sages: Walter Benjamin, Gershom Scholem, Baruch Spinoza, the rabbis of the Talmud.

Shapiro's early work, *January,* published when he was only eighteen years old, *Poems from Deal,* and *A Man Holding an Acoustic Panel,* are full of witty paradox and non sequiturs, coupled with more than a hint of Ashberyian Dada. Yet in his 1971 collection *A Man Holding an Acoustic Panel* Shapiro had already begun to develop the mode more typical of his later work, the philosophical meditation with personal or erotic overtones. Thus, in his "Ode to Timaeus," after Plato's dialogue of the same name, Shapiro lyrically explores the nature of desire:

> The best is gymnastic;
> next best like a cloud or sailboat;
> least best is a drastic
> screwing you can't do without.
>
> Two things alone cannot be
> united without a third satisfactorily;
> so it shakes man and woman
>
> together till she grows large again
> Such is the origin
> of all that is human.

Another typical element in Shapiro's work is its autobiographical slant, imaginatively transfigured and centered on his family, his violin (as a young man Shapiro was a professional violinist), and his compensatory fantasy life:

> There are no umbrellas, there are only frosty parachutes,
> Little angels who instruct him how to fly.
> He must not struggle too much with his hands,
> Which having practiced the violin now dog-paddle in air.
> High above the invigorated gulf the air walks down its
>   own road.

The sister jumps up in a dual column of wind.
Inside, Mother serves breakfast; the bluejay gulps at the
    feeding-station.
The family now knows he can fly, but still father
    knows best.

This element gets its most moving exposure in "Friday Night Quartet" (*To an Idea*), a sequence that memorializes Shapiro's mother. Here Shapiro is at his most straightforward and touching; still, his understatement avoids any bathos or sentimentality the subject matter might invite:

Lying on the angiogram cot, strapped down and hot
    and bloody,
My mother said, The worst words in the English language
Are these David—Don't move.
And what do you think the best words are: Here's
    some water.

Shapiro's collection *After a Lost Original* shifts the autobiographical focus to the next generation, to Shapiro's relation with his son. In "To My Son" the poet offers himself as a sacrifice of love in the Oedipal struggle:

I love you so much
I am going to let you kill me . . .

I fear every narrow road
on which we will eventually meet
But do not banish me so fast, my son
Your clubfoot that I have pierced
is more beautiful, to me, than your mother's breast.

Shapiro's best work springs from his reflection on the restlessness of imagination and desire, a theme he renders at times scherzando and at other times with a melancholy tremolo. This restlessness impels a metonymic drift from term to term, at once the subject matter and the formal principle of a poem like "The Devil's Trill Sonata" in *Lateness:*

The elevator slips so far, so fast
Surely the ladder then is an improvement
On the elevator in this respect. And don't forget the
    fireman's pole
Or Rapunzel, whose hair was a staircase.

This passage performs a (literal) slippage through the semantic field of "things that go up and down," graduating rapidly to the phallic fireman's pole and Rapunzel's fetishistic torrent of blond hair.

Behind or beyond the play of desire, however, there lies nothing graspable. When this play is momentarily arrested, the word is seen to refer only to other words. Even the master signifier, God or the name of the father, is caught up in this speech chain, spun out above a void. Thus, Shapiro writes in "A Prayer," from *House, Blown Apart,*

Our father, emphasis on our elder betters
With the pronouns not possessed but stolen like
    a royal teacup

Thy will be done, since we have little faith that
    ours ever could

On earth and heaven: two truncated rhomboids
Give us this day, give us one day, give it
Like water, and also give us water
Snow, music, and house I now avoid, as one avoids
certain words, and they are words.

Poetry, as the poems in *After a Lost Original* suggest, is inseparable from parody, hypothetical reconstruction, reduplication, necessary ruin. But this sober assessment has its corollary in the urgency of poetry as remembrance, repair, and resistance. Poetry comes down to us as sorrowful ashes, for it stakes itself in the fire of history:

are you in the
"forgetting movement"
No I'm in the remembrance
movement and poetry
is fire in the house.

—Tyrus Miller

SHAPIRO, Harvey

Nationality: American. **Born:** Chicago, Illinois, 27 January 1924. **Education:** Yale University, New Haven, Connecticut, B.A. 1947; Columbia University, New York, M.A. 1948. **Military Service:** U.S. Army Air Force 1943–45: Distinguished Flying Cross. **Family:** Married Edna Lewis Kaufman in 1953; two sons. **Career:** Instructor in English, Cornell University, Ithaca, New York, 1949–50, 1951–52; creative writing fellow, Bard College, Annandale-on-Hudson, New York, 1950–51; assistant editor, *Commentary,* New York, 1955–56; editor, *New Yorker,* 1956–57; editor, *New York Times Book Review,* 1975–83. Editor, 1957–64, assistant editor, 1964–75, deputy editor, 1983–94, and since 1994 consulting editor, *New York Times Magazine.* **Awards:** YMHA Poetry Center award, 1952; Swallow Press award, 1954; Rockefeller grant, 1968. **Address:** 43 Pierrepont Street, Brooklyn, New York 11201, U.S.A.

PUBLICATIONS

Poetry

The Eye. Denver, Swallow, 1953.
The Book and Other Poems. Cummington, Massachusetts, Cummington Press, 1955.
Mountain, Fire, Thornbush. Denver, Swallow, 1961.
Battle Report: Selected Poems. Middletown, Connecticut, Wesleyan University Press, 1966.
This World. Middletown, Connecticut, Wesleyan University Press, 1971.
Lauds. New York, Sun, 1975.
Lauds and Nightsounds. New York, Sun, 1978.
The Light Holds. Middletown, Connecticut, Wesleyan University Press, 1984.

National Cold Storage Company: New and Selected Poems. Middletown, Connecticut, Wesleyan University Press, 1988.
A Day's Portion. Brooklyn, Hanging Loose Press, 1994.
Selected Poems. Middletown, Connecticut, Wesleyan University Press, and Manchester, England, Carcanet, 1997.

*

Critical Studies: By David Ignatow, in *The Nation* (New York), 24 April 1967; ''Rebels in the Kingdom'' by Jascha Kessler, in *Midstream* (New York), April 1972; *Figures of Capable Imagination* by Harold Bloom, New York, Seabury Press, 1976; ''Light from the Mountain'' by David Ray, in *New Letters Review of Books* (Kansas City, Missouri), 11(1), 1988; ''I Sing the City Eclectic'' by Matthew Flamm, in *The Nation* (New York), 13 June 1994; ''Zen Records'' by Lawrence Joseph, in *The Nation,* 19 December 1997; ''Looking for the Way: The Poetry of Harvey Shapiro'' by Norman Finkelstein, in *Religion and Literature,* autumn 1998.

Harvey Shapiro comments:

My earliest poetry, as sampled in *The Eye* (Swallow, 1953), comes out of several influences, several traditions. As between Chaucer's note words, small articulations, and Milton's large sounds, big lines, blocks of vowels, organ stops, etc., I was a Milton man. It was that sound that led me into poetry. And it was that sound that got me reading Hart Crane, one of the first American poets I began to study seriously. (I did my master's essay at Columbia on his *White Buildings.*) It was Crane's sound and technique that interested me, not his (sadly) optimistic message, as it was his ability to cut city scenes and modern nervosities into Elizabethan blank verse.

Concurrent interests: French symbolist poetry (Rimbaud, Baudelaire) and always a side interest in William Carlos Williams, just then beginning to emerge. This was an interest that pulled against all the others but was to become dominant. My worst poems of that period came out of my hankering for large sound—poems of meaningless bombast—and attempts to reproduce French symbolism—just literary.

To move on. In an attempt to work out of the literary (it was about that time I dropped teaching English at universities), I went back to my childhood and early adolescent interest in Jewish subjects and beliefs. Here too I could see a division between the Hebraic (Milton) and the Yiddish (Chaucer), and my poems came mainly from the Hebraic. At least that was true when I was working from the past. When I was working from the present, I consciously aped Yiddish poetry and speech rhythms and locutions, as remembered from my home.

My Jewish poems were more than a celebration of Jewishness. They were also a searching for the primitive, to get behind the Bible stories and Hebrew school to basic irrational, primitive myth.

Those poems probably represented a ghetto for me, one I made for myself, in part to protect myself during that time I was shifting from job to job, hard put to find a way to support my growing family. So it was a fictive security inside a world of real insecurity.

Which brings me to the present. I work now mainly in free form, though sometimes my lines jump off from a basic four beats. Sometimes they are William Carlos Williams lines (phrase units designed to move swiftly).

The Williams influence is more than technical. Through him and through Charles Reznikoff I have learned to find my subject matter in the streets of my own life mostly. Actually the shift in my manner was dictated by new subject matter clamoring to be heard, as it is for every

poet. The Jewish influence remains in my constant search for the way, the way of right living. But here the way is constantly in the present and has always to be sought; it is not given. Urban mystic. My poems are private when set against the public declarations of many of my contemporaries, but I think they could only have been written today and that they are an accurate reading of our time.

*   *   *

Harvey Shapiro's mature poetry knows how to profit from walking naked, without florid effects or prosodic contrivances. Yet his poems are constructed on solid foundations, in particular the spare, urban poetry of older Brooklyn poets like George Oppen and Charles Reznikoff. From these one-time members of the objectivist movement, the 1930s brainchild of William Carlos Williams, Shapiro learned to keep his eye and intellect trained on the object of his imaginative gaze. He resisted the facile transcendence that by the 1970s had become the characteristic aesthetic gesture of mainstream American poetry. At the same time Shapiro updated objectivist practice, accessing the more directly personal material made available by the confessional poets:

> Not wanting to invent emotion
> I pursued the flat literal,
> Saying wife, children, job
> over and over.

His domestic verse cuts across the sentiment usually associated with poems on the home and family, sparing neither himself nor others. It grapples with marital strife, postmarital affairs, and generational conflict: ''I spent one hour with one son at his shrink / discussing (my choice) why he seemed to hate me.''

As a career newspaperman, Shapiro shares with Williams, the pediatrician-poet, the opportunistic poetics of an overworked professional. His muse speaks in spurts and snatches, late at night with a whiskey bottle, or during business hours:

> I am on the lookout for
> A great illumining,
> Prepared to recognize it
> Instantly and put it to use
> Even among the desks
> And chairs of the office, should
> It come between nine and five.

This makes for a jagged, rib-jabbing poetry. His ideal medium is the loosely knit sequence of brief images or aphoristic fragments—splinters of urban life that are made to yield larger meanings beneath the pressure of his intellect.

Shapiro's poems are the determinedly private meditations of a man engaged daily in the public use of language. Their aim is self-knowledge rather than transformation or catharsis. They are the product of his need to understand ''[his] way of being in the world,'' as he says in ''A Jerusalem Notebook'':

> not perfect freedom or the pitch
> of madness, but that the particulars
> of my life become manifest
> to me walking these dark streets.

As such, they are frank and unmediated, an insomniac's catalog of lust, "ego demons," and night terrors.

Shapiro's gallows humor, his uncensored treatment of sex, and his mordant asides on middle-aged and middle-class life may not be to everyone's taste. Yet bleak and unpretty as his poems often are,

> now and then a voice cuts through
> saying something right: No sound
> is dissonant which tells of life.

—Martin McKinsey

SHAUGHNESSY, Brenda

Nationality: American. **Born:** Okinawa, Japan, 1970. **Education:** Columbia University, New York, M.F.A. in poetry.

PUBLICATIONS

Poetry

Interior with Sudden Joy. New York, Farrar Straus, 1999.

*   *   *

Brenda Shaughnessy's poems in *Interior with Sudden Joy* are lively but dense and are sexually charged. Most have a first-person narrator who reflects upon relationships and private experiences. Shaughnessy sometimes uses unusual words like "scopophilia" and concocted words like "aracholescence." Because she employs odd images and comparisons, her meanings are often difficult to discern, and it is sometimes necessary for the reader to puzzle over her poetry.

In "Still Life, with Glozinia" the narrator proposes to draw a picture of the listener ("I will make something of you both pigment / and insecticide"), suggesting underlying ill intent. The poet draws an analogy with nuns who make a wine with berries and gloxinia that turns their insides "all blue." Like them, the speaker is cold and unable to paint or move her subject. Various other poems are addressed to a difficult lover. Shaughnessy invokes a loved one in "Letter to the Crevice Novice," suggesting that he or she is like a vampire who would kill to keep love alive for centuries and that "love was death / enough." A question arises about the depth of this love since the novice perceives love only superficially. "Fetish: The Historical Orphan" bemoans the glacial love of one addressed as "Czarina," who causes the speaker pain; the speaker wishes for "a fusing of the retinas, to see yourself as I see you." "What's Uncanny" deals with a lover with whom there is "too much choreography . . . Too little dance." "Mistress Formika" relates the pleasure and pain of love: "Can this be too much pleasure in one so smart, debauched / and thin?" But quarreling also ensues. "Illumine" asks for intimacy and emotional closure, and in "Postfeminism" the poet speaks of two types of people: "Hot with mixed / light drunk with insult. You and me." "Arachnolescence" is a dark poem about fantasies of pain the speaker will inflict upon a lover who is an "arachno-demigod." "Rise" relates the resumption of an affair, yet

the end of the poem strikes a bitter note: "you lie with me, smelling / of almonds, as the poisoned do."

In Shaughnessy's comic, voyeuristic poem "Panoption" the speaker, looking through a telescope on a viewing deck, sees a roommate experimenting with a vibrator. Several possibilities emerge: to confess in detail to the roommate, to keep watching, or to stay home and watch a potential viewer of the speaker. "Lacquer" is about the poet's mother, who writes her diary in Japanese, a language not understood by the daughter. The poem is emblematic of the failure of communication.

As she incorporates curious words into a private diction, Shaughnessy's art becomes resonant of poets like John Ashbery. Her poetry is both idiosyncratic and sensuous and, like that of Dorothy Tanning, is indebted to the surrealists. At times Shaughnessy's poetry is self-conscious and enigmatic. Witty and lively, Shaughnessy celebrates female sexuality as the theme of the joy and sorrow of love informs her poems.

—Shirley J. Paolini

SHELTON, Richard

Nationality: American. **Born:** Boise, Idaho, 24 June 1933. **Education:** Harding College, Searcy, Arkansas, 1951–53; Abilene Christian College, Texas, B.A. in English 1958; University of Arizona, Tucson, M.A. 1960. **Military Service:** U.S. Army, 1956–58. **Family:** Married Lois Bruce in 1956; one son. **Career:** Teacher, Lowell School, Bisbee, Arizona, 1958–60; director, Ruth Stephan Poetry Center, Tucson, 1964–65. Instructor, 1960–64, assistant professor, 1969–73, associate professor, 1973–79, director of the creative writing program, 1979–81, professor of English, 1979–91, and since 1991 Regent's Professor, University of Arizona, Tucson. **Awards:** International Poetry Forum United States award, 1970; Borestone Mountain award, 1970, 1971, 1972; National Endowment for the Arts fellowship, 1976, 1991; Governor's award, 1991; Western States award, 1992; Southwestern award for literary excellence, 1994; Arizona Library Association's Adult Author award, 1994. **Address:** Department of English, University of Arizona, Tucson, Arizona 85721, U.S.A.

PUBLICATIONS

Poetry

Journal of Return. San Francisco, Kayak, 1969.
The Tattooed Desert. Pittsburgh, University of Pittsburgh Press, 1971.
The Heroes of Our Time. Lincoln, Nebraska, Best Cellar Press, 1972.
Of All the Dirty Words. Pittsburgh, University of Pittsburgh Press, 1972.
Calendar: A Cycle of Poems. Phoenix, Arizona, Baleen Press, 1972.
Among the Stones. Pittsburgh, Monument Press, 1973.
Chosen Place. Crete, Nebraska, Best Cellar Press, 1975.
You Can't Have Everything. Pittsburgh, University of Pittsburgh Press, 1975.
Desert Water. Pittsburgh, Monument Press, 1977.
The Bus to Veracruz. Pittsburgh, University of Pittsburgh Press, 1978.

Selected Poems 1969–1981. Pittsburgh, University of Pittsburgh Press, 1982.

A Kind of Glory. Port Townsend, Washington, Copper Canyon Press, 1982.

Hohokam. Tucson, Arizona, Sun/Gemini Press, 1986.

The Other Side of the Story. Lewiston, Idaho, Confluence Press, 1987.

Plays

Screenplays: *Sonoran: The Hidden Desert,* 1979; *Another Day,* 1981; *The Sound of Water,* 1983.

Other

Going Back to Bisbee. Tucson, University of Arizona Press, 1992.

*

Critical Studies: In *Chicago Tribune Magazine,* 22 January 1970; in *Prairie Schooner* (Lincoln, Nebraska), summer 1972; in *Poetry* (Chicago), July 1972, July 1973, and April 1978; in *San Francisco Chronicle,* 27 May 1973; by Dave Smith, in *Los Angeles Times,* 19 February 1978; by Philip Allan Friedman, in *Gramercy Review* (New York), summer 1979; *Rereadings* by Michael Hogan, Crete, Nebraska, Best Cellar Press, 1979; by Victor Contoski, in *Western American Literature* (Logan, Utah), 14(1), 1979; ''Southwestern Gothic: On the Frontier between Landscape and Locale'' by Scott P. Sanders, in *Frontier Gothic,* n.p., Farleigh Dickinson University Press, 1993; ''Poetic Space: Richard Shelton'' by Carolyn Kizer, in *Proses,* Port Townsend, Washington, Copper Canyon Press, 1994.

Richard Shelton comments:

I hope my work reflects something of the Sonora Desert, in which I have lived for more than thirty years.

*   *   *

At age twenty-five Richard Shelton moved from Texas to southern Arizona (Tucson), where he has lived ever since, teaching literature courses at the University of Arizona and writing book after book of his perceptions and responses to the desert climate and terrain he has called his ''chosen place.'' Shelton is now an inveterate Southwesterner, with deep, often spiritual affinity for the rocks and saguaro cactus of the desert, the mountains, the sea one hundred miles below him in the Gulf of California. These are his usual subjects in the many books he has written since his first publication, *Journal of Return.* The sea and desert are the extremes of his personal mythology. They frame the earth for him, an earth of silences, of ghostly night animals, of rocks that exchange brief whispers about the moon on nights of the long dry season. Tucson is ringed with mountains, the Tucson Mountains, Mount Lemmon, Mica Mountain, and others, and they are a third dimension of nature for him, an urge of nature to thrust up into the sky, a dream of the rocks that lie scattered on the desert floor. The night sky is a brilliance of immense stars in Shelton's poems, under which dark, quiet, sometimes desperate lives are endured.

Shelton's verse technique consolidates several extreme tendencies of modern American poetry—the spiritual visions of nature to be found in Robinson Jeffers's and William Stafford's work together with Robert Lowell's painful self-excoriations—but the result for Shelton is often more discord and discontinuity than wholeness of vision. The desert remains for him an ambiguous metaphor; either it is a spiritual paradise or it is the hell of exiled human life. As a result his poetry never leaps fully into one or the other possibility, but it seems suspended between a potential vision of desert infinities and an obsession with his own lifelong unhappiness and skepticism, as expressed in ''Mexico'':

> I never find what I am looking for
> and each time I return older
> with my ugliness intact
> but with the knowledge that if it isn't there
> in the darkness under Scorpio
> it isn't anywhere

He writes as though his own individuality will never quite hatch out to the larger realm of nature he longs to be part of.

This alone would be sufficiently interesting drama or poetry, but for Shelton it tends to sever his poetry from its intended depth and freedom. His canon has no perceptible growth or development of vision but rather moves through cycles of restatement and reexamination of his dilemma. At his best he can render the desert world with striking immediacy, particularly where he feels himself to be its interpreter and voice, as in ''The Kingdom of the Moon'':

> the moon commands the desert cold
> a word so harsh
> it splits the tongue
> of the true aloe
>
> the moon pulls stones
> to the surface
> and directs the ghosts
> of dry rivers in their paths
> toward the sea

In ''Burning'' he says,

> today the rain kept
> coming back as if it had
> nowhere else to go
>
> and each time
> the desert welcomed it
> the gates of the desert
> never rust but they open
> only to the voice of rain

Shelton's poetry must be judged carefully. If it is at times didactic, sentimental, indeterminate, or merely repetitious, these limitations are along the way of a large and beautiful intention: to capture a region and to impose upon it a human witness and contact of extraordinary thoroughness and sensitivity. Many of his poems will drop away in time, but what remains of his canon will be durable lyrics that are essentially American in their effort to find spiritual jointure with the land.

Though Shelton's poetry has not continued to grow much, he has taken to prose for further self-exploration. In the personal memoir *Going Back to Bisbee,* modeled on Steinbeck's *Travels with Charley,* we go along in his old blue Dodge, ''Blue Boy,'' back to the mining town of Bisbee, Arizona, where the young Shelton had his first teaching job at Lowell Junior High. The mountain he lived on is now a bald pit mined out by Phelps Dodge. Bisbee is where the poet's consciousness and concerns for desert nature were formed, and he recalls his two years there with pain and pride as the place that made him what he is.

—Paul Christensen

SHETTY, Manohar

Nationality: Indian. **Born:** Bombay, 5 November 1953. **Education:** St. Peter's High School, Panchgani; University of Bombay, B.A. 1974. **Career:** Since 1974 a journalist. Sub-editor, *For You,* Bombay, 1974–75, *Indian Express,* Bombay, 1977–80; editor, *Keynote,* Bombay, 1982; chief sub-editor, *Sunday Mid-day,* Bangalore, 1983–85; editor, *Goa Today,* Goa, 1987–93. **Awards:** Homi Bhabha fellow, 1995–97; Fundacao Oriente fellow, 1989–99. **Address:** Panoramic Apartments, La Marvel Colony, Dona Paula, Goa 403 004, India.

PUBLICATIONS

Poetry

A Guarded Space. Bombay, Newground, 1981.
Borrowed Time. Bombay, Praxis, 1988.
Domestic Creatures: Poems. Oxford, Oxford University Press, 1994.

Other

Editor, *Ferry Crossing—Short Stories from Goa.* New Delhi, Penguin India, 1998.

*

Critical Studies: ''Manohar Shetty: Guarded Spaces'' by Bruce King, in *SPAN* (Murdoch, Australia), 20, April 1985; ''The Poet's India II'' by Bruce King, in *Modern Indian Poetry in English,* New Delhi, Oxford University Press, 1987; ''Sudeep Sen, on the New Generation of Indian Poets: Agha Shahid Ali, Manohar Shetty, Meena Alexander, Vijay Nambisan,'' in *Poetry Review,* spring 1993.

*   *   *

In Manohar Shetty's poetic world bats sweep ''through moon-gilded windows, / Gliding across the walls / Like giant bowties'' (''Bats''), a cockroach ''tumbles out / Like a family secret'' (''Domestic Creatures''), and moored boats ''lurch closer, bodies chafe / And whisper, wince at each / Touch of the wind'' (''The Boats''). Shetty's distinctive analogical vision elicits the uncanny from the most everyday materials, but his greatest strength is as an innovative formalist. Accomplished rhymes, often internal—''Till one lax season an axe / Convulsed the boughs'' (''Familiarities'')—and deft syntactic balancing acts—''Unfinished houses resemble / Abandoned ruins, and this one / With stunted columns and jagged / Supports like a child's drawing / Has been left out to soak in / The monsoon'' (''Bearings'')—make for a disciplined verse whose precise rhythms effortlessly carry a diction that bristles with little surprises.

Shetty's poetic range is carefully restricted to an immediately observable reality. He appears refreshingly secure in his circumscribed subject, declining to agonize over criteria of ''Indianness.'' (Yet his writing is awash with local light and color, especially from the sea of his native Bombay, whose defining presence is registered in some of his strongest poems.) His techniques, too, are strictly limited. He has perfected a semiregular three-to-four-stress line that allows for infinitely extensible semantic units, particularly when conjoined with his signature preference for the participle, as in ''Ants'':

> Livid seethings outnumbering
> Harnessed thrashing beasts,
> They advance, planned cordons
> Dredging the land, multiplying,
> Communicating silently.

The same technique can be seen in ''Neighbourhood'':

> Her consuming eye shifting
> To an old man moving
> With a brimming tin-can past
> A slumped dog, its paws
> Cycling slowly in the air,
> Jaws grinding wide in a yawn

In the latter poem a routine village scene is transfixed in a single, multiply enjambed sentence of forty-one lines. There can be no doubt that as a craftsman Shetty has found his métier.

Just below the composed surfaces of Shetty's work tugs a deep tension between the pains of sentience and the apparent peace of the nonhuman. ''Mannequin'' brings to life a department store model in her ''transparent cage'' who laments that she ''cannot go beyond / This fixed fond smile.'' A related monologue, ''Scarecrow,'' is spoken by a stick figure sentenced by his master to remain immobile amid the flux of nature; at the very end of the poem the all-seeing scarecrow pronounces ambiguously, ''But the long night is never over. / Buried in the scorched earth / At my master's foot, the scorpion / Unfolds a heraldic emblem.'' In ''Departures'' the speaker, leaving home on a long journey, observes a moth on the windowpane of the bus. The moth's stillness (''Wrapped in peace, its wings / A neat canvas tent, distance / Never came to an end; live / Minuscule mummy in a pyramid / Of sky, trees and fertile air!'') gives measure, balance, and ultimately solace to the speaker's lonely displacement: ''I felt like a stone / Tensing in the air—hanging fast / To my light exemplar / Still rooted to glass.''

For Western readers Shetty's achievement is to have domesticated, through meticulous observation, an unruly and potentially exotic habitat. (*Domestic Creatures* is the title of a rich 1994 compendium of his poems.) But he is always alive to the deranging possibilities of the commonplace. Thus, in ''One Morning'' he writes, ''I woke to honey / Startled into sunlight / Pouring in from a sky so vivid / It seemed unravelled / From a bolt of blue silk.'' The poem ends with these lines:

I sat in the bus crushed
Between people, the short trip

Past landmarks so inured to
They looked unreal, as when
Staring in intense fatigue
At a familiar word
It appears an alien script.

So, too, Shetty's poems work to unsettle and realign our perceptions of the familiar. Within his small sphere his originality is striking, his characteristic compression elegant and memorable.

—Minnie Singh

SHUMAKER, Peggy

Nationality: American. **Born:** La Mesa, California, 22 March 1952. **Education:** University of Arizona, Tucson, B.A. 1974, M.F.A. 1979. **Career:** Graduate assistant instructor, University of Arizona, Tucson, 1976–79; writer-in-residence, Arizona Commission on the Arts, 1979–85; faculty associate in creative writing, Arizona State University, 1983–85; visiting assistant professor in creative writing, University of Alaska Fairbanks, 1985–86; director of creative writing, department of English, Old Dominion University, Norfolk, Virginia, 1986–88; codirector of creative writing, department of English, 1988–99, head of department of English, 1991–93, associate professor and professor, 1993–99, and since 1999 professor emeritus, University of Alaska Fairbanks. Director, Old Dominion University Literary Festival, 1987–88; featured poet, Writers at Work Conference, Park City, Utah, 1989, Port Townsend Writers Conference, Washington, 1993, Artspeak, Wyoming Arts Council, 1995, and Quartz Mountain Oklahoma Art Institute, 1995; coordinator, Midnight Sun Writers Series, 1989–95, and Alaskan Poetry Festival, 1990; literary judge, WESTAF Western States Book Awards, 1995, *Nimrod*/Pablo Neruda Prize for Poetry, 1995, and National Foundation for Advancement in the Arts, 1999; since 1994 member, Western Literature Presenting Network. Member, 1990, board of directors, vice president, 1991–92, president, 1992–93, and board adviser, 1993–94, Associated Writing Programs. **Award:** NEA Fellowship, 1989. **Address:** 100 Cushman Street, Suite 210, Fairbanks, Alaska 99701, U.S.A.

PUBLICATIONS

Poetry

Esperanza's Hair. Tuscaloosa, University of Alabama Press, 1985.
The Circle of Totems. Pittsburgh, University of Pittsburgh Press, 1988.
Braided River (chapbook). Anchorage, Limner Press, 1993.
Wings Moist from the Other World. Pittsburgh, University of Pittsburgh Press, 1994.

*

Critical Study: "Inherently Restless" by Marjorie K. Cole, in *American Book Review,* 11(6), January 1990.

*   *   *

Peggy Shumaker's poetry represents the period style that defines much of the work produced in university writing programs since the 1970s. She writes primarily in free verse, and her thematic concerns include coming to terms with survival in abusive relationships, personal emergence and identification in the larger context of contemporary feminism, correcting and clearing up the half-truths of the past—especially her own—and protesting environmental abuses, particularly in her adopted state of Alaska.

Born in La Mesa, California, Shumaker attended the University of Arizona and has directed the writing programs both at Old Dominion University in Norfolk, Virginia, and at the University of Alaska. Shumaker has also served as president of the Associated Writing Programs, the increasingly influential national service organization for creative writing programs and the students and teachers associated with them.

In the representative poem "Calvinism" Shumaker critically speculates on inherited faith and the mother-daughter relationship:

When the knob on my calf
reached the size of an egg,
my mother held a double-edged blade
in the blue-gas flame.
Look away when I lance it,
she did too, so the putrid spray
hit only her earlobe and the left lens
of her glasses . . .

Moving from unadorned (albeit gruesome) reportage to a forced revelation, Shumaker sees in her own discomfort the suffering and contamination of others:

    . . . I misheard her, *abscess,*
and pictured instead, in my leg,
the bottomless hole
sinners fall into, evil ones
cast into my leg, and me
walking around with muscles full
of other folks' deceptions.

The poem continues with an account of the treatment of the speaker's ailment. This in turn sets up the wished-for, if unlikely, personal revelation at the poem's end. As the last gauze dressing that "tempted the poison out of the wound" is removed, the poet offers this declaration:

    . . . and I knew
about limbo, a dance involving a broomstick
and flesh bending back, and I knew about belief,
and the boiling oblivion.

The poem resonates if the reader can supply much substance among the thinnest of connections drawn between witchcraft and witchhunts, a mother's home remedies, and the poet's boil. Arguably, this writing is as much personal anecdote as it is poetry, but it is also very representative of its time.

—Robert McDowell

SHUTTLE, Penelope (Diane)

Nationality: British. **Born:** Staines, Middlesex, 12 May 1947. **Education:** Staines Grammar School, 1952–59; Matthew Arnold County Secondary School, 1959–65. **Family:** Married Peter Redgrove, *q.v.,* in 1980; one daughter. **Career:** Part-time shorthand typist, 1965–69. Judge for numerous awards and competitions. **Awards:** Arts Council grant, 1969, 1972, 1985; Greenwood poetry prize, 1972; Eric Gregory award, 1974. Lives in Falmouth, Cornwall. **Agent:** David Higham Associates Ltd., 5–8 Lower John Street, London WlR 4HA, England.

PUBLICATIONS

Poetry

Nostalgia Neurosis. Aylesford, Kent, St. Albert's Press, 1968.
Branch. Rushden, Northamptonshire, Sceptre Press, 1971.
Midwinter Mandala. New Malden, Surrey, Headland, 1973.
The Hermaphrodite Album, with Peter Redgrove. London, Fuller D'Arch Smith, 1973.
Moon Meal. Rushden, Northamptonshire, Sceptre Press, 1973.
Autumn Piano and Other Poems. Liverpool, Rondo, 1974.
Photographs of Persephone. Feltham, Middlesex, Quarto Press, 1974.
The Songbook of the Snow and Other Poems. Ilkley, Yorkshire, Janus Press, 1974.
The Dream. Knotting, Bedfordshire, Sceptre Press, 1975.
Webs on Fire. London, Gallery Press, 1975.
Period. London, Words, 1976.
Four American Sketches. Knotting, Bedfordshire, Sceptre Press, 1976.
The Orchard Upstairs. Oxford, Oxford University Press, 1980; New York, Oxford University Press, 1981.
The Child-Stealer. Oxford, Oxford University Press, 1983.
The Lion from Rio. Oxford, Oxford University Press, 1986.
Adventures with My Horse. Oxford, Oxford University Press, 1988.
Taxing the Rain. Oxford, Oxford University Press, 1994.
Selected Poems, 1980–1996. Oxford, Oxford University Press, n.d.
A Leaf out of His Book. Oxford, Carcanet/Oxford Poets, 1999.

Plays

Radio Plays: *The Girl Who Lost Her Glove,* 1975; *The Dauntless Girl,* 1978.

Novels

An Excusable Vengeance, in New Writers 6. London, Calder and Boyars, 1967.
All the Usual Hours of Sleeping. London, Calder and Boyars, 1969.

Wailing Monkey Embracing a Tree. London, Calder and Boyars, 1974.
The Terrors of Dr. Treviles, with Peter Redgrove. London, Routledge, 1974.
The Glass Cottage: A Nautical Romance, with Peter Redgrove. London, Routledge, 1976.
Jesusa. Falmouth, Cornwall, Granite Press, 1976.
Rainsplitter in the Zodiac Garden. London, Boyars, 1977; Nantucket, Massachusetts, Longship Press, 1978.
The Mirror of the Giant. London, Boyars, 1980.

Short Story

Prognostica. Knotting, Bedfordshire, Martin Booth, 1980.

Other

The Wise Wound: Menstruation and Everywoman, with Peter Redgrove. London, Gollancz, 1978; as *The Wise Wound: Eve's Curse and Everywoman,* New York, Marek, 1979; revised edition, London, Grafton, 1986.
Alchemy for Women: Personal Transformation through Dreams and the Female Cycle, with Peter Redgrove. N.p., Rider Books, 1995.

*

Critical Study: ''Peter Redgrove and Penelope Shuttle: The Joys and Perils of Collaboration'' by Erika Duncan, in *Book Forum* (Niantic, Connecticut), 7(4), 1986.

Penelope Shuttle comments:

When I was about eight or nine, I'd walk home from school along two tree-lined roads, Rookery Road and Acacia Avenue. I liked to choose a leaf that looked and felt special to me, and place it, as an offering or decoration or comment, at the root of another tree.

Writing poetry, I'm participating in the natural environment of the imagination.

But why *his* Book?

Women poets are now relishing and exploring the paradox inherent in a male muse. Recently Carol Rumens said: ''Some of my muses are male, some are female. It doesn't seem to me to be a very radical or schizophrenic thing to play it both ways, because I think every human being combines different elements of their gender and also perhaps the other gender.''

The Muse changes sex, the Muse is all ages.

In 1986, realizing that I was fully and passionately engaged maternally with my daughter, I made the decision to have no more children. A few months later I experienced a series of rich yet disturbing dreams featuring a young boy of about eight or nine, the same age at which I'd offered leaves to trees. He was my unconceived son, and the dreams announced a bereavement for that unmade life. But all those energies, physical and spiritual, that go into pregnancy, birth and child rearing, concentrated themselves into poetry. My unborn son became one of my muses, an unspoilt male spirit, not yet a grown man with all a man's troubled focus.

Also, the Book is Cornwall. I've lived here since 1970 and to my mind it is a masculine country. Despite the tourist layer wrapped around the region like a Cornish pastry crust, Cornwall has very high unemployment levels, and life can be as hard here for many people as the granite underfoot. Various poems here consider Cornwall, its history, its present, its alternative future.

His Book is also the book of nature. The poem sequence *Verdant* is about the carvings of pagan green men that you find in many churches. Their foliate faces remind us of vitalities and knowledge previous to Christian culture.

The title poem is for my companion Peter Redgrove. It evokes the inner and outer landscapes we've shared during our many years together, taking leaves out of one another's books. See my long stepped poem ''Geologies'' with its connection to Peter's early poem ''Minerals of Cornwall, Stones of Cornwall'' and how in his poem ''Abattoir Bride'' he says, ''And there is a leaf-marriage too . . .''

*   *   *

Although Penelope Shuttle is the author of some extraordinary novels, she is by nature a poet. For a long time her gift manifested itself surrealistically in works of intense emotional oppression. Like her coauthor and husband, Peter Redgrove, Shuttle dared when she was very young to open her imagination to the teachings of the unconscious. In all her writings she remains passionately committed primarily to exploring hidden regions of the woman's psyche in a dream imagery wholly her own.

Shuttle's early, disturbing writing can now be seen in relation to her mature development. The collections of poetry that appeared after 1980 are remarkable achievements both in matter and style. In *The Orchard Upstairs* the prevalent symbols are directly related to the poet's sensual experience of pregnancy and childbearing. These delicate poems tell the truth ''but tell it slant.'' This is especially the case in the title poem, which sets up a dichotomy between outside and inside, destruction and creation, male and female, while all the time recognizing their vital interconnectedness:

Outside, the wind and the rain,
a darkness lurching against the threadbare house:
inside, the orchard upstairs . . .

The orchard, the womb, the bearer of ''fruits,'' sacrifices itself in the act of giving birth to the child. In so doing the woman suffers not only physically but also through loss of innocence and, indeed, loss of her pregnant self:

A small speck or stain
on my heart.
It is my sadness for the lost room,
the pillaged house.

The loss finds compensation in the gain of a child, the daughter whose presence haunts the poems of *The Child-Stealer*. Here childbearing is still the theme, but it alternates with a second theme, that of childhood, both the poet's own and her daughter's. The child stealer is the witch of menstruation who carries away the unborn, the figure of Lilith in a myth of life and death in which death is not evil but a necessary, wise opposite. Childhood is understood in a Blakean light, but Shuttle's taut language intercepts sentimentality:

In the boundless afternoon
the children are walking
with their gentle grammar on their lips

from door to door
the little ones go, brightly tranquil,
repenting nothing.

How safe their journey,
their placid marching,
famous and simple voyage.

The reader is persuaded that these impossible children, these stolen ones who will never be, are indeed in the poet's imagination real enough to undertake the crusade they are seen to embody. It is as if by writing the poem Shuttle had created children in her mind that she could not create in her body.

The Lion from Rio pursues the theme of wife, mother, husband, and child in poems more explicitly sexual, in some cases charmingly anecdotal. At her best, however, Shuttle is a symbolist of female experience. Her mental landscape peacefully assimilates house, garden, and ''flaxen river,'' through which cavort her emblems of physical energy: horse, snake (occasionally hedgehog), and the lion of life itself.

The poem ''Horse of the Month'' suggests that the title of Shuttle's fourth collection, *Adventures with My Horse,* will center on the theme of menstruation. The collection is actually full of animals, real and symbolic, described with wit and a refreshing zest for language. Like Redgrove, Shuttle subscribes to some innocent romantic inversions, so that serpent and pregnant sow are saviors in an Eden presided over by Selena the moon rather than the sun god Apollo. That there is scarcely room for evil in this imaginary womb-enclosed world is something to be pondered. But Shuttle triumphs in poems like ''Dressing the Child,'' in which a river becomes the knitted sleeve of a continuously reborn and conscientiously mothered child-earth:

Wide spindling river,
out-of-fashion green and cream
woollen river cast on huge brown needles,
bare tree-trunks garter-stitching
the currents, purling the banks,
armholing the bridges, casting-off barges.
The winter river is a long coarse sleeve
of flecked and brindled wool
into which I shove your thundery arm, the cuff
of ribbed bushes scratchy-tight on your wrist.

—Anne Stevenson

SILKO, Leslie Marmon

Nationality: American. **Born:** 1948. **Education:** Attended Board of Indian Affairs schools, Laguna, New Mexico, and a Catholic school in Albuquerque; University of New Mexico, Albuquerque, B.A. (summa cum laude) in English 1969; studied law briefly. **Family:** Has two sons. **Career:** Taught for two years at Navajo Community College, Tsaile, Arizona; lived in Ketchikan, Alaska, for two years; taught at University of New Mexico. Since 1978 professor of English, University of Arizona, Tucson. **Awards:** National Endowment for the Arts award, 1974; *Chicago Review* award, 1974; Pushcart prize, 1977; MacArthur Foundation grant, 1983. **Address:** Department of English, University of Arizona, Tucson, Arizona 85721, U.S.A.

PUBLICATIONS

Poetry

Laguna Woman. Greenfield Center, New York, Greenfield Review Press, 1974.
Storyteller (includes short stories). New York, Seaver, 1981.

Play

Lullaby, with Frank Chin, adaptation of the story by Silko (produced San Francisco. 1976).

Novels

Ceremony. New York, Viking Press, 1977.
Almanac of the Dead. New York, Simon and Schuster, 1991.
Yellow Woman. New Brunswick, New Jersey, Rutgers University Press, 1993.
Gardens in the Dunes. New York, Simon and Schuster, 1999.

Other

The Delicacy and Strength of Lace: Letters Between Leslie Marmon Silko and James A. Wright, edited by Anne Wright. St. Paul, Minnesota, Graywolf Press, 1986.
Sacred Water: Narratives and Pictures. Tucson, Flood Plain, 1993.
Yellow Woman and a Beauty of the Spirit: Essays on Native American Life Today. New York, Simon and Schuster, 1996.

*

Manuscript Collection: University of Arizona, Tucson.

Critical Studies: *Leslie Marmon Silko* by Per Seyersted, Boise, Idaho, Boise State University, 1980; *Four American Indian Literary Masters* by Alan R. Velie, Norman, University of Oklahoma Press, 1982; *Place and Vision: The Function of Landscape in Native American Fiction* by Robert M. Nelson, New York, P. Lang, 1993; ''Northamerican Silences: History, Identity, and Witness in the Poetry of Gloria Anzaldua, Cherrie Moraga, and Leslie Marmon Silko'' by Kate Adams, in *Listening to Silences: New Essays in Feminist Criticism,* edited by Elaine Hedges and Shelley Fisher Fishkin, New York, Oxford University Press, 1994; *Shifting the Ground: Four American Women Writers' Revisions of Nature, Gender, and Race* (dissertation) by Nancy Rachel Stein, Rutgers University, New Brunswick, 1994; ''New Dreaming: Joy Harjo, Wendy Rose, Leslie Marmon Silko'' by Jeanne Perreault, in *Deferring a Dream: Literary Sub-Versions of the American Columbiad,* edited by Gert Buelens and Ernst Rudin, Basel, Switzerland, Birkhauser, 1994; ''The Construction of Gender and Ethnicity in the Poetry of Leslie Silko and Louise Erdrich'' by Susan Perez Castillo, in *ICLA '91*

Tokyo: The Force of Vision, II: Visions in History; Visions of the Other, edited by Earl Miner and others, Tokyo, International Comparative Literature Association, 1995; ''Toward an Ecology of Justice: Transformative Ecological Theory and Practice'' by Joni Adamson Clarke, in *Reading the Earth: New Directions in the Study of Literature and Environment,* edited by Michael P. Branch and others, Moscow, University of Idaho Press, 1998; *Leslie Marmon Silko: A Collection of Critical Essays* edited by Louise K. Bennett and James L. Thorson, Albuquerque, University of New Mexico Press, 1999.

*   *   *

Leslie Marmon Silko's reputation rests upon her ability as a storyteller, and her output of poems has been relatively small. Her poems are a central part of her work as a writer, however, and she often uses the forms of poetry even in the middle of such works of prose fiction as *Ceremony.* She makes little use of simile and metaphor in her verse, with image and narration being the key elements. Her autobiographical book *Storyteller* is an interesting combination of old photographs, conventional short stories, and story poems. Silko herself denies that some of her poems are poems, seeing them instead as stories placed on the page with line breaks that help to replicate more clearly the motion of a storytelling voice.

The world of Silko's poetry is shaped by her Native American consciousness. Born in Albuquerque, New Mexico, she was brought up at Laguna among relatives whose roots went back many generations into traditional ways. Though regarded as one of the most acculturated of the pueblos, Laguna still possesses a strong sense of history and continuity. On the other hand, because Laguna adopted many European ways and a number of whites who married into the pueblo (Silko's ''great-grandpa Marmon'' among them), it is not surprising that it has produced not only Silko but also several other significant writers whose concerns are those of the ''half-breed,'' the person of mixed blood. Rather than viewing this heritage as a curse, Silko has used European literary forms to move toward the strength of the Laguna earth and the stories of her family. These stories are both personal reminiscences and ancient myths, and at times the two blend. The boundary lines between the real world and the world of legends and between the modern and the ancient but continuing past are extremely thin in all of her work. Indeed, her sense of time is not at all a European one. The reader feels that in her poems all things are very much interconnected. Her world is a world of both tremendous changes brought by Western civilization and a lastingly strong natural environment, of which the Native American is part and in which everything is possessed of the power to be and become.

Change is an important theme in Silko's work. ''Bear Story'' tells how the bears can call people to them and make them become bears themselves. There are characters in Laguna and other Southwestern Indian stories, the stories she grew up with and the ones she always returns to, who are changers, who make others change, and who can change themselves. The coyote is a prime example. The earthy, ironic humor in ''Toe'osh: A Laguna Coyote Story'' has made it one of her most often quoted poems.

Silko is also a writer who celebrates the strength of women, and the title of her first collection of poetry, *Laguna Woman,* underscores her identification with her own sex. Whether it is Silko herself, the mythic Yellow Woman, or her own grandmother, Marie Anaya Marmon, the women in Silko's poems are strong, independent, even wildly indomitable.

In such poems as ''Where Mountain Lion Lay Down with Deer''
we see Silko's non-Western sense of time. Things from the past and
the present coexist and change one another:

> I smell the wind for my ancestors
>   pale blue leaves
>   crushes wild mountain smell.
> Returning
>   up the gray stone cliff
>   where I descended
>   a thousand years ago
> Returning to faded black stone
> where mountain lion lay down with deer.

The image of the mountain lion and the deer may remind one of the
biblical lion and lamb, but the animals have different roles in this
place, are charged with a different mythic power. Silko says later in
the same poem that

> The old ones who remember me are gone
>   the old songs are all forgotten
> and the story of my birth.
> How I danced in snow-frost moonlight
>   distant stars to the end of the Earth . . .

Her words are not a lament, however. They do not convey a sense of
loss but rather a deep continuity that goes beyond conventional ideas
of individual reality. Although she is a child of more than one culture,
her voice clearly speaks for the Native American way, not a way that
is gone but one that continues beyond time, changing and unchanged.

—Joseph Bruchac

SILLIMAN, Ron(ald Glenn)

Nationality: American. **Born:** Pasco, Washington, 5 August 1946.
Education: Merritt College, 1965, 1969–72; San Francisco State
College (now University), 1966–69; University of California, Berkeley, 1969–71. **Family:** Married 1) Rochelle Nameroff in 1965 (divorced 1972); 2) Krishna Evans in 1986; two sons. **Career:** Editorial
assistant, Mecca Publications, San Francisco, 1972; director of research and education, Committee for Prisoner Humanity and Justice,
San Rafael, California, 1972–76; project manager, Tenderloin
Ethnographic Research Project, San Francisco, 1977–78; director of
outreach, Central City Hospitality House, San Francisco, 1979–81;
lecturer, San Francisco State University, 1981; visiting lecturer,
University of California, San Diego, 1982; writer-in-residence, New
College of California, San Francisco, 1982; director of public relations and development, 1982–86, and poet-in-residence, 1983–90,
California Institute of Integral Studies, San Francisco; executive
director, Center for Social Research, Berkeley, California, 1986–89;
service marketing specialist, ComputerLand Corporation, Pleasanton,
California, 1989–94. Since 1994 service products marketing manager, Vanstar Corporation. Editor, *Tottel's,* Oakland and San Francisco, 1970–81; executive editor, 1986–89, and later member of the
editorial collective, *Socialist Review,* Berkeley. **Awards:** Hart Crane

and Alice Crane Williams award, 1968; Joan Lee Yang award, 1970,
1971; National Endowment for the Arts fellowship, 1979; California
Arts Council grant, 1979, 1980; Poetry Center book award, 1985.
Address: 262 Orchard Road, Paoli, Pennsylvania 19301–1116, U.S.A.

PUBLICATIONS

Poetry

Moon in the Seventh House. Milwaukee, Wisconsin, Gunrunner
    Press, 1968.
Three Syntactic Fictions for Dennis Schmitz. N.p., Bloodbooks, 1969.
Crow. Ithaca, New York, Ithaca House, 1971.
Mohawk. Bowling Green, Ohio, Doones Press, 1973.
Nox. Providence, Rhode Island, Burning Deck Press, 1974.
Sitting Up, Standing Up, Taking Steps. Berkeley, California, Tuumba
    Press, 1978.
Ketjak. San Francisco, This, 1978.
Tjanting. Berkeley, California, Figures, 1981.
Bart. Hartford, Connecticut, Potes and Poets Press, 1982.
ABC. Berkeley, California, Tuumba Press, 1983.
Paradise. Providence, Rhode Island, Burning Deck Press, 1985.
The Age of Huts. New York, Roof, 1986.
Lit. Elmwood, Connecticut, Potes and Poets Press, 1987.
What. Great Barrington, Massachusetts, Figures, 1988.
Manifest. Tenerife, Canary Islands, Zasterle Press, 1990.
Toner. Hartford, Connecticut, Potes and Poets Press, 1992.
Demo to Ink. Tucson, Arizona, Chax Press, 1992.
Jones. N.p, Generator Press, 1993.
N/O. New York, Roof, 1994.
Xing. N.p., Meow Press, 1996.

Play

Screenplay: *Beyond Prisons,* 1973.

Other

The New Sentence. New York, Roof, 1987.
Leningrad/American Writers in the Soviet Union, with others. N.p.,
    Mercury House, 1991.

Editor, *A Symposium on Clark Coolidge.* Milwaukee, Wisconsin,
    Membrane Press, 1978.
Editor, *In the American Tree.* Orono, Maine, National Poetry Founda-
    tion, 1986.
Editor, *Unfinished Business: Twenty Years of Socialist Review.* N.p.,
    Verso Press, 1991.

*

Manuscript Collection: University of California, San Diego.

Critical Studies: ''After Sentence, Sentence'' by Michael Davidson,
in *American Book Review* (New York), September-October 1982;
''The Crisis at Present: Talk Poems and the New Poet's Prose,'' in
Poet's Prose: The Crisis in American Verse, by Stephen Fredman,
Cambridge, Cambridge University Press, 1983; ''The Word As

Such'' by Marjorie Perloff, in *American Poetry Review* (Philadelphia), 13(3), May-June 1984; ''From the Language Poets'' by Robert Creeley, in *San Francisco Chronicle,* 28 September 1986; ''Ron Silliman'' by Rae Armantrout, in *Postmodern Fiction: A Bio- Bibliographical Guide,* edited by Larry McCaffery, New York, Greenwood Press, 1986; ''Contemporary Poetry, Alternate Routes'' by Jerome J. McGann, in *Critical Inquiry* (Chicago), 13(3), spring 1987; ''Ron Silliman: Non-Hierarchical Perception,'' in *Open Form and the Feminine Imagination,* by Stephen-Paul Martin, Washington, D.C., Maisonneuve Press, 1988; ''A Paradigm Lost: Ron Silliman's Paradise & the Archaeology of Language'' by Stephen-Paul Martin, in *Sagetrieb* (Orono, Maine), 8(1–2), spring-fall 1989; ''Contemporary American Poetry and the Pseudo Avant-Garde'' by Keith Tuma, in *Chicago Review* (Chicago), 36(3–4), 1989; ''The Alphabet, Spelt from Silliman's Leaves'' by Anne Mack and J.J. Rome, in *South Atlantic Quarterly* (Durham, North Carolina), 89(4), fall 1990; ''Parataxis and Narrative: The New Sentence in Theory and Practice'' by Bob Perelman, in *American Literature* (Durham, North Carolina), 65(2), June 1993; ''A Taxable Matter'' by C.D. Wright, in *A Field Guide to Contemporary Poetry and Poetics,* edited by Stuart Friebert, David Walker, and David Young, Oberlin, Ohio, Oberlin College, 1997; ''Poetics, Polemic, and the Question of Intelligibility'' by Benjamin Friedlander, in *Postmodern Culture* (Charlottesville, Virginia), 9(1), September 1998.

*   *   *

During the 1980s Ron Silliman earned recognition as perhaps the foremost among the West Coast language poets, both on the strength of his role as a crusader for the cause and for the scale and mastery of his own poetry. Silliman has energetically championed his colleagues, assembling the definitive anthology, *In the American Tree.* Furthermore, he has repeatedly taken every public opportunity to draw attention to other poets' work. Some of these notices are collected in *The New Sentence,* which also contains Silliman's key theoretical writings. It is important to emphasize the demeanor with which Silliman has involved himself in the American poetry scene, for his own work is conspicuously guided by egalitarian principles committed to poetry as a collaboration between the writer and reader. Whereas some of his compatriots share this belief, they nevertheless produce unyielding hermetic poetry. Silliman, by contrast, is not only the most accessible poet of the language school but also one of the most approachable poets writing in North America.

Silliman is a poet of the quotidian, writing in the tradition of Whitman, Williams, and Ginsberg. The milieu is recognizably that of the San Francisco Bay, its buses and streets, work sites, galleries, cafés, and lofts. Silliman has long been active as a political organizer in San Francisco, and his writing displays an ease of reference and meticulousness of detail that reflect this. (Appropriately, Silliman celebrated the publication of his long book *Tjanting* by reading it aloud on a San Francisco street corner during the busiest hours of the workday.) Silliman's observationally precise style aspires to the ''film-eye'' chronicles of early Bolshevism, as in Dziga Vertov's 1928 film *The Man with a Movie Camera,* but the man behind the tripod, superimposed on the urban flux, now becomes the poet with a pocket notebook, with the page as the fulcrum between the inner thought and outer view. Consider, for instance, these lines from *What:*

Chewing gum disrupts
the rhythm of the writing.

The way legs jut up
when the chair's too short.
Place where I bit
the inside of my lip.
Sometimes, wearing my reading glasses,
the outer world a soft, amiable fuzz,
I'm quite alone. Times Square
is not a square at all. Say ''scalding''
with a long *a.* Incest
amid Siamese twins. Dystopia
for vacant skies, for amber weights
of blame. Fur burdened fountain's travesties
above the routed veins. And then
went down on the snips
of old lines parodied. CHiPs
in a row at an officer's funeral
hot under the midday valley sun.
Old Miz Johnson, whose lawn I mowed,
'62–63, kept a flag in a box
back in her bedroom closet
which she referred to as
''my son.'' Woman strives to appear stylish
in light pink pantsuit and neckbrace.
Tilting his VFW cap jauntily forward
he begs for spare change. Three teens sit parked
in a large pink Caddy, passing a doobie
between them. Fresh clipped nails
feel like fuzzy fingers. Why
am I telling you this?

Silliman's work deviates from the utopian propensities of a Whitman or a Ginsberg insofar as he politicizes the paratactic function of random or unmotivated juxtapositions. Connections between sentences are generally connotative rather than syllogistic, so that the persons and situations are not specifically framed as illustrations subordinate to a theme. Instead, the formal structure mirrors a public space, which is a blend of motivated relations (couples, families, workers, organized groups) and strictly aleatory aggregates (passengers on a given bus, pedestrians crossing a street, customers in line in a store). In the cited passage, for instance, the notion of citizenship is clearly invoked by the presence of law enforcement officers, the veteran, and the mother of a soldier killed in action. Each is presented objectively, dispassionately, yet taken together they are instances of the ''dystopia'' referred to in a parody of the American song ''Oh beautiful for spacious skies and amber waves of grain . . .'' This in turn yields a pastiche of the opening of Pound's *The Cantos* (itself celebrated for being an English version of a Latin rendering of a Greek text), ''And then went down to the sea in ships'' becoming in Silliman's hands ''down on the snips / of old lines parodied.'' The implication is that citizenship is no substitute for community, and that state-administered consumer capitalism sanctions individualization only in parodic forms, clichés within a grand cliché.

Another characteristic of Silliman's work in the above passage is the poet's inclusion of himself as one among many figures in the poem, reflecting on his bodily disposition and his compositional strategies but not otherwise invested with special authority. He even implies that his own poetic praxis is not immune to the pressures of dominant ideology. Consequently his overtures to the creative intervention of the reader constitute an ongoing plea that is not so much interpersonal as transpersonal.

Silliman's work may be read as a grand refusal of the chronic strategies of authorial domination. This is not to imply that the work is disordered but rather that Silliman has elected to abide with one of the most daring propositions of "open," or "processual," poetics-namely, that form and content are mutually implicated at all points of the text, as in a hologram. Silliman has frequently relied on the mathematical Fibonacci sequence for compositional organization. This device is explicit and inescapably part of the reader's experience in the books *Ketjak* and *Tjanting*, but in later works like *Lit* the Fibonacci sequence is operative but unintrusive. One might conclude that Silliman's original tendency to formalist experimentalism has been attenuated by more explicit thematic concerns. The prominence of these concerns in *What* and *Paradise* can be retrospectively gleaned, however, in even the earliest pieces in *The Age of Huts*, which displays flamboyantly experimental texts such as "Sunset Debris," a bravura piece consisting entirely of questions that resolve seamlessly into the formalist strategy but that also make the kind of sense we look to content for: "What if each word has a purpose? What is a construct? How do our lives absorb stress? When is an act complete?" The patient sagacity of such questions, which are sustained for thirty pages, continues to echo throughout Silliman's work, making his poetry one of the most user-friendly literary utopias.

—Jed Rasula

SIMIC, Charles

Nationality: American. **Born:** Belgrade, Yugoslavia, 9 May 1938; immigrated to the United States in 1954; naturalized, 1971. **Education:** Oak Park High School, Illinois; University of Chicago, 1956–59; New York University, 1959–61, 1963–65, B.A. 1967. **Military Service:** U.S. Army, 1961–63. **Family:** Married Helen Dubin in 1964; one daughter and one son. **Career:** Proofreader, Chicago *Sun-Times;* member of the department of English, California State College, Hayward, 1970–73. Since 1973 distinguished professor of English, University of New Hampshire, Durham. Editorial assistant, *Aperture* magazine, New York, 1966–69. **Awards:** P.E.N. award, for translation, 1970, 1980; Guggenheim fellowship, 1972; National Endowment for the Arts fellowship, 1974, 1979; Edgar Allan Poe award, 1975; American Academy award, 1976; Harriet Monroe poetry award, 1980; Poetry Society of America di Castignola award, 1980; Fulbright fellowship, 1982; Ingram Merrill fellowship, 1983; MacArthur fellowship, 1984; Pulitzer prize, 1990. **Address:** Department of English, University of New Hampshire, Durham, New Hampshire 03824, U.S.A.

PUBLICATIONS

Poetry

What the Grass Says. San Francisco, Kayak, 1967.
Somewhere among Us a Stone Is Taking Notes. San Francisco, Kayak, 1969.
Dismantling the Silence. New York, Braziller, and London, Cape, 1971.
White. New York, New Rivers Press, 1972; revised edition, Durango, Colorado, Logbridge Rhodes, 1980.
Return to a Place Lit by a Glass of Milk. New York, Braziller, 1974.

Biography and a Lament: Poems 1961–1967. Hartford, Connecticut, Bartholomew's Cobble, 1976.
Charon's Cosmology. New York, Braziller, 1977.
Brooms: Selected Poems. Barry, Glamorgan, Edge Press, 1978.
School for Dark Thoughts. Pawlet, Vermont, Banyan Press, 1978.
Classic Ballroom Dances. New York, Braziller, 1980.
Shaving at Night. San Francisco, Meadow Press, 1982.
Austerities. New York, Braziller, 1982; London, Secker and Warburg, 1983.
Weather Forecast for Utopia and Vicinity: Poems 1967–1982. Barrytown, New York, Station Hill Press, 1983.
The Chicken Without a Head. Portland, Oregon, Trace, 1983.
Selected Poems 1963–1983. New York, Braziller, 1985; London, Secker and Warburg, 1986; revised edition, Braziller, 1990.
Unending Blues. San Diego, Harcourt Brace, 1986.
The World Doesn't End: Prose Poems. San Diego, Harcourt Brace, 1989.
In the Room We Share (includes prose). New York, Paragon House, 1990.
The Book of Gods and Devils. San Diego, Harcourt Brace, 1990.
Hotel Insomnia. San Diego, Harcourt Brace, 1992.
A Wedding in Hell. San Diego, Harcourt Brace, 1994.
Frightening Toys. London, Faber and Faber, 1995.
Walking the Black Cat. San Diego, Harcourt Brace, 1996.
Looking for Trouble. London, Faber and Faber, 1997
Jackstraws. San Diego, Harcourt Brace, 1999.
Selected Early Poems. New York, Braziller, 1999.

Recording: *School for Dark Thoughts,* Watershed, 1978.

Other

The Uncertain Certainty: Interviews, Essays, and Notes on Poetry. Ann Arbor, University of Michigan Press, 1985.
Wonderful Words, Silent Truth. Ann Arbor, University of Michigan Press, 1990.
Dimestore Alchemy. New York, Ecco Press, 1992.
Unemployed Fortune Teller. Ann Arbor, University of Michigan Press, 1994.
Orphan Factory. Ann Arbor, University of Michigan Press, 1998.
The Fly in the Soup. Ann Arbor, University of Michigan Press, 1999.

Editor and Translator, with C.W. Truesdale, *Fire Gardens,* by Ivan V. Lilac. New York, New Rivers Press, 1970.
Editor and Translator, *Four Yugoslav Poets: Ivan V. Lilac, Brank Miljkovic, Milorad Pavic, Ljubomir Simovic* New York, Lillabulero Press, 1970.
Editor and Translator, *The Little Box: Poems,* by Vasko Popa. Washington, D.C., Charioteer Press, 1970.
Editor, with Mark Strand, *Another Republic: 17 European and South American Writers.* New York, Ecco Press, 1976.
Editor and Translator, *Homage to the Lame Wolf: Selected Poems 1956–1975,* by Vasko Popa. Oberlin, Ohio, Oberlin College, 1979; enlarged edition, 1987.
Editor and Co-translator, *Selected Poems of Tomaz Salamun.* New York, Ecco Press, 1988.
Editor, *The Essential Campion.* New York, Ecco Press, 1988.

Translator, *Key to Dream According to Djordje.* Chicago, Elpenor, 1978.

Translator, with Peter Kastmiler, *Atlantis: Selected Poems of Slavko Mihalic.* Greenfield Center, New York, Greenfield Review Press, 1987.

Translator, *Roll Call of Mirrors: Selected Poems,* by Ivan V. Lilac. Middletown, Connecticut, Wesleyan University Press, 1988.

Translator, *Some Other Wine and Light,* by Aleksandar Ristovic. Washington, D.C., Charioteer Press, 1989.

Translator, *Bandit Wind,* by Slavko Janevski. Takoma Park, Maryland, Dryad Press, 1991.

Translator, *The Horse Has Six Legs, An Anthology of Serbian Poetry.* St. Paul, Minnesota, Graywolf, 1992.

Translator, *Night Mail,* by Novica Tadic. Oberlin, Ohio, Field, 1992.

Translator, *Devil's Lunch*, by Aleksandar Ristovic. London, Faber and Faber, 1999.

*

Critical Studies: "Immanent Distance: Silence and the Poetry of Charles Simic" by Bruce Bond, in *Mid-American Review* (Bowling Green, Ohio), 8(1), 1988; "Writing Things: Literary Property in Heidegger and Simic" by Kevin Hart, in *New Literary History* (Baltimore, Maryland), autumn 1989; "An Interview with Charles Simic" with Andrew Liebs, in *Single Hound* (Portsmouth, New Hampshire) 2(2), 1990; "The Secret World of Charles Simic" by Marci Janas, in *Contemporary Poetry and Poetics* (Oberlin, Ohio), spring 1991; "The Poet on a Roll" by Ileana A. Orlich, in *Centennial Review* (East Lansing, Michigan), spring 1992; "Simic's *Cabbage*" by Philip Miller, in *Explicator* (Washington, D.C.), summer, 1993.

Charles Simic comments:

Simic has been called a surrealist, magic realist, and plain old realist. Although born in Yugoslavia, he thinks of himself as a New England writer in the tradition of Emily Dickinson and Nathaniel Hawthorne.

*   *   *

At the opening of Charles Simic's book-length poem *White,* the author hesitates before the blank page, poised for another "raid on the inarticulate":

Out of poverty
to begin again

With the color of the bride
And that of blindness,

Touch what I can
Of the quick

Speak and then wait,
As if this light

Will continue to linger
On the threshold

This passage aptly summarizes Simic's poetic project as it voices his desire to articulate a mythic primeval world existing in a silence beyond speech, a world that he has elsewhere described as being "one notch below language . . . that place of original action and desire . . . a world where magic is possible, where chance reigns, where metaphors have their supreme logic, where imagination is free and truthful." In the figure of the bride the passage hints at the fulfillment, at once ritual and erotic, that the approach to this archetypal realm promises. Yet the poem, in the rigor of its terse, minimalist lines no less than in its open acknowledgment of the poverty of the poet's language and imagination, promises no shortcut to transcendence. If the mute world is to speak, the poet must listen as much as he talks, and if illumination is to come, it is likely to pass in a moment. More ominously, the mention of blindness hints that it may not come at all.

In the mid-1960s, when he first began publishing poetry, Simic's obsession with this silent world, with what used to be called the sublime, effectively bracketed him with the group of American poets loosely known as the deep imagists, the most prominent of whom were Robert Bly and W.S. Merwin. Like them, Simic could point to the influence of Theodore Roethke and the surrealists on the visionary, dreamlike structures of his poems. (Like Bly and Merwin, Simic also would become a prolific translator of his influences, especially eastern European poets like Vasko Popa and Ivan Lilac.) Following the deep imagists, much of Simic's early verse seeks to reach toward a realm of pastoral stillness through a concentrated effort of attention. In "Evening" he writes,

The snail gives off stillness.
The weed is blessed.
At the end of a long day
The man finds joy, the water peace.

Let all be simple. Let all stand still
Without a final direction.
That which brings you into the world
To take you away at death
Is one and the same;
The shadow long and pointy
Is its church

Yet the successful rapprochement with such a blissful silence is comparatively rare in Simic's work. There are other elements in his poetic voice: a sense of humor at once dark and playful, an unflinching recognition of the political horrors of the twentieth century that was acquired during the poet's childhood in wartime Yugoslavia, and a consequent suspicion of the very cosmos he would interrogate. These elements give Simic's poems a jaggedly ironic edge and save him from the occasional complacencies of his deep imagist counterparts.

This ambivalent tone is well captured in the title poem of Simic's first major collection, *Dismantling the Silence,* wherein the archetypal poetic encounter with the sublime is rendered as a clinical, macabre dissection suffused with dread:

Take down its ears first
Carefully so they don't spill over.
With a sharp whistle slit its belly open.
If there are ashes in it, close your eyes
And blow them whichever way the wind is pointing.
If there's water, sleeping water,
Bring the root of a plant that hasn't drunk for a month.

When you reach the bones,

And you haven't got a pack of dogs with you,
And you haven't got a pine coffin
And a wagon pulled by oxen to make them rattle,
Slip them quickly under your skin,
Next time you pick up your sack,
You'll hear them setting your teeth on edge . . .

It is this dread, concentrated around the ghostly, disembodied objects of an unpeopled universe, that defines the world of Simic's early poetry. It is a landscape that seems at once lost in a distant past—the anthropomorphic world of primitive folklore—and curiously contemporary—the stuff of postapocalyptic nightmare. Through this landscape Simic's detached, precise voice picks its ironic way, interrogating one discarded artifact after another, searching for an answer to the bloody riddle of modern history. Often, as in ''Fork,'' the answer seems to point to a primal ignorance and violence shared by humans and animals alike:

This strange thing must have crept
Right out of hell
It resembles a bird's foot
Worn around the cannibal's neck.

As you hold it in your hand,
As you stab with it into a piece of meat,
It is possible to imagine the rest of the bird:
Its head which like your fist
Is large, bald, beakless and blind.

Such poems, balanced as they are between a terse, matter-of-fact narrator and a stark, surrealist imagery, carry a tremendous visceral jolt. But they run the risk of burning out their reader, who may be able to endure only so many of these metaphoric shocks before becoming jaded. Hence, in later works Simic has moved away from the hypersurrealist image, the mordant one-liner, which in his early work was expected to carry the weight of the entire poem. Simic's later verse is quieter, more relaxed, and if it is no less pessimistic, its despair seems diffused throughout the poem rather than concentrated in a single moment of shock. For the Kafkaesque slaughterhouse of wartime Europe a poem like ''The Partial Explanation'' substitutes the curious emptiness and alienation of postwar America:

Seems like a long time
Since the waiter took my order
Grimy little luncheonette,
The snow falling outside.
Seems like it has grown darker
Since I last heard the kitchen door
Behind my back
Since I last noticed
Anyone pass on the street.

A glass of ice water
Keeps me company
At this table I chose myself
Upon entering

And a longing
Incredible longing
To eavesdrop

On the conversation
Of cooks

Though the settings of these poems remain strangely anonymous, virtually unplaceable in place or time, Simic's universe has gradually acquired a sprinkling of human occupants, and his later poetry has seemed to reach out to such characters in gestures of genuine, if somewhat muted, empathy. In a poem like ''Toward Nightfall,'' from the 1986 collection *Unending Blues,* all of the familiar elements of Simic's verse are assembled—the scaffolds, the bare trees, the smell of spilled blood, the monsters (this time on movie posters)—but the poem ends by reflecting the weight of these elements upon a human center:

The old man never learned
To read well, and so
Reads on in that half-whisper,
And in that half light
Verging on the dark,
About that day's tragedies
Which supposedly are not
Tragedies in the absence of
Figures endowed with
Classic nobility of soul.

With their spare, even tranquil, movement these poems bring a new, intersubjective dimension to the silence that has never been far from the surface in Simic's work, offering an alternative to the minimalist rigor of his earlier verse.

Simic's 1989 collection of sixty-seven prose poems, *The World Doesn't End,* won him the Pulitzer Prize. In paragraphs that stun through their suddenness of juxtaposition, these poems feel fresh, characteristically bizarre, and simultaneously logical and illogical. The world of these poems is like ''the old river . . . [that] in its confusion sometimes forgets and flows backwards.'' Heaven is full of ''little shrunken deaf ears instead of stars.'' With echoes of Rimbaud and Socrates, these are among Simic's most dynamic and extreme poems: ''It's so quiet in the world. One can hear the old river, which in its confusion sometimes forgets and flows backwards.''

At times Simic's particular surrealistic clarity pushes the very boundaries of consciousness to verge on the terrain of the sleepless. His 1992 collection, *Hotel Insomnia,* invites us with this accord: ''Sleeplessness is like metaphysics. Be there.'' Once inside, we find an labyrinthian atmosphere charged with symbolic resonances, ''the infinite number of lines / That join to me things and beings, / so that a diagram / Of any moment in my life / Looks like a child's scribble.'' Simic's is a blasted world in which poems can easily resonate as prayers. Fragmented dreams, melancholy, and bleak humor color the poems in *A Wedding in Hell,* in which some images—a blackened window, a cockroach, a stopped clock—recur with a grim and unsettling staccato even as they are saturated in the soft infinities of imagination. His poetry in this collection resounds ''like the wind / Between the cold winter stars. / A creaky door / Way out in the darkness. / Some kind of small bird / Trapped by a cat / And calling on heaven to witness.''

In *Walking the Black Cat* Simic focuses on the way in which chance and luck infuse the commonplace world, even with its illusions. Disorientation is still his guiding state, but the juxtaposition of life and death via allusions to authors—most notably, in the title, Edgar Allan Poe—sets the poems in a populated sphere. In ''Relaxing in a Madhouse'' Moses, Socrates, Lincoln, and Adam and Eve all share a space with the ''general who was busy with the ant farm in his head.'' For Simic the charm of the black cat, archetypally one of bad luck, is its constancy, its potency, its necessity. He is as happily aligned with superstition as Eliot's Madame Sosostris, and in ''My Magician'' he masquerades as the magician's dummy: ''Through a row of wooden teeth / We spoke of God the Father. / Then we vanished into a deck of cards.''

Jackstraws persists in this manner of injecting the ordinary world with the temper and tension of emotional storms, sometimes with a cryptic sense of play. Although Simic's staid persona is one of a tortured survivor, he can be strangely, almost whimsically, compassionate toward such minutiae as the dramatics of insects. Life for Simic is random guesswork, a precarious world in which vulnerabilities are so intense that the self shimmers like an eerie, perpetual, and mildly consoling storm.

—Anthony G. Stocks and Martha Sutro

SIMMONS, James (Stewart Alexander)

Nationality: British. **Born:** Londonderry, Northern Ireland, 14 February 1933. **Education:** Foyle College, Londonderry; Campbell College, Belfast; University of Leeds, Yorkshire, B.A. (honors) in English 1958. **Family:** Married 1) Laura Stinson in 1956 (divorced 1977); four daughters and one son; 2) Imelda Foley in 1981 (separated 1988), one daughter; 3) Janice Fitzpatrick, one son. **Career:** Teacher at Friends School, Lisburn, Northern Ireland, Ahmadu Bello University, Zaria, Nigeria, 1963–66, and New University of Ulster, Coleraine, 1968–84. Writer-in-residence, Queens University, Belfast, 1989–92. Founded the Poets' House in 1991 with Janice Fitzpatrick. Editor, *Poetry and Audience,* Leeds, 1957–58. Founder, *Honest Ulsterman,* 1963, and Poor Genius Record Company, 1976. **Awards:** Eric Gregory award, 1962; Cholmondeley award, 1977; Irish Publishers' award, 1986, for *Selected Poems 1956–1986.* **Address:** 15 Kerr Street, Portrush, Northern Ireland.

PUBLICATIONS

Poetry

Ballad of a Marriage. Belfast, Festival, 1966.
Late But in Earnest. London, Bodley Head, 1967.
Ten Poems. Belfast, Festival, 1968.
In the Wilderness and Other Poems. London, Bodley Head, 1969.
Songs for Derry, music by the author. Belfast, Ulsterman, 1969.
No Ties. Belfast, Ulsterman, 1970.
Energy to Burn. London, Bodley Head, 1971.
No Land Is Waste, Dr. Eliot. Richmond, Surrey, Keepsake Press, 1972.
The Long Summer Still to Come. Belfast, Blackstaff Press, 1973.
West Strand Visions. Belfast, Blackstaff Press, 1974.
Memorials of a Tour in Yorkshire. Belfast, Ulsterman, 1975.
Judy Garland and the Cold War. Belfast, Blackstaff Press, 1976.
The Selected James Simmons, edited by Edna Longley. Belfast, Blackstaff Press, 1978.

Constantly Singing. Belfast, Blackstaff Press, 1980.
From the Irish. Belfast, Blackstaff Press, 1985.
Selected Poems 1956–1986. Newcastle upon Tyne, Bloodaxe, 1986.
Sex, Rectitude and Loneliness. Belfast, Lapwing Press, 1992.
Mainstream. Galway, Salmon/Poolbeg, 1994.
Elegies. Matnooth, Sotto Voce Press, 1994.
The Company of Children. Cliffs of Mother, County Clare, Ireland, Salmon, 1999.

Recordings: *City and Eastern,* Outlets; *Pubs,* BBC; *Love in the Post,* Poor Genius; *The Ballad of Claudy,* Poor Genius; *The Rosyrevor Sessions,* Spring Records, 1987.

Plays

Aikin Mata, with Tony Harrison, adaptation of *Lysistrata* by Aristophanes (produced Zaria, Nigeria, 1965). Ibadan, Oxford University Press, 1966.
The Cattle Rustling. Belfast, Fortnight Publications, 1991.

Other

Sean O'Casey. London, Macmillan, 1983; New York, Grove Press, 1984.
At 6 O'Clock in the Silence, edited by Janice Fitzpatrick. Belfast, Lapwing Press, 1993.

Editor, with A.R. Mortimer, *Out on the Edge.* Leeds, Leeds University, 1958.
Editor, *New Poems from Ulster.* Coleraine, New University of Ulster, 1974.
Editor, *Ten Irish Poets: An Anthology.* Cheadle, Cheshire, Carcanet, 1974.
Editor, *Soundings 3: Annual Anthology of New Irish Writing.* Belfast, Blackstaff Press, 1975.

*

Manuscript Collections: University of Texas, Austin; New University of Ulster, Coleraine.

Critical Studies: Interview with Robert Chapman, in *Confrontations* (New York), spring 1975; by Paul Durcan, in Cork *Examiner,* 3 July 1978; by Alan Hollinghurst, in *Encounter* (London), February-March 1981; by Peter Porter, in *The Observer* (London), 31 August 1985; by Anthony Bradley, in *The Irish Literary Supplement,* November 1987; *The Thoughtful Songs of James Simmons* by Tony Knowland, in *Poets of Northern Ireland,* edited by Elmer Andrews, London, MacMillan, 1993.

James Simmons comments:

(1980) I see myself in the mainstream of English poetry, following Shakespeare, as most of the poets I admire do—Blake, Hopkins, Hardy, Burns, Yeats, etc. Ewan MacColl reviving the old ballads opened up the possibility of better songs and also a sense of serious writing, tragedy, being possible in a popular form. For all their self-indulgence the new songwriters (Dylan, Mitchell, Newman, etc.) have a sort of excitement that seems to be lacking in contemporary poetry. The new fashion for reading poetry aloud has turned out to be boring in most cases. Find myself getting curmudgeonly about ''experiment,'' for it so often seems a way for bad poets to disguise their limitations. Do not feel much inclined to argue the toss anymore.

(1995) The title of my new large collection endorses my previous remarks. I call it *Mainstream*. Marriage to Janice and running her school of poetry have renewed energy. I meet and work with many young poets, Irish and American, and many established poets who teach here: James McAuley, Paul Durcan, Seamus Heaney, Bill Matthews, Derek Mahon, Sherod Santos. I hope to explore free verse more.

Irish poetry is in danger of becoming an extension of the Tourism Board. Radical voices are not welcome. There is a sad fashion for teasing, obscure poetry that has little passion or intellect. Watch out for Martin Mooney and Catriona Clutterbuck.

My poems get longer and more complicated—but lucid and humane. I am pleased that Edgar Lee Masters and Elizabeth Bishop are seen as central to American poetry. I also salute the new work of Jean Valentine and Tess Gallagher, Lynne McMahon and Sharon Olds.

*   *   *

James Simmons is a curiously vulnerable poet despite his rambunctious style and the projected, even cultivated, persona of the good-humoredly lecherous boozer: ''Our youth was gay but rough, / much drink and copulation. / If that seems not enough / blame our miseducation.'' His rhymes thump steadily home, giving the careless reader an impression of verbal insensitivity, and the humor is sometimes so robust that a superficial reading can leave one unaware of the quality of Simmons's sensibility, which may well account for the unfortunate reception given to his collections by certain reviewers. The poem ''One of the Boys,'' from which the four lines quoted above are taken, can be seen as a joyfully iconoclastic romp: ''the great careers all tricks, / the fine arts all my arse, / business and politics / a cruel farce.'' But the final lines get under the surface of this defensive philistinism to point to its emptiness and the subconscious awareness of its emptiness in its practitioners:

> Though fear of getting fired
> may ease, and work is hated
> less, we are tired, tired
> and incapacitated.
> On golf courses, in bars,
> crutched by the cash we earn,
> we think of nights in cars
> with energy to burn.

There is a sympathetic understanding here of a tragic sense of loss, which reminds me obliquely of the purport of a line in Philip Larkin's poem ''Mr. Bleaney'': ''That how we live measures our own nature.''

Though ''One of the Boys'' is heavily rhymed, the rhymes can be seen to underpin the poem and are by no means intrusive. But while this poem succeeds, Simmons's style and stance are replete with the dangers of the sentimental ''good-natured tart'' variety, and the poems can involve a great deal of casuistry. This can be seen in ''The Wife-Swappers,'' for example, when the poet attempts to equate, and therefore justify, a taste for lechery with an honest harmlessness. It could be said, of course, that Donne, too, indulged in such sophistry, but he employed considerably more wit and subtlety, if that can be considered a defense. It all comes down to the fact, I suppose, that Simmons sees the poet as an entertainer and moralist, and while he never fails to entertain (no mean achievement), the entertainer sometimes elbows out the moralist.

Yet, for the most part, not very far from the clowning and posturing surface of his more swashbuckling poems there is always a hint of carpe diem or an awareness of values missed: ''Your dumbness on a walk / was better than my clown's talk. / You showed me what you meant . . .'' (''Goodbye Sally''). At its best Simmons's poetry can express an understanding of and empathy with certain aspects of the human tragedy that are only considered minor because they occur with such frequency and are common to so many. Notice how in ''Antigone's Hour'' he moderates the often heavy beat of his poetry to a minor key, as it were, so that the tragic element is, in fact, in the very ordinariness of what is often seen as an extraordinary situation:

> All risks are a tribute
> to the adventurous dead.
> Gathering fine small flowers
> was all they wanted said . . .
>
> No guards observed them
> acting the clown.
> Their own doubts what to do
> next let them down.

The real strength of Simmons's poetry resides in his basic humanity and in his sympathy and preference for the human condition, however fallible and whatever its faults, as in ''Stephano Remembers'': ''We were distracted by too many things . . . / the wine, the jokes, the music, fancy gowns / We were no good as murderers, we were clowns.'' The constant use of the clown as an archetype is a clue here.

—John Cotton

SIMPSON, Louis (Aston Marantz)

Nationality: American. **Born:** Jamaica, British West Indies, 27 March 1923. **Education:** Munro College, Jamaica, 1933–40, Cambridge Higher Schools Certificate, 1939; Columbia University, New York, B.S. 1948, A.M. 1950. Ph.D. 1959. **Military Service:** U.S. Army, 1943–45: Purple Heart and Bronze Star. **Family:** Married 1) Jeanne Claire Rogers in 1949 (divorced 1954), one son; 2) Dorothy Roochvarg in 1955 (divorced 1979), one son and one daughter; 3) Miriam Bachner in 1985 (divorced 1998). **Career:** Editor, Bobbs-Merrill Publishing Company, New York, 1950–55; instructor, Columbia University, 1955–59; professor of English, University of California, Berkeley, 1959–67. Professor of English, 1967–91, distinguished professor, 1991–93, and since 1993 professor emeritus, State University of New York, Stony Brook. **Awards:** American Academy in Rome fellowship, 1957; *Hudson Review* fellowship, 1957; Edna St. Vincent Millay award, 1960; Guggenheim fellowship, 1962, 1970; American Council of Learned Societies grant, 1963; Pulitzer prize, 1964; Columbia University medal for Excellence, 1965; American Academy award, 1976; Institute of Jamaica Centenary award, 1980;

National Jewish Book award, 1981; Elmer Holmes Bobst award, 1987; Harold Morton Landon award for translation, 1997. D.H.L.: Eastern Michigan University, Ypsilanti, 1977. D.Litt.: Hampden Sydney College, 1990. **Address:** P.O. Box 119, Setauket, New York 11733–0119, U.S.A.

PUBLICATIONS

Poetry

The Arrivistes: Poems 1940–1949. New York, Fine Editions Press, 1949.

Good News of Death and Other Poems. New York, Scribner, 1955.

A Dream of Governors. Middletown, Connecticut, Wesleyan University Press, 1959.

At the End of the Open Road. Middletown, Connecticut Wesleyan University Press, 1963.

Five American Poets, with others, edited by Thom Gunn and Ted Hughes. London, Faber, 1963.

Selected Poems. New York, Harcourt Brace, 1965; London, Oxford University Press, 1966.

Adventures of the Letter 1. London, Oxford University Press, and New York, Harper, 1971.

The Invasion of Italy. Northampton, Massachusetts, Main Street, 1976.

Searching for the Ox. New York, Morrow, and London, Oxford University Press, 1976.

Armidale. Brockport, New York, BOA, 1979.

Caviare at the Funeral. New York, Watts, 1980; Oxford, Oxford University Press, 1981.

The Best Hour of the Night. New Haven, Connecticut, Ticknor and Fields, 1983.

People Live Here: Selected Poems 1949–1983. Brockport, New York, BOA, 1983; London, Secker and Warburg, 1985.

Poems. Merrick, New York, Cross-Cultural Communications, 1989.

Collected Poems. New York, Paragon House, 1990.

In the Room We Share. New York, Paragon House, 1990.

Wei Wei and Other Friends. Francestown, New Hampshire, Typographeum, 1990.

Jamaica Poems. Lewisburg, Pennsylvania, Press of Appletree Alley, 1993.

The King My Father's Wreck. Brownsville, Oregon, Story Line Press, 1995.

There You Are: Poems. Brownsville, Oregon, Story Line Press, 1995.

Recordings: *Louis Simpson Reads from His Own Works,* Carillon, 1961; *Today's Poets 1,* with others, Folkways, 1967; *Physical Universe.* Watershed. 1985.

Plays

The Father Out of the Machine: A Masque, in *Chicago Review,* winter, 1950.

Good News of Death, in *Hudson Review* (New York), summer 1952.

Andromeda, in *Hudson Review* (New York), winter 1956.

The Breasts of Tiresias, adaptation of the play by Apollinaire, in *Modern French Theatre,* edited by Michael Benedikt and George E. Wellwarth. New York, Dutton, 1964; as *Modern French Plays,* London, Faber, 1965.

Novel

Riverside Drive. New York, Atheneum, 1962.

Other

James Hogg: A Critical Study. Edinburg, Oliver and Boyd, and New York, St. Martin's Press, 1962.

Air with Armed Men (autobiography). London, London Magazine Editions, 1972; as *North of Jamaica,* New York, Harper, 1972.

Three on the Tower: The Lives and Works of Ezra Pound, T.S. Eliot, and William Carlos Williams. New York, Morrow, 1975.

A Revolution in Taste: Studies of Dylan Thomas, Allen Ginsberg, Sylvia Plath, and Robert Lowell. New York, Macmillan, 1978; as *Studies of Dylan Thomas, Allen Ginsberg, Sylvia Plath, and Robert Lowell,* London, Macmillan, 1979.

A Company of Poets. Ann Arbor, University of Michigan Press, 1981.

The Character of the Poet. Ann Arbor, University of Michigan Press, 1986.

Selected Prose. New York, Paragon House, 1989.

Ships Going into the Blue: Essays and Notes on Poetry. Ann Arbor, University of Michigan Press, 1994.

Editor, with Donald Hall and Robert Pack, *The New Poets of England and America.* New York, Meridian, 1957; London, New English Library, 1974.

Editor, *An Introduction to Poetry.* New York, St. Martin's Press, 1986.

Editor, *Modern Poets of France: A Bilingual Anthology.* Ashland, Oregon, Story Line Press, 1997.

*

Bibliography: *Louis Simpson: A Reference Guide* by William H. Roberson, Boston, Hall, 1980.

Manuscript Collection: Library of Congress, Washington, D.C.

Critical Studies: *Louis Simpson* by Ronald Moran, New York, Twayne, 1972, and *Four Poets and the Emotive Imagination* by Moran and George S. Lensing, Baton Rouge, Louisiana State University Press, 1976; *The World's Hieroglyphic Beauty: Five American Poets* by Peter Stitt, Athens, University of Georgia Press, 1985; *On Louis Simpson: Depths beyond Happiness* edited by Hank Lazer, Ann Arbor, University of Michigan Press, 1988; ''Great Experiments: The Poetry of Louis Simpson'' by Henry Taylor, in *Hollins Critic* (Hollins College, Virginia), 27(3), June 1990; ''Re-Viewing Louis Simpson'' by James. M. Cox, in *Southern Review* (Baton Rouge, Louisiana), 31(1), winter 1995.

Louis Simpson comments:

I have written about many subjects: war, love, American landscape, and history. For several years I have been writing in free form. Influences: many poets, English and American—particularly Eliot and Whitman. I believe that poetry rises from the inner life of the poet and is expressed in original images and rhythms. Also, the language of poetry should be closely related to the language in which men actually think and speak.

(1980) My earliest published work was in traditional forms. At the end of the 1950s I began writing in irregular, unrhymed lines; I was attempting to write verse that would sound like speech. My subjects have frequently been taken from life, and in many of my poems there is a narrative or dramatic element. I aim at transparency, to let the action, feeling, and idea come through with no interference. Writing well is like meditating; it requires rising above the merely personal.

(1990) I would like my poems to seem as true as a story by Chekhov . . . or a poem by Chaucer.

*   *   *

Louis Simpson's *Selected Poems* contained portions from his previous volumes as well as a dozen works in "New Poems." Two earlier volumes, published only four years apart, revealed his remarkable growth. Dealing with war, love, history, the emptiness of modern life, and the American in Europe, *A Dream of Governors* was knowing and intelligent but somewhat too formal, avoiding simultaneously the pressure of passion and the perspective of vision.

At the End of the Open Road, which received the Pulitzer, was a different matter entirely. Partly under the influence of the deep imagists, led by Robert Bly, Simpson found the key to the meaning and power of his themes. The development of the poem from the routine to the timeless, from situation to response, was no longer a matter of mere machinery but rather of vital shock. It was not simply that his style was getting more experimental but rather that his flexibility was a sign of growth in the character and thought of the speaker, an openness to life whereby the poet risked being changed by what he experienced. Simpson was on his way to becoming a major poet.

We have in this volume another group of poems about America, but they are much more penetrating than those in *A Dream of Governors.* "In California," for example, begins, "Here I am, troubling the dream coast / With my New York face." "In the Suburbs" begins, "There's no way out. / You were born to waste your life." There are three poems at the end inspired by Whitman, who is also hailed in "In California." Simpson knows that "the Open Road goes [now] to the used-car lot" and that, since the past keeps repeating itself, it cannot be canceled out; finally, "At the end of the open road we come to ourselves." Simpson had come a long way from the somewhat easy stance of Sherwood Anderson in "Hot Night on Water Street" and "The Boarder" from *A Dream of Governors.* America's emptiness was now seen in its historical context, and thus the poet's satire had cause and direction.

There also is a group of four wonderful love poems—"Summer Morning," "The Silent Lover," "Birch," and "The Sea and the Forest"—which are by far more meaningful and passionate than Simpson's earlier erotic lyrics. In the first named, for example, the speaker remembers having been with a girl in a hotel room fifteen years earlier, and he feels the weight of the intervening time, concluding, "So I have spoiled my chances. / For what? Sheer laziness, / The thrill of an assignation, / My life that I hold in secret." Finally, there is the remarkable piece called "American Poetry," a marvel of concise meaning, which I quote in full:

Whatever it is, it must have
A stomach that can digest
Rubber, coal, uranium, moons, poems.

Like the shark, it contains a shoe.

It must swim for miles through the desert
Uttering cries that are almost human.

Simpson had digested the indigestible and was now embarked on his long swim through the desert.

Two years later in "The Laurel Tree," from "New Poems," we find Simpson realizing that "I must be patient with shapes / Of automobile fenders and ketchup bottles. / These things are the beginning / of things not visible to the naked eye." In "Things," in the confrontation between the speaker and an unearthly visitor, the latter tells him, "Things which to us in the pure state are mysteries, / Are your simplest articles of household use." The speaker replies, "I have suspected / The Mix-master knows more than I do, / The air conditioner is the better poet."

The spirituality of the mundane is surely a Whitmanesque-not to say Zen—theme, and Simpson returned in his next book, *Adventures of the Letter I,* to his obsession with America. In "Doubting," for example, he says, "I look on the negro as myself, I accuse myself / of sociopathic tendencies, I accuse my accusers." Here he has wittily captured the authentic Whitman mood and cadence, but then the feeling falls and he becomes depressed. Once more he must learn to be patient, he says, and "to breathe in, breathe out, / and to sit by the bed and watch."

Adventures of the Letter I is a marvelous and varied book, fulfilling all of Simpson's earlier promise and carrying it a stage further. It begins, for example, with a strange and fablelike section on Volhynia in which the poet creates an imaginary version of that part of the Ukraine his mother came from. There also is a section called "Individuals," which contains an effective narrative portrait, "Vandergast and the Girl," reminiscent in subject and tone of Edwin Arlington Robinson. In order to digest the trash of ordinary life, to see the light of meaning in the trivial, Simpson had to go into himself and learn to be patient, trusting "in silence" and not believing "in ideas / unless they are unavoidable" ("An American Peasant").

In *Searching for the Ox,* a book in which Simpson moves out on his own to develop what he sees as a plain, transparent narrative and dramatic style, the desert swim seems at moments to be wavering. There is, on the one hand, an emphasis in his preface to this volume on the rendering of human experience and of the world we live in, but there is also a strange note of detachment at the conclusion when he recalls his former selves as they appear in some of these poems: "But I have changed; I am different from the boy and the man I used to be . . . These changes cry out for a life that does not change. The less we are at home in the world, the more we bear witness to that other life." Paying attention to his cue, we are not surprised to find that the style of this book is not simply clear and direct, the language of speech, but that it also is curiously level, limpid, and even deliberately flat. The recurring theme of homelessness, of feeling out of the world, becomes more intelligible when we read, for example, "When I look back at myself / it is like looking through a window / and seeing another person" ("The Springs at Gadara") or "At dusk when the lamps go on / I have stayed outside and watched / the shadow-life of the interior, / feeling myself apart from it" ("Searching for the Ox").

Passion and trust in silence and patience alike were at a low ebb. One could only hope that the consequent shrinking of the ordinary would prove temporary, for there were a number of suggestions that Simpson's intention was otherwise. He explained that the book's title had its origin in a series of Zen illustrations whose message is the mastery and elimination of self (in the oriental sense of "ego"), a message that is not coincidentally related to Eliot's "objective correlative.'' The result for Simpson is a poetry that focuses on ordinary life not simply to reflect it but even more to evoke feelings and ideas about it, if not to like life then to see it in the scheme of things as part of a larger vision. As with Eliot's often misunderstood concept, the intent is not to be passionless but to allow the object to embody and evoke the passion. His confessed models are—in addition to Whitman—Wordsworth, Chekhov, and William Carlos Williams. He would reject any either/or choice between art and life, between pure beauty or pure alienation.

Simpson clearly is engaged in a significant struggle, and his next two major collections, *Caviare at the Funeral* and *The Best Hour of the Night,* bear its marks. Although he continues to explore memories of his Jamaican childhood, relates his mother's tales of her own childhood, and puzzles over the mysteries of time and art, he nevertheless continues also to plumb the emptiness of the ordinary without transformation, still in a dry, flat tone. It is not simply the emptiness of the lives of shop girls, soldiers on leave, or cocktail waitresses and of the gas stations, bars, and hotels where their stories are played out, but it also includes suburban couples as well, their adulteries and the shopping malls and restaurants where they live their lives. Rarely does the speaker accuse himself, reserving for himself instead the role of wry observer.

An exception is ''Armidale,'' a prose piece about a visit to Australia, and the four poems that accompany it in *Caviare at the Funeral.* There is a vigor here, partly produced by the frontierlike milieu of the place and partly by the moving effect of this milieu upon the speaker. Another exception is ''Physical Universe,'' from *The Best Hour of the Night,* which, although narrated in the third person, represents the speaker finding a Zen-like delight once again in the ordinary, a delight he is, unfortunately, somewhat less likely to find in the lives of his neighbors. But perhaps it is, nevertheless, a good sign that reintegration is on the way.

This impression is borne out by Simpson's 1990 volume *In the Room We Share,* a collection of forty-nine poems plus a prose memoir of his and his wife's visit to Italy to attend to his aging and ailing mother. What we see here is the more frequent success—despite the occasional risk of flatness—of Simpson's quest to transform ordinary life embodied in ordinary language into a transcendent vision. In ''Harry and Grace,'' for example, while the speaker acknowledges that he has material for the expected satire of life in the Hamptons on Long Island, he deliberately rejects this approach and, responding to a flight of geese in the flashing sunset, takes his place in line for the usual outdoor cookout. ''The People Next Door'' finds the speaker, without losing his sense of difference, laughing with those who laugh and mourning with those who mourn. In ''Summer Comes to the Three Villages'' God smells the smoke of summer ''and pronounces it good.'' In his memoir, when his mother objects to his radical desertion of ''beauty'' and escapism, he replies that ''as in a Chekhov story it should show the poetry in common things.'' We see that Simpson has discovered how to mine this rich ore more consistently.

Wei Wei and Other Friends, also published in 1990, is a chapbook containing three new poems. ''The Saying,'' a short poem about meeting a man at a party who reminds the speaker of someone he knew during his Paris days, has a touch of whimsy, the man protesting that he does not know what the speaker is talking about. ''Wei Wei'' is a five-page portrait of Marjorie, a woman who ''served during World War II / as liaison with Chiang Kaishek'' and who bores her visitors with her rambling stories of that time. The speaker's mind glazes over, and he wanders off to her reproachful glance. She drives people away because she expects so much attention, and he finds

himself unable to express his condolences when her husband dies: ''Life isn't like a novel, with people / rushing into each other's arms / and asking to be forgiven.'' ''Three Chimneys,'' just over a page in length, is a portrait of three sisters—Carol, Beverly, and Jo Ann. The focus is on the last woman, who is a dental assistant, and her boyfriend. The speaker is sitting in the dentist's chair, awaiting Dr. Weiss and his drill. It would seem that Jo Ann is not yet ready for marriage, for her boyfriend only wants to sit and watch television, while she likes to read books. The speaker concludes dryly, ''I think it's more personal. / Sex. It usually is.''

While this work continues Simpson's vein of suburban observations, his 1993 volume *Jamaica Poems* returns to his early life in Jamaica. Because it begins with a prose memoir, which is continued in *The King My Father's Wreck* (1995), and contains fourteen poems published in his previous volumes, it serves as a useful compendium of his work on the theme.

There You Are, another work published in 1995, is divided into three sections plus an opening poem, ''To a Russian Poet,'' which laments the oncoming commercialization of post-Soviet Russia and concludes with the Zen koan ''What's the sound of one hand clapping?'' ''Objects of the Stream,'' prefaced with a William James quotation about the persistence of memory in the present, contains memories of school days, the 1960s, student uprisings, and Existentialism, among other things. This section also includes the title poem, a hallucinatory depiction of French Jews being rounded up for Auschwitz: ''So tomorrow, there you are, / And they walk you to the station . . .'' The middle section, ''The Walker on Main Street,'' returns to life in the contemporary suburbs and is prefaced with a quotation from Chaucer about plain speaking. Here the poet evokes his underlying mundane/transcendent theme, the title poem describing a strange man who used to walk through the town dressed always in the same winter clothing even in summer. The concluding section, ''A Clearing,'' is prefaced with a quotation from Amos Oz about the difficulty of renouncing all desire. The title poem tells of the speaker's time as a visiting professor in Australia and of leaving a party to walk outside in the night: ''I had ceased to exist. / There was only whatever it was / that was looking at the sky / and listening to the wind.'' We have returned to the Zen koan with which the volume began, showing that Simpson remains one of our most significant lyric poets.

—Norman Friedman

SIMPSON, R(onald) A(lbert)

Nationality: Australian. **Born:** Melbourne, Victoria, 1 February 1929. **Education:** Royal Melbourne Institute of Technology, Associateship Diploma of Art; Melbourne Teachers' College, Primary Teachers' Certificate 1951. **Family:** Married Pamela Bowles in 1955; one son and one daughter. **Career:** Primary school teacher, Melbourne, and in England, 1951–57; art teacher in secondary schools in Melbourne, 1958–61; sub-editor, Department of Education, Melbourne, 1962–67; lecturer in art, 1968–71, and senior lecturer, 1972–87, Chisholm Institute of Technology, Melbourne. Poetry editor, *The Bulletin,* Sydney, 1963–65. Since 1969 poetry editor, *The Age,* Melbourne. **Awards:** Australian Arts Council travel grant, 1977; fellowship, 1986; FAW Christopher Brennan award, 1992. **Address:** 29 Omama Road, Murrumbeena, Melbourne, Victoria 3163, Australia.

PUBLICATIONS

Poetry

The Walk along the Beach. Sydney, Edwards and Shaw, 1960.
This Real Pompeii. Brisbane, Jacaranda Press, 1964.
After the Assassination and Other Poems. Brisbane, Jacaranda Press, 1968.
Diver. St. Lucia, University of Queensland Press, 1972.
Poems from Murrumbeena. St. Lucia, University of Queensland Press, 1976.
The Forbidden City. Sydney, Edwards and Shaw, 1979.
Selected Poems. St. Lucia, University of Queensland Press, 1981.
Words for a Journey: Poems 1980–1985. Melbourne, Melbourne University Press, 1986.
Dancing Table: Poems and Drawings 1986–1991. Melbourne, Penguin Books, 1992.
The Impossible: And Other Poems. Wollongong, New South Wales, Five Islands Press, 1998.
The Midday Clock. Melbourne, Macmillan/The Age, 1999.

Other

Editor, *Poems from "The Age" 1967–79.* Melbourne, Hyland House, 1979.

*

Manuscript Collection: National Library of Australia, Canberra.

Critical Studies: *The Literature of Australia* edited by Geoffrey Dutton, Melbourne, Penguin, 1976; "On UQP's Selection" by Graham Rowlands, in *Overland* (Melbourne), 88, July 1982; "Mixed Motives, Mixed Diction: Recent Australian Poetry" by Chris Wallace-Crabbe, in *Journal of Commonwealth Literature* (East Sussex, England), 19(1), 1984.

R.A. Simpson comments:

As a poet I use words in an effort to understand and clarify experiences. I get my main joy from poetry in the use of words; the struggle for clarification is the painful region. My early poetry was stiff and formal. I believe, and hope, that my recent work shows greater ease and freedom. My background as an art teacher contributed to my experiments in concrete poetry, an area I no longer find interesting.

I do not see myself merely as an Australian poet, though there are obvious Australian attitudes in my poetry and I have used Australian themes. Most present-day Australian poets would seriously believe that the best poetry being written today here and overseas reflects some kind of international style, a sense of the poet's responsibility to human beings in general. Australian poets feel part of the larger flow of ideas and are now making significant contributions.

*   *   *

One of a group of Melbourne poets who came to prominence in the 1950s and then became influential in the 1960s, R.A. Simpson has carefully maintained certain essential characteristics more consistently than have his fellow poets Vincent Buckley, Chris Wallace-Crabbe, and Evan Jones, all of whom have modified their original

formal regularity and slightly academic (or at least cloistered) affectations of irony and equipoise. In his first collection, *The Walk along the Beach,* Simpson quite firmly demonstrated a mind concerned with paring language down, with understatement, and with letting the image work with a minimum of encumbrances. The early poems were often overtly concerned, however, with the heritage of a Roman Catholic boyhood, the subsequent loss of faith, and the aftermath of guilt. Indeed, even as late as Simpson's poetry in *Diver,* the innate direction of mind is through channels of justification or expiation. Though there may be no God for Simpson, there is still an implied judgment.

The verse style that worries its way through these concerns is, however, strangely tight-lipped and reticent. At its weakest it seems hesitant, hardly daring to indulge even in connectives. At its best it is a strikingly taut and resonant instrument capable of playing upon (and preying upon) those central nervous gropings and ambivalences that our own speech can enmesh us in. Simpson's poetry is not graceful or elegant. It is self-guarded, and it keeps catching itself off guard. Both in the 1960s and the 1970s it remained outside the current fashions, but its essential honesty sustains it. It is a poetry one can return to many times and always with a gain.

The later collections *The Forbidden City* and *Words for a Journey* maintain Simpson's tightness and restraint but are enhanced by something of the sparkle of travel and the honing of his sense of quiet wit. There are still macabre overtones, but there is also an element of gentle play that has mellowed the poet's voice. His later work seems somehow more gregarious without losing any sense of honesty or intensity. In many ways *Dancing Table: Poems & Drawings 1986–1991,* published in 1992, sharpens the rueful wit and observation of its predecessors. The more his works look toward mortality and loss, the more the sense of play resurfaces, with life seen as a balancing act and the dancing table as a hollow board. His prizewinning collection *The Impossible* and the volume *The Midday Clock* reinforce the grave playfulness of Simpson's later work and seem to reach a new audience for his characteristic ruefulness and wit.

—Thomas W. Shapcott

SINCLAIR, Iain

Nationality: British. **Born:** Cardiff, 11 June 1943. **Education:** Cheltenham College, 1956–61; London School of Film Technique; Trinity College, Dublin; Courtauld Institute, London. **Family:** Married Mary Annabel Rose Hadman in 1967; two daughters and one son. **Career:** Former poetry consultant, Paladin Publishers, London. Since 1979 book dealer in London. **Agent:** John Parker, MBA Literary Agents Ltd., 45 Fitzroy Street, London W1P SHR. **Address:** 28 Albion Drive. London E8 4ET, England.

PUBLICATIONS

Poetry

Back Garden Poems. London, Albion Village Press, 1970.
Muscat's Würm. London, Albion Village Press, 1972.
The Birth Rug. London, Albion Village Press, 1973.
Lud Heat. London, Albion Village Press, 1975.
Brown Clouds. Newcastle upon Tyne, Pig Press, 1977.

The Penances. London, Many Press, 1977.
Suicide Bridge. London, Albion Village Press, 1979.
Fluxions. London, Albion Drive, 1983.
Flesh Eggs and Scalp Metal. London, Hoarse Commerce, 1983.
Autistic Poses. London, Hoarse Commerce, 1985.
Significant Wreckage. Child Okeford, Dorset, Words, 1988.
Flesh Eggs and Scalp Metal: Selected Poems 1970–1987. London, Paladin, 1989.
Jack Elam's Other Eye. London, Hoarse Commerce, 1991.
The Ebbing of the Kraft. Cambridge, Equipage, 1997.

Plays

An Explanation, with Christopher Bamford (produced Dublin, 1963).
Cords, with Christopher Bamford (produced Dublin, 1964).

Novels

White Chappell, Scarlet Tracings. Uppingham, Goldmark, 1987.
Downriver (or, The Vessels of Wrath). London, Paladin, 1991.
Radon Daughters. London, Jonathan Cape, 1994.
Slow Chocolate Autopsy, with Dave McKean. London, Phoenix House, 1997.

Other

The Kodak Mantra Diaries: Allen Ginsberg in London. London, Albion Village Press, 1971.
Lights Out for the Territory. London, Granta, 1997.
Crash. London, BFI Publishing, 1999.
Liquid City, with Marc Atkins. London, Reaktion, 1999.
Dark Lanthorns. Uppingham, Goldmark, 1999.
Rodinsky's Room, with Rachel Lichtenstein. London, Granta, 1999.
Sorry Meniscus: Excursions to the Millennium Dome. London, Profile, 1999.

Editor, *The Conductors of Chaos: Anthology.* London, Picador, 1996.
Editor, with Douglas Oliver and Denise Riley, *Penguin Modern Poets 10.* London, Penguin, 1996.

*

Critical Study: "A Cartography of Absence: The Work of Iain Sinclair" by Simon Perril, in *Comparative Criticism,* 19, 1997.

*   *   *

With its mixture of the esoteric and the earthy and its combination of poetic and prose forms, which give his work its unique range of tones and textures, Iain Sinclair had finally by the 1990s become almost a cult figure, proving that a poet from the underground could make it to the surface.

Sinclair's roots as a writer belong in the late 1960s inheritance from American beat and Black Mountain lyricism, but he was not well known in the alternative British poetries of the time. Perhaps this was because his early occupation was as a documentary filmmaker, a point worth noting since precise perception and the ability to "frame" significant slices of life have fed the realist side of his writing, which provides interesting contrasts with the use of arcane knowledge and free prosodic forms derived from Charles Olson. His first substantial

book was the prose log of the making, in 1968, of an Allen Ginsberg documentary and was published by his own Albion Village Press as *The Kodak Mantra Diaries.* Along with stills and transcripts, this not altogether reverent account is still a valuable source of information about Ginsberg and about both the official and unofficial faces of late 1960s radicalism, the backdrop for Sinclair's writing. The exercise was valuable for Sinclair, who honed his prose writing to a style similar to that of the so-called new journalism, which adapted fictional pace and tension to reportage. It also established Sinclair as a maker of books.

Sinclair's major trilogy (for a number of years it looked as if the third might never appear) consists of the books *Lud Heat* (1975), *Suicide Bridge* (1979), and *White Chappell, Scarlet Tracings* (1987). *Lud Heat*'s central thesis is that Hawksmoor's London churches emanate psychic energies that affect the population. (Peter Ackroyd borrowed this for his novel *Hawksmoor,* for which he is satirized in Sinclair's later work.) The work charts his own mundane life, as a council grass cutter working near the churches, in diary form. He bears witness to the films of Stan Brakage and the homicidally obsessed sculpture of his friend and poet B. Catling. Sinclair dramatizes himself as cosmic victim when apparently random events emerge as patterned and preordained. Essays on ritual murder sites and on the churches provide the patterning.

In *Suicide Bridge* the focus becomes more mythic, and the verse is more confidently handled as narrative. Sinclair cleverly takes Blake's sons of Albion from the prophetic books and replicates Blake's modeling of them upon real characters. Thus, Blake's Hand and Hyle—the Hunt brothers and Hayley—are refigured as modern embodiments of instinctive East London evil, the Kray Twins. This imposition of "myth" carries with it a danger that Sinclair recognizes in his introductory essay: behind his identification of an ancient place and a particular named person could be the modern energy of fascism. On the other hand, another long essay, "The Horse. The Man. The Talking Head," attempts to chart both occult forces and contemporary conspiracy theories (the focus is on the strange paranoid existence of Howard Hughes) and to align the two, so that by the end America's White House-underworld-CIA-big business-showbiz nexus is figured as literally demonic. Indeed, the first of the sons to die, Kotope, is a capitalist with underworld connections. His is the paranoia of bullet-proof Rolls Royce windshields, traveling through London in a vain pursuit of an occult grail. "The Manner of His Dying" is pastiche William Burroughs: "Six Arabs on the Doorstep" mow him down and then dissolve into shrubbery. But death, as for many of the murder victims, fulfills him. He becomes the place and "erects one final, animal, vision of the city, / . . . and is gone."

These two handsomely produced Albion Village books became, along with Allen Fisher's extensive *Place* project, models for a notational obsession with place and topology in some radical poetry of the 1970s, but they did not receive much contemporary recognition, although Sinclair was anthologized in *The New British Poetry* (1988). Sinclair's work was also taken up by the so-called Cambridge school of poetry—despite the fact that one of its practitioners is satirized in *Suicide Bridge* as Skofeld—and his work was again later anthologized in *A Various Art* (1987), where he oddly shares space and apparent allegiances with poets like J.H. Prynne. Between *Suicide Bridge* and these anthologies Sinclair published very little and was even rumored to have given up writing.

Working as a bookseller and perhaps seeing Ackroyd's borrowings of his work as symptomatic of the parasitism of the literary world, Sinclair eventually turned to fiction, in turn "borrowing" Ackroyd's device in *Hawksmoor* of presenting a double narrative—contemporary set against historical. The earlier books had been obsessed with murder and with the still unsolved mystery of the East End Ripper murders of the 1880s. Stephen Knight's *Jack the Ripper: The Final Solution* was a timely piece of journalistic detective work, and it is not surprising that its theory that a vast conspiracy, involving both Walter Sickert and Queen Victoria's physician, Sir William Gull, was responsible for the murders was assimilated into Sinclair's novel *White Chappell, Scarlet Tracings.* A narrative based on the life of Gull and other Victorians ("their behaviour is dictated by sources other than historical record," a note tells us) contrasts with the surprisingly seedy world of contemporary bookselling and the obsession of a character called "the author" with solving the murders. The sole runner-up for the *Guardian* fiction prize of 1987, the novel is too esoteric and allusive to be treated singularly and needs to be seen as the fictional conclusion to the notational *Lud Heat* and the mythic *Suicide Bridge,* to which it presents an interesting formal variation. Indeed, it is difficult to conceive how a writer who really does believe that words are magic would have much patience with the kind of textual unities that contemporary fiction favors any more than his poetry has commerce with the empirical and rational lyricism of the dominant orthodoxy of British verse.

This highlights the essential difficulty for a reader who does not share a belief in what Sinclair calls the "complex and secretly-worked system of parallels, analogues and models." Despite Sinclair's occasional skepticism toward his own pattern making, does the reader merely accept this occult knowledge and learning as some readers of Yeats accommodate *A Vision,* as a convenient superstructure for fictive elaboration? To do so is to take Sinclair's work less than seriously.

The success of the novel led Paladin to issue a selected poems, *Flesh Eggs and Scalp Metal,* and Penguin to feature him in its Modern Poets series. These are valuable for collecting his short later poems, notable for their terse "street detail" (to use the title of one) of East End lowlife. The poems seem occasional, as though his greatest energies are now reserved for fiction, including a great ragbag of London, *Downriver.* Nonetheless, his work as poetry consultant at Paladin and as editor of *The Conductors of Chaos* (1996) attempted to gain the kind of visibility that he now enjoys for other writers of the alternative British poetries, drawing on his own association with the Cambridge school and upon Catling's involvement in the vibrant performance writing scene.

Sinclair has increasingly not operated as a poet. He can be observed in the British media talking about Cronenberg's *Crash,* on which he has written a critical work, or about the beauty of the automobile, revealed by his own circumnavigation of London's orbital motorway. Perhaps this only brings him back to the cultural arena of *The Kodak Mantra Diaries.* In any case, his poetry has always included that which is not poetry.

—Robert Sheppard

SISSON, C(harles) H(ubert)

Nationality: British. **Born:** Bristol, 22 April 1914. **Education:** University of Bristol, 1931–34, B.A. (honors) in philosophy and English literature 1934; University of Berlin and University of Freiburg, 1934–35; Sorbonne, Paris, 1935–36. **Military Service:** British Army Intelligence Corps in India, 1942–45. **Family:** Married Nora Gilbertson in 1937; two daughters. **Career:** Assistant principal, 1936–42, principal, 1945–53, assistant secretary, 1953–62, and under secretary, 1962–68, Ministry of Labour, London; assistant under secretary of state, 1968–71, and director of Occupational Safety and Health, 1971–73, Department of Employment, London. Co-editor, *PN Review,* Manchester, 1976–83. **Awards:** Senior Simon Research fellowship, University of Manchester, 1956. D.Litt.: University of Bristol, 1980. Fellow, Royal Society of Literature, 1975. Companion of Honour, 1993. **Agent:** Laurence Pollinger Ltd., 16 Maddox Street, London W1R OEU. **Address:** Moorfield Cottage, The Hill, Langport, Somerset TA10 9PU, England.

PUBLICATIONS

Poetry

Versions and Perversions of Heine. London, Gaberbocchus, 1955.
Poems. Fairwarp, Sussex, Peter Russell, 1959.
Twenty-One Poems. Privately printed, 1960.
The London Zoo. London, Abelard Schuman, 1961.
Numbers. London, Methuen, 1965.
Catullus. London, MacGibbon and Kee, 1966; New York, Orion Press, 1967.
The Discarnation; or, How the Flesh Became Word and Dwelt among Us. Privately printed, 1967.
Metamorphoses. London, Methuen, 1968.
Roman Poems. Privately printed, 1968.
In the Trojan Ditch: Collected Poems and Selected Translations. Cheadle, Cheshire, Carcanet, 1974.
The Corridor. Hitchin, Hertfordshire, Mandeville Press, 1975.
Anchises. Manchester, Carcanet, 1976.
Exactions. Manchester, Carcanet, 1980.
Selected Poems. Manchester, Carcanet, 1981; Redding Ridge, Connecticut, Black Swan, 1982.
Night Thoughts and Other Poems. Oxford, Inky Parrot, 1983.
Collected Poems 1943–1983. Manchester, Carcanet, 1984.
God Bless Karl Marx! Manchester, Carcanet, 1987.
16 Sonnets. London, H. and C. Laserprint, 1990.
Antidotes. Manchester, Carcanet, 1991.
Nine Sonnets. Warwick, Greville Press, 1991.
The Pattern. London, Enitharmon, 1993.
What and Who. Manchester, Carcanet, 1994.
Poems, Selected. Manchester, Carcanet, 1995; as *Selected Poems,* New York, New Directions, 1996.
Collected Poems. Manchester, Carcanet, 1998.

Novels

An Asiatic Romance. London, Gaberbocchus, 1953.
Christopher Homm. London, Methuen, 1965.

Other

The Spirit of British Administration and Some European Comparisons. London, Faber, and New York, Praeger, 1959.
Art and Action. London, Methuen, 1965.
Essays. Privately printed, 1967.

English Poetry 1900–1950: An Assessment. London, Hart Davis, 1971.

The Case of Walter Bagehot. London, Faber, 1972.

David Hume. Edinburgh, Ramsay Head Press, 1976.

The Avoidance of Literature: Collected Essays, edited by Michael Schmidt. Manchester, Carcanet, 1978.

Anglican Essays. Manchester, Carcanet, 1983.

On the Look-Out: A Partial Autobiography. Manchester, Carcanet, 1989.

In Two Minds: Guesses at Other Writers. Manchester, Carcanet, 1990.

English Perspectives: Essays on Liberty and Government. Manchester, Carcanet, 1992.

Is There a Church of England? Reflections on Permanence and Progression. Manchester, Carcanet, 1993.

Editor, *A South African Album,* by David Wright. Cape Town, Philip, 1976.

Editor, *The English Sermon 1650–1750.* Manchester, Carcanet, 1976.

Editor, *Selected Poems,* by Jonathan Swift. Manchester, Carcanet, 1976.

Editor, *Jude the Obscure,* by Hardy. London, Penguin, 1978.

Editor, *Autobiographical and Other Papers,* by Philip Mairet. Manchester, Carcanet, 1981.

Editor, *The Rash Act,* by Ford Madox Ford. Manchester, Carcanet, 1982.

Editor, *Selected Poems,* by Christina Rossetti. Manchester, Carcanet, 1984.

Editor, *Selected Writings,* by Jeremy Taylor. Manchester, Carcanet, 1990.

Editor, *Poems and Essays on Poetry,* by Edgar Allan Poe. Manchester, Carcanet, 1995.

Translator, *The Poetic Art: A Translation of Horace's Ars Poetica.* Cheadle, Cheshire, Carcanet, 1975.

Translator, *De Rerum Natura: The Poem on Nature,* by Laucretius. Manchester, Carcanet, 1976.

Translator, *Some Tales of La Fontaine.* Manchester, Carcanet, 1979.

Translator, *The Divine Comedy,* by Dante. Manchester, Carcanet, 1980; Chicago, Regnery, 1981; New York, Oxford University Press, 1993.

Translator, *The Song of Roland.* Manchester, Carcanet, 1983.

Translator, *The Regrets,* by Joachim Du Bellay. Manchester, Carcanet, 1984.

Translator, *The Aeneid,* by Virgil. Manchester, Carcanet, 1986.

Translator, *Britannicus, Phaedra, Ahaliah.* Oxford, Oxford University Press, 1987.

Translator, *Collected Translations.* Manchester, Carcanet, 1996.

*

Manuscript Collection: University of Bristol.

Critical Studies: By Martin Seymour-Smith, in *X* (London), 2(3), 1961, in *Agenda* (London), summer-autumn 1970, and in *Guide to Modern World Literature,* London, Wolfe, 1973; by Donald Davie, in *Listener* (London), 9 May 1974; by Robert Nye, in *Times Literary Supplement* (London), 29 November 1974; by David Wright, in *Agenda* (London), autumn 1975; by John Pilling, in *Critical Quarterly* (Manchester), spring 1979; "C.H. Sisson Issue" of *PN Review* (Manchester), spring 1984; "The Poetry of Hell and the Poetry of Paradise: Food for Thought for Translators, Critics, Poets and Other Readers" by Valeria Tinkler-Villani, in *Bulletin of the John Rylands University Library of Manchester* (Manchester, England), 76(1), spring 1994; "Time's Workings: The Stringent Art of C.H. Sisson" by E.M. Knottenbelt, in *In Black and Gold: Contiguous Traditions in Post-War British and Irish Poetry,* edited by C.C. Barfoot, Amsterdam, Rodopi, 1994.

C.H. Sisson comments:

My verse is about things that I am, at the moment of writing, just beginning to understand. When I have understood them, or have that impression, the subject has gone, and I have to find another. Or stop. Generally my resolution is to stop, but another subject is found in time, and I begin again. I began by stopping, so to speak, for having written some verse as an adolescent. I gave up at twenty because I had a great respect for poetry and did not think I could write it. The war and exile produced a few hesitant verses, wrung from me, but I stopped again without really having begun. A more productive start was about 1950, when I was already on the declining side *del cammin di nostra vita.* No wonder, therefore, that my themes have often been age, decline, and death, with the occasional desperate hopes of the receding man. Naturally some facility has come with practice, and the risk now is less from stopping than from going on. One comes to understand too much, or to think one does.

As to verse forms, whether they are what is called regular or not, it is a small matter. I have written in both kinds. What matters is the rhythm, which is the identifying mark of the poem. If that fails, there is no need for a poem; better shut up.

Influences: all one's interests bear, in unexpected ways, on what one writes. Still more, one's poetry may be prophetic of interests one is about to have. The influence of other poets, generally in youth, is deadly while it lasts. There is, however, a deliberate, mature learning that is beneficial. For this purpose I have found translations of the greatest value, with the Latins as the great, though not the only, masters. What I aim at is to make plain statements and not more of them than I need. "It is the nature of man that puzzles me"; I should like to leave a few recognizable, not novel, indications. The man that was the same in Neolithic and in Roman times, as now, is of more interest than the freak of circumstances. This truth lies at the bottom of a well of rhythm.

*   *   *

In his collection *God Bless Karl Marx!* C.H. Sisson speaks of mankind, himself included, as "treaders of the obvious way." With a life as a career civil servant, it seems a particularly apt description of this apparently conventional man. As any reader of his poems soon discovers, however, appearances belie the truth. Though many of his themes—death, procreation, politics, society—are poetically conventional enough, Sisson is, in fact, an unusually original mind among poets today. This is because his most enduring theme and obsession is the questioning of the reality of consciousness itself: "What is the cure for the disease / Of consciousness?" He does not stop at merely the subverting question but asserts his negative discoveries in a curiously positive, yet never sanctimonious, fashion: "The swindle of the world, the mind / Visited upon humankind, / Reason, ha, ha!"

Sisson reminds one very much of the pessimist Hardy's demand that in order to discover the best we should first have a good look at the worst. Even so, there is nothing morbid—and surprisingly little pure despair—in Sisson's poetry. This has a good deal to do with his remarkably plain but hard-edged style, his pure diction, his acute wit, and his lack of self-pity. The very essence of his style is passion annealed, purified, and clarified to such a degree of limpidity that even his gloomiest diagnoses seem bathed in a curious and personal light, which is odd for such a disbeliever in the reality of the self.

"How superficial is the mind of man!''; uncertainty remains the "end of all," and "no word covers a square inch unharmed''; "I advise / The young who would be wise / They should all read examples / Of the philosophers." One of the principal concerns of Sisson is epistemology—how we know what we think we know:

> . . . I sought to find
> What errors might be in a human mind
> And to embrace them all, the skimpy ghosts

All through his work is this ceaseless exploration against despair, an excavating at the very roots of consciousness. "There is no question, as it has come to me, of filling note-books with what one knows already," he writes in the foreword to *Collected Poems 1943–1983*. Yet how, when all is said and done, can Sisson continue to write engaging poetry when his main preoccupation is, to borrow I.A. Richards's phrase, "the meaning of meaning" or, as Sisson might adapt it, "the meaninglessness of meaning"? The answer is quite simply, as I have said, that he has a personal voice of remarkable clarity, totally unmannered but stunningly direct in real authority. Indeed, to reverse the sense, he seems to speak with the authority of the real, and it is his great achievement to do so not by following William Carlos Williams's famous dictum of "no ideas but in things" but by using judiciously both the concrete image and the most precise abstraction. His utterance is instinct with passion, but it is a passion that moves like water under ice.

If there is one image that is both abstract and concrete at the same time and that engages all of Sisson's love, it is England—the England of tradition, faith, and fact. In his poem "Sisson's Goodnight" he would have you understand that "but once I dabbled in the Creed / And England always has my love." This patriotic belief is shored against his own corroding skepticism by the experience that has taught him in the end to be sure at least of this: "For now I know, only the past is true." Sisson's idea of England is not capricious or theoretical, however, but visionary. This is demonstrated conclusively in a late, small poem called "Aller Church," where, though he is walking "under the half-edge of Sedgemoor" in Somerset, he asks, "When shall I see England again?" and realizes that he must content himself not with a precise answer but with the assertion that "this world is not yours." England, if it is anything, is an imaginative, though not imaginary, experience, and, as with the visitations of the muse, it is infrequent but creative when it occurs.

Sisson is not an eccentric but an original. A principal feature of his originality is an obsessive and almost bleak self-criticism:

> His youthful walk
> And grey moustache
> Conceal a heart
> Which cannot feel.

The deadness of the heart in old age, the lust attendant upon both youth and age, a highly ambivalent eschatology, a profound disbelief in the self or in "personality," a strong sense not so much of original sin as of the sheer ignorance of humans about anything, and a

mercilessly honest way of looking at himself and society ("Iago was an honest man; / I have that reputation'')—these are the concerns that have conspired, or driven, Sisson to develop a poetry that is as complete "a criticism of life" as ever Matthew Arnold could have dreamed of when he gave his famous definition to the world. In Sisson's words, "the conscious task" of his poetry "becomes the rejection of whatever appears with the face of familiarity" so that, though any one of his themes may be familiar enough, their bleakly oblique or their dismally direct presentations are somehow always unfamiliar. It is an unfamiliarity—in the words of Donald Davie an "unadvertised drama" of truth and experience—that is set free by a controlled passion transmuted into an instrument of the profoundest irony. Sisson has a thoroughly unsentimental intelligence that also has authored some of the finest and most effective prose of its age, and his work is the most serious corrective available to flabby, facile, or false versifying in our time.

In *Antidotes* Sisson's tight-lipped skepticism shows a slight shift toward didacticism, sometimes with a whiff of dogma: "The only hope the living have / Is Christ, and never mind the dead." This didacticism finds formal excellence in, for example, "The Quandary," actually a soliloquy that shows what a fine traditional metrical craftsman he is. But there is a problem in that his restless, passionate, but despairing nature—productive though it is of beautiful if bleak utterance—is unable to celebrate unreservedly and so must either repeat itself, like a needle stuck in a worn groove, or obsessively question words and the reality of reality:

> —Only another lie
> As once there was in youth:
> Then, that the body spoke,
> Now, that old age is truth.

Elsewhere he says, "When we name that, we say what we cannot know" and "How, in the end, can anybody say / That his life had this or that thing in it, / Or that it failed or succeeded, caught, / As all time is, in multiples of nought?''

Sisson surely is our greatest, purest nihilist, yet he is driven by such passion as to make his nihilism believable by making poetry of it. This happens, for instance, in the spare, grim, sad "Thurloxton," where feeling redeems nihilism and makes it poetry.

Until I had read the later work of Sisson, I would not have believed it possible to make so much beauty out of so much doubt. In *What and Who,* published for his eightieth birthday, Sisson's great crisis of identity continues to be obsessively explored, but as in *Antidotes,* so in this volume there is wonderful and beautiful relief to be found from time to time. He is, as one blurb says, "one of Britain's finest living writers," though not, given his remorseless negativity, ever likely to be one of its most popular.

—William Oxley

SKINNER, Knute (Rumsey)

Nationality: American. **Born:** St. Louis, Missouri, 25 April 1929. **Education:** Culver-Stockton College, Canton, Missouri, 1947–49; University of Northern Colorado, Greeley, A.B. in speech and drama

1951; Middlebury College, Vermont, M.A. in English 1954; University of Iowa, Iowa City, Ph.D. in English 1958. **Family:** Married 1) Jeanne Pratt in 1953 (divorced 1954), one son; 2) Linda Kuhn in 1961 (divorced 1977), two sons; 3) Edna Faye Kiel in 1978. **Career:** English teacher, Boise High School, Idaho, 1951–54; instructor in English, University of Iowa, 1955–56, 1957–58, 1960–61; assistant professor of English, Oklahoma College for Women, Chickasha, 1961–62. Part-time lecturer, 1962–70, associate professor, 1971–73, professor of English, 1973–97, and since 1997 professor emeritus, Western Washington University, Bellingham. Poetry editor, Southern Illinois University Press, Carbondale, 1975–76; editor and publisher, Signpost Press, Bellingham, 1977–95; co-editor, 1977–86, and editor, 1993–95, *Bellingham Review*. Since 1996 associate editor, *New Series: Departures.* **Awards:** Huntington Hartford Foundation fellowship, 1961; National Endowment for the Arts grant, 1975; Millay Colony for the Arts fellowship, 1976. **Address:** Killaspuglonane, Lahinch, County Clare, Ireland.

PUBLICATIONS

Poetry

Stranger with a Watch. Francestown, New Hampshire, Golden Quill Press, 1965.
A Close Sky over Killaspuglonane. Dublin, Dolmen Press, 1968; St. Louis, Burton Press, 1975.
In Dinosaur Country. Greeley, Colorado, Pierian Press, 1969.
The Sorcerers: A Laotian Tale. Bellingham, Washington, Goliards Press, 1972.
Hearing of the Hard Times. Stafford, Virginia, Northwoods Press, 1981.
The Flame Room. Tacoma, Washington, Folly Press, 1983.
Selected Poems. Leek, Staffordshire, Aquila, 1985.
Learning to Spell 'Zucchini.' Galway. Salmon. 1988.
The Bears and Other Poems. Galway, Salmon, 1991.
What Trudy Knows and Other Poems. Galway, Salmon, 1994.
The Cold Irish Earth: New and Selected Poems of Ireland, 1965–1995. Liscannor, County Clare, Salmon, 1996.
An Afternoon Quiet and Other Poems. Johnstown, Ohio, Pudding House, 1998.

*

Manuscript Collection: Humanities Research Center, University of Texas, Austin; The Center for Pacific Northwest Studies, Western Washington University, Bellingham.

Critical Studies: ''From Ireland the American'' by Gregory FitzGerald, in *Ann Arbor Review* (Michigan), summer 1968; by Thomas Churchill, in *Concerning Poetry* (Bellingham, Washington), fall 1968; ''Killaspuglonane'' by Harry Chambers, in *Phoenix* (Manchester), summer 1969; X.J. Kennedy in *Concerning Poetry* (Bellingham, Washington), fall 1969.

Knute Skinner comments:
I have attempted to embody (emphasis on ''body'') love and death. In other poems I have analyzed character. In a few I have attempted to enter nature and have gone so far as to find spirit in a cow. I am no longer as interested in the distant and abstract as I am in my immediate surroundings. Some of my poems are set in Killaspuglonane, my adopted townland, and *Learning to Spell 'Zucchini'* deals in part with friends and relatives. My influences are varied and usual. In two collections, *The Bears* and *What Trudy Knows,* the speakers are all fictional characters narrating brief episodes in tense dramatic situations. I began by writing rhymed stanzas and now write mostly free verse—though I still use rhyme, meter, syllabic or accentual, if the poem asks for it.

*   *   *

Knute Skinner creates from remarkably disparate sources. His poems of love, death, and isolation in *Stranger with a Watch* are powerfully underscored by a wry and acid humor that etches at the surface of experience to reveal inner situations and private struggles. He writes elegies for the living as well as the dead, mourning the mourners. In his constant interplay of mind and senses and in his perception of physical decay and time he recalls Hardy, Housman, and Yeats. There is ironic laughter at twisted circumstance; there is understatement, wordplay, and a combination of metaphysical and sensual imagery; there is concern with madness, prophecy, and the stripping of poetic language to its bones and marrow. In form Skinner ranges widely and easily from lyric to epigram, from sonnet to ballad to free style, but his vision is peculiarly his own. By his criticism he reveals how things are and thereby implies how they ought to be— how love should not be a commodity, how men should not journey alone, how formality and self-consciousness should not divert people from genuine feeling. Through his poems the reader catches glimpses of lost connections—of time, places, and people that are not what they were—and a sense of love's fragility and ineffability.

In *A Close Sky over Killaspuglonane* Skinner allies himself with his Irish heritage, reflecting the land, the people, and the traditions of County Clare. Here he writes most strongly out of a sense of place. He can be chillingly honest, as in ''The Cold Irish Earth,'' which causes him to ''shudder,'' and though his ''coat hangs drying now / by the kitchen range,'' he knows that, when ''a cold rain falls,'' ''down at Healy's Cross / the Killaspuglonane graveyard / is wet to the bone.'' In ''The Cow'' he comes upon ''surely the whitest cow I shall ever see,'' a poem lifting the reader to such a level of wonder that, like the speaker, he can only hold his breath and read on about this cow that grows whiter in the sunlight ''until she seems like a moon reflecting the sun, / a cow-shaped moon newly materialized / to dazzle upon the rise of a grassy hill.'' As the cow becomes transfigured into a ''goddess,'' the speaker yearns to approach, to pay homage while he wonders,

> Would I be touched to some extent by the sunlight,
> and would my eyes be blinded with revelation?
> Or would I find cowdung beneath my feet
> and would she and I eat grass for the rest of our lives?

Out of this world's ingredients, then, Skinner can create a transcendent vision or a lyrical moment, whether it be a cow imbued with divine spirit or a longing to ''dissolve this skin.''

In ''This Skin'' the speaker, a child-man, asks a simple and haunting question, ''Why can't I have the rain for a body?'' ''Imagine

Grass,'' the concluding poem in *A Close Sky over Killaspuglonane,* is a work that astonishes with the scope of its vision as it orbits from this planet into the distant reaches of space and mind only to return with reverence to that miracle ''. . . somewhere in the measured mass / of everything, imagine grass.''

In *Dinosaur Country* displays an exuberant sense of life through humor that can be gentle, whimsical, or uproarious. Without flinching, Skinner reintroduces ''gross'' material into the life experience via poetry. His poems include ''Blackheads,'' ''Phlegm,'' and ''Urine,'' and he presents ''A Poem for the Class of 69'' (in the concrete poetic style). His laughter is compelling and human, reminding the reader that nothing is ugly or alien unless he makes it so.

In *Hearing of the Hard Times* Skinner returns to Ireland, to inner and outer weather. He reminds us again that what is close by is just as deserving of attention—and maybe more so—than the world of political events. Thus, in ''A Four Days' Rain'' the speaker conversationally tells of ''a sheep rotting on the hill where that mare / washes her hooves in the wet grass / . . . / It was there on polling day.'' The reader is invited to ''Take my coat if you'd like to see for yourself,'' and the poem concludes with a masterful understatement, equating both worlds: ''Sometime after they returned the party to power / the dogs buried one of its legs / in with the turnips.''

Skinner unquestionably possesses a gift for stripping and compressing language, for capturing a situation—and the reader's attention—through quiet understatement, as in ''Two Sentences'' (from *The Flame Room*):

> My father died with small
> change in his pocket.
> He was never president
> of my mother's fan club.

At the same time he can achieve effortlessly the conversational quality of an Irish farmer while expressing gratitude for the seemingly ordinary life. In ''Costly Thy Habit As Thy Purse Can Buy,'' after morning rising the ''I'' addresses the reader:

> And you? Perhaps you'd as soon not ask
> what will happen next,
> for none of it sounds extraordinary, does it?
>
> No, not at all—is that
> what you're going to say?
> Not extraordinary to have a cat and a dog
>
> always there in the morning?
> Nor to have children who may or may not rise early
> and who vary their greetings?
>
> Nor to drink orange juice sleepily in the kitchen?
> Nor to open the curtains and be surprised at the weather,
> whatever it is?

Ending this way, the poem invites the reader to respond and to recognize his own blessings. Skinner's poems must be counted among them.

—Carl Lindner

SKRZYNECKL, Peter

Nationality: Australian. **Born:** Imhert, Germany, 6 April 1945; immigrated to Australia in 1949. **Education:** St. Patrick's College, Strathfield, New South Wales; University of New England, Armidale, New South Wales; University of Sydney. **Family:** Married Kate Magrath in 1980; two daughters and one son. **Career:** Formerly a primary school teacher. Since 1987 lecturer in English, University of Western Sydney, Macarthur, New South Wales. **Awards:** Captain Cook Bicentenary award, 1970; Grace Leven award, 1972; Henry Lawson award, for short story, 1985. **Agent:** Curtis Brown Ltd., P.O. Box 19, Paddington, Sydney, New South Wales 2122, Australia. **Address:** 6 Sybil Street, Eastwood, New South Wales 2122, Australia.

PUBLICATIONS

Poetry

There, behind the Lids. Sydney, Lyrebird, 1970.
Headwaters. Sydney, Lyrebird, 1972.
Immigrant Chronicle. St. Lucia, University of Queensland Press, 1975.
The Aviary: Poems 1975–1977. Sydney, Edwards and Shaw, 1978.
The Polish Immigrant. Brisbane, Phoenix, 1982.
Night Swim. Sydney, Hale and Iremonger, 1989.
Easter Sunday. Sydney, HarperCollins, 1993.

Novel

The Beloved Mountain. Sydney, Hale and Iremonger, 1988.

Short Stories

The Wild Dogs. St. Lucia, University of Queensland Press, 1987.
Rock 'n' Roll Heroes. Sydney, Hale & Iremonger, 1992.
The Cry of the Goldfinch. Sydney and New York, Anchor, 1996.

Other

Editor, *Joseph's Coat: An Anthology of Multicultural Writing.* Sydney, Hale and Iremonger, 1985.
Editor, *The Breaking Line.* Sydney, Youngstreet Poets, 1995.
Editor, *Influence: Australian Voices.* Sydney and New York, Anchor, 1997.

*

Manuscript Collection: University of New England, Armidale, New South Wales; Australian Defence Forces Academy, Canberra, Australia.

Critical Studies: ''Return to the Homeland after 40-Year Journey'' by Peter Fuller, in *Migration* (Canberra), October/November 1988; ''Peaks and Troughs of New Fiction,'' in *The Age* (Melbourne), 15 October 1988; *The Poetry of Peter Skrzynecki* by Barry Spurr, Sydney, Pascal Press, 1992; ''Asking What Life's Purpose Should Be,'' in *New England Review* (Armidale, New South Wales), 1993;

"Peter Skrzynecki: 'The Revelation of a Landfall'" by Michael Griffith, in *Southerly* (Sydney), 54(3), September 1994.

Peter Skrzynecki comments:

I have always been interested in the human and physical landscapes of existence—in the exile of immigrants from Europe after World War II and their settlement in this new, strange land. My poetry has mostly been concerned with this generation and also with the expression of my fascination for the physical and spiritual features of Australia.

(1995) The notion of spirituality has crept into my work more, the grapplings between pure states of being and our human frailties. The concept of dark or evil forces, also, with our abandonment of original self. The paradox of extremes, of joy, grief. These concepts find their outlets either in poetry or prose.

                    *   *   *

Peter Skrzynecki is perhaps the most traditional of the contemporary Australian poets, standing in a direct line of descent that may be traced through the lyric poets of the previous generation—Campbell, Wright, Stewart, McAuley, Robinson—back to Slessor, Shaw Neilson, and Brennan.

This is remarkable in a way, given Skrzynecki's Polish/Ukrainian background and his migration to Australia as a child. It is this experience that provides the subject for much of his best poetry and the note of loss that is its most powerful characteristic. Yet it is precisely this elegiac note that sounds through the Australian lyric tradition, and since the experience of migration and displacement, however distant, is at its source, it is not surprising that the tradition should prove fertile ground for later comers. There is a second point of convergence, for, like the earlier "nature poets," Skrzynecki turns to the landscape for identification that the old culture and the old ways of life no longer afford him.

The landscape that dominates Skrzynecki's early poetry, and that haunts the later, is that of the New England plateau in northern New South Wales, where he took up his first teaching position. Finely observed and presented with a clarity that owes something to the particular qualities of the region's light, but more to the poet's sense of being an outsider looking on a strange new world, this landscape is both alluring and menacing. It is appealing in its intensity and yet unrevealing, as if some vital part of it were beyond the poet's reach. In "Bullock Skull," from the collection *Night Swim,* Skrzynecki compares such a landscape to "a distant planet / once glimpsed at the edge of a dream":

grey paddocks sheeted with frost
and cattle standing mutely
under shrouds of rising mist;
sheep feeding beside yellowdust roads
or the edge of granite ravines—
crimson lowries streaking through forests
and over waters of the Styx.

The river in question is actually called the Styx, and so the symbolism is unforced. But often in the early poetry, particularly in *Headwaters,* Skrzynecki deliberately heightens the symbolic effect through mythological, biblical, or cosmological associations, allegorizing the landscape in a way that dramatizes his own sense of exclusion even as he presses his claim to possess it imaginatively. The following is from "Wallamumbi":

In the ancient forest of gorges
He listened to the whisper of birds:
Heard the chant of midnight prophecies
And a name spelt out into the darkness of gullies;
Saw the migration of men and wings
Along the frozen river in the Kingdom of the Dead:
The begin-all, end-all landscape
From which no one before him had returned,
Where all mists rise, frost hardens bone,
And each granite boulder, like a stationary planet,
Becomes a landmark under a galaxy of tableland stars.

In his later poetry Skrzynecki eschews this kind of inflation in favor of a quiet insistence on the significance of ordinary things. At the same time his subjects are usually observed from an elegiac perspective. They are significant because they have been remembered, so that absence and loss are an essential part of their meaning. His mastery of the elegy (he uses the form more extensively than any of his contemporaries) and his sure command of rhythm and line impart a processional quality to his recollections:

For nineteen years
we departed
each morning, shut the house
like a well-oiled lock,
hid the key
under a rusty bucket:
to school and work—
over that still too-narrow bridge,
around the factory
that was always burning down.

This quality is also evident in Skrzynecki's elegiac catalogs, his habit of enumeration suggesting both a desire to preserve the past and an awareness that it falls some way short of a living inheritance:

For nineteen years
we lived together—
kept pre-war Europe alive
with photographs and letters,
heated discussions
and embracing gestures:
visitors that ate
kielbasa, salt herrings
and rye bread, drank
raw vodka or cherry brandy
and smoked like
a dozen Puffing Billies.

Naturalized more
than a decade ago
we became citizens of the soil
that was feeding us—
inheritors of a key
that'll open no house
when this one is pulled down.

These stanzas are from "10 Mary Street," one of the poems on the migrant experience collected in *The Polish Immigrant*. Skrzynecki explores the psychological consequences of migration with great insight and sensitivity. Perhaps the most telling effect, since it defines his own perspective as a poet, is the strain placed on the relationship between parent and child. The strength his parents still draw from the old ways stands in marked contrast to the sense of guilt and unworthiness caused by his own defection from those ways. Many of Skrzynecki's elegies celebrate heroic parental figures, their value heightened by the awareness of what it is in them that is lost or unavailable to the son. The portraits tend to have the quality of icons. Both the form and the attitude of veneration it implies may derive from the poet's orthodox Roman Catholic upbringing. Hence the opening of "Feliks Skrzynecki":

> My gentle father
> kept pace only with the Joneses
> of his own mind's making—
> loved his garden like an only child,
> spent years walking its perimeter
> from sunrise to sleep.
> Alert, brisk and silent,
> he swept its paths
> ten times around the world.

The rhythm of Skrzynecki's elegiac catalogs is like a bell tolling out the measure of loss, but his poetic icons present a counterbalance, gathering their elements into a vision of order and value. Their power is particularly felt in Skrzynecki's volume *Night Swim,* a collection again haunted by the specter of loss—in this case the breakdown of the poet's first marriage—but one that also celebrates his rediscovery of his children and his new marriage. The landscape here is suburban for the most part, the detail humble and ordinary, but in such poems as "Burning Off," "A Green Memento," or "Weeding" these suburban settings are transfigured by a religious spirit of affirmation:

> Sweat stains our limbs
> in the sunset's light. A shiver ripples
> along the downhill breeze.
> We tug at knotted roots
> like a pair of servants
> working on hands and knees.
> The child within you
> has not yet started to move—
> though you laugh
> and strain at the toil.
> We turn up roots, white as flesh,
> and our fingers touch
> in the warm, black soil.

—Ivor Indyk

SLAVITT, David (Rytman)

Nationality: American. **Born:** White Plains, New York, 23 March 1935. **Education:** Phillips Academy, Andover, Massachusetts, graduated 1952; Yale University, New Haven, Connecticut, 1952–56, B.A.

(magna cum laude) 1956; Columbia University, New York, M.A. 1957. **Family:** Married 1) Lynn Meyer in 1956 (divorced 1977), three children; 2) Janet Abrahm in 1978. **Career:** Instructor, Georgia Institute of Technology, Atlanta, 1957–58; associate editor, 1958–65, and movie editor, 1964–65, *Newsweek* magazine, New York; associate professor of English, Temple University, Philadelphia, 1978–80. Lecturer in English and comparative literature, Columbia University, New York, 1985–86; teacher of creative writing, Rutgers University, Camden, New Jersey, 1987; associate fellow, Trumbull College, Yale University; lecturer in English, University of Pennsylvania, 1990–96; lecturer, Princeton University, 1996. Book reviewer for *Philadelphia Inquirer, Chicago Tribune, Newsday,* and *New York Times.* **Awards:** Pennsylvania Council on the Arts fellowship, 1985, 1987; National Endowment for the Arts fellowship, 1988; American Academy award, 1989; Rockefeller Foundation artist's residence, 1989; PEN/Book-of-the-Month Club Citation for Distinguished Translation, 1991, for *Ovid's Poetry of Exile;* Arts and Humanities grant, Project on Death in America, 1999. **Address:** 523 South 41st Street, Philadelphia, Pennsylvania 19104, U.S.A.

PUBLICATIONS

Poetry

Suits for the Dead. New York, Scribner, 1961.
The Carnivore. Chapel Hill, University of North Carolina Press, 1965.
Day Sailing and Other Poems. Chapel Hill, University of North Carolina Press, 1969.
Child's Play. Baton Rouge, Louisiana State University Press, 1972.
Vital Signs: New and Selected Poems. New York, Doubleday, 1975.
Rounding the Horn. Baton Rouge, Louisiana State University Press, 1978.
Dozens. Baton Rouge, Louisiana State University Press, 1981.
Big Nose. Baton Rouge, Louisiana State University Press, 1983.
The Walls of Thebes. Baton Rouge, Louisiana State University Press, 1986.
Equinox and Other Poems. Baton Rouge, Louisiana State University Press, 1989.
Eight Longer Poems. Baton Rouge, Louisiana State University Press, 1990.
Crossroads. Baton Rouge, Louisiana, Louisiana State University Press, 1994.
A Gift. Baton Rouge, Louisiana, Louisiana State University Press, 1996.
Epic and Epigram: Two Elizabethan Entertainments. Baton Rouge, Louisiana, Louisiana State University Press, 1997.
PS3569.LC: Poems. Baton Rouge, Louisiana, Louisiana State University Press, 1998.
Falling from Silence. Baton Rouge, Louisiana, Louisiana State University Press, 2001.

Plays

King Saul (produced New York, 1967).
The Cardinal Sins (produced New York, 1969).

Novels

Rochelle; or, Virtue Rewarded. London, Chapman and Hall, 1966; New York, Delacorte Press, 1967.

The Exhibitionist (as Henry Sutton). New York, Geis, 1967; London, Geis, 1968.

Feel Free. New York, Delacorte Press, 1968; London, Hodder and Stoughton, 1969.

The Voyeur (as Henry Sutton). New York, Geis, and London, Hodder and Stoughton, 1969.

Vector (as Henry Sutton). New York, Geis, 1970; London, Hodder and Stoughton, 1971.

Anagrams. London, Hodder and Stoughton, 1970; New York, Doubleday, 1971.

ABCD. New York, Doubleday, 1972; London, Hamish Hamilton, 1974.

The Liberated (as Henry Sutton). New York, Doubleday, 1973; London, W.H. Allen, 1974.

The Outer Mongolian. New York, Doubleday, 1973.

The Killing of the King. New York, Doubleday, and London, W.H. Allen, 1974.

King of Hearts. New York, Arbor House, 1976.

That Golden Woman (as Henry Lazarus). New York, Fawcett, 1976; London, Sphere, 1977.

The Sacrifice (as Henry Sutton). New York, Grosset and Dunlap, 1978; London, Sphere, 1980.

Jo Stern. New York, Harper, 1978.

The Idol (as David Benjamin). New York, Putnam, 1978.

The Proposal (as Henry Sutton). New York, Charter, 1980.

Cold Comfort. New York, Methuen, 1980.

Ringer. New York, Dutton, 1982; London, Severn House, 1983.

Alice at 80. New York, Doubleday, 1984; London, Severn House, 1985.

The Agent, with Bill Adler. New York, Doubleday, 1986.

The Hussar. Baton Rouge, Louisiana State University Press, 1987.

Salazar Blinks. New York, Atheneum, 1988.

Lives of the Saints. New York, Atheneum, 1990.

Short Stories Are Not Real Life. Baton Rouge, Louisiana, Louisiana State University Press, 1991.

Turkish Delights. Baton Rouge, Louisiana, Louisiana State University Press, 1993.

The Cliff. Baton Rouge, Louisiana, Louisiana State University Press, 1994.

Get Thee to a Nunnery: Two Divertimentos from Shakespeare. North Haven, Connecticut, Catbird Press, 1999.

Other

Understanding Social Life: An Introduction to Social Psychology, with Paul F. Secord and Carl W. Backman. New York, McGraw Hill, 1976.

Physicians Observed. New York, Doubleday, 1987.

Virgil. New Haven Connecticut, Yale University Press, 1991.

Editor, *Land of Superior Mirages: New and Selected Poems,* by Adrien Stoutenberg. Baltimore, Maryland, Johns Hopkins University Press, 1986.

Translator, *The Eclogues of Virgil.* New York, Doubleday, 1971.

Translator, *The Eclogues and the Georgics of Virgil.* New York, Doubleday, 1972.

Translator, *The Tristia of Ovid.* Cleveland, Ohio, Bellflower Press, 1986.

Translator, *Ovid's Poetry of Exile.* Baltimore, Maryland, Johns Hopkins University Press, 1989.

Translator, *Seneca: The Tragedies Vol. I.* Baltimore, Johns Hopkins University Press, 1992.

Translator, *The Fables of Avianus.* Baltimore, John Hopkins University Press, 1993.

Translator, *The Metamorphoses of Ovid.* Baltimore, Johns Hopkins University Press, 1994.

Translator, *Seneca: The Tragedies Vol. II.* Baltimore, Johns Hopkins University Press, 1994.

Translator, *Sixty-one Psalms of David.* Oxford University Press, 1996.

Translator, *The Myth of Prudentius.* Baltimore, Maryland, John Hopkins University Press, 1996.

Translator, *The Oresteia of Aeschylus.* Philadelphia, Pennsylvania, Philadelphia, Pennsylvania, University of Pennsylvania Press, 1997.

Translator, *Broken Columns: Two Roman Epic Fragments (Statius and Claudian).* Philadelphia, Pennsylvania, University of Pennsylvania Press, 1997.

Translator, *Epinician Odes and Dithyrambs of Bacchylides.* Philadelphia, Pennsylvania, University of Pennsylvania Press, 1998.

Translator, *A Crown for the King* by Ibn Gabirol. Oxford University Press, 1998.

Translator, *Celebrating Ladies: The Thesmophoriazusae of Aristophanes.* Philadelphia, Pennsylvania, University of Pennsylvania Press, 1998.

Translator, *The Persians of Aeschylus.* Philadelphia, Pennsylvania, University of Pennsylvania Press, 1998.

Translator, *Three Amusements of Ausonius.* Philadelphia, Pennsylvania, University of Pennsylvania Press, 1998.

Translator, *João Pinto Delgado's Poem of Queen Esther.* Oxford University Press, 1999.

Translator, *The Voyage of the Argo of Valerius Flaccus.* Baltimore, Maryland, John Hopkins University Press, 1999.

Translator, *The Book of the Twelve Prophets.* Oxford University Press, 2000.

Translator, *Sonets of Love and Death of Jean de Sponde.* Evanston, Illinois, Northwestern University Press, 2000.

Translator, *The Latin Odes of Jean Dorat.* Alexandria, Virginia, Orchises Press, 2000.

*

Manuscript Collection: Beinecke Library, Yale University, New Haven, Connecticut.

Critical Studies: Interview in *The Writer's Voice* edited by George Garrett and John Graham, New York, Morrow, 1973; "The Fun of the End of the World: David R. Slavitt's Poems" by Henry Taylor, in *Virginia Quarterly Review* (Charlottesville), winter 1990; "Years of Iron: Ovid's Poetry of Exile" by Bernard Knox, in *The New Republic* (Washington, D.C.); "An Amoeban Contest Where Nobody Loses: The Eclogues of Virgil Translated by David R. Slavitt" by George Garrett, in *Compulsory Figures,* Baton Rouge, Louisiana, Louisiana State University Press, 1992; "The Tristia of Ovid" by George

Garrett, in *My Silk Purse and Yours: The Publishing Scene and American Literary Art,* St. Louis, University Of Missouri Press, 1992; in *The Classical Journal*, February 1993.

David Slavitt comments:

As I look back over a career that has now included some seventy-odd books, I am struck by its improbability. My model, of course, was Robert Penn Warren, who was one of my teachers at Yale and whose accomplishments as a poet, novelist, and essayist, while individually impressive, are together almost unmatched in American literature. His was a liberating example, and I was then lucky enough to find as friends such writers as George Garrett, Fred Chappell, Richard Dillard, and Kelly Cherry, all of whom are poets first of all but also men and women of letters who have taken delight in discovering what each of the genres can reveal about the human condition.

*   *   *

In 1961, in the introduction to David Slavitt's first book of poems, John Hall Wheelock said that "one of the distinguishing characteristics of Mr. Slavitt's poetry is a severe restraint in the use of figurative language. It is the brilliance and clarity of his work, its brisk pace and taut resonance of line, its ironic and sardonic counterpoint, and, above all, its dramatic tensions, rather than any striking use of imagery or metaphor, that make it memorable." Slavitt's later books have borne out this description of his poetry, for he is a classicist, not one of the Eliot generation of neoclassicists who still depended so heavily on the "romantic image" but rather a genuine classicist, one who uses reason and wit to order his experience, to explain it, to describe it rather than (like a romantic) to embody it or transcend it.

The voice of Slavitt's poetry is that of a man talking, an intelligent and urbane man, a man of wit and of no little wisdom who speaks of life and more increasingly of death, often playfully, more often seriously. It is not surprising that his version of Virgil's *Eclogues* and *Georgics,* not strictly a translation of Virgil's poetic musings but rather an application of Slavitt's own striking voice and vision to those musings, is his finest book of poems. They are audacious, even arrogant, and brilliant throughout, a genuine translation of Virgil's approach to things into Slavitt's own well-honed modern classical idiom and a commentary on his approach as well.

As aware as any classical poet ever was of poetry as a self-conscious confidence trick, Slavitt is also aware of its necessity and its real value. In this version of the eighth eclogue, he says,

> Madness—
> schizoid, of course—but it works, and you and I
> can read, hear, give ourselves up to the poem,
> and all our hurts too are healed, at least for a time.
> We're all like dogs. A bone, a sop, distracts,
> or the howl of another dog. We take it up,
> one or two at a time, and then whole packs,
> pouring out a grief we never felt
> or sharing a real grief with all the others,
> which becomes a public occasion, a communion,
> a kind of celebration, a kind of prayer.

Slavitt's translation of Ovid's *Tristia* extends his long-distance communion with the classical mind into darker ground, bringing new (and quite modern) life to those seldom read, bitter, often self-pitying poems. And his translation of Ovid's *Metamorphoses* allows him to bring to life again the bright wonders of these poems. In later collections such as *Equinox, Eight Longer Poems,* and *Crossroads,* Slavitt continues his conversations with himself, his family and friends, and his readers in a dazzling variety of voices and forms. His works demonstrate how unique he is as a contemporary American poet of wit and intellect and how much he seems, volume by volume, to share with Auden the same range of erudition and interest and the same disregard for literary fashions or conventions. But the darkness that pervades the Ovid poems shapes these new poems, too, although not without consolation or resolution. In "Equinox," a poem to his sister after the murder of their mother, he concludes,

> We don't
> believe in souls up there spinning around
> forever like Laika but emptiness, cold
> and darkness are good enough. I'd call that heaven.

Or as Slavitt puts it in "Scream," the closing poem of *Crossroads,* "Defiance, at that pitch, is a kind of prayer." Writing in a romantic time, Slavitt has gone his own clear-eyed way, and it has proven to be a way well worth going.

—R.H.W. Dillard

SMITH, Dave

Nationality: American. **Born:** David Jeddie Smith, Portsmouth, Virginia, 19 December 1942. **Education:** University of Virginia, Charlottesville, 1961–65, B.A. in English 1965; College of William and Mary, Williamsburg, Virginia, 1966; Southern Illinois University, Edwardsville, M.A. 1969; Ohio University, Athens, Ph.D. in English 1976. **Military Service:** United States Air Force, 1969–72; Staff Sergeant. **Family:** Married Deloras Mae Weaver in 1966; one son and two daughters. **Career:** Teacher of English and French, and football coach, Poquoson High School, Virginia, 1965–67; part-time instructor, Christopher Newport College, Newport News, Virginia, 1970–72, Thomas Nelson, Community College, Hampton, Virginia, 1970–72, and College of William and Mary, 1971; instructor, Western Michigan University, Kalamazoo, 1974–75; assistant professor, Cottey College, Nevada, Missouri, 1975–76; assistant professor, 1976–79, director of the creative writing program, 1976–80, and associate professor of English, 1979–81, University of Utah, Salt Lake City; associate professor of English, University of Florida, Gainesville, 1981; professor of English, Virginia Commonwealth University, Richmond, 1981–90. Professor of English, 1990–98, and since 1998 Boyd Professor of English, Louisiana State University, Baton Rouge. Visiting Professor of English, State University of New York, Binghamton, 1980, and The Writing Seminars, Johns Hopkins University, Baltimore, Maryland, Fall 1999. Editor, *Sou'wester* magazine, Edwardsville, Illinois, 1967–68; founding editor, *Back Door* magazine, Poquoson, Virginia and Athens, Ohio, 1969–79; poetry editor, *Rocky Mountain Review,* Temple, Arizona, 1978–80; columnist, *American Poetry Review.* Philadelphia, 1978–82. Since 1990 co-editor, *Southern Review,* Baton Rouge. **Awards:** *Kansas Quarterly* prize, 1975; Breadloaf Writers Conference John Atherton fellowship, 1975; Borestone Mountain award, 1976; National Endowment for the Arts fellowship, 1976, 1981; *Southern Poetry Review* prize, 1977; American Academy award, 1979; *Portland Review* prize, 1979;

Guggenheim fellowship, 1982; Lyndhurst fellowship, 1987–89; Virginia prize in poetry, 1989. **Member:** The Fellowship of Southern Writers, 1996. **Agent:** Timothy Seldes, Russell and Volkening Inc., 50 West 29th Street, New York, New York 10001. **Address:** Department of English, Louisiana State University, Baton Rouge, Louisiana 70803, U.S.A.

PUBLICATIONS

Poetry

Bull Island. Poquoson, Virginia, Back Door Press, 1970.
Mean Rufus Throw Down. Fredonia, New York, Basilisk Press, 1973.
The Fisherman's Whore. Athens, Ohio University Press, 1974.
Drunks. Edwardsville, Illinois, Sou'wester, 1974.
Cumberland Station. Urbana, University of Illinois Press, 1976.
In Dark, Sudden with Light. Athens, Ohio, Croissant, 1977.
Goshawk, Antelope. Urbana, University of Illinois Press, 1979.
   Dream Flights. Urbana, University of Illinois Press, 1981.
Blue Spruce. Syracuse, Tamarack, 1981.
Homage to Edgar Allan Poe. Baton Rouge, Louisiana State University Press, 1981.
In the House of the Judge. New York, Harper, 1983.
Gray Soldiers. Winston-Salem, North Carolina, Stuart Wright, 1983.
The Roundhouse Voices: Selected and New Poems. New York, Harper, 1985.
Three Poems. Child Okeford, Dorset, Words Press, 1988.
Cuba Night. New York, Morrow, 1990.
Night Pleasures: New and Selected Poems. Newcastle upon Tyne, Bloodaxe Books, 1992.
Fate's Kite: Poems 1991–1995. Baton Rouge, Louisiana State University Press, 1996.
Floating on Solitude: Three Books of Poems. Urbana, University of Illinois Press, 1996.
Tremble. Tuscaloosa, Alabama, Black Warrior Review, 1997.
The Wick of Memory: New and Selected Poems 1970–2000. Baton Rouge, Louisiana State University Press, 2000

Recording: *The Colors of Our Age,* Watershed, 1988.

Novel

Onliness. Baton Rouge, Louisiana State University Press, 1981.

Short Stories

Southern Delights. Athens, Ohio, Croissant, 1984.

Other

Local Assays: On Contemporary American Poetry. Urbana, University of Illinois Press, 1985.

Editor, *The Pure Clear Word: Essays on the Poetry of James Wright.* Urbana, University of Illinois Press, 1982.

Editor, with David Bottoms, *The Morrow Anthology of Younger American* Poets. New York, Morrow, 1985.
Editor, *The Essential Poe.* New York, Ecco Press, 1990.

*

Manuscript Collection: Ohio University Rare Books Library, Athens, Ohio.

Critical Studies: By Robert DeMott, in *American Poets since World War II* edited by Donald J. Greiner, Detroit, Gale, 1980; "The Mind's Assertive Flow," in *New Yorker,* July 1980, and *Part of Nature, Part of Us,* Cambridge, Massachusetts, Harvard University Press, 1981, both by Helen Vendler; by Alan Bold, in *Times Literary Supplement* (London), November 1981; *The Giver of Morning: On the Poetry of Dave Smith* (includes bibliography) edited by Bruce Weigl, Birmingham, Alabama, Thunder City Press, 1982; "Unfold the Fullness: Dave Smith's Poetry and Fiction" by Thom Swiss, in *Sewanee Review* (Tennessee), Summer 1983, "A Secret You Can't Break Free" by the author, in *A World Unsuspected,* edited by Alex Harris, Chapel Hill, University of North Carolina Press, 1987; "Southern Weather" by Helen Vendler, in *New Yorker,* 1 April 1990; interview with Dave Smith by Ernest Suarez, in *Contemporary Literature* (Madison, Wisconsin), 37(3), Fall 1996.

Dave Smith comments:

The poems I have written are attempts to conflate the lyric and the narrative. I believe we make meaning by telling a tale, and poetry without meaning does not exist. But poetry is also song. I have wanted to find meaning and song in the prosaic and ordinary moments of our lives, in the local place and in the colorfully immediate. I began by wanting a language in the poem that was neither excessively and artificially poetic nor slack and crude as most talk, in most circumstances, usually is. I wanted a rough, measured music swelling out of and defining a narrative occasion in the way a particular man's talk, once heard, carries the full weight and shape of idiosyncratic character. All this rests on my assumption that poetry emerges from the individual spirit in crisis, that poetry matters because it is the death wrestler, the courage giver. Poetry is an entertainment, but it exists to give us pleasure in all the ways enumerated by Dr. Samuel Johnson: the pleasures of memory, of landscape, of diversion, of identity, of event, and of knowledge. Such pleasures arrive only from the struggle with words to know what can be known, to reveal and reinforce the human bond, the human responsibility in this world. I would be pleased to think my poems had such an effect on readers.

*   *   *

Dave Smith began writing almost jealously, defiantly about "his" Virginia country, a peninsula surrounded by the Poquoson River and Chesapeake Bay. As he once said in an interview, he told stories about tough, hardworking watermen and women "because they seemed to me in some respects exemplars of virtues I admired"—stoic courage, passion, a certain dignity, and a certain integrity. He wanted to write poems like "The Seafarer," *The Wanderer,* and *Beowulf* and "not merely because of the tough and lonely language, the odd and visceral music."

Smith wrote initially about tidewater Virginia as if it were Troy, a place of elemental struggles and defeats. The man in "Hard Times,

But Carrying On'' is representative, his eyes "once blue and pure / as the Bay'' now "turned thick with grim / trails of tasteless oil'':

> Even so,
> he works his hole with craft,
> eats fish for lunch at noon and dots
>
> it with a single swallow of rye, then
> drags back hard on the surging
> net, while all around the bags
> crank up slack as widow's dugs in rain.

The surface of Smith's early poems is hard and tense, the people's struggles occasioned not by political or spiritual forces but by natural ones—wind, water, and sun. In "March Storm" and "Among the Oyster Boats at Plum Tree Cave" these forces are antagonists in a wild, passionate drama that leaves everyone exhausted, spent. In "Cumberland Station" the reader learns why people often leave that country with some relief. Later, in *Goshawk, Antelope*, Smith turned with equal vigor to the myths and perils of the far West, Wyoming and Utah, where he lived for several years during the late 1970s.

Subsequent collections, including a sequence called "Homage to Edgar Allan Poe" and another called "Men with/without Women"—with its echoes of Hemingway's early collection of stories—indicate quite different powers as a poet, among them a gift for lyricism. "Waking under Spruce with My Love," which begins another sequence, is representative of this later style:

> I can feel the sheet luff on my thighs, the emptiness
> cool and pleasant inside my body . . .
> I think this must be the silence that love always is . . .

This group of poems ends fittingly with "Wedding Song," a witty, clear-eyed tribute to the occasion, reflecting again Smith's strong sense of history and topography.

During the 1980s Smith began to move from the tough regionalism of the early poems to a subtler language, with indebtedness to Louis Simpson and Richard Hugo, Robert Penn Warren and James Wright, all of whom Smith wrote about in *Local Assays*. A poem to Wright, written about the same time, is appropriately entitled "Outside Martins Ferry, Ohio." "In the House of the Judge," the title poem of a collection published in 1983, employs a narrative structure similar to Warren's in exploring the spirit of place, a residence in a small Pennsylvania town. It is characteristic of Smith's later work, in which he confronts the reader with an unexpected and elemental question in the middle of the poem: "How many hours must a man watch snow shift the world before he sees it is only a dream / of useless hope stamped and restamped by the ash-steps of those we / can do no justice to except in loving them?" The long breath and casual structure of this sentence may pose problems for the reader, at times making one wonder where the poem is headed and if the writer is in control of his language and subject matter.

Many of the poems Smith chose for *The Roundhouse Voices: Selected and New Poems* were revised, and some were expanded. In the new poems for that volume and in *Cuba Night*—"Bible School" and "Southern Crescent," for example—he returns to the preoccupations of the early poems, to his native Virginia, and to experiences of family, early childhood, and adolescence as he moves toward maturity in a familiar landscape. As always, the voice in these newer poems is Smith's own, with a respect for place and for the best of what is new in contemporary language and song. Whatever he writes about takes on the look of his territory. Even "Pregnant," for example, that uncomfortable state of being, calls up references to a particular natural setting—"Think of the verbs by which they go: waddle, lumber, loll, / shudder, slide, shuffle, wander— / as if theirs is the aimless pulsing of summer-shallowed / streams through the mountain's / dreaming crowd of spruce."

Smith's collection *Fate's Kite* consists of eighty-nine thirteen-line poems in unrhymed, loosely iambic pentameter. These fine, bluesy poems act as containers for the poet's endless obsession with certain subjects—abandoned cars, compost piles, racial tension. This is the matter of his southern inscape, a matter that echoes other old places, Seamus Heaney's Ireland, for example, places such as the "leached childhood field you longed to hunt" ("Field Dressing"), where Smith seems to exact a spiritual longing of near peril: "Lord, admit / us, we lived here, almost happy, almost yours."

The Wick of Memory: New and Selected Poems, 1970–2000 marks Smith's early influences, most notably Robert Lowell, and his later progressions. Smith turns from meditations on oyster boats, where "the currents carried / cloisters of murk, / miracles that bloom / luminous and unseen, sweet things to be / brought up, bejeweled, culled from husks," to poems with quirky and surprising attention to the south. "The Holy Mother of Connecticut Avenue," the book's first poem, is probably one of the most electric: "death's hot shit piled up around us, a stinking smoke / coiled like BO out of skinless wires, on floorboards licked, / as if all we wanted was flame-touched at last." Smith's experiments and innovations with grammar and rhythm might be too risky at times, but the poems never fail to explore a deeply imagined world.

—Michael True and Martha Sutro

SMITH, John (Charles)

Pseudonyms: C. Busby Smith. **Nationality:** British. **Born:** High Wycombe, Buckinghamshire, 5 April 1924. **Education:** St. James's Elementary School, Gerrards Cross, Buckinghamshire. **Career:** Director, 1946–58, managing director, 1959–71, and since 1972 advisory director, Christy and Moore Ltd. literary agents, London. Editor, *Poetry Review*, London, 1962–65. **Awards:** *Adam International* prize, 1953. **Address:** 3 Adelaide Court, 15 Adelaide Crescent, Hove, Sussex, England.

PUBLICATIONS

Poetry

Gates of Beauty and Death (as C. Busby Smith). London, Fortune Press, 1948.
The Dark Side of Love. London, Hogarth Press, 1952.
The Birth of Venus. London, Hutchinson, 1954.
Excursus in Autumn. London, Hutchinson, 1958.
A Letter to Lao Tze. London, Hart Davis, 1961.
A Discreet Immorality. London, Hart Davis, 1965.
Five Songs of Resurrection. Privately printed, 1967.

Four Ritual Dances. Privately printed, 1968.
Entering Rooms. London, Chatto and Windus-Hogarth Press, 1973.
A Landscape of My Own: Selected Poems 1948–1982. London, Robson, 1982.
Songs for Simpletons. London, Robson, 1984.
Poems for Paul Klee. Oxford, Alembic Press, 1990.

Plays

The Mask of Glory (produced Gerrards Cross, Buckinghamshire, 1956.)
Mr. Smith's Apocalypse: A Jazz Cantata, music by Michael Garrick (produced Farnham, Surrey, 1969). London, Robbins Music, 1970.
The Stirring, music by Michael Garrick (produced Manchester, 1984).
Zodiac of Angels, music by Michael Garrick (produced Manchester, 1988).

Other

Jan le Witt: An Appreciation of His Work, with Herbert Read and Jean Cassou. London, Routledge, 1971.
The Broken Fiddlestick (for children). London, Longman, 1971.
The Early Bird and the Worm (for children). London, Burke, 1972.
The Arts Betrayed. London, Herbert Press, and New York, Universe, 1978.
Cheesemaking in Scotland: A History. Clydebank, Scottish Dairy Association, 1995.

Editor, with William Kean Seymour, *The Pattern of Poetry.* London, Burke, 1963.
Editor, *My Kind of Verse.* London, Burke, 1965; New York, Macmillan, 1968.
Editor, *Modern Love Poems.* London, Studio Vista, 1966.
Editor, with William Kean Seymour, *Happy Christmas.* Philadelphia, Westminster Press, and London, Burke, 1968.
Editor, *My Kind of Rhymes.* London, Burke, 1972.
Editor, *The Poets' Gift: Poems by the Crabbe Memorial Poetry Competition Judges, 1955–1985.* Hadleigh, Suffolk Poetry Society, 1986.
Editor, *A Feast of Poetry.* London, Burke, 1988.

*

Critical Study: In *Literary Review,* 38(2), winter 1995.

John Smith comments:

As briefly as possible, I would describe my poetry as lyrical, metaphysical, formal, sardonic.

*   *   *

The title poem of one of John Smith's early collections is "The Birth of Venus," an attractively Audenesque mythological piece:

Somewhat incredible seems the fable
    Of this great lady from the sea;
Could one so flushed with love be able
    To store such rich propensity

In that damp element, cold and dead?
    Could Love arise from the grey sea-bed
Or rank weed nourish such potency? . . .

Venus, most near and dear of all
    Those Goddesses whose lives we scan,
Keep for all time our hearts in thrall
    Wherein, at your birth, Love began.
        However great or proud he be
        Without you, Goddess from the sea,
    How pitiably small is man . . .

Love, human and divine, has remained Smith's central subject.

Smith is essentially a philosophical poet, his attention to love's human presence or absence always wedded to an awareness of its metaphysical significance. At times this awareness leads him into the use of excessively abstract language as he follows through a train of thought with a thoroughness that can lead to an uncomfortable rhythmic flatness:

I have said that all gifts are God given, yet deny God,
And is this not a contradiction in terms? . . .
. . . I think we have to acknowledge
That a difference between the God I deny and ourselves
Lies in our love of innocence, his love of redemption.

It is typical of Smith, however, that in the very same poem ("The Holiness of the Heart's Affections") he should achieve a poetic idiom for the presentation of philosophical ideas that is both genuinely poetic and lucid in its articulation of complex processes of thought. It is of Eliot that we are then reminded:

Desire, or the implementation of desire,
Is it that which finally is divine: not that which is,
But that which would be, is about to become,
Which was not and is not and will not be,
Existing only in transubstantial state
Of apprehension never of comprehension?
And is this not in the last resort what love is,
Refined and essential, or brutal in the act:
A fusion of twin unjoinable lonelinesses?

The last striking phrase, reminiscent of the seventeenth-century Metaphysicals, is a key to much that is best in Smith's poems of human love. Especially fine is "The Face of Love," which examines such ideas with a formal grace and clarity of mind suggestive of Marvell, echoes of whom are quite often to be heard in Smith's work:

. . .
If, on a rash day, in an empty hall
        One of two lovers were constrained to draw
The other's likeness on the distempered wall
        So that a stranger might see what he saw,

The hand would falter and the bright eyes cloud
        With tears; a shock of grief his breath would smother.
Yet in that loss he'd know himself most proud:
        True lovers grow invisible to each other,

> And their twin absences achieve that state
> 　　　Of love itself where no shape breaks between.
> Each with the other fuses to create
> 　　　One face of love that sees not nor is seen.

On the other hand, a number of poems on the parting of lovers (e.g., ''Gone,'' ''Ending,'' ''The Realization,'' and ''First, Goodbye'') take part of their particular poignancy from the implicit sense of the continuing presence of separation at the very heart of the closest of relationships. ''The Holiness of the Heart's Affections'' finds Smith denying ''the presumptuous dogma that God is Love / In the glory of its reversal that Love is God.'' Love can be worshiped, however, only in full knowledge of its unattainability.

In *Songs for Simpletons* Smith's mythological imagination reasserts itself in a remarkable sequence of twenty-five lyrics that are densely allusive for all their seemingly simple language (the very title deliberately sets off appropriately Blakean resonances) and that, in the author's own words, concern themselves with ''the dichotomy between Eros and Agape.'' The Jack and Jill of these poems occupy an archetypal world of emotion and act, where brutality and tenderness coexist, where sexual passion and spiritual mystery are elementally bound together. The sequence is a considerable and individual achievement and deserves more attention than it has received.

Elsewhere in Smith's work the reader is likely to be struck by such fables of existence and faith as ''Prologue'' or by sustained meditations such as ''Snow'' or ''Thoughts from Torcello.'' A series of poems on works of art or painters (e.g., ''Monet,'' ''Bellini's Ecstasy of St. Francis in the Frick Museum and the Trees on the Way to Boston, 1978'') gives full play to the poet's repeated encounters with the idea and presence of that God in whom he does not believe.

Smith's work is uneven, and a first encounter with it is probably best made in selection. For the period up to 1982 *A Landscape of My Own* fits the bill very well. The reader of the poems in that volume and in the later *Songs for Simpletons* will find in Smith a poet with a thorough and an alert mind and a largeness of subject that reward exploration.

—Glyn Pursglove

SMITH, Ken(neth John)

Nationality: British. **Born:** Rudston, East Yorkshire, 4 December 1938. **Education:** Hull and Knaresborough grammar schools; University of Leeds, Yorkshire (assistant editor, *Poetry and Audience*), B.A. in English literature 1963. **Military Service:** Royal Air Force, 1958–60. **Family:** Married Ann Minnis in 1960 (dissolved 1978); two daughters and one son. **Career:** Teacher at an elementary school, Dewsbury, Yorkshire, 1963–64, and Batley Technical and Art College, Yorkshire, 1964–65; tutor, Exeter College of Art, Devon, 1965–69; instructor in creative writing, Slippery Rock State College, Pennsylvania, 1969–72; visiting poet, Clark University, and College of the Holy Cross, both in Worcester, Massachusetts, 1972–73; Yorkshire Arts Fellow, Leeds University, 1976–78; writer-in-residence, Kingston Polytechnic, Surrey, 1979–81, and Wormwood Scrubs Prison, London, 1985–87. Co-editor, *Stand,* Newcastle upon Tyne, 1963–69; editor, *South West Review,* Exeter, 1976–79; since the mid-1990s co-editor, *Stone Soup,* London. **Awards:** Gregory award, 1964; Arts Council bursary, 1975, 1978, award, 1988; Lannan

Foundation award for poetry, 1997; Cholmondeley award, 1998. **Address:** 78 Friars Road, London E6 ILL, England.

PUBLICATIONS

Poetry

Eleven Poems. Leeds, Northern House, 1964.
The Pity. London, Cape, 1967.
Academic Board Poems. Harpford, Devon, Peeks Press, 1968.
A Selection of Poems. Gillingham, Kent, Arc, 1969.
Work, Distances. Chicago, Swallow Press, 1972.
The Wild Rose. Memphis, Stinktree, 1973.
Hawk Wolf. Knotting Bedfordshire, Sceptre Press, 1975.
Frontwards in a Backwards Movie. Todmorden, Lancashire, Arc, 1975.
Wasichi. London, Aloes, 1975.
Anus Mundi. Hardwick, Massachusetts, Four Zoas Press, 1976.
Island Called Henry the Navigator. Glen Ellyn, Illinois, Cat's Pajamas Press, 1976.
Blue's Rocket. Privately printed, 1976.
Tristan Crazy. Newcastle upon Tyne, Bloodaxe, 1978.
Tales of the Hunter. Boston, Night House, 1979.
Fox Running. London, Rolling Moss, 1980.
The Joined-Up Writing. Croydon, Surrey, X Press, 1980.
What I'm Doing Now (and for the Rose Lady) (30/4/80). London, Oasis, 1980.
Burned Books. Newcastle upon Tyne, Bloodaxe, 1981.
The Poet Reclining: Selected Poems 1962–1980. Newcastle upon Tyne, Bloodaxe, 1982.
Abel Baker Charlie Delta Epic. Sonnets. Newcastle upon Tyne, Bloodaxe, 1982.
The Quick Brown Fox. Leamington, Other Branch Readings, 1984.
Terra. Newcastle upon Tyne, Bloodaxe, 1986.
Wormwood. Newcastle upon Tyne, Bloodaxe, 1987.
The heart, the border. Newcastle upon Tyne, Bloodaxe, 1990.
Tender to the Queen of Spain. Newcastle upon Tyne, Bloodaxe, 1993.
Wild Root. Newcastle upon Tyne, Bloodaxe, 1998.
Wire through the Heart. Budapest, Ister, 2000.

Short Stories

A Book of Chinese Whispers. Newcastle upon Tyne, Bloodaxe, 1987.

Other

Inside Time, with Dave Wait. London, Harrap, 1989.
Berlin; Coming in from the Cold. London, Hamish Hamilton, 1990

Editor, with Judi Benson, *Klaonica: Poems for Bosnia.* London, Bloodaxe, 1993.
Editor, with Matthew Sweeney, *Beyond Bedlam.* London, Anvil, 1997.

*

Critical Study: ''Salvaged from the Ruins: Ken Smith's Constellations'' by Stan Smith, in *British Poetry from the 1950s to the 1990s:*

Politics and Art, edited by Gary Day and Brian Docherty, London, Macmillan, and New York, St. Martin's Press, 1997.

Ken Smith comments:

Over the years my work has developed in response to the different environments in which I have arrived as much as to travel and the spaces between; mine are portable roots, some in Yorkshire, some in America, some in Devon, some now in London. Exeter, the city I most lived in, provided me with the figure of *The Wanderer* from the Anglo-Saxon *Exeter Book;* I have identified as much with him and his homelessness as with the irony of his poem having had in the cathedral library a home for the past nine hundred years. Writing is for me the act of discovering roots and pasts behind the present I find myself in as if by some marvelous accident. I am located in the work I do and in the daily rediscovery of language, the magic liquid that connects me to all else. I live in that as much as anywhere. Devon also made available to me the ancient silences of Dartmoor, that marvelous museum of all that has happened to us, a museum I do not encourage anyone to visit. By Kestor, above Chagford, among the stony leavings of the iron makers, is where I go whenever I have a decision to make, and there I feel the strongest root into the sullen past. On other days I am gregarious and have moved recently closer and closer to dramatic expression. Community, environment, and all the minutiae of gesture and inflexion—these are all my concerns still.

Themes: environment (hence nature), domestic, human relations and human attitudes, the rural in conflict with the urban, our subjective world implanted in an indifferent objectivity. Usual verse forms: free, intuitively worked, organic. General sources: any, many accidental and incidental, but environment and history, the sense of being alive, etc. Literary sources: many and scattered, too many to mention but mostly twentieth-century.

Among other things, I want to express the way we live and comment on it: the way we live in society, the way our environment is and we with it, how we form community—the minute ways in which the shapes of our lives are expressed in habits, gestures, buildings, our conscious and unconscious reactions to weather, landscape, each other—how we bind our lives down to the smallest detail distinguishing individual or community. So in this sense I am interested in custom and in speech and so in language and so in process. The poem itself is a process more than a product of this interest. I want a language that enacts and makes living, that is living rather than merely representative, a language metaphoric in itself.

*   *   *

Ken Smith's first collection, *The Pity,* seemed to identify him as a nature poet, a category he has since resisted. The northern landscapes of his early poems have more to do with suffering than celebration and nothing whatever to do with magic or prettification. In "Family Group," for example, his father is seen "stumping / through pinewoods, hunched and small, feeling / the weather on him. Work angled him, / fingers were crooked with frost, stiffened." Throughout Smith's work figures move endlessly, haunted by an unmapped Eden that is glimpsed but never gained "in the north" of Smith's imagination.

These preoccupations led Smith away from English literary models into travels in America and the wealth of small press works gathered in *The Poet Reclining: Selected Poems 1962–1980.* This selection reveals the development of an imagination that compels its poems to perform their subjects, subordinating detail to voice, aiming to reproduce rather than gloss experience. Smith's work of the late 1960s and the 1970s is often characterized by restrained vocabulary, refusal of abstraction, and extreme economy of metaphor. In place of pyrotechnics, his ear gives the plainest syllable its due, with discreet parallelism and subtle pacing: "It was a life bound / to the land, to silence / of another kind, it was / the other place" ("Another Part of His Childhood"). With *Burned Books* he adds a dimension of ellipsis to his resources. In the fragmentary narrative of a vanished state, as apparently told in part by the former President Perdu, seeming incoherence emerges as one of Smith's major subjects.

The pivotal work in Smith's career is *Fox Running,* a nightmare tour of London. Its hero, the eponymous Fox, pursues an aimless but unstoppable course along the subways, bus routes, and concealed byways of the city, haunted by loss, unable to break the circle of his desperation: "His single ticket to the city, a room / nights howling in the shower, / sleeping drunk inside the wardrobe, / dreamless, pissing in the sink." Switching between a narrative voice and the comments of Fox himself, the poem cuts a swathe through the city's subject matter—racism, violence, bureaucracy, imminent holocaust, the underlife's economy of drugs and whiskey, the offcuts of conversation. Its force derives from the energy and unsparing accuracy Smith brings to that most harrowing of derelictions, the stage when an original grievance is supplanted by the agonies of the present.

Terra again takes London, then under Margaret Thatcher, as its stage, incorporating the marriage of technology and state terrorism. After "Mister Mayhew's Visit," "the poor / are pushing to the windows like the fog," while "all the best words have moved to Surrey." "In Silvertown, Chasing the Dragon" speaks of a government ". . . known as sh, / they own the miles of wire, the acids / that devour forests and white words out, / and they are listening in the telephone . . . ." Combining satire, anger, black humor, and what literature, though not experience, describes as surrealism, Smith emerges in the "London Sonnets" and the extraordinary manic aria of "Departure's Speech" as one of the few poets to have taken the measure of the 1980s. The decade seems to have stimulated a new suggestiveness and authority in his work, and this is sustained in his book *Wormwood.*

Wormwood, like his prose work *Inside Time,* is the product of Smith's period as writer-in-residence at H.M. Prison, Wormwood Scrubs. In a grim sense, prison has proved to be Smith's ideal subject. Even nonprison poems such as "Serbian Letter" and "The Rope" have a claustral atmosphere, while the "hulks" of Wormwood Scrubs enforce a community of solitaries, villains, madmen, losers, and unfortunates whose fury, grief, and longing have much in common with the dispossession and isolation that dog Smith's earlier work. Smith moves inward and downward, finding in jail a radical confirmation of life's crueler facts. The speaker in the prose section "Wormwood," for example, goes "down the steps in chains and down the stairs in cuffs, and backwards down the up escalator shackled to the jailer, and at last in a bodybag down the well under the cellar under the basement under the crypt under the undercroft and still some down to go." At times a blend of voices is created, so that the letter *I* asks to be assigned not to an individual but to a common longing:

That world you speak of, friend,
lives in another song in a tune
I can't recall, another tale
told at the road's turn where wind

moves among beeches. I know.
I was there. The wind told me.

This lyric extreme is not permitted to disguise the limits to sympathy or the need for self-preservation that underwrites solitude: ''Some whose eyes I don't meet, / hands I don't shake.'' This frankness in turn lends value to the image of release into miraculous ordinariness: ''I want rain, the lamefoot doves / crowding city monuments, the traffic / and the grainy flush of air in the tubes.''

Smith stands apart from the common practices of postwar British poetry, belonging neither to the mainstream nor its experimental wings. His concern for poetry as a form of speech suggests a kinship with some American poets, but his enthusiasms in transatlantic poetry—Robert Bly, James Wright, John Haynes, and W.S. Merwin-are not those that might be expected. He looks back into elements of the English romantic tradition and beyond it to Chaucer and Anglo-Saxon. There is a constant and often satisfying negotiation between craft and impulse, between habits of puritan economy and the urge to compose the literally singing line; the result is the engraving of a voice that meanwhile continues to develop. At its best his work speaks from the commonwealth of experience across time and distance, often with the mysterious simplicity of ballads or the blues, sturdy, beautiful, and memorable.

—Sean O'Brien

SMITH, Vivian (Brian)

Nationality: Australian. **Born:** Hobart, Tasmania, 3 June 1933. **Education:** University of Tasmania, Hobart, M.A. 1956; University of Sydney, Ph.D. 1971. **Family:** Married Sybille Gottwald in 1960; two daughters and one son. **Career:** Lecturer in French, University of Tasmania, 1955–67. Lecturer. 1967–74, senior lecturer, 1974–82, and reader in English, 1982–96, University of Sydney. Literary editor, *Quadrant,* Sydney, 1975–90. **Awards:** Grace Leven prize, 1982; New South Wales Premier's prize, 1983; Patrick White literary award, 1997. **Member:** Fellow, Academy of Humanities of Australia; Australian Society of Authors. **Address:** 19 McLeod Street, Mosman, New South Wales 2088, Australia.

PUBLICATIONS

Poetry

The Other Meaning. Sydney, Edwards and Shaw, 1956.
An Island South. Sydney, Angus and Robertson, 1967.
Familiar Places. Sydney, Angus and Robertson, 1978.
Tide Country. Sydney, Angus and Robertson, 1982.
Selected Poems. Sydney. Angus and Robertson. 1985.
New Selected Poems. Sydney, Angus and Robertson, 1995.

Other

James McAuley. Melbourne, Lansdowne Press, 1965; revised edition, 1970.
Les Vigé en Australie (for children). Melbourne, Longman, 1967.

Vance Palmer. Melbourne, Oxford University Press, 1971.
The Poetry of Robert Lowell. Sydney, Sydney University Press, 1974.
Vance and Nettie Palmer. New York, Twayne, 1975.
Tasmania and Australian Poetry. Hobart, University of Tasmania, 1984.

Editor, *Australian Poetry 1969.* Sydney, Angus and Robertson, 1969.
Editor, *Letters of Vance and Nettie Palmer 1915–1963.* Canberra, National Library of Australia, 1977.
Editor, *Young St. Poets Anthology.* Sydney, Wentworth, 1981.
Editor, with Peter Coleman and Lee Shrubb, *Quadrant: Twenty Five Years.* St. Lucia, University of Queensland Press, 1982.
Editor, with Margaret Scott, *Effects of Light: The Poetry of Tasmania.* Hobart, Tasmania, Twelvetrees, 1985.
Editor, *Australian Poetry 1986 [1988]: The Finest of Recent Australian Poetry.* Sydney, Angus and Robertson, 2 vols., 1986–88.
Editor, *Nettie Palmer: Her Private Journal ''Fourteen Years,'' Poems, Reviews and Literary Essays.* St. Lucia, University of Queensland Press, 1988.
Editor, *Sydney's Poems.* Sydney, Primavera Press, 1992.

*

Manuscript Collections: Australian National Library, Canberra; Australian Defence Force Academy, Canberra.

Critical Studies: ''The Poetry of *The Other Meaning*'' by Margaret Irvin, in Poetry (Sydney), February 1969; *Bread and Wine* by Kenneth Slessor, Sydney, Angus and Robertson, 1970; *Commonwealth Literature* by William Walsh, London, Oxford University Press, 1973; *A Map of Australian Verse* by James McAuley, Melbourne, Oxford University Press, 1976; ''Two Poets'' by Elaine Lindsay, in *Twenty-Four Hours* (Sydney), January 1979; *Modern Australian Poetry 1920–1970* by Herbert C. Jaffa, Detroit, Gale, 1979; ''A Style That Needs No Change: Vivian Smith's *Tide Country*'' by Les A. Murray, in *Catholic Weekly* (Surrey Hills, New South Wales), 26 December 1982; ''The Lyrical Poetry of Vivian Smith'' by Elizabeth Perkins, in *Quadrant* (Sydney), March 1983; ''Individualism and Diversity: A Tasmanian Fosterage'' by Margaret Scott, in *Island Magazine* (Sandy Bay, Tasmania), 15, winter 1983; ''The Poetry of Vivian Smith'' by Michael Haig, in *The Age* (Melbourne), 5(7), November 1985; ''Patience and Surprise: The Poetry of Vivian Smith'' by Neil Rowe, in *Southerly* (Surrey Hills, New South Wales), 2, 1986; ''And Here They Rest in Place'' by Jennifer Strauss, in *Overland* (Mt. Eliza, Victoria), 103, 1986; ''The Poetry of Vivian Smith'' by Carmel Gaffney, in *Quadrant* (Sydney), July 1989; by Gary Catalano, in *Quadrant* (France), 39(12), December 1995; ''Still Life: Art and Nature in Vivian Smith's Poetry'' by David McCooey, in *Australian Literary Studies* (St. Lucia, Queensland), 17(2); October 1995; Vivian Smith issue of *Southerly* (Surrey Hills, New South Wales), 56(2), winter 1996.

Vivian Smith comments:

(1980) Within the context of Australian poetry I am, I suppose, something of a regionalist, since most of my poems are about Hobart and Tasmania, though Sydney too has been one of the poles of my inspiration. I write in free and traditional forms, and my lyrics try to affirm both the sense of a personal inner world and the inescapable presence of the actual. There are two areas of influence in my work.

The first is that of the Australian poets who most impressed me when I first started to write, particularly Judith Wright and Kenneth Slessor with their focus on landscape and especially the sea, an inescapable element for a Tasmanian. The second is that of the French and German poets whose work I studied closely and lectured on for many years. Although I have lived in Sydney for the last 12 years, Tasmania, with its special qualities of light, vegetation, and landscape, is still the focal point of my work, and I have tried to capture something of its peculiar essence, which is colonial, Europeanized, astringent, secluded, peaceful, and wild. Hobart still seems to me more like a European town or city than any other place in Australia and the most beautiful of all the capital cities.

Looking back over my poems, I find that they are concerned with various attitudes of mind, how to go on living fully and humanly without dogma or theory but without becoming a victim of unstructured experience. In other words, they are concerned with the nature and meaning of belief.

(1990) The above still seems to me to be an accurate statement about aspects of my work, though critics are now writing about its universal and philosophical qualities rather than its regionalism or its earlier preoccupation with history and landscape.

(1995) My new poems have been increasingly concerned with the scrutiny of modes and codes of behavior, the odd, the unexpectedly poignant, observed in the animal as well as the human world ("Dung Beetles," "At the Parrot House," "Taronga Park"). The language has become grittier, the rhythmic structure more complex. *New Selected Poems* contains a series of prose poems of memories of Hobart in the 1940s as well as many unrhymed free forms. I am aiming all the time for control and intensity.

*   *   *

In Australia in the 1950s there appeared to be a blossoming of young, fresh poetic talent, predominantly regional in origin: David Rowbotham in Queensland, Randolph Stow in Western Australia, and, in Tasmania, Christopher Koch and Vivian Smith. In his first volume, *The Other Meaning,* Smith showed a sensitive response to his environment. The "other meaning" he sought was some aspect of the transient that gave it either definition or awareness.

In *An Island South* the influence of the then predominantly academic poets of dry wit in England and America is more apparent, but since that volume Smith has published only occasional poems. His work has a reticence that sometimes underplays the deftness of observation and precision of control that give his best work a true luminosity. Though his themes have tended to remain persistently close to immediate response, he has appreciably hardened the texture of his poems to a gemlike precision. If he does not appear to have justified the early anticipations of his admirers, his work has grown in its own terms and with honesty and quiet dignity.

Tide Country, which was awarded the important Grace Leven poetry prize in 1982, shows Smith's work at its most assured. The poetry is precise and well controlled, yet capable of an eloquence less reliant upon its lyric forms than the poet's intensity of response to his chosen material, which remains close to observed experience transformed by mature insight and a vast reservoir of cultural values. *New Selected Poems,* published in 1994, demonstrates no great changes but gathers together later poems from occasional journals and other sources.

—Thomas W. Shapcott

SMITH, William Jay

Nationality: American. **Born:** Winnfield, Louisiana, 22 April 1918. **Education:** Blow School, St. Louis, 1924–31; Cleveland High School, 1931–35; Washington University, St. Louis, 1935–41, B.A. 1939, M.A. in French 1941; Institut de Touraine, Tours, France, 1938; Columbia University, New York, 1946–47; Wadham College, Oxford (Rhodes Scholar), 1947–48; University of Florence, 1948–50. **Military Service:** U.S. Naval Reserve, 1941–45: Lieutenant. **Family:** Married 1) the poet Barbara Howes in 1947 (divorced 1965), two sons; 2) Sonja Haussmann in 1966, one stepson. **Career:** Assistant in French, Washington University, 1939–41; instructor in English and French, 1946–47, and visiting professor of writing, School of the Arts, and acting chairman, Writing Division, 1973–75, Columbia University; instructor in English, 1951, and poet-in-residence and lecturer in English, 1959–64, 1966–67, Williams College, Williamstown, Massachusetts. Writer-in-residence, 1965–66, professor of English, 1967–68 and 1970–80, and since 1980 professor emeritus, Hollins College, Virginia. Consultant in poetry, 1968–70, and honorary consultant, 1970–76, Library of Congress, Washington, D.C.; lecturer, Salzburg Seminar in American Studies, 1975; Fulbright Lecturer, Moscow State University, 1981; poet-in-residence, Cathedral of St. John the Divine, New York, 1985–88. Editorial consultant, Grove Press, New York, 1958–60; poetry reviewer, *Harper's,* New York, 1962–66; editor, *The Journal of Literary Translation,* New York, 1973–89. Democratic member, Vermont House of Representatives, 1960–62. **Awards:** Young Poets prize, 1945, and Union League Civic and Arts Foundation prize, 1964 (*Poetry,* Chicago); Alumni citation, Washington University, 1963; Ford fellowship, for drama, 1964; Henry Bellamann Major award, 1970; Loines award, 1972; National Endowment for the Arts grant, 1972, 1995; National Endowment for the Humanities grant, 1975, 1989; Gold Medal of Labor (Hungary), 1978; New England Poetry Club Golden Rose, 1979; Ingram Merrill Foundation grant, 1982; Camargo Foundation fellow, 1986; Médaille de Vermeil, French Academy, 1991; René Vásquez Díaz prize, Swedish Academy; Pro Cultura Hungarica medal, 1993. D.Litt.: New England College, Henniker, New Hampshire, 1973. **Member:** Member, 1975, and vice president for literature, 1986–89, American Academy of Arts and Letters. **Agent:** George Nicholson, Sterling Lord Literistic Inc., 65 Bleeker Street, New York, New York 10012. **Address:** 63 Luther Shaw Road, Cummington, Massachusetts 01026, U.S.A., and 52–56 rue d'Alleray, 75015 Paris, France.

PUBLICATIONS

Poetry

Poems. New York, Banyan Press, 1947.
Celebration at Dark. London, Hamish Hamilton, and New York, Farrar Straus, 1950.
Snow. New York, Schlosser Paper Corporation, 1953.
The Stork: A Poem Announcing the Safe Happy Arrival of Gregory Smith. New York, Caliban Press, 1954.
Typewriter Birds. New York, Caliban Press, 1954.
The Bead Curtain: Calligrams. Privately printed, 1957.
The Old Man on the Isthmus. Privately printed, 1957.
Poems 1947–1957. Boston, Little Brown, 1957.

Two Poems. Pownal, Vermont, Mason Hill Press, 1959.

A Minor Ode to the Morgan Horse. Privately printed, 1961.

Prince Souvanna Phouma: An Exchange Between Richard Wilbur and William Jay Smith. Williamstown, Massachusetts, Chapel Press, 1963.

Morels. Privately printed, 1964.

Quail in Autumn. Privately printed, 1965.

The Tin Can and Other Poems. New York, Delacorte Press, 1966.

A Clutch of Clerihews. Privately printed, 1966.

Winter Morning. Privately printed, 1967.

Imaginary Dialogue. Privately printed, 1968.

Hull Bay, St. Thomas. Privately printed, 1970.

New and Selected Poems. New York, Delacorte Press, 1970.

A Rose for Katherine Anne Porter. New York, Albondocani Press, 1970.

At Delphi: For Allen Tate on His Seventy-Fifth Birthday, 19 November 1974. Williamstown, Massachusetts, Chapel Press, 1974.

Venice in the Fog. Greensboro, North Carolina, Unicorn Press, 1975.

Song for a Country Wedding. Privately printed, 1976.

Verses on the Times, with Richard Wilbur. New York, Gutenberg Press, 1978.

Journey to the Dead Sea. Omaha, Nebraska, Abattoir, 1979.

The Tall Poets. Winston-Salem, North Carolina, Palaemon Press, 1979.

Mr. Smith. New York, Delacorte Press, 1980.

The Traveler's Tree: New and Selected Poems. New York, Persea, 1980; Manchester, Carcanet, 1981.

Oxford Doggerel. Privately printed, 1983.

Collected Translations: Italian, French, Spanish, Portuguese. Minneapolis, New Rivers Press, 1985.

The Tin Can. Roslyn, New York, Stone House Press, 1988.

Journey to the Interior. Roslyn, New York, Stone House Press, 1988.

Plain Talk: Epigrams, Epitaphs, Satires, Nonsense, Occasional, Concrete and Quotidian Poems. New York, Center for Book Arts, 1988.

Collected Poems 1939–1989. New York, Scribner, 1990.

American Primitive. Roslyn, New York, Stone House Press, 1990.

Winter Morning. St. Louis, Missouri, Washington University Libraries, 1990.

Ode on the Occasion of the Centennial Ball, 30 January 1991. New York, The Century Association, 1991.

A Toast to James Thomas Flexner on His Eight-Fifth Birthday, 13 January 1992. Roslyn, New York, Stone House Press, 1992.

The Cyclist. Roslyn, New York, Stone House Press, 1995.

The World below the Window: Poems 1937–1997. Baltimore, Maryland, Johns Hopkins University Press, 1998.

The Cherokee Lottery: A Sequence of Poems. Willimantic, Connecticut, Curbstone Press, 2000.

Christmas Card Poems (with Barbara Howes): *Lachrymae Christi and In the Old Country,* 1948; *Poems: The Homecoming and The Piazza,* 1949; *Two French Poems: The Roses of Saadi and Five Minute Watercolor,* 1950—all privately printed.

Artists' Books: *Marine,* poem in English, with oil on paper illustrations by Julius Baltazar, Paris, Julius Baltazar, 1994; *The Pyramid of the Louvre,* concrete typewriter poem with collages by Bertrand Dorny, Paris, Bertrand Dorny, 1995; *Lily in Autumn,* poem in English, with oil on paper illustrations by Julius Baltazar, Paris,

Julius Baltazar, 1995; *Le Jeune Cyclist* (The Cyclist), translated by Sonja Haussmann, with five engravings by Albert Dupont, Paris, L'Inéditeur, 1996; *Le Sentier* (The Trail), concrete poem translated by Alain Bosquet, with engraving by Albert Dupont, Paris, L'Inéditeur, 1999.

Poetry (for children)

Laughing Time. Boston, Little Brown, 1955; London, Faber, 1956.

Boy Blue's Book of Beasts. Boston, Little Brown, 1957.

Puptents and Pebbles: A Nonsense ABC. Boston, Little Brown, 1959; London, Faber, 1960.

Typewriter Town. New York, Dutton, 1960.

What Did I See? New York, Crowell Collier, 1962.

My Little Book of Big and Little (Little Dimity, Big Gumbo, Big and Little). Riverside, New Jersey, Rutledge, 3 vols., 1963.

Ho for a Hat! Boston, Little Brown, 1964; revised edition, 1989.

If I Had a Boat. New York, Macmillan, 1966; Kingswood, Surrey, World' s Work, 1967.

Mr. Smith and Other Nonsense. New York, Delacorte Press, 1968.

Around My Room and Other Poems. New York, Lancelot Press, 1969.

Grandmother Ostrich and Other Poems. New York, Lancelot Press, 1969.

Laughing Time and Other Poems. New York, Lancelot Press, 1969.

Laughing Time: Nonsense Poems. New York, Delacorte Press, 1980.

The Key. New York, Children's Book Council, 1982.

Laughing Time: Collected Nonsense. New York, Farrar Straus, 1990.

Birds and Beasts. Boston, Godine, 1990.

Big and Little. Honesdale, Pennsylvania, Boyds Mill Press, 1992.

Around My Room. New York, Farrar Straus, 2000.

Plays

The Straw Market, music by the author (produced Washington, D.C., 1965; New York, 1969).

Army Brat: A Dramatic Narrative for Three Voices (produced New York, 1980; Washington, D.C., 1982).

Other

The Spectra Hoax (criticism). Middletown, Connecticut, Wesleyan University Press, 1961.

The Skies of Venice. New York, Andre Emmerich Gallery, 1961.

Children and Poetry: A Selective Annotated Bibliography, with Virginia Haviland. Washington, D.C., Library of Congress, 1969; revised edition, 1979.

Louise Bogan: A Woman's Words. Washington, D.C., Library of Congress, 1972.

The Streaks of the Tulip: Selected Criticism. New York, Delacorte Press, 1972.

Green. St. Louis, Washington University Libraries, 1980.

Army Brat: A Memoir. New York, Persea, 1980.

Editor and Translator, *Selected Writings of Jules Laforgue.* New York, Grove Press, 1956.

Editor, *Herrick.* New York, Dell, 1962.

Editor, with Louise Bogan, *The Golden Journey: Poems for Young People.* Chicago, Reilly and Lee, 1965; London, Evans, 1967; revised edition, Chicago, Contemporary Books, 1990.

Editor, *Poems from France* (for children). New York, Crowell, 1967.

Editor, *Poems from Italy* (for children). New York, Crowell, 1972.

Editor, *Light Verse and Satires,* by Witter Bynner. New York, Farrar Straus, and London, Faber, 1978.

Editor, *A Green Place: Modern Poems* (for children). New York, Delacorte Press, 1982.

Editor, with Emanuel Brasil, *Brazilian Poetry 1950–1980.* Middletown, Connecticut, Wesleyan University Press, 1983; London, Harper, 1984.

Editor, with J.S. Holmes, *Dutch Interior: Post-War Poetry of the Netherlands and Flanders.* New York, Columbia University Press, 1984.

Editor, with Dana Gioia, *Poems from Italy.* Minneapolis, New Rivers Press, 1985.

Editor, with F.D. Reeve, *An Arrow in the Wall: Selected Poetry and Prose of Andrei Voznesensky.* New York, Holt, and London, Secker and Warburg, 1986.

Editor, *Life Sentence: Selected Poems,* by Nina Cassian. New York, Norton, 1990.

Editor, *Songs of Childhood,* by Federico García Lorca. Roslyn, New York, Stone House Press, 1994.

Editor, *What You Have Almost Forgotten: Selected Poems,* by Gyula Illyés. Budapest, Kortárs Kiadó, and Willimantic, Connecticut, Curbstone Press, 1999.

Translator, *Scirroco,* by Romualdo Romano. New York, Farrar Straus, 1951.

Translator, *Poems of a Multimillionaire,* by Valery Larbaud. New York, Bonacio and Saul, 1955.

Translator, *Children of the Forest* (for children), by Elsa Beskow. New York, Delacorte Press, 1969.

Translator, *Two Plays by Charles Bertin: Christopher Columbus and Don Juan.* Minneapolis, University of Minnesota Press, 1970.

Translator, *The Pirate Book* (for children), by Lennart Hellsing. New York, Delacorte Press, and London, Benn, 1972.

Translator, *Chairs above the Danube,* by Szabolcs Várady. Privately printed, 1977.

Translator, *Saga,* by Andrei Voznesensky. Privately printed, 1978.

Translator, with Max Hayward, *The Telephone* (for children), by Kornei Chukovsky. New York, Delacorte Press, 1977.

Translator, with Leif Sjöberg, *Agadir,* by Artur Lundkvist. Pittsburgh, International Poetry Forum, 1979.

Translator, with Ingvar Schousboe, *The Pact: My Friendship with Isak Dinesen,* by Thorkild Bjørnvig. Baton Rouge, Louisiana State University Press, 1983; London, Souvenir Press, 1984.

Translator, *Moral Tales,* by Jules Laforgue. New York, New Directions, 1985; London, Picador, 1987.

Translator, with Leif Sjöberg, *Wild Bouquet: Nature Poems,* by Henry Martinson. Kansas City, Missouri, Bookmark Press, 1985.

Translator, *Collected Translations: Italian, French, Spanish, Portuguese.* Minneapolis, New Rivers Press, 1985.

Translator, with Edwin Morgan and others, *Eternal Moment: Selected Poems,* by Sándor Weöres. Minneapolis, New Rivers Press, and London, Anvil Press, 1988.

Translator, with Sonja Haussmann Smith, *The Madman and the Medusa,* by Tchicaya U Tam'Si. Charlottesville, Virginia, University Press of Virginia, 1989.

Translator, *Epitaph for Vysotsky,* by Andrei Voznesensky. Roslyn, New York, Stone House Press, 1990.

Translator, *Poetry,* by Nina Cassian. Roslyn, New York, Stone House Press, 1990.

Translator, *Christopher Columbus,* by Charles Bertin. Roslyn, New York, Stone House Press, 1991.

Translator, *Snail,* by Federico García Lorca. Privately printed, 1994.

Translator, *Berlin: The City and the Court,* by Jules Laforgue. New York, Turtle Point Press, 1995.

Translator, with Leif Sjöberg, *The Forest of Childhood: Poems from Sweden.* Minneapolis, New Rivers Press, 1997.

*

Bibliography: "William Jay Smith: A Bibliographical Checklist" by Timothy D. Murray, Newark, University of Delaware Library.

Manuscript Collection: Washington University, St. Louis; concrete poetry in the Ruth and Marvin Sackner Archive of Concrete and Visual Poetry, Miami Beach, Florida; the Berg Collection, New York Public Library, Special Collections; University of Delaware, Newark; Special Collections, Amherst College, Amherst, Massachusetts.

Critical Studies: "William Jay Smith," in *Modern Verse in English, 1900–1950,* edited by David Cecil and Allen Tate, London, Eyre and Spottiswoode, and New York, Macmillan, 1958; "William Jay Smith," in *The Hollins Poets,* edited by Louis D. Rubin, Charlottesville, University Press of Virginia, 1967; "The Lightness of William Jay Smith" by Dorothy Judd Hall, in *Southern Humanities Review* (Auburn, Alabama), summer 1968; "A Poet Named Smith" by Jean G. Lawlor, in *Washington Post* (Washington, D.C.), 9 March 1969, "An Interview with William Jay Smith" by Elizavietta Ritchie, in *Voyages* (Washington, D.C.), winter 1970; "The Dark Train and the Green Place: The Poetry of William Jay Smith" by Josephine Jacobsen, in *Hollins Critic* (Virginia), February 1975; *Children's Literature in the Elementary School,* 3rd edition, by Charlotte S. Huck and Doris A. Young, New York, Holt Rinehart, 1976; *Children and Books,* 6th edition, by May Hill Arbuthnot, Zena Sutherland, and Dianne L. Monson, Chicago, Scott Foresman, 1981; "Ars Poetica: 1 Heartlessness: American Primitive" by James Fenton, in *Independent* (London), 28 January 1990; "Enter the Dark House" by Henry Taylor, in *Michigan Quarterly Review* (Ann Arbor, Michigan), 30(4), fall 1991; "Narrowing Our 'Soul-From Soul Abyss': Inward Journeys of Robert Frost, Richard Wilbur, and William Jay Smith" by Dorothy Judd Hall, in *His 'Incalculable' Influence on Others: Essays on Robert Frost in Our Time,* edited by Earl J. Wilcox, Victoria, British Columbia, University of Victoria Press, 1994; by Dana Gioia, in *The Oxford Companion to Twentieth Century Poetry,* edited by Ian Hamilton, Oxford University Press, 1994; "Darkness in the Light Verse of William Jay Smith," in *Light,* summer 1996, and "William Jay Smith at Eighty: An Interview," in *New Letters,* 65(3), 1999, both by Robert Phillips; "The Pleasures of Formal Poetry" by Elizabeth Frank, in *Atlantic Monthly,* September 1998.

William Jay Smith comments:

I am a lyric poet, alert, I hope, as one of my fellow poets, Stanley Kunitz, has put it, "to the changing weathers of a landscape, to the motions of the mind, to the complications and surprises of the human comedy." I believe that poetry should communicate; it is, by its very nature, complex, but its complexity should not prevent its making an immediate impact on the reader. Great poetry must have resonance; it must resound with the mystery of the human psyche and possess always its own distinct, identifiable, and haunting music. Since 1965 certain of my poems have been written in long unrhymed lines because the material with which I have been dealing has seemed to lend itself to this form, which is often close to, but always different from, prose. I have always used a great variety of verse forms, especially in my poetry for children. I believe that poetry begins in childhood and that a poet who can remember his own childhood exactly can, and should, communicate to children.

*   *   *

William Jay Smith's first book, *Poems,* announced a poet of exotic subjects, high patina, and exquisite music, a combination suggestive of early Wallace Stevens. Poems such as ''The Peacock of Java,'' ''On the Islands Which Are Solomon's,'' and ''Of Islands'' transform a seascape of atolls that ''brings, even / To the tree of heaven, heaven.'' Other poems, like ''The Barber'' and ''The Closing of the Rodeo,'' initiate Smith's satirical rendering of the American commonplace, while ''Cupidon'' reflects his interest in incremental ballad form and fantasy. This early work seemed a deft performance in the then dominant metaphysical style, but Smith has always sounded a note of his own, his lightness, dexterity, elegance, and wit reflecting not only the prevailing influence of Eliot, Tate, and Ransom but also earlier poets who had influenced them.

During World War II Smith served as a liaison officer aboard a Free French naval vessel, and he began his civilian career as a teacher of French literature at Columbia. He published a distinguished translation of Valery Larbaud in 1955 and of Jules Laforgue in 1956. The qualities of formal versification, precarious poise, and wit in his early verse seem akin to those of Laforgue, the dream work suggestive of Larbaud. Further clues to his own verse are offered in Smith's two critical studies. *The Spectra Hoax* is an entertaining reconstruction of the successful leg-pull by Witter Bynner and Arthur Davidson Ficke, who not only concocted a fictitious school of poets in 1916–18 but, writing pseudonymously as its members, also begat better poems than when they used their own names and wrote in more conventional styles. The following year Smith's introduction to a selection of the poems of Robert Herrick described that poet as ''a master of understatement [who] knows what to omit,'' ''a perfect miniaturist; nothing is too small for him to notice or too great to reduce in size.'' These and other occasional essays are collected in *The Streaks of the Tulip: Selected Criticism.*

Smith's translations and studies of English, French, and American poets suggest the range and sources of his fascination with satire, fantasy, and wordplay, his comprehension of the true seriousness of successful light verse, and his devotion, until his late work, to brief lyrics, conventional forms, aesthetic distance from his subjects, and a burnished surface, as in his little poem ''Tulip,'' which offers ''magnificence within a frame.'' Similar qualities animate his several books of verse for children. He has written, ''I believe that poetry begins in childhood and that a poet who can remember his own childhood exactly can, and should, communicate to children.'' One such communication, *Typewriter Town* (1960), anticipated by several years the vogue for concrete poetry among writers for adults.

These qualities and Smith's characteristic lightness of touch are blended into an unmistakably American idiom in *Poems 1947–1957,* especially in ''Letter,'' ''Death of a Jazz Musician,'' and ''American Primitive'':

Look at him there in his stovepipe hat,
His high-top shoes, and his handsome collar;
Only my Daddy could look like that,
And I love my Daddy like he loves his Dollar.

The screen door bangs, and it sounds so funny—
There he is in a shower of gold;
His pockets are stuffed with folding money,
His lips are blue, and his hands feel cold.

He hangs in the hall by his black cravat,
The ladies faint, and the children holler:
Only my Daddy could look like that,
And I love my Daddy like he loves his dollar.

Beginning with *The Tin Can and Other Poems* Smith, like most of the poets of his generation, moved on from the style he had mastered to a new, freer prosody, in which the dark side of experience is presented in a more unmediated way than in poems like ''American Primitive,'' which had enclosed it in a play of wit and form:

O dreadful night! . . . What train will come? . . . What
    tree is that?
        . . . a sycamore—the mottled bark stripped bare,
Desolate in winter light against the track, and I
    continue on to the mudflats
By the roaring river where garbage, chicken coops, and
    houses rush
        by me on mud-crested waves,
And at my feet are dead fish—catfish, gars—and there
    in a little inlet
Come on a deserted camp, the tin can in which the hoboes
    brewed their
        coffee stained bitter black
As the cinders sweeping ahead under a milkweed-colored
    sky along a
        darkening track
            And gaze into a slough's green stagnant foam,
                and know that the way out is never back,
                                    but down,
                        down . . .
            What train will come
                to bear me back
                across so wide a town?

At least one reviewer of *The Tin Can* suggested that the hitherto elegant Smith had succumbed to the prosier incantations of Allen Ginsberg. As with Ginsberg, this loose, rolling line makes possible the inclusion in Smith's work of many grubby realities that, like Herrick, he had earlier tended to omit or to transfigure. Smith's sensibility, however, has little in common with the beat bard's, and a likelier *point d'origine* for these poems is in the free verse and surreal observations of the contemporary by Larbaud. Smith's long, unrhymed line makes possible an amplitude of feeling as well as inclusiveness of subject, and in it he has continued to explore both his descent into the inarticulate and the terrifying (''My voice goes out like a funicular over an abyss, and my hands hang at my sides, clenching the void; / My dreams are filled with bitter oranges and carrots, signifying calumny and sorrow'') and his intimations of the unity of all things, as in "The Tin Can," a poem of withdrawal from the world and the resultant gift of vision to the spirit.

Collected Poems 1939–1989 offers a generous selection from Smith's previous books, including a section of his light verse, and a group of poems written since *The Traveler's Tree,* his last major volume. In "Sitting Bull in Serbia," written in free verse, the old rebel chief, now in Buffalo Bill's Wild West Show, passes on to "Black George, leader of the Serbian revolt" his defiant vision of "the Earth's Great Spirit." Himself part Choctaw, Smith writes in "The Players" of a band of Seminoles who appear in costumes stolen from an itinerant Shakespearean company to reject a proffered treaty: "There will be no surrender, General. There will be no peace; / only the murderer who waits, only the poetry that kills."

In observance of the indefatigable poet's eightieth birthday a larger volume, *The World below the Window: Poems 1937–1997,* appeared in 1998, with new poems that address aging, finding little or varying comfort: "The naked mirror man is old and gray . . . / He'll lean upon a stick within the year; / the fire subsides but still the ashes glow: / to feel so young and yet so old appear" ("The Ironies of Age"). In "Journey to the Interior" the poet "has gone into the forest" where "trees around grow toothpick thin / and a deepening dustcloud swirls about / and every road leads on within / and none leads out." It is a bleakness somewhat assuaged in "The Cyclist," in which, witnessing a fatal accident that recalls the death of another young girl, his daughter, the poet seems to hear her say, "All that turns returns—returns, and is forgiven, understood; / as you approach life's end, you will see / the circle is complete."

The Cherokee Lottery (2000) expands the number of poems in this sequence to eighteen. This is the most ambitious treatment in verse of the dispossession of the Indians since Robert Penn Warren's narrative poem *Chief Joseph of the Nez Perce* (1983) and Daniel Hoffman's *Brotherly Love* (1982), on William Penn's treaty with the Lenni-Lenape and their betrayal by his successors. In his memoir *Army Brat* Smith traces his descent form Chief Moshulatubbe and writes of the influence of his Choctaw heritage on his work:

> I like to think that the still center from which I believe my poetry springs has much in common with the reverential attitude of the Native American towards the elements, the sensory and spiritual connection between earth and sky . . . The visual element in my work may owe something to my Choctaw heritage . . . I found it reassuring that while I had been brought up on an Army garrison founded as an outpost in the Indian Wars, I had forebears . . . on the outside and in the enemy's camp.

Smith's poem, dramatizing the forced evacuation of the southern and Midwestern tribes to Oklahoma, is episodic. The Cherokee and Choctaw chiefs appear and speak in their own voices; Sequoyah invents an alphabet, giving writing to the Cherokees; an old Choctaw laments the forced abandonment of his tribe's funeral customs. In other sections we see the Indians through the eyes of others: Tocqueville sees nursing mothers, the old and the sick, uncomplaining, on rafts floating downriver; an army officer witnesses the suffering on the Trail of Tears as, starving, the forced marchers tear apart pumpkins in a field. Interspersed among descriptions are lyrical passages, as in the concluding lines about Sequoyah, whose name is with us yet in "a giant evergreen":

> Its rings record lost kingdoms, ancient wars,
> through raging fires it stood and bears the scars,
> yet climbs the mountainside to touch the stars.

The artists George Catlin and Charles Banks Wilson regard the subjects they drew and painted, Wilson depicting their lingering survivors like "the last pureblood Kaw / . . . seated in his driveway listening / on earphones to peyote music,"

> and now, with no one left to understand his native tongue,
> he told me, "God gave the Kaw this language, so when
> I talk to people, I speak English,

> but when I talk to God, I speak his language."

The lottery of the title is the subject of the second poem: "When the Cherokees refused to leave / the state set up a lottery / to rid them of their land." After the drawing by which their land was apportioned to the whites and the tribe ejected at bayonet point,

> no one spoke,
> no one cried: only the dogs
> howled as if they alone
> could voice the nation's grief . . .

The final poem, "Full Circle: The Connecticut Casino," is juxtaposed with the Cherokee lottery:

> It was with this Casino that the Mashantucket
>   Pequot Nation
> finally tricked the Great White Father Trickster
> or outfoxed the Great White Fox
> . . .
> and all the gold stolen from the Cherokees in Georgia
> seeming to return now to the Pequots in Connecticut

The poem ends with a vision of "that far-off land / where people speak / only the truth / and where all races live together / in lasting peace and perfect harmony."

The shifting points of view, varied forms, and changing rhythms keep the sequence lively. The complexity of the sequence, which is tragic in feeling, is in its structure, not in its accessible texture. The poems, with all of their sometimes bizarre conjunctions, are yet historically accurate. *The Cherokee Lottery* is a major work, a dramatic moral reckoning, made vivid in verse, of an injustice in American history.

Over a period of more than sixty years Smith has written a body of work perhaps unrivaled in its range: formal lyrics, free verse meditations, distinguished translations of contemporary and nineteenth-century poets from the French, Italian, Romanian, and Hungarian, delightful children's poetry, discriminating criticism, a lively memoir, and the sequence *The Cherokee Lottery*. What has been constant in Smith's work is his range of tone, embracing the elegant, the absurd, the grotesque, the tragic, and the visionary in verse, whether formal or free, characterized by poise and resonance.

—Daniel Hoffman

SMITHER, Elizabeth (Edwina)

Nationality: New Zealander. **Born:** Elizabeth Edwina Harrington, New Plymouth, 15 September 1941. **Education:** New Plymouth Girls' High School, 1955–59; extra-mural studies at Victoria University, Wellington, and Massey University, Palmerston North, 1959–60; New Zealand Library School, Wellington, 1962. **Family:** Married Michael Duncan Smither in 1963 (divorced 1984); one daughter and two sons. **Career:** Library assistant, 1959–62, cataloguer, 1962–63, children's librarian, 1963–64, and since 1979 fiction librarian, New Plymouth Public Library. **Awards:** New Zealand Literary Fund bursary, 1977, 1988, and traveling bursary, 1984; Freda Buckland award, 1983; University of Auckland literary fellowship, 1984; Scholarship in Letters, 1987, 1992; New Zealand Book award for poetry, 1990 **Address:** 19-A Mount View Place, New Plymouth, New Zealand.

PUBLICATIONS

Poetry

Here Come the Clouds. Martinborough, Taylor, 1975.
You're Very Seductive, William Carlos Williams. Dunedin, McIndoe, 1978.
Little Poems. New Plymouth, T.J. Mutch, 1979.
The Sarah Train (for children). Eastbourne, Hawk Press, 1980.
Casanova's Ankle. Auckland, Oxford University Press, 1981.
The Legend of Marcello Mastraoianni's Wife. Auckland, Auckland University Press-Oxford University Press, 1981.
Shakespeare Virgins. Auckland, Auckland University Press, 1985.
Professor Musgrove's Canary. Auckland, Oxford University Press, 1986.
Gorilla, Guerilla. Auckland, Earl of Seacliff Art Workshop, 1986.
Animaux. Wellington, Modern House, 1988.
A Pattern of Marching. Auckland, Auckland University Press, 1989.
A Cortège of Daughters. Newcastle upon Tyne, Cloud Press, 1993.
The Tudor Style: Poems New & Selected. Auckland, Auckland University Press, 1993.
The Lark Quartet. Auckland, Auckland University Press, 1999.

Novels

First Blood. London, Hodder and Stoughton, 1983.
Brother-Love, Sister-Love. Auckland, Hodder and Stoughton, 1986.

Short Stories

Nights at the Embassy. Auckland, Auckland University Press, 1990.
Mr. Fish and Other Stories. Dunedin, McIndoe, 1994.
The Mathematics of Jane Austen. Auckland, Godwit, 1997.

Other

Tug Brothers (for children). Auckland, Oxford University Press, 1983.
Taranaki, with David Hill, photographs by Jane Dove. Auckland, Hodder and Stoughton, 1987.
The Journal Box. Auckland, Auckland University Press, 1996.

Editor, with David Hill, *The Seventies Connection.* Dunedin, McIndoe, 1980.
Editor, with C.K. Stead and Kendrick Smithyman, *The New Gramophone Room: Poetry and Fiction.* Auckland, University of Auckland, 1985.

*

Manuscript Collection: Hocken Library, University of Otago, Dunedin.

Critical Studies: "A Way of Understanding Ourselves" by Elizabeth Caffin, in *Landfall 118* (Christchurch), 1976; "Maurice Shadbolt Talks to Elizabeth Smither," in Pilgrims 5 and 6 (Christchurch), 1978; "*The Legend of Marcello Mastroianni's Wife,* and *Casanova's Ankle,* Elizabeth Smither" by Shawna Macivor, in *Landfall 141* (Christchurch), 1982; "Elizabeth Smither interview by the Editor" by David Dowling, in *Landfall 151* (Christchurch), 1984; "Smithereens" by Bill Manhire, in *Listener* 127, 4 June 1990; "Tremendous Forgeries, Confabulations and Graphologies Elliptical: The Lyric/Anti-Lyric Poetry of Sharon Thesen and Elizabeth Smither" by Pamela Banting, in *Australian and New Zealand Studies in Canada* (Prince George, British Columbia), 6, fall 1991.

Elizabeth Smither comments:

Poetry, to me, remains the most exciting form, the most compressed and vital; formal or informal, it perpetually re-creates itself to new demands. Other mediums have evasive techniques, but poetry is direct, forcing a confrontation between the world and the self. For me there is no forward planning or even knowledge of the subject; technique is created at the moment of writing. I write to find out everything. The best poems are both intensely personal and impersonal, teaching something about the true nature of personality. I see poetry always expanding, in advance of theory, like the universe itself, and if few poets write the poems they want, the chase is the greatest pleasure.

*   *   *

Elizabeth Smither began writing effectively when she was about thirty and fairly quickly found her voice and a reputation, so that she is substantially a poet without any juvenilia. She has done some traveling beyond New Zealand, where her home is not in one of the larger cities but in a provincial port, a Sleepy Hollow backed by a lush pastoral scene that is dominated by a spectacularly dead volcano. It is a place grounded in a long-term history of Maori settlement and a short-term history of European settlement but one with a notable passage to it of nineteenth-century colonial warfare. There is little recourse to local history in Smither's poems, although she has explored something of it in her prose, and there is scarcely more to do with either landscape or seascape or evident awareness of the transforming of the area as the oil rigs on- and offshore work away at their surroundings, the natural gas enterprises breed, and the petrochemical plants riot over the paddocks. In neither earlier nor later books does much occur that may be confidently thought to come from family or immediate social experience. There is some from family and some from friendships, but there is much from the poet's imaginative response to literature. What is impressive about her work is that it is a poetry of imagination. Where the poetry is of experience, it is likely to have some qualifying or mediating effect, again from literature or from a quiet Roman Catholicism.

Smither's poems are rarely long lined, and they are customarily shortish pieces that do not reach halfway down the page. They have a peculiar punctuation, of a kind that M.K. Joseph, another Catholic poet, used at one stage in his career. The syntax is disrupted in a modestly venturesome way, which one may judge is aimed at evoking an illusion of immediacy, as of a slightly breathless utterance. This is the case whether the poet is assumed to be speaking in her own person, in one or another of her male or female personae, or through a speaker whose sex is in neither way assertive. The voice of the later poems, including those of *Casanova's Ankle,* is more likely to be a woman's and so too the viewpoint.

Smither's poems are sympathetic and empathetic, able to command that quick, shrewd comment that delights the reader simply because it is so aptly shrewd or provocative. They are not poems of wit in any usual sense, any more than they are in a usual sense self-centered. She may be in them, but she is also distant from them. She may advertize that she attaches herself to modernist modes, like those of Williams, Lowell, or Kinnell, but she is also distanced from such modes, not fully committed to them. To be more venturesome would become her.

Smither is a conservative modernist. If you look at her evident Catholicism, you see the Catholicism of family custom plus an awareness of tradition—Saint Teresa, Saint Ignatius, Saint Paul—and something of latter-day religion, Teilhard de Chardin perhaps but not as late as Hans Küng. The poems of faith are poems of rapprochement, of subjective-objective or attachment-detachment, records of an impulse to reconcile at least two modes of tradition. She effects a reconciliation that complements by way of one particular universe of discourse the compromises apparent in her favored strategies as a "maker."

The matter of playing off traditions is one thing. Recurring to compressed statements is another, in which the calculated, quizzical relating of tenor and vehicle in metaphor continues to result not so much in conveying a metaphoric statement as in exciting a sense of incongruity without, as one might expect, a consequent nuance of comedy. Yet this approach is increasingly more likely to dispose toward irony. Prosy reality reimagined is heightened, disturbingly heightened even if Smither has from the start pinned and still usually pins her poetics on and over a firm basis of sentences. It is only when the sentences cumulate that the exposition becomes something other, a deceptive something other.

The heavy haulers pull their sometimes fantastically sculpted pieces of machinery to the industrial sites. Lights blaze from gantry and rig between sea and mountain. As Wallace Stevens did in Hartford, Smither sits to work with her back to the window.

—Kendrick Smithyman

SNODGRASS, W(illiam) D(eWitt)

Nationality: American **Born:** Wilkinsburg, Pennsylvania, 5 January 1926. **Education:** Geneva College, Beaver Falls, Pennsylvania, 1943–44, 1946; University of Iowa, Iowa City, 1946–55, B.A. 1949, M.A. 1951, M.F.A. 1953. **Military Service:** U.S. Navy, 1944–46. **Family:** Married 1) Lila Jean Hank in 1946 (divorced 1953), one daughter; 2) Janice Wilson in 1954 (divorced 1966), one son and one stepdaughter; 3) Camille Rykowski in 1967 (divorced 1978); 4) Kathleen Brown in 1985. **Career:** Instructor in English, Cornell University, Ithaca, New York, 1955–57, University of Rochester, New York, 1957–58, and Wayne State University, Detroit, 1959–67; professor of English and speech, Syracuse University, New York 1968–77. Visiting professor, 1979, and distinguished professor of creative writing and contemporary literature, 1980–94, University of Delaware, Newark. visiting teacher, Morehead Writers Conference, Kentucky, summer 1955, Antioch Writers Conference, Yellow Springs, Ohio, summers 1958–59, Narrative Poetry Workshop, State University of New York, Binghamton, 1977, Old Dominion University, Norfolk Virginia, 1978–79, Cranbrook Writers' Conference, Birmingham, Michigan, 1981, San Miguel Poetry Week, San Miguel de Allende, Mexico, 1998–2000. **Awards:** Ingram Merrill Foundation award, 1958, and fellowship, 1979; *Hudson Review* fellowship, 1958; Longview award, 1959; Poetry Society of America special citation, 1960; Yaddo Resident award, 1960, 1961, 1965, 1976, 1977; American Academy grant, 1960; Pulitzer prize, 1960; Guinness award (U K), 1961; Ford fellowship, for drama, 1963; Miles award, 1966; National Endowment for the Arts grant, 1966; Guggenheim fellowship, 1972; Academy of American Poets fellowship, 1973; Centennial Medal (Romania), 1977; Harold Morton Landon Translation award, Academy of American Poets, 1999, for *Selected Translations.* Honorary doctorate: Allegheny College, 1991. **Member:** American Academy, 1972; Fellow, Academy of American Poets, 1973. **Address:** R.D. 1, Box 51, Erieville, New York 13061, U.S.A.

PUBLICATIONS

Poetry

Heart's Needle. New York, Knopf, 1959; Hessle, Yorkshire, Marvell Press, 1960.

After Experience: Poems and Translations. New York, Harper, and London, Oxford University Press, 1968.

Remains (as S.S. Gardons). Mount Horeb, Wisconsin, Perishable Press, 1970; revised edition (as W.D. Snodgrass), Brockport, New York, BOA Editions, 1985.

The Führer Bunker: A Cycle of Poems in Progress. Brockport, New York, BOA Editions, 1977.

If Birds Build with Your Hair. New York, Nadja, 1979.

These Trees Stand. New York, Carol Joyce, 1981.

Heinrich Himmler. Cumberland, Iowa, Pterodactyl Press, 1982.

The Boy Made of Meat. Concord, New Hampshire, Ewert, 1983.

Magda Goebbels. Winston-Salem, North Carolina, Palaemon, 1983.

D.D. Byrde Callying Jennie Wrenn. Concord, New Hampshire, Ewert, 1984.

W.D. Meets Mr. Evil. . . San Diego, Brighton Press, 1985.

The House the Poet Built. San Diego, Brighton Press, 1986.

The Kinder Capers. New York, Nadja, 1986.

A Locked House. Concord, New Hampshire, Ewert, 1986.

Selected Poems 1957–1987. New York, Soho Press, 1987.

W.D.'s Midnight Carnival. Encinitas, California, ARTRA, 1988.

To Shape a Song. New York, Nadja, 1988.

Lullaby: The Comforting of Cock Robin. New York, Nadja, 1988.

The Death of Cock Robin. Newark, University of Delaware Press, 1989.

Autumn Variations. New York, Nadja, 1990.

Each in His Season. Brockport, New York, BOA Editions, 1993.

The Fuhrer Bunker: The Complete Cycle. Brockport, New York, BOA Editions, 1995.

After-Images: Autobiographical Sketches. Rochester, New York, BOA Editions, 1999.

Recording: *Calling from the Wood's Edge,* Watershed, 1985.

Play

The Führer Bunker (produced Norfolk, Virginia, 1980; New York, 1981).

Other

In Radical Pursuit: Critical Essays and Lectures. New York, Harper, 1975.

Editor, *Syracuse Poems 1969.* Syracuse, Syracuse University Department of English, 1969.

Translator, with Lore Segal, *Gallows Songs,* by Christian Morgenstern. Ann Arbor, University of Michigan Press, 1967.

Translator, *Six Troubadour Songs.* Providence, Rhode Island, Burning Deck, 1977.

Translator, *Traditional Hungarian Songs.* Baltimore, Seluzicki, 1978.

Translator, *Six Minnesinger Songs.* Providence, Rhode Island, Burning Deck, 1983.

Translator, *The Four Seasons.* New York, Targ, 1984.

Translator, *Five Romanian Ballads.* Bucharest, Romania, Cartea Romaneasca, 1993.

Translator, *Selected Translations.* Rochester, New York, BOA Editions, 1998.

*

Bibliography: *W.D. Snodgrass: A Bibliography* by William White, Detroit, Wayne State University Press, 1960.

Manuscript Collection: University of Delaware Library, Newark, Delaware.

Critical Studies: *W.D. Snodgrass* by Paul L. Gaston, Boston, Twayne, 1978; *Everything Human: The Poetry of W.D. Snodgrass* edited Stephen Haven, Ann Arbor, University of Michigan Press, 1993; ''The Strength of Departure in Snodgrass's 'Leaving the Motel''' by Coreen Dwyer Wees, in *Notes on Contemporary Literature* (Carrollton, Georgia), 24(2), March 1994; *W.D. Snodgrass in Conversation with Philip Hoy* by Philip Hoy, London, Between the Lines, 1998; *Tuned and under Tension: The Recent Poetry of W.D. Snodgrass* edited by Philip Raisor, Newark, University of Delaware Press, 1999.

W.D. Snodgrass comments:

I am usually called a ''confessional'' poet or else an ''academic'' poet. Such terms seem to me not very helpful. I first became known for poems of a very personal nature, especially those about losing a daughter in a divorce. Many of those early poems were in formal meters and had an ''open'' surface. All through my career, however, I have written both free verse and formal meters. At first I published more of the formal work because it seemed more successful to me. Recently my free (or apparently free) verse seems more

successful, so I publish more of it. My poems now are much less directly personal and often experiment with multiple voices or with musical devices. My work almost always goes very slowly and involves long periods of gestation and revision. This is not because I am particularly perfectionistic but because it takes me so long to get through the conscious areas of beliefs and half-truths into the subrational areas where it may be possible to make a real discovery.

*   *   *

Since the publication in 1959 of the Pulitzer prizewinning *Heart's Needle,* W.D. Snodgrass has established himself as one of the most prolific, versatile, and accomplished poets of his generation. Quick to recognize the personal and confessional nature of the poems of this first volume, critics pointed out that Snodgrass was following the example of his teachers, Randall Jarrell and Robert Lowell. Like them, Snodgrass developed a hard and refined craft that used rigidly controlled forms to objectify his personal pain and to transform it into art. By doing so he seemed to be saying, ''Don't look at me; look at what I've been able to do with me, to make of me.'' Nonetheless, he has not been content to write about himself only. Instead, he has embarked on major efforts to engage historical forces and to account for what he sees as the basic human tragedy. At his best he is both family centered and metaphysical. The bitterness and disappointment he sees as part of life stems from the limitations of human existence.

In his first two volumes, *Heart's Needle* and *After Experience,* Snodgrass is racked by guilt, not only for the sense of a failed life as father and husband but also for placing the lives of his family on display. In ''The First Leaf,'' from *Heart's Needle,* he says to his daughter,

> Now I can earn a living
> By turning out elegant strophes.
> Your six-year teeth lie on my desk
> Like a soldier's trophies.

The tone of this and most of the work in his first volume is ironic and bitter, but although his poems are steeped in life's pain and grief, he refuses to be self-indulgent. Above all he seeks to examine motivation and to seek forgiveness wherever possible. Such is his theme in the exquisite sequence of poems that give the volume its title and that express pain and sorrow in brilliantly controlled forms, as in the following—

> Winter again and it is snowing;
> Although you are still three,
> You are already growing
> Strange to me

—or in the line ''Whom equal weakness binds together / none shall separate.''

The effort to transform personal sorrow into art takes on a new dimension in Snodgrass's second volume, *After Experience.* He ransacks other poetic traditions for vehicles and models to express private grief. A good portion of the volume is composed of translations of poems by Rilke, de Nerval, Rimbaud, and Eichendorff that use symbols to objectify and generalize the poets' personal experiences, as in Rilke's ''The Panther'' or Eichendorff's ''On My Child's Death.'' The first half, however, is composed of poems that remind us of those of *Heart's Needle,* many written during the same time but not included in that volume. Poems such as ''Partial Eclipse,'' ''September,'' and ''Reconstructions'' provide additional perspective on the poet's shattered marriage. Another portion of the volume includes poems that comment on paintings by modern masters whose work has had significant influence on the poet's sensibilities: Matisse, Vuillard, Manet, Monet, and van Gogh. The poem based on Vuillard's *The Mother and Sister of the Artist* is particularly important to Snodgrass, who sees in it a portrait of a domineering mother and a frail and sickly daughter, which reminds him of his own mother and sister. This relationship becomes the core of his writing in his next volume, *Remains.*

The material of *Remains* was so sensitive that Snodgrass published it under the pseudonym S.S. Gardons, which is ''Snodgrass'' spelled backwards. In the volume Snodgrass takes a harsh and unforgiving look at his parents and their treatment of their children, particularly of his sister, whose death at the age of twenty-five he blames on them. In ''The Mother'' he pictures a woman obsessed with power and evil (''If evil did not exist, she would create it / To die in righteousness''), and in ''Diplomacy: The Father'' he pictures a man devoid of will who scavenges human weaknesses to gain personal advantage over others and who surrounds himself with an air of meanness and emptiness. What pity or compassion the poet feels is for his sister, and in poems such as ''The Mouse,'' ''Viewing the Body,'' ''Disposal,'' and ''Fourth of July'' he presents her as the victim of the inadequate parents. Throughout her life neglected and demeaned, only at her funeral is she accorded ''a place of honor.''

The publication of *The Führer Bunker* in 1977 demonstrated that Snodgrass was developing into a poet of diverse and prodigious talent. The volume is a total break from his previous work and represents a bold and ambitious attempt to transcend the limits of personal experience and to rise to the level of dramatic poetry. The awful sense of guilt and responsibility of the individual, the sense of a Hitler in himself and in all of us, provided the motivation to search into the heart of what Hannah Arendt called in her book *Eichmann in Jerusalem* ''the banality of evil.'' Through the interior monologues of Hitler, his senior officials, and his mistress, Eva Braun, the volume tells the story of the last days of the survival of the Third Reich. As if reacting to charges of excessive concern for his own personal life, Snodgrass immerses himself in historical fact. Presented as a work in progress to which he has continued to add, including *Magda Goebbels* and *Heinrich Himmler,* Snodgrass apparently believed that some truth of human nature is inherent in these events. In the monologues of the characters monstrous acts mingle with the utter banality of daily life.

Two other volumes, *If Birds Build with Your Hair* and *A Locked House,* represent a return to the personal and confessional mode. The poems reflect the experience of another failed marriage, more heart-rending than the first. This marriage apparently was supposed to last the poet's lifetime, but his wife turns to another, younger man and the poet's life turns to ashes. In *If Birds Build with Your Hair* the bitterness of this disappointment is sharply felt in poems such as ''Old Apple Trees,'' ''Cherry Saplings,'' and ''Setting Out,'' and in *A Locked House* in ''Mutability,'' ''The Last Time,'' and ''A Valediction.''

Although he has worked on additional volumes, most of Snodgrass's later work is in his *Selected Poems 1957–1987,* which contains not only generous selections from his earlier work but also new work published separately as a cycle of poems called *The Kinder Capers,* which includes *The House the Poet Built,* and selections from

The Death of Cock Robin, poems written to accompany paintings by DeLoss McGraw. These latter works represent a totally new departure for Snodgrass and suggest the kind of originality that Berryman discovered when he wrote *The Dream Songs.* Inspired by McGraw's drawings and picking up story lines and poetic forms from Mother Goose, Snodgrass has written powerful poems in which he displays a new inventive magic and comic play with language and verse forms as well as a playfulness in relation to himself as poet. Although apparently keyed to children, these poems are much too complex and innovative to be left only to the young, and they should be read by adults of all ages.

—Richard Damashek

SNYDER, Gary (Sherman)

Nationality: American. **Born:** San Francisco, California, 8 May 1930. **Education:** Lincoln High School, Portland, Oregon; Reed College, Portland, B.A. in anthropology 1951; Indiana University, Bloomington, 1951–52; University of California, Berkeley, 1953–56; studied Buddhism in Japan, 1956, 1959–64, 1965–68. **Family:** Married 1) Alison Gass in 1950 (divorced 1952); 2) Joanne Kyger, *q.v.,* in 1960 (divorced 1965); 3) Masa Uehara in 1967 (divorced), two sons; 4) Carole Koda in 1991. **Career:** General lookout, Mt. Baker Forest, 1952–53; seaman 1957–58; lecturer in English, University of California, Berkeley, 1964–65. Since 1985 professor of English, University of California, Davis. **Awards:** Bess Hokin prize, 1964, and Levinson prize, 1968 (*Poetry,* Chicago); Bollingen grant, for Buddhist Studies, 1965; American Academy prize, 1966; Guggenheim fellowship, 1968; Pulitzer Prize, 1975; Before Columbus Foundation award, 1984; Bollingen prize for poetry, 1997. **Address:** c/o North Point Press, 850 Talbot Avenue, Berkeley, California 94706, U.S.A.

PUBLICATIONS

Poetry

Riprap. Kyoto, Origin Press, 1959.
Myths and Texts. New York, Totem, 1960.
Hop, Skip, and Jump. Berkeley, California, Oyez, 1964.
Nanao Knows. San Francisco, Four Seasons, 1964.
The Firing. New York, R.L. Ross, 1964.
Across Lamarack Col. Privately printed, 1964.
Riprap, and Cold Mountain Poems. San Francisco, Four Seasons, 1965.
Six Sections from Mountains and Rivers without End. San Francisco, Four Seasons, 1965; London, Fulcrum Press, 1968; enlarged edition, Four Seasons, 1970.
Dear Mr. President, with Philip Whalen. Privately printed, 1965.
Three Worlds, Three Realms, Six Roads. Marlboro, Vermont, Griffin Press, 1966.
A Range of Poems. London, Fulcrum Press, 1966.
The Back Country. London, Fulcrum Press, 1967; New York, New Directions, 1968.
The Blue Sky. New York, Phoenix Book Shop, 1969.
Sours of the Hills. New York, Portents, 1969.

Regarding Wave. Iowa City, Windhover Press, 1969; enlarged edition, New York, New Directions, 1970; London, Fulcrum Press, 1971.

Anasazi. Santa Barbara, California, Yes Press, 1971.

Manzanita. Kent, Ohio, Kent State University Libraries, 1971.

Clear Cut. Detroit, Alternative Press, n.d.

Manzanita (collection). Bolinas, California, Four Seasons, 1972.

The Fudo Trilogy: Spell Against Demons, Smokey the Bear Sutra, The California Water Plan. Berkeley, California, Shaman Drum, 1973.

Turtle Island. New York, New Directions, 1974.

All in the Family. Davis, University of California Library, 1975.

Songs for Gaia. Port Townsend, Washington, Copper Canyon Press, 1979.

True Night, illustrated by Bob Giorgio. Privately printed, 1980.

Axe Handles. Berkeley, California, North Point Press, 1983.

Tree Zen, with D. Steven Conkle. Columbus, Ohio, Broken Stone, 1984.

Left Out in the Rain: New Poems 1947–1985. Berkeley, California, North Point Press, 1986.

The Fates of Rocks and Trees. San Francisco, James Linden, 1986.

No Nature: New and Selected Poems. New York, Pantheon Books, 1993.

North Pacific Lands & Waters: A Further Six Sections. Waldron Island, Brooding Heron Press, 1993.

Mountains and Rivers without End. Washington, D.C., Counterpoint, 1996.

Three on Community. Boise, Idaho, Limberlost Press, 1996.

Recordings: *Today's Poets 4,* with others, Folkways; *This Is Our Body,* Watershed, 1989.

Other

Earth House Hold: Technical Notes and Queries to Fellow Dharma Revolutionaries. New York, New Directions, and London, Cape, 1969.

Four Changes. Privately printed, 1969.

On Bread and Poetry: A Panel Discussion, with Lew Welch and Philip Whalen. Bolinas, California, Grey Fox Press, 1977.

The Old Ways: Six Essays. San Francisco, City Lights, 1977.

He Who Hunted Birds in His Father's Village: The Dimensions of a Haida Myth. Bolinas, California, Grey Fox Press, 1979.

The Real Work: Interviews and Talks 1964–1979, edited by Scott McLean. New York, New Directions, 1980.

Passage Through India. Bolinas, California, Grey Fox Press, 1984.

Good Wild Sacred. Madley, Hereford, Five Seasons Press, 1984.

Gary Snyder Papers. Davis, California, University of California, Davis, 1995.

The Practice of the Wild. San Francisco, North Point Press, 1990.

A Place in Space: Ethics, Aesthetics, and Watersheds: New and Selected Prose. Washington, D.C., Counterpoint, 1995.

The Gary Snyder Reader: Prose, Poetry, and Translations, 1952–1998. Washington, D.C., Counterpoint, 1999.

Editor, with Gutetsu Kanetsuki, *The Wooden Fish: Basic Sutras and Gathas of Rinzai Zen.* Kyoto, First Zen Institute of America in Japan, 1961.

*

Bibliography: *Gary Snyder* by Katherine McNeill, New York, Phoenix, 1980; revised edition, 1983.

Manuscript Collection: University of California, Davis.

Critical Studies: "Gary Snyder Issue" of *In Transit,* 1969; *The Tribal Dharma: An Essay on the Work of Gary Snyder* by Kenneth White, Dyfed, Unicorn, 1975; *Gary Snyder* by Bob Steuding, Boston, Twayne, 1976; *Gary Snyder* by Bert Almon, Boise, Idaho, Boise State University, 1979; *Critical Essays on Gary Snyder* edited by Patrick D. Murphy, Boston, Massachusetts, G.K. Hall, 1990; *Gary Snyder and the American Unconscious: Inhabiting the Ground* by Tim Dean, New York, St. Martin's Press, 1991; *Gary Snyder: Dimensions of a Life* edited by Jon Halper, San Francisco, Sierra Club Books, 1991; *Understanding Gary Snyder* by Patrick D. Murphy, Columbia, South Carolina, University of South Carolina Press, 1992; *Journeys Toward the Original Mind: The Long Poems of Gary Snyder* by Robert Schuler, New York, Peter Lang, 1994; "The Circumambulation of Mt. Tamalpais" by David Robertson, in *Western American Literature* (Logan, Utah), 30(1), spring 1995; *Poststructuralist Environmentalism and Beyond: Eco-Consciousness in Snyder, Kingsolver, and Momaday* (dissertation) by Yong-ki Kang, Indiana University, Pennsylvania, 1996; "Gary Snyder" by John P. O'Grady, in *Updating the Literary West,* edited by Max Westbrook, Fort Worth, Texas, Western Literature Association, 1997; *Identity, Masculinity, and Femininity in the Poetry of Gary Snyder* (dissertation) by Maura Ruth Gage, University of South Florida, 1997; "Ecopoetical Poetry: The Example of Gary Snyder and Wendell Berry" by Lothar Honnighausen, in *Poetics in the Poem: Critical Essays on American Self-Reflexive Poetry,* edited by Dorothy Z. Baker, New York, Peter Lang, 1997; "Semiotic Shepherds: Gary Snyder, Frank O'Hara, and the Embodiment of an Urban Pastoral" by Timothy G. Gray, in *Contemporary Literature* (Madison, Wisconsin), 39(4), winter 1998; "The Path to Endless: Gary Snyder in the Mid-1990s" by Susan Kalter, in *Texas Studies in Literature and Language* (Austin, Texas), 41(1), spring 1999; "Wilderness and the Agrarian Principle: Gary Snyder, Wendell Berry, and the Ethical Definition of the 'Wild'" by David M. Robinson, in *Isle* (Reno, Nevada), 6(1), winter 1999.

*   *   *

Gary Snyder is a poet and an environmentalist of the American West and of the Asian Far East, a highly literate primitive (he calls himself "archaic") who loves the worlds of the California Sierras, the American Indian, and Zen Buddhism. It is not an accident that fellow poet and environmentalist Wendell Berry is a friend.

A characteristic example of Snyder's literate primitivism occurs in "Milton by Firelight," written in 1955, in which tension exists between the author of *Paradise Lost* and a single jack miner. Snyder sides with the miner:

What use, Milton, a silly story,
Of our lost general parents, eaters of fruit? . . .
In ten thousand years the Sierras
Will be dry and dead, home of the scorpion.
Ice-scratched slabs and bent trees.
No paradise, no fall,
Only the weathering land

The wheeling sky,
Man, with his Satan
Scouring the chaos of the mind.

"The Bath" is one of the most attractive poems in *The Back Country*. In it Snyder celebrates exuberantly the pleasures of bathing his two small sons and his wife. The question is asked,

is this our body?
                                        and thrice the answer
this is our body

The fourth answer is not italicized but begins the line:

This is our body.

The poem is a pleasant excursion into male-female difference and identity, a therapeutic exercise in accepting one's own body, a religious statement.

"The Bath" is properly republished in *Turtle Island*, the Indian name for what thousands of years later became known to the white man as America. This book, which won a Pulitzer prize in 1975, owes much to Eugene Odum, whose *Fundamentals of Ecology* appeared in 1971, and to Zen Buddhism, which Snyder has practiced for most of his adult life.

Besides "The Bath," other good poems in *Turtle Island* include "I Went into the Maverick Bar," "Night Herons," "Straight Creek-Great Bum," and "What Happened Here Before." In "I Went into the Maverick Bar" the poet enters a bar that lives in the past, as the speaker once lived, something he now rejects. "Night Herons" apotheosizes the "ever-fresh and lovely dawn." "Straight Creek-Great Burn" celebrates a flight of birds: "never a leader / They arc and loop." "What Happened Here Before," as Sherman Paul wrote in a perspicuous review in *Parnassus,* "reminds us of our brief sovereignty."

Axe Handles, as the jacket blurb tells us, is the first collection of new poems after *Turtle Island*. The title poem recalls Wendell Berry's earlier "The Gathering," in which the son inherits a tradition from the father. As Snyder concludes, "How we go on." Two other poems in *Axe Handles* refer directly or indirectly to Berry. "What I Have Learned" continues the dialogue begun in Berry's "The Gathering." It begins with

What have I learned but
the proper use of certain tools,

and it ends with the Heraclitean

Seeing in silence:
never the same twice,
but when you get it right,
                        you pass it on.

The second poem, which is called "Berry Territory," begins with Berry's wife, Tanya:

Under dead leaves Tanya finds a tortoise
        matching the leaves—legs pulled in—

and then

Wendell, crouched down,
        Sticks his face in a woodchuck hole
        "Hey, smell that, it's a fox'."

It ends with "Some home." This is a love poem for close friends and wild animals. "Changing Diapers" is another love poem, this one to a Snyder baby. Its last stanza opens out from an intimate task to a wide perspective:

No trouble, friend,
You and me and Geronimo
Are men.

"Arts Council" is both personal and impersonal, personal because Snyder has for many years been on the California Arts Council, part of that time as its chairman, and impersonal because Snyder and his colleagues cannot take themselves too seriously, for their tasks are essentially irrelevant. I quote the poem in full:

Because there is no art
        There are artists

Because there are no artists
        We need money

Because there is no money
        We give

Because there is no we
        There is art

"For All," the last poem in *Axe Handles,* effectively summarizes Snyder's view of allegiance:

I pledge allegiance to the soil
of Turtle Island
one ecosystem
in diversity
under the sun

With joyful interpenetration for all.

Left Out in the Rain: New Poems 1947–1985 collects more than 150 poems that did not appear in previous books. The volume begins with a teenager's approach to what becomes a lifelong subject, the archaic. "Elk Trails," written on Mount Saint Helens, in Washington State, begins,

Ancient, world-old Elk paths
Narrow, dusty Elk paths
Wide-trampled, muddy,
Aimless . . . wandering . . .
Everchanging Elk paths

The last poem in the book is "Sherry in July," a title that immediately proclaims Julius Caesar, a lifelong interest in linguistics, and drinking:

Julius Caesar, cut from his mother's womb
    Caedere to cut off (caesura)
    Sanskrit *Khidati*—tear—
(Jack Wilson, Wovoka, Paiute ''Cutter'')
Caesar to Kaiser to Tsesari, Tsar.
    and a town in Spain, Caesaris
    —Xeres—Jerez—
    have some sherry.

Snyder's 1992 collection, *No Nature: New and Selected Poems*, is another attempt at an overview, this time of poems spanning thirty years. The hallmarks of Snyder's focus continue to be environmentalism and nature, Eastern languages, and religion. For him ''no nature'' is a claim that the division between humanity and nature is false. ''Taste all, and hand the knowledge down,'' he encourages. The interrelatedness of matter and spirit is the force of the poems in this volume. ''Axe Handles'' attempts to articulate truths without reducing itself to truisms:

And I see: Pound was an ace,
Chen was an axe, I am an axe
And my son a handle, soon
To be shaping again, model
And tool, craft of culture,
How we go on.

Some of the poems express a mildness that comes with experience, age, and establishment. In ''The Sweat'' Snyder is reconciled:

Older is smarter and more tasty.
Minds tough and funny—many lovers—
At the end of days of talking
Science, writing, values, spirit, politics, poems—

In 1956, moved by a Chinese scroll painting, Snyder began a long poem that ultimately took forty years to write. Including details from the varied range of his life's experiences, he touches on hitchhiking Route 99 from Oregon to San Francisco, trail work in the Sierras, Zen studies, and working on the high seas. He writes, ''In my small spare time, I read geology and geomorphology. I came to see the yogic implications of 'mountains' and 'rivers' as the play between the tough spirit of willed self-discipline and the generous and loving spirit of concern for all beings.''

Snyder's impulse is the creation of poetry that sings of the whole earth, in keeping with the sweeping tradition of Ezra Pound's *The Cantos* or William Carlos Williams's *Patterson*. Snyder tirelessly addresses the existence and nuance of the real and the true: Dogen's painted Zen hunger for a rice cake, the Chinese scroll ''Endless Streams and Mountains,'' the poet's own Sierra foothills. Even in the history of rocks, the poet finds ''lime-rich wave-wash soothing shales and silts / a thousand miles of chest-deep reef . . .''

Snyder's take on high-rise occupants, ''cliffdwellers,'' has a distinctly populist feel:

Towers, up there the
Clean crisp white dress white skin
women and men
Who occupy sunnier niches,
Higher up on the layered stratigraphy cliffs, get

More photosynthesis, flow by more ostracods,
get more sushi,
Gather more flesh, have delightful
Cascading laughs . . .

The most interesting and successfully imagined sections of this long poem involve Snyder's construction of a world of wild nature beneath the structures of civilization, as in ''Walking the New York Bedrock/Alive in the Sea of Information'':

Squalls From the steps leading down to the subway. Blue-chested runner, a female, on car streets, Red lights block traffic but she like the Bean of a streetlight in the whine of the Skilsaw, she runs right through. A cross street leads toward a river North goes to the woods South takes you fishing Peregrines nest at the thirty-fifth floor . . .

—James K. Robinson and Martha Sutro

SORRENTINO, Gilbert

Nationality: American. **Born:** Brooklyn, New York, 27 April 1929. **Education:** New York public schools; Brooklyn College, 1950–51, 1955–57. **Military Service:** U.S. Army Medical Corps, 1951–53. **Family:** Married 1) Elsene Wiessner (divorced); 2) Vivian Victoria Ortiz; two sons and one daughter. **Career:** Re-insurance clerk, Fidelity and Casualty Company, New York, 1947–48; messenger, American Houses Inc., 1948–49; freight checker, Ace Assembly Agency, New York, 1954–56; packer, Bennett Brothers, New York, 1956–57; shipping room supervisor, Thermo-fax Sales, 1957–60. Editor, *Neon* magazine, 1956–60, and Grove Press, 1965–70, both New York; book editor, *Kulchur*, New York, 1961–63; taught at Columbia University, New York, 1965; Aspen Writers Workshop, Colorado, 1967; Sarah Lawrence College, Bronxville, New York, 1971–72; New School for Social Research, New York, 1976–79, 1980–82; Edwin S. Quain Professor of Literature, University of Scranton, Pennsylvania, 1979. Since 1982 professor of English, Stanford University, California. **Awards:** Guggenheim fellowship, 1973, 1987; National Endowment for the Arts grant, 1974, 1978; Fels award, 1975; Ariadne Foundation grant, 1975; Creative Artist Public Service grant, 1975; John Dos Passos prize, 1981; American Academy award, 1985; Lannan Literary award for fiction, 1992. **Agent:** Mel Berger, William Morris Agency, 1350 Avenue of the Americas, New York, New York 10019. **Address:** Department of English, Stanford University, Stanford. California 94305–2087 U.S.A.

PUBLICATIONS

Poetry

The Darkness Surrounds Us. Highlands, North Carolina, Jargon, 1960.
Black and White. New York, Totem, 1964.
The Perfect Fiction. New York, Norton, 1968.
Corrosive Sublimate. Los Angeles, Black Sparrow Press, 1971.
A Dozen Oranges. Santa Barbara, California, Black Sparrow Press, 1976.

White Sail. Santa Barbara, California, Black Sparrow Press, 1977.
The Orangery. Austin, University of Texas Press, 1978.
Selected Poems 1958–1980. Santa Barbara, California, Black Sparrow Press, 1981.

Play

Flawless Play Restored: The Masque of Fungo. Los Angeles, Black Sparrow Press, 1974.

Novels

The Sky Changes. New York, Hill and Wang, 1966.
Steelwork. New York, Pantheon, 1970.
Imaginative Qualities of Actual Things. New York, Pantheon, 1971.
Splendide-Hôtel. New York, New Directions, 1973.
Mulligan Stew. New York, Grove Press, 1979; London, Boyars, 1980.
Aberration of Starlight. New York, Random House, 1980; London, Boyars, 1981.
Crystal Vision. Berkeley, California, North Point Press, 1981; London, Boyars, 1982.
Blue Pastoral. Berkeley, California, North Point Press, 1983; London, Boyars, 1985.
Odd Number. Berkeley, California, North Point Press, 1985.
Rose Theatre. Elmwood Park, Illinois, Dalkey Archive, 1987.
Misterioso. Elmwood Park. Illinois, Dalkey Archive, 1989.
Under the Shadow. Elmwood Park, Illinois, Dalkey Archive, 1991.
Red the Fiend. New York, Fromm International Publishing Company, 1995.
Pack of Lies: A Trilogy. Normal, Illinois, Dalkey Archive, 1997.

Short Stories

A Beehive Arranged on Humane Principles. New York, Grenfell Press, 1986.

Other

Something Said (essays). Berkeley, California, North Point Press, 1984.

Translator, *Sulpiciae Elegidia/Elegiacs of Sulpicia.* Mount Horeb, Wisconsin, Perishable Press, 1977.

*

Manuscript Collection: University of Delaware, Newark, New Jersey; Stanford University, Stanford, California.

Critical Studies: In *Grosseteste Review 6* (Pensnett, Staffordshire), 1–4, 1973; *Vort 6* (Silver Spring, Maryland), fall 1974; *The Review of Contemporary Fiction* (Elmwood Park, Illinois), spring 1981; in *From the Margin: Writings in Italian Americana*, edited by Anthony Julian Tamburri, Paolo A. Giordano, and Fred L. Gardaphe, West Lafayette, Indiana, Purdue University Press, 1991; "The Artist As Accidental Tourist in Gilbert Sorrentino's *Blue Pastoral*," by Jaye Berman Montresor, in *Studies in American Humor* (San Marcos, Texas), 3(1), 1994.

Gilbert Sorrentino comments:

I do not champion a "poetry of statement" and I despise narrative in verse. What I look for in my work is a verse dense in its particulars but flexible in its total structure.

* * *

The concept that language must "inform" or carry messages is a concept abandoned by poets at least as far back as Rimbaud. I subscribe to this belief and distrust a poetry of narrative and "content," and, in so far as I have been able, I have attempted to make the language of my fiction function in the way that the language of my verse functions, i.e. *poetically.*

Gilbert Sorrentino's title *Corrosive Sublimate* provides a clue to his work. In the tradition of those who believe that poetry makes nothing happen or that it should not mean but be, Sorrentino makes stark, nonmetaphoric statements about the corrupt urban world, about his own personal pain, about the reality of death. Written in an open-ended way, usually signaled by his use of the single, open parenthesis, his work invites the reader simply to experience the poem; there is no morality, no vision, simply the thing itself (the "corrosive" reality). Sorrentino speaks of the photograph often, as if to say that this alone stops, or seems to stop, time, though, like the poem, it contains no "meaning." The eye, memory, and feeling, however, transform the photo; so, too, imagination transforms language (the "sublimate"), which is dead until experienced: "The dead cannot be told anything so we revere them / The past is static. That is a photo. / But mine— even the dead / sit up flaking in their graves—mine / is the heart / that fell apart / at the junction unremembered."
"Four Songs" treats questions of art and reality:

It's better not to think
that when the wind blows
in the white curtains
it's the real thing.

When the wind invisible
touches the curtains
stop it short as in
some photograph.

Some photograph show
the shape of the wind
the color is the white
color of the curtains.

Against the silence and
white wind and white curtains
imagine in a blank room
one perfect heart.

"The Handbook of Versification" concerns the reality of the word itself and the nonreferential nature of poetry:

One thought the recurring "image" in the poet's song an
instant of consciousness.

Clear, clear day, in sun, one's majority upon one, it
is seen to be simple obsession, and helpless,
The mind careening through the infinite spaces of itself
Snags on some plain word:
Through and between whose familiar letters the true
true image of what happened: of the blank world.

Nevertheless, many of Sorrentino's poems are photos, glossies on this blank world, and his language is hard and clear, often New York vernacular, his subjects the surfaces of New York. Like the title of his novel *Steelwork,* his poems are scaffolds that assert only the forms of reality, the forms of New York. "I speak now, tell you a bright truth," writes the poet; "this is a bitter city"—one of violence, frustration, and empty dreams. Although Sorrentino may localize his dislikes—e.g., cults (the "moony people") and the mobile middle classes and intellectuals numb with anger and fear—he says of New York, "When you leave this town, you / Is just campin out." As he travels across America ("See America First"), he laments the poverty and unending violence and filth. Sorrentino would have us recover "certain portions of the heart" and heed the possibilities of a unique identity. In a sardonic fashion he warns, "Heed the story of the man / who took the garbage out / and threw himself away" ("Beautiful Soup"). Of psychiatrists he asks, "Who's the character in the armchair / drinking cheap wine / . . . glum as hell," and of marriage he writes, "you get hurt, fierce . . . dear God." Sorrentino's New York is specific—he writes of El Bronx, Broadway, the Van Wyck Expressway—and his is a world peopled by Jung, Artaud, Stevens, Baudelaire, Apollinaire, Thomas Blackburn, Robert Creeley, Dexter Gordon, Sarah Vaughan, Louis Armstrong, and Bunk Johnson.

Although some of Sorrentino's poems extend to specific survivors of American history—veterans, Indians, miners—his finest poems are the personal ones, those occasional moments of bittersweet nostalgia for the past and his own lost innocence. Bartering death's inevitability is the fecundity of memory. "Toward the End of Winter" concerns the poet's thirty-eighth birthday; he is "aware / of the birth of all time lost and buried." "Brought almost to tears / by the simple presence of myself in my own flesh, in the chair, / my familiar things around," he listens to a sentimental old song on the phonograph. As it arouses many associations, he sees "every act, each careful gesture / in tableau," and, ultimately, "the singer enmeshed with the reality / of her voice in her own presence, of flesh . . . / there is no truth / but in dear event, shaken, sudden . . . / I miss everybody."

Many of Sorrentino's poems maintain an irony and self-mockery, along with the pain of lost innocence. Of "Marjorie" he says, "Now there must be / stretch marks beneath her fitted girdle," and he muses, "I had the very bud of her, beauty and clarity day clear"; he concludes, "God / all the things destroyed / since I last kissed her / on what bitter corner / in the Bronx." Awareness alone is redemptive; one must seek out of life "some few moments / of bitter understanding" that "we were children / Of loveless worlds, or precisely, one world / and found that (or searched for that) / absolutely alone."

The new poems in *Selected Poems* include many of Sorrentino's flashy and flippant New York types, once again characterized by his bitter cynicism, puns, and local jargon—the man with "various patches on his tight tight pants," a former harlot from Perth Amboy whose "nights fell to their knees" as "Bibi stared into emptiness." For all of them terror lurks in the trivial.

Sorrentino's basic assumption that the world means nothing but what it is ("Behind this world is nothing / This world reveals itself

completely") also characterizes the new poems, and he takes to task Wordsworthian idealism. He will not write of daffodils but of daisies, and for his persona the flowers, at best, will be nothing but boring; the spectator in nature, like anywhere else, remains isolated and afraid. "Daisies are just white," he writes, "nothing makes them change."

Despite the predominant cynicism of these tough and realistic poems, Sorrentino remains fascinated with the magic of things, not because they mean anything but because they stir the imagination, the stuff of life itself: "The cucumber impaled upon the picket / Has no meaning whatsoever although it points" to an infinite number of associations, many of which the poet suggests. He concludes that what he most admires are the "sets of data that makes a feast of lightning / occur . . . the bright and beautiful nonsequitur . . . / lurking mysterious but plain enormities hilarious / In their candor in their cruelty. Worlds of steel."

That language fails to connect with a knowable reality and that this imposes an enormous frustration upon the writer are among the few observations one can make with any certainty about *Under the Shadows.* The volume appears to be a collection of seemingly unrelated narratives but in fact is a poetic collage of past and present reveries. Its fifty-nine sections have the texture of muted colors that advance and recede, depending upon one's point of access. Sorrentino displays the mind at work, the inner and outer world of conscious thought and memory. Interestingly, however, while using the form of seemingly disconnected fragments, he repeats figures and situations (a snowman, a scantily dressed woman near a window, women in white near a dark lake) and incorporates puns and self-conscious reminders of his role as a writer, particularly familiar in the work of Donald Barthelme and Robert Coover. "Maps," which begins with a concrete object-become-symbol, will be especially familiar to Barthelme devotees, but here Sorrentino focuses on the artist's/historian's/individual's sanity and irrationality in attempting to fix an image reflecting human experience.

It is similarly difficult trying to classify the genre of Sorrentino's later work. *Red the Fiend* is a monstrous tale of a sadistic Brooklyn family that turns an innocent child ("Red") into an unhappy and unloving "fiend." Although the book is relentlessly repulsive in its details, Sorrentino's poetic prose evokes a unique response in the reader. One feels a great sadness and even affection for the boy, who matures to vulgar sexuality and utter cynicism. Red is a devil because he has been the scapegoat for everyone in his family—his witchlike grandmother (with her always handy leather belt), passive grandfather, cheerless mother, and sometimes-visiting alcoholic father. The novel is a disturbing study of the destruction of hope and of any virtue we associate with childhood.

—Lois Gordon

SOTO, Gary

Nationality: American. **Born:** Fresno, California, 12 April 1952. **Education:** California State University, Fresno, B.A. 1974; University of California, Irvine, M.F.A. 1976. **Family:** Married Carolyn Oda in 1975; one daughter. **Career:** Formerly associate professor of English and ethnic studies, University of California, Berkeley; served as Elliston Poet, University of Cincinnati, and The Martin Luther

King/Cesar Chavez/Rosa Parks Visiting Professor of English, Wayne State University; currently distinguished professor of creative writing, University of California, Riverside. **Awards:** The Discovery-*The Nation* prize, 1975; International Poetry Forum award, 1976; Guggenheim fellowship, 1979; National Endowment for the Arts fellowship, 1982; Bess Hokin prize, and Levinson award, 1984 (*Poetry,* Chicago); American Book award, for prose, 1985; California Arts Council fellowship, 1989; Andrew Carnegie medal, 1993; National Book Award finalist, 1995; Hispanic Heritage award, 1999. **Address:** 43 The Crescent, Berkeley, California 94708, U.S.A.

PUBLICATIONS

Poetry

The Elements of San Joaquin. Pittsburgh, University of Pittsburgh Press, 1977.
The Tale of Sunlight. Pittsburgh, University of Pittsburgh Press, 1978.
Where Sparrows Work Hard. Pittsburgh, University of Pittsburgh Press, 1981.
Black Hair. Pittsburgh, University of Pittsburgh Press, 1985.
Who Will Know Us? San Francisco, Chronicle, 1990.
A Fire in My Hands. New York, Scholastic, 1990.
Who Will Know Us? San Francisco, Chronicle Books, 1990.
Home Course in Religion. San Francisco, Chronicle Books, 1992.
Neighborhood Odes. New York, Harcourt Brace, 1992.
Canto Familiar/Familiar Song. New York, Harcourt Brace, 1994.
New & Selected Poems. San Francisco, Chronicle Books, 1995.
Junior College. San Francisco, Chronicle Books, 1997.
A Natural Man. San Francisco, Chronicle Books, 1999.

Novels

Summer on Wheel. New York, Scholastic, 1996.
Buried Onions. New York, Harcourt Brace, 1997.
Nickel and Dime. Albuquerque, University of New Mexico, 2000.

Plays

Novio Boy. New York, Harcourt Brace, 1997.
Nerdlandia. New York, Putnam, 1999.

Other

Living up the Street: Narrative Recollections. San Francisco, Strawberry Hill Press, 1985.
Small Faces. Houston, Texas, Arte Publico, 1986.
The Cat's Meow (for children). San Francisco, Strawberry Hill Press, 1987.
Lesser Evils: Ten Quartets (essays). Houston, Texas, Arte Publico, 1988.
A Summer Life (essays). Hanover, New Hampshire, University Press of New England, 1990.
Taking Sides. New York, Harcourt Brace, 1991.
Pacific Crossing. New York, Harcourt Brace, 1992.
Local News. New York, Harcourt Brace, 1993.
Too Many Tamales. New York, Putnam, 1993.

Crazy Weekend. New York, Scholastic, 1994.
Jesse. New York, Harcourt Brace, 1994.
Chato's Kitchen. New York, Putnam, 1995.
Old Man and His Door. New York, Putnam, 1996.
Snapshots from the Wedding. New York, Putnam, 1997.
Petty Crimes (short stories). New York, Harcourt Brace, 1998.

Editor, *Entrance: Four Chicano Poets.* Greenfield Center, New York, Greenfield Review Press, 1976.
Editor, *California Childhood: Recollections and Stories of the Golden State.* Berkeley, California, Creative Arts, 1988.
Editor, *Pieces of the Heart,* San Francisco, Chronicle Books, 1993.

*

Critical Studies: By Patricia de la Fuente, in *Revista Chicano-Riquena* (Houston, Texas), 11(2), 1983; by Alberto Rios, in *Contemporary Latin American Culture: Unity and Diversity,* Tempe, Arizona, Center for Latin American Studies, 1984; by Hector A. Torres, in *Critica: A Journal of Critical Essays* (San Diego, California), spring 1988; by Ute Erben and Rudolf Erben, in *MELUS: The Journal of the Society for the Study of the Multi-Ethnic Literature of the United States* (Amherst, Massachusetts), fall 1991–92; by Don Lee, in *Ploughshares* (Boston, Massachusetts), spring 1995; in *Updating the Literary West* by Robin Ganz, Fort Worth, Texas, Western Literature Association, 1997; *The Calvanist Roots of the Modern Era* by Michael Tomasek Manson, Hanover, New Hampshire, University Press of New England, 1997.

*   *   *

Few poems are as closely linked to twentieth-century agrarian reality as those of Gary Soto. Yet his subjects are not the familiar Midwest farmers of Sandburg or the independent tillers of rocky soil found in Frost. Instead, Soto presents the worlds of Chicano workers whose lands are seldom their own and whose visions of America are those of ones looking up from the bottom, not out over wide expanses of possibility. It is somewhat ironic that a poet such as Soto, with the concerns of an existentialist Cesar Chavez, should find himself regularly published in the *New Yorker* and in beautiful volumes from a university press. But despite their poverty, their despair, and the ugliness of their surroundings, his characters inhabit a world that is precisely visioned and full of a fierce love for life. Further, Soto's diction is classically spare and his images exact in creating this dangerous world, as in his poem "The Street," from *The Tale of Sunlight:*

One could say a bottle
That emptied like a cough
Turned over, slashed at a face,
And later a car tire.

One could say the wound tears again
Opening like an eye
From a sleep
That is never deep enough.

The poor are unshuffled cards of leaves

Reordered by wind, turned over on a wish
To reveal their true suits.
They never win.

With such clear similes and such technical virtuosity, which both gives the reader a distance from the experience and renders it that much more achingly alive, it is perhaps less surprising that Soto's message of solidarity with some of the most wretched of the American earth should be found on upper-class coffee tables and that it should be carefully read.

There is an aggressive imagination in Soto, an imagination linked strongly to the most basic things of life and of the body. The first poem in *The Elements of San Joaquin* sets a tone that Soto has followed throughout his work. It gives us the picture of a man who is overworked and locked in a seemingly hopeless existence, yet he is not a man who is without worth, not a man we cannot care about:

On the road of factories
Gray as the clouds
That drifted
Above them
Leonard was among men
Whose arms
Were bracelets
Of burns
And whose families
Were a pain
They could not
Shrug off . . .

Somehow that which is bitter in life becomes a richness, a resonance. The short lines and enumerated details that draw our attention to each word are characteristic of all of his poetry and, I think, of his vision. The careful description, the exactness, and the somatic nature of the simile are also characteristic of all of Soto's work, including the later autobiographical prose essays that read like poetry.

With his unashamed love for people, for relatives, and for the wounded rising too close to the surface at times, Soto can come close to sentimentality. But he almost always manages to save himself from lapsing too far into overt pity by his control and by the distance he keeps, a distance like that of the documentary filmmaker who allows the images and the lives of people to shine through in a structure that lets them speak for themselves. Soto speaks with a concern reminiscent of the most political of the Latin American poets, yet he avoids the traps of rhetoric and overstatement that weaken many of the poems of writers such as Neruda. He also avoids appearing grandiose by concentrating—like an intense ray of sun that burns off a man's finger—his images on small incidents, on individuals rather than world-shaking events. These lines from his poem ''The Space'' are a sort of creed for Soto, spoken in the voice of a character he calls Manuel Zaragoza, whose dramatic monologues give the poet even more distance to explore his favorite subject matter, the vision of the ordinary and oppressed:

I say it is enough
To be where the smells
Of creatures
Braid like rope

And to know if
The grasses' rustle
Is only
A lizard passing.

—Joseph Bruchac

SOUSTER, (Holmes) Raymond

Nationality: Canadian. **Born:** Toronto, Ontario, 15 January 1921. **Education:** University of Toronto Schools; Humberside Collegiate Institute, Toronto, 1938–39. **Military Service:** Royal Canadian Air Force, 1941–45. **Family:** Married Rosalia Lena Geralde in 1947. **Career:** Staff member, Canadian Imperial Bank of Commerce, Toronto, 1939–84; poet-in-residence, University College, University of Toronto, 1984–85. Editor, *Direction,* Sydney, Nova Scotia, 1943–46; co-editor, *Contact,* Toronto, 1952–54; editor, *Combustion,* Toronto, 1957–60. Chair, League of Canadian Poets, 1968–72. **Awards:** Governor-General's award, 1964; President's Medal, University of Western Ontario, 1967; Centennial Medal, 1967; Silver Jubilee Medal, 1977; City of Toronto Book award, 1979; officer, Order of Canada, 1995. **Address:** 39 Baby Point Road, Toronto, Ontario M6S 2G2, Canada.

PUBLICATIONS

Poetry

Unit of Five, with others edited by Ronald Hambleton. Toronto, Ryerson Press, 1944.
When We Are Young. Montreal, First Statement Press, 1946.
Go to Sleep, World. Toronto, Ryerson Press, 1947.
City Hall Street. Toronto, Ryerson Press, 1951.
Cerberus, with Louis Dudek and Irving Layton. Toronto, Contact Press, 1952.
Shake Hands with the Hangman: Poems 1940–1952. Toronto, Contact Press, 1953.
A Dream That Is Dying. Toronto, Contact Press, 1954.
Walking Death. Toronto, Contact Press, 1954.
For What Time Slays. Toronto, Contact Press, 1955.
Selected Poems, edited by Louis Dudek. Toronto, Contact Press, 1956.
Crêpe-Hanger's Carnival: Selected Poems 1955–58. Toronto, Contact Press, 1958.
Place of Meeting: Poems 1958–1960. Toronto, Gallery Editions, 1962.
A Local Pride. Toronto, Contact Press, 1962.
12 New Poems. Lanham, Maryland, Goosetree Press, 1964.
The Colour of the Times: The Collected Poems of Raymond Souster. Toronto, Ryerson Press, 1964.
Ten Elephants on Yonge Street. Toronto, Ryerson Press, 1965.
As Is. Toronto, Oxford University Press, 1967.
Lost and Found: Uncollected Poems. Toronto, Clarke Irwin, 1968.
So Far So Good: Poems 1938–1968. Ottawa, Oberon Press, 1969.
The Years. Ottawa, Oberon Press, 1971.

Selected Poems, edited by Michael Macklem. Ottawa, Oberon Press, 1972.

Change-Up: New Poems. Ottawa, Oberon Press, 1974.

Double-Header. Ottawa, Oberon Press, and London, Dobson, 1975.

Rain-Check. Ottawa, Oberon Press, 1975; London, Dobson, 1976.

Extra Innings. Ottawa, Oberon Press, and London, Dobson, 1977.

Hanging In: New Poems. Ottawa, Oberon Press, 1979.

Collected Poems 1940–1993. Ottawa, Oberon Press, 8 vols., 1980–99.

Going the Distance: New Poems 1979–1982. Ottawa, Oberon Press, 1983.

Jubilee of Death: The Raid on Dieppe. Ottawa, Oberon Press, 1984.

Queen City, photographs by Bill Brooks. Ottawa, Oberon Press, 1984.

Flight of the Roller Coaster (for children). Ottawa, Oberon, 1985.

Into This Dark Earth, with James Deahl. Toronto, Unfinished Monument Press, 1985.

It Takes All Kinds. Ottawa, Oberon Press, 1986.

The Eyes of Love. Ottawa, Oberon Press, 1987.

Asking for More. Ottawa, Oberon Press, 1988.

Running out the Clock. Ottawa, Oberon Press, 1991.

Riding the Long Black Horse. Ottawa, Oberon Press, 1993.

Old Bank Notes. Ottawa, Oberon Press, 1993.

No Sad Songs Wanted Here. Ottawa, Oberon Press, 1995.

Close to Home. Ottawa, Oberon Press, 1996.

Of Time & Toronto. Ottawa, Oberon Press, 2000.

Recording: *Raymond Souster,* Ontario Institute for Studies in Education, 1971.

Novels

The Winter of Time (as Raymond Holmes). Toronto, Export, 1949.

On Target (as John Holmes). Toronto, Village Book Store Press, 1973

Other

From Hell to Breakfast, with Douglas Alcorn. Toronto, Intruder Press, 1980.

Editor, *Poets 56: Ten Younger English-Canadians.* Toronto, Contact Press, 1956.

Editor, *Experiment: Poems 1923–1929,* by W.W.E. Ross. Toronto, Contact Press, 1958.

Editor, *New Wave Canada: The New Explosion in Canadian Poetry.* Toronto, Contact Press, 1966.

Editor, with John Robert Colombo, *Shapes and Sounds: Poems of W.W.E. Ross.* Toronto, Longman, 1968.

Editor, with Douglas Lochhead, *Made in Canada: New Poems of the Seventies.* Ottawa, Oberon Press, 1970.

Editor, with Richard Woollatt, *Generation Now* (textbook). Toronto, Longman, 1970.

Editor, with Richard Woollatt, *Sights and Sounds* (textbook). Toronto, Macmillan, 1973.

Editor, with Douglas Lochhead, *100 Poems of Nineteenth Century Canada* (textbook). Toronto, Macmillan, 1974.

Editor, with Richard Woollatt, *These Loved, These Hated Lands* (textbook). Toronto, Doubleday, 1975.

Editor, *Vapour and Blue: The Poetry of William Wilfred Campbell.* Sutton West, Ontario, Paget Press, 1978.

Editor, *Comfort of the Fields: The Best Known Poems of Archibald Lampman.* Sutton West, Ontario, Paget Press, 1979.

Editor, with Richard Woollatt, *Poems of a Snow-Eyed Country.* Don Mills, Ontario, Academic Press, 1980.

Editor, *Powassan's Drum: Selected Poems of Duncan Campbell Scott.* Ottawa, Tecumseh Press, 1985.

Editor, with Douglas Lochhead, *Windflower: The Selected Poems of Bliss Carman.* Ottawa, Tecumseh Press, 1985.

Editor, *An Acadian Easter: The Collected Poems of Francis Sherman.* Ottawa, Borealis Press, 1999.

*

Bibliography: *Raymond Souster: A Descriptive Bibliography* by Bruce Whiteman, Ottawa, Oberon Press, 1984.

Manuscript Collections: Rare Book Room, University of Toronto Library; McLellan Library, McGill University, Montreal; Lakehead University, Thunder Bay, Ontario.

Critical Studies: ''Groundhog among the Stars'' by Louis Dudek, in *Canadian Literature* (Vancouver), autumn 1964; ''To Souster from Vermont'' by Hayden Carruth, in *Tamarack Review* (Toronto), winter 1965; introduction by Michael Macklem to *Selected Poems,* 1972; *From There to Here,* Erin, Ontario, Press Porcépic, 1974, and *Louis Dudek and Raymond Souster,* Vancouver, Douglas and McIntyre, 1980, Seattle, University of Washington Press, 1981, both by Frank Davey; ''Raymond Souster: The Quiet Chronicler'' by Bruce Meyer and Brian O'Riordan, in *Waves* (Richmond Hill, Ontario), 11(4), spring 1983; ''Baseball and the Canadian Imagination'' by George Bowering, in *Canadian Literature* (Vancouver, British Columbia), 108, spring 1986; *The Place of American Poets in the Development of Irving Layton, Louis Dudek and Raymound Souster* (dissertation) by Sabrina Lee Reed, N.p., 1989; by Bruce Whiteman, in *ECW's Biographical Guide to Canadian Poets,* edited by Robert Lecker, Jack David, and Ellen Quigley, Toronto, ECW, 1993.

Raymond Souster comments:

Whoever I write to, I want to make the substance of the poems so immediate, so real, so clear, that the reader feels the same exhilaration—be it fear or joy—that I derived from the experience, object, or mood that triggered the poem in the first place.... I like to think I am ''talking out'' my poems rather than consciously dressing them up in the trappings of the academic school. For many years I held to the theory that all poetry must be written out of a sudden spontaneous impulse in which the poet is unbearably moved to write down the words of that vision. Now I am more inclined to echo the view of Guiseppe Ungaretti when he says, ''Between one flower gathered and the other given, the inexpressible Null.''

*   *   *

Raymond Souster's poetic career has spanned five decades, and his *Collected Poems* comprise six volumes. Souster's early work is his best known, and the pieces most often found in anthologies date from the 1940s and 1950s. These are short lyrics, usually set in the city of Toronto, which nostalgically recall scenes of childhood or empathetically depict the solitary misfits who inhabit the city streets. Souster's later work, employing documentary material in longer forms, is less well known.

A strong documentary impulse runs throughout Souster's work. He articulates his view of the poet's role in "Poems Are Happening":

Poems are happening all around us,
but we don't see them,
or else can't hear them.

That's perhaps why they have to wave
and cry out like fools
until the poet comes along.

Throughout his writing career Souster has made it his task to record the overlooked poetic moments of everyday life. He makes poetry of his immediate environment, and since he has lived all his life in Toronto, this city is the setting for much of his work. Many poems evoke specific details of the city's landscape—streets, buildings, parks, landmarks. In a sense the body of Souster's lyric verse can be read as a documentary of Toronto and of the changes the city has undergone during his life.

Souster's lyrics can be roughly divided into the personal and the social. The personal lyrics explore a variety of themes; there are love poems and poems for friends and celebrations of the simple pleasures of life, such as jazz and baseball. The most distinctively characteristic of Souster's personal poems are those evoking the past, especially his own childhood, seeking in memories of a simpler, more innocent past "a lost but recovered joy" ("Yonge Street Saturday Night"). Like many modernist poets, Souster frequently expresses despair at the materialism and spiritual aridity of the modern world, and the nostalgic tone that marks much of his work reflects a desire to escape the painful realities of contemporary life: "the world, like us, / is tired, very tired of reality, / seeks to hide from it every chance it gets" ("Sunday Night Walk"). Reality, however, is ultimately inescapable, the past irrecoverable. Some solace is offered by the natural world, which Souster frequently celebrates in imagist lyrics. The nature he portrays is what survives in the modern urban environment—garden flowers and trees, birds, city animals such as squirrels, raccoons, and domestic cats, of which he seems particularly fond. He frequently juxtaposes such natural images with images of the inorganic city, as in "Dandelion":

Dandelion, if it wasn't
for your impudence
this dull split length of concrete
would never have burst into blossom
even once in its lustreless lifetime.

Nature retains its vitality in the inhospitable city, but the human figures who populate Souster's Toronto are less hardy. His social poetry focuses primarily on the victims of modern society, the misfits and outcasts who populate the city's streets and who are ignored by the competitive, self-absorbed crowds that surround them, for example, the old newspaper vendor who is a fixture on a corner in the financial district and the derelicts, drunks, drug addicts, and bag ladies who survive on the margins of urban society.

The strength of Souster's lyric verse lies in the simplicity of his style and the precision and clarity of his imagery. His concrete diction and conversational tone are effective in articulating the poems that "are happening all around us." His greatest weakness is a tendency toward sentimentality. This is a danger particularly in his sympathetic portraits of urban outcasts, although he generally guards against the temptation to self-indulgent pity and allows his unfortunate subjects to retain their human dignity.

Beginning in the early 1960s, Souster began to explore the possibilities of documentary verse, producing several "found poems" constructed from historical documents and writing a series called "Pictures from a Long-Lost World" that dramatize historical moments. A few of these works recall Canadian history, but most focus on European history, in particular, events of World Wars I and II. Several of the World War I poems embody the recollections of Souster's father of his service in the 1914–18 conflict. More focus on World War II, however, Souster's own war. Souster served in the Canadian air force from 1941 to 1945, and although he did not see active service, arriving in Europe only as the war ended, his wartime experience has clearly been a major influence on his life and work. Many of his early lyrics recall his air force days in Nova Scotia and England. Some of Souster's "Pictures from a Long-Lost World" are based on actual historical photographs, others focus on individual moments, and several are narrative poems that recount specific incidents, often in the voice of one of the participants. These poems present a somewhat ambivalent attitude toward war. While condemning warfare, they celebrate heroism, especially heroic sacrifice in the face of insurmountable odds, and they convey a feeling of nostalgia for more heroic times. Some of the pictures of the past are very effective, in particular "Mauthausen, 1942," a stark evocation of the barbaric treatment of prisoners in Auschwitz.

The longer narrative pieces are less successful because of the amount of factual material they must accommodate. This problem is particularly apparent in Souster's most ambitious long poem, "Jubilee of Death." This book-length work tells the story of the disastrous Allied raid on Dieppe, France, in August 1942, giving particular attention to the prominent role played by Canadian troops. The poem is divided into four parts—"Preparation," "The Landing," "Withdrawal," "Surrender"—in which various participants in the action, ranging from Winston Churchill through various levels of the military command down to private soldiers, tell their own stories of the Dieppe landing in their own voices. Souster's dramatic technique is effective in conveying the complexity of the motivations and political pressures that led to the undertaking of this suicidal mission, as well as the chaotic experience of the landing itself. The volume and complexity of the factual information the story requires detract from the narrative's effectiveness, however.

In a brief poem entitled "Confession" Souster writes,

I'm not sure I'm ready for epics—
there are far too many little songs
the rest have left unsung.

Souster's attempts at epic, in "Jubilee of Death" and the longer "Pictures from a Long-Lost World," are interesting, but they are less effective than his "little songs." His greatest achievement lies in the shorter lyric poems, in which he captures in simple language and sharp, clear images significant moments of human experience.

—Linda Lamont-Stewart

SOYINKA, Wole

Nationality: Nigerian. **Born:** Akinwande Oluwole Soyinka, in Abeokuta, 13 July 1934. **Education:** St. Peter's School, Ake, Abeokuta, 1938–43; Abeokuta Grammar School, 1944–45; Government College, Ibadan, 1946–50; University College, Ibadan (now University of Ibadan), 1952–54; University of Leeds, Yorkshire, 1954–57, B.A. (honors) in English. **Family:** Married; four children. **Career:** Play reader, Royal Court Theatre, London, 1957–59; Rockefeller Research Fellow in drama, University of Ibadan, 1961–62; lecturer in English, University of Ife, Ile-Ife, 1963–64; senior lecturer in English, University of Lagos, 1965–67; head of the department of theater arts, University of Ibadan, 1969–72 (appointment made in 1967); professor of comparative literature, and head of the department of dramatic arts, University of Ife, 1975–85. Visiting fellow, Churchill College, Cambridge, 1973–74; visiting professor, University of Ghana, Legon, 1973–74, University of Sheffield, 1974, Yale University, New Haven, Connecticut, 1979–80, and Cornell University, Ithaca, New York, 1986. Since 1988 Goldwin Smith professor for African Studies and Theatre Arts, Cornell University. Founding director, 1960 Masks Theatre, 1960, and Orisun Theatre, 1964, Lagos and Ibadan, and Unife Guerilla Theatre, Ile-Ife, 1978; co-editor, *Black Orpheus,* 1961–64; editor, *Transition* (later *Ch'indaba*) magazine, Accra, Ghana, 1975–77. Secretary-General, Union of Writers of the African Peoples, 1975. Tried and acquitted of armed robbery, 1965; political prisoner, detained by the Federal Military Government, Lagos and Kaduna, 1967–69. **Awards:** Dakar Festival award, 1966; John Whiting award, 1967; Jock Campbell award (*New Statesman*), for fiction, 1968; Nobel prize for literature, 1986; Benson Medal, 1990; Premio Letterario Internazionalle Mondello, 1990. D.Litt: University of Leeds, 1973, Yale University, University of Montpellier, France, University of Lagos, and University of Bayreuth, 1989. Fellow, Royal Society of Literature (U.K.); member, American Academy, and Academy of Arts and Letters of the German Democratic Republic. Named Commander, Federal Republic of Nigeria, 1986, Order of La Legion d'Honneur, France, 1989, and Order of the Republic of Italy, 1990; Akogun of Isara, 1989; Akinlatun of Egbaland, 1990. **Agent:** Morton Leavy, Leavy Rosensweig and Hyman, 11 East 44th Street, New York, New York 10017; or Triharty (Nig.) Ltd. Agency Division, 4, Ola-ayeni Street, Ikeja, Lagos, Nigeria. (U.K. Correspondent: Cognix Ltd., Media Suite, 3 Tyers Gate, London SE1 3HX). **Address:** P.O. Box 935, Abeokuta, Ogun, Nigeria.

PUBLICATIONS

Poetry

Idanre and Other Poems. London, Methuen, 1967; New York, Hill and Wang, 1968.
Poems from Prison. London, Collings, 1969.
A Shuttle in the Crypt. London, Eyre Methuen-Collings, and New York, Hill and Wang, 1972.
Ogun Abibimañ . London, Collings, 1976.
Mandela's Earth and Other Poems. New York, Random House, 1988; London, Deutsch, 1989.
Early Poems. Oxford, Oxford University Press, 1997.

Plays

The Swamp Dwellers (produced London, 1958; New York, 1968). Included in *Three Plays,* 1963; in *Five Plays,* 1964.
The Lion and the Jewel (produced Ibadan, 1959; London, 1966). Ibadan, London, and New York, Oxford University Press, 1963.
The Invention (produced London, 1959).
A Dance of the Forests (produced Lagos, 1960). Ibadan, London, and New York, Oxford University Press, 1963.
The Trials of Brother Jero (produced Ibadan, 1960; Cambridge, 1965; London, 1966; New York, 1967). Included in *Three Plays,* 1963; in *Five Plays,* 1964.
Camwood on the Leaves (broadcast 1960). London, Eyre Methuen, 1973; in *Camwood on the Leaves, and Before the Blackout,* 1974.
The Republican and The New Republican (satirical revues; produced Lagos, 1963).
Three Plays. Ibadan, Mbari, 1963; as *Three Short Plays,* London, Oxford University Press, 1969.
The Strong Breed (produced Ibadan, 1964; London, 1966; New York, 1967). Included in *Three Plays,* 1963; in *Five Plays,* 1964
Childe Internationale (produced Ibadan, 1964). Ibadan, Fountain, 1987.
Kongi's Harvest (produced Ibadan, 1964; New York, 1968). Ibadan, London, and New York, Oxford University Press, 1967.
Five Plays: A Dance of the Forests, The Lion and the Jewel, The Swamp Dwellers, The Trials of Brother Jero, The Strong Breed. Ibadan, London, and New York, Oxford University Press, 1964.
Before the Blackout (produced Ibadan, 1965; Leeds, 1981). Ibadan, Orisun, 1971; in *Camwood on the Leaves, and Before the Blackout,* 1974.
The Road (produced London, 1965; also director: produced Chicago, 1984). Ibadan, London, and New York, Oxford University Press, 1965.
Rites of the Harmattan Solstice (produced Lagos, 1966).
Madmen and Specialists (produced Waterford, Connecticut, and New York, 1970; revised version, also director: produced Ibadan, 1971). London, Methuen, 1971; New York, Hill and Wang, 1972.
The Jero Plays: The Trials of Brother Jero, and Jero's Metamorphosis. London, Eyre Methuen, 1973.
Jero's Metamorphosis (produced Lagos, 1975). Included in *The Jero Plays,* 1973.
The Bacchae: A Communion Rite, adaptation of the play by Euripides (produced London, 1973). London, Eyre Methuen, 1973; New York, Norton, 1974.
Collected Plays: 1. *A Dance of the Forests, The Swamp Dwellers, The Strong Breed, The Road, The Bacchae.* London and New York, Oxford University Press, 1973. 2. *The Lion and the Jewel, Kongi's Harvest, The Trials of Brother Jero, Jero's Metamorphosis, Madmen and Specialists.* London and New York, Oxford University Press, 1974.
Camwood on the Leaves, and Before the Blackout: Two Short Plays. New York, Third Press, 1974.
Death and the King's Horseman (also director: produced Ile-Ife, 1976; Chicago, 1979; also director: produced New York, 1987). London, Eyre Methuen, 1975; New York, Norton, 1976.
Opera Wonyosi, adaptation of *The Threepenny Opera* by Brecht (also director: produced Ile-Ife, 1977). Bloomington, Indiana University Press, and London, Collings, 1981.
Golden Accord (produced Louisville, 1980).
Priority Projects (revue; produced on Nigeria tour, 1982).

Requiem for a Futurologist (also director: produced Ile-Ife, 1983). London, Collings, 1985.

A Play of Giants (also director: produced New Haven, Connecticut, 1984). London, Methuen, 1984.

Six Plays (includes *The Trials of Brother Jero, Jero's Metamorphosis, Camwood on the Leaves, Death and the King's Horseman, Madmen and Specialists, Opera Wonyosi*). London, Methuen. 1984.

From Zia with Love. London, Methuen, 1992.

The Beatification of Area Boy (produced Leeds, England, 1996). London, Methuen, 1995.

Wole Soyinka: Plays 2. London, Methuen, 1999.

Screenplay: *Kongi's Harvest,* 1970.

Radio Plays: *Camwood on the Leaves,* 1960; *The Detainee,* 1965; *Die Still, Dr. Godspeak,* 1981; *A Scourge of Hyacinths,* 1990; *Nineteen Ninety-Four,* 1993.

Television Plays: *Joshua: A Nigerian Portrait,* 1962 (Canada); *Culture in Transition,* 1963 (USA).

Novels

The Interpreters. London, Deutsch, 1965; New York, Macmillan, 1970.

Season of Anomy. London, Collings, 1973; New York, Third Press, 1974.

Other

The Man Died: Prison Notes. London, Eyre Methuen-Collings, and New York, Harper, 1972.

In Person: Achebe, Awoonor, and Soyinka at the University of Washington. Seattle, University of Washington African Studies Program, 1975.

Myth, Literature, and the African World. London, Cambridge University Press, 1976.

Aké: The Years of Childhood (autobiography). London, Collings, 1981; New York, Vintage, 1983.

The Critic and Society (essay). Ile-Ife, University of Ife Press, 1981.

The Past Must Address Its Present (lecture). N.p., Nobel Foundation, 1986; as *This Past Must Address Its Present,* New York, Anson Phelps Institute, 1988.

Art, Dialogue and Outrage: Essays on Literature and Culture. Ibadan, New Horn, 1988.

Isara: A Voyage Around "Essay." New York, Random House, 1989; London, Methuen, 1990.

Ibadan—The Penkelemes Years. London, Methuen, 1994.

Democracy and the University Idea: The Student Factor (lecture). Lagos, Obafemi Awalowo Foundation, 1996.

The Open Sore of a Continent: A Personal Narrative of the Nigerian Crisis. New York, Oxford University Press, 1997.

The Burden of Memory, the Muse of Forgiveness. New York, Oxford University Press, 1999.

Editor, *Poems of Black Africa.* London, Secker and Warburg, and New York, Hill and Wang, 1975.

Translator, *The Forest of a Thousand Daemons: A Hunter's Saga,* by D.O. Fagunwa. London, Nelson, 1968; New York, Humanities Press, 1969.

*

Bibliography: *Wole Soyinka: A Bibliography* by B. Okpu, Lagos, Libriservice, 1984.

Critical Studies: *Wole Soyinka* by Gerald Moore, London, Evans, and New York, Africana, 1971, revised edition, Evans, 1978; *The Writing of Wole Soyinka* by Eldred D. Jones, London, Heinemann, 1973, revised edition, 1983, 2nd revised edition, London, Curry, 1988; *Three Nigerian Poets: A Critical Study of the Poetry of Soyinka, Clark, and Okigbo* by Nyong J. Udoeyop, Ibadan, Ibadan University Press, 1973; *Critical Perspectives on Wole Soyinka* edited by James Gibbs, Washington, D.C., Three Continents Press, 1980, London, Heinemann, 1981; *Wole Soyinka*, London, Macmillan, and New York, Grove Press, 1986, and "Essential Soyinka: Sketches and Plays, Satire and Poetry: Soyinka's Recent Work on the Theatre," in *West Africa*, 3899, June 1992, both by Gibbs; *A Writer and His Gods: A Study of the Importance of Yoruba Myths and Religious Ideas in the Writing of Wole Soyinka* by Stephan Larsen, Stockholm, University of Stockholm, 1983; *Wole Soyinka: An Introduction to His Writing* by Obi Maduakar, London, Garland, 1986; *Before Our Very Eyes: Tribute to Wole Soyinka* edited by Dapo Adelugba, Ibadan, Spectrum, 1987; *Index of Subjects, Proverbs and Themes in the Writings of Wole Soyinka* by Greta M.K. Coger, New York, Greenwood, 1988; "Black Mortality" by David Dabydeen, in *Poetry Review* (London), 79(1), spring 1989; "Discourse Styles and Forms in New Literatures in English: A Reading of Wole Soyinka's 'Idanre'" by Pushpinder Syal, in *ARIEL* (Calgary, Alberta), 22(4), October 1991; "The Syntax and Semantics of Idanre Noun Phrases: A Linguistic Spectacle" by Mabel Osakwe, in *Language and Style* (Flushing, New York), 24(3), summer 1991; "Ogun Widens His Haunt: Wole Soyinka's New Poems," in *Callaloo* (Baltimore, Maryland), 14(3), summer 1991, and *The Poetry of Wole Soyinka*, Lagos, Nigeria, Malthouse, 1994, both by Tanure Ojaide; "Because of Humanity: The Ring of Patriotic Anguish in Wole Soyinka's Poetry" by J.O.J. Nwachukwu-Agbada, in *Commonwealth Essays and Studies* (Dijon, France), 14(2), spring 1992; "On the Making of Wole Soyinka's Poetry: A Literary Inquiry into His Sources" by Gboyega Kolawole, in *Journal of Asian and African Studies* (Tokyo), 44, 1992; "Soyinka's Use of 'the Displaced Myth' in Idanre" by M.S. Nagarajan, in *Indian Response to African Writing,* edited by A. Ramakrishna Rao and C.R. Visweswara Rao, New Delhi, Prestige, 1993; "The Ogun Consciousness in Modern Creative Man: A Reading of Wole Soyinka's 'Idanre'" by Edward C. Okwu, in *The Gong and the Flute: African Literary Development and Celebration,* edited by Kalu Ogbaa, Westport, Connecticut, Greenwood, 1994; "Wole Soyinka and the Atunda Ideal: A Reading of Soyinka's Poetry" by Niyi Osundare, in *Wole Soyinka: An Appraisal,* edited by Adwale Maja-Pearce, Oxford, Heinemann, 1994; "The Politics of the Shuttle: Wole Soyinka's Poetic Space" by Jeff Thomson, in *Research in African Literatures* (Columbus, Ohio), 27(2), summer 1996; "Wole Soyinka's 'Dawn' and the Cults of Ogun" by Yaw Adu-Gyamfi, in *ARIEL* (Canada), 28(4), October 1997; "Post-Civil War Nigerian Poetry: The Ibadan Experience" by Oyeniyi Okunoye, in *Africa* (Rome, Italy), 53(2), June 1998.

Theatrical Activities: Director: **Plays**—by Brecht, Chekhov, Clark, Easmon, Eseoghene, Ogunyemi, Shakespeare, Synge, and his own works; *L'Espace et la Magie,* Paris, 1972; *The Biko Inquest* by Jon Blair and Norman Fenton, Ile-Ife, 1978, and New York, 1980. Actor: **Plays**—Igwezu in *The Swamp Dwellers,* London, 1958; Obaneji and Forest Father in *A Dance of the Forests,* Lagos and Ibadan, 1960; Dauda Touray in *Dear Parent and Ogre* by R. Sarif Easmon, Ibadan, 1961; in *The Republican,* Lagos, 1963; **Film**— *Kongi's Harvest,* 1970; **Radio**—Konu in *The Detainee,* 1965.

* * *

Wole Soyinka's first volume of collected poems, *Idanre and Other Poems,* is a significant guide to the direction of the author's work. He first made his name as a writer of light satirical verse in poems like "Telephone Conversation," "The Immigrant," and "The Other Immigrant," all of which he excluded from this collection. A preoccupation with more somber themes is represented by "Requiem" (also, and more surprisingly, excluded from the collected poems), in which he explores the continuing but tenuous relationship between the dead and the living in a series of delicate images suggestive of barely perceptible contact: "You leave your faint depressions / Skim-flying still, on the still pond's surface. / Where darkness crouches, egret wings / Your love is gossamer." This preoccupation with death and the beyond—particularly with death at high speed on the road—is one of the features of his later poetry and drama. His poem "Death in the Dawn" ends with the startled recognition by a victim of a car crash of his sudden transformation: "Brother / Silenced in the startled hug of / Your invention—is this mocked grimace / This closed contortion—I?" Several pictures of this kind occur in Soyinka's prose, poetry, and drama. Indeed, one of the impressive features is his consistency between genres and over the whole period of his writing.

In a magazine interview Soyinka spoke about the "personal intimacy which I have developed with a certain aspect of the road . . . it concerns the reality of death . . ." For him death on the road is a kind of sacrifice to "progress," a notion that Soyinka treats with extreme skepticism. But sacrifice—self-sacrifice, or martyrdom—is another theme with which Soyinka has become increasingly concerned. Society often destroys its greatest benefactors. Indeed, it is ironic that society advances through the willingness of sensitive souls to suffer martyrdom if necessary. This is the central theme both of his play *The Strong Breed* and of "The Dreamer," a poem based on the idea of the Crucifixion. The dreamer, like Eman in *The Strong Breed,* is martyred in his prime, but in the final stanza of the poem there is the suggestion that out of his bitter suffering a new and powerful growth arises:

The burden bowed the boughs to earth
A girdle for the sea
And bitter pods gave voices birth
A ring of stones
And throes and thrones
And incense on the sea.

This theme, that society needs such victims for its own salvation, is an important one in Soyinka's writing. The captain in his play *A Dance of the Forests* is emasculated and sold into slavery for sticking to his principles, in this case a refusal to fight in a causeless war. Nowhere is Soyinka's growing concern with man's incorrigible urge

for self-destruction through war better portrayed than in the long poem "Idanre." In this work he pictures Ogun, who has become the dominant figure in his writing, as having been invited by men to fight on their behalf but as being unable to distinguish friend from foe:

He strides sweat encrusted
Bristles on risen tendons

Porcupine and barbed. Again he turns
Into his men, butcher's axe
Rises and sinks

Behind it, a guest no one
Can recall.

Soyinka was forced to act out his poetic theme when, as a result of his abortive efforts to avert the Nigerian civil war with a trip across the embattled frontiers, he was arrested and detained by the federal military government. A period of solitary confinement was the gestation period for the spate of writing that followed Soyinka's release nearly two years later. The title of his volume *A Shuttle in the Crypt* (two of the poems had been smuggled out and separately published by Rex Collings as *Poems from Prison*), with its suggestion of confined, energetic activity, symbolizes both Soyinka's imprisoned state, an active mind frustrated by inactivity, as well as his refusal to accept mental defeat. He relives his predicament in his admiring tribute to the imprisoned Nelson Mandela, for whom he constructs the same "survival kit" he had made for himself in *A Shuttle in the Crypt*:

. . . Do you tame geckos?
Do grasshoppers break your silences?
Bats' radar pips pinpoint your statuesque
Gaze transcending distances at will?

Soyinka's writings after his release, both prose and poetry, are characterized by a more activist message. In the prose work *The Man Died* he says, "These men are not merely evil, I thought. They are the mindlessness of evil made flesh. One should never stumble into their hands but seek the power to destroy them . . . To seek the power to destroy them is to fulfill a moral task." In "Flowers for My Land," one of the two smuggled poems later included in *A Shuttle in the Crypt,* he writes,

Come, let us
With the mangled kind
Make pact, no less
Against the lesser
Leagues of death, and mutilations of the mind.
Take justice
In your hands who can
Or dare.

"Flowers for My Land" does not really represent the mood of the entire collection, which is more introspective—"a map of the course trodden by the mind," as Soyinka describes the collection in the preface—but it does foreshadow the sharper edge of his other postprison writings.

One African leader who dared to take justice into his own hands was Samora Machel, president of Mozambique, who virtually declared war against the minority regime of Rhodesia, an act that inspired Soyinka's long poetic work *Ogun Abibimañ*. The work is a celebration of Machel's symbolic act and, in the pause before real and uncompromising battle was joined, a vision of the imminent war of liberation in which both parts of the continent—hitherto the separate territories of Shaka in the east and Ogun in the west—would unite to overthrow the white tyranny: "Our histories meet, the forests merge / With the savannah . . . / and Ogun treads the earth of Shaka!" The poem sweeps along with a heady exhilaration, brushing aside all restraining considerations. It is too late for love, too late for reflection: "Can love outrace the random bullet / To possess the heart of black despair? / Remember Sharpville—not as aberration / Of the single hour, but years and generations." Will the war be won? Will the right weapons be found even after, in a desperate search for them, men have rifled "our sacred groves to yield, in need, thighbones / Honed to drinking points . . . ?" No one knows. Even those fighting on the side of right will be imperfect men, and mistakes will be made, but there is no other way. As Soyinka asks with typically irreverent irony, "If man cannot, what god dare claim perfection?"

Soyinka's ideas have not fundamentally changed. Prison hardened his tone, but the poet remains the protagonist of freedom against tyranny, of the force of life against the forces of death. His involvement with the prodemocracy forces ranged against military rule in Nigeria and on the side of the thwarted president-elect, Mashood Abiola, produced another typical piece of bravura when, in defiance of the military authorities, he slipped out of the country in 1994, even though his travel documents had been confiscated.

Because Soyinka's work is an attempt to formulate a meaning out of the contradictory forces that govern human life and actions, Ogun, who unites these two qualities without separating them, is an apt symbol. The poet himself effects a similar fusion in his work between African and European influences. European dramatic and poetic conventions are fused with African conventions and ways of thought to produce an original type of poetry. He invokes the pantheon of Yoruba gods to forge a new ethic whose validity is not confined to Africa. He imbues English with a verve and an expansiveness that spring from the imagist nature of Yoruba speech. This is what makes Soyinka both an African and a world writer.

—Eldred D. Jones

SPACKS, Barry (Bernard)

Nationality: American. **Born:** Philadelphia, Pennsylvania, 21 February 1931. **Education:** University of Pennsylvania, Philadelphia, B.A. (honors) 1952; Indiana University, Bloomington, M.A. 1956; Pembroke College, Cambridge (Fulbright scholar), 1956–57. **Military Service:** U.S. Army Signal Corps, 1952–54. **Family:** Married Patricia Meyer in 1955 (divorced 1979); one daughter. **Career:** Assistant professor, University of Florida, Gainesville, 1957–59; professor of English, Massachusetts Institute of Technology, Cambridge, 1960–83. Visiting professor of English, University of Kentucky, Lexington, 1978–79, and University of California, Berkeley, 1980. Since 1981 member of faculty, University of California, Santa Barbara. **Awards:** St. Botolph's award, 1971; Commonwealth Club of California Medal, 1982. **Agent:**

Lynn Nesbit, International Creative Management, 40 West 57th Street, New York, New York 10019. **Address:** 1111 Bath Street, Santa Barbara, California 93101, U.S.A.

PUBLICATIONS

Poetry

Twenty Poems. Santa Barbara, California, Sun Press, 1967.
The Company of Children. New York, Doubleday, 1969.
Something Human. New York, Harper's Magazine Press, 1972.
Teaching the Penguins to Fly. Boston, Godine, 1975.
Imagining a Unicorn. Athens, University of Georgia Press, 1978.
Spacks Street: New and Selected Poems. Baltimore, Johns Hopkins University Press, 1982.
Brief Sparrow. Los Angeles, Illuminati, 1988.

Novels

The Sophomore. Englewood Cliffs, New Jersey, Prentice Hall, 1968; London, Collins, 1969.
Orphans. New York, Harper's Magazine Press, 1972.

*   *   *

Barry Spacks is not widely known, and he is not regarded as part of a school or movement. So far as I know, he does not give readings and does not publicize himself. But what he does do is write steadily and well, producing poems that are craftsmanlike, pleasant to read, and genuine in feeling and tone. He writes on many subjects, often drawn from his life as a professor of English, but it is perhaps fair to say that his real subject is the life of the poet and his responsibilities and rights. Either directly stated or implied throughout his work are the themes of the right of the poet to remain free, to say what he feels, to indulge himself in nostalgia, speculation, dream, fantasy, and metaphor. Spacks is a likable writer ("unpretentious" is the word one is tempted to overuse in describing him), at home with himself and his life. His lyrics reveal an American poet-professor singing of the vagaries of the quotidian in a world that amuses, touches, and delights him.

Spacks's subjects are as numerous as his poems: his boyhood, his daughter, famous writers he has seen in Boston (Berryman, Neruda, Borges), a student killed while hang gliding, lustful thoughts in a Laundromat, a Buster Keaton film. But he is particularly good at turning casual occasions into poems. He has the ability to take a small incident, an almost everyday occurrence, and turn it into a small and unpretentious but nevertheless satisfying work. Grading papers late at night and mistaking the reflection of his light for someone else's, two friends cooking dinner, finding a design of leaves on the pavement, seeing his old professor drunk in a bar, landing at an airport, finding a Yiddish newspaper on the Riverside line—such subjects furnish the basis for his meditative (perhaps "ruminative" is more accurate) lyrics. But this intellectual cud chewing results in a very personal light verse, accomplished and sensitive in its handling of the stuff of everyday life.

Spacks has a good ear for language, and his poems are virtually without a false note. There is no rhetoric or bombast and little wordplay. The verse, often rhymed or in stanzas but moving toward more free verse in his later work, is clean and hard-edged, each word carefully chosen and placed. In his best poems one feels delight and almost surprise in seeing things come together, and what sometimes seems inconsequential at the outset suddenly resolves into a striking image or idea. In one of his best poems, ''Like a Prism,'' the prism image comes to be a symbol of equality of opportunity; in ''Teaching the Penguins to Fly'' a whimsical idea becomes a wry comment on 1960s-like notions of social liberation.

Spacks's images are often striking, with a playful or even surrealistic quality, such as the comparison of the sea to the ''sound of 12,000 women scrubbing bloody chainmail.'' Or consider these opening lines from ''For a Pregnant Lady'':

> Doing my usual thing: vacuuming Death Valley;
>   stitching up some weekday shrouds;
>   when all at once your nowhere-near-born child
> gazes through my window, nose against the glass;

These lines would seem to follow the little *ars poetica* he outlines in ''Wit and Whimsy'':

> Rule one: make precious
> little sense.
>
> Rule two: commit
> no permanence.
>
> Rule three: ignore
> rule four.

But there is more to Spacks than gently breaking the rules. In poems like ''New Copley in the Gallery'' and ''The Parent Birds'' he assembles intricate machines that function smoothly. In his later work his subjects seem more topical, as in the ecological ''Malediction,'' perhaps reflecting his fuller sense of his roles as father, poet, professor, and citizen.

The title poem of *Spacks Street: New and Selected Poems* was first collected in his previous volume. It is a poem about fame, about the poet's understated anxieties about his ambitions, his goals in life, and the importance of what he does as a poet. He imagines a street named after him and someone recalling his youth on that street, and he says, ''God, if they only could see me today, / the old gang / back on Spacks Street!'' His ambivalence about the distance between his dreams and their realization goes back at least as far as ''A Quiet Day,'' which mentions ''a wife assisting the long divorce of her husband / from his large dreams.'' In another poem, ''The Downright Poet,'' he ironically views the poet and his pretensions in relation to society: ''always for him much is laughable, / namely Himself, and Others.''

Among the best of the later poems is ''A Marriage,'' about divorce, ''The Shaver,'' a feeling memorial to his father-in-law, and ''Six Small Songs for a Silver Flute,'' short imagist/haiku lyrics about love. In his poems of the 1980s Spacks sustained his love for the life of the poet and of the poet-teacher, continuing to find delight in the small surprises of daily life. If these poems have little chance of changing the world or the direction of modern poetry (and I suspect that their creator has no such hopes), they are nevertheless very accomplished, sensitive poems.

—Donald Barlow Stauffer

SPARK, Muriel (Sarah)

Nationality: British. **Born:** Muriel Sarah Camberg, Edinburgh, 1918. **Education:** James Gillespie's School for Girls and Heriot Watt College, both Edinburgh. **Family:** Married S.O. Spark in 1937 (dissolved by 1943); one son. **Career:** Worked in the Political Intelligence Department of the British Foreign Office during World War II. General secretary of the Poetry Society, and editor of the *Poetry Review,* London, 1947–49. **Awards:** *The Observer* story prize, 1951; Italia prize, for radio drama, 1962; James Tait Black memorial prize, for fiction, 1966; F.N.A.C. prize (France), 1987; Bram Stoker award, 1988; Royal Bank of Scotland-Saltire Society award, 1988; T.S. Eliot award, Ingersoll Foundation, 1992; David Cohen British Literature prize, 1997; Gold Pen award, 1998. C.Litt.: Royal Society of Literature, 1991. D.Litt.: University of Strathclyde, Glasgow, 1971; University of Edinburgh, 1989; University of Aberdeen, 1995; University of St. Andrews, 1998. Honorary degrees: University of Heriot Watt, 1995; University of Oxford, 1999. Honorary fellow, Royal Society of Literature, 1963, and Royal Society of Edinburgh; honorary member, American Academy of Arts and Letters, 1978. D.B.E. (Dame Commander of the Order of the British Empire). Commandeur de l'Ordre des Arts et des Lettres, France, 1996. **Agent:** David Higham Associates Ltd., 5–8 Lower John Street, Golden Square, London W1R 4HA, England.

PUBLICATIONS

Poetry

Out of a Book (as Muriel Camberg). Leith, Midlothian, Millar and Burden, 1933.
The Fanfarlo and Other Verse. Aldington, Kent, Hand and Flower Press, 1952.
Collected Poems I. London, Macmillan, 1967; New York, Knopf, 1968.
Going Up to Sotheby's and Other Poems. London, Granada, 1982.

Plays

Doctors of Philosophy (produced London, 1962). London, Macmillan, 1963; New York, Knopf, 1966.

Radio Plays: *The Party Through the Wall,* 1957; *The Interview,* 1958; *The Dry River Bed,* 1959; *The Ballad of Peckham Rye,* 1960; *Danger Zone,* 1961.

Novels

The Comforters. London, Macmillan, and Philadelphia, Lippincott, 1957.
Robinson. London, Macmillan, and Philadelphia, Lippincott, 1958.
Memento Mori. London, Macmillan, and Philadelphia, Lippincott, 1959.
The Ballad of Peckham Rye. London, Macmillan, and Philadelphia, Lippincott, 1960.
The Bachelors. London, Macmillan, 1960; Philadelphia, Lippincott, 1961.
The Prime of Miss Jean Brodie. London, Macmillan, 1961; Philadelphia, Lippincott, 1962.

The Girls of Slender Means. London, Macmillan, and New York, Knopf, 1963.

The Mandelbaum Gate. London, Macmillan, and New York, Knopf, 1965.

The Public Image. London, Macmillan, and New York, Knopf, 1968.

The Driver's Seat. London, Macmillan, and New York, Knopf, 1970.

Not to Disturb. London, Macmillan, 1971; New York, Viking Press, 1972.

The Hothouse by the Fast River. London, Macmillan, and New York, Viking Press, 1973.

The Abbess of Crewe. London, Macmillan, and New York, Viking Press, 1974.

The Takeover. London, Macmillan, and New York, Viking Press, 1976.

Territorial Rights. London, Macmillan, and New York, Coward McCann, 1979.

Loitering with Intent. London, Bodley Head, and New York, Coward McCann, 1981.

The Only Problem. London, Bodley Head, and New York, Coward McCann, 1984.

A Far Cry from Kensington. London, Constable, and Boston, Houghton Mifflin, 1988.

Symposium. London, Constable, and Boston, Houghton Mifflin, 1990.

Reality and Dreams. London, Constable, 1996; Boston, Houghton Mifflin, 1997.

Short Stories

The Go-Away Bird and Other Stories. London, Macmillan, 1958; Philadelphia, Lippincott, 1960.

Voices at Play (includes the radio plays *The Party Through the Wall, The Interview, The Dry River Bed, The Danger Zone*). London, Macmillan, 1961; Philadelphia, Lippincott, 1962.

Collected Stories I. London, Macmillan, 1967; New York, Knopf, 1968.

Bang-Bang You're Dead and Other Stories. London, Granada, 1982.

The Stories of Muriel Spark. New York, Dutton, 1985; London, Bodley Head, 1987.

The Collected Stories. London, Penguin, 1994.

Open to the Public, New & Collected Stories. New York, New Directions, 1997.

Other

Child of Light: A Reassessment of Mary Wollstonecraft Shelley. London, Tower Bridge, 1951; revised edition, as *Mary Shelley,* New York, Dutton, 1987; London, Constable, 1988.

Emily Brontë: Her Life and Work, with Derek Stanford. London, Owen, 1953; New York, British Book Centre, 1960.

John Masefield. London, Nevill, 1953; revised edition, London, Hutchinson, 1992.

The Very Fine Clock (for children). New York, Knopf, 1968; London, Macmillan, 1969.

Curriculum Vitae. London, Constable, 1992; Boston, Houghton Mifflin, 1993.

The French Window and The Small Telephone (for children). London, Colophon Press, 1993.

The Essence of the Brontës. London, Peter Owen Ltd., 1993.

Editor, *A Selection of Poems,* by Emily Brontë. London, Grey Walls Press, 1952.

Editor, *The Brontë Letters.* London, Nevill, 1954; as *The Letters of the Brontës: A Selection,* Norman, University of Oklahoma Press, 1954.

Editor, with Derek Stanford, *Letters of John Henry Newman.* London, Owen, 1957.

*

Bibliography: *Iris Murdoch and Muriel Spark: A Bibliography* by Thomas T. Tominaga and Wilma Schneidermeyer, Metuchen, New Jersey, Scarecrow Press, 1976.

Critical Studies: *Muriel Spark* by Karl Malkoff, New York, Columbia University Press, 1968; *Muriel Spark* by Patricia Stubbs, London, Longman, 1973; *Muriel Spark* by Peter Kemp, London, Elek, 1974, New York, Barnes and Noble, 1975; *Muriel Spark* by Alan Massie, Edinburgh, Ramsay Head Press, 1979; *The Faith and Fiction of Muriel Spark* by Ruth Whittaker, London, Macmillan, 1982; *Comedy and the Woman Writer: Woolf, Spark, and Feminism* by Judy Little, Lincoln, University of Nebraska Press, 1983; *Muriel Spark: An Odd Capacity for Vision* edited by Alan Bold, London, Vision Press, and New York, Barnes and Noble, 1984, and *Muriel Spark* by Bold, London, Methuen, 1986; *Muriel Spark* by Velma B. Richmond, New York, Ungar, 1984; *Muriel Spark* by Norman Page, London, Macmillan, 1990; ''The Ancestral Laughter of the Streets: Humor in Muriel Spark's Earlier Works'' by Regina Barreca, in her *New Perspectives on Women and Comedy,* Philadelphia, Gordon and Breach, 1992; *The Women of Muriel Spark* by Judy Sproxton, London, Constable, 1992; *Critical Essays on Muriel Spark,* New York, Hall, and Toronto, Macmillan, 1992; ''The First Half of Muriel Spark'' by Roger Kimball, in *New Criterion* (New York), 11(8), April 1993; ''The Deliberate Cunning of Muriel Spark'' in *The Scottish Novel since the Seventies: New Visions, Old Dreams,* edited by Gavin Wallace and Randall Stevenson, Edinburgh, Edinburgh University Press, 1993; ''Muriel Spark and the Oxymoronic Vision'' by Joseph Hynes, in *Contemporary British Women Writers: Narrative Strategies,* New York, St Martin's Press, 1993; '''We All Have Something to Hide': Muriel Spark, Autobiography, and the Influence of Newman on the Career of a Novlist'' by Leon Litvack, in *Durham University Journal* (New Elvet, Durham), 86(55), July 1994; ''Muriel Spark and Gothic'' by Christopher MacLachlan, in *Studies in Scottish Fiction: 1945 to the Present,* edited by Susanne Hagemann, Frankfurt, Peter Lang, 1996; ''Portraits of the Artists As Young Defiers: James Joyce and Muriel Spark'' by Sharon Felton, in *Tennessee Philological Bulletin* (Chattanooga, Tennessee), 33, 1996; ''The Remarkable Fictions of Muriel Spark'' by Gerard Carruthers, in *A History of Scottish Women's Writing,* edited by Douglas Gifford and Dorothy McMillan, Edinburgh, Edinburgh University Press, 1997; ''The End of History: Cultural Change According to Muriel Spark'' by Rod Mengham, in his *An Introduction to Contemporary Fiction: International Writing in English since 1970,* Cambridge, England, Polity, 1999.

*   *   *

''What's good enough for Archimedes / Ought to be good enough for me'' (''Elementary'')—Muriel Spark's verse mocks the inadequacy of scientific definition and rejoices in ''an odd capacity for vision.'' Though "Against the Transcendentalists" elevates "poets" over "visionaries" and hopes ". . . that if Byzantium / Should appear in Kensington / The city will fit the size / Of the perimeter of my eyes / And of the span of my hand," the poem paradoxically celebrates the miracle these limits create—"The flesh made word." And the Kensington that obsesses a number of other poems is "Kensington of dreadful night" ("The Pearl-Miners"), where the persona invokes "latent Christ" ("Elegy in a Kensington Churchyard"). Sometimes the miraculous becomes merely the talking steel chairs of familiar satire on human interchangeability with artifacts ("A Visit"). Conversely, the elegant colloquialism of "Fruitless Fable," a chronicle of Mr. Chiddicott's sudden enslavement by his "perfected tea-machine," raises the poem from mock-heroic moral fable ("Alas, the transience of bliss—") to genuine fantasy. Occasionally fantasy dramatizes obsession with ". . . my other / who sounds my superstition like a bagpipe" ("Intermittence") or with ". . . the momentary name I gave / To a slight stir in a fictitious grave" ("Evelyn Cavallo").

Spark's most ambitious fusion of obsession with fantasy creates the "tremorous metropolis" of "The Ballad of the Fanfarlo," a hallucinatory "settlement of fever" in which vocal traffic lights and ether bowls seem as ordinary or extraordinary as everything else. This nightmare continuation of Baudelaire's prose satire traces the quest of the romantic poet Samuel Cramer for his alter ego, Manuela de Monteverde, and the dancer Fanfarlo but significantly changes the tone of the original. Baudelaire's Cramer ultimately edits a socialist journal and presumably no longer signs Manuela's name to "quelques folies romantiques," while Spark's hero, either true to his early vision or atoning for his defection, is willing to endure the horrors of "No-Man's Sanatorium" in his quest. Despite a generous epigraph from Baudelaire, the poem's atmosphere and stanza form suggest "The Ancient Mariner" and, at times, "Sir Patrick Spens" as filtered through Coleridge's "Dejection: An Ode": "The new moon like a pair of surgical forceps / With the old moon in her jaws." Only in such passages, when Spark defines romantic art through parody, does the poem achieve the simultaneous re-creation and mockery of Baudelaire toward which it aims.

Cramer is funnier in a brief appearance as a visiting journalist in "The Nativity" when he replies to rumors of mysterious happenings at the inn: "No good to me if it's local." "The Nativity," Spark's longest religious poem, precariously blends faith and fantasy in a portrait of bizarre wise men: "You with the nose on top of your head, smell out / The principalities of heaven for all of us." Riddling wit defines the limits of religious mystery in shorter works—"Conundrum," "Holy Water Rondel," and "Faith and Works" ("We are the truest saint alive / As near as two and two make five"). Even an apparently secular exercise like "The Rout," which, in the manner of Marianne Moore, fuses a news article about a battle between bees and wasps in a village church with a dispatch from Cromwell, reinforced by quotations from Lawrence and *The Pocket Book of British Insects: The Honey Bee,* produces not only the eloquent parody of "the murder of innumerable bees" but also an elegant questioning of man's relation to the rest of creation. Like Spark's seemingly casual treatment of religion, the moralizing is always implicit, offhand. However complex her tone, Spark's forms are generally traditional. The more controlled the verse, the more the strictness of the pattern causes a concentration in theme that becomes incantatory, as in "Edinburgh Villanelle":

These eyes that saw the saturnine

Waters no provident whim made wine
Fail to infuriate the dull
Heart of Midlothian, never mine

—Burton Kendle

SPARSHOTT, Francis (Edward)

Nationality: Canadian. **Born:** Chatham, Kent, England, 19 May 1926; immigrated to Canada, 1950, naturalized, 1970. **Education:** King's School, Rochester, Kent, 1934–43; Corpus Christi College, Oxford, 1943–44, 1947–50, B.A. 1950, M.A. 1950. **Military Service:** British Army Intelligence Corps, 1944–47: Sergeant. **Family:** Married Kathleen Elizabeth Vaughan in 1953; one daughter. **Career:** Lecturer in philosophy, University of Toronto, 1950–55; lecturer in classics, 1955–70, and assistant professor, 1955–62, associate professor, 1962–64, professor, 1964–82, chair of department of philosophy, Victoria College, and university professor, 1982–91, University of Toronto. Visiting professor, Northwestern University, Evanston, Illinois, 1958–59, University of Illinois, Urbana, 1966, and Sir George Williams University, Montreal, 1971. President, Canadian Philosophical Association, 1975–76, and League of Canadian Poets, 1977–79; president, American Society for Aesthetics, 1981–82. **Awards:** President's Medal, University of Western Ontario, for poetry, 1959, for essay, 1962; American Council of Learned Societies fellowship, 1961; Canada Council fellowship, 1970; Killam fellowship, 1977; Canadian Broadcasting Corporation prize, 1981; Royal Society of Canada Centennial Medal, 1982; Connaught senior fellowship, 1984. Fellow, Royal Society of Canada, 1977. **Address:** 50 Crescentwood Road, Scarborough, Ontario M1N 1E4, Canada.

PUBLICATIONS

Poetry

A Divided Voice. Toronto, Oxford University Press, 1965.
A Cardboard Garage. Toronto, Clarke Irwin, 1969.
The Naming of the Beasts. Windsor, Ontario, Black Moss, 1979.
The Rainy Hills: Verses after a Japanese Fashion. Privately printed, 1979.
New Fingers for Old Dikes. Toronto, League of Canadian Poets, 1981.
The Hanging Gardens of Etobicoke. Toronto, Childe Thursday, 1983.
The Cave of Trophonius. Ilderton, Ontario, Brick, 1983.
Storms and Screens. Toronto, Childe Thursday, 1986.
Sculling to Byzantium. Toronto, Childe Thursday, 1989.
Views from the Zucchini Gazebo. Toronto, Childe Thursday, 1994.
Home from the Air. Toronto, Childe Thursday, 1997.

Other

An Enquiry into Goodness and Related Concepts, with Some Remarks on the Nature and Scope of Such Enquiries. Toronto, University of Toronto Press, and Chicago, University of Chicago Press, 1958.
The Structure of Aesthetics. Toronto, University of Toronto Press, and London, Routledge, 1963.
The Concept of Criticism. Oxford, Clarendon Press, 1967.

A Book by Cromwell Kent (humor). Scarborough, Ontario, Vanity Press, 1970.
Looking for Philosophy. Montreal, McGill-Queen's University Press, 1972.
The Theory of the Arts. Princeton, New Jersey, Princeton University Press, 1982.
Off the Ground: First Steps to a Philosophical Consideration of the Dance. Princeton, New Jersey, Princeton University Press. 1988.
Taking Life Seriously: A Study of the Argument of the Nicomachean Ethics. Toronto, University of Toronto Press, 1994.
A Measured Pace: Toward a Philosophical Understanding of the Arts of Dance. Toronto, University of Toronto Press, 1995.
The Future of Aesthetics. Toronto, University of Toronto Press, 1998.

*

Bibliography: "Francis Sparshott: A Bibliograhpy of His Writings," in *Journal of Aesthetic Education,* 31(2), 1997.

Manuscript Collection: Pratt Library, Victoria College, University of Toronto.

Critical Studies: "Francis Sparshott" by E.A. Trott, in *Profiles in Canadian Literature,* vol. 6, Toronto, Dundurn Press, 1986; "Off the Ground: First Steps to a Philosophical Consideration of Dance by Francis Sparshott" by Gerald E. Myers, in *Philosophy and Phenomenological Research,* 52(1), March 1992.

*   *   *

Although Francis Sparshott remains relatively unknown as a poet, he became known internationally as a professor of philosophy at the University of Toronto and as one of Canada's foremost theoreticians of aesthetics. The search for value and meaning that informs much of his philosophical writing extends to his poetry, and the most successful of his poems draw heavily from philosophy, often taking the form of a dialogue between mythical, modern, and historical characters and events.

In "Rhetoric for a Divided Voice" Sparshott proclaims that, muselike, "behind my brain / Distant voices sing." In his panhistorical search for meaning and value Sparshott does indeed invoke the voices of diverse historical, mythical, and contemporary characters, for example, Mu'Allaqa of Imr Al-Qais, Charon, Jacques Derrida, Farrah Fawcett, and Walt Whitman. Their faint voices inevitably remain unheard, however. In "The Wall" Sparshott laments this condition, suggesting that our search for meaning and value is not only eternal but also ultimately elusive:

We walk away from our lives   backward   through
     time garden
as though life were a painting on a wall   and we moving
slowly away seeing at first mere splashes
of dense colour   thrilling & huge   but meaningless.

An inability to locate meaning in either the objects, events, or personalities of contemporary society frequently manifests itself in an idealization of youth or, in a more general sense, in a fictive idyllic past. In "Stations of Loss" growing older is described as "nothing really, / folks do it every day / who can't do anything else at all hardly. / It is only not to be young again / that's hard, that's hard,"

while "Reflex" bitterly reflects upon youth's passing—"I never felt ready / to give up the earth."

If meaning is beyond our grasp, then what sustains us in Sparshott's poetry is the quest, the journey toward meaning. The poet has, for example, described his poem "The Cave of Trophonius" as a "trip of the shaman through the universe." This pronouncement applies equally to poems such as "Migrants," "Neanderthal National Anthem," and "Lines for a Future Astronaut," which are indeed peopled with travelers, migrants, explorers, and wanderers of all kinds. In "Legends," for example, a returning explorer tells his anxious companions that the Canadian coast "doesn't end . . . / it goes all the way round." Thus, even the journey provides not answers but more questions.

Stylistically, imagism lends itself well to the travel narrative of a Sparshott explorer, hence its function as the primary stylistic feature of his poetry, graceful meditations on the material things that we see on our journeys through life. The essential features of imagism—the avoidance of clichéd language, the use of the vernacular, the eclectic, sometimes banal, choice of subject, and the attempt at suggestion rather than complete presentation—appear in most of Sparshott's collections of poetry. An example is his poem "Still Life with Campanulas":

Silence was brushed over surrendered farms
     from fragile bells. Cars in their black park
     turned slow, teased from cold coils a sudden spark.

The attempt to adopt a literary style that successfully accommodates both his philosophical and theological training as well as his preoccupation with the search for meaning continues in Sparshott's experimentation with the haiku form. His work in the form culminated in the publication in 1979 of his collection of haiku titled *The Rainy Hills.*

The quest for value and meaning is not without its lighter side, and Sparshott's poems are frequently imbued with a sense of humor and irreverence. His poems offer witty insights into the everyday machinations of contemporary society ("Penguins and Eskimos"), blend the sacred with the profane ("The 64,000 Drachma Question"), or delight in a playful manipulation of language ("Cyclic Poems"). In the poem "Stations of Loss," for example, we are told that God "blew it," while in one of his more amusing poems, "Bookkeeping," Sparshott nonchalantly explains the sorry plight that those who cannot read their own handwriting face daily:

What was it cost me four dollars April twentynine
I can't read the entry
on a good day it looks like milk or mail
mornings like this mire or perhaps ruin
most of the time it looks like misc
what kind of entry is that for a man's accounts.

Sparshott's poetry is not widely read in Canada because of its sometimes inconsistent and uninventive use of language and technique and its too frequent slips into parody. Nevertheless, it demonstrates an eclectic mix of themes, styles, and techniques and warrants consideration of the poet in the international context of twentieth-century poetry.

—Thomas Hastings

SPIRES, Elizabeth (Kay)

Nationality: American. **Born:** Lancaster, Ohio, 28 May 1952. **Education:** Vassar College, Poughkeepsie, New York, 1970–74, B.A. 1974; Johns Hopkins University, Baltimore, Maryland, 1978–79, M.A. 1979. **Family:** Married novelist Madison Smartt Bell in 1985; one daughter. **Career:** Visiting assistant professor, Washington College, Chestertown, Maryland, 1981; freelance writer, Columbus, Ohio, and Baltimore, Maryland, 1977–80; writer-in-residence, Loyola College, Baltimore, Maryland, 1981–82. Professor of English, 1982–86, 1988–97, and since 1996 chair for distinguished achievement, Goucher College, Towson, Maryland. **Awards:** National Endowment for the Arts fellowship, 1981, 1992; Amy Lowell Traveling scholarship, 1986; Sara Teasdale Poetry award, 1990; Guggenheim fellowship, 1992; Whiting Writers award, 1996; Witter Bynner Prize for Poetry, American Academy of Art & Letters, 1998; Maryland Library Association Author award, 1998. Member, Academy of American Poets. **Agent:** Jane Gelfman, Gelfman Schneider Literary Agents, Inc., 250 West 57th Street, New York, New York 10107, U.S.A. **Address:** 6208 Pinehurst Road, Baltimore, Maryland 21212, U.S.A.

PUBLICATIONS

Poetry

Globe. Middletown, Connecticut, Wesleyan University Press, 1981.
Swan's Island. New York, Holt, 1985.
Annonciade. New York, Viking, 1989.
Worldling. New York, Norton, 1995.

Other

With One White Wing (for children). New York, Margaret K. McElderry Books/Simon and Schuster, 1995.
The Mouse of Amherst (for children). New York, Farrar, Straus & Giroux, 1998.
Riddle Road (for children). New York, Margaret K. McElderry Books/Simon and Schuster, 1999.

Editor, *The Instance of Knowing: The Occasional Prose of Josephine Jacobsen*. Ann Arbor, Michigan, University of Michigan Press, 1997.

*

Critical Studies: ''Post-American Style'' by Tony Whedon, in *The Iowa Review* (Iowa City), 23(1), 1993; in *Partisan Review* (New York), fall 1994; interview in *Southwest Review* (Dallas), winter 1995, and profile in *Ploughshares* (Boston), winter, 1999–2000, both by A.V. Christie.

*   *   *

Supple free verse shapes Elizabeth Spires's quietly remarkable poetry, on occasion its lines judiciously tapped into place by rhyme and meter. There are several directions ein the movement of her work.

In one, life for the poet comes to position itself more and more consciously within ''the shaded porch of generation, / big enough for everyone,'' as her account of identity moves from childhood to parenthood and gains a broader and historically colored perspective. In another lost love bends in transit from bitterness and pain into knowledge and from there into a conjugal haven. The painful loss of a lover and separation from a son through divorce are balanced thematically in poems about consolidation with a new partner, aided by the birth of a daughter. Finally, the poetry juggles the tension between the longing for heaven and the longing for reconciliation with death in the way only a lapsed Roman Catholic appears to know the ineradicable stir of these longings. All three strands can be seen in both the early and late work as Spires pulls the fabric of her poetry firmly and authoritatively beyond the prosaic and into the true territory of the lyric, into myth and fable.

Consciously or unconsciously, this ambitious and comprehensive design plays out within a consistently developing imagery. The mirrors and lights of a boardwalk, a fun house show, and the prostitutes of the photographer Bellocq's Storyville all learn to coexist with the mirrors, bells, and monasteries of a later preoccupation, as the colorful objects of public spectacle, a pervasive interest, turn increasingly inward and, one might say, upward. Choice, or rather choosing as a consequence of what the self sees imaginatively, makes an early appearance, as in the concluding lines from ''Mirrors.'' Even in the heat of love the representations we make to others are always, perhaps only, representations we make to ourselves:

> When you bend over me, asking
> why I cried out, I see
> my face in your eyes, the jetty's
> yellow beacon flashing
> a warning on the walls around us.
> Any promises we make
> will be promises to ourselves.

In later poems the mirroring of self and other becomes increasingly complex. While the lines quoted above point to the ways in which even loving selves remain isolated, later poems affirm and fissure that loving dialectic as both expansion and suffocation. In other exercises of reflection and split consciousness there are poems that explore mirroring indirectly through the device of the dramatic monologue. In ''The Comb and The Mirror'' the mermaid speaker reports on love's spell in which ''self gives back the self / in love's unreflecting mirror,'' but the angle of her attraction is a fatal embrace. In other mirrors women, like those in ''Storyville Portraits,'' helplessly see themselves contracting:

> . . . *Who reflects who?*
> thinks the woman in the mirror,
> her life narrowing before her,
> a series of identical rooms,
> each smaller than the one before,
> so that she grows smaller and more terrified

In still other poems implied mirrors are ubiquitous—the shield of children's bodies reflecting the sun, the poet's face swimming in the tea plate she holds, and so on. Mirrors in lakes and seas also bind us to a material nature reflecting back a material selfhood, while other mirrors refract family likeness, sister to sister, or an older self—one's own or one's daughter's—back to a younger self.

In "The Travellers" and in poems like "Waving Goodbye" and "Stonington Self-Portrait" the doubled and dissolving self of the mirror watcher extends to other connecting meditations. In these the pairing is not only that of the self and watcher but also Spires's characterization of time, in which the present reflects the past or future. A "now" peels back to a "then," and a long ago shades a present that is relentlessly other, often some inexplicable relative of the dead but changeless.

Mysteriously, what the gaze dwells on frequently becomes something else, an interior image, an alter ego. An example is the heron/angel in "Two Watchers" who echoes the mysterious heron self seen in the earlier "Patchy Fog," who with "hungering heron eye" waits

> until the morning's
> curtain parts and shafts of sunlight make
> the heron cry, cry out, to see itself defined,
> bright burning outline in sky's water, and beat
> its wings and fly, smoke into smoke, toward heaven,
> mind that masterminds the pond's closed circle.

Reflection, which has been a basic figure from *Annonciade* onward, moves to become transformation.

This does not happen with anything approaching an angelic certainty, however, as the heaven toward which the heron directs his flight clouds over intermittently. In *Annonciade* Spires mixes prose and poetry in a piece called "Falling Away," the name for the experience of lapsed religious belief. The work returns in memory to a classroom in which "the crucifix above the front blackboard [hangs] in a face-off with the big round clock on the back wall." At age eleven the speaker's task is to imagine heaven and hell and to measure eternity. In the clock of her own time, in a recurring nightmare, the speaker returns "in my adult mind and body among children" still trying to master the earlier lesson: "Standing in the dark hallway, I'm thinking how I'll finally see through the keyhole into that polarized world of good and evil, guilt and absolution, that even a fallen-away Catholic can't escape. After all I have all time. Have all eternity."

True to this project, sensing the presence of the transcendent and faithful to its definitions, Spires's poems attempt to see behind the mirror into the object's real weightiness, beneath its skin, and over the horizon into those other layers of being. Whether the layers are celestial or simply other is not a question that can be safely answered. But a generous risk taking is in this poet's nature. The final poem of her book *Worldling* does not hesitate for a moment to invoke a larger, more visionary economy. Reading a parable about human mutability to her daughter at night, she says,

> Our only paradise is here,
> and we are rich as misers, rich in change!
> We hold in our empty hands a currency of days
> that we must spend down to the very last,
> no holding back allowed. But sleep now.
> And I'll sleep, too, to wake with you,
> wake to the everlasting present of our life.

—Lorrie Goldensohn

STAINER, Pauline

Nationality: British. **Born:** Burslem, 5 March 1941. **Education:** St. Anne's College, Oxford, 1960–63, B.A. 1963; Southampton University, M.Phil. 1967. **Awards:** Hawthornden fellowship, 1987; winner of Skoob Index on Censorship Competition, 1992; National Poetry Competition prize winner, 1992. **Address:** Casa di Scrittori, 40 Debden Road, Saffron Walden, Essex CB11 4AB, England.

PUBLICATIONS

Poetry

The Honeycomb. Newcastle upon Tyne, Bloodaxe, 1989.
Little Egypt. N.p., The Brotherhood of Ruralists, 1991.
Sighting the Slave-ship. Newcastle upon Tyne, Bloodaxe, 1992.
The Ice-Pilot Speaks. Newcastle upon Tyne, Bloodaxe, 1994.
The Wound-Dresser's Dream. Newcastle upon Tyne, Bloodaxe, 1996.
Parable Island. Newcastle upon Tyne, Bloodaxe, 1999.

Recording: *Words from Jerusalem* (videotape), British Broadcasting Corporation, 1995.

Other

Translator, with Ase-Marie Nesse, *The No-Man's Tree.* Guildford, Surrey, Making Waves, n.d.

*

Critical Studies: By Patricia McCarthy, in *Agenda* (London), 31(2), summer 1993; in *Poetry Review,* 84(1), spring 1994; by John Burnside, in *Poetry Review,* 85(2), summer 1995.

*   *   *

I first encountered the poetry of Pauline Stainer at the adjudication of the Stroud International Poetry Competition in 1981. Her poem "The Honeycomb" was awarded second prize, and it was obvious that she had been robbed. "The Honeycomb" was clearly the outstanding poem on offer that day, and so I found deep pleasure when some years later her first collection was published with the title *The Honeycomb.* Why did it take so long? It is a story of poetic injustice, although Stroud did make amends in 1984 when it awarded her first prize.

As an example of the extended use of an image, "The Honeycomb" is a small masterpiece. It begins,

> They had made love early in the high bed,
> Not knowing the honeycomb stretched
> Between lathe and plaster of the outer wall.

The poem then continues to throb with the activity of the bees in their comb: "their vibration swelled the room." This, together with the voluptuous sweetness of the honey "in the virgin wax," parallels the lovemaking in the room, leading to a beautifully apt conclusion:

> Now winters later, burning the beeswax candle,
> Could he forget his tremulous first loving
> In the humming dawn.

As an introduction to the writing skills and the sensuous use of language in Stainer's poetry, "The Honeycomb" sets the tone.

Since then, however, this direct style has developed into a more oblique one. In "The Ice Pilot Speaks" we find an extended presentation of a series of coded messages lit with brilliant flashes of vivid imagery—

> The bisque-doll
> on the seabed
> mouthing the Titanic

—or, in a scene of a visceral hell—

> Loki is bound
> with his own entrails
> but who will wear
> this smoking scarlet?

From this the reader is expected to construct a cumulative vision and sense. The method works beautifully in such poems as "Leper at Dunwich" and "Kinga Chapel" and is superb in "War Requiem," where the effect is electric:

> against the flicker
> of the crematorium
>
> the orchestra
> disrobing in the shower room

But in the longer "The Ice Pilot Speaks" I feel that Stainer demands too much of her readers. The clues are too teasing and demand too esoteric a knowledge. It is as if the reader is witnessing the flickerings, however brilliant, on the walls of a Platonic cave of the mind, offering only a glimpse of a higher reality.

Stainer's strength is in her powerful visual imagery. It is not surprising that this often expresses itself in poems about painters and paintings. In her "Turner Is Lashed to the Mast" she catches the very essence of his art:

> how water
> makes the wind visible,
> how the sea strikes
> like a steel gauntlet.

She does the same for Stanley Spencer in "The Infinite Act":

> the disciples shoal
> along the malthouse wall,
> principalities and powers
> smoke their bayonets

—John Cotton

STALLWORTHY, Jon (Howie)

Nationality: British. Born: London, 18 January 1935. Education: Dragon School, Oxford, 1940–48; Rugby School, Warwickshire, 1948–53; Magdalen College, Oxford (Newdigate prize, 1958), 1955–59, B.A. 1958, B.Litt. 1961. Military Service: Oxfordshire and Buckinghamshire Light Infantry, Royal West African Frontier Force, 1953–55. Family: Married Gillian Waldock in 1960; one daughter and two sons. Career: Editor, Oxford University Press, London, 1959–71, and Clarendon Press, Oxford, 1972–74; deputy academic publisher, Oxford University Press, Oxford, 1974–77; John Wendell Anderson Professor of English, Cornell University, Ithaca, New York, 1977–86. Fellow, Wolfson College, reader in English literature, 1986–92, and since 1992 professor of English literature, Oxford. Chatterton Lecturer, British Academy, 1970; visiting fellow, All Souls College, Oxford, 1971–72. Awards: Duff Cooper memorial award, 1974; W.H. Smith & Son literary award, 1975; E.M. Forster award, 1976; Southern Arts literary prize, 1998. Fellow, Royal Society of Literature, 1971, and British Academy, 1990. Address: Long Farm, Elsfield Road, Old Marston, Oxford, England.

PUBLICATIONS

Poetry

The Earthly Paradise. Privately printed, 1958.
The Astronomy of Love. London, Oxford University Press, 1961.
Out of Bounds. London, Oxford University Press, 1963.
The Almond Tree. London, Turret, 1967.
A Day in the City. Exeter, Exeter Books, 1967.
Root and Branch. London, Chatto and Windus-Hogarth Press, and New York, Oxford University Press, 1969.
Positives. Dublin, Dolmen Press, 1969.
A Dinner of Herbs. Exeter, Rougemont Press, 1970.
Hand in Hand. London, Chatto and Windus-Hogarth Press, and New York, Oxford University Press, 1974.
The Apple Barrel: Selected Poems 1956–1963. London, Oxford University Press, 1974.
A Familiar Tree. London, Chatto and Windus-Oxford University Press, and New York, Oxford University Press, 1978.
The Anzac Sonata: New and Selected Poems. London, Chatto and Windus, 1986; New York, Norton, 1987.
The Guest from the Future. Oxford, Perpetua Press, 1989.
Rounding the Horn: Collected Poems. Manchester, Carcanet, 1998.

Other

Between the Lines: Yeats's Poetry in the Making. Oxford, Clarendon Press, 1963.
Vision and Revision in Yeats's "Last Poems." Oxford, Clarendon Press, 1969.
Wilfred Owen. London, Chatto and Windus-Oxford University Press, 1974; New York, Oxford University Press, 1975.
Poets of the First World War. London, Oxford University Press, 1974
Louis MacNeice. London and Boston, Faber, 1995.
Singing School: The Making of a Poet. London, John Murray, 1998.

Editor, *Yeats: Last Poems: A Casebook.* London, Macmillan, 1968; Nashville, Aurora, 1970.

Editor, with Seamus Heaney and Alan Brownjohn, *New Poems 1970–1971.* London, Hutchinson, 1971.

Editor, *The Penguin Book of Love Poetry.* London, Penguin, 1973; as *A Book of Love Poetry,* New York, Oxford University Press, 1974.

Editor, *The Complete Poems and Fragments,* by Wilfred Owen. London, Chatto and Windus-Oxford University Press, 1983; New York, Norton, 2 vols., 1984.

Editor, *The Oxford Book of War Poetry.* Oxford and New York, Oxford University Press, 1984.

Editor, *The Poems of Wilfred Owen.* London, Hogarth Press, 1985; New York, Norton, 1986.

Editor, *First Lines: Poems Written in Youth from Herbert to Heaney.* London, Carcanet, 1987.

Editor, *Henry Reed: Collected Poems.* London and New York, Oxford University Press, 1991.

Editor, *Wilfred Owen: The War Poems.* London, Chatto and Windus, 1994.

Editor, with Margaret Ferguson and Mary Jo Salter, *The Norton Anthology of Poetry,* 4th edition. New York, Norton, 1996.

Editor, with M.H. Abrams and others, *The Norton Anthology of English Literature,* 7th edition. New York, Norton, 1999.

Translator, with Jerzy Peterkiewicz, *Five Centuries of Polish Poetry,* revised edition. London, Oxford University Press, 1970.

Translator, with Peter France, *The Twelve and Other Poems,* by Alexander Blok. London, Eyre and Spottiswoode, and New York, Oxford University Press, 1970; as *Selected Poems,* London, Penguin, 1974.

Translator, with Peter France, *Selected Poems,* by Boris Pasternak. London, Allen Lane, and New York, Norton, 1983.

*

Manuscript Collection: Bodleian Library, Oxford.

Critical Studies: "Playing with Words" by the author, in *Times Educational Supplement* (London), August 1976; by Harry Marten, in *Contemporary Literature* (Madison, Wisconsin), summer 1979; by the author, in *World Authors 1975–1980,* edited by Vineta Colby, New York, Wilson, 1985; in *Ecstatic Occasions, Expedient Forms,* edited by David Lehman, New York, Macmillan, 1988; interview with Jon Stallworthy by Sophie Ahmeen, in *Plum Review,* 4, fall-winter 1992; by Peter MacDonald, in *Times Literary Supplement* (London), 8 January 1999.

Jon Stallworthy comments:

When a poet is asked to "make a statement," he should respond with a poem, but I am tongue-tied in police stations, so will echo Keats: "I am certain of nothing but the holiness of the heart's affection." The changing seasons of "the heart's affection" have prompted the best of the poems I have written since, at the age of seven, I set myself to learn how to make poems as a carpenter makes tables and chairs. I count myself a maker, and such other things as I have made with words—studies of Yeats "at work," translations of poems by Blok and Pasternak—have been made with one purpose in view: to learn how to make better poems. And what is a poem? When my daughter asked that question, I found my tongue:

                    A POEM IS
something that someone is saying

no louder, Pip, than my "goodnight"—
words with a tune, which outstaying
their speaker travel as far
as that amazing, vibrant light
from a long-extinguished star.

*   *   *

Martin Seymour-Smith has rightly described Jon Stallworthy as "a quiet poet, a fastidious craftsman." Though his forms are somewhat experimental in the later verse, he remains a traditionalist in subject matter, as indicated by his persistent preoccupation with family, England, and "good form." The sarcastic tone of "A Poem about Poems about Vietnam," from the 1960s, suggests his impatience with self-dramatization and showbiz.

As "an elegist for the British Empire," Stallworthy has written nostalgically, if occasionally satirically, about its institutions and personalities. These poems include—from the early collections— "Poem upon the Quincentenary of Magdalen College" and "Epilogue to an Empire 1600–1900" (for Trafalgar Day), as well as the later "Great Britain" and elegies to Margaret and Geoffrey Keynes.

In "The Peshawar Vale Hunt," characteristic in tone of Stallworthy's lament for a bygone era, a patron at the Horseshoe Bar of the Club raises his glass in mock salute to a photograph of hunters, circa 1910, saying,

                    If they could see
themselves now, groups on the grass
in their insolent poses! History
has put down the mighty

from their family seats; tumbled them, arse
over crop, out of the saddle.

Later in the poem, however, when the gentlemen in the photograph speak for themselves, they provide their own—and perhaps Stallworthy's—apologia for long-ago indiscretions:

Empire builder, with your back to the wall,
have you any last word to say?
"It is better to ride fiercely, and fall,
than never to ride at all."

"Here Comes Sir George" similarly challenges scornful contemporaries to recognize the skill of a provincial civil service officer, "the last of the titans."

Stallworthy's best poems make skillful use of incidents from his private life, as in "The Almond Tree," about his son, and "Making a Bed," for his wife. His most ambitious work also centers on family history in the sequence published as *A Familiar Tree.* Here he traces the movement of the Stallworthys over two centuries, from England to islands in the South Pacific to New Zealand and back to England, recording the family's continuities and conflicts in the midst of adventures and religious quests. In the opening poem, "At the Church of St. John Baptist, Preston Bissett," the speaker prays for guidance as he begins a verse chronicle of seven generations:

Let me go down to them and learn
what they learnt on their journeys.

And to the looted cavern
of the skull, let me restore
their sights, their broken speech, before
from these worn steps or steps like these
speechless to the speechless I return.

Some works are in a lighter vein, which Stallworthy inevitably handles well. The middle-aged speaker in "Elegy for a Mis-Spent Youth" decries his lack of assertiveness, years ago, as his thoughts return

to the attic over the square . . .
    your dress over the back
of a chair, and the bed
where, nightly, drowsy with the fair
exchange of love and with the smell
of chestnut wicks lighting the square,
we never lay and never shall

Editor and biographer of Wilfred Owen, Stallworthy has also written verse about the poet and World War I. "The Anzac Sonata," the title poem in his 1986 volume of new and selected poems, describes the lives of family members victimized by violence, beginning with the death of a young man in the Mediterranean in 1915. In a characteristically elegiac mood, the poem intersperses the harsh details of their lives with this refrain:

Another time,
    another place . . .
Lift and tighten
    the horsehair bow,
shuttle rosin
    to and fro.

In the midst of suffering there are also reasons for joy in almost any life, Stallworthy seems to say, and the sonata concludes with this appropriate musical notation:

At the last stroke
    of the coda,

hold the note
    there, that first note.
jubilant from
    the fiddle's throat.

—Michael True

STEAD, C(hristian) K(arlson)

Nationality: New Zealander. **Born:** Auckland, 17 October 1932. **Education:** Mount Albert Grammar School; Auckland University, B.A. 1954, M.A. (honors) 1955; Bristol University (Michael Hiatt Baker Scholar), Ph.D. 1961. **Family:** Married Kathleen Elizabeth Roberts in 1955; two daughters and one son. **Career:** Lecturer in English, University of New England, New South Wales, 1956–57; lecturer, 1959–61, senior lecturer, 1962–64, associate professor, 1964–68, and professor of English, 1969–86, University of Auckland. Chair, New Zealand Literary Fund, 1973–75; chair, New Zealand Authors' Fund, 1988–91; vice president, New Zealand PEN, 1989–90. **Awards:** Poetry Awards Incorporated prize (U.S.A.), 1955; Readers award (*Landfall*), 1959; Katherine Mansfield award, for fiction and for essay, 1961, and fellowship, 1972; Nuffield traveling fellowship, 1965; Jessie Mackay poetry award, 1973; New Zealand Book award, for poetry, 1976, for fiction, 1986, 1996; New Zealand Arts Council scholarship, 1987. Litt.D.: University of Auckland, 1982. C.B.E. (Commander, Order of the British Empire), 1985. **Address:** 37 Tohunga Crescent, Parnell, Auckland 1, New Zealand.

PUBLICATIONS

Poetry

Whether the Will Is Free: Poems 1954–62. Auckland, Paul's Book Arcade, 1964.
Crossing the Bar. Auckland, Auckland University Press-Oxford University Press, 1972.
Quesada: Poems 1972–1974. Auckland, The Shed, 1975.
Walking Westward. Auckland, The Shed, 1979.
Geographies. Auckland, Auckland University Press-Oxford University Press, 1982.
Poems of a Decade. Dunedin, Pilgrims South Press, 1983.
Paris. Auckland, Auckland University Press-Oxford University Press, 1984.
Between. Auckland, Auckland University Press, 1988.
Voices. Wellington, Government Printing Office, 1990.
Straw into Gold: Poems New & Selected. Auckland, Auckland University Press, and Todmorton, England, Arc, 1997.
The Right Thing. Auckland, Auckland University Press, and Todmorton, England, Arc, 2000.

Novels

Smith's Dream. Auckland, Longman Paul, 1971.
All Visitors Ashore. Auckland, Collins, and London, Harvill Press, 1984.
The Death of the Body. London, Collins, 1986.
Sister Hollywood. London, Collins, 1989; New York, St. Martins' Press, 1990.
The End of the Century at the End of the World. London, Harvill Press, 1992.
The Singing Whakapapa. Auckland and Sydney, Penguin Books, 1994.
Villa Vittoria. Auckland and Sydney, Penguin Books, 1997.
Taking about O'Dwyer. Auckland, Penguin Books, 1999; Sydney, HarperCollins, and London, Harvill Press, 2000.

Short Stories

Five for the Symbol. Auckland, Longman Paul, 1981.
The Blind Blond with Candles in Her Hair. Auckland and Sydney, Penguin Books, 1998.

Other

The New Poetic: Yeats to Eliot. London, Hutchinson, 1964; New York, Harper, 1966.

In the Glass Case: Essays on New Zealand Literature. Auckland, Auckland University Press-Oxford University Press, 1981.

Pound, Yeats, Eliot and the Modernist Movement. London, Macmillan, and New Brunswick, New Jersey, Rutgers University Press, 1986.

Answering to the Language: Essays on Modern Writers. Auckland, Auckland University Press, 1989.

Editor, *New Zealand Short Stories: Second Series.* London, Oxford University Press, 1966.

Editor, *Measure for Measure: A Casebook.* London, Macmillan, 1971.

Editor, *The Letters and Journals of Katherine Mansfield: A Selection.* London, Allen Lane, 1977.

Editor, *Collected Stories,* by Maurice Duggan. Auckland, Auckland University Press-Oxford University Press, 1981.

Editor, with Elizabeth Smither and Kendrick Smithyman, *The New Gramophone Room: Poetry and Fiction.* Auckland, University of Auckland, 1985.

Editor, *The Faber Book of Contemporary South Pacific Stories.* London, Faber, 1994.

*

Manuscript Collection: Alexander Turnbull Library, Wellington.

Critical Studies: By James Bertram, in *Islands 2* (Christchurch), 1972; by Peter Crisp, in *New Argot* (Auckland), 1975; by Rob Jackaman, in *Landfall* 114 (Christchurch), 1975; by Ken Arvidson, in *Journal of New Zealand Literature 1,* 1983; interview with Michael Harlow, in *Landfall 132* (Christchurch), 1983; *"Poems of a Decade, C.K. Stead: Two Responses"* by Dell Boldt and Mike Doyle, in *Landfall 152* (Christchurch), December 1984, and "A Study of Two Long Poems by C.K. Stead" (thesis) by Boldt, Palmerston North, Massey University, 1984; in *Ariel* (Calgary, Alberta), 16(4), October 1985; "A Deckchair of Words," in *Landfall 159* (Christchurch), September 1986, and "Stead's Dream," in *Landfall 163* (Christchurch), September 1987, both by Reginald Berry; "Modernist Making and Self-Making" by A. Walton Litz, in *Times Literary Supplement* (London), 10 October 1986; interview in *Talking about Ourselves,* edited by Harry Ricketts, Wellington, Mallinson Rendel, 1986; in *The Writer Written* by Jean-Pierre Durix. New York, Greenwood Press, 1987; in *The Government of the Tongue* by Seamus Heaney, London, Faber, 1988; by Dennis McEldowney, in *Landfall 173* (Christchurch), March 1990; "C.K. Stead and Fleur Adcock, A Conversation," in *Landfall 181* (Christchurch), March 1992; *C.K. Stead and Three Modes of New Zealand Poetry* (dissertation) by Allan Robert Phillipson, University of British Columbia, 1997; *Travels with Stead in Space and Time* by Lawrence Jones, New Zealand Books, March 2000.

C.K. Stead comments:

I am always troubled that I cannot write more poems than I do, that although I am a fairly conscientious and hardworking person, the Muse will not warm to these virtues, in fact, seems bored by them. I do not take the view that poets who write more than I do are less demanding of themselves, that "more means worse." I envy their fluency and still hope one day to learn the trick.

Reviewers tell me, with an emphasis that varies, of course, from approval to disapproval, that my poems are disciplined. This seems to suggest labor, conscious effort, self-control—all the qualities that go, for example, into my critical prose. But for me the discipline by which poems are achieved is quite different and still something I do not properly understand. I have to step out of the world in which I fill various roles (critic, professor, committee member, family man, etc.) and in which the clock rules. I have to sink back into myself to a point where all the trappings, all the things that are accidental, are lost. Then what is dredged up will sometimes seem worth polishing and putting on display.

Although I have on one occasion worked a poem into being through literally hundreds of drafts, an experience that was itself a kind of "possession" and not at all pleasant, it is usually true for me that hard labor does not help and that Keats's dictum holds: "if poetry come not as naturally as the leaves to the tree it might as well not come at all." To be in that rare state where poetry comes naturally is for me the greatest felicity. I am always afraid that it will never happen again.

I am a self-regarding younger son. My natural tone is secure but not definitive. I am a liberal, fitted neither for moralizing nor for command. But when I am able to dig deep enough, I discover another self who, though not very likable, is perhaps the best of the poet in me. I conceive of this person as German, romantic, authoritarian, detached yet full of passion, above all a musician. To learn that a poet I admire (Yeats, for instance, or the New Zealander James K. Baxter) could not sing in tune shocks me almost to disbelief.

When I write poetry I very often have in mind the image of a place, and whatever the subject or "approach" of the poem, that image will carry through into the final form. But I also have the feeling that if a poem is merely personal it may be trivial, and I often catch myself, in the process of writing, nudging the personal vision toward some kind of general or public utterance.

In my earlier poems influences are clearly apparent, but I do not think I am much influenced any longer by other poets, though I continue of course to be stimulated by them. For better or worse, I seem to have found my own form. Though I still write occasionally in formal stanzas, more often I find myself writing a cluster of short pieces, all springing out of one mood, one experience, one preoccupation, which together make up the poem. I like to write with as little punctuation as possible, accommodating line lengths and syntax to one another in a free-flowing verse sentence in which words echo one another and the pauses and runs of sound parallel the sense.

To be invited to write about oneself is, of course, a trap. What can a poet say about his own work except that he does the best he can and that he hopes someone else will enjoy it?

*　　*　　*

In 1965 C.K. Stead named truth, generosity, and delight as the qualities he would like his poems to manifest, although in such a way that the three would not readily be separable. His idea of truth, of "responses to occasions" and of fidelity to experience that cannot presume to think itself total but may justly be selective, is more than simply being honest. His poems should be true as long as they recognize that poetry serves "Art before Principle, because Art serves the world which Principle admonishes."

Stead later qualified this view. The importance of principle increased and intensified under the influence of a more resolute political commitment prompted by Vietnam. This change informed poems (Stead refers to the poems of the first section of his *Crossing the Bar*) with a troubled and indignant or outraged sense of the inhumanity of men, the irresponsible reductiveness of those for whom responsibility was properly their occupation. The poems are inclined to be short lined, declarative, direct. Their tensions are of patently different orders from those of *Whether the Will Is Free*. In the matter of tension as such, as well as in such ploys as regarding Washington, D.C., as a modern Rome, he may be reflecting Allen Tate, one whom he did not name as an influence in his 1970 statement for the first edition of *Contemporary Poets*.

Stead's poems of protest are naturally enough concerned with intimations of the consequences of power politics, particularly the denial of identity and of individual rights. "Anonymous" and "anonymity" are words his reader has to register. Vexatious questioning of identity is old hat but a continuous business. It is also to be affirmed as a matter of principle but as principle is affirmed through the means of the art. The second qualification to Stead's 1965 view may be traced in an article on James K. Baxter's later poems, the *Jerusalem Sonnets*. In Baxter's sonnets Stead found an eminent value, "their creation of a personality . . . a heightened sense of life." He went on to talk about "the world fresh to our awakening senses."

Stead's poetry increasingly moved to the cultivation of personality, to assert a heightened sense of life threatened by the devious contrivings of men of affairs and the unpredictability of everyday accidents (a smashed car, a neck broken while swimming). There were fresh awakenings to the possibilities of whatever part of the world his poems found their scenes in, which came to be varied indeed. The scenes, the occasions, and Stead's technical resources along with them grew astonishingly. In the 1950s he was accomplished, resourceful, but fairly conservative. His "Pictures in a Gallery Undersea," which put to work his expertise in the so-called new poetic, was an accomplished suite that readers have seen as a tribute to Eliot but that Stead himself regards as more of a tribute to Pound. The success of "Pictures" made him more confident, and he extended his range in forms, tonalities, and personae. He enhanced the facts, the truth, of his poems by splendidly marrying the occasions, his feelings (which may be rich and complex), and his formidable intelligence and delightful ingenuities.

When Stead wrote about John Mulgan in *Islands,* he subtitled his article "A Question of Identity." The first part of the article is about Stead identifying with places known to the young Mulgan and how Mulgan became part of the making of Stead. In the same issue Stead published a set of poems under the title "Scoria" that in parts connect with or overlap with scenes of Mulgan's childhood. Literature in a place, or the placing of literature as part of the process of identifying and finding identity, is an apparent impulse. Throughout his career he has returned to inquire into and effectively to reorganize his own past. "Only what lies behind," he said years ago, "falls into shape." "Scoria" seeks out shapes of childhood, events of childhood, stories of its places, and along with these makes an unprecedented (for Stead) use of early New Zealand writers. It is a sustained exercise in recovery and discovery, in which part of the discovery is again finding appropriate forms. Once more one remembers Tate saying, "The form is the meaning."

At one time Stead's poetry could be seen shifting from comment on experience to being direct experience, culminating in what is known as his works in open form, which conform to the principles he expounded in 1979. Nonetheless, he proposed to his reader that what was to be directly experienced was necessarily varied in its kinds, both in kinds of directness and kinds of experience as he transmitted it. His complex reality came to encompass an active sense of the "mythological" in a usual way of understanding that word, giving a fresh vitality to truth, generosity, and delight. It encompassed as well a sense of what was open to mythologizing, such as a cultivated man might have as response to the material and immaterial facts of being in Paris.

This Stead did in the ten-part sequence *Paris,* moving away from "openness" in practices that range widely in what turns out to be not so large a body of work as one would have credited. It gives an impression that derives from the accumulation of varied effects in such distinctly different modes. The poems are eminently regulated, where liberty is not license and discourse knows well what it is doing and what point is to be made.

Stead retired from his teaching post in 1986. In 1988 he wrote in *Between* about the local and special of his time and place and his extended family, as well as presenting another twenty radical "responses" to Catullus. (The 1982 work *Geographies* has fifteen Catullus pieces.) *Voices,* commissioned for the New Zealand sesquicentennial of 1990, is a suite of fifty-one parts spoken from 1820 (a missionary) to 1990 (an address to the first governor). The author's note to the work talks of "historical fiction." The talk here of history has to do with family as well as public concerns and of personal history, which is aware how close these matters may stand to mythologizing.

—Kendrick Smithyman

STEELE, Timothy (Reid)

Nationality: American. **Born:** Burlington, Vermont, 22 January 1948. **Education:** Stanford University, California, B.A. 1970; Brandeis University, Waltham, Massachusetts, M.A. 1972, Ph.D. 1977. **Family:** Married 1) Catherine Fuller in 1969 (divorced 1973); 2) Victoria Lee Erpelding in 1979. **Career:** Lecturer, California State University, Hayward, 1973–74, Stanford University, 1975–77, University of California, Los Angeles, 1977–83, and University of California, Santa Barbara, 1986. Since 1987 professor, California State University, Los Angeles. **Awards:** Wallace Stegner fellowship (Stanford University), 1972–73; Guggenheim fellowship, 1984–85; Lavan award, 1986; Commonwealth Club of California Medal, 1986; Los Angeles P.E.N. Center literary award, 1987; California Arts Council grant, 1993. **Address:** 1801 Preuss Road, Los Angeles, California 90035, U.S.A.

PUBLICATIONS

Poetry

Uncertainties and Rest. Baton Rouge, Louisiana State University Press, 1979.
The Prudent Heart. Los Angeles, Symposium Press, 1983.
Nine Poems. Florence, Kentucky, R.L. Barth, 1984.
On Harmony. Omaha, Nebraska, Abbatoir, 1984.
Short Subjects. Florence, Kentucky, R.L. Barth, 1985.
Sapphics against Anger and Other Poems. New York, Random House, 1986.
Beatitudes. Child Okeford, Dorset, Words Press, 1988.

The Color Wheel. Baltimore, John Hopkins University Press, 1994.
Sapphics and Uncertainties: Poems 1970–1986. Fayetteville, University of Arkansas Press, 1995.

Other

Missing Measures: Modern Poetry and the Revolt against Meter. Fayetteville, University of Arkansas Press, 1990.
All the Fun's in How You Say a Thing: An Explanation of Meter and Versification. Athens, Ohio University Press, 1999.

Editor, *The Poems of J.V. Cunningham.* Athens, Ohio, Swallow Press/Ohio University Press, 1997.

*

Critical Studies: ''Reciprocals'' by Wyatt Prunty, in *Southern Review* (Baton Rouge, Louisiana), 17(3), July 1981; ''Return to Metaphor: From Deep Imagist to New Formalist'' by Paul Lake, in *Southwest Review* (Dallas, Texas), 74(4), autumn 1989; ''The Poetry of Timothy Steele'' by Kevin Walzer, in *Tennessee Quarterly,* 2(3), winter 1996.

Timothy Steele comments:

Because comparatively few poets today write in meters, rhymes, and stanzas, my use of these has resulted in my being labeled a ''formalist.'' But I find this term meaningless and objectionable. It suggests, among other things, an interest in style rather than substance, whereas I believe that the two are mutually vital in any successful poem. I employ the traditional instruments of verse simply because I love the symmetries and surprises that they produce and because meter especially allows me to render feelings and ideas more flexibly, precisely, and memorably than I otherwise could. This preference is personal and aesthetic, however; I have never imagined that it provided me with access to cultural or spiritual virtue. And despite allegations to the contrary about *Missing Measures,* I have never said that vers libre is somehow wrong and immoral or that meter is somehow right and pure. The experimental school of Pound, Eliot, Lawrence, and Williams has its own beauties and achievements. But we can prize them justly and build on them, it seems to me, only if we retain a knowledge and appreciation of the time-tested principles of standard versification. Free verse cannot be free unless there is something for it to be free of.

*   *   *

Usually regarded as one of the New Formalists who have returned to traditional stanzaic verse and meter in reaction to free verse and modernist open form, Timothy Steele is a complex poet in style and sensibility. His cultural politics are not the conservatism of nostalgia often associated with formalism; rather, they are an insistence on the reality of experience, the truth of the moment, the good of the ordinary in contrast to the exploration of extremes and the idealization of radical states of being. His early emphasis on the experience of the actual world in *Uncertainties and Rest* seems part of an American tradition. But the symbolism of contentedly raking ''the last leaves'' and ''the dead grass'' on Sunday afternoon is the opposite of the usual celebration of the physical world: ''I gather what

I want, and leave the rest / To the vague sounds of traffic, far away.'' Steele intellectualizes the necessity of avoiding the dangers of pursuing experience, and when he does, his poetry can be as argumentative as that of any seventeenth-century Metaphysical: ''Formality's a renewable disguise, / Well-worded distance . . . . We do not overanalyze; / We take on faith what we have been.'' His poems are also filled with literary echoes and allusions, which are part of their meaning. His models are as varied as Martial, Donne, and Larkin. Although he avoids the autobiographical and confessional, the poems are about himself and his feelings, experiences, and ideas and about what he observes: ''To be respected / And loved made sense to me once, but of late / I'm drawn by more workable conceits.'' If the tone is low pressure, the logical pressure can be intense. There is at times a formality but seldom a mask or distancing. Rather than seeing Steele as a conservative, one might regard him as someone who, having experimented with cultural liberation, has learned the need for caution, prudence, the acceptance of limitation, and the enjoyment of the average and who, along with this, has learned the need for definitions or precisions, which include common sense and common experience: ''Culture? It's life humanely felt. / (See too Politeness, Mercy, Hope.)''

If Steele's verse is defensively rational, there appears to be a past—alluded to in such poems as ''Wait,'' ''For Ying Lew,'' and ''Cowboy''—of drugs, breakdown, ambition, and romantic hurt: ''There's scarcely time to sort out the debris, / I'm coming down too fast.'' The formerly and still potentially volcanic Steele rejects the personal costs of romanticism and modernism. ''Baker Beach at Sunset'' is explicit about this:

> . . . Friends say

> That there's still gold in modernist motifs—
> But I've learned what too much self-scrutiny
> Does to the spirit. Secondhand beliefs,
> The palpitating soul.

Most of Steele's *Nine Poems,* a limited edition of 150 copies, and *Short Subjects,* consisting of a rhymed ''Dedication for my sister, who likes epigrams'' and ten four-line epigrams, are republished in *Sapphics against Anger and Other Poems.* Steele's poems have increasingly grown beyond the early personal scenes, with their wounded wisdom, to greater complexities, and in doing so they require larger, more challenging forms. A sapphic stanza is an unrhymed stanza of Greek origin consisting of three sapphic lines (composed of two trochees and a dactyl followed by two more trochees) and a final line termed an adonic (a dactyl and a trochee). A spondee may replace the trochee in the first and second line at the second and fifth foot or in line three at the third foot. Steele chooses or invents new forms for each poem, particularly favoring intricately rhymed nine-line stanzas, with one unrhymed line, and tetrameters.

In *Sapphics against Anger* the title poem is concerned with the destructiveness of uncontrolled emotions:

> ''That fellow, at the slightest provocation,
> Slammed phone receivers down, and waved his arms like
> A madman. What Attila did to Europe,
>   What Genghis Khan did

> To Asia, that poor dope did to his marriage.''

> May I, that is, put learning to good purpose,
> Mindful that melancholy is a sin, though
>   Stylish at present.

While praising "the prudent heart" and holding introspection at a distance as potentially self-damaging, Steele seems unable to forget himself, his desires, and the past. Although he knows that reaching for the ideal is illusionary and leads to frustration, Steele remains haunted. Each poem is more a declaration of intent than a record of contentment: "Old letters are reproaches, mute petitions / Unlosable in some desk drawer . . . they speak of / Now-jettisoned ambitions / And insecurities which passed for love . . . climates favorable to / Illusions not illusions any longer." Steele battens down the hatches tightly against self-destructive internal tempests and defends a small, tight territory of the self and what the self holds dear. "Snapshots for Posterity" out-Larkins Larkin in regarding an infant as an emblem of possible future despair: "May you one day chant, / 'Vanity, vanity,' / As a charm against / The chartering of hopes."

While having a taste for pastiche, tongue-in-cheek allusions, and the investing of significance in the trivia of ordinary life, Steele is more at home with abstract and philosophical ideas than with hedonist pleasures. His poems require thought, analysis, and awareness. The Donne-like display of philosophical terms, distinctions, analogies, and logic chopping is evidence of a mind shaping experience by conceptualizing and drawing conclusions. Steele is a strongly metaphysical poet who thinks in verse; his poems have a logical, argumentative structure. In "Love Poem," for example, the chaotic formlessness of silence and self-conscious alienation is rejected in favor of order, self-definition, form, and articulation:

> If, like poor Pierrot, I've anxiously
>   Dwelt in my life, the spell is broken.
> Awakened to your touch and voice, I see
> That evil is the formless and unspoken,
> And that peace rests in form and nomenclature,
> Which render our two natures—formerly
> Discomfited, self-conscious—second nature.

Sapphics against Anger includes "Chanson Philosophique," a jeu d'esprit in which nominalist and realist perspectives on identity are ingeniously opposed to reach the paradoxical conclusion that whatever happens "has occurred / often and never."

For Steele the excesses of romantic art and emotion reflect dangerously unformed personalities. Knowing but fearing the obsessive and the uncharted, he aspires to clarity, structure, controlled boundaries, and the defined. While his case against the formlessness of romanticism is similar to that made by the modernists, he regards modernism as a further descent into the inferno of chaos and desire. Decisions must be taken, ambitions curbed, an identity established. In a poem about *Last Tango in Paris,* he says, "All life conspires to define us, / Weighing us down with who we are," but "Blisses anonymously pursued / Destroy us" or are never enjoyed. Only "in some less fallen world" might life gracefully contain the strong emotions given formal shape by classical art:

> Like-what?—like Haydn's symphonies,
> Structures of balanced contradictions,
> For all their evident restrictions,
> Crazy with lightness and desire.

Such poetics explain the explosive contrary elements present but controlled in Steele's poems.

The Color Wheel describes the poet's experience living and teaching in Los Angeles. The city becomes a figure for conditions of life that are disorienting, cut off from the past, but not without moral and aesthetic interest. "December in Los Angeles" begins with the lines "The tulip bulbs rest darkly in the fridge / To get the winter they can't get outside . . . ." Memory and artifice, the memory of a rural childhood and the daedal craft of his art, enable Steele to construct a life in the postmodern desert. Because the city is in perpetual flux, the poet must exercise his skills of adaptation:

> A *miracle!* we say, astonished at life,
>   And, given time, our briefcase in hand,
> We hurry to work and savor clattering
>   Through the makeshift tunnel that detours
> The sidewalk out around a construction sight,
>   The fresh plywood springy underfoot.

The syllabism brings an experimental aspect to the verse, quite in keeping with the shifting look and feel of Los Angeles. At such moments Steele reminds us that American formalism can have its Emersonian side, an openness to the flight of events, a restlessness and whimsicality in its lines.

—Bruce King and Lee Oser

STEPANCHEV, Stephen

Nationality: American. **Born:** Mokrin, Yugoslavia, 30 January 1915; immigrated to the United States, 1922; naturalized, 1938. **Education:** University of Chicago, A.B. 1937 (Phi Beta Kappa), M.A. 1938; New York University, Ph.D. 1950. **Military Service:** U.S. Army, 1941–45; Bronze Star. **Career:** Instructor in English, Purdue University, Lafayette, Indiana, 1938–41; New York University, 1946–47, 1948–49; member of the English department, 1949–64, and professor of English, Queens College, Flushing, New York, 1964–85. Fulbright professor of American literature, University of Copenhagen, spring 1957. **Awards:** Society of Midland Authors prize (*Poetry,* Chicago), 1937; National Endowment for the Arts grant, 1968; Oscar Blumental prize (*Poetry,* Chicago), 1995; Poet Laureate of the Borough of Queens, New York City, 1997–2000. **Address:** 140–60 Beech Avenue, Apartment 3C, Flushing, New York 11355, U.S.A.

PUBLICATIONS

Poetry

Three Priests in April. Baltimore, Contemporary Poetry, 1956.
Spring in the Harbor. Flushing, New York, Amity Press, 1967.
Vietnam. Los Angeles, Black Sparrow Press, 1968.
A Man Running in the Rain. Los Angeles, Black Sparrow Press, 1969.
The Mind. Los Angeles, Black Sparrow Press, 1972.
The Mad Bomber. Los Angeles, Black Sparrow Press, 1972.
Mining the Darkness. Los Angeles, Black Sparrow Press, 1975.
Medusa and Others. Los Angeles, Black Sparrow Press, 1975.
The Dove in the Acacia (bilingual edition, translation by Rasa Popov).
     Vrsac, Yugoslavia, KOV, 1977.

What I Own. Santa Barbara, California, Black Sparrow Press, 1978.
Descent. Roslyn, New York, Stone House Press, 1988.
Seven Horizons. Washington, D.C., Orchises Press, 1997.

Other

Dreiser among the Critics: A Study of American Reactions to the Work of a Literary Naturalist, 1900–1949. Folcroft, Pennsylvania, Folcroft Library Editions, 1972.
American Poetry since 1945: A Critical Survey. New York, Harper, 1965.
The Walt Whitman Lectures, with John Tytell. Flushing, New York, Friends of the Queens College Library, 1993.

Editor, *The People's College on the Hill: Fifty Years at Queens College, 1937–1987.* Flushing, New York, Queens College Press, 1990.

*

Critical Study: In *Poetry,* CLXV(3), December 1994.

*   *   *

A New York poet-professor, Stephen Stepanchev writes lucid, urbane poems that depict dreams or cityscapes, remember parents or childhood, recount quarrels with a lover, or observe a fellow victim of life with sympathy. Mostly they are first-person poems, and usually the speaker is a wry, detached observer: "The telephone squatted all day / In the equilibrium of indifference. / No one called that wrong number, / Me, poking among dead men's words" ("A Visit"). The poems rely for their energy on a rapid montage of images rendered in a succession of simple declarative sentences without much rhythmic intensity. (Like much contemporary image-centered poetry, they might well be translations.) The images are usually clever, seldom memorable. "November withdraws like a junkie," he writes, or "I was of two minds, like traffic," or "I live in the rice paddies of my desperation." One registers the effect, admires the invention, and passes on unmoved. Sometimes one cannot even admire; "Yesterday I poured gasoline all over myself / And flamed like a monk / To move you" seems both lurid and unpleasantly exploitative.

Still, the general effect is an agreeable one, well represented by the following complete poem, from *The Mad Bomber,* called "In the Gallery":

Repetition makes a garden,
But these roses are, clearly, unemployed.
Nature does so much better than this painter
I am expected to admire. My attention
Wanders to a gallery guest whose hair
Is a lair of lights, whose face dreams
Like a wheat field, and whose eyes glisten
With tears induced by her contact lenses.
I mix her in my martini and drink
Her down at the window overlooking the East
River, where the moon is breaking up in shivers.

—Seamus Cooney

STEPHENS, Alan (Archer)

Nationality: American. **Born:** Greeley, Colorado, 19 December 1925. **Education:** University of Colorado, Boulder, 1946–48; University of Denver, Colorado, A.B., M.A. 1950; Stanford University, California; University of Missouri, Columbia, Ph.D. 1954. **Military Service:** U.S. Army Air Force, 1943–45. **Family:** Married Frances Jones in 1948; three sons. **Career:** Assistant professor of English, Arizona State University, Tempe, 1954–58; assistant professor, 1959–63, associate professor, 1963–67, and then professor of English, University of California, Santa Barbara. **Awards:** Swallow Press New Poetry Series award, 1957. **Address:** Department of English, University of California, Santa Barbara, California 93106, U.S.A.

PUBLICATIONS

Poetry

The Sum. Denver, Swallow, 1958.
Between Matter and Principle. Denver, Swallow, 1963.
The Heat Lightning. Brunswick, Maine, Bowdoin College Museum of Art, 1967.
Tree Meditation and Others. Chicago, Swallow Press, 1970.
White River Poems. Chicago, Swallow Press, 1975.
In Plain Air: Poems 1958–1980. Chicago, Swallow Press, 1982.
Goodbye Matilija. Albuquerque, New Mexico, Living Batch Press, 1992.
The White Boat and Some Other Poems. Kalamazoo, Michigan, The Buckner Press, 1995.
Away from the Road: Poems. Albuquerque, New Mexico, Living Batch Press, 1998.

Other

Editor, *Selected Poems,* by Barnabe Googe. Denver, Swallow, 1961.

*

Critical Study: "Matthew Flamm Praises Alan Stephens's *Tree Meditation and Others,*" in *Poetry East* (Chicago), 34, fall 1992.

Alan Stephens comments:

The longer one goes on writing poems the more clear it becomes that the best work is done only with the help of a stroke or two of good luck.

*   *   *

Alan Stephens is a nature poet. His main interest has been to render nature faithfully, but as a realization of a meditative response that answers to the sensibility in natural objects. He seeks an effect similar to that of Wordsworth's early "Influence of Natural Objects." Stephens has remarked about his own poems that they are "descriptive meditations rather than meditative descriptions . . ." To this end he wishes his poetry naked, the form invariably open, the expression spare. His utterances are, however, either clipped directions, like a dramatist's for the setting of scenes, or discursive meanderings, too often simple only for being denuded of figurative speech. An example is the following stanza from ''A Breath'':

> A quiet, cool, spring morning—
> the sun up, and its light
> crossing things without emphasis,
> merely bringing out the pale colors.

Of course, the limitations of this manner are sometimes quite successfully accommodated to a larger context, as in ''Home Rock.''

While society and socially conscious or sophisticated speech are almost entirely absent from Stephens's quiet poetry, his work is effective in those instances in which domestic man is projected against a natural backdrop. In such cases he usually works with a motif of black and white, of darkness and tenuously comforting light. Meditating on the omnivorous incursion of dark space even into his own beard, the speaker of ''To Fran'' achieves this minimal consolation:

> it must be we belong in it—at once remotely
> and intimately; the way a sheepherder's fire at night belongs
> in the distance on a desert upland.

And returning from the moonlit night and ''the black shadow of the house,'' the speaker of ''Sounds'' reports that ''I go back in, and hunch over / The familiar hiss of my pencil tip / Racing across the lighted page.''

—David M. Heaton

STERN, Gerald

Nationality: American. **Born:** Pittsburgh, Pennsylvania, 22 February 1925. **Education:** University of Pittsburgh, B.A. 1947; Columbia University, New York, M.A. 1949. **Military Service:** U.S. Army Air Corps. **Family:** Married Patricia Miller in 1952 (divorced); one daughter and one son. **Career:** Instructor, Temple University, Philadelphia, 1957–63; professor, Indiana University of Pennsylvania, Indiana, 1963–67, and Somerset County College, Somerville, New Jersey, 1968–82; faculty member, Writers' Workshop, University of Iowa, Iowa City, 1982–94. Visiting poet, Sarah Lawrence College, Bronxville, New York, 1977; visiting professor, University of Pittsburgh, 1978, Columbia University, 1980, Bucknell University, Lewisburg, Pennsylvania, spring 1988, and New York University, fall 1989; distinguished chair, University of Alabama, University, 1984; Fanny Hurst Professor, Washington University, St. Louis, fall 1985; Bain Swiggert Chair, Princeton University, New Jersey, fall 1989; poet-in-residence, Bucknell University, spring 1994. Since 1973 consultant in literature, Pennsylvania Arts Council, Harrisburg. **Awards:** National Endowment for the Arts grant, 1976, 1981, 1987; Lamont Poetry Selection award, 1977; State of Pennsylvania creative writing grant, 1979; Pennsylvania Governor's award, 1980; Guggenheim fellowship, 1980; Bess Hokin award (*Poetry,* Chicago), 1980; Bernard F. Connor award, 1981; Melville Caine award, 1982; Jerome J. Shestack prize, 1984; fellowship, Academy of American Poets, 1993. **Address:** Creative Writing Program, Department of English, University of Iowa, Iowa City, Iowa 52242, U.S.A.

PUBLICATIONS

Poetry

The Naming of Beasts and Other Poems. West Branch, Iowa, Cummington Press, 1973.
Rejoicings. Fredericton, New Brunswick, Fiddlehead, 1973; Los Angeles, Metro, 1984.
Lucky Life. Boston, Houghton Mifflin, 1977.
The Red Coal. Boston, Houghton Mifflin, 1981.
Paradise Poems. New York, Random House, 1984.
Lovesick. New York, Harper, 1987.
Leaving Another Kingdom: Selected Poems. New York, Harper, 1990.
Two Long Poems. Pittsburgh, Carnegie Mellon University Press. 1990.
Bread without Sugar. New York, Norton, 1992.
Odd Mercy. New York, Norton, 1995.
This Time: New and Selected Poems. New York, Norton, 1998.
Last Blue: Poems. New York, Norton, 2000.

Recording: *Rotten Angel,* Watershed, 1989.

*

Critical Studies: Gerald Stern issue of *Poetry East* (Ripon, Wisconsin), fall 1988; *Making the Light Come: The Poetry of Gerald Stern* by Jane Somerville, Detroit, Wayne State University Press, 1990; ''Explaining, Explaining: A Conversation with Gerald Stern, Parts I & II'' by Leslie Kelen, in *Boulevard,* 7(2–3), spring 1992; ''American Latitude'' by Calvin Bedient, in *Southern Review* (Baton Rouge, Louisiana), 29(4), autumn 1993; ''New Jerusalems: Contemporary Jewish American Poets and the Puritan Tradition'' by Jonathan N. Barron, in *The Calvinist Roots of the Modern Era,* edited by Aliki Barnstone, Michael Tomasek Manson, and Carol J. Singley, Hanover, New Hampshire, University Press of New England, 1997; ''The Poetry of Gerald Stern'' by Mark Hillringhouse, in *Literary Review* (Madison, New Jersey), 40(2), winter 1997; *The Terror of Our Days: Sylvia Plath, William Heyen, Gerald Stern, and Jerome Rothenberg Poetically Respond to Holocaust* (dissertation) by Harriet Abbey Leibowitz Parmet, Lehigh University, 1998; interview with Gary Pacernick, in *American Poetry Review* (Philadelphia), 27(4), July-August 1998.

Gerald Stern comments:

(1980) If I could choose one poem of mine to explain my stance, or my artistic position, it would be ''The One Thing in Life,'' which appears in *Lucky Life.* In this poem I stake out a place for myself, so to speak, that was overlooked or ignored or disdained, a place no one else wanted. I mean this in a psychological and metaphorical and philosophical sense. The poem is short, so I will quote it:

> Wherever I go now I lie down on my own bed of straw
> and bury my face in my own pillow.
> I can stop in any city I want to
> and pull the stiff blanket up to my chin.
> It's easy now, walking up a flight of carpeted stairs
> and down a hall past the painted fire doors.
> It's easy bumping my knees on a rickety table

and bending down to a tiny sink.
There is a sweetness buried in my mind;
there is water with a small cave behind it;
there's a mouth speaking Greek.
It is what I keep to myself; what I return to;
the one thing that no one else wanted.

When I think about the place "no one else wanted," I think of an abandoned or despised area. I think of weeds, a ruin, a desert, but I think of these things not as remote in time or place from that which is familiar and cherished and valuable—our civilization—but as things that lie just under the surface and just out of eyesight. And I think especially of the dynamic and ironic interpenetration of the two. Thus, my poetry is concerned a great deal with opposites—city-country, present-past, civilization-savagery, powerful-weak, well known-obscure—and is often dualistic in nature, though it is not informed in any formal sense by a philosophical or religious principle of dualism. (I clearly favor the "weaker" of the two, but I have affection for both.) Ultimately the "abandoned" place is a state of mind, or an energy state or a condition, that is within me, and I merely am reaching out for "examples" to approximate this state.

Another aspect of the poetry is that of rebirth or regeneration. A great many of my poems are concerned with rebirth, and I find that the spring season, the time of rebirth, and those holidays and celebrations, religious and otherwise, that relate to rebirth are important in my poems: "God of Rain, God of Water" and "The Sensitive Knife" from *Lucky Life* and "In Kovalchick's Garden" and "The Blessed" from *Rejoicings*.

I have been living for the last 10 years on the Delaware River, near Easton, Pennsylvania, less than two hours away from Philadelphia or New York City. I find myself spending a lot of time in the city and writing about it, as well as in the country, and I find that the relationship of these two is an embodiment of my underlying myth, so that I am living life symbolically even as I live it literally. Thus when I write of the literal, I am simultaneously writing symbolically, and the language, which is precise and descriptive, takes on overtones and layers. Several critics, confused by my exact and literal observations, insofar as what I was describing was not common knowledge, mistakenly described me as a surrealist poet.

I find, especially recently, that I am moved a great deal by Jewish mysticism and Chasidism, but I am not unaware that these are parts of huge historical systems that involve commitments and obligations and that I am in a sense "tasting" from the banquet of Judaism those delicacies that suit me. I do believe, though, that, even if I do not practice the ritual, I realize, whether I mention him specifically or not, the lot of the Jew in history and embody him and his spirit in my poems.

I have discovered that my poetry is prized because it comes so much to life orally, and I have discovered that I am a success as a reader. I put it this way because I did not start off intending my poems to be part of the oral revolution of recent American poetry. I believe my poems stand by themselves on the page, but I am delighted, also, to find how well they work out loud.

I am not sure who my precursors are, who has influenced me the most. I am delighted to live in an age without masters. Many commentators have remarked about the closeness to Whitman, particularly in the formal structure, but I ascribe that to our mutual reading in the Scriptures, and as regards anaphora and other poetic devices or strategies, they come more from my reading of the prophets and Psalms than from "Song of Myself." Indeed, though I love Whitman, I feel closer if anything to Dickinson, just as I feel as close to Elizabeth Bishop as I do to Theodore Roethke.

(1990) Since I have moved to Iowa in the early 1980s, there has been a shifting both in the music and the content of my poetry, though I do not know whether to ascribe it to the changed geographic locality or a change that results inevitably from the passing of time. I move around a lot. I am not fixed with family and location the way I formerly was, so the voyage is different. I think my poems now are more baroque, more afield, and sometimes less given to explication as they grow less rooted, and they may be more philosophical, even religious, in tone, even as they retain the same political base. They are, if anything, though, a modification, not a radical reversal. The loyalties are the same, the voice is the same, and, if anything, there is even more of an obsession with the past, with Jewish roots, with time, and a commitment to the world as it is, the beloved physical world that is our gift.

(1995) My most recent poems go into areas whose source, frankly, I am unsure of. I search for more and more freedom; I let the spirit take me. Yet I continue to love the concrete and the particular. In terms of form, I would put it that my language, and even my syntax, even as it reaches for new structures, is deeply grounded, and I am thinking joyously and deliberately about form in a stronger way than I have for years, as I try to re-create it.

But what is important to me in poetry is what I understand and what I say, and as I get ready to finish six decades of life on this beautiful earth, I find myself returning more and more to the idea of justice, even as I did in my second decade. And I see justice not only as reflecting moral states and systems but as that which is altogether and only and specifically human, thus the rarest and most original thing amongst our billions of stars. I see it, therefore, as having metaphysical and mystical overtones and as something not banal but hardly expressed as yet, that imagined state that the great early prophets, Isaiah and Amos and Jesus, already understood as they tried to drag us with them in their great love for us. My poetry is about this.

It is, therefore, a life-and-death matter. But it is always, and only, music. It is only music I am interested in. The music of poetry.

*   *   *

Gerald Stern's deeply felt poetry is written in the confessional mode practiced by such other contemporary poets as Ginsberg and Ferlinghetti, and in company with them he continues the American romantic tradition of Walt Whitman, with its emphasis on the writer himself as a contemporary everyman and its celebration of place. But Stern uses his narrative and emotional self-portraiture to create a uniquely detailed central figure or speaker, and his America is rendered with biblical intensity and a Judaic sense of time and loss.

Van Gogh ("Against the Whirling Lines, / Small and powerful in the hands of the Blue God," from "Self-Portrait") becomes a vivid counterpart figure for Stern himself as wanderer and artist. But as Stern travels in his own personal landscape, the journeys are usually return journeys and the places visited effaced by time. "Straus Park," with its specific references, is an especially vivid example:

If you know about the Babylonian Jews
coming back to their stone houses in Jerusalem . . .
then you must know how I felt when I saw Stanley's
    Cafeteria
boarded up and the sale sign out.

"On the Island," "Four Sad Poems on the Delaware," and "County Line Road" present similar metaphors of time in rural settings, and Stern brings both the rural and urban aspects of his world together in "One Foot in the River": "Going to New York I carry the river in my head / and match it with the flow on 72nd Street and the flow on Broadway."

Like Whitman and the poets of the beat generation, Stern makes considerable use of repetition for rhetorical effect. But the repetitions work in other ways as well. In the central poem "Lucky Life" they emphasize an ironic optimism and the importance of survival without illusion, but it is survival enhanced by tradition and by the recurring rituals of everyday life. The return journeys are, of course, also repetitions. The final lines of "Let Me Please Look into My Window" seem to summarize Stern's view of all such wanderings: "Let me wake up happy, let me know where I am, let me lie still, / as we turn left, as we cross the water, as we leave the light."

—Gaynor F. Bradish

STEVENS, Peter

Nationality: Canadian. **Born:** Manchester, Lancashire, England, 17 November 1927. **Education:** Burnage High School, Manchester, graduated 1946; Nottingham University, B.A. (honors) in English, Cert.Ed. 1951; McMaster University, Hamilton, Ontario, 1963–64, M.A. 1963; University of Saskatchewan, Saskatoon, Ph.D. 1968. **Family:** Married June Sidebotham in 1957; two daughters and one son. **Career:** Schoolteacher in England, 1951–57; chair of the department of English, Hillfield College, Hamilton, Ontario, 1957–64; lecturer, Extension Division, McMaster University, 1961–64; assistant professor of English, University of Saskatchewan, 1964–69. Associate professor, 1969–73, professor of English, 1973–97, and since 1997 professor emeritus, University of Windsor, Ontario. Poetry editor, *Canadian Forum,* Toronto, 1968–73; director and editor, Sesame Press, Windsor, 1974–81; jazz columnist, *Windsor Star,* 1973–90; poetry editor, *Literary Review of Canada,* 1993–98. **Awards:** Canada Council award, 1969. **Address:** 2055 Richmond Street, Windsor, Ontario, N8Y 1L3, Canada.

PUBLICATIONS

Poetry

Plain Geometry. Toronto, Ganglia Press, 1968.
Nothing But Spoons. Montreal, Delta Canada, 1969.
A Few Myths. Vancouver, Talonbooks, 1971.
Breadcrusts and Glass. Fredericton, New Brunswick, Fiddlehead, 1972.
Family Feelings and Other Poems. Guelph, Ontario, Alive Press, 1974.
Momentary Stay. London, Ontario, Killaly Press, 1974.
And the Dying Sky Like Blood: A Bethune Collage for Several Voices. Ottawa, Borealis Press, 1974.
The Bogman Pavese Tactics. Fredericton, New Brunswick, Fiddlehead, 1977.
And All That Jazz. Toronto, League of Canadian Poets, 1980.
Coming Back. Windsor, Ontario, Sesame Press, 1981.

Revenge of the Mistresses. Windsor, Ontario, Black Moss Press, 1981.
Out of the Willow Trees. Saskatoon, Saskatchewan, Thistledown Press, 1986.
Swimming in the Afternoon: Selected Poems of Peter Stevens. Windsor, Ontario, Black Moss Press, 1992.
Rip Rap: Yorkshire Ripper Poems. Windsor, Ontario, Black Moss Press, 1995.
Thinking into the Dark. Calgary, Alberta, Bayeux Arts Press, 1997.
Attending to This World. Windsor, Ontario, Black Moss Press, 1998.

Other

Modern English-Canadian Poetry: A Guide to Information Sources Detroit, Gale, 1978.
Miriam Waddington and Her Work. Toronto, ECW Press, 1984.
Dorothy Livesay: Patterns in a Poetic Life. Toronto, ECW Press, 1992.

Editor, *The McGill Movement: A.J.M Smith, F.R. Scott, and Leo Kennedy.* Toronto, Ryerson Press, 1969.
Editor, with J.L. Granatstein, *Forum: Canadian Life and Letters 1920–1970: Selections from "The Canadian Forum."* Toronto, University of Toronto Press, 1972.
Editor, *The First Day of Spring: Stories and Other Prose,* by Raymond Knister. Toronto, University of Toronto Press, 1976.

*

Manuscript Collections: University of Saskatchewan, Saskatoon; McMaster University, Hamilton, Ontario.

Critical Studies: By Robert Thacker, in *Biography,* 17(1), winter 1994; in *Canadian Literature,* 144, 1995.

Peter Stevens comments:

I deal with the local landscape and places: the prairie, its place in my own personal and family life, its past, its geologic history, its mythology. I write usually in free verse paragraphs and have experimented with some concrete forms, a method of using anagrams I call Anagrammatics. General influences are simply Canada and being Canadian. Canadian writers I admire and whose work has probably made an impression on mine are Al Purdy and Earle Birney. I admire the technical facility of Auden and early Ezra Pound. I have paid attention to the North Americanness of W.C. Williams, particularly as it emerges in a Canadian manner in the poetry of W.W.E. Ross and Raymond Souster. More recently I have responded in my work to four American poets: Henry Taylor, Jack Gilbert, Stephen Dunn, and Stephen Dobyns.

*   *   *

Peter Stevens is a poet who at once reflects the immigrant tradition and the strong regionalism of Canadian poetry. Emigrating from Britain to Canada, he brought with him a poetic sensibility influenced by the low-toned English writing of the 1950s. That sensibility has since been modified by Canadian experience, not only of daily life but also of the literary ambience. The result is a manner that is undramatic, deliberately uncolorful but, rather like an early spring landscape on the prairies where Stevens spent much of his time in Canada, slowly revealing of subtleties of perception and tone, pleasing gradations in the range of gray and brown.

Stevens finally settled in Windsor, Ontario, and became the center of a small poetic group there, and for a time he enjoyed a certain national standing as poetry editor of *Canadian Forum.* It is with southern Ontario poets that his affinities seem to lie.

Significantly, Stevens himself recognizes the influence on him of Canadian imagists like W.W.E. Ross and Raymond Souster. As with these poets, there is little metaphorical or adjectival color in Stevens's poems. The images are meant to speak dryly for themselves, as in the opening lines of ''Fuschia'':

> blood drops belled
> hanging in hedges
> above the bay curved
> under cliffs I remember
> an island in my past . . . .

Indeed, there are times when Stevens is very explicit about the role of the poet as observer rather than commentator. This is evident, for example, in the poem ''Seeing Is Seeing Is Believing,'' from his early collection *Breadcrusts and Glass:*

> A stalker lurches across the snow.
> His shadow stretches inhuman long
> across snow's glistening crust of ice.
>
> A rabbit sits stark still, then spurts away
> to black trees, dark lines blacker on the white,
> as this dense shadow slides into his eye.
>
> All I see is rabbit flashing into shadows
> away from stealthy shadow: no comment.
> The eye does not speak, it does not think . . .

While many poems seem to show Stevens's thoughtful perception of the natural world and little more, others have more depth. An example of the latter is *And the Dying Sky like Blood,* a suite based on the life and death of Norman Bethune, a Canadian hero in China. Here a social conscience and a political indignation are extended. There are other poems that show Stevens to be sharply aware of the anomalies and frustrations of the artistic life (a whole suite was written on painters), and in these there emerge an ironic, almost acerbic view of the self and, at times, a curious, questioning consciousness of literature as pretension. There is a strain of poetic populism in much of his work that leads Stevens at times to incorporate jazz themes and vulgar erotic elements into his poems.

—George Woodcock

STEVENSON, Anne (Katherine)

Nationality: American. **Born:** Cambridge, England, 3 January 1933. **Education:** University High School, Ann Arbor, Michigan, 1947–50; University of Michigan, Ann Arbor (Hopwood award, 1951, 1952,

1954), B.A. 1954 (Phi Beta Kappa), M.A. 1962; Radcliffe Institute, Cambridge, Massachusetts, 1970–71. **Family:** Married 1) R.L. Hitchcock in 1955 (divorced), one daughter; 2) Mark Elvin in 1962 (divorced), two sons; 3) Michael Farley (divorced); 4) Peter Lucas in 1987. **Career:** Schoolteacher, Lillesden School, Hawkhurst, Kent, 1955–56, Westminster School, Georgia, 1959–60, and Cambridge School, Weston, Massachusetts, 1961–62; advertising manager, A.& C. Black publishers, London, 1956–57; tutor, Extra-Mural Studies, University of Glasgow, 1970–73; counselor, Open University, Paisley, Renfrew, 1972–73; writing fellow, University of Dundee, 1973–75; fellow, Lady Margaret Hall, Oxford, 1975–77; writer-in-residence, Bulmershe College, Reading, Berkshire, 1977–78, and University of Edinburgh, 1987–89. Co-founder, with Michael Farley and Alan Halsey, Poetry Bookshop, Hay-on-Wye, Powys, 1979. Northern Arts Literary Fellow, Newcastle and Durham, 1981–82 and 1984–85. Founding co-editor, *Other Poetry,* Leicester, 1978–83, Mid-Day Publications, Oxford, and Other Poetry Editions. Member of the Literature Panel, Arts Council, 1983–85; board member, Poetry Book Society, London, 1986–88. **Awards:** Scottish Arts Council bursary, 1973; Southern Arts bursary, 1978; Welsh Arts Council bursary, 1981; Athena award, University of Michigan, 1990. Fellow, Royal Society of Literature, 1978, and University of Michigan Institute for the Humanities, 1993. **Address:** 30 Logan Street, Langley Park, Durham DH7 9YN, England.

PUBLICATIONS

Poetry

Living in America. Ann Arbor, Michigan, Generation Press, 1965.
Reversals. Middletown, Connecticut, Wesleyan University Press, 1969.
Correspondences: A Family History in Letters. Middletown, Connecticut, Wesleyan University Press, and London, Oxford University Press, 1974.
Travelling behind Glass: Selected Poems 1963–1973. London, Oxford University Press, 1974.
A Morden Tower Reading 3. Newcastle upon Tyne, Morden Tower, 1977.
Cliff Walk. Richmond, Surrey, Keepsake Press, 1977.
Enough of Green. London, Oxford University Press, 1977.
Sonnets for Five Seasons. Hereford, Five Seasons Press, 1979.
Minute by Glass Minute. Oxford, Oxford University Press, 1982.
Green Mountain, Black Mountain. Boston, Rowan Tree Press, 1982.
Turkish Rondo. Loughton, Essex, Piatkus, 1982.
Making Poetry. Oxford, Pisces Press, 1983.
A Legacy. Durham, Taxus Press, 1983.
Black Grate Poems. Oxford, Inky Parrot Press, 1984.
The Fiction-Makers. Oxford, Oxford University Press, 1985.
Winter Time. Ashington, Northumberland, MidNAG, 1986.
Selected Poems, 1956–1986. Oxford and New York, Oxford University Press, 1987.
The Other House. Oxford, Oxford University Press, 1990.
Four and a Half Dancing Men. Oxford and New York, Oxford University Press, 1993.
The Collected Poems of Anne Stevenson, 1955–1995. Oxford and New York, Oxford University Press, 1996.
Once upon a Time This Morning. New York, Greenwillow Books, 1997.

Plays

Radio Plays: *Correspondences,* 1975; *Child of Adam,* 1976.

Other

Elizabeth Bishop. New York, Twayne, 1966; London, Collins, 1967.
Bitter Fame: A Life of Sylvia Plath. Boston, Houghton Mifflin, and London, Viking, 1989.
Five Looks at Elizabeth Bishop. London, Bellew, 1998.
Between the Iceberg and the Ship: Selected Essays. Ann Arbor, University of Michigan Press, 1998.

Editor, *Selected Poems,* by Frances Bellerby. London, Enitharmon Press, 1986.
Editor, *The Poetry Book Society.* London, Hutchinson, 1991.
Editor, with Dannie Abse, *The Gregory Anthology.* London, Hutchinson, 1995.

*

Critical Studies: By Dorothy Donnelly, in *Michigan Quarterly Review* (Ann Arbor), fall 1966 and April 1971; by Jay Parini, in *Lines Review* 50 (Edinburgh), September 1974, and in *Ploughshares* (Cambridge), autumn 1978; "The Transitory Walker: Feeling for Continuities in the Poetry" by Dewi Stephen Jones, in *New Welsh Review* (Lampeter), autumn 1989; "The Plath Myth and the Reviewing of Bitter Fame" by Olwyn Hughes, in *Poetry Review* (London), 80(3), autumn 1990; "Dark Corners: On Poetry and Melancholy" by Stephen Wilson, in *Encounter,* 74(3), April 1990; "A Chev'ril Glove" by the author, in *The Poet's Voice and Craft,* edited by C.B. McCully, Manchester, Carcanet, 1994; "A Woman of Letters: History vs. Fiction in Anne Stevenson's 'Correspondences'—A Family History in Letters" by Tiina Sarisalmi, in *English Studies and History,* edited by David Robertson, Tampere, Finland, University of Tampere, 1994; "Responses to Elizabeth Bishop: Anne Stevenson, Eavan Boland and Jo Shapcott" by David G. Williams, in *English* (Leicester, England), 44(180), autumn 1995; "Poems of Innocence and Experience" by Richard Tillinghast, in *Michigan Quarterly Review* (Ann Arbor), 37(4), fall 1998.

Anne Stevenson comments:

Each of my collections, I suspect, represents a chapter in a quest for a poetry both personal and responsible, at once truthful, passionate, and carefully crafted. In the 1960s I was questioning the assumptions I had grown up with: what was good, what was evil, what was love, what was responsibility, by what freedom of will could I choose my life? In *Correspondences* I set forth the drama of my own (and some of America's) internal contradictions. I emerged into the near nihilism of *Enough of Green* when I was living in Oxford and then rejected academia for the visionary release of *Minute by Glass Minute* in the Welsh border country. For a time I considered myself to be a "religious poet," but ultimately I decided the attractions of absolute belief were a delusion. *The Fiction-Makers* is a set of variations on a theme by Shakespeare-cum-Bentham: all the world's a stage, and all we can truly believe—even, perhaps, in mathematics and the natural sciences—are our own ideas. Writing a biography of Sylvia Plath convinced me that poetry today is at a turning point. Nostalgic wistfulness, individual self-pity, political idealism, angst, fury, vindictiveness, all the emotional magnets of the romantics, are, in the last analysis, fictions. They have been replaced in poetry, in the twentieth century, chiefly by abstract experiment with language, which, of course, is starvation fare for poets. *The Other House* is an attempt at a new departure; it is a slender book of poems, but I like to think it makes its peace with language and that it finally turns away from the mirrors of self-interest and begins to look out the window.

*   *   *

"We were the very landscape / We walked through," Anne Stevenson wrote in her first volume, *Living in America.* The correspondence of physical and moral landscapes has recurred throughout her work, whether the "landscape without regrets" of the Sierra Nevada (*Reversals*), the modest frugality of Cambridge and the Fens, or the isolation and asperity of the northeast coast of Scotland, which is the setting for most of the poems in *Enough of Green.* "Living in America" describes a continent that threatens its residents, its two shores "hurrying towards each other" while "desperately the inhabitants hoped to be saved in the middle, / Pray to the mountains and deserts to keep them apart." "The Suburb" gives human face to this fear—a sullen and domesticated defeatism that says, "Better / to lie still and let the babies run through me"—while "The Women" quietly records a similar suppression in its picture of "women, waiting, waiting for their husbands, / sit[ting] among dahlias all the afternoons, / while quiet processional seasons drift and subside at their doors like dunes."

But much of Stevenson's poetry has been a revolt against this tyranny of the environment over the self. *Correspondences: A Family History in Letters* traces 150 years in the life of the Chandler family on both sides of the Atlantic. In the last letter of the volume the fictitious poetess Kay Boyd writes to her father from London of her flight from the United States: "'Nowhere is safe.' / It is a poem I can't continue. / It is America I can't contain." Flight here involves refusing "the tug back" of "allegiance to innocence which is not there," deliberately leaving it unclear whether it is innocence or allegiance that is lacking. The "correspondences" of the title are in one sense those between the unsustainable poetic project and the unimaginable magnitude of America. But in the letters themselves new correspondences emerge as successive generations live through corresponding dilemmas, flights, and returns, sometimes unwittingly using the same language to describe their plights. Thus Kay's sister, Eden, writes to her of a recurring nightmare after their mother's death, asking her to come home in words that echo their ancestor Reuben Chandler, a prodigal son writing in 1832 to his father, a Vermont minister, of his own wish to return. Kay's desire to "make amends for what was not said," not just in her own relationship with her parents but also through all the fraught generations of her family, to "do justice to the living, to the dead," likewise recalls the earlier father writing to his errant daughter in Yorkshire, mourning a husband lost at sea. Preferring, in her father's words, "the precarious apartments of the world / to the safer premises of the spirit," his daughter nevertheless chooses a fall from grace that brings a profounder suffering than he, in his naive self-righteousness, can ever know. Kay Boyd, having the last word in the book, makes it clear that this is a price worth paying.

Travelling behind Glass attempts to justify this peripatetic living as a conscious moral choice. The title poem toys with residence, imagining "a heart at grass" among the "predictable greens" of an accepted landscape but opts instead for "the paranoid howl of the / highway," where the "carapace" of the car becomes a symbol of the freewheeling will that prefers even the risk of madness to domesticity.

The theme of renunciation is reiterated in *Enough of Green*. This volume makes it clear that it is precisely the green world of the senses (''love grown rank as seeding grass'') that has to be renounced in favor of the steely, ascetic discipline of an art that has replaced the Christian God as taskmaster. There is in all of Stevenson's poetry an extremist's desire for the sterility and outrage of the puritan's scalpel. What makes the Scottish landscape so attractive is its sense of life as stress and erosion, an attrition that uncovers the essential contours of a mind and a place.

There is a certain relentlessness of imagination, a dogged, insistent quality, to Stevenson's poetry, but it is protected from the stridency of those ''intense shrill / ladies and gaunt, fanatical burnt out old women,'' whose fate she clearly fears in ''Coming Back to Cambridge'' and elsewhere, by both an elegiac sadness and a sly, wicked wit. The former is revealed in those poems that speak of love as the ''remorseless joy of dereliction'' (''Ragwort''), a song made out of deprivation and loss; the latter appears in a poem such as ''Theme with Variations,'' with its cool worldliness.

Minute by Glass Minute uses landscape as the embodiment of contrary impulses. The sequence at its heart, ''Green Mountain, Black Mountain,'' contrasts the cold, green mountains of Vermont, where Stevenson spent her childhood, with the ''lusher Black Mountains of South Wales (rich in history and myth, but new to me)'' of later residence. In part an elegy for her American parents, it speculates on the dialectical tension of Old and New Worlds, puritan and hedonistic impulses, a landscape threaded with history compared with one still apparently inviolate. ''Threads,'' as a trope that links meaning, handwriting, stitching, and affiliation, runs through the sequence, raising questions about the larger impulse to establish connections, stitch together significances, that pervades the volume. The landscapes of the volume are damp, bedrizzled, and misted, and even summer is ''steamy'' with wet. Weather gets in the way of an eye that wants simplicity and transparency of meanings. In one poem Stevenson charges Blake with romantic obfuscation: ''How dare you inflict imagination on us! / What halo does the world deserve?'' But Stevenson also recognizes her own incompetence before a world that refuses meanings, where ''even my cat knows more about death than I do.'' She is driven to quiet fury by the inadequacy of words, unable to paint ''the mudness of mud'' or the ''cloudness of clouds.'' But this poem, ''If I Could Paint Essences,'' sums up the antitheses of her vision, admitting that just as she arrives at the ''true sightness of seeing'' she unexpectedly wants to play on ''cellos of metaphor'': ''And in such imaginings I lose sight of sight.'' Whatever else might be said, it is certainly true that Stevenson does not, in *Minute by Glass Minute,* lose sight either of words or of things.

—Stan Smith

STONE, Ruth

Nationality: American. **Born:** Roanoke, Virginia, 8 June 1915. **Education:** University of Illinois, Urbana; Harvard University, Cambridge, Massachusetts; Radcliffe Institute (now Bunting Institute), Cambridge, Massachusetts, 1963–65. **Family:** Married Walter B. Stone (died 1959); three daughters. **Career:** Seminar teacher, Radcliffe College, Cambridge, Massachusetts, 1963–65, and Wellesley College, Massachusetts, 1965; member of the department of English,

Brandeis University, Waltheim, Massachusetts, 1965–66; poet-in-residence, University of Wisconsin, Madison 1967–69; artist-in-residence, University of Illinois, Urbana 1971–73; visiting professor, Indiana University, Bloomington, 1973–74; Creative Writing Chair, Center College, Danville, Kentucky, winter 1975; Hurst Visiting Professor, Brandeis University, 1975; visiting professor, University of Virginia, Charlottesville, 1977–78; Regents Lecturer, spring 1978, and visiting lecturer, fall 1978, spring 1981, University of California, Davis; poet-in-residence, fall 1984, and visiting professor, fall 1985, spring 1986, New York University; adjunct professor, Cooper Union, New York, 1986; visiting professor, fall 1989, spring 1990, Old Dominion University, Norfolk, Virginia. Since 1990 professor of English and creative writing, State University of New York, Binghamton. **Awards:** Bess Hokin prize (*Poetry,* Chicago), 1954; *Kenyon Review* fellowship, 1956; Shelley memorial prize, 1964; Guggenheim fellowship, 1972, 1975–76; Delmore Schwartz award, 1983–84; Whiting award, 1986; Paterson prize, 1988. **Address:** R.F.D. 3, Brandon, Vermont 05733, U.S.A.

PUBLICATIONS

Poetry

In an Iridescent Time. New York, Harcourt Brace, 1959.
Topography and Other Poems. New York, Harcourt Brace, 1971.
Unknown Messages. Hindsboro, Illinois, Nemesis Press, 1973.
Cheap: New Poems and Ballads. New York, Harcourt Brace, 1975.
American Milk. Fanwood, New Jersey, From Here Press, 1986.
Second-Hand Coat: Poems New and Selected. Boston, Godine, 1987.
The Solution. Towson, Maryland, Alembic Press, 1989.
Who Is the Widow's Muse. Cambridge, Massachusetts, Yellow Moon Press, 1991.
Simplicity. Northampton, Massachusetts, Paris Press, 1995.
Ordinary Words. Ashfield, Massachusetts, Paris Press, 1999.

Recordings: *Ways of Survival,* Watershed, 1986; *A Movable Feast,* National Public Radio, 1987.

*

Critical Studies: ''On the Poetry of Ruth Stone: Selections and Commentary'' by Harvey Gross, in *Iowa Review* (Iowa City), 3, spring 1972; ''Interview: Ruth Stone'' by Sandra M. Gilbert, in *California Quarterly* (Davis), 10, Autumn 1975, and ''Sex Wars: Not the Fun Kind'' by Gilbert and Susan Gubar, in *New York Times Book Review,* 27, December 1987; ''A Room of Their Own'' by Patricia Blake, in *Time* (New York), 22 December 1980; ''On Ruth Stone'' by various authors, in *Extended Outlooks: The Iowa Review Collection of Contemporary Women Writers,* edited by Jane Cooper, Gwen Head, Adelaide Morris, and Marcia Southwick, New York, Collier, 1982; ''Six Women Poets'' by Geoffrey H. Hartman, in *Easy Pieces,* New York, Columbia University Press, 1985; ''Entire Histories'' by Donald Hall, in *Hungry Mind Review* (St. Paul, Minnesota), spring 1988; ''The Quiet Roar of Oxymorons'' by Frances Mayes, in *San Jose Mercury News,* 10 July 1988; ''Mourning Becomes Electric: Ruth Stone Digs Up the Past'' by Robyn Selman, in *Village Voice* (New York), 1 November 1988; ''Art in Obscurity'' by Julie Fay, in *Women's Review of Books* (Wellesley, Massachusetts), 6, July 1989; *The House Is Made of Poetry: The Art of Ruth Stone* edited by Wendy

Barker and Sandra Gilbert, Carbondale, Southern Illinois University Press, 1996; interview with J.F. Battaglia, in *Boulevard,* 12(1–2), winter 1997.

Ruth Stone comments:

I think my work is a natural response to my life. What I see and feel changes like a prism, moment to moment; a poem holds and illuminates. It is a small drama. I think, too, my poems are a release, a laughing at the ridiculous and songs of mourning, celebrating marriage and loss, all the sad baggage of our lives. It is so overwhelming, so complex. Outside the window here is teeming with life from far down in the soil to far up in the sky. Poems are a way of seeking patterns within this complexity.

*   *   *

Although at age forty-four she was no beginner when she published her first book, *In an Iridescent Time,* in 1959, Ruth Stone was working largely within the elegant, formal conventions of that era, showing her respect for the likes of Ransom and Stevens. Thus, along with many other women poets of the 1950s—for example, Sylvia Plath and Adrienne Rich—she began her career by expressing a female vision through a male medium.

Nevertheless, within the largely regular forms of these early poems there is heard a complex woman's voice compounded of the artful naïveté of fable and tale and the deceptive simplicity of a sophisticated artist. The voice is as responsive to marriage, family, and human solitude as it is to animals, landscapes, and seasons. Given to gorgeous diction, eloquent syntax, and powerful statement, along with occasional colloquialisms, the book contains nothing callow or unformed, although today it appears marked by a somewhat overdone artfulness. This impression is confirmed by Stone's own changes as she has developed and explored the various possibilities of her special voice.

There was a conspicuous silence of twelve years before Stone's next book, *Topography and Other Poems,* appeared, and the single most determinative cause of the hiatus—as well as of its fruit—must have been her poet-scholar husband's unexpected suicide in 1959 when they were in England, leaving Stone and her three daughters to fend for themselves. She returns repeatedly here and in subsequent volumes to this devastating experience, and without either over- or underplaying it she somehow manages to survive and grow strong, as Hemingway's Frederic Henry says, in the broken places. Thus, there is a deepening of her emotional range, accompanied as we would expect by a corresponding roughening of rhythm and diction.

The more general poetic and political rebellions of the 1960s were no doubt operative as well, but Stone never becomes programmatic. A Keatsian poet "of Sensations rather than of Thoughts"—although like Keats she is certainly not without thought—so busy is she with her responses to the pressures of the lived life that she cannot afford time for philosophizing or moralizing.

Stone's second volume deals with her first attempts to absorb her husband's death, her reactions to the people around her, her return with her daughters to the seasons of Vermont, her subsequent travels, and her continuing growth as a poet, mother, and person. She begins using more direct speech and unrhymed free verse lines of variable length, not, however, without her characteristic touches of elegance. In "Changing (For Marcia)" she writes to her eldest child, noticing the changes in her, and reflects, "Love cannot be still; / Listen. It's folly and wisdom; / Come and share."

That Stone had regained her voice and creative will at this time was shown four years later by the publication of *Cheap: New Poems and Ballads.* Here we find her risking relationships with others while still trying to deal with her husband's death and the loss of their life together, and she mines an iron vein of mordant wit to make bearable the bitterness. Some of her lines strike a late Plathian note of barely contained hysteria: "I hid sometimes in the closet among my own clothes" ("Loss"). But near a barn young bulls are bellowing ("Communion"), and solace is found in the germinative force of nature. "Cocks and Mares" concludes with a marvelous evocation of female power in wild mares.

Second-Hand Coat: Poems New and Selected, which came out in 1987, contains forty-six new poems. Along with exploring her evolving feelings about her lost husband, Stone probes more deeply into her childhood years and early family memories. Once again she balances between "fertility/futility" ("Pine Cones"), and in addition she reaches a new level of outrageous fantasy and satire. In "Some Things You'll Need to Know . . ." a "poetry factory" is described in which "the antiwar and human rights poems / are processed in the white room. / Everyone there wears sterile gauze."

The Solution, a chapbook of eighteen poems that came out two years later, in 1989, adds yet another new note—the emergence of Stone's other self, her doppelgänger, as in "The Rotten Sample." "Bird in the Gilbert's Tree" is truly remarkable, beginning with the question "What is that bird saying?" and continuing on to give in verbal form what is strictly nonverbal, a tour de force worthy of Lewis Carroll: "And you, my consort, my basket, / my broody decibels, / my lover in the lesser scales; / this is our tree, our vista, / our bagworms."

Who Is the Widow's Muse? makes of the doppelgänger a dramatic and structural device in a sequence of fifty-two relatively short lyrics (perhaps for a year's cycle), plus a prefatory poem as introduction. Here the muse, a realistic—not to say caustic—voice, serves to limit and control the operatic tendency of the widow's voice in her endless quest for ways to come to terms with her husband's death. As a result the tone is a miraculous blend of desolation and laughter, a unique achievement. At the end, when the widow wants to write "one more" poem about her loss, the muse "shakes her head" and, in an almost unbearably compassionate gesture, "took the widow in her arms." The poem concludes, "'Now say it with me', the muse said. / 'Once and for all . . . he is forever dead'." Thus is Stone solving, in her own particular way, the problem of expressing a female vision through a female idiom.

Stone's 1995 volume *Simplicity* contains the poems of *The Solution* as well as a hundred pages of later work. Some still deal with her husband, but the rest derive from an independent inspiration, although it is of a rather somber mood, for at the age of eighty Stone has grown into a deep knowledge of suffering and survival. Her range is broad as well, shifting in a moment from the common to the cosmic, from the ordinary to the surreal. Riding a train or bus, she notes the passage of weather and the seasons, the isolation of those beside her, and the small towns and shops sliding by. She is the poet of hope in the midst of doom, of love as it encounters death, and of the apocalypse forthcoming in the mundane. "The Artist" is revelatory, showing the painter in his own painting—an old oriental scroll—climbing a mountain to reach a temple. Although he has been walking all day, he will not get there before dark, "and yet there is no way to stop him. He is / still going up and he is still only half way."

Four years later Stone published *Ordinary Words,* a new, beautiful full-length collection. Although she continues with many of her customary themes—her husband's death, a woman's poetry, the transcendent in the midst of the mundane, a mordant view of country life—she also reaches more toward a strange, unsettling, and profound theme of hysteria, chaos, and madness. So we read in ''This'' of a ''glaze of vision fragmented.'' In ''The Dark,'' about her sister's death from cancer, ''we come to know / violent chaos at the pure brutal heart,'' and in ''How They Got Her to Quiet Down'' we learn of the madness of Aunt Mabel. The theme is found in other poems, for example, in ''So What'' (''For me the great truths are laced with hysteria'') and in ''Aesthetics of the Cattle Farm'' (''A small funereal woods / into which a farmer dragged / the diseased cattle and left / them to fall to their knees''). Nevertheless there remains the balancing impulse, as in her description of a hummingbird ''entering the wild furnace of the flower's heart'' (''Hummingbirds'') or in her touching descriptions in ''The Ways of Daughters'' or in ''At the Museum, 1938,'' which concludes, ''Outside, the great elms along the streets in Urbana, / their green arched cathedral canopies; the continuous / singing of birds among their breathing branches.'' And we see her now hard-earned intensity working equally well in both modes.

—Norman Friedman

STRAND, Mark

Nationality: American. **Born:** Summerside, Prince Edward Island, Canada, 11 April 1934; came to the United States in 1938. **Education:** Antioch College, Yellow Springs, Ohio, B.A. 1957; Yale University, New Haven, Connecticut (Cook prize and Bergin prize, 1959), B.F.A. 1959; University of Florence (Fulbright Fellow), 1960–61; University of Iowa, Iowa City, M.A. 1962. **Family:** Married 1) Antonia Ratensky in 1961 (divorced 1973), one daughter; 2) Julia Rumsey Garretson in 1976. **Career:** Instructor, University of Iowa, 1962–65; Fulbright Lecturer, University of Brazil, Rio de Janeiro, 1965–66; assistant professor, Mount Holyoke College, South Hadley, Massachusetts, 1967; visiting professor, University of Washington, Seattle, 1968, 1970; adjunct associate professor, Columbia University, New York, 1969–72; visiting professor, Yale University, 1969; associate professor, Brooklyn College, New York, 1970–72; Bain-Swiggett Lecturer, Princeton University, New Jersey, 1973; Hurst Professor, Brandeis University, Waltham, Massachusetts, 1974–75; visiting professor, University of Virginia, Charlottesville, 1976 and 1978, California State University, Fresno, 1977, University of California, Irvine, 1978, Wesleyan University, Middletown, Connecticut, 1979, Harvard University, Cambridge, Massachusetts, 1980; visiting professor, University of Utah, Salt Lake City, 1981–86; Elliot Coleman Professor of Poetry, The Writing Seminars, Johns Hopkins University, Baltimore, Maryland, 1994–98. Since 1998 Andrew MacLeish Distinguished Service Professor, University of Chicago. Poetry editor, 1995–99, *The New Republic*. **Awards:** Ingram Merrill Foundation fellowship, 1966; National Endowment for the Arts grant, 1967, 1977, 1986. Rockefeller award, 1968; Guggenheim fellowship, 1974; Edgar Allan Poe award, 1974; American Academy award, 1975; Academy of American Poets fellowship, 1979; MacArthur Foundation fellowship, 1987; Utah Governor's award in the arts, 1992; Bobbitt National prize for poetry, 1992; Bollingen prize for poetry, 1993; Bingham prize for poetry, 1999; Pulitzer prize for poetry, 1999. Member, American Academy. United States Poet Laureate, 1990–91. **Member:** American Academy and Institute of Arts & Letters, 1980; American Academy of Arts and Sciences, 1995. **Address:** c/o Harry Ford, Knopf Inc., 201 East 50th Street, New York, New York 10022, U.S.A.

PUBLICATIONS

Poetry

Sleeping with One Eye Open. Iowa City, Stone Wall Press, 1964.
Reasons for Moving. New York, Atheneum, 1968.
Darker. New York, Atheneum, 1970.
The Story of Our Lives. New York, Atheneum, 1973.
The Sargentville Notebook. Providence, Rhode Island, Burning Deck, 1973.
Elegy for My Father. Iowa City, Windhover Press, 1973.
The Late Hour. New York, Atheneum, 1978.
Selected Poems. New York, Atheneum, 1980.
The Continuous Life. New York, Knopf, 1990.
Selected Poems. New York, Knopf, 1990.
Dark Harbor. New York, Knopf, 1993.
Blizzard of One. New York, Knopf, 1998.

Short Stories

Mr. and Mrs. Baby and Other Stories. New York, Knopf, 1985; London, Chatto and Windus. 1986.

Other

The Monument. New York, Ecco Press, 1978.
The Planet of Lost Things (for children). New York, Potter, 1982.
The Night Book (for children). New York, Potter, 1985.
Rembrandt Takes a Walk (for children). New York, Potter, 1986.
Prose. Portland, Oregon, Charles Seluzicki, 1987.
William Bailey. New York, Abrams, 1987.
Hopper. Hopewell, New Jersey, Ecco Press, 1994.

Editor, *The Contemporary American Poets: American Poetry since 1940.* Cleveland, World, 1969.
Editor, *New Poetry of Mexico.* New York, Dutton, 1970; London, Secker and Warburg, 1972.
Editor and Translator, *The Owl's Insomnia: Selected Poems of Rafael Alberti.* New York, Atheneum, 1973.
Editor and Translator, *Souvenir of the Ancient World: Selected Poems of Carlos Drummond de Andrade.* New York, Antaeus, 1976.
Editor, with Charles Simic, *Another Republic: 17 European and South American Writers.* New York, Ecco Press, 1976.
Editor, *Art of the Real: Nine American Figurative Painters.* New York, Potter, 1983; London, Aurum Press, 1984.
Editor, with Thomas Colchie, *Travelling in the Family: Selected Poems of Carlos Drummond de Andrade.* New York, Random House, 1986.
Editor, with David Lehman, *The Best American Poetry 1991.* New York, Macmillan, 1991.
Editor, *The Golden Ecco Anthology.* Hopewell, New Jersey, Ecco Press, 1994.

Translator, *18 Poems from the Quechua*. Cambridge, Massachusetts, Halty Ferguson, 1971.

Translator, *Texas,* by Jorge Luis Borges. Austin, University of Texas Humanities Research Center, 1975.

*

Manuscript Collection: Lilly Library, University of Indiana, Bloomington.

Critical Studies: "Mark Strand: *Darker*" by James Crenner, in *Seneca Review* (Geneva, New York), April 1971; "A Conversation with Mark Strand," in *Ohio Review* (Athens), winter 1972; "Dark and Radiant Peripheries: Mark Strand and A.R. Ammons" by Harold Bloom, in *Southern Review* (Baton Rouge, Louisiana), winter 1972; "Beginnings and Endings" by Robert McKlitsch, in *Literary Review* (Rutherford, New Jersey), spring 1978; by Linda Gregerson, in *Parnassus* (New York), 1982; *Mark Strand and the Poet's Place in Contemporary Culture* by David Kirby, Columbia, University of Missouri Press, 1990; "Poetry Chronicle: Amy Clampitt, Louise Glück, Mark Strand," in *Raritan* (New Brunswick, New Jersey), 10(3), winter 1991, and "Reading As Poets Read: Following Mark Strand," in *Philosophy and Literature* (Baltimore, Maryland), 20(1), April 1996, both by Charles Berger; by Harold Bloom, in *Gettysburg Review* (Gettysburg, Pennsylvania), 4(2), spring 1991.

*   *   *

Mark Strand is one of the finest, most controlled of lyric poets, his poems written with an impeccable and seemingly effortless technique. They are fascinating not only as superbly finished poetry but also for the artistic strategies they employ and, despite his own completely distinct voice, for the other writers and artists they do not echo but evoke. The quintessential Strand can be found in the concluding part of "Seven Poems," from *Darker:*

I have a key
so I open the door and walk in.
It is dark and I walk in.
It is darker and I walk in.

Spare and windblown, these lines are stripped of everything nonessential. The utter simplicity of action and language, the repetitions, the subtle alternations in sentence structure (especially the shift to the comparative "darker"), and the placings of the "I" work to wondrous and mysterious effect. The voice is unmistakably Strand, yet the repetitions, the simple denotative words tricked into unexpected connotations, and the darkness are reminiscent of Samuel Beckett.

The four lines are also a touchstone for other important aspects of Strand's poetry. The symmetry of the last two lines shows an exquisite sense of balance, and precarious balances between dichotomies, opposites, and contradictions—such as absence/presence, dark/light, life/death, night/day, indoor/outdoor—are basic to his technique. The contraries, like the vocabulary, are simple, but they are artfully arranged, rearranged, and varied to create patterns of meaning and complication. An example central to man and artist is "I empty myself of my life and my life remains" ("The Remains," from *Darker*). Since the romantic beguilement with it, the subject-object dichotomy has provided the magic caesura that allows such contraries to merge or reverse themselves, and across that same caesura is the

work of Beckett and Harold Pinter also written and "reality," as in Strand, so brilliantly undermined.

This undermining or transformation of the landscape of reality is accomplished as well by the suppression, implicit in lyric poetry, of narrative fact and dramatic situation. The entire volume of Strand's *The Story of Our Lives,* with its deliberate allusion to storytelling, makes use of this method. Like Beckett, a virtuoso with endings and beginnings, and Pinter, who tells *Betrayal* backward, Strand manipulates narrative time and the sequence of events and deliberately excludes needed information. In *The Story of Our Lives* Strand begins with "Elegy for My Father," the end of one of the stories, moves to a poem called "To Begin," and ends the final poem, "The Untelling," with the line "He sat and began to write."

The telling, not telling, or retelling of stories is explored extensively in this volume. The "Elegy for My Father," with its ambiguous and intensifying refrain, "Nothing could stop you," is one kind of story. "To Begin" recounts the true beginning, the struggle to write. "The Room" is an ambiguous dramatic situation that recalls in its oblique angle of vision Robbe-Grillet's *Jealousy* and his screenplay for Resnais's *Last Year at Marienbad.* The surface story is presented and dismissed in the poem "The Story of Our Lives," which is followed by "Inside the Story." The climax of the volume comes with the brilliant construction and deconstruction of a narrative in "The Untelling." Here an account of a memory is told four times. Each time its telling is not right, and at the close of the poem the fifth attempt is about to commence. The story in its four variations is haunting and surreal, as these lines suggest:

Although I have tried to return, I have always
ended here, where I am now. The lake
still exists, and so does the lawn, though the people
who slept there that afternoon have not been seen since.

Many parallels come to mind. Among them are the strangely shifting landscapes of Georges Seurat, the novels of John Hawkes, the theater work of Robert Wilson, and Pinter's screenplay for *The Go-Between.* Strand, who once studied to be a painter, has also written about Edward Hopper in an essay titled "Hopper: The Loneliness Factor," in which he argues that several of Hopper's paintings are constructed around the dominant shape of a "nonexistent vanishing point"; the works cannot resolve their conflicts within their own boundaries. Interestingly akin to Hopper's paintings, Strand's poetry creates a central disquiet that resonates, often chillingly, beyond the lines on the page. Even poems written thirty years into his career seem to work and rework the conditions of his well-known "Keeping Things Whole" from the 1964 volume *Sleeping with One Eye Open:* "In a field / I am the absence / of field. / This is / always the case. / Wherever I am / I am what is missing."

In his 1990 collection *The Continuous Life,* his first after a decade-long hiatus, the poet reminds us, in longer-lined poems and a few short prose narratives, that events do not necessarily lead to meaningful ends. Like the weltanschauung of Kafka or Beckett, Strand's is depopulated and prone to extinctions, untellings, and an ongoingness rooted in vacancy. "A.M." says,

Another day has come,
Another fabulous escape from the damages of night,
so even the gulls, in the ragged circle of their flight,
Above the sea's long lanes that flash and fall, scream their
    approval.

How well the sun's rays probe
The rotting carcass of a skate, how well
They show the worms and swarming flies at work,
How well they shine upon the fatal sprawl
Of everything on earth.

A surrealistic emptiness pervades the forty-five sections of Strand's long poem *Dark Harbor,* a collection that utilizes different tones, genres, and stances to create a full world of mysterious shapes and serene disappearances and that reads like a night of dreams: ''And yet all you want is to rise out of the shade / Of yourself into the cooling blaze of summer night / When the moon shines and the earth itself / Is covered and silent in the stoniness of its sleep.'' Many of the sections of the book concern themselves with aging and decline and with the role of poetry in the world: ''Rivers, mountains, animals, all find their true place, / / But only while Orpheus sings. When the song is over / The world resumes its old flaws.'' The poet of *Dark Harbor* always seems to find himself in the twilit world of fragile beauty and peril.

The collection *Blizzard of One* evokes a more crowded world than the one we usually see in Strand, with poems dedicated to his poet and painter friends and with a looser, more unabashed verve swinging within the lines of the poems. Love passing, mortality, the sad frontier of nostalgia, and the eroticism of our lone interiors are still his concerns, but he seems to see them with flourish. In the book's second poem, ''The Beach Hotel,'' he writes,

Oh, look, the ship is sailing without us! And the wind
Is from the east, and the next ship leaves in a year.
Let's go back to the beach hotel where the rain never stops,
Where the garden, green and shadow-filled, says, in the rarest
Of whispers, ''Beware of encroachment.'' We can stroll, can visit
The dead decked out in their ashen pajamas, and after a tour
Of the birches, can lie on the rumpled bed, watching
The ancient moonlight creep across the floor. The window panes
Will shake, and waves of darkness, cold, uncalled-for, grim,
Will cover us. And into the close and mirrored catacombs of sleep
We'll fall, and there in the tided light discover the bones,
The dust, the bitter remains of someone who might have been
    Had we not taken his place.

—Gaynor F. Bradish and Martha Sutro

STRAUSS, Jennifer

Nationality: Australian. **Born:** Jennifer Wallace, Heywood, Victoria, 30 January 1933. **Education:** University of Melbourne, 1951–54, B.A. (honors) 1954; University of Glasgow, 1957–58; Monash University, Ph.D. 1991. **Family:** Married Werner Strauss in 1958; three sons. **Career:** Lecturer, University of Melbourne, 1961–63. Lecturer, 1964–71, senior lecturer, 1971–91, and since 1991 associate professor, Monash University, Melbourne. Visiting scholar, University of North Carolina, Chapel Hill, 1974, and Australian National University, Canberra, 1988; visiting professor, Centre for Medieval Studies, University of Toronto, Ontario, 1982; member of literature committee, Ministry for the Arts, Victoria, 1983–85. Chair, Premier's Literary Awards Committee, 1989–91. **Awards:** *Westerly* Sesquicentenary

prize, 1979. **Address:** 2/12 Tollington Avenue, East Malvern, Victoria 3145, Australia.

PUBLICATIONS

Poetry

Children and Other Strangers. Melbourne, Nelson, 1975.
Winter Driving. Melbourne, Sisters, 1981.
Labour Ward. Melbourne Pariah Press, 1988.
Tierra del Fuego: New and Selected Poems. Altona North, Victoria, Pariah Press, 1997.

Other

''*Stop Laughing! I'm Being Serious:*'' *Studies in Seriousness and Wit in Contemporary Australian Literature.* Townsville, Foundation for the Study of Australian Literature, 1990.
Boundary Conditions: The Poetry of Gwen Harwood. St. Lucia, University of Queensland Press, 1992.
Judith Wright. Melbourne and New York, Oxford University Press, 1995.

Editor, with Bruce Moore and Jan Noble, *Middle English Verse: An Anthology.* Melbourne, Monash University, 1976; revised edition, with Charles A. Stevenson, 1985.
Editor, *The Oxford Book of Australian Love Poems.* Melbourne, Oxford University Press, 1993.
Editor, with Bruce Bennett and Chris Wallace-Crabbe, *The Oxford Literary History of Australia.* Melbourne, Oxford University Press, 1998.
Editor, *Family Ties: Australian Poems of the Family.* Melbourne, Oxford University Press, 1998.

*

Manuscript Collection: Australian Defence Force Academy, Canberra.

Critical Studies: ''Pensive Seductions: New Collections by Four Women Poets'' by Yvonne Rousseau, in *The Age Monthly Review* (Melbourne), February 1989; ''What the Witness Spoke: Jennifer Strauss, Labour Ward'' by Noel Rowe, in *Southerly,* 52(1), 1992.

Jennifer Strauss comments:
    People—their psychological states and social conditions—interest me more than landscape, and the direction of that interest has been influenced by feminist thought. If all my poems are personal, very few are unequivocally autobiographical. Mostly I write because things disturb rather than distress. I want to make something out of that disturbance, which is not necessarily caused by obvious disorder. The wrong kind of order can be the most disturbing of all. And the poem does not exorcise the original feeling; poems are neither problem solvers nor dissolvers.
    I have never been able to produce a finished poem by making up my mind to write a (any) poem at a particular time, much less by making up my mind to write in a particular form. I can only write when a particular poetic idea germinates in the kinds of experiences in which there are intersections of thought and feeling, past and present, particular and type. The idea of a poem is not an idea at all in a

philosophical or even discursive sense. It is a dimly perceived shape, and the defining of that shape is a process of discovering as much as of making. My output is small. I write the kind of poems I can. I admire a great many other kinds.

* * *

The phrase ''a little winter sun,'' from ''The Pain of Others,'' could be seen as a definitive image of Jennifer Strauss's poetic world. Though she is eloquent in her exploration of private and public worlds, rarely in her poetry does the intimate world of a loving family escape the shadow of wider realities. Into a peaceful kitchen, for example, ''the morning paper / Spills its daily due / Of blood and bastardry,'' and refuge is only sought, not found, in a child's sunlit nursery, for ''dark in the quiet pulsing of your blood / I hear the jackboots thud the wild world over'' (''For Nicholas, One Year Old''). In a later poem, ''Models,'' a children's game and reflections on history coalesce in a tellingly ironic comment on human nature:

Makers of cities
Makers of wars
The boys are playing.
They are painting the tanks.
For more than an hour now
They have not quarrelled.

In ''Collage: The Personal Is Political'' the connections between domestic and political violence are relentlessly probed through the fate of children at the hands of abusing parents and warring governments. The demand ''LET THERE BE JUSTICE'' raises the question of degrees of guilt and degrees of punishment:

Let there be trials
the parents will go to jail
and so they should
and so they should
the pilots may have nightmares
and so they should
but the torturers
will draw their pay
the generals wear their medals

The combination of sensibility and hard logic, of a refined and taut poetics, has always been a mark of Strauss's work. While her development has increasingly been toward a wry disengagement from the often close personal voice of the earlier poetry, awareness of the frailty of love and of institutionalized violence remains a strong current in her work. One process of this disengagement can be seen in the increasing use, in her second and third volumes, of characters from literature, history, and myth in dramatic monologues(''Guinevere Dying,'' Jezebel's maid in ''A Just Cause,'' ''Wife to Horatio,'' the ''Bluebeard Rescripted'' poems). The sun in their often bleak landscapes derives from individual courage, stoicism, and self-awareness, as in ''Labour Ward,'' where the brevity of a journey combines birth, rebirth, and death:

In grief,
Joy's a foreign country.

It's there, but you need a visa.
No-one will issue it;
You must bear it yourself.

''Epitaphs for Casualties,'' a section heading from Strauss's first volume, might serve as a cover title for many of her poems, in which defiance and a grim humor often serve as saving graces. ''Pine-Cones and My Grandmother'' praises the ''sharp-tongued'' woman who ''taught to a timid child / Something of fortitude, / Not to flinch / At barbs on the wire fence. / 'If the head gets through, / The rest,' she said / 'Will follow.''' The adult voice applies the wisdom differently, escaping conventions that her grandmother accepted and requiring the head to take second place, for her heart ''has made up its mind / To get through the fence.'' With similar defiance the speaker in the monologue ''Wife to Horatio,'' explaining a successful retreat from the dark intricacies of life in Elsinore, has acted to safeguard the future. Her daughter Ophelia is ''playing by the river,'' but

There'll be no drowning here.
I've seen to it that she knows how to swim.

There is no such comfort in action for the persona of the moving, biting ''Guenevere Dying.'' Measured, ironic, uncompromising, this is one of Strauss's most striking poems. Wild Cornish Gwen, first caught in ''the sweet cage'' of love, is saved from death only to be caged again in a convent. Merlin, Arthur, and Lancelot all betray her. The priest permits her to see the sky from her cell '''not . . . to pleasure the rotting flesh / But to nourish the labouring soul.''' A pear tree, her wedding gift, is the symbol for her life. Although it is beautiful, it is barren, and Arthur condemns it as lacking in utility: ''We owe the land / Good husbandry!'' When the tree is burned, its ashes ''blew through the casement onto my marriage bed.'' In Gwen's rescue from the fires of martyrdom, woman and nature are joined ('''A brand plucked from the burning,''' admonishes the priest; '''I am bruised all over on men's imperatives,''' Gwen reflects):

Men slaughter men with sword and lance
'Honourably': trees and women they burn—
Always afraid of female blood.
Barren, barren . . .
         Burning, burning . . .

A casualty of ''Crown, Honour, Chivalry,'' Gwen speaks her own bitter epitaph. Throughout the poem the association of women with the natural world resonates against the imperatives of the masculine world, where Gwen's ''honest desire . . . starved in that garden of cultivated souls.'' Imagery, logic, and language speak for the higher culture of the natural order denied in ''good husbandry,'' the barbarism and cruelty of the court and church.

Another deathbed monologue, this by a casualty of similar orthodoxies, is that of a nineteenth-century Viennese physician, ''Ignaz Semmelweis.'' A pioneer in the treatment of puerperal fever, Semmelweis also dies incarcerated (in an insane asylum), his death proof of his theory of sepsis. The evil against which he fights is the belief that childbirth is ''accursed . . . from Eve downwards,'' that women as midwives, uncontaminated by work in the dissection rooms, must go:

They don't punish enough. Better believe
God vindictive
Than a doctor dirty.

Here and in "The Anabaptist Cages, Munster," the collection *Labour Ward* juxtaposes images of the cruelty and ignorance of the past with those of the present ("The Snapshot Album of the Innocent Tourist"). A series of love lyrics are not exempt from a form of irony. In these disruptions of an established mood come from the speaker, varying from the darkness of "Search and Destroy" ("was it the language / of love or of war?") to "Aubade," a gentle morning song that ends with the poet's "faithless fingers" itching to transcribe experience.

—Nan Bowman Albinski

STRYK, Lucien

Nationality: American. **Born:** Kolo, Poland, 7 April 1924. **Education:** Indiana University, Bloomington, B.A. 1948; University of Maryland, College Park, M.F.S. 1950; Sorbonne, Paris; University of London; University of Iowa, Iowa City, M.F.A. 1956. **Military Service:** U.S. Army, 1943–45. **Family:** Married; two children. **Career:** Professor emeritus of English, Northern Illinois University, DeKalb. Visiting lecturer, Niigata University, Japan, 1956–58, and Yamaguchi University, Japan, 1962–63; Fulbright lecturer, Iran, 1961–62. **Awards:** Grove Press fellowship, 1960; Yale University-Asia Society grant, 1961; Ford Foundation faculty fellowship, University of Chicago, 1963; Isaac Rosenbaum award (*Voices*), 1964; Swallow Press award, 1965; National Translation grant, 1969; National Endowment for the Arts award, 1975; Illinois Governor's award, 1979; Illinois Arts Council award, 1983; Rockefeller fellowship, 1984; Illinois Teachers of English Author of the Year award, 1992. **Address:** c/o Ohio University Press, Athens, Ohio 45701, U.S.A.

PUBLICATIONS

Poetry

Taproot. Oxford, Fantasy Press, 1953.
The Trespasser. Oxford, Fantasy Press, 1956.
Notes for a Guidebook. Denver, Swallow, 1965.
The Pit and Other Poems. Chicago, Swallow Press, 1969.
Awakening. Chicago, Swallow Press, 1973.
Selected Poems. Chicago, Swallow Press, 1976.
Three Zen Poems. Knotting, Bedfordshire, Sceptre Press, 1976.
The Duckpond. London, J. Jay/Omphalos Press, 1978.
Zen Poems. Cambridge, Embers Handpress, 1980.
Cherries. Bristol, Rhode Island, Ampersand Press, 1983.
Willows. Cambridge, Embers Handpress, 1983.
Collected Poems 1953–1983. Athens, Swallow Press-Ohio University Press, 1984.
Bells of Lombardy. DeKalb, Northern Illinois University Press, 1986.
Of Pen and Ink and Paper Scraps. Athens, Swallow Press-Ohio University Press, 1989.

Where We Are: Selected Poems and Zen Translations. London, Skoob, 1995.
And Still Birds Sing: New & Collected Poems. Athens, Swallow Press-Ohio University Press, 1998.

Recordings: *Zen Poems*, Folkways, 1980; *Selected Poems*, Folkways, 1983.

Other

Zen: Poems, Prayers, Sermons, Anecdotes, Interviews, with Takashi Ikemoto. New York, Doubleday, 1965.
Encounter with Zen: Writings on Poetry and Zen. Athens, Swallow Press-Ohio University Press, 1981.

Editor, *Heartland: Poets of the Midwest.* DeKalb, Northern Illinois University Press, 1967; *Heartland 2,* 1975.
Editor, *World of the Buddha: A Reader.* New York, Doubleday, 1968.
Editor and translator, with Takashi Ikemoto, *Afterimages: Zen Poems of Shinkichi Takahashi.* Chicago, Swallow Press, and London, Alan Ross, 1970.
Editor, and translator with Takashi Ikemoto, *The Penguin Book of Zen Poetry.* Chicago, Swallow Press, and London, Allen Lane, 1977; revised edition, as *Zen Poetry: Let the Spring Breeze Enter,* New York, Grove Press, 1995.
Editor, *Prairie Voices: A Collection of Illinois Poets.* Peoria, Illinois, Spoon River Poetry Press, 1980.

Translator, with Takashi Ikemoto and Taigan Takayama, *Zen Poems of China and Japan: The Crane's Bill.* New York, Grove/Atlantic, 1981.
Translator, with Takashi Ikemoto, *Twelve Death Poems of the Chinese Zen Masters.* Providence, Rhode Island, Hellcoal Press, 1973.
Translator, *Three Zen Poems after Shinkichi Takahashi.* Knotting, Bedfordshire, Sceptre Press, 1976.
Co-Translator, *Haiku of the Japanese Masters.* Derry, Pennsylvania, Rook Press, 1977.
Co-Translator, *The Duckweed Way: Haiku of Issa.* Derry, Pennsylvania, Rook Press, 1977.
Translator, *Bird of Time: Haiku of Basho.* Vermillion, South Dakota, Flatlands Press, 1983.
Translator, *Traveler My Name: Haiku of Basho.* Norwich, Embers Handpress, 1984.
Translator, *On Love and Barley: Haiku of Basho.* Honolulu, University of Hawaii Press, and London, Penguin, 1985.
Translator, *Triumph of the Sparrow: Zen Poems of Shinkichi Takahashi.* Urbana. University of Illinois Press. 1986.

*

Bibliography: "Lucien Stryk: A Bibliography" by Craig S. Abbott, in *Analytical & Enumerative Bibliography* (DeKalb, Illinois), 5(3–4), 1991.

Manuscript Collection: Mugar Memorial Library, Boston University.

Critical Studies: Interviews in *Modern Poetry Studies* (Buffalo, New York), 10(1), 1980, *Loblolly* (Gary, Texas), 2, 1985, and *American*

Poetry Review (Philadelphia), March/April 1990; *Zen, Poetry, the Art of Lucien Stryk* edited by Susan Porterfield, Athens, Ohio, Swallow Press, 1993, and ''Portrait of a Poet As a Young Man: Lucien Stryk'' by Porterfield, in *Midwestern Miscellany* (East Lansing, Michigan), 22, 1994; *West Meets East in Lucien Stryk's Poetry* (dissertation) by Brigitte Debord, University of Arkansas, 1995.

Lucien Stryk comments:

I consider myself primarily a poet with a strong interest in oriental philosophy. Some critics have associated me with other poets and schools, but frankly I like to think of myself as an independent.

I do not think a grown-up poet can do much about the content of his verse: he either has or has not worthy concerns, he is either small or large minded, and such things as his politics and social attitudes generally get into this verse one way or another. My chief concern as a poet is to make something, something firmly enough crafted to assure its life for longer than one hurried reading. How to get this done is the main study of my life. I suppose that what some critics have called my economy of statement has to a certain degree been influenced by my work as a translator of Zen poetry, but I am far from certain about that.

Anyhow, I try for a firm line and, most important of all, image and/or metaphor without which, so far as I am concerned, there cannot be poetry. Whatever else he is—and he had better be much more—the poet is an active, finely tuned sensorium, his eye working perfectly with his ear and his fingers touching delicately. When the poet is that, and when his theme is worthy, he may produce a good poem. Yet the making of a good poem is never less than a mystery, and no poet would really want it to be anything less, however much he despairs.

*   *   *

Lucien Stryk has written that the poet's ideal is ''to get 'beyond poetry,' . . . to avoid the hateful evidence of our will to impress.'' Whether the subject be boyhood and domestic incidents, admired works of art, the horrors of the Pacific theater of World War II, or his experiences throughout the northern hemisphere, Stryk has sought an unadorned poetry depending on clarity of image. Known for translations of and writings about oriental literature, Stryk has found a discipline—personal as well as aesthetic—in Zen. As he says in the watershed poem ''Awakening,'' Zen provided ''the moment of my / pointing.'' Writing out of the heightened, cleansed consciousness of his discipline, he says, ''I am always happy, / . . . / fully aware.''

Such calm has not come easily. Stryk's first two books were indulgently artful, and one senses that self-justification has often challenged his determination to become a self-effaced, ''awakened'' man. In ''Away,'' for example, when the poet longs for picturesque foreign places, he is immediately chastised: ''Down, down, and breathe!'' His ''feet go faster faster, / suddenly fly off''; calm returns, and he bows ''to Master Takayama / who smiles all the way from Japan.'' Indeed, one might argue that Stryk's great poems result from—perhaps portray—successful resolution of artistic and spiritual dilemmas.

Especially during the 1960s and 1970s, Stryk achieved poems that, while admirable by many standards, steadied with *muga,* an unrestrained identification with their objects, an unclouded vision. ''It is joy,'' he writes in ''Zen: The Rocks of Sesshu,'' ''that lifts those pigeons to / Stitch the clouds / With circling, light flashing from underwings.'' ''Awakening,'' a later, equally impressive sequence, images not only the mind-clearing exhilaration of Zen but also the self-dissolution (''mind pointing / like a torch, I cannot see beyond /

the frost, out nor in'') that reveals the immensity of the void inherent in even the most familiar things:

Softness everywhere,
snow a smear,
air a gray sack.

Time. Place. Thing.
Felt between
skin and bone, flesh.

Just as important, poems not dealing directly with Zen present the discoveries of a startled mind: ''Étude,'' which tells the miracle of a plain woman's playing of Chopin; ''Memo to the Builder,'' which calls for a house that would allow birds to ''make a whir- / / ring thoroughfare / Of a room or two'' so that ''the wild, the rare / Not only happen . . . . But / Be the normal''; poems like ''Amputee,'' ''Clown,'' and ''Busker,'' which quickly and surely focus the wit, pathos, or mystique of a person; ''The Goose,'' which remembers a bird killed by the poet's car and the maddening grief that followed; and ''Rites of Passage,'' a lovely evocation of a son's inevitable separation from his father.

The same sensibility—words that ''hide nothing except the art behind them''—has yielded vivid poems about World War II, based on Stryk's as well as others' experiences and ranging in mood from anger to reconciliation. ''The Pit'' recalls the gruesome work of burying bloated corpses during combat and concludes, ''Ask anyone who / Saw it: nobody won that war.'' On the other hand, ''Letter to Jean-Paul Baudot, at Christmas,'' a poem of irresistible pathos, tells of cannibalism among French resistance fighters and of one man's annual retching when snow reminds him of the horror:

I see you on the first snow of the year
spreadeagled, face buried in that stench.
I write once more, Jean-Paul, though you don't

answer, because I must: today men do far worse.
Yours in hope of peace, for all of us,
before the coming of another snow.

And recollections of World War II have inspired some of the most moving of Stryk's later work, for example, ''Rooms,'' in which he also eulogizes his mother, and ''Park of the Martyrs of Liberty,'' the eighteenth of the twenty-six parts of the sequence ''Bells of Lombardy,'' set in Bellagio, Italy.

It is tempting to speculate what a reader of the future might find distinctive about Stryk's poems. Their international scope would have to be part of the answer. Stryk has set almost half of his mature poems in recognizable foreign countries, not only Japan but also England, Sweden, Spain, France, Italy, Russia, and Iran. One sees women in a Japanese mine ''bent over / Feedbelts circling like blood,'' a beggar woman inside her crate in Iran, ''cracked almsbowl up, / Ten *rials* a snapshot, jaw clenched miserably / For an extra five,'' and ''the bronzed Spaniard'' who upstages the orators of London's Hyde Park with his acrobatics.

The drama of Stryk's fathoming unfamiliar people, places, and even animals—of his learning to replace tourists' eyes intoxicated with the exotic with the less romanticized vision of the knowledgeable, often disillusioned, but also awakened and hopeful man—has shaped an art that reveals, as Stryk has said it must, "the full range of [a man's] life."

—Jay S. Paul

STUART, Dabney

Nationality: American. **Born:** Richmond, Virginia, 4 November 1937. **Education:** Davidson College, North Carolina, 1956–60, A.B. 1960; Harvard University, Cambridge, Massachusetts (Summer Poetry Prize, 1962), A.M. 1962. **Family:** Married Sandra Westcott (third marriage) in 1983; one daughter and two sons. **Career:** Instructor in English, College of William and Mary, Williamsburg, Virginia, 1961–65; instructor, 1965–66, assistant professor, 1966–69, associate professor, 1969–74, professor, 1974–91, and since 1991 S. Blount Mason Professor of English, Washington and Lee University, Lexington, Virginia. Visiting professor, Middlebury College, Vermont, 1968–69, and Ohio University, Athens, spring 1975; resident poet, Trinity College, Hartford, Connecticut, 1978; visiting poet, University of Virginia, Charlottesville, 1981, 1982–83. Poetry editor, *Shenandoah,* Lexington, 1966–76, and editor-in-chief, 1988–95; member of the editorial board, Poets in the South, 1974–82; poetry editor, *New Virginia Review,* 1983. **Awards:** Poetry Society of America Dylan Thomas prize, 1965; National Endowment for the Arts grant, 1969, fellowship 1974, 1982; Borestone Mountain award, 1969, 1974, 1977; Virginia Governor's award, 1979; Guggenheim fellowship, 1987–88; Virginia Individual Artist fellowship, 1995; residency at Bellagio Study and Conference Center, spring 2000. **Address:** Department of English, Washington and Lee University, Lexington, Virginia 24450, U.S.A.

PUBLICATIONS

Poetry

The Diving Bell. New York, Knopf, 1966.
A Particular Place. New York, Knopf, 1969.
Corgi Modern Poets in Focus 3, with others, edited by Dannie Abse, London, Corgi, 1971.
The Other Hand. Baton Rouge, Louisiana State University Press, 1974.
Friends of Yours, Friends of Mine. Richmond, Virginia, Rainmaker Press, 1974.
Round and Round: A Triptych. Baton Rouge, Louisiana State University Press, 1977.
Rockbridge Poems. Emory, Virginia, Iron Mountain Press, 1981.
Common Ground. Baton Rouge, Louisiana State University Press, 1982.
Don't Look Back. Baton Rouge, Louisiana State University Press, 1987.
Narcissus Dreaming. Baton Rouge, Louisiana State University Press, 1990.
Light Years: New and Selected Poems. Baton Rouge, Louisiana State University Press, 1994.
Second Sight. St. Louis, University of Missouri Press, 1996.
Long Gone. Baton Rouge, Louisiana State University Press, 1997.
Strains of the Old Man. Abingdon, Virginia, Sow's Ear Press, 1999.
Settlers. Baton Rouge, Louisiana State University Press, 1999.

Short Stories

Sweet Lucy Wine: Stories. Baton Rouge, Louisiana State University Press, 1992.
The Way to Cobbs Creek. St. Louis, University of Missouri Press, 1997.

Other

Nabokov: The Dimensions of Parody. Baton Rouge, Louisiana State University Press, 1978.

*

Manuscript Collections: Virginia Commonwealth University, Richmond; Washington and Lee University, Lexington, Virginia.

Critical Studies: By X.J. Kennedy, in *Shenandoah* (Lexington, Virginia), autumn 1966; John Unterecker, in *Shenandoah* (Lexington, Virginia), autumn 1969; Dannie Abse, in *Corgi Modern Poets in Focus 3,* 1971; by the author, in *Contemporary Poetry in America,* edited by Miller Williams, New York, Random House, 1973; D.E. Richardson, in *Southern Review* (Baton Rouge, Louisiana), autumn 1976; Stephen Dobyns, in *Washington Post Book World,* 7 November 1982; Fred Chappell, in Roanoke *Times* (Virginia), 27 March 1983, and 30 August 1987; "Ghostlier Demarcations, Keener Sounds" by Barbara Fialkowski, in *Poets in the South* (Tampa, Florida), fall 1984; Robert Gingher, in Greensboro *News and Record* (North Carolina), 7 June 1987; Paul Ramsey, in *Chronicles* (Rockford, Illinois), March 1989; "Every Poet in His Humor," in *The Georgia Review* (Athens), winter 1990, and "Not As a Leaf: Southern Poetry and the Innovation of Tradition," in *The Georgia Review* (Athens), fall 1997, both by Fred Chappell; "A Dream Not of Wholeness, but of Endless Dreaming" by Gilbert Allen, and "The Long Mirror: Dabney Stuart's Film Allusions" by Fred Chappell, in the Dabney Stuart issue of *Kentucky Poetry Review,* 27(1), spring 1991; by Warren Werner in *The Chatahoochee Review* (Dunwoody), winter 1991; by Greg Johnson in *The Georgia Review* (Athens), winter 1992–93; by Haines Sprunt in *The Hollins Critic* (Roanoke), June 1993; "Six Davidson Poets: The Consolation of Some memorable Language" by Barbara Mayer, in *The Davidson Journal* (Davidson, North Carolina), fall 1993; "The Poetry of Grown Men" by Brendan Galvin, in *Tar River Poetry,* spring 1995; "Poetry Chronicle" by R.S. Gwynn, in *Hudson Review,* XLIX(2), summer 1996; "Six Soloists" by Betty Adcock, in *Southern Review* (Baton Rouge, Louisiana), 32(4), winter 1996.

Dabney Stuart comments:

My work ranges formally from traditional English patterns to associative, nonmetrical verse. My more recent poems, since and including *Common Ground,* have been characterized by a combination of aspects of both strains in individual poems, including the use of irregularly patterned half rhymes, acrostic structures, and nonce forms. I have been consistently involved with certain themes and subject matter: family relationships, particularly those involving parents and children, levels of consciousness mirrored in language, the unforeseen and ubiquitous past, shifting perspective, cultural icons, isolation, dreams, the hidden self. The work of Alice Miller (*Prisoners of Childhood, Thou Shalt Not Be Aware*), Margaret Mahler, certain seventeenth-century poets, Paul Cezanne, and others have significantly aided me in developing an understanding of the sources of my work and the ways of its maturation. See my autobiographical statement, "Knots into Webs," in volume 105 of the *Dictionary of Literary Biography*.

*   *   *

In his first book, *The Diving Bell*, Dabney Stuart revealed himself as a skillful and intelligent poet. His command of language and his confident handling of relatively traditional forms are combined with a gentle candor that enables many of the poems in the volume to transcend the category of Lowellesque confessional verse into which they run the risk of falling. There is nothing trite about his contribution to this genre, however. For example, he speaks of the small daughter he seldom sees as a conjurer—"Your voice a wand, you called the olive grapes"—but he later adds,

Yet, deserting your role,
You called me by my name—
I'd rather
have been that metaphor, your father.

Here language is both image and instrument. Stuart's second book, *A Particular Place*, advances into more adventurous territory. In fact, it includes a number of poems about place, contemplative in tone and dwelling on stone and water, air, and stillness. But it also explores deeper regions of symbol and myth and psychic landscapes in poetry that owes little to traditional forms. Consider, for example, these lines from "The Charles River":

On summer evenings here
Lovers may kiss to Stravinsky:
Le sacre du printemps.
If they lie close enough
To the bank, the music and the river
Lapping the stones
Become one sound . . .

Although some of the poems are more successful than others, the ones that do succeed achieve a haunting resonance.

Stuart's later books *The Other Hand* and *Round and Round* continue to work within the formal and thematic boundaries set by his first two books. That is, most of the poems are written in free verse and tend toward fairly short lines, while thematically the poems are still immersed in the contemplative, second-generation deep image poetry Stuart used in *A Particular Place*. The changes that occur in the work in these two books primarily involve tone. Stuart begins to exhibit a wider range of tonal expression, from the caustic to the contemplative. These lines from the poem "Mystic" offer an example of his manipulation of tone: "I have seen God O Yes / Don't fondle me with doubt / or any lower case vanity . . ." *Songs for Champagne Saturday* also does not offer any major deviation from the work of his earlier volumes. The poems here are competent and interesting but not particularly memorable.

Common Ground, however, shows Stuart moving beyond the earlier books and charting new terrain in which to work. The poems now usually have a longer, more sonically interesting line. The exploration in *Round and Round* begins to have an effect on his tone. For instance, Stuart occasionally begins to use a highly authoritative

tone, as in the end to "Turntables," where he writes about a newborn: "His small body, new in the air, / filling it; / The human music. The awful human music." He is also capable, however, of successfully returning to a more meditative voice, as in "Snorkeling in the Caribbean." Filled by numerous fine poems, *Common Ground* is work that fulfills the promise his first book offered and is thus a turning point in his career.

The poems that have followed—in *Don't Look Back* and *Narcissus Dreaming* and the newer work in his selected poems, *Light Years*—all profit from what Stuart apparently learned while writing *Common Ground*. *Don't Look Back* has several very strong poems, including "Casting," "Taking the Wheel," and the title poem. Ranging over primarily personal terrain, the poems are emotional, yet they are still shaped by the precision that guided Stuart's early work. Many of the poems of *Narcissus Dreaming* are also powerful. Consider, for instance, the closing lines of the title poem. Narcissus, fishing in a place where the surface ripples wrinkle his reflection, finally gets a bite, and so he reels in his line and pulls in his reflection, "a laid out suit / of clothes lifted / by its center," which he then "lowers" into "the boat" and "takes . . . upon himself,"

drenched, obscene,
a perfectly imperfect fit,
leaving the water
imageless, opaque,
other.

Firm control of tone and a staccato rhythm fueled by disjointed, surprising line breaks create several memorable poems in this book.

In his collections *Long Gone* and *Settlers* Stuart has begun to experiment a bit more with tone, imagery, and subject matter. Although some critics have speculated that his experimentation has been out of an attempt to emulate some of the celebrated experiments of younger poets with form and language, a more plausible answer is that Stuart is exploring, experimenting, and, indeed, changing as a poet. Perhaps *Settlers* is most indicative of these changes. While tonal control and consistency—a reliance upon the precisely rendered image—was a mainstay of Stuart's career up until the late 1990s, this collection, which focuses primarily on familial difficulties and transitions, uses sharp shifts in tone in order to highlight the painful disruptions the poems consider. Although it is fair to say that Stuart does not seem as comfortable writing in more experimental modes, his range as a poet and his formal control would seem to argue that he can add these sudden, almost filmic shifts to his repertoire.

—Fleur Adcock and Tod Marshall

SUKNASKI, Andrew, Jr.

Pseudonyms: Jessy Kid Dalton. **Nationality:** Canadian. **Born:** Wood Mountain, Saskatchewan, 30 July 1942. **Education:** Ambassador School, Wood Mountain; L.V. Rogers High School, Nelson, British Columbia; Kootenay School of Art, Nelson, 1962–63, 1966–67, diploma in fine arts 1967; University of Victoria, British Columbia, 1964–65; Montreal Museum of Fine Arts School of Art and Design, 1965; Notre Dame University, Nelson, 1966–67; University of British Columbia, Vancouver, 1967–68; Simon Fraser University, Burnaby,

British Columbia, 1968–69. **Career:** Founder and editor, *Elfin Plot,* 1969–74, and *Sundog,* 1973–76, and Deodar Shadow Press, 1970–71, Anak Press, 1971–76, and Sundog Press, 1973–78, all Wood Mountain. Since 1982 editor, *Three Legged Coyote,* Wood Mountain. Writer-in-residence, St. John's College, University of Manitoba, Winnipeg, 1977–78. **Awards:** Canada Council grant, 1971, 1972, 1973, 1976, 1978, 1980, 1982; Canadian Authors Association prize, 1978; Saskatchewan Culture and Youth grant, 1981. **Address:** Wood Mountain, Saskatchewan S0H 4L0, Canada.

PUBLICATIONS

Poetry

This Shadow of Eden, Once. Wood Mountain, Deodar Shadow Press, 1970.
Circles. Wood Mountain, Deodar Shadow Press, 1970.
In Mind ov Xrossroads ov Mythologies. Wood Mountain, Anak Press, 1971.
Rose Way in the East. Toronto, Ganglia Press, 1972.
Old Mill. Vancouver, Blewointmentpress, 1972.
The Nightwatchman. Wood Mountain, Anak Press, 1972.
The Zen Pilgrimage. Wood Mountain, Anak Press, 1972.
Y th Evolution into Ruenz. Wood Mountain, Anak Press, 1972.
Four Parts Sand: Concrete Poems, with others. Ottawa, Oberon Press, 1972.
Wood Mountain Poems. Wood Mountain, Anak Press, 1973; expanded edition, edited by Al Purdy, Toronto, Macmillan, 1976.
Suicide Notes, Book One. Wood Mountain, Sundog Press, 1973.
Phillip Well. Prince George, British Columbia, College of New Caledonia, 1973.
These Fragments I've Gathered for Ezra. Edinburg, Texas, Funch Press, 1973.
Leaving. Seven Person, Alberta, Repository Press, 1974.
On First Looking Down from Lion's Gate Bridge. Wood Mountain, Anak Press, 1974; revised edition, Windsor, Ontario, Black Moss Press, 1976.
Blind Man's House. Wood Mountain, Anak Press, 1975.
Leaving Wood Mountain. Wood Mountain, Sundog Press. 1975.
Writing on Stone: Poemdrawings 1966–1976. Wood Mountain, Anak Press, 1976.
Octomi. Saskatoon, Thistledown Press, 1976.
Almighty Voice. Toronto, Dreadnaught Press, 1977.
Moses Beauchamp. Winnipeg, Turnstone Press, 1978.
The Ghosts Call You Poor. Toronto, Macmillan, 1978.
Two for Father, with George Morrissette. Wood Mountain, Sundog Press, 1978.
East of Myloona. Saskatoon, Thistledown Press, 1979.
In the Name of Narid: New Poems. Erin, Ontario, Porcupine's Quill, 1981.
Montage for an Interstellar Cry. Winnipeg, Turnstone Press, 1982.
The Land They Gave Away: Selected and New Poems. Edmonton, NeWest Press, 1982.
Silk Trail. Toronto, Nightwood, 1985.

Play

Don'tcha Know the North Wind and You in My Hair, with others (produced Saskatoon, 1978).

Other

Translator, *The Shadow of Sound,* by Andrei Voznesensky. Prince George, British Columbia, College of New Caledonia, 1975.

*

Critical Studies: "Writing along the Road to Wood Mountain" by Eli Mandel, in *Another Time,* Erin, Ontario, Press Porcépic, 1977; "Shadows of Our Ancestors" by Harvey Spak, and "Ghostly Voices" by Stephen Scobie, both in *NeWest ReView* (Edmonton), October 1978; by Kristjana Gunnars, in *Arts Manitoba* (Winnipeg), fall 1983; "Voices from the Canadian Steppes: Ukrainian Elements in Andrew Suknaski's Poetry" by Jars Balan, in *Studia Ucrainica* (Ottawa), 4, 1988; "Andrew Suknaski's 'Wood Mountain Time' and the Chronotype of Multiculturalism" by Dawn Morgan, in *Mosaic,* 29(3), September 1996.

Andrew Suknaski, Jr., comments:

(1980) 1. Concerns: the meaning of home and a vaguely divided guilt; guilt for what happened to the Indian, his land taken, imprisoned on his reserve; and guilt because to feel this guilt is a betrayal of what you ethnically are, the son of a homesteader and his wife who must be rightfully honored in one's mythology.

2. Origins: mythic mainsprings—the meaning of self: self your place of birth, self the proximity of the buried to the living of that place, self in home . . . being your dreamtime (tribal history, the ancestral way of life—that place where you leave going beyond to become faceless . . . mind and heart telescoped, forever yearning to return . . . home).

3. Naming the lost: in the western prairie labyrinth where the poet as art casualty must retie the severed threads: guilt, betrayal, and populist myth on the margins of the dreaming utopia that victimizes one naming the lost to arrest niggling visions of where the godly becomes monstrous, where reality becomes myth . . . as Leslie Fiedler warns, where myth often victimizes the innocent as one's humanity is shortchanged by the ticket taker at the circus gate—that point of entry to our nightmares and otherness.

(1985) 4. Definition of West: divining for West/part 2 of celestial mechanics/life fragment in progress . . . drift of word, humanity, and myth from Sanskrit *Narayan,* "Man-Path," to *Amurru,* "Westerners"—mountain Amorites west from Akkad and Sumer; drift of etymon anchoring mythic West and mariners . . . from Islamic trade secret in name of Al-Gharb, "The West," edge of the known world to become Phoenician *Algarve* guarded by Pillars of Hercules; from ne plus ultra to plus ultra . . . "More Beyond"/dream . . . there is a beyond . . . perhaps another place and North West Passage; the search, the beginning in journeys beyond and back home by water . . . binary home/old and new . . . the new West . . . from dream of ancient vestal virgins illuminating heart of the old city to counterfeit dream of new vestal virgins—the brokers of Wall Street . . . West no longer a simple definition but a lifelong project and projection along the map of word and flesh.

*　　*　　*

"If Canada ever needed an argument in defence of the regional writer, Andrew Suknaski is it," a reviewer once wrote. Suknaski has taken the Canadian prairies as his subject. Of Polish-Ukrainian parentage, he was born on a farm outside the village of Wood Mountain in southwestern Saskatchewan. He writes about his background and about prairie life in the past and present: the endless plains, Indians, eastern European settlers, Mounties, Canadians, Americans. Reading *Wood Mountain Poems* makes one aware of the curious psychological fact that, if space has expanded in this region, time has contracted, so that the past and the present are ever present while Toronto and Vancouver are light-years distant.

The poems in *The Ghosts Call You Poor* take the form of jottings, rambling letters, and documentations, among other things, but all are concerned with what sociologists call ''marginalized people.'' The Indians and Métis are preeminently among such people, as Suknaski shows in ''Dreaming of the Northwest Passage'':

the native showed us the way
the native drew the first map on sand and earth
the northern esquimaux drew in snow
and did with small shale cairns
what contour lines do
to indicate mountains
for scottish and british explorers

the indian showed us the way to the heart
of the prairie
and distant mountains

There is more rhetoric than drama in Suknaski's poetry, more feeling for great masses of people than for individuals, more a sense of summing up a patchwork past than a sense of signaling the presence of a new society or a significant new beginning. Only in one of his lesser-known books, *Leaving,* does Suknaski write about his travels throughout Europe and the East. The poems here have a bright, light quality that is entirely lacking in the dark and somber prairie poems.

Montage for an Interstellar Cry offers an elaborate montage that is rather like a radio documentary poem for many voices. It covers such particulars as MX missile testing, Wood Mountain, Pinochet's Chile, prehistoric man, the Maritime-born astronomer Simon Newcomb, and the frustrations of life at the fringes of cities. The work resonates with the sounds of the prairies in the past and the present. The sense of place has been caught in the sense of eternity.

Silk Trail is another prairie documentary that goes from a creation myth through inchoate silence to the presence of animals and then to the aboriginal inhabitants and their Turtle Island. It ends with the arrival of the Canadian Pacific Railway's ''silk trains,'' which provided pretty much nonstop travel for precious bales of raw silk being taken from the East Coast to the West. Thus the prairies are caught in a silken web as well as in Suknaski's imagination.

It is difficult to imagine what if anything someone from a region other than the three Prairie Provinces of Alberta, Saskatchewan, and Manitoba—and perhaps the northern U.S. plains—could make of Suknaski's books of poetry. Perhaps his poetry does not ''travel.'' But through his verse one may travel to the prairies and glean a sense of what life is like in this region, which the widely traveled newspaperman Harrison Salisbury called ''the most exciting in the world.''

George Woodcock, the poet and critic, was so impressed with Suknaski's achievement that he created a word to describe it. Woodcock called it ''geo-poetry'' to draw attention to its preoccupation

with geographical and related factors. Thus, Suknaski is the geo-poet of the Canadian prairies.

—John Robert Colombo

SURENDRAN, C.P.

Nationality: Indian. **Born:** Kerala, 1959. **Education:** University of Delhi, M.A. in English literature. **Career:** Lecturer of English, Calicut University. Since 1986 journalist, became senior assistant editor, *Times of India.*

PUBLICATIONS

Poetry

Posthumous Poetry. New Delhi and New York, Penguin Books India, 1999.

*   *   *

There is a big city feel about C.P. Surendran's poetry. He is cut off from family, alienated from religion, living on his own, sharing the disillusionment and disquiet that can accompany modern freedom, skepticism, and individualism. Life appears to consist mostly of drink, drugs, and lust. He was introduced by Dom Moraes as being fiery, raw, and filled with loneliness, alienation, and anger. A journalist, he brought a hard-boiled, disillusioned tough-guy attitude to the Indian poetry scene. His half of the *Gemini II* volume begins with a reply to Wallace Stevens's famous ''Sunday Morning.'' In Surendran's version there is only flesh, as opposed to the earth on which it lives. There is an ambiguity throughout the poem; its subject may be the speaker's vision of the world as a place of flesh and lust, but the poem may also be about a violent relationship with a woman. The poem is both a reply to Stevens's hedonism of the imagination and also itself a metaphor in which man's violence toward nature is repeated in his relationship with women. In the first stanza there is a pun on ''sole''/ ''soul,'' which reappears later in the volume: ''Heel in my hand, / I outstare the sole of the beast / Twisting in my fist.'' The implication is that the soul is where we touch the earth (the bed); there is only the flesh upon the physical.

Many of the poems use religious titles—''Renunciation,'' ''Annunciation,'' ''First Signs, Last Rites,'' ''Requiem of the Rose,'' ''Lazarus''—but they do so ironically. They offer a portrait of someone with a Roman Catholic background who is familiar with the classics of modern literature and who lives by himself with his cat after the breakup of his relationship with a woman he still desires. Life feels meaningless. Religion and notions of the spirit are no longer believable, yet human relations have failed, and he is left with his anger. In ''Surprise'' we read, ''I'm leaving, she says'' and ''The day falls from the cross / Dies on the floor.'' His salvation and redemption from life die when she leaves. He drinks too much, making meals for himself is disagreeable, and he knows that eventually he will die. In ''Renunciation'' he wakes up to ''breakfast for one. Beer and wine . . . Lunch is a conceit of three, My cat, / Your snapshot, and me.'' He often speaks of himself as dead, or he imagines his death. He cannot be like those in the past who lived among large, extended Indian families and who as they grew old accepted their role as elders to be cared for. Seeing old people, he knows, in "Geriatrics, Geriatricks," that he does not want the humiliations of age, with its "meekness without remission . . . The emptying avenues of flesh and bone . . . Take me, dear Lord, / before my time." Weekends alone are hell. In "Saturday Poems" he "sits, wishing / Monday were here." He watches television, gets drunk, "remains / Bedridden, thinking of her thighs." He "wants Monday like a woman." These are poems of the anguish of modern urban secular life, with its expectation of fulfillment and experience of dissatisfaction. This is the world of unrest that Hindu and Buddhist spirituality try to avoid.

Surendran's solution is, rather romantically, found in poetry. He has made clear his poetic purpose ("therapeutic") and his assumed readership. He has said, "The dangerously funny thing about arty-farty writing is that it is not meant for your consumer: the salaried man or woman who is pretending to have a good time in the big bleak cities of India, but is unable to make sense of his huge spatial and temporal dislocation." According to Surendran, "I am seeking a whole new constituency of readership," and he says, "My poetry understands and respects that I write to heal, not impress." His manner is aggressive and attention getting and the argument minimal, but he has a clear notion of what he is doing.

The ironically titled *Posthumous Poetry* is prefaced by Surendran's explanation that the poems are "posthumous" to the breakup of his marriage, the collapse of communism, the failure of the Naxalites, and the betrayal of revolution by friends who have chosen to go abroad to earn money. There is an inconsistency in this, for he claims that he was always skeptical of politics, ideas, and life, so that such betrayals should not have shocked him. In fact, they should have confirmed the correctness of his skepticism. In addition, Surendran's poetry tires through the continual use of a heightened voice and through a style in which many sentences are fragments intended as images or in which an extremely abbreviated speech conveys macho knowingness. The repetition of telegraphese can be as artificial as any older poetic diction. Surendran's introduction to *Posthumous Poetry* claims that "all tragedies are trite; there's no grief death cannot resolve," which is itself, depending on how one reads it, trite or false. In the face of such a disillusioning world, he claims that only poetry is true, absolute, "like dead men talking."

Surendran's manner is off-putting. The introduction to *Posthumous Poetry,* for example, is a digressive attack on everything: "If Christ were to swim on the cross again, how many of us would watch Him without a remote in hand? The question applies to Catholics as well." Even the title of the volume, justifiable in itself, has its element of sensationalism. What has died are a former marriage, his belief (which he claims never really to have had) in ideas and politics, and the radicalism (which he supposedly never believed in) of his friends. In the first poem Surendran explains that he is trying to "get one word right . . . But death doesn't matter. / It's metaphor." There is not only metaphor, but there are also rhyme and harmonization. The "metaphor" of the concluding line rhymes with the unusual "Ms Christopher" in the first line and with "matter" in line four, and the *r* sound is also at the "right" at the end of line three. This is lyric poetry disguising itself as popular tabloid sensationalism.

The second poem of the volume, "Goal Keeper," uses the problems of an athlete as a metaphor for man in the universe: "Implosion of all time in a moment's dare / And miss; a whiff of eternal loss." Surendran uses images from modern culture, including television, and he combines the characteristics of modern urban life

with the eternal problems of being human and with our relationship to the world in which we live. *Posthumous Poetry* claims that in a world of nothingness, disillusionment, boredom, failure, and death there can be no answer except to tell the truth in poetry that challenges erasure.

—Bruce King

SUTHERLAND, (Roderick) Fraser

Nationality: Canadian. **Born:** Pictou, Nova Scotia, 5 December 1946. **Education:** University of King's College, Halifax, Nova Scotia, 1965–66; Carleton University, Ottawa, Ontario, 1966–69, Bachelor of Journalism 1969. **Family:** Married Alison Sutherland in 1978; one son. **Career:** Columnist and Ottawa correspondent, *Pictou Advocate,* 1965–69; reporter, *Halifax Chronicle-Herald,* 1966, *Wall Street Journal*-Canadian Dow Jones News Service, Ottawa, 1967, *The Globe and Mail,* Toronto, 1968, *The Toronto Daily Star,* 1969; staff writer, Maclean-Hunter Business Publications and *Canadian Travel Courier,* Toronto, 1969–70; instructor, Writers' Federation of Nova Scotia Students' Summer Workshop, 1978, 1979; editorial board member, *Writing* magazine, Nelson, British Columbia, 1982–83; instructor, School of Writing, David Thompson University Centre, Nelson, British Columbia, 1982–83; managing editor, *Books in Canada,* Toronto, 1984–86; Canadian poetry reviewer, *The Globe and Mail,* Toronto, 1984–88 and since 1993; literary editor, *The Idler,* Toronto, 1986; editor, *Funk & Wagnalls Canadian College Dictionary,* 1992–96; contributing editor, *Fitzhenry & Whiteside Canadian Thesaurus,* 1995–98; editor, *Nelson Canadian Dictionary,* 1996; revising editor, *Random House College Thesaurus,* 1996; lexicographer, *Encarta World English Dicttionary,* 1996–99; contributing editor, *Gage Intermediate Dictionary,* 1997; Canadian editor, *Collins Pocket Reference Canadian Dictionary,* 1997; senior contributing editor, *Webster's American Family Dictionary,* 1997–98; contributing editor, *Gage Canadian School Dictionary,* 1998–99. Since 1974 freelance editor. **Awards:** The Canada Council writing grant, 1973, 1975, 1979, 1988; Ontario Arts Council writing grant, 1975, 1986, 1987, 1988; guest, Spanish Association for Canadian Studies, Madrid, and meeting of the Italian Association for Canadian Studies, Acireale, Italy, 1988. **Address:** 39 Helena Avenue, Toronto, Ontario M66 2H3, Canada.

PUBLICATIONS

Poetry

Strange Ironies. Fredericton, Fiddlehead, 1972.
In the Wake Of. Ottawa and Kingston, Northern Journey, 1974.
Within the Wound. Ottawa and Montreal, Northern Journey, 1976.
Madwomen. Windsor, Black Moss, 1978.
Whitefaces. Windsor, Black Moss, 1986.
Jonestown. Toronto, McClelland and Stewart, 1996.
Peace and War, with Goran Simic. Toronto, Privately printed, 1998.

Short Stories

In the Village of Alias. Porters Lake, Nova Scotia, Pottersfield, 1986.

Other

The Monthly Epic: A History of Canadian Magazines. Toronto, Fitzhenry and Whiteside, 1989.
John Glassco: An Essay and Bibliography. Toronto, ECW, 1996.

*

Fraser Sutherland comments:

Whether I have written them or not, the poems I would like to write would have the beauty, autonomy, and otherness of a bird, beast, or tree. When I review what I have done, however, it is like reading the work of an eccentric, half-familiar stranger. He has satirical and documentary impulses. He is lugubrious, with flashes of levity, and is obsessed with illness and wounds. Although usually rejecting end rhymes, he is technically conservative. He is, or was, profoundly hung up on women in a quasi-Freudian or Jungian sort of way. He is attracted to psychopaths, not so much by their way of life as by their language. He cannot abide to live where he came from, rural Nova Scotia, and cannot stop writing about it.

In the course of a life I suppose that all the writing I have admired, and some I did not, has influenced me. But here are the twentieth-century poets whose work, whole or in part, I most favor: Auden, Elizabeth Bishop, Constantine Cavafy, Carlos Drummond de Andrade, Paul Éluard, Robert Graves, Ted Hughes, Irving Layton, Philip Larkin, Les A. Murray, Alden Nowlan, Fernando Pessoa, Ezra Pound, Al Purdy, Jules Supervielle, W.B. Yeats. Some composite of these, I like to imagine, might yield the greatest modern poem, though probably a macaronic one.

*   *   *

These days the notion that the poet could be or should be a man of letters is unfashionable. When it is revived, Fraser Sutherland will be described as a man of letters. At a time when poets are writing in hypertext, Sutherland finds employment as a book publisher's editor and consultant on lexicography. While academic critics are subverting the text, his desire is to establish it in the context of his life and society. When internationalists and globalists abound, he is concerned to describe the qualities and contradictions of life in the rural Maritimes, where he spent his early years, and to draw attention to the literature of Canada as an autonomous country in the world. With poets singing or performing their works on television and making them available on Internet cafés, Sutherland is happy muttering his lines, giving poetry readings to poetry lovers, printing his poems in small press publications, and expressing deeply held convictions in the face of a compromising and corrupting society.

The title of Sutherland's first book expresses some of the contradictions in the character of the poet specifically and in human nature generally. Called *Strange Ironies* (1972), it includes a number of strong poems, notably ''The Matuschka Case.'' The title *Within the Wound* (1976) suggests a descent into personal pain; the poet is driven to depths not always apparent. His poem ''Auden's Face'' is interesting in that it stays on the surface yet surmises the depths, saying, ''Much of the poetry's dispensable, but observe his face.'' Sutherland wrote about the pain and suffering of Frida Kahlo in a poem that preceded popular interest in her painting. He is not above having a bit of fun in the poem ''On Foreign Women,'' finding an ironic contrast between the feminine reality and the stereotypical responses to it.

As the poet Al Purdy noted about the poems in *Madwomen* (1978), ''There seem to be several people industriously scribbling away at these examples of literary genesis.'' There is the commentator on art who is not really urbane, the observer of women who is no Don Juan, the traveler who refuses to be the tourist, and the observer of the world who sees its foibles and failures through dry eyes that once held tears and may yet again.

Many poets burst into bloom in their youth and then droop with age. Other poets cautiously but resolutely push out their buds from the earth and head for the sun. Sutherland is one of the latter, and his poems have increased in subtlety and depth. *Whitefaces* (1986), his strongest collection, finds him writing poems that seem not at all as grimy and grumpy as the early poems, although no less honest and direct. In the title poem he writes,

> If I, a whiteface, am bored,
> think of the depthless boredom a blackface
> feels enveloped by white.

''Forms of Loss'' is philosophic about life's shortcomings: ''Loss is given us, and we take it.'' There is about Sutherland's work the sense of something unfulfilled, a feeling held in common with fellow Maritime poet Alden Nowlan. This can be seen, for example, in ''Insofar as Weather'':

> I am somewhere in the mist.
> You find me, you take me home.
> What happens then? We decide.
> I go, you stay. Unsaid . . .

The sense of the unfulfilled is an inevitable feeling: ''But afterward, / each of us is different.'' Our own and other peoples' lives may be difficult, but experiences leave more than simple scars. Communication itself is chancy. Here are four lines from ''Loyalty to an Old Idea'':

> Though you are years, a continent away,
> though these lines are written
> in a language you cannot understand,
> they're written for you, a moment's utterance . . .

What is interesting about the conceit of this poem is the poet's commitment to continue to write lines, even though they may not be read or, if they are read, not understood or, if understood, disregarded. It is a very human response and the one that impelled him to write the book-length poem *Jonestown* (1996) to place in the context of everyday life the unbelievable events surrounding the mass suicide of nine hundred followers of the Reverend Jim Jones in Guyana in 1978. The gruesome story of mass obsession is presented in the present tense through snatches of prose, free verse, documentary-like description, and the direct speech of some of its seventy-one characters. It is Sutherland's epic, and like the epic it focuses on events and stands apart from any overt moral condemnation of the hubris that led to the human tragedy.

Peace and War (1998) is a joint collection of fifty-four poems written by Sutherland and the Toronto-based Bosnian writer Goran Simić (in the translations of Amela Simić). These are among Sutherland's finest works. Some of the poems, like the extended comparison titled ''Myself & Napoleon Bonaparte'' (''His family was long established in Corsica. / Mine in Nova Scotia.''), are straightforward and playful. Yet I think it is true to say that, if Simić is war-weary, Sutherland is world-weary. As he writes in "Beginning,"

> To feel that lonely-aching hotel room
> until I come to myself and strangely then
> am grasped by others. To find new streets,
> cafés, restaurants, and parks, a different soil,
> to say, it's me, I'm here as indifference shatters.
> Then, far from myself, I can tell you:
> You don't know about me I'm more than you think.

The poet is right. He is an underestimated poet of subtlety and depth, the most humane of the poets of English Canada.

—John Robert Colombo

SUTHERLAND-SMITH, James (Alfred)

Nationality: British. **Born:** Aberdeen, Scotland, 17 June 1948. **Education:** Leeds University, 1968–71, B.A. in political studies 1971; Matlock College of Education, Derbyshire, 1973–74, Post-graduate Certificate in Education (English and History); University of East Anglia, 1988–89, M.A. in Teaching English as a Foreign Language. **Family:** Married Viera Schlosserova; one stepdaughter. **Career:** Articled clerk, WH Barnes (Accountants), London, 1972–73; teacher, Priory Road Middle School, Wimbledon, London, 1974–76, Jizan Secondary School, Saudi Arabia, 1976–77; language teacher, Inlingua, London, 1977–80, Azzawiya Oil Refinery, Libya, 1980–82, National Guard Training School, Riyadh, Saudi Arabia, 1982–86; head of language unit, Qatar Public Telecommunications, Doha, Qatar, 1986–88; lecturer, Safarik University, Presov, Slovakia, 1989–95. Since 1995 British Council English Language Advisor, East Slovakia. **Awards:** Gregory award, 1978; National Poetry Competition prizes, 1982, 1983, 1986, 1987, 1989; Cheltenham Festival Poetry Competition prizes, 1982, 1986, 1988; Cardiff International Poetry Competition prize, 1992; *Stand* Magazine Competition prize, 1996; Exeter International Poetry Competition prizes, 1996, 1997; Bridport Literary Festival Competition prizes, 1996, 1998. **Address:** Lesnicka 18, Solivar, 080 05 Presov, Slovakia.

PUBLICATIONS

Poetry

Four Poetry and Audience Poets, with others. Leeds, Poetry and Audience, 1971.
A Poetry Quintet. London, Gollancz, 1976.
A Singer from Sabiya. London, The Many Press, 1979.
Naming of the Arrow. London, Salamander Imprint, 1980.
The Country of Rumour. London, The Many Press, 1984.
At the Skin Resort. Todmorden, England, Arc Publications, 1999.

Recording: Iluzie, Modry Peter, 1991.

Other

Translator, *Not Waiting for Miracles.* Levoca, Slovakia, Modry Peter, 1993.
Translator, with Martin Solotruk, *Tightrope Walker: Selected Poems by Jan Ondrus.* Bratislava, Slovakia, Studna, 1998.
Translator, *Lojko, the Alarm Clock: Some Tales for Children by Vladimir Smihula.* Presov, Slovakia, Privatpress, 1999.

*

James Sutherland-Smith comments:

My early poetry was written under the influence of Eliot and then Robert Graves. At Leeds University I was impressed by the work and presence of Geoffrey Hill, although I think I was more inclined to imitate the poems of Roy Fuller in *New Poems* and Derek Mahon in *Crossing the Water.* Later on I discovered the poems of Osip Mandelstam and the memoirs of his widow, Nadezhda Mandelstam.

My early poetry was concerned with making striking images and making each poem sound all of a piece. Through the Penguin Modern European Poets series I understood that a poem did not have to be representational of a feeling, opinion, or scene but became more alive as an exploration of language that gradually focused feeling or thought. This occasionally made my poems difficult for English readers. An example is the sequence "Naming of the Arrow," which was inspired by a hearing of the poet Nikita Stanescu's "Elegies" in London in 1972.

From 1980 I have lived almost all the time abroad, in the Middle East and in Slovakia. I have also traveled extensively. My profession is that of a language teacher, and this combined with the need to communicate in a simplified form has made my poetry plainer. The Middle East prompted poems that attempt to deal with a failure to become part of the culture while my work of the last six years deals with the experience of the collapse of communism and how it has changed not only eastern Europe but the sensibility of a Western liberal, too.

*   *   *

Ranging across international settings clarified by their titles—from "Wandsworth Bridge" to "Swimming in the Red Sea before a Sandstorm"—James Sutherland-Smith's early poems are nevertheless curiously indefinite about their various localities, grappling instead with internal circumstances of placement and poetic self-definition. "Fantasia: London and Ocean," from his first full-length collection, *A Singer from Sabiya,* expresses the desire of these poems to communicate by a series of movements more visceral than those of speech: "We should have dolphin radar / Not telephones." Struggling with and against artifice to become like "Dante's pebbles," whose "nature is not hidden / By the water's polish" ("A Gift of Stones, Light and Water"), the often awkwardly burdened language of these poems pits itself against the commonplaces of English as familiar tongue and seeks to "move as if from discourse / Grimy with abuse to clarity" ("The Café in the Desert").

Sutherland-Smith's early poems search for clarity in the contradictory plenitude of ascetic abandon or search for an erotic and tactile mobility beyond the stasis of words. The results are not always clear. The horses in "Mist and Horses outside Sittingbourne," for instance, are "united / When their colour is compromised / Between light and dark in monotones / Arcane as waxy phosphorus / Sealed away in an airtight jar,'' and in ''Bear,'' from *Naming of the Arrow,* the animal is ''muzzled by largactil'' (a proprietary name for chlorpromazine, a tranquilizer used in the treatment of certain mental disorders as well as for the control of vomiting). Nor are the results always erotic, as the stilted lines of ''The Maiden in the Wood'' bear witness to (''dancing / In the wood's taut unaltered radiance'') or as the tedious recourse to figures of engorged nipples in ''A Sensuous Language'' testifies. Nevertheless, the struggle for a more sparse precision produces in the early poems some distinctively phrased observations, as in ''Late Autumn,'' for instance, when ''forests have shed / Their intimate vocabulary'' and become ''a slaughtered army or a species / Shot for its fur, strung on a wire,'' and force is revealed as ''no more than a breeze turning / The weathervane or hands touching.'' By carefully considering, say, the mineral life of chalk—''the calcium slush / Of skeletons hardened and raised / Still dead'' (''Chalkland'')—or in attempting to articulate how ''saying more means less and less'' in ''Brush and Ink: Some Japanese Pictures,'' the more successful of these poems begin to validate the ambition that motivates them and so prepare for the more precise definition of later works.

With the 1984 appearance of *The Country of Rumour,* Sutherland-Smith's poems are more comfortable in their observance of life—mostly Middle Eastern desert life—and more confident in their articulation. Often simpler in execution, more immediate in presentation, and less obscure in diction—even at times homely—these poems allow geographical surrounds to complement their intelligibility, rooting themselves more securely in the exotic environment of their production. The first poem, ''Exile,'' begins, ''Here there is no hardship except the worst / Which is the absence of your voice,'' and it ends, ''Outside / The mimosa declines into blossom. / Orioles mourn in the olive groves.'' In the poem ''In the Harbour at Leptis Magna,'' ''An octopus unfolds like a dishcloth / Then mottles to the colour of the sand / And seagrass it undulates upon.'' Looking with ''clear childish eyes'' and coming to resemble ''a kind of Zeppelin with flippers,'' the octopus seems to the speaker ''more bird than Minerva's chipped emblem'' that presides ''dumb as a dead language'' over the ''buried two-thirds / Of this Roman monument to force.'' The speaker is ''not detained'' from entering the water, though ''an Arab followed to make sure / I left with nothing which was not mine.'' Though still perhaps unnecessarily dense in their layers of allusion and still suffering from moments of obtuseness, these poems no longer struggle as awkwardly with their formal containers, and the collection culminates with a charmingly uncluttered series of ''Sonnets from Zawai,'' most notable of which is the opening trilogy devoted to cooking chickens.

Later poems, which add to Middle Eastern materials a concern with affairs in eastern Europe, especially Slovakia (from whose language Sutherland-Smith has published English translations), are even more firmly rooted in observations of a foreignness. These poems appear to have lost much of the linguistic desperation attending some of their earlier counterparts, and many have matured into a grace comfortable enough to accommodate the political and social changes taking place around them or, perhaps more impressively, to accommodate cultural rhythms that persist through change. They turn to consideration of subjects like anti-Semitism, in ''A New Age,'' or, as in ''After Partition,'' describe listening to a radio from which ''a foxtrot / Slithers out from the Thirties, a time before / Innocence became not just impossible / But absurd.'' From ''A Snail in Istanbul'' or ''A Violin Playing in Cairo'' to ''An Execution in Riyadh'' or ''Wild Plums in Slovakia,'' the later poems open themselves to a continuance and change from which they educe a more locally intimate sense of joy and suffering. Increasingly concerned with the weight and passage of history bearing down alongside everyday occurrence, a number of these poems appear to have absorbed through local circumstance something akin to W.H. Auden's later appreciation of our complex occupancy in time, as in ''Replacing Russian'':

> Where I ply my trade, one hundred miles west
> Of what was said to be an evil empire,
> A man hefts on to his shoulder a length
> Of two-by-four and strolls off, his fly undone.

—Brain Macaskill

SWARD, Robert (S.)

Nationality: American; Canadian Landed Immigrant. **Born:** Chicago, Illinois, 23 June 1933. **Education:** Von Steuben High School, Chicago; San Diego Junior College, California, 1951; University of Illinois, Urbana, 1953–56, B.A. (honors) 1956 (Phi Beta Kappa); Bread Loaf School of English, Middlebury, Vermont, summers 1956–58; University of Iowa, Iowa City, M.A. 1958; University of Bristol (Fulbright Fellow), 1960–61. **Military Service:** U.S. Navy in Korea, 1951–53. **Family:** Married 1) Sondra Hirch in 1956, one daughter; 2) Diane Kaldes in 1960 (divorced 1969), two daughters and one son; 3) Judith Essenson in 1969 (divorced 1972) one daughter; 4) Irina Schestakowich in 1975, one son; lives with Gloria K. Alford since 1988. **Career:** Research fellow, 1956–58, and poet-in-residence, spring 1967, University of Iowa; lecturer in English, Connecticut College, New London, 1958–59; writer-in-residence, Cornell University, Ithaca, New York, 1962–64, Aspen Writers' Conference, Colorado, summer 1967, and University of Victoria, British Columbia, 1969–73; from 1979 participant, Writers in the Schools programs, Ontario; from 1984 associate fellow, Strong College, York University, Toronto. Visiting writer, University of California, Santa Cruz, since 1986, Monterey Peninsula College, 1986–88, Cultural Council of Santa Cruz County, since 1986, Cabrillo College, Aptos, California, since 1988, Foothill Writers' Conference, summers 1988–89, and Foothill College, Los Altos, California. Founding editor, Soft Press, 1970–77, and editor, Hancock House Editions, 1976–79, both in Victoria. Since 1979 freelance writer: book reviewer, Toronto *Star,* and broadcaster, CBC Radio. **Awards:** Dylan Thomas award, 1958; Yaddo fellowship, summers 1959–69; MacDowell Colony fellowship, summers 1959–72; Fulbright scholarship, 1960–61; D.H. Lawrence fellowship, 1966; Guggenheim fellowship, 1966; Canada Council grant, 1973, 1981, 1982, 1983; Ontario Arts Council grant, 1982, 1983, 1984; Montalvo Literary Arts award, 1989. **Address:** P.O. Box 7062, Santa Cruz, California 95061–7062, U.S.A.

PUBLICATIONS

Poetry

Advertisements. Chicago, Odyssey, 1958.
Uncle Dog and Other Poems. London, Putnam, 1962.
Kissing the Dancer and Other Poems. Ithaca, New York, Cornell University Press, 1964.

Thousand-Year-Old Fiancée and Other Poems. Ithaca, New York, Cornell University Press, 1965.

In Mexico and Other Poems. London, Ambit, 1966.

Horgbortom Stringbottom, I Am Yours, You Are History. Chicago, Swallow Press, 1970.

Quorum, with Noah, by Charles Doyle. Victoria, British Columbia, Soft Press, 1970.

Songs from the Jurassic Shales. Victoria, British Columbia, Soft Press, 1970.

Hannah's Cartoon. Victoria, British Columbia, Soft Press, 1970.

Gift. Victoria, British Columbia, Soft Press, 1970.

Raspberry (as Dr. Soft). Victoria, British Columbia, Soft Press, 1971.

Risk. Victoria, British Columbia, Soft Press, 1971.

Four Poems. Wichita, Kansas, J. Meechem, 1973.

Letter to a Straw Hat. Victoria, British Columbia, Soft Press, 1974.

Five Iowa Poems and One Iowa Print. Iowa City, Stone Wall Press, 1975.

Honey Bear on Lasqueti Island, B.C. Victoria, British Columbia, Soft Press, 1978.

Six Poems. Toronto, League of Canadian Poets, 1980.

Twelve Poems. Toronto, Island House, 1982.

Half a Life's History: Poems New and Selected (1957–1983). Toronto, Aya Press, 1983.

Movies: Left to Right. London, South Western Ontario Poetry Publications, 1983.

The Three Roberts: Premier Performance, with Robert Priest and Robert Zend. Toronto, HMS Press, 1984.

The Three Roberts on Love, with Robert Priest and Robert Zend. Toronto, Dreadnaught Press, 1984.

The Three Roberts on Childhood, with Robert Priest and Robert Zend. St. Catharines, Ontario, Moonstone Press, 1985.

Poet Santa Cruz. Santa Cruz, California, Jazz Press, 1985.

Four Incarnations, New & Selected Poems, 1957–1991. Minneapolis, Coffee House Press, 1991.

Family, with Charles Atkinson, Tillie Shaw, and David Swanger. Concord, California, Select Poets Series, 1994.

Uncivilizing, A Collection of Poetry. Toronto, Insomniac Press, 1997.

Recording: *Thousand-Year-Old Fiancée and Other Poems,* Aural, 1965.

Novels

The Jurassic Shales. Toronto, Coach House Press, 1975.

A Much-Married Man. Victoria, British Columbia, Ekstasis Editions, 1996.

Other

The Toronto Islands: An Illustrated History. Toronto, Dreadnaught, 1983.

Editor, with Tim Groves and Mario Martinelli, *Vancouver Island Poems.* Victoria, British Columbia, Soft Press, 1973.

Editor, *Cheers for Muktananda.* Victoria, British Columbia, Soft Press, 1976.

*

Bibliography: By John Gill, in *New: American and Canadian Poetry* (Trumansburg, New York), 1973.

Manuscript Collections: Washington University Library, St. Louis; National Library of Canada, Ottawa; University of Victoria; Toronto City Archives, City Hall; University of California at Santa Cruz Library, Special Collection.

Critical Studies: ''The Voices Have Range'' by John Malcolm Brinnin, in *New York Times Book Review,* 25 October 1964; introduction by William Meredith to *Kissing the Dancer and Other Poems,* 1964; *A Controversy of Poets* edited by Paris Leary and Robert Kelly, New York, Doubleday, 1965; ''Robert Sward: A Mysticism of Objects'' by Laurence Lieberman, in *Carleton Miscellany,* spring 1967; ''A Poetry Chronicle'' by Constance Urdang, in *Poetry* (Chicago), 17 February 1972; introduction by Earle Birney to *Poems New and Selected (1957–1983),* 1983; ''Off the Wall Approach'' by Ann Struthers, in *Des Moines Sunday Register,* 10 May 1992; ''Profile: Poet Robert Sward'' by John Laue, in *Monterey Bay Writer,* summer 1994.

Robert Sward comments:

Born on the Jewish North Side of Chicago, bar mitzvahed, sailor, amnesiac, university professor (Cornell, Iowa, Connecticut College), newspaper editor, food reviewer, father of five children, husband to four wives, I have had a writing career that has been described by critic Virginia Lee as a ''long and winding road.''

1. Switchblade Poetry: Chicago Style.

I began writing poetry in Chicago at age fifteen when I was named corresponding secretary for a gang of young punks and hoodlums called the Semcoes. A ''social athletic club,'' we met at various locations two Thursdays a month. My job was to write postcards to inform my brother thugs—who carried switchblade knives and stole cars for fun and profit—as to when, where, and why we were meeting.

Rhyming couplets seemed the appropriate form to notify characters like light-fingered Foxman, cross-eyed Harris, and Irving ''Koko,'' of upcoming meetings. An example of my switchblade juvenilia:

The Semcoes meet next Thursday night
at Speedway Koko's. Five bucks dues, Foxman, or fight.

Koko was a young boxer whose father owned Chicago's Speedway Wrecking Company and whose basement was filled with punching bags and pinball machines. Koko and the others joked about my affliction—the writing of poetry—but were so astonished that they criticized me mainly for my inability to spell.

2. Sailor Librarian: San Diego.

At seventeen I graduated from high school, gave up my job as soda jerk, and joined the navy. The Korean War was under way, my mother had died, and Chicago seemed an oppressive place to be.

My thanks to the U.S. Navy. They taught me how to type (sixty words a minute), organize an office, and serve as a librarian. In 1952 I served in Korea aboard a 300-foot-long, flat-bottomed Landing Ship Tank (LST). A yeoman third class, I became overseer of twelve hundred paperback books, a sturdy upright typewriter, and a couple of filing cabinets.

The best thing about duty on an LST is the ship's speed—eight to ten knots. It takes approximately one month for an LST to sail between San Diego and Pusan, Korea. That month I read Melville's *Moby Dick,* Whitman's *Leaves of Grass,* Thoreau's *Walden,* Isak Dinesen's *Winter's Tales,* the King James Version of the Bible, Shakespeare's *Hamlet, King Lear,* and a biography of Abraham Lincoln.

While at sea, I began writing poetry as if poems, to paraphrase Thoreau, were secret letters from some distant land. I sent one poem to a girl named Lorelei, with whom I was in love. Lorelei had a job at the Dairy Queen. Shortly before enlisting in the navy, I spent fifteen dollars of my soda jerk money taking her up in a single-engine sight-seeing airplane so we could kiss and—at the same time—get a good look at Chicago from the air. Beautiful Lorelei never responded to my poem. Years later, at the University of Iowa's workshop, I learned that much of what I had been writing—love poems inspired by a combination of lust and loneliness—belonged, loosely speaking, to a tradition, the venerable tradition of unrequited love.

3. Mr. Amnesia: Cambridge.

In 1962, after ten years of writing poetry, my book *Uncle Dog and Other Poems* was published by Putnam in England. That was followed by two books from Cornell University Press, *Kissing the Dancer* and *Thousand-Year-Old Fiancée.* Then in 1966 I was invited to do fourteen poetry readings in a two-week stretch at places like Dartmouth, Amherst, and the University of Connecticut.

The day before I was scheduled to embark on the reading series I was hit by a speeding MG in Cambridge, Massachusetts. I lost my memory for a period of about twenty-four hours. Just as I saw the world fresh while cruising to a war zone, so I now caught a glimpse of what a city like Cambridge can look like when one's inner slate, so to speak, is wiped clean. For the record, I went ahead—with bandages—and did all fourteen readings.

4. Santa Claus: Santa Cruz.

In December 1985, recently returned to the United States after some years in Canada, a freelance writer, in search of a story, I sought and found employment as a rent-a-Santa Claus. Imagine walking into the local community center and suddenly, at the sight of four hundred children, feeling transformed from one's skinny, sad-eyed self into an elf, having to chant the prescribed syllables, ''Ho, Ho, Ho.''

What is poetry? For me it is the restrained music of a switchblade knife. It is an amphibious warship magically transformed into a basketball court and then transformed again into a movie theater showing a film about the life of Joan of Arc. It is the vision of an amnesiac bleeding from a head injury, witnessing the play of sunlight on a redbrick wall.

Poetry comes to a bearded Jewish wanderer pulling on a pair of high rubber boots with white fur, and a set of musical sleigh bells, over blue, fleece-lined sweatpants. It comes to the father of five children bearing gifts for four hundred and, choked up, unable to speak, alternately laughing and sobbing the three traditional sylla-bles—''Ho, Ho, Ho''—hearing at the same time in his heart the more plaintive, tragic ''Oi vay, Oi vay, Oi vay.''

*   *   *

A striking feature of Robert Sward's poetry is its range. He is a master of unique observation, gifted with emotional recall, capable of

goofy humor as well as experiments in disdain, and properly turned off by war and the diplomatic posture of his native America. Sward's ''Statement of Poetics''—a poem that appeared in *New: American & Canadian Poetry 20*—may indicate his attitudes accurately enough, though it may also indicate his disdain for unanswerable poetic questions. He is outrageous as often as not, seeming capable of walking on words halfway between the double exposures of put-on and truth:

Talk

people talking, getting that
into one's poetry that
is my poetics. Love
hate lies laughing stealings
self-confession self-destruction
get them all get
them all into writing.
No one has to
read them. No one
has to publish them.
I am more and
more for unpublished poetry.

Sward's delight with language is evident in all of his poetry, and the reader senses a healthy dose of play at work in every poem. He revels in the power of the final word, which he uses with delight against the innocent as well as those who have crossed him. He writes in ''Mothers-in-Law,'' both of whom he lost through divorce, that the first of them ''required, upon departure, / The services of three gentlemen with shoehorns / To get her back into her large black / Studebaker.'' The reader experiences vicarious pleasure imagining the lady in question thumbing through Sward's book. It may be the play of an adolescent nature, but how grand to have a poet awaken the childishness within us.

Indeed, if we accept spontaneity as a primary quality of child-hood, Sward's childishness is virtually unequaled. The poetry that results is sometimes half-baked, but it is so direct of statement that we unquestionably feel the poet's complete, warty presence. I will take this kind of unguarded, risky stuff any day in preference to the urbane, sophisticated verse of poets half his age who write only within a limited range of highly selected posturings. Sward is willing to let his reader hate him, yet he himself escapes the pit of self-hatred. At times his spontaneity works against him, as in the polemic ''In Mexico,'' where after describing his opposition to American war policies, he concludes, ''What a country! / For even / Your stupidity, / The Charm / Of Your / Tastelessness, / Vitality, / Greed / / *America, get out / of Vietnam, / The Dominican Republic, / Africa, Europe / Southeast Asia* / / Has begun to smell / Has begun to smell / I would say / Like the Pentagon, / Like senility / Like death.'' I believe that poems written without deference to academic standards should rise above such standards and not be vulnerable to the kind of bitchy complaint that the subject's ''stupidity'' and ''charm'' are not capa-ble of their verbs. Further, the abstract image is not even linguistically interesting unless Sward intends a different subject. In any case, spontaneity in this instance results in dull rhetoric.

For each of his few failed risks, however, Sward has many poems that win against the odds, his only form the integrity of his voice. The language is tight and the words comprehensible, and he can move up off the page, out of the words, like a man coming into sunlight. I admire his fullness and will end with excerpts from two distinctly different poems, "San Cristobal" and "Risk":

Pine cones, aspen,
Starlight, the light
World one way, then another
The light rising,
The light drawn up into stars

Voice is light,
The world is light
The stars, their hands
Striking through

It's a calculated risk, whatever you do.
    A man has cancer of the rectum. You
    take out his rectum and
maybe he dies of heart failure.
Or he's fine and goes on for 20 years.

—Geof Hewitt

SWEENEY, Matthew

Nationality: Irish. **Born:** County Donegal, 6 October 1952. **Education:** Gormanston College, County Meath, 1965–70; University College, Dublin, 1970–72; Polytechnic of North London, 1977–78, B.A. (honors) in English and German; University of Freiburg, West Germany, 1977–78. **Family:** Married Rosemary Barber in 1979; two children. **Career:** Writer-in-residence, Farnham College, Surrey, 1984, 1985; external advisor in creative writing, West Surrey College of Art and Design, Farnham, 1986–89; publicist and events assistant, Poetry Society, London, 1988–90; poet-in-residence, Hereford & Worcester, 1991; writer-in-residence, South Bank Centre, 1994–95. **Awards:** Prudence Farmer award, 1984; University of East Anglia writing fellowship, 1986; Cholmondeley award, 1987; Arts Council of Great Britain Bursary in creative writing, 1992. **Address:** 11 Dombey Street, London, WC1N 3PB, England.

PUBLICATIONS

Poetry

Without Shores. Leicester, Omens, 1978.
A Dream of Maps. Dublin, Raven Arts Press, 1981.
A Round House. Dublin, Raven Arts Press, and London, Allison and Busby, 1983.
The Lame Waltzer. Dublin, Raven Arts Press, and London, Allison and Busby, 1985.
Blue Shoes. London, Secker and Warburg, 1989.
Cacti. London, Secker and Warburg, 1992.
The Flying Spring Onion (for children). London, Faber, 1992.
The Blue Taps (for children). London, Prospero Poets, 1994.
Fatso in the Red Suit (for children). London, Faber, 1995.
The Bridal Suite (for children). London, Cape, 1997.
A Smell of Fish. London, Cape, 2000.

Other

The Chinese Dressing Gown (for children). Dublin, Raven Arts Press, 1987.
The Snow Vulture (for children). London, Faber, 1992.
Writing Poetry: And Getting Published. London, Hodder Headline, and Lincolnwood, Illinois, NTC Publishing Group, 1997.

Editor, *One for Jimmy: An Anthology from the Hereford and Worcester Poetry Project.* N.p., Hereford and Worcester County Council, 1992.
Editor, *Emergency Kit: Poems for Strange Times,* by Jo Shapcott. London, Faber, 1996.
Editor, with Ken Smith and Felix Post, *Beyond Bedlam: Poems Written out of Mental Distress.* London, Anvil Press Poetry, 1997.

*

Critical Study: "The Permanent City: The Younger Irish Poets" by Gerald Dawe, in *The Irish Writer and the City,* edited by Maurice Harmon, Gerards Cross, Buckinghamshire, Smythe, and Totowa, New Jersey, Barnes and Noble, 1984.

*   *   *

Matthew Sweeney's work does not sit comfortably in the canon of contemporary British or Irish poetry, and for a time his work did not receive the international recognition it has long deserved. There is little figurative language and almost no rhetoric in a typical Sweeney poem, and he bears a more fruitful comparison with certain American and eastern European poets. Curiously, his great strength and uniqueness among his contemporaries was inadvertently summed up in a negative review of his work by one particularly shrill Irish critic, who complained that his work was "uncontaminated by simile or metaphor." Indeed, although Sweeney can and does turn out remarkable similes with consummate skill, he will never attract readers who come to poetry for the easy glitter of surface tropes. Instead, he achieves his considerable effects by subtle shifts of tonal register within highly distilled, suggestive narratives and dramatic monologues. Furthermore, his poems are pervaded by a potent mixture of horror and humor reminiscent of Kafka and Beckett.

In "The Coffin Shop," for example, Sweeney depicts as truly repellent creatures the morticians who "recognise the recently alone," adding with typical quirkiness, "Their eyes are expressive as pandas / who have mastered maths . . ." But the humor in no way dilutes or softens the subtle horror of the final lines: "They poke the velvet cushions for the head, / they stand back and turn to face you / —you'd hardly decline if you could."

Sweeney has the uncanny ability to remind us of nightmares we had forgotten; childhood terrors, fear of bodily decrepitude, and the apocalypse are all embodied in his finely wrought parables. This darkness and bizarre wit often emerge slowly, welling up as the poem progresses, as in "Where Fishermen Can't Swim," the title of which sums up that potent blend of menace and fatalism—the intimation of disaster—that underscores so many of his best poems. The poem is set in Sweeney's native Donegal, where one morning "a lobster boat cast off, whose engine / croaked before the rocks were by.'' The youngest of the crew jumps out onto a rock to push the boat off and laughs when he cannot jump back, at which point the narrative takes a nightmarish turn: ''But exactly when did he realise / that the boat would float no nearer . . .'' The structure of this last phrase is repeated as Sweeney details the crew's desperate efforts to save the boy as the tide rises: ''that all those pulls on the engine cord / would yield no shudders; that no rope / or lifebelt existed to be thrown; / that those flares were lost in cloud; / that the radio would bring a copter / an hour later? He had forty minutes— / to cling while the waves attacked, / to feel the rock gradually submerge. / And they had forty minutes of watching, / shouting into the radio, till he cried / out, sank from view, and stayed there.'' The rising sea is effectively mimed in the grammatical structures of the poem.

One of the most unexpected aspects of Sweeney's work is his formalism. Whereas many poets employ rhyme and meter in a clearly recognizable way in order to demonstrate their facility with language, Sweeney seems to take great pains to disguise difficult forms and rhymes. Perhaps this is because Sweeney, unlike many British and Irish poets, uses the aleatory qualities of form in composition in order to gain access to scenes or pictures that lie beneath waking consciousness. If the form exerts a subliminal effect on the reader, so much the better.

Particularly interesting in this regard is Sweeney's use of that most difficult of forms, the sestina. Many readers of the collection *Blue Shoes* will be surprised to discover that it contains two sestinas, ''The Monk's Watch'' and ''The Queue.'' In both cases the repetition of words demanded by the form is skillfully camouflaged by the compelling flow of narrative. Similarly, poems like ''The U Boat'' and ''Postcard of a Hanging'' are so deftly and subtly rhymed that the form never intrudes and there remains after reading only a lingering sense of precision.

''Postcard of a Hanging'' is one of Sweeney's best poems, revealing a moral complexity beneath its disturbing humor. It takes the form of a dramatic monologue spoken by a friend imagining ''you'' (perhaps the poet) receiving the grim postcard of the title. He pictures the recipient's disgust, with the image fading as he gradually surmises that the photograph is merely a trick, ''a decadent oriental gimmick / to put liberals off their breakfast / of an egg, toast, jam and the rest.'' The second of the poem's three stanzas deals with the message on the reverse of the card, hinting at the sender's culinary and erotic adventures, in stark contrast to the banality of ''an egg, toast, jam and the rest.'' When we return in the last stanza to reinspect the disturbing image, it is as if the poet's—and reader's—faith in the narrator's humanity has been subtly destabilized:

And you turned to the picture again,
a colour print—a gallows, two men,
one hooded, one holding a noose
of whitest rope, for the moment loose,
and low in the foreground a crowd
of men mainly, silently loud,
all eastern, except for two or three—
one of whom, if you look closely, is me.

Few poets writing in English can so gracefully guide us to the heart of darkness.

—Michael Donaghy

SZIRTES, George

Nationality: British. **Born:** Budapest, Hungary, 29 November 1948; immigrated to England in 1956. **Education:** Kingsbury County Grammar School, 1960–68; Harrow School of Art, 1968–69; Leeds College of Art, 1969–72, B.A. in fine art 1972; Goldsmiths' College, London, 1972–73, A.T.C. 1973. **Family:** Married Clarissa Upchurch in 1970; one son and one daughter. **Career:** Part-time teacher in colleges and schools, 1973–75; head of art, Hitchin Girls School, Hertfordshire, 1975–81; head of art, 1981–87, and since 1987 part-time staff member, St. Christopher School, Letchworth, Hertfordshire. Proprietor, Starwheel Press, Hitchin. Since 1987 freelance writer and translator. Senior lecturer in poetry, Norfolk Institute of Art and Design, 1991. **Awards:** Faber memorial prize, 1980; Arts Council grant, 1984; Cholmondeley award, 1987. Fellow, Royal Society of Literature, 1982; Déry prize for translation, 1991; Gold Star of the Hungarian Republic for translation, 1991. **Address:** 16 Damgate Street, Wymondham, Norfolk NR18 OBQ, England.

PUBLICATIONS

Poetry

Poems. Leeds, Perkin, 1972.
The Iron Clouds. Hitchin, Hertfordshire, Dodman Press, 1975.
Visitors. Hitchin, Hertfordshire, Mandeville Press, 1976.
A Mandeville Troika, with Neil Powell and Peter Scupham. Hitchin, Hertfordshire, Mandeville Press, 1977.
An Illustrated Alphabet. Hitchin, Hertfordshire, Mandeville Press, 1978.
At the Sink. London, Keepsake Press, 1978.
Silver Age. Hitchin, Hertfordshire, Dodman Press, 1978.
The Slant Door. London, Secker and Warburg, 1979.
Sermon on a Ship. Hitchin, Hertfordshire, Dodman Press, 1980.
Homage to Cheval. Berkhamsted, Hertfordshire, Priapus, 1981.
November and May. London, Secker and Warburg, 1981.
The Kissing Place. Hitchin, Hertfordshire, Starwheel Press, 1982.
Short Wave. London, Secker and Warburg, 1984.
The Photographer in Winter. London, Secker and Warburg, 1986.
Metro. Oxford, Oxford University Press, 1988.
Bridge Passages. Oxford, Oxford University Press, 1991.
Blind Field. Oxford, Oxford University Press, 1994.
Selected Poems, 1976–1996. Oxford and New York, Oxford University Press, 1996.
Portrait of My Father in an English Landscape. Oxford and New York, Oxford University Press, 1998.

Other

The Red All Over Riddle Book (for children). London, Faber, 1997.

Editor, *A Starwheel Portfolio, The Transparent Room, Strict Seasons, Spring Offensive, Cloud Station, States of Undress* (verse and etching portfolios). Hitchin, Hertfordshire, Starwheel Press, 6 vols., 1978–84.

Editor, *The Blood of the Walsungs: Selected Poems,* by Ottó Orbán. Newcastle upon Tyne, Bloodaxe, Budapest, Corvina, and Chester Springs, Pennsylvania, Dufour, 1993.

Editor, *Collected Poems,* by Freda Downie. Newcastle upon Tyne, Bloodaxe, 1995.

Editor and translator, *New Life,* by Zsuzsa Rakovsky. Oxford, Oxford University Press, 1994.

Editor and translator, with George Gömöri, *The Colonnade of Teeth: Modern Hungarian Poetry.* Newcastle upon Tyne, Bloodaxe, and Chester Springs, Pennsylvania, Dufour, 1996.

Translator, *The Tragedy of Man,* by Imre Madách. New York, Puski, 1988.

Translator, *Through the Smoke,* selected poems by István Vas. Budapest and London, Corvina, 1989.

Translator, *Anna Édes,* by Dezsö Kosztolányi. London, Quartet, 1991; New York, New Directions, 1993.

Translator, *The Melancholy of Resistance,* by László Krasznahorkai. London, Quartet, 1998.

Translator, *The Adventures of Sindbad,* by Gyula Krúdy. Budapest and New York, CEU Press, 1998.

*

Critical Studies: Reviews by Peter Porter, in *The Observer* (London), 19 August 1979, 22 January 1984, 1 June 1986, and 9 August 1988; by Christopher Hope, in *London Magazine,* March 1980; by William Palmer, in *Poetry Review* (London), December 1981; by Carol Rumens, in *Quarto* (London), February 1982; by Ian Bamforth, in *Edinburgh Review,* spring 1982; by Tim Dooley, in *Times Literary Supplement* (London), 13 January 1984; by Michael Hulse, in *Literary Review* (London), January 1984; by Barbara Hardy, in *Books and Bookmen* (London), April 1986; by Anne Stevenson, in *The Sunday Times* (London), 14 September 1986; by John Lucas, in *New Statesman* (London), 26 August 1988; by Sean O'Brien, in *Poetry Review* (London), 1988; by Peter Forbes, in *The Listener* (London), 1 December 1988; by John Whitworth, in *Poetry Review* (London), 85(2), summer 1995.

George Szirtes comments:

In 1985 I wrote, "I think at whatever point the reader picks up my poetry he will find a conflict between two states of mind." These I called "the possibility of happiness" and "apprehension of disaster." The early poems in *The Slant Door* made repeated references to pictures, often paintings, as points of arrest between these states. Sometimes the setting would be domestic; other times exotic. The effect would often entail conflating the two. This seemed to define the territory I could best move in.

I think I thought of art—perhaps I still do—as the only way of organizing nebulous experience. Precisely because of that it is not to be trusted. *November and May* concentrates less on the finished object, more on the process of making. In one poem, "The Silver Tree," a group of girls in a winter classroom are making an artificial tree out of twigs and silver paper. The poem imagines the tree fatally embracing them and the girls hanging like fruit "until / Imaginary gods pass by and cut them down." In other poems faces turn into maps, mice nibble at paintings, a car turns into a piece of architecture by Gaudí, a piano gets up and prepares for breakfast.

The act of arrest is faintly erotic. The dead, starved, and aged retain all the sensuality of healthy youth. In my third book, *Short Wave,* there are variations on the notion of history as Eros. Household props, specific rooms, streets and squares become ways of preserving passionate fictions. The sofa on which my mother leaned when she was young and where "a young man like a strong wind hung / About her shoulders and her undone lips" has come unstuffed. It turns into bubbles, "delicate and blinding." In one short poem a "kitchen grows a beard of fragrance / curling with pomade and vinegar." The victim in a poem about Goya "is tossed in a blanket / By cheerful bosomy girls." He is soon shot and "blazes / like an indulgent omen." The title poem seeks some center to experience by turning the dial on the radio through a sequence of stations to locate "that Balkan baritone / who tells me what the world believes of me." History is a voluptuous white noise full of secret puns. In "Assassins" the Russians commemorate Burns night while celebrating "their history of combustions."

The shortwave frequencies lead back to my birthplace, Budapest. In *The Photographer in Winter,* written after my first return visit in 1984, the paintings of the first book give way, as the title suggests, to photographs. In the same way invention yields to dreamlike documentation. The title poem follows the photographer about her business. Pictures break up, turn into snow; the world disintegrates at our fingers' ends as we click the shutter. The camera shows now an X ray, now the self-conscious posing of a model. "The Courtyards" describes a block of Budapest flats during the 1956 uprising, and looks to locate a home in the eyes of a blind woman who carries the keys to the elevator. A series of poems about railway journeys notices multiple reflections in the window and follows "fantastic trains like twists of barley" into Chinese ice palaces, where everything is "frozen, formal / Furious and unattainable." In "The Swimmers" a church floor dissolves to reveal the dead writhing like eels and rising "hearing nothing— / No names, no objects, no singing, nothing but sea."

Metro continues the Hungarian theme using the metaphor of the underground train. A psychopomp figure leads one into the world of 1944, bearing a moldered cross "through tunnels tight as fingers in a glove." This history provides a particularly ghostly Eros for children to encounter in their sleep as they turn to the wall "through which / Symbols pass and cool their blood." An uncle disappears when the glove closes about him and drops him in a ditch: "The ditch becomes a pit, / the pit a symbol, the symbol a desire." Stalin's mustache grows enormous, like foliage on a wall, streets are "hard cores of pleasure," doorways are "ripe fruit, stay soft and open, exhaling a fragrance of drains or tobacco." The whole poem runs through 780 lines, as the train hesitates at the doors of Ravensbruck. Other poems in the book are related to and divided either side of it.

Bridge Passages, my third "Hungarian" book, is set mostly in 1989, when I spent eight months in Budapest. The poems in it are the closest I have got to reportage (which is not very close) in that they respond on a daily level to the rapid political changes of the time. The poems are, as usual, formal-informal, with tight stanzas and rhyming structures, the syntax running through the line breaks. In spring an early fly "scrambles up / fizzing furiously, leans / against the glass, revving up his motor, / then into gear and upwards." He "gropes / towards his notion of the good, / his personal heap, however much it stinks." In the new politics "the lost flesh settles down against the bone / with the lightness of a cushion." There are poems conflating the events in Tiananmen Square, Heroes Square Budapest, and Wajda's film "Ashes and Diamonds," poems in which rain types out the nonsense language of flies and human lovers. It is a restless mixture of a book, with a series of poems based on my early experiences of England (see particularly "A Picture of My Parents with Their First Television") and a number of translations from the Hungarian.

By this time I was spending much of my time translating. In fact, I had been including translated poems in my own collections since *The Photographer in Winter*. As I translated fiction, drama, verse, and essays, I was often disoriented by being billed as a Hungarian poet despite never having written a line in Hungarian. The disorientation was partly symbolic. After three books of pre-Hungary and three post-, I returned to the theme of photography for my most recent book of poems, *Blind Field*. The book balances two concerns: one aesthetic, the other, broadly speaking, humane. The photography-film poems are fantasies on the idea of truth, with references to Arbus and Raymond Chandler. The Gulf War, freak shows, Renaissance Florence, the early years of the century, the sheer voluptuousness of looking at any or all of these things are themes that move through the first section of the book. The last section refers to more immediate family histories: dining in an old restaurant, my father's great aunt and her habit of presenting him with small cakes on a doily. I suppose this reflects the peculiar melancholy of the central European quotidian. Between these two sections comes "Transylvania," a poem in terza rima about a visit to my mother's hometown, Cluj-Napoca. At its center is an ice-skating scene that may hold it together. The skaters are "lines of ink / impossible to read now. A fountain jets / snow. The bandstand is a skating rink / full of toy soldiers." Above the double time scale of summer now/winter then, "vague herds / of cloud, meander like soldiers on patrol / at a border station between two absurd / countries."

And this is where I am now, somewhere between two histories and two traditions. A few declarative sentences to end with: I admire the following twentieth-century poets in particular: Eliot, Auden, Ransom, Stevens, Roethke, MacNeice, Bishop, and Hecht. Before that Herbert, Marvell, Pope, Clare, and Browning. Wordsworth can sometimes move me to tears, but I am not alone in that. I have a ridiculous fondness for oddities like Crashaw, Diaper, and Beddoes and suspect Ransom may belong among these. The modern Hungarians Sándor Weöres and Ágnes Nemes Nagy seem to me great poets, but I have translated some other very good ones, including Vas, Orbán, and Rakovsky. Among my contemporaries I most admire Peter Porter, James Fenton, Joseph Brodsky, Derek Walcott, Seamus Heaney, and Derek Mahon. They seem to me to display conspicuous courage, humanity, and grace, though I like many others almost as well. There are fashions in these things I try not to pay too much attention to. I do not, alas, expect to be worn on T-shirts. (Stanzas printed on the backs of central European railway tickets would be more my style.) I am doing a selected poems for publication in 1996. It will be interesting to see what shape the remnants make. In the meantime I shall endeavor to translate less.

*   *   *

His early training as a student of the fine arts has helped shape George Szirtes's poetry in ways more subtle than are usually appreciated by literary assessors not used to drawing accurate parallels and distinctions between poetry and the visual arts. Szirtes is not conspicuously a visual poet, one who sees the surface of the world with a painter's eye and whose descriptions of it are therefore more detailed. Although his career as a poet has coincided with the rise to prominence of the so-called Martian school of poetry, he has not been attracted to this cartouche way of celebrating visual likeness. He has, indeed, a good eye, but it is the shape made by thought and the composed structure of language that he has stressed in his poems. A poem may be invented almost as if it were being planned on ruled paper, and it is one of Szirtes's strengths that his poetry recognizes that, since words are symbols, ideas are just as much true gifts to the poet as are scenes and objects.

Szirtes's Hungarian origins (he went to England in 1956, at the age of eight, with his parents) may have given him a wider range of sympathies. Among these is surrealism perhaps and a fondness for fables and folk legends, but a deeply rooted English tradition lies behind much of his work. While a student at Leeds, he came under the influence of Martin Bell, a poet of great erudition and a brilliant translator from the French. From Bell, and later from his own reading and involvement in English literature, Szirtes took a central path—the vision of the English mystics, including the Caroline poets, Christopher Smart, William Blake, and Samuel Palmer.

Much of Szirtes's verse is set indoors, in the lush wonderland of the domestic hearth, full of voices, furniture, bric-a-brac, and the remembrance of dreams. His book *The Slant Door* is lulled by a dreamy resonance that occasionally overpowers the syntax and structure of the verse. Its surrealist tone is never obtrusive, though it can be surprising, as in "The Bird Cage, 1851," in which a genre scene of a girl stooping to kiss and pout at a caged bird in a conservatory becomes an image of immanent menace:

The glass is vibrant with its rainbows; flowerpots
Perched sullenly on the rough sill glow brick-red.
The bird's small feet are sharp and her beak cuts
The pouted fruitage of the lady's head.

November and May and *Short Wave* show how strongly Szirtes's talent has developed. The poems in these volumes add a dramatic force to the richness of their language, and he is now the master of traditional forms and stanzas and of regular meters, as well as of freer tropes. He has a fine and corrosive wit and rather unexpectedly produces many excellent parodies and satires. Examples are "The Cosmo Guide to Culture," "Homage to the Postman Cheval," and "Slow Tango for Six Horses."

It is difficult to place Szirtes in the league of today's poets, as can be seen from his exclusion from such a taste-setting anthology as the *Penguin Book of Contemporary British Poetry*. Serious readers, however, have reason to believe that Szirtes's talent is one of the strongest.

—Peter Porter

T

TABAN LO LIYONG

Nationality: Sudanese. **Born:** Kajo Kaji, in 1939. **Education:** Bobi Full Primary School, 1945–51; Gulu High School, 1952–54; Sir Samuel Baker School, 1955–57; National Teachers College, Kyambogo, 1958–59, teachers certificate; Knoxville College, Tennessee, 1962–63; Howard University, Washington, D.C., B.A. in literature and journalism 1966; University of Iowa (International Writers Workshop Fellow), Iowa City, M.F.A. 1968. **Family:** Married 1) Lucy Apiyo in 1964, two children; 2) Janet Khemisa Michael in 1978, four children. **Career:** Tutorial fellow, Institute of African Studies, 1968–69, and lecturer in English, 1969–75, University of Nairobi; exchange lecturer, University of Dar es Salaam, Tanzania, 1972; chair and senior lecturer, Literature Department, University of Papua New Guinea, Port Moresby, 1975–77; senior public relations officer, 1978–79, senior lecturer, College of Adult Education and Training, 1980–82, and staff member, 1985–93, Literature Unit, College of Education, University of Juba. Visiting professor of literature, 1995, since 1996 professor of literature, and since 1998 professor and head of the Centre for African Studies, University of Venda, South Africa. Visiting professor, National Museum of Ethnology at Osaka, 1993–94; inaugural visiting professor, Curtin University, Perth, Australia, 1994–95; visiting summer lecturer, University of Western Australia, January 1995. Elected representative of Kajo Kaji Constituency, 1982–85, and chair of Committee of Culture and Information, 1982–83, Southern Peoples Regional Assembly, Juba; chair, Committee of Legislation and Economic Affairs, 1983–85, and acting deputy speaker, 1984–85, Peoples Regional Assembly, Equatorial Region. Founder and editor, with Alan Ogot, *MILA,* Nairobi, 1969. **Address:** Faculty of Arts, University of Venda, Private Bag x5050, Thohoyandou, 1950, Venda, South Africa.

PUBLICATIONS

Poetry

Eating Chiefs: Lwo Culture from Lolwe to Malkal. London, Heinemann, 1970; New York, Humanities Press, 1971.
Frantz Fanon's Uneven Ribs: With Poems More and More. London, Heinemann, 1971.
Another Nigger Dead. London, Heinemann, 1972.
Ballads of Underdevelopment: Poems and Thoughts. Kampala, East African Literature Bureau, 1974.
The Cows of Shambat, Sudanese Poems. Harare, Zimbabwe Publishing House, 1992.
Words That Melt a Mountain. Nairobi, East African Educational Publishers, 1996.
Homage to Onyame. Lagos, Malthouse Press, 1997.
Carrying Knowledge up a Palm Tree. Lawrenceville, New Jersey, Third World Press, 1998.

Novels

Meditations in Limbo. Nairobi, Equatorial, 1970.
Meditations. London, Rex Collings, 1978.

Short Stories

Fixions and Other Stories. London, Heinemann, 1969.
The Uniformed Man. Nairobi, East African Publishing House, 1971.

Other

The Last Word: Cultural Synthesism. Nairobi, East African Publishing House, 1969.
Popular Culture of East Africa: Oral Literature. Nairobi, Longman, 1972.
Thirteen Offensives Against Our Enemies. Nairobi, East African Literature Bureau, 1973.
The Universal Variety of Negritude. Port Moresby, University of Papua New Guinea Press, 1976.
Another Last Word. Nairobi, Heinemann, 1990.
Culture Is Rutan. Nairobi, Longman, 1991.
Reconstituting the Sudan(s). Florida Hill, Vivlia Publishers, 1998.

Editor, *Sir Apolo Kagwa Discovers England,* by Ham Mukasa, translated by Ernest Millar. London, Heinemann, 1975.
Editor, *Women in Folktales and Short Stories of Africa.* Pietersburg, Azalea Publishers, 1997.

*

Critical Studies: "New Poetry: Taban lo Liyong" by Paddy Kitchen, in *The Scotsman* (Edinburgh), 11 December 1971; "A Collection of Lwo Tales: Eating Chiefs by Taban lo Liyong" in *Target* (Nairobi), January 1972; "Taban lo Liyong: *Another Nigger Dead*" by Eldred D. Jones, in *African Literature Today,* 6, 1972; "The Tabanic Genre" by Chris Wanjala, in *Standpoints on African Literature: A Critical Anthology,* edited by Wanjala, Nairobi, East African Literature Bureau, 1973; "Poet Who Speaks in Riddles: *Another Nigger Dead* by Taban lo Liyong" by Patrick de Souza, in *New Nation* (Singapore), 13 January 1973; "Taban lo Liyong," in *Understanding African Poetry: A Study of Ten Poets,* by Ken Goodwin, London, Heinemann, 1982; "Bibliyongraphy, or Six Tabans in Search of an Author" by Peter Nazareth, in *The Writing of East and Central Africa,* edited by G.D. Killam, London, Heinemann, 1984; "Characteristics of Absurdist African Literature: Taban lo Liyong's Fixions-A Study in the Absurd," in *African Studies Review* (Atlanta, Georgia), 27(1), March 1984, and "Taban lo Liyong's *The Uniformed Man:* A Reconstructivist and Metafictional Parody of Modernism," in *Language and Style* (Flushing, New York), 24(3), summer 1991, both by F. Odun Balogun; "Black Consciousness in East and South African Poetry: Unity and Divergence in the Poetry of Taban Lo Liyong and Sipho Sepamla" by Ezenwa-Ohaeto, in *Presence Africaine* (Paris, France), 140, 1986; "Cultural Synthesis: A Language Plan for the 1980s" by Carol M. Eastman, in *ACLALS Bulletin,* 7(6), 1986; "Taban lo Liyong's Short Stories: A Western Form of Art?" by Frank Schulze, in *World Literature Written in English* (Singapore), 26(2), autumn 1986; "Yet Another Word with Taban" by Wahome Mutahi, in *African Literature Association Bulletin,* 18(3), summer 1992; "Taban Lo Liyong in South Africa" by Stephen Gray, in *ALA Bulletin,* 23(4), autumn 1997.

Taban lo Liyong comments:

Banana bye-laws
This shall be proclaimed from
The Papal Sea and the Imam's Minaret
The Jewish Synagogue and the Gentile's Rooftop
The Philistine's Market-place and Kaffir's Palaver
The Military Police's HQ and the Witchdoctor's Den:

The new bye-law is this:
No banana shall be called a banana
Unless it is dressed.

Previously, somethings had passed for bananas
Whereas they were not:
Some were green, yellow, brown, pink, black:
These couldn't all have been bananas.

Henceforth,
In order to qualify for a banana
It must be dressed in the specified jacket
Which jacket must be watertight expandable
And made from the best Thai silk.

And the qualified banana-lucky fellow-
Must wear his jacket up to his neck
And it must remain in place all night
Or till the party comes to a close.
Previously all those raw, unseemly naked so-called bananas
Attended parties undressed with disastrous consequences:
Hence the need for this sartorial regulation.

So, boys, if you cultivate bananas
And would like to take them to parties
Make sure you have a wardrobe of jackets
Of the finest make, appropriate size and fit
And party givers must check
Quite early before the party begins
That the jackets are in position
And that the banana is dressed for partying

On no ground should an undressed banana
Be permitted to attend a party:
The penalty for this is death
By the slow wasting away of the trunk.

Given under my seal
He who lives for ever
Akhenaten II, Beloved of Isis
King of Upper and Lower Worlds
Wearer of the Double Diadems
Under Constant Protection of the Ureaus
In His Twelfth Year of Accession:
Good Health and Peace to all.

*   *   *

Taban lo Liyong is a prolific writer. After what he calls the "First Harvest"—a spate of collections published in the 1970s, most of which are no longer available in bookshops—he produced a "Second Harvest" of several titles, four of them poetry, that have been published or prepared for publication, while a "Third Harvest" is being gathered. In itself this seasonal division points both to his originality and to his rootedness in the tradition of his agricultural forebears. Inspired by both traditional forms and modern experiment, he produces subtle and often very funny poems out of, and very much beyond, the pain and confusion that afflict the Sudanese community to which he belongs.

Taban lo Liyong's suspicion of conventional thinking and standard attitudes is obvious in almost everything he writes. It is particularly clear in lines such as

Normalcy, normalcy, normalcy
I detest thee.
Borne of the Joneses who mean well;
The priests of old and juju witches;
The advertising men;
Or, the modern psychiatrists,
I detest thee, normalcy.

It is also to be found in his distrust of the negritude movement: "Yet Sedar Senghor maintains / we are the people of passion."
One of his first published collections, *Eating Chiefs,* testifies to his interest in the cultural tradition of his Luo people. Over the years he has collected and retold creatively an impressive number of tales or epics. While his poems are oriented toward the present and the future, they draw on tradition, not only through references to traditional characters and events and in his fablelike use of animals but also in their form. He uses epigrams that are close to riddles, or he tells moral lessons, often in long "epicaresque" narratives that use to the full the oral devices of repetitions and scansion, sometimes in balanced sentences that acquire the status of proverbs.

Taban lo Liyong is a thinker-poet, but by self-definition he is a "law-less" not a "rule-full" poet. He is a poet within the tradition established by his ancestors, though in the same poem ("The Best Poets," in *Frantz Fanon's Uneven Ribs*) he goes on to mention the American poets e.e. cummings and Ezra Pound as "the best artisans / with ears for sounds" and ends with an amused flourish:

they write
marv'lously
modernly

like me.

Taban lo Liyong is also a teacher-poet. His use of paradoxes and his elusiveness prompt the reader to an increased degree of alertness. From the way they begin, his poems rarely say exactly what readers expect them to say. A true disciple of Nietzsche, he delights in paradoxes, in developing apparently contradictory statements. In fact, he often shifts unobtrusively from one standpoint to another so that the altered perspective makes for a completely different perception. The tone is somehow bent in midcourse and the meaning of key terms twisted around, and eventually the reader is left questioning previously accepted ideas. For instance, he begins the first poem in *Another Nigger Dead* with fairly sarcastic references to tragedy in relation to "African coups":

it is not tragedy
if the risks are not mammoth

it is no tragedy
if only few common peoples lives are involved.

Yet tragedy gradually emerges as a major teaching force in man's life. Those who have read too much Sartre or Artaud are, he maintains, "well indoctrinated against shedding tears," "emancipated from feelings," and therefore free to be callous. In a completely different register, the shorter poem that begins "Don't follow the big wheel" records and questions a number of easy slogans and ends with the terseness of a positive exhortation: "Do." In his subtle oscillation between positive and negative poles it is often difficult to determine at which point irony comes into play.

Taban lo Liyong is often bitingly ironical, but his irony does not indicate an absence of concern. In his verse the private man is not kept separate from the public one, and candid autobiographical revelations occur next to his censure of social ills. He is a committed writer and in his way a political activist, but he is one who keeps his tongue firmly in his cheek for fear of its turning into wood, one who makes it a rule always to be utterly unpredictable.

During the 1980s and 1990s Sudan has been torn by fierce civil war fed, to some extent, by international interests. In such a time writers may seem helpless. To Hölderlin's question of the point of writing poetry in times of crises, Taban lo Liyong has given a definite answer: to laugh and make us laugh, to prompt awareness through laughter, as did the fools of old.

—Christine Pagnoulle

TARN, Nathaniel

Nationality: American. **Born:** Paris, France, 30 June 1928. **Education:** Cambridge University, B.A. (honors) 1948, M.A. 1952; Sorbonne and École des Hautes Études, Paris, Cert. C.F.R.E.; University of Chicago, M.A. 1952, Ph.D. 1957; London School of Economics; School of Oriental and African Studies, University of London. **Family:** Divorced: two children; married Janet Rodney in 1981. **Career:** Has worked as an anthropologist in Guatemala, Alaska, and Burma. Former member of the faculty, University of Chicago, and University of London; visiting professor, State University of New York, Buffalo, and Princeton University, New Jersey, 1969–70; professor of comparative literature, 1970–85, and since 1985 emeritus professor, Rutgers University, New Brunswick, New Jersey; visiting professor, University of Pennsylvania, Philadelphia, 1976, and Jilin University, China, 1982. General editor, Cape Editions, and director, Cape Goliard publishers, London, 1967–69. **Awards:** Guinness prize, 1963; Wenner Gren fellowship, 1978, 1980; Commonwealth of Pennsylvania fellowship, 1984; Rockefeller Foundation fellowship, 1988. **Address:** P.O. Box 8187, Santa Fe, New Mexico 87504, U.S.A.

PUBLICATIONS

Poetry

Old Savage/Young City. London, Cape, 1964; New York, Random House, 1965.
Penguin Modern Poets 7, with Richard Murphy and Jon Silkin. London, Penguin, 1966.
Where Babylon Ends. London, Cape Goliard Press, and New York, Grossman, 1968.
The Beautiful Contradictions. London, Cape Goliard Press, 1969; New York, Random House, 1970.
October: A Sequence of Ten Poems Followed by Requiem Pro Duabus Filiis Israel. London, Trigram Press, 1969.
The Silence. Milan, M'Arte, 1970.
A Nowhere for Vallejo: Choices, October. New York, Random House, 1971; London, Cape, 1972.
Lyrics for the Bride of God: Section: The Artemision. Santa Barbara, California, Tree, 1973.
The Persephones. Santa Barbara, California, Tree, 1974.
Lyrics for the Bride of God. New York, New Directions, and London, Cape, 1975.
Narrative of This Fall. Los Angeles, Black Sparrow Press, 1975.
The House of Leaves. Santa Barbara, California, Black Sparrow Press, 1976.
From Alashka: The Ground of Our Great Admiration of Nature, with Janet Rodney. London, Permanent Press, 1977.
The Microcosm. Milwaukee, Membrane Press, 1977.
Birdscapes, with Seaside. Santa Barbara, California, Black Sparrow Press, 1978.
The Forest, with Janet Rodney. Mount Horeb, Wisconsin, Perishable Press, 1978.
Atitlan/Alashka: New and Selected Poems, with Janet Rodney. Boulder, Colorado, Brillig Works Press, 1979.
The Land Songs. Plymouth, Blue Guitar, 1981.
Weekends in Mexico. London, Oxus Press, 1982.
The Desert Mothers. Grenada, Mississippi, Salt Works Press, 1984.
At the Western Gates. Santa Fe, Tooth of Time, 1985.
Palenque: Selected Poems 1972–1984. London and Plymouth, Devon, Oasis/Shearsman Press, 1986.
Seeing America First. Minneapolis, Coffee House Press, 1989.
The Mothers of Matagalpa. London, Oasis, 1989.
Flying the Body. Los Angeles, Arundel Press, 1993.
Caja del Rio. Tucson, Arizona, Chax Press, 1993.
The Architextures 1–7: The Man of Music. Sherman Oaks, California, Ninja Press, 1999.
The Architextures 1–70. Tucson, Arizona, Chax Press, 2000.
Three Letters from the City: The St. Petersburg Poems 1968–1998. Santa Fe, New Mexico, Weaselsleeves Press, 2000.

Recordings: *I Think This May Be Eden,* Spoken Engine, 1994.

Other

Views from the Weaving Mountain: Selected Essays in Poetics & Anthropology. Albuquerque, University of New Mexico Press, 1991.
Scandals in the House of Birds: Shamans and Priests on Lake Atitlan. New York, Marsilio, 1997.

Editor and Translator with others, *Con Cuba: An Anthology of Cuban Poetry of the Last Sixty Years.* London, Cape Goliard Press, and New York, Grossman, 1969.
Editor and Translator with others, *Selected Poems: A Bilingual Edition,* by Pablo Neruda. London, Cape, 1970; New York, Delacorte Press, 1972.
Editor, *Multitude of One,* by Natasha Tarn. New York, Grenfell Press, 1994.

Translator, *The Heights of Macchu Picchu*, by Pablo Neruda. London, Cape, 1966; New York, Farrar Straus, 1967.

Translator, *Stelae*, by Victor Segalen. Santa Barbara, California, Unicorn Press, 1969.

Translator, *Zapotec Struggles*, edited by Howard Campbell et al. Washington D.C., Smithsonian Institute Press, 1993.

*

Bibliography: *Nathaniel Tarn: A Descriptive Bibliography* by Lee Bartlett, Jefferson, North Carolina, McFarland, 1987.

Critical Studies: In *Le Belle Contradizzioni,* Milan, Munt Press, 1973; ''Nathaniel Tarn Symposium'' in *Boundary 2* (Binghamton, New York), fall 1975; ''The House of Leaves'' by A. Kingsley Weatherhead, in *Credences 4* (Kent, Ohio), 1977; by Ted Enslin and Rochelle Ratner, in *American Book Review 2* (New York), 5, 1980; *Translating Neruda* by John Felstiner, Stanford, California, Stanford University Press, 1980; ''America As Desired: Nathaniel Tarn's Poetry of the Outsider As Insider'' by Doris Sommer, in *American Poetry I* (Albuquerque), 4, 1984; ''Il Mito come Metalinguaggio nella Poesia de Nathaniel Tarn'' by Fedora Giordano, in *Letteratura d'America* (Rome), 5(22), 1984; by George Economu, in *Sulfur* (Ypsilanti, Michigan), 14, 1985; by Gene Frumkin, in *Artspace* (Albuquerque), 10(1), 1985; in *Talking Poetry,* Albuquerque, University of New Mexico Press, 1987, and *The Sun Is But a Morning Star: Studies in West Coast Poetry and Poetics,* Albuquerque, University of New Mexico Press, 1989, both by Lee Bartlett; ''Nathaniel Tarn: The Body As River,'' in *Poetry Flash* (San Francisco), 227, 1992; ''Bringing the World to Little England: Cape Editions, Cape Goliard and Poetry in the Sixties'' by Shamoon Zamir, in *Comparative Criticism* (England), 19, 1997; Nathaniel Tarn section in *Xcp* (Minneapolis, Minnesota), 5, 1999.

Nathaniel Tarn comments:

The primary question today concerns the survivability of poetry. We must look for it not in the horizontal deployment of an ever shrinking population of readers at any given historical moment but in a vertical time-depth, poetry surviving as a diachronic passage of culture from one generation of readers to another. For me such time-depth is literally without limit. I take at face value the idea that poetry, whenever it truly inhabits any one of us, reaches back to whatever we can envisage as the beginning of all and any time, encompassing the poetry voiced by any human from that beginning onward.

Further, as poet—and anthropologist used to the notion of all good coming from the ancestors—I think of the poet's virtually sole important function as being that of a carrier of a vocal link between the living and the dead, speaking with the living as the orators of the dead and addressing the dead on the part of all life in return. The time-bound voices of any given set of the living in this model would be but the very briefest of flashes in the cosmic pan.

In study, work, and personal life Buddhist philosophy has always been a guiding light. I am suggesting that, ideotypically, the pure time-space of poetry can be taken as the breathed or voiced component of a reach for wisdom—many would call it a path—in which nothing need be lost and everything can be recuperated at any moment and at any place in the practice of a constant and summarily attentive presence.

It follows that poetry can only be obliterated if the human is obliterated and that, unless this latter circumstance were to occur, there can be no fear whatsoever of poetry ever being lost. Nor, I hope, need it be pointed out that such a view categorically does not lift poetry out of our daily life into some woolly or smoky divine empyrean; on the contrary, it affords poetry the very best vantage point from which to survey all politics from the cosmic to the regional and local, no subject in any time or space whatsoever being alien to it.

I have always argued for three levels of operation of the poetic voice. First, a surface level, the ''vocal,'' involves the individual poet's voice qua individual, and as we know from the present scene, that level is enormously competitive. Should a poet remain at that level, there can be no access whatsoever to the vantage point I have described. Next, it is usually held that under the individual voice lies a silence out of which that voice emerges; this I would take as the second level of operation. But it is not a primordial silence, for under it, in turn, there seems to be some kind of third level that, for want of a better term, I call the ''choral.'' The easiest way to describe this level is to refer to a sense many have that the truer they are being in referring to themselves, the more their voice appears to sound like the voice of all. This level, then, is communal, and it is the absolute opposite of competitive. One way of speaking of this might be to posit that on level one the self acts in reciprocity to others, on level two in reciprocity to self, and on level three in nonreciprocity, reciprocity dying out since where there is no self there can be no other.

My model goes on to postulate that, in fact, one cannot reside or dwell in either level one or level three uniquely. Levels one and three are both illusions, reciprocal illusions if you will, the first representing the war of ego or self with others in a babel of voices, the third representing the ideal peace of nonself with all creation. Neither of these by themselves are possibilities for long, because when you dwell within one, it is impossible even to conceive of the existence of the other, and the process can therefore not be rounded out. In fact, the model eventually proposes silence, the level that initially would seem to be by definition alien to the poet, as the only reality in which poetry can ultimately dwell.

I see specific menaces to the immediate future of poetry. These range from macro- to microsociological issues. Among the first, one might wonder on present evidence whether the promised information highway involving all possible media is not the incarnate reign of quantity over quality. If so, whether it, together with an ever growing attrition of language and a thriving, universally distributed illiteracy, will not seriously endanger the art as we know it. I am not certain either way.

Among the micro issues I also see quantity over quality as the main aspect of the picture. The myth that there can no longer be, in our present state of cultural evolution, any mute, inglorious Miltons falters where quantity drowning out quality can be demonstrated at every turn, both in publishing and in the production and reception of writing. As Kenneth Rexroth pointed out some time ago, you have the choice, past a certain age, between suicide, black hole depression, or a megaton weight of passive aggression on all sides as your only defenses. The intrusion of allegedly ''creative'' writing into the university since the end of World War II has created and goes on creating a huge quantity of students, all carrying poets' batons in their knapsacks who, once golden youth is over, are doomed—such are the conditions of true poetry as well as conditions in the immediate market—to the most abject disappointment and suffering. It is, alas, the case that where too many laboratory animals are crowded into too small a cage they start lacerating each other. We should cease misleading youth in this way and abolish all writing programs as well as all the cultural bureaucracies that feed off them.

I would also suggest the abolition of all awards and prizes. You may have noticed that the word "poet" no longer exists. We now have "renowned poet," "famous poet," "distinguished poet," "much-awarded poet," "massively prized poet," "interminably honored poet," etc. Like all inflation, this masks a currency devaluation. In a society that does not truly value poetry, the poet disappears behind the award. The award is frantically crying out for an attention no longer freely granted to the poet.

This same intrusion of allegedly "creative" writing into the university has created a situation of intellectual incest rather than marriage. As many have pointed out, poet no longer talks to or listens to anyone else but other poet. The result is that, on the one hand, we have a highly redundant workforce of traditional academic poets servicing the M.F.A. industry and, on the other, an avant-garde rapidly approaching that status in the same academy. In the latter's work a massive crisis of the signified brought about by pathologically devoted self-rapture with the signifier and interminable pottering with contemporary critical theory is in effect rapidly reaching the same dead end as that reached by the traditionalists. Superspecialized technocrats of complexity are bound to suffer the same fate as the dinosaurs.

On a more hopeful note, I would see the continued attention to song in the many elements of the population that refuse to succumb to the domination of the academy, or do not have the means even to attend it, as one reflection of where importance lies. The pluralism and multiculturalism of America—seen not as the United States alone but as the whole continent from Alaska to Tierra del Fuego—may be one of our choicest guarantees that the immediate future is more enticing than it looks from these perspectives.

*   *   *

I remember on the shores of the most beautiful lake in
    the world
whose name in its own language means abundance of waters
as if the volcanoes surrounding it had broken open the earth
there in the village of Saint James of Compostela one
    cold night
not the cereus-scented summer nights in which a voice I
    never traced
sang those heartbreaking serenades to no one known
a visiting couple gave birth in the market place
the father gnawing the cord like a rat to free the child
and before leaving in the morning they were given the
    freedom of the place
        I mean the child was given

A child of nowhere, Nathaniel Tarn has been given, and has given himself, a freedom of place that is rare among contemporary poets. Anglo-French by birth, a dual citizen, his childhood was bilingual, and he was educated on both sides of the English Channel. In the 1950s and 1960s he had a short career as a self-described "25th-rate" French surrealist poet and a more successful run as an up-and-coming young English poet, becoming associated with the so-called Group as well as editor of the extraordinary Cape editions.

Furthermore, he was an anthropologist, a student of Claude Lévi-Strauss in Paris and Robert Redfield in Chicago, writing monographs on the Atitlán region of Guatemala. He was also a Buddhist scholar and author of, among other writings, a book on the monastic politics of Burma. In 1970 Tarn followed his literary affinities and moved to the United States, where he became an American poet and citizen. As an anthropologist he continued to write on Guatemala and as a Buddhist scholar to be involved with the Tibetan diaspora.

This range of Tarn's is mirrored in four major book-length poems: in a poetry of place in which the place is always changing (*The Beautiful Contradictions*); a love poetry in which the object of desire undergoes countless transformations (*Lyrics for the Bride of God*); a deeply personal poetry that the poet allows to be spoken by others (*A Nowhere for Vallejo*), a collage of lines and invented lines by the Peruvian poet, in Spanish and English translation, mingled with the voice of Tarn—and *From Alashka*, written with Janet Rodney, perhaps the century's only collaborative poem that does not identify the individual contributions. Moreover the poetry has, in the poet's words, frequent "unconscious thrusts, sudden irruptions into the body of the work, almost like spirit-cult possessions," in which the poet speaks in other voices and sometimes other languages.

What holds this together is Tarn's ecstatic vision, his continuing enthusiasm for the stuff of the world. It is a poetry whose native tongue is myth, and it rolls out in long lines of sacred hymns that oscillate between the demotic and the hieratic (as heir to Christopher Smart and Blake, to Whitman and the Neruda of *The Heights of Macchu Picchu,* which he translated) and sequences of short poems, small, linked bursts of sharp image and speech (tying Tarn to Williams and contemporary practitioners like Snyder and Kelly).

Since the death of Kenneth Rexroth, Tarn is the major celebrant of heterosexual love in the language. His combination of ingenious metaphor and sexual exuberance has not been heard in English since the seventeenth century. (Indeed, much of Tarn's American work may be read as an epic elaboration of Donne's erotic geography of the "new found land.") Like Rexroth, he is the author of travel narratives that restore the adjective "readable" to poetry. And like Rexroth and MacDiarmid, his poetry encompasses Eastern philosophy, world myth, revolutionary politics, and precise descriptions of the natural world. (His poems are filled with birds.)

Not an exile longing for the abandoned home but a nomad longing for the idea of home, Tarn exemplifies the American condition and the Jewish condition. Tarn, both American and Jewish, has declared that *sparagmos* ("the falling to pieces / the tearing to pieces / of the world as body") is "the inescapable theme of our time." (He can at times be as indignant as Pound at the destroyers of culture and of the wilderness.) His poetry, along with that of few others, sets course for a mythical unity—the *hierosgamos,* marriage of earth and sky, when history will be forever in the present tense, somewhere will be everywhere, and the author everyone:

            . . . that the branch may break
that the long voyage may end for the planet
and the furthest point of death be returned from
the separation into dead and live
summer and winter, and only green be seen above ground
        that he might go home

—Eliot Weinberger

TATE, James (Vincent)

Nationality: American. **Born:** Kansas City, Missouri, 8 December 1943. **Education:** University of Missouri, Kansas City, 1963–64; Kansas State College, Pittsburgh, B.A. 1965; University of Iowa, Iowa City, M.F.A. 1967. **Career:** Visiting lecturer, University of Iowa, 1965–67, and University of California, Berkeley, 1967–68; assistant professor, Columbia University, New York, 1969–71, and Emerson College, Boston, 1970–71. Since 1971 member of the English Department, University of Massachusetts, Amherst. Since 1967 poetry editor, *Dickinson Review,* North Dakota. Currently associate editor, Pym Randall Press, Cambridge, Massachusetts, and Barn Dream Press; consultant, Coordinating Council of Literary Magazines. **Awards:** Yale Series of Younger Poets award, 1966; National Endowment for the Arts grant, 1968, 1969, and fellow, 1980; American Academy award, 1974; Guggenheim fellowship, 1976; Pulitzer prize for poetry, 1992, for *Selected Poems,* National Book award for poetry, 1994, for *Worshipful Company of Fletchers;* Tanning prize, Academy of American Poets, 1995. **Address:** Department of English, University of Massachusetts, Amherst, Massachusetts 01002, U.S.A.

PUBLICATIONS

Poetry

Cages. Iowa City, Shepherds Press, 1966.
The Destination. Cambridge, Massachusetts, Pym Randall Press, 1967.
The Lost Pilot. New Haven, Connecticut, Yale University Press, 1967.
The Torches. Santa Barbara, California, Unicorn Press, 1968; revised edition, 1971.
Notes of Woe. Iowa City, Stone Wall Press, 1968.
Mystics in Chicago. Santa Barbara, California, Unicorn Press, 1968.
Camping in the Valley. Chicago, Madison Park Press, 1968.
Row with Your Hair. San Francisco, Kayak, 1969.
Is There Anything. Fremont, Michigan, Sumac Press, 1969.
Shepherds of the Mist. Los Angeles, Black Sparrow Press, 1969.
The Oblivion Ha-Ha. Boston, Little Brown, 1970.
Amnesia People. Girard, Kansas, Little Balkans, 1970.
Deaf Girl Playing. Cambridge, Massachusetts, Pym Randall Press, 1970.
Are You Ready Mary Baker Eddy?, with Bill Knott. San Francisco, Cloud Marauder Press, 1970.
The Immortals. Santa Barbara, California, Unicorn Press, 1970.
Wrong Songs. Cambridge, Massachusetts, Halty Ferguson, 1970.
Hints to Pilgrims. Cambridge, Massachusetts, Halty Ferguson, 1971; revised edition, Amherst, University of Massachusetts Press, 1982.
Nobody Goes to Visit the Insane Anymore. Santa Barbara, California, Unicorn Press, 1971.
Absences: New Poems. Boston, Little Brown, 1972.
Apology for Eating Geoffrey Movius' Hyacinth. Santa Barbara, California, Unicorn Press, 1972.
Viper Jazz. Middletown, Connecticut, Wesleyan University Press, 1976.
Riven Doggeries. New York, Ecco Press, 1979.

The Land of Little Sticks. Worcester, Massachusetts, Metacom Press, 1981.
Constant Defender. New York, Ecco Press, 1983.
Just Shades. University, Alabama, Parallel, 1985.
Reckoner. Middletown, Connecticut, Wesleyan University Press, 1986.
Distance from Loved Ones. Middletown, Connecticut, Wesleyan University Press, 1990.
Selected Poems. Middletown, Connecticut, Wesleyan University Press, 1991.
Worshipful Company of Fletchers: Poems. Hopewell, New Jersey, Ecco Press, 1994.

Novel

Lucky Darryl, with Bill Knott. New York, Release Press, 1977.

Short Stories

Hottentot Ossuary. Cambridge, Massachusetts, Temple Bar Bookshop, 1974.

Other

The Route As Briefed. Ann Arbor, University of Michigan Press, 1999.

Editor, with David Lehman, *The Best American Poetry 1997.* New York, Scribner, 1997.

*

Manuscript Collection: Humanities Research Center, University of Texas, Austin.

Critical Studies: "James Tate and Sidney Goldfarb and the Inexhaustible Nature of the Murmur" by R.D. Rosen, in *American Poetry Since 1960-Some Critical Perspectives,* edited by Robert B. Shaw, Chester Springs, Pennsylvania, Dufour, 1974; in *American Poetry Observed: Poets on Their Work,* edited by Joe David Bellamy, Urbana, University of Illinois Press, 1984; "The Desperate Buck and Wing: James Tate and the Failure of Ritual" by Donald Revell, in *Western Humanities Review* (Salt Lake City, Utah), 38(4), winter 1984; James Tate issue of *Ploughshares* (Boston), 11(1), 1985; "The Masters Can Only Make Us Laugh: Authority in the Poetry of James Tate" by Lee Upton, in *South Atlantic Review* (Atlanta), 55(4), November 1990; James Tate issue of *Denver Quarterly* (Denver), 33(3), fall 1998.

James Tate comments:
I am in the tradition of the impurists: Whitman, Williams, Neruda. I am trying to combine words in such a way as to lend a new life, a new hope, to that which is lifeless and hopeless. If the vision in the poems is occasionally black, it is so in order to see more clearly the fabric of which that blackness is made and thereby understand the source. If the source is understood, there is the possibility of correcting it.

In my poems it seems one of the recurring themes must be the agony of communication itself; despair and hatred are born out of this failure to communicate. The poem is man's noblest effort because it is utterly useless.

I use the image as a kind of drill to penetrate the veils of illusion we complacently call the real world, the world of shadows through which we move so confidently. I want to split that world and release the energy of a higher reality. There is nothing I will not do, because I see a new possibility each day.

* * *

James Tate, the son of pioneers, is from Missouri, the "show-me" state. As such, he inherits the antic skepticism of Mark Twain as well as the prismatic images and adamantine syllabics of Marianne Moore. For instance, the eight-syllable lines of "The Shop Keeper" from *The Lost Pilot,* Tate's first collection, inventory the life of the merchant who "just broke a two dollar / thing":

> You close the door and leave to find
> your home. Afraid to think of what
> business is coming to, you
> think of sleep, dishwater, gaslamps,
> cypress, eggshells, hell; what you are
>
> coming to—bells, rags, big Sunday.

"You," which along with "you are" frames the stanza, is no more than his stock, and the poet is no more substantial than his eggshell images. This specular "you" allows Tate not only to reckon himself along with his shopkeeper but also lets him echo the old-timer's anxiety ("what is the world coming to?") and tap out his pentameter journey home. Several of the best poems in *The Lost Pilot* are apostrophes that conjure up the absent, such as the titular elegy to his piloting father, who died around his son's age (twenty-three) in World War II. The memorial tercets of "The Lost Pilot" preserve a tender Whitmanesque anaphora: "If I could cajole / you to come back . . . / . . . I would touch you . . . I would touch your face . . . I would / discover you, and I would not / turn you in." But the ageless father, orbiting like John Glenn, cannot hear his apostrophizing son, who "cannot get off the ground." As in Vaughan's elegy to Herbert and his generation—"They have all Gone into the World of Light"—Tate takes his gravity- and grave-defying father's place on earth.

With *Absences* (1972) Tate hangs up his shingle as a nihilist. Nothingness, of course, was in the air. The French existentialists Sartre and Camus were colonizing American universities, and the American surrealists, Mark Strand and W.S. Merwin in particular, were making much of the nothing of shadows and mirrors. But Tate's negations, less philosophical than countercultural, are attempts at purging the suburb from him and his poetry. Nearing the untrustworthy age of thirty, Tate fears not the void but saying "exactly what is expected of me." The sequence "Absences" thwarts these expectations:

> We should all be behind bars.
> I am the commuter
> no matter how unreachably far away.
> . . .
> I can imagine a wife
> serving dinner
> of light bulbs & garbage cans.
> How do you like your mashed potatoes?
> With pins in them.

> Pretty soon I am talking
> to the secretary
> of her personal secretary,
> a faithful wife, in herself,
>
> a jaspered morning.

The surrealist violence here pierces both sitcom living and confessional poetry. But the Christian guilt, which needs a crime (adultery) to explain it, comes from John Berryman, the dark descendant of Whitman and Williams whose *Dream Songs* haunts Tate's work. The "wife" and the "secretary" are one, and both remain conventional while providing the commuter with a "jaspered," if guilt-ridden, moment. Tate reckons, "I have sung 200 songs . . . addressed to WOMAN to WOMAN to WOMAN." Tate's "woman" (not "a woman") is too often the gaily apostrophized earth mother or airhead: "Rubberducky that part of woman / that has to be going to the store / . . . sexual eggs, I touch you." But when Tate lets women be subjects rather than simply vehicles for his subjectivity, he writes with conviction and pathos. In "A Friend Told Me" Tate addresses his ex-love:

> stood there on the step,
> snow turning scarlet
> on your velvet hat,
> wishing a larger pain
> would soak you up.

The missing "you" in Tate's address mirrors the woman's blushing wish to disappear. To be sure, this wish reflects Tate's own embarrassment. But the woman remains a suffering, self-conscious character whom the narrator does not soak up.

In Tate's *Reckoner* the suburbanites are as two-dimensional, and Tate as hyperdimensional, as ever. In fact, Tate's patented surrealist diction is really comic hyperbole that, like Huck Finn's tall tales and colorful diction, keep his verse from collapsing into expectations. In "Jelka Revisited" the stunned commuters who have just lost their luggage on the plane (note the distance traveled since "The Lost Pilot") stand "pig-headed in Poisonville, bleeding lemonade / onto the drip-dry tarmac." They are not "eyeless in Gaza, spilling lemonade onto their clothes." In "The Dead Man's Medicine" we learn that "some orphans are stricken / with typhoid, and that is going to blemish our jubilee." It is not simply "the children are sick" or merely a "party." This hyperbolic diction both inflates the once minimal lines of Tate's verse and gives his poetry a festive, holiday atmosphere. But we also find Tate more talkative, less anxious about rattling on like his neighbors:

> Disconsolate bunglers, incalculable cloves,
> the Ship sang. Ginger scurvy.
> Then I took one of them around to see chlorophyll
> working in the meadow, and later bought him
> a porkpie hat. Night was coming on, hell,
> night had come and gone and I was still
> reading, reading my way through the library.

The dark night of the soul has passed from Tate's accommodating, but still pleasantly surprising, later style, nearer Ashbery's than Berryman's. "Hell" is just another cuss word. But people should not expect to recognize themselves too clearly in Tate's poems. Once a

Missourian, always a Missourian; the leopard cannot change its spots. In these famished times, however, "the famous bones / of the spotted leopard / are all they have."

—John Shoptaw

TAYLOR, Andrew (McDonald)

Nationality: Australian. **Born:** Warrnambool, Victoria, 19 March 1940. **Education:** Scotch College, Melbourne, graduated 1957; University of Melbourne, 1958–61, B.A. (honors) 1961, M.A. (honors) 1971; State University of New York, Buffalo, 1970–71. **Family:** Married 1) Jill Burriss in 1964 (divorced 1978), one son; 2) Beate Josephi in 1980, one daughter. **Career:** Tutor, 1962–63, and Lockie Fellow, 1966–68, University of Melbourne; teacher, British Institute, Rome, 1964–65; American Council of Learned Societies Fellow, State University of New York, Buffalo, 1970–71. Lecturer, 1971–74, and senior lecturer in English, 1975–92, University of Adelaide. Since 1992 Foundation Professor of English, Edith Cowan University, Western Australia. Member, Literary Board of Australian Council, 1978–81. **Awards:** Australian Council of Learned Societies Fellowship, 1970; Commonwealth poetry prize, 1986; Premier's award for poetry, 1995, for *Sandstone*. Member of the Order of Australia. **Address:** Edith Cowan University, Mount Lawley, Western Australia 6050, Australia.

PUBLICATIONS

Poetry

The Cool Change. St. Lucia, University of Queensland Press, 1971.
Ice Fishing. St. Lucia, University of Queensland Press, 1973.
The Invention of Fire. St. Lucia, University of Queensland Press, 1976.
The Cat's Chin and Ears: A Bestiary. Sydney, Angus and Robertson, 1976.
Parabolas: Prose Poems. Brisbane, Makar Press, 1976.
The Crystal Absences, The Trout. Sydney, Island Press, 1978.
Selected Poems 1960–1980. St. Lucia, University of Queensland Press, 1982; revised edition, *1960–1985,* 1988.
Travelling. St. Lucia, University of Queensland Press, 1986.
Folds in the Map. St. Lucia, University of Queensland Press, 1991.
Sandstone. St. Lucia, University of Queensland Press, 1995.

Plays

The Letters of Amalie Dietrich (opera libretto; produced Adelaide, 1988).
Borossa (opera libretto; produced Adelaide, 1988).

Other

Bernie the Midnight Owl (for children). Ringwood, Victoria, Penguin, 1984.
Reading Australian Poetry. St. Lucia, University of Queensland Press, 1987.

Editor, *Byron: Selected Poems.* Melbourne, Cassell, 1971.

Editor, with Ian Reid, *Number Two Friendly Street.* Adelaide, Adelaide University Union Press, 1978.
Editor, with Judith Rodriguez, *Poems from the Australian's 20th Anniversary Competition.* Sydney, Angus and Robertson, 1985.
Editor, *Unsettled Areas: Recent Short Fiction: A South Australian Collection.* Adelaide, Wakefield Press, 1986.
Editor, with Russell McDougall, *(Un)Common Ground: Essays on the New Literatures in English.* Adelaide, Flinders University, 1990.

Translator, with Beate Josephi, *Miracles of Disbelief: Selected Poems from the German of Christine Lavant, Ingeborg Bachmann, Sarah Kirsch, Ursula Krechel.* Canberra, Leros Press, 1985.

*

Manuscript Collection: National Library of Australia, Canberra.

Critical Studies: "On UQP's Selection" by Graham Rowlands, in *Overland* (Melbourne), 88, July 1982; by Heimo Ertl, in *Voices from Distant Lands: Poetry in the Commonwealth,* edited by Konrad Gross and Wolfgang Klooss, Wurzburg, Konigshausen and Neumann, 1983; "Recent Australian Poetry: The Ordinary and the Extraordinary: Rhyll McMaster, Andrew Taylor, Bruce Beaver, Robert Harris and Jan Owen" by Alan Gould, in *Quadrant* (Victoria, Australia), 30(10), October 1986.

Andrew Taylor comments:

(1980) Looking back across them, I find that my poems are about the ordinary things of life. They grow out of such things as happiness, a response to the weather, and the more traumatic occurrences that a normal life is prey to: breakup of a marriage, separation from a child, a new being in love, travel, etc. The larger historical dramas and the political scenarios are not for me.

On the other hand, I do not see my poetry as particularly domestic. I try to convey the way the mundane particulars of my life, because they are so pressing to me, conform to larger patterns that express common experience and give it importance. As a result, my poems are an attempt at finding the myth within which we live. (Lévi-Strauss suggests that the number of myths is small but the forms they take almost infinite.) My poems are thus the result of a lot of listening to what is within me.

I have tried to make colloquial speech say what it rarely says in talk. This has meant moving away from the more formal phrasing and cadences of my first book toward a plainer speech that says more interesting things. This has also meant a move toward longer poems, toward multiples, though, rather than narratives.

I suppose you could say I am a city poet rather than a rural or a nature poet, even though the country and the sea are an inexhaustible source of images for me. It is in cities that, for me anyway, most life is lived. I find that in Australia it is still possible to live in a city without totally losing touch with the country.

(1985) Supplement: since writing the above I have traveled extensively and am continuing to do so. This has inevitably had some effect on my poetry, although I have tried to maintain its Australian quality.

(1990) Life in Australia is now far less insular than it was when I began writing. Although much of my time is now spent in other countries, I feel that this is not the threat to nationality I might once have felt it to be. Instead, it is a challenge to redefine nationality on a less parochial basis, the product of a global revolution in travel and communication.

(1995) Since moving to Western Australia in 1992, I have found myself stimulated by the extraordinary Indian Ocean coastline and the countryside to explore connections between my present life and my childhood spent on eastern Australia's southern coast. My most recent poetry has thus taken, probably temporarily, a semiautobiographical turn.

Australian society has changed greatly since I was young. The emphasis on multiculturalism, the diminution of racism and ignorance, and an eager pursuit of cultural and racial plurality have made the country an exciting place for a writer. Although the circumstances of my life still enable me to travel often and extensively, much of the diversity and stimulus Australians once had to seek abroad is now available at home.

*   *   *

Andrew Taylor's account of influences on his work, set forth in a paper for a seminar at Macquarie University in 1979, confirmed him as one of the Australian poets growing up in the 1950s and 1960s for whom the surprises in their formative reading came from U.S. poetry. Taylor has shown this influence in an increasing freedom with verse forms and an openness to personally associative progressions within his poems. He surely absorbed these lessons the more readily because, from first publication, his has been an emotionally interpreted world.

Copiously detailed in rendering place and mood, the early poems use solid, richly worked forms—long stanzas, discursive chunks of twenty lines or more, often the three-beat Eliot line. They show openness in their willing use of rhyme, which rarely comes into tyrannical prominence. The academic emerges in a well-bred air of always being informed, but Taylor's real business is listening for the personal suggestiveness that living gives to things. His voice is never raised, and the tone is intimate. The tenderness of his love poems is distinctive, as in ''the fur coat.'' His second book deliberately explores the breaking up of form. In its five parts, the last three referring to a stay in the United States, there are sequences of short numbered segments. Although the poems derive their clearest human appeal from crises in relationships—the death of a father, a love affair—Taylor keeps his world rich with things and weather and is liable at any moment to let a gentle, rather introverted humor play among them.

Perhaps Taylor's most tonally ambitious work is the ''Cathedral'' section of *The Invention of Fire,* a celebration of continuing life in love and art. The sequence works very differently from the ''Beyond Silence'' assemblages of tiny poems that have attracted much notice. The nine ''Cathedral'' poems have wide literary and historical references, tend to lyrical but intense conclusions, and only (it seems) by a lack of vigilance and sudden pressure allow a nakedly personal cry to emerge:

The whole roof
bursts into earth
at the (careful
of skin cancer you say)
touch of summer

villages have burnt like banknotes

for the profit of sunburn lotion
   & you've taken our son away

in the vault's wreckage
small pieces of sky
glitter.

The Crystal Absences, The Trout is a sustained love discourse written over two months. It is a fluid, continuous, eager, and intimate communication of memories—current emotional notes—and strains toward a reunion. The labored solidity of Taylor's early manner has given way to a protean short line that registers alertness, while his optimism and unaffectedness keep even intense perceptions from weighing and slowing the poem:

a life in the world
     a barefoot
and sure walk over stones
the *feel* of a place we know
because it's now thoroughly ours
thus thoroughly other
and can never be known
       ourselves
at home in that mystery
     Parsifal's
divine stupidity
    a shaman's
trust in flight
    a man's
and a woman's trust in each other
a child's confidence in love.

Taylor's staying power and the continuing relevance of his 1980s and 1990s poetry have impressively confirmed his choices. These years also have seen forays into libretto writing, in a collaboration with the composer Ralph Middenway, and the publication of *Selected Poems,* also reissued with additions, and new books of poetry. Taylor's book on Australia's principal twentieth-century poets, *Reading Australian Poetry,* is probably the most thoughtful available overview. It follows Judith Wright's *Preoccupations in Australian Poetry,* published twenty years earlier, in method and usefulness to students and also in illustrating how thoroughly time can dispense with minor figures. *Travelling,* from the mid-1980s, is a ripe achievement. It includes poems on nature and civilization written from Taylor's memories of more than a decade of travels, mainly to Germany and other central European countries, with his wife, the writer Beate Josephi and his collaborator in a distinguished translation from German of four women poets, and their daughter. In a discussion with David Malouf (''Nature''), wielding the ghazel with a Holub-like gentle mordancy (''Regret about the Wolves''), and traversing Prague, Adelaide, New York, and the cities of what was then Yugoslavia, Taylor shows a versatility that flourishes on the multiplicity of material and comparisons.

Folds in the Map is less closely meditated and suffers from its miscellaneous organization, starting with various reminiscences that include a series on a long-cherished home and an anthology of objects—''Spoons,'' ''Dish Drainers,'' ''Letterboxes,'' ''Pencils,'' ''Stapler,'' ''Spade,'' and so on. The latter are polished—especially the parody ''Thirteen ways of looking at a mirror''—and a good deal happier than the third section, which consists of five lightish, uncomfortable pieces about occupying a chairman's office. The fourth part manages dullness even in what should have been a good bet, "Learning how to win at tennis" as miserere, but four elegiac poems end the section with growing conviction.

The fifth part makes amends. Apart from "London," a less than successful essay in the tetrameter couplet form that Peter Porter adopted from Bishop King, these poems once again take up Taylor's truest vein—observations of landscape, culture, and relationships. Mysteries in the continuity of the European literary enterprise are developed in the opening lines of "In the landscape of the Bros. Grimm":

> I've come home to a landscape
> not my own. Towers of grass
> crane over me and the air
> is always twilight, a misty avenue
> of birdsong that will never sleep
> before I do.

It is the context of history that gives "The Lizards of Tuscany" a finesse and joy unchallenged by the merely urban "Ants" and the comically zoomorphic "Stapler" earlier in the collection.

Among a variety of meditations, the coastal scenery—near Warrnambool, Taylor's childhood home, it seems—is constantly invoked in *Sandstone*. This sea note at the end of "Testament" is perhaps a debt to Shakespeare:

> I'm a child. We're in a rowboat
> and we've taken the floorboards up
> in the dark, my father holding a flashlight
> while we pick the pearls of my mother's
> broken necklace from the sludge
> of the hull. We will never
> find them all, the smallest buds
> in the gathering dark, as the wind
> rises and our boat rocks, water
> and wind, slapping the boards.

Michael Sharkey pinpoints urbanity and tenderness as Taylor's leading qualities. With appreciation of these should go the recognition that he has won from scholarship and experiment a fine balance between ease of talk and emotional tension.

—Judith Rodriguez

TAYLOR, Henry (Splawn)

Nationality: American. **Born:** Loudoun County, Virginia, 21 June 1942. **Education:** University of Virginia, Charlottesville, 1960–65, B.A. in English 1965; Hollins College, Roanoke, Virginia, 1965–66, M.A. in English and Creative Writing 1966. **Family:** Married 1) Sarah Spencer Bean in 1965 (divorced 1967); 2) Frances Carney in 1968 (divorced 1995), two sons; 3) Sarah Spencer in 1995. **Career:** Instructor, Roanoke College, Salem, Virginia, 1966–68; assistant professor, University of Utah, Salt Lake City, 1968–71; associate professor, 1971–75, and since 1975 professor, The American University, Washington, D.C. Writer-in-residence, Hollins College, Roanoke,

Virginia, spring 1978; distinguished poet-in-residence, Wichita State University, Kansas, spring 1994, and Randolph-Macon Woman's College, 1997. **Awards:** National Endowment for the Arts fellowship, 1978, 1986; Witter Bynner Poetry award, 1984; Pulitzer prize, 1986, for *The Flying Change*. **Member:** Academy of American Poets, Fellowship of Southern Writers. **Address:** P.O. Box 23, Lincoln, Virginia 20161–0023, U.S.A.

PUBLICATIONS

Poetry

The Horse Show at Midnight: Poems. Baton Rouge, Louisiana State University Press, 1966.
Breakings. San Luis Obispo, California, The Solo Press, 1971.
An Afternoon of Pocket Billiards. Salt Lake City, University of Utah, 1975; with *The Horse Show at Midnight,* Baton Rouge, Louisiana State University Press, 1992.
The Flying Change. Baton Rouge, Louisiana State University Press, 1985.
Understanding Fiction: Poems, 1986–1996. Baton Rouge, Louisiana State University Press, 1996.
Brief Candles: 101 Clerihews. Baton Rouge, Louisiana State University Press, 2000.

Other

Compulsory Figures: Essays on Recent American Poets. Baton Rouge, Louisiana State University Press, 1992.

Editor, with Frank N. Magill, *Magill's (Masterplots) Literary Annual 1972, 1973, 1974.* Englewood Cliffs, Salem Press, 1972, 1974, 1975.
Editor, *The Water of Light: A Miscellany in Honor of Brewster Ghiselin.* Salt Lake City, University of Utah Press, 1976.

Translator, with Robert A. Brooks, *The Children of Herakles* by Euripides. New York, Oxford University Press, 1981.
Translator, *The Weevil [Plautus],* in *Complete Roman Drama.* Baltimore, Maryland, Johns Hopkins University Press, 1995.
Translator, *Leaves from the Dry Tree,* by Vladimir Levchev. Merrick, New York, Cross-Cultural Communications, 1997.
Translator, *Electra,* by Sophocles. Philadelphia, University of Pennsylvania Press, 1998.
Translator, *Black Book of the Endangered Species,* by Vladimir Levchev. Washington, D.C., Word Works, 1999.

*

Bibliography: *Henry Taylor: A Bibliographic Chronicle, 1961–87* by Stuart Wright, in *Bulletin of Bibliography* 45(2), June 1988.

Henry Taylor comments:
The landscape of rural northern Virginia, and the equestrian sports that thrive there, have both been central to my life and my writing. Though it has been years since I rode competitively, the images and sensations of those days, and the recollection that I have communicated deeply with other creatures without using any words, have given me my own sense of the place of language in human experience. Possibly under the additional influence of my Quaker

faith and upbringing, I try to encourage the poem's tendency to drift from speech toward a more nearly silent existence. But my belief in what I am doing always meets a severe test in any statement of mine about what I have done or am doing.

However, there can be no doubt of the importance to my work of various writers and mentors, including but certainly not limited to Fred Bornhauser, R.H.W. Dillard, Fred Chappell, Kelly Cherry, George Garrett, May Sarton, David Slavitt, Carolyn Kizer, William Jay Smith, Robert Watson, Richard Bausch, Robert Bausch, Maxine Kumin, and others whose work, example, and friendship have helped me toward better work and better commitment to it.

*   *   *

Over the years the poetry of Henry Taylor has revealed itself to be very much of a piece. Although he first became known for witty parodies of other poets, which Robert Bly published in *The Sixties,* and has continued to write poems which arise from an essentially classical sense of satire and humor, his is a poetry that draws its real strength not so much from his formal skills, his intelligence, and his wit, all of which are considerable, but rather from an inescapable moral and metaphysical tension that informs it line by line. The characters and speakers of Taylor's poems are always pulling away from something and being drawn back to it, seeking something lost or never found while accepting a life without it, or being perpetually wounded by the inexorable movement of time but forcing themselves to examine and reexamine its wearing away of their lives.

The title poem of his Pulitzer prizewinning third book, *The Flying Change* (1985), brings this tension sharply into focus as it describes a riding maneuver in which a horse can change leads during a moment of suspension in the air, a maneuver made more difficult by the weight of the rider. "The aim of teaching a horse to move beneath you is to remind him how he moved when he was free," the poems says, but it goes on to extend that perception into a meditation about time and loss and freedom:

A single leaf turns sideways in the wind
in time to save a remnant of the day;
I am lifted like a whipcrack to the moves
I studied on that barbered stretch of ground,
before I schooled myself to drift away

from skills I still possess, but must outlive.
Sometimes when I cup water in my hands
and watch it slip away and disappear,
I see that age will make my hands a sieve;
but for a moment the shifting world suspends

its flight and leans toward the sun once more,
as if to interrupt its mindless plunge
through works and days that will not come again.
I hold myself immobile in bright air,
sustained in time astride the flying change.

Even in the poems of his precocious first collection, *The Horse Show at Midnight* (1966), which was published before his twenty-fourth birthday, Taylor wrote of characters (often much older than himself) who are striding the flying change, learning their limitations,

understanding what they can do and charting the boundaries of what they cannot, living, as he puts it in "A Blind Man Locking His House," in "the weather of despair" without giving in to despair. In his second book, *An Afternoon of Pocket Billiards* (1975), he continued his exploration of the tension between freedom and restraint in a more directly personal vein. Early in the collection, for example, he writes in "Goodbye to the Old Friends" of his turning away from the traditions and Quaker beliefs of his family, but later in the book, in "Return to the Old Friends," he finds himself back among the Friends, trying to recall "the force I was opposing/in my father's calm eyes as I fled rejoicing," even as he takes up again the burden of the past and the healing fact of his belief.

Time and again in his poems Taylor returns to the image of home as the place where one's wild freedom is painfully broken but also as the place toward which one blindly makes one's way through the dangerous dark. No wonder that so many of the central metaphors of his most personal work are drawn from the schooling of horses, the art of restraining wildness without losing its beauty and power. It also is not surprising that his is a poetry which, even though it is often violent and nakedly realistic, is usually written in traditional forms. Not since Edwin Arlington Robinson has an American poet consistently written narratives of such unrestrained emotional force in such disciplined and formal verse.

Taylor's later poems of lost and recovered love, which have appeared in journals, make it clear that he is continuing to explore and develop the central themes of his work. "Understanding Fiction," the tentative title of his next collection, shows that he has lost none of his sense of humor and daring. Together, these books should make clear what the Pulitzer revealed to many readers who were unfamiliar with his work—that Henry Taylor is a poet whose deeply felt, superbly crafted poems form a body of work which cannot be ignored in any serious assessment of contemporary American poetry.

—R.H.W. Dillard

THESEN, Sharon

Nationality: Canadian. **Born:** Tisdale, Saskatchewan, 1 October 1946. **Education:** Simon Fraser University, Burnaby, British Columbia, B.A. 1970, M.A. 1974. **Family:** Married 1) Brian Fawcett in 1966 (divorced), one son; 2) Peter Thompson. **Career:** Has worked as a dental assistant, cab driver, and record librarian. Since c. 1970 English teacher, Capilano College, Vancouver, British Columbia. Poetry editor, *Capilano Review,* 1978–89. **Address:** 2785 West 18th Avenue, Vancouver, British Columbia V6L 1B4, Canada.

PUBLICATIONS

Poetry

Artemis Hates Romance. Toronto, Coach House Press, 1980.
Radio New France Radio. Vancouver, Slug Press, 1982.
Holding the Pose. Toronto, Coach House Press, 1983.
Confabulations: Poems for Malcolm Lowry. Lantzville, British Columbia, Oolichan, 1984.

The Beginning of the Long Dash. Toronto, Coach House Press, 1987.
The Pangs of Sunday. Toronto, McClelland and Stewart, 1990.
Aurora. Toronto, Coach House Press, 1995.
News & Smoke: Selected Poems. Burnaby, British Columbia, Talonbooks, 1999.
A Pair of Scissors and Other Poems. Toronto, House of Anansi Press, 2000.

Other

Editor, *Selected Poems: The Vision Tree* by Phyllis Webb. Vancouver, Talonbooks, 1982.
Editor, *The New Long Poem Anthology.* Toronto, Coach House Press, 1991.
Editor, with Ralph Maud, *Charles Olson and Frances Boldereff: A Modern Correspondence,* by Charles Olson. Hanover, New Hampshire, University Press of New England, 1999.

*

Manuscript Collection: McGill University, Montreal.

Critical Studies: ''Knots of Energy: The Contest of Discourses in Sharon Thesen's Poetry'' by Rob Dunham, and ''The Barren Reach of Modern Desire: Intertextuality in Sharon Thesen's 'The Beginning of the Long Dash''' by Steven Scobie, both in *Sagetrieb* (Orono, Maine), 7(1), spring 1988; ''Writing through the Margins: Sharon Thesen's and Bill Manhire's Apparently Lyrical Poetry'' by Douglas Barbour, in *Australian and New Zealand Studies in Canada* (Prince George, British Columbia), 4, fall 1990; ''Tremendous Forgeries, Confabulations and Graphologies Elliptical: The Lyric/Anti-Lyric Poetry of Sharon Thesen and Elizabeth Smither'' by Pamela Banting, in *Australian and New Zealand Studies in Canada* (Prince George, British Columbia), 6, fall 1991; by Andrew Stubbs, in *Canadian Writers and Their Works,* edited by Robert Lecker, Jack David, and Ellen Quigley, Toronto, Ontario, ECW, 1995.

*   *   *

In her first book, *Artemis Hates Romance,* Sharon Thesen warns that ''the defoliated / imagination is the end / of all lyric'' (''Day Dream''). The flowering of Thesen's writing, witnessed in the volumes of poetry published beginning in 1980, is a clear indication that her own imagination is in full bloom. Thesen's lyricism, however, is not unremittingly bright and fragrant, for it lives in and grows out of a world marked by limitation and loss.

Thesen's early volumes in particular are characterized by fairly grim explorations of the limits of love, loneliness, anger, and despair. In a 1988 interview in the *Malahat Review* she calls these works her ''mad,'' ''sad,'' and ''bad'' books. In *Artemis Hates Romance* Thesen vents her rage and sorrow at the failures of romantic relationships, stating that ''there is no / metaphor for love that is not / redness & pain'' (''Wilkinson Road Poems'') and that the appearance of love ''brings dread to the heart, / knowledge / unasked for'' (''The Argument Begins with A''). In a poem called ''Dedication'' Thesen's anger is specifically targeted at '''honeybunch,''' otherwise addressed as ''you stupid fucker'' and ''you slimy hogstool,'' for his part in arresting her career as a poet: ''you never thought I'd do / it did

ya . . . / it's no goddamn thanks to you, hiding my / typewriter and always wanting fancy dinners all the time.''

Holding the Pose is a quieter work, inhabited by cheating hearts and icy hearts, brokenhearted skies and rain, dim places and painful yellow tulips. Early in the volume, in a poem entitled ''Discourse,'' Thesen concludes with irony that ''finally there's not / all that much / you can say,'' and yet she continues to write ''another word written, and another'' in ''the daily effort to solve / the puzzled heart'' (''Hello Goodbye''). Declaring that ''it is my own pain / I write'' (''X''), Thesen in this book sifts through her memories in order to heal herself and her imagination. Her meditations on the painful past are not maudlin or self-pitying, however, for in ''Praxis'' she firmly tells herself, and the reader, to ''imagine a future better / than now'' and to ''stop crying. Get up. Go out. Leap / the mossy garden wall / the steel fence or whatever / the case may be.''

Confabulations, is a series of poems for and about the deceased poet Malcolm Lowry. In the *Malahat Review* interview Thesen explains that the work is ''a confabulation with a kind of suffering that I identified with and understood deeply'' and that Lowry provided ''a persona through which I could speak that material without having to write confessional autobiographical poetry.'' These poems are a powerful evocation of Lowry's struggles with both alcohol and language and of Thesen's struggles with the darkness of her own world (which is also ours). ''This world / scissored your mind,'' she writes, ''bone-dry shreds of ecstacy / & terror igniting / your fragile nests.'' In his own voice Thesen's Lowry declares, ''I wake up / weeping the whole grief of the world / strangling my vocabulary.'' The volume's most haunting phrase, ''where I am it is dark,'' speaks not only of Lowry's nightmare world but also of the one we all live in and share.

The Beginning of the Long Dash marks the beginning of a change of tone in Thesen's work; she herself has called it her ''glad'' book. This change is particularly evident in ''The Landlord's Flower Beds,'' where the roses are ''white, / yellow, red, pink, all colors / of the rainbow'' and where they ''almost / pull you out of bed at night.'' Flowers also perform a vital function in ''The Occasions.'' Here the ''pale pink roses / are the tenderest things,'' and ''sitting with them you understand / the perfection of all things,'' though that understanding proves in the end to be transitory.

This volume also contains a number of poem sequences, a tangible indication of Thesen's expanding vision as she moves from a personal into a larger cultural milieu. The title poem, for example, is a philosophical meditation on the state of the world (social, moral, political) as the twentieth century was drawing to a close and is framed as a contemplation on the Christmas and New Year's season. In Thesen's fin de siècle world ''the five most compelling words / are *sex, free, cure, money,* and *baldness,* / a chain of conditions ranging from heaven to hell,'' and ''there's nothing to eat / but images to hunger for.'' The poem's title refers to the National Research Council Official Time Signal indicating 10:00 Pacific Standard Time, and as Thesen explains in the *Malahat Review* interview, it has a double meaning. On the one hand it signals that ''there's lots of time,'' but on the other hand it can be read metaphorically: ''it's a long dash all right, but toward what are we headed?''

If the new poems in Thesen's volume *The Pangs of Sunday* are any indication, the poet herself has headed in different directions. Alongside typically wry lyrics like ''The Scalpel,'' ''Elegy, the Fertility Specialist,'' and ''Emergency,'' in which Thesen declares succinctly that ''human love / is not so easy as speech / will allow,'' there are poems at once surreal and ordinary. Animals accompany the poet to corner letter boxes and the grocery store, and "when I put on / a fancy dinner, a few animals / are under the table staring at the guests." Empty pineapple shells "attract the wrong sort of chicken / who wear black thongs and carry a knife," the "crawfish garnish / outmanoeuvre[s]" Napoleon, and "adjacent recipes / clash by night" in the surreal kitchen ("Chicken in a Pensive Shell"). Finally, as the volume closes, the poet rides her "lovely horse / into the perfume department / at Eaton's," declaring, "We tried not to break anything / but also we were not abstract." In this new material and throughout her previous work Thesen moves through all our ordinary days, making unusual, even startling connections. Hers is a poetry of careful observation, of precise statement. It challenges the way we see ourselves and see the world and ourselves in the world.

—Susan Schenk

THOMAS, D(onald) M(ichael)

Nationality: British. **Born:** Redruth, Cornwall, 27 January 1935. **Education:** Redruth Grammar School; University High School, Melbourne; New College, Oxford, B.A. (honors) in English 1958, M.A. 1961. **Military Service:** British Army (national service), 1953–54. **Family:** Married twice; two sons and one daughter. **Career:** Teacher, Teignmouth Grammar School, Devon, 1959–63; senior lecturer in English, Hereford College of Education, 1964–78. Visiting lecturer in English, Hamline University, St. Paul, Minnesota, 1967; lecturer in creative writing, American University, Washington, D.C., 1982. **Awards:** Richard Hillary memorial prize, 1960; British Arts Council award, for translation, 1975, for novel, 1980; Cholmondeley award, for poetry, 1978; *Guardian-Gollancz* Fantasy Novel prize, 1979; *Los Angeles Times* prize, for fiction, 1981; Cheltenham prize, for novel, 1981; Silver Pen award, 1982. **Address:** The Coach House, Rashleigh Vale, Truro, Cornwall TR1 1TJ, England.

PUBLICATIONS

Poetry

Personal and Possessive. London, Outposts, 1964.
Penguin Modern Poets 11, with D.M. Black and Peter Redgrove. London, Penguin, 1968.
Two Voices. London, Cape Goliard Press, and New York, Grossman, 1968.
The Lover's Horoscope: Kinetic Poem. Laramie, Wyoming, Purple Sage, 1970.
Logan Stone. London, Cape Goliard Press, and New York, Grossman, 1971.
The Shaft. Gillingham, Kent, Arc, 1973.
Lilith-Prints. Cardiff, Second Aeon, 1974.
Symphony in Moscow. Richmond, Surrey, Keepsake Press, 1974.
Love and Other Deaths. London, Elek, 1975.
The Rock. Knotting, Bedfordshire, Sceptre Press, 1975.
Orpheus in Hell. Knotting, Bedfordshire, Sceptre Press 1977.
The Honeymoon Voyage. London, Secker and Warburg, 1978.

Protest: A Poem after a Medieval Armenian Poem by Frik. Privately printed, 1980.
Dreaming in Bronze. London, Secker and Warburg, 1981.
Selected Poems. London, Secker and Warburg, and New York, Viking Press, 1983.
News from the Front, with Sylvia Kantaris. Todmorden, Lancashire, Arc, 1983.
The Puberty Tree, New & Selected Poems. Newcastle upon Tyne, Bloodaxe, 1992.

Plays

The White Hotel, adaptation of his own novel (produced Edinburgh, 1984).

Radio Plays: *You Will Hear Thunder, 1981; Boris Godunov,* from play by Pushkin, 1984.

Novels

The Flute-Player. London, Gollancz, and New York, Dutton, 1979.
Birthstone. London, Gollancz, 1980.
The White Hotel. London, Gollancz, and New York, Viking Press, 1981.
Russian Nights: Ararat. London, Gollancz, and New York, Viking Press, 1983.
Swallow. London, Gollancz, and New York, Viking, 1984.
Sphinx. London, Gollancz, 1986; New York, Viking, 1987.
Summit. London, Gollancz, 1987; New York, Viking, 1988.
Lying Together. London, Gollancz, and New York, Viking, 1990.
Flying in to Love. London, Bloomsbury, 1991.
Pictures at an Exhibition. London, Bloomsbury, 1993.
Eating Pavlova. London, Bloomsbury, 1994.
Lady with a Laptop: A Novel. New York, Carroll and Graf, 1996.

Other

The Devil and the Floral Dance (for children). London, Robson, 1978.
Memories and Hallucinations: A Memoir. London, Gollancz, and New York, Viking, 1988.
Alexander Solzhenitsyn: A Century in His Life. London, Little Brown, and New York, St. Martin's Press, 1998.

Editor, *The Granite Kingdom: Poems of Cornwall.* Truro, Cornwall, Barton, 1970.
Editor, *Poetry in Crosslight.* London, Longman, 1975.
Editor, *Songs from the Earth: Selected Poems of John Harris, Cornish Miner, 1820–84.* Padstow, Cornwall, Lodenek Press, 1977.

Translator, *Requiem, and Poem Without a Hero,* by Anna Akhmatova. London, Elek, 1976; Athens, Ohio University Press, 1977.
Translator, *Way of All the Earth,* by Anna Akhmatova. London, Secker and Warburg, and Athens, Ohio University Press, 1979.
Translator, *Invisible Threads,* by Evtushenko. New York, Macmillan, 1981.

Translator, *The Bronze Horseman and Other Poems,* by Pushkin. London, Secker and Warburg, and New York, Viking Press, 1982.

Translator, *A Dove in Santiago,* by Yevgeny Yevtushenko. London, Secker and Warburg, 1982; New York, Viking Press, 1983.

Translator, *You Will Hear Thunder: Poems,* by Anna Akhmatova. London, Secker and Warburg, and Athens, Ohio University Press-Swallow Press, 1985.

Translator, *Boris Gudunov* by Alexander Pushkin. Leamington Spa, Sixth Chamber Press, 1985.

*

Critical Studies: By David Brooks, in *Helix* (Victoria, Australia), 21–22, spring 1985; "Subject in/of/to History and His Story" by Linda Hutcheon, in *Diacritics* (Baltimore, Maryland), 16(1), spring 1986; "The Phalaris Syndrome: Alain Robbe-Grillet vs. D.M. Thomas" by K.J. Phillips, in *Women and Violence in Literature: An Essay Collection,* edited by Katherine Anne Ackley, New York, Garland, 1990; *The Eschatological and the Other: Literature toward the End* (dissertation) by Steven Lane Pugmire, University of Washington, 1993; "Translation and Plagiarism: Puskin and D.M. Thomas" by Lauren G. Leighton, in *Slavic and East European Journal* (Tucson, Arizona), 38(1), spring 1994; by Rachel Wetzsteon, in *British Writers: Supplement IV,* edited by George Stade and Carol Howard, New York, Scribner, 1997.

D.M. Thomas comments:

(1974) My poetry does not move far from love and death. Early poems (see *Penguin Modern Poets 11*) use science fiction themes as images of desire and separation. More recently, my most obsessive themes have been sexuality, family deaths, and a search for lost roots.

*   *   *

To follow the work of D.M. Thomas from his first Outposts booklet, *Personal and Possessive,* through *Dreaming in Bronze* is to encounter an impressive development and variety. The early erotic poetry gives way to the series of science fiction poems that established his reputation and then moves on to a poetry of a more subtle and tender exploration of relationships and emotions. He is a poet who keeps his readers on the alert, never quite letting them know what to expect next. In *The Honeymoon Voyage* we find robust reworkings of Brazilian and Japanese myths, together with poems that hark back to his family and roots in Cornwall. One is reminded of Fernando Pessoa, the Portuguese poet who invented three other poets to write in modes other than his own, for Thomas could well do the same if he were so minded.

For all of Thomas's versatility, however, there is a common factor in his work: he is essentially a narrative poet. Thomas is more than that, of course, but he can maintain a narrative flow and thrust that carry the reader along. It is this ability that gives his science fiction poems their strength, and in this he reminds us of the Victorian narrative poets, especially Browning, in such science fiction monologues as "Tithonus," "Cygnus," and "Hera's Spring." They are, in addition, remarkably atmospheric poems, not only in their exotic settings but also in the depth of feeling they convey of desire and separation: "Believe me, dear, though it will seem strange / to you, I have wept too for all these / things you mention" ("Hera's Spring").

Yet even in Thomas's shorter poems it is the narrative thread, however tenuous, that holds them together and helps to give them unity and coherence. It is the same narrative skill that finds him adapting style, language, and rhythm to match the characters and situations he depicts. Thomas is a fine craftsman, and his style, while often deceptively unobtrusive, is clearly adapted and related to his subject matter. A case in point is "Under Carn Brea," a series of Cornish portraits ranging from the ribald Mona—"Groaned, bumped and thumped and showed how far / Snapped suspenders sank back in the fat. / 'I'n it shameful!' Whooped her anguish"—to the gentle depths of the understanding of Perry, who was to become a near recluse on the death of her husband—"It would have been a shocking waste of life / But it was Perry's self, and nothing else." This is true also of his prose. Witness the superb pastiche of Sigmund Freud's style in *The White Hotel.*

In *Dreaming in Bronze* we find a strongly personal element emerging, so that even in his historical reconstructions Thomas's memories and experiences intrude and merge to construct his own highly charged and sensual fables. The dangers of an emotionally erotic self-indulgence are inherent in this and can be observed in such poems as "Big Deaths, Little Deaths" and in his collaboration with Sylvia Kantaris in *News from the Front.* It is as if Thomas has taken this joint exercise as a competition in flying, and it is well written if you like that kind of thing. But it is this element of risk that makes Thomas one of the more exciting poets writing today. At his best his talent for a creative empathy and selective use of detail succeeds in evoking the complex of emotions that underlie the situations of which he writes.

—John Cotton

THOMAS, Lorenzo

Nationality: American (emigrated from Panama in 1948). **Born:** Republic of Panama, 31 August 1944. **Education:** Queens College (now City University of New York), B.A. 1967; graduate study at Pratt Institute. **Military Service:** U.S. Naval Reserve, 1968–72; served in Vietnam. **Career:** Assistant reference librarian, Pratt Institute, New York, 1967–68; writer-in-residence, Texas Southern University, Houston, 1973; creative writing teacher, Black Arts Center, Houston, 1973–75. Since 1976 correspondent, *Living Blues,* Chicago. Has worked with the Poetry-in-the-Schools program in New York, Texas, Oklahoma, Florida, Arkansas, and Georgia. **Awards:** Dwight Durling prize in poetry, 1963; Poets Foundation award, 1966, 1974; Committee on Poetry grant, 1973; Lucille Medwick award, 1974; National Endowment for the Arts creative writing fellowship, 1983; Houston Festival Foundation Arts award, 1984. **Address:** P.O. Box 14645, Houston, Texas 77021, U.S.A.

PUBLICATIONS

Poetry

A Visible Island. N.p., Adlib Press, 1967.
Fit Music: California Songs. New York, Angel Hair Books, 1972.
Dracula. New York, Angel Hair Books, 1973.

Framing the Sunrise. N.p., Sun Be/Am Associates, 1975.
Sound Science. N.p., Sun Be/Am Associates, 1978.
The Bathers: Selected Poems. New York, Reed, 1978.
Chances Are Few. Berkeley, California, Blue Wind Press, 1979.

Other

Extraordinary Measures: Afrocentric Modernism and Twentieth-Century American Poetry. Tuscaloosa, University of Alabama Press, 2000.

Editor, *ANKH: Getting It Together.* N.p., Hope Development, 1974.
Editor, *Sing the Sun Up: Creative Writing Ideas from African American Literature.* New York, Teachers and Writers Collaborative, 1998.

*

Critical Studies: Interview with Charles H. Rowell, in *Callaloo* (Baltimore, Maryland), 4(1–3), 1981, and with Hermine Pinson, in *Callaloo* (Baltimore, Maryland), 22(2), spring 1999.

*   *   *

Beginning with his first published collection, *A Visible Island,* Lorenzo Thomas has dealt with a range of important contemporary issues in a variety of poetics. His Panamanian past as well as his identity as a politicized African-American writer, coupled with an intense interest in how poetry is connected to everyday language, have led to Thomas's production of an important body of writing. His work as a teenager in the Umbra workshop on the Lower East Side of New York involved him from an early age in an intense aesthetic and political environment. Other writers such as Brenda Walcott and Lennox Raphael helped create a vibrant dialogue in a community that was formative for the young Thomas's work. The civil rights movement, the ethnically diverse city of New York, and the development of African identity, as well as various avant-garde artistic groups, shaped Thomas's early poetics and have continued to influence him. It is important also to note Thomas's service in Vietnam, which had a profound influence on his attitude about the marginalized and their involvement in the nation.

Thomas's interest in the early work of Amiri Baraka as well as in the French surrealist André Breton and the Martinican were important to his early collections. Magical realist textures, a strong sense of African identity, and an intense interest in folk cultures are also significant in the early books. Of course, important to an exploration of any of these issues for a displaced Panamanian is the concept of diasporic exile, a theme that Thomas explores with particular effectiveness in the early poem "The Unnatural Life." Other poems grapple with African identity and the ways in which it is frequently "masked" in contemporary American social life, how the African exile deals with his lot in a country that again and again marginalizes him.

A later poem shows how Thomas has attempted to continue the exploration of the themes of his earlier work while embracing contemporary culture and its impact on forming attitudes and perspectives on important subjects. Consider, for example, these lines:

Watch who ends up in contestant's row
I like it when the colored people win

It always was all women years ago
Once in a while maybe a young Marine
Lcpl in dress uniform
Every other word he said was "sir"
Probably a newlywed on top of that

The poem builds to end with the refrain "I like it when the colored people win." Besides the thematic issue of the marginalization of African-Americans, the poem also illustrates Thomas's formal range. Like Gwendolyn Brooks, he is a poet who is comfortable writing about highly polemical subjects in a variety of poetic styles. Sometimes he uses rhyme and sometimes free verse, but his work is always propelled by an attention to the possibilities of the vernacular.

Whatever the poetics that are prominent in any given poem, Thomas is a clear example of a contemporary African-American poet who has managed to keep political concerns alive without compromising his devotion to craft. As he has commented, "Poetry is an often effective remedy for the sometimes life-threatening ailment of spontaneous speech. Poetry is formulaic language, a cure for blurting." Thomas's work enacts just such a cure, aspiring toward natural-sounding language, incorporating the vernacular, yet always aware of its aesthetic effects. That Thomas's work frequently succeeds—while dealing with some of the most divisive of political topics—speaks to his great abilities.

—Tod Marshall

THOMAS, R(onald) S(tuart)

Nationality: Welsh. **Born:** Cardiff, Glamorgan, 29 March 1913. **Education:** County School, Holyhead; University College, Bangor; St. Michael's College, Llandaff; University of Wales, Cardiff, B.A. in classics 1935. **Family:** Married Mildred Eldridge in 1940; one son. **Career:** Ordained deacon, 1937, priest, 1937: curate of Chirk, Denbigh, 1936–40; curate of Hanmer, Flintshire, 1940–42; rector of Manafon, Montgomery, 1942–54; vicar of St. Michael's, Eglwysfach, Denbigh, 1954–67, and of St. Hywyn, Aberdaron, with St. Mary, Bodferin, 1967–78; rector of Rhiw, with Llanfaelrhys, 1972–78. **Awards:** Heinemann award, 1955; Queen's Gold Medal for Poetry, 1964; Welsh Arts Council award, 1968, 1976; Cholmondeley award, 1978; Lannan Lifetime Achievement award for poetry, 1996. **Address:** Sarn-y-Plas, Y Rhiw, Pwllheli, Gwynedd, Wales.

PUBLICATIONS

Poetry

The Stones of the Field. Carmarthen, Druid Press, 1946.
An Acre of Land. Newtown, Montgomeryshire Printing Company, 1952.
The Minister. Newtown, Montgomeryshire Printing Company, 1953.
Song at the Year's Turning: Poems 1942–1954. London, Hart Davis, 1955.
Poetry for Supper. London, Hart Davis, 1958; Chester Springs, Pennsylvania, Dufour, 1961.
Judgement Day. London, Poetry Book Society, 1960.

Tares. London, Hart Davis, and Chester Springs, Pennsylvania, Dufour, 1961.

Penguin Modern Poets 1, with Lawrence Durrell and Elizabeth Jennings. London, Penguin, 1962.

The Bread of Truth. London, Hart Davis, and Chester Springs, Pennsylvania, Dufour, 1963.

Pietà. London, Hart Davis, 1966.

Not That He Brought Flowers. London, Hart Davis, 1968.

Pergamon Poets 1, with Roy Fuller, edited by Evan Owen. Oxford, Pergamon Press, 1968.

Postcard: Song. N.p., Fishpaste, 1968.

The Mountains. New York, Chilmark Press, 1968.

H'm. London, Macmillan, and New York, St. Martin's Press, 1972.

Selected Poems 1946–1968. London, Hart Davis MacGibbon, 1973; New York, St. Martin's Press, 1974.

What Is a Welshman? Llandybie, Dyfed, Christopher Davies, 1974.

Laboratories of the Spirit. London, Macmillan, 1975; Boston, Godine, 1976.

The Way of It. Sunderland, Ceolfrith Press, 1977.

Frequencies. London, Macmillan, 1978.

Between Here and Now. London, Macmillan, 1981.

Poet's Meeting. Stratford-upon-Avon, Celandine, 1983.

Later Poems: A Selection. London, Macmillan, 1983.

The Poems of R.S. Thomas. Fayetteville, University of Arkansas Press, 1985.

Destinations. Stratford-upon-Avon, Celandine, 1985.

Experimenting with an Amen. London, Macmillan, 1986.

Selected Poems 1946–1968. Newcastle upon Tyne, Bloodaxe, 1986.

Welsh Airs. Bridgend, Glamorgan, Poetry Wales Press, and Chester Springs, Pennsylvania, Dufour, 1987.

The Echoes Return Slow. London, Macmillan, 1988.

Three Poems. Child Okeford, Dorset, Words Press, 1988.

Later Poems: A Selection. London, Macmillan, 1989.

Mass for Hard Times. Newcastle upon Tyne, Bloodaxe, 1992.

Collected Poems, 1945–1990. London, Phoenix, 1993.

No Truce with the Furies. Newcastle upon Tyne, Bloodaxe, and Chester Springs, Pennsylvania, Dufour, 1995.

R.S. Thomas. London, J.M. Dent, 1996.

Love Poems. London, Phoenix, 1996.

Other

Words and the Poet (lecture). Cardiff, University of Wales Press, 1964.

Young and Old (for children). London, Chatto and Windus, 1972.

Selected Prose, edited by Sandra Anstey. Bridgend, Glamorgan, Poetry Wales Press, 1983; Chester Springs, Pennsylvania, Dufour. 1984.

Ingrowing Thoughts. Bridgend, Glamorgan, Poetry Wales Press, 1985.

Neb. Caenorfon, Gwasg Gwynedd, 1985.

Pe Medrwn yr Iaith: Ac Ysgrifau Eraill. Abertawe, Christopher Davies, 1988.

Autobiographies. London, J.M. Dent, 1997.

Editor, *The Batsford Book of Country Verse.* London, Batsford, 1961.

Editor, *The Penguin Book of Religious Verse.* London, Penguin, 1963.

Editor, *Selected Poems,* by Edward Thomas. London, Faber, 1964.

Editor, *A Choice of George Herbert's Verse.* London, Faber, 1967.

Editor, *A Choice of Wordsworth's Verse.* London, Faber, 1971.

Editor, *Between Sea and Sky: Images of Bardsey,* by P. Hope Jones. Llandysul, Gomer, 1998.

*

Critical Studies: In *Welsh Anvil* (Llandybie), 1949, 1952; in *Critical Quarterly* (Manchester), ii, 4, 1960; in *A Review of English Literature* (Leeds), iii, 4, 1960; in *Anglo-Welsh Review* (Pembroke Dock, Wales), xiii, 31, 1963; *R.S. Thomas* by R. George Thomas, London, Longman, 1964; R.S. Thomas issue of *Poetry Wales* (Llandybie), winter 1972; *R.S. Thomas* by William Moelwyn Merchant, Cardiff, University of Wales Press, and Mystic, Connecticut, Verry, 1979; *Yeats, Eliot, and R.S. Thomas: Riding the Echo* by A.E. Dyson, London, Macmillan, 1981; *Critical Writings on R.S. Thomas* edited by Sandra Anstey, Bridgend, Glamorgan, Poetry Wales Press, 1982; *R.S. Thomas, Poet of the Hidden God: Meaning and Meditation in the Poetry of R.S. Thomas* by D.Z. Phillips, London, Macmillan, 1986; *The Poetry of R.S. Thomas* by J.P. Ward, Bridgend, Glamorgan, Poetry Wales Press, 1987; *Miraculous Simplicity,* Fayetteville, University of Arkansas Press, 1992; *The Page's Drift: R.S. Thomas at Eighty,* Bridgend, Glamorgan, Seren, 1993; *'Texts against Chaos': Anglo-Welsh Identity in the Poetry of R.S. Thomas, Raymond Garlick, and Roland Mathias* (dissertation) by Megan Sue Lloyd, University of Kentucky, 1993; *The Religious Poetry of R.S. Thomas* (dissertation) by Janice Darlene Peterson, University of Alberta, 1993; *Approaches to the Study of R.S. Thomas's Selected Poems, 1946–1968* by Ellie Jones, Cardiff, National Language Unit of Wales, 1994; ''Why the Most Famous Welsh Poet Writes in English'' by Rosemary Markham, in *Contemporary Review* (Surrey, England), 264(1538), March 1994; *R.S. Thomas: Conceding an Absence: Images of God Explored* by Elaine Shepherd, New York, St. Martin's Press, 1996; ''Through the Looking Glass: R.S. Thomas's The Echoes Return Slow As Poetic Autobiography'' by David Lloyd, in *Twentieth Century Literature* (Hempstead, New York), 42(4), winter 1996; *R.S. Thomas: Conceding an Absence* by Elaine Shepherd, Houndmills, England, Macmillan, and New York, St. Martin's Press, 1996; ''Vernon Watkins and R.S. Thomas'' by Dennis Brown, in *British Poetry from the 1950s to the 1990s: Politics and Art,* edited by Gary Day, London, Macmillan, and New York, St. Martin's Press, 1997; ''Dualism and Theodicy in R.S. Thomas' Poetry'' by Christine Meilicke, in *Literature & Theology* (England), 12(4), December 1998.

*   *   *

Consciously or unconsciously, R.S. Thomas has taken on something of the mantle of an Old Testament prophet. That is why he was drawn early on to translate ''The Cry of Elisha after Elijah'' from the Welsh of Thomas Williams. But he has taken on only ''something of the mantle,'' and the something is the prophetic tone and surge of the Hebrew prophets as mediated through the King James Version of the Bible. The other reason for his attraction to this poem of Williams is its ambiguity in the face of the mystery of God, which has become Thomas's lifelong theme: ''Cold is my cry; our bond was broken . . . / My understanding is darkened, / It is no gain to inquire.'' His other theme is that of the natural world, for in the beginning Thomas was very much a Welsh Wordsworth: ''Just an ordinary man of the bald Welsh hills, / Who pens a few sheep in a gap of cloud.'' ''Michael'' and ''The Leech Gatherer'' lie behind Thomas's ''Iago Prytherch,'' and, as with Wordsworth, there is great identification with peasant and place in Thomas's early poems.

It has rightly been said that there is much bitterness in Thomas's poetry, whether against modern man ("He's a new man now, part of the machine, / His nerves of metal and his blood oil") or against the remnants of the agrarian folk of Wales like Iago Prytherch, with his "frightening . . . vacancy of mind." But what is not so frequently pointed out is the huge compassion for the hill people, the peasants and sheep farmers, in their lonely struggle for subsistence and even for those victims of the more contemporary world like the displaced young girl in "The Evacuee," who "grew, a small bird in the nest / Of welcome . . ." and whom "the men watched . . . and, nodding, smiled / With earth's charity, patient and strong." Stan Smith's claim that "this is pastoral poetry with a sour edge . . ." severely understates the nature of the poetry of Thomas. The "sour edge" is everywhere in the details and images of the poetry: "Docking mangels, chipping the green skin / From the yellow bones with a half-witted grin / Of satisfaction . . ."; ". . . the table unlaid and bare / As a boar's backside." But one simply cannot say that Thomas's final plea for Iago Prytherch, so reminiscent of Roy Campbell's "The Serf"— "Remember him, then, for he, too, is a winner of wars, / Enduring like a tree under the curious stars"—is anything but a tribute to his universalizing compassion. The same is true of his "Death of a Peasant":

> You remember Davies? He died, you know,
> With his face to the wall, as the manner is
> Of the poor peasant in his stone croft . . .

Yes, there is bitterness. His description of his own country and people is bitter:

> There is no present in Wales,
> And no future . . .
> And an impotent people,
> Sick with inbreeding,
> Worrying the carcase of an old song.

But such bitterness is no more the whole spirit of this poet than any single play gives the whole of Shakespeare.

As Richard Poole put it, commenting on the work of Thomas years after these early poems, "Here was the real thing—language with a tough directness of utterance and a thrilling beauty, and a voice at once personal and universal." This expresses the real poet in his wholeness. Thomas is a major poet because his genius is multifaceted and universal. He embraces politics, Welsh nationalism, the shortcomings of science and the materialism of the consumer society, and, above all, the long struggle with the problem of faith in the modern world. As the years have gone by, his work has grown ever more philosophical. Indeed, through his resorting to the great philosophers for help with the problems of faith and reality, he makes palpable in as concrete a way as possible the thorniest of abstractions. At the heart of his poetry, especially in his later years, is a relentless questioning.

Though a priest, Thomas is not a great religious poet in the tradition of, say, Herbert or Traherne or the biblical poet-prophets, for he does not, cannot, bear sufficient witness to the reality of God or the religious experience. As Robert Minhinnick has rightly said, "Dylan Thomas, pondering the estuarine splendours of his adopted home, gets tantalisingly closer to faith." Thomas, however, bears perpetual witness to the absence of God, the emptiness of Christ's churches, the constantly unanswered (as he sees it) cries of prayer. In truth his poetry reveals, more than anything, a hymn to doubt and the existential agony of modern man. Paradoxically, if he were not so profoundly honest, Thomas might settle for the cop-out of atheism: "I have heard the still, small voice / and it was that of the bacteria / demolishing my cosmos . . . / I am alone on the surface / of a turning planet"; and "He looked over / the world's edge and nausea / engulfed him" (from *The Echoes Return Slow*). In "Via Negativa" we read of "that great absence / In our lives, the empty silence / Within . . ."

Thomas has become the national monument of Anglo-Welsh literature, as many critics put it, an "icon." This in fact is how reviewer Glenda Beagan described him before going on to sum up: "Perhaps the vertiginous repulsion/fascination of the later poems could not have come about without that preliminary hard-core of rootedness in earth, those specifics of place, since, for matter to be recognised as the scaffolding of spirit, it must first be fully apprehended as matter in its own right." That, I think, is about right as a summing up of the vast, doubt-filled corpus of this major and, if not "religious," certainly spiritually obsessed poet.

—William Oxley

THWAITE, Anthony (Simon)

Nationality: British. **Born:** Chester, Cheshire, 23 June 1930. **Education:** Leeds; Sheffield; the United States, 1940–44; at Kingswood School, Bath; Christ Church, Oxford, B.A. (honors) 1955, M.A. 1959. **Military Service:** 1949–51. **Family:** Married Ann Harrop (i.e., the writer Ann Thwaite) in 1955; four daughters. **Career:** Visiting lecturer in English literature, Tokyo University, Japan, 1955–57; radio producer, BBC, London, 1957–62; literary editor, *The Listener,* London, 1962–65; assistant professor of English, University of Libya, Benghazi, 1965–67; literary editor, *New Statesman,* London, 1968–72; visiting professor, University of Kuwait, 1974; co-editor, *Encounter,* London, 1973–85; poetry adviser, Secker and Warburg publishers, London, 1971–86; poet-in-residence, Vanderbilt University, Nashville, Tennessee, 1992. Editorial director, 1986–95, and until 1995 editorial consultant, Andre Deutsch publishers, London. **Awards:** Richard Hillary memorial prize, 1968; Henfield Writing fellowship, University of East Anglia, Norwich, summer 1972; Cholmondeley award, 1983; Japan Foundation fellowship, University of Tokyo, 1985–86. Honorary fellow, Westminster College, Oxford, 1991. D. Litt.: University of Hull, 1989. Fellow, Royal Society of Literature, 1978. O.B.E. (Officer, Order of the British Empire), 1990. **Address:** The Mill House, Low Tharston, Norfolk NR15 2YN, England.

PUBLICATIONS

Poetry

(Poems). Oxford, Fantasy Press, 1953.
Home Truths. Hessle, Yorkshire, Marvell Press, 1957.
Poems. Privately printed, Tokyo, 1957.
The Owl in the Tree. London, Oxford University Press, 1963.

The Stones of Emptiness: Poems 1963–66. London, Oxford University Press, 1967.

Penguin Modern Poets 18, with A. Alvarez and Roy Fuller. London, Penguin, 1970.

Points. London, Turret, 1972.

Inscriptions: Poems 1967–72. London, Oxford University Press, 1973.

Jack. Hitchin, Hertfordshire, Cellar Press, 1973.

New Confessions. London, Oxford University Press, 1974.

A Portion for Foxes. London, Oxford University Press, 1977.

Victorian Voices. Oxford and New York, Oxford University Press, 1980.

Telling Tales. Sidcot, Somerset, Gruffyground Press, 1983.

Poems 1953–1983. London, Secker and Warburg, 1984.

Letter from Tokyo. London, Century Hutchinson, 1987.

Poems 1953–1988. London, Century Hutchinson, 1989.

The Dust of the World. London, Sinclair-Stevenson, 1994.

Selected Poems 1956–1996. London, Enitharmon Press, 1997.

A Different Country: New Poems. London, Enitharmon Press, 2000.

Other

Essays on Contemporary English Poetry: Hopkins to the Present Day. Tokyo, Kenkyusha, 1957; revised edition, as *Contemporary English Poetry: An Introduction,* London, Heinemann, 1959; Chester Springs, Pennsylvania, Dufour, 1961.

Japan in Colour, photographs by Roloff Beny. London, Thames and Hudson, and New York, McGraw Hill, 1967.

The Deserts of Hesperides: An Experience of Libya. London, Secker and Warburg, and New York, Roy, 1969.

Poetry Today 1960–1973. London, Longman, 1973; revised edition, as *Poetry Today: A Critical Guide to British Poetry 1960–1984,* 1985; revised edition, as *Poetry Today, 1960–1995,* 1995.

Roloff Beny in Italy, with Peter Porter. London, Thames and Hudson, and New York, Harper, 1974.

Beyond the Inhabited World: Roman Britain (for children). London, Deutsch, 1976; New York, Seabury Press, 1977.

Twentieth-Century English Poetry. London, Heinemann, and New York, Barnes and Noble, 1978.

Odyssey: Mirror of the Mediterranean, photographs by Roloff Beny. London, Thames and Hudson, and New York, Harper, 1981.

Six Centuries of Verse. London, Thames TV-Methuen, 1984.

Using the Past: Contemporary Poets and History (lecture). Tokyo, English Literary Society of Japan, 1985.

Anthony Thwaite in Conversation with Peter Dale and Ian Hamilton. London, Between the Lines, 1999.

Editor, with Hilary Corke and William Plomer, *New Poems 1961.* London, Hutchinson, 1961.

Editor, and Translator with Geoffrey Bownas, *The Penguin Book of Japanese Verse.* London, Penguin, 1964; revised edition, 1998.

Editor, with Peter Porter, *The English Poets: From Chaucer to Edward Thomas.* London, Secker and Warburg, 1974.

Editor, *Poems for Shakespeare 3.* London, Globe Playhouse, 1974.

Editor, with Fleur Adcock, *New Poetry 4.* London, Hutchinson, 1978.

Editor, *Larkin at Sixty.* London, Faber, 1982.

Editor, with Howard Sergeant, *The Gregory Awards Anthology 1981–1982.* Manchester, Carcanet, 1982.

Editor, with John Mole, *Poetry 1945 to 1980.* London, Longman, 1983.

Editor, *Collected Poems,* by Philip Larkin. London, Faber, 1988: New York, Farrar Straus, 1989.

Editor, *Selected Letters,* by Philip Larkin. London, Faber, 1992; New York, Farrar, Straus, 1993.

Editor, *Selected Poems,* by Henry Wadsworth Longfellow. London, Everyman's Library, 1993.

*

Manuscript Collections: Brynmor Jones Library, University of Hull; Brotherton Library, University of Leeds.

Critical Studies: *British Poetry between the Movement and Modernism: Anthony Thwaite and Philip Larkin* by Hans Osterwalder, Heidelberg, Germany, Carl Winter Universitätsverlag, 1991; by Penelope Fitzgerald, in *New Criterion,* 11(7), March 1993; by John Simon, in *Book World,* 23(50), 12 December 1993.

*   *   *

Paradox confronts the reader of the work of Anthony Thwaite. He is a man with strong domestic ties who is impelled to uproot himself in search of new horizons, a creature of habit who resents it, inwardly longing for a change of scene, a modern poet with a deep and abiding sense of the past, a formal, austere artist troubled by a lurking unease, an inveterate collector who admits to the futility of life. Thwaite sets down his contradictions with dispassionate honesty, blending them into a body of work striking in its range and conviction, at once urbane and challenging.

Collecting is the most obvious of Thwaite's traits, and it is described and mulled over in several poems. Wherever Thwaite goes, he takes ''luggage'' with him, as ''Personal Effects'' testifies: ''an affluent magpie in a nest that creaks / With impedimenta.'' In ''The Antiquarian'' he asks himself the reason for this compulsive hoarding but finds no definite answer. Further reading suggests that, in fact, these random collections of objects serve him as evidence of the physical world and more subtly as talismans, proofs, and reminders of past ages. By them history is made a continuum in which the endless cycle of man's rise, brief glory, and inevitable fall are mirrored in a pattern of centuries. This linking of past and present in an unbroken sequence enables Thwaite to unite them in ''The Letters of Synesius,'' with the laconic epistles of the fourth-century bishop interwoven with the poet's current asides and the barbarian invaders given modern parallels as tourists and oil tycoons. This ability to project himself into a figure from the past surfaces again in *Victorian Voices,* a series of monologues by factual and fictitious personalities of the age. Thwaite excels in these portraits, whether presenting the children's author drawing homilies from nature, the doomed rebellion of a novelist's wife, or the engaging roguery of the anonymous Irish beggar. *Victorian Voices* is possibly the most sustained of Thwaite's collections and is undeniably impressive, but one hesitates to call it his best. A certain sameness of tone denies it that range and diversity characteristic of the poet's finest work.

Thwaite is fascinated by history and by the message that is decoded from the archaeological fragments he assembles. Burrowing in the ruins of Jamestown or eyeing the crumbling cliff edges of Dunwich, he finds proof of mankind's fragility, the slow wearing away of all things under the pressure of time. The images reappear in

"The Stones of Emptiness," the desert boulders of the title poem emphasizing the wilderness ("They define the void. They assert / How vast the distance are, featureless, bare . . ."). Dust is seen as the one unalterable substance, the common denominator to which everything must be reduced.

Dust is the dominant theme in the collection *The Dust of the World,* in which Thwaite once more examines the inevitability of decay and the transience of human civilization and struggles to find "a meaning in our mess." Here, in verses that range over his experiences as a lecturer in Japan and the United States, as a visitor to Asia and eastern Europe, and as an archaeologist on digs and a wanderer around museums, Thwaite provides his own commentary on the frailty of mankind. "Levelling" and "Under the Campus" find him reminded of his own mortality while confronting the litter of past ages; in "Accumulations" he baulks at the incredible mass of literature and artifacts on which the dust settles so relentlessly. The horrors of war invade his mind in "Sarajevo II" and in "Franklin and Nashville: 1864," where he reveals the ugly reality of death beneath the textbook utterances. Elsewhere he shows a wry amusement in his memories of poetry festivals, and in "Memoir" and "The Notebooks" he explores the nature and origins of literary self-expression. *The Dust of the World* also includes moving elegies of fellow writers and the author's boyhood recollections of World War II. In this collection, as in all of his work, Thwaite finds himself caught in a painful search for the right words, forever striving to encapsulate the essence of a moment that is doomed to fade and vanish. *The Dust of the World* is further evidence of his skill in achieving this seemingly impossible task.

Recent years have seen Thwaite increasingly involved in critical and editorial work. His editing of the *Collected Poems* and *Selected Letters* of his friend and fellow poet, the late Philip Larkin, and his *Selected Poems* of Longfellow, are testimony to his ability in this field, while in *Poetry Today, 1960–95* he provides his own thoughtful assessment of his contemporaries. A highly accomplished, disciplined writer with an awareness of tradition and the "rules of poetry," Thwaite remains unconvinced by the protest and performance movements of the 1960s and by what he sees as the overt politicizing of the form. *Selected Poems 1956–1996* brings together classic examples of his earlier writing—"Mr. Cooper," "The Letters of Synesius," "Dust," "Victorian Voices," among others—with new, previously unpublished poems that once more present the deepest of feelings in neat, well-structured forms. "Changing Ties," in which the poet reflects on the difference between the black and the flowery ties he swaps while traveling from a funeral to a wedding ("Leaving what was, moving towards what is") manages to convey a great deal in a handful of lines. This, one feels, is the essence of poetry, and it is a terrain that Thwaite knows better than most.

—Geoff Sadler

TILLINGHAST, Richard (Williford)

Nationality: American. **Born:** Memphis, Tennessee, 25 November 1940. **Education:** University of the South, Sewanee, Tennessee (assistant editor, *Sewanee Review*), A.B. 1962; Harvard University, Cambridge, Massachusetts (Woodrow Wilson Fellow), A.M. 1963,

Ph.D. 1970. **Family:** Married 1) Nancy Walton Pringle in 1965 (divorced 1970); 2) Mary Graves in 1973, three sons and one daughter. **Career:** Professor of English, University of California, Berkeley, 1968–73; instructor, San Quentin Prison College Program, 1975–78; visiting assistant professor, University of the South, 1979–80; Briggs-Copeland Lecturer, Harvard University, 1980–83. Since 1983 professor of English, University of Michigan, Ann Arbor. Faculty associate, Michigan Institute for the Humanities, 1988–89 and 1993–94. **Awards:** Sinclair-Kennedy travel grant, 1966–67; Creative Arts Institute grant, 1970; National Endowment for the Humanities grant, 1980; Breadloaf Conference fellowship, 1982; Michigan Arts Council grant, 1985; Millay Colony residency, 1985; Yaddo Writers' Retreat residency, 1986; Michigan Council for the Arts grant, 1986; American Research Institute fellowship, 1990; Amy Lowell travel grant, 1990–91; travel grants to Northern Ireland from the British Council, 1992–94; Ann Stanford prize for poetry, 1992. **Address:** University of Michigan, Department of English, Haven Hall, Ann Arbor, Michigan 48109–1003, U.S.A.

PUBLICATIONS

Poetry

The Keeper. Cambridge, Massachusetts, Pym Randall Press, 1968.
Sleep Watch. Middletown, Connecticut, Wesleyan University Press, 1969.
The Knife and Other Poems. Middletown, Connecticut, Wesleyan University Press, 1980.
Sewanee in Ruins. Sewanee, Tennessee, University Press, 1981.
Fossils, Metal, and the Blue Limit. Bennington, Vermont, White Creek Press, 1982.
Our Flag Was Still There. Middletown, Connecticut, Wesleyan University Press, 1984.
The Stonecutter's Hand. Boston, David R. Godine, 1995.
Today in the Café Trieste. Galway, Ireland, Salmon Publishing, and Chester Springs, Pennsylvania, Dufour, 1997.

Other

Robert Lowell: Damaged Grandeur. Ann Arbor, University of Michigan Press, 1995.

Editor, *A Visit to the Gallery: The University of Michigan Museum of Art.* Ann Arbor, University of Michigan Press, 1997.

*

Critical Studies: "Five Sleepers" by Robert Watson, in *Poetry* (Chicago), March 1970; "The Future of Confession" by Alan Williams, in *Shenandoah* (Lexington, Virginia), summer 1970; "At the First Doorway of the Lost Life" by James Atlas, in *Chicago Review,* autumn 1970; by Bruce Bennett, in *New York Times Book Review,* 10 May 1981; by Jay Parini, in *Quest,* September 1981; by Alan Williamson, in *Parnassus* (New York), winter 1981; "Reflections on *The Knife*" by Andrea Blaugrund, in *Harvard Advocate* (Cambridge, Massachusetts), December 1981; by Paul Breslin, in *New York Times Book Review,* 22 July 1982; by Wyatt Prunty, in

Southern Review (Baton Rouge, Louisiana), fall 1984; ''No Vers Is Libre'' by Scott Ward, in *Shenandoah* (Lexington, Virginia), 45(3), fall 1995.

Richard Tillinghast comments:

I see poetry as a kind of invocation of the spiritual realities inherent in things—the hidden and mysterious significance of colors, sounds, smells, textures. It is something like the speech of animals and plants, if they could speak. As an early, oral, nonrational art, unashamedly archaic in its origins, poetry still carries some of the magic of the early days of the human race. At its best it is consistent with the grace, naturalness, solidity, charm, thrill, and sense of necessity that are found in the earliest human accomplishments: hunting, fire building, cooking, cultivation of the soil, fishing, and weaving. To mention poetry in the same breath with these things must also remind one of the practice, skill, and expertise that are necessary for the accomplishment of good writing.

*   *   *

Richard Tillinghast's *Sleep Watch* amazed its readers with a startling, ingenious way of seeing things. Here is an animal describing God's bungling of the Creation: ''Later on when he saw that things had gone wrong / . . . it rested him to look at us / And I found I could love him in his weakness / as I never could before / the beauty left his face . . .'' Here is ''Waking on the Train'': ''after the commuters / cigars windows being jerked open / your body begins to know it hasn't slept / It thinks of all the parts of itself / that would touch a bed . . .''

Many of Tillinghast's poems touch on that dreamlike area of consciousness between waking and sleeping. Everything real is in doubt, and that may be desirable. ''Is everything sliding?'' he asks in a poem called ''Everything Is Going to Be All Right,'' and he answers, ''Nothing / to worry about— / Getting lost means sliding in all directions.''

American fashions in poetry—Eastern mysticism, nature worship, confession—hover dangerously about Tillinghast's work, but they are kept at bay by his delicate obliqueness, plus a hawk's eye for metaphor: ''I put the cap back onto the pen / the way a court reunites a / mother and child,'' and ''I am alert at once / and think of the cat / coasting on its muscles . . .''

One of the best poems in *Sleep Watch* is about rising from a childhood illness to confront the world of health. The poet senses an undefined disappointment in his parents, for he has not given them cause to mourn: ''For them I am closing the door to the place / where the dead children are stored / where the pets have gone to heaven.''

A certain self-consciousness has led Tillinghast to develop his own style. He uses spaces where one would normally expect punctuation, allowing his poems to lie on the page between breathing intervals, like directions for speech. There is an abundance of self-consciousness and sensitivity, and Tillinghast has given us a brilliant tour of his complex psyche.

Tillinghast addresses the complexity of transformation with an abundance of self-consciousness and sensitivity. His book *Our Flag Was Still There* compiles long meditations on the relationship between the present and the past, in one poem with the difficult history southern college students address, in another with a broken-down van.

But *The Stonecutter's Hand* is perhaps Tillinghast's most substantial contribution to contemporary poetry to date. From Turkey to Belgrade to Dublin to Manhattan, the poems consider a wide scope with a historical consciousness that can feel both emotional and intellectual. Self-effacing, he begins the book's opener, ''Anatolian Journey,'' with the lines ''Impedimenta of the self / Left behind somewhere.'' Although he moves through many worlds in this collection, he works with both the language of country and the language of earth, an earth that does not subscribe to maps and boundaries: ''in the morning wake to / Acres of sunflowers / warmer than any human welcome; / Haystacks domed like the domes of whitewashed mosques, / And the Black Sea rising out of itself / like the fragrance of remoteness.'' Tillinghast ultimately chooses various forms of remoteness because they sharpen his attention to the numinousness of the precise and immediate world in which each poem lives.

—Anne Stevenson and Martha Sutro

TOMLINSON, (Alfred) Charles

Nationality: British. **Born:** Stoke-on-Trent, Staffordshire, 8 January 1927. **Education:** Longton High School; Queens' College, Cambridge, B.A. in English 1948, M.A.; Royal Holloway and Bedford Colleges, University of London, M.A. 1955. **Family:** Married Brenda Raybould in 1948; two daughters. **Career:** Lecturer, 1957–68, reader, 1968–82, professor of English, 1982–92, and since 1992 emeritus professor and senior research fellow, University of Bristol. Visiting professor, 1962–63, and Witter Bynner Lecturer, 1976, University of New Mexico, Albuquerque; O'Connor Professor of Literature, Colgate University, Hamilton, New York, 1967–68, 1989; visiting professor, Princeton University, New Jersey, 1981; Southey Lecturer, University of Bristol, 1982; Clark Lecturer, Cambridge University, 1982; Kenneth Allott Lecturer, University of Liverpool, 1983; Lamont Professor, Union College, Schenectady, New York, 1987; visiting professor, McMaster University, Hamilton, Ontario, 1987; Edmund Blunden Lecturer, Hong Kong, 1987; honorary professor, University of Keele, 1989; Stubbs Lecturer, Toronto, 1992; St. Jerome Lecture on translation, National Translation Centre, Norwich, 1995. Artist: individual shows—Oxford University Press, London, 1972; Clare College, Cambridge, 1975; Arts Council tour, 1978; Poetry Society, London, 1983; Regent's Park College Gallery, Oxford, 1986; Colby College, Waterville, Maine, 1987; and McMaster University, Hamilton, Ontario, 1987. **Awards:** Bess Hokin prize, 1956; Levinson prize, 1960; Oscar Blumenthal prize, 1960; Union League Civic and Arts Foundation prize, 1961; Inez Boulton prize, 1964; and Frank O'Hara prize, 1968 (*Poetry,* Chicago); University of New Mexico D.H. Lawrence fellowship, 1963; National Translation Centre grant, 1968; Institute of International Education fellowship, 1968; Cholmondeley award, 1979; Wilbur award for poetic achievement, 1982; Cittadella Premio Europeo, Italy, 1991; Bennett award, New York, 1993; Research residency, Rockefeller Study Center, Bellagio, Italy, 1991. Hon. D.Litt.: University of Keele, Staffordshire, 1981; Colgate University, Hamilton, New York, 1981; University of New Mexico, Albuquerque, 1986. Fellow, Royal Society of Literature, 1974; honorary fellow, Queens' College, Cambridge, 1974; honorary fellow, Royal Holloway and Bedford New College, University of London, 1991; foreign honorary member, American Academy of Arts and Sciences, 1998. **Address:** Brook Cottage, Ozleworth Bottom, Wotton-under-Edge, Gloucestershire GL12 7QB, England.

PUBLICATIONS

Poetry

Relations and Contraries. Aldington, Kent, Hand and Flower Press, 1951.

The Necklace. Oxford, Fantasy Press, 1955; revised edition, London, Oxford University Press, 1966.

Solo for a Glass Harmonica. San Francisco, Poems in Folio, 1957.

Seeing Is Believing. New York, McDowell Obolensky, 1958; London, Oxford University Press, 1960.

A Peopled Landscape. London, Oxford University Press, 1963.

Poems: A Selection, with Tony Connor and Austin Clarke. London and New York, Oxford University Press, 1964.

American Scenes and Other Poems. London, Oxford University Press, 1966.

The Matachines. Cerillos, New Mexico, San Marcos Press, 1968.

To Be Engraved on the Skull of a Cormorant. London, Unaccompanied Serpent, 1968.

Penguin Modern Poets 14, with Alan Brownjohn and Michael Hamburger. London, Penguin, 1969.

The Way of a World. London, Oxford University Press, 1969.

America West Southwest. Cerillos, New Mexico, San Marcos Press, 1969.

Renga, with others. Paris, Gallimard, 1970; translated by the author, New York, Braziller, 1972; London, Penguin, 1979.

Words and Images. London, Convent Garden Press, 1972.

Written on Water. London, Oxford University Press, 1972.

The Way In and Other Poems. London, Oxford University Press, 1974.

The Shaft. London, Oxford University Press, 1978.

Selected Poems 1951–1974. London, Oxford University Press, 1978.

Oppositions: Debate with Mallarmé for Octavio Paz. Santa Barbara, California, Unicorn Press, n.d.

Stone Speech. Ashington, Northumberland, MidNAG, n.d.

On Water. Ashington, Northumberland, MidNAG, n.d.

Airborn/Hijos del Air, with Octavio Paz. Mexico, Martin Pescador, 1979; London, Anvil Press Poetry, 1981.

The Flood. Oxford and New York, Oxford University Press, 1981.

Notes from New York and Other Poems. Oxford, Oxford University Press, 1984.

Collected Poems 1951–1981. Oxford, Oxford University Press, 1985; revised edition, 1987.

Eden: Graphics and Poetry. Bristol, Redcliffe, 1985.

The Return. Oxford, Oxford University Press, 1987.

Annunciations. Oxford, Oxford University Press, 1989.

Selected Poems. Toronto, Exile, 1989.

The Door in the Wall. Oxford, Oxford University Press, 1992.

Jubilation. Oxford and New York, Oxford University Press, 1995.

Selected Poems 1955–1997. Oxford, Oxford University Press, and New York, New Directions, 1997.

The Vineyard above the Sea. Oxford, Carcanet, 1999.

Other

The Poem As Initiation. Hamilton, New York, Colgate University Press, 1968.

In Black and White (graphics). Cheadle, Cheshire, Carcanet, 1976.

Some Americans: A Personal Record. Berkeley, University of California Press, 1981.

Isaac Rosenberg of Bristol (lecture). Bristol, Bristol Historical Association, 1982.

Poetry and Metamorphosis (lectures). Cambridge and New York, Cambridge University Press, 1983.

The Sense of the Past: Three Twentieth-Century Poets (lecture). Liverpool, Liverpool University Press, 1983.

Translations. Oxford, Oxford University Press, 1983.

Editor, *Marianne Moore: A Collection of Critical Essays.* Englewood Cliffs, New Jersey, Prentice Hall, 1969.

Editor, *William Carlos Williams: Critical Anthology.* London, Penguin, 1972.

Editor, *Selected Poems,* by William Carlos Williams. London, Penguin, 1976; revised edition, New York, New Directions, 1985.

Editor and Translator, *Selected Poems,* by Octavio Paz. London, Penguin, 1979.

Editor, *The Oxford Book of Verse in English Translation.* Oxford, Oxford University Press, 1980.

Editor, *Poems of George Oppen.* Newcastle upon Tyne, Cloud Press, 1991.

Editor, *Eros English'd: Erotic poems from the Greek and Latin.* Bristol, Bristol Classical Press, 1991.

Translator, *Versions from Fyodor Tyutchev, 1803–1873.* London, Oxford University Press, 1960.

Translator, with Henry Gifford, *Castilian Ilexes: Versions from Antonio Machado.* London, Oxford University Press, 1963.

Translator, with Henry Gifford, *Ten Versions from Trilce,* by César Vallejo. Cerillos, New Mexico, San Marcos Press, 1970.

Translator, *Selected Poems of Attilio Bertolucci.* Newcastle upon Tyne, Bloodaxe, 1993.

*

Manuscript Collections: British Library, London; State University of New York, Buffalo; Harry S. Ransom Manuscript Center at Austin, University of Texas.

Critical Studies: ''Negotiation: American Scenes and Other Poems,'' in *Essays in Criticism* (Oxford), July 1967, ''Philip Larkin and Charles Tomlinson: Realism and Art,'' in *The Present Age* edited by Boris Ford, London, Penguin, 1983, and *Passionate Intellect: The Poetry of Charles Tomlinson,* Kirkham, Liverpool University Press, 1999, all by Michael Kirkham; ''The Poetry of Charles Tomlinson,'' in *Agenda 9* (London), 1970, and ''Charles Tomlinson,'' in *Twentieth Century Poetry,* Milton Keynes, Buckinghamshire, Open University Press, 1976, both by Michael Edwards; by Calvin Bedient, in *Eight Contemporary Poets,* London and New York, Oxford University Press, 1974; by Michael Schmidt, in *PN Review 5* (Manchester), 1, 1977; interview with Alan Ross, in *London Magazine,* January 1981; *Charles Tomlinson: Man and Artist* edited by Kathleen O'Gorman, Columbia, University of Missouri Press, 1988; *The World As Event: The Poetry of Charles Tomlinson* by Brian John, Montreal, McGill University-Queen's University Press, 1989; *Charles Tomlinson and the Objective Tradition* by Richard Swigg, Lewisburg, Pennsylvania, Bucknell University Press, and London and Toronto, Associated

University Presses, 1994; *Escritores britanicos en Alcala, I: British Writers at Alcala* edited by Ricardo J. Sola Buil and Luis Alberto Lazaro, Alcala de Henares, Spain, Universidad de Alcala de Henares, 1995; Charles Tomlinson issue of *Agenda* (London), 33(2), summer 1995; "Charles Tomlinson: An Eden in Arden" by Rainer Lengeler, in *Poetry in the British Isles: Non-Metropolitan Perspectives,* edited by Hans-Werner Ludwig and Lothar Fietz, Cardiff, University of Wales Press, 1995; "Charles Tomlinson and the Automobile: Shifting Perspectives and a Moving Frame" by Judith P. Saunders, in *Sagetrieb* (Orono, Maine), 14(3), winter 1995; "Louis Zukofsky, Charles Tomlinson, and the 'Objective Tradition'" by Michael Hennessy, in *Contemporary Literature* (Madison, Wisconsin), 37(2), summer 1996; "The Civility of Relationships: Charles Tomlinson and the Conversion of American Modernism" by Michel Delville, in *Symbiosis* (England), 1(1), April 1997; "Two Extremes of a Continuum: On Translating Ted Hughes and Charles Tomlinson into Spanish" by Jordi Doce, in *Forum for Modern Language Studies* (Scotland), 33(1), January 1997; *Charles Tomlinson* by Timothy Clark, Northcote House, 1999.

Charles Tomlinson comments:

My theme is relationship. The hardness of crystals, the facets of cut glass, but also the shifting of light, energizing weather that is the result of the combination of sun and frost—these are the images for a certain mental climate, components for the moral landscape of my poetry in general. One critic has described that climate as Augustan. But it is an Augustanism that has felt the impact of French poetry— Baudelaire to Valéry—and of modern American poetry. A phenomenological poetry, with roots in Wordsworth and in Ruskin, is what I take myself to be writing. Translation has been an accompanying discipline, and so have drawing and painting.

*   *   *

Charles Tomlinson is widely spoken of as one of the earliest English poets to learn from American poets, yet in his work as a whole, that is, in most of its parts, these influences get transmuted into something that is very English. In a wonderful British countertradition he is an eccentric of the normal—eccentric in his unflagging urgency and resolutely normal in the opposition to poetic inflation—as in the poem "Through Binoculars" from *The Necklace:*

To see thus
Is to ignore the revenge of light on shadow,
To confound both in a brittle and false union

This fictive extension into madness
Has a kind of bracing effect:
That normality is, after all, desirable
One can no longer doubt having experienced its opposite.

In three of Tomlinson's initial volumes, *Relations and Contraries, The Necklace,* and *Seeing Is Believing,* he uses generic American modernist diction, rhythms, tones, and subjects, and like American poets he is haunted by Laforgue, Mallarmé, and Valéry. There are lines, phrases, and structures that evoke Marianne Moore, Wallace Stevens, Pound, and Eliot, and yet by and large the poems are his own. This generalized modernism made Tomlinson seem like a classic very early in his career.

The borrowed style gradually disappeared during the 1950s as Tomlinson put his apprenticeship behind him, but a major trait of his mature work can be found in his earliest poetry. This is a passion for definition that in the course of his work gets less and less abstract, further from the definitions of taste and style—in the manner of young artists announced as revelations from on high—and the analysis of light, sound, and silence in the most abstract terms borrowed from physics, space, and time. He is, in fact, interested in their interaction, as if he wanted to make sense of the space-time of modern physics. What survives from this is sharp observation of nature, cities, architecture, and foreign scenes, accompanied by clearheaded analysis along with very little personal reference, rage, passion, or wild delight. The characteristic voice is that of the reliable and imaginative observer whose sense of reality and whose reasonable and far-reaching conclusions can be trusted. Like Wordsworth he is an inveterate drawer of morals from what he sees, and like Herbert he is querulous, discursive, and loyally unorthodox, full of subtly persuasive redefinition.

In terms that have a bearing on his own artistic goals, Tomlinson praises the revolutionary composer Arnold Schoenberg, in exile in America:

But to redeem
         both the idiom and the instrument
                  was reserved
to this exiled Jew—to bring
         by fiat
                  certainty from possibility.

It is typical of Tomlinson's struggle against entrapment by his own strong drive for stability and normalcy that the circle of self and world widen with themes of exile and foreignness, and this is why we find many poems on travel, some of his best work in fact.

We also find a remarkable range of types of poems: modern ballads like "Of Lady Grange" from *The Way In and Other Poems;* flawless adaptions of eighteenth-century moralized narratives in a series of poems on the French Revolution in *The Shaft;* and a life of Denham, also from *The Shaft,* that does not contain a false note. Other poems, such as "Class" and "The Rich," sound like Larkin. The following lines are from the latter:

I like the rich—the way
they say 'I'm not made of money':
their favorite pastoral
is to think they're not rich at all—
poorer, perhaps, than you or me,
for they have the imagination of that fall
into the pinched decency
we take for granted.

It is characteristic that Tomlinson is not interested in the easy wisecrack that ends with the second line, and the sentence drives on for a larger, richer picture that includes the self-reflexive speaker's world. This range, along with the American poems in the style of William Carlos Williams and Robert Creeley and the international style in his collaboration on *Renga,* a cycle of poems with Octavio Paz, Eduardo Sanguineti, and Jacques Roubaud, gives an accurate measure of the depth of his "myriad-mindedness" and therefore of his need for diversity of form and content. There is no hunger to keep in fashion in his many changes, for he is an inventor and not a follower.

Tomlinson's carrying rhythm is a *vers libéré*, not quite free verse, that suggests an iambic pentameter norm as its background rhythmic ghost. It becomes closer to a regular iambic meter in the two books of the late 1980s, *The Return* and *Annunciations*. These lines from "Carrara Revisited," from the latter book, are quite regular:

> Only in flight could you gather at a glance
> So much of space and depth as from this height;
> Yet flight would blur the unbroken separation
> Of fragile sounds from solid soundless—
> The chime of metal against distant stone,
> The crumple and the crumble of devastation
> Those quarries filter up at us.

But while this meter is his most common, Tomlinson's departures are highly significant, most notably with the use of Williams's so-called triadic line. Like Williams he can use it for searching and meditative purposes as well as for his surgically apt description. These lines are from "The Impalpabilities" in *A Peopled Landscape:*

> It is the sense
>   of things that we must include
>   because we do not understand them
> the impalpabilities
>   in the marine dark
>   the chords
> that will not resolve themselves
>   but hang
>   in an orchestral undertow

The brilliant use of Williams's highly personal invention is full and adequate to Tomlinson's needs. (If the lines sound like anyone of the older generation, it is Marianne Moore.)

Many poets regard Tomlinson's inventive use of off-rhyme as one of his greatest gifts to the craft. An example of this brilliance is seen in the so-called analyzed rhyme in the following lines that begin "The Oaxaca Bus" from *American Scenes:*

> *Fiat Voluntas Tua:*
> over the head of the dri*v*er
> an al*tar*. No end *to it,*
> the beginning seems *to be*
> Our L*a*dy of Soli*tude*
> blessing the cr*ow*d . . .

Technical questions lead to aesthetic ones, and a recurrent symbol, like stolen theology incorporated into art, is the notion of Eden that appears regularly from *Seeing Is Believing* to *Annunciations.* Despite the diversity and increasing maturity of his work, Eden remains Tomlinson's symbol for the perfection that only art can imagine and embody. It is not an idea as fully developed as Yeats's Byzantium, but it is a reminder of the extraordinary potency of art in its dual nature as the lost and the promised, that which is most to be desired and necessary to renounce.

—Barry Goldensohn

TRANTER, John (Ernest)

Nationality: Australian. **Born:** Cooma, New South Wales, 29 April 1943. **Education:** Moruya Intermediate High School; Hurlstone Agricultural High School, graduated 1960; Sydney University, B.A. 1970. **Family:** Married Lynette Maree in 1968; one daughter and one son. **Career:** Darkroom technician, 1967–68, script editor and writer, then radio drama and features producer, 1974–77, and coordinator, Radio Helicon arts program, 1987–88, Australian Broadcasting Commission, Sydney and Brisbane; Asian editor, Angus and Robertson publishers, Singapore, 1971–73; sub-editor, Special Broadcasting Service Multicultural Television, Sydney, 1981–86; visiting fellow, Australian National University, Canberra, 1981; guest lecturer, University of Sydney, and Macquarie University, Sydney, both 1982, Australian National University and New South Wales Institute of Technology, Broadway, 1982–83, and Canberra College of Advanced Education, 1983; editor, External Course Development Section, New South Wales Department of Technical and Further Education, 1983–84. Writer-in-residence, New South Wales Institute of Technology, 1983, Macquarie University, 1985, Australian National University, 1987, and Rollins College, Florida, 1992. Publisher and editor, Transit Poetry, Sydney, 1980–83; poetry editor, *Bulletin,* 1990–93. **Awards:** Australia Council fellowship, 1974, 1978, 1979, 1980, 1982, 1984, 1985, 1986, 1990, 1991; Grace Leven prize, 1988; New South Wales Premier's award, 1988; Australian Artists Creative fellowship, 1991–93; Literature Board fellowship, 1994–97. **Address:** Literature Board, Australia Council, P.O. Box 788, Strawberry Hills, New South Wales 2012, Australia.

PUBLICATIONS

Poetry

Parallax and Other Poems. Sydney, South Head Press, 1970.
Red Movie and Other Poems. Sydney, Angus and Robertson, 1972.
The Blast Area. Brisbane, Makar Press, 1974.
The Alphabet Murders: Notes from a Work in Progress. Sydney, Angus and Robertson, 1975.
Crying in Early Infancy: One Hundred Sonnets. Brisbane, Makar Press, 1977.
Dazed in the Ladies Lounge. Sydney, Island Press, 1979.
Selected Poems. Sydney, Hale and Iremonger, 1982.
Gloria. Privately printed, 1986.
Under Berlin: New Poems 1988. St. Lucia, University of Queensland Press, 1988.
Days in the Capital. Canberra, National Library of Australia, 1992.
The Floor of Heaven. New York, HarperCollins, 1992.
At the Florida. St. Lucia, University of Queensland Press, 1993.

Plays

Radio Plays and Scripts: *Looking for Hunter,* 1974; *Le Morte d'Arthur,* from the work by Thomas Malory, 1974; *Knight-Prisoner: The Life of Sir Thomas Malory,* 1974; *Sideshow People,* 1976; *The Poetry of Frank O'Hara,* 1976(?).

Other

Editor, *The New Australian Poetry*. Brisbane, Makar Press, 1979.
Editor, *The Tin Wash Dish*. N.p., ABC Books, 1988.
Editor, with Philip Mead, *Penguin Book of Modern Australian Poetry*. Melbourne, Penguin, 1992.
Editor, *Martin Johnston—Selected Poems and Prose*. St. Lucia, University of Queensland Press, 1993.
Editor, with Philip Mead, *The Bloodaxe Book of Modern Australian Poetry*. Newcastle upon Tyne, Bloodaxe, 1994.

*

Manuscript Collection: Australian National Library, Canberra.

Critical Studies: "Opening a Murder List" by Alan Gould, in *Nation Review* (Melbourne), 4–10 June 1976; "Poems That Go Angst in the Night" by Martin Duwell, in *The Australian* (Sydney), 11–12 September 1982; "Tranter's Plots" by Kate Lilley, in *Australian Literary Studies* (Brisbane), 14(1), May 1989; "Casual Slaughters" by Andrew Riemer, in *The Sydney Morning Herald* (Sydney), 19 September 1992; "Playful Poetry of Florida" by Martin Duwell, in *The Australian* (Sydney), 13–14 November 1993; "Feral Symbolists: Robert Adamson, John Tranter, and the Response to Rimbaud" by David Brooks, in *Australian Literary Studies* (St. Lucia, Queensland), 16(3), May 1994; in *In Other Words: Interviews with Australian Poets* by Barbara Williams, Amsterdam, Rodopi, 1998.

John Tranter comments:

Australian reviewers have called my work complex, technically assured, cynical, humorless, humorous, too concerned with avant-garde ideas, conservative, and experimental. Though I like a poem to be moving, I dislike gush; though I admire wit and skill, I like to have a good time.

*   *   *

In 1968 John Tranter achieved publication of a substantial collection of poems, *Parallax,* through the slightly devious means of a special issue of the magazine *Poetry Australia.* It was one way of sidestepping the Commonwealth Literary Fund (then the major funding body), which had refused support for the manuscript. It is always easy in retrospect to illustrate the insensitivity of any official patronizing and funding body, but in the instance of Tranter the action does seem extraordinary. Reread years later, *Parallax* almost bends over backward to present a conservative front, though it does so with integrity. Its direction, however, is clearly toward an absorption of the then recently available American experiments in formal innovation and the so-called drug culture. *Parallax* remains a reprimand to orthodox conservatism. The elements that spoke compromise can now be seen as the least creatively helpful for the young poet, and the elements that pointed toward innovation and genuine growth were, in fact, modified by the existing cultural climate even though their freshness remains stimulating.

It was with the publication of his volume *Red Movie* in 1972 that Tranter spelled out the real dimension of his innovative talent. The early poems had shown an eclectic voracity for stimuli—from Bly to Slessor, from Ginsberg to Beaver—but *Red Movie* made eclecticism a

virtue. The work, especially the title poem, remains a pivotal experiment in language, in making language rub against itself, in making it rub against a culture, a commerce, an environment. Although its surface mimics, perhaps even mocks, American preoccupations with surreal and telescopic forms, its essential laconism is peculiarly Australian. It was succeeded by a follow-up series of poems, some of them successful, some blatant (and provocative) in their failure, but Tranter's *Crying in Early Infancy* became for the late 1970s what *Red Movie* was for the first half of the decade—the quintessential statement. Subtitled, significantly enough, "One Hundred Sonnets," it shows a renewal of interest in older forms that was part of late-1970s culture, though the deeply ironic undertones are particularly Australian and personal. These sonnets are indeed classic in their combination of "sounding against each other" and sounding upon the admass culture of the generation. Nothing in Australian writing quite precedes their constructive use of negative associations to build up a resonance of deep vulnerability. In *Crying in Early Infancy* Tranter brought what is perhaps the most intelligent verbal equipment of his generation to a point of creative breakthrough and of challenge. The challenge is enormous, partly because the alternatives now presented to Tranter are so sharp; his tone of wry mockery may become dangerously brittle and his cautious exploration of the self self-defeating. He is, essentially, a city poet, thoroughly urban in his preoccupations. No other poet of his generation is so well equipped to define whole areas of poetic territory as Tranter, and possibly no other is so sharply aware of the risks.

With the publication of his award-winning volume *Under Berlin: New Poems 1988* Tranter has been generally recognized as having reached out into new territory. Although the book is still clearly imbued with a sense of urban reality, expressed in the dislocations of media glare and eclecticism, there is in it a new openness to personal and emotional response. A quiet, elegiac tone underlies the games playing and the teasing voice, which results in a new plangency. This does not undercut Tranter's characteristic sharpness, but it does reinforce the vulnerable humanity that had first gained a footing in his earlier, and still central, *Crying in Early Infancy. Under Berlin* is a more mature work, however, and it gives a striking indication of a rich vein of development, making Tranter surely one of the most inventive of contemporary Australian poets.

The Floor of Heaven (1992), *Days in the Capital* (1992), and *At the Florida* (1993) appeared in quick succession and hard on the heels of *The Penguin Book of Modern Australian Poetry* (1991), edited by Tranter and Philip Mead. The lucidity and introspective tone of the award-winning *The Floor of Heaven* helped prepare the way for some of the underlying narrative anguish of *At the Florida.* The latter work affronted some because of its "American cool" and its violence and also because the narrative technique had been pared of anything in the least "poetic." The work does perhaps point toward a new direction for Tranter-prose fiction. In 1993 Tranter also published his edition of selected poetry and prose of Martin Johnston, and in 1994 there appeared *The Bloodaxe Book of Modern Australian Poetry,* edited by Tranter and Mead. Such a prolific burst of activity heralded an undoubtedly significant turn in Tranter's already notable career: from self-proclaimed leader of the Generation of '68 to the almost urbane man of letters, proficient in a range of forms, editorially sharp, and constantly inventive within his declared parameters, which have broadened to include his own version of the long narrative poem, one of the recurring challenges of the decade.

—Thomas W. Shapcott

TRINIDAD, David (Allen)

Nationality: American. **Born:** Los Angeles, 20 July 1953. **Education:** California State University, Northridge, B.A. in English 1979; Brooklyn College, New York, M.F.A. in creative writing 1990. **Career:** Poetry workshop instructor, Beyond Baroque Literary/Arts Center, Venice, California, 1987–88, The Poetry Project at St. Mark's Church, New York, 1990–91, The Writer's Voice, West Side YMCA Center for the Arts, New York, 1989–96, Hudson Valley Writers' Center, Tarrytown, New York, 1991, and Rutgers University, New Brunswick, New Jersey, since 1996; adjunct lecturer, Department of English, Brooklyn College, New York, 1988–92. Since 1996 director, Writers at Rutgers Reading Series, Department of English, Rutgers University, New Brunswick, New Jersey, and core faculty, M.F.A. Creative Writing Program, New School for Social Research, New York. Visiting faculty, Bard College, Annandale-on-Hudson, New York, 1998. Editor/publisher, Sherwood Press, Los Angeles, 1981–84; editor, *Brooklyn Review,* Brooklyn College, 1989–90. **Awards:** Dorland Mountain Colony fellowship, 1979; Michael Tuck Foundation fellowship, Brooklyn College, 1988; Fund for Poetry award, New York, 1988, 1996; Blue Mountain Center fellowship, New York, 1992; artists' fellowship, New York Foundation for the Arts, 1997. **Address:** 401 West Broadway, New York, New York 10012, U.S.A.

PUBLICATIONS

Poetry

Pavane. Los Angeles, Sherwood Press, 1981.
Monday, Monday. Los Angeles, Cold Calm Press, 1985.
Living Doll. Los Angeles, Illuminati, 1986.
November. New York, Hanuman Books, 1987.
A Taste of Honey, with Bob Flanagan. Los Angeles, Cold Calm Press, 1990.
Hand over Heart: Poems 1981–1988. New York, Amethyst Press, 1991; London, Serpent's Tail, 1994.
Answer Song. New York, High Risk Books, and London, Serpent's Tail, 1994.
Essay with Movable Parts. Normal, Illinois, Thorngate Road Press, 1998.
Plasticville. Chappaqua, New York, Turtle Point Press, 2000.

Short Stories

Three Stories. New York, Hanuman Books, 1988.

Other

Editor, *Powerless: Selected Poems 1973–1990,* by Tim Dlugos. New York, High Risk Books, and London, Serpent's Tail, 1996.

*

Manuscript Collection: David Trinidad Archive, Downtown Collection, Fales Library, New York University.

Critical Studies: "Subjectivity and Disappointment in Contemporary American Poetry" by David Kaufmann, in *Ploughshares* (Cambridge, Massachusetts), 17(4), winter 1991–92; by David Yezzi, in *Parnassus* (New York), 18–19(1–2), 1993; by Gary Sullivan, in *City Pages,* 14 December 1994; "Pop Culture and Poetry: An Interview with David Trinidad" by Richard Marranca and Vasiliki Koros, in *Literary Review* (Madison, New Jersey), 42(2), winter 1999.

*　　*　　*

With a Whitmanesque generosity of spirit, David Trinidad embraces the seemingly prosaic elements of daily life, shaping the stuff of sitcoms and hit songs, shopping trips and love affairs into a poetics of longing. His spare, direct language, grounded in narratives of love and in the iconography of popular culture, reveals an awareness charged with affection and regret.

Trinidad's lines are pure, clean, and uncluttered, describing moments of intense clarity. "The Boy," from *Pavane,* is typical of the poet's mood and approach. The autobiographical account of an adolescent boy's homoerotic awakening, it begins on a note of wistful remembrance or dream: "Looking back, / I think that he must have been an angel." Obsessed with this figure of a thin blond boy ("I couldn't stop staring"), the speaker in the poem recounts that one night, toward summer's end, the silent boy appeared in his room and entered his bed. "But perhaps I am not remembering / correctly," he immediately adds, concluding with the question whether the apparition was actual or whether

> . . . it was me, not blond
> but dark, who sat all summer
> on that sunny corner: seventeen
> and struggling to outlast
> my own restlessness.

The nostalgia with which the poet views his early self develops into a more complex and nuanced awareness in "Red Parade," from *Plasticville.* Deceptively simple, the poem explores the tragedy and pathos of artistic ambition. In the first lines Trinidad is sulking on the couch, "depressed because my / book wasn't nominated / for a gay award." When his partner Ira comes home with red tulips to cheer him up, the poet associates the flowers first with the Barbie outfits he loves to collect and then, seeing them as Sylvia Plath's "bowl of red blooms," with the destructive trajectory of that poet's life:

> . . . Poor
>
> Sylvia, who so
> desperately wanted awards,
> and only won them
>
> after she was dead.

The sudden contrast between his own ambition and Plath's nudges Trinidad from self-pity toward gratitude for the love that surrounds him. "You guys," he concludes, addressing Ira and their dog Byron: "My / spirits are lifted by their / tulips, kisses, licks."

In much of his work Trinidad revels in the material of popular culture. "In My Room," from *Plasticville,* is a litany of titles of 1960s-era pop songs strung together with the phrases "in my room I listened to" or simply "I listened to." Devoid of artifice, the poem is an irresistible evocation of both a particular time and the more universal loneliness of adolescence. Several other pieces from *Plasticville* employ similar pastiche techniques. "Fortunes" arranges fortune cookie adages into rhymed couplets, and "Chatty Cathy Villanelle" cleverly exploits the intricately repeated patterns of the villanelle form in its use of the talking doll's rote phrases. "The Love Machine" cuts and pastes sentences from Jacqueline Susann's novel of the same name into a grotesque yet strangely moving comment on sex. "Garbo's Trolls," written in terza rima, recounts how art dealer Sam Green, a friend of the reclusive film star Greta Garbo, bent to retrieve a cocktail peanut that had rolled under Garbo's couch and found

a plastic gnome with thick

orange Dynel hair and coal-
black eyes, peeking out at
me.

Discovering a whole group of trolls hidden there, he becomes intrigued. Whenever he has the chance, he checks under the couch and finds that the trolls are obviously rearranged, played with. The secret of the trolls becomes as weirdly obsessive as the myth of Garbo herself.

Indeed, obsession is Trinidad's theme. Poems saturated with snippets of pop songs and TV commercials, references to movie stars, sitcom plots, and toy accessories convey, through their very excess, the obsessive's insatiable need for connection. Yet there is an element of banality, too, in such excess, and occasionally Trinidad's work presents what is merely trite without illuminating it. In a sense, however, this is consistent with the all-embracing reach of his poetic vision: what is a plastic, kitschy, mass-produced—aesthetic junk food can also bring pleasure and is worthy of our attention.

—Elizabeth Shostak

TSALOUMAS, Dimitris

Nationality: Greek. **Born:** Leros, Greece, 13 October 1921. **Education:** University of Melbourne, B.A., Dip.Ed. **Family:** Married Ilse Wulff in 1958; two daughters and two sons. **Career:** Teacher with the Victoria Education Department and in secondary schools, 1958–82. Writer-in-residence, Oxford University, 1989. **Awards:** Australia Council grant, 1982, fellowship, 1984; National Book Council award, 1983; Patrick White award, 1994; Wesley M. Wright prize, 1994. **Address:** 72 Glenhuntly Road, Elwood, Victoria 3184, Australia.

PUBLICATIONS

Poetry

Resurrection 1967, and Triptych for a Second Coming (in Greek). Melbourne, Arion, 1974.
Observations of a Hypochondriac (in Greek). Privately printed, 1974.
The House with the Eucalypts (in Greek). Athens-Melbourne, AKE Press, 1975.

The Sick Barber and Other Characters (in Greek). Athens, Ikaros, 1979.
The Son of Sir Sakis: A Roman Tale for Advanced Children (in Greek). Privately printed, 1979.
The Book of Epigrams (in Greek). Thessaloniki, Nea Poreia, 1981; enlarged edition, 1982; in Greek and English, translated by Philip Grundy, St. Lucia, University of Queensland Press, 1985.
The Observatory: Selected Poems (in Greek and English), translated by Philip Grundy. St. Lucia, University of Queensland Press, 1983.
Falcon Drinking: The English Poems. St. Lucia, University of Queensland Press, 1988.
Portrait of a Dog. Ringwood, Victoria, University of Queensland Press, 1991.
The Barge. St. Lucia, Queensland, University of Queensland Press, 1993.
To Taxidi: 1963–1992. Athena, Ekdoseis Sokole, and Melbourne, Owl, 1995.
Six Improvisations on the River. Beeston, Nottingham, Shoestring Press, 1995.
The Harbour. St. Lucia, Queensland, University of Queensland Press, 1998.
Stoneland Harvest: New & Selected Poems. Beeston, Nottingham, Shoestring Press, 1999.

Other

Editor and Translator, *Contemporary Australian Poetry* (in English and Greek). Thessaloniki, Nea Poreia, 1985; St. Lucia, University of Queensland Press, 1986.
Editor, *Selected Poems 1972–1986,* by Manfred Jurgensen. Newstead, Queensland, Albion Press, 1987.

*

Critical Studies: "Dimitris Tsaloumas Observed" by Judith Rodriguez, in *Meanjin* (Melbourne), January 1983; "The Poetry of Dimitris Tsaloumas" by R.F. Brissenden, in *The Age Monthly Review* (Melbourne), March 1983; "A Greek Poet in Australia" by Bruce Beaver, in *Quadrant* (Sydney), December 1983; "En utvandrad Grekisk poet" by Artur Lundkvist, in *Svenska Dagbladet* (Stockholm), July 1985; "Salt and Gravel" by Peter Levi, in *Times Literary Supplement* (London), 4 October 1985; "A Different Perspective" by David Constantine, in *Poetry Review* (London), 1(2), 1986; "Notes on the Poetry of Dimitris Tsaloumas" by John Barnes, Martin Duwell, M.G. Meraklis, and Chris Fifis, in *Meridian* (Melbourne), 6(2), October 1987; "Occasions of Metaphor" by Vincent O'Sullivan, in *The Age Monthly Review* (Melbourne), March 1989; *Dimitris Tsaloumas, Poet* by Con Castan, Melbourne, Elikia, 1990; "Poetry Born in Exile" by Andrew Reimer, in *The Age Monthly Review* (Melbourne), 18 July 1993; "Floating on Currents of Creativity" by Martin Duwell, in *The Australian,* August 1993; "'The Glint and the Shadow': The Poetry of Dimitris Tsaloumas" by Enrique Martinez, in *Australian Literature Today,* edited by R.K. Dhawan and David Kerr, New Delhi, Indian Society for Commonwealth Studies, 1993; "Exilens Dubbla Sprak: Dimitri Tsaloumas—Poeten Fran Vindarnas Oar" by Sun

Axelsson, in *Bonniers Litterara Magasin* (Stockholm), 65(4), 1996; ''Poetry and the Immigrant Experience'' by Rajeev S. Patke, in *Crossing Cultures: Essays on Literature and Culture of the Asia-Pacific,* edited by Bruce Bennett and others, London, Skoob, 1996.

Dimitris Tsaloumas comments:

I began to write at the comparatively young age of twenty or thereabouts. I wish I had not. It would have spared me all the regret that I was to experience in the following years. It was my passion for music that had driven me to it—music of a special kind that, I felt, could have come only from me. But it did not, so I stopped trying. It was not until the early 1960s that I resumed writing, mainly because what I was after was not coming from anybody else either. I do not know the extent of my success, if any, but I have been trying ever since, never for a moment deviating from the straight pursuit of that ideal, never allowing anything to interfere with it, neither expediency nor fashion. I worked in complete obscurity for twenty years. Few people knew of me in Greece and even fewer in Australia. It did not seem to bother me much. I was reasonably happy in what I was doing.

What I mean by ''music'' is something perhaps too complex for one word to express, but music in general has most of the things that make up the nature of my ideal: harmony of parts, order and discipline, the power of rhythm, a universality of language and meaning. For me the implications of this last characteristic are of particular importance. I think that no matter how personal the emotional basis of an experience is the work of art that results from it should both retain and project it beyond into something wider, more comprehensive. Humanity is vast, and poets should range far and wide over that vastness. I have always found the intimately personal stifling. Furthermore, I believe that a true poet's quest is founded on a faith that can only be sustained through a struggle with meaning (yes!) or the creation of new meaning out of the old. Each creative act should be a rebirth, the reaffirmation of that faith. There is nothing new in this, but the rebirth of faith is discovery, and I believe that poetry can only survive by the miracle of such a renewal.

*   *   *

With the publication in 1983 of *The Observatory,* Dimitris Tsaloumas appeared as a revelation to Australians. Here was a mature and profoundly significant poet who had been living and writing in their country for more than thirty years, but in the Greek language, and who had a powerful independence of mind. It was not merely that Tsaloumas was a poet of the diaspora but that within his own terms he had created a body of writing commanding attention. The book was the first significant landmark of the evolving multiculturalism of Australia, yet at the same time it stressed an individuality and a style that placed Tsaloumas in the forefront of contemporary poetry in any country.

In the success of *The Observatory,* which won the National Book Council award for 1983, Tsaloumas was assisted by the distinguished collaboration of the translator Philip Grundy, and their second venture, *The Book of Epigrams,* reinforced both the powerful wit and the severity of the poet's resonant lyricism. In addition, his remarkable anthology of contemporary Australian poetry, with his own translations into Greek, demonstrated a sure understanding of Australian literary developments and was awarded high praise in Greece. As if to demonstrate further his versatility in both languages, *Falcon Drinking,* a volume of English-language poems, was launched at the Adelaide Festival Writers Week in 1988. Two further volumes of poems in English, *Portrait of a Dog* and *The Barge,* both published in the early 1990s, showed an increasing assurance in his adopted language. Here the acerbic attack and satirical edge noted in the translations in *The Book of Epigrams* have become savagely domesticated, and *The Barge* added to the poet's corpus with work of a more reflective vigor. His later collection *The Harbour* (1998) consolidated Tsaloumas's mastery of English in almost magisterial resonance but without any loss of his characteristic acerbic wit. It was awarded the John Bray Biennial Poetry prize at the Adelaide Festival in 2000.

Although he has drawn upon both Greek and Australian motifs, Tsaloumas has always avoided the superficial themes of nostalgia and alienation. His is a genuinely committed voice, but the politics are universal, and as we have discovered, the commitment transcends even the remarkable claims of specific languages. His work is intensely informed by a sensitivity to cadence that has made him acclaimed as a major Greek poet and, in his adopted country, an outstanding Australian one.

—Thomas W. Shapcott

TURCO, Lewis (Putnam)

Nationality: American. **Born:** Buffalo, New York, 2 May 1934. **Education:** Suffield Academy, Connecticut, 1947–49; Meriden High School, Connecticut, 1949–52; University of Connecticut, Storrs, 1956–59, B.A. 1959; University of Iowa, Iowa City, 1959–60, 1962, M.A. 1962. **Military Service:** U.S. Navy, 1952–56. **Family:** Married Jean Cate Houdlette in 1956; one son and one daughter. **Career:** Graduate assistant and part-time instructor of English, University of Connecticut, Storrs, spring 1959; editorial assistant, University of Iowa Writers Workshop, 1959–60; instructor of English, 1960–64, and Poetry Center founding director, 1961–64, Cleveland State University; assistant professor of English, Hillsdale College, Michigan, 1964–65. Assistant professor, 1965–68, associate professor, 1968–71, professor of English, 1965–96, poet-in-residence, 1995, and since 1996 professor emeritus, State University of New York, Oswego. Visiting professor of English, State University of New York, Potsdam, 1968–69; since 1975 Faculty Exchange Scholar, State University of New York; Bingham poet-in-residence, University of Louisville, Kentucky, 1982; writer-in-residence, Ashland University, Ashland, Ohio, spring 1991. Participant, New York Council for the Humanities ''Speakers in the Humanities Program,'' 1992–95. **Awards:** Yaddo fellowship, 1959, 1977; Academy of American Poets prize, 1960; Bread Loaf Writers fellowship, 1961; Helen Bullis prize (*Poetry Northwest*), 1972; National Endowment for the Arts-P.E.N. prize, for fiction, 1983; Melville Cane award, 1986; winner, *Silverfish Review* Chapbook Competition, 1989; First Place, Cooper House Chapbook Competition, 1990, for *Murmurs in the Walls;* Distinguished Alumnus award, Alumni Association of the University of Connecticut, 1992; installed in the Meriden, Connecticut Hall of Fame, 1993; Bordighera Bilingual Poetry prize, Sonia Raiziss-Giop Charitable Foundation, 1997; John Ciardi award for lifetime achievement in poetry, 1999. **Agent:** John Joen, Mathom Press Enterprises, Box 362, Oswego, New York 13126–0362, or (booking agent) Bill Thompson, Briarwood Writers Alliance, 61 Briarwood Circle, Needham Heights, Massachusetts 02194, U.S.A. **Address:** P.O. Box 161, Dresden, Maine 04342–0161, U.S.A.

PUBLICATIONS

Poetry

Day after History. Arlington, Virginia, Samisdat, 1956.
First Poems. Francestown, New Hampshire, Golden Quill Press, 1960.
The Sketches of Lewis Turco and Livevil: A Mask. Cleveland, American Weave Press, 1962.
Awaken, Bells Falling: Poems 1959–1967. Columbia, University of Missouri Press, 1968.
The Inhabitant. Northampton, Massachusetts, Despa Press, 1970.
Pocoangelini: A Fantography and Other Poems. Northampton, Massachusetts, Despa Press, 1971.
The Weed Garden. Orangeburg, South Carolina, Peaceweed Press, 1973.
Courses in Lambents (as Wesli Court). Oswego, New York, Mathom, 1977.
Curses and Laments (as Wesli Court). Stevens Point, Wisconsin, Song Magazine Press, 1978.
A Cage of Creatures. Potsdam, New York, Banjo Press, 1978.
Seasons of the Blood. Rochester, New York, Mammoth Press, 1980.
American Still Lifes. Oswego, New York, Mathom, 1981.
The Airs of Wales (as Wesli Court). Philadelphia, Poetry Newsletter Press, 1981.
The Compleat Melancholick. Minneapolis, Bieler Press, 1985.
A Maze of Monsters. Livingston, Alabama, Livingston University Press, 1986.
The Shifting Web: New and Selected Poems. Fayetteville, University of Arkansas Press, 1989.
A Family Album. Eugene, Oregon, Silverfish Review Press, 1990.
Murmurs in the Walls. Oklahoma City, Cooper House, 1992.
Legends of the Mists. Kew Gardens, New Spirit Press, 1993.
A Book of Fears. West Lafayette, Indiana, Bordighera, 1998.

Broadsides, cards, etc.: *At Yule,* 1958; *O Well,* 1963; *Pocoangelini 8,* 1965; *The Burning Bush,* 1966; *Image Tinged with No Color,* 1966; *School Drawing,* 1966; *My Country Wife,* 1966; *Nativity,* 1967; *The Children and the Unicorn,* 1968; *The Glass Nest,* 1968; *Burning the News,* 1968; *The Sign,* 1970; *A Carol for Melora's First Xmas,* 1971; *The Magi,* 1972; *Nursery Rime,* 1973; *The Fences,* 1973; *The Pond,* 1974; *The Vista,* 1975; *The House,* 1976; *Epitaph IV,* 1978; *Epitaph V,* 1978; *Gnomic Verses,* 1978; *The Habitation,* 1978; *Albums,* 1979; *The Covered Bridge,* 1979; *Prothalamion,* 1980; *Millpond,* 1981; *The Summons,* 1981; *Winter,* 1982; *Lineage,* 1983; *Company,* 1983; *Lorrie,* 1984; *First Snow,* 1985; *Fading Things,* 1986; *An Amherst Christmas,* 1987; *The Birdsong Blues,* 1988; *The Xmas Blues,* 1989; *A Voice in an Old House,* 1990; *Sapphic Stanzas in Falling Measures,* 1991; *Villanelle of the First Day,* 1992; *Theme and Variation,* 1993; *The View from a Winter Garret,* 1994.

Recordings: *Raceway and Other Poems,* Library of Congress Archive, 1959; *Poems,* Cleveland State University, 1961; *Recent Poems,* Library of Congress Archive, 1979.

Plays

Dreams of Stone and Sun (produced Storrs, Connecticut, 1959); published in *Theatre Journal* (Oswego, New York), Fall 1971.
The Elections Last Fall (produced Oswego, New York, 1969); published in *Polemic 6* (Cleveland). 1961.
The Fog (opera libretto), music by Walter Hekster. Amsterdam, Donemus, 1987.

Ballet Scenario: *While the Spider Slept,* 1965.

Radio Play: *Vincent,* 1987.

Other

The Book of Forms: A Handbook of Poetics. New York, Dutton, 1968; revised edition, as *The New Book of Forms,* Hanover, New Hampshire, University Press of New England, 1986.
The Literature of New York (bibliography). Oneonta, New York State English Council, 1970.
Creative Writing in Poetry. Albany, State University of New York, 1970.
Poetry: An Introduction Through Writing. Reston, Virginia, Reston Publishing Company, 1973.
Freshman Composition and Literature. Saratoga Springs, New York, Empire State College, 1973.
Murgatroyd and Mabel (for children; as Wesli Court). Oswego, New York, Mathom, 1978.
Visions and Revisions of American Poetry. Fayetteville, University of Arkansas Press, 1986.
Dialogue: A Socratic Dialogue on the Art of Writing Dialogue in Fiction. Cincinnati, Ohio, Writer's Digest, 1989.
Dialogue. London, Robinson Publishing, 1991.
The Public Poet, Five Lectures on the Art and Craft of Poetry. Ashland, Ashland University Poetry Press, 1991.
Emily Dickinson, Woman of Letters. Albany, State University of New York Press, 1993.
Shaking the Family Tree: A Remembrance. West Lafayette, Indiana, Bordighera, 1998.
The Book of Literary Terms: The Genres of Fiction, Drama, Nonfiction, Literary Criticism, and Scholarship. Hanover, New Hampshire, University Press of New England, 1999.

Editor, *The Spiritual Autobiography of Luigi Turco.* Ann Arbor, Michigan, University Microfilms Books, 1969.
Editor, *That Band from Indiana,* by Charlie Davis. Oswego, New York, Mathom, 1982.
Editor, *The Life and Poetry of Manoah Bodman: Bard of the Berkshires.* Lanham, Maryland, University Press of America, 1999.

*

Bibliography: "Lewis Turco: A Bibliography of His Works and of Criticism of Them," in *F.W. Crumb Memorial Library Bibliographies,* Potsdam, State University of New York, 1972; in *A Bibliographic Guide to the Literature of Contemporary American Poetry, 1970–75,* by Phillis Gershator, Metuchen, New Jersey, Scarecrow Press, 1976; in *Dictionary of Italian-American Poets,* by Ferdinando F. Alfonsi, New York, Peter Lang, 1989.

Manuscript Collection: Wilbur Cross Library, University of Connecticut, Storrs.

Critical Studies: "The Formalism of Lewis Turco" by Hyatt H. Waggoner, in *Concerning Poetry* (Bellingham, Washington), fall 1969; "The Progress of Lewis Turco" by William Heyen, in *Modern Poetry Studies* (Buffalo), 5(2), 1976; "Sympathetic Magic" by the author, in *American Poets in 1976*, edited by William Heyen, Indianapolis, Bobbs Merrill, 1976; introduction by H.R. Coursen to *American Still Lifes,* 1981; "Making the Language Dance and Go Deep" by Donald Masterson, in *Cream City Review* (Milwaukee), 1983; "A Certain Slant of Light: The Poetry of Lewis Turco" by Herbert R. Coursen, Jr., in *The Hollins Critic* (Hollins, Virginia), XXVIII, 2 April 1991; "The Mirror Image: A Retrospective Image of Lewis Turco" by De Villo Sloan, in *Voices in Italian Americana,* III(1), spring 1992; "Terra Imaginaria" by Gene Van Troyer, in *The English Record,* XLIII(2), 1992.

Lewis Turco comments:

I consider that poetry is the genre of language art. The poet concentrates on language as substance, in much the same manner as the sculptor concentrates on stone as shape or the dancer on the body as motion. Like writers in the other literary genres, the poet may use either of the two modes, prose, which is unmetered language, or verse, which is metered language (according to the O.E.D.). Any of the genres may be written in either of the modes; that is to say, there may be prose or verse fiction, prose or verse drama, prose or verse essay, prose or verse poetry.

These distinctions between genre and mode, it seems to me, ought to be obvious, but that people continue to confuse the two is evident in their continued use of the contradiction in terms "free verse" and in the often asked question, What is the difference between prose and poetry? There is only one logical answer to the latter: prose is a mode, and poetry is a genre. And of course verse cannot be free if it is metered language.

It is always my intention to know as much as I possibly can about all the genres and about both the modes, so that I may write whatever I please, however I please, shaping the language as well as I am capable of doing for any purposes I wish. I am not interested in a style; I am interested in all styles. Not in one form but in every form, including the experimental. I do not care to inhabit a conceptual or artistic prison by limiting myself to techniques agonists approve for some reason of literary theory or manifesto of poetics. I will throw nothing away before I discover what I may do with it.

But these are pragmatics and rationalities. All worthwhile writing has emotional and irrational imponderables as well. I tried to address these in

A DEDICATION

for John Brinnin and Don Justice,
on a line by Joel Sloman

> If it is true that
> "the sea worm is a decorated flute
>   that pipes in the most ancient mode"—
>
> and if it is true, too, that
> the salt content of mammalian blood

is exactly equivalent
to the salinity of the oceans
at the time life emerged onto the land;

>   and if it is true
> that man is the only mammal with a
>   capacity for song, well, then,
>   that explains why the baroque
>   worm swims in our veins, piping, and why
>   we dance to his measure inch by
> equivocal inch. And it explains why
> this song, even as it explains nothing.
>   —from *The Shifting Web*

*   *   *

Lewis Turco has been cited by many as his generation's best practitioner of formal verse, a distinction that from some is an honor, while from others it is an insult. Nevertheless, the judgment is misleading. Turco's work is not a compendium of exercises in poetical technique. In fact, his vision—here dark and brooding, there deceptively light, even witty—has led him into almost as many camps of American poetry as exist.

The more obviously formal period is found in Turco's first two collections. Their less successful work is overly flat and prosaic, as in "Narcissus to His Fleshly Shade," or is too repetitive, which dulls the image, as in the opening sentence of "The Old Professor and the Sphinx." Yet a great deal from this period is strong. The Audenesque "An Immigrant Ballad" wonderfully contrasts the profane and the sacred: "The girl was pleased: she'd saved a soul / (O light a stogie with a coal)." "A Tale of Rivers and a Boy" is at once like a fairy tale and syntactically innovative, while "My Country Wife" is rich in sound.

Turco's second period is mildly experimental. *The Inhabitant,* the poems of which are allegorical, is made up of alternating prose poems and lyrics. In the lyrics punctuation is often missing and syntax skewed. Throughout, the poet persistently narrows his vision, aiming in each prose poem at the larger picture and then focusing in each lyric on a smaller, but no less important, specific aspect. Many of the prose poems, such as "The Guestroom," are engaging and melodic.

After *The Inhabitant* Turco published volumes in a variety of styles, from a collection based for the most part on the tarot to the dramatic monologues of the "Bordello" sequence. His group of poems "Pocoangelini" has a folktale flavor, while "The Sketches," more than two dozen related poems, contain some of Turco's most contemporary diction, as in "'scram on home or I'll bop your nose'" ("Gene").

In *American Still Lifes* Turco's chief concern and metaphor is nature. No longer are humans important—except for those in the poems who perceive nature—and the poems are characterized by a haikulike quality. Even when the poems are about objects associated with people, as in "The Tavern" or "The Meetinghouse," the reader strongly feels the absence of human beings.

The title *The Shifting Web* suggests that Turco is as aware of the shifts in style, theme, and form as are those who follow his career. In this volume there are hefty selections from eleven of his twelve collections—his first, *Day after History,* is not represented—arranged thematically rather than chronologically. The section of new poems opens with "Reflections at Forty-Nine," an understated observation from the vantage point of midlife and midcareer. In these poems Turco's voice is controlled, offering a nearly emotionless account of aging and leaving an understanding of what has occurred, although it is neither identified nor articulated. In the following poems the elegiac tone and theme continue, with house, home, domestic scenes, and family situations as Turco's chief metaphors for life and the status quo threatened by time.

Despite the sense of doom that permeates these poems, the section closes with the upbeat "Poem," in which the relationship between poets and poems is likened to that between a child and a kite. Like a kite, the poem is at once elusive yet attached to the poet, able to be held or to escape. In the paradoxical relationship between poet and poem, between child and kite—in short, between the creator and the creation—Turco seems to find relief, if not hope. The poet and poem become one; the child follows the kite in its escape into the sky just as the poet is released from the trials of this world during the act of creating.

In two later chapbooks, *A Family Album* and *Murmurs in the Walls,* Turco adopts the personas of various members of an extended family. Together these collections, the poems of which are composed of syllabic verse, reveal not only self-portraits of a distinctly American family, one as old as the nation itself, but also a lyrical record of that family's personal experiences, among them a marriage in which love has died, a celebration of Independence Day, watching bears in a junkyard, and the emptiness of old age.

Turco has composed a series of some sixty centones based on Emily Dickinson's correspondence with her friends and relatives. Collected as "A Sampler of Hours" in *Emily Dickinson, Woman of Letters,* the centones vacillate from the surrealistic to the contemplative, from the bitingly realistic to the naive. While expertly retaining Dickinson's voice and principal themes, these experiments bridge the gaps between the past and present, the female and male, and prose and poetry, and the best of them reveal a passionate contemporary sensibility at work despite the nineteenth-century prose on which they are based.

—Jim Elledge

TURNBULL, Gael (Lundin)

Nationality: Scottish. **Born:** Edinburgh, 7 April 1928. **Education:** Cambridge University, B.A. 1948; University of Pennsylvania, Philadelphia, M.D. 1951. **Family:** Married 1) Jonnie May Draper in 1952 (divorced 1983), three daughters; 2) Pamela Jill Iles in 1983. **Career:** Medical practitioner, 1952–89. Editor, with Michael Shayer, *Migrant* magazine, Worcester, and Ventura, California, 1959–60. **Awards:** Union League and Arts Foundation prize (*Poetry,* Chicago), 1965; Alice Hunt Bartlett prize, 1968. **Address:** 12 Strathearn Place, Edinburgh EH9 2AL, Scotland.

PUBLICATIONS

Poetry

Trio, with Eli Mandel and Phyllis Webb. Toronto, Contact Press, 1954.
The Knot in the Wood and Fifteen Other Poems. London, Revision Press, 1955.
Bjarni Spike-Helgi's Son and Other Poems. Ashland, Massachusetts, Origin Press, 1956.

A Libation. Glasgow, The Poet, 1957.
With Hey, Ho. . . . Worcester and Ventura, California, Migrant Press, 1961.
To You, I Write. Worcester and Ventura, California, Migrant Press, 1963.
A Very Particular Hill. Edinburgh, Wild Hawthorn Press, 1963.
Twenty Words, Twenty Days: A Sketchbook and a Morula. Birmingham, Migrant Press, 1966.
Walls. Privately printed, 1967.
Briefly. Nottingham, Tarasque Press, 1967.
A Trampoline: Poems 1952–1964. London, Cape Goliard Press, 1968.
Seven from Stifford's. Privately printed, 1968.
I, Maksoud. Exeter, University of Exeter, 1969.
Scantlings: Poems 1964–1969. London, Cape Goliard Press, 1970.
Finger Cymbals. Edinburgh, Satis, 1971.
A Sea Story. Saffron Walden, Essex, Byways, 1973(?).
A Random Sapling. Newcastle upon Tyne, Pig Press, 1974.
Wulstan. Bradford, Yorkshire, Blue Tunnel, 1975.
Witley Court Revisited. Malvern, Worcestershire, Migrant Press, 1975.
Residues: Down the Sluice of Time. Pensnett, Staffordshire, Grosseteste, 1976.
Thronging the Heart. Belper, Derbyshire, Aggie Weston's, 1976.
What Makes the Weeds Grow Tall. Hereford, Five Seasons Press, 1978.
If a Glance Could Be Enough. Edinburgh, Satis, 1978.
The Small Change. Malvern, Worcestershire, Migrant Press, 1980.
Rain in Wales. Edinburgh, Satis, 1981.
Nine Intersections. Twickenham, Middlesex, Circle Press, 1982.
A Gathering of Poems 1950–1980. London, Anvil Press Poetry, 1983.
From the Language of the Heart. Glasgow, Mariscat Press, 1983; enlarged edition, Lexington, Kentucky, Gnomon, 1985.
Traces. Twickenham, Middlesex, Circle Press, 1983.
Circus. Malvern, Worcestershire, Peacock Press, 1984.
Spaces. Edinburgh, Satis, 1986.
A Winter Journey. Durham, Pig Press, 1987.
Strands: As from a Fleece. London, Circle Press, 1990.
While Breath Persist. Erin, Ontario, The Porcupine's Quill, 1992.
For Whose Delight. Glasgow, Mariscat Press, 1995.
Transmutations. Nottingham, Shoestring Press, 1997.
A Rattle of Scree. Kirkcaldy, Akros, 1997.
Amorous Greeting. Staines, Vennel Press, 1998.

Other

A Year and a Day. Glasgow, Mariscat Press, 1985.

Translator, with Jean Beaupré, *Nine Poems,* by Hector de Saint-Denys-Garneau. Privately printed, 1955.
Translator, with Jean Beaupré, *Eight Poems,* by Roland Giguère. Privately printed, 1955.
Translator, with Jean Beaupré, *Seven Poems,* by Giles Hénault. Privately printed, 1955.
Translator, with Jean Beaupré, *Six Poems,* by Paul-Marie Lapointe. Privately printed, 1955.
Translator, with Jean Beaupré and Jill Iles, *Twelve Poems,* by Jean Follain. Nailsworth, Gloucestershire, Moschatel Press, n.d.

*

Manuscript Collections: Mitchell Library, Glasgow; National Library of Scotland, Edinburgh.

Critical Studies: "Gael Turnbull's Poetry" by Kenneth Cox, in *Scripsi* (Melbourne), June 1984; "Heart of Saying: The Poetry of Gael Turnbull" by David Miller in *New British Poetries,* Manchester, Manchester University Press, 1993; by M. Simpson, in *Critical Survey* (Oxford, England), 8(3), 1996.

* * *

Gael Turnbull has a place in literary history because of his work with *Migrant*—both the magazine and the press—in the late 1950s and early 1960s. He was responsible for providing a platform for many forward-looking poets at a time when their outlets were limited, and he acted as a contact point for writers on both sides of the Atlantic. His work in this respect should never be overlooked. But Turnbull has also been a consistently good poet himself, though never getting the attention he deserves.

What is always apparent from a reading of any of Turnbull's scattered pamphlets and his handful of major collections is the accessibility of his writing. He is never obscure and offers a consistent and civilized point of view as a central theme of his work. One of his chief accomplishments, the long poem "Twenty Words, Twenty Days," perhaps stands as a demonstration of form and content coming together in such a way as to provide the reader with an overall view of the man and poet. Turnbull decided to take a word at random from the dictionary on each day between 17 November and 6 December 1963 and then build a section of the poem around it. This kind of device could lead some poets into a hit-or-miss affair of impressions, loose word associations, and inconsequential details, but Turnbull lays a solid base of meaning for his observations of each day's events. His work as a doctor, his family commitments, his activities as a publisher, and his awareness of himself as a poet are all intertwined in the poem, as they are in real life. The language is clear and direct, and the rhythm, subtly constructed from the natural flow of ordinary speech, keeps the whole moving in a relaxed manner. Although the poem looks deceptively casual on the page, there is no doubt at all that it is well constructed, and it never loses control of what it wants to say.

"Twenty Words, Twenty Days" was originally published as a pamphlet, but it is, quite naturally, central to *A Gathering Of Poems,* described by Turnbull as a "comprehensive collection" of his work between 1950 and 1980. Also of importance is "Residues: Down the Sluice of Time," another long piece that impresses with its combination of technique and content. The reader is made aware of the importance of people, both past and present, to Turnbull's work. He can write effectively about landscapes and nature, but the relationship of people to both is always stressed. These lengthy poems are difficult to illustrate in short extracts, and it would be unfair to do so anyway because of their completeness. They need to be read in full if one is to understand them properly.

But it would be wrong to overlook Turnbull's shorter poems. Many of them are, it is true, fairly straightforward and simple, but they are none the worse for it. He is not afraid of a charming kind of innocence or of sounding almost naive. And he sometimes writes in the manner of old songs and nursery rhymes:

Daft about Sally—
who's daft enough to be

sometimes, when she fancies,
a bit daft about me.

Turnbull can also be satirical, as in "Thighs Gripping," and sharp about social matters, as in "At Mareta":

The poor are starving at Mareta,
not exclusively at Mareta
but particularly.

The shorter poems I have mentioned, together with many others, stand on their own merits, but it needs to be said that some of Turnbull's minor pieces have to be seen in context to take on meaning. Placed on a page on their own, they can seem slight, but read in relation to other, similar poems, they have more substance. The small collection *A Winter Journey* has a number of short statements that benefit from being seen as a part, rather than the whole, of something:

As the darkness hardens
in the tightening frost
and the last flakes of snow
sift from the impoverished air,
scree drifts of stars appear
and thicken, flinty bright

It is all there, the easy rhythm, the liking for direct language, the delight in the natural world, and it is like listening to the familiar voice of a friend one has come to know and trust. It makes the reader realize that Turnbull's work represents a point of view that has remained true and steady. The same voice can be heard in all of the poems. He may not be a major poet, and his writing never gives the impression that he has deliberately aimed for that status, but at his best he is a skilled and wonderfully readable writer.

—Jim Burns

TURNER, Brian (Lindsay)

Nationality: New Zealander. **Born:** Dunedin in 1944. **Education:** Otago Boys' High School, 1957–61. **Family:** Divorced; one son. **Career:** Customs officer, Customs Department, Dunedin, 1962–64, and Christchurch, 1964–66; trade and university sales representative, and editor, Oxford University Press, Wellington, 1968–74; radio journalist, Radio Otago, Dunedin, 1974; managing editor, John McIndoe Ltd., Dunedin, 1975–83, 1985–86. **Awards:** Commonwealth poetry prize, 1978; Robert Burns fellowship (University of Otago), 1984; John Cowie Reid Memorial prize, 1985; New Zealand Book award for poetry, 1993; Scholarship in Letters, 1994. **Address:** 410 Highgate Roslyn, Dunedin, New Zealand.

PUBLICATIONS

Poetry

Ladders of Rain. Dunedin, McIndoe, 1978.
Ancestors. Dunedin, McIndoe, 1981.
Listening to the River. Dunedin, McIndoe, 1983.

Bones. Dunedin, McIndoe, 1985.
All That Blue Can Be. Dunedin, McIndoe, 1989.
Beyond. Dunedin, McIndoe, 1992.

Other

Images of Coastal Otago, photographs by Michael de Hamel. Dunedin, McIndoe, 1982.
New Zealand High Country: Four Seasons, photographs by Gordon Roberts. Wellington, Millwood Press, 1983.
Opening Up, with Glenn Turner. Auckland, Hodder and Stoughton, 1987.
The Last River's Song, photographs by Lloyd Godman. Dunedin, McIndoe, 1989.
The Guide to Trout Fishing in Otago. Dunedin, Otago Acclimatisation Society, 1994.
The Australian Terrace House. Melbourne, Angus and Robertson, 1995.

*

Critical Study: By Lawrence Dale, in *Landfall,* 44(3), September 1990.

Brian Turner comments:

People and places, past and present—the way they color one's life and the color they give to our existence—are constant themes in my poetry. My poetry has been described, variously, as "taut," "spare," "frank," "traditional," "regional," and my voice as "strongly individual" and "highly distinctive." In essence I am a lyric poet.

Vincent O'Sullivan has written that "reading [my] poems is to enter a world where natural things stand starkly, and emotions are felt as directly as the rocks and streams and mountains to which constantly he returns. It is difficult to think of any New Zealand writer who is so at ease with them . . . His lines are precise, honest, warm, undogmatic."

I am interested in the inner responses of people to the natural world around them and in their responses to each other. My work contains a significant number of love poems.

Somewhere I have been termed "the quintessential Otago poet of his day"—a flattering, resonant description that makes me chortle.

*   *   *

Brian Turner is known principally as a regional poet, an observer of the often rugged terrain and wildlife of Otago, the province of New Zealand's South Island that is his home. He has gained a much wider reputation for the directness, honesty, and vividness of work that habitually puts human matters into natural and challenging contact with a deeply known land.

Turner has poems on hawks that recall Hughes, on landscape that recall Heaney. But his eye and voice are distinctly his own in their strength and sensitivity to their own habitation and in their quirkily derogatory wit. In Turner's "Hawk" the bird

is prying Director,
is the smarmy Al Capone
of the air; the shushing wing-beat
harbours the sound

of cruising limousines . . .

In "Carrot" he says to the vegetable,

You know, carrot,
you grate on my nerves.

I understand
your angry new-born look
when you are wrenched
from the earth's warm haven.

His moon is "buxom" and his mountains "white-rumped," his clouds "hump in full view," and his bumblebee is a "goofy flyer."

While such a list omits Turner's clarity and sensitivity of description, it demonstrates how emphatically he rejects mannered pastoralism. Refreshingly egalitarian too, he writes poems for grass, pebbles, radishes, potatoes ("scabby testicles"), a craven pet dog, a sleeping cat, a slaughtered pig, and even a runner struggling uphill in training. He mocks the conventional platitudes and deprecates the more conventional subjects. "Dismiss all talk of 'rare beauty' / or 'lyric fastness' as piffle," he writes, insisting simply that "there *are* always the hills" ("Always the Hills" from *Ladders of Rain*).

Turner deprecates himself too, as "Nature Man," as fantasist ("I might have been like Wyatt Earp"), and as lover. In "Take It As It Comes," a very funny poem of an amorous encounter, an interior monologue wickedly mocks male self-consciousness at such moments:

I shrug off my shirt.
Burly men do it better, I'm sure,
but shrugging is manly
so I shrug away and cough . . .

In "Country Matters" distraction at the key moment comes from

    a fat frog
            croaking and staring pop-eyed
like a lovesick money-lender . . .

In this good-humored self-mockery, pragmatism, and refusal to sentimentalize, Turner could be called (were it not nearly defamatory to do so in New Zealand these days) an unrepentantly masculine poet. There is a male quality in his honesty, generosity, delicacy of feeling, loyalty, and capacity for self-criticism, as well as in his wit, bawdiness, and energy. He is also a love poet whose forthrightness, tenderness, and insight are without equal among contemporary New Zealand writers of either gender. The following is from "Love Poem":

Fretful I melt in the sensate
and lovely river of your body
and you leave me desolate,
afraid . . .

Turner also has written outstanding poems of personal relations, including poems for his father (movingly charting a changing relationship), for children, for past lovers, for friends, and, perhaps most memorably, for ancestors. The continuity of human and family contact with the land has become one of his central themes, notably in *Ancestors* and *Bones,* while *Beyond* has added the complexities of time and memory.

Such lack of concern for convention, along with his almost defiant regionalism, could make Turner seem a provincial primitivist, a sort of down under John Clare, if it were not for the high sophistication of his reading and his craft. Williams, Berryman, Lowell, Ashbery, Gass, Raymond Chandler, Larkin, James K. Baxter, and Paul Durkin, among others, are studied and incorporated as naturally and directly as the rivers, hills, and vegetables that are the other sort of soil for Turner's poetic roots. He shows himself increasingly able to write not only of impulses from vernal woods but also of the mind of man, and his volumes *All That Blue Can Be* and *Beyond* have a metaphysical and at times even mystical quality, as well as a subtly refined technical confidence.

On the surface Turner's poems are lucid in sense, vigorous in tone, and full of a sinewy rhythmic energy, but complex structures and sound patterns often lie beneath, as in ''Drain'':

The sun glints through the trees
and the sky is suddenly blue, not
blue, then blue again; and
close to tears, you remember
you used to think
that you were lost. Back

you go, back to
the drain
before it fills again
with all that isn't blue
and can't be
if you are
all that blue can be.

The lucidity remains and is a welcome strength. Turner is not interested in ciphers or trickeries, and he even likes to give thematic coherence to his volumes.

Because he lives at a distance from literary centers, Turner's distinctive and substantial work has not been widely recognized, despite his having won the Commonwealth poetry prize in 1978 and the New Zealand Book award for poetry for *Beyond*. Among other achievements he is an excellent sportsman and sports writer, and perhaps it is the balance such experience brings that saves his work from any merely literary indulgence.

It is important to see, however, that Turner's strengths are more than the sum of his omissions. Certainly he is never indulgent or phony in craft or content, but more significantly he writes with an integrity of experience and language drawn from the land he so positively inhabits. His nature poetry is thus of that best kind, which works as directly as the sun and the rain. His poems, which are centered in human emotions, relationships, and memories, treat their growth and decay as naturally and caringly as if they were trees and grass, as in ''Remind Me Tomorrow'':

I know, I know,
nothing's true
except what you happen to believe in.
I believe in the brief wind
that functions intermittently
and noses like a hedgehog
in a scurry of leaves:
I believe
trees listen and gossip and say

If we can live with the wind
you can live with anyone.

—Roger Robinson

TUWHARE, Hone

Nationality: New Zealander. **Born:** Kaikohe, 21 October 1922. **Education:** Campbell's Kindergarten, Victoria Park; Kaikohe Primary School; Avondale Primary School; Mangere Central Primary School; Beresford Street School, Auckland; Seddon Memorial Technical College, Auckland, 1939–41; Otahuhu Technical College, 1941. **Military Service:** Maori Battalion, 1945, and the New Zealand Second Divisional Cavalry, 1945–47. **Family:** Married Jean Tuwhare in 1949; three sons. **Career:** Formerly member, Wellington Boilermakers Union, Amalgamated Society of Railway Servants, Wellington Public Service Association, Freezing Workers Union, Wellington Tramway Workers Union, and district executive, Communist Party of New Zealand; president, Te Manhoe Local, New Zealand Workers Union, 1962–64. Since 1964 member, Auckland Boilermakers Union. President, Birkdale Maori Cultural Committee, Auckland, 1966–68; councillor, Borough of Birkenhead, Auckland, 1968–70; organizer of the Maori Artists and Writers Conference, Te Kaha, 1973. **Awards:** Internal Affairs Department travel grant, 1956; New Zealand Award for Achievement, 1965; Robert Burns Centennial fellowship, University of Otago, 1969. **Address:** c/o Longman Paul Ltd., Milford, Auckland, New Zealand.

PUBLICATIONS

Poetry

No Ordinary Sun. Auckland, Blackwood and Janet Paul, 1964.
Come Rain Hail. Dunedin, University of Otago Bibliography Room, 1970.
Sapwood and Milk. Dunedin, Caveman Press, 1972.
Something Nothing. Dunedin, Caveman Press, 1973.
Making a Fist of It (includes stories). Dunedin, Jackstraw Press, 1978.
Selected Poems. Dunedin, McIndoe, 1980.
Year of the Dog. Dunedin, McIndoe, 1982.
Mihi: Collected Poems. Auckland, Penguin, 1987.
Short Back & Sideways. Auckland, New Zealand, Godwit, 1992.
Deep River Talk: Collected Poems. Honolulu, University of Hawaii Press, 1994.
Shape-Shifter. Wellington, New Zealand, Steele Roberts, 1997.

Recording: *Wind Song and Rain,* Kiwi, 1975.

*

Critical Studies: By M.P. Jackson, in *Landfall* 74 (Christchurch), June 1965; ''The Poetry of Hone Tuwhare'' by Ron Tamplin, in *New Quarterly Cave* (Hamilton, New Zealand), 1(4), 1976; ''No Ordinary Rain: The Poetry of Hone Tuwhare'' by Ingrid Glienke, in *Voices from Distant Lands: Poetry in the Commonwealth,* edited by Konrad Gross and Wolfgang Klooss, Wurzburg, Konigshausen & Neumann, 1983; ''Hone Tuwhare, the Carvet Poet'' by Tia Barrett, in *Commonwealth Essays and Studies* (Dijon, France), 7(2), spring 1985; ''Ready to

Move: Interview with Hone Tuwhare'' by Bill Manhire, in *Landfall* (Dunedin, New Zealand), 42(3), September 1988.

Hone Tuwhare comments:

Strongly influenced by translated works of Mayakovsky, Mao Tse-tung, García Lorca, Louis Aragon, Pablo Neruda, and Shakespeare, and R.A.K. Mason of New Zealand, together with a close study of *Nga Moteatea me nga harikari o te Iwi Maori*, a collection of untranslated Maori songs. Also the Old Testament.

* * *

Hone Tuwhare is the first Maori to achieve a reputation for poetry written in English. The fact that he is a Maori and that elements of the native culture find their way into his work has helped him attract wider attention than most New Zealand poets receive. In addition, Tuwhare is an attractive personality who reads his poetry well in public and is frequently in demand and on tour. His work is already studied widely in schools, and his books go on being reprinted.

Tuwhare's early work (which appeared, however, when he was already in his early forties) is lyrical, with a strongly aural quality, full of assonance and half rhyme within a tightly written free verse form. Trees, mountains, rivers, sun, wind, and rain are personified and addressed directly; the universe is animate. This is a Maori quality, yet it is also "literary," even artificial, and there is a sense sometimes of confusion between the two. The weaker poems can descend into whimsy, or they may at times remind the reader of the faded nineteenth-century language into which Maori poetry was customarily translated by early scholars. Tuwhare is often more effective when he speaks directly and plainly than when he seeks after images and conceits. For example, "Tree let your arms fall / raise them not sharply in supplication / to the bright enhaloed cloud" is weaker, being more literary, than the directness (especially in the second and third lines) of "o voiceless land, let me echo your desolation. / The mana of my house has fled, / the marae is but a paddock of thistle." (*Mana* means "pride" or "prestige," and *marae* is the word for the meeting ground of the tribe. Both words are entirely familiar to European New Zealanders.)

Distinct from the predominant lyricism of the early work there is a strong, personal, anecdotal style, humorous, generous in feeling, colloquial in language, that has come to predominate in Tuwhare's later books. Some reviewers have regretted the change, but it seems clear that the gains outweigh any losses.

Some subjects suit Tuwhare better than others in that they get the best, the most authentic, out of him linguistically, and this is especially so of poems dealing with the countryside and with occasions that take him back to his own family. Into such poems he works a physical quality of experience that all New Zealanders recognize but that few of European background can translate so directly into words: "I bend / my back. Ankle deep in water how reassuring / to hear the knock and rattle of cockle in the / flax kit as I strain black sand away." Tuwhare is particularly good in poems dealing with bereavement, exploiting the Maori custom in which the corpse is addressed by the mourner and kinship is claimed.

There is something of Maori oratory in the direct speech of all of Tuwhare's work, and his humor is a unifying quality, making the reader feel that a consistent personality runs through the poems. Tone of voice is an intangible element that often makes the difference between success and failure in poetry, and there is in Tuwhare's tone

at its best a distinct combination of qualities, at once informal, colloquial New Zealand English but with a decorum recognizably Maori:

Eat the gifts of the sea raw. That's basic.
Wrap yourself around some of it. Now take this cluster
of mussels for example:

I prise a couple loose, and with one in each palm see,
I clap my hands and crack their hairy heads together
Then I go *shlup,* and spit the broken bits out after.

Read in Tuwhare's rich, breathy voice, such poems become admirable performing scripts.

—C.K. Stead

TWICHELL, Chase

Nationality: American. **Born:** New Haven, Connecticut, 20 August 1950. **Education:** Trinity College, Hartford, Connecticut, 1970–73, B.A. 1973; University of Iowa, Iowa City, 1974–76, M.F.A. 1976. **Family:** Married Russell Banks in 1989. **Career:** Editor, Pennyroyal Press, West Hatfield, Massachusetts, 1976–85; visiting assistant professor, Hampshire College, Amherst, Massachusetts, 1983–85; associate professor, University of Alabama, Tuscaloosa, 1985–88; lecturer, Princeton University, New Jersey, 1989–2000; instructor, M.F.A. Program in Creative Writing, Goddard College, 1997–99. Since 1999 faculty member, M.F.A. Program for Writers, Warren Wilson College. Founder, Ausable Press, 1999. **Awards:** National Endowment for the Arts fellowship, 1987, 1993; Guggenheim fellowship, 1990; literature award, American Academy of Arts and Letters, 1994; Alice Fay Di Castagnola award, Poetry Society of America, 1997, for *The Snow Watcher.* **Member:** Academy of American Poets. **Agent:** Ellen Levine, Suite 1801, 15 East 26th Street, New York, New York 10010, U.S.A.

PUBLICATIONS

Poetry

Northern Spy. Pittsburgh, University of Pittsburgh Press, 1981.
The Odds. Pittsburgh, University of Pittsburgh Press, 1986.
Perdido. New York, Farrar Straus, 1991; London, Faber, 1992.
The Ghost of Eden. Princeton, New Jersey, Ontario Review Press, and London, Faber, 1995.
The Snow Watcher. Princeton, New Jersey, Ontario Review Press, 1998; London, Bloodaxe, 1999.

Other

Editor, with Robin Behn, *The Practice of Poetry: Writing Exercises from Poets Who Teach.* New York, HarperCollins, 1992.

*

Critical Studies: "The One Clear Unspoken Sign: Four Young Poets" by Louie Skipper, in *Black Warrior Review* (Tuscaloosa,

Alabama), 12(2), spring 1986; ''About Chase Twichell'' by David Daniel, in *Ploughshares* (Boston), 19(4), winter 1993–94.

*   *   *

Chase Twichell's poems move through the natural world much as a biologist moves over the landscape collecting and cataloging specimens. Their chronicle of personal experience is similarly meticulous and edgy with the tone of the tough, unsentimental conclusions for which the author is noted.

In *The Odds* (1986) Twichell embellishes the crisp style of her debut volume, *Northern Spy* (1981), by opening herself to the first-person narrative. Central to the collection are two longer poems, ''My Ruby of Lasting Sadness,'' which looks back on youthful romance, and ''A Suckling Pig,'' a relentless depiction of psychological and physical excesses among a privileged set of New England friends. ''Her agony,'' Gerald Stern has said, ''is the certain delicate moment where the mind realizes its isolation, its loneliness and its longing.''

Twichell's most intense encounters with her agony may be found in the poems of her third volume, *Perdido* (1991). Much of this book dwells on the subject of love, springing from love's occasions to full awareness of that ''certain delicate moment.'' Sex is an especially vibrant bridge from the mundane to revelation. In ''Remember Death,'' for example, the narrator looks past the shoulder of her lover ''up into the high vaults / of the Church of the Falling Leaf.'' She notes but chooses to endure the sticks hurting her back and the wasps departing and returning to their nest above. She observes and does her best to give in to the conflicting energies of the moment and let life happen.

In ''The Condom Tree'' this impulse triggers a reevaluation of a childhood memory. Again the door opens on the occasion of sex. During lovemaking the narrator closes her eyes and travels back to her tenth year, when, one day by the river, she came on a young maple tree the older children of the neighborhood had adorned with condoms: ''. . . was it beautiful,'' the poet asks, ''caught in that dirty floral light, / or was it an ugly thing?'' Such basic questions of value and certainty always emerge from the core of this poet's explorations. ''Her poems,'' C.K. Williams has written, ''manifest a sharp ironic awareness of what's expected of a woman's sensitivity, and a gratifying willingness to play off these expectations in illuminating ways.'' The observation seems accurate. In ''The Condom Tree'' the poet recalls that the tree was ''beautiful first, and ugly afterward'':

That must be right,
though in the remembering
its value has been changed again,
and now that flowering
dapples the two of us
with its tendered shadows,
dapples the rumpled bed as it slips
out of the damp present
into our separate pasts.

In memory and experience value is always changing. Twichell's clearest message is to accept responsibility and to remain open to, and aware of, the world's ever changing pulse.

—Robert McDowell

U-V

UPDIKE, John (Hoyer)

Nationality: American. **Born:** Shillington, Pennsylvania, 18 March 1932. **Education:** Public schools in Shillington; Harvard University, Cambridge, Massachusetts, A.B. (summa cum laude) 1954; Ruskin School of Drawing and Fine Arts, Oxford (Knox Fellow), 1954–55. **Family:** Married 1) Mary Pennington in 1953 (dissolved), two daughters and two sons; 2) Martha Bernhard in 1977. **Career:** Staff reporter, *New Yorker,* 1955–57; writer since 1957. **Awards:** Guggenheim fellowship, 1959; Rosenthal award, 1960; National Book award, 1964; O. Henry award, 1966; Foreign Book prize (France), 1966; New England Poetry Club Golden Rose, 1979; MacDowell Medal, 1981; Pulitzer prize, 1982, 1991; American Book award, 1982; National Book Critics Circle award, for fiction, 1982, 1991, for criticism, 1984; Union League Club Abraham Lincoln award, 1982; National Arts Club Medal of Honor, 1984; National Medal of the Arts, 1989; Howells medal, 1995; Campion award, 1997; Hemingway Literary Light award, 1999. **Member:** American Academy, 1976. **Address:** Beverly Farms, Beverly, Massachusetts 01915, U.S.A.

PUBLICATIONS

Poetry

The Carpentered Hen and Other Tame Creatures. New York, Harper, 1958; as *Hoping for a Hoopoe,* London, Gollancz, 1959.
Telephone Poles and Other Poems. New York, Knopf, and London, Deutsch, 1963.
Verse. New York, Fawcett, 1965.
Dog's Death. Cambridge, Massachusetts, Lowell House, 1965.
The Angels. Pensacola, Florida, King and Queen Press, 1968.
Bath after Sailing. Monroe, Connecticut, Pendulum Press, 1968.
Midpoint and Other Poems. New York, Knopf, and London, Deutsch, 1969.
Seventy Poems. London, Penguin, 1972.
Six Poems. New York, Aloe, 1973.
Query. New York, Albondocani Press, 1974.
Cunts (Upon Receiving the Swingers Life Club Membership Solicitation). New York, Hallman, 1974.
Tossing and Turning. New York, Knopf, and London, Deutsch, 1977.
Sixteen Sonnets. Cambridge, Massachusetts, Halty Ferguson, 1979.
An Oddly Lovely Day Alone. Richmond, Virginia, Waves Press, 1979.
Five Poems. Cleveland, Bits Press, 1980.
Spring Trio. Winston-Salem, North Carolina, Palaemon Press, 1982.
Jester's Dozen. Northridge, California, Lord John Press, 1984.
Facing Nature. New York, Knopf, 1985; London, Deutsch, 1986.
A Pear like a Potato. Northridge, California, Santa Susana Press, 1986.
Two Sonnets. Austin, Texas, Wind River Press, 1987.
The Afterlife. Leamington, Warwickshire, Sixth Chamber Press, 1987.
On the Move. Cleveland, Bits Press, 1988.
Getting the Words Out. Northridge, California, Lord John Press, 1988.
Mites & Other Poems in Miniature. Northridge, California, Lord John Press, 1990.
Recent Poems, 1986–1990. Helsinki, Eurographica, 1990.
Collected Poems 1953–1993. London, Penguin, 1993.
In the Cemetery High above Shillington. Concord, New Hampshire, William Ewert, 1995.

Plays

Three Texts from Early Ipswich: A Pageant. Ipswich, Massachusetts, 17th Century Day Committee, 1968.
Buchanan Dying. New York, Knopf, and London, Deutsch, 1974.

Novels

The Poorhouse Fair. New York, Knopf, and London, Gollancz, 1959.
Rabbit, Run. New York, Knopf, 1960; London, Deutsch, 1961.
The Centaur. New York, Knopf, and London, Deutsch, 1963.
Of the Farm. New York, Knopf, 1965.
Couples. New York, Knopf, and London, Deutsch, 1968.
Rabbit Redux. New York, Knopf, 1971; London, Deutsch, 1972.
A Month of Sundays. New York, Knopf, and London, Deutsch, 1975.
Marry Me: A Romance. New York, Knopf, 1976; London, Deutsch, 1977, and reprinted, Hamish Hamilton, 1993.
The Coup. New York, Knopf, 1978; London, Deutsch, 1979.
Rabbit Is Rich. New York, Knopf, 1981; London, Deutsch, 1982.
The Witches of Eastwick. New York, Knopf, and London, Deutsch, 1984.
Roger's Version. New York, Knopf, and London, Deutsch, 1986.
S, A Novel. New York, Knopf, and London, Deutsch, 1988.
Rabbit at Rest. New York, Knopf, and London, Deutsch, 1990.
A Rabbit Omnibus: Three Angstrom Novels. London, Deutsch, 1990.
Memories of the Ford Adminstration. New York, Knopf, and London, Penguin, 1992.
Brazil. London, Penguin, 1994.
In the Beauty of the Lilies. New York, Knopf, 1996.
Toward the End of Time. New York, Knopf, 1997.
Gertrude and Claudius. New York, Knopf, 2000.

Short Stories

The Same Door. New York, Knopf, 1959; London, Deutsch, 1962.
Pigeon Feathers and Other Stories. New York, Knopf, and London, Deutsch, 1962.
Olinger Stories: A Selection. New York, Knopf, 1964.
The Music School. New York, Knopf, 1966, and reprinted as *The Music School: Short Stories,* 1991; London, Deutsch, 1967.
Penguin Modern Stories 2, with others. London, Penguin, 1969.
Bech: A Book. New York, Knopf, and London, Deutsch, 1970.
The Indian. Marvin, South Dakota, Blue Cloud Abbey, 1971.
Museums and Women and Other Stories. New York, Knopf, 1972; London, Deutsch, 1973.
Warm Wine: An Idyll. New York, Albondocani Press, 1973.

Couples: A Short Story. Cambridge, Massachusetts, Halty Ferguson, 1976.

Too Far to Go: The Maples Stories. New York, Fawcett, 1979; as *Your Lover Just Called: Stories of Joan and Richard Maple,* London, Penguin, 1980.

Problems and Other Stories. New York, Knopf, 1979; London, Deutsch, 1980.

Three Illuminations in the Life of an American Author. New York, Targ, 1979.

The Chaste Planet. Worcester, Massachusetts, Metacom Press, 1980.

The Beloved. Northridge, California, Lord John Press, 1982.

Bech Is Back. New York, Knopf, 1982; London, Deutsch, 1983.

Getting Older. Helsinki, Eurographica, 1985.

Going Abroad. Helsinki, Eurographica, 1987.

Trust Me. New York, Knopf, and London, Deutsch, 1987.

More Stately Mansions. Jackson, Mississippi, Nouveau Press, 1987.

The Afterlife and Other Stories. Lodon, Hamish Hamilton, 1995.

Bech at Bay. New York, Knopf, and London, Hamish Hamilton, 1998.

Other

The Magic Flute (for children), with Warren Chappell. New York, Knopf, 1962.

The Ring (for children), with Warren Chappell. New York, Knopf, 1964.

Assorted Prose. New York, Knopf, and London, Deutsch, 1965.

A Child's Calendar. New York, Knopf, 1965.

On Meeting Authors. Newburyport, Massachusetts, Wickford Press, 1968.

Bottom's Dream: Adapted from William Shakespeare's "A Midsummer Night's Dream" (for children). New York, Knopf, 1969.

A Good Place. New York, Aloe, 1973.

Picked-Up Pieces. New York, Knopf, 1975; London, Deutsch, 1976.

Hub Fans Bid Kid Adieu. Northridge, California, Lord John Press, 1977.

Ego and Art in Walt Whitman. New York, Targ, 1978.

Talk from the Fifties. Northridge, California, Lord John Press, 1979.

People One Knows: Interviews with Insufficiently Famous Americans. Northridge, California, Lord John Press, 1980.

Hawthorne's Creed. New York, Targ, 1981.

Hugging the Shore: Essays and Criticism. New York, Knopf, 1983; London, Deutsch, 1984; reprinted, Hopewell, New Jersey, Ecco Press, 1994.

Confessions of a Wild Bore (essay). Newton, Iowa, Tamazunchale Press, 1984.

Emersonianism (lecture). Cleveland, Bits Press, 1984.

The Art of Adding and the Art of Taking Away: Selections from John Updike's Manuscripts, edited by Elizabeth A. Falsey. Cambridge, Massachusetts, Harvard College Library, 1987.

Self-Consciousness: Memoirs. New York, Knopf, and London, Deutsch, 1989.

Just Looking: Essays on Art. New York, Knopf, and London, Deutsch, 1989.

Brother Grasshopper. Worcester, Massachusetts, Metacom Press, 1990.

The Alligators. Mankato, Minnesota, Creative Education, 1990.

Odd Jobs: Essays and Criticism. New York, Knopf, 1991; London, Penguin, 1992.

The Complete Henry Bech. London and New York, Penguin, 1992.

Concerts at Castle Hill: John Updike's Middle Initial Reviews Local Music in Ipswich, Massachusetts, from 1961 to 1965. Northridge, California, Lord John Press, 1993.

Conversations with John Updike. Jackson, University of Mississippi Press, 1994.

A Helpful Alphabet of Friendly Objects (for children). New York, Knopf, 1994.

Golf Dreams. New York, Knopf, 1996.

More Matter. New York, Knopf, 1999.

Editor, *Pens and Needles,* by David Levine. Boston, Gambit, 1970.

Editor, with Shannon Ravenel, *The Best American Short Stories 1984.* Boston, Houghton, Mifflin, 1984; as *The Year's Best American Short Stories,* London, Severn House, 1985.

Editor, *A Century of Arts and Letters.* New York, Columbia University Press, 1998.

Editor, with Katrina Kenison, *Best American Short Stories of the Century,* Boston, Houghton Mifflin, 1999.

*

Bibliography: *John Updike: A Bibliography* by C. Clarke Taylor, Kent, Ohio, Kent State University Press, 1968; *An Annotated Bibliography of John Updike Criticism 1967–1973, and a Checklist of His Works* by Michael A. Olivas, New York, Garland, 1975; *John Updike: A Comprehensive Bibliography with Selected Annotations* by Elizabeth A. Gearhart, Norwood, Pennsylvania, Norwood Editions, 1978; *John Updike: A Bibliography of Research and Criticism, 1970–1986* by Cameron Northouse, Dallas, Contemporary Research Associates, 1988; *John Updike: A Bibliography, 1967–1993* by Jack De Bellis, Westport, Connecticut, Greenwood Press, 1994.

Manuscript Collection: Harvard University, Cambridge, Massachusetts.

Critical Studies: Interviews in *Life* (New York), 4 November 1966, *Paris Review,* winter 1968, and *New York Times Book Review,* 10 April 1977; *John Updike* by Charles T. Samuels, Minneapolis, University of Minnesota Press, 1969; *John Updike* by Robert Detweiler, New York, Twayne, 1972, revised edition, 1984; *John Updike: A Collection of Critical Essays* edited by David Thorburn and Howard Eiland, Englewood Cliffs, New Jersey, Prentice Hall, 1979; *John Updike* by Suzanne H. Uphaus, New York, Ungar, 1980; *The Other John Updike: Poems/Short Stories/Prose/Play* by Donald J. Greiner, Athens, Ohio University Press, 1981; *Critical Essays on John Updike* edited by William R. Macnaughton, Boston, Hall, 1982; *Updike's Novels: Thorns Spell A Word* by Jeff H. Campbell, Wichita Falls, Texas, Midwestern State University Press, 1987; *John Updike* edited by Harold Bloom, New York, Chelsea House, 1987; *John Updike* by Judie Newman, London, Macmillan, 1988; *The Survivor in Contemporary American Fiction: Saul Bellow, Bernard Malamud, John Updike, Kurt Vonnegut, Jr.* by Sukhbir Singh, Delhi, B.R. Publishing Corporation, 1991; *Something and Nothingness: The Fiction of John Updike & John Fowles* by John Neary, Carbondale, Southern Illinois University Press, 1992; *Updike's Version: Rewriting The Scarlet Letter* by James A. Schiff, Columbia, University of Missouri Press, 1992; *John Updike: A Study of the Short Fiction* by Robert M. Luscher, New York, Twayne, 1993; *New Essays on Rabbit, Run* by Stanley Trachtenberg, Cambridge, Cambridge University Press, 1993; in *Rabbit Tales: Poetry and Politics in John Updike's Rabbit Novels,* Tuscaloosa, University of Alabama Press, 1998; *John Updike* *and Religion* edited by James Yerkes, Grand Rapids, Michigan, Eerdsman, 1999.

John Updike comments:

(1970) I began as a writer of light verse and have tried to carry over into my serious or lyric verse something of the strictness and liveliness of the lesser form. My extensive prose writing has consumed much of the energy that might have gone into my development as a poet, though my long poem ''Midpoint'' is an attempt to catch up.

(1985) In my most recent collection, *Facing Nature,* I am proudest of the sonnets and the seven linked ''odes'' to natural processes.

(1990) I am looking forward to assembling my *Collected Poems* for publication in 1993.

(1999) I am looking forward to collecting my recent poems for publication in 2001.

*   *   *

It is perhaps inevitable that, as one of the most distinguished of America's post-World War II novelists, John Updike the poet should have been undervalued, at least outside the United States. Despite his belief in and practice of (from time to time) light verse and his virtuosic abilities (including parodic skills) in it, the finest of his serious poems stand in relationship to his light verse something like the way the composer Shostakovich's symphonies, impressive public utterances, do to the confessional intimacy of his string quartets.

Updike's first volume, *The Carpentered Hen and Other Tame Creatures,* shows a characteristic delight in the handling of language, deftness in manipulating regular forms, and pleasure in mocking the more absurd pronouncements of such constant pundits of the passing moment as journalists and advertising men. In ''Duet with Muffled Brakes,'' for instance, he satirizes the claim made in the *New Yorker* (for which Updike once worked and where many of his early poems, stories, and prose pieces first appeared) that the meeting of Mr. Rolls with Mr. Royce made engineering history. There are serious poems, too, like ''Ex-Basketball Player,'' which touch on one of the central themes of Updike's poetry, the quick passage of youthful prowess and the inevitability of the aging process.

Updike's next collection, *Telephone Poles,* again contains some dazzlingly brilliant light verse parodying ''occasional poems'' (in the narrow sense of the term). They include the hilarious ''Recital,'' based on an actual headline in the *New York Times,* ''Roger Baobo Gives Recital on Tuba,'' in which Updike indulges in wildly improbable, witty rhyming. Other poems in the lighter section celebrate Agatha Christie and Beatrix Potter for their ''perfect craft'' and Dr. Johnson for his role as a great revivifier of language.

In the more important serious section Updike deals with themes familiar to readers of his novels: the pleasures of the ordinary, the sense of ever impending mutability that hangs over all things, and, in the title poem, the importance of humans' resourcefulness in adapting nature to their needs. In ''Seven Stanzas at Easter'' he deals with those who seek to mystify Christianity, dismissing the facile use of mythic symbolism in the Resurrection story with ''make no mistake: if He rose at all / it was as His body.''

The long title poem of *Midpoint* is autobiographical, taking the reader through a self-examination of the poet's life to the age of thirty-seven, when he is preparing to face the reverse slope of the ''Hill of Life,'' as he calls it. Grimy photographs of the poet at various stages of his career, drawings, and humorous mathematical formulae are used to enliven the central sections. The poem concludes in mock eighteenth-century style:

The time is gone, when Pope could ladle Wit
In couplet droplets, and decanter it.
Wordsworth's sweet brooding, Milton's pride,
And Tennyson's unease have all been tried;
Fin-de-siècle sickliness became
High-stepping Modernism, then went lame.
Art offers now, not cunning and exile,
But blank explosions and a hostile simile.
    Deepest in the thicket, thorns spell a word.
Born laughing, I've believed in the Absurd,
Which brought me this far; henceforth, if I can,
I must impersonate a serious man.

In the second part of *Midpoint* Updike is serious in a collection of moving lyrical poems. In ''Topsfield Fair,'' for instance, looking at turkeys, rabbits, cattle, pigeons, and the ''mute meek monkey,'' he observes that

Our hearts go out to them, then stop:
our fellows in mortality, like us
stiff-thrust into marvellous machines
tight-packed with chemical commands
to breathe, blink, feed, sniff, mate,
and, stuck like stamps in species, go out of date.

Tossing and Turning contains poems recalling Updike's boyhood in Shillington, Pennsylvania, and his days at Harvard, ''vast village where the wise enjoy the young.'' A prevailing tone is expressed by the lady in ''South of the Alps,'' in which, driving along, the poet says that her ''. . . hand fell heavy on my arm and grasped, / 'Tell me—why doesn't anything last?''' There are also two poems, ''Cunt'' and ''Pussy,'' that explicitly celebrate sexual love with a startlingly explicit, imaginative intensity.

If little fresh ground is broken in Updike's collection *Facing Nature,* the celebration of the ordinary in American life is no less skilled and the technique no less spikily varied. And the melancholy tone, if anything, is more pervasive, as in ''The Moons of Jupiter'':

So, in a city, as we hurry along
Or swiftly ascend to the sixtieth floor,
Enormity suddenly dawns and we become
Beamwalker treading a handsbreadth of steel,
The winds of space shining around our feet.

The poetry is restlessly lively in imagery, energetic in rhythmic variety, and constantly echoing the hollow at the heart of things. Although Updike never lets us forget the ''cityscape / whose mass would crush us were we once / to stop the inward chant, *This not real,''* he frequently, and deliciously, relieves his, and our, angst with such refreshing nonsense as

The cars in Caracas
create a ruckukus,
a four-wheeled fracacas,
taxaxis and trackus.

Cacaphono-comic,

1219

the tracaffic is farcic;
its weaves leads the stomach
to turn Caracarsick.

—Maurice Lindsay

VALENTINE, Jean

Nationality: American. **Born:** Chicago, Illinois, 27 April 1934. **Education:** Milton Academy, 1949–52; Radcliffe College, Cambridge Massachusetts, 1952–56, B.A. (cum laude) 1956. **Family:** Married James Chace in 1957 (divorced 1968); two daughters. **Career:** Poetry workshop teacher, Swarthmore College, Pennsylvania, 1968–70, Barnard College, New York, 1968, 1970, Yale University, New Haven, Connecticut, 1970, 1973–74, Hunter College, New York, 1970–75; member of the faculty, Sarah Lawrence College, Bronxville, New York; after 1974, member of the department of writing, Columbia University, New York. **Awards:** Yale Series of Younger Poets award, 1965; National Endowment for the Arts grant, 1972; Guggenheim fellowship, 1976. **Address:** Department of Writing, Columbia University, New York, New York 10027, U.S.A.

PUBLICATIONS

Poetry

Dream Barker and Other Poems. New Haven, Connecticut, Yale University Press, 1965.
Pilgrims. New York, Farrar Straus, 1969.
Ordinary Things. New York, Farrar Straus, 1974.
Turn. Oberlin, Ohio, Pocket Pal Press, 1977.
The Messenger. New York, Farrar Straus, 1979.
Home, Deep, Blue: New and Selected Poems. Cambridge, Massachusetts, Alice James, 1988.
Night Lake. Lewisburg, Pennsylvania, The Press of Appletree Alley, 1992.
The River at Wolf. Cambridge, Massachusetts, Alice James Books, 1992.
The Under Voice: Selected Poems. Upper Fairhill, Galway, Ireland, Salmon, 1995.
Growing Darkness, Growing Light. Pittsburgh, Pennsylvania, Carnegie Mellon University Press, 1997.
The Cradle of the Real Life. Hanover, New Hampshire, University Press of New England, 2000.

Recording: *The Resurrected,* Watershed, 1989.

*

Manuscript Collection: Lamont Library, Harvard University, Cambridge, Massachusetts.

Critical Studies: "On Jean Valentine: A Continuum of Turning" by Philip Booth, in *American Poetry Review* (Philadelphia), 9(1), 1980; "Standing in the Whole Stare" by Alberta Turner, in *Field* (Oberlin, Ohio), 40, spring 1989.

*   *   *

In Jean Valentine's first book, *Dream Barker* (1965), her poems transform dreams into living experience by means of luminous language that echoes the unconscious mind's revelations. In the later volumes *Ordinary Things* (1974) and *The Messenger* (1979) she almost reverses this process to show life as veiled and inconclusive, as suggestive rather than definitive, as dreamlike. The elliptical yet lucid craft of these poems presents experience as only imperfectly graspable. The poems ride lightly on the waves of thought, more textures than statements. While in *Dream Barker* she refers openly to events such as first love, wedding, childbirth, and parenthood, by the 1970s her poems have become mistier and more private in their references. No premature conclusion mars the sense of emotional atmosphere as more important than external incident. She does not try to evade the pain of existence, and it is perhaps her sensitivity to pain that necessitates the oblique approach. She writes of the loss of love, separations, a child's death, or war without raising her voice, always without bitterness or self-aggrandizement.

Valentine's reluctance in her 1970s work to refer overtly to her personal life evidently led to her interest in translation, a way of speaking through another poet's voice but leaving the reader to decide the extent of affinity between the two writers. *Ordinary Things* includes her translation of the Dutch poet Huub Oosterhuis's "Twenty Days' Journey," a moving meditation on the death of someone the poet has deeply loved. She seems attracted to the poem's dream-nightmare quality of grief, which is completely consuming yet is delicately expressed: "my body turns to mist but still stays alive, / an eye that will not close."

This sense of love enduring beyond personal absence or presence also marks Valentine's own long poem "Fidelities," in which she is reading a letter from a lover. As she reads, her room becomes his, and the park is both present and remembered, becoming another field in which both are walking. Her world is softened and subdued, bounded by solitude, memories, and letters, peaceful days providing perspective on her life. Friendship is a major motif of *The Messenger,* and in memory she befriends her parents and old acquaintances and cradles and resolves her feelings for them. The poems are sometimes titled merely with a date, and they often quote the words of others in gently free-associative style, usually with a fragmented structure that is faithful to flickering thought.

But thought no longer flickers in the new poems that accompany Valentine's selected work in the 1988 volume *Home, Deep, Blue.* Here a decided change is revealed, a remission of the subdued, near hesitant mood. More confidence and bravery, less fear of stepping out into experience, result in bolder syntax and images stronger in outline and in bright colors, with brown, blue, and white gold occurring in just the first two poems of the volume. Dream and memory remain prime motivators, but a new earthiness invigorates her reflections. The title "Awake, This Summer" encapsulates her rejuvenation; she has awakened, it seems, from circumstances that quelled her spirit and enchained her words. The season is summer; it is ripeness and love—new, blest, thoroughly enjoyed.

This becomes even clearer in Valentine's collection *The River at Wolf* (1992). Many of the poems in this volume are set in the American West, some having been written at Ucross, a writers' retreat near Sterling, Wyoming, and all of them, even those on her mother's death, exude a sunlit physicality that strengthens her perennially tender thoughtfulness and sensitivity. Dreams themselves enact more vivid dramas, inviting freer interpretations. ''Barrie's Dream, the Wild Geese'' begins with ''I dreamed about Elizabeth Bishop and Robert Lowell'' and continues,

> he was talking, and talking to us
> he was saying, 'She is the best—'
> Then the geese flew over,
> and he stopped talking. Everyone stopped talking,
> because of the geese.

It is true that Lowell thought Bishop to be ''the best,'' but here one sees that Valentine is the best, not only to the lover-dreamer. Her diction is ever tactful, and her perfect landings after a free-associative swing, ''consciousness of this big form,'' enable the release of unconscious mind out of its hiding place into conscious light.

> The sound of their wings!
> Oars rowing laborious, wood against wood: it was
> a continuing thought, no, it was a labor,
> how to accept your lover's love. Who could do it alone?
> Under our radiant sleep they were bearing us all night long.

The wild goose is the Chinese poet's symbol for freedom. While Valentine's expressive powers have always been rare and great, now added to them are exuberance and the creative freedom to fly even higher.

Both creative ascent and descent into the depths of life's mysteriousness mark *Growing Darkness, Growing Light* (1997). Here Valentine reverts to and expands her earlier thematics on dreams. A dream, as a Native American epigraph explains, opens up the transitional space between the rationality of daylight and the darkly irrational unconscious as well as the moment of death, in which the mind breaks into dissociative fragments. The poet's compassion and desire confront the dissolution of the self as she meditates on the afflicted ''soul,'' a frequently repeated term. AIDS, cancer, Ireland's bloody politics, and the deaths of poet-friends are seen through the dream lens that both heightens felt pain and makes it bearable through energized language. Death is the ''deep black unfold,'' as unknowable to us as to the unconscious patient in an intensive care unit.

A sense of meaning's elusiveness and the struggle with death expressed in dream language also suffuses Valentine's 2000 collection, *The Cradle of the Real Life*. Each of these lyrics, often quite short, elliptically sketches a fragment of a mythic scene or a *cri de coeur*, like a single Matissean brushstroke. The worst horrors— bereavements, separations, orphans abused, the pain of those dying, the nightmare lives of women in bad marriages, prison, or the madhouse—are veiled, unspoken as if unspeakable, left for the reader to imagine. A heart subdued by suffering and loss shows through the lines.

The theologian Martin Buber's concept of ''Thou'' is cited in the epigraph as the ''cradle of the Real Life.'' For Valentine ''Thou'' suggests not so much God as the ''Other'' that might be a lover, force,

power, divinity, or life itself beyond individual consciousness. The world now appears wintry and uncertain to the poet. She is constrained yet moved by beauty and sadness in an almost oriental contemplativeness. A final haiku-like poem reads:

> Snow falling
> off the Atlantic
>
> out toward strangeness
>
> you
> a breath on a coal

The absence of verbs and cohesive syntax seems to signal the impossibility of defining the real or of taking any kind of gross action. Affirmation remains, however. The ''you'' or ''Thou'' allied with the energy of Logos, the divine creative Word, becomes living and personal, sending out poetic sparks in the face of oblivion.

—Jane Augustine

VAN DUYN, Mona (Jane)

Nationality: American. **Born:** Waterloo, Iowa, 9 May 1921. **Education:** University of Northern Iowa, Cedar Falls, B.A. 1942; University of Iowa, Iowa City, M.A. 1943. **Family:** Married Jarvis Thurston in 1943. **Career:** Instructor in English, University of Iowa, 1944–46, and University of Louisville, Kentucky, 1946–50; lecturer in English, 1950–67, adjunct professor of poetry workshops, 1983, and Visiting Hurst Professor, 1987, Washington University, St. Louis; lecturer, Salzburg Seminar in American Studies, 1973. Poetry consultant, Olin Library Modern Literature Collection, Washington University. Editor, with Jarvis Thurston, *Perspective: A Quarterly of Literature*, St. Louis, 1947–67. **Awards**: Eunice Tietjens memorial prize, 1956, and Harriet Monroe memorial prize, 1968 (*Poetry*, Chicago); Helen Bullis prize (*Poetry Northwest*), 1964; National Endowment for the Arts grant, 1966, 1985; National Council for the Arts grant, 1967; Borestone Mountain poetry prize, 1968; Hart Crane memorial award, 1968; Bollingen prize, 1971; National Book award, 1971; Guggenheim fellowship, 1972; Loines award, 1976; Academy of American Poets fellowship, 1981; Cornell College Sandburg prize, 1982; Shelley memorial prize, 1987; Pulitzer prize, 1991, for *Near Changes*; Golden Plate award, American Academy of Achievement, 1992; U.S. Poet Laureate, 1992–93; St. Louis award, Arts and Education Council, 1994. D.Litt.: Washington University, 1971; Cornell College, Mt. Vernon, Iowa, 1972; University of North Iowa, 1991; University of the South, Sewanee, 1993; George Washington University, 1993, and Georgetown University, 1993. **Member:** Academy of American Poets, 1983. Chancellor, Academy of American Poets, 1985. **Address:** 7505 Teasdale Avenue, St. Louis, Missouri 63130, U.S.A.

PUBLICATIONS

Poetry

Valentines to the Wide World. Iowa City, Cummington Press, 1959.
A Time of Bees. Chapel Hill, University of North Carolina Press, 1964.

To See, To Take. New York, Atheneum, 1970.
Bedtime Stories. Champaign, Illinois, Ceres Press, 1972.
Merciful Disguises: Poems Published and Unpublished. New York, Atheneum, 1973.
Letters from a Father and Other Poems. New York, Atheneum, 1982.
Near Changes. New York, Knopf, 1990.
If It Be Not I: Collected Poems, 1959–1982. New York, Knopf, 1993.
Firefall: Poems. New York, Knopf, 1993.

Recording: *Mona Van Duyn and Elliott Coleman Reading Their Poems in the Coolidge Auditorium,* Gertrude Clarke Whittal Poetry and Literature Fund, 1971; *Mona Van Duyn Reading Her Poems,* Gertrude Clarke Whittal Poetry and Literature Fund, Library of Congress, 1990.

Other

Matters of Poetry. Washington D.C., Library of Congress, 1993.

*

Manuscript Collection: Olin Library, Washington University, St. Louis.

Critical Studies: "Mona Van Duyn and the Politics of Love" by Lorrie Goldensohn, in *Ploughshares* (Cambridge, Massachusetts), 4(3), 1978; by Constance Hunting, in *Parnassus* (New York), 16(2), 1991; interview with Marianne Abel, in *Iowa Woman,* 11(3), autumn 1991; "Life Work" by Robert B. Shaw, in *Shenandoah* (Lexington, Virginia), 44(1), spring 1994; "Strangers May Run: The Nation's First Woman Poet Laureate" by Judith Hall, in *Antioch Review* (Yellow Springs, Ohio), 52(1), winter 1994.

*   *   *

The awarding of the Bollingen prize in 1971 to Mona Van Duyn and her receipt of the National Book award in poetry that same year brought long overdue general recognition to this fine poet, whose insight, humor, and technical skill had seemed for a long time to be appreciated largely only in her native Midwest. Many national awards followed, and in June 1992 she was appointed poet laureate and consultant in poetry at the Library of Congress.

The appeal of her poems comes from the double sense of their adherence to the formal tradition of poetry while at the same time they get "down to the bone" of human experience. "The wintry work of living, our flawed art" is a basic theme. Her poetic craft emanates from, in fact is identical with, the conscious intelligence that everyone has and uses to shape everyday happenstance into meaningful experience: "The world blooms and we all bend and bring / from ground and sea and mind its handsome harvests." Poetry making thus becomes a metaphor for activities of living minds. "Join us with charity," she says in "To My Godson, On His Christening," "whose deeds, like the little poet's metaphors, / are good only in brave approximations, / who design, in walled-up workrooms, beautiful doors." In "Three Valentines to the Wide World" she calls the beauty of the world "merciless and intemperate" and suggests that against "that rage" we must "pit love and art, which are compassionate." The tension in Van Duyn's poems rises from two dualisms: the world seen as cruel but lovely, a "brilliant wasting"; and the tension between strict forms (often long-lined, slant-rhymed quatrains) and

proselike statements that vary from Yeatsian elegance to Midwestern colloquialism.

Love and art pitted against the merciless world is a theme that enables Van Duyn to range wide and deep. She can be philosophical, ironic, elegiac, or penetratingly personal as she explores the tensions in this intermingling, which appear notably in poems on marriage. In one section of "Toward a Definition of Marriage" the marital relationship is described in literary terms:

> It is closest to picaresque, but essentially artless . . .
> How could its structure be more than improvising,
> when it never ends, but line after line plod on . . .
> But it's known by heart now; it rounded the steeliest shape
>   to shapeliness, it was so loving an exercise.

The expanded parallelism between life and poetry is brilliantly developed in "An Essay on Criticism," in which the poet adapts Pope's eighteenth-century title and heroic couplet form to meditate philosophically while opening a package of dried onion soup in her kitchen. No tears fall from chopping real onions, and poetic words, abstract on the page, can wait for centuries until water is added from a later reader's tears to enliven them. But the poet's tears fall now, caused by life—a friend's confession of a secret love—not by poetry, and these tears, reminders of mortality, command her to command us that ". . . we must care right away!"

Caring deeply for her own childhood pain and for that of her ill and dying parents, she records family history in the persona poems of *Bedtime Stories* (1972) and in the elegies of *Letters from a Father* (1982), of which "The Stream," on her mother's death, poignantly expresses primal loss. In this volume concentration on family life is counterbalanced, as all along in her work, by poems based on travel, rendering a sense of wide-ranging life through observations of Spain, France, the Missouri Ozarks, and Maine, where she and her husband spent many summers. In the collection *Firefall* (1993) the elegiac mode predominates as friends die and old age comes on. But sure of her always supple craft, she also enjoys playing with poetic tradition by creating "minimalist sonnets" of fourteen very short lines broken into quatrains with a final two- or six-line stanza. These are terse, sometimes witty, sometimes reminiscent of Emily Dickinson.

The final elegiac poems are the strongest among the strong poems here. In "The Delivery" a cruel incident of childhood is seen as delivering her own self to her, a kind of birth. "Falls" invokes memories of firefall in Yosemite Park and of Niagara Falls, with both fire and water symbolizing her own creative livingness even as it implicitly falls toward death. The poem ends with lovely lines epitomizing her poetic triumph yet in depth of spirit almost suggesting an epitaph: "May one who comes upon a final book / and hunts in husks for kernel hints of me / find Niagara's roar still sacred to dim ears, / Firefall still blazing bright in memory." Let it be so.

—Jane Augustine

VAN WINCKEL, Nance

Nationality: American. **Born:** Roanoke, Virginia, 24 October 1951. **Education:** University of Wisconsin, Milwaukee, 1970–73, B.A. 1973; Eastern Washington University, Cheney, 1974–75; University of Denver, Colorado, 1975–76, M.A. 1976. **Family:** Married Robert

Fredrik Nelson in 1985. **Career:** Instructor of English, Marymount College, Salina, Kansas, 1976–79; assistant professor of English, Lake Forest College, Illinois, 1979–90. Since 1990 professor of English, Eastern Washington University, Cheney, and since 1999 fiction instructor, Vermont College. Journalist, *The Milwaukee Journal,* 1974; associate editor, *The Denver Quarterly,* 1976; president, Associated Kansas Writing Programs, 1978; associate editor, *The Ark River Review,* 1979–81. Editor, 1990–96, *Willow Springs,* and since 1993 associate editor, Eastern Washington University Press. **Awards:** National Endowment for the Humanities fellowship, 1981; Illinois Arts Council Literary fellowships, 1983, 1985, 1987; National Endowment for the Arts literary fellowship, 1989; Society of Midland Authors First Book award, 1989, for *Bad Girl, with Hawk;* Poetry Society of America Gordon Barber award, 1989; Northwest Institute grant (for literary research), 1991, 1993, 1994; Paterson fiction prize, 1998, for *Quake;* Washington State Governor's award for literature, 1999, for *After a Spell.* **Address:** 12506 South Gardner, Cheney, Washington 99004, U.S.A.

PUBLICATIONS

Poetry

The 24 Doors. Minneapolis, Minnesota, Bieler Press, 1985.
Bad Girl, with Hawk. Urbana, University of Illinois Press, 1988.
The Dirt. Oxford, Ohio, Miami University Press, 1994.
After a Spell. Oxford, Ohio, Miami University Press, 1997.

Short Stories

Limited Lifetime Warranty. Columbia, University of Missouri Press, 1994.
Quake. Columbia, University of Missouri Press, 1994.
Curtain Creek Farm. New York, Persea Books, 2000.

*

Critical Study: By Thomas Palakeel, in *North Dakota Quarterly,* 62(2), spring 1995.

*   *   *

In the introductory epigraphs to *Bad Girl, with Hawk* (1988) and *The Dirt* (1994) Nance Van Winckel quotes, respectively, Wallace Stevens and Rainer Maria Rilke, two poets from whom she has learned a great deal. Her poems often have a ruminative, lyrical quality one might associate with Rilke and, as with Stevens, a rigorous attention to the melodic possibilities of the line. She tends to use narrative to focus on single events rather than as exposition for extended stories.

Bad Girl, with Hawk, though less unified than *The Dirt,* contains many strong poems. "Holding Together," for example, demonstrates Van Winckel's skill at working pleasurable sounds into her lines. More subtle than in Stevens, the simple diction and near conversational manner of this poem actually enfold a rich rhythmic and sonic texture:

And in the pond our old friend the fish—
whose tail fin long ago snapped off—
he treads water, watches

for opportunities. And when they come,
cautionless, he envelopes them
with the long horizon of his body.

Although Van Winckel often uses a midlength free verse line, as in the above, she also writes adeptly in other forms, from shorter-lined free verse poems to blank verse.

Bad Girl, with Hawk contains a variety of poems, including brief lyrics and narratives as well as several pieces that possess a mythical quality, including "Basket with Blue Ox," "She Who Hunts," and "All He Asks," which are some of the strongest in the book. Thematically the book ranges from poems remembering childhood ("But I shrug off the red sweater / she's knit around me. It's not in me / to keep my shoulders always warm") to a shrewd consideration of culture in "Outdoor Movie," in which Moses splits the sea in front of "the black shining bubbles / of Hudsons and DeSotos," and a compelling description of the natural world ("Outside, a confusion of chickory / and cornflowers blow sunlight / to pieces). Such variation clearly shows the versatility of Van Winckel's talent, but the book does not cohere as tightly as a completely successful collection should.

In *Bad Girl, with Hawk,* as in her later work, Van Winckel writes poems of fairly short length. "Lost in Riverview Trailer Court," a poem of fourteen irregular stanzas on three pages, is the book's longest. This brevity is connected to the lyrical-narrative style in which she writes. The difficulty of maintaining the intensity of the lyrical moment and the fact that Van Winckel is not interested in relying too heavily on narrative, perhaps reserving such attention for her short stories, make for shorter poems.

Van Winckel's second collection, *The Dirt,* is an outstanding, tightly organized book. It achieves its synthesis through tying together poems that deal with themes of memory, loss, desire, and hope. The music of the lines is richer, more ambitious than in the first collection, as is Van Winckel's use of syntax to propel the lines in interesting ways. The poem "Nicholas by the River" is a good example of these two qualities:

Two heaps of clothes by an old stump,
and Nicholas neck-deep in that water
too cold for our own good. Shimmering
when he said he wasn't sure but thought
maybe it was a man he wanted,
though I was what he had
under his hands in that blue current—
darker and rougher in the middle
over the deep spots.

Sometimes, as in the above, the poems rely on brief narrated events. At other times Van Winckel combines narrative with a more lyrical, meditative voice, as at the end of "Levitation":

We could never
have dreamed such a pure departure
from the foolishness of our lives,

nor the dark expanse our lungs took in,
or the strange strength that came rushing
from nowhere into our hands.

The collection *After a Spell* was published in 1997. This book continues Van Winckel's work with a midlength free verse line, but the narrative compulsion that played such a strong role in her earlier poems has diminished. More specifically, although the poems in the book utilize narrative, they are less linear, more disjunctive. It sometimes seems as if we have interrupted a series of events and caught only a glimpse of things. Consider, for example, these lines from ''Cockadoodledo (Woman Selling Dogs in the Village)'':

In this town everyone sleeps late.
A tireless wind
in the night-wear, and how tardily
their fields are sown.

Once a man's language and mine
intersected across 17 words. No three
made a sentence.

Other poems in the book are more traditionally narrative, and still others make myths out of the narrators' pasts. In all of these cases, however, the tales Van Winckel's narrators tell—or allow us to enter in media res—are engaging and illustrative of her vivid imagination.

Van Winckel is a versatile and talented writer. The strong voices that compel her poems, coupled with her studious attention to craft, have served to elevate her work and establish her as a significant American poet.

—Tod Marshall

VAS DIAS, Robert (Leonard Michael)

Nationality: American. **Born:** London, England, 19 January 1931. **Education:** Grinnell College, Iowa, B.A. 1953; Columbia University, New York, 1959–61. **Military Service:** U.S. Army, 1953–55. **Family:** Married Susan McClintock in 1961 (divorced 1989); one son. **Career:** Assistant editor, Prentice Hall publishers, New York, 1955–56; staff editor, Allyn and Bacon publishers, Boston, 1956–57; freelance editor, 1957–65; instructor in English, Long Island University, Brooklyn, New York, 1964–66; instructor, American Language Institute, New York University, 1966–71; tutor and poet-in-residence, Thomas Jefferson College, Grand Valley State College, Allendale, Michigan, 1971–74; lecturer, Antioch International Writing Program, London, 1977–81. Since 1981 lecturer, University of Maryland European Division. Director, Aspen Writers Workshop, Colorado, 1964–67; director of the National Poetry Centre, and general secretary, Poetry Society, London, 1975–78. Associate editor, *Sumac,* Fremont, Michigan, 1970–72, and *Mulch,* Amherst, Massachusetts, 1973–74; editor, *Atlantic Review,* London, 1978–80. Since 1972 publisher, Permanent Press, London and New York; since 1983 co-editor, *Ninth Decade* (now *Tenth Decade*), London. **Awards:**

Creative Artists Public Service grant, 1975; C. Day Lewis fellowship, 1980. **Address:** 5 B, Compton Avenue, Conconbury, London N1 2XD, England.

PUBLICATIONS

Poetry

Ribbed Vision. Privately printed, 1963.
The Counted. New York, Caterpillar, 1967.
*The Life of Parts; or, Thanking You for the Book on Building
    Birdfeeders.* Mount Horeb, Wisconsin, Perishable Press, 1972.
Speech Acts and Happenings. Indianapolis, Bobbs Merrill, 1972.
Making Faces. London, Joe DiMaggio Press, 1975.
Ode. Omaha, Abattoir, 1977.
Poems Beginning: ''The World.'' London, Oasis, 1979.
Time Exposures. London, Oasis, 1999.

Other

Editor, *Inside Outer Space: New Poems of the Space Age.* New York,
    Doubleday, 1970.

*

Manuscript Collection: University of Virginia, Charlottesville.

Critical Studies: By Linda Wagner, in *Red Cedar Review* (East Lansing, Michigan), 1973; by Toby Olson, in *Margins 28–30* (Milwaukee), 1976; by Lee Harwood, in *Poetry Information 15* (London), 1976.

Robert Vas Dias comments:

(1985) Though born in England, I grew up and lived in the U.S.A for thirty-four years, and a large proportion of my work has been published there. I have now been living in London for the past decade, so one could say I am thoroughly mid-Atlantic, whatever that means. I have never considered myself a member of a school or group, but I do recognize affinities of approach between my work and that of the Black Mountain poets, the American objectivists, and certain poets living or who used to live in New York. My poems reflect the congruences and incongruities of my daily life, and therefore they often express the tension between a conscious and an instinctual apperception. I like the way the literal particular, the expositional, the familiar, can shade into the numinous. The language is as I find it.

*   *   *

Robert Vas Dias writes a poetry of crisp understatement, often in segments arranged unexpectedly. He has long expressed a mock-serious view of the world, a world much like that of William Carlos Williams, David Ignatow, and Paul Blackburn in that his images are those of winter birds, children, junkyards, movies, trees, and boats. The substance of Vas Dias's poetry is the commonplace and the stance often the stoic, but the real métier of the poetry—and, one suspects, of the poet's philosophy—is the play within the language and the structure.

Although W.H. Auden defined a poet as one who loves to play with words, the affinities between Vas Dias's verbal constructs and the writing of Gertrude Stein are more noticeable. In *Making Faces* Vas Dias creates high jinks of word repetition and association, with shifting meaning jumping to sprung meaning, all caught within a heavily rhythmic context. The title poem, with its play on "face" ("defaced with the face I face"), introduces a collection in which nearly every poem moves from a root noun, which is also used as verb, to unlikely extensions, clichés, compounds, and misreadings, as variant as the single face in the process of "making faces." The comic use of the theme of the contemporary poet's identity, which has dominated American poetry for some time, is refreshing. What is impressive is Vas Dias's ability to achieve thematic coherence through what looks to be only wordplay. Among the strongest poems are "Poem Starting with Words Written on a Postcard" (using "state" and forms of "to be," with the opening line "I miss you because I am in another state"), "The Gift of Snakes" (here the wordplay leads to darker associations in theme), and the funny, sexual "Poem of Places and Tongues."

In the earlier collection *Speech Acts and Happenings* Vas Dias wrote a more conventional poetry, satisfying his need for invention through creating various speakers. While there are some poems in his later work about other personae, tapping his ability to re-create the idioms of characters he has conceived, most of the later poems express the Vas Dias sense of language and theme. Thus, in some ways his later work is less virtuoso and closer to the poet himself. We see his deep sense of loss over Paul Blackburn's death, his feeling of displacement—at least temporarily—as he returns to his childhood home of England, and his melancholy, tempered with tranquility, in winter. Although we come to know his friends and his fears, the process of knowing the persona in the poems is not arduous or tiresome but rather lively, interesting, and convincing.

Other poems and collections evince this same kind of preoccupation with the sense of play in language and the poet's responsibility to name. "Time Exposure" gives the reader glimpses of the poet's persona as he moves back into moments of his past, always near the threatening, alluring water. Earth and flight are juxtaposed as other constants in his search for self. The chapbook *Ode* is a prose poem montage expressing loss, suiting the definition of "ode" to the content of the poem. Heavily emotional, inventive in its mixed forms, the poem sequence juxtaposes guidebook explanations of the losses of cultural landmarks with the poet's often oblique poem commentaries. "Blackfriars Convent had been washed away by 1754" appears just before "left window in the row / of windows left / in the wall standing / lights behind me quick / as the vandal sun runs / behind the winter / wall of trees." Effective as a sound and image poem, the verse also repeats words and designs used in other poems within the sequence. Again, the reader must be impressed with the spare control.

Poems Beginning: "The World" is just that, a group of poems that have to do with the ponderous themes the phrase suggests. Vas Dias's shifting rhythms and generally taut voice, coupled with his sense of play, make the collection effective. When he writes, "we're afloat but hardly," the reader shares the grimace, not a lament. Whether Vas Dias is writing his way through the world or making faces, his poems are striking examples of the poet creating his own world through his own sense of language, and that is what poets and poems have been about since the beginning. It did, after all, start with the word.

—Linda W. Wagner-Martin

VIERECK, Peter (Robert Edwin)

Nationality: American. **Born:** New York City, 5 August 1916. **Education:** Horace Mann School for Boys, New York; Harvard University, Cambridge, Massachusetts, B.S. (summa cum laude) 1937 (Phi Beta Kappa), M.A. 1939, Ph.D. 1942; Christ Church, Oxford (Henry Fellow), 1937–38. **Military Service:** U.S. Army, 1943–45, and instructor in history, U.S. Army University, Florence, Italy, 1945. **Family:** Married 1) Anya de Markov in 1945 (divorced 1970), one son and one daughter; 2) Betty Martin Falkenberg in 1972. **Career:** Teaching assistant, 1941–42, instructor in German, and tutor in history and literature, 1946–47, Harvard University; assistant professor of history, 1947–48, and visiting professor of Russian history, 1948–49, Smith College, Northampton, Massachusetts. Associate professor, 1948–55, professor of history, 1955–65, Alumnae Foundation Chair of interpretive studies, 1965–79, and since 1979 William R. Kenan, Jr., chair of history, Mount Holyoke College, South Hadley, Massachusetts. Visiting lecturer in American Culture, Oxford University, 1953; Whittall Lecturer in poetry, Library of Congress, Washington, D.C., 1954, 1963, 1979; Fulbright Lecturer, University of Florence, 1955; Elliston Lecturer, University of Cincinnati, Ohio, 1956; visiting professor, University of California, Berkeley, 1957, 1964, and City College of New York, 1964; State Department Cultural Exchange Lecturer in the U.S.S.R., 1961; visiting research scholar, 20th Century Fund, U.S.S.R., 1962–63; visiting scholar, American Academy in Rome, 1949–50, 1977–78, and Rockefeller Studies Center, Bellagio, 1977. Poetry Workshop director, New York Writers Conference, 1965–67. **Awards:** Eunice Tietjens prize (*Poetry,* Chicago), 1948; Guggenheim fellowship, 1948; Pulitzer prize, 1949; Rockefeller grant, 1958; Horace Mann School award, 1958; Twentieth Century Fund scholarship, 1962; National Endowment for the Arts fellowship, 1969; Sadin prize (*New York Quarterly*), 1977; Columbia University Translation Center prize, 1978; Artists Foundation fellowship, 1978; New England Golden Rose award, 1981; Varouja prize, 1983; Ingram Merrill Foundation fellow in poetry, 1985. L.H.D.: Olivet College, Michigan, 1959. **Address:** 12 Silver Street, South Hadley, Massachusetts 01075, U.S.A.

PUBLICATIONS

Poetry

Terror and Decorum: Poems 1940–1948. New York, Scribner, 1948.
Strike through the Mask! New Lyrical Poems. New York, Scribner, 1950.
The First Morning: New Poems. New York, Scribner, 1952.
The Persimmon Tree: New Pastoral and Lyric Poems. New York, Scribner, 1956.

New and Selected Poems 1932–1967. Indianapolis, Bobbs Merrill, 1967.

Archer in the Marrow: The Applewood Cycles 1967–1987. New York, Norton, 1987.

Tide and Continuities: Last and First Poems, 1995–1938. Fayetteville, University of Arkansas Press, 1995.

Play

The Tree Witch (produced Cambridge, Massachusetts, 1961). Published as *The Tree Witch: A Poem and a Play (First of All a Poem),* New York, Scribner, 1961.

Other

Metapolitics: From the Romantics to Hitler. New York, Knopf, 1941; revised edition, as *Metapolitics: The Roots of the Nazi Mind,* New York, Putnam, 1961; revised edition, Baton Rouge, Louisiana State University Press, 1979.

Conservatism Revisited: The Revolt Against Revolt, 1815–1949. New York, Scribner, 1949; London, Lehmann, 1950.

Shame and Glory of the Intellectuals: Babbitt Jr. vs. the Rediscovery of Values. Boston, Beacon Press, 1953; revised edition, New York, Putnam, 1965.

Dream and Responsibility: Four Test Cases of the Tension Between Poetry and Society. Washington, D.C., University Press of Washington, 1953.

The Unadjusted Man: A New Hero for Americans: Reflections on the Distinction Between Conforming and Conserving. Boston, Beacon Press, 1956; revised edition, New York, Putnam, 1962.

Conservatism: From John Adams to Churchill. Princeton, New Jersey, Van Nostrand, 1956.

Inner Liberty: The Stubborn Grit in the Machine (lecture). Wallingford, Pennsylvania, Pendle Hill Pamphlets, 1957.

Conservatism Revisited and the New Conservatism: What Went Wrong? New York, Macmillan, 1962; revised edition, Baton Rouge, Louisiana State University Press, 1980.

*

Critical Studies: *Peter Viereck* by Marie Henault, New York, Twayne, 1969; "The 'God Is Like Kilroy' Passage in Peter Viereck's 'Kilroy'" by Peter P. Clarke, in *Notes on Contemporary Literature* (Carrollton, Georgia), 14(4), September 1984.

*   *   *

A poet is some one who skims ever weightier
Stones ever farther on water.

Tides and Continuities (1995), from which the lines above are taken, attests to the increasing ambition, range, technical expertise, and overall achievement of Peter Viereck's verse. Because Viereck's later works, whether originals or revisions, draw heavily from his earlier poetry, much of it in out-of-print volumes, it is crucial to assess his entire writing career.

A nervous daring informs Viereck's characteristic verse, especially in his first books. The more ambitious later work regrettably

sacrifices some of this excitement and does not always create a language or unifying tone appropriate to its ambition, a problem apparent in the 1987 *Archer in the Marrow* and its coda, "Crossbow," published in *Tides and Continuities.* Occasionally the cleverness of the early poems overreaches itself. For example, strained sound effects inadvertently trivialize the image of Nazi evil "hiking in shorts through tyranny's Tyrols" ("Crass Times Redeemed by Dignity of Souls"). But Viereck's gambles generally succeed, and his sound patterns can create the illusion of a new etymology: ". . . Aeneas on the boat from Troy / Before harps cooled the arson into art" ("Lot's Wife"). This bravado works best in his epic treatment in "Kilroy" and in "To a Sinister Potato," where echoes of "Ode on a Grecian Urn" heighten the bizarre grandeur of the parody: "O vast earth-apple, waiting to be fried. / Of all life's starers the most many-eyed. / What furtive purpose hatched you long ago / In Indiana or in Idaho?" The zest animating these poems, from *Terror and Decorum,* not only legitimates his frequent comic rhymes or his bastardized Spenserian language, as in "Ballad of the Jollie Gleeman," but also supports the tender, frightening "Six Theological Cradle Songs," which use nursery jingles and childhood games to dramatize the terror implicit in mortality. Sometimes, as in an elegy for Hart Crane, Viereck concentrates his frenzy to achieve powerful gnomic wit: ". . . and he found / New York was the clerks his daddy hired / Plus gin plus sea; then Hart felt tired. / Drank both and drowned" ("Look, Hart, That Horse You Ride Is Wood").

The later volumes provide less outrageous fun as they attempt a variety of ambitious themes. The straightforward comic verse may falter, as in "Full Circle," a series of parodies of new critics and modern poets, including Viereck himself. But he develops impressive poems with unusual personae. "To My Isis" wittily conveys Viereck's range, from "Whatever simmers . . . birch or trout" to ". . . Mud I also mimic: Let salivating warthogs gambol by. / Preening their bristles. All gross masks I'll try. / But hairy spiders. These I can't stomach." His most striking impersonations, wisely retained in *Tides and Continuities,* are of trees. An oak threatens a willow: "Your chance of passing next week's Woodlore Test / Is—bear it oakly—not the best. / You know the price! The beaver foreman claims / He needs just one more trunk to mend his dams." ("The Slacker Need Not Apologize"). A stage direction states, "Beavers in over-alls drag away storm-felled oak." (Viereck's frequent subtitles and end notes and his epigraphs suggest a nervous editor, eager to help but unwilling to compromise the integrity of the text by altering it.) The willow ultimately survives: "Mere echo (—strummer?), mad (—or wild with truth?) / But contours of the winds lured far too far. / I'm left behind when even God flies south / (If 'God' means all climate I ignore)." The dashes, question marks, and parentheses heighten the struggling uncertainty implicit in the dialectic of the poem. Here, or in a debate between Goethe and Crane in "Decorum and Terror," Viereck dramatizes viewpoints both limited and belligerent that fuse into a compassionate, accepting overview. His teasingly show-off rhymes—"Courtiers prance/Otto Kahn's" or "Barrack/Weimaric/Pyrrhic/wreck"—make both speakers less than Olympian and prepare for the final triumphant rhyme of "Viereck," which asserts both the poet's mastery of his poem and the fusion of classical decorum and romantic terror that are its antagonists.

Viereck's vegetation poems delicately convey both imagined states of nonhuman consciousness and their human analogues. "The Slacker Apologizes," for example, makes credible the boast of a "crass young weed":

Last night my stamen
Could hear her pistil sigh . . .
My pollen's shy
Deep nuzzling tells her: weeds must love or die.

Viereck wisely emphasized many individual lines and passages from his earlier volumes in *Archer in the Marrow,* a long poem of more than two hundred pages that dramatizes the desire to "self-surpass" through the help of woman ("God's image made human by Eve") and art ("Art wasn't art but lifeblood . . ."). A series of debates by man, God, and the son (the latter two are man's "imagined inner voices") provide the structure of the poem. Ultimately and triumphantly, the son fuses with Dionysius—"Look: goatfoot Jesus on the village green"—an image suggesting man's potential for liberation from the constraints of both traditional Christianity and modern science. Epigraphs from Nietzsche emphasize the many Nietzschean motifs in the poem; indeed, *Archer in the Marrow* attempts, among other laudable goals, to rescue Nietzsche from twentieth-century distortions. A wealth of similar echoes from artists as diverse as Sophocles and Duke Ellington suggests the range of Viereck's vision of the nature of man, from his "lungfish ancestor" to Adolf Eichmann.

On one level *Archer in the Marrow* seems a commonplace book compiled by an intelligence of a very high order. (The overall effect of *Tides and Continuities* is much the same, though made more painful by its many references to illness and hospital procedures). Viereck's verse, buttressed by the essay "Form in Poetry," elaborate notes, and a glossary of allusions, offers variations on three thousand years of attempts to define man. But at times the literary and philosophical excerpts threaten to overwhelm the poem, as they do *Tides and Continuities,* the quotations sometimes conveying powers of thought and imagery superior to Viereck's. His wit occasionally strains to develop themes that demand greater elevation of language: "Flesh being gene-scrawled for neither music nor justice, / Let's improvise them, no matter what the script, / Parching on Scylla / or drowning on Charybdis, / We're Proteus dodging blueprints of Procrustes." The individual lines may capture images of man's makeshift grandeur, but the rhymes seem forced and weaken the poem, and sometimes the conflicting voices, indicated by changes in typeface, suggest more a glib flyting than a philosophical clash: "A case of folie-à-deux?— *'No, folie-à-Dieu'* / No, folie-adieu."

The title of *Tides and Continuities* says it all. The first lengthy section of poems, "Mostly Hospital and Old Age," is Viereck's testament: "Begun in hospitals in my seventies. Their theme: old age and its coming to terms with the archetypal trio: Persephone, Dionysius, Pluto." These dramatizations of warring, occasionally reconciled forces within man allow Viereck to display the richness of his erudition and to embody the metrical theories that have always interested him. The volume seems to be his version of *The Cantos,* especially when the speaker sounds cantankerous, or of *The Waste Land,* an impression reinforced by the copious notes and the ambition of a work that moves from man's "landlocked landfish" beginnings to his control by the medical establishment. At times the verse convincingly conveys a quirky speaker's consciousness as it displays the art and wit acquired during a long life in an attempt to define and ward off, if not defeat, the enemy. Judged less charitably, the same verse seems more the poet's obsessive display of anger, learning, and metrical theories, as in these lines from "At My Hospital Window":

—Your exorcist-spells of slant-rhyme knickknacks
Are duds," death cackles. "To hide from my *nox*

(Since Thanatos' mother is night-goddess Nyx)
Is SACRILEGE. Here I come. Ready or—
Not.

Perhaps the strongest new poem in the volume is "Pluto Incognito," in which a janitor's voice fuses with Pluto's during a "tumor autopsy—dead brain cells are galvanized awake for an instant by the surgeon scalpel . . . the whole resultant Pluto monologue flashes by in that instant . . ." Admittedly, the poem has its share of flat lines ("The erotic being their most addictive narcotic") and strained wit ("Because her art-of-love out Ovids Ovid / I gave her anklets pluto-crats would covet . . ."), but at times the daring of Viereck's vision finds seemingly inevitable expression as the speaker attacks those "calling my royal dreams plebeian tumors," a witty rebuke of science and a powerful defense of art. Even more successfully outrageous is the following:

Brer Zeus yanked a girl from a migraine.
(None called Athena his tumor.)
Me too? Is the sharp kiss jabbing my brain
The girl I'm horny for?

The lines convey that fusion of learning and colloquialism, wit and psychological realism that represents Viereck at his best. His poetry continues to celebrate individual human consciousness amid the recurring patterns of birth, death, and birth that threaten its significance. Perhaps only the artist possesses the blend of courage and grace to make a difference:

Though life ails just a day faster than art allays,
Though age rots art before it can learn to sing true,
Sing anyhow. Continue.

—Burton Kendle

VOIGT, Ellen Bryant

Nationality: American. **Born:** Danville, Virginia, 9 May 1943. **Education:** Converse College, Spartanburg, South Carolina, B.A. 1964; University of Iowa, Iowa City, M.F.A. 1966. **Family:** Married Francis George Wilhelm Voigt in 1965; one daughter and one son. **Career:** Technical writer, College Pharmacy, University of Iowa, 1965–66; assistant professor of literature and writing, Iowa Wesleyan College, Mt. Pleasant, Iowa, 1966–69; teacher of literature and writing, 1970–79, and director of writing program, 1976–79, Goddard College, Plainfield, Vermont; associate professor of creative writing, Massachusetts Institute of Technology, Cambridge, 1979–82. Since 1981 faculty member, M.F.A. program for writers, Warren Wilson College, Swannanoa, North Carolina. Visiting writer, Newcombe College, Tulane University, 1996, Virginia Commonwealth University, 1996–97, and University of Cincinnati, 1997. Faculty member, Aspen Writers' Conference, Breadloaf Writers' Conference, Indiana Writers' Conference, Napa Valley Writers' Conference, and Ropewalk Writers' Conference. Advisory editor, *Arion's Dolphin,* 1971–75. Also professional pianist. **Awards:** Vermont Council on the Arts grant, 1974–75; National Endowment for the Arts grant, 1976–77; Guggenheim fellowship, 1978–79; Alice Fay Di Castagnola award, Poetry Society of America, 1983; Sara Teasdale award, Wellesley

College, 1986; Gretchen Warren Poetry award, New England Poetry Society, 1986; Lila Wallace-Reader's Digest award, 1999–2002; Vermont State poet, 1999–2003. **Address:** P.O. Box 128, Marshfield, Vermont 05658, U.S.A.

PUBLICATIONS

Poetry

Claiming Kin. Middletown, Connecticut, Wesleyan University Press, 1976.
The Forces of Plenty. New York, Norton, 1983.
The Lotus Flowers. New York. Norton. 1987.
Two Trees. New York, Norton, 1992.
Kyrie. New York, Norton, 1995.

Other

The Flexible Lyric. Athens, University of Georgia Press, 1999.

Editor, with George Orr, *Poets Teaching Poets: Self and the World.* Ann Arbor, University of Michigan Press, 1996.

*

Manuscript Collection: Middlebury College, Middlebury, Vermont.

Critical Studies: "Pain and Plenitude: First and Second Books by Maria Flook and Ellen Bryant Voigt" by Carolyne Wright, in *Literary Review* (Madison, New Jersey), 30(1), fall 1986; "Air and Earth: Recent Books by Jorie Graham and Ellen Bryant Voigt" by James Ulmer, in *Black Warrior Review* (Tuscaloosa, Alabama), 15(2), spring 1989; "Four Salvers Salvaging: New Work by Voigt, Olds, Dove, and McHugh" by Peter Harris, in *Virginia Quarterly Review* (Charlottesville, Virginia), 64(2), spring 1988; "The Free Verse Line" by Jonathan Holden, in *The Line in Postmodern Poetry,* edited by Robert Joseph Frank and Henry M. Sayre, Urbana, University of Illinois Press, 1988; "Speculations on a Southern Snipe" by Dave Smith, in *The Future of Southern Letters,* edited by Jefferson Humphries and John Lowe, New York, Oxford University Press, 1996; by Ernest Suarez, in *Five Points* (Atlanta, Georgia), 3(1), fall 1998.

*   *   *

Ellen Bryant Voigt's poems concern themselves with separation and connection. She is a careful observer of both nature and human behavior, and her vision is clear and compassionate at the same time.

Her first book, *Claiming Kin,* seeks parallels everywhere between human life and nature. It is nature, for example, that gives us a model for hope. Perhaps we, like the snake, may "rise up in new skins / a full confusion of green . . ." ("Snakeskin"). On the other hand, nature's more ominous lessons are acknowledged as well. The black widow spider, for example, ties sensuality and fertility to death. Voigt's nature poems complement the poems in which she attempts to claim and come to terms with her human kin. Many of her poems concern the family, which she characterizes as "the circle of fire." In the long poem "Sister" the speaker returns to her family to deal with

her mother's illness and finds herself reexamining the tangle of feelings that comprise her relationship with her sister:

> When we were little
> I used to wish you dead;
> then hold my breath and sweat
> to hear yours
> release, intake, relax into sleep.

In *The Forces of Plenty,* her second volume, Voigt examines many of the same themes, but whereas her writing has become more confident, her stance has, perhaps wisely, become less so. She moves away from the exuberant lushness of *Claiming Kin,* with its ". . . thick pythons, / slack and drowsy, who droop down / like untied sashes / from the trees" ("Tropics") and its emphasis on what joins, to look more closely at what separates. Ironically, as the speaker remarks in "January," it is our very ability to reflect on nature that separates us from it:

> If I think I am apart from this, I am a fool.
> And if I think the black engine of the stove
> can raise in me the same luminous waking,
> I am still a fool,
> since I am the one who keeps the fire.

A sense of mortality pervades the book, which includes several elegies, making life and happiness more precious and more fragile. In "Year's End" two parents' relief at their own child's recovery from illness is tempered by the knowledge that a friend's child has just died, and they listen to their own child's breath "like refugees who listen to the sea, / unable to fully rejoice, or fully grieve."

The Lotus Flowers incorporates and finds salvation in some of the hard truths first observed in *The Forces of Plenty.* In "The Farmer," for example, a man stung by a swarm of bees is saved by ". . . the years of smaller doses— / like minor disappointments, / instructive poison, something he could use." These poems, however, are even more deeply rooted in personal experience and in Voigt's rural southern background. There is a tinge of melancholy about the past, a lament for the loss of innocence, as in "Nightshade," in which the daughter cannot forgive her father for accidentally poisoning the dog and says that "without pure evil in the world, / there was no east or west, no polestar / and no ratifying dove . . ." In its concern with place and pattern, the title poem is a culmination of this book's themes. The shape made by the girls on their pallets—"spokes in a wheel"—echoes the shapes of the constellations they study, and the stars in these constellations mirror the lotus flowers, now "folded / into candles," through which the girls had earlier rowed. In this poem the opposition between nature and humanity, innocence and knowledge, individual and community seems temporarily resolved.

The resolution shifts, however, in *Two Trees,* the most austere and foreboding of Voigt's books. Although, like her previous volumes, it contains poems of family and nature, it is most concerned with the spiritual aspects of the subjects, and music and myth provide its major subjects and metaphors. The emphasis here is on what separates—the music that "keeps the girl apart / as she prefers . . ." ("Variations: At the Piano") or "beauty that divides us" ("First Song")—and on the loss of innocence. The title poem retells the expulsion from paradise and the eternal longing that results: "while the mind cried out / for that addictive tree it had tasted, / and for that other crown still visible over the wall." A sense of resignation pervades the book. What makes us human is not an ability to control our fate but our need to struggle and reach out to one another: ''The one who can sings to the one who can't / who waits in the pit, like Procne among the slaves, / as the gods decide how all such stories end . . .'' (''Song and Story''). Her innovative adaptation of musical variations, in which three sets of poems called ''variations'' expand aspects of a titled poem, skillfully merges theme and technique and makes of this collection a haunting whole.

Voigt's style has grown more flexible with each book in order to accommodate her increasingly complex vision. Her subjects range from the intimacies of daily life to the exploration of our place in the universe. She is a poet who dares to say that ''nothing is learned / by turning away . . . .'' (''Talking the Fire Out'' from *The Forces of Plenty*).

—Kathleen Aguero

WADDINGTON, Miriam

Nationality: Canadian. **Born:** Miriam Dworkin, Winnipeg, Manitoba, 23 December 1917. **Education:** Machray School, Winnipeg; Lisgar Institute, Ottawa; University of Toronto, B.A. 1939, diploma in social work 1942, M.A. 1968; University of Pennsylvania, Philadelphia, M.S.W. 1945. **Family:** Married Patrick Donald Waddington in 1939 (divorced 1965); two sons. **Career:** Caseworker, Jewish Family Service, Toronto, 1942–44, 1957–60, and Philadelphia Child Guidance Clinic, 1944–45; assistant director, Jewish Child Welfare Bureau, Montreal, 1945–46; lecturer and supervisor, McGill School of Social Work, Montreal, 1946–49; caseworker, Montreal Children's Hospital Speech Clinic, 1950–52, and John Howard Society, 1955–57; staff member, Montreal Children's Hospital, 1952–54; supervisor, North York Family Service, 1960–62. Member of the English Department, 1964–73, professor of literature, 1973–83, and since 1983 emeritus professor, York University, Toronto. Writer-in-residence, University of Ottawa, 1974, Windsor Public Library, 1983, and Metropolitan Toronto Reference Library, 1986. Advisory editor, Journal of the Otto Rank Association, 1973–83; poetry editor, *Poetry Toronto,* 1981–82. **Awards:** Canada Council fellowship, 1962, 1968, 1971, 1979; J.I. Segal award, 1973, 1987. D.Litt.: Lakehead University, Thunder Bay, Ontario, 1975; York University, 1985. **Address:** Department of English, York University, Toronto, Ontario M3J 1P3, Canada.

PUBLICATIONS

Poetry

Green World. Montreal, First Statement Press, 1945.
The Second Silence. Toronto, Ryerson Press, 1955.
The Season's Lovers. Toronto, Ryerson Press, 1958.
The Glass Trumpet. Toronto, Oxford University Press, 1966.
Call Them Canadians. Ottawa, Queen's Printers and National Film Board, 1968.
Say Yes. Toronto, Oxford University Press, 1969.
Dream Telescope. London, Anvil Press Poetry, 1972.
Driving Home: Poems New and Selected. Toronto, Oxford University Press, 1972; London, Anvil Press Poetry, 1973.
The Price of Gold. Toronto, Oxford University Press, 1976.
Mister Never. Winnipeg, Turnstone Press, 1978.
The Visitants. Toronto, Oxford University Press, 1981; New York, Oxford University Press, 1982.
Collected Poems. Toronto, Oxford University Press, 1986.
The Last Landscape. Toronto and Oxford, Oxford University Press, 1992.
Canada: Romancing the Land. Toronto, Key Porter Books, 1996.

Plays

Radio Documentaries: *Chekov,* 1958; *Poe,* 1962.

Short Stories

Summer at Lonely Beach: Selected Short Stories. Oakville, Ontario, Mosaic Press, 1982.

Other

A.M. Klein. Toronto, Copp Clark, 1970.
The Function of Folklore in the Poetry of A.M. Klein (lecture). St. John's, Newfoundland, Memorial University, 1983.
Apartment 7: Essays New and Selected. Toronto, Oxford University Press, 1989.
Cercando Fragole in Giugno E Altre Poesie (in Italian and English). Bologna, CLUEB, 1993.

Editor, *Essays, Poems, Controversies,* by John Sutherland. Toronto, McClelland and Stewart, 1973.
Editor, *The Collected Poems of A.M. Klein.* Toronto, McGraw Hill Ryerson, and New York, McGraw Hill, 1974.

*

Bibliography: By Laurie Ricou, in *The Annotated Bibliography of Canada's Major Authors 6,* edited by Robert Lecker and Jack David, Toronto, ECW Press, 1985.

Manuscript Collection: Public Archives of Canada, Ottawa.

Critical Studies: "The Lyric Craft of Miriam Waddington" by Ian Sowton, in *Dalhousie Review* (Halifax, Nova Scotia), summer 1958; "Into My Green World: The Poetry of Miriam Waddington" by Laurence R. Ricou, in *Essays on Canadian Writing* (Toronto), fall 1978; *Twelve Voices* by Jon Pearce, Ottawa, Borealis Press, 1980; *Miriam Waddington* by Cathy Matyas, Toronto, Dundurn Press, 1982; *Miriam Waddington and Her Work* by Peter Stevens, Toronto, ECW Press, 1984; "Miriam Waddington: An Afternoon" by Marvyne Jenoff, in *Waves* (Richmond Hill, Ontario), 14(1–2), fall 1985; *Transformation Poetics: Refiguring the Female Subject in the Early Poetry and Life Writing of Dorothy Livesay and Miriam Waddington* (dissertation), York University, 1997.

Miriam Waddington comments:

About my poetry: the key to it is the language. My Canadian English takes its cue from the prairies where I was born and conceals more than it reveals. Some concealments: the social, mythic, and linguistic reverberations of the Yiddish and Russian cultures of my childhood, plus the austerity and Scottish accents of my early teachers.

*   *   *

In the early 1940s there were few opportunities in Canada to publish a book of poetry. Miriam Waddington's first collection, *Green World,* was published by John Sutherland's First Statement Press in Montreal, where two active literary groups were about to launch the magazines *First Statement* and *Preview.* These writers wanted to see an end to the colonial attitudes that had dominated

Canadian writing through the Canadian Authors Association publication *Canadian Poetry Magazine.*

Between the appearance of *Green World* in 1943 and *Collected Poems* in 1986, Waddington published ten books of poetry. Sharp observation, wit, and compassion have remained constant. A change to short lines in *The Glass Trumpet* was unconscious and connected with new ways of looking at the world, a matter of zeitgeist, the poet says. Using spaces instead of commas was deliberate and concerned the appearance of a poem on the page. She later began to like commas again, her wish for precise meaning taking precedence.

Early poems were about birth, mothering, and love, with a few poems about social issues. But with degrees in social work, Waddington became involved with the deprived and dispossessed, and she turned her poetry to subjects of social significance. She met and became fast friends with Dorothy Livesay, who had ''ignored maple leaves'' to write about the desperate condition of people caught in a social revolution. Waddington became a compassionate outsider who saw more and more human misery in her work. As time went on, she wrote more frequently about courts and prisons, and with the publication of *The Season's Lovers* she realized that she was not in the mainstream of Canadian literature because her poetry could not be called metaphysical and mythic. *The Season's Lovers* dealt with ''the realities of crippled lives, poverty, and the strange innocence of the weak and rejected.''

The exploration of what it means to be Canadian has been a favorite theme of Waddington's. *Driving Home: Poems New and Selected* contains many poems examining her identity as a Canadian, including the following:

CANADIANS

Here are
our signatures:
geese fish eskimo
faces girl-guide
cookies ink-drawings
tree-plantings summer
storms and winter
emanations.

We look
like a geography
but just scratch us
and we bleed like
history are full
of modest misery
sensitive
to double-talk double-take
(and double-cross)
in a country
too wide
to be single in.

Waddington says in the afterword to *Collected Poems* that her attitude to poetry is the same as it was fifty years earlier when she wrote in the 1938 poem ''Unheard Melodies,''

I the tender and brooding outsider
Concern myself with subtle melodies

Fashioning usual themes
In unknown obscure lives.

—Patience Wheatley

WAGONER, David (Russell)

Nationality: American. **Born:** Massillon, Ohio, 5 June 1926. **Education:** Pennsylvania State University, University Park, B.A. 1947; Indiana University, Bloomington, M.A. in English 1949. **Military Service:** U.S. Navy, 1944–46. **Family:** Married 1) Elizabeth Arensman in 1950 (divorced 1952); 2) Patricia Parrott in 1961 (divorced 1982), two daughters; 3) Robin Heather Seyfried in 1982. **Career:** Instructor, DePauw University, Greencastle, Indiana, 1949–50, and Pennsylvania State University, 1950–53. Assistant professor, 1954–57, associate professor, 1958–66, and since 1966, professor of English, University of Washington, Seattle. Elliston Professor of poetry, University of Cincinnati, 1968; editor, Princeton University Press Contemporary Poetry Series, 1977–81. Since 1966 editor, *Poetry Northwest,* Seattle; since 1983 poetry editor, University of Missouri Press, Columbia. **Awards:** Guggenheim fellowship, 1956; Ford fellowship, for drama, 1964; American Academy grant, 1967; Morton Dauwen Zabel prize, 1967, Oscar Blumenthal prize, 1974, Eunice Tietjens memorial prize, 1977, and English-Speaking Union prize, 1980 (*Poetry,* Chicago); National Endowment for the Arts grant, 1969; Fels prize, 1975; Sherwood Anderson award, 1980; Union League prize, 1987; Ruth Lilly poetry prize, 1991; Levinson prize, 1994; Ohioana Book award, 1997, for *Walt Whitman Bathing.* **Member:** Academy of American Poets; Chancelor, 1978. **Address:** Department of English, University of Washington, Seattle, Washington 98195, U.S.A.

PUBLICATIONS

Poetry

Dry Sun, Dry Wind. Bloomington, Indiana University Press, 1953.
A Place to Stand. Bloomington, Indiana University Press, 1958.
Poems. Portland, Oregon, Portland Art Museum, 1959.
The Nesting Ground. Bloomington, Indiana University Press, 1963.
Five Poets of the Pacific Northwest, with others edited by Robin Skelton. Seattle, University of Washington Press, 1964.
Staying Alive. Bloomington, Indiana University Press, 1966.
New and Selected Poems. Bloomington, Indiana University Press, 1969.
Working Against Time. London, Rapp and Whiting, 1970.
Riverbed. Bloomington, Indiana University Press, 1972.
Sleeping in the Woods. Bloomington, Indiana University Press, 1974.
A Guide to Dungeness Spit. Port Townsend, Washington, Graywolf Press, 1975.
Travelling Light. Port Townsend, Washington, Graywolf Press, 1976.
Collected Poems 1956–1976. Bloomington, Indiana University Press, 1976.
Who Shall Be the Sun? Poems Based on the Lore, Legends, and Myths of Northwest Coast and Plateau Indians. Bloomington, Indiana University Press, 1978.
In Broken Country. Boston, Little Brown, 1979.
Landfall. Boston, Little Brown, 1981.

First Light. Boston, Little Brown, 1983.

Through the Forest: New and Selected Poems, 1977–1987. New York, Atlantic Monthly Press, 1987.

Walt Whitman Bathing: Poems. Urbana, University of Illinois Press, 1996.

Traveling Light: Collected and New Poems. Urbana, University of Illinois Press, 1999.

Recording: *David Wagoner Reads from 'The Escape Artist,'* American Audio Prose Library, 1981; *The Poets among Us,* Writing on Air, 1998.

Plays

An Eye for an Eye for an Eye (produced Seattle, 1973).

Screenplay: *The Escape Artist,* 1981.

Novels

The Man in the Middle. New York, Harcourt Brace, 1954; London, Gollancz, 1955.

Money, Money, Money. New York, Harcourt Brace, 1955.

Rock. New York, Viking Press, 1958.

The Escape Artist. New York, Farrar Straus, and London, Gollancz, 1965.

Baby, Come On Inside. New York, Farrar Straus, 1968.

Where Is My Wandering Boy Tonight? New York, Farrar Straus, 1970.

The Road to Many a Wonder. New York, Farrar Straus, 1974.

Tracker. Boston, Little Brown, 1975.

Whole Hog. Boston, Little Brown, 1976.

The Hanging Garden. Boston, Little Brown, 1980; London, Hale, 1982.

Other

Editor, *Straw for the Fire: From the Notebooks of Theodore Roethke 1943–1963.* New York, Doubleday, 1972.

*

Manuscript Collections: Olin Library, Washington University, St. Louis; University of Washington, Seattle.

Critical Studies: "The Poetry of David Wagoner" by Robert Boyers, in *Kenyon Review* (Gambier, Ohio), 1970; "An Interview with David Wagoner," in *Crazy Horse 12* (Marshall, Minnesota), 1972; "A Conversation with David Wagoner," in *Yes* (Avoca, New York), 4(1), 1973; "On David Wagoner," in *Salmagundi* (Saratoga Springs, New York), spring-summer 1973, and "Pelting Dark Windows," in *Parnassus* (New York), spring-summer 1977, both by Sanford Pinsker; *Three Pacific Northwest Poets: William Stafford, Richard Hugo, and David Wagoner* by Sanford Pinsker, Boston, Twayne, 1987; *David Wagoner* by Ron McFarland, Boise, Idaho, Boise State University Press, 1989; *Treading Softly, Speaking Low: Contemporary American Poetry in the Didactic Mode* by Joanna Durczak, Lubin, 1994; by Laurie Ricou, in *Updating the Literary West*, Fort Worth, Texas, Western Literature Association, 1997; *The*

World of David Wagoner by Ron McFarland, Moscow, University of Idaho Press, 1997.

David Wagoner comments:

I have an affinity for the dramatic lyric, in tones ranging from the loud and satiric through the quiet and conversational.

*   *   *

While it is true that Theodore Roethke, his undergraduate teacher at Pennsylvania State University, was instrumental in bringing David Wagoner to the Pacific Northwest, one could argue that he would have found his way there anyway. After spending his formative years in Whiting, Indiana, an industrial suburb of Chicago that is hard to surpass for disfigured earth, Dantesque fire, and polluted water and air, Wagoner understandably found his place in one of the few regions in America that still has some unspoiled wilderness and some unspoiled people, American Indians.

Wagoner is one of America's most prolific and versatile writers. Not only has he published twenty volumes of poetry, but he also has produced ten substantial novels. The novelist's feeling for detail enriches the poetry, not only in such mythical narrative poems as "The Return of Icarus," "The Labors of Thor," and "Beauty and the Beast" but also in his dramatic and lyric poems. His versatility is patent. His themes are important ones: survival, anger at those who violate the natural world, a Chaucerian delight in human oddity. He manages tones from gaiety to meditative seriousness. He is rarely self-importantly solemn.

Because Wagoner has been publishing poetry for well over four decades, a considerable achievement is available for assessment. After his first two volumes—nothing from the first and little from the second appears in *Collected Poems 1956–1976*—Wagoner moved beyond the influence of Roethke and Edgar Lee Masters to find his own forms. They include the mock instruction manuals best exemplified by "Advice to the Orchestra," "The Singing Lesson," "Staying Alive," "Sleeping in the Woods," and "Meeting a Bear"; elegies far from Theocritus, such as the mordant "For a Forest Clear-Cut by the Weyerhaeuser Company"; and mythic poems based on American Indian materials.

"Staying Alive" is one of the best American poems since World War II, a profoundly sensible set of instructions to one lost in the woods and valuable to anyone anywhere who is interested in staying alive. "Sleeping in the Woods" goes on from "Staying Alive" to show Wagoner achieving his peculiar harmony with the natural world. The poem opens with

> Not having found your way out of the woods, begin
> Looking for somewhere to bed down at nightfall
> Though you have nothing
> But parts of yourself to lie on . . .

In "Talking to Barr Creek" Wagoner succeeds at what Matthew Arnold failed to do in "A Summer Night," realistically aspiring to a harmony with nature not beyond human possibility. At the end of the poem the speaker prays:

> Grant me your endless, ungrudging impulse
> Forward, the lavishness of your light movements,
> Your constant inconstancy . . .
> Your sudden stillness . . .

Teach me your spirit, going yet staying, being
Born, vanishing, enduring.

For a man so attuned to the wild natural world where American
Indians still live, it seems almost a matter of course that Wagoner's
work should include a book prompted by Indian myths. The final two
stanzas of the title poem of *Who Shall Be the Sun?* give an idea of
Wagoner's sensitive, respectful handling of Indian lore:

The People said, "We shall have no sun at all!"
But Snake whispered, "I have dreamed I was the sun."
Raven, Hawk, and Coyote mocked him by torchlight:
"You cannot scream or howl! You cannot run or fly!
You cannot burn, dazzle or blacken the earth!
How can you be the sun?" "By dreaming," Snake
    whispered.

He rose then out of the rich night.
He coiled in a ball, low in the sky.
Slowly he shed the Red Skin of Dawn,
The Skin of the Blue Noontime, the Skin of Gold,
And last the Skin of Darkness, and the People
Slept in their lodges, safe, till he coiled again.

Through the Forest: New and Selected Poems, 1977–1987
consists of about half the poems each from *In Broken Country,*
Landfall, and *First Light,* with twenty-four new poems. The arrangement of *Through the Forest* is wonderfully playful. Far from the usual
custom of ordering poems chronologically as written or published,
they appear mixed like a deck of shuffled cards, though not without
method. In fact, some of the new poems, which make up about one-
seventh of the book, are clumped together.

"Making a Fire in the Rain" is a good example of the poetry in
In Broken Country. It illustrates the poet expressing lyrically and
realistically his wry honesty. The final stanza admits defeat:

The rain is too much, suddenly, the wind deadly,
The stones too blunt, and the fire too close for comfort,
I get up no wiser, though now cured like a salmon,
And climb to the road—turning for one more look
At that obstinate tongue of light dwindling to nothing.
The smoke sweeps off downstream in a toppling column.

In *Landfall* a number of poems contemplate small insects and
birds and great waters and trees. One favorite is "Return to the
Swamp," with its lines "What did I hope to find? This crystal-
gazing / . . . / How can I shape, again, something from nothing?"

The collection *First Light* is Wagoner's most intense, perhaps
stimulated by the courtship of and marriage to his second wife. A
representative poem is "Loon Mating," which ends,

And now the haunting uprisen mating call,
And again, and now the beautiful sane laughter.

An appropriate example of the new poems in *Through the Forest*
is Wagoner's "Eulogy for Richard Hugo (1923–1982)," in praise of
his poet friend. The last stanza is eloquent and successful, even in its
true and slant rhymes:

He spent his days in search of a hometown
Where he could be class hero and class clown,
Unknown and famous, friendly and alone:
Wearing his old school colors: the gray and white
Of ashes, he lies there now, its laureate.

In the collection *Walt Whitman Bathing,* Wagoner, like Whitman,
finds his inspiration in the landscape of America. Dense and probing,
these poems seem to need to account for the material of the poet's world:

Above the river, over the broad hillside
and down the slope in clusters and strewn throngs,
cross-tangled and intermingled,
wildflowers are blooming, seemingly all at once.

These are poems that enact an intricate emotional life but maintain a
detachment necessary for Wagoner's particular discretion. Separation from trivialities and passing concerns is critical for this poet, as in
"By a River":

Your choice was always clear: not the long struggle
Upstream against the current, against the constant
Headlong pummeling of snow-melt and downpour
Nor the leaf-slow easy drifting
Downstream . . .
but simply staying
Here by the river where you watch and wait
For what appears, moves past, and vanishes.

Wagoner occasionally tends toward surrealism, but his work is
mainly rooted in the natural or, as in his consideration of the
experience of American Indians, in the archetypal and the mythic.
With his evenness of tone and his plain Midwestern diction, he recalls
Sandburg and sometimes Frost. This is a voice that endures in its
direct call to immediate, lyrical experience.

—James K. Robinson and Martha Sutro

WAH, Fred(erick James)

Nationality: Canadian. **Born:** Swift Current, Saskatchewan, 23
January 1939. **Education:** University of British Columbia, Vancouver,
1958–63, B.A. 1963; University of New Mexico, Albuquerque,
1963–64; State University of New York, Buffalo, 1964–67, M.A.
1967. **Family:** Married Pauline Butling in 1962; two daughters.
Career: Instructor, English, 1967–78, 1984–85, professional writing
program, 1985–88, and chairman, Arts I, 1967–78, Selkirk College,
Castlegar, British Columbia; coordinator and instructor, writing
program, David Thompson University Centre, Nelson, British Columbia, 1978–84; coordinator and teacher of writing workshops,
Kootenay School of Writing, Nelson and Vancouver, British Columbia, 1984–88. Since 1989 professor, English, University of Calgary.
Associate editor, *Tish,* 1961–63; editor, *Sum,* 1963–66; associate
editor, *Magazine of Further Studies,* 1966–70; editor, *Scree,* 1972–74;
since 1970 associate editor, *Open Letter,* and since 1992 editorial
board, *Ariel.* **Awards:** MacMillan prize for poetry, University of
British Columbia, 1963; Canada Council fellowship, 1967, Research
Travel grant, 1969, Arts grant I, 1977–78, and Senior Arts award,

1986; Governor-General's award, 1986, for *Waiting for Saskatchewan;* Department of External Affairs grant, 1990, 1992; Stephan G. Stephanson award, 1991, for *So Far.* **Address:** 2702 Chalice Road Northwest, Calgary, Alberta T2L 1C7, Canada.

PUBLICATIONS

Poetry

Lardeau. Toronto, Island Press, 1965.
Mountain. Buffalo, Audit Press, 1967.
Among. Toronto, Coach House Press, 1972.
Tree. Vancouver, Vancouver Community Press, 1972.
Earth. Canton, New York, Institute of Further Studies, 1974.
Pictograms from the Interior of B.C. Vancouver, Talonbooks, 1975.
Loki Is Buried at Smoky Creek: Selected Poetry. Vancouver, Talonbooks, 1980.
Owners Manual. Lantzville, Island Writing Series, 1981.
Breathin' My Name With a Sigh. Vancouver, Talonbooks, 1981.
Grasp the Sparrow's Tail. Kyoto, n.p., 1982.
Waiting for Saskatchewan. Winnipeg, Turnstone Press, 1985.
Rooftops. N.p., Blackberry Books, 1987.
Music at the Heart of Thinking. Red Deer, Red Deer College Press, 1987.
Limestone Lakes Utaniki. Red Deer, Red Deer College Press, 1989.
So Far. Vancouver, Talonbooks, 1991.
Alley Alley Home Free. Red Deer, Red Deer College Press, 1992.
Diamond Grill. Edmonton, NeWest Publishers, 1996.

Other

Faking It: Poetics & Hybridity, Critical Writing 1984–1999. Edmonton, NeWest Publishers, 2000.

Editor, *Place, Anyplace.* Castlegar, Cotinneh Books, 1973.
Editor, *Net Work, Selected Writings of Daphne Marlatt.* Vancouver, Talonbooks, 1980.
Editor, with Frank Davey, *Swift Current.* Toronto, Coach House Press, 1986.
Editor, with Roy Miki, *Beyond the Orchard: Essays on The Martyrology.* Vancouver, West Coast Line, 1997.

*

Manuscript Collection: Simon Fraser University, Burnaby, British Columbia.

Critical Studies: In *From There to Here: A Guide to English-Canadian Literature Since 1960* by Frank Davey, Vancouver, Press Porcepic, 1974; "Fred Wah: A Poetry of Dialogue" by Smaro Kamboureli, in *Line 4,* 1984; "The Undersigned: Ethnicity and Signature-Effects in Fred Wah's Poetry," in *West Coast Line* (Vancouver), 2, fall 1990, and *Translation Poetics: Composing the Body Canadian* (dissertation), both by Pamela Banting, University of Alberta, 1991; "'Mother/Father Things I Am Also': Fred Wah, Breathin' His Name with a Sigh" by Susan Rudy Dorscht, in *Inside the Poem: Essays and Poems in Honour of Donald Stephens,* edited by W.H. New, Toronto, Oxford University Press, 1992; "Making

Race Opaque: Fred Wah's Poetics of Opposition and Differentiation" by Jeff Derksen, in *West Coast Line* (Vancouver), 29(3), winter 1995–96.

*   *   *

Fred Wah began his writing career as a member of the *Tish* group on the campus of the University of British Columbia in the early 1960s. He was influenced by the Black Mountain poets of the day and then joined the editorial board of the journal *Open Letter.* In the 1970s and 1980s he held creative writing positions at the David Thompson University Centre in Nelson, British Columbia, a lively center for new writers, especially those associated with western Canada. In 1984 Wah teamed up with Frank Davey to launch a computer network called SwiftCurrent, described as "the world's first on-line electronic literary magazine." Writers in Canadian cities had a home page long before the Internet made the term a household word. Despite the interest in computers and communication, it is the prairie experience that has been Wah's mainstay, as is the case with his fellow Saskatchewan poet Andrew Suknaski.

In his early work Wah wrote with great simplicity. For instance, the poetic epigram of *Tree* (1972) reads as follows: "Go to the forest, Tree / please wait for me there." In later works he moved from simplicity to complexity, from lucidity to density, and from defining things to finding things. *Loki Is Buried at Smoky Creek* (1980) bears an introduction by George Bowering that quotes Davey on Wah: "The concept which dominates Wah's writing is that the geographic and human particulars which immediately surround a man not only contain all place and all history but together form a place that is for that man the true centre of the cosmos." The poem "What to Do When You Get There" certainly conveys a sense of being somewhere, although it is not clear exactly where:

get into a corner or something
take the 90 degree horizon
and with what you still carry from your trip
put it together privately
. . .
laugh a little bit at the perspective
its large
and when things rise in you like this
come to the surface with a force of their own
then let them
sit in the warmth
be in the middle of the large

Wah received the Governor-General's award for poetry for his book *Waiting for Saskatchewan* (1985). Many readers regard the book as Wah's crowning achievement. This is only fitting because the prose and poetry of the book celebrate the poet's native province, its present and particularly its past. At the same time the poet reaches out in the book to embrace his own past. Born in Swift Current, Saskatchewan, the son of a Chinese immigrant, he explored and innovated until he had a sense of who he was and where he stood. The book is structured in the sense that sections are called "Haibun" and "Elite." In the former a passage of prose is followed by a haikulike line of poetry. Nostalgia for the everyday life of the 1960s is characteristic: "Someday I'll grow them, prairie hollyhocks again, / on a stucco wall." In the latter section, which is perhaps more powerful, there are prose impressions of everyday life in Swift

Current. The lines of the poems move toward free association and are quite often difficult to follow, though one senses the hectic eloquence of the person in the act of uttering the words and making the right connections:

> and the origins grandparents countries places converged
> europe asia railroads carpenters nailed grain elevators
> . . .
> I want it back, wait in this snowblown winter night
> for that latitude of itself its own largeness
> my body to get complete
> it still owes me, it does

"Out of Wah's synaptic leaps a wonderful new music springs, a source, primary materials every reader needs," noted bpNichol of the poems found in Wah's book *Music at the Heart of Thinking* (1987). Will the synapses continue to leap? It seems that the meaning of the poems is growing elusive. "No. 42" includes such lines as these:

> Is that the flesh made word
> or is that the flesh-made word?
>
> Le mot juste or just tomatoes?
>
> Telling you, you telling me, field waiting.

Art as play? There are signs that Wah's later poems (now texts) are more theoretically based than are the earlier ones, which are derived from experience as well as theory. In "One Makes (the) Difference" in *Alley Alley Home Free* (1992), Wah writes as follows: "A text is a place where a labyrinth of continually revealing meanings are available, a place that offers more possibility than we can be sure we know, sometimes more than we know." What is worthwhile about Wah's work is the sense of someone who is straining to know more about himself and his portion of the earth.

—John Robert Colombo

WAINWRIGHT, Jeffrey

Nationality: British. **Born:** Stoke-on-Trent, Staffordshire, 19 February 1944. **Education:** Florence County Primary Junior School; Longton High School, 1955–62; University of Leeds, B.A. 1965, M.A. 1967. **Family:** Married Judith Batt in 1967; one son and one daughter. **Career:** Lecturer in American literature, University College of Wales, Aberystwyth, 1967–72. Since 1973 lecturer, then senior lecturer in English, Manchester Polytechnic. Visiting instructor, Long Island University, New York, 1970–71. **Address:** 11 Hesketh Avenue, Didsbury, Manchester M20 8QN, England.

PUBLICATIONS

Poetry

The Important Man. Newcastle upon Tyne, Northern House, 1970.
Heart's Desire. Manchester, Carcanet, 1978.
Selected Poems. Manchester. Carcanet, 1985.

The Red-Headed Pupil. Manchester, Carcanet, 1994.
Out of the Air. Manchester, Carcanet, 1999.

Play

The Mystery of the Charity of Joan of Arc, adaptation of a work by Charles Peguy (produced Stratford upon Avon, 1984). Manchester, Carcanet, 1986.

Other

Translator, *The Satin Slipper* by Paul Claudel (play broadcast BBC Radio 3, 1988).
Translator, *Le Cid* by Pierre Corneille (play broadcast BBC Radio 3, 1994).

*

Critical Studies: Introduction by the author to *Heart's Desire* in *Poetry Book Society Bulletin* (London), spring 1978; "Am I Doing It Right?" by the author, in *The Poet's Voice and Craft,* edited by C.B. McCully, Manchester, Carcanet, 1994.

Jeffrey Wainwright comments:

I do not think the responsibilities of poetry toward play, toward words as sound images that are only provisionally attached or supposedly free of referents, preclude an attempt to say something in a poem, however oblique, composite, or provisional. The strength that poetry—having absorbed the discursiveness of neoclassicism, the subjectivity of romanticism, and the fragmentation of modernism—now possesses is the opportunity to combine so many different aspects of experience, knowledge, and ways of speaking and to mix them in a way that is richer, more linguistically—that is to say humanly—diverse than any of the argufying discourses it might feed from. Descartes, a child's bedtime memories, geology and evolution (popularly apprehended), a bit of argot, and verbal playfulness can coexist here as in no other form outside the literary. Of course we strive to think our way through discrete subjects and to impose on ourselves the appropriate rules of enquiry and contemplation, and it is right that we do so. But that effort is part of the whole contingent jostle of our mental states that bear the impression of the language about us. The capacity of the poem to speak something of this mix of the mind is what interests me most at present, though not, I hope, as an interior monologue but as part of the exchanges in which we seek for sense.

*   *   *

"History, which is Eternal Life, is what / We need to celebrate." From his early poems on the battles of Waterloo and Jutland in *The Important Man* to "Thomas Müntzer" in *Heart's Desire,* Jeffrey Wainwright has been drawn to historical subjects. He treats them in a language sparse and plain enough to be easily underestimated. But Wainwright is a poet of vision. His poems show that social reality is everywhere a construct made by human beings and therefore capable of being changed by them, and his gift is in writing of the particular human activity or transaction in a way that reveals the larger power relations and social constructions that inform what is apparently personal. Without depending on rhetorical or analytical language, he can show that questions of politics, class, wealth, or power are not optional extras to understanding or simply the province of the committed but rather are implicit in all we do. It follows that the psychology of human actions, even theology, is all of a piece with politics, and Wainwright is as interested in states of mind, emotion, and beliefs as in material action.

Müntzer was a sixteenth-century Protestant reformer and leader in the Peasants' War. Reviled as a madman and liar for daring to propose that ''God made / All men free with his own blood shed,'' Wainwright shows Müntzer as one whose vision is inseparable from his struggle for justice, and the poem conveys the power of his exultant faith. Inspired by God's ''promised rainbow'' at the Battle of Frankenhausen, he says, ''I thought I could catch their bullets in my hands.'' Vision and courage like his are the preconditions of social justice but not the sufficient means, for what they confront in the poem is the material power of those who monopolize wealth and learning. One cannot catch bullets. Wainwright is not afraid to show the heroic visionary as sometimes ridiculous, self-punishing, and self-indulgent, perhaps necessarily so. The pursuit of paradise on earth is both idealism and action, both hopeful and terrible. As another poem, ''Before Battle,'' puts it, ''We wade so deep in our desire for good.''

The title sequence in *Heart's Desire* treats the same themes in more personal terms. Poems of love and grief show how we may ''escape ourselves alone,'' for love is the first move beyond the self. ''Heart's desire'' comes close to being an oxymoron, in which the most inward and personal are yoked to what points beyond the self, for desires must be formed and chosen. In forming them we may actually have to fight ''our dealing hearts and flying brain.'' These limpid lyrics are carefully woven out of the repetitions of a few nouns—''desire,'' ''dream,'' ''heart,'' ''light''—which, like all of the most common and familiar words in the language, bear the most complex charges of meaning. *Selected Poems* draws heavily on *Heart's Desire,* and in the handful of later poems collected in the volume Wainwright restates his preoccupations with love, death, and war and with the connections between what is supposedly private and what is public and historical.

Wainwright's spare language suggests utterance wrung from silence. It suggests human beings reduced to vulnerable simplicity and truthfulness by the pressure of immediate and particular circumstances, driven to speech by the need to become conscious of their situations. His socialism, too, is the stronger for its near reticence, its being allowed to emerge in the reader's own construction of the poem's juxtaposed images.

—R.J.C. Watt

WAKOSKI, Diane

Nationality: American. **Born:** Whittier, California, 3 August 1937. **Education:** University of California, Berkeley, B.A. in English 1960. **Family:** Married 1) S. Shepard Sherbell in 1965 (divorced 1967); 2) Michael Watterlond in 1973 (divorced 1975); 3) Robert J. Turney in 1982. **Career:** Clerk, British Book Centre, New York, 1960–63; English teacher, Junior High School 22, New York, 1963–66; lecturer, New School for Social Research, New York, 1969. Poet-in-residence, California Institute of Technology, Pasadena, spring 1972; University of Virginia, Charlottesville, autumn 1972–73; Willamette University Salem, Oregon, spring 1974; University of California,

Irvine, fall 1974; Hollins College, Virginia, 1974; Lake Forest College, Illinois, 1974; Colorado College, Colorado Springs, 1974; Macalester College, St. Paul, 1975; Michigan State University, East Lansing, spring 1975; University of Wisconsin, Madison, fall 1975; Whitman College, Walla Walla, Washington, fall 1976; University of Washington, Seattle, spring-summer 1977; University of Hawaii, Honolulu, fall 1978; and Emory University, Atlanta 1980–81. United States Information Agency lecturer, Romania, Hungary, and Yugoslavia, 1976. Since 1976, writer-in-residence, Michigan State University. **Awards:** Bread Loaf Writers Conference Robert Frost fellowship, 1966; Cassandra Foundation award, 1970; New York State Council on the Arts grant, 1971; Guggenheim grant, 1972; National Endowment for the Arts grant, 1973; Fulbright fellowship, 1984; Michigan Arts Council grant, 1988; Michigan Arts Foundation award, 1989; William Carlos Williams prize, 1989; University Distinguished Professorship, 1990; honorary member Phi Beta Kappa, 1998. **Address:** 607 Division, East Lansing, Michigan 48823, U.S.A.

PUBLICATIONS

Poetry

Coins and Coffins. New York, Hawk's Well Press, 1962.
Four Young Lady Poets, with others, edited by LeRoi Jones. New York, Totem-Corinth, 1962.
Dream Sheet. New York, Software Press, 1965.
Discrepancies and Apparitions. New York, Doubleday, 1966.
The George Washington Poems. New York, Riverrun Press, 1967.
Greed Parts One and Two. Los Angeles, Black Sparrow Press, 1968.
The Diamond Merchant. Cambridge, Massachusetts, Sans Souci Press, 1968.
Inside the Blood Factory. New York, Doubleday, 1968.
A Play and Two Poems, with Robert Kelly and Ron Loewinsohn. Los Angeles, Black Sparrow Press, 1968.
Thanking My Mother for Piano Lessons. Mount Horeb, Wisconsin, Perishable Press, 1969.
Greed Parts 3 and 4. Los Angeles, Black Sparrow Press, 1969.
The Moon Has a Complicated Geography. Palo Alto, California, Odda Tala Press, 1969.
The Magellanic Clouds. Los Angeles, Black Sparrow Press, 1970.
Greed Parts 5–7. Los Angeles, Black Sparrow Press, 1970.
The Lament of the Lady Bank Dick. Cambridge, Massachusetts, Sans Souci Press, 1970.
Love, You Big Fat Snail. San Francisco, Tenth Muse, 1970.
Black Dream Ditty for Billy ''The Kid'' Seen in Dr. Generosity's Bar Recruiting for Hell's Angels and Black Mafia. Los Angeles, Black Sparrow Press, 1970.
The Wise Men Drawn to Kneel in Wonder at the Fact So of Itself. Los Angeles, Black Sparrow Press, 1970.
Exorcism. Boston, My Dukes, 1971.
This Water Baby: For Tony. Santa Barbara, California, Unicorn Press. 1971.
On Barbara's Shore. Los Angeles, Black Sparrow Press, 1971.
The Motorcycle Betrayal Poems. New York, Simon and Schuster, 1971.
The Pumpkin Pie, Or Reassurances Are Always False, Tho We Love Them, Only Physics Counts. Los Angeles, Black Sparrow Press, 1972.

The Purple Finch Song. Mount Horeb, Wisconsin, Perishable Press, 1972.

Sometimes a Poet Will Hijack the Moon. Providence, Rhode Island, Burning Deck, 1972.

Smudging. Los Angeles, Black Sparrow Press, 1972.

The Owl and the Snake: A Fable. Mount Horeb, Wisconsin, Perishable Press, 1973.

Greed Parts 8, 9, 11. Los Angeles, Black Sparrow Press, 1973.

Dancing on the Grave of a Son of a Bitch. Los Angeles, Black Sparrow Press, 1973.

Stilllife: Michael, Silver, Flute, and Violets. Storrs, University of Connecticut, 1973.

Winter Sequences. Los Angeles, Black Sparrow Press, 1973.

Trilogy: Coins and Coffins, Discrepancies and Apparitions, The George Washington Poems. New York, Doubleday, 1974.

Looking for the King of Spain. Los Angeles, Black Sparrow Press, 1974.

The Wandering Tattler. Mount Horeb, Wisconsin, Perishable Press, 1974.

Abalone. Los Angeles, Black Sparrow Press, 1974.

Virtuoso Literature for Two and Four Hands. New York, Doubleday, 1975.

The Fable of the Lion and the Scorpion. Milwaukee, Pentagram Press, 1975.

Waiting for the King of Spain. Santa Barbara, California, Black Sparrow Press, 1976.

The Laguna Contract of Diane Wakoski. Madison, Wisconsin, Crepuscular Press, 1976.

George Washington's Camp Cups. Madison, Wisconsin, Red Ozier Press, 1976.

The Last Poem, with *Tough Company,* by Charles Bukowski. Santa Barbara, California, Black Sparrow Press, 1976.

The Ring. Santa Barbara, California, Black Sparrow Press, 1977.

Overnight Projects with Wood. Madison, Wisconsin, Red Ozier Press, 1977.

Spending Christmas with the Man from Receiving at Sears. Santa Barbara, California, Black Sparrow Press, 1977.

The Man Who Shook Hands. New York, Doubleday, 1978.

Pachelbel's Canon. Santa Barbara, California, Black Sparrow Press, 1978.

Trophies. Santa Barbara, California, Black Sparrow, Press, 1979.

Cap of Darkness, Including Looking for the King of Spain and Pachelbel's Canon. Santa Barbara, California, Black Sparrow Press, 1980.

Making a Sacher Torte: Nine Poems, Twelve Illustrations, with Ellen Lanyon. Mount Horeb, Wisconsin, Perishable Press, 1981.

Saturn's Rings. New York, Targ, 1982.

The Lady Who Drove Me to the Airport. Worcester, Massachusetts, Metacom Press, 1982.

Divers. N.p., Barbarian Press, 1982.

The Magician's Feastletters. Santa Barbara, California, Black Sparrow Press, 1982.

Looking for Beethoven in Las Vegas. New York, Red Ozier Press, 1983.

The Collected Greed: Parts 1–13. Santa Barbara, California, Black Sparrow Press, 1984.

The Managed World. New York, Red Ozier Press, 1985.

Why My Mother Likes Liberace. Tucson, Arizona, Sun/Gemini Press, 1985.

The Rings of Saturn. Santa Barbara, California, Black Sparrow Press, 1986.

Emerald Ice: Selected Poems 1962–1987. Santa Rosa, California, Black Sparrow Press, 1988.

The Archaeology of Movies and Books:

  Medea the Sorceress. Santa Rosa, California, Black Sparrow Press. 1991.

  Jason the Sailor. Santa Rosa, California, Black Sparrow Press, 1993.

  The Emerald City of Las Vegas. Santa Rosa, California, Black Sparrow Press, 1995.

  The Ice Queen. Tuscaloosa, Alabama, Parallel Editions, 1994.

Jason the Sailor. Santa Rosa, California, Black Sparrow Press, 1993.

The Emerald City of Las Vegas. Santa Rosa, California, Black Sparrow Press, 1995.

Argonaut Rose. Santa Rosa, California, Black Sparrow Press, 1998.

Trying to Convince Robert That a Woman He Doesn't Like Is Beautiful. Fresno, California, Wake Up Heavy Press, 2000.

The Butcher's Apron: New and Selected Poems. Santa Rosa, California, Black Sparrow Press, 2000.

Other

Form Is an Extension of Content. Los Angeles, Black Sparrow Press, 1972.

Creating a Personal Mythology. Los Angeles, Black Sparrow Press, 1975.

Variations on a Theme. Santa Barbara, California, Black Sparrow Press, 1976.

Toward a New Poetry. Ann Arbor, University of Michigan Press, 1980.

Unveilings, photographs by Lynn Stern. New York, Hudson Hill Press, 1989.

*

Manuscript Collection: University of Arizona Library, Tucson.

Critical Studies: "A Terrible War: A Conversation with Diane Wakoski" by Philip Gerber and Robert Gemmett, in *Far Point 4* (Winnipeg), Spring-Summer 1970; "Symposium on Diane Wakoski," in *Margins* (Milwaukee), January/February/March 1976; "Diane Wakoski's Personal Mythology: Dionysian Music, Created Presence" by Taffy Wynne Martin, in *Boundary 2* (Binghamton, New York), 10(3), Spring 1982; "Diane Wakoski: Disentangling the Woman from the Moon," in *Women as Mythmakers: Poetry and Visual Art by Twentieth-Century Women,* by Estella Lauter, Bloomington, Indiana University Press, 1984; "Wakoski's Poems: Moving Past Confession" by Linda W. Wagner, in *Still the Frame Holds,* edited by Sheila Roberts, San Bernardino, Borgo Press, 1993; "Language: The Poet as Master and Servant" by David Young, in *A Field Guide to Contemporary Poetry and Poetics,* edited by Stuart Friebert, David Walker, and Young, Oberlin, Ohio, Oberlin College, 1997; "Diane Wakoski" by Joanne Allred, in *Updating the Literary West,* Fort Worth, Texas, Western Literature Association, 1997; "Gods and Heroes Revised: Mythological Concepts of Masculinity in Contemporary Women's Poetry" by Christa Buschendorf, in *Amerikastudien* (Mainz, Germany), 43(4), 1998.

Diane Wakoski comments:

I think of myself as a narrative poet, a poet creating both a personal narrative and a personal mythology. I write long poems and emotional ones. My themes are loss, imprecise perception, justice, truth, the duality of the world, and the possibilities of magic, transformation, and the creation of beauty out of ugliness. My language is dramatic, oral, and as American as I can make it, with the appropriate plain surfaces and rich vocabulary. I am impatient with stupidity, bureaucracy, and organizations. Poetry, for me, is the supreme art of the individual using a huge, magnificent range of language to show how special, different, and wonderful his perceptions are. With verve and finesse. With discursive precision. And with utter contempt for pettiness of imagination or spirit.

* * *

One of the most important and controversial poets in the United States, Diane Wakoski is also one of the most prolific. Early appraisals of her work as a product of her association with the deep image poets of New York and later efforts to discount it as confessional or angry and self-pitying have all proved inadequate or unjust. Like Whitman, she uses the autobiographical self to create an American voice, but, like Wallace Stevens, she has made the human imagination the real subject of her work. In her efforts to show how the mind may work to acknowledge or create beauty in virtually any situation, she has found the storyteller's narration as useful as the image and the actor's use of masks and roles more telling than the cri de coeur. The self in her body of work has become an instrument to awaken the imaginative consciousness of others. Paradoxically, this intellectual poet, who makes no secret of her love for classical music or her wide-ranging interests in science and mythology, is well received, not because she "spills her guts" (to use Anne Sexton's famous phrase), but because her digressive style allows so many points of entry into the webs of thought and feeling she creates.

Wakoski has devised an idiosyncratic form of the long poem that allows her to be discursive or imagistic, factual or mythical, mundane or visionary, and to shift from one of these levels to another without losing her audience by relying primarily on common language and ordinary rhythms of speech. Varying line lengths are used to make melody, determine tempo, and draw attention to key words. In her series titled The Archaeology of Movies and Books, which uses the Greek tales of Jason and Medea and the city of Las Vegas as focal points, she includes not only her trademark poems but also intersperses excerpts from books on quantum physics and gambling. In addition, there are prose letters to presumably fictional men, Jonathan and Craig, wherein "Diane," as Postmistress, Moon Woman, Lady of the Light, can discuss anything she considers relevant to the poems or the quoted passages. In Argonaut Rose Wakoski links cafés from the Atlantic to the Pacific, Vienna to Point Dume, exploring a connection between Medea's story and her own decision as a teenage single mother to give up her children. As she reports telling one young man late in the book, "'human is anger, and also / living beyond anger.'" The books are Foucaultian not only in their digging for the personal and cultural elements (both classical and popular) that have shaped the consciousness of "Diane" as an American but also in laying bare the "discipline of self" she pursues so actively and self-consciously on our behalf.

From the beginning Wakoski has been interested in mythology as a source of identity, a target for critique, and an ongoing creative enterprise. Her best works have always engaged the most enduring problems of the relationships between ourselves and other human beings, nature, or the cultural ideas (such as justice, power, or beauty) that order human lives. One of her most ambitious books, The Collected Greed, containing poems that had appeared in chapbooks from 1968 to 1984, shows both the continuity of her poetic interests and the seriousness of her effort to develop a distinctive aesthetic stance (analogous to Baudelaire's "aesthetique du mal") capable of treating the less attractive sides of human lives. Her poems confronting "the man's world" in the historical figure of George Washington and her singular creation of a fantasy figure called the "King of Spain" are only the most obvious manifestations of a pervasive tendency to filter ordinary experience through the perspective of mythic characters. Although her later poems are still filled with real and imagined people, Wakoski has taken increasing pleasure in the phenomena of nature, for example, in the lady slipper that she loves "more than jewels or gold or men" or in the mushroom's inky "cap of darkness." (The latter is a phrase she has also used to refer to her invisible Athena-like helmet for combating the ghost of greed, which she defines as the inability to choose.) The title poem of her 1988 collection of selected poems, "Emerald Ice," presents a jewel the color of fresh basil with the "liquid hardness" of ice to epitomize her poetry of the previous thirty years.

Perhaps Wakoski's most impressive achievement has been to imagine a female self who is painfully aware of imperfections—her own as well as her culture's—but who can nonetheless celebrate the adequacy of the poet's imagination and also dream of a poetic "territory" that is "inexorably" her own. Wakoski's talent, courage, conscience, breadth of vision, and insight into human weakness seem likely to make this remarkably coherent oeuvre one of the hallmarks of our time.

—Estella Lauter

WALCOTT, Derek (Alton)

Nationality: British. **Born:** Castries, St. Lucia, West Indies, 23 January 1930. **Education:** St. Mary's College, Castries, 1941–47; University College of the West Indies, Mona, Jamaica, 1950–54, B.A. 1953. **Family:** Married 1) Fay Moyston in 1954 (divorced 1959), one son; 2) Margaret Ruth Maillard in 1962 (divorced), two daughters; 3) Norline Metivier in 1982 (divorced). **Career:** Teacher, St. Mary's College, Castries, 1947–50 and 1954, Grenada Boy's Secondary School, St. George's, 1953–54, and Jamaica College, Kingston, 1955; feature writer, *Public Opinion*, Kingston, 1956–57; feature writer, 1960–62, and drama critic, 1963–68, *Trinidad Guardian*, Port-of-Spain. Co-founder, St. Lucia Arts Guild, 1950, and Basement Theatre, Port-of-Spain; founding director, Little Carib Theatre Workshop (later Trinidad Theatre Workshop), 1959–76. Assistant professor of creative writing, 1981, and since 1985 visiting professor, Boston University. Visiting professor, Columbia University, New York, 1981, and Harvard University, Cambridge, Massachusetts, 1982, 1987. **Awards:** Rockefeller grant, 1957, 1966, and fellowship, 1958; Arts Advisory Council of Jamaica prize, 1960; Guinness award, 1961; Ingram Merrill Foundation grant, 1962; Borestone Mountain award, 1964, 1977; Royal Society of Literature Heinemann award, 1966, 1983; Cholmondeley award, 1969; Audrey Wood fellowship, 1969; Eugene O'Neill Foundation fellowship, 1969; Gold Hummingbird Medal (Trinidad), 1969; Obie award, for drama, 1971; Jock

Campbell award (*New Statesman*), 1974; Guggenheim award, 1977; *American Poetry Review* award, 1979; Welsh Arts Council International Writers prize, 1980; MacArthur fellowship, 1981; *Los Angeles Times* prize, 1986; Queen's Gold Medal for Poetry, 1988; Nobel prize for literature, 1992. D.Litt.: University of the West Indies, Mona, 1973. Fellow, Royal Society of Literature, 1966. O.B.E. (Officer, Order of the British Empire), 1972. **Member:** Honorary member, American Academy, 1979. **Agent:** Bridget Aschenberg, International Famous Agency, 1301 Avenue of The Americas, New York, New York 10019, U.S.A. **Address:** 165 Duke of Edinburgh Avenue, Diego Martin, Trinidad and Tobago.

PUBLICATIONS

Poetry

25 Poems. Port-of-Spain, Guardian Commercial Printery, 1948.
Epitaph for the Young: XII Cantos. Bridgetown, Barbados Advocate, 1949.
Poems. Kingston, Jamaica, City Printery, 1951.
In a Green Night: Poems 1948–1960. London, Cape, 1962.
Selected Poems. New York, Farrar Straus, 1964.
The Castaway and Other Poems. London, Cape, 1965.
The Gulf and Other Poems. London, Cape, 1969; as *The Gulf,* New York, Farrar Straus, 1970.
Another Life. New York, Farrar Straus, and London, Cape, 1973.
Sea Grapes. London, Cape, and New York, Farrar Straus, 1976.
The Star-Apple Kingdom. New York, Farrar Straus, 1979; London, Cape, 1980.
Selected Poetry, edited by Wayne Brown. London, Heinemann, 1981.
The Fortunate Traveller. New York, Farrar Straus, 1981; London, Faber, 1982.
The Caribbean Poetry of Derek Walcott and the Art of Romare Bearden. New York, Limited Editions Club, 1983.
Midsummer. New York, Farrar Straus, and London, Faber, 1984.
Collected Poems 1948–1984. New York, Farrar Straus, and London, Faber, 1986.
The Arkansas Testament. New York, Farrar Straus, 1987; London, Faber, 1988.
Omeros. New York, Farrar Straus, 1989.
Collected Poems. London, Faber, 1990.
Poems 1965–1980. London, Cape, 1992.
Derek Walcott: Selected Poems. Harlow, Longman, 1993.
The Bounty. London, Faber, and New York, Farrar Straus, 1997.

Plays

Cry for a Leader (produced St. Lucia, 1950).
Senza Alcun Sospetto (broadcast 1950; as *Paolo and Francesca,* produced St. Lucia, 1951?).
Henri Christophe: A Chronicle (also director: produced Castries, 1950; London, 1952). Bridgetown, Barbados Advocate, 1950.
Robin and Andrea, published in *Bim* (Christ Church, Barbados), December 1950.
Three Assassins (produced St. Lucia, 1951?).
The Price of Mercy (produced St. Lucia, 1951?).
Harry Dernier (as *Dernier,* broadcast 1952; as *Harry Dernier,* also director: produced Mona, 1952). Bridgetown, Barbados Advocate, 1952.

The Sea at Dauphin (produced Trinidad, 1954; London, 1960; New York, 1978). Mona, University College of the West Indies Extra-Mural Department, 1954; in *Dream on Monkey Mountain and Other Plays,* 1970.
Crossroads (produced Jamaica, 1954).
The Charlatan (also director: produced Mona, 1954?; revised version, music by Fred Hope and Rupert Dennison, produced Port-of-Spain, 1973; revised version, music by Galt MacDermot, produced Los Angeles, 1974; revised version produced Port-of-Spain, 1977).
The Wine of the Country (also director: produced Mona, 1956).
The Golden Lions (also director: produced Mona, 1956).
Ione: A Play with Music (produced Kingston, 1957). Mona, University College of the West Indies Extra-Mural Department, 1957.
Ti-Jean and His Brothers (produced Castries, 1957; revised version, also director: produced Port-of-Spain, 1958; Hanover, New Hampshire, 1971; also director: produced New York, 1972; London, 1986). Included in *Dream on Monkey Mountain and Other Plays,* 1970.
Drums and Colours (produced Port-of-Spain, 1958). Published in *Caribbean Quarterly* (Mona), vol. 7, nos. I and 2, 1961.
Malcochon; or, The Six in the Rain (produced Castries, 1959; as *Six in the Rain,* produced London, 1960; as *Malcochon,* produced New York, 1969). Included in *Dream on Monkey Mountain and Other Plays,* 1970.
Jourmard; or, A Comedy till the Last Minute (produced St. Lucia, 1959; New York, 1962).
Batai (carnival show; also director: produced Port-of-Spain, 1965).
Dream on Monkey Mountain (also director: produced Toronto, 1967; Waterford, Connecticut, 1969; New York, 1970). Included in *Dream on Monkey Mountain and Other Plays,* 1970.
Franklin: A Tale of the Islands (produced Georgetown, Guyana, 1969; revised version, also director: produced Port-of-Spain, 1973)
In a Fine Castle (also director: produced Mona, 1970; Los Angeles, 1972). Excerpt, as *Conscience of a Revolutionary,* published in *Express* (Port-of-Spain), 24 October 1971.
Dream on Monkey Mountain and Other Plays (includes *Ti-Jean and His Brothers, Malcochon, The Sea at Dauphin,* and the essay "What the Twilight Says"). New York, Farrar Straus, 1970; London, Cape, 1972.
The Joker of Seville, music by Galt MacDermot, adaptation of the play by Tirso de Molina (produced Port-of-Spain, 1974). With *O Babylon!,* New York, Farrar Straus, 1978; London, Cape, 1979.
O Babylon!, music by Galt MacDermot (also director: produced Port-of-Spain, 1976; London, 1988). With *The Joker of Seville,* New York, Farrar Straus, 1978; London, Cape, 1979.
Remembrance (also director: produced St. Croix, U.S. Virgin Islands, 1977; New York, 1979; London, 1980). With *Pantomime,* New York, Farrar Straus, 1980.
The Snow Queen (television play), excerpt published in *People* (Port-of-Spain), April 1977.
Pantomime (produced Port-of-Spain, 1978; London, 1979; Washington, D.C., 1981; New York, 1986). With *Remembrance,* New York, Farrar Straus, 1980.
Marie Laveau, music by Galt MacDermot (also director: produced St. Thomas, U.S. Virgin Islands, 1979). Excerpts published in *Trinidad and Tobago Review* (Tunapuna), Christmas 1979.
The Isle Is Full of Noises (produced Hartford, Connecticut, 1982).

Beef, No Chicken (produced New Haven, Connecticut, 1982; London, 1989). Included in *Three Plays,* 1986.

Three Plays (includes *The Last Carnival; Beef, No Chicken; A Branch of the Blue Nile*). New York, Farrar Straus, 1986.

The Odyssey: A Stage Version. New York, Farrar Straus, 1993.

The Capeman: A Musical, with Paul Simon (produced New York, 1997). New York, Farrar Straus, 1998.

Radio Plays: *Senza Alcun Sospetto,* 1950; *Dernier,* 1952.

Other

The Poet in the Theatre. London, Poetry Book Society, 1990.

The Antilles: Fragments of Epic Memory: The Nobel Lecture. London, Faber, 1993.

Homage to Robert Frost, with Joseph Brodsky and Seamus Heaney. New York, Farrar Straus, 1996.

What the Twilight Says: Essays. London, Faber, and New York, Farrar Straus, 1998.

Tiepolo's Hound. New York, Farrar Straus, 2000.

*

Bibliography: *Derek Walcott: An Annotated Bibliography of His Works* by Irma E. Goldstraw, New York, Garland, 1984.

Critical Studies: *Derek Walcott: Memory As Vision* by Edward Baugh, London, Longman, 1978; *Derek Walcott: Poet of the Islands* by Ned Thomas, Cardiff, Welsh Arts Council, 1980; *Derek Walcott* by Robert D. Hamner, Boston, Twayne, 1981; *Derek Walcott* by Harold Bloom, New York, Chelsea House, 1988; *The Art of Derek Walcott,* edited by Stewart Brown, Bridgend, Glamorgan, Seren, 1989; *Derek Walcott's Poetry: American Mimicry* by Rei Terrada, Boston, Northeastern University Press, 1992; *Critical Perspectives on Derek Walcott,* edited by Robert Hamner, Colorado Springs, Colorado, Three Continents Press, 1993; *Derek Walcott and West Indian Drama* by Bruce King, Oxford, Oxford University Press, 1995; "Derek Walcott and Alejo Carpentier: Nature, History, and the Caribbean Writer" by David Mikics, in *Magical Realism: Theory, History, Community,* edited by Lois Parkinson Zamora and Wendy B. Faris, Durham, North Carolina, Duke University Press, 1995; "Value Judgments on Art and the Question of Macho Attitudes: The Case of Derek Walcott" by Elaine Savory, in *Postcolonial Literatures: Achebe, Ngugi, Desai, Walcott,* edited by Michael Parker and Roger Starkey, New York, St. Martin's Press, 1995; *Caliban Takes Up His Pen: The Epic Poetry of Kamau Brathwaite, Derek Walcott, and Andrew Salkey* (dissertation) by Michelle Diane Derose, University of Iowa, 1996; "Derek Walcott's Poetics of Cultural Identity" by Steven P. Sondrup, in *Dedalus* (Lisbon, Portugal), 6, 1996; "Caliban or Crusoe? Straddling the Paradigms of 'Post'-Colonial Identity: Derek Walcott and Jean Arasanayagam" by Neloufer de Mel, in *Nationalism vs. Internationalism: (Inter)National Dimensions of Literatures in English,* edited by Wolfgang Zach and Ken L. Goodwin, Tubingen, Germany, Stauffenburg, 1996; *Epic of the Dispossessed: Derek Walcott's 'Omeros'* by Robert D. Hamner, Columbia, University of Missouri Press, 1997; Derek Walcott issue of *South Atlantic Quarterly* (Durham, North Carolina), 96(2), spring 1997; "Derek Walcott and the Value of Poetry" by J. Roger Kurtz, in *Rendezvous,* 31(2), spring 1997; *Taking Everything In: Poetic Personal and Poetic Voice in the Poems of Derek Walcott* (dissertation) by Anne L. Knee,

Ohio State University, 1998; "On the (False) Idea of Exile: Derek Walcott and Grace Nichols" by Aleid Fokkema, in *(Un)Writing Empire,* edited by Theo D'haen, Amsterdam, Rodopi, 1998; *Novelty in Verse: Bakhtin and the Multivocal Epics of Pound, H.D., and Walcott* (dissertation) by Mara Noelle Scanlon, University of Wisconsin, Madison, 1998; *Beating a Restless Drum: The Poetics of Kamau Brathwaite and Derek Walcott* by June Bobb, Trenton, New Jersey, Africa World Press, 1998; *Derek Walcott* by John Thieme, Manchester, England, Manchester University Press, 1999.

Theatrical Activities: Director: many of his own plays.

* * *

Derek Walcott's main concern has been to understand what he is and how he has been made by his family, his community, his life, and his choice of vocation as a poet. His poetry is often autobiographical, but other central concerns are the existence of evil, especially in the form of political tyranny and racial hatred, and his relationship to time, death, and God. Alongside poems about family, friends, loves, and a generation attempting to be artists are poems concerned with his estrangement—as a brown, English-speaking, Anglicized, Methodist-raised Protestant (with two English grandparents)—from the black, patois-speaking, French Catholic culture of Saint Lucia in the West Indies. For Walcott European art, particularly poetry, is a means to redeem the inarticulate and unformed society into which he was born, creating the self in the process of writing about the problems of being a Caribbean poet. But to become an artist and an English-language poet working in the tradition of European art and poetry, while it is his vocation and overriding purpose in life, by its very nature further distances him from the local community and life he would celebrate. He is also consciously in the tradition of Whitman, Neruda, Saint-John Perse, and others who asked what New World poetry might be. Many of Walcott's early poems attempt to see both sides of his racial heritage. Walcott's volumes after *The Castaway* note his increasing alienation from the actual society of Saint Lucia while presenting him as part of Caribbean history, whether representative of a group of artists, a generation discovering West Indianness, or the alienated, nonconforming "red" (colored) among blacks and whites. He often later returns to the same story, adding disillusionment, divorces, exile, nostalgia, and a larger body of acquaintances and places, commenting on the continuing injustices of a world in which the powerful enslave and suppress the weak.

Each of Walcott's books of poems has a title suggestive of some inner unity, and they appear to grow one from another. *The Gulf* includes poems representative of the gulf between North America and the Caribbean, the exile and the native, the poet and the masses, and Walcott's youthful hopes and his middle age. The feeling of being part of a community of Caribbean writers who, having to leave the region in order to survive, became estranged from the lands they write about is forcefully expressed in "Homecoming: Anse La Raye": "but never guessed you'd come / to know there are homecomings without home." Partly a Caribbean "Portrait of the Brown Artist as a Young Man," *Another Life* mythologizes a generation of artists who discovered the West Indies, opposed the philistines, and through creativity, sex, and love lived fully and memorably. As well as a virtuoso display in its range of verse forms, the poem is a magnificent tribute to an era when three friends of different social backgrounds could share the excitement of discovering themselves and culture. He complains that independence has not improved the position of the common worker or the artist, and he encloses "in this circle of hell" the ministers of culture "who explain to the peasant why he is African."

Walcott's highly complex, incantatory style changed in the mid-1970s, for a time becoming surprisingly taut and angry, with metaphor compressed into what appears to be plain speech. As he wrote in *Sea Grapes* more directly about local political issues and learned to trust his voice, the language of the verse also was transformed, coming closer to dialect and pidgin. His poems from *Sea Grapes* onward imply that he was forced from the Caribbean he loves because of his opposition to the black nationalist demand for a folk culture and the militant left's identification with the urban, proletarian masses. He views the former as reactionary, an attempt to create an artificial national culture, and he criticizes black power advocates and Marxists for importing foreign ideologies into the Caribbean and for glorifying illiteracy.

Walcott's writing has always been committed to a liberal humanism. "The Schooner *Flight*," an extended poem in eleven parts from *The Star-Apple Kingdom*, projects autobiography onto a story of "a rusty head sailor with sea-green eyes / that they nickname Shabine, the patois for / any red nigger," who travels throughout the Caribbean to escape both local black power politicians and his women. The poem laments the short-lived West Indian Federation (1958–62), with its concept of a Caribbean union that the politicians destroyed to raise themselves to local power. "Forest of Europe" sees analogies between oppression in America, the Caribbean, and Russia. Walcott's claim is that tyranny and oppression are common to human history—as witnessed by slavery, the destruction of American Indians, and the Nazi extermination of European Jewry—and that true poets speak against such regimes. The poets are united in telling the truth about oppression and celebrating the survival of the human spirit. Poets are a brotherhood, learning from one another their craft, their truths, and how to survive. Many poems are addressed to writers and create an international community.

The Fortunate Traveller includes a poetic meditation on differences between "North and South." While the globe cracks "like a begging bowl," the North destroys its surplus grain. Seeing parallels between the diasporas of Jews and blacks, Walcott plays with the notion that he might be part Jew, and he notes that even now in small-town Virginia the cashier avoids a black man's hand. It is an irony of his later work that the "red man" fleeing black dominance should, in the United States, find himself regarded as black. Several poems refer to and imitate American poetry and art as an alien culture, about which Walcott has feelings of ambivalence. In *Midsummer,* a powerful linked sequence of fifty-four poems in long Virgilian lines, Walcott returns to the tropics and compares his memories to what he has become: "And this is the lot of all wanderers, this is their fate, / that the more they wander, the more the world grows wide"; "You were distressed by your habitat, you shall not find peace / till you and your origins reconcile"; and "The midsummer sea, the hot pitchroad, this grass, these shacks that made me."

The contrasting influences of Caribbean and European culture have in the later poems become two worlds, at times two poetic manners, dictions, and personalities. They are two separate lives expressed formally in the two halves, "Here" and "Elsewhere," of *The Arkansas Testament*. The poems written in Saint Lucia use a wide variety of language as Walcott muses on his past, how loved landmarks of his nostalgia have changed and how he has failed to be the poet of his "home" and people. Now he is at home nowhere. The poems show Walcott using rhyme, tight form, and a public manner to create a thinking, less lyrical voice concerned with the relationship of politics, religion, and society. Injustice, racism, and imperialism exist as far apart in time and place as the Roman Empire, Hitler's Germany, Russia, and the United States. In Arkansas for a reading, he contrasts the American contribution to democracy to the haunted, historically shaped racial vision of its blacks, in which every white is a probable enemy. How can he be an American poet in a society that still celebrates the Confederate states and in which blacks still suffer such injustice? Oppression and injustice "will never end," for "the original sin is in our seed."

There have always been creative tensions in Walcott's work between the local and the universal, between varieties of English, and between the spoken word and literary form. This was originally expressed in the obvious polarities of race, color, place, culture, and heritage. There has been, however, a vision of the Caribbean as the inheritor of all of the world's major cultures, past and present, which exist side by side rather than in conflict. In this view the Caribbean makes a palette of experiences and models available to the artist considering the history, arts, and people of the region. *Epitaph for the Young* and the sonnet sequence "Tales of the Islands" (in *Selected Poems* and *In a Green Night*) are less imitations than ways of indicating that the classical past was similar to and remains contemporary with the Caribbean, just as *Another Life* shows the discovery of modern culture by a generation of Saint Lucians as similar to the outburst of modern art in late nineteenth-century Europe. Whereas others have tried to resist or reject what they consider imperialist, colonialist, or alien, Walcott has incorporated into his poetry most of what is available to him, thus enriching rather than limiting what it is to be a Caribbean poet.

Omeros is less an imitation Homeric epic than a long, fragmented modern poem unified by various stories, themes, and images and a self-conscious structure. The method is itself a statement about Caribbean art, history, and culture in which Walcott appears within a mixture of lyricism, autobiography, fiction, story, drama, comment, and satire. The best known internationally of Walcott's works, it is also one of the more difficult, for the focus unexpectedly shifts, the narrator changes, and the stories it tells unpredictably interweave, disappear, and return. It is about Saint Lucia (the Helen of the West Indies), its history, people, and landscape, about black Saint Lucians who have Homeric names and whose lives bear some resemblance to their archetypes, about the Afro-Caribbean dream of Africa, about the English who fought for and settled on the island, about the twilight and passing of the British Empire, about local politics, and about Walcott's own life and the nature of writing. The twelve-syllable rhymed lines move in and out of meter and proselike cadences within three-line stanzas in a variety of complex ways so as to mix the heightening of lyric poetry with the more relaxed tension of narrative. Although its stories span several continents and many periods of time and use a wide variety of kinds of English, *Omeros* is a further, grander development of Walcott's notion of using European art to give classical status to West Indian subject matter. The work also reflects Walcott's increasing concern with homecoming. Life is seen as an epic, an adventurous journey into the world, and an exile, and as in works such as his play *The Odyssey* there is a celebration of return, of coming home.

The Bounty celebrates life while lamenting that it ends in death. The bounty includes all gifts from God: the natural world and its creatures; the beauty of Saint Lucia and Trinidad; being a writer, the gift of poetry; even the ship *Bounty,* which brought breadfruit from the Pacific to the Caribbean. The poems are filled with unexpected analogies, the making of analogies being part of the bounty of all creation, as can be seen by the ant that will eventually help turn the dead into bread. ''The Bounty,'' a sequence of seven poems that form an elegy commemorating the poet's mother, comprises the first part of the volume. The second part, with thirty-seven poems, includes elegies to Joseph Brodsky and other friends who have died. At times Walcott seems in purgatory, with life in Boston being an exile from the paradise of Saint Lucia. With the building of a house in Saint Lucia, he has seemingly concluded his odyssey after years of wandering, but there are also confessions of continuing restlessness and desire.

Walcott's book *Tiepolo's Hound* consists of a long poem accompanied by twenty-six full-color reproductions of his own paintings. A verse biography of Camille Pissarro, who was born and raised in Saint Thomas but who moved to France to have a career as a painter and who became one of the best known of the impressionists, ''Tiepolo's Hound'' is also about the relationship of memory to art, the life of the artist, exile, the nature of modern art, and the relationship of Caribbean and other New World arts to Europe and to other cultures. That Pissarro's family were Jews who had fled to France from the Inquisition and then later fled an outburst of French anti-Semitism to settle in Saint Thomas illustrates Walcott's claim that the Caribbean is a mosaic of peoples, arts, and cultures, outcast from their origins, and that the region's cultural heritage includes the French along with the African. Walcott's concern is with the dog in a painting, which for him becomes a symbol of making great art from the ordinary world and which throughout the poem is echoed by and contrasted to actual dogs. Eventually the poet comes across a sick, starving mongrel in the Caribbean that he realizes should be the object of his love rather than the white hound (or muse) of the painting. Like many of Walcott's poems, ''Tiepolo's Hound'' moves from being a biography of Pissarro to focus on Walcott, concluding with his travels to Spain, Italy, and France and the new friends he has made. Walcott imagines Pissarro as, like himself, someone who discovers that his talents are in an art for which there is little local interest and with which he could not support himself. ''Tiepolo's Hound'' shows how the past crystallizes into images that become more and more distant from their origins and that take on a life of their own.

—Bruce King

WALDMAN, Anne (Lesley)

Nationality: American. **Born:** Millville, New Jersey, 2 April 1945. **Education:** Bennington College, Vermont, B.A. in English 1966. **Family:** Married Reed Eyre Bye in 1980 (divorced); one son. **Career:** Assistant director, 1966–68, and director, 1968–78, St. Mark's Church-in-the-Bowery Poetry Project, New York. Since 1974, founding co-director, with Allen Ginsberg, Jack Kerouac School of Disembodied Poetics, Naropa Institute, Boulder, Colorado. Associated with Stevens Institute of Technology, Hoboken, New Jersey, 1981–82, New College of California, San Francisco, 1982, York University, Toronto, 1984, Institute of American Indian Arts, Santa Fe, New Mexico, 1985, University of Maine, Portland, summer 1986, and Naropa Institute of Halifax, Nova Scotia, summers 1986, 1987. Co-director, Schule für Dichtung, Vienna, Austria, 1999. Member of the board of directors, Giorno Poetry Systems Institute,

and Eye and Ear Theatre, both New York. **Awards:** Dylan Thomas award, 1967; Cultural Artists grant, 1976; National Endowment for the Arts grant, 1980; Shelly Memorial award, 1996. **Address:** Naropa University, 2130 Arapahoe Avenue, Boulder, Colorado 80302, U.S.A.

PUBLICATIONS

Poetry

On the Wing. New York, Boke, 1967.
Giant Night. New York, Angel Hair, 1968.
O My Life! New York, Angel Hair, 1969.
Baby Breakdown. Indianapolis, Bobbs Merrill, 1970.
Up Through the Years. New York, Angel Hair, 1970.
Giant Night: Selected Poems. New York, Corinth, 1970.
Icy Rose. New York, Angel Hair, 1971.
No Hassles. New York, Kulchur, 1971.
Memorial Day, with Ted Berrigan. New York, Poetry Project, 1971.
Holy City. Privately printed, 1971.
Goodies from Anne Waldman. London, Strange Faeces Press, 1971.
Light and Shadow. Privately printed, 1972.
The West Indies Poems. New York, Boke, 1972.
Spin Off. Bolinas, California, Big Sky, 1972.
Self Portrait, with Joe Brainard. New York, Siamese Banana Press, 1973.
Life Notes: Selected Poems. Indianapolis, Bobbs Merrill, 1973.
The Contemplative Life. Detroit, Alternative Press, n.d.
Fast Speaking Woman. Detroit, Red Hanrahan Press, 1974.
Fast Speaking Woman and Other Chants. San Francisco, City Lights, 1975; revised edition, 1978.
Sun the Blond Out. Berkeley, California, Arif, 1975.
Journals and Dreams. New York, Stonehill, 1976.
Shaman. Boston, Munich, 1977.
4 Travels, with Reed Bye. New York, Sayonara, 1978.
To a Young Poet. Boston, White Raven, 1979.
Countries. West Branch, Iowa, Toothpaste Press, 1980.
Cabin. Calais, Vermont, Z Press, 1982.
First Baby Poems. Boulder, Colorado, Rocky Ledge, 1982; augmented edition, New York, Hyacinth Girls, 1983.
Make-Up on Empty Space. West Branch, Iowa, Toothpaste Press, 1984.
Skin Meat Bones. Minneapolis, Coffee House Press, 1985.
Invention. New York, Kulchur, 1985.
The Romance Thing. Flint, Michigan, Bamberger, 1987.
Blue Mosque. New York, United Artists, 1987.
Helping the Dreamer: Selected Poems 1966–1988. Minneapolis, Coffee House Press. 1989.
Not a Male Pseudonym. New York, Tender Buttons, 1990.
Lokapala. New York, Rocky Ledger, 1991.
Fait Accompli. N.p., Last Generation, 1992.
Iovis: All Is Full of Jove. Minneapolis, Coffee House Press, 1993.
Troubairitz. N.p., Fifth Planet Press, 1993.
Kill or Cure. New York, Penguin Poets, 1994.
Kin. New York, Granary Books, 1997.
Iovis II: All Is Full of Jove. Minneapolis, Minnesota, Coffee House Press, 1997.
Au Lit, Holy or Transgressions of the Maghreb, with Eleni Sikelianos and Laird Hunt. Erie, Colorado, Amokeproff Press, 1998.

Homage to Allen G. New York, Granary Books, 1998.
Young Manhattan, with Bill Berkson. Boulder, Colorado, Erudite Fangs, 1999.

Recordings: *John Giorno and Anne Waldman,* Giorno, 1978; *Fast Speaking Woman,* S Press Tapes, *Uh-Oh Plutonium!,* Hyacinth Girls, 1982; *Crack in the World,* Sounds True, 1986; *Made Up in Texas,* Paris, 1986.

Other

Editor, *The World Anthology: Poems from the St. Mark's Poetry Project,* and *Another World.* Indianapolis, Bobbs Merrill, 1969–71.
Editor, with Marilyn Webb, *Talking Poetics from Naropa Institute.* Boulder, Colorado, Shambala, 2 vols., 1978–79.
Editor, *Nice to See You: Homage to Ted Berrigan.* Minneapolis, Coffee House Press, 1988.
Editor, with Andrew Schelling, *Disembodied Poetics: Annals of the Jack Kerouac School.* Albuquerque, University of New Mexico Press, 1994.
Editor, *The Beat Book.* Boston, Shambhala, 1996.

Translator, with Andrew Schelling, *Songs of the Sons & Daughters of Buddha.* Boston, Shambhala, 1996.

*

Critical Studies: By Alicia Ostriker, in *Partisan Review* (New Brunswick, New Jersey), spring-summer 1971, and *Parnassus* (New York), fall-winter, 1974; by Gerard Malanga, in *Poetry* (Chicago), January 1974; by Richard Morris, in *Margins* (Milwaukee, Wisconsin), October-November 1974; by Aram Saroyan, in *New York Times Book Review,* April 1976; *The Beats: Literary Bohemians in Postwar America* edited by Ann Charters, Detroit, Gale, 2 vols., 1983; "Shamanic Ritual As Poetic Model: The Case of Maria Sabine and Anne Waldman" by Daniel C. Noel, in *Journal of Ritual Studies* (Pittsburgh, Pennsylvania), 1(1), winter 1987; by Lee Bartlett in his *Talking Poetry: Conversations in the Workshop with Contemporary Poets,* Albuquerque, University of New Mexico Press, 1987; Anne Waldman issue of *Talisman* (Jersey City, New Jersey), 13, fall 1994; "Gods and Heroes Revised: Mythological Concepts of Masculinity in Contemporary Women's Poetry" by Christa Buschendorf, in *Amerikastudien* (Mainz, Germany), 43(4), 1998; "Iovis Omnia Plena" by Alice Notley, in *Chicago Review* (Chicago), 44(1), 1998.

*   *   *

"Poetry should be a joy . . . a pleasure . . . . The whole thing of the suffering poet . . . it's so unnecessary. You can get so intense that you can't produce. There's work to be done." Whatever else it may or may not do, Anne Waldman's poetry keeps this promise. Most often her poems find their inspiration and shape in an implicitly celebratory display of the diverse pleasures of things—life in New York, world travel, sex and friendships, even her own fantasies and dreams. The high-spiritedness, rich humor, and eager openness that sustain her work derive less from the idealism than from the affluence of the 1960s. But then she cannot help it if she is lucky. What matters is that she improves upon her luck, for the imaginative persuasiveness of her best poems recalls Whitman's insight that "the most affluent man is he that confronts all the shows he sees by equivalents out of the stronger wealth of himself." For Waldman poetry justifies itself as the show of life, and the pleasures it offers are inherent in the process whereby the impulses of life are released into living forms.

If Waldman dismisses the "suffering poet," it is almost always in the spirit of one for whom suffering can properly show itself only indirectly, as the elusive and finally unappeasable passion that both nourishes and chastens the poet's creative play—"There is work to be done." Nowhere is this element in her work more crucial than in her best-known poem, "Fast Speaking Woman," which goes like this, with very little variation of pattern, for nearly six hundred lines:

> I'm a witch woman
> I'm a beggar woman
> I'm a shade woman
> I'm a shadow woman
> I'm a leaf woman
> I'm a leaping woman

This remarkable piece could never hold our attention for six lines, let alone six hundred, were it not for its creative recklessness, at once desperate and playful. This is chiefly a matter of Waldman's splendidly uninhibited aesthetic opportunism, so that each line seems generated by some underplayed excess of the matter and movement of preceding ones. The imaginative power of the poem inheres in the immediacy of its language yet remains apart, its freshness not just unharmed but actually enriched by any show it has made.

"Fast Speaking Woman" is something of a tour de force, but even in its extremity it is characteristic of the aims and methods of Waldman's work. She is committed to the classic American mode of open-form, or projective, verse, though, despite the idiomatic pungency and speed of her language, the music of her poetry is closer to that of song than of speech. This is especially true of the "chants" in the collection *Fast Speaking Woman,* but even her less regular pieces, the best of which, I think, are in *Baby Breakdown* ("I Am Not a Woman" and "Conversational Poem") and, especially, *Journals and Dreams* ("Blues Cadet," "Mirror Meditation," "My Lady," and "When the World Was Steady"), strike the ear not as speech but as snatches of song stitched into even more various musical patterns, a variousness in music that answers to and resolves a rich contradictoriness of feeling and perception.

From its beginnings the open-form tradition has rested on some form of belief in the correspondence between inner and outer worlds, but one must go back to Whitman to find precedent for Waldman's astonishingly unstudied practical faith that discoveries of the self are revelations of a world and vice versa. The epigraph to "Fast Speaking Woman" is "I is other," and what counts in her work is less the tenacity than the nonchalance of her exploration of the truth of this. She neither apologizes for her egotism nor worries about her otherness. Coming from any poet this is exhilarating, but coming from a woman it is truly revolutionary. The word "woman" appears in nearly every line of "Fast Speaking Woman," yet it receives little rhythmic or semantic stress. It is treated simply as the natural point of departure and return for each excursus of self, as if nothing better could or need be imagined than to create a world in terms of a woman's acts of self-realization. The form of the poem gives the game away more unmistakably than others, but it is far from the only one to play that game with extraordinary inventiveness and grace.

—John Hinchey

WALDROP, Rosmarie

Also wrote as Rosmarie Keith. **Nationality:** American. **Born:** Kitzingen/Main, Germany, 24 August 1935. **Education:** Universität Würzburg, 1954–56; Université d'Aix-Marseilles, 1956–57; Universität Freiburg, 1957–58; University of Michigan, 1959–66, M.A. 1960, Ph.D. 1966. **Family:** Married Keith Waldrop in 1959. **Career:** Assistant professor, Wesleyan University, Middletown, Connecticut, 1964–70; poet-in-the-schools, Rhode Island, 1971–72; visiting poet, Southeastern Massachusetts University, 1977; visiting lecturer, 1977–78, and visiting associate professor, 1983, 1990–91, 1993, Brown University, Providence, Rhode Island; visiting lecturer, Tufts University, Medford, Massachusetts, 1979–81. Since 1968 co-editor and publisher, Burning Deck Press. Co-founder, playwright, and director, Wastepaper Theater, Providence, 1973–83. **Awards:** Hopwood award, 1963; Humboldt award, 1970–71, 1975; Howard award, 1974–75; Translation Center award, 1978; National Endowment for the Arts fellowship, 1980, 1994; Rhode Island Governor's Arts award, 1988; Fund for Poetry, 1990; PEN Book of the Month Club Citation in Translation, 1991; DAAD Berlin Artists Program, 1993; Landon Translation award, 1994; Lila Wallace-Reader's Digest award, 1999–2001. **Address:** 71 Elmgrove Avenue, Providence, Rhode Island 02906, U.S.A.

PUBLICATIONS

Poetry

The Aggressive Ways of the Casual Stranger. New York, Random House, 1972.
The Road Is Everywhere or Stop This Body. Columbia, Missouri, Open Places, 1978.
When They Have Senses. Providence, Burning Deck, 1980.
Nothing Has Changed. Windsor, Vermont, Awede Press, 1981.
Differences for Four Hands. Philadelphia, Singing Horse Press, 1984.
Streets Enough to Welcome Snow. Barrytown, New York, Station Hill, 1986.
The Reproduction of Profiles. New York, New Directions, 1987.
Peculiar Motions. Berkeley, California, Kelsey Street Press, 1990.
Lawn of Excluded Middle. New York, Tender Buttons, 1993.
A Key into the Language of America. New York, New Directions, 1994.
Another Language: Selected Poems. Jersey City, New Jersey, Talisman House, 1997.
Well Well Reality, with Keith Waldrop. Sausalito, California, Post-Apollo Press, 1998.
Split Infinites. Philadelphia, Singing Horse Press, 1998.
Reluctant Gravities. New York, New Directions, 1999.

Novels

The Hanky of Pippin's Daughter. Barrytown, New York, Station Hill, 1986.
A Form/of Taking/It All. Barrytown, New York, Station Hill, 1990.

Other

Against Language? The Hague, Netherlands, Mouton, 1971

Editor, with Keith Waldrop, *A Century in Two Decades.* Providence, Burning Deck, 1982.

Translator, *Bodies and Shadows* by Peter Weiss. New York, Delacorte, 1969.
Translator, *Elya* by Edmond Jabès. Bolinas, California, Tree Books, 1973.
Translator, *The Book of Questions* by Edmond Jabès. Middletown, Connecticut, Wesleyan University Press, 1976.
Translator, *The Book of Yukel/Return to the Book* (volumes II and III of *The Book of Questions*) by Edmond Jabès. Middletown, Connecticut, Wesleyan University Press, 1983.
Translator, *Yaël/Elya/Aely* (volumes IV, V, and VI of *The Book of Questions*) by Edmond Jabès. Middletown, Connecticut, Wesleyan University Press, 1984.
Translator, with Harriett Watts, *The Vienna Group: Six Major Austrian Poets.* Barrytown, New York, Station Hill Press, 1985.
Translator, *Paul Celan, Collected Prose.* Manchester, Carcanet, and New York, Sheep Meadow, 1986
Translator, with Tod Kabza, *Archeology of the Mother: A Selection of Poems by Alain Veinstein.* Peterborough, Cambridgeshire, Spectacular Diseases, 1986.
Translator, *The Book of Dialogue* by Edmond Jabès. Middletown, Connecticut, Wesleyan University Press, 1987.
Translator, *The Book of Shares* by Edmond Jabès. Chicago, University of Chicago Press, 1989.
Translator, *Some Thing Black* by Jacques Roubaud. Elmwood Park, Illinois, Dalkey Archive Press, 1990.
Translator, *The Book of Resemblances* by Edmond Jabès. Middletown, Connecticut, Wesleyan University Press, 1990.
Translator, *Intimations The Desert* (volume II of *The Book of Resemblances*) by Edmond Jabès. Middletown, Connecticut, Wesleyan University Press, 1991.
Translator, *From the Book to the Book* by Edmond Jabès. Middletown, Connecticut, Wesleyan University Press, 1991.
Translator, *Rimbaud in Abyssinia* by Alain Borer. New York, William Morrow, 1991.
Translator, *Dawn* by Joseph Guglielmi. Peterborough, Cambridgeshire, Spectacular Diseases, 1991.
Translator, *The Ineffaceable The Unperceived* (volume III of *The Book of Resemblances*) by Edmond Jabès. Middletown, Connecticut, Wesleyan University Press, 1992.
Translator, *The Book of Margins* by Edmond Jabès. Chicago, University of Chicago Press, 1993.
Translator, *A Foreigner Carrying in the Crook of His Arm a Tiny Book* by Edmond Jabès. Middletown, Connecticut, Wesleyan University Press, 1993.
Translator, *Heiligenanstalt* by Friederike Mayröcker. Providence, Burning Deck, 1994.
Translator, *The Plurality of Worlds of Lewis* by Jacques Roubaud. Normal, Illinois, Dalkey Archive Press, 1995.
Translator, *Mountains in Berlin: Selected Poems by Elke Erb.* Providence, Burning Deck, 1995.
Translator, *The Little Book of Unsuspected Subversion* by Edmond Jabès. Stanford, California, Stanford University Press, 1996.
Translator, with Harriett Watts, *With Each Clouded Peak* by Friederike Mayröcker. Los Angeles, Sun and Moon Press, 1998.

*

Critical Studies: "The Ambition of Senses" by Craig Watson, in *Montemora #8* (New York), 1981; "Non-Euclidean Narrative Combustion" by Joan Retallack, in *Parnassus* (New York), summer 1988; interview with Edward Foster, in *Talisman* (Jersey City, New Jersey), 6, spring 1991; "Syntextural Investigations" by Jonathan Monroe, in *Diacritics 26,* fall/winter 1996; *Wittgenstein's Ladder* by Marjorie Perloff, Chicago, University of Chicago Press, 1996; "Rosmarie Waldrop's Shorter American Memory" by Kornelia Freitag, in *The Construction and Contestation of American Cultures and Identities in the Early National Period,* edited by Udeo Hebel, Heidelberg, Verlag, 1999.

*   *   *

Rosmarie Waldrop began her writing life with a little book of prose called *Against Language?* This was her manifesto to the world that language, such as we use every day and pour into our daily newspapers and novels and poems, was exhausted. When the fund of words and expressions is exhausted, the mind itself goes brittle, social vision shrinks, and life is more or less imprisoned in the triteness of a used-up consciousness. It is the duty of writers, she tells us in this manifesto, to go to the edges of language, to work out what is for now the unsayable, the unknowable, and to revive speech. Here is how she puts her argument in the conclusion:

> . . . the poets who are seriously dissatisfied with our conventions of language (and do not just take this attitude as an excuse or because it is fashionable) are working at the borders of the unsayable and unknowable. They are trying to explore the areas bordering pure spirit or the void, unformed matter or energy, and their realm of 'things' considered as having a self-sufficient being alien to man. And since our language is our world, changing the language seems a possibility of changing our ways of seeing and thus to some extent changing what is seeable and knowable.

This attractive program was set forth some few years before the public became aware of language poetry, the school of American poets who studied Wittgenstein and Derrida and pursued the notion that language is a finite realm within a broader human consciousness. It could be said that these poets wanted to explore the rest of consciousness beyond "the city of words." The theory goes that, if the speaker deranges syntax—Rimbaud's suggestion—and explodes grammatical structure—in which sexism, white bias, imperialist master class illusions, and subject-object dichotomies (Cartesian thinking) are concealed—it is possible to liberate the tongue so as to enter the hinterlands of knowledge obscured by the walls of conventional language.

These absolutes are not new to poetry. Emerson spoke of an attitude to nature that would free the voices within and restore wholeness of vision. Pound's notion of the image as a glimpse at the gods in nature and Olson's "human universe" prepared the way for Waldrop's pronouncements. She tells us that poetry has always borrowed from the arts and music, but she adds that it must also borrow from autism and mathematics so as to gain the ground that consciousness otherwise excludes. Autism gives us a window into daydreams, and mathematics is "pure relation."

The result is an eerie mode of lyric, in prose poem format, in which subtleties are uncovered, as in Waldrop's squibs in *The Reproduction of Profiles:*

You told me, if something is not used it is meaningless, and took my temperature which I had thought to save for a more difficult day. In the mirror, every night, the same face, a bit more threadbare, a dress worn too long. The moon was out in the cold, along with the restless, dissatisfied wind that seemed to change the location of the sycamores. I expected reproaches because I had mentioned the word love, but you only accused me of stealing your pencil, and sadness disappeared with sense. You made a ceremony out of holding your head in your hands because, you said, it could not be contained in itself.

Implicit here and elsewhere in Waldrop's poetry is the principle that things are alive in their own dynamics and that they make relations and forms from an imagination in nature. The poet is witness, an imitator of natural creativity, not a copyist. By subduing some of the instrumental logic of the self, nature regains its original autonomy and instructs the human soul.

Beneath Waldrop and her language peers is a steadily building faith in nature religion. The codes in which they write this new logic of expression, with its strange Piranesi staircases going nowhere, rising and falling in goalless antiprogress, suggest a new, secular Latin prayer book, a priesthood of nature mystics in America. The more we hear of "reenchantment" in contemporary discourse, the easier it is to believe that language mysticism is the means by which the old spells, visions, and reverence for otherness are returning to mind.

Consider the following passage in "Overshadowed," from *The Aggressive Ways of the Casual Stranger:*

Spidery running
a phantom child
all the dead are eager
to be remembered
the concave world where
souls smelled
and pleasure came in a net full of fish
glassy
desolate

This is a lyric at the edge, but it is also about something, Waldrop's childhood years growing up in Germany. We get glimpses here and there of cold, removed parents, the German rituals that are now tainted in retrospect by visions of the Holocaust. Waldrop does not write the equivalent of Sylvia Plath's "Daddy," which draws its fire from conventional logic. Instead, she writes from several ongoing conscious tracks of thought, picking a few details from one, merging them with a few from another. The style is similar to the recollective mode of Lyn Hejinian and to Leslie Scalopino, Susan Howe, and other language masters.

Here is another sample of the mode from "Menstruation," also in *The Aggressive Ways of the Casual Stranger:*

My appetite's for waking
chill crystals in the clouds
pebble seeds
Flaubert devoted years to
accumulation of details

worthless
next to a bare wall
I insist on living
with words
vicarious birth vicarious existence
each month my womb cries
its mouth swollen

What one often hears in Waldrop's poetry are the words ''sleep,'' ''waiting,'' ''mist,'' ''grey,'' and ''solitude'' and mathematical terms like ''equation'' and ''correspondence.'' But she also has a fine, inventive ear for new phrases, like these from ''Kind Regards,'' included in *Streets Enough to Welcome Snow:*

Your air of kind regards
kind randomness
of a museum
canvas sneakers
along with raspberry lips

*

lately you say I've had an awkward
pull
toward the past tense
my remarks renovate
details in oil

If there is a plot, it is the regaining of Waldrop's own autonomy in a marriage, the working up of a separate consciousness with its own vision of the world. She writes often about an Amerindian woman named Saltwoman, her alter ego. The surprising function of this figure is that Waldrop makes her from the kind of sleep talk she writes, and it holds our attention. It works perhaps more deeply and strongly than conventional taste will sometimes want to admit.

—Paul Christensen

WALKER, Ted

Nationality: British. **Born:** Edward Joseph Walker, Lancing, Sussex, 28 November 1934. **Education:** Steyning Grammar School; St. John's College, Cambridge, B.A. (honors) in modern languages 1956, M.A. 1977. **Military Service:** Royal Naval Volunteer Reserve. **Family:** Married 1) Lorna Benfell in 1956 (died 1987), two daughters and two sons; 2) Audrey Joan Hicks in 1988. **Career:** Assistant French master, North Paddington Secondary School, 1956–58; head of French, Southall Technical School, Middlesex, 1958–63; head of modern languages, William Fletcher School, Bognor Regis, Sussex, 1963–65; assistant master of French, Spanish, and English literature, and head of general studies, Chichester High School, Sussex, 1965–70. Poet-in-residence, assistant professor, associate professor, and professor of creative writing, 1971–92, and since 1992 emeritus professor, New England College, Arundel, Sussex. Founder with John Cotton and editor since 1962, *Priapus,* Berkhamsted, Hertfordshire. **Awards:** Eric Gregory award, 1964; Cholmondeley award, 1966; Alice Hunt Bartlett prize, 1968; Arts Council travel grant, 1978; P.E.N. Ackerley prize, for autobiography, 1983; Campion prize;

Society of Authors travel bursary; Southern Arts Society literature bursary. D.Litt.: Southampton University, 1995. Fellow, Royal Society of Literature. **Agent:** David Higham Associates Ltd., 5–8 Lower John Street, London W1R 4HA. **Address:** Argyll House, The Square, Eastergate, Chichester, West Sussex PO20 6UP, England.

PUBLICATIONS

Poetry

Those Other Growths. Leeds, Northern House, 1964.
Fox on a Barn Door: Poems 1963–4. London, Cape, 1965; New York, Braziller, 1966.
The Solitaries: Poems 1964–5. London, Cape, and New York, Braziller, 1967.
The Night Bathers: Poems 1966–8. London, Cape, 1970.
Gloves to the Hangman: Poems 1969–72. London, Cape, 1973.
Burning the Ivy: Poems 1973–77. London, Cape, 1978.
The Lion's Cavalcade (for children). London, Cape, 1980.
Hands at a Live Fire: Selected Poems. London, Secker and Warburg, 1987.
The Last of England. London, Cape, 1992.
Grandad's Seagulls (for children). London, Blackie Children's, 1994.
Mangoes on the Moon: Poems 1992–1998. London, London Magazine Editions, 1999.

Recording: *Modern Poetry,* with John Wain, BFA, 1972.

Plays

Radio Scripts: *The Final Miracle,* 1979; *The Third Person,* 1980; *The Trotliners,* 1981; *A Hill in Southern England,* 1982; *Before Crufts,* 1983; *A Portrait of William Plomer,* 1983; *Big Jim and the Figaro Club,* 1987.

Television Plays: *Big Jim and the Figaro Club,* 1980 (film), 1981 (series); *The Gaffer,* 1983; *A Family Man,* 1984; *Marshwood Vale; The Gaffer; Barbed Water; Wind in the Willows,* 1995.

Short Stories

You've Never Heard Me Sing: Selected Short Stories 1968–1983. London, Heinemann, 1985.

Other

The High Path (autobiography). London, Routledge, 1985.
In Spain. London, Secker and Warburg, 1987.

*

Manuscript Collection: Lockwood Memorial Library, State University of New York, Buffalo.

Critical Study: ''Ted Walker, Seamus Heaney, and Kenneth White: Three New Poets'' by John Press, in *Southern Review* (Baton Rouge, Louisiana), 5, 1969.

Ted Walker comments:

My poetry seems to deal with loneliness and isolation. Since I live in the country, my imagery tends to be rural and even regional. My territory is Sussex and the Sussex coast.

* * *

Much of Ted Walker's poetry is in the great tradition of English nature poetry, which stretches in modern times from Wordsworth to Ted Hughes. In Walker's case it is a poetry that, while one of close and accurate detail, looks beyond external nature to observe parallels and draw implications related to the human condition: "regret / the vacant seemliness / by which we live. For which we lost / that proper, vital gift of waste" ("Crocuses"). The territory of Walker's poetry is the seashore, with its inlets and breakwaters, and the isolated, lonely areas of the English countryside, including the creatures that inhabit them. He draws a parallel between the ultimate solitude of the human soul when confronting the universe in which it finds itself and the dissatisfaction of humans in contrast to the aptness and completeness of the rest of the animal kingdom in relation to their environment. The isolation of the situations depicted in the poems reflects man looking both within himself and out toward "that God I won't believe in" for something beyond immediate experience to meet spiritual loneliness. It is not without significance that the title of one of Walker's early collections is *The Solitaries.*

In *The Night Bathers* there is a shift of emphasis. The same qualities of precise observation and craftsmanship are present, but the poet has grown older, and the past is beginning to haunt the present and enrich and give it depth of meaning. The title poem explores the poet's relationship with his son as a reflection of the relationship between himself and his own father:

when he was young to understand
why, momently out of the night
and purposeful beyond the reach
of all his worry, I had swum
deep into banks of sea-fret
too far to have to answer him.

There also is a clearly observable growth in Walker's technical mastery, which allows him to relax his earlier tight control and use a language closer to the colloquial. This development continues in his collection *Gloves to the Hangman,* including such poems as "Letter to Barbados," which has an ease of expression that gives the work an immediacy of reception without any diminution of strength: "Dear far-off brother. Thank you for yours, / And for the gift you send of little shells."

In the collection *Burning the Ivy* we find Walker using his skill to write poetry of a more directly personal dimension. The personae are abandoned, and a more vulnerable area of feeling and emotion is explored and expressed, often tellingly so as in the elegy for William Plomer, "After the Funeral," and the poem for Paul Coltman on his retirement, "For His Old English Master." There is a feeling of getting nearer to the truth of things here than in the earlier assaults on the universal design of things, splendid as the earlier works are.

In *It could be that it was Walker's striving toward this truth that led him to all but abandon poetry for prose and drama, as he did with such splendid and moving effect in his autobiographical The High Path* and in a television play about his father. He has published relatively little poetry since *Burning the Ivy,* but after several years of poetic silence Walker emerged in 1999 with a welcome collection, *Mangoes on the Moon.* He prefaces the new book with

When uninspired, a poet should stay mute;
My muse went AWOL, so I pawned my lute.

The first part of this Lazarus-like collection consists of poems written about his stay in Australia. In them he catches with his old precision the matey, relaxed comradeship of the hearty outdoor, beachside, camping, barbie life he enjoyed there:

Weeks later, content to be lazing
By savage waters, laid back as hippies,
We browse—not according to the clock,
But whenever burnt-meat barbie smells
Bring the memory of hunger back.

The second part of the book is full of Walker's movingly and deeply felt memories of his first wife, his father, and his grandchildren and of old friends, as in "For Andrew Young":

While your Woodbine ash lengthened and drooped
But would not fall to soil your clerical chest,
ignorance burned inside me; and stray wisps
Of stupidity dried my discomforted lips.
'What do you know of Prehistory?' you offered.

As shown in "For His Dead Wife," Walker's ability to rouse deep emotions and feelings is still with him:

Forgive me, that you looked the bride
You'd been; who slept at peace, alone,
Warm after love.

He has not lost his touch nor his writing hand its cunning.

—John Cotton

WALLACE-CRABBE, Chris(topher Keith)

Nationality: Australian. **Born:** Richmond, Victoria, 6 May 1934. **Education:** Scotch College; University of Melbourne, Victoria, B.A. 1956, M.A. (Lockie Fellow) 1964; Yale University, New Haven, Connecticut (Harkness Fellow), 1965–67. **Military Service:** Royal Australian Air Force, 1952–53. **Family:** Married Sophie Feil; one son and one daughter. **Career:** Junior technical officer, Royal Mint, Melbourne, 1951–52; journalist in Victoria, 1953–54; clerical officer, Gas and Fuel Corporation, 1954–55; teacher, Haileybury College, Brighton, Victoria, 1957–58. Senior lecturer in English, 1968–76, reader in English, from 1976, since 1988 professor of English, and since 1989 director of the Australian Centre, University of Melbourne. Visiting senior fellow, Linacre College, Oxford, 1983–84; visiting professor of Australian studies, Harvard University, Cambridge, Massachusetts, 1988–90. **Awards:** Farmer's prize, 1969;

Grace Leven prize, 1986; Dublin prize, 1987. **Address:** 910 Drummond Street, North Carlton, Victoria 3054, Australia.

PUBLICATIONS

Poetry

No Glass Houses. Melbourne, Ravenswood Press, 1956.
The Music of Division. Sydney, Angus and Robertson, 1959.
Eight Metropolitan Poems. Adelaide, Australian Letters, 1962.
In Light and Darkness. Sydney, Angus and Robertson, 1964.
The Rebel General. Sydney, Angus and Robertson, 1967.
Where the Wind Came. Sydney, Angus and Robertson, 1971.
Selected Poems 1955–1972. Sydney, Angus and Robertson, 1973.
Act in the Noon. Melbourne, Cotswold Press, 1974.
The Shapes of Gallipoli. Melbourne, Cotswold Press, 1975.
The Foundations of Joy. Sydney, Angus and Robertson, 1976.
The Emotions Are Not Skilled Workers. Sydney, Angus and Robertson, 1979; London, Angus and Robertson, 1980.
The Amorous Cannibal and Other Poems. Oxford, Oxford University Press, 1985.
I'm Deadly Serious. Oxford, Oxford University Press, 1988.
For Crying Out Loud. Oxford and New York, Oxford University Press, 1990.
Rungs of Time. Oxford and New York, Oxford University Press, 1993.
Selected Poems, 1956–1994. Oxford and New York, Oxford University Press, 1995.
Whirling. Oxford and New York, Oxford University Press, 1998.

Recording: *Chris Wallace-Crabbe Reads from His Own Work,* University of Queensland Press, 1973.

Novel

Splinters. Adelaide, Rigby, 1981.

Other

Melbourne or the Bush: Essays on Australian Literature and Society. Sydney, Angus and Robertson, 1973.
Toil and Spin: Two Directions in Modern Poetry. Melbourne, Hutchinson, 1979.
Three Absences in Australian Writing. Townsville, Queensland, Foundation for Australian Literature Studies, 1983.
Poetry and Belief. Hobart, University of Tasmania, 1990.
Falling into Language. Melbourne and New York, Oxford University Press, 1990.

Editor, *Six Voices: Contemporary Australian Poets.* Sydney, Angus and Robertson, 1963; Westport, Connecticut, Greenwood Press, 1979.
Editor, *The Australian Nationalists.* Melbourne, Oxford University Press, 1971.
Editor, *Australian Poetry '71.* Sydney, Angus and Robertson, 1971.
Editor, *The Golden Apples of the Sun: Twentieth Century Australian Poetry.* Melbourne, Melbourne University Press, 1980.
Editor, *Clubbing of the Gunfire: 101 Australian War Poems.* Melbourne, Melbourne University Press, 1984.
Editor, with others, *Multicultural Australia: The Challenge of Change.* Newham, Victoria, Scribe, 1991.
Editor, with Kerry Fattley, *From the Republic of Conscience: An International Anthology of Poetry.* Flemington, Victoria, Aird Books, with Amnesty International, 1992.
Editor, *Author, Author!* Melbourne, Oxford University Press, 1998.
Editor, with Hal Bolitho, *Approaching Australia.* Cambridge, Massachusetts, Harvard Chair of Australian Studies, 1998.

*

Critical Studies: ''A Modest Radiance'' by E.A.M. Colman, in *Westerly* (Nedlands, Western Australia), 1969; ''To Move in Light: The Poetry of Chris Wallace-Crabbe'' by Peter Steele, in *Meanjin* (Melbourne), 1970; ''Transition and Advance'' by James Tulip, in *Southerly* (Sydney), 1972; ''Stop Laughing, This Is Serious'' by Jennifer Strauss, in *Townsville,* 1990; ''Leisure and Grief: The Recent Poetry of Chris Wallace-Crabbe'' by David McCooey, in *Australian Literary Studies* (St. Lucia, Queensland, Australia), 17(4), October 1996; interview with Paul Kane, in *Antipodes* (Austin, Texas), 12(2), December 1998; in *In Other Words: Interviews with Australian Poets,* by Barbara Williams, Amsterdam, Rodopi, 1998.

Chris Wallace-Crabbe comments:

(1985) My early poetry explored the nature of social order and of intellectual coherence in a world in which religious sanctions seemed irrelevant; my concern at this stage was to make poetic structures that testified to the strength that was inherent in human reason and (hopefully) to humorous resilience as a way of meeting the contradictions of experience. Later, finding my early poetry rather too stiff, rigorous, and explicit, I came to seek more supple rhythms and more autonomous images—a poetry that was more fully charged with the physical world. And a poetry that questioned the English language.

Over the past few years I have increasingly been trying to come to terms with violence: political, personal, and intrapersonal. I am interested in the paradox that we tend most profoundly to worship vitality for its own sake, while we are bound at the same time to deplore such vitality as manifests itself in the form of violence. Poetry, like other constructive activities, issues from forces that are potentially destructive. The self, when it is most vital, is not reducible to a moral agent. These are the central concerns that I have been trying to dramatize in my recent poems. At the same time, inevitably, my poetry has been growing less formal, less architecturally shaped, and more sinuous, more shifting, more various in its effects and directions. Psychomachia concerns me greatly, especially in its lyrical forms.

My current attitude to poetry is best summed up in A.D. Hope's haunting line ''What questions are there that we fail to ask?'' That, and my sense that the language I use subverts itself, but not nearly so fast as it subverts me. My latest poems, family romances of mental structure, play out despairing comedies with words that keep falling away. How, but with wit, can one survive as ''the gene's blind way of making another gene''? And another lyric answers, ''Ah, that would be telling / Just as he always does.''

*   *   *

Chris Wallace-Crabbe's volume of poems *The Music of Division* confirmed the promise first indicated by the appearance of his work in Australian literary journals beginning in the early 1950s. This work was unusual in an Australian context in that it avoided the overindulgence and exuberance normally associated with a young writer. *The Music of Division* exhibited a coolness and a quality of apparent detachment that looked forward to the early 1960s rather than back to the more romantic 1950s of Australian poetry. In this first volume the most notable poems are based upon observation of political forces, particularly as they implicate individual personalities in the tension between public and private responses. This preoccupation is developed and expanded in later books such as *In Light and Darkness* and *The Rebel General* and is perhaps taken to its furthest stretch in the prizewinning long poem "Blood Is the Water," included in the volume *Where the Wind Came.*

Such a continuous preoccupation with and development of the themes of power and political motivation have, interestingly enough, led Wallace-Crabbe away from an earlier detachment to an increasing relaxation and a sense of full humanness in his writing. He himself has written, "After stoical-formalist beginnings, I seek a poetry of Romantic fullness and humanity. I want to see how far lyrical, Dionysian impulses can be released and expressed without loss of intelligence." His *Selected Poems 1955–1972,* published in his fortieth year, would seem to mark a significant watershed in his work. It is worth noting that this volume commences with a series of "Meditations," which imply that the poet is reaching out in new directions, perhaps more fully exploring the vein of lyricism that has glittered tantalizingly throughout the volumes that preceded it and are abridged into it. The almost ruthless severity of the abridgment still indicates, however, that Wallace-Crabbe exercises a powerful and severe intelligence in the organization of his compositions.

After publishing his collection *The Emotions Are Not Skilled Workers* in 1979, Wallace-Crabbe in the early 1980s appeared to fall back into a generational gap, his work apparently overshadowed by that of a newly maturing generation that included John Tranter and Alan Wearne, poets who found different solutions to the subjects of political and social interaction so clearly at the center of Wallace-Crabbe's poetic concerns. But in his collections *The Amorous Cannibal* and *I'm Deadly Serious,* both published in England rather than Australia, Wallace-Crabbe reestablished his personal voice with a new precision and élan. Perhaps in addressing himself to a larger English-speaking audience he found personal quiddity to be as important as lean, precise observation. Certainly in these newer poems the old public/private, Dionysian/Apollonian tensions persist, but they do so in terms of a more relaxed, even sensuous delight in the uncanny way language invents us. The result loses none of the large-scale view but rather enhances it through a sort of integration with a vernacular never before quite so accepted or so well placed. Prior to the publication of his *Selected Poems, 1956–1994* by Oxford University Press in 1995, his two previous collections, *For Crying Out Loud* and *Rungs of Time,* consolidated this sense of newfound creative energy and ways of balancing urbanity and knowledgeability with an attentive eye for the enjoyableness of things as well as their awfulness. The later *Whirling* (1998) seems to generate a further momentum, but the profound elegy "A Threshold for My Son" throws its shadows over the book, tempering its robustness with an underlying vulnerability.

—Thomas W. Shapcott

WARD, Diane (Lee)

Nationality: American. **Born:** Washington, D.C., 9 November 1956. **Education:** Corcoran School of Art, Washington, D.C., 1975–77. **Family:** Married Chris Hauty in 1988; two sons. **Awards:** National Endowment for the Arts fellowship, 1980; San Francisco State Poetry Center's Book of the Year award, 1984; California Arts Council fellowship in literature, 1988–89. **Address:** 1013B 21st Street, Santa Monica, California 90403, U.S.A.

PUBLICATIONS

Poetry

On Duke Ellington's Birthday. Privately published, 1977.
Trop-i-dom. Washington, D.C., Jawbone, 1977.
The Light American. Washington, D.C., Jawbone, 1978.
Theory of Emotion. New York, Segue/O Press, 1978.
Never without One. New York, Roof Books, 1984.
Relation. New York, Roof Books, 1989.
Imaginary Movie. Elmwood, Connecticut, Potes and Poets Press, 1992.
Exhibition. Elmwood, Connecticut, Potes and Poets Press, 1995.
Human Ceiling. New York, Roof Books, 1995.

*

Diane Ward comments:

I was trained as a visual artist and approach my writing—imagery, form, process—informed by the tools and concerns I developed as a visual artist.

My early, and continuing, influences are the writings of a variety of visual artists, Gertrude Stein, Virginia Woolf, Francis Ponge, Gaston Bachelard, William Burroughs, the New York school poets (especially Bernadette Mayer, Alice Notley, Clark Coolidge). These are only a handful of the many writers/artists who have continued to be a presence in my writing/life.

*   *   *

Diane Ward is often associated with the language poetry group. Her work possesses most of the external attributes of language-oriented poetry, including an attention to the material quality of words, a highly experimental and self-reflexive stance, and the use of an essentially abstract, quasi-expository rhetoric. Unlike many language poets, however, Ward does not focus primarily on the act of writing itself but instead conceives of poetry as a means of accounting for the complex dialectics of language and desire. "Absolution," from her 1989 collection *Relation,* begins,

My arms are given
clean away, heaven forgiven.

I live in arms, touched
by sentence, treble up, sentence.

Reaching out across the states,
statements, clear mess of states.

Perhaps the most pervasive influence on Ward's poetry is that of Gertrude Stein, whose cubist poetic prose in *Tender Buttons* prefigures Ward's abstract descriptions of private experience as well as her constant blurring of the distinction between the psychological and the physical world. More generally, Ward seeks to account for the complex verbal and gestural strategies used by people in relating to one another, or simply to themselves, in seemingly casual situations. Her explorations of the human consciousness, however, are far from being merely anecdotal, and her most particular talent lies in a cold-eyed investigation of basic patterns of behavior and of the multiple correspondences between inner and outer landscapes, private and public architectures. "Pronouncing," a prose poem contained in *Never without One,* is a typical example of Ward's antilyrical landscapes, in which her interest in the meanders of the human mind is often subordinated to an analysis of medium and perspective:

> Arrested modesty fades once out on the town. An iced commodity a motion fanning out over every position a body could play. Order replaces disorder. A direction cuddles up to a slice of this magnet world. The chord continues climbing. Total elevators lay down to cherish the thought.

Ward's poems are characterized by a sense of what Jean Baudrillard has called "the loss of the real," a condition in which the old modernist tension between reality and illusion, the "authentic" original and the copy, has been dissipated. As a result they depict a world in which the self, confronted with "window oddities painted like painting," is liable to mistake "the forest for trees and tree-like devices." "Pronouncing" is also emblematic of Ward's rejection of narrative linearity. Like most of her poems, it consists of a series of discrete but interrelated moments forming a continuous verbal choreography much like the "on-call improvised emotional flow" described in "Immediate Content Recognition," which stands as both an illustration of and a commentary on Ward's poetic project:

> an aura surrounds each phrase stumbled through
> not like bubbles around words in comic strips
> or even thought bubbles
> or static on the radio
> more of a disembodied mouth making perfect choreographed
>   words without sounds and each twitch
> twist and frown composed for the moment

The screen tests of Ward's collection *Imaginary Movie* suggest that the demise of traditional categories of representation, as well as the problem of artistic composition and its relationship to an increasingly elusive "real," have not ceased to occupy her mind. By putting the accent on the changing present of human consciousness, the instability of thought, and the impossibility of attending to a single representation of the same phenomenon, they further testify to Ward's desire to represent reality in a state of flux. Ultimately, they create a performative moment in which the process of perception itself is their subject matter:

> noxious clouds on the horizon
> same blue gray everyday
> now war *is* like tv:

> inversion presses down

> the hills' perspective disappears
> until you forget they were
> what was ever there

—Michel Delville

WARREN, Rosanna

Nationality: American. **Born:** Fairfield, Connecticut, 27 July 1953. **Education:** Accademia delle Belle Arti, Rome, 1971–72; Skowhegan School of Painting and Sculpture, 1974; New York Studio School, 1975; Yale University, B.A. (summa cum laude) 1976; Johns Hopkins University, M.A. 1980. **Family:** Married Stephen Scully in 1981; two daughters and one stepson. **Career:** Private art teacher, 1977–78; clerical worker, St. Martin's Press, New York, 1977–78; assistant professor of English, Vanderbilt University, Nashville, 1981–82. Visiting assistant professor, 1982–88, and since 1989 assistant professor of English and modern foreign languages, Boston University. Poet-in-residence, Robert Frost Farm, 1990. **Awards:** Yaddo fellowship, 1980; Nation Discovery Award in Poetry, 92nd Street YMHA-YWCA, New York, 1980; Newton Arts Council award, 1983; Ingram Merrill grant for poetry, 1983, 1993; Guggenheim fellowship, 1985–86; grant, American Council of Learned Societies, 1989–90; Lavan Younger Poets prize, Academy of American Poets, 1992; Lamont Poetry prize, Academy of American Poets, 1993; Lila Wallace Writers' Fund award, 1994; Witter Bynner prize, Academy of Arts and Letters, 1994. **Address:** University Professors Program, Boston University, 745 Commonwealth Avenue, Boston, Massachusetts 02215, U.S.A.

PUBLICATIONS

Poetry

Snow Day. Winston-Salem, North Carolina, Palaemon Press, 1981.
Each Leaf Shines Separate. New York, Norton, 1984.
Stained Glass. New York, Norton, 1993.

Novel

The Joey Story. New York, Random House, 1963.

Other

Editor, *The Art of Translation: Voices from the Field.* Boston, Northeastern University Press, 1989.
Editor, with William Arrowsmith, *Cuttlefish Bones,* by Eugenio Montale. New York, Norton, 1993.
Editor, with Stephen Scully, *Suppliant Women,* by Euripides. New York, Oxford University Press, 1995.
Editor, with William Arrowsmith, *Satura: 1962–1970,* by Eugenio Montale. New York, Norton, 1998.

*

Critical Studies: By Andre Lefevere, in *Comparative Literature Studies,* 28(1), 1991; by Larry Moffi, in *Poet Lore,* 89(1), spring 1994.

*   *   *

Rosanna Warren's poetry is essentially personal. She is an elegiac poet. Her poems are often described as somber and austere, with an air of resignation, although they are not at all passive. Warren's primary theme, with variations, is death and mourning, and she uses literature, historical and current events, photographs, and the fine arts as inspiration for her work. Her preoccupation with death is a means of revealing how utterly fragile, yet resilient life is.

In ''Song'' readers find themselves encased in the quiet and solemn beauty of a graveyard:

Let bland sky
be your canopy. Fringe the bedspread with the wall of
    lapsing stones.
Here faith has cut
in upright granite ''Meet me in Heaven'' at the grave of
    each child lost the same year,
three, buried here a century ago . . .

I turn away. I shall meet you nowhere, in no transfig-
    ured hour.
On soft matted soil
blueberries crawl, each separate berry a small, not globe of
    tinctured sun
Crushed on the tongue
it releases a pang of flesh. Tender flesh, slipped from its
    skin preserves its blue hear
down my throat.

Some of Warren's poems are simple elegies. ''The Broken Pot,'' one of her more uplifting works, is a tribute to her mother, Eleanor Clark, author of *Rome and a Villa.* The poem ends,

receding colonnades scooped out of solitude
the internal city a habitable beauty subsisting on
    disappearance
monument to which I turn now with my tribute of broken
    shards, my symbolon
from the original vessel in whose clay we share.

Other poems are genuinely sorrowful yet not at all mournful. Instead, they convey a feeling of vague sadness. For example, the poem ''Noon'' is filled with the activities and sounds of a summer day yet leaves readers feeling hollow and melancholic:

Someone's hammer raps the air,
    duet with its own knocked echo. Here is the precise
dead heart of the living day, the hollow core, the pit
around which light thickens, and we eat.

It may be that the subject of many of Warren's mournful poems is her father, the novelist and poet Robert Penn Warren. Thus, in the elegy ''From New Hampshire,'' published in the collection *Stained Glass,* Warren is clearly mourning someone she loves. Yet the sadness associated with her mourning seems light and bearable:

I think you have taken a long late evening walk
Your heavy shoes glisten with dew
I hear your footsteps pause on the dirt road
and I know you are picking out
the dark mass of the sleeping mountain from the dark
mass of night and testing the heaviness of each.

In certain poems, however, her experience of death is expressed in stark, almost physical, terms. Thus, ''Elegist'' reads,

More marrow to suck, more elegies to whistle through the
digestive tract. So help me God to another dollop of death,
come on strong with the gravy and black eyed peas . . .
preserve the drool in ink: Death since you nourish me, I'll
flatter you inordinately. Consumers both, with claws cocked
and molars prompt at the fresh-dug grave, reaper and elegist,
my throat an open sepulchre, my tongue forever groping
forever young.

Warren has also found subjects for her poems in the tragedies of the news. ''The Cost,'' for example, is about a baby found in a trash can at the city zoo, and ''Child Model'' describes the mother of a young Eskimo boy. Following the depiction of a sealskin grave–crèche, the poet concludes by speaking directly to the deceased child:

We clutch you, ancient child: we need to think you're saved as
if one face unmarred in Kodachrome rescued all others who
have died ugly, bruised, disqualified.

Warren's haunting ''Departure'' reminds us of past terrors:

''I can only speak to people who-''
Unspeaking, unspoken, the full-breasted woman tied to a
    dead man upside down
stands center stage with a lamp in her hand, shed
    kerosene glow
on the marching band.
That's Cupid, the dark swarf who tightens her rope; this is
    art, this is love, that's the classical shape
of proscenium arch. This is Germany, May '32 ''can only
    speak to people who
already carry, consciously or unconsciously, within them-''

In a review of *Stained Glass* the critic Robert Shaw observed that he was so accustomed to gritting his teeth at unwarranted cheerfulness in poems that he was actually searching Warren's poems for a ''silver lining.'' Indeed, her poems may exude a tragic conception of life, but they are by no means fundamentally nihilistic or pessimistic. As a poet of death and mourning, Warren is nevertheless fully aware of the magnificent richness of life.

—Christine Miner Minderovic

WARSH, Lewis (David)

Nationality: American. **Born:** New York City, 9 November 1944.
Education: City College of New York, B.A. 1966, M.A. 1975.
Family: Married Bernadette Mayer in 1975 (divorced 1985); two

daughters and one son. **Career:** Teacher, St. Marks Church-in-the-Bowery Poetry Project, New York, 1973–75 and 1992–94, Naropa Institute, Boulder, Colorado, 1978, New England College, Henniker, New Hampshire, 1979–80, Queens College, Queens, New York, 1984–86, and Fairleigh Dickinson University, Teaneck, New Jersey, 1987–88. Since 1984 adjunct associate professor, Long Island University, Brooklyn, New York. Editor, *Angel Hair* magazine and Angel Hair Books, New York, 1966–77, and *Boston Eagle*, 1972–74. Since 1977 editor and publisher, *United Artists* magazine and United Artists Books, New York. **Awards:** Poets Foundation award, 1972; Creative Artists Public Service grant, 1978; National Endowment for the Arts grant, 1980; Coordinating Council of Literary Magazines Editor's Fellowship award, 1981; New York Foundation of the Arts award, 1988; Fund for Poetry grant, 1994. **Address:** 701 President Street, Brooklyn, New York 11215, U.S.A.

PUBLICATIONS

Poetry

The Suicide Rates. Eugene, Oregon, Toad Press, 1967.
Highjacking. New York, Boke, 1968.
Moving through Air. New York, Angel Hair, 1968.
Chicago, with Tom Clark. New York, Angel Hair, 1969.
Two Poems. Windsor, Ontario, Orange Bear Reader, 1971.
Dreaming As One. New York, Corinth, 1971.
Long Distance. London, Ferry Press, 1971.
Today. New York, Adventures in Poetry, 1974.
Immediate Surrounding. Lancaster, Massachusetts, Other, 1974.
Blue Heaven. New York, Kulchur, 1978.
Hives. New York, United Artists, 1979.
Methods of Birth Control. College Park, Maryland, Sun and Moon, 1983.
The Corset. Detroit, In Camera, 1986.
Information from the Surface of Venus. New York, United Artists, 1987.
Avenue of Escape. New York, Long New Books, 1995.
Money under the Table. San Francisco, Trip Street Press, 1997.

Novels

Agnes and Sally. New York, Fiction Collective, 1984.
A Free Man. Los Angeles, Sun and Moon Press, 1990.

Other

Part of My History. Toronto, Coach House Press, 1972.
The Maharajah's Son (autobiography). New York, Angel Hair, 1977.

Editor, *Another Smashed Pinecone,* by Bernadette Mayer. Brooklyn, New York, United Artists Books, 1998.

Translator, *Night of Loveless Nights,* by Robert Desnos. New York, Ant's Forefoot, 1973.

*

Manuscript Collections: New York University Library; San Diego State University Library.

Critical Study: Lewis Warsh issue of *Talisman* (Jersey City, New Jersey), 18, fall 1998

*　　*　　*

In the last line of "Brothers Levernoch," Lewis Warsh writes, "People who are discontented shock me." The voice that speaks in his poems is almost always content. Although the poems are personal, or seem to be, they are not "confessional" in the usual sense of the term. Warsh is the calm and detached observer. Immediate autobiography, things remembered from long ago, newspaper reports, accounts of his family—all enter on equal footing. The most common events assert themselves as worthy of complete and careful attention. The writing itself is almost colorless. There is nothing flashy or stylish. The careless reader will miss the mastery.

Warsh seldom commits a generalization. One of the largest collections of his work, *Blue Heaven* (the title presumably taken from the song), opens with a poem about the pleasures and dangers of thinking:

> Thoughts make men strangers
> and create great moments of urgency,
> as well as nervousness, when a thought
> moves you to wake up and light a cigarette
> and lie back on pillow, content
> in thinking, in playing the thought through,
> that's the only way for it to die!

To the extent that he thinks in his poetry, Warsh is willing to let his thought have this quality, as one of the media, along with perception, of existence. The danger of thought is that it can become so absorbing that one misses other important things—the cigarette, the pillow. After a certain point he is willing to let everything go to its proper death. In "Single File," he writes, "All my poems / no center / everything scattered / many voices trailing off / empty illusions / of emotions and thoughts / incredible pipe dreams / disappearing / beneath waves." To many poets this would be cause for despair, but to Warsh it is merely the way things are.

Inside these limits, in which irony is raised to a total sense of the world, he is capable of immense variety. He does not play endless variations on two or three successful themes or forms. He can be epigrammatic or tightly imagistic, but he is also effective in looser, anecdotal poems. He has written some strong prose poems, and some of his poems seem to cry out for a musical setting: "At times like this / we leave our fears behind and enter / a world / where what we see / doesn't exist, where words / dance out along the curb / like playful cubs / and the heart sings on / —to High Heavens—regardless."

There are no poems that can be called typical, a remarkable fact in a poet who might best be called a formalist. Though he does not work in conventional forms, his poems turn again and again on the recognition of formal connections. This can be seen perhaps most clearly in a poem like "Footnote," which is an exploration of the formal relationship between the Percy Shelley-Harriet Westbrook-Thomas Hogg circle and the Friedrich Nietzsche-Lou Salome-Paul Ree circle. An awareness of relationships of this kind, on both the most minute and on the grandest scales, generates the energy of his poetry. It is one of the truest kinds of intelligence, and the pleasure of reading Warsh's work is that he generously makes his intelligence available.

—Don Byrd

WATERMAN, Andrew (John)

Nationality: British. **Born:** London, 28 May 1940. **Education:** Trinity School, Croydon, 1951–57; University of Leicester, 1963–66, B.A. (honors) in English 1966; Worcester College, Oxford, 1966–68. **Family:** Married Angela Marilyn Hannah Eagle in 1982 (second marriage; dissolved 1985); one son. **Career:** Lecturer, 1968–78, and since 1978 senior lecturer in English, University of Ulster, Coleraine. **Awards:** Cholmondeley award, 1977; Arvon Foundation prize, 1981. **Address:** 15 Hazelbank Road, Coleraine, County Londonderry, Northern Ireland.

PUBLICATIONS

Poetry

Last Fruit. Hitchin, Hertfordshire, Mandeville Press, 1974.
Living Room. London, Marvell Press, 1974.
From the Other Country. Manchester, Carcanet, 1977.
Over the Wall. Manchester, Carcanet, 1980.
Out for the Elements. Manchester, Carcanet, 1981.
Selected Poems. Manchester, Carcanet, 1986.
In the Planetarium. Manchester, Carcanet, 1990.
The End of the Pier Show. Manchester, Carcanet, 1995.

Other

Editor, *The Poetry of Chess.* London, Anvil Press Poetry, 1981.

*

Critical Studies: "Mature Students: Peter Scupham and Andrew Waterman," in *British Poetry since 1970* edited by Peter Jones and Michael Schmidt, Manchester, Carcanet, and New York, Persea, 1980, and "Waterman and the Elements," in *Helix 17* (Ivanhoe, Australia), 1984, both by Neil Powell.

Andrew Waterman comments:

Some of one's poems are personal and autobiographical; others range into themes or times remote from one's immediate life and circumstances. From my own point of view, however, all I write feels finally of a piece, however disparate the superficial materials. England, where I grew up and which I frequently revisit, and Ireland, where I have lived and worked since 1968, both supply my poetry with settings and subject material. I find a poem begins with a sort of fermenting in one's mind of some detail or occasion, perhaps in itself trivial, anything from a view across a field or supermarket to a scrap of conversation or personal incident or encounter, until a pressure evolves so that one feels nagged to get out pencil and paper and start jotting, crossing out, trying again; and only the labor of working itself discovers what, if anything, is there that can be won into poetry. One tries to intuit the right rhythm and shape, pick up imaginative glints as one works. The process is comparable not to working from a blueprint

but to starting with material like a sculptor with a mass of stone and a sense of a harmonious finished statue that might, with luck, be conjured from this material. At the start one is not sure of the exact form of the finished work—only that it is possible. At the end the rubble one has chipped away litters one's draft sheets, and the poem is "finished," a contraption of words that floats free of one, with luck embodying a pattern of feelings and perceptions that will speak to and please other people, an imaginative world that imaginations can inhabit.

*   *   *

Andrew Waterman's poetry has a sharp awareness of the typical and the commonplace, particularly when he is quoting and inventing the direct speech of others. In his own voice the same colloquial language often holds people at a distance, reducing them to types: "an old dear yammering," "Annes, Pams, Joyces." Such long perspectives have their use, for they enable him to take in big sweeps of history and social change, and the wider the view the more convincing he becomes. When dealing with particular issues, such as the peasant fixities being swept away by the television and computer society, Waterman strikes familiar attitudes reminiscent of Leavis in a tone like Larkin's. But when more ambitious, he can be powerfully discursive and subtly symbolical at the same time, as in "Playing through Old Games of Chess" in *Over the Wall,* where one hundred years of change are counterpointed against chess games and history is shown as the product of a complex logic of interlocking choices. In *From the Other Country,* his first book-length collection, the articulate stops just short of the prolix, and he is prepared to tolerate the occasional flaccid phrase (an airplane, for example, is a "hushed cylinder of steel") for the sake of broad and bold effects.

Outspoken in both his criticism and his liking of "stunted" Northern Ireland, Waterman claims the privileges of both insider and outsider, "among, not of, all this." He can have it both ways, not just in allegiance to place and culture but also to class, occupation, and friends. In many poems about the tangled wastes of love, selfishness, and cross-purposes, he writes of emotion indulged but also mistrusted ("fatuities of poignancy"), or he combines the wistful with the ruthless ("growth is a process perpetually / of abandonment, amputation"). He evokes a well-dramatized instability here, several feeling and thinking sensibilities inhabiting the same self, generated by a language that veers abruptly between the racy and the poetically heightened. He is closer to American confessional verse than many of his British contemporaries are willing to go, and his personal poems include some of his greatest successes as well as failures.

The inanimate world in Waterman has a life of its own ("furniture settling ton by ton into fitted carpets"). Lines suggesting the autonomy of nature are often used to show up the human world, for the charm of the nonhuman is that it promises meaning but seldom grants it, unlike his acquaintances "touting problems, all queueing for further transfusions." Poems in *Over the Wall* thrive energetically on unashamed rage at the nuisance value of friends whose "dingy mouths keep working" and who "terribly foul / your bed" or of more predictable targets like the "write-off in residence" and the "Hairy Scrotum School" of poets. But Waterman is now a master of form, wittily controlling stanzas that, though elaborate, have naturalness of rhythm and freedom of movement.

The title poem of *Out for the Elements* marks Waterman's full poetic maturity. In a stanza form based loosely on the sonnet, he sustains for fifteen hundred lines an intelligent, discursive meditation in a manner that stands comparison with Auden's ''Letter to Lord Byron.'' In this spacious and immensely readable poem there is for the first time room for his various subjects—social observation, Northern Ireland, autobiography—happily to coexist, held together by a mellower and more flexible tone than before. Without posturing he can keep ''faith with the bruised common heart.''

—R.J.C. Watt

WATERS, Michael (George)

Nationality: American. **Born:** New York City, 23 November 1949. **Education:** State University of New York, Brockport, 1967–70, 1971–72, B.A. 1971, M.A. 1972; University of Nottingham, England, 1970–71; University of Iowa, Iowa City, 1972–74, M.F.A. 1974; Ohio University, Athens, 1975–77, Ph.D. 1977. **Family:** Married 1) Robin Irwin 1972 (divorced 1992), one daughter; 2) Mihaela Moscaliuc in 1999. **Career:** Instructor, Ohio University, Athens, 1977–78; visiting professor, University of Athens, Greece, 1981–82; writer-in-residence, Sweet Briar College, Sweet Briar, Virginia, 1987–89; visiting professor, University of Maryland, 1995. Since 1978 professor, Salisbury State University, Maryland. **Awards:** National Endowment for the Arts fellowship, 1984; Pushcart prizes, 1984, 1990; Towson State University prizes for literature, 1985, 1990; Individual Artist awards, Maryland State Arts Council, 1990, 1992, 1997. **Address:** Department of English, Salisbury State University, Salisbury, Maryland 21801, U.S.A.

PUBLICATIONS

Poetry

Fish Light. Ithaca, New York, Ithaca House, 1975.
Not Just Any Death. Brockport, New York, BOA Editions, 1979.
Anniversary of the Air. Pittsburgh, Carnegie-Mellon University Press, 1985.
The Burden Lifters. Pittsburgh, Carnegie-Mellon University Press, 1989.
Bountiful. Pittsburgh, Carnegie-Mellon University Press, 1992.
Green Ash, Red Maple, Black Gum. Brockport, New York, BOA Editions, 1997.
New & Selected Poems. Brockport, New York, BOA Editions, 2000.

Other

Editor, *Dissolve to Island: On the Poetry of John Logan.* Houston, Ford-Brown Company, 1984.
Editor, with A. Pulin, Jr., *Contemporary American Poetry (7th edition).* Boston, Houghton Mifflin, 2000.

*

Critical Studies: In *The Post-Confessionals: Conversations with American Poets of the Eighties* edited by Earl G. Ingersoll, Judith Kitchen, and Stan Sanvel Rubin, Rutherford, Fairleigh Dickinson

University Press, 1989; ''Loss and Redemption'' by Floyd Collins, in *Gettysburg Review* (Gettysburg, Pennsylvania), 11(4), winter 1998.

*   *   *

The rise of American creative writing programs in the latter half of the twentieth century has exerted conflicting influence on the art itself. On the one hand, these programs have trained and nurtured enthusiastic readers who might never have come to poetry for more than a passing experience. On the other hand, they have often insulated the art from society's larger conditions, encouraging a contemporary version of art for art's sake—or of art for therapy's sake or imitation in the name of art. This latter influence has generated a few recognizable period styles—the poem of autobiographical meditation, the poem of solipsistic exposition—yet it is the poetry that both acknowledges and transcends these limitations that we come to read over again.

Like the majority of poets of his generation, Michael Waters has often made his living by teaching in the academy. But unlike many of his peers, Waters in his poetry never loses sight of the multifaceted connections between his immediate experience and that of the world beyond the university. Water's intelligence has been described as ''restless,'' and that seems right enough, but I would add that it is expansive too. If the poet's business is largely empathy, then Waters opens himself to humanity's triumphs and trials without hesitation, and his consummate skill enables him to perform the role of a most reliable witness. In his poems Waters roams widely for inspiration, from a mid-nineteenth-century free love settlement, to a keeper of lighthouses, to Saint Paul himself. Throughout his several volumes one encounters a healthy, refreshing curiosity about others. The poems most directly emerge out of Waters's urban background and extensive travels in Greece, Costa Rica, Thailand, and elsewhere. Often they are formal, arranged in taut stanzas and making effective use of both end and internal rhyme. Most significantly, even when they begin in personal experience, they often connect with—and help to make sense of—the experience of others.

In ''Burning the Dolls,'' from *The Burden Lifters,* Waters draws on an odd bit of American history. At a free love settlement in 1851 in Oneida, New York, the commune's children voted to burn their dolls because they represented motherhood. One of the girls speaks throughout the poem:

And when the burning was done,
      when her white, Sunday dress
         was transformed to ash
and each perfect, grasping

finger melted upon the coals,
      when her varnished face burst
         in the furnace of my soul,
the waxy lips forever lost,

then I knew I'd no longer pray,
      even with fire haunting me,
         because I hadn't resembled
closely enough my mother,

hadn't withheld my burgeoning

desire, so like a doll
          concealing what I'd learned
I burned and burned and burned.

The dexterity of Water's method can be seen in the internal rhyme of "mother"/"desire," linking the end of the third stanza above to the fourth stanza (line two) and in the emphatic concluding rhyme ("learned"/"burned"), which through repetition becomes a grim chant. The poem is also notable for its haunting depiction of lost innocence and inherited consequences, the resignation that often accompanies the bearing of legacies into a new generation and beyond. Waters consistently and skillfully explores responsibilities and consequences such as these, and by doing so he merits our closest attention.

—Robert McDowell

WATSON, Robert (Winthrop)

Nationality: American. **Born:** Passaic, New Jersey, 26 December 1925. **Education:** Williams College, Williamstown, Massachusetts, B.A. 1946; University of Zurich (Swiss-American Exchange Fellow), 1947; Johns Hopkins University, Baltimore, M.A. 1950, Ph.D. in English 1955. **Military Service:** U.S. Naval Reserve, 1943–45. **Family:** Married Elizabeth Ann Rean in 1952; one son and one daughter. **Career:** Instructor, Williams College, 1946, 1947–48, 1952–53, and Johns Hopkins University, 1950–52. Member of the faculty since 1953, and since 1963 professor of English, University of North Carolina, Greensboro. Visiting poet, California State University, Northridge, 1968–69. **Awards:** *American Scholar* prize, 1959; National Endowment for the Arts grant, 1973; American Academy award, 1977. **Address:** 9-D Fountain Manor Drive, Greensboro, North Carolina 27405, U.S.A.

PUBLICATIONS

Poetry

A Paper Horse. New York, Atheneum, 1962.
Advantages of Dark. New York, Atheneum, 1966.
Christmas in Las Vegas. New York, Atheneum, 1971.
Watson on the Beach. Greensboro, North Carolina, SB Press, 1972.
Selected Poems. New York, Atheneum, 1974.
Island of Bones. Greensboro, North Carolina, Unicorn Press, 1977.
Night Blooming Cactus. New York, Atheneum, 1980.
The Pendulum, New and Selected Poems. Baton Rouge, Louisiana State University Press, 1995.

Play

A Plot in the Palace, in *First Stage* (Lafayette, Indiana), 1964.

Novels

Three Sides of the Mirror. New York, Putnam, 1966.
Lily Lang. New York, St. Martin's Press, 1977.

Other

Editor, with Gibbons Ruark, *The Greensboro Reader.* Chapel Hill, University of North Carolina Press, 1964.

*

Manuscript Collection: Jackson Library, University of North Carolina, Greensboro.

Critical Studies: By Thomas Lask in *New York Times,* 11 December 1971; by Grover Smith, in *Above Ground Review* (Arden, North Carolina), winter 1971; by Sister Bernetta Quinn, in *Georgia Review* (Athens), fall 1977; by James Finn Cotter, in *Hudson Review* (New York), summer 1981; "Robert Watson Issue" of *Greensboro Review* (North Carolina), summer 1989; "Robert Watson: Everything We Cannot See Is Here," in *Compulsory Figures: Essays on Recent American Poetry* by Henry Taylor, Baton Rouge, Louisiana State University Press, 1992.

Robert Watson comments:

I am primarily a poet, but in my spare time I also enjoy writing fiction and drama. Though I have written some criticism and reviews, I write informative prose only at the point of a gun.

With few exceptions, the statements made by poets in our time about their work seem pretentious, silly, boring, or all three at once. Theories get much attention, more than the poems from which they come; no theories for me. And if I try to detail characteristics of my poetry, then I am writing my obituary. In vague terms I try to make my work as musical (in the poetic sense), alive, and intimate as I can and try to get in the way people feel about their lives and their world. I do dramatic, lyric, and narrative poems in a wide variety of forms, most of my own invention. What does not seem to fit poems I put in prose fiction.

*   *   *

Robert Watson's poetry is energetic and economical, splendidly suited to the difficult art of creating characters in verse. Watson's first book, *A Paper Horse,* established these facts with far more authority and consistency than is usual in first collections. The book demonstrates a mastery of staccato compression in a variety of formal approaches that range from free verse to strict rhyme and meter. Most of the poems are soliloquies by a variety of characters particularly qualified to speak of the loss of youth, freedom, or love. The surface bleakness of the characters' lives is mitigated by Watson's compassion for them and by his strong and distinctive style.

Watson's style has a density of texture that is nevertheless accessible, for he uses what sounds like the language of real speech in compressed syntactical arrangements. He often places repetitive parallel clauses so that essential grammatical elements, such as subjects, can be omitted without loss of clarity. When this method is combined with a strongly audible metrical pattern, the results include distinctive but plausible speech and unusual power.

Watson's style remains much the same in *Advantages of Dark,* but the collection extends the range of starting points for his poetry. In addition to soliloquies, there are a number of satires of contemporary life, some of which portray with harrowing humor the willful recalcitrance of everyday inanimate objects. The book also contains an ambitious long poem, "The City of Passaic," that uses the lives of a number of its inhabitants to evoke the life of the city where Watson was born. "Lines for a President" also deserves mention as one of the very few convincing and genuine American poems on the assassination of John F. Kennedy.

Christmas in Las Vegas is something of a return to the bleakness of *A Paper Horse*. In his accustomed style, which suddenly appears to have been developed for just this purpose, Watson explores the brittle brilliance of modern urban life, in which people are almost indistinguishable from the machines that have enslaved them. The somber tones of this collection, paradoxically deepened by the relentless presence of artificial light, are more profound than any Watson had previously struck.

Love and the apparent perversity of the external world are only two of the recurrent themes in Watson's shorter poems. Others, such as the seductiveness of self-delusion, the related conviction that elsewhere is better than here, or the difficulty of locating the boundary between life and death, turn up not only in the short poems but also in the several longer ones, ranging roughly between 80 and 240 lines, that have constituted an important part of each of Watson's collections. Since the appearance of "Watson on the Beach" in his first book and of the aforementioned "City of Passaic," Watson has continued to explore the possibilities of this difficult form, as in "Victoria Woodhull," a superb characterization of a historical personage, and in "Island of Bones," collected in *Night Blooming Cactus*. Set in Key West and more fragmentary in structure than most of Watson's earlier poems, "Island of Bones" is a sturdy and absorbing reminder of Watson's continuing restlessness and invention.

—Henry Taylor

WAYMAN, Tom

Nationality: Canadian. **Born:** Thomas Ethan Wayman, Hawkesbury, Ontario, 13 August 1945. **Education:** University of British Columbia, Vancouver, 1962–66, B.A. 1966; University of California, Irvine, 1966–68, M.F.A. 1968. **Career:** Instructor in English, Colorado State University, Fort Collins, 1968–69; worked at construction, demolition, and factory jobs, and as a teacher's aide, 1969–75; writer-in-residence, University of Windsor, Ontario, 1975–76; assistant professor of English, Wayne State University, Detroit, 1976–77; writer-in-residence, University of Alberta, Edmonton, 1978–79; faculty member, David Thompson University Centre School of Writing, Nelson, British Columbia, 1980–82; writer-in-residence, Simon Fraser University, Burnaby, British Columbia, spring 1983; instructor, Kwantlen College, Surrey, British Columbia, fall 1983; faculty member, Kootenay School of Writing, Vancouver, British Columbia, 1984–87; instructor, Kwantlen College, Surrey, British Columbia, 1988–89; professor, English department, Okanagan University College, Kelowna, British Columbia, 1990–91, 1992–95; faculty member, writing studio, Kootenay School of the Arts, 1991–92, 1996–98; writer-in-residence, University of Toronto, 1996. Since 1998 faculty member, English Department, Kwantlen University College, Surrey, British Columbia. **Awards:** Helen Bullis prize (*Poetry Northwest*) 1972; Borestone Mountain poetry award, 1972, 1973, 1974, 1976; Canadian Authors Association prize, 1975; Canada Council senior grant, 1975, 1977; A.J.M. Smith prize, Michigan State University, 1976; U.S. Bicentennial award, 1976. **Address:** P.O. Box 163, Winlaw, British Columbia V0G 2J0, Canada.

PUBLICATIONS

Poetry

Mindscapes, with others, edited by Ann Wall. Toronto, Anansi, 1971.
Waiting for Wayman. Toronto, McClelland and Stewart, 1973.
For and against the Moon: Blues, Yells, and Chuckles. Toronto, Macmillan, 1974.
Money and Rain: Tom Wayman Live! Toronto, Macmillan, 1975.
Routines. Seattle, Black Eye Press, 1976.
Transport. Toronto, Dreadnaught Press, 1976.
Kitchener/Chicago/Saskatoon. Windsor, Ontario, Flat Singles Press, 1977
Free Time: Industrial Poems. Toronto, Macmillan, 1977.
A Planet Mostly Sea: Two Poems. Winnipeg, Turnstone Press, 1979.
Introducing Tom Wayman: Selected Poems 1973–1980. Princeton, New Jersey, Ontario Review Press, 1980.
Living on the Ground: Tom Wayman Country. Toronto, McClelland and Stewart, 1980.
The Nobel Prize Acceptance Speech: New and Selected Poems. Saskatoon, Thistledown Press, 1981.
Counting the Hours: City Poems. Toronto, McClelland and Stewart, 1983.
The Face of Jack Munro. Madeira Park, British Columbia, Harbour, 1986.
In a Small House on the Outskirts of Heaven. Madeira Park, British Columbia, Harbour, 1989.
Did I Miss Anything? Selected Poems 1973–1993. Madeira Park, British Columbia, Harbour, 1993.
The Astonishing Weight of the Dead. Vancouver, Polestar, 1994.
I'll Be Right Back: New and Selected Poems 1980–1996. Princeton, New Jersey, Ontario Review Press, 1997.
The Colours of the Forest. Madeira Park, British Columbia, Harbour, 1999.

Other

Inside Job: Essays on the New Work Writing. Madeira Park, British Columbia, Harbour, 1983.
A Country Not Considered: Canada, Culture, Work. Toronto, Anansi, 1993.

Editor, *Beaton Abbot's Got the Contract: An Anthology of Working Poems.* Edmonton, NeWest Press, 1974.
Editor, *A Government Job at Last: An Anthology of Working Poems, Mainly Canadian.* Vancouver, MacLeod, 1976.
Editor, *Going for Coffee: Poetry on the Job.* Madeira Park, British Columbia, Harbour, 1981.
Editor, with Calvin Wharton, *East of Main: An Anthology of Poems from East Vancouver.* Vancouver, Pulp Press, 1989.
Editor, *Paperwork: Contemporary Poems from the Job.* Madeira Park, British Columbia, Harbour, 1991.

Critical Studies: "Tom Wayman: An Introduction" by Paul Delany, in *Little Magazine* (New York), winter 1975–76; "Way Out with Wayman: The Engaged Voice" by Marlowe Anderson, in CV 2 (Winnipeg), January 1976; "The Condition of Being Alive: Tom

Wayman's Poetry'' by Jenné Andrews, in *Colorado Review* (Fort Collins), fall 1985; ''Waiting for Wayman to Get Off Work'' by Phil Hall, in *Quarry* (Kingston, Ontario), December 1987; ''Tom Wayman: Working Poet'' by Doug Smith, in *Canadian Forum,* 74(843), 1 October 1995; *Tom Wayman and His Works,* monograph by John Harris, Toronto, ECW Press, 1997.

Tom Wayman comments:

What I want to do with my poems, and with the poems by others that I encourage and collect, is bring into Canadian literature a poetry of everyday life based on the central experience of that life for most people—daily work. By ''work'' I mean what men and women do for a living, whether paid or unpaid, blue- or white-collar. I consider this experience central because I believe the work we do profoundly affects every other aspect of our existence—our standard of living, how much time and energy we have off the job, who our friends are, and more. Even our attitudes to such traditionally ''poetic'' subjects as love, death, and nature are very strongly influenced by the conditions and content of our daily work. An accurate description of contemporary Canadian jobs and how these affect our lives is virtually taboo at present in our entertainment and fine arts media. I find it discouraging that the literary arts—which are touted, and funded, as epitomizing the human spirit—should help perpetuate the taboo against accurately depicting the central and governing life experience of most Canadians. My efforts as a writer are dedicated to revealing the many dimensions to how work is currently organized and the tangible and intangible implications of such jobs for human beings.

*   *   *

Tom Wayman is one of the few Canadian political poets, and it is perhaps to his advantage as a poet that his politics is somewhat distanced from the contemporary Canadian scene. His is the politics of the North American 1960s, when Wayman was personally involved in the radical student movement in California and when, as he has said, he later lived by ''hustle, construction labouring, unemployment insurance, and welfare.'' It is, reaching even farther back, the turn-of-the-century politics of the unpolitical, stemming from the antigovernment propaganda of the Industrial Workers of the World (IWW), or Wobblies, and the anarchist movement of that time.

Wayman's is a politics with its own kind of realism, accepting defeat without disillusionment and having—at least in the imagination—its own imperatives of action. This is suggested in Wayman's early and moving poem ''The Dream of the Guerillas'': ''And night quiet / after the dream. / Street lights burn on. / The slogans are calm as dim walls. The clock, the clock says: now / the guerillas are coming and you must go with them.''

Wayman's radicalism is mingled with a great deal of nostalgia, and he looks to the lost causes of the past as well as to the losing causes of the present. He has actually been a member of the moribund IWW, and he ends a 1977 poem on the continuity of submerged libertarian ideals (''The Ghosts of the Anarchists Speak of George Woodcock'') by having a Spanish anarchist say,

Still, we don't win So now what happened here
must be written down   Not that anybody could list
all the arguments, the wind, the food,
the sweat and thinking and fighting

that led us to try this and try that
to be successful here and fail there. But we need
true words that tell what we did
so compactly, so magnificently
they are like a seed you hold in your hand
and see in it all the intricate beauty
of the strong dark flowers that will come.

Wayman first emerged out of publication in magazines when a group of his poems was printed, with work by three other writers, in *Mindscapes.* The volumes he has published since then, including *Waiting for Wayman, Money and Rain: Tom Wayman Live!,* and *Living on the Ground: Tom Wayman Country,* have projected, as their titles suggest, not only a resolutely minority political attitude but also a highly idiosyncratic personality. There is a great deal of the dramatic in Wayman's poetic method. A comic person named Wayman faces the world as a Schweikian guerrilla, and in this role he dominates a whole series of poems devoted to exposing the enormities of the world against which the poet clumsily and futilely but relentlessly fights.

But underlying the comedy, and expressed in other poems with a good deal of sincere pathos, is a recognition of the misery and pain of the economically and politically oppressed, who represent the greater part of the world's population. Despite this recognition Wayman does not give way to despair, but he no longer rises high in the heavens of hope and no longer sees self-sacrifice as an imperative: ''I no longer believe my pain / will help another human being.''

In his book *In a Small House on the Outskirts of Heaven* Wayman remarks in an afterword, ''Personally, I find it discouraging that the literary arts—which are touted (and funded—as epitomizing the human spirit)—should help perpetuate the taboo against accurately depicting daily work and thus contributing to human pain. I find it offensive each new anthology of Canadian poetry, prose or drama that once again offers a literary poetry of a country—in which nobody works.'' Wayman himself has written a great deal about work and how it should fulfill and satisfy a person but how in modern society it usually results in a person's feeling degraded.

Wayman is not only a good urban poet with a red Wobbly card in his wallet, however. He is also a man sensitive to his environment and avid to spend his leisure in it, and some of his finest poems are about backpacking through the Canadian wilderness. *In a Small Town on the Outskirts of Heaven* as well as his earlier books contain remarkable lyrical and elegiac pieces about the mountain and island country and the cityscapes Wayman has loved. ''Vancouver Winter,'' which is almost Eliotian in its clear luminosity, is brief enough to quote entirely:

Like cats at a window
the houses along the wet street
look out on the downpour.
       In the window of a house
a cat. In the cat's eye
       drenched asphalt, the line of houses,
smoke from the chimneys streaming
toward the ground
through the sodden air.

There is a broad sweep to Wayman that someone has not unjustly compared to Walt Whitman. He is vigorous, protean in fancy, and more self-critical than most poets of his highly productive kind. Facility is his temptation, but it has rarely led him away from true feeling.

—George Woodcock

WEARNE, Alan (Richard)

Nationality: Australian. **Born:** Melbourne, 23 July 1948. **Education:** Monash University, Melbourne, 1967–68; La Trobe University, Bundoora, Victoria, B.A. 1973; Rusden College, Dip.Ed. 1977. **Career:** Has worked as a high school teacher in Melbourne, and for the Australian Public Service. Labour candidate for Victorian State Parliament, 1979. Poetry editor, *Meanjin,* 1984–87. **Awards:** Australia Council fellowship, 1974, 1978, 1984, 1986, 1987; National Book Council award, 1987; Australian Literary Society Gold Medal, 1987. **Address:** 83 Edgevale Road, Kew, Melbourne, Victoria 3103, Australia.

PUBLICATIONS

Poetry

Public Relations. Brisbane, Makar Press, 1972.
New Devil, New Parish. St. Lucia, University of Queensland Press, 1976.
The Nightmarkets (novel in verse). Melbourne and New York, Penguin, 1986.
Out Here (novella in verse). Newcastle upon Tyne, Bloodaxe, 1987.

Novel

Kicking in Danger: A Damien Chubb Footy Mystery. North Fitzroy, Victoria, Black Pepper, 1997.

Other

The Puzzles of Childhood by Manning Clark. Melbourne, Department of Discussion Programs, Council of Adult Education, 1990.
George Johnston, A Biography by Garry Kinnane. Melbourne, Department of Discussion Programs, Council of Adult Education, 1991.

*　　*　　*

Manuscript Collection: Fryer Library, University of Queensland.

Critical Study: "Melways to His Melbourne: Alan Wearne's 'The Nightmarkets'" by Peter Craven, in *Meanjin* (Parkville, Victoria), 46(3), September 1987.

Alan Wearne comments:

I write large-scale works, although within these works sections can be as small as, say, six lines. One hundred lines for me is, however, a small poem. My most famous work is *The Nightmarkets,* a verse novel that has achieved a certain fame in Australia but that overseas publishers seem to be too scared to take on board. Penguin U.K. tried thinking about the idea for a while but gave up. This annoys me, but I can understand.

There are poets whom I wish I could write like, let alone be as good as: Hardy, Stevens, Edwin Muir. But I would much rather write like myself. Anything too influenced is, at best, an unintentional parody and, at worst, decidedly second rate.

My gods are many, but Shakespeare, Browning, Byron, Frank O'Hara, Auden, Meredith (of *Modern Love),* Clough (of "Amours de Voyage"), James K. Baxter, Tennyson rate quite highly. Also Kenneth Koch, Philip Larkin, Stevie Smith, etc.

I know a little Portuguese but not enough to come to grips with Carlos Drummond de Andrade, Fernando Pessoa, and Luis de Camoes as much as I would like to in the original.

Poetry is still in luck, sheltered from any Booker prize-type bullshit. Australian poetry is still lucky in that it has not the uniform "creative writing school" drabness that afflicts the United States. There is, however, a lot of garbage being written in Australia today, and, rhyming, blank, or free, doggerel is doggerel!

*　　*　　*

The long narrative poem is Alan Wearne's métier. *Out Here* and *The Nightmarkets* are both sequences of dramatic monologues in different voices that explain focal events through differing realities. His shorter poems (one is entitled "Extracts from a Competent Novel") seem to be a flexing of his poetic muscle in preparation for these extended narratives. Browning and Meredith, among the mentors he cites, are the clearest influences, but his flexibility in using contrasting verse forms and the number of his characters make Wearne's long poems truly novelistic.

In *The Nightmarkets* Wearne's characters are differentiated by the use of rhyme and poetic structures. *Out Here,* however, relies on language for contrast. The catalyst for the speakers' stories in *Out Here* is the self-inflicted stabbing of a teenage boy, but as the title reflects, the core of the poem is not the re-creation of this event (a response to his parents' impending separation) but an examination of the values of a particular place, an affluent middle-class suburb. The titles of individual poems continue the emphasis on place: "Like It's Some Ghost Town," "Home," "Homes," "Out There." In the first poem a schoolteacher passes judgment on place and people: "that area hasn't community / hasn't responsibility: / who won't serve, but want to / be served."

Through multiple voices Wearne builds up a picture of the empty materialism of suburban life as viewed by both insiders and outsiders. The boy's mother, closest to understanding her life when she confesses that she "had kids not opinions," fights through her husband's infidelities to maintain her self-perception as "brisk . . . poised . . . efficient." Her narrative breaks down at the end, a combination of stoicism and sentiment: "leave me darling, but recall: *I just / wanna stay here and love you* remember it?" The father's narrative, situated as he is between the wife and mistress, perceptively describes the latter as his "exhilarating / dead-end," likening her to her own place: "organized efficient, neat / living-room, clean kitchen, / bathroom: the bedroom is / total shambles." While the wife and mistress fall back on clichés from popular songs to express their feelings, he turns to the masculine equivalent of friendship, in particular to his older brother, a retired football hero. The son and his girlfriend are better educated than their elders but lack experience and power, so that the only mature voice from "out here" is the last, her father's.

The sequence of voices within the poem controls and balances the narratives. The first line of the first poem, "I viewed the eddies of the Viney maelstrom," establishes the detachment and sophistication of the schoolteacher. Mother, father, and mistress are followed by two other voices from ''outside,'' the grandfather and aunt. The grandfather, a contractor responsible for the estate but living elsewhere, upholds a crude conservatism, defends his life (''built and begat''), and surveys his family of daughters, respecting only the strong one who argues with him. The aunt, independent, radical, outspoken, despairing of her ''object-addicted, middle-ground, / mothering big sister,'' explicitly rejects the false sentimentality of the wife and mistress: ''hey, little girl, do you still / run to his arms and seek / as these songs? . . . sister that's shit!'' The voices of the youngsters are placed seventh and eighth, positions indicative of their insignificance in the lives of the adults and of the relative unimportance of the stabbing, which is swallowed by family separation.

The Nightmarkets uses fewer speakers (six) but has a much wider number of characters. Here the theme is time (1980) more than place (Melbourne) as the radicals and others of the late 1960s and the 1970s make their way in a changing world in which ''the enemy still is greed'' and we hear the ''endless insulting chant: / Leave it to the market forces / *leave it to the market forces*'' (''Melbourne 1980''). Wearne's spectrum here includes the upper-class establishment, the suburban middle class, inner-city radicals, and the fringes of the underworld. Old friendships and political and sexual alliances are the filaments that stretch across a city.

The major voices are those of Ian Metcalfe, a journalist, and his brother Robert, a union official and an aspiring Labor politician, both 1970s political activists. For Robert, Wearne uses a form he describes as ''formal yet adventurous'':

> The fight is the cause
> is the fight;
>
>   which gelled as I addressed
> my branch, 'What I Believe and Why,' 'Mate?' asked that
>   resident academic,
>   could these events be termed ''seeds of a white collar''
>   consciousness?'

Ian's form, the sixteen-line Meredith sonnet (one serves as an epigraph to the volume) with ''outrageous rhymes,'' successfully renders a character defending his youthful idealism, hating any compromise that he makes, and still living the ''pot'' culture of the 1970s. These lines are from ''The Division of O'Dowd''

> . . . (The sea might remind us
> . . . of love civilization, etcetera, M. Arnold-style,
> but we opt
>   for a counter-meal, fish, of course, at the Steam
> Packet.)
>   I'd on a windcheater while she took from the
> backseat her jacket
>   used on such occasions. We walked by Hobson's Bay till
> the sun stopped.

The voice of the prostitute Terri is a series of twelve-line sonnets; of the conservative politician John McTaggart, prose; of his mother, a more formally rendered sonnet; of Robert's ex-girlfriend, now McTaggart's lover, the journalist Sue Dobbo, free verse in the first instance and rhymed couplets in the second (when she has

resigned some of her freedom to accept the role of official biographer to her lover.)

Through these characters Wearne examines 1980s greed and the obsession with market forces at a time of political confusion between the 1975 dismissal of Gough Whitlam's Labor government, a watershed in Australian politics, and the 1983 election of another Labor government. Ian's role as an investigative journalist brings all of the characters together, and his connection with Terri allows Wearne to draw parallels between political life and life in a high-class brothel (the Crystal Palace). While these are not explicitly drawn throughout, they are articulated in Ian's final monologue, at his last meeting with Terri:

> . . . We stood apart in an alcove, testing
>   the order of business. Love was in the previous
> minutes;
>   correspondence, though important, had been limited;
> you'd tell
>   we'd get each other's vote of thanks. As for the
> future? As for the future, we can muster the numbers
>   required for control

Wearne's interest in people is given full play in *The Nightmarkets,* where even the most briefly heard voice has individuality. The narrative action is limited, but the delineation of character is deft and compelling.

—Nan Bowman Albinski

WEBB, Phyllis

Nationality: Canadian. **Born:** Victoria, British Columbia, 8 April 1927. **Education:** University of British Columbia, Vancouver, B.A. in English and philosophy 1949; McGill University, Montreal, 1953. **Career:** Secretary, Montreal, 1956; teaching assistant, English Department, University of British Columbia, Vancouver, 1960–64; program organizer, 1964–67, and executive producer, 1967–69, Canadian Broadcasting Corporation, Toronto; guest lecturer, University of British Columbia, 1976–77, Banff Centre, Alberta, 1981; writer-in-residence, University of Alberta, 1980–81; adjunct professor, Creative Writing Department, University of Victoria, British Columbia, 1989–93. **Awards:** Canadian Government Overseas award, 1957; Canada Council bursary, 1963, and award, 1969, 1981, 1987; Governor-General's award, 1983; Governor General's award, 1982. Officer of the Order of Canada, 1992. **Address:** R.R. 2, Mt. Baker Circle, C-9, Ganges, British Columbia V0S 1E0, Canada.

PUBLICATIONS

Poetry

Trio, with Gael Turnbull and Eli Mandel. Toronto, Contact Press, 1954.
Even Your Right Eye. Toronto, McClelland and Stewart, 1956.
The Sea Is Also a Garden. Toronto, Ryerson Press, 1962.
Naked Poems. Vancouver, Periwinkle Press, 1965.

Selected Poems 1954–1965, edited by John Hulcoop. Vancouver, Talonbooks, 1971.
Wilson's Bowl. Toronto, Coach House Press, 1980.
Sunday Water: Thirteen Anti Ghazals. Lantzville, British Columbia, Island, 1982.
The Vision Tree: Selected Poems, edited by Sharon Thesen. Vancouver, Talonbooks, 1982.
Water and Light: Ghazals and Anti Ghazals. Toronto, Coach House Press. 1984.
Hanging Fire. Toronto, Coach House, 1990.

Other

Talking. Montreal, Quadrant, 1982.
Nothing but Brush Strokes: Selected Prose. Edmonton, NeWest, 1995.

*

Bibliography: By Cecelia Frey, in *The Annotated Bibliography of Canada's Major Authors,* vol.6, edited by Robert Lecker and Jack David, Toronto, ECW Press, 1985.

Manuscript Collections: National Library of Canada, Ottawa; Talonbooks Archives, Vancouver; Simon Fraser University Library, Bumaby, British Columbia.

Critical Studies: "The Structure of Loss" by Helen Sonthoff, in *Canadian Literature* (Vancouver), summer 1961; "Phyllis Webb and the Priestess of Motion" in *Canadian Literature* (Vancouver), spring 1967, introduction to *Selected Poems 1954–1965,* 1971, *Phyllis Webb and Her Works,* Toronto, ECW Press, 1991, and "Webb's Book of Revelation: Lifting the Lid off 'Krakatoa' and 'Spiritual Storm,'" in *Inside the Poems: Essays and Poems in Honour of Donald Stephens,* edited by W.H. New, Toronto, Oxford University Press, 1992, all by John Hulcoop; introduction by Sharon Thesen to *The Vision Tree,* 1982; "I and I: Phyllis Webb's 'I Daniel,'" in *Open Letter* (Toronto), 2–3, summer-fall 1985, and "Surviving the Paraph-Raise," in *Signature, Event, Cantext,* Edmonton, Alberta, NeWest Press, 1989, both by Stephen Scobie; "Proceeding before the Amorous Invisible: Phyllis Webb and the Ghazal" by Susan Glickman, in *Canadian Literature* (Vancouver), winter 1987; "Phyllis Webb As a Post-Duncan Poet" in *Sagetrieh* (Orono, Maine), 7(1), 1988, and "You Devise. We Devise," in *West Coast Line,* both by Pauline Butling, 6, winter 1991–92; *Aspects of the Spiritual in Three Canadian Women Poets: Anne Wilkinson, Gwendolyn MacEwen, and Phyllis Webb* (dissertation), McMaster University University, 1992, and "Phyllis Webb: The Voice that Breaks," in *Canadian Poetry* (London, Ontario), 32, spring-summer 1993, both by Liza Potvin; "'Oh for the Carp of a Critic': Research in the Phyllis Webb Papers" by Lorna Knight, in *West Coast Line,* 26(2), fall 1992; *Self-Deconstructing Lyric: Coleridge, Dickinson, Williams and Webb* (dissertation) by Raymond Gilbert Wilton, University of Alberta, 1994; *The Feminist Romantic: The Revisionary Rhetoric of 'Double Negative,' 'Naked Poems,' and 'Gyno-Text'* (dissertation) by Susan Lee Drodge, Memorial University of Newfoundland, 1996; "A Question of Form: Phyllis Webb's Water and Light: Ghazals and Anti Ghazals" by Shirley Chew, in *The Contact and the Culmination,* edited by Marc Delrez and Benedicte Ledent, Liege, Belgium, L3, 1997; "Feminist

Ecocritique As Forensic Archaeology: Digging in Critical Grave-yards and Phyllis Webb's Gardens" by Diana M.A. Relke, in *Canadian Poetry,* 42, spring-summer 1998.

*   *   *

Phyllis Webb is a poet of austere dedication whose relatively small number of finely crafted poems have slowly attracted the attention of readers. Her work also has influenced other poets and helped to change the course of poetry in Canada during the years in which she has been steadily honing her craft.

Webb's first poems appeared at the beginning of the 1950s in *Contemporary Verse,* Alan Crawley's historic little magazine. Since then she has published only sparsely. She always seems reluctant to release a poem into print or speech, and her works, when they do appear, have been honed to an extraordinary intellectual spareness. Yet her image as a diffident and reclusive poet is not entirely justified. She has at times been politically active on the left, as when at the age of twenty-two she stood unsuccessfully as a social democratic candidate in the British Columbia provincial elections. In the mid-1960s, working for the Canadian Broadcasting Corporation, she devised and was the first producer of the highly regarded program *Ideas.* The venerable program continued to flourish long after Webb retired from the world of public action to her retreat on Salt Spring Island, a place of relative seclusion in the channel between Vancouver Island and mainland British Columbia.

Webb shared her first volume, *Trio,* with two poets remarkably unlike herself, Gael Turnbull and Eli Mandel. Her first individual volume, *Even Your Right Eye,* appeared in 1956, and while *The Sea Is Also a Garden* and the sparse *Naked Poems* were issued together in the early 1960s, her *Selected Poems* of 1971 included nothing published after 1965. There was a long gap before her next collection, *Wilson's Bowl,* appeared in 1980. This was followed in 1982 by *The Vision Tree: Selected Poems* and *Sunday Water: Thirteen Anti Ghazals* and in 1984 by *Water and Light: Ghazals and Anti Ghazals.* *Hanging Fire* appeared in 1990. *The Vision Tree,* the book nearest to a volume of collected poems, represents the work of more than thirty years in a mere 154 pages.

Webb's later books have finally established her among Canada's leading poets, although her influence on younger poets had been evident long before. Northrop Frye described *Wilson's Bowl* as "a landmark in Canadian poetry," and *The Vision Tree* won her the establishment recognition of a Governor-General's award. She continues to write in seclusion, to polish, and, very often, to discard.

For Webb, in fact, growing in maturity as a poet has meant withdrawal for long periods, a narrowing of the circle of the creative self in keeping with the solipsistic character of much of her verse. More than twenty-five years ago she said that "the public and the person are inevitably / one and the same self." But while this may have been true of the Webb who campaigned as a socialist candidate, it has not been true for many years of the poet who has become concerned with personal emotions, the loneliness of living, the knife-edge paths on which we painfully dance our way to death. She no longer sees art as a "remedy," as a "patched, matched protection for Because."

The result is perhaps foreshadowed in the early poem "Is Our Distress":

This our inheritance
is our distress

born of the weight of eons
it skeletons our flesh,
bearing us on
we wear it
though it bears us.

The philosophic pessimism—in unguarded moments breaking down into self-pity—that these lines suggest has tended to control the development of thought in Webb's poems. It has led her to move from the elaborate and the assured toward the simplified view of anarchists like Kropotkin, the view that the less one demands of existence, the less one has to defend. One question in ''Some Final Questions,'' a section of *Naked Poems,* reads

Now, you are sitting doubled up in pain.
What's that for?

doubled up I feel
small like these poems
the area of attack
is diminished

The *Naked Poems* are indeed reductive in terms of verse as well as life. They were prepared for by a work in *The Sea Is Also a Garden,* ''Poetics against an Angel of Death,'' in which Webb says,

Last night I thought I would not wake again
but now with this June morning I run ragged to elude
The Great Iambic Pentameter
who is the Hound of Heaven in our stress
because I want to die
writing Haiku
or, better,
long lines, clean and syllabic as knotted bamboo. Yes!

Indeed, Webb's poems at this point became quasi-haiku, small, simple, as packed with meaning as stone artifacts, and punctuated by periods of stubborn silence. These ''naked poems,'' as austerely beautiful as weathered bones, are crucial to her career. In the later poems of *Wilson's Bowl* and in their successors Webb emerged into what is, in fact, a structure of ''long lines, clean and syllabic as knotted bamboo.'' The poems of this last period are no longer minimalist. They expand not only formally into complex patterns of sound but also in thought, in what Webb herself has called ''the dance of the intellect in the syllables,'' and there is a return on an apolitical level to the humane considerations of her earliest phase as she weaves the problems of self and other into pieces like her ''Kropotkin Poems'':

The Memoirs of a Revolutionist before me, things fall
together now. Pine needles, arbutus bark, the tide
comes in, path to the beach lights with sun-fall.
Highest joys? The simple profundity of a deadman works
at my style. I am impoverished. He the White Christ.
Not a case of identification. Easier to see myself
in the white cat asleep on the bed. Exile. I live

alone. I have a phone. I shall go to Russia. One
more day run round and the 'good masterpiece of work'
does not come. I scribble. I approach some distant dream.
I wait for moonlight reflecting on the night sea. I can
wait. We shall see.

Webb, more than most other poets, has forced herself to know the limitations of her talent, and in this way she has learned its full powers. The stark, elliptical beauty of the collection *Hanging Fire* places her, with Douglas Barbour and Fred Wah, in the forefront of the Canadian language poets. Some titles of the poems she calls ''?'' are used as triggers for meditations, which are sometimes on the sounds of the words themselves. Wit, insight, and musical instinct combine to penetrate and then illuminate what was unknown before.

—George Woodcock and Patience Wheatley

WEDDE, Ian

Nationality: New Zealander. **Born:** Blenheim, 17 October 1946. **Education:** Auckland University, M.A. (honors) 1968. **Family:** Married Rosemary Beauchamp in 1967; three sons. **Career:** Formerly forester, factory worker, gardener, and postman. British Council teacher, Jordan, 1969–70; poetry reviewer, *London Magazine,* 1970–71; broadcasting editor, New Zealand Broadcasting Corporation, 1972; writer-in-residence, Victoria University, Wellington, 1984; art critic, Wellington *Evening Post,* 1983–90. **Awards:** Robert Burns fellowship, University of Otago, 1972; Arts Council bursary, 1974, and travel award, 1983; New Zealand Book award, for fiction, 1977, and for verse, 1978; Victoria University writing fellowship, 1984. **Address:** 118-A Maidavale Road, Roseneath, Wellington 1, New Zealand.

PUBLICATIONS

Poetry

Homage to Matisse. London, Amphedesma Press, 1971.
Made Over. Auckland, Stephen Chan, 1974.
Pathway to the Sea. Christchurch, Hawk Press, 1974.
Earthly: Sonnets for Carlos. Akaroa, New Zealand, Amphedesma Press, 1975.
Don't Listen. Christchurch, Hawk Press, 1977.
Spells for Coming Out. Auckland, Auckland University Press, 1977.
Castaly and Other Poems. Auckland, Auckland University Press-Oxford University Press, 1980; Oxford, Oxford University Press, 1981.
Tales of Gotham City. Auckland, Auckland University Press-Oxford University Press, 1984.
Georgicon. Wellington, Victoria University Press, 1984.
Driving into the Storm: Selected Poems. Auckland, Oxford University Press, 1987.
Tendering. Auckland, Auckland University Press, 1988.
The Drummer. Auckland, Auckland University Press, 1993.

Plays

Eyeball Eyeball (produced Packakariki, 1983).
Double or Quit: The Life and Times of Percy Topliss (produced on tour, England, 1984).

Radio Plays: *Stations,* music by Jack Body, 1969; *Pukeko,* music by John Rimmer, 1972.

Novels

Dick Seddon's Great Dive. Auckland, Islands, 1976.
Symmes Hole. Auckland, Penguin, and London, Faber, 1986.

Short Stories

The Shirt Factory and Other Stories. Wellington, Victoria University Press, 1981.
Survival Arts. Auckland, Penguin, and London, Faber, 1988.

Other

How to Be Nowhere: Essays and Texts, 1971–1994. Wellington, Victoria University Press, 1995.

Editor, with Harvey McQueen, *The Penguin Book of Contemporary New Zealand Verse.* Auckland, Penguin, 1985; revised edition, with McQueen and Miriama Evans, 1989.
Editor, with Gregory Burke, *Now See Hear! Art, Language, and Translation.* Wellington, Victoria University Press, 1990.
Editor, *Dream Collectors: One Hundred Years of Art in New Zealand.* Wellington, Te Papa Press, 1998.

Editor and translator, with Fawwas Tuqan, *Selected Poems,* by Mahmud Darwish. Cheadle. Cheshire, Carcanet, 1974.

*

Critical Studies: "Loathing the Golden Arches: Ian Wedde and Postmodernism" by Cynthia Brophy, in *Landfall* (Dunedin, New Zealand), 42(1), March 1988; by Jonathan Lamb, in *Dirty Silence: Aspects of Language and Literature in New Zealand,* edited by Graham McGregor and Mark Williams, Auckland, Oxford University Press, 1991; "Beyond All Law: Ian Wedde's New Zealand Settlers" by John McLaren, in *Australian and New Zealand Studies in Canada* (Prince George, British Columbia), 7, June 1992; by Linda Hardy, in *Asian and Pacific Inscriptions: Identities, Ethnicities, Nationalities,* edited by Suvendrini Perera, Victoria, Australia, Meridian, 1995; "The Re-Emergence of a Nation: Ian Wedde's 'Symmes Hole'" by Laura Moss, in *Revue Frontenac Review,* 12, 1995.

Ian Wedde comments:

Poems are ways out of solipsism, not necessarily the poet's. If the poems are any good, then the poet through writing and the readers through reading are transported. Poems are not mirrors but creations, where "creations" is understood as a kind of present participle. I am myself skeptical about the perfectibility of people; I think they change to remain the same. For this reason, and because of what I have said above about poetry and because poetry is not discrete but a function of people, I am not interested in poems as objects, potentially perfectible, but as processes that involve us. Naturally, the ways in which they do this are not unimportant. But the notion that poems order the world interests me only insofar as they may be said to do this by bringing us, through the intercourse in which they involve us, to cognition of varieties of the world's disorder. This disorder, after all, can be every bit as shapely as the most exquisite *poème bien fait,* so called. My own impulse in writing poems is to inquire rather than describe. At the same time I am attracted by the idea of a *forma formans,* a shape or the ghost of a shape that, as Yves Bonnefoy has pointed out in his notes on translating Yeats, can determine the as yet uncertain content of which it becomes, reciprocally, an aspect. Mathematics can show us an exact principle of symmetry shared by one of the very oldest creatures, the nautilus, by a Greek temple, by innumerable supermarkets. With luck, poetry can offer us a similarly continuous and vital perspective.

*   *   *

Ian Wedde is one of a group of New Zealand poets who are graduates in English from the University of Auckland and who have been influenced by the American modernist tradition as it flows from Pound, early Eliot, and William Carlos Williams through Charles Olson, Robert Duncan, and Robert Creeley. This is a major shift of emphasis in New Zealand poetry, and probably most readers would concede Wedde's place as the leading exponent. At the same time, unlike some of his contemporaries, Wedde does not seem trapped in a narrow and restrictive mode but experiments freely. Most often he lets the feeling determine the shape of the poem, but in an unusual departure he has written a sequence of sonnets in which there is a tight, though discreet and well-concealed, rhyme pattern, a free flow of idea and image, and a predominance of speaking voice, as in Lowell's sonnets. All of this is contained within an exact syllabic count, ten syllables to the line, yet with no line permitted to fall into the old traditional iambic beat. This 1975 sequence, *Earthly: Sonnets for Carlos,* remains one of Wedde's major achievements.

As a young man Wedde spent time traveling outside New Zealand, and his experiences in Italy and the Middle East, particularly in Jordan, provided the occasion for a number of striking poems. In this connection his translation, in collaboration with Fawwas Tuqan, of the poems of Mahmud Darwish should be mentioned.

Wedde is consistently at the center of his own poetry, creating himself (it might be said) as he goes. He is sensitive, voluble, and full of energy. There is always the sense that more is being registered than can be mastered, more felt than finds expression, and this is the right sort of imbalance for the production of poetry. His poems may sometimes seem overcharged, producing a hectic, even agitating effect, but this is preferable to a smooth Parnassian surface and inevitable in poems that aim to be highly active and to involve the reader in their activity. Wedde's poems are "open," not merely in the sense of finding their forms as they go but also in being deliberately less than complete statements. Readers are invited in, their imaginations engaged to do that part of the work the poet leaves for them. This, I think, is what Wedde means when he writes in an anthology of younger New Zealand poets that "the reduction of quests and discoveries to their essentials makes them more charismatic, more dependent upon the mysterious triggers which we all share to greater or lesser extent, which can propel us violently or as though in a dream into previously unknown or unimagined or misunderstood territories and times." The judgment involved in such a strategy has to be exact.

Wedde's temperament is affirmative. He is expansive, rhapsodic, apostrophizing, ecstatic, which means that he is in more or less constant occupation of that area where a fine line divides the celebratory from the effusive and sentimental. In this, it should be said, he is with Keats, and like Keats he is on dangerous ground. High spirits anywhere can be as offensive to the mean in heart as to the genuinely oppressed, and, New Zealand being on the whole a dour, repressive society, Wedde is likely to run into critical trouble. But if this affirmative energy is the quality that makes him vulnerable, it is also his greatest strength, the source of the continual vitality and sense of freshness in his language or, as Arnold said of Keats, of that ''indescribable *gusto* in the voice'':

> & what's better to do than celebrate
> the fact? Look
>   the dark bloom's left your eyes
> spring's ripe
> the horizon the blue sky
> the air pours towards you   the bean flower's sweet
> again   that fucking ferryman grates
> his rowlocks in mid channel again   high
> clouds are spinning like tops again & I
> couldn't ever have enough of all that
>
> & you again & again & again:
> waking, quickening, travelling through one
> world after another   through all the weird
> stations of the earthly paradise named
> for one impossible diamond-backed dream
> or another, as though no one else cared

Wedde also has appeared in a new, semiofficial guise as an anthologist of New Zealand poetry, and here his determination to base his selections partly on ethnicity and gender while at the same time declining to relinquish the traditional view that poems in anthologies should be chosen for their excellence, or at least for accomplishment, has involved him in many painful contradictions. This is particularly the case in the representation of poetry translated from Maori, a language he does not know. His introduction to *The Penguin Book of Contemporary New Zealand Verse* is a model of obliquity and lends some weight to those who have argued that the rich confusions of his own poetry are not so much a matter of choice as the reflection of a mind in receipt of more copious impressions, and subject to greater and more diverse moral pressures, than it can easily bring to order. But Wedde has added considerably to the range of New Zealand poetry, and to imagine the scene without him is to imagine it seriously depleted.

—C.K. Stead

WEIGL, Bruce (Allan)

Nationality: American. **Born:** Lorain, Ohio, 27 January 1949. **Education:** Oberlin College, Ohio, A.B. in English 1974; University of New Hampshire, Durham, M.A. in Writing/American and British Literature 1975; University of Utah, Salt Lake City, Ph.D. in Writing/ American and British Literature 1979. **Military Service:** U.S. Army 1967–70; in Vietnam 1967–68: Bronze Star. **Family:** Married Jean Kondo Weigl in 1972; one son. **Career:** Teaching assistant, University of New Hampshire, Durham, 1974–75; instructor, English, Lorain Community College, Elyria, Ohio, 1976–77; teaching fellow, University of Utah, Salt Lake City, 1977–79; assistant professor of English and director of creative writing, 1979–81; assistant professor of English, 1981–85, and associate professor of English, 1984–86, Old Dominion University, Norfolk, Virginia. Associate professor of English, 1986–90, and since 1990 professor of English and director of M.F.A. in writing, Pennsylvania State University, University Park. Reader and consultant, University of Missouri Press, Wamsetter Press, and Longwood Publishers; reader and editor, The Associated Writing Program; associate editor, *Intervention*, 1982–84; contributing editor and review columnist, *Poet Lore;* consultant/reviewer, *Choice;* advising/contributing editor, *The James Dickey Newsletter.* **Awards:** Yaddo Foundation fellowship, 1976; Academy of American Poets prize, 1978; *Pushcart* prize, 1980–81, 1993; Breadloaf fellowship in poetry, Bread Loaf Writers Conference, 1981; Tu Do Cien Kien award for contributions to American culture, Vietnam Veterans of America, 1987; National Endowment for the Arts fellowship, 1988; Best American Poetry prize, 1994. **Address:** English Department, Pennsylvania State University, University Park, 1251 South Garner Street, State College, Pennsylvania 16801, U.S.A.

PUBLICATIONS

Poetry

Executioner. Tucson, Ironwood Press, 1976.
A Sack Full of Old Quarrels. Cleveland, Cleveland State University Poetry Center, 1977.
A Romance. Pittsburgh, University of Pittsburgh Press, 1979.
The Monkey Wars. Athens, University of Georgia Press, 1985.
Song of Napalm. New York, Atlantic Monthly Press, 1988.
What Saves Us. Evanston, Illinois, Triquarterly Books, 1992.
Sweet Lorain. Evanston, Illinois, Triquarterly Books, 1996.
After the Others: Poems. Evanston, Illinois, Northwestern University Press, 1999.
Archeology of the Circle: New and Selected Poems. New York, Grove Press, 1999.

Other

The Circle of Hanh: A Memoir. New York, Grove Press, 2000.

Editor, *The Giver of Morning: On Dave Smith.* Houston, Thunder City Press, 1983.
Editor, *The Imagination as Glory: On the Poetry of James Dickey.* Urbana, University of Illinois Press, 1984.
Editor, with others, *Pushcart Prize XI Anthology: Best of the Small Presses 12.* Wainscott, New York, Pushcart Press, 1987.
Editor, *Not on the Map,* by Kevin Bowen. Dublin, Dedalus Press, and Chester Springs, Pennsylvania, Dufour, 1996.
Editor, *Charles Simic: Essays on the Poetry.* Ann Arbor, University of Michigan Press, 1996.
Editor, with Kevin Bowen, *Writing between the Lines: An Anthology on War and Its Social Consequences.* Amherst, University of Massachusetts Press, 1997.

Editor, *Angel Riding a Beast: Poems,* by Liliana Ursu. Evanston, Illinois, Northwestern University Press, 1998.

Editor, with Kevin Bowen and Ba Chung Nguyen, *Mountain River: Vietnamese Poetry from the Wars, 1948–1993: A Bilingual Collection.* Amherst, University of Massachusetts Press, 1998.

Translator, with Nguyen Thanh, *Poems from Captured Documents.* Amherst, University of Massachusetts Press, 1994.

*

Critical Studies: "A Sense-Making Perspective in Recent Poetry by Vietnam Veterans," in *American Poetry Review* (Philadelphia), November/December 1986, and "'What Shall We Give Our Children?' Fatherhood Poems by Veterans," in *The United States and Viet Nam from War to Peace,* edited by Richard M. Slabey, Jefferson, North Carolina, McFarland, 1995, both by Lorrie Smith; in *American Literature and the Experience of Vietnam,* Athens, University of Georgia Press, 1991, and in *Vietnam Authors in Their Generation· Re-Thinking America,* Athens, University of Georgia Press, 1991, both by Philip D. Beidler; in *Fourteen Landing Zones: Approaches to Vietnam War Literature* by Philip K. Jason, Iowa City, University of Iowa Press, 1991; "Bruce Weigl: Out of the Landscape of His Past" by Edward J. Reilly, in *Journal of American Culture,* 16(3), fall 1993; in *Radical Visions: Poetry by Vietnam Veterans,* by Vincente F. Gotera, Athens, University of Georgia Press, 1993; "Agendas for Vietnam War Poetry: Reading the War As Art, History, Therapy, and Politics" by Stephen P. Hidalgo, in *Journal of American Culture,* 16(3), fall 1993; "Unmixed Purities" by Nance Van Winckel, in *Shenandoah* (Lexington, Virginia), fall 1993; in *The Art and Craft of Poetry* by Michael J. Bugeja, Cincinnati, Writer's Digest Books, 1994.

Bruce Weigl comments:

Why I Write Like I Write: Notes toward an *Ars Poetica.*

"Fanatics have their dreams . . ."—John Keats

The paradox of my particular pathology as a writer is that the war ruined my life and in return gave me my art. The war robbed me of my boyhood and forced me, at eighteen years old, to bear too much witness to the world, to what men were capable of doing to other men, to children and to women.

The war took away my life and gave me poetry in return. The war taught me irony; that I among the others would survive is ironic. All of my heroes are dead. That is the particular paradox of my experience as a writer. The fate the world has given to me is to write so beautifully as to draw the others into horror.

I was up North on Highway One past Hue. I must have had some bad water because I got sick. I shit and vomited. In my stomach a black snake grew. They sent me to the rear, to An Khe, where I slept in twisted sheets on a cot until some man threw a book at me and said, "Read this boy." I was eighteen. This was called the Republic of Vietnam. Republic. God save us.

I had never read a book straight through in my life. I could not say the names in this book even out loud to myself, but I kept reading, the dream of the suffering horse pulling me into the story. I read Raskolnikov's letter over and over. Something snapped into place in my brain.

"I fear in my heart that you may have been visited by the latest unfashionable belief," Pulcheria wrote to her son. Somehow she was writing to me as well. I do not know why the words made sense, in 1968, the war raging all around us, the air filled with screams. The world conspired to put me there, in that war, in that province of blood, at that moment, so the man could drop that book into my bunk without looking at me. Book that was my link to another world, that was my bridge into a space blown wide open with light that filled my brain.

I came from a house of no books. I ran away from the steel mill town and its grit to the war. I was not headed in the direction of books, but there was a moment reading and rereading *Crime and Punishment* that morning, my stomach raw from bad water, my nerves blown out, my life on a kind of wire or string, that I must have glimpsed the enormous possibilities of expression because I was jarred out of one way of thinking into another, and from that moment the enormity and the impossibility of the struggle at hand revealed itself as a kind of splendor or order that vanished as quickly as it appeared. I have looked for it ever since. It has become my way to find it in the darker corners where it wants to weld something hurtful to something human. I come from a long line of violence. In my poems I try to find a shape for the litany of terror in order to bring it into comprehension. The impossible. The terrible beauty of our lives: that we use them up, that the hunger fades. The impossible. Say it clearly and you make it beautiful, no matter what.

*　　*　　*

Bruce Weigl's special gift is an ability to bring a scene immediately to life, as in the opening lines of the title poem of *What Saves Us*:

We were wrapped around each other
in the back of my father's car parked
in the empty lot of the high school
of our failure, sweat on her neck
like oil.

This narrative gift informs Weigl's poems about growing up among the coal mines and blast furnaces of Pennsylvania and Ohio and, later, among the battlefields and street women of Vietnam during the Tet offensive. These are the subjects and settings of his earlier poems, but he later moves to the struggle to reclaim his life.

The married narrator of one poem tells his wife that "not even your good love" can blot out the war. He still lives among the victims, the boys who "fell before me in heaps, their arms / and legs flailing ridiculously through the smoke and flash," and the Vietnamese girl in the famous photograph,

running from her village, napalm
stuck to her dress like jelly,
her hands reaching for the no one
who waits in waves of heat before her.

These lines are from the title poem of Weigl's fifth collection, *Song of Napalm,* accurately described by Russell Banks as "the story of an American innocent's descent into hell and his excruciating return to life on the surface" amid breakdown, recovery, and a return to Hanoi twenty years later. To this body of work Weigl has added a substantial and fascinating collection of poems by Vietnamese soldiers, translated into English.

"Inside me the war had eaten a hole," says the voice in "On the Anniversary of Her Grace." In harsh times at home and abroad, the narrator of "The Forms of Eleventh Street" concludes that what saved him

> were the Latin prayers
> come back from the years
> like desire,
> and the many mouths
> open in absolution,
> and the nakedness,
> the belt flashing,
> the fists from nowhere
> the abandonment of love.

The world of Weigl's poems is harsh, even brutal, where ugliness and beauty flare out in unlikely places and are inextricably intertwined with

> one heart robbing another
> in a rented room, a great sadness
> and a great happiness, at the same time, descending.

The continual juxtaposition of present circumstance and memories from the past, such as his young son's bed-wetting and his own experience years before ("The Confusion of Planes We Must Wander in Sleep"), gives resonance to his rather sparse narratives. Characteristically, his poems conclude with a brief reflection exactly appropriate to the scene:

> what we pass on is not always a gift,
> not always grace or strength or music, but sometimes a
>   burden, . . .
> because even the weaknesses are a kind of beauty
> for the way they bind us into what love, finally, must be.

In such poems Weigl conveys the precise tone and character of a era that left an indelible mark on the American psyche. It is an impressive poetic achievement.

—Michael True

WEISS, Theodore (Russell)

Nationality: American. **Born:** Reading, Pennsylvania, 16 December 1916. **Education:** Muhlenberg College, Allentown, Pennsylvania, B.A. 1938; Columbia University, New York, M.A. 1940. **Family:** Married Renée Karol in 1941. **Career:** Instructor in English, University of Maryland, College Park, 1941, University of North Carolina, Chapel Hill, 1942–44, and Yale University, New Haven, Connecticut, 1944–46; assistant professor, 1946–52, associate professor, 1952–55, and professor of English, 1958–66, Bard College Annandale-on-Hudson, New York; lecturer, New School for Social Research, New York, 1955–56; visiting professor of poetry, Massachusetts Institute of Technology, Cambridge, 1961–62; lecturer, New York City YMHA, 1965–67; poet-in-residence, 1966–67, professor of English and creative writing, 1968–77, Paton Professor, 1977–87,

guest, Institute for Advanced Studies, 1986–87, and since 1987 emeritus professor, Princeton University, New Jersey. Hurst Professor, Washington University, St. Louis, 1978; lecturer for the United States Information Service in Southeast Asia, Hungary, and Denmark, 1979–80; poet-in-residence, Monash University, Clayton, Victoria, 1982; professor of English, Cooper Union, New York, 1988. Since 1943 founding editor, *Quarterly Review of Literature;* member, Wesleyan University Press Poetry Board, 1964–70; general editor, Princeton University Press Contemporary Poets series, 1974–78. Since 1964 honorary fellow, Ezra Stiles College, Yale University. **Awards:** Ford fellowship, 1953; Wallace Stevens award, 1956; National Endowment for the Arts grant, 1967, 1969; Ingram Merrill Foundation grant, 1974; Brandeis University Creative Arts award, 1977; Guggenheim fellowship, 1986–87; Shelley memorial award, 1989; PEN Club Special Achievement award for publishing, 1997; Williams/Derwood award for poetry, 1999. D.Litt.: Muhlenberg College, 1968; Bard College, 1973. **Address:** 26 Haslet Avenue, Princeton, New Jersey 08540, U.S.A.

PUBLICATIONS

Poetry

The Catch. New York, Twayne, 1951.
Outlanders. New York, Macmillan, 1960.
Gunsight. New York, New York University Press, 1962.
The Medium. New York, Macmillan, 1965.
The Last Day and the First. New York, Macmillan, 1968.
The World before Us: Poems 1950–1970. New York, Macmillan, 1970.
Fireweeds. New York, Macmillan, 1976.
Views and Spectacles: Selected Poems. London, Chatto and Windus, 1978.
The Aerialist. Princeton, New Jersey, Pilgrim Press, 1978.
Views and Spectacles: New and Selected Shorter Poems. New York, Macmillan, 1979.
Recoveries. New York, Macmillan, and London, Collier Macmillan, 1982.
A Slow Fuse: New Poems. New York, Macmillan, 1984.
From Princeton One Autumn Afternoon: Collected Poems. New York, Macmillan, 1987.
A Sum of Destructions. Baton Rouge, Louisiana State University Press, 1994.
Selected Poems: 1950–1995. Evanston, Illinois, Triquarterly Press, 1995.

Recording: *Theodore Weiss Reads from His Own Work,* CMS, 1975.

Other

Gerard Manley Hopkins, Realist on Parnassus. Privately printed, 1940.
The Breath of Clowns and Kings: A Study of Shakespeare. New York, Atheneum, and London, Chatto and Windus, 1971.
The Man from Porlock: Engagements 1944–1981. Princeton, New Jersey, Princeton University Press, 1982.
Toward a Classical Modernity and a Modern Classicism. Portree, Isle of Skye, Aquila, 1982.

Editor, *Selections from the Note-hooks of Gerard Manley Hopkins.* New York, New Directions, 1945.

Editor, with Renée Weiss, *Contemporary Poetry.* Princeton, New Jersey, Princeton University Press, 1975.

*

Manuscript Collection: Princeton University Library, New Jersey.

Critical Studies: By Harry Berger, in *The Fat Abbot* (New Haven, Connecticut), summer-fall 1961; Richard Howard, in *Alone with America,* New York, Atheneum, 1969, London, Thames and Hudson, 1970, revised edition, Atheneum, 1980, and in *Perspective* (St. Louis), 1969; Helen J.F. de Aquilar, in *Parnassus* (New York), 1980; interview, with Colette Inez, in *First Person Singular* edited by Joyce Carol Oates, Princeton, New Jersey, Ontario Review Press, 1983; Willard Spiegelman, in *Parnassus* (New York), fall-winter 1984.

Theodore Weiss comments:

Many years ago, in *A Controversy of Poets,* I wrote, "I am concerned in a proudly snippety time with the sustained poem." Though I have written many short poems since then, I see no reason to disagree with the above sentiment. In that statement I went on to regret "poetry's surrender of immense sectors of the world to prose, most of all the novel . . ." In the last fifteen-twenty years, I am happy to say, more and more poets have turned to the narrative and the dramatic, including the dramatic monologue. I continue to believe that "poetry can and must renew its older, larger interest in people and a world past the poet's self-preoccupations."

In "A Note" introducing my collected poems I stressed my sense of one's work as a growing, changing, yet fundamentally single thing. I said (here I quote the bulk of "A Note"):

Since writing for me has constituted something like a work in progress and since with time poems may show weaknesses as well as new possibilities, I have attended to these developments. Revision has been an increasingly integral part of my writing life. One early long [book-length] poem here was some twenty years in the making. A making which has continued in this latest round. Thus reverberations, deliberate and inevitable, sound throughout the volume. For, to some deep degree, each new poem is a reinforcement and realization drawn up out of and for its predecessors.

Over a lifetime the voice of a writer, as it changes, with luck also grows more unmistakably his or her own: the changes, bearing out earlier premises and promises, come home again. That voice strengthens itself by its very accommodating of others and the other. So from the start I was after a voice that could give voice to the many people inside and out, to the drama of their collision as . . . to the larger music of their harmony . . . An ideal I have held before me is a poetry, a language, absorbed in an exploiting its own immense resources yet, at the same time, transparent to the world at large.

*   *   *

Theodore Weiss is a formidable figure. For more than fifty years he has edited the *Quarterly Review of Literature.* His book *The Breath of Clowns and Kings* is probably the best study of Shakespeare's early work that we have. *The Man from Porlock,* a collection of essays, offers unexpected insights into such twentieth-century writers as Wallace Stevens, Ezra Pound, Yvor Winters, and Philip Larkin. The approach here is not dissimilar in some respects to that of C.S. Lewis, a comparison that Weiss might welcome. Biography, intentionality, personal recollection—all perform functions the New Critics of yesteryear would have fulfilled through verbal analysis.

Weiss's techniques succeed, however, because the prose in which they are deployed is easy and unforced. One is always conscious of a personal voice. Indeed, Weiss's criticism is so well written that it seems to spill over into his poetry. One could, in fact, say that much of his poetry is itself a kind of criticism. It is unfailingly literary, preoccupied with art and artistic effect, and powered by a highly evident interest in language. Weiss brought out his first book at an age unusually mature for a poet. Perhaps because of this, it is an especially attractive venture. It opens with "The Hook," a poem commemorating a young sculptress—"the woman who at last— / 'I do not use live models'—sculptured fish . . .''

There is a lyrical energy in the poem that is characteristic of Weiss's work taken as a whole. Run-on lines and composite words are typical, almost a matter of mannerisms. They testify that one of Weiss's poetic ancestors is Gerard Manley Hopkins. The use of short lines and stepped verse betoken William Carlos Williams to be another. Like this latter poet, Weiss aspires after the long poem. Also like Williams, however, Weiss has more gift for energy of phrase than for construction. The result is that the mind is often dazzled by local rhetoric while failing to grasp the larger works as entities. This is especially true of the ambitious poem *Gunsight,* which fills a volume of fifty-five pages. On the back cover of the volume there is an apt description of the poem within. "[*Gunsight*] is a narrative-dramatic psychological fantasy that records the sensations and memories of a wounded soldier as he undergoes surgery." The comment gives us a good idea of the subject matter, but it also suggests dispersion, for "narrative-dramatic psychological fantasy" seems to indicate a fairly mixed genre. At no point is a situation located with the degree of precision we find, for instance, in Robert Lowell's *Life Studies* or in Galway Kinnell's "The Avenue Bearing the Initial of Christ into the New World." Rather, there is a kind of lyric haze, with detail that never quite coalesces into scene or setting: "You zigzag like a furled-out, wind-flopt moth. / The breakers, toppled, hurl you onto roaring/ rocks . . ." *Gunsight* is, like its progenitor, Williams's *Paterson,* best read as a series of interconnected lyrics rather than as a single poem with a unifying tendency and a plot.

Weiss scores especially when his scholarship intersects with what seems to be a natural disposition toward elegy and regret. "Two for Heinrich Bleucher," from his collection of 1965, recalls a friend and colleague—"one, apart, till now squinting through the fumes . . ." The poem is ratified in the collection *A Slow Fuse.* Blücher, as the name is now spelled, is commemorated once more, along with Hannah Arendt, in possibly the most sustained verse its author has accomplished:

> At once I'm in a living
> room, its windows flung wide open
> to the sky, as if, someone unfolding
> a letter—
>   pressed inside its leaves
> a tiny, faded flower, mountain laurel,
> what is left of one particular morning—
> morning, atop this autumn afternoon,

its blazoning forth;
   gusts rousing
out of trees and braided with day's ric-
ochet from mountains hulked behind,
a couple dally, once more fledglings
nestled like the larks that towered round
them, rue-and-laurel-interwoven wreath . . .

This is a symphony of recollection and evocation. The tribute is so splendid as to compel belief in the quality of the couple thus invoked. Here the wide-ranging scholarship and empathy with the dead conjoin. The transitions have the inevitability we would expect of so practiced an editor, and the pattern of sound in the verse has a richness and variety that suggest, in no merely derivative sense, the major romantics. This volume, together with *The Catch,* would have been enough to set Weiss in the forefront of contemporary poets. With the oeuvre of the intervening years, including the opulent contribution of criticism, Weiss is certain, when future scholars come to review our literature, to appear a key to the age.

—Philip Hobsbaum

WEISSBORT, Daniel

Nationality: British. **Born:** London, 1 May 1935. **Education:** St. Paul's School, London, 1948–52; Queens' College, Cambridge, 1953–56, B.A. (honors) 1956, M.A. **Family:** Married Jill Anderson in 1961 (divorced 1979); two daughters and one son. **Career:** Director, Albion Knitwear, London, 1957–61. Advisory director, Poetry International, London, 1970–73; director, Carcanet Press, Oxford, later Cheadle, Cheshire, and Manchester, 1972–80. Visiting professor of comparative literature, 1974–75, since 1975 director of translation workshop, since 1980 professor of English and comparative literature, acting director of international writing program, 1986, and chair of comparative literature, 1987, University of Iowa, Iowa City. Member of the Poetry Society General Council, London, 1972–74. Co-founding editor, with Ted Hughes, *Modern Poetry in Translation,* London, 1965–83. Member of the Executive Board, American Literary Translators Association, 1982–86. **Awards:** Arts Council bursary, for translation, 1971, 1972; University of Iowa writing fellowship, 1973; Glatstein memorial prize (*Poetry,* Chicago), 1978; National Endowment for the Arts translation fellowship, 1981; Arts Council literature award, 1984. **Agent:** John Johnson, 45–47 Clerkenwell Green, London EC1R OHT, England. **Address:** Department of Comparative Literature, University of Iowa, Iowa City, Iowa 52242, U.S.A.

PUBLICATIONS

Poetry

The Leaseholder. Oxford, Carcanet, 1971.
In an Emergency. Oxford, Carcanet, 1972.
Soundings. Manchester, Carcanet, 1977.
Leaseholder: New and Collected Poems 1965–1985. Manchester, Carcanet, 1986.
Inscription. New York, Cross-Cultural Communications, 1990.
Fathers. Newcastle, Northern House, 1991.

Lake: New and Selected Poems. New York, Sheep Meadow Press, 1993.
Nietzsche's Attaché Case. Manchester, Carcanet, 1993.
Eretskelev (Dogland). Jerusalem, Carmel Publishing House, 1994.
What Was All the Fuss About? London, Anvil Press Poetry, and Chester Springs, Pennsylvania, Dufour, 1998.

Other

Editor and translator, *Natalya Gorbanevskaya: Poems, Trial, Prison.* Oxford, Carcanet, 1972.
Editor and translator, *Post-War Russian Poetry.* London, Penguin, 1974.
Editor and translator, with John Glad, *Russian Poetry: The Modern Period.* Iowa City, University of Iowa Press, 1978.
Editor, *Translating Poetry: The Double Labyrinth.* London, Macmillan, and Iowa City, University of Iowa Press, 1989.
Editor, *The Poetry of Survival: Post-War Poets of Central and Eastern Europe.* London, Anvil Press Poetry, and New York, St. Martin's Press, 1990.
Editor, with Max Hayward and Albert C. Todd, *20th Century Russian Poetry: Silver and Steel: An Anthology,* selected by Yevgeny Yevtushenko. New York, Doubleday, 1993.

Translator, *The Soviet People and Their Society,* by Pierre Sorlin. London, Pall Mall Press, and New York, Praeger, 1968.
Translator. *Guerillas in Latin America: The Technique of the Counter-State,* by Luis Mercier Vega. London, Pall Mall Press, and New York, Praeger, 1969.
Translator, *Scrolls: Selected Poems of Nikolai Zabolotsky.* London, Cape, 1971.
Translator, *A History of the People's Democracies: Eastern Europe since Stalin,* by François Fetjö. London, Pall Mall Press, 1971.
Translator, *The Rare and Extraordinary History of Holy Russia,* by Gustave Doré. London, Alcove Press, 1972.
Translator, *Nose! Nose? No-se! and Other Plays,* by Andrei Amalriki. New York, Harcourt Brace, 1973.
Translator, with Anthony Rudolf, *The War Is Over: Selected Poems,* by Evgeny Vinokurov. Cheadle, Cheshire, Carcanet, 1976.
Translator, *From the Night and Other Poems,* by Lev Mak. Ann Arbor, Michigan, Ardis, 1978.
Translator, *Ivan the Terrible and Ivan the Fool,* by Yevgeny Yevtushenko. London, Gollancz, 1979.
Translator, *Missing Person,* by Patrick Modiano. London, Cape, 1980.
Translator, *The World about Us,* by Claude Simon. Princeton, New Jersey, Ontario Review Press, 1983.
Translator, with Tomislav Longinovic, *Red Knight: Serbo-Croatian Women's Songs.* London, Menard/Kings, 1992.
Translator, with Anthony Rudolf and Audrey Jones, *Theme & Version: Plath & Ronsard,* by Yves Bonnefoy. London, Menard Press, and Berkeley, California, SPD, 1995.
Translator, *Selected Poems: Translated from the Russian,* by Nikolai Zabolotskii. Manchester, Carcanet, 1999.

*

Critical Studies: By Paul Oppenheimer, in *American Book Review,* 13(2), June 1991; by David Malcolm, in *Polish Review,* 38(1), 1993; by Michael Beard, in *North Dakota Quarterly,* 61(1), winter 1993.

Daniel Weissbort comments:

Writing poetry, for me, is trying to find a language I lost before birth. This is an obscure enterprise, to say the least, and I have discovered few guides. For me, writing poetry is indispensable to listening rather than the other way round. I have written here and there and feel I have some acquaintance now with my proper topography, but only some. Whereas others—the poets I most admire in our times, poets I have even translated, those of the first postwar generation of Middle Europe—write of what most concerns us, of our history, our mythology, of the fate of humankind and of this planet, I cannot see much beyond the space that opens up, again and again, around my head. But the language I reach for perhaps shares something with theirs. In recent years I have come to feel that my situation between languages, as it were, is beginning to resemble a country in its own right.

*   *   *

Daniel Weissbort aims at expressing himself through a type of poetry that approximates most closely to normal human speech. Over the years he has gradually perfected a method of writing that edits out all consciously ''poetic'' elements from his verse. Weissbort's style is shorn of elaboration in favor of a blunt, matter-of-fact utterance that comes as near as is possible to speaking thoughts aloud. Yet behind the apparent artlessness of his work lie a strong poetic intelligence and an organization and structure whose details are not always immediately evident to the reader.

Weissbort's is the poetry of unease, depicting as it does the vain struggles of the poet-narrator to impose an orderly routine on the continually threatening chaos of his life and the world about him. He is a prolific editor and translator of Russian literature, and his early collections—*The Leaseholder, In an Emergency,* and *Soundings*—tend at times to portray him as a character out of Goncharov or Dostoyevsky, a sad, ineffectual figure with his gloomy drinking bouts, low self-esteem, and the forebodings that dog his brief moments of happiness. Guilt and loss are presented as recurring themes, and love itself is seen as fragile and elusive, not entirely to be trusted. Even in the ecstasies of physical passion Weissbort is still painfully aware that he remains separate and apart: ''With each caress I lose you more / —pleasure's no guarantee at all—.'' Writing, it seems, serves him as an escape, an unreal ordering of experience in which, unlike life, he feels at home. Initiated into love and its pain, Weissbort looks back ruefully to his unattached innocence and finds himself writing comfortably in the absence of his beloved. Safety of this kind, however, cannot endure for long. Relationships and responsibilities break in upon him, disrupting his illusory calm and the poems he describes as ''fantasies of growing up.''

Leaseholder, a collection of Weissbort's poems from 1965 onward, blends work from the earlier volumes with later productions and reveals a stronger character than its predecessors. The Weissbort encountered here is less prone to self-pity and despair; he is a mature man who has met and survived the constant attacks of life to make it into his second half century. All the same, he remains vulnerable and introspective, his poems continually stressing man's essential fragility in a hostile universe, the helplessness of the well-meaning individual confronted by the complexities of love, loss, and death. In ''Rehearsal'' the restraint of his lines emphasizes the pain of a remembered incident that prefigured eventual separation: ''You leave. The thunderous prison silence / of your absence swallows up all sound. / I rehearse, abruptly shut the door, / and you rehearse not

looking round.'' Elsewhere he laments the loss of parents and friends, contemplating the void they have left and struggling to accept the fact that they are dead. Broodings on the terrifying finality of death haunt Weissbort's poems, the last part of *Leaseholder* concentrating on the gradual decline of his beloved mother. Forced to witness the slow disintegration as she loses her ability to communicate, then her sanity, and eventually her life, the poet explores in unsentimental but moving words the tragic nature of her death and his close spiritual identification with her: ''She was a kind of me, although / she didn't know it as I did. / And so, as I watched her breaking down, / it was as if I watched myself.'' The death of his mother is the creative force behind many of the later poems, Weissbort torn between incomprehension of the terrible reality—he speaks to her through the coffin as she is carried for burial—and bitter resentment at being left alone.

Threatened himself by reminders of his own mortality, Weissbort recalls the cancer operation that almost killed him, a piece of bone excised for ''the right to move on.'' Observing the world, he finds tokens of death and loss everywhere; the felling of a tree, an empty house, separation of lovers, or children growing up—all are noted as aspects of the same lurking malaise. This said, he handles the trauma and unease with a certain amount of detachment, avoiding the lure of self-pity as he sets down thoughts and experiences in his pared, unliterary style. Insight into his motives is keen and perceptive, and he is able to assess his own work with objectivity: ''I tried to write aphoristically / without embellishment. / Now pithiness does not become me.'' His Jewishness, an understated but significant element in his writing, surfaces with sad recollections of his childhood in Britain and in his idealized vision of America in ''A Dream of Tall Buildings.'' In ''Pity the Poor Racist'' Weissbort uses a gentle, self-mocking irony to ridicule his would-be enemy, revealing at once the murderous stupidity of racism and the sad, flawed natures of its adherents: ''Pity him . . . that he was not able to erect barriers, / that diversity became a creed, / that the idea of universal refuge instead of refuge for the elect / prevailed . . . oh, pity him, though he / is without pity.''

The loss of loved ones and a continuing examination of the self and its relationship with others inform the poems of the later collections. In *Fathers* Weissbort recalls his conversations with his long dead parent and the feelings of constraint and distance that held them apart from each other, and he speculates ruefully on his own flawed role as a father to his children. The wistful memories of ''What He Told Me'' and ''Suddenly over the Lake'' and the overwhelming, unexpected emotion of ''All You Needed'' are effectively contrasted with the murder of a marauding bat in ''Defending,'' and the grim vision of age and decay is experienced in ''Sanatorium.''

Some of these poems, together with earlier collections, reappear in *Nietzsche's Attaché Case,* where they are imaginatively used afresh as part of longer narrative works. ''Lake'' has Weissbort questioning the meaning of his life in an extended poem that incorporates the memories of ''Suddenly over the Lake,'' from *Fathers,* while ''What He Told Me'' and other poems are brilliantly reworked in ''The Gate,'' in which the author explores his feelings for both his parents with a moving honesty. In his later collection *What Was All the Fuss About?* Weissbort gathers poems written over the previous ten years. Individually and as a unit, they show him digging even deeper into everyday experience, past memories and dreams. His understatement is remarkable, matched by the wonderful immediacy of his writing, which details the thoughts and feelings of a given moment almost as it arrives. ''A Fool Rises!'' sees him pondering the decline of his body, while in ''Taking His Name'' he admits his lack of religious faith.

Whether contemplating the passing flight of a bumblebee, listening as the fridge outpaces his heartbeat in the night, or analyzing the aches and pains of approaching old age, Weissbort hooks the reader's attention with his short, hard-hitting verses.

While aware of his Jewish heritage, Weissbort remains suspicious of utopias and of religious beliefs that result in aggression. "Tribes" condemns the sanctified violence in the Middle East ("and finally the beatitudes are sung / over rivers flowing with blood"), and in "What Fools!" the poet presents the Promised Land as "a land lit by a fearful dawn, / a gulag-land." In spite of this, biblical images continue to appear in his work, most ironically as he recalls the death of Mr. Wathen, the teacher who changed Weissbort's name as being "too German" ("Mr. Wathen raised his brolly and strode / confidently into the Finchley Road. // Like Moses crossing the Red Sea, I thought.") Death and our response to its ever present threat remain at the center of his work, in his recollections of his father's death and in the poignant clutch of poems in memory of his late mother. Himself forced to confront the threat of cancer and a lifesaving operation, Weissbort examines his work and its meaning in "Born Again" and "I'd Like to Talk of This and That." The latter poem best sums up the essence of his writing. Weissbort would like to write about politics and history but instead must articulate "what I'm feeling, / what I'm feeling right now, for example, / about my continuing existence. // It seems that to define that feeling / is the least I can do." At the time of writing, one suspects that it is something he does better than anyone else.

Weissbort's poetry probes deeper than most, and his vision is both acute and honest. If some of the revelations are painful, they also are rewarding, and they confirm his position as an important, innovative stylist.

—Geoff Sadler

WELCH, James

Nationality: American. **Born:** Browning, Montana, in 1940. **Education:** University of Montana, Missoula, B.A.; Northern Montana College, Harve. **Awards:** National Endowment for the Arts grant, 1969; *Los Angeles Times* prize, for fiction, 1987. **Address:** c/o W.W. Norton and Co., 500 Fifth Avenue, New York, New York 10110, U.S.A.

PUBLICATIONS

Poetry

Riding the Earthboy 40. Cleveland, World, 1971; revised edition, New York, Harper, 1975.

Recording: *Sandra McPherson and James Welch Reading from Their Work,* Gertrude Clarke Whittal Poetry and Literature Fund, Library of Congress, 1979.

Novels

Winter in the Blood. New York, Harper, 1974.
The Death of Jim Loney. New York, Harper, 1979; London, Gollancz, 1980.
Fools Crow. New York, Viking, 1986.

The Indian Lawyer. New York, Penguin, 1990.
The Heartsong of Charging Elk: A Novel. New York, Doubleday, 2000.

Other

Killing Custer: The Battle of the Little Bighorn and the Fate of the Plains Indians, with Paul Stekler. New York, Norton, 1994.

Editor, with Ripley S. Hugg and Lois M. Welch, *The Real West Marginal Way: A Poet's Autobiography* by Richard Hugo. New York, Norton, 1986.
Editor, *Tribes: Stories and Poems.* Boston, Emerson College, 1994.

*

Critical Studies: *Four American Indian Literary Masters* by Alan R. Velie, Norman, University of Oklahoma Press, 1982; *James Welch* by Peter Wild, Boise, Idaho, Boise State University, 1983; *James Welch* by Ron McFarland, Lewiston, Idaho, Confluence Press, 1986; *Place and Vision: The Function of Landscape in Native American Fiction* by Robert M. Nelson, New York, P. Lang, 1993; "Ecological Restoration As Post-Colonial Ritual of Community in Three Native American Novels" by Christopher Norden, in *Studies in American Indian Literatures* (Virginia), 6(4), winter 1994; *Issues of Identity in the Writing of N. Scott Momaday, James Welch, Leslie Silko and Louise Erdrich* (dissertation) by Sidner John Larson, University of Arizona, 1994; "Finding Lost Generations: Recovering Omitted History in 'Winter in the Blood'" by Paul Eisenstein, in *MELUS* (Amherst, Massachusetts), 19(3), fall 1994; "About James Welch" by Don Lee, in *Ploughshares* (Boston), 20(1), spring 1994; *Between Voice and Text: Bicultural Negotiation in the Contemporary Native American Novel* (dissertation) by James Allison Gray, University of Wisconsin, Madison, 1995; "The Art of Hybridization—James Welch's 'Fools Crow'" by Hans Bak, in *American Studies in Scandinavia* (Copenhagen), 27(1), 1995; "A Literary Criticism: Mixed Blood Reading" by A. B. McClure, in *Wicazo SA Review* (Rapid City, South Dakota), 11(2), fall 1995; *Healing through Traditional Stories and Storytelling in Contemporary Native-American Fiction* (dissertation) by Jian Shi, Lehigh University, 1995; in *Western American Literature* (Logan, Utah), 32(1), spring 1997, and in *Updating the Literary West,* Forth Worth, Texas Christian University Press, both by William W. Bevis; "George Custer, Norman Maclean, and James Welch: Personal History and the Redemption of Defeat" by O. Alan Weltzien, in *Arizona Quarterly* (Tucson, Arizona), 52(4), winter 1996; "New Warriors, New Legends: Basketball in Three Native American Works of Fiction" by Peter Donahue, in *American Indian Culture and Research Journal* (Los Angeles), 21(2), 1997.

*   *   *

James Welch is a poet whose Native American background helped shape his only volume of poetry, *Riding the Earthboy 40,* a book that was one of the strongest first volumes of poetry published in the United States in the 1970s. As is the case with other fine young American Indian writers such as Simon Ortiz, Leslie Silko, Duane Niatum, and Ray Youngbear, Welch brings to his writing a deep consciousness of the earth that makes his poems exciting and alive, full of depth and mystery. This consciousness, mingled with a sense of loss, makes for some of the most powerful moments in his poems, as in the last lines of "Thanksgiving at Snake Butte":

> On top, our horses broke, loped through
> a small stand of stunted pine, then jolted
> to a nervous walk. Before us lay
> the smooth stones of our ancestors, the fish,
> the lizard, snake and bent-kneed
>
> bowman—etched by something crude,
> by a wandering race, driven by their names
> for time: its winds, its rain, its snow
> and the cold moon tugging at the crude figures
> in this, the season of their loss.

Welch's poems frequently revolve around contemporary Indian experience but without the sentimental overlay too many bad non-Indian poets have brought to their writings about Native Americans. The images in Welch's poems are like the northwest winds of a Montana winter, hard, crystal cold, and powerful, as in "Christmas Comes to Moccasin Flat"—"Christmas comes like this: Wise men / unhurried, candles bought on credit (poor price / for calves), warriors face down in wine sleep. / Winds cheat to pull heat from smoke . . ."—or in "Going to Remake This World":

> From my window, I see bundled Doris Horseman,
> black in the blowing snow, her raving son,
> Horace, too busy counting flakes to hide his face.
> He doesn't know. He kicks my dog
> and glares at me, too dumb to thank the men
> who keep him on relief and his mama drunk . . .

His poem "The Man from Washington" is already a minor classic, with its picture of a Bureau of Indian Affairs bureaucrat, "a slouching dwarf with rainwater eyes . . ." who promises

> that life would go on as usual,
> that treaties would be signed, and everyone—
> man, woman and child—would be inoculated
> against a world in which we had no part,
> a world of money, promise and disease.

With irony and honesty Welch has approached being both an Indian and a poet in contemporary American and has come out of it with poems that are always memorable and, in some cases, close to great.

—Joseph Bruchac

WELLS, Robert

Nationality: British. **Born:** Oxford, 17 August 1947. **Education:** King's College, Cambridge, 1965–68. **Family:** Married; one son and one daughter. **Career:** Forester in North Devon; teacher of English in Italy and Iran; English teacher, Leicester University, 1979–82. **Address:** c/o Carcanet Press, Fourth Floor, Conavon Court, 12–16 Blackfriars Street, Manchester M3 5BQ, England.

PUBLICATIONS

Poetry

Shade Mariners, with Dick Davis and Clive Wilmer. Cambridge, Gregory Spiro, 1970.
The Winter's Task. Manchester, Carcanet, 1977.
Selected Poems. Manchester, Carcanet, 1986.
Lusus. Manchester, Carcanet, 1999.

Other

Translator, *The Georgics,* by Virgil. Manchester, Carcanet, 1982.
Translator, *The Idylls,* by Theocritus. Manchester, Carcanet, 1988.

*

Critical Study: "'Incidentals of Remoteness': Robert Wells and the Idea of Pastoral" by Rodney Edgecombe, in *English Studies in Africa* (Johannesburg, South Africa), 32(1), 1989.

*　　*　　*

Robert Wells was first published in company with Dick Davis and Clive Wilmer in the booklet *Shade Mariners,* and his output since then certainly cannot be described as prolific. A selection of his work was included in two anthologies edited by Michael Schmidt—*Ten English Poets* (1976) and *Some Contemporary Poets of Britain and Ireland* (1983). In addition, there is a *Selected Poems* that includes poems from his critically well received earlier book, *The Winter's Task,* and also selections from his translations. Another volume, *Lusus,* was published in 1999.

Wells has chosen not to publish imitative juvenilia or otherwise to dazzle his readers with a showy, youthful brilliance. Instead, we find in his still-too-few poems a quiet yet confident ability to render a variety of feelings in words with precision and clarity. Wells does not adopt a persona in his work. He is a man whose attention is focused on a landscape or place outside himself and who renders that place as itself while simultaneously remaining aware of his own sensations in relation to it. This can be seen, for example, in the early "The Wind Blows," which succinctly expresses the small particulars of a sunny landscape through a subtle and delicate use of rhythm:

> The wind blows. Winds blow the
> Hill green and grey. Olives
> Are alive with light. Fat grow the
> Grapes green-misted with a mist that lives.

Wells is the contemplative artist. If this appears to set him apart from many active inventors of a contemporary idiom, it nonetheless allows him a distinctly recognizable style of his own, formally restrained yet unforced and natural in tone, as in "Shape of Air":

> It has lighted on you, this shape of air.
> I don't want you to know that it is there:
> Not yours or mine, as by the gate you stand
> That divides the mountain from the worked land

Wells's modest and decorous stylishness always remains true to his feeling for words and rhythms. His poems are often laconic and, at times, almost lapidary in their brevity. One such poem, "Not like the Fields," quoted here in full, uses understatement to express an unruly emotion and two types of nature:

> His nature was mild like the fields.
> It was the soft turf under his tread,
> The alteration of weather.
> But desire was in his nature too
> And that was not like the fields.

If these poems have antecedents, then Edward Thomas has to be named. Wells is one of a line of English poets who never strain for effects, rhetorical or otherwise, and without whom we would be lacking some of our most authentic talents of the last half of the twentieth century, Norman Cameron, James Reeves, and Philip Larkin among them.

The distinctive flavor of Wells's poems is found in a mix of the rigor of epigram and a naturally meditative sensibility. He is a poet who takes us into his confidence and who, on a first reading, can appear vulnerable and, on a second, curiously impersonal. An example is "For Pasolini," addressed to the great Italian filmmaker, which is both personal in tone and yet extremely objective in content:

> Vecchio ragazzo di Casarsa, dear protagonist,
> Where shall we find the like of your intelligence?
> The hunters who come here on Sunday with their
>   dogs and guns
> Are not enough to keep the forest paths open.
> Two years untrodden, and bramble will cover the track,
> The broom lean across.

The later poem "Richard Wilson in Wales," which takes another subject from art, provides us with insight into the work of the eighteenth-century painter of landscape:

> His mind was a lake trapped in a mountain hollow,
> A thin trickle spilling over stones to a river
> That wound where in youth he tracked it, to Italy—
> The fields where the Graces showed themselves
>   and danced.
> The mountain shuts out the view and dulls the water

> But the clouds are touched with a remembered light.

Wells has translated both the *Georgics* of Virgil and the idylls of Theocritus with distinction. This should hardly come as a surprise, for his own poems, in their concise directness, have clearly learned from some of the elements of classical literature. In the introduction to his translation of the *Georgics,* highly praised by Peter Levi as "the best Virgil's *Georgics* since Dryden's," Wells unintentionally supplies us with an insight into his own passionate delight in Virgil and also what poetry can do in the world:

> Virgil's clarity is not a clarity of surface—it has not that sharpness of edge and line that Ezra Pound has taught us to look for. To read Virgil is like looking down through very clear water; one is barely conscious of the surface, but the objects on the riverbed are made to shine. Bathed in his sensibility the world has a subdued brightness, like pebbles under water, all their colours enlivened. I have tried to render something of this.

Wells's translation of the idylls of Theocritus also is impressive and includes a memorable version of "The Lovesongs," simultaneously cool and passionate, as in the following song:

> My right eye twitched for luck. Shall I see her now?
> I shall settle myself against this pine as I sing.
> She may take some notice; she isn't made of steel.

We should value Wells's poetry if we set any store by Thomas Hardy's phrase defining poetry as "closeness of phrase to vision," which is precisely what Wells aims for and, at times, achieves.

—Jonathan Barker

WENDT, Albert

Nationality: Samoan. **Born:** Apia, Western Samoa, 27 October 1939; member of the Aiga Sa-Tuala. **Education:** New Plymouth Boys High School, New Zealand, graduated 1957; Ardmore Teacher's College, diploma in teaching, 1959; Victoria University, Wellington, 1960–64, M.A. (honors) in history 1964. **Family:** Married Jennifer Elizabeth Whyte in 1964; two daughters and one son. **Career:** Teacher, 1964–69, and principal, 1969–73, Samoa College, Apia; senior lecturer, 1974–75, assistant director of Extension Services, 1976–77, and professor of Pacific literature, 1982–87, University of the South Pacific, Suva, Fiji. Since 1988 professor of English, University of Auckland. Since 1978 director, University of the South Pacific Centre, Apia, Western Samoa. Editor, *Bulletin,* now *Samoa Times,* Apia, 1966, and Mana Publications, Suva, Fiji, 1974–80. Coordinator, Unesco Program on Oceanic Cultures, 1975–79. **Awards:** *Landfall* prize, 1963; Wattie award, 1980; Commonwealth Book prize for Southeast Asia and Pacific, 1992. **Agent:** Tim Curnow, Curtis Brown (Australia) Pty. Ltd., 27 Union Street, Paddington, New South Wales 2021, Australia. **Address:** Department of English, University of Auckland, Private Bag, Auckland, New Zealand.

PUBLICATIONS

Poetry

Inside Us the Dead: Poems 1961 to 1974. Auckland, Longman Paul, 1976.
Shaman of Visions. Auckland, Auckland University Press, 1984; Oxford, Oxford University Press, 1985.
Photographs. Auckland, Auckland University Press, 1995.

Plays

Comes the Revolution (produced Suva, Fiji, 1972).
The Contract (produced Apia, Western Samoa, 1972).

Novels

Sons for the Return Home. Auckland, Longman Paul, 1973; London, Penguin, 1987.
Pouliuli. Auckland, Longman Paul, 1977; Honolulu, University Press of Hawaii, 1980; London, Penguin, 1987.

Leaves of the Banyan Tree. Auckland, Longman Paul, 1979; London, Allen Lane, 1980; as *The Banyan,* New York, Doubleday, 1984.
Ola. Auckland, Penguin Books, 1991.
Black Rainbow. Auckland, Penguin Books, 1992.

Short Stories

Flying-Fox in a Freedom Tree. Auckland, Longman Paul, 1974.
The Birth and Death of the Miracle Man. London, and New York. Viking, 1986.
The Best of Albert Wendt's Short Stories. Auckland, Random House New Zealand, 1999.

Other

Editor, *Some Modern Poetry from Fiji [Western Samoa, the New Hebrides, the Solomon Islands, Vanuatu].* Suva, Fiji, Mana, 5 vols., 1974–75.
Editor, *Lali: A Pacific Anthology.* Auckland, Longman Paul, 1980.
Editor, *Nuanua: Pacific Writing in English since 1980.* Honolulu, University of Hawaii, 1995.

*

Critical Studies: ''Towards a New Oceania'' by the author, in *Mana Review* (Suva, Fiji), 1(1), January 1976; chapter on Wendt in *South Pacific Literature: From Myth to Fabulation,* by Subramani, Suva, Fiji, University of the South Pacific, 1985; ''Blue Myth Brooding in Orchid: A Third-World Reappraisal of Island Poetics,'' in *Journal of West Indian Literature* (Kingston, Jamaica), 1(2), June 1987, and ''Anthopologists and Other Frauds,'' in *Comparative Literature* (Eugene, Oregon), 46(2), spring 1994, both by Graham Huggan; ''Intertextuality in the Fiction of Camus and Wendt'' by Evelyn Ellerman, and ''Allegories of the Novel in Albert Wendt's 'Pouliuli''' by Joseph Chadwick, both in *Comparative Literature East and West: Traditions and Trends,* edited by Cornelia Moore and Raymond A. Moody, Honolulu, University of Hawaii Press, 1989; ''Fables of Interculturality: Some Contemporary South Pacific Narratives'' by Hartwig Isernhagen, in *Commonwealth Essays and Studies* (Dijon, France), 12(2), spring 1990; ''The Attempt 'To Snare the Void and Give It Word''' by Jean-Pierre Durix, in *International Literature in English: Essays on the Major Writers,* edited by Robert L. Ross, New York, Garland, 1991; ''Multi-Ethnic Literature in the Classroom: Whose Standards?'' by Sandra Kiser Tawake, in *World Englishes* (Tarrytown, New York), 10(3), winter 1991; ''A Tribute to the Fa'a Samoa: Albert Wendt's 'Birth and Death of the Miracle Man''' by Valerie O'Rourke, in *World Literature Today* (Norman, Oklahoma), 66(1), winter 1992; Albert Wendt issue of *Commonwealth Essays and Studies* (Dijon, France),16(2), spring 1993; ''Toward a New Tourism: Albert Wendt and Becoming Attractions'' by Robert Chi, in *Cultural Critique* (Cary, North Carolina), 37, fall 1997; ''Man and His/Story in the Poetry of Albert Wendt'' by Carole Froude-Durix, in *The Contact and the Culmination,* edited by Marc Delrez and Benedicte Ledent, Liege, Belgium, L3, 1997; ''Imagining the Future: Restructuring Identity in 'Pouliuli' and 'Maiba''' by Sarah J. Doetschman, in *World Literature Today* (Norman, Oklahoma), 72(1), winter 1998; ''Return to Exile: Locating Home'' by Juniper Ellis, in *Jouvert* (Raleigh, North Carolina), 2(2), 1998; in *Spiritcarvers: Interviews*

with Eighteen Writers from New Zealand, edited by Antonella Sarti, Amsterdam, Rodopi, 1998.

* * *

''I belong to Oceania,'' says the Samoan poet Albert Wendt, ''and it nourishes my spirit, helps to define me, and feeds my imagination.'' But while the vivid myths and legends and the lush tropical landscapes of Wendt's native Polynesian islands may inspire and sustain the poet, they may also flatter to deceive him. Removed both from the geographical mainland and from the perceived cultural mainstream, third world island poets such as Wendt may well feel that they are living in a state of perpetual exile, a feeling exacerbated by the knowledge that their geographical and cultural environment has historically been the subject of other people's myths. Much of Wendt's poetry is a reaction against the tyranny of European myths of a South Sea island paradise that not only distort, or ignore altogether, the actual experiences of island life—experiences that bear the scars, both physical and mental, of colonial intrusion—but that also impair the vision of native island poets whose creativity is compromised by the stock images and inherited clichés of their colonial education.

Not surprisingly, then, colonialism is the favored target for Wendt's satirical verse, whose most bitter invective is directed toward the injustices of a system that has continued to have a profound impact on island life and on the islanders' perceptions of themselves long after the statutory declaration of political independence. Wendt's poetry takes cynical delight in the irony that the celebrated *Fa'a-Samoa,* or ''Samoan way of life,'' is shot through with the contradictions of colonialism, as in ''The Faa-Somoa Is Perfect, They Sd'':

> its true, they sd, our samoa
> is a paradise, we venerate our royalty,
> our pastors and leaders and our beloved dead
>
> god gave us the faa-samoa and
> only he can take it away, they sd
> amen, i sd
>
> their imported firstclass whisky
> was alive with corpses: my uncle
> and his army of hungry kids,
> malnutritioned children in dirty wards,
> an old woman begging in the bank,
> my generation migrating overseas
> for jobs, while politicians
> and merchants brag obesely
> in the RSA, and pastors bang
> out sermons about the obedient
> and righteous life—aiafu
> all growing fat in
> a blind man's paradise

The historical forces of colonialism have to be reckoned with, but they have yet to be defeated. The long autobiographical poem ''Inside Us the Dead'' provides a particularly good example of Wendt's attempt to come to terms with an often traumatic past in which the disjointed events of history are transmuted into, if never fully redeemed by, the regenerative patterns of indigenous myth.

Like the prose fiction for which he is better known, Wendt's poetry is hybrid in form, reflecting the multiple heritage of his oceanic culture. The interweaving of Polynesian oral and European literary traditions, along with the ironic juxtaposition of elements from high- and lowbrow culture, are most in evidence in Wendt's longer poems. A striking example can be found in the bizarre "Where the Mind Is." Here Wendt exercises his skill in the grotesque by producing a series of offbeat, and often thoroughly unsavory, metaphors for the workings of the poetic imagination, whose activities are compared to the moronic acrobatics of "Tarzan the Swinging Poet," to the indiscriminate consumption of pseudo-American "Buddies," and to the lurid fantasies of a modern-day Marquis de Sade. Wendt's most effective combination of European and Polynesian material is in the rightly acclaimed "Inside Us the Dead," where "imported" (Christian) and indigenous (pagan) symbols come together to illustrate the poem's main theme of fruitless sacrifice:

> No sanctuary
> from the sun-black seed
> inside and self's cell—
> coral lacerating the promise,
> self-inflicted wounds at the altar
> of power will not heal.

The tortured self-consciousness of "Inside Us the Dead" and the warped cynicism of "Where the Mind Is" might be considered typical of what the Fijian critic Subramani has called Wendt's "crippled cosmos," a nightmarish world inhabited by the freaks and monsters of a deeply troubled, even pathologically disturbed, mind. But while many of Wendt's poems frighten us with their gleeful self-destructiveness, others delight us with their ready wit or move us with their elegiac tributes to the past, as does "Dawn to Night":

> Above your head the round light dangles.
> I watch you as the night ticks around us
> and remember those times
>
> in the room of our youth:
> dark skies until you walked in
> and I glowed with your joy.

Wendt's best poems combine some or even all of these elements. In the powerful "Nightmare to Waking," for example, the poet's exorcism of a malevolent ancestral past allows for the exalted vision of a "reborn" future:

> My life
> to begin where the nightmare ended
> and crosses stand like islands:
> Upolu, Savaii, Apolima, and Manono
> are scented with morning.

Poetry such as this is technically accomplished, but it is also courageous. Wendt's brutal honesty sets an example for the increasing number of writers in the South Pacific region whose "individual journeys into the Void . . . are creating a new Oceania."

—Graham Huggan

WEVILL, David (Anthony)

Nationality: Canadian. **Born:** Yokohama, Japan, 15 March 1935. **Education:** Trinity College School, Port Hope, Ontario; Fisher Park High School, Ottawa; Caius College, Cambridge, B.A. 1957. **Family:** Married Assia Gutman in 1960. **Career:** Lecturer in English, University of Mandalay, Burma, 1958–60; fellow, National Translation Center, Austin, Texas, after 1968. Member of the Department of English, University of Texas, Austin. **Awards:** Eric Gregory award, 1963; Richard Hillary memorial prize, 1965; Arts Council triennial prize, 1965, and bursary, 1965, 1966 (Great Britain); Guggenheim fellowship, 1981–82; Canada Council grant, 1989. **Address:** Department of English, University of Texas, Austin, Texas 78712, U.S.A.

PUBLICATIONS

Poetry

Penguin Modern Poets 4, with David Holbrook and Christopher Middleton. London, Penguin, 1963.
Birth of a Shark. London, Macmillan, and New York, St. Martin's Press, 1964.
A Christ of the Ice-Floes. London, Macmillan, and New York, St. Martin's Press, 1966.
Firebreak. London, Macmillan, 1971.
Where the Arrow Falls. London, Macmillan, 1973; New York, St. Martin's Press, 1974.
Other Names for the Heart: New and Selected Poems, 1964–1984. Toronto, Exile, 1985.
Figure of Eight. Toronto, Exile, 1987; Plymouth, Devon, Shearsman. 1988.
Child Eating Snow. Toronto, Exile, 1994.

Other

Casual Ties. Austin, Texas, Curbstone, 1983.

Translator, with Edwin Morgan, *Sándor Weöres and Ferenc Juhász: Selected Poems.* London, Penguin, 1970.

*

Critical Study: "David Wevill's *A Christ of the Ice-Floes:* Vision of the Elemental World" by Anthony Saroop, in *Pluck 1* (Edmonton, Alberta), 1967.

David Wevill comments:

I have tried to create complete poems, not just passing observations. So far I think I have succeeded only in a few poems. I do not know what direction a poem will take until it is finished. The theme therefore is unconscious. I have been much taken with Spanish poetry: Lorca, Neruda, Machado, Paz. They have a terseness that I admire and am only just perhaps starting to achieve. I do not use any particular verse form; the poem takes its own form. I cannot point to any particular influences; these have been many, as much, say, from prose and painting as from other poetry. Landscape is in my poetry, not as nature, but in the North American or Spanish sense as something "out there."

*   *   *

David Wevill took the title for his collection *Where the Arrow Falls* from a North American Indian legend that told the story of three brothers who shot arrows into the air on the promise that they would build their kingdoms on the spots where the projectiles landed. Two of the three brothers were successful in finding their arrows. The third never found his arrow, and he spent his entire life traveling and searching for the elusive key to his dreams. Throughout Wevill's poetry the metaphor, indeed the motif, of the search becomes the keynote. In some poems he searches for solace from his sadness, for answers to the questions that perplex and haunt him, while in others he searches for the three lost women of his life: a mother, a wife, and a lover. Only in his volume *Figure of Eight* does he come to the conclusion that the circuitous search is neither linear nor temporal but circular; the goal is the search itself. In the final section of *Figure of Eight,* in the poem "Full Moon Story," as the wanderer's story and experience wind back upon themselves like a Möbius strip, Wevill comes to the realization that

> The world seen through glass
> only resembles the world we
> cut so easily . . .
>
> . . . Somewhere at the heart of it all
> someone suffers, writhes, hangs limp
> and comes to life in a dream
> I can't imagine.

The overwhelming sense of suffering that pervades Wevill's poetry seems to be the hard-won and bitterly endured process of the pain of purification, the result of which is a spiritual stillness. It is an almost oriental sense of equilibrium or calm in which the individual finds himself and his own existence in tune with a world that, ultimately, cannot share his subjective agony. Simply put, the search in Wevill's work is the process of rising above one's own subjectivity. In "The Text," which concludes *Other Names for the Heart: New and Selected Poems, 1964–1984,* he writes,

> He touches the tip of the cigarette to the circle,
> and the circle burns, expands. Its black edge eats
> the words he had written, eats into the text of
> the sun, the beginning of his day, and stops for no
> reason at the O of Odysseus, whose journey is not
> yet complete, and therefore not fully begun: as
> one must know the end before he begins: the stillness
> in the movement of the heart.

Wevill's sense of sadness, which earlier critics had described as "intense personal responses intellectualized," has become more carefully delineated in his later volumes. The responses have become less intellectual and more philosophical so that the persona of the poems is a man who is in search of questions and answers, not only cerebrally but also emotionally. The reader, however, must not look for pragmatic interpretations and solutions to the problems the poems confront. Instead, the beauty and the strength of Wevill's work, as in Leonard Cohen's poetry, lies in its elusiveness, in the poet's desire to make the ethereal understandable. In the title poem "Other Names for the Heart" Wevill writes passionately about an attempted suicide of the composer Robert Schumann:

> and sometimes, when the light is good
> we move as music, we compose ourselves
> in patterns of exact time
>
> and dance as blood, the piano
> silent, the melody in ourselves.
>
> But it takes the courage of gods
> and we are human. It requires
>
> what our eyes must refuse to see
> to see ourselves . . .
>
> what they rescued was a question answered.

"The stillness in the movement of the heart" appears to be the answer not only to the question of Schumann but also to the question Wevill has asked of his own life.

In one of Wevill's earliest and most enigmatic poems, the title poem from *A Christ of the Ice-Floes,* the persona finds himself in a "halfway season," perhaps on the verge of confronting his own suffering, and remakes "himself in the image of March," a naive and innocent young man who discovers that the world is a place of changes that neither need nor offer any justification. Like Peter Redgrove, his contemporary and associate in Philip Hobsbaum's Group workshop of the early 1960s, Wevill began as a poet concerned with entropy and energy, with effects more than the causes. "Birth of a Shark," Wevill's early masterpiece from his book by the same title, focuses on the raw energy and instinctual curiosity of a young shark that confronts a group of swimmers. It is a poem that owes more to E.J. Pratt's "The Shark" than to Redgrove's earliest work:

> What had become of the young shark?
> It was time for the ocean to move on,
> Somehow, sheathed in the warm current
> He'd lost his youthful bite, and fell
> Shuddering among the feelers of kelp
> And dragging weeds. His belly touched sand,
> The shark ran aground on his own shadow.

Unlike his British counterparts in the Group, Wevill's early poetry was less concerned with the minute details of nature (what some critics have called "The Group Poem") and more interested in emotional responses to place, landscape, season, and element. This difference may be attributable to the fact that Wevill was and still is a Canadian, both in nationality and in poetic outlook, and, like many of his Canadian contemporaries, such as Gwendolyn MacEwen, the narration of the external world gradually metamorphoses itself in his canon into a critical examination of the internal needs and struggles of the individual. The leap between the naturalistic work of his first two volumes and the more philosophical speculations of those of the 1980s is not so great considering that it was made via the route of dream, mythology, and primitive spiritualism in *Firebreak* and *Where the Arrow Falls.*

In "The Story of Colours," from *Other Names for the Heart,* Wevill analyzes his position in the world and makes an effort to come to terms with his losses:

> The philosopher on his walk
> comes upon them, looks away and
> passes on. And he is the one
> who will suffer the memory of what he has seen
>
> forever, his passion, compassion,
> life, lived in praise of light, light's heart
> broken in him by this accident. The eyes
> are telltales only. They have not the power
>
> to bring summer down from the hills,
> to heal what grows cold. The days
> wander like torches lost in the dark. They
> waver, shine brilliantly, and almost lose heart.

The Wevill of the later poetry, however, does not lose heart; in fact, he finds it. His later poems are tender, domestic at times, less searching, and more accepting, with a kind of Iberian resignation that dwells on the border between solace and grief. His dead, he realizes in "Figure of Eight," are dead, and his life must continue. The searcher becomes the survivor, and the survivor becomes the sage among the shadows:

> The light has hands and turns itself
> so slowly from frown to smile
> the day latening toward the coast
> in sunlight on a clear road with the tape-deck playing
> the light back to you
> > > the evening *raga* sung
> in the raw voice of the sea
> the three descending notes repeating
> > > > naming you again
> asking you to return. And you are gone.
>
> *En la bendita soledad, tu sombra.*
> In the blessed solitude, your shadow also.

—Bruce Meyer

WHALEN, Philip (Glenn)

Nationality: American. **Born:** Portland, Oregon, 20 October 1923. **Education:** Reed College, Portland, B.A. in literature and languages 1951. **Military Service:** U.S. Army Air Force, 1943–46. **Career:** Lecturer and teacher: ordained as Zen Buddhist priest, 1973: Shuso (Acting Head Monk), Zen Mountain Center, 1975. Lecturer, San Francisco Zen Center and Zen Mountain Center, Tassajara Springs, California. Head Monk, Dharma Sangha, Santa Fe, New Mexico, 1984. Head of practice, 1989–91, and since 1991 abbot, One Mountain Temple, San Francisco. **Awards:** Poets Foundation award, 1962; Ratcliff award, 1964; American Academy grant, 1965, 1992; Commission on Poetry grant, 1968, 1970, 1971; Morton Dauwen Zabel award, 1986; Fund for Poetry award, 1987, 1992. **Address:** 57 Hartford Street, San Francisco, California, 94114, U.S.A.

PUBLICATIONS

Poetry

Three Satires. Privately printed, 1951.
Self-Portrait, from Another Direction. San Francisco, Auerhahn Press, 1959.
Like I Say. New York, Totem-Corinth, 1960.
Memoirs of an Interglacial Age. San Francisco, Auerhahn Press, 1960.
Hymnus ad Patrem Sinensis. San Francisco, Four Seasons, 1963.
Monday in the Evening: 21 Vlll 61. Milan, East 128, 1963.
Three Mornings. San Francisco, Four Seasons, 1964.
Goddess. Privately printed, 1964.
Every Day. Eugene Oregon, Coyote, 1965.
Dear Mr. President, with Gary Snyder. Privately printed, 1965.
Highgrade: Doodles, Poems. Eugene, Oregon, Coyote, 1966.
The Education Continues Along. Eugene, Oregon, Toad Press, 1967.
T/O. San Francisco, Dave Haselwood, 1967.
On Bear's Head: Selected Poems. New York, Harcourt Brace, 1969.
Severance Pay: Poems 1967–1969. San Francisco, Four Seasons, 1970.
Scenes of Life at the Capital. Bolinas, California, Grey Fox Press, 1971.
The Kindness of Strangers: Poems 1969–1974. Bolinas, California, Four Season, 1975.
Decompressions: Selected Poems. Bolinas, California, Grey Fox Press, 1977.
Enough Said: Fluctuat nec Mergitur: Poems 1974–1979. San Francisco, Grey Fox Press, 1980.
Heavy Breathing. San Francisco, Four Seasons, 1983.
Overtime. Newark, New Jersey, Penguin, 1999.
Some of These Days. N.p., Desert Rose Press, 1999.

Recording: *By and Large: Philip Whalen Reading His Work,* UBIK Sound, 1987.

Novels

You Didn't Even Try. San Francisco, Coyote, 1967; published with *Imaginary Speeches for a Brazen Head,* as *Two Novels,* Somerville, Massachusetts, Zephyr Press, 1985.
Imaginary Speeches for a Brazen Head. Los Angeles, Black Sparrow Press, 1972; published with *You Didn't Even Try,* as *Two Novels,* Somerville, Massachusetts, Zephyr Press, 1985.

Other

The Invention of the Letter: A Beastly Morality (for children). New York, Carp and Whitefish Press, 1967.
Prolegomena to a Study of the Universe. Berkeley, California, Poltroon Press, 1976.
On Bread and Poetry: A Panel Discussion, with Lew Welch and Gary Snyder. Bolinas, California, Grey Fox Press, 1977.

Off the Wall: Interviews with Philip Whalen, edited by Donald Allen. Bolinas, California, Four Seasons, 1978.
The Diamond Noodle. Berkeley, California, Poltroon Press, 1979.

*

Manuscript Collections: Columbia University, New York; Reed College, Portland, Oregon.

Critical Studies: "Whalen Issue" of *Intransit* (Eugene, Oregon), 1967; introduction by Kevin Power to *Prolegomena to a Study of the Universe,* 1976; introduction by Paul Christensen to *Two Novels,* 1985; *All Come to This: The Life and Works of Lew Welch in the Context of the Twentieth Century* (dissertation) by Eric Paul Shaffer, University of California, Davis, 1992; "The Circumambulation of Mt. Tamalpais" by David Robertson, in *Western American Literature* (Logan, Utah), 30(1), spring 1995.

Philip Whalen comments:

I try to write in colloquial American speech, but I often fail because many of the subjects I am interested in—Buddhism, Chinese and Japanese literature and painting and architecture, formal symphonic music, the history of science, historiography, archaeology—are not much discussed by my fellow Americans. I try to do the best I can. I began studying English poetry at an early age, and I continue to work at it.

*   *   *

Many contemporary American poets, including Allen Ginsberg, W.S. Merwin, Gary Snyder, and Lucien Stryk, have been deeply affected by Zen, but none so much as Philip Whalen, who went to live in a Zen commune in California. Whalen turned to Zen rather late in life, but when he did he committed himself completely. With shaved head and saffron robes, Whalen became a unique figure on the poetic scene.

Whalen has always been different from everyone else, and he has felt proud of it. In an early poem, "Further Notice," he proclaims, "I shall be myself— / Free, a genius, an embarrassment / Like the Indian, the buffalo / Like Yellowstone National Park." In his early writings, however, Whalen's sense of his singularity often led to feelings of alienation and even, in his frequent references to his "own gross shape," to self-loathing. It also led to producing some exceedingly shrill political verse.

Whalen's Zen awakening changed his approach. Though still believing, as he states in his fine "Birthday Poem," that "the world is wicked by definition; my job is to stay aware of it," Whalen came to use methods of expression and poetic subjects that are more subtle. In his preface to *Decompressions* Whalen remarks, "I have a hunch that if I write a really good poem today about the weather, about a flower or any apparently 'irrelevant' . . . subject, that the revolution will be hastened considerably more than if I composed a pamphlet attacking the government and the capitalist system." Thus, instead of overt political statements, his later work offers insights gained by and expressed in the traditional Zen manner, as in his arresting poem "Never Apologize, Never Explain":

A pair of strange new birds in the maple tree
Peer through the windows,

Mother and father visiting me:
    "You are unmarried,
    No child begot
    Now we are birds, now you've
        forgotten us
    Although in dreams we visit you
        in human shape"

They speak Homer's language
Sing like Aeschylus

The life of a poet: less than 2/3rds of a second

In "Science and Language" Whalen writes, "It is impossible to write in English about Japanese / Persons, places and things," but his own work, in poems like "Eamd," belies this. Nevertheless, his subject matter is most frequently American and is usually centered on "the ruined city / San Francisco." What is perhaps most remarkable about his work is the contrast made between its Zen sensibility and its contemporary American setting, a society in which, as "In the Night" says, we "fall upward / Into a fake superiority."

Zen offers Whalen a genuine superiority. It is a discipline that requires much of a man and of a writer, and it is one that makes a person constantly aware of his own shortcomings. Nevertheless, in Zen, as in the poetic imagination, there always exists the potential for human perfection. All of this is captured succinctly in "For Kai Snyder":

7:V:60 (an interesting *lapsus calami*)
A few minutes ago I tried a somersault; couldn't do it
I was afraid and I couldn't remember how.
I fell over on one shoulder,
Rolled about and nearly went over backwards
And finally hurt my chest.
What kind of psychomotor *malebolge* had I got into . . .
"This is old age, &c."

After thinking it all over
Imagining how it might be done
I performed three forward somersaults, 7:V:70
Aged 46 years 6 months and 37 days.

—Dennis Lynch

WHITE, Kenneth

Nationality: British. **Born:** Glasgow, Lanarkshire, 28 April 1936. **Education:** University of Glasgow, M.A. (honors) in French and German 1959; University of Munich; University of Paris. **Family:** Married Marie-Claude Charlut. **Career:** Lecturer in English, Sorbonne, Paris, 1962–63, and Faculty of Letters, Pau, France, 1967–68; lecturer in French, University of Glasgow 1963–67. Lecturer in English, Institut Charles V, 1969–83, and since 1983 professor of 20th-century poetics, Sorbonne, University of Paris. Founder, *Jargon Papers,* Glasgow, *Feuillage,* Pau, *The Feathered Egg,* Paris, and the *Cahiers de Gèopoètique,* organ of the Institut International de Gèopoètique.

Awards: *Prix Médicis Étranger,* 1983; French Academy Grand Prix de Rayonnement, 1985; de Vigny prize, 1987. **Address:** Gwenved, Chemin du Goaquer, 22560 Trebeurden, France.

PUBLICATIONS

Poetry

Wild Coal. Paris, Club des Etudiants d'Anglais, 1963.
En Toute Candeur (includes essays). Paris, Mercure de France, 1964.
The Cold Wind of Dawn. London, Cape, 1966.
The Most Difficult Area. London, Cape Goliard Press, and New York, Grossman, 1968.
A Walk along the Shore. Guildford, Surrey, Circle Press, 1977.
Mahamudra (bilingual edition). Paris, Mercure de France, 1979.
Ode fragmentée à la Bretagne blanche. Bordeaux, William Blake, 1980.
Le Grand Rivage (bilingual edition). Paris, Nouveau Commerce, 1980.
Scènes d'un monde flottant (bilingual edition). Paris, Grasset, 1983.
Terre de diamant (bilingual edition). Paris, Grasset, 1983.
Atlantica: Mouvements et méditations (bilingual edition). Paris, Grasset, 1986.
The Bird Path: Collected Longer Poems. Edinburgh, Mainstream, 1989.
Handbook for the Diamond Country: Collected Shorter Poems 1960–1990. Edinburgh, Mainstream, 1990.
Limites et marges. Paris, Mercure de France, 2000.

Fiction

Letters from Courgounel. London, Cape, 1966.
Les Limbes incandescents. Paris, Denoël, 1976.
Dérives. Paris, Nadeau, 1978.
L'Écosse avec Kenneth White. Paris, Flammarion, 1980.
Le Visage du vent d'est. Paris, Presses d'Aujourd'hui, 1980.
La Route bleue. Paris, Grasset, 1983; as *The Blue Road,* Edinburgh, Mainstream, 1990.

Other

The Tribal Dharma: An Essay on the Work of Gary Snyder. Dyfed, Unicom, 1975.
The Life-Technique of John Cowper Powys. Swansea, Galloping Dog Press, 1978.
Segalen: Théorie et pratique du voyage. Paris, Eibel, 1979.
La Figure du dehors. Paris, Grasset, 1982.
Une Apocalypse tranquille: Crise et creation dans la culture occidentale. Paris, Grasset, 1985.
Mahamudra: La grande geste. Paris, Mercure de France, 1987.
Travels in the Drifting Dawn. Edinburgh, Mainstream, 1989.
"Rivages": Lectures de Kenneth White. Nimes, Editions Terriers, 1987.
Orcades. Rennes, Apogée, 1998.
Corsica: L'itinéraire des rives et des monts. Ajaccio, France, La Marge Edition, 1998.

Editor, *Edimbourgh.* Paris, Autrement, 1986.
Editor, *Ecosse.* Paris, Autremont, 1988.

Translator, *Selected Poems,* by André Breton. London, Cape Goliard Press, 1969.
Translator, *Ode to Charles Fourier,* by André Breton. London, Cape Goliard Press, 1969.

*

Manuscript Collection: National Library of Scotland, Edinburgh.

Critical Studies: *The Truth of Poetry* by Michael Hamburger, London, Weidenfeld and Nicolson, 1969, New York, Harcourt Brace, 1970; by Hans Berge, in *Raster* (Amsterdam), autumn 1970; by Robert Bréchon, in *Critique* (Paris), April 1979; "Kenneth White: Portrait de l'artiste en jeune pin" by M. Duclos, in *Poetes Anglais Contemporains,* edited by J. Genet and R. Gallet, Caen, Centre de Recherches de Litt. & Ling., 1982; "Kenneth White: A Re-Sourcing of Western Culture" by Tony McManus, and "A Pict in Roman Gaul: Kenneth White and France" by Graham Dunstan Martin, both in *Chapman,* 59, January 1990; "Poetry after God: The Reinvention of the Sacred in the Work of Eugene Guillevic and Kenneth White" by Gavin Bowd, in *Dalhousie French Studies* (Canada), 39–40, summer-fall 1997; "Roots of the Geo-Poetic: Going beyond Linguistic Man" by H.W. Fawkner, in *Moderna Sprak* (Goteborg, Sweden), 91(1), 1997; "Kenneth White: Modernite Geopoetique et Postmodernite" by Olivier Penot-Lacassagne, in *Oeuvres & Critiques* (Tubingen, Germany), 23(1), 1998.

Kenneth White comments:

(1980) I can call myself a poet providing the word be adequately defined. I like Elie Faure's description: "The poet is he who never ceases to have confidence precisely because he does not attach himself to any port . . . but pursues . . . a form that flies through the tempest and is lost unceasingly in the eternal becoming."

The theme of my poetry (and prose) is the way to the complete and utter realization of myself, which I see as the real and central content of art, without which it degenerates into a collection of more or less formally or psychologically interesting comments or objects. With a play on words and with the knowledge that whiteness is the synthesis of all colors, I tend for the moment to call this "complete realization of myself" whiteness and to translate moments of unity by terms indicative of whiteness. My aim, beyond the temporary realizations of whiteness, is to ground this idea, this myth (as program), to situate the ecstasy extensively, and find, discover, create a "white world."

In more philosophical terms, I see myself living in a world of separation and scission, and my aim, my desire, is to move beyond this world of separation into unity. I find the theme in Hegel, who speaks of the early Greek world as "an immaculate world unadulterated by any scission." While the Hegelian synthesis, however, is purely intellectual, ideal, my aim is concrete realization.

In this direction I have been influenced, or confirmed, by Whitman and Nietzsche (critique of present civilization, affirmation of life, will to self-realization). Both of these also mean the end of a certain Western culture and, as I see it, an opening to the East, which can help us to discover a deeper West, create in the West a civilization more existentially alive, more integrated, rather than merely mechanically active and essentially incoherent.

It is in the East that I find the terms and the vocabulary (and examples) more consonant with my search. In *L'Esprit Synthetique de la Chine,* Liou Kia-Hway speaks of the aim of Eastern life-thought, as contrasted with the radical dualism and abstraction of the West, as "a concrete totality which suffers no separation," penetrating beyond the dualism into the "ground of being."

The way I see myself traveling toward this ground realization is the *sunyavada,* which Linnart Mäll, in his *Terminologia Indica,* translates as "The Zero Way"—"a quite original way of thought, so original it seems impossible to compare it with anything else."

My traveling on this way I express through poems and prose, the poems in general expressing more intense moments of concentration, the prose recounting the traveling, attempting a synthesis of information interspersed with moments of higher unity. The poems are characterized perhaps by intuitive rhythm, inner form, simplicity (i.e., a highly organized complexity without elaboration), and a recurrent iconography (gulls and recent convergent image of the Rosy Gull), which makes for a characteristic world. They are meant to satisfy demands, desires such as Bash expresses—"There are many who write verse, but few who keep to the rules of the heart"—understanding "heart" here not sentimentally but as a psychosensual/intellectual synthesis, the poem itself being such a synthesis, uniting a content of ontological significance with an aesthetic of delight. "Before a poet can write haiku," writes Otsuji, and the same goes for poems in general as I understand them, "he must find a unity within his life which must come from the effort to discover his true self."

How far do I think I have traveled on my way? After passing through "the most difficult area," I would say, with Paul Klee, "a little nearer to the heart of creation than is normal but still too far away."

*   *   *

If we except the more ecstatic passages, *Letters from Gourgounel* contains some of Kenneth White's most achieved writing, for in the prose of the book we see his language engaging with substantial, particular experience more fully than has been the general rule in his poetry. It is not simply that much of his earlier poetry was too content with routine romantic gestures and unsubstantiated claims ("the deep-down poetry I trade my life for" or "I speak in knowledge to all men / the great things and the beautiful I bring"). It is rather that in his poetry he has set himself the difficult task of exploring those areas of experience in which emptiness and silence may be sensed not in terms of negation but in terms of a more positive approach to a sense of immanence and revelation. Thus we have references to such phenomena as "this light that is / the limit of austerity / and makes words blind," statements like "at the limits of saying / the soul flies to the mouth / and the poem is born," and poems such as "In the Emptiness" that assert, in the emptiness, an experience of "reality right to the bone."

The general difficulty, then, is to reconcile the mystic's pull toward wordlessness and the poet's ineradicable dependence on words. In particular, the poetry's frequent resort to assertion, to statements about experience, may be characterized both by abstractions and by a lack of clear focus upon such concrete details as are mentioned. The difficulty for White is how to solve such a problem in a manner that is germane to his sensibility. There are several poems (e.g., "Extraordinary Moment" and "Sesshu") that seem to indicate a possible solution. These poems clearly have learned from oriental models, and their strength is that their focus on particulars is sharp and their implications are clear without being overly spelled out.

—Robin Fulton

WHITTEMORE, (Edward) Reed (II)

Nationality: American. **Born:** New Haven, Connecticut, 11 September 1919. **Education:** Yale University, New Haven, A.B. 1941; Princeton University, New Jersey, 1945–46. **Military Service:** U.S. Army Air Force, 1941–45: Captain. **Family:** Married Helen Lundeen in 1952; two daughters and two sons. **Career:** Member of the department of English, 1947–62, chair of the department, 1962–64, and professor of English, 1962–67, Carleton College, Northfield, Minnesota; Bain-Swiggett Lecturer, Princeton University, 1968; professor of English, 1968–84, and since 1984 emeritus professor, University of Maryland, College Park. Editor, *Furioso,* various locations, 1939–53, *Carleton Miscellany,* Northfield, Minnesota, 1960–64, and *Delos* magazine, College Park, Maryland, 1988–92. Program associate, National Institute of Public Affairs, 1966–68. Literary editor, *New Republic,* Washington, D.C., 1969–73. Consultant in poetry, 1964–65, and interim consultant, 1984–85, Library of Congress, Washington, D.C. Poet Laureate for Maryland, 1985–88. **Awards:** Emily Clark Balch prize (*Virginia Quarterly Review*), 1962; National Endowment for the Arts grant, 1968; American Academy award of Merit, 1971. Litt. D.: Carleton College, 1971. **Address:** 4526 Albion Road, College Park, Maryland 20740, U.S.A.

PUBLICATIONS

Poetry

Heroes and Heroines. New York, Reynal, 1946.
An American Takes a Walk and Other Poems. Minneapolis, University of Minnesota Press, 1956.
The Self-Made Man and Other Poems. New York, Macmillan, 1959.
The Boy from Iowa: Poems and Essays. New York, Macmillan, 1962
Return, Alpheus: A Poem for the Literary Elders of Phi Beta Kappa. Williamsburg, Virginia, King and Queen Press, 1965.
Poems, New and Selected. Minneapolis, University of Minnesota Press, 1967.
50 Poems 50. Minneapolis, University of Minnesota Press, 1970.
The Mother's Breast and the Father's House. Boston, Houghton Mifflin, 1974.
The Feel of Rock: Poems of Three Decades. Washington, D.C., Dryad Press, 1982.
The Past, the Future, the Present: Poems Selected and New. Fayetteville, University of Arkansas Press, 1990.

Other

Little Magazines. Minneapolis, University of Minnesota Press, 1963.
The Fascination of the Abomination: Poems, Stories, and Essays. New York, Macmillan, 1963.
Ways of Misunderstanding Poetry. Washington, D.C., Library of Congress, 1965.
From Zero to the Absolute: Essays. New York, Crown, 1967.
William Carlos Williams: Poet from Jersey. Boston, Houghton Mifflin, 1975.
The Poet as Journalist: Life at the New Republic. Washington, D.C., New Republic, 1976.
Poets and Anthologists: A Look at the Current Poet-Packaging Process (lecture). Washington, D.C., Library of Congress, 1986.

Pure Lives: The Early Biographers. Baltimore, Johns Hopkins University Press, 1988.
Whole Lives: Shapers of Modern Biography. Baltimore, Johns Hopkins University Press, 1989.
Six Literary Lives. St. Louis, University of Missouri Press, 1993.

Editor, *Browning.* New York, Dell, 1960.

*

Critical Study: "A Note on Reed Whittemore" by Roger Hecht, in *Sewanee Review* (Sewanee, Tennessee), 71, 1963.

*   *   *

Reed Whittemore was among the first poets of his generation to make full use of the graceful and natural rhythms of William Carlos Williams's poetry. In his editorship of *Furioso* and the *Carleton Miscellany,* as well as in his career as teacher and biographer, Whittemore influenced the course of American language for more than forty years. For one poem in particular, the first and among the most powerful discussions of the idiocy and waywardness of the nuclear age, he deserves a permanent place in American poetry. That memorable lyric, "Lines Composed upon Reading an Announcement by Civil Defense Authorities Recommending That I Build a Bomb Shelter in My Backyard," concludes on this sensible note:

But I'll not, no not do it, not go back
And lie there in that dark under the weight
Of all that earth on that old door for my state.
I know too much to think now that if I creep
From the grown-up's house to the child's house I'll keep.

The Self-Made Man, Whittemore's longest poem, with echoes of Stevens's "The Comedian as the Letter C," extends the range of his ironic vision. It treats the Emersonian ideal with both mockery and tragic insight, as when the hero asks, "Where in my chatter, where in my banter / Where, where in this impious figure before you / Is God's wrath?" Among the New England worthies satirized in the poem is Mary Baker Eddy, in this memorable refrain from section 6:

Mary Baker of New Hampshire,
Mary Baker of New Hampshire.
I speak it twice; the rhythm stamps her
Simple Mary of New Hampshire.

Although capable of the clearest observation, as in "The Party," about children's seriousness at play, Whittemore later turned away from more complex emotions, and many of his poems after about 1960 can only be regarded with disappointment, as if there were some failure of nerve or energy. A terrible darkness broods among the light Horatian satires about cultural conferences and New York sophisticates, but inevitably the speaker refuses to face the deeper implications of his ironic view. Why were all the obvious opportunities ignored, one wonders, as in "Dead Walk," for example, or "The Storing of Soul"? Beside the fully realized humor of the early poems, one must set the frequently moving but inadequately rendered sadness of the later ones. Only occasionally is the sureness and grace evident again, as in the following from "The Feel of Rock":

My father went broke on a shaded street.
My mother drank there.
My brothers removed themselves; they were complete.
I kept my room and slicked down my hair . . .
I did not know until grown how alone,
In bed in a dark room,
One could be, one had been, little father clone.

—Michael True

WIENERS, John (Joseph)

Nationality: American. **Born:** Boston, Massachusetts, 6 January 1934. **Education:** Boston College, A.B. in English 1954; Black Mountain College, North Carolina, 1955–56; State University of New York, Buffalo (teaching fellow), 1965–67. **Career:** Library clerk, Lamont Library, Harvard University, Cambridge, Massachusetts, 1955–57; actor and stage manager, Poets Theatre, Cambridge, 1956; assistant bookkeeper, 8th Street Bookshop, New York, 1962–63; subscriptions editor, Jordan Marsh Company, Boston, 1963–65; class leader, Beacon Hill Free School, Boston, 1973. Co-founding editor, *Measure,* Boston. **Awards:** Poets Foundation grant, 1961; New Hope Foundation award, 1963; National Endowment for the Arts grant, 1966, 1968; fellowship, 1986; American Academy award, 1968; Committee on Poetry grant, 1970, 1971, 1972; Guggenheim fellowship, 1986. **Address:** c/o Raymond Foye Editions, Chelsea Hotel, 222 West 23rd Street, No. 807, New York, New York 10011–2301, U.S.A.

PUBLICATIONS

Poetry

The Hotel Wentley Poems. San Francisco, Auerhahn Press, 1958; revised edition, San Francisco, Dave Haselwood, 1965.
Ace of Pentacles. New York, Carr, 1964.
You Talk of Going But Don't Even Have a Suitcase. Spoleto, Italy, Spoleto Festival, 1965.
Chinoiserie. San Francisco, Dave Haselwood, 1965.
Hart Crane, Harry Crosby, I See You Going over the Edge. Detroit, Artists' Workshop Press, 1966.
Pressed Wafer. Buffalo, Gallery Upstairs Press, 1967.
King Solomon's Magnetic Quiz. Pleasant Valley, New York, Kriya Press, 1967.
Long Distance. Mount Horeb, Wisconsin, Perishable Press, 1968.
Selected Poems. London, Cape, 1968.
L'Abysse. New York, Minkoff, 1968.
On Looking in the Mirror. New York, Brownstone Press, 1968.
Unhired. Mount Horeb, Wisconsin, Perishable Press, 1968.
A Letter to Charles Olson. New York, Charters, 1968.
Idyll. Santa Barbara, California, Unicorn Press, 1968.
To Do. Stony Brook, New York, Stony Brook Poetics Foundation, 1968.
Asylum Poems. New York, Angel Hair, 1969.
Invitation. Santa Barbara, California, Unicorn Press, 1970.
Youth. New York, Phoenix Book Shop, 1970.
Nerves. London, Cape Goliard Press, and New York, Grossman, 1970.
Larders. Cambridge, Massachusetts, Restau Press, 1970.

Reading in Bed. San Francisco, White Rabbit Press, 1970.

First Poem after Silence since Thanksgiving. San Francisco, Butterfly, 1970.

Selected Poems. London, Cape, and New York, Grossman, 1972.

Playboy. Boston, Good Gay Poets, 1972.

We Were There! New York, Athanor, 1973.

God Is the Organ of Novelty. Cambridge, Massachusetts, Pomegranate Press, 1973.

Yes, Youth Are Marching On Against the World. Philadelphia, Middle Earth Bookstore, 1973.

Behind the State Capitol; or, Cincinnati Pike. Boston, Good Gay Poets, 1975.

Collected Poems 1958–1984. Santa Barbara, California, Black Sparrow Press, 1986.

Cultural Affairs in Boston: Poetry and Prose. Santa Rosa, California, Black Sparrow Press, 1988.

Plays

Still-Life (produced New York, 1961).

Of Asphodel, in Hell's Despite (produced New York, 1963). New York, Judson Poet's Theatre, n.d.

Anklesox and Five Shoelaces (produced New York, 1966).

Television Documentary: *The Spirit of Romance,* with Robert Duncan, 1965.

Other

A Memory of Black Mountain College. Cambridge, Massachusetts Institute of Technology Press, 1969.

Woman. Canton, New York, Institute of Further Studies, 1972.

The Lanterns along the Wall. Buffalo, Other Publications, 1972.

Hotels. New York, Angel Hair, 1974.

A Superficial Estimation. New York and Madras, India, Hanuman, 1986.

Conjugal Contraries and Quart. New York and Madras, India, Hanuman, 1986.

The Journal of John Wieners Is to Be Called 707 Scott Street for Billie Holiday, 1959. Los Angeles, Sun and Moon Press, 1996.

*

Bibliography: ''John Wieners: A Checklist'' by George F. Butterick, in *Athanor 3* (Clarkson, New York), summer-fall 1973.

Manuscript Collections: Bancroft Library, University of California, Berkeley; State University of New York, Buffalo; University of California, San Diego; Frank Melville, Jr., Memorial Library, State University of New York, Stony Brook; New York University; Homer Babidge Library, University of Connecticut, Storrs.

Critical Studies: By Denise Levertov, in *Poetry* (Chicago), February 1965; by Robert Duncan, in *The Nation* (New York), 31 May 1965; by Lewis Warsh, in *Boston Phoenix,* January 1973; interview, in *Gay Sunshine* (San Francisco), March 1973; John Wieners issue of *Mirage* (San Francisco), 1985; by Anselm Hollo, in *American Book Review,* 11(6), January 1990.

John Wieners comments:

(1970) My themes are heartfelt ones of youth and manly desire. Their subjects are despair, frustration, ideal satisfaction, with biblical and classical referential echoes. Their forms are declarative, orderly, and true, without invention. General sources are Edna St. Vincent Millay, United States prose writers of the twentieth century, lyricists in the Greek anthology, Homer, Sappho, Horace, Virgilius, the songs of Geoffrey Chaucer, and subsequent strains of the English tradition. Characteristic stylistic devices are the direct address of German lieder, Near Eastern intimacy, and Chinese abbreviation.

(1974) Poetry since sixteen has been an obsession, every day, every minute, hearkening to the form of poetry. Its practitioners and personables continue to remain fixed as divinities equal to those of the French novelists since 1945 or the Pleiades of court presentation. I have kept the sun and myself upon a balcony bent under its power to lead my attainment toward magnitudinous worldly success and ultimately the presentation toward one person of its worth. For what would it matter if I could not be of use or of importance to this possible derelict in the world's eyes, but to my heart, husband-god, king-emperor? And yet not that. Simply a poor person in need of myself.

Along its possession blossom many rewards, leisure, conversation, books, friends, entertainment for the ultimate collected editions to merit his devotion.

*   *   *

Perhaps the most appealing thing about John Wieners's poems is the vulnerability they express. He has produced some of the most poignant lyrics of their kind. His dominant theme is dolor, loss of love, and rapture. His is a poetry of feeling rather than will, small chapels for devotion. He is preoccupied with glamour and unattainable desire, yet he is saved from self-pity by service to a poetry larger than even his despair: ''It is eternal audience / and my feet hardened, my heart / blackened, nodding and / bowing before it.'' He avoids triteness by the almost perfect timing, the exquisite phrasing. His best poems are relieved from sentimentality by precarious rhyme, perilous syntax, and dramatic poise. He is capable of the most precise syncopations: ''Yet so tenuous, so fine / this thing is, I am / sitting on the hard bed . . .'' The casual lines only heighten the authenticity of his voice. The despair is so matter-of-fact that not only do we ache for the pity of it but we believe that to be overcome by such despair is inevitable for the poet. That is the awe which is awful. It is a single tone played repeatedly, as in Housman. Wieners is easily the torch singer he once said he wished he could be. No one has sung so convincingly of the haunted underside of life save Billie Holiday, his heroine, or perhaps Edith Piaf, whose fragility his resembles. How out of the sordid and decadent he is able to raise the purest strains is his specialization, his accomplishment. We remain before his poems as the poet does before his image of himself—''all morning / long. / With my hand over my mouth.''

Along with *The Hotel Wentley Poems,* Wieners's finest collection remains *Ace of Pentacles.* There are some excellent poems in *Nerves,* a few otherwise uncollected ones in *Selected Poems,* and fewer still in *Behind the State Capitol,* a collection of ''cinema decoupages; verses, abbreviated prose insights'' that takes its title from the poet's residence below Beacon Hill in Boston, behind the state capitol building. Wieners has not been his own best representative, as *Selected Poems* too often attests. Not only did he leave out some of his finest poems—''Long Nook,'' ''A Poem for Trapped

Things,'' ''Moon Poems,'' ''Not Complete Enough,'' ''My Mother,'' ''The Meadow Where All Things Grow,'' ''Hart Crane, Harry Crosby,'' ''Billie''—but many of those included have been revised, and not always with success.

Whether through loss of confidence or false notions of improvement, in almost every case the alterations are for the poorer. The changes usually result from a misguided effort to attain a more ''poetic'' effect, most often through the elimination of articles and copulas or from the compression of openly whispered lines into more regular stanzas, but the effect is to eliminate the spoken directness and accuracy of the original. For example, the poet adds the title ''153 Avenue C'' (on New York's Lower East Side, where the poem was written) to previously untitled lines but takes away their perfectly understated horror by removing the copulas of natural speech. Other changes are simply strange if not inept, and they are endemic throughout the volume. In *Behind the State Capitol,* produced from copy apparently prepared by the poet himself, typing eccentricities have been allowed to stand, contributing nothing but confusion. The poet has forsaken his own genius and the stark simplicity of the original statements, so forthright they cannot be doubted or denied. He has lost the touch that enabled him to revise so successfully ''A Poem for Painters'' (if one compares the original version with that in the 1958 *Hotel Wentley Poems*), which contains his most famous lines and the summarization of his consistent theme:

> My poems contain no
> wilde beestes, no
> lady of the lake, music
> of the spheres, or organ chants.
>
> Only the score of a man's
> struggle to stay with
> what is his own, what
> lies within him to do.

Wieners has continued to be loyal to his ''voices,'' those to whom *Ace of Pentacles* was dedicated, only now, with youth gone, there are more of them crowding about, incessant, obscuring the flame. The clear, elegant voice and the lyric perfection of the early poems have been lost to the multiple personalities, and the consequence is warring diction, abuse of rhyme, and linguistic excess. The *dérèglement* Rimbaud prepared us for has occurred.

—George F. Butterick

WIER, Dara

Nationality: American. **Born:** Dara Ann Dixon, New Orleans, 30 December 1949. **Education:** Louisiana State University, Baton Rouge, 1967–70; Longwood College, Farmville, Virginia, 1970–71, B.S. 1971; Bowling Green University, Ohio, 1972–74, M.F.A. 1974. **Family:** One son and one daughter. **Career:** Assistant professor, Hollins College, Virginia, 1975–80; associate professor, University of Alabama, Tuscaloosa, 1980–85. Since 1985 professor, University of Massachusetts, Amherst. Visiting poet, University of Utah, Salt Lake City, 1980, and University of Texas, Austin, 1983; Richard Hugo Memorial Chairholder, University of Montana, Missoula, 1992. **Awards:** National Endowment for the Arts fellowship, 1980;

Guggenheim fellowship, 1991–92. **Address:** 504 Montague Road, Amherst, Massachusetts 01002, U.S.A.

PUBLICATIONS

Poetry

Blood Hook & Eye. Austin, University of Texas press, 1977.
The 8-Step Grapevine. Pittsburgh, Pennsylvania, Carnegie Mellon University Press, 1980.
All You Have in Common. Pittsburgh, Pennsylvania, Carnegie Mellon University Press, 1984.
The Book of Knowledge. Pittsburgh, Pennsylvania, Carnegie Mellon University Press, 1988.
Blue for the Plough. Pittsburgh, Pennsylvania, Carnegie Mellon University Press, 1992.
Our Master Plan. Pittsburgh, Pennsylvania, Carnegie Mellon University Press, 1999.
Voyages in English. Pittsburgh, Pennsylvania, Carnegie Mellon University Press, 2001.

*

Critical Studies: ''History and the Transpersonal Talent: Or, 'I'm Just Tired of Reading Guys''' by Richard Katrovas, in *New England Review and Bread Loaf Quarterly* (Middlebury, Vermont), 11(3), spring 1989; ''Thinking This, Knowing That, in the Present'' by William Harmon, in *Parnassus* (New York), 16(1), 1990.

*   *   *

Dara Wier's poetry is driven by wit and verbal energy. Taking its cues from a range of contemporary poets, Wier's early work drew favorable comparisons to both Anne Sexton and John Berryman. Wier's verbal energy, however, ties her to a much more experimental poetics than either Berryman or Sexton pursued. Frequently Wier's poems cascade down the page in one or two cumulative or periodic sentences; they occasionally eschew formal rules of grammar and syntax and usually are energetic and lively. In addition, the wildly associative capabilities of her work coupled with a penchant for the humorous tie her poetry to that of Ashbery and her colleague at the University of Massachusetts, James Tate. Having drawn all of these comparisons, however, it is important to underscore that, although she is still a relatively young poet, Wier's work is promising and driven by an idiosyncratic, original vision.

Wier's first mature work can be found in *Our Master Plan*. The poetry up until then is sometimes verbally engaging and sometimes compelling for its emotional candor, but it is seldom as energetic as the later poems. Traces of her contemporaries Sharon Olds and Louise Glück can be found in the early work. To put it another way, although one can see Wier reaching for her individual vision, the earlier poems seldom reach the heights of the later poetry. *Our Master Plan* is an exceptional book. Incorporating history and contemporary events and objects, the poems achieve a kaleidoscope of wit and emotion. Consider, for example, these lines from the opening of ''If I Were a Raptor Cruising through the Timetables of History'':

> I would want you to come with me into those years
> in which it is recorded that nothing happened in

Daily Life, so maybe we could stir something up.
We could listen for the syllables in a famous Arab's
Epic and watch tea appear in China.
Maybe we could warn the alchemists to take better care
of their products.
Like drop-ins to a seance we might enter those eras
in which it is recorded nothing happened in Music.
And say this is impossible.

The energy is apparent. If there is a weakness to the poetry—and to this poem in particular—it is that Wier occasionally conjures up associations that are not always realized in a satisfying manner. Throughout history a raptor has suggested a predatory quality, and although Wier leaves it as a final, conclusive image (''And we'd have to pack our own lunch / because there were no chickens in Babylon''), perhaps this aspect could be better integrated into the poem.

But such quibbles are just quibbles. Wier's collection *Voyages in English* frequently achieves a verbal splendor, a collapsing energy of syntax and imagery that shoves a reader through the poem in a manner reminiscent of William Everson and Ann Waldman. ''Perhaps Died and Gone to Heaven'' is a good example:

And when they rolled me over
great storms moved across my breasts
and a terrible accident lay on my ankles,
stories of extortion covered half my neck
and a birth announcement blazed across my face . . .

The poem builds to the following conclusion:

. . . and when they searched past the roots of my hair
they felt the stirrings of a liquid music
and found the vault where lost objects are sent
and where words which are not spoken wait
and they turned back to their experiments
and their trials and left it.

Wier's poetry is driven by a ''liquid music'' that both takes in the world and skirts at breathtaking speed just over the surface of it. Her utilization of a capacious syntax and the energy of accretive sentence structures make for a poetry of force and energy.

—Tod Marshall

WILBUR, Richard (Purdy)

Nationality: American. **Born:** New York City, 1 March 1921. **Education:** Amherst College, Massachusetts, B.A. 1942, A.M. 1952; Harvard University, Cambridge, Massachusetts, A.M. 1947. **Military Service:** U.S. Army, 1943–45: Sergeant. **Family:** Married Charlotte Ward in 1942; one daughter and three sons. **Career:** Member of the Society of Fellows, 1947–50, and assistant professor of English, 1950–54, Harvard University; associate professor of English, Wellesley College, Massachusetts, 1955–57; professor of English, Wesleyan University, Middletown, Connecticut, 1957–77; writer-in-residence, Smith College, Northampton, Massachusetts,

1977–86. General editor, Laurel Poets series, Dell Publishing Company, New York. State Department cultural exchange representative to the U.S.S.R., 1961. **Awards:** Guggenheim fellowship, 1952, 1963; American Academy in Rome fellowship, 1954; Pulitzer prize, 1957, 1989; National Book award, 1957; Edna St. Vincent Millay memorial award, 1957; Ford fellowship, for drama, 1960; Melville Cane award, 1962; Bollingen prize, for translation, 1963, for poetry, 1971; Sarah Josepha Hale award, 1968; Brandeis University Creative Arts award, 1970; Henri Desfeuilles prize, 1971; Shelley memorial award, 1973; Harriet Monroe award, 1978; P.E.N. translation award, 1983; Drama Desk award, for translation, 1983; St. Botolph's Club Foundation award, 1983; Camargo Foundation fellowship, 1985; *Los Angeles Times* prize, 1988; Birmingham-Southern University Grand Master award, 1989; Aiken-Taylor award, 1988; Gold medal for poetry, American Academy of Arts & Letters, 1991; MacDowell medal, 1992; National Arts Club medal of honor for literature, 1994; Pen/Manheim medal for translation, 1994; National medal of arts, 1994. L.H.D.: Lawrence University, Appleton, Wisconsin, 1960; Washington University, St. Louis, 1964; Williams College, Williamstown, Massachusetts, 1975; Rochester University, Rochester, New York, 1976; Carnegie Mellon University, Pittsburgh, 1980; State University of New York, Pottsdam, 1986; Skidmore College, Saratoga Springs, New York, 1987. D.Litt.: Amherst College, 1967; Clark University, Worcester, Massachusetts, 1970; American International College, Springfield, Massachusetts, 1974; Marquette University, Milwaukee, 1977; Wesleyan University, 1977; Lake Forest College, Illinois, 1982. Member, American Academy of Arts and Sciences; president, 1974–76, and chancellor, 1976–78, 1980–81, American Academy of Arts & Letters; chancellor emeritus, Academy of American Poets; Chevalier, Ordre National des Palmes Académiques, 1983; United States Poet Laureate, 1987–88. **Agent:** Gilbert Parker, William Morris Agency, 1325 Avenue of the Americas, New York, New York 10019. **Address:** 87 Dodwells Road, Cummington, Massachusetts 01026, U.S.A.

PUBLICATIONS

Poetry

The Beautiful Changes and Other Poems. New York, Reynal, 1947.
Ceremony and Other Poems. New York, Harcourt Brace, 1950.
Things of This World. New York, Harcourt Brace, 1956; one section reprinted as *Digging to China,* New York, Doubleday, 1970.
Poems 1943–1956. London, Faber, 1957.
Advice to a Prophet and Other Poems. New York, Harcourt Brace, 1961; London, Faber, 1962.
The Poems of Richard Wilbur. New York, Harcourt Brace, 1963.
The Pelican from a Bestiary of 1120. Privately printed, 1963.
Prince Souvanna Phouma: An Exchange Between Richard Wilbur and William Jay Smith. Williamstown, Massachusetts, Chapel Press, 1963.
Complaint. New York, Phoenix Book Shop, 1968.
Walking to Sleep: New Poems and Translations. New York, Harcourt Brace, 1969; London, Faber, 1971.
Seed Leaves: Homage to R.F. Boston, Godine, 1974.
The Mind-Reader: New Poems. New York, Harcourt Brace, 1976; London, Faber, 1977.
Verses on the Times, with William Jay Smith. New York, Gutenberg Press, 1978.

Seven Poems. Omaha, Nebraska, Abattoir, 1981.

Pedestrian Flight: Twenty-one Clerihews for the Telephone. Winston-Salem, North Carolina, Palaemon Press, 1981.

A Finished Man. Cleveland, Bits Press, 1985.

New and Collected Poems. San Diego, Harcourt Brace, 1988; London, Faber, 1989.

Bone Key and Other Poems. West Chester, Aralia Press, 1998.

Mayflies: New Poems and Translations. New York, Harcourt Brace, 2000.

Recordings: *Poems,* Spoken Arts, 1959; *Richard Wilbur Reading His Poetry,* Caedmon, 1972.

Plays

The Misanthrope, translation of the play by Molière (produced Cambridge, Massachusetts, 1955; New York, 1956). New York, Harcourt Brace, 1955; London, Faber, 1958; revised version, music by Margaret Pine (produced New York, 1977).

Candide (lyrics only, with others), book by Lillian Hellman, music by Leonard Bernstein, adaptation of the novel by Voltaire (produced New York, 1956; London, 1959). New York, Random House, 1957.

Tartuffe, translation of the play by Molière (produced Milwaukee, Wisconsin, 1964; New York, 1965). New York, Harcourt Brace, 1963; London, Faber, 1964.

School for Wives, translation of the play by Molière (produced New York, 1971). New York, Harcourt Brace, 1971.

The Learned Ladies, translation of the play by Molière (produced Williamstown, Massachusetts, 1977; London, 1981). New York, Harcourt Brace, 1978.

Andromache, translation of the play by Racine. New York, Harcourt Brace, 1982.

Molière: Four Comedies (includes *The Misanthrope, Tartuffe, School for Wives,* and *The Learned Ladies*). New York, Harcourt Brace, 1982.

Phaedra, translation of the play by Racine (produced Stratford, Ontario, 1990). San Diego, Harcourt Brace, 1986.

On Freedom's Ground (cantata), with William Schuman (produced New York, 1986).

The School for Husbands, translation of the play by Molière. New York, Harcourt Brace, 1992.

Sganarelle, or The Imaginary Cuckold, translation of the play by Molière. New York, Dramatists Play Service, 1993.

Amphitryon, translation of the play by Molière. New York, Dramatists Play Service, 1995.

Don Juan, translation of the play by Molière. New York, Dramatists Play Service, 1998.

Other

Emily Dickinson: Three Views, with Louise Bogan and Archibald MacLeish. Amherst, Massachusetts, Amherst College Press, 1960.

Loudmouse (for children). London, Crowell Collier, and New York, Collier Macmillan, 1963.

Opposites (for children), drawings by the author. New York, Harcourt Brace, 1973.

Responses: Prose Pieces 1953–1976. New York, Harcourt Brace, 1976.

The Whale and Other Uncollected Translations. Brockport, New York, BOA, 1982.

On My Own Work. Portree, Isle of Skye, Aquila, 1983.

Conversations with Richard Wilbur, edited by William Butts. University, University Press of Mississippi, 1990.

More Opposites (for children). New York, Harcourt Brace, 1991.

A Game of Catch (for children). San Diego, Harcourt Brace, 1994.

The Disappearing Alphabet (for children). New York, Harcourt Brace, 1998.

Editor, with Louis Untermeyer and Karl Shapiro, *Modern American and Modern British Poetry,* revised shorter edition. New York, Harcourt Brace, 1955.

Editor, *A Bestiary* (anthology). New York, Pantheon, 1955.

Editor, *Complete Poems of Poe.* New York, Dell, 1959.

Editor, with Alfred B. Harbage, *Poems of Shakespeare.* London, Penguin, 1966; revised edition, as *The Narrative Poems, and Poems of Doubtful Authenticity,* 1974.

Editor, *Selected Poems,* by Witter Bynner. New York, Farrar Straus, and London, Faber, 1978.

Translator, *The Funeral of Bobo,* by Joseph Brodsky. Ann Arbor, Michigan, Ardis, 1974.

*

Bibliography: *Richard Wilbur: A Bibliographical Checklist* by John P. Field, Kent, Ohio, Kent State University Press, 1971.

Manuscript Collections: Amherst College, Massachusetts; Lockwood Memorial Library, State University of New York, Buffalo.

Critical Studies: *Richard Wilbur* by Donald L. Hill, New York, Twayne, 1967; *Richard Wilbur* by Paul F. Cummins, Grand Rapids, Michigan, Eerdmans, 1971; "On Richard Wilbur" by William Heyen, summer 1973, "Verse Translation and Richard Wilbur" by Raymond Oliver, spring 1975, and "Richard Wilbur: The Quarrel with Poe" by Bruce F. Michelson, spring 1978, all in *Southern Review* (Baton Rouge, Louisiana); "The Motions of the Mind" by Anthony Hecht, in *Times Literary Supplement* (London), 20 May 1977; "The Cheshire Smile: On Richard Wilbur" by Mary Kinzie, in *American Poetry Review* (Philadelphia), May-June 1977; "Richard Wilbur's World" by Robert B. Shaw, in *Parnassus* (New York), spring-summer 1977; "Reconsideration: The Poetry of Richard Wilbur" by Frank McConnell, in *New Republic* (Washington, D.C.), 29 July 1978; *Richard Wilbur's Creation* edited by Wendy Salinger, Ann Arbor, University of Michigan Press, 1983; *Wilbur's Poetry: Music in a Scattering Time* by Bruce Michelson, Amherst, University of Massachusetts Press, 1991; *Richard Wilbur: A Reference Guide* by Frances Butler, N.p., G.K. Hall & Company, 1991; *The Happiest Intellection: Richard Wilbur's Poetry* (master's thesis) by Harriet Milsted Doty, Wake Forest University, 1993; Richard Wilbur issue of *Christianity and Literature* (Carrollton, Georgia), 42(4), summer 1993; *To Tread Mind Fields: Controversy and the Poetry of Richard Wilbur* (master's thesis) by Gus Pollock, Southern Illinois University at Edwardsville, 1993; *Richard Wilbur and the Poetry of Apocalyptic Interstices* (dissertation) by Randall D. Compton, University of North Texas, 1994; "Richard Purdy Wilbur: A Review of the Research and Criticism" by Frances Bixler and Jane Hoogestraat, in *Resources for American Literary Study* (University Park, Pennsylvania), 20(1), 1994; *The Radical Integration of Science, Religion, and Poetry in the*

Writings of Loren Eiseley and Richard Wilbur (dissertation) by Betty Ritz Rogers, University of North Carolina at Greensboro, 1995; *Ecstasy within Discipline: The Poetry of Richard Wilbur* by John B. Hougen, Atlanta, Scholars Press, 1995; *A Reader's Guide to the Poetry of Richard Wilbur* by Rodney Stenning Edgecombe, Tuscaloosa, University of Alabama Press, 1995; ''Modern Poetry after Modernism: The Example of Richard Wilbur'' by James Longenbach, in *The Future of Modernism,* edited by Hugh Witemeyer, Ann Arbor, University of Michigan Press, 1997; ''The Reflexive Art of Richard Wilbur'' by J.M. Reibetanz, in *University of Toronto Quarterly*, 67(2), spring 1998; Richard Wilbur issue of *War, Literature, and the Arts* (U.S. Air Force Academy, Colorado), 10(1), spring-summer 1998.

Richard Wilbur comments:

Poetry, for me, is an exasperating and clarifying play with certain images and themes that I cannot escape and prefer not to state here in prose. As the title of my selected prose (*Responses*) would suggest, I have generally written criticism on invitation, but also out of an appreciative involvement with the subject. My translations also have largely come about through a sense of affinity, a desire to put whatever knacks I may have at the service of some admired original.

*   *   *

Richard Wilbur's poetry is graceful, at times elegant, and it is highly literary and deeply felt. It awakens the child or the lover in the reader and shows, with an unerring sense of language and image, the sturdiness of nature and the mystery of the world and love. He knows his craft, and metered poetry and rhyme seemingly come effortlessly to him. His subjects—human relationships, nature, tradition, and divinity—are ones he has explored many times in his poetry, indeed, using his favorite images to see anew a moment in time or a scene in nature. Anyone who admires Frost's poetry or who takes pleasure in a poet who can imbue a stalk of corn, a spider web, a stand of trees, a gambler, and a bully with both an immediacy and transcendence will want to read Wilbur's verse. For readers bred on Shakespeare and fond of Molière, Mallarmé, and the Greeks, Wilbur is a must read. He is steeped in literary traditions but is unostentatious in his use of metaphor and allusion. In 1987 Wilbur became the second U.S. poet laureate, succeeding Robert Penn Warren. Wilbur was well suited to the role, skilled at rendering occasional poems that escape the ceremonial pomp so often marring such ventures.

Wilbur's verse meets the criteria he set forth in an essay in 1966 by which poetry should be judged. In ''Poetry and Happiness'' he wrote, ''When the sensibility is sufficient to the expression of the world, and when the world, in turn, is answerable to the poet's mind and heart, then the poet is happy, and can make his reader so.'' Wilbur has often been accused of wanting passion in his poetry, of writing a poetry that is too academic and that lacks the scope and grandeur of subject that distinguishes the greatest poets. Nonetheless, Wilbur has held to his own standard while at the same time defending his practice. He continues to strike the difficult balance between solipsism and the scientific objectivity upon which his best poetry depends.

Wilbur's poem ''Cottage Street, 1953'' (*The Mind-Reader*) answers the critic who holds that the play of the mind upon an object has become unfashionable, that only the noisy iconoclasm of the beats or the naked outpourings of the psyche by the confessional poets can excite emotions proper to poetry. The poem also implicitly sustains Wilbur's belief that even in this day a baroque fountain in the Villa Sciarra, a Delacroix painting, or a boy grown into a man asking forgiveness of his dead dog are as significant subjects for verse as man's passions or private confessions.

''Cottage Street, 1953'' recalls a gathering shortly after Sylvia Plath's unsuccessful suicide attempt. It takes place in the Cambridge kitchen of Edna Ward, Wilbur's mother-in-law, and Wilbur and Plath's mother are present. In an atmosphere of strain Ward, Wilbur, and Plath's mother struggle to cheer up Plath. Wilbur concludes his poem by affirming the love of Ward over the denial of Plath:

> And Edna Ward shall die in fifteen years,
> After her eight-and-eighty summers of
> Such grace and courage as permit no tears,
> The thin hand reaching out, the last word *love*.
>
> Outliving Sylvia who, condemned to live,
> Shall study for a decade, as she must,
> To state at last her brilliant negative
> In poems free and helpless and unjust.

Wilbur's poems acknowledge pain. His early poems protesting World War II and his occasional poems on the Vietnam War decry war's disorder. The complex and infinitely rich ''Castles and Distances'' brilliantly knits blood and love together:

> Oh, it is hunters alone
> Regret the beastly pain, it is they who love the foe
> That quarries out their force, and every arrow
> Is feathered soft with wishes to atone;
> Even the surest sword in sorrow
> Bleeds for its spoiling blow.

Some of the lines in the poem make us feel the ''harpoon's hurt,'' the piteous eyes of the ''hounded stag,'' the seeming wantonness of slaughter, but others recast the pain, not softening but altering it, reminding us that pain and joy can exist together. Neither can be eliminated; experience will not allow the simple, albeit brilliant, denial of Sylvia Plath.

To complain that Wilbur is ''shy'' or ''restrained'' or ''too charitable'' is to misunderstand the intent of his poems, which is not to distort but rightly to see the tensions that inform our sense of the world, to set isolated moments in perspective. Wilbur's is a world of balanced discord.

In ''Poetry and Happiness'' Wilbur acknowledges his debt to John Crowe Ransom and defends his choice to write stanzaically formal verse, full of practiced metrical irregularities that set forth contrapuntally thesis and antithesis and that reach a resolution appropriately ironic to suit the disordered world mirrored in the poems. He observes that his poetry has grown plainer over the years, more direct and less precocious, with fewer of the jaunty verbal techniques of a poet-juggler. His manner moves slightly away from the ironic meditative lyric of ''Caserta Garden'' and ''A Baroque Wall-Fountain in the Villa Sciarra'' toward the dramatic poem, as in ''Two Voices in a Meadow,'' which presents the speaking voices of a milkweed plant and a stone. The common theme of his poetry has to do with ''the proper relation between the tangible world and the intuitions of the spirit.''

The poems in *Walking to Sleep* and *The Mind-Reader* evolve in the direction Wilbur described in his earlier essay while remaining constant to his themes and sensibility. Most often he is fascinated by a highly kinesthetic poetry. In ''Grace'' he writes of the pause and the leap, saying, ''And Nijinsky hadn't the words to make the laws / For learning to loiter in air; he 'merely' said, / 'I merely leap and pause.'''' Wilbur's poetry searches for the words Nijinsky lacked. Frequently Wilbur develops his poems by arresting the reader's eye and taking it through a minute study of the object—be it from nature, history, legend, or his personal past—that the poem contemplates. As he unfolds the object to the seer, he uses a language of such studied movement and rest that we delight at the variety of ways in which a thing can move, and we marvel at the final figure of the poem that balances the conflicting motions. Poems such as ''Lightness,'' ''The Juggler,'' and ''On the Marginal Way'' typify this method.

Thinking about the relationship between ideas and poetry, Wilbur writes, ''What poetry does with ideas is redeem them from abstraction and submerge them in sensibility.'' ''Love Calls Us to the Things of This World'' discovers the corporeal in the spiritual and makes us marvel at the poet's fanciful meditation on a line of laundry hanging in the sun. ''The Eye'' and ''The Fourth of July,'' both in *The Mind-Reader,* make ideas live. His diction in this collection remains academic, but he experiments more with a colloquial speech. ''Piccola Commedia'' can be seen to have descended from ''A Black November Turkey'' (*Poems, 1943–1956*). He demurs from speaking directly of his life; his personal poems speak obliquely, and he mostly relies on humor and the fanciful to distance himself. ''The Writer'' is an excellent illustration of how Wilbur depicts a private family moment with affection, light humor, and candor. The blank verse poems ''In Limbo'' and ''The Mind-Reader,'' along with ''Walking to Sleep,'' depart from most of Wilbur's verse in their length and sustained characterization of himself, but their concern with perspective, irony, minute detail, and a speech of varied kinds immediately relates them thematically and tonally to the body of his writing.

Wilbur's *New and Collected Poems* contains a collection of all of his earlier volumes of poetry—arranged, unaltered, and with no omissions and in reverse chronological order—along with twenty-seven new poems, including the lyrics for the cantata ''On Freedom's Ground.'' The cantata was done in collaboration with William Schuman and performed at Lincoln Center in 1986 in celebration of the centennial of the Statue of Liberty. Wilbur's new poems are somewhat plainer in style. ''The Ride,'' ''Lying,'' ''Leaving,'' ''A Finished Man,'' and ''For W.H. Auden'' represent the range and accomplishments of the best of them. ''The Ride'' is beautiful and haunting in its simplicity, recalling the speaker's dream ride on the back of a horse through a snowstorm and ''shattering vacancies'' and

On into what was not,

Till the weave of the storm grew thin,
With a threading of cedar-smoke,
And the ice-blind pane of an inn
Shimmered, and I awoke.

How shall I now get back?
To the inn-yard where he stands,
Burdened with every lack,
And waken the stable-hands

To give him, before I think
That there was no horse at all,
Some hay, some water to drink,
A blanket and a stall?

The mythopoetic qualities of the dream and the care of the speaker for the horse and, in even stranger ways, for himself are deeply affecting.

''Lying'' captures another aspect of Wilbur's poetic sensibility. It expresses his belief that finally there is no invention but only a ''bearing witness / To what each morning brings again to light.'' This poem sums up Wilbur's artistic credo, using words and images and discursive turns that show him at his best, an exact witness of nature and man's changing ways. ''Leaving'' casts the poet's eye upon the ending of a garden party and his leave-taking, seeing the hostess and her guests and the gamboling children and himself as if they were figures in a charade or a masque in which all have briefly taken on a larger self, a part they would not have played had they glimpsed themselves as he does in his moment of parting. ''A Finished Man'' echoes some of the language and rhythms of Yeats's ''The Tower'' and mocks the learned, ceremonial public man who is brought back to a campus to dedicate a monumental gym. ''For W.H. Auden'' demonstrates Wilbur's technical mastery and offers an elegiac verse in praise of Auden. Many of the new poems show Wilbur's humility, his humor, his deep connections to nature and people, and his love of words.

Mayflies, a slender volume published in 2000, gathers together all of the poems Wilbur has written since *New and Collected Poems,* published twelve years earlier, along with some new translations. The volume continues the trend toward greater simplicity and grace. Poems such as ''A Barred Owl,'' ''Zea'' (a poem on cornstalks), ''For C.'' (written for his wife), and ''A Wall in the Woods: Cummington'' have all of the elegance and beauty and poignancy so characteristic of Wilbur. ''Bonds'' and several exceedingly short poems display the acuity of his mind in a playful but serious way. Most of the poems in the collection have a striking simplicity, a quietly witty turn, a sense of deep moral fiber, and great personal caring for people and nature. Critics will undoubtedly complain that this brilliant, elegant poet has always worked in much the same range and has lacked the scope and daring of the greatest poets. The poetry of his late period has none of the lust and force of Yeats's late verse or the religious turn of T.S. Eliot, nor does it show the wrenching emotions of a soul in pain. His poetry is quieter, more firmly planted, but it is also quizzical and full of wonder for the world he inhabits and the people most dear to him, his wife and daughter. And finally the notes at the end and the translations again show us the man of learning who painstakingly keeps educating his reader to past traditions, older meanings, and other poets in his craft. He continues to demonstrate that he has one of the finest metrical ears and best sense of the musicality in language of any poet writing today.

—Carol Simpson Stern

WILD, Peter

Nationality: American. **Born:** Northampton, Massachusetts, 25 April 1940. **Education:** University of Arizona, Tucson, 1958–62, 1965–67, B.A. 1962, M.A. 1967; University of California, Irvine, 1967–69, M.F.A. 1969. **Family:** Married 1) Sylvia Ortiz in 1966; 2) Rosemary Harrold in 1981. **Career:** Assistant professor of English, Sul Ross State University, Alpine, Texas, 1969–71; assistant professor, 1971–73, associate professor, 1973–79, and since 1979 professor of English,

University of Arizona. Since 1974 contributing editor, *High Country News,* Lander, Wyoming; since 1983 consulting editor, *Diversions.*
Awards: *Writer's Digest* prize, 1964; Hart Crane and Alice Crane Williams Memorial Fund grant, 1969; *Ark River Review* prize, 1972; Ohio State University President's prize, 1982. **Address:** 1547 East Lester, Tucson, Arizona 85719, U.S.A.

PUBLICATIONS

Poetry

The Good Fox. Glassboro, New Jersey, Goodly, 1967.
Sonnets. San Francisco, Cranium Press, 1967.
The Afternoon in Dismay. Cincinnati, Art Association of Cincinnati, 1968.
Mica Mountain Poems. Ithaca, New York, Lillabulero Press, 1968.
Joining Up and Other Poems. Sacramento, California, Runcible Spoon, 1968.
Mad Night with Sunflowers. Sacramento, California, Runcible Spoon, 1968.
Love Poems. Northwood Narrows, New Hampshire, Lillabulero Press, 1969.
Three Nights in the Chiricahuas. Madison, Wisconsin, Abraxas Press, 1969.
Poems. Portland, Oregon, Prensa de Lagar, 1969.
Fat Man Poems. Belmont, Massachusetts, Hellric, 1970.
Terms and Renewals. San Francisco, Two Windows Press, 1970.
Grace. Pennington, New Jersey, Stone Press, 1971.
Dilemma. Poquoson, Virginia, Back Door Press, 1971.
Wild's Magical Book of Cranial Effusions. New York, New Rivers Press, 1971.
Peligros. Ithaca, New York, Ithaca House, 1972.
New and Selected Poems. New York, New Rivers Press, 1973.
Cochise. New York, Doubleday, 1973.
The Cloning. New York, Doubleday, 1974.
Tumacacori. Berkeley, California, Two Windows Press, 1974.
Health. Berkeley, California, Two Windows Press, 1974.
Chihuahua. New York, Doubleday, 1976.
The Island Hunter. Tannersville, New York, Tideline Press, 1976.
Pioneers. Tannersville, New York, Tideline Press, 1976.
The Cavalryman. Tannersville, New York, Tideline Press, 1976.
House Fires. Santa Cruz, California, Greenhouse Review Press, 1977.
Gold Mines. Iola, Wisconsin, Wolfsong Press, 1978.
Barn Fires. Point Reyes, California, Floating Island, 1978.
Zuni Butte. Bisbee, Arizona, San Pedro Press, 1978.
The Lost Tribe. Iola, Wisconsin, Wolfsong Press, 1979.
Jeanne d'Arc: A Collection of New Poems. Memphis, St. Luke's Press, 1980.
Rainbow. Des Moines, Iowa, Blue Buildings Press, 1980.
Wilderness. St. Paul, Minnesota, New Rivers Press, 1980.
Heretics. Madison, Wisconsin, Ghost Pony Press, 1981.
Bitterroots. Tucson, Blue Moon Press, 1982.
The Peaceable Kingdom. Rochester, New York, Adler Press, 1983.
Getting Ready for a Date. Madison, Wisconsin, Ghost Pony Press, 1984.
The Light on Little Mormon Lake. Point Reyes, California, Floating Island, 1984.
The Brides of Christ. Vienna, Austria, Mosaic, 1991.
Easy Victory. Tucson, University of Arizona Press, 1994.

Other

Pioneer Conservationists of Western [and Eastern] *America.* Missoula, Montana, Mountain Press, 2 vols., 1979–83.
Enos Mills. Boise, Idaho, Boise State University, 1979.
Clarence King. Boise, Idaho, Boise State University, 1981.
James Welch. Boise, Idaho, Boise State University, 1983.
Barry Lopez. Boise, Idaho, Boise State University, 1984.
John Haines. Boise, Idaho, Boise State University, 1985.
John Nicholas. Boise, Idaho, Boise State University, 1986.
The Saguaro Forest. Flagstaff, Arizona, Northland Press, 1986.
John C. Van Dyke: The Desert. Boise, Idaho, Boise State University, 1988.
Alvar Núñez Cabeza de Vaca. Boise, Idaho, Boise State University, 1991.
Ann Zwinger. Boise, Idaho, Boise State University, 1993.
The Opal Desert: Explorations of Fantasy and Reality in the American Southwest. Austin, University of Texas Press, 1999.

Editor, with Frank Graziano, *New Poetry of the American West.* Durango, Colorado, Logbridge Rhodes, 1982.

*

Manuscript Collection: University of Arizona, Tucson.

Critical Studies: "Eight Chapbooks," in *The Dragonfly* (Pocatello, Idaho), fall and winter 1970; "Keeping Us Mad" by B. Salchert, in *Wisconsin Review* (Oshkosh), spring 1972; "Lillabulero's Pamphlets," in *Greenfield Review* (Greenfield Center, New York), June 1972; "Mud Men, Mud Women" by Robert Peters, in *Margins* (Milwaukee, Wisconsin), October-November 1974; "Peter Wild: Ways of Promise" by Philip Allan Friedman, in *Gramercy Review* (Los Angeles), summer 1978; interview, in *Blue Moon News* (Tucson), 1980; "Going Wild: Poems of the Idaho-Montana Border," in *Redneck Review of Literature,* 15, fall 1988, and "Discovering Peter Wild: Contemporary Poet of the Southwest," in *New Mexico Humanities Review* (Socorro, New Mexico), 32, 1989, both by James Maguire; *Peter Wild* by Edward Butscher, Boise, Boise State University, 1992; "Pressed in the Spirit: Recent Poetry by Peter Cooley and Peter Wild" by Mark Dawson, in *Black Warrior Review* (Tuscaloosa, Alabama), 19(2), spring-summer 1993.

Peter Wild comments:

Both figuratively and in reality, I have always felt a necessity to spend a great deal of time in the open, in the outdoors. Hence, the deterioration of the natural environment, overpopulation, and the erosion of man's cultural diversity are conditions of great concern to me. Furthermore, due to a strong sense of place, as a resident of the American Southwest, a region of the Anglo, Mexican, and American Indian, I often hold conflicting sympathies and allegiances. This is not to imply that I consider myself either a nature poet or a regional poet—a poet must write for all men—but in general it may be of help for a reader to remember that the above connects and circumstances of my life undoubtedly underlie and temper much of my writing.

*   *   *

In 1973, at the age of thirty-three, Peter Wild published a new and selected poems. It appeared only six years after he had first published his poetry. Why this premature act? Of course, it was partly because of a strong interest in Wild's poetry and a highly successful debut in the world of writing. As William Matthews wrote in the introduction, ''The effect is of a baroque telegram, or the wildest photo caption you'll ever read.'' Wild's poems were realistic enough to use vivid details, as in the short poem ''Talking with the Cook When the First Man Comes to Coffee'':

> In the sky
> gauze patches
> soak over our wounds
> that drip sparks,
> flying in a second to the horizon.
>
> we dig our needle
> heels in against it, our spurs
> founder in the dust
> up to our knees, the calf
> gone mad on his white
> intestine of a rope.
>
> until the first hand
> closes around the cup,
> a scar covered with hair
> and the light shines out
>   from the tips of our boots.

But each poem also revealed a sense of the inner world of magic, the unconscious, a dreamworld. It was a kind of surrealism very attractive to readers and critics from many different backgrounds. In a poem called ''Last Night Emily Dickinson,'' Wild fuses our dreamworld, a kind of comic book image of a literary figure, and the natural world. Goats are watching the phenomena:

> Last night Emily Dickinson
>   flew over my house
> on a fried chicken liver,
>   mushy grass hair
>   unloosed
> and her apron tucked up
>   under her white knees.
>
> . . .
> she shot
>   over the dark margin of the trees
> like a comet
>   bound to explode:
> and in the pale light of it
>   I saw their bloodless faces
> white like the heads of tapeworms
> turn in a even sweep
>   to watch her go
>
> we set our teeth
>   but the explosion
>   never came
> so we went back to bed;
> there were only grease spots
> on the window panes
> in the imminent darkness

> like a butterfly
>   my heart tore
>   in two.

I quote portions of this poem at length because it shows the Wild who is a magic realist, a poet writing in and out of the real world, with a normal, expected psychological dimension juxtaposed against the distortion of both reality and fantasy.

Since that time, however, Wild has been evolving into a very different poet. He has become a genuine surrealist, working beyond the attractive vision of snakes as dragons, then dragon kites, men whose sense of the real world is so strong that their boots glow in the morning air, or a fast-food Emily Dickinson, leaving more grease than good taste in the pop consumer's life. This turning away from easy, though brilliant and attractive, writing has lost Wild many of his earlier readers. His poems now demand a quite different facility from readers and never grant the jigsaw puzzle satisfaction of his earlier work. In a later book, *The Peaceable Kingdom,* there is a poem that seems to address this very issue, for surely Wild, like many poets whose work has grown and changed so that it is scarcely recognizable to his early readers, must be plagued with people wanting him to remain the same. In ''Favors'' he begins, ''The moon wants to talk to me / but I have nothing to say to him. / Is he a bill collector scratching at the door, / telephoning late at night?'' The poem goes on to describe the pesky bill collector following him, and he begins to see the man in different disguises and other identities. He concludes the poem with

>   Or at last
> recognize him, the scrannel St. Bernard
> who lives in the basement of the abandoned Mormon
>   church
> coming out to tip over our garbage cans, feed there.
> ''Ethel,'' I shout from the back porch, ''get me
> my shotgun, the one with birdshot in it,''
>   and blast him away
> a balloon losing its air with first and final voice,
> doing the whole neighborhood a favor.

I think that what has happened to Wild over the years is that his political sense of conscience (he is a member of the Sierra Club and closely involved with environmental issues) has invaded his more orderly and aesthetic surrealism from the past, giving his vision a new complexity, one that brooks nothing simple and easy. He begins a poem called ''Babylon'' with the lines ''The poor would love to live here / in this garage of sparkling whitewash, / your storage room.'' It is one of many poems that do not make easy constructs or present witty comments on life. These poems, even more than John Ashbery's, often seem to start in one place and end without any logical connections. But perhaps the greatest change to be seen in Wild's work is that he no longer makes an attempt to gratify the reader psychologically. This is a risky step for the poet to take, but one the reader who wants more than delightful images must be very gratified to observe. Perhaps publishing a premature *New and Selected Poems* at such an early age, then, was a gesture of commitment on his part to leave behind an old vision, not one he would renounce but one he wished to move forward from. It may be one he wishes his readers also to leave behind as pleasant history, while we look at the new and dangerous future ahead of us.

—Diane Wakoski

WILLIAMS, C(harles) K(enneth)

Nationality: American. **Born:** Newark, New Jersey, 4 November 1936. **Education:** Bucknell University, Lewisburg, Pennsylvania; University of Pennsylvania, Philadelphia, 1955–59, B.A. 1959. **Family:** Married 1) Sarah Jones in 1965; 2) Catherine Mauger in 1975; one daughter and one son. **Career:** Since 1972 contributing editor, *American Poetry Review,* Philadelphia. Visiting professor, Franklin and Marshall College, Lancaster, Pennsylvania, 1977, University of California, Irvine, 1978; Boston University, 1979, Columbia University, New York, 1981–85, Brooklyn College, New York, 1982–83, George Mason University, Fairfax, Virginia, 1985–95, University of California, Berkeley, 1986, and New York University, since 1995. **Awards:** Guggenheim fellowship, 1974; National Endowment for the Arts fellowship, 1985 and 1993; National Book Critics Circle prize, 1987; Morton Dauwen Zabel prize, 1989; Lila Wallace Reader's Digest Writers' award, 1993; Harriet Monroe prize, *Poetry,* 1993; PEN/Voelker Career Achievement award, 1998; Berlin prize, American Academy in Berlin, 1998, American Academy of Arts and Letters literature award, 1999. **Address:** 82 Rue d'Hauteville, 75010 Paris, France.

PUBLICATIONS

Poetry

A Day for Anne Frank. Philadelphia, Falcon Press, 1968.
Lies. Boston, Houghton Mifflin, 1969.
I Am the Bitter Name. Boston, Houghton Mifflin, 1972.
With Ignorance. Boston, Houghton Mifflin, 1977.
The Lark, The Thrush, The Starling. Providence, Rhode Island, Burning Deck, 1983.
Tar. New York, Random House, 1983.
Flesh and Blood. New York, Farrar Straus, 1987; Newcastle upon Tyne, Bloodaxe, 1988.
Poems 1963–1983. New York, Farrar Straus, and Newcastle upon Tyne, Bloodaxe, 1988.
Helen. Alexandria, Orchises Press, 1991.
A Dream of Mind. New York, Farrar Straus, and Newcastle upon Tyne, Bloodaxe, both 1992.
Selected Poems. New York, Farrar Straus, 1994.
The Vigil. New York, Farrar Straus, 1997.
Repair. New York, Farrar Straus, 1999.

Recording: *Tar and Other Poems,* Watershed, 1985.

Plays

Screenplay: *Criminals,* directed by Joseph Strick, 1994.

Other

Poetry and Consciousness. Ann Arbor, University of Michigan Press, 1998.

Editor, *Selected and Last Poems,* by Paul Zweig. Middletown, Connecticut, Wesleyan University Press, 1989.
Editor, *The Essential Hopkins.* Hopewell, New Jersey, Ecco Press, 1993.

Translator, with Gregory W. Dickerson, *Women of Trachis,* by Sophocles. New York, Oxford University Press, 1978; London, Oxford University Press, 1979.
Translator, *The Bacchae of Euripides.* New York, Farrar Straus, 1991.
Translator, with Renata Gorczynski and Benjamin Ivry, *Canvas,* by Adam Zagajewski. New York, Farrar, Straus and Giroux, and London, Faber and Faber, both 1991.
Translator, with John Montague and Margaret Guiton, *The Selected Poems of Francis Ponge,* by Francis Ponge. Winston-Salem, North Carolina, Wake Forest State University, 1994.

*

Critical Studies: By Richard Howard in *Kenyon Review* (Gambier, Ohio), summer 1970, and in *American Poetry Review* (Philadelphia), November 1972; by L.E. Sissman, in *Boston Sun-Globe,* 18 July 1972; by Morris Dickstein, in *Parnassus* (New York), fall 1972, and in *New York Times,* 10 July 1977; by Stanley Plumly, in *American Poetry Review* (Philadelphia), January 1978; by Dave Smith, in *Western Humanities Review* (Salt Lake City), autumn 1978; by Dan Bogen in *The Nation* (New York), 30 May 1987; by Linda Greggerson, in *Poetry* (Chicago), February 1988; by Michael Hoffman, in *Times Literary Supplement,* 20 January 1989; by J.D. McClatchy, in *Poetry* (Chicago), April 1989; by Michael Donaghy, in *Poetry Review,* September 1989; by Ciaran Carson, in *Irish Review,* September 1989; by Alan Jenkins, in *The Sunday Observer* (London), 8 June 1989; by Sherrod Santos, in *Parnassus* (New York), 1991; by Edward Hirsch, in *The New Republic,* 17 August 1992; by Fred Merchant, in *Harvard Review* (Cambridge), May 1993; ''Mid-Course Corrections: Some Notes on Genre'' by Carl Dennis, in *Denver Quarterly,* 29(2), fall 1994; interview by Keith S. Norris, in *New England Review* (Hanover, New Hampshire), 17(2), spring 1995.

*   *   *

In C.K. Williams's best poems the words hold together line by line and sustain the emotion of what is being said. Furthermore, it becomes clear that it is insight, or vision, that is central and that feeling, like the almost ceaseless questioning that takes place in Williams's poems, is a means by which he opens up a space for vision. There is a metaphysical, even spiritual, dimension to Williams's work in the way his poems address themselves to ultimate questions, extreme situations, and moments of vision, and indeed they address themselves to divinity itself in a manner that could be characterized equally as ambivalent and probing. The poems also show an interest in personal being in all of its aspects and possibilities—physical, psychological, and spiritual—and have an ethical, humane concern for the vulnerability of human life, especially in relation to the machinations of political power. The vigor, vividness, idiosyncratic detail, and strong emotional content are partial aspects of a writing that needs to be seen in terms of questioning, questing, probing, and seeing in the sense of seeing with insight. In the long achieved poem ''With Ignorance,'' from the book of the same title, he writes,

> What would release be? Being forgiven? No, never
>   forgiven, never only forgiven.
> To be touched, somehow, with presence, so that the only
>   sign is a step, towards or away?

Or not even a step, because the walls, of self, of dread, can
    never release,
can never forgive stepping away, out of the willed or
    refused, out of the lie or the fear
of the self that still holds back and refuses, resists, and
    turns back again and again into the willed.
What could it be, though? The first, hectic rush past guilt
    and remorse?
What if we could find a way through the fires that aren't
    with us and the terrors that are?
What would be there? Would we be thrown back into
    perhaps or not yet or not needed or done?

The poem finds a temporary, partial resolution in the notion of
blessing:

Willed or unwilled, word or sign, the word suddenly filled
    with its own breath.
Self and other the self within other and the self still moved
    through its word,
consuming itself, still, and consuming, still being rage, war,
    the fear, the aghast,
but bless, bless still, even the fear, the loss, the gutting of
    word, the gutting even of hunger,
but still to bless and bless, even the turn back, the refusal,
    to bless and to bless.

This prepares a space for the final epiphanic movement of the poem:

There was a light in a room. You came to it, leaned to it,
    reaching, touching,
and watching you, I saw you give back to the light a light
    more than light
and to the silence you gave more than silence, and, in the
    silence, I heard it.

Williams's long lines can sometimes be relaxed in pace and
rhythm and conversational in tone, but mostly there is a rushed,
breathless immediacy to his words, the sentences continuing on and
on. At times it is as if there were always more to say, while at other
times it is as if the poet wished to keep deferring any kind of an
ending. This sense of urgency of Williams's poems becomes the
theme, in a fictionalized form, in "Yours," from the collection *I Am
the Bitter Name.* When the poems fail, it is usually because the words
are carried along by the emotion in such a way that there are whole
passages loosely strung together and unable to embody any effective
force. It must also be said that the short poems in the collection *Flesh
and Blood* often seem to end before the anecdotal impulse—also
present in much of Williams's other work—has pushed, or been
pushed, through to something beyond anecdote. In addition, the
language in these poems is too often without the pressure, the
intensity, of his best work. A comparison with Charles Reznikoff's
personal or observational poems is instructive, because Reznikoff's
precise, economical use of language makes Williams's less successful poems look verbose. Too, Reznikoff's eye for telling or charged
details is surer than Williams's. These criticisms cannot be made,
however, of the long elegiac piece "Le Petit Salvié," which concludes *Flesh and Blood.* This must be included among Williams's
finest poems, together with such pieces as "One of the Muses" (from

Tar), "With Ignorance," and the beautiful poems adapted from
Issa—*The Lark, The Thrush, The Starling.*

—David Miller

WILLIAMS, Emmett

Nationality: American. **Born:** Greenville, South Carolina, 4 April
1925. **Education:** Kenyon College, Gambier, Ohio, B.A. 1949;
University of Paris. **Military Service:** U.S. Army, 1943–46. **Family:**
Married 1) Laura Powell MacCarteney in 1949, two daughters and
one son; 2) Ann Nöel Stevenson in 1970, one son. **Career:** Lived in
Europe, 1949–66: on the staff of *European Stars & Stripes,* in
Darmstadt; assistant to the ethnologist Paul Radin, in Lugano; associated with the Darmstadt group of concrete poets; founding member of
the Domaine Poetique, Paris, and the international Fluxus group since
1962. Editor-in-chief, Something Else Press, New York, 1966–70;
artist-in-residence, Fairleigh Dickinson University, Madison, New
Jersey, 1968, and University of Kentucky, Lexington, 1969; professor
of art, School of Critical Studies, California Institute of the Arts,
Valencia, 1970–72; guest professor, Nova Scotia College of Art and
Design, Halifax, 1972–74; artist-in-residence, Mount Holyoke Col-
lege, South Hadley, Massachusetts, 1975–77; artist-in-residence,
research fellow, Carpenter Center for the Visual Arts, Harvard
University, Cambridge, Massachusetts, 1977–80; artist-in-residence
Berliner Kunstler Programm, 1980. Artist-in-residence and guest
professor, Hochschule der Kunste, Berlin, and Hochschule für bildender
Künste, Hamburg, 1981–85. Co-founder and director, International
Symposium of the Arts, Warsaw, 1987–88. Artist-in-residence,
Machida-shi Museum of Graphic Arts, Tokyo, 1987, and Malindi
Artists' Proof, Malindi, Kenya, 1990 and 1992. Since 1990 president,
The Artists' Museum, Lodz, Poland. **Awards:** National Endowment
for the Arts fellowship, 1979. **Address:** Koblenzerstr 17, 10715
Berlin, Germany.

PUBLICATIONS

Poetry

Konkretionen. Darmstadt, Gemmany, Material, 1958.
13 Variations on 6 Words by Gertrude Stein (1958). Cologne, Galerie
    der Spiegel, 1965.
Rotapoems. Stuttgart, Hansjörg Mayer, 1966.
The Last French-Fried Potato and Other Poems. New York, Some-
    thing Else Press, 1967.
Sweethearts. Stuttgart, Hansjörg Mayer, 1967; New York, Something
    Else Press, 1968.
The Book of Thorn and Eth. Stuttgart, Hansjörg Mayer, 1968.
The Boy and the Bird. Stuttgart, Hansjörg Mayer, and New York,
    Wittenborn, 1968; new edition, illustrated by the author, Stuttgart
    and London, Hansjörg Mayer, 1979.
A Valentine for Nöel. Stuttgart, Hansjörg Mayer, 1973.
Selected Shorter Poems 1950–1970. Stuttgart, Hansjörg Mayer, 1974;
    New York, New Directions, 1975.
The Voyage. Stuttgart, Hanjorg Mayer, 1975.
Faustzeichnungen, illustrated by the author. Berlin, Rainer, 1983.
A Little Night Book, illustrated by Keith Godard. New York, Works,
    1983.

Deutsche Gedichte und Lichtskulpturen, illustrated by the author. Berlin, Rainer Verlag, 1988.
La Dernière Pomme Frite et Autres Poemes des Fifties et Sixties. Geneva, Centre de Gravure Contemporaine, 1989.
Aleph, Alpha, and Alfalfa. Berlin, Haus am Lutzowplatz, 1993.

Plays

Ja, Es war noch da (produced Darmstadt, Germany, 1960). Published in Nota 4 (Munich), 1960; as *Yes It Was Still There* (produced New York, 1965).
A Cellar Song for 5 Voices (produced New York, 1961).
4-Directional Song of Doubt for 5 Voices (produced Wiesbaden, Germany, 1962).
The Ultimate Poem (produced Arras, France, 1964).

Other

Six Variations upon a Spoerri Landscape: A Suite of Lithographs. Halifax, Nova Scotia College of Art and Design Lithography Workshop, 1973.
Zodiac (lithographs). Tokyo, Gallery Birthday Star, 1974.
Schemes and Variations (autobiographical essays and illustrations). Berlin, Nationalgalerie, and Stuttgart and London, Hansjörg Mayer, 1981.
Holdup (photodrama), with Keith Godard. New York, Works, 1981.
Chicken Feet, Duck Limbs, and Dada Handshakes. Vancouver, Western Front, 1984.
schutzengel/l'ange gardien/guardian angel/angelo custode. Cologne, Edition Hundertmark, 1985.
My Life in Flux—and Vice Versa. London and New York, Thames and Hudson, 1991.

Editor, *Poésie et cetera américaine.* Paris, Biennale, 1963.
Editor, *An Anthology of Concrete Poetry.* New York, Something Else Press, 1967.
Editor, *Store Days,* by Claes Oldenburg. New York, Something Else Press, 1967.
Editor, "Language Happenings," in *Open Poetry: Four Anthologies of Expanded Poems.* New York, Simon and Schuster, 1973.
Editor, with Ann Nöel, *Mr. Fluxus: A Collective Portrait of George Maciunas 1931–1978.* London, Thames and Hudson, 1997.

Translator, *An Anecdoted Topography of Chance. . . ,* by Daniel Spoerri. New York, Something Else Press, 1966.
Translator, *The Mythological Travels of a Modern Sir John Mandeville* by Daniel Spoerri. New York, Something Else Press, 1970.
Translator, *Mythology and Meatballs: A Greek Island Diary-Cookbook,* by Daniel Spoerri. Berkeley, California, Aris, 1982.

*

Bibliography: In *Schemes and Variations,* 1981; *An Annotated Bibliography* by P. Frank Brattleboro, Vermont, Something Else Press, 1983.

Manuscript Collections: Sohm Archive, Staatsgalerie, Stuttgart; Sackner Archive, Miami Beach, Florida.

Critical Studies: *Concrete Poetry: A World View* by M.E. Solt, Bloomington, University of Indiana, 1968; "A Blurb for Emmett" by R. Hamilton, in *Collected Words* (London), 1982; "All Han Zon Dek!" by S. MacDonald, in *Afterimage* (Rochester, New York), 12(6), 1985; "Fluxus Today and Yesterday" by J. Pijnappel, in *Art & Design* (London), 28, 1992; "Poetry As Life and Life As Fiesta" by A. Arias-Misson, in *American Poetry Review* (Philadelphia), April-May 1992.

*　　*　　*

Emmett Williams's name is better known than his poetry, and one reason for this is that he edited *An Anthology of Concrete Poetry,* which has outsold its competitors (including an anthology of mine). At the same time most of his poetry remains unpublished, particularly in his native country. Unlike other American writers of his generation, Williams became closely involved in the 1950s with the European intermedia avant-garde, epitomized by the so-called Darmstadt Circle, in which he figured prominently. By the 1960s he was an initiator of Fluxus, an international post-Dada, mixed-means movement that won considerable attention at the time but that has escaped most historians of contemporary art and literature. Thus, to an unusual degree his writing reflects the experimental tradition in the nonliterary arts. For instance, he echoed not Dylan Thomas but rather Kurt Schwitters in his early performance poems, to use the term that refers to poems whose most appropriate form is not the printed page but rather live performance.

It was Williams's good fortune to learn that English-language poetry could be composed in radically alternative ways, different not only from the academic poetry of the time but also from the declamatory expressionism of, say, Allen Ginsberg. Instead, Williams pioneered the art of concrete poetry, in which the poet eschews conventional syntax and related devices to organize language in other ways. Rather than using free form, Williams favored such severe constraints as repetition, permutation, and linguistic minimalism. His masterpiece, the book-length *Sweethearts,* consists of one word (the title) whose eleven letters are visually distributed over 150 or so sequentially expressive pages, the work as a whole relating the evolution of a relationship between a man and a woman. Like Williams's other work, *Sweethearts* is extremely witty, and like much else in experimental writing, it must be seen and read for its magic to be believed.

—Richard Kostelanetz

WILLIAMS, Hugo (Mordaunt)

Nationality: British. **Born:** Windsor, Berkshire, 20 February 1942; son of the actor and playwright Hugh Williams. **Education:** Eton College, 1955–59. **Family:** Married Hermine Demoriane in 1965; one daughter. **Career:** Editorial assistant, 1960–61, and assistant editor, 1961–70, *London Magazine;* staff writer, *Telegraph Magazine,* London, 1965; Henfield Fellow, University of East Anglia, Norwich, 1981; television critic and poetry editor, *New Statesman,* London, 1983–88; theater critic, *Sunday Correspondent,* London, 1989–91. Since 1993 film critic for *Harper's,* New York, and *Queen's,* London. Teaches at University of East Anglia, works as a film critic, and writes the "Freelance Column" for the *Times Literary Supplement.* **Awards:** Eric Gregory award, 1965; Arts Council bursary,

1966; Cholmondeley award, 1970; Faber memorial prize, 1979. **Address:** 3 Raleigh Street, London N1 8NW, England.

PUBLICATIONS

Poetry

Symptoms of Loss. London and New York, Oxford University Press, 1965.
Poems. London, The Review, 1969.
Sugar Daddy. London and New York, Oxford University Press, 1970.
Cherry Blossom. London, Poem-of-the-Month Club, 1972.
Some Sweet Day. London and New York, Oxford University Press, 1975.
Love-Life. London, Whizzard Press, 1979.
Writing Home. Oxford, Oxford University Press, 1985.
First Poems. Edinburgh, Tragara Press, 1985.
Selected Poems. Oxford, Oxford University Press, 1989.
Self-Portrait with a Slide. Oxford, Oxford University Press, 1990.
Dock Leaves. London, Faber, 1994.
Billy's Rain. London, Faber, 1999.

Recording: *British Poets of Our Times,* with Adrian Henri, Argo.

Play

Screenplay: *Flight to Berlin,* with Christopher Petit, 1984.

Other

All the Time in the World (travel). London, Alan Ross, 1966; Philadelphia, Chilton, 1968.
No Particular Place to Go (travel). London, Cape, 1981.
Freelancing: Adventures of a Poet. London and Boston, Faber, 1995.

Editor, *"London Magazine" Poems, 1961–1966.* London, Alan Ross. 1966.

*

Critical Studies: Interview with Mark Wormald, in *Oxford Poetry,* 4(3), September 1989; by Robert Crawford, in *London Review of Books,* 17(4), 23 February 1995..

*   *   *

The poems of Hugo Williams are atypical of much contemporary British poetry in their candid ability to express emotion. Some critics have complained that his poems veer into sentiment, but the fact remains that they are noticeably open to feeling in a way that, say, the poems of Philip Larkin certainly are and those of other, younger poets are not. He is also unusual in that many of his poems form part of an ongoing autobiography. His work has a stylistic and rhythmic lightness of touch in which traditional verse forms evolve into something recognizably his own.

When Williams first came to notice in the late 1960s, he was grouped with the poets Michael Fried, Ian Hamilton, David Harsent, and Colin Falck, who (along with other poets) published in the *Review* little magazine. A typical *Review* poem was generally short, imagistic, and focused precisely on a single emotion or situation. The idea of a "school" was short-lived and misleading however, and the poets involved soon developed along their own separate ways.

Williams's first book, *Symptoms of Loss*, hardly fits the *Review* stereotype. It also does not suffer from the derivative style of many first books but achieves a distinctive individual tone throughout. *Symptoms of Loss* opens and closes with impressively original poems, from the opening "Still Hot from Filing," a meditation on a newly cut front door key, to the final poem, "The Butcher," which is characteristic of his work in a number of ways:

> He is a rosy young man with white eyelashes
> Like a bullock. He always serves me now.
>
> I think he knows about my life. How we prefer
> To eat in when it's cold. How someone
> With a foreign accent can only cook veal.
> He writes the price on the grease-proof packet
>
> And hands it to me courteously. His smile
> Is the official seal on my marriage.

The language is simple, favoring coolly expressed plain statements of fact, and the poem provides us with a brief glimpse into part of a continuing autobiography. The specific everyday things of life such as "grease-proof" paper and the courteous smile with which the meat is handed over are clearly noted. There is a sense of distance between the two involved in the transaction, yet a sense of relationship too. But the everydayness of the poem is deceptive and can suddenly veer off into unusual flights of (pre-Martian) fantastic imagery and wit, as when the butcher is described as "like a bullock" or when a smile becomes "the official seal on my marriage." This first book showed Williams to have already a fully realized tone and approach of his own. The apprenticeship that led to the maturity of *Symptoms of Loss* can be followed in the early poems gathered in the 1985 limited edition *First Poems*.

In many ways marriage and married life are Williams's key themes and a thread running through his early books. He is an original and disarmingly direct love poet, managing to be both honest and engaging, as in "Sugar Daddy," from the book of the same name, in which he confesses, "I'm blood brother, / Sugar-daddy, millionaire to you. / I want to buy you things."

Love-Life was a book centered around the single theme of love— not often particularly happy—from the perspective of marriage. In "Bachelors" we find a sense of the responsibilities of marriage and the view of bachelors as both "denimed Romeos" and "amateurs of passion," knowing little of the reality of love. This somber note is found elsewhere in the book, yet expressed with an almost throwaway lightness of touch that, neither too overcrafted nor too rhythmically loose, brought something new to poetry. Another poem, "Present Continuous," gives us a specific image of loss based on possessions in "fifty pairs of shoes / Still hang around the window on the stairs, / The changing fashions of your years with me." Other poems touch on Williams's interest in clothes, a self-consciously dandiacal aspect (perhaps inherited from his "father's forty-seven suits") unusual in contemporary British poetry and highly suspected and misunderstood by the more puritan of literary critics.

Both *Love-Life* and Williams's next, and best, book, *Writing Home,* explore aspects of his youth. *Writing Home* takes as its theme his relationship with his father, the stage and film actor Hugh

Williams. The book enabled Williams, as it did Robert Lowell in his autobiographical *Life Studies,* to introduce more deeply personal material taken direct from his own family history. The forms of the poems are rhythmically supple, at once fluid and seemingly throwaway, entertained and entertaining, yet moving too. *Writing Home* has a unified tone throughout. Even in the formal elegy ''Death of an Actor'' it is amused, ironic without malice, good mannered to the reader, and possessing real humor, elegance, and wit.

The book charts the boyhood and youth of Williams. The opening poem, ''At Least a Hundred Words,'' deals with the letters written by the boys at a boarding school to their parents at homes far away. The poems in *Writing Home* are letters written by the adult poet to his past:

What shall we say in our letters home?
That we're perfectly all right?
That we stand on the playground with red faces
and our hair sticking up?

The two major pieces of the book are the sequences ''An Actor's War'' and ''Death of an Actor,'' the latter a formal elegy for his father. But the book is also self-mockingly funny at the expense of Williams's younger self, as in ''Early Work'' on his conscious teenage attempts to imitate popular hairstyles, ''a turmoil of popular styles and prejudices, / stiff with unreality and fear.'' Williams also perfectly captures schoolboy angst in ''A Picture of a Girl in a Bikini,'' when he is summoned to the headmaster's study:

Inside is the worst news in the world,
my copy of Man Junior with a picture of a girl
in a bikini playing with a beach ball.
I must have left it under my mattress.
The Headmaster looks at me in disbelief
and asks, 'What is the meaning of this?'

The book was a risk, dealing with personal autobiography directly and honestly (there is a poem on his father—''Out of work at fifty, smoking fifty a day''), but it was his most successful and impressive achievement to date.

Self-Portrait with a Slide, Williams's next book, included the reemergence, in a number of poems, of Sonny Jim, a lanky and cheerful children's character from an early breakfast cereal ad. He was first introduced as a Williams persona in *Sugar Daddy,* and Sonny Jim poems have appeared in books regularly since then. Sonny Jim is self-conscious, boyish, humorous, and vulnerable, an innocent adrift in a complex world. The poems, interspersed among others in *Self-Portrait with a Slide,* create a thread running through the book.

Whereas *Writing Home* concentrated on Williams's relationship with his father, his book *Dock Leaves* takes as its central theme poems occasioned by memories following the death of his mother, the actress and dramatist Margaret Vyner. The return to personal material is fruitful and makes the book another high point for Williams's readers. Early in the book we find ''Margaret Vyner,'' consisting of prose passages on important events in the external world juxtaposed with brief glimpses of the progress of the child from the age of eleven in Sydney in 1925 through her time as a chorus girl, the realization of her ambition to go to Europe, her work as a model, and her eventual marriage to Williams's father. The prose poem ends in the year 1946 with an image of the four-year-old poet carrying about ''my mother's empty Patou scent bottle in the shape of a crown.''

The poems of *Dock Leaves* evoke the boyhood of Williams and present scenes from his life in relation to his mother with ease and a characteristic lightness of touch. The reader is offered sensitive and dispassionate views of a personal happiness and of a boy growing up from childhood to adolescence, of girlfriends, and of the eventual responsibilities of adulthood. ''The Age of Steam'' brilliantly re-creates a farewell at a railway station in the 1950s. His mother kisses her son good-bye:

A last gasp of *Moment Supreme*
as she leans over me, then nothing at all
but the ribbon of her smell unravelling,
the station clock moving on with a little jerk,
the whistle blowing.

The method of a poem such as this is very close to the early success of ''The Butcher'' of 1965 and demonstrates the stylistic consistency of Williams's work. Throughout *Dock Leaves* we meet a lucid and careful artistry that aims to present us with realistically portrayed incidents from a personal past. The poem ''Joy,'' with its metaphorical understanding that for every pain there is a joy to balance it—''that there was nothing / worse in all the world / than stinging nettle stings / and nothing better / than cool dock leaves''—could serve as the coda of the book.

Billy's Rain, published in 1999, is a book to read in tandem with the earlier *Love-Life.* Both books deal with the reality and the complexities of human sexual love. But while *Love-Life* centers on marriage, *Billy's Rain* is a book about a love affair. The book was a critical success on publication and received the T.S. Eliot prize, the premier British poetry award. At the presentation, made by T.S. Eliot's widow Valerie, Blake Morrison, who was chairman of the judges, spoke of the book's ''seeming artlessness, its unflinching candour and its cumulative power.''

Billy's Rain is a book-length sequence of fifty-one poems that chart the development of a love affair from beginning to end. The book has a narrative flow that lends a compelling edge to the poems and holds the reader's attention throughout. The reader is taken into the confidence of the writer and lives through his experience. The story is told in a fair and curiously balanced way, with a lack of self-dramatization. The language takes pride in seeming artlessly plain while also showing that only a true master could construct these poems, as in the subtleties of ''Siren Song,'' which ends,

Once in a while she'll pick up the phone
and her voice sings to me out of the past.
The hair on the back of my neck stands up
as I catch her smell for a second.

Williams expresses brilliantly the highs and lows of the affair, while keeping his characteristic lightness of touch and his sense of humor intact. ''Her News,'' which comes toward the end of the book, when the affair is over, has a twist at the end and reconfirms the strengths of marriage, with all of its affection and its arguments:

But no, I couldn't go through all that again,
not without my own wife being there,
not without her getting cross about everything.

The poems of Williams express real emotions from the past and the present plainly and honesty and with a limpid deftness of rhythm.

He has, rightly, been called a writer able to celebrate the moment, and his poems are sure to endure.

—Jonathan Barker

WILLIAMS, Jonathan (Chamberlain)

Nationality: American. **Born:** Asheville, North Carolina, 8 March 1929. **Education:** St. Albans School, Washington, D.C., 1941–47; Princeton University, New Jersey, 1947–49; Atelier 17, New York, 1949–50; Institute of Design, Chicago, 1951; Black Mountain College, North Carolina, 1951–56. **Military Service:** Conscientious Objector: U.S. Army Medical Corps, 1952–53. **Career:** Since 1951 executive director, The Jargon Society, Inc., publishers, Highlands, North Carolina. Scholar-in-residence Aspen Institute, Colorado, 1962, 1967–68, poet-in-residence, Maryland Institute College of Art, Baltimore, 1968–69, University of Kansas, Lawrence, 1971, and University of Delaware, Newark, 1977; visiting poet, Wake Forest University, North Carolina School of the Arts, Salem College, Winston-Salem State University, all North Carolina, all 1973, and University of California, San Diego, 1982. Since 1980 curator, Jargon Society Archive, State University of New York, Buffalo. Since 1960 vice president, Cast-Iron Lawn-Deer Owners of America. **Awards:** Guggenheim fellowship, 1957; Longview Foundation grant, 1960; National Endowment for the Arts grant 1968, 1969, 1970, 1972, 1978, 1981; Coordinating Council of Little Magazines award, 1974; Carey-Thomas award, for publishing, 1977; inductee, North Carolina Literary Hall of Fame, Southern Pines, North Carolina, 1998. D.H.L.: Maryland Institute College of Art, 1969. **Address:** P.O. Box 10, Highlands, North Carolina 28741, U.S.A.; or, Corn Close, Dentdale, Sedbergh, Cumbria, LA10 15QG, England.

PUBLICATIONS

Poetry

Sixmas. Privately printed, 1950.
Tactilopera. Privately printed, 1951.
Garbage Litters the Iron Face of the Sun's Child. San Francisco, Jargon, 1951.
Red/Gray. Black Mountain, North Carolina, Jargon, 1952.
Four Stoppages. Stuttgart, Jargon, 1953.
Lord! Lord! Lord! Highlands, North Carolina, Jargon, 1959.
The Empire Finals at Verona. Highlands, North Carolina, Jargon, 1959.
Amen Huzza Selah. Black Mountain, North Carolina, Jargon, 1960.
Elegies and Celebrations. Highlands, North Carolina, Jargon, 1962.
In England's Green & (A Garland and a Clyster). San Francisco, Auerhahn Press, 1962.
Emblems for the Little Dells and Nooks and Corners of Paradise. London, Jargon, 1962.
Lullabies Twisters Gibbers Drags. Highlands, North Carolina Nantahala Foundation, 1963; as *The Macon County North Carolina Meshuga Sound Society, Jonathan Williams, Musical Director, Presents: Lullabies, Twisters, Gibbers, Drags (a là manière de M.*

Louis Moreau Gottschalk, late of the City of New Orleans), London, Jargon, 1963.
Davenport Gap. Highlands, North Carolina, Jargon, 1963.
Green Corn thru a Cow or Where Were You When the Culture Explosion Hit the Fan? Privately printed, 1965.
Petite Concrete Suite. Detroit, Fenian Head Centre Press, 1965.
Twelve Jargonelles from the Herbalist's Notebook. Bloomington, Indiana University Design Department, 1965.
Ten Jargonelles from the Herbalist's Notebook. Urbana, University of Illinois Design Department, 1966.
Four Jargonelles from the Herbalist's Notebook. Cambridge, Massachusetts, Lowell, 1966.
Paean to Dvorak, Deemer, and McClure. San Francisco, Dave Haselwood, 1966.
Affilati Attrezzi Per I Giardini di Catullo (bilingual edition). Milan, Lerici Editore, 1966.
Crafts of the Southern Highlands. New York, Craft Horizons, 1966.
Mahler Becomes Politics, Beisbol. London, Marlborough Gallery, 1967.
50! Epiphytes, -taphs, -tomes, -grams, -thets! 50! London, Poet and Printer, 1967.
A French 75! San Francisco, Dave Haselwood, 1967.
Polycotyledonous Poems. Stuttgart, Hansjorg Mayer, 1967.
The Lucidities: Sixteen in Visionary Company. London, Turret, 1967.
Eight Jargonelles from the Herbalist's Notebook. Bloomington, Indiana University Design Department, 1967.
LTGD. Bloomington, Indiana University Design Department, 1967.
Les Six Pak. Aspen, Colorado, Aspen Institute, 1967.
Sharp Tools for Catullan Gardens. Bloomington, Indiana University Fine Arts Department, 1968.
A Bestiary for Anti-Laodiceans, Lamed-Vovniks and Lacandons. Aspen, Colorado, Aspen Institute, 1968.
Ripostes. Stuttgart, Domberger, 1968.
An Ear in Bartram's Tree: Selected Poems 1957–67. Chapel Hill, University of North Carolina Press, 1969.
On Arriving at the Same Age as Jack Benny. Urbana, Illinois, Finial Press, 1969.
Six Rusticated, Wall-Eyed Poems. Baltimore, Maryland Institute Press, 1969.
The Apocryphal Oracular Yeah-Sayings of Mae West. Baltimore, Maryland Institute Press, 1969.
The New Architectural Monuments of Baltimore City. Baltimore, Maryland Institute Press, 1971.
The Patagonian Declaration of Independence. Urbana, University of Illinois Design Department, 1971.
Strung Out with Elgar on a Hill. Urbana, Illinois, Finial Press, 1971.
Blues and Roots, Rue and Bluets: A Garland for the Appalachians. New York, Grossman, 1971.
The Loco Logodaedalist in Situ: Selected Poems 1968–70. London, Cape Goliard Press, 1971; New York, Grossman, 1972.
Epitaph, with Thomas Meyer. Dentdale, Cumbria, Jargon, 1972.
Fruits Confits, with Thomas Meyer. Privately printed, 1972.
Lord Decca Dent's Weaponry Guide to the Devices of the Pentland Hills Oral Rearmament Society. Wilsden, Bradford, Yorkshire, Blue Tunnel, 1973.
Andrew Marvell Wanders in the Grassy Deeps along the Wharfe at Nun Appleton House and Attains a Small At-one-ment. Cambridge, Massachusetts, Pomegranate Press, 1973.
Clipped Greens. Dentdale, Cumbria, Finial Press, 1973.

Adventures with a Twelve-Inch Pianist Beyond the Blue Horizon. Roswell, New Mexico, DBA, 1973.

Who Is Little Enis? Highlands, North Carolina, Jargon, 1974.

Five from Up t'Dale. Kendal, Cumbria, Finial Press, 1974.

Hasidic Exclamation on Stevie Smith's Poem "Not Waving But Drowning." Storrs, University of Connecticut Library, 1974.

Pairidaeza. Dentdale, Cumbria, Jargon, 1975.

My Quaker-Atheist Friend. London, Larry and Ruby Wallrich, 1975.

Joyfull News out of the Newfounde World. Highlands, North Carolina, Jargon, 1975.

Gists from a Presidential Report on Hardcornponeography. Highlands, North Carolina, Jargon, 1975.

A Wee Tot for Catullus. Nailsworth, Gloucestershire, Moschatel Press, 1975.

A Celestial Centennial Reverie for Charles Edward Ives. Roswell, New Mexico, DBA, 1975.

Imaginary Postcards. London, Trigram Press, 1975.

gAy BC's. Champaign, Illinois, Finial Press, 1976.

In the Field at the Solstice. Champaign, Illinois, Finial Press, 1976.

Untinears and Antennae for Maurice Ravel. St. Paul, Minnesota, Truck Press, 1977.

An Omen for Stevie Smith. New Haven, Connecticut, Yale University Sterling Library, 1977.

A Blue Ridge Weather Prophet. Frankfort, Kentucky, Gnomon Press, 1977.

Super-Duper Zuppa Inglese. Belper, Derbyshire, Aggie Weston's 1977.

A Blue Ridge Weather Prophet Makes Twelve Stitches in Time on the Twelfth Day of Christmas. Frankfort, Kentucky, Gnomon Press, 1977.

E.A.N. Privately printed, 1977.

5 Entries in the Commonplace Book of Jonathan Williams Dated Early 1978. Rocky Mount, North Carolina Wesleyan College, 1978.

A Hairy Coat near Yanwath Yat. Rocky Mount, North Carolina Wesleyan College, 1978.

Elite/Elate Poems: Poems 1971–1975. Highlands, North Carolina, Jargon, 1979.

JW, on the Road Selling That Old Orphic Snake-Oil in the Jargon-Sized Bottles, 1951–1978. Washington, D.C., Visual Press, 1979.

Shankum Naggum. Rocky Mount, North Carolina Wesleyan College Friends of the Library, 1979.

The Delian Seasons. Bradford, Yorkshire, Topia Press, 1979.

Glees, Swarthy Monotonies, Rince Cochon, and Chozzerai for Simon. Roswell, New Mexico, DBA, 1980.

Homage Umbrage Quibble and Chicane. Roswell, New Mexico, DBA, 1980.

Poem on His Name, on His Birthday, February 18, 1980. Rocky Mount, North Carolina Wesleyan College, 1980.

An Arabesk for Frederick Delius at the Year's End. Buffalo, State University of New York, 1981.

Get Hot or Get Out: A Selection of Poems 1957–1981. Metuchen, New Jersey, Scarecrow Press, 1982.

Niches Inches: New and Selected Poems 1957–1981. Privately printed, 1982.

Lexington Nocturne: A Poem by Jonathan Williams as Interpreted by Keith Smith. Rochester, New York, Keith Smith, 1983.

"And He Hath Sown . . ." Rocky Mount, North Carolina Wesleyan College, 1983.

62 Climerikews to Amuse Mr. Lear. Roswell, New Mexico, DBA/JCA, 1983.

The Fifty-Two Clerihews of Clara Hughes. Atlanta, Georgia, Pynyon Press, 1983.

In the Azure over the Squalor: Ransackings and Shorings. New York, Jordan Davies, 1983; revised edition, Highlands, North Carolina, Otis, 1984; enlarged edition, Frankfort, Kentucky, Gnomon Press, 1985; enlarged edition, as *Quote Unquote*, Berkeley, California, Ten Speed Press, 1989.

Taoist Foretaste of Spring. Privately printed, 1985.

Dear World, Forget It! Love, Mnemosyne: A Range of Letters, 1984–85. Roswell, New Mexico, DBA/JCA, 1985.

Calling All Jargonauts! Calling All Lapsed Lamed-Vovniks!!! Highlands, North Carolina, Jargon, 1986.

Noah Webster to Wee Lorine Niedecker. Minneapolis, Origin, 1986.

A Discrete Sign on the Steinway in the Phillips Memorial Gallery. Minneapolis, Hermetic Press, 1986.

An Announcement: Elizabeth Crommelin Melby Davies. New York, Jennifer Melby and Jordan Davies, 1986.

Week Number 4 from Jonathan Williams's Day Book "An Enchiridion of Asps." Rocky Mount, North Carolina Wesleyan College, 1987.

Jonathan Williams: Week No. 5. Milwaukee, Woodland Pattern, 1987.

Rivulets and Sibilants of Dent. Bradford, Yorkshire, Topia Press, 1987.

Uncle Gus Flaubert Rates the Jargon Society in 101 Laconic Présale, Sage Sentences. Hanes Foundation, Rare Book Collection/University Library, Chapel Hill, University of North Carolina, 1989.

Aposiopeses. Minneapolis, Granary, 1988.

Dementations on Shank's Mare. New Haven, Connecticut, Truck Press, 1988.

Metafours for Mysophobes. Twickenham, Middlesex, North and South, 1990.

Quantulumcumque. Asheville, North Carolina, French Broad Press. 1991.

Only Forty Minutes More. Highlands, North Carolina, The Press of Otis the Lamed-Vovnik, 1991.

Anathma Maranatha. New York, The Press of Richard Minsky, 1993.

No-No-Nse-Nse. Mount Horeb, Wisconsin, The Perishable Press, 1993.

Horny & Ornery. Highlands, North Carolina, The Press of Otis the Lamed-Vovnik, 1994.

St. Swithin's Swivet. Woodchester, Gloucestershire, John Furnival Editions, 1999.

Recording: *Get Hot or Get Out*, Watershed, 1982.

Other

Lines about Hills above Lakes. Fort Lauderdale, Florida, Roman, 1964.

Descant on Rawthey's Madrigal: Conversations with Basil Bunting. Lexington, Kentucky, Gnomon Press, 1968.

The Appalachian Photographs of Doris Ulmann. Highlands, North Carolina, Jargon, 1971.

Clarence John Laughlin: The Personal Eye. New York, Aperture, 1973.

The Family Album of Lucybelle Crater. Highlands, North Carolina, Jargon, 1974.

How What? Collages, Texts, Photographs. Dublin, Georgia, Mole Press, 1975.

Portrait Photographs. Frankfort, Kentucky, Gnomon Press, and London, Coracle, 1979.

Jonathan Williams: A Poet Collects (exhibition catalog). Winston-Salem, North Carolina, Southeastern Center for Contemporary Art, 1981.

The Magpie's Bagpipe (essays). Berkeley, California, North Point Press, 1982.

Lord Stodge's Cood Thing Guide to Over 100 English Delights. Roswell, New Mexico, DBA/JCA, 1985.

The Concise Dentdale Dictionary of English Place-Names. Highland, North Carolina, Otis, 1987.

Le Garage Ravi de Rocky Mount (essay). Rocky Mount, North Carolina, Wesleyan College Press, 1988.

Jonathan Williams' Quote Book 1992–93. Highlands, North Carolina, Press of Otis the Lamed-Vovnik, 1994.

Letters to Mencken from the Land of Pink Lichen. New York, Dim Gray Bar Press, 1994.

26 Enlarged, Engorged Polaroids. Dentdale, Cumbria, Press of Otis the Lamed-Vovnik, 1994.

Long Taters: Johnathan Williams' Quote Book 1994. Highlands, North Carolina, Press of Otis the Lamed-Vovnik, 1996.

Editor, *Edward Dahlberg: A Tribute.* New York, David Lewis, 1970.

Editor, *Epitaphs for Lorine: 33 Poets Celebrate Lorine Niedecker.* Highlands, North Carolina, Jargon, 1973.

Editor, *The Sleep of Reason,* by Lyle Bonge. Highlands, North Carolina, Jargon, 1974.

Editor, *Madeira and Toasts for Basil Bunting's 75th Birthday.* Highlands, North Carolina, Jargon, 1977.

Editor, *I Shall Save One Land Unvisited: Eleven Southern Photographers.* Frankfort, Kentucky, Gnomon Press, 1978.

Editor, *Donald B. Anderson at 70.* Highlands, North Carolina, Jargon, 1989.

*

Bibliography: *Jonathan Williams: A Bibliographical Checklist of His Writings, 1950–1988* by James S. Jaffe, privately printed, 1989.

Manuscript Collections: Jargon Society Archive, University of North Carolina, Chapel Hill, and State University of New York, Buffalo.

Critical Studies: Introduction to *An Ear in Bartram's Tree: Selected Poems 1957–67,* 1969, and *Jonathan Williams, Poet,* Cleveland, Asphodel Book Shop, 1969, both by Guy Davenport; "The Sound of Our Speaking" by Robert Morgan, in *The Nation* (New York), 6 September 1971; by Herbert Leibowitz, in *New York Times Book Review,* 21 November 1971; by Raymond Gardner, in *The Guardian* (London), 3 July 1972; in *Vort 4* (Silver Spring, Maryland), 1973; *Fiftieth Birthday Celebration for Jonathan Williams* edited by Jonathan Greene, Frankfort, Kentucky, Truck-Gnomon Press, 1979; "A Quarter Century of The Jargon Society: An Interview with Jonathan Williams" by William Corbett, in *The Art of Literary Publishing: Editors on Their Craft,* edited by Bill Henderson, Wainscott, New York, Pushcart, 1980; "Piping Down the Valleys Wild" by X.J. Kennedy, in *Parnassus* (New York), 12(1), fall-winter 1984; interview by Jim Cory, in *James White Review,* 11(1), 1993; interview by Leverett T. Smith, in *North Carolina Literary Review,* 2(2), 1995.

Jonathan Williams comments:

(1980) I am primarily a poet, but since we do not live for ourselves alone, I have always assumed (since 1951) that the publishing of my poetic enthusiasms was part of the job. And the reading of poems aloud to audiences, which I have done approximately twelve hundred times from Vancouver to Wien.

I have been called a Black Mountain poet, a beat poet, a southern-poetry-today poet, a light poet, an informalist poet, a formalist poet, a concrete poet, a found object poet, a relentlessly and tiresomely avant-garde poet. To my knowledge all I am is a poet; like anyone else, I write as I can.

The masters of delectation and precision are my mentors: Blake, Marvell, Buson, Archilochos, Martial, Catullus, Dickinson, Ono no Komachi, Basho, and Whitman. From more immediate times: Pound, William Carlos Williams, Robinson Jeffers, Kenneth Patchen, Kenneth Rexroth, Charles Olson, Ian Hamilton Finlay, Stevie Smith, Basil Bunting, J.V. Cunningham, James Laughlin . . . I use all the devices I know, all the tricks in Orpheus's black bag; if it is possible to move rocks and trees, it is just possible to keep ice from forming in other human hearts. Poems are passionate things to give courage to those who respond to their messages. I write for those who long for the saving grace of the language. I never write for Laodiceans. The gentle reader and I are going to go round and round. Richard of St. Victor teaches us that in art and in life there are more things to love than we could possibly have imagined. "Odi et amo," said Catullus. I want Catullus in the poems and Willie Mays and Thomas Jefferson and Charles Ives and Apollo and hill farmers and people who talk trash. The language is airy, earthy, Regency, witty, offensive, etc., whatever it needs to be. This is your friendly local, ecological Logodaedalist talking.

*   *   *

Like most folk remedies, Jonathan Williams's poems have a little vinegar in them. They can either be celebratory, as witness his many epitaphs, or meant to increase circulation by chaffing. He recognizes that poems can be jokes in their compression and timing and that timing can have a greater effectiveness than sincerity or moral indignation. God is pun. No ear bends our own closer to the intricacies of words, the multiplicity of play possible in a word, than Williams's. More a lodestone than semiprecious, he has a nose for irony and finds it everywhere in the world around him.

Williams is a public-spirited private man who keeps gravestones swept clean and foibles clear of hypocrisy. Since sexuality is one of the most abused of our notions, it gets a good deal of Williams's attention. A man of judgment, he honors and condemns. He is an incessant observer, constantly contrasting haut monde with down home. He knows the *moeurs* of his people, and he sizes up a culture in a flash:

come on,
Gene

the

Boogers
got

Lummy Jean Licklighter

in an attic
over near Viper!

For Williams the first American poem might have been the one carved by Daniel Boone on a tree after he killed his first bear, unless it was the one on the tree at the colony at Roanoke. Poetry occurs wherever people have invested in words, whatever they have trusted to the permanence of letters. His is a poetry of use, whether as cenotaph or whammy-diddle, such as that whittled by his acquaintance Sam Ward. I hear America singing: "o the Smokies are ok but me / I go for Theosophy, / higher things, Hindu-type philosophy, / none of this licker and sex . . ." Wherever there is man there are sneezes, scratching, and foibles.

In terms of contemporary literature Williams is a Ben Franklin, another active man in the world, or else like the women in "Aunt Creasy, On Work": "shucks / I make the livin / uncle / just makes the livin worthwhile." The subjects are not just American or Appalachian either. The following is from "Bessie from the Hebrides":

well then, what do you do
with all the steel wool
you steal?

well then,
I'm knittin'
a kettle!

He can scowl and scold when he wants to ("Cobwebbery"), but it is a modest enough goal he is after: "The poet, as ever, has little to offer but the veracity of his ears and eyes, in the hope he has kept them sharp and affectionate." Yet neighborhoods, universities, cities may rise or fall on such a principle.

Williams has a primitivism combined with a nobility of outlook and refined exactitude. He is rarely introspective, and all the searching, one senses, goes on before he discovers the poem. He and Twain would have conversed famously. He is rarely descriptive, seldom prescriptive, but unusually perceptive. Is he a Luddite? Was Samuel Johnson? There seems to be a forgiving quality before any hauteur has a chance to take hold. He is one of the few poets about whom it could be said that he has never bored a reader. That is because there is nothing he does not find interesting. Inertia does not stand a chance. He picks up, shakes, sniffs, squints at, and puts back something exactly where he has found it or slightly atilt in a new light. He handles every word, every name, to see if it rattles, to find if it reverberates with primary or secondary meanings.

Williams has been the ideal reader for some fifty of our best writers and musicians and photographers, including Bunting, Dahlberg, Olson, William Carlos Williams, Mingus, Meatyard, Siskind. It is no wonder that he has fifty "cosmic" readers in return who are loyal to him like the initiates of a cargo cult. Perhaps loyalty more than any other value besides wit is what he commands. What sort of man sets out to be an epigrammatist for our times? One who insists on the last word, a man fearful of his own oblivion, an upholder of the value of friendship, a thrifty man cleansed of cynicism. Heaven knows, it requires as much energy to chisel an inscription as to let loose a heart.

—George F. Butterick

WILLIAMS, Miller

Nationality: American. **Born:** Hoxie, Arkansas, 8 April 1930. **Education:** Arkansas State College, Conway, B.S. in biology 1951; University of Arkansas, Fayetteville, M.S. in zoology 1952. **Family:** Married 1) Lucille Day in 1951 (divorced): 2) Rebecca Jordan Hall in 1969; two daughters and one son. **Career:** Taught biology at McNeese State College, Lake Charles, Louisiana, and Millsaps College, Jackson, Mississippi; instructor, 1962–63, and assistant professor of English, 1964–66, Louisiana State University, Baton Rouge; associate professor of English, Loyola University, New Orleans, 1966–70; Fulbright professor of American studies, National University of Mexico, 1970. Co-director, graduate program in creative writing, 1971–80, associate professor, 1971–73, director, program in translation, 1974–80, professor of English, 1973–87, and chair of the comparative literature program, 1977–80, and since 1987 professor, University of Arkansas. Visiting professor, University of Chile, Santiago, 1963–64. Poetry editor, Louisiana State University Press, 1966–68; editor, *New Orleans Review,* 1968–69; since 1978 contributing editor, *Translation Review,* Richardson, Texas; founding director, University of Arkansas Press, 1980–97; president, American Literary Translators Association, 1979–81. **Awards:** Henry Bellaman award, 1957; Bread Loaf Writers Conference fellowship, 1961; Amy Lowell traveling scholarship, 1963; Arts Fund award, 1973; American Academy in Rome fellowship 1976; Poets' prize for *Living on the Surface,* 1991; Charity Randall citation for contribution to poetry as a spoken art, 1993; John William Corrington award for literary excellence, 1994; Academy award for literature, American Academy of Arts and Letters, 1995. H.H.D.: Lander College, Greenwood, South Carolina, 1983. D.H.L.: Hendrix College, 1995. **Address:** Department of English, University of Arkansas, Fayetteville, Arkansas 72701, U.S.A.

PUBLICATIONS

Poetry

A Circle of Stone. Baton Rouge, Louisiana State University Press, 1964.
Recital (bilingual edition). Valparaiso, Chile, Ediciones Océano, 1964.
So Long at the Fair. New York, Dutton, 1968.
The Only World There Is. New York, Dutton, 1971.
Halfway from Hoxie: New and Selected Poems. New York, Dutton, 1973.
Why God Permits Evil: New Poems. Baton Rouge, Louisiana State University Press, 1977.
Distractions. Baton Rouge, Louisiana State University Press, 1981.
The Boys on Their Bony Mules. Baton Rouge, Louisiana State University Press, 1983.

Imperfect Love. Baton Rouge, Louisiana State University Press, 1986.

Living on the Surface: New and Selected Poems. Baton Rouge, Louisiana State University Press, 1989.

Adjusting to the Light. Columbia, University of Missouri Press, 1992.

Points of Departure. Champaign, University of Illinois Press, 1995.

The Ways We Touch. Champaign, University of Illinois Press, 1997.

Some Jazz a While: Collected Poems. Champaign, University of Illinois Press, 1999.

Other

The Poetry of John Crowe Ransom. New Brunswick, New Jersey, Rutgers University Press, 1972.

Railroad: Trains and Train People in American Culture, with James A. McPherson. New York, Random House, 1976.

Patterns of Poetry: An Encyclopedia of Forms. Baton Rouge, Louisiana State University Press, 1986.

Editor, *19 Poetas de Hoy en los EEUU.* Valparaiso, Chile, United States Information Agency, 1966.

Editor, with John William Corrington, *Southern Writing in the Sixties: Fiction and Poetry.* Baton Rouge, Louisiana State University Press, 2 vols., 1966–67.

Editor, *Chile: An Anthology of New Writing.* Kent, Ohio, Kent State University Press, 1968.

Editor, *The Achievement of John Ciardi: A Comprehensive Selection of His Poems with a Critical Introduction.* Chicago, Scott Foresman, 1969.

Editor, *Contemporary Poetry in America.* New York, Random House, 1973.

Editor with John Ciardi, *How Does a Poem Mean?,* revised edition. Boston, Houghton Mifflin, 1975.

Editor, *A Roman Collection: Stories, Poems, and Other Good Pieces by the Writing Residents of the American Academy in Rome.* Columbia, University of Missouri Press, 1980.

Editor, *Ozark, Ozark: A Hillside Reader.* Columbia, University of Missouri Press, 1981.

Translator, *Poems and Antipoems,* by Nicanor Parra. New York, New Directions, 1967; London, Cape, 1968.

Translator, *Emergency Poems,* by Nicanor Parra. New York, New Directions, 1972; London, Boyars, 1977.

Translator, *Sonnets of Giuseppe Belli.* Baton Rouge, Louisiana State University Press, 1981.

*

Manuscript Collection: Special Collections, University of Arkansas Library, Fayetteville.

Critical Studies: ''About Miller Williams'' by James Whitehead, in *Dickinson Review* (North Dakota), spring 1973; ''Translating the Dialect: Miller Williams' Romanesco,'' by John DuVal, in *Translation Review* (Richardson, Texas), 32–33, 1990; *Miller Williams and the Poetry of the Particular* edited by Michael Burns, Columbia, University of Missouri Press, 1991; ''Never Confuse a Fact with Truth: The Poetry of Miller Williams'' by Robert Morgan, in *Mississippi Quarterly* (Mississippi State, Mississippi), 46(1), winter 1992–93.

Miller Williams comments:

I am not sure that one ought to discuss one's poetry in public; it seems somehow not quite decent, and, besides, almost anyone will have a better perspective on a body of poems than the poet. It may mean something if I say that I distrust the romantic vision and dislike the classical. Beyond this, the poems are there to be read for what they have to say and how they say it.

*   *   *

Miller Williams is a poet of the American small town, its streets and neighborhoods, its bus stations and shabby factories. Simple logic reveals, however, that a town ultimately takes its character from the character of its people. Williams has learned this lesson early and learned it well, for a strength throughout his career has been his adeptness at portraiture. In the introduction to Williams's first book of poems, *A Circle of Stone,* Howard Nemerov links him to the character-portrait tradition of Edgar Lee Masters, and one may as well add to that tradition those of Edwin Arlington Robinson and John Crowe Ransom. Where Williams is most successful at these portraits, he achieves a balance between the subtle irony of Masters or Ransom and the more blatant irony of Robinson. ''On the Death of a Middle Aged Man,'' perhaps Williams's best-known early poem, strikes such a balance.

A reader learns quickly of the character's unambiguous feeling toward his unambiguous name:

Beverly
who wished his mother wanting a girl again
had called him something at best ambiguous
like Francis or Marion

Williams achieves subtle irony, however, in giving ambiguity a large role in the poem, in the question, for example, of whether the sexual encounters of Beverly's sweetheart, Helen, really ''counted'' since they were with her older brother and her minister. Ambiguity enriches the poem, too, in Williams's statement that Beverly ''went for eleven years to the Packard plant / and bent to Helen who punched the proper holes / how many bodies.'' This bending to connotes both a romantic gesture, bowing, and a sexual one, bending toward or bending over someone in the act of lovemaking. Williams retains this ambiguity in his *Halfway from Hoxie: New and Selected Poems,* when he changes ''bent to'' to ''turn for,'' the act of turning suggestive again both of a romantic gesture and a sexual one, as in ''turning a trick.''

Williams's work calls to mind—in addition to Masters, Robinson, and Ransom—such Latin American surrealists as Nicanor Parra, whose poems Williams translated and published as *Emergency Poems.* Taking ideas and images to their zany extremes seems a surrealist method for which Williams has a flair. ''I Got out of the House for the First Time,'' ''Toast to Floyd Collins,'' and ''And Then,'' all new poems in *Halfway from Hoxie,* use repetition to create a sense of lost equilibrium and absurdity, with ''And Then'' conveying a more serious tone than the first two:

Your toothbrush won't remember your mouth
Your shoes won't remember your feet

Your wife one good morning

will remember your weight
will feel unfaithful
throwing the toothbrush away
dropping the shoes in the Salvation Army box
will set your picture in the living room

someone wearing a coat you would not have worn
will ask was that your husband
she will say yes

Williams's stylistic range encompasses an ornate but energetic formalism, a flat, prosaic free verse and a more sharply hewn free verse. In "Leaving New York in the Penn Central to Metuchen" (*Halfway from Hoxie*), Williams uses alliteration in his rhymed couplets to such a degree that it might be called overused if the lines did not evoke so well the motion of a subway train: "Go buck, go hiss and the bright balled works / tremble and turn. Go clank and the car jerks."

More than a handful of poems, however, leave behind rhythm when they leave behind rhyme. "Lying," from *Distractions,* lacks the vitality that a stronger sense of music would give it. The casualness of the lines approaches the mood of someone passing time, but one cannot help but feel that the language itself lacks energy:

Standing beside a library in Brooklyn
I wait for my ride to come. I turn some pages.
A man puts his foot on a fire hydrant
and bends to tie his shoe. I see a gun.

Yet Williams can, as "And Then" illustrates, shape his free verse to musical ends, avoiding the prosaic and giving that free verse an almost incantatory power.

Two of Williams's finest poems, both from *Distractions,* depart from his typical sardonic tone. In "Rebecca, for Whom Nothing Has Been Written Page after Page," Williams addresses a granddaughter and tries to explain that, despite his esteem for language, language cannot do justice to a description of her. This theme is not new, yet Williams's tone succeeds in establishing an intimacy rare in his own work and a degree of intimacy rare in the work of many other poets. After acknowledging the serviceability of language, Williams writes elegiacally of its limitations:

What phrase explains, what simile can guess
a daughter's daughter? We half know who you are,
moment by moment, remembering what you were
as you grow past, becoming by quick revisions
an image in the door.

The sardonic tone also is gone in "Evening: A Studio in Rome," and while it would be hard to prove a cause-and-effect relationship, the change in tone seems to allow Williams to write movingly of a city just as he can write movingly of small towns. This meditative poem, in contrast to some of his others, is more luxurious, more willing to take its time in fleshing out the moment:

The window here is hung in the west wall.
It lays on the opposite wall a square of light.
Sliced by the lopsided slats of the broken blind,

the light hangs like a painting. Now, and now,
the shadow of a swallow shoots across it.

One recognizes Williams's deftness with alliteration, here the "sw" in "swallow" breaking up nicely the "sh" in "shadow" and in "shoots." What is new, however, is the acute perception of the swallow's shadow on the wall: "Now, and now." Such patience also provides the poet with his final passage, one that seems to indicate that Williams's good poems have gotten better:

This minute Rome is dark
as only Rome is dark, as if somebody
could go out reaching toward it, and find no Rome.

—Martin McGovern

WILMER, Clive

Nationality: British. **Born:** Harrogate, Yorkshire, 10 February 1945. **Education:** Emanuel School, 1956–63; King's College, Cambridge, 1964–67 and 1968–71, B.A. (honors) in English 1967, M.A. in English 1971. **Family:** Married Diane Redmond in 1971 (divorced 1987); one daughter and one son. **Career:** Teacher of English, British Institute of Florence, 1968, and Oxford School of English, Padua, 1971–72; assistant lecturer, University of Padua, Verona, 1971–72; freelance teacher and journalist, Cambridge, 1972–73; teacher of English, Bell School of Languages, Cambridge, 1973–86; visiting professor in creative writing, University of California, Santa Barbara, 1986. Since 1986 freelance teacher, writer, and broadcaster. Presenter, *Poet of the Month* radio program, 1989–92; member of the faculty, University of Cambridge, 1992; research associate, Corpus Christi College, Oxford, 1997–99; research fellow and poet-in-residence, Anglia Polytechnic University, 1998–2000; associate teaching officer, Fitzwilliam and Sidney Sussex Colleges, Cambridge, 1999. Editor, *Numbers,* 1986–90. Member, organizing committee of exhibition for centenary of Ezra Pound, *Pound's Artists* (Kettle's Yard, Cambridge, and London), 1985. **Awards:** Arts Council grant, 1979; Artisjus translation prize (Hungary), 1980; Author's Foundation grant, 1993; Mikimoto Memorial Ruskin Lecturer, University of Lancaster, 1996; honorary fellowship, Anglia Polytechnic University, 1997; Hungarian PEN Club Memorial Medal for Translation, Budapest, 1998. **Member:** Companion, Guild of St. George, 1995. **Agent:** Michael Thomas, A.M. Heath and Co. Ltd., 79 St. Martin's Lane, London WC2N 4AA. **Address:** 57 Norwich Street, Cambridge CB2 1ND, England.

PUBLICATIONS

Poetry

Shade Mariners, with Dick Davis and Robert Wells. Cambridge, Gregory Spiro, 1970.
The Dwelling-Place. Manchester, Carcanet, 1977.
Devotions. Manchester, Carcanet, 1982.
A Catalogue of Flowers. Florence, Kentucky, R.L. Barth, 1986.

Amores. Wivenhoe, Essex, L. Bell, 1986.
The Infinite Variety. Florence, Kentucky, R.L. Barth, 1989.
Of Earthly Paradise. Manchester, Carcanet, 1992.
Selected Poems. Manchester, Carcanet, 1995.
The Falls. Tonbridge, Kent, Worple Press, 2000.

Other

Poets Talking: Poet of the Month Interviews from BBC Radio 3. Manchester, Carcanet, 1994.

Editor, *The Occasions of Poetry: Essays in Criticism and Autobiography,* by Thom Gunn. London, Faber, and New York, Farrar Straus, 1982.
Editor, *Unto This Last, and Other Writings,* by John Ruskin. Harmondsworth, Penguin, 1986.
Editor, *Selected Poems and Translations,* by Dante Gabriel Rossetti. Manchester, Carcanet, 1991.
Editor, *News From Nowhere and Other Writings,* by William Morris. Harmondsworth, Penguin, 1993.
Editor, with Charles Moseley, *Cambridge Observed: An Anthology.* Cambridge, Colt Books, 1998.
Editor, *With the Grain: Essays on Thomas Hardy and Modern British Poetry,* by Donald Davie. Manchester, Carcanet, 1998.
Editor, with George Gömöri, *The Life and Work of Miklós Radnóti: Essays.* Boulder, Colorado, East European Monographs, 1999.

Translator, with George Gömöri, *Forced March: Selected Poems,* by Miklós Radnóti. Manchester, Carcanet, 1979.
Translator, with George Gömöri, *Night Song of the Personal Shadow: Selected Poems,* by György Petri. Newcastle upon Tyne, Bloodaxe, 1990.
Translator, with George Gömöri, *My Manifold City,* by George Gömöri. Cambridge, Alba Press, 1998.
Translator, with George Gömöri, *Eternal Monday: New and Selected Poems,* by György Petri. Newcastle upon Tyne, Bloodaxe, 1999.

*

Critical Studies: By John Mole, in *Times Literary Supplement* (London), 13 January 1978; by Peter Gilbert, in *Jewish Quarterly* (London), summer-autumn 1980; by Martin Dodsworth, in *The Guardian* (London), 19 August 1982; in *PN Review 30* (Manchester), 9(4), and in *Times Literary Supplement* (London), 4 December 1992, both by Thom Gunn; by Tim Dooley, in *Times Literary Supplement* (London), 7 January 1983; by Ruth Padel in *The Times Saturday Review* (London), 23 January 1993; by Vernon Scannell in *Sunday Telegraph* (London), 14 March 1993; by Roger Garfitt, in *Poetry Review,* 84(2), summer 1994.

Clive Wilmer comments:

My work is formal, usually in a traditional way, but by no means always so. Form is a matter of artifice and therefore derives from our human sense of order. Language is a means of communicating to others the meaning our experience has for us. Poetry is language at its most intense and most formal. It is something that stands aside from the current of everyday life in an attempt to understand. Behind what I write I always feel a kind of dialogue going on between art and nature,

between the flux of undifferentiated matter and the human need for meaning and permanence.

*   *   *

Clive Wilmer's poetry is largely traditional, often unfashionable, and, in view of what it attempts, remarkably successful. Without embarrassment Wilmer can rework a story from *Ivanhoe,* write of chivalry, honor, and Renaissance courtesy as if they still lived, and use foursquare hymn stanzas without slipping into protective irony or parody. And he can usually do these things without making his reader cringe. Yet he is not an anachronism or a purveyor of nostalgia; he has his own kind of involvement with the present and even has some lessons for those with more up-to-date assumptions.

Wilmer's first strength is as an elegist and epitaphist. His preoccupation is not with death but with the dead and their relation to the living, and he is less concerned with the dead themselves than with their works, the legacy that forms the preconditions of our own entry into meaning. Fascinated by their lapidary force, Wilmer writes verse as strikingly unegotistical, as empty of the posturing lyric "I," as powerful tombstone inscriptions. He is not ashamed to praise and admire greatly, to celebrate virtues and achievements, and he can do so without gush because celebration for him does not entail the suspension of rationality and judgment. In his introduction to Thom Gunn's critical essays, Wilmer quotes Gunn on Yvor Winters: "The conveying [of experience] has little meaning without the evaluation." Wilmer admires both as poets of "contained energy." For him, as for Gunn, Thomas Hardy, William Carlos Williams, and Ben Jonson, all poetry is occasional, and the true poet is "true to his occasions," more interested in the world than in himself. We are apparently back in a world of stable certainties and moral virtues and with a poetry that acknowledges the charm and moving power of abstract as well as concrete language. Wilmer is a Christian who can put his trust in "a simple, disembodied word, the truth," but if that seems far too unproblematic in the late twentieth century, the word "disembodied" suggests the losses, as well as the satisfactions, of abstract certainty and faith.

In his critical writing Wilmer has defended the use of archaisms in poetry. Sometimes his own language seems worn smooth, overfamiliar, or merely imitative of, say, eighteenth-century effects. But more often his poetry demonstrates the validity of his perception that the conventional epithet can be more painful, more pathos laden, than the sharp new phrase. Meaning, after all, is a matter of employing conventional signs. Wilmer is more modern than he appears. His "devotional" poetry, more interested in the text than its writer, finds a way out of the traps of expressionism. Poem after poem shows people rapt out of themselves by becoming absorbed in some work or pursuit: a boy staring at the riches of the seabed or a bird-watcher patiently awaiting his prey's return, becoming "less than himself and more." Likewise, to the intelligent Christian the play of difference is no decentering nightmare but rather another perception of babel, for in the world we inhabit language is "shattered into vagrant syllables" and we can only dream of a world where "the sense / Of things would be the things themselves and words / Would gem the melismatic harmony / Rarely, articulating it." He is well aware of the circuitous approach of language to truth and meaning or of the human to the divine.

The middle section of *Devotions* shows that Wilmer is no traditionalist merely for the sake of being so, for here he sets aside his taut traditional stanzas and metrics and experiments with counterpoising half lines by weight. *Amores,* a short poem published on a single folded sheet, is more personal than most of his work, being reflections on the memory of a past episode of love, and its minimal appearance reinforces the poignancy of the subject: ''Three afternoons of love, and you must go. / I miss you, scarcely knowing whom I miss.''

Wilmer's best work has dignity, emotional force, elegance, and even grandeur. The poems avoid sonority or self-satisfaction by admitting into themselves all of the forces—desolation, terror, malignity, slaughter—that would destroy their scheme of values and then by fending them off, thus conveying the precious fragility of what they seek to create—''A clearing, where love grows, and rests.''

—R.J.C. Watt

WILSON, Keith

Nationality: American. **Born:** Clovis, New Mexico, 26 December 1927. **Education:** U.S. Naval Academy, Annapolis, Maryland, B.S. 1950; University of New Mexico, Albuquerque, M.A. 1956. **Military Service:** U.S. Navy, 1950–54: Lieutenant; Korean War combat veteran. **Family:** Married Heloise Brigham in 1958; four daughters and one son. **Career:** Instructor, University of Nevada, Reno, 1956–57; technical writer, Sandia Corporation, Albuquerque, 1958–60; instructor, University of Arizona, Tucson, 1960–65. Professor of English and poet-in-residence, from 1965, now emeritus professor, New Mexico State University, Las Cruces. Fulbright Professor, University of Cluj, Romania, 1974–75; distinguished visiting professor and writer, Bowling Green State University, Ohio, spring 1991; distinguished visiting writer, 1998, the U.S. Naval Academy. Consultant to Coordinating Council for Literary Magazines, 1972–74; consultant to National Endowment for the Arts to Voice of America, 1975; master poet for New Mexico Poetry in the School Program. **Awards:** University of New Mexico D.H. Lawrence fellowship, 1972; P.E.N. American Center grant, 1972; Westhafer award, 1972, National Endowment for the Arts grant, 1974; New Mexico Governor's award, 1988; Premio Fronteriza, Border Book Festival, 1997. **Address:** 1500 South Locust, Las Cruces, New Mexico 88001, U.S.A.

PUBLICATIONS

Poetry

Sketches for a New Mexico Hill Town. Concord, Massachusetts, Wine Press, 1966.
The Old Car and Other Blackpoems. Sacramento, California, Grande Ronde Press, 1968.
II Sequences. Portland, Oregon, Wine Press, 1968.
Graves Registry and Other Poems. New York, Grove Press, 1969.
Psalms for Various Voices. Las Cruces, New Mexico, Tolar Creek Syndicate, 1969.
Homestead. San Francisco, Kayak, 1970.
The Old Man and Others: Some Faces for America. Las Cruces, New Mexico State University Press, 1970.
The Shadow of Our Bones. Portland, Oregon, Trask House, 1971.
Rocks. Oshkosh, Wisconsin, Road Runner Press, 1971.
MidWatch: Graves Registry Part IV and V. Fremont, Michigan, Sumac Press, 1972.

Song of Thantog. New York, Athanor, 1972.
Thantog: Songs of a Jaguar Priest. Dennis, Massachusetts, Salt-Works Press, 1977.
While Dancing Feet Shatter the Earth. Logan, Utah State University Press, 1978.
The Streets of San Miguel. Tucson, Arizona, Maguey Press, 1978.
Desert Cenote. Fort Kent, Maine, Great Raven Press, 1978.
The Shaman Deer. Dennis, Massachusetts, Salt-Works Press, 1978.
Retablos. Albuquerque, San Marcos Press, 1980.
Stone Roses: Poems from Transylvania. Logan, Utah State University Press, 1983.
Lovesongs and Mandalas: Some Poems for Family and Friends. Navada, Iowa, San Marcos Press, 1984.
Meeting in Jal. Nobbs, New Mexico, Hawk Press, 1985.
Lion's Gate: Selected Poems 1963–1986. El Paso, Texas, Cinco Puntos Press, 1987.
The Winds of Pentecost. Las Cruces, New Mexico, Blue Mesa Press, 1988.
Graves Registry. Livingston, Montana, Clark City Press, 1992.
The Way of the Dove. Las Cruces, New Mexico, Whole Notes Press, 1994.
Études. Boise, Idaho, Lumberlast Press, 1994.

*

Critical Studies: By William Winthrop, in *New Mexican* (Santa Fe), 25 August 1968; in *San Marcos Review* (Albuquerque), February 1978.

Keith Wilson comments:

I hold with, or to, a number of concepts of the new American poetry.

Three major areas of concern: (1) New Mexico Southwest, (2) the sea, (3) emotional geography. I often use methods derived, in part at least, from Charles Olson's projective verse. He, Robert Duncan, and Robert Creeley have been large influences on me, as have both William Carlos Williams and, from childhood, Robert Burns.

*   *   *

Keith Wilson's poems are filled with the history, geography, and climate of their locales and even more steeped in the ghosts that cling to these settings. History in his poems is more of a spiritual experience than a matter for pedantry. His most comprehensive collection, *Lion's Gate: Selected Poems 1963–1986,* samples all of the major locales he has written about and includes work from all of his major collections.

One of these collections, *Homestead,* traces both his personal and his historical awareness of the American Southwest. The poems celebrate the strengths and mark the weaknesses of the people of this harsh but lovely land, where violence may be the snake under a nearby stone, ready to strike, sometimes at random, or, as in ''The Drug Store,'' have its source in human actions:

one night, a fat old man
while teasing a baby
tossed him high
into the smokefilled
air inside & the great

fan cut the boy's
head off.

the man caught
the trunk
& carried it to
its mother.

There is also the brutality done in the name of religion, as, for example, in "Teofilo's Father":

Brothers carried him in honor
through the streets of our village:
for three days they sang & marched,
bearing the corpse until the smell
drove all but the devout away.

This poem about the death of a Penitente not only captures the harm done in the name of faith but also hints at the cultural differences that often divide humanity at the same time they enrich the world. In "Teofilo Orozco" Teofilo's son, the author's boyhood friend, returns, like the author, from time in the service, but when they met,

. . . as I shook
his hand I saw the blue tattooed cross,
the slashed rays of the Pachuco, man
of violence, hater of gringos.

As Teofilo's friends watch, they shake hands, probably for the last time.

Wilson's work is full of quick, vivid character sketches of people who enrich the Southwest landscape, for example, an old man at peace with a rattlesnake under his house and another who raises but cannot bring himself to slaughter his farm animals. Perhaps the most vivid personage of all is the land itself, as shown in these lines from "The Voices Of My Desert":

New Mexico is a myth, an ancient whirlpool
of time where moments stand still just before
being sucked down to other planes, other hours.

In "New Mexico: Paso Por Aqui" the poet tells us that

This is an old land, dry & brittle.
Its charms are bones, hollowed to whistles,
dancing feet hidden by rising dust.

Wilson's poetry also reflects on his experiences as a naval officer in the 1950s. *Graves Registry* treats the Korean War, and *MidWatch: Graves Registry Part IV and V* extends his reflections on war and man's attraction to violence to the Vietnam War. These poems face up to the most unpleasant aspects of human existence and contain powerful images: fountains of flesh rising from bombings, faces blown away by a single bullet. They also strive toward affirmation in the face of the horrendous evidence of history.

A later collection, *Stone Roses: Poems from Transylvania,* chronicles a year Wilson spent in the mid-1970s as a lecturer at Babes-Bolyai University "in the ancient principality of Transylvania," a part of Romania. Here violence springs less from war than from the harshness and difficulty of life, but even so, as in New Mexico, the author bumps into his past, into earlier selves. The following is from "The Minaret in Constanta":

Slowly
I raised my head

saw the gate I had dreamed of
since childhood, without understanding, encrusted
with lions . . .

I sat on that terrace, drank cognac in reverence
for whatever that night long ago might have meant
to that me who lived a little while ago and remembered
so long a night, candles, her lips, and lions.

Wilson's poems are ultimately heartening, for he brings compassion rather than self-righteous anger to human follies. It is this sense of our own complicity in history, whether through repetition or reincarnation, that makes his preoccupation with his own ancestral past and the historical roots of place, in New Mexico, Korea, or Romania, valuable. This is not nostalgia at work but rather a desire to learn from the past, to help something new rise from the ruins of the old: "It was the purpose of these poems to show / the glories of war, sadnesses of peace. / Replace them both."

—Duane Ackerson

WITHEFORD, Hubert

Nationality: New Zealander. **Born:** Wellington, 18 March 1921. **Education:** Victoria University of Wellington, M.A. 1943. **Family:** Married Noel Brooke Anderson in 1941; one son. **Career:** Staff member, New Zealand Prime Minister's Office, Wellington, 1939–45, New Zealand War History Branch, Wellington, 1945–53. Staff member, 1954–67, head of Overseas Section, Reference Division, 1968–78, and director of Reference Division, 1978–81.

PUBLICATIONS

Poetry

Shadow of the Flame, Poems, 1942–47. Auckland, Pelorus Press, 1950.
The Falcon Mask. Christchurch, Pegasus Press, 1951.
The Lightning Makes a Difference. London, Brookside Press, 1962.
A Native, Perhaps Beautiful. Christchurch, Caxton, 1967.
A Possible Order. Harrow, Middlesex, Ravine Press, 1980.
A Blue Monkey for the Tomb. London and Boston, Faber, 1994.

*   *   *

Hubert Witheford began to publish in Wellington in the 1940s while he was a student in history at the University of Victoria. His early poems were heavy with symbolism and were rhetorical in tone and form, but they had an abstract intellectual quality that marked them out from the more typically romantic poetry of his contemporary James K. Baxter. This can be seen, for example, in ''Bright Sunlight'':

> The flower unfolding and the burning tombs
> At the far sun of lonely flame are kindled
> Beneath whose power as in earth's final light
> The citizens of chaos come to justice.

Witheford quickly assimilated T.S. Eliot's view of literary history, that in the seventeenth century there had been a ''dissociation of sensibility,'' from which modernism was at last rescuing poetry in English. He also was among the first New Zealand poets to appreciate and write intelligently about Pound's *Cantos*. This led to a gradual shift in his own poetry in the direction of wit, though for some time there was a continuing element of mysteriousness, even mysticism. In the early 1950s Witheford moved to London, where he was employed in the Central Office of Information. For many years he worked almost entirely in isolation, cut off from his potential readers at home and without establishing any significant British reputation.

There was a gap of ten years between Witheford's second and third books, and it is in this period that the full shift into his mature style occurs. The iambic beat is largely gone. The lines are shorter, or at least more varied, the cadences closer to those of speech, and the statements more direct. The wit that was evident in his student prose writings now finds its way into the poems, especially those of his fourth book, *A Native, Perhaps Beautiful,* still probably his best. It is as much as anything a matter of tone, as shown in excerpts from ''The Displacement'' and from ''Towards a Completely Flat Surface'':

> I know without opening my eyes
> It is ugly,
> It is mine.

> I take a drink from an undeniable
> Sportsman in a white polo-neck jersey

''Barbarossa,'' a recollection of the earthquake that destroyed the town of Napier in his childhood, revives the legend of the great soldier-king Frederick Barbarossa, who ''sits in his armour'' in a cave, waiting to rise from the dead, as the burghers of Napier sit ''squashed in their ancient Fords'' under the ''half a hill / Spilt on the coast road.''

After his retirement from the British civil service in 1981, Witheford went back to live in New Zealand, but his attempt to return to his roots proved a failure, and he was there only long enough to earn a place (his identity thinly disguised) in the intimate memoirs of a noted New Zealand woman poet. The publication of *A Blue Monkey for the Tomb* (1994) by Faber & Faber, still the most prestigious of British publishing houses, seems to mark Witheford finally as an expatriate writer whose identity, like Fleur Adcock's, has become more British than New Zealand.

Witheford's new poems are stripped, direct, sometimes witty, often gloomy, domestic in subject, and lacking entirely the plush language of his early work, but lacking also its sense of mysteriousness and consequent space for the reader to reach into or beyond the first strike of sense. The effect, as in ''Going into Winter,'' is somewhat bleak, not unlike the poems of the similarly retired and retiring British civil servant C.H. Sisson:

> Each morning
> I wake earlier
> Mourning
> The chances
> That will never happen again,

> Welcoming
> The deluded sparrows
> Who think it is dawn.

—C.K. Stead

WOODS, John (Warren)

Nationality: American. **Born:** Martinsville, Indiana, 12 July 1926. **Education:** Indiana University, Bloomington, B.S. 1949, M.A. 1955; University of Iowa, Iowa City, 1957–58. **Military Service:** Served in the U.S. Air Force, 1944–46. **Family:** Married Emily Newbury in 1951 (died 1983); two sons. **Career:** Assistant professor, 1955–61, associate professor, 1961–65, and professor of English, 1965–92, Western Michigan University, Kalamazoo. Visiting professor of English, University of California, Irvine, 1967–68; poet-in-residence, Purdue University, West Lafayette, Indiana, 1975. **Awards:** Bread Loaf Writers Conference Robert Frost fellowship, 1962; Yaddo fellowship, 1963, 1964; Theodore Roethke prize (*Poetry Northwest*), 1968; National Endowment for the Arts grant, 1969, and fellowship, 1982. **Address:** 6411 Hampton Street, Portage, Michigan 49002.

PUBLICATIONS

Poetry

The Deaths at Paragon, Indiana. Bloomington, Indiana University Press, 1955.

On the Morning of Color. Bloomington, Indiana University Press, 1961.

The Cutting Edge. Bloomington, Indiana University Press, 1966.

Keeping Out of Trouble. Bloomington, Indiana University Press, 1968.

Turning to Look Back: Poems 1955–1970. Bloomington, Indiana University Press, 1972.

The Knees of Widows. Kalamazoo, Michigan, Westigan Review Press, 1972.

Voyages to the Inland Sea II: Essays and Poems, with Felix Pollack and James Hearst, edited by John Judson. La Crosse, University of Wisconsin Center for Contemporary Poetry, 1972.

Alcohol. Grand Rapids, Michigan, Pilot Press, 1973.

A Bone Flicker. La Crosse, Wisconsin, Juniper, 1973.

Striking the Earth. Bloomington, Indiana University Press, 1976.

Thirty Years on the Force. La Crosse, Wisconsin, Juniper, 1977.

The Night of the Game. Bloomington, Indiana, Raintree Press, 1982.

The Valley of Minor Animals. Port Townsend, Washington, Dragon Gate, 1982.

The Salt Stone: Selected Poems. Port Townsend, Washington, Dragon Gate, 1985.
Black Marigolds. Gainesville, University of Florida Press, 1994.

Other

Translator, *The Dog King,* by Christoph Ransmayr. New York, Knopf, 1997.

*

Critical Studies: By Richard Hugo, in *Northwest Review* (Eugene, Oregon), 1967; by David Etter, in *Chicago Review,* winter 1972; "In the Grip of Days: The Poetry of John Woods" by Henry Taylor, in *Hollins Critic* (Virginia), 23(4), October 1986.

John Woods comments:

All that is important about my poetry to the general reader lies in the poetry itself. If, Dear General Reader, we might sit down together over a bottle, we might begin a friendship, an enemyship, a love affair, whatever. Until then, the great whirling mass of particulars that make up You, and Me, can only meet at the interface of my poems.

*   *   *

John Woods, a master of contemporary idiom, sets his poems in the twentieth-century Midwest. Through three generations of Indiana farm folk, "between the two wars of father and son," he expresses human hopes and anxieties with an exceptional poetic sense of place and of time. The grandfather's recollection of genealogy is vague yet certain:

> I don't know where we came from.
> So many graves stay open too long,
> so many girls lie back tonight
> trying to be secret rivers in the limestone.

Woods has discovered a language needing no support of learned notes for characters who "think back along their bones." Generations die back into the Indiana corn knowing, instinctively, that Adonis is violently stoned red before regeneration. Wood chooses apt items for his own totem:

> I shaped a man, my totem animal,
> from branches, murky soil, and pasture dung . . .
> From a bird stoned red beneath an elm,
> I took a wing for tongue.

Woods indeed takes a wing for tongue. His language is lively, his imagery precise, and his rhythms range from the conversational tempo of the elegiac poems on life before death to a swift tumble of images in the wry, humorous asides on life's perplexities.

Turning to Look Back and *The Salt Stone* amply represent Woods's poetic range. His first group in both collections, "The Deaths at Paragon," gathers elegiac poems on generation and death. Sophisticated love poems, both lithe and muscular, follow in "In Time of Apples." Poems of social commentary are gathered in "Red

Telephones," and formal lyrics, including a fine sestina, in "Barley Tongues."

—Edward Callan

WRIGHT, C(arolyn) D.

Nationality: American. **Born:** Mountain Home, Arkansas, 6 January 1949. **Education:** Memphis State University, Memphis, Tennessee, 1969–71, B.A. 1971; University of Arkansas, Fayetteville, 1973–76, M.F.A. 1976. **Family:** Married Forrest Gander in 1982; one son. **Career:** Graduate teaching assistant, University of Arkansas, Fayetteville, 1973–76; poet-in-the-schools, Office of Arkansas Arts and Humanities, 1976–78; office manager, The Poetry Center, San Francisco State University, 1980–82. Since 1983 professor, Brown University, Providence, Rhode Island. Co-editor, Lost Roads Publishers, Providence, Rhode Island. **Awards:** National Endowment for the Arts fellowship, 1982, 1988; Witter Bynner Poetry prize, 1986; Guggenheim fellowship, 1987; General Electric award for younger writers, 1988; Whiting Foundation award, 1989; Rhode Island Governor's award for the Arts, 1990; Poetry Center Book award, 1992; Lila Wallace Writers' award, 1992; State Poet of Rhode Island, 1994; Lannan Literary award, 1999; artist grant, Foundation for Contemporary Performing Arts, 1999. Bunting Institute fellowship, 1987. **Address:** English Department, x1852, Brown University, Providence, Rhode Island 02912, U.S.A.

PUBLICATIONS

Poetry

Alla Breve Loving. Spokane, Washington, Mill Mountain Press, 1976.
Room Rented by a Single Woman. Fayetteville, Arkansas, Lost Roads Publishers, 1977.
Terrorism. Fayetteville, Arkansas, Lost Roads Publishers, 1978.
Translations of the Gospel Back into Tongues. Albany, New York, State University of New York Press, 1981.
Further Adventures with You. Pittsburgh, Carnegie-Mellon Press, 1986.
String Light. Athens, Georgia, University of Georgia Press, 1992.
Just Whistle. Berkeley, California, Kelsey Street Press, 1993.
The Lost Roads Project: A Walk-In Book of Arkansas. Fayetteville, University of Arkansas Press, 1994.
Tremble. Hopewell, New Jersey, Ecco Press, 1996.
Deepstep Come Shining. Port Townsend, Washington, Copper Canyon Press, 1998.

Recording: *C.D. Wright* (videotape), The Poetry Center at San Francisco State University, 1992.

Other

The Reader's Map of Arkansas. Fayetteville, University of Arkansas Press, 1995.

Editor, *The Lost Roads Project: A Walk-In Book of Arkansas.* Fayetteville, University of Arkansas Press, 1995.

*

Critical Study: ''Politics and the Personal Lyric in the Poetry of Joy Harjo and C.D. Wright'' by Jenny Goodman, in *Melus: Theory, Culture, and Criticism,* 19(2), summer 1994.

C.D. Wright comments:

Poetry is my central station. All that can converge in a given individual intersects there for me, under the big clock. Many of my influences are extraliterary-friends, trees. Others answer to other arts—music, photography. Other disciplines—folklore, recent history. Still others, to temperament—leftist. And of course a lifetime of reading helter-skelter through the layers of time and translation, only gaining consistency and some pattern, from rural to urban, with contemporary American poetry. I still try to sustain a certain tolerance toward the whole field even as my own writing seems to be shifting allegiances. I try not to forfeit what can never be recovered—my hardheaded, idiomatic bedrock. I try not to remain ignorant of the ever changing present tense of poetry. Some say the genre is anachronistic. I say these people, their lives, have become too prosaic.

* * *

In the prose text ''hills,'' which introduces her 1986 collection *Further Adventures with You,* C.D. Wright explains that her poems ''are about desire, conflict, the dearth of justice for all. About persons of small means. They are succinct but otherwise orthodox novels in which the necessary characters are brought out, made intimate, . . . engage in dramatic action and leave the scene forever with or without a resolution in hand or sight. Each on the space of a page or less.'' This statement captures several qualities common to all of the work of this Arkansas-born poet, whose earliest writing was dialect based and regional in focus: its storytelling impulse, its focus on everyday things and events, its backdrop of melancholia and brooding violence, its necessarily elliptical brevity. Yet in a crucial respect Wright's later work has superseded the *ars poetica* she offers in ''hills,'' for the relation between poetry and prose in her writing has become more complex, and her lineated stories veer demonstratively toward less orthodox forms.

Typical of Wright's earlier ''orthodox novels'' is the poem ''Vanish,'' from *Translations of the Gospels Back into Tongues* (1981). This is a poem of memory, loss, and desire, all states of absence that Wright's poem comes to occupy, offering its lineaments of story to mark the place which the vanishing experience had occupied and now leaves bare. The poem offers fragmentary recollections of an encounter between a girl and a sailor, perhaps before the funeral of the girl's brother. The encounter ended long ago without issue, and the sailor and girl have separated. The poem's first-person voice shifts over the course of the poem's thirty-one lines from the aged sailor to the now mature girl. ''Vanish'' begins,

> Because I did not die
> I sit in the captain's chair
> Going deaf in one ear, blind in the other.
> I live because the sea does.

By the end, however, the girl's fading memories swallow up the sailor's voice, consigning it to the near oblivion of the sea swell:

> Because I did not marry
> I wash by the light of the body.
> Soap floats out of my mind.
> I have almost forgotten
> The sailor whose name I did not catch,
> His salty tongue on my ear,
> A wave on a shell.

Only between these two drifting buoys of consciousness may the broken pieces of their common story surface, traces of the shipwrecked possibilities of love.

Wright's stories are often mediated through a wounded interiority or a dreaming mind, as in the title poem of her 1986 book *Further Adventures with You:*

> We are on a primeval river in a reptilian den.
>
> There are birds you don't want to tangle with, trees you
>   cannot identify . . .
>
> Somehow we spend the evening with Mingus
> in a White Castle. Or somewhere. Nearly drunk. He says
>   he would like to play for the gang.

The dream—with its expression of unspoken wishes, its mobilization of childhood memories and ephemera of the day, its enigmatic yoking of distant scenes—serves as an apt model for the lyric consciousness implicit in Wright's poetry generally and not only in her ''dream poems.'' For dreams, despite their apparent incoherence, are ways of revisiting what in our waking lives is irrecoverable, whether because of passing time or by our failure to attend to it as it was lived. Poetry, too, may be such a mode of dreamlike remembrance. As Wright suggests in ''the box this comes in,'' an allegorical ''deviation on poetry,'' a meditation on poetry via the image of an antique box, ''Within the limits of this diminutive wooden world, I have made do with the cracks of light and tokens of loss and recovery that came my way.''

Both *Further Adventures with You* and *String Light,* however, exhibit Wright's discovery of nonverse forms, which in turn seem to shift the center of gravity of her poetry from states of desire toward the experiential richness of language forms as such. Thus, in her sequence ''The Ozark Odes'' the section entitled ''Arkansas Towns'' is dedicated purely to the delightful and strange place-names of Wright's home state:

> Acorn
> Back Gate
> Bald Knob
> Ben Hur
> Biggers
> Blue Ball

—all the way up to ''Whisp,'' ''Yellville,'' and ''Zent.'' Similarly, the prose poems subjoined to ''What No One Could Have Told Them'' isolate a single detail—a toddler urinating, a child yawning—and repeat it in new word contexts until the detail takes on luminosity as language, independent of its humble content. Wright's numerous prose poems, and above all the Kerouac-like "sketching" of "The Night I Met Little Floyd" and "The Next Time I Crossed the Line into Oklahoma," both in *String Light,* bear out the distinction she drew in "hills": whereas her poems are based on narrative, her prose "is about language if it is about any one thing."

—Tyrus Miller

WRIGHT, Charles (Penzel, Jr.)

Nationality: American. **Born:** Pickwick Dam, Tennessee, 25 August 1935. **Education:** Davidson College, North Carolina, 1953–57, B.A. 1957; University of Iowa, Iowa City, 1961–63, M.F.A. 1963; University of Rome (Fulbright fellow), 1963–64. **Military Service:** U.S. Army Intelligence Corps, 1957–61: Captain. **Family:** Married Holly McIntire in 1969; one son. **Career:** Professor of English, University of California, Irvine, 1966–83. Since 1983 professor of English, University of Virginia, Charlottesville. Fulbright lecturer, University of Padua, 1968–69; visiting lecturer, University of Iowa, 1974–75, Princeton University, New Jersey, 1978, and Columbia University, New York, 1978; distinguished visiting professor, Universita' Degli Studi, Florence, Italy, spring 1992. **Awards:** Eunice Tietjens award (*Poetry,* Chicago), 1969; National Endowment for the Arts grant, 1974; Guggenheim fellowship, 1975; Poetry Society of America Melville Cane award, 1976; Academy of American Poets Edgar Allan Poe award, 1976; American Academy grant, 1977; P.E.N. translation prize, 1979; Ingram Merrill fellowship, 1980; National Book award, 1983; Brandeis University Creative Arts award, 1987; award of merit medal, American Academy of Arts and Letters, 1992; Distinguished Contribution to Letters award, Ingram Merrill Foundation, 1993; Ruth Lilly prize, 1993; *Los Angeles Times* book prize, 1997; National Book Critics Circle prize, 1997; Pulitzer prize, 1998; Ambassador Book award, 1998; Antico Fattore Premio (Italy), 1998; Library Lion, New York Public Library, 1999. **Address:** 940 Locust Avenue, Charlottesville, Virginia 22901, U.S.A.

PUBLICATIONS

Poetry

The Voyage. Iowa City, Patrician Press, 1963.
6 Poems. London, Freed, 1965.
The Dream Animal. Toronto, Anansi, 1968.
Private Madrigals. Madison, Wisconsin, Abraxas Press, 1969.
The Grave of the Right Hand. Middletown, Connecticut, Wesleyan University Press, 1970.
The Venice Notebook. Boston, Bam Dream Press, 1971.
Backwater. Santa Ana, California, Golem Press, 1973.
Hard Freight. Middletown, Connecticut, Wesleyan University Press, 1973.
Bloodlines. Middletown, Connecticut, Wesleyan University Press, 1975.
Colophons. Iowa City, Windhover Press, 1977.
China Trace. Middletown, Connecticut, Wesleyan University Press, 1977.

Wright: A Profile. Iowa City, Grilled Flowers Press, 1979.
Dead Color. Salem, Oregon, Seluzicki, 1980.
The Southern Cross. New York, Random House, 1981.
Country Music: Selected Early Poems. Middletown, Connecticut, Wesleyan University Press, 1982.
Four Poems of Departure. Portland, Oregon, Trace, 1983.
The Other Side of the River. New York, Random House, 1984.
Five Journals. New York, Red Ozier Press, 1986.
Zone Journals. New York, Farrar Straus, 1988.
The World of the 10,000 Things. New York, Farrar Straus, 1990.
Xionia. Iowa City, Iowa, Windhover Press, 1990.
Chickamauga. New York, Farrar Straus, 1995.
Black Zodiac. New York, Farrar Straus, 1997.
Appalachia. New York, Farrar Straus, 1998.
North American Bear. Sutton Hoo Press, 1999.
Negative Blue. New York, Farrar Straus, 2000.

Recording: *The Tongue Is a White Water,* Watershed, 1985.

Other

Halflife: Improvisations and Interviews, 1977–1987. Ann Arbor, University of Michigan Press, 1988.
Quarter Notes. Ann Arbor, University of Michigan Press, 1995.

Translator, *The Storm and Other Poems,* by Eugenio Montale. Oberlin, Ohio, Oberlin College, 1978.
Translator, *Motets,* by Eugenio Montale. Iowa City, Windhover Press, 1981.
Translator, *Orphic Songs,* by Dino Campana. Oberlin, Ohio, Oberlin College, 1984.

*

Bibliography: In *Bulletin of Bibliography* (Westport, Connecticut), 43(1), March 1986.

Critical Studies: Interview, in *Field 17* (Oberlin, Ohio), fall 1977; by Helen Vendler, in *New Yorker,* 29 October 1979, and in *Part of Nature, Part of Us,* Cambridge, Massachusetts, Harvard University Press, 1980, and *The Music of What Happens,* Cambridge, Massachusetts, Harvard University Press, 1988, both by Vendler; interview, in *Poetry West* (Salt Lake City, Utah), summer 1981; Calvin Bedient, in *Parnassus* (New York), summer 1982; George F. Butterick, in *Dictionary of Literary Biography Yearbook 1982,* edited by Richard Ziegfeld, Detroit, Gale, 1983; in *The Still Performance* by James McCorkle, Charlottesville, University Press of Virginia, 1989; "Slide-Wheeling around the Curves" by Calvin Bedient, in *The Southern Review* (Baton Rouge, Louisiana) winter 1991; by James McCorkle in *The Still Performance: Writing, Self, and Interconnection in Five Postmodern American Poets,* Charlottesville, Univeristy Press of Virginia, 1992; interview,in *North Carolina Literary Review,* spring 1994; "Metaphysics of the Image in Charles Wright and Paul Cezanne" in *Southern Review,* winter 1994; *The Point Where All Things Meet,* edited by Tom Andrews, Oberlin, Oberlin College Press, 1995; in *Some Necessary Angels,* New York, Columbia University Press, 1997; "A Poetry of Transcendence" by Floyd Collins, in *Gettsbug Review,* winter 1997; in *Uncertainty + Plenitude*, Iowa City, University of Iowa Press, 1997; in *The Muse of Abandonment*

Lewisburg, Bucknell University Press, 1998; in *Five Points: A Journal of Literature and Art* (Atlanta, Georgia), spring-summer 1998.

*   *   *

We sometimes admire poetry for its powers of representation and sometimes for its self-contained formal and musical appeal. Charles Wright's work is notable for its balancing of these impulses; he nearly always manages to have it both ways. His southern heritage makes him both a powerful storyteller and a writer unafraid of ornate, carnivalesque language. His integrity makes him an indefatigable investigator of experience and truth, while his fascination with poetic form and verbal expressiveness drives him to greater and greater forms of experimentation. The result is a sizable and impressively consistent poetic canon taking shape as one of the truly distinctive bodies of poetry created in the second half of the twentieth century.

Wright's first four collections, gathered in a selected form as *Country Music*, show him finding and consolidating his powers as a poet. He writes short poems, prose poems, striking longer sequences, portraits (often titled "Homages"), and self-portraits. Personal memories—of childhood, of Italy (especially Verona and Venice), where he served in the U.S. Army and later returned to teach, and of California, where he lived and taught until 1983—play a role, but they are always mixed with a detached impulse to meditate, to isolate and arrange the details of experience as a means of creating beauty. The great romantic issue of transcendence, the symbolist urge to attain the visionary, is never very far away:

> There is a shine you move towards, the shine
> Of water; you want it to step from,
> And out of, wearing its strings and slick confetti.
> You come to the sea, but turn back, its surgy retractions
> Too slippery and out of place,
> Wrecked looking-glass, bundles of grief.
> And inland, the necklace of lakes—High Lonesome
> And pendant, the 40s its throat,
> Its glint like icicles against the skin . . . ?
> There's no one to wear it now, or hand it down.
> The river will have it, shine
> Of the underlight, shine of the lost quarter;
> The river, rope of remembering, unbroken shoe,
> The flushed and unwavering mirror . . .

This is the eighteenth section of the sequence "Skins" from the collection called *Bloodlines*. It is an acceptance of the element of water, an expression of faith in the visionary possibilities of this world. Its combination of highly fanciful figures—confetti, necklace, shoe—and of more mundane and recognizable details—slipperiness, reflection, the shine of water—illustrates the carefully mixed nature of Wright's style. The expert handling of line, pause, syntax, and sound, in this case to achieve an elevated, incantatory mode of speech, is also characteristic.

The title of the first selected poems, *Country Music*, with its epigraph from Hemingway ("The country was always better than the people"), is not casual. Wright's feeling for place, whether the American South, West, or Northwest or the Italy of Lake Garda and the Adige River, is intense and compelling. "Blackwater Mountain," a poem in *Hard Freight*, begins with a careful evocation of a place and time: "That time of evening, weightless and disparate, / When the loon cries, when the small bass / Jostle the lake's reflections, when / The green of the oak begins / To open its robes to the dark . . ." The middle of the poem suggests that the poet is recalling duck hunting with his father, particularly one unsuccessful search for a wounded duck. It ends with these lines:

> I stand where we stood before and aim
> My flashlight down to the lake. A black duck
> Explodes to my right, hangs, and is gone.
> He shows me the way to you;
> He shows me the way to a different fire
> Where you, black moon, warm your hands.

One senses the influence of Montale here in the organizing of the experience and the deliberate openness to mystery, but even more striking is the poem's effective grounding in its sure sense of place, past and present. The lake and duck are not literary; they belong to experience and draw their authenticity from the poet's reverence for the natural world.

In the collections since *Country Music*, brought together in *The World of the 10,000 Things*, Wright has moved into more and more ambitious and original poetic forms. Many of the poetic structures cultivate a challenging capaciousness. *The Southern Cross* opens with the dazzling eight-page poem "Homage to Paul Cézanne," and it closes with the seventeen-page title poem. This latter piece, with unnumbered sections and long, often broken (i.e., stepped-down) lines mixing memory, reflection, speculation, and often quite varying tones, is a sort of journal-become-poem. It turns out to have been the prototype for much of Wright's later work, poems that risk the prosaic and the garrulous while managing both an impressive music and a strict economy. *The Other Side of the River* tends to restrict these poems to a length of three pages or so as a rule, while *Zone Journals* lets them go. Made up of just ten poems, it has as its centerpiece the forty-seven-page "A Journal of the Year of the Ox," which, for all its length, does not feel different in kind from the poems around it. Again, the titles are not casual, and one feels that Wright is reinventing the journal as poem and the poem as journal, accomplishing a form of great flexibility and inclusiveness.

"A Journal of English Days," for example, is a twelve-page poem that covers a period spent in England from September to December. The speaker visits a number of places, returning often to Kensington Church Walk, where Pound lived. He ponders the weather, memory, the changing details of the season, an England sometimes seen through the eyes of fellow artists ("Chelsea Embankment, 5 p.m. Whistler pastels squished / Down the fluted water, orange, / Tamarind, apricot / jade on the slate slip of the river"), and, as always, he conducts his search for stability and reassurance, for some truth or divinity behind the intriguing brocade of nature. The poem's close is typical in its duality, a weary dismissing of the search, on the one hand, followed by a recollected moment of vision, on the other:

> How sweet to think that Nature is solvency,
>   that something empirically true
> Lies just under the dead leaves
> That will make us anchorites in the dark
> Chambers of some celestial perpetuity—
>   nice to think that,
> Given the bleak alternative,
> Though it hasn't proved so before,
>   and won't now

No matter what things we scrape aside—
        God is an abstract noun.

—Flashback: a late September Sunday,
        the V & A courtyard,
Holly and I at one end,
Bronze Buddha under some falling leaves at the other:
Weightlessness of the world's skin
        undulating like a balloon
Losing its air around us, down drifting down
Through the faint hiss of eternity
Emptying somewhere else
        O emptying elsewhere
This afternoon, skin
That recovers me and slides me in like a hand
As I unclench and spread
        finger by finger inside the Buddha's eye . . .

Suddenly God is not an abstract noun, and the search is rewarded, temporarily and on precarious verbal terms, by a moment of vision and wholeness.

It might be said that Wright is reconstituting Pound's failed program along new and successful lines: more centered, less bookish, more ready to mend what is broken and relinquish authority in areas where it will not hold firm. Certainly his temperament is more suited to the tasks at hand. Whereas Gertrude Stein accurately characterized Pound as a "village explainer," Wright's postmodern temper is more that of a listener and observer: attentive, modest, but firmly committed to a music that realizes poetry's highest aims, the aims of Dante.

—David Young

WRIGHT, Jay

Nationality: American. **Born:** Albuquerque, New Mexico, 25 May 1935. **Education:** University of New Mexico, Albuquerque; University of California, Berkeley, B.A.; Rutgers University, New Brunswick, New Jersey, M.A.; further study at Union Theological Seminary. **Career:** Poet-in-residence, Talladega University, Tougaloo University, Texas Southern University, and Dundee University, Scotland. Instructor, Yale University, New Haven, Connecticut, 1975–79. **Awards:** National Council on the Arts grant, 1967; Hodder fellow in playwriting, Princeton University; fellow in creative writing, Dundee University; Academy of American Poets fellowship for distinguished poetic achievement, 1996. **Address:** c/o Princeton University Press, 41 William Street, Princeton, New Jersey 08540–5237, U.S.A.

PUBLICATIONS

Poetry

Death As History. Millbrook, New York, Kriya Press, 1967.
The Homecoming Singer. New York, Corinth Books, 1971.
Soothsayers and Omens. New York, Seven Woods Press, 1976.
Dimensions of History. Santa Cruz, California, Kayak, 1976.
The Double Invention of Komo. Austin, University of Texas Press, 1980.
Elaine's Book. Charlottesville, University Press of Virginia, 1986.

Explications/Interpretations. Charlottesville, University Press of Virginia, 1984.
Selected Poems of Jay Wright. Princeton, New Jersey, Princeton University Press, 1987.
Boleros. Princeton, New Jersey, Princeton University Press, 1991.

Play

Balloons, A Comedy in One Act. Boston, Baker's Plays, 1968.

*

Critical Studies: *The Forerunners: Black Poets in America* by Woodie King, Washington, D.C., Howard University Press, 1975; "The Early Poetry of Jay Wright" by Gerald Barrax, and "The Descent of Nommo: Literacy as Method in Jay Wright's 'Benjamin Banneker Helps to Build a City'" by Vera M. Kutzinski, both in *Callaloo* (Charlottesville, Virginia), 6(3), fall 1983; "The Clarity of Being Strange: Jay Wright's The Double Invention of Komo" by Michael Tomasek Manson, in *Black Literature Forum,* 24, fall 1990; "From a Goat Path in Africa: An Approach to the Poetry of Jay Wright" by Isidore Okpewho, in *Callaloo* (Charlottesville, Virginia), 14(3), summer 1991; "Jay Wright's Poetics: An Appreciation" by Ron Welburn, in *Melus* (Amherst, Massachusetts), 18, fall 1993.

*   *   *

Ever since Ezra Pound undertook his descent into the troubadour mind in the early twentieth century, American writers have been making pilgrimages to obscure cultures to bring back lore and insight in an effort to expand the visionary powers of the mind. Charles Olson made a trek to the Yucatán Peninsula to study Mayan culture in 1950, and the beats scattered into Mexico, India, Japan, and North Africa in search of new ideas. Carlos Casteneda put his stamp on the 1960s with *The Teachings of Don Juan,* in which he became the willing initiate into the mysteries of a peyote cult among the Yaqui Indians of the southern Sonoran Desert. In Jay Wright's attempt to find a new source of religious ideas, he has plumbed the work of French anthropologists studying the Dogon and Bambara cultures of West Africa.

In *The Double Invention of Komo* Wright undertakes the task of imagining his own initiation into the rites of Komo as practiced by the Bambara, a people located on the upper Niger River and the subject of the book *Les Fondements de la societé d'initiation du Komo,* by the anthropologists Germaine Dieterlen and Yousouf Tata Cissé, on which Wright's poem is based. In an afterword to his poem Wright tells us that the initiate into the Komo religion attempts "to go 'beyond the pool,' to understand the universe within which the human spirit 'imbibes abstract things.'" Wright has done this to bring about the "necessary transformation of an enhanced world of intransigent act," to redeem us from our own errors and ignorance.

The claim Wright makes is familiar after a century of rebirths and conversions to other religions. This is one more piece in the jigsaw puzzle of twentieth-century art, in which Christianity's boundaries are scaled and other religions sympathetically explored. The goal is self-liberation, the transcendence of personal identity to gain the larger cosmos of nature and otherness. Here is some of the language of the poem's close:

I forget my name;
I forget my mother's and father's names.

I am about to be born.
I forget where I come from
and where I am going.
I cannot distinguish
right from left, front from rear.
Show me the way of my race
and of my fathers . . .

You take me to kneel, forehead to earth, before Komo.
You present me to sacred things.
I am reborn into a new life.
My eyes open to Komo.

The task is boldly undertaken, but there are structural and psychological problems posed here that the poem does not fully resolve. How is it that a poet of modern urban consciousness, with the whole range of English at his command, can hope to duplicate the modes of ritual descent as performed by rural Africans? The nature of ritual and of tribal cohesion depends upon body language, repeated gestures, grunts, and mantras, yet this poem weighs in with a large dictionary to accomplish the same ends. The mind is here, but the body's powers to read signs and make meanings from gestures and animal noises is minimized. What we have is a sort of orchestral transcription of the music from an African finger harp.

It simply does not work to bring such articulate skills to the person of a man who says that

All day, I stub in my father's fields
or whistle in the market over
my mother's pots, adept in the provisions
of belonging.
At night, I lodge
near the most familiar limbs.
On my bed,
I am fused to my brother's steel spine.
The wind's bugle covers my day's breath.

This language comes from a culture of self-consciousness. The diversity, density, and multiple layerings of the words used attest to the autonomy and hypertrophy of the self that has arisen out of centuries of social evolution in the West. How can this weight of alien psychology be crammed into the mouth of a tribal youth who has no bearings in such a world?

Unhappily, the poem never moves beyond the paradox of its strategy. It strains to possess the feeling of the rituals underhand, but Wright keeps his personal identity out of the poem. The fact that he is himself an African-American might have helped to convince us of some innate, a priori resonance between his and the Bambara imagination. Perhaps not. In the end the poem seems to prove the reverse of its intention—that one cannot easily leap from one's own culture to grasp the reality of another's. The poem is stuck in its own metaphysical and linguistic provinciality, with much intelligent laboring exerted for a noble but unreached goal:

Down below the love bed,
the knit bones of the dead
cock their conch ears
to another soul's implosion.
My monody impels you to the shore,
where I enroll among the thorns

clutched in the rocks.
I will, by my heart's hunker-down
harzard, examine your twilight eyes
and will.

Boleros is a more effective use of Wright's powers. In it he keeps himself apart from the mythological landscape of Mexico, which he traces to Indian roots and from there to Asian Indian and Catholic European ideas. This is Wright country; he was born in New Mexico and raised there and in California. He has a passion for how the ritual mind works, and the ecumenical bent of Wright's thinking is put to good use in threading together a world religious system from the faith of Mexico's southern *indios*. The plot of the book is a travel memoir of the poet and his wife moving from one world (Scotland, New England) to the other (Mexico), from Protestant rationality to the depths of the Mayan and Aztec worlds, with their layerings of Spanish Catholicism and other New World elements.

Wright is buoyant and clearheaded in *Boleros,* and he stays out of the psychological traps of his earlier book. He enjoys his role as an intelligent guide to both worlds:

Here,
as we stand in the Mayan evening,
I know I should be able to say
something simple,
such as, it is the same moon,
that the triad—moon, earth,
and that star in Taurus—
sounds right again.
Where is my synodic certainty?
I know less than the ancients
who were accustomed to a late moon
            and its difficult omens.

"I am learning," Wright says later in the same poem. Indeed, he is a tireless worker in the quest to bring passion and sensuality to American belief. The story of religion in the twentieth century may one day be its central motif. Wright's early years in New York were spent among some of the brightest talents of the postmodern religious renaissance, and it is no accident that he should emerge as another of its principal voices.

—Paul Christensen

WRIGHT, Judith (Arundell)

Nationality: Australian. **Born:** Armidale, New South Wales, 31 May 1915. **Education:** Blackfriar Correspondence School, New South Wales; New England Girls School, Armidale; University of Sydney. **Family:** Married J.P. McKinney (died 1966); one daughter. **Career:** Secretary and clerk, 1938–42; clerk, Universities Commission, 1943–44; university statistician, University of Queensland, St. Lucia, 1945–48. Commonwealth Literary Fund Lecturer, Australia, 1949, 1962; honors tutor in English, University of Queensland, 1967. Member, Australia Council, 1973–74. **Awards:** Grace Leven prize, 1950, 1972; Commonwealth Literary Fund fellowship, 1964; Australia Britannica award, 1964; Australian Academy of the Humanities fellowship, 1970; Australian National University Creative Arts fellowship, 1974; Senior Writers fellowship, 1977; Fellowship of Australian Writers Robert Frost memorial award, 1977; Asan World prize, 1984. D.Litt.: University of Queensland, 1962; University of New England, Armidale, 1963; Sydney University, 1977; Monash University, Clayton, Victoria, 1977; Australian National University, Canberra, 1981; Griffith University, Nathan, Queensland, 1988; University of Melbourne, 1988; Premier's prize, New South Wales, 1987; The Queen's prize for poetry, 1992. **Address:** "Yven," Little River Road, Braidwood, New South Wales 2622, Australia. **Died:** 25 June 2000.

PUBLICATIONS

Poetry

The Moving Image. Melbourne, Meanjin Press, 1946.
Woman to Man. Sydney, Angus and Robertson, 1949.
The Gateway. Sydney, Angus and Robertson, 1953.
The Two Fires. Sydney, Angus and Robertson, 1955.
Australian Bird Poems. Adelaide, Australian Letters, 1961.
Birds. Sydney, Angus and Robertson, 1962.
(Poems), selected and introduced by the author. Sydney, Angus and Robertson, 1963.
Five Senses: Selected Poems. Sydney, Angus and Robertson, 1963.
City Sunrise. Brisbane, Shapcott Press, 1964.
The Other Half. Sydney, Angus and Robertson, 1966.
Poetry from Australia: Pergamon Poets 6, with Randolph Stow and William Hart-Smith, edited by Howard Sergeant. Oxford, Pergamon Press, 1969.
Collected Poems 1942–1970. Sydney, Angus and Robertson, 1971.
Alive: Poems 1971–72. Sydney, Angus and Robertson, 1973.
Fourth Quarter and Other Poems. Sydney, Angus and Robertson, 1976; London, Angus and Robertson, 1977.
The Double Tree: Selected Poems 1942–1976. Boston, Houghton Mifflin, 1978.
Journeys, with others, edited by Fay Zwicky. Melbourne, Sisters, 1982.
Phantom Dwelling. Sydney, Angus and Robertson, 1985; London, Virago Press, 1986.
A Human Pattern (selected poems). Sydney, Angus and Robertson, 1990; Manchester, Carcanet, 1992.
Collected Poems. Sydney, Angus and Robertson, and Manchester, Carcanet, 1994.

Recording: *Judith Wright Reads from Her Own Work,* University of Queensland Press, 1973.

Short Stories

The Nature of Love. Melbourne, Sun, 1966.

Other

Australian Poetry (lecture). Armidale, New South Wales, University of New England, 1955 (?).
King of the Dingoes (for children). Melbourne, Oxford University Press, 1958; London, Angus and Robertson, 1959.
The Generations of Men. Melbourne, Oxford University Press, 1959.

The Day the Mountains Played (for children). Brisbane, Jacaranda Press, 1960; London, Angus and Robertson, 1963.
Range the Mountains High (for children). Melbourne, Lansdowne Press, and London, Angus and Robertson, 1962; revised edition, Lansdowne Press, 1971.
Country Towns (for children). Melbourne, Oxford University Press, 1963; London, Oxford University Press, 1964.
Charles Harpur. Melbourne, Lansdowne Press, 1963; revised edition, Melbourne and London, Oxford University Press, 1977.
Shaw Neilson (biography and selected verse). Sydney, Angus and Robertson, 1963.
Preoccupations in Australian Poetry. Melbourne and London, Oxford University Press, 1965.
The River and the Road (for children). Melbourne, Lansdowne Press, 1966; London, Angus and Robertson, 1967; revised edition, Lansdowne Press, 1971.
Henry Lawson. Melbourne, London, and New York, Oxford University Press, 1967.
Conservation As an Emerging Concept. Sydney, Australian Conservation Foundation, 1970.
Because I Was Invited (essays). Melbourne, Oxford University Press, 1975; London, Oxford University Press, 1976.
Charles Harpur. Melbourne and London, Oxford University Press, 1977.
The Coral Battleground. Melbourne, Nelson, 1977.
The Cry for the Dead. Melbourne, Oxford, and New York, Oxford University Press, 1981.
We Call for a Treaty. Sydney, Collins/Fontana, 1985.
Born of the Conquerors (essays). Canberra, Aboriginal Studies Press, 1991.
Going on Talking (essays). Springwood, New South Wales, Butterfly Books, 1992.

Editor, *Australian Poetry 1948.* Sydney, Angus and Robertson, 1949.
Editor, *A Book of Australian Verse.* Melbourne and London, Oxford University Press, 1956; revised edition, 1968.
Editor, *New Land, New Language: An Anthology of Australian Verse.* Melbourne and London, Oxford University Press, 1957.
Editor, with A.K. Thomson, *The Poet's Pen.* Brisbane, Jacaranda Press, 1965.
Editor, with Val Vallis, *Witnesses of Spring: Unpublished Poems,* by Shaw Neilson. Sydney, Angus and Robertson, 1970.
Editor, with others, *Report of the National Estate.* Canberra, Government Publishing Service, 1974.
Editor, with others, *Reef, Rainforest, Mangroves, Man.* Cairns, Wildlife Preservation Society of Queensland, 1980.

*

Bibliography: *Judith Wright: A Bibliography,* Adelaide, Libraries Board of South Australia, 1968; *Judith Wright* by Shirley Walker, Melbourne, Oxford University Press, 1981.

Critical Studies: *Focus on Judith Wright* by W.N. Scott, Brisbane, University of Queensland Press, 1967; *Critical Essays on Judith Wright* edited by A.K. Thomson, Brisbane, Jacaranda Press, 1968; *Judith Wright* by A.D. Hope, Melbourne, Oxford University Press, 1975; *Judith Wright: An Appreciation* edited by N. Simms, Hamilton, New Zealand, Outrigger Press, 1976; *The Poetry of Judith Wright: A Search for Unity,* Melbourne, Arnold, 1980, and "The Cry for the

Dead—Judith Wright and the Aborigines,'' in *The Writer's Sense of the Past: Essays on Southeast Asian and Australian Literature,* edited by Kirpal Singh, Singapore, Singapore University Press, 1987, both by Shirley Walker; ''The Australianness of Judith Wright: Landscape: Metaphor and Analogy'' by Anne Godschalk, in *Dutch Quarterly Review of Anglo-American Letters* (Amsterdam), 12(4), 1982; ''The Poetry of Judith Wright: An Attempt at Interpretation'' by Dilip Kumar Sen, in *Journal of the Department of English* (Calcutta), 18(1), 1982–83; ''Judith Wright and the Colonial Experience'' by Alur Janakiram, in *The Colonial and the Neo-Colonial Encounters in Commonwealth Literature,* edited by H.H. Anniah Gowda, Mysore, Prasaragana University, 1983; ''Judith Wright's Most Famous Poem: An Explication'' by Ralf Norman, in *Three Lectures on Literature in English,* edited by Roger D. Sell, Abo, Abo Akademie, 1983; ''The Sense of Reality in Judith Wright's Poetry'' by Maryvonne Nedeljkovic, in *Commonwealth Essays and Studies* (Dijon, France), 8(2), spring 1986; ''Another Side of Paradise: A.D. Hope and Judith Wright'' by Fay Zwicky, in *Southerly* (Southerly, Australia), 48(1), March 1988; ''Setting Her Signature on the Land: The Poetry of Judith Wright'' by Nancy Potter, in *Antipodes* (Brooklyn, New York), 3(1), spring 1989; ''Re-Reading Judith Wright'' by John Salter, in *New Literatures Review* (Wollongong, NSW, Australia), 18, winter 1989; ''Time and Change in Judith Wright'' by Radharani Chakravarty, in *Commonwealth Review* (New Delhi), 2(1–2), 1990–91; ''An Ecological Vision,'' in *International Literature in English: Essays on the Major Writers,* edited by Robert L. Ross, New York, Garland, 1991, and ''Place and Moral Commitment: Judith Wright and Christina Stead,'' in *Perceiving Other Worlds,* edited by Edwin Thumboo, Singapore, Times Academy, 1991, both by Bruce Bennett; ''Ulysses in New England: A Tribute to Judith Wright'' by Peter Skrzynecki, in *Southerly* (Southerly, Australia), 52(3), September 1992; ''Within the Bounds of Feminine Sensibility? The Poetry of Rosemary Dobson, Gwen Harwood, and Judith Wright'' by Jennifer Strauss, in *Still the Frame Holds: Essays on Women Poets and Writers,* edited by Sheila Roberts and Yvonne Pacheco Tevis, San Bernardino, Borgo, 1993; ''The Poetry of Judith Wright: Inventing Australia, Inventing the Self'' by Nela Bureu, in *Miscelanea* (Saragossa, Spain), 16, 1995; ''Judith Wright's Nature Poetry—The Problem of Living 'Through a Web of Language''' by Robert Zeller, in *Antipodes* (Austin, Texas), 12(1), June 1998.

Judith Wright commented:

The background of my work lies in my main life concerns, as an Australian whose family on both sides were early comers to a country that was one of the last to be settled by the whites and were from the beginning farmers and pastoralists. Brought up in a landscape once of extraordinary beauty, but despised by its settlers because of its unfamiliarity, I have I suppose been trying to expiate a deep sense of guilt over what we have done to the country, to its first inhabitants of all kinds, and are still and increasingly doing. This is one aspect of the sources of my work. I have never for long been an urban dweller, and the images I use and also my methods no doubt reflect my ties to the landscape I live in. I tend to use ''traditional''—i.e., biological—rhythms more than free or new forms, which I see as better adapted to urban living and urban tensions and problems.

Another strong influence on my work has been my relationship with my husband, whose philosophical investigation of the sources and development of Western thought I shared in till his death. As a woman poet, the biological aspect of feminine experience has naturally been of importance in my work also. I expect my poetry is of a kind that no urban technological society will produce again, but I have tried to remain faithful to my own experience and outlook rather than engage in experimental verse for which it does not fit me.

Over the years since 1970 I have been increasingly concerned with questions of conservation and the situation of Australian Aborigines, and my participation in active organizations on both issues is reflected in my work during this time.

* * *

Judith Wright, one of Australia's most distinguished and best-loved poets and an ardent conservationist, unites in her poetry a vision of wholeness, a synthesis of body, mind, and spirit that stands counter to the alienation of modern life. Ever aware of the ''link between the decline of our inner and of our outer worlds,'' she continually seeks to forge this lost unity against ''our decaying capacities for imagination, vision and creation,'' our separation from the natural world. In poems on untouched nature she pursues this quest to ''name and know / beyond the flowers I gather / the one that does not wither— / the truth from which they grow'' (''The Forest,'' *Five Senses*). Wright evokes the spontaneity of nature in the personification that takes place in ''The Wattle-Tree'' when the tree breaks ''into the truth I had no voice to speak: / into a million images of the Sun, my God'' (*The Two Fires*). She also credits this spontaneity to an earlier Australian poet, seeking like him to ''live . . . fed on by unseen poetry . . . [and] give these heavy words away'' (''For John Shaw Neilson,'' *The Other Half*). The search for the essence of a reality implicit in the everyday reaches an epiphany of loving communion with the landscape and its ''ravelled shore'' and ''contours of dunes'' when, in ''Jet Flight over Derby,''

I lost my foreign words
and spoke in tongues like birds.

The desire to go beyond language resulted in a new form of expression in *Phantom Dwelling*. In ''Brevity'' Wright heralds a change to pared-down forms in the two concluding sections of the volume, confiding that ''these days I don't draw / very deep breaths'':

I used to love Keats, Blake.
Now I try haiku
for its honed brevities,
its inclusive silences.

Issa. Shiki. Buson. Bash
Few words and with no rhetoric.
Enclosed by silence
as is the thrush's call.

In the minimalist poems that follow Wright achieves her contact with that ''unseen poetry,'' as in ''Caddis-Fly'' (''Small twilight helicopter'') or ''Fox'' (''Fox, fox! / Behind him follows the crackle of his name'').

But while nature, and in particular the landscape of the Australian bush, is a loved and constant subject of Wright's poetry, so too are human feelings and actions. Though rarely particularizing its subjects, her poems of human love can capture tenderness and wonder in their universal aspects, as in one of her best-known poems, ''Woman to Man,'' a moving meditation on an unborn child:

This is our hunter and our chase,
the third who lay in our embrace.
This is the strength that your arm knows,
the arc of flesh that is my breast,
the precise crystals of our eyes.

The poetic control and precision of language in this and its companion poems counterpoise the two acts of creation, producing some of Wright's most successful work.

In "Bullocky" and "Brother and Sisters" Wright captures the world of the pioneers. In other poems, among them the early "Nigger's Leap, New England" and "The Bora Ring," the spirits of the Aborigines haunt their land and its settlers, "the tribal story / lost in an alien tale." Those living in "Dark Ones" also haunt:

On the other side of the road
the dark ones stand.
Something leaks in our blood
like the ooze from a wound.

These "night ghosts of a land / only by day possessed," silently watching as "faces of pale stone" turn aside, and the association of the Aborigines with the land describe one of the other symptoms of alienation that Wright often confronts. In her poetry, as in her prose, she reminds white Australians that their refusal to acknowledge the Aborigines' spiritual rights to land lies at the heart of their own loss of contact with the natural world. Her own love of the "unseen poetry" of nature, and its significance as a creative, spiritual force, gives her particular respect for those who sustained and nurtured it as a spiritual force of their own.

It is appropriate that "Patterns," the final poem of *Phantom Dwelling*—the last of a sequence entitled "The Shadow of Fire (Ghazals)"—should bring together in a series of couplets the renewing and destructive forms of fire, Wright's recurrent image of the spirit. While the dual aspects have been opposed in earlier poems, here the emphasis is on reconciling these opposites. Even the "thousand suns" of nuclear explosion are contained in the Heraclitean philosophy of flux, itself not a stranger in her work:

All's fire, said Heraclitus; measures of it
kindle as others fade. All changes yet all's one.

We are born of ethereal fire and we return there.
Understand the Logos; reconcile opposing principles . . .

'Twisted are the hearts of men—dark powers possess them.
Burn the distant evildoer, the unseen sinner.'

That prayer to Agni, fire-god, cannot be prayed.
We are all of us born of fire, possessed by darkness.

Here the word (Logos) has been absorbed into the principle of reconciliation, as the poem balances light and dark, destruction and salvation, evil and good; fire is the "ethereal" source of life as well as the apocalypse. "Patterns" includes and transcends all of the earlier images of fire, that of the wattle tree, of the creative fire that derives from homely images ("Cleaning Day"), of the napalm of Vietnam, of "the contained argument of the bomb" ("The Precipice"). It is entirely consistent that Wright should forge the broken links of outer and inner worlds by combining these oppositions in a poem of

Christian symbolism, classical philosophy, and modern science ("Strontium in the bones . . . is said to be 'a good conductor of electricity'") and in a form that is based on the Persian verse form of the ghazal. From a poet whose life work has been the definition of light and darkness, the fusion of the broken, this is a poem that brings the universe itself into an embracing and forgiving whole.

—Nan Bowman Albinski

WRIGHT, Kit

Nationality: British. **Born:** Kent in 1944. **Education:** Berkhamsted School, Hertfordshire; New College, Oxford. **Career:** Teacher in a comprehensive school, London; lecturer in English, Brock University, St. Catharines, Ontario, 3 years. Education secretary, Poetry Society, London, 1970–75; fellow-commoner in creative arts, Trinity College, Cambridge, 1977–79. **Awards:** Geoffrey Faber memorial prize, 1978; Poetry Society Alice Hunt Bartlett prize, 1978; Arts Council bursary, 1985. **Address:** c/o Viking Kestrel, 27 Wrights Lane, London W8 5TZ, England.

PUBLICATIONS

Poetry

Treble Poets 1, with Stephen Miller and Elizabeth Maslen. London, Chatto and Windus, 1974.
The Bear Looked over the Mountain. London, Salamander Imprint, 1977.
Bump-Starting the Hearse. London, Hutchinson, 1983.
From the Day Room. Liverpool, Windows Press, 1983.
Real Rags and Red. London, Century Hutchinson, 1988.
Poems 1974–1983. London, Century Hutchinson, 1988.
Short Afternoons. London, Century Hutchinson, 1989.

Poetry (for children)

Arthur's Father [Granny, Sister, Uncle]. London, Methuen, 4 vols., 1978.
Rabbiting On and Other Poems. London, Fontana, 1978.
Hot Dog and Other Poems. London, Kestrel, 1981.
Professor Potts Meets the Animals of Africa. London, Watts, 1981.
Cat among the Pigeons. London, Viking Kestrel, 1987.
Tigerella. London, Scholastic Children's Books, 1993.
Dolphinella. London, Deutsch Children's Books, 1995.

Other (for children)

Great Snakes! London, Viking, 1994.

Editor, *Soundings: A Selection of Poems for Speaking Aloud.* London, Heinemann, 1975.
Editor, *Poems for 9-Year-Olds and Under.* London, Kestrel, 1984.
Editor, *Poems for Over 10-Year-Olds.* London, Viking Kestrel, 1984.
Editor, *Funnybunch: A New Puffin Book of Funny Verse.* London, Viking, 1993.

*

Critical Studies: In *Poetry Review,* 85(1), spring 1995; by Robert Potts, in *Times Literary Supplement* (London), 4814, 1995.

*   *   *

Rumor has it that Kit Wright writes lyrics for musical reviews and the like, and I can well believe it. Many of his poems have that breezily rhythmical, easily rhyming quality that shouts out for a catchy tune. Sometimes he even provides a chorus or two:

> She's got
> Red boots on, she's got
> Red boots on,
> Kicking up the winter
> Till the winter is gone.

What is certain is that there is more to it than this, and if Wright's rhythms and rhymes have literary forebears, then one must be Auden. The echoes are present:

> Coming out of nowhere,
> Into nowhere sped,
> Blind as time, my darling,
> Blind nothing in its head.

What are Wright's own are his wit, his insights into our urban life, and the refreshing contemporaneity of his language. The language does not eschew transatlantic overtones, while at the same time making sure that it is the genuine article and not the language that never was of the popular entertainer.

> I light the last one from the pack. Outside
> An evening of wind and rain drivels and blusters
> Against my sidestreet window.

Add to all of this Wright's sense of fun and one gets sudden glimpses of a world that, however bizarre, is never far from the world we know. The poetry is sometimes brittlely bright, as in ''Humpty's Fatalism''—''I was a tough old egg / Philip Marlow / hanging in / sunny side up''—but at other times it gets its effects by contrasting the language used and the theme expressed—''I was thinking about her all the way from Troy / (I slipped town when the Greek Horse showed).'' But the poems are never far from pushing at the nerve of real feeling, as in ''Elizabeth'' or ''What were you going to say'':

> What were you going to say
> On the path above the sea
> When we stared down at the bay

> And suddenly
> The film of the bright day
> Snapped at the end of a reel.

It is certainly this facility, together with his lively inventiveness, that makes Wright's collections of verse for young people so deservedly popular.

These qualities are even more apparent in Wright's second collection, *Bump-Starting the Hearse.* There are, of course, the wildly and hilariously scurrilous pieces such as ''Underneath the Archers'' (''Everyone's on about Walter's willy / Down at The Bull tonight''). But alongside are poems such as ''The Day Room,'' about a mental hospital, and ''The Specialist'':

> Imagine you dreamed this
> stone-cold dream
> and woke and the whole cold
> thing were true

Such poems induce those shudders that used to be described as ''some one walking over your grave.''

A ''light verse master'' is how Peter Porter has described Wright, and so he is. But while his poetry amuses and entertains, it also disturbs, making us look at the commonplace with fresh insight and sharpness of feeling even when it is at its most self-deprecating.

In his 1989 collection *Short Afternoons* the serious concerns and the darker side of Wright's work are more to the fore. The remarkable facility to rhyme is still present—''Garter''/''Charter''/''Sparta''; ''skyline''/''by-line''; ''listening''/''glistening''—but this must not lull the reader into the idea that it heralds light verse. There are, of course, still splendidly bawdy pieces, like ''Star and Garter,'' but alongside are deeply moving and concerned pieces such as ''A Pastoral Disappointment'' and ''Unlikely Obbligato of Andersontown.'' In his mixture of the scurrilous, light, and seriously sympathetic Wright shows a healthy, Shakespearean disregard for Aristotle's unities.

Wright is also a considerable poet for young people. His poems for children are an integral part of his work and should not be overlooked. He is one of that honorable company who have not descended to the patronizing Christmas cracker and music hall jokes that others pass off as verse. The rhyming and rhythm are as carefully and properly crafted as in his poems for adults, which accounts for their popular appeal. In this respect ''Zoe's Ear-Rings'' is a tour de force, while the earlier poem ''A Visit to the Aquarium'' begins with a superb evocation of eelishness that is the stuff of real poetry.

—John Cotton

Y

YAP, Arthur

Nationality: Singaporean. **Born:** Singapore, 11 January 1943. **Education:** University of Singapore, 1962–65, B.A. (honors) 1965; TTC Singapore, Cert. Ed. 1967; University of Leeds, England, 1974–75, M.A. 1975; National University of Singapore, 1982–84, Ph.D. 1984. **Career:** Education officer, Ministry of Education, Singapore, 1965–78. Since 1979 senior lecturer, National University of Singapore. **Awards:** National Book Development Council of Singapore's Poetry award, 1976, 1982, 1988; Southeast Asia Write award, 1983; Singapore's Cultural Medallion for poetry, 1983; Mont-Blanc-CFA award, Singapore, 1998. **Address:** 40 Lloyd Road, #02–48, Singapore 239107.

PUBLICATIONS

Poetry

Only Lines. Singapore, Federal Publications, 1971.
Five Takes. Singapore, University of Singapore Press, 1974.
Commonplace. Singapore, Heinemann, 1978.
Down the Line. Singapore, Heinemann, 1980.
Man Snake Apple. Singapore, Heinemann, 1986.
The Space of City Trees: Selected Poems. London, SKOOB, 2000.

Recording: *Singapore Poetry in English,* National University of Singapore, 1998.

Short Stories

Singapore Short Stories. Singapore, Heinemann, 1978.

Other

A Brief Critical Survey of Prose Writings in Singapore and Malaysia. Singapore, Educational Publications Bureau, 1971.
English Grammar and Usage. Singapore, Federal Publications, 1981.
Thematic Structure in Poetic Discourse. Singapore, Copinter, 1987.

Editor, *Language Education in Multilingual Societies.* Singapore, RELC, 1978.

*

Manuscript Collection: Central Library, National University of Singapore, Kent Ridge, Singapore.

Critical Studies: "Beyond Responsibility" by D.J. Enright, in *Times Literary Supplement* (London), 24 November 1978; "To Much Eliot and Alas, No Ulysses" by Anthony Burgess, in *Straits Times* (Singapore), 9 August 1983; "The 'Second Tongue' Myth: English Poetry in Polylingual Singapore" by Jan B. Gordon, in *ARIEL* (Calgary, Alberta), 15(4), October 1984; "Towards a Creative Use of the Alien Tongue: A Study of Singapore Literature in the English Language" by Miyuki Kosetsu, in *Southeast Asian Studies* (Kyoto, Japan), 22(1), June 1984; "The Sense of Place in Singaporean and Malaysian Poetry in English with Special Reference to Wong Phui Nam and Arthur Yap" by Anne Brewster, in *A Sense of Place in the New Literatures in English,* edited by Peggy Nightingale, St. Lucia, University of Queensland Press, 1986.

*   *   *

Painter and short story writer as well as poet, Arthur Yap belongs to the generation of Singaporeans whose careers coincide with the development of that modern state. The history of modern Singapore has been a period of self-reliance, enterprise, pragmatic endeavor, material prosperity, and rapid change, to all of which the poetry has reacted with oblique but persistent irony, sharp observation, wry nostalgia, and enormous and genuinely original linguistic liveliness. Among poets there also has been, however, a reflective ambivalence about the solicitations for an affirmative public commitment to everything that nation building requires of its writers. In their laconic precision images like the following, from Yap's "local colour" and "elementary pieces," are characteristic:

> the artist is neither here nor there
> he mistakes grassroots for his hair
> now the strands have sprouted in the air
> flanking an attap hut as a cultural stair
>
> the fluidity of air
> tranquil even as water,
> scatters hope like litter.

Yap's poetry is marked by certain distinctive features that have remained more or less constant. As in "dawn," he has an acute eye for nuanced detail of gesture and tone in the human world and of evanescence and mutability in the natural world:

> dawn in the quiet key of light
> utters a whole paragraph of hues
> in the early mutter of an aviary.

His pared-down minimalism of grammar and imagery is more a matter of a temperamental preference for economy of means and a distaste for display rather than an affiliation with an international idiom, although the addiction to lowercase letters and other related syntactic effects is not without recollections of e.e. cummings. This can be seen in the following lines from "until":

> until anthony passed away
> i never saw cheeriest optimism
> a person leaving hospital,
> family carrying bags & he himself.

Yap's witty self-consciousness about the oddities and quiddities of language use, evidence of his training and professional interest in linguistics, can enter quite directly into poems like "the grammar of a dinner," "words," "a lesson on the definite article," "parts of speech," and "group dynamics i." This leads to occasional patches of arid or riddling self-absorption, but more often it creates situations that are funny as well as insightful, as in "2 Mothers in a HDB Playground." Yap is very good with ventriloquistic effects, showing skill in portraying people through their linguistic idiosyncrasies. He can also be whimsical, playful, and self-indulgent. Part of "letter from a youth to his prospective employer" goes like this:

> i am reasonably qualified;
> quite handsome; my lack of experience compensated
> by my prodigal intelligence: i shall not expect
> to marry the typewriter: it's decision-making
> i am after; that's what i am: a leader of tomorrow;
> so why don't you make it today? my personality
> is personable: & all opportunities being equal:
> i am equal to any most opportune moment . . .

Yap's poetry also shows a tendency toward abstraction, which is corroborated by the paintings reproduced in the volume *Commonplace*. Poems often take off at a speculative tangent from a perceived concrete detail to go on a journey whose rewards depend on how much the reader can bring to the work by way of tolerance and stamina for nimble, imaginative free play. In brief, the style is a daring and difficult one, ever willing to take chances. It cannot be denied that for every exhilarating poem that works there are a handful of trial pieces reading like experiments that did not quite come off. But the sum total of his achievement is a considerable body of poetry that is witty, humane, and inimitable.

The principal contribution of Yap's poetry to Singaporean writing is to show how individuality can be sustained independently of the pressures to conform to conventional importunities. It practices what can best be described as a highly personal impersonality and a very disengaged engagement. It resists the times with what the moment has to offer, and its eccentric resistance redefines "the centre":

> on Sunday it isn't whether the sun
> & shadows have been well constructed,
> they are a detachable presence.
> the other days have the colours of the world.
> Sunday's recitation is by omission
> rather than by commission.
> if you had asked, the roadsweeper
> would have lent you his road.
> it is the day the wheel is re-invented
> to a halt.

Along with the very different work of his contemporaries and colleagues, the older Edwin Thumboo and the slightly younger Lee Tzu Pheng, Yap's poems constitute the best part of the diverse body of contemporary Singaporean writing. In their significance and interest they are comparable to the best poetry written in the past few decades from anywhere in the English-speaking world.

—Rajeev S. Patke

YATES, J(oel) Michael

Nationality: Canadian. **Born:** Fulton, Missouri, United States, 10 April 1938. **Education:** Westminster College, Fulton; University of Kansas City, Missouri (Poetry prize, 1960), B.A. 1960, M.A. 1961; University of Michigan, Ann Arbor (Hopwood award, for poetry, 1964, for drama, 1964), 1962–64. **Family:** Married Ann West in 1970 (divorced); three daughters. **Career:** Promotional director, Public Radio Corporation, Houston, 1961–62; teaching fellow, University of Michigan, 1962–63; taught at Ohio University, Athens, 1964–65, and University of Alaska, Fairbanks, 1965–66; assistant professor, 1966–69, and associate professor of English, 1969–71, University of British Columbia, Vancouver; taught at University of Arkansas, Fayetteville, fall 1972, and University of Texas, Dallas, 1976–77. Editor-in-chief, 1966–67, and poetry editor, 1966–71, *Prism International,* and member of the editorial board, Prism International Press, Mission, British Columbia, 1966–71; founding editor, with Andreas Schroeder, *Contemporary Literature in Translation,* Vancouver, 1968–81; member of the editorial board, *Mundus Artium,* Athens, Ohio; general editor, *Campus Canada;* president, Sono Nis Press, Vancouver, later Victoria, British Columbia, 1968–76; Head of Special Projects Division, University of British Columbia Press, 1977–78; sales representative, Mitchell Press, from 1978; public relations consultant, Canadian Broadcasting Corporation, Vancouver, 1980. Works for Department of the Attorney General, British Columbia Provincial Government. Member of the editorial board, *Canadian Fiction Magazine.* **Awards:** International Broadcasting award, 1961, 1962; Canada Council grant, 1968, 1969, 1971, and Senior Arts award, 1972, 1974. **Address:** c/o Sono Nis Press, 1745 Blanchard Street, Victoria, British Columbia V8W 2J8. Canada.

PUBLICATIONS

Poetry

Spiral of Mirrors. Francestown, New Hampshire, Golden Quill Press, 1967.
Hunt in an Unmapped Interior and Other Poems. Francestown, New Hampshire, Golden Quill Press, 1967.
Canticle for Electronic Music. Victoria, British Columbia, Charles Morriss, 1967.
Parallax, with Bob Flick. Victoria, British Columbia, Charles Morriss, 1968.
The Great Bear Lake Meditations. Ottawa, Oberon Press, 1970.
Nothing Speaks for the Blue Moraines: New and Selected Poems. Vancouver, Sono Nis Press, 1973.
Breath of the Snow Leopard. Vancouver, Sono Nis Press, 1974.
The Qualicum Physics. San Francisco, Kanchenjunga Press, 1975.
Esox Nobilior non Esox Lucius. Fredericton, New Brunswick, Fiddlehead, 1978.
Fugue Brancusi. Victoria, British Columbia, Sono Nis Press, 1983.
The Queen Charlotte Islands Meditations. Moonbeam, Ontario, Penumbra Press, 1983.
The Completely Collapsible Portable Man: Selected Shorter Lyrics. Oakville, Ontario, Mosaic Press, 1984.
Schedules of Silence: The Collected Longer Poems. Vancouver, Pulp Press, 1986.

Plays

Subjunction (produced Fairbanks, Alaska, 1965).

Night Freight (broadcast, 1968; produced Toronto, 1972). Toronto, Playwrights, 1972.

Theatre of War (produced Winnipeg, Manitoba, 1970).

The Calling (produced Minneapolis, 1973). Toronto, Playwrights, 1971.

The Abstract Beast: New Fiction and Drama (includes the plays *The Abstract Beast, The Border, The Broadcaster, The Calling, The Panel, Smokestack in the Desert, Theatre of War*). Vancouver, Sono Nis Press, 1971.

Search for the Tse-Tse Fly (produced Montreal, 1974). In *Quarks*, 1975.

Quarks (includes *The Net, Search for the Tse-Tse Fly, The Calling*). Toronto, Playwrights, 1975.

Screenplay: *The Grand Edit*, 1966.

Radio Plays: *The Broadcaster*, 1968; *Theatre of War*, 1968; *The Calling*, 1968; *Night Freight*, 1968; *The Panel*, 1969; *The Abstract Beast*, 1969; *Smokestack in the Desert*, 1970; *Poet in an Arctic Landscape*, 1970; *The Border*, 1971; *Realia*, 1975; *The Net*, 1975; *Search for the Tse-Tse Fly*, 1975; *Sinking of the North West Passage*, 1975; *The Secret of State*, 1976; *Pluto's Republic*, 1977.

Television Plays: *Smokestack in the Desert*, 1975; *Search for the Tse-Tse Fly*, 1975.

Short Stories

Man in the Glass Octopus. Vancouver, Sono Nis Press, 1968.

Fazes in Elsewhen: New and Selected Fiction. Vancouver, Intermedia Press, 1977.

Torque [Torpor]: Collected Fiction 1960–1987. Vancouver, Aresenal Pulp Press, vol. 1, 1987; Vancouver, Cacanadadada Press, vol. 2, 1988.

Other

Line Screw: My Twelve Riotous Years Working behind Bars in Some of Canada's Toughest Jails, An Unrepentant Memoir. Toronto, McClelland and Stewart, 1993.

Editor, with Andreas Schroeder, *Contemporary Poetry of British Columbia.* Vancouver, Sono Nis Press, 2 vols., 1970–72.

Editor, with Charles Lillard, *Volvox: Poetry from the Unofficial Languages of Canada in English Translation.* Vancouver, Sono Nis Press, 1971.

Editor, *Contemporary Fiction of British Columbia.* Vancouver, Sono Nis Press, 1971.

Editor, *Light Like a Summons: Five Poets.* Vancouver, Cacanadadada, 1989.

*

J. Michael Yates comments:

1. For me an image is one of an infinite number of entrances into an arena where something ineffable is going on. If the thing I am after were statable, probably it would be better said in expository prose.

The issues most often taken up by good poetry usually require use of the silences between and behind words. For this mode of communication metaphor, indirection are the best engines.

2. With each piece I attempt to cause a structure, a system, of images whose parts belong dissonantly to a whole whose meaning cannot be stated. I mean Stravinsky's dissonance. In *Poetics of Music* he suggests that dissonance is only a transitional element; consonance must be achieved one way or another, either in the instrumentation or in the ear of the listener. The latter is my way—to give the reader the "thing" I am talking about, frame by frame, and ask him to project it inside him in the manner that most entertains him. Different and isolate as each of us is, it seems the only honesty.

3. Ideally, fifteen readers will make fifteen very different (and fifteen equally justifiable) poems from a piece I have written. As I am different from you at any moment, I differ from myself through successive moments; even the most familiar things change with changes in the coordinates of consciousness and time. I could not possibly re-create the coordinates of consciousness that produced a given piece and thereby tell you what it means.

4. Ideally, a reader would come to a poem relaxed, with open consciousness, no preconceptions or suspicions that the poem is a locked door and someone somewhere—probably the treacherous bastard author-is hiding the key. The parts of a poem that persist inside a reader arrive there via personal correspondences. Exterior interpretations remain merely exterior. Belief in one's own associations is difficult, very difficult. But only those will translate the poem from "mine" to "yours."

5. Ideally, one would read a poem as if he were the first reader in history to read a poem—and as if no one on earth were reading a poem at that moment. Impossible. Necessary.

6. Ideally, I write as if no one has ever written a poem. As if no one is writing now. Ridiculous. Imperative.

7. Understanding is a sweet, vague Renaissance dream that never came true. According to me, poems are not to be understood but responded to. Understanding promises universal truth. Naive. I am a rare user and no pusher at all of either reality or its "ism." I do not assume a representative universe. As if one could come to an understanding about such things.

*   *   *

An overview of the work of J. Michael Yates is complicated by the diversity of forms in which he has written and by his marked experimentation. This said, there are themes and images common to all of Yates's output, from the early poems to the plays of *The Abstract Beast* and the late on-line poems. Also common to his work is a certain self-consciousness arising from his experimentation, from a sense of self-as-artist, and from an attitude to language simultaneously deconstructive and mythic.

Yates is preoccupied with the notion that the ideas of the writer are his whole world and reality. This fascination with a state of being in which the mind becomes a substitute for, or a performance of, the "real" is perhaps seen most clearly in *Man in the Glass Octopus,* but it is prefigured in the early poems of *Hunt in an Unmapped Interior* (whose title suggests it) and continues into the endless series of lenses viewing lenses of the *Parallax* poems. It also prompts the recurrent images of animals eating animals, cameras filming cameras, and mirrors mirroring mirrors, with which the poems are filled. It explains as well the persona of the author/narrator as Adam naming Creation, a trope in the early poems that flirted with a notion then popular in

Canadian literary criticism and discussed, for example, by D.G. Jones. In Yates's poetry the idea is extended until the mind of Adam becomes the mind of God, itself an insubstantial mirror of Yates's own consciousness. Finally, it is embodied in the name of the press Yates founded: Sono Nis (the I is not). As his work has moved onto the Internet and into visual poetry involving color and font, even the printed page has become disembodied, the power of the word to capture the "I" ever more feeble and the process of writing/reading more necessary.

Each of these notions is introduced in *Hunt in an Unmapped Interior,* a collection of poems strongly reminiscent of Wallace Stevens, in which the short pieces are deft and incisive and the longer ones ruminative. *Canticle for Electronic Music* is disappointing after this auspicious beginning, for Yates has difficulty in sustaining the longer poems. *The Great Bear Lake Meditations* is a more mature work, in which the Adam persona is accepted and in which Yates's love of words becomes congruent with his deconstructive impulse; if the poet's only reality is the imagination, then words becomes signs of nothing other than aspects of his imagination. In *Parallax* Yates gropes toward but fails to quite reach a further refinement in which if "words are better than talk . . . [then] silence [is] better than words." Building upon camera imagery, the poems attempt the visual. But to create a "silent" poem is ultimately to produce a blank page, and these poems, however compelling, are "at the verge of total desire that ends in the half-act." Yates has somehow moved closer to this early objective in his later writings that move between genres and also move into Web-based calligraphies that represent "speaking" words, "speaking images," and silent connections. Lists of words "sound themselves," but the act of conjuring meaning is a personal act on the part of the reader; the writer no longer seems to direct it.

In *The Abstract Beast* Yates began to look toward these new forms, modifying his poems into the prose they always approached and into highly successful short radio plays (which would be less successful in production on the stage). In *Man in the Glass Octopus* Yates became less obsessive about myth, the result being a collection that, with the exception of some unfortunately reprinted early pieces, is as inventive as it is exciting. Some thinness does arise in the stories, and the plays are sometimes inconclusive, but the collection signals an important shift.

Yates's new work, however, has returned in many ways to self-consciousness, perhaps again in response to experimentation, this time in a new medium. That Yates has moved to publishing on the Internet is a signal of his continuing interest in style, innovation, and the interface between imagination and its physical expression.

—Reid Gilbert

YAU, John

Nationality: American. **Born:** 1950. **Career:** Art critic and independent curator. Distinguished visiting critic, Pratt Institute (Graduate School of Art), 1985–90, Maryland Institute, College of Art, spring 1986, and School of Visual Arts, 1988–90; visiting poet, Brown University, spring 1992; visiting scholar, Getty Center, winter 1993; visiting professor, University of California, Berkeley, spring 1994 and spring 1995. Ahmanson Curatorial Fellow, Museum of Contemporary Art, Los Angeles, 1993–96. **Awards:** National Endowment

for the Arts fellowship, 1977–78; Ingram Merrill Foundation fellowship, 1979–80, 1985–86; New York Foundation for the Arts award, 1988; Lavan award, 1988; General Electric Foundation award, 1988; Brendan Gill award, 1992; Jerome Shestack prize, 1993. **Address:** c/o Black Sparrow Press, 24 Tenth Street, Santa Rosa, California 95401, U.S.A.

PUBLICATIONS

Poetry

Crossing Canal Street. Binghamton, New York, Bellevue Press, 1976.
The Reading of an Ever-Changing Tale. Clinton, New York, Nobodaddy Press, 1977.
Sometimes. New York, Sheep Meadow Press, 1979.
The Sleepless Night of Eugene Delacroix. New York, Release Press, 1980.
Notarikon. New York, Jordan Davies, 1981.
Broken Off by the Music. Providence, Rhode Island, Burning Deck, 1981.
Corpse and Mirror. New York, Holt Rinehart, 1983.
Radiant Silhouette: New and Selected Work 1974–1988. Santa Rosa, California, Black Sparrow Press, 1989.
Dragon's Blood. Colombes, France, Collectif Generacion, 1989.
Big City Primer: Reading New York at the End of the Twentieth Century. New York, Timken Publishers, 1991.
Edificio Sayonara. Santa Rosa, California, Black Sparrow Press, 1992.
Postcards from Trakl. New York, ULAE, 1994.
Berlin Diptychon. New York, Timken, 1995.
Forbidden Entries. Santa Rosa, California, Black Sparrow Press, 1996.

Short Stories

Hawaiian Cowboys. Santa Rosa, California, Black Sparrow Press, 1994.
My Symptoms. Santa Rosa, California, Black Sparrow Press, 1998.

Other

In the Realm of Appearances: The Art of Andy Warhol. Hopewell, New Jersey, Ecco Press, 1993.
A.R. Penck. New York, Abrams, 1993.
The United States of Jasper Johns. Cambridge, Massachusetts, Zoland Books, 1996.

Editor, with David Kermani, *Fairfield Porter: The Collected Poems with Selected Drawings.* New York, Tibor de Nagy, 1985.
Editor, *In Pursuit of the Invisible: Selections from the Collection of Janice and Mickey Cartin: An Exhibition at the Loomis Chaffee School.* West Stockbridge, Massachusetts, Hard Press, 1996.
Editor, with others, *Original Sin: The Visionary Art of Joe Coleman.* New York, HECK, 1997.
Editor, *An Anthology of Fetish Fiction.* New York, Four Walls Eight Windows, 1998.

*

Bibliography: "John Yau: Contributions toward a Bibliography" by Ed Foster, in *Talisman, 5,* Fall 1990.

Critical Studies: "Reconstructing Asian-American Poetry: A Case for Ethnopoetics" by Shirley Lim, in *MELUS* (Amherst, Massachusetts), 14(2), summer 1987; John Yau issue of *Talisman* (Jersey City, New Jersey), 5, fall 1990; "'Chaos Goes Uncourted': John Yau's Dis-Orienting Poetics" by Priscilla Wald, in *Cohesion and Dissent in America,* edited by Carol Colatrella and Joseph Alkana, Albany, State University of New York, 1994; "A Bughouse Interaction" by Eric Peterson, in *Bughouse,* 2, summer 1994; *Word and Flesh: Materiality, Violence and Asian-American Poetics* (dissertation) by Juliana Chu Chang, University of California, Berkeley, 1995.

*   *   *

John Yau is a poet who, like John Ashbery, has earned much of his living in the world of the visual arts, writing art criticism, curating exhibitions, teaching at the Pratt Institute and the School of Visual Arts, and often collaborating with artists on book, print, and mixed-media projects. It is not surprising then to find that Yau's poems are often as much a product of his visual sense of the world as they are of his awareness of his double heritage from both oriental and occidental cultures.

Yau often uses the technique of surrealism disguised as imagism in his poems, as in "A Suite of Imitations Written after Reading Translations of Poems by Li He and Li Shang-yin":

When she left she took everything—her hair
Was a dream filled with colors gone by noon.
Yet, if nothing can be retrieved, I am still pulled
Toward this woman, who is still asleep, locked
Away in another life; her hair
Piled up like red peonies at noon.

But even more characteristic of Yau's later work is the attempt to bring stereotypical images from the pop culture of the oriental into satirical play, as well as to co-opt American myths to his own purposes. He does this in a series of poems called "Genghis Chan: Private Eye," for example, or in a poem like

"Sam Spade Haiku"

Perfect oval	Dark intermissions
Unlaced leather smile	Satin waist nipper
Tall drink of water	Coal blue lips
Fist full of trouble	Pink alabaster burden

These aspects of his work reveal Yau to be a New York school poet of the younger generation who, like Frank O'Hara, might be looking for a poetics that would allow him to create poems of greater immediacy. The surrealist prose poems have not stopped or even changed, and, in fact, Yau has always moved back and forth between sparsely imagist formations on the page, as in the early poem "Shimmering Pediment"—

An overloaded circuit—lightning
jammed the horizon, and for days
The echoes remained in my eyes

—or in the later "Radiant Silhouette I"—

Blue leather harness slips off glistening shoulders
A row of whispers burns on the windowsill

—to the denser texture of prose poems such as those in *Corpse and Mirror,* like "Carp and Goldfish," or the later "Spin, Spell, Spill":

I lift the velvet tourniquet closer to the whale lamp and review the fabled grains, their yellowing history murmuring behind my salvaged eyes. The sky is not quite the color of dawn. It is January, and you are in Bozeman, Montana. I thought I would begin this while you were in the air above the floor plan of the clouds, their exhumed disarray and brittle gleam.

This often seems more like prose than poetry, but the focus is always directed toward lyrical images—of women, of light, of the burdens of love—that seem to represent the incommunicable. In "Bare Sheets II" Yau says,

None of the many words we summoned to our sides fitted what we said to each other. Words and phrases, like small birds, their pulsing colors, rose up and scattered in every direction. Frantic wings tore the remaining stars further and further apart. Although winter had claimed the city, the bay windows were still open. Night or something known by that name was soaking through the last porous layers of language we had left, the ones we imagined keeping from each other. It is time to start removing our skin, you whispered, its alphabet of disguises.

As with the poems of Ashbery, O'Hara, and Kenneth Koch, the subject of Yau's poems is frequently love and its failure. But more important is the emphasis on the failure of communication, of words losing their power, and perhaps, especially as might be found in Ashbery, a sense that old values, old meanings have collapsed and that words are only empty repositories. The frequent surrealist gesture of satire against language itself, and especially poetry, is a trait Yau shares with these older poets. He uses it in a more lyrical way than his predecessors, however, perhaps because of the invocation of Chinese poetry.

—Diane Wakoski

YOUNG, Al(bert James)

Nationality: American. **Born:** Ocean Springs, Mississippi, 31 May 1939. **Education:** University of Michigan, Ann Arbor (co-editor, *Generation* magazine), 1957–61; Stanford University, California (Stegner Creative Writing Fellow), 1966–67; University of California, Berkeley, A.B. in Spanish 1969. **Family:** Married Arline June Belch in 1963; one son. **Career:** Freelance musician, 1958–64; disc jockey, KJAZ-FM, Alameda, California, 1961–65; instructor and linguistic consultant, San Francisco Neighborhood Youth Corps Writing Workshop, 1968–69; writing instructor, San Francisco Museum of Art Teenage Workshop, 1968–69; Jones Lecturer in creative writing, Stanford University, 1969–74; screenwriter, Laser Films, New York, 1972, Stigwood Corporation, London and New York, 1972, Verdon Productions, Hollywood, 1976, First Artists Ltd.,

Burbank, California, 1976–77, and Universal, Hollywood, 1979; writer-in-residence, University of Washington, Seattle, 1981–82. Since 1979 director, Associated Writing Programs. Founding editor, *Loveletter,* San Francisco, 1966–68. Since 1972 co-editor, *Yardbird Reader,* Berkeley, California; contributing editor, since 1972, *Changes,* New York, and since 1973, *Umoja,* New Mexico; since 1981 editor and publisher, with Ishmael Reed, *Quilt,* Berkeley; vice president, Yardbird Publishing Cooperative. **Awards:** National Endowment for the Arts grant, 1968, 1969, 1974; San Francisco Foundation Joseph Henry Jackson Award, 1969; Guggenheim fellowship, 1974; Pushcart prize, 1980; Before Columbus Foundation award, 1982. **Agent:** Lynn Nesbit, International Creative Management, 40 West 57th Street, New York, New York 10019. **Address:** 514 Bryant Street, Palo Alto, California 94301, U.S.A.

PUBLICATIONS

Poetry

Dancing. New York, Corinth, 1969.
The Song Turning Back into Itself. New York, Holt Rinehart, 1971.
Some Recent Fiction. San Francisco, San Francisco Book Company, 1974.
Geography of the Near Past. New York, Holt Rinehart, 1976.
The Blues Don't Change: New and Selected Poems. Baton Rouge, Louisiana State University Press, 1982.
Heaven: Collected Poems, 1956–1990. Berkeley, California, Creative Arts, 1989.
Straight No Chaser. Berkeley, California, Creative Arts Book Company, 1994.
Conjugal Visits: And Other Poems in Verse and Prose. Berkeley, California, Creative Arts Book Company, 1996.

Recording: *By Heart and by Ear,* Watershed, 1986; *Our Souls Have Grown Deep Like the Rivers,* Rhino/Word Beat, 2000.

Plays

Screenplays: *Nigger, 1972; Sparkle,* 1972.

Novels

Snakes. New York, Holt Rinehart, 1970; London, Sidgwick and Jackson, 1971.
Who Is Angelina? New York, Holt Rinehart, 1975; London, Sidgwick and Jackson, 1978.
Sitting Pretty. New York, Holt Rinehart, 1976.
Ask Me Now. New York, McGraw Hill, and London, Sidgwick and Jackson, 1980.
Seduction by Light. New York, Delta, 1988.

Other

Bodies and Soul: Musical Memoirs. Berkeley, California, Creative Arts, 1981.
Kinds of Blue: Musical Memoirs. Berkeley, California, Creative Arts, 1984.
Things Ain't What They Used to Be: Musical Memoirs. Berkeley, California, Creative Arts, 1987.

Mingus/Mingus: Two Memoirs, with Janet Coleman. Berkeley, California Creative Arts, 1989.
Drowning in the Sea of Love: Musical Memoirs. Hopewell, New Jersey, 1995.

Editor, with Ishmael Reed, *Yardbird Lives!* New York, Grove Press, 1978.
Editor, with Ishmael Reed, *Quilt 2–3.* Berkeley, California Reed and Young's Quilt, 2 vols., 1981–82.
Editor, *African American Literature: A Brief Introduction and Anthology.* New York, HarperCollins College Publishers, 1996.

*

Bibliography: In *New Black Voices,* edited by Abraham Chapman, New York, New American Library, 1972.

Critical Studies: ''Reader's Report'' by Martin Levin, in *New York Times Book Review,* 17 May 1970; ''Growing Up Black'' by L.E. Sissman, in the *New Yorker,* 11 July 1970; ''Jazzed Up,'' in the *Times Literary Supplement* (London), 30 July 1971; ''Artistry and Theme in Al Young's 'Snakes''' by Douglass Bolling, in *Negro American Literature Forum* (Terre Haute, Indiana), 8, 1974; ''Search for 'Soul Space': A Study of Al Young's 'Who Is Angelina?' and the Dimensions of Freedom'' by Elizabeth Schultz, in *The Afro-American Novel since 1960,* edited by Peter Bruck and Wolfgang Karrer, Amsterdam, Gruner, 1982; *The Writer's Mind: Interviews with American Authors* edited by Irv Broughton, Fayetteville, University of Arkansas Press, 1990; *Music As Medium for Maturation in Three Afro-American Novels* (dissertation) by Michael Charles Carroll, University of Nebraska, Lincoln, 1992.

Al Young comments:

I see my poetry as being essentially autobiographical in subject matter and detail, characterized by a marked personal and lyrical mysticism as well as a concern with social and spiritual problems of contemporary man in a technological environment that grows hourly more impersonal and unreal. My favorite themes are those of love, the infinite changeability of the world as well as its eternal changelessness, and the kind of meaning (both private and universal) that flowers out of everyday life. My influences in general have been black culture and popular speech (southern rural and urban U.S.) and music in particular (jazz, Afro-American folk and popular music, the music of Charles Mingus and John Coltrane, which defies categorization, Caribbean music of both English- and Spanish-speaking peoples), American Indian poetry and song, Hindu philosophy. Some poets I admire and have consciously learned from: Li Po, Nicolas Guillen, Rabindranath Tagore, the poetry of the Bible, Federico Garcia Lorca, Kenneth Patchen, Blaise Cendrars, early T.S. Eliot, Rimbaud, Brecht, LeRoi Jones, Mayakovsky, Denise Levertov, Léopold Senghor, Kenneth Rexroth, Cervantes, Diane Wakoski, and Nicanor Parra. Besides being as necessary as food, water, air, sunlight, and sleep, poetry is my way of celebrating spirit, in all of its infinite forms (charted and uncharted), as the central, unifying force in creation.

*   *   *

Al Young's 1976 book *Geography of the Near Past* contains five poems satirically representing ''art as a hustle.'' Purporting to be dictations by O.O. Gabugah, ''a militant advocate of the oral tradition,'' the poems are full of posturing and the rhetoric of racial politics. Technically facile, they ridicule not the literary method of poets like Gabugah but rather their dedication to the notion of art as weapon. Nothing could be further from the practice of Young himself, who calls poetry a

magic wafer you take
into your mouth
&
swallow for dear life

To Young poetry is a means ''to swim against / world current / knowing it to be as much a dream / as it is drama on the highest stage.'' The trick is to know that ''each universe is only / an ever-shifting sea / in the surfacing eyes of former fish.'' Inevitably, then, poetry for Young takes an autobiographical subject seeking authenticity in the flux of process.

A first step occurs in poems of controlled focus, where accidental details of ordinary life gain meaning by association. The sequence of a day's ordinary events becomes a love letter in ''Dear Arl,'' and in ''A Dance for Li Po'' bringing home groceries stimulates reflection on the variety of good places the poet has been over the years. The continuity of associative time converts memory into the principle of a fluid reality in ''The Song Turning Back into Itself.'' Here the images of circling in time and space lead into a statement of the power of song to create new versions of love and loneliness while also organizing past experience of those states. There is, too, the sense, shared with musicians, of the capacity of art to generate identity through the expression of a lyrical mysticism. It is appropriate that the sequence concludes with a jazz-inspired flyaway song in which the poet soars over rooftops.

As though for the time being his aesthetic needs no further statement, Young's poems in *Geography of the Near Past* return to detailing the small incident so that he can plumb it for significance. A series of poems on the cities of Manhattan, Boston, Providence, Detroit, and Denver relate moments of intense feeling, with the verse renouncing commentary or explication in favor of the re-creation of a moment's mood. The moments are brief, the mood without ambiguity, but there is no mistaking the effect. It is that of poetry performing its ancient function of discovery.

Young's writing reflects his ear for and practice as a jazz musician, and many of his poems attempt to translate blues and jazz into language. What he calls ''a laughter in the blood that dances'' in his collection *The Blues Don't Change* is manifested as spontaneity, freshness, and a kind of improvisational spirituality. Humor and light rhythms infuse his sensuous attention to words.

Young's grace and scope of subject have vastly increased with the progression of his career. In the nearly three hundred poems gathered in *Heaven: Collected Poems, 1956–1990,* the geography reaches from Detroit to Stockholm, Los Angeles, Mississippi, Poland, Paris, and Brooklyn. The first poems reflect Young's early concerns—''dilettante'' militias, jazz, and the basic distinctions between black and white experience: ''When white people speak of being uptight / they're talking about dissolution & deflection / but when black people say uptight / they mean everything's all right.'' The unlimited range of Young's heart shows through in every broad and affectionate gesture he makes toward the world. For him the way through barriers and rejections born of difference is by love and acceptance: ''Nor must you let the great haters / of our time /

rattle in your heart.'' Young claims as influences a wildly diverse group, including Li Po, Nijinsky, Lorca, Mayakovsky, Frank O'Hara, and Amiri Baraka (LeRoi Jones). Through great attachments and confluences this poet has established a generous voice of the collective that shines with rhythm and expanse.

—John M. Reilly and Martha Sutro

YOUNG, David (Pollock)

Nationality: American. **Born:** Davenport, Iowa, 14 December 1936. **Education:** Carleton College, Northfield, Minnesota, B.A. 1958; Yale University, New Haven, Connecticut, M.A. 1959, Ph.D. 1965. **Family:** Married 1) Chloe Hamilton in 1963 (died 1985), one daughter and one son; 2) Georgia Newman in 1989. **Career:** Instructor, 1961–65, assistant professor, 1965–69, associate professor, 1969–73, since 1973 professor of English, and since 1986 Longman Professor, Oberlin College, Ohio. Since 1969 editor, *Field: Contemporary Poetry and Poetics,* Oberlin. Co-owner, Triskelion Press, Oberlin. **Awards:** Tane award (Massachusetts Review), 1965; National Endowment for the Arts grant, 1967, and fellowship, 1981; International Poetry Forum United States award, 1968; Guggenheim fellowship, 1978; Ohio State University Press/The Journal award, 1994. **Address:** Oberlin College, Department of English, Rice Hall, Oberlin, Ohio 44074, U.S.A.

PUBLICATIONS

Poetry

Sweating Out the Winter. Pittsburgh, University of Pittsburgh Press, 1969.
Thoughts of Chairman Mao. Oberlin, Ohio, Triskelion Press, 1970.
Boxcars. New York, Ecco Press, 1973.
Work Lights: Thirty-Two Prose Poems. Cleveland, Cleveland State Poetry Center, 1977.
The Names of a Hare in English. Pittsburgh, University of Pittsburgh Press, 1979.
Foraging. Middletown, Connecticut, Wesleyan University Press, 1986.
Earthshine. Middletown, Connecticut, Wesleyan University Press, 1988.
The Planet on the Desk: Selected and New Poems, 1960–1990. Middletown, Connecticut, Wesleyan University Press, 1991.
Night Thoughts and Henry Vaughan. Columbus, Ohio State University Press, 1994.
At the White Window. Columbus, Ohio State University Press, 2000.

Other

Something of Great Constancy: The Art of ''A Midsummer Night's Dream.'' New Haven, Connecticut, Yale University Press, 1966.
The Heart's Forest: A Study of Shakespeare's Pastoral Plays. New Haven, Connecticut, Yale University Press, 1972.
Troubled Mirror: A Study of Yeats's ''The Tower.'' Iowa City, University of Iowa Press, 1987.

The Action to the Word: Structure and Style in Shakespearean Tragedy. New Haven, Connecticut, Yale University Press, 1990.
Seasoning: A Poet's Year: With Seasonal Recipes. Columbus, Ohio State University Press, 1999.

Editor, *Twentieth Century Interpretations of "Henry IV, Part Two:" A Collection of Critical Essays.* Englewood Cliffs, New Jersey, Prentice Hall, 1968.
Editor, with Stuart Friebert, *A Field Guide to Contemporary Poetry and Poetics.* New York, Longman, 1980; revised edition, Oberlin, Ohio, Oberlin College Press, 1997.
Editor, with Stuart Friebert, *The Longman Anthology of Contemporary American Poetry, 1950–1980.* New York, Longman, 1983; revised edition, 1989.
Editor, with Keith Hollaman, *Magical Realist Fiction.* New York, Longman, 1984.
Editor and Translator, *The Dimension of the Present Moment: Essays,* by Miroslav Holub. London, Faber, 1990.
Editor, with Stuart Friebert, *Models of the Universe: An Anthology of the Prose Poem.* Oberlin, Ohio, Oberlin College Press, 1995.

Translator, *Six Poems from Wang Wet.* Oberlin, Ohio, Triskelion Press, 1969.
Translator, *Magic Strings: Nine Poems from Li Ho.* Oberlin, Ohio, Pocket Pal Press, 1976.
Translator, *Duino Elegies,* by Rainer Maria Rilke. New York, Norton, 1978.
Translator, *Wang Wei, Li Po, Tu Fu, Li Ho: Four T'ang Poets.* Oberlin, Ohio, Oberlin College, 1980; revised edition, as *Five T'ang Poets: Wang Wei, Li Po, Tu Fu, Li Ho, Li Shing-yin,* 1990.
Translator, with Stuart Friebert and David Walker, *Valuable Nail: Selected Poems,* by Günter Eich. Oberlin, Ohio, Oberlin College, 1981.
Translator, with Dana Hábová, *Interferon: or, On Theater,* by Miroslav Holub. Oberlin, Ohio, Oberlin College, 1982.
Translator, *Sonnets to Orpheus,* by Rainer Maria Rilke. Middletown, Connecticut, Wesleyan University Press, 1987.
Translator, *The Heights of Macchu Picchu,* by Pablo Neruda. N.p., Songs Before Zero Press, 1987.
Translator, with Dana Hábová, *Vanishing Lung Syndrome,* by Miroslav Holub. London, Faber, and Oberlin, Ohio, Oberlin College, 1990.
Translator, *Selected Poems of Rainer Maria Rilke: The Book of Fresh Beginnings.* Oberlin, Ohio, Oberlin College Press, 1994.
Translator, with Jiann I. Lin, *The Clouds Float North: The Complete Poems of Yu Xuanji.* Middletown, Conneticut, Wesleyan University Press, 1998.

*

David Young comments:

My collections of poetry, I find, tend to be more and more unified by recurrent figures and themes. Since I depend very much on what is called "inspiration" in writing my poetry, it is gratifying to be able to shape the materials presented to me in that fashion into larger wholes that benefit from mirroring and echoing. *Foraging* is filled with images of mushrooms (and mushroom hunting, a hobby of mine) and ghosts. Both of these leading motifs relate to the way the imagination reuses and recycles what is lost, decayed, or difficult to accept. *Earthshine* is four poems, two long and two short, but really all one integrated text, the most unified book I have been able to manage.

*　　*　　*

David Young is a poet in the middle tradition. Neither conservative nor avant-garde, he writes in a style both modest and accomplished and addresses the great, familiar themes: death, history, desire, memory, the pressure of reality, the seductions of language, the claims of the imagination. A Shakespeare scholar, an editor of several anthologies and of the prominent journal *Field,* and a translator of Rilke, Miroslav Holub, Günter Eich, and several Chinese poets, Young displays his erudition only subtly. His many allusions are not obtrusive, and the poems do not depend on them. His important poems unite emotion and intellect, showing how feeling can be embedded in ideas and ideas in feeling and how both depend on the visible world.

Young's work has developed profoundly during his career. His lines have gradually become more subtle and gracious, his language more balanced and eloquent, his subject matter denser and more important. His first book, *Sweating Out the Winter,* is uneven. Keen images sometimes float on poems that do not cohere. A clear, rather plain diction and a spare line are often inappropriately wedded to spurious surrealism or youthful silliness. The worst poem asks, "Will Tarzan swing in time / down on his tall vine / to knock the nasty priest . . . ?" We hope so, for "crocodiles slaver / lying in wait." The poem is about the relationship between art and reality, but in this case Young has not found the mise-en-scène in which to embed his theoretical concerns. But other poems in the same collection foreshadow the patient and tender notation that grounds ideas in Young's later work.

In his second collection, *Boxcars,* Young often tries the confines of an even smaller, plainer poem, derived in part from William Stafford. Some of these are quietly effective. Among the best is "Ohio," which defines human limitation in terms of landscape:

Looking across a field
at a stand of trees
—more than a windbreak
less than a forest—
is pretty much all
the view we have

Even so, the poem concludes that "there's a lot to see"; you could "sit all day" with "that view before you." Other poems in the volume seem strained and dated, however. There are still remnants of surrealism, the wrong mode for this poet. An example is a poem about the body as a "whole world," where there are "gangsters in the stomach," "babies screaming in the back," and "a big party in the groin," to which, fortunately, the reader is "not invited."

When they are not innate, surrealistic gestures can be a cover for the failure to observe accurately. Experimental flings can be a substitute for hard thought. But during the 1980s Young began to put his love for the play of language in the service of serious pleasure. Surprise becomes a necessity of the poem, not an escapade, as surface and substance unite.

Young's major treatise on the relations of language and meaning is the long title poem of *The Names of a Hare in English.* It opens with a thirteenth-century poem of the same title that lists more than seventy names for the hare. The old text instigates a brilliant meditation on "language, that burrow, warren, camouflage" that will "deceive you and survive you." Filled with the names of plants, animals, and stars, the poem proposes that "names bind us to strange forms of life." There are moments when these "baskets of epithets spilled down the page" become "a path to the heart."

Among Young's other important poems is "Mesa Verde," from *Foraging*. The setting is Chaco Canyon in New Mexico. Young's speaker longs to be inhabited by the past, to be entered by the dead and revivified by their presence. He calls on Anasazi, a Pueblo name for "the ancients":

> Climb into me, Anasazi,
> take my tongue and language,
> tell how you came to farm the corn,
> hoarding the snow-melt, learned
> to be weavers, potters, masons
> in the huge American daylight . . .

The voice of Anasazi enters the poem to inscribe the history of the Pueblo people, who can now be observed only in the museum where

> smaller than hummingbirds
> these people kneel and climb in little models
> weaving their tiny baskets
> hoarding their dollhouse ears of corn.

Young toys with the idea that we all "crouch below some diorama / while sunlight moves across a mesa . . ." The poem closes as "the hummingbird comes to rest, midair, / and the mind meshes with other minds / lost patterns of thought that hang / over the mesas, across the hillsides," while the sun "carries the day away / through dry and shining air."

Young's mature work is consistently fine. He seems to have found what he needs: luxurious syntax, mellow language, a firm yet fluid landscape, humility, authenticity, dignity.

—Jane Somerville

Z

ZEPHANIAH, Benjamin

Nationality: British. **Born:** Birmingham, in 1958; grew up in Jamaica. **Family:** Married in 1990. **Career:** Performer. **Awards:** Honorary doctorates: University of North London, 1998; University of West of England, 1999. **Agent:** Sandra Boyce Management, 1 Kingsway House, Albion Road, London N16 0TA, England.

PUBLICATIONS

Poetry

Pen Rhythm. London, Page One, 1980.
The Dread Affair: Collected Poems. London, Arena, 1985.
City Psalms. Newcastle upon Tyne, Bloodaxe, 1992.
Talking Turkeys (for children). London, Viking/Penguin, 1994.
Out of the Night. Gloucester, New Clarion Press, 1994.
Funky Chickens (for children). London, Puffin/Penguin, 1996.
Propa Propaganda. Newcastle upon Tyne, Bloodaxe, 1996.
School's Out. Edinburgh, AK Press, 1997.

Recordings: *Dub Ranting,* Radical Wallpaper, 1982; *Rasta,* Upright, 1983; *Big Boy Don't Make Girls Cry,* Upright, 1984; *Free South Africa/Stop de War,* Upright, 1986; *Us and Dem,* Mango, 1990; *Crisis,* Working Playtime, 1992; *Back to Roots,* Acid Jazz, 1995; *Belly of de Beast,* Ariwa, 1996; *Dancing Tribes* (with Back to Base), MP Records, 1999.

Plays

Playing the Right Tune (produced London, 1985).
Job Rocking (produced London, 1987).
Streetwise (produced London, 1990).

Radio Plays: *Hurricane Dub,* 1989; *Our Teachers Gone Crazy,* 1990.

Television Play: *Dread Poets Society,* 1991.

Novels

Face. London, Bloomsbury, 1999.

Other

Ina Liverpool. Liverpool, African Arts Collective, n.d.
Rasta Time in Palestine. Liverpool, Shakti, 1990.

Editor, *The Bloomsbury Book of Love Poems.* London, Bloomsbury, 1999.

*

Critical Study: ''Chanting down Babylon: Three Rastafarian Dub Poets'' by Darren J. Middleton, in *'This Is How We Flow': Rhythm in*

Black Cultures, edited by Angela M.S. Nelson, Columbia, University of South Carolina Press, 1999.

Theatrical Activities: Actor: **Film**—*Didn't You Kill My Brother?,* 1987; *Farendg,* 1989; *Dread Poets Society,* 1991.

Benjamin Zephaniah comments:

Zephaniah is a great believer in oral poetry. He is continually touring, taking his poetry to people who do not have books readily available and to countries where the illiteracy rate is high. His work is mainly political or social commentary and can go to both extremes, from humorous to serious drama. Zephaniah also believes that it is not good enough for one to stand on stage proclaiming one's ideas but that the artist must work with organizations to make those ideas a reality.

Zephaniah's motto is Increase the peace by any means necessary.

* * *

Benjamin Zephaniah is black, red, and dread. His themes are drawn from the news, from the front pages, from the pubs and streets, and from the black British politics of today. In a very old-fashioned way, he is a poet fighting injustice with words, and what is the point of having a poet if he tells the stories just as you or I would have told them?

Zephaniah came from Jamaica by way of Handsworth Green in Birmingham. His childhood has already become the subject of a mythology of its own; one newspaper had his family too poor to afford a comb so that they used a fork instead. He was composing and performing poetry before he could read and write effectively, and he still performs everything from memory. I remember that, when I asked him for a copy of his ''Green Poem,'' Zephaniah said that he did not have a copy and that if I wanted one I would have to take it down from dictation. After being told off for spelling ''dis,'' ''dem,'' and ''dat'' with ''th,'' I got the hang of it. The rhythm solves it.

It is not easy for Zephaniah to reach an audience among which his words will strike new chords. Over the years he has become a regular performer at literature festivals up and down the country, but the audiences in these places are typically white and middle class. Although they enjoy the business of a comic poet painting the vices and follies of humankind, they do not get near an understanding of the roots of the poetry or the heart of the man. Where the audiences do intuit what he means—the people in the pubs and clubs of the inner cities, the South Wales valleys, the streets of Liverpool—they do not laugh from the heart at ''Dis Policeman Keeps on Kicking Me to Death.'' Theirs is a laugh of empathy with bits on the miners' strike, urban riots, and the poll tax, with Thatcherism wrapped up in it, a different laugh from the one at the Cheltenham Literature Festival.

Younger audiences sometimes miss a dimension of Zephaniah's work. Able to enjoy the flow of language in his performances, they do not, however, always have a mature grasp of the issues involved. For some time he has addressed children's audiences directly and for the purpose of entertaining them. The publication of *Talking Turkeys* in 1994 proved to be a great success, with immediate requests for more poetry for children, which, as in the way of the world, adults love too.

It is often assumed that establishment poets do not rate Zephaniah seriously, but I am not sure that this is true. They have at least heard of him, even though he may not have heard of them. There is a view sometimes whispered that his poems do not work on paper. I think it is true that one needs to know his speech patterns and his voice before the rhythms become plain in reading the work. But I can think of dozens of poets whose work only became clear to me once I had heard them reading it. In the late 1980s Zephaniah was nominated but not finally accepted for honorary chairs in poetry at both Oxford and Cambridge, losing out to the worthy Seamus Heaney in one case. At best he suspects that snobbery about the properness of his poetry is to blame. At worst, who knows?

—R.T. Mole

ZIMMER, Paul (Jerome)

Nationality: American. **Born:** Canton, Ohio, 18 September 1934. **Education:** Kent State University, Kent, Ohio, 1952–53, 1956–59, B.A. 1968. **Military Service:** U.S. Army, 1954–55. **Family:** Married Suzanne Koklauner in 1959; one daughter and one son. **Career:** Macy's book department manager, San Francisco, 1961–63; manager, San Francisco News Company, 1963–65; manager, UCLA Bookstore, Los Angeles, 1965–67; associate director, University of Pittsburgh Press, and editor, Pitt Poetry series, 1967–78; director, University of Georgia Press, Athens, 1978–84; director, University of Iowa Press, Iowa City, 1984–97. Poet-in-residence, Chico State College, California, spring 1970. **Awards:** Borestone Mountain award, 1971; National Endowment for the Arts grant, 1974, 1982; Helen Bullis memorial award (*Poetry Northwest*), 1975; Pushcart prize, 1977, 1981; American Academy award, 1985. **Address:** R.R. 1, Box 108, Soldiers Grove, Wisconsin 54655–9702, U.S.A.

PUBLICATIONS

Poetry

A Seed on the Wind. Privately printed, 1960.
The Ribs of Death. New York, October House, 1967.
The Republic of Many Voices. New York, October House, 1969.
The Zimmer Poems. Washington, D.C., Dryad Press, 1976.
With Wanda: Town and Country Poems. Washington, D.C., Dryad Press, 1980.
The Ancient Wars. Pittsburgh, Slow Loris Press, 1981.
Earthbound Zimmer. Milton, Massachusetts, Chowder, 1983.
Family Reunion: Selected and New Poems. Pittsburgh, University of Pittsburgh Press, 1983.
Big Blue Train. Fayetteville, University of Arkansas Press, 1983.
The American Zimmer. Athens, Georgia, Night Owl Press, 1984.
Live with Animals. Bristol, Rhode Island, Ampersand Press, 1987.
The Great Bird of Love. Urbana, University of Illinois Press, 1989.
Crossing to Sunlight: Selected Poems. Athens, University of Georgia Press, 1996.

*

Critical Studies: By Hayden Carruth, in *Hudson Review* (New York), summer 1968; by Robert Boyers, in *Partisan Review* (New Brunswick, New Jersey), 1969; by James Den Boer, in *Voyages* (Washington, D.C.), spring 1970; by the author, in *American Poets in 1976,* edited by William Heyen, Indianapolis, Bobbs Merrill, 1976, and in *Gravida* (New York), 1979; *Zimmer As Poet, Poet As Zimmer* edited by Jan Susina, Houston, Texas, Ford Brown, 1986; in *The Writer's Mind: Interviews with American Authors,* edited by Irv Broughton, Fayetteville, University of Arkansas Press, 1990; "The Atomic Test Poems of Paul Zimmer" by John Gery, in *War, Literature, and the Arts* (U.S. Air Force Academy, Colorado), 6(1), spring-summer 1994; "Enactments of Desire" by Floyd Collins, in *Gettysburg Review* (Gettysburg, Pennsylvania), 10(2), summer 1997.

Paul Zimmer comments:

I have been working on poems for close to four decades now. As I age, I find it increasingly difficult to make coherent general statements about my work, except that I am very happy that I have been able to continue writing poetry.

It is always important for a poet to be able to consider most recent writing to be their best and most mature work. I continue to claim this, and I find it satisfying that I can still feel this way. Of course I have more experience; thus there seems to be less concoction, less nervous humor, more substance, more confidence in the work.

It is not easy to be a poet in this busy and indifferent world. I am grateful for my career, but, like most poets, I wish I had more time to devote to the work.

*   *   *

Paul Zimmer is quite an interesting manifestation of what happens to an American poet who feels the weight of Walt Whitman's gift, the freedom to sing the song of the self. This ingenious poet clearly feels more comfortable with a mask than the pure voice of self. The quotation from Thomas Hardy beginning his *Family Reunion: Selected and New Poems* invokes a literary tradition quite different from the one an American poet must grapple with. And clearly he longs for a more civilized garden, containing clothed rather than naked selves. In creating the "Zimmer Poems," along with another series, the "Wanda Poems," he has found a way of distancing himself by existing only in the third person, as in "Zimmer in Grade School":

But I could never hide anything. . . .

Even now
When I hide behind elaborate masks
It is always known that I am Zimmer.

As one reads through the Zimmer poems, it seems that if there is any sense of self in the poems it is a sense of a failed human, of someone humiliated constantly and almost without anything to brag about or praise. Conversely, Wanda, of the Wanda poems, is someone beautiful and other for the Zimmer persona to love.

Zimmer is the figure we look for. If he is the autobiographical Paul Zimmer, he is also a cartoon. And it is not always clear if Zimmer is a cartoon because all people are cartoons, or if it is because Zimmer himself is so much more absurd than other men. There is a gesture of contempt for the art of poetry itself when this confusion occurs, and it becomes a serious reminder that the poet, Paul Zimmer, has invented the Zimmer poems not out of self-disgust but out of frustration with a poetic tradition he does not wholly embrace. His satire of Whitman in "Leaves of Zimmer" makes this clear:

You Zimmer! Whimpering, heavy, mumbling, lewd;
Does America sing you a sad song?
It is a trifle! Resign yourself!
Nothing is without flaw.
Confess that you feel small buds unclutching again!
Confess that the rich sod turns up to you always as
  your lover!
By God! Accept nothing less than this for affection:
The stars dangling like green apples on the distant peaks;
The sea foam combing itself through rocks;
No foofoo can strip you of this!
No mountebanks can take this away!
If one is deprived then all are deprived;
America will love us all or it will not love.

There is an abrasive self-hatred apparent in many of the Zimmer poems that is not Paul Zimmer hating Paul Zimmer but rather the poet Paul Zimmer chafing and angry, hating an unwanted poetic tradition he is so much a part of that he cannot cast it off. His resolution, the invention of the Zimmer poems, is an ingenious one, although its success is not complete. Often when he seems most trapped, he writes himself imaginatively into another world, pleasing the reader with his wit just as the whining Zimmer was starting to irritate him. This happens, for example, in ''Zimmer Imagines Heaven'':

I sit with Joseph Conrad in Monet's garden.
We are listening to Yeats chant his poems,
A breeze stirs through Thomas Hardy's moustache,
John Skelton has gone to the house for beer,
Wanda Landowska lightly fingers a clavichord . . .

Though in this poem the poet starts with the preferred world of European artists, he ends the poem with Alice B. Toklas serving him a meal after he has listened with pleasure to some American poetry along with a play by Shakespeare. One wishes that Zimmer did not hate his American self so much, but the poet, Paul Zimmer, has created quite an interesting embroidery out of his struggle.

—Diane Wakoski

ZWICKY, (Julia) Fay

Nationality: Australian. **Born:** Julia Fay Rosefield, Melbourne, 4 July 1933. **Education:** University of Melbourne, 1950–54, B.A. (honors). **Family:** Married 1) Karl Zwicky in 1957 (divorced), one son and one daughter; 2) James Mackie in 1990 (divorced). **Career:** Concert pianist, 1950–65; senior lecturer in English, University of Western Australia, Perth, 1972–87. Member of literature board, Australia Council, Sydney, 1978–81; poetry editor, *Westerly,* Perth, 1974–83 and 1993–98, and *Patterns,* Fremantle, 1974–83; associate editor, since 1988, *Overland,* Melbourne, and since 1989, *Southerly,* Sydney. **Awards:** New South Wales Premier's award, 1982; Western Australian Literary award, for nonfiction, 1987; Western Australian Premier's award for poetry, 1991, 1999. **Agent:** Australian Literary Management, 2A Armstrong Street, Middle Park, Victoria 3206. **Address:** 30 Goldsmith Road, Claremont, Western Australia 6010, Australia.

PUBLICATIONS

Poetry

Isaac Babel's Fiddle. Adelaide, Maximus, 1975.
Kaddish and Other Poems. St. Lucia, University of Queensland Press, 1982.
Ask Me. St. Lucia, University of Queensland Press, 1990.
A Touch of Ginger, with Dennis Haskell. Applecross, Folio, 1991.
Poems 1970–1992. St. Lucia, University of Queensland Press, 1993.
The Gatekeeper's Wife. Sydney, Brandl and Schlesinger, 1997.

Short Stories

Hostages. Fremantle, Western Australia, Fremantle Arts Centre Press, 1983.

Other

The Lyre in the Pawnshop: Essays on Literature and Survival 1974–1984. Nedlands, University of Western Australia Press, 1986.

Editor, *Quarry: A Selection of Western Australian Poetry.* Fremantle, Western Australia, Fremantle Arts Centre Press, 1981.
Editor, *Journeys: Judith Wright, Rosemary Dobson, Gwen Harwood, Dorothy Hewett.* Melbourne, Sisters, 1982.
Editor, *Procession: Youngstreet Poets Three.* Sydney, Hale and Iremonger, 1987.

*

Critical Studies: ''Finding a Voice in 'This Fiercely Fathered and Unmothered World': The Poetry of Fay Zwicky'' by Joan Kirby, in *Poetry and Gender,* edited by David Brooks and Brenda Walker, St. Lucia, University of Queensland Press, 1989; ''Fay Zwicky: The Poet As Moralist'' by Ivor Indyk, and ''On the Shifting Sands of Our Experience: Fay Zwicky's Poetry'' by Elsa Linguanti, both in *Southerly* (Sydney), 54(3), September 1994; in *In Other Words: Interviews with Australian Poets,* by Barbara Williams, Amsterdam, Rodopi, 1998.

Fay Zwicky comments:

Certain themes run with obdurate consistency through the three collections spanning a period of twenty years or so. Chief among these is probably an affirmation of the human speaking voice, often discerned in opposition to the oppressive silence of an inarticulate culture.

Some poems in the first book, *Isaac Babel's Fiddle,* weave a densely textured mythic structure around the settlement in Australia of my Jewish ancestors in the middle of the nineteenth century. The sense of exile implicit in the migrant assimilation process is linked with an awareness of being bound to a diminishing past while remaining ambiguously ironic about the preservation of constraining traditions. Under masks and a variety of voices, the poems explore the lot of the traditionally silent female who is also a member of an ethnic minority group and thus doubly sentenced.

Finding a voice also informs the looser lines of poems in *Kaddish and Other Poems.* These have more breathing space, take more risks with form, and, as in the title poem with its four distinctively symphonic movements, take their shape from musical models.

Several poems set up an argument either as internal monologue or as exploration of traditional mythological characters. In the ''Ark Voices'' sequence a capricious God is questioned about survival, its penalties and obligations. Other poems are concerned with identity in a contemporary context and the artist's ambiguous role in keeping faith with the history of human suffering in a heedless society.

The third collection, *Ask Me,* ranges further afield with poems written after visits to China, India, and America. Several deal with experiences as a hospice worker, and two long elegies provide a climax to the growing sense of life's fragility. The speaking voice has become less urgent, the irony less lacerating. Although there are fewer masks and ''literary'' allusions, a more colloquial emphasis, these poems continue to articulate the dimensions of a vision apparent in earlier work questioning the limits of speech and silence.

*   *   *

Fay Zwicky's poetry might well take as its epigraph the line from fellow musician-poet Gwen Harwood that asserts, ''a fire-talented tongue will choose its truth.'' It will also choose its mode of telling, and Zwicky's sometimes fierce truths are diversely told—confrontationally, obliquely, passionately, wittily, astringently, compassionately. *Ask Me,* the title of her 1990 collection, characteristically challenges the indifferent shrug of ''Don't ask me,'' declaring an allegiance to engagement, a preparedness to answer. As shown in ''In Memory of Vincent Buckley,'' Zwicky's humanist commitment to communication informs the value that she places on poetry's power to celebrate

those blessed moments of the ordinary,
rarer than ornaments of beaten gold and twice as rare
to those intransigent for truth amid imposture.

The commitment to communication has also informed Zwicky's important critical writings. ''Language,'' she has argued, ''is the product of a deep-rooted web of potential for empathy between people, a shared structure.'' The disintegration of language and of the social fabric go together, leaving those unwilling or unable to resist with ''the despair and frustration of being unable to communicate or to love, the impotence of refusing responsibility for the word.'' Writers must ''put in a word for life,'' the speaker in ''Lot's Wife (Take 18)'' declares, while the entire volume of *Kaddish* has as its basis that idea that to fail to speak is to fail to love. *Kaddish* opens with a ritual prayer for Zwicky's dead father in which the poet finally voices and memorializes a contentious love, and it closes with a ritualized plea to be forgiven for the poems that have died ''under each inert hour of my silence . . . the many I have frozen with irony.''

To place a negative value on irony is to challenge the contemporary critical wisdom of Zwicky's academic education, but then much of her work has challenged assumptions prevalent in the discursive constructions of both Australian and female identity. ''Speeches and Silences,'' her 1983 *Quadrant* essay, begins by questioning in general the valorization of silence as reaching beyond words to ''ineffable purity of vision'' before proceeding to argue that the exaltation of strong, silent stoicism puts Australians at particular at risk of being left ''wordless / In a dumb landscape.'' This, she argues, is particularly oppressive for women, because stoic silence is construed as a masculine virtue, ''leaving the female to flounder without the longed-for verbal signposts needed for the articulation of feeling.''

Like many contemporary women poets, Zwicky has raided the world of patriarchal myth in order to provide a voice for the silent or to question the distribution of power. Probably her greatest achievement in the mythic mode lies in the wonderfully sensuous, pragmatic, and exuberant pathos of the voices with which Mrs. Noah and the animals address God in ''Ark Voices.'' Yet in her very articulation of what it means to be ''speechless and unspoken to,'' her refusal to reciprocate the language of tyranny, and her insistence on compassion, Mrs. Noah achieves a speaking presence capable of being translated into the joyful enumerator of names in ''Southern Spell.'' Certainly Zwicky herself has managed to find words for a long-term, and by no means simple, engagement with her personal and cultural heritage, with the love she can deny neither her Jewish father nor the patriarchs of Western thought and religion, and through this engagement she has come to the kind of crone's wisdom that illuminates *The Gatekeeper's Wife.* For if the ego demands speech, the communicative life demands that we be able to listen, and having listened, the poet has obligations to the kind of commemorative contract (''Remember me'' . . . ''I do / I will'') that Zwicky accepts as the conclusion of her elegy ''For Jim.''

Less formal in mode than *Kaddish,* Zwicky's later elegies are vulnerable to the weight of time. It is not only the lost lover who was her first husband who is remembered in ''Akibat'' but also the lost self-as-bride, the lost time and (Indonesian) place of love's beginning. But if loss is something that cannot be denied by one ''intransigent for truth,'' it is also something not merely balanced against, but inextricably intermingled with, happiness, with the ''earth's sweet mulch'' that is celebrated in ''Learning,'' the autobiographical poem at the heart of *The Gatekeeper's Wife.* It is not nostalgia that rules as this ''teacher'' looks to learn afresh

Without adjectives to reckon how
verbs to work out why
nouns to know what
learning the new heart's tenses,
surprises concordances, and how O
how not to fear the fatherless dark.

—Jennifer Strauss

ZWICKY, Jan

Nationality: Canadian. **Born:** Calgary, Alberta, 10 May 1955. **Education:** University of Calgary, Alberta, 1972–76, B.A. 1976; University of Toronto, Ontario, 1976–81, M.A. 1977, Ph.D. 1981. **Career:** Variously employed as musician and seasonal instructor in philosophy at such institutions as Princeton University, University of Western Ontario, and University of Alberta. Since 1996 associate professor of philosophy, University of Victoria. **Awards:** Governor General's award, 1999.

PUBLICATIONS

Poetry

Where Have We Been. London, Ontario, Brick Books, 1982.
Wittgenstein Elegies. London, Ontario, Brick Books, 1986.
The New Room. Toronto, Coach House Press, 1989.

Lyric Philosophy. Toronto, University of Toronto Press, 1992.
Songs for Relinquishing the Earth. London, Ontario, Brick Books, 1998.

*

Critical Studies: ''Scaffoldings of Weary Words: Jan Zwicky's 'Wittgenstein Elegies''' by John Harris, in *Essays on Canadian Writing* (Toronto), 37, spring 1989; by J. Bruin, in *History of European Ideas,* 18(6), 1994; by Alex Neill, in *Journal of Aesthetics and Art Criticism,* 52(3), summer 1994.

*   *   *

Although many of her concerns have remained constant, Jan Zwicky's style has evolved in specificity and precision since her early work. Zwicky's imagery has always been unshowy and effective, but a comparison between ''After Summer,'' from *Where Have We Been,* and ''Recovery,'' from *Songs for Relinquishing the Earth,* shows how the language has been heightened and tightened:

Poised between summer's slack heat
and the corded knot of winter's passion, even
love lies on us lightly, and with gentleness.
High clouds at sunset. Single leaves
on still water.

And when at last grief has dried you out, nearly
weightless, like a little bone, one day,
no reason in particular, the world decides to tug:
twinge under the breastbone, the sudden thought
you might stand up, walk to the door and
keep on going . . .

The context within which the poems are presented has changed as well. As a book, *Where Have We Been* lacks many of the elements that often accompany poetry collections; there are no dedications, acknowledgments, or other peripheral personal material. But *Songs for Relinquishing the Earth* originated as a self-crafted book, each copy sewn by hand for a reader in response to an individual request. Word of mouth led to formal publication, and the work is dedicated to Zwicky's fellow poet Don McKay.

From beginning to end, Zwicky likes to site her reflections in gardens and open spaces amid the flight of birds and the ebb and flow of weather and the seasons. Consistent, too, has been her preoccupation with music and philosophy. The latter comes to the fore in *Wittgenstein Elegies,* whose point of departure is Wittgenstein's *Philosophical Remarks* (1930), which Zwicky notes was ''an attempt to demonstrate that all things of genuine value utterly superseded the world of 'facts.''' Wittgenstein has been misunderstood, she asserts. He did not in fact banish transcendence from the realm of the discussable, only put it in its proper place. What is clear is that Zwicky finds Wittgenstein's gnomic utterances to be poetically stimulating, just as Martin Heidegger's very different style has proved to be suggestive for other poets.

Zwicky humanizes Wittgenstein by interweaving his life and tragedies with those of another Austrian, the great expressionist poet Georg Trakl. In doing so, she manipulates format, quoting from both in italicized passages and placing material in the left margin to, as she says, ''give some indication of the play of voices among Wittgenstein's

public personae, Trakl, Wittgenstein's interior monologue, and the narrator.'' In ''The Death of Georg Trakl'' she says,

The lovely logic, winter mornings with sunshine
Unrecoverable, buried in the background
Medium of understanding hidden
Nothing can be explained or deduced
It is all before us.

From the relatively abstract language of *Wittgenstein Elegies,* Zwicky moves into the imagistic music of *The New Room.* Among a few long poems in sections, including ''Seven Elegies: Robert William Zwicky (1927–1987),'' there are fine lyrics such as ''Practising Bach,'' in which she observes

One cardinal, sweet against the snow
as candy, as a long-stemmed rose.
But it is sparrows who
are brown as bread, empty the feeder
hourly, divest us of those seeds:
smooth, striped,
unique and numberless as days.

Zwicky's intelligence and syntactic variety combine in her best book to date, *Songs for Relinquishing the Earth.* Her dual interests in music and philosophy complement each other here, and many of the poems involve both, including a sequence about the parallel lives of Bruckner and Kant. Composers—Brahms, Bartók, Hindemith—interpret the world for her. In ''Beethoven: Op. 127, Adagio'' we hear

A-flat: cream's richness,
    like a good field in April, a blackness
        you wanted to eat,

or in August, the string's breath thick
    with heat and dust, like
        being able to breathe weight . . .

In the note on Hindemith's *Trauermusik* that ends the book, Zwicky says that the composition's lack of a leading note in its closing measures ''tells us, in the relinquishing that is the end of mourning, we must pass through—as through a ghost, that absence in ourselves.'' But one product of emerging on the other side is perception, precarious but necessary. In ''March Nineteenth'' from *The New Room* she calls it

. . . this fragile window
opening and opening
on small unsteady stars.

—Fraser Sutherland

NOTES ON ADVISERS AND CONTRIBUTORS

ABSE, Dannie. See his own entry. **Essay:** Gjertrud Schnackenberg

ACKERSON, Duane. Freelance writer. Former editor, *The Dragonfly* magazine. Author of several verse pamphlets, including *UA Flight to Chicago*, 1971, *Inventory*, 1971, *Old Movie House*, 1972, *Weathering*, 1974, *The Eggplant*, 1977, and *The Bird at the End of the Universe*, 1997, as well as fiction in magazines and anthologies. Editor of anthologies of poetry. **Essays:** Ai; Jimmy Santiago Baca; Madeline DeFrees; Roland Flint; David Jaffin; Tom McKeown; David St. John; Keith Wilson.

ADCOCK, Fleur. See her own entry. **Essay:** Dabney Stuart.

AGUERO, Kathleen. Associate professor of freshman composition, Pine Manor College, Chestnut Hill, Massachusetts. Author of *Thirsty Day*, 1977, and *The Real Weather*, 1987. Editor of *Critical Challenges in Contemporary American Poetry* (with Marie Harris), 1987, *Ear to the Ground: An Anthology of Contemporary American Poetry* (with Harris), 1989, and *Daily Fare: Essays from the Multicultural Experience*, 1993. **Essays:** Forrest Gander; Ellen Bryant Voigt.

AITCHISON, James. See his own entry. **Essay:** Maurice Lindsay.

ALBINSKI, Nan Bowman. Senior research associate, A-NZ Studies Center, Pennsylvania State University, University Park. Author of *Women's Utopias in British and American Fiction*, 1988, and numerous articles on utopian, Australian, and New Zealand fiction. **Essays:** Dorothy Hewett; Jannifer Maiden; Cilla McQueen; Jennifer Strauss; Alan Wearne; Judith Wright.

ALLEN, Donald. Editor-in-chief, Grey Fox Press, Bolinas, California. Former editor (1957-59), with Barney Rosset, and West Coast editor (1960-70), *The Evergreen Review*. Editor of the anthologies *The New American Poetry 1945-60*, 1960, *New American Story*, 1965, *New Writing in the U.S.A.* (with Robert Creeley), 1967, *Poetics of the New American Poetry*, 1973, and *The Postmoderns* (with George F. Butterick), 1982. Editor or translator of works by Lorca, Ionesco, Olson, Lew Welch, Kerouac, Dorn, Creeley, Ginsberg, and Frank O'Hara.

ANDRE, Michael. Executive director, Unmuzzled Ox Books and Magazine, New York. Author of the poetry books *Get Serious, My Regrets, Studying the Ground for Holes, Letters Home, Jabbing the Ass Hole Is High Comedy,* and *It as It.* Also author of *The Poets' Encyclopedia* and articles in *Art News* and *Village Voice.* **Essays:** Bill Bissett; Maxine Chernoff; Gene Fowler.

ARNOLD, Stephen H. Professor emeritus and former chair, Department of Comparative and Film Studies, University of Alberta. Former editor of *African Literature Association Bulletin.* Author of *Critical Perspectives on Mongo Beti*, 1998. **Essay:** Niyi Osundare.

AUGUSTINE, Jane. Associate professor of English emerita, Pratt Institute, Brooklyn, New York. Author of *Lit by the Earth's Dark Blood*, 1977, *Journeys*, 1985, and *French Window*, 1998, as well as fiction in *Images of Women in Literature*, 4th edition, 1986, and poetry in literary magazines. Editor of *The Gift by H.D.: The Complete Text*, 1998. **Essays:** Marilyn Hacker; Judith Johnson; Richard Kostelanetz; Rochelle Owens; Jean Valentine; Mona Van Duyn.

BAKER, Houston A., Jr. Greenfield Professor of English, University of Pennsylvania, Philadelphia. Author of the poetry books *No*

Matter Where You Travel You Still Be Black, 1979, *Spirit Run*, 1982, and *Blues Journeys Home*, 1985. Also author of *Long Black Song: Essays in Black American Literature and Culture*, 1972, *Singers of Daybreak: Studies in Black American Literature*, 1974, *A Many-Colored Coat of Dreams: The Poetry of Countée Cullen*, 1974, *The Journey Back: Issues in Black Literature and Criticism*, 1980, *Blues, Ideology, and Afro-American Literature*, 1985, *Modernism and the Harlem Renaissance*, 1987, and *Afro-American Poetics: Revisions of Harlem and the Black Aesthetic*, 1988. Editor of *Black Literature in America*, 1971, *Twentieth-Century Interpretations of "Native Son,"* 1972, *English Literature: Opening Up the Canon* (with Leslie A. Fiedler), 1981, *Three American Literatures: Essays in Chicano, Native American, and Asian-American Literature for Teachers of American Literature*, 1982, *Narrative of the Life of Frederick Douglass*, 1982, and *Afro-American Literary Study in the 1990s* (with Patricia Redmond), 1989. **Essay:** James A. Emanuel.

BARKER, Jonathan. Principal literature officer, British Council, London. Author of critical articles and reviews in *Agenda, PN Review, Poetry Wales, Times Literary Supplement*, and other journals. Editor of *The Arts Council Poetry Library Catalogue*, 6th edition, 1981, *Selected Poems of W.H. Davies*, 1985, *Poetry Book Society Anthology 1986-87*, 1986, *The Art of Edward Thomas*, 1987, *Thirty Years of the Poetry Book Society, 1956-86*, 1988, *Collected Poems of Norman Cameron* (with Warren Hope), 1990, and *Poetry in Britain and Ireland since 1970: A Select Bibliography*, 1995. **Essays:** Fred D'Aguiar; Alistair Elliot; Donald Justice; Glyn Maxwell; Jamie McKendrick; Robert Wells; Hugo Williams.

BARRETT, Renu. Archivist, McMaster University Library, Hamilton, Ontario, and member of the executive, Hamilton Poetry Centre. Compiler of the annotated bibliographies *Two Centuries of Oliver Goldsmith: Eighteenth and Nineteenth Century Editions in McMaster University Library*, 1976, and *Canadian Pamphlets*, 1976-77. **Essays:** Peter Didsbury; Judith Fitzgerald; Chenjerai Hove; Thomas McCarthy; Don McKay.

BERTRAM, James. Emeritus professor of English, Victoria University of Wellington, New Zealand, and general editor, "New Zealand Writers and Their Work" series. Author of *Charles Brasch*, 1976, *Dan Davin*, 1983, *Flight of the Phoenix: Critical Notes on New Zealand Writers*, 1985, and several books on China. Editor of *New Zealand Letters of Thomas Arnold the Younger*, 2 vols., 1966, 1980. **Essay:** Ruth Dallas.

BIRKETT, Jennifer. Professor of French studies, University of Birmingham. Author of *The Sins of the Fathers: Decadence in France and Europe, 1870-1914*, 1986. Editor and translator of *The Body and the Dream: French Erotic Fiction 1464-1900*, 1983, and editor of *Determined Women: The Construction of the Female Subject, 1900-1990* (with Elizabeth Harvey), 1990. **Essays:** Anne Cluysenaar; Elaine Feinstein.

BIRNEY, Earle. See his own entry.

BODE, Walter. Former assistant editor, Viking Penguin, New York. **Essays:** Irving Feldman; Daniel Halpern.

BOLDEN, B.J. Associate professor of English, Chicago State University, and director, Gwendolyn Brooks Center for Black Literature and Creative Writing. Author of *Urban Rage in Bronzeville: Social Commentary in the Poetry of Gwendolyn Brooks, 1945-1960*, as well as essays on Lucille Clifton, Sonia Sanchez, and Ntozake Shange. **Essays:** Lucille Clifton; Wanda Coleman; Sonia Sanchez.

BORKLUND, Elmer. Professor of English, Pennsylvania State University, University Park, and former associate editor, *Chicago Review.* Author of *Contemporary Literary Critics,* 1977 (2nd edition, 1982), and articles in *Modern Philology, Commentary, New York Herald-Tribune Book Week,* and *Journal of General Education.* **Essay:** James Michie.

BOYERS, Robert. Professor of English and Tisch Professor of Arts and Letters, Skidmore College, Saratoga Springs, New York, and editor, *Salmagundi* magazine. Author of *Excursions: Selected Literary Essays,* 1976, *Lionel Trilling: Negative Capability and the Wisdom of Avoidance,* 1977, *F.R. Leavis: Judgment and the Discipline of Thought,* 1978, *R.P. Blackmur,* 1981, *Atrocity and Amnesia: The Political Novel since 1945,* 1985, and *After the Avant-Garde,* 1988. Editor of *Robert Lowell: The Poet in His Time* (with Michael London), 1969, *Contemporary Poetry in America,* 1975, *The Salmagundi Reader* (with Peggy Boyers), 1983, and several collections of articles. **Essay:** Alan Dugan.

BRADISH, Gaynor F. Former adjunct associate professor, Union College, Schenectady, New York. Author of the introduction to Arthur Kopit's *Oh Dad, Poor Dad . . . ,* 1960. Director of *Asylum* by Kopit, New York, 1963, and of many plays for drama workshops and university groups. Died. **Essays:** Gerald Stern; Mark Strand.

BRANTLEY, Jennifer. Assistant professor in the English Department, University of Wisconsin-River Falls. Author of an article on Gloria Naylor in *Everything Got Four Sides: The Early Novels of Gloria Naylor* and of an article in *Women's Life Writing* and author of poetry published in *13th Moon, Hurricane Alice, Women and Language, genre, Kaleidoscope,* and other magazines. Reviewer for *Literary Magazine Review.* **Essay:** Judith Minty.

BRATHWAITE, Edward Kamau. See his own entry. **Essays:** Wilson Harris; Ian McDonald; Anthony McNeill; The Mighty Sparrow; Mervyn Morris; Bruce St. John.

BREINER, Laurence A. Associate professor of English, Boston University, Massachusetts. Author of *An Introduction to West Indian Poetry,* as well as articles on Caribbean literature. **Essays:** Edward Baugh; Wayne Brown.

BROUGHTON, W.S. Senior lecturer in English, Massey University, Palmerston North, New Zealand. **Essay:** Michael Jackson.

BROWN, Lloyd W. Member of the Department of Comparative Literature, University of Southern California, Los Angeles. Author of *Amiri Baraka,* 1980, *Women Writers in Black Africa,* 1981, and *West Indian Poetry,* 1984. Editor of *The Black Writer in Africa and the Americas,* 1973. **Essay:** Edward Kamau Brathwaite.

BRUCE, George. See his own entry. **Essays:** James Aitchison; Tom Buchan; Stewart Conn; Robin Fulton; Duncan Glen; Pete Morgan; Alastair Reid.

BRUCHAC, Joseph. Editor, *Greenfield Review,* Greenfield Center, New York. Author of numerous collections of poetry, including *Near the Mountains,* 1987, and *Langes Gedächtnis/Long Memory,* 1989, as well as novels, collections of traditional Native American stories, and a book of interviews with Native American poets. Editor of *Songs from This Earth on Turtle's Back,* 1983, *New Voices from the*

Longhouse, 1989, and many other books. **Essays:** Chinua Achebe; Dennis Brutus; Syl Cheyney-Coker; Michael Echeruo; Lyn Lifshin; John Okai; Leslie Marmon Silko; Gary Soto; James Welch.

BUCKINGHAM, Hugh. Senior lecturer in English, Richmond College, Surrey. **Essays:** Fiona Pitt-Kethley; Peter Reading.

BURNS, Jim. See his own entry. **Essays:** Barry MacSweeney; Harold Norse; Gael Turnbull.

BURWELL, Rose Marie. Professor of English, Northern Illinois University, DeKalb. Author of *A Chronological Catalogue of the Reading of D.H. Lawrence,* 1970 (addenda in *D.H. Lawrence Review,* 1973), and several articles on Joyce Carol Oates. Contributor to *A D.H. Lawrence Handbook,* 1982. **Essay:** Joyce Carol Oates.

BUTTERICK, George F. Former curator of literary archives and lecturer in English, University of Connecticut, Storrs. Author of *A Guide to the Maximus Poems of Charles Olson,* 1978, *Editing the Maximus Poems: Supplementary Notes,* 1983, and several books of poetry, including *The Collected Poems,* edited by Richard Blevius, 1988. Editor of *The Postmoderns: The New American Poetry Revised,* 1982, and works by Vincent Ferrini and by Charles Olson. Died 1988. **Essays:** Joanne Kyger; John Wieners; Jonathan Williams.

BYRD, Don. Member of the Department of English, State University of New York, Albany. Author of the poetry books *Aesop's Garden,* 1976, *Technics of Travel,* 1981, and *The Great Dimestore Centennial,* 1986, as well as the critical works *Charles Olson's Maximum,* 1980, and *The Poetics of the Common Knowledge,* 1994. **Essays:** Amiri Baraka; Robert Creeley; Michael Davidson; Jackson Mac Low; Simon Oritz; Michael Palmer; Ed Sanders; Lewis Warsh.

CALLAN, Edward. Distinguished university professor emeritus, Western Michigan University, Kalamazoo. Author of *Yeats on Yeats,* 1981, *Alan Paton,* revised edition, 1982, *Auden: A Carnival of Intellect,* 1983, and other books and articles. **Essay:** John Woods.

CAMPBELL, Katie. Writer and freelance journalist, London. Author of *What He Really Wants Is a Dog* (short stories), 1989, and *Let Us Leave Them Believing* (poetry), 1991. **Essays:** Fleur Adcock; Gillian Clarke; Lorna Goodison; Jenny Joseph; Sharon Olds; Marge Piercy.

CAREW, Rivers. Former chief subeditor (1987-93), BBC World Service, London, and editor (1964-69), *Dublin Magazine.* Author of *Figures out of Mist* (with Timothy Brownlow), 1966, as well as verse in *The Penguin Book of Irish Verse,* 1970, and in periodicals. **Essays:** Helen Dunmore; Herbert Lomas; Michael Longley.

CARRUTH, Hayden. See his own entry. **Essays:** Carol Bergé; Arthur Gregor; Kenneth Koch.

CATON, James. Former lecturer, Buffalo State College, New York. **Essays:** Beverly Dahlen; Christopher Dewdney.

CHAMBERS, D.D.C. Associate professor of English, Trinity College, Toronto. Editor of *A Few Friends: Poems for Thom Gunn's 60th Birthday,* 1989, and two books of poetry by Thomas Traherne. **Essays:** Leonard Cohen; David Helwig.

CHARTERS, Ann. Professor of English, University of Connecticut, Storrs. Author of *Nobody: The Story of Bert Williams,* 1970, *Kerouac: A*

Biography, 1973, *I Love: The Story of Vladimir Mayakovsky and Lili Brik* (with Samuel Charters), 1979, and a study of ragtime. Editor of *The Beats: Literary Bohemians in Postwar America,* 2 vols., 1983, *The Story and Its Writer,* 1990, *The Portable Beat Reader,* 1992, *The Kerouac Reader,* 1995, and *Selected Kerouac Letters,* 1995. **Essay:** Alice Notley.

CHRISTENSEN, Paul. Professor of modern literature, Texas A&M University, College Station. Author of several books of poetry as well as *Charles Olson: Call Him Ishmael,* 1979. Editor of *In Love, In Sorrow: The Complete Correspondence of Charles Olson and Edward Dahlberg,* 1990, and *Minding the Underworld: Clayton Eshleman and Late Postmodernism,* 1991. **Essays:** Bill Berkson; Charles Bernstein; Robert Bly; David Bromige; Albert Goldbarth; Lyn Hejinian; Edward Hirsch; T.R. Hummer; Naomi Shihab Nye; Richard Shelton; Rosmarie Waldrop; Jay Wright.

CLARENCE, Judy. Librarian, California State University, Hayward. Poetry reviewer for *Library Journal* and author of the books of poetry *Kitchen Sonnets* (with Minnie Elmer), 1965, and *Running out of Colors* (1972). **Essays:** Elaine Equi; Caroline Finkelstein.

CLARKE, Austin. Poet, playwright, and literary critic. Died 1974. **Essays:** Pearse Hutchinson; Desmond O'Grady.

CLUYSENAAR, Anne. See her own entry. **Essays:** Roy Fisher; Christopher Pilling.

COLLERAN, Jeanne. Associate professor of English, John Carroll University, Cleveland, Ohio. Author of numerous articles on contemporary literature and postcolonial fiction and drama. **Essays:** Harry Clifton; James McAuley.

COLOMBO, John Robert. See his own entry. **Essays:** George Bowering; Elizabeth Brewster; Anne Carson; Victor Coleman; Cyril Dabydeen; Frank Davey; Greg Gatenby; Kristjana Gunnars; Don Gutteridge; Daryl Hine; Rita Joe; Robert Kroetsch; Dennis Lee; Douglas LePan; Jay Macpherson; Seymour Mayne; Steve McCaffery; David McFadden; A. F. Moritz; Rona Murray; Richard Outram; Gianna Patriarca; Andrew Suknaski, Jr., Fraser Sutherland; Fred Wah.

COOKSON, William. Editor, *Agenda* magazine, London. Author of the poetry books *Dream Traces,* 1975, *Spell,* 1986, and *Vestiges (1955-1995),* 1995, as well as *A Guide to the Cantos of Ezra Pound,* 1984. Editor of *Ezra Pound: Selected Prose, 1909-1965,* 1973, and *Agenda—An Anthology 1959-1993,* 1994. **Essays:** Anne Beresford; John Burnside.

COOLEY, John R. Associate professor of English, Western Michigan University, Kalamazoo. Author of *Savages and Naturals: Black Portraits by White Writers in Modern American Literature,* 1982, *The Great Unknown: The Journals of the Historic First Expedition down the Colorado River,* 1988, and articles on Hardy, Welty, Stephen Crane, Hemingway, and O'Neill. **Essays:** Hayden Carruth; Leonard Nathan.

COONEY, Seamus. Professor of English and graduate director, Western Michigan University, Kalamazoo. Author of articles on Byron, Scott, Lawrence, Binyon, and Austin Clarke. Editor of *By the Well of Living and Seeing: New and Selected Poems* by Charles Reznikoff, *Poems 1918-1975: The Complete Poems of Charles Reznikoff,* 1989, and of *Men without Art,* by Wyndham Lewis.

Essays: Cid Corman; Theodore Enslin; Jonathan Greene; Stephen Stepanchev.

COPPOLA, Carlo. Professor of modern languages and literatures and professor of linguistics, Oakland University, Rochester, Michigan. Cofounder, *Journal of South Asian Literature,* and editor of *Marxist Influences and South Asian Literature,* 1974. **Essay:** Kaiser Haq.

CORCORAN, Neil. Member of the Department of English, University of Sheffield. Author of *The Song of Deeds: A Study of "The Anathemata" of David Jones,* 1982, *Seamus Heaney,* 1986, and reviews in *PN Review, Times Literary Supplement,* and *London Review of Books.* **Essays:** James Fenton; Thom Gunn; Tony Harrison; Geoffrey Hill; Peter Levi; John Matthias; Andrew Motion; Tom Paulin; Craig Raine; Christopher Reid.

COTTON, John. See his own entry. **Essays:** Moniza Alvi; Elizabeth Bartlett; Alan Brownjohn; Jim Burns; Wendy Cope; Vicki Feaver; Roger Garfitt; John Gohorry; Philip Gross; David Holbrook; Glyn Hughes; Mick Imlah; Sylvia Kantaris; James Kirkup; Lotte Kramer; Edward Lucie-Smith; Gerda Mayer; John Mole; Rodney Pybus; Carol Rumens; Carole Satyamurti; Peter Scupham; Fred Sedgwick; Jo Shapcott; James Simmons; Pauline Stainer; D.M. Thomas; Ted Walker; Kit Wright.

CURTIS, Tony. See his own entry. **Essays:** Norman Dubie; Raymond Garlick; Jeremy Hooker; Sheenagh Pugh.

DAMASHEK, Richard. Member of the Communications Division, Richland Community College, Decatur, Illinois. Author of articles on Randall Jarrell and Ingmar Bergman and reviews in *Books Abroad* and other periodicals. **Essays:** Philip Booth; R.H.W. Dillard; Laurence Lieberman; Thomas Lux; Paul Petrie; W.D. Snodgrass.

DAVIES, J.M.Q. Senior lecturer in English, Northern Territory University, Casuarina, Australia. **Essays:** Bruce Beaver; Geoffrey Lehmann.

DAY, Aidan. Professor of nineteenth-century and contemporary literature, University of Edinburgh. Author of *Jokerman: Reading the Lyrics of Bob Dylan,* 1988, *Romanticism,* 1995, and *Angela Carter: The Rational Glass,* 1998. Coeditor of *The Tennyson Archive,* 31 vols., 1987-93. **Essay:** Bob Dylan.

DAY, Cynthia. Freelance writer, Syracuse, New York. Author of work in *Ironwood, Literary Review,* and *En Passant.* **Essay:** Peter Meinke.

DELVILLE, Michel. F.N.R.S. research assistant, University of Liege, Belgium. Author of articles in various journals, including *The Southern Literary Journal* and *The Prose Poem: An International Journal.* Also author of the pamphlet *Giacomo Joyce: fragments d'un discours inachevé,* 1994, as well as chapters in *Post-War Literature in English,* edited by Hans Bertens, 1995, and *Trajectories of the Fantastic,* edited by M. Morrison, 1995. **Essay:** Diane Ward.

DIGGORY, Terence. Courtney and Steven Ross Professor of Interdisciplinary Studies, Skidmore College, Saratoga Springs, New York. Author of *Yeats and American Poetry: The Tradition of the Self,* 1983, and *William Carlos Williams and the Ethics of Painting,* 1991, and coeditor, with Stephen Paul Miller, of *The Scene of My Selves:*

New Work on New York School Poets, 2000. **Essays:** Jack Gilbert; Linda Gregg.

DILLARD, R.H.W. See his own entry. **Essays:** Diane Ackerman; John Engels; George Garrett; Julia Randall; David Slavitt; Henry Taylor.

DONAGHY, Michael. See his own entry. **Essays:** Thomas Disch; Carol Ann Duffy; Matthew Sweeney.

DORSINVILLE, Max. Professor of English, McGill University, Montreal. Author of *Caliban without Prospero: An Essay on Quebec and Black Literature,* 1974, *Le Pays Natal: Essais sur les littératures du tiers-monde et du Québec,* 1983, *Solidarités: Tiers-Monde et littérature comparée,* 1988, and articles in *PMLA, Canadian Literature,* and *Livres et Auteurs Québecois.* **Essay:** Joan Finnigan.

DOUGHERTY, David C. Professor of English, Loyola College, Baltimore. Author of *James Wright,* 1987, as well as articles on Robinson Jeffers, Saul Bellow, Raymond Chandler, John Updike, and Walker Percy and reviews in the *Baltimore Sunday Sun.* **Essay:** Galway Kinnell.

DOWLING, David. Senior lecturer in English, Massey University, Palmerston North, New Zealand. Author of *Introducing Bruce Mason,* 1983, *Bloomsbury Aesthetics and the Novels of Forster and Woolf,* 1984, *Fictions of Nuclear Disaster,* 1986, *William Faulkner,* 1989, and *Mrs. Dalloway,* 1990. Editor of *Novelists on Novelists,* 1983, *Every Kind of Weather: Bruce Mason,* 1986, and *Katherine Mansfield: Dramatic Sketches,* 1988. **Essays:** Charles Doyle; Lauris Edmond; Vincent O'Sullivan.

DRAIN, Sheila Haney. Member of the English Department, John Carroll University, Cleveland, Ohio. Author of poetry in *The Deciduous Review* and *The Carroll Quarterly.* **Essay:** Harry Clifton.

DUDEK, Louis. See his own entry. **Essay:** D.G. Jones.

DULAI, Surjit S. Professor of English, Michigan State University, East Lansing, and editor, *Journal of South Asian Literature.* **Essays:** Alamgir Hashmi; Jayanta Mahapatra; Vikram Seth.

DUNN, Douglas. See his own entry.

EKELUND, Doug. Freelance writer. Producer of documentaries for community access television. **Essay:** Gary Geddes.

ELLEDGE, Jim. Professor of English, Illinois State University, Normal. Author of the poetry books *Nothing Nice,* 1987, *Various Envies,* 1989, *Earth As It Is,* 1994, *Into the Arms of the Universe,* 1995, and *Four Chapters of Coming Forth by Day,* 1999, as well as poems, fiction, and critical essays in journals, books, and anthologies. Also author of *James Dickey: A Bibliography, 1947-1974,* 1979, *Weldon Kees: A Critical Introduction,* 1985, *Frank O'Hara: To Be True to a City,* 1990, *Standing "Between the Dead and the Living": The Elegiac Technique of Wilfred Owen's War Poems,* 1992, *The Little Magazine in Illinois: A Directory,* 1993, *Sweet Nothings: An Anthology of Rock and Roll in American Poetry,* 1994, and, with Susan Swartwout, *Real Things: An Anthology of Popular Culture in American Poetry.* **Essays:** James Bertolino; Ronald Johnson; David Ray; Lewis Turco.

EMANUEL, James A. See his own entry.

ENRIGHT, Mary. Librarian, Poetry Library, London.

FOSTER, Edward. Professor of English and American literature, Stevens Institute of Technology, Hoboken, New Jersey, and founding editor, Talisman House, Publishers. Author of *All Acts Are Simply Acts,* 1995, *boy in the key of e,* 1998, and *Answerable to None: Berrigan, Bronk, and the American Real,* 1999, as well as studies of the beats, the Black Mountain poets, William Saroyan, and Jack Spicer. **Essays:** Paul Hoover; Carl Phillips.

FRASER, G.S. Reader in modern English literature, University of Leicester, 1964-79. Author of several books of verse (collected as *Poems,* 1981), travel books, and critical studies of Yeats, Dylan Thomas, Pound, Durrell, and Pope. Also author of *The Modern Writer and His World,* 1953, *Vision and Rhetoric,* 1959, *Metre, Rhythm and Free Verse,* 1970, and *A Stranger and Afraid: The Autobiography of an Intellectual,* 1983. Editor of works by Keith Douglas and Robert Burns and of verse anthologies. Died 1980.

FRIEDMAN, Norman. Emeritus professor of English, Queens College, City University of New York. Author of *E.E. Cummings: The Art of His Poetry,* 1960, *Poetry: An Introduction to Its Form and Art* (with C.A. McLaughlin), 1961, *Logic, Rhetoric, Style* (with McLaughlin), 1963, *E.E. Cummings: The Growth of a Writer,* 1964, *Form and Meaning in Fiction,* 1975, *The Magic Badge* (poems), 1985, *The Intrusions of Love* (poems), 1992, and *(Re)valuing Cummings : Further Essays on the Poet, 1962-1993,* 1996. Editor of *E.E. Cummings: A Collection of Critical Essays,* 1971. **Essays:** Richard Howard; Vern Rutsala; Louis Simpson; Ruth Stone.

FULTON, Robin. See his own entry. **Essay:** Kenneth White.

GALL, Sally M. Librettist, poet, critic, and scholar. Author of *The Modern Poetic Sequence* (with M.L. Rosenthal), 1983, *Ramon Guthrie's Maximum Security Ward: An American Classic,* 1984, and more than forty articles in collections and journals. Editor of *Maximum Security Ward and Other Poems* by Guthrie, 1984. **Essay:** Frederick Morgan.

GARDNER, Thomas. Associate professor of English, Virginia Polytechnic, Blacksburg. Author of *Discovering Ourselves in Whitman: The Contemporary American Long Poem,* 1989, and articles on contemporary poets in *Contemporary Literature, The Georgia Review, American Poetry, Sagetrieb,* and other journals. **Essay:** Robert Hass.

GASPAR, Robert. Freelance writer. **Essays:** Brendan Galvin; Garrett Hongo.

GERMAIN, Edward B. Instructor in English, Phillips Academy, Andover, Massachusetts. Editor of *Flag of Ecstasy: Selected Poems of Charles Henri Ford,* 1972, *Shadows of the Sun: The Diaries of Harry Crosby,* 1977, and *English and American Surrealist Poetry,* 1977. **Essays:** Robert Dana; Charles Henri Ford; Lee Harwood; Thylias Moss; Ron Padgett.

GERVAIS, Marty. See his own entry as C.H.Gervais. **Essay:** James Reaney.

GIBBS, James. Senior lecturer, University of the West of England, Bristol. Author of *Wole Soyinka,* 1986, and *Wole Soyinka: A Bibliography of Primary and Secondary Sources* (with Ketu H. Katrak and Henry Louis Gates, Jr.), 1986. Editor of *Critical Perspectives on Wole Soyinka,* 1980, and *A Handbook for African Writers,* 1986, and coeditor of *African Writers' Handbook,* 1999, and *African Theatre in Development,* 1999. **Essay:** Jack Mapanje.

GILBERT, Reid. Professor of English and drama, Capilano College, Vancouver, and member of the editorial board, *Canadian Theatre Review* and *Theatre Research in Canada.* Author of the play *A Glass Darkly,* 1972, and articles in *Theatre Research in Canada, Canadian Theatre Review, Theatre Journal, Theatre Research International,* and other journals. **Essays:** Daphne Marlatt; J. Michael Yates.

GIOIA, Dana. See his own entry. **Essay:** Ted Kooser.

GLOVER, Michael. Freelance writer and editor. Reviewer for *Books and Bookmen, British Book News, PN Review, Melbourne Age, Observer,* and *School Librarian.* **Essays:** Judith Kazantzis; Douglas Livingstone; Anthony Rudolf; Michael Schmidt.

GOLDENSOHN, Barry. Professor of English, Skidmore College, Saratoga Springs, New York. Author of the poetry books *St. Venus Eve,* 1972, *Uncarving the Block,* 1978, *The Marrano,* 1988, *Dance Music* (chapbook), 1992, and *East Long Pond* (chapbook). **Essays:** Rodney Jones; Robert Pinsky; Charles Tomlinson.

GOLDENSOHN, Lorrie. Teacher of poetry and fiction writing, Vassar College, Poughkeepsie, New York. Author of *The Tether* (poems), 1984, and *Elizabeth Bishop: The Biography of a Poetry,* 1992. **Essays:** Olga Broumas; Jane Cooper; Elizabeth Spires.

GORDON, Lois. Professor of English and comparative literature, Fairleigh Dickinson University, Teaneck, New Jersey. Author of *Stratagems to Uncover Nakedness: The Dramas of Harold Pinter,* 1969, *Donald Barthelme,* 1981, *Robert Coover: The Universal Fictionmaking Process,* 1983, *American Chronicle: Six Decades in American Life 1920-1980,* 1987, *American Chronicle, Seven Decades in American Life, 1920-1989,* 1990, *The World of Samuel Beckett,* 1996, *American Chronicle: Year by Year through the Twentieth Century,* 1999, and numerous articles on contemporary authors and American culture. **Essays:** Richard Eberhart; W.S. Merwin; Adrienne Rich; Gilbert Sorrentino.

GREENBERG, Alvin. Professor of English, Macalester College, St. Paul, Minnesota. Author of several volumes of poetry, including *Heavy Wings,* 1988, and *Why We Live with Animals,* 1990; the novels *Going Nowhere,* 1971, and *The Invention of the West,* 1976; and short stories, including *The Man in the Cardboard Mask,* 1985. **Essay:** Margaret Randall.

GRIFFITHS, Bill. Former secretary and chairman, Association of Little Presses, and founder, SULPhA (Seaham Unaligned Literary and Philosophical Association). Author of *Anglo-Saxon Magic,* 1996, and *North East Dialect,* 1999, as well as several books of poetry, including *Cycles,* 1973, *Building: The New London Hospital,* 1980, *Tract against the Giants: Selected Poems,* 1984, *Star Fish Jail,* 1993, and *Split Cities,* 1999. Translator from Old English of *Guthlac B,* 1986, *The Land Ceremonies Charm,* 1986, *The Nine Herbs Charm,* 1987, and *The Old English Poem 'Phoenix,'* 1990. **Essay:** Tom Pickard.

HALL, Donald. See his own entry.

HALPERN, Daniel. See his own entry.

HARNETT, Ruth. Lecturer in English, Rhodes University, Grahamstown, South Africa. **Essay:** Guy Butler.

HASTINGS, Thomas. Instructor, University of British Columbia, Vancouver. **Essay:** Francis Sparshott.

HATLEN, Burton. Professor of English, University of Maine, Orono. Editor, *Sagetrieb,* a journal devoted to scholarship on poetry in the imagist/objectivist tradition. Author of *George Oppen: Man and Poet,* 1981, *I Wanted to Tell You* (poems), 1987, and articles on Pound, H.D., Williams, Olson, Duncan, Spicer, Levertov, Whitman, and Shakespeare. **Essays:** Rae Armantrout; Tony Hoagland; Fanny Howe.

HEATON, David M. Associate professor of English and university ombudsman, Ohio University, Athens. Author of poetry and poetry translations as well as articles on Ted Hughes, Alan Sillitoe, and George P. Elliott. **Essays:** Marvin Bell; Stanley Plumly; Alan Stephens.

HELLER, Michael. See his own entry. **Essay:** Hugh Seidman.

HEWITT, Geof. Founding editor, Kumquat Press, Enosburg, Vermont. Author of several books of poetry and editor of poetry anthologies. **Essays:** Peter Davison; Robert Sward.

HILL, Douglas. Author of science fiction for children and adults, several works of nonfiction, and poetry in periodicals and anthologies. Editor of *Tribune 40,* 1977, and collections of fantasy writing. **Essay:** Bernard Kops.

HINCHEY, John. Member of the Department of English, Swarthmore College, Pennsylvania. **Essay:** Anne Waldman.

HINES, Susan C. Instructor in English literature, Georgia State University, Atlanta. **Essay:** George McWhirter.

HOBSBAUM, Philip. See his own entry. **Essays:** Francis Berry; Kate Clanchy; Jeni Couzyn; U.A. Fanthorpe; Zulfikar Ghose; Lavinia Greenlaw; Christopher Levenson; Sarah Maguire; Derek Mahon; Matthew Mead; Robert Nye; Frank Ormsby; Don Paterson; William Peskett; Peter Porter; F.T. Prince; Robin Robertson; Theodore Weiss.

HOEY, Allen. Professor, Department of Language and Literature, Bucks City Community College, Newtown, Pennsylvania. Author of the poetry books *A Fire in the Cold House of Being,* 1987, and *What Persists,* 1992, as well as poems in many journals, including *The Georgia Review, The Hudson Review, Poetry,* and *The Southern Review.* Contributor since 1991 to *Contemporary Literary Criticism.* **Essays:** Hayden Carruth; Robert Hass; Jane Hirshfield.

HOFFMAN, Daniel. See his own entry. **Essays:** A.R. Ammons; William Meredith; William Jay Smith.

HOLM, Janis Butler. Associate professor of English, Ohio University, Athens. Consulting editor, *Wide Angle: A Quarterly Journal of Film History, Theory, Criticism, and Practice.* Author of articles on cultural perceptions of gender. Editor of *The Mirrhor of Modestie.* **Essay:** Carolyn Rodgers.

HSU, Ruth Y. Assistant professor, Department of English, University of Hawaii, Manoa. Author of articles on contemporary poets, including Derek Walcott, in *Verse,* and Li-Young Lee, in *Dictionary of Literary Biography: American Poets since World War II.* **Essay:** Garrett Hongo.

HUDSON, Theodore R. Editorial consultant and former graduate professor of English, Howard University, Washington, D.C. Author of *From LeRoi Jones to Amiri Baraka: The Literary Works,* 1973, and numerous articles. **Essays:** Lucille Clifton; Haki R. Madhubuti; E. Ethelbert Miller; Sonia Sanchez.

HUGGAN, Graham. Assistant professor of English, Harvard University, Cambridge, Massachusetts. Author of "'Blue Myth Brooding in Orchid': A Third World Reappraisal of Island Poetics," in *Journal of West Indian Literature,* 2(1), 1987, "Decolonizing the Map: Post-Colonialism, Post-Structuralism and the Cartographic Connection," in *Ariel,* 20(4), 1989, and other essays on postcolonial literature and literary theory. **Essay:** Albert Wendt.

INDYK, Ivor. Senior lecturer in Australian literature, University of Sydney. Assistant editor of *Southerly* journal. Contributor to the *Penguin New Literary History of Australia,* 1988. **Essay:** Peter Skrzynecki.

JAMES, Charles L. Professor of English, Swarthmore College, Pennsylvania. Author of *The Black Writer in America* (bibliography), 1969. Editor of *From the Roots: Short Stories by Black Americans,* 1970. **Essays:** Gwendolyn Brooks; Mari Evans; Michael S. Harper; Ishmael Reed.

JONES, Eldred D. Emeritus professor of English, University of Sierra Leone, Freetown. Author of *Othello's Countrymen: The Africans in English Renaissance Drama,* 1955, *The Elizabethan Image of Africa,* 1971, and *The Writing of Wole Soyinka,* 1973 (revised 1982, 1988). Editor of *A Krio-English Dictionary* (with Clifford N. Fyle), 1980, and the annual *African Literature Today.* Series editor of New Perspectives on African Literature. **Essay:** Wole Soyinka.

KAPLAN, Susan. Freelance writer. **Essay:** William Pitt Root.

KEATON, Rebekah. English and humanities instructor, Genesee Community College, SUNY. **Essay:** Mary Jo Bang.

KENDLE, Burton. Professor of English, Roosevelt University, Chicago. Author of articles on D.H. Lawrence, John Cheever, William March, Tennessee Williams, and others and on screenwriting. **Essays:** Robert Pack; Muriel Spark; Peter Viereck.

KING, Bruce. Author of *The New English Literatures: Cultural Nationalism in a Changing World,* 1980, *Modern Indian Poetry in English,* 1987, *Three Indian Poets: Ezekiel, Ramanujan and Moraes,* 1990, *V.S. Napaul,* 1993, *Derek Walcott and West Indian Drama,* 1995, *Derek Walcott: A Caribbean Life,* 2000, and books on Shakespeare, Marvell, and Dryden. Editor of books on the New English literatures and Dryden. **Essays:** John Agard; Agha Shahid Ali; James Berry; Bernardine Evaristo; Alamgir Hashmi; Tabish Khair; Jayanta Mahapatra; Bibhu Padhi; Vikram Seth; Timothy Steele; C.P. Surendran; Derek Walcott.

KINSELLA, Thomas. See his own entry.

KOHLI, Devindra. Professor of English, University of Kashmir, Srinagar, and founding coeditor of *The Indian Literary.* Visiting professor at various universities in Germany, including the universities of Frankfurt, Bonn, Munich, Duisburg, Essen, and Halle-Wittenberg. Author of *Virgin Whiteness,* 1968, and *Kamala Das,* 1975, as well as articles in *Malahat Review, Gravesiana, Journal of Commonwealth Literature, Times Literary Supplement,* and *Journal of South Asian Literature.* Editor of *Indian Writers at Work,* 1991, and coeditor of *Heritage of English,* 1980. **Essays:** Keki N. Daruwalla; Kamala Das; Adil Jussawalla; Shiv K. Kumar.

KORGES, James. Freelance writer. Author of *Erskine Caldwell,* 1969. Editor of *Critique: Studies in Modern Fiction,* 1962-70. Died 1975. **Essay:** Edgar Bowers.

KOSTELANETZ, Richard. See his own entry. **Essays:** Clark Coolidge; Kenneth Goldsmith; Emmett Williams.

KRAPF, Norbert. Professor of English and director of the Poetry Center, C.W. Post College, Long Island University, Greenvale, New York. Author of several collections of poetry, including *A Dream of Plum Blossoms,* 1985, *East of New York City,* 1986, and *Somewhere in Southern Indiana: Poems of Midwest Origins,* 1993, as well as fiction, translations, and articles in journals. Editor of *Under Open Sky: Poets on William Cullen Bryant,* 1986. Editor and translator of *Beneath the Cherry Sapling: Legends from Franconia,* 1988, and *Shadows on the Sundial: Selected Early Poems of Rainer Maria Rilke,* 1990. **Essays:** William Heyen; Robert Morgan.

KUGLER, B.T. Codirector, Harper House Children's Service, Hertfordshire, England. Author of articles in *British Journal of Psychiatry, Psychiatry Research,* and other journals and collections. **Essays:** John Fuller; David Harsent.

LAMONT-STEWART, Linda. Instructor, York University, Toronto. Author of essays and reviews on contemporary Canadian fiction and poetry. **Essays:** Irving Layton; Raymond Souster.

LANDIS, Joan Hutton. Chair of the academic faculty and professor of English, Curtis Institute of Music, Philadelphia. Author of poems in *New York Times Book of Verse, The Far Point, Transatlantic Review, Quadrille,* and other journals, as well as essays and reviews on modern poetry and Shakespeare in *Salmagundi, Midway, Transatlantic Review, Hamlet Studies, Shakespeare Quarterly,* and *Modern Language Studies.* **Essay:** John Peck.

LAUTER, Estella. Chair, English Department, University of Wisconsin, Oshkosh. Author of *Women as Mythmakers: Poetry and Art by Twentieth-Century Women,* 1984. **Essay:** Diane Wakoski.

LEHMANN, Geoffrey. See his own entry. **Essays:** Robert Gray; Kevin Hart; Geoff Page.

LEUSMANN, Harald. Member, English Department, Ball State University, Muncie, Indiana. Author of articles in various publications, including *Wasafiri* and *World Literature Today.* **Essay:** Anthony Kellman.

LINDBERG, Stanley W. Professor of English, University of Georgia, Athens, and editor, *The Georgia Review.* Author of *The Annotated McGuffrey,* 1976, and *Van Nostrand's Plain English Handbook,* 1980. Editor of *The Plays of Frederick Reynolds,* 1983, *Necessary Fictions: Selected Stories from the Georgia Review* (with Stephen Corey), 1986, and *Keener Sounds: Selected Poems from the Georgia Review* (with Corey), 1987. **Essay:** Reg Saner.

LINDNER, Carl. Professor of English, University of Wisconsin-Parkside, Kenosha. Author of poetry chapbooks *Vampire* and *The Only Game* and the book of poetry *Shooting Baskets in a Dark Gymnasium.* **Essays:** Michael Anania; Philip Dacey; Edward Field; Knute Skinner.

LINDSAY, Maurice. See his own entry. **Essays:** George Bruce; Valerie Gillies; Frank Kuppner; Alasdair Maclean; John Updike.

LUCAS, Rose. Lecturer in literature, Monash University, Caulfield East, Victoria, Australia. **Essay:** J.S. Harry.

LUCIE-SMITH, Edward. See his own entry. **Essay:** Hamish Henderson.

LYNCH, Dennis. Former instructor, Great Books Foundation, Chicago. Author of articles on William Stafford and other American writers in various periodicals, including *American Poetry Review, Modern Poetry Studies,* and *New Republic.* **Essays:** Lawrence Ferlinghetti; Donald Finkel; Jim Harrison; Philip Whalen.

MACASKILL, Brian. Associate professor of English, John Carroll University, Cleveland, Ohio. Author of articles in *Contemporary Literature, Modern Fiction Studies, Novel: A Forum on Fiction,* and other journals. **Essays:** Simon Armitage; Jeremy Cronin; James Sutherland-Smith.

MACNAB, Roy. See his own entry. **Essays:** Patrick Cullinan; R.N. Currey; Anthony Delius; Stephen Gray.

MAGEE, Wes. See his own entry. **Essays:** John Cotton; Blake Morrison; Lawrence Sail.

MARIE, Jacquelyn. Women's Studies/Reference Librarian, McHenry Library, University of California, Santa Cruz. Author of articles on Buchi Emecheta, Harryette Mullen; Michelle Roberts, Anna Livia, and others. **Essay:** Harryette Mullen.

MARKOTIC, Nicole. Member of the English Department, University of Calgary, Alberta. Author of *Connect the Dots* (poetry), 1994, *Yellow Pages: A Novel of Telephonic Intentions,* 1995, and articles in *Tessera, Canadian Poetry, Open Letter,* and other journals. **Essay:** Jeff Derksen.

MARSHALL, Tod. Teacher, Department of English, Gonzaga University, Spokane, Washington. Author of essays on contemporary poetry in *The American Poetry Review, The Georgia Review, The Boston Review,* and elsewhere. **Essays:** Billy Collins; R.H.W. Dillard; Brenda Hillman; Donald Revell; Dabney Stuart; Lorenzo Thomas; Nance Van Winckel; Dara Wier.

MATHIAS, Roland. See his own entry. **Essay:** Leslie Norris.

MATHUR, Ashok. Copublisher of *disOrientation chapbooks* (an alternative-format poetry series) and member of the editorial collective *absinthe* (a literary journal). Author of the book of poems *Loveruage,* 1994. **Essay:** Erin Mouré.

MATTHEWS, William. See his own entry. **Essays:** Gary Gildner; Jorie Graham; Judith Moffett; James Scully.

MAXWELL, Glyn. See his own entry. **Essays:** David Dabydeen; Selima Hill; Jeremy Reed.

MAYO, E.L. Professor of English, Drake University, Des Moines, Iowa, 1947-75. Author of several books of poetry, including *Collected Poems,* edited by David Ray, 1981. Died. **Essays:** Anselm Hollo; Robert Mezey.

McCARTHY, Thomas. Librarian of Cork Corporation and poetry editor of *Stet* magazine, Cork. Author of many books of poetry, including *Seven Winters in Paris,* 1989, and the novel *Without Power,* 1991. **Essays:** Anthony Cronin; Paul Durcan; Patrick Galvin; Richard Murphy; Eiléan Ní Chuilleanáin.

McDOWELL, Robert. Publisher and editor, Story Line Press, Brownsville, Oregon. Author of *Quiet Money* (poetry), 1987, *The Diviners* (poetry), 1995, and *Sound and Form in Modern Poetry* (with Harvey Gross), 1995. Editor of *Poetry after Modernism,* 1990. **Essays:** Lucie Brock-Broido; David Dooley; Reginald Gibbons; Donald Hall; Mark Jarman; Yusef Komunyakaa; Li-Young Lee; David Lehman; Susan Mitchell; Alberto Ríos; Peggy Shumaker; Chase Twichell; Michael Waters.

McELROY, George. Former lecturer, Indiana University Northwest, Gary. Author of textbooks and of reviews in *Opera News.* **Essay:** Pritish Nandy.

McGOVERN, Martin. Author of poetry in *North American Review, Poetry,* and other journals, as well as criticism in *Sewanee Review, Chicago Review,* and *Montana Review.* **Essay:** Miller Williams.

McKINSEY, Martin. Author and translator of poems in numerous magazines and anthologies. **Essays:** Bill Knott; Frederick Seidel; Harvey Shapiro.

MELTZER, David. See his own entry. **Essays:** John Brandi; Victor Hernández Cruz; Diane Di Prima; Jack Hirschman; Susan Howe; Nathaniel Mackey.

MEYER, Bruce. Member of the Department of English, University of Windsor, Ontario. Author of *In Their Words: Interviews with Fourteen Canadian Writers.* Editor of *Arrivals: Canadian Poetry in the Eighties, The Selected Poems of Frank Prewett,* and *Separate Islands: Contemporary British and Irish Poetry.* **Essays:** Lorna Crozier; C.H. Gervais; John Newlove; David Wevill.

MILLER, David. Freelance writer, London. Author of *Darkness Enfolding,* 1989, *Messages,* 1989, and *W.H. Hudson and the Elusive Paradise,* 1990. **Essay:** C.K. Williams.

MILLER, Julie. Former member of the Department of English, Ohio University, Athens. **Essays:** Rita Dove; Alice Fulton; Josephine Jacobsen.

MILLER, Tyrus. Assistant professor, Department of Comparative Literature and English, Yale University, New Haven, Connecticut. Author of *Earthworks* (poems); articles in *Textual Practice, Hambone,* and *Paideuma*; and essays on Mina Loy, C. Day Lewis, and Walter Benjamin in edited volumes. **Essays:** Barbara Guest; David Shapiro; C.D. Wright.

MILLS, Ralph J., Jr. Professor of English, University of Illinois at Chicago. Author of several books of poetry, including *March Light,* 1983, *Each Branch: Poems 1976-1985,* 1986, *A While,* 1989, and *A Window in Air: Poems,* 1993. Also author of *Contemporary American Poetry,* 1965, *Creation's Very Self,* 1969, *Cry of the Human: Essays on Contemporary American Poetry,* 1975, and books on Theodore Roethke, Richard Eberhart, Edith Sitwell, and Kathleen Raine. Editor of Roethke's prose and letters, as well as works by David Ignatow. **Essay:** Stephen Berg.

MINDEROVIC, Christine Miner. Freelance writer. Author of essays on literature, art, and dance for various publications. **Essays:** Mark Doty; Peter Gizzi; Wesley C. McNair; Rosanna Warren.

MIOLA, Robert. Professor of English, Loyola College, Baltimore. **Essays:** Charles Edward Eaton; Anthony Hecht; Philip Levine.

MOLE, R.T. Literature officer, Arts Council of Wales. Author of *A History of Ponthir Cricket Club,* 1985. **Essay:** Benjamin Zephaniah.

MONTAGUE, John. See his own entry. **Essays:** Barry Callaghan; Ciaran Carson; Thomas Kinsella; Carolyn Kizer; Paula Meehan.

MORGAN, Edwin. See his own entry. **Essays:** David Black; Ian Hamilton Finlay; Tom Leonard; Liz Lochhead.

MORRISON, Blake. See his own entry.

NAGARAJAN, S. Former professor of English, University of Hyderabad, India. **Essays:** Nissim Ezekiel; Arvind Krishna Mehrotra; Dom Moraes; R. Parthasarathy.

NELSON, Rudolph L. Associate professor of English, State University of New York, Albany. **Essay:** Edwin Honig.

NEWLOVE, John. See his own entry. **Essay:** Joe Rosenblatt.

NICHOLSON, Colin. Senior lecturer in English, University of Edinburgh. Editor of *Alexander Pope: Essays for the Tercentenary,* 1988, and *Margaret Laurence: Critical Essays on the Fiction,* 1990. **Essays:** Ron Butlin; Eunice De Souza.

O'BRIEN, Sean. See his own entry. **Essays:** Kathleen Jamie; Ken Smith.

O'DONOGHUE, Bernard. Lecturer in English, Magdalen College, Oxford, and poetry reviewer for *Times Literary Supplement* and *Poetry Review.* Author of the poetry books *Razorblades and Pencils,* 1984, *Poaching Rights,* 1987, and *The Absent Signifier,* 1990. **Essays:** David Constantine; Peter Fallon; Paul Muldoon; Dennis O'Driscoll.

OJAIDE, Tanure. Professor of African-American and African studies, University of North Carolina at Charlotte; formerly teacher at the University of Maiduguri, Nigeria. Author of several collections of poetry, including *The Fate of Vultures,* 1990, *The Blood of Peace,* 1991, *Daydreams of Ants,* 1997, and *Invoking the Warrior Spirit: New and Selected Poems,* 1999; books of literary essays, including *Poetic Imagination in Black Africa,* 1996; and the memoir *Great Boys: An African Childhood,* 1998. **Essays:** Frank Chipasula; Kojo Laing.

O'NEILL, Michael. Professor of English, University of Durham, and editor of *Poetry Durham.* Author of *The Human Mind's Imaginings: Conflict and Achievement in Shelley's Poetry, Percy Bysshe Shelley: A Literary Life,* 1989, *The Stripped Bed* (poetry), 1990, *Auden, MacNeice, Spender: The Thirties Poetry* (with Gareth Reeves), 1992, and *Romanticism and the Self-Conscious Poem,* 1997. Editor of *Shelley: Longman Critical Reader,* 1993, *The Defence of Poetry Fair Copies,* 1994, *Keats: Bicentenary Readings,* 1997, and *Literature of the Romantic Period: A Biographical Guide,* 1998. Coeditor of *Fair-Copy Manuscripts of Shelley's Poems in European and American Libraries,* 1997. Winner of Cholmondeley award for poetry, 1990. **Essays:** Eavan Boland; Robert Crawford; Michael Donaghy; Mark Ford; Michael Hofmann; John Montague; Bernard O'Donoghue.

OSER, Lee. Member of the English Department, Yale University, New Haven, Connecticut. Author of poetry and criticism in various journals. **Essay:** Timothy Steele.

OWENS, Derek. Poet, visual artist, and teacher of composition and literature at the college level. **Essay:** Bob Perelman.

OXLEY, William. See his own entry. **Essays:** Dannie Abse; Dick Davis; Dana Gioia; John Heath-Stubbs; P.J. Kavanagh; Kathleen Raine; Peter Russell; Vernon Scannell; C.H. Sisson; R.S. Thomas.

PAGNOULLE, Christine. Lecturer in English, University of Liege, Belgium. Author of *Malcolm Lowry: Voyage au Fond de Nos Abîmes,* 1977, and *David Jones: A Commentary on the Poetic Fragments,* 1987. Translator of poems by contemporary authors. **Essays:** Duncan Bush; Tony Curtis; Jackie Kay; Taban lo Liyong.

PAOLINI, Shirley J. Professor of literature, University of Houston-Clear Lake, Texas. Author of *Confessions of Sin and Love in the Middle Ages: Augustine's Confessions and Dante's Divina Commedia* (1985) and *Creativity, Culture and Values: Comparative Essays in Literary Aesthetics* (1990); of essays in *Antipodes, Tamkang Review,* and *Humanities and the Good Life;* and of articles in *Reference Guide to Short Fiction* and *Contemporary World Writers.* General editor for the series New Connections: Studies in Interdisciplinarity, published by Peter Lang. **Essays:** Joyce Peseroff; Brenda Shaughnessy.

PARISI, Joseph. Editor-in-chief, *Poetry* magazine, Chicago. Author of *Viewer's Guide to "Voices and Visions,"* 1987, and *Marianne Moore: The Art of a Modernist,* 1990. Editor of *The "Poetry" Anthology 1912-1977* (with Daryl Hine), 1978. **Essay:** Alfred Corn.

PARKER, Derek. Former editor of *Poetry Review,* London. Author of many books, including *The Fall of Phaeton* (poetry), 1954, *Byron and His World,* 1968, *John Donne and His World,* 1974, and *Nijinsky: God of the Dance,* 1988, as well as travel guides and works on astrology, the chorus girl, and popular entertainers. Editor of anthologies of poetry and fiction. **Essays:** Alex Comfort; Christopher Fry.

PATKE, Rajeev S. Associate professor, Department of English, National University of Singapore. Author of *The Long Poems of Wallace Stevens,* 1985. Coeditor of *Institutions in Cultures: Theory and Practice,* 1996. **Essays:** Gieve Patel; Arthur Yap.

PAUL, Jay S. Professor and chair of English, Christopher Newport University, Newport News, Virginia. Author of *Going Home in Flood Time,* 1999, as well as poetry, fiction, essays, and reviews in periodicals. **Essays:** Nikki Giovanni; John Knoepfle; Heather McHugh; Linda Pastan; Lucien Stryk.

PEREIRA, Ernest. Professor of English, University of South Africa, Pretoria, and former president, English Academy of Southern Africa. Author of articles in journals, encyclopedias, and *The Dictionary of South African Biography.* Editor of the anthologies *The Poet's Circle, Contemporary South African Plays,* and *Tellers of Tales, Singers of Songs.* Coeditor of *Companion to South African English Literature, African Poems of Thomas Pringle* (with Michael Chapman), and *The Unknown Pauline Smith* (a selection of miscellaneous prose writings). **Essays:** Perseus Adams; Mazisi Kunene; Chris Mann; Oswald Mtshali.

PERLOFF, Marjorie. Sadie D. Patek Professor of Humanities Emerita, Stanford University, California. Author of *Rhyme and Meaning in the Poetry of Yeats,* 1970, *The Poetic Art of Robert Lowell,* 1973, *Frank O'Hara: Poet among Painters,* 1977, *The Other Tradition: Towards a Postmodern Poetry,* 1980, *George Oppen, Man and Poet,* 1981, *The Poetics of Indeterminacy,* 1982, *The Dance of the Intellect: Studies in the Poetry of the Pound Tradition,* 1985, *The Futurist Moment,* 1986, *Poetic License: Essays in Modern and Postmodern Poetics,* 1989, *Radical Artifice: Writing Poetry in the*

Age of Media, 1991, *Wittgenstein's Ladder: Poetic Language and the Strangeness of the Ordinary,* 1996, and *Poetry On and Off the Page: Essays for Emergent Occasions,* 1998. Editor of *Postmodern Genres,* 1989, and *John Cage: Composed in America* (with Charles Junkerman), 1994. Member, editorial board, *American Poetry: The Twentieth Century,* 2000. **Essays:** David Antin; John Ashbery; Kathleen Fraser.

PETERSEN, Kirsten Holst. Member of the Commonwealth Literature Division, University of Aarhus, Denmark, and reviewer for *Danida.* Author of *A Critical View of John Pepper Clark's Selected Poems,* 1981. Editor of *Enigma of Values* (with Anna Rutherford), 1975, *Cowries and Kobos: The West African Oral Tale and Short Story* (with Rutherford), 1981, and *Displaced Persons* (with Rutherford), 1988. **Essays:** John Pepper Clark; Roy Macnab; Grace Nichols; Sipho Sepamla.

PLOMER, William. Author of novels, short stories, and poetry, including *Celebrations* (verse), 1972, *The Autobiography,* 1975, and *Electric Delights* (selections), edited by Rupert Hart-Davis, 1978. Died 1973.

PORTER, Peter. See his own entry. **Essay:** George Szirtes.

POSMENTIER, Sonya B. Teacher, Roeper School, Bloomfield Hills, Michigan. **Essays:** Mimi Khalvati; Ruth Padel.

PRESS, John. Former officer of the British Council. Author of several books of poetry, including *A Girl with Beehive Hair,* 1986, as well as the critical works *Rule and Energy,* 1963, *A Map of Modern English Verse,* 1969, *The Lengthening Shadows,* 1971, *John Betjeman,* 1974, *Poets of World War I,* 1983, and *Poets of World War II,* 1983. **Essays:** Robert Conquest; J.C. Hall; Edward Lowbury.

PURSGLOVE, Glyn. Lecturer in English, University College, Swansea. Author of *Francis Warner and Tradition: An Introduction to the Plays,* 1981, and *Francis Warner's Poetry,* 1988. Editor of *Distinguishing Poetry: Writings on Poetry by William Oxley,* 1989, and *Tasso's "Aminta" and Other Poems by Henry Reynolds.* **Essays:** Alison Brackenbury; Peter Dale; Kenward Elmslie; David Gascoyne; John Hollander; Glyn Jones; Robert Kelly; Brendan Kennelly; Brad Leithauser; Roland Mathias; William Oxley; Robert L. Peters; Anne Ridler; John Smith.

RASULA, Jed. Professor of English, Queen's University, Kingston, Ontario, and associate editor, *Sulfur* magazine. Author of *Tabula Rasula,* 1986, and articles on contemporary poetry in *Sagetrieb, Credence, Poetics Journal, Hudson Review, Contemporary Literature, Boundary 2,* and other journals. **Essays:** Robin Blaser; Ron Silliman.

RAVENSCROFT, Arthur. Former senior lecturer in English literature, University of Leeds, and founding editor, *Journal of Commonwealth Literature.* Author of *Chinua Achebe,* 1969 (revised 1977), *Nigerian Writers and the African Past,* 1978, and *"Teaching Words" in African Literature,* 1986. Coauthor of *A Guide to 20th-Century English, Irish and Commonwealth Literature,* 1983. Translator of *Journal of Jan Van Riebeeck* (with C.K. Johnman), vol. 3, 1958. Died 1989.

RAY, David. See his own entry. **Essays:** Ed Dorn; Patricia Goedicke.

RECTOR, Liam. Author of *The Sorrow of Architecture* (poetry), 1984, *American Prodigal* (poetry), 1994, and poems, essays, and reviews in many journals. Editor of *The Day I Was Older: On the Poetry of Donald Hall,* 1989. **Essays:** Frank Bidart; Molly Peacock.

REIBETANZ, John. Professor of English, Victoria College, University of Toronto. Author of *The Lear World,* 1977, *Ashbourn,* 1986, and *Morning Watch,* 1995. **Essays:** Don Coles; Pier Giorgio Di Cicco.

REIBETANZ, Julia. Professor, Department of English, University of Toronto. Author of *A Reading of Eliot's Four Quartets,* 1983. **Essays:** Rachel Hadas; P.K. Page.

REILLY, John M. Professor of English, Howard University, Washington, D.C. Author of many articles on African-American literature, popular crime writing, and social fiction, as well as bibliographical essays in *Black American Writers,* 1978, and *American Literary Scholarship.* Editor of *Richard Wright: The Critical Reception,* 1978, and the reference book *Twentieth-Century Crime and Mystery Writers,* 1980 (2nd edition, 1985). **Essays:** Alvin Aubert; Clarence Major; Al Young.

RIACII, Alan. See his own entry. **Essay:** Murray Edmond.

RICKARDS, Colin. Press correspondent in Latin America and the Caribbean for twelve years. Author of *Caribbean Power,* 1963, *The Man from Devil's Island,* 1968, and several books about the American West. **Essay:** Louise Bennett.

ROBINSON, James K. Professor of English, University of Cincinnati. Editor of *The Mayor of Casterbridge* by Hardy and of several anthologies. **Essays:** Wendell Berry; Tess Gallagher; Louise Glück; Gary Snyder; David Wagoner.

ROBINSON, Roger. Professor of English and assistant vice-chancellor, Victoria University of Wellington, New Zealand. Coeditor of *Oxford Companion to New Zealand Literature,* 1998. **Essays:** Peter Bland; Alistair Campbell; Bill Manhire; Brian Turner.

RODDICK, Alan. Public health dentist, Christchurch, New Zealand. Author of *The Eye Corrects: Poems 1955-1965,* and *Allen Curnow,* 1980. Editor of two books of poetry by Charles Brasch. **Essays:** Jenny Bornholdt; Kevin Ireland.

RODRIGUEZ, Judith. See her own entry. **Essays:** Caroline Caddy; Alan Gould; Antigone Kefalá; Philip Mead; Mudrooroo; Les Murray; Gig Ryan; Andrew Taylor.

SADLER, Geoff. Freelance writer of Western novels, as Jeff Sadler and Wes Calhoun, and of a trilogy of plantation novels, as Geoffrey Sadler. Author of a five-volume history of Chesterfield librarians and of *Journey to Freedom* (with Antoni Snarski), 1990, *Shirebrook: Birth of a Colliery* (with Ernest I. Roberts), 1991, *Shirebrook in Old Picture Postcards,* 1993, *Shirebrook,* 1994, and *Shirebrook: A Second Selection,* 1995. Editor of *Twentieth Century Western Writers,* 1991, and *Write First Time: An Anthology of Work by the Shirebrook and District Writers' Group,* 1992. **Essays:** Gavin Bantock; Kevin Crossley-Holland; Maureen Duffy; Ruth Fainlight; Adrian Henri; Brian Jones; Christopher Logue; Wes Magee; Roger McGough; Adrian Mitchell; Philip Oakes; Brian Patten; Anthony Thwaite; Daniel Weissbort.

SCHENK, Susan. Assistant professor of English, University of Western Ontario, London, and editor of Brick Books. **Essay:** Sharon Thesen.

SCHMIDT, Michael. See his own entry.

SCHROEDER, Andreas. Member of the editorial board, *Canadian Fiction* magazine, Prince George, British Columbia. Author of several collections of poetry, as well as novels, short stories, and other books. Editor of poetry and short story anthologies. **Essay:** Michael Bullock.

SCHULTZ, Susan M. Assistant professor of English, University of Hawaii, Honolulu. Author of *Another Childhood* (poetry chapbook), 1993; articles on modern and contemporary poetry in *Arizona Quarterly, Raritan, Sagetrieb, Talisman,* and other journals; and reviews in *Postmodern Culture* and *American Book Review.* Editor of *The Tribe of John: Ashbery and Contemporary Poetry,* 1995. **Essays:** Sudesh Mishra; Olive Senior.

SCUPHAM, Peter. See his own entry. **Essay:** Neil Powell.

SEDGWICK, Fred. See his own entry. **Essays:** Douglas Dunn; Ian Hamilton; Michael Hulse; William Scammell.

SERGEANT, Howard. Founding editor of *Outposts* magazine and Outposts Publications. Author of four books of poetry and three books about poetry. Editor of many anthologies and collections of poetry. Died 1987. **Essays:** Taner Baybars; Kwes Brew; Marcus Cumberlege; Harry Guest; Philip Hobsbaum; Gabriel Okara; Paul Roche.

SEYMOUR-SMITH, Martin. Freelance writer. Former poetry editor of various journals and literary adviser to Hodder and Stoughton publishers. Author of numerous books, including the poetry collections *Tea with Miss Stockport: 24 Poems,* 1963, and *Reminiscences of Norma: Poems 1963-1970,* 1971. **Essay:** Alejandrino G. Hufana.

SHAPCOTT, Thomas W. See his own entry. **Essays:** Robert Adamson; Bruce Dawe; Rosemary Dobson; Laurie Duggan; Peter Goldsworthy; Rodney Hall; Coral Hull; John Kinsella; Anthony Lawrence; Kate Llewellyn; David Malouf; Rhyll McMaster; Jan Owen; Dorothy Porter; Judith Rodriguez; Pete Rose; David Rowbotham; R.A. Simpson; Vivian Smith; John Tranter; Dimitris Tsaloumas; Chris Wallace-Crabbe.

SHARMA, J.N. Professor of English, University of Jodhpur, India. Author of *International Fiction of Henry James,* 1979. **Essay:** Sam Cornish.

SHEPPARD, Robert. Author of several books of poetry, including *Empty Diaries,* 1998; a collection of essays, *Far Language,* 1999; poems in the anthologies *The New British Poetry,* 1988, *Floating Capital,* 1991, and *Other,* 1999; and reviews in *New Statesman/New Society, Times Literary Supplement,* and *PN Review.* **Essays:** Bob Cobbing; Tom Raworth; Iain Sinclair.

SHOPTAW, John. Member of the Department of English, Princeton University, New Jersey. **Essays:** Leslie Scalapino; James Tate.

SHOSTAK, Elizabeth. Teacher of literature and writing at Northeastern University and Boston University. Contributing editor of *Boston Book Review.* **Essays:** Ian Duhig; Martin Espada; Sianne Ngal; David Trinidad.

SHUCARD, Alan. Professor and chair of the English Department, University of Wisconsin-Parkside, Kenosha, and general editor of Twayne Critical History of Poetry series. Author of several books of poetry, a study of Countée Cullen, and the books *American Poetry: The Puritans through Walt Whitman,* and *Modern American Poetry, 1865-1950* (with Fred Moramarco and William Sullivan), 1989. **Essay:** Louise Erdrich.

SILKIN, Jon. See his own entry. **Essays:** Jon Glover; Michael Hamburger.

SINGH, Minnie. Assistant professor of English, Loyola College, Baltimore. **Essays:** Sujata Bhatt; Imtiaz Dharker; Saleem Peeradina; Manohar Shetty.

SLOANE, Sarah. Associate professor of English, Colorado State University, Fort Collins. Author of *Digital Fictions: Storytelling in a Material World,* 2000, and of numerous essays, poems, and reviews. **Essays:** Judy Grahn; Elma Mitchell.

SMITH, A.J.M. Former professor of English, Michigan State University, East Lansing. Author of six books of poetry, including *The Classic Shade: Selected Poems,* 1978, as well as books on Robert Bridges, E.J. Pratt, and Canadian literature. Editor of many general collections of poetry and specialized collections of Canadian writing. Died 1980. **Essay:** Jay Macpherson.

SMITH, Anna. Lecturer, Department of English, University of Canterbury, Christchurch, New Zealand. Author of *Julia Kristeva: Readings in Exile and Estrangement* and an essay on Keri Hulme in *Opening the Book: New Essays on New Zealand Literature,* edited by Michele Leggot and Mark Williams, 1995. **Essays:** Anne French; Keri Hulme; Alan Riach.

SMITH, Stan. Professor of English, University of Dundee; director, with R.J.C. Watt, of Auden Concordance Project; and general editor of Longman Critical Reader series and Longman Studies in Twentieth-Century Literature series. Author of *A Sadly Contracted Hero: The Comic Self in Post-War American Fiction,* 1981, *Inviolable Voice: History and Twentieth-Century Poetry,* 1982, *W.H. Auden,* 1985, *Edward Thomas,* 1986, *W.B. Yeats: A Critical Introduction,* 1990, and *The Origins of Modernism: Eliot, Pound, Yeats and the Rhetorics of Renewal,* 1994. **Essays:** Seamus Heaney; Christopher Middleton; John Montague; Peter Redgrove; Anne Stevenson.

SMITHYMAN, Kendrick. See his own entry. **Essays:** Elizabeth Smither; C.K. Stead.

SOAR, Geoffrey. Honorary research librarian, University College London Library. Author of *Interaction & Overlap: From the Little Magazine & Small Press Collection at University College London* (with David Miller), 1994. **Essays:** Edwin Morgan; Tom Pickard.

SOMERVILLE, Jane. Professor of English, West Virginia University, Parkersburg. Author of *Making the Light Come: The Poetry of Gerald Stern,* 1990, and poetry and essays in various journals. Editor of *Gambit: A Journal of the Ohio Valley.* **Essays:** Russell Edson; Jack Marshall; David Young.

SQUIRES, Radcliffe. Former professor of English, University of Michigan, Ann Arbor. Author of numerous poetry collections, including *Gardens of the World,* 1981, and *The Envoy,* 1983, as well as *The Major Themes of Robert Frost,* 1963, *Allen Tate: A Literary Biography,* 1971, and other books. Died. **Essay:** Brewster Ghiselin.

SRIVASTAVA, Aruna. Assistant professor of English, University of Calgary, Alberta. **Essays:** Meena Alexander; Mongane Wally Serote.

STAUFFER, Donald Barlow. Associate professor emeritus of English, State University of New York, Albany. Author of *A Short History of American Poetry,* 1974, and *The Merry Mood: Poe's Uses of Humor,* 1982. **Essays:** Stanley Burnshaw; Gregory Corso; Gregory Orr; Barry Spacks.

STEAD, C.K. See his own entry. **Essays:** Allen Curnow; Sam Hunt; Andrew Johnston; Gregory O'Brien; Alistair Paterson; Hone Tuwhare; Ian Wedde; Hubert Witheford.

STERN, Carol Simpson. Dean of Graduate School and professor and chair of Department of Performance Studies, Northwestern University, Evanston, Illinois. Author of *Performance: Texts and Contexts* (with Bruce Henderson), 1993. **Essays:** A. Alvarez; Peter Everwine; Sanda Gilbert; Erica Jong; Susan Musgrave; Stephen Sandy; Richard Wilbur.

STEVENSON, Anne. See her own entry. **Essays:** Richard Kell; Penelope Shuttle; Richard Tillinghast.

STEWART, Douglas. Former literary editor of the *Bulletin,* Sydney, and literary adviser to Angus and Robertson publishers, Sydney. Author of many books of poetry, as well as plays, short stories, and nonfiction. Editor of anthologies of Australian poetry and short stories. Died 1985.

STOCKS, Anthony G. Freelance writer. **Essays:** Margaret Atwood; Linton Kwesi Johnson; Charles Simic.

STRAUSS, Jennifer. See her own entry. **Essays:** Philip Salom; John A. Scott; Thomas W. Shapcott; Fay Zwicky.

SULLIVAN, Rosemary. Professor of English, University of Toronto. Author of *Theodore Roethke: The Garden Master,* 1975, *The Space a Name Makes* (poetry), 1986, *Blue Panic* (poetry), 1991, *By Heart: Elizabeth Smart/A Life,* 1991, and articles on Roethke, Samuel Beckett, Robert Lowell, Margaret Atwood, and P.K. Page. Editor of *Elements of Fiction* (with Robert Scholes), 1982, *Stories [More Stories] by Canadian Women,* 2 vols., 1984, 1987, and *Poetry by Canadian Women,* 1989. **Essay:** Patrick Lane.

SUTHERLAND, Fraser. See his own entry. **Essays:** Marilyn Bowering; Robert Bringhurst; George Clarke; John Robert Colombo; Don Domanski; Michael Harris; George Johnston; Florence McNeil; Jan Zwicky.

SUTRO, Martha. Visiting professor, English Department, University of Montana, Missoula. **Essays:** Fleur Adcock; A.R. Ammons; Margaret Atwood; Marvin Bell; John Pepper Clark; Tom Clark; Cid Corman; Alfred Corn; Rita Dove; Kathleen Fraser; Tess Gallagher; Reginald Gibbons; Louise Gluck; Patricia Goedicke; Jorie Graham; Seamus Heaney; Charles Simic; Dave Smith; Gary Snyder; Mark Strand; Richard Tillinghast; David Wagoner; Al Young.

SYLVESTER, William. Professor of English and comparative literature, State University of New York, Buffalo. Author of *Honky in the Woodpile,* 1982, *Dig the Flower Children,* 1983, *Listen to the Ice,* 1984, and poetry and criticism in various journals. **Essays:** Maya Angelou; Andrew Crozier; Johanna Drucker; Daniel Hoffman; Michael McClure; David Meltzer; Lisel Mueller.

SYMONS, Julian. Former reviewer, *Sunday Times,* London, and *Manchester Evening News.* Author of several poetry collections, including *The Object of an Affair and Other Poems,* 1974, and *Seven*

Poems for Sarah, 1979, as well as plays, novels, short stories, and other books. Died 1994. **Essay:** Alan Ross.

TAGGART, John. Member of Department of English, Shippensburg University, Pennsylvania, and editor of *Maps* poetry magazine. Author of many books of poetry and articles on the objectivist poets. **Essay:** Toby Olson.

TATE, Allen. Poet, novelist, and literary critic. Author of many books, including *Collected Essays,* 1959, *Memoirs and Opinions,* 1975, *The Fathers and Other Fiction,* 1976, and *Collected Poems,* 1977. Died 1979.

TAYLOR, Henry. See his own entry. **Essays:** Fred Chappell; Samuel Hazo; Greg Pape; Mary Jo Salter; Robert Watson.

TAYLOR, Myron. Former associate professor of English, State University of New York, Albany. Author of articles on Shakespeare in *The Christian Scholar, Studies in English,* and *Shakespeare Quarterly.* Died 1989. **Essay:** Daniel Berrigan.

TERRY, Arthur. Emeritus professor of literature, University of Essex, Colchester. Author of *Catalan Literature,* 1972, a study of Antonio Machado, and two volumes of essays on modern Catalan poetry. Editor of *An Anthology of Spanish Poetry 1500-1700,* 2 vols., 1965-68, *Selected Poems of Ausias March,* 1976, and *Seventeenth-Century Spanish Poetry: The Power of Artifice,* 1993. **Essay:** Laurence Lerner.

THORN, Michael. Novelist, biographer, and schoolteacher. Author of *Pen Friends,* 1988. **Essay:** E.A. Markham.

THWAITE, Anthony. See his own entry.

TOWNS, Saundra. Lecturer in English, Bernard Baruch College, City University of New York. Author of *Lillian Hellman,* 1989, and of essays and reviews in *The Nation, Black Books Bulletin, Black World, Black Position,* and other periodicals. **Essays:** June Jordan; Raymond R. Patterson.

TRUE, Michael. Professor of English, Assumption College, Worcester, Massachusetts. Author of *Homemade Social Justice,* 1982, *Justice-Seekers, Peacemakers: 32 Portraits in Courage,* 1985, *Worcester Area Writers, 1680-1980,* 1987, *To Construct Peace: 30 More Justice Seekers,* 1991, *Ordinary People: Family Life and Global Values,* 1992, *An Energy Field More Intense Than War: The Nonviolent Tradition and American Literature,* 1995, and articles in *Commonweal, America, The Progressive, New Republic, Boston Globe, Harvard Divinity Bulletin, American Writers,* and *Contemporary Literary Criticism.* Editor of *Daniel Berrigan: Poetry, Drama, Prose,* 1988. **Essays:** Stephen Dobyns; Stephen Dunn; Joy Harjo; X.J. Kennedy; Stanley Kunitz; Dave Smith; Jon Stallworthy; Bruce Weigl; Reed Whittemore.

VAS DIAS, Robert. See his own entry. **Essays:** John Ash; Michael Heller.

VENDLER, Helen. Kenan Professor of English, Harvard University, Cambridge, Massachusetts. Author of *Yeats's Vision and the Later Plays,* 1963, *On Extended Wings: Wallace Stevens' Longer Poems,* 1969, *The Poetry of George Herbert,* 1975, *Part of Nature, Part of Us: Modern American Poets,* 1980, *The Odes of John Keats,* 1983, *Wallace Stevens: Words Chosen out of Desire,* 1984, *Voices and Visions: The Poet in America,* 1987, *The Music of What Happens:*

Poems, Poets, Critics, 1988, and *Soul Says: On Recent Poetry,* 1995. Editor of *The Harvard Book of Contemporary American Poetry,* 1985.

VENKATACHARI, K. Research officer and editor, Institute of Asian Studies, Barkarpura, Hyderabad, India. **Essay:** Arun Kolatkar.

WAGNER-MARTIN, Linda W. Hanes Professor of English, University of North Carolina, Chapel Hill. Author of *The Poems of William Carlos Williams,* 1964, *The Prose of William Carlos Williams,* 1970, *Denise Levertov,* 1967, *Hemingway and Faulkner: Inventors, Masters,* 1975, *Introducing Poems,* 1976, *John Dos Passos,* 1979, *Ellen Glasgow: Beyond Convention,* 1982, *Sylvia Plath: A Biography,* 1987, *The Modern American Novel 1914-1945,* 1989, *Telling Women's Lives: The New Biography,* 1994, *Favored Strangers: Gertrude Stein and Her Family,* 1995, *The Mid-Century American Novel, 1935-1965,* 1997, and *Sylvia Plath: A Literary Life,* 1999. Editor of *Critical Essays on Sylvia Plath,* 1984, *Sylvia Plath: The Critical Heritage,* 1988, *Critical Essays on Anne Sexton,* 1989, and *The Oxford Companion to Women Writers in the United States,* 1999. **Essays:** Lorna Cervantes; Carolyn Forché; Robert Vas Dias.

WAKOSKI, Diane. See her own entry. **Essays:** Clayton Eshleman; James Koller; Maxine Kumin; Mary Oliver; Michael Ondaatje; Carl Rakosi; Jerome Rothenberg; Peter Wild; John Yau; Paul Zimmer.

WALTON, Priscilla L. Assistant professor, University of Lethbridge, Alberta. Author of critical essays in various journals, including *North Dakota Quarterly, Ariel, Scripta Mediterranea,* and *Comparative Literature in Canada.* **Essay:** Ntozake Shange.

WATT, R.J.C. Lecturer in English and dean of students, Faculty of Arts and Social Sciences, University of Dundee. Author of an introductory study of Hopkins and of articles on modern poetry, textual problems in Shakespeare, and literary computing. **Essays:** Henry Graham; Medbh McGuckian; Sean O'Brien; Jeffrey Wainwright; Andrew Waterman; Clive Wilmer.

WEINBERGER, Eliot. Essayist, editor, and translator. Author of *Works on Paper* and *19 Ways of Looking at Wang Wei.* Editor and translator of *The Collected Poems of Octavio Paz, Altazor* by Vicente Huidobro, and a dozen other books of Latin American poetry and prose. **Essay:** Nathaniel Tarn.

WERNER, Theresa. Editor and freelance writer, London. **Essay:** Lauris Edmond.

WHEALE, Nigel. Member of the faculty, Cambridgeshire College of Arts and Technology. Author of the poetry books *Answerable*

Love, 1977, and *Simples,* 1979, as well as reviews in the *Times Literary Supplement, Poetry Review,* and *JEGP.* **Essay:** J.H. Prynne.

WHEATLEY, Patience. Coordinator of the Living Archives series, published by the League of Canadian Poets. Author of the poetry books *A Hinge of Spring,* 1986, and *Good-bye to the Sugar Refinery,* 1989. **Essays:** Douglas Barbour; Roo Borson; Fred Cogswell; Miriam Waddington; Phyllis Webb.

WILLY, Margaret. Lecturer, British Council and Morley College, London. Author of the poetry books *The Invisible Sun,* 1946, and *Every Star a Tongue,* 1951, as well as critical studies of Chaucer, Traherne, Fielding, Browning, Crashaw, Vaughan, Emily Brontë, and English diarists. Editor of two anthologies and of plays by Goldsmith. **Essays:** D.J. Enright; Phoebe Hesketh; Elizabeth Jennings; Robert Minhinnick.

WILSON, Joseph. Associate professor of creative writing, Anna Maria College, Paxton, Massachusetts. Author of poetry in literary journals. **Essay:** Michael Dennis Browne.

WOODCOCK, George. Former associate professor of English, University of British Columbia, Vancouver, and contributing editor of *Dissent,* New York. Author of numerous poetry collections, including *Tolstoy at Yasnaya Polyana & Other Poems,* 1991, and *The Cherry Tree on Cherry Street and Other Poems,* 1994, as well as plays and other books. Died 1995. **Essays:** Margaret Avison; Louis Dudek; P.K. Page; Al Purdy; Peter Stevens; Tom Wayman; Phyllis Webb.

WRIGHT, Derek. Associate professor of English, Northern Territory University, Darwin. Author of *Ayi Kwei Armah's Africa: The Sources of His Fiction,* 1989, *Wole Soyinka Revisited,* 1993, and *The Novels of Nuruddin Farah,* 1994. Editor of *Critical Perspectives on Ayi Kwei Armah,* 1990, and *New African Writing & Criticism,* 1995. **Essays:** Kofi Awoonor; Lenrie Peters.

YABES, Leopoldo Y. Former professor of literature and Philippine studies, University of the Philippines, Quezon City. Author of more than twenty books, including *The University and the Fear of Ideas,* 1956, *Philippine Literature in English,* 1958, *The Filipino Struggle for Intellectual Freedom,* 1959, *Jose Rizal on His Centenary,* 1963, and *The Ordeal of a Man of Academe,* 1967. Editor of *Philippine Short Stories,* 2 vols., 1975-81, and other books. Died 1988. **Essay:** Ricaredo Demetillo.

YOUNG, David. See his own entry. **Essays:** Sandra McPherson; Dennis Schmitz; Charles Wright.

YOUNG, Steven. Member of Department of English, Pomona College, Claremont, California. Theater director and actor. **Essays:** Michael Benedikt; Tom Clark.

NATIONALITY INDEX

Below is the list of entrants divided by nationality. The nationalities were chosen largely from information supplied by the entrants. A small number of poets submitted two nationalities (e.g., American and British) and thus are listed under both. It should be noted that "British" was used for all English entrants and for any other British entrant who chose that designation over a more specific one, such as "Scottish."

American

Diane Ackerman
Ai
Meena Alexander
A.R. Ammons
Michael Anania
Maya Angelou
David Antin
Rae Armantrout
John Ashbery
Alvin Aubert
Jimmy Santiago Baca
Mary Jo Bang
Amiri Baraka
Marvin Bell
Michael Benedikt
Stephen Berg
Carol Bergé
Bill Berkson
Charles Bernstein
Daniel Berrigan
Wendell Berry
James Bertolino
Frank Bidart
Robert Bly
Philip Booth
Roo Borson
Edgar Bowers
John Brandi
Lucie Brock-Broido
Gwendolyn Brooks
Olga Broumas
Michael Dennis Browne
Stanley Burnshaw
Hayden Carruth
Lorna Dee Cervantes
Fred Chappell
Maxine Chernoff
Tom Clark
Lucille Clifton
Wanda Coleman
Billy Collins
Robert Conquest
Clark Coolidge
Jane Cooper
Cid Corman
Alfred Corn
Sam Cornish
Gregory Corso
Robert Creeley
Philip Dacey
Beverly Dahlen
Robert Dana
Michael Davidson

Peter Davison
Madeline DeFrees
Diane di Prima
R.H.W. Dillard
Thomas M. Disch
Stephen Dobyns
Michael Donaghy
David Dooley
Ed Dorn
Mark Doty
Rita Dove
Johanna Drucker
Norman Dubie
Alan Dugan
Stephen Dunn
Bob Dylan
Charles Edward Eaton
Richard Eberhart
Russell Edson
Kenward Elmslie
James A. Emanuel
John Engels
Theodore Enslin
Elaine Equi
Louise Erdrich
Clayton Eshleman
Martin Espada
Mari Evans
Peter Everwine
Ruth Fainlight
Irving Feldman
Lawrence Ferlinghetti
Edward Field
Donald Finkel
Caroline Finkelstein
Roland Flint
Carolyn Forché
Charles Henri Ford
Gene Fowler
Kathleen Fraser
Alice Fulton
Tess Gallagher
Brendan Galvin
Forrest Gander
George Garrett
Brewster Ghiselin
Reginald Gibbons
Jack Gilbert
Sandra M. Gilbert
Gary Gildner
Dana Gioia
Nikki Giovanni
Peter Gizzi
Louise Glück

Patricia Goedicke
Albert Goldbarth
Kenneth Goldsmith
Jorie Graham
Judy Grahn
Jonathan Greene
Linda Gregg
Arthur Gregor
Barbara Guest
Marilyn Hacker
Rachel Hadas
Donald Hall
Daniel Halpern
Joy Harjo
Michael S. Harper
Jim Harrison
Robert Hass
Samuel Hazo
Anthony Hecht
Lyn Hejinian
Michael Heller
William Heyen
Brenda Hillman
Edward Hirsch
Jack Hirschman
Jane Hirshfield
Tony Hoagland
Daniel Hoffman
John Hollander
Garrett Hongo
Edwin Honig
Paul Hoover
Richard Howard
Fanny Howe
Susan Howe
T.R. Hummer
Josephine Jacobsen
David Jaffin
Mark Jarman
Judith Johnson
Ronald Johnson
Rodney Jones
Erica Jong
June Jordan
Donald Justice
Robert Kelly
X.J. Kennedy
Galway Kinnell
Carolyn Kizer
John Knoepfle
Bill Knott
Kenneth Koch
James Koller
Yusef Komunyakaa

Coral Hull
Antigone Kefalá
John Kinsella
Anthony Lawrence
Geoffrey Lehmann
Kate Llewellyn
Jennifer Maiden
David Malouf
Rhyll McMaster
Philip Mead
Mudrooroo
Les Murray
Jan Owen
Geoff Page
Dorothy Porter
Peter Porter
Judith Rodriguez
Peter Rose
David Rowbotham
Gig Ryan
Philip Salom
Thomas W. Shapcott
R.A. Simpson
Peter Skrzyneckl
Vivian Smith
Jennifer Strauss
Andrew Taylor
John Tranter
Chris Wallace-Crabbe
Alan Wearne
Judith Wright
Fay Zwicky

Bangladeshi
Kaiser Haq

Barbadian
Edward Kamau Brathwaite
Anthony Kellman
Bruce St. John

British
Dannie Abse
Fleur Adcock
John Agard
A. Alvarez
Moniza Alvi
Simon Armitage
John Ash
Gavin Bantock
Elizabeth Bartlett
Taner Baybars
Anne Beresford
Francis Berry
James Berry
D.M. Black
Peter Bland
Alison Brackenbury
Alan Brownjohn
George Bruce
Dennis Brutus
Michael Bullock

Jim Burns
Kate Clanchy
Bob Cobbing
Alex Comfort
Stewart Conn
David Constantine
Wendy Cope
John Cotton
Kevin Crossley-Holland
Andrew Crozier
Marcus Cumberlege
R.N. Currey
Tony Curtis
Fred D'Aguiar
Peter Dale
Dick Davis
Peter Didsbury
Charles Doyle
Carol Ann Duffy
Maureen Duffy
Ian Duhig
Helen Dunmore
Douglas Dunn
Alistair Elliot
D.J. Enright
Bernardine Evaristo
U.A. Fanthorpe
Vicki Feaver
Elaine Feinstein
James Fenton
Ian Hamilton Finlay
Roy Fisher
Mark Ford
Christopher Fry
John Fuller
Robin Fulton
Roger Garfitt
Raymond Garlick
David Gascoyne
Zulfikar Ghose
Duncan Glen
Jon Glover
John Gohorry
Henry Graham
Lavinia Greenlaw
Philip Gross
Harry Guest
Thom Gunn
J.C. Hall
Michael Hamburger
Ian Hamilton
Wilson Harris
Tony Harrison
David Harsent
Lee Harwood
John Heath-Stubbs
Adrian Henri
Phoebe Hesketh
Geoffrey Hill
Selima Hill

Philip Hobsbaum
David Holbrook
Jeremy Hooker
Glyn Hughes
Michael Hulse
Elizabeth Jennings
Brian Jones
Glyn Jones
Jenny Joseph
Sylvia Kantaris
P.J. Kavanagh
Judith Kazantzis
Richard Kell
James Kirkup
Bernard Kops
Lotte Kramer
Frank Kuppner
Laurence Lerner
Peter Levi
Christopher Logue
Herbert Lomas
Edward Lowbury
Edward Lucie-Smith
Barry MacSweeney
Wes Magee
Sarah Maguire
Derek Mahon
E.A. Markham
Roland Mathias
Glyn Maxwell
Gerda Mayer
Roger McGough
Jamie McKendrick
Cilla McQueen
Matthew Mead
James Michic
Christopher Middleton
Robert Minhinnick
Adrian Mitchell
John Mole
Dom Moraes
Pete Morgan
Blake Morrison
Andrew Motion
Robert Nye
Sean O'Brien
Philip Oakes
William Oxley
Brian Patten
Tom Paulin
William Peskett
Tom Pickard
Christopher Pilling
Fiona Pitt-Kethley
Neil Powell
F.T. Prince
J.H. Prynne
Sheenagh Pugh
Rodney Pybus
Craig Raine

Anne Cluysenaar
Anthony Cronin
Paul Durcan
Peter Fallon
Patrick Galvin
Seamus Heaney
Pearse Hutchinson
Brendan Kennelly
Thomas Kinsella
Michael Longley
James J. McAuley
Thomas McCarthy
Medbh McGuckian
Paula Meehan
John Montague
Paul Muldoon
Richard Murphy
Eiléan Ní Chuilleanáin
Bernard O'Donoghue
Dennis O'Driscoll
Desmond O'Grady
Frank Ormsby
Ruth Padel
Tom Raworth
Matthew Sweeney

Jamaican
Edward Baugh
Louise Bennett
Lorna Goodison
Linton Kwesi Johnson
Anthony McNeill
Mervyn Morris
Olive Senior

Malawian
Frank Chipasula
Jack Mapanje

Mexican
Michael Schmidt

New Zealander
Jenny Bornholdt
Alistair Campbell
Allen Curnow

Ruth Dallas
Lauris Edmond
Murray Edmond
Anne French
Keri Hulme
Sam Hunt
Kevin Ireland
Michael Jackson
Andrew Johnston
Bill Manhire
Gregory O'Brien
Vincent O'Sullivan
Alistair Paterson
Elizabeth Smither
C.K. Stead
Brian Turner
Hone Tuwhare
Ian Wedde
Hubert Witheford

Nigerian
Chinua Achebe
John Pepper Clark
Michael Echeruo
Gabriel Okara
Niyi Osundare
Wole Soyinka

Pakistani
Alamgir Hashmi

Puerto Rican
Victor Hernández Cruz

Samoan
Albert Wendt

Scottish
James Aitchison
Tom Buchan
John Burnside
Ron Butlin
Robert Crawford
Valerie Gillies
Michael Harris
Hamish Henderson
Mick Imlah

Kathleen Jamie
Jackie Kay
Tom Leonard
Maurice Lindsay
Liz Lochhead
Alasdair Maclean
Elma Mitchell
Edwin Morgan
Don Paterson
Alan Riach
Gael Turnbull

Sierra Leonean
Syl Cheyney-Coker

Singaporean
Arthur Yap

South African
Perseus Adams
Guy Butler
Jeremy Cronin
Patrick Cullinan
Anthony Delius
Stephen Gray
Mazisi Kunene
Douglas Livingstone
Roy Macnab
Chris Mann
Oswald Mtshali
Sipho Sepamla
Mongane Wally Serote

Sudanese
Taban lo Liyong

Trinidadian
Wayne Brown
The Mighty Sparrow

Welsh
Duncan Bush
Gillian Clarke
Leslie Norris
R.S. Thomas

Zimbabwean
Chenjerai Hove

TITLE INDEX

The following list includes the titles of all books listed in the Poetry section of the entries in the book. The name in parenthesis is meant to direct the reader to the appropriate entry where full publication information is given.

Black Grate Poems (Stevenson), 1984
Black Hair (Soto), 1985
Black Holes, Black Stockings (Broumas), 1985
Black Huntsman (Layton), 1951
Black Judgement (Giovanni), 1968
Black Love (Brooks), 1982
Black Magic: Collected Poetry 1961-1967 (Baraka), 1970
Black Man Abroad: The Toulouse Poems (Emanuel), 1978
Black Marigolds (Woods), 1994
Black Mesa Poems (Baca), 1989
Black Night Window (Newlove), 1968
Black Orchid (Haq), 1996
Black Orchid (Moritz), 1981
Black Pride (Madhubuti), 1968
Black Riviera (Jarman), 1990
Black South-Easter (Delius), 1966
Black Spiders (Jamie), 1982
Black Steel: Joe Frazier and Muhammad Ali (Brooks), 1971
Black Sugar: Trisexual Poems (Reed, J.), 1992
Black Torch (MacSweeney), 1978
Black Water: Approaching Zukovsky (Adamson), 1999
Black Wings, White Dead (Bullock), 1978
Black Zodiac (Wright, Charles), 1997
Blackberries (Heyen), 1996
Blackberry Light (Heyen), 1981
Blackberry Season (Owen), 1993
Blackbird: Elegy for William Gordon Calvert, Being Book Two
     of Black Torch (MacSweeney), 1980
Blackest Rose (Meltzer), 1964
Blacks (Brooks), 1987
Blaenau Observed (Garlick), 1957
Blake's Newton (Palmer), 1972
Blast Area (Tranter), 1974
Blazing Fruit (McGough), 1990
Bleecker Street (Reed, J.), 1980
Bleeding Heart Yard (Scammell), 1992
blew trewz (Bissett), 1970
Blind Field (Szirtes), 1994
Blind Man's House (Suknaski), 1975
Blind Photographer: Poems and Sketches (Rosenblatt), 1973
Blind Swimmer: Selected Early Poems, 1970-1975 (Lux), 1996
Blizzard of One (Strand), 1998
Blizzard Voices (Kooser), 1986
Block Island (Berrigan), 1985
Blonds on Bikes (Bowering, G.), 1997
Blood and Family (Kinsella), 1988
Blood Harvest (Dana), 1987
Blood Hook & Eye (Wier), 1977
Blood in the Desert's Eyes: Poems (Cheyney-Coker), 1990
Blood Lord (Seidman), 1974
Blood Mountain (Engels), 1977
Blood of Adonis (Hazo), 1971
Blood Pressure: Poems (Gilbert), 1988
Blood Rights (Hazo), 1968
Blood Road (Lifshin), 1989
Blood, Tin, Straw (Olds), 1999
Bloodfire (Chappell), 1978
Bloodlight for Malachi McNair (McWhirter), 1974
Bloodlines (Wright; Charles), 1975
Bloomingdale Papers (Carruth), 1974

Bloomsday (Mac Low), 1984
Blue (Clark, T.), 1974
Blue and The Brown Poems (Finlay), 1968
Blue Bamboo (Kirkup), 1994
Blue Ceiling (Hollo), 1992
Blue Coffee: Poems, 1985-1996 (Mitchell), 1996
Blue Dust, New Mexico (Lifshin), 1982
Blue Fingers (Lifshin), 1974
Blue for the Plough (Wier), 1992
Blue Heaven (Warsh), 1978
Blue Horses Nuzzle Tuesday (Lifshin), 1983
Blue Is the Hero: Poems 1960-1975 (Berkson), 1976
Blue Like the Heavens: New and Selected Poems (Gildner), 1984
Blue Madonna (Lifshin), 1974
Blue Monkey for the Tomb (Witheford), 1994
Blue Mosque (Waldman), 1987
Blue Notes (Duggan), 1990
Blue Pastures (Oliver), 1995
Blue Propeller (Layton), 1955
Blue Rags (Meltzer), 1974
Blue Rain (Campbell), 1967
Blue Ridge Weather Prophet (Williams, J.), 1977
Blue Ridge Weather Prophet Makes Twelve Stitches in Time on
     the Twelfth Day of Christmas (Williams, J.), 1977
Blue Roofs of Japan: A Score for Interpenetrating Voices
     (Bringhurst), 1986
Blue Shoes (Sweeney), 1989
Blue Sky (Snyder), 1969
Blue Spruce (Smith, D.), 1981
Blue Stairs (Guest, B.), 1968
Blue Talaria (Reed, J.), 1976
Blue Taps (Sweeney), 1994
Blue Tattoo (Lifshin), 1995
Blue Tit Tilts at the Edge of the Sea: Selected Poems 1964-1974
     (Hall, D.), 1975
Blue Wine and Other Poems (Hollander), 1979
Blue-Fly in His Head (Heath-Stubbs), 1962
Bluebeard's Castle (Fisher), 1973
Blues and Roots, Rue and Bluets: A Garland for the
     Appalachians (Williams, J.), 1971
Blues Book for Blue Black Magical Women (Sanchez), 1974
Blues Don't Change: New and Selected Poems (Young, A.), 1982
Blues: For All the Changes: New Poems (Giovanni), 1999
Blues in Black and White (Emanuel), 1992
Blues Is You in Me (Sepamla), 1976
Blue's Rocket (Smith, K.), 1976
Blur in Between: Poems 1960-61 (Purdy), 1962
Boat in the Forest (Lux), 1992
Boatman (Macpherson), 1957
Boats Are Home (Kennelly), 1980
Boatyard (Finlay), 1969
Bob Cobbing's Girlie Poems: collected poems 5 (Cobbing), 1983
Bob Cob's Rag Bag (Cobbing), 1977
Bob Jubile (Cobbing), 1990
Body (Benedikt), 1968
Body Rags (Kinnell), 1969
Body Servant: Poems of Exile (Kirkup), 1971
Body Traffic (Dobyns), 1991
Bog Poems (Heaney), 1975
Bogman Pavese Tactics (Stevens), 1977